HOLY BIBLE

• • • • •

Presented to

_____

_____

by

_____

_____

Date and Occasion

_____

_____

• • • • •

NKJV FOUNDATION
STUDY BIBLE

NKJV FOUNDATION
STUDY BIBLE

NEW KING JAMES
VERSION®

THOMAS NELSON
Since 1798

www.ThomasNelson.com

15 16 17 18 19 20 21 22 /DSC/ 16 15 14 13 12 11 10 9 8 7 6 5 4 3 2

Table of Contents

Abbreviations of Books of the Bible

The Old Testament

Genesis	Gen.	Ecclesiastes	Eccl.
Exodus	Ex.	Song of Solomon	Song
Leviticus	Lev.	Isaiah	Is.
Numbers	Num.	Jeremiah	Jer.
Deuteronomy	Deut.	Lamentations	Lam.
Joshua	Josh.	Ezekiel	Ezek.
Judges	Judg.	Daniel	Dan.
Ruth	Ruth	Hosea	Hos.
1 Samuel	1 Sam.	Joel	Joel
2 Samuel	2 Sam.	Amos	Amos
1 Kings	1 Kin.	Obadiah	Obad.
2 Kings	2 Kin.	Jonah	Jon.
1 Chronicles	1 Chr.	Micah	Mic.
2 Chronicles	2 Chr.	Nahum	Nah.
Ezra	Ezra	Habakkuk	Hab.
Nehemiah	Neh.	Zephaniah	Zeph.
Esther	Esth.	Haggai	Hag.
Job	Job	Zechariah	Zech.
Psalms	Ps.	Malachi	Mal.
Proverbs	Prov.		

The New Testament

Matthew	Matt.	1 Timothy	1 Tim.
Mark	Mark	2 Timothy	2 Tim.
Luke	Luke	Titus	Titus
John	John	Philemon	Philem.
Acts	Acts	Hebrews	Heb.
Romans	Rom.	James	James
1 Corinthians	1 Cor.	1 Peter	1 Pet.
2 Corinthians	2 Cor.	2 Peter	2 Pet.
Galatians	Gal.	1 John	1 John
Ephesians	Eph.	2 John	2 John
Philippians	Phil.	3 John	3 John
Colossians	Col.	Jude	Jude
1 Thessalonians	1 Thess.	Revelation	Rev.
2 Thessalonians	2 Thess.		

Introduction to the
NKJV Foundation Study Bible

As its name implies, the *NKJV Foundation Study Bible* is designed to provide a foundation for Bible study. It is intended for both beginning and experienced students of the Scriptures who want a Bible that contains the key features of a study Bible in a convenient, compact, and concise form.

- The full text of the New King James Version is used, in a format that shows paragraphs, poetry, and other special formats. Based on the time-honored King James Version, the NKJV is preferred by many Bible readers for its unparalleled accuracy, beauty, and clarity. The NKJV uses up-to-date English while maintaining the literary quality of the KJV.

- Concise study notes are based on the notes originally prepared for *The NKJV Study Bible,* providing succinct comments on passages of Scripture.

- Theological notes draw attention to the most important doctrinal content of the Bible. These notes are signified by a bold roman heading followed by a dash. They are indexed in the back of the Bible both by title and by location.

- New King James Version translators' footnotes offer clarification and information about original language texts.

- In-text subject headings help to organize and illuminate Bible reading and study.

- Words of Jesus are printed in red to assist identification.

- Book introductions give background information about each of the Bible's 66 books.

- Cross-references direct attention to other passages for further study of words and concepts in Scripture. Conceptual cross-references are indicated by square brackets.

- A concordance provides an alphabetical listing of important passages by key words.

- Full-color maps of Bible lands are included in the back of the Bible.

Preface to the New King James Version®

Purpose

In the preface to the 1611 edition, the translators of the Authorized Version, known popularly as the King James Bible, state that it was not their purpose "to make a new translation ... but to make a good one better." Indebted to the earlier work of William Tyndale and others, they saw their best contribution to consist in revising and enhancing the excellence of the English versions which had sprung from the Reformation of the sixteenth century. In harmony with the purpose of the King James scholars, the translators and editors of the present work have not pursued a goal of innovation. They have perceived the Holy Bible, New King James Version, as a continuation of the labors of the earlier translators, thus unlocking for today's readers the spiritual treasures found especially in the Authorized Version of the Holy Scriptures.

A Living Legacy

For nearly four hundred years, and throughout several revisions of its English form, the King James Bible has been deeply revered among the English-speaking peoples of the world. The precision of translation for which it is historically renowned, and its majesty of style, have enabled that monumental version of the word of God to become the mainspring of the religion, language, and legal foundations of our civilization.

Although the Elizabethan period and our own era share in zeal for technical advance, the former period was more aggressively devoted to classical learning. Along with this awakened concern for the classics came a flourishing companion interest in the Scriptures, an interest that was enlivened by the conviction that the manuscripts were providentially handed down and were a trustworthy record of the inspired Word of God. The King James translators were committed to producing an English Bible that would be a precise translation, and by

no means a paraphrase or a broadly approximate rendering. On the one hand, the scholars were almost as familiar with the original languages of the Bible as with their native English. On the other hand, their reverence for the divine Author and His Word assured a translation of the Scriptures in which only a principle of utmost accuracy could be accepted.

In 1786 Catholic scholar Alexander Geddes said of the King James Bible, "If accuracy and strictest attention to the letter of the text be supposed to constitute an excellent version, this is of all versions the most excellent." George Bernard Shaw became a literary legend in the twentieth century because of his severe and often humorous criticisms of our most cherished values. Surprisingly, however, Shaw pays the following tribute to the scholars commissioned by King James: "The translation was extraordinarily well done because to the translators what they were translating was not merely a curious collection of ancient books written by different authors in different stages of culture, but the Word of God divinely revealed through His chosen and expressly inspired scribes. In this conviction they carried out their work with boundless reverence and care and achieved a beautifully artistic result." History agrees with these estimates. Therefore, while seeking to unveil the excellent *form* of the traditional English Bible, special care has also been taken in the present edition to preserve the work of *precision* which is the legacy of the 1611 translators.

Complete Equivalence in Translation

Where new translation has been necessary in the New King James Version, the most complete representation of the original has been rendered by considering the history of usage and etymology of words in their contexts. This principle of complete equivalence seeks to preserve *all* of the information

in the text, while presenting it in good literary form. Dynamic equivalence, a recent procedure in Bible translation, commonly results in paraphrasing where a more literal rendering is needed to reflect a specific and vital sense. For example, complete equivalence truly renders the original text in expressions such as "lifted her voice and wept" (Gen. 21:16); "I gave you cleanness of teeth" (Amos 4:6); "Jesus met them, saying, 'Rejoice!'" (Matt. 28:9); and "Woman, what does your concern have to do with Me?" (John 2:4). Complete equivalence translates fully, in order to provide an English text that is both accurate and readable.

In keeping with the principle of complete equivalence, it is the policy to translate interjections which are commonly omitted in modern language renderings of the Bible. As an example, the interjection *behold*, in the older King James editions, continues to have a place in English usage, especially in dramatically calling attention to a spectacular scene, or an event of profound importance such as the Immanuel prophecy of Isaiah 7:14. Consequently, *behold* is retained for these occasions in the present edition. However, the Hebrew and Greek originals for this word can be translated variously, depending on the circumstances in the passage. Therefore, in addition to *behold*, words such as *indeed, look, see,* and *surely* are also rendered to convey the appropriate sense suggested by the context in each case.

In faithfulness to God and to our readers, it was deemed appropriate that all participating scholars sign a statement affirming their belief in the verbal and plenary inspiration of Scripture, and in the inerrancy of the original autographs.

Devotional Quality

The King James scholars readily appreciated the intrinsic beauty of divine revelation. They accordingly disciplined their talents to render well-chosen English words of their time, as well as a graceful, often musical arrangement of language, which has stirred the hearts of Bible readers through the years. The translators, the committees, and the editors of the present edition, while sensitive to the late-twentieth-century English idiom, and while adhering faithfully to the Hebrew, Aramaic, and Greek texts, have sought to maintain those lyrical and devotional qualities that are so highly regarded in the Authorized

Version. This devotional quality is especially apparent in the poetic and prophetic books, although even the relatively plain style of the Gospels and Epistles cannot strictly be likened, as sometimes suggested, to modern newspaper style. The Koine Greek of the New Testament is influenced by the Hebrew background of the writers, for whom even the gospel narratives were not merely flat utterance, but often song in various degrees of rhythm.

The Style

Students of the Bible applaud the timeless devotional character of our historic Bible. Yet it is also universally understood that our language, like all living languages, has undergone profound change since 1611. Subsequent revisions of the King James Bible have sought to keep abreast of changes in English speech. The present work is a further step toward this objective. Where obsolescence and other reading difficulties exist, present-day vocabulary, punctuation, and grammar have been carefully integrated. Words representing ancient objects, such as *chariot* and *phylactery*, have no modern substitutes and are therefore retained.

A special feature of the New King James Version is its conformity to the thought flow of the 1611 Bible. The reader discovers that the sequence and selection of words, phrases, and clauses of the new edition, while much clearer, are so close to the traditional that there is remarkable ease in listening to the reading of either edition while following with the other.

In the discipline of translating biblical and other ancient languages, a standard method of transliteration, that is, the English spelling of untranslated words, such as names of persons and places, has never been commonly adopted. In keeping with the design of the present work, the King James spelling of untranslated words is retained, although made uniform throughout. For example, instead of the spellings *Isaiah* and *Elijah* in the Old Testament, and *Esaias* and *Elias* in the New Testament, *Isaiah* and *Elijah* now appear in both Testaments.

King James doctrinal and theological terms, for example, *propitiation, justification,* and *sanctification,* are generally familiar to English-speaking peoples. Such terms have been retained except where the original language

indicates need for a more precise translation.

Readers of the Authorized Version will immediately be struck by the absence of several pronouns: *thee, thou,* and *ye* are replaced by the simple *you,* while *your* and *yours* are substituted for *thy* and *thine* as applicable. *Thee, thou, thy* and *thine* were once forms of address to express a special relationship to human as well as divine persons. These pronouns are no longer part of our language. However, reverence for God in the present work is preserved by capitalizing pronouns, including *You, Your,* and *Yours,* which refer to Him. Additionally, capitalization of these pronouns benefits the reader by clearly distinguishing divine and human persons referred to in a passage. Without such capitalization the distinction is often obscure, because the antecedent of a pronoun is not always clear in the English translation.

In addition to the pronoun usages of the seventeenth century, the *-eth* and *-est* verb endings, so familiar in the earlier King James editions, are now obsolete. Unless a speaker is schooled in these verb endings, there is common difficulty in selecting the correct form to be used with a given subject of the verb in vocal prayer. That is, should we use *love, loveth,* or *lovest? do, doeth, doest,* or *dost? have, hath,* or *hast?* Because these forms are obsolete, contemporary English usage has been substituted for the previous verb endings.

In older editions of the King James Version, the frequency of the connective *and* far exceeded the limits of present English usage. Also, biblical linguists agree that the Hebrew and Greek original words for this conjunction may commonly be translated otherwise, depending on the immediate context. Therefore, instead of *and,* alternatives such as *also, but, however, now, so, then,* and *thus* are accordingly rendered in the present edition, when the original language permits.

The real character of the Authorized Version does not reside in its archaic pronouns or verbs or other grammatical forms of the seventeenth century, but rather in the care taken by its scholars to impart the letter and spirit of the original text in a majestic and reverent style.

The Format

The format of the New King James Version is designed to enhance the vividness and devotional quality of the Holy Scriptures:

- Subject headings assist the reader to identify topics and transitions in the biblical content.
- Words or phrases in *italics* indicate expressions in the original language which require clarification by additional English words, as also done throughout the history of the King James Bible.
- Oblique type in the New Testament indicates a quotation from the Old Testament.
- Prose is divided into paragraphs to indicate the structure of thought.
- Poetry is structured as contemporary verse to reflect the poetic form and beauty of the passage in the original language.
- The covenant name of God was usually translated from the Hebrew as LORD or GOD (using capital letters as shown) in the King James Old Testament. This tradition is maintained. In the present edition the name is so capitalized whenever the covenant name is quoted in the New Testament from a passage in the Old Testament.

The Old Testament Text

The Hebrew Bible has come down to us through the scrupulous care of ancient scribes who copied the original text in successive generations. By the sixth century A.D. the scribes were succeeded by a group known as the Masoretes, who continued to preserve the sacred Scriptures for another five hundred years in a form known as the Masoretic Text. Babylonia, Palestine, and Tiberias were the main centers of Masoretic activity; but by the tenth century A.D. the Masoretes of Tiberias, led by the family of ben Asher, gained the ascendancy. Through subsequent editions, the ben Asher text became in the twelfth century the only recognized form of the Hebrew Scriptures.

Daniel Bomberg printed the first Rabbinic Bible in 1516–17; that work was followed in 1524–25 by a second edition prepared by Jacob ben Chayyim and also published by Bomberg. The text of ben Chayyim was adopted in most subsequent Hebrew Bibles, including those used by the King James translators. The ben Chayyim text was also used for the first two editions of Rudolph Kittel's *Biblia Hebraica* of 1906 and 1912. In 1937 Paul

Kahle published a third edition of *Biblia Hebraica*. This edition was based on the oldest dated manuscript of the ben Asher text, the Leningrad Manuscript B19a (A.D. 1008), which Kahle regarded as superior to that used by ben Chayyim.

For the New King James Version the text used was the 1967/1977 Stuttgart edition of the *Biblia Hebraica*, with frequent comparisons being made with the Bomberg edition of 1524–25. The Septuagint (Greek) Version of the Old Testament and the Latin Vulgate also were consulted. In addition to referring to a variety of ancient versions of the Hebrew Scriptures, the New King James Version draws on the resources of relevant manuscripts from the Dead Sea caves. In the few places where the Hebrew was so obscure that the 1611 King James was compelled to follow one of the versions, but where information is now available to resolve the problems, the New King James Version follows the Hebrew text. Significant variations are recorded in the New King James translators' notes.

The New Testament Text

There is more manuscript support for the New Testament than for any other body of ancient literature. Over five thousand Greek, eight thousand Latin, and many more manuscripts in other languages attest the integrity of the New Testament. There is only one basic New Testament used by Protestants, Roman Catholics, and Orthodox, by conservatives and liberals. Minor variations in hand copying have appeared through the centuries, before mechanical printing began about A.D. 1450.

Some variations exist in the spelling of Greek words, in word order, and in similar details. These ordinarily do not show up in translation and do not affect the sense of the text in any way. Other manuscript differences such as omission or inclusion of a word or a clause, and two paragraphs in the Gospels, should not overshadow the overwhelming degree of *agreement* which exists among the ancient records. Bible readers may be assured that the most important differences in English New Testaments of today are due, not to manuscript divergence, but to the way in which translators view the task of translation: How literally should the text be rendered? How does the translator view the matter of biblical inspiration? Does the translator adopt a paraphrase when a literal

rendering would be quite clear and more to the point? The New King James Version follows the historic precedent of the Authorized Version in maintaining a literal approach to translation, except where the idiom of the original language cannot be translated directly into our tongue.

The King James New Testament was based on the traditional text of the Greek-speaking churches, first published in 1516, and later called the Textus Receptus or Received Text. Although based on the relatively few available manuscripts, these were representative of many more which existed at the time but only became known later. In the late nineteenth century, B. Westcott and F. Hort taught that this text had been officially edited by the fourth-century church, but a total lack of historical evidence for this event has forced a revision of the theory. It is now widely held that the Byzantine Text that largely supports the Textus Receptus has as much right as the Alexandrian or any other tradition to be weighed in determining the text of the New Testament.

Since the 1880s most contemporary translations of the New Testament have relied upon a relatively few manuscripts discovered chiefly in the late nineteenth and early twentieth centuries. Such translations depend primarily on two manuscripts, Codex Vaticanus and Codex Sinaiticus, because of their greater age. The Greek text obtained by using these sources and the related papyri (our most ancient manuscripts) is known as the Alexandrian Text. However, some scholars have grounds for doubting the faithfulness of Vaticanus and Sinaiticus, since they often disagree with one another, and Sinaiticus exhibits excessive omission.

A third viewpoint of New Testament scholarship holds that the best text is based on the consensus of the majority of existing Greek manuscripts. This text is called the Majority Text. Most of these manuscripts are in substantial agreement. Even though many are late, and none is earlier than the fifth century, usually their readings are verified by papyri, ancient versions, quotations from the early church fathers, or a combination of these. The Majority Text is similar to the Textus Receptus, but it corrects those readings which have little or no support in the Greek manuscript tradition.

Today, scholars agree that the science of New Testament textual

criticism is in a state of flux. Very few scholars still favor the Textus Receptus as such, and then often for its historical prestige as the text of Luther, Calvin, Tyndale, and the King James Version. For about a century most have followed a Critical Text (so called because it is edited according to specific principles of textual criticism) which depends heavily upon the Alexandrian type of text. More recently many have abandoned this Critical Text (which is quite similar to the one edited by Westcott and Hort) for one that is more eclectic. Finally, a small but growing number of scholars prefer the Majority Text, which is close to the traditional text except in the Revelation.

In light of these facts, and also because the New King James Version is the fifth revision of a historic document translated from specific Greek texts, the editors decided to retain the traditional text in the body of the New Testament and to indicate major Critical and Majority Text variant readings in the translators' notes. Although these variations are duly indicated in the translators' notes of the present edition, it is most important to emphasize that fully eighty-five percent of the New Testament text is the same in the Textus Receptus, the Alexandrian Text, and the Majority Text.

New King James Translators' Notes

Significant textual explanations, alternate translations, and New Testament citations of Old Testament passages are supplied in the New King James translators' notes.

Important textual variants in the Old Testament are identified in a standard form.

The textual notes in the present edition of the New Testament make no evaluation of readings, but do clearly indicate the manuscript sources of readings. They objectively present the facts without such tendentious remarks as "the best manuscripts omit" or "the most reliable manuscripts read." Such notes are value judgments that differ according to varying viewpoints on the text. By giving a clearly defined set of variants the New King James Version benefits readers of all textual persuasions.

Where significant variations occur in the New Testament Greek manuscripts, textual notes are classified as follows:

NU-Text
These variations from the traditional text generally represent the Alexandrian or Egyptian type of text described previously in "The New Testament Text." They are found in the Critical Text published in the twenty-seventh edition of the Nestle-Aland Greek New Testament (N) and in the United Bible Societies' fourth edition (U), hence the acronym, "NU-Text."

M-Text
This symbol indicates points of variation in the Majority Text from the traditional text, as also previously discussed in "The New Testament Text." It should be noted that M stands for whatever reading is printed in the published *Greek New Testament According to the Majority Text,* whether supported by overwhelming, strong, or only a divided majority textual tradition.

The textual notes reflect the scholarship of the past two centuries and will assist the reader to observe the variations between the different manuscript traditions of the New Testament. Such information is generally not available in English translations of the New Testament.

THE
OLD TESTAMENT

THE FIRST BOOK OF MOSES CALLED
GENESIS

▶ **AUTHOR:** Nowhere in the Book of Genesis is the author named. Although the events of the book end 300 years before Moses was born, the rest of the Bible and most church historians attribute the authorship of Genesis to Moses. Both the Old and New Testaments have many references to Moses as its author (Ex. 7:14; Lev. 1:1–2; Num. 33:2; Deut. 1:1; Dan. 9:11–13; Mal. 4:4; Matt. 8:4; Mark 12:26; Luke 16:29; John 7:19; Acts 26:22; Rom. 10:19). Both early Jewish and Christian writers name Moses as the author.

▶ **TIME:** c. 4000–1804 B.C.   ▶ **KEY VERSE:** Gen. 3:15

▶ **THEME:** After the initial story of the world's creation, Genesis (beginnings) covers two basic subjects: God and man. God creates man. Man disobeys God and alienates himself from God. Genesis is the story then of the subsequent interactions between God and man that bring them back together into a right relationship. As such, the book points to the beginnings of the way of change, of restoration, and of a new way of life. Genesis sets the tone for the rest of the Bible with clear teaching on following God's call, believing in His promises, and being obedient to His commands. The main characters who dominate the story are the patriarchs: Abraham, Isaac, Jacob, and Joseph.

The History of Creation

1 In the ᵃbeginning ᵇGod created the heavens and the earth. ²The earth was ᶜwithout form, and void; and darkness *was** on the face of the deep. ᵈAnd the Spirit of God was hovering over the face of the waters.

³ᵉThen God said, ᶠ"Let there be ᵍlight"; and there was light. ⁴And God saw the light, that *it was* good; and God divided the light from the darkness. ⁵God called the light Day, and the ʰdarkness He called Night. So the evening and the morning were the first day.

⁶Then God said, ⁱ"Let there be a firmament in the midst of the waters, and let it divide the waters from the waters." ⁷Thus God made the firmament, ʲand divided the waters which *were* under the firmament from the waters which *were* ᵏabove the firmament; and it was so. ⁸And God called the

---

* **1:2** Words in italic type have been added for clarity. They are not found in the original Hebrew or Aramaic.

1:1 Creation—Biblical revelation begins with a simple, strong, and sublime affirmation. Instead of arguing the existence of God, it declares that the very existence of the universe depends on the creative power of God. The world we live in was created by God and belongs to Him. His absolute ownership requires our faithful stewardship of all things.
1:1 In the beginning. No information is given to us about what happened before the creation of the physical universe, though John 1:1 speaks of this time. It is possible that the rise, rebellion, and judgment of Satan transpired before the events of this chapter. **God.** This standard Hebrew term for deity *Elohim* is in the form called the plural of majesty or plural of intensity. In contrast to the ordinary plural (gods), this plural means "the fullness of deity" or "God—very God." Furthermore, the use of the plural allows for the later revelation of the Trinity (see 11:7; Matt. 28:19; John 1:1–3).
1:3 Let there be light. These words express a principal theme of the Bible: God bringing light into darkness (see Is. 9:1–2). Here, God produced physical light. The New Testament records God sending His Son to be the light of the world (John 8:12), bringing release from the spiritual darkness of bondage to sin. In the end, there will no longer be any darkness at all and we will be face to face with the source of light (Rev. 21:23).
1:7 divided the waters. The description of upper and lower waters is somewhat mysterious; it has been theorized that this is simply a reference to the division between the water of the seas and rivers on the surface of the earth and the water vapor which is part of the atmosphere.

1:1 ᵃ [John 1:1–3] ᵇ Acts 17:24   **1:2** ᶜ Jer. 4:23 ᵈ Is. 40:13, 14   **1:3** ᵉ Ps. 33:6, 9 ᶠ 2 Cor. 4:6 ᵍ [Heb. 11:3]   **1:5** ʰ Ps. 19:2; 33:6; 74:16; 104:20; 136:5   **1:6** ⁱ Jer. 10:12   **1:7** ʲ Prov. 8:27–29 ᵏ Ps. 148:4

firmament Heaven. So the evening and the
morning were the second day.
9 Then God said, [l]“Let the waters under
the heavens be gathered together into one
place, and [m]let the dry *land* appear”; and
it was so. 10 And God called the dry *land*
Earth, and the gathering together of the
waters He called Seas. And God saw that
it was good.
11 Then God said, “Let the earth [n]bring
forth grass, the herb *that* yields seed, *and*
the [o]fruit tree *that* yields fruit according to its kind, whose seed *is* in itself, on
the earth”; and it was so. 12 And the earth
brought forth grass, the herb *that* yields
seed according to its kind, and the tree *that*
yields fruit, whose seed *is* in itself according to its kind. And God saw that *it was*
good. 13 So the evening and the morning
were the third day.
14 Then God said, “Let there be [p]lights
in the firmament of the heavens to divide
the day from the night; and let them be
for signs and [q]seasons, and for days and
years; 15 and let them be for lights in the
firmament of the heavens to give light on
the earth”; and it was so. 16 Then God made
two great lights: the [r]greater light to rule
the day, and the [s]lesser light to rule the
night. *He made* [t]the stars also. 17 God set
them in the firmament of the [u]heavens to
give light on the earth, 18 and to [v]rule over
the day and over the night, and to divide
the light from the darkness. And God saw
that *it was* good. 19 So the evening and the
morning were the fourth day.
20 Then God said, “Let the waters abound
with an abundance of living creatures, and
let birds fly above the earth across the
face of the firmament of the heavens.” 21 So
[w]God created great sea creatures and every
living thing that moves, with which the waters abounded, according to their kind, and
every winged bird according to its kind.
And God saw that *it was* good. 22 And God
blessed them, saying, [x]“Be fruitful and multiply, and fill the waters in the seas, and let
birds multiply on the earth.” 23 So the evening and the morning were the fifth day.
24 Then God said, “Let the earth bring
forth the living creature according to its
kind: cattle and creeping thing and beast
of the earth, *each* according to its kind”;
and it was so. 25 And God made the beast
of the earth according to its kind, cattle
according to its kind, and everything that
creeps on the earth according to its kind.
And God saw that *it was* good.
26 Then God said, [y]“Let Us make man in
Our image, according to Our likeness; [z]let
them have dominion over the fish of the
sea, over the birds of the air, and over the
cattle, over all* the earth and over every
creeping thing that creeps on the earth.”
27 So God created man [a]in His *own* image;
in the image of God He created him; [b]male
and female He created them. 28 Then God
blessed them, and God said to them, [c]“Be
fruitful and multiply; fill the earth and
[d]subdue it; have dominion over the fish of
the sea, over the birds of the air, and over
every living thing that moves on the earth.”
29 And God said, “See, I have given you
every herb *that* yields seed which *is* on the
face of all the earth, and every tree whose
fruit yields seed; [e]to you it shall be for food.

* **1:26** Syriac reads *all the wild animals of.*

1:11–12 ***seed . . . kind.*** God not only created plant life; He also set in motion the process that makes plant life reproduce.

1:14 ***for signs and seasons.*** Some have mistakenly viewed these words as a biblical basis for astrology. The signs in this case relate to phases of the moon and the relative positions of stars that mark the passage of time from the vantage point of earth. The two words form a pair that may be translated *seasonal signs.*

1:16 ***He made the stars also.*** This is a remarkable statement. In the ancient Middle East, other religions worshiped, deified, and mystified the stars. Israel's neighbors revered the stars and looked to them for guidance. In contrast, the biblical creation story gives the stars only the barest mention, as though the writer shrugged and said, *And, oh, yes, He also made the stars.* Such a statement showed great contempt for ancient Babylonian astrology (Ps. 29; 93).

1:24 ***living creature.*** This expression contains the word sometimes used for the soul, but the word can also mean “life,” “being,” “living thing,” or “person,” depending on the context. The same phrase is used for man in 2:7.

1:26 ***in Our image.*** Since God is spirit (John 4:24), there can be no “image” or “likeness” of Him in the normal sense of these words. The traditional view of this passage is that God's image in man is in specific moral, ethical, and intellectual abilities. A more recent view, based on a possible interpretation of Hebrew grammar and the knowledge of the Middle East, interprets the phrase as meaning “Let Us make man *as* Our image.” In ancient times an emperor might command statues of himself to be placed in remote parts of his empire. These symbols would declare that these areas were under his power and reign. So God placed humans as living symbols of Himself on earth to represent His reign. This interpretation fits well with the command that follows—to reign over all that God has made.

1:28 ***fill the earth and subdue it.*** The word translated *subdue* means “bring into bondage.” This harsh term is used elsewhere of military conquest (Zech. 9:15) and of God subduing our iniquities (Mic. 7:19). Since this direction was given before the fall, it appears that the need to subdue the earth is not because of sin but because God left part of the arranging and ordering of the creation as work for mankind to do. Whatever the case, subdue does not mean “destroy” or “ruin.” It does mean to “act as managers who have

1:9 [l] Job 26:10 [m] Ps. 24:1, 2; 33:7; 95:5 **1:11** [n] Heb. 6:7 [o] 2 Sam. 16:1 **1:14** [p] Ps. 74:16; 136:5–9 [q] Ps. 104:19 **1:16** [r] Ps. 136:8 [s] Ps. 8:3 [t] Job 38:7 **1:17** [u] Gen. 15:5 **1:18** [v] Jer. 31:35 **1:21** [w] Ps. 104:25–28 **1:22** [x] Gen. 8:17 **1:26** [y] [Eph. 4:24] [z] Gen. 9:2 **1:27** [a] Gen. 5:2 [b] Matt. 19:4 **1:28** [c] Gen. 9:1, 7 [d] 1 Cor. 9:27 **1:29** [e] Gen. 9:3

[30]Also, to [f]every beast of the earth, to every [g]bird of the air, and to everything that creeps on the earth, in which *there is* life, *I have given* every green herb for food"; and it was so. [31]Then [h]God saw everything that He had made, and indeed *it was* very good. So the evening and the morning were the sixth day.

2 Thus the heavens and the earth, and [a]all the host of them, were finished. [2b]And on the seventh day God ended His work which He had done, and He rested on the seventh day from all His work which He had done. [3]Then God [c]blessed the seventh day and sanctified it, because in it He rested from all His work which God had created and made.

[4d]This *is* the history* of the heavens and the earth when they were created, in the day that the LORD God made the earth and the heavens, [5]before any [e]plant of the field was in the earth and before any herb of the field had grown. For the LORD God had not [f]caused it to rain on the earth; and *there was* no man [g]to till the ground; [6]but a mist went up from the earth and watered the whole face of the ground.

[7]And the LORD God formed man *of* the [h]dust of the ground, and [i]breathed into his [j]nostrils the breath of life; and [k]man became a living being.

Life in God's Garden

[8]The LORD God planted [l]a garden [m]eastward in [n]Eden, and there He put the man whom He had formed. [9]And out of the ground the LORD God made [o]every tree grow that is pleasant to the sight and good for food. [p]The tree of life *was* also in the midst of the garden, and the tree of the knowledge of good and [q]evil.

[10]Now a river went out of Eden to water the garden, and from there it parted and became four riverheads. [11]The name of the first *is* Pishon; it *is* the one which skirts [r]the whole land of Havilah, where *there is* gold. [12]And the gold of that land *is* good. [s]Bdellium and the onyx stone *are* there. [13]The name of the second river *is* Gihon; it *is* the one which goes around the whole land of Cush. [14]The name of the third river *is* [t]Hiddekel;* it *is* the one which goes toward the east of Assyria. The fourth river *is* the Euphrates.

[15]Then the LORD God took the man and put him in the garden of Eden to tend and keep it. [16]And the LORD God commanded the man, saying, "Of every tree of the garden you may freely eat; [17]but of the tree of the knowledge of good and evil [u]you shall not eat, for in the day that you eat of it [v]you shall surely [w]die."

[18]And the LORD God said, "*It is* not good that man should be alone; [x]I will make him a helper comparable to him." [19y]Out of the ground the LORD God formed every beast of the field and every bird of the air,

---

* **2:4** Hebrew *toledoth*, literally *generations*
* **2:14** Or *Tigris*

---

the authority to run everything as God planned." This command applies equally to male and female.

2:2 He rested on the seventh day. God did not rest because of fatigue, but because of His accomplishment. God is never weary (Is. 40:28–29). The verb translated "rested" is related to the word for Sabbath, which means "rest." God's rest on the seventh day showed that He was satisfied with the work He had done.

2:4 the LORD God. This is a significant term. The word translated *God* is the same word as in 1:1. The word translated *LORD* is the proper name of God, Yahweh (or Jehovah; see Ex. 3:14–15). The God of chapter 1 and the LORD God of chapter 2 are one and the same.

2:6 mist. The precise meaning of this word is uncertain. Obviously it refers to some manner of irrigation before the Lord brought the cycles of rain into being.

2:7 the breath of life. Although God created light with a mere word (1:3), He created man by fashioning a body out of mud and clay, transforming the clay into something new, and then breathing life into it. This "breath of life" is something which only God can bestow. Medical knowledge enables doctors to keep a human body "alive," keeping the heart pumping and the vital organs functioning, but it does not enable them to keep or to call back the breath of life. Some have speculated that the "breath of life" is the human soul, but later on, animals are also described as having the "breath of life" in their nostrils (7:22), which would seem to indicate that this is simply a reference to the miracle of living, breathing flesh.

2:15–17 The First Covenant—In biblical times the purpose of a covenant was to establish an agreement between two persons or groups. The elements of a covenant included a promise on the part of one person and the conditions that needed to be fulfilled on the part of the other person in order for the promises to be carried out by both parties to the covenant. The Edenic covenant is the first covenant mentioned in the Bible. God gave Adam a place in His creation and charged him with the responsibility of caring for the garden. The only condition in the covenant was that Adam could not allow himself to eat of the fruit of the tree of the knowledge of good and evil or he would die. This covenant was terminated by Adam's disobedience which also resulted in man's spiritual and physical death. God then established a new covenant with Adam in Genesis 3:14–21.

2:17 shall surely die. These emphatic words are made of two forms of the verb meaning "to die." The point is not that the guilty person would drop dead on the instant, but that death would surely happen—there is no escape (Heb. 9:27).

2:18 It is not good. Until this point, everything in creation was very good.

2:19 to see what he would call them. In giving each

1:30 [f]Ps. 145:15 [g]Job 38:41   **1:31** [h][Ps. 104:24]
2:1 [a]Ps. 33:6   **2:2** [b]Ex. 20:9–11; 31:17   **2:3** [c][Is. 58:13]
2:4 [d]Gen. 1:1   **2:5** [e]Gen. 1:11, 12 [f]Gen. 7:4 [g]Gen. 3:23
2:7 [h]Gen. 3:19, 23 [i]Job 33:4 [j]Gen. 7:22 [k]1 Cor. 15:45
2:8 [l]Is. 51:3 [m]Gen. 3:23, 24 [n]Gen. 4:16   **2:9** [o]Ezek. 31:8 [p][Gen. 3:22] [q][Deut. 1:39]   **2:11** [r]Gen. 25:18
2:12 [s]Num. 11:7   **2:14** [t]Dan. 10:4   **2:17** [u]Gen. 3:1, 3, 11, 17 [v]Gen. 3:3, 19 [w]Rom. 5:12   **2:18** [x]1 Cor. 11:8, 9
2:19 [y]Gen. 1:20, 24

and ᶻbrought *them* to Adam to see what he would call them. And whatever Adam called each living creature, that *was* its name. **20**So Adam gave names to all cattle, to the birds of the air, and to every beast of the field. But for Adam there was not found a helper comparable to him.

21And the LORD God caused a ᵃdeep sleep to fall on Adam, and he slept; and He took one of his ribs, and closed up the flesh in its place. **22**Then the rib which the LORD God had taken from man He made into a woman, ᵇand He ᶜbrought her to the man.

23And Adam said:

"This *is* now ᵈbone of my bones
And flesh of my flesh;
She shall be called Woman,
Because she was ᵉtaken out of Man."

24f Therefore a man shall leave his father and mother and ᵍbe joined to his wife, and they shall become one flesh.

25h And they were both naked, the man and his wife, and were not ⁱashamed.

The Temptation and Fall of Man

3 Now ᵃthe serpent was ᵇmore cunning than any beast of the field which the LORD God had made. And he said to the woman, "Has God indeed said, 'You shall not eat of every tree of the garden'?"

2And the woman said to the serpent, "We may eat the ᶜfruit of the trees of the garden; **3**but of the fruit of the tree which *is* in the midst of the garden, God has said, 'You shall not eat it, nor shall you ᵈtouch it, lest you die.'"

4eThen the serpent said to the woman, "You will not surely die. **5**For God knows that in the day you eat of it your eyes will be opened, and you will be like God, knowing good and evil."

6So when the woman ᶠsaw that the tree *was* good for food, that it *was* pleasant to the eyes, and a tree desirable to make *one* wise, she took of its fruit ᵍand ate. She also gave to her husband with her, and he ate. **7**Then the eyes of both of them were opened, ʰand they knew that they *were* naked; and they sewed fig leaves together and made themselves coverings.

8And they heard ⁱthe sound of the LORD God walking in the garden in the cool of the day, and Adam and his wife ʲhid themselves from the presence of the LORD God among the trees of the garden.

9Then the LORD God called to Adam and said to him, "Where *are* you?"

---

animal its name, Adam demonstrated his right as God's agent (1:26–28), the one set in place as lord of the created order.

2:20 *helper comparable to him.* Some have felt that calling the woman man's helper indicates that she is inferior in value, but this is far from true. In fact, the term "help" is used to describe God Himself, when He comes to our aid. The word "helper" indicates role, not value or position. The helper Adam needed was not merely a servant or a slave, nor another man exactly like himself. He needed a complement, equal in value and with the same intelligence, personality, spirituality, and ethical and moral sense; but with different qualities and a different role, a helper who could join with him in his work of subduing the earth.

2:21 *He took one of his ribs.* God's use of Adam's rib was fitting. He might have started over with dust and clay. But by using a part of Adam himself, the identification of Adam with his partner would be ensured. As Martin Luther observed, God might have taken a bone from a toe, and thus signified that Adam was to rule over her; or He might have taken a bone from his head to indicate her rule over him. But by taking a bone from his side, God implied equality and mutual respect.

2:24 *one flesh.* This phrase suggests both a physical, sexual bonding and a lifelong relationship. They are still separate persons, but together they are as one (Eph. 5:31). In the New Testament, Jesus refers to this text as the foundation of the biblical view of marriage (Matt. 19:5). A married couple functions as "we," rather than "me and you." They are a new unit, separate from the family units they each came from. This does not mean that they will no longer relate to their extended families, but that their "one flesh" is a unit distinct from either family.

3:1 *the serpent.* With no introduction, Satan appears

in the garden of Eden. This is the first clue in Scripture of creation outside the one Adam and Eve experienced. It is interesting to note that Eve expressed no surprise at the serpent speaking to her in intelligible language.

3:3 *You shall not eat it, nor shall you touch it.* Some interpreters suggest that the woman was already sinning by adding to the word of God, for these words were not part of God's instructions in 2:17. Scripture, however, always refers to the eating of the fruit as the sin, and never comments on Eve's addition. Her words reflected the original command well enough, and indeed they would have ensured that the command would be kept.

3:5 *you will be like God.* God's fullness of knowledge was only one of the superiorities that set Him apart from the woman. But the serpent combined all of God's superiority over the woman into this one audacious appeal to her pride.

3:6–7 Sin's Consequences—At first Adam's sin does not appear to be all that significant. All he did was take a bite of some fruit. But Scripture takes it very seriously. Adam's sin was one of disobedience and rebellion. God told Adam not to eat the fruit of the "tree of the knowledge of good and evil" under penalty of death (2:17). That action of eating the fruit changed Adam's whole nature as well as his relationship with God. Adam became a sinner and as such he died. His spiritual death was immediate, the physical death progressive. Adam, who began the human race, then became the source of sin for the world. We

2:19 ᶻPs. 8:6   2:21 ᵃ1 Sam. 26:12   2:22 ᵇ1 Tim. 2:13 ᶜHeb. 13:4   2:23 ᵈGen. 29:14 ᵉ1 Cor. 11:8, 9
2:24 ᶠMatt. 19:5 ᵍMark 10:6–8   2:25 ʰGen. 3:7, 10 ⁱIs. 47:3   3:1 ᵃ1 Chr. 21:1 ᵇ2 Cor. 11:3   3:2 ᶜGen. 2:16, 17
3:3 ᵈEx. 19:12, 13   3:4 ᵉ[2 Cor. 11:3]   3:6 ᶠ1 John 2:16 ᵍ1 Tim. 2:14   3:7 ʰGen. 2:25   3:8 ⁱJob 38:1 ʲJob 31:33

[10]So he said, "I heard Your voice in the garden, [k]and I was afraid because I was naked; and I hid myself."
[11]And He said, "Who told you that you *were* naked? Have you eaten from the tree of which I commanded you that you should not eat?"
[12]Then the man said, [l]"The woman whom You gave *to be* with me, she gave me of the tree, and I ate."
[13]And the LORD God said to the woman, "What *is* this you have done?"
The woman said, [m]"The serpent deceived me, and I ate."
[14]So the LORD God said to the serpent:

"Because you have done this,
You *are* cursed more than all cattle,
And more than every beast of the field;
On your belly you shall go,
And [n]you shall eat dust
All the days of your life.
15 And I will put enmity
Between you and the woman,
And between [o]your seed and [p]her Seed;
[q]He shall bruise your head,
And you shall bruise His heel."

[16]To the woman He said:

"I will greatly multiply your sorrow and your conception;
[r]In pain you shall bring forth children;
[s]Your desire *shall be* for your husband,
And he shall [t]rule over you."

[17]Then to Adam He said, [u]"Because you have heeded the voice of your wife, and have eaten from the tree [v]of which I commanded you, saying, 'You shall not eat of it':

[w]"Cursed *is* the ground for your sake;
[x]In toil you shall eat *of* it
All the days of your life.
18 Both thorns and thistles it shall bring forth for you,
And [y]you shall eat the herb of the field.
19 [z]In the sweat of your face you shall eat bread
Till you return to the ground,
For out of it you were taken;
[a]For dust you *are,*
And [b]to dust you shall return."

[20]And Adam called his wife's name [c]Eve, because she was the mother of all living.
[21]Also for Adam and his wife the LORD God made tunics of skin, and clothed them.
[22]Then the LORD God said, "Behold, the man has become like one of Us, to know good and evil. And now, lest he put out his hand and take also of the tree of life, and eat, and live forever"—[23]therefore the LORD God sent him out of the garden of Eden [d]to till the ground from which he was taken. [24]So [e]He drove out the man; and He placed [f]cherubim [g]at the east of the garden of Eden, and a flaming sword which turned every way, to guard the way to the tree of [h]life.

---

are all sinners by nature because Adam sinned (Rom. 5:12–14). We inherit sin from Adam in our natures in the same way we inherit many of our physical characteristics from our parents. Sin is a universal part of our spiritual inheritance.

3:14–21 The Covenant with Adam—The Adamic covenant is the second covenant God made with man. It sets forth conditions that will be in effect until the curse of death is lifted (Is. 11:6–10; Rom. 8:18–23). In Christ's death and resurrection we have the beginning (firstfruits) of the lifting of the curse. The ultimate lifting of the curse will happen as Christ establishes His final reign on earth.

3:14 *to the serpent.* The Lord turned first to the serpent and brought judgment upon him. God did not excuse the woman because she was deceived, but He did bring the harsher judgment on the one who had deceived her.

3:15 Christ—This passage is sometimes referred to as the "preaching of Messiah in the garden of Eden," because it introduces the One who will deliver mankind from the power of the Tempter. The seed of the serpent, those of the human race who choose evil and thus give themselves into the control of the Evil One, would hate and destroy the Seed of the woman, who was Jesus Christ. But in that very act, Evil condemned itself. Jesus rose triumphant from the grave, having paid the blood atonement for the sin of the world and conquered death forever. Thus the Seed of woman crushed the head of the serpent.

3:16 *your sorrow and your conception.* The woman's joy in conceiving and bearing children would be saddened by the pain of it. ***desire . . . rule.*** The word *desire* can also mean "an attempt to usurp authority or control" as in 4:7. The last two lines of this verse could be paraphrased, "You will now have a tendency to try to dominate your husband and he will have the tendency to act as a tyrant." Each strives for control and neither lives in the best interest of the other (Phil. 2:3–4). The antidote is in the restoration of mutual respect and dignity through Jesus Christ (Eph. 5:21–23).

3:17–19 *Cursed is the ground . . . In the sweat of your face.* Humans sometimes tend to look upon work itself as a curse, but it is important to remember that work in itself is part of the "very good" creation. The curse on the ground simply means that work is now painful and tiresome toil instead of the pure satisfaction that it was designed to be. ***to dust you shall return.*** The word of God was sure: God had stated that they would certainly die (2:17). Now they were served notice concerning the process of aging and decay that was already at work (5:5; 6:3).

3:22 *tree of life.* Adam and Eve apparently had free access to this tree before the fall, and by continuing to eat its fruit they would live forever. The penalty for sin was not instant death, but banishment from this tree and eventual death and decay. One day this tree will be planted anew and its fruit will be for the healing of the nations (Rev. 22:2).

3:10 [k]Gen. 2:25 **3:12** [l][Prov. 28:13] **3:13** [m]2 Cor. 11:3 **3:14** [n]Deut. 28:15–20 **3:15** [o]John 8:44 [p]Is. 7:14 [q]Rom. 16:20 **3:16** [r]John 16:21 [s]Gen. 4:7 [t]1 Cor. 11:3 **3:17** [u]1 Sam. 15:23 [v]Gen. 2:17 [w]Rom. 8:20–22 [x]Eccl. 2:23 **3:18** [y]Ps. 104:14 **3:19** [z]2 Thess. 3:10 [a]Gen. 2:7; 5:5 [b]Job 21:26 **3:20** [c]2 Cor. 11:3 **3:23** [d]Gen. 4:2; 9:20 **3:24** [e]Ezek. 31:3, 11 [f]Ps. 104:4 [g]Gen. 2:8 [h]Gen. 2:9

Cain Murders Abel

4 Now Adam knew Eve his wife, and she conceived and bore Cain, and said, "I have acquired a man from the LORD." ²Then she bore again, this time his brother Abel. Now ᵃAbel was a keeper of sheep, but Cain was a tiller of the ground. ³And in the process of time it came to pass that Cain brought an offering of the fruit ᵇof the ground to the LORD. ⁴Abel also brought of ᶜthe firstborn of his flock and of ᵈtheir fat. And the LORD respected ᵉAbel and his offering, ⁵but He did not respect Cain and his offering. And Cain was very angry, and his countenance fell.

⁶So the LORD said to Cain, "Why are you angry? And why has your countenance fallen? ⁷If you do well, will you not be accepted? And if you do not do well, sin lies at the door. And its desire *is* for you, but you should rule over it."

⁸Now Cain talked with Abel his brother;* and it came to pass, when they were in the field, that Cain rose up against Abel his brother and ᶠkilled him.

⁹Then the LORD said to Cain, "Where *is* Abel your brother?"

He said, ᵍ"I do not know. *Am* I ʰmy brother's keeper?"

¹⁰And He said, "What have you done? The voice of your brother's ⁱcries out to Me from the ground. ¹¹So now ʲyou *are* cursed from the earth, which has opened its mouth to receive your brother's blood from your hand. ¹²When you till the ground, it shall no longer yield its strength to you. A fugitive and a vagabond you shall be on the earth."

¹³And Cain said to the LORD, "My punishment *is* greater than I can bear! ¹⁴Surely You have driven me out this day from the face of the ground; ᵏI shall be ˡhidden from Your face; I shall be a fugitive and a vagabond on the earth, and it will happen *that* ᵐanyone who finds me will kill me."

¹⁵And the LORD said to him, "Therefore,* whoever kills Cain, vengeance shall be taken on him ⁿsevenfold." And the LORD set a ᵒmark on Cain, lest anyone finding him should kill him.

The Family of Cain

¹⁶Then Cain ᵖwent out from the ᑫpresence of the LORD and dwelt in the land of Nod on the east of Eden. ¹⁷And Cain knew his wife, and she conceived and bore Enoch. And he built a city, ʳand called the name of the city after the name of his son—Enoch. ¹⁸To Enoch was born Irad; and Irad begot Mehujael, and Mehujael begot Methushael, and Methushael begot Lamech.

¹⁹Then Lamech took for himself ˢtwo wives: the name of one *was* Adah, and the name of the second *was* Zillah. ²⁰And Adah bore Jabal. He was the father of those who dwelt in tents and have livestock. ²¹His brother's name *was* Jubal. He was the father of all those who play the harp and flute. ²²And as for Zillah, she also bore Tubal-Cain, an instructor of every craftsman in bronze and iron. And the sister of Tubal-Cain *was* Naamah.

²³Then Lamech said to his wives:

"Adah and Zillah, hear my voice;
Wives of Lamech, listen to my speech!
For I have killed a man for wounding me,
Even a young man for hurting me.
²⁴ ᵗIf Cain shall be avenged sevenfold,
Then Lamech seventy-sevenfold."

* **4:8** Samaritan Pentateuch, Septuagint, Syriac, and Vulgate add *"Let us go out to the field."*
* **4:15** Following Masoretic Text and Targum; Septuagint, Syriac, and Vulgate read *Not so.*

4:3 *Cain brought an offering.* Genesis does not explain how the practice of sacrificial worship began, but it is clear that Adam and Eve's two sons understood the custom. Some people assume that Cain's offering was unsuitable because it was not a blood offering, and blood is required for the forgiveness of sins (Heb. 9:22). But nothing in this chapter indicates that Cain and Abel were coming to God for forgiveness. Their sacrifices were acts of worship, and as such a bloodless offering was not necessarily inappropriate (see Lev. 6:14–23). Apparently the deficiency was in Cain's heart, not in the actual offering. Abel's offering was "more excellent" than Cain's because of his faith in the Lord (Heb. 11:4).

4:8 *killed him.* The murder was stunning in its lack of precedent, its suddenness, and its finality. Jesus spoke of this ghastly event as a historical fact (Matt. 23:35).

4:17 *Cain knew his wife.* The identity of Cain's wife has long been a source of puzzlement and argument to the readers and critics of the Book of Genesis. Some have postulated that God created other humans outside of the garden of Eden, but the Scriptures give no such indication, and in fact Adam refers to his wife as "the mother of all living" (3:20). It makes the most sense to assume that Cain married one of his sisters. While this idea seems repugnant to us today, it must be remembered that Adam and Eve's children had a near perfect gene pool, and there would not have been any genetic complications with close intermarrying. God's strict prohibition against siblings and other close relatives marrying did not come until much later (Lev. 18); even Abraham's wife Sarah was his half sister. ***Enoch.*** The fact that Cain named a city after his son indicates the rapid and dramatic increase in population.

4:2 ᵈLuke 11:50, 51 **4:3** ᵇNum. 18:12 **4:4** ᶜNum. 18:17 ᵈLev. 3:16 ᵉHeb. 11:4 **4:8** ᶠ[1 John 3:12–15] **4:9** ᵍJohn 8:44 ʰ1 Cor. 8:11–13 **4:10** ⁱHeb. 12:24 **4:11** ʲGen. 3:14 **4:14** ᵏPs. 51:11 ˡIs. 1:15 ᵐNum. 35:19, 21, 27 **4:15** ⁿGen. 4:24 ᵒEzek. 9:4, 6 **4:16** ᵖ2 Kin. 13:23; 24:20 ᑫJon. 1:3 **4:17** ʳPs. 49:11 **4:19** ˢGen. 2:24; 16:3 **4:24** ᵗGen. 4:15

A New Son

25And Adam knew his wife again, and she bore a son and named him Seth, "For God has appointed another seed for me instead of Abel, whom Cain killed." 26And as for Seth, vto him also a son was born; and he named him Enosh.* Then *men* began wto call on the name of the LORD.

The Family of Adam

5 This is the book of the agenealogy of Adam. In the day that God created man, He made him in bthe likeness of God. 2He created them cmale and female, dblessed them and called them Mankind in the day they were created. 3And Adam lived one hundred and thirty years, and begot *a son* ein his own likeness, after his image, and named him fSeth. 4After he begot Seth, gthe days of Adam were eight hundred years; hand he had sons and daughters. 5So all the days that Adam lived were nine hundred and thirty years; iand he died.

6Seth lived one hundred and five years, and begot Enosh. 7After he begot jEnosh, Seth lived eight hundred and seven years, and had sons and daughters. 8So all the days of Seth were nine hundred and twelve years; and he died.

9Enosh lived ninety years, and begot Cainan.* 10After he begot Cainan, Enosh lived eight hundred and fifteen years, and had sons and daughters. 11So all the days of Enosh were nine hundred and five years; and he died.

12Cainan lived seventy years, and begot Mahalalel. 13After he begot Mahalalel, Cainan lived eight hundred and forty years, and had sons and daughters. 14So all the days of Cainan were nine hundred and ten years; and he died.

15Mahalalel lived sixty-five years, and begot Jared. 16After he begot Jared, Mahalalel lived eight hundred and thirty years,

and had sons and daughters. 17So all the days of Mahalalel were eight hundred and ninety-five years; and he died.

18Jared lived one hundred and sixty-two years, and begot kEnoch. 19After he begot Enoch, Jared lived eight hundred years, and had sons and daughters. 20So all the days of Jared were nine hundred and sixty-two years; and he died.

21Enoch lived sixty-five years, and begot Methuselah. 22After he begot Methuselah, Enoch lwalked with God three hundred years, and had sons and daughters. 23So all the days of Enoch were three hundred and sixty-five years. 24And mEnoch walked with God; and he *was* not, for God ntook him.

25Methuselah lived one hundred and eighty-seven years, and begot Lamech. 26After he begot Lamech, Methuselah lived seven hundred and eighty-two years, and had sons and daughters. 27So all the days of Methuselah were nine hundred and sixty-nine years; and he died.

28Lamech lived one hundred and eighty-two years, and had a son. 29And he called his name oNoah, saying, "This *one* will comfort us concerning our work and the toil of our hands, because of the ground pwhich the LORD has cursed." 30After he begot Noah, Lamech lived five hundred and ninety-five years, and had sons and daughters. 31So all the days of Lamech were seven hundred and seventy-seven years; and he died.

32And Noah was five hundred years old, and Noah begot qShem, Ham, rand Japheth.

The Wickedness and Judgment of Man

6 Now it came to pass, awhen men began to multiply on the face of the earth, and

---

* **4:26** Greek *Enos* * **5:9** Hebrew *Qenan*

4:25 Seth. While it is certain that Adam and Eve had other daughters, and possibly other sons as well, the death of righteous Abel and the banishment of their firstborn, Cain, had left them with no one to carry on their line for good and for the promise of the Messiah. Seth is specifically mentioned among Adam and Eve's children because it would be through his descendants that the Messiah would come. His name is related to a Hebrew verb meaning "to place" or "to set" for he was appointed to take this special place in the plan of God.
4:26 men began to call on the name of the LORD. These words can hardly mean that only now did people begin to pray to God. Rather, the verb *call* means "to make proclamation." That is, this is the beginning of preaching, of witnessing, and testifying in the name of the Lord (12:8).
5:3 one hundred and thirty years. The long lives of the people of the early chapters of Genesis have led to considerable speculation. One suggestion is that these ages were possible because of tremendously different climate and environmental conditions that were in effect before the flood.

5:5 and he died. God created humans for eternity; if Adam and Eve had not disobeyed, they would have lived forever. There is a profound sadness in Adam's death, for it reminds us of Adam's mortality—and hence our own.
5:21–24 for God took him. Only Enoch and Elijah were taken by God without experiencing death (2 Kin. 2:11). This was both a testimony of Enoch's deep faith in God (Heb. 11:5–6) and a strong reminder at the beginning of biblical history that for God's people, there is life in God's presence after our physical bodies have died.

4:25 uGen. 5:3 **4:26** vGen. 5:6 wZeph. 3:9 **5:1** aGen. 2:4; 6:9 bGen. 1:26; 9:6 **5:2** cMark 10:6 dGen. 1:28; 9:1 **5:3** e1 Cor. 15:48, 49 fGen. 4:25 **5:4** gLuke 3:36–38 hGen. 5:8; 4:25 **5:5** i[Heb. 9:27] **5:7** jGen. 4:26 **5:18** kJude 14, 15 **5:22** lGen. 6:9; 17:1; 24:40; 48:15 **5:24** m2 Kin. 2:11 nHeb. 11:5 **5:29** oLuke 3:36 pGen. 3:17–19; 4:11 **5:32** qGen. 6:10; 7:13 rGen. 10:21 **6:1** aGen. 1:28

daughters were born to them, ²that the sons of God saw the daughters of men, that they *were* beautiful; and they ᵇtook wives for themselves of all whom they chose.

³And the LORD said, ᶜ"My Spirit shall not ᵈstrive* with man forever, ᵉfor he *is* indeed flesh; yet his days shall be one hundred and twenty years." ⁴There were giants on the earth in those ᶠdays, and also afterward, when the sons of God came in to the daughters of men and they bore *children* to them. Those *were* the mighty men who *were* of old, men of renown.

⁵Then the LORD* saw that the wickedness of man *was* great in the earth, and *that* every ᵍintent of the thoughts of his heart *was* only evil continually. ⁶And ʰthe LORD was sorry that He had made man on the earth, and ⁱHe was grieved in His ʲheart. ⁷So the LORD said, "I will ᵏdestroy man whom I have created from the face of the earth, both man and beast, creeping thing and birds of the air, for I am sorry that I have made them." ⁸But Noah ˡfound grace in the eyes of the LORD.

Noah Pleases God

⁹This is the genealogy of Noah. ᵐNoah was a just man, perfect in his generations. Noah ⁿwalked with God. ¹⁰And Noah begot three sons: ᵒShem, Ham, and Japheth.

¹¹The earth also was corrupt ᵖbefore God, and the earth was ᵍfilled with violence. ¹²So God ʳlooked upon the earth, and indeed it was corrupt; for ˢall flesh had corrupted their way on the earth.

The Ark Prepared

¹³And God said to Noah, ᵗ"The end of all flesh has come before Me, for the earth is filled with violence through them; ᵘand behold, ᵛI will destroy them with the earth. ¹⁴Make yourself an ark of gopherwood; make rooms in the ark, and cover it inside and outside with pitch. ¹⁵And this is how you shall make it: The length of the ark *shall be* three hundred cubits, its width fifty cubits, and its height thirty cubits. ¹⁶You shall make a window for the ark, and you shall finish it to a cubit from above; and set the door of the ark in its side. You shall make it *with* lower, second, and third *decks*. ¹⁷ʷAnd behold, I Myself am bringing ˣfloodwaters on the earth, to destroy from under heaven all flesh in which *is* the breath of life; everything that *is* on the earth shall ʸdie. ¹⁸But I will establish My ᶻcovenant with you; and ᵃyou

---

* **6:3** Septuagint, Syriac, Targum, and Vulgate read *abide*. * **6:5** Following Masoretic Text and Targum; Vulgate reads *God;* Septuagint reads *LORD God.*

6:2 sons of God . . . daughters of men. This passage is very difficult to interpret. Some believe that the "sons of God" were the men of the righteous line of Seth, while the "daughters of men" were Cain's offspring. This does not account for the fact that their offspring were giants, men of extraordinary size and talents; it is also problematic in that it assumes that Cain's descendants were universally more sinful than Seth's descendants. Since Noah was the only descendant of Seth who was considered righteous, this is obviously not accurate. A second view is that the "sons of God" were angelic beings. The phrase "sons of God" is used elsewhere in Scripture to refer to angelic beings (Job 1:6), but it seems impossible since angels in heaven do not marry (Matt. 22:30). It may be, however, that these "sons of God" were some of the rebellious angels who had joined Satan (2 Pet. 2:4; Jude 6); they took on human form (as Satan was apparently able to take on the form of a snake), and out of perverted lust, seduced human women. The problem with this theory is that verse 4 says that these unions produced children. Nothing in the rest of Scripture would indicate that angels reproduce, or that a spirit being could mate with a human being. Nor is there any reference to half-man/half-spirit beings. Whichever view one settles on, it is clear that what happened here was corrupt and one of the reasons for the flood.

6:11 corrupt. The verb translated *corrupt* has the idea of being ruined, spoiled, or destroyed. Sinful people were bringing ruin to the world that belonged to the living God (Ps. 24:1).

6:11–13 Disobedience—In the beginning, God pronounced His creative work good. But with the entrance of sin and decadence on the scene, the world became corrupt in His sight. It was not merely

that some individuals or groups had corrupted their ways, but a matter of pervasive perversity. Because sin is repugnant to His holiness, God declared His purpose of destroying both mankind and the earth he had polluted. Defying God's will affects our environment as well as ourselves. Judgment for disobedience is only averted through repentance and fresh submission to God.

6:14 ark. The word *ark* simply means "box." The same word is used for the box in which the baby Moses was placed in the Nile (Ex. 2:3), and for the gold-covered chest which contained the stone tablets of the covenant (Ex. 25:10). We usually picture Noah's ark as a huge ship, with curved bow and stern, but it was very likely more like a large box. It was not designed for navigation, but simply to stay safely afloat.

6:15 cubits. A cubit was supposed to be the measurement of a man's forearm, from the tip of the bent elbow to the fingertips. This is naturally a somewhat imprecise measurement, but it is generally considered to equal about 18 inches. Hence the ark was about 450 feet long, 75 feet wide, and 45 feet high.

6:17 I Myself. The Hebrew text places significant emphasis on the personal role of God in the ensuing storm.

6:18–19 covenant. This is the first time the word *covenant* is used in the Bible. The details of this covenant

---

6:2 ᵇ Deut. 7:3, 4 **6:3** ᶜ [Gal. 5:16, 17] ᵈ 2 Thess. 2:7 ᵉ Ps. 78:39 **6:4** ᶠ Num. 13:32, 33 **6:5** ᵍ Gen. 8:21 **6:6** ʰ 1 Sam. 15:11, 29 ⁱ Is. 63:10 ʲ Mark 3:5 **6:7** ᵏ Gen. 7:4, 23 **6:8** ˡ Gen. 19:19 **6:9** ᵐ 2 Pet. 2:5 ⁿ Gen. 5:22, 24 **6:10** ᵒ Gen. 5:32; 7:13 **6:11** ᵖ Rom. 2:13 ᵍ Ezek. 8:17 **6:12** ʳ Ps. 14:2; 53:2, 3 ˢ Ps. 14:1–3 **6:13** ᵗ 1 Pet. 4:7 ᵘ Gen. 6:17 ᵛ 2 Pet. 2:4–10 **6:17** ʷ 2 Pet. 2:5 ˣ 2 Pet. 3:6 ʸ Luke 16:22 **6:18** ᶻ Gen. 8:20—9:17; 17:7 ᵃ Gen. 7:1, 7, 13

shall go into the ark—you, your sons, your wife, and your sons' wives with you. 19And of every living thing of all flesh you shall bring *b*two of every *sort* into the ark, to keep *them* alive with you; they shall be male and female. 20Of the birds after their kind, of animals after their kind, and of every creeping thing of the earth after its kind, two of every *kind* *c*will come to you to keep *them* alive. 21And you shall take for yourself of all food that is eaten, and you shall gather *it* to yourself; and it shall be food for you and for them."

22*d*Thus Noah did; *e*according to all that *f*God commanded him, so he did.

The Great Flood

7 Then the *a*LORD said to Noah, *b*"Come into the ark, you and all your household, because I have seen *that* you *are* righteous before Me in this generation. 2You shall take with you seven each of every *d*clean animal, a male and his female; *e*two each of animals that *are* unclean, a male and his female; 3also seven each of birds of the air, male and female, to keep the species alive on the face of all the earth. 4For after *f*seven more days I will cause it to rain on the earth *g*forty days and forty nights, and I will destroy from the face of the earth all living things that I have made." 5*h*And Noah did according to all that the LORD commanded him. 6Noah *was* *i*six hundred years old when the floodwaters were on the earth.

7*i*So Noah, with his sons, his wife, and his sons' wives, went into the ark because of the waters of the flood. 8Of clean animals, of animals that *are* unclean, of birds, and of everything that creeps on the earth, 9two by two they went into the ark to Noah, male and female, as God had commanded Noah. 10And it came to pass after seven days that the waters of the flood were on

the earth. 11In the six hundredth year of Noah's life, in the second month, on *k*that day all *l*the fountains of the great deep were broken up, and the *m*windows of heaven were opened. 12*n*And the rain was on the earth forty days and forty nights.

13On the very same day Noah and Noah's sons, Shem, Ham, and Japheth, and Noah's wife and the three wives of his sons with them, entered the ark— 14*o*they and every beast after its kind, all cattle after their kind, every creeping thing that creeps on the earth after its kind, and every bird after its kind, every bird of every *p*sort. 15And they *q*went into the ark to Noah, two by two, of all flesh in which *is* the breath of life. 16So those that entered, male and female of all flesh, went in *r*as God had commanded him; and the LORD shut him in.

17*s*Now the flood was on the earth forty days. The waters increased and lifted up the ark, and it rose high above the earth. 18The waters prevailed and greatly increased on the earth, *t*and the ark moved about on the surface of the waters. 19And the waters prevailed exceedingly on the earth, and all the high hills under the whole heaven were covered. 20The waters prevailed fifteen cubits upward, and the mountains were covered. 21*u*And all flesh died that moved on the earth: birds and cattle and beasts and every creeping thing that creeps on the earth, and every man. 22All in *v*whose nostrils *was* the breath of the spirit* of life, all that *was* on the dry *land*, died. 23So He destroyed all living things which were on the face of the ground: both man and cattle, creeping thing and bird of the air. They were destroyed from the earth. Only *w*Noah and those who *were* with him in the ark remained *alive*. 24*x*And the waters

---

* 7:22 Septuagint and Vulgate omit *of the spirit.*

---

were given after the flood (9:9). Here, in the midst of judgment, the Lord stooped down to meet the needs of His servant (Ps. 40:1; 113:6) and to enter into a binding oath with him.

7:9 they went into the ark to Noah. The gathering and cooperation of the animals must have been arranged by God. It appears that after Noah and his wife and sons entered the ark, the animals followed of their own accord.

7:11 fountains of the great deep . . . windows of heaven. Until this time, no rain had fallen on the earth, but it was watered by a mist (2:5–6). This description of the first rain portrays a thundering, catastrophic event, accompanied by violent upheaval of the earth's crust and geysers of water bursting from the depths. The violence and the amount of water involved are more than enough to account for many peculiarities of the earth's surface, such as the formation of the Grand Canyon. The flood also explains the enormous quantity of fossilized remains of plants, animals, and shellfish that are buried in layers of rock over the entire surface of the earth and even on the tops of mountains.

7:16 shut him in. The Lord who had drawn them now

closed the door on them. That shut door was a symbol of closure, safety, and God's deliverance.

7:19 the high hills under the whole heaven were covered. This explicit declaration, accompanied by the assertion in verse 21 that every living thing died, makes it clear that this was no localized event, but in actuality a worldwide catastrophic flood (see 8:5). Jesus affirmed the historicity of the "days of Noah" when he compared them to the end days (Matt. 24:37–38; Luke 17:26–27). Peter similarly used the story of Noah and the flood as a pattern for the final judgment (1 Pet. 3:20; 2 Pet. 2:5; 3:5–6).

6:19 *b* Gen. 7:2, 8, 9, 14–16 **6:20** *c* Gen. 7:9, 15
6:22 *d* Gen. 7:5; 12:4, 5 *e* Gen. 7:5, 9, 16 *f* [1 John 5:3]
7:1 *a* Matt. 11:28 *b* Matt. 24:38 *c* Gen. 6:9 **7:2** *d* Lev. 11
e Lev. 10:10 **7:4** *f* Gen. 7:10 *g* Gen. 7:12, 17 **7:5** *h* Gen.
6:22 **7:6** *i* Gen. 5:4, 32 **7:7** *j* Matt. 24:38 **7:11** *k* Matt.
24:39 *l* Gen. 8:2 *m* Ps. 78:23 **7:12** *n* Gen. 7:4, 17
7:14 *o* Gen. 6:19 *p* Gen. 1:21 **7:15** *q* Gen. 6:19, 20; 7:9
7:16 *r* Gen. 7:2, 3 **7:17** *s* Gen. 7:4, 12; 8:6 **7:18** *t* Ps.
104:26 **7:21** *u* Gen. 6:7, 13, 17; 7:4 **7:22** *v* Gen. 2:7
7:23 *w* 2 Pet. 2:5 **7:24** *x* Gen. 8:3, 4

prevailed on the earth one hundred and fifty days.

Noah's Deliverance

8 Then God *ᵃ*remembered Noah, and every living thing, and all the animals that *were* with him in the ark. *ᵇ*And God made a wind to pass over the earth, and the waters subsided. 2*ᶜ*The fountains of the deep and the windows of heaven were also *ᵈ*stopped, and *ᵉ*the rain from heaven was restrained. 3And the waters receded continually from the earth. At the end *ᶠ*of the hundred and fifty days the waters decreased. 4Then the ark rested in the seventh month, the seventeenth day of the month, on the mountains of Ararat. 5And the waters decreased continually until the tenth month. In the tenth *month,* on the first *day* of the month, the tops of the mountains were seen.

6So it came to pass, at the end of forty days, that Noah *ᵍ*opened the window of the ark which he had made. 7Then he sent out a raven, which kept going to and fro until the waters had dried up from the earth. 8He also sent out from himself a dove, to see if the waters had receded from the face of the ground. 9But the dove found no resting place for the sole of her foot, and she returned into the ark to him, for the waters *were* on the face of the whole earth. So he put out his hand and took her, and drew her into the ark to himself. 10And he waited yet another seven days, and again he sent the dove out from the ark. 11Then the dove came to him in the evening, and behold, a freshly plucked olive leaf *was* in her mouth; and Noah knew that the waters had receded from the earth. 12So he waited yet another seven days and sent out the dove, which did not return again to him anymore.

13And it came to pass in the six hundred and first year, in the first *month,* the first *day* of the month, that the waters were dried up from the earth; and Noah removed the covering of the ark and looked,

and indeed the surface of the ground was dry. 14And in the second month, on the twenty-seventh day of the month, the earth was dried.

15Then God spoke to Noah, saying, 16"Go out of the ark, *ʰ*you and your wife, and your sons and your sons' wives with you. 17Bring out with you every living thing of all flesh that *is* with you: birds and cattle and every creeping thing that creeps on the earth, so that they may abound on the earth, and *ᶦ*be fruitful and multiply on the earth." 18So Noah went out, and his sons and his wife and his sons' wives with him. 19Every animal, every creeping thing, every bird, *and* whatever creeps on the earth, according to their families, went out of the ark.

God's Covenant with Creation

20Then Noah built an *ʲ*altar to the LORD, and took of *ᵏ*every clean animal and of every clean bird, and offered *ˡ*burnt offerings on the altar. 21And the LORD smelled *ᵐ*a soothing aroma. Then the LORD said in His heart, "I will never again *ⁿ*curse the ground for man's sake, although the *ᵒ*imagination of man's heart *is* evil from his youth; *ᵖ*nor will I again destroy every living thing as I have done.

22 "While the earth *ᑫ*remains,
    Seedtime and harvest,
    Cold and heat,
    Winter and summer,
    And *ʳ*day and night
    Shall not cease."

9 So God blessed Noah and his sons, and said to them: *ᵃ*"Be fruitful and multiply, and fill the earth.* 2*ᵇ*And the fear of you and the dread of you shall be on every beast of the earth, on every bird of the air, on all that move *on* the earth, and on all the fish of the sea. They are given into your hand. 3*ᶜ*Every moving thing that lives shall be food for you. I have given you *ᵈ*all

---

* **9:1** Compare Genesis 1:28

8:14 the earth was dried. After more than a full year, the waters had returned to their place (7:11). As in the beginning, God brought the waters of earth into their place (1:9–13). The flood began in Noah's 600th year, in the 2nd month, on day 17 (7:11) and ended in Noah's 601st year, in the 2nd month, on day 27 (8:14).
8:20 an altar. This is the first mention of sacrificial worship since the days of Cain and Abel (4:3–5); yet we may assume that the principle of sacrificial worship was perpetuated through the line of faithful people (ch. 5).
8:22 While the earth remains. The words of this verse are a poem of powerful effect. These words might easily have become a song of faith, the response of the people of God to the promise He made (v. 21). Later in Israel's history, the prophets recalled God's great promise to Noah (Is. 54:9–10).
9:1–19 God's Promise to Noah—Only when we think of God as Creator, as well as Redeemer, can we begin to understand His covenant of redemption

as being related to the covenant of creation (Gen. 1:26–30; 2:15–17). God doesn't abandon His creation. On the contrary, though evil has corrupted it, He graciously (for it is undeserved) establishes a covenantal relationship with Noah's descendants as well as with every beast of the earth. This note of universality is given further expression by Hosea (2:18) and Jonah (4:11). When Paul encourages Roman believers about struggles in this life, he reminds them that they are not alone, but assures them that the whole creation also groans and suffers, eagerly anticipating that final

---

8:1 *ᵃ*Gen. 19:29 *ᵇ*Ex. 14:21; 15:10 **8:2** *ᶜ*Gen. 7:11 *ᵈ*Deut. 11:17 *ᵉ*Job 38:37 **8:3** *ᶠ*Gen. 7:24 **8:6** *ᵍ*Gen. 6:16 **8:16** *ʰ*Gen. 7:13 **8:17** *ᶦ*Gen. 1:22, 28; 9:1, 7 **8:20** *ʲ*Gen. 12:7 *ᵏ*Lev. 11 *ˡ*Ex. 10:25 **8:21** *ᵐ*Ex. 29:18, 25 *ⁿ*Gen. 3:17; 6:7, 13, 17 *ᵒ*Gen. 6:5; 11:6 *ᵖ*Gen. 9:11, 15 **8:22** *ᑫ*Is. 54:9 *ʳ*Jer. 33:20, 25 **9:1** *ᵃ*Gen. 1:28, 29; 8:17; 9:7, 19; 10:32 **9:2** *ᵇ*Ps. 8:6 **9:3** *ᶜ*Deut. 12:15; 14:3, 9, 11 *ᵈ*Rom. 14:14, 20

things, even as the egreen herbs. 4fBut you shall not eat flesh with its life, *that is,* its blood. 5Surely for your lifeblood I will demand *a reckoning;* gfrom the hand of every beast I will require it, and hfrom the hand of man. From the hand of every iman's brother I will require the life of man.

6 "Whoever jsheds man's blood,
    By man his blood shall be shed;
  kFor in the image of God
    He made man.
7 And as for you, lbe fruitful and
      multiply;
    Bring forth abundantly in the
      earth
    And multiply in it."

8Then God spoke to Noah and to his sons with him, saying: 9"And as for Me, mbehold, I establish nMy covenant with you and with your descendants* after you, 10oand with every living creature that *is* with you: the birds, the cattle, and every beast of the earth with you, of all that go out of the ark, every beast of the earth. 11Thus pI establish My covenant with you: Never again shall all flesh be cut off by the waters of the flood; never again shall there be a flood to destroy the earth."

12And God said: q"This *is* the sign of the covenant which I make between Me and you, and every living creature that *is* with you, for perpetual generations: 13I set rMy rainbow in the cloud, and it shall be for the sign of the covenant between Me and the earth. 14It shall be, when I bring a cloud over the earth, that the rainbow shall be seen in the cloud; 15and sI will remember My covenant which *is* between Me and you and every living creature of all flesh; the waters shall never again become a flood to destroy all flesh. 16The rainbow shall be in the cloud, and I will look on it to remember tthe everlasting covenant between God and every living creature of all flesh that *is* on the earth." 17And God said to Noah, "This *is* the sign of the covenant which I

have established between Me and all flesh that *is* on the earth."

Noah and His Sons

18Now the sons of Noah who went out of the ark were Shem, Ham, and Japheth. uAnd Ham *was* the father of Canaan. 19vThese three *were* the sons of Noah, wand from these the whole earth was populated.

20And Noah began *to be* xa farmer, and he planted a vineyard. 21Then he drank of the wine yand was drunk, and became uncovered in his tent. 22And Ham, the father of Canaan, saw the nakedness of his father, and told his two brothers outside. 23zBut Shem and Japheth took a garment, laid *it* on both their shoulders, and went backward and covered the nakedness of their father. Their faces *were* turned away, and they did not see their father's nakedness.

24So Noah awoke from his wine, and knew what his younger son had done to him. 25Then he said:

a"Cursed *be* Canaan;
   A bservant of servants
   He shall be to his brethren."

26And he said:

c"Blessed *be* the LORD,
   The God of Shem,
   And may Canaan be his servant.
27 May God denlarge Japheth,
   eAnd may he dwell in the tents of Shem;
   And may Canaan be his servant."

28And Noah lived after the flood three hundred and fifty years. 29So all the days of Noah were nine hundred and fifty years; and he died.

Nations Descended from Noah

10 Now this *is* the genealogy of the sons of Noah: Shem, Ham, and Japheth.

---

* **9:9** Literally *seed*

---

redemption from the curse of sin. The promise given here is to never destroy the earth again by flood (v. 11). The rainbow is then a testimony of the existence of this promise.

9:4 blood. This restriction gets more attention in Leviticus (see Lev. 17:11–12). Blood represents the animal's life. It may be used in sacrifice, for all life belongs to the Lord.

9:6 image of God. Sin did not destroy man as the image of God. God values human life more highly than animal life because only humankind possesses God's image.

9:9 covenant. This is the second occurrence in Genesis of the important concept of covenant (6:18). God promised that He would establish His covenant with Noah and here He accomplished this great work.

9:26–27 Shem. Shem was given precedence over his brothers. Eber and Abram were descended from Shem (11:10–30), so Shem's blessing is ultimately a blessing on Israel.

9:29 and he died. Noah's death was the end of an era. Only he and his family spanned two worlds, that of the earth before and after the flood. His long life (950 years) gave him opportunity to transmit to his many descendants the dramatic story that he had lived out with his family. Peoples in places and cultures the world over have memories and stories of a great flood in antiquity. The details differ, but the stories remain.

9:3 e Gen. 1:29 **9:4** f 1 Sam. 14:33, 34 **9:5** g Ex. 21:28 h Gen. 4:9, 10 i Acts 17:26 **9:6** j Lev. 24:17 k Gen. 1:26, 27 **9:7** l Gen. 9:1, 19 **9:9** m Gen. 6:18 n Is. 54:9 **9:10** o Ps. 145:9 **9:11** p Is. 54:9 **9:12** q Gen. 9:13, 17; 17:11 **9:13** r Ezek. 1:28 **9:15** s Lev. 26:42, 45 **9:16** t Gen. 17:13, 19 **9:18** u Gen. 9:25–27; 10:6 **9:19** v Gen. 5:32 w 1 Chr. 1:4 **9:20** x Gen. 3:19, 23; 4:2 **9:21** y Prov. 20:1 **9:23** z Ex. 20:12 **9:25** a Deut. 27:16 b Josh. 9:23 **9:26** c Gen. 14:20; 24:27 **9:27** d Gen. 10:2–5; 39:3 e Eph. 2:13; 14; 3:6

ᵃAnd sons were born to them after the flood.

2ᵇThe sons of Japheth *were* Gomer, Magog, Madai, Javan, Tubal, Meshech, and Tiras. 3The sons of Gomer *were* Ashkenaz, Riphath,* and Togarmah. 4The sons of Javan *were* Elishah, Tarshish, Kittim, and Dodanim.* 5From these ᶜthe coastland *peoples* of the Gentiles were separated into their lands, everyone according to his language, according to their families, into their nations.

6ᵈThe sons of Ham *were* Cush, Mizraim, Put,* and Canaan. 7The sons of Cush *were* Seba, Havilah, Sabtah, Raamah, and Sabtechah; and the sons of Raamah *were* Sheba and Dedan.

8Cush begot ᵉNimrod; he began to be a mighty one on the earth. 9He was a mighty ᶠhunter before the LORD; therefore it is said, "Like Nimrod the mighty hunter ᵍbefore the LORD." 10ʰAnd the beginning of his kingdom was ⁱBabel, Erech, Accad, and Calneh, in the land of Shinar. 11From that land he went to ʲAssyria and built Nineveh, Rehoboth Ir, Calah, 12and Resen between Nineveh and Calah (that *is* the principal city).

13Mizraim begot Ludim, Anamim, Lehabim, Naphtuhim, 14Pathrusim, and Casluhim ᵏ(from whom came the Philistines and Caphtorim).

15Canaan begot Sidon his firstborn, and ˡHeth; 16ᵐthe Jebusite, the Amorite, and the Girgashite; 17the Hivite, the Arkite, and the Sinite; 18the Arvadite, the Zemarite, and the Hamathite. Afterward the families of the Canaanites were dispersed. 19ⁿAnd the border of the Canaanites was from Sidon as you go toward Gerar, as far as Gaza; then as you go toward Sodom, Gomorrah, Admah, and Zeboiim, as far as Lasha. 20These *were* the sons of Ham, according to their families, according to their languages, in their lands *and* in their nations.

21And *children* were born also to Shem, the father of all the children of Eber, the brother of Japheth the elder. 22The ᵒsons of Shem *were* Elam, Asshur, ᵖArphaxad, Lud, and Aram. 23The sons of Aram *were* Uz, Hul, Gether, and Mash.* 24Arphaxad begot �q Salah,* and Salah begot Eber. 25ʳTo Eber were born two sons: the name of one *was* Peleg, for in his days the earth was divided; and his brother's name *was* Joktan. 26Joktan begot Almodad, Sheleph, Hazarmaveth, Jerah, 27Hadoram, Uzal, Diklah, 28Obal,* Abimael, Sheba, 29Ophir, Havilah, and Jobab. All these *were* the sons of Joktan. 30And their dwelling place was from Mesha as you go toward Sephar, the mountain of the east. 31These *were* the sons of Shem, according to their families, according to their languages, in their lands, according to their nations.

32ˢThese *were* the families of the sons of Noah, according to their generations, in their nations; ᵗand from these the nations were divided on the earth after the flood.

The Tower of Babel

11 Now the whole earth had one language and one speech. 2And it came to pass, as they journeyed from the east, that they found a plain in the land ᵃof Shinar, and they dwelt there. 3Then they said to one another, "Come, let us make bricks and bake *them* thoroughly." They had brick for stone, and they had asphalt for mortar. 4And they said, "Come, let us build ourselves a city, and a tower ᵇwhose top *is* in the heavens; let us make a ᶜname for ourselves, lest we ᵈbe scattered abroad over the face of the whole earth."

5ᵉBut the LORD came down to see the

---

* **10:3** Spelled *Diphath* in 1 Chronicles 1:6 * **10:4** Spelled *Rodanim* in Samaritan Pentateuch and 1 Chronicles 1:7 * **10:6** Or *Phut* * **10:23** Called *Meshech* in Septuagint and 1 Chronicles 1:17 * **10:24** Following Masoretic Text, Vulgate, and Targum; Septuagint reads *Arphaxad begot Cainan, and Cainan begot Salah* (compare Luke 3:35, 36). * **10:28** Spelled *Ebal* in 1 Chronicles 1:22

10:2 The sons of Japheth. The listing of Japheth's descendants is briefer than the others. Among the persons and peoples mentioned is Javan, an ancient name for the Greek people. It is thought that many of Japheth's descendants migrated to Europe.

10:6 The sons of Ham. Cush is the ancient name for Ethiopia; Mizraim is a name for Egypt.

10:7–11 Nimrod. Like Lamech the descendant of Cain, Nimrod's infamy was proverbial. His territory was in the lands of the east, the fabled ancient cities of Mesopotamia. The prophet Micah would later use the name Nimrod to describe the region of Assyria, which would come under God's judgment (Mic. 5:5–6).

10:21–24 Eber. This is the name that gives rise to the term *Hebrew*, which is first used of Abram in 14:13. Eber descended from Shem, the one of Noah's sons who was appointed to carry on the messianic line. Abram was a direct descendant of Eber.

10:32 the families of the sons of Noah. Although not every ancient people group is listed in this "Table of the Nations," its clear teaching is that all the varied peoples of the earth, no matter of what land or language, are descended from Noah.

11:2 the land of Shinar. This is the region of ancient Babylon in Mesopotamia (10:10).

11:4 Pride—God divided the human race into different language groups because they had refused to obey His command to fill the earth, and had become united for an evil purpose. This does not mean that God wants the world to remain divided. Christ came

10:1 ᵃGen. 9:1, 7, 19   **10:2** ᵇ1 Chr. 1:5–7   **10:5** ᶜPs. 72:10   **10:6** ᵈ1 Chr. 1:8–16   **10:8** ᵉMic. 5:6   **10:9** ᶠJer. 16:16   ᵍGen. 21:20   **10:10** ʰMic. 5:6   ⁱGen. 11:9   **10:11** ʲMic. 5:6   **10:14** ᵏ1 Chr. 1:12   **10:15** ˡGen. 23:3   **10:16** ᵐGen. 14:7; 15:19–21   **10:19** ⁿNum. 34:2–12   **10:22** ᵒ1 Chr. 1:17–28   ᵖLuke 3:36   **10:24** �q Gen. 11:12   **10:25** ʳ1 Chr. 1:19   **10:32** ˢGen. 10:1   ᵗGen. 9:19; 11:8   **11:2** ᵃGen. 10:10; 14:1   **11:4** ᵇDeut. 1:28; 9:1   ᶜGen. 6:4   ᵈDeut. 4:27   **11:5** ᵉGen. 18:21

city and the tower which the sons of men had built. [6]And the LORD said, "Indeed [f]the people are one and they all have [g]one language, and this is what they begin to do; now nothing that they [h]propose to do will be withheld from them. [7]Come, [i]let Us go down and there [j]confuse their language, that they may not understand one another's speech." [8]So [k]the LORD scattered them abroad from there [l]over the face of all the earth, and they ceased building the city. [9]Therefore its name is called Babel, [m]because there the LORD confused the language of all the earth; and from there the LORD scattered them abroad over the face of all the earth.

Shem's Descendants

[10n]This is the genealogy of Shem: Shem was one hundred years old, and begot Arphaxad two years after the flood. [11]After he begot Arphaxad, Shem lived five hundred years, and begot sons and daughters. [12]Arphaxad lived thirty-five years, [o]and begot Salah. [13]After he begot Salah, Arphaxad lived four hundred and three years, and begot sons and daughters. [14]Salah lived thirty years, and begot Eber. [15]After he begot Eber, Salah lived four hundred and three years, and begot sons and daughters. [16p]Eber lived thirty-four years, and begot [q]Peleg. [17]After he begot Peleg, Eber lived four hundred and thirty years, and begot sons and daughters. [18]Peleg lived thirty years, and begot Reu. [19]After he begot Reu, Peleg lived two hundred and nine years, and begot sons and daughters. [20]Reu lived thirty-two years, and begot [r]Serug. [21]After he begot Serug, Reu lived two hundred and seven years, and begot sons and daughters. [22]Serug lived thirty years, and begot Nahor. [23]After he begot Nahor, Serug lived two hundred years, and begot sons and daughters. [24]Nahor lived twenty-nine years, and begot [s]Terah. [25]After he begot Terah, Nahor lived one hundred and nineteen years, and begot sons and daughters. [26]Now Terah lived seventy years, and [t]begot Abram, Nahor, and Haran.

Terah's Descendants

[27]This is the genealogy of Terah: Terah begot [u]Abram, Nahor, and Haran. Haran begot Lot. [28]And Haran died before his father Terah in his native land, in Ur of the Chaldeans. [29]Then Abram and Nahor took wives: the name of Abram's wife was [v]Sarai, and the name of Nahor's wife, [w]Milcah, the daughter of Haran the father of Milcah and the father of Iscah. [30]But [x]Sarai was barren; she had no child. [31]And Terah [y]took his son Abram and his grandson Lot, the son of Haran, and his daughter-in-law Sarai, his son Abram's wife, and they went out with them from [z]Ur of the Chaldeans to go to [a]the land of Canaan; and they came to Haran and dwelt there. [32]So the days of Terah were two hundred and five years, and Terah died in Haran.

Promises to Abram

12 Now the [a]LORD had said to Abram:

"Get [b]out of your country,
From your family
And from your father's house,
To a land that I will show you.

---

to reconcile the world to God (2 Cor. 5:19), and when we are in Christ we are not only reconciled to God, but to one another (Eph. 2:11–19). The unity God destroyed by judgment at Babel was restored by grace on the Day of Pentecost. On that day people from different nations came together to hear the gospel in their own languages.
11:7 let Us go down. The plural "Us" in this passage is similar to the language of 1:26–28. The plural pronoun emphasizes the majesty of the speaker.
11:9 Babel. There is a pun in this name that no Hebrew reader would miss. The verb for confuse sounds similar to the name of the city. **confused . . . scattered.** Because of their pride and arrogance, God scattered the peoples of the earth and confused their language, but one day peoples of all languages and cultures will unite to celebrate the grace of God's risen Son, lifting their voices together in praise of the Lamb (Rev. 5:8–14).
11:10–25 the genealogy. This genealogy shows that Abram was a descendant of Noah through Shem, just as Noah was a descendant of Adam through Seth. It is interesting to note that while the people mentioned in this genealogy lived to be very old, they did not reach the great ages of the peoples before the flood. Instead, their lives appear to be growing progressively shorter.
11:28 Ur of the Chaldeans. For generations, scholars

have believed this to be the famous Ur located near the ancient delta in the Persian Gulf where the Tigris and Euphrates Rivers flow together. More recently, some scholars have noted the tablets at Ebla that speak of an Ur in the region of north Syria and suggest that this is the city of Haran's death.
11:29 Sarai. The name Sarai means "princess," implying a person of noble birth. Later we learn that Sarai was Abram's half sister (20:12).
12:1 LORD. Even though the name Yahweh (translated LORD) is not explained until Exodus 3:14–15, it is used here to make it clear to the readers that this was the same God who later formed the nation of Israel, and who was the Creator (2:4).
12:1–3 God's Covenant with Abram—The covenant with Abram is the first covenant that pertains to the rule of God. It is unconditional, and depends

11:6 [f]Gen. 9:19 [g]Gen. 11:1 [h]Ps. 2:1 **11:7** [i]Gen. 1:26 [j]Ex. 4:11 **11:8** [k][Luke 1:51] [l]Gen. 10:25, 32 **11:9** [m]1 Cor. 14:23 **11:10** [n]Gen. 10:22–25 **11:12** [o]Luke 3:35 **11:16** [p]1 Chr. 1:25 **11:20** [r]Luke 3:35 **11:24** [s]Josh. 24:2 **11:26** [t]1 Chr. 1:26 **11:27** [u]Gen. 11:31; 17:5 **11:29** [v]Gen. 17:15; 20:12 [w]Gen. 22:20, 23; 24:15 **11:30** [x]Gen. 16:1, 2 **11:31** [y]Gen. 12:1 [z]Acts 7:4 [a]Gen. 10:19 **12:1** [a]Acts 7:2, 3 [b]Gen. 13:9

2 cI will make you a great nation;
   dI will bless you
   And make your name great;
   eAnd you shall be a blessing.
3 fI will bless those who bless you,
   And I will curse him who curses you;
   And in gyou all the families of the
      earth shall be hblessed."

4So Abram departed as the LORD had spoken to him, and Lot went with him. And Abram was seventy-five years old when he departed from Haran. 5Then Abram took Sarai his wife and Lot his brother's son, and all their possessions that they had gathered, and ithe people whom they had acquired in jHaran, and they kdeparted to go to the land of Canaan. So they came to the land of Canaan. 6Abram lpassed through the land to the place of Shechem, mas far as the terebinth tree of Moreh.* nAnd the Canaanites were then in the land.

7oThen the LORD appeared to Abram and said, p"To your descendants I will give this land." And there he built an qaltar to the LORD, who had appeared to him. 8And he moved from there to the mountain east of Bethel, and he pitched his tent with Bethel on the west and Ai on the east; there he built an altar to the LORD and rcalled on the name of the LORD. 9So Abram journeyed, sgoing on still toward the South.*

Abram in Egypt

10Now there was ta famine in the land, and Abram uwent down to Egypt to dwell there, for the famine was vsevere in the land. 11And it came to pass, when he was close to entering Egypt, that he said to Sarai his wife, "Indeed I know that you are wa woman of beautiful countenance. 12Therefore it will happen, when the Egyptians see you, that they will say, 'This is his wife';

and they xwill kill me, but they will let you live. 13yPlease say you are my zsister, that it may be well with me for your sake, and that I* may live because of you."

14So it was, when Abram came into Egypt, that the Egyptians saw the woman, that she was very beautiful. 15The princes of Pharaoh also saw her and commended her to Pharaoh. And the woman was taken to Pharaoh's house. 16He atreated Abram well for her sake. He bhad sheep, oxen, male donkeys, male and female servants, female donkeys, and camels.

17But the LORD cplagued Pharaoh and his house with great plagues because of Sarai, Abram's wife. 18And Pharaoh called Abram and said, d"What is this you have done to me? Why did you not tell me that she was your wife? 19Why did you say, 'She is my sister'? I might have taken her as my wife. Now therefore, here is your wife; take her and go your way." 20eSo Pharaoh commanded his men concerning him; and they sent him away, with his wife and all that he had.

Abram Inherits Canaan

13 Then Abram went up from Egypt, he and his wife and all that he had, and aLot with him, bto the South.* 2cAbram was very rich in livestock, in silver, and in gold. 3And he went on his journey dfrom the South as far as Bethel, to the place where his tent had been at the beginning, between Bethel and Ai, 4to the eplace in the altar which he had made there at first. And there Abram fcalled on the name of the LORD.

5Lot also, who went with Abram, had

* 12:6 Hebrew *Alon Moreh*   * 12:9 Hebrew *Negev*
* 12:13 Literally *my soul*   * 13:1 Hebrew *Negev*

---

only on God who obligates Himself in grace, indicated by the unconditional declaration, "I will." The Abrahamic covenant is also the basis of other covenants and it promises blessings in three areas: (1) *national*—"I will make you a great nation," (2) *personal*—"I will bless you and make your name great; and (3) *universal*—"in you all the families of the earth shall be blessed." The Abrahamic covenant is an important link in all that God began to do, has done throughout history, and will continue to do until the consummation of history. God blesses Abram and all his descendants through the Messiah, who is Abram's progeny and provides salvation for the entire world.

12:2–3 *I will bless you.* There are seven elements in God's promise to Abram. The number seven is often used in Scripture to suggest fullness and completeness.

12:7 *To your descendants.* The land of Canaan was a gift to the descendants of Abram. God owned the land (Ps. 24:1); it was His to do with as He pleased. The people of Canaan had lost their right to occupy the land due to their awful depravity (see 15:16). Thus God declared that this land would become the land of Israel (15:18–21; 17:6–8).

12:8 *called on the name of the LORD.* This was not a

private prayer but a public proclamation. Abram was telling others about the Lord.

12:11 *woman of beautiful countenance.* Sarai's physical beauty was remarkable considering her age. She was ten years younger than Abram, or about 65 (12:4; 17:17).

12:13 *my sister.* Sarai was Abram's half sister, the daughter of his father but not of his mother (20:12).

12:17 *the LORD plagued Pharaoh.* This is the first example of the cursing and blessing element of God's promise (see 12:2–3).

12:2 c Deut. 26:5 d Gen. 22:17; 24:35 e Gen. 28:4
12:3 f Num. 24:9 g Acts 3:25; [Gal. 3:8] h Is. 41:27
12:5 i Gen. 14:14 j Gen. 11:31 k Gen. 13:18 12:6 l Heb. 11:9 m Deut. 11:30 n Gen. 10:18, 19 12:7 o Gen. 17:1; 18:1 p Gen. 13:15; 15:18; 17:8; Acts 7:5; Gal. 3:16 q Gen. 13:4; 18; 22:9 12:8 r Gen. 4:26; 13:4; 21:33 12:9 s Gen. 13:1, 3; 20:1; 24:62 12:10 t Gen. 26:1 u Ps. 105:13 v Gen. 43:1 12:11 w Gen. 12:14; 26:7; 29:17 12:12 x Gen. 20:11; 26:7 12:13 y Gen. 20:1–18; 26:6–11 z Gen. 20:12 12:16 a Gen. 20:14 b Gen. 13:2 12:17 c 1 Chr. 16:21 12:18 d Gen. 20:9, 10; 26:10 12:20 e [Prov. 21:1] 13:1 a Gen. 12:4; 14:12, 16 b Gen. 12:9 13:2 c Gen. 24:35; 26:14 13:3 d Gen. 12:8, 9 13:4 e Gen. 12:7, 8; 21:33 f Ps. 116:17

flocks and herds and tents. [6]Now [g]the land was not able to support them, that they might dwell together, for their possessions were so great that they could not dwell together. [7]And there was [h]strife between the herdsmen of Abram's livestock and the herdsmen of Lot's livestock. [i]The Canaanites and the Perizzites then dwelt in the land.

[8]So Abram said to Lot, [j]"Please let there be no strife between you and me, and between my herdsmen and your herdsmen; for we are brethren. [9][k]Is not the whole land before you? Please [l]separate from me. [m]If you take the left, then I will go to the right; or, if you go to the right, then I will go to the left."

[10]And Lot lifted his eyes and saw all [n]the plain of Jordan, that it was well watered everywhere (before the LORD [o]destroyed Sodom and Gomorrah) [p]like the garden of the LORD, like the land of Egypt as you go toward [q]Zoar. [11]Then Lot chose for himself all the plain of Jordan, and Lot journeyed east. And they separated from each other. [12]Abram dwelt in the land of Canaan, and Lot [r]dwelt in the cities of the plain and [s]pitched his tent even as far as Sodom. [13]But the men of Sodom [t]were exceedingly wicked and [u]sinful against the LORD.

[14]And the LORD said to Abram, after Lot [v]had separated from him: "Lift your eyes now and look from the place where you are—[w]northward, southward, eastward, and westward; [15]for all the land which you see [x]I give to you and [y]your descendants* forever. [16]And [z]I will make your descendants as the dust of the earth; so that if a man could number the dust of the earth, then your descendants also could be numbered. [17]Arise, walk in the land through its length and its width, for I give it to you."

[18][a]Then Abram moved his tent, and went and [b]dwelt by the terebinth trees of Mamre,* [c]which are in Hebron, and built an [d]altar there to the LORD.

Lot's Captivity and Rescue

14 And it came to pass in the days of Amraphel king [a]of Shinar, Arioch king of Ellasar, Chedorlaomer king of [b]Elam, and Tidal king of nations,* [2]that they made war with Bera king of Sodom, Birsha king of Gomorrah, Shinab king of [c]Admah, Shemeber king of Zeboiim, and the king of Bela (that is, [d]Zoar). [3]All these joined together in the Valley of Siddim [e](that is, the Salt Sea). [4]Twelve years [f]they served Chedorlaomer, and in the thirteenth year they rebelled.

[5]In the fourteenth year Chedorlaomer and the kings that were with him came and attacked [g]the Rephaim in Ashteroth Karnaim, [h]the Zuzim in Ham, [i]the Emim in Shaveh Kiriathaim, [6][j]and the Horites in their mountain of Seir, as far as El Paran, which is by the wilderness. [7]Then they turned back and came to En Mishpat (that is, Kadesh), and attacked all the country of the Amalekites, and also the Amorites who dwelt [k]in Hazezon Tamar.

[8]And the king of Sodom, the king of Gomorrah, the king of Admah, the king of Zeboiim, and the king of Bela (that is, Zoar) went out and joined together in battle in the Valley of Siddim [9]against Chedorlaomer king of Elam, Tidal king of nations,* Amraphel king of Shinar, and Arioch king of Ellasar—four kings against five. [10]Now the Valley of Siddim was full of [l]asphalt pits; and the kings of Sodom and Gomorrah fled; some fell there, and the remainder fled [m]to the mountains. [11]Then they took [n]all the goods of Sodom and Gomorrah, and all their provisions, and went their way. [12]They also took Lot, Abram's [o]brother's son [p]who dwelt in Sodom, and his goods, and departed.

[13]Then one who had escaped came and told Abram the [q]Hebrew, for [r]he dwelt by the terebinth trees of Mamre* the Amorite, brother of Eshcol and brother of Aner; [s]and they were allies with Abram. [14]Now [t]when Abram heard that [u]his brother was taken captive, he armed his three hundred and eighteen trained servants who were [v]born in his own house, and went in pursuit [w]as far as Dan. [15]He divided his forces against

---

* **13:15** Literally *seed*, and so throughout the book
* **13:18** Hebrew *Alon Mamre*   * **14:1** Hebrew *goyim*   * **14:9** Hebrew *goyim*   * **14:13** Hebrew *Alon Mamre*

13:7 The Canaanites and the Perizzites. As in 12:6, the point of this phrase is that the land was already populated; Abram and Lot did not come into an empty region but had to compete for land for their rapidly growing herds and flocks.

13:14–17 This section forms part of the set of texts that set the stage for the Abrahamic covenant (see the list at 15:1–21). This section builds on 12:1–3,7, the passage in which God first gave His great promise to Abram.

14:3 the Valley of Siddim. This valley is most likely submerged under the waters of the Dead Sea today.

14:14 three hundred and eighteen. The fact that Abram could find this many fighting men from among his own servants is an indication of the great wealth and honor that the Lord had given him (12:2–3).

13:6 [g]Gen. 36:7   **13:7** [h]Gen. 26:20   [i]Gen. 12:6; 15:20, 21   **13:8** [j]1 Cor. 6:7   **13:9** [k]Gen. 20:15; 34:10   [l]Gen. 13:11, 14   [m][Rom. 12:18]   **13:10** [n]Gen. 19:17–29   [o]Gen. 19:24   [p]Gen. 2:8, 10   [q]Deut. 34:3   **13:12** [r]Gen. 19:24, 25, 29   [s]Gen. 14:12; 19:1   **13:13** [t]Gen. 18:20, 21   [u]Gen. 6:11; 39:9   **13:14** [v]Gen. 13:11   [w]Gen. 28:14   **13:15** [x]Acts 7:5   [y]2 Chr. 20:7   **13:16** [z]Gen. 22:17   **13:18** [a]Gen. 26:17   [b]Gen. 14:13   [c]Gen. 23:2; 35:27   [d]Gen. 8:20; 22:8, 9   **14:1** [a]Gen. 10:10; 11:2   [b]Is. 11:11; 21:2   [c]Deut. 29:23   [d]Gen. 13:10; 19:22   **14:3** [e]Num. 34:12   **14:4** [f]Gen. 9:26   **14:5** [g]Gen. 15:20   [h]Deut. 2:20   [i]Deut. 2:10   **14:6** [j]Deut. 2:12, 22   **14:7** [k]2 Chr. 20:2   **14:10** [l]Gen. 11:3   **14:11** [n]Gen. 14:16, 21   **14:12** [o]Gen. 11:27; 12:5   [p]Gen. 13:12   **14:13** [q]Gen. 39:14; 40:15   [r]Gen. 13:18   [s]Gen. 14:24; 21:27, 32   **14:14** [t]Gen. 19:29   [u]Gen. 13:8; 14:12   [v]Gen. 12:5; 15:3; 17:27   [w]Deut. 34:1

them by night, and he and his servants ˣattacked them and pursued them as far as Hobah, which *is* north of Damascus. ¹⁶So he ʸbrought back all the goods, and also brought back his brother Lot and his goods, as well as the women and the people.

¹⁷And the king of Sodom ᶻwent out to meet him at the Valley of Shaveh (that *is,* ªthe King's Valley), ᵇafter his return from the defeat of Chedorlaomer and the kings who *were* with him.

Abram and Melchizedek

¹⁸Then ᶜMelchizedek king of Salem brought out ᵈbread and wine; he *was* ᵉthe priest of ᶠGod Most High. ¹⁹And he blessed him and said:

ᵍ"Blessed be Abram of God Most High,
ʰPossessor of heaven and earth;
20 And ⁱblessed be God Most High,
   Who has delivered your enemies into
      your hand."

And he ʲgave him a tithe of all.

²¹Now the king of Sodom said to Abram, "Give me the persons, and take the goods for yourself."

²²But Abram ᵏsaid to the king of Sodom, "I ˡhave raised my hand to the LORD, God Most High, ᵐthe Possessor of heaven and earth, ²³that ⁿI *will take* nothing, from a thread to a sandal strap, and that I will not take anything that *is* yours, lest you should say, 'I have made Abram rich'— ²⁴except only what the young men have eaten, and the portion of the men who went with me: Aner, Eshcol, and Mamre; let them take their portion."

God's Covenant with Abram

15 After these things the word of the LORD came to Abram ªin a vision, saying, ᵇ"Do not be afraid, Abram. I *am* your ᶜshield, your exceedingly ᵈgreat reward."

²ᵉBut Abram said, "Lord GOD, what will You give me, ᶠseeing I go childless, and the heir of my house *is* Eliezer of Damascus?" ³Then Abram said, "Look, You have given me no offspring; indeed ᵍone born in my house is my heir!"

⁴And behold, the word of the LORD *came* to him, saying, "This one shall not be your heir, but one who ʰwill come from your own body shall be your heir." ⁵Then He brought him outside and said, "Look now toward heaven, and ⁱcount the ʲstars if you are able to number them." And He said to him, ᵏ"So shall your ˡdescendants be."

⁶And he ᵐbelieved in the LORD, and He ⁿaccounted it to him for righteousness.

⁷Then He said to him, "I *am* the LORD, who ᵒbrought you out of ᵖUr of the Chaldeans, ᑫto give you this land to inherit it."

⁸And he said, "Lord GOD, ʳhow shall I know that I will inherit it?"

⁹So He said to him, "Bring Me a three-year-old heifer, a three-year-old female goat, a three-year-old ram, a turtledove,

---

14:18 *Melchizedek.* This name means "my king is righteous." Melchizedek was a contemporary of Abram who worshiped the living God. He is described as the "king of Salem," an older, shorter name for Jerusalem. The word is based on the root from which the word *shalom* (peace) comes. Melchizedek is a mysterious figure, apparently appearing from nowhere, and with no explanation of his family or background. He is a priest of God Most High, even though there is no indication that he is of Abram's family or is a descendant of Shem. The writer of Hebrews compares Melchizedek with another priest, the Lord Jesus Christ (see Heb. 5:9; Ps. 110:4).

14:20 *blessed be God Most High.* When we bless God, we acknowledge Him as the source of all our blessings (Ps. 103:1–2). *tithe.* This is the first mention of tithing in the Bible. Even though there is no word of tithing as a command until much later (Deut. 14:22), the concept of a tenth belonging to God was apparently known. Abram's gift indicates that he considered Melchizedek a true priest of the living God; in giving this gift Abram was giving to the Lord.

14:22 *the LORD, God Most High.* Abraham identified Yahweh, translated here as "the LORD," with the most high God for whom Melchizedek was priest. This is a clear statement that he and Melchizedek worshiped the same God.

15:1–21 This section is one of the texts that present the Abrahamic covenant (see 17:1–22; 18:1–15; 22:15–18; 26:23–24; 35:9–15; compare also 12:1–3,7; 13:14–17).

15:2 *Eliezer of Damascus.* This man had the honor of being Abram's heir because Abram and Sarai had no child of their own. Some have wondered if Eliezer is also the unnamed servant of Abraham who went on the quest for a wife for Isaac (24:2–5).

15:6 *he believed.* Almost ten years had passed since the original promises were given. As Abram grew older and still had no children, it was natural for him to wonder how the promises could be fulfilled. In answer to Abram's questions, God, who had revealed Himself in word, and who had faithfully protected him and sustained him, again pledged His word of promise. Abram believed and his faith was accounted to him as righteousness. Some have thought that in Old Testament times people were saved by their good deeds rather than by faith, but this idea is mistaken. Abram was not saved because of righteous living or obedience, but by believing in God and so being declared righteous by Him. The only valid work is the work of faith (John 6:28–29; James 2:2).

15:9 *Bring Me.* Abram prepared the sacrifice, but God enacted the sign (v. 17). This emphasizes the unilateral, unconditional nature of the covenant.

14:15 ˣ Is. 41:2, 3   **14:16** ʸ Gen. 31:18   **14:17** ᶻ 1 Sam. 18:6 ª 2 Sam. 18:18 ᵇ Heb. 7:1   **14:18** ᶜ Heb. 7:1–10 ᵈ Gen. 18:5 ᵉ Ps. 110:4 ᶠ Acts 16:17   **14:19** ᵍ Ruth 3:10 ʰ Gen. 14:22   **14:20** ⁱ Gen. 24:27 ʲ Heb. 7:4   **14:22** ᵏ Gen. 14:2, 8, 10 ˡ Dan. 12:7 ᵐ Gen. 14:19   **14:23** ⁿ 2 Kin. 5:16   **15:1** ª Dan. 10:1 ᵇ Gen. 21:17; 26:24 ᶜ Deut. 33:29 ᵈ Prov. 11:18   **15:2** ᵉ Gen. 17:18 ᶠ Acts 7:5   **15:3** ᵍ Gen. 14:14   **15:4** ʰ 2 Sam. 7:12   **15:5** ⁱ Ps. 147:4 ʲ Jer. 33:22 ᵏ Ex. 32:13 ˡ Gen. 17:19   **15:6** ᵐ Rom. 4:3, 9, 22 ⁿ Ps. 32:2; 106:31   **15:7** ᵒ Gen. 12:1 ᵖ Gen. 11:28, 31 ᑫ Ps. 105:42, 44   **15:8** ʳ Luke 1:18

and a young pigeon." [10]Then he brought all these to Him and, [s]cut them in two, down the middle, and placed each piece opposite the other; but he did not cut [t]the birds in two. [11]And when the vultures came down on the carcasses, Abram drove them away.

[12]Now when the sun was going down, [u]a deep sleep fell upon Abram; and behold, horror *and* great darkness fell upon him. [13]Then He said to Abram: "Know certainly [v]that your descendants will be strangers in a land *that is* not theirs, and will serve them, and [w]they will afflict them four hundred years. [14]And also the nation whom they serve [x]I will judge; afterward [y]they shall come out with great possessions. [15]Now as for you, [z]you shall go [a]to your fathers in peace; [b]you shall be buried at a good old age. [16]But [c]in the fourth generation they shall return here, for the iniquity [d]of the Amorites [e]is not yet complete."

[17]And it came to pass, when the sun went down and it was dark, that behold, there appeared a smoking oven and a burning torch that [f]passed between those pieces. [18]On the same day the LORD [g]made a covenant with Abram, saying:

[h]"To your descendants I have given this land, from the river of Egypt to the great river, the River Euphrates— [19]the Kenites, the Kenezzites, the Kadmonites, [20]the Hittites, the Perizzites, the Rephaim, [21]the Amorites, the Canaanites, the Girgashites, and the Jebusites."

Hagar and Ishmael

16 Now Sarai, Abram's wife, [a]had borne him no *children.* And she had [b]an Egyptian maidservant whose name was [c]Hagar. [2][d]So Sarai said to Abram, "See

now, the LORD [e]has restrained me from bearing *children.* Please, [f]go in to my maid; perhaps I shall obtain children by her." And Abram [g]heeded the voice of Sarai. [3]Then Sarai, Abram's wife, took Hagar her maid, the Egyptian, and gave her to her husband Abram to be his wife, after Abram [h]had dwelt ten years in the land of Canaan. [4]So he went in to Hagar, and she conceived. And when she saw that she had conceived, her mistress became [i]despised in her eyes. [5]Then Sarai said to Abram, "My wrong *be* upon you! I gave my maid into your embrace; and when she saw that she had conceived, I became despised in her eyes. [j]The LORD judge between you and me."

[6][k]So Abram said to Sarai, "Indeed your maid *is* in your hand; do to her as you please." And when Sarai dealt harshly with her, [l]she fled from her presence.

[7]Now the [m]Angel of the LORD found her by a spring of water in the wilderness, [n]by the spring on the way to [o]Shur. [8]And He said, "Hagar, Sarai's maid, where have you come from, and where are you going?"

She said, "I am fleeing from the presence of my mistress Sarai."

[9]The Angel of the LORD said to her, "Return to your mistress, and [p]submit yourself under her hand." [10]Then the Angel of the LORD said to her, [q]"I will multiply your descendants exceedingly, so that they shall not be counted for multitude." [11]And the Angel of the LORD said to her:

"Behold, you *are* with child,
[r]And you shall bear a son.
You shall call his name Ishmael,
Because the LORD has heard your
    affliction.

15:12 horror . . . darkness. These two words give great emphasis to the meaning "an overwhelmingly dark terror." This kind of reaction to the indescribable holiness of the Lord (Is. 6:3; 40:25) is natural—Abram was about to experience the presence of the Almighty. This was a moment of profound dread and holy awe.

15:13 four hundred years. Moses wrote down the story of Abram's life from the vantage point of the generation who fulfilled this prophecy (Ex. 12:40–42).

15:17 between those pieces. This last element has profound implications. In solemn agreements between equals (parity treaties), both parties would pass between the bloody pieces of slain animals and birds. The symbol would be evident to all: "May I become like this if I do not keep my part of the agreement." But Abram was not to walk this grisly pathway. Only God made the journey in the symbols of smoke and fire. The fulfillment of the promise of God to Abram, the Abrahamic covenant, is as sure as the ongoing life of the Lord.

15:18 this land. God's promise to Abram included his descendants and the Promised One, the Seed of Genesis 3:15. But the promise also included the land of Canaan. God removed the people of Israel from the land of Canaan several times, but He never revoked His everlasting promise (17:8). The promise will be fulfilled

in its fullness when Jesus Christ returns (Is. 9:1–7). **the river of Egypt.** The "river of Egypt" may refer to the Nile, or it may be what is called today the Wadi el Arish, a smaller watercourse at the natural boundary of Egypt and the land of Israel. **the River Euphrates.** This is the northern arm of the Euphrates in Syria.

15:20 Rephaim. A people of unusually tall stature; they are called giants in 2 Samuel 21:15–22 (see Num. 13:33; Deut. 2:11; 3:11).

16:2 go in to my maid. This seems to have been an accepted practice in the ancient Middle East. If a woman was unable to bear children, she might use her servant as a surrogate mother, and adopt the child as her own.

16:11 Ishmael. The name Ishmael uses the divine name El, and means "God hears."

15:10 [s] Jer. 34:18 [t] Lev. 1:17   **15:12** [u] Gen. 2:21; 28:11   **15:13** [v] Ex. 1:11 [w] Ex. 12:40   **15:14** [x] Ex. 6:6 [y] Ex. 12:36   **15:15** [z] Job 5:26 [a] Gen. 25:8; 47:30 [b] Gen. 25:8   **15:16** [c] Ex. 12:41 [d] 1 Kin. 21:26 [e] Matt. 23:32   **15:17** [f] Jer. 34:18, 19   **15:18** [g] Gen. 24:7 [h] Gen. 12:7; 17:8   **16:1** [a] Gen. 11:30; 15:2, 3 [b] Gen. 12:16; 21:9 [c] Gal. 4:24   **16:2** [d] Gen. 30:3 [e] Gen. 20:18 [f] Gen. 30:3, 9 [g] Gen. 3:17   **16:3** [h] Gen. 12:4, 5   **16:4** [i] [Prov. 30:21, 23]   **16:5** [j] Gen. 31:53   **16:6** [k] 1 Pet. 3:7 [l] Ex. 2:15   **16:7** [m] Gen. 21:17, 18; 22:11, 15; 31:11 [n] Gen. 20:1; 25:18 [o] Ex. 15:22   **16:9** [p] [Titus 2:9]   **16:10** [q] Gen. 17:20   **16:11** [r] Luke 1:13, 31

12 sHe shall be a wild man;
His hand *shall be* against every man,
And every man's hand against him.
tAnd he shall dwell in the presence of
all his brethren."

13Then she called the name of the LORD
who spoke to her, You-Are-the-God-Who-
Sees; for she said, "Have I also here seen
Him uwho sees me?" 14Therefore the well
was called vBeer Lahai Roi;* observe, *it is*
wbetween Kadesh and Bered.

15So xHagar bore Abram a son; and
Abram named his son, whom Hagar bore,
Ishmael. 16Abram *was* eighty-six years old
when Hagar bore Ishmael to Abram.

The Sign of the Covenant

17 When Abram was ninety-nine years
old, the LORD aappeared to Abram
and said to him, b"I *am* Almighty God;
cwalk before Me and be dblameless. 2And
I will make My ecovenant between Me
and you, and fwill multiply you exceedingly." 3Then Abram fell on his face, and
God talked with him, saying: 4"As for Me,
behold, My covenant is with you, and you
shall be a gfather of many nations. 5No longer shall hyour name be called Abram, but
your name shall be Abraham; ifor I have
made you a father of many nations. 6I will
make you exceedingly fruitful; and I will
make nations jof you, and kkings shall
come from you. 7And I will lestablish My
covenant between Me and you and your
descendants after you in their generations,
for an everlasting covenant, mto be God to
you and nyour descendants after you. 8Also
oI give to you and your descendants after
you the land pin which you are a stranger,

all the land of Canaan, as an everlasting
possession; and qI will be their God."
9And God said to Abraham: "As for you,
ryou shall keep My covenant, you and your
descendants after you throughout their
generations. 10This *is* My covenant which
you shall keep, between Me and you and
your descendants after you: sEvery male
child among you shall be circumcised;
11and you shall be circumcised in the flesh
of your foreskins, and it shall be ta sign of
the covenant between Me and you. 12He
who is eight days old among you ushall
be circumcised, every male child in your
generations, he who is born in your house
or bought with money from any foreigner
who is not your descendant. 13He who is
born in your house and he who is bought
with your money must be circumcised, and
My covenant shall be in your flesh for an
everlasting covenant. 14And the uncircumcised male child, who is not circumcised in
the flesh of his foreskin, that person vshall
be cut off from his people; he has broken
My covenant."

15Then God said to Abraham, "As for
Sarai your wife, you shall not call her name
Sarai, but Sarah *shall be* her name. 16And
I will bless her and also give you a son by
her; then I will bless her, wand she shall
be *a mother xof* nations; ykings of peoples
shall be from her."

17Then Abraham fell on his face zand
laughed, and said in his heart, "Shall *a
child* be born to a man who is one hundred
years old? And shall Sarah, who is ninety
years old, bear *a child*?" 18And Abraham

---

* **16:14** Literally *Well of the One Who Lives and
Sees Me*

17:4 covenant. While the peoples who descended
directly from Abram (the nation of Israel, the Midianites, Ishmaelites, and Edomites) were certainly
numerous, Abram was "father of many" in a much
broader sense yet. The message of the New Testament reveals that God's promise to Abram is to be fulfilled in the community of faith in every nation. The
promise was so certain that his name was changed
to Abraham, as an everlasting reminder of God's
gracious covenant. Furthermore, the emphatic "as
for Me" underscores the identity of the all-sufficient
God who takes the initiative for establishing the covenantal relationship. This relationship is both spiritual
and personal, anticipating the divine pledge, "and I
will be their God." The wonder of it all is that we who
believe in Jesus Christ are part of that "multitude of
nations" who share in the faith of Abraham "who is
the father of us all."
17:5 Abram . . . Abraham. This name change is significant. Abram means "exalted father." Abraham
means "father of many"—a direct reflection of his
new role.
17:8 the land . . . an everlasting possession. The
promise clearly included the Israelite people *and*
the land of Canaan. The two are linked in the language of the covenant in chapter 15. Even though
God removed Israel more than once from the

land, He promised them ultimate possession of
Canaan.
17:13 circumcised. Circumcision in and of itself did
not make people acceptable to God. It was meant as a
tangible symbol of God's covenant in their lives, as an
outward sign standing for the inward reality of a thorough commitment to God. In the New Testament, the
apostle Paul speaks of having a "circumcised heart,"
pointing to the fact that a circumcised body means
nothing if the heart is not in accord (Rom. 2:25–29).
17:15 Sarai . . . Sarah. Both names come from the
same root, meaning "princess." No explanation is
given for the change in Sarah's name, but like the
name change from Abram to Abraham (vv. 4–5) the
new name accompanied a new relationship with God.

16:12 s Gen. 21:20 t Gen. 25:18 **16:13** u Gen.
31:42 **16:14** v Gen. 24:62 w Num. 13:26 **16:15** x Gal.
4:22 **17:1** a Gen. 12:7; 18:1 b Gen. 28:3; 35:11 c 2 Kin.
20:3 d Deut. 18:13 **17:2** e Gen. 15:18 f Gen. 12:2; 13:16;
15:5; 18:18 **17:4** g [Rom. 4:11, 12, 16] **17:5** h Neh.
9:7 i Rom. 4:17 **17:6** j Gen. 17:16; 35:11 k Matt.
1:6 **17:7** l [Gal. 3:17] m Gen. 26:24; 28:13 n Rom. 9:8;
Gal. 3:16 **17:8** o Acts 7:5 p Gen. 23:4; 28:4 q Lev. 26:12
17:9 r Ex. 19:5 **17:10** s Acts 7:8 **17:11** t Ex. 12:13, 48
17:12 u Lev. 12:3 **17:14** v Ex. 4:24–26 **17:16** w Gen.
18:10 x Gen. 35:11 y Gen. 17:6; 36:31 **17:17** z Gen. 17:3;
18:12; 21:6

^asaid to God, "Oh, that Ishmael might live before You!"

¹⁹Then God said: "No, ^bSarah your wife shall bear you a son, and you shall call his name Isaac; I will establish My ^ccovenant with him for an everlasting covenant, *and* with his descendants after him. ²⁰And as for Ishmael, I have heard you. Behold, I have blessed him, and will make him fruitful, and ^dwill multiply him exceedingly. He shall beget ^etwelve princes, ^fand I will make him a great nation. ²¹But My ^gcovenant I will establish with Isaac, ^hwhom Sarah shall bear to you at this ⁱset time next year." ²²Then He finished talking with him, and God went up from Abraham.

²³So Abraham took Ishmael his son, all who were born in his house and all who were bought with his money, every male among the men of Abraham's house, and circumcised the flesh of their foreskins that very same day, as God had said to him. ²⁴Abraham *was* ninety-nine years old when he was circumcised in the flesh of his foreskin. ²⁵And Ishmael his son *was* thirteen years old when he was circumcised in the flesh of his foreskin. ²⁶That very same day Abraham was circumcised, and his son Ishmael; ²⁷and ^jall the men of his house, born in the house or bought with money from a foreigner, were circumcised with him.

The Son of Promise

18 Then the LORD appeared to him by the ^aterebinth trees of Mamre,* as he was sitting in the tent door in the heat of the day. ²^bSo he lifted his eyes and looked, and behold, three men were standing by him; ^cand when he saw *them*, he ran from the tent door to meet them, and bowed himself to the ground, ³and said, "My Lord, if I have now found favor in Your sight, do not pass on by Your servant. ⁴Please let ^da little water be brought, and wash your feet, and rest yourselves under the tree. ⁵And ^eI will bring a morsel of bread, that ^fyou may refresh your hearts. After that you may pass by, ^ginasmuch as you have come to your servant."

They said, "Do as you have said."

⁶So Abraham hurried into the tent to Sarah and said, "Quickly, make ready three measures of fine meal; knead *it* and make cakes." ⁷And Abraham ran to the herd, took a tender and good calf, gave *it* to a young man, and he hastened to prepare it. ⁸So ^hhe took butter and milk and the calf which he had prepared, and set *it* before them; and he stood by them under the tree as they ate.

⁹Then they said to him, "Where *is* Sarah your wife?"

So he said, "Here, ⁱin the tent."

¹⁰And He said, "I will certainly return to you ^jaccording to the time of life, and behold, ^kSarah your wife shall have a son." (Sarah was listening in the tent door which *was* behind him.) ¹¹Now ^lAbraham and Sarah were old, well advanced in age; *and* Sarah ^mhad passed the age of childbearing.* ¹²Therefore Sarah ⁿlaughed within herself, saying, ^o"After I have grown old, shall I have pleasure, my ^plord being old also?"

¹³And the LORD said to Abraham, "Why did Sarah laugh, saying, 'Shall I surely bear *a child*, since I am old?' ¹⁴^qIs anything too hard for the LORD? ^rAt the appointed time I will return to you, according to the time of life, and Sarah shall have a son."

¹⁵But Sarah denied *it*, saying, "I did not laugh," for she was afraid.

And He said, "No, but you did laugh!"

Abraham Intercedes for Sodom

¹⁶Then the men rose from there and looked toward Sodom, and Abraham went with them ^sto send them on the way. ¹⁷And the LORD said, ^t"Shall I hide from Abraham what I am doing, ¹⁸since Abraham shall surely become a great and mighty nation, and all the nations of the earth shall be ^ublessed in him? ¹⁹For I have known him, in order ^vthat he may command his children and his household after him, that they keep the way of the LORD, to do righteousness and justice, that the LORD may bring to Abraham what He has spoken to

---

* **18:1** Hebrew *Alon Mamre*   * **18:11** Literally *the manner of women had ceased to be with Sarah*

17:19 *Isaac*. The name Isaac means "laughter" (see 21:1–6).

18:1 *the LORD appeared*. This was the fifth time the Lord appeared to Abraham since he came into the land of Canaan (12:7; 13:14–17; 15:1–21; 17:1–22).

18:2–3 *three men*. Verse 1 states that the Lord appeared to Abraham, then the next verse refers to "three men." It seems clear from verses 1, 13, and 17 that one of the three was the Lord Himself, and from 19:1 on the other two are referred to as angels. Apparently all three were in human form, and were able to eat the meal that Abraham had prepared. Many have speculated that this was an appearance of the preincarnate Christ.

18:19 *For I have known him*. Some translations

say, "I have chosen him." The language speaks of the intimate relationship which motivates the Lord to accomplish His purpose in Abraham (22:12).

17:18 ^aGen. 18:23   **17:19** ^bGen. 18:10; 21:2; [Gal. 4:28]   ^cGen. 22:16   **17:20** ^dGen. 16:10   ^eGen. 25:12–16   ^fGen. 21:13, 18   **17:21** ^gGen. 26:2–5   ^hGen. 21:2   ⁱGen. 18:14   **17:27** ^jGen. 18:19   **18:1** ^aGen. 13:18; 14:13   **18:2** ^bHeb. 13:2   ^cGen. 19:1   **18:4** ^dGen. 19:2; 24:32; 43:24   **18:5** ^eJudg. 6:18, 19; 13:15, 16   ^fJudg. 19:5   ^gGen. 19:8; 33:10   **18:8** ^hGen. 19:3   **18:9** ⁱGen. 24:67   **18:10** ^j2 Kin. 4:16   ^kRom. 9:9   **18:11** ^lGen. 17:17   ^mGen. 31:35   **18:12** ⁿGen. 17:17   ^oLuke 1:18   ^p1 Pet. 3:6   **18:14** ^qJer. 32:17   ^rGen. 17:21; 18:10   **18:16** ^sRom. 15:24   **18:17** ^tPs. 25:14   **18:18** ^u[Acts 3:25, 26; Gal. 3:8]   **18:19** ^v[Deut. 4:9, 10; 6:6, 7]

him." **20**And the LORD said, "Because ʷthe outcry against Sodom and Gomorrah is great, and because their ˣsin is very grave, **21**ʸI will go down now and see whether they have done altogether according to the outcry against it that has come to Me; and if not, ᶻI will know."

22Then the men turned away from there ᵃand went toward Sodom, but Abraham still stood before the LORD. **23**And Abraham ᵇcame near and said, ᶜ"Would You also ᵈdestroy the ᵉrighteous with the wicked? **24**Suppose there were fifty righteous within the city; would You also destroy the place and not spare it for the fifty righteous that were in it? **25**Far be it from You to do such a thing as this, to slay the righteous with the wicked, so that ᶠthe righteous should be as the wicked; far be it from You! ᵍShall not the Judge of all the earth do right?"

26So the LORD said, ʰ"If I find in Sodom fifty righteous within the city, then I will spare all the place for their sakes."

27Then Abraham answered and said, "Indeed now, I who am ⁱbut dust and ashes have taken it upon myself to speak to the Lord: **28**Suppose there were five less than the fifty righteous; would You destroy all of the city for lack of five?"

So He said, "If I find there forty-five, I will not destroy it."

29And he spoke to Him yet again and said, "Suppose there should be forty found there?"

So He said, "I will not do it for the sake of forty."

30Then he said, ʲ"Let not the Lord be angry, and I will speak: Suppose thirty should be found there?"

So He said, "I will not do it if I find thirty there."

31And he said, "Indeed now, I have taken it upon myself to speak to the Lord: Suppose twenty should be found there?"

So He said, "I will not destroy it for the sake of twenty."

32Then he said, "Let not the Lord be angry, and I will speak but once more: Suppose ten should be found there?"

ᵏAnd He said, "I will not destroy it for the sake of ten." **33**So the LORD went His way as soon as He had finished speaking with Abraham; and Abraham returned to his place.

Sodom's Depravity

19 Now ᵃthe two angels came to Sodom in the evening, and ᵇLot was sitting in the gate of Sodom. When Lot saw them, he rose to meet them, and he bowed himself with his face toward the ground. **2**And he said, "Here now, my lords, please ᶜturn in to your servant's house and spend the night, and ᵈwash your feet; then you may rise early and go on your way."

And they said, ᵉ"No, but we will spend the night in the open square."

3But he insisted strongly; so they turned in to him and entered his house. ᶠThen he made them a feast, and baked ᵍunleavened bread, and they ate.

4Now before they lay down, the men of the city, the men of Sodom, both old and young, all the people from every quarter, surrounded the house. **5**ʰAnd they called to Lot and said to him, "Where are the men who came to you tonight? ⁱBring them out to us that we ʲmay know them carnally."

6So ᵏLot went out to them through the doorway, shut the door behind him, **7**and said, "Please, my brethren, do not do so wickedly! **8**ˡSee now, I have two daughters who have not known a man; please, let me bring them out to you, and you may do to them as you wish; only do nothing to these men, ᵐsince this is the reason they have come under the shadow of my roof."

9And they said, "Stand back!" Then they said, "This one ⁿcame in to stay here, ᵒand he keeps acting as a judge; now we will deal worse with you than with them." So they pressed hard against the man Lot, and came near to break down the door. **10**But the men reached out their hands and pulled Lot into the house with them, and shut the door. **11**And they ᵖstruck the men who were at the doorway of the house with blindness, both small and great, so that they became weary trying to find the door.

Sodom and Gomorrah Destroyed

12Then the men said to Lot, "Have you anyone else here? Son-in-law, your sons, your daughters, and whomever you have in the city—ᵈtake them out of this place! **13**For we will destroy this place, because the ʳoutcry against them has grown great before the face of the LORD, and ˢthe LORD has sent us to destroy it."

---

do righteousness and justice. One idea in two words—"genuine righteousness."
19:2 my lords. This is a greeting of respect for special visitors.
19:5 know them. This term usually refers to sexual relations between a man and a woman (4:1); here it is referring to homosexual activity, which God has declared is an abomination (Lev. 18:22).

18:20 ʷGen. 4:10; 19:13 ˣGen. 13:13 **18:21** ʸGen. 11:5 ᶻDeut. 8:2; 13:3 **18:22** ᵃGen. 18:16; 19:1 **18:23** ᵇ[Heb. 10:22] ᶜNum. 16:22 ᵈJob 9:22 ᵉGen. 20:4 **18:25** ᶠIs. 3:10, 11 ᵍDeut. 1:16, 17; 32:4 **18:26** ʰJer. 5:1 **18:27** ⁱ[Gen. 3:19] **18:30** ʲJudg. 6:39 **18:32** ᵏJames 5:16 **19:1** ᵃGen. 18:2, 16, 22 ᵇGen. 18:1–5 **19:2** ᶜ[Heb. 13:2] ᵈGen. 18:4; 24:32 ᵉLuke 24:28 **19:3** ᶠGen. 18:6–8 ᵍEx. 12:8 **19:5** ʰIs. 3:9 ⁱJudg. 19:22 ʲGen. 4:1 **19:6** ᵏJudg. 19:23 **19:8** ˡJudg. 19:24 ᵐGen. 18:5 **19:9** ⁿ2 Pet. 2:7, 8 ᵒEx. 2:14 **19:11** ᵖGen. 20:17, 18 **19:12** ᵈ2 Pet. 2:7, 9 **19:13** ʳGen. 18:20 ˢ1 Chr. 21:15

14So Lot went out and spoke to his sons-
in-law, [t]who had married his daughters,
and said, [u]"Get up, get out of this place; for
the LORD will destroy this city!" [v]But to his
sons-in-law he seemed to be joking.
15When the morning dawned, the angels urged Lot to hurry, saying, [w]"Arise,
take your wife and your two daughters
who are here, lest you be consumed in the
punishment of the city." 16And while he
lingered, the men [x]took hold of his hand,
his wife's hand, and the hands of his two
daughters, the [y]LORD being merciful to
him, [z]and they brought him out and set
him outside the city. 17So it came to pass,
when they had brought them outside, that
he* said, [a]"Escape for your life! [b]Do not
look behind you nor stay anywhere in the
plain. Escape [c]to the mountains, lest you
be destroyed."
18Then Lot said to them, "Please, [d]no, my
lords! 19Indeed now, your servant has found
favor in your sight, and you have increased
your mercy which you have shown me by
saving my life; but I cannot escape to the
mountains, lest some evil overtake me and
I die. 20See now, this city *is* near *enough* to
flee to, and it *is* a little one; please let me
escape there (*is* it not a little one?) and my
soul shall live."
21And he said to him, "See, [e]I have favored you concerning this thing also, in
that I will not overthrow this city for which
you have spoken. 22Hurry, escape there.
For [f]I cannot do anything until you arrive
there."
Therefore [g]the name of the city was
called Zoar.
23The sun had risen upon the earth when
Lot entered Zoar. 24Then the LORD rained
[h]brimstone and [i]fire on Sodom and Gomorrah, from the LORD out of the heavens. 25So
He overthrew those cities, all the plain,
all the inhabitants of the cities, and [j]what
grew on the ground.
26But his wife looked back behind him,
and she became [k]a pillar of salt.
27And Abraham went early in the
morning to the place where [l]he had stood
before the LORD. 28Then he looked toward
Sodom and Gomorrah, and toward all the
land of the plain; and he saw, and behold,
[m]the smoke of the land which went up like
the smoke of a furnace. 29And it came to
pass, when God destroyed the cities of the
plain, that God [n]remembered Abraham,
and sent Lot out of the midst of the overthrow, when He overthrew the cities in
which Lot had dwelt.

The Descendants of Lot

30Then Lot went up out of Zoar and
[o]dwelt in the mountains, and his two
daughters were with him; for he was
afraid to dwell in Zoar. And he and his two
daughters dwelt in a cave. 31Now the firstborn said to the younger, "Our father *is* old,
and *there is* no man on the earth [p]to come
in to us as is the custom of all the earth.
32Come, let us make our father drink wine,
and we will lie with him, that we [q]may preserve the lineage of our father." 33So they
made their father drink wine that night.
And the firstborn went in and lay with her
father, and he did not know when she lay
down or when she arose.
34It happened on the next day that the
firstborn said to the younger, "Indeed I lay
with my father last night; let us make him
drink wine tonight also, and you go in *and*
lie with him, that we may preserve the lineage of our father." 35Then they made their
father drink wine that night also. And the
younger arose and lay with him, and he did
not know when she lay down or when she
arose.
36Thus both the daughters of Lot were
with child by their father. 37The firstborn
bore a son and called his name Moab; [r]he *is*
the father of the Moabites to this day. 38And
the younger, she also bore a son and called
his name Ben-Ammi; [s]he *is* the father of the
people of Ammon to this day.

* **19:17** Septuagint, Syriac, and Vulgate read *they*.

19:16 *the LORD being merciful to him.* This is the whole point of the story. God could have destroyed the city of Sodom with no word to Lot or Abraham (18:17). But because of His mercy, God's angels grabbed Lot and his family and brought them forcibly to safety. In this passage, Lot appears weak, indecisive, and unsure of whether he really wants to be rescued. However, the New Testament speaks a good word for Lot's character, calling him a "righteous man" and telling us that he was grieved by the sin he saw in Sodom and Gomorrah (2 Pet. 2:6–8).

19:22 *Zoar.* This name means "insignificant in size."

19:23–26 *brimstone and fire.* This may be simply a supernatural judgment on the cities, but some have also theorized that the fire and brimstone which "rained" down on them may have been from a volcanic eruption. In any case, it is clear that the destruction was a judgment from God, and that it was under His control.

19:26 *pillar of salt.* Near the Dead Sea, which is believed to now cover the site of Sodom and Gomorrah, there are numerous rock salt formations, including pillars about the size of a human. Jesus referred to the fate of Lot's wife as a historical fact (Luke 17:32).

19:36–38 *Moab . . . Ben-Ammi.* The shameful act of incest led to the births of two sons whose descendants (the Moabites and the Ammonites) would greatly trouble Israel.

19:14 [t]Matt. 1:18 [u]Num. 16:21, 24, 26, 45 [v]Ex. 9:21 **19:15** [w]Rev. 18:4 **19:16** [x]2 Pet. 2:7 [y]Luke 18:13 [z]Ps. 34:22 **19:17** [a]Jer. 48:6 [b]Matt. 24:16–18 [c]Gen. 14:10 **19:18** [d]Acts 10:14 **19:21** [e]Job 42:8, 9 **19:22** [f]Ex. 32:10 [g]Gen. 13:10; 14:2 **19:24** [h]Deut. 29:23 [i]Lev. 10:2 **19:25** [j]Ps. 107:34 **19:26** [k]Luke 17:32 **19:27** [l]Gen. 18:22 **19:28** [m]Rev. 9:2; 18:9 **19:29** [n]Gen. 8:1; 18:23 **19:30** [o]Gen. 19:17, 19 **19:31** [p]Gen. 16:2, 4; 38:8, 9 **19:32** [q][Mark 12:19] **19:37** [r]Deut. 2:9 **19:38** [s]Deut. 2:19

Abraham and Abimelech

20 And Abraham journeyed from ^athere to the South, and dwelt between ^bKadesh and Shur, and ^cstayed in Gerar. ²Now Abraham said of Sarah his wife, ^d"She *is* my sister." And Abimelech king of Gerar sent and ^etook Sarah.

³But ^fGod came to Abimelech ^gin a dream by night, and said to him, ^h"Indeed you *are* a dead man because of the woman whom you have taken, for she *is* a man's wife."

⁴But Abimelech had not come near her; and he said, "Lord, ⁱwill You slay a righteous nation also? ⁵Did he not say to me, 'She *is* my sister'? And she, even she herself said, 'He *is* my brother.' ^jIn the integrity of my heart and innocence of my hands I have done this."

⁶And God said to him in a dream, "Yes, I know that you did this in the integrity of your heart. For ^kI also withheld you from sinning ^lagainst Me; therefore I did not let you touch her. ⁷Now therefore, restore the man's wife; ^mfor he *is* a prophet, and he will pray for you and you shall live. But if you do not restore *her*, ⁿknow that you shall surely die, you ^oand all who *are* yours."

⁸So Abimelech rose early in the morning, called all his servants, and told all these things in their hearing; and the men were very much afraid. ⁹And Abimelech called Abraham and said to him, "What have you done to us? How have I offended you, ^pthat you have brought on me and on my kingdom a great sin? You have done deeds to me ^qthat ought not to be done." ¹⁰Then Abimelech said to Abraham, "What did you have in view, that you have done this thing?"

¹¹And Abraham said, "Because I thought, surely ^rthe fear of God *is* not in this place; and ^sthey will kill me on account of my wife. ¹²But indeed ^t*she is* truly my sister. She *is* the daughter of my father, but not the daughter of my mother; and she became my wife. ¹³And it came to pass, when ^uGod caused me to wander from my father's house, that I said to her, 'This *is* your kindness that you should do for me: in every place, wherever we go, ^vsay of me, "He *is* my brother." '"

¹⁴Then Abimelech ^wtook sheep, oxen, and male and female servants, and gave *them* to Abraham; and he restored Sarah his wife to him. ¹⁵And Abimelech said, "See, ^xmy land *is* before you; dwell where it pleases you." ¹⁶Then to Sarah he said, "Behold, I have given your brother a thousand *pieces* of silver; ^yindeed this vindicates you* ^zbefore all who *are* with you and before everybody." Thus she was rebuked.

¹⁷So Abraham prayed ^ato God; and God ^bhealed Abimelech, his wife, and his female servants. Then they bore *children*; ¹⁸for the LORD ^chad closed up all the wombs of the house of Abimelech because of Sarah, Abraham's wife.

Isaac Is Born

21 And the LORD ^avisited Sarah as He had said, and the LORD did for Sarah ^bas He had spoken. ²For Sarah ^cconceived and bore Abraham a son in his old age, ^dat the set time of which God had spoken to him. ³And Abraham called the name of his son who was born to him—whom Sarah bore to him—^eIsaac. ⁴Then Abraham ^fcircumcised his son Isaac when he was eight days old, ^gas God had commanded him. ⁵Now ^hAbraham was one hundred years old when his son Isaac was born to him. ⁶And Sarah said, ⁱ"God has made me laugh, *and* all who hear ^jwill laugh with me." ⁷She also said, "Who would have said to Abraham that Sarah would nurse children? ^kFor I have borne *him* a son in his old age."

Hagar and Ishmael Depart

⁸So the child grew and was weaned. And Abraham made a great feast on the same day that Isaac was weaned.

⁹And Sarah saw the son of Hagar ^lthe

---

* **20:16** Literally *it is a covering of the eyes for you*

20:2 She is my sister. The complete truth told in such a way as to deceive or mislead is still a falsehood. Abraham's words were true: "She is my sister," but the message he intended to convey was false: "She is not married to me." His intent was deceit and the consequences he reaped were the same as if he had directly lied. A man speaks the real truth when he speaks the truth in his heart (Ps. 15:2).

20:3 God came . . . in a dream. Presumably, Abimelech was a pagan king. Yet God warned him of the wrong he was about to commit. This is another instance of the protective care that the Lord gives His people (31:24; Num. 22:12–20).

20:12 indeed she is truly my sister. Later the law would prohibit the marriage of people so closely related, but in the early years of the earth it was apparently acceptable for half siblings to marry (see note at 4:17).

21:1 And the LORD visited Sarah as He had said. The Bible stresses that the Lord causes conceptions; that

children are a gift of the Lord (Ps. 127:3). The verb *visit* is an extraordinary choice here, indicating that Lord entered directly into the affairs of His people.

21:3 Isaac. Isaac means "He (God) is laughing (now)." At one time Abraham and Sarah had both laughed at the improbability of having a son in their old age

---

20:1 ^aGen. 18:1 ^bGen. 12:9; 16:7, 14 ^cGen. 26:1, 6
20:2 ^dGen. 12:11–13; 26:7 ^eGen. 12:15 **20:3** ^fPs. 105:14 ^gJob 33:15 ^hGen. 20:7 **20:4** ⁱGen. 18:23–25 **20:5** ^j2 Kin. 20:3 **20:6** ^k1 Sam. 25:26, 34 ^lGen. 39:9 ^m1 Sam. 2:17 ⁿNum. 16:32, 33 **20:9** ^pGen. 26:10; 39:9 ^qGen. 34:7 **20:11** ^rProv. 16:6 ^sGen. 12:12; 26:7 **20:12** ^tGen. 11:29 **20:13** ^uGen. 12:1–9, 11 ^vGen. 12:13; 20:5 **20:14** ^wGen. 12:16 **20:15** ^xGen. 13:9; 34:10; 47:6 **20:16** ^yGen. 26:11 ^zMal. 2:9 **20:17** ^aJob 42:9 ^bGen. 21:2 **20:18** ^cGen. 12:17 **21:1** ^a1 Sam. 2:21 ^b[Gal. 4:23, 28] **21:2** ^cHeb. 11:11, 12 ^dGen. 17:21; 18:10, 14 **21:3** ^eGen. 17:19, 21 **21:4** ^fActs 7:8 ^gGen. 17:10, 12 **21:5** ^hGen. 17:1, 17 **21:6** ⁱIs. 54:1 ^jLuke 1:58 **21:7** ^kGen. 18:11, 12 **21:9** ^lGen. 16:1, 4, 15

Egyptian, whom she had borne to Abraham, ^mscoffing. ¹⁰Therefore she said to Abraham, ⁿ"Cast out this bondwoman and her son; for the son of this bondwoman shall not be heir with my son, *namely* with Isaac." ¹¹And the matter was very displeasing in Abraham's sight ^obecause of his son.

¹²But God said to Abraham, "Do not let it be displeasing in your sight because of the lad or because of your bondwoman. Whatever Sarah has said to you, listen to her voice; for ^pin Isaac your seed shall be called. ¹³Yet I will also make ^qa nation of the son of the bondwoman, because he *is* your seed."

¹⁴So Abraham rose early in the morning, and took bread and a skin of water; and putting *it* on her shoulder, he gave *it* and the boy to Hagar, and ^rsent her away. Then she departed and wandered in the Wilderness of Beersheba. ¹⁵And the water in the skin was used up, and she placed the boy under one of the shrubs. ¹⁶Then she went and sat down across from *him* at a distance of about a bowshot; for she said to herself, "Let me not see the death of the boy." So she sat opposite *him*, and lifted her voice and wept.

¹⁷And ^sGod heard the voice of the lad. Then the ^tangel of God called to Hagar out of heaven, and said to her, "What ails you, Hagar? Fear not, for God has heard the voice of the lad where he *is*. ¹⁸Arise, lift up the lad and hold him with your hand, for ^uI will make him a great nation."

¹⁹Then ^vGod opened her eyes, and she saw a well of water. And she went and filled the skin with water, and gave the lad a drink. ²⁰So God ^wwas with the lad; and he grew and dwelt in the wilderness, ^xand became an archer. ²¹He dwelt in the Wilderness of Paran; and his mother ^ytook a wife for him from the land of Egypt.

A Covenant with Abimelech

²²And it came to pass at that time that ^zAbimelech and Phichol, the commander

of his army, spoke to Abraham, saying, ^a"God *is* with you in all that you do. ²³Now therefore, ^bswear to me by God that you will not deal falsely with me, with my offspring, or with my posterity; but that according to the kindness that I have done to you, you will do to me and to the land in which you have dwelt."

²⁴And Abraham said, "I will swear."

²⁵Then Abraham rebuked Abimelech because of a well of water which Abimelech's servants ^chad seized. ²⁶And Abimelech said, "I do not know who has done this thing; you did not tell me, nor had I heard *of it* until today." ²⁷So Abraham took sheep and oxen and gave them to Abimelech, and the two of them ^dmade a covenant. ²⁸And Abraham set seven ewe lambs of the flock by themselves.

²⁹Then Abimelech asked Abraham, ^e"What *is the meaning of* these seven ewe lambs which you have set by themselves?"

³⁰And he said, "You will take *these* seven ewe lambs from my hand, that ^fthey may be my witness that I have dug this well." ³¹Therefore he ^gcalled that place Beersheba,* because the two of them swore an oath there.

³²Thus they made a covenant at Beersheba. So Abimelech rose with Phichol, the commander of his army, and they returned to the land of the Philistines. ³³Then *Abraham* planted a tamarisk tree in Beersheba, and ^hthere called on the name of the LORD, ⁱthe Everlasting God. ³⁴And Abraham stayed in the land of the Philistines many days.

Abraham's Faith Confirmed

22 Now it came to pass after these things that ^aGod tested Abraham, and said to him, "Abraham!"

And he said, "Here I am."

---

* **21:31** Literally *Well of the Oath* or *Well of the Seven*

(17:17; 18:12); now with the birth of the promised child their laughter took on a happier meaning.

21:12 listen to her voice. As painful as the situation was, God confirmed that Sarah was right that Ishmael would have to leave. Only Isaac was the child of promise, the one through whom the covenant would be fulfilled. This complicated situation was part of the price Abraham had to pay for trying to bring about God's promises in his own time. Nevertheless, God is merciful and He did not abandon Hagar and Ishmael.

21:17 God heard. What wonderful words these are! There is no pain of His people that He does not see or hear about (Is. 40:27–28; Heb. 2:10,18; 4:15). Even though Ishmael was not the son of promise, God still had His hand on his life.

21:23 kindness. This exceedingly important term, sometimes translated *loyal love* or *lovingkindness* is often used in the Psalms to describe God's character. Here we see its proper context in a binding relationship. The term basically describes covenant loyalty (24:12).

21:27 covenant. This is a binding agreement between two equals, similar to today's business contracts.

21:28–31 seven ewe lambs . . . Beersheba. The Hebrew number seven is similar in sound to the verb meaning "to swear" (v. 24). Thus Beersheba would be the well where they swore and the well of the seven ewe lambs.

21:34 the land of the Philistines. The name Palestine comes from the word for Philistine.

21:9 ^m [Gal. 4:29]   **21:10** ⁿ Gal. 3:18; 4:30   **21:11** ^o Gen. 17:18   **21:12** ^p Matt. 1:2; Luke 3:34; [Rom. 9:7, 8]; Heb. 11:18   **21:13** ^q Gen. 16:10; 17:20; 21:18; 25:12–18   **21:14** ^r John 8:35   **21:17** ^s Ex. 3:7   ^t Gen. 22:11   **21:18** ^u Gen. 16:10; 21:13; 25:12–16   **21:19** ^v Num. 22:31   **21:20** ^w Gen. 28:15; 39:2, 3, 21   ^x Gen. 16:12   **21:21** ^y Gen. 24:4   **21:22** ^z Gen. 20:2, 14; 26:26   ^a Gen. 26:28   **21:23** ^b Josh. 2:12   **21:25** ^c Gen. 15, 18, 20–22   **21:27** ^d Gen. 26:31; 31:44   **21:29** ^e Gen. 33:8   **21:30** ^f Gen. 31:48, 52   **21:31** ^g Gen. 21:14; 26:33   **21:33** ^h Gen. 4:26; 12:8; 13:4; 26:25   ⁱ Deut. 32:40; 33:27   **22:1** ^a Heb. 11:17

2Then He said, "Take now your son, *b*your only *son* Isaac, whom you *c*love, and go *d*to the land of Moriah, and offer him there as a *e*burnt offering on one of the mountains of which I shall tell you."

3So Abraham rose early in the morning and saddled his donkey, and took two of his young men with him, and Isaac his son; and he split the wood for the burnt offering, and arose and went to the place of which God had told him. 4Then on the third day Abraham lifted his eyes and saw the place afar off. 5And Abraham said to his young men, "Stay here with the donkey; the lad* and I will go yonder and worship, and we will *f*come back to you."

6So Abraham took the wood of the burnt offering and *g*laid *it* on Isaac his son; and he took the fire in his hand, and a knife, and the two of them went together. 7But Isaac spoke to Abraham his father and said, "My father!"

And he said, "Here I am, my son."

Then he said, "Look, the fire and the wood, but where *is* the lamb for a burnt offering?"

8And Abraham said, "My son, God will provide for Himself the *h*lamb for a *i*burnt offering." So the two of them went together.

9Then they came to the place of which God had told him. And Abraham built an altar there and placed the wood in order; and he bound Isaac his son and *j*laid him on the altar, upon the wood. 10And Abraham stretched out his hand and took the knife to slay his son.

11But the *k*Angel of the LORD called to him from heaven and said, "Abraham, Abraham!"

So he said, "Here I am."

12And He said, *l*"Do not lay your hand on the lad, or do anything to him; for *m*now I know that you fear God, since you have not *n*withheld your son, your only *son*, from Me."

13Then Abraham lifted his eyes and looked, and there behind *him was* a ram caught in a thicket by its horns. So Abraham went and took the ram, and offered it up for a burnt offering instead of his son. 14And Abraham called the name of the place, The-LORD-Will-Provide;* as it is said *to* this day, "In the Mount of the LORD it shall be provided."

15Then the Angel of the LORD called to Abraham a second time out of heaven, 16and said: *o*"By Myself I have sworn, says the LORD, because you have done this thing, and have not withheld your son, your only *son*— 17blessing I will *p*bless you, and multiplying I will multiply your descendants *q*as the stars of the heaven *r*and as the sand which *is* on the seashore; and *s*your descendants shall possess the gate of their enemies. 18t*In your seed all the nations of the earth shall be blessed, *u*because you have obeyed My voice." 19So Abraham returned to his young men, and they rose and went together to *v*Beersheba; and Abraham dwelt at Beersheba.

The Family of Nahor

20Now it came to pass after these things that it was told Abraham, saying, "Indeed *w*Milcah also has borne children to your brother Nahor: 21x*Huz his firstborn, Buz his brother, Kemuel the father *y*of Aram, 22Chesed, Hazo, Pildash, Jidlaph, and Bethuel." 23And *z*Bethuel begot Rebekah.* These eight Milcah bore to Nahor, Abraham's brother. 24His concubine, whose name was Reumah, also bore Tebah, Gaham, Thahash, and Maachah.

---

* **22:5** Or *young man*   * **22:14** Hebrew *YHWH Yireh*   * **22:23** Spelled *Rebecca* in Romans 9:10

22:5 worship, and . . . come back to you. Abraham's comment to his servants is a significant avowal of his faith in God. Even though he was going to sacrifice his son, he was confident that they both would return.
22:8 God will provide. Abraham's faith in God's promise is shown in his response to a very real and terrible test. Many times this is seen as a test of the quality of Abraham's love for God—who would he choose, God or his son? However, there is no sign that Abraham made this mistake. He knew beyond a shadow of doubt that Isaac was given to him directly by God, the son of promise. Therefore it was right that he should love his son of promise as a gift from God. God's covenant said that a great nation would descend from Isaac, therefore it would be so. Abraham's test was not "whom do you love most?" but "do you really believe Me?" The answer was a resounding, "Yes!" Abraham carried his faith to the knife edge on his son's flesh. God had promised, and it would be so, even if Isaac had to be raised from the dead to make His words come to pass (Heb. 11:17–19).
22:9 bound Isaac his son. Surely Isaac could have struggled or run away at this point, but there is no evidence that he did so. Apparently Isaac's faith and trust both in God and in his father was sufficient to stand the test.
22:14 The-LORD-Will-Provide. As God provided a ram to take the place of Abraham's son, so one day He would provide His own Son to take our place. Some believe that Mount Moriah later became part of the city of Jerusalem, and was the site of Solomon's temple.
22:17 bless . . . multiply. In the Hebrew, this is stated by doubling the verbs, a Hebrew idiom that powerfully emphasizes the certainty of the action.
22:18 seed. Here this is a grand play on words. The seed was Isaac, and by extension the Jewish nation.

22:2 *b* Gen. 22:12, 16 *c* John 5:20 *d* 2 Chr. 3:1 *e* Gen. 8:20; 31:54   **22:5** *f* [Heb. 11:19]   **22:6** *g* John 19:17   **22:8** *h* John 1:29, 36 *i* Ex. 12:3–6   **22:9** *j* [Heb. 11:17–19]   **22:11** *k* Gen. 16:7–11; 21:17, 18; 31:11   **22:12** *l* 1 Sam. 15:22 *m* James 2:21, 22 *n* Gen. 22:2, 16   **22:16** *o* Ps. 105:9   **22:17** *p* Gen. 17:16; 26:3, 24 *q* Gen. 15:5; 26:4 *r* Gen. 13:16; 32:12 *s* Gen. 24:60   **22:18** *t* Gen. 12:3; 18:18; 26:4; [Acts 3:25, 26]; Gal. 3:8, 9, 16, 18 *u* Gen. 18:19; 22:3, 10; 26:5   **22:19** *v* Gen. 21:31   **22:20** *w* Gen. 11:29; 24:15   **22:21** *x* Job 1:1 *y* Job 32:2   **22:23** *z* Gen. 24:15

Sarah's Death and Burial

23 Sarah lived one hundred and twenty-seven years; *these were* the years of the life of Sarah. ²So Sarah died in ªKirjath Arba (that *is,* ᵇHebron) in the land of Canaan, and Abraham came to mourn for Sarah and to weep for her.

³Then Abraham stood up from before his dead, and spoke to the sons of ᶜHeth, saying, ⁴ᵈ"I *am* a foreigner and a visitor among you. ᵉGive me property for a burial place among you, that I may bury my dead out of my sight."

⁵And the sons of Heth answered Abraham, saying to him, ⁶"Hear us, my lord: You *are* ᶠa mighty prince among us; bury your dead in the choicest of our burial places. None of us will withhold from you his burial place, that you may bury your dead."

⁷Then Abraham stood up and bowed himself to the people of the land, the sons of Heth. ⁸And he spoke with them, saying, "If it is your wish that I bury my dead out of my sight, hear me, and meet with Ephron the son of Zohar for me, ⁹that he may give me the cave of ᵍMachpelah which he has, which *is* at the end of his field. Let him give it to me at the full price, as property for a burial place among you."

¹⁰Now Ephron dwelt among the sons of Heth; and Ephron the Hittite answered Abraham in the presence of the sons of Heth, all who ʰentered at the gate of his city, saying, ¹¹ⁱ"No, my lord, hear me: I give you the field and the cave that *is* in it; I give it to you in the presence of the sons of my people. I give it to you. Bury your dead!"

¹²Then Abraham bowed himself down before the people of the land; ¹³and he spoke to Ephron in the hearing of the people of the land, saying, "If you *will give it,* please hear me. I will give you money for the field; take *it* from me and I will bury my dead there."

¹⁴And Ephron answered Abraham, saying to him, ¹⁵"My lord, listen to me; the land *is worth* four hundred ʲshekels of silver. What *is* that between you and me? So

bury your dead." ¹⁶And Abraham listened to Ephron; and Abraham ᵏweighed out the silver for Ephron which he had named in the hearing of the sons of Heth, four hundred shekels of silver, currency of the merchants.

¹⁷So ˡthe field of Ephron which *was* in Machpelah, which *was* before Mamre, the field and the cave which *was* in it, and all the trees that *were* in the field, which *were* within all the surrounding borders, were deeded ¹⁸to Abraham as a possession in the presence of the sons of Heth, before all who went in at the gate of his city.

¹⁹And after this, Abraham buried Sarah his wife in the cave of the field of Machpelah, before Mamre (that *is,* Hebron) in the land of Canaan. ²⁰So the field and the cave that *is* in it ᵐwere deeded to Abraham by the sons of Heth as property for a burial place.

A Bride for Isaac

24 Now Abraham ªwas old, well advanced in age; and the LORD ᵇhad blessed Abraham in all things. ²So Abraham said ᶜto the oldest servant of his house, who ᵈruled over all that he had, "Please, ᵉput your hand under my thigh, ³and I will make you ᶠswear by the LORD, the God of heaven and the God of the earth, that ᵍyou will not take a wife for my son from the daughters of the Canaanites, among whom I dwell; ⁴ʰbut you shall go ⁱto my country and to my family, and take a wife for my son Isaac."

⁵And the servant said to him, "Perhaps the woman will not be willing to follow me to this land. Must I take your son back to the land from which you came?"

⁶But Abraham said to him, "Beware that you do not take my son back there. ⁷The LORD God of heaven, who ʲtook me from my father's house and from the land of my family, and who spoke to me and swore to me, saying, ᵏ'To your descendants* I give this land,' ˡHe will send His angel before you, and you shall take a wife for my

* **24:7** Literally *seed*

Specifically the Seed was one descendant of Abraham, Jesus the Messiah.

23:13 *I will give you money for the field.* Abraham would not have been offering "money" as we think of it today; minted coins were not invented until at least 650 B.C. Instead, trading was done by barter, or with precious metals by weight.

23:15 *What is that between you and me?* The dialogue in this chapter gives a wonderfully detailed example of the bargaining process of the day. Abraham clearly understood Ephron's generous statement as a politely phrased way of setting his price.

23:20 *field . . . cave . . . were deeded to Abraham.* It is interesting to note that the only piece of the Promised Land that Abraham ever personally possessed was this field and cave to bury his wife.

24:2 *the oldest servant.* Some have thought that this might be Eliezer of Damascus, the one who had

been named as Abraham's heir before the births of Ishmael and Isaac.

24:3 *the daughters of the Canaanites.* This was not an issue of racism, as is sometimes thought—it was theological. The Canaanite peoples worshiped the false gods Baal and Asherah (Deut. 7:3).

23:2 ª Josh. 14:15; 15:13; 21:11 ᵇ Gen. 13:18; 23:19 **23:3** ᶜ Gen. 10:15; 15:20 **23:4** ᵈ [Gen. 17:8] ᵉ Acts 7:5, 16 **23:6** ᶠ Gen. 13:2; 14:14; 24:35 **23:9** ᵍ Gen. 25:9 **23:10** ʰ Gen. 23:18; 34:20, 24 **23:11** ⁱ 2 Sam. 24:21–24 **23:15** ʲ Ex. 30:13 **23:16** ᵏ Jer. 32:9, 10 **23:17** ˡ Gen. 25:9; 49:29–32; 50:13 **23:20** ᵐ Jer. 32:10, 11 **24:1** ª Gen. 18:11; 21:5 ᵇ Gen. 12:2; 13:2; 24:35 **24:2** ᶜ Gen. 15:2 ᵈ Gen. 24:10; 39:4–6 ᵉ Gen. 47:29 **24:3** ᶠ Gen. 14:19, 22 ᵍ Deut. 7:3 **24:4** ʰ Gen. 28:2 ⁱ Gen. 12:1 **24:7** ʲ Gen. 12:1; 24:3 ᵏ Gen. 12:7; 13:15; 15:18; 17:8 ˡ Ex. 23:20, 23; 33:2

son from there. **8**And if the woman is not willing to follow you, then *m*you will be released from this oath; only do not take my son back there." **9**So the servant put his hand under the thigh of Abraham his master, and swore to him concerning this matter.

10Then the servant took ten of his master's camels and departed, *n*for all his master's goods *were in* his hand. And he arose and went to Mesopotamia, to *o*the city of Nahor. **11**And he made his camels kneel down outside the city by a well of water at evening time, the time *p*when women go out to draw *water.* **12**Then he *q*said, "O LORD God of my master Abraham, please *r*give me success this day, and show kindness to my master Abraham. **13**Behold, *here s*I stand by the well of water, and *t*the daughters of the men of the city are coming out to draw water. **14**Now let it be that the young woman to whom I say, 'Please let down your pitcher that I may drink,' and she says, 'Drink, and I will also give your camels a drink'—*let* her *be the one* You have appointed for Your servant Isaac. And *u*by this I will know that You have shown kindness to my master."

15And it happened, *v*before he had finished speaking, that behold, *w*Rebekah, who was born to Bethuel, son of *x*Milcah, the wife of Nahor, Abraham's brother, came out with her pitcher on her shoulder. **16**Now the young woman *y*was very beautiful to behold, a virgin; no man had known her. And she went down to the well, filled her pitcher, and came up. **17**And the servant ran to meet her and said, "Please let me drink a little water from your pitcher."

18z*So she said, "Drink, my lord." Then she quickly let her pitcher down to her hand, and gave him a drink. **19**And when she had finished giving him a drink, she said, "I will draw *water* for your camels also, until they have finished drinking." **20**Then she quickly emptied her pitcher into the trough, ran back to the well to draw *water,* and drew for all his camels. **21**And the man, wondering at her, remained silent so as to know whether *a*the LORD had made his journey prosperous or not.

22So it was, when the camels had finished drinking, that the man took a golden *b*nose ring weighing half a shekel, and two bracelets for her wrists weighing ten *shekels* of gold, **23**and said, "Whose daughter *are* you? Tell me, please, is there room *in* your father's house for us to lodge?"

24So she said to him, *c*"I *am* the daughter of Bethuel, Milcah's son, whom she bore to Nahor." **25**Moreover she said to him, "We have both straw and feed enough, and room to lodge."

26Then the man *d*bowed down his head and worshiped the LORD. **27**And he said, *e*"Blessed *be* the LORD God of my master Abraham, who has not forsaken *f*His mercy and His truth toward my master. As for me, being on the way, the LORD *g*led me to the house of my master's brethren." **28**So the young woman ran and told her mother's household these things.

29Now Rebekah had a brother whose name *was* *h*Laban, and Laban ran out to the man by the well. **30**So it came to pass, when he saw the nose ring, and the bracelets on his sister's wrists, and when he heard the words of his sister Rebekah, saying, "Thus the man spoke to me," that he went to the man. And there he stood by the camels at the well. **31**And he said, "Come in, *i*O blessed of the LORD! Why do you stand outside? For I have prepared the house, and a place for the camels."

32Then the man came to the house. And he unloaded the camels, and *j*provided straw and feed for the camels, and water to *k*wash his feet and the feet of the men who *were* with him. **33**Food was set before him to eat, but he said, *l*"I will not eat until I have told about my errand."

And he said, "Speak on."

34So he said, "I *am* Abraham's servant. **35**The LORD *m*has blessed my master greatly, and he has become great; and He has given him flocks and herds, silver and gold, male and female servants, and camels and donkeys. **36**And Sarah my master's wife *n*bore a son to my master when she was old; and *o*to him he has given all that he has. **37**Now my master *p*made me swear, saying, 'You shall not take a wife for my son from the daughters of the Canaanites, in whose land I dwell; **38**q*but you shall go to my father's house and to my family, and take a wife for my son.'

24:12 O LORD God of my master Abraham. This language does not mean that the servant himself did not believe in God. The servant was making his appeal on the basis of God's covenant loyalty to Abraham.

24:15 Providence—Abraham sent his servant to choose Isaac's bride, confident that his servant would be led by the Lord and that in God's providence he would make the right choice. The servant prayed for very specific guidance, and God sent him Rebekah. He was impressed not only with her physical beauty, but also with her kind, generous, and hospitable character. His decision was confirmed when her parents gave their consent and she agreed to return with him. Today we must remember to seek the Lord's guidance and trust in His providence just as Abraham's servant, Rebekah, and her family did.

24:8 *m* Josh. 2:17–20   **24:10** *n* Gen. 24:2, 22   *o* Gen. 11:31, 32; 22:20; 27:43; 29:5   **24:11** *p* Ex. 2:16   **24:12** *q* Ex. 3:6, 15   *r* Neh. 1:11   **24:13** *s* Gen. 24:43   *t* Ex. 2:16   **24:14** *u* Judg. 6:17, 37   **24:15** *v* Is. 65:24   *w* Gen. 24:45; 25:20   *x* Gen. 22:20, 23   **24:16** *y* Gen. 12:11; 26:7; 29:17   **24:18** *z* [1 Pet. 3:8, 9]   **24:21** *a* Gen. 24:12–14, 27, 52   **24:22** *b* Ex. 32:2, 3   **24:24** *c* Gen. 22:23; 24:15   **24:26** *d* Ex. 4:31   *e* Ex. 18:10   *f* Gen. 32:10   *g* Gen. 24:21, 48   **24:29** *h* Gen. 29:5, 13   **24:31** *i* Judg. 17:2   **24:32** *j* Gen. 43:24   *k* Gen. 19:2   **24:33** *l* John 4:34   **24:35** *m* Gen. 13:2; 24:1   **24:36** *n* Gen. 21:1–7   *o* Gen. 21:10; 25:5   **24:37** *p* Gen. 24:2–4   **24:38** *q* Gen. 24:4

[39r]And I said to my master, 'Perhaps the woman will not follow me.' [40s]But he said to me, 'The LORD, [t]before whom I walk, will send His angel with you and prosper your way; and you shall take a wife for my son from my family and from my father's house. [41u]You will be clear from this oath when you arrive among my family; for if they will not give her to you, then you will be released from my oath.'

[42]"And this day I came to the well and said, [v]'O LORD God of my master Abraham, if You will now prosper the way in which I go, [43w]behold, I stand by the well of water; and it shall come to pass that when the virgin comes out to draw water, and I say to her, "Please give me a little water from your pitcher to drink," [44]and she says to me, "Drink, and I will draw for your camels also,"—let her be the woman whom the LORD has appointed for my master's son.'

[45x]"But before I had finished [y]speaking in my heart, there was Rebekah, coming out with her pitcher on her shoulder; and she went down to the well and drew water. And I said to her, 'Please let me drink.' [46]And she made haste and let her pitcher down from her shoulder, and said, 'Drink, and I will give your camels a drink also.' So I drank, and she gave the camels a drink also. [47]Then I asked her, and said, 'Whose daughter are you?' And she said, 'The daughter of Bethuel, Nahor's son, whom Milcah bore to him.' So I put the nose ring on her nose and the bracelets on her wrists. [48z]And I bowed my head and worshiped the LORD, and blessed the LORD God of my master Abraham, who had led me in the way of truth to [a]take the daughter of my master's brother for his son. [49]Now if you will [b]deal kindly and truly with my master, tell me. And if not, tell me, that I may turn to the right hand or to the left."

[50]Then Laban and Bethuel answered and said, [c]"The thing comes from the LORD; we cannot [d]speak to you either bad or good. [51e]Here is Rebekah before you; take her and go, and let her be your master's son's wife, as the LORD has spoken."

[52]And it came to pass, when Abraham's servant heard their words, that [f]he worshiped the LORD, bowing himself to the earth. [53]Then the servant brought out [g]jewelry of silver, jewelry of gold, and clothing, and gave them to Rebekah. He also gave [h]precious things to her brother and to her mother.

[54]And he and the men who were with him ate and drank and stayed all night. Then they arose in the morning, and he said, [i]"Send me away to my master."

[55]But her brother and her mother said, "Let the young woman stay with us a few days, at least ten; after that she may go."

[56]And he said to them, "Do not hinder me, since the LORD has prospered my way; send me away so that I may go to my master."

[57]So they said, "We will call the young woman and ask her personally." [58]Then they called Rebekah and said to her, "Will you go with this man?"

And she said, "I will go."

[59]So they sent away Rebekah their sister [j]and her nurse, and Abraham's servant and his men. [60]And they blessed Rebekah and said to her:

"Our sister, may you become
[k]The mother of thousands of ten thousands;
[l]And may your descendants possess
The gates of those who hate them."

[61]Then Rebekah and her maids arose, and they rode on the camels and followed the man. So the servant took Rebekah and departed.

[62]Now Isaac came from the way of [m]Beer Lahai Roi, for he dwelt in the South. [63]And Isaac went out [n]to meditate in the field in the evening; and he lifted his eyes and looked, and there, the camels were coming. [64]Then Rebekah lifted her eyes, and when [o]she saw Isaac she dismounted from her camel; [65]for she had said to the servant, "Who is this man walking in the field to meet us?"

The servant said, "It is my master." So she took a veil and covered herself.

[66]And the servant told Isaac all the things that he had done. [67]Then Isaac brought her into his mother Sarah's tent; and he [p]took Rebekah and she became his wife, and he loved her. So Isaac [q]was comforted after his mother's death.

24:50 The thing comes from the LORD. It appears that the family of Bethuel and Laban also worshiped the living God, or at least acknowledged Him along with other gods (see 31:19; Josh. 24:2).

24:60 they blessed Rebekah. These words are not mere sentiment, nor are they a magical charm, but a prayer for God's blessing on her life. **gates.** The possession of the gates of one's enemies meant power over them (22:17).

24:67 he loved her. The love of Isaac for Rebekah is a wonderful fulfillment and illustration of God's original purpose for marriage. Realizing it was not good for man to be alone (2:18), the Creator graciously created Eve, a helper for Adam. God Himself then performed history's first wedding. Isaac

and Rebekah serve not only as a lovely example of godly marriage, but also as a beautiful picture of the love between Christ and the church in the New

24:39 [r] Gen. 24:5 **24:40** [s] Gen. 24:7 [t] Gen. 5:22, 24; 17:1
24:41 [u] Gen. 24:8 **24:42** [v] Gen. 24:12 **24:43** [w] Gen. 24:13 **24:45** [x] Gen. 24:15 [y] 1 Sam. 1:13 **24:48** [z] Gen. 24:26, 52 [a] Gen. 22:23; 24:27 **24:49** [b] Josh. 2:14
24:50 [c] Ps. 118:23 [d] Gen. 31:24, 29 **24:51** [e] Gen. 20:15 **24:52** [f] Gen. 24:26, 48 **24:53** [g] Ex. 3:22; 11:2; 12:35 [h] 2 Chr. 21:3 **24:54** [i] Gen. 24:56, 59; 30:25
24:59 [j] Gen. 35:8 **24:60** [k] Gen. 17:16 [l] Gen. 22:17; 28:14 **24:62** [m] Gen. 16:14; 25:11 **24:63** [n] Josh. 1:8
24:64 [o] Josh. 15:18 **24:67** [p] Gen. 25:20; 29:20 [q] Gen. 23:1, 2; 38:12

Abraham and Keturah

25 Abraham again took a wife, and her name was [a]Keturah. [2]And [b]she bore him Zimran, Jokshan, Medan, Midian, Ishbak, and Shuah. [3]Jokshan begot Sheba and Dedan. And the sons of Dedan were Asshurim, Letushim, and Leummim. [4]And the sons of Midian were Ephah, Epher, Hanoch, Abidah, and Eldaah. All these were the children of Keturah.

[5]And [c]Abraham gave all that he had to Isaac. [6]But Abraham gave gifts to the sons of the concubines which Abraham had; and while he was still living he [d]sent them eastward, away from Isaac his son, to [e]the country of the east.

Abraham's Death and Burial

[7]This is the sum of the years of Abraham's life which he lived: one hundred and seventy-five years. [8]Then Abraham breathed his last and [f]died in a good old age, an old man and full of years, and [g]was gathered to his people. [9]And [h]his sons Isaac and Ishmael buried him in the cave of [i]Machpelah, which is before Mamre, in the field of Ephron the son of Zohar the Hittite, [10]the field which Abraham purchased from the sons of Heth. [k]There Abraham was buried, and Sarah his wife. [11]And it came to pass, after the death of Abraham, that God blessed his son Isaac. And Isaac dwelt at [l]Beer Lahai Roi.

The Families of Ishmael and Isaac

[12]Now this is the [m]genealogy of Ishmael, Abraham's son, whom Hagar the Egyptian, Sarah's maidservant, bore to Abraham. [13]And [n]these were the names of the sons of Ishmael, by their names, according to their generations: The firstborn of Ishmael, Nebajoth; then Kedar, Adbeel, Mibsam, [14]Mishma, Dumah, Massa, [15]Hadar,* Tema, Jetur, Naphish, and Kedemah. [16]These were the sons of Ishmael and these were their names, by their towns and their settlements, [o]twelve princes according to their nations. [17]These were the years of the life of Ishmael: one hundred and thirty-seven years; and [p]he breathed his last and died, and was gathered to his people. [18][q](They dwelt from Havilah as far as Shur, which is east of Egypt as you go toward Assyria.) He died [r]in the presence of all his brethren.

[19]This is the [s]genealogy of Isaac, Abraham's son. [t]Abraham begot Isaac. [20]Isaac was forty years old when he took Rebekah as wife, [u]the daughter of Bethuel the Syrian of Padan Aram, [v]the sister of Laban the Syrian. [21]Now Isaac pleaded with the LORD for his wife, because she was barren; [w]and the LORD granted his plea, [x]and Rebekah his wife conceived. [22]But the children struggled together within her; and she said, "If all is well, why am I like this?" [y]So she went to inquire of the LORD.

[23]And the LORD said to her:

[z]"Two nations are in your womb,
Two peoples shall be separated from
    your body;
One people shall be stronger than [a]the
    other,
[b]And the older shall serve the younger."

[24]So when her days were fulfilled for her to give birth, indeed there were twins in her womb. [25]And the first came out red. He was [c]like a hairy garment all over; so they called his name Esau.* [26]Afterward his brother came out, and [d]his hand took hold of Esau's heel; so [e]his name was called Jacob.* Isaac was sixty years old when she bore them.

[27]So the boys grew. And Esau was [f]a

---

* 25:15 Masoretic Text reads Hadad. * 25:25 Literally Hairy * 25:26 Literally Supplanter

---

Testament. Rebekah, like the church, loved her bridegroom without first seeing him (compare Gen. 24:58 with 1 Pet. 1:8). Like the church, Rebekah was prayed for by her bridegroom (Gen. 24:63; Rom. 8:34). Isaac, having previously been presented for offering on Mount Moriah (Gen. 22:1–14), was content to await the arrival of his bride. He was an early portrayal of the Son of God who now awaits the arrival of His bride in heaven (Heb. 10:12–14).

25:1 took a wife. In 1 Chronicles 1:32, Keturah is described as Abraham's concubine. It is not really known exactly what position she had in Abraham's household, or when the relationship began. Her sons had a status similar to that of Ishmael, Abraham's son by Hagar (ch. 16), but without Ishmael's particular blessing (Gen. 16:10–16).

25:2 Midian. This son was the father of the Midianites, some of whom later bought Joseph from his brothers (37:28,36).

25:11 God blessed. God blessed Isaac because He had already established "an everlasting covenant" with him (17:19; Heb. 11:17). Later God renewed the covenant with Isaac personally (26:2–5).

25:21 pleaded. The Hebrew verb here indicates that Isaac prayed passionately for his wife. For examples of passionate prayer, see Ex. 8:30; 2 Sam. 21:14; 24:25.
25:25 Esau. This name sounds like the Hebrew word that means "hairy."
25:26 Jacob. The Hebrew word that means "heel" sounds similar to the name Jacob. The name may mean either "he who grasps at the heel (of another)" or "He (the Lord) is at his heels (is his protector)."

25:1 [a] 1 Chr. 1:32, 33   **25:2** [b] 1 Chr. 1:32, 33   **25:5** [c] Gen. 24:35, 36   **25:6** [d] Gen. 21:14   [e] Judg. 6:3   **25:8** [f] Gen. 15:15; 47:8, 9   [g] Gen. 25:17; 35:29; 49:29, 33   **25:9** [h] Gen. 35:29; 50:13   [i] Gen. 23:9, 17; 49:30   **25:10** [j] Gen. 23:3–16   [k] Gen. 49:31   **25:11** [l] Gen. 16:14   **25:12** [m] Gen. 11:10, 27; 16:15   **25:13** [n] 1 Chr. 1:29–31   **25:16** [o] Gen. 17:20   **25:17** [p] Gen. 25:8; 49:33   **25:18** [q] 1 Sam. 15:7   [r] Gen. 16:12   **25:19** [s] Gen. 36:1, 9   [t] Matt. 1:2   **25:20** [u] Gen. 22:23; 24:15, 29, 67   [v] Gen. 24:29   **25:21** [w] 1 Chr. 5:20   [x] Rom. 9:10–13   **25:22** [y] 1 Sam. 1:15; 9:9; 10:22   **25:23** [z] Gen. 17:4–6, 16; 24:60   [a] 2 Sam. 8:14   [b] Rom. 9:12   **25:25** [c] Gen. 27:11, 16, 23   **25:26** [d] Hos. 12:3   [e] Gen. 27:36   **25:27** [f] Gen. 27:3, 5

skillful hunter, a man of the field; but Jacob was [g]a mild man, [h]dwelling in tents.
28And Isaac loved Esau because he [i]ate *of*
his game, [j]but Rebekah loved Jacob.

Esau Sells His Birthright

29Now Jacob cooked a stew; and Esau
came in from the field, and he *was* weary.
30And Esau said to Jacob, "Please feed me
with that same red *stew*, for I *am* weary."
Therefore his name was called Edom.*
31But Jacob said, "Sell me your birthright as of this day."
32And Esau said, "Look, I *am* about to
die; so [k]what *is* this birthright to me?"
33Then Jacob said, "Swear to me as of
this day."
So he swore to him, and [l]sold his birthright to Jacob. 34And Jacob gave Esau
bread and stew of lentils; then [m]he ate and
drank, arose, and went his way. Thus Esau
[n]despised *his* birthright.

Isaac and Abimelech

26 There was a famine in the land, besides [a]the first famine that was in
the days of Abraham. And Isaac went to
[b]Abimelech king of the Philistines, in Gerar.
2Then the LORD appeared to him and
said: [c]"Do not go down to Egypt; live in
[d]the land of which I shall tell you. 3[e]Dwell
in this land, and [f]I will be with you and
[g]bless you; for to you and your descendants
[h]I give all these lands, and I will perform
[i]the oath which I swore to Abraham your
father. 4And [j]I will make your descendants
multiply as the stars of heaven; I will give
to your descendants all these lands; [k]and in
your seed all the nations of the earth shall
be blessed; 5[l]because Abraham obeyed My
voice and kept My charge, My commandments, My statutes, and My laws."
6So Isaac dwelt in Gerar. 7And the men
of the place asked about his wife. And
[m]he said, "She *is* my sister"; for [n]he was
afraid to say, "*She is* my wife," *because*
he thought, "lest the men of the place kill
me for Rebekah, because she *is* [o]beautiful
to behold." 8Now it came to pass, when he
had been there a long time, that Abimelech king of the Philistines looked through
a window, and saw, and there was Isaac,
showing endearment to Rebekah his wife.
9Then Abimelech called Isaac and said,
"Quite obviously she *is* your wife; so how
could you say, 'She *is* my sister'?"
Isaac said to him, "Because I said, 'Lest
I die on account of her.'"
10And Abimelech said, "What *is* this
you have done to us? One of the people
might soon have lain with your wife, and
[p]you would have brought guilt on us." 11So
Abimelech charged all *his* people, saying,
"He who [q]touches this man or his wife shall
surely be put to death."
12Then Isaac sowed in that land, and
reaped in the same year [r]a hundredfold;
and the LORD [s]blessed him. 13The man [t]be-
gan to prosper, and continued prospering
until he became very prosperous; 14for he
had possessions of flocks and possessions
of herds and a great number of servants.
So the Philistines [u]envied him. 15Now the
Philistines had stopped up all the wells
[v]which his father's servants had dug in the
days of Abraham his father, and they had
filled them with earth. 16And Abimelech
said to Isaac, "Go away from us, for [w]you
are much mightier than we."
17Then Isaac departed from there and
pitched his tent in the Valley of Gerar, and
dwelt there. 18And Isaac dug again the
wells of water which they had dug in the
days of Abraham his father, for the Philistines had stopped them up after the death
of Abraham. [x]He called them by the names
which his father had called them.
19Also Isaac's servants dug in the valley,
and found a well of running water there.
20But the herdsmen of Gerar [y]quarreled
with Isaac's herdsmen, saying, "The water
is ours." So he called the name of the well
Esek,* because they quarreled with him.
21Then they dug another well, and they
quarreled over that *one* also. So he called

* **25:30** Literally *Red* * **26:20** Literally *Quarrel*

25:30 *Edom.* This name means "red." The nickname is here connected to the red stew for which he traded his birthright; many have speculated that Esau may have had ruddy skin, or even red hair since the name stuck and even became the name of his land and the nation of his descendants (36:8).

26:1 *Philistines.* The Philistines are thought to have come to the coastland of Canaan following their defeat by the Egyptians around 1200 B.C. The Egyptians called them the "Sea Peoples"; they were apparently Greek peoples who migrated eastward (see 1 Sam. 4:1; 2 Sam. 5:17).

26:3 *bless you.* The Lord fulfilled His promise to Abraham concerning Isaac (17:19). He established His everlasting covenant with Isaac, just as He had with Abraham.

26:7 *sister.* Rebekah was Isaac's close relative, but she was not his sister (she was his first cousin once removed). Isaac was even more deceitful than his father Abraham (20:2,12).

26:12–13 *blessed.* God's special work for Abraham was extended to the son.

25:27 [g] Job 1:1, 8 [h] Heb. 11:9 **25:28** [i] Gen. 27:4, 19, 25, 31 [j] Gen. 27:6–10 **25:32** [k] Mark 8:36, 37 **25:33** [l] Heb. 12:16 **25:34** [m] Eccl. 8:15 [n] Heb. 12:16, 17 **26:1** [a] Gen. 12:10 [b] Gen. 20:1, 2 **26:2** [c] Gen. 12:7; 17:1; 18:1; 35:9 [d] Gen. 12:1 **26:3** [e] Heb. 11:9 [f] Gen. 28:13, 15 [g] Gen. 12:2 [h] Gen. 12:7; 13:15; 15:18 [i] Gen. 22:16 **26:4** [j] Gen. 15:5; 22:17 [k] Gen. 12:3; 22:18; Gal. 3:8 **26:5** [l] Gen. 22:16, 18 **26:7** [m] Gen. 12:13; 20:2, 12, 13 [n] Prov. 29:25 [o] Gen. 12:11; 24:16; 29:17 **26:10** [p] Gen. 20:9 **26:11** [q] Ps. 105:15 **26:12** [r] Matt. 13:8, 23 [s] Gen. 24:1; 25:8, 11; 26:3 **26:13** [t] [Prov. 10:22] **26:14** [u] Gen. 37:11 **26:15** [v] Gen. 21:25, 30 **26:16** [w] Ex. 1:9 **26:18** [x] Gen. 21:31 **26:20** [y] Gen. 21:25

its name Sitnah.* ²²And he moved from there and dug another well, and they did not quarrel over it. So he called its name Rehoboth,* because he said, "For now the LORD has made room for us, and we shall ᶻbe fruitful in the land."

²³Then he went up from there to Beersheba. ²⁴And the LORD ᵃappeared to him the same night and said, ᵇ"I *am* the God of your father Abraham; ᶜdo not fear, for ᵈI *am* with you. I will bless you and multiply your descendants for My servant Abraham's sake." ²⁵So he ᵉbuilt an altar there and ᶠcalled on the name of the LORD, and he pitched his tent there; and there Isaac's servants dug a well.

²⁶Then Abimelech came to him from Gerar with Ahuzzath, one of his friends, ᵍand Phichol the commander of his army. ²⁷And Isaac said to them, "Why have you come to me, ʰsince you hate me and have ⁱsent me away from you?"

²⁸But they said, "We have certainly seen that the LORD ʲis with you. So we said, 'Let there now be an oath between us, between you and us; and let us make a covenant with you, ²⁹that you will do us no harm, since we have not touched you, and since we have done nothing to you but good and have sent you away in peace. ᵏYou *are* now the blessed of the LORD.'"

³⁰ˡSo he made them a feast, and they ate and drank. ³¹Then they arose early in the morning and ᵐswore an oath with one another; and Isaac sent them away, and they departed from him in peace.

³²It came to pass the same day that Isaac's servants came and told him about the well which they had dug, and said to him, "We have found water." ³³So he called it Shebah.* ⁿTherefore the name of the city *is* Beersheba* to this day.

³⁴ᵒWhen Esau was forty years old, he took as wives Judith the daughter of Beeri the Hittite, and Basemath the daughter of Elon the Hittite. ³⁵And ᵖthey were a grief of mind to Isaac and Rebekah.

Isaac Blesses Jacob

27 Now it came to pass, when Isaac was ᵃold and ᵇhis eyes were so dim that he could not see, that he called Esau his older son and said to him, "My son."

And he answered him, "Here I am."

²Then he said, "Behold now, I am old. I ᶜdo not know the day of my death. ³ᵈNow therefore, please take your weapons, your quiver and your bow, and go out to the field and hunt game for me. ⁴And make me savory food, such as I love, and bring *it* to me that I may eat, that my soul ᵉmay bless you before I die."

⁵Now Rebekah was listening when Isaac spoke to Esau his son. And Esau went to the field to hunt game and to bring *it*. ⁶So Rebekah spoke to Jacob her son, saying, "Indeed I heard your father speak to Esau your brother, saying, ⁷'Bring me game and make savory food for me, that I may eat it and bless you in the presence of the LORD before my death.' ⁸Now therefore, my son, ᶠobey my voice according to what I command you. ⁹Go now to the flock and bring me from there two choice kids of the goats, and I will make ᵍsavory food from them for your father, such as he loves. ¹⁰Then you shall take *it* to your father, that he may eat *it*, and that he ʰmay bless you before his death."

¹¹And Jacob said to Rebekah his mother, "Look, ⁱEsau my brother *is* a hairy man, and I *am* a smooth-*skinned* man. ¹²Perhaps my father will ʲfeel me, and I shall seem to be a deceiver to him; and I shall bring ᵏa curse on myself and not a blessing."

¹³But his mother said to him, ˡ"*Let* your curse *be* on me, my son; only obey my voice, and go, get *them* for me." ¹⁴And he went and got *them* and brought *them* to his mother, and his mother ᵐmade savory food, such as his father loved. ¹⁵Then Rebekah took the ⁿchoice clothes of her elder son Esau, which *were* with her in the house, and put them on Jacob her younger son. ¹⁶And she put the skins of the kids of the goats on his hands and on the smooth part of his neck. ¹⁷Then she gave the savory food and the bread, which she had prepared, into the hand of her son Jacob.

* **26:21** Literally *Enmity* * **26:22** Literally *Spaciousness* * **26:33** Literally *Oath* or *Seven* • Literally *Well of the Oath* or *Well of the Seven*

26:25 called on the name of the LORD. Isaac followed the practice of his father (12:8). At this altar Isaac not only prayed to the Lord, he also affirmed the reality of the living God in this special land (12:8; 21:33).

26:34 Hittite. Because the Hittites believed in many different gods, Esau's marriages were unacceptable for one belonging to God's covenant family.

27:4 my soul. This phrase is simply a substitute for the personal pronoun "I."

27:8 obey my voice . . . what I command you. Rebekah certainly appears calculating and devious in this passage, but God had told her before they were even born that the younger son would have precedence over the older (25:23). He had not, however, told her to make sure that it happened, and the results of her deception were family strife and the loss of her younger son.

26:22 ᶻGen. 17:6; 28:3; 41:52 **26:24** ᵃGen. 26:2 ᵇGen. 17:7, 8; 24:12 ᶜGen. 15:1 ᵈGen. 26:3, 4 **26:25** ᵉGen. 12:7, 8; 13:4, 18; 22:9; 33:20 ᶠPs. 116:17 **26:26** ᵍGen. 21:22 **26:27** ʰJudg. 11:7 ⁱGen. 26:16 **26:28** ʲGen. 21:22, 23 **26:29** ᵏGen. 24:31 **26:30** ˡGen. 19:3 **26:31** ᵐGen. 21:31 **26:33** ⁿGen. 21:31; 28:10 **26:34** ᵒGen. 28:8; 36:2 **26:35** ᵖGen. 27:46; 28:1, 8 **27:1** ᵃGen. 35:28 ᵇGen. 48:10 **27:2** ᶜ[Prov. 27:1] **27:3** ᵈGen. 25:27, 28 **27:4** ᵉDeut. 33:1 **27:8** ᶠGen. 27:13, 43 **27:9** ᵍGen. 27:4 **27:10** ʰGen. 27:4; 48:16 **27:11** ⁱGen. 25:25 **27:12** ʲGen. 27:21, 22 ᵏDeut. 27:18 **27:13** ˡGen. 43:9 **27:14** ᵐProv. 23:3 **27:15** ⁿGen. 27:27

¹⁸So he went to his father and said, "My father."

And he said, "Here I am. Who *are* you, my son?"

¹⁹Jacob said to his father, "I *am* Esau your firstborn; I have done just as you told me; please arise, sit and eat of my game, °that your soul may bless me."

²⁰But Isaac said to his son, "How *is it* that you have found *it* so quickly, my son?"

And he said, "Because the LORD your God brought *it* to me."

²¹Isaac said to Jacob, "Please come near, that I ᵖmay feel you, my son, whether you *are* really my son Esau or not." ²²So Jacob went near to Isaac his father, and he felt him and said, "The voice *is* Jacob's voice, but the hands *are* the hands of Esau." ²³And he did not recognize him, because �q his hands were hairy like his brother Esau's hands; so he blessed him. ²⁴Then he said, "*Are* you really my son Esau?"

He said, "I *am*."

²⁵He said, "Bring *it* near to me, and I will eat of my son's game, so ʳthat my soul may bless you." So he brought *it* near to him, and he ate; and he brought him wine, and he drank. ²⁶Then his father Isaac said to him, "Come near now and kiss me, my son." ²⁷And he came near and ˢkissed him; and he smelled the smell of his clothing, and blessed him and said:

"Surely, ᵗthe smell of my son
    Is like the smell of a field
    Which the LORD has blessed.
28 Therefore may ᵘGod give you
    Of ᵛthe dew of heaven,
    Of ʷthe fatness of the earth,
    And ˣplenty of grain and wine.
29 ʸLet peoples serve you,
    And nations bow down to you.
    Be master over your brethren,
    And ᶻlet your mother's sons bow down
        to you.
ᵃCursed *be* everyone who curses you,
And blessed *be* those who bless you!"

Esau's Lost Hope

³⁰Now it happened, as soon as Isaac had finished blessing Jacob, and Jacob had scarcely gone out from the presence of Isaac his father, that Esau his brother came in from his hunting. ³¹He also had made savory food, and brought it to his father, and said to his father, "Let my father arise and ᵇeat of his son's game, that your soul may bless me."

³²And his father Isaac said to him, "Who *are* you?"

So he said, "I *am* your son, your firstborn, Esau."

³³Then Isaac trembled exceedingly, and said, "Who? Where *is* the one who hunted game and brought *it* to me? I ate all *of it* before you came, and I have blessed him— ᶜ*and* indeed he shall be blessed."

³⁴When Esau heard the words of his father, ᵈhe cried with an exceedingly great and bitter cry, and said to his father, "Bless me—me also, O my father!"

³⁵But he said, "Your brother came with deceit and has taken away your blessing."

³⁶And *Esau* said, ᵉ"Is he not rightly named Jacob? For he has supplanted me these two times. He took away my birthright, and now look, he has taken away my blessing!" And he said, "Have you not reserved a blessing for me?"

³⁷Then Isaac answered and said to Esau, ᶠ"Indeed I have made him your master, and all his brethren I have given to him as servants; with ᵍgrain and wine I have sustained him. What shall I do now for you, my son?"

³⁸And Esau said to his father, "Have you only one blessing, my father? Bless me—me also, O my father!" And Esau lifted up his voice ʰand wept.

³⁹Then Isaac his father answered and said to him:

"Behold, ⁱyour dwelling shall be of the
        fatness of the earth,
    And of the dew of heaven from above.
40 By your sword you shall live,
    And ʲyou shall serve your brother;
    And ᵏit shall come to pass, when you
        become restless,
    That you shall break his yoke from
        your neck."

Jacob Escapes from Esau

⁴¹So Esau ˡhated Jacob because of the blessing with which his father blessed him, and Esau said in his heart, ᵐ"The days of mourning for my father are at hand; ⁿthen I will kill my brother Jacob."

⁴²And the words of Esau her older son were told to Rebekah. So she sent and called Jacob her younger son, and said to him, "Surely your brother Esau °comforts

---

27:18–29 Falsehood—Jacob may have felt justified in deceiving his father, since Esau had already sold him the birthright. Esau had clearly demonstrated his contempt of the position (including the spiritual responsibility) which was his by right, while Jacob valued and desired it. However, lofty purposes and aspirations cannot justify deceit and trickery. We must be content to leave the fulfillment of God's promises in His hand and wait for His time.
27:29 *peoples serve you.* Isaac predicted that Jacob's descendants would obtain supremacy over

27:19 °Gen. 27:4   **27:21** ᵖGen. 27:12   **27:23** �q Gen.
27:16   **27:25** ʳGen. 27:4, 10, 19, 31   **27:27** ˢGen.
29:13   ᵗSong 4:11   **27:28** ᵘHeb. 11:20   ᵛDeut. 33:13,
28   ʷGen. 45:18   ˣDeut. 7:13; 33:28   **27:29** ʸGen. 9:25;
25:23   ᶻGen. 37:7, 10; 49:8   ᵃGen. 12:2, 3   **27:31** ᵇGen.
27:4   **27:33** ᶜGen. 25:23; 28:3, 4   **27:34** ᵈ[Heb. 12:17]
27:36 ᵉGen. 25:26, 32–34   **27:37** ᶠ2 Sam. 8:14   ᵍGen.
27:28, 29   **27:38** ʰHeb. 12:17   **27:39** ⁱHeb. 11:20
27:40 ʲGen. 25:23; 27:29   ᵏ2 Kin. 8:20–22   **27:41** ˡGen.
26:27; 32:3–11; 37:4, 5, 8   ᵐGen. 50:2–4, 10   ⁿObad. 10
27:42 °Ps. 64:5

himself concerning you *by intending* to kill you. [43]Now therefore, my son, obey my voice: arise, flee to my brother Laban [p]in Haran. [44]And stay with him a [q]few days, until your brother's fury turns away, [45]until your brother's anger turns away from you, and he forgets what you have done to him; then I will send and bring you from there. Why should I be bereaved also of you both in one day?"

[46]And Rebekah said to Isaac, [r]"I am weary of my life because of the daughters of Heth; [s]if Jacob takes a wife of the daughters of Heth, like these *who are* the daughters of the land, what good will my life be to me?"

28 Then Isaac called Jacob and [a]blessed him, and charged him, and said to him: [b]"You shall not take a wife from the daughters of Canaan. [2c]Arise, go to [d]Padan Aram, to the house of [e]Bethuel your mother's father; and take yourself a wife from there of the daughters of [f]Laban your mother's brother.

[3] "May [g]God Almighty bless you,
And make you [h]fruitful and multiply you,
That you may be an assembly of peoples;
[4] And give you [i]the blessing of Abraham,
To you and your descendants with you,
That you may inherit the land
[j]In which you are a stranger,
Which God gave to Abraham."

[5]So Isaac sent Jacob away, and he went to Padan Aram, to Laban the son of Bethuel the Syrian, the brother of Rebekah, the mother of Jacob and Esau.

Esau Marries Mahalath

[6]Esau saw that Isaac had blessed Jacob and sent him away to Padan Aram to take himself a wife from there, *and that* as he blessed him he gave him a charge, saying, "You shall not take a wife from the daughters of Canaan," [7]and that Jacob had obeyed his father and his mother and had gone to Padan Aram. [8]Also Esau saw [k]that the daughters of Canaan did not please his father Isaac. [9]So Esau went to Ishmael and [l]took [m]Mahalath the daughter of Ishmael, Abraham's son, [n]the sister of Nebajoth, to be his wife in addition to the wives he had.

Jacob's Vow at Bethel

[10]Now Jacob [o]went out from Beersheba and went toward [p]Haran. [11]So he came to a certain place and stayed there all night, because the sun had set. And he took one of the stones of that place and put it at his head, and he lay down in that place to sleep. [12]Then he [q]dreamed, and behold, a ladder *was* set up on the earth, and its top reached to heaven; and there [r]the angels of God were ascending and descending on it. [13s]And behold, the LORD stood above it and said: [t]"I *am* the LORD God of Abraham your father and the God of Isaac; [u]the land on which you lie I will give to you and your [v]descendants. [14]Also your descendants shall be as the dust of the earth; you shall spread abroad [w]to the west and the east, to the north and the south; and [x]in you and in your seed all the families of the earth shall be blessed. [15]Behold, [y]I *am* with you and will [z]keep you wherever you go, and will [a]bring you back to this land; for [b]I will not leave you [c]until I have done what I have spoken to you."

[16]Then Jacob awoke from his sleep and said, "Surely the LORD is in [d]this place, and I did not know *it*." [17]And he was afraid and said, "How awesome *is* this place! This *is* none other than the house of God, and this *is* the gate of heaven!"

[18]Then Jacob rose early in the morning, and took the stone that he had put at his head, [e]set it up as a pillar, [f]and poured oil on top of it. [19]And he called the name of [g]that place Bethel;* but the name of that city had been Luz previously. [20h]Then Jacob made a vow, saying, "If [i]God will be

---

* **28:19** Literally *House of God*

---

other peoples. Jesus, as the King of kings, and a descendant of Jacob, ultimately fulfilled this prediction (1 Tim. 6:14–16).

27:46 *daughters of Heth.* Intermarrying with the pagan women of Canaan was dangerous because they would bring their pagan gods and pagan worship into their new homes.

28:2 *Padan Aram.* This is a region of Haran in northern Aram (Syria) near the Euphrates River.

28:3 *God Almighty.* This Hebrew name *El Shaddai* is used by or in the hearing of Abraham, Isaac, and Jacob (35:11). God later identified Himself to Moses with this same name (Ex. 6:3).

28:9 *Mahalath.* This daughter of Ishmael is probably the same woman as Basemath (36:3). Her name means "dance."

28:10–15 *Jacob's Dream*—The ladder of Jacob's dream reminds us of Jesus' words about the angels

"ascending and descending upon the Son of Man" (John 1:51), vividly depicting Himself as the Way into the heavenlies. Certainly Jacob did not deserve such

27:43 [p] Gen. 11:31; 25:20; 28:2, 5　**27:44** [q] Gen. 31:41
27:46 [r] Gen. 26:34, 35; 28:8　[s] Gen. 24:3　**28:1** [a] Gen.
27:33　[b] Gen. 24:3　**28:2** [c] Hos. 12:12　[d] Gen. 25:20
[e] Gen. 22:23　[f] Gen. 24:29; 27:43; 29:5　**28:3** [g] Gen.
17:16; 35:11; 48:3　[h] Gen. 26:4, 24　**28:4** [i] Gen. 12:2, 3;
22:17　[j] Gen. 17:8; 23:4; 36:7　**28:8** [k] Gen. 24:3; 26:34,
35; 27:46　**28:9** [l] Gen. 26:34, 35　[m] Gen. 36:2, 3　[n] Gen.
25:13　**28:10** [o] Hos. 12:12　[p] Gen. 12:4, 5; 27:43; 29:4
28:12 [q] Gen. 31:10; 41:1　[r] John 1:51　**28:13** [s] Gen. 35:1;
48:3　[t] Gen. 26:24　[u] Gen. 13:15, 17; 26:3; 35:12　[v] Gen. 13:16;
22:17　**28:14** [w] Gen. 13:14, 15　[x] Gen. 12:3; 18:18; 22:18;
26:4　**28:15** [y] Gen. 26:3, 24; 31:3　[z] Gen. 48:16　[a] Gen. 35:6;
48:21　[b] Deut. 7:9; 31:6, 8　[c] Num. 23:19　**28:16** [d] Ex. 3:5
28:18 [e] Gen. 31:13, 45　[f] Lev. 8:10–12　**28:19** [g] Judg. 1:23,
26　**28:20** [h] Judg. 11:30　[i] Gen. 28:15

with me, and keep me in this way that I am going, and give me *i*bread to eat and clothing to put on, ²¹so that *k*I come back to my father's house in peace, *l*then the LORD shall be my God. ²²And this stone which I have set as a pillar *m*shall be God's house, *n*and of all that You give me I will surely give a tenth to You."

Jacob Meets Rachel

29 So Jacob went on his journey *a*and came to the land of the people of the East. ²And he looked, and saw a *b*well in the field; and behold, there *were* three flocks of sheep lying by it; for out of that well they watered the flocks. A large stone *was* on the well's mouth. ³Now all the flocks would be gathered there; and they would roll the stone from the well's mouth, water the sheep, and put the stone back in its place on the well's mouth.

⁴And Jacob said to them, "My brethren, where *are* you from?"

And they said, "We *are* from *c*Haran."

⁵Then he said to them, "Do you know *d*Laban the son of Nahor?"

And they said, "We know him."

⁶So he said to them, *e*"Is he well?"

And they said, "*He is* well. And look, his daughter Rachel *f*is coming with the sheep."

⁷Then he said, "Look, *it is* still high day; *it is* not time for the cattle to be gathered together. Water the sheep, and go and feed *them*."

⁸But they said, "We cannot until all the flocks are gathered together, and they have rolled the stone from the well's mouth; then we water the sheep."

⁹Now while he was still speaking with them, *g*Rachel came with her father's sheep, for she was a shepherdess. ¹⁰And it came to pass, when Jacob saw Rachel the daughter of Laban his mother's brother, and the sheep of Laban his mother's brother, that Jacob went near and *h*rolled the stone from the well's mouth, and watered the flock of Laban his mother's brother.

¹¹Then Jacob *i*kissed Rachel, and lifted up his voice and wept. ¹²And Jacob told Rachel that he *was* *j*her father's relative, and that he *was* Rebekah's son. *k*So she ran and told her father.

¹³Then it came to pass, when Laban heard the report about Jacob his sister's son, that *l*he ran to meet him, and embraced him and kissed him, and brought him to his house. So he told Laban all these things. ¹⁴And Laban said to him, *m*"Surely you *are* my bone and my flesh." And he stayed with him for a month.

Jacob Marries Leah and Rachel

¹⁵Then Laban said to Jacob, "Because you *are* my relative, should you therefore serve me for nothing? Tell me, *n*what *should* your wages *be*?" ¹⁶Now Laban had two daughters: the name of the elder *was* Leah, and the name of the younger *was* Rachel. ¹⁷Leah's eyes *were* delicate, but Rachel was *o*beautiful of form and appearance.

¹⁸Now Jacob loved Rachel; so he said, *p*"I will serve you seven years for Rachel your younger daughter."

¹⁹And Laban said, "*It is* better that I give her to you than that I should give her to another man. Stay with me." ²⁰So Jacob *q*served seven years for Rachel, and they seemed *only* a few days to him because of the love he had for her.

²¹Then Jacob said to Laban, "Give me my wife, for my days are fulfilled, that I may *r*go in to her." ²²And Laban gathered together all the men of the place and *s*made a feast. ²³Now it came to pass in the evening, that he took Leah his daughter and brought her to Jacob; and he went in to her. ²⁴And Laban gave his maid *t*Zilpah to his daughter Leah *as* a maid. ²⁵So it came to pass in the morning, that behold, it *was* Leah. And he said to Laban, "What is this you have done to me? Was it not for Rachel that I served you? Why then have you *u*deceived me?"

²⁶And Laban said, "It must not be done

---

grace after cheating his brother out of the blessings of Isaac. Indeed, he was already suffering by being banished from the fellowship of his family. Nevertheless, God mercifully confirmed the covenant promises made to Abraham and Isaac concerning the land and the descendants. His words, "I am with you and will keep you" speak of God's personal presence for protection and guidance, anticipating Jacob's return to the land, so that all the promises might be fulfilled. Surely the grace of God goes far beyond our small expectations.

28:22 *a tenth.* Jacob promised to give a tenth of his possessions to God. Abraham had given the same proportion to Melchizedek, the priest of the most high God. Later the Mosaic law required giving a tenth to God (Deut. 14:22).

29:5 *son.* This term is being used in a loose sense. Nahor was actually the grandfather of Laban (22:20–23; 24:15,50).

29:6 *Rachel.* This name is a term of endearment meaning "ewe lamb."

29:21–25 *Deception*—Many times we see God's prohibitions as mere taboos. We somehow imagine that God says no just because He can, instead of acknowledging both His goodwill towards us, and His wisdom. God does not merely prohibit lying

28:20 *i* 1 Tim. 6:8   **28:21** *k* Judg. 11:31   *l* Deut. 26:17
28:22 *m* Gen. 35:7, 14   *n* Gen. 14:20   **29:1** *a* Num.
23:7   **29:2** *b* Gen. 24:10, 11   **29:4** *c* Gen. 11:31; 28:10
29:5 *d* Gen. 24:24, 29; 28:2   **29:6** *e* Gen. 43:27   *f* Ex. 2:16,
17   **29:9** *g* Ex. 2:16   **29:10** *h* Ex. 2:17   **29:11** *i* Gen.
33:4; 45:14, 15   **29:12** *j* Gen. 13:8; 14:14, 16; 28:5   *k* Gen.
24:28   **29:14** *m* Gen. 2:23; 37:27
29:15 *n* Gen. 30:28; 31:41   **29:17** *o* Gen. 12:11, 14; 26:7
29:18 *p* Gen. 31:41   **29:20** *q* Gen. 30:26   **29:21** *r* Judg.
15:1   **29:22** *s* John 2:1, 2   **29:24** *t* Gen. 30:9, 10
29:25 *u* 1 Sam. 28:12

so in our country, to give the younger before the firstborn. 27 [v]Fulfill her week, and
we will give you this one also for the service which you will serve with me still another seven years.”
28 Then Jacob did so and fulfilled her
week. So he gave him his daughter Rachel
as wife also. 29 And Laban gave his maid
[w]Bilhah to his daughter Rachel as a maid.
30 Then *Jacob* also went in to Rachel, and
he also [x]loved Rachel more than Leah. And
he served with Laban [y]still another seven
years.

The Children of Jacob

31 When the LORD [z]saw that Leah *was*
unloved, He [a]opened her womb; but Rachel
was barren. 32 So Leah conceived and bore
a son, and she called his name Reuben;*
for she said, “The LORD has surely [b]looked
on my affliction. Now therefore, my husband will love me.” 33 Then she conceived
again and bore a son, and said, “Because
the LORD has heard that I *am* unloved,
He has therefore given me this *son* also.”
And she called his name Simeon.* 34 She
conceived again and bore a son, and said,
“Now this time my husband will become
attached to me, because I have borne him
three sons.” Therefore his name was called
Levi.* 35 And she conceived again and bore
a son, and said, “Now I will praise the
LORD.” Therefore she called his name [c]Ju-
dah.* Then she stopped bearing.

30 Now when Rachel saw that [a]she bore
Jacob no children, Rachel [b]envied
her sister, and said to Jacob, “Give me children, [c]or else I die!”
2 And Jacob's anger was aroused against
Rachel, and he said, [d]“*Am* I in the place of
God, who has withheld from you the fruit
of the womb?”
3 So she said, “Here is [e]my maid Bilhah;
go in to her, [f]and she will bear *a child* on
my knees, [g]that I also may have children
by her.” 4 Then she gave him Bilhah her
maid [h]as wife, and Jacob went in to her.
5 And Bilhah conceived and bore Jacob a
son. 6 Then Rachel said, “God has [i]judged
my case; and He has also heard my voice
and given me a son.” Therefore she called
his name Dan.* 7 And Rachel's maid Bilhah
conceived again and bore Jacob a second
son. 8 Then Rachel said, “With great wres-
tlings I have wrestled with my sister, *and*
indeed I have prevailed.” So she called his
name Naphtali.*
9 When Leah saw that she had stopped
bearing, she took Zilpah her maid and
[j]gave her to Jacob as wife. 10 And Leah's
maid Zilpah bore Jacob a son. 11 Then Leah
said, “A troop comes!”* So she called his
name Gad.* 12 And Leah's maid Zilpah bore
Jacob a second son. 13 Then Leah said, “I
am happy, for the daughters [k]will call me
blessed.” So she called his name Asher.*
14 Now Reuben went in the days of wheat
harvest and found mandrakes in the field,
and brought them to his mother Leah.
Then Rachel said to Leah, [l]“Please give me
some of your son's mandrakes.”
15 But she said to her, [m]“*Is it* a small matter that you have taken away my husband?
Would you take away my son's mandrakes
also?”
And Rachel said, “Therefore he will
lie with you tonight for your son's mandrakes.”
16 When Jacob came out of the field in
the evening, Leah went out to meet him
and said, “You must come in to me, for I
have surely hired you with my son's mandrakes.” And he lay with her that night.
17 And God listened to Leah, and she
conceived and bore Jacob a fifth son.
18 Leah said, “God has given me my wages,
because I have given my maid to my husband.” So she called his name Issachar.*
19 Then Leah conceived again and bore Jacob a sixth son. 20 And Leah said, “God has
endowed me *with* a good endowment; now
my husband will dwell with me, because
I have borne him six sons.” So she called
his name Zebulun.* 21 Afterward she bore
a [n]daughter, and called her name Dinah.
22 Then God [o]remembered Rachel, and
God listened to her and [p]opened her womb.
23 And she conceived and bore a son, and
said, “God has taken away [q]my reproach.”

* 29:32 Literally *See, a Son* * 29:33 Literally *Heard* * 29:34 Literally *Attached* * 29:35 Literally *Praise* * 30:6 Literally *Judge* * 30:8 Literally *My Wrestling* * 30:11 Following Qere, Syriac, and Targum; Kethib, Septuagint, and Vulgate read *in fortune.* • Literally *Troop* or *Fortune* * 30:13 Literally *Happy* * 30:18 Literally *Wages* * 30:20 Literally *Dwelling*

---

because He can, it is because it is destructive. Jacob learned through experience that trickery and deceit bring complicated and painful consequences. False dealing destroys trust in a relationship, and once trust has been broken it is difficult, if not impossible, to entirely restore it.

29:31 *unloved.* God was kind to Leah in her predicament. Even though she was the unloved wife, it was through her son Judah that the messianic line was carried out.

30:14 *mandrakes.* This is a plant which was regarded as an aid to conception. Its aroma was associated with lovemaking (Song 7:13).

30:22 *remembered . . . listened to her . . . opened.* These three verbs emphasize conception as a gift from God.

29:27 [v] Judg. 14:2 **29:29** [w] Gen. 30:3–5 **29:30** [x] Deut. 21:15–17 [y] Gen. 30:26; 31:41 **29:31** [z] Ps. 127:3 [a] Gen. 30:1 **29:32** [b] Deut. 26:7 **29:35** [c] Matt. 1:2 **30:1** [a] Gen. 16:1, 2; 29:31 [b] Gen. 37:11 [c] [Job 5:2] **30:2** [d] 1 Sam. 1:5 **30:3** [e] Gen. 16:2 [f] Gen. 50:23 [g] Gen. 16:2, 3 **30:4** [h] Gen. 16:3, 4 **30:6** [i] Lam. 3:59 **30:9** [j] Gen. 30:4 **30:13** [k] Luke 1:48 **30:14** [l] Gen. 25:30 **30:15** [m] [Num. 16:9, 13] **30:21** [n] Gen. 34:1 **30:22** [o] 1 Sam. 1:19, 20 [p] Gen. 29:31 **30:23** [q] Luke 1:25

²⁴So she called his name Joseph,* and said, ʳ"The Lᴏʀᴅ shall add to me another son."

Jacob's Agreement with Laban

²⁵And it came to pass, when Rachel had borne Joseph, that Jacob said to Laban, ˢ"Send me away, that I may go to ᵗmy own place and to my country. ²⁶Give *me* my wives and my children ᵘfor whom I have served you, and let me go; for you know my service which ᵛI have done for you."

²⁷And Laban said to him, "Please *stay*, if I have found favor in your eyes, *for* I have learned by experience that the Lᴏʀᴅ has blessed me for your sake." ²⁸Then he said, ʷ"Name me your wages, and I will give *it*." ²⁹So *Jacob* said to him, ˣ"You know how I have served you and how your livestock has been with me. ³⁰For what you had before I *came was* little, and it has increased to a great amount; the Lᴏʀᴅ has blessed you since my coming. And now, when shall I also ʸprovide for my own house?"

³¹So he said, "What shall I give you?" And Jacob said, "You shall not give me anything. If you will do this thing for me, I will again feed and keep your flocks: ³²Let me pass through all your flock today, removing from there all the speckled and spotted sheep, and all the brown ones among the lambs, and the spotted and speckled among the goats; and ᶻ*these* shall be my wages. ³³So my ᵃrighteousness will answer for me in time to come, when the subject of my wages comes before you: every one that *is* not speckled and spotted among the goats, and brown among the lambs, will be considered stolen, if *it is* with me."

³⁴And Laban said, "Oh, that it were according to your word!" ³⁵So he removed that day the male goats that were ᵇspeckled and spotted, all the female goats that were speckled and spotted, every one that had *some* white in it, and all the brown ones among the lambs, and gave *them* into the hand of his sons. ³⁶Then he put three days' journey between himself and Jacob, and Jacob fed the rest of Laban's flocks.

³⁷Now ᶜJacob took for himself rods of green poplar and of the almond and chestnut trees, peeled white strips in them, and exposed the white which *was* in the rods. ³⁸And the rods which he had peeled, he set before the flocks in the gutters, in the watering troughs where the flocks came to drink, so that they should conceive when they came to drink. ³⁹So the flocks conceived before the rods, and the flocks brought forth streaked, speckled, and spotted. ⁴⁰Then Jacob separated the lambs, and made the flocks face toward the streaked and all the brown in the flock of Laban; but he put his own flocks by themselves and did not put them with Laban's flock.

⁴¹And it came to pass, whenever the stronger livestock conceived, that Jacob placed the rods before the eyes of the livestock in the gutters, that they might conceive among the rods. ⁴²But when the flocks were feeble, he did not put *them* in; so the feebler were Laban's and the stronger Jacob's. ⁴³Thus the man ᵈbecame exceedingly prosperous, and ᵉhad large flocks, female and male servants, and camels and donkeys.

Jacob Flees from Laban

31 Now *Jacob* heard the words of Laban's sons, saying, "Jacob has taken away all that was our father's, and from what was our father's he has acquired all this ᵃwealth." ²And Jacob saw the ᵇcountenance of Laban, and indeed it *was* not ᶜfavorable toward him as before. ³Then the Lᴏʀᴅ said to Jacob, ᵈ"Return to the land of your fathers and to your family, and I will ᵉbe with you."

⁴So Jacob sent and called Rachel and Leah to the field, to his flock, ⁵and said to them, ᶠ"I see your father's countenance, that it *is* not *favorable* toward me as before; but the God of my father ᵍhas been with me. ⁶And ʰyou know that with all my might I have served your father. ⁷Yet your father has deceived me and ⁱchanged my wages ʲten times, but God ᵏdid not allow him to hurt me. ⁸If he said thus: 'The speckled shall be your wages,' then all the flocks

---

* **30:24** Literally *He Will Add*

30:25 own place. Even though Jacob had lived for twenty years with Laban's family, he had not adopted that place as his own. He never forgot that the promise and covenant of God were for the land of Canaan, and he knew that he must return.
30:27 blessed. God had promised to bless others through Abraham's descendants (12:2–3). Now God blessed Laban through Jacob.
30:37 rods of green poplar. Just what significance these sticks hold is unknown. Some have theorized that they were simply symbols of Jacob's faith in God. Whatever the case, God blessed Jacob by causing Laban's stock to give birth to speckled and spotted young.
31:7 deceived me. Jacob had surely lived up to his name, deceiving his old father and tricking his

brother out of the birthright. But in Laban he met his match, and tasted some of his own medicine. The consequences of dishonesty reach both ways. Because of his own trickery, Jacob had to flee from his home. He apparently never saw his mother again, and

---

30:24 ʳ Gen. 35:16–18 **30:25** ˢ Gen. 24:54, 56 ᵗ Gen. 18:33 **30:26** ᵘ Gen. 29:18–20, 27, 30 ᵛ Gen. 26:24; 39:3 **30:28** ʷ Gen. 29:15; 31:7, 41 **30:29** ˣ Gen. 31:6, 38–40 **30:30** ʸ [1 Tim. 5:8] **30:32** ᶻ Gen. 31:8 **30:33** ᵃ Ps. 37:6 **30:35** ᵇ Gen. 31:9–12 **30:37** ᶜ Gen. 31:9–12 **30:43** ᵈ Gen. 12:16; 30:30 ᵉ Gen. 13:2; 24:35; 26:13, 14 **31:1** ᵃ Ps. 49:16 **31:2** ᵇ Gen. 4:5 ᶜ Deut. 28:54 **31:3** ᵈ Gen. 28:15, 20, 21; 32:9 ᵉ Gen. 46:4 **31:5** ᶠ Gen. 31:2, 3 ᵍ Is. 41:10 **31:6** ʰ Gen. 30:29; 31:38–41 **31:7** ⁱ Gen. 29:25; 31:41 ʲ Num. 14:22 ᵏ Job 1:10

bore speckled. And if he said thus: [i]'The streaked shall be your wages,' then all the flocks bore streaked. 9So God has [m]taken away the livestock of your father and given *them* to me.

10"And it happened, at the time when the flocks conceived, that I lifted my eyes and saw in a dream, and behold, the rams which leaped upon the flocks *were* streaked, speckled, and gray-spotted. 11Then [n]the Angel of God spoke to me in a dream, saying, 'Jacob.' And I said, 'Here I am.' 12And He said, 'Lift your eyes now and see, all the rams which leap on the flocks *are* streaked, speckled, and gray-spotted; for [o]I have seen all that Laban is doing to you. 13I *am* the God of Bethel, [p]where you anointed the pillar *and* where you made a vow to Me. Now [q]arise, get out of this land, and return to the land of your family.' "

14Then Rachel and Leah answered and said to him, [r]"Is there still any portion or inheritance for us in our father's house? 15Are we not considered strangers by him? For [s]he has sold us, and also completely consumed our money. 16For all these riches which God has taken from our father are *really* ours and our children's; now then, whatever God has said to you, do it."

17Then Jacob rose and set his sons and his wives on camels. 18And he carried away all his livestock and all his possessions which he had gained, his acquired livestock which he had gained in Padan Aram, to go to his father Isaac in the land of [t]Canaan. 19Now Laban had gone to shear his sheep, and Rachel had stolen the [u]household idols that were her father's. 20And Jacob stole away, unknown to Laban the Syrian, in that he did not tell him that he intended to flee. 21So he fled with all that he had. He arose and crossed the river, and [v]headed toward the mountains of Gilead.

Laban Pursues Jacob

22And Laban was told on the third day that Jacob had fled. 23Then he took [w]his brethren with him and pursued him for seven days' journey, and he overtook him in the mountains of Gilead. 24But God [x]had come to Laban the Syrian in a dream by night, and said to him, "Be careful that you [y]speak to Jacob neither good nor bad."

25So Laban overtook Jacob. Now Jacob had pitched his tent in the mountains, and

Laban with his brethren pitched in the mountains of Gilead.

26And Laban said to Jacob: "What have you done, that you have stolen away unknown to me, and [z]carried away my daughters like captives *taken* with the sword? 27Why did you flee away secretly, and steal away from me, and not tell me; for I might have sent you away with joy and songs, with timbrel and harp? 28And you did not allow me to kiss my sons and my daughters. Now [b]you have done foolishly in *so* doing. 29It is in my power to do you harm, but the [c]God of your father spoke to me [d]last night, saying, 'Be careful that you speak to Jacob neither good nor bad.' 30And now you have surely gone because you greatly long for your father's house, *but* why did you [e]steal my gods?"

31Then Jacob answered and said to Laban, "Because I was [f]afraid, for I said, 'Perhaps you would take your daughters from me by force.' 32With whomever you find your gods, [g]do not let him live. In the presence of our brethren, identify what I have of yours and take *it* with you." For Jacob did not know that Rachel had stolen them.

33And Laban went into Jacob's tent, into Leah's tent, and into the two maids' tents, but he did not find *them*. Then he went out of Leah's tent and entered Rachel's tent. 34Now Rachel had taken the household idols, put them in the camel's saddle, and sat on them. And Laban searched all about the tent but did not find *them*. 35And she said to her father, "Let it not displease my lord that I cannot [h]rise before you, for the manner of women *is* with me." And he searched but did not find the household idols.

36Then Jacob was angry and rebuked Laban, and Jacob answered and said to Laban: "What *is* my trespass? What *is* my sin, that you have so hotly pursued me? 37Although you have searched all my things, what part of your household things have you found? Set *it* here before my brethren and your brethren, that they may judge between us both! 38These twenty years I *have* been with you; your ewes and your female goats have not miscarried their young, and I have not eaten the rams of your flock. 39[i]That which was torn *by beasts* I did not bring to you; I bore the loss of it. [j]You required it from my hand, *whether* stolen

---

his relationship with his father and his only brother was broken. Lying not only harms the liar, but it also affects those he lies to. Because of Laban's trickery, Jacob was saddled with an unloved wife, quarreling sons, and constant domestic strife.

31:19 idols. Laban's family may have been polytheistic (believing in many gods), as Abraham's father Terah evidently was (Josh. 24:1–3). Considering the evidence of verses 25–50 it seems likely that they worshiped Yahweh along with other "lesser gods." In this culture, the possession of the idols was the right

31:8 [l] Gen. 30:32   **31:9** [m] Gen. 31:1, 16   **31:11** [n] Gen. 16:7–11; 22:11, 15; 31:13; 48:16   **31:12** [o] Ex. 3:7   **31:13** [p] Gen. 28:16–22; 35:1, 6, 15   [q] Gen. 31:3; 32:9   **31:14** [r] Gen. 2:24   **31:15** [s] Gen. 29:15; 20, 23, 27   **31:18** [t] Gen. 17:8; 33:18; 35:27   **31:19** [u] Judg. 17:5   **31:21** [v] 2 Kin. 12:17   **31:23** [w] Gen. 13:8   **31:24** [x] Gen. 20:3; 31:29; 46:2–4   [y] Gen. 24:50; 31:7, 29   **31:26** [z] 1 Sam. 30:2   **31:28** [a] Gen. 31:55   [b] 1 Sam. 13:13   **31:29** [c] Gen. 28:13; 31:5, 24, 42, 53   [d] Gen. 31:24   **31:30** [e] Judg. 17:5; 18:24   **31:31** [f] Gen. 26:7; 32:7, 11   **31:32** [g] Gen. 44:9   **31:35** [h] Lev. 19:32   **31:39** [i] Ex. 22:10   [j] Ex. 22:10–13

by day or stolen by night. [40]*There* I was! In the day the drought consumed me, and the frost by night, and my sleep departed from my eyes. [41]Thus I have been in your house twenty years; I [k]served you fourteen years for your two daughters, and six years for your flock, and [l]you have changed my wages ten times. [42][m]Unless the God of my father, the God of Abraham and [n]the Fear of Isaac, had been with me, surely now you would have sent me away empty-handed. [o]God has seen my affliction and the labor of my hands, and [p]rebuked you last night."

Laban's Covenant with Jacob

[43]And Laban answered and said to Jacob, "*These* daughters *are* my daughters, and *these* children *are* my children, and *this* flock *is* my flock; all that you see *is* mine. But what can I do this day to these my daughters or to their children whom they have borne? [44]Now therefore, come, [q]let us make a covenant, [r]you and I, and let it be a witness between you and me."

[45]So Jacob [s]took a stone and set it up *as* a pillar. [46]Then Jacob said to his brethren, "Gather stones." And they took stones and made a heap, and they ate there on the heap. [47]Laban called it Jegar Sahadutha,* but Jacob called it Galeed.* [48]And Laban said, [t]"This heap *is* a witness between you and me this day." Therefore its name was called Galeed, [49]also [u]Mizpah,* because he said, "May the LORD watch between you and me when we are absent one from another. [50]If you afflict my daughters, or if you take *other* wives besides my daughters, *although* no man *is* with us—see, God *is* witness between you and me!"

[51]Then Laban said to Jacob, "Here is this heap and here is *this* pillar, which I have placed between you and me. [52]This heap *is* a witness, and *this* pillar *is* a witness, that I will not pass beyond this heap to you, and you will not pass beyond this heap and this pillar to me, for harm. [53]The God of Abraham, the God of Nahor, and the God of their father [v]judge between us." And Jacob [w]swore by [x]the Fear of his father Isaac. [54]Then Jacob offered a sacrifice on the mountain, and called his brethren to eat bread. And they ate bread and stayed all night on the mountain. [55]And early in the morning Laban arose, and [y]kissed his sons and daughters and [z]blessed them. Then Laban departed and [a]returned to his place.

Esau Comes to Meet Jacob

32 So Jacob went on his way, and [a]the angels of God met him. [2]When Jacob saw them, he said, "This *is* God's [b]camp." And he called the name of that place Mahanaim.*

[3]Then Jacob sent messengers before him to Esau his brother [c]in the land of Seir, [d]the country of Edom. [4]And he commanded them, saying, [e]"Speak thus to my lord Esau, 'Thus your servant Jacob says: "I have dwelt with Laban and stayed there until now. [5][f]I have oxen, donkeys, flocks, and male and female servants; and I have sent to tell my lord, that [g]I may find favor in your sight." ' "

[6]Then the messengers returned to Jacob, saying, "We came to your brother Esau, and [h]he also is coming to meet you, and four hundred men *are* with him." [7]So Jacob was greatly afraid and [i]distressed; and he divided the people that *were* with him, and the flocks and herds and camels, into two companies. [8]And he said, "If Esau comes to the one company and attacks it, then the other company which is left will escape."

[9][j]Then Jacob said, [k]"O God of my father Abraham and God of my father Isaac, the LORD [l]who said to me, 'Return to your country and to your family, and I will deal well with you': [10]I am not worthy of the least of all the [m]mercies and of all the truth which You have shown Your servant; for I crossed over this Jordan with [n]my staff, and now I have become two companies. [11]oDeliver me, I pray, from the hand of my brother, from the hand of Esau; for I fear him, lest he come and attack me *and* [p]the mother with the children. [12]For [q]You said, 'I will surely treat you well, and make your descendants as the [r]sand of the sea, which cannot be numbered for multitude.' "

---

* **31:47** Literally, in Aramaic, *Heap of Witness*
• Literally, in Hebrew, *Heap of Witness*
* **31:49** Literally *Watch*   * **32:2** Literally *Double Camp*

---

of the principal heir. Rachel probably did not steal the idols in order to worship them, but because they represented ownership of her father's property.
31:44 covenant. This instance of a covenant was an agreement between two equals.
31:49 Mizpah. This name means "outlook point," a place to keep watch. God above had His eyes on both men to make them keep their covenant.
31:53 The God of Abraham. The wording in Laban's oath suggests that Abraham, Nahor, and their father Terah all worshiped the same One True God. Joshua records the fact that Terah at least worshiped other gods as well (Josh. 24:1–3). It is possible that they were henotheistic—worshiping God not as the only God but as the most important and powerful among many.

32:11 Deliver me, I pray. Jacob did not pray in generalities. He named his concerns openly, and concluded with another appeal to God's promises. Christians

31:41 [k]Gen. 29:20, 27–30 [l]Gen. 31:7   **31:42** [m]Ps. 124:1, 2 [n]Is. 8:13 [o]Ex. 3:7 [p]1 Chr. 12:17   **31:44** [q]Gen. 21:27, 32; 26:28 [r]Josh. 24:27   **31:45** [s]Gen. 28:18; 35:14   **31:48** [t]Josh. 24:27   **31:49** [u]Judg. 10:17; 11:29   **31:53** [v]Gen. 16:5 [w]Gen. 21:23 [x]Gen. 31:42   **31:55** [y]Gen. 29:11, 13; 31:28, 43 [z]Gen. 28:1 [a]Num. 24:25   **32:1** [a]Num. 22:31   **32:2** [b]Josh. 5:14   **32:3** [c]Gen. 14:6; 33:14, 16 [d]Gen. 25:30; 36:6–9   **32:4** [e]Prov. 15:1   **32:5** [f]Gen. 30:43 [g]Gen. 33:8, 15   **32:6** [h]Gen. 33:1   **32:7** [i]Gen. 32:11; 35:3   **32:9** [j][Ps. 50:15] [k]Gen. 28:13; 31:42 [l]Gen. 31:3, 13   **32:10** [m]Gen. 24:27 [n]Job 8:7   **32:11** [o]Ps. 59:1, 2 [p]Hos. 10:14   **32:12** [q]Gen. 28:13–15 [r]Gen. 22:17

13So he lodged there that same night, and took what came to his hand as sa present for Esau his brother: 14two hundred female goats and twenty male goats, two hundred ewes and twenty rams, 15thirty milk camels with their colts, forty cows and ten bulls, twenty female donkeys and ten foals. 16Then he delivered *them* to the hand of his servants, every drove by itself, and said to his servants, "Pass over before me, and put some distance between successive droves." 17And he commanded the first one, saying, "When Esau my brother meets you and asks you, saying, 'To whom do you belong, and where are you going? Whose *are* these in front of you?' 18then you shall say, 'They *are* your servant Jacob's. It *is a* present sent to my lord Esau; and behold, he also *is* behind us.' " 19So he commanded the second, the third, and all who followed the droves, saying, "In this manner you shall speak to Esau when you find him; 20and also say, 'Behold, your servant Jacob *is* behind us.' " For he said, "I will tappease him with the present that goes before me, and afterward I will see his face; perhaps he will accept me." 21So the present went on over before him, but he himself lodged that night in the camp.

Wrestling with God

22And he arose that night and took his two wives, his two female servants, and his eleven sons, uand crossed over the ford of Jabbok. 23He took them, sent them over the brook, and sent over what he had. 24Then Jacob was left alone; and va Man wrestled with him until the breaking of day. 25Now when He saw that He did not prevail against him, He touched the socket of his hip; and wthe socket of Jacob's hip was out of joint as He wrestled with him. 26And xHe said, "Let Me go, for the day breaks."

But he said, y"I will not let You go unless You bless me!"

27So He said to him, "What *is* your name?"

He said, "Jacob."

28And He said, z"Your name shall no longer be called Jacob, but Israel;* for you have astruggled with God and bwith men, and have prevailed."

29Then Jacob asked, saying, "Tell *me* Your name, I pray."

And He said, c"Why *is* it *that* you ask about My name?" And He dblessed him there.

30So Jacob called the name of the place Peniel:* "For eI have seen God face to face, and my life is preserved." 31Just as he crossed over Penuel* the sun rose on him, and he limped on his hip. 32Therefore to this day the children of Israel do not eat the muscle that shrank, which *is* on the hip socket, because He touched the socket of Jacob's hip in the muscle that shrank.

Jacob and Esau Meet

33 Now Jacob lifted his eyes and looked, and there, aEsau was coming, and with him were four hundred men. So he divided the children among Leah, Rachel, and the two maidservants. 2And he put the maidservants and their children in front, Leah and her children behind, and Rachel and Joseph last. 3Then he crossed over before them and bbowed himself to the ground seven times, until he came near to his brother.

4cBut Esau ran to meet him, and embraced him, dand fell on his neck and kissed him, and they wept. 5And he lifted his eyes and saw the women and children, and said, "Who *are* these with you?"

So he said, "The children ewhom God has graciously given your servant." 6Then the maidservants came near, they and their children, and bowed down. 7And Leah also came near with her children, and they bowed down. Afterward Joseph and Rachel came near, and they bowed down.

8Then Esau said, "What *do you mean by* fall this company which I met?"

And he said, "*These are* gto find favor in the sight of my lord."

9But Esau said, "I have enough, my brother; keep what you have for yourself."

10And Jacob said, "No, please, if I hhave now found favor in your sight, then receive my present from my hand, inasmuch as I have seen your face as though I had seen

* **32:28** Literally *Prince with God*   * **32:30** Literally *Face of God*   * **32:31** Same as *Peniel,* verse 30

---

today can likewise base their prayers on God's proven character and His promises in the Bible.

32:24 *A Man wrestled with him.* Some believe that the Man who wrestled with Jacob was the preincarnate Jesus Christ. Others believe the Man was the Angel of God (21:17; 31:11). In any case, Jacob wrestled with a manifestation of God (vv. 28–30), and because of God's mercy he survived.

32:28 *Israel.* Before Jacob wrestled with the angel, his name, "one who supplants," described a man who was deceitful in character. Afterwards he was given the new status of a champion, "one who strives (or prevails) with God," or "prince with God."

32:30 *God face to face.* The dramatic name ("face of God") given to the location shows the awesome

nature of the encounter. Here God's messenger in human form was the same as God Himself, a fact which Jacob recognized to his amazement. In Hebrew thought, the penalty for seeing God face to face was death (Ex. 33:20), yet Jacob had passed through such an experience and had survived.

32:13 s Gen. 43:11   **32:20** t [Prov. 21:14]   **32:22** u Deut. 3:16   **32:24** v Hos. 12:2–4   **32:25** w 2 Cor. 12:7   **32:26** x Luke 24:28   y Hos. 12:4   **32:28** z Gen. 35:10   a Hos. 12:3, 4   b Gen. 25:31; 27:33   **32:29** c Judg. 13:17, 18   d Gen. 35:9   **32:30** e Gen. 16:13   **33:1** a Gen. 32:6   **33:3** b Gen. 18:2; 42:6   **33:4** c Gen. 32:28   d Gen. 45:14, 15   **33:5** e Gen. 48:9   **33:8** f Gen. 32:13–16   g Gen. 32:5   **33:10** h Gen. 43:3

the face of God, and you were pleased with me. ¹¹Please, take ⁱmy blessing that is brought to you, because God has dealt ʲgraciously with me, and because I have enough." ᵏSo he urged him, and he took *it.*

¹²Then Esau said, "Let us take our journey; let us go, and I will go before you."

¹³But Jacob said to him, "My lord knows that the children *are* weak, and the flocks and herds which are nursing *are* with me. And if the men should drive them hard one day, all the flock will die. ¹⁴Please let my lord go on ahead before his servant. I will lead on slowly at a pace which the livestock that go before me, and the children, are able to endure, until I come to my lord ˡin Seir."

¹⁵And Esau said, "Now let me leave with you *some* of the people who *are* with me."

But he said, "What need is there? ᵐLet me find favor in the sight of my lord." ¹⁶So Esau returned that day on his way to Seir. ¹⁷And Jacob journeyed to ⁿSuccoth, built himself a house, and made booths for his livestock. Therefore the name of the place is called Succoth.*

Jacob Comes to Canaan

¹⁸Then Jacob came safely to ᵒthe city of ᵖShechem, which *is* in the land of Canaan, when he came from Padan Aram; and he pitched his tent before the city. ¹⁹And ᑫhe bought the parcel of land, where he had pitched his tent, from the children of Hamor, Shechem's father, for one hundred pieces of money. ²⁰Then he erected an altar there and called it ʳEl Elohe Israel.*

The Dinah Incident

34 Now ᵃDinah the daughter of Leah, whom she had borne to Jacob, went out to see the daughters of the land. ²And when Shechem the son of Hamor the Hivite, prince of the country, saw her, he ᵇtook her and lay with her, and violated her. ³His soul was strongly attracted to Dinah the daughter of Jacob, and he loved the young woman and spoke kindly to the young woman. ⁴So Shechem ᶜspoke to his father Hamor, saying, "Get me this young woman as a wife."

⁵And Jacob heard that he had defiled Dinah his daughter. Now his sons were with his livestock in the field; so Jacob ᵈheld his peace until they came. ⁶Then Hamor the father of Shechem went out to Jacob to speak with him. ⁷And the sons of Jacob came in from the field when they heard *it;* and the men were grieved and very angry, because

he ᵉhad done a disgraceful thing in Israel by lying with Jacob's daughter, ᶠa thing which ought not to be done. ⁸But Hamor spoke with them, saying, "The soul of my son Shechem longs for your daughter. Please give her to him as a wife. ⁹And make marriages with us; give your daughters to us, and take our daughters to yourselves. ¹⁰So you shall dwell with us, and the land shall be before you. Dwell and trade in it, and acquire possessions for yourselves in it."

¹¹Then Shechem said to her father and her brothers, "Let me find favor in your eyes, and whatever you say to me I will give. ¹²Ask me ever so much ᵍdowry and gift, and I will give according to what you say to me; but give me the young woman as a wife."

¹³But the sons of Jacob answered Shechem and Hamor his father, and spoke ʰdeceitfully, because he had defiled Dinah their sister. ¹⁴And they said to them, "We cannot do this thing, to give our sister to one who is ⁱuncircumcised, for ʲthat *would be* a reproach to us. ¹⁵But on this *condition* we will consent to you: If you will become as we *are,* if every male of you is circumcised, ¹⁶then we will give our daughters to you, and we will take your daughters to us; and we will dwell with you, and we will become one people. ¹⁷But if you will not heed us and be circumcised, then we will take our daughter and be gone."

¹⁸And their words pleased Hamor and Shechem, Hamor's son. ¹⁹So the young man did not delay to do the thing, because he delighted in Jacob's daughter. He *was* ᵏmore honorable than all the household of his father.

²⁰And Hamor and Shechem his son came to the ˡgate of their city, and spoke with the men of their city, saying: ²¹"These men *are* at peace with us. Therefore let them dwell in the land and trade in it. For indeed the land *is* large enough for them. Let us take their daughters to us as wives, and let us give them our daughters. ²²Only on this *condition* will the men consent to dwell with us, to be one people: if every male among us is circumcised as they *are* circumcised. ²³*Will* not their livestock, their property, and every animal of theirs *be* ours? Only let us consent to them, and they will dwell with us." ²⁴And all who

---

* **33:17** Literally *Booths*   * **33:20** Literally *God, the God of Israel*

33:11 *Please, take my blessing.* Before, Jacob had done all he could to take Esau's blessing (25:29–34; 27:1–45). Now a wiser man, Jacob wanted to bless his brother with what God had given him.

33:20 *he erected an altar there.* The name Jacob gave this altar reflected his mature faith in "God, the God of Israel." The God of Jacob's fathers was now Jacob's personal God, for He had fulfilled His promises and protected him (28:13–15).

33:11 ⁱ 1 Sam. 25:27; 30:26 ʲEx. 33:19 ᵏ 2 Kin. 5:23
33:14 ˡGen. 32:3; 36:8 **33:15** ᵐRuth 2:13 **33:17** ⁿJosh. 13:27 **33:18** ᵒJohn 3:23 ᵖJosh. 24:1 **33:19** ᑫJohn 4:5
33:20 ʳGen. 35:7 **34:1** ᵃGen. 30:21 **34:2** ᵇGen. 20:2
34:4 ᶜJudg. 14:2 **34:5** ᵈ2 Sam. 13:22 **34:7** ᵉJudg. 20:6 ᶠ2 Sam. 13:12 **34:12** ᵍEx. 22:16, 17 **34:13** ʰGen. 31:7 **34:14** ⁱEx. 12:48 ʲJosh. 5:2–9 **34:19** ᵏ1 Chr. 4:9
34:20 ˡRuth 4:1, 11

[m]went out of the gate of his city heeded Hamor and Shechem his son; every male was circumcised, all who went out of the gate of his city.

25Now it came to pass on the third day, when they were in pain, that two of the sons of Jacob, [n]Simeon and Levi, Dinah's brothers, each took his sword and came boldly upon the city and killed all the males. 26And they [o]killed Hamor and Shechem his son with the edge of the sword, and took Dinah from Shechem's house, and went out. 27The sons of Jacob came upon the slain, and plundered the city, because their sister had been defiled. 28They took their sheep, their oxen, and their donkeys, what was in the city and what was in the field, 29and all their wealth. All their little ones and their wives they took captive; and they plundered even all that was in the houses.

30Then Jacob said to Simeon and Levi, [p]"You have [q]troubled me [r]by making me obnoxious among the inhabitants of the land, among the Canaanites and the Perizzites; [s]and since I am few in number, they will gather themselves together against me and kill me. I shall be destroyed, my household and I." 31But they said, "Should he treat our sister like a harlot?"

Jacob's Return to Bethel

35 Then God said to Jacob, "Arise, go up to [a]Bethel and dwell there; and make an altar there to God, [b]who appeared to you [c]when you fled from the face of Esau your brother."

2And Jacob said to his [d]household and to all who were with him, "Put away [e]the foreign gods that are among you, [f]purify yourselves, and change your garments. 3Then let us arise and go up to Bethel; and I will make an altar there to God, [g]who answered me in the day of my distress [h]and has been with me in the way which I have gone." 4So they gave Jacob all the foreign gods which were in their hands, and the [i]earrings which were in their ears; and Jacob hid them under [j]the terebinth tree which was by Shechem.

5And they journeyed, and [k]the terror of God was upon the cities that were all around them, and they did not pursue the sons of Jacob. 6So Jacob came to [l]Luz (that is, Bethel), which is in the land of Canaan, he and all the people who were with him. 7And he [m]built an altar there and called the place El Bethel,* because [n]there God appeared to him when he fled from the face of his brother.

8Now [o]Deborah, Rebekah's nurse, died, and she was buried below Bethel under the terebinth tree. So the name of it was called Allon Bachuth.*

9Then [p]God appeared to Jacob again, when he came from Padan Aram, and [q]blessed him. 10And God said to him, "Your name is Jacob; [r]your name shall not be called Jacob anymore, [s]but Israel shall be your name." So He called his name Israel. 11Also God said to him: [t]"I am God Almighty. [u]Be fruitful and multiply; [v]a nation and a company of nations shall proceed from you, and kings shall come from your body. 12The [w]land which I gave Abraham and Isaac I give to you; and to your descendants after you I give this land." 13Then God [x]went up from him in the place where He talked with him. 14So Jacob [y]set up a pillar in the place where He talked with him, a pillar of stone; and he poured a drink offering on it, and he poured oil on it. 15And Jacob called the name of the place where God spoke with him, [z]Bethel.

Death of Rachel

16Then they journeyed from Bethel. And when there was but a little distance to go to Ephrath, Rachel labored in childbirth,

---

* **35:7** Literally *God of the House of God*
* **35:8** Literally *Terebinth of Weeping*

34:25 killed all the males. Jacob's sons were correct that God did not want them to intermarry with the pagan Canaanite families. According to later Levitical law, they were even correct that rape was punishable by death. However, their treacherous pretended friendship and the massacre of all the men of Shechem, along with their greedy looting of all the Shechemites' goods, was clearly not a justifiable execution of justice, and God condemned their violence and anger (49:5–7).

35:2 foreign gods. Jacob's command included the idols that Rachel had stolen (31:22–35) as well as any idols among his servants. These were not gods Jacob himself had been worshiping, but he had apparently been allowing others in his household to do so.

35:10–12 Israel shall be your name. The renewal of God's covenant with Jacob was introduced by confirming Jacob's change of name to Israel, the one who "wrestled with God and prevailed." The promises made to Abraham and Isaac were once again repeated, underscoring the continuity of the covenant. Furthermore, a rather significant phrase is added, "be fruitful and multiply," which incorporated the creation ordinance, thus exhibiting the continuity with the covenant of creation. The covenant Lord is the God of creation and of redemption.

35:16 Ephrath. This is an alternative name for the region around Bethlehem (v. 19; 48:7; Ruth 1:2; Mic. 5:2). The King of Glory would one day be born near the birthplace of Benjamin (Matt. 2:1).

34:24 [m] Gen. 23:10, 18   **34:25** [n] Gen. 29:33, 34; 42:24; 49:5–7   **34:26** [o] Gen. 49:5, 6   **34:30** [p] Gen. 49:6   [q] Josh. 7:25   [r] Ex. 5:21   [s] Deut. 4:27   **35:1** [a] Gen. 28:19; 31:13   [b] Gen. 28:13   [c] Gen. 27:43   **35:2** [d] Josh. 24:15   [e] Gen. 24:2, 14, 23   [f] Ex. 19:10, 14   **35:3** [g] Gen. 32:7, 24   [h] Gen. 28:15, 20; 31:3, 42   **35:4** [i] Hos. 2:13   [j] Josh. 24:26   **35:5** [k] Ex. 15:16; 23:27   **35:6** [l] Gen. 28:19, 22; 48:3   **35:7** [m] Eccl. 5:4   [n] Gen. 28:13   **35:8** [o] Gen. 24:59   **35:9** [p] Josh. 5:13   [q] Gen. 32:29   **35:10** [r] Gen. 17:5   [s] Gen. 32:28   **35:11** [t] Ex. 6:3   [u] Gen. 9:1, 7   [v] Gen. 17:5, 6, 16; 28:3; 48:4   **35:12** [w] Gen. 12:7; 13:15; 26:3, 4; 28:13; 48:4   **35:13** [x] Gen. 17:22; 18:33   **35:14** [y] Gen. 28:18, 19; 31:45   **35:15** [z] Gen. 28:19

and she had hard labor. [17]Now it came to pass, when she was in hard labor, that the midwife said to her, "Do not fear; [a]you will have this son also." [18]And so it was, as her soul was departing (for she died), that she called his name Ben-Oni;* but his father called him Benjamin.* [19]So [b]Rachel died and was buried on the way to [c]Ephrath (that is, Bethlehem). [20]And Jacob set a pillar on her grave, which is the pillar of Rachel's grave [d]to this day.

[21]Then Israel journeyed and pitched his tent beyond [e]the tower of Eder. [22]And it happened, when Israel dwelt in that land, that Reuben went and [f]lay with Bilhah his father's concubine; and Israel heard about it.

Jacob's Twelve Sons

Now the sons of Jacob were twelve: [23]the sons of Leah were [g]Reuben, Jacob's firstborn, and Simeon, Levi, Judah, Issachar, and Zebulun; [24]the sons of Rachel were Joseph and Benjamin; [25]the sons of Bilhah, Rachel's maidservant, were Dan and Naphtali; [26]and the sons of Zilpah, Leah's maidservant, were Gad and Asher. These were the sons of Jacob who were born to him in Padan Aram.

Death of Isaac

[27]Then Jacob came to his father Isaac at [h]Mamre, or [i]Kirjath Arba* (that is, Hebron), where Abraham and Isaac had dwelt. [28]Now the days of Isaac were one hundred and eighty years. [29]So Isaac breathed his last and died, and [j]was gathered to his people, being old and full of days. And [k]his sons Esau and Jacob buried him.

The Family of Esau

36 Now this is the genealogy of Esau, [a]who is Edom. [2b]Esau took his wives from the daughters of Canaan: Adah the daughter of Elon the [c]Hittite; [d]Aholibamah the daughter of Anah, the daughter of Zibeon the Hivite; [3]and [e]Basemath, Ishmael's daughter, sister of Nebajoth. [4]Now [f]Adah bore Eliphaz to Esau, and Basemath bore Reuel. [5]And Aholibamah bore Jeush, Jaalam, and Korah. These were the sons of Esau who were born to him in the land of Canaan.

[6]Then Esau took his wives, his sons, his daughters, and all the persons of his household, his cattle and all his animals, and all his goods which he had gained in the land of Canaan, and went to a country away from the presence of his brother Jacob. [7g]For their possessions were too great for them to dwell together, and [h]the land where they were strangers could not support them because of their livestock. [8]So Esau dwelt in [i]Mount Seir. [j]Esau is Edom.

[9]And this is the genealogy of Esau the father of the Edomites in Mount Seir. [10]These were the names of Esau's sons: [k]Eliphaz the son of Adah the wife of Esau, and Reuel the son of Basemath the wife of Esau. [11]And the sons of Eliphaz were Teman, Omar, Zepho,* Gatam, and Kenaz. [12]Now Timna was the concubine of Eliphaz, Esau's son, and she bore [l]Amalek to Eliphaz. These were the sons of Adah, Esau's wife.

[13]These were the sons of Reuel: Nahath, Zerah, Shammah, and Mizzah. These were the sons of Basemath, Esau's wife.

[14]These were the sons of Aholibamah, Esau's wife, the daughter of Anah, the daughter of Zibeon. And she bore to Esau: Jeush, Jaalam, and Korah.

The Chiefs of Edom

[15]These were the chiefs of the sons of Esau. The sons of Eliphaz, the firstborn son of Esau, were Chief Teman, Chief Omar, Chief Zepho, Chief Kenaz, [16]Chief Korah,* Chief Gatam, and Chief Amalek. These were the chiefs of Eliphaz in the land of Edom. They were the sons of Adah.

[17]These were the sons of Reuel, Esau's son: Chief Nahath, Chief Zerah, Chief Shammah, and Chief Mizzah. These were the chiefs of Reuel in the land of Edom. These were the sons of Basemath, Esau's wife.

[18]And these were the sons of Aholibamah, Esau's wife: Chief Jeush, Chief Jaalam, and Chief Korah. These were the chiefs who descended from Aholibamah, Esau's wife, the daughter of Anah. [19]These were the sons of Esau, who is Edom, and these were their chiefs.

The Sons of Seir

[20m]These were the sons of Seir [n]the Horite who inhabited the land: Lotan, Shobal, Zibeon, Anah, [21]Dishon, Ezer,

---

* **35:18** Literally Son of My Sorrow • Literally Son of the Right Hand   * **35:27** Literally Town of Arba   * **36:11** Spelled Zephi in 1 Chronicles 1:36   * **36:16** Samaritan Pentateuch omits Chief Korah.

35:27 Jacob came to his father Isaac. After more than 20 years of exile Jacob finally visited his father. Sadly, his mother Rebekah was probably dead since she is not mentioned.

36:12 Amalek. Esau's grandson Amalek founded a people that later would trouble the Israelites (Num. 14:39–45).

35:17 [a]Gen. 30:24   **35:19** [b]Gen. 48:7   [c]Mic. 5:2
35:20 [d]1 Sam. 10:2   **35:21** [e]Mic. 4:8   **35:22** [f]Gen. 49:4   **35:23** [g]Ex. 1:1–4   **35:27** [h]Gen. 13:18; 18:1; 23:19   [i]Josh. 14:15   **35:29** [j]Gen. 15:15; 25:8; 49:33   [k]Gen. 25:9; 49:31   **36:1** [a]Gen. 25:30   **36:2** [b]Gen. 26:34; 28:9   [c]2 Kin. 7:6   [d]Gen. 36:25   **36:3** [e]Gen. 28:9   **36:4** [f]1 Chr. 1:35   **36:7** [g]Gen. 13:6, 11   [h]Gen. 17:8; 28:4   **36:8** [i]Gen. 32:3   [j]Gen. 36:1, 19   **36:10** [k]1 Chr. 1:35   **36:12** [l]Num. 24:20   **36:20** [m]1 Chr. 1:38–42   [n]Gen. 14:6

and Dishan. These *were* the chiefs of the
Horites, the sons of Seir, in the land of
Edom.
22 And the sons of Lotan were Hori and
Hemam.* Lotan's sister *was* Timna.
23 These *were* the sons of Shobal: Alvan,*
Manahath, Ebal, Shepho,* and Onam.
24 These *were* the sons of Zibeon: both
Ajah and Anah. This *was the* Anah who
found the water* in the wilderness as he
pastured [o]the donkeys of his father Zibeon.
25 These *were* the children of Anah: Dishon
and Aholibamah the daughter of Anah.
26 These *were* the sons of Dishon:* Hemdan,* Eshban, Ithran, and Cheran. 27 These
were the sons of Ezer: Bilhan, Zaavan, and
Akan.* 28 These *were* the sons of Dishan:
[p]Uz and Aran.
29 These *were* the chiefs of the Horites:
Chief Lotan, Chief Shobal, Chief Zibeon,
Chief Anah, 30 Chief Dishon, Chief Ezer,
and Chief Dishan. These *were* the chiefs of
the Horites, according to their chiefs in the
land of Seir.

The Kings of Edom

31 [q]Now these *were* the kings who
reigned in the land of Edom before any
king reigned over the children of Israel:
32 Bela the son of Beor reigned in Edom,
and the name of his city *was* Dinhabah.
33 And when Bela died, Jobab the son of
Zerah of Bozrah reigned in his place.
34 When Jobab died, Husham of the land
of the Temanites reigned in his place.
35 And when Husham died, Hadad the son
of Bedad, who attacked Midian in the field
of Moab, reigned in his place. And the
name of his city *was* Avith. 36 When Hadad died, Samlah of Masrekah reigned in
his place. 37 And when Samlah died, Saul
of [r]Rehoboth-*by*-the-River reigned in his
place. 38 When Saul died, Baal-Hanan the
son of Achbor reigned in his place. 39 And
when Baal-Hanan the son of Achbor died,
Hadar* reigned in his place; and the name
of his city *was* Pau.* His wife's name *was*
Mehetabel, the daughter of Matred, the
daughter of Mezahab.

The Chiefs of Esau

40 And these *were* the names of the chiefs
of Esau, according to their families and
their places, by their names: Chief Timnah,
Chief Alvah,* Chief Jetheth, 41 Chief Aholibamah, Chief Elah, Chief Pinon, 42 Chief
Kenaz, Chief Teman, Chief Mibzar, 43 Chief
Magdiel, and Chief Iram. These *were* the
chiefs of Edom, according to their dwelling
places in the land of their possession. Esau
was the father of the Edomites.

Joseph Dreams of Greatness

37 Now Jacob dwelt in the land [a]where
his father was a stranger, in the land
of Canaan. 2 This *is* the history of Jacob.
Joseph, *being* seventeen years old, was
feeding the flock with his brothers. And
the lad *was* with the sons of Bilhah and
the sons of Zilpah, his father's wives; and
Joseph brought a [b]bad report of them to his
father.
3 Now Israel loved Joseph more than all
his children, because he *was* [c]the son of
his old age. Also he [d]made him a tunic of
many colors. 4 But when his brothers saw
that their father loved him more than all
his brothers, they [e]hated him and could not
speak peaceably to him.
5 Now Joseph had a dream, and he told
it to his brothers; and they hated him even
more. 6 So he said to them, "Please hear this
dream which I have dreamed: 7 [f]There we
were, binding sheaves in the field. Then
behold, my sheaf arose and also stood upright; and indeed your sheaves stood all
around and bowed down to my sheaf."
8 And his brothers said to him, "Shall you

* **36:22** Spelled *Homam* in 1 Chronicles 1:39 * **36:23** Spelled *Alian* in 1 Chronicles 1:40 • Spelled *Shephi* in 1 Chronicles 1:40 * **36:24** Following Masoretic Text and Vulgate (*hot springs*); Septuagint reads *Jamin;* Targum reads *mighty men;* Talmud interprets as *mules.* * **36:26** Hebrew *Dishan* • Spelled *Hamran* in 1 Chronicles 1:41 * **36:27** Spelled *Jaakan* in 1 Chronicles 1:42 * **36:39** Spelled *Hadad* in Samaritan Pentateuch, Syriac, and 1 Chronicles 1:50 • Spelled *Pai* in 1 Chronicles 1:50 * **36:40** Spelled *Aliah* in 1 Chronicles 1:51

36:40–43 ***Esau was the father of the Edomites.*** Although Esau was not the heir of God's everlasting covenant with the family of Abraham, God still blessed his family and made them into a nation.

37:1 ***a stranger.*** The Lord had promised that this land would become a permanent possession of Abraham's family (12:7). To the third generation, that promise was still not realized. Jacob and his family were still aliens in the land.

37:2 ***a bad report.*** Since Joseph in general demonstrated his integrity (see ch. 39), he was probably not slandering his brothers, but accurately reporting some negligence on their part.

37:3 ***a tunic of many colors.*** This is the traditional translation. The Hebrew phrase may simply mean a garment with long sleeves. The robe was certainly distinctive in some way, and probably costly.

37:4 ***hated him.*** Because fallen and unregenerate man hates God, he displays hatred in his relations with others. The hatred of Joseph's brothers is attributed primarily to the love which Jacob had for his youngest son. As a result of their hatred the brothers were not able to speak kindly to Joseph, and the hatred led to a plot to kill him. Jesus remarked that the world's hatred of His people is a reflection of hatred against Himself (John 15:18). Love is the leading characteristic of the godly as hatred is the mark of the worldly person.

36:24 [o] Lev. 19:19 **36:28** [p] Job 1:1 **36:31** [q] 1 Chr. 1:43 **36:37** [r] Gen. 10:11 **37:1** [a] Gen. 17:8; 23:4; 28:4; 36:7 **37:2** [b] 1 Sam. 2:22–24 **37:3** [c] Gen. 44:20 [d] Gen. 37:23, 32 **37:4** [e] Gen. 27:41; 49:23 **37:7** [f] Gen. 42:6, 9; 43:26; 44:14

indeed reign over us? Or shall you indeed have dominion over us?" So they hated him even more for his dreams and for his words.

9Then he dreamed still another dream and told it to his brothers, and said, "Look, I have dreamed another dream. And this time, gthe sun, the moon, and the eleven stars bowed down to me."

10So he told it to his father and his brothers; and his father rebuked him and said to him, "What is this dream that you have dreamed? Shall your mother and I and hyour brothers indeed come to bow down to the earth before you?" 11And ihis brothers envied him, but his father jkept the matter in mind.

Joseph Sold by His Brothers

12Then his brothers went to feed their father's flock in Shechem. 13And Israel said to Joseph, "Are not your brothers feeding the flock in kShechem? Come, I will send you to them."

So he said to him, "Here I am."

14Then he said to him, "Please go and see if it is well with your brothers and well with the flocks, and bring back word to me." So he sent him out of the Valley of lHebron, and he went to Shechem.

15Now a certain man found him, and there he was, wandering in the field. And the man asked him, saying, "What are you seeking?"

16So he said, "I am seeking my brothers. mPlease tell me where they are feeding their flocks."

17And the man said, "They have departed from here, for I heard them say, 'Let us go to Dothan.'" So Joseph went after his brothers and found them in nDothan.

18Now when they saw him afar off, even before he came near them, othey conspired against him to kill him. 19Then they said to one another, "Look, this dreamer is coming! 20pCome therefore, let us now kill him and cast him into some pit; and we shall say, 'Some wild beast has devoured him.' We shall see what will become of his dreams!"

21But qReuben heard it, and he delivered him out of their hands, and said, "Let us not kill him." 22And Reuben said to them, "Shed no blood, but cast him into this pit which is in the wilderness, and do not lay a hand on him"—that he might deliver him out of their hands, and bring him back to his father.

23So it came to pass, when Joseph had come to his brothers, that they rstripped Joseph of his tunic, the tunic of many colors that was on him. 24Then they took him and cast him into a pit. And the pit was empty; there was no water in it.

25sAnd they sat down to eat a meal. Then they lifted their eyes and looked, and there was a company of tIshmaelites, coming from Gilead with their camels, bearing spices, ubalm, and myrrh, on their way to carry them down to Egypt. 26So Judah said to his brothers, "What profit is there if we kill our brother and vconceal his blood? 27Come and let us sell him to the Ishmaelites, and wlet not our hand be upon him, for he is xour brother and your flesh." And his brothers listened. 28Then zMidianite traders passed by; so the brothers pulled Joseph up and lifted him out of the pit, aand sold him to the Ishmaelites for btwenty shekels of silver. And they took Joseph to Egypt.

29Then Reuben returned to the pit, and indeed Joseph was not in the pit; and he ctore his clothes. 30And he returned to his brothers and said, "The lad dis no more; and I, where shall I go?"

31So they took eJoseph's tunic, killed a kid of the goats, and dipped the tunic in the blood. 32Then they sent the tunic of many colors, and they brought it to their father and said, "We have found this. Do you know whether it is your son's tunic or not?"

33And he recognized it and said, "It is my son's tunic. A fwild beast has devoured him. Without doubt Joseph is torn to pieces." 34Then Jacob gtore his clothes, put sackcloth on his waist, and hmourned for his son many days. 35And all his sons and all his daughters iarose to comfort him; but he refused to be comforted, and he said,

37:17 **Dothan.** This is about ten miles north of Shechem, near Mount Gilboa.
37:21 **Let us not kill him.** Reuben, as the firstborn son and principal heir, had the most to lose if Joseph's dreams came true. Yet Reuben intervened to spare Joseph's life. This was something of a contrast with his earlier wicked actions (35:22).
37:25 **Ishmaelites.** The Ishmaelites of this passage were wandering traders. The name (referring to descendants of Ishmael, the son of Abraham and Hagar) is loosely equivalent with the name Midianite (Midian was another son of Abraham, by Keturah). Probably the families of the two half brothers had a strong alliance and were so closely associated that the names became interchangeable (v. 28).
37:28 **twenty shekels of silver.** The standard price for a slave in later Israelite law was 30 shekels of silver.

37:29 **tore his clothes.** Tearing one's clothes was a common expression of grief and dismay. Reuben's grief was genuine feeling for his younger brother mixed with fear that he, the oldest brother, would be blamed.

37:9 gGen. 46:29; 47:25 **37:10** hGen. 27:29 **37:11** iActs 7:9 jDan. 7:28 **37:13** kGen. 33:18–20 **37:14** lGen. 13:18; 23:2, 19; 35:27 **37:16** mSong 1:7 **37:17** n2 Kin. 6:13 **37:18** oMark 14:1 **37:20** pProv. 1:11 **37:21** qGen. 42:22 **37:23** rMatt. 27:28 **37:25** sProv. 30:20 tGen. 16:11, 12; 37:28, 36; 39:1 uJer. 8:22 **37:26** vGen. 37:20 **37:27** w1 Sam. 18:17 xGen. 42:21 yGen. 29:14 **37:28** zJudg. 6:1–3; 8:22, 24 aPs. 105:17 bMatt. 27:9 **37:29** cJob 1:20 **37:30** dGen. 42:13, 36 **37:31** eGen. 37:3, 23 **37:33** fGen. 37:20 **37:34** g2 Sam. 3:31 hGen. 50:10 **37:35** i2 Sam. 12:17

"For *i*I shall go down into the grave to my son in mourning." Thus his father wept for him.

³⁶Now *k*the Midianites* had sold him in Egypt to Potiphar, an officer of Pharaoh *and* captain of the guard.

Judah and Tamar

38 It came to pass at that time that Judah departed from his brothers, and *a*visited a certain Adullamite whose name *was* Hirah. ²And Judah *b*saw there a daughter of a certain Canaanite whose name *was* *c*Shua, and he married her and went in to her. ³So she conceived and bore a son, and he called his name *d*Er. ⁴She conceived again and bore a son, and she called his name *e*Onan. ⁵And she conceived yet again and bore a son, and called his name *f*Shelah. He was at Chezib when she bore him.

⁶Then Judah *g*took a wife for Er his firstborn, and her name *was* *h*Tamar. ⁷But *i*Er, Judah's firstborn, was wicked in the sight of the Lᴏʀᴅ, *j*and the Lᴏʀᴅ killed him. ⁸And Judah said to Onan, "Go in to *k*your brother's wife and marry her, and raise up an heir to your brother." ⁹But Onan knew that the heir would not be *l*his; and it came to pass, when he went in to his brother's wife, that he emitted on the ground, lest he should give an heir to his brother. ¹⁰And the thing which he did displeased the Lᴏʀᴅ; therefore He killed *m*him also.

¹¹Then Judah said to Tamar his daughter-in-law, *n*"Remain a widow in your father's house till my son Shelah is grown." For he said, "Lest he also die like his brothers." And Tamar went and dwelt *o*in her father's house.

¹²Now in the process of time the daughter of Shua, Judah's wife, died; and Judah *p*was comforted, and went up to his sheepshearers at Timnah, he and his friend Hirah the Adullamite. ¹³And it was told Tamar, saying, "Look, your father-in-law is going up *q*to Timnah to shear his sheep." ¹⁴So she took off her widow's garments, covered *herself* with a veil and wrapped herself, and *r*sat in an open place which *was* on the way to Timnah; for she saw *s*that Shelah was grown, and she was not given to him as a wife. ¹⁵When Judah saw her, he thought she *was* a harlot, because she had covered her face. ¹⁶Then he turned to her by the way, and said, "Please let me come in to you"; for he did not know that she *was* his daughter-in-law.

So she said, "What will you give me, that you may come in to me?"

¹⁷And he said, *t*"I will send a young goat from the flock."

So she said, *u*"Will you give *me* a pledge till you send *it*?"

¹⁸Then he said, "What pledge shall I give you?"

So she said, *v*"Your signet and cord, and your staff that *is* in your hand." Then he gave *them* to her, and went in to her, and she conceived by him. ¹⁹So she arose and went away, and *w*laid aside her veil and put on the garments of her widowhood.

²⁰And Judah sent the young goat by the hand of his friend the Adullamite, to receive *his* pledge from the woman's hand, but he did not find her. ²¹Then he asked the men of that place, saying, "Where is the harlot who *was* openly by the roadside?"

And they said, "There was no harlot in this *place*."

²²So he returned to Judah and said, "I cannot find her. Also, the men of the place said there was no harlot in this *place*."

²³Then Judah said, "Let her take *them* for herself, lest we be shamed; for I sent this young goat and you have not found her."

38:1–30 At first glance it appears that the story of Judah and Tamar is an intrusion into the story of Joseph, but it is here for a reason. It provides a stunning contrast between the morals of Judah and Joseph. It illustrates the further disintegration of Jacob's family. If this process continued, Jacob's family, the family of promise, would become like the people of Canaan.
38:8 to your brother's wife. In order to maintain the family line and the name of the deceased, it was the custom in ancient times for the dead man's brother to marry the widow and father a child that would carry on the man's family. This is called *levirate* marriage, from the Latin word meaning "husband's brother." The custom became part of the Mosaic law (Deut. 25:5–10; Ruth 4:1–12).
38:15–18 Fornication—God designed sexual relations to be enjoyed exclusively within the framework of marriage: one man, for one woman, mutually committed for life. Outside of this framework, all sexual relations are sin. This is not because God wants to deprive His people of pleasure, but because He wants to protect them from the painful and destructive

consequences of sin. Sexual union is not only a union of the body, but of the whole person (1 Cor. 6:15–20). Illicit sexual relations defile the temple of God, breed both physical and social disease, and serve as a source for many other sins.
38:18 signet. This was an ancient means of identification. The signet was distinctively etched in stone, metal, or ivory. To confirm a business transaction, or make an order official, the signet was pressed into soft clay, leaving its distinctive impression. Basically, Judah gave Tamar the equivalent of a modern credit card.

37:35 *j* Gen. 25:8; 35:29; 42:38; 44:29, 31 **37:36** *k* Gen. 39:1 **38:1** *a* 2 Kin. 4:8 **38:2** *b* Gen. 34:2 *c* 1 Chr. 2:3 **38:3** *d* Gen. 46:12 **38:4** *e* Num. 26:19 **38:5** *f* Num. 26:20 **38:6** *g* Gen. 21:21 *h* Ruth 4:12 **38:7** *i* Gen. 46:12 *j* 1 Chr. 2:3 **38:8** *k* Deut. 25:5, 6 **38:9** *l* Deut. 25:6 **38:10** *m* Gen. 46:12 **38:11** *n* Ruth 1:12, 13 *o* Lev. 22:13 **38:12** *p* 2 Sam. 13:39 **38:13** *q* Josh. 15:10, 57 **38:14** *r* Prov. 7:12 *s* Gen. 38:11, 26 **38:17** *t* Ezek. 16:33 *u* Gen. 38:20 **38:18** *v* Gen. 38:25; 41:42 **38:19** *w* Gen. 38:14

²⁴And it came to pass, about three months after, that Judah was told, saying, "Tamar your daughter-in-law has ˣplayed the harlot; furthermore she *is* with child by harlotry."

So Judah said, "Bring her out ʸand let her be burned!"

²⁵When she *was* brought out, she sent to her father-in-law, saying, "By the man to whom these belong, I *am* with child." And she said, ᶻ"Please determine whose these *are*—the signet and cord, and staff."

²⁶So Judah ᵃacknowledged *them* and said, ᵇ"She has been more righteous than I, because ᶜI did not give her to Shelah my son." And he ᵈnever knew her again.

²⁷Now it came to pass, at the time for giving birth, that behold, twins *were* in her womb. ²⁸And so it was, when she was giving birth, that *the one* put out *his* hand; and the midwife took a scarlet *thread* and bound it on his hand, saying, "This one came out first." ²⁹Then it happened, as he drew back his hand, that his brother came out unexpectedly; and she said, "How did you break through? *This* breach *be* upon you!" Therefore his name was called ᵉPerez.* ³⁰Afterward his brother came out who had the scarlet *thread* on his hand. And his name was called ᶠZerah.

Joseph a Slave in Egypt

39 Now Joseph had been taken ᵃdown to Egypt. And ᵇPotiphar, an officer of Pharaoh, captain of the guard, an Egyptian, ᶜbought him from the Ishmaelites who had taken him down there. ²ᵈThe LORD was with Joseph, and he was a successful man; and he was in the house of his master the Egyptian. ³And his master saw that the LORD *was* with him and that the LORD ᵉmade all he did to prosper in his hand. ⁴So Joseph ᶠfound favor in his sight, and served him. Then he made him ᵍoverseer of his house, and all *that* he had he put under his authority. ⁵So it was, from the time *that* he had made him overseer of his house and all that he had, that ʰthe LORD blessed the Egyptian's house for Joseph's sake; and the blessing of the LORD was on all that he had in the house and in the field. ⁶Thus he left all that he had in Joseph's hand, and he did not know what he had except for the bread which he ate.

Now Joseph ⁱwas handsome in form and appearance.

⁷And it came to pass after these things that his master's wife cast longing eyes on Joseph, and she said, ʲ"Lie with me."

⁸But he refused and said to his master's wife, "Look, my master does not know what *is* with me in the house, and he has committed all that he has to my hand. ⁹*There is* no one greater in this house than I, nor has he kept back anything from me but you, because you *are* his wife. ᵏHow then can I do this great wickedness, and ˡsin against God?"

¹⁰So it was, as she spoke to Joseph day by day, that he ᵐdid not heed her, to lie with her *or* to be with her.

¹¹But it happened about this time, when Joseph went into the house to do his work, and none of the men of the house *was* inside, ¹²that she ⁿcaught him by his garment, saying, "Lie with me." But he left his garment in her hand, and fled and ran outside. ¹³And so it was, when she saw that he had left his garment in her hand and fled outside, ¹⁴that she called to the men of her house and spoke to them, saying, "See, he has brought in to us a ᵒHebrew to mock us. He came in to me to lie with me, and I cried out with a loud voice. ¹⁵And it happened, when he heard that I lifted my voice and cried out, that he left his garment with me, and fled and went outside."

¹⁶So she kept his garment with her until his master came home. ¹⁷Then she ᵖspoke to him with words like these, saying, "The Hebrew servant whom you brought to us came in to me to mock me; ¹⁸so it happened, as I lifted my voice and cried out, that he left his garment with me and fled outside."

---

* **38:29** Literally *Breach* or *Breakthrough*

38:26 She has been more righteous than I. Judah, one of the heirs of the everlasting covenant with the living God, was put to shame by a Canaanite woman. To his credit, Judah confessed his sins.

38:29 Perez. Perez was in the lineage of David, and eventually Jesus the Messiah (Ruth 4:18; Matt. 1:3).

39:2 The LORD was with Joseph. This key phrase of this section is repeated (vv. 21,23). This phrase indicates that God cared for, protected, and blessed Joseph.

39:4 found favor. Joseph's life illustrates the principle that one who is faithful in little will be given charge over much (Matt. 25:21; 1 Cor. 4:2).

39:5 the LORD blessed the Egyptian's house. God blessed Potiphar's house because of Joseph, just as He had blessed Laban because of Jacob.

39:9 sin against God. Joseph rejected the solicitation to sin, regarding it both as a wicked act of treachery against his master, and as a defiling and rebellious act before a holy God. Because Joseph's conscience was bound by God and His truth, he was able to resist this evil suggestion more than once. Pleasing God was more important to Joseph than engaging in the pleasures of sin for a season. His fear and reverence of God was the directing power of his life.

38:24 ˣ Judg. 19:2 ʸ Lev. 20:14; 21:9   **38:25** ᶻ Gen. 37:32; 38:18   **38:26** ᵃ Gen. 37:33 ᵇ 1 Sam. 24:17 ᶜ Gen. 38:14 ᵈ Job 34:31, 32   **38:29** ᵉ Gen. 46:12   **38:30** ᶠ 1 Chr. 2:4   **39:1** ᵃ Gen. 12:10; 43:15 ᵇ Gen. 37:36 ᶜ Gen. 37:28; 45:4   **39:2** ᵈ Acts 7:9   **39:3** ᵉ Ps. 1:3   **39:4** ᶠ Gen. 18:3; 19:19; 39:21 ᵍ Gen. 24:2, 10; 39:8, 22; 41:40   **39:5** ʰ Gen. 18:26; 30:27   **39:6** ⁱ 1 Sam. 16:12   **39:7** ʲ 2 Sam. 13:11   **39:9** ᵏ Prov. 6:29, 32 ˡ Ps. 51:4   **39:10** ᵐ Prov. 1:10   **39:12** ⁿ Prov. 7:13   **39:14** ᵒ Gen. 14:13; 41:12   **39:17** ᵖ Ex. 23:1

[19]So it was, when his master heard the words which his wife spoke to him, saying, "Your servant did to me after this manner," that his [q]anger was aroused. [20]Then Joseph's master took him and [r]put him into the [s]prison, a place where the king's prisoners were confined. And he was there in the prison. [21]But the LORD was with Joseph and showed him mercy, and He [t]gave him favor in the sight of the keeper of the prison. [22]And the keeper of the prison [u]committed to Joseph's hand all the prisoners who were in the prison; whatever they did there, it was his doing. [23]The keeper of the prison did not look into anything that was under Joseph's authority,* because the [v]LORD was with him; and whatever he did, the LORD made it prosper.

The Prisoners' Dreams

40 It came to pass after these things that the [a]butler and the baker of the king of Egypt offended their lord, the king of Egypt. [2]And Pharaoh was [b]angry with his two officers, the chief butler and the chief baker. [3c]So he put them in custody in the house of the captain of the guard, in the prison, the place where Joseph was confined. [4]And the captain of the guard charged Joseph with them, and he served them; so they were in custody for a while.

[5]Then the butler and the baker of the king of Egypt, who were confined in the prison, [d]had a dream, both of them, each man's dream in one night and each man's dream with its own interpretation. [6]And Joseph came in to them in the morning and looked at them, and saw that they were sad. [7]So he asked Pharaoh's officers who were with him in the custody of his lord's house, saying, [e]"Why do you look so sad today?"

[8]And they said to him, [f]"We each have had a dream, and there is no interpreter of it."

So Joseph said to them, [g]"Do not interpretations belong to God? Tell them to me, please."

[9]Then the chief butler told his dream to Joseph, and said to him, "Behold, in my dream a vine was before me, [10]and in the vine were three branches; it was as though

it budded, its blossoms shot forth, and its clusters brought forth ripe grapes. [11]Then Pharaoh's cup was in my hand; and I took the grapes and pressed them into Pharaoh's cup, and placed the cup in Pharaoh's hand."

[12]And Joseph said to him, [h]"This is the interpretation of it: The three branches [i]are three days. [13]Now within three days Pharaoh will [j]lift up your head and restore you to your place, and you will put Pharaoh's cup in his hand according to the former manner, when you were his butler. [14]But [k]remember me when it is well with you, and [l]please show kindness to me; make mention of me to Pharaoh, and get me out of this house. [15]For indeed I was [m]stolen away from the land of the Hebrews; [n]and also I have done nothing here that they should put me into the dungeon."

[16]When the chief baker saw that the interpretation was good, he said to Joseph, "I also was in my dream, and there were three white baskets on my head. [17]In the uppermost basket were all kinds of baked goods for Pharaoh, and the birds ate them out of the basket on my head."

[18]So Joseph answered and said, [o]"This is the interpretation of it: The three baskets are three days. [19p]Within three days Pharaoh will lift off your head from you and [q]hang you on a tree; and the birds will eat your flesh from you."

[20]Now it came to pass on the third day, which was Pharaoh's [r]birthday, that he [s]made a feast for all his servants; and he [t]lifted up the head of the chief butler and of the chief baker among his servants. [21]Then he [u]restored the chief butler to his butlership again, and [v]he placed the cup in Pharaoh's hand. [22]But he [w]hanged the chief baker, as Joseph had interpreted to them. [23]Yet the chief butler did not remember Joseph, but [x]forgot him.

Pharaoh's Dreams

41 Then it came to pass, at the end of two full years, that [a]Pharaoh had a dream; and behold, he stood by the river.

---

* **39:23** Literally *his hand*

39:20 into the prison. Surprisingly, Potiphar did not simply kill Joseph outright. It is possible that knowledge of Joseph's character (or his own wife's character) caused him to suspect that the story was not wholly true.

39:21 mercy. This word can be translated *loyal love* (Ps. 13:5). God faithfully kept His promises by staying with His people (12:1–3; 50:24).

39:23 the LORD made it prosper. Because of God's blessing, everything Joseph did prospered (Ps. 1:1–3).

40:8 interpretations belong to God. Joseph not only announced his faith, he then quickly acted upon it. Joseph had received dreams and visions as a younger man, and he had understood their meaning (37:5–11).

40:22 he hanged the chief baker. Pharaoh was

clearly a ruthless ruler who rewarded those who served him well, but destroyed those he perceived as threats.

39:19 [q] Prov. 6:34, 35 **39:20** [r] Ps. 105:18 [s] Gen. 40:3, 15; 41:14 **39:21** [t] Acts 7:9, 10 **39:22** [u] Gen. 39:4; 40:3, 4 **39:23** [v] Gen. 39:2, 3 **40:1** [a] Neh. 1:11 **40:2** [b] Prov. 16:14 **40:3** [c] Gen. 39:1, 20, 23; 41:10 **40:5** [d] Gen. 37:5; 41:1 **40:7** [e] Neh. 2:2 **40:8** [f] Gen. 41:15 [g] [Dan. 2:11, 20–22, 27, 28, 47] **40:12** [h] Dan. 2:36; 4:18, 19 [i] Gen. 40:18; 42:17 **40:13** [j] 2 Kin. 25:27 **40:14** [k] Luke 23:42 [l] Josh. 2:12 **40:15** [m] Gen. 37:26–28 [n] Gen. 39:20 **40:18** [o] Gen. 40:12 **40:19** [p] Gen. 40:13 [q] Deut. 21:22 **40:20** [r] Matt. 14:6–10 [s] Mark 6:21 [t] Gen. 40:13, 19 **40:21** [u] Gen. 40:13 [v] Neh. 2:1 **40:22** [w] Gen. 40:19 **40:23** [x] Eccl. 9:15, 16 **41:1** [a] Gen. 40:5

2 Suddenly there came up out of the river
seven cows, fine looking and fat; and they
fed in the meadow. 3 Then behold, seven
other cows came up after them out of the
river, ugly and gaunt, and stood by the *oth-*
er cows on the bank of the river. 4 And the
ugly and gaunt cows ate up the seven fine
looking and fat cows. So Pharaoh awoke.
5 He slept and dreamed a second time; and
suddenly seven heads of grain came up on
one stalk, plump and good. 6 Then behold,
seven thin heads, blighted by the [b]east
wind, sprang up after them. 7 And the seven
thin heads devoured the seven plump and
full heads. So Pharaoh awoke, and indeed,
it was a dream. 8 Now it came to pass in the
morning [c]that his spirit was troubled, and
he sent and called for all [d]the magicians of
Egypt and all its [e]wise men. And Pharaoh
told them his dreams, but *there was* no one
who could interpret them for Pharaoh.

9 Then the [f]chief butler spoke to Pharaoh, saying: "I remember my faults this
day. 10 When Pharaoh was [g]angry with
his servants, [h]and put me in custody in the
house of the captain of the guard, *both* me
and the chief baker, 11 [i]we each had a dream
in one night, he and I. Each of us dreamed
according to the interpretation of his *own*
dream. 12 Now there *was* a young [j]Hebrew
man with us there, a [k]servant of the captain of the guard. And we told him, and he
[l]interpreted our dreams for us; to each man
he interpreted according to his *own* dream.
13 And it came to pass, just [m]as he interpreted for us, so it happened. He restored me to
my office, and he hanged him."

14 [n]Then Pharaoh sent and called Joseph,
and they [o]brought him quickly [p]out of the
dungeon; and he shaved, [q]changed his
clothing, and came to Pharaoh. 15 And Pharaoh said to Joseph, "I have had a dream,
and *there is* no one who can interpret it.
[r]But I have heard it said of you *that* you can
understand a dream, to interpret it."

16 So Joseph answered Pharaoh, saying,
[s]"*It is* not in me; [t]God will give Pharaoh an
answer of peace."

17 Then Pharaoh said to Joseph: "Behold,
[u]in my dream I stood on the bank of the
river. 18 Suddenly seven cows came up out
of the river, fine looking and fat; and they
fed in the meadow. 19 Then behold, seven
other cows came up after them, poor and
very ugly and gaunt, such ugliness as I
have never seen in all the land of Egypt.
20 And the gaunt and ugly cows ate up the
first seven, the fat cows. 21 When they had
eaten them up, no one would have known
that they had eaten them, for they *were* just
as ugly as at the beginning. So I awoke.
22 Also I saw in my dream, and suddenly
seven heads came up on one stalk, full and
good. 23 Then behold, seven heads, withered, thin, *and* blighted by the east wind,
sprang up after them. 24 And the thin heads
devoured the seven good heads. So [v]I told
this to the magicians, but *there was* no one
who could explain *it* to me."

25 Then Joseph said to Pharaoh, "The
dreams of Pharaoh *are* one; [w]God has
shown Pharaoh what He *is* about to do:
26 The seven good cows *are* seven years,
and the seven good heads *are* seven years;
the dreams *are* one. 27 And the seven thin
and ugly cows which came up after them
are seven years, and the seven empty
heads blighted by the east wind are [x]sev-
en years of famine. 28 [y]This *is* the thing
which I have spoken to Pharaoh. God has
shown Pharaoh what He *is* about to do.
29 Indeed [z]seven years of great plenty will
come throughout all the land of Egypt;
30 but after them seven years of famine will
[a]arise, and all the plenty will be forgotten
in the land of Egypt; and the famine [b]will
deplete the land. 31 So the plenty will not be
known in the land because of the famine
following, for it *will be* very severe. 32 And
the dream was repeated to Pharaoh twice
because the [c]thing *is* established by God,
and God will shortly bring it to pass.

33 "Now therefore, let Pharaoh select a
discerning and wise man, and set him over
the land of Egypt. 34 Let Pharaoh do *this,*
and let him appoint officers over the land,
[d]to collect one-fifth *of the produce* of the
land of Egypt in the seven plentiful years.
35 And [e]let them gather all the food of those
good years that are coming, and store up

41:8 *magicians.* The Hebrew term is related to the word for *stylus*, a writing instrument. Thus the magicians were associated in some manner with writing and knowledge, no doubt of the occult. ***wise men.*** These were a class of scholars associated with the courts of the ancient Middle East. They were either functionaries of pagan religions, or merely observers and interpreters of life.

41:14 *shaved.* Egyptian men not only shaved their faces, but their entire bodies and heads. Egyptian officials scorned the "hairy" Canaanites, including the Hebrews (43:32). While he lived in Egypt Joseph apparently adopted the dress and manner of the Egyptians.

41:16 *God.* Joseph praised the power of the living God in the pagan court of Pharaoh. He would not take any credit to himself, nor did he try to use the situation to plead for his own release.

41:32 *God, and God.* Joseph made it clear that he was speaking about the one God, not the numerous false gods that filled the Egyptian court, or Pharaoh himself who was believed to be a god (22:1; 42:18).

41:6 [b] Ex. 10:13 **41:8** [c] Dan. 2:1, 3; 4:5, 19 [d] Ex. 7:11, 22 [e] Matt. 2:1 **41:9** [f] Gen. 40:1, 14, 23 **41:10** [g] Gen. 40:2, 3 [h] Gen. 39:20 **41:11** [i] Gen. 40:5 **41:12** [j] Gen. 39:14; 43:32 [k] Gen. 37:36 [l] Gen. 40:12 **41:13** [m] Gen. 40:21, 22 **41:14** [n] Ps. 105:20 [o] Dan. 2:25 [p] [1 Sam. 2:8] [q] 2 Kin. 25:27–29 **41:15** [r] Dan. 5:16 **41:16** [s] Dan. 2:30 [t] Dan. 2:22, 28, 47 **41:17** [u] Gen. 41:1 **41:24** [v] Is. 8:19 **41:25** [w] Dan. 2:28, 29, 45 **41:27** [x] 2 Kin. 8:1 **41:28** [y] [Gen. 41:25, 32] **41:29** [z] Gen. 41:47 **41:30** [a] Gen. 41:54, 56 [b] Gen. 47:13 **41:32** [c] Num. 23:19 **41:34** [d] [Prov. 6:6–8] **41:35** [e] Gen. 41:48

grain under the authority of Pharaoh, and
let them keep food in the cities. 36 Then that
food shall be as a reserve for the land for
the seven years of famine which shall be
in the land of Egypt, that the land [f]may not
perish during the famine."

Joseph's Rise to Power

37 So [g]the advice was good in the eyes of
Pharaoh and in the eyes of all his servants.
38 And Pharaoh said to his servants, "Can
we find *such a one* as this, a man [h]in whom
is the Spirit of God?"
39 Then Pharaoh said to Joseph, "Inasmuch as God has shown you all this, *there*
is no one as discerning and wise as you.
40 [i]You shall be over my house, and all my
people shall be ruled according to your
word; only in regard to the throne will I
be greater than you." 41 And Pharaoh said
to Joseph, "See, I have [j]set you over all the
land of Egypt."
42 Then Pharaoh [k]took his signet ring off
his hand and put it on Joseph's hand; and
he [l]clothed him in garments of fine linen
[m]and put a gold chain around his neck.
43 And he had him ride in the second [n]char-
iot which he had; [o]and they cried out before
him, "Bow the knee!" So he set him [p]over
all the land of Egypt. 44 Pharaoh also said
to Joseph, "I *am* Pharaoh, and without your
consent no man may lift his hand or foot
in all the land of Egypt." 45 And Pharaoh
called Joseph's name Zaphnath-Paaneah.
And he gave him as a wife [q]Asenath, the
daughter of Poti-Pherah priest of On. So
Joseph went out over *all* the land of Egypt.
46 Joseph was thirty years old when he
[r]stood before Pharaoh king of Egypt. And
Joseph went out from the presence of Pharaoh, and went throughout all the land of
Egypt. 47 Now in the seven plentiful years
the ground brought forth abundantly. 48 So
he gathered up all the food of the seven
years which were in the land of Egypt,
and laid up the food in the cities; he laid up
in every city the food of the fields which
surrounded them. 49 Joseph gathered very
much grain, [s]as the sand of the sea, until
he stopped counting, for *it was* immeasurable.
50 [t]And to Joseph were born two sons
before the years of famine came, whom
Asenath, the daughter of Poti-Pherah
priest of On, bore to him. 51 Joseph called
the name of the firstborn Manasseh:* "For
God has made me forget all my toil and all
my [u]father's house." 52 And the name of the
second he called Ephraim:* "For God has
caused me to be [v]fruitful in the land of my
affliction."
53 Then the seven years of plenty which
were in the land of Egypt ended, 54 [w]and
the seven years of famine began to come,
[x]as Joseph had said. The famine was in
all lands, but in all the land of Egypt there
was bread. 55 So when all the land of Egypt
was famished, the people cried to Pharaoh
for bread. Then Pharaoh said to all the
Egyptians, "Go to Joseph; [y]whatever he
says to you, do." 56 The famine was over all
the face of the earth, and Joseph opened
all the storehouses* and [z]sold to the Egyptians. And the famine became severe in the
land of Egypt. 57 [a]So all countries came to
Joseph in Egypt to [b]buy *grain*, because the
famine was severe in all lands.

Joseph's Brothers Go to Egypt

42 When [a]Jacob saw that there was
grain in Egypt, Jacob said to his
sons, "Why do you look at one another?"
2 And he said, "Indeed I have heard that
there is grain in Egypt; go down to that
place and buy for us there, that we may
[b]live and not die."
3 So Joseph's ten brothers went down to
buy grain in Egypt. 4 But Jacob did not send
Joseph's brother Benjamin with his brothers, for he said, [c]"Lest some calamity befall
him." 5 And the sons of Israel went to buy
grain among those who journeyed, for the
famine was [d]in the land of Canaan.

*41:51 Literally *Making Forgetful* *41:52 Literally *Fruitfulness* *41:56 Literally *all that was in them*

41:38 *in whom is the Spirit of God.* Even if he did not follow God himself, Pharaoh was at least acknowledging that Joseph was extraordinarily wise, and that the power of his God was obvious in his life.

41:39 *discerning and wise.* Joseph is an illustration of the instructions Paul gave Colosse: "Walk in wisdom toward those who are outside" (Col. 4:5). Pharaoh recognized that Joseph's wisdom was not the ordinary powers of a clever man, but something unique and outside of himself. Joseph was wise because he listened to God, not just because of his extraordinary intelligence and perspicacity. God's wisdom is moral. It discerns between good and evil. It is seen through prudence in secular affairs and comes through personal experience with the Lord.

41:45 *Zaphnath-Paaneah.* This Egyptian name probably means something like "the god speaks and lives." ***Asenath.*** This name means "belonging to (the goddess) Neith." ***Poti-Pherah.*** This name means "he whom Ra (the sun god) gave." Even though his father-in-law was the priest of a pagan god, Joseph and Asenath's sons were worshipers of the Lord, not Ra.

42:4 *Benjamin.* Jacob still played favorites, but this time there is no mention of jealousy among the other brothers as there had been before (37:8).

41:36 [f]Gen. 47:15, 19 **41:37** [g]Acts 7:10 **41:38** [h]Num. 27:18 **41:40** [i]Ps. 105:21 **41:41** [j]Dan. 6:3
41:42 [k]Esth. 3:10 [l]Esth. 8:2, 15 [m]Dan. 5:7, 16, 29
41:43 [n]Gen. 46:29 [o]Esth. 6:9 [p]Gen. 42:6 **41:45** [q]Gen. 46:20 **41:46** [r]1 Sam. 16:21 **41:49** [s]Gen. 22:17
41:50 [t]Gen. 46:20; 48:5 **41:51** [u]Ps. 45:10 **41:52** [v]Gen. 17:6; 28:3; 49:22 **41:54** [w]Acts 7:11 [x]Gen. 41:30
41:55 [y]John 2:5 **41:56** [z]Gen. 42:6 **41:57** [a]Ezek. 29:12 [b]Gen. 27:28, 37; 42:3 **42:1** [a]Acts 7:12 **42:2** [b]Gen. 43:8
42:4 [c]Gen. 42:38 **42:5** [d]Acts 7:11

6 Now Joseph *was* governor [e]over the
land; and it was he who sold to all the people of the land. And Joseph's brothers came
and [f]bowed down before him with *their*
faces to the earth. 7 Joseph saw his brothers and recognized them, but he acted as
[g]a stranger to them and spoke roughly to
them. Then he said to them, "Where do you
come from?"
And they said, "From the land of Canaan
to buy food."
8 So Joseph recognized his brothers, but
they did not recognize him. 9 Then Joseph
[h]remembered the dreams which he had
dreamed about them, and said to them,
"You *are* spies! You have come to see the
nakedness of the land!"
10 And they said to him, "No, my lord, but
your servants have come to buy food. 11 We
are all one man's sons; we *are* honest *men;*
your servants are not spies."
12 But he said to them, "No, but you have
come to see the nakedness of the land."
13 And they said, "Your servants *are*
twelve brothers, the sons of one man in the
land of Canaan; and in fact, the youngest *is*
with our father today, and one [i]*is* no more."
14 But Joseph said to them, "It *is* as I spoke
to you, saying, 'You *are* spies!' 15 In this *manner* you shall be tested: [j]By the life of Pharaoh, you shall not leave this place unless
your youngest brother comes here. 16 Send
one of you, and let him bring your brother;
and you shall be kept in prison, that your
words may be tested to see whether *there is*
any truth in you; or else, by the life of Pharaoh, surely you *are* spies!" 17 So he put them
all together in prison [k]three days.
18 Then Joseph said to them the third day,
"Do this and live, [l]*for* I fear God: 19 If you
are honest *men,* let one of your brothers
be confined to your prison house; but you,
go and carry grain for the famine of your
houses. 20 And [m]bring your youngest brother to me; so your words will be verified, and
you shall not die."
And they did so. 21 Then they said to one
another, [n]"We *are* truly guilty concerning
our brother, for we saw the anguish of
his soul when he pleaded with us, and we
would not hear; [o]therefore this distress has
come upon us."
22 And Reuben answered them, saying,
[p]"Did I not speak to you, saying, 'Do not
sin against the boy'; and you would not
listen? Therefore behold, his blood is now
[q]required of us." 23 But they did not know
that Joseph understood *them,* for he spoke
to them through an interpreter. 24 And he
turned himself away from them and [r]wept.
Then he returned to them again, and talked
with them. And he took [s]Simeon from them
and bound him before their eyes.

The Brothers Return to Canaan

25 Then Joseph [t]gave a command to fill
their sacks with grain, to [u]restore every
man's money to his sack, and to give them
provisions for the journey. [v]Thus he did for
them. 26 So they loaded their donkeys with
the grain and departed from there. 27 But
as [w]one *of them* opened his sack to give his
donkey feed at the encampment, he saw his
money; and there it was, in the mouth of
his sack. 28 So he said to his brothers, "My
money has been restored, and there it is,
in my sack!" Then their hearts failed *them*
and they were afraid, saying to one another, "What *is* this *that* God has done to us?"
29 Then they went to Jacob their father in
the land of Canaan and told him all that had
happened to them, saying: 30 "The man *who*
is lord of the land [x]spoke roughly to us, and
took us for spies of the country. 31 But we
said to him, 'We *are* honest *men;* we are not
spies. 32 We *are* twelve brothers, sons of our
father; one *is* no *more,* and the youngest *is*
with our father this day in the land of Canaan.' 33 Then the man, the lord of the country, said to us, [y]'By this I will know that you
are honest *men:* Leave one of your brothers
here with me, take *food for* the famine of
your households, and be gone. 34 And bring
your [z]youngest brother to me; so I shall
know that you *are* not spies, but *that* you
are honest *men.* I will grant your brother to
you, and you may [a]trade in the land.'"
35 Then it happened as they emptied their
sacks, that surprisingly [b]each man's bundle of money *was* in his sack; and when
they and their father saw the bundles of
money, they were afraid. 36 And Jacob their
father said to them, "You have [c]bereaved
me: Joseph is no *more,* Simeon is no *more,*

42:6 ***bowed down before him.*** God fulfilled the dreams He gave to Joseph at the age of 17 (37:5–11).
42:9 ***You are spies.*** Joseph set out to learn whether his brothers had changed for the better. Would they betray each other when under pressure?
42:18 ***I fear God.*** Joseph gave his brothers a clue about who he was.
42:22 ***Did I not speak to you.*** Joseph's brothers were fearful because they knew they were guilty before God and that they deserved any punishment that God might choose to send. They must have been troubled by feelings of guilt for years, and even though they did not realize who Joseph really was, they immediately attributed their troubles to their guilt.
42:25 ***money.*** This refers to a certain weight of silver. Coins had not been invented at this time.

42:6 [e] Gen. 41:41, 55 [f] Gen. 37:7–10; 41:43 **42:7** [g] Gen. 45:1, 2 **42:9** [h] Gen. 37:5–9 **42:13** [i] Gen. 37:30; 42:32; 44:20 **42:15** [j] 1 Sam. 1:26; 17:55 **42:17** [k] Gen. 40:4, 7, 12 **42:18** [l] Lev. 25:43 **42:20** [m] Gen. 42:34; 43:5; 44:23 **42:21** [n] Hos. 5:15 [o] Prov. 21:13 **42:22** [p] Gen. 37:21, 22, 29 [q] Gen. 9:5, 6 **42:24** [r] Gen. 43:30; 45:14, 15 [s] Gen. 34:25, 30; 43:14, 23 **42:25** [t] Gen. 44:1 [u] Gen. 43:12 [v] [Rom. 12:17, 20, 21] **42:27** [w] Gen. 43:21, 22 **42:30** [x] Gen. 42:7 **42:33** [y] Gen. 42:15, 19, 20 **42:34** [z] Gen. 42:20; 43:3, 5 [a] Gen. 34:10 **42:35** [b] Gen. 43:12, 15, 21 **42:36** [c] Gen. 43:14

and you want to take *d*Benjamin. All these things are against me."

37 Then Reuben spoke to his father, saying, "Kill my two sons if I do not bring him *back* to you; put him in my hands, and I will bring him back to you."

38 But he said, "My son shall not go down with you, for *e*his brother is dead, and he is left alone. *f*If any calamity should befall him along the way in which you go, then you would *g*bring down my gray hair with sorrow to the grave."

Joseph's Brothers Return with Benjamin

43 Now the famine *was* *a*severe in the land. 2And it came to pass, when they had eaten up the grain which they had brought from Egypt, that their father said to them, "Go *b*back, buy us a little food."

3 But Judah spoke to him, saying, "The man solemnly warned us, saying, 'You shall not see my face unless your *c*brother *is* with you.' 4If you send our brother with us, we will go down and buy you food. 5But if you will not send *him*, we will not go down; for the man said to us, 'You shall not see my face unless your brother *is* with you.'"

6 And Israel said, "Why did you deal *so* wrongfully with me *as* to tell the man whether you had still *another* brother?"

7 But they said, "The man asked us pointedly about ourselves and our family, saying, '*Is* your father still alive? Have you *another* brother?' And we told him according to these words. Could we possibly have known that he would say, 'Bring your brother down'?"

8 Then Judah said to Israel his father, "Send the lad with me, and we will arise and go, that we may *d*live and not die, both we and you *and* also our little ones. 9I myself will be surety for him; from my hand you shall require him. *e*If I do not bring him *back* to you and set him before you, then let me bear the blame forever. 10For if we had not lingered, surely by now we would have returned this second time."

11 And their father Israel said to them, "If it *must be* so, then do this: Take some of the best fruits of the land in your vessels and *f*carry down a present for the man—a little *g*balm and a little honey, spices and myrrh, pistachio nuts and almonds. 12Take double money in your hand, and take back

in your hand the money *h*that was returned in the mouth of your sacks; perhaps it was an oversight. 13Take your brother also, and arise, go back to the man. 14And may God *i*Almighty *j*give you mercy before the man, that he may release your other brother and Benjamin. *k*If I am bereaved, I am bereaved!"

15 So the men took that present and Benjamin, and they took double money in their hand, and arose and went *l*down to Egypt; and they stood before Joseph. 16When Joseph saw Benjamin with them, he said to the *m*steward of his house, "Take *these* men to my home, and slaughter an animal and make ready; for *these* men will dine with me at noon." 17Then the man did as Joseph ordered, and the man brought the men into Joseph's house.

18 Now the men were *n*afraid because they were brought into Joseph's house; and they said, "*It is* because of the money, which was returned in our sacks the first time, that we are brought in, so that he may make a case against us and seize us, to take us as slaves with our donkeys."

19 When they drew near to the steward of Joseph's house, they talked with him at the door of the house, 20and said, "O sir, *o*we indeed came down the first time to buy food; 21but *p*it happened, when we came to the encampment, that we opened our sacks, and there, *each* man's money *was* in the mouth of his sack, our money in full weight; so we have brought it back in our hand. 22And we have brought down other money in our hands to buy food. We do not know who put our money in our sacks."

23 But he said, "Peace *be* with you, do not be afraid. Your God and the God of your father has given you treasure in your sacks; I had your money." Then he brought *q*Simeon out to them.

24 So the man brought the men into Joseph's house, and *r*gave *them* water, and they washed their feet; and he gave their donkeys feed. 25Then they made the present ready for Joseph's coming at noon, for they heard that they would eat bread there.

26 And when Joseph came home, they brought him the present which *was* in their hand into the house, and *s*bowed down before him to the earth. 27Then he asked them about *their* well-being, and said, "*Is* your father well, the old man *t*of whom you spoke? *Is* he still alive?"

43:8 Send the lad with me. Judah promised that he would keep Benjamin safe. Judah had changed tremendously (38:1). Instead of leaving the family, he protected his brother and was concerned about his father's welfare.

43:23 Your God and the God of your father. Surprisingly, the steward expressed his own faith in the God of Joseph and Jacob.

43:26 bowed. For the second time (42:6) the brothers of Joseph bowed down to him, just as his dreams had predicted (37:5–11).

42:36 *d* [Rom. 8:28, 31]   **42:38** *e* Gen. 37:22; 42:13; 44:20, 28 *f* Gen. 42:4; 44:29 *g* Gen. 37:35; 44:31   **43:1** *a* Gen. 41:54, 57; 42:5; 45:6, 11   **43:2** *b* Gen. 42:2; 44:25   **43:3** *c* Gen. 42:20; 43:5; 44:23   **43:8** *d* Gen. 42:2; 47:19   **43:9** *e* Gen. 42:37; 44:32   **43:11** *f* Gen. 32:20; 33:10; 43:25, 26 *g* Jer. 8:22   **43:12** *h* Gen. 42:25, 35; 43:21, 22   **43:14** *i* Gen. 17:1; 28:3; 35:11; 48:3 *j* Ps. 106:46 *k* Esth. 4:16   **43:15** *l* Gen. 39:1; 46:3, 6   **43:16** *m* Gen. 24:2; 39:4; 44:1   **43:18** *n* Gen. 42:28   **43:20** *o* Gen. 42:3, 10   **43:21** *p* Gen. 42:27, 35   **43:23** *q* Gen. 42:24   **43:24** *r* Gen. 18:4; 19:2; 24:32   **43:26** *s* Gen. 37:7, 10; 42:6; 44:14   **43:27** *t* Gen. 29:6; 42:11, 13; 43:7; 45:3

28And they answered, "Your servant our father *is* in good health; he *is* still alive." uAnd they bowed their heads down and prostrated themselves.

29Then he lifted his eyes and saw his brother Benjamin, vhis mother's son, and said, "*Is* this your younger brother wof whom you spoke to me?" And he said, "God be gracious to you, my son." 30Now xhis heart yearned for his brother; so Joseph made haste and sought *somewhere* to weep. And he went into *his* chamber and ywept there. 31Then he washed his face and came out; and he restrained himself, and said, "Serve the zbread."

32So they set him a place by himself, and them by themselves, and the Egyptians who ate with him by themselves; because the Egyptians could not eat food with the aHebrews, for that *is* an abomination to the Egyptians. 33And they sat before him, the firstborn according to his cbirthright and the youngest according to his youth; and the men looked in astonishment at one another. 34Then he took servings to them from before him, but Benjamin's serving was dfive times as much as any of theirs. So they drank and were merry with him.

Joseph's Cup

44 And he commanded the asteward of his house, saying, b"Fill the men's sacks with food, as much as they can carry, and put each man's money in the mouth of his sack. 2Also put my cup, the silver cup, in the mouth of the sack of the youngest, and his grain money." So he did according to the word that Joseph had spoken. 3As soon as the morning dawned, the men were sent away, they and their donkeys. 4When they had gone out of the city, *and* were not yet far off, Joseph said to his steward, "Get up, follow the men; and when you overtake them, say to them, 'Why have you crepaid evil for good? 5*Is* not this *the one* from which my lord drinks, and with which he indeed practices divination? You have done evil in so doing.'"

6So he overtook them, and he spoke to them these same words. 7And they said to him, "Why does my lord say these words? Far be it from us that your servants should do such a thing. 8Look, we brought back to you from the land of Canaan dthe money which we found in the mouth of our sacks. How then could we steal silver or gold from your lord's house? 9With whomever of your servants it is found, elet him die, and we also will be my lord's slaves."

10And he said, "Now also *let* it *be* according to your words; he with whom it is found shall be my slave, and you shall be blameless." 11Then each man speedily let down his sack to the ground, and each opened his sack. 12So he searched. He began with the oldest and left off with the youngest; and the cup was found in Benjamin's sack. 13Then they ftore their clothes, and each man loaded his donkey and returned to the city.

14So Judah and his brothers came to Joseph's house, and he was still there; and they gfell before him on the ground. 15And Joseph said to them, "What deed *is* this you have done? Did you not know that such a man as I can certainly practice divination?"

16Then Judah said, "What shall we say to my lord? What shall we speak? Or how shall we clear ourselves? God has hfound out the iniquity of your servants; here iwe are, my lord's slaves, both we and *he* also with whom the cup was found."

17But he said, i"Far be it from me that I should do so; the man in whose hand the cup was found, he shall be my slave. And as for you, go up in peace to your father."

Judah Intercedes for Benjamin

18Then Judah came near to him and said: "O my lord, please let your servant speak a word in my lord's hearing, and kdo not let your anger burn against your servant; for you *are* even like Pharaoh. 19My lord asked his servants, saying, 'Have you a father or a brother?' 20And we said to my lord, 'We have a father, an old man, and la child of *his* old age, *who is* young; his brother is mdead, and he nalone is left of his mother's children, and his ofather loves him.' 21Then you said to your servants, p'Bring him down to me, that I may set my eyes on him.' 22And

---

43:32 *an abomination.* This word can indicate the strongest revulsion, something that might cause physical illness (46:34). The Egyptians (who carefully shaved their entire bodies) may have been repulsed by the "hairy" Hebrews.

44:15 *can certainly practice divination.* This curious verse is not very clear in meaning. Clearly a God-fearing man like Joseph who knew that only God can interpret dreams and visions (40:8) would not have been one to dabble in the occult. He may just have been trying to frighten his brothers by appearing to know things supernaturally (this would certainly have been backed up by his uncanny knowledge of their birth order in 43:33).

44:17 *go up in peace to your father.* Joseph was testing his brothers again, to see if they had changed in their attitude to the son of their father's favorite wife. Would they leave Benjamin a slave in Egypt as they had Joseph?

43:28 u Gen. 37:7, 10 **43:29** v Gen. 35:17, 18 w Gen. 42:13 **43:30** x 1 Kin. 3:26 y Gen. 42:24; 45:2, 14, 15; 46:29 **43:31** z Gen. 43:25 **43:32** a Gen. 41:12 b Gen. 46:34 **43:33** c Gen. 27:36; 42:7 **43:34** d Gen. 35:24; 45:22 **44:1** a Gen. 43:16 b Gen. 42:25 **44:4** c 1 Sam. 25:21 **44:8** d Gen. 43:21 **44:9** e Gen. 31:32 **44:13** f 2 Sam. 1:11 **44:14** g Gen. 37:7, 10 **44:16** h [Num. 32:23] i Gen. 44:9 **44:17** j Prov. 17:15 **44:18** k Ex. 32:22 **44:20** l Gen. 37:3; 43:8; 44:30 m Gen. 42:38 n Gen. 46:19 o Gen. 42:4 **44:21** p Gen. 42:15, 20

we said to my lord, *q*'The lad cannot leave his father, for *if* he should leave his father, *his father* would die.' 23But you said to your servants, 'Unless your youngest brother comes down with you, you shall see my face no more.'

24"So it was, when we went up to your servant my father, that we told him the words of my lord. 25And *r*our father said, 'Go back *and* buy us a little food.' 26But we said, 'We cannot go down; if our youngest brother is with us, then we will go down; for we may not see the man's face unless our youngest brother *is* with us.' 27Then your servant my father said to us, 'You know that *s*my wife bore me two sons; 28and the one went out from me, and I said, *t*"Surely he is torn to pieces"; and I have not seen him since. 29But if you *u*take this one also from me, and calamity befalls him, you shall bring down my gray hair with sorrow to the grave.'

30"Now therefore, when I come to your servant my father, and the lad *is* not with us, since *v*his life is bound up in the lad's life, 31it will happen, when he sees that the lad *is* not *with us*, that he will die. So your servants will bring down the gray hair of your servant our father with sorrow to the grave. 32For your servant became surety for the lad to my father, saying, *w*'If I do not bring him *back* to you, then I shall bear the blame before my father forever.' 33Now therefore, please *x*let your servant remain instead of the lad as a slave to my lord, and let the lad go up with his brothers. 34For how shall I go up to my father if the lad *is* not with me, lest perhaps I see the evil that would come upon my father?"

Joseph Revealed to His Brothers

45 Then Joseph could not restrain himself before all those who stood by him, and he cried out, "Make everyone go out from me!" So no one stood with him *a*while Joseph made himself known to his brothers. 2And he *b*wept aloud, and the Egyptians and the house of Pharaoh heard *it*.

3Then Joseph said to his brothers, *c*"I am Joseph; does my father still live?" But his brothers could not answer him, for they were dismayed in his presence. 4And Joseph said to his brothers, "Please come near to me." So they came near. Then he said: "I *am* Joseph your brother, *d*whom you sold into Egypt. 5But now, do not therefore be grieved or angry with yourselves because you sold me here; *e*for God sent me before you to preserve life. 6For these two years the *f*famine *has been* in the land, and *there are* still five years in which *there will be* neither plowing nor harvesting. 7And God *g*sent me before you to preserve a posterity for you in the earth, and to save your lives by a great deliverance. 8So now *it was* not you *who* sent me here, but *h*God; and He has made me *i*a father to Pharaoh, and lord of all his house, and a *j*ruler throughout all the land of Egypt.

9"Hurry and go up to my father, and say to him, 'Thus says your son Joseph: "God has made me lord of all Egypt; come down to me, do not tarry. 10*k*You shall dwell in the land of Goshen, and you shall be near to me, you and your children, your children's children, your flocks and your herds, and all that you have. 11There I will *l*provide for you, lest you and your household, and all that you have, come to poverty; for *there are* still five years of famine."'

12"And behold, your eyes and the eyes of my brother Benjamin see that *it is* *m*my mouth that speaks to you. 13So you shall tell my father of all my glory in Egypt, and of all that you have seen; and you shall hurry and *n*bring my father down here."

14Then he fell on his brother Benjamin's neck and wept, and Benjamin wept on his neck. 15Moreover he *o*kissed all his brothers and wept over them, and after that his brothers talked with him.

16Now the report of it was heard in Pharaoh's house, saying, "Joseph's brothers have come." So it pleased Pharaoh and his servants well. 17And Pharaoh said to Joseph, "Say to your brothers, 'Do this: Load your animals and depart; go to the land of Canaan. 18Bring your father and

---

45:1–4 Real Love—A profound comparison can be made between the life of Joseph and the life of Christ. Both Joseph and Jesus were persecuted unjustly (Gen. 37:11–28; Matt. 26:59). Both were lost to their brothers for a while (Gen. 45:1–15; Rom. 10:1–4). Both later forgave and restored their repentant brothers (Gen. 45:1–15; Zech. 8:1–8).

45:3 I am Joseph. Joseph must have said this in Hebrew, finally dropping the ruse of the interpreter (42:23).

45:5 God sent me. God often permits the wicked to carry out their evil plans in order to fulfill some larger purpose He has for the objects of their violence and cruelty. Since it is not possible for us to see the whole picture from God's perspective, we must exercise faith and believe that the God of all the earth will do right and that all things do work together for good to those who love God, who are called according to His

purpose. Joseph was able to freely forgive his brothers partly because he recognized that their sin had been turned by God into something good.

45:10 You shall dwell in the land of Goshen. This was God's plan. He had told Abraham that his descendants would live in a foreign land (15:13–16).

44:22 *q* Gen. 43:3, 5 **44:25** *r* Gen. 43:2 **44:27** *s* Gen. 30:22–24; 35:16–18; 46:19 **44:28** *t* Gen. 37:31–35 **44:29** *u* Gen. 42:36, 38; 44:31 **44:30** *v* [1 Sam. 18:1; 25:29] **44:32** *w* Gen. 43:9 **44:33** *x* Ex. 32:32 **45:1** *a* Acts 7:13 **45:2** *b* Gen. 43:30; 46:29 **45:3** *c* Acts 7:13 **45:4** *d* Gen. 37:28; 39:1 **45:5** *e* Gen. 45:7, 8; 50:20 **45:6** *f* Gen. 43:1; 47:4, 13 **45:7** *g* Gen. 45:5; 50:20 **45:8** *h* [Rom. 8:28] *i* Is. 22:21 *j* Gen. 41:43; 42:6 **45:10** *k* Gen. 46:28, 34; 47:1, 6 **45:11** *l* Gen. 47:12 **45:12** *m* Gen. 42:23 **45:13** *n* Acts 7:14 **45:15** *o* Gen. 48:10

your households and come to me; I will give you the best of the land of Egypt, and you will eat ᵖthe fat of the land. ¹⁹Now you are commanded—do this: Take carts out of the land of Egypt for your little ones and your wives; bring your father and come. ²⁰Also do not be concerned about your goods, for the best of all the land of Egypt *is* yours.'"

²¹Then the sons of Israel did so; and Joseph gave them �q carts, according to the command of Pharaoh, and he gave them provisions for the journey. ²²He gave to all of them, to each man, ʳchanges of garments; but to Benjamin he gave three hundred *pieces* of silver and ˢfive changes of garments. ²³And he sent to his father these *things:* ten donkeys loaded with the good things of Egypt, and ten female donkeys loaded with grain, bread, and food for his father for the journey. ²⁴So he sent his brothers away, and they departed; and he said to them, "See that you do not become troubled along the way."

²⁵Then they went up out of Egypt, and came to the land of Canaan to Jacob their father. ²⁶And they told him, saying, "Joseph *is* still alive, and he *is* governor over all the land of Egypt." ᵗAnd Jacob's heart stood still, because he did not believe them. ²⁷But when they told him all the words which Joseph had said to them, and when he saw the carts which Joseph had sent to carry him, the spirit ᵘof Jacob their father revived. ²⁸Then Israel said, "It *is* enough. Joseph my son *is* still alive. I will go and see him before I die."

Jacob's Journey to Egypt

46 So Israel took his journey with all that he had, and came to ᵃBeersheba, and offered sacrifices ᵇto the God of his father Isaac. ²Then God spoke to Israel ᶜin the visions of the night, and said, "Jacob, Jacob!"

And he said, "Here I am."

³So He said, "I *am* God, ᵈthe God of your father; do not fear to go down to Egypt, for I will ᵉmake of you a great nation there. ⁴ᶠI will go down with you to Egypt, and I will also surely ᵍbring you up *again;* and ʰJoseph will put his hand on your eyes."

⁵Then ⁱJacob arose from Beersheba; and the sons of Israel carried their father Jacob, their little ones, and their wives, in the carts ʲwhich Pharaoh had sent to carry him. ⁶So they took their livestock and their goods, which they had acquired in the land of Canaan, and went to Egypt, ᵏJacob and all his descendants with him. ⁷His sons and his sons' sons, his daughters and his sons' daughters, and all his descendants he brought with him to Egypt.

⁸Now ˡthese *were* the names of the children of Israel, Jacob and his sons, who went to Egypt: ᵐReuben *was* Jacob's firstborn. ⁹The ⁿsons of Reuben *were* Hanoch, Pallu, Hezron, and Carmi. ¹⁰ᵒThe sons of Simeon *were* Jemuel,* Jamin, Ohad, Jachin,* Zohar,* and Shaul, the son of a Canaanite woman. ¹¹The sons of ᵖLevi *were* Gershon, Kohath, and Merari. ¹²The sons of ᑫJudah *were* ʳEr, Onan, Shelah, Perez, and Zerah (but Er and Onan died in the land of Canaan). ˢThe sons of Perez were Hezron and Hamul. ¹³The sons of Issachar *were* Tola, Puvah,* Job,* and Shimron. ¹⁴The ᵗsons of Zebulun *were* Sered, Elon, and Jahleel. ¹⁵These *were* the ᵘsons of Leah, whom she bore to Jacob in Padan Aram, with his daughter Dinah. All the persons, his sons and his daughters, *were* thirty-three.

¹⁶The sons of Gad *were* Ziphion,* Haggi, Shuni, Ezbon,* Eri, Arodi,* and Areli. ¹⁷ᵛThe sons of Asher *were* Jimnah, Ishuah, Isui, Beriah, and Serah, their sister. And the sons of Beriah *were* Heber and Malchiel. ¹⁸ʷThese *were* the sons of Zilpah, ˣwhom Laban gave to Leah his daughter; and these she bore to Jacob: sixteen persons.

¹⁹The ʸsons of Rachel, ᶻJacob's wife, *were* Joseph and Benjamin. ²⁰ᵃAnd to Joseph in the land of Egypt were born Manasseh and Ephraim, whom Asenath, the daughter of Poti-Pherah priest of On, bore to him. ²¹ᵇThe sons of Benjamin *were* Belah, Becher, Ashbel, Gera, Naaman, ᶜEhi, Rosh, ᵈMuppim, Huppim,* and Ard. ²²These *were* the sons of Rachel, who were born to Jacob: fourteen persons in all.

* **46:10** Spelled *Nemuel* in 1 Chronicles 4:24 • Called *Jarib* in 1 Chronicles 4:24 • Called *Zerah* in 1 Chronicles 4:24 * **46:13** Spelled *Puah* in 1 Chronicles 7:1 • Same as *Jashub* in Numbers 26:24 and 1 Chronicles 7:1 * **46:16** Spelled *Zephon* in Samaritan Pentateuch, Septuagint, and Numbers 26:15 • Called *Ozni* in Numbers 26:16 • Spelled *Arod* in Numbers 26:17 * **46:21** Called *Hupham* in Numbers 26:39

46:1 *Israel took his journey.* Jacob's journey to Egypt began a four-hundred-year sojourn away from the promised land of Canaan. Jacob entered Egypt with his twelve sons and their families; Jacob's descendants would leave Egypt as a small nation.

46:2 *Israel . . . Jacob.* The fact that these names are used interchangeably indicates that the earlier negative connotations of the name Jacob had faded (31:11; 32:28; 35:10).

46:11 *Gershon, Kohath, and Merari.* These sons of Levi became the founders of the Levitical families (Ex. 6:16–19). Aaron and Moses descended from Kohath (Ex. 6:20–25).

45:18ᵖ Gen. 27:28; 47:6   **45:21**ᑫ Gen. 45:19; 46:5   **45:22**ʳ 2 Kin. 5:5 ˢ Gen. 43:34   **45:26**ᵗ Job 29:24   **45:27**ᵘ Judg. 15:19   **46:1**ᵃ Gen. 21:31, 33; 26:32, 33; 28:10 ᵇ Gen. 26:24, 25; 28:13; 31:42; 32:9   **46:2**ᶜ Gen. 15:1; 22:11; 31:11   **46:3**ᵈ Gen. 17:1; 28:13 ᵉ Deut. 26:5   **46:4**ᶠ Gen. 28:15; 31:3; 48:21 ᵍ Gen. 15:16; 50:12, 24, 25 ʰ Gen. 50:1   **46:5**ⁱ Acts 7:15 ʲ Gen. 45:19–21   **46:6**ᵏ Deut. 26:5   **46:8**ˡ Ex. 1:1–4 ᵐ Num. 26:4, 5   **46:9**ⁿ Ex. 6:14   **46:10**ᵒ Ex. 6:15   **46:11**ᵖ 1 Chr. 6:1, 16   **46:12**ᑫ 1 Chr. 2:3; 4:21 ʳ Gen. 38:3, 7, 10 ˢ Gen. 38:29   **46:14**ᵗ Num. 26:26   **46:15**ᵘ Gen. 35:23; 49:31   **46:17**ᵛ 1 Chr. 7:30   **46:18**ʷ Gen. 30:10; 37:2 ˣ Gen. 29:24   **46:19**ʸ Gen. 35:24 ᶻ Gen. 44:27   **46:20**ᵃ Gen. 41:45, 50–52; 48:1   **46:21**ᵇ 1 Chr. 7:6; 8:1 ᶜ Num. 26:38 ᵈ Num. 26:39

23The son of Dan *was* Hushim.* 24*e*The sons of Naphtali *were* Jahzeel,* Guni, Jezer, and Shillem.* 25*f*These *were* the sons of Bilhah, *g*whom Laban gave to Rachel his daughter, and she bore these to Jacob: seven persons in all.

26*h*All the persons who went with Jacob to Egypt, who came from his body, *i*besides Jacob's sons' wives, *were* sixty-six persons in all. 27And the sons of Joseph who were born to him in Egypt *were* two persons. *j*All the persons of the house of Jacob who went to Egypt were seventy.

Jacob Settles in Goshen

28Then he sent Judah before him to Joseph, *k*to point out before him *the way* to Goshen. And they came *l*to the land of Goshen. 29So Joseph made ready his *m*chariot and went up to Goshen to meet his father Israel; and he presented himself to him, and *n*fell on his neck and wept on his neck a good while.

30And Israel said to Joseph, *o*"Now let me die, since I have seen your face, because you *are* still alive."

31Then Joseph said to his brothers and to his father's household, *p*"I will go up and tell Pharaoh, and say to him, 'My brothers and those of my father's house, who *were* in the land of Canaan, have come to me. 32And the men *are* *q*shepherds, for their occupation has been to feed livestock; and they have brought their flocks, their herds, and all that they have.' 33So it shall be, when Pharaoh calls you and says, *r*'What is your *s*occupation?' 34that you shall say, 'Your servants' occupation has been with livestock *t*from our youth even till now, both we *and* also our fathers,' that you may dwell in the land of Goshen; for every shepherd is *u*an abomination to the Egyptians."

47 Then Joseph *a*went and told Pharaoh, and said, "My father and my brothers, their flocks and their herds and all that they possess, have come from the land of Canaan; and indeed they *are* in *b*the land of Goshen." 2And he took five men from among his brothers and *c*presented them to Pharaoh. 3Then Pharaoh said to his brothers, *d*"What *is* your occupation?"

And they said to Pharaoh, *e*"Your servants *are* shepherds, both we *and* also our fathers." 4And they said to Pharaoh, *f*"We have come to dwell in the land, because your servants have no pasture for their flocks, *g*for the famine *is* severe in the land of Canaan. Now therefore, please let your servants *h*dwell in the land of Goshen."

5Then Pharaoh spoke to Joseph, saying, "Your father and your brothers have come to you. 6*i*The land of Egypt *is* before you. Have your father and brothers dwell in the best of the land; let them dwell *j*in the land of Goshen. And if you know *any* competent men among them, then make them chief herdsmen over my livestock."

7Then Joseph brought in his father Jacob and set him before Pharaoh; and Jacob *k*blessed Pharaoh. 8Pharaoh said to Jacob, "How old *are* you?"

9And Jacob said to Pharaoh, *l*"The days of the years of my pilgrimage *are* *m*one hundred and thirty years; *n*few and evil have been the days of the years of my life, and *o*they have not attained to the days of the years of the life of my fathers in the days of their pilgrimage." 10So Jacob *p*blessed Pharaoh, and went out from before Pharaoh.

11And Joseph situated his father and his

---

* **46:23** Called *Shuham* in Numbers 26:42
* **46:24** Spelled *Jahziel* in 1 Chronicles 7:13 • Spelled *Shallum* in 1 Chronicles 7:13

46:26–27 sixty-six . . . seventy. When Joseph, his two sons, and Jacob himself are added, the number of males in Jacob's family equals seventy.
46:34 every shepherd is an abomination to the Egyptians. God used the racial and ethnic prejudice of the Egyptians as a way of preserving the ethnic and spiritual identity of His own people. Jacob's family was already intermarrying with the Canaanites (ch. 38) and was in danger of losing its identity as the people of God.
47:5–6 Pharaoh. There is some uncertainty concerning the identity of this pharaoh. Many believe he was Amenhotep I of the eleventh dynasty. Prior to his reign Egypt had suffered political and economic chaos for 200 years. Irrigation and building projects fell into ruin, and civil war raged. But Pharaoh Amenhotep was able to reunite Egypt, rebuilding the country and developing world trade. One of the reasons for his success no doubt stemmed from the fact that he was a generous man as we are told here. Not only was he generous to his own people, but he was kind to Israel. God had already promised to bless those who blessed the descendants of Abraham (Gen. 12:3). The lesson is clear. If a pagan king can experience

God's blessing for his generosity, how much more can born-again believers know the riches of heaven for their generosity? Solomon reminds us of this principle: "The generous soul will be made rich" (Prov. 11:25).
47:8 How old are you? Pharaoh's question suggests that the long ages of the patriarchal family were truly exceptional, even for this period. Jacob's final 147 years (47:28) were fewer than the 175 years of Abraham (25:7) and the 180 years of Isaac (35:28), but still a significant age.

46:24 *e* Num. 26:48   **46:25** *f* Gen. 30:5, 7 *g* Gen. 29:29   **46:26** *h* Ex. 1:5 *i* Gen. 35:11   **46:27** *j* Deut. 10:22   **46:28** *k* Gen. 31:21 *l* Gen. 47:1   **46:29** *m* Gen. 41:43 *n* Gen. 45:14, 15   **46:30** *o* Luke 2:29, 30   **46:31** *p* Gen. 47:1   **46:32** *q* Gen. 47:3   **46:33** *r* Gen. 47:2, 3 *s* Gen. 47:3   **46:34** *t* Gen. 30:35; 34:5; 37:17 *u* Gen. 43:32   **47:1** *a* Gen. 46:31 *b* Gen. 45:10; 46:28; 50:8   **47:2** *c* Acts 7:13   **47:3** *d* Gen. 46:33 *e* Gen. 46:32, 34   **47:4** *f* Deut. 26:5 *g* Gen. 43:1 *h* Gen. 46:34   **47:6** *i* Gen. 20:15; 45:10, 18; 47:11 *j* Gen. 47:4   **47:7** *k* Gen. 47:10; 48:15, 20   **47:9** *l* [Heb. 11:9, 13] *m* Gen. 47:28 *n* [Job 14:1] *o* Gen. 5:5; 11:10, 11; 25:7, 8; 35:28   **47:10** *p* Gen. 47:7

brothers, and gave them a possession in the land of Egypt, in the best of the land, in the land of *a*Rameses, *r*as Pharaoh had commanded. 12Then Joseph provided his father, his brothers, and all *s*his father's household with bread, according to the number in *their* families.

Joseph Deals with the Famine

13Now *there was* no bread in all the land; for the famine *was* very severe, *t*so that the land of Egypt and the land of Canaan languished because of the famine. 14*u*And Joseph gathered up all the money that was found in the land of Egypt and in the land of Canaan, for the grain which they bought; and Joseph brought the money into Pharaoh's house.

15So when the money failed in the land of Egypt and in the land of Canaan, all the Egyptians came to Joseph and said, "Give us bread, for *v*why should we die in your presence? For the money has failed."

16Then Joseph said, "Give your livestock, and I will give you *bread* for your livestock, if the money is gone." 17So they brought their livestock to Joseph, and Joseph gave them bread *in exchange* for the horses, the flocks, the cattle of the herds, and for the donkeys. Thus he fed them with bread *in exchange* for all their livestock that year.

18When that year had ended, they came to him the next year and said to him, "We will not hide from my lord that our money is gone; my lord also has our herds of livestock. There is nothing left in the sight of my lord but our bodies and our lands. 19Why should we die before your eyes, both we and our land? Buy us and our land for bread, and we and our land will be servants of Pharaoh; give *us* seed, that we may *w*live and not die, that the land may not be desolate."

20Then Joseph *x*bought all the land of Egypt for Pharaoh; for every man of the Egyptians sold his field, because the famine was severe upon them. So the land became Pharaoh's. 21And as for the people, he moved them into the cities,* from *one* end of the borders of Egypt to the *other* end. 22*y*Only the land of the *z*priests he did not buy; for the priests had rations *allotted to them* by Pharaoh, and they ate their rations which Pharaoh gave them; therefore they did not sell their lands.

23Then Joseph said to the people, "Indeed I have bought you and your land this day for Pharaoh. Look, *here is* seed for you, and you shall sow the land. 24And it shall come to pass in the harvest that you shall give one-fifth to Pharaoh. Four-fifths shall be your own, as seed for the field and for your food, for those of your households and as food for your little ones."

25So they said, "You have saved *a*our lives; let us find favor in the sight of my lord, and we will be Pharaoh's servants." 26And Joseph made it a law over the land of Egypt to this day, *that* Pharaoh should have one-fifth, *b*except for the land of the priests only, *which* did not become Pharaoh's.

Joseph's Vow to Jacob

27So Israel *c*dwelt in the land of Egypt, in the country of Goshen; and they had possessions there and *d*grew and multiplied exceedingly. 28And Jacob lived in the land of Egypt seventeen years. So the length of Jacob's life was one hundred and forty-seven years. 29When the time *e*drew near that Israel must die, he called his son Joseph and said to him, "Now if I have found favor in your sight, please *f*put your hand under my thigh, and *g*deal kindly and truly with me. *h*Please do not bury me in Egypt, 30but *i*let me lie with my fathers; you shall carry me out of Egypt and *j*bury me in their burial place."

And he said, "I will do as you have said." 31Then he said, "Swear to me." And he swore to him. So *k*Israel bowed himself on the head of the bed.

Jacob Blesses Joseph's Sons

48 Now it came to pass after these things that Joseph was told, "Indeed your father *is* sick"; and he took with him his two sons, *a*Manasseh and Ephraim. 2And Jacob was told, "Look, your son Joseph is coming to you"; and Israel strengthened himself and sat up on the bed. 3Then Jacob said to Joseph: "God *b*Almighty appeared to me at *c*Luz in the land of Canaan and blessed me, 4and said to me, 'Behold, I will *d*make you fruitful and multiply you, and I will make of you a multitude of people, and *e*give this land to your descendants after you *f*as an everlasting possession.'

* **47:21** Following Masoretic Text and Targum; Samaritan Pentateuch, Septuagint, and Vulgate read *made the people virtual slaves.*

47:20 the land. Pharaoh's ownership of all the land of Egypt would one day lead to gross abuses of power (see the Book of Exodus).

47:29 deal kindly and truly with me. In other words, "demonstrate to me the utmost covenant loyalty." Jacob showed his vigorous faith in God's promises by asking to be buried in the land promised to his descendants.

47:11 *q*Ex. 1:11; 12:37 *r*Gen. 47:6, 27 **47:12** *s*Gen. 45:11; 50:21 **47:13** *t*Gen. 41:30 **47:14** *u*Gen. 41:56; 42:6 **47:15** *v*Gen. 47:19 **47:19** *w*Gen. 43:8 **47:20** *x*Jer. 32:43 **47:22** *y*Ezra 7:24 *z*Gen. 41:45 **47:25** *a*Gen. 33:15 **47:26** *b*Gen. 47:22 **47:27** *c*Gen. 47:11 *d*Gen. 17:6; 26:4; 35:11; 46:3 **47:29** *e*Deut. 31:14 *f*Gen. 24:2–4 *g*Gen. 24:49 *h*Gen. 50:25 **47:30** *i*2 Sam. 19:37 *j*Gen. 49:29; 50:5–13 **47:31** *k*1 Kin. 1:47 **48:1** *a*Gen. 41:51, 56; 46:20; 50:23 **48:3** *b*Gen. 43:14; 49:25 *c*Gen. 28:13, 19; 35:6, 9 **48:4** *d*Gen. 46:3 *e*Ex. 6:8 *f*Gen. 17:8

5And now your gtwo sons, Ephraim and Manasseh, who were born to you in the land of Egypt before I came to you in Egypt, *are* mine; as Reuben and Simeon, they shall be mine. 6Your offspring whom you beget after them shall be yours; they will be called by the name of their brothers in their inheritance. 7But as for me, when I came from Padan, hRachel died beside me in the land of Canaan on the way, when *there was* but a little distance to go to Ephrath; and I buried her there on the way to Ephrath (that is, Bethlehem)."

8Then Israel saw Joseph's sons, and said, "Who *are* these?"

9Joseph said to his father, "They *are* my sons, whom God has given me in this *place.*"

And he said, "Please bring them to me, and iI will bless them." 10Now jthe eyes of Israel were dim with age, *so that* he could not see. Then Joseph brought them near him, and he kkissed them and embraced them. 11And Israel said to Joseph, l"I had not thought to see your face; but in fact, God has also shown me your offspring!"

12So Joseph brought them from beside his knees, and he bowed down with his face to the earth. 13And Joseph took them both, Ephraim with his right hand toward Israel's left hand, and Manasseh with his left hand toward Israel's right hand, and brought *them* near him. 14Then Israel stretched out his right hand and mlaid *it* on Ephraim's head, who *was* the younger, and his left hand on Manasseh's head, nguiding his hands knowingly, for Manasseh *was* the ofirstborn. 15And phe blessed Joseph, and said:

"God, qbefore whom my fathers
    Abraham and Isaac walked,
The God who has fed me all my life
    long to this day,
16 The Angel rwho has redeemed me
    from all evil,
Bless the lads;
Let smy name be named upon them,
And the name of my fathers Abraham
    and Isaac;
And let them tgrow into a multitude in
    the midst of the earth."

17Now when Joseph saw that his father ulaid his right hand on the head of Ephraim, it displeased him; so he took hold of his father's hand to remove it from Ephraim's head to Manasseh's head. 18And Joseph said to his father, "Not so, my father, for this *one is* the firstborn; put your right hand on his head."

19But his father refused and said, v"I know, my son, I know. He also shall become a people, and he also shall be great; but truly whis younger brother shall be greater than he, and his descendants shall become a multitude of nations."

20So he blessed them that day, saying, x"By you Israel will bless, saying, 'May God make you as Ephraim and as Manasseh!'" And thus he set Ephraim before Manasseh.

21Then Israel said to Joseph, "Behold, I am dying, but yGod will be with you and bring you back to the land of your fathers. 22Moreover zI have given to you one portion above your brothers, which I took from the hand aof the Amorite with my sword and my bow."

Jacob's Last Words to His Sons

49 And Jacob called his sons and said, "Gather together, that I may atell you what shall befall you bin the last days:

2 "Gather together and hear, you sons of
    Jacob,
  And listen to Israel your father.

3 "Reuben, you are cmy firstborn,
  My might and the beginning of my
    strength,
  The excellency of dignity and the
    excellency of power.
4 Unstable as water, you shall not excel,
  Because you dwent up to your father's
    bed;
  Then you defiled *it*—
  He went up to my couch.

5 "Simeon and Levi *are* brothers;
  Instruments of cruelty *are in* their
    dwelling place.
6 eLet not my soul enter their council;
  Let not my honor be united fto their
    assembly;
  gFor in their anger they slew a man,
  And in their self-will they hamstrung
    an ox.
7 Cursed *be* their anger, for *it is* fierce;
  And their wrath, for it is cruel!

48:5–7 Ephraim and Manasseh. As firstborn, Reuben should have received a double portion of the inheritance, but he had forfeited his birthright by his sins (35:22). By adopting Ephraim and Manasseh as his own sons, Jacob gave the double portion to Joseph.

48:22 one portion above. Jacob promised Joseph that he would one day return to the land of Canaan. The promise was fulfilled after Joseph's death (50:24–26).

49:5–7 Simeon and Levi. This prophecy was fulfilled when the Israelites settled in the Promised Land. Simeon's allotment was scattered within the larger portion of the tribe of Judah, and Levi's allotment was scattered cities throughout the land (Josh. 21).

48:5 g Josh. 13:7; 14:4 **48:7** h Gen. 35:9, 16, 19, 20 **48:9** i Gen. 27:4; 47:15 **48:10** j Gen. 27:1 k Gen. 27:27; 45:15; 50:1 **48:11** l Gen. 45:26 **48:14** m Matt. 19:15 n Gen. 48:19 o Josh. 17:1 **48:15** p [Heb. 11:21] q Gen. 17:1; 24:40 **48:16** r Gen. 22:11, 15–18; 28:13–15; 31:11 s Amos 9:12 t Num. 26:34, 37 **48:17** u Gen. 48:14 **48:19** v Gen. 48:14 w Num. 1:33, 35 **48:20** x Ruth 4:11, 12 **48:21** y Gen. 28:15; 46:4; 50:24 **48:22** z Josh. 24:32 a Gen. 34:28 **49:1** a Deut. 33:1, 6–25 b Is. 2:2; 39:6 **49:3** c Gen. 29:32 **49:4** d Gen. 35:22 **49:6** e Prov. 1:15, 16 f Ps. 26:9 g Gen. 34:26

*h*I will divide them in Jacob
And scatter them in Israel.

8 "Judah,*i* you *are he* whom your brothers
      shall praise;
    *j*Your hand *shall be* on the neck of your
      enemies;
    *k*Your father's children shall bow down
      before you.
9 Judah *is* *l*a lion's whelp;
    From the prey, my son, you have
      gone up.
    *m*He bows down, he lies down as a
      lion;
    And as a lion, who shall rouse him?
10 *n*The scepter shall not depart from
      Judah,
    Nor *o*a lawgiver from between his feet,
    *p*Until Shiloh comes;
    *q*And to Him *shall be* the obedience of
      the people.
11 Binding his donkey to the vine,
    And his donkey's colt to the choice
      vine,
    He washed his garments in wine,
    And his clothes in the blood of
      grapes.
12 His eyes *are* darker than wine,
    And his teeth whiter than milk.

13 "Zebulun*r* shall dwell by the haven of
      the sea;
    He *shall become* a haven for ships,
    And his border shall *s*adjoin Sidon.

14 "Issachar*t* is a strong donkey,
    Lying down between two burdens;
15 He saw that rest *was* good,
    And that the land *was* pleasant;
    He bowed *u*his shoulder to bear *a
      burden*,
    And became a band of slaves.

16 "Dan*v* shall judge his people
    As one of the tribes of Israel.
17 *w*Dan shall be a serpent by the way,
    A viper by the path,
    That bites the horse's heels
    So that its rider shall fall backward.
18 *x*I have waited for your salvation,
    O Lord!

19 "Gad,*y* a troop shall tramp upon him,
    But he shall triumph at last.

20 "Bread from *z*Asher *shall be* rich,
    And he shall yield royal dainties.

21 "Naphtali*a* *is* a deer let loose;
    He uses beautiful words.

22 "Joseph *is* a fruitful bough,
    A fruitful bough by a well;
    His branches run over the wall.
23 The archers have *b*bitterly grieved
      him,
    Shot *at him* and hated him.
24 But his *c*bow remained in strength,
    And the arms of his hands were made
      strong
    By the hands of *d*the Mighty *God* of
      Jacob
    e(From there *f*is the Shepherd, *g*the
      Stone of Israel),
25 *h*By the God of your father who will
      help you,
    *i*And by the Almighty *j*who will bless
      you
    With blessings of heaven above,
    Blessings of the deep that lies
      beneath,
    Blessings of the breasts and of the
      womb.
26 The blessings of your father
    Have excelled the blessings of my
      ancestors,
    *k*Up to the utmost bound of the
      everlasting hills.
    *l*They shall be on the head of
      Joseph,
    And on the crown of the head of
      him who was separate from his
      brothers.

27 "Benjamin is a *m*ravenous wolf;
    In the morning he shall devour the
      prey,
    *n*And at night he shall divide the
      spoil."

28All these *are* the twelve tribes of Israel,
and this *is* what their father spoke to them.
And he blessed them; he blessed each one
according to his own blessing.

49:10 *scepter.* With these words, Jacob predicted that a royal line would rise from Judah's descendants. Shiloh is an obscure word, probably meaning "the one to whom it belongs." In other words, Judah's descendants would be the rulers of Israel until the coming of "Shiloh," the One to whom all royal authority belongs. In this context, Shiloh, like "the Seed," is a reference to the coming Messiah.
49:11–12 *wine . . . blood.* The imagery in this verse describes the warfare that the Messiah will wage to establish His reign (Ps. 2; 110; Rev. 19:11–21).
49:24 *Shepherd.* The image of God as a shepherd occurs many times in Scripture. This term would have had great significance for a family of shepherds. God shepherded and cared for their families just as they shepherded and cared for their own flocks. God is the one Good Shepherd (Ps. 23; John 10).

49:28 *the twelve tribes of Israel.* Jacob's blessings are prophecies about the destiny of each tribe. Some of the blessings are obscure, but the blessings on Judah and Joseph are clear prophecies from God

49:7 *h* Josh. 19:1, 9; 21:1–42   **49:8** *i* Deut. 33:7 *j* Ps. 18:40 *k* 1 Chr. 5:2   **49:9** *l* [Rev. 5:5] *m* Num. 23:24; 24:9 **49:10** *n* Num. 24:17; Matt. 1:3; 2:6; Luke 3:33; Rev. 5:5 *o* Ps. 60:7 *p* Is. 11:1 *q* Ps. 2:6–9; 72:8–11   **49:13** *r* Deut. 33:18, 19 *s* Gen. 10:19   **49:14** *t* 1 Chr. 12:32   **49:15** *u* 1 Sam. 10:9   **49:16** *v* Deut. 33:22   **49:17** *w* Judg. 18:27 **49:18** *x* Is. 25:9   **49:19** *y* Deut. 33:20   **49:20** *z* Deut. 33:24   **49:21** *a* Deut. 33:23   **49:23** *b* Gen. 37:4, 24   **49:24** *c* Job 29:20 *d* Ps. 132:2, 5 *e* Gen. 45:11; 47:12 *f* [Ps. 23:1; 80:1] *g* Is. 28:16   **49:25** *h* Gen. 28:13; 32:9; 35:3; 43:23; 50:17 *i* Gen. 17:1; 35:11 *j* Deut. 33:13 **49:26** *k* Deut. 33:15 *l* Deut. 33:16   **49:27** *m* Judg. 20:21, 25 *n* Zech. 14:1

Jacob's Death and Burial

29Then he charged them and said to them: "I °am to be gathered to my people; ᵖbury me with my fathers ᑫin the cave that *is* in the field of Ephron the Hittite, 30in the cave that *is* in the field of Machpelah, which *is* before Mamre in the land of Canaan, ʳwhich Abraham bought with the field of Ephron the Hittite as a possession for a burial place. 31sThere they buried Abraham and Sarah his wife, ᵗthere they buried Isaac and Rebekah his wife, and there I buried Leah. 32The field and the cave that *is* there *were* purchased from the sons of Heth." 33And when Jacob had finished commanding his sons, he drew his feet up into the bed and breathed his last, and was gathered to his people.

50 Then Joseph ᵃfell on his father's face and ᵇwept over him, and kissed him. 2And Joseph commanded his servants the physicians to ᶜembalm his father. So the physicians embalmed Israel. 3Forty days were required for him, for such are the days required for those who are embalmed; and the Egyptians ᵈmourned for him seventy days.

4Now when the days of his mourning were past, Joseph spoke to ᵉthe household of Pharaoh, saying, "If now I have found favor in your eyes, please speak in the hearing of Pharaoh, saying, 5f'My father made me swear, saying, "Behold, I am dying; in my grave ᵍwhich I dug for myself in the land of Canaan, there you shall bury me." Now therefore, please let me go up and bury my father, and I will come back.'"

6And Pharaoh said, "Go up and bury your father, as he made you swear."

7So Joseph went up to bury his father; and with him went up all the servants of Pharaoh, the elders of his house, and all the elders of the land of Egypt, 8as well as all the house of Joseph, his brothers, and his father's house. Only their little ones, their flocks, and their herds they left in the land of Goshen. 9And there went up with him both chariots and horsemen, and it was a very great gathering.

10Then they came to the threshing floor of Atad, which *is* beyond the Jordan, and they ʰmourned there with a great and very solemn lamentation. ⁱHe observed seven days of mourning for his father. 11And when the inhabitants of the land, the Canaanites, saw the mourning at the threshing floor of Atad, they said, "This *is* a deep mourning of the Egyptians." Therefore its name was called Abel Mizraim,* which *is* beyond the Jordan.

12So his sons did for him just as he had commanded them. 13For ʲhis sons carried him to the land of Canaan, and buried him in the cave of the field of Machpelah, before Mamre, which Abraham ᵏbought with the field from Ephron the Hittite as property for a burial place. 14And after he had buried his father, Joseph returned to Egypt, he and his brothers and all who went up with him to bury his father.

Joseph Reassures His Brothers

15When Joseph's brothers saw that their father was dead, ˡthey said, "Perhaps Joseph will hate us, and may actually repay us for all the evil which we did to him." 16So they sent *messengers* to Joseph, saying, "Before your father died he commanded, saying, 17'Thus you shall say to Joseph: "I beg you, please forgive the trespass of your brothers and their sin; ᵐfor they did evil to you."' Now, please, forgive the trespass of the servants of ⁿthe God of your father." And Joseph wept when they spoke to him.

18Then his brothers also went and °fell down before his face, and they said, "Behold, we *are* your servants."

19Joseph said to them, ᵖ"Do not be afraid, ᑫfor *am* I in the place of God? 20ʳBut as for you, you meant evil against me; *but* sGod meant it for good, in order to bring it about as *it is* this day, to save many people alive. 21Now therefore, do not be afraid; ᵗI will provide for you and your little ones." And he comforted them and spoke kindly to them.

Death of Joseph

22So Joseph dwelt in Egypt, he and his father's household. And Joseph lived

---

* 50:11 Literally *Mourning of Egypt*

---

about their destinies (compare Moses' blessing of the tribes of Israel, Deut. 33).
50:5–6 swear. Bound by an oath, Joseph requested leave to bury his father in Canaan in a place ready for his remains. It seems today that we do not take vows as seriously as Joseph took his promise to his father, and everything from casual promises to solemn marriage vows are broken with little remorse. Honoring vows, both in small matters and significant, honors God because He asks us to put away lying and speak truth (Eph. 4:25). Broken vows result in broken hearts and ruined relationships, blasted memories, ineffective lives and testimonies. Even a foolish or wrong vow cannot be lightly set aside, but must be repented

of before God. We must learn to promise wisely, and honor our promises faithfully.
50:20 God meant it for good. God transformed the

49:29 ° Gen. 15:15; 25:8; 35:29 ᵖ Gen. 47:30 ᑫ Gen. 23:16–20; 50:13   **49:30** ʳ Gen. 23:3–20   **49:31** s Gen. 23:19, 20; 25:9 ᵗ Gen. 35:29; 50:13   **50:1** ᵃ Gen. 46:4, 29 ᵇ 2 Kin. 13:14   **50:2** ᶜ Gen. 50:26   **50:3** ᵈ Deut. 34:8   **50:4** ᵉ Esth. 4:2   **50:5** ᶠ Gen. 47:29–31 ᵍ Is. 22:16   **50:10** ʰ Acts 8:2 ⁱ 1 Sam. 31:13   **50:13** ʲ Acts 7:16 ᵏ Gen. 23:16–20   **50:15** ˡ [Job 15:21]   **50:17** ᵐ [Prov. 28:13] ⁿ Gen. 49:25   **50:18** ° Gen. 37:7–10; 41:43; 44:14   **50:19** ᵖ Gen. 45:5 ᑫ 2 Kin. 5:7   **50:20** ʳ Ps. 56:5 s [Acts 3:13–15]   **50:21** ᵗ [Matt. 5:44]

one hundred and ten years. ²³Joseph saw Ephraim's children ᵘto the third *generation*. ᵛThe children of Machir, the son of Manasseh, ʷwere also brought up on Joseph's knees.

²⁴And Joseph said to his brethren, "I am dying; but ˣGod will surely visit you, and bring you out of this land to the land ʸof which He swore to Abraham, to Isaac, and to Jacob." ²⁵Then ᶻJoseph took an oath from the children of Israel, saying, "God will surely visit you, and ᵃyou shall carry up my ᵇbones from here." ²⁶So Joseph died, *being* one hundred and ten years old; and they embalmed him, and he was put in a coffin in Egypt.

---

evil of a group of men into an exceedingly great work. Joseph not only saved the lives of numerous people in the ancient world, he also testified to the power and goodness of the living God.

50:24 to Abraham, to Isaac, and to Jacob. This phrase is the standard way of referring to God's covenant with Abraham's family (50:24; Ex. 2:24; 3:16). The recital of the three names reaffirms the certainty of the promise and God's commitment to fulfill it.

50:25 carry up my bones. Hundreds of years later,

Moses would keep the Israelites' oath by taking Joseph's bones with the people into the wilderness (Ex. 13:19). Finally, Joshua would bury the bones of Joseph at Shechem (Josh. 24:32).

50:23 ᵘ Job 42:16 ᵛ Num. 26:29; 32:39 ʷ Gen. 30:3 **50:24** ˣ Ex. 3:16, 17 ʸ Gen. 26:3; 35:12; 46:4 **50:25** ᶻ Ex. 13:19 ᵃ Deut. 1:8; 30:1–8 ᵇ Ex. 13:19

THE SECOND BOOK OF MOSES CALLED
EXODUS

▶ **AUTHOR:** Exodus has been attributed to Moses since the time of Joshua (cf. 20:25; Josh. 8:30–32), and there is a great deal of both internal and external evidence that supports Moses as the author. The claims in Joshua are backed by similar testimony from Malachi (4:4), the disciples (John 1:45), Paul (Rom. 10:5), and Christ (Mark 7:10; 12:26; Luke 20:37; John 5:46–47; 7:19,22–23). Portions of the book itself claim the authorship of Moses (ch. 15; 17:8–14; 20:1–17; 24:4,7,12; 31:18; 34:1–27). The author of Exodus must have been a man familiar with the customs and climate of Egypt. Its consistency of style points to a single author and its ancient literary devices support its antiquity.

▶ **TIME:** c. 1875–1445 B.C.   ▶ **KEY VERSES:** Ex. 19:5–6

▶ **THEME:** The main character of Exodus is clearly Moses. God gives him the job of leading the exodus from Egypt. Moses also takes on the job of establishing, at God's direction, the essential elements of the Jewish patterns of life and worship. He is simultaneously God's designated representative of the people to God and God's messenger and representative to the people. The critical events in Exodus are the Passover and the giving of the Ten Commandments. The remainder of the Old Testament continually refers back to God's deliverance of Israel from Egypt and the law as delivered at Sinai. In these events God's identity and purpose is revealed. There are many signs and wonders of His power. Aspects of His nature and His expectations of the people also become increasingly clear.

Israel's Suffering in Egypt

1 Now ^athese *are* the names of the children of Israel who came to Egypt; each man and his household came with Jacob: ²Reuben, Simeon, Levi, and Judah; ³Issachar, Zebulun, and Benjamin; ⁴Dan, Naphtali, Gad, and Asher. ⁵All those who were descendants* of Jacob were ^bseventy* persons (for Joseph was in Egypt *already*). ⁶And ^cJoseph died, all his brothers, and all that generation. ^{7d}But the children of Israel were fruitful and increased abundantly, multiplied and grew exceedingly mighty; and the land was filled with them.

⁸Now there arose a new king over Egypt, ^ewho did not know Joseph. ⁹And he said to his people, "Look, the people of the children of Israel *are* more and ^fmightier than we; ^{10g}come, let us ^hdeal shrewdly with them, lest they multiply, and it happen, in the event of war, that they also join our enemies and fight against us, and so go up out of the land." ¹¹Therefore they set taskmasters over them ⁱto afflict them

* **1:5** Literally *who came from the loins of* • Dead Sea Scrolls and Septuagint read *seventy-five* (compare Acts 7:14).

1:1 *Israel.* Originally, Israel was called Jacob. His twelve sons became the founders of the twelve tribes of the nation Israel.

1:2–4 The sons are listed according to their mothers and their ages. Reuben, Simeon, Levi, Judah, Issachar, and Zebulun were all sons of Leah. Benjamin was the son of Rachel. Dan and Naphtali were sons of Bilhah, the maid of Rachel. Gad and Asher were sons of Zilpah, the maid of Leah (for each son's birth, see Gen. 29:31–35; 35:16–20,23–26).

1:8 *a new king.* This king did not remember Joseph, his privileged position in the older pharaoh's administration, his administrative skill that saved the Egyptians from starvation, and his enrichment of the pharaoh's treasury. This pharaoh was probably one of the Hyksos kings who descended from foreign invaders. Ethnically they were a minority in Egypt,

and they may have perceived the growing numbers of Hebrews as a personal challenge.

1:11–22 *to afflict them.* Long before the sons of Israel came to Egypt, Abraham received a remarkable revelation from the Lord (Gen. 15:13–16): his descendants would be strangers in a foreign land and would be enslaved and oppressed for four hundred years. "In all their affliction He was afflicted" (Is. 63:9). At the point when Israel's afflictions became unbearable they cried for help, and God responded in faithfulness to His promise.

1:11 *Pithom and Raamses.* These storage cities are mentioned according to the names by which they

---

1:1 ^aGen. 46:8–27   **1:5** ^bGen. 46:26, 27   **1:6** ^cGen. 50:26   **1:7** ^dActs 7:17   **1:8** ^eActs 7:18, 19   **1:9** ^fGen. 26:16   **1:10** ^gPs. 83:3, 4   ^hActs 7:19   **1:11** ⁱEx. 3:7; 5:6

with their [j]burdens. And they built for Pharaoh [k]supply cities, Pithom [l]and Raamses.
12But the more they afflicted them, the
more they multiplied and grew. And they
were in dread of the children of Israel. 13So
the Egyptians made the children of Israel
[m]serve with rigor. 14And they [n]made their
lives bitter with hard bondage—[o]in mortar,
in brick, and in all manner of service in the
field. All their service in which they made
them serve *was* with rigor.

15Then the king of Egypt spoke to the
[p]Hebrew midwives, of whom the name of
one *was* Shiphrah and the name of the other Puah; 16and he said, "When you do the
duties of a midwife for the Hebrew wom-
en, and see *them* on the birthstools, if it *is*
a [q]son, then you shall kill him; but if it *is*
a daughter, then she shall live." 17But the
midwives [r]feared God, and did not do [s]as
the king of Egypt commanded them, but
saved the male children alive. 18So the king
of Egypt called for the midwives and said
to them, "Why have you done this thing,
and saved the male children alive?"

19And [t]the midwives said to Pharaoh,
"Because the Hebrew women *are* not like
the Egyptian women; for they *are* lively
and give birth before the midwives come
to them."

20[u]Therefore God dealt well with the
midwives, and the people multiplied and
grew very mighty. 21And so it was, because
the midwives feared God, [v]that He provided households for them.

22So Pharaoh commanded all his people,
saying, [w]"Every son who is born* you shall
cast into the river, and every daughter you
shall save alive."

Moses Is Born

2 And [a]a man of the house of Levi went
and took *as wife* a daughter of Levi.
2So the woman conceived and bore a son.
And [b]when she saw that he *was* a beautiful
child, she hid him three months. 3But when
she could no longer hide him, she took an
ark of [c]bulrushes for him, daubed it with
[d]asphalt and [e]pitch, put the child in it, and
laid *it* in the reeds [f]by the river's bank.
4[g]And his sister stood afar off, to know
what would be done to him.

5Then the [h]daughter of Pharaoh came
down to bathe at the river. And her maidens walked along the riverside; and when
she saw the ark among the reeds, she sent
her maid to get it. 6And when she opened
it, she saw the child, and behold, the baby
wept. So she had compassion on him, and
said, "This is one of the Hebrews' children."

7Then his sister said to Pharaoh's daughter, "Shall I go and call a nurse for you from
the Hebrew women, that she may nurse the
child for you?"

8And Pharaoh's daughter said to her,
"Go." So the maiden went and called the
child's mother. 9Then Pharaoh's daughter said to her, "Take this child away and
nurse him for me, and I will give *you* your
wages." So the woman took the child and
nursed him. 10And the child grew, and she
brought him to Pharaoh's daughter, and he
became [i]her son. So she called his name
Moses,* saying, "Because I drew him out
of the water."

Moses Flees to Midian

11Now it came to pass in those days,
[j]when Moses was grown, that he went out
to his brethren and looked at their burdens. And he saw an Egyptian beating a
Hebrew, one of his brethren. 12So he looked

* **1:22** Samaritan Pentateuch, Septuagint, and Targum add *to the Hebrews.* * **2:10** Literally *Drawn Out*

---

were known in later times. The Pharaoh Ramses (whose name presumably relates to the name of one of these cities) was not yet in power.

1:15 ***king of Egypt.*** This king was probably not the Hyksos king alluded to in verses 8–14. This king, perhaps Thutmose I (c. 1539–1514 B.C.), ruled Egypt when Moses was born (2:1–10). ***Hebrew midwives.*** The names of these women (Shiphrah—"beautiful one," and Puah—"splendid one") are preserved in this account because they were godly women with a courageous faith. At the same time, the names of the pharaohs—the "important" people of the day—are omitted.

1:17 ***feared.*** The Hebrew term for "fear" is the word regularly used for piety, obedience, and the true worship of God (20:20; Gen. 22:12).

2:2 ***bore a son.*** This was not their first child; both Miriam and Aaron were older than Moses (v. 4; 7:7).

2:6 ***one of the Hebrews' children.*** A Hebrew baby would have been circumcised on the eighth day. Although circumcision was practiced in Egypt, it was not done to infants. Upon unwrapping the infant's clothing, the women would have seen his special mark.

2:10 ***Because I drew him out.*** In Hebrew, the name Moses means "he who draws out." In this manner, Moses' name can refer the reader to the living God, who is the true Deliverer, and also to Moses, who was used by God to deliver the Israelites from the Red Sea (chs. 14–15). The one who was drawn out of water would be the means of drawing the Israelite nation out of water.

2:11 ***when Moses was grown.*** The years of Moses' experience in the pharaoh's court are not detailed. Yet Stephen, the New Testament martyr, reported the long-held and surely accurate tradition: "Moses was learned in all the wisdom of the Egyptians, and was mighty in words and deeds" (Acts 7:22). The

1:11 [j] Ex. 1:14; 2:11; 5:4–9; 6:6 [k] 1 Kin. 9:19 [l] Gen. 47:11 **1:13** [m] Gen. 15:13 **1:14** [n] Num. 20:15 [o] Ps. 81:6 **1:15** [p] Ex. 2:6 **1:16** [q] Acts 7:19 **1:17** [r] Prov. 16:6 [s] Dan. 3:16, 18 **1:19** [t] Josh. 2:4 **1:20** [u] [Prov. 11:18] **1:21** [v] 1 Sam. 2:35 **1:22** [w] Acts 7:19 **2:1** [a] Ex. 6:16–20 **2:2** [b] Acts 7:20 **2:3** [c] Is. 18:2 [d] Gen. 14:10 [e] Gen. 6:14 [f] Is. 19:6 **2:4** [g] Num. 26:59 **2:5** [h] Acts 7:21 **2:10** [i] Acts 7:21 **2:11** [j] Heb. 11:24–26

this way and that way, and when he saw no one, he [k]killed the Egyptian and hid him in the sand. [13]And [l]when he went out the second day, behold, two Hebrew men [m]were fighting, and he said to the one who did the wrong, "Why are you striking your companion?"

[14]Then he said, [n]"Who made you a prince and a judge over us? Do you intend to kill me as you killed the Egyptian?"

So Moses [o]feared and said, "Surely this thing is known!" [15]When Pharaoh heard of this matter, he sought to kill Moses. But [p]Moses fled from the face of Pharaoh and dwelt in the land of [q]Midian; and he sat down by [r]a well.

[16s]Now the priest of Midian had seven daughters. [t]And they came and drew water, and they filled the [u]troughs to water their father's flock. [17]Then the [v]shepherds came and [w]drove them away; but Moses stood up and helped them, and [x]watered their flock.

[18]When they came to [y]Reuel their father, [z]he said, "How is it that you have come so soon today?"

[19]And they said, "An Egyptian delivered us from the hand of the shepherds, and he also drew enough water for us and watered the flock."

[20]So he said to his daughters, "And where is he? Why is it that you have left the man? Call him, that he may [a]eat bread."

[21]Then Moses was content to live with the man, and he gave [b]Zipporah his daughter to Moses. [22]And she bore him a son. He called his name [c]Gershom,* for he said, "I have been [d]a stranger in a foreign land."

[23]Now it happened [e]in the process of time that the king of Egypt died. Then the children of Israel [f]groaned because of the bondage, and they cried out; and [g]their cry came up to God because of the bondage. [24]So God [h]heard their groaning, and God [i]remembered His [j]covenant with Abraham, with Isaac, and with Jacob. [25]And God [k]looked upon the children of Israel, and God [l]acknowledged them.

Moses at the Burning Bush

3 Now Moses was tending the flock of [a]Jethro his father-in-law, [b]the priest of Midian. And he led the flock to the back of the desert, and came to [c]Horeb, [d]the mountain of God. [2]And [e]the Angel of the LORD appeared to him in a flame of fire from the midst of a bush. So he looked, and behold, the bush was burning with fire, but the bush was not consumed. [3]Then Moses said, "I will now turn aside and see this [f]great sight, why the bush does not burn."

[4]So when the LORD saw that he turned aside to look, God called [g]to him from the midst of the bush and said, "Moses, Moses!"

And he said, "Here I am."

[5]Then He said, "Do not draw near this place. [h]Take your sandals off your feet, for the place where you stand is holy ground." [6]Moreover He said, [i]"I am the God of your father—the God of Abraham, the God of Isaac, and the God of Jacob." And Moses hid his face, for [j]he was afraid to look upon God.

[7]And the LORD said: [k]"I have surely seen the oppression of My people who are in

---

* **2:22** Literally *Stranger There*

---

training Moses received was the best education the world had to offer at the time. He would have learned three languages: Egyptian, Akkadian, and Hebrew. When Moses came into the presence of Pharaoh to demand freedom for his people, he was no "uneducated slave," but had received an education on a par with the king's.

2:15 the land of Midian. This is the region of the Sinai Peninsula and Arabian deserts where the semi-nomadic Midianites lived (for the Abrahamic origin of this people group, see Gen. 25:1).

2:16 the priest of Midian. This man appears to have been a foreigner who had come to worship the true and living God.

2:18 Reuel. Reuel is also called Jethro (4:18).

2:19 An Egyptian. Moses apparently still dressed and spoke as an Egyptian, rather than as a Hebrew.

2:22 Gershom. Gershom means "a stranger there." Moses was doubly removed from his land. He and his people, the Israelites, were strangers in Egypt, and now he was estranged even from his people.

2:23 the king of Egypt died. The death of Pharaoh (likely Thutmose III, who died about 1447 B.C.) meant that Moses could return to Egypt (4:19).

3:1 Horeb. This alternate name for Mount Sinai means "desolate place." Yet because of God's appearance on the mountain, this desolate place would become holy. Usually the site of this mountain is

identified as Jebel el-Musa, a mountain in the southern Sinai Peninsula.

3:2 Angel. The word angel simply means "messenger" (Mal. 1:1). In the Old Testament, the term "the Angel of the LORD" is used numerous times, and is identified with God as well as being distinguished from Him. In this passage, having mentioned that the Angel of the Lord appeared to Moses, it is immediately established that it was the Lord Himself (v. 4).

3:6 the God of your father. God identified Himself as the God worshiped by Abraham, Isaac, and Jacob. In announcing these names, the Lord was assuring Moses that the covenant He had made with them was still intact.

2:12 [k] Acts 7:24, 25 **2:13** [l] Acts 7:26–28 [m] Prov. 25:8 **2:14** [n] Acts 7:27, 28 [o] Judg. 6:27 **2:15** [p] Acts 7:29 [q] Ex. 3:1 [r] Gen. 24:11; 29:2 **2:16** [s] Ex. 3:1; 4:18; 18:12 [t] Gen. 24:11, 13, 19; 29:6–10 [u] Gen. 30:38 **2:17** [v] Gen. 47:3 [w] Gen. 26:19–21 [x] Gen. 29:3, 10 **2:18** [y] Num. 10:29 [z] Ex. 3:1; 4:18 **2:20** [a] Gen. 31:54; 43:25 **2:21** [b] Ex. 4:25; 18:2 **2:22** [c] Ex. 4:20; 18:3, 4 [d] Acts 7:29 **2:23** [e] Acts 7:34 [f] Deut. 26:7 [g] James 5:4 **2:24** [h] Ex. 6:5 [i] Gen. 15:13; 22:16–18; 26:2–5; 28:13–15 [j] Gen. 12:1–3; 15:14; 17:1–14 **2:25** [k] Ex. 4:31 [l] Ex. 3:7 **3:1** [a] Ex. 4:18 [b] Ex. 2:16 [c] Ex. 17:6 [d] Ex. 18:5 **3:2** [e] Deut. 33:16 **3:3** [f] Acts 7:31 **3:4** [g] Deut. 33:16 **3:5** [h] Josh. 5:15 **3:6** [i] [Matt. 22:32] [j] 1 Kin. 19:13 **3:7** [k] Ex. 2:23–25

Egypt, and have heard their cry *because of their taskmasters, *mfor I know their sorrows. 8So *nI have come down to *odeliver them out of the hand of the Egyptians, and to bring them up from that land to *pa good and large land, to a land *qflowing with milk and honey, to the place of *rthe Canaanites and the Hittites and the Amorites and the Perizzites and the Hivites and the Jebusites. 9Now therefore, behold, *sthe cry of the children of Israel has come to Me, and I have also seen the *toppression with which the Egyptians oppress them. 10uCome now, therefore, and I will send you to Pharaoh that you may bring My people, the children of Israel, out of Egypt."

11But Moses said to God, *v"Who *am I that I should go to Pharaoh, and that I should bring the children of Israel out of Egypt?"

12So He said, *w"I will certainly be with you. And this *shall be a *xsign to you that I have sent you: When you have brought the people out of Egypt, you shall serve God on this mountain."

13Then Moses said to God, "Indeed, *when I come to the children of Israel and say to them, 'The God of your fathers has sent me to you,' and they say to me, 'What *is His name?' what shall I say to them?"

14And God said to Moses, "I AM WHO I AM." And He said, "Thus you shall say to the children of Israel, *y'I AM has sent me to you.'" 15Moreover God said to Moses, "Thus you shall say to the children of Israel: 'The LORD God of your fathers, the God of Abraham, the God of Isaac, and the God of Jacob, has sent me to you. This *is *zMy name forever, and this *is My memorial to all generations.' 16Go and *agather the elders of Israel together, and say to them, 'The LORD God of your fathers, the God of Abraham, of Isaac, and of Jacob, appeared to me, saying, *b"I have surely visited you and *seen what is done to you in Egypt; 17and I have said *cI will bring you up out of the affliction of Egypt to the land of the Canaanites and the Hittites and the Amorites and the Perizzites and the Hivites and the Jebusites, to a land flowing with milk and honey."' 18Then *dthey will heed your voice; and *eyou shall come, you and the elders of Israel, to the king of Egypt; and you shall

say to him, 'The LORD God of the Hebrews has *fmet with us; and now, please, let us go three days' journey into the wilderness, that we may sacrifice to the LORD our God.' 19But I am sure that the king of Egypt *gwill not let you go, no, not even by a mighty hand. 20So I will *hstretch out My hand and strike Egypt with *iall My wonders which I will do in its midst; and *jafter that he will let you go. 21And *kI will give this people favor in the sight of the Egyptians; and it shall be, when you go, that you shall not go empty-handed. 22lBut every woman shall ask of her neighbor, namely, of her who dwells near her house, *marticles of silver, articles of gold, and clothing; and you shall put *them on your sons and on your daughters. So *nyou shall plunder the Egyptians."

Miraculous Signs for Pharaoh

4 Then Moses answered and said, "But suppose they will not believe me or listen to my voice; suppose they say, 'The LORD has not appeared to you.'"

2So the LORD said to him, "What *is that in your hand?"

He said, "A rod."

3And He said, "Cast it on the ground." So he cast it on the ground, and it became a serpent; and Moses fled from it. 4Then the LORD said to Moses, "Reach out your hand and take *it by the tail" (and he reached out his hand and caught it, and it became a rod in his hand), 5"that they may *abelieve that the *bLORD God of their fathers, the God of Abraham, the God of Isaac, and the God of Jacob, has appeared to you."

6Furthermore the LORD said to him, "Now put your hand in your bosom." And he put his hand in his bosom, and when he took it out, behold, his hand *was leprous, *clike snow. 7And He said, "Put your hand in your bosom again." So he put his hand in his bosom again, and drew it out of his bosom, and behold, *dit was restored like his *other flesh. 8"Then it will be, if they do not believe you, nor heed the message of the *efirst sign, that they may believe the message of the latter sign. 9And it shall be, if they do not believe even these two signs, or listen to your voice, that you shall take

---

3:14 I AM WHO I AM. The One who spoke to Moses declared Himself to be the Eternal One—uncaused and independent. Only the Creator of all things can call Himself the I AM in the absolute sense; all other creatures are in debt to Him for their existence. But in addition, God the Creator declares His relationship with the people of Israel. The future tense of the Hebrew verb related to God's name is used in verse 12: The I AM *will be* with His people. Thus God declares His covenantal relationship with Israel by His name.

3:15 The LORD. LORD in capital letters is the form translators have chosen to represent the Hebrew name YHWH (also transliterated Yahweh, or Jehovah). The Hebrew word meaning "I Am" used in verse 14 is very similar.

4:6–7 leprous. The term *leprosy* included a wide variety of skin diseases.

3:7 *l* Ex. 1:11 *m* Ex. 2:25 **3:8** *n* Gen. 15:13–16; 46:4; 50:24, 25 *o* Ex. 6:6–8; 12:51 *p* Deut. 1:25; 8:7–9 *q* Jer. 11:5 *r* Gen. 15:19–21 **3:9** *s* Ex. 2:23 *t* Ex. 1:11, 13, 14 **3:10** *u* [Mic. 6:4] **3:11** *v* Ex. 4:10; 6:12 **3:12** *w* Gen. 31:3 *x* Ex. 4:8; 19:3 **3:14** *y* [John 8:24, 28, 58] **3:15** *z* Ps. 30:4; 97:12; 102:12; 135:13 **3:16** *a* Ex. 4:29 *b* Ex. 2:25; 4:31 **3:17** *c* Gen. 15:13–21; 46:4; 50:24, 25 **3:18** *d* Ex. 4:31 *e* Ex. 5:1, 3 *f* Num. 23:3, 4, 15, 16 **3:19** *g* Ex. 5:2 **3:20** *h* Ex. 6:6; 9:15 *i* Deut. 6:22 *j* Ex. 11:1; 12:31–37 **3:21** *k* Ex. 11:3; 12:36 **3:22** *l* Ex. 11:2 *m* Ex. 33:6 *n* Job 27:17 **4:5** *a* Ex. 4:31; 19:9 *b* Ex. 3:6, 15 **4:6** *c* Num. 12:10 **4:7** *d* Deut. 32:39 **4:8** *e* Ex. 7:6–13

water from the river* and pour *it* on the dry *land.* *The water which you take from the river will become blood on the dry *land.*"

¹⁰Then Moses said to the LORD, "O my Lord, I *am* not eloquent, neither before nor since You have spoken to Your servant; but ᵍI *am* slow of speech and slow of tongue."

¹¹So the LORD said to him, ʰ"Who has made man's mouth? Or who makes the mute, the deaf, the seeing, or the blind? *Have* not I, the LORD? ¹²Now therefore, go, and I will be ᶦwith your mouth and teach you what you shall say."

¹³But he said, "O my Lord, ʲplease send by the hand of whomever *else* You may send."

¹⁴So ᵏthe anger of the LORD was kindled against Moses, and He said: "Is not Aaron the Levite your ˡbrother? I know that he can speak well. And look, ᵐhe is also coming out to meet you. When he sees you, he will be glad in his heart. ¹⁵Now ⁿyou shall speak to him and ᵒput the words in his mouth. And ᵖI will be with your mouth and with his mouth, and I will teach you what you shall do. ¹⁶So he shall be your spokesman to the people. And he himself shall be as a mouth for you, and ᑫyou shall be to him as God. ¹⁷And you shall take this rod in your hand, with which you shall do the signs."

Moses Goes to Egypt

¹⁸So Moses went and returned to ʳJethro his father-in-law, and said to him, "Please let me go and return to my brethren who *are* in Egypt, and see whether they are still alive."

And Jethro said to Moses, ˢ"Go in peace."

¹⁹Now the LORD said to Moses in ᵗMidian, "Go, return to ᵘEgypt; for all the men who ᵛsought your life are dead." ²⁰Then Moses ʷtook his wife and his sons and set

them on a donkey, and he returned to the land of Egypt. And Moses took ˣthe rod of God in his hand.

²¹And the LORD said to Moses, "When you go back to Egypt, see that you do all those ʸwonders before Pharaoh which I have put in your hand. But ᶻI will harden his heart, so that he will not let the people go. ²²Then you shall ᵃsay to Pharaoh, 'Thus says the LORD: ᵇ"Israel *is* My son, ᶜMy firstborn. ²³So I say to you, let My son go that he may serve Me. But if you refuse to let him go, indeed ᵈI will kill your son, your firstborn."'"

²⁴And it came to pass on the way, at the ᵉencampment, that the LORD ᶠmet him and sought to ᵍkill him. ²⁵Then ʰZipporah took ᶦa sharp stone and cut off the foreskin of her son and cast *it* at *Moses'** feet, and said, "Surely you *are* a husband of blood to me!" ²⁶So He let him go. Then she said, "*You are* a husband of blood!"—because of the circumcision.

²⁷And the LORD ʲsaid to Aaron, "Go into the wilderness ᵏto meet Moses." So he went and met him ᵏon the mountain of God, and kissed him. ²⁸So Moses ˡtold Aaron all the words of the LORD who had sent him, and all the ᵐsigns which He had commanded him. ²⁹Then Moses and Aaron ⁿwent and gathered together all the elders of the children of Israel. ³⁰ᵒAnd Aaron spoke all the words which the LORD had spoken to Moses. Then he did the signs in the sight of the people. ³¹So the people ᵖbelieved; and when they heard that the LORD had ᑫvisited the children of Israel and that He ʳhad looked on their affliction, then ˢthey bowed their heads and worshiped.

* 4:9 That is, the Nile   * 4:25 Literally *his*

4:19 who sought your life. God promised Abraham that those who persecuted Israel would be judged (Gen. 12:3), and it is clear from history that God fulfilled His promise. In Exodus 14, the Egyptians attempted to destroy the Israelites by driving them into the Red Sea, but instead were drowned themselves. Those who threw Daniel to the lions were devoured by those same beasts (Dan. 6). Haman plotted to destroy all the Jews in Persia, and ended up signing his own death warrant (Esth. 7). "The LORD preserves all who love Him" (Ps. 145:20).

4:21 Pharaoh. This pharaoh was most likely Amenhotep II (c. 1447–1421). **I will harden his heart.** Some interpret these words to mean that God would confirm what Pharaoh had stubbornly determined to do. In the first five plagues, the hardening was attributed to Pharaoh (7:13,22; 8:15,19,32; 9:7). Then for the sixth plague, God hardened a heart that had already rejected Him (9:12). Others insist that God had determined Pharaoh's negative response to Moses long before Pharaoh could harden his heart. These interpreters point to this verse and to 9:16, in which God says that He raised up Pharaoh for the purpose of demonstrating His power.

4:24 sought to kill him. The precise meaning of this passage is unclear. Apparently someone in Moses' family was not circumcised, despite God's command. It is possible that Moses had kept one of his sons uncircumcised in order to please his Midianite family. (The Midianites practiced adult male circumcision at the time of marriage, rather than infant circumcision as the Hebrews did.) Moses' neglect of the sign of God's covenant was very serious, especially for the future leader of God's people.

4:9 ᶠEx. 7:19, 20   **4:10** ᵍEx. 3:11; 4:1; 6:12   **4:11** ʰPs. 94:9; 146:8   **4:12** ᶦIs. 50:4   **4:13** ʲJon. 1:3   **4:14** ᵏNum. 11:1, 33   ˡNum. 26:59   ᵐEx. 4:27   **4:15** ⁿEx. 4:12, 30; 7:1, 2   ᵒNum. 23:5, 12   ᵖDeut. 5:31   **4:16** ᑫEx. 7:1, 2   **4:18** ʳEx. 2:21; 3:1; 4:18   ˢJudg. 18:6   **4:19** ᵗEx. 3:1; 18:1   ᵘGen. 46:3, 6   ᵛEx. 2:15, 23   **4:20** ʷEx. 18:2–5   ˣNum. 20:8, 9, 11   **4:21** ʸEx. 3:20; 11:9, 10   ᶻJohn 12:40   **4:22** ᵃEx. 5:1   ᵇHos. 11:1   ᶜJer. 31:9   **4:23** ᵈEx. 11:5; 12:29   **4:24** ᵉGen. 42:27   ᶠNum. 22:22   ᵍGen. 17:14   **4:25** ʰEx. 2:21; 18:2   ᶦJosh. 5:2, 3   **4:27** ʲEx. 4:14   ᵏEx. 3:1; 18:5; 24:13   **4:28** ˡEx. 4:15, 16   ᵐEx. 4:8, 9   **4:29** ⁿEx. 3:16; 12:21   **4:30** ᵒEx. 4:15, 16   **4:31** ᵖEx. 3:18; 4:8, 9; 19:9   ᑫGen. 50:24   ʳEx. 2:25; 3:7   ˢGen. 24:26

First Encounter with Pharaoh

5 Afterward Moses and Aaron went in and told Pharaoh, "Thus says the LORD God of Israel: 'Let My people go, that they may hold ᵃa feast to Me in the wilderness.'"

²And Pharaoh said, ᵇ"Who *is* the LORD, that I should obey His voice to let Israel go? I do not know the LORD, ᶜnor will I let Israel go."

³So they said, ᵈ"The God of the Hebrews has ᵉmet with us. Please, let us go three days' journey into the desert and sacrifice to the LORD our God, lest He fall upon us with ᶠpestilence or with the sword."

⁴Then the king of Egypt said to them, "Moses and Aaron, why do you take the people from their work? Get *back* to your ᵍlabor." ⁵And Pharaoh said, "Look, the people of the land *are* ʰmany now, and you make them rest from their labor!"

⁶So the same day Pharaoh commanded the ⁱtaskmasters of the people and their officers, saying, ⁷"You shall no longer give the people straw to make ʲbrick as before. Let them go and gather straw for themselves. ⁸And you shall lay on them the quota of bricks which they made before. You shall not reduce it. For they are idle; therefore they cry out, saying, 'Let us go *and* sacrifice to our God.' ⁹Let more work be laid on the men, that they may labor in it, and let them not regard false words."

¹⁰And the taskmasters of the people and their officers went out and spoke to the people, saying, "Thus says Pharaoh: 'I will not give you straw. ¹¹Go, get yourselves straw where you can find it; yet none of your work will be reduced.'" ¹²So the people were scattered abroad throughout all the land of Egypt to gather stubble instead of straw. ¹³And the taskmasters forced *them* to hurry, saying, "Fulfill your work, your daily quota, as when there was straw." ¹⁴Also the ᵏofficers of the children of Israel, whom Pharaoh's taskmasters had set over them, were ˡbeaten *and* were asked, "Why have you not fulfilled your task in making brick both yesterday and today, as before?"

¹⁵Then the officers of the children of Israel came and cried out to Pharaoh, saying, "Why are you dealing thus with your servants? ¹⁶There is no straw given to your servants, and they say to us, 'Make brick!' And indeed your servants *are* beaten, but the fault *is* in your *own* people."

¹⁷But he said, "You *are* idle! Idle! Therefore you say, 'Let us go *and* sacrifice to the LORD.' ¹⁸Therefore go now *and* work; for no straw shall be given you, yet you shall deliver the quota of bricks." ¹⁹And the officers of the children of Israel saw *that* they *were* in trouble after it was said, "You shall not reduce *any* bricks from your daily quota."

²⁰Then, as they came out from Pharaoh, they met Moses and Aaron who stood there to meet them. ²¹ᵐAnd they said to them, "Let the LORD look on you and judge, because you have made us abhorrent in the sight of Pharaoh and in the sight of his servants, to put a sword in their hand to kill us."

Israel's Deliverance Assured

²²So Moses returned to the LORD and said, "Lord, why have You brought trouble on this people? Why *is* it You have sent me? ²³For since I came to Pharaoh to speak in Your name, he has done evil to this people; neither have You delivered Your people at all."

6 Then the LORD said to Moses, "Now you shall see what I will do to Pharaoh. For ᵃwith a strong hand he will let them go, and with a strong hand ᵇhe will drive them out of his land."

²And God spoke to Moses and said to him: "I *am* the LORD. ³ᶜI appeared to Abraham, to Isaac, and to Jacob, as ᵈGod Almighty, but *by* My name ᵉLORD* I was not known to them. ⁴ᶠI have also established My covenant with them, ᵍto give them the land of Canaan, the land of their pilgrimage, ʰin which they were strangers. ⁵And ⁱI have also heard the groaning of the children of

---

* **6:3** Hebrew *YHWH*, traditionally *Jehovah*

5:2 *Who is the LORD.* Later these words would haunt Pharaoh (12:31–32). Meanwhile, Pharaoh believed himself to be a god in his own right, and certainly felt no need to cave in to the demands of a god who claimed to be the champion of his slave labor force.

5:7–9 *Let them go and gather straw for themselves.* It is easy to rationalize our cruel treatment of others when it is in our selfish interest to do so. We often hear "Pharaoh's reasoning" about minority peoples or people on welfare today. Of course laziness and discontent is a genuine problem for some who are on welfare, or who feel oppressed (just as it is for some who were born into wealth and privilege), but too often we turn off the concern we should have for the poor and oppressed with the comfortable conviction that somehow they deserve their problems. If we continue in this attitude, we may be sure that God will judge our sin. God cares deeply for the

weak, the poor, and the downtrodden; if we are genuine disciples we will share His concern.

5:23 *speak in Your name.* It seems that Moses expected Pharaoh to cave in as soon as he heard the use of the Lord's name Yahweh (3:13–15; 5:1). Yet God had warned Moses that Pharaoh would do the opposite (3:19; 4:21).

6:4 *My covenant.* This is a reference to the Abrahamic covenant celebrated in Genesis (Gen. 12:1–3,7; 15:12–21; 17:1–16; 22:15–18).

5:1 ᵃEx. 3:18; 7:16; 10:9   **5:2** ᵇ2 Kin. 18:35 ᶜEx. 3:19; 7:14   **5:3** ᵈEx. 3:18; 7:16 ᵉNum. 23:3 ᶠEx. 9:15   **5:4** ᵍEx. 1:11; 2:11; 6:6   **5:5** ʰEx. 1:7, 9   **5:6** ⁱEx. 1:11; 3:7; 5:10, 13, 14   **5:7** ʲEx. 1:14   **5:14** ᵏEx. 5:6 ˡIs. 10:24   **5:21** ᵐEx. 6:9; 14:11; 15:24; 16:2   **6:1** ᵃEx. 3:19 ᵇEx. 12:31, 33, 39   **6:3** ᶜGen. 17:1; 35:9; 48:3 ᵈGen. 28:3; 35:11 ᵉPs. 68:4; 83:18   **6:4** ᶠGen. 12:7; 15:18; 17:4, 7, 8; 26:3; 28:4, 13 ᵍLev. 25:23 ʰGen. 28:4   **6:5** ⁱEx. 2:24

Israel whom the Egyptians keep in bondage, and I have remembered My covenant.
6Therefore say to the children of Israel: [j]'I
am the LORD; [k]I will bring you out from
under the burdens of the Egyptians, I will
[l]rescue you from their bondage, and I will
redeem you with an outstretched arm and
with great judgments. 7I will [m]take you as
My people, and [n]I will be your God. Then
you shall know that I *am* the LORD your
God who brings you out [o]from under the
burdens of the Egyptians. 8And I will bring
you into the land which I [p]swore to give to
Abraham, Isaac, and Jacob; and I will give
it to you *as* a heritage: I *am* the LORD.'" 9So
Moses spoke thus to the children of Israel;
[q]but they did not heed Moses, because of
[r]anguish of spirit and cruel bondage.
10And the LORD spoke to Moses, saying,
11"Go in, tell Pharaoh king of Egypt to let
the children of Israel go out of his land."
12And Moses spoke before the LORD,
saying, "The children of Israel have not
heeded me. How then shall Pharaoh heed
me, for [s]I *am* of uncircumcised lips?"
13Then the LORD spoke to Moses and
Aaron, and gave them a [t]command for the
children of Israel and for Pharaoh king of
Egypt, to bring the children of Israel out of
the land of Egypt.

The Family of Moses and Aaron

14These *are* the heads of their fathers'
houses: [u]The sons of Reuben, the firstborn
of Israel, *were* Hanoch, Pallu, Hezron, and
Carmi. These are the families of Reuben.
15[v]And the sons of Simeon *were* Jemuel,*
Jamin, Ohad, Jachin, Zohar, and Shaul the
son of a Canaanite woman. These *are* the
families of Simeon. 16These *are* the names
of [w]the sons of Levi according to their generations: Gershon, Kohath, and Merari.
And the years of the life of Levi *were* one
hundred and thirty-seven. 17[x]The sons of
Gershon *were* Libni and Shimi according
to their families. 18And [y]the sons of Kohath
were Amram, Izhar, Hebron, and Uzziel.
And the years of the life of Kohath *were*
one hundred and thirty-three. 19[z]The sons
of Merari *were* Mahli and Mushi. These
are the families of Levi according to their
generations.
20Now [a]Amram took for himself
[b]Jochebed, his father's sister, as wife; and
she bore him [c]Aaron and Moses. And the
years of the life of Amram *were* one hundred and thirty-seven. 21[d]The sons of Izhar
were Korah, Nepheg, and Zichri. 22And
[e]the sons of Uzziel *were* Mishael, Elzaphan,
and Zithri. 23Aaron took to himself Elishe-
ba, daughter of [f]Amminadab, sister of
Nahshon, as wife; and she bore him [g]Na-
dab, Abihu, [h]Eleazar, and Ithamar. 24And
[i]the sons of Korah *were* Assir, Elkanah,
and Abiasaph. These are the families of
the Korahites. 25Eleazar, Aaron's son, took
for himself one of the daughters of Putiel
as wife; and [j]she bore him Phinehas. These
are the heads of the fathers' houses of the
Levites according to their families.
26These *are the same* Aaron and Moses to whom the LORD said, "Bring out the
children of Israel from the land of Egypt
according to their [k]armies." 27These *are*
the ones who spoke to Pharaoh king of
Egypt, [l]to bring out the children of Israel
from Egypt. These *are the same* Moses and
Aaron.

Aaron Is Moses' Spokesman

28And it came to pass, on the day the
LORD spoke to Moses in the land of Egypt,
29that the LORD spoke to Moses, saying, "I
am the LORD. [m]Speak to Pharaoh king of
Egypt all that I say to you."
30But Moses said before the LORD, "Behold, [n]I *am* of uncircumcised lips, and how
shall Pharaoh heed me?"
7 So the LORD said to Moses: "See, I have
made you [a]*as* God to Pharaoh, and
Aaron your brother shall be [b]your prophet. 2You [c]shall speak all that I command
you. And Aaron your brother shall tell
Pharaoh to send the children of Israel out
of his land. 3And [d]I will harden Pharaoh's
heart, and [e]multiply My [f]signs and My
wonders in the land of Egypt. 4But [g]Pha-
raoh will not heed you, so [h]that I may lay
My hand on Egypt and bring My armies
and My people, the children of Israel, out
of the land of Egypt [i]by great judgments.
5And the Egyptians [j]shall know that I *am*
the LORD, when I [k]stretch out My hand on
Egypt and [l]bring out the children of Israel
from among them."
6Then Moses and Aaron [m]did *so;* just as

* **6:15** Spelled *Nemuel* in Numbers 26:12

6:14–27 *their fathers'.* The family history of Moses, Aaron, and Miriam is important because all of Israel's future priests would come from this family.

7:1 *your prophet.* As Moses was the prophet of the Lord, so Aaron became Moses' prophet. Aaron would speak for Moses, for a prophet was the "mouth" of the one who sent him.

7:3 *I will harden Pharaoh's heart.* It was a part of God's plan that Pharaoh would be inflexibly stubborn, thus setting the scene for God to deliver His people by powerful signs and wonders.

6:6 *j* Deut. 6:12 *k* Deut. 26:8 *l* Deut. 7:8 **6:7** *m* 2 Sam. 7:24 *n* Ex. 29:45, 46 *o* Ex. 5:4, 5 **6:8** *p* Gen. 15:18; 26:3 **6:9** *q* Ex. 5:21 *r* Ex. 2:23 **6:12** *s* Jer. 1:6 **6:13** *t* Deut. 31:14 **6:14** *u* Gen. 46:9 **6:15** *v* Gen. 46:10 **6:16** *w* Gen. 46:11 **6:17** *x* 1 Chr. 6:17 **6:18** *y* 1 Chr. 6:2, 18 **6:19** *z* 1 Chr. 6:19; 23:21 **6:20** *a* Ex. 2:1, 2 *b* Num. 26:59 *c* Num. 26:59 **6:21** *d* 1 Chr. 6:37, 38 **6:22** *e* Lev. 10:4 **6:23** *f* Ruth 4:19, 20 *g* Lev. 10:1 *h* Ex. 28:1 **6:24** *i* Num. 26:11 **6:25** *j* Num. 25:7, 11 **6:26** *k* Ex. 7:4; 12:17, 51 **6:27** *l* Ps. 77:20 **6:29** *m* Ex. 6:11; 7:2 **6:30** *n* Ex. 4:10; 6:12 **7:1** *a* Ex. 4:16 *b* Ex. 4:15, 16 **7:2** *c* Ex. 4:15 **7:3** *d* Ex. 4:21; 9:12 *e* Ex. 11:9 *f* Deut. 4:34 **7:4** *g* Ex. 3:19, 20; 10:1; 11:9 *h* Ex. 9:14 *i* Ex. 6:6; 12:12 **7:5** *j* Ps. 9:16 *k* Ex. 9:15 *l* Ex. 3:20; 6:6; 12:51 **7:6** *m* Ex. 7:2

the LORD commanded them, so they did. [7]And Moses was [n]eighty years old and [o]Aaron eighty-three years old when they spoke to Pharaoh.

Aaron's Miraculous Rod

[8]Then the LORD spoke to Moses and Aaron, saying, [9]"When Pharaoh speaks to you, saying, [p]'Show a miracle for yourselves,' then you shall say to Aaron, [q]'Take your rod and cast it before Pharaoh, and let it become a serpent.'" [10]So Moses and Aaron went in to Pharaoh, and they did so, just [r]as the LORD commanded. And Aaron cast down his rod before Pharaoh and before his servants, and it [s]became a serpent.

[11]But Pharaoh also [t]called the wise men and [u]the sorcerers; so the magicians of Egypt, they also [v]did in like manner with their enchantments. [12]For every man threw down his rod, and they became serpents. But Aaron's rod swallowed up their rods. [13]And Pharaoh's heart grew hard, and he did not heed them, as the LORD had said.

The First Plague: Waters Become Blood

[14]So the LORD said to Moses: [w]"Pharaoh's heart is hard; he refuses to let the people go. [15]Go to Pharaoh in the morning, when he goes out to the [x]water, and you shall stand by the river's bank to meet him; and [y]the rod which was turned to a serpent you shall take in your hand. [16]And you shall say to him, [z]'The LORD God of the Hebrews has sent me to you, saying, "Let My people go, [a]that they may serve Me in the wilderness"; but indeed, until now you would not hear! [17]Thus says the LORD: "By this [b]you shall know that I am the LORD.

Behold, I will strike the waters which are in the river with the rod that is in my hand, and [c]they shall be turned [d]to blood. [18]And the fish that are in the river shall die, the river shall stink, and the Egyptians will [e]loathe to drink the water of the river."'"

[19]Then the LORD spoke to Moses, "Say to Aaron, 'Take your rod and [f]stretch out your hand over the waters of Egypt, over their streams, over their rivers, over their ponds, and over all their pools of water, that they may become blood. And there shall be blood throughout all the land of Egypt, both in buckets of wood and pitchers of stone.'" [20]And Moses and Aaron did so, just as the LORD commanded. So he [g]lifted up the rod and struck the waters that were in the river, in the sight of Pharaoh and in the sight of his servants. And all the [h]waters that were in the river were turned to blood. [21]The fish that were in the river died, the river stank, and the Egyptians [i]could not drink the water of the river. So there was blood throughout all the land of Egypt.

[22][j]Then the magicians of Egypt did [k]so with their enchantments; and Pharaoh's heart grew hard, and he did not heed them, [l]as the LORD had said. [23]And Pharaoh turned and went into his house. Neither was his heart moved by this. [24]So all the Egyptians dug all around the river for water to drink, because they could not drink the water of the river. [25]And seven days passed after the LORD had struck the river.

The Second Plague: Frogs

8 And the LORD spoke to Moses, "Go to Pharaoh and say to him, 'Thus says the LORD: "Let My people go, [a]that they may serve Me. [2]But if you [b]refuse to let them go,

---

7:7 eighty . . . eighty-three. These men had already lived as long as the average lifetime of our day before their principal life work had begun. Moses and Aaron each lived another forty years as leaders of the nation of Israel.

7:9–10 Miracles—A miracle could be defined as the temporary suspension of some natural law (like turning a staff into a snake), or the manipulation of natural forces (such as weather) over which humans ordinarily have no jurisdiction. We tend to look for miracles only for their immediate results (healing, retribution, etc.), but in the Bible miracles are always for a "sign." The focus isn't on the actual miracle, but on the supernatural as a sign of God's working in the situation. This is clearly seen in the miracles of Jesus. If His purpose had just been physical healing, He would have set up a clinic and systematically healed everyone. Instead, His miracles were for a sign, to let people know who and what He was (John 20:30–31).

7:11 wise men . . . sorcerers . . . magicians. The king's wise men were his counselors, men of learning and insight. In ancient times, the "wise men" of a court were often associated with occult practices. The power of these men may have been in trickery and sleight-of-hand illusions, or demonic power. Later the royal courts of Israel had wise men (1 Kin. 4:34; Prov.

25:1), but the black arts of sorcery, divination, and astrology were forbidden (Deut. 18:9–14).

7:12 his rod . . . serpents. The text does not say whether this was a genuine transformation or a trick of Pharaoh's evil sorcerers. Whatever the case, their serpents were no match for the serpent of God's sign.

7:15 to the water . . . the river's bank. Pharaoh went to the waters of the Nile not to bathe but to be empowered. Pharaoh's bath in the Nile was a sacred Egyptian rite connected to his claim of divinity. The plague on the waters of the Nile was a direct attack on the Egyptian religion.

7:23 turned and went into his house. Pharaoh showed his utter disdain for the revelation of God's power and his complete lack of concern for the suffering of his own people.

7:7 [n] Deut. 29:5; 31:2; 34:7 [o] Num. 33:39   **7:9** [p] Is. 7:11 [q] Ex. 4:2; 3, 17   **7:10** [r] Ex. 7:9 [s] Ex. 4:3   **7:11** [t] Gen. 41:8 [u] 2 Tim. 3:8 [v] Ex. 7:22; 8:7, 18   **7:14** [w] Ex. 8:15; 10:1, 20, 27   **7:15** [x] Ex. 2:5; 8:20 [y] Ex. 4:2, 3; 7:10   **7:16** [z] Ex. 3:13, 18; 4:22 [a] Ex. 3:12, 18; 4:23; 5:1, 3; 8:1   **7:17** [b] Ex. 5:2; 7:5; 10:2 [c] Ex. 4:9; 7:20 [d] Rev. 11:6; 16:4, 6   **7:18** [e] Ex. 7:24   **7:19** [f] Ex. 8:5, 6, 16; 9:22; 10:12, 21; 14:21, 26   **7:20** [g] Ex. 17:5 [h] Ps. 78:44; 105:29, 30   **7:21** [i] Ex. 7:18   **7:22** [j] Ex. 7:11 [k] Ex. 8:7 [l] Ex. 3:19; 7:3   **8:1** [a] Ex. 3:12, 18; 4:23; 5:1, 3   **8:2** [b] Ex. 7:14; 9:2

behold, I will smite all your territory with cfrogs. ³So the river shall bring forth frogs abundantly, which shall go up and come into your house, into your dbedroom, on your bed, into the houses of your servants, on your people, into your ovens, and into your kneading bowls. ⁴And the frogs shall come up on you, on your people, and on all your servants.'''"

⁵Then the LORD spoke to Moses, "Say to Aaron, e'Stretch out your hand with your rod over the streams, over the rivers, and over the ponds, and cause frogs to come up on the land of Egypt.'" ⁶So Aaron stretched out his hand over the waters of Egypt, fthe frogs came up and covered the land of Egypt. ⁷gAnd the magicians did so with their enchantments, and brought up frogs on the land of Egypt.

⁸Then Pharaoh called for Moses and Aaron, and said, h"Entreat the LORD that He may take away the frogs from me and from my people; and I will let the people igo, that they may sacrifice to the LORD."

⁹And Moses said to Pharaoh, "Accept the honor of saying when I shall intercede for you, for your servants, and for your people, to destroy the frogs from you and your houses, *that* they may remain in the river only."

¹⁰So he said, "Tomorrow." And he said, "*Let it be* according to your word, that you may know that jthere is no one like the LORD our God. ¹¹And the frogs shall depart from you, from your houses, from your servants, and from your people. They shall remain in the river only."

¹²Then Moses and Aaron went out from Pharaoh. And Moses kcried out to the LORD concerning the frogs which He had brought against Pharaoh. ¹³So the LORD did according to the word of Moses. And the frogs died out of the houses, out of the courtyards, and out of the fields. ¹⁴They gathered them together in heaps, and the land stank. ¹⁵But when Pharaoh saw that there was lrelief, mhe hardened his heart and did not heed them, as the LORD had said.

The Third Plague: Lice

¹⁶So the LORD said to Moses, "Say to Aaron, 'Stretch out your rod, and strike the dust of the land, so that it may become lice throughout all the land of Egypt.'" ¹⁷And they did so. For Aaron stretched out his hand with his rod and struck the dust of the earth, and nit became lice on man and beast. All the dust of the land became lice throughout all the land of Egypt.

¹⁸Now othe magicians so worked with their enchantments to bring forth lice, but they pcould not. So there were lice on man and beast. ¹⁹Then the magicians said to Pharaoh, "This *is* qthe finger of God." But Pharaoh's rheart grew hard, and he did not heed them, just as the LORD had said.

The Fourth Plague: Flies

²⁰And the LORD said to Moses, s"Rise early in the morning and stand before Pharaoh as he comes out to the water. Then say to him, 'Thus says the LORD: t"Let My people go, that they may serve Me. ²¹Or else, if you will not let My people go, behold, I will send swarms *of flies* on you and your servants, on your people and into your houses. The houses of the Egyptians shall be full of swarms *of flies*, and also the ground on which they *stand*. ²²And in that day uI will set apart the land of vGoshen, in which My people dwell, that no swarms *of flies* shall be there, in order that you may wknow that I *am* the LORD in the midst of the xland. ²³I will make a difference* between My people and your people. Tomorrow this ysign shall be."'" ²⁴And the LORD did so. zThick swarms *of flies* came into the house of Pharaoh, *into* his servants' houses, and into all the land of Egypt. The land was corrupted because of the swarms *of flies*.

²⁵Then Pharaoh called for Moses and Aaron, and said, "Go, sacrifice to your God in the land."

* **8:23** Literally *set a ransom* (compare Exodus 9:4 and 11:7)

8:7 the magicians . . . with their enchantments. We do not know how or in what quantities the magicians produced frogs, but doing so hardly helped the situation. Clearly the power they had was not strong enough to counteract the plagues God sent.
8:8 called for Moses and Aaron. Note that Pharaoh did not turn to his magicians to relieve the land of the frogs.
8:15 Instability—The action of this Egyptian pharaoh is a case study in instability. He gave permission for the people to go and then changed his mind more than once. He alternated between denying the power of God and actually admitting his sin. Pharaoh was a rebel against God, tossed about by his own lack of integrity. Believers can take warning from Pharaoh's behavior. The apostle James informs us that a double-minded man is unstable in all his ways (James 1:8). But stability isn't something we

achieve by sheer willpower. Real integrity and stability come from the security of our relationship with God.
8:18 the magicians . . . enchantments . . . but they could not. Perhaps the lack of announcement meant they had no time to prepare. The magicians could not duplicate God's work, further proof that this was no trick, but the hand of God.

8:2 c Rev. 16:13   **8:3** d Ps. 105:30   **8:5** e Ex. 7:19
8:6 f Ps. 78:45; 105:30   **8:7** g Ex. 7:11, 22   **8:8** h Ex.
8:28; 9:28; 10:17   i Ex. 10:8, 24   **8:10** j Ex. 9:14; 15:11
8:12 k Ex. 8:30; 9:33; 10:18; 32:11   **8:15** l Eccl. 8:11   m Ex.
7:14, 22; 9:34   **8:17** n Ps. 105:31   **8:18** o Ex. 7:11, 12; 8:7
p Dan. 5:8   **8:19** q Ex. 7:5; 10:7   r Ex. 8:15   **8:20** s Ex. 7:15;
9:13   t Ex. 3:18; 4:23; 5:1, 3; 8:1   **8:22** u Ex. 9:4, 6, 26; 10:23;
11:6, 7; 12:13   v Gen. 50:8   w Ex. 7:5, 17; 10:2; 14:4   x Ex. 9:29
8:23 y Ex. 4:8   **8:24** z Ps. 78:45; 105:31

26 And Moses said, "It is not right to do
so, for we would be sacrificing [a]the abomination of the Egyptians to the LORD our
God. If we sacrifice the abomination of the
Egyptians before their eyes, then will they
not stone us? 27 We will go [b]three days' journey into the wilderness and sacrifice to the
LORD our God as [c]He will command us."
28 So Pharaoh said, "I will let you go, that
you may sacrifice to the LORD your God in
the wilderness; only you shall not go very
far away. [d]Intercede for me."
29 Then Moses said, "Indeed I am going
out from you, and I will entreat the LORD,
that the swarms *of flies* may depart tomorrow from Pharaoh, from his servants, and
from his people. But let Pharaoh not [e]deal
deceitfully anymore in not letting the people go to sacrifice to the LORD."
30 So Moses went out from Pharaoh and
[f]entreated the LORD. 31 And the LORD did
according to the word of Moses; He removed the swarms *of flies* from Pharaoh,
from his servants, and from his people. Not
one remained. 32 But Pharaoh [g]hardened
his heart at this time also; neither would
he let the people go.

The Fifth Plague: Livestock Diseased

9 Then the LORD said to Moses, [a]"Go in
to Pharaoh and tell him, 'Thus says the
LORD God of the Hebrews: "Let My people
go, that they may [b]serve Me. 2 For if you
[c]refuse to let *them* go, and still hold them,
3 behold, the [d]hand of the LORD will be on
your cattle in the field, on the horses, on the
donkeys, on the camels, on the oxen, and on
the sheep—a very severe pestilence. 4 And
[e]the LORD will make a difference between
the livestock of Israel and the livestock of
Egypt. So nothing shall die of all *that* belongs to the children of Israel."'" 5 Then the
LORD appointed a set time, saying, "Tomorrow the LORD will do this thing in the land."
6 So the LORD did this thing on the next
day, and [f]all the livestock of Egypt died; but
of the livestock of the children of Israel, not
one died. 7 Then Pharaoh sent, and indeed,
not even one of the livestock of the Israelites was dead. But the [g]heart of Pharaoh
became hard, and he did not let the people go.

The Sixth Plague: Boils

8 So the LORD said to Moses and Aaron,
"Take for yourselves handfuls of ashes
from a furnace, and let Moses scatter it toward the heavens in the sight of Pharaoh.
9 And it will become fine dust in all the land
of Egypt, and it will cause [h]boils that break
out in sores on man and beast throughout
all the land of Egypt." 10 Then they took
ashes from the furnace and stood before
Pharaoh, and Moses scattered *them* toward heaven. And *they* caused [i]boils that
break out in sores on man and beast. 11 And
the [j]magicians could not stand before Moses because of the [k]boils, for the boils were
on the magicians and on all the Egyptians.
12 But the LORD hardened the heart of Pharaoh; and he [l]did not heed them, just [m]as
the LORD had spoken to Moses.

The Seventh Plague: Hail

13 Then the LORD said to Moses, [n]"Rise
early in the morning and stand before
Pharaoh, and say to him, 'Thus says the
LORD God of the Hebrews: "Let My people
go, that they may [o]serve Me, 14 for at this
time I will send all My plagues to your very
heart, and on your servants and on your
people, [p]that you may know that *there*
is none like Me in all the earth. 15 Now if
I had [q]stretched out My hand and struck
you and your people with [r]pestilence,
then you would have been cut off from
the earth. 16 But indeed for [s]this *purpose* I
have raised you up, that I may [t]show My
power *in* you, and that My [u]name may be
declared in all the earth. 17 As yet you exalt
yourself against My people in that you will
not let them go. 18 Behold, tomorrow about
this time I will cause very heavy hail to
rain down, such as has not been in Egypt
since its founding until now. 19 Therefore
send now *and* gather your livestock and

8:26 ***the abomination of the Egyptians.*** Moses employed the ethnic and cultural sensibilities of the Egyptians to free the Israelites (Gen. 43:32; 46:34). The sacrificial animals of Israel would include sheep, something the Egyptians regarded as detestable.

9:11 ***for the boils were upon the magicians.*** The reference to the hapless magicians is almost humorous. Not only were they powerless, but they also suffered from the plague.

9:16 ***for this purpose I have raised you up.*** God used Pharaoh's stubbornness and disobedience to demonstrate His power. Pharaoh was not only an evil ruler in a powerful state; he was an evil man, ungodly, and unrighteous. Pharaoh set himself up as a god who maintained the stability of his kingdom. The Lord's judgment on him was an appropriate response to this fraud.

9:17 ***you exalt yourself.*** Pharaoh was behaving like the king of Tyre (Ezek. 28:1–10) and Satan, whom the king of Tyre emulated (Ezek. 28:11–19).

9:19 ***gather your livestock.*** The fact that God was judging Pharaoh does not mean that He was unmerciful. The Lord could have destroyed Pharaoh and his people in a moment (v. 15), but instead He warned them of the calamities about to befall them. Apparently some of the Egyptians took the word of the Lord seriously.

8:26 [a] Gen. 43:32; 46:34 **8:27** [b] Ex. 3:18; 5:3 [c] Ex. 3:12 **8:28** [d] Ex. 8:8, 15, 29, 32; 9:28 **8:29** [e] Ex. 8:8, 15 **8:30** [f] Ex. 8:12 **8:32** [g] Ex. 4:21; 8:8, 15 **9:1** [a] Ex. 4:23; 8:1 [b] Ex. 7:16 **9:2** [c] Ex. 8:2 **9:3** [d] Ex. 7:4 **9:4** [e] Ex. 8:22 **9:6** [f] Ps. 78:48, 50 **9:7** [g] Ex. 7:14; 8:32 **9:9** [h] Rev. 16:2 **9:10** [i] Deut. 28:27 **9:11** [j] [Ex. 8:18, 19] [k] Job 2:7 **9:12** [l] Ex. 7:13 [m] Ex. 4:21 **9:13** [n] Ex. 8:20 [o] Ex. 9:1 **9:14** [p] Ex. 8:10 **9:15** [q] Ex. 3:20; 7:5 [r] Ex. 5:3 **9:16** [s] [Rom. 9:17, 18] [t] Ex. 7:4, 5; 10:1; 11:9; 14:17 [u] 1 Kin. 8:43

all that you have in the field, for the hail shall come down on every man and every animal which is found in the field and is not brought home; and they shall die." ' "

20He who ᵛfeared the word of the LORD among the ʷservants of Pharaoh made his servants and his livestock flee to the houses. 21But he who did not regard the word of the LORD left his servants and his livestock in the field.

22Then the LORD said to Moses, "Stretch out your hand toward heaven, that there may be ˣhail in all the land of Egypt—on man, on beast, and on every herb of the field, throughout the land of Egypt." 23And Moses stretched out his rod toward heaven; and ʸthe LORD sent thunder and hail, and fire darted to the ground. And the LORD rained hail on the land of Egypt. 24So there was hail, and fire mingled with the hail, so very heavy that there was none like it in all the land of Egypt since it became a nation. 25And the ᶻhail struck throughout the whole land of Egypt, all that was in the field, both man and beast; and the hail struck every herb of the field and broke every tree of the field. 26ᵃOnly in the land of Goshen, where the children of Israel were, there was no hail.

27And Pharaoh sent and ᵇcalled for Moses and Aaron, and said to them, ᶜ"I have sinned this time. ᵈThe LORD is righteous, and my people and I are wicked. 28ᵉEntreat the LORD, that there may be no more mighty thundering and hail, for it is enough. I will let you ᶠgo, and you shall stay no longer."

29So Moses said to him, "As soon as I have gone out of the city, I will ᵍspread out my hands to the LORD; the thunder will cease, and there will be no more hail, that you may know that the ʰearth is the LORD's. 30But as for you and your servants, ⁱI know that you will not yet fear the LORD God."

31Now the flax and the barley were struck, ʲfor the barley was in the head and the flax was in bud. 32But the wheat and the spelt were not struck, for they are late crops.

33So Moses went out of the city from Pharaoh and ᵏspread out his hands to the LORD; then the thunder and the hail

ceased, and the rain was not poured on the earth. 34And when Pharaoh saw that the rain, the hail, and the thunder had ceased, he sinned yet more; and he hardened his heart, he and his servants. 35So ˡthe heart of Pharaoh was hard; neither would he let the children of Israel go, as the LORD had spoken by Moses.

The Eighth Plague: Locusts

10 Now the LORD said to Moses, "Go in to Pharaoh; ᵃfor I have hardened his heart and the hearts of his servants, ᵇthat I may show these signs of Mine before him, 2and that ᶜyou may tell in the hearing of your son and your son's son the mighty things I have done in Egypt, and My signs which I have done among them, that you may ᵈknow that I am the LORD."

3So Moses and Aaron came in to Pharaoh and said to him, "Thus says the LORD God of the Hebrews: 'How long will you refuse to ᵉhumble yourself before Me? Let My people go, that they may ᶠserve Me. 4Or else, if you refuse to let My people go, behold, tomorrow I will bring ᵍlocusts into your territory. 5And they shall cover the face of the earth, so that no one will be able to see the earth; and ʰthey shall eat the residue of what is left, which remains to you from the hail, and they shall eat every tree which grows up for you out of the field. 6They shall ⁱfill your houses, the houses of all your servants, and the houses of all the Egyptians—which neither your fathers nor your fathers' fathers have seen, since the day that they were on the earth to this day.' " And he turned and went out from Pharaoh.

7Then Pharaoh's ʲservants said to him, "How long shall this man be ᵏa snare to us? Let the men go, that they may serve the LORD their God. Do you not yet know that Egypt is destroyed?"

8So Moses and Aaron were brought again to Pharaoh, and he said to them, "Go, serve the LORD your God. Who are the ones that are going?"

9And Moses said, "We will go with our young and our old; with our sons and our daughters, with our flocks and our herds we will go, for ˡwe must hold a feast to the LORD."

10Then he said to them, "The LORD had

9:27 I have sinned. This was a stunning admission for such a proud man. Sadly, these words of contrition would not hold. Pharaoh repeated them later (10:16–17), only to take them back in the end.

10:1 I have hardened his heart. Three verbs are used in Exodus to describe God's hardening of Pharaoh's heart. Usually the verb meaning "to make hard" is used (4:21). In 7:3 the verb "to make stiff" is used. Here the Hebrew verb that means "to make heavy" or "to make insensitive" is used.

10:3 refuse to humble yourself. Pharaoh's pride was his undoing. He believed himself to be a god and paraded himself like one. God resists the

proud but gives grace to the humble (Ps. 18:27; 1 Pet. 5:5).

9:20 ᵛ [Prov. 13:13] ʷ Ex. 8:19; 10:7 **9:22** ˣ Rev. 16:21 **9:23** ʸ Josh. 10:11 **9:25** ᶻ Ps. 78:47, 48; 105:32, 33 **9:26** ᵃ Ex. 8:22, 23; 9:4, 6; 10:23; 11:7; 12:13 **9:27** ᵇ Ex. 8:8 ᶜ Ex. 9:34; 10:16, 17 ᵈ 2 Chr. 12:6 **9:28** ᵉ Ex. 8:8, 28; 10:17 ᶠ Ex. 8:25; 10:8, 24 **9:29** ᵍ Is. 1:15 ʰ Ps. 24:1 **9:30** ⁱ [Is. 26:10] **9:31** ʲ Ruth 1:22; 2:23 **9:33** ᵏ Ex. 8:12; 9:29 **9:35** ˡ Ex. 4:21 **10:1** ᵃ John 12:40 ᵇ Ex. 7:4; 9:16 **10:2** ᶜ Joel 1:3 ᵈ Ex. 7:5, 17; 8:22 **10:3** ᵉ [1 Kin. 21:29] ᶠ Ex. 4:23; 8:1; 9:1 **10:4** ᵍ Rev. 9:3 **10:5** ʰ Ex. 9:32 **10:6** ⁱ Ex. 8:3, 21 **10:7** ʲ Ex. 7:5; 8:19; 9:20; 12:33 ᵏ Ex. 23:33 **10:9** ˡ Ex. 5:1; 7:16

better be with you when I let you and your
little ones go! Beware, for evil is ahead of
you. 11Not so! Go now, you *who are* men,
and serve the LORD, for that is what you
desired." And they were driven [m]out from
Pharaoh's presence.
12Then the LORD said to Moses, [n]"Stretch
out your hand over the land of Egypt for
the locusts, that they may come upon the
land of Egypt, and [o]eat every herb of the
land—all that the hail has left." 13So Moses
stretched out his rod over the land of Egypt,
and the LORD brought an east wind on the
land all that day and all *that* night. When
it was morning, the east wind brought the
locusts. 14And [p]the locusts went up over
all the land of Egypt and rested on all the
territory of Egypt. *They were* very severe;
[q]previously there had been no such locusts
as they, nor shall there be such after them.
15For they [r]covered the face of the whole
earth, so that the land was darkened; and
they [s]ate every herb of the land and all the
fruit of the trees which the hail had left. So
there remained nothing green on the trees
or on the plants of the field throughout all
the land of Egypt.
16Then Pharaoh called [t]for Moses and
Aaron in haste, and said, [u]"I have sinned
against the LORD your God and against
you. 17Now therefore, please forgive my
sin only this once, and [v]entreat the LORD
your God, that He may take away from me
this death only." 18So he [w]went out from
Pharaoh and entreated the LORD. 19And
the LORD turned a very strong west wind,
which took the locusts away and blew them
[x]into the Red Sea. There remained not one
locust in all the territory of Egypt. 20But the
LORD [y]hardened Pharaoh's heart, and he
did not let the children of Israel go.

The Ninth Plague: Darkness

21Then the LORD said to Moses, [z]"Stretch
out your hand toward heaven, that there
may be darkness over the land of Egypt,
darkness *which* may even be felt." 22So
Moses stretched out his hand toward heav-
en, and there was [a]thick darkness in all the
land of Egypt [b]three days. 23They did not
see one another; nor did anyone rise from
his place for three days. [c]But all the children of Israel had light in their dwellings.
24Then Pharaoh called to Moses and
[d]said, "Go, serve the LORD; only let your
flocks and your herds be kept back. Let
your [e]little ones also go with you."
25But Moses said, "You must also give us
sacrifices and burnt offerings, that we may
sacrifice to the LORD our God. 26Our [f]live-
stock also shall go with us; not a hoof shall
be left behind. For we must take some of
them to serve the LORD our God, and even
we do not know with what we must serve
the LORD until we arrive there."
27But the LORD [g]hardened Pharaoh's
heart, and he would not let them go. 28Then
Pharaoh said to him, [h]"Get away from me!
Take heed to yourself and see my face no
more! For in the day you see my face you
shall die!"
29So Moses said, "You have spoken well.
[i]I will never see your face again."

Death of the Firstborn Announced

11 And the LORD said to Moses, "I will
bring one more plague on Pharaoh
and on Egypt. [a]Afterward he will let you
go from here. [b]When he lets *you* go, he
will surely drive you out of here altogether. 2Speak now in the hearing of the people,
and let every man ask from his neighbor
and every woman from her neighbor, articles of silver and [c]articles of gold." 3[d]And
the LORD gave the people favor in the
sight of the Egyptians. Moreover the man
[e]Moses *was* very great in the land of Egypt,
in the sight of Pharaoh's servants and in
the sight of the people.
4Then Moses said, "Thus says the LORD:
[f]'About midnight I will go out into the midst
of Egypt; 5and [g]all the firstborn in the land
of Egypt shall die, from the firstborn of
Pharaoh who sits on his throne, even to
the firstborn of the female servant who *is*

10:12–16 Repentance—In Exodus 9 and 10 there are two vivid examples of "foxhole religion" recorded for us. This kind of "faith" freely acknowledges the person and power of God during a terrible crisis, and then promptly forgets all about Him when the danger passes. Just like little children, we want to avert punishment by saying, "I'm sorry, I'm sorry!" and then go about our business as usual. God is not interested in empty "I've sinned" confessions. Only true repentance from the heart is acceptable to God.

10:20 *But the LORD hardened Pharaoh's heart.* See 3:19; 4:21; 5:2; 7:3,13–14.

10:22 *thick darkness.* This calamity was another direct attack on the Egyptian religious system. They worshiped many gods, but none so much as the sun. An enshrouding darkness that lasted three days was a clear statement that their gods, their Pharaoh with his supposed control of nature, and all Pharaoh's counselors were, in reality, helpless before the God of Israel.

10:27 *But the LORD hardened Pharaoh's heart.* See 3:19; 4:21; 5:2; 7:3,13–14.

11:3 *favor.* After all that had happened, we might suppose that the Egyptians would have universally hated the Hebrews. Instead, most of the people felt positively towards them, even Pharaoh's own servants.

10:11 [m] Ex. 10:28 **10:12** [n] Ex. 7:19 [o] Ex. 10:5, 15 **10:14** [p] Ps. 78:46; 105:34 [q] Joel 1:4, 7; 2:1–11 **10:15** [r] Ex. 10:5 [s] Ps. 105:35 **10:16** [t] Ex. 8:8 [u] Ex. 9:27 **10:17** [v] 1 Kin. 13:6 **10:18** [w] Ex. 8:30 **10:19** [x] Joel 2:20 **10:20** [y] Ex. 4:21; 10:1; 11:10 **10:21** [z] Ex. 9:22 **10:22** [a] Ps. 105:28 [b] Ex. 3:18 **10:23** [c] Ex. 8:22, 23 **10:24** [d] Ex. 8:8, 25; 10:8 [e] Ex. 10:10 **10:26** [f] Ex. 10:9 **10:27** [g] Ex. 4:21; 10:1, 20; 14:4, 8 **10:28** [h] Ex. 10:11 **10:29** [i] Heb. 11:27 **11:1** [a] Ex. 12:31, 33, 39 [b] Ex. 6:1; 12:39 **11:2** [c] Ex. 3:22; 12:35, 36 **11:3** [d] Ex. 3:21; 12:36 [e] Deut. 34:10–12 **11:4** [f] Ex. 12:12, 23, 29 **11:5** [g] Ex. 4:23; 12:12, 29

behind the handmill, and all the firstborn of the animals. [6h]Then there shall be a great cry throughout all the land of Egypt, [i]such as was not like it *before,* nor shall be like it again. [7j]But against none of the children of Israel [k]shall a dog move its tongue, against man or beast, that you may know that the LORD does make a difference between the Egyptians and Israel.' [8]And [l]all these your servants shall come down to me and bow down to me, saying, 'Get out, and all the people who follow you!' After that I will go out." [m]Then he went out from Pharaoh in great anger.

[9]But the LORD said to Moses, [n]"Pharaoh will not heed you, so that [o]My wonders may be multiplied in the land of Egypt." [10]So Moses and Aaron did all these wonders before Pharaoh; [p]and the LORD hardened Pharaoh's heart, and he did not let the children of Israel go out of his land.

The Passover Instituted

12 Now the LORD spoke to Moses and Aaron in the land of Egypt, saying, [2a]"This month *shall be* your beginning of months; it *shall be* the first month of the year to you. [3]Speak to all the congregation of Israel, saying: 'On the [b]tenth of this month every man shall take for himself a lamb, according to the house of *his* father, a lamb for a household. [4]And if the household is too small for the lamb, let him and his neighbor next to his house take *it* according to the number of the persons; according to each man's need you shall make your count for the lamb. [5]Your lamb shall be [c]without blemish, a male of the first year. You may take *it* from the sheep or from the goats. [6]Now you shall keep it until the [d]fourteenth day of the same month. Then the whole assembly of the congregation of Israel shall kill it at twilight. [7]And they shall take *some* of the blood and put *it* on the two doorposts and on the lintel of the houses where they eat it. [8]Then they shall eat the flesh on that [e]night; [f]roasted in fire, with [g]unleavened bread *and* with bitter *herbs* they shall eat it. [9]Do not eat it raw, nor boiled at all with water, but [h]roasted in fire—its head with its legs and its entrails. [10i]You shall let none of it remain until morning, and what remains of it until morning you shall burn with fire. [11]And thus you shall eat it: *with* a belt on your waist, your sandals on your feet, and your staff in your hand. So you shall eat it in haste. [j]It *is* the LORD's Passover.

[12]'For I [k]will pass through the land of Egypt on that night, and will strike all the firstborn in the land of Egypt, both man and beast; and [l]against all the gods of Egypt I will execute judgment: [m]I am the LORD. [13]Now the blood shall be a sign for you on the houses where you *are.* And when I see the blood, I will pass over you; and the plague shall not be on you to destroy *you* when I strike the land of Egypt. [14]'So this day shall be to you [n]a memorial; and you shall keep it as a feast to the LORD throughout your generations. You shall keep it as a [o]feast [p]by an everlasting

---

11:7 *a difference between the Egyptians and Israel.* The institution of the Passover accentuated this great distinction. The Lord in His mercy protected His people even as He executed judgment on those who opposed Him.

11:9–10 *wonders.* We tend to think that if God would only send a miracle, people would have to believe. Sadly, history shows that this is not true. Often these individuals who have seen God's mightiest miracles have responded by displaying a total lack of faith. Pharaoh had all the proof one could want of who God was, and did not believe. The Pharisees saw a man raised from the dead, and wanted to kill both the man and his healer (John 11:53; 12:9–11). God desires us to believe His word by faith, and not be dependent on supernatural and external signs and wonders. Miracles are signs, just as the creation itself is a sign of God's power and authority (Rom. 1:19–20), but a person whose heart is hardened toward God will not be any more impressed with a miracle than with a sunset.

12:1–14 The Passover—There was only one Passover. The Passover feast has always been one of the primary elements of Jewish religious tradition and is their way of remembering the "pass over" by the Lord, sparing the people of a visit by "the destroyer" (v. 23). By celebrating it, Jews remember one of the key elements of their history. It points to their national identity and to their deliverance as a community of faith. One could say that it was a defining moment of their faith. For the Christian, the event clearly foreshadows the cross of Christ. He is our Passover Lamb who delivers us from death by taking it all on Himself.

The parallels between Exodus 12 and the Christian communion service are noteworthy (1 Cor. 11:23–26). **12:2 *your beginning of months.*** This month, called Abib in 13:4 corresponds to April/May and is also called Nisan. The Hebrew people began to mark time in relation to the time of their departure from Egypt. **12:5 *without blemish.*** Sacrifice was not a way to get rid of unwanted animals. Only the very best lambs were suitable. The Passover lamb sacrificed for the Israelites was meant as a picture of the coming death of the perfect, sinless Savior, Jesus Christ.

12:8 *unleavened bread . . . bitter herbs.* The Passover meal is full of symbolism, the unleavened bread reminded them that the first Passover was eaten in haste, ready for flight. The bitter herbs were a reminder of the bitterness of the slavery from which they were rescued.

12:12 *I will pass through . . . I will execute.* The repetition of the pronoun "I" emphasizes that God did this, not an angel or some other agent.

12:13 *sign.* The term "sign" can mean a reminder, memorial, or symbol, as it does here, or a miracle that points to the power of God.

11:6 [h] Ex. 12:30 [i] Ex. 10:14 **11:7** [j] Ex. 8:22 [k] Josh. 10:21 **11:8** [l] Ex. 12:31–33 [m] Heb. 11:27 **11:9** [n] Ex. 3:19; 7:4; 10:1 [o] Ex. 7:3; 9:16 **11:10** [p] Rom. 2:5 **12:2** [a] Deut. 16:1 **12:3** [b] Josh. 4:19 **12:5** [c] [1 Pet. 1:19] **12:6** [d] Lev. 23:5 **12:8** [e] Num. 9:12 [f] Deut. 16:7 [g] 1 Cor. 5:8 **12:9** [h] Deut. 16:7 **12:10** [i] Ex. 16:19; 23:18; 34:25 **12:11** [j] Ex. 12:13, 21, 27, 43 **12:12** [k] Ex. 11:4, 5 [l] Num. 33:4 [m] Ex. 6:2 **12:14** [n] Ex. 13:9 [o] Lev. 23:4, 5 [p] Ex. 12:17, 24; 13:10

ordinance. [15a]Seven days you shall eat unleavened bread. On the first day you shall remove leaven from your houses. For whoever eats leavened bread from the first day until the seventh day, [r]that person shall be cut off from Israel. [16]On the first day *there shall be* [s]a holy convocation, and on the seventh day there shall be a holy convocation for you. No manner of work shall be done on them; but *that* which everyone must eat—that only may be prepared by you. [17]So you shall observe *the Feast of* Unleavened Bread, for [t]on this same day I will have brought your armies [u]out of the land of Egypt. Therefore you shall observe this day throughout your generations as an everlasting ordinance. [18v]In the first *month*, on the fourteenth day of the month at evening, you shall eat unleavened bread, until the twenty-first day of the month at evening. [19]For [w]seven days no leaven shall be found in your houses, since whoever eats what is leavened, that same person shall be cut off from the congregation of Israel, whether *he is* a stranger or a native of the land. [20]You shall eat nothing leavened; in all your dwellings you shall eat unleavened bread.'"

[21]Then [x]Moses called for all the [y]elders of Israel and said to them, [z]"Pick out and take lambs for yourselves according to your families, and kill the Passover *lamb.* [22a]And you shall take a bunch of hyssop, dip *it* in the blood that *is* in the basin, and [b]strike the lintel and the two doorposts with the blood that *is* in the basin. And none of you shall go out of the door of his house until morning. [23c]For the LORD will pass through to strike the Egyptians; and when He sees the [d]blood on the lintel and on the two doorposts, the LORD will pass over the door and [e]not allow [f]the destroyer to come into your houses to strike you. [24]And you shall [g]observe this thing as an ordinance for you and your sons forever. [25]It will come to pass when you come to the land which the LORD will give you, [h]just as He promised, that you shall keep this service. [26i]And it shall be, when your children say to you, 'What do

you mean by this service?' [27]that you shall say, [j]'It *is* the Passover sacrifice of the LORD, who passed over the houses of the children of Israel in Egypt when He struck the Egyptians and delivered our households.'" So the people [k]bowed their heads and worshiped. [28]Then the children of Israel went away and [l]did *so;* just as the LORD had commanded Moses and Aaron, so they did.

The Tenth Plague: Death of the Firstborn

[29m]And it came to pass at midnight that [n]the LORD struck all the firstborn in the land of Egypt, from the firstborn of Pharaoh who sat on his throne to the firstborn of the captive who *was* in the dungeon, and all the firstborn of [o]livestock. [30]So Pharaoh rose in the night, he, all his servants, and all the Egyptians; and there was a great cry in Egypt, for *there was* not a house where *there was* not one dead.

The Exodus

[31]Then he [p]called for Moses and Aaron by night, and said, "Rise, go out from among my people, [q]both you and the children of Israel. And go, serve the LORD as you have [r]said. [32s]Also take your flocks and your herds, as you have said, and be gone; and bless me also."

[33t]And the Egyptians [u]urged the people, that they might send them out of the land in haste. For they said, "We *shall* all *be* dead." [34]So the people took their dough before it was leavened, having their kneading bowls bound up in their clothes on their shoulders. [35]Now the children of Israel had done according to the word of Moses, and they had asked from the Egyptians [v]articles of silver, articles of gold, and clothing. [36w]And the LORD had given the people favor in the sight of the Egyptians, so that they granted them *what they requested.* Thus [x]they plundered the Egyptians.

[37]Then [y]the children of Israel journeyed from [z]Rameses to Succoth, about [a]six

---

12:29–33 the LORD struck all the firstborn. In the Passover we have a summary of God's eternal plan of salvation. Jesus, the final sacrifice, was killed at the time of the Passover feast; His blood provides salvation from eternal death. Note some similarities between the first and final Passover: (1) the blood of an innocent sacrifice must be shed, (2) the sacrifice must be blameless, and (3) the shed blood must be applied by faith.
12:29 and all the firstborn of livestock. Though not nearly as awful as the death of firstborn children, the death of the livestock was a blow to the Egyptians economically. These deaths were also attacks on the power of their gods (v. 12).
12:32 and bless me also. At last Pharaoh capitulated (10:9,26). The death of his son—and the deaths of firstborn sons everywhere—must have shattered him to the core of his being.
12:36 plundered the Egyptians. Newly freed slaves do not usually make their escape with their masters

pushing the family silver into their hands. Far from wanting to keep the Israelites in bondage, the rest of Egypt couldn't wait to get rid of them.
12:37 Rameses. The reference to Rameses most likely relates to the store city Raamses, mentioned in 1:11, perhaps Tel el-Maskhuta further to the east. *six hundred thousand men.* This number of men would

12:15 [q] Lev. 23:6 [r] Gen. 17:14   **12:16** [s] Lev. 23:2, 7, 8
12:17 [t] Ex. 12:14; 13:3, 10 [u] Num. 33:1   **12:18** [v] Lev.
23:5–8   **12:19** [w] Ex. 12:15; 23:15; 34:18   **12:21** [x] [Heb.
11:28] [y] Ex. 3:16 [z] Num. 9:4   **12:22** [a] Heb. 11:28 [b] Ex. 12:7
12:23 [c] Ex. 11:4; 12:12, 13 [d] Ex. 24:8 [e] Rev. 7:3; 9:4 [f] Heb.
11:28   **12:24** [g] Ex. 12:14, 17; 13:5, 10   **12:25** [h] Ex. 3:8, 17
12:26 [i] Ex. 10:2; 13:8, 14, 15   **12:27** [j] Ex. 12:11 [k] Ex. 4:31
12:28 [l] [Heb. 11:28]   **12:29** [m] Ex. 11:4, 5 [n] Num. 8:17;
33:4 [o] Ex. 9:6   **12:31** [p] Ex. 10:28, 29 [q] Ex. 8:25; 11:1 [r] Ex.
10:9   **12:32** [s] Ex. 10:9, 26   **12:33** [t] Ex. 10:7 [u] Ps. 105:38
12:35 [v] Ex. 3:21, 22; 11:2, 3   **12:36** [w] Ex. 3:21 [x] Gen. 15:14
12:37 [y] Num. 33:3, 5 [z] Gen. 47:11 [a] Ex. 38:26

hundred thousand men on foot, besides children. [38]A [b]mixed multitude went up with them also, and flocks and herds—a great deal of [c]livestock. [39]And they baked unleavened cakes of the dough which they had brought out of Egypt; for it was not leavened, because [d]they were driven out of Egypt and could not wait, nor had they prepared provisions for themselves.

[40]Now the sojourn of the children of Israel who lived in Egypt* *was* [e]four hundred and thirty years. [41]And it came to pass at the end of the four hundred and thirty years—on that very same day—it came to pass that [f]all the armies of the LORD went out from the land of Egypt. [42]It *is* [g]a night of solemn observance to the LORD for bringing them out of the land of Egypt. This *is* that night of the LORD, a solemn observance for all the children of Israel throughout their generations.

Passover Regulations

[43]And the LORD said to Moses and Aaron, "This *is* [h]the ordinance of the Passover: No foreigner shall eat it. [44]But every man's servant who is bought for money, when you have [i]circumcised him, then he may eat it. [45i]A sojourner and a hired servant shall not eat it. [46]In one house it shall be eaten; you shall not carry any of the flesh outside the house, [k]nor shall you break one of its bones. [47l]All the congregation of Israel shall keep it. [48]And [m]when a stranger dwells with you *and wants* to keep the Passover to the LORD, let all his males be circumcised, and then let him come near and keep it; and he shall be as a native of the land. For no uncircumcised person shall eat it. [49n]One law shall be for the native-born and for the stranger who dwells among you."

[50]Thus all the children of Israel did; as the LORD commanded Moses and Aaron, so they did. [51o]And it came to pass, on that very same day, that the LORD brought the children of Israel out of the land of Egypt [p]according to their armies.

The Firstborn Consecrated

13 Then the LORD spoke to Moses, saying, [2a]"Consecrate to Me all the firstborn, whatever opens the womb among the children of Israel, *both* of man and beast; it is Mine."

The Feast of Unleavened Bread

[3]And Moses said to the people: [b]"Remember this day in which you went out of Egypt, out of the house of bondage; for [c]by strength of hand the LORD brought you out of this *place*. [d]No leavened bread shall be eaten. [4e]On this day you are going out, in the month Abib. [5]And it shall be, when the LORD [f]brings you into the [g]land of the Canaanites and the Hittites and the Amorites and the Hivites and the Jebusites, which He [h]swore to your fathers to give you, a land flowing with milk and honey, [i]that you shall keep this service in this month. [6i]Seven days you shall eat unleavened bread, and on the seventh day *there shall be* a feast to the LORD. [7]Unleavened bread shall be eaten seven days. And [k]no leavened bread shall be seen among you, nor shall leaven be seen among you in all your quarters. [8]And you shall [l]tell your son in that day, saying, 'This is *done* because of what the LORD did for me when I came up from Egypt.' [9]It shall be as [m]a sign to you

---

* **12:40** Samaritan Pentateuch and Septuagint read *Egypt and Canaan.*

---

indicate a total population of perhaps three million men, women, and children (Num. 1:46).

12:38 *mixed multitude*. Apparently a number of Egyptians and perhaps other non-Hebrews joined the flight out of Egypt. Some of these people later caused trouble when things did not go as smoothly as expected (Num. 11:4).

12:39 *unleavened cakes*. The symbolism in this has to do with the haste of their departure, not (as some have supposed) that there is something evil in leaven itself. If leaven were intrinsically evil, the Israelites would have been forbidden to eat leaven at any time. In the New Testament, leaven is often used as a symbolic way of speaking about sin, but again, leaven in and of itself is not evil.

12:40 *four hundred and thirty years*. If the Exodus took place around 1446 B.C., Jacob's arrival in Egypt would have been around 1876 B.C.

12:46 *nor shall you break one of its bones*. Not breaking the bones of the lamb foreshadowed Jesus' death. None of the Savior's bones were broken, even though He suffered a horrible death (Ps. 34:20; John 19:33–36).

13:1–22 *Consecrate to Me*. Before the dramatic story of the crossing of the Red Sea there is a record

of foundational institutions that the Lord gave to Israel. These are: (1) the consecration of the firstborn (vv. 1–2); (2) the Feast of Unleavened Bread (vv. 3–10); and (3) the law concerning the firstborn (vv. 11–16). This is followed by the Lord's command to the Israelites to travel in an unexpected direction (vv. 17–22).

13:9 *sign*. A similar commandment is found in Deuteronomy 6:8. Jews would fasten a small box containing passages of Scripture to their foreheads or arms during prayer, to serve as a memorial. The physical symbol was designed to be a reminder of the inner reality of making God's law the guiding rule of all we do.

12:38 [b] Num. 11:4 [c] Deut. 3:19   **12:39** [d] Ex. 6:1; 11:1; 12:31–33   **12:40** [e] Acts 7:6   **12:41** [f] Ex. 3:8, 10; 6:6; 7:4   **12:42** [g] Deut. 16:1, 6   **12:43** [h] Num. 9:14   **12:44** [i] Gen. 17:12, 13   **12:45** [i] Lev. 22:10   **12:46** [k] [John 19:33, 36]   **12:47** [l] Ex. 12:6   **12:48** [m] Num. 9:14   **12:49** [n] Num. 15:15, 16   **12:51** [o] Ex. 12:41; 20:2 [p] Ex. 6:26   **13:2** [a] Luke 2:23   **13:3** [b] Deut. 16:3 [c] Ex. 3:20; 6:1 [d] Ex. 12:8, 19   **13:4** [e] Ex. 12:2; 23:15; 34:18   **13:5** [f] Ex. 3:8, 17 [g] Gen. 17:8 [h] Ex. 6:8 [i] Ex. 12:25, 26   **13:6** [i] Ex. 12:15–20   **13:7** [k] Ex. 12:19   **13:8** [l] Ex. 10:2; 12:26; 13:14   **13:9** [m] Deut. 6:8; 11:18

on your hand and as a memorial between your eyes, that the LORD's law may be in your mouth; for with a strong hand the LORD has brought you out of Egypt. [10]*n*You shall therefore keep this ordinance in its season from year to year.

The Law of the Firstborn

[11]"And it shall be, when the LORD *o*brings you into the land of the *p*Canaanites, as He swore to you and your fathers, and gives it to you, [12]*q*that you shall set apart to the LORD all that open the womb, that is, every firstborn that comes from an animal which you have; the males *shall be* the LORD's. [13]But *r*every firstborn of a donkey you shall redeem with a lamb; and if you will not redeem *it*, then you shall break its neck. And all the firstborn of man among your sons *s*you shall redeem. [14]*t*So it shall be, when your son asks you in time to come, saying, 'What *is* this?' that you shall say to him, *u*'By strength of hand the LORD brought us out of Egypt, out of the house of bondage. [15]And it came to pass, when Pharaoh was stubborn about letting us go, that *v*the LORD killed all the firstborn in the land of Egypt, both the firstborn of man and the firstborn of beast. Therefore I sacrifice to the LORD all males that open the womb, but all the firstborn of my sons I redeem.' [16]It shall be as *w*a sign on your hand and as frontlets between your eyes, for by strength of hand the LORD brought us out of Egypt."

The Wilderness Way

[17]Then it came to pass, when Pharaoh had let the people go, that God did not lead them *by* way of the land of the Philistines, although that *was* near; for God said, "Lest perhaps the people *x*change their minds when they see war, and *y*return to Egypt." [18]So God *z*led the people around *by* way of the wilderness of the Red Sea. And the children of Israel went up in orderly ranks out of the land of Egypt.

[19]And Moses took the *a*bones of *b*Joseph with him, for he had placed the children of Israel under solemn oath, saying, *c*"God

will surely visit you, and you shall carry up my bones from here with you."*

[20]So *d*they took their journey from *e*Succoth and camped in Etham at the edge of the wilderness. [21]And *f*the LORD went before them by day in a pillar of cloud to lead the way, and by night in a pillar of fire to give them light, so as to go by day and night. [22]He did not take away the pillar of cloud by day or the pillar of fire by night *from* before the people.

The Red Sea Crossing

14 Now the LORD spoke to Moses, saying: [2]"Speak to the children of Israel, *a*that they turn and camp before *b*Pi Hahiroth, between *c*Migdol and the sea, opposite Baal Zephon; you shall camp before it by the sea. [3]For Pharaoh will say of the children of Israel, *d*'They *are* bewildered by the land; the wilderness has closed them in.' [4]Then *e*I will harden Pharaoh's heart, so that he will pursue them; and I *f*will gain honor over Pharaoh and over all his army, *g*that the Egyptians may know that I *am* the LORD." And they did so.

[5]Now it was told the king of Egypt that the people had fled, and *h*the heart of Pharaoh and his servants was turned against the people; and they said, "Why have we done this, that we have let Israel go from serving us?" [6]So he made ready his chariot and took his people with him. [7]Also, he took *i*six hundred choice chariots, and all the chariots of Egypt with captains over every one of them. [8]And the LORD *j*hardened the heart of Pharaoh king of Egypt, and he pursued the children of Israel; and *k*the children of Israel went out with boldness. [9]So the *l*Egyptians pursued them, all the horses *and* chariots of Pharaoh, his horsemen and his army, and overtook them camping by the sea beside Pi Hahiroth, before Baal Zephon.

[10]And when Pharaoh drew near, the children of Israel lifted their eyes, and behold, the Egyptians marched after them. So they were very afraid, and the children of Israel

---

* 13:19 Genesis 50:25

13:13 *firstborn of a donkey.* Donkeys were unclean animals, and could not be used as a sacrifice. Instead they were redeemed with a lamb. Similarly, a firstborn son was redeemed. God would never allow human sacrifice. Later the Lord claimed the Levites for Himself in exchange for the firstborn sons of the people (Num. 3:40–51).

13:18 *way of the wilderness.* The route the Israelites traveled from Egypt to Canaan has been disputed. The traditional route has the people moving in a southerly direction along the western shore of the Sinai Peninsula until they reached Mount Sinai in the far south central region of the peninsula. ***Red Sea.*** This translation comes from the Septuagint (the Greek translation of the Old Testament); the Hebrew phrase means "Sea of Reeds." This phrase may refer

to the ancient northern extension of the Red Sea. Many believe that it was one of the marshy lakes of the region.

13:19 *the bones of Joseph.* The story of the last wish of Joseph and his death is found in Genesis 50:22–26.

13:10 *n* Ex. 12:14, 24   **13:11** *o* Ex. 13:5 *p* Num. 21:3
13:12 *q* Lev. 27:26   **13:13** *r* Ex. 34:20 *s* Num. 3:46, 47;
18:15, 16   **13:14** *t* Deut. 6:20 *u* Ex. 13:3, 9   **13:15** *v* Ex.
12:29   **13:16** *w* Ex. 13:9   **13:17** *x* Ex. 14:11 *y* Deut. 17:16
13:18 *z* Num. 33:6   **13:19** *a* Gen. 50:24, 25 *b* Ex. 1:6; Deut.
33:13–17 *c* Ex. 4:31   **13:20** *d* Num. 33:6–8 *e* Ex. 12:37
13:21 *f* Deut. 1:33   **14:2** *a* Ex. 13:18 *b* Num. 33:7 *c* Jer. 44:1
14:3 *d* Ps. 71:11   **14:4** *e* Ex. 4:21; 7:3; 14:17 *f* Ex. 9:16; 14:17,
18, 23 *g* Ex. 7:5; 14:25   **14:5** *h* Ps. 105:25   **14:7** *i* Ex. 15:4
14:8 *j* Ex. 14:4 *k* Num. 33:3   **14:9** *l* Josh. 24:6

[m]cried out to the LORD. [11][n]Then they said to Moses, "Because *there were* no graves in Egypt, have you taken us away to die in the wilderness? Why have you so dealt with us, to bring us up out of Egypt? [12][o]Is this not the word that we told you in Egypt, saying, 'Let us alone that we may serve the Egyptians'? For *it would have been* better for us to serve the Egyptians than that we should die in the wilderness."

[13]And Moses said to the people, [p]"Do not be afraid. [q]Stand still, and see the [r]salvation of the LORD, which He will accomplish for you today. For the Egyptians whom you see today, you shall [s]see again no more forever. [14][t]The LORD will fight for you, and you shall [u]hold your peace."

[15]And the LORD said to Moses, "Why do you cry to Me? Tell the children of Israel to go forward. [16]But [v]lift up your rod, and stretch out your hand over the sea and divide it. And the children of Israel shall go on dry *ground* through the midst of the sea. [17]And I indeed will [w]harden the hearts of the Egyptians, and they shall follow them. So I will [x]gain honor over Pharaoh and over all his army, his chariots, and his horsemen. [18]Then the Egyptians shall know that I *am* the LORD, when I have gained honor for Myself over Pharaoh, his chariots, and his horsemen."

[19]And the Angel of God, [y]who went before the camp of Israel, moved and went behind them; and the pillar of cloud went from before them and stood behind them. [20]So it came between the camp of the Egyptians and the camp of Israel. Thus it was a cloud and darkness *to the one*, and it gave light by night *to the other*, so that the one did not come near the other all that night.

[21]Then Moses stretched out his hand over the sea; and the LORD caused the sea to go *back* by a strong east wind all that night, and [z]made the sea into dry *land*, and the waters were [a]divided. [22]So [b]the children of Israel went into the midst of the sea on the dry *ground*, and the waters *were* [c]a wall to them on their right hand and on their left.

[23]And the Egyptians pursued and went after them into the midst of the sea, all Pharaoh's horses, his chariots, and his horsemen. [24]Now it came to pass, in the morning [d]watch, that [e]the LORD looked down upon the army of the Egyptians through the pillar of fire and cloud, and He troubled the army of the Egyptians. [25]And He took off* their chariot wheels, so that they drove them with difficulty; and the Egyptians said, "Let us flee from the face of Israel, for the LORD [f]fights for them against the Egyptians."

[26]Then the LORD said to Moses, "Stretch out your hand over the sea, that the waters may come back upon the Egyptians, on their chariots, and on their horsemen." [27]And Moses stretched out his hand over the sea; and when the morning appeared, the sea [g]returned to its full depth, while the Egyptians were fleeing into it. So the LORD [h]overthrew the Egyptians in the midst of the sea. [28]Then [i]the waters returned and covered the chariots, the horsemen, *and* all the army of Pharaoh that came into the sea after them. Not so much as one of them remained. [29]But [j]the children of Israel had walked on dry *land* in the midst of the sea, and the waters *were* a wall to them on their right hand and on their left.

[30]So the LORD [k]saved Israel that day out of the hand of the Egyptians, and Israel [l]saw the Egyptians dead on the seashore. [31]Thus Israel saw the great work which the LORD had done in Egypt; so the people feared the LORD, and [m]believed the LORD and His servant Moses.

The Song of Moses

15 Then [a]Moses and the children of Israel sang this song to the LORD, and spoke, saying:

"I will [b]sing to the LORD,
For He has triumphed gloriously!

---

* **14:25** Samaritan Pentateuch, Septuagint, and Syriac read *bound*.

14:11–12 Why. This marks the first of ten episodes of Israel's unbelief, beginning at the Red Sea, and concluding at Kadesh Barnea (Num. 14:22). Because of these ten events an entire generation was prevented from entering the Promised Land. The New Testament book of Hebrews recalls these events, using the Promised Land as a picture of heaven and warning that disobedience and unbelief will still keep people out of the final land of "rest" (Heb. 4).

14:13 the salvation of the LORD. The Hebrew word for salvation comes from a term that has to do with room or space. The people were under great pressure, squeezed between the waters before them and the armies of Pharaoh behind them. Salvation relieved the pressure in a most dramatic way.

14:19 Angel of God. The term "Angel of God" is an alternative expression for the angel of the Lord. The pillar of cloud is later strongly associated with the Lord Himself (33:9–11).

14:25 the LORD fights for them. This was the confession the Lord demanded; word spread widely that the Lord fought for the Israelites.

14:31 the people . . . believed the LORD. The same wording is used of Abraham's saving faith in Genesis 15:6 (see also Rom. 4). The people were transformed spiritually even as they were delivered physically.

14:10 [m] Neh. 9:9 **14:11** [n] Ps. 106:7, 8 **14:12** [o] Ex. 5:21; 6:9 **14:13** [p] 2 Chr. 20:15, 17 [q] Ps. 46:10, 11 [r] Ex. 14:30; 15:2 [s] Deut. 28:68 **14:14** [t] Deut. 1:30; 3:22 [u] Is. 30:15] **14:16** [v] Num. 20:8, 9, 11 **14:17** [w] Ex. 14:8 [x] Ex. 14:4 **14:19** [y] [Is. 63:9] **14:21** [z] Ps. 66:6; 106:9; 136:13, 14 [a] Is. 63:12, 13 **14:22** [b] Ex. 15:19 [c] Ex. 14:29; 15:8 **14:24** [d] Judg. 7:19 [e] Ex. 13:21 **14:25** [f] Ex. 7:5; 14:4, 14, 18 **14:27** [g] Josh. 4:18 [h] Ex. 15:1, 7 **14:28** [i] Ps. 78:53; 106:11 **14:29** [j] Ps. 66:6; 78:52, 53 **14:30** [k] Ps. 106:8, 10 [l] Ps. 58:10; 59:10 **14:31** [m] John 2:11; 11:45 **15:1** [a] Ps. 106:12 [b] Is. 12:1–6

The horse and its rider
He has thrown into the sea!
2 The LORD *is* my strength and csong,
And He has become my salvation;
He *is* my God, and dI will praise Him;
My efather's God, and I fwill exalt Him.
3 The LORD *is* a man of gwar;
The LORD *is* His hname.
4 iPharaoh's chariots and his army He
has cast into the sea;
jHis chosen captains also are drowned
in the Red Sea.
5 The depths have covered them;
kThey sank to the bottom like a stone.
6 "Your lright hand, O LORD, has become
glorious in power;
Your right hand, O LORD, has dashed
the enemy in pieces.
7 And in the greatness of Your
mexcellence
You have overthrown those who rose
against You;
You sent forth nYour wrath;
It oconsumed them plike stubble.
8 And qwith the blast of Your nostrils
The waters were gathered together;
rThe floods stood upright like a heap;
The depths congealed in the heart of
the sea.
9 sThe enemy said, 'I will pursue,
I will overtake,
I will tdivide the spoil;
My desire shall be satisfied on them.
I will draw my sword,
My hand shall destroy them.'
10 You blew with Your wind,
The sea covered them;
They sank like lead in the mighty
waters.
11 "Who uis like You, O LORD, among the
gods?
Who *is* like You, vglorious in holiness,
Fearful in wpraises, xdoing wonders?

12 You stretched out Your right hand;
The earth swallowed them.
13 You in Your mercy have yled forth
The people whom You have redeemed;
You have guided *them* in Your
strength
To zYour holy habitation.
14 "The apeople will hear *and* be afraid;
bSorrow will take hold of the
inhabitants of Philistia.
15 cThen dthe chiefs of Edom will be
dismayed;
eThe mighty men of Moab,
Trembling will take hold of them;
fAll the inhabitants of Canaan will
gmelt away.
16 hFear and dread will fall on them;
By the greatness of Your arm
They will be ias still as a stone,
Till Your people pass over, O LORD,
Till the people pass over
jWhom You have purchased.
17 You will bring them in and kplant
them
In the lmountain of Your inheritance,
In the place, O LORD, *which* You have
made
For Your own dwelling,
The msanctuary, O Lord, *which* Your
hands have established.
18 "Then LORD shall reign forever and
ever."

19For the ohorses of Pharaoh went with
his chariots and his horsemen into the sea,
and pthe LORD brought back the waters of
the sea upon them. But the children of Israel went on dry *land* in the midst of the sea.

The Song of Miriam

20Then Miriam qthe prophetess, rthe sister of Aaron, stook the timbrel in her hand;
and all the women went out after her twith

15:2 My father's God. The Israelites had worshiped,
believed, and obeyed. Today, Christians are part of
Abraham's line because they also believe, obey, and
worship the same God (Gal. 3:6–7). Many faithful
believers have preceded us.
15:3 The LORD is His name. Other supposed gods
had secret names that only guilds of priests knew.
By knowing a god's secret name, a priest supposedly
had special access to that god. But the living God had
made His name known to all, and salvation is found
in His name alone.
15:11 Who is like You? Many times, the Bible uses
the language of incomparability to describe the true
God. In a world in which there are many supposed
gods, the Lord is unique. He alone is God. He is not
just better than other gods; there *are* no other gods.
No person, god, or thing can be compared to the one
true God (Ps. 96:4; Is. 40:25–26; Mic. 7:18).
15:18 The LORD shall reign forever and ever. Ultimately, the salvation of Israel from Egypt points to
the coming reign of the living God on earth over His
redeemed people.
This victory song ends with the assertion of the

eternal rule of the Lord, promising the kingdom
of God rather than the conquering of neighboring
lands. Its emphasis is spiritual, not material. Now that
deliverance from slavery in Egypt had been accomplished, the Hebrews would be formed by God into a
nation which was designed to be a witness to the rest
of the world of God's character and authority.
15:20 prophetess. Although there is no record of
women serving as priests in ancient Israel, women
did serve as prophetesses (Deborah, Judg. 4:4; the

15:2 c Is. 12:2 d Gen. 28:21, 22 e Ex. 3:6, 15, 16 f Is.
25:1 **15:3** g Rev. 19:11 h Ps. 24:8; 83:18 **15:4** i Ex.
14:28 j Ex. 14:7 **15:5** k Neh. 9:11 **15:6** l Ps. 17:7; 118:15
15:7 m Deut. 33:26 n Ps. 78:49, 50 o Ps. 59:13 p Is. 5:24
15:8 q Ex. 14:21, 22, 29 r Ps. 78:13 **15:9** s Judg. 5:30 t Is.
53:12 **15:11** u 1 Kin. 8:23 v Is. 6:3 w 1 Chr. 16:25 x Ps.
77:11, 14 **15:13** y [Ps. 77:20] z Ps. 78:54 **15:14** a Josh.
2:9 b Ps. 48:6 **15:15** c Gen. 36:15, 40 d Deut. 2:4 e Num.
22:3, 4 f Josh. 5:1 g Josh. 2:9–11, 24 **15:16** h Josh. 2:9
i 1 Sam. 25:37 j Jer. 31:11 **15:17** k Ps. 44:2; 80:8, 15 l Ps.
2:6; 78:54, 68 m Ps. 68:16; 76:2; 132:13, 14 **15:18** n Is.
57:15 **15:19** o Ex. 14:23 p Ex. 14:28 **15:20** q Judg. 4:4
r Num. 26:59 s 1 Sam. 18:6 t Judg. 11:34; 21:21

timbrels and with dances. ²¹And Miriam ᵘanswered them:

> ᵛ"Sing to the LORD,
> For He has triumphed gloriously!
> The horse and its rider
> He has thrown into the sea!"

Bitter Waters Made Sweet

²²So Moses brought Israel from the Red Sea; then they went out into the Wilderness of ʷShur. And they went three days in the wilderness and found no ˣwater. ²³Now when they came to ʸMarah, they could not drink the waters of Marah, for they *were* bitter. Therefore the name of it was called Marah.* ²⁴And the people ᶻcomplained against Moses, saying, "What shall we drink?" ²⁵So he cried out to the LORD, and the LORD showed him a tree. ᵃWhen he cast *it* into the waters, the waters were made sweet.

There He ᵇmade a statute and an ordinance for them, and there ᶜHe tested them, ²⁶and said, ᵈ"If you diligently heed the voice of the LORD your God and do what is right in His sight, give ear to His commandments and keep all His statutes, I will put none of the ᵉdiseases on you which I have brought on the Egyptians. For I *am* the LORD ᶠwho heals you."

²⁷ᵍThen they came to Elim, where there *were* twelve wells of water and seventy palm trees; so they camped there by the waters.

Bread from Heaven

16 And they ᵃjourneyed from Elim, and all the congregation of the children of Israel came to the Wilderness of Sin, which is between Elim and ᵇSinai, on the fifteenth day of the second month after they departed from the land of Egypt. ²Then the whole congregation of the children of Israel ᶜcomplained against Moses and Aaron in the wilderness. ³And the children of Israel said to them, ᵈ"Oh, that we had died by the hand of the LORD in the land of Egypt, ᵉwhen we sat by the pots of

meat *and* when we ate bread to the full! For you have brought us out into this wilderness to kill this whole assembly with hunger."

⁴Then the LORD said to Moses, "Behold, I will rain ᶠbread from heaven for you. And the people shall go out and gather a certain quota every day, that I may ᵍtest them, whether they will ʰwalk in My law or not. ⁵And it shall be on the sixth day that they shall prepare what they bring in, and ⁱit shall be twice as much as they gather daily."

⁶Then Moses and Aaron said to all the children of Israel, ʲ"At evening you shall know that the LORD has brought you out of the land of Egypt. ⁷And in the morning you shall see ᵏthe glory of the LORD; for He ˡhears your complaints against the LORD. But ᵐwhat *are* we, that you complain against us?" ⁸Also Moses said, "*This shall be seen* when the LORD gives you meat to eat in the evening, and in the morning bread to the full; for the LORD hears your complaints which you make against Him. And what *are* we? Your complaints *are* not against us but ⁿagainst the LORD."

⁹Then Moses spoke to Aaron, "Say to all the congregation of the children of Israel, ᵒ'Come near before the LORD, for He has heard your complaints.'" ¹⁰Now it came to pass, as Aaron spoke to the whole congregation of the children of Israel, that they looked toward the wilderness, and behold, the glory of the LORD ᵖappeared in the cloud.

¹¹And the LORD spoke to Moses, saying, ¹²�q"I have heard the complaints of the children of Israel. Speak to them, saying, ʳ'At twilight you shall eat meat, and ˢin the morning you shall be filled with bread. And you shall know that I *am* the LORD your God.'"

¹³So it was that ᵗquails came up at evening and covered the camp, and in the morning ᵘthe dew lay all around the camp.

---

* 15:23 Literally *Bitter*

---

wife of Isaiah, Is. 8:3; Huldah, 2 Kin. 22:14). As a prophetess, Miriam spoke authoritatively from God. However, it is apparent that neither she nor Aaron had the level of intimacy with God that Moses had.

15:24 complained. The people's recent deliverance from the Egyptian armies makes this complaint seem fickle and a true test of God's mercy. We are like the Israelites far too often, turning from praise to complaint at a moment's notice.

15:27 Elim. Elim means "place of trees." The wells and palms of this oasis would have been a welcome relief from the barren wasteland.

16:1 Wilderness of Sin. The location of this wasteland is uncertain; its position between Elim and Sinai depends on the location of Mount Sinai. (The name Sin has nothing to do with the English word "sin.")

16:5 twice as much. Gathering extra food on the sixth day would allow for the Sabbath rest (v. 25).

16:10 the glory of the LORD. This is one of the grand appearances of God recorded in Exodus. We do not know exactly what the people saw in the cloud, but the sight certainly made them aware of God's majestic and somewhat ominous presence (Ps. 97:2–5).

15:21 ᵘ 1 Sam. 18:7 ᵛ Ex. 15:1 **15:22** ʷ Gen. 16:7; 20:1; 25:18 ˣ Num. 20:2 **15:23** ʸ Num. 33:8 **15:24** ᶻ Ex. 14:11; 16:2 **15:25** ᵃ 2 Kin. 2:21 ᵇ Josh. 24:25 ᶜ Deut. 8:2, 16 **15:26** ᵈ Deut. 7:12, 15 ᵉ Deut. 28:27, 58, 60 ᶠ Ex. 23:25 **15:27** ᵍ Num. 33:9 **16:1** ᵃ Num. 33:10, 11 ᵇ Ex. 12:6, 51; 19:1 **16:2** ᶜ 1 Cor. 10:10 **16:3** ᵈ Lam. 4:9 ᵉ Num. 11:4, 5 **16:4** ᶠ [John 6:31–35] ᵍ Deut. 8:2, 16 ʰ Judg. 2:22 **16:5** ⁱ Lev. 25:21 **16:6** ʲ Ex. 6:7 **16:7** ᵏ John 11:4, 40 ˡ Num. 14:27; 17:5 ᵐ Num. 16:11 **16:8** ⁿ 1 Sam. 8:7 **16:9** ᵒ Num. 16:16 **16:10** ᵖ Num. 16:19 **16:12** �q Ex. 16:8 ʳ Ex. 16:6 ˢ Ex. 16:7 **16:13** ᵗ Num. 11:31 ᵘ Num. 11:9

[14]And when the layer of dew lifted, there, on the surface of the wilderness, was [v]a small round [w]substance, *as* fine as frost on the ground. [15]So when the children of Israel saw *it*, they said to one another, "What is it?" For they did not know what it *was*.

And Moses said to them, [x]"This *is* the bread which the LORD has given you to eat. [16]This is the thing which the LORD has commanded: 'Let every man gather it [y]according to each one's need, one [z]omer for each person, *according to the* number of persons; let every man take for *those* who *are* in his tent.'"

[17]Then the children of Israel did so and gathered, some more, some less. [18]So when they measured *it* by omers, [a]he who gathered much had nothing left over, and he who gathered little had no lack. Every man had gathered according to each one's need. [19]And Moses said, "Let no one [b]leave any of it till morning." [20]Notwithstanding they did not heed Moses. But some of them left part of it until morning, and it bred worms and stank. And Moses was angry with them. [21]So they gathered it every morning, every man according to his need. And when the sun became hot, it melted.

[22]And so it was, on the sixth day, *that* they gathered twice as much bread, two omers for each one. And all the rulers of the congregation came and told Moses. [23]Then he said to them, "This *is what* the LORD has said: 'Tomorrow *is* [c]a Sabbath rest, a holy Sabbath to the LORD. Bake what you will bake *today*, and boil what you will boil; and lay up for yourselves all that remains, to be kept until morning.'" [24]So they laid it up till morning, as Moses commanded; and it did not [d]stink, nor were there any worms in it. [25]Then Moses said, "Eat that today, for today *is* a Sabbath to the LORD; today you will not find it in the field. [26e]Six days you

shall gather it, but on the seventh day, the Sabbath, there will be none."

[27]Now it happened *that some* of the people went out on the seventh day to gather, but they found none. [28]And the LORD said to Moses, "How long [f]do you refuse to keep My commandments and My laws? [29]See! For the LORD has given you the Sabbath; therefore He gives you on the sixth day bread for two days. Let every man remain in his place; let no man go out of his place on the seventh day." [30]So the people rested on the seventh day.

[31]And the house of Israel called its name Manna.* And [g]it *was* like white coriander seed, and the taste of it *was* like wafers *made* with honey.

[32]Then Moses said, "This *is* the thing which the LORD has commanded: 'Fill an omer with it, to be kept for your generations, that they may see the bread with which I fed you in the wilderness, when I brought you out of the land of Egypt.'" [33]And Moses said to Aaron, [h]"Take a pot and put an omer of manna in it, and lay it up before the LORD, to be kept for your generations." [34]As the LORD commanded Moses, so Aaron laid it up [i]before the Testimony, to be kept. [35]And the children of Israel [j]ate manna [k]forty years, [l]until they came to an inhabited land; they ate manna until they came to the border of the land of Canaan. [36]Now an omer *is* one-tenth of an ephah.

Water from the Rock

17 Then [a]all the congregation of the children of Israel set out on their journey from the Wilderness of [b]Sin, according to the commandment of the LORD, and camped in Rephidim; but *there was* no water for the people to [c]drink. [2d]Therefore

---

* **16:31** Literally *What?* (compare Exodus 16:15)

16:14 *a small round substance as fine as frost on the ground.* There have been many attempts to explain manna as a naturally occurring substance that still might be found in the desert, suggesting that it was some kind of plant or animal secretion. However, it is clear from the wording of these verses that this was not so. The description of the manna was necessary precisely because it was *not* a naturally occurring substance, or something they had ever seen before (Num. 11:1–15).
16:15–18 God's Provision—It is easy to think we trust in God and believe He will supply all of our needs when we have food, shelter, and clothing. It is more difficult when the food is low, the clothing has disappeared, and there is no money to pay the rent. Sometimes God allows us to be in this kind of position so that we will have to learn to consciously rely on His providence. When we really place our lives in His hands, we will experience a depth of relationship which is worth far more than all the security in the world.
16:19 *Let no one leave any of it.* The Israelites' daily dependence on manna was an act of faith in God's provision.

16:26 *Six days . . . the Sabbath.* The characteristics of manna were a built-in reminder of the importance of the Sabbath day in the life of the people of Israel.
16:31 *coriander seed . . . honey.* Apparently the manna was very tasty. It must also have been very nutritious since it was the staple of the Israelites for a full generation.
16:32 *to be kept for your generations.* This pot of manna was not only a reminder of God's miraculous provision, but a miracle in itself since it did not spoil as did the extra manna Israelites gathered for themselves.

16:14 [v]Num. 11:7, 8 [w]Ps. 147:16 **16:15** [x]1 Cor. 10:3 **16:16** [y]Ex. 12:4 [z]Ex. 16:32, 36 **16:18** [a]2 Cor. 8:15 **16:19** [b]Ex. 12:10; 16:23; 23:18 **16:23** [c]Gen. 2:3 **16:24** [d]Ex. 16:20 **16:26** [e]Ex. 20:9, 10 **16:28** [f]2 Kin. 17:14 **16:31** [g]Num. 11:7–9 **16:33** [h]Heb. 9:4 **16:34** [i]Num. 17:10 **16:35** [j]Deut. 8:3, 16 [k]Num. 33:38 [l]Josh. 5:12 **17:1** [a]Ex. 16:1 [b]Num. 33:11–15 [c]Ex. 15:22 **17:2** [d]Num. 20:2, 3, 13

the people contended with Moses, and said, "Give us water, that we may drink."

So Moses said to them, "Why do you contend with me? Why do you *e*tempt the LORD?"

3And the people thirsted there for water, and the people *f*complained against Moses, and said, "Why *is* it you have brought us up out of Egypt, to kill us and our children and our *g*livestock with thirst?"

4So Moses *h*cried out to the LORD, saying, "What shall I do with this people? They are almost ready to *i*stone me!"

5And the LORD said to Moses, *j*"Go on before the people, and take with you some of the elders of Israel. Also take in your hand your rod with which *k*you struck the river, and go. 6*l*Behold, I will stand before you there on the rock in Horeb; and you shall strike the rock, and water will come out of it, that the people may drink."

And Moses did so in the sight of the elders of Israel. 7So he called the name of the place *m*Massah* and Meribah,* because of the contention of the children of Israel, and because they tempted the LORD, saying, "Is the LORD among us or not?"

Victory over the Amalekites

8*n*Now Amalek came and fought with Israel in Rephidim. 9And Moses said to Joshua, "Choose us some men and go out, fight with Amalek. Tomorrow I will stand on the top of the hill with *o*the rod of God in my hand." 10So Joshua did as Moses said to him, and fought with Amalek. And Moses, Aaron, and Hur went up to the top of the hill. 11And so it was, when Moses *p*held up his hand, that Israel prevailed; and when he let down his hand, Amalek prevailed. 12But Moses' hands *became* heavy; so they took a stone and put *it* under him, and he sat on it. And Aaron and Hur supported his

hands, one on one side, and the other on the other side; and his hands were steady until the going down of the sun. 13So Joshua defeated Amalek and his people with the edge of the sword.

14Then the LORD said to Moses, *q*"Write this *for* a memorial in the book and recount *it* in the hearing of Joshua, that *r*I will utterly blot out the remembrance of Amalek from under heaven." 15And Moses built an altar and called its name, The-LORD-Is-My-Banner;* 16for he said, "Because the LORD has *s*sworn: the LORD *will have* war with Amalek from generation to generation."

Jethro's Advice

18 And *a*Jethro, the priest of Midian, Moses' father-in-law, heard of all that *b*God had done for Moses and for Israel His people—that the LORD had brought Israel out of Egypt. 2Then Jethro, Moses' father-in-law, took *c*Zipporah, Moses' wife, after he had sent her back, 3with her *d*two sons, of whom the name of one *was* Gershom (for he said, *e*"I have been a stranger in a foreign land")* 4and the name of the other *was* Eliezer* (for *he said,* "The God of my father *was* my *f*help, and delivered me from the sword of Pharaoh"); 5and Jethro, Moses' father-in-law, came with his sons and his wife to Moses in the wilderness, where he was encamped at *g*the mountain of God. 6Now he had said to Moses, "I, your father-in-law Jethro, am coming to you with your wife and her two sons with her."

7So Moses *h*went out to meet his father-in-law, bowed down, and *i*kissed him. And they asked each other about *their* well-being, and they went into the tent.

---

* 17:7 Literally *Tempted* • Literally *Contention*
* 17:15 Hebrew *YHWH Nissi* * 18:3 Compare Exodus 2:22 * 18:4 Literally *My God Is Help*

17:7 Is the LORD among us. The people had seen God's power in the plagues, the Exodus, the crossing of the Red Sea, and the provision of manna. Every day they saw the pillar of His presence. We can wonder at their lack of faith until we look at our own weakness.
17:8 Amalek. The people of Amalek were descendants of Esau, and thus relatives of the Hebrews (Gen. 36:12). Their attack on Israel was unprovoked. The Israelites—and the Lord—regarded this attack as particularly heinous (vv. 14–16).
17:14 Write this. Some people allege that the first five books of the Old Testament were not actually written down until centuries after Moses' death. Others concede that Moses may have written certain small sections, such as the one to which this verse seems to refer (24:4). However, strong tradition supports the assertion that Moses really wrote all of the first five books (except for the account of his own death); ancient Jews, including Jesus, referred to this portion of the Scripture as "the books of Moses."
17:16 the LORD has sworn. This Hebrew phrase is somewhat obscure, but appears to mean "Surely there is a hand on the throne of the LORD." In this

phraseology, the Creator of the universe is pictured as seated on His throne while raising His hand in a solemn oath. It is a fearful thing for the wicked to fall into the hands of the just and righteous Judge of the universe.
18:6 her two sons. Zipporah's two sons stayed with Moses and became part of the families of Israel. However, the subsequent history of the family of Gershom involved a return to idols and inappropriate priesthood (Judg. 18:30).
18:7 bowed down, and kissed him. The ancient Middle Eastern acts of bowing and kissing were not acts of worship, but signs of respect and reminders of obligations between two people.

17:2 *e* [Deut. 6:16] 17:3 *f* Ex. 16:2, 3 *g* Ex. 12:38
17:4 *h* Ex. 14:15 *i* John 8:59; 10:31 17:5 *j* Ezek. 2:6
k Num. 20:8 17:6 *l* Num. 20:10, 11 17:7 *m* Num.
20:13, 24; 27:14 17:8 *n* Gen. 36:12 17:9 *o* Ex. 4:20
17:11 *p* [James 5:16] 17:14 *q* Ex. 24:4; 34:27 *r* 1 Sam. 15:3
17:16 *s* Gen. 22:14–16 18:1 *a* Ex. 2:16, 18; 3:1 *b* [Ps.
106:2, 8] 18:2 *c* Ex. 2:21; 4:20–26 18:3 *d* Acts 7:29
e Ex. 2:22 18:4 *f* Gen. 49:25 18:5 *g* Ex. 3:1, 12; 4:27;
24:13 18:7 *h* Gen. 18:2 *i* Ex. 4:27

8And Moses told his father-in-law all that the LORD had done to Pharaoh and to the Egyptians for Israel's sake, all the hardship that had come upon them on the way, and how the LORD had *i*delivered them. 9Then Jethro rejoiced for all the *k*good which the LORD had done for Israel, whom He had delivered out of the hand of the Egyptians. 10And Jethro said, *l*"Blessed be the LORD, who has delivered you out of the hand of the Egyptians and out of the hand of Pharaoh, and who has delivered the people from under the hand of the Egyptians. 11Now I know that the LORD is *m*greater than all the gods; *n*for in the very thing in which they behaved *o*proudly, He was above them." 12Then Jethro, Moses' father-in-law, took* a burnt *p*offering and other sacrifices to offer to God. And Aaron came with all the elders of Israel *q*to eat bread with Moses' father-in-law before God.

13And so it was, on the next day, that Moses *r*sat to judge the people; and the people stood before Moses from morning until evening. 14So when Moses' father-in-law saw all that he did for the people, he said, "What is this thing that you are doing for the people? Why do you alone sit, and all the people stand before you from morning until evening?"

15And Moses said to his father-in-law, "Because *s*the people come to me to inquire of God. 16When they have *t*a difficulty, they come to me, and I judge between one and another; and I make known the statutes of God and His laws."

17So Moses' father-in-law said to him, "The thing that you do is not good. 18Both you and these people who are with you will surely wear yourselves out. For this thing is too much for you; *u*you are not able to perform it by yourself. 19Listen now to my voice; I will give you counsel, and God will be with you: Stand *v*before God for the people, so that you may *w*bring the difficulties to God. 20And you shall *x*teach them the statutes and the laws, and show them the way in which they must walk and *y*the work they must do. 21Moreover you shall select from all the people *z*able men, such

as *a*fear God, *b*men of truth, *c*hating covetousness; and place such over them to be rulers of thousands, rulers of hundreds, rulers of fifties, and rulers of tens. 22And let them judge the people at all times. *d*Then it will be that every great matter they shall bring to you, but every small matter they themselves shall judge. So it will be easier for you, for *e*they will bear the burden with you. 23If you do this thing, and God so commands you, then you will be able to endure, and all this people will also go to their *f*place in peace."

24So Moses heeded the voice of his father-in-law and did all that he had said. 25And *g*Moses chose able men out of all Israel, and made them heads over the people: rulers of thousands, rulers of hundreds, rulers of fifties, and rulers of tens. 26So they judged the people at all times; the *h*hard cases they brought to Moses, but they judged every small case themselves. 27Then Moses let his father-in-law depart, and *i*he went his way to his own land.

Israel at Mount Sinai

19 In the third month after the children of Israel had gone out of the land of Egypt, on the same day, *a*they came to the Wilderness of Sinai. 2For they had departed from *b*Rephidim, had come to the Wilderness of Sinai, and camped in the wilderness. So Israel camped there before *c*the mountain.

3And *d*Moses went up to God, and the LORD *e*called to him from the mountain, saying, "Thus you shall say to the house of Jacob, and tell the children of Israel: 4*f*'You have seen what I did to the Egyptians, and how *g*I bore you on eagles' wings and brought you to Myself. 5Now *h*therefore, if you will indeed obey My voice and *i*keep My covenant, then *j*you shall be a special treasure to Me above all people; for all the earth is *k*Mine. 6And you shall be to Me a *l*kingdom of priests and a *m*holy nation.'

---

* **18:12** Following Masoretic Text and Septuagint; Syriac, Targum, and Vulgate read offered.

18:11 Now I know that the LORD is greater. Jethro's words imply that he had once regarded the Lord as one among many gods, or perhaps as the principal deity over the lesser. Here he declares full faith in God as the supreme Deity.

18:21 covetousness. Jethro's five qualifications for judges are similar to the qualifications for elders in the New Testament (1 Tim. 3:1–13). In particular, the men recommended by Jethro were to be God-fearing and haters of dishonesty. As such they would not be susceptible to bribery, and justice would not be perverted. God takes no bribes (Deut. 10:17), so neither must a judge. A bribe blinds the eyes. Human justice must reflect divine justice, which is impartial (Rom. 2:11).
19:5–8 God Gives His Covenant—The covenant with Moses is the second covenant that pertains to the rule of God. It is different than the Abrahamic

covenant in that it is conditional. It is introduced by the conditional formula "if you will indeed obey My voice . . . you shall be a special treasure to Me." This covenant was given to the nation Israel so

18:8 *i*Ex. 15:6, 16 **18:9** *k* [Is. 63:7–14] **18:10** *l* Gen. 14:20 **18:11** *m* 2 Chr. 2:5 *n* Ex. 1:10, 16, 22; 5:2, 7 *o* Luke 1:51 **18:12** *p* Ex. 24:5 *q* Deut. 12:7 **18:13** *r* Matt. 23:2 **18:15** *s* Lev. 24:12 **18:16** *t* Ex. 24:14 **18:18** *u* Num. 11:14, 17 **18:19** *v* Ex. 4:16; 20:19 *w* Num. 9:8; 27:5 **18:20** *x* Deut. 5:1 *y* Deut. 1:18 **18:21** *z* Acts 6:3 *a* 2 Sam. 23:3 *b* Ezek. 18:8 *c* Deut. 16:19 **18:22** *d* Deut. 1:17 *e* Num. 11:17 **18:23** *f* Ex. 16:29 **18:25** *g* Deut. 1:15 **18:26** *h* Job 29:16 **18:27** *i* Num. 10:29, 30 **19:1** *a* Num. 33:15 **19:2** *b* Ex. 17:1 *c* Ex. 3:1, 12; 18:5 **19:3** *d* Acts 7:38 *e* Ex. 3:4 **19:4** *f* Deut. 29:2 *g* Is. 46:3 **19:5** *h* Ex. 15:26; 23:22 *i* Deut. 5:2 *j* Ps. 135:4 *k* Ex. 9:29 **19:6** *l* [1 Pet. 2:5, 9] *m* Deut. 7:6; 14:21; 26:19

These *are* the words which you shall speak to the children of Israel."

7So Moses came and called for the *n*elders of the people, and laid before them all these words which the LORD commanded him. 8Then *o*all the people answered together and said, "All that the LORD has spoken we will do." So Moses brought back the words of the people to the LORD. 9And the LORD said to Moses, "Behold, I come to you *p*in the thick cloud, *q*that the people may hear when I speak with you, and believe you forever."

So Moses told the words of the people to the LORD.

10Then the LORD said to Moses, "Go to the people and *r*consecrate them today and tomorrow, and let them wash their clothes. 11And let them be ready for the third day. For on the third day the LORD will come down upon Mount Sinai in the sight of all the people. 12You shall set bounds for the people all around, saying, 'Take heed to yourselves *that* you do *not* go up to the mountain or touch its base. *s*Whoever touches the mountain shall surely be put to death. 13Not a hand shall touch him, but he shall surely be stoned or shot *with an arrow*; whether man or beast, he shall not live.' When the trumpet sounds long, they shall come near the mountain."

14So Moses went down from the mountain to the people and sanctified the people, and they washed their clothes. 15And he said to the people, "Be ready for the third day; *t*do not come near *your* wives."

16Then it came to pass on the third day, in the morning, that there were *u*thunderings and lightnings, and a thick cloud on the mountain; and the sound of the trumpet was very loud, so that all the people who *were* in the camp *v*trembled. 17And *w*Moses

brought the people out of the camp to meet with God, and they stood at the foot of the mountain. 18Now *x*Mount Sinai *was* completely in smoke, because the LORD descended upon *y*it in fire. *z*Its smoke ascended like the smoke of a furnace, and *a*whole mountain* quaked greatly. 19And when the blast of the trumpet sounded long and became louder and louder, *b*Moses spoke, and *c*God answered him by voice. 20Then the LORD came down upon Mount Sinai, on the top of the mountain. And the LORD called Moses to the top of the mountain, and Moses went up.

21And the LORD said to Moses, "Go down and warn the people, lest they break through *d*to gaze at the LORD, and many of them perish. 22Also let the *e*priests who come near the LORD *f*consecrate themselves, lest the LORD *g*break out against them."

23But Moses said to the LORD, "The people cannot come up to Mount Sinai; for You warned us, saying, *h*'Set bounds around the mountain and consecrate it.'"

24Then the LORD said to him, "Away! Get down and then come up, you and Aaron with you. But do not let the priests and the people break through to come up to the LORD, lest He break out against them." 25So Moses went down to the people and spoke to them.

The Ten Commandments

20 And God spoke *a*all these words, saying:

2 *b*"I am the LORD your God, who brought you out of the land of Egypt, *c*out of the house of bondage.

* **19:18** Septuagint reads *all the people.*

that those who believed God's promises given to Abraham in the Abrahamic covenant (Gen. 12:1–3) would know how they should live. The Mosaic covenant in its entirety governs three areas of their lives: (1) the commandments governed their personal lives (Ex. 20:1–26); (2) the law governed their social lives particularly as they related to one another (Ex. 21:1—24:11); and (3) the ordinances governed their religious lives so that the people would know how to approach God (Ex. 24:12—31:18). The Mosaic covenant did not replace the Abrahamic covenant. It was added alongside the Abrahamic covenant so that the people of Israel would know how to live until "the Seed," Christ, comes and makes the complete and perfect sacrifice. The Mosaic covenant was never given so that by keeping it people could be saved, but so that they might realize that they cannot do what God wants, even when God writes it down on stone tablets. The law was given that man might realize that he is helpless and that his only hope is to receive the righteousness of God by faith in Jesus (Gal. 3:17–24).

19:16 *the sound of the trumpet was very loud.* Amazingly, one of the heavenly visitors played the trumpet rather than someone in the camp of Israel

(compare Is. 27:13; 1 Cor. 15:52; 1 Thess. 4:16). No wonder they trembled (20:18–19).

19:18 *the LORD descended.* Even though we know God is everywhere, language such as this gives us a greater appreciation of His merciful grace.

20:1 *And God spoke.* The following words of God are known as the law of Moses, but this is only because they were delivered to the people from God through Moses, not because Moses invented them.

20:1–17 The Ten Commandments—The first four Commandments (20:1–11) lay out the basics of the relationship with God. God is not a mere abstraction or figment of imagination. He is the God who spoke dramatically to the patriarchs and continues to speak to us. Our responsibility is to have a relationship with

19:7 *n* Ex. 4:29, 30   **19:8** *o* Deut. 5:27; 26:17   **19:9** *p* Ex. 19:16; 20:21; 24:15   *q* Deut. 4:12, 36   **19:10** *r* Lev. 11:44, 45   **19:12** *s* Heb. 12:20   **19:15** *t* [1 Cor. 7:5]   **19:16** *u* Heb. 12:18, 19   *v* Heb. 12:21   **19:17** *w* Deut. 4:10   **19:18** *x* Deut. 4:11   *y* Ex. 3:2; 24:17   *z* Gen. 15:17; 19:28   *a* Ps. 68:8   **19:19** *b* Heb. 12:21   *c* Ps. 81:7   **19:21** *d* 1 Sam. 6:19   **19:22** *e* Ex. 19:24; 24:5   *f* Lev. 10:3; 21:6–8   *g* 2 Sam. 6:7, 8   **19:23** *h* Ex. 19:12   **20:1** *a* Deut. 5:22   **20:2** *b* Hos. 13:4   *c* Ex. 13:3

3 d"You shall have no other gods before Me.

4 e"You shall not make for yourself a carved image—any likeness *of anything* that *is* in heaven above, or that *is* in the earth beneath, or that *is* in the water under the earth; 5f you shall not bow down to them nor serve them. gFor I, the LORD your God, *am* a jealous God, hvisiting the iniquity of the fathers upon the children to the third and fourth *generations* of those who hate Me, 6but ishowing mercy to thousands, to those who love Me and keep My commandments.

7 j"You shall not take the name of the LORD your God in vain, for the LORD kwill not hold *him* guiltless who takes His name in vain.

8 l"Remember the Sabbath day, to keep it holy. 9mSix days you shall labor and do all your work, 10but the nseventh day *is* the Sabbath of the LORD your God. *In it* you shall do no work: you,

nor your son, nor your daughter, nor your male servant, nor your female servant, nor your cattle, onor your stranger who *is* within your gates. 11For pin six days the LORD made the heavens and the earth, the sea, and all that *is* in them, and rested the seventh day. Therefore the LORD blessed the Sabbath day and hallowed it.

12 q"Honor your father and your mother, that your days may be rlong upon the land which the LORD your God is giving you.

13 s"You shall not murder.

14 t"You shall not commit uadultery.

15 v"You shall not steal.

16 w"You shall not bear false witness against your neighbor.

17 x"You shall not covet your neighbor's house; yyou shall not covet your neighbor's wife, nor his male servant, nor his female servant, nor his ox, nor his donkey, nor anything that *is* your neighbor's."

Him whereby we explicitly recognize Him, listen to what He says and then obey. What He wants isn't all that complicated. He is the Creator and Master of the world, as we know it. Any view of God that makes Him less, falls short of what is required to make the relationship between God and man work. For example if God is not the creator and sustainer of the world, then the perspective of Genesis 1:28 and our responsibility as stewards of His creation don't make much sense.

The last six Commandments (20:12–17) give us the basics for living—with our families, our neighbors and our communities. Disregarding and disobeying any of these commands leads to the breakdown and possible destruction of those relationships. The relationship between a parent and a child can only go downhill if the basic respect for the parent has not been created and maintained. Adultery clearly has enormous potential to destroy a marriage because it creates distrust where trust should be. Trust is one of the foundational blocks of the marriage relationship.

While many would like to say that these Commandments are limiting, confining and outdated, in reality, they provide the basis for a society to function harmoniously. Only when a culture places limits on itself, is it able to prosper. Followed correctly, these Commandments provide safety and freedom, the same way a fish functions best within the confines of water. In the water it lives and prospers. On land it dies.

20:3 *no other gods.* God is not to be viewed as one god among many, or even as the highest among many. He is the one and only.

20:4 *not make . . . any likeness.* This command has often been misunderstood as a prohibition against all kinds of art. In fact, God used many "likenesses" of created things to beautify His tabernacle, including carved images and woven pictures. The prohibition was not against art, but against attempting to "picture" God. Any statue, icon, painting, or image of any sort which is meant to be a representation of God can only detract from His glory. God does not want

His people to worship a picture of "what He might look like," He wants all our worship for Himself alone.

20:5 *a jealous God.* In other words, He has a zeal for the truth that He alone is God, and He is jealous of any rivals.

20:6 *showing mercy to thousands.* The contrasting of the phrases "third and fourth generations" (v. 5) with "thousands" demonstrates that God's mercy is greater than His wrath. The lingering effects of righteousness will last far longer than the lingering effects of wrath.

20:7 *in vain.* Using God's name in vain is trivializing His name by regarding it as insignificant, trying to advance evil purposes by coaxing God to violate His character and purposes, or even simply using it thoughtlessly, without any attempt to realize of whom we are speaking.

20:8–11 *Remember the Sabbath day.* The word Sabbath means "rest." The command to rest and remember the Lord on the seventh day goes back to the pattern set at the time of creation (Gen. 2:2–3).

20:12 *Honor your father and your mother.* The term "honor" means "to treat with significance." Many times we equate "honor" with "obey," but in fact the two are not synonyms. Adult children or children of ungodly parents can find ways to honor when they cannot in good conscience obey.

20:14 *adultery.* God regards the sanctity of marriage as a sacred trust similar to the sanctity of life (v. 13). The marriage relationship is a symbol of God's faithfulness to us.

20:16 *false witness.* This command is an essential foundation for a just and effective judicial system.

20:3 d Jer. 25:6; 35:15 **20:4** e Deut. 4:15–19; 27:15 **20:5** f Is. 44:15, 19 g Deut. 4:24 h Num. 14:18, 33 **20:6** i Deut. 7:9 **20:7** j Lev. 19:12 k Mic. 6:11 **20:8** l Lev. 26:2 **20:9** m Luke 13:14 **20:10** n Gen. 2:2, 3 o Neh. 13:16–19 **20:11** p Ex. 31:17 **20:12** q Lev. 19:3 r Deut. 5:16, 33; 6:2; 11:8, 9 **20:13** s Rom. 13:9 **20:14** t Matt. 5:27 u Deut. 5:18 **20:15** v Lev. 19:11, 13 **20:16** w Deut. 5:20 **20:17** x [Eph. 5:3, 5] y [Matt. 5:28]

The People Afraid of God's Presence

18Now zall the people awitnessed the thunderings, the lightning flashes, the sound of the trumpet, and the mountain bsmoking; and when the people saw it, they trembled and stood afar off. 19Then they said to Moses, c"You speak with us, and we will hear; but dlet not God speak with us, lest we die."

20And Moses said to the people, e"Do not fear; ffor God has come to test you, and gthat His fear may be before you, so that you may not sin." 21So the people stood afar off, but Moses drew near hthe thick darkness where God was.

The Law of the Altar

22Then the LORD said to Moses, "Thus you shall say to the children of Israel: 'You have seen that I have talked with you ifrom heaven. 23You shall not make anything to be jwith Me—gods of silver or gods of gold you shall not make for yourselves. 24An altar of kearth you shall make for Me, and you shall sacrifice on it your burnt offerings and your peace offerings, lyour sheep and your oxen. In every mplace where I record My name I will come to you, and I will nbless you. 25And oif you make Me an altar of stone, you shall not build it of hewn stone; for if you puse your tool on it, you have profaned it. 26Nor shall you go up by steps to My altar, that your qnakedness may not be exposed on it.'

The Law Concerning Servants

21 "Now these are the judgments which you shall aset before them: 2bIf you buy a Hebrew servant, he shall serve six years; and in the seventh he shall go out free and pay nothing. 3If he comes in by himself, he shall go out by himself; if he comes in married, then his wife shall go out with him. 4If his master has given him a wife, and she has borne him sons or daughters, the wife and her children shall be her master's, and he shall go out by himself. 5cBut if the servant plainly says, 'I love my master, my wife, and my children; I will not go out free,' 6then his master shall bring him to the djudges. He shall also bring him to the door, or to the doorpost, and his master shall pierce his ear with an awl; and he shall serve him forever.

7"And if a man esells his daughter to be a female slave, she shall not go out as the male slaves do. 8If she does not please her master, who has betrothed her to himself, then he shall let her be redeemed. He shall have no right to sell her to a foreign people, since he has dealt deceitfully with her. 9And if he has betrothed her to his son, he shall deal with her according to the custom of daughters. 10If he takes another wife, he shall not diminish her food, her clothing, fand her marriage rights. 11And if he does not do these three for her, then she shall go out free, without paying money.

The Law Concerning Violence

12g"He who strikes a man so that he dies shall surely be put to death. 13However, hif he did not lie in wait, but God idelivered him into his hand, then jI will appoint for you a place where he may flee.

14"But if a man acts with kpremeditation against his neighbor, to kill him by treachery, lyou shall take him from My altar, that he may die.

15"And he who strikes his father or his mother shall surely be put to death.

16m"He who kidnaps a man and nsells him, or if he is ofound in his hand, shall surely be put to death.

17"And phe who curses his father or his mother shall surely be put to death.

18"If men contend with each other, and one strikes the other with a stone or with his fist, and he does not die but is confined to his bed, 19if he rises again and walks about outside qwith his staff, then he who struck him shall be acquitted. He shall only pay for the loss of his time, and shall provide for him to be thoroughly healed.

20"And if a man beats his male or female servant with a rod, so that he dies under his hand, he shall surely be punished. 21Notwithstanding, if he remains alive a day or

---

20:20 *His fear.* God did not want His people to live in terror of Him, as though He were an irrational, uncontrolled, violent force, ready to be unleashed on innocent people without provocation. Rather, God wanted His people to respect the obvious hazards of wanton sin. Appropriate fear of God in this sense would make them circumspect, reverent, obedient, and worshipful, so that they might not sin.

20:26 *your nakedness.* The pagan worship of the Canaanites involved sexually perverse acts. Nothing obscene or unseemly was permitted in the pure worship of the living God.

21:1 *the judgments.* Also translated "ordinances," this word describes God's response to a specific action, something like an umpire's call. The judgments of God set forth here are responses to specific situations; the Ten Commandments are more general laws, a code for living rather than a response to a certain problem.

20:18 z Heb. 12:18, 19 a Rev. 1:10, 12 b Ex. 19:16, 18 **20:19** c Heb. 12:19 d Deut. 5:5, 23–27 **20:20** e [Is. 41:10, 13] f [Deut. 13:3] g Is. 8:13 **20:21** h Ex. 19:16 **20:22** i Deut. 4:36; 5:24, 26 **20:23** j Ex. 32:1, 2, 4 **20:24** k Ex. 20:25; 27:1–8 l Ex. 24:5 m 2 Chr. 6:6 n Gen. 12:2 **20:25** o Deut. 27:5 p Josh. 8:30, 31 **20:26** q Ex. 28:42, 43 **21:1** a Deut. 4:14; 6:1 **21:2** b Jer. 34:14 **21:5** c Deut. 15:16, 17 **21:6** d Ex. 12:12; 22:8, 9 **21:7** e Neh. 5:5 **21:10** f [1 Cor. 7:3, 5] **21:12** g [Matt. 26:52] **21:13** h Deut. 19:4, 5 i 1 Sam. 24:4, 10, 18 j Num. 35:11 **21:14** k Deut. 19:11, 12 l 1 Kin. 2:28–34 **21:16** m Deut. 24:7 n Gen. 37:28 o Ex. 22:4 **21:17** p Mark 7:10 **21:19** q 2 Sam. 3:29

two, he shall not be punished; for he *is* his 'property.

²²"If men fight, and hurt a woman with child, so that she gives birth prematurely, yet no harm follows, he shall surely be punished accordingly as the woman's husband imposes on him; and he shall ˢpay as the judges *determine.* ²³But if *any* harm follows, then you shall give life for life, ²⁴teye for eye, tooth for tooth, hand for hand, foot for foot, ²⁵burn for burn, wound for wound, stripe for stripe.

²⁶"If a man strikes the eye of his male or female servant, and destroys it, he shall let him go free for the sake of his eye. ²⁷And if he knocks out the tooth of his male or female servant, he shall let him go free for the sake of his tooth.

Animal Control Laws

²⁸"If an ox gores a man or a woman to death, then ᵘthe ox shall surely be stoned, and its flesh shall not be eaten; but the owner of the ox *shall be* acquitted. ²⁹But if the ox tended to thrust with its horn in times past, and it has been made known to his owner, and he has not kept it confined, so that it has killed a man or a woman, the ox shall be stoned and its owner also shall be put to death. ³⁰If there is imposed on him a sum of money, then he shall pay ᵛto redeem his life, whatever is imposed on him. ³¹Whether it has gored a son or gored a daughter, according to this judgment it shall be done to him. ³²If the ox gores a male or female servant, he shall give to their master ʷthirty shekels of silver, and the ˣox shall be stoned.

³³"And if a man opens a pit, or if a man digs a pit and does not cover it, and an ox or a donkey falls in it, ³⁴the owner of the pit shall make *it* good; he shall give money to their owner, but the dead *animal* shall be his. ³⁵"If one man's ox hurts another's, so that it dies, then they shall sell the live ox and divide the money from it; and the dead ox they shall also divide. ³⁶Or if it was known that the ox tended to thrust in time past, and its owner has not kept it confined, he shall surely pay ox for ox, and the dead animal shall be his own.

Responsibility for Property

22 "If a man steals an ox or a sheep, and slaughters it or sells it, he shall

ᵃrestore five oxen for an ox and four sheep for a sheep. ²If the thief is found ᵇbreaking in, and he is struck so that he dies, *there shall be* ᶜno guilt for his bloodshed. ³If the sun has risen on him, *there shall be* guilt for his bloodshed. He should make full restitution; if he has nothing, then he shall be ᵈsold for his theft. ⁴If the theft is certainly ᵉfound alive in his hand, whether it is an ox or donkey or sheep, he shall ᶠrestore double.

⁵"If a man causes a field or vineyard to be grazed, and lets loose his animal, and it feeds in another man's field, he shall make restitution from the best of his own field and the best of his own vineyard.

⁶"If fire breaks out and catches in thorns, so that stacked grain, standing grain, or the field is consumed, he who kindled the fire shall surely make restitution.

⁷"If a man ᵍdelivers to his neighbor money or articles to keep, and it is stolen out of the man's house, ʰif the thief is found, he shall pay double. ⁸If the thief is not found, then the master of the house shall be brought to the ⁱjudges *to see* whether he has put his hand into his neighbor's goods.

⁹"For any kind of trespass, *whether it concerns* an ox, a donkey, a sheep, or clothing, *or* for any kind of lost thing which *another* claims to be his, the ʲcause of both parties shall come before the judges; *and* whomever the judges condemn shall pay double to his neighbor. ¹⁰If a man delivers to his neighbor a donkey, an ox, a sheep, or any animal to keep, and it dies, is hurt, or driven away, no one seeing *it,* ¹¹then an ᵏoath of the LORD shall be between them both, that he has not put his hand into his neighbor's goods; and the owner of it shall accept *that,* and he shall not make *it* good. ¹²But ˡif, in fact, it is stolen from him, he shall make restitution to the owner of it. ¹³If it is ᵐtorn to pieces *by a beast, then* he shall bring it as evidence, *and* he shall not make good what was torn.

¹⁴"And if a man borrows *anything* from his neighbor, and it becomes injured or dies, the owner of it not *being* with it, he shall surely make *it* good. ¹⁵If its owner *was* with it, he shall not make *it* good; if it *was* hired, it came for its hire.

Moral and Ceremonial Principles

¹⁶ⁿ"If a man entices a virgin who is not betrothed, and lies with her, he shall surely

---

21:24 eye for eye, tooth for tooth. Here we encounter the best known statement of the "law of retaliation." The idea here is not to foster revenge, but to curtail it. The natural, sinful human response is "a head for an eye, a jaw for a tooth, an arm for a hand." This law says *"no more than* eye for eye, tooth for tooth."

22:1–4 the sun has risen on him. There is a difference between struggling with an intruder at the moment when he is caught red-handed, and hunting him up in order to kill him later on. The law made a

distinction between self-defense and murder as retaliation.

21:21 ʳLev. 25:44–46   **21:22** ˢEx. 18:21, 22; 21:30   **21:24** ᵗLev. 24:20   **21:28** ᵘGen. 9:5   **21:30** ᵛNum. 35:31   **21:32** ʷZech. 11:12, 13 ˣEx. 21:28   **22:1** ᵃ2 Sam. 12:6   **22:2** ᵇMatt. 6:19; 24:43 ᶜNum. 35:27   **22:3** ᵈEx. 21:2   **22:4** ᵉEx. 21:16 ᶠProv. 6:31   **22:7** ᵍLev. 6:1–7 ʰEx. 22:4   **22:8** ⁱEx. 21:6, 22; 22:28   **22:9** ʲDeut. 25:1   **22:11** ᵏHeb. 6:16   **22:12** ˡGen. 31:39   **22:13** ᵐGen. 31:39   **22:16** ⁿDeut. 22:28, 29

pay the bride-price for her *to be* his wife. [17]If her father utterly refuses to give her to him, he shall pay money according to the [o]bride-price of virgins.

[18][p]"You shall not permit a sorceress to live.

[19][q]"Whoever lies with an animal shall surely be put to death.

[20][r]"He who sacrifices to *any* god, except to the LORD only, he shall be utterly destroyed.

[21][s]"You shall neither mistreat a stranger nor oppress him, for you were strangers in the land of Egypt.

[22][t]"You shall not afflict any widow or fatherless child. [23]If you afflict them in any way, *and* they [u]cry at all to Me, I will surely [v]hear their cry; [24]and My [w]wrath will become hot, and I will kill you with the sword; [x]your wives shall be widows, and your children fatherless.

[25][y]"If you lend money to *any of* My people *who are* poor among you, you shall not be like a moneylender to him; you shall not charge him [z]interest. [26][a]If you ever take your neighbor's garment as a pledge, you shall return it to him before the sun goes down. [27]For that *is* his only covering, it *is* his garment for his skin. What will he sleep in? And it will be that when he cries to Me, I will hear, for I *am* [b]gracious.

[28][c]"You shall not revile God, nor curse a [d]ruler of your people.

[29]"You shall not delay *to offer* [e]the first of your ripe produce and your juices. [f]The firstborn of your sons you shall give to Me. [30][g]Likewise you shall do with your oxen *and* your sheep. It shall be with its mother [h]seven days; on the eighth day you shall give it to Me.

[31]"And you shall be [i]holy men to Me: [j]you shall not eat meat torn *by beasts* in the field; you shall throw it to the dogs.

Justice for All

23 "You [a]shall not circulate a false report. Do not put your hand with the wicked to be an [b]unrighteous witness. [2][c]You shall not follow a crowd to do evil; [d]nor shall you testify in a dispute so as to turn aside after

many to pervert *justice.* [3]You shall not show partiality to a [e]poor man in his dispute.

[4][f]"If you meet your enemy's ox or his donkey going astray, you shall surely bring it back to him again. [5][g]If you see the donkey of one who hates you lying under its burden, and you would refrain from helping it, you shall surely help him with it.

[6][h]"You shall not pervert the judgment of your poor in his dispute. [7][i]Keep yourself far from a false matter; [j]do not kill the innocent and righteous. For [k]I will not justify the wicked. [8]And [l]you [m]shall take no bribe, for a bribe blinds the discerning and perverts the words of the righteous.

[9]"Also you shall not oppress a stranger, for you know the heart of a stranger, because you were strangers in the land of Egypt.

The Law of Sabbaths

[10][n]"Six years you shall sow your land and gather in its produce, [11]but the seventh *year* you shall let it rest and lie fallow, that the poor of your people may eat; and what they leave, the beasts of the field may eat. In like manner you shall do with your vineyard *and* your olive grove. [12][o]Six days you shall do your work, and on the seventh day you shall rest, that your ox and your donkey may rest, and the son of your female servant and the stranger may be refreshed.

[13]"And in all that I have said to you, [p]be circumspect and [q]make no mention of the name of other gods, nor let it be heard from your mouth.

Three Annual Feasts

[14][r]"Three times you shall keep a feast to Me in the year: [15][s]You shall keep the Feast of Unleavened Bread (you shall eat unleavened bread seven days, as I commanded you, at the time appointed in the month of Abib, for in it you came out of Egypt; [t]none shall appear before Me empty); [16][u]and [v]the Feast of Harvest, the firstfruits of your labors which you have sown in the field; and the Feast of Ingathering at the end of the year, when you have gathered in *the fruit of* your labors from the field.

22:18 *You shall not permit a sorceress to live.* The Bible does not record any executions of sorcerers or sorceresses, but it does recount the deadly consequences of false worship (ch. 32; Num. 25).

23:1 *false report.* Malicious talk is everywhere condemned in Scripture (see James 3:1–12).

23:3 *show partiality to a poor man.* God's support of the poor did not overrule His justice. Here God anticipated that some would use poverty as an excuse for greedy, even criminal activity.

23:11 *rest and lie fallow.* Letting the land rest allowed the poor to glean any produce that might grow during the fallow year. It also gave the land time to rejuvenate for greater productivity in subsequent years. The year of rest was an act of faith, for the Israelites would have to trust God to meet their needs.

22:17 [o] Gen. 34:12   **22:18** [p] 1 Sam. 28:3–10   **22:19** [q] Lev. 18:23; 20:15, 16   **22:20** [r] Ex. 32:8; 34:15   **22:21** [s] Deut. 10:19   **22:22** [t] [James 1:27]   **22:23** [u] [Luke 18:7] [v] Ps. 18:6   **22:24** [w] Ps. 69:24 [x] Ps. 109:9   **22:25** [y] Lev. 25:35–37 [z] Ps. 15:5   **22:26** [a] Deut. 24:6, 10–13   **22:27** [b] Ex. 34:6, 7   **22:28** [c] Eccl. 10:20 [d] Acts 23:5   **22:29** [e] Ex. 23:16, 19 [f] Ex. 13:2, 12, 15   **22:30** [g] Deut. 15:19 [h] Lev. 22:27   **22:31** [i] Lev. 11:44; 19:2 [j] Ezek. 4:14   **23:1** [a] Ps. 101:5 [b] Deut. 19:16–21   **23:2** [c] Gen. 7:1 [d] Lev. 19:15   **23:3** [e] Deut. 1:17; 16:19   **23:4** [f] [Rom. 12:20]   **23:5** [g] Deut. 22:4   **23:6** [h] Eccl. 5:8   **23:7** [i] Eph. 4:25 [j] Matt. 27:4 [k] Rom. 1:18   **23:8** [l] Prov. 15:27; 17:8, 23 [m] Ex. 22:21   **23:10** [n] Lev. 25:1–7   **23:12** [o] Luke 13:14   **23:13** [p] 1 Tim. 4:16 [q] Josh. 23:7   **23:14** [r] Ex. 23:17; 34:22–24   **23:15** [s] Ex. 12:14–20 [t] Ex. 22:29; 34:20   **23:16** [u] Ex. 34:22 [v] Deut. 16:13

17w"Three times in the year all your males shall appear before the Lord GOD.*

18x"You shall not offer the blood of My sacrifice with yleavened bread; nor shall the fat of My sacrifice remain until morning. 19z The first of the firstfruits of your land you shall bring into the house of the LORD your God. aYou shall not boil a young goat in its mother's milk.

The Angel and the Promises

20b"Behold, I send an Angel before you to keep you in the way and to bring you into the place which I have prepared. 21Beware of Him and obey His voice; cdo not provoke Him, for He will dnot pardon your transgressions; for eMy name is in Him. 22But if you indeed obey His voice and do all that I speak, then fI will be an enemy to your enemies and an adversary to your adversaries. 23gFor My Angel will go before you and hbring you in to the Amorites and the Hittites and the Perizzites and the Canaanites and the Hivites and the Jebusites; and I will cut them off. 24You shall not ibow down to their gods, jnor serve them, knor do according to their works; kbut you shall utterly overthrow them and completely break down their sacred pillars.

25"So you shall lserve the LORD your God, and mHe will bless your bread and your water. And nI will take sickness away from the midst of you. 26oNo one shall suffer miscarriage or be barren in your land; I will pfulfill the number of your days.

27"I will send qMy fear before you, I will rcause confusion among all the people to whom you come, and will make all your enemies turn their backs to you. 28And sI will send hornets before you, which shall drive out the Hivite, the Canaanite, and the Hittite from before you. 29tI will not drive them out from before you in one year, lest the land become desolate and the beasts of the field become too numerous for you. 30Little by little I will drive them out from

before you, until you have increased, and you inherit the land. 31And uI will set your bounds from the Red Sea to the sea, Philistia, and from the desert to the River.* For I will vdeliver the inhabitants of the land into your hand, and you shall drive them out before you. 32wYou shall make no covenant with them, nor with their gods. 33They shall not dwell in your land, lest they make you sin against Me. For if you serve their gods, xit will surely be a snare to you."

Israel Affirms the Covenant

24 Now He said to Moses, "Come up to the LORD, you and Aaron, aNadab and Abihu, band seventy of the elders of Israel, and worship from afar. 2And Moses alone shall come near the LORD, but they shall not come near; nor shall the people go up with him."

3So Moses came and told the people all the words of the LORD and all the judgments. And all the people answered with one voice and said, c"All the words which the LORD has said we will do." 4And Moses dwrote all the words of the LORD. And he rose early in the morning, and built an altar at the foot of the mountain, and twelve epillars according to the twelve tribes of Israel. 5Then he sent young men of the children of Israel, who offered fburnt offerings and sacrificed peace offerings of oxen to the LORD. 6And Moses gtook half the blood and put it in basins, and half the blood he sprinkled on the altar. 7Then he htook the Book of the Covenant and read in the hearing of the people. And they said, "All that the LORD has said we will do, and be obedient." 8And Moses took the blood, sprinkled it on the people, and said, "This is ithe blood of the covenant which the LORD has made with you according to all these words."

---

* 23:17 Hebrew YHWH, usually translated LORD
* 23:31 Hebrew Nahar, the Euphrates

23:17 Lord GOD. Here two names for God, Adonai (translated as Lord), and Yahweh (translated as GOD), are used together. This expression emphasizes God's sovereignty.
23:20 Angel. The statement "My name is in Him" (v. 21) shows that this messenger is the Angel of the Lord, who is none other than God Himself; with the promise of His presence and protection comes the warning "obey His voice," for the Lord is a holy God who cannot dwell in the presence of sin. Obedience is the evidence of reality of the covenant relationship. The Angel of the Lord "encamps all around those who fear Him" (Ps. 34:7).
23:26 suffer miscarriage or be barren. God reminded His people that He was the one who controlled reproduction—not the fertility cults of the pagan Canaanites.
24:6 blood. This blood anticipated the death of the coming Messiah, Jesus. His blood could do what the blood of bulls and goats could never accomplish; His death opened the way for direct

communication with God (12:7; Rom. 3:23–26; Heb. 10:4,10).
24:8 the blood of the covenant. Just as their houses were protected from the Passover by the sign of blood (ch. 12), now the people were brought into a covenant relationship with the Lord with a sign of blood. This is a picture of our own relationship with God, brought about by the blood of Jesus (1 Pet. 1:2).

23:17 wDeut. 16:16 **23:18** xEx. 34:25 yDeut. 16:4
23:19 zDeut. 26:2, 10 aDeut. 14:21 **23:20** bEx. 3:2;
13:15; 14:19 **23:21** cPs. 78:40, 56 dDeut. 18:19 eIs.
9:6 **23:22** fDeut. 30:7 **23:23** gEx. 23:20 hJosh. 24:8,
11 **23:24** iEx. 20:5; 23:13, 33 jDeut. 12:30, 31 kNum.
33:52 **23:25** lDeut. 6:13 mDeut. 28:5 nEx. 15:26
23:26 oDeut. 7:14; 28:4 p1 Chr. 23:1 **23:27** qEx. 15:16
rDeut. 7:23 **23:28** sJosh. 24:12 **23:29** tDeut. 7:22
23:31 uGen. 15:18 vJosh. 21:44 **23:32** wEx. 34:12,
15 **23:33** xPs. 106:36 **24:1** aLev. 10:1, 2 bNum. 11:16
24:3 cEx. 19:8; 24:7 **24:4** dDeut. 31:9 eGen. 28:18
24:5 fEx. 18:12; 20:24 **24:6** gHeb. 9:18 **24:7** hHeb.
9:19 **24:8** i[Luke 22:20]

On the Mountain with God

⁹Then Moses went up, also Aaron, Nadab, and Abihu, and seventy of the elders of Israel, ¹⁰and they ʲsaw the God of Israel. And *there was* under His feet as it were a paved work of ᵏsapphire stone, and it was like ˡvery heavens in *its* clarity. ¹¹But on the nobles of the children of Israel He ᵐdid not lay His hand. So ⁿthey saw God, and they ᵒate and drank.

¹²Then the LORD said to Moses, ᵖ"Come up to Me on the mountain and be there; and I will give you ᑫtablets of stone, and the law and commandments which I have written, that you may teach them."

¹³So Moses arose with ʳhis assistant Joshua, and Moses went up to the mountain of God. ¹⁴And he said to the elders, "Wait here for us until we come back to you. Indeed, Aaron and ˢHur *are* with you. If any man has a difficulty, let him go to them." ¹⁵Then Moses went up into the mountain, and ᵗa cloud covered the mountain.

¹⁶Now ᵘthe glory of the LORD rested on Mount Sinai, and the cloud covered it six days. And on the seventh day He called to Moses out of the midst of the cloud. ¹⁷The sight of the glory of the LORD *was* like ᵛa consuming fire on the top of the mountain in the eyes of the children of Israel. ¹⁸So Moses went into the midst of the cloud and went up into the mountain. And ʷMoses was on the mountain forty days and forty nights.

Offerings for the Sanctuary

25 Then the LORD spoke to Moses, saying: ²"Speak to the children of Israel, that they bring Me an offering. ᵃFrom everyone who gives it willingly with his heart you shall take My offering. ³And this *is* the offering which you shall take from them: gold, silver, and bronze; ⁴blue, purple, and scarlet *thread,* fine linen, and goats' *hair;* ⁵ram skins dyed red, badger skins, and acacia wood; ⁶ᵇoil for the light, and ᶜspices for the anointing oil and for the sweet incense; ⁷onyx stones, and stones to be set in the ᵈephod and in the breastplate. ⁸And let them make Me a ᵉsanctuary, that ᶠI may dwell among them. ⁹According to all that I show you, *that is,* the pattern of the tabernacle and the pattern of all its furnishings, just so you shall make *it.*

The Ark of the Testimony

¹⁰ᵍ"And they shall make an ark of acacia wood; two and a half cubits *shall be* its length, a cubit and a half its width, and a cubit and a half its height. ¹¹And you shall overlay it with pure gold, inside and out you shall overlay it, and shall make on it a molding of ʰgold all around. ¹²You shall cast four rings of gold for it, and put *them* in its four corners; two rings *shall be* on one side, and two rings on the other side. ¹³And you shall make poles *of* acacia wood, and overlay them with gold. ¹⁴You shall put the poles into the rings on the sides of the ark, that the ark may be carried by them. ¹⁵ⁱThe poles shall be in the rings of the ark; they shall not be taken from it. ¹⁶And you shall put into the ark ʲthe Testimony which I will give you.

¹⁷ᵏ"You shall make a mercy seat of pure gold; two and a half cubits *shall be* its length and a cubit and a half its width. ¹⁸And you shall make two cherubim of gold; of hammered work you shall make them at the two ends of the mercy seat. ¹⁹Make one cherub at one end, and the other cherub at the other end; you shall make the cherubim at the two ends of it of one *piece* with the mercy seat. ²⁰And ˡthe cherubim shall stretch out *their* wings above, covering the mercy seat with their wings, and they shall face one another; the faces of the cherubim *shall be* toward the mercy seat. ²¹ᵐYou shall put the mercy seat on top of the ark, and ⁿin the ark you shall put

---

24:9–17 God of Israel. This vision of God was a great privilege. The elders of the people saw God standing on a structure resembling a transparent sapphire platform, which emphasized His grandeur. Blue was one of the colors favored by some members of ancient Near Eastern royalty. God's glory is the manifestation of all His divine characteristics, including power and holiness, which for Israel were represented by the billowing consuming fire (Heb. 12:29).

24:12 Come up to Me. Only Moses could draw near to God at that time. Today, we are all called to draw near to God through Jesus (see Heb. 4:14–16).

25:2 everyone who gives it willingly. God does not need the gifts of His people, but He desires us to give to Him as an expression of true worship.

25:9 the pattern. The language of these verses suggests that there is a heavenly pattern that the earthly tabernacle was designed to resemble (see v. 40; 26:30; 27:8; Acts 7:44; Heb. 8:5).

25:10 ark. In contrast to the idolatry of Israel's neighbors, the shrine of the living God had no likeness or idol of any sort (20:2–6). **cubit.** This measurement was represented by the length of a man's arm from elbow to extended middle finger. The commonly accepted estimate for the cubit is eighteen inches. Therefore, the ark was about four feet long and two and one quarter feet wide and high.

25:17 mercy seat. This English phrase translates a Hebrew noun derived from the verb meaning "atone for," "to cover over," or "to make propitiation." The mercy seat was the lid of the ark, the place where God's spirit rested.

24:10 ʲ[John 1:18; 6:46] ᵏEzek. 1:26 ˡMatt. 17:2
24:11 ᵐEx. 19:21 ⁿGen. 32:30 ᵒ1 Cor. 10:18 **24:12** ᵖEx. 24:2, 15 ᑫEx. 31:18; 32:15 **24:13** ʳEx. 32:17 **24:14** ˢEx. 17:10, 12 **24:15** ᵗEx. 19:9 **24:16** ᵘEx. 16:10; 33:18 **24:17** ᵛDeut. 4:26, 36; 9:3 **24:18** ʷEx. 34:28
25:2 ᵃEx. 35:4–9, 21 **25:6** ᵇEx. 27:20 ᶜEx. 30:23
25:7 ᵈEx. 28:4, 6–14 **25:8** ᵉHeb. 9:1, 2 ᶠ[2 Cor. 6:16]
25:10 ᵍEx. 37:1–9 **25:11** ʰEx. 37:2 **25:15** ⁱ1 Kin. 8:8 **25:16** ʲHeb. 9:4 **25:17** ᵏEx. 37:6 **25:20** ˡ1 Kin. 8:7
25:21 ᵐEx. 26:34; 40:20 ⁿEx. 25:16

the Testimony that I will give you. ²²And ^othere I will meet with you, and I will speak with you from above the mercy seat, from ^pbetween the two cherubim which *are* on the ark of the Testimony, about everything which I will give you in commandment to the children of Israel.

The Table for the Showbread

²³^q"You shall also make a table of acacia wood; two cubits *shall be* its length, a cubit its width, and a cubit and a half its height. ²⁴And you shall overlay it with pure gold, and make a molding of gold all around. ²⁵You shall make for it a frame of a handbreadth all around, and you shall make a gold molding for the frame all around. ²⁶And you shall make for it four rings of gold, and put the rings on the four corners that *are* at its four legs. ²⁷The rings shall be close to the frame, as holders for the poles to bear the table. ²⁸And you shall make the poles of acacia wood, and overlay them with gold, that the table may be carried with them. ²⁹You shall make ^rits dishes, its pans, its pitchers, and its bowls for pouring. You shall make them of pure gold. ³⁰And you shall set the ^sshowbread on the table before Me always.

The Gold Lampstand

³¹^t"You shall also make a lampstand of pure gold; the lampstand shall be of hammered work. Its shaft, its branches, its bowls, its *ornamental* knobs, and flowers shall be *of one piece*. ³²And six branches shall come out of its sides: three branches of the lampstand out of one side, and three branches of the lampstand out of the other side. ³³^uThree bowls *shall be* made like almond *blossoms* on one branch, *with* an *ornamental* knob and a flower, and three bowls made like almond *blossoms* on the other branch, *with* an *ornamental* knob and a flower—and so for the six branches that come out of the lampstand. ³⁴^vOn the lampstand itself four bowls *shall be* made like almond *blossoms, each with* its *ornamental* knob and flower. ³⁵And *there shall be* a knob under the *first* two branches of the same, a knob under the *second* two

branches of the same, and a knob under the *third* two branches of the same, according to the six branches that extend from the lampstand. ³⁶Their knobs and their branches *shall be of one piece;* all of it *shall be* one hammered piece of pure gold. ³⁷You shall make seven lamps for it, and ^wthey shall arrange its lamps so that they ^xgive light in front of it. ³⁸And its wick-trimmers and their trays *shall be* of pure gold. ³⁹It shall be made of a talent of pure gold, with all these utensils. ⁴⁰And ^ysee to it that you make *them* according to the pattern which was shown you on the mountain.

The Tabernacle

26 "Moreover ^ayou shall make the tabernacle *with* ten curtains *of* fine woven linen and blue, purple, and scarlet *thread;* with artistic designs of cherubim you shall weave them. ²The length of each curtain *shall be* twenty-eight cubits, and the width of each curtain four cubits. And every one of the curtains shall have the same measurements. ³Five curtains shall be coupled to one another, and *the other* five curtains *shall be* coupled to one another. ⁴And you shall make loops of blue *yarn* on the edge of the curtain on the selvedge of *one* set, and likewise you shall do on the outer edge of *the other* curtain of the second set. ⁵Fifty loops you shall make in the one curtain, and fifty loops you shall make on the edge of the curtain that *is* on the end of the second set, that the loops may be clasped to one another. ⁶And you shall make fifty clasps of gold, and couple the curtains together with the clasps, so that it may be one tabernacle.

⁷^b"You shall also make curtains of goats' hair, to be a tent over the tabernacle. You shall make eleven curtains. ⁸The length of each curtain *shall be* thirty cubits, and the width of each curtain four cubits; and the eleven curtains shall all have the same measurements. ⁹And you shall couple five curtains by themselves and six curtains by themselves, and you shall double over the sixth curtain at the forefront of the tent. ¹⁰You shall make fifty loops on the edge of the curtain that is outermost in *one* set, and fifty loops on the edge of the curtain of

---

25:22 I will meet with you. God dwells with His people in the space-time reality in which He created them, and communicates with them in the language with which He endowed them. He is not aloof and He is not silent. His words are an extension of Himself and reflect His nature. They are altogether pure and without blemish, and they are fully authoritative. At the same time, His words reach out to man and are rooted in love, issued from the mercy seat. He speaks them Himself or has them spoken by His authority. He preserves them. He writes them or has them written under His superintendence. God is the ultimate Author of His own Word. This Word is and remains His living and abiding Voice.
25:29 pure gold. All of the implements for making bread were also to be costly and wonderfully

designed to physically represent their holiness. They were "set apart" to God.
25:30 the showbread. Twelve loaves representing the twelve tribes of Israel were placed in two rows with six loaves in each row (Lev. 24:5–9). It was called showbread because it was placed symbolically before the face of God.
25:39 talent. A talent weighed about 75 pounds.
26:1 tabernacle. The word tabernacle simply means "tent."

25:22 ᵒ Ex. 29:42, 43; 30:6, 36   ᵖ Num. 7:89   25:23 �q Ex. 37:10–16   25:29 ʳ Ex. 37:16   25:30 ˢ Lev. 24:5–9
25:31 ᵗ Zech. 4:2   25:33 ᵘ Ex. 37:19   25:34 ᵛ Ex. 37:20–22   25:37 ʷ Lev. 24:3, 4   ˣ Num. 8:2   25:40 ʸ [Heb. 8:5]
26:1 ᵃ Ex. 36:8–19   26:7 ᵇ Ex. 36:14

the second set. ¹¹And you shall make fifty bronze clasps, put the clasps into the loops, and couple the tent together, that it may be one. ¹²The remnant that remains of the curtains of the tent, the half curtain that remains, shall hang over the back of the tabernacle. ¹³And a cubit on one side and a cubit on the other side, of what remains of the length of the curtains of the tent, shall hang over the sides of the tabernacle, on this side and on that side, to cover it.

¹⁴c"You shall also make a covering of ram skins dyed red for the tent, and a covering of badger skins above that.

¹⁵"And for the tabernacle you shall ^dmake the boards of acacia wood, standing upright. ¹⁶Ten cubits *shall be* the length of a board, and a cubit and a half *shall be* the width of each board. ¹⁷Two tenons *shall be* in each board for binding one to another. Thus you shall make for all the boards of the tabernacle. ¹⁸And you shall make the boards for the tabernacle, twenty boards for the south side. ¹⁹You shall make forty sockets of silver under the twenty boards: two sockets under each of the boards for its two tenons. ²⁰And for the second side of the tabernacle, the north side, *there shall be* twenty boards ²¹and their forty sockets of silver: two sockets under each of the boards. ²²For the far side of the tabernacle, westward, you shall make six boards. ²³And you shall also make two boards for the two back corners of the tabernacle. ²⁴They shall be coupled together at the bottom and they shall be coupled together at the top by one ring. Thus it shall be for both of them. They shall be for the two corners. ²⁵So there shall be eight boards with their sockets of silver—sixteen sockets—two sockets under each of the boards.

²⁶"And you shall make bars of acacia wood: five for the boards on one side of the tabernacle, ²⁷five bars for the boards on the other side of the tabernacle, and five bars for the boards of the side of the tabernacle, for the far side westward. ²⁸The ^emiddle bar shall pass through the midst of the boards from end to end. ²⁹You shall overlay the boards with gold, make their rings of gold *as* holders for the bars, and overlay the bars with gold. ³⁰And you shall raise up the tabernacle ^faccording to its pattern which you were shown on the mountain.

^{31g}"You shall make a veil woven of blue, purple, and scarlet *thread*, and fine woven linen. It shall be woven with an artistic design of cherubim. ³²You shall hang it upon the four pillars of acacia *wood* overlaid with gold. Their hooks *shall be* gold, upon

four sockets of silver. ³³And you shall hang the veil from the clasps. Then you shall bring ^hthe ark of the Testimony in there, behind the veil. The veil shall be a divider for you between ⁱthe holy *place* and the Most Holy. ^{34j}You shall put the mercy seat upon the ark of the Testimony in the Most Holy. ^{35k}You shall set the table outside the veil, and ^lthe lampstand across from the table on the side of the tabernacle toward the south; and you shall put the table on the north side.

^{36m}"You shall make a screen for the door of the tabernacle, *woven of* blue, purple, and scarlet *thread*, and fine woven linen, made by a weaver. ³⁷And you shall make for the screen ⁿfive pillars of acacia *wood*, and overlay them with gold; their hooks *shall be* gold, and you shall cast five sockets of bronze for them.

The Altar of Burnt Offering

27 "You shall make ^aan altar of acacia wood, five cubits long and five cubits wide—the altar shall be square—and its height *shall be* three cubits. ²You shall make its horns on its four corners; its horns shall be of one piece with it. And you shall overlay it with bronze. ³Also you shall make its pans to receive its ashes, and its shovels and its basins and its forks and its firepans; you shall make all its utensils of bronze. ⁴You shall make a grate for it, a network of bronze; and on the network you shall make four bronze rings at its four corners. ⁵You shall put it under the rim of the altar beneath, that the network may be midway up the altar. ⁶And you shall make poles for the altar, poles of acacia wood, and overlay them with bronze. ⁷The poles shall be put in the rings, and the poles shall be on the two sides of the altar to bear it. ⁸You shall make it hollow with boards; ^bas it was shown you on the mountain, so shall they make *it*.

The Court of the Tabernacle

⁹c"You shall also make the court of the tabernacle. For the south side *there shall be* hangings for the court *made of* fine woven linen, one hundred cubits long for one side. ¹⁰And its twenty pillars and their twenty sockets *shall be* bronze. The hooks of the pillars and their bands *shall be* silver. ¹¹Likewise along the length of the north side *there shall be* hangings one hundred *cubits* long, with its twenty pillars and their twenty sockets of bronze, and the hooks of the pillars and their bands of silver.

27:9–18 *court of the tabernacle.* The courtyard separated the ceremonies of worship from common areas. It was arranged to keep people and stray animals from wandering into the tabernacle. Entering the tent could only be a deliberate act.

26:14 ^c Ex. 35:7, 23; 36:19   **26:15** ^d Ex. 36:20–34   **26:28** ^e Ex. 36:33   **26:30** ^f Acts 7:44   **26:31** ^g Matt. 27:51   **26:33** ^h Ex. 25:10–16; 40:21 ⁱ Heb. 9:2, 3   **26:34** ^j Ex. 25:17–22; 40:20   **26:35** ^k Ex. 40:22 ^l Ex. 40:24   **26:36** ^m Ex. 36:37   **26:37** ⁿ Ex. 36:38   **27:1** ^a Ex. 38:1   **27:8** ^b Ex. 25:40; 26:30   **27:9** ^c Ex. 38:9–20

12"And along the width of the court on
the west side *shall be* hangings of fifty
cubits, with their ten pillars and their ten
sockets. 13The width of the court on the
east side *shall be* fifty cubits. 14The hangings on *one* side *of the gate shall be* fifteen
cubits, *with* their three pillars and their
three sockets. 15And on the other side *shall*
be hangings of fifteen *cubits, with* their
three pillars and their three sockets.
16"For the gate of the court *there shall be*
a screen twenty cubits long, *woven of* blue,
purple, and scarlet *thread,* and fine woven
linen, made by a weaver. It *shall have* four
pillars and four sockets. 17All the pillars
around the court shall have bands of silver; their [d]hooks *shall be* of silver and their
sockets of bronze. 18The length of the court
shall be one hundred cubits, the width fifty throughout, and the height five cubits,
made of fine woven linen, and its sockets of
bronze. 19All the utensils of the tabernacle
for all its service, all its pegs, and all the
pegs of the court, *shall be* of bronze.

The Care of the Lampstand

20"And [e]you shall command the children of Israel that they bring you pure oil
of pressed olives for the light, to cause the
lamp to burn continually. 21In the tabernacle of meeting, [f]outside the veil which *is*
before the Testimony, [g]Aaron and his sons
shall tend it from evening until morning
before the LORD. [h]*It shall be* a statute forever to their generations on behalf of the
children of Israel.

Garments for the Priesthood

28 "Now take [a]Aaron your brother, and
his sons with him, from among the
children of Israel, that he may minister to
Me as [b]priest, Aaron *and* Aaron's sons:
[c]Nadab, Abihu, [d]Eleazar, and Ithamar.
2And [e]you shall make holy garments for
Aaron your brother, for glory and for beauty. 3So [f]you shall speak to all *who are* gifted
artisans, [g]whom I have filled with the spirit of wisdom, that they may make Aaron's
garments, to consecrate him, that he may
minister to Me as priest. 4And these *are* the
garments which they shall make: [h]a breastplate, [i]an ephod,* [j]a robe, [k]a skillfully woven tunic, a turban, and [l]a sash. So they
shall make holy garments for Aaron your
brother and his sons, that he may minister
to Me as priest.

The Ephod

5"They shall take the gold, blue, purple, and scarlet *thread,* and the fine linen,
6[m]and they shall make the ephod of gold,
blue, purple, *and* scarlet *thread,* and fine
woven linen, artistically worked. 7It shall
have two shoulder straps joined at its two
edges, and *so* it shall be joined together.
8And the intricately woven band of the
ephod, which *is* on it, shall be of the same
workmanship, *made of* gold, blue, purple,
and scarlet *thread,* and fine woven linen.
9"Then you shall take two onyx [n]stones
and engrave on them the names of the
sons of Israel: 10six of their names on one
stone and six names on the other stone, in
order of their [o]birth. 11With the work of an
[p]engraver in stone, *like* the engravings of
a signet, you shall engrave the two stones
with the names of the sons of Israel. You
shall set them in settings of gold. 12And you
shall put the two stones on the shoulders of
the ephod *as* memorial stones for the sons
of Israel. So [q]Aaron shall bear their names
before the LORD on his two shoulders [r]as a
memorial. 13You shall also make settings
of gold, 14and you shall make two chains of
pure gold like braided cords, and fasten the
braided chains to the settings.

The Breastplate

15[s]"You shall make the breastplate of
judgment. Artistically woven according to
the workmanship of the ephod you shall
make it: of gold, blue, purple, and scarlet
thread, and fine woven linen, you shall
make it. 16It shall be doubled into a square:
a span *shall be* its length, and a span *shall*
be its width. 17[t]And you shall put settings of
stones in it, four rows of stones: *The first* row
shall be a sardius, a topaz, and an emerald;

* 28:4 That is, an ornamented vest

27:20 *pure oil of pressed olives.* All that was used in the tabernacle and sacrifices must be pure and without blemish in order to honor God's holiness. ***the lamp to burn continually.*** The oil for the lampstand was the gift of the children of Israel. It had to be pure oil, as a symbol of our need to call upon the Lord from a pure heart (2 Tim. 2:22). The lamps were to burn continuously, a reminder of the perpetual need of the sinner for the light of God's word, "a lamp to my feet and a light to my path" (Ps. 119:105).

28:3 *all who are gifted artisans.* This expression literally means "those who are wise at heart." The same expression is used of the skillful women who did the weaving (35:25).

28:5–14 *ephod.* The ephod has been described as a cape or vest made of fine linen with brilliant colors. Its two main sections covered the chest and back, with seams at the shoulders and a band at the waist.

28:16 *span.* The span was determined as the length from the tip of the thumb to the tip of the small finger on an outstretched hand. It is generally estimated as nine inches, or half a cubit.

27:17 [d]Ex. 38:19 **27:20** [e]Lev. 24:1–4 **27:21** [f]Ex. 26:31, 33 [g]Ex. 30:8 [h]Lev. 3:17; 16:34 **28:1** [a]Num. 3:10; 18:7 [b]Heb. 5:4 [c]Lev. 10:1 [d]Ex. 6:23 **28:2** [e]Ex. 29:5, 29; 31:10; 39:1–31 **28:3** [f]Ex. 31:6; 36:1 [g]Ex. 31:3; 35:30, 31 **28:4** [h]Ex. 28:15 [i]Ex. 28:6 [j]Ex. 28:31 [k]Ex. 28:39 [l]Lev. 8:7 **28:6** [m]Ex. 39:2–7 **28:9** [n]Ex. 35:27 **28:10** [o]Gen. 29:31—30:24; 35:16–18 **28:11** [p]Ex. 35:35 **28:12** [q]Ex. 28:29, 30; 39:6, 7 [r]Josh. 4:7 **28:15** [s]Ex. 39:8–21 **28:17** [t]Ex. 39:10

this shall be the first row; 18the second row *shall be* a turquoise, a sapphire, and a diamond; 19the third row, a jacinth, an agate, and an amethyst; 20and the fourth row, a beryl, an onyx, and a jasper. They shall be set in gold settings. 21And the stones shall have the names of the sons of Israel, twelve according to their names, *like* the engravings of a signet, each one with its own name; they shall be according to the twelve tribes.

22"You shall make chains for the breastplate at the end, like braided cords of pure gold. 23And you shall make two rings of gold for the breastplate, and put the two rings on the two ends of the breastplate. 24Then you shall put the two braided *chains* of gold in the two rings which are on the ends of the breastplate; 25and the *other* two ends of the two braided *chains* you shall fasten to the two settings, and put them on the shoulder straps of the ephod in the front.

26"You shall make two rings of gold, and put them on the two ends of the breastplate, on the edge of it, which is on the inner side of the ephod. 27And two *other* rings of gold you shall make, and put them on the two shoulder straps, underneath the ephod toward its front, right at the seam above the intricately woven band of the ephod. 28They shall bind the breastplate by means of its rings to the rings of the ephod, using a blue cord, so that it is above the intricately woven band of the ephod, and so that the breastplate does not come loose from the ephod.

29"So Aaron shall ᵘbear the names of the sons of Israel on the breastplate of judgment over his heart, when he goes into the holy *place*, as a memorial before the Lᴏʀᴅ continually. 30And ᵛyou shall put in the breastplate of judgment the Urim and the Thummim,* and they shall be over Aaron's heart when he goes in before the Lᴏʀᴅ. So Aaron shall bear the judgment of the children of Israel over his heart before the Lᴏʀᴅ continually.

Other Priestly Garments

31ʷ"You shall make the robe of the ephod all of blue. 32There shall be an opening for his head in the middle of it; it shall have a woven binding all around its opening, like the opening in a coat of mail, so that it does not tear. 33And upon its hem you shall make pomegranates of blue, purple, and scarlet, all around its hem, and bells of gold between them all around: 34a golden bell and a pomegranate, a golden bell and a pomegranate, upon the hem of the robe all around. 35And it shall be upon Aaron when he ministers, and its sound will be heard when he goes into the holy *place* before the Lᴏʀᴅ and when he comes out, that he may not die.

36ˣ"You shall also make a plate of pure gold and engrave on it, *like* the engraving of a signet:

HOLINESS TO THE LORD.

37And you shall put it on a blue cord, that it may be on the turban; it shall be on the front of the turban. 38So it shall be on Aaron's forehead, that Aaron may ʸbear the iniquity of the holy things which the children of Israel hallow in all their holy gifts; and it shall always be on his forehead, that they may be ᶻaccepted before the Lᴏʀᴅ.

39"You shall ᵃskillfully weave the tunic of fine linen *thread*, you shall make the turban of fine linen, and you shall make the sash of woven work.

40ᵇ"For Aaron's sons you shall make tunics, and you shall make sashes for them. And you shall make hats for them, for glory and ᶜbeauty. 41So you shall put them on Aaron your brother and on his sons with him. You shall ᵈanoint them, ᵉconsecrate them, and sanctify them, that they may minister to Me as priests. 42And you shall make ᶠfor them linen trousers to cover their nakedness; they shall reach from the waist to the thighs. 43They shall be on Aaron and on his sons when they come into the tabernacle of meeting, or when they come near ᵍthe altar to minister in the holy *place*, that they ʰdo not incur iniquity and die. ⁱ*It shall be* a statute forever to him and his descendants after him.

Aaron and His Sons Consecrated

29 "And this is what you shall do to them to hallow them for ministering to Me as priests: ᵃTake one young bull and two

* **28:30** Literally *the Lights and the Perfections* (compare Leviticus 8:8)

28:30 the Urim and the Thummim. These translated Hebrew words mean "Lights" and "Perfections." Together their names may mean "perfect knowledge" or a similar idea. It is not known exactly what the Urim and Thummim were, or how they were used. Some have suggested that they were two stones used for the casting of lots.

28:42 trousers. The command to wear trousers protected the modesty of the priests. Given the sexually preoccupied worship of Israel's neighbors, this provision was decidedly countercultural.

29:1–9 hallow them. The outward purification process was used to symbolize the inward purity which was demanded of the priests of Israel, the

intermediaries between the people and their holy God. Obviously the priests were not perfectly pure; it was only God's gracious act of accepting blood sacrifices that allowed the priests to stand in His presence on behalf of the people. The outward washings of the priests showed that they were doing everything possible to live their lives in the way they

28:29 ᵘEx. 28:12   **28:30** ᵛLev. 8:8   **28:31** ʷEx. 39:22–26   **28:36** ˣEx. 39:30, 31   **28:38** ʸ[1 Pet. 2:24] ᶻLev. 1:4; 22:27; 23:11   **28:39** ᵃEx. 35:35; 39:27–29 **28:40** ᵇEzek. 44:17, 18 ᶜEx. 28:2   **28:41** ᵈLev. 10:7 ᵉLev. 8   **28:42** ᶠEx. 39:28   **28:43** ᵍEx. 20:26 ʰNum. 9:13; 18:22 ⁱEx. 27:21   **29:1** ᵃ[Heb. 7:26–28]

rams without blemish, 2 and [b]unleavened
bread, unleavened cakes mixed with oil,
and unleavened wafers anointed with oil
(you shall make them of wheat flour). 3 You
shall put them in one basket and bring
them in the basket, with the bull and the
two rams.
4 "And Aaron and his sons you shall
bring to the door of the tabernacle of meeting, [c]and you shall wash them with water.
5 [d]Then you shall take the garments, put
the tunic on Aaron, and the robe of the
ephod, the ephod, and the breastplate, and
gird him with the [e]intricately woven band
of the ephod. 6 [f]You shall put the turban on
his head, and put the holy crown on the turban. 7 And you shall take the anointing [g]oil,
pour *it* on his head, and anoint him. 8 Then
[h]you shall bring his sons and put tunics on
them. 9 And you shall gird them with sashes, Aaron and his sons, and put the hats on
them. [i]The priesthood shall be theirs for a
perpetual statute. So you shall [j]consecrate
Aaron and his sons.
10 "You shall also have the bull brought
before the tabernacle of meeting, and [k]Aar-
on and his sons shall put their hands on
the head of the bull. 11 Then you shall kill
the bull before the LORD, *by* the door of
the tabernacle of meeting. 12 You shall take
some of the blood of the bull and put *it* on
[l]the horns of the altar with your finger, and
[m]pour all the blood beside the base of the
altar. 13 And [n]you shall take all the fat that
covers the entrails, the fatty lobe *attached*
to the liver, and the two kidneys and the fat
that *is* on them, and burn *them* on the altar.
14 But [o]the flesh of the bull, with its skin and
its offal, you shall burn with fire outside
the camp. It *is* a sin offering.
15 [p]"You shall also take one ram, and
Aaron and his sons shall [q]put their hands
on the head of the ram; 16 and you shall kill
the ram, and you shall take its blood and
[r]sprinkle *it* all around on the altar. 17 Then
you shall cut the ram in pieces, wash its
entrails and its legs, and put *them* with its
pieces and with its head. 18 And you shall
burn the whole ram on the altar. It *is* a
[s]burnt offering to the LORD; it *is* a sweet
aroma, an offering made by fire to the
LORD.

19 [t]"You shall also take the other ram, and
Aaron and his sons shall put their hands on
the head of the ram. 20 Then you shall kill
the ram, and take some of its blood and put
it on the tip of the right ear of Aaron and
on the tip of the right ear of his sons, on
the thumb of their right hand and on the
big toe of their right foot, and sprinkle the
blood all around on the altar. 21 And you
shall take some of the blood that is on the
altar, and some of [u]the anointing oil, and
sprinkle *it* on Aaron and on his garments,
on his sons and on the garments of his sons
with him; and [v]he and his garments shall
be hallowed, and his sons and his sons'
garments with him.
22 "Also you shall take the fat of the ram,
the fat tail, the fat that covers the entrails,
the fatty lobe *attached to* the liver, the two
kidneys and the fat on them, the right thigh
(for it *is* a ram of consecration), 23 [w]one loaf
of bread, one cake *made with* oil, and one
wafer from the basket of the unleavened
bread that *is* before the LORD; 24 and you
shall put all these in the hands of Aaron
and in the hands of his sons, and you shall
[x]wave them *as* a wave offering before the
LORD. 25 [y]You shall receive them back from
their hands and burn *them* on the altar as
a burnt offering, as a sweet aroma before
the LORD. It *is* an offering made by fire to
the LORD.
26 "Then you shall take [z]the breast of the
ram of Aaron's consecration and wave it
as a wave offering before the LORD; and it
shall be your portion. 27 And from the ram
of the consecration you shall consecrate
[a]the breast of the wave offering which is
waved, and the thigh of the heave offering
which is raised, of *that* which *is* for Aaron
and of *that* which is for his sons. 28 It shall
be from the children of Israel *for* Aaron
and his sons [b]by a statute forever. For it is a
heave offering; [c]it shall be a heave offering
from the children of Israel from the sacrifices of their peace offerings, *that is*, their
heave offering to the LORD.
29 "And the [d]holy garments of Aaron
[e]shall be his sons' after him, [f]to be anointed in them and to be consecrated in them.
30 [g]That son who becomes priest in his
place shall put them on for [h]seven days,

---

had been commanded by God. Likewise, in the New Testament era, the only reason that Christians can stand before God as believer-priests is because God graciously accepts Christ's sacrifice on behalf of our sins.

29:9 *consecrate.* The verb translated *consecrate* in this verse literally means "to fill one's hand." A king was handed a rod as the symbol of his political power; so the hand of the priest was filled with spiritual power.

29:18 *burnt offering.* Aaron and his sons needed to offer sacrifices for themselves as much as for their fellow Israelites (Heb. 5:1–4).

29:24 *wave offering.* This offering made it clear that everything was owed to God, but some was received back as God's gift (Lev. 7:30; 10:14).

29:2 [b]Lev. 2:4; 6:19–23 **29:4** [c]Ex. 40:12 **29:5** [d]Ex. 28:2 [e]Ex. 28:8 **29:6** [f]Lev. 8:9 **29:7** [g]Ex. 25:6; 30:25–31 **29:8** [h]Ex. 28:39, 40 **29:9** [i]Num. 3:10; 18:7; 25:13 [j]Ex. 28:41 **29:10** [k]Lev. 1:4; 8:14 **29:12** [l]Lev. 8:15 [m]Ex. 27:2; 30:2 **29:13** [n]Lev. 1:8; 3:3, 4 **29:14** [o]Lev. 4:11, 12, 21 **29:15** [p]Lev. 8:18 [q]Lev. 1:4–9 **29:16** [r]Ex. 24:6 **29:18** [s]Ex. 20:24 **29:19** [t]Lev. 8:22 **29:21** [u]Ex. 30:25, 31 [v][Heb. 9:22] **29:23** [w]Lev. 8:26 **29:24** [x]Lev. 7:30; 10:14 **29:25** [y]Lev. 8:28 **29:26** [z]Lev. 7:31, 34; 8:29 **29:27** [a]Num. 18:11, 18 **29:28** [b]Lev. 10:15 [c]Lev. 3:1; 7:34 **29:29** [d]Ex. 28:2 [e]Num. 20:26, 28 [f]Num. 18:8 **29:30** [g]Num. 20:28 [h]Lev. 8:35

when he enters the tabernacle of meeting to minister in the holy *place.*

31"And you shall take the ram of the consecration and *i*boil its flesh in the holy place. 32Then Aaron and his sons shall eat the flesh of the ram, and the *j*bread that *is* in the basket, *by* the door of the tabernacle of meeting. 33*k*They shall eat those things with which the atonement was made, to consecrate *and* to sanctify them; *l*but an outsider shall not eat *them,* because they *are* holy. 34And if any of the flesh of the consecration offerings, or of the bread, remains until the morning, then *m*you shall burn the remainder with fire. It shall not be eaten, because it *is* holy.

35"Thus you shall do to Aaron and his sons, according to all that I have commanded you. *n*Seven days you shall consecrate them. 36And you *o*shall offer a bull every day *as* a sin offering for atonement. *p*You shall cleanse the altar when you make atonement for it, and you shall anoint it to sanctify it. 37Seven days you shall make atonement for the altar and sanctify it. And the altar shall be most holy. *q*Whatever touches the altar must be holy.*

The Daily Offerings

38"Now this *is* what you shall offer on the altar: *r*two lambs of the first year, *s*day by day continually. 39One lamb you shall offer *t*in the morning, and the other lamb you shall offer at twilight. 40With the one lamb shall be one-tenth *of an ephah* of flour mixed with one-fourth of a hin of pressed oil, and one-fourth of a hin of wine *as* a drink offering. 41And the other lamb you shall *u*offer at twilight; and you shall offer with it the grain offering and the drink offering, as in the morning, for a sweet aroma, an offering made by fire to the LORD. 42*This shall be* *v*a continual burnt offering throughout your generations *at* the door of the tabernacle of meeting before the LORD, *w*where I will meet you to speak with you.

43And there I will meet with the children of Israel, and *the tabernacle* *x*shall be sanctified by My glory. 44So I will consecrate the tabernacle of meeting and the altar. I will also *y*consecrate both Aaron and his sons to minister to Me as priests. 45*z*I will dwell among the children of Israel and will *a*be their God. 46And they shall know that *b*I *am* the LORD their God, who *c*brought them up out of the land of Egypt, that I may dwell among them. I *am* the LORD their God.

The Altar of Incense

30 "You shall make *a*an altar to burn incense on; you shall make it of acacia wood. 2A cubit *shall be* its length and a cubit its width—it shall be square—and two cubits *shall be* its height. Its horns *shall be* of one piece with it. 3And you shall overlay its top, its sides all around, and its horns with pure gold; and you shall make for it a molding of gold all around. 4Two gold rings you shall make for it, under the molding on both its sides. You shall place *them* on its two sides, and they will be holders for the poles with which to bear it. 5You shall make the poles of acacia wood, and overlay them with gold. 6And you shall put it before the *b*veil that *is* before the ark of the Testimony, before the *c*mercy seat that *is* over the Testimony, where I will meet with you.

7"Aaron shall burn on it *d*sweet incense every morning; when *e*he tends the lamps, he shall burn incense on it. 8And when Aaron lights the lamps at twilight, he shall burn incense on it, a perpetual incense before the LORD throughout your generations. 9You shall not offer *f*strange incense on it, or a burnt offering, or a grain offering; nor shall you pour a drink offering on it. 10And *g*Aaron shall make atonement upon its horns once a year with the blood of the sin offering of atonement; once a year he shall

---

* **29:37** Compare Numbers 4:15 and Haggai 2:11–13

29:40 ephah...hin. One-tenth of an ephah was about two quarts; one-fourth of a hin was about one quart.
29:45 dwell among the children. Man is God's special creation, created in His image and likeness. A part of that image and likeness is the uniqueness of personality that allows communion with God. He did not create a race of robots but rather endowed man with a will so that he might choose fellowship with God. In Israel, fellowship with God centered in the tabernacle and especially in the mercy seat which symbolized His presence. Today, believers have fellowship with God through the indwelling of the Holy Spirit. In eternity He will dwell in the midst of His people more fully than ever before.
30:7 sweet incense. Burning incense was a privilege restricted to those who were allowed to approach God.
30:9 strange incense. The incense offered to God was to be made from a special recipe consecrated to be used only in the worship at the tabernacle. No other incense was acceptable.
30:10 atonement. The sacrificial blood of the sin

offering (Lev. 16:18) was applied to the incense altar to indicate that even this article needed cleansing to preserve its ideal holiness because of man's willful or accidental sin. The Hebrew word for "atonement" involves the covering or canceling of sin, resulting in the offender being reconciled to God. Without blood being shed there can be no forgiveness (Heb. 9:22). The atonement made annually for this small altar is a reminder that everything in God's service must be holy to the Lord (Zech. 14:20).

29:31 *i* Lev. 8:31   **29:32** *j* Matt. 12:4   **29:33** *k* Lev. 10:14, 15, 17   *l* Lev. 22:10   **29:34** *m* Lev. 7:18; 8:32   **29:35** *n* Lev. 8:33–35   **29:36** *o* Heb. 10:11   *p* Ex. 30:26–29; 40:10, 11   **29:37** *q* Num. 4:15; Hag. 2:11–13; Matt. 23:19   **29:38** *r* Num. 28:3–31; 29:6–38   *s* Dan. 12:11   **29:39** *t* Ezek. 46:13–15   **29:41** *u* 2 Kin. 16:15   **29:42** *v* Ex. 30:8   *w* Ex. 25:22; 33:7, 9   **29:43** *x* 1 Kin. 8:11   **29:44** *y* Lev. 21:15   **29:45** *z* [Rev. 21:3]   *a* Gen. 17:8   **29:46** *b* Ex. 16:12; 20:2   *c* Lev. 11:45   **30:1** *a* Ex. 37:25–29   **30:6** *b* Ex. 26:31–35   *c* Ex. 25:21, 22   **30:7** *d* 1 Sam. 2:28   *e* Ex. 27:20, 21   **30:9** *f* Lev. 10:1   **30:10** *g* Lev. 16:3–34

make atonement upon it throughout your generations. It is most holy to the LORD."

The Ransom Money

[11]Then the LORD spoke to Moses, saying: [12h]"When you take the census of the children of Israel for their number, then every man shall give [i]a ransom for himself to the LORD, when you number them, that there may be no [j]plague among them when you number them. [13k]This is what everyone among those who are numbered shall give: half a shekel according to the shekel of the sanctuary [l](a shekel is twenty gerahs). [m]The half-shekel shall be an offering to the LORD. [14]Everyone included among those who are numbered, from twenty years old and above, shall give an offering to the LORD. [15]The [n]rich shall not give more and the poor shall not give less than half a shekel, when you give an offering to the LORD, to make atonement for yourselves. [16]And you shall take the atonement money of the children of Israel, and [o]shall appoint it for the service of the tabernacle of meeting, that it may be [p]a memorial for the children of Israel before the LORD, to make atonement for yourselves."

The Bronze Laver

[17]Then the LORD spoke to Moses, saying: [18a]"You shall also make a laver of bronze, with its base also of bronze, for washing. You shall [r]put it between the tabernacle of meeting and the altar. And you shall put water in it, [19]for Aaron and his sons [s]shall wash their hands and their feet in water from it. [20]When they go into the tabernacle of meeting, or when they come near the altar to minister, to burn an offering made by fire to the LORD, they shall wash with water, lest they die. [21]So they shall wash their hands and their feet, lest they die. And [t]it shall be a statute forever to them—to him and his descendants throughout their generations."

The Holy Anointing Oil

[22]Moreover the LORD spoke to Moses, saying: [23]"Also take for yourself [u]quality spices—five hundred shekels of liquid [v]myrrh, half as much sweet-smelling cinnamon (two hundred and fifty shekels),

two hundred and fifty shekels of sweet-smelling [w]cane, [24]five hundred shekels of [x]cassia, according to the shekel of the sanctuary, and a [y]hin of olive oil. [25]And you shall make from these a holy anointing oil, an ointment compounded according to the art of the perfumer. It shall be [z]a holy anointing oil. [26a]With it you shall anoint the tabernacle of meeting and the ark of the Testimony; [27]the table and all its utensils, the lampstand and its utensils, and the altar of incense; [28]the altar of burnt offering with all its utensils, and the laver and its base. [29]You shall consecrate them, that they may be most holy; [*]whatever touches them must be holy.[*] [30c]And you shall anoint Aaron and his sons, and consecrate them, that they may minister to Me as priests.

[31]"And you shall speak to the children of Israel, saying: 'This shall be a holy anointing oil to Me throughout your generations. [32]It shall not be poured on man's flesh; nor shall you make any other like it, according to its composition. [d]It is holy, and it shall be holy to you. [33e]Whoever compounds any like it, or whoever puts any of it on an outsider, [f]shall be cut off from his people.'"

The Incense

[34]And the LORD said to Moses: [g]"Take sweet spices, stacte and onycha and galbanum, and pure frankincense with these sweet spices; there shall be equal amounts of each. [35]You shall make of these an incense, a compound [h]according to the art of the perfumer, salted, pure, and holy. [36]And you shall beat some of it very fine, and put some of it before the Testimony in the tabernacle of meeting [i]where I will meet with you. [j]It shall be most holy to you. [37]But as for the incense which you shall make, [k]you shall not make any for yourselves, according to its composition. It shall be to you holy for the LORD. [38l]Whoever makes any like it, to smell it, he shall be cut off from his people."

Artisans for Building the Tabernacle

31 Then the LORD spoke to Moses, saying: [2a]"See, I have called by name Bezalel the [b]son of Uri, the son of Hur, of the tribe of Judah. [3]And I have [c]filled him

---

[*] **30:29** Compare Numbers 4:15 and Haggai 2:11–13

30:12 ransom. The idea is to pay a price for one's life. The Israelites had to acknowledge that their lives were from God and governed by Him by giving Him an offering of money.

30:19 wash their hands and their feet. The continual washing was symbolic of the need to be cleansed from sin regularly.

31:3 filled him with the Spirit of God. We often think of the "filling of the Spirit" only in connection with Acts 2, but passages such as this one help us to see the continuity of God's work among His people through the ages. In this case, the Spirit empowered uniquely gifted people to design and

build a tabernacle befitting a holy and magnificent God.

30:12 [h] Num. 1:2; 26:2 [i] [1 Pet. 1:18, 19] [j] 2 Sam. 24:15 **30:13** [k] Matt. 17:24 [l] Num. 3:47 [m] Ex. 38:26 **30:15** [n] [Eph. 6:9] **30:16** [o] Ex. 38:25–31 [p] Num. 16:40 **30:18** [q] Ex. 38:8 [r] Ex. 40:30 **30:19** [s] Ex. 40:31, 32 **30:21** [t] Ex. 28:43 **30:23** [u] Ezek. 27:22 [v] Prov. 7:17 [w] Song 4:14 **30:24** [x] Ps. 45:8 [y] Ex. 29:40 **30:25** [z] Ex. 37:29; 40:9 **30:26** [a] Lev. 8:10 **30:29** [b] Ex. 29:37 [*] Lev. 6:18; Num. 4:15; Hag. 2:11–13 **30:30** [c] Lev. 8:12 **30:32** [d] Ex. 30:25, 37 **30:33** [e] Ex. 30:38 [f] Gen. 17:14 **30:34** [g] Ex. 25:6; 37:29 **30:35** [h] Ex. 30:25 **30:36** [i] Ex. 29:42 [j] Lev. 2:3 **30:37** [k] Ex. 30:32 **30:38** [l] Ex. 30:33 **31:2** [a] Ex. 35:30—36:1 [b] 1 Chr. 2:20 **31:3** [c] 1 Kin. 7:14

with the Spirit of God, in wisdom, in under-standing, in knowledge, and in all *manner of* workmanship, [4]to design artistic works, to work in gold, in silver, in bronze, [5]in cutting jewels for setting, in carving wood, and to work in all *manner of* workmanship. [6]"And I, indeed I, have appointed with him [d]Aholiab the son of Ahisamach, of the tribe of Dan; and I have put wisdom in the hearts of all the [e]gifted artisans, that they may make all that I have commanded you: [7f]the tabernacle of meeting, [g]the ark of the Testimony and [h]the mercy seat that *is* on it, and all the furniture of the tabernacle—[8i]the table and its utensils, [j]the pure *gold* lampstand with all its utensils, the altar of incense, [9k]the altar of burnt offering with all its utensils, and [l]the laver and its base— [10m]the garments of ministry,* the holy garments for Aaron the priest and the garments of his sons, to minister as priests, [11n]and the anointing oil and [o]sweet incense for the holy *place.* According to all that I have commanded you they shall do."

The Sabbath Law

[12]And the LORD spoke to Moses, saying, [13]"Speak also to the children of Israel, saying: [p]'Surely My Sabbaths you shall keep, for it *is* a sign between Me and you throughout your generations, that *you* may know that I *am* the LORD who [q]sanctifies you. [14r]You shall keep the Sabbath, therefore, for *it is* holy to you. Everyone who profanes it shall surely be put to death; for [s]whoever does *any* work on it, that person shall be cut off from among his people. [15]Work shall be done for [t]six days, but the [u]seventh is the Sabbath of rest, holy to the LORD. Whoever does *any* work on the Sabbath day, he shall surely be put to death. [16]Therefore the children of Israel shall keep the Sabbath, to observe the Sabbath throughout their generations *as* a perpetual covenant. [17]It *is* [v]a sign between Me and the children of Israel forever; for [w]in six days the LORD made the heavens and the earth, and on the seventh day He rested and was refreshed.'"

[18]And when He had made an end of speaking with him on Mount Sinai, He gave Moses [x]two tablets of the Testimony, tablets of stone, written with the finger of God.

The Gold Calf

32 Now when the people saw that Moses [a]delayed coming down from the mountain, the people [b]gathered together to Aaron, and said to him, [c]"Come, make us gods that shall [d]go before us; for *as for* this Moses, the man who [e]brought us up out of the land of Egypt, we do not know what has become of him."

[2]And Aaron said to them, "Break off the [f]golden earrings which *are* in the ears of your wives, your sons, and your daughters, and bring *them* to me." [3]So all the people broke off the golden earrings which *were* in their ears, and brought *them* to Aaron. [4g]And he received *the* gold from their hand, and he fashioned it with an engraving tool, and made a molded calf.

Then they said, "This *is* your god, O Israel, that [h]brought you out of the land of Egypt!"

[5]So when Aaron saw *it,* he built an altar before it. And Aaron made a [i]proclamation and said, "Tomorrow *is* a feast to the LORD." [6]Then they rose early on the next day, offered burnt offerings, and brought peace offerings; and the people [j]sat down to eat and drink, and rose up to play.

[7]And the LORD said to Moses, [k]"Go, get down! For your people whom you brought out of the land of Egypt [l]have corrupted *themselves.* [8]They have turned aside quickly out of the way which [m]I commanded them. They have made themselves a molded calf, and worshiped it and sacrificed to it, and said, [n]'This *is* your god, O Israel, that brought you out of the land of Egypt!'" [9]And the LORD said to Moses, [o]"I

* **31:10** Or *woven garments*

31:18 the finger of God. This verse underscores the divine origin of the law. Scholars of religion have long spoken of Israel's religious ideas as its unique contribution to civilization, much as the Greeks developed philosophy and the Romans displayed a genius for organization and empire-building. Yet such a comparison misses the point of Scripture. The Bible speaks not of the genius of Israel, but of the finger of God. The Ten Commandments were not the product of man, but the revelation of the Lord.

32:1–35 The Gold Calf—The story of the Israelites' worship of the golden calf reveals both the unfaithfulness of the Israelites and God's great mercy. Even though the people had so quickly broken their promise to obey Him, God forgave their sin and began again with them.

32:2–3 golden earrings. These were part of the treasure from Egypt that should have been used for building the tabernacle (35:20–29).

32:4 a molded calf. This was an ominous worship symbol. Not only were the cow and the bull worshiped in Egypt, but the bull was a familiar embodiment of Baal seen in Canaan. It appears that the worship of the Lord had been blended with the symbols of Baal and other fertility gods. In this one scene, the people broke the first three of God's commandments.

31:6 [d]Ex. 35:34 [e]Ex. 28:3; 35:10, 35; 36:1 **31:7** [f]Ex. 36:8 [g]Ex. 37:1–5 [h]Ex. 37:6–9 **31:8** [i]Ex. 37:10–16 [j]Ex. 37:17–24 **31:9** [k]Ex. 38:1–7 [l]Ex. 38:8 **31:10** [m]Ex. 39:1, 41 **31:11** [n]Ex. 30:23–33 [o]Ex. 30:34–38 **31:13** [p]Ezek. 20:12, 20 [q]Lev. 20:8 **31:14** [r]Ex. 20:8 [s]Num. 15:32–36 **31:15** [t]Ex. 20:9–11 [u]Gen. 2:2 **31:17** [v]Ex. 31:13 [w]Gen. 1:31; 2:2, 3 **31:18** [x][Ex. 24:12; 32:15, 16] **32:1** [a]Ex. 24:18; Deut. 9:9–12 [b]Ex. 17:1–3 [c]Acts 7:40 [d]Ex. 13:21 [e]Ex. 32:8 **32:2** [f]Ex. 11:2; 35:22 **32:4** [g]Ex. 20:3, 4, 23 [h]Ex. 29:45, 46 **32:5** [i]2 Kin. 10:20 **32:6** [j]Num. 25:2 **32:7** [k]Deut. 9:8–21 [l]Gen. 6:11, 12 **32:8** [m]Ex. 20:3, 4, 23 [n]1 Kin. 12:28 **32:9** [o][Acts 7:51]

have seen this people, and indeed it *is* a stiff-necked people! ¹⁰Now therefore, ᵖlet Me alone, that �q My wrath may burn hot against them and I may consume them. And ᴦI will make of you a great nation."

¹¹ˢThen Moses pleaded with the LORD his God, and said: "LORD, why does Your wrath burn hot against Your people whom You have brought out of the land of Egypt with great power and with a mighty hand? ¹²ᵗWhy should the Egyptians speak, and say, 'He brought them out to harm them, to kill them in the mountains, and to consume them from the face of the earth'? Turn from Your fierce wrath, and ᵘrelent from this harm to Your people. ¹³Remember Abraham, Isaac, and Israel, Your servants, to whom You ᵛswore by Your own self, and said to them, ʷ'I will multiply your descendants as the stars of heaven; and all this land that I have spoken of I give to your descendants, and they shall inherit it forever.'"* ¹⁴So the LORD ˣrelented from the harm which He said He would do to His people.

¹⁵And ʸMoses turned and went down from the mountain, and the two tablets of the Testimony *were* in his hand. The tablets *were* written on both sides; on the one *side* and on the other they were written. ¹⁶Now the ᶻtablets *were* the work of God, and the writing *was* the writing of God engraved on the tablets.

¹⁷And when Joshua heard the noise of the people as they shouted, he said to Moses, "*There is* a noise of war in the camp." ¹⁸But he said:

"*It is* not the noise of the shout of
    victory,
Nor the noise of the cry of defeat,
But the sound of singing I hear."

¹⁹So it was, as soon as he came near the camp, that ᵃhe saw the calf *and* the dancing. So Moses' anger became hot, and he cast the tablets out of his hands and broke them at the foot of the mountain. ²⁰ᵇThen he took the calf which they had made, burned *it* in the fire, and ground *it* to powder; and he scattered *it* on the water and made the children of Israel drink *it*. ²¹And Moses said to Aaron, ᶜ"What did this people do to you that you have brought so great a sin upon them?"

²²So Aaron said, "Do not let the anger of my lord become hot. ᵈYou know the people, that they *are set* on evil. ²³For they said to me, 'Make us gods that shall go before us; *as for* this Moses, the man who brought us out of the land of Egypt, we do not know what has become of him.' ²⁴And I said to them, 'Whoever has any gold, let them break *it* off.' So they gave *it* to me, and I cast it into the fire, and this calf came out."

²⁵Now when Moses saw that the people *were* ᵉunrestrained (for Aaron ᶠhad not restrained them, to *their* shame among their enemies), ²⁶then Moses stood in the entrance of the camp, and said, "Whoever *is* on the LORD's side—*come* to me!" And all the sons of Levi gathered themselves together to him. ²⁷And he said to them, "Thus says the LORD God of Israel: 'Let every man put his sword on his side, and go in and out from entrance to entrance throughout the camp, and ᵍlet every man kill his brother, every man his companion, and every man his neighbor.' " ²⁸So the sons of Levi did according to the word of Moses. And about three thousand men of the people fell that day. ²⁹ʰThen Moses said, "Consecrate yourselves today to the LORD, that He may bestow on you a blessing this day, for every man has opposed his son and his brother."

³⁰Now it came to pass on the next day that Moses said to the people, ⁱ"You have committed a great sin. So now I will go up to the LORD; ʲperhaps I can ᵏmake atonement for your sin." ³¹Then Moses ˡreturned to the LORD and said, "Oh, these people have committed a great sin, and have ᵐmade for themselves a god of gold! ³²Yet now, if You will forgive their sin—but if not, I pray, ⁿblot me ᵒout of Your book which You have written."

---

* **32:13** Genesis 13:15 and 22:17

32:14 the LORD relented. Here is a wonderful example of the interaction of faithful intercessory prayer and the purpose of the Lord. He uses our prayer combined with His own determination to make His will come to pass.

32:25–26 were unrestrained. Obedience to God is many times just the opposite of "what everybody else is doing." Humans are very prone to giving in to peer pressure at the crucial moment. We often care more about what those around us think than about what God thinks. Aaron and the other Levites fell into this trap initially, but when Moses gave them another chance to say where their loyalties really lay, they chose the path of obedience. Even though almost "everybody was doing it," they were willing to say, "No, this is wrong. We were wrong." The Levites were not innocent, but God blessed them for their repentance and their obedience.

32:27–28 his brother ... his companion ... his neighbor. This terrible massacre is hard for us to reconcile with our feelings, but we must realize that sin is loathsome, and deserving of death. The Levites were used by God to execute His judgment in this instance, but they were not given general authority to kill sinners.

32:32–33 blot me out of Your book. Like Paul many centuries later, Moses could almost wish himself to be cursed, if by being so he could secure the salvation of his people (Rom. 9:3).

32:10 ᵖDeut. 9:14, 19   �q Ex. 22:24   ᴦNum. 14:12
32:11 ˢDeut. 9:18, 26–29   **32:12** ᵗNum. 14:13–19
ᵘEx. 32:14   **32:13** ᵛ[Heb. 6:13]   ʷGen. 12:7; 13:15;
15:7, 18; 22:17; 26:4; 35:11, 12   **32:14** ˣ2 Sam. 24:16
32:15 ʸDeut. 9:15   **32:16** ᶻEx. 31:18   **32:19** ᵃDeut.
9:16, 17   **32:20** ᵇDeut. 9:21   **32:21** ᶜGen. 26:10
32:22 ᵈDeut. 9:24   **32:25** ᵉEx. 33:4, 5   ᶠ2 Chr. 28:19
32:27 ᵍNum. 25:5–13   **32:29** ʰEx. 28:41   **32:30** ⁱ1 Sam.
12:20, 23   ʲ2 Sam. 16:12   ᵏNum. 25:13   **32:31** ˡDeut. 9:18
ᵐEx. 20:23   **32:32** ⁿPs. 69:28   ᵒDan. 12:1

33And the LORD said to Moses, p"Whoever has sinned against Me, I will qblot him out of My book. 34Now therefore, go, lead the people to the place of which I have rspoken to you. sBehold, My Angel shall go before you. Nevertheless, tin the day when I visit for punishment, I will uvisit punishment upon them for their sin."

35So the LORD plagued the people because of vwhat they did with the calf which Aaron made.

The Command to Leave Sinai

33 Then the LORD said to Moses, "Depart and go up from here, you aand the people whom you have brought out of the land of Egypt, to the land of which I swore to Abraham, Isaac, and Jacob, saying, b'To your descendants I will give it.' 2cAnd I will send My Angel before you, dand I will drive out the Canaanite and the Amorite and the Hittite and the Perizzite and the Hivite and the Jebusite. 3Go up eto a land flowing with milk and honey; for I will not go up in your midst, lest fI consume you on the way, for you are ga stiff-necked people."

4And when the people heard this bad news, hthey mourned, iand no one put on his ornaments. 5For the LORD had said to Moses, "Say to the children of Israel, 'You are a stiff-necked people. I could come up into your midst in one moment and consume you. Now therefore, take off your ornaments, that I may jknow what to do to you.'" 6So the children of Israel stripped themselves of their ornaments by Mount Horeb.

Moses Meets with the LORD

7Moses took his tent and pitched it outside the camp, far from the camp, and kcalled it the tabernacle of meeting. And it came to pass that everyone who lsought the LORD went out to the tabernacle of meeting which was outside the camp. 8So it was, whenever Moses went out to the tabernacle, that all the people rose, and each man stood mat his tent door and watched Moses until mhe had gone into the tabernacle. 9And it came to pass, when Moses entered the tabernacle, that the pillar of cloud descended and stood at the door of the tabernacle, and the LORD ntalked with Moses. 10All the people saw the pillar of cloud standing at the tabernacle door, and all the people rose and oworshiped, each man in his tent door. 11So pthe LORD spoke to Moses face to face, as a man speaks to his friend. And he would return to the camp, but qhis servant Joshua the son of Nun, a young man, did not depart from the tabernacle.

The Promise of God's Presence

12Then Moses said to the LORD, "See, rYou say to me, 'Bring up this people.' But You have not let me know whom You will send with me. Yet You have said, s'I know you by name, and you have also found grace in My sight.' 13Now therefore, I pray, tif I have found grace in Your sight, ushow me now Your way, that I may know You and that I may find grace in Your sight. And consider that this nation is vYour people."

14And He said, w"My Presence will go with you, and I will give you xrest."

15Then he said to Him, y"If Your Presence does not go with us, do not bring us up from here. 16For how then will it be known that Your people and I have found grace in Your sight, zexcept You go with us? So we ashall be separate, Your people and I, from all the people who are upon the face of the earth."

17So the LORD said to Moses, b"I will also do this thing that you have spoken; for you have found grace in My sight, and I know you by name."

18And he said, "Please, show me cYour glory."

19Then He said, "I will make all My

32:34 in the day. This may refer to the day of the Lord, proclaimed by later prophets (Joel 2; Zeph. 1).

33:5 stiff-necked. Contrary to popular belief, God did not choose the Hebrew people because of their righteousness or willingness to serve Him (Deut. 9:7). In fact, one of Israel's besetting sins was obstinacy (vv. 3,5), and God saw them as a rebellious and stiff-necked people. The opposite of being obstinate is to have a "circumcised heart" (Deut. 10:16). Such a heart is inclined to obey the Word of God. God's presence with His people was in response to His covenantal promise: if they obeyed Him they would be His "special treasure" (Ex. 19:5).

33:6 stripped themselves of their ornaments. These ornaments were probably associated with the idolatrous worship of the golden calf. Their removal was a mark of genuine repentance and renewal.

33:8 all the people rose, and ... stood. In contrast to their former wickedness, the people now responded reverently to the living God.

33:11 his servant Joshua. The word translated servant here does not mean slave, but rather a minister, one who does spiritual service.

33:17 I know you by name. God's grace was accompanied by His intimate knowledge of and care for Moses.

32:33 p [Ezek. 18:4; 33:2, 14, 15] q Ex. 17:14 **32:34** r Ex. 3:17 s Ex. 23:20 t Deut. 32:35 u Ps. 89:32 **32:35** v Neh. 9:18 **33:1** d Ex. 32:1, 7, 13 b Gen. 12:7 **33:2** c Ex. 32:34 d Josh. 24:11 **33:3** e Ex. 3:8 f Num. 16:21, 45 g Ex. 32:9; 33:5 **33:4** h Num. 14:1, 39 i Ezra 9:3 **33:5** j [Ps. 139:23] **33:7** k Ex. 29:42, 43 l Deut. 4:29 **33:8** m Num. 16:27 **33:9** n Ps. 99:7 **33:10** o Ex. 4:31 **33:11** p Num. 12:8 q Ex. 24:13 **33:12** r Ex. 3:10; 32:34 s Ex. 33:17 **33:13** t Ex. 34:9 u Ps. 25:4; 27:11; 86:11; 119:33 v Deut. 9:26, 29 **33:14** w Is. 63:9 x Josh. 21:44; 22:4 **33:15** y Ex. 33:3 **33:16** z Num. 14:14 a Ex. 34:10 **33:17** b [James 5:16] **33:18** c [1 Tim. 6:16]

[d]goodness pass before you, and I will proclaim the name of the LORD before you. [e]I will be gracious to whom I will be [f]gracious, and I will have compassion on whom I will have compassion." [20]But He said, "You cannot see My face; for [g]no man shall see Me, and live." [21]And the LORD said, "Here is a place by Me, and you shall stand on the rock. [22]So it shall be, while My glory passes by, that I will put you [h]in the cleft of the rock, and will [i]cover you with My hand while I pass by. [23]Then I will take away My hand, and you shall see My back; but My face shall [j]not be seen."

Moses Makes New Tablets

34 And the LORD said to Moses, [a]"Cut two tablets of stone like the first *ones*, and [b]I will write on *these* tablets the words that were on the first tablets which you broke. [2]So be ready in the morning, and come up in the morning to Mount Sinai, and present yourself to Me there [c]on the top of the mountain. [3]And no man shall [d]come up with you, and let no man be seen throughout all the mountain; let neither flocks nor herds feed before that mountain."

[4]So he cut two tablets of stone like the first *ones*. Then Moses rose early in the morning and went up Mount Sinai, as the LORD had commanded him; and he took in his hand the two tablets of stone.

[5]Now the LORD descended in the [e]cloud and stood with him there, and [f]proclaimed the name of the LORD. [6]And the LORD passed before him and proclaimed, "The LORD, the LORD [g]God, merciful and gracious, longsuffering, and abounding in [h]goodness and [i]truth, [7][j]keeping mercy for thousands, [k]forgiving iniquity and transgression and sin, [l]by no means clearing *the guilty*, visiting the iniquity of the fathers upon the children and the children's children to the third and the fourth generation."

[8]So Moses made haste and [m]bowed his head toward the earth, and worshiped. [9]Then he said, "If now I have found grace in Your sight, O Lord, [n]let my Lord, I pray, go among us, even though we *are* a [o]stiff-necked people; and pardon our iniquity and our sin, and take us as [p]Your inheritance."

The Covenant Renewed

[10]And He said: "Behold, [q]I make a covenant. Before all your people I will [r]do marvels such as have not been done in all the earth, nor in any nation; and all the people among whom you *are* shall see the work of the LORD. For it *is* [s]an awesome thing that I will do with you. [11][t]Observe what I command you this day. Behold, [u]I am driving out from before you the Amorite and the Canaanite and the Hittite and the Perizzite and the Hivite and the Jebusite. [12][v]Take heed to yourself, lest you make a covenant with the inhabitants of the land where you are going, lest it be a snare in your midst. [13]But you shall [w]destroy their altars, break their *sacred* pillars, and [x]cut down their wooden images [14](for you shall worship [y]no other god, for the LORD, whose [z]name *is* Jealous, *is* a [a]jealous God), [15]lest you make a covenant with the inhabitants of the land, and they [b]play the harlot with their gods and make sacrifice to their gods, and *one of them* [c]invites you and you [d]eat of his sacrifice, [16]and you take of [e]his daughters for your sons, and his daughters [f]play the harlot with their gods and make your sons play the harlot with their gods.

[17][g]"You shall make no molded gods for yourselves.

[18]"The Feast of [h]Unleavened Bread you shall keep. Seven days you shall eat unleavened bread, as I commanded you, in the appointed time of the [i]month of Abib; for in the month of Abib you came out from Egypt.

[19][j]"All that open the womb *are* Mine, and every male firstborn among your livestock,

---

33:22–23 My hand. The use of words such as hand, back, and face is a way of describing God, who is Spirit, in terms familiar to humans.

34:6 merciful and gracious ... abounding in goodness and truth. God is overwhelmingly gracious. John's description of the coming of Jesus echoes this passage, describing the Messiah as "full of grace and truth" (John 1:14,17). To see Jesus is to see the Father (John 1:18).

34:7 forgiving iniquity. God is a God of unlimited grace, mercy, and forgiveness. But man is not automatically forgiven—He will by no means leave the guilty unpunished. We receive forgiveness from God only when we repent and seek reconciliation with Him. The second covenant with Israel (34:10) included relief from the judgment of the people's sins to allow them to be taught their need and seek forgiveness.

34:15 play the harlot. This is probably more than a figure of speech. Unfaithfulness to the Lord was often manifested in sexual rites with temple prostitutes

(male and female), acts of supposed union with Baal, Asherah, and other pagan deities.

34:16 take of his daughters for your sons. The quickest way for the Israelites to become corrupted with the false worship of the Canaanites would have been to marry into it.

33:19 [d]Ex. 34:6, 7 [e][Rom. 9:15, 16, 18] [f][Rom. 4:4, 16] **33:20** [g][Gen. 32:30] **33:22** [h]Is. 2:21 [i]Ps. 91:1, 4 **33:23** [j][John 1:18] **34:1** [a][Ex. 24:12; 31:18; 32:15, 16, 19] [b]Deut. 10:2, 4 **34:2** [c]Ex. 19:11, 18, 20 **34:3** [d]Ex. 19:12, 13; 24:9–11 **34:5** [e]Ex. 19:9 [f]Ex. 33:19 **34:6** [g]Neh. 9:17 [h]Rom. 2:4 [i]Ps. 108:4 **34:7** [j]Ex. 20:6 [k]Ps. 103:3, 4 [l]Job 10:14 **34:8** [m]Ex. 4:31 **34:9** [n]Ex. 33:12–16 [o]Ex. 33:3 [p]Ps. 33:12; 94:14 **34:10** [q]Deut. 5:2 [r]Ps. 77:14 [s]Ps. 145:6 **34:11** [t]Deut. 6:25 [u]Ex. 23:20–33; 33:2 **34:12** [v]Ex. 23:32, 33 **34:13** [w]Deut. 12:3 [x]2 Kin. 18:4 **34:14** [y][Ex. 20:3–5] [z][Is. 9:6; 57:15] [a][Deut. 4:24] **34:15** [b]Judg. 2:17 [c]Num. 25:1, 2 [d]1 Cor. 8:4, 7, 10 **34:16** [e]Gen. 28:1 [f]Num. 25:1, 2 **34:17** [g]Ex. 20:4, 23; 32:8 **34:18** [h]Ex. 12:15, 16 [i]Ex. 12:2; 13:4 **34:19** [j]Ex. 13:2; 22:29

whether ox or sheep. [20]But [k]the firstborn of a donkey you shall redeem with a lamb. And if you will not redeem *him*, then you shall break his neck. All the firstborn of your sons you shall redeem.

"And none shall appear before Me [l]empty-handed.

[21m]"Six days you shall work, but on the seventh day you shall rest; in plowing time and in harvest you shall rest.

[22]"And you shall observe the Feast of Weeks, of the firstfruits of wheat harvest, and the Feast of Ingathering at the year's end.

[23n]"Three times in the year all your men shall appear before the Lord, the Lord God of Israel. [24]For I will [o]cast out the nations before you and enlarge your borders; neither will any man covet your land when you go up to appear before the Lord your God three times in the year.

[25]"You shall not offer the blood of My sacrifice with leaven, [p]nor shall the sacrifice of the Feast of the Passover be left until morning.

[26a]"The first of the firstfruits of your land you shall bring to the house of the Lord your God. You shall not boil a young goat in its mother's milk."

[27]Then the Lord said to Moses, "Write [r]these words, for according to the tenor of these words I have made a covenant with you and with Israel." [28s]So he was there with the Lord forty days and forty nights; he neither ate bread nor drank water. And [t]He wrote on the tablets the words of the covenant, the Ten Commandments.*

The Shining Face of Moses

[29]Now it was so, when Moses came down from Mount Sinai (and the [u]two tablets of the Testimony *were* in Moses' hand when he came down from the mountain), that Moses did not know that the skin of his face shone while he talked with Him. [30]So when Aaron and all the children of Israel saw Moses, behold, [v]the skin of his face shone, and they were afraid to come near him. [31]Then Moses called to them, and Aaron and all the rulers of the congregation returned to him; and Moses talked with them. [32]Afterward all the children of Israel came near, [w]and he gave them as commandments all that the Lord had spoken with him on Mount Sinai. [33]And when Moses had finished speaking with them,

he put [x]a veil on his face. [34]But [y]whenever Moses went in before the Lord to speak with Him, he would take the veil off until he came out; and he would come out and speak to the children of Israel whatever he had been commanded. [35]And whenever the children of Israel saw the face of Moses, that the skin of Moses' face shone, then Moses would put the veil on his face again, until he went in to speak with Him.

Sabbath Regulations

35 Then Moses gathered all the congregation of the children of Israel together, and said to them, [a]"These *are* the words which the Lord has commanded *you* to do: [2]Work shall be done for [b]six days, but the seventh day shall be a holy day for you, a Sabbath of rest to the Lord. Whoever does any work on it shall be put to [c]death. [3d]You shall kindle no fire throughout your dwellings on the Sabbath day."

Offerings for the Tabernacle

[4]And Moses spoke to all the congregation of the children of Israel, saying, [e]"This *is* the thing which the Lord commanded, saying: [5]'Take from among you an offering to the Lord. [f]Whoever *is* of a willing heart, let him bring it as an offering to the Lord: [g]gold, silver, and bronze; [6h]blue, purple, and scarlet *thread*, fine linen, and [i]goats' *hair*; [7]ram skins dyed red, badger skins, and acacia wood; [8]oil for the light, [j]and spices for the anointing oil and for the sweet incense; [9]onyx stones, and stones to be set in the ephod and in the breastplate.

Articles of the Tabernacle

[10k]'All *who are* gifted artisans among you shall come and make all that the Lord has commanded: [11]the tabernacle, its tent, its covering, its clasps, its boards, its bars, its pillars, and its sockets; [12m]the ark and its poles, *with* the mercy seat, and the veil of the covering; [13]the [n]table and its poles, all its utensils, [o]and the showbread; [14]also [p]the lampstand for the light, its utensils, its lamps, and the oil for the light; [15q]the incense altar, its poles, [r]the anointing oil, [s]the sweet incense, and the screen for the door at the entrance of the tabernacle;

---

* 34:28 Literally *Ten Words*

34:28 forty days and forty nights. A person can survive without food for weeks, but no one can go entirely without water for more than three or four days. This fact has been used to cast doubt on the truth of this passage, but we must recall that there is no reason to think that God could not keep His servant hydrated in any way He chose.

34:33 *a veil on his face.* Paul taught that Moses wore the veil because the glow faded, a sign of imperfect glory (2 Cor. 3:7,13).

34:20 [k] Ex. 13:13 [l] Ex. 22:29; 23:15 **34:21** [m] Ex. 20:9; 23:12; 31:15; 35:2 **34:23** [n] Ex. 23:14–17 **34:24** [o] [Ex. 33:2] **34:25** [p] Ex. 12:10 **34:26** [q] Ex. 23:19 **34:27** [r] Deut. 31:9 **34:28** [s] Ex. 24:18 [t] Ex. 34:1, 4 **34:29** [u] Ex. 32:15 **34:30** [v] 2 Cor. 3:7 **34:32** [w] Ex. 24:3 **34:34** [x] [2 Cor. 3:13, 14] **34:34** [y] [2 Cor. 3:13–16] **35:1** [a] Ex. 34:32 **35:2** [b] Lev. 23:3 [c] Num. 15:32–36 **35:3** [d] Ex. 12:16; 16:23 **35:4** [e] Ex. 25:1, 2 **35:5** [f] Ex. 25:2 [g] Ex. 38:24 **35:6** [h] Ex. 36:8 [i] Ex. 36:14 **35:8** [j] Ex. 25:6; 30:23–25 **35:10** [k] Ex. 31:2–6; 36:1, 2 **35:11** [l] Ex. 26:1, 2; 36:14 **35:12** [m] Ex. 25:10–22 **35:13** [n] Ex. 25:23 [o] Ex. 25:30 **35:14** [p] Ex. 25:31 **35:15** [q] Ex. 30:1 [r] Ex. 30:25 [s] Ex. 30:34–38

16tthe altar of burnt offering with its bronze grating, its poles, all its utensils, *and* the laver and its base; 17uthe hangings of the court, its pillars, their sockets, and the screen for the gate of the court; 18the pegs of the tabernacle, the pegs of the court, and their cords; 19vthe garments of ministry,* for ministering in the holy *place*—the holy garments for Aaron the priest and the garments of his sons, to minister as priests.'"

The Tabernacle Offerings Presented

20And all the congregation of the children of Israel departed from the presence of Moses. 21Then everyone came wwhose heart was stirred, and everyone whose spirit was willing, *and* they xbrought the LORD's offering for the work of the tabernacle of meeting, for all its service, and for the holy garments. 22They came, both men and women, as many as had a willing heart, *and* brought yearrings and nose rings, rings and necklaces, all zjewelry of gold, that is, every man who *made* an offering of gold to the LORD. 23And aevery man, with whom was found blue, purple, and scarlet *thread*, fine linen, and goats' hair, red skins of rams, and badger skins, brought *them*. 24Everyone who offered an offering of silver or bronze brought the LORD's offering. And everyone with whom was found acacia wood for any work of the service, brought *it*. 25All the women *who were* bgifted artisans spun yarn with their hands, and brought what they had spun of blue, purple, *and* scarlet, and fine linen. 26And all the women whose hearts stirred with wisdom spun yarn of goats' hair. 27cThe rulers brought onyx stones, and the stones to be set in the ephod and in the breastplate, 28and dspices and oil for the light, for the anointing oil, and for the sweet incense. 29The children of Israel brought a efreewill offering to the LORD, all the men and women whose hearts were willing to bring *material* for all kinds of work which the LORD, by the hand of Moses, had commanded to be done.

The Artisans Called by God

30And Moses said to the children of Israel, "See, fthe LORD has called by name Bezalel the son of Uri, the son of Hur, of the tribe of Judah; 31and He has filled him with the Spirit of God, in wisdom and understanding, in knowledge and all manner of workmanship, 32to design artistic works, to work in gold and silver and bronze, 33in cutting jewels for setting, in carving wood, and to work in all manner of artistic workmanship.

34"And He has put in his heart the ability to teach, *in* him and gAholiab the son of Ahisamach, of the tribe of Dan. 35He has hfilled them with skill to do all manner of work of the engraver and the designer and the tapestry maker, in blue, purple, and scarlet *thread*, and fine linen, and of the weaver—those who do every work and those who design artistic works.

36 "And Bezalel and Aholiab, and every agifted artisan in whom the LORD has put wisdom and understanding, to know how to do all manner of work for the service of the bsanctuary, shall do according to all that the LORD has commanded."

The People Give More than Enough

2Then Moses called Bezalel and Aholiab, and every gifted artisan in cwhose heart the LORD had put wisdom, everyone whose heart was stirred, to come and do the work. 3And they received from Moses all the doffering which the children of Israel ehad brought for the work of the service of making the sanctuary. So they continued bringing to him freewill offerings every morning. 4Then all the craftsmen who were doing all the work of the sanctuary came, each from the work he was doing, 5and they spoke to Moses, saying, f"The people bring much more than enough for the service of the work which the LORD commanded *us* to do."

6So Moses gave a commandment, and they caused it to be proclaimed throughout the camp, saying, "Let neither man nor woman do any more work for the offering of the sanctuary." And the people were restrained from bringing, 7for the material they had was sufficient for all the work to be done—indeed too gmuch.

Building the Tabernacle

8hThen all the gifted artisans among them who worked on the tabernacle made ten curtains woven of fine linen, and of

---

* 35:19 Or *woven garments*

35:31–35 Spirit of God. The work of the Holy Spirit is often thought to have begun at Pentecost (Acts 2), but in fact the Holy Spirit of God was at work long before that time. The Old Testament shows that He was active in creation (Gen. 1:2; Job 33:4). The Spirit came upon men for prophetic utterance (1 Sam. 10:10) and for all divine revelation (2 Sam. 23:2). Men were endowed with special functions by the power of the Holy Spirit (Ex. 31:3; Judg. 11:29; 13:25; 14:6). Bezalel is a good example of a man indwelt by the Spirit of God in the Old Testament (37:1–9).

36:8—37:29 Servant—Not only ability was required

for service in building the tabernacle. God also wanted willing hearts (36:2). Even if we do not feel

35:16 fEx. 27:1–8   **35:17** uEx. 27:9–18   **35:19** vEx. 31:10; 39:1, 41   **35:21** wEx. 25:2; 35:5, 22, 26, 29; 36:2   xEx. 35:24   **35:22** yEx. 32:2, 3   zEx. 11:2   **35:23** a1 Chr. 29:8   **35:25** bEx. 28:3; 31:6; 36:1   **35:27** cEzra 2:68   **35:28** dEx. 30:23   **35:29** e1 Chr. 29:9   **35:30** fEx. 31:1–6   **35:34** gEx. 31:6   **35:35** h1 Kin. 7:14   **36:1** aEx. 28:3; 31:6; 35:10, 35   bEx. 25:8   **36:2** c1 Chr. 29:5, 9, 17   **36:3** dEx. 35:5   eEx. 35:27   **36:5** f[2 Cor. 8:2, 3]   **36:7** g1 Kin. 8:64   **36:8** hEx. 26:1–14

blue, purple, and scarlet *thread; with* artistic designs of cherubim they made them. 9The length of each curtain *was* twenty-eight cubits, and the width of each curtain four cubits; the curtains *were* all the same size. 10And he coupled five curtains to one another, and *the other* five curtains he coupled to one another. 11He made loops of blue *yarn* on the edge of the curtain on the selvedge of one set; likewise he did on the outer edge of *the other* curtain of the second set. 12*i*Fifty loops he made on one curtain, and fifty loops he made on the edge of the curtain on the end of the second set; the loops held one *curtain* to another. 13And he made fifty clasps of gold, and coupled the curtains to one another with the clasps, that it might be one tabernacle.

14*j*He made curtains of goats' *hair* for the tent over the tabernacle; he made eleven curtains. 15The length of each curtain *was* thirty cubits, and the width of each curtain four cubits; the eleven curtains *were* the same size. 16He coupled five curtains by themselves and six curtains by themselves. 17And he made fifty loops on the edge of the curtain that is outermost in one set, and fifty loops he made on the edge of the curtain of the second set. 18He also made fifty bronze clasps to couple the tent together, that it might be one. 19*k*Then he made a covering for the tent of ram skins dyed red, and a covering of badger skins above *that.*

20For the tabernacle *l*he made boards of acacia wood, standing upright. 21The length of each board *was* ten cubits, and the width of each board a cubit and a half. 22Each board had two tenons *m*for binding one to another. Thus he made for all the boards of the tabernacle. 23And he made boards for the tabernacle, twenty boards for the south side. 24Forty sockets of silver he made to go under the twenty boards: two sockets under each of the boards for its two tenons. 25And for the other side of the tabernacle, the north side, he made twenty boards 26and their forty sockets of silver: two sockets under each of the boards. 27For the west side of the tabernacle he made six boards. 28He also made two boards for the two back corners of the tabernacle. 29And they were coupled at the bottom and coupled together at the top by one ring. Thus he made both of them for the two corners. 30So there were eight

boards and their sockets—sixteen sockets of silver—two sockets under each of the boards.

31And he made *n*bars of acacia wood: five for the boards on one side of the tabernacle, 32five bars for the boards on the other side of the tabernacle, and five bars for the boards of the tabernacle on the far side westward. 33And he made the middle bar to pass through the boards from one end to the other. 34He overlaid the boards with gold, made their rings of gold *to be* holders for the bars, and overlaid the bars with gold.

35And he made *o*a veil of blue, purple, and scarlet *thread,* and fine woven linen; it was worked *with* an artistic design of cherubim. 36He made for it four pillars of acacia *wood,* and overlaid them with gold, with their hooks of gold; and he cast four sockets of silver for them.

37He also made a *p*screen for the tabernacle door, of blue, purple, and scarlet *thread,* and fine woven linen, made by a weaver, 38and its five pillars with their hooks. And he overlaid their capitals and their rings with gold, but their five sockets *were* bronze.

Making the Ark of the Testimony

37 Then *a*Bezalel made *b*the ark of acacia wood; two and a half cubits *was* its length, a cubit and a half its width, and a cubit and a half its height. 2He overlaid it with pure gold inside and outside, and made a molding of gold all around it. 3And he cast for it four rings of gold *to be set* in its four corners: two rings on one side, and two rings on the other side of it. 4He made poles of acacia wood, and overlaid them with gold. 5And he put the poles into the rings at the sides of the ark, to bear the ark. 6He also made the *c*mercy seat of pure gold; two and a half cubits *was* its length and a cubit and a half its width. 7He made two cherubim of beaten gold; he made them of one piece at the two ends of the mercy seat: 8one cherub at one end on this side, and the other cherub at the *other* end on that side. He made the cherubim at the two ends of *one piece* with the mercy seat. 9The cherubim spread out *their* wings above, *and* covered the *d*mercy seat with their wings. They faced one another; the faces of the cherubim were toward the mercy seat.

---

that we are particularly good at anything, we must remember that every talent we possess, no matter how small, is a gift from God. He gives us these gifts so that we will have something to give back to Him. We should look at ourselves, not saying, "I don't have any great skill, I'll just sit and watch," but rather, "Here's what I have—where shall I start?"

37:1–9 Bezalel. Bezalel carefully reproduced the pattern given to Moses (25:10–22). Obviously this pattern wasn't just a "design suggestion" from God.

Each detail had to be just like the plan because each part was a symbol or reminder of their relationship with God, His character, and His holiness.

36:12 *i* Ex. 26:5   **36:14** *j* Ex. 26:7   **36:19** *k* Ex. 26:14
36:20 *l* Ex. 26:15–29   **36:22** *m* Ex. 26:17   **36:31** *n* Ex.
26:26–29   **36:35** *o* Ex. 26:31–37   **36:37** *p* Ex. 26:36
37:1 *a* Ex. 35:30; 36:1   *b* Ex. 25:10–20   **37:6** *c* Ex. 25:17
37:9 *d* Ex. 25:20

Making the Table for the Showbread

¹⁰He made ᵉthe table of acacia wood; two cubits *was* its length, a cubit its width, and a cubit and a half its height. ¹¹And he overlaid it with pure gold, and made a molding of gold all around it. ¹²Also he made a frame of a handbreadth all around it, and made a molding of gold for the frame all around it. ¹³And he cast for it four rings of gold, and put the rings on the four corners that *were* at its four legs. ¹⁴The rings were close to the frame, as holders for the poles to bear the table. ¹⁵And he made the poles of acacia wood to bear the table, and overlaid them with gold. ¹⁶He made of pure gold the utensils which were on the table: its ᶠdishes, its cups, its bowls, and its pitchers for pouring.

Making the Gold Lampstand

¹⁷He also made the ᵍlampstand of pure gold; of hammered work he made the lampstand. Its shaft, its branches, its bowls, its *ornamental* knobs, and its flowers were of the same piece. ¹⁸And six branches came out of its sides: three branches of the lampstand out of one side, and three branches of the lampstand out of the other side. ¹⁹There were three bowls made like almond *blossoms* on one branch, with an *ornamental* knob and a flower, and three bowls made like almond *blossoms* on the other branch, with an *ornamental* knob and a flower—and so for the six branches coming out of the lampstand. ²⁰And on the lampstand itself *were* four bowls made like almond *blossoms, each with* its *ornamental* knob and flower. ²¹*There was* a knob under the *first* two branches of the same, a knob under the *second* two branches of the same, and a knob under the *third* two branches of the same, according to the six branches extending from it. ²²Their knobs and their branches were of one piece; all of it *was* one hammered piece of pure gold. ²³And he made its seven lamps, its ʰwick-trimmers, and its trays of pure gold. ²⁴Of a talent of pure gold he made it, with all its utensils.

Making the Altar of Incense

²⁵ⁱHe made the incense altar of acacia wood. Its length *was* a cubit and its width a cubit—*it was* square—and two cubits *was* its height. Its horns were of *one piece* with it. ²⁶And he overlaid it with pure gold: its top, its sides all around, and its horns. He also made for it a molding of gold all around it. ²⁷He made two rings of gold for it under its molding, by its two corners on both sides, as holders for the poles with which to bear it. ²⁸And he ʲmade the poles of acacia wood, and overlaid them with gold.

Making the Anointing Oil and the Incense

²⁹He also made ᵏthe holy anointing oil and the pure incense of sweet spices, according to the work of the perfumer.

Making the Altar of Burnt Offering

38 He made ᵃthe altar of burnt offering of acacia wood; five cubits *was* its length and five cubits its width—*it was* square—and its height *was* three cubits. ²He made its horns on its four corners; the horns were of *one piece* with it. And he overlaid it with bronze. ³He made all the utensils for the altar: the pans, the shovels, the basins, the forks, and the firepans; all its utensils he made of bronze. ⁴And he made a grate of bronze network for the altar, under its rim, midway from the bottom. ⁵He cast four rings for the four corners of the bronze grating, *as* holders for the poles. ⁶And he made the poles of acacia wood, and overlaid them with bronze. ⁷Then he put the poles into the rings on the sides of the altar, with which to bear it. He made the altar hollow with boards.

Making the Bronze Laver

⁸He made ᵇthe laver of bronze and its base of bronze, from the bronze mirrors of the serving women who assembled at the door of the tabernacle of meeting.

Making the Court of the Tabernacle

⁹Then he made ᶜthe court on the south side; the hangings of the court *were of* fine woven linen, one hundred cubits long. ¹⁰There *were* twenty pillars for them, with twenty bronze sockets. The hooks of the pillars and their bands *were* silver. ¹¹On the north side *the hangings were* one hundred cubits *long,* with twenty pillars and their twenty bronze sockets. The hooks of the pillars and their bands *were* silver. ¹²And on the west side *there were* hangings of fifty cubits, with ten pillars and their ten sockets. The hooks of the pillars and their bands *were* silver. ¹³For the east side *the hangings were* fifty cubits. ¹⁴The hangings of one side *of the gate were* fifteen cubits *long, with* their three pillars and their three sockets, ¹⁵and the same for the other side of the court gate; on this side and that *were* hangings of fifteen cubits, *with* their three pillars and their three sockets. ¹⁶All the hangings of the court all around *were of* fine woven linen. ¹⁷The sockets for the pillars *were* bronze, the hooks of the pillars and their bands *were* silver, and the overlay of their capitals *was* silver; and all the pillars of the court had bands of silver. ¹⁸The screen for the gate of the court *was* woven of blue, purple, and scarlet *thread,* and of fine woven linen. The

---

length *was* twenty cubits, and the height along its width *was* five cubits, corresponding to the hangings of the court. ¹⁹And *there were* four pillars *with* their four sockets of bronze; their hooks *were* silver, and the overlay of their capitals and their bands *was* silver. ²⁰All the ᵈpegs of the tabernacle, and of the court all around, *were* bronze.

Materials of the Tabernacle

²¹This is the inventory of the tabernacle, ᵉthe tabernacle of the Testimony, which was counted according to the commandment of Moses, for the service of the Levites, ᶠby the hand of ᵍIthamar, son of Aaron the priest.

²²ʰBezalel the son of Uri, the son of Hur, of the tribe of Judah, made all that the LORD had commanded Moses. ²³And with him *was* ⁱAholiab the son of Ahisamach, of the tribe of Dan, an engraver and designer, a weaver of blue, purple, and scarlet *thread*, and of fine linen.

²⁴All the gold that was used in all the work of the holy *place*, that is, the gold of the ʲoffering, was twenty-nine talents and seven hundred and thirty shekels, according to ᵏthe shekel of the sanctuary. ²⁵And the silver from those who were ˡnumbered of the congregation *was* one hundred talents and one thousand seven hundred and seventy-five shekels, according to the shekel of the sanctuary: ²⁶ᵐa bekah for each man (*that is,* half a shekel, according to the shekel of the sanctuary), for everyone included in the numbering from twenty years old and above, for ⁿsix hundred and three thousand, five hundred and fifty *men*. ²⁷And from the hundred talents of silver were cast ᵒthe sockets of the sanctuary and the bases of the veil: one hundred sockets from the hundred talents, one talent for each socket. ²⁸Then from the one thousand seven hundred and seventy-five *shekels* he made hooks for the pillars, overlaid their capitals, and ᵖmade bands for them.

²⁹The offering of bronze *was* seventy talents and two thousand four hundred shekels. ³⁰And with it he made the sockets for the door of the tabernacle of meeting, the bronze altar, the bronze grating for it, and all the utensils for the altar, ³¹the sockets for the court all around, the bases for the court gate, all the pegs for the tabernacle, and all the pegs for the court all around.

Making the Garments of the Priesthood

39 Of the ᵃblue, purple, and scarlet *thread* they made ᵇgarments of ministry,* for ministering in the holy *place*, and made the holy garments for Aaron, ᶜas the LORD had commanded Moses.

Making the Ephod

²ᵈHe made the ᵉephod of gold, blue, purple, and scarlet *thread*, and of fine woven linen. ³And they beat the gold into thin sheets and cut *it into* threads, to work *it* in with the blue, purple, and scarlet *thread*, and the fine linen, *into* artistic designs. ⁴They made shoulder straps for it to couple *it* together; it was coupled together at its two edges. ⁵And the intricately woven band of his ephod that *was* on it *was* of the same workmanship, *woven of* gold, blue, purple, and scarlet *thread*, and *of* fine woven linen, as the LORD had commanded Moses.

⁶ᶠAnd they set onyx stones, enclosed in settings of gold; they were engraved, as signets are engraved, with the names of the sons of Israel. ⁷He put them on the shoulders of the ephod *as* ᵍmemorial stones for the sons of Israel, as the LORD had commanded Moses.

Making the Breastplate

⁸ʰAnd he made the breastplate, artistically woven like the workmanship of the ephod, of gold, blue, purple, and scarlet *thread*, and of fine woven linen. ⁹They made the breastplate square by doubling it; a span *was* its length and a span its width when doubled. ¹⁰ⁱAnd they set in it four rows of stones: a row with a sardius, a topaz, and an emerald was the first row; ¹¹the second row, a turquoise, a sapphire,

* **39:1** Or *woven garments*

38:22–23 Responsibility—No higher tribute can be paid than "Well done—you've finished." Bezalel and his assistant, Aholiab, were called, Spirit-endowed, and commissioned for one work and one work alone. Neither of these individuals ever became celebrities, but God does not measure our effectiveness in His kingdom work by how many times we make the headlines in the local media. God cares about whether we obey Him faithfully, not whether other people approve of us. It is easy to make verbal commitments that sound really good, but God isn't looking for fine words. He complimented Bezalel and Aholiab on finishing their assignment, not on their fine start or their good intentions (39:43).
38:24 All the gold. The weight of all the gold used in the work may have been about a ton. The talent weighed about 75 pounds, and equaled 3,000 shekels.
38:25 the silver. The quantity of silver was enormous, about 7,000 pounds.

38:26 a bekah for each man. The census of Numbers 14:6 puts the number of men over the age of 20 at 603,550.
38:27–28 the sanctuary. Although the tabernacle was a tent, it was not a makeshift dwelling. It was a glorious shrine that symbolized the presence of the living God in the midst of the people.
38:29 bronze. About 5,000 pounds of bronze were used.

38:20 ᵈEx. 27:19   **38:21** ᵉActs 7:44   ᶠNum. 4:28, 33
ᵍLev. 10:6, 16   **38:22** ʰEx. 31:2, 6   **38:23** ⁱEx. 31:6; 36:1
38:24 ʲEx. 35:5, 22   ᵏEx. 30:13, 24   **38:25** ˡEx. 30:11–16
38:26 ᵐEx. 30:13, 15   ⁿNum. 1:46; 26:51   **38:27** ᵒEx.
26:19, 21, 25, 32   **38:28** ᵖEx. 27:17   **39:1** ᵃEx. 25:4;
35:23   ᵇEx. 31:10; 35:19   ᶜEx. 28:4   **39:2** ᵈEx. 28:6–14
ᵉEx. 8:7   **39:6** ᶠEx. 28:9–11   **39:7** ᵍEx. 28:12, 29
39:8 ʰEx. 28:15–30   **39:10** ⁱEx. 28:17

and a diamond; 12the third row, a jacinth, an agate, and an amethyst; 13the fourth row, a beryl, an onyx, and a jasper. *They were* enclosed in settings of gold in their mountings. 14*There were* itwelve stones according to the names of the sons of Israel: according to their names, *engraved like* a signet, each one with its own name according to the twelve tribes. 15And they made chains for the breastplate at the ends, like braided cords of pure gold. 16They also made two settings of gold and two gold rings, and put the two rings on the two ends of the breastplate. 17And they put the two braided *chains* of gold in the two rings on the ends of the breastplate. 18The two ends of the two braided *chains* they fastened in the two settings, and put them on the shoulder straps of the ephod in the front. 19And they made two rings of gold and put *them* on the two ends of the breastplate, on the edge of it, which *was* on the inward side of the ephod. 20They made two *other* gold rings and put them on the two shoulder straps, underneath the ephod toward its front, right at the seam above the intricately woven band of the ephod. 21And they bound the breastplate by means of its rings to the rings of the ephod with a blue cord, so that it would be above the intricately woven band of the ephod, and that the breastplate would not come loose from the ephod, as the LORD had commanded Moses.

Making the Other Priestly Garments

22kHe made the lrobe of the ephod of woven work, all of blue. 23And *there was* an opening in the middle of the robe, like the opening in a coat of mail, *with* a woven binding all around the opening, so that it would not tear. 24They made on the hem of the robe pomegranates of blue, purple, and scarlet, and of fine woven *linen*. 25And they made mbells of pure gold, and put the bells between the pomegranates on the hem of the robe all around between the pomegranates: 26a bell and a pomegranate, a bell and a pomegranate, all around the hem of the robe to minister in, as the LORD had commanded Moses.

27nThey made tunics, artistically woven of fine linen, for Aaron and his sons, 28oa turban of fine linen, exquisite hats of fine linen, pshort trousers of fine woven linen,

29qand a sash of fine woven linen with blue, purple, and scarlet *thread*, made by a weaver, as the LORD had commanded Moses.

30rThen they made the plate of the holy crown of pure gold, and wrote on it an inscription *like* the engraving of a signet:

sHOLINESS TO THE LORD.

31And they tied to it a blue cord, to fasten *it* above on the turban, as the LORD had commanded Moses.

The Work Completed

32Thus all the work of the tabernacle of the tent of meeting was tfinished. And the children of Israel did uaccording to all that the LORD had commanded Moses; so they did. 33And they brought the tabernacle to Moses, the tent and all its furnishings: its clasps, its boards, its bars, its pillars, and its sockets, 34the covering of ram skins dyed red, the covering of badger skins, and the veil of the covering; 35the ark of the Testimony with its poles, and the mercy seat; 36the table, all its utensils, and the vshowbread; 37the pure *gold* lampstand with its lamps (the lamps set in order), all its utensils, and the oil for light; 38the gold altar, the anointing oil, and the sweet incense; the screen for the tabernacle door; 39the bronze altar, its grate of bronze, its poles, and all its utensils; the laver with its base; 40the hangings of the court, its pillars and its sockets, the screen for the court gate, its cords, and its pegs; all the utensils for the service of the tabernacle, for the tent of meeting; 41and the garments of ministry,* to minister in the holy *place:* the holy garments for Aaron the priest, and his sons' garments, to minister as priests.

42According to all that the LORD had commanded Moses, so the children of Israel wdid all the work. 43Then Moses looked over all the work, and indeed they had done it; as the LORD had commanded, just so they had done it. And Moses xblessed them.

The Tabernacle Erected and Arranged

40 Then the LORD aspoke to Moses, saying: 2"On the first day of the bfirst month you shall set up cthe tabernacle of the tent of meeting. 3dYou shall put in it the

---

* 39:41 Or *woven garments*

39:32–43 so they did. Because it was so important in God's plan for His people, both in the wilderness and today, the tabernacle had to be constructed in exact accordance with the divine pattern. It was the place where His glory would actually dwell and where they could meet Him. Because they had done just as the Lord had commanded, "Moses blessed them." A mood of celebration pervades these verses. One can sense the pride of accomplishment coupled with the reverence for all of these holy objects.

40:2 first month. This was the month of Abib, also called Nisan (12:2; 13:4). The tabernacle was

completed nine months after the arrival of the people at Mount Sinai (19:1) and two weeks before the second celebration of the Passover (v. 17).

39:14 *j* Rev. 21:12   **39:22** *k* Ex. 28:31–35   *l* Ex. 29:5
39:25 *m* Ex. 28:33   **39:27** *n* Ex. 28:39, 40   **39:28** *o* Ex.
28:4, 39   *p* Ex. 28:42   **39:29** *q* Ex. 28:39   **39:30** *r* Ex.
28:36, 37   *s* Zech. 14:20   **39:32** *t* Ex. 40:17   *u* Ex. 25:40;
39:42, 43   **39:36** *v* Ex. 23–30   **39:42** *w* Ex. 35:10
39:43 *x* Lev. 9:22, 23   **40:1** *a* Ex. 25:1—31:18   **40:2** *b* Ex.
12:2; 13:4   *c* Ex. 26:1, 30; 40:17   **40:3** *d* Num. 4:5

ark of the Testimony, and partition off the ark with the veil. [4e]You shall bring in the table and [f]arrange the things that are to be set in order on it; [g]and you shall bring in the lampstand and light its lamps. [5h]You shall also set the altar of gold for the incense before the ark of the Testimony, and put up the screen for the door of the tabernacle. [6]Then you shall set the [i]altar of the burnt offering before the door of the tabernacle of the tent of meeting. [7]And [j]you shall set the laver between the tabernacle of meeting and the altar, and put water in it. [8]You shall set up the court all around, and hang up the screen at the court gate.

[9]"And you shall take the anointing oil, and [k]anoint the tabernacle and all that is in it; and you shall hallow it and all its utensils, and it shall be holy. [10]You shall [l]anoint the altar of the burnt offering and all its utensils, and consecrate the altar. [m]The altar shall be most holy. [11]And you shall anoint the laver and its base, and consecrate it.

[12n]"Then you shall bring Aaron and his sons to the door of the tabernacle of meeting and wash them with water. [13]You shall put the holy [o]garments on Aaron, [p]and anoint him and consecrate him, that he may minister to Me as priest. [14]And you shall bring his sons and clothe them with tunics. [15]You shall anoint them, as you anointed their father, that they may minister to Me as priests; for their anointing shall surely be [q]an everlasting priesthood throughout their generations."

[16]Thus Moses did; according to all that the LORD had commanded him, so he did.

[17]And it came to pass in the first month of the second year, on the first day of the month, that the [r]tabernacle was raised up. [18]So Moses raised up the tabernacle, fastened its sockets, set up its boards, put in its bars, and raised up its pillars. [19]And he spread out the tent over the tabernacle and put the covering of the tent on top of it, as the LORD had commanded Moses. [20]He took [s]the Testimony and put it into the ark, inserted the poles through the rings of the ark, and put the mercy seat on top of the ark. [21]And he brought the ark into the tabernacle, [t]hung up the veil of the covering, and partitioned off the ark of the Testimony, as the LORD had commanded Moses.

[22u]He put the table in the tabernacle of meeting, on the north side of the tabernacle, outside the veil; [23v]and he set the bread in order upon it before the LORD, as the LORD had commanded Moses. [24w]He put the lampstand in the tabernacle of meeting, across from the table, on the south side of the tabernacle; [25]and [x]he lit the lamps before the LORD, as the LORD had commanded Moses. [26y]He put the gold altar in the tabernacle of meeting in front of the veil; [27z]and he burned sweet incense on it, as the LORD had commanded Moses. [28a]He hung up the screen at the door of the tabernacle. [29b]And he put the altar of burnt offering before the door of the tabernacle of the tent of meeting, and [c]offered upon it the burnt offering and the grain offering, as the LORD had commanded Moses. [30d]He set the laver between the tabernacle of meeting and the altar, and put water there for washing; [31]and Moses, Aaron, and his sons would [e]wash their hands and their feet with water from it. [32]Whenever they went into the tabernacle of meeting, and when they came near the altar, they washed, [f]as the LORD had commanded Moses. [33g]And he raised up the court all around the tabernacle and the altar, and hung up the screen of the court gate. So Moses [h]finished the work.

The Cloud and the Glory

[34i]Then the [j]cloud covered the tabernacle of meeting, and the [k]glory of the LORD filled the tabernacle. [35]And Moses [l]was not able to enter the tabernacle of meeting, because the cloud rested above it, and the glory of the LORD filled the tabernacle. [36m]Whenever the cloud was taken up from above the tabernacle, the children of Israel would go onward in all their journeys. [37]But [n]if the cloud was not taken up, then they did not journey till the day that it was taken up. [38]For [o]the cloud of the LORD was above the tabernacle by day, and fire was over it by night, in the sight of all the house of Israel, throughout all their journeys.

40:20–21 the Testimony . . . the mercy seat. The Testimony was the stone tablets of the Ten Commandments (25:16). The mercy seat was the cover of the ark (25:17–22).

40:34 cloud . . . glory. When the Lord came near in 19:20, the people were terrified, but this time they were overjoyed. The glory of the Lord filling the tabernacle demonstrated His presence with the Israelites, His significance to them, and His awe-inspiring wonder.

40:35 the cloud rested above it. God is not "far away in heaven," occasionally looking at the earth. He lives among His people, and He desires to communicate with them (John 1:14).

40:38 the cloud of the LORD. The Book of Exodus ends with the picture of the gracious God hovering

protectively over His people. He allowed His presence to be felt and seen.

40:4 [e] Ex. 26:35; 40:22 [f] Ex. 25:30; 40:23 [g] Ex. 40:24, 25 **40:5** [h] Ex. 40:26 **40:6** [i] Ex. 39:39 **40:7** [j] Ex. 30:18; 40:30 **40:9** [k] Ex. 30:26 **40:10** [l] Ex. 30:26–30 [m] Ex. 29:36, 37 **40:12** [n] Lev. 8:1–13 **40:13** [o] Ex. 29:5; 39:1, 41 [p] Ex. 28:41] **40:15** [q] Num. 25:13 **40:17** [r] Ex. 40:2 **40:20** [s] Ex. 25:16 **40:21** [t] Ex. 26:33 **40:22** [u] Ex. 26:35 **40:23** [v] Ex. 40:4 **40:24** [w] Ex. 26:35 **40:25** [x] Ex. 25:37; 30:7, 8; 40:4 **40:26** [y] Ex. 30:1, 6; 40:5 **40:27** [z] Ex. 30:7 **40:28** [a] Ex. 26:36; 40:5 **40:29** [b] Ex. 40:6 [c] Ex. 29:38–42 **40:30** [d] Ex. 30:18; 40:7 **40:31** [e] Ex. 30:19, 20 **40:32** [f] Ex. 30:19 **40:33** [g] Ex. 27:9–18; 40:8 [h] [Heb. 3:2–5] **40:34** [i] Num. 9:15 [j] 1 Kin. 8:10, 11 [k] Lev. 9:6, 23 **40:35** [l] 1 Kin. 8:11 **40:36** [m] Num. 9:17 **40:37** [n] Num. 9:19–22 **40:38** [o] Ex. 13:21

THE THIRD BOOK OF MOSES CALLED
LEVITICUS

▶ **AUTHOR:** Moses is declared to be the author of Leviticus fifty-six times within the book. External evidence supporting the authorship of Moses includes (1) a uniform ancient testimony, (2) parallels found in the Ras Shamra Tablets dating from 1400 B.C., and (3) the testimony of Christ (Matt. 8:2–4 and Lev. 14:1–4; Matt. 12:4 and Lev. 24:9; Luke 2:22).

▶ **TIME:** c. 1405 B.C.   ▶ **KEY VERSES:** Lev. 20:7–8

▶ **THEME:** Leviticus is God's guidebook for His newly redeemed people. It shows them how to worship and live holy lives. The instructions for the sacrificial system point to a holy God and what He requires from people who would serve Him. The laws of holiness and sanctification provide basic instructions for living in a community. Together the two groups of laws are a framework for relationship between God and man. Blessings result from obedience to these laws and discipline is the result of disobedience.

The Burnt Offering

1 Now the LORD [a]called to Moses, and spoke to him [b]from the tabernacle of meeting, saying, [2]"Speak to the children of Israel, and say to them: [c]'When any one of you brings an offering to the LORD, you shall bring your offering of the livestock—of the herd and of the flock.

[3]'If his offering is a burnt sacrifice of the herd, let him offer a male [d]without blemish; he shall offer it of his own free will at the door of the tabernacle of meeting before the LORD. [4e]Then he shall put his hand on the head of the burnt offering, and it will be [f]accepted on his behalf [g]to make atonement for him. [5]He shall kill the [h]bull before the LORD; [i]and the priests, Aaron's sons, shall bring the blood [j]and sprinkle the blood all around on the altar that is by the door of the tabernacle of meeting. [6]And he shall [k]skin the burnt offering and cut it into its pieces. [7]The sons of Aaron the priest shall put [l]fire on the altar, and [m]lay the wood in order on the fire. [8]Then the priests, Aaron's sons, shall lay the parts, the head, and the fat in order on the wood that is on the fire upon the altar; [9]but he shall wash its entrails and its legs with water. And the priest shall burn all on the altar as a burnt sacrifice, an offering made by fire, a [n]sweet aroma to the LORD.

[10]'If his offering is of the flocks—of the sheep or of the goats—as a burnt sacrifice, he shall bring a male [o]without

---

1:1–17 offering to the LORD. Leviticus continues the Exodus narrative of the dedication of the tabernacle by indicating how the liberated Israelites are to worship their God. This book deals with the voluntary sacrifices for thanksgiving, communion, or cleansing from sin. These offerings from the herd or flock represented the labor and financial investment of the owner, and were a continual reminder that a price always has to be paid for sin.

1:3 burnt sacrifice. The "burnt sacrifice" was the only offering that was entirely consumed on the altar. It foreshadows the total sacrifice of Christ on the cross, as well as representing wholehearted, unreserved worship where nothing is withheld or left over. It reminds us that nothing must be held back for ourselves; it all belongs to Him. **male without blemish.** Offering a perfect animal was a real sacrifice, not just "something they didn't really need or want." These perfect animals were valuable for breeding or for sale. The principle still holds. God's people are to offer their best, of their own free will, and with joy.

1:4 he shall put his hand upon the head of the burnt offering. Each worshiper brought his or her own offering and laid his own hand on the animal's head. No one could send another to act on his behalf. In the same way, no one today can send someone else to accept Christ's atonement for him; we must each come to Christ ourselves, acknowledging our own sin before Him.

1:9 sweet aroma. Never does Scripture represent God as eating the offerings brought to Him, as the pagan gods were thought to do. When a sacrifice was done in faith with a free will, it was accepted by the Lord as desirable, or sweet.

1:1 a Ex. 19:3; 25:22   b Ex. 40:34   **1:2** c Lev. 22:18, 19
1:3 d Eph. 5:27   **1:4** e Lev. 3:2, 8, 13; 4:15   f [Rom. 12:1]
g 2 Chr. 29:23, 24   **1:5** h Mic. 6:6   i 2 Chr. 35:11   j [Heb. 12:24]   **1:6** k Lev. 7:8   **1:7** l Mal. 1:10   m Gen. 22:9
1:9 n Gen. 8:21   **1:10** o Lev. 1:3

blemish. [11][p]He shall kill it on the north side of the altar before the LORD; and the priests, Aaron's sons, shall sprinkle its blood all around on the altar. [12]And he shall cut it into its pieces, with its head and its fat; and the priest shall lay them in order on the wood that *is* on the fire upon the altar; [13]but he shall wash the entrails and the legs with water. Then the priest shall bring *it* all and burn *it* on the altar; it *is* a burnt sacrifice, an [q]offering made by fire, a sweet aroma to the LORD.

[14]'And if the burnt sacrifice of his offering to the LORD *is* of birds, then he shall bring his offering of [r]turtledoves or young pigeons. [15]The priest shall bring it to the altar, wring off its head, and burn *it* on the altar; its blood shall be drained out at the side of the altar. [16]And he shall remove its crop with its feathers and cast it [s]beside the altar on the east side, into the place for ashes. [17]Then he shall split it at its wings, *but* [t]shall not divide *it* completely; and the priest shall burn it on the altar, on the wood that *is* on the fire. [u]It *is* a burnt sacrifice, an offering made by fire, a sweet aroma to the LORD.

The Grain Offering

2 'When anyone offers [a]a grain offering to the LORD, his offering shall be *of* fine flour. And he shall pour oil on it, and put [b]frankincense on it. [2]He shall bring it to Aaron's sons, the priests, one of whom shall take from it his handful of fine flour and oil with all the frankincense. And the priest shall burn [c]*it as* a memorial on the altar, an offering made by fire, a sweet aroma to the LORD. [3][d]The rest of the grain offering *shall be* Aaron's and his [e]sons'. [f]*It is* most holy of the offerings to the LORD made by fire.

[4]'And if you bring as an offering a grain offering baked in the oven, *it shall be* unleavened cakes of fine flour mixed with oil, or unleavened wafers [g]anointed with oil. [5]But if your offering *is* a grain offering *baked* in a pan, *it shall be of* fine flour, unleavened, mixed with oil. [6]You shall break it in pieces and pour oil on it; it *is* a grain offering.

[7]'If your offering *is* a grain offering *baked* in a [h]covered pan, it shall be made *of* fine flour with oil. [8]You shall bring the grain offering that is made of these things to the LORD. And when it is presented to the priest, he shall bring it to the altar. [9]Then the priest shall take from the grain offering [i]a memorial portion, and burn *it* on the altar. *It is* an [j]offering made by fire, a sweet aroma to the LORD. [10]And [k]what is left of the grain offering *shall be* Aaron's and his sons'. *It is* most holy of the offerings to the LORD made by fire.

[11]'No grain offering which you bring to the LORD shall be made with [l]leaven, for you shall burn no leaven nor any honey in any offering to the LORD made by fire. [12][m]As for the offering of the firstfruits, you shall offer them to the LORD, but they shall not be burned on the altar for a sweet aroma. [13]And every offering of your grain offering [n]you shall season with salt; you shall not allow [o]the salt of the covenant of your God to be lacking from your grain offering. [p]With all your offerings you shall offer salt.

[14]'If you offer a grain offering of your firstfruits to the LORD, [q]you shall offer for the grain offering of your firstfruits green heads of grain roasted on the fire, grain beaten from [r]full heads. [15]And [s]you shall put oil on it, and lay frankincense on it. It *is* a grain offering. [16]Then the priest shall burn [t]the memorial portion: *part* of its beaten grain and *part* of its oil, with all the frankincense, as an offering made by fire to the LORD.

2:1 *oil . . . frankincense.* Olive oil was a primary part of the diet and a prominent symbol of blessing and prosperity. Frankincense was a costly incense from South Arabia and East Africa, an imported luxury that would have to be bought with money. By including frankincense, as well as the animals and grain they could raise on their land, every aspect of Israel's wealth was made a part of the offerings to God.

2:3 *shall be Aaron's and his sons'.* A significant portion of the priest's daily food came from this part of the grain offering. Only the consecrated priests were allowed to eat it, and only within the tabernacle.

2:8–9 *priest.* There were always two individuals involved when the ancient Hebrew brought his sacrifice to God. One was the offerer himself and the other was the officiating priest, who was the "bridge builder" between men and God. Jesus, as a better priest and a better sacrifice, once for all time bridged the gap between God and man, and through Him we can have direct access to God, to confess our sins and receive forgiveness.

2:11 *leaven.* Leaven and honey were prohibited because both cause fermentation, which represents corruption.

2:13 *salt of the covenant of your God.* Salt was to be used in every grain offering. This was a reminder of the covenant that God had made with Israel at Sinai, and was a symbol of faithfulness to God and His covenant. There is an old saying, "he has eaten my salt," which means that you have taken someone into your home, given them shelter, food, and hospitality. The idea of the "salt" of God's covenant was well understood.

1:11 [p] Lev. 1:5 **1:13** [q] Num. 15:4–7; 28:12–14 **1:14** [r] Lev. 5:7, 11; 12:8 **1:16** [s] Lev. 6:10 **1:17** [t] Gen. 15:10 [u] Lev. 1:9, 13 **2:1** [a] Num. 15:4 [b] Lev. 5:11 **2:2** [c] Lev. 2:9; 5:12; 6:15; 24:7 **2:3** [d] Lev. 7:9 [e] Lev. 6:6; 10:12, 13 [f] Num. 18:9 **2:4** [g] Ex. 29:2 **2:7** [h] Lev. 7:9 **2:9** [i] Lev. 2:2, 16; 5:12; 6:15 [j] Ex. 29:18 **2:10** [k] Lev. 2:3; 6:16 **2:11** [l] Lev. 6:16, 17 **2:12** [m] Lev. 23:10, 11, 17, 18 **2:13** [n] [Col. 4:6] [o] Num. 18:19 [p] Ezek. 43:24 **2:14** [q] Lev. 23:10, 14 [r] 2 Kin. 4:42 **2:15** [s] Lev. 2:1 **2:16** [t] Lev. 2:2

The Peace Offering

3 'When his offering *is* a *a*sacrifice of a peace offering, if he offers *it* of the herd, whether male or female, he shall offer it *b*without blemish before the LORD. 2And *c*he shall lay his hand on the head of his offering, and kill it *at* the door of the tabernacle of meeting; and Aaron's sons, the priests, shall *d*sprinkle the blood all around on the altar. 3Then he shall offer from the sacrifice of the peace offering an offering made by fire to the LORD. *e*The fat that covers the entrails and all the fat that *is* on the entrails, 4the two kidneys and the fat that *is* on them by the flanks, and the fatty lobe *attached* to the liver above the kidneys, he shall remove; 5and Aaron's sons *f*shall burn it on the altar upon the *g*burnt sacrifice, which *is* on the wood that *is* on the fire, *as* an *h*offering made by fire, a *i*sweet aroma to the LORD.

6'If his offering as a sacrifice of a peace offering to the LORD *is* of the flock, *whether* male or female, *j*he shall offer it without blemish. 7If he offers a *k*lamb as his offering, then he shall *l*offer it *m*before the LORD. 8And he shall lay his hand on the head of his offering, and kill it before the tabernacle of meeting; and Aaron's sons shall sprinkle its blood all around on the altar. 9Then he shall offer from the sacrifice of the peace offering, as an offering made by fire to the LORD, its fat *and* the whole fat tail which he shall remove close to the backbone. And the fat that covers the entrails and all the fat that *is* on the entrails, 10the two kidneys and the fat that *is* on them by the flanks, and the fatty lobe *attached* to the liver above the kidneys, he shall remove; 11and the priest shall burn *them* on the altar *as* *n*food, an offering made by fire to the LORD.

12'And if his *o*offering *is* a goat, then *p*he shall offer it before the LORD. 13He shall lay his hand on its head and kill it before

the tabernacle of meeting; and the sons of Aaron shall sprinkle its blood all around on the altar. 14Then he shall offer from it his offering, as an offering made by fire to the LORD. The fat that covers the entrails and all the fat that *is* on the entrails, 15the two kidneys and the fat that *is* on them by the flanks, and the fatty lobe *attached* to the liver above the kidneys, he shall remove; 16and the priest shall burn them on the altar *as* food, an offering made by fire for a sweet aroma; *q*all the fat *is* the LORD's.

17'*This shall be* a *r*perpetual statute throughout your generations in all your dwellings: you shall eat neither fat nor *s*blood.'"

The Sin Offering

4 Now the LORD spoke to Moses, saying, 2"Speak to the children of Israel, saying: *a*'If a person sins unintentionally against any of the commandments of the LORD *in anything* which ought not to be done, and does any of them, 3b*if the anointed priest sins, bringing guilt on the people, then let him offer to the LORD for his sin which he has sinned *c*a young bull without blemish as a *d*sin offering. 4He shall bring the bull *e*to the door of the tabernacle of meeting before the LORD, lay his hand on the bull's head, and kill the bull before the LORD. 5Then the anointed priest shall *f*take some of the bull's blood and bring it to the tabernacle of meeting. 6The priest shall dip his finger in the blood and sprinkle some of the blood seven times before the LORD, in front of the *g*veil of the sanctuary. 7And the priest shall *h*put some of the blood on the horns of the altar of sweet incense before the LORD, which is in the tabernacle of meeting; and he shall pour *i*the remaining blood of the bull at the base of the altar of the burnt offering, which is at the door of the tabernacle of meeting. 8He shall take from it all the fat of the bull as the sin offering. The fat that covers the entrails and

---

3:1 *peace offering.* The Hebrew word for "peace" means "wholeness, completeness, soundness, health." When a person possesses all of these attributes, he is at peace. The peace offerings were a time of celebrating and enjoying the gift of peace with God. Yet it was only after Christ's death and resurrection, when He became our perfect peace offering (Col. 1:20) that we could really have perfect peace with God. The sacrifices had to be made over and over, but Christ's death was once, for all time.

3:3–4 *two kidneys, and the fat that is on them . . . the fatty lobe.* The fat was one of the most prized portions of the meat, and the kidneys were considered the seat of the emotions. The liver was an essential organ for telling the future in the pagan cultures surrounding Israel. Giving all of these things to God symbolized giving Him the best, giving Him the hopes, dreams, and desires of life; recognizing that He alone has control of the future, and that He will reveal it in His own way, at His own time.

3:5 *upon the burnt sacrifice.* The peace offering nor-

mally followed the burnt offering, which was entirely consumed on the altar. Being reconciled to God through the burnt offering, the worshiper was in a position to fellowship with God. Repentance and reconciliation must always come before genuine fellowship.

3:9 *the whole fat tail.* The tail of the Palestinian broad-tailed sheep is almost entirely fat and can weigh more than 16 pounds. This explains its special mention in the regulations for offering the fat of the sheep.

3:1 *a* Lev. 7:11, 29 *b* Lev. 1:3; 22:20–24 **3:2** *c* Lev. 1:4, 5; 16:21 *d* Lev. 1:5 **3:3** *e* Lev. 1:8; 3:16; 4:8, 9 **3:5** *f* Ex. 29:13 *g* 2 Chr. 35:14 *h* Num. 28:3–10 *i* Num. 15:8–10 **3:6** *j* Lev. 3:1; 22:20–24 **3:7** *k* Num. 15:4, 5 *l* 1 Kin. 8:62 *m* Lev. 17:8, 9 **3:11** *n* Num. 28:2 **3:12** *o* Num. 15:6–11 *p* Lev. 3:1, 7 **3:16** *q* Lev. 7:23–25 **3:17** *r* Lev. 6:18; 7:36; 17:7; 23:14 *s* Lev. 7:23, 26; 17:10, 14 **4:2** *a* Lev. 5:15–18 **4:3** *b* Lev. 8:12 *c* Lev. 3:1; 9:2 *d* Lev. 9:7 **4:4** *e* Lev. 1:3, 4; 4:15 **4:5** *f* Lev. 16:14 **4:6** *g* Ex. 40:21, 26 **4:7** *h* Lev. 4:18, 25, 30, 34; 8:15; 9:9; 16:18 *i* Ex. 40:5, 6; Lev. 5:9

all the fat which *is* on the entrails, 9the two
kidneys and the fat that *is* on them by the
flanks, and the fatty lobe *attached* to the
liver above the kidneys, he shall remove,
10[j]as it was taken from the bull of the sacrifice of the peace offering; and the priest
shall burn them on the altar of the burnt
offering. 11[k]But the bull's hide and all its
flesh, with its head and legs, its entrails
and offal— 12the whole bull he shall carry
outside the camp to a clean place, [l]where
the ashes are poured out, and [m]burn it on
wood with fire; where the ashes are poured
out it shall be burned.

13'Now [n]if the whole congregation of Israel sins unintentionally, [o]and the thing
is hidden from the eyes of the assembly,
and they have done *something against*
any of the commandments of the LORD *in*
anything which should not be done, and
are guilty; 14when the sin which they have
committed becomes known, then the assembly shall offer a young bull for the sin,
and bring it before the tabernacle of meeting. 15And the elders of the congregation
[p]shall lay their hands on the head of the
bull before the LORD. Then the bull shall
be killed before the LORD. 16[q]The anointed
priest shall bring some of the bull's blood
to the tabernacle of meeting. 17Then the
priest shall dip his finger in the blood and
sprinkle *it* seven times before the LORD, in
front of the veil. 18And he shall put *some* of
the blood on the horns of the altar which *is*
before the LORD, which *is* in the tabernacle
of meeting; and he shall pour the remaining blood at the base of the altar of burnt
offering, which is at the door of the tabernacle of meeting. 19He shall take all the fat
from it and burn *it* on the altar. 20And he
shall do [r]with the bull as he did with the
bull as a sin offering; thus he shall do with
it. [s]So the priest shall make atonement for
them, and it shall be forgiven them. 21Then
he shall carry the bull outside the camp,
and burn it as he burned the first bull. It *is*
a sin offering for the assembly.

22'When a ruler has sinned, and [t]done
something unintentionally *against* any of
the commandments of the LORD his God
in anything which should not be done, and
is guilty, 23or [u]if his sin which he has committed comes to his knowledge, he shall
bring as his offering a kid of the goats, a
male without blemish. 24And [v]he shall lay
his hand on the head of the goat, and kill
it at the place where they kill the burnt offering before the LORD. It *is* a sin offering.
25[w]The priest shall take some of the blood
of the sin offering with his finger, put *it*
on the horns of the altar of burnt offering,
and pour its blood at the base of the altar
of burnt offering. 26And he shall burn all its
fat on the altar, like [x]the fat of the sacrifice
of the peace offering. [y]So the priest shall
make atonement for him concerning his
sin, and it shall be forgiven him.

27[z]'If anyone of the common people
sins unintentionally by doing *something*
against any of the commandments of the
LORD *in anything* which ought not to be
done, and is guilty, 28or [a]if his sin which
he has committed comes to his knowledge,
then he shall bring as his offering a kid of
the goats, a female without blemish, for
his sin which he has committed. 29[b]And he
shall lay his hand on the head of the sin offering, and kill the sin offering at the place
of the burnt offering. 30Then the priest
shall take *some* of its blood with his finger,
put *it* on the horns of the altar of burnt offering, and pour all *the remaining* blood at
the base of the altar. 31[c]He shall remove all
its fat, [d]as fat is removed from the sacrifice
of the peace offering; and the priest shall
burn it on the altar for a [e]sweet aroma to
the LORD. [f]So the priest shall make atonement for him, and it shall be forgiven him.

32'If he brings a lamb as his sin offering,
[g]he shall bring a female without blemish.
33Then he shall [h]lay his hand on the head
of the sin offering, and kill it as a sin offering at the place where they kill the burnt
offering. 34The priest shall take *some* of the
blood of the sin offering with his finger, put
it on the horns of the altar of burnt offering, and pour all *the remaining* blood at the
base of the altar. 35He shall remove all its
fat, as the fat of the lamb is removed from
the sacrifice of the peace offering. Then the
priest shall burn it on the altar, [i]according
to the offerings made by fire to the LORD.
[j]So the priest shall make atonement for his
sin that he has committed, and it shall be
forgiven him.

4:11–12 ***the whole bull.*** Burning the whole bull ensured that the priest did not profit in any way from his own sin or the atonement for his sin. Carrying it outside the camp was another way of symbolizing the seriousness and pollution of sin.

4:13–21 ***the whole congregation.*** Interestingly, not only individuals bring a sin offering to God, but the whole congregation as well. We are used to thinking of individuals coming under conviction and repenting, but how can a whole community come to this way of thinking? A congregation or community can begin to realize that they have misrepresented God, or fallen short of their God-given responsibilities, and together repent and ask for forgiveness, even though the members repenting may not have been the actual people who made the bad decisions that created the problem. Groups need to turn around and redirect their actions, just as much as individuals do,

4:10 [j] Lev. 3:3–5 **4:11** [k] Ex. 29:14 **4:12** [l] Lev. 4:21; 6:10, 11; 16:27 [m] [Heb. 13:11, 12] **4:13** [n] Num. 15:24–26 [o] Lev. 5:2–4, 17 **4:15** [p] Lev. 1:3, 4 **4:16** [q] Lev. 4:5 **4:20** [r] Lev. 4:3 [s] Num. 15:25 **4:22** [t] Lev. 4:2, 13, 27 **4:23** [u] Lev. 4:14; 5:4 **4:24** [v] [Is. 53:6] **4:25** [w] Lev. 4:7, 18, 30, 34 **4:26** [x] Lev. 3:3–5 [y] Lev. 4:20 **4:27** [z] Num. 15:27 **4:28** [a] Lev. 4:23 **4:29** [b] Lev. 1:4; 4:4, 24 **4:31** [c] Lev. 3:14 [d] Lev. 3:3, 4 [e] Ex. 29:18 [f] Lev. 4:26 **4:32** [g] Lev. 4:28 **4:33** [h] Num. 8:12 **4:35** [i] Lev. 3:5 [j] Lev. 4:26, 31

The Trespass Offering

5 'If a person sins in [a]hearing the utterance of an oath, and *is* a witness, whether he has seen or known *of the matter*—if
he does not tell *it*, he [b]bears guilt.
2'Or [c]if a person touches any unclean
thing, whether *it is* the carcass of an unclean beast, or the carcass of unclean livestock, or the carcass of unclean creeping
things, and he is unaware of it, he also shall
be unclean and [d]guilty. 3Or if he touches
[e]human uncleanness—whatever uncleanness with which a man may be defiled,
and he is unaware of it—when he realizes
it, then he shall be guilty.
4'Or if a person swears, speaking
thoughtlessly with *his* lips [f]to do evil or
[g]to do good, whatever *it is* that a man may
pronounce by an oath, and he is unaware
of it—when he realizes *it*, then he shall be
guilty in any of these *matters*.
5'And it shall be, when he is guilty in any
of these *matters*, that he shall [h]confess that
he has sinned in that *thing*; 6and he shall
bring his trespass offering to the LORD for
his sin which he has committed, a female
from the flock, a lamb or a kid of the goats
as a sin offering. So the priest shall make
atonement for him concerning his sin.
7[i]'If he is not able to bring a lamb, then
he shall bring to the LORD, for his trespass
which he has committed, two [j]turtledoves
or two young pigeons: one as a sin offering
and the other as a burnt offering. 8And he
shall bring them to the priest, who shall offer *that* which *is* for the sin offering first,
and [k]wring off its head from its neck, but
shall not divide *it* completely. 9Then he
shall sprinkle *some* of the blood of the sin
offering on the side of the altar, and the
[l]rest of the blood shall be drained out at the
base of the altar. It *is* a sin offering. 10And
he shall offer the second *as* a burnt offering according to the [m]prescribed manner.
So [n]the priest shall make atonement on his
behalf for his sin which he has committed,
and it shall be forgiven him.
11'But if he is [o]not able to bring two turtledoves or two young pigeons, then he
who sinned shall bring for his offering
one-tenth of an ephah of fine flour as a
sin offering. [p]He shall put no oil on it, nor
shall he put frankincense on it, for it *is* a
sin offering. 12Then he shall bring it to the
priest, and the priest shall take his handful of it [q]as a memorial portion, and burn
it on the altar [r]according to the offerings
made by fire to the LORD. It *is* a sin offering. 13[s]The priest shall make atonement for
him, for his sin that he has committed in
any of these matters; and it shall be forgiv-
en him. [t]*The rest* shall be the priest's as a
grain offering.'"

Offerings with Restitution

14Then the LORD spoke to Moses, saying: 15[u]"If a person commits a trespass, and
sins unintentionally in regard to the holy
things of the LORD, then [v]he shall bring to
the LORD as his trespass offering a ram
without blemish from the flocks, with your
valuation in shekels of silver according to
[w]the shekel of the sanctuary, as a trespass
offering. 16And he shall make restitution
for the harm that he has done in regard to
the holy thing, [x]and shall add one-fifth to it
and give it to the priest. [y]So the priest shall
make atonement for him with the ram of

---

and this is one of the ways that God changes whole societies.

5:3 ***human uncleanness.*** Body fluids, a person's waste, and contact with a corpse were all causes of uncleanness. The ancient Israelites knew nothing about microbiology, but God, who knows everything, gave them laws that prevented disease and made them distinct from their neighbors.

5:4 ***swears . . . and he is unaware of it.*** Certainly a person would know when he makes a vow, but he might not be immediately aware of how rash his vow is, or that the long term consequences are undesirable. Whether the vow was made with good intentions, but not carried out, or made with wicked intentions, but not carried out, the person who made the vow is still responsible to repent of his foolishness when he becomes aware of it.

5:7 ***two turtledoves.*** Part of the purification offering was burned on the altar, and part was not burned. When offering birds, the worshiper brought two in order to accomplish this.

5:11 ***one-tenth of an ephah.*** This was approximately two quarts.

5:13 ***The rest shall be the priest's.*** Part of the offering was burned on the altar, as was part of the animal sacrifices. The rest belonged to the priests, as did the remainder of the animal sacrifices brought by ordinary citizens, except for their burnt offerings.

5:15 ***commits a trespass, and sins unintentionally . . . trespass offering.*** This refers both to the objective responsibility of a sinner for his or her actions and the subjective feeling of guilt experienced by the sinner. The offering righted the wrong of the offense and cleared the conscience of the sinner.

5:15—6:7 ***person commits a trespass.*** The trespass offering covers both offenses against God (5:15–19) and against people (6:1–7). The offense may be unintentional, or quite deliberate, but regardless of the motive, such actions make the perpetrator guilty. The quickest way to mend relationships with God and with fellow human beings is to honestly admit our guilt and wrongdoing, pay back or repair where we can, and ask forgiveness of those we have sinned against. This responsibility cannot be sidestepped.

5:1 [a] Prov. 29:24 [b] Num. 9:13 **5:2** [c] Num. 19:11–16 [d] Lev. 5:17 **5:3** [e] Lev. 5:12, 13, 15 **5:4** [f] Acts 23:12 [g] [James 5:12] **5:5** [h] Prov. 28:13 **5:7** [i] Lev. 12:6, 8; 14:21 [j] Lev. 1:14 **5:8** [k] Lev. 1:15–17 **5:9** [l] Lev. 4:7, 18, 30, 34 **5:10** [m] Lev. 1:14–17 [n] Lev. 4:20, 26; 5:13, 16 **5:11** [o] Lev. 14:21–32 [p] Num. 5:15 **5:12** [q] Lev. 2:2 [r] Lev. 4:35 **5:13** [s] Lev. 4:26 [t] Lev. 2:3; 6:17, 26 **5:15** [u] Lev. 4:2; 22:14 [v] Ezra 10:19 [w] Ex. 30:13 **5:16** [x] Num. 5:7 [y] Lev. 4:26

the trespass offering, and it shall be for-given him.

[17]"If a person sins, and commits any of these things which are forbidden to be done by the commandments of the LORD, [z]though he does not know *it*, yet he is [a]guilty and shall bear his iniquity. [18b]And he shall bring to the priest a ram without blemish from the flock, with your valua-tion, as a trespass offering. So the priest shall make atonement for him regarding his ignorance in which he erred and did not know *it*, and it shall be forgiven him. [19]It is a trespass offering; [c]he has certainly trespassed against the LORD."

6 And the LORD spoke to Moses, say-ing: [2]"If a person sins and [a]commits a trespass against the LORD by [b]lying to his neighbor about [c]what was delivered to him for safekeeping, or about a pledge, or about a robbery, or if he has [d]extorted from his neighbor, [3]or if he [e]has found what was lost and lies concerning it, and [f]swears falsely—in any one of these things that a man may do in which he sins: [4]then it shall be, because he has sinned and is guilty, that he shall restore [g]what he has stolen, or the thing which he has extorted, or what was delivered to him for safekeep-ing, or the lost thing which he found, [5]or all that about which he has sworn falsely. He shall [h]restore its full value, add one-fifth more to it, *and* give it to whomever it be-longs, on the day of his trespass offering. [6]And he shall bring his trespass offering to the LORD, [i]a ram without blemish from the flock, with your valuation, as a tres-pass offering, to the priest. [7j]So the priest shall make atonement for him before the LORD, and he shall be forgiven for any one

of these things that he may have done in which he trespasses."

The Law of the Burnt Offering

[8]Then the LORD spoke to Moses, saying, [9]"Command Aaron and his sons, saying, 'This is the [k]law of the burnt offering: The burnt offering *shall be* on the hearth upon the altar all night until morning, and the fire of the altar shall be kept burning on it. [10]And the priest shall put on his linen garment, and his linen trousers he shall put on his body, and take up the ashes of the burnt offering which the fire has con-sumed on the altar, and he shall put them [m]beside the altar. [11]Then [n]he shall take off his garments, put on other garments, and carry the ashes outside the camp [o]to a clean place. [12]And the fire on the altar shall be kept burning on it; it shall not be put out. And the priest shall burn wood on it every morning, and lay the burnt of-fering in order on it; and he shall burn on it the [p]fat of the peace offerings. [13]A fire shall always be burning on the [q]altar; it shall never go out.

The Law of the Grain Offering

[14]'This *is* the law of the grain offering: The sons of Aaron shall offer it on the al-tar before the LORD. [15]He shall take from it his handful of the fine flour of the grain offering, with its oil, and all the frankin-cense which *is* on the grain offering, and shall burn *it* on the altar *for* a sweet aroma, as a memorial to the LORD. [16]And the re-mainder of it Aaron and his sons shall eat; with unleavened bread it shall be eaten in a holy place; in the court of the tabernacle of meeting they shall eat it. [17]It shall not be

---

5:17 *though he does not know it, yet is he guilty.* Ignorance does not make an offense harmless. The offender was still guilty and bore responsibility for his sin. He might also be troubled in conscience, though he might never learn the exact nature of his offense. This raises the concept that a person can be aware of a break in his fellowship with God, without being sure what caused this break.

5:18 *erred and did not know it.* This was not a sin of rebellion, but one for which the offender earnestly desired to atone, though he did not know what it was.

5:19 *he has certainly trespassed against the LORD.* The fact that the priest declared him forgiven, and the peace of conscience that the worshiper had, declares that he was indeed guilty of some trespass; it was not his imagination. It is possible for a Christian to have an overactive conscience that keeps the believer in a constant state of anxiety about unknown sins. It is good to remember that God knows all about this, and if we confess our feelings of guilt, He will either show us our true guilt and grant us forgiveness and a clear conscience, or show us the error in our thinking regarding what He expects from us.

6:5–6 *restore.* Restitution and a one-fifth fine were evidence of genuine repentance. Then the offender could bring the ram for the trespass offering and be forgiven for the sin of swearing falsely in God's

name. Jesus preserved this order for the person who remembered at the altar that he had offended his brother (Matt. 5:23).

6:10 *trousers.* The breeches were linen trousers that prevented immodest exposure as the priest ascended and descended the altar ramp. This mod-esty communicated to the Israelites that human sexuality could not influence God. That idea was central feature of Baal worship, which continually tempted the Israelites. The priests of Baal would use obscene gestures and actions in the pagan worship of their depraved god.

6:13 *fire shall always be burning.* There are at least three reasons the priests are instructed to keep the fire burning. The original fire on the altar came from God, perpetual fire symbolized perpetual worship, and perpetual fire was a reminder of the continual need for atonement and reconciliation with God.

5:17 [z] Lev. 4:2, 13, 22, 27 [a] Lev. 5:1, 2 **5:18** [b] Lev. 5:15 **5:19** [c] Ezra 10:2 **6:2** [a] Num. 5:6 [b] Lev. 19:11 [c] Ex. 22:7, 10 [d] Prov. 24:28 **6:3** [e] Deut. 22:1–4 [f] Ex. 22:11 **6:4** [g] Lev. 24:18, 21 **6:5** [h] Lev. 5:16 **6:6** [i] Lev. 1:3; 5:15 **6:7** [j] Lev. 4:26 **6:9** [k] Ex. 29:38–42 **6:10** [l] Ex. 28:39–43 [m] Lev. 1:16 **6:11** [n] Ezek. 44:19 [o] Lev. 4:12 **6:12** [p] Lev. 3:3, 5, 9, 14 **6:13** [q] Lev. 1:7

baked with leaven. I have given it *as* their portion of My offerings made by fire; it *is* most holy, like the sin offering and the ʳtrespass offering. ¹⁸ˢAll the males among the children of Aaron may eat it. ᵗ*It shall be* a statute forever in your generations concerning the offerings made by fire to the LORD. ᵘEveryone who touches them must be holy.'"*

¹⁹And the LORD spoke to Moses, saying, ²⁰ᵛ"This *is* the offering of Aaron and his sons, which they shall offer to the LORD, *beginning* on the day when he is anointed: one-tenth of an ʷephah of fine flour as a daily grain offering, half of it in the morning and half of it at night. ²¹It shall be made in a ˣpan with oil. *When it is* mixed, you shall bring it in. The baked pieces of the grain offering you shall offer *for* a sweet aroma to the LORD. ²²The priest from among his sons, ʸwho is anointed in his place, shall offer it. *It is* a statute forever to the LORD. ᶻIt shall be wholly burned. ²³For every grain offering for the priest shall be wholly burned. It shall not be eaten."

The Law of the Sin Offering

²⁴Also the LORD spoke to Moses, saying, ²⁵"Speak to Aaron and to his sons, saying, 'This *is* the law of the sin offering: ᵃIn the place where the burnt offering is killed, the sin offering shall be killed before the LORD. It *is* most holy. ²⁶ᵇThe priest who offers it for sin shall eat it. In a holy place it shall be eaten, in the court of the tabernacle of meeting. ²⁷ᶜEveryone who touches its flesh must be holy.* And when its blood is sprinkled on any garment, you shall wash that on which it was sprinkled, in a holy place. ²⁸But the earthen vessel in which it is boiled ᵈshall be broken. And if it is boiled in a bronze pot, it shall be both scoured and rinsed in water. ²⁹All the males among the priests may eat it. It *is* most holy. ³⁰ᵉBut no sin offering from which *any* of the blood is brought into the tabernacle of meeting, to make atonement in the holy ᶠ*place*,* shall be ᵍeaten. It shall be ʰburned in the fire.

The Law of the Trespass Offering

7 'Likewise ᵃthis *is* the law of the trespass offering (it *is* most holy): ²In the place where they kill the burnt offering they shall kill the trespass offering. And its blood he shall sprinkle all around on the altar. ³And he shall offer from it all its fat. The fat tail and the fat that covers the entrails, ⁴the two kidneys and the fat that *is* on them by the flanks, and the fatty lobe *attached* to the liver above the kidneys, he shall remove; ⁵and the priest shall burn them on the altar *as* an offering made by fire to the LORD. It *is* a trespass offering. ⁶ᵇEvery male among the priests may eat it. It shall be eaten in a holy place. ᶜIt *is* most holy. ⁷ᵈThe trespass offering *is* like the sin offering; *there is* one law for them both: the priest who makes atonement with it shall have *it.* ⁸And the priest who offers anyone's burnt offering, that priest shall have for himself the skin of the burnt offering which he has offered. ⁹Also ᵉevery grain offering that is baked in the oven and all that is prepared in the covered pan, or in a pan, shall be the priest's who offers it. ¹⁰Every grain offering, *whether* mixed with oil or dry, shall belong to all the sons of Aaron, to one *as much* as the other.

The Law of Peace Offerings

¹¹ᶠ'This *is* the law of the sacrifice of peace offerings which he shall offer to the LORD: ¹²If he offers it for a thanksgiving, then he shall offer, with the sacrifice of thanksgiving, unleavened cakes mixed with oil, unleavened wafers ᵍanointed with oil, or cakes of blended flour mixed with oil. ¹³Besides the cakes, *as* his offering he shall offer ʰleavened bread with the sacrifice of thanksgiving of his peace offering. ¹⁴And from it he shall offer one cake from each offering *as* a heave offering to the LORD. ⁱIt shall belong to the priest who sprinkles the blood of the peace offering.

---

* **6:18** Compare Numbers 4:15 and Haggai 2:11–13
* **6:27** Compare Numbers 4:15 and Haggai 2:11–13
* **6:30** The Most Holy Place when capitalized

6:20 *half of it in the morning . . . half of it at night.* The idea of a morning and evening appointment with God is ancient. It is a precious privilege, open to every believer because Jesus opened the door into the presence of God when He died on the cross for our sins.

6:22 *a statute forever.* This grain offering and the burnt offering were sacrificed daily—with some interruptions, most notably during the exile—until the destruction of the temple in A.D. 70. Even in the periods of Judah's worst apostasy, the evidence suggests that the daily offerings continued, though often for incorrect or inadequate reasons (Is. 1:10–17; Jer. 7:8–15; Mic. 6:6–8).

7:1–7 *trespass offering.* The guilt or trespass offering was "most holy," showing how seriously and carefully God considers the acts of reparation made by His people. The priest was to eat it in a holy place. It was his to eat, as part of God's provision for him, but he was to remember where it came from. The price of atonement has never been cheap in God's eyes, even when it was as incomplete as the offering of a goat or lamb.

6:17 ʳ Lev. 7:7 **6:18** ˢ Lev. 6:29; 7:6 ᵗ Lev. 3:17 ᵘ Ex. 29:37; Num. 4:15; Hag. 2:11–13 **6:20** ᵛ Ex. 29:2 ʷ Ex. 16:36 **6:21** ˣ Lev. 2:5; 7:9 **6:22** ʸ Lev. 4:3 ᶻ Ex. 29:25 **6:25** ᵃ Lev. 1:1, 3, 5, 11 **6:26** ᵇ [Ezek. 44:28, 29] **6:27** ᶜ Ex. 29:37; Num. 4:15; Hag. 2:11–13 **6:28** ᵈ Lev. 11:33; 15:12 **6:30** ᵉ Lev. 4:7, 11, 12, 18, 21; 10:18; 16:27 ᶠ Ex. 26:33 ᵍ Lev. 6:16, 23, 26 ʰ Lev. 16:27 **7:1** ᵃ Lev. 5:14—6:7 **7:6** ᵇ Lev. 6:16–18, 29 ᶜ Lev. 2:3 **7:7** ᵈ Lev. 6:24–30; 14:13 **7:9** ᵉ Lev. 2:3, 10 **7:11** ᶠ Lev. 3:1; 22:18, 21 **7:12** ᵍ Num. 6:15 **7:13** ʰ Amos 4:5 **7:14** ⁱ Num. 18:8, 11, 19

15j"The flesh of the sacrifice of his peace offering for thanksgiving shall be eaten the same day it is offered. He shall not leave any of it until morning. 16But kif the sacrifice of his offering *is* a vow or a voluntary offering, it shall be eaten the same day that he offers his sacrifice; but on the next day the remainder of it also may be eaten; 17the remainder of the flesh of the sacrifice on the third day must be burned with fire. 18And if *any* of the flesh of the sacrifice of his peace offering is eaten at all on the third day, it shall not be accepted, nor shall it be limputed to him; it shall be an mabomination *to* him who offers it, and the person who eats of it shall bear guilt.

19"The flesh that touches any unclean thing shall not be eaten. It shall be burned with fire. And as for the *clean* flesh, all who are clean may eat of it. 20But the person who eats the flesh of the sacrifice of the peace offering that *belongs* to the nLORD, owhile he is unclean, that person pshall be cut off from his people. 21Moreover the person who touches any unclean thing, *such as* qhuman uncleanness, *an* runclean animal, or any sabominable unclean thing,* and who eats the flesh of the sacrifice of the peace offering that *belongs* to the LORD, that person tshall be cut off from his people.'"

Fat and Blood May Not Be Eaten

22And the LORD spoke to Moses, saying, 23"Speak to the children of Israel, saying: u'You shall not eat any fat, of ox or sheep or goat. 24And the fat of an animal that dies *naturally*, and the fat of what is torn by wild beasts, may be used in any other way; but you shall by no means eat it. 25For whoever eats the fat of the animal of which men offer an offering made by fire to the LORD, the person who eats *it* shall be cut off from his people. 26vMoreover you shall not eat any blood in any of your dwellings, *whether* of bird or beast. 27Whoever eats any blood, that person shall be cut off from his people.'"

The Portion of Aaron and His Sons

28Then the LORD spoke to Moses, saying, 29"Speak to the children of Israel, saying: w'He who offers the sacrifice of his peace offering to the LORD shall bring his offering to the LORD from the sacrifice of his peace offering. 30xHis own hands

shall bring the offerings made by fire to the LORD. The fat with the breast he shall bring, that the ybreast may be waved *as* a wave offering before the LORD. 31zAnd the priest shall burn the fat on the altar, but the abreast shall be Aaron's and his sons'. 32bAlso the right thigh you shall give to the priest *as* a heave offering from the sacrifices of your peace offerings. 33He among the sons of Aaron, who offers the blood of the peace offering and the fat, shall have the right thigh for *his* part. 34For cthe breast of the wave offering and the thigh of the heave offering I have taken from the children of Israel, from the sacrifices of their peace offerings, and I have given them to Aaron the priest and to his sons from the children of Israel by a statute forever.'"

35This *is* the consecrated portion for Aaron and his sons, from the offerings made by fire to the LORD, on the day when *Moses* presented them to minister to the LORD as priests. 36The LORD commanded this to be given to them by the children of Israel, don the day that He anointed them, *by* a statute forever throughout their generations.

37This *is* the law eof the burnt offering, fthe grain offering, gthe sin offering, hthe trespass offering, ithe consecrations, and ithe sacrifice of the peace offering, 38which the LORD commanded Moses on Mount Sinai, on the day when He commanded the children of Israel kto offer their offerings to the LORD in the Wilderness of Sinai.

Aaron and His Sons Consecrated

8 And the LORD spoke to Moses, saying: 2a"Take Aaron and his sons with him, and bthe garments, cthe anointing oil, a dbull as the sin offering, two erams, and a basket of unleavened bread; 3and gather all the congregation together at the door of the tabernacle of meeting."

4So Moses did as the LORD commanded him. And the congregation was gathered together at the door of the tabernacle of meeting. 5And Moses said to the congregation, "This *is* what the LORD commanded to be done."

6Then Moses brought Aaron and his sons and fwashed them with water. 7And

---

* 7:21 Following Masoretic Text, Septuagint, and Vulgate; Samaritan Pentateuch, Syriac, and Targum read *swarming thing* (compare 5:2).

7:34 the breast of the wave offering and the thigh of the heave offering. This present was a contribution to the officiating priest as his portion of the peace offerings for thanksgiving. The offering was waved before the Lord as an acknowledgment that He is the giver of all gifts.

8:6–13 Purification—Moses carried out the Lord's command (Ex. 29:4) by purifying Aaron and his sons for the priesthood. The purification process began with an outward washing of water which symbolized an inward purity. The believer today also shows

7:15j Lev. 22:29, 30   **7:16**k Lev. 19:5–8   **7:18**l Num. 18:27 m Lev. 11:10, 11, 41; 19:7   **7:20**n [Heb. 2:17] o Num. 19:13 p Gen. 17:14   **7:21**q Lev. 5:2, 3, 5 r Lev. 11:24, 28 s Ezek. 4:14 t Lev. 7:20   **7:23**u Lev. 3:17; 17:10–15   **7:26**v Acts 15:20, 29   **7:29**w Lev. 3:1; 22:21 **7:30**x Lev. 3:3, 4, 9, 14 y Ex. 29:24, 27   **7:31**z Lev. 3:5, 11, 16 a Deut. 18:3   **7:32**b Num. 6:20   **7:34**c Lev. 10:14, 15   **7:36**d Lev. 8:12, 30   **7:37**e Lev. 6:9 f Lev. 6:14 g Lev. 6:25 h Lev. 7:1 i Lev. 29:1 j Lev. 7:11   **7:38**k Lev. 1:1, 2   **8:2**a Ex. 29:1–3 b Lev. 28:2, 4 c Ex. 30:24, 25 d Ex. 29:10 e Ex. 29:15, 19   **8:6**f Heb. 10:22

he ᵍput the tunic on him, girded him with the sash, clothed him with the robe, and put the ephod on him; and he girded him with the intricately woven band of the ephod, and with it tied *the ephod* on him. ⁸Then he put the breastplate on him, and he ʰput the Urim and the Thummim* in the breastplate. ⁹ⁱAnd he put the turban on his head. Also on the turban, on its front, he put the golden plate, the holy crown, as the LORD had commanded Moses.

¹⁰ʲAlso Moses took the anointing oil, and anointed the tabernacle and all that *was* in it, and consecrated them. ¹¹He sprinkled some of it on the altar seven times, anointed the altar and all its utensils, and the laver and its base, to consecrate them. ¹²And he ᵏpoured some of the anointing oil on Aaron's head and anointed him, to consecrate him.

¹³ˡThen Moses brought Aaron's sons and put tunics on them, girded them with sashes, and put hats on them, as the LORD had commanded Moses.

¹⁴ᵐAnd he brought the bull for the sin offering. Then Aaron and his sons ⁿlaid their hands on the head of the bull for the sin offering, ¹⁵and Moses killed *it*. ᵒThen he took the blood, and put *some* on the horns of the altar all around with his finger, and purified the altar. And he poured the blood at the base of the altar, and consecrated it, to make atonement for it. ¹⁶ᵖThen he took all the fat that *was* on the entrails, the fatty lobe *attached to* the liver, and the two kidneys with their fat, and Moses burned *them* on the altar. ¹⁷But the bull, its hide, its flesh, and its offal, he burned with fire outside the camp, as the LORD ᑫhad commanded Moses.

¹⁸ʳThen he brought the ram as the burnt offering. And Aaron and his sons laid their hands on the head of the ram, ¹⁹and Moses killed *it*. Then he sprinkled the blood all around on the altar. ²⁰And he cut the ram into pieces; and Moses ˢburned the head, the pieces, and the fat. ²¹Then he washed the entrails and the legs in water. And Moses burned the whole ram on the altar. It *was* a burnt sacrifice for a sweet aroma, an offering made by fire to the LORD, ᵗas the LORD had commanded Moses.

²²And ᵘhe brought the second ram, the ram of consecration. Then Aaron and his sons laid their hands on the head of the ram, ²³and Moses killed *it*. Also he took some of ᵛits blood and put it on the tip of Aaron's right ear, on the thumb of his right hand, and on the big toe of his right foot. ²⁴Then he brought Aaron's sons. And Moses put *some* of the ʷblood on the tips of their right ears, on the thumbs of their right hands, and on the big toes of their right feet. And Moses sprinkled the blood all around on the altar. ²⁵ˣThen he took the fat and the fat tail, all the fat that *was* on the entrails, the fatty lobe *attached to* the liver, the two kidneys and their fat, and the right thigh; ²⁶ʸand from the basket of unleavened bread that was before the LORD he took one unleavened cake, a cake of bread *anointed with* oil, and one wafer, and put *them* on the fat and on the right thigh; ²⁷and he put all *these* ᶻin Aaron's hands and in his sons' hands, and waved them *as* a wave offering before the LORD. ²⁸ᵃThen Moses took them from their hands and burned *them* on the altar, on the burnt offering. They *were* consecration offerings for a sweet aroma. That *was* an offering made by fire to the LORD. ²⁹And ᵇMoses took the ᶜbreast and waved it *as* a wave offering before the LORD. It was Moses' ᵈpart of the ram of consecration, as the LORD had commanded Moses.

³⁰Then ᵉMoses took some of the anointing oil and some of the blood which *was* on the altar, and sprinkled *it* on Aaron, on his garments, on his sons, and on the garments of his sons with him; and he consecrated Aaron, his garments, his sons, and the garments of his sons with him.

³¹And Moses said to Aaron and his sons, ᶠ"Boil the flesh *at* the door of the tabernacle of meeting, and eat it there with the bread that *is* in the basket of consecration offerings, as I commanded, saying, 'Aaron and his sons shall eat it.' ³²ᵍWhat remains of the flesh and of the bread you shall burn with fire. ³³And you shall not go outside the door of the tabernacle of meeting *for* seven days, until the days of your consecration are ended. For ʰseven days he shall consecrate you.

---

* **8:8** Literally *the Lights and the Perfections* (compare Exodus 28:30)

---

his inward reality (his acceptance of Christ and the presence of the Holy Spirit) with his outward actions. These acts of obedience do not create the inward reality, but they confirm it.

8:8 the Urim and the Thummim. These were the sacred lots used to determine the will of God. What they looked like and how they were used is not known. Apparently, the high priest phrased questions so the answers would be yes, or no, depending on how the lots came up.

8:12 anointed him. The high priests of Israel, beginning here with Aaron, were anointed, as were the kings of Israel (1 Sam. 10:1; 16:13) and at least one of the prophets (1 Kin. 19:16). Jesus combines in His

person the offices of High Priest, King, and Prophet, so He is *the* Anointed One, which is the meaning of the names Messiah (Hebrew) and Christ (Greek).

8:7 ᵍ Ex. 39:1–31　**8:8** ʰ Ex. 28:30　**8:9** ⁱ Ex. 28:36, 37; 29:6　**8:10** ʲ Ex. 30:26–29; 40:10, 11　**8:12** ᵏ Ps. 133:2　**8:13** ˡ Ex. 29:8, 9　**8:14** ᵐ Ezek. 43:19　ⁿ Lev. 4:4　**8:15** ᵒ Lev. 4:7　**8:16** ᵖ Ex. 29:13　**8:17** ᑫ Lev. 4:11, 12　**8:18** ʳ Ex. 29:15　**8:20** ˢ Lev. 1:8　**8:21** ᵗ Ex. 29:18　**8:22** ᵘ Ex. 29:19, 31　**8:23** ᵛ Lev. 14:14　**8:24** ʷ [Heb. 9:13, 14, 18–23]　**8:25** ˣ Ex. 29:22　**8:26** ʸ Ex. 29:23　**8:27** ᶻ Ex. 29:24　**8:28** ᵃ Ex. 29:25　**8:29** ᵇ Ps. 99:6　ᶜ Ex. 29:27　ᵈ Ex. 29:26　**8:30** ᵉ Ex. 29:21; 30:30　**8:31** ᶠ Ex. 29:31, 32　**8:32** ᵍ Ex. 29:34　**8:33** ʰ Ex. 29:30, 35

34iAs he has done this day, so the LORD has commanded to do, to make atonement for you. 35Therefore you shall stay at the door of the tabernacle of meeting day and night for seven days, and jkeep the charge of the LORD, so that you may not die; for so I have been commanded." 36So Aaron and his sons did all the things that the LORD had commanded by the hand of Moses.

The Priestly Ministry Begins

9 It came to pass on the aeighth day that Moses called Aaron and his sons and the elders of Israel. 2And he said to Aaron, "Take for yourself a young bbull as a sin offering and a ram as a burnt offering, without blemish, and offer them before the LORD. 3And to the children of Israel you shall speak, saying, c"Take a kid of the goats as a sin offering, and a calf and a lamb, both of the first year, without blemish, as a burnt offering, 4also a bull and a ram as peace offerings, to sacrifice before the LORD, and da grain offering mixed with oil; for etoday the LORD will appear to you.'"

5So they brought what Moses commanded before the tabernacle of meeting. And all the congregation drew near and stood before the LORD. 6Then Moses said, "This is the thing which the LORD commanded you to do, and the glory of the LORD will appear to you." 7And Moses said to Aaron, "Go to the altar, foffer your sin offering and your burnt offering, and make atonement for yourself and for the people. gOffer the offering of the people, and make atonement for them, as the LORD commanded."

8Aaron therefore went to the altar and killed the calf of the sin offering, which was for himself. 9Then the sons of Aaron brought the blood to him. And he dipped his finger in the blood, put it on the horns of the altar, and poured the blood at the base of the altar. 10hBut the fat, the kidneys, and the fatty lobe from the liver of the sin offering he burned on the altar, as the LORD had commanded Moses. 11iThe flesh and the hide he burned with fire outside the camp.

12And he killed the burnt offering; and Aaron's sons presented to him the blood, jwhich he sprinkled all around on the altar. 13kThen they presented the burnt offering to him, with its pieces and head, and he burned them on the altar. 14lAnd he washed the entrails and the legs, and burned them with the burnt offering on the altar.

15mThen he brought the people's offering, and took the goat, which was the sin offering for the people, and killed it and offered it for sin, like the first one. 16And he brought the burnt offering and offered it naccording to the prescribed manner. 17Then he brought the grain offering, took a handful of it, and burned it on the altar, obesides the burnt sacrifice of the morning.

18He also killed the bull and the ram as psacrifices of peace offerings, which were for the people. And Aaron's sons presented to him the blood, which he sprinkled all around on the altar, 19and the fat from the bull and the ram—the fatty tail, what covers the entrails and the kidneys, and the fatty lobe attached to the liver; 20and they put the fat on the breasts. qThen he burned the fat on the altar; 21but the breasts and the right thigh Aaron waved ras a wave offering before the LORD, as Moses had commanded.

22Then Aaron lifted his hand toward the people, sblessed them, and came down from offering the sin offering, the burnt offering, and peace offerings. 23And Moses and Aaron went into the tabernacle of meeting, and came out and blessed the people. Then the glory of the LORD appeared to all the people, 24and tfire came out from before the LORD and consumed the burnt offering and the fat on the altar. When all the people saw it, they ushouted and fell on their vfaces.

The Profane Fire of Nadab and Abihu

10 Then aNadab and Abihu, the sons of Aaron, beach took his censer and put fire in it, put incense on it, and offered cprofane fire before the LORD, which He

---

8:35 so that you may not die. This statement was a reminder that it is dangerous to approach God carelessly, without reverence, or ignore His instructions. Two of Aaron's sons failed to heed this warning and died (ch. 10).

9:4 the LORD will appear to you. The purpose of all worship is to fellowship with God. The sacrifices were not an end in themselves; they allowed the worshiper to meet with God without being destroyed. The Israelites looked forward and we look back to Christ's atonement, which made the way for us to come freely into God's presence.

9:15 the goat, which was the sin offering. This goat was offered for atonement of the people as a general acknowledgment that they would always need to make things right with God before they could worship Him, and is referred to again in ch. 16. The bull for the sin offering (4:14) was for a specific sin, rather than dealing with sin nature (that is, our ability to sin).

9:22 Aaron . . . blessed them. The ultimate function of the priests was to bless the people. The purpose of the priest's sacrifices was to cleanse the priests so they could bless the people, and the purpose of the people's sacrifices was to cleanse the people to receive this blessing from God.

10:1–2 profane fire. Aaron and his sons served the Lord as high priests in the worship of the tabernacle. They had been properly appointed, purified, clothed,

8:34i [Heb. 7:16]   **8:35**j Deut. 11:1   **9:1**a Ezek. 43:27   **9:2**b Lev. 4:1–12   **9:3**c Lev. 4:23, 28   **9:4**d Lev. 2:4 e Ex. 29:43   **9:7**f [Heb. 5:3–5; 7:27] g Lev. 4:16, 20   **9:10**h Lev. 8:16   **9:11**i Lev. 4:11, 12; 8:17   **9:12**j Lev. 1:5; 8:19   **9:13**k Lev. 8:20   **9:14**l Lev. 8:21   **9:15**m [Is. 53:10]   **9:16**n Lev. 1:1–13   **9:17**o Ex. 29:38, 39   **9:18**p Lev. 3:1–11   **9:20**q Lev. 3:5, 16   **9:21**r Lev. 7:30–34   **9:22**s Luke 24:50   **9:24**t Judg. 6:21   u Ezra 3:11 v 1 Kin. 18:38, 39   **10:1**a Num. 3:2–4 b Lev. 16:12 c Ex. 30:9

had not commanded them. ²So ᵈfire went out from the LORD and devoured them, and they died before the LORD. ³And Moses said to Aaron, "This is what the LORD spoke, saying:

'By those ᵉwho come near Me
I must be regarded as holy;
And before all the people
I must be glorified.'"

So Aaron held his peace.

⁴Then Moses called Mishael and Elzaphan, the sons of Uzziel the uncle of Aaron, and said to them, "Come near, ᶠcarry your brethren from before the sanctuary out of the camp." ⁵So they went near and carried them by their tunics out of the camp, as Moses had said.

⁶And Moses said to Aaron, and to Eleazar and Ithamar, his sons, "Do not uncover your heads nor tear your clothes, lest you die, and ᵍwrath come upon all the people. But let your brethren, the whole house of Israel, bewail the burning which the LORD has kindled. ⁷ʰYou shall not go out from the door of the tabernacle of meeting, lest you die, ⁱfor the anointing oil of the LORD is upon you." And they did according to the word of Moses.

Conduct Prescribed for Priests

⁸Then the LORD spoke to Aaron, saying: ⁹ʲ"Do not drink wine or intoxicating drink, you, nor your sons with you, when you go into the tabernacle of meeting, lest you die. It shall be a statute forever throughout your generations, ¹⁰that you may ᵏdistinguish between holy and unholy, and between unclean and clean, ¹¹ˡand that you may teach the children of Israel all the statutes which the LORD has spoken to them by the hand of Moses."

¹²And Moses spoke to Aaron, and to Eleazar and Ithamar, his sons who were left: ᵐ"Take the grain offering that remains of the offerings made by fire to the LORD, and eat it without leaven beside the altar; ⁿfor it is most holy. ¹³You shall eat it in a ᵒholy place, because it is your due and your sons' due, of the sacrifices made by fire to the LORD; for ᵖso I have been commanded.

¹⁴ᵃThe breast of the wave offering and the thigh of the heave offering you shall eat in a clean place, you, your sons, and your ʳdaughters with you; for they are your due and your sons' ˢdue, which are given from the sacrifices of peace offerings of the children of Israel. ¹⁵ᵗThe thigh of the heave offering and the breast of the wave offering they shall bring with the offerings of fat made by fire, to offer as a wave offering before the LORD. And it shall be yours and your sons' with you, by a statute forever, as the LORD has commanded."

¹⁶Then Moses made careful inquiry about ᵘthe goat of the sin offering, and there it was—burned up. And he was angry with Eleazar and Ithamar, the sons of Aaron who were left, saying, ¹⁷ᵛ"Why have you not eaten the sin offering in a holy place, since it is most holy, and God has given it to you to bear ᵂthe guilt of the congregation, to make atonement for them before the LORD? ¹⁸See! ˣIts blood was not brought inside the holy place;* indeed you should have eaten it in a holy place, ʸas I commanded."

¹⁹And Aaron said to Moses, "Look, ᶻthis day they have offered their sin offering and their burnt offering before the LORD, and such things have befallen me! If I had eaten the sin offering today, ᵃwould it have been accepted in the sight of the LORD?" ²⁰So when Moses heard that, he was content.

Foods Permitted and Forbidden

11 Now the LORD spoke to Moses and Aaron, saying to them, ²"Speak to the children of Israel, saying, ᵃ"These are the animals which you may eat among all the animals that are on the earth: ³Among the animals, whatever divides the hoof, having cloven hooves and chewing the cud—that you may eat. ⁴Nevertheless these you shall ᵇnot eat among those that chew the cud or those that have cloven hooves: the camel, because it chews the cud but does not have cloven hooves, is unclean to you; ⁵the rock hyrax, because it chews

---

* 10:18 The Most Holy Place when capitalized

---

anointed, and ordained. Initially they did everything that the Lord commanded through Moses. But when Nadab and Abihu disobeyed God in the very performance of their duties, the Lord swiftly punished them with a consuming fire. Being blessed with a thriving ministry is no excuse to go off and do things our own way. God doesn't take such actions lightly, and neither should we.

10:3 By those who come near Me . . . I must be glorified. Although this passage refers specifically to the priests of Israel, it is still a good concept for all believers. We are close to God, we remember that He is holy, that He paid a great price to redeem us, and it is our purpose to glorify Him.

11:3 chewing the cud. Ruminants, like cows, sheep, goats, deer, and antelope, eat only plants, mainly

grasses and grains. No meat-eating animal chews the cud.

11:4 the camel. Some of Israel's neighbors considered the camel a great delicacy.

11:5–6 rock hyrax . . . hare. The rock hyrax, or coney, lives in colonies among the rocks. It is about the size

---

10:2 ᵈ Num. 11:1; 16:35 **10:3** ᵉ Ex. 19:22 **10:4** ᶠ Acts 5:6, 10 **10:6** ᵍ 2 Sam. 24:1 **10:7** ʰ Lev. 8:33; 21:12 ⁱ Lev. 8:30 **10:9** ʲ Ezek. 44:21 **10:10** ᵏ Ezek. 22:26; 44:23 **10:11** ˡ Deut. 24:8 **10:12** ᵐ Num. 18:9 ⁿ Lev. 21:22 **10:13** ᵒ Num. 18:10 ᵖ Lev. 2:3; 6:16 **10:14** ᵠ Num. 18:11 ʳ Lev. 22:13 ˢ Num. 18:10 **10:15** ᵗ Lev. 7:29, 30, 34 **10:16** ᵘ Lev. 9:3, 15 **10:17** ᵛ Lev. 6:24–30 ᵂ Ex. 28:38 **10:18** ˣ Lev. 6:30 ʸ Lev. 6:26, 30 **10:19** ᶻ Lev. 9:8, 12 ᵃ [Is. 1:11–15] **11:2** ᵃ Deut. 14:4 **11:4** ᵇ Acts 10:14

the cud but does not have cloven hooves, *is* unclean to you; ⁶the hare, because it chews the cud but does not have cloven hooves, *is* unclean to you; ⁷and the swine, though it divides the hoof, having cloven hooves, yet does not chew the cud, ^c*is* unclean to you. ⁸Their flesh you shall not eat, and their carcasses you shall not touch. ^dThey *are* unclean to you.

^{9e}'These you may eat of all that *are* in the water: whatever in the water has fins and scales, whether in the seas or in the rivers—that you may eat. ¹⁰But all in the seas or in the rivers that do not have fins and scales, all that move in the water or any living thing which *is* in the water, they *are* an ^fabomination to you. ¹¹They shall be an abomination to you; you shall not eat their flesh, but you shall regard their carcasses as an abomination. ¹²Whatever in the water does not have fins or scales—that *shall be* an abomination to you.

^{13g}'And these you shall regard as an abomination among the birds; they shall not be eaten, they *are* an abomination: the eagle, the vulture, the buzzard, ¹⁴the kite, and the falcon after its kind; ¹⁵every raven after its kind, ¹⁶the ostrich, the short-eared owl, the sea gull, and the hawk after its kind; ¹⁷the little owl, the fisher owl, and the screech owl; ¹⁸the white owl, the jackdaw, and the carrion vulture; ¹⁹the stork, the heron after its kind, the hoopoe, and the bat.

²⁰'All flying insects that creep on *all* fours *shall be* an abomination to you. ²¹Yet these you may eat of every flying insect that creeps on *all* fours: those which have jointed legs above their feet with which to leap on the earth. ²²These you may eat: ^hthe locust after its kind, the destroying locust after its kind, the cricket after its kind, and the grasshopper after its kind. ²³But all *other* flying insects which have four feet *shall be* an abomination to you.

Unclean Animals

²⁴'By these you shall become unclean; whoever touches the carcass of any of them shall be unclean until evening; ²⁵whoever

carries part of the carcass of any of them ⁱshall wash his clothes and be unclean until evening. ²⁶*The carcass* of any animal which divides the foot, but is not cloven-hoofed or does not chew the cud, *is* unclean to you. Everyone who touches it shall be unclean. ²⁷And whatever goes on its paws, among all kinds of animals that go on *all* fours, those *are* unclean to you. Whoever touches any such carcass shall be unclean until evening. ²⁸Whoever carries *any such* carcass shall wash his clothes and be unclean until evening. It *is* unclean to you.

²⁹'These also *shall be* unclean to you among the creeping things that creep on the earth: the mole, ^jthe mouse, and the large lizard after its kind; ³⁰the gecko, the monitor lizard, the sand reptile, the sand lizard, and the chameleon. ³¹These *are* unclean to you among all that creep. Whoever ^ktouches them when they are dead shall be unclean until evening. ³²Anything on which *any* of them falls, when they are dead shall be unclean, whether *it is* any item of wood or clothing or skin or sack, whatever item *it is*, in which *any* work is done, ^lit must be put in water. And it shall be unclean until evening; then it shall be clean. ³³Any ^mearthen vessel into which *any* of them falls ⁿyou shall break; and whatever *is* in it shall be unclean: ³⁴in such a vessel, any edible food upon which water falls becomes unclean, and any drink that may be drunk from it becomes unclean. ³⁵And everything on which *a part* of *any such* carcass falls shall be unclean; whether *it is* an oven or cooking stove, it shall be broken down; *for* they *are* unclean, and shall be unclean to you. ³⁶Nevertheless a spring or a cistern, *in which there is* plenty of water, shall be clean, but whatever touches any such carcass becomes unclean. ³⁷And if a part of *any such* carcass falls on any planting seed which is to be sown, it *remains* clean. ³⁸But if water is put on the seed, and if *a part* of *any such* carcass falls on it, it *becomes* unclean to you.

³⁹'And if any animal which you may eat dies, he who touches its carcass shall be

---

of the rabbit, and like the rabbit, appears to chew constantly, but it is not a true ruminant, nor does it have a hoof.

11:7 the swine. The swine is the best known of the unclean animals. We know now that pigs can pass some diseases to humans, and that inadequately cooked meat is one way these diseases are transferred. Pigs were sacrificed to pagan deities, and God was carefully steering His people away from these corrupted cultures.

11:8 their carcasses you shall not touch. In the case of these unclean animals, eating their meat or touching their dead bodies caused an Israelite to be unclean, or ritually impure. However, touching a live animal did not make the Israelites unclean, and they were allowed to use camels and donkeys as beasts of burden.

11:11-12 abomination. The phrasing is careful,

deliberate, and repetitive to remove any possibility of finding any exception anywhere. *Abomination* is a stronger word than *unclean*, and implies not just avoidance, but repulsion.

11:20 creep on all fours. This phrase is an idiom for crawling on the ground, as insects do on their six legs. Many insects move about in filth and eat refuse.

11:21 jointed legs above their feet. The joints are the enlarged third legs of locusts and grasshoppers that enable them to leap. Locusts and grasshoppers do not live in filth or eat dung; they eat only plants.

11:7 ^c Is. 65:4; 66:3, 17 **11:8** ^d Is. 52:11 **11:9** ^e Deut. 14:9 **11:10** ^f Lev. 7:18, 21 **11:13** ^g Is. 66:17 **11:22** ^h Matt. 3:4 **11:25** ⁱ Num. 19:10, 21, 22; 31:24 **11:29** ^j Is. 66:17 **11:31** ^k Hag. 2:13 **11:32** ^l Lev. 15:12 **11:33** ^m Lev. 6:28 ⁿ Lev. 15:12

ᵒunclean until evening. ⁴⁰ᵖHe who eats of its carcass shall wash his clothes and be unclean until evening. He also who carries its carcass shall wash his clothes and be unclean until evening.

⁴¹'And every creeping thing that creeps on the earth *shall be* an abomination. It shall not be eaten. ⁴²Whatever crawls on its belly, whatever goes on *all* fours, or whatever has many feet among all creeping things that creep on the earth—these you shall not eat, for they *are* an abomination. ⁴³ᑫYou shall not make yourselves abominable with any creeping thing that creeps; nor shall you make yourselves unclean with them, lest you be defiled by them. ⁴⁴For I *am* the LORD your ʳGod. You shall therefore consecrate yourselves, and ˢyou shall be holy; for I *am* holy. Neither shall you defile yourselves with any creeping thing that creeps on the earth. ⁴⁵ᵗFor I *am* the LORD who brings you up out of the land of Egypt, to be your God. ᵘYou shall therefore be holy, for I *am* holy.

⁴⁶'This *is* the law of the animals and the birds and every living creature that moves in the waters, and of every creature that creeps on the earth, ⁴⁷ᵛto distinguish between the unclean and the clean, and between the animal that may be eaten and the animal that may not be eaten.'"

The Ritual After Childbirth

12 Then the LORD spoke to Moses, saying, ²"Speak to the children of Israel, saying: 'If a ᵃwoman has conceived, and borne a male child, then ᵇshe shall be unclean seven days; ᶜas in the days of her customary impurity she shall be unclean. ³And on the ᵈeighth day the flesh of his foreskin shall be circumcised. ⁴She shall then continue in the blood of *her*

purification thirty-three days. She shall not touch any hallowed thing, nor come into the sanctuary until the days of her purification are fulfilled.

⁵'But if she bears a female child, then she shall be unclean two weeks, as in her customary impurity, and she shall continue in the blood of *her* purification thirty-six days.

⁶ᵉ'When the days of her purification are fulfilled, whether for a son or a daughter, she shall bring to the priest a ᶠlamb of the first year as a burnt offering, and a young pigeon or a turtledove as a ᵍsin offering, to the door of the tabernacle of meeting. ⁷Then he shall offer it before the LORD, and make atonement for her. And she shall be clean from the flow of her blood. This *is* the law for her who has borne a male or a female.

⁸ʰ'And if she is not able to bring a lamb, then she may bring two turtledoves or two young pigeons—one as a burnt offering and the other as a sin offering. ⁱSo the priest shall make atonement for her, and she will be clean.'"

The Law Concerning Leprosy

13 And the LORD spoke to Moses and Aaron, saying: ²"When a man has on the skin of his body a swelling, ᵃa scab, or a bright spot, and it becomes on the skin of his body *like* a leprous* sore, ᵇthen he shall be brought to Aaron the priest or to one of his sons the priests. ³The priest shall examine the sore on the skin of the body; and if the hair on the sore has turned white, and the sore appears *to be* deeper than the skin of his body, it *is* a leprous sore. Then the priest shall examine him, and pronounce

---

* **13:2** Hebrew *saraath*, disfiguring skin diseases, including leprosy, and so in verses 2–46 and 14:2–32

11:44–45 be holy. Our Lord calls us to personal holiness, and holy living can only come from a life which spends time with the Lord, meditating on who He is, seeking His power to be like Him. We will make mistakes and sin all of our lives, which God never does; when He asks us to be holy because He is holy, it is a goal that we grow toward. Even though we never finish, we still overcome many, many areas of sin, and this growth shows others that we serve a holy God, because they see His characteristics in us.

12:2 conceived, and borne a male child...unclean. The child did not cause the mother to be unclean. God had ordained and blessed childbirth from the beginning, even before the sin in the garden (Gen. 1:28). It was the blood and other fluids in childbirth that made the mother ritually unclean for a period of time, just as other bodily fluids caused people to be unclean.

12:4 blood of her purification thirty-three days. There is a practical as well as a ceremonial aspect to these instructions. The eighth day marked the end of the mother's uncleanness with regard to everyday objects and activities; she would no longer make them unclean by touching them. But her personal uncleanness continued. This corresponds with the

medical characteristics of childbirth, and the need for special care and rest for the mother. (There is no reason given why this period is double with the birth of a female child.)

12:8 if she is not able to bring a lamb. Mary, following the birth of Jesus and the days of her purification, went to the temple in Jerusalem and offered a pair of doves because she was poor. **be clean.** The law of purification after childbirth demonstrates that all aspects of human existence are touched by sin. Childbirth itself is not sinful, and having children was one of the good commands that the Lord gave Adam and Eve in the garden. Yet pain in childbirth was one of the curses of the fall, and this time of purification can be viewed as a reminder that humans are still dealing with a sin nature that needs God's mercy and purification.

13:2 a man. The Hebrew word for "a man" means "human being," that is, anyone.

11:39 ᵒ Hag. 2:11–13   **11:40** ᵖ Lev. 17:15; 22:8   **11:43** ᑫ Lev. 20:25   **11:44** ʳ Ex. 6:7   ˢ 1 Pet. 1:15, 16   **11:45** ᵗ Ex. 6:7; 20:2   ᵘ Lev. 11:44   **11:47** ᵛ Ezek. 44:23   **12:2** ᵃ Lev. 15:19   ᵇ Luke 2:22   ᶜ Lev. 18:19   **12:3** ᵈ Gen. 17:12   **12:6** ᵉ Luke 2:22   ᶠ [John 1:29]   ᵍ Lev. 5:7   **12:8** ʰ Lev. 5:7   ⁱ Lev. 4:26   **13:2** ᵃ Is. 3:17   ᵇ Mal. 2:7

him unclean. 4But if the bright spot *is* white on the skin of his body, and does not appear *to be* deeper than the skin, and its hair has not turned white, then the priest shall isolate *the one who has* the sore cseven days. 5And the priest shall examine him on the seventh day; and indeed *if* the sore appears to be as it was, *and* the sore has not spread on the skin, then the priest shall isolate him another seven days. 6Then the priest shall examine him again on the seventh day; and indeed *if* the sore has faded, *and* the sore has not spread on the skin, then the priest shall pronounce him clean; it *is only* a scab, and he dshall wash his clothes and be clean. 7But if the scab should at all spread over the skin, after he has been seen by the priest for his cleansing, he shall be seen by the priest again. 8And *if* the priest sees that the scab has indeed spread on the skin, then the priest shall pronounce him unclean. It *is* leprosy.

9"When the leprous sore is on a person, then he shall be brought to the priest. 10eAnd the priest shall examine *him;* and indeed *if* the swelling on the skin *is* white, and it has turned the hair white, and *there is* a spot of raw flesh in the swelling, 11it *is* an old leprosy on the skin of his body. The priest shall pronounce him unclean, and shall not isolate him, for he *is* unclean.

12"And if leprosy breaks out all over the skin, and the leprosy covers all the skin of *the one who has* the sore, from his head to his foot, wherever the priest looks, 13then the priest shall consider; and indeed *if* the leprosy has covered all his body, he shall pronounce *him* clean *who has* the sore. It has all turned fwhite. He *is* clean. 14But when raw flesh appears on him, he shall be unclean. 15And the priest shall examine the raw flesh and pronounce him to be unclean; *for* the raw flesh *is* unclean. It *is* leprosy. 16Or if the raw flesh changes and turns white again, he shall come to the priest. 17And the priest shall examine him; and indeed *if* the sore has turned white, then the priest shall pronounce *him* clean *who has* the sore. He *is* clean.

18"If the body develops a gboil in the skin, and it is healed, 19and in the place of the boil there comes a white swelling or a bright spot, reddish-white, then it shall be shown to the priest; 20and *if,* when the priest sees it, it indeed appears deeper than the skin, and its hair has turned white, the priest shall pronounce him unclean. It *is* a leprous sore which has broken out of the boil. 21But if the priest examines it, and indeed *there are* no white hairs in it, and it *is* not deeper than the skin, but has faded,

then the priest shall isolate him seven days; 22and if it should at all spread over the skin, then the priest shall pronounce him unclean. It *is* a leprous sore. 23But if the bright spot stays in one place, *and* has not spread, it *is* the scar of the boil; and the priest shall pronounce him clean.

24"Or if the body receives a hburn on its skin by fire, and the raw *flesh* of the burn becomes a bright spot, reddish-white or white, 25then the priest shall examine it; and indeed *if* the hair of the bright spot has turned white, and it appears deeper than the skin, it *is* leprosy broken out in the burn. Therefore the priest shall pronounce him unclean. It *is* a leprous sore. 26But if the priest examines it, and indeed *there are* no white hairs in the bright spot, and it *is* not deeper than the skin, but has faded, then the priest shall isolate him seven days. 27And the priest shall examine him on the seventh day. If it has at all spread over the skin, then the priest shall pronounce him unclean. It *is* a leprous sore. 28But if the bright spot stays in one place, *and* has not spread on the skin, but has faded, it *is* a swelling from the burn. The priest shall pronounce him clean, for it *is* the scar from the burn.

29"If a man or woman has a sore on the head or the beard, 30then the priest shall examine the sore; and indeed if it appears deeper than the skin, *and there is* in it thin yellow hair, then the priest shall pronounce him unclean. It *is* a scaly leprosy of the head or beard. 31But if the priest examines the scaly sore, and indeed it does not appear deeper than the skin, and *there is* no black hair in it, then the priest shall isolate *the one who has* the scale seven days. 32And on the seventh day the priest shall examine the sore; and indeed *if* the scale has not spread, and there is no yellow hair in it, and the scale does not appear deeper than the skin, 33he shall shave himself, but the scale he shall not shave. And the priest shall isolate *the one who has* the scale another seven days. 34On the seventh day the priest shall examine the scale; and indeed *if* the scale has not spread over the skin, and does not appear deeper than the skin, then the priest shall pronounce him clean. He shall wash his clothes and be clean. 35But if the scale should at all spread over the skin after his cleansing, 36then the priest shall examine him; and indeed *if* the scale has spread over the skin, the priest need not seek for yellow hair. He *is* unclean. 37But if the scale appears to be at a standstill, and there is black hair grown up in it, the scale has healed. He *is* clean, and the priest shall pronounce him clean.

13:11 *shall not isolate him.* Isolation, or quarantine, was for the purpose of protecting the community until a diagnosis was reached. In this case, the patient was already diagnosed as "unclean," which meant he had to live outside the camp (v. 46).

13:4 c Lev. 14:8 **13:6** d Lev. 11:25; 14:8 **13:10** e Num. 12:10, 12 **13:13** f Ex. 4:6 **13:18** g Ex. 9:9; 15:26 **13:24** h Is. 3:24

³⁸"If a man or a woman has bright spots on the skin of the body, *specifically* white bright spots, ³⁹then the priest shall look; and indeed *if* the bright spots on the skin of the body *are* dull white, it *is* a white spot *that* grows on the skin. He *is* clean.

⁴⁰"As for the man whose hair has fallen from his head, he *is* bald, *but* he *is* clean. ⁴¹He whose hair has fallen from his forehead, he *is* bald on the forehead, *but* he *is* clean. ⁴²And if there is on the bald head or bald ^jforehead a reddish-white sore, it *is* leprosy breaking out on his bald head or his bald forehead. ⁴³Then the priest shall examine it; and indeed *if* the swelling of the sore *is* reddish-white on his bald head or on his bald forehead, as the appearance of leprosy on the skin of the body, ⁴⁴he is a leprous man. He *is* unclean. The priest shall surely pronounce him unclean; his sore *is* on his ^jhead.

⁴⁵"Now the leper on whom the sore *is*, his clothes shall be torn and his head ^kbare; and he shall ^lcover his mustache, and cry, ^m'Unclean! Unclean!' ⁴⁶He shall be unclean. All the days he has the sore he shall be unclean. He *is* unclean, and he shall dwell alone; his dwelling *shall be* ⁿoutside the camp.

The Law Concerning Leprous Garments

⁴⁷"Also, if a garment has a leprous plague* in it, *whether it is* a woolen garment or a linen garment, ⁴⁸whether *it is in* the warp or woof of linen or wool, whether in leather or in anything made of leather, ⁴⁹and if the plague is greenish or reddish in the garment or in the leather, whether in the warp or in the woof, or in anything made of leather, it *is* a leprous plague and shall be shown to the priest. ⁵⁰The priest shall examine the plague and isolate *that which has* the plague seven days. ⁵¹And he shall examine the plague on the seventh day. If the plague has spread in the garment, either in the warp or in the woof, in the leather *or* in anything made of leather, the plague *is* an ^oactive leprosy. It *is*

unclean. ⁵²He shall therefore burn that garment in which is the plague, whether warp or woof, in wool or in linen, or anything of leather, for it *is* an active leprosy; *the garment* shall be burned in the fire.

⁵³"But if the priest examines *it*, and indeed the plague has not spread in the garment, either in the warp or in the woof, or in anything made of leather, ⁵⁴then the priest shall command that they wash *the thing* in which *is* the plague; and he shall isolate it another seven days. ⁵⁵Then the priest shall examine the plague after it has been washed; and indeed *if* the plague has not changed its color, though the plague has not spread, it *is* unclean, and you shall burn it in the fire; it continues eating away, *whether* the damage *is* outside or inside. ⁵⁶If the priest examines *it*, and indeed the plague has faded after washing it, then he shall tear it out of the garment, whether out of the warp or out of the woof, or out of the leather. ⁵⁷But if it appears again in the garment, either in the warp or in the woof, or in anything made of leather, it *is a* spreading *plague;* you shall burn with fire that in which is the plague. ⁵⁸And if you wash the garment, either warp or woof, or whatever is made of leather, if the plague has disappeared from it, then it shall be washed a second time, and shall be clean.

⁵⁹"This *is* the law of the leprous plague in a garment of wool or linen, either in the warp or woof, or in anything made of leather, to pronounce it clean or to pronounce it unclean."

The Ritual for Cleansing Healed Lepers

14 Then the LORD spoke to Moses, saying, ²"This shall be the law of the leper for the day of his cleansing: He ^ashall be brought to the priest. ³And the priest shall go out of the camp, and the priest shall examine *him;* and indeed, *if* the leprosy is

* **13:47** A mold, fungus, or similar infestation, and so in verses 47–59

13:45–46 *clothes shall be torn . . . mustache.* These actions were signs of mourning, for chronic skin diseases isolated the patients from life and family as if they had died. It is easy to see how leprosy became a metaphor for sin. Like serious skin diseases, sin is dangerous and ultimately fatal, often difficult to diagnose, and incurable without God's intervention.
13:47 *leprous plague.* This would include any mold, mildew, or other fungus growths on clothing.
13:50–58 *priest shall examine the plague.* The procedures for diagnosing a problem with a garment were similar to those for diagnosing human skin ailments. The fact that a garment was considered worth saving after a piece had been torn out of it was an economic consideration, reflecting the value of cloth.
14:1–9 *cleansing.* It is likely that the sprigs of hyssop were tied to the cedar with the scarlet thread. With that in one hand and the living bird in the other,

the priest would dip them all in the blood and water mixture in the pottery bowl and shake them over the head of the person to be cleansed. It may seem like a rather messy procedure, but being purified from sin has never been a tidy process. In the end, it took Christ's death on the cross to cleanse His followers. The bird which was released is a reminder of the real freedom and joy that any forgiven sinner experiences.
14:2 *He shall be brought to the priest.* The priest was responsible for the diagnosis, and he was the one who administered the sacrifices and rituals that celebrated the return of the person to the community

---

13:42 ^j 2 Chr. 26:19 **13:44** ^j Is. 1:5 **13:45** ^k Lev. 10:6; 21:10 ^l Ezek. 24:17, 22 ^m Lam. 4:15 **13:46** ⁿ Num. 5:1–4; 12:14 **13:51** ^o Lev. 14:44 **14:2** ^a Matt. 8:2, 4

healed in the leper, [4]then the priest shall command to take for him who is to be cleansed two living *and* clean birds, [b]cedar wood, [c]scarlet, and [d]hyssop. [5]And the priest shall command that one of the birds be killed in an earthen vessel over running water. [6]As for the living bird, he shall take it, the cedar wood and the scarlet and the hyssop, and dip them and the living bird in the blood of the bird *that was* killed over the running water. [7]And he shall [e]sprinkle it [f]seven times on him who is to be cleansed from the leprosy, and shall pronounce him clean, and shall let the living bird loose in the open field. [8]He who is to be cleansed [g]shall wash his clothes, shave off all his hair, and [h]wash himself in water, that he may be clean. After that he shall come into the camp, and [i]shall stay outside his tent seven days. [9]But on the [j]seventh day he shall shave all the hair off his head and his beard and his eyebrows—all his hair he shall shave off. He shall wash his clothes and wash his body in water, and he shall be clean.

[10]"And on the eighth day [k]he shall take two male lambs without blemish, one ewe lamb of the first year without blemish, three-tenths *of an ephah* of fine flour mixed with oil as [l]a grain offering, and one log of oil. [11]Then the priest who makes *him* clean shall present the man who is to be made clean, and those things, before the LORD, *at* the door of the tabernacle of meeting. [12]And the priest shall take one male lamb and [m]offer it as a trespass offering, and the log of oil, and [n]wave them *as* a wave offering before the LORD. [13]Then he shall kill the lamb [o]in the place where he kills the sin offering and the burnt offering, in a holy place; for [p]as the sin offering *is* the priest's, so *is* the trespass offering. [q]It *is* most holy. [14]The priest shall take *some* of the blood of the trespass offering, and the priest shall

put *it* [r]on the tip of the right ear of him who is to be cleansed, on the thumb of his right hand, and on the big toe of his right foot. [15]And the priest shall take *some* of the log of oil, and pour *it* into the palm of his own left hand. [16]Then the priest shall dip his right finger in the oil that *is* in his left hand, and shall [s]sprinkle some of the oil with his finger seven times before the LORD. [17]And of the rest of the oil in his hand, the priest shall put *some* on the tip of the right ear of him who is to be cleansed, on the thumb of his right hand, and on the big toe of his right foot, on the blood of the trespass offering. [18]The rest of the oil that *is* in the priest's hand he shall put on the head of him who is to be cleansed. [t]So the priest shall make atonement for him before the LORD.

[19]"Then the priest shall offer [u]the sin offering, and make atonement for him who is to be cleansed from his uncleanness. Afterward he shall kill the burnt offering. [20]And the priest shall offer the burnt offering and the grain offering on the altar. So the priest shall make atonement for him, and he shall be [v]clean.

[21]"But [w]if he is poor and cannot afford it, then he shall take one male lamb *as* a trespass offering to be waved, to make atonement for him, one-tenth *of an ephah* of fine flour mixed with oil as a grain offering, a log of oil, [22]xand two turtledoves or two young pigeons, such as he is able to afford: one shall be a sin offering and the other a burnt offering. [23]yHe shall bring them to the priest on the eighth day for his cleansing, to the door of the tabernacle of meeting, before the LORD. [24]zAnd the priest shall take the lamb of the trespass offering and the log of oil, and the priest shall wave them *as* a wave offering before the LORD. [25]Then he shall kill the lamb of the trespass offering, [a]and the priest shall take *some* of the blood of the trespass offering and put *it* on the tip

---

of Israel. Jesus was aware of these laws when He touched the leper and healed him, and then directed the leper to show himself to the priest (Matt. 8:4).

14:4 cedar wood, scarlet, and hyssop. Cedar is both durable and resistant to decay, scarlet is a reminder of blood, and hyssop is an aromatic herb used for flavor, fragrance, and medicine. Each of these items would have been a reminder of the blood that cleansed, the decay that was stopped, and the sweetness of good health.

14:5 running water. This is literally "living water," water from a spring or stream rather than water from a cistern, vessel, or pool. Living water symbolizes life. Jesus told the woman at the well to ask for living water (John 4:7–14).

14:9–32 shave . . . wash. What is termed leprosy was apparently a number of skin diseases which were infectious, and thus were an apt picture of sin, which also corrupts the flesh, and is spread through social contact. The picture of isolating, analyzing, and finally cleansing these skin diseases is similar to the process of recognizing, repenting, and being forgiven for sin. Blood is necessary in both cases, and in

both cases the touch of the Holy Spirit, symbolized by oil, is present.

14:10 the eighth day. The eighth day was the day of circumcision for a newborn male, and the cleansed person was starting again, almost like being born again into the community.

14:21–32 if he is poor. God's legislation for Israel showed special concern for the poor. In these sacrifices the poor Israelite still had to bring a lamb for the trespass offering, but for the sin offering or burnt offering he was allowed to bring turtledoves or pigeons. The grain offering was reduced from three-tenths to one-tenth of an ephah of fine flour.

14:4 b Num. 19:6 c Ex. 25:4 d Ps. 51:7 **14:7** e Num. 19:18, 19 f Ps. 51:2 **14:8** g Num. 8:7 h [Heb. 10:22] i Num. 5:2, 3; 12:14, 15 **14:9** j Num. 19:19 **14:10** k Matt. 8:4 l Lev. 2:1 **14:12** m Lev. 5:6, 18; 6:6; 14:19 n Ex. 29:22–24, 26 **14:13** o Ex. 29:11 p Lev. 6:24–30; 7:7 q Lev. 2:3; 7:6; 21:22 **14:14** r Lev. 8:23, 24 **14:16** s Lev. 4:6 **14:18** t Lev. 4:26; 5:6 **14:19** u Lev. 5:1, 6; 12:7 **14:20** v Lev. 14:8, 9 **14:21** w Lev. 5:7, 11; 12:8; 27:8 **14:22** x Lev. 12:8; 15:14, 15 **14:23** y Lev. 14:10, 11 **14:24** z Lev. 14:12 **14:25** a Lev. 14:14, 17

of the right ear of him who is to be cleansed, on the thumb of his right hand, and on the big toe of his right foot. 26And the priest shall pour some of the oil into the palm of his own left hand. 27Then the priest shall sprinkle with his right finger *some* of the oil that *is* in his left hand seven times before the LORD. 28And the priest shall put *some* of the oil that *is* in his hand on the tip of the right ear of him who is to be cleansed, on the thumb of the right hand, and on the big toe of his right foot, on the place of the blood of the trespass offering. 29The rest of the oil that *is* in the priest's hand he shall put on the head of him who is to be cleansed, to make atonement for him before the LORD. 30And he shall offer one of *b*the turtledoves or young pigeons, such as he can afford— 31such as he is able to afford, the one *as* a sin offering and the other *as* a burnt offering, with the grain offering. So the priest shall make atonement for him who is to be cleansed before the LORD. 32This *is* the law *for one* who had a leprous sore, who cannot afford *c*the usual cleansing."

The Law Concerning Leprous Houses

33And the LORD spoke to Moses and Aaron, saying: 34*d*"When you have come into the land of Canaan, which I give you as a possession, and *e*I put the leprous plague* in a house in the land of your possession, 35and he who owns the house comes and tells the priest, saying, 'It seems to me that there is *f*some plague in the house,' 36then the priest shall command that they empty the house, before the priest goes *into it* to examine the plague, that all that *is* in the house may not be made unclean; and afterward the priest shall go in to examine the house. 37And he shall examine the plague; and indeed *if* the plague *is* on the walls of the house with ingrained streaks, greenish or reddish, which appear to be deep in the wall, 38then the priest shall go out of the house, to the door of the house, and shut up the house seven days. 39And the priest shall come again on the seventh day and look; and indeed *if* the plague has spread on the walls of the house, 40then the priest shall command that they take away the stones in which *is* the plague, and they shall cast them into an unclean place outside the city. 41And he shall cause the house to be scraped inside, all around, and the dust

that they scrape off they shall pour out in an unclean place outside the city. 42Then they shall take other stones and put *them* in the place of *those* stones, and he shall take other mortar and plaster the house.

43"Now if the plague comes back and breaks out in the house, after he has taken away the stones, after he has scraped the house, and after it is plastered, 44then the priest shall come and look; and indeed *if* the plague has spread in the house, it *is* *g*an active leprosy in the house. It *is* unclean. 45And he shall break down the house, its stones, its timber, and all the plaster of the house, and he shall carry *them* outside the city to an unclean place. 46Moreover he who goes into the house at all while it is shut up shall be unclean until *h*evening. 47And he who lies down in the house shall *i*wash his clothes, and he who eats in the house shall wash his clothes.

48"But if the priest comes in and examines *it*, and indeed the plague has not spread in the house after the house was plastered, then the priest shall pronounce the house clean, because the plague is healed. 49And *j*he shall take, to cleanse the house, two birds, cedar wood, scarlet, and hyssop. 50Then he shall kill one of the birds in an earthen vessel over running water; 51and he shall take the cedar wood, the hyssop, the scarlet, and the living bird, and dip them in the blood of the slain bird and in the running water, and sprinkle the house seven times. 52And he shall cleanse the house with the blood of the bird and the running water and the living bird, with the cedar wood, the hyssop, and the scarlet. 53Then he shall let the living bird loose outside the city in the open field, and *k*make atonement for the house, and it shall be clean.

54"This *is* the law for any *l*leprous sore and scale, 55for the *m*leprosy of a garment *n*and of a house, 56for a swelling and a scab and a bright spot, 57to *p*teach when *it is* unclean and when *it is* clean. This *is* the law of leprosy."

The Law Concerning Bodily Discharges

15 And the LORD spoke to Moses and Aaron, saying, 2"Speak to the children of Israel, and say to them: *a*'When

* **14:34** Decomposition by mildew, mold, dry rot, etc., and so in verses 34–53

14:34 *leprous plague in a house.* This is the same term used of serious skin diseases in chapter 13. All of these conditions were harmful, whether on human skin, clothing, or the wall of a house.

14:54–57 *the law for any leprous sore.* The uncleanness of leprosy required action. If it could not be removed, the thing that carried the uncleanness had to be removed from among God's people. In the same way, the uncleanness of sin requires action, but God has provided an infinitely stronger remedy through the blood of Christ.

14:30 *b* Lev. 14:22; 15:14, 15   **14:32** *c* Lev. 14:10   **14:34** *d* Deut. 7:1; 32:49 *e* [Prov. 3:33]   **14:35** *f* [Ps. 91:9, 10]   **14:44** *g* Lev. 13:51   **14:46** *h* Lev. 11:24; 15:5   **14:47** *i* Lev. 14:8   **14:49** *j* Lev. 14:4   **14:53** *k* Lev. 14:20   **14:54** *l* Lev. 13:30; 26:21   **14:55** *m* Lev. 13:47–52 *n* Lev. 14:34   **14:56** *o* Lev. 13:2   **14:57** *p* Deut. 24:8   **15:2** *a* Num. 5:2

any man has a discharge from his body, his discharge *is* unclean. ³And this shall be his uncleanness in regard to his discharge—whether his body runs with his discharge, or his body is stopped up by his discharge, it *is* his uncleanness. ⁴Every bed is unclean on which he who has the discharge lies, and everything on which he sits shall be unclean. ⁵And whoever ᵇtouches his bed shall ᶜwash his clothes and ᵈbathe in water, and be unclean until evening. ⁶He who sits on anything on which he who has the ᵉdischarge sat shall wash his clothes and bathe in water, and be unclean until evening. ⁷And he who touches the body of him who has the discharge shall wash his clothes and bathe in water, and be unclean until evening. ⁸If he who has the discharge ᶠspits on him who is clean, then he shall wash his clothes and bathe in water, and be unclean until evening. ⁹Any saddle on which he who has the discharge rides shall be unclean. ¹⁰Whoever touches anything that was under him shall be unclean until evening. He who carries *any of* those things shall wash his clothes and bathe in water, and be unclean until evening. ¹¹And whomever the one who has the discharge touches, and has not rinsed his hands in water, he shall wash his clothes and bathe in water, and be unclean until evening. ¹²The ᵍvessel of earth that he who has the discharge touches shall be broken, and every vessel of wood shall be rinsed in water.

¹³'And when he who has a discharge is cleansed of his discharge, then ʰhe shall count for himself seven days for his cleansing, wash his clothes, and bathe his body in running water; then he shall be clean. ¹⁴On the eighth day he shall take for himself ⁱtwo turtledoves or two young pigeons, and come before the LORD, to the door of the tabernacle of meeting, and give them to the priest. ¹⁵Then the priest shall offer them, ʲthe one *as* a sin offering and the other *as* a burnt offering. ᵏSo the priest shall make atonement for him before the LORD because of his discharge.

¹⁶'If any man has an emission of semen, then he shall wash all his body in water, and be unclean until evening. ¹⁷And any

garment and any leather on which there is semen, it shall be washed with water, and be unclean until evening. ¹⁸Also, when a woman lies with a man, and *there is* an emission of semen, they shall bathe in water, and ᵐbe unclean until evening.

¹⁹ⁿ'If a woman has a discharge, *and* the discharge from her body is blood, she shall be set apart seven days; and whoever touches her shall be unclean until evening. ²⁰Everything that she lies on during her impurity shall be unclean; also everything that she sits on shall be unclean. ²¹Whoever touches her bed shall wash his clothes and bathe in water, and be unclean until evening. ²²And whoever touches anything that she sat on shall wash his clothes and bathe in water, and be unclean until evening. ²³If *anything* is on *her* bed or on anything on which she sits, when he touches it, he shall be unclean until evening. ²⁴And ᵒif any man lies with her at all, so that her impurity is on him, he shall be unclean seven days; and every bed on which he lies shall be unclean.

²⁵'If ᵖa woman has a discharge of blood for many days, other than at the time of her *customary* impurity, or if it runs beyond her *usual time of* impurity, all the days of her unclean discharge shall be as the days of her *customary* impurity. She *shall be* unclean. ²⁶Every bed on which she lies all the days of her discharge shall be to her as the bed of her impurity; and whatever she sits on shall be unclean, as the uncleanness of her impurity. ²⁷Whoever touches those things shall be unclean; he shall wash his clothes and bathe in water, and be unclean until evening.

²⁸'But ᵠif she is cleansed of her discharge, then she shall count for herself seven days, and after that she shall be clean. ²⁹And on the eighth day she shall take for herself two turtledoves or two young pigeons, and bring them to the priest, to the door of the tabernacle of meeting. ³⁰Then the priest shall offer the one *as* a sin offering and the other *as* a ʳburnt offering, and the priest shall make atonement for her before the LORD for the discharge of her uncleanness.

³¹'Thus you shall ˢseparate the children

15:18 bathe in water . . . unclean. God's plan from the beginning includes sexual intercourse between a man and his wife; this is not sinful in God's eyes. The uncleanness and requirements of washing were a ritual cleansing, a reminder of the holiness of God, not a prohibition of intimate relationships.

15:19 woman . . . discharge. There are rules for cleansing, but no sacrifice was required. Menstruation was not regarded as sinful.

15:25–27 blood for many days. If a woman had a flow of blood at any time other than her normal monthly period, or if this was unusually long, her uncleanness continued the whole time and passed to all she touched. The woman with a hemorrhage who touched Jesus secretly (Luke 8:43–48) was in this situation.

15:28–30 cleansed of her discharge. The woman was to bring the smallest allowable sacrifice for the atonement of sins she may have committed during the period of her uncleanness.

15:31–33 separate . . . from their uncleanness. Hygiene and health were important by-products, but the focus of these regulations concerning

15:5 ᵇ Lev. 5:2; 14:46 ᶜ Lev. 14:8, 47 ᵈ Lev. 11:25; 17:15
15:6 ᵉ Deut. 23:10 **15:8** ᶠ Num. 12:14 **15:12** ᵍ Lev. 6:28; 11:32, 33 **15:13** ʰ Lev. 14:8; 15:28 **15:14** ⁱ Lev. 14:22, 23, 30, 31 **15:15** ʲ Lev. 14:30, 31 ᵏ Lev. 14:19, 31 **15:16** ˡ Lev. 22:4 **15:18** ᵐ [1 Sam. 21:4] **15:19** ⁿ Lev. 12:2 **15:24** ᵒ Lev. 18:19; 20:18 **15:25** ᵖ Matt. 9:20 **15:28** ᵠ Lev. 15:13–15 **15:30** ʳ Lev. 5:7 **15:31** ˢ Deut. 24:8

of Israel from their uncleanness, lest they die in their uncleanness when they [t]defile My tabernacle that *is* among them. [32u]This *is* the law for one who has a discharge, [v]and *for him* who emits semen and is unclean thereby, [33w]and for her who is indisposed because of her *customary* impurity, and for one who has a discharge, either man [x]or woman, [y]and for him who lies with her who is unclean.'"

The Day of Atonement

16 Now the LORD spoke to Moses after [a]the death of the two sons of Aaron, when they offered *profane fire* before the LORD, and died; [2]and the LORD said to Moses: "Tell Aaron your brother [b]not to come at *just* any time into the Holy *Place* inside the veil, before the mercy seat which *is* on the ark, lest he die; for [c]I will appear in the cloud above the mercy seat.

[3]"Thus Aaron shall [d]come into the Holy *Place*: [e]with *the blood of* a young bull as a sin offering, and *of* a ram as a burnt offering. [4]He shall put the [f]holy linen tunic and the linen trousers on his body; [g]he shall be girded with a linen sash, and with the linen turban he shall be attired. These *are* holy garments. Therefore he shall wash his body in water, and put them on. [5]And he shall take from [h]the congregation of the children of Israel two kids of the goats as a sin offering, and one ram as a burnt offering.

[6]"Aaron shall offer the bull as a sin offering, which *is* for himself, and [i]make atonement for himself and for his house. [7]He shall take the two goats and present them before the LORD *at* the door of the tabernacle of meeting. [8]Then Aaron shall cast lots for the two goats: one lot for the LORD and the other lot for the scapegoat. [9]And Aaron shall bring the goat on which the LORD's lot fell, and offer it *as* a sin offering. [10]But the goat on which the lot fell to be the scapegoat shall be presented alive before the LORD, to make [j]atonement upon it, *and* to let it go as the scapegoat into the wilderness.

[11]"And Aaron shall bring the bull of the sin offering, which is for himself, and make atonement for [k]himself and for his house, and shall kill the bull as the sin offering which *is* for himself. [12]Then he shall take [l]a censer full of burning coals of fire from the altar before the LORD, with his hands full of [m]sweet incense beaten fine, and bring *it* inside the veil. [13n]And he shall put the incense on the fire before the LORD, that the cloud of incense may cover the [o]mercy seat that *is* on the Testimony, lest he [p]die. [14q]He shall take some of the blood of the bull and [r]sprinkle *it* with his finger on the mercy seat on the east *side*; and before the mercy seat he shall sprinkle some of the blood with his finger seven times.

[15s]"Then he shall kill the goat of the sin offering, which *is* for the people, bring its blood [t]inside the veil, do with that blood as he did with the blood of the bull, and sprinkle it on the mercy seat and before the mercy seat. [16]So he shall [u]make atonement for the Holy *Place*, because of the uncleanness of the children of Israel, and because of their transgressions, for all their sins; and so he shall do for the tabernacle of meeting which remains among them in the midst of their uncleanness. [17]There shall be [v]no man in the tabernacle of meeting when he goes in to make atonement in the Holy *Place*, until he comes out, that he may make atonement for himself, for his household, and for all the assembly of Israel. [18]And he shall go out to the altar that *is* before the LORD, and make atonement for [w]it, and shall take some of the blood of the bull and some of the blood of the goat, and put it on the horns of the altar all around. [19]Then he shall sprinkle some of the blood on it with his finger seven times, cleanse it, and [x]consecrate it from the uncleanness of the children of Israel.

[20]"And when he has made an end of atoning for the Holy *Place*, the tabernacle of meeting, and the altar, he shall bring the

---

uncleanness was on keeping God's tabernacle undefiled. Ceremonial laws in regard to natural impurity seem strange to us, because these ceremonies were made obsolete by the perfect sacrifice of Christ. But in the Old Testament one form of blasphemy was the defilement of sanctuary worship by certain forms of ceremonial impurity.

16:2 come at just any time. This refers to the arrogant attitude in which Aaron's sons had approached to offer unauthorized sacrifice. God is holy, and must not be approached carelessly. After Christ opened the way for all believers to approach God at any time, it is perhaps easy to forget that we still approach with reverence and awe. It was because of the terrible price of the cross that we have this privilege, not because God has suddenly become casual.

16:6 for himself. After atoning for himself the high priest could offer the sacrifice to atone for the people. The author of Hebrews places great emphasis on this point in discussing the superior priesthood of

Jesus, who did not have to offer a sacrifice for Himself before He could be the sacrifice of atonement, one time for all people (Heb. 7:26; 9:11–28; 10:19–22).

16:15–19 the goat . . . for the people. Aaron offered the goat for the people, and the other actions involved in this sacrifice made it clear that the sins of the people had a defiling effect on the tabernacle. If not removed, the sins would have caused the ministry to be ineffective in atoning for the people.

15:31 [t] Num. 5:3; 19:13, 20   **15:32** [u] Lev. 15:2 [v] Lev. 15:16   **15:33** [w] Lev. 15:19 [x] Lev. 15:25 [y] Lev. 15:24   **16:1** [a] Lev. 10:1, 2   **16:2** [b] Ex. 30:10 [c] Ex. 25:21, 22; 40:34   **16:3** [d] [Heb. 9:7, 12, 24, 25] [e] Lev. 4:3   **16:4** [f] Ex. 28:39, 42, 43 [g] Ex. 30:20   **16:5** [h] Lev. 4:14   **16:6** [i] [Heb. 5:3; 7:27, 28; 9:7]   **16:10** [j] [1 John 2:2]   **16:11** [k] [Heb. 7:27; 9:7]   **16:12** [l] Lev. 10:1 [m] Ex. 30:34–38   **16:13** [n] Ex. 30:7, 8 [o] Ex. 25:21 [p] Ex. 28:43   **16:14** [q] [Heb. 9:25; 10:4] [r] Lev. 4:6, 17   **16:15** [s] [Heb. 2:17] [t] [Heb. 6:19; 7:27; 9:3, 7, 12]   **16:16** [u] Ex. 29:36; 30:10   **16:17** [v] Luke 1:10   **16:18** [w] Ex. 29:36   **16:19** [x] Ezek. 43:20

live goat. ^{21}Aaron shall lay both his hands on the head of the live goat, ^{y}confess over it all the iniquities of the children of Israel, and all their transgressions, concerning all their sins, ^{z}putting them on the head of the goat, and shall send *it* away into the wilderness by the hand of a suitable man. ^{22}The goat shall ^{a}bear on itself all their iniquities to an uninhabited land; and he shall ^{b}release the goat in the wilderness.

^{23}"Then Aaron shall come into the tabernacle of meeting, ^{c}shall take off the linen garments which he put on when he went into the Holy *Place*, and shall leave them there. ^{24}And he shall wash his body with water in a holy place, put on his garments, come out and offer his burnt offering and the burnt offering of the people, and make atonement for himself and for the people. ^{25d}The fat of the sin offering he shall burn on the altar. ^{26}And he who released the goat as the scapegoat shall wash his clothes ^{e}and bathe his body in water, and afterward he may come into the camp. ^{27f}The bull *for* the sin offering and the goat *for* the sin offering, whose blood was brought in to make atonement in the Holy *Place*, shall be carried outside the camp. And they shall burn in the fire their skins, their flesh, and their offal. ^{28}Then he who burns them shall wash his clothes and bathe his body in water, and afterward he may come into the camp.

^{29}"*This* shall be a statute forever for you: ^{g}In the seventh month, on the tenth *day* of the month, you shall afflict your souls, and do no work at all, *whether* a native of your own country or a stranger who dwells among you. ^{30}For on that day *the priest* shall make atonement for you, to ^{h}cleanse you, *that* you may be clean from all your sins before the LORD. ^{31i}It *is* a sabbath of solemn rest for you, and you shall afflict your souls. *It is* a statute forever. ^{32j}And the priest, who is anointed and ^{k}consecrated to minister as priest in his father's place, shall make atonement, and put on the linen clothes, the holy garments; ^{33}then he shall make atonement for the Holy Sanctuary,* and he shall make atonement for the tabernacle of meeting and for the altar, and he shall make atonement for the priests and for all the people of the assembly. ^{34l}This shall be an everlasting statute for you, to make atonement for the children of Israel, for all their sins, ^{m}once a year." And he did as the LORD commanded Moses.

The Sanctity of Blood

17 And the LORD spoke to Moses, saying, ^{2}"Speak to Aaron, to his sons, and to all the children of Israel, and say to them, 'This *is* the thing which the LORD has commanded, saying: ^{3}"Whatever man of the house of Israel who ^{a}kills an ox or lamb or goat in the camp, or who kills *it* outside the camp, ^{4}and does not bring it to the door of the tabernacle of meeting to offer an offering to the LORD before the tabernacle of the LORD, the guilt of bloodshed shall be ^{b}imputed to that man. He has shed blood; and that man shall be cut off from among his people, ^{5}to the end that the children of Israel may bring their sacrifices ^{c}which they offer in the open field, that they may bring them to the LORD at the door of the tabernacle of meeting, to the priest, and offer them

---

* **16:33** That is, the Most Holy Place

16:21 *Aaron shall lay both his hands on the head of the live goat.* Sending the goat into the wilderness was a public ceremony. Everyone could see Aaron symbolically placing the sins of the people on the goat's head. All of the ways that people could offend God were placed on the head of the goat, which took them away from the camp, away from the people, away from God.

16:22 *goat shall bear on itself.* This is the origin of the common expression "scapegoat." The goat was not guilty of the sins, but he bore them anyway, allowing the guilty to escape the consequences of their sins. In Jesus' bearing the sins of the human race, and in His death outside the city (outside the camp), He fulfilled this annual ritual of the Day of Atonement. Not only was Jesus the perfect High Priest, He was the perfect Sacrifice.

16:29 *In the seventh month.* The Day of Atonement fell between mid-September and mid-October.

16:29–34 The Day of Atonement—This whole process of animal sacrifice seems foreign to us. There is no enjoyment in seeing an animal killed. Special underwear and extra washings do not fit our religious experience. It is easy for us to wonder why this was necessary. What is the big deal anyway? The primary reason we have trouble with this is that we have such a superficial understanding of sin and God's attitude

toward it. We tend to think of sin as a kind of correctable mistake, easily taken care of. Why be so upset about it?

The Day of Atonement pointed the Israelites to the seriousness of sin. They were able to see that sin was an affront to God that had to be dealt with. It is like cancer. If it is not treated, death is the ultimate consequence. At its core, sin is rebellion against God. This ceremony stood as a permanent reminder of these truths. It pointed to God's holiness, to the drastic measures needed to deal with sin. Our souls are to be cleansed thoroughly and the sacrifices on the Day of Atonement accomplished this cleansing for the Israelite community. As such it was the most important day in the Jewish religious calendar.

17:5 *sacrifices . . . in the open field.* Such sacrifices were strictly forbidden. All sacrifices were to be clearly and unequivocally made to God alone, and in His way.

16:21 ^{y} Lev. 5:5; 26:40 ^{z} [Is. 53:6] **16:22** ^{a} [Is. 53:6, 11, 12] ^{b} Lev. 14:7 **16:23** ^{c} Ezek. 42:14; 44:19 **16:25** ^{d} Lev. 1:8; 4:10 **16:26** ^{e} Lev. 15:5 **16:27** ^{f} Heb. 13:11 **16:29** ^{g} Lev. 23:27–32 **16:30** ^{h} Jer. 33:8 **16:31** ^{i} Lev. 23:27, 32 **16:32** ^{j} Lev. 4:3, 5, 16; 21:10 ^{k} Ex. 29:29, 30 **16:34** ^{l} Lev. 23:31 ^{m} [Heb. 9:7, 25, 28] **17:3** ^{a} Deut. 12:5, 15, 21 **17:4** ^{b} Rom. 5:13 **17:5** ^{c} Deut. 12:1–27

as peace offerings to the LORD. [6]And the priest [d]shall sprinkle the blood on the altar of the LORD *at* the door of the tabernacle of meeting, and [e]burn the fat for a sweet aroma to the LORD. [7]They shall no more offer their sacrifices [f]to demons, after whom they [g]have played the harlot. This shall be a statute forever for them throughout their generations."'

[8]"Also you shall say to them: 'Whatever man of the house of Israel, or of the strangers who dwell among you, [h]who offers a burnt offering or sacrifice, [9]and does not [i]bring it to the door of the tabernacle of meeting, to offer it to the LORD, that man shall be cut off from among his people.

[10][i]'And whatever man of the house of Israel, or of the strangers who dwell among you, who eats any blood, [k]I will set My face against that person who eats blood, and will cut him off from among his people. [11]For the [l]life of the flesh *is* in the blood, and I have given it to you upon the altar [m]to make atonement for your souls; for [n]it *is* the blood *that* makes atonement for the soul.' [12]Therefore I said to the children of Israel, 'No one among you shall eat blood, nor shall any stranger who dwells among you eat blood.'

[13]"Whatever man of the children of Israel, or of the strangers who dwell among you, who [o]hunts and catches any animal or bird that may be eaten, he shall [p]pour out its blood and [q]cover it with dust; [14]for it is the life of all flesh. Its blood sustains its life. Therefore I said to the children of Israel,

'You shall not eat the blood of any flesh, for the life of all flesh is its blood. Whoever eats it shall be cut off.'

[15s]"And every person who eats what died *naturally* or what was torn *by beasts, whether he is* a native of your own country or a stranger, [t]he shall both wash his clothes and [u]bathe in water, and be unclean until evening. Then he shall be clean. [16]But if he does not wash *them* or bathe his body, then [v]he shall bear his guilt."

Laws of Sexual Morality

18 Then the LORD spoke to Moses, saying, [2]"Speak to the children of Israel, and say to them: [a]'I am the LORD your God. [3b]According to the doings of the land of Egypt, where you dwelt, you shall not do; and [c]according to the doings of the land of Canaan, where I am bringing you, you shall not do; nor shall you walk in their ordinances. [4d]You shall observe My judgments and keep My ordinances, to walk in them: I *am* the LORD your God. [5]You shall therefore keep My statutes and My judgments, which if a man does, he shall live by them: I *am* the LORD.

[6]'None of you shall approach anyone who is near of kin to him, to uncover his nakedness: I *am* the LORD. [7]The nakedness of your father or the nakedness of your mother you shall not uncover. She *is* your mother; you shall not uncover her nakedness. [8]The nakedness of your [e]father's wife you shall not uncover; it *is* your father's nakedness. [9f]The nakedness of your sister,

---

17:7 to demons . . . played the harlot. Pagan deities in the form of goats, like satyrs, were a part of the cultures surrounding the Israelites. Israel's worship of other gods, and God's attitude toward it was likened to the way a husband would feel if his wife became a prostitute. This was a picture of betrayal that the Israelites could understand. **statute forever.** Because this was a permanent rule, it becomes clear that it was not an injunction against slaughtering animals for meat, but referred to sacrifices. When Israel's worship was centered in Jerusalem, some families lived more than a hundred miles from the temple. They could not have traveled so far to kill animals for meat, although they did make the journey for sacrifices.
17:10 any blood. Eating blood was forbidden in the strongest possible terms.
17:13 cover it with dust. Blood was to be treated respectfully, and covering it with earth was a token of burial.
18:2 the LORD. This is the translation of the name for God, sometimes called Yahweh, the name by which God revealed Himself to Moses (Ex. 6:2–8). In using this name, God was basing His claim to the Israelites' devotion on His willingness to reveal Himself to them, to redeem them and to be their God.
18:4 My judgments . . . My ordinances. "Judgments" refers to judicial decisions involving situations that might not be addressed in the statutes. "Ordinances" are decrees, laws, and acts of a permanent nature.
18:5 if a man does, he shall live. God gave the law

as a means of life on all levels—physical, moral, spiritual, and relational.
18:6 None . . . anyone who is near of kin . . . uncover his nakedness. This term covers cases such as incest between father and daughter and between brother and full sister, even though they are absent from the following list. To uncover someone's nakedness is to have sexual intercourse with that person.
18:7 The nakedness of your father . . . you shall not uncover. The point of this passage is that committing incest with the wife of one's father is symbolically to uncover the father's nakedness too, because the two are one flesh through marriage.
18:8 father's wife. Even if your father's wife is not your mother, it is still wrong to have sexual relations with her. In Israel at that time multiple wives or concubines were still part of society, as well as a second wife coming into the family through death or divorce of the first wife.
18:9 your sister. Though this may seem redundant, God wanted to make it abundantly clear that a sister who did not share the same pair of parents as her

---

17:6 [d] Lev. 3:2 [e] Num. 18:17　**17:7** [f] Deut. 32:17 [g] Ezek. 23:8　**17:8** [h] Lev. 1:2, 3; 18:26　**17:9** [i] Lev. 14:23
17:10 [j] Gen. 9:4 [k] Lev. 20:3, 5, 6　**17:11** [l] Gen. 9:4 [m] [Matt. 26:28] [n] [Heb. 9:22]　**17:13** [o] Lev. 7:26 [p] Deut. 12:16, 24 [q] Ezek. 24:7　**17:14** [r] Gen. 9:4　**17:15** [s] Ex. 22:31 [t] Lev. 11:25 [u] Lev. 15:5　**17:16** [v] Lev. 5:1　**18:2** [a] Ex. 6:7
18:3 [b] Ezek. 20:7, 8 [c] Lev. 18:24–30; 20:23　**18:4** [d] Ezek. 20:19　**18:8** [e] Gen. 35:22　**18:9** [f] Deut. 27:22

the daughter of your father, or the daughter of your mother, *whether* born at home or elsewhere, their nakedness you shall not uncover. ¹⁰The nakedness of your son's daughter or your daughter's daughter, their nakedness you shall not uncover; for theirs *is* your own nakedness. ¹¹The nakedness of your father's wife's daughter, begotten by your father—she *is* your sister—you shall not uncover her nakedness. ¹²ᵍYou shall not uncover the nakedness of your father's sister; she *is* near of kin to your father. ¹³You shall not uncover the nakedness of your mother's sister, for she *is* near of kin to your mother. ¹⁴ʰYou shall not uncover the nakedness of your father's brother; you shall not approach his wife; she *is* your aunt. ¹⁵You shall not uncover the nakedness of your daughter-in-law—she *is* your son's wife—you shall not uncover her nakedness. ¹⁶You shall not uncover the nakedness of your brother's wife; it *is* your brother's nakedness. ¹⁷You shall not uncover the nakedness of a woman and her ⁱdaughter, nor shall you take her son's daughter or her daughter's daughter, to uncover her nakedness. They *are* near of kin to her. It *is* wickedness. ¹⁸Nor shall you take a woman ʲas a rival to her sister, to uncover her nakedness while the other is alive.

¹⁹'Also you shall not approach a woman to uncover her nakedness as ᵏlong as she is in her ˡcustomary impurity. ²⁰ᵐMoreover you shall not lie carnally with your ⁿneighbor's wife, to defile yourself with her. ²¹And you shall not let any of your descendants ᵒpass through ᵖthe fire to qMolech, nor shall you profane the name of your God: I *am* the LORD. ²²You shall not lie with ʳa male as with a woman. It *is* an abomination. ²³Nor shall you mate with any ˢanimal, to defile yourself with it. Nor shall any woman stand before an animal to mate with it. It *is* perversion.

²⁴ᵗ'Do not defile yourselves with any of these things; ᵘfor by all these the nations are defiled, which I am casting out before you. ²⁵For ᵛthe land is defiled; therefore I ʷvisit the punishment of its iniquity upon it, and the land ˣvomits out its inhabitants. ²⁶ʸYou shall therefore keep My statutes and My judgments, and shall not commit *any* of these abominations, *either* any of your own nation or any stranger who dwells among you ²⁷(for all these abominations the men of the land have done, who *were* before you, and thus the land is defiled), ²⁸lest ᶻthe land vomit you out also when you defile it, as it vomited out the nations that *were* before you. ²⁹For whoever commits any of these abominations, the persons who commit *them* shall be cut off from among their people. ³⁰'Therefore you shall keep My ordinance, so ᵃthat *you* do not commit *any* of these abominable customs which were committed before you, and that you do not defile yourselves by them: ᵇI *am* the LORD your God.'"

Moral and Ceremonial Laws

19 And the LORD spoke to Moses, saying, ²"Speak to all the congregation of the children of Israel, and say to them: ᵃ'You shall be holy, for I the LORD your God *am* holy.

³ᵇ'Every one of you shall revere his mother and his father, and ᶜkeep My Sabbaths: I *am* the LORD your God.

⁴ᵈ'Do not turn to idols, ᵉnor make for yourselves molded gods: I *am* the LORD your God.

⁵'And ᶠif you offer a sacrifice of a peace offering to the LORD, you shall offer it of your own free will. ⁶It shall be eaten the same day you offer *it*, and on the next day. And if any remains until the third day, it shall be burned in the fire. ⁷And if it is eaten at all on the third day, it *is* an abomination. It shall not be accepted. ⁸Therefore

---

brother was still off limits. This would cover husbands of multiple wives and illegitimate children. Sexual sin is serious with long reaching consequences, and it is clearly forbidden within the family.

18:20 with your neighbor's wife. Adultery is forbidden in Exodus 20:14 and its penalty is given in Leviticus 20:10.

18:21 your descendants . . . to Molech. God forbids child sacrifice right along with incest. This is destructive behavior with far-reaching consequences, and all followers of the Lord will abhor it as God does.

18:22 lie with a male. Homosexuality here is labeled an abomination, something detestable to God both ritually (as a part of the Canaanite religion) and morally. To abominate something is to be repulsed by it, and when God is repulsed, it is a clear message that homosexuality is not part of His plan for human relationships.

18:23 any animal. Bestiality is labeled a perversion, something out of the natural order and a defilement. It, too, was a feature of some of the religions of Israel's neighbors.

18:24–30 defile. The land had become so defiled by

the perverted practices of the Canaanites that it was vomiting them out. For that reason, the land would be available to Israel to settle. The Israelites, however, needed to be careful to live as God's holy people, or the land would vomit them out as well.

19:3 keep My Sabbaths. The weekly Sabbath was an acknowledgment that not everything depended on the Israelites' efforts. It was an acknowledgment of God's lordship and His grace.

19:5 peace offering. The peace offering was a free-will offering.

18:12 ᵍ Lev. 20:19   18:14 ʰ Lev. 20:20   18:17 ⁱ Lev. 20:14   18:18 ʲ 1 Sam. 1:6, 8   18:19 ᵏ Ezek. 18:6 ˡ Lev. 15:24; 20:18   18:20 ᵐ [Prov. 6:25–33] ⁿ Lev. 20:10   18:21 ᵒ Lev. 20:2–5 ᵖ 2 Kin. 16:3 q 1 Kin. 11:7, 33 18:22 ʳ Lev. 20:13   18:23 ˢ Ex. 22:19   18:24 ᵗ Matt. 15:18–20 ᵘ Deut. 18:12   18:25 ᵛ Num. 35:33, 34 ʷ Jer. 5:9 ˣ Lev. 18:28; 20:22   18:26 ʸ Lev. 18:5, 30 18:28 ᶻ Jer. 9:19   18:30 ᵃ Lev. 18:3; 22:9 ᵇ Lev. 18:2 19:2 ᵃ Lev. 11:44; 20:7, 26   19:3 ᵇ Ex. 20:12 ᶜ Ex. 16:23; 20:8; 31:13   19:4 ᵈ Ex. 20:4 ᵉ Ex. 34:17   19:5 ᶠ Lev. 7:16

everyone who eats it shall bear his iniquity, because he has profaned the hallowed *offering* of the LORD; and that person shall be cut off from his people.

9g'When you reap the harvest of your land, you shall not wholly reap the corners of your field, nor shall you gather the gleanings of your harvest. 10And you shall not glean your vineyard, nor shall you gather *every* grape of your vineyard; you shall leave them for the poor and the stranger: I *am* the LORD your God.

11h'You shall not steal, nor deal falsely, inor lie to one another. 12And you shall not iswear by My name falsely, knor shall you profane the name of your God: I *am* the LORD.

13l'You shall not cheat your neighbor, nor rob *him*. mThe wages of him who is hired shall not remain with you all night until morning. 14You shall not curse the deaf, nnor put a stumbling block before the blind, but shall fear your God: I *am* the LORD.

15'You shall do no injustice in ojudgment. You shall not pbe partial to the poor, nor honor the person of the mighty. In righteousness you shall judge your neighbor. 16You shall not go about *as* a qtalebearer among your people; nor shall you rtake a stand against the life of your neighbor: I *am* the LORD.

17s'You shall not hate your brother in your heart. tYou shall surely rebuke your neighbor, and not bear sin because of him. 18uYou shall not take vengeance, nor bear any grudge against the children of your people, vbut you shall love your neighbor as yourself: I *am* the LORD.

19'You shall keep My statutes. You shall not let your livestock breed with another kind. You shall not sow your field with mixed seed. Nor shall a garment of mixed linen and wool come upon you.

20'Whoever lies carnally with a woman who *is* wbetrothed to a man as a concubine, and who has not at all been redeemed nor given her freedom, for this there shall be scourging; *but* they shall not be put to death, because she was not free. 21And he shall bring his trespass offering to the LORD, to the door of the tabernacle of meeting, a ram as a trespass offering. 22The priest shall make atonement for him with the ram of the trespass offering before the LORD for his sin which he has committed. And the sin which he has committed shall be forgiven him.

23'When you come into the land, and have planted all kinds of trees for food, then you shall count their fruit as uncircumcised. Three years it shall be as uncircumcised to you. *It* shall not be eaten. 24But in the fourth year all its fruit shall be holy, a praise to the LORD. 25And in the fifth year you may eat its fruit, that it may yield to you its increase: I *am* the LORD your God.

26'You shall not eat *anything* with the blood, nor shall you practice divination or soothsaying. 27You shall not shave around the sides of your head, nor shall you disfigure the edges of your beard. 28You shall not xmake any cuttings in your flesh for the dead, nor tattoo any marks on you: I *am* the LORD.

29y'Do not prostitute your daughter, to cause her to be a harlot, lest the land fall into harlotry, and the land become full of wickedness.

19:10 *for the poor and the stranger.* Providing for the poor and the alien who could not own land was a priority in ancient Israel. The generosity of God's people was rooted in God's generosity toward the Israelites.

19:16 *talebearer.* A talebearer is one who is not only a gossip, but one who is actively seeking to destroy another's reputation.

19:17 *hate . . . in your heart.* Jesus addressed this principle in the Sermon on the Mount (Matt. 5:21–24).

19:18 *take vengeance.* Vengeance belongs to God (Deut. 32:35); His vengeance is entirely just. It is easy for human vengeance to be carried out too zealously, leaving the by products of bitterness and hatred. Instead, we are to do good to those who hate us and pray for those who persecute us (Matt. 5:44). ***love.*** The word "love" is first found in Genesis 22:2, where God told Abraham to offer up his son whom he loved as a burnt sacrifice upon Mount Moriah, and the first mention of love in the New Testament is God proclaiming that Jesus is His beloved Son (Matt. 3:17). Family love is something people find easy to understand. Even if it is not very strong in one's nuclear family, the longing for love shows us that we understand what it is to be. To take this love one step further, that a parent would allow a child to die for the good of others, stretches the concept of love. And yet it is that very love that caused God to send His Son to die for the whole world.

19:20 *a woman . . . a concubine.* The slave woman had a low social standing and few rights, and may not have had the freedom to cry out when approached sexually. Therefore, she remained guiltless. Because she was a slave, the man escaped death, but remained guilty before God. Atonement was necessary for him to receive forgiveness.

19:26 *divination.* God, and not a demon or impersonal force, is all powerful and directs the future. Practicing divination reveals a lack of trust in God to bring the best in the future in His timing.

19:27–28 *beard . . . cuttings in your flesh . . . nor tattoo any marks.* The human body was designed by God to be beautiful. Disfiguring the body for the dead, or as a sign of mourning, is dishonoring to God. Some disfiguring was a part of pagan religions, and was forbidden to God's people for any reason.

19:29 *cause her to be a harlot.* Sexual relations are sacred. Forcing a daughter to violate that sanctity defiled her against her will.

19:9 g Deut. 24:19–22 **19:11** h Ex. 20:15, 16 i Eph. 4:25 **19:12** j Deut. 5:11 k Lev. 18:21 **19:13** l Ex. 22:7–15, 21–27 m Deut. 24:15 **19:14** n Deut. 27:18 **19:15** o Deut. 16:19 p Ex. 23:3, 6 **19:16** q Prov. 11:13; 18:8; 20:19 r 1 Kin. 21:7–19 **19:17** s [1 John 2:9, 11; 3:15] t Matt. 18:15 **19:18** u [Deut. 32:35] v Mark 12:31 **19:20** w Deut. 22:23–27 **19:28** x Jer. 16:6 **19:29** y Deut. 22:21; 23:17, 18

30 'You shall keep My Sabbaths and [z]rev-
erence My sanctuary: I *am* the LORD.
31 'Give no regard to mediums and familiar spirits; do not seek after [a]them, to be
defiled by them: I *am* the LORD your God.
32 [b]'You shall rise before the gray headed
and honor the presence of an old man, and
[c]fear your God: I *am* the LORD.
33 'And [d]if a stranger dwells with you
in your land, you shall not mistreat him.
34 [e]The stranger who dwells among you
shall be to you as one born among you,
and [f]you shall love him as yourself; for you
were strangers in the land of Egypt: I *am*
the LORD your God.
35 'You shall do no injustice in judgment,
in measurement of length, weight, or volume. 36 You shall have [g]honest scales,
honest weights, an honest ephah, and an
honest hin: I *am* the LORD your God, who
brought you out of the land of Egypt.
37 [h]'Therefore you shall observe all My
statutes and all My judgments, and perform them: I *am* the LORD.' "

Penalties for Breaking the Law

20 Then the LORD spoke to Moses, saying, 2 [a]"Again, you shall say to the
children of Israel: [b]'Whoever of the children of Israel, or of the strangers who dwell
in Israel, who gives *any* of his descendants
to Molech, he shall surely be put to death.
The people of the land shall [c]stone him
with stones. 3 [d]I will set My face against
that man, and will cut him off from his
people, because he has given *some* of his
descendants to Molech, to defile My sanctuary and profane My holy name. 4 And if
the people of the land should in any way
hide their eyes from the man, when he
gives *some* of his descendants to Molech,
and they do not kill him, 5 then I will set My
face against that man and against his family; and I will cut him off from his people,
and all who prostitute themselves with him
to commit harlotry with Molech.
6 'And [e]the person who turns to mediums
and familiar spirits, to prostitute himself
with them, I will set My face against that
person and cut him off from his people.
7 [f]Consecrate yourselves therefore, and be
holy, for I *am* the LORD your God. 8 And you
shall keep [g]My statutes, and perform them:
[h]I *am* the LORD who sanctifies you.
9 'For [i]everyone who curses his father or
his mother shall surely be put to death. He
has cursed his father or his mother. [j]His
blood *shall be* upon him.
10 [k]'The man who commits adultery with
another man's wife, *he* who commits adultery with his neighbor's wife, the adulterer
and the adulteress, shall surely be put to
death. 11 The man who lies with his [l]fa-
ther's wife has uncovered his father's nakedness; both of them shall surely be put
to death. Their blood *shall be* upon them.
12 If a man lies with his [m]daughter-in-law,
both of them shall surely be put to death.
They have committed perversion. Their
blood *shall be* upon them. 13 [n]If a man lies
with a male as he lies with a woman, both
of them have committed an abomination.
They shall surely be put to death. Their
blood *shall be* upon them. 14 If a man marries a woman and her [o]mother, it *is* wickedness. They shall be burned with fire,
both he and they, that there may be no
wickedness among you. 15 If a man mates
with an [p]animal, he shall surely be put to
death, and you shall kill the animal. 16 If a
woman approaches any animal and mates
with it, you shall kill the woman and the
animal. They shall surely be put to death.
Their blood *is* upon them.
17 'If a man takes his [q]sister, his father's
daughter or his mother's daughter, and
sees her nakedness and she sees his nakedness, it *is* a wicked thing. And they shall be
cut off in the sight of their people. He has
uncovered his sister's nakedness. He shall
bear his guilt. 18 [r]If a man lies with a woman
during her sickness and uncovers her nakedness, he has exposed her flow, and she
has uncovered the flow of her blood. Both
of them shall be cut off from their people.
19 'You shall not uncover the nakedness
of your [s]mother's sister nor of your [t]fa-
ther's sister, for that would uncover his
near of kin. They shall bear their guilt. 20 If
a man lies with his [u]uncle's wife, he has

19:31 *mediums . . . familiar spirits.* In principle this is no different than divination. Its practice involves consulting the spirits of the dead, or other spirits, both of which are strictly forbidden. It demonstrates lack of faith and rebellion against God and His ways.

19:35–36 *injustice in judgment, in measurement.* Injustice in legal transactions or in business are equally wrong. God is just and generous, and His people are to be the same.

20:2–5 *gives any of his descendants to Molech . . . put to death . . . stone him.* The penalty for child sacrifice, whether carried out by an alien or a citizen of Israel, was death, either carried out by the justice system or by God Himself. Children are a trust and blessing from God, and killing them in a pagan ritual is a wickedness that God will not overlook.

20:8 *who sanctifies you.* To be sanctified is to be "set apart." The worshiper was set apart to God, from all other allegiances.

20:9 *His blood shall be upon him.* This statement assured the executioners that they were not guilty of shedding the offender's blood.

19:30 [z] Lev. 26:2 **19:31** [a] Lev. 20:6, 27 **19:32** [b] 1 Tim. 5:1 [c] Lev. 19:14 **19:33** [d] Ex. 22:21 **19:34** [e] Ex. 12:48 [f] Deut. 10:19 **19:36** [g] Deut. 25:13–15 **19:37** [h] Lev. 18:4, 5 **20:2** [a] Lev. 18:2 [b] Lev. 18:21 [c] Deut. 17:2–5 **20:3** [d] Lev. 17:10 **20:6** [e] Lev. 19:31 **20:7** [f] Lev. 19:2 **20:8** [g] Lev. 19:19, 37 [h] Ex. 31:13 **20:9** [i] Ex. 21:17 [j] 2 Sam. 1:16 **20:10** [k] Ex. 20:14 **20:11** [l] Lev. 18:7, 8 **20:12** [m] Lev. 18:15 **20:13** [n] Lev. 18:22 **20:14** [o] Lev. 18:17 **20:15** [p] Lev. 18:23 **20:17** [q] Lev. 18:9 **20:18** [r] Lev. 15:24; 18:19 **20:19** [s] Lev. 18:13 [t] Lev. 18:12 **20:20** [u] Lev. 18:14

uncovered his uncle's nakedness. They shall bear their sin; they shall die childless. 21If a man takes his ᵛbrother's wife, it *is* an unclean thing. He has uncovered his brother's nakedness. They shall be childless.

22‘You shall therefore keep all My ʷstatutes and all My judgments, and perform them, that the land where I am bringing you to dwell ˣmay not vomit you out. 23ʸAnd you shall not walk in the statutes of the nation which I am casting out before you; for they commit all these things, and ᶻtherefore I abhor them. 24But ᵃI have said to you, "You shall inherit their land, and I will give it to you to possess, a land flowing with milk and honey." I *am* the LORD your God, ᵇwho has separated you from the peoples. 25ᶜYou shall therefore distinguish between clean animals and unclean, between unclean birds and clean, ᵈand you shall not make yourselves abominable by beast or by bird, or by any kind of living thing that creeps on the ground, which I have separated from you as unclean. 26And you shall be holy to Me, ᵉfor I the LORD *am* holy, and have separated you from the peoples, that you should be Mine.

27ᶠ‘A man or a woman who is a medium, or who has familiar spirits, shall surely be put to death; they shall stone them with stones. Their blood *shall be* upon them.'"

Regulations for Conduct of Priests

21 And the LORD said to Moses, "Speak to the priests, the sons of Aaron, and say to them: ᵃ‘None shall defile himself for the dead among his people, 2except for his relatives who are nearest to him: his mother, his father, his son, his daughter, and his brother; 3also his virgin sister who is near to him, who has had no husband, for her he may defile himself. 4*Otherwise* he shall not defile himself, *being* a chief man among his people, to profane himself.

5ᵇ‘They shall not make any bald *place* on their heads, nor shall they shave the edges of their beards nor make any cuttings in their flesh. 6They shall be ᶜholy to their God and not profane the name of their God, for they offer the offerings of the LORD made by fire, *and* the ᵈbread of their God; ᵉtherefore they shall be holy. 7ᶠThey shall not take a wife *who is* a harlot or a defiled woman, nor shall they take a woman ᵍdivorced from her husband; for *the priest** is holy to his God. 8Therefore you shall consecrate him, for he offers the bread of your God. He shall be holy to you, for ʰI the LORD, who ⁱsanctify you, *am* holy. 9The daughter of any priest, if she profanes herself by playing the harlot, she profanes her father. She shall be ʲburned with fire.

10‘He who *is* the high priest among his brethren, on whose head the anointing oil was ᵏpoured and who is consecrated to wear the garments, shall not ˡuncover his head nor tear his clothes; 11nor shall he go ᵐnear any dead body, nor defile himself for his father or his mother; 12ⁿnor shall he go out of the sanctuary, nor profane the sanctuary of his God; for the ᵒconsecration of the anointing oil of his God *is* upon him: I *am* the LORD. 13And he shall take a wife in her virginity. 14A widow or a divorced woman or a defiled woman *or* a harlot— these he shall not marry; but he shall take a virgin of his own people as wife. 15Nor shall he profane his posterity among his people, for I the LORD sanctify him.'"

16And the LORD spoke to Moses, saying, 17"Speak to Aaron, saying: 'No man of your descendants in *succeeding* generations, who has *any* defect, may approach to offer the bread of his God. 18For any man who has a ᵖdefect shall not approach: a man blind or lame, who has a marred *face* or any *limb* ᵍtoo long, 19a man who has a broken foot or broken hand, 20or is a hunchback or a dwarf, or *a man* who has a defect in his eye, or eczema or scab, or is a eunuch. 21No man of the descendants of Aaron the priest, who has a defect, shall come near to offer the offerings made by fire to the LORD. He has a defect; he shall not come near to offer the bread of his God. 22He may eat the bread of his God, *both* the most holy and the holy; 23only he shall not go near the ʳveil or approach the altar, because he has a defect, lest ˢhe profane My sanctuaries; for I the LORD sanctify them.'"

---

* **21:7** Literally *he*

20:21 takes his brother's wife. It may be assumed that this passage refers to taking his brother's wife while his brother is still living. Deuteronomy 25:5–10 gives a fairly detailed directive for a brother marrying his brother's childless widow and giving the firstborn the name of the dead brother, so that his family line will be maintained.

21:5 not make any bald place . . . cuttings in their flesh. These were pagan customs, and all Israel was forbidden to observe them (19:27).

21:9 profanes herself by playing the harlot. Prostitution, the ultimate promiscuity, was the opposite of holiness, the ultimate faithfulness. The daughter was to reflect her father's holiness to God.

21:22 He may eat. Physical defect did not imply

a moral defect. The person afflicted was to receive his food as the other priests did, from the sacrifices.

20:21 ᵛ Lev. 18:16   **20:22** ʷ Lev. 18:26; 19:37
ˣ Lev. 18:25, 28   **20:23** ʸ Lev. 18:3, 24 ᶻ Deut.
9:5   **20:24** ᵃ Ex. 3:17; 6:8; 13:5; 33:1–3 ᵇ Ex. 19:5; 33:16
20:25 ᶜ Lev. 10:10; 11:1–47 ᵈ Lev. 11:43   **20:26** ᵉ Lev.
19:2   **20:27** ᶠ Lev. 19:31   **21:1** ᵃ Ezek. 44:25
21:5 ᵇ Deut. 14:1   **21:6** ᶜ Ex. 22:31 ᵈ Lev. 3:11 ᵉ Is. 52:11
21:7 ᶠ Ezek. 44:22 ᵍ Deut. 24:1, 2   **21:8** ʰ Lev. 11:44,
45 ⁱ Lev. 8:12, 30   **21:9** ʲ Deut. 22:21   **21:10** ᵏ Lev.
8:12 ˡ Lev. 10:6, 7   **21:11** ᵐ Num. 19:14   **21:12** ⁿ Lev.
10:7 ᵒ Ex. 29:6, 7   **21:18** ᵖ Lev. 22:19–25 ᵍ Lev. 22:23
21:23 ʳ Lev. 16:2 ˢ Lev. 21:12

²⁴And Moses told *it* to Aaron and his sons, and to all the children of Israel.

22 Then the LORD spoke to Moses, saying, ²"Speak to Aaron and his sons, that they ᵃseparate themselves from the holy things of the children of Israel, and that they ᵇdo not profane My holy name *by* what they ᶜdedicate to Me: I *am* the LORD. ³Say to them: 'Whoever of all your descendants throughout your generations, who goes near the holy things which the children of Israel dedicate to the LORD, ᵈwhile he has uncleanness upon him, that person shall be cut off from My presence: I *am* the LORD.

⁴'Whatever man of the descendants of Aaron, who *is* a ᵉleper or has ᶠa discharge, shall not eat the holy offerings ᵍuntil he is clean. And ʰwhoever touches anything made unclean *by* a corpse, or ⁱa man who has had an emission of semen, ⁵or ʲwhoever touches any creeping thing by which he would be made unclean, or ᵏany person by whom he would become unclean, whatever his uncleanness may be— ⁶the person who has touched any such thing shall be unclean until evening, and shall not eat the holy *offerings* unless he ˡwashes his body with water. ⁷And when the sun goes down he shall be clean; and afterward he may eat the holy *offerings*, because ᵐit *is* his food. ⁸ⁿWhatever dies *naturally* or is torn *by* beasts he shall not eat, to defile himself with it: I *am* the LORD. ⁹'They shall therefore keep ᵒMy ordinance, ᵖlest they bear sin for it and die thereby, if they profane it: I the LORD sanctify them.

¹⁰ᑫ'No outsider shall eat the holy *offering*; one who dwells with the priest, or a hired servant, shall not eat the holy thing. ¹¹But if the priest ʳbuys a person with his money, he may eat it; and one who is born in his house may eat his food. ¹²If the priest's daughter is married to an outsider, she may not eat of the holy offerings. ¹³But if the priest's daughter is a widow or divorced, and has no child, and has returned to her father's house as in her youth, she may eat her father's food; but no outsider shall eat it.

¹⁴'And if a man eats the ˢholy *offering* unintentionally, then he shall restore a holy *offering* to the priest, and add one-fifth to it. ¹⁵They shall not profane the holy *offerings* of the children of Israel, which they offer to the LORD, ¹⁶or allow them to bear the guilt of trespass when they eat their holy *offerings*; for I the LORD sanctify them.' "

Offerings Accepted and Not Accepted

¹⁷And the LORD spoke to Moses, saying, ¹⁸"Speak to Aaron and his sons, and to all the children of Israel, and say to them: ᵗ'Whatever man of the house of Israel, or of the strangers in Israel, who offers his sacrifice for any of his vows or for any of his freewill offerings, which they offer to the LORD as a burnt offering— ¹⁹ᵘ*you shall offer* of your own free will a male without blemish from the cattle, from the sheep, or from the goats. ²⁰ᵛWhatever has a defect, you shall not offer, for it shall not be acceptable on your behalf. ²¹And ʷwhoever offers a sacrifice of a peace offering to the LORD, ˣto fulfill *his* vow, or a freewill offering from the cattle or the sheep, it must be perfect to be accepted; there shall be no defect in it. ²²ʸThose *that are* blind or broken or maimed, or have an ulcer or eczema or scabs, you shall not offer to the LORD, nor make ᶻan offering by fire of them on the altar to the LORD. ²³Either a bull or a lamb that has any limb ᵃtoo long or too short you may offer *as* a freewill offering, but for a vow it shall not be accepted.

²⁴'You shall not offer to the LORD what is bruised or crushed, or torn or cut; nor shall you make any offering *of them* in your land. ²⁵Nor ᵇfrom a foreigner's hand shall you offer any of these as ᶜthe bread of your God, because their ᵈcorruption *is* in them, *and* defects *are* in them. They shall not be accepted on your behalf.' "

²⁶And the LORD spoke to Moses, saying:

22:3 *all your descendants throughout your generations.* This statement made the restriction as broad as possible in any one generation, and as broad as possible through all time. ***cut off from My presence.*** The individual was not executed or banished from the community, but was permanently barred from ministering as a priest.

22:7 *it is his food.* The sacrifices brought by the Israelites were a major part of the daily provisions of the priests.

22:8 *dies naturally or is torn by beasts.* An ordinary Israelite was unclean until evening if he ate such animals (17:15–16), but a priest was not to eat them at all.

22:11 *buys a person . . . he may eat.* Strangers, guests, and hired servants were forbidden to eat of the holy gifts, but slaves and their children were considered as a part of the priest's family, and could eat of the consecrated food.

22:18 *strangers in Israel.* Resident aliens in Israel

were permitted to worship God with the Israelites, and were subject to the same regulations about sacrifices.

22:21 *it must be perfect to be accepted.* This is a very clear directive, yet the prophet Malachi addressed the problem of defective sacrifices in his day (Mal. 1:7–14). God called that "despising" His name.

22:2 ᵃ Num. 6:3 ᵇ Lev. 18:21 ᶜ Ex. 28:38 **22:3** ᵈ Lev. 7:20, 21 **22:4** ᵉ Num. 5:2 ᶠ Lev. 15:2 ᵍ Lev. 14:2; 15:13 ʰ Num. 19:11 ⁱ Lev. 15:16, 17 **22:5** ʲ Lev. 11:23–28 ᵏ Lev. 15:7, 19 **22:6** ˡ Lev. 15:5 **22:7** ᵐ Num. 18:11, 13 **22:8** ⁿ Lev. 7:24; 11:39, 40; 17:15 **22:9** ᵒ Lev. 18:30 ᵖ Ex. 28:43 **22:10** ᑫ Ex. 29:33 **22:11** ʳ Ex. 12:44 **22:14** ˢ Num. 18:32 **22:18** ᵗ Lev. 1:2, 3, 10 **22:19** ᵘ Lev. 1:3 **22:20** ᵛ Deut. 15:21; 17:1 **22:21** ʷ Lev. 3:1, 6 ˣ Num. 15:3, 8 **22:22** ʸ Mal. 1:8 ᶻ Lev. 1:9, 13; 3:3, 5 **22:23** ᵃ Lev. 21:18 **22:25** ᵇ Num. 15:15, 16 ᶜ Lev. 21:6, 17 ᵈ Mal. 1:14

²⁷ᵉ"When a bull or a sheep or a goat is born, it shall be seven days with its mother; and from the eighth day and thereafter it shall be accepted as an offering made by fire to the LORD. ²⁸*Whether it is* a cow or ewe, do not kill both her ᶠand her young on the same day. ²⁹And when you ᵍoffer a sacrifice of thanksgiving to the LORD, offer *it* of your own free will. ³⁰On the same day it shall be eaten; you shall leave ʰnone of it until morning: I *am* the LORD.

³¹ⁱ"Therefore you shall keep My commandments, and perform them: I *am* the LORD. ³²ʲYou shall not profane My holy name, but ᵏI will be hallowed among the children of Israel. I *am* the LORD who ˡsanctifies you, ³³ᵐwho brought you out of the land of Egypt, to be your God: I *am* the LORD."

Feasts of the LORD

23 And the LORD spoke to Moses, saying, ²"Speak to the children of Israel, and say to them: 'The feasts of the LORD, which you shall proclaim *to be* ᵃholy convocations, these *are* My feasts.

The Sabbath

³ᵇ'Six days shall work be done, but the seventh day *is* a Sabbath of solemn rest, a holy convocation. You shall do no work *on it*; it *is* the Sabbath of the LORD in all your dwellings.

The Passover and Unleavened Bread

⁴ᶜ'These *are* the feasts of the LORD, holy convocations which you shall proclaim at their appointed times. ⁵ᵈOn the fourteenth *day* of the first month at twilight *is* the LORD's Passover. ⁶And on the fifteenth day of the same month *is* the Feast of Unleavened Bread to the LORD; seven days you must eat unleavened bread. ⁷ᵉOn the first day you shall have a holy convocation; you

shall do no customary work on it. ⁸But you shall offer an offering made by fire to the LORD for seven days. The seventh day *shall be* a holy convocation; you shall do no customary work *on it.*'"

The Feast of Firstfruits

⁹And the LORD spoke to Moses, saying, ¹⁰"Speak to the children of Israel, and say to them: ᶠ'When you come into the land which I give to you, and reap its harvest, then you shall bring a sheaf of ᵍthe firstfruits of your harvest to the priest. ¹¹He shall ʰwave the sheaf before the LORD, to be accepted on your behalf; on the day after the Sabbath the priest shall wave it. ¹²And you shall offer on that day, when you wave the sheaf, a male lamb of the first year, without blemish, as a burnt offering to the LORD. ¹³Its grain offering *shall be* two-tenths *of an ephah* of fine flour mixed with oil, an offering made by fire to the LORD, for a sweet aroma; and its drink offering *shall be* of wine, one-fourth of a hin. ¹⁴You shall eat neither bread nor parched grain nor fresh grain until the same day that you have brought an offering to your God; *it shall be* a statute forever throughout your generations in all your dwellings.

The Feast of Weeks

¹⁵'And you shall count for yourselves from the day after the Sabbath, from the day that you brought the sheaf of the wave offering: seven Sabbaths shall be completed. ¹⁶Count ⁱfifty days to the day after the seventh Sabbath; then you shall offer ʲa new grain offering to the LORD. ¹⁷You shall bring from your dwellings two wave *loaves* of two-tenths *of an ephah*. They shall be of fine flour; they shall be baked with leaven. *They are* ᵏthe firstfruits to the LORD. ¹⁸And you shall offer with the bread seven lambs of the first year, without blemish, one

---

22:31 commandments. As Christians, it is important to understand the relationship between grace and law. A focus on the law without grace leads to rule oriented life, where our actions may be decent enough, but our heart is hard toward God. But if the focus is only on grace, we may be without the guidelines necessary to keep us from just doing what is right in our own eyes. Certain directives are given to us because even when we are born again, we are not all wise. The best way to balance all of this is to consider the whole counsel of God by reading and seeking to understand the whole Bible.

23:3 Six days shall work be done. Work was given to the human race in the garden of Eden. It is one of the ways humans bear the image of God, and is not a curse on the race. Even after the fall it remains God's good gift. **a Sabbath of solemn rest . . . in all your dwellings.** The regular seventh day of rest is for our refreshment, and a day of solemn, joyful worship. It was not to be observed only in the sanctuary, it was to be celebrated in every household. The writer of Hebrews (ch. 4) calls belief in the saving work of

Jesus, "entering His rest," and compares that to the Sabbath rest.

23:5 fourteenth day of the first month. This month would fall between mid-March and mid-April. The Passover celebrated Israel's exodus from Egypt (Ex. 12:1–28).

23:6–8 Feast of Unleavened Bread. This festival immediately followed Passover, and later in Israel's history, it involved pilgrimages to the central sanctuary; first in Shiloh, and later in Jerusalem.

23:10 sheaf of the firstfruits. This bundle of the first harvested barley belonged to God as a special offering, acknowledging God's provision for the harvest.

22:27 ᵉ Ex. 22:30   **22:28** ᶠ Deut. 22:6, 7   **22:29** ᵍ Lev. 7:12   **22:30** ʰ Lev. 7:15   **22:31** ⁱ Deut. 4:40   **22:32** ʲ Lev. 18:21   ᵏ Lev. 10:3   ˡ Lev. 20:8   **22:33** ᵐ Lev. 19:36, 37   **23:4** ᶜ Ex. 23:14–16   **23:5** ᵈ Ex. 12:1–28   **23:7** ᵉ Ex. 12:16   **23:10** ᶠ Ex. 23:19; 34:26   ᵍ [Rom. 11:16]   **23:11** ʰ Ex. 29:24   **23:16** ⁱ Acts 2:1   ʲ Num. 28:26   **23:17** ᵏ Num. 15:17–21

young bull, and two rams. They shall be
as a burnt offering to the LORD, with their
grain offering and their drink offerings, an
offering made by fire for a sweet aroma to
the LORD. 19 Then you shall sacrifice [l]one
kid of the goats as a sin offering, and two
male lambs of the first year as a sacrifice of
a [m]peace offering. 20 The priest shall wave
them with the bread of the firstfruits *as* a
wave offering before the LORD, with the
two lambs. [n]They shall be holy to the LORD
for the priest. 21 And you shall proclaim on
the same day *that* it is a holy convocation
to you. You shall do no customary work *on*
it. It shall be a statute forever in all your
dwellings throughout your generations.
22 [o]'When you reap the harvest of your
land, you shall not wholly reap the corners
of your field when you reap, nor shall you
gather any gleaning from your harvest.
You shall leave them for the poor and for
the stranger: I *am* the LORD your God.'"

The Feast of Trumpets

23 Then the LORD spoke to Moses, saying,
24 "Speak to the children of Israel, saying:
'In the [p]seventh month, on the first *day* of
the month, you shall have a sabbath-*rest*,
[q]a memorial of blowing of trumpets, a holy
convocation. 25 You shall do no customary
work *on it;* and you shall offer an offering
made by fire to the LORD.'"

The Day of Atonement

26 And the LORD spoke to Moses, saying:
27 [r]"Also the tenth *day* of this seventh month
shall be the Day of Atonement. It shall be a
holy convocation for you; you shall afflict
your souls, and offer an offering made by
fire to the LORD. 28 And you shall do no
work on that same day, for it *is* the Day
of Atonement, [s]to make atonement for
you before the LORD your God. 29 For any
person who is not [t]afflicted *in soul* on that
same day [u]shall be cut off from his people.
30 And any person who does any work on
that same day, [v]that person I will destroy
from among his people. 31 You shall do no
manner of work; *it shall be* a statute forever throughout your generations in all your
dwellings. 32 It *shall be* to you a sabbath
of *solemn* rest, and you shall afflict your
souls; on the ninth *day* of the month at evening, from evening to evening, you shall
celebrate your sabbath."

The Feast of Tabernacles

33 Then the LORD spoke to Moses, saying,
34 "Speak to the children of Israel, saying:
[w]'The fifteenth day of this seventh month
shall be the Feast of Tabernacles *for* seven
days to the LORD. 35 On the first day *there*
shall be a holy convocation. You shall do
no customary work *on it.* 36 *For* seven days
you shall offer an [x]offering made by fire
to the LORD. [y]On the eighth day you shall
have a holy convocation, and you shall offer an offering made by fire to the LORD. It
is a [z]sacred assembly, *and* you shall do no
customary work *on it.*
37 [a]'These *are* the feasts of the LORD
which you shall proclaim *to be* holy convocations, to offer an offering made by fire to
the LORD, a burnt offering and a grain offering, a sacrifice and drink offerings, everything on its day— 38 [b]besides the Sabbaths
of the LORD, besides your gifts, besides
all your vows, and besides all your freewill offerings which you give to the LORD.
39 'Also on the fifteenth day of the seventh month, when you have [c]gathered in
the fruit of the land, you shall keep the feast
of the LORD *for* seven days; on the first day
there shall be a sabbath-*rest*, and on the
eighth day a sabbath-*rest*. 40 And [d]you shall
take for yourselves on the first day the fruit
of beautiful trees, branches of palm trees,
the boughs of leafy trees, and willows of
the brook; [e]and you shall rejoice before the
LORD your God for seven days. 41 [f]You shall
keep it as a feast to the LORD for seven days
in the year. *It shall be* a statute forever in
your generations. You shall celebrate it in
the seventh month. 42 [g]You shall dwell in
booths for seven days. [h]All who are native
Israelites shall dwell in booths, 43 [i]that your
generations may [j]know that I made the
children of Israel dwell in booths when [k]I
brought them out of the land of Egypt: I *am*
the LORD your God.'"
44 So Moses [l]declared to the children of
Israel the feasts of the LORD.

23:24 *In the seventh month.* This holiday falls in mid-September. It was a reminder of God's goodness, which was expressed in the covenant, and asked God to continue to remember that covenant.

23:26–32 Atonement—The Day of Atonement was a time to set aside all the thoughts and actions that typically fill the day and consider one's relationship with God. This was to be a time of humbleness, which would preclude any self-righteousness or merely comparing oneself with others. It was a time to remember that even people who want to follow God need to have their lives realigned with Him. Christians regularly take time to think of these things as they remember the Lord's death until He comes again, with the bread and the cup of communion.

23:27 *Day of Atonement.* The day was not given this name in chapter 16, but this was the day of all days, when complete atonement was made for all Israel.

23:40 *boughs of leafy trees.* The leafy tree is thought to be the myrtle.

23:19 [l] Num. 28:30 [m] Lev. 3:1 **23:20** [n] Deut. 18:4 **23:22** [o] Lev. 19:9, 10 **23:24** [p] Num. 29:1 [q] Lev. 25:9 **23:27** [r] Num. 29:7 **23:28** [s] Lev. 16:34 **23:29** [t] Jer. 31:9 [u] Num. 5:2 **23:30** [v] Lev. 20:3–6 **23:34** [w] Num. 29:12 **23:36** [x] Num. 29:12–34 [y] Num. 29:35–38 [z] Deut. 16:8 **23:37** [a] Lev. 23:2, 4 **23:38** [b] Num. 29:39 **23:39** [c] Ex. 23:16 **23:40** [d] Neh. 8:15 [e] Deut. 12:7; 16:14, 15 **23:41** [f] Num. 29:12 **23:42** [g] [Is. 4:6] [h] Neh. 8:14–16 **23:43** [i] Deut. 31:13 [j] Ex. 10:2 [k] Lev. 22:33 **23:44** [l] Lev. 23:2

Care of the Tabernacle Lamps

24 Then the LORD spoke to Moses, saying: [2a]"Command the children of Israel that they bring to you pure oil of pressed olives for the light, to make the lamps burn continually. [3]Outside the veil of the Testimony, in the tabernacle of meeting, Aaron shall be in charge of it from evening until morning before the LORD continually; *it shall be* a statute forever in your generations. [4]He shall be in charge of the lamps on [b]the pure *gold* lampstand before the LORD continually.

The Bread of the Tabernacle

[5]"And you shall take fine flour and bake twelve [c]cakes with it. Two-tenths *of an ephah* shall be in each cake. [6]You shall set them in two rows, six in a row, [d]on the pure *gold* table before the LORD. [7]And you shall put pure frankincense on *each* row, that it may be on the bread for a [e]memorial, an offering made by fire to the LORD. [8f]Every Sabbath he shall set it in order before the LORD continually, *being taken* from the children of Israel by an everlasting covenant. [9]And [g]it shall be for Aaron and his sons, [h]and they shall eat it in a holy place; for it *is* most holy to him from the offerings of the LORD made by fire, by a perpetual statute."

The Penalty for Blasphemy

[10]Now the son of an Israelite woman, whose father *was* an Egyptian, went out among the children of Israel; and this Israelite *woman's* son and a man of Israel fought each other in the camp. [11]And the Israelite woman's son [i]blasphemed the name *of the* LORD and [j]cursed; and so they [k]brought him to Moses. (His mother's name *was* Shelomith the daughter of Dibri, of the tribe of Dan.) [12]Then they [l]put him in custody, [m]that the mind of the LORD might be shown to them.

[13]And the LORD spoke to Moses, saying, [14]"Take outside the camp him who has cursed; then let all who heard *him* [n]lay their hands on his head, and let all the congregation stone him.

[15]"Then you shall speak to the children of Israel, saying: 'Whoever curses his God [o]shall bear his sin. [16]And whoever [p]blasphemes the name of the LORD shall surely be put to death. All the congregation shall certainly stone him, the stranger as well as him who is born in the land. When he blasphemes the name *of the* LORD, he shall be put to death.

[17q]'Whoever kills any man shall surely be put to death. [18r]Whoever kills an animal shall make it good, animal for animal.

[19]'If a man causes disfigurement of his neighbor, as [s]he has done, so shall it be done to him— [20]fracture for [t]fracture, [u]eye for eye, tooth for tooth; as he has caused disfigurement of a man, so shall it be done to him. [21]And whoever kills an animal shall restore it; but whoever kills a man shall be put to death. [22]You shall have [v]the same law for the stranger and for one from your own country; for I *am* the LORD your God.'"

[23]Then Moses spoke to the children of Israel; and they took outside the camp him who had cursed, and stoned him with stones. So the children of Israel did as the LORD commanded Moses.

The Sabbath of the Seventh Year

25 And the LORD spoke to Moses on Mount [a]Sinai, saying, [2]"Speak to the children of Israel, and say to them: 'When you come into the land which I give you, then the land shall [b]keep a sabbath to the LORD. [3]Six years you shall sow your field, and six years you shall prune your vineyard, and gather its fruit; [4]but in the [c]seventh year there shall be a sabbath of solemn [d]rest for the land, a sabbath to the LORD. You shall neither sow your field nor prune your vineyard. [5e]What grows of its own accord of your harvest you shall not reap, nor gather the grapes of your untended vine, *for* it is a year of rest for the land. [6]And the sabbath *produce* of the land shall be food for you: for you, your male and female servants, your hired man, and the stranger who dwells with you, [7]for your livestock and the beasts that *are* in your land—all its produce shall be for food.

The Year of Jubilee

[8]'And you shall count seven sabbaths of years for yourself, seven times seven years; and the time of the seven sabbaths of years shall be to you forty-nine years.

24:19–20 *eye for eye.* This law is also found in Exodus 21:23–25. Its purpose is not to require the injured party to inflict equal bodily harm on the one who had injured him, but to restrict him from inflicting greater harm than he received.

24:22 *the same law.* These laws are repeated here in order to answer the question of whether these laws apply to non-Israelites. The answer is yes, they also apply to the stranger in the land.

25:5 *shall not reap.* Reaping and gathering for storage and selling were not permitted. However, harvesting for daily needs was allowed.

24:2 [a] Ex. 27:20, 21   **24:4** [b] Ex. 25:31; 31:8; 37:17
24:5 [c] Ex. 25:30; 39:36; 40:23   **24:6** [d] 1 Kin. 7:48
24:7 [e] Lev. 2:2, 9, 16   **24:8** [f] 1 Chr. 9:32   **24:9** [g] Matt.
12:4 [h] Ex. 29:33   **24:11** [i] Ex. 22:28 / Is. 8:21 [k] Ex. 18:22,
26   **24:12** [l] Num. 15:34 [m] Num. 27:5   **24:14** [n] Deut.
13:9; 17:7   **24:15** [o] Lev. 20:17   **24:16** [p] [Mark 3:28, 29]
24:17 [q] Ex. 21:12   **24:18** [r] Lev. 24:21   **24:19** [s] Ex. 21:24
24:20 [t] Ex. 21:23 [u] [Matt. 5:38, 39]   **24:22** [v] Ex. 12:49
25:1 [a] Lev. 26:46   **25:2** [b] Lev. 26:34, 35   **25:4** [c] Deut.
15:1 [d] [Heb. 4:9]   **25:5** [e] 2 Kin. 19:29

9Then you shall cause the trumpet of the Jubilee to sound on the tenth *day* of the seventh month; [f]on the Day of Atonement you shall make the trumpet to sound throughout all your land. 10And you shall consecrate the fiftieth year, and [g]proclaim liberty throughout all the land to all its inhabitants. It shall be a Jubilee for you; and each of you shall return to his possession, [h]and each of you shall return to his family. 11That fiftieth year shall be a Jubilee to you; in it [i]you shall neither sow nor reap what grows of its own accord, nor gather *the grapes* of your untended vine. 12For it *is* the Jubilee; it shall be holy to you; [j]you shall eat its produce from the field.

13[k]'In this Year of Jubilee, each of you shall return to his possession. 14And if you sell anything to your neighbor or buy from your neighbor's hand, you shall not [l]oppress one another. 15[m]According to the number of years after the Jubilee you shall buy from your neighbor, and according to the number of years of crops he shall sell to you. 16According to the multitude of years you shall increase its price, and according to the fewer number of years you shall diminish its price; for he sells to you *according* to the number *of the years* of the crops. 17Therefore [n]you shall not oppress one another, [o]but you shall fear your God; for I *am* the LORD your God.

Provisions for the Seventh Year

18[p]'So you shall observe My statutes and keep My judgments, and perform them; [q]and you will dwell in the land in safety. 19Then the land will yield its fruit, and [r]you will eat your fill, and dwell there in safety. 20'And if you say, [s]"What shall we eat in the seventh year, since [t]we shall not sow nor gather in our produce?" 21Then I will [u]command My blessing on you in the [v]sixth year, and it will bring forth produce enough for three years. 22[w]And you shall sow in the eighth year, and eat [x]old produce until the ninth year; until its produce comes in, you shall eat *of* the old *harvest.*

Redemption of Property

23'The land shall not be sold permanently, for [y]the land *is* Mine; for you *are* [z]strangers and sojourners with Me. 24And in all the land of your possession you shall grant redemption of the land.

25[a]'If one of your brethren becomes poor, and has sold *some* of his possession, and if [b]his redeeming relative comes to redeem it, then he may redeem what his brother sold. 26Or if the man has no one to redeem it, but he himself becomes able to redeem it, 27then [c]let him count the years since its sale, and restore the remainder to the man to whom he sold it, that he may return to his possession. 28But if he is not able to have *it* restored to himself, then what was sold shall remain in the hand of him who bought it until the Year of Jubilee; [d]and in the Jubilee it shall be released, and he shall return to his possession.

29'If a man sells a house in a walled city, then he may redeem it within a whole year after it is sold; *within* a full year he may redeem it. 30But if it is not redeemed within the space of a full year, then the house in the walled city shall belong permanently to him who bought it, throughout his generations. It shall not be released in the Jubilee. 31However, the houses of villages which have no wall around them shall be counted as the fields of the country. They may be redeemed, and they shall be released in the Jubilee. 32Nevertheless [e]the cities of the Levites, *and* the houses in the cities of their possession, the Levites may redeem at any time. 33And if a man purchases a house from the Levites, then the house that was sold in the city of his possession shall be released in the Jubilee; for the houses in the cities of the Levites *are* their possession among the children of Israel. 34But [f]the field of the common-land of their cities may not be [g]sold, for it *is* their perpetual possession.

Lending to the Poor

35'If one of your brethren becomes poor, and falls into poverty among you, then

---

25:10 return. This word could also be translated "liberty." It meant specifically that all debts were canceled, all Israelites who had sold themselves into slavery were freed, and all the land reverted to its original owners, from the time the land was divided by Joshua. The same phrase occurs in Isaiah 61:1, the passage Jesus read in the synagogue in Nazareth at the beginning of His earthly ministry. Jesus declares liberty to all who have lost their inheritance and become slaves to sin.

25:11 Jubilee. The fiftieth, or jubilee, year, followed a Sabbath year of rest, so this meant that there were two years of rest in a row for the land.

25:17 fear your God. Fear of God includes respect of man, who is God's highest creation. A deep respect of the life of man, who is created in God's image and likeness, is stressed in Scriptures. This text prohibits taking advantage of or oppressing others, and for the

Christian there is the added reminder that we are not to injure those "for whose sake Christ died" (1 Cor. 8:11).

25:23 sojourners with Me. The principle governing all of these laws was that the land did not belong to Israel; it belonged to God.

25:9 [f] Lev. 23:24, 27   **25:10** [g] Jer. 34:8, 15, 17   [h] Num. 36:4   **25:11** [i] Lev. 25:5   **25:12** [j] Lev. 25:6, 7   **25:13** [k] Lev. 25:10; 27:24   **25:14** [l] Lev. 19:13   **25:15** [m] Lev. 27:18, 23   **25:17** [n] Lev. 25:14   [o] Lev. 19:14, 32; 25:43   **25:18** [p] Lev. 19:37   [q] Deut. 12:10   **25:19** [r] Lev. 26:5   **25:20** [s] Matt. 6:25, 31   [t] Lev. 25:4, 5   **25:21** [u] Deut. 28:8   [v] Ex. 16:29   **25:22** [w] 2 Kin. 19:29   [x] Josh. 5:11   **25:23** [y] Ex. 19:5   [z] Ps. 39:12   **25:25** [a] Ruth 2:20; 4:4, 6   [b] Ruth 3:2, 9, 12   **25:27** [c] Lev. 25:50–52   **25:28** [d] Lev. 25:10, 13   **25:32** [e] Num. 35:1–8   **25:34** [f] Num. 35:2–5   [g] Acts 4:36, 37

you shall [h]help him, like a stranger or a sojourner, that he may live with you. 36[i]Take no usury or interest from him; but [j]fear your God, that your brother may live with you. 37You shall not lend him your money for usury, nor lend him your food at a profit. 38[k]I am the LORD your God, who brought you out of the land of Egypt, to give you the land of Canaan *and* to be your God.

The Law Concerning Slavery

39'And if *one of* your brethren *who dwells* by you becomes poor, and sells himself to you, you shall not compel him to serve as a slave. 40As a hired servant *and* a sojourner he shall be with you, *and* shall serve you until the Year of Jubilee. 41And *then* he shall depart from you—he and his children [l]with him—and shall return to his own family. He shall return to the possession of his fathers. 42For they *are* [m]My servants, whom I brought out of the land of Egypt; they shall not be sold as slaves. 43[n]You shall not rule over him [o]with rigor, but you [p]shall fear your God. 44And as for your male and female slaves whom you may have—from the nations that are around you, from them you may buy male and female slaves. 45Moreover you may buy [q]the children of the strangers who dwell among you, and their families who are with you, which they beget in your land; and they shall become your property. 46And [r]you may take them as an inheritance for your children after you, to inherit *them as* a possession; they shall be your permanent slaves. But regarding your brethren, the children of Israel, you shall not rule over one another with rigor.

47'Now if a sojourner or stranger close to you becomes rich, and *one of* your brethren *who dwells* by him becomes poor, and sells himself to the stranger *or* sojourner close to you, or to a member of the stranger's family, 48after he is sold he may be redeemed again. One of his brothers may redeem him; 49or his uncle or his uncle's son may redeem him; or *anyone* who is near of kin to him in his family may redeem him; or if he is able he may redeem himself. 50Thus he shall reckon with him

who bought him: The price of his release shall be according to the number of years, from the year that he was sold to him until the Year of Jubilee; *it shall be* [s]according to the time of a hired servant for him. 51If *there are* still many years *remaining*, according to them he shall repay the price of his redemption from the money with which he was bought. 52And if there remain but a few years until the Year of Jubilee, then he shall reckon with him, *and* according to his years he shall repay him the price of his redemption. 53He shall be with him as a yearly hired servant, and he shall not rule with rigor over him in your sight. 54And if he is not redeemed in these *years*, then he shall be released in the Year of Jubilee—he and his children with him. 55For the children of Israel *are* servants to Me; they *are* My servants whom I brought out of the land of Egypt: I *am* the LORD your God.

Promise of Blessing and Retribution

26 'You shall [a]not make idols for yourselves;

neither a carved image nor a *sacred* pillar shall you rear up for yourselves;

nor shall you set up an engraved stone in your land, to bow down to it;

for I *am* the LORD your God.

2 [b]You shall keep My Sabbaths and reverence My sanctuary:

I *am* the LORD.

3 [c]If you walk in My statutes and keep My commandments, and perform them,

4 [d]then I will give you rain in its season, [e]the land shall yield its produce, and the trees of the field shall yield their fruit.

5 [f]Your threshing shall last till the time of vintage, and the vintage shall last till the time of sowing;

you shall eat your bread to the full, and [g]dwell in your land safely.

6 [h]I will give peace in the land, and [i]you shall lie down, and none will make you afraid;

25:44–46 permanent slaves. The fact that God made laws to govern the current practices of slavery does not mean that He approved of slavery. He made laws about divorce, too, but He also said that He hates divorce.

26:1 engraved stone. A sacred pillar was a stone or wooden column erected to represent a pagan god or goddess. It was not a likeness, but a symbol. Together, the four terms used in this verse cover all the possibilities for pagan images.

26:4–5 rain in its season . . . threshing . . . time of vintage . . . sowing. Not only would God provide the rain when needed, He would provide abundant harvests. The grain harvest was finished by early to mid-June, and the grape harvest began about two months later. Having two months to thresh the grain

indicated a large harvest. Likewise sowing could not occur until after the first rains softened the ground, usually in mid-October. A two-month grape harvest would be a bumper crop. This is the first of the three blessings from God.

26:6–10 peace in the land. Neither animal nor human adversaries would be successful against

25:35 [h] Deut. 15:7–11; 24:14, 15　**25:36** [i] Ex. 22:25 [j] Neh. 5:9　**25:38** [k] Lev. 11:45; 22:32, 33　**25:41** [l] Ex. 21:3　**25:42** [m] [Rom. 6:22]　**25:43** [n] Eph. 6:9 [o] Ex. 1:13, 14 [p] Mal. 3:5　**25:45** [q] [Is. 56:3, 6, 7]　**25:46** [r] Is. 14:2　**25:50** [s] Job 7:1　**26:1** [a] Ex. 20:4, 5　**26:2** [b] Lev. 19:30　**26:3** [c] Deut. 28:1–14　**26:4** [d] Is. 30:23 [e] Ps. 67:6　**26:5** [f] Amos 9:13 [g] Lev. 25:18, 19　**26:6** [h] Is. 45:7 [i] Job 11:19

I will rid the land of [j]evil beasts,
and [k]the sword will not go through your land.
7 You will chase your enemies, and they shall fall by the sword before you.
8 [l]Five of you shall chase a hundred, and a hundred of you shall put ten thousand to flight;
your enemies shall fall by the sword before you.

9 'For I will [m]look on you favorably and [n]make you fruitful, multiply you and confirm My [o]covenant with you.
10 You shall eat the [p]old harvest, and clear out the old because of the new.
11 [q]I will set My tabernacle among you, and My soul shall not abhor you.
12 [r]I will walk among you and be your God, and you shall be My people.
13 I *am* the LORD your God, who brought you out of the land of Egypt, that *you* should not be their slaves;
I have broken the bands of your [s]yoke and made you walk upright.

14 'But if you do not obey Me, and do not observe all these commandments,
15 and if you despise My statutes, or if your soul abhors My judgments, so that you do not perform all My commandments, *but* break My covenant,
16 I also will do this to you:
I will even appoint terror over you, [t]wasting disease and fever which shall [u]consume the eyes and [v]cause sorrow of heart.
And [w]you shall sow your seed in vain, for your enemies shall eat it.
17 I will set [x]My face against you, and [y]you shall be defeated by your enemies.
[z]Those who hate you shall reign over you, and you shall [a]flee when no one pursues you.

18 'And after all this, if you do not obey Me, then I will punish you [b]seven times more for your sins.
19 I will [c]break the pride of your power;
I [d]will make your heavens like iron and your earth like bronze.
20 And your [e]strength shall be spent in vain;
for your [f]land shall not yield its produce, nor shall the trees of the land yield their fruit.

21 'Then, if you walk contrary to Me, and are not willing to obey Me, I will bring on you seven times more plagues, according to your sins.
22 [g]I will also send wild beasts among you, which shall rob you of your children, destroy your livestock, and make you few in number;
and [h]your highways shall be desolate.

23 'And if [i]by these things you are not reformed by Me, but walk contrary to Me,
24 [j]then I also will walk contrary to you, and I will punish you yet seven times for your sins.
25 And [k]I will bring a sword against you that will execute the vengeance of the covenant;

Israel. This is the second of the three blessings from God.

26:11–13 *I will walk among you.* The third blessing was the promise of His presence within Israel, actively walking among them and looking out for their welfare.

26:12–13 *be your God.* The image in these verses is a dramatic one, reminding the Israelites that God would be their intimate associate continually. He would walk with them, support them in times of difficulty and danger, and abundantly provide for both their physical and spiritual needs. To be God's people meant that the Israelites had to obey God's laws scrupulously, to be holy as God is holy, and to be a witness of God among the pagan nations.

26:14–15 *not observe all these commandments.* As with the blessings, the curses are presented in an "if-then" format.

26:16–17 *terror . . . wasting disease and fever.* Fear, illness, poor harvest, and enemies in the land would be God's first attempts to draw Israel back to Himself.

26:18–20 *heavens like iron.* The second series of curses were characterized as "seven times more." Rain was essential to the whole nation, both the fall and spring rains.

26:19 *pride of your power.* The pride of power will often cause a person or nation to trust in its own strength and accomplishments rather than to submit to God and give Him the honor and glory. The punishment for this pride was drought—skies like iron, with not even a hint of rain. This can be true on a personal level as well as a national level if one forgets that it is God who has given the position of significance. Then the iron heavens make it seem as if prayers are not heard, and the parched spirit cries out for God's touch again.

26:21–22 *seven times more plagues.* The third series of curses are again increased "seven times," so that the land is plagued with wild beasts that attack both their children and their domestic animals.

26:23–26 *a sword . . . pestilence . . . hand of the enemy . . . eat and not be satisfied.* The fourth series of curses are also increased "seven times." When enemies invaded the land, the people living in unwalled villages fled to walled cities, and if the city was besieged, the overcrowding created prime conditions for epidemics and famine.

26:6 [j] 2 Kin. 17:25 [k] Ezek. 14:17 **26:8** [l] Deut. 32:30 **26:9** [m] Ex. 2:25 [n] Gen. 17:6, 7 [o] Gen. 17:1–7 **26:10** [p] Lev. 25:22 **26:11** [q] Ex. 25:8; 29:45, 46 **26:12** [r] [2 Cor. 6:16] **26:13** [s] Gen. 27:40 **26:16** [t] Deut. 28:22 [u] 1 Sam. 2:33 [v] Ezek. 24:23; 33:10 [w] Judg. 6:3–6 **26:17** [x] Ps. 34:16 [y] Deut. 28:25 [z] Ps. 106:41 [a] Prov. 28:1 **26:18** [b] 1 Sam. 2:5 **26:19** [c] Is. 25:11 [d] Deut. 28:23 **26:20** [e] Ps. 127:1 [f] Gen. 4:12 **26:22** [g] Deut. 32:24 [h] Judg. 5:6 **26:23** [i] Amos 4:6–12 **26:24** [j] Lev. 26:28, 41 **26:25** [k] Ezek. 5:17

when you are gathered together within your cities [l]I will send pestilence among you;
and you shall be delivered into the hand of the enemy.
26 [m]When I have cut off your supply of bread, ten women shall bake your bread in one oven, and they shall bring back your bread by weight, [n]and you shall eat and not be satisfied.

27 'And after all this, if you do not obey Me, but walk contrary to Me,
28 then I also will walk contrary to you in fury;
and I, even I, will chastise you seven times for your sins.
29 [o]You shall eat the flesh of your sons, and you shall eat the flesh of your daughters.
30 [p]I will destroy your high places, cut down your incense altars, and cast your carcasses on the lifeless forms of your idols;
and My soul shall abhor you.
31 I will lay your [q]cities waste and [r]bring your sanctuaries to desolation, and I will not [s]smell the fragrance of your sweet aromas.
32 [t]I will bring the land to desolation, and your enemies who dwell in it shall be astonished at it.
33 [u]I will scatter you among the nations and draw out a sword after you;
your land shall be desolate and your cities waste.
34 [v]Then the land shall enjoy its sabbaths as long as it lies desolate and you *are* in your enemies' land;
then the land shall rest and enjoy its sabbaths.
35 As long as *it* lies desolate it shall rest—
for the time it did not rest on your [w]sabbaths when you dwelt in it.

36 'And as for those of you who are left, I will send [x]faintness into their hearts in the lands of their enemies;
the sound of a shaken leaf shall cause them to flee;
they shall flee as though fleeing from a sword, and they shall fall when no one pursues.
37 [y]They shall stumble over one another, as it were before a sword, when no one pursues;
and [z]you shall have no *power* to stand before your enemies.
38 You shall [a]perish among the nations, and the land of your enemies shall eat you up.
39 And those of you who are left [b]shall waste away in their iniquity in your enemies' lands;
also in their [c]fathers' iniquities, which are with them, they shall waste away.

40 '*But* [d]if they confess their iniquity and the iniquity of their fathers, with their unfaithfulness in which they were unfaithful to Me, and that they also have walked contrary to Me,
41 and *that* I also have walked contrary to them and have brought them into the land of their enemies;
if their [e]uncircumcised hearts are [f]humbled, and they [g]accept their guilt—
42 then I will [h]remember My covenant with Jacob, and My covenant with Isaac and My covenant with Abraham I will remember;
I will [i]remember the land.
43 [j]The land also shall be left empty by them, and will enjoy its sabbaths while it lies desolate without them;
they will accept their guilt, because they [k]despised My judgments and because their soul abhorred My statutes.
44 Yet for all that, when they are in the land of their enemies, [l]I will not cast them away, nor shall I abhor them, to utterly destroy them and break My covenant with them;
for I *am* the LORD their God.
45 But [m]for their sake I will remember the covenant of their ancestors, [n]whom I

26:29 *eat the flesh of your sons . . . daughters.* The fifth and final curse, "seven times for your sins," was cannibalism. This actually happened centuries later during a siege of Samaria, and later still in Jerusalem (2 Kin. 6:28–29; Lam. 2:20; 4:10).

26:30 *high places . . . idols.* The high places and images or incense altars were dedicated to the worship of pagan gods.

26:33 *scatter.* This threat was fulfilled in the Babylonian exile of 587–536 B.C.

26:36–37 *faintness into their hearts.* Survivors would not enjoy relief or peace of mind after escaping the disasters. They would still be timid, even when no one pursued them.

26:38–39 *perish among the nations.* Having been exiled to foreign lands, the people were not to think they were beyond God's punitive reach.

26:42 *My covenant.* God's covenant with the patriarchs took precedence over the covenant at Sinai (Gal. 3:15–18). Even when Israel violated the Sinai covenant, God honored the patriarchal covenant.

26:44–45 *I will not cast them away . . . remember the covenant.* Ultimately, God's character is grace, mercy, love and redemption. On that basis, God would remember the covenant and redeem them because He is God.

26:25 [l] Deut. 28:21 **26:26** [m] Ps. 105:16 [n] Mic. 6:14 **26:29** [o] 2 Kin. 6:28, 29 **26:30** [p] 2 Chr. 34:3 **26:31** [q] 2 Kin. 25:4, 10 [r] Ps. 74:7 [s] Is. 1:11–15 **26:32** [t] Jer. 9:11; 18:16 **26:33** [u] Deut. 4:27 **26:34** [v] 2 Chr. 36:21 **26:35** [w] Lev. 25:2 **26:36** [x] Ezek. 21:7, 12, 15 **26:37** [y] 1 Sam. 14:15, 16 [z] Josh. 7:12, 13 **26:38** [a] Deut. 4:26 **26:39** [b] Ezek. 4:17; 33:10 [c] Ex. 34:7 **26:40** [d] Neh. 9:2 **26:41** [e] Acts 7:51 [f] 2 Chr. 12:6, 7, 12 [g] Dan. 9:7 **26:42** [h] Ex. 2:24; 6:5 [i] Ps. 136:23 **26:43** [j] Lev. 26:34, 35 [k] Lev. 26:15 **26:44** [l] Deut. 4:31 **26:45** [m] [Rom. 11:28] [n] Lev. 22:33; 25:38

brought out of the land of Egypt °in the sight of the nations, that I might be their God:

I *am* the LORD.'"

⁴⁶ᵖThese *are* the statutes and judgments and laws which the LORD made between Himself and the children of Israel ᑫon Mount Sinai by the hand of Moses.

Redeeming Persons and Property Dedicated to God

27 Now the LORD spoke to Moses, saying, ²"Speak to the children of Israel, and say to them: ᵃ'When a man consecrates by a vow certain persons to the LORD, according to your valuation, ³if your valuation is of a male from twenty years old up to sixty years old, then your valuation shall be fifty shekels of silver, ᵇaccording to the shekel of the sanctuary. ⁴If it *is* a female, then your valuation shall be thirty shekels; ⁵and if from five years old up to twenty years old, then your valuation for a male shall be twenty shekels, and for a female ten shekels; ⁶and if from a month old up to five years old, then your valuation for a male shall be five shekels of silver, and for a female your valuation shall be three shekels of silver; ⁷and if from sixty years old and above, if *it is* a male, then your valuation shall be fifteen shekels, and for a female ten shekels.

⁸'But if he is too poor to pay your valuation, then he shall present himself before the priest, and the priest shall set a value for ᶜhim; according to the ability of him who vowed, the priest shall value him.

⁹'If *it is* an animal that men may bring as an offering to the LORD, all that *anyone* gives to the LORD shall be holy. ¹⁰He shall not substitute it or exchange it, good for bad or bad for good; and if he at all exchanges animal for animal, then both it and the one exchanged for it shall be ᵈholy. ¹¹If *it is* an unclean animal which they do not offer as a sacrifice to the LORD, then he shall present the animal before the priest; ¹²and the priest shall set a value for it, whether it is good or bad; as you, the priest, value it, so

it shall be. ¹³ᵉBut if he *wants* at all *to* redeem it, then he must add one-fifth to your valuation.

¹⁴'And when a man dedicates his house *to be* holy to the LORD, then the priest shall set a value for it, whether it is good or bad; as the priest values it, so it shall stand. ¹⁵If he who dedicated it *wants to* redeem his house, then he must add one-fifth of the money of your valuation to it, and it shall be his.

¹⁶'If a man dedicates to the LORD *part* of a field of his possession, then your valuation shall be according to the seed for it. A homer of barley seed *shall be valued* at fifty shekels of silver. ¹⁷If he dedicates his field from the Year of Jubilee, according to your valuation it shall stand. ¹⁸But if he dedicates his field after the Jubilee, then the priest shall ᶠreckon to him the money due according to the years that remain till the Year of Jubilee, and it shall be deducted from your valuation. ¹⁹And if he who dedicates the field ever wishes to redeem it, then he must add one-fifth of the money of your valuation to it, and it shall belong to him. ²⁰But if he does not want to redeem the field, or if he has sold the field to another man, it shall not be redeemed anymore; ²¹but the field, ᵍwhen it is released in the Jubilee, shall be holy to the LORD, as a ʰdevoted field; it shall be ⁱthe possession of the priest.

²²'And if a man dedicates to the LORD a field which he has bought, which is not the field of ʲhis possession, ²³then the priest shall reckon to him the worth of your valuation, up to the Year of Jubilee, and he shall give your valuation on that day *as a* holy *offering* to the LORD. ²⁴ᵏIn the Year of Jubilee the field shall return to him from whom it was bought, to the one who *owned* the land as a possession. ²⁵And all your valuations shall be according to the shekel of the sanctuary: ˡtwenty gerahs to the shekel.

²⁶'But the ᵐfirstborn of the animals, which should be the LORD's firstborn, no man shall dedicate; whether *it is* an ox or sheep, it *is* the LORD's. ²⁷And if *it is* an unclean animal, then he shall redeem *it* according to your valuation, and ⁿshall add

---

27:2–8 by a vow . . . shall value. While people could dedicate themselves or their children to the Lord (1 Sam. 1:11,22) only the Levites were allowed to serve God as priests. Therefore, those others vowed in service to the Lord had to be redeemed, and the value of his service was given to the sanctuary.

27:8 too poor. Fifty shekels might have represented about four years' earnings. If a person was too poor to pay this price, the priest set a price that the person could pay.

27:14–24 dedicates. Consecrating or dedicating property to the Lord, and then buying it back with cash if one wants to use it for oneself is a curious idea to modern people. We tend to consider dedication of something to God as using it in a way that pleases Him, and the line between "God's" and "mine"

may be very fuzzy. We are familiar with offering praises or tithes to God as worship, but think of the way we handle property as "good" or "poor" stewardship. A passage like this reminds us that we are not to be casual in worship. Are we offering to God or not? Is it His, or do we want it back at no cost to ourselves?

27:16 homer of barley. A homer was a donkey load.

26:45 ° Ps. 98:2   **26:46** ᵖ [John 1:17]   ᑫ Lev. 25:1
27:2 ᵃ Num. 6:2   **27:3** ᵇ Ex. 30:13   **27:8** ᶜ Lev. 5:11;
14:21–24   **27:10** ᵈ Lev. 27:33   **27:13** ᵉ Lev. 6:5; 22:14;
27:15, 19   **27:18** ᶠ Lev. 25:15, 16, 28   **27:21** ᵍ Lev.
25:10, 28, 31   ʰ Lev. 27:28   ⁱ Num. 18:14   **27:22** ʲ Lev.
25:10, 25   **27:24** ᵏ Lev. 25:10–13, 28   **27:25** ˡ Ex. 30:13
27:26 ᵐ Ex. 13:2, 12; 22:30   **27:27** ⁿ Lev. 27:11, 12

one-fifth to it; or if it is not redeemed, then it shall be sold according to your valuation.

28 o'Nevertheless no devoted *offering* that a man may devote to the LORD of all that he has, *both* man and beast, or the field of his possession, shall be sold or redeemed; every devoted *offering is* most holy to the LORD. 29pNo person under the ban, who may become doomed to destruction among men, shall be redeemed, *but* shall surely be put to death. 30And qall the tithe of the land, *whether* of the seed of the land *or* of the fruit of the tree, *is* the LORD's. It *is* holy to the LORD. 31rIf a man wants at all to redeem *any* of his tithes, he shall add one-fifth to it. 32And concerning the tithe of the herd or the flock, of whatever spasses under the rod, the tenth one shall be holy to the LORD. 33He shall not inquire whether it is good or bad, tnor shall he exchange it; and if he exchanges it at all, then both it and the one exchanged for it shall be holy; it shall not be redeemed.'"

34uThese *are* the commandments which the LORD commanded Moses for the children of Israel on Mount vSinai.

27:28 *devoted offering.* Devoting a possession was a stronger act than dedication. Nothing devoted could be redeemed; persons devoted (under the ban) were to be put to death. No private citizen would have had the power to put himself or anyone else "under the ban."
27:31 *redeem any of his tithes.* For a person living a distance from the sanctuary, it may have been more practical to redeem the tithe than to bring the crops to the sanctuary.
27:32 *under the rod.* Sheep and goats were inspected when they passed under the rod that the shepherd placed across the entrance to the fold. This was a time to determine if the animals were under any distress from disease or injury, and was also the time that some of them were set aside for the Lord.

27:28 o Josh. 6:17–19   **27:29** p Num. 21:2   **27:30** q Gen. 28:22   **27:31** r Lev. 27:13   **27:32** s Jer. 33:13   **27:33** t Lev. 27:10   **27:34** u Lev. 26:46   v [Heb. 12:18–29]

THE FOURTH BOOK OF MOSES CALLED
NUMBERS

▶ **AUTHOR:** The Jews, Samaritans, and the early church testify to Moses' authorship. Several New Testament passages attribute events cited from Numbers to Moses (John 3:14; Acts 7; 13; 1 Cor. 10:1–11; Heb. 3–4), and there are more than eighty claims within Numbers that state that the Lord spoke to Moses (1:1). Numbers 33:2 says that Moses recorded their journeys at the Lord's command. As an eyewitness who kept detailed records, and the central character of the events in the book, no one was better qualified to write this book than Moses.

▶ **TIME:** c. 1444–1405 B.C.   ▶ **KEY VERSES:** Num. 14:22–23

▶ **THEME:** At Sinai, this newly resurrected nation of Israel receives its laws, its system of sacrifices, and its national charter. The people then should be ready to take the next step into the Promised Land, but they aren't. Numbers largely has Israel in a holding pattern. While the book records further steps taken in organizing the nation, its central narrative is that of the refusal of the people to go into Canaan. But God still doesn't give up on His people. He continues to discipline them in an effort to have a new generation ready to fulfill His plan. In this context Numbers points to God's sovereignty, His patience, and His desire to bless His people.

The First Census of Israel

1 Now the LORD spoke to Moses ^{a}in the Wilderness of Sinai, ^{b}in the tabernacle of meeting, on the ^{c}first *day* of the second month, in the second year after they had come out of the land of Egypt, saying: 2^d"Take a census of all the congregation of the children of Israel, by their families, by their fathers' houses, according to the number of names, every male ^{e}individually, 3from ^{f}twenty years old and above—all who *are able to* go to war in Israel. You and Aaron shall number them by their armies. 4And with you there shall be a man from every tribe, each one the head of his father's house.

5"These are the names of the men who shall stand with you: from Reuben, Elizur the son of Shedeur; 6from Simeon, Shelumiel the son of Zurishaddai; 7from Judah, Nahshon the son of Amminadab; 8from Issachar, Nethanel the son of Zuar; 9from Zebulun, Eliab the son of Helon; 10from the sons of Joseph: from Ephraim, Elishama the son of Ammihud; from Manasseh, Gamaliel the son of Pedahzur; 11from Benjamin, Abidan the son of Gideoni; 12from Dan, Ahiezer the son of Ammishaddai; 13from Asher, Pagiel the son of Ocran;

14from Gad, Eliasaph the son of ^{g}Deuel;* 15from Naphtali, Ahira the son of Enan." 16^{h}These *were* ^{i}chosen from the congregation, leaders of their fathers' tribes, ^{j}heads of the divisions in Israel.

17Then Moses and Aaron took these men who had been mentioned ^{k}by name, 18and they assembled all the congregation together on the first *day* of the second month; and they recited their ^{l}ancestry by families, by their fathers' houses, according to the number of names, from twenty years old and above, each one individually. 19As the LORD commanded Moses, so he numbered them in the Wilderness of Sinai.

20Now the ^{m}children of Reuben, Israel's oldest son, their genealogies by their families, by their fathers' house, according to the number of names, every male individually, from twenty years old and above, all who *were able to* go to war: 21those who were numbered of the tribe of Reuben *were* forty-six thousand five hundred.

22From the ^{n}children of Simeon, their genealogies by their families, by their fathers' house, of those who were

* **1:14** Spelled *Reuel* in 2:14

1:1 *Wilderness of Sinai.* The setting of the Book of Numbers is the wilderness. Not only did the Israelites live in the wilderness, but they as a nation were traveling through a time of spiritual emptiness. They were starting all over in their relationship with God after a time of slavery. The empty wilderness kept them dependent, and kept them from being

1:1 ^{a}Ex. 19:1 ^{b}Ex. 25:22 ^{c}Num. 9:1; 10:11   **1:2** ^{d}Num. 26:2, 63, 64 ^{e}Ex. 30:12, 13; 38:26   **1:3** ^{f}Ex. 30:14; 38:26   **1:14** ^{g}Num. 7:42   **1:16** ^{h}Num. 7:2 ^{i}Num. 16:2 ^{j}Ex. 18:21, 25   **1:17** ^{k}Is. 43:1   **1:18** ^{l}Ezra 2:59   **1:20** ^{m}Num. 2:10, 11; 26:5–11; 32:6, 15, 21, 29   **1:22** ^{n}Num. 2:12, 13; 26:12–14

numbered, according to the number of names, every male individually, from twenty years old and above, all who *were able to* go to war: [23]those who were numbered of the tribe of Simeon *were* fifty-nine thousand three hundred.

[24]From the [o]children of Gad, their genealogies by their families, by their fathers' house, according to the number of names, from twenty years old and above, all who *were able to* go to war: [25]those who were numbered of the tribe of Gad *were* forty-five thousand six hundred and fifty.

[26]From the [p]children of Judah, their genealogies by their families, by their fathers' house, according to the number of names, from twenty years old and above, all who *were able to* go to war: [27]those who were numbered of the tribe of Judah *were* [q]seventy-four thousand six hundred.

[28]From the [r]children of Issachar, their genealogies by their families, by their fathers' house, according to the number of names, from twenty years old and above, all who *were able to* go to war: [29]those who were numbered of the tribe of Issachar *were* fifty-four thousand four hundred.

[30]From the [s]children of Zebulun, their genealogies by their families, by their fathers' house, according to the number of names, from twenty years old and above, all who *were able to* go to war: [31]those who were numbered of the tribe of Zebulun *were* fifty-seven thousand four hundred.

[32]From the sons of Joseph, the [t]children of Ephraim, their genealogies by their families, by their fathers' house, according to the number of names, from twenty years old and above, all who *were able to* go to war: [33]those who were numbered of the tribe of Ephraim *were* forty thousand five hundred.

[34]From the [u]children of Manasseh, their genealogies by their families, by their fathers' house, according to the number of names, from twenty years old and above, all who *were able to* go to war: [35]those who were numbered of the tribe of Manasseh *were* thirty-two thousand two hundred.

[36]From the [v]children of Benjamin, their genealogies by their families, by their fathers' house, according to the number of names, from twenty years old and above, all who *were able to* go to war: [37]those who were numbered of the tribe of Benjamin *were* thirty-five thousand four hundred.

[38]From the [w]children of Dan, their genealogies by their families, by their fathers' house, according to the number of names, from twenty years old and above, all who *were able to* go to war: [39]those who were numbered of the tribe of Dan *were* sixty-two thousand seven hundred.

[40]From the [x]children of Asher, their genealogies by their families, by their fathers' house, according to the number of names, from twenty years old and above, all who *were able to* go to war: [41]those who were numbered of the tribe of Asher *were* forty-one thousand five hundred.

[42]From the children of Naphtali, their genealogies by their families, by their fathers' house, according to the number of names, from twenty years old and above, all who *were able to* go to war: [43]those who were numbered of the tribe of Naphtali *were* fifty-three thousand four hundred.

[44y]These are the ones who were numbered, whom Moses and Aaron numbered, with the leaders of Israel, twelve men, each one representing his father's house. [45]So all who were numbered of the children of Israel, by their fathers' houses, from twenty years old and above, all who *were able to* go to war in Israel— [46]all who were numbered were [z]six hundred and three thousand five hundred and fifty.

[47]But [a]the Levites were not numbered among them by their fathers' tribe; [48]for the LORD had spoken to Moses, saying: [49b]"Only the tribe of Levi you shall not number, nor take a census of them among the children of Israel; [50c]but you shall appoint the Levites over the tabernacle of the Testimony, over all its furnishings, and over all things that belong to it; they shall carry the tabernacle and all its furnishings; they shall attend to it [d]and camp around the tabernacle. [51e]And when the tabernacle is to go forward, the Levites shall take it down; and when the tabernacle is to be set up, the Levites shall set it [f]up. [g]The outsider who comes near shall be put to death. [52]The children of Israel shall pitch their tents, everyone by his own camp, [h]everyone by his own standard, according to their armies; [53i]but the Levites shall camp around the tabernacle of the Testimony, that there may be no [j]wrath on the congregation of the children of Israel; and the Levites shall [k]keep charge of the tabernacle of the Testimony."

[54]Thus the children of Israel did; according to all that the LORD commanded Moses, so they did.

---

distracted with the normal affairs of caring for land and animals.

1:44–46 all who were numbered. The number of able-bodied men who were at least twenty years old would indicate a population of between two and five million, including the women, children, and older or infirm men who were not counted in this census.

1:50 the tabernacle. The term *tabernacle* points to the temporary and portable nature of the tent.

1:24 [o] Num. 26:15–18   **1:26** [p] 2 Sam. 24:9   **1:27** [q] 2 Chr. 17:14   **1:28** [r] Num. 2:5, 6   **1:30** [s] Num. 2:7, 8; 26:26, 27   **1:32** [t] Num. 26:28–37   **1:34** [u] Num. 2:20, 21; 26:28–34   **1:36** [v] Num. 26:38–41   **1:38** [w] Gen. 30:6; 46:23   **1:40** [x] Num. 2:27, 28; 26:44–47   **1:44** [y] Num. 26:64   **1:46** [z] Ex. 12:37; 38:26   **1:47** [a] Num. 2:33; 3:14–22; 26:57–62   **1:49** [b] Num. 2:33; 26:62   **1:50** [c] Ex. 38:21   [d] Num. 3:23, 29, 35, 38   **1:51** [e] Num. 4:5–15; 10:17, 21   [f] Num. 10:21   [g] Num. 3:10, 38; 4:15, 19, 20; 18:22   **1:52** [h] Num. 2:2, 34; 24:2   **1:53** [i] Num. 1:50   [j] Lev. 10:6   [k] 1 Chr. 23:32

The Tribes and Leaders by Armies

2 And the LORD spoke to Moses and Aaron, saying: ^{2a}"Everyone of the children of Israel shall camp by his own standard, beside the emblems of his father's house; they shall camp ^bsome distance from the tabernacle of meeting. ³On the ^ceast side, toward the rising of the sun, those of the standard of the forces with Judah shall camp according to their armies; and ^dNahshon the son of Amminadab *shall be* the leader of the children of Judah." ⁴And his army was numbered at seventy-four thousand six hundred.

⁵"Those who camp next to him *shall be* the tribe of Issachar, and Nethanel the son of Zuar *shall be* the leader of the children of Issachar." ⁶And his army was numbered at fifty-four thousand four hundred.

⁷"Then *comes* the tribe of Zebulun, and Eliab the son of Helon *shall be* the leader of the children of Zebulun." ⁸And his army was numbered at fifty-seven thousand four hundred. ⁹"All who were numbered according to their armies of the forces with Judah, one hundred and eighty-six thousand four hundred—^ethese shall break camp first.

¹⁰"On the ^fsouth side *shall be* the standard of the forces with Reuben according to their armies, and the leader of the children of Reuben *shall be* Elizur the son of Shedeur." ¹¹And his army was numbered at forty-six thousand five hundred.

¹²"Those who camp next to him *shall be* the tribe of Simeon, and the leader of the children of Simeon *shall be* Shelumiel the son of Zurishaddai." ¹³And his army was numbered at fifty-nine thousand three hundred.

¹⁴"Then *comes* the tribe of Gad, and the leader of the children of Gad *shall be* Eliasaph the son of Reuel."* ¹⁵And his army was numbered at forty-five thousand six hundred and fifty. ¹⁶"All who were numbered according to their armies of the forces with Reuben, one hundred and fifty-one thousand four hundred and fifty—^gthey shall be the second to break camp.

^{17h}"And the tabernacle of meeting shall move out with the camp of the Levites ⁱin the middle of the camps; as they camp, so they shall move out, everyone in his place, by their standards.

¹⁸"On the west side *shall be* the standard of the forces with Ephraim according to their armies, and the leader of the children of Ephraim *shall be* Elishama the son of Ammihud." ¹⁹And his army was numbered at forty thousand five hundred.

²⁰"Next to him *comes* the tribe of Manasseh, and the leader of the children of Manasseh *shall be* Gamaliel the son of Pedahzur." ²¹And his army was numbered at thirty-two thousand two hundred.

²²"Then *comes* the tribe of Benjamin, and the leader of the children of Benjamin *shall be* Abidan the son of Gideoni." ²³And his army was numbered at thirty-five thousand four hundred. ²⁴"All who were numbered according to their armies of the forces with Ephraim, one hundred and eight thousand one hundred—^jthey shall be the third to break camp.

²⁵"The standard of the forces with Dan *shall be* on the north side according to their armies, and the leader of the children of Dan *shall be* Ahiezer the son of Ammishaddai." ²⁶And his army was numbered at sixty-two thousand seven hundred.

²⁷"Those who camp next to him *shall be* the tribe of Asher, and the leader of the children of Asher *shall be* Pagiel the son of Ocran." ²⁸And his army was numbered at forty-one thousand five hundred.

²⁹"Then *comes* the tribe of Naphtali, and the leader of the children of Naphtali *shall be* Ahira the son of Enan." ³⁰And his army was numbered at fifty-three thousand four hundred. ³¹"All who were numbered of the forces with Dan, one hundred and fifty-seven thousand six hundred—^kthey shall break camp last, with their standards."

³²These *are* the ones who were numbered of the children of Israel by their fathers' houses. ^lAll who were numbered according to their armies of the forces *were* six hundred and three thousand five hundred and fifty. ³³But ^mthe Levites were not numbered among the children of Israel, just as the LORD commanded Moses.

³⁴Thus the children of Israel ⁿdid according to all that the LORD commanded Moses; ^oso they camped by their standards and so they broke camp, each one by his family, according to their fathers' houses.

---

* **2:14** Spelled *Deuel* in 1:14 and 7:42

2:1–2 *by his own standard.* A person's identity was not only derived from his or her tribe, but also from his or her place in relation to the tabernacle. This is a chapter on design and order; it speaks to the importance of knowing one's duties in relation to the holy and living God.

2:3–9 *On the east side, toward the rising of the sun.* The east side was the favored side, facing the rising sun. The Israelites were not a seafaring people; in effect they turned their backs to the sea, so the word for "back" could mean "west" or "the sea."

2:17 *tabernacle . . . the Levites in the middle.* In the line of march the tabernacle was in a central position—a symbol not only of Israel's protection of the holy objects, but also of the presence of God among His people.

2:2 ^a Num. 1:52; 24:2   ^b Josh. 3:4   **2:3** ^c Num. 10:5   ^d 1 Chr. 2:10   **2:9** ^e Num. 10:14   **2:10** ^f Num. 10:6   **2:16** ^g Num. 10:18   **2:17** ^h Num. 10:17, 21   ⁱ Num. 1:53   **2:24** ^j Num. 10:22   **2:31** ^k Num. 10:25   **2:32** ^l Ex. 38:26   **2:33** ^m Num. 1:47; 26:57–62   **2:34** ⁿ Num. 1:54   ^o Num. 24:2, 5, 6

The Sons of Aaron

3 Now these *are* the [a]records of Aaron
and Moses when the LORD spoke with
Moses on Mount Sinai. 2 And these *are*
the names of the sons of Aaron: Nadab,
the [b]firstborn, and [c]Abihu, Eleazar, and
Ithamar. 3 These *are* the names of the sons
of Aaron, [d]the anointed priests, whom he
consecrated to minister as priests. 4 [e]Nadab
and Abihu had died before the LORD when
they offered profane fire before the LORD
in the Wilderness of Sinai; and they had
no children. So Eleazar and Ithamar ministered as priests in the presence of Aaron
their father.

The Levites Serve in the Tabernacle

5 And the LORD spoke to Moses, saying:
6 [f]"Bring the tribe of Levi near, and present
them before Aaron the priest, that they
may serve him. 7 And they shall attend to
his needs and the needs of the whole congregation before the tabernacle of meeting,
to do [g]the work of the tabernacle. 8 Also
they shall attend to all the furnishings of
the tabernacle of meeting, and to the needs
of the children of Israel, to do the work of
the tabernacle. 9 And [h]you shall give the Levites to Aaron and his sons; they *are* given
entirely to him* from among the children
of Israel. 10 So you shall appoint Aaron and
his sons, [i]and they shall attend to their
priesthood; [j]but the outsider who comes
near shall be put to death."
11 Then the LORD spoke to Moses, saying:
12 "Now behold, [k]I Myself have taken the
Levites from among the children of Israel
instead of every firstborn who opens the
womb among the children of Israel. Therefore the Levites shall be [l]Mine, 13 because
[m]all the firstborn *are* Mine. [n]On the day
that I struck all the firstborn in the land of
Egypt, I sanctified to Myself all the firstborn in Israel, both man and beast. They
shall be Mine: I *am* the LORD."

Census of the Levites Commanded

14 Then the LORD spoke to Moses in the
Wilderness of Sinai, saying: 15 "Number the
children of Levi by their fathers' houses,
by their families; you shall number [o]every
male from a month old and above."
16 So Moses numbered them according
to the word of the LORD, as he was commanded. 17 [p]These were the sons of Levi
by their names: Gershon, Kohath, and
Merari. 18 And these *are* the names of the
sons of [q]Gershon by their families: [r]Libni
and Shimei. 19 And the sons of [s]Kohath by
their families: [t]Amram, Izehar, Hebron,
and Uzziel. 20 [u]And the sons of Merari by
their families: Mahli and Mushi. These *are*
the families of the Levites by their fathers'
houses.
21 From Gershon *came* the family of the
Libnites and the family of the Shimites;
these *were* the families of the Gershonites.
22 Those who were numbered, according to
the number of all the males from a month
old and above—of those who were numbered *there were* seven thousand five hundred. 23 [v]The families of the Gershonites
were to camp behind the tabernacle westward. 24 And the leader of the father's house
of the Gershonites *was* Eliasaph the son of
Lael. 25 [w]The duties of the children of Gershon in the tabernacle of meeting *included*
[x]the tabernacle, [y]the tent with [z]its covering,
the [a]screen for the door of the tabernacle of
meeting, 26 [b]the screen for the door of the
court, [c]the hangings of the court which
are around the tabernacle and the altar,
and [d]their cords, according to all the work
relating to them.
27 [e]From Kohath *came* the family of the
Amramites, the family of the Izharites, the
family of the Hebronites, and the family of
the Uzzielites; these *were* the families of the
Kohathites. 28 According to the number of
all the males, from a month old and above,
there were eight thousand six* hundred
keeping charge of the sanctuary. 29 [f]The
families of the children of Kohath were to
camp on the south side of the tabernacle.
30 And the leader of the fathers' house of the
families of the Kohathites *was* Elizaphan
the son of [g]Uzziel. 31 [h]Their duty *included*
[i]the ark, [j]the table, [k]the lampstand, [l]the
altars, the utensils of the sanctuary with
which they ministered, [m]the screen, and all
the work relating to them.
32 And Eleazar the son of Aaron the
priest *was to be* chief over the leaders of

---

* **3:9** Samaritan Pentateuch and Septuagint read *Me.* * **3:28** Some manuscripts of the Septuagint read *three.*

3:1–10 *sons of Aaron.* The priests had privileged access to God. In the New Covenant this is no longer confined only to a particular group of God's people. All Christians comprise God's new temple and constitute "a holy priesthood, to offer up spiritual sacrifices acceptable to God through Jesus Christ" (1 Pet. 2:5).

3:5–10 *Aaron and his sons.* The Levites could care for the holy things, but only the priests, who ministered in the tabernacle, drew near to God. Only the high priest entered the Most Holy Place.

3:11–13 *I sanctified to Myself.* God is directly involved in redemption. When God redeemed and saved His people, it was by His own person.

3:1 [a] Ex. 6:16–27 **3:2** [b] Ex. 6:23 [c] Num. 26:60, 61 **3:3** [d] Ex. 28:41 **3:4** [e] 1 Chr. 24:2 **3:6** [f] Num. 8:6–22; 18:1–7 **3:7** [g] Num. 1:50; 8:11, 15, 24, 26 **3:9** [h] Num. 8:19; 18:6, 7 **3:10** [i] Ex. 29:9 [j] Num. 1:51; 3:38; 16:40 **3:12** [k] Num. 3:41; 8:16; 18:6 [l] Num. 3:45; 8:14 **3:13** [m] Ex. 13:2 [n] Num. 8:17 **3:15** [o] Num. 3:39; 26:62 **3:17** [p] Ex. 6:16–22 **3:18** [q] Num. 4:38–41 [r] Ex. 6:17 **3:19** [s] Num. 4:34–37 [t] Ex. 6:18 **3:20** [u] Ex. 6:19 **3:23** [v] Num. 1:53 **3:25** [w] Num. 4:24–26 [x] Ex. 25:9 [y] Ex. 26:1 [z] Ex. 26:7, 14 [a] Ex. 26:36 **3:26** [b] Ex. 27:9, 12, 14, 15 [c] Ex. 27:16 [d] Ex. 35:18 **3:27** [e] 1 Chr. 26:23 **3:29** [f] Num. 1:53 **3:30** [g] Lev. 10:4 **3:31** [h] Num. 4:15 [i] Ex. 25:10 [j] Ex. 25:23 [k] Ex. 25:31 [l] Ex. 27:1; 30:1 [m] Ex. 26:31–33

the Levites, *with* oversight of those who kept charge of the sanctuary.

33From Merari *came* the family of the Mahlites and the family of the Mushites; these *were* the families of Merari. 34And those who were numbered, according to the number of all the males from a month old and above, *were* six thousand two hundred. 35The leader of the fathers' house of the families of Merari *was* Zuriel the son of Abihail. *n*These *were* to camp on the north side of the tabernacle. 36And *o*the appointed duty of the children of Merari *included* the boards of the tabernacle, its bars, its pillars, its sockets, its utensils, all the work relating to them, 37and the pillars of the court all around, with their sockets, their pegs, and their cords.

38*p*Moreover those who were to camp before the tabernacle on the east, before the tabernacle of meeting, *were* Moses, Aaron, and his sons, *q*keeping charge of the sanctuary, *r*to meet the needs of the children of Israel; but *s*the outsider who came near was to be put to death. 39*t*All who were numbered of the Levites, whom Moses and Aaron numbered at the commandment of the LORD, by their families, all the males from a month old and above, *were* twenty-two thousand.

Levites Dedicated Instead of the Firstborn

40Then the LORD said to Moses: *u*"Number all the firstborn males of the children of Israel from a month old and above, and take the number of their names. 41*v*And you shall take the Levites for Me—I *am* the LORD—instead of all the firstborn among the children of Israel, and the livestock of the Levites instead of all the firstborn among the livestock of the children of Israel." 42So Moses numbered all the firstborn among the children of Israel, as the LORD commanded him. 43And all the firstborn males, according to the number of names from a month old and above, of those who were numbered of them, were twenty-two thousand two hundred and seventy-three.

44Then the LORD spoke to Moses, saying: 45*w*"Take the Levites instead of all the firstborn among the children of Israel, and the livestock of the Levites instead of their livestock. The Levites shall be Mine: I *am* the LORD. 46And for *x*the redemption of the two hundred and seventy-three of the firstborn of the children of Israel, *y*who are more than the number of the Levites, 47you shall take *z*five shekels for each one *a*individually; you shall take *them* in the currency of the shekel of the sanctuary, *b*the shekel of twenty gerahs. 48And you shall give the money, with which the excess number of them is redeemed, to Aaron and his sons."

49So Moses took the redemption money from those who were over and above those who were redeemed by the Levites. 50From the firstborn of the children of Israel he took the money, *c*one thousand three hundred and sixty-five *shekels*, according to the shekel of the sanctuary. 51And Moses *d*gave their redemption money to Aaron and his sons, according to the word of the LORD, as the LORD commanded Moses.

Duties of the Sons of Kohath

4 Then the LORD spoke to Moses and Aaron, saying: 2"Take a census of the sons of *a*Kohath from among the children of Levi, by their families, by their fathers' house, 3*b*from thirty years old and above, even to fifty years old, all who enter the service to do the work in the tabernacle of meeting.

4*c*"This *is* the service of the sons of Kohath in the tabernacle of meeting, *relating to* *d*the most holy things: 5When the camp prepares to journey, Aaron and his sons shall come, and they shall take down *e*the covering veil and cover the *f*ark of the Testimony with it. 6Then they shall put on it a covering of badger skins, and spread over *that* a cloth entirely of *g*blue; and they shall insert *h*its poles.

7"On the *i*table of showbread they shall spread a blue cloth, and put on it the dishes, the pans, the bowls, and the pitchers for

---

3:38 *keeping charge.* "Keeping charge of the sanctuary" was committed to a particular group of people, and no one else was to intrude on that task. Believers, as part of the body of Christ, also have certain duties. These roles are not rigid, but they are definite, planned, and created by God for the good of the whole church. The teamwork of the whole body creates a harmonious whole, and if one fails in his duty, the whole team suffers (1 Cor. 12).

3:40–42 *Number all the firstborn males.* When God passed over the homes of the Hebrew families who had obeyed His commands in the Passover (Ex. 12:23–51), He declared the surviving firstborn Hebrew children—and also the firstborn of animals—to be His. The animals were sacrificed, the firstborn were redeemed (paid for), at first by the Levites who took the place of all the other firstborn, and

then by a set sum of money for those that numbered more than the Levites. It is a clear statement of fact that people belong to God.

4:3 *from thirty years old.* According to 8:24, the Levites were to be twenty-five years old, which seems like a contradiction to this passage. It is possible that the difference reflects a time of apprenticeship.

3:35 *n* Num. 1:53; 2:25 **3:36** *o* Num. 4:31, 32
3:38 *p* Num. 1:53 *q* Num. 18:5 *r* Num. 3:7, 8 *s* Num.
3:10 **3:39** *t* Num. 3:43; 4:48; 26:62 **3:40** *u* Num. 3:15
3:41 *v* Num. 3:12, 45 **3:45** *w* Num. 3:12, 41 **3:46** *x* Ex.
13:13, 15 *y* Num. 3:39, 43 **3:47** *z* Lev. 27:6 *a* Num. 3:
18, 20 *b* Ex. 30:13 **3:50** *c* Num. 3:46, 47 **3:51** *d* Num.
3:48 **4:2** *a* Num. 3:27–32 **4:3** *b* Num. 4:23, 30, 35; 8:24
4:4 *c* Num. 4:15 *d* Num. 4:19 **4:5** *e* Ex. 26:31 *f* Ex. 25:10,
16 **4:6** *g* Ex. 39:1 *h* Ex. 25:13 **4:7** *i* Ex. 25:23, 29, 30

pouring; and the [i]showbread* shall be on it. [8]They shall spread over them a scarlet cloth, and cover the same with a covering of badger skins; and they shall insert its poles. [9]And they shall take a blue cloth and cover the [k]lampstand of the light, [l]with its lamps, its wick-trimmers, its trays, and all its oil vessels, with which they service it. [10]Then they shall put it with all its utensils in a covering of badger skins, and put it on a carrying beam.

[11]"Over [m]the golden altar they shall spread a blue cloth, and cover it with a covering of badger skins; and they shall insert its poles. [12]Then they shall take all the [n]utensils of service with which they minister in the sanctuary, put them in a blue cloth, cover them with a covering of badger skins, and put them on a carrying beam. [13]Also they shall take away the ashes from the altar, and spread a purple cloth over it. [14]They shall put on it all its implements with which they minister there—the fire-pans, the forks, the shovels, the basins, and all the utensils of the altar—and they shall spread on it a covering of badger skins, and insert its poles. [15]And when Aaron and his sons have finished covering the sanctuary and all the furnishings of the sanctuary, when the camp is set to go, then [o]the sons of Kohath shall come to carry them; [p]but they shall not touch any holy thing, lest they die.

"[q]These are the things in the tabernacle of meeting which the sons of Kohath are to carry.

[16]"The appointed duty of Eleazar the son of Aaron the priest is [r]the oil for the light, the [s]sweet incense, [t]the daily grain offering, the [u]anointing oil, the oversight of all the tabernacle, of all that is in it, with the sanctuary and its furnishings."

[17]Then the LORD spoke to Moses and Aaron, saying: [18]"Do not cut off the tribe of the families of the Kohathites from among the Levites; [19]but do this in regard to them, that they may live and not die when they approach [v]the most holy things: Aaron and his sons shall go in and appoint each of them to his service and his task. [20w]But they shall not go in to watch while the holy things are being covered, lest they die."

Duties of the Sons of Gershon

[21]Then the LORD spoke to Moses, saying: [22]"Also take a census of the sons of Gershon, by their fathers' house, by their families. [23x]From thirty years old and above,

even to fifty years old, you shall number them, all who enter to perform the service, to do the work in the tabernacle of meeting. [24]This is the [y]service of the families of the Gershonites, in serving and carrying: [25z]They shall carry the [a]curtains of the tabernacle and the tabernacle of meeting with its covering, the covering of [b]badger skins that is on it, the screen for the door of the tabernacle of meeting, [26]the screen for the door of the gate of the court, the hangings of the court which are around the tabernacle and altar, and their cords, all the furnishings for their service and all that is made for these things: so shall they serve.

[27]"Aaron and his sons shall assign all the service of the sons of the Gershonites, all their tasks and all their service. And you shall appoint to them all their tasks as their duty. [28]This is the service of families of the sons of Gershon in the tabernacle of meeting. And their duties shall be [c]under the authority* of Ithamar the son of Aaron the priest.

Duties of the Sons of Merari

[29]"As for the sons of [d]Merari, you shall number them by their families and by their fathers' house. [30e]From thirty years old and above, even to fifty years old, you shall number them, everyone who enters the service to do the work of the tabernacle of meeting. [31]And [f]this is [g]what they must carry as all their service for the tabernacle of meeting: [h]the boards of the tabernacle, its bars, its pillars, its sockets, [32]and the pillars around the court with their sockets, pegs, and cords, with all their furnishings and all their service; and you shall [i]assign to each man by name the items he must carry. [33]This is the service of the families of the sons of Merari, as all their service for the tabernacle of meeting, under the authority* of Ithamar the son of Aaron the priest."

Census of the Levites

[34j]And Moses, Aaron, and the leaders of the congregation numbered the sons of the Kohathites by their families and by their fathers' house, [35]from thirty [k]years old and above, even to fifty years old, every-one who entered the service for work in the tabernacle of meeting; [36]and those who were numbered by their families were two

---

* **4:7** Literally the continual bread   * **4:28** Literally hand   * **4:33** Literally hand

4:16 The appointed duty of Eleazar. God made arrangements for the priest to approach Him in the way He prescribed. If the priests did not do their job, no one else could do it for them. It was a big responsibility, and the well-being of the whole nation depended upon their faithfulness.

4:21–28 perform the service. There are various tasks given to us in the kingdom of God which appear to be of minor importance. Daily faithfulness in the

4:7 [j] Lev. 24:5–9   **4:9** [k] Ex. 25:31   [l] Ex. 25:37, 38   **4:11** [m] Ex. 30:1–5   **4:12** [n] Ex. 25:9   **4:15** [o] Deut. 31:9   [p] 2 Sam. 6:6, 7   [q] Num. 3:31   **4:16** [r] Lev. 24:2   [s] Ex. 30:34   [t] Ex. 29:38   [u] Ex. 30:23–25   **4:19** [v] Num. 4:4   **4:20** [w] Num. 19:21   **4:23** [x] Num. 4:3   **4:24** [y] Num. 7:7   **4:25** [z] Num. 3:25, 26   [a] Ex. 36:8   [b] Ex. 26:14   **4:28** [c] Num. 4:33   **4:29** [d] Num. 3:33–37   **4:30** [e] Num. 4:3; 8:24–26   **4:31** [f] Num. 3:36, 37   [g] Num. 7:8   [h] Ex. 26:15   **4:32** [i] Ex. 25:9; 38:21   **4:34** [j] Num. 4:2   **4:35** [k] Num. 4:47

thousand seven hundred and fifty. 37 These *were* the ones who were numbered of the families of the Kohathites, all who might serve in the tabernacle of meeting, whom Moses and Aaron numbered according to the commandment of the LORD by the hand of Moses.

38 And those who were numbered of the sons of Gershon, by their families and by their fathers' house, 39 from thirty years old and above, even to fifty years old, everyone who entered the service for work in the tabernacle of meeting— 40 those who were numbered by their families, by their fathers' house, were two thousand six hundred and thirty. 41 [l]These *are* the ones who were numbered of the families of the sons of Gershon, of all who might serve in the tabernacle of meeting, whom Moses and Aaron numbered according to the commandment of the LORD.

42 Those of the families of the sons of Merari who were numbered, by their families, by their fathers' house, 43 from thirty years old and above, even to fifty years old, everyone who entered the service for work in the tabernacle of meeting— 44 those who were numbered by their families were three thousand two hundred. 45 These *are* the ones who were numbered of the families of the sons of Merari, whom Moses and Aaron numbered [m]according to the word of the LORD by the hand of Moses.

46 All who were [n]numbered of the Levites, whom Moses, Aaron, and the leaders of Israel numbered, by their families and by their fathers' houses, 47 [o]from thirty years old and above, even to fifty years old, everyone who came to do the work of service and the work of bearing burdens in the tabernacle of meeting— 48 those who were numbered were eight thousand five hundred and eighty.

49 According to the commandment of the LORD they were numbered by the hand of Moses, [p]each according to his service and according to his task; thus were they numbered by him, [q]as the LORD commanded Moses.

Ceremonially Unclean Persons Isolated

5 And the LORD spoke to Moses, saying: 2 "Command the children of Israel that they put out of the camp every [a]leper, everyone who has a [b]discharge, and whoever becomes [c]defiled by a corpse. 3 You shall put out both male and female; you shall put them outside the camp, that they may not defile their camps [d]in the midst of which I dwell." 4 And the children of Israel did so, and put them outside the camp; as the LORD spoke to Moses, so the children of Israel did.

Confession and Restitution

5 Then the LORD spoke to Moses, saying, 6 "Speak to the children of Israel: [e]'When a man or woman commits any sin that men commit in unfaithfulness against the LORD, and that person is guilty, 7 [f]then he shall confess the sin which he has committed. He shall make restitution for his trespass [g]in full, plus one-fifth of it, and give *it* to the one he has wronged. 8 But if the man has no relative to whom restitution may be made for the wrong, the restitution for the wrong *must go* to the LORD for the priest, in addition to [h]the ram of the atonement with which atonement is made for him. 9 Every [i]offering of all the holy things of the children of Israel, which they bring to the priest, shall be [j]his. 10 And every man's holy things shall be [k]his; whatever any man gives the priest shall be his.'"

Concerning Unfaithful Wives

11 And the LORD spoke to Moses, saying, 12 "Speak to the children of Israel, and say to them: 'If any man's wife goes astray and behaves unfaithfully toward him, 13 and a man [l]lies with her carnally, and it is hidden from the eyes of her husband, and it is concealed that she has defiled herself, and *there was* no witness against her, nor was she [m]caught— 14 if the spirit of jealousy comes upon him and he becomes [n]jealous of his wife, who has defiled herself; or if

---

little things is the best preparation for greater trusts. Mary, the mother of Jesus is an example of this. Her response to the angel when she was told that she would be the mother of Jesus was, "Behold the maidservant of the Lord . . ." (Luke 1:38). She had found favor in the way she conducted her daily life, and God chose her for a unique and blessed role.

5:3 *not defile their camps . . . I dwell.* Ritual purity was important because God wanted the Israelites to remember that He lived among them. They needed to think of Him walking around in the camp and live in such a way that there was not something offensive for God to discover.

5:6 *unfaithfulness against the LORD.* Not only did God deal with ritual impurity, He was also concerned about how the people treated each other. To label sin as "acting unfaithfully" kept the real issue right in front. When we mistreat our fellow citizens, God cares, and He takes it personally. He made us; He made them. We each belong to Him, and we are not to wrong other people.

5:12 *wife goes astray.* The wife belonged to her husband. If she was unfaithful, she could be stoned. If she was not guilty, and he acted on his unsubstantiated suspicions, he would be guilty of murder. The woman had a serious responsibility to her husband because the reliability of family lines depended upon

4:41 [l]Num. 4:22 **4:45** [m]Num. 4:29 **4:46** [n]1 Chr. 23:3–23 **4:47** [o]Num. 4:3, 23, 30 **4:49** [p]Num. 4:15, 24, 31 [q]Num. 4:1, 21 **5:2** [a]Lev. 13:3, 8, 46 [b]Lev. 15:2 [c]Lev. 21:1 **5:3** [d]Lev. 26:11, 12 **5:6** [e]Lev. 5:14—6:7 **5:7** [f]Lev. 5:5; 26:40, 41 [g]Lev. 6:4, 5 **5:8** [h]Lev. 5:15; 6:6, 7; 7:7 **5:9** [i]Ex. 29:28 [j]Lev. 7:32–34; 10:14, 15 **5:10** [k]Lev. 10:13 **5:13** [l]Lev. 18:20; 20:10 [m]John 8:4 **5:14** [n]Prov. 6:34

the spirit of jealousy comes upon him and he becomes jealous of his wife, although she has not defiled herself— ¹⁵then the man shall bring his wife to the priest. He shall ^obring the offering required for her, one-tenth of an ephah of barley meal; he shall pour no oil on it and put no frankincense on it, because it *is* a grain offering of jealousy, an offering for remembering, for ^pbringing iniquity to remembrance.

¹⁶'And the priest shall bring her near, and set her before the ^qLORD. ¹⁷The priest shall take holy water in an earthen vessel, and take some of the dust that is on the floor of the tabernacle and put *it* into the water. ¹⁸Then the priest shall stand the woman before the LORD, uncover the woman's head, and put the offering for remembering in her hands, which *is* the grain offering of jealousy. And the priest shall have in his hand the bitter water that brings a curse. ¹⁹And the priest shall put her under oath, and say to the woman, "If no man has lain with you, and if you have not gone astray to uncleanness *while* under your husband's *authority,* be free from this bitter water that brings a curse. ²⁰But if you have gone astray *while* under your husband's *authority,* and if you have defiled yourself and some man other than your husband has lain with you"— ²¹then the priest shall ^rput the woman under the oath of the curse, and he shall say to the woman—^s"the LORD make you a curse and an oath among your people, when the LORD makes your thigh rot and your belly swell; ²²and may this water that causes the curse ^tgo into your stomach, and make *your* belly swell and *your* thigh rot."

'Then^u the woman shall say, "Amen, so be it."

²³'Then the priest shall write these curses in a book, and he shall scrape *them* off into the bitter water. ²⁴And he shall make the woman drink the bitter water that brings a curse, and the water that brings the curse shall enter her *to become* bitter. ²⁵^vThen the priest shall take the grain offering of jealousy from the woman's hand, shall ^wwave the offering before the LORD, and bring it to the altar; ²⁶and the priest shall take a handful of the offering, ^xas its memorial portion, burn *it* on the altar, and afterward make the woman drink the water. ²⁷When he has made her drink the water, then it shall be, if she has defiled herself and behaved unfaithfully toward her husband, that the water that brings a ^ycurse will enter her *and become* bitter, and her belly will swell, her thigh will rot, and the woman ^zwill become a curse among her people. ²⁸But if the woman has not defiled herself, and is clean, then she shall be free and may conceive children.

²⁹'This *is* the law of jealousy, when a wife, *while* under her husband's *authority,* ^agoes astray and defiles herself, ³⁰or when the spirit of jealousy comes upon a man, and he becomes jealous of his wife; then he shall stand the woman before the LORD, and the priest shall execute all this law upon her. ³¹Then the man shall be free from iniquity, but that woman ^bshall bear her guilt.'"

The Law of the Nazirite

6 Then the LORD spoke to Moses, saying, ²"Speak to the children of Israel, and say to them: 'When either a man or woman consecrates an offering to take the vow of a Nazirite, ^ato separate himself to the LORD, ^{3b}he shall separate himself from wine and *similar* drink; he shall drink neither vinegar made from wine nor vinegar

---

her faithfulness. It is obvious if a woman is pregnant, but it is not obvious who the father is. By bringing the whole sorry problem to God, the Israelites could be sure of justice.

5:15 bring his wife to the priest. Determining if a woman had been unfaithful to her husband, when she had not been caught in wrongdoing, was more difficult than detecting skin diseases. But because God was in the camp, the issue could be resolved by the priest, in the presence of God. Again, it reminded the Israelites that nothing was hidden from God.

5:18 bitter water that brings a curse. This was not a magic potion, but dust from the floor of the tabernacle and holy water. The woman held in her own hands the grain offering for jealousy. These things reminded everyone that they were standing in the presence of God, and that it was He who would determine if the woman bore any guilt.

5:21 your thigh rot and your belly swell. These words speak symbolically of a miscarriage (of an illegitimate child) if the woman was pregnant, and the inability to conceive again. In the biblical world, a woman who was unable to bear children was regarded as being under a curse; in this case it would have been true.

5:31 woman shall bear her guilt. Throughout the Bible God compares idolatry with marital unfaithfulness, so it is clear that this is a subject that touches close to the heart of every man and woman. God is faithful to His people, and they are to be true to Him. In the same way, as a daily picture of this faithfulness, the husband and wife are to be true and faithful to each other. The law recognizes the volatility of unfaithfulness, provides a limit to unjust accusations, and underlines the seriousness of the moral lapse that comes with adultery. A guilty woman would indeed bear her guilt, but a faithful woman would be exonerated.

6:1–8 Self-Denial—To serve God by abstaining from legitimate things is the Christian's privilege today as well. It is not that God is looking for sacrifice, but He is looking for a willing heart that will lay aside the good to spend time on the best.

5:15 ^o Lev. 5:11 ^p 1 Kin. 17:18 **5:16** ^q Heb. 13:4 **5:21** ^r Josh. 6:26 ^s Jer. 29:22 **5:22** ^t Ps. 109:18 ^u Deut. 27:15–26 **5:25** ^v Lev. 8:27 ^w Lev. 2:2, 9 **5:26** ^x Lev. 2:2, 9 **5:27** ^y Jer. 24:9; 29:18, 22; 42:18 ^z Num. 5:21 **5:29** ^a Num. 5:19 **5:31** ^b Lev. 20:17, 19, 20 **6:2** ^a Judg. 13:5 **6:3** ^b Luke 1:15

made from *similar* drink; neither shall he drink any grape juice, nor eat fresh grapes or raisins. ⁴All the days of his separation he shall eat nothing that is produced by the grapevine, from seed to skin.

⁵'All the days of the vow of his separation no ᶜrazor shall come upon his head; until the days are fulfilled for which he separated himself to the LORD, he shall be holy. *Then* he shall let the locks of the hair of his head grow. ⁶All the days that he separates himself to the LORD ᵈhe shall not go near a dead body. ⁷ᵉHe shall not make himself unclean even for his father or his mother, for his brother or his sister, when they die, because his separation to God *is* on his head. ⁸ᶠAll the days of his separation he shall be holy to the LORD.

⁹'And if anyone dies very suddenly beside him, and he defiles his consecrated head, then he shall ᵍshave his head on the day of his cleansing; on the seventh day he shall shave it. ¹⁰Then ʰon the eighth day he shall bring two turtledoves or two young pigeons to the priest, to the door of the tabernacle of meeting; ¹¹and the priest shall offer one as a sin offering and *the* other as a burnt offering, and make atonement for him, because he sinned in regard to the corpse; and he shall sanctify his head that same day. ¹²He shall consecrate to the LORD the days of his separation, and bring a male lamb in its first year ⁱas a trespass offering; but the former days shall be lost, because his separation was defiled.

¹³'Now this *is* the law of the Nazirite: ʲWhen the days of his separation are fulfilled, he shall be brought to the door of the tabernacle of meeting. ¹⁴And he shall present his offering to the LORD: one male lamb in its first year without blemish as a burnt offering, one ewe lamb in its first year without blemish ᵏas a sin offering, one ram without blemish ˡas a peace offering, ¹⁵a basket of unleavened bread, ᵐcakes of fine flour mixed with oil, unleavened wafers ⁿanointed with oil, and their grain offering with their ᵒdrink offerings.

¹⁶'Then the priest shall bring *them*

before the LORD and offer his sin offering and his burnt offering; ¹⁷and he shall offer the ram as a sacrifice of a peace offering to the LORD, with the basket of unleavened bread; the priest shall also offer its grain offering and its drink offering. ¹⁸ᵖThen the Nazirite shall shave his consecrated head *at* the door of the tabernacle of meeting, and shall take the hair from his consecrated head and put *it* on the fire which is under the sacrifice of the peace offering.

¹⁹'And the priest shall take the ᵠboiled shoulder of the ram, one ʳunleavened cake from the basket, and one unleavened wafer, and ˢput *them* upon the hands of the Nazirite after he has shaved his consecrated *hair*, ²⁰and the priest shall wave them as a wave offering before the LORD; ᵗthey *are* holy for the priest, together with the breast of the wave offering and the thigh of the heave offering. After that the Nazirite may drink wine.'

²¹"This is the law of the Nazirite who vows to the LORD the offering for his separation, and besides that, whatever else his hand is able to provide; according to the vow which he takes, so he must do according to the law of his separation."

The Priestly Blessing

²²And the LORD spoke to Moses, saying: ²³"Speak to Aaron and his sons, saying, 'This is the way you shall bless the children of Israel. Say to them:

24 "The LORD ᵘbless you and ᵛkeep you;
25 The LORD ʷmake His face shine upon you,
    And ˣbe gracious to you;
26 ʸThe LORD lift up His countenance upon you,
    And ᶻgive you peace."'

²⁷ᵃ"So they shall put My name on the children of Israel, and ᵇI will bless them."

Offerings of the Leaders

7 Now it came to pass, when Moses had finished ᵃsetting up the tabernacle, that

---

6:21 *the law of the Nazirite.* Not to be confused with a Nazarene (one from Nazareth), the Nazirite vows were practiced both in the Old and New Testament. It is likely that John the Baptist was a Nazirite, probably all of his life.

6:23 *bless the children of Israel.* This special blessing shows the love and mercy of God toward His chosen people. God's keeping power, His shining personal presence, His eye contact, and His own peace would be a blessing that would mark the Israelites as belonging to God Himself, and they would be called with His name.

7:1 *when Moses had finished setting up the tabernacle.* This phrasing places the events of this chapter before the taking of the census in chapters 1–4. The tabernacle was completed on the first day of the first month of the second year. The census began one month later.

7:1–11 *brought their offering.* The tabernacle from the beginning to the end was constructed and furnished by willing hearts and hands. God wants us to give to His work because we are eager to, not because we are required. Jesus directed, "Give, and it will be given to you; good measure, pressed down, shaken together, and running over" (Luke 6:38). We can never outgive God.

6:5 ᶜ 1 Sam. 1:11   **6:6** ᵈ Num. 19:11–22   **6:7** ᵉ Num. 9:6   **6:8** ᶠ [2 Cor. 6:17, 18]   **6:9** ᵍ Lev. 14:8, 9   **6:10** ʰ Lev. 5:7; 14:22; 15:14, 29   **6:12** ⁱ Lev. 5:6   **6:13** ʲ Acts 21:26   **6:14** ᵏ Lev. 4:2, 27, 32   ˡ Lev. 3:6   **6:15** ᵐ Lev. 2:4   ⁿ Ex. 29:2   ᵒ Num. 15:5, 7, 10   **6:18** ᵖ Acts 21:23, 24   **6:19** ᵠ 1 Sam. 2:15   ʳ Ex. 29:23, 24   ˢ Lev. 7:30   **6:20** ᵗ Ex. 29:27, 28   **6:24** ᵘ Deut. 28:3–6   ᵛ John 7:11   **6:25** ʷ Dan. 9:17   ˣ Mal. 1:9   **6:26** ʸ Ps. 4:6; 89:15   ᶻ Lev. 26:6   **6:27** ᵃ Is. 43:7   ᵇ Num. 23:20   **7:1** ᵃ Ex. 40:17–33

he *b*anointed it and consecrated it and all its furnishings, and the altar and all its utensils; so he anointed them and consecrated them. 2Then *c*the leaders of Israel, the heads of their fathers' houses, who *were* the leaders of the tribes and over those who were numbered, made an offering. 3And they brought their offering before the LORD, six covered carts and twelve oxen, a cart for *every* two of the leaders, and for each one an ox; and they presented them before the tabernacle.

4Then the LORD spoke to Moses, saying, 5"Accept *these* from them, that they may be used in doing the work of the tabernacle of meeting; and you shall give them to the Levites, *to* every man according to his service." 6So Moses took the carts and the oxen, and gave them to the Levites. 7Two carts and four oxen *d*he gave to the sons of Gershon, according to their service; 8*e*and four carts and eight oxen he gave to the sons of Merari, according to their service, under the authority* of Ithamar the son of Aaron the priest. 9But to the sons of Kohath he gave none, because theirs *was f*the service of the holy things, *g*which they carried on their shoulders.

10Now the leaders offered *h*the dedication *offering* for the altar when it was anointed; so the leaders offered their offering before the altar. 11For the LORD said to Moses, "They shall offer their offering, one leader each day, for the dedication of the altar."

12And the one who offered his offering on the first day *was i*Nahshon the son of Amminadab, from the tribe of Judah. 13His offering *was* one silver platter, the weight of which *was* one hundred and thirty *shekels*, and one silver bowl of seventy shekels, according to *j*the shekel of the sanctuary, both of them full of fine flour mixed with oil as a *k*grain offering; 14one gold pan of ten *shekels*, full of *l*incense; 15*m*one young bull, one ram, and one male lamb *n*in its first year, as a burnt offering; 16one kid of the goats as a *o*sin offering; 17and for *p*the sacrifice of peace offerings: two oxen, five rams, five male goats, and five male lambs in their first year. This *was* the offering of Nahshon the son of Amminadab.

18On the second day Nethanel the son of Zuar, leader of Issachar, presented *an offering.* 19For his offering he offered one silver platter, the weight of which *was* one hundred and thirty shekels, and one silver bowl of seventy shekels, according to the shekel of the sanctuary, both of them full of fine flour mixed with oil as a grain offering; 20one gold pan of ten *shekels*, full of incense; 21one young bull, one ram, and one

male lamb in its first year, as a burnt offering; 22one kid of the goats as a sin offering; 23and as the sacrifice of peace offerings: two oxen, five rams, five male goats, and five male lambs in their first year. This *was* the offering of Nethanel the son of Zuar.

24On the third day Eliab the son of Helon, leader of the children of Zebulun, *presented an offering.* 25His offering *was* one silver platter, the weight of which *was* one hundred and thirty *shekels*, and one silver bowl of seventy shekels, according to the shekel of the sanctuary, both of them full of fine flour mixed with oil as a grain offering; 26one gold pan of ten *shekels*, full of incense; 27one young bull, one ram, and one male lamb in its first year, as a burnt offering; 28one kid of the goats as a sin offering; 29and for the sacrifice of peace offerings: two oxen, five rams, five male goats, and five male lambs in their first year. This *was* the offering of Eliab the son of Helon.

30On the fourth day *q*Elizur the son of Shedeur, leader of the children of Reuben, *presented an offering.* 31His offering *was* one silver platter, the weight of which *was* one hundred and thirty *shekels*, and one silver bowl of seventy shekels, according to the shekel of the sanctuary, both of them full of fine flour mixed with oil as a grain offering; 32one gold pan of ten *shekels*, full of incense; 33one young bull, one ram, and one male lamb in its first year, as a burnt offering; 34one kid of the goats as a sin offering; 35and as the sacrifice of peace offerings: two oxen, five rams, five male goats, and five male lambs in their first year. This *was* the offering of Elizur the son of Shedeur.

36On the fifth day *r*Shelumiel the son of Zurishaddai, leader of the children of Simeon, *presented an offering.* 37His offering *was* one silver platter, the weight of which *was* one hundred and thirty *shekels*, and one silver bowl of seventy shekels, according to the shekel of the sanctuary, both of them full of fine flour mixed with oil as a grain offering; 38one gold pan of ten *shekels*, full of incense; 39one young bull, one ram, and one male lamb in its first year, as a burnt offering; 40one kid of the goats as a sin offering; 41and as the sacrifice of peace offerings: two oxen, five rams, five male goats, and five male lambs in their first year. This *was* the offering of Shelumiel the son of Zurishaddai.

42On the sixth day *s*Eliasaph the son of Deuel,* leader of the children of Gad, *presented an offering.* 43His offering *was* one silver platter, the weight of which *was* one

---

* **7:8** Literally *hand*   * **7:42** Spelled *Reuel* in 2:14

7:1 *b* Lev. 8:10, 11   **7:2** *c* Num. 1:4   **7:7** *d* Num. 4:24–28   **7:8** *e* Num. 4:29–33   **7:9** *f* Num. 4:15   *g* Num. 4:6–14   **7:10** *h* 2 Chr. 7:5, 9   **7:12** *i* Num. 2:3   **7:13** *j* Ex. 30:13

k Lev. 2:1   **7:14** *l* Ex. 30:34, 35   **7:15** *m* Lev. 1:2   *n* Ex. 12:5   **7:16** *o* Lev. 4:23   **7:17** *p* Lev. 3:1   **7:30** *q* Num. 1:5; 2:10   **7:36** *r* Num. 1:6; 2:12; 7:41   **7:42** *s* Num. 1:14; 2:14; 10:20

hundred and thirty *shekels*, and one silver bowl of seventy shekels, according to the shekel of the sanctuary, both of them full of fine flour mixed with oil as a grain offering; 44one gold pan of ten *shekels*, full of incense; 45one young bull, one ram, and one male lamb in its first year, as ᵗa burnt offering; 46one kid of the goats as a sin offering; 47and as the sacrifice of peace offerings: two oxen, five rams, five male goats, and five male lambs in their first year. This *was* the offering of Eliasaph the son of Deuel.

48On the seventh day ᵘElishama the son of Ammihud, leader of the children of Ephraim, *presented an offering.* 49His offering *was* one silver platter, the weight of which *was* one hundred and thirty *shekels*, and one silver bowl of seventy shekels, according to the shekel of the sanctuary, both of them full of fine flour mixed with oil as a grain offering; 50one gold pan of ten *shekels*, full of incense; 51one young bull, one ram, and one male lamb in its first year, as a burnt offering; 52one kid of the goats as a sin offering; 53and as the sacrifice of peace offerings: two oxen, five rams, five male goats, and five male lambs in their first year. This *was* the offering of Elishama the son of Ammihud.

54On the eighth day ᵛGamaliel the son of Pedahzur, leader of the children of Manasseh, *presented an offering.* 55His offering *was* one silver platter, the weight of which *was* one hundred and thirty *shekels*, and one silver bowl of seventy shekels, according to the shekel of the sanctuary, both of them full of fine flour mixed with oil as a grain offering; 56one gold pan of ten *shekels*, full of incense; 57one young bull, one ram, and one male lamb in its first year, as a burnt offering; 58one kid of the goats as a sin offering; 59and as the sacrifice of peace offerings: two oxen, five rams, five male goats, and five male lambs in their first year. This *was* the offering of Gamaliel the son of Pedahzur.

60On the ninth day ʷAbidan the son of Gideoni, leader of the children of Benjamin, *presented an offering.* 61His offering *was* one silver platter, the weight of which *was* one hundred and thirty *shekels*, and one silver bowl of seventy shekels, according to the shekel of the sanctuary, both of them full of fine flour mixed with oil as a grain offering; 62one gold pan of ten *shekels*, full of incense; 63one young bull, one ram, and one male lamb in its first year, as a burnt offering; 64one kid of the goats as a sin offering; 65and as the sacrifice of peace offerings: two oxen, five rams, five male goats, and five male lambs in their first year. This *was* the offering of Abidan the son of Gideoni.

66On the tenth day ˣAhiezer the son of Ammishaddai, leader of the children of Dan, *presented an offering.* 67His offering *was* one silver platter, the weight of which *was* one hundred and thirty *shekels*, and one silver bowl of seventy shekels, according to the shekel of the sanctuary, both of them full of fine flour mixed with oil as a grain offering; 68one gold pan of ten *shekels*, full of incense; 69one young bull, one ram, and one male lamb in its first year, as a burnt offering; 70one kid of the goats as a sin offering; 71and as the sacrifice of peace offerings: two oxen, five rams, five male goats, and five male lambs in their first year. This *was* the offering of Ahiezer the son of Ammishaddai.

72On the eleventh day ʸPagiel the son of Ocran, leader of the children of Asher, *presented an offering.* 73His offering *was* one silver platter, the weight of which *was* one hundred and thirty *shekels*, and one silver bowl of seventy shekels, according to the shekel of the sanctuary, both of them full of fine flour mixed with oil as a grain offering; 74one gold pan of ten *shekels*, full of incense; 75one young bull, one ram, and one male lamb in its first year, as a burnt offering; 76one kid of the goats as a sin offering; 77and as the sacrifice of peace offerings: two oxen, five rams, five male goats, and five male lambs in their first year. This *was* the offering of Pagiel the son of Ocran.

78On the twelfth day ᶻAhira the son of Enan, leader of the children of Naphtali, *presented an offering.* 79His offering *was* one silver platter, the weight of which *was* one hundred and thirty *shekels*, and one silver bowl of seventy shekels, according to the shekel of the sanctuary, both of them full of fine flour mixed with oil as a grain offering; 80one gold pan of ten *shekels*, full of incense; 81one young bull, one ram, and one male lamb in its first year, as a burnt offering; 82one kid of the goats as a sin offering; 83and as the sacrifice of peace offerings: two oxen, five rams, five male goats, and five male lambs in their first year. This *was* the offering of Ahira the son of Enan.

84This *was* ᵃthe dedication *offering* for the altar from the leaders of Israel, when it was anointed: twelve silver platters, twelve silver bowls, and twelve gold pans. 85Each silver platter *weighed* one hundred and thirty *shekels* and each bowl seventy *shekels*. All the silver of the vessels *weighed* two thousand four hundred *shekels*, according to the shekel of the sanctuary. 86The twelve gold pans full of incense *weighed* ten *shekels* apiece, according to the shekel of the sanctuary; all the gold of the pans *weighed* one hundred and twenty *shekels*. 87All the oxen for the burnt offering *were* twelve

young bulls, the rams twelve, the male lambs in their first year twelve, with their grain offering, and the kids of the goats as a sin offering twelve. 88And all the oxen for the sacrifice of peace offerings were twenty-four bulls, the rams sixty, the male goats sixty, and the lambs in their first year sixty. This *was* the dedication *offering* for the altar after it was *b*anointed.

89Now when Moses went into the tabernacle of meeting *c*to speak with Him, he heard *d*the voice of One speaking to him from above the mercy seat that *was* on the ark of the Testimony, from *e*between the two cherubim; thus He spoke to him.

Arrangement of the Lamps

8 And the LORD spoke to Moses, saying: 2"Speak to Aaron, and say to him, 'When you *a*arrange the lamps, the seven *b*lamps shall give light in front of the lampstand.'" 3And Aaron did so; he arranged the lamps to face toward the front of the lampstand, as the LORD commanded Moses. 4*c*Now this workmanship of the lampstand *was* hammered gold; from its shaft to its flowers it *was* *d*hammered work. *e*According to the pattern which the LORD had shown Moses, so he made the lampstand.

Cleansing and Dedication of the Levites

5Then the LORD spoke to Moses, saying: 6"Take the Levites from among the children of Israel and cleanse them *ceremonially*. 7Thus you shall do to them to cleanse them: *f*Sprinkle water of purification on them, and *g*let them shave all their body, and let them wash their clothes, and *so* make themselves clean. 8Then let them take a young bull with *h*its grain offering of fine flour mixed with oil, and you shall take another young bull as a sin offering. 9*i*And you shall bring the Levites before the tabernacle of meeting, *j*and you shall gather together the whole congregation of the children of Israel. 10So you shall bring the Levites before the LORD, and the children of Israel *k*shall lay their hands on the Levites; 11and Aaron shall offer the Levites before the LORD *like* a *l*wave offering from the children of Israel, that they may perform the work of the LORD. 12*m*Then the Levites shall lay their hands on the heads of the young bulls, and you shall offer one as a sin offering and the other as a burnt offering to the LORD, to make atonement for the Levites.

13"And you shall stand the Levites before Aaron and his sons, and then offer them *like* a wave offering to the LORD. 14Thus you shall *n*separate the Levites from among the children of Israel, and the Levites shall be *o*Mine. 15After that the Levites shall go in to service the tabernacle of meeting. So you shall cleanse them and *p*offer them *like* a wave offering. 16For they *are* *q*wholly given to Me from among the children of Israel; I have taken them for Myself *r*instead of all who open the womb, the firstborn of all the children of Israel. 17*s*For all the firstborn among the children of Israel *are* Mine, *both* man and beast; on the day that I struck all the firstborn in the land of Egypt I sanctified them to Myself. 18I have taken the Levites instead of all the firstborn of the children of Israel. 19And *t*I have given the Levites as a gift to Aaron and his sons from among the children of Israel, to do the work for the children of Israel in the tabernacle of meeting, and to make atonement for the children of Israel, *u*that there be no plague among the children of Israel when the children of Israel come near the sanctuary."

20Thus Moses and Aaron and all the congregation of the children of Israel did to the Levites; according to all that the LORD commanded Moses concerning the Levites, so the children of Israel did to them. 21*v*And the Levites purified themselves and washed their clothes; then Aaron presented them *like* a wave offering before the LORD, and Aaron made atonement for them

---

7:89 *heard the voice.* The tabernacle is referred to as the "tabernacle of meeting," because it was here that the Lord communicated with His people. Moses knew that it was the Lord he was hearing, and he took that word very seriously. The Word of God is still something that God's people can hear, usually through the Bible, sometimes in creation (Rom. 1), and sometimes through the work of the Holy Spirit. This is usually a strong impression that God wants you to pay attention to something, wait, change a decision, or pray. The leading of the Holy Spirit will never contradict Scripture, so it is exceedingly important for believers to maintain a familiarity with the Bible, so they can know God and hear Him.

8:10–12 *shall lay their hands on.* The sons of Israel who laid their hands on the Levites in this ancient symbol of dedication were showing their support for and agreement with the special role that the Levites had been set aside for. This would be an event that everyone could look back on and remember as an important, solemn time of dedication and asking for God's blessing.

8:16 *wholly given to Me.* The Hebrew words for this phrase are an emphatic doubling: "given, given."

8:19 *no plague.* God's holiness would not bear an improper approach. But in His mercy He provided the protective hedge of the Levites, to keep the Israelites from coming near the sanctuary in an unauthorized way, and thus causing a plague.

7:88 *b* Num. 7:1, 10   **7:89** *c* [Ex. 33:9, 11]   *d* Ex. 25:21, 22   *e* Ps. 80:1; 99:1   **8:2** *a* Lev. 24:2–4   *b* Ex. 25:37; 40:25   **8:4** *c* Ex. 25:31   *d* Ex. 25:18   *e* Ex. 25:40   **8:7** *f* Num. 19:9, 13, 17, 20   *g* Lev. 14:8; 9   **8:8** *h* Lev. 2:1   **8:9** *i* Ex. 29:4; 40:12   *j* Lev. 8:3   **8:10** *k* Lev. 1:4   **8:11** *l* Num. 18:6   **8:12** *m* Ex. 29:10   **8:14** *n* Num. 16:9   *o* Num. 3:12, 45; 16:9   **8:15** *p* Num. 8:11, 13   **8:16** *q* Num. 3:9   *r* Num. 3:12, 45   **8:17** *s* Ex. 12:2, 12, 13, 15   **8:19** *t* Num. 3:9   *u* Num. 1:53; 16:46; 18:5   **8:21** *v* Num. 8:7

to cleanse them. ²²ᵂAfter that the Levites went in to do their work in the tabernacle of meeting before Aaron and his sons; ˣas the LORD commanded Moses concerning the Levites, so they did to them.

²³Then the LORD spoke to Moses, saying, ²⁴"This *is* what *pertains* to the Levites: ʸFrom twenty-five years old and above one may enter to perform service in the work of the tabernacle of meeting; ²⁵and at the age of fifty years they must cease performing this work, and shall work no more. ²⁶They may minister with their brethren in the tabernacle of meeting, ᶻto attend to needs, but they *themselves* shall do no work. Thus you shall do to the Levites regarding their duties."

The Second Passover

9 Now the LORD spoke to Moses in the Wilderness of Sinai, in the first month of the second year after they had come out of the land of Egypt, saying: ²"Let the children of Israel keep ᵃthe Passover at its appointed ᵇtime. ³On the fourteenth day of this month, at twilight, you shall keep it at its appointed time. According to all its rites and ceremonies you shall keep it." ⁴So Moses told the children of Israel that they should keep the Passover. ⁵And ᶜthey kept the Passover on the fourteenth day of the first month, at twilight, in the Wilderness of Sinai; according to all that the LORD commanded Moses, so the children of Israel did.

⁶Now there were *certain* men who were ᵈdefiled by a human corpse, so that they could not keep the Passover on that day; ᵉand they came before Moses and Aaron that day. ⁷And those men said to him, "We *became* defiled by a human corpse. Why are we kept from presenting the offering of the LORD at its appointed time among the children of Israel?"

⁸And Moses said to them, "Stand still, that ᶠI may hear what the LORD will command concerning you."

⁹Then the LORD spoke to Moses, saying, ¹⁰"Speak to the children of Israel, saying: 'If anyone of you or your posterity is unclean because of a corpse, or *is* far away on a journey, he may still keep the LORD's Passover. ¹¹On ᵍthe fourteenth day of the second month, at twilight, they may keep it. They shall ʰeat it with unleavened bread and bitter herbs. ¹²ⁱThey shall leave none of it until morning, ʲnor break one of its bones. ᵏAccording to all the ordinances of the Passover they shall keep it. ¹³But the man who *is* clean and is not on a journey, and ceases to keep the Passover, that same person ˡshall be cut off from among his people, because he ᵐdid not bring the offering of the LORD at its appointed time; that man shall ⁿbear his sin.

¹⁴'And if a stranger dwells among you, and would keep the LORD's Passover, he must do so according to the rite of the Passover and according to its ceremony; ᵒyou shall have one ordinance, both for the stranger and the native of the land.' "

The Cloud and the Fire

¹⁵Now ᵖon the day that the tabernacle was raised up, the cloud ᑫcovered the tabernacle, the tent of the Testimony; ʳfrom evening until morning it was above the tabernacle like the appearance of fire. ¹⁶So it was always: the cloud covered it by *day*, and the appearance of fire by night. ¹⁷Whenever the cloud ˢwas taken up from above the tabernacle, after that the children of Israel would journey; and in the place where the cloud settled, there the children of Israel would pitch their tents. ¹⁸At the command of the LORD the children of Israel would journey, and at the command of the LORD they would camp; ᵗas long as the cloud stayed above the tabernacle they remained encamped. ¹⁹Even when the cloud continued long, many days above the tabernacle, the children of Israel ᵘkept the charge of the LORD and did not journey. ²⁰So it was, when the cloud was

---

8:24 From twenty-five years old. According to 4:3, the Levites were to be thirty years old, which seems like a contradiction to this passage. It is possible that the difference reflects a time of apprenticeship.

9:1 the first month of the second year. This phrasing places the events of this chapter before the taking of the census. (See note at 7:1.)

9:1–5 keep the Passover. When the first Passover was celebrated in Egypt, the command was given to commemorate it throughout Israel's generations (Ex. 12:14). This would be the second time that the Israelites had observed this special commemorative event. Passover had greater significance than any Israelite of that day could imagine, however wonderful the exodus events were. Redemption from Egypt was a picture of greater redemption yet to be, when the blood of Christ would speak of better things than the blood applied to the doors in Egypt. Christ is now our eternal Passover (1 Cor. 5:7).

9:12 nor break one of its bones. It is fitting to remember that when the Savior was crucified as our "Passover Lamb," none of His bones were broken (John 19:36).

9:15–23 the cloud. The cloud was a dramatic symbol of the active presence of God with His people, hovering over them in protection, moving ahead of them for direction, and coming near at night as fire for comfort in the darkness.

8:22 ᵂNum. 8:15 ˣNum. 8:5 **8:24** ʸNum. 4:3 **8:26** ᶻNum. 1:53 **9:2** ᵃLev. 23:5 ᵇ2 Chr. 30:1–15 **9:5** ᶜJosh. 5:10 **9:6** ᵈNum. 5:2; 9:11–22 ᵉNum. 27:2 **9:8** ᶠNum. 27:5 **9:11** ᵍ2 Chr. 30:2, 15 ʰEx. 12:8 **9:12** ⁱEx. 12:10 ʲEx. 12:46 ᵏEx. 12:43 **9:13** ˡEx. 12:15, 47 ᵐNum. 9:7 ⁿNum. 5:31 **9:14** ᵒEx. 12:49 **9:15** ᵖEx. 40:33, 34 ᑫIs. 4:5 ʳEx. 13:21, 22; 40:38 **9:17** ˢEx. 40:36–38 **9:18** ᵗ1 Cor. 10:1 **9:19** ᵘNum. 1:53; 3:8

above the tabernacle a few days: according
to the command of the LORD they would remain encamped, and according to the command of the LORD they would journey. 21So
it was, when the cloud remained only from
evening until morning: when the cloud was
taken up in the morning, then they would
journey; whether by day or by night, whenever the cloud was taken up, they would
journey. 22*Whether it was* two days, a
month, or a year that the cloud remained
above the tabernacle, the children of Israel
[v]would remain encamped and not journey;
but when it was taken up, they would journey. 23At the command of the LORD they
remained encamped, and at the command
of the LORD they journeyed; they [w]kept the
charge of the LORD, at the command of the
LORD by the hand of Moses.

Two Silver Trumpets

10 And the LORD spoke to Moses, saying: 2"Make two silver trumpets for
yourself; you shall make them of hammered work; you shall use them for [a]call-
ing the congregation and for directing the
movement of the camps. 3When [b]they blow
both of them, all the congregation shall
gather before you at the door of the tabernacle of meeting. 4But if they blow *only*
one, then the leaders, the [c]heads of the divisions of Israel, shall gather to you. 5When
you sound the [d]advance, [e]the camps that
lie on the east side shall then begin their
journey. 6When you sound the advance the
second time, then the camps that lie [f]on the
south side shall begin their journey; they
shall sound the call for them to begin their
journeys. 7And when the assembly is to be
gathered together, [g]you shall blow, but not
[h]sound the advance. 8[i]The sons of Aaron,
the priests, shall blow the trumpets; and
these shall be to you as an ordinance forever throughout your generations.

9[j]"When you go to war in your land
against the enemy who [k]oppresses you,
then you shall sound an alarm with the
trumpets, and you will be [l]remembered
before the LORD your God, and you will
be saved from your enemies. 10Also [m]in
the day of your gladness, in your appointed feasts, and at the beginning of your
months, you shall blow the trumpets over
your burnt offerings and over the sacrifices
of your peace offerings; and they shall be
[n]a memorial for you before your God: I *am*
the LORD your God."

Departure from Sinai

11Now it came to pass on the twentieth
day of the second month, in the second
year, that the cloud [o]was taken up from
above the tabernacle of the Testimony.
12And the children of Israel set out from
[p]the Wilderness of Sinai on [q]their journeys;
then the cloud settled down in the [r]Wilder-
ness of Paran. 13So they started out for the
first time [s]according to the command of the
LORD by the hand of Moses.

14The standard of the camp of the
children of Judah [t]set out first according to their armies; over their army was
[u]Nahshon the son of Amminadab. 15Over
the army of the tribe of the children of Issachar *was* Nethanel the son of Zuar. 16And
over the army of the tribe of the children of
Zebulun *was* Eliab the son of Helon.

17Then [v]the tabernacle was taken down;
and the sons of Gershon and the sons of
Merari set out, [w]carrying the tabernacle.

18And [x]the standard of the camp of Reuben set out according to their armies; over
their army *was* Elizur the son of Shedeur.
19Over the army of the tribe of the children
of Simeon *was* Shelumiel the son of Zurishaddai. 20And over the army of the tribe
of the children of Gad *was* Eliasaph the son
of Deuel.

21Then the Kohathites set out, carrying
the [y]holy things. (The tabernacle would be
prepared for their arrival.)

22And [z]the standard of the camp of the
children of Ephraim set out according to
their armies; over their army *was* Elishama the son of Ammihud. 23Over the army
of the tribe of the children of Manasseh
was Gamaliel the son of Pedahzur. 24And
over the army of the tribe of the children of
Benjamin *was* Abidan the son of Gideoni.

25Then [a]the standard of the camp of the
children of Dan (the rear guard of all the
camps) set out according to their armies;
over their army *was* Ahiezer the son of
Ammishaddai. 26Over the army of the tribe
of the children of Asher *was* Pagiel the son
of Ocran. 27And over the army of the tribe

9:23 *At the command.* Like the children of Israel, our existence often seems to us like a wilderness. Most often we want to *move,* to *do,* to *know.* Without waiting and following God's directions, His Word, His plan, we miss His best, and lessons are lost or delayed. How blessed to wait for God's direction, to obey Him in both stops and starts in all of life! No words spoken, no money spent, no job taken, no engagement ring given or received, without knowing we will be keeping God's charge.

10:2 *two silver trumpets.* The two silver trumpets were different from the curved ram's horn trumpets (Lev. 25:9). Made of hammered silver, these instruments were straight with a flaring bell, like the post horns of medieval Europe. Since they did not have valves, they would have been played like a bugle.

9:22 [v]Ex. 40:36, 37 **9:23** [w]Num. 9:19 **10:2** [a]Is. 1:13 **10:3** [b]Jer. 4:5 **10:4** [c]Ex. 18:21 **10:5** [d]Joel 2:1 [e]Num. 2:3 **10:6** [f]Num. 2:10 **10:7** [g]Num. 10:3 [h]Joel 2:1 **10:8** [i]Num. 31:6 **10:9** [j]Josh. 6:5 [k]Judg. 2:18; 4:3; 6:9; 10:8, 12 [l]Gen. 8:1 **10:10** [m]Lev. 23:24 [n]Num. 10:9 **10:11** [o]Num. 9:17 **10:12** [p]Ex. 19:1 [q]Ex. 40:36 [r]Gen. 21:21 **10:13** [s]Num. 10:5, 6 **10:14** [t]Num. 2:3–9 [u]Num. 1:7 **10:17** [v]Num. 1:51 [w]Num. 4:21–32; 7:7–9 **10:18** [x]Num. 2:10–16 **10:21** [y]Num. 4:4–20; 7:9 **10:22** [z]Num. 2:18–24 **10:25** [a]Num. 2:25–31

of the children of Naphtali *was* Ahira the son of Enan.

28bThus *was* the order of march of the children of Israel, according to their armies, when they began their journey.

29Now Moses said to cHobab the son of dReuel* the Midianite, Moses' father-in-law, "We are setting out for the place of which the LORD said, e'I will give it to you.' Come with us, and fwe will treat you well; for gthe LORD has promised good things to Israel."

30And he said to him, "I will not go, but I will depart to my *own* land and to my relatives."

31So *Moses* said, "Please do not leave, inasmuch as you know how we are to camp in the wilderness, and you can be our heyes. 32And it shall be, if you go with us—indeed it shall be—that iwhatever good the LORD will do to us, the same we will do to you."

33So they departed from jthe mountain of the LORD on a journey of three days; and the ark of the covenant of the LORD kwent before them for the three days' journey, to search out a resting place for them. 34And lthe cloud of the LORD *was* above them by day when they went out from the camp.

35So it was, whenever the ark set out, that Moses said:

m"Rise up, O LORD!
Let Your enemies be scattered,
And let those who hate You flee before
    You."

36And when it rested, he said:

"Return, O LORD,
To the many thousands of Israel."

The People Complain

11 Now awhen the people complained, it displeased the LORD; bfor the LORD heard *it*, and His anger was aroused. So the cfire of the LORD burned among them, and consumed *some* in the outskirts of the camp. 2Then the people dcried out to Moses, and when Moses eprayed to the LORD, the fire was quenched. 3So he called the

name of the place Taberah,* because the fire of the LORD had burned among them.

4Now the fmixed multitude who were among them yielded to gintense craving; so the children of Israel also wept again and said: h"Who will give us meat to eat? 5iWe remember the fish which we ate freely in Egypt, the cucumbers, the melons, the leeks, the onions, and the garlic; 6but now jour whole being *is* dried up; *there is* nothing at all except this manna *before* our eyes!"

7Now kthe manna *was* like coriander seed, and its color like the color of bdellium. 8The people went about and gathered *it*, ground *it* on millstones or beat *it* in mortar, cooked *it* in pans, and made cakes of it; and lits taste was like the taste of pastry prepared with oil. 9And mwhen the dew fell on the camp in the night, the manna fell on it.

10Then Moses heard the people weeping throughout their families, everyone at the door of his tent; and nthe anger of the LORD was greatly aroused; Moses also was displeased. 11oSo Moses said to the LORD, "Why have You afflicted Your servant? And why have I not found favor in Your sight, that You have laid the burden of all these people on me? 12Did I conceive all these people? Did I beget them, that You should say to me, p'Carry them in your bosom, as a qguardian carries a nursing child,' to the land which You rswore to their fathers? 13sWhere am I to get meat to give to all these people? For they weep all over me, saying, 'Give us meat, that we may eat.' 14tI am not able to bear all these people alone, because the burden *is* too heavy for me. 15If You treat me like this, please kill me here and now—if I have found favor in Your sight—and udo not let me see my wretchedness!"

The Seventy Elders

16So the LORD said to Moses: "Gather to Me vseventy men of the elders of Israel,

---

* **10:29** Septuagint reads *Raguel* (compare Exodus 2:18).   * **11:3** Literally *Burning*

10:29 *Reuel.* Also called Jethro (Ex. 3:1), Reuel was the priest of Midian who befriended Moses and gave his daughter Zipporah to him as his wife.

11:1 *complained.* Murmuring and complaining demonstrated a lack of trust in God's plan, provision, and judgment. Such attitudes are no more pleasing to God now than they were then, although He does not discipline complainers with fire from heaven.

11:4 *mixed multitude.* The presence of a mixed multitude, or rabble, indicates that there were people in the camp who had escaped from slavery or poverty in Egypt, but were not Israelites. They seem to have been the instigators of dissatisfaction, who made discomfort an excuse to agitate rebellion against God. God's people have always had the responsibility to keep their ears tuned to God's voice instead of the voices of the unbelievers around them.

11:10 *weeping.* Instead of thankfulness, the Israelites

complained against what they had been given and asked for more. This is a serious sin (Ps. 78:17), and in response God chastened them. We ought to learn from the example of the Israelites in the wilderness and make thankfulness our lifestyle (Phil. 4:4).

10:28 b Num. 2:34   **10:29** c Judg. 4:11   d Ex. 2:18; 3:1; 18:12   e Gen. 12:7   f Judg. 1:16   g Ex. 3:8   **10:31** h Job 29:15   **10:32** i Judg. 1:16   **10:33** j Ex. 3:1   k Deut. 1:33   **10:34** l Ex. 13:21   **10:35** m Ps. 68:1, 2; 132:8   **11:1** a Num. 14:2; 16:11; 17:5   b Ps. 78:21   c Lev. 10:2   **11:2** d Num. 12:11, 13; 21:7   e [James 5:16]   **11:4** f Ex. 12:38   g 1 Cor. 10:6   h [Ps. 78:18]   **11:5** i Ex. 16:3   **11:6** j Num. 21:5   **11:7** k Ex. 16:14, 31   **11:8** l Ex. 16:31   **11:9** m Ex. 16:13, 14   **11:10** n Ps. 78:21   **11:11** o Deut. 1:12   **11:12** p Is. 40:11   q Is. 49:23   r Gen. 26:3   **11:13** s Mark 8:4   **11:14** t Ex. 18:18   **11:15** u Rev. 3:17   **11:16** v Ex. 18:25; 24:1, 9

whom you know to be the elders of the people and [w]officers over them; bring them to the tabernacle of meeting, that they may stand there with you. [17]Then I will come down and talk with you there. [x]I will take of the Spirit that *is* upon you and will put *the same* upon them; and they shall bear the burden of the people with you, that you may not bear *it* yourself alone. [18]Then you shall say to the people, 'Consecrate yourselves for tomorrow, and you shall eat meat; for you have wept [y]in the hearing of the LORD, saying, "Who will give us meat to eat? For *it was* well with us in Egypt." Therefore the LORD will give you meat, and you shall eat. [19]You shall eat, not one day, nor two days, nor five days, nor ten days, nor twenty days, [20z]but *for* a whole month, until it comes out of your nostrils and becomes loathsome to you, because you have [a]despised the LORD who is among you, and have wept before Him, saying, [b]"Why did we ever come up out of Egypt?"'"

[21]And Moses said, [c]"The people whom I *am* among *are* six hundred thousand men on foot; yet You have said, 'I will give them meat, that they may eat *for* a whole month.' [22d]Shall flocks and herds be slaughtered for them, to provide enough for them? Or shall all the fish of the sea be gathered together for them, to provide enough for them?"

[23]And the LORD said to Moses, [e]"Has the LORD's arm been shortened? Now you shall see whether [f]what I say will happen to you or not."

[24]So Moses went out and told the people the words of the LORD, and he [g]gathered the seventy men of the elders of the people and placed them around the tabernacle. [25]Then the LORD came down in the cloud, and spoke to him, and took of the Spirit that *was* upon him, and placed *the same* upon the seventy elders; and it happened, [h]when the Spirit rested upon them, that [i]they prophesied, although they never did *so* again.*

[26]But two men had remained in the camp: the name of one *was* Eldad, and the name of the other Medad. And the Spirit rested upon them. Now they *were* among those listed, but who [j]had not gone out to the tabernacle; yet they prophesied in the camp. [27]And a young man ran and told Moses, and said, "Eldad and Medad are prophesying in the camp."

[28]So Joshua the son of Nun, Moses' assistant, *one* of his choice men, answered and said, "Moses my lord, [k]forbid them!"

[29]Then Moses said to him, "Are you zealous for my sake? [l]Oh, that all the LORD's people were prophets *and* that the LORD would put His Spirit upon them!" [30]And Moses returned to the camp, he and the elders of Israel.

The LORD Sends Quail

[31]Now a [m]wind went out from the LORD, and it brought quail from the sea and left *them* fluttering near the camp, about a day's journey on this side and about a day's journey on the other side, all around the camp, and about two cubits above the surface of the ground. [32]And the people stayed up all that day, all night, and all the next day, and gathered the quail (he who gathered least gathered ten [n]homers); and they spread *them* out for themselves all around the camp. [33]But while the [o]meat *was* still between their teeth, before it was chewed, the wrath of the LORD was aroused against the people, and the LORD struck the people with a very great plague. [34]So he called the name of that place Kibroth Hattaavah,* because there they buried the people who had yielded to craving.

[35p]From Kibroth Hattaavah the people moved to Hazeroth, and camped at Hazeroth.

Dissension of Aaron and Miriam

12 Then [a]Miriam and Aaron spoke [b]against Moses because of the Ethiopian woman whom he had married; for [c]he had married an Ethiopian woman. [2]So they said, "Has the LORD indeed spoken only through [d]Moses? [e]Has He not spoken through us also?" And the LORD [f]heard *it*. [3](Now the man Moses *was* very humble, more than all men who *were* on the face of the earth.)

[4g]Suddenly the LORD said to Moses, Aaron, and Miriam, "Come out, you three, to the tabernacle of meeting!" So the three came out. [5h]Then the LORD came down in the pillar of cloud and stood *in* the door of

---

* **11:25** Targum and Vulgate read *did not cease.*
* **11:34** Literally *Graves of Craving*

11:26 Eldad . . . Medad. These two men prophesied, even though they had not joined the other elders at the tabernacle. They were not obedient, but neither were they presumptuous, and the Lord showed that He still wanted them as leaders.
11:34 Kibroth Hattaavah. The place was called "Graves of Craving," for the greedy people buried there.
11:35 Hazeroth. This place of rest is called "Enclosures."
12:5 the LORD came down. The language of this verse is more directly physical than usual. God came down, stood, and then called Aaron and Miriam forward.

God's presence had been in the camp, but this was apparently distinctly more direct.

11:16 [w] Deut. 16:18   **11:17** [x] 1 Sam. 10:6   **11:18** [y] Ex. 16:7   **11:20** [z] Ps. 78:29; 106:15   [a] 1 Sam. 10:19   [b] Num. 21:5   **11:21** [c] Gen. 12:2   **11:22** [d] 2 Kin. 7:2   **11:23** [e] Is. 50:2; 59:1   [f] Num. 23:19   **11:24** [g] Num. 11:16   **11:25** [h] 2 Kin. 2:15   [i] Joel 2:28   **11:26** [j] Jer. 36:5   **11:28** [k] [Mark 9:38–40]   **11:29** [l] 1 Cor. 14:5   **11:31** [m] Ex. 16:13   **11:32** [n] Ezek. 45:11   **11:33** [o] Ps. 78:29–31; 106:15   **11:35** [p] Num. 33:17   **12:1** [a] Num. 20:1   [b] Num. 11:1   [c] Ex. 2:21   **12:2** [d] Num. 16:3   [e] Mic. 6:4   [f] Ezek. 35:12, 13   **12:4** [g] [Ps. 76:9]   **12:5** [h] Ex. 19:9; 34:5

the tabernacle, and called Aaron and Miriam. And they both went forward. 6Then He said,

"Hear now My words:
If there is a prophet among you,
I, the LORD, make Myself known to
him *i*in a vision;
I speak to him *j*in a dream.
7 Not so with *k*My servant Moses;
*l*He *is* faithful in all *m*My house.
8 I speak with him *n*face to face,
Even *o*plainly, and not in dark sayings;
And he sees *p*the form of the LORD.
Why then *q*were you not afraid
To speak against My servant Moses?"

9So the anger of the LORD was aroused against them, and He departed. 10And when the cloud departed from above the tabernacle, *r*suddenly Miriam became *s*leprous, as *white as* snow. Then Aaron turned toward Miriam, and there she was, a leper. 11So Aaron said to Moses, "Oh, my lord! Please *t*do not lay *this* sin on us, in which we have done foolishly and in which we have sinned. 12Please *u*do not let her be as one dead, whose flesh is half consumed when he comes out of his mother's womb!"

13So Moses cried out to the LORD, saying, "Please *v*heal her, O God, I pray!"

14Then the LORD said to Moses, "If her father had but *w*spit in her face, would she not be shamed seven days? Let her be *x*shut out of the camp seven days, and afterward she may be received *again.*" 15ySo Miriam was shut out of the camp seven days, and the people did not journey till Miriam was brought in *again.* 16And afterward the people moved from *z*Hazeroth and camped in the Wilderness of Paran.

Spies Sent into Canaan

13 And the LORD spoke to Moses, saying, 2a"Send men to spy out the land of Canaan, which I am giving to the children of Israel; from each tribe of their fathers you shall send a man, every one a leader among them."

3So Moses sent them *b*from the Wilderness of Paran according to the command of the LORD, all of them men who *were* heads of the children of Israel. 4Now these *were* their names: from the tribe of Reuben, Shammua the son of Zaccur; 5from the

tribe of Simeon, Shaphat the son of Hori; 6cfrom the tribe of Judah, *d*Caleb the son of Jephunneh; 7from the tribe of Issachar, Igal the son of Joseph; 8from the tribe of Ephraim, Hoshea* the son of Nun; 9from the tribe of Benjamin, Palti the son of Raphu; 10from the tribe of Zebulun, Gaddiel the son of Sodi; 11from the tribe of Joseph, *that is,* from the tribe of Manasseh, Gaddi the son of Susi; 12from the tribe of Dan, Ammiel the son of Gemalli; 13from the tribe of Asher, Sethur the son of Michael; 14from the tribe of Naphtali, Nahbi the son of Vophsi; 15from the tribe of Gad, Geuel the son of Machi.

16These *are* the names of the men whom Moses sent to spy out the land. And Moses called *e*Hoshea* the son of Nun, Joshua.

17Then Moses sent them to spy out the land of Canaan, and said to them, "Go up this *way* into the South, and go up to *f*the mountains, 18and see what the land is like: whether the people who dwell in it *are* strong or weak, few or many; 19whether the land they dwell in *is* good or bad; whether the cities they inhabit *are* like camps or strongholds; 20whether the land *is* rich or poor; and whether there are forests there or not. *g*Be of good courage. And bring some of the fruit of the land." Now the time *was* the season of the first ripe grapes.

21So they went up and spied out the land *h*from the Wilderness of Zin as far as *i*Rehob, near the entrance of *j*Hamath. 22And they went up through the South and came to *k*Hebron; Ahiman, Sheshai, and Talmai, the descendants of *l*Anak, *were* there. (Now Hebron was built seven years before Zoan in Egypt.) 23mThen they came to the Valley of Eshcol, and there cut down a branch with one cluster of grapes; they carried it between two of them on a pole. *They* also *brought* some of the pomegranates and figs. 24The place was called the Valley of Eshcol,* because of the cluster which the men of Israel cut down there. 25And they returned from spying out the land after forty days.

26Now they departed and came back to Moses and Aaron and all the congregation of the children of Israel in the Wilderness

---

* **13:8** Septuagint and Vulgate read *Oshea.*
* **13:16** Septuagint and Vulgate read *Oshea.*
* **13:24** Literally *Cluster*

12:8 face to face, even plainly. These verses speak of the completely intimate relationship that God had with Moses.

12:16 the Wilderness of Paran. Paran had been the destination of the people since they set out from Mount Sinai. The journey had been marred by discontent, complaining, and rebellion.

13:16 Joshua. Hoshea means "salvation." Joshua means "the Lord saves." Moses may have changed Joshua's name to emphasize that it was the Lord, not any particular leader, that they were dependent on. Jesus is another form of the name Joshua.

12:6 *i* Gen. 46:2 *j* Gen. 31:10 **12:7** *k* Josh. 1:1 *l* Heb. 3:2, 5 *m* 1 Tim. 1:12 **12:8** *n* Deut. 34:10 *o* [1 Cor. 13:12] *p* Ex. 33:19–23 *q* 2 Pet. 2:10 **12:10** *r* Deut. 24:9 *s* 2 Kin. 5:27; 15:5 **12:11** *t* 2 Sam. 19:19; 24:10 **12:12** *u* Ps. 88:4 **12:13** *v* Ps. 103:3 **12:14** *w* Deut. 25:9 *x* Lev. 13:46 **12:15** *y* Deut. 24:9 **12:16** *z* Num. 11:35; 33:17, 18 **13:2** *a* Deut. 1:22; 9:23 **13:3** *b* Num. 12:16; 32:8 **13:6** *c* Num. 34:19 *d* Josh. 14:6, 7 **13:16** *e* Ex. 17:9 **13:17** *f* Judg. 1:9 **13:20** *g* Deut. 31:6, 7, 23 **13:21** *h* Num. 20:1; 27:14; 33:36 *i* Josh. 19:28 *j* Josh. 13:5 **13:22** *k* Josh. 15:13, 14 *l* Josh. 11:21, 22 **13:23** *m* Deut. 1:24, 25

of Paran, at ^nKadesh; they brought back word to them and to all the congregation, and showed them the fruit of the land. ^27Then they told him, and said: "We went to the land where you sent us. It truly flows with ^omilk and honey, ^pand this *is* its fruit. ^28Nevertheless the ^qpeople who dwell in the land *are* strong; the cities *are* fortified *and* very large; moreover we saw the descendants of ^rAnak there. ^29^sThe Amalekites dwell in the land of the South; the Hittites, the Jebusites, and the Amorites dwell in the mountains; and the Canaanites dwell by the sea and along the banks of the Jordan."

^30Then ^tCaleb quieted the people before Moses, and said, "Let us go up at once and take possession, for we are well able to overcome it."

^31^uBut the men who had gone up with him said, "We are not able to go up against the people, for they *are* stronger than we." ^32^vAnd they gave the children of Israel a bad report of the land which they had spied out, saying, "The land through which we have gone as spies *is* a land that devours its inhabitants, and ^wall the people whom we saw in it *are* men of *great* stature. ^33There we saw the giants* (^xthe descendants of Anak came from the giants); and we were ^ylike grasshoppers in our own sight, and so we were ^zin their sight."

Israel Refuses to Enter Canaan

14 So all the congregation lifted up their voices and cried, and the people ^awept that night. ^2^bAnd all the children of Israel complained against Moses and Aaron, and the whole congregation said to them, "If only we had died in the land of Egypt! Or if only we had died in this wilderness! ^3Why has the LORD brought us to this land to fall by the sword, that our wives and ^cchildren should become victims? Would it not be better for us to return to Egypt?" ^4So they said to one another, ^d"Let us select a leader and ^ereturn to Egypt."

^5Then Moses and Aaron fell on their faces before all the assembly of the congregation of the children of Israel.

^6But Joshua the son of Nun and Caleb the son of Jephunneh, *who were* among those who had spied out the land, tore their clothes; ^7and they spoke to all the congregation of the children of Israel, saying: ^f"The land we passed through to spy out *is* an exceedingly good land. ^8If the LORD ^gdelights in us, then He will bring us into this land and give it to us, ^h'a land which flows with milk and honey.'* ^9Only ^ido not rebel against the LORD, ^jnor fear the people of the land, for ^kthey *are* our bread; their protection has departed from them, ^land the LORD *is* with us. Do not fear them."

^10^mAnd all the congregation said to stone them with stones. Now ^nthe glory of the LORD appeared in the tabernacle of meeting before all the children of Israel.

Moses Intercedes for the People

^11Then the LORD said to Moses: "How long will these people ^oreject Me? And how long will they not ^pbelieve Me, with all the signs which I have performed among them? ^12I will strike them with the pestilence and disinherit them, and I will ^qmake of you a nation greater and mightier than they."

^13And ^rMoses said to the LORD: ^s"Then the Egyptians will hear *it*, for by Your might You brought these people up from among them, ^14and they will tell *it* to the inhabitants of this land. They have ^theard that You, LORD, *are* among these people; that You, LORD, are seen face to face and Your cloud stands above them, and You go before them in a pillar of cloud by day and in a pillar of fire by night. ^15Now *if* You kill these people as one man, then the nations which have heard of Your fame will speak, saying, ^16'Because the LORD was not ^uable to bring this people to the land which He swore to give them, therefore He killed them in the wilderness.' ^17And now, I pray, let the power of my Lord be great, just as You have spoken, saying, ^18^v'The LORD is longsuffering and abundant in mercy, forgiving iniquity and transgression; but He

---

* **13:33** Hebrew *nephilim*   * **14:8** Exodus 3:8

13:27 *flows with milk and honey.* This phrase brought visions of pleasure and plenty to the Israelites. Canaan was a good land, a land with pasture for sheep and goats, with orchards and vineyards. The orchards and beekeeping went hand in hand, and thriving orchards meant honey. This was a land that was already developed and prospering.

14:3 *our wives and children should become victims.* Not only did the Israelites complain against Moses and Aaron, they dishonored God, saying that He would heartlessly bring them to a place where they would die along with their wives and children.

14:11 *How long.* This chapter records perhaps the saddest and most far-reaching event in the history of Israel, surpassed only by the crucifixion of their own Messiah. The miracles performed in the Exodus

did not convince the Israelites of God's trustworthiness, and the miracles of Christ did not convince the leaders of the day that He was the promised Messiah (Matt. 16:1–4).

13:26 ^nDeut. 1:19   **13:27** ^oEx. 3:8, 17; 13:5; 33:3 ^pDeut. 1:25   **13:28** ^qDeut. 1:28; 9:1, 2 ^rJosh. 11:21, 22   **13:29** ^sJudg. 6:3   **13:30** ^tNum. 14:6, 24 **13:31** ^uDeut. 1:28; 9:1–3   **13:32** ^vNum. 14:36, 37 ^wAmos 2:9   **13:33** ^xDeut. 1:28; 9:2 ^yIs. 40:22 ^z1 Sam. 17:42 **14:1** ^aDeut. 1:45   **14:2** ^bEx. 16:2; 17:3   **14:3** ^cDeut. 1:39   **14:4** ^dNeh. 9:17 ^eActs 7:39   **14:7** ^fNum. 13:27 **14:8** ^gDeut. 10:15 ^hNum. 13:27   **14:9** ^iDeut. 1:26; 9:7, 23, 24 ^jNum. 7:18 ^kNum. 24:8 ^lDeut. 20:1, 3, 4; 31:6–8 **14:10** ^mEx. 17:4 ^nEx. 16:10   **14:11** ^oHeb. 3:8 ^pDeut. 9:23   **14:12** ^qEx. 32:10   **14:13** ^rPs. 106:23 ^sEx. 32:12 **14:14** ^tDeut. 2:25   **14:16** ^uDeut. 9:28   **14:18** ^vEx. 34:6, 7

by no means clears *the guilty,* ʷvisiting the iniquity of the fathers on the children to the third and fourth *generation.*'* ¹⁹ˣPardon the iniquity of this people, I pray, ʸaccording to the greatness of Your mercy, just ᶻas You have forgiven this people, from Egypt even until now."

²⁰Then the LORD said: "I have pardoned, ᵃaccording to your word; ²¹but truly, as I live, ᵇall the earth shall be filled with the glory of the LORD— ²²ᶜbecause all these men who have seen My glory and the signs which I did in Egypt and in the wilderness, and have put Me to the test now ᵈthese ten times, and have not heeded My voice, ²³they certainly shall not ᵉsee the land of which I swore to their fathers, nor shall any of those who rejected Me see it. ²⁴But My servant ᶠCaleb, because he has a different spirit in him and ᵍhas followed Me fully, I will bring into the land where he went, and his descendants shall inherit it. ²⁵Now the Amalekites and the Canaanites dwell in the valley; tomorrow turn and ʰmove out into the wilderness by the Way of the Red Sea."

Death Sentence on the Rebels

²⁶And the LORD spoke to Moses and Aaron, saying, ²⁷"How long *shall I bear with* this evil congregation who complain against Me? ʲI have heard the complaints which the children of Israel make against Me. ²⁸ᵏSay to them, 'As I live,' says the LORD, 'just as you have spoken in My hearing, so I will do to you: ²⁹The carcasses of you who have complained against Me shall fall in this wilderness, ˡall of you who were numbered, according to your entire number, from twenty years old and above. ³⁰ᵐExcept for Caleb the son of Jephunneh and Joshua the son of Nun, you shall by no means enter the land which I swore I would make you dwell in. ³¹ⁿBut your little ones, whom you said would be victims, I will bring in, and they shall know the land which ᵒyou have despised. ³²But *as for* you, ᵖyour carcasses shall fall in this wilderness. ³³And your sons shall ᑫbe shepherds

in the wilderness ʳforty years, and ˢbear the brunt of your infidelity, until your carcasses are consumed in the wilderness. ³⁴ᵗAccording to the number of the days in which you spied out the land, ᵘforty days, for each day you shall bear your guilt one year, *namely* forty years, ᵛand you shall know My rejection. ³⁵ʷI the LORD have spoken this. I will surely do so to all ˣthis evil congregation who are gathered together against Me. In this wilderness they shall be consumed, and there they shall die.' "

³⁶Now the men whom Moses sent to spy out the land, who returned and made all the congregation complain against him by bringing a bad report of the land, ³⁷those very men who brought the evil report about the land, ʸdied by the plague before the LORD. ³⁸ᶻBut Joshua the son of Nun and Caleb the son of Jephunneh remained alive, of the men who went to spy out the land.

A Futile Invasion Attempt

³⁹Then Moses told these words to all the children of Israel, ᵃand the people mourned greatly. ⁴⁰And they rose early in the morning and went up to the top of the mountain, saying, ᵇ"Here we are, and we will go up to the place which the LORD has promised, for we have sinned!"

⁴¹And Moses said, "Now why do you transgress the command of the LORD? For this will not succeed. ⁴²ᶜDo not go up, lest you be defeated by your enemies, for the LORD *is* not among you. ⁴³For the Amalekites and the Canaanites *are* there before you, and you shall fall by the sword; ᵈbecause you have turned away from the LORD, the LORD will not be with you."

⁴⁴ᵉBut they presumed to go up to the mountaintop. Nevertheless, neither the ark of the covenant of the LORD nor Moses departed from the camp. ⁴⁵Then the Amalekites and the Canaanites who dwelt in that mountain came down and attacked them, and drove them back as far as ᶠHormah.

* 14:18 Exodus 34:6, 7

14:19 Pardon . . . I pray. This passage records the divine testing of Moses. God was not speaking lightly when He offered to smite the Israelites and start over with another group, new descendants from Moses. But Moses needed to know his own heart about the Israelites. As frustrating as they had been, they were still a living history of the mighty hand of God, and Moses did not want the story of their rescue to end with annihilation in the wilderness. Moses' response was what God wanted to hear, and in passionately and humbly asking for their pardon, Moses had no room for bitterness toward the people who were so difficult to lead.

14:23 they certainly shall not see the land. God pardoned those who turned against Him, but there was a price to pay. They would not see the land that they had complained was impossible to possess.

There is often a lifelong consequence to sin, even with forgiveness.

14:45 Hormah. The name of this place is very apt; it means "utter destruction."

14:18 ʷEx. 20:5   **14:19** ˣEx. 32:32; 34:9 ʸPs. 51:1; 106:45 ᶻPs. 78:38   **14:20** ᵃMic. 7:18–20   **14:21** ᵇPs. 72:19 **14:22** ᶜDeut. 1:35 ᵈGen. 31:7   **14:23** ᵉNum. 26:65; 32:11 **14:24** ᶠJosh. 14:6, 8, 9 ᵍNum. 32:12   **14:25** ʰDeut. 1:40   **14:27** ⁱEx. 16:28 ʲEx. 16:12   **14:28** ᵏHeb. 3:16–19   **14:29** ˡNum. 1:45, 46; 26:64   **14:30** ᵐDeut. 1:36–38   **14:31** ⁿDeut. 1:39 ᵒPs. 106:24   **14:32** ᵖNum. 26:64, 65; 32:13   **14:33** ᑫPs. 107:40 ʳDeut. 2:14 ˢEzek. 23:35   **14:34** ᵗNum. 13:25 ᵘEzek. 4:6 ᵛ[Heb. 4:1] **14:35** ʷNum. 23:19 ˣ1 Cor. 10:5   **14:37** ʸ[1 Cor. 10:10] **14:38** ᶻJosh. 14:6, 10   **14:39** ᵃEx. 33:4   **14:40** ᵇDeut. 1:41–44   **14:42** ᶜDeut. 1:42; 31:17   **14:43** ᵈ2 Chr. 15:2 **14:44** ᵉDeut. 1:43   **14:45** ᶠNum. 21:3

Laws of Grain and Drink Offerings

15 And the LORD spoke to Moses, saying,
2[a]“Speak to the children of Israel, and
say to them: ‘When you have come into the
land you are to inhabit, which I am giving
to you, 3and you [b]make an offering by fire
to the LORD, a burnt offering or a sacrifice,
[c]to fulfill a vow or as a freewill offering or
[d]in your appointed feasts, to make a [e]sweet
aroma to the LORD, from the herd or the
flock, 4then [f]he who presents his offering
to the LORD shall bring [g]a grain offering of
one-tenth *of an ephah* of fine flour mixed
[h]with one-fourth of a hin of oil; 5[i]and one-
fourth of a hin of wine as a drink offering
you shall prepare with the burnt offering
or the sacrifice, for each [j]lamb. 6[k]Or for a
ram you shall prepare as a grain offering
two-tenths *of an ephah* of fine flour mixed
with one-third of a hin of oil; 7and as a
drink offering you shall offer one-third of
a hin of wine as a sweet aroma to the LORD.
8And when you prepare a young bull as a
burnt offering, or as a sacrifice to fulfill a
vow, or as a [l]peace offering to the LORD,
9then shall be offered [m]with the young bull
a grain offering of three-tenths *of an ephah*
of fine flour mixed with half a hin of oil;
10and you shall bring as the drink offering
half a hin of wine as an offering made by
fire, a sweet aroma to the LORD.

11[n]‘Thus it shall be done for each young
bull, for each ram, or for each lamb or
young goat. 12According to the number that
you prepare, so you shall do with everyone
according to their number. 13All who are
native-born shall do these things in this
manner, in presenting an offering made by
fire, a sweet aroma to the LORD. 14And if
a stranger dwells with you, or whoever *is*
among you throughout your generations,
and would present an offering made by
fire, a sweet aroma to the LORD, just as you
do, so shall he do. 15[o]One ordinance *shall be*
for you of the assembly and for the stranger
who dwells *with you,* an ordinance forever
throughout your generations; as you are, so
shall the stranger be before the LORD. 16One
law and one custom shall be for you and for
the stranger who dwells with you.’ ”*

17Again the LORD spoke to Moses,
saying, 18[p]“Speak to the children of Israel,
and say to them: ‘When you come into the
land to which I bring you, 19then it will be,
when you eat of [q]the bread of the land, that
you shall offer up a heave offering to the
LORD. 20[r]You shall offer up a cake of the
first of your ground meal *as* [s]a heave offering; as a heave offering of the threshing
floor, so shall you offer it up. 21Of the first
of your ground meal you shall give to the
LORD a heave offering throughout your
generations.

Laws Concerning Unintentional Sin

22[t]‘If you sin unintentionally, and do not
observe all these commandments which
the LORD has spoken to Moses— 23all that
the LORD has commanded you by the hand
of Moses, from the day the LORD gave
commandment and onward throughout
your generations— 24then it will be, [u]if it
is unintentionally committed, without the
knowledge of the congregation, that the
whole congregation shall offer one young
bull as a burnt offering, as a sweet aroma
to the LORD, [v]with its grain offering and its
drink offering, according to the ordinance,
and [w]one kid of the goats as a sin offering.
25[x]So the priest shall make atonement for
the whole congregation of the children of
Israel, and it shall be forgiven them, for it
was unintentional; they shall bring their
offering, an offering made by fire to the
LORD, and their sin offering before the
LORD, for their unintended sin. 26It shall
be forgiven the whole congregation of the
children of Israel and the stranger who
dwells among them, because all the people
did it unintentionally.

27‘And [y]if a person sins unintentionally,
then he shall bring a female goat in its first
year as a sin offering. 28[z]So the priest shall
make atonement for the person who sins
unintentionally, when he sins unintentionally before the LORD, to make atonement
for him; and it shall be forgiven him.
29[a]You shall have one law for him who sins
unintentionally, *for* him who is native-born
among the children of Israel and for the
stranger who dwells among them.

* **15:16** Compare Exodus 12:49

15:2 ***When you have come into the land.*** These words may seem inappropriate following God's punishment for disobedience. But His overall purpose had not changed, and the children would enter the land the parents had rejected.

15:5 ***wine.*** The wine was poured out on the altar in an accompaniment to the burnt offering. It was another way of giving freely back to God that which the worshiper valued. Paul refers to himself as being poured out like a drink offering (2 Tim. 4:6). There is a sense of being finished, emptied of himself, and physically spent, as he does his final work. In the same way, the wine was emptied for God; it was used up. It was not waved, nor was a portion saved for the priests.

15:19–21 ***offer up a heave offering.*** By holding up the very first produce from a harvest, or the first cake made from the first grain of the season, the worshiper thanked God as the giver of all good gifts.

15:2 [a] Lev. 23:10 **15:3** [b] Lev. 1:2, 3 [c] Lev. 7:16; 22:18, 21 [d] Lev. 23:2, 8, 12, 38 [e] Ex. 29:18 **15:4** [f] Lev. 2:1; 6:14 [g] Ex. 29:40 [h] Num. 28:5 **15:5** [i] Num. 28:7, 14 [j] Lev. 1:10; 3:6 **15:6** [k] Num. 28:12, 14 **15:8** [l] Lev. 7:11 **15:9** [m] Num. 28:12, 14 **15:11** [n] Num. 28 **15:15** [o] Num. 9:14; 15:29 **15:18** [p] Deut. 26:1 **15:19** [q] Josh. 5:11, 12 **15:20** [r] Lev. 23:10, 14, 17 [s] Lev. 2:14; 23:10, 16 **15:22** [t] Lev. 4:2 **15:24** [u] Lev. 4:13 [v] Num. 15:8–10 [w] Lev. 4:23 **15:25** [x] [Heb. 2:17] **15:27** [y] Lev. 4:27–31 **15:28** [z] Lev. 4:35 **15:29** [a] Num. 15:15

Law Concerning Presumptuous Sin

30*b*'But the person who does *anything* presumptuously, *whether he is* native-born or a stranger, that one brings reproach on the LORD, and he shall be cut off from among his people. 31Because he has *c*despised the word of the LORD, and has broken His commandment, that person shall be completely cut off; his guilt *shall be* upon him.'"

Penalty for Violating the Sabbath

32Now while the children of Israel were in the wilderness, *d*they found a man gathering sticks on the Sabbath day. 33And those who found him gathering sticks brought him to Moses and Aaron, and to all the congregation. 34They put him *e*under guard, because it had not been explained what should be done to him. 35Then the LORD said to Moses, *f*"The man must surely be put to death; all the congregation shall *g*stone him with stones outside the camp." 36So, as the LORD commanded Moses, all the congregation brought him outside the camp and stoned him with stones, and he died.

Tassels on Garments

37Again the LORD spoke to Moses, saying, 38"Speak to the children of Israel: Tell *h*them to make tassels on the corners of their garments throughout their generations, and to put a blue thread in the tassels of the corners. 39And you shall have the tassel, that you may look upon it and *i*remember all the commandments of the LORD and do them, and that you *j*may not *k*follow the harlotry to which your own heart and your own eyes are inclined, 40and that you may remember and do all My commandments, and be *l*holy for your God. 41I *am* the LORD your God, who brought you out of the land of Egypt, to be your God: I *am* the LORD your God."

Rebellion Against Moses and Aaron

16 Now *a*Korah the son of Izhar, the son of Kohath, the son of Levi, with

*b*Dathan and Abiram the sons of Eliab, and On the son of Peleth, sons of Reuben, took *men;* 2and they rose up before Moses with some of the children of Israel, two hundred and fifty leaders of the congregation, *c*representatives of the congregation, men of renown. 3*d*They gathered together against Moses and Aaron, and said to them, "*You take* too much upon yourselves, for *e*all the congregation *is* holy, every one of them, *f*and the LORD *is* among them. Why then do you exalt yourselves above the assembly of the LORD?"

4So when Moses heard *it,* he *g*fell on his face; 5and he spoke to Korah and all his company, saying, "Tomorrow morning the LORD will show who *is* *h*His and *who is* *i*holy, and will cause *him* to *j*come near to Him. That one whom He chooses He will cause to come near to Him. 6Do this: Take censers, Korah and all your company; 7put fire in them and put incense in them before the LORD tomorrow, and it shall be *that* the man whom the LORD chooses *is* the holy one. *You take* too much upon yourselves, you sons of Levi!"

8Then Moses said to Korah, "Hear now, you sons of Levi: 9*Is it* *k*a small thing to you that the God of Israel has *l*separated you from the congregation of Israel, to bring you near to Himself, to do the work of the tabernacle of the LORD, and to stand before the congregation to serve them; 10and that He has brought you near *to Himself,* you and all your brethren, the sons of Levi, with you? And are you seeking the priesthood also? 11Therefore you and all your company *are* gathered together against the LORD. *m*And what *is* Aaron that you complain against him?"

12And Moses sent to call Dathan and Abiram the sons of Eliab, but they said, "We will not come up! 13*Is it* a small thing that you have brought us up out of *n*a land flowing with milk and honey, to kill us in the wilderness, that you should *o*keep acting like a prince over us? 14Moreover *p*you have not brought us into *q*a land flowing with milk and honey, nor given us inheritance of fields and vineyards. Will you

15:30–31 presumptuously. Moses spoke of unfaithfulness when he reminded the people of their presumption at Kadesh (Deut. 1:43). Their presumption was overstepping the limits of what God allowed, and doing it defiantly. If they had trusted God, they would have been happy to do things His way. Christians need to be on guard, lest they too be guilty of presumptuous sin. Consider the words of David, "Keep back Your servant also from presumptuous sins" (Ps. 19:13).
15:39 follow the harlotry. A harlot is a prostitute. Prostitution of the heart is unfaithfulness to God, in the same way that prostitution is unfaithfulness to the sanctity of marriage.
16:1 Korah. Korah was already set aside in a special position; he was a Levite. His sin was greater than jealousy of his cousins, the priests. He had set himself against God, and led others to do the same.

16:1–3 they rose up. Churches, organizations, marriages, and homes can all be affected by complaining, by rebelling against those whom God has appointed to lead. Great blessing and joy and guidance come from turning such feelings over to God and obeying Him and those whom He has designated.

15:30 *b* Deut. 1:43; 17:12   **15:31** *c* Prov. 13:13
15:32 *d* Ex. 31:14, 15; 35:2, 3   **15:34** *e* Lev. 24:12
15:35 *f* Ex. 31:14, 15   *g* Lev. 24:14   **15:38** *h* Matt. 23:5
15:39 *i* Ps. 103:18   *j* Deut. 29:19   *k* James 4:4   **15:40** *l* [Lev. 11:44, 45]   **16:1** *a* Ex. 6:21   *b* Num. 26:9   **16:2** *c* Num. 1:16; 26:9   **16:3** *d* Ps. 106:16   *e* Ex. 19:6   *f* Ex. 29:45
16:4 *g* Num. 14:5; 20:6   **16:5** *h* [2 Tim. 2:19]   *i* Lev. 21:6–8, 12   *j* Ezek. 40:46; 44:15, 16   **16:9** *k* Is. 7:13   *l* Deut. 10:8
16:11 *m* Ex. 16:7, 8   **16:13** *n* Num. 11:4–6   *o* Ex. 2:14
16:14 *p* Num. 14:1–4   *q* Ex. 3:8

put out the eyes of these men? We will not come up!"

¹⁵Then Moses was very angry, and said to the LORD, ʳ"Do not respect their offering. ˢI have not taken one donkey from them, nor have I hurt one of them."

¹⁶And Moses said to Korah, "Tomorrow, you and all your company be present ᵗbefore the LORD—you and they, as well as Aaron. ¹⁷Let each take his censer and put incense in it, and each of you bring his censer before the LORD, two hundred and fifty censers; both you and Aaron, each *with* his censer." ¹⁸So every man took his censer, put fire in it, laid incense on it, and stood at the door of the tabernacle of meeting with Moses and Aaron. ¹⁹And Korah gathered all the congregation against them at the door of the tabernacle of meeting. Then ᵘthe glory of the LORD appeared to all the congregation.

²⁰And the LORD spoke to Moses and Aaron, saying, ²¹ᵛ"Separate yourselves from among this congregation, that I may ʷconsume them in a moment."

²²Then they ˣfell on their faces, and said, "O God, ʸthe God of the spirits of all flesh, shall one man sin, and You be angry with all the ᶻcongregation?"

²³So the LORD spoke to Moses, saying, ²⁴"Speak to the congregation, saying, 'Get away from the tents of Korah, Dathan, and Abiram.'"

²⁵Then Moses rose and went to Dathan and Abiram, and the elders of Israel followed him. ²⁶And he spoke to the congregation, saying, ᵃ"Depart now from the tents of these wicked men! Touch nothing of theirs, lest you be consumed in all their sins." ²⁷So they got away from around the tents of Korah, Dathan, and Abiram; and Dathan and Abiram came out and stood at the door of their tents, with their wives, their sons, and their little ᵇchildren.

²⁸And Moses said: ᶜ"By this you shall know that the LORD has sent me to do all these works, for *I have* not *done them* ᵈof my own will. ²⁹If these men die naturally like all men, or if they are ᵉvisited by the common fate of all men, *then* the LORD

has not sent me. ³⁰But if the LORD creates ᶠa new thing, and the earth opens its mouth and swallows them up with all that belongs to them, and they ᵍgo down alive into the pit, then you will understand that these men have rejected the LORD."

³¹ʰNow it came to pass, as he finished speaking all these words, that the ground split apart under them, ³²and the earth opened its mouth and swallowed them up, with their households and ⁱall the men with Korah, with all *their* goods. ³³So they and all those with them went down alive into the pit; the earth closed over them, and they perished from among the assembly. ³⁴Then all Israel who *were* around them fled at their cry, for they said, "Lest the earth swallow us up *also!*"

³⁵And ʲa fire came out from the LORD and consumed the two hundred and fifty men who were offering incense.

³⁶Then the LORD spoke to Moses, saying: ³⁷"Tell Eleazar, the son of Aaron the priest, to pick up the censers out of the blaze, for ᵏthey are holy, and scatter the fire some distance away. ³⁸The censers of ˡthese men who sinned against their own souls, let them be made into hammered plates as a covering for the altar. Because they presented them before the LORD, therefore they are holy; ᵐand they shall be a sign to the children of Israel." ³⁹So Eleazar the priest took the bronze censers, which those who were burned up had presented, and they were hammered out as a covering on the altar, ⁴⁰to *be* a memorial to the children of Israel ⁿthat no outsider, who *is* not a descendant of Aaron, should come near to offer incense before the LORD, that he might not become like Korah and his companions, just as the LORD had said to him through Moses.

Complaints of the People

⁴¹On the next day ᵒall the congregation of the children of Israel complained against Moses and Aaron, saying, "You have killed the people of the LORD." ⁴²Now it happened, when the congregation had gathered against Moses and Aaron, that they

---

16:24 Get away. The Lord was giving the people a chance to show to whom they really had allegiance: God, or Korah and his followers.

16:32 all the men with Korah. The whole families of Dathan and Abiram were swallowed up, but some of Korah's descendants did not follow him, and were not destroyed. Some of them contributed a considerable number of psalms (see Ps. 42). God is always merciful, even when dealing with the flagrant troublemakers.

16:37 pick up the censers. Just as He spared the relatives of Korah who were not in rebellion, so, also, did He save the censers. They were holy because they had been dedicated to God, but they would not be used as incense burners again.

16:41 complained against Moses and Aaron. Incredibly, even after watching the dramatic destruction of the rebels, the congregation blamed the very

leaders who had pleaded for the Lord to spare the rest of the congregation (v. 20). Obviously the people still strongly identified with Korah and his followers, and did not comprehend what they had just witnessed. Witnessing the destructiveness of sin does not always make people wake up and change their ways.

16:15 ʳGen. 4:4, 5 ˢ1 Sam. 12:3 **16:16** ᵗ1 Sam. 12:3, 7
16:19 ᵘNum. 14:10 **16:21** ᵛGen. 19:17 ʷEx. 32:10;
33:5 **16:22** ˣNum. 14:5 ʸNum. 27:16 ᶻGen. 18:23–32;
20:4 **16:26** ᵃGen. 19:12, 14, 15, 17 **16:27** ᵇNum. 26:11
16:28 ᶜJohn 5:36 ᵈJohn 5:30 **16:29** ᵉEx. 20:5
16:30 ᶠJob 31:3 ᵍ[Ps. 55:15] **16:31** ʰNum. 26:10
16:32 ⁱNum. 26:11 **16:35** ʲNum. 11:1–3; 26:10
16:37 ᵏLev. 27:28 **16:38** ˡHab. 2:10 ᵐNum. 17:10
16:40 ⁿNum. 3:10 **16:41** ᵒNum. 14:2

turned toward the tabernacle of meeting; and suddenly *p*the cloud covered it, and the glory of the LORD appeared. 43Then Moses and Aaron came before the tabernacle of meeting.

44And the LORD spoke to Moses, saying, 45"Get away from among this congregation, that I may consume them in a moment."

And they fell on their faces.

46So Moses said to Aaron, "Take a censer and put fire in it from the altar, put incense *on it*, and take it quickly to the congregation and make atonement for them; *q*for wrath has gone out from the LORD. The plague has begun." 47Then Aaron took *it* as Moses commanded, and ran into the midst of the assembly; and already the plague had begun among the people. So he put in the incense and made atonement for the people. 48And he stood between the dead and the living; *r*so the plague was stopped. 49Now those who died in the plague were fourteen thousand seven hundred, besides those who died in the Korah incident. 50So Aaron returned to Moses at the door of the tabernacle of meeting, for the plague had stopped.

The Budding of Aaron's Rod

17 And the LORD spoke to Moses, saying: 2"Speak to the children of Israel, and get from them a rod from each father's house, all their leaders according to their fathers' houses—twelve rods. Write each man's name on his rod. 3And you shall write Aaron's name on the rod of Levi. For there shall be one rod for the head of *each* father's house. 4Then you shall place them in the tabernacle of meeting before *a*the Testimony, *b*where I meet with you. 5And it shall be *that* the rod of the man *c*whom I choose will blossom; thus I will rid Myself of the complaints of the children of Israel, *d*which they make against you."

6So Moses spoke to the children of Israel, and each of their leaders gave him a rod apiece, for each leader according to their fathers' houses, twelve rods; and the rod of Aaron *was* among their rods. 7And Moses placed the rods before the LORD in *e*the tabernacle of witness.

8Now it came to pass on the next day that Moses went into the tabernacle of witness, and behold, the *f*rod of Aaron, of the house of Levi, had sprouted and put forth buds, had produced blossoms and yielded ripe almonds. 9Then Moses brought out all the rods from before the LORD to all the children of Israel; and they looked, and each man took his rod.

10And the LORD said to Moses, "Bring *g*Aaron's rod back before the Testimony, to be kept *h*as a sign against the rebels, *i*that you may put their complaints away from Me, lest they die." 11Thus did Moses; just as the LORD had commanded him, so he did.

12So the children of Israel spoke to Moses, saying, "Surely we die, we perish, we all perish! 13*j*Whoever even comes near the tabernacle of the LORD must die. Shall we all utterly die?"

Duties of Priests and Levites

18 Then the LORD said to Aaron: *a*"You and your sons and your father's house with you shall *b*bear the iniquity *related to* the sanctuary, and you and your sons with you shall bear the iniquity *associated with* your priesthood. 2Also bring with you your brethren of the *c*tribe of Levi, the tribe of your father, that they may be *d*joined with you and serve you while you and your sons *are* with you before the tabernacle of witness. 3They shall attend to your needs and *e*all the needs of the tabernacle; *f*but they shall not come near the articles of the sanctuary and the altar, *g*lest they die—they and you also. 4They shall be joined with you and attend to the needs of the tabernacle of meeting, for all the work of the tabernacle; *h*but an outsider shall not come near you. 5And you shall attend to the duties of the sanctuary and *i*the duties of the altar, *i*that there *may* be no more wrath on the children of Israel. 6Behold, I Myself have *k*taken your brethren the Levites from among the children of Israel;

16:48 *he stood between the dead and the living.* Aaron stood between the living and the dead to stop the plague—just like the Savior, who stands in the gap between life and death.

17:12 *we perish.* The Israelites were overshadowed by despondency. Aware of God's righteous judgments against their constant grumbling, they were gripped by fear. They knew they were guilty, they knew that God would punish them, and the warm light of peace had left their lives. When this happens, let us remember that there is still one way back into the sunshine. Repentance leads to the happy experience of the remission of sins and peace with God (Luke 24:47).

17:13 *Shall we all utterly die?* Finally the people realized that God had revealed His will through His miraculous actions among them. They suddenly saw their presumption and God's opinion of it.

18:1 *bear the iniquity related to the sanctuary . . . priesthood.* The priests stood as intermediaries between God and man. If the people had no advocate before the Lord, they would die in their offenses. The priests had a formidable responsibility, for if they did not do their job, the whole community suffered.

16:42 *p* Ex. 40:34 **16:46** *q* Num. 18:5 **16:48** *r* Num. 25:8 **17:4** *a* Ex. 25:16 *b* Ex. 25:22; 29:42, 43; 30:36 **17:5** *c* Num. 16:5 *d* Num. 16:11 **17:7** *e* Ex. 38:21 **17:8** *f* [Ezek. 17:24] **17:10** *g* Heb. 9:4 *h* Deut. 9:7, 24 *i* Num. 17:5 **17:13** *j* Num. 1:51, 53; 18:4, 7 **18:1** *a* Num. 17:13 *b* Ex. 28:38 **18:2** *c* Num. 1:47 *d* Num. 3:5–10 **18:3** *e* Num. 3:25, 31, 36 *f* Num. 16:40 *g* Num. 4:15 **18:4** *h* Num. 3:10 **18:5** *i* Lev. 24:3 *j* Num. 8:19; 16:46 **18:6** *k* Num. 3:12, 45

they are a gift to you, given by the LORD, to do the work of the tabernacle of meeting. [7]Therefore *m*you and your sons with you shall attend to your priesthood for everything at the altar and *n*behind the veil; and you shall serve. I give your priesthood *to you* as a *o*gift for service, but the outsider who comes near shall be put to death."

Offerings for Support of the Priests

[8]And the LORD spoke to Aaron: "Here, *p*I Myself have also given you charge of My heave offerings, all the holy gifts of the children of Israel; I have given them *q*as a portion to you and your sons, as an ordinance forever. [9]This shall be yours of the most holy things *reserved* from the fire: every offering of theirs, every *r*grain offering and every *s*sin offering and every *t*trespass offering which they render to Me, *shall be* most holy for you and your sons. [10]*u*In a most holy *place* you shall eat it; every male shall eat it. It shall be holy to you.

[11]"This also *is* yours: *v*the heave offering of their gift, with all the wave offerings of the children of Israel; I have given them to you, and your sons and daughters with you, as an ordinance forever. *w*Everyone who is clean in your house may eat it.

[12]*x*"All the best of the oil, all the best of the new wine and the grain, *y*their firstfruits which they offer to the LORD, I have given them to you. [13]Whatever first ripe fruit is in their land, *z*which they bring to the LORD, shall be yours. Everyone who is clean in your house may eat it.

[14]*a*"Every devoted thing in Israel shall be yours.

[15]"Everything that first opens *b*the womb of all flesh, which they bring to the LORD, whether man or beast, shall be yours; nevertheless the firstborn of man you shall surely redeem, and *c*the firstborn of unclean animals you shall redeem. [16]And those redeemed of the devoted things you shall redeem when one month old, *d*according to your valuation, for five shekels of silver, according to the shekel of the sanctuary, which *is* *e*twenty gerahs. [17]*f*But the firstborn of a cow, the firstborn of a sheep, or the firstborn of a goat you shall not redeem; they *are* holy. *g*You shall sprinkle their blood on the altar, and burn their fat *as* an offering made by fire for a sweet aroma to the LORD. [18]And their flesh

shall be yours, just as the *h*wave breast and the right thigh are yours.

[19]"All the heave offerings of the holy things, which the children of Israel offer to the LORD, I have given to you and your sons and daughters with you as an ordinance forever; *i*it *is* a covenant of salt forever before the LORD with you and your descendants with you."

[20]Then the LORD said to Aaron: "You shall have *j*no inheritance in their land, nor shall you have any portion among them; *k*I *am* your portion and your inheritance among the children of Israel.

Tithes for Support of the Levites

[21]"Behold, *l*I have given the children of Levi all the tithes in Israel as an inheritance in return for the work which they perform, *m*the work of the tabernacle of meeting. [22]*n*Hereafter the children of Israel shall not come near the tabernacle of meeting, *o*lest they bear sin and die. [23]But the Levites shall perform the work of the tabernacle of meeting, and they shall bear their iniquity; *it shall be* a statute forever, throughout your generations, that among the children of Israel they shall have no inheritance. [24]For the tithes of the children of Israel, which they offer up *as* a heave offering to the LORD, I have given to the Levites as an inheritance; therefore I have said to them, 'Among the children of Israel they shall have no inheritance.'"

The Tithe of the Levites

[25]Then the LORD spoke to Moses, saying, [26]"Speak thus to the Levites, and say to them: 'When you take from the children of Israel the tithes which I have given you from them as your inheritance, then you shall offer up a heave offering of it to the LORD, *p*a tenth of the tithe. [27]And your heave offering shall be reckoned to you as though *it were* the grain of the *q*threshing floor and as the fullness of the winepress. [28]Thus you shall also offer a heave offering to the LORD from all your tithes which you receive from the children of Israel, and you shall give the LORD's heave offering from it to Aaron the priest. [29]Of all your gifts you shall offer up every heave offering due to the LORD, from all the best of them, the consecrated part of them.' [30]Therefore you shall say to them: 'When you have lifted

---

18:19 as an ordinance forever. The priests lived off the produce of the land as God provided for them through the gifts of His people. Instead of inheriting land, God was their inheritance. They would be well supplied as long as the people were faithful, and this would be a good incentive to the priests to be responsible.

18:6 *i* Num. 3:9　**18:7** *m* Num. 3:10; 18:5　*n* Heb. 9:3, 6　*o* 1 Pet. 5:2, 3　**18:8** *p* Lev. 6:16, 18; 7:28–34　*q* Ex. 29:29; 40:13, 15　**18:9** *r* Lev. 2:2, 3; 10:12, 13　*s* Lev. 6:25, 26　*t* Lev. 7:7　**18:10** *u* Lev. 6:16, 26　**18:11** *v* Deut. 18:3–5　*w* Lev. 22:1–16　**18:12** *x* Ex. 23:19　*y* Ex. 22:29　**18:13** *z* Ex. 22:29; 23:19; 34:26　**18:14** *a* Lev. 27:1–33　**18:15** *b* Ex. 13:2　*c* Ex. 13:12–15　**18:16** *d* Lev. 27:6　*e* Ex. 30:13　**18:17** *f* Deut. 15:19　*g* Lev. 3:2, 5　**18:18** *h* Ex. 29:26–28　**18:19** *i* 2 Chr. 13:5　**18:20** *j* Josh. 13:14, 33　*k* Ezek. 44:28　**18:21** *l* Lev. 27:30–33　*m* Num. 3:7, 8　**18:22** *n* Num. 1:51　*o* Lev. 22:9　**18:26** *p* Neh. 10:38　**18:27** *q* Num. 15:20

up the best of it, then *the rest* shall be accounted to the Levites as the produce of the
threshing floor and as the produce of the
winepress. 31 You may eat it in any place,
you and your households, for it *is* [r]your
reward for your work in the tabernacle of
meeting. 32 And you shall [s]bear no sin because of it, when you have lifted up the best
of it. But you shall not [t]profane the holy
gifts of the children of Israel, lest you die.'"

Laws of Purification

19 Now the LORD spoke to Moses and
Aaron, saying, 2 "This *is* the ordinance of the law which the LORD has commanded, saying: 'Speak to the children of
Israel, that they bring you a red heifer without blemish, in which there *is* no [a]defect
[b]*and* on which a yoke has never come. 3 You
shall give it to Eleazar the priest, that he
may take it [c]outside the camp, and it shall
be slaughtered before him; 4 and Eleazar
the priest shall take some of its blood with
his finger, and [d]sprinkle some of its blood
seven times directly in front of the tabernacle of meeting. 5 Then the heifer shall be
burned in his sight: [e]its hide, its flesh, its
blood, and its offal shall be burned. 6 And
the priest shall take [f]cedar wood and [g]hys-
sop and scarlet, and cast *them* into the
midst of the fire burning the heifer. 7 [h]Then
the priest shall wash his clothes, he shall
bathe in water, and afterward he shall
come into the camp; the priest shall be
unclean until evening. 8 And the one who
burns it shall wash his clothes in water,
bathe in water, and shall be unclean until
evening. 9 Then a man *who is* clean shall
gather up [i]the ashes of the heifer, and store
them outside the camp in a clean place; and
they shall be kept for the congregation of
the children of Israel [j]for the water of purification;* it *is* for purifying from sin. 10 And
the one who gathers the ashes of the heifer
shall wash his clothes, and be unclean until
evening. It shall be a statute forever to the
children of Israel and to the stranger who
dwells among them.

11 [k]'He who touches the dead body of anyone shall be unclean seven days. 12 [l]He shall
purify himself with the water on the third
day and on the seventh day; *then* he will
be clean. But if he does not purify himself
on the third day and on the seventh day, he
will not be clean. 13 Whoever touches the
body of anyone who has died, and [m]does
not purify himself, [n]defiles the tabernacle
of the LORD. That person shall be cut off
from Israel. He shall be unclean, because
[o]the water of purification was not sprinkled on him; [p]his uncleanness *is* still on
him.

14 'This *is* the law when a man dies in
a tent: All who come into the tent and all
who *are* in the tent shall be unclean seven
days; 15 and every [q]open vessel, which has
no cover fastened on it, *is* unclean. 16 [r]Who-
ever in the open field touches one who is
slain by a sword or who has died, or a bone
of a man, or a grave, shall be unclean seven
days.

17 'And for an unclean *person* they shall
take some of the [s]ashes of the heifer burnt
for purification from sin, and running water shall be put on them in a vessel. 18 A
clean person shall take [t]hyssop and dip *it*
in the water, sprinkle *it* on the tent, on all
the vessels, on the persons who were there,
or on the one who touched a bone, the slain,
the dead, or a grave. 19 The clean *person*
shall sprinkle the unclean on the third day
and on the seventh day; [u]and on the seventh day he shall purify himself, wash his
clothes, and bathe in water; and at evening
he shall be clean.

20 'But the man who is unclean and does
not purify himself, that person shall be cut
off from among the assembly, because he
has [v]defiled the sanctuary of the LORD.
The water of purification has not been
sprinkled on him; he *is* unclean. 21 It shall
be a perpetual statute for them. He who
sprinkles the water of purification shall
wash his clothes; and he who touches the

* **19:9** Literally *impurity*

19:2 *red heifer.* The animal sacrificed for making the waters of purification was different than sacrifices for sins or thanksgivings. It was a female, not a male, its color was specified, it was killed outside the camp, and cedar and hyssop, used in purification ceremonies, were added to the burning heifer.

19:9 *the water of purification.* It is not that this water was "magic," but it was prepared in obedience to God's commands, and was an outward symbol of the inner work that God does to remove impurity. It is important to recognize that the rituals and celebrations were designed by God to create an awareness in His people of their spiritual needs, and ultimately to prepare them for Christ. All of the washings and sacrifices were still powerless to change hearts. That is a spiritual work done by God alone.

19:20 *does not purify himself.* The issues of uncleanness were so serious that the one who applied the waters of purification became unclean also. Refusing to accept the need for cleansing was not just the act of an uncouth person who didn't care about germs. Every time someone dies, it is a reminder that death came into the world through sin (Rom. 5:12–14). The ritual for cleansing was a way of addressing the fact that it was sin that made this happen: the world is not the way God created it to be, and humans are in continual need of being reconciled to their Creator.

18:31 [r][Luke 10:7] **18:32** [s]Lev. 19:8; 22:16 [t]Lev. 22:2, 15 **19:2** [a]Lev. 22:20–25 [b]Deut. 21:3 **19:3** [c]Lev. 4:12, 21 **19:4** [d]Lev. 4:6 **19:5** [e]Ex. 29:14 **19:6** [f]Lev. 14:4, 6, 49 [g]Ex. 12:22 **19:7** [h]Lev. 11:25; 15:5; 16:26, 28 **19:9** [i][Heb. 9:13, 14] [j]Num. 19:13, 20, 21 **19:11** [k]Lev. 21:1, 11 **19:12** [l]Num. 19:19; 31:19 **19:13** [m]Lev. 22:3–7 [n]Lev. 15:31 [o]Num. 8:7; 19:9 [p]Lev. 7:20; 22:3 **19:15** [q]Num. 31:20 **19:16** [r]Num. 19:11; 31:19 **19:17** [s]Num. 19:9 **19:18** [t]Ps. 51:7 **19:19** [u]Lev. 14:9 **19:20** [v]Num. 19:13

water of purification shall be unclean until evening. 22wWhatever the unclean *person* touches shall be unclean; and xthe person who touches *it* shall be unclean until evening.'"

Moses' Error at Kadesh

20 Thena the children of Israel, the whole congregation, came into the Wilderness of Zin in the first month, and the people stayed in bKadesh; and cMiriam died there and was buried there.

2dNow there was no water for the congregation; eso they gathered together against Moses and Aaron. 3And the people fcontended with Moses and spoke, saying: "If only we had died gwhen our brethren died before the LORD! 4hWhy have you brought up the assembly of the LORD into this wilderness, that we and our animals should die here? 5And why have you made us come up out of Egypt, to bring us to this evil place? It *is* not a place of grain or figs or vines or pomegranates; nor *is* there any water to drink." 6So Moses and Aaron went from the presence of the assembly to the door of the tabernacle of meeting, and ithey fell on their faces. And jthe glory of the LORD appeared to them.

7Then the LORD spoke to Moses, saying, 8k"Take the rod; you and your brother Aaron gather the congregation together. Speak to the rock before their eyes, and it will yield its water; thus lyou shall bring water for them out of the rock, and give drink to the congregation and their animals." 9So Moses took the rod mfrom before the LORD as He commanded him.

10And Moses and Aaron gathered the assembly together before the rock; and he said to them, n"Hear now, you rebels! Must we bring water for you out of this rock?" 11Then Moses lifted his hand and struck the rock twice with his rod; oand water came out abundantly, and the congregation and their animals drank.

12Then the LORD spoke to Moses and Aaron, "Because pyou did not believe Me, to qhallow Me in the eyes of the children of Israel, therefore you shall not bring this assembly into the land which I have given them."

13rThis *was* the water of Meribah,* because the children of Israel contended with the LORD, and He was hallowed among them.

Passage Through Edom Refused

14sNow Moses sent messengers from Kadesh to the king of tEdom. u"Thus says your brother Israel: 'You know all the hardship that has befallen us, 15vhow our fathers went down to Egypt, wand we dwelt in Egypt a long time, xand the Egyptians afflicted us and our fathers. 16yWhen we cried out to the LORD, He heard our voice and zsent the Angel and brought us up out of Egypt; now here we are in Kadesh, a city on the edge of your border. 17Please alet us pass through your country. We will not pass through fields or vineyards, nor will we drink water from wells; we will go along the King's Highway; we will not turn aside to the right hand or to the left until we have passed through your territory.'"

18Then bEdom said to him, "You shall not pass through my *land*, lest I come out against you with the sword."

19So the children of Israel said to him, "We will go by the Highway, and if I or my livestock drink any of your water, cthen I will pay for it; let me only pass through on foot, nothing *more*."

20Then he said, d"You shall not pass through." So Edom came out against them with many men and with a strong hand.

---

* **20:13** Literally *Contention*

20:1 *in the first month.* No year is associated with this month; most likely it is the fortieth year, the end of the sojourn in the wilderness.
20:2 *no water.* Having no water was the subject of the first crisis that the Israelites had on their journey out of Egypt (Ex. 17). The same problem, forty years later, provokes the same ingratitude and anger from the people.
20:11 *struck the rock twice.* The first time God brought water from the rock, He asked Moses to strike it. This time He asked Moses to speak to it. In his anger at the Israelites' attitude, Moses spoke roughly to the Israelites and struck the rock. Even Moses could mess things up by responding in anger.
20:11,23–24 *because you rebelled.* Up to this point, Moses' obedience had been impeccable. It may seem that his anger was so understandable that God was overly harsh in His discipline of Moses. But Moses was the only representative of God to the people. It was only with Moses that God had spoken face to face, and Moses had a grave responsibility to only communicate what God actually said. Moses' attitude was displeasing to God, and his actions went beyond

what God had directed. Anger and presumption are still two quick ways to break our fellowship with God.
20:13 *Meribah.* This is the same name that was given 40 years earlier to the location of the first water crisis (Ex. 17:7). The word means "contention."
20:14 *your brother Israel.* The Edomites were descendants of Jacob's brother Esau. Because of this relationship, Moses had a special basis of appeal, and for the same reason, the Israelites were not to fight the Edomites.

19:22 wHag. 2:11–13 xLev. 15:5 **20:1** dNum. 13:21; 33:36 bNum. 13:26 cEx. 15:20 **20:2** dEx. 17:1 eNum. 16:19, 42 **20:3** fEx. 17:2 gNum. 11:1, 33; 14:37; 16:31–35, 49 **20:4** hEx. 17:3 **20:6** iNum. 14:5; 16:4, 22, 45 jNum. 14:10 **20:8** kEx. 4:17, 20; 17:5, 6 lNeh. 9:15 **20:9** mNum. 17:10 **20:10** nPs. 106:33 **20:11** o[1 Cor. 10:4] **20:12** pDeut. 1:37; 3:26, 27; 34:5 qLev. 10:3 **20:13** rDeut. 33:8 **20:14** sJudg. 11:16, 17 tGen. 36:31–39 uDeut. 2:4 **20:15** vGen. 46:6 wEx. 12:40 xDeut. 26:6 **20:16** yEx. 2:23; 3:7 zEx. 3:2; 14:19 **20:17** aNum. 21:22 **20:18** bNum. 24:18 **20:19** cDeut. 2:6, 28 **20:20** dJudg. 11:17

21Thus Edom *e*refused to give Israel passage through his territory; so Israel *f*turned away from him.

Death of Aaron

22Now the children of Israel, the whole congregation, journeyed from *g*Kadesh *h*and came to Mount Hor. 23And the LORD spoke to Moses and Aaron in Mount Hor by the border of the land of Edom, saying: 24"Aaron shall be *i*gathered to his people, for he shall not enter the land which I have given to the children of Israel, because you rebelled against My word at the water of Meribah. 25*j*Take Aaron and Eleazar his son, and bring them up to Mount Hor; 26and strip Aaron of his garments and put them on Eleazar his son; for Aaron shall be gathered *to his people* and die there." 27So Moses did just as the LORD commanded, and they went up to Mount Hor in the sight of all the congregation. 28*k*Moses stripped Aaron of his garments and put them on Eleazar his son; and *l*Aaron died there on the top of the mountain. Then Moses and Eleazar came down from the mountain. 29Now when all the congregation saw that Aaron was dead, all the house of Israel mourned for Aaron *m*thirty days.

Canaanites Defeated at Hormah

21 The *a*king of Arad, the Canaanite, who dwelt in the South, heard that Israel was coming on the road to Atharim. Then he fought against Israel and took *some* of them prisoners. 2*b*So Israel made a vow to the LORD, and said, "If You will indeed deliver this people into my hand, then *c*I will utterly destroy their cities." 3And the LORD listened to the voice of Israel and delivered up the Canaanites, and they utterly destroyed them and their cities. So the name of that place was called Hormah.*

The Bronze Serpent

4Then they journeyed from Mount Hor by the Way of the Red Sea, to *d*go around the land of Edom; and the soul of the people became very discouraged on the way. 5And the people *e*spoke against God and against Moses: "Why have you brought us up out of Egypt to die in the wilderness? For *there is* no food and no water, and our soul loathes

this worthless bread." 6So *f*the LORD sent *g*fiery serpents among the people, and they bit the people; and many of the people of Israel died.

7*h*Therefore the people came to Moses, and said, "We have *i*sinned, for we have spoken against the LORD and against you; *j*pray to the LORD that He take away the serpents from us." So Moses prayed for the people.
8Then the LORD said to Moses, *k*"Make a *l*fiery *serpent*, and set it on a pole; and it shall be that everyone who is bitten, when he looks at it, shall live." 9So *m*Moses made a bronze serpent, and put it on a pole; and so it was, if a serpent had bitten anyone, when he looked at the bronze serpent, he lived.

From Mount Hor to Moab

10Now the children of Israel moved on and *n*camped in Oboth. 11And they journeyed from Oboth and camped at Ije Abarim, in the wilderness which *is* east of Moab, toward the sunrise. 12oFrom there they moved and camped in the Valley of Zered. 13From there they moved and camped on the other side of the Arnon, which *is* in the wilderness that extends from the border of the Amorites; for *p*the Arnon *is* the border of Moab, between Moab and the Amorites. 14Therefore it is said in the Book of the Wars of the LORD:

> "Waheb in Suphah,*
> The brooks of the Arnon,
> 15 And the slope of the brooks
> That reaches to the dwelling of *q*Ar,
> And lies on the border of Moab."

16From there *they went* *r*to Beer, which *is* the well where the LORD said to Moses, "Gather the people together, and I will give them water." 17Then Israel sang this song:

> *s*"Spring up, O well!
> All of you sing to it—
> 18 The well the leaders sank,
> Dug by the nation's nobles,
> By the *t*lawgiver, with their staves."

And from the wilderness *they went* to Mattanah, 19from Mattanah to Nahaliel,

---

* 21:3 Literally *Utter Destruction*   * 21:14 Ancient unknown places; Vulgate reads *What He did in the Red Sea.*

21:5 *loathes this worthless bread.* As the psalmist later observed, "How often they provoked Him in the wilderness, and grieved Him in the desert!" (Ps. 78:40). In their contempt of the food, the people were actually spurning God who had given them this food. It is a sharp reminder to believers to do all things without grumbling (Phil. 2:14) so the glory of the Lord will be evident to those who are watching.
21:8 *fiery serpent . . . when he looks at it, shall live.* Jesus pointed to this stunning image in His dialogue with Nicodemus (John 3:14–15). Jesus was nailed to the cross, and those who look at it—who realize, "the cross is the price for *my* sins"—will receive eternal life. Each Israelite who looked at the bronze snake

knew that the snake bites were the penalty for his own sinful attitudes. In both cases, only God has the cure.

20:21 *e* Deut. 2:27, 30 *f* Judg. 11:18   **20:22** *g* Num. 33:37 *h* Num. 21:4   **20:24** *i* Gen. 25:8   **20:25** *j* Num. 33:38   **20:28** *k* Ex. 29:29, 30 *l* Num. 33:38   **20:29** *m* Deut. 34:8   **21:1** *a* Judg. 1:16   **21:2** *b* Gen. 28:20 *c* Deut. 2:34   **21:4** *d* Judg. 11:18   **21:5** *e* Num. 20:4, 5   **21:6** *f* 1 Cor. 10:9 *g* Deut. 8:15   **21:7** *h* Num. 11:2 *i* Lev. 26:40 *j* Ex. 8:8   **21:8** *k* [John 3:14, 15] *l* Is. 14:29; 30:6   **21:9** *m* John 3:14, 15   **21:10** *n* Num. 33:43, 44   **21:12** *o* Deut. 2:13   **21:13** *p* Num. 22:36   **21:15** *q* Deut. 2:9, 18, 29   **21:16** *r* Judg. 9:21   **21:17** *s* Ex. 15:1   **21:18** *t* Is. 33:22

from Nahaliel to Bamoth, ²⁰and from Ba-moth, *in* the valley that *is* in the country of Moab, to the top of Pisgah which looks ^udown on the wasteland.*

King Sihon Defeated

²¹Then ^vIsrael sent messengers to Sihon king of the Amorites, saying, ²²^w"Let me pass through your land. We will not turn aside into fields or vineyards; we will not drink water from wells. We will go by the King's Highway until we have passed through your territory." ²³^xBut Sihon would not allow Israel to pass through his territory. So Sihon gathered all his people together and went out against Israel in the wilderness, ^yand he came to Jahaz and fought against Israel. ²⁴Then ^zIsrael defeated him with the edge of the sword, and took possession of his land from the Arnon to the Jabbok, as far as the people of Ammon; for the border of the people of Ammon *was* fortified. ²⁵So Israel took all these cities, and Israel ^adwelt in all the cities of the Amorites, in Heshbon and in all its villages. ²⁶For Heshbon *was* the city of Sihon king of the Amorites, who had fought against the former king of Moab, and had taken all his land from his hand as far as the Arnon. ²⁷Therefore those who speak in proverbs say:

"Come to Heshbon, let it be built;
Let the city of Sihon be repaired.

²⁸ "For ^bfire went out from Heshbon,
A flame from the city of Sihon;
It consumed ^cAr of Moab,
The lords of the ^dheights of the Arnon.
²⁹ Woe to you, ^eMoab!
You have perished, O people of
^fChemosh!
He has given his ^gsons as fugitives,
And his ^hdaughters into captivity,
To Sihon king of the Amorites.

³⁰ "But we have shot at them;
Heshbon has perished ⁱas far as Dibon.
Then we laid waste as far as Nophah,
Which *reaches* to ^jMedeba."

³¹Thus Israel dwelt in the land of the Amorites. ³²Then Moses sent to spy out ^kJazer; and they took its villages and drove out the Amorites who *were* there.

King Og Defeated

³³^lAnd they turned and went up by the way to ^mBashan. So Og king of Bashan went out against them, he and all his peo-ple, to battle ⁿat Edrei. ³⁴Then the LORD said to Moses, ^o"Do not fear him, for I have delivered him into your hand, with all his people and his land; and ^pyou shall do to him as you did to Sihon king of the Am-orites, who dwelt at Heshbon." ³⁵^qSo they defeated him, his sons, and all his people, until there was no survivor left him; and they took possession of his land.

Balak Sends for Balaam

22 Then ^athe children of Israel moved, and camped in the plains of Moab on the side of the Jordan *across from* Jericho.

²Now ^bBalak the son of Zippor saw all that Israel had done to the Amorites. ³And ^cMoab was exceedingly afraid of the peo-ple because they *were* many, and Moab was sick with dread because of the chil-dren of Israel. ⁴So Moab said to ^dthe elders of Midian, "Now this company will lick up everything around us, as an ox licks up the grass of the field." And Balak the son of Zippor *was* king of the Moabites at that time. ⁵Then ^ehe sent messengers to Balaam the son of Beor at ^fPethor, which *is* near the River* in the land of the sons of his people,* to call him, saying: "Look, a people has come from Egypt. See, they cover the face of the earth, and are settling next to me! ⁶^gTherefore please come at once, ^hcurse this people for me, for they *are* too mighty for me. Perhaps I shall be able to defeat them and drive them out of the land, for I know that he whom you bless *is* blessed, and he whom you curse is cursed."

⁷So the elders of Moab and the elders of

---

* **21:20** Hebrew *Jeshimon*   * **22:5** That is, the Euphrates • Or *the people of Amau*

21:21 king of the Amorites. The Amorites were one of the peoples that God had commissioned Israel to destroy (Ex. 33:2; 34:11).

21:21–24 Saying No to God—A stubborn "no" to an innocent and reasonable request can produce a counter-reaction. It is not that it is wrong to ever say "no," but the key fault on the part of the Amorites was a hard-hearted refusal to consider a request that would cost them nothing to grant. With God's wis-dom, we need to consider our words carefully, and "if it is possible, as much as depends on you, live peace-ably with all men" (Rom. 12:18).

21:27–32 people of Chemosh. This song begins with a recital of the earlier victory of the Amorites over the people of Moab and their god Chemosh. After defeat-ing Sihon and the Amorites, Israel became a formida-ble threat to Moab. The Moabites were pointing out that the Moabites' god did not help them. Now that

the Amorites had been defeated, it was clear that the God of Israel was greater than the gods of both the Moabites and the Amorites.

22:5 Balaam. Balak hired Balaam to destroy Israel by spiritual means. He thought that Balaam could cause Israel's "gods" to stop protecting them.

22:6 he whom you curse is cursed. The reality is that

21:20 ^u Num. 23:28   **21:21** ^v Deut. 2:26–37
21:22 ^w Num. 20:16, 17   **21:23** ^x Deut. 29:7 ^y Judg. 11:20
21:24 ^z Amos 2:9   **21:25** ^a Amos 2:10   **21:28** ^b Jer.
48:45, 46 ^c Is. 15:1 ^d Num. 22:41; 33:52   **21:29** ^e Jer.
48:46 ^f Judg. 11:24 ^g Is. 15:2, 5 ^h Is. 16:2   **21:30** ⁱ Num.
32:3, 34 ^j Is. 15:2   **21:32** ^k Jer. 48:32   **21:33** ^l Deut.
29:7 ^m Deut. 3:1 ⁿ Josh. 13:12   **21:34** ^o Deut. 3:2 ^p Num.
21:24   **21:35** ^q Deut. 3:3, 4; 29:7   **22:1** ^a Num. 33:48,
49   **22:2** ^b Judg. 11:25   **22:3** ^c Ex. 15:15   **22:4** ^d Num.
25:15–18; 31:1–3   **22:5** ^e 2 Pet. 2:15 ^f Deut. 23:4
22:6 ^g Num. 22:17; 23:7, 8 ^h Num. 22:12; 24:9

Midian departed with the [i]diviner's fee in their hand, and they came to Balaam and spoke to him the words of Balak. [8]And he said to them, [j]"Lodge here tonight, and I will bring back word to you, as the LORD speaks to me." So the princes of Moab stayed with Balaam.

[9k]Then God came to Balaam and said, "Who *are* these men with you?"

[10]So Balaam said to God, "Balak the son of Zippor, king of Moab, has sent to me, *saying,* [11]'Look, a people has come out of Egypt, and they cover the face of the earth. Come now, curse them for me; perhaps I shall be able to overpower them and drive them out.'"

[12]And God said to Balaam, "You shall not go with them; you shall not curse the people, for [l]they *are* blessed."

[13]So Balaam rose in the morning and said to the princes of Balak, "Go back to your land, for the LORD has refused to give me permission to go with you."

[14]And the princes of Moab rose and went to Balak, and said, "Balaam refuses to come with us."

[15]Then Balak again sent princes, more numerous and more honorable than they. [16]And they came to Balaam and said to him, "Thus says Balak the son of Zippor: 'Please let nothing hinder you from coming to me; [17]for I will certainly [m]honor you greatly, and I will do whatever you say to me. [n]Therefore please come, curse this people for me.'"

[18]Then Balaam answered and said to the servants of Balak, [o]"Though Balak were to give me his house full of silver and gold, [p]I could not go beyond the word of the LORD my God, to do less or more. [19]Now therefore, please, you also [q]stay here tonight, that I may know what more the LORD will say to me."

[20r]And God came to Balaam at night and said to him, "If the men come to call you,

rise *and* go with them; but [s]only the word which I speak to you—that you shall do." [21]So Balaam rose in the morning, saddled his donkey, and went with the princes of Moab.

Balaam, the Donkey, and the Angel

[22]Then God's anger was aroused because he went, [t]and the Angel of the LORD took His stand in the way as an adversary against him. And he was riding on his donkey, and his two servants *were* with him. [23]Now [u]the donkey saw the Angel of the LORD standing in the way with His drawn sword in His hand, and the donkey turned aside out of the way and went into the field. So Balaam struck the donkey to turn her back onto the road. [24]Then the Angel of the LORD stood in a narrow path between the vineyards, *with* a wall on this side and a wall on that side. [25]And when the donkey saw the Angel of the LORD, she pushed herself against the wall and crushed Balaam's foot against the wall; so he struck her again. [26]Then the Angel of the LORD went further, and stood in a narrow place where there *was* no way to turn either to the right hand or to the left. [27]And when the donkey saw the Angel of the LORD, she lay down under Balaam; so Balaam's anger was aroused, and he struck the donkey with his staff.

[28]Then the LORD [v]opened the mouth of the donkey, and she said to Balaam, "What have I done to you, that you have struck me these three times?"

[29]And Balaam said to the donkey, "Because you have abused me. I wish there were a sword in my hand, [w]for now I would kill you!"

[30x]So the donkey said to Balaam, "*Am* I not your donkey on which you have ridden, ever since *I became* yours, to this day? Was I ever disposed to do this to you?"

And he said, "No."

God's blessing on Israel could not be tampered with. It is important to remember that the Creator God is the source of all blessing and that no evil can stand against God's blessing and protection.

22:8 *as the LORD speaks to me.* Balaam speaks of the Lord as if he were intimate with Him. No doubt he had heard of the Lord, and no doubt the Lord did give him the words to say when Balaam looked at the Israelites. But Balaam did not give the Lord God any greater place in his own life than he gave to pagan gods, as is evidenced by his subsequent actions.

22:18 *the LORD my God.* This is not a confession of faith on Balaam's part, but a bold and false claim to be a medium of Israel's "god." Balaam was motivated by greed, not by a desire to please the Lord (2 Pet. 2:15; Jude 11).

22:22 *God's anger was aroused because he went.* God had given Balaam permission to go, after he asked the second time, and yet God was angry. This is a little puzzling, but if we remember that God is not whimsical, it makes sense. God had already told Balaam "no," and when Balak's leaders came to him

again, Balaam came to God again, saying in essence, "but now there is a lot of money and power available, so let me run this by You again . . . ." He was treating the Lord as if He were any little demon god, who is appealed to by money and divination rituals. Balaam did not comprehend that he was dealing with the real, powerful, awesome, and almighty God, until he encountered the angel with his drawn sword. God had a plan, and He was going to use Balaam to sabotage Balak's plans in a way that would definitely communicate to Balak exactly who the Israelites' God was, and what His plan was for His people. But Balaam needed to understand that it was the Lord who was in charge, not Balaam and his divination methods.

22:7 [i] 1 Sam. 9:7, 8 **22:8** [j] Num. 22:19 **22:9** [k] Gen. 20:3 **22:12** [l] [Rom. 11:28] **22:17** [m] Num. 24:11 [n] Num. 22:6 **22:18** [o] Num. 22:38; 24:13 [p] 1 Kin. 22:14 **22:19** [q] Num. 22:8 **22:20** [r] Num. 22:9 [s] Num. 22:35; 23:5, 12, 16, 26; 24:13 **22:22** [t] Ex. 4:24 **22:23** [u] Josh. 5:13 **22:28** [v] 2 Pet. 2:16 **22:29** [w] [Prov. 12:10] **22:30** [x] 2 Pet. 2:16

31 Then the LORD [y]opened Balaam's eyes, and he saw the Angel of the LORD standing in the way with His drawn sword in His hand; and he bowed his head and fell flat on his face. 32 And the Angel of the LORD said to him, "Why have you struck your donkey these three times? Behold, I have come out to stand against you, because *your* way is [z]perverse before Me. 33 The donkey saw Me and turned aside from Me these three times. If she had not turned aside from Me, surely I would also have killed you by now, and let her live."

34 And Balaam said to the Angel of the LORD, [a]"I have sinned, for I did not know You stood in the way against me. Now therefore, if it displeases You, I will turn back."

35 Then the Angel of the LORD said to Balaam, "Go with the men, [b]but only the word that I speak to you, that you shall speak." So Balaam went with the princes of Balak.

36 Now when Balak heard that Balaam was coming, [c]he went out to meet him at the city of Moab, [d]which *is* on the border at the Arnon, the boundary of the territory. 37 Then Balak said to Balaam, "Did I not earnestly send to you, calling for you? Why did you not come to me? Am I not able [e]to honor you?"

38 And Balaam said to Balak, "Look, I have come to you! Now, have I any power at all to say anything? [f]The word that God puts in my mouth, that I must speak." 39 So Balaam went with Balak, and they came to Kirjath Huzoth. 40 Then Balak offered oxen and sheep, and he sent *some* to Balaam and to the princes who *were* with him.

Balaam's First Prophecy

41 So it was, the next day, that Balak took Balaam and brought him up to the [g]high places of Baal, that from there he might observe the extent of the people.

23 Then Balaam said to Balak, [a]"Build seven altars for me here, and prepare for me here seven bulls and seven rams."

2 And Balak did just as Balaam had spoken, and Balak and Balaam [b]offered a bull and a ram on *each* altar. 3 Then Balaam said to Balak, [c]"Stand by your burnt offering, and I will go; perhaps the LORD will come [d]to meet me, and whatever He shows me I will tell you." So he went to a desolate height. 4 [e]And God met Balaam, and he said to Him, "I have prepared the seven altars, and I have offered on *each* altar a bull and a ram."

5 Then the LORD [f]put a word in Balaam's mouth, and said, "Return to Balak, and thus you shall speak." 6 So he returned to him, and there he was, standing by his burnt offering, he and all the princes of Moab.

7 And he [g]took up his oracle and said:

"Balak the king of Moab has brought
me from Aram,
From the mountains of the east.
[h]'Come, curse Jacob for me,
And come, [i]denounce Israel!'

8 "How[j] shall I curse whom God has not
cursed?
And how shall I denounce *whom* the
LORD has not denounced?
9 For from the top of the rocks I see him,
And from the hills I behold him;
There! [k]A people dwelling alone,
[l]Not reckoning itself among the
nations.

10 "Who[m] can count the dust* of Jacob,
Or number one-fourth of Israel?
Let me die [n]the death of the righteous,
And let my end be like his!"

11 Then Balak said to Balaam, "What have you done to me? [o]I took you to curse my enemies, and look, you have blessed *them* bountifully!"

12 So he answered and said, [p]"Must I not take heed to speak what the LORD has put in my mouth?"

Balaam's Second Prophecy

13 Then Balak said to him, "Please come with me to another place from which you may see them; you shall see only the outer part of them, and shall not see them all; curse them for me from there." 14 So he brought him to the field of Zophim, to the top of Pisgah, [q]and built seven altars, and offered a bull and a ram on *each* altar.

15 And he said to Balak, "Stand here by your burnt offering while I meet* *the LORD* over there."

16 Then the LORD met Balaam, and [r]put

*23:10 Or *dust cloud* *23:15 Following Masoretic Text, Targum, and Vulgate; Syriac reads *call;* Septuagint reads *go and ask God.*

23:5 *the LORD put a word in Balaam's mouth.* Even though Balaam was not a true servant of God, the words that Balaam spoke were truly God's blessing.
23:7–10 *took up his oracle.* The words that Balaam spoke, however unwillingly, certainly affirmed God's providence for the nation Israel. It is curious how the Lord used a mercenary and devious diviner to clearly speak the blessing on Israel, but that too was a part of God's providence. Balaam was claiming to speak for the Lord; the Lord would make sure that Balaam indeed spoke for Him.

22:31 [y]Gen. 21:19 **22:32** [z][2 Pet. 2:14, 15] **22:34** [a]2 Sam. 12:13 **22:35** [b]Num. 22:20 **22:36** [c]Gen. 14:17 [d]Num. 21:13 **22:37** [e]Num. 22:17; 24:11 **22:38** [f]1 Kin. 22:14 **22:41** [g]Num. 21:28 **23:1** [a]Num. 23:29 **23:2** [b]Num. 23:14, 30 **23:3** [c]Num. 23:15 [d]Num. 23:4, 16 **23:4** [e]Num. 23:16 **23:5** [f]Deut. 18:18 **23:7** [g]Deut. 23:4 [h]Num. 22:6, 11, 17 [i]1 Sam. 17:10 **23:8** [j]Num. 22:12 **23:9** [k]Deut. 32:8; 33:28 [l]Ex. 33:16 **23:10** [m]Gen. 13:16; 22:17; 28:14 [n]Ps. 116:15 **23:11** [o]Num. 22:11 **23:12** [p]Num. 22:38 **23:14** [q]Num. 23:1, 2 **23:16** [r]Num. 22:35; 23:5

a word in his mouth, and said, "Go back to Balak, and thus you shall speak." ¹⁷So he came to him, and there he was, standing by his burnt offering, and the princes of Moab were with him. And Balak said to him, "What has the LORD spoken?"

¹⁸Then he took up his oracle and said:

ˢ"Rise up, Balak, and hear!
Listen to me, son of Zippor!

¹⁹ "God ᵗ is not a man, that He should lie,
Nor a son of man, that He should repent.
Has He ᵘsaid, and will He not do?
Or has He spoken, and will He not make it good?

²⁰ Behold, I have received a command to bless;
ᵛHe has blessed, and I cannot reverse it.

²¹ "Heʷ has not observed iniquity in Jacob,
Nor has He seen wickedness in Israel.
The LORD his God is with him,
ˣAnd the shout of a King is among them.

²² ʸGod brings them out of Egypt;
He has ᶻstrength like a wild ox.

²³ "For there is no sorcery against Jacob,
Nor any divination against Israel.
It now must be said of Jacob
And of Israel, 'Oh, ᵃwhat God has done!'

²⁴ Look, a people rises ᵇlike a lioness,
And lifts itself up like a lion;
ᶜIt shall not lie down until it devours the prey,
And drinks the blood of the slain."

²⁵Then Balak said to Balaam, "Neither curse them at all, nor bless them at all!"

²⁶So Balaam answered and said to Balak, "Did I not tell you, saying, ᵈ'All that the LORD speaks, that I must do'?"

Balaam's Third Prophecy

²⁷Then Balak said to Balaam, "Please come, I will take you to another place; perhaps it will please God that you may curse them for me from there." ²⁸So Balak took Balaam to the top of Peor, that ᵉoverlooks the wasteland.* ²⁹Then Balaam said to Balak, "Build for me here seven altars, and prepare for me here seven bulls and seven rams." ³⁰And Balak did as Balaam had said, and offered a bull and a ram on every altar.

24 Now when Balaam saw that it pleased the LORD to bless Israel, he did not go

as at ᵃother times, to seek to use sorcery, but he set his face toward the wilderness. ²And Balaam raised his eyes, and saw Israel ᵇencamped according to their tribes; and ᶜthe Spirit of God came upon him.

³ᵈThen he took up his oracle and said:

"The utterance of Balaam the son of Beor,
The utterance of the man whose eyes are opened,

⁴ The utterance of him who hears the words of God,
Who sees the vision of the Almighty,
Who ᵉfalls down, with eyes wide open:

⁵ "How lovely are your tents, O Jacob!
Your dwellings, O Israel!

⁶ Like valleys that stretch out,
ᶠLike gardens by the riverside,
Like aloes ᵍplanted by the LORD,
Like cedars beside the waters.

⁷ He shall pour water from his buckets,
And his seed shall be ʰin many waters.

"His king shall be higher than ⁱAgag,
And his ʲkingdom shall be exalted.

⁸ "Godᵏ brings him out of Egypt;
He has strength like a wild ox;
He shall ˡconsume the nations, his enemies;
He shall ᵐbreak their bones
And ⁿpierce them with his arrows.

⁹ 'Heᵒ bows down, he lies down as a lion;
And as a lion, who shall rouse him?'*

ᵖ"Blessed is he who blesses you,
And cursed is he who curses you."

¹⁰Then Balak's anger was aroused against Balaam, and he ᵠstruck his hands together; and Balak said to Balaam, ʳ"I called you to curse my enemies, and look, you have bountifully blessed them these three times! ¹¹Now therefore, flee to your place. ˢI said I would greatly honor you, but in fact, the LORD has kept you back from honor."

¹²So Balaam said to Balak, "Did I not also speak to your messengers whom you sent to me, saying, ¹³'If Balak were to give me his house full of silver and gold, I could not go beyond the word of the LORD, to do good or bad of my own will. What the LORD says, that I must speak'? ¹⁴And now, indeed, I am going to my people. Come, ᵗI will advise you what this people will do to your people in the ᵘlatter days."

* 23:28 Hebrew Jeshimon   * 24:9 Genesis 49:9

23:18 ˢJudg. 3:20   23:19 ᵗMal. 3:6 ᵘ1 Kin. 8:56
23:20 ᵛNum. 22:12   23:21 ʷ[Rom. 4:7, 8] ˣPs. 89:15–18
23:22 ʸNum. 24:8 ᶻDeut. 33:17   23:23 ᵃPs. 31:19; 44:1
23:24 ᵇGen. 49:9 ᶜGen. 49:27   23:26 ᵈNum. 22:38
23:28 ᵉNum. 21:20   24:1 ᵃNum. 23:3, 15   24:2 ᵇNum.
2:2, 34 ᶜNum. 11:25   24:3 ᵈNum. 23:7, 18   24:4 ᵉEzek.

1:28   24:6 ᶠJer. 17:8 ᵍPs. 104:16   24:7 ʰJer. 51:13
ⁱ1 Sam. 15:8, 9 ʲ2 Sam. 5:12   24:8 ᵏNum. 23:22 ˡNum.
14:9; 23:24 ᵐPs. 2:9 ⁿPs. 45:5   24:9 ᵒGen. 49:9 ᵖGen.
12:3; 27:29   24:10 ᵠEzek. 21:14, 17 ʳNum. 23:11
24:11 ˢNum. 22:17, 37   24:14 ᵗ[Mic. 6:5] ᵘGen. 49:1

Balaam's Fourth Prophecy

¹⁵So he took up his oracle and said:

"The utterance of Balaam the son of
Beor,
And the utterance of the man whose
eyes are opened;
¹⁶ The utterance of him who hears the
words of God,
And has the knowledge of the Most
High,
Who sees the vision of the Almighty,
Who falls down, with eyes wide open:

¹⁷ "ᵛI see Him, but not now;
I behold Him, but not near;
ʷA Star shall come out of Jacob;
ˣA Scepter shall rise out of Israel,
And batter the brow of Moab,
And destroy all the sons of tumult.*

¹⁸ "And ʸEdom shall be a possession;
Seir also, his enemies, shall be a
possession,
While Israel does valiantly.
¹⁹ ᶻOut of Jacob One shall have dominion,
And destroy the remains of the city."

²⁰Then he looked on Amalek, and he
took up his oracle and said:

"Amalek *was* first among the nations,
But *shall be* last until he perishes."

²¹Then he looked on the Kenites, and he
took up his oracle and said:

"Firm is your dwelling place,
And your nest is set in the rock;
²² Nevertheless Kain shall be burned.
How long until Asshur carries you
away captive?"

²³Then he took up his oracle and said:

"Alas! Who shall live when God does
this?
²⁴ But ships *shall come* from the coasts
of ᵃCyprus,*
And they shall afflict Asshur and
afflict ᵇEber,
And so shall *Amalek,** until he
perishes."

²⁵So Balaam rose and departed and ᶜre-
turned to his place; Balak also went his
way.

Israel's Harlotry in Moab

25 Now Israel remained in ᵃAcacia
Grove,* and the ᵇpeople began to
commit harlotry with the women of Moab.
²ᶜThey invited the people to ᵈthe sacrifices of their gods, and the people ate and
ᵉbowed down to their gods. ³So Israel was
joined to Baal of Peor, and ᶠthe anger of the
LORD was aroused against Israel.
⁴Then the LORD said to Moses, ᵍ"Take
all the leaders of the people and hang the
offenders before the LORD, out in the sun,
ʰthat the fierce anger of the LORD may turn
away from Israel."
⁵So Moses said to ᶦthe judges of Israel,
ʲ"Every one of you kill his men who were
joined to Baal of Peor."
⁶And indeed, one of the children of Israel came and presented to his brethren
a Midianite woman in the sight of Moses
and in the sight of all the congregation of
the children of Israel, ᵏwho *were* weeping
at the door of the tabernacle of meeting.

---

* **24:17** Hebrew *Sheth* (compare Jeremiah 48:45)
* **24:24** Hebrew *Kittim* • Literally *he* or *that one*
* **25:1** Hebrew *Shittim*

**24:17–19 *I see him, but not now: . . . a Star shall
come out of Jacob.*** This poetic language clearly
refers to the Messiah. The pagan Balaam had a vision
of the coming of the Hebrew Messiah, the Lord Jesus
Christ. He was visible from afar, He was like a star,
radiant and beautiful. And He is the victor over His
enemies, including Moab—the nation that hired
Balaam to curse Israel.
24:19 *dominion.* At this point Balaam should have
repented of his involvement with Balak. It was clear
that the Lord God was in control, not Balaam, and
that the Lord's curses were not for hire. This should
be a great encouragement to believers in our day,
because we can trust in a God who has promised to
bless those who trust in Him. Our God will not change
His mind and forget those who have put their faith
in Him.
24:22 *until Asshur carries you away captive.*
Asshur is Assyria. This nation did take the rebellious
Northern Kingdom of Israel captive in 772 B.C.
25:1–3 *commit harlotry.* Right on the edge of the
Promised Land the Israelites had shown unfaithfulness to God again. It was not just that they had illicit
sex with women outside their nation. They had participated in the licentious worship of the Baal of Peor.
Worshiping idols on the side is not just a little slip, like
eating between meals. They had enough information

to know how seriously offended God would be, and
they just did not care. Such behavior is always likened to adultery, and this was something that God
rebuked His people for repeatedly (Is. 1:21; Jer. 3:1;
Ezek. 16; Hos. 2:5).
25:1 *the women of Moab.* What the men of Moab
could not do, the women were able to accomplish.
They trapped the Israelite men in sexual immorality and false worship. The principal instigator of
this sorry affair was none other than Balaam (31:16).
Perhaps the most sobering aspect is the fact that
the Moabites were descendants of Lot, through his
daughter's incestuous relationship with her father,
after their long sojourn in Sodom (Gen. 19). Sexual
perversion had a long history in this group.
25:4–5 *fierce anger of the LORD.* This was the most
serious challenge to God's authority yet. The people
had been seduced into joining the worship of Baal.
And it was Baal worship that they had been sent to
Canaan to eliminate.

24:17 ᵛRev. 1:7 ʷMatt. 2:2 ˣGen. 49:10 **24:18**ʸ2 Sam.
8:14 **24:19**ᶻAmos 9:11, 12 **24:24**ᵃGen. 10:4 ᵇGen.
10:21, 25 **24:25**ᶜNum. 21:34; 31:8 **25:1**ᵃJosh.
2:1 ᵇRev. 2:14 **25:2**ᶜHos. 9:10 ᵈEx. 34:15 ᵉEx. 20:5
25:3ᶠPs. 106:28, 29 **25:4**ᵍDeut. 4:3 ʰNum. 25:11
25:5ᶦEx. 18:21 ʲDeut. 13:6, 9 **25:6**ᵏJoel 2:17

7Now *l*when Phinehas *m*the son of Eleazar, the son of Aaron the priest, saw *it*, he rose from among the congregation and took a javelin in his hand; 8and he went after the man of Israel into the tent and thrust both of them through, the man of Israel, and the woman through her body. So *n*the plague was *o*stopped among the children of Israel. 9And *p*those who died in the plague were twenty-four thousand.

10Then the LORD spoke to Moses, saying: 11*a*"Phinehas the son of Eleazar, the son of Aaron the priest, has turned back My wrath from the children of Israel, because he was zealous with My zeal among them, so that I did not consume the children of Israel in *r*My zeal. 12Therefore say, *s*'Behold, I give to him *t*My covenant of peace; 13and it shall be to him and *u*his descendants after him a covenant of *v*an everlasting priesthood, because he was *w*zealous for his God, and *x*made atonement for the children of Israel.'"

14Now the name of the Israelite who was killed, who was killed with the Midianite woman, *was* Zimri the son of Salu, a leader of a father's house among the Simeonites. 15And the name of the Midianite woman who was killed *was* Cozbi the daughter of *y*Zur; he *was* head of the people of a father's house in Midian.

16Then the LORD spoke to Moses, saying: 17*z*"Harass the Midianites, and attack them; 18for they harassed you with their *a*schemes by which they seduced you in the matter of Peor and in the matter of Cozbi, the daughter of a leader of Midian, their sister, who was killed in the day of the plague because of Peor."

The Second Census of Israel

26 And it came to pass, after the *a*plague, that the LORD spoke to Moses and Eleazar the son of Aaron the priest, saying: 2*b*"Take a census of all the congregation of the children of Israel *c*from twenty years old and above, by their fathers' houses, all who are able to go to war in Israel." 3So Moses and Eleazar the priest spoke with them *d*in the plains of Moab by the Jordan, *across from* Jericho, saying: 4*"Take a census of the people from twenty years old and above, just as the LORD *e*commanded Moses and the children of Israel who came out of the land of Egypt."

5*f*Reuben *was* the firstborn of Israel.

The children of Reuben *were: of* Hanoch, the family of the Hanochites; *of* Pallu, the family of the Palluites; 6*of* Hezron, the family of the Hezronites; *of* Carmi, the family of the Carmites. 7These *are* the families of the Reubenites: those who were numbered of them were forty-three thousand seven hundred and thirty. 8And the son of Pallu *was* Eliab. 9The sons of Eliab *were* Nemuel, Dathan, and Abiram. These *are* the Dathan and Abiram, *g*representatives of the congregation, who contended against Moses and Aaron in the company of Korah, when they contended against the LORD; 10*h*and the earth opened its mouth and swallowed them up together with Korah when that company died, when the fire devoured two hundred and fifty men; *i*and they became a sign. 11Nevertheless *j*the children of Korah did not die.

12The sons of Simeon according to their families *were: of* Nemuel,* the family of the Nemuelites; *of* Jamin, the family of the Jaminites; *of* Jachin,* the family of the Jachinites; 13*of* Zerah,* the family of the Zarhites; *of* Shaul, the family of the Shaulites. 14These *are* the families of the Simeonites: twenty-two thousand two hundred.

15The sons of Gad according to their families *were: of* Zephon,* the family of the Zephonites; *of* Haggi, the family of the Haggites; *of* Shuni, the family of the Shunites; 16*of* Ozni,* the family of the Oznites; *of* Eri, the family of the Erites; 17*of* Arod,* the family of the Arodites; *of* Areli, the family of the Arelites. 18These *are* the families of the sons of Gad according to those who were numbered of them: forty thousand five hundred.

19*k*The sons of Judah *were* Er and Onan; and Er and Onan died in the land of Canaan. 20And *l*the sons of Judah according to their families were: *of* Shelah, the family of the Shelanites; *of* Perez, the family of the Parzites; *of* Zerah, the family of the Zarhites. 21And the sons of Perez *were: of* Hezron, the family of the Hezronites; *of* Hamul, the family of the Hamulites.

---

* **26:12** Spelled *Jemuel* in Genesis 46:10 and Exodus 6:15 • Called *Jarib* in 1 Chronicles 4:24 * **26:13** Called *Zohar* in Genesis 46:10 * **26:15** Called *Ziphion* in Genesis 46:16 * **26:16** Called *Ezbon* in Genesis 46:16 * **26:17** Spelled *Arodi* in Samaritan Pentateuch, Syriac, and Genesis 46:16

25:7 Phinehas the son of Eleazar. For this decisive and courageous act, Phinehas is praised, not only in this book, but in Psalm 106:30–31. In the psalm, it says that this act was "accounted to him for righteousness." **26:2 Take a census of all the congregation.** The plague is over, the old generation has all died. This is a new beginning and a new census. Despite all the people who had died in the wilderness, the total population was not significantly different than the first census.

25:7 *l*Ps. 106:30 *m*Ex. 6:25 **25:8** *n*Ps. 106:30 *o*Num. 16:46–48 **25:9** *p*Deut. 4:3 **25:11** *q*Ps. 106:30 *r*[Ex. 20:5] **25:12** *s*[Mal. 2:4, 5; 3:1] *t*Is. 54:10 **25:13** *u*1 Chr. 6:4–15 *v*Ex. 40:15 *w*Acts 22:3 *x*[Heb. 2:17] **25:15** *y*Num. 31:8 **25:17** *z*Num. 31:1–3 **25:18** *a*Rev. 2:14 **26:1** *a*Num. 25:9 **26:2** *b*Num. 1:2; 14:29 *c*Num. 1:3 **26:3** *d*Num. 22:1; 31:12; 33:48; 35:1 **26:4** *e*Num. 1:1 **26:5** *f*Ex. 6:14 **26:9** *g*Num. 1:16; 16:1, 2 **26:10** *h*Num. 16:32–35 *i*Num. 16:38–40 **26:11** *j*Ex. 6:24 **26:19** *k*Gen. 38:2; 46:12 **26:20** *l*1 Chr. 2:3

22These *are* the families of Judah according to those who were numbered of them: seventy-six thousand five hundred.

23The sons of Issachar according to their families *were: of* Tola, the family of the Tolaites; of Puah,* the family of the Punites;* 24of Jashub, the family of the Jashubites; of Shimron, the family of the Shimronites. 25These *are* the families of Issachar according to those who were numbered of them: sixty-four thousand three hundred.

26mThe sons of Zebulun according to their families *were:* of Sered, the family of the Sardites; of Elon, the family of the Elonites; of Jahleel, the family of the Jahleelites. 27These *are* the families of the Zebulunites according to those who were numbered of them: sixty thousand five hundred.

28nThe sons of Joseph according to their families, by Manasseh and Ephraim, *were:* 29The sons of oManasseh: of pMachir, the family of the Machirites; and Machir begot Gilead; of Gilead, the family of the Gileadites. 30These *are* the sons of Gilead: *of* Jeezer,* the family of the Jeezerites; of Helek, the family of the Helekites; 31*of* Asriel, the family of the Asrielites; *of* Shechem, the family of the Shechemites; 32*of* Shemida, the family of the Shemidaites; *of* Hepher, the family of the Hepherites. 33Now qZelophehad the son of Hepher had no sons, but daughters; and the names of the daughters of Zelophehad *were* Mahlah, Noah, Hoglah, Milcah, and Tirzah. 34These *are* the families of Manasseh; and those who were numbered of them *were* fifty-two thousand seven hundred.

35These *are* the sons of Ephraim according to their families: of Shuthelah, the family of the Shuthalhites; of Becher,* the family of the Bachrites; of Tahan, the family of the Tahanites. 36And these *are* the sons of Shuthelah: of Eran, the family of the Eranites. 37These *are* the families of the sons of Ephraim according to those who were numbered of them: thirty-two thousand five hundred.

These *are* the sons of Joseph according to their families.

38rThe sons of Benjamin according to their families were: of Bela, the family of the Belaites; of Ashbel, the family of the Ashbelites; of sAhiram, the family of the Ahiramites; 39of tShupham,* the family of the Shuphamites; of Hupham,* the family of the Huphamites. 40And the sons of Bela were Ard* and Naaman; uof Ard, the family of the Ardites; of Naaman, the family of the Naamites. 41These *are* the sons of Benjamin according to their families; and those

who were numbered of them *were* forty-five thousand six hundred.

42These *are* the sons of Dan according to their families: of Shuham,* the family of the Shuhamites. These *are* the families of Dan according to their families. 43All the families of the Shuhamites, according to those who were numbered of them, *were* sixty-four thousand four hundred.

44vThe sons of Asher according to their families *were:* of Jimna, the family of the Jimnites; of Jesui, the family of the Jesuites; of Beriah, the family of the Beriites. 45Of the sons of Beriah: of Heber, the family of the Heberites; of Malchiel, the family of the Malchielites. 46And the name of the daughter of Asher *was* Serah. 47These *are* the families of the sons of Asher according to those who were numbered of them: fifty-three thousand four hundred.

48wThe sons of Naphtali according to their families *were:* of Jahzeel,* the family of the Jahzeelites; of Guni, the family of the Gunites; 49of Jezer, the family of the Jezerites; of xShillem, the family of the Shillemites. 50These *are* the families of Naphtali according to their families; and those who were numbered of them *were* forty-five thousand four hundred.

51yThese *are* those who were numbered of the children of Israel: six hundred and one thousand seven hundred and thirty.

52Then the LORD spoke to Moses, saying: 53z"To these the land shall be adivided as an inheritance, according to the number of names. 54bTo a large *tribe* you shall give a larger inheritance, and to a small *tribe* you shall give a smaller inheritance. Each shall be given its inheritance according to those who were numbered of them. 55But the land shall be cdivided by lot; they shall inherit according to the names of the tribes of their fathers. 56According to the lot their inheritance shall be divided between the larger and the smaller."

57dAnd these *are* those who were numbered of the Levites according to their families: of Gershon, the family of the Gershonites; of Kohath, the family of the

---

* **26:23** Hebrew *Puvah* (compare Genesis 46:13 and 1 Chronicles 7:1); Samaritan Pentateuch, Septuagint, Syriac, and Vulgate read *Puah*. • Samaritan Pentateuch, Septuagint, Syriac, and Vulgate read *Puaites*.   * **26:30** Called *Abiezer* in Joshua 17:2   * **26:35** Called *Bered* in 1 Chronicles 7:20   * **26:39** Masoretic Text reads *Shephupham*, spelled *Shephuphan* in 1 Chronicles 8:5. • Called *Huppim* in Genesis 46:21   * **26:40** Called *Addar* in 1 Chronicles 8:3   * **26:42** Called *Hushim* in Genesis 46:23   * **26:48** Spelled *Jahziel* in 1 Chronicles 7:13

26:51 *those who were numbered.* The totals of the twelve tribes are very similar. Some had increased, some had decreased. The final figure shows a slight decrease, from 603,550 to 601,730.

26:26 m Gen. 46:14   **26:28** n Gen. 46:20   **26:29** o Josh. 17:1   p 1 Chr. 7:14, 15   **26:33** q Num. 27:1; 36:11   **26:38** r Gen. 46:21   s 1 Chr. 8:1, 2   **26:39** t 1 Chr. 7:12   **26:40** u 1 Chr. 8:3   **26:44** v Gen. 46:17   **26:48** w 1 Chr. 7:13   **26:49** x 1 Chr. 7:13   **26:51** y Num. 1:46; 11:21   **26:53** z Josh. 11:23; 14:1   a Num. 33:54   **26:54** b Num. 33:54   **26:55** c Num. 33:54; 34:13   **26:57** d Gen. 46:11

Kohathites; of Merari, the family of the Merarites. ⁵⁸These *are* the families of the Levites: the family of the Libnites, the family of the Hebronites, the family of the Mahlites, the family of the Mushites, and the family of the Korathites. And Kohath begot Amram. ⁵⁹The name of Amram's wife *was* ᵉJochebed the daughter of Levi, who was born to Levi in Egypt; and to Amram she bore Aaron and Moses and their sister Miriam. ⁶⁰ᶠTo Aaron were born Nadab and Abihu, Eleazar and Ithamar. ⁶¹And ᵍNadab and Abihu died when they offered profane fire before the LORD.

⁶²ʰNow those who were numbered of them were twenty-three thousand, every male from a month old and above; ⁱfor they were not numbered among the other children of Israel, because there was ʲno inheritance given to them among the children of Israel.

⁶³These *are* those who were numbered by Moses and Eleazar the priest, who numbered the children of Israel ᵏin the plains of Moab by the Jordan, *across from* Jericho. ⁶⁴ˡBut among these there was not a man of those who were numbered by Moses and Aaron the priest when they numbered the children of Israel in the ᵐWilderness of Sinai. ⁶⁵For the LORD had said of them, "They ⁿshall surely die in the wilderness." So there was not left a man of them, ᵒexcept Caleb the son of Jephunneh and Joshua the son of Nun.

Inheritance Laws

27 Then came the daughters of ᵃZelophehad the son of Hepher, the son of Gilead, the son of Machir, the son of Manasseh, from the families of Manasseh the son of Joseph; and these *were* the names of his daughters: Mahlah, Noah, Hoglah, Milcah, and Tirzah. ²And they stood before Moses, before Eleazar the priest, and before the leaders and all the congregation, *by* the doorway of the tabernacle of meeting, saying: ³"Our father ᵇdied in the wilderness; but he was not in the company of those who gathered together against the LORD, ᶜin company with Korah, but he died in his own sin; and he had no sons. ⁴Why

should the name of our father be ᵈremoved from among his family because he had no son? ᵉGive us a possession among our father's brothers."

⁵So Moses ᶠbrought their case before the LORD.

⁶And the LORD spoke to Moses, saying: ⁷"The daughters of Zelophehad speak *what is* right; ᵍyou shall surely give them a possession of inheritance among their father's brothers, and cause the inheritance of their father to pass to them. ⁸And you shall speak to the children of Israel, saying: 'If a man dies and has no son, then you shall cause his inheritance to pass to his daughter. ⁹If he has no daughter, then you shall give his inheritance to his brothers. ¹⁰If he has no brothers, then you shall give his inheritance to his father's brothers. ¹¹And if his father has no brothers, then you shall give his inheritance to the relative closest to him in his family, and he shall possess it.'" And it shall be to the children of Israel ʰa statute of judgment, just as the LORD commanded Moses.

Joshua the Next Leader of Israel

¹²Now the LORD said to Moses: ⁱ"Go up into this Mount Abarim, and see the land which I have given to the children of Israel. ¹³And when you have seen it, you also ʲshall be gathered to your people, as Aaron your brother was gathered. ¹⁴For in the Wilderness of Zin, during the strife of the congregation, you ᵏrebelled against My command to hallow Me at the waters before their eyes." (These *are* the ˡwaters of Meribah, at Kadesh in the Wilderness of Zin.)

¹⁵Then Moses spoke to the LORD, saying: ¹⁶"Let the LORD, ᵐthe God of the spirits of all flesh, set a man over the congregation, ¹⁷ⁿwho may go out before them and go in before them, who may lead them out and bring them in, that the congregation of the LORD may not be ᵒlike sheep which have no shepherd."

¹⁸And the LORD said to Moses: "Take Joshua the son of Nun with you, a man ᵖin whom *is* the Spirit, and ᵠlay your hand on him; ¹⁹set him before Eleazar the priest

---

27:1–5 the daughters of Zelophehad. In ancient Israel, women did not inherit land. Yet because their case made sense, Moses took the issue to the Lord.

27:7 speak what is right. Justice was done to women regarding inheritance because Moses took the case to God, and His truth was used as the foundation for the decree. Only as we base our decisions in life on God's truth, as expressed in the Bible and in Jesus Himself, will we be acting in truth. Any other way can bring injustice and decisions regretted because they spring from error.

27:18 Holy Spirit—Joshua was "a man in whom is the Spirit." In the Old Testament, only a few people had the Holy Spirit. It was not until after Jesus' resurrection that the Holy Spirit indwelt every believer. The way that God speaks to the heart of man, apart

from the written Word, has generally been through the quiet voice of the Holy Spirit. Joshua apparently was a man led by the voice of the Spirit of God. He is not pictured as seeing visions or being led by angels, yet his leadership was effective and faithful.

26:59 ᵉEx. 2:1, 2; 6:20 **26:60** ᶠNum. 3:2 **26:61** ᵍLev. 10:1, 2 **26:62** ʰNum. 3:39 ⁱNum. 1:49 ʲNum. 18:20, 23, 24 **26:63** ᵏNum. 26:3 **26:64** ˡNum. 14:29–35 ᵐNum. 1:1–46 **26:65** ⁿNum. 14:26–35 ᵒNum. 14:30 **27:1** ᵈNum. 26:33; 36:1, 11 **27:3** ᵇNum. 14:35; 26:64, 65 ᶜNum. 16:1, 2 **27:4** ᵈDeut. 25:6 ᵉJosh. 17:4 **27:5** ᶠEx. 18:13–26 **27:7** ᵍNum. 36:2 **27:11** ʰNum. 35:29 **27:12** ⁱNum. 33:47 **27:13** ʲDeut. 10:6; 34:5, 6 **27:14** ᵏPs. 106:32, 33 ˡEx. 17:7 **27:16** ᵐNum. 16:22 **27:17** ⁿDeut. 31:2 ᵒZech. 10:2 **27:18** ᵖGen. 41:38 ᵠDeut. 34:9

and before all the congregation, and *r*inaugurate him in their sight. 20And *s*you shall give *some* of your authority to him, that all the congregation of the children of Israel *t*may be obedient. 21*u*He shall stand before Eleazar the priest, who shall inquire before the LORD for him *v*by the judgment of the Urim. *w*At his word they shall go out, and at his word they shall come in, he and all the children of Israel with him—all the congregation."

22So Moses did as the LORD commanded him. He took Joshua and set him before Eleazar the priest and before all the congregation. 23And he laid his hands on him *x*and inaugurated him, just as the LORD commanded by the hand of Moses.

Daily Offerings

28 Now the LORD spoke to Moses, saying, 2"Command the children of Israel, and say to them, 'My offering, *a*My food for My offerings made by fire as a sweet aroma to Me, you shall be careful to offer to Me at their appointed time.'

3"And you shall say to them, *b*'This *is* the offering made by fire which you shall offer to the LORD: two male lambs in their first year without blemish, day by day, as a regular burnt offering. 4The one lamb you shall offer in the morning, the other lamb you shall offer in the evening, 5and *c*onetenth of an ephah of fine flour as a *d*grain offering mixed with one-fourth of a hin of pressed oil. 6*It is e*a regular burnt offering which was ordained at Mount Sinai for a sweet aroma, an offering made by fire to the LORD. 7And its drink offering *shall be* one-fourth of a hin for each lamb; *f*in a holy *place* you shall pour out the drink to the LORD as an offering. 8The other lamb you shall offer in the evening; as the morning grain offering and its drink offering, you shall offer *it* as an offering made by fire, a sweet aroma to the LORD.

Sabbath Offerings

9'And on the Sabbath day two lambs in their first year, without blemish, and twotenths *of an ephah* of fine flour as a grain offering, mixed with oil, with its drink offering— 10*this is g*the burnt offering for every Sabbath, besides the regular burnt offering with its drink offering.

Monthly Offerings

11*h*'At the beginnings of your months you shall present a burnt offering to the

LORD: two young bulls, one ram, and seven lambs in their first year, without blemish; 12*i*three-tenths *of an ephah* of fine flour as a grain offering, mixed with oil, for each bull; two-tenths *of an ephah* of fine flour as a grain offering, mixed with oil, for the one ram; 13and one-tenth *of an ephah* of fine flour, mixed with oil, as a grain offering for each lamb, as a burnt offering of sweet aroma, an offering made by fire to the LORD. 14Their drink offering shall be half a hin of wine for a bull, one-third of a hin for a ram, and one-fourth of a hin for a lamb; this *is* the burnt offering for each month throughout the months of the year. 15Also *j*one kid of the goats as a sin offering to the LORD shall be offered, besides the regular burnt offering and its drink offering.

Offerings at Passover

16*k*'On the fourteenth day of the first month *is* the Passover of the LORD. 17*l*And on the fifteenth day of this month *is* the feast; unleavened bread shall be eaten for seven days. 18On the *m*first day *you shall* have a holy convocation. You shall do no customary work. 19And you shall present an offering made by fire as a burnt offering to the LORD: two young bulls, one ram, and seven lambs in their first year. *n*Be sure they are without blemish. 20Their grain offering shall be of fine flour mixed with oil: three-tenths *of an ephah* you shall offer for a bull, and two-tenths for a ram; 21you shall offer one-tenth *of an ephah* for each of the seven lambs; 22also *o*one goat *as* a sin offering, to make atonement for you. 23You shall offer these besides the burnt offering of the morning, which *is* for a regular burnt offering. 24In this manner you shall offer the food of the offering made by fire daily for seven days, as a sweet aroma to the LORD; it shall be offered besides the regular burnt offering and its drink offering. 25And *p*on the seventh day you shall have a holy convocation. You shall do no customary work.

Offerings at the Feast of Weeks

26'Also *q*on the day of the firstfruits, when you bring a new grain offering to the LORD at your *Feast of* Weeks, you shall have a holy convocation. You shall do no customary work. 27You shall present a burnt offering as a sweet aroma to the LORD: *r*two young bulls, one ram, and seven lambs in their first year, 28with their grain offering of fine flour mixed with oil: three-tenths *of an ephah* for each bull,

---

28:26 *Feast of Weeks.* The Feast of Weeks occurred 50 days after Passover and the Feast of Unleavened Bread.

27:19 *r* Deut. 3:28; 31:3, 7, 8, 23   **27:20** *s* Num. 11:17
t Josh. 1:16–18   **27:21** *u* 1 Sam. 23:9; 30:7   *v* Ex. 28:30
w 1 Sam. 22:10   **27:23** *x* Deut. 3:28; 31:7, 8   **28:2** *a* Lev.

3:11; 21:6, 8   **28:3** *b* Ex. 29:38–42   **28:5** *c* Ex.
16:36   *d* Lev. 2:1   **28:6** *e* Ex. 29:42   **28:7** *f* Ex. 29:42
28:10 *g* Ezek. 46:4   **28:11** *h* Num. 10:10   **28:12** *i* Num.
15:4–12   **28:15** *j* Num. 15:24; 28:3, 22   **28:16** *k* Lev.
23:5–8   **28:17** *l* Lev. 23:6   **28:18** *m* Lev. 23:7
28:19 *n* Deut. 15:21   **28:22** *o* Num. 28:15   **28:25** *p* Lev.
23:8   **28:26** *q* Deut. 16:9–12   **28:27** *r* Lev. 23:18, 19

two-tenths for the one ram, [29]and one-tenth for each of the seven lambs; [30]*also* one kid of the goats, to make atonement for you. [31]sBe sure they are without blemish. You shall present *them* with their drink offerings, besides the regular burnt offering with its grain offering.

Offerings at the Feast of Trumpets

29 'And in the seventh month, on the first *day* of the month, you shall have a holy convocation. You shall do no customary work. For you *a*it is a day of blowing the trumpets. [2]You shall offer a burnt offering as a sweet aroma to the LORD: one young bull, one ram, *and* seven lambs in their first year, without blemish. [3]Their grain offering *shall be* fine flour mixed with oil: three-tenths *of an ephah* for the bull, two-tenths for the ram, [4]and one-tenth for each of the seven lambs; [5]also one kid of the goats *as* a sin offering, to make atonement for you; [6]besides *b*the burnt offering with its grain offering for the New Moon, *c*the regular burnt offering with its grain offering, and their drink offerings, *d*according to their ordinance, as a sweet aroma, an offering made by fire to the LORD.

Offerings on the Day of Atonement

[7]e'On the tenth *day* of this seventh month you shall have a holy convocation. You shall *f*afflict your souls; you shall not do any work. [8]You shall present a burnt offering to the LORD as a sweet aroma: one young bull, one ram, *and* seven lambs in their first year. *g*Be sure they are without blemish. [9]Their grain offering *shall be of* fine flour mixed with oil: three-tenths *of an ephah* for the bull, two-tenths for the one ram, [10]and one-tenth for each of the seven lambs; [11]also one kid of the goats *as* a sin offering, besides *h*the sin offering for atonement, the regular burnt offering with its grain offering, and their drink offerings.

Offerings at the Feast of Tabernacles

[12]i'On the fifteenth day of the seventh month you shall have a holy convocation.

You shall do no customary work, and you shall keep a feast to the LORD seven days. [13]jYou shall present a burnt offering, an offering made by fire as a sweet aroma to the LORD: thirteen young bulls, two rams, *and* fourteen lambs in their first year. They shall be without blemish. [14]Their grain offering *shall be of* fine flour mixed with oil: three-tenths *of an ephah* for each of the thirteen bulls, two-tenths for each of the two rams, [15]and one-tenth for each of the fourteen lambs; [16]also one kid of the goats *as* a sin offering, besides the regular burnt offering, its grain offering, and its drink offering.

[17]'On the *k*second day *present* twelve young bulls, two rams, fourteen lambs in their first year without blemish, [18]and their grain offering and their drink offerings for the bulls, for the rams, and for the lambs, by their number, *l*according to the ordinance; [19]also one kid of the goats *as* a sin offering, besides the regular burnt offering with its grain offering, and their drink offerings.

[20]'On the third day *present* eleven bulls, two rams, fourteen lambs in their first year without blemish, [21]and their grain offering and their drink offerings for the bulls, for the rams, and for the lambs, by their number, *m*according to the ordinance; [22]also one goat *as* a sin offering, besides the regular burnt offering, its grain offering, and its drink offering.

[23]'On the fourth day *present* ten bulls, two rams, *and* fourteen lambs in their first year, without blemish, [24]and their grain offering and their drink offerings for the bulls, for the rams, and for the lambs, by their number, according to the ordinance; [25]also one kid of the goats *as* a sin offering, besides the regular burnt offering, its grain offering, and its drink offering.

[26]'On the fifth day *present* nine bulls, two rams, *and* fourteen lambs in their first year without blemish, [27]and their grain offering and their drink offerings for the bulls, for the rams, and for the lambs, by their number, according to the ordinance; [28]also one goat *as* a sin offering, besides

---

29:1–40 holy convocation. This chapter regulates offerings to the Lord during the three sacred festivals of the seventh month: the Feast of Trumpets, the Day of Atonement, and the Feast of Tabernacles. The Feast of Trumpets marked the beginning of Israel's civil year. It was a day of preparation for the next two celebrations. The Day of Atonement was a solemn day on which sins were confessed and special sacrifices made for the holy place, the priests, and the people. The Feast of Tabernacles was a time of rejoicing.
29:1 a day of blowing the trumpets. The celebration of the Feast of Trumpets involved blowing ram's horns. Later this festival became identified with the New Year festival.
29:11 offering for atonement. The Day of Atone-

ment, or Yom Kippur, was regarded as the most holy day of all. Leviticus 16 describes it as a day of fasting, rather than feasting.
29:12 feast to the LORD seven days. The celebration of the Feast of Tabernacles, or Succoth, included both sacrifices and eight days of "no work." In later years Israelites lived in tents or booths during this celebration, to commemorate the years that their ancestors lived in tents in the desert.

28:31 s Num. 28:3, 19 **29:1** a Lev. 23:23–25
29:6 b Num. 28:11–15 c Num. 28:3 d Num. 15:11, 12
29:7 e Lev. 16:29–34; 23:26–32 f Is. 58:5 **29:8** g Num.
28:19 **29:11** h Lev. 16:3, 5 **29:12** i Deut. 16:13–15
29:13 j Ezra 3:4 **29:17** k Lev. 23:36 **29:18** l Num. 15:12;
28:7, 14; 29:3, 4, 9, 10 **29:21** m Num. 29:18

the regular burnt offering, its grain offering, and its drink offering.

29‘On the sixth day *present* eight bulls, two rams, *and* fourteen lambs in their first year without blemish, 30and their grain offering and their drink offerings for the bulls, for the rams, and for the lambs, by their number, according to the ordinance; 31also one goat *as* a sin offering, besides the regular burnt offering, its grain offering, and its drink offering.

32‘On the seventh day *present* seven bulls, two rams, *and* fourteen lambs in their first year without blemish, 33and their grain offering and their drink offerings for the bulls, for the rams, and for the lambs, by their number, according to the ordinance; 34also one goat *as* a sin offering, besides the regular burnt offering, its grain offering, and its drink offering.

35‘On the eighth day you shall have a [n]sacred assembly. You shall do no customary work. 36You shall present a burnt offering, an offering made by fire as a sweet aroma to the LORD: one bull, one ram, seven lambs in their first year without blemish, 37and their grain offering and their drink offerings for the bull, for the ram, and for the lambs, by their number, according to the ordinance; 38also one goat *as* a sin offering, besides the regular burnt offering, its grain offering, and its drink offering.

39‘These you shall present to the LORD at [o]your appointed feasts (besides your [p]vowed offerings and your freewill offerings) as your burnt offerings and your grain offerings, as your drink offerings and your peace offerings.’ ”

40So Moses told the children of Israel everything, just as the LORD commanded Moses.

The Law Concerning Vows

30 Then Moses spoke to [a]the heads of the tribes concerning the children of Israel, saying, “This *is* the thing which the LORD has commanded: 2[b]If a man makes a vow to the LORD, or [c]swears an oath to bind himself by some agreement, he shall not break his word; he shall [d]do according to all that proceeds out of his mouth.

3“Or if a woman makes a vow to the LORD, and binds *herself* by some agreement while in her father’s house in her youth, 4and her father hears her vow and the agreement by which she has bound herself, and her father

holds his peace, then all her vows shall stand, and every agreement with which she has bound herself shall stand. 5But if her father overrules her on the day that he hears, then none of her vows nor her agreements by which she has bound herself shall stand; and the LORD will release her, because her father overruled her.

6“If indeed she takes a husband, while bound by her vows or by a rash utterance from her lips by which she bound herself, 7and her husband hears *it*, and makes no response to her on the day that he hears, then her vows shall stand, and her agreements by which she bound herself shall stand. 8But if her husband [e]overrules her on the day that he hears *it*, he shall make void her vow which she took and what she uttered with her lips, by which she bound herself, and the LORD will release her.

9“Also any vow of a widow or a divorced woman, by which she has bound herself, shall stand against her.

10“If she vowed in her husband’s house, or bound herself by an agreement with an oath, 11and her husband heard *it*, and made no response to her *and* did not overrule her, then all her vows shall stand, and every agreement by which she bound herself shall stand. 12But if her husband truly made them void on the day he heard *them*, then whatever proceeded from her lips concerning her vows or concerning the agreement binding her, it shall not stand; her husband has made them void, and the LORD will release her. 13Every vow and every binding oath to afflict her soul, her husband may confirm it, or her husband may make it void. 14Now if her husband makes no response whatever to her from day to day, then he confirms all her vows or all the agreements that bind her; he confirms them, because he made no response to her on the day that he heard *them*. 15But if he does make them void after he has heard *them*, then he shall bear her guilt.”

16These *are* the statutes which the LORD commanded Moses, between a man and his wife, and between a father and his daughter in her youth in her father’s house.

Vengeance on the Midianites

31 And the LORD spoke to Moses, saying: 2[a]“Take vengeance on the Midianites for the children of Israel. After ward you shall [b]be gathered to your people.”

30:2 *If a man makes a vow.* The key issue is clear: One who makes a vow shall not break his word. Vows that are made to the Lord must be carried out.
30:3 *if a woman.* In Israelite culture, an unmarried woman was under the protection of her father. If she made a vow, she might bring her father into an obligation that he did not want to fulfill, or could not fulfill. The same was true of a married woman (v. 6). Her vows would involve her husband, so the husband or father had to agree to the vow.

31:2 *Midianites.* The Midianites were descendants of Abraham and his wife Keturah, but were not part of the covenant that God had with Abraham, Isaac, and Jacob.

29:35 [n] Lev. 23:36   **29:39** [o] Lev. 23:1–44 [p] Lev. 7:16; 22:18, 21, 23; 23:38   **30:1** [a] Num. 1:4, 16; 7:2   **30:2** [b] Lev. 27:2 [c] Matt. 14:9 [d] Job 22:27   **30:8** [e] [Gen. 3:16]   **31:2** [a] Num. 25:17 [b] Num. 27:12, 13

³So Moses spoke to the people, saying, "Arm some of yourselves for war, and let them go against the Midianites to take vengeance for the LORD on ᶜMidian. ⁴A thousand from each tribe of all the tribes of Israel you shall send to the war."

⁵So there were recruited from the divisions of Israel one thousand from *each* tribe, twelve thousand armed for war. ⁶Then Moses sent them to the war, one thousand from *each* tribe; he sent them to the war with Phinehas the son of Eleazar the priest, with the holy articles and ᵈthe signal trumpets in his hand. ⁷And they warred against the Midianites, just as the LORD commanded Moses, and ᵉthey killed all the ᶠmales. ⁸They killed the kings of Midian with *the rest of* those who were killed—ᵍEvi, Rekem, ʰZur, Hur, and Reba, the five kings of Midian. ⁱBalaam the son of Beor they also killed with the sword.

⁹And the children of Israel took the women of Midian captive, with their little ones, and took as spoil all their cattle, all their flocks, and all their goods. ¹⁰They also burned with fire all the cities where they dwelt, and all their forts. ¹¹And ʲthey took all the spoil and all the booty—of man and beast.

Return from the War

¹²Then they brought the captives, the booty, and the spoil to Moses, to Eleazar the priest, and to the congregation of the children of Israel, to the camp in the plains of Moab by the Jordan, *across from* Jericho. ¹³And Moses, Eleazar the priest, and all the leaders of the congregation, went to meet them outside the camp. ¹⁴But Moses was angry with the officers of the army, *with* the captains over thousands and captains over hundreds, who had come from the battle.

¹⁵And Moses said to them: "Have you kept ᵏall the women alive? ¹⁶Look, ˡthese *women* caused the children of Israel, through the ᵐcounsel of Balaam, to trespass against the LORD in the incident of Peor, and ⁿthere was a plague among the congregation of the LORD. ¹⁷Now therefore, ᵒkill every male among the little ones, and kill every woman who has known a man intimately. ¹⁸But keep alive ᵖfor yourselves

all the young girls who have not known a man intimately. ¹⁹And as for you, �q remain outside the camp seven days; whoever has killed any person, and ʳwhoever has touched any slain, purify yourselves and your captives on the third day and on the seventh day. ²⁰Purify every garment, everything made of leather, everything woven of goats' *hair,* and everything made of wood."

²¹Then Eleazar the priest said to the men of war who had gone to the battle, "This *is* the ordinance of the law which the LORD commanded Moses: ²²Only the gold, the silver, the bronze, the iron, the tin, and the lead, ²³everything that can endure fire, you shall put through the fire, and it shall be clean; and it shall be purified ˢwith the water of purification. But all that cannot endure fire you shall put through water. ²⁴ᵗAnd you shall wash your clothes on the seventh day and be clean, and afterward you may come into the camp."

Division of the Plunder

²⁵Now the LORD spoke to Moses, saying: ²⁶"Count up the plunder that was taken—of man and beast—you and Eleazar the priest and the chief fathers of the congregation; ²⁷and ᵘdivide the plunder into two parts, between those who took part in the war, who went out to battle, and all the congregation. ²⁸And levy a tribute for the LORD on the men of war who went out to battle: ᵛone of every five hundred of the persons, the cattle, the donkeys, and the sheep; ²⁹take *it* from their half, and ʷgive *it* to Eleazar the priest as a heave offering to the LORD. ³⁰And from the children of Israel's half you shall take ˣone of every fifty, drawn from the persons, the cattle, the donkeys, and the sheep, from all the livestock, and give them to the Levites ʸwho keep charge of the tabernacle of the LORD." ³¹So Moses and Eleazar the priest did as the LORD commanded Moses.

³²The booty remaining from the plunder, which the men of war had taken, was six hundred and seventy-five thousand sheep, ³³seventy-two thousand cattle, ³⁴sixty-one thousand donkeys, ³⁵and thirty-two thousand persons in all, of women who had not known a man intimately.

31:7–16 Unfaithfulness—Moses was ordered to campaign against the Midianites because of their wicked involvement in the seduction of Israel (25:17–18). He was angry with the officers of the army because they had not carried out the Lord's directive concerning the women who had caused Israel to act unfaithfully toward the Lord. There was no excuse for the officers' unfaithfulness. The plague that followed the seduction of Israel should have been enough to make them aware of the great responsibility they had to obey God's directives.

31:27 *divide the plunder.* The division of the plunder, or booty, among those who had gone to war and

those who had not, set a standard for future battles. The proportion that was regarded as the Lord's also became a standard.

31:3 ᶜ Josh. 13:21   **31:6** ᵈ Num. 10:9   **31:7** ᵉ Deut. 20:13   ᶠ Gen. 34:25   **31:8** ᵍ Josh. 13:21   ʰ Num. 25:15   ⁱ Josh. 13:22   **31:11** ʲ Deut. 20:14   **31:15** ᵏ Deut. 20:14   **31:16** ˡ Num. 25:2   ᵐ Rev. 2:14   ⁿ Num. 25:9   **31:17** ᵒ Deut. 7:2; 20:16–18   **31:18** ᵖ Deut. 21:10–14   **31:19** q Num. 5:2   ʳ Num. 19:11–22   **31:23** ˢ Num. 19:9, 17   **31:24** ᵗ Lev. 11:25   **31:27** ᵘ Josh. 22:8   **31:28** ᵛ Num. 31:30, 47   **31:29** ʷ Deut. 18:1–5   **31:30** ˣ Num. 31:42–47   ʸ Num. 3:7, 8, 25, 31, 36; 18:3, 4

36And the half, the portion for those who had gone out to war, was in number three hundred and thirty-seven thousand five hundred sheep; 37and the LORD's tribute of the sheep was six hundred and seventy-five. 38The cattle *were* thirty-six thousand, of which the LORD's tribute *was* seventy-two. 39The donkeys *were* thirty thousand five hundred, of which the LORD's tribute *was* sixty-one. 40The persons *were* sixteen thousand, of which the LORD's tribute *was* thirty-two persons. 41So Moses gave the tribute *which was* the LORD's heave offering to Eleazar the priest, *z*as the LORD commanded Moses.

42And from the children of Israel's half, which Moses separated from the men who fought— 43now the half belonging to the congregation was three hundred and thirty-seven thousand five hundred sheep, 44thirty-six thousand cattle, 45thirty thousand five hundred donkeys, 46and sixteen thousand persons— 47and *a*from the children of Israel's half Moses took one of every fifty, drawn from man and beast, and gave them to the Levites, who kept charge of the tabernacle of the LORD, as the LORD commanded Moses.

48Then the officers who *were* over thousands of the army, the captains of thousands and captains of hundreds, came near to Moses; 49and they said to Moses, "Your servants have taken a count of the men of war who *are* under our command, and not a man of us is missing. 50Therefore we have brought an offering for the LORD, what every man found of ornaments of gold: armlets and bracelets and signet rings and earrings and necklaces, *b*to make atonement for ourselves before the LORD." 51So Moses and Eleazar the priest received the gold from them, all the fashioned ornaments. 52And all the gold of the offering that they offered to the LORD, from the captains of thousands and captains of hundreds, was sixteen thousand seven hundred and fifty shekels. 53c(The men of war had taken spoil, every man for himself.) 54And Moses and Eleazar the priest received the gold from the captains of thousands and of hundreds, and brought it into the tabernacle of meeting *d*as a memorial for the children of Israel before the LORD.

The Tribes Settling East of the Jordan

32 Now the children of Reuben and the children of Gad had a very great multitude of livestock; and when they saw the land of *a*Jazer and the land of *b*Gilead, that indeed the region *was* a place for livestock, 2the children of Gad and the children of Reuben came and spoke to Moses, to Eleazar the priest, and to the leaders of the congregation, saying, 3"Ataroth, Dibon, Jazer, *c*Nimrah, *d*Heshbon, Elealeh, *e*Shebam, Nebo, and *f*Beon, 4the country *g*which the LORD defeated before the congregation of Israel, *is* a land for livestock, and your servants have livestock." 5Therefore they said, "If we have found favor in your sight, let this land be given to your servants as a possession. Do not take us over the Jordan."

6And Moses said to the children of Gad and to the children of Reuben: "Shall your brethren go to war while you sit here? 7Now why will you *h*discourage the heart of the children of Israel from going over into the land which the LORD has given them? 8Thus your fathers did *i*when I sent them away from Kadesh Barnea *j*to see the land. 9For *k*when they went up to the Valley of Eshcol and saw the land, they discouraged the heart of the children of Israel, so that they did not go into the land which the LORD had given them. 10So the LORD's anger was aroused on that day, and He swore an oath, saying, 11"Surely none of the men who came up from Egypt, *m*from twenty years old and above, shall see the land of which I swore to Abraham, Isaac, and Jacob, because *n*they have not wholly followed Me, 12except Caleb the son of Jephunneh, the Kenizzite, and Joshua the son of Nun, *o*for they have wholly followed the LORD.' 13So the LORD's anger was aroused against Israel, and He made them *p*wander in the wilderness forty years, until *q*all the generation that had done evil in the sight of the LORD was gone. 14And look! You have risen in your fathers' place, a brood of sinful men, to increase still more the *r*fierce anger of the LORD against Israel. 15For if you *s*turn away from following Him, He will once again leave them in the wilderness, and you will destroy all these people."

16Then they came near to him and said: "We will build sheepfolds here for our

31:52 **sixteen thousand seven hundred and fifty shekels.** The officers' gift was over 400 pounds of gold.
32:5 **If we have found favor.** Although an inheritance on the east side of the Jordan was not part of God's promise, the respectful request of the Reubenites and Gadites was granted, because they came humbly, not rebelliously.
32:8–13 **Thus your fathers did.** To discourage obedience of God's orders and so prevent His people from entering upon the full enjoyment of the promises is a serious sin. Let us never forget that without an obedient faith, it is impossible to please God (Heb. 11:6).

31:41 *z* Num. 5:9, 10; 18:8, 19   31:47 *a* Num. 31:30   31:50 *b* Ex. 30:12–16   31:53 *c* Deut. 20:14   31:54 *d* Ex. 30:16   32:1 *a* Num. 21:32 *b* Deut. 3:13   32:3 *c* Num. 32:36 *d* Josh. 13:17, 26 *e* Num. 32:38 *f* Num. 32:38   32:4 *g* Num. 21:24, 34, 35   32:7 *h* Num. 13:27—14:4   32:8 *i* Num. 13:3, 26 *j* Deut. 1:19–25   32:9 *k* Deut. 1:24, 28   32:10 *l* Deut. 1:34–36   32:11 *m* Num. 14:28, 29; 26:63–65 *n* Num. 14:24, 30   32:12 *o* Deut. 1:36   32:13 *p* Num. 14:33–35 *q* Num. 26:64, 65   32:14 *r* Deut. 1:34   32:15 *s* Deut. 30:17, 18

livestock, and cities for our little ones, [17]but [t]we ourselves will be armed, ready *to go* before the children of Israel until we have brought them to their place; and our little ones will dwell in the fortified cities because of the inhabitants of the land. [18u]We will not return to our homes until every one of the children of Israel has received his inheritance. [19]For we will not inherit with them on the other side of the Jordan and beyond, [v]because our inheritance has fallen to us on this eastern side of the Jordan."

[20]Then [w]Moses said to them: "If you do this thing, if you arm yourselves before the LORD for the war, [21]and all your armed men cross over the Jordan before the LORD until He has driven out His enemies from before Him, [22]and [x]the land is subdued before the LORD, then afterward [y]you may return and be blameless before the LORD and before Israel; and [z]this land shall be your possession before the LORD. [23]But if you do not do so, then take note, you have sinned against the LORD; and be sure [a]your sin will find you out. [24b]Build cities for your little ones and folds for your sheep, and do what has proceeded out of your mouth."

[25]And the children of Gad and the children of Reuben spoke to Moses, saying: "Your servants will do as my lord commands. [26c]Our little ones, our wives, our flocks, and all our livestock will be there in the cities of Gilead; [27d]but your servants will cross over, every man armed for war, before the LORD to battle, just as my lord says."

[28]So Moses gave command [e]concerning them to Eleazar the priest, to Joshua the son of Nun, and to the chief fathers of the tribes of the children of Israel. [29]And Moses said to them: "If the children of Gad and the children of Reuben cross over the Jordan with you, every man armed for battle before the LORD, and the land is subdued before you, then you shall give them the land of Gilead as a possession. [30]But if they do not cross over armed with you, they shall have possessions among you in the land of Canaan."

[31]Then the children of Gad and the children of Reuben answered, saying: "As the LORD has said to your servants, so we will do. [32]We will cross over armed before the LORD into the land of Canaan, but the possession of our inheritance *shall remain* with us on this side of the Jordan."

[33]So [f]Moses gave to the children of Gad, to the children of Reuben, and to half the tribe of Manasseh the son of Joseph, [g]the kingdom of Sihon king of the Amorites and the kingdom of Og king of Bashan, the land with its cities within the borders, the cities of the surrounding country. [34]And the children of Gad built [h]Dibon and Ataroth and [i]Aroer, [35]Atroth and Shophan and [j]Jazer and Jogbehah, [36k]Beth Nimrah and Beth Haran, [l]fortified cities, and folds for sheep. [37]And the children of Reuben built [m]Heshbon and Elealeh and Kirjathaim, [38n]Nebo and [o]Baal Meon [p](*their* names being changed) and Shibmah; and they gave *other* names to the cities which they built.

[39]And the children of [q]Machir the son of Manasseh went to Gilead and took it, and dispossessed the Amorites who *were* in it. [40]So Moses [r]gave Gilead to Machir the son of Manasseh, and he dwelt in it. [41]Also [s]Jair the son of Manasseh went and took its small towns, and called them [t]Havoth Jair.* [42]Then Nobah went and took Kenath and its villages, and he called it Nobah, after his own name.

Israel's Journey from Egypt Reviewed

33 These *are* the journeys of the children of Israel, who went out of the land of Egypt by their armies under the [a]hand of Moses and Aaron. [2]Now Moses wrote down the starting points of their journeys at the command of the LORD. And these *are* their journeys according to their starting points:

[3]They [b]departed from Rameses in [c]the first month, on the fifteenth day of the first month; on the day after the Passover the children of Israel went out [d]with boldness in the sight of all the Egyptians. [4]For the Egyptians were burying all *their* firstborn, [e]whom the LORD had killed among them. Also [f]on their gods the LORD had executed judgments.

[5g]Then the children of Israel moved from Rameses and camped at Succoth. [6]They departed from [h]Succoth and camped at Etham, which *is* on the edge of the wilderness. [7i]They moved from Etham and turned back to Pi Hahiroth, which *is* east of Baal Zephon; and they camped

---

* **32:41** Literally *Towns of Jair*

32:31 *so we will do.* Reuben and Gad gladly affirmed their allegiance to the Lord and their consideration of the remainder of the community of Israel. The benevolence of Reuben and Gad is a beautiful picture of the mutual ties between God's people. Truly, we are one body.

32:17 [t] Josh. 4:12, 13   **32:18** [u] Josh. 22:1–4
32:19 [v] Josh. 12:1; 13:8   **32:20** [w] Deut. 3:18

32:22 [x] Deut. 3:20   [y] Josh. 22:4   [z] Deut. 3:12, 15, 16, 18
32:23 [a] Is. 59:12   **32:24** [b] Num. 32:16   **32:26** [c] Josh. 1:14
32:27 [d] Josh. 4:12   **32:28** [e] Josh. 1:13   **32:33** [f] Deut.
3:8–17; 29:8   [g] Num. 21:24, 33, 35   **32:34** [h] Num. 33:45,
46   [i] Deut. 2:36   **32:35** [j] Num. 32:1, 3   **32:36** [k] Num.
32:3   [l] Num. 32:24   **32:37** [m] Num. 21:27   **32:38** [n] Is.
46:1   [o] Ezek. 25:9   [p] Ex. 23:13   **32:39** [q] Gen. 50:23
32:40 [r] Deut. 3:12, 13, 15   **32:41** [s] Deut. 3:14   [t] Judg.
10:4   **33:1** [a] Ps. 77:20   **33:3** [b] Ex. 12:37   [c] Ex. 12:2; 13:4
[d] Ex. 14:8   **33:4** [e] Ex. 12:29   [f] Is. 19:1   **33:5** [g] Ex. 12:37
33:6 [h] Ex. 13:20   **33:7** [i] Ex. 14:1, 2, 9

near Migdol. [8]They departed from before Hahiroth* and [i]passed through the midst of the sea into the wilderness, went three days' journey in the Wilderness of Etham, and camped at Marah. [9]They moved from Marah and [k]came to Elim. At Elim were twelve springs of water and seventy palm trees; so they camped there.

[10]They moved from Elim and camped by the Red Sea. [11]They moved from the Red Sea and camped in the [l]Wilderness of Sin. [12]They journeyed from the Wilderness of Sin and camped at Dophkah. [13]They departed from Dophkah and camped at Alush. [14]They moved from Alush and camped at [m]Rephidim, where there was no water for the people to drink.

[15]They departed from Rephidim and camped in the [n]Wilderness of Sinai. [16]They moved from the Wilderness of Sinai and camped [o]at Kibroth Hattaavah. [17]They departed from Kibroth Hattaavah and [p]camped at Hazeroth. [18]They departed from Hazeroth and camped at [q]Rithmah. [19]They departed from Rithmah and camped at Rimmon Perez. [20]They departed from Rimmon Perez and camped at Libnah. [21]They moved from Libnah and camped at Rissah. [22]They journeyed from Rissah and camped at Kehelathah. [23]They went from Kehelathah and camped at Mount Shepher. [24]They moved from Mount Shepher and camped at Haradah. [25]They moved from Haradah and camped at Makheloth. [26]They moved from Makheloth and camped at Tahath. [27]They departed from Tahath and camped at Terah. [28]They moved from Terah and camped at Mithkah. [29]They went from Mithkah and camped at Hashmonah. [30]They departed from Hashmonah and [r]camped at Moseroth. [31]They departed from Moseroth and camped at Bene Jaakan. [32]They moved from [s]Bene Jaakan and [t]camped at Hor Hagidgad. [33]They went from Hor Hagidgad and camped at Jotbathah. [34]They moved from Jotbathah [u]and camped at Abronah. [35]They departed from Abronah and camped at Ezion Geber. [36]They moved from Ezion Geber and camped in the [v]Wilderness of Zin, which is Kadesh. [37]They moved from [w]Kadesh and camped at Mount Hor, on the boundary of the land of Edom.

[38]Then [x]Aaron the priest went up to Mount Hor at the command of the LORD, and died there in the fortieth year after the children of Israel had come out of the land of Egypt, on the first day of the fifth month. [39]Aaron was one hundred and twenty-three years old when he died on Mount Hor.

[40]Now [y]the king of Arad, the Canaanite, who dwelt in the South in the land of Canaan, heard of the coming of the children of Israel.

[41]So they departed from Mount Hor and camped at Zalmonah. [42]They departed from Zalmonah and camped at Punon. [43]They departed from Punon and [z]camped at Oboth. [44][a]They departed from Oboth and camped at Ije Abarim, at the border of Moab. [45]They departed from Ijim* and camped [b]at Dibon Gad. [46]They moved from Dibon Gad and camped at [c]Almon Diblathaim. [47]They moved from Almon Diblathaim [d]and camped in the mountains of Abarim, before Nebo. [48]They departed from the mountains of Abarim and [e]camped in the plains of Moab by the Jordan, across from Jericho. [49]They camped by the Jordan, from Beth Jesimoth as far as the [f]Abel Acacia Grove* in the plains of Moab.

Instructions for the Conquest of Canaan

[50]Now the LORD spoke to Moses in the plains of Moab by the Jordan, across from Jericho, saying, [51]"Speak to the children of Israel, and say to them: [g]"When you have crossed the Jordan into the land of Canaan, [52][h]then you shall drive out all the inhabitants of the land from before you, destroy all their engraved stones, destroy all their molded images, and demolish all their high places; [53]you shall dispossess the inhabitants of the land and dwell in it, for I have given you the land to [i]possess. [54]And [j]you shall divide the land by lot as an inheritance among your families; to the larger you shall give a larger inheritance, and to the smaller you shall give a smaller inheritance; there everyone's inheritance shall be whatever falls to him by lot. You shall inherit according to the tribes of your

---

* 33:8 Many Hebrew manuscripts, Samaritan Pentateuch, Syriac, Targum, and Vulgate read from Pi Hahiroth (compare verse 7).
* 33:45 Same as Ije Abarim, verse 44
* 33:49 Hebrew Abel Shittim

33:53 for I have given you the land to possess. It was God's land, and He had transferred it from the Canaanites to the Israelites. Though the land was promised to the nation as a gift, it did not come into the possession of the people without their involvement. Israel had to drive out the inhabitants, destroy their high places, their figures, stones, and molten images. Still, the land was God's gracious gift to His people. In spite of all of our striving, we have only what we receive from the hand of the Lord.

33:8 [j] Ex. 14:22; 15:22, 23   **33:9** [k] Ex. 15:27   **33:11** [l] Ex. 16:1   **33:14** [m] Ex. 17:1; 19:2   **33:15** [n] Ex. 16:1; 19:1, 2   **33:16** [o] Num. 11:34   **33:17** [p] Num. 11:35   **33:18** [q] Num. 12:16   **33:30** [r] Deut. 10:6   **33:32** [s] Deut. 10:6   **33:34** [u] Deut. 2:8   **33:36** [v] Num. 20:1; 27:14   **33:37** [w] Num. 20:22, 23; 21:4   **33:38** [x] Num. 20:25, 28   **33:40** [y] Num. 21:1   **33:43** [z] Num. 21:10   **33:44** [a] Num. 21:11   **33:45** [b] Num. 32:34   **33:46** [c] Jer. 48:22   **33:47** [d] Deut. 32:49   **33:48** [e] Num. 22:1; 31:12; 35:1   **33:49** [f] Num. 25:1   **33:51** [g] Josh. 3:17   **33:52** [h] Deut. 7:2, 5; 12:3   **33:53** [i] Deut. 11:31   **33:54** [j] Num. 26:53–56

fathers. 55But if you do not drive out the inhabitants of the land from before you, then it shall be that those whom you let remain *shall be* [k]irritants in your eyes and thorns in your sides, and they shall harass you in the land where you dwell. 56Moreover it shall be *that* I will do to you as I thought to do to them.'"

The Appointed Boundaries of Canaan

34 Then the LORD spoke to Moses, saying, 2"Command the children of Israel, and say to them: 'When you come into [a]the land of Canaan, this *is* the land that shall fall to you as an inheritance—the land of Canaan to its boundaries. 3[b]Your southern border shall be from the Wilderness of Zin along the border of Edom; then your southern border shall extend eastward to the end of [c]the Salt Sea; 4your border shall turn from the southern side of [d]the Ascent of Akrabbim, continue to Zin, and be on the south of [e]Kadesh Barnea; then it shall go on to [f]Hazar Addar, and continue to Azmon; 5the border shall turn from Azmon [g]to the Brook of Egypt, and it shall end at the Sea.

6'As for the [h]western border, you shall have the Great Sea for a border; this shall be your western border.

7'And this shall be your northern border: From the Great Sea you shall mark out your *border* line to [i]Mount Hor; 8from Mount Hor you shall mark out *your border* [j]to the entrance of Hamath; then the direction of the border shall be toward [k]Zedad; 9the border shall proceed to Ziphron, and it shall end at [l]Hazar Enan. This shall be your northern border.

10'You shall mark out your eastern border from Hazar Enan to Shepham; 11the border shall go down from Shepham to [m]Riblah on the east side of Ain; the border shall go down and reach to the eastern side of the Sea [n]of Chinnereth; 12the border shall go down along the Jordan, and it shall end at [o]the Salt Sea. This shall be your land with its surrounding boundaries.'"

13Then Moses commanded the children of Israel, saying: [p]"This *is* the land which you shall inherit by lot, which the LORD has commanded to give to the nine tribes and

to the half-tribe. 14[q]For the tribe of the children of Reuben according to the house of their fathers, and the tribe of the children of Gad according to the house of their fathers, have received *their inheritance;* and the half-tribe of Manasseh has received its inheritance. 15The two tribes and the half-tribe have received their inheritance on this side of the Jordan, *across from* Jericho eastward, toward the sunrise."

The Leaders Appointed to Divide the Land

16And the LORD spoke to Moses, saying, 17"These *are* the names of the men who shall divide the land among you as an inheritance: [r]Eleazar the priest and Joshua the son of Nun. 18And you shall take one [s]leader of every tribe to divide the land for the inheritance. 19These *are* the names of the men: from the tribe of Judah, Caleb the son of Jephunneh; 20from the tribe of the children of Simeon, Shemuel the son of Ammihud; 21from the tribe of Benjamin, Elidad the son of Chislon; 22a leader from the tribe of the children of Dan, Bukki the son of Jogli; 23from the sons of Joseph: a leader from the tribe of the children of Manasseh, Hanniel the son of Ephod, 24and a leader from the tribe of the children of Ephraim, Kemuel the son of Shiphtan; 25a leader from the tribe of the children of Zebulun, Elizaphan the son of Parnach; 26a leader from the tribe of the children of Issachar, Paltiel the son of Azzan; 27a leader from the tribe of the children of Asher, Ahihud the son of Shelomi; 28and a leader from the tribe of the children of Naphtali, Pedahel the son of Ammihud."

29These *are* the ones the LORD commanded to divide the inheritance among the children of Israel in the land of Canaan.

Cities for the Levites

35 And the LORD spoke to Moses in [a]the plains of Moab by the Jordan *across from* Jericho, saying: 2[b]"Command the children of Israel that they give the Levites cities to dwell in from the inheritance of their possession, and you shall *also* give the Levites [c]common-land around the cities. 3They shall have the cities to dwell in; and their common-land shall be for their cattle,

33:55–56 But if you do not. If the idolatrous Canaanites were allowed to live among God's people, they would be a constant enticement to sin. If the Israelites fell into the same sin as the Canaanites, their punishment would be the same.
34:1–12 the land of Canaan to its boundaries. Chapter 34 serves as a detailed display of the grandeur of the land that God was about to give to His people.
34:16–29 These are the names of the men. The listing of the men serves several purposes. It gives authenticity to the record, it memorializes these individuals in the history of Israel, and it serves as a legal

arrangement so that the transfer of the land to the tribes would be done in order.

33:55 [k] Josh. 23:13 **34:2** [a] Gen. 17:8 **34:3** [b] Josh. 15:1–3 [c] Gen. 14:3 **34:4** [d] Josh. 15:3 [e] Num. 13:26; 32:8 [f] Josh. 15:3, 4 **34:5** [g] Josh. 15:4, 47 **34:6** [h] Ezek. 47:20 **34:7** [i] Num. 33:37 **34:8** [j] Num. 13:21 [k] Ezek. 47:15 **34:9** [l] Ezek. 47:17 **34:11** [m] 2 Kin. 23:33 [n] Deut. 3:17 **34:12** [o] Num. 34:3 **34:13** [p] Josh. 14:1–5 **34:14** [q] Num. 32:33 **34:17** [r] Josh. 14:1, 2; 19:51 **34:18** [s] Num. 1:4, 16 **35:1** [a] Num. 33:50 **35:2** [b] Josh. 14:3, 4; 21:2, 3 [c] Lev. 25:32–34

for their herds, and for all their animals. 4The common-land of the cities which you will give the Levites *shall extend* from the wall of the city outward a thousand cubits all around. 5And you shall measure outside the city on the east side two thousand cubits, on the south side two thousand cubits, on the west side two thousand cubits, and on the north side two thousand cubits. The city *shall be* in the middle. This shall belong to them as common-land for the cities.

6"Now among the cities which you will give to the Levites *you shall appoint* dsix cities of refuge, to which a manslayer may flee. And to these you shall add forty-two cities. 7So all the cities you will give to the Levites *shall be* eforty-eight; these *you shall give* with their common-land. 8And the cities which you will give *shall be* ffrom the possession of the children of Israel; gfrom the larger *tribe* you shall give many, from the smaller you shall give few. Each shall give some of its cities to the Levites, in proportion to the inheritance that each receives."

Cities of Refuge

9Then the LORD spoke to Moses, saying, 10"Speak to the children of Israel, and say to them: h'When you cross the Jordan into the land of Canaan, 11then iyou shall appoint cities to be cities of refuge for you, that the manslayer who kills any person accidentally may flee there. 12iThey shall be cities of refuge for you from the avenger, that the manslayer may not die until he stands before the congregation in judgment. 13And of the cities which you give, you shall have ksix cities of refuge. 14lYou shall appoint three cities on this side of the Jordan, and three cities you shall appoint in the land of Canaan, *which* will be cities of refuge. 15These six cities shall be for refuge for the children of Israel, mfor the stranger, and for the sojourner among them, that anyone who kills a person accidentally may flee there.

16n'But if he strikes him with an iron implement, so that he dies, he *is* a murderer; the murderer shall surely be put to death. 17And if he strikes him with a stone in the hand, by which one could die, and he does die, he *is* a murderer; the murderer shall surely be put to death. 18Or *if* he strikes him with a wooden hand weapon, by which one could die, and he does die, he *is* a murderer; the murderer shall surely be put to death. 19oThe avenger of blood himself shall put the murderer to death; when he meets him, he shall put him to death. 20pIf he pushes him out of hatred or, qwhile lying in wait, hurls something at him so that he dies, 21or in enmity he strikes him with his hand so that he dies, the one who struck *him* shall surely be put to death. He *is* a murderer. The avenger of blood shall put the murderer to death when he meets him.

22'However, if he pushes him suddenly rwithout enmity, or throws anything at him without lying in wait, 23or uses a stone, by which a man could die, throwing *it* at him without seeing *him*, so that he dies, while he was not his enemy or seeking his harm, 24then sthe congregation shall judge between the manslayer and the avenger of blood according to these judgments. 25So the congregation shall deliver the manslayer from the hand of the avenger of blood, and the congregation shall return him to the city of refuge where he had fled, and the shall remain there until the death of the high priest uwho was anointed with the holy oil. 26But if the manslayer at any time goes outside the limits of the city of refuge where he fled, 27and the avenger of blood finds him outside the limits of his city of refuge, and the avenger of blood kills the manslayer, he shall not be guilty of blood, 28because he should have remained in his city of refuge until the death of the high priest. But after the death of the high priest the manslayer may return to the land of his possession.

29'And these *things* shall be va statute of judgment to you throughout your generations in all your dwellings. 30Whoever kills a person, the murderer shall be put to death on the wtestimony of witnesses; but one witness is not *sufficient* testimony against a person for the death *penalty*. 31Moreover you shall take no ransom for the life of a murderer who *is* guilty of death, but he shall surely be put to death. 32And you shall take no ransom for him who has fled to his city of refuge, that he may return to dwell in the land before the death of the priest.

35:29–34 *statute of judgment.* The practice of blood vengeance was common in the ancient Near East. Divine law was formulated to control and limit blood vengeance in Israel (vv. 9–34). God's Word differed significantly from the surrounding cultures. The difference of practice was due to Israel's unique view of man created in God's image. These directives regarding blood vengeance are referred to here as a "statute of judgment," coming from a word meaning "to engrave." The Word of God was written, given to govern and direct their conduct "in all their dwellings." We can be truly grateful that the revelation of God comes to us in a permanently accessible form.

35:30–34 *Whoever kills a person.* The people were not to confuse accidental manslaughter with premeditated murder.

35:6 d Josh. 20:2, 7, 8; 21:3, 13 **35:7** e Josh. 21:41 **35:8** f Josh. 21:3 g Num. 26:54; 33:54 **35:10** h Josh. 20:1–9 **35:11** i Ex. 21:13 **35:12** j Deut. 19:6 **35:13** k Num. 35:6 **35:14** l Deut. 4:41 **35:15** m Num. 15:16 **35:16** n Lev. 24:17 **35:19** o Num. 35:21, 24, 27 **35:20** p Gen. 4:8 q Ex. 21:14 **35:22** r Ex. 21:13 **35:24** s Josh. 20:6 **35:25** t Josh. 20:6 u Ex. 29:7 **35:29** v Num. 27:11 **35:30** w Deut. 17:6; 19:15

³³So you shall not pollute the land where you *are;* for blood ˣdefiles the land, and no atonement can be made for the land, for the blood that is shed on it, except ʸby the blood of him who shed it. ³⁴Therefore ᶻdo not defile the land which you inhabit, in the midst of which I dwell; for ᵃI the LORD dwell among the children of Israel.'"

Marriage of Female Heirs

36 Now the chief fathers of the families of the ᵃchildren of Gilead the son of Machir, the son of Manasseh, of the families of the sons of Joseph, came near and ᵇspoke before Moses and before the leaders, the chief fathers of the children of Israel. ²And they said: ᶜ"The LORD commanded my lord *Moses* to give the land as an inheritance by lot to the children of Israel, and ᵈmy lord was commanded by the LORD to give the inheritance of our brother Zelophehad to his daughters. ³Now if they are married to any of the sons of the *other* tribes of the children of Israel, then their inheritance will be ᵉtaken from the inheritance of our fathers, and it will be added to the inheritance of the tribe into which they marry; so it will be taken from the lot of our inheritance. ⁴And when ᶠthe Jubilee of the children of Israel comes, then their inheritance will be added to the inheritance of the tribe into which they marry; so their inheritance will be taken away from the inheritance of the tribe of our fathers."

⁵Then Moses commanded the children of Israel according to the word of the LORD, saying: ᵍ"What the tribe of the sons of Joseph speaks is right. ⁶This *is* what the LORD commands concerning the daughters of Zelophehad, saying, 'Let them marry whom they think best, ʰbut they may marry only within the family of their father's tribe.' ⁷So the inheritance of the children of Israel shall not change hands from tribe to tribe, for every one of the children of Israel shall keep the inheritance of the tribe of his fathers. ⁸And ʲevery daughter who possesses an inheritance in any tribe of the children of Israel shall be the wife of one of the family of her father's tribe, so that the children of Israel each may possess the inheritance of his fathers. ⁹Thus no inheritance shall change hands from *one* tribe to another, but every tribe of the children of Israel shall keep its own inheritance."

¹⁰Just as the LORD commanded Moses, so did the daughters of Zelophehad; ¹¹ᵏfor Mahlah, Tirzah, Hoglah, Milcah, and Noah, the daughters of Zelophehad, were married to the sons of their father's brothers. ¹²They were married into the families of the children of Manasseh the son of Joseph, and their inheritance remained in the tribe of their father's family.

¹³These *are* the commandments and the judgments which the LORD commanded the children of Israel by the hand of Moses ˡin the plains of Moab by the Jordan, *across from* Jericho.

36:5–13 *only within the family of their father's tribe.* This beautiful example of concern for fair treatment of Zelophehad's daughters, consideration for the well-being of the tribe, and obedience to Moses' decision is a happy ending to this book that is so full of hard-heartedness and disobedience.

35:33 ˣ Ps. 106:38 ʸ Gen. 9:6   **35:34** ᶻ Lev. 18:24, 25 ᵃ Ex. 29:45, 46   **36:1** ᵃ Num. 26:29 ᵇ Num. 27:1–11 **36:2** ᶜ Josh. 17:4 ᵈ Num. 27:1, 5–7   **36:3** ᵉ Num. 27:4 **36:4** ᶠ Lev. 25:10   **36:5** ᵍ Num. 27:7   **36:6** ʰ Num. 36:11, 12   **36:7** ʲ 1 Kin. 21:3   **36:8** ʲ 1 Chr. 23:22 **36:11** ᵏ Num. 26:33; 27:1   **36:13** ˡ Num. 26:3; 33:50

THE FIFTH BOOK OF MOSES CALLED
DEUTERONOMY

AUTHOR: Numerous external and internal evidences support the authorship of Moses. The Old Testament attributes Deuteronomy to Moses (Josh. 1:7; Judg. 3:4; 1 Kin. 2:3; 2 Kin. 14:6; Ezra 3:2; Neh. 1:7; Ps. 103:7; Dan. 9:11; Mal. 4:4), and there is evidence from Joshua and 1 Samuel to indicate that these laws existed in the form of codified written statutes that influenced the Israelites in Canaan. Christ quoted Deuteronomy when He was being tempted (Matt. 4:4,7,10) and attributed it to Moses (Matt. 19:7–9; Mark 7:10; Luke 20:28; John 5:45–47) as do the more than eighty citations of Deuteronomy in the New Testament. Internally, the book includes about forty claims to Moses as the author (1:1–5; 4:44–46; 29:1; 31:9,24–26). The political and geographic details of Deuteronomy indicate a firsthand knowledge of the events.

TIME: c. 1405 B.C.   **KEY VERSES:** Deut. 30:19–20

THEME: Deuteronomy is a series of addresses that Moses gives to the nation of Israel just before it enters the Promised Land. In many ways it can be seen as the coach's speech given to a team just before it takes the field. The book reviews and reiterates what has been taught in the previous books of Moses in the same way that a coach's last instructions contain a review of the basic game plan and what has been covered in practice. The purpose of that speech is to focus on what to do and then create the motivation to carry it out. For the Israelites much of the previous instruction was somewhat hypothetical. Many of the laws assumed the occupation of the land. Now, as they stand looking over the Jordan River, they're within reach of moving from the hypothetical to the real and practical. God has renewed His marvelous covenant with them. Now is the time to live up to its requirements.

The Previous Command to Enter Canaan

1 These *are* the words which Moses spoke to all Israel *a*on this side of the Jordan in the wilderness, in the plain* opposite Suph,* between Paran, Tophel, Laban, Hazeroth, and Dizahab. ²*It is* eleven days' *journey* from Horeb by way of Mount Seir *b*to Kadesh Barnea. ³Now it came to pass *c*in the fortieth year, in the eleventh month, on the first *day* of the month, *that* Moses spoke to the children of Israel according to all that the LORD had given him as commandments to them, ⁴*d*after he had killed Sihon king of the Amorites, who dwelt in Heshbon, and Og king of Bashan, who dwelt at Ashtaroth *e*in* Edrei.

⁵On this side of the Jordan in the land of Moab, Moses began to explain this law, saying, ⁶"The LORD our God spoke to us *f*in Horeb, saying: 'You have dwelt long

*g*enough at this mountain. ⁷Turn and take your journey, and go to the mountains of the Amorites, to all the neighboring *places* in the plain,* in the mountains and in the lowland, in the South and on the seacoast, to the land of the Canaanites and to Lebanon, as far as the great river, the River Euphrates. ⁸See, I have set the land before you; go in and possess the land which the LORD swore to your fathers—to *h*Abraham, Isaac, and Jacob—to give to them and their descendants after them.'

Tribal Leaders Appointed

⁹"And *i*I spoke to you at that time, saying: 'I alone am not able to bear you. ¹⁰The LORD your God has multiplied you, *j*and here you

---

* **1:1** Hebrew *arabah* • One manuscript of the Septuagint, also Targum and Vulgate, read *Red Sea.*   * **1:4** Septuagint, Syriac, and Vulgate read *and* (compare Joshua 12:4).   * **1:7** Hebrew *arabah*

1:2 *eleven days' journey.* A journey that might have taken Israel less than two weeks to complete lasted forty years because of unbelief and disobedience (Num. 13–14).
1:5 *law.* The Hebrew word translated "law" basically means "instruction."

1:1 *a* Deut. 4:44–46   **1:2** *b* Num. 13:26; 32:8   **1:3** *c* Num. 33:38   **1:4** *d* Num. 21:23, 24, 33–35   *e* Josh. 13:12
1:6 *f* Ex. 3:1, 12   *g* Ex. 19:1, 2   **1:8** *h* Gen. 12:7; 15:5; 22:17; 26:3; 28:13   **1:9** *i* Ex. 18:18, 24   **1:10** *j* Gen. 15:5; 22:17

are today, as the stars of heaven in multitude. ¹¹ᵏMay the LORD God of your fathers make you a thousand times more numerous than you are, and bless you *l*as He has promised you! ¹²ᵐHow can I alone bear your problems and your burdens and your complaints? ¹³Choose wise, understanding, and knowledgeable men from among your tribes, and I will make them heads over you.' ¹⁴And you answered me and said, 'The thing which you have told *us* to do *is* good.' ¹⁵So I took ⁿthe heads of your tribes, wise and knowledgeable men, and made them heads over you, leaders of thousands, leaders of hundreds, leaders of fifties, leaders of tens, and officers for your tribes.

¹⁶"Then I commanded your judges at that time, saying, 'Hear *the cases* between your brethren, and ojudge righteously between a man and his pbrother or the stranger who is with him. ¹⁷ᵃYou shall not show partiality in judgment; you shall hear the small as well as the great; you shall not be afraid in any man's presence, for rthe judgment *is* God's. The case that is too hard for you, sbring to me, and I will hear it.' ¹⁸And I commanded you at that time all the things which you should do.

Israel's Refusal to Enter the Land

¹⁹"So we departed from Horeb, tand went through all that great and terrible wilderness which you saw on the way to the mountains of the Amorites, as the LORD our God had commanded us. Then uwe came to Kadesh Barnea. ²⁰And I said to you, 'You have come to the mountains of the Amorites, which the LORD our God is giving us. ²¹Look, the LORD your God has set the land before you; go up *and* possess *it*, as the LORD God of your fathers has spoken to you; vdo not fear or be discouraged.'

²²"And every one of you came near to me and said, 'Let us send men before us, and let them search out the land for us, and bring back word to us of the way by which we should go up, and of the cities into which we shall come.'

²³"The plan pleased me well; so wI took twelve of your men, one man from *each*

tribe. ²⁴xAnd they departed and went up into the mountains, and came to the Valley of Eshcol, and spied it out. ²⁵They also took *some* of the fruit of the land in their hands and brought *it* down to us; and they brought back word to us, saying, 'It *is* a ygood land which the LORD our God is giving us.'

²⁶z"Nevertheless you would not go up, but rebelled against the command of the LORD your God; ²⁷and you acomplained in your tents, and said, 'Because the LORD bhates us, He has brought us out of the land of Egypt to deliver us into the hand of the Amorites, to destroy us. ²⁸Where can we go up? Our brethren have discouraged our hearts, saying, c"The people *are* greater and taller than we; the cities *are* great and fortified up to heaven; moreover we have seen the sons of the dAnakim there."'

²⁹"Then I said to you, 'Do not be terrified, eor afraid of them. ³⁰fThe LORD your God, who goes before you, He will fight for you, according to all He did for you in Egypt before your eyes, ³¹and in the wilderness where you saw how the LORD your God carried you, as a gman carries his son, in all the way that you went until you came to this place.' ³²Yet, for all that, hyou did not believe the LORD your God, ³³iwho went in the way before you jto search out a place for you to pitch your tents, to show you the way you should go, in the fire by night and in the cloud by day.

The Penalty for Israel's Rebellion

³⁴"And the LORD heard the sound of your words, and was angry, kand took an oath, saying, ³⁵l"Surely not one of these men of this evil generation shall see that good land of which I swore to give to your fathers, ³⁶mexcept Caleb the son of Jephunneh; he shall see it, and to him and his children I am giving the land on which he walked, because ⁿhe wholly followed the LORD.' ³⁷oThe LORD was also angry with me for your sakes, saying, 'Even you shall not go in there. ³⁸pJoshua the son of Nun, qwho stands before you, he shall go in there. rEncourage him, for he shall cause Israel to inherit it.

1:13 wise, understanding. The qualities of the leaders reflect the attributes of God. Wisdom is the ability to judge fairly and understand and make wise use of facts. Discernment or understanding is the ability to find the hidden or obscure aspects of a situation.

1:20 Amorites. The Amorites were one of the groups Israel encountered in their approach to the Promised Land. This term is often a general designation for the Canaanites.

1:26–28 you complained. An attitude of complaining and criticism toward the circumstances in our lives keeps us from seeing God's hand in the situation. Our situation may indeed be difficult, but God has promised that He will never leave us nor forsake us. Paul said that he had learned how to be content in every circumstance. He made it a habit to give thanks in all things, and knew how to be contented with

little, and how to be contented with much. He knew that he could do anything through Christ, who gives us strength (Phil. 4:13).

1:28 the Anakim. The Anakim were an ancient people known for their great size (Num. 13:28).

1:11 *k* 2 Sam. 24:3 *l* Gen. 15:5   **1:12** *m* 1 Kin. 3:8, 9   **1:15** *n* Ex. 18:25   **1:16** *o* Deut. 16:18 *p* Lev. 24:22   **1:17** *q* Prov. 24:23–26 *r* 2 Chr. 19:6 *s* Ex. 18:22, 26   **1:19** *t* Deut. 2:7; 8:15; 32:10 *u* Num. 13:26   **1:21** *v* Josh. 1:6, 9   **1:23** *w* Num. 13:2, 3   **1:24** *x* Num. 13:21–25   **1:25** *y* Num. 13:27   **1:26** *z* Num. 14:1–4   **1:27** *a* Ps. 106:25 *b* Deut. 9:28   **1:28** *c* Deut. 9:1, 2 *d* Num. 13:28   **1:29** *e* Num. 14:9   **1:30** *f* Ex. 14:14   **1:31** *g* Is. 46:3, 4; 63:9   **1:32** *h* Jude 5   **1:33** *i* Ex. 13:21 *j* Num. 10:33   **1:34** *k* Deut. 2:14, 15   **1:35** *l* Num. 14:22, 23   **1:36** *m* [Josh. 14:9] *n* Num. 32:11, 12   **1:37** *o* Deut. 3:26; 4:21; 34:4   **1:38** *p* Num. 14:30 *q* 1 Sam. 16:22 *r* Deut. 31:7, 23

³⁹s‘Moreover your little ones and your children, who ᵗyou say will be victims, who today ᵘhave no knowledge of good and evil, they shall go in there; to them I will give it, and they shall possess it. ⁴⁰ᵛBut *as for you,* turn and take your journey into the wilderness by the Way of the Red Sea.’

⁴¹"Then you answered and said to me, ʷ‘We have sinned against the LORD; we will go up and fight, just as the LORD our God commanded us.’ And when everyone of you had girded on his weapons of war, you were ready to go up into the mountain. ⁴²"And the LORD said to me, ‘Tell them, ˣ"Do not go up nor fight, for I *am* not among you; lest you be defeated before your enemies."’ ⁴³So I spoke to you; yet you would not listen, but ʸrebelled against the command of the LORD, and ᶻpresumptuously went up into the mountain. ⁴⁴And the Amorites who dwelt in that mountain came out against you and chased you ᵃas bees do, and drove you back from Seir to Hormah. ⁴⁵Then you returned and wept before the LORD, but the LORD would not listen to your voice nor give ear to you. ⁴⁶ᵇ"So you remained in Kadesh many days, according to the days that you spent *there.*

The Desert Years

2 ᵃ"Then we turned and journeyed into the wilderness of the Way of the Red Sea, ᵇas the LORD spoke to me, and we skirted Mount Seir for many days.

²"And the LORD spoke to me, saying: ³‘You have skirted this mountain ᶜlong enough; turn northward. ⁴And command the people, saying, ᵈ"You *are about to* pass through the territory of ᵉyour brethren, the descendants of Esau, who live in Seir; and they will be afraid of you. Therefore watch yourselves carefully. ⁵Do not meddle with them, for I will not give you *any* of their land, no, not so much as one footstep, ᶠbecause I have given Mount Seir to Esau *as* a possession. ⁶You shall buy food from them with money, that you may eat; and you shall also buy water from them with money, that you may drink.

⁷"For the LORD your God has blessed you in all the work of your hand. He knows your trudging through this great wilderness. ᵍThese forty years the LORD your God *has been* with you; you have lacked nothing."’

⁸"And when we passed beyond our brethren, the descendants of Esau who dwell in Seir, away from the road of the plain, away from ʰElath and Ezion Geber, we ᶦturned and passed by way of the Wilderness of Moab. ⁹Then the LORD said to me, ‘Do not harass Moab, nor contend with them in battle, for I will not give you *any* of their land *as* a possession, because I have given ʲAr to ᵏthe descendants of Lot *as* a possession.’"

¹⁰ˡ(The Emim had dwelt there in times past, a people as great and numerous and tall as ᵐthe Anakim. ¹¹They were also regarded as giants,* like the Anakim, but the Moabites call them Emim. ¹²ⁿThe Horites formerly dwelt in Seir, but the descendants of Esau dispossessed them and destroyed them from before them, and dwelt in their place, just as Israel did to the land of their possession which the LORD gave them.)

¹³"‘Now rise and cross over ᵒthe Valley of the Zered.’ So we crossed over the Valley of the Zered. ¹⁴And the time we took to come ᵖfrom Kadesh Barnea until we crossed over the Valley of the Zered *was* thirty-eight years, �q until all the generation of the men of war was consumed from the midst of the camp, ʳjust as the LORD had sworn to them. ¹⁵For indeed the hand of the LORD was against them, to destroy them from the midst of the camp until they were consumed.

¹⁶"So it was, when all the men of war had finally perished from among the people, ¹⁷that the LORD spoke to me, saying: ¹⁸‘This day you are to cross over at Ar, the

* **2:11** Hebrew *rephaim*

1:39 *your children, who you say will be victims.* The most outrageous of Israel's complaints against God was that He had wanted their children to die (Num. 14:31). But the Lord demonstrated His love and faithfulness to His people by protecting those younger than 20 so that they could inherit the land.

1:44 *Hormah.* This name means "destruction," and probably refers to a site south of the Amorite hill country by Kadesh Barnea that was later called by that name.

2:7 *God has blessed.* The Israelites could not have survived forty years in the wilderness without the miraculous provision of God. That care has been an inspiration and encouragement to God's people throughout history. Those who receive God's bounty with a thankful heart find that it is enough, no matter how difficult the circumstances, and those who complain never recognize His blessing at all.

2:8 *we turned and passed by way.* The Israelites turned away from the way of the Red Sea, on which these cities were located and turned to the wilderness of Moab, which was the area east of Moab (Num. 33:44).

2:9 *Ar.* Ar is a synonym for the region of Moab. The Moabites were related to the Israelites through Lot (Gen. 19:37).

2:13 *Zered.* The brook of Zered was east of the Dead Sea at the border between Edom and Moab.

2:15 *hand.* The term "hand" suggests God's personal involvement both in acts of deliverance (Ex. 15:6) and in chastisement.

1:39 ˢ Num. 14:31 ᵗ Num. 14:3 ᵘ Is. 7:15, 16   **1:40** ᵛ Num. 14:25   **1:41** ʷ Num. 14:40   **1:42** ˣ Num. 14:41–43   **1:43** ʸ Num. 14:44 ᶻ Deut. 17:12, 13   **1:44** ᵃ Ps. 118:12   **1:46** ᵇ Deut. 2:7, 14   **2:1** ᵃ Deut. 1:40 ᵇ Num. 14:25   **2:3** ᶜ Deut. 2:7, 14   **2:4** ᵈ Num. 20:14–21 ᵉ Deut. 23:7   **2:5** ᶠ Gen. 36:8   **2:7** ᵍ Deut. 8:2–4   **2:8** ʰ Judg. 11:18 ᶦ Num. 21:4   **2:9** ʲ Deut. 2:18, 29 ᵏ Gen. 19:36–38   **2:10** ˡ Gen. 14:5 ᵐ Deut. 9:2   **2:12** ⁿ Deut. 2:22   **2:13** ᵒ Num. 21:12   **2:14** ᵖ Num. 13:26 �q Deut. 1:34, 35 ʳ Num. 14:35

boundary of Moab. [19]And *when* you come near the people of Ammon, do not harass them or meddle with them, for I will not give you *any* of the land of the people of Ammon *as* a possession, because I have given it to *s*the descendants of Lot *as* a possession.'"

[20](That was also regarded as a land of giants;* giants formerly dwelt there. But the Ammonites call them *t*Zamzummim, [21]*u*a people as great and numerous and tall as the Anakim. But the LORD destroyed them before them, and they dispossessed them and dwelt in their place, [22]just as He had done for the descendants of Esau, *v*who dwelt in Seir, when He destroyed *w*the Horites from before them. They dispossessed them and dwelt in their place, even to this day. [23]And *x*the Avim, who dwelt in villages as far as Gaza—*y*the Caphtorim, who came from Caphtor, destroyed them and dwelt in their place.)

[24]" 'Rise, take your journey, and *z*cross over the River Arnon. Look, I have given into your hand *a*Sihon the Amorite, king of Heshbon, and his land. Begin to possess *it*, and engage him in battle. [25]*b*This day I will begin to put the dread and fear of you upon the nations under the whole heaven, who shall hear the report of you, and shall *c*tremble and be in anguish because of you.'

King Sihon Defeated

[26]"And I *d*sent messengers from the Wilderness of Kedemoth to Sihon king of Heshbon, *e*with words of peace, saying, [27]*f*'Let me pass through your land; I will keep strictly to the road, and I will turn neither to the right nor to the left. [28]You shall sell me food for money, that I may eat, and give me water for money, that I may drink; *g*only let me pass through on foot, [29]*h*just as the descendants of Esau who dwell in Seir and the Moabites who dwell in Ar did

for me, until I cross the Jordan to the land which the LORD our God is giving us.'

[30]*i*"But Sihon king of Heshbon would not let us pass through, for *j*the LORD your God *k*hardened his spirit and made his heart obstinate, that He might deliver him into your hand, as *it is* this day.

[31]"And the LORD said to me, 'See, I have begun to *l*give Sihon and his land over to you. Begin to possess *it*, that you may inherit his land.' [32]*m*Then Sihon and all his people came out against us to fight at Jahaz. [33]And *n*the LORD our God delivered him over to us; so *o*we defeated him, his sons, and all his people. [34]We took all his cities at that time, and we *p*utterly destroyed the men, women, and little ones of every city; we left none remaining. [35]We took only the livestock as plunder for ourselves, with the spoil of the cities which we took. [36]*q*From Aroer, which *is* on the bank of the River Arnon, and *from* *r*the city that *is* in the ravine, as far as Gilead, there was not one city too strong for us; *s*the LORD our God delivered all to us. [37]Only you did not go near the land of the people of Ammon— anywhere along the River *t*Jabbok, or to the cities of the mountains, or *u*wherever the LORD our God had forbidden us.

King Og Defeated

3 "Then we turned and went up the road to Bashan; and *a*Og king of Bashan came out against us, he and all his people, to battle *b*at Edrei. [2]And the LORD said to me, 'Do not fear him, for I have delivered him and all his people and his land into your hand; you shall do to him as you did to *c*Sihon king of the Amorites, who dwelt at Heshbon.'

[3]"So the LORD our God also delivered into our hands Og king of Bashan, with all his people, and we attacked him until he

---

* 2:20 Hebrew *rephaim*

2:23 Avim . . . Gaza . . . Caphtorim . . . Caphtor. The Avim lived in villages between the Jordan and the Mediterranean coast. Gaza was a Philistine city on the Mediterranean coast. The Caphtorim were a group of tribes that came by sea to the coasts of Canaan and Egypt. Caphtor is possibly the same as Crete (Gen. 10:14).
2:24 River Arnon. The river Arnon was the traditional border between Moab and Ammon.
2:26 Wilderness of Kedemoth. This desert within the territory of Sihon was located on its eastern border, east of the Dead Sea.
2:32 Jahaz. Jahaz was located north of Kedemoth (Is. 15:4).
2:34–35 utterly destroyed. By the law of the ban, every living thing, human and animal, was to be put to death. Sometimes, as in this case, the Lord permitted the Israelites to take livestock and property as spoil, and sometimes the Lord permitted the women and children to be spared. Canaanite idolatry had reached such abominable levels that the Lord was

not willing to put up with it any longer. He intended to put an end to it, and also to prevent the Israelites from being corrupted by the Canaanites.
2:36–37 Aroer . . . Gilead . . . Jabbok. Aroer was a city on the northern bank of the river Arnon at the border between Sihon and Moab. Gilead was the northern boundary of Sihon. Jabbok was the river Jacob crossed on his way back to Canaan (Gen. 32:22).
3:1 Bashan . . . Og. Bashan was the region east of the Sea of Galilee. The territory of Og may have extended south of the river Yarmuk into Gilead.

2:19 *s* Gen. 19:38   **2:20** *t* Gen. 14:5   **2:21** *u* Deut. 2:10
2:22 *v* Gen. 36:8 *w* Gen. 14:6; 36:20–30   **2:23** *x* Josh. 13:3
y Gen. 10:14   **2:24** *z* Judg. 11:18 *a* Deut. 1:4   **2:25** *b* Ex.
23:27 *c* Ex. 15:14–16   **2:26** *d* Num. 21:21–32 *e* Deut. 20:10
2:27 *f* Judg. 11:19   **2:28** *g* Num. 20:19   **2:29** *h* Deut.
23:3, 4   **2:30** *i* Num. 21:23 *j* Josh. 11:20 *k* Ex. 4:21
2:31 *l* Deut. 1:3, 8   **2:32** *m* Num. 21:23   **2:33** *n* Deut. 7:2
o Num. 21:24   **2:34** *p* Lev. 27:28   **2:36** *q* Deut. 3:12; 4:48
r Josh. 13:9, 16 *s* Ps. 44:3   **2:37** *t* Gen. 32:22 *u* Deut. 2:5, 9,
19   **3:1** *a* Num. 21:33–35 *b* Deut. 1:4   **3:2** *c* Num. 21:34

had no survivors remaining. ⁴And we took all his cities at that time; there was not a city which we did not take from them: sixty cities, ^dall the region of Argob, the kingdom of Og in Bashan. ⁵All these cities *were* fortified with high walls, gates, and bars, besides a great many rural towns. ⁶And we utterly destroyed them, as we did to Sihon king ^eof Heshbon, utterly destroying the men, women, and children of every city. ⁷But all the livestock and the spoil of the cities we took as booty for ourselves.

⁸"And at that time we took the ^fland from the hand of the two kings of the Amorites who *were* on this side of the Jordan, from the River Arnon to Mount ^gHermon ⁹(the Sidonians call ^hHermon Sirion, and the Amorites call it Senir), ¹⁰ⁱall the cities of the plain, all Gilead, and ^jall Bashan, as far as Salcah and Edrei, cities of the kingdom of Og in Bashan.

^{11k}"For only Og king of Bashan remained of the remnant of ^lthe giants.* Indeed his bedstead *was* an iron bedstead. (*Is it not in* ^mRabbah of the people of Ammon?) Nine cubits *is* its length and four cubits its width, according to the standard cubit.

The Land East of the Jordan Divided

¹²"And this ⁿland, *which* we possessed at that time, ^ofrom Aroer, which *is* by the River Arnon, and half the mountains of Gilead and ^pits cities, I gave to the Reubenites and the Gadites. ^{13a}The rest of Gilead, and all Bashan, the kingdom of Og, I gave to half the tribe of Manasseh. (All the region of Argob, with all Bashan, was called the land of the giants.* ^{14r}Jair the son of Manasseh took all the region of Argob, ^sas

far as the border of the Geshurites and the Maachathites, and ^tcalled Bashan after his own name, Havoth Jair,* to this day.)

¹⁵"Also I gave ^uGilead to Machir. ¹⁶And to the Reubenites ^vand the Gadites I gave from Gilead as far as the River Arnon, the middle of the river as *the* border, as far as the River Jabbok, ^wthe border of the people of Ammon; ¹⁷the plain also, with the Jordan as *the* border, from Chinnereth ^xas far as the east side of the Sea of the Arabah ^y(the Salt Sea), below the slopes of Pisgah.

¹⁸"Then I commanded you at that time, saying: 'The LORD your God has given you this land to possess. ^zAll you men of valor shall cross over armed before your brethren, the children of Israel. ¹⁹But your wives, your little ones, and your livestock (I know that you have much livestock) shall stay in your cities which I have given you, ²⁰until the LORD has given ^arest to your brethren as to you, and they also possess the land which the LORD your God is giving them beyond the Jordan. Then each of you may ^breturn to his possession which I have given you.'

²¹"And ^cI commanded Joshua at that time, saying, 'Your eyes have seen all that the LORD your God has done to these two kings; so will the LORD do to all the kingdoms through which you pass. ²²You must not fear them, for ^dthe LORD your God Himself fights for you.'

Moses Forbidden to Enter the Land

²³"Then ^eI pleaded with the LORD at that time, saying: ²⁴'O Lord GOD, You have begun to show Your servant ^fYour greatness

---

* **3:11** Hebrew *rephaim*   * **3:13** Hebrew *rephaim*
* **3:14** Literally *Towns of Jair*

3:8 Mount Hermon. Mount Hermon is in the mountain range in the north between Canaan and Lebanon.
3:9–11 Sidonians. The Sidonians were Phoenicians, a well-known ancient seafaring people.
3:10 Salcah. Salcah was a city located at the eastern border of Bashan.
3:11 bedstead. "Bedstead" could also be translated *sarcophagus,* that is, *stone coffin.* **Rabbah.** Rabbah was on the site of Amman, the capital of modern Jordan. **cubit.** The ordinary cubit is about eighteen inches. Nine cubits is about thirteen feet, and four cubits is about six feet.
3:14 Geshurites . . . Maachathites. The Geshurites lived east of the Sea of Galilee and south of Mount Hermon. The Maachathites were descended from Abraham's brother Nahor.
3:17 Chinnereth. Chinnereth is another name for the Sea of Galilee.
3:23–25 pleaded with the LORD. Moses was a man of prayer and a man of God. He had repeatedly interceded with God for the rebellious Israelites, and God had answered those prayers. Yet this request of Moses to enter the Promised Land was answered with a decided "no," and with the command not to mention the matter again. We usually don't know

why God says "no" to things that seem not only reasonable, but right and good to us. It is hard to give thanks for the answer we did not want, but we must learn that "no" can also be the hand of our loving Heavenly Father. Most of the time we won't see, this side of heaven, how grateful we ought to be for the "no" of God.
3:24 O Lord GOD. The Hebrew word for "Lord," or "Master," is followed by the personal name of God (Yahweh, here translated "GOD"). The respect and humbleness in calling God "Master," the long companionship revealed in calling God by the covenant name, and the pleading, just to see the Promised Land, poignantly speak of Moses' longing.

3:4 ^dDeut. 3:13, 14   **3:6** ^eDeut. 2:24, 34, 35
3:8 ^fJosh. 12:6; 13:8–12   ^g1 Chr. 5:23   **3:9** ^h1 Chr. 5:23   **3:10** ⁱDeut. 4:49   ^jJosh. 12:5; 13:11   **3:11** ^kAmos 2:9   ^lDeut. 2:11, 20   ^mJer. 49:2   **3:12** ⁿNum. 32:33   ^oDeut. 2:36   ^pNum. 34:14   **3:13** ^qJosh. 13:29–31; 17:1   **3:14** ^r1 Chr. 2:22   ^sJosh. 13:13   ^tNum. 32:41   **3:15** ^uNum. 32:39, 40   **3:16** ^v2 Sam. 24:5   ^wNum. 21:24   **3:17** ^xNum. 34:11, 12   ^yGen. 14:3   **3:18** ^zNum. 32:20   **3:20** ^aDeut. 12:9, 10   ^bJosh. 22:4   **3:21** ^c[Num. 27:22, 23]   **3:22** ^dEx. 14:14   **3:23** ^e[2 Cor. 12:8, 9]   **3:24** ^fDeut. 5:24; 11:2

and Your mighty hand, for gwhat god *is* *there* in heaven or on earth who can do *anything* like Your works and Your mighty *deeds?* 25I pray, let me cross over and see hthe good land beyond the Jordan, those pleasant mountains, and Lebanon.'

26"But the LORD iwas angry with me on your account, and would not listen to me. So the LORD said to me: 'Enough of that! Speak no more to Me of this matter. 27jGo up to the top of Pisgah, and lift your eyes toward the west, the north, and the south, and the east; behold *it* with your eyes, for you shall not cross over this Jordan. 28But kcommand Joshua, and encourage him and strengthen him; for he shall go over before this people, and he shall cause them to inherit the land which you will see.'

29"So we stayed in lthe valley opposite Beth Peor.

Moses Commands Obedience

4 "Now, O Israel, listen to athe statutes and the judgments which I teach you to observe, that you may live, and go in and possess the land which the LORD God of your fathers is giving you. 2bYou shall not add to the word which I command you, nor take from it, that you may keep the commandments of the LORD your God which I command you. 3Your eyes have seen what the LORD did at cBaal Peor; for the LORD your God has destroyed from among you all the men who followed Baal of Peor. 4But you who held fast to the LORD your God *are* alive today, every one of you.

5"Surely I have taught you statutes and judgments, just as the LORD my God commanded me, that you should act according to *them* in the land which you go to possess. 6Therefore be careful to observe *them;* for this *is* dyour wisdom and your understanding in the sight of the peoples who will hear all these statutes, and say,

'Surely this great nation *is* a wise and understanding people.'

7"For ewhat great nation *is there* that has fGod so near to it, as the LORD our God *is* to us, for whatever *reason* we may call upon Him? 8And what great nation *is there* that has *such* statutes and righteous judgments as are in all this law which I set before you this day? 9Only take heed to yourself, and diligently gkeep yourself, lest you hforget the things your eyes have seen, and lest they depart from your heart all the days of your life. And iteach them to your children and your grandchildren, 10*especially concerning* ithe day you stood before the LORD your God in Horeb, when the LORD said to me, 'Gather the people to Me, and I will let them hear My words, that they may learn to fear Me all the days they live on the earth, and *that* they may teach their children.'

11"Then you came near and stood at the foot of the mountain, and the mountain burned with fire to the midst of heaven, with darkness, cloud, and thick darkness. 12kAnd the LORD spoke to you out of the midst of the fire. You heard the sound of the words, but saw no form; lyou only *heard* a voice. 13mSo He declared to you His covenant which He commanded you to perform, nthe Ten Commandments; and oHe wrote them on two tablets of stone. 14And pthe LORD commanded me at that time to teach you statutes and judgments, that you might observe them in the land which you cross over to possess.

Beware of Idolatry

15q"Take careful heed to yourselves, for you saw no rform when the LORD spoke to you at Horeb out of the midst of the fire, 16lest you sact corruptly and tmake for yourselves a carved image in the form of any figure: uthe likeness of male or female,

---

3:29 Beth Peor. This was a pagan site dedicated to Baal of Peor (Num. 25:3–5) and was the scene of Israel's first disastrous encounter with the sexually centered worship of Baal (4:3).

4:1 listen. The exhortation to listen includes an encouragement to obey (4:9; 5:1; 6:3–4).

4:6 in the sight of the peoples. By living in obedience to God, Israel would become a countercultural force, showing the way of God in both society and government.

4:9 your children. One of the purposes of the family is to pass on from generation to generation the acts of God among men. In times where the written record did not exist, or where people could not read, the wonderful acts of God were repeated in stories and conversations. With the Bible readily available, we don't have to rely on our memories alone to recall the things that God has done, but we are still responsible to make these things known to our children. It is also important to tell our children about the times that the Lord has answered our prayers, convicted our conscience, and blessed us with His peace. The best role model a child can have is a parent whose heart is centered on the Lord.

4:12 heard . . . but saw no form. The Lord revealed His glory to the Israelites, but they saw no visual image other than darkness and fire. They did hear God's voice, however (v. 15). This verse reminds us that God is Spirit (John 4:24).

4:15–19 you saw no form. There was no way of describing or giving shape with any image to the experience of God's presence at Sinai (Ex. 20:18). Since Israel had not seen the form of God, they could not represent Him in any way. Although people were created in the likeness of God (Gen. 1:26–27), no image created in human likeness could represent God, nor could any animal or the majestic heavenly

3:24 9 2 Sam. 7:22   3:25 h Deut. 4:22   3:26 i Num. 20:12; 27:14   3:27 j Num. 23:14; 27:12   3:28 k Num. 27:18, 23   3:29 l Deut. 4:46; 34:6   4:1 a [Rom. 10:5]   4:2 b Prov. 30:6   4:3 c Num. 25:1–9   4:6 d [2 Tim. 3:15]   4:7 e [2 Sam. 7:23]   f [Is. 55:6]   4:9 9 Prov. 4:23   h Deut. 29:2–8   i Gen. 18:19   4:10 j Ex. 19:9, 16, 17   4:12 k Deut. 5:4, 22   l 1 Kin. 19:11–18   4:13 m Deut. 9:9, 11   n Ex. 34:28   o Ex. 24:12   4:14 p Ex. 21:1   4:15 q Josh. 23:11   r Is. 40:18   4:16 s Deut. 9:12; 31:29   t Ex. 20:4, 5   u Rom. 1:23

17the likeness of any animal that *is* on the earth or the likeness of any winged bird that flies in the air, 18the likeness of anything that creeps on the ground or the likeness of any fish that *is* in the water beneath the earth. 19And *take heed,* lest you vlift your eyes to heaven, and *when* you see the sun, the moon, and the stars, wall the host of heaven, you feel driven to xworship them and serve them, which the LORD your God has given to all the peoples under the whole heaven as a heritage. 20But the LORD has taken you and ybrought you out of the iron furnace, out of Egypt, to be zHis people, an inheritance, as you are this day. 21Furthermore athe LORD was angry with me for your sakes, and swore that bI would not cross over the Jordan, and that I would not enter the good land which the LORD your God is giving you as an inheritance. 22But cI must die in this land, dI must not cross over the Jordan; but you shall cross over and possess ethat good land. 23Take heed to yourselves, lest you forget the covenant of the LORD your God which He made with you, fand make for yourselves a carved image in the form of anything which the LORD your God has forbidden you. 24For gthe LORD your God *is* a consuming fire, ha jealous God.

25"When you beget children and grandchildren and have grown old in the land, and act corruptly and make a carved image in the form of anything, and ido evil in the sight of the LORD your God to provoke Him to anger, 26jI call heaven and earth to witness against you this day, that you will soon utterly perish from the land which you cross over the Jordan to possess; you will not prolong *your* days in it, but will be utterly destroyed. 27And the LORD kwill scatter you among the peoples, and you will be left few in number among the nations where the LORD will drive you. 28And lthere you will serve gods, the work of men's hands, wood and stone, mwhich neither see nor hear nor eat nor smell. 29nBut from there you will seek the LORD your

God, and you will find *Him* if you seek Him with all your heart and with all your soul. 30When you are in distress, and all these things come upon you in the olatter days, when you pturn to the LORD your God and obey His voice 31(for the LORD your God *is* a merciful God), He will not forsake you nor qdestroy you, nor forget the covenant of your fathers which He swore to them.

32"For rask now concerning the days that are past, which were before you, since the day that God created man on the earth, and *ask* sfrom one end of heaven to the other, whether *any* great *thing* like this has happened, or *anything* like it has been heard. 33tDid *any* people *ever* hear the voice of God speaking out of the midst of the fire, as you have heard, and live? 34Or did God *ever* try to go *and* take for Himself a nation from the midst of *another* nation, uby trials, vby signs, by wonders, by war, wby a mighty hand and xan outstretched arm, yand by great terrors, according to all that the LORD your God did for you in Egypt before your eyes? 35To you it was shown, that you might know that the LORD Himself *is* God; zthere is none other besides Him. 36aOut of heaven He let you hear His voice, that He might instruct you; on earth He showed you His great fire, and you heard His words out of the midst of the fire. 37And because bHe loved your fathers, therefore He chose their descendants after them; and cHe brought you out of Egypt with His Presence, with His mighty power, 38ddriving out from before you nations greater and mightier than you, to bring you in, to give you their land *as* an inheritance, as *it is* this day. 39Therefore know this day, and consider *it* in your heart, that ethe LORD Himself *is* God in heaven above and on the earth beneath; *there is* no other. 40fYou shall therefore keep His statutes and His commandments which I command you today, that it may go well with you and with your children after you, and that you may prolong *your* days in the land which the LORD your God is giving you for all time."

---

bodies. The Israelites could know God's creation, His power, and His character, but they would have to be satisfied to know Him without any visual image.

4:24 *a consuming fire . . . jealous.* God is free to destroy disobedient and rebellious people. Israel had witnessed His righteous anger during the wilderness journey as well as in Canaan (Num. 16; Heb. 12:19). "Jealous" means that God will tolerate no rivalry or unfaithfulness. This word can also be translated *zealous.* God is zealous for His holiness.

4:26 *heaven and earth.* All creation would act as God's witness against a rebellious and obstinate people. God's invisible attributes, His eternal power and divine nature are all clearly seen in creation (Rom. 1:20), so that man is without excuse. The creation belongs to God just as much as man does, and God uses it for His eternal purposes, one of which is to stand as a witness to the disobedient.

4:27 *scatter you among the peoples.* This is a

prophetic warning of the exiles that would take place in 722 and 586 B.C.

4:40 *that it may go well with you.* The promise of blessing in the land was conditional—it required obedience.

4:19 v Deut. 17:3 w 2 Kin. 21:3 x [Rom. 1:25] **4:20** y Jer. 11:4 z Deut. 7:6; 27:9 **4:21** a Num. 20:12 b Num. 27:13, 14 **4:22** c 2 Pet. 1:13–15 d Deut. 3:27 e Deut. 3:25 **4:23** f Deut. 4:16 **4:24** g Deut. 9:3 h Ex. 20:5; 34:14 **4:25** i 2 Kin. 17:17 **4:26** j Deut. 30:18, 19 **4:27** k Deut. 28:62 **4:28** l Jer. 16:13 m Ps. 115:4–7; 135:15–17 **4:29** n [2 Chr. 15:4] **4:30** o Hos. 3:5 p Joel 2:12 **4:31** q Jer. 30:11 r Job 8:8 s Matt. 24:31 **4:33** t Deut. 5:24–26 **4:34** u Deut. 7:19 v Ex. 7:3 w Ex. 13:3 x Ex. 6:6 y Deut. 26:8 **4:35** z Mark 12:32 **4:36** a Heb. 12:19, 25 **4:37** b Deut. 7:7, 8; 10:15; 33:3 c Ex. 13:3, 9, 14 **4:38** d Deut. 7:1 **4:39** e Josh. 2:11 **4:40** f Lev. 22:31

Cities of Refuge East of the Jordan

41Then Moses gset apart three cities on this side of the Jordan, toward the rising of the sun, 42hthat the manslayer might flee there, who kills his neighbor unintentionally, without having hated him in time past, and that by fleeing to one of these cities he might live: 43iBezer in the wilderness on the plateau for the Reubenites, Ramoth in Gilead for the Gadites, and Golan in Bashan for the Manassites.

Introduction to God's Law

44Now this is the law which Moses set before the children of Israel. 45These are the testimonies, the statutes, and the judgments which Moses spoke to the children of Israel after they came out of Egypt, 46on this side of the Jordan, jin the valley opposite Beth Peor, in the land of Sihon king of the Amorites, who dwelt at Heshbon, whom Moses and the children of Israel kdefeated after they came out of Egypt. 47And they took possession of his land and the land lof Og king of Bashan, two kings of the Amorites, who were on this side of the Jordan, toward the rising of the sun, 48mfrom Aroer, which is on the bank of the River Arnon, even to Mount Sion* (that is, nHermon), 49and all the plain on the east side of the Jordan as far as the Sea of the Arabah, below the oslopes of Pisgah.

The Ten Commandments Reviewed

5 And Moses called all Israel, and said to them: "Hear, O Israel, the statutes and judgments which I speak in your hearing today, that you may learn them and be careful to observe them. 2aThe LORD our God made a covenant with us in Horeb. 3The LORD bdid not make this covenant with our fathers, but with us, those who are here today, all of us who are alive. 4cThe LORD talked with you face to face on the mountain from the midst of the fire. 5dI stood between the LORD and you at that time, to declare to you the word of the LORD; for eyou were afraid because of the fire, and you did not go up the mountain. He said:

6 f'I am the LORD your God who brought you out of the land of Egypt, out of the house of bondage.

7 g'You shall have no other gods before Me.

8 h'You shall not make for yourself a carved image—any likeness of anything that is in heaven above, or that is in the earth beneath, or that is in the water under the earth; 9you shall not ibow down to them nor serve them. For I, the LORD your God, am a jealous God, visiting the iniquity of the fathers upon the children to the third and fourth generations of those who hate Me, 10jbut showing mercy to thousands, to those who love Me and keep My commandments.

11 k'You shall not take the name of the LORD your God in vain, for the LORD will not hold him guiltless who takes His name in vain.

12 l'Observe the Sabbath day, to keep it holy, as the LORD your God commanded you. 13mSix days you shall labor and do all your work, 14but the seventh day is the nSabbath of the LORD your God. In it you shall do no work: you, nor your son, nor your daughter, nor your male servant, nor your female servant, nor your ox, nor your donkey, nor any of your cattle, nor your stranger who is within your gates, that your male servant and your female servant may rest as well as you. 15oAnd remember that you were a slave in the land of Egypt, and the LORD your God brought you out from there pby a mighty hand and by an outstretched arm; therefore the LORD your God commanded you to keep the Sabbath day.

16 q'Honor your father and your mother, as the LORD your God has commanded you, rthat your days may be long, and that it may be well with syou in the land which the LORD your God is giving you.

17 t'You shall not murder.

---

* 4:48 Syriac reads Sirion (compare 3:9).

5:6–21 Commandments—The Ten Commandments are the basis for holy living—not just a list of rules, but an explanation of what God expects of us. Loving God comes first. Setting aside a day to focus on God is essential for maintaining this relationship. The way we feel about God will affect the way we feel about people, and this will have a direct effect on how we treat others. Even though these three ideas summarize the Commandments, it is also essential to examine each individual command and think about how it applies to our lives. It is not easy to faithfully obey these simple statements.

5:11 take . . . in vain. Taking the name of the Lord in vain refers to the abuse, misuse, blasphemy, cursing, or manipulation of the Lord's name. Something

"vain" is empty or without value, significance, or meaning.

5:12 the Sabbath. The primary significance of the Sabbath was that it belonged to the Lord.

4:41 g Num. 35:6 **4:42** b Deut. 19:4 **4:43** i Josh. 20:8
4:46 j Deut. 3:29 k Num. 21:24 **4:47** l Num. 21:33–35
4:48 m Deut. 2:36; 3:12 n Deut. 3:9 **4:49** o Deut. 3:17
5:2 a Ex. 19:5 **5:3** b Heb. 8:9 **5:4** c Ex. 19:9 **5:5** d Gal. 3:19 e Ex. 19:16 **5:6** f Ex. 20:2–17 **5:7** g Hos. 13:4
5:8 h Ex. 20:4 **5:9** i Ex. 34:7, 14–16 **5:10** j Dan. 9:4
5:11 k Ex. 20:7 **5:12** l Ex. 20:8 **5:13** m Ex. 23:12; 35:2
5:14 n [Heb. 4:4] **5:15** o Deut. 15:15 p Deut. 4:34, 37
5:16 q Lev. 19:3 r Deut. 6:2 s Deut. 4:40 **5:17** t Matt. 5:21

18 u'You shall not commit adultery.

19 v'You shall not steal.

20w'You shall not bear false witness against your neighbor.

21 x'You shall not covet your neighbor's wife; and you shall not desire your neighbor's house, his field, his male servant, his female servant, his ox, his donkey, or anything that *is* your neighbor's.'

22"These words the LORD spoke to all your assembly, in the mountain from the midst of the fire, the cloud, and the thick darkness, with a loud voice; and He added no more. And yHe wrote them on two tablets of stone and gave them to me.

The People Afraid of God's Presence

23z"So it was, when you heard the voice from the midst of the darkness, while the mountain was burning with fire, that you came near to me, all the heads of your tribes and your elders. 24And you said: 'Surely the LORD our God has shown us His glory and His greatness, and awe have heard His voice from the midst of the fire. We have seen this day that God speaks with man; yet he bstill lives. 25Now therefore, why should we die? For this great fire will consume us; cif we hear the voice of the LORD our God anymore, then we shall die. 26dFor who is there of all flesh who has heard the voice of the living God speaking from the midst of the fire, as we have, and lived? 27You go near and hear all that the LORD our God may say, and etell us all that the LORD our God says to you, and we will hear and do it.'

28"Then the LORD heard the voice of your words when you spoke to me, and the LORD said to me: 'I have heard the voice of the words of this people which they have spoken to you. fThey are right in all that they have spoken. 29gOh, that they had such a heart in them that they would fear Me and halways keep all My commandments, ithat it might be well with them and with their children forever! 30Go and say to them, "Return to your tents." 31But as for you, stand here by Me, jand I will speak to you all the commandments, the statutes, and the judgments which you shall teach them, that they may observe *them* in the land which I am giving them to possess.'

32"Therefore you shall be careful to do as the LORD your God has commanded you; kyou shall not turn aside to the right hand or to the left. 33You shall walk in lall the ways which the LORD your God has commanded you, that you may live mand *that it may be* well with you, and *that* you may prolong *your* days in the land which you shall possess.

The Greatest Commandment

6 "Now this *is* athe commandment, *and these are* the statutes and judgments which the LORD your God has commanded to teach you, that you may observe *them* in the land which you are crossing over to possess, 2bthat you may fear the LORD your God, to keep all His statutes and His commandments which I command you, you and your son and your grandson, all the days of your life, cand that your days may be prolonged. 3Therefore hear, O Israel, and be careful to observe *it*, that it may be well with you, and that you may dmultiply greatly eas the LORD God of your fathers has promised you—f'a land flowing with milk and honey.'*

* **6:3** Exodus 3:8

5:18 adultery. Adultery was a betrayal not only of a commitment, but of a relationship. Anyone who treated marriage lightly would also treat his or her relationship with God lightly.

5:21 covet. This command deals specifically with an attitude, rather than an action. Covetousness is self-centered dissatisfaction, which does not reflect loving concern for the well-being of others. Loving God and loving others are closely connected (Matt. 22:37–39).

5:22 wrote them in two tablets . . . gave them. The two tablets were two complete copies of the law. Usually two copies were made of ancient Middle Eastern treaties. One was retained by each of the contracting parties. But God gave both copies to Moses, signifying that God Himself would be with the Israelites. God and the Israelites kept their copies in the same place because they lived together.

5:25–26 why should we die . . . LORD our God. The Israelites' fear was an important part of understanding their sin and need for help in meeting the requirements of God. The living God is powerful, great, and holy, and He wants us to be like Him, so each sinner needs to realize the need for God's mercy.

5:29 heart in them. The people were impressed with what they saw and heard, but their hearts were unchanged.

6:2 fear. The fear of the Lord includes awe for His greatness and holiness, love for Him, and submission to His will. Initially, the fear of God may involve fright, knowing that God has the right to punish us for our sins. But when we look at His holiness and love, there is a joy in knowing God, who not only sees us for who we really are, but helps us to be who He wants us to be.

6:3 God of your fathers. God was their God, generation after generation, and He expected them to follow Him, from generation to generation as well.

5:18 u Ex. 20:14   **5:19** v [Rom. 13:9]   **5:20** w Ex. 20:16; 23:1   **5:21** x Ex. 20:17   **5:22** y Deut. 4:13   **5:23** z Ex. 20:18, 19   **5:24** a Ex. 19:19   b Deut. 4:33   **5:25** c Deut. 18:16   **5:26** d Deut. 4:33   **5:27** e Ex. 20:19   **5:28** f Deut. 18:17   **5:29** g Ps. 81:13   h Deut. 11:1   i Deut. 4:40   **5:31** j [Gal. 3:19]   **5:32** k Deut. 17:20; 28:14   **5:33** l Deut. 10:12   m Deut. 4:40   **6:1** a Deut. 12:1   **6:2** b [Eccl. 12:13]   c Deut. 4:40   **6:3** d Deut. 7:13   e Gen. 22:17   f Ex. 3:8, 17

4g"Hear, O Israel: The LORD our God, the LORD *is* one!* 5hYou shall love the LORD your God with all your heart, iwith all your soul, and with all your strength.

6"And jthese words which I command you today shall be in your heart. 7kYou shall teach them diligently to your children, and shall talk of them when you sit in your house, when you walk by the way, when you lie down, and when you rise up. 8lYou shall bind them as a sign on your hand, and they shall be as frontlets between your eyes. 9mYou shall write them on the doorposts of your house and on your gates.

Caution Against Disobedience

10"So it shall be, when the LORD your God brings you into the land of which He swore to your fathers, to Abraham, Isaac, and Jacob, to give you large and beautiful cities nwhich you did not build, 11houses full of all good things, which you did not fill, hewn-out wells which you did not dig, vineyards and olive trees which you did not plant—owhen you have eaten and are full— 12*then* beware, lest you forget the pLORD who brought you out of the land of Egypt, from the house of bondage. 13You shall qfear the LORD your God and serve Him, and rshall take oaths in His name. 14You shall not go after other gods, sthe gods of the peoples who *are* all around you 15(for tthe LORD your God *is* a jealous God

uamong you), lest the anger of the LORD your God be aroused against you and destroy you from the face of the earth.

16v"You shall not tempt the LORD your God was you tempted *Him* in Massah. 17You shall xdiligently keep the commandments of the LORD your God, His testimonies, and His statutes which He has commanded you. 18And you yshall do *what is* right and good in the sight of the LORD, that it may be well with you, and that you may go in and possess the good land of which the LORD swore to your fathers, 19zto cast out all your enemies from before you, as the LORD has spoken.

20a"When your son asks you in time to come, saying, 'What *is the meaning of* the testimonies, the statutes, and the judgments which the LORD our God has commanded you?' 21then you shall say to your son: 'We were slaves of Pharaoh in Egypt, and the LORD brought us out of Egypt bwith a mighty hand; 22and the LORD showed signs and wonders before our eyes, great and severe, against Egypt, Pharaoh, and all his household. 23Then He brought us out from there, that He might bring us in, to give us the land of which He swore to our fathers. 24And the LORD commanded us to observe all these statutes, cto fear the LORD our God, dfor our good always, that

---

* **6:4** Or *The LORD is our God, the LORD alone* (that is, the only one)

6:4 Hear, O Israel. This verse is the celebrated Shema, the basic confession of faith in Judaism (Matt. 22:37; Mark 12:29; Luke 10:27). The first word, "hear," is the Hebrew word *shema*. The people are to hear and respond properly to God. He is their God, and He alone is the Lord.

6:4–9 Passing on the Faith—In the days leading up to the end of Moses' leadership, he laid out the essentials of raising a family to follow God. Moses knew that these instructions were a foundational element in Israel's future. The only way the Israelites could maintain the land they were going to possess was to make sure that the faith would be passed on to each succeeding generation. Nothing has changed. Today we need to heed the same instructions.

In a family's life the teaching of God is to be a constant, daily effort. God is to be made a part of everyday life. It is the responsibility of a parent to be constantly looking for opportunities to teach children about God's instructions for living. God's instructions should be like clothing. They should be put on the minute we get up and kept on all day. They are to be our constant companions. Sharing our faith should be a natural part of daily communication with our children. We should also remember that these instructions come in the text subsequent to the command to love God with all of our heart and soul and strength. How else can we love Him better than by obeying and following Him and teaching our children to do the same?

6:5 shall love. Moses repeatedly exhorted the Israelites to respond to God's love with devotion. God commanded His people to choose Him with all their

being, and in the process to deny all other supposed deities.

6:8–9 hand . . . frontlets . . . doorposts . . . gates. In later years the Jews interpreted these instructions by wearing phylacteries (boxes containing Scripture) when they prayed. They attached a small vessel called a mezuzah, which contained these verses, to the doorpost. The purpose of this whole passage is to emphasize that God's ways are to be a part of our conversations, our homes, and every activity. They are to be as close to us and as visible as our hand or our forehead.

6:20–24 your son asks. The answer to the Israelite child's question would include four components: we were slaves in Egypt, the Lord brought us out with a mighty hand, He gave us land, and we have a challenge to responsible action. This is a powerful teaching tool, and one that applies to all Christians. We are to teach our children that we were slaves to sin, the Lord Jesus brought us out with a mighty hand, He has given us a Kingdom, and we have a challenge to responsible action.

6:4 g[1 Cor. 8:4, 6]   **6:5** hMatt. 22:37   i2 Kin. 23:25   **6:6** jDeut. 11:18–20   **6:7** kDeut. 4:9; 11:19   **6:8** lProv. 3:3; 6:21; 7:3   **6:9** mDeut. 11:20   **6:10** nJosh. 24:13   **6:11** oDeut. 8:10; 11:15; 14:29   **6:12** pDeut. 8:11–18   **6:13** qMatt. 4:10   rDeut. 5:11   **6:14** sDeut. 13:7   **6:15** tEx. 20:5   uEx. 33:3   **6:16** vLuke 4:12   w[1 Cor. 10:9]   **6:17** xDeut. 11:22   **6:18** yEx. 15:26   **6:19** zNum. 33:52, 53   **6:20** aDeut. 13:8, 14   **6:21** bEx. 13:3   **6:24** cDeut. 6:2   dJer. 32:39

^eHe might preserve us alive, as *it is* this day. ²⁵Then ^fit will be righteousness for us, if we are careful to observe all these commandments before the LORD our God, as He has commanded us.'

A Chosen People

7 "When the LORD your God brings you into the land which you go to ^apossess, and has cast out many ^bnations before you, ^cthe Hittites and the Girgashites and the Amorites and the Canaanites and the Perizzites and the Hivites and the Jebusites, seven nations greater and mightier than you, ²and when the LORD your God delivers ^dthem over to you, you shall conquer them *and* utterly destroy them. ^eYou shall make no covenant with them nor show mercy to them. ³Nor shall you make marriages with them. You shall not give your daughter to their son, nor take their daughter for your son. ⁴For they will turn your sons away from following Me, to serve other gods; ^gso the anger of the LORD will be aroused against you and destroy you suddenly. ⁵But thus you shall deal with them: you shall ^hdestroy their altars, and break down their *sacred* pillars, and cut down their wooden images,* and burn their carved images with fire.

⁶"For you *are* a holy people to the LORD your God; ⁱthe LORD your God has chosen you to be a people for Himself, a special treasure above all the peoples on the face of the earth. ⁷The LORD did not set His ^jlove on you nor choose you because you were more in number than any other people, for you were ^kthe least of all peoples; ⁸but ^lbecause the LORD loves you, and because He would keep ^mthe oath which He swore to your fathers, ⁿthe LORD has brought you out with a mighty hand, and redeemed you from the house of bondage, from the hand of Pharaoh king of Egypt.

⁹"Therefore know that the LORD your God, He *is* God, ^othe faithful God ^pwho keeps covenant and mercy for a thousand generations with those who love Him and keep His commandments; ¹⁰and He repays those who hate Him to their face, to destroy them. He will not be ^qslack with him who

hates Him; He will repay him to his face. ¹¹Therefore you shall keep the commandment, the statutes, and the judgments which I command you today, to observe them.

Blessings of Obedience

¹²"Then it shall come to pass, because you listen to these judgments, and keep and do them, that the LORD your God will keep with you the covenant and the mercy which He swore to your fathers. ¹³And He will ^rlove you and bless you and multiply you; ^sHe will also bless the fruit of your womb and the fruit of your land, your grain and your new wine and your oil, the increase of your cattle and the offspring of your flock, in the land of which He swore to your fathers to give you. ¹⁴You shall be blessed above all peoples; there shall not be a male or female ^tbarren among you or among your livestock. ¹⁵And the LORD will take away from you all sickness, and will afflict you with none of the ^uterrible diseases of Egypt which you have known, but will lay *them* on all those who hate you. ¹⁶Also you shall destroy all the peoples whom the LORD your God delivers over to you; your eye shall have no pity on them; nor shall you serve their gods, for that ^v*will be a* snare to you.

¹⁷"If you should say in your heart, 'These nations are greater than I; how can I dispossess them?'— ¹⁸you shall not be afraid of them, *but* you shall ^wremember well what the LORD your God did to Pharaoh and to all Egypt: ¹⁹^xthe great trials which your eyes saw, the signs and the wonders, the mighty hand and the outstretched arm, by which the LORD your God brought you out. So shall the LORD your God do to all the peoples of whom you are afraid. ²⁰^yMoreover the LORD your God will send the hornet among them until those who are left, who hide themselves from you, are destroyed. ²¹You shall not be terrified of them; for the LORD your God, the great and awesome God, *is* among you. ²²And the LORD your God will drive out those nations before you ^zlittle by

---

* 7:5 Hebrew *Asherim*, Canaanite deities

7:1 Hittites ... Girgashites ... Amorites ... Canaanites ... Perizzites ... Hivites ... Jebusites. The Hittites came originally from Asia Minor (Gen. 23:10). The Girgashites are an unknown people (Gen. 10:16; 1 Chr. 1:14). The Amorites were the native population of Canaan that had settled in the mountains. The Canaanites were the native population that had settled in the coastland, the Perizzites were the native population that had settled in the hill country, and the Hivites were the native population that had settled south of the Lebanon mountains. The Jebusites (perhaps an offshoot of the Hittites) were the native population settled near what later became Jerusalem. **7:2 covenant.** Covenant refers to any treaty with the Canaanite nations that might undermine God's covenant with Israel.

7:22 little by little. God's plan was that the land would be conquered in two stages. The first was a broad, rapid conquest under Joshua, and the second was a gradual, area by area conquest.

6:24 ^e Deut. 4:1 **6:25** ^f [Rom. 10:3, 5] **7:1** ^a Deut. 6:10 ^b Gen. 15:19–21 ^c Ex. 33:2 **7:2** ^d Num. 31:17 ^e Josh. 2:14 **7:3** ^f 1 Kin. 11:2 **7:4** ^g Deut. 6:15 **7:5** ^h Ex. 23:24; 34:13 **7:6** ⁱ Ex. 19:5, 6 **7:7** ^j Deut. 4:37 ^k Deut. 10:22 **7:8** ^l Deut. 10:15 ^m Luke 1:55, 72, 73 ⁿ Ex. 13:3, 14 **7:9** ^o 1 Cor. 1:9 ^p Neh. 1:5 **7:10** ^q [2 Pet. 3:9, 10] **7:13** ^r John 14:21 ^s Deut. 28:4 **7:14** ^t Ex. 23:26 **7:15** ^u Ex. 9:14; 15:26 **7:16** ^v Judg. 8:27 **7:18** ^w Ps. 105:5 **7:19** ^x Deut. 4:34; 29:3 **7:20** ^y Josh. 24:12 **7:22** ^z Ex. 23:29, 30

little; you will be unable to destroy them at once, lest the beasts of the field become *too* numerous for you. [23]But the LORD your God will deliver them over to you, and will inflict defeat upon them until they are destroyed. [24]And [a]He will deliver their kings into your hand, and you will destroy their name from under heaven; [b]no one shall be able to stand against you until you have destroyed them. [25]You shall burn the carved images of their gods with fire; you shall not [c]covet the silver or gold *that is* on them, nor take *it* for yourselves, lest you be snared by it; for it *is* an abomination to the LORD your God. [26]Nor shall you bring an abomination into your house, lest you be doomed to destruction like it. You shall utterly detest it and utterly abhor it, [d]for it *is* an accursed thing.

Remember the LORD Your God

8 "Every commandment which I command you today [a]you must be careful to observe, that you may live and [b]multiply, and go in and possess the land of which the LORD swore to your fathers. [2]And you shall remember that the LORD your God [c]led you all the way these forty years in the wilderness, to humble you *and* [d]test you, [e]to know what *was* in your heart, whether you would keep His commandments or not. [3]So He humbled you, [f]allowed you to hunger, and [g]fed you with manna which you did not know nor did your fathers know, that He might make you know that man shall [h]not live by bread alone; but man lives by every *word* that proceeds from the mouth of the LORD. [4][i]Your garments did not wear out on you, nor did your foot swell these forty years. [5][j]You should know in your heart that as a man chastens his son, *so* the LORD your God chastens you.

[6]"Therefore you shall keep the commandments of the LORD your God, [k]to walk in His ways and to fear Him. [7]For the LORD your God is bringing you into a good land, [l]a land of brooks of water, of fountains and springs, that flow out of valleys and hills; [8]a land of wheat and barley, of vines and

fig trees and pomegranates, a land of olive oil and honey; [9]a land in which you will eat bread without scarcity, in which you will lack nothing; a land whose stones *are* iron and out of whose hills you can dig copper. [10][m]When you have eaten and are full, then you shall bless the LORD your God for the good land which He has given you.

[11]"Beware that you do not forget the LORD your God by not keeping His commandments, His judgments, and His statutes which I command you today, [12][n]lest—*when* you have eaten and are full, and have built beautiful houses and dwell *in them;* [13]and *when* your herds and your flocks multiply, and your silver and your gold are multiplied, and all that you have is multiplied; [14]when your heart is lifted up, and you [p]forget the LORD your God who brought you out of the land of Egypt, from the house of bondage; [15]who [q]led you through that great and terrible wilderness, [r]in which *were* fiery serpents and scorpions and thirsty land where there was no water; [s]who brought water for you out of the flinty rock; [16]who fed you in the wilderness with [t]manna, which your fathers did not know, that He might humble you and that He might test you, [u]to do you good in the end— [17]then you say in your heart, 'My power and the might of my hand have gained me this wealth.'

[18]"And you shall remember the LORD your God, [v]for *it is* He who gives you power to get wealth, [w]that He may establish His covenant which He swore to your fathers, as *it is* this day. [19]Then it shall be, if you by any means forget the LORD your God, and follow other gods, and serve them and worship them, [x]I testify against you this day that you shall surely perish. [20]As the nations which the LORD destroys before you, [y]so you shall perish, because you would not be obedient to the voice of the LORD your God.

Israel's Rebellions Reviewed

9 "Hear, O Israel: You *are* to cross over the Jordan today, and go in to dispossess

---

8:3 man shall not live by bread alone. Humans have a spiritual nature that can be satisfied only by the spiritual nutrients of God's word. Jesus used these words to rebuke Satan when Jesus was tempted in the wilderness (Matt. 4:4; Luke 4:1–4). **proceeds from the mouth of the LORD.** The Bible is valuable because it is the word of God. It is inspired by God not only in the sense that it is relating true events, but because God knows the kinds of things that people need to know to follow Him in a world of sin, uncertainty, and death. God's word is man's only wisdom and hope. When people study it, rely on it, and apply it, the word will prove to be both wise and right. For God is as good as His every word, and God's every word is as good as the One from whom it comes.

8:16 test you, to do you good. Through the whole experience in Egypt and the wilderness, the Lord was

leading His children into decisions that would bring out their true nature. Difficult as the tests were, the Lord knew what was necessary to reveal to the Israelites not only His character, but theirs as well.

8:17 My power. Moses warned the people that prosperity and wealth often lead to an exaltation of self and a rejection of God.

7:24 [a] Josh. 10:24, 42; 12:1–24 [b] Josh. 23:9 **7:25** [c] Prov. 23:6 **7:26** [d] Deut. 13:17 **8:1** [a] Deut. 4:1; 6:24 [b] Deut. 30:16 **8:2** [c] Amos 2:10 [d] Ex. 16:4 [e] [John 2:25] **8:3** [f] Ex. 16:2, 3 [g] Ex. 16:12, 14, 35 [h] Matt. 4:4 **8:4** [i] Neh. 9:21 **8:5** [j] 2 Sam. 7:14 **8:6** [k] [Deut. 5:33] **8:7** [l] Deut. 11:9–12 **8:10** [m] Deut. 6:11, 12 **8:12** [n] Hos. 13:6 **8:14** [o] 1 Cor. 4:7 [p] Ps. 106:21 **8:15** [q] Is. 63:12–14 [r] Num. 21:6 [s] Num. 20:11 **8:16** [t] Ex. 16:15 [u] [Heb. 12:11] **8:18** [v] Hos. 2:8 [w] Deut. 7:8, 12 **8:19** [x] Deut. 4:26; 30:18 **8:20** [y] [Dan. 9:11, 12]

nations greater and mightier than yourself, cities great and fortified up to heaven, [2]a people great and tall, the [a]descendants of the Anakim, whom you know, and *of whom* you heard *it said,* 'Who can stand before the descendants of Anak?' [3]Therefore understand today that the LORD your God *is* He who [b]goes over before you *as a* [c]consuming fire. [d]He will destroy them and bring them down before you; [e]so you shall drive them out and destroy them quickly, as the LORD has said to you.

[4f]"Do not think in your heart, after the LORD your God has cast them out before you, saying, 'Because of my righteousness the LORD has brought me in to possess this land'; but *it is* [g]because of the wickedness of these nations *that* the LORD is driving them out from before you. [5]It is not because of your righteousness or the uprightness of your heart *that* you go in to possess their land, but because of the wickedness of these nations *that* the LORD your God drives them out from before you, and that He may fulfill the [i]word which the LORD swore to your fathers, to Abraham, Isaac, and Jacob. [6]Therefore understand that the LORD your God is not giving you this good land to possess because of your righteousness, for you *are* a [j]stiff-necked people.

[7]"Remember! Do not forget how you [k]provoked the LORD your God to wrath in the wilderness. [l]From the day that you departed from the land of Egypt until you came to this place, you have been rebellious against the LORD. [8]Also [m]in Horeb you provoked the LORD to wrath, so that the LORD was angry *enough* with you to have destroyed you. [9n]When I went up into the mountain to receive the tablets of stone, the tablets of the covenant which the LORD made with you, then I stayed on the mountain forty days and [o]forty nights. I neither ate bread nor drank water. [10p]Then the LORD delivered to me two tablets of stone written with the finger of God, and on them *were* all the words which the LORD had spoken to you on the mountain from the midst of the fire [q]in the day of

the assembly. [11]And it came to pass, at the end of forty days and forty nights, *that* the LORD gave me the two tablets of stone, the tablets of the covenant.

[12]"Then the LORD said to me, [r]'Arise, go down quickly from here, for your people whom you brought out of Egypt have acted corruptly; they have [s]quickly turned aside from the way which I commanded them; they have made themselves a molded image.'

[13]"Furthermore [t]the LORD spoke to me, saying, 'I have seen this people, and indeed [u]they are a stiff-necked people. [14v]Let Me alone, that I may destroy them and [w]blot out their name from under heaven; [x]and I will make of you a nation mightier and greater than they.'

[15y]"So I turned and came down from the mountain, and [z]the mountain burned with fire; and the two tablets of the covenant *were* in my two hands. [16]And [a]I looked, and behold, you had sinned against the LORD your God—had made for yourselves a molded calf! You had turned aside quickly from the way which the LORD had commanded you. [17]Then I took the two tablets and threw them out of my two hands and [b]broke them before your eyes. [18]And I [c]fell down before the LORD, as at the first, forty days and forty nights; I neither ate bread nor drank water, because of all your sin which you committed in doing wickedly in the sight of the LORD, to provoke Him to anger. [19d]For I was afraid of the anger and hot displeasure with which the LORD was angry with you, to destroy you. [e]But the LORD listened to me at that time also. [20]And the LORD was very angry with Aaron *and* would have destroyed him; so I prayed for Aaron also at the same time. [21]Then I took your sin, the calf which you had made, and burned it with fire and crushed it *and* ground *it* very small, until it was as fine as dust; and I [f]threw its dust into the brook that descended from the mountain.

[22]"Also at [g]Taberah and [h]Massah and [i]Kibroth Hattaavah you provoked the LORD to wrath. [23]Likewise, [j]when the LORD sent

---

9:4–6 *to possess this land.* The conquest of Canaan was both a judgment on the wickedness of the native population and a promise fulfilled to Abraham, Isaac, and Jacob (Gen. 15:18–21). The land was a gift of grace, not a gift given because of the merits of the Israelites.
9:7 *Do not forget.* In addition to remembering the grace of God, the people also had to remember how vulnerable they were to apostasy (1:6—3:29).
9:9 *nor drank water.* A person cannot go more than approximately three days without water and survive. God supernaturally preserved Moses during the forty days.
9:10 *finger of God.* The Ten Commandments were written on stone by the hand of God. This visual picture of God writing His words is so personal. There is another time that God writes on tablets, and that is on the tablet of the human heart (2 Cor. 3:3). This, too, is intensely personal and life changing. In the end, His

followers can only put the words of the stone tablets into effect after the Spirit of the living God has written on their hearts.
9:19 *the LORD listened to me.* For Moses' prayer, see verses 26–29. Daniel's prayer for the nation resembled Moses' intercession (Dan. 9:3–23).

9:2 [a] Num. 13:22, 28, 33   **9:3** [b] Josh. 3:11; 5:14   [c] Deut. 4:24   [d] Deut. 7:24   [e] Ex. 23:31   **9:4** [f] Deut. 8:17   [g] Lev. 18:3, 24–30   **9:5** [h] [Titus 3:5]   [i] Gen. 50:24   **9:6** [j] Deut. 31:27   **9:7** [k] Num. 14:22   [l] Ex. 14:11   **9:8** [m] Ex. 32:1–8   **9:9** [n] Deut. 5:2–22   [o] Ex. 24:18   **9:10** [p] Deut. 4:13   [q] Ex. 19:17   **9:12** [r] Ex. 32:7, 8   [s] Deut. 31:29   **9:13** [t] Ex. 32:9   [u] Deut. 9:6   **9:14** [v] Ex. 32:10   [w] Deut. 29:20   [x] Num. 14:12   **9:15** [y] Ex. 32:15–19   [z] Ex. 19:18   **9:16** [a] Ex. 32:19   **9:17** [b] Ex. 32:19   **9:18** [c] Ex. 34:28   **9:19** [d] Ex. 32:10, 11   [e] Ex. 32:14   **9:21** [f] Ex. 32:20   **9:22** [g] Num. 11:1, 3   [h] Ex. 17:7   [i] Num. 11:4, 34   **9:23** [j] Num. 13:3

you from Kadesh Barnea, saying, 'Go up and possess the land which I have given you,' then you rebelled against the commandment of the LORD your God, and [k]you did not believe Him nor obey His voice. [24]lYou have been rebellious against the LORD from the day that I knew you.

[25m]"Thus I prostrated myself before the LORD; forty days and forty nights I kept prostrating myself, because the LORD had said He would destroy you. [26]Therefore I prayed to the LORD, and said: 'O Lord GOD, do not destroy Your people and [n]Your inheritance whom You have redeemed through Your greatness, whom You have brought out of Egypt with a mighty hand. [27]Remember Your servants, Abraham, Isaac, and Jacob; do not look on the stubbornness of this people, or on their wickedness or their sin, [28]lest the land from which You brought us should say, "Because the LORD was not able to bring them to the land which He promised them, and because He hated them, He has brought them out to kill them in the wilderness." [29]Yet they *are* Your people and Your inheritance, whom You brought out by Your mighty power and by Your outstretched arm.'

The Second Pair of Tablets

10 "At that time the LORD said to me, 'Hew for yourself two tablets of stone like the first, and come up to Me on the mountain and make yourself an [a]ark of wood. [2]And I will write on the tablets the words that were on the first tablets, which you broke; and [b]you shall put them in the ark.'

[3]"So I made an ark of acacia wood, hewed two tablets of stone like the first, and went up the mountain, having the two tablets in my hand. [4]And He wrote on the tablets according to the first writing, the Ten Commandments, [c]which the LORD had spoken to you in the mountain from the midst of the fire in the day of the assembly; and the LORD gave them to me. [5]Then I turned and [d]came down from the mountain, and [e]put the tablets in the ark which I had made; [f]and there they are, just as the LORD commanded me."

[6](Now the children of Israel journeyed from the wells of Bene Jaakan to Moserah, where Aaron [g]died, and where he was buried; and Eleazar his son ministered as priest in his stead. [7h]From there they journeyed to Gudgodah, and from Gudgodah to Jotbathah, a land of rivers of water. [8]At that time [i]the LORD separated the tribe of Levi [j]to bear the ark of the covenant of the LORD, [k]to stand before the LORD to minister to Him and [l]to bless in His name, to this day. [9m]Therefore Levi has no portion nor inheritance with his brethren; the LORD *is* his inheritance, just as the LORD your God promised him.)

[10]"As at the first time, [n]I stayed in the mountain forty days and forty nights; [o]the LORD also heard me at that time, *and* the LORD chose not to destroy you. [11p]Then the LORD said to me, 'Arise, begin your journey before the people, that they may go in and possess the land which I swore to their fathers to give them.'

The Essence of the Law

[12]"And now, Israel, [q]what does the LORD your God require of you, but to fear the LORD your God, to walk in all His ways and to [r]love Him, to serve the LORD your God with all your heart and with all your soul, [13]*and* to keep the commandments of the LORD and His statutes which I command you today [s]for your good? [14]Indeed heaven and the highest heavens belong to the [t]LORD your God, *also* the earth with all that *is* in it. [15]The LORD delighted only in your fathers, to love them; and He chose their descendants after them, you above all peoples, as *it is* this day. [16]Therefore circumcise the foreskin of your [u]heart, and be [v]stiff-necked no longer. [17]For the LORD your God *is* [w]God of gods and [x]Lord of lords, the great God, [y]mighty and awesome, who [z]shows no partiality nor takes a bribe. [18a]He administers justice for the fatherless and the widow, and loves the stranger, giving him food and clothing. [19]Therefore love the stranger, for you were strangers in the land of Egypt. [20b]You shall fear the LORD your God; you shall serve Him, and to Him you shall hold fast, and take oaths in His name. [21]He *is* your praise, and He *is* your God, who has done for you

---

9:26–29 I prayed. Moses took God's judgment seriously. Nevertheless he asked God for what he felt was important. He appealed to God's faithfulness, mercy, and honor. It is always all right to beseech the Lord for what seems right to us from our point of view, but as we pray, we remember that God knows more than we do, and we can trust Him to take the best course of action.

10:3 acacia wood. The acacia or shittim tree is still found in the Sinai peninsula, but in smaller numbers than when the Israelites passed through. Some varieties produce an attractive, highly figured hardwood.

10:19 Therefore love the stranger. God's good provision for their own needs should have motivated the

Israelites to love the stranger among them. To love and provide for the disadvantaged was in fact following God's example.

9:23 [k] Ps. 106:24, 25 **9:24** [l] Deut. 9:7; 31:27 **9:25** [m] Deut. 9:18 **9:26** [n] Deut. 32:9 **10:1** [a] Ex. 25:10 **10:2** [b] Ex. 25:16, 21 **10:4** [c] Ex. 20:1; 34:28 **10:5** [d] Ex. 34:29 [e] Ex. 40:20 [f] 1 Kin. 8:9 **10:6** [g] Num. 20:25–28; 33:38 **10:7** [h] Num. 33:32–34 **10:8** [i] Num. 3:6 [j] Num. 4:5, 15; 10:21 [k] Deut. 18:5 [l] Num. 6:23 **10:9** [m] Deut. 18:1, 2 **10:10** [n] Deut. 9:18 [o] Ex. 32:14 **10:11** [p] Ex. 33:1 **10:12** [q] Mic. 6:8 [r] Deut. 6:5 **10:13** [s] Deut. 6:24 **10:14** [t] [Neh. 9:6] **10:16** [u] Jer. 4:4 [v] Deut. 9:6, 13 **10:17** [w] Dan. 2:47 [x] Rev. 19:16 [y] Deut. 7:21 [z] Acts 10:34 **10:18** [a] Ps. 68:5; 146:9 **10:20** [b] Matt. 4:10

these great and awesome things which your eyes have seen. [22]Your fathers went down to Egypt with seventy persons, and now the LORD your God has made you as the stars of heaven in multitude.

Love and Obedience Rewarded

11 "Therefore you shall love the LORD your God, and keep His charge, His statutes, His judgments, and His commandments always. [2]Know today that I do not speak with your children, who have not known and who have not seen the chastening of the LORD your God, His greatness and His mighty hand and His outstretched arm— [3]His signs and His acts which He did in the midst of Egypt, to Pharaoh king of Egypt, and to all his land; [4]what He did to the army of Egypt, to their horses and their chariots: [a]how He made the waters of the Red Sea overflow them as they pursued you, and how the LORD has destroyed them to this day; [5b]what He did for you in the wilderness until you came to this place; [6]and what He did to Dathan and Abiram the sons of Eliab, the son of Reuben: how the earth opened its mouth and swallowed them up, their households, their tents, and all the substance that was in their possession, in the midst of all Israel— [7]but your eyes have [c]seen every great act of the LORD which He did.

[8]"Therefore you shall keep every commandment which I command you today, that you may [d]be strong, and go in and possess the land which you cross over to possess, [9]and [e]that you may prolong your days in the land [f]which the LORD swore to give your fathers, to them and their descendants,' [g]'a land flowing with milk and honey.' [10]For the land which you go to possess is not like the land of Egypt from which you have come, where you sowed your seed and watered it by foot, as a vegetable garden; [11h]but the land which you cross over to possess is a land of hills and valleys, which drinks water from the rain of heaven, [12]a land for which the LORD your God cares; [i]the eyes of the LORD your God are always on it, from the beginning of the year to the very end of the year.

[13]'And it shall be that if you earnestly obey My commandments which I command

you today, to love the LORD your God and serve Him with all your heart and with all your soul, [14]then [i]I* will give you the rain for your land in its season, [k]the early rain and the latter rain, that you may gather in your grain, your new wine, and your oil. [15l]And I will send grass in your fields for your livestock, that you may [m]eat and be filled.' [16]Take heed to yourselves, [n]lest your heart be deceived, and you turn aside and [o]serve other gods and worship them, [17]lest [p]the LORD's anger be aroused against you, and He [q]shut up the heavens so that there be no rain, and the land yield no produce, and [r]you perish quickly from the good land which the LORD is giving you.

[18]"Therefore [s]you shall lay up these words of mine in your heart and in your [t]soul, and [u]bind them as a sign on your hand, and they shall be as frontlets between your eyes. [19v]You shall teach them to your children, speaking of them when you sit in your house, when you walk by the way, when you lie down, and when you rise up. [20w]And you shall write them on the doorposts of your house and on your gates, [21]that [x]your days and the days of your children may be multiplied in the land of which the LORD swore to your fathers to give them, like [y]the days of the heavens above the earth.

[22]"For if [z]you carefully keep all these commandments which I command you to do—to love the LORD your God, to walk in all His ways, and [a]to hold fast to Him— [23]then the LORD will [b]drive out all these nations from before you, and you will [c]dispossess greater and mightier nations than yourselves. [24d]Every place on which the sole of your foot treads shall be yours: [e]from the wilderness and Lebanon, from the river, the River Euphrates, even to the Western Sea,* shall be your territory. [25]No man shall be able to [f]stand against you; the LORD your God will put the [g]dread of you and the fear of you upon all the land where you tread, just as He has said to you.

[26h]"Behold, I set before you today a

---

* **11:9** Exodus 3:8   * **11:14** Following Masoretic Text and Targum; Samaritan Pentateuch, Septuagint, and Vulgate read He.   * **11:24** That is, the Mediterranean

---

11:1 keep His charge. Loving God is in response to His love for us. We are directed to love God, but God first demonstrates His love for us. He rescued the Israelites from slavery to the Egyptians; He rescues us from slavery to sin (Rom. 6:20). Our first response is to return this love He has shown us. Our second response is to keep His commandments, to do the things He says to do. Love oils the wheels of obedience and makes obedience a blessing, not a burden.

11:9–12 not like the land of Egypt. Agriculture in Egypt depended on irrigation, the annual flooding of the Nile.

11:14 early rain . . . latter rain. The early rain

encouraged the sprouting of seed and new growth. The late rain brought crops to maturity.

11:4 [a] Ps. 106:11   **11:5** [b] Ps. 106:16–18   **11:7** [c] Deut. 10:21; 29:2   **11:8** [d] Josh. 1:6, 7   **11:9** [e] Deut. 4:40; 5:16, 33; 6:2   [f] Deut. 9:5   [g] Ex. 3:8   **11:11** [h] Deut. 8:7   **11:12** [i] 1 Kin. 9:3   **11:14** [j] Deut. 28:12   [k] Joel 2:23   **11:15** [l] Ps. 104:14   [m] Deut. 6:11   **11:16** [n] Job 31:27   [o] Deut. 8:19   **11:17** [p] Deut. 6:15; 9:19   [q] 2 Chr. 6:26; 7:13   [r] Deut. 4:26   **11:18** [s] Deut. 6:6–9   [t] Ps. 119:2, 34   [u] Deut. 6:8   **11:19** [v] Deut. 4:9, 10; 6:7   **11:20** [w] Deut. 6:9   **11:21** [x] Deut. 4:40   [y] Ps. 72:5; 89:29   **11:22** [z] Deut. 11:1   [a] Deut. 10:20   **11:23** [b] Deut. 4:38   [c] Deut. 9:1   **11:24** [d] Josh. 1:3; 14:9   [e] Gen. 15:18   **11:25** [f] Deut. 7:24   [g] Deut. 2:25   **11:26** [h] Deut. 30:1, 15, 19

blessing and a curse: [27]the blessing, if you obey the commandments of the LORD your God which I command you today; [28]and the [i]curse, if you do not obey the commandments of the LORD your God, but turn aside from the way which I command you today, to go after other gods which you have not known. [29]Now it shall be, when the LORD your God has brought you into the land which you go to possess, that you shall put the [k]blessing on Mount Gerizim and the [l]curse on Mount Ebal. [30]Are they not on the other side of the Jordan, toward the setting sun, in the land of the Canaanites who dwell in the plain opposite Gilgal, [m]beside the terebinth trees of Moreh? [31]For you will cross over the Jordan and go in to possess the land which the LORD your God is giving you, and you will possess it and dwell in it. [32]And you shall be careful to observe all the statutes and judgments which I set before you today.

A Prescribed Place of Worship

12 "These [a]are the statutes and judgments which you shall be careful to observe in the land which the LORD God of your fathers is giving you to possess, [b]all the days that you live on the earth. [2c]You shall utterly destroy all the places where the nations which you shall dispossess served their gods, [d]on the high mountains and on the hills and under every green tree. [3]And [e]you shall destroy their altars, break their sacred pillars, and burn their wooden images with fire; you shall cut down the carved images of their gods and destroy their names from that place. [4]You shall not [f]worship the LORD your God with such things.

[5]"But you shall seek the [g]place where the LORD your God chooses, out of all your tribes, to put His name for His [h]dwelling place; and there you shall go. [6i]There you shall take your burnt offerings, your sacrifices, your tithes, the heave offerings of your hand, your vowed offerings, your

freewill offerings, and the [j]firstborn of your herds and flocks. [7]And [k]there you shall eat before the LORD your God, and [l]you shall rejoice in all to which you have put your hand, you and your households, in which the LORD your God has blessed you.

[8]"You shall not at all do as we are doing here today—[m]every man doing whatever is right in his own eyes— [9]for as yet you have not come to the [n]rest and the inheritance which the LORD your God is giving you. [10]But when you cross over the Jordan and dwell in the land which the LORD your God is giving you to inherit, and He gives you [o]rest from all your enemies round about, so that you dwell in safety, [11]then there will be the place where the LORD your God chooses to make His name abide. There you shall bring all that I command you: your burnt offerings, your sacrifices, your tithes, the heave offerings of your hand, and all your choice offerings which you vow to the LORD. [12]And [p]you shall rejoice before the LORD your God, you and your sons and your daughters, your male and female servants, and the [q]Levite who is within your gates, since he has no portion nor inheritance with you. [13]Take heed to yourself that you do not offer your burnt offerings in every place that you see; [14]but in the place which the LORD chooses, in one of your tribes, there you shall offer your burnt offerings, and there you shall do all that I command you.

[15]"However, [r]you may slaughter and eat meat within all your gates, whatever your heart desires, according to the blessing of the LORD your God which He has given you; [s]the unclean and the clean may eat of it, [t]of the gazelle and the deer alike. [16u]Only you shall not eat the blood; you shall pour it on the earth like water. [17]You may not eat within your gates the tithe of your grain or your new wine or your oil, of the firstborn of your herd or your flock, of any of your offerings which you vow, of your freewill offerings, or of the heave offering of your

---

12:1–4 altars . . . pillars. The sacred pillars were monuments dedicated to one of the gods. They represented the power of fertility. The poles refer to the altars dedicated to the goddess Asherah, who was frequently associated with Baal.
12:5 seek. Whatever one seeks is the object of one's desire and devotion. Once they were settled in the land, the different tribes would be spread out, but they would still find God in their midst, in the place that God chose. This place was to be the object of their desire, God Himself the object of their devotion.
12:6 sacrifices. The Hebrew word for sacrifice always designates the offering of an animal. The contribution of the hand was one which the priest lifted up to signify that it was a gift to the Lord (Ex. 29:27; Lev. 7:34). The priest took his share and the worshiper and his family ate the rest. A votive offering was made in the fulfillment of a vow (Lev. 7:16; Num. 6:21). A freewill offering was voluntary (Ex. 35:27–29; Lev. 7:16).
12:7 eat . . . rejoice. The communal offerings were to

be eaten and enjoyed by those who offered them. It was a time of celebration before the Lord.
12:8 whatever is right in his own eyes. In the wilderness the people did not develop a common focus on the Lord. Moses challenged the new generation to act with common faithfulness and obedience.
12:17 eat within your gates. Aspects of God's worship were designed for community celebration, and were not to be done in the privacy of the home.

11:27 [i] Deut. 28:1–14　**11:28** [j] Deut. 28:15–68　**11:29** [k] Josh. 8:33　[l] Deut. 27:13–26　**11:30** [m] Gen. 12:6　**12:1** [a] Deut. 6:1　[b] Deut. 4:9, 10　**12:2** [c] Ex. 34:13　[d] 2 Kin. 16:4; 17:10, 11　**12:3** [e] Num. 33:52　**12:4** [f] Deut. 12:31　**12:5** [g] Ex. 20:24　[h] Ex. 15:13　**12:6** [i] Lev. 17:3, 4　[i] Deut. 14:23　**12:7** [k] Deut. 14:26　[l] Deut. 12:12, 18　**12:8** [m] Judg. 17:6; 21:25　**12:9** [n] Deut. 3:20; 25:19　**12:10** [o] Josh. 11:23　**12:12** [p] Deut. 12:18; 26:11　[q] Deut. 10:9; 14:29　**12:15** [r] Deut. 12:21　[s] Deut. 12:22　[t] Deut. 14:5　**12:16** [u] Gen. 9:4

hand. [18]But you must eat them before the LORD your God in the place which the LORD your God chooses, you and your son and your daughter, your male servant and your female servant, and the Levite who *is* within your gates; and you shall rejoice before the LORD your God in all to which you put your hands. [19]Take heed to yourself that you do not forsake the Levite as long as you live in your land.

[20]"When the LORD your God [v]enlarges your border as He has promised you, and you say, 'Let me eat meat,' because you long to eat meat, you may eat as much meat as your heart desires. [21]If the place where the LORD your God chooses to put His name is too far from [w]you, then you may slaughter from your herd and from your flock which the LORD has given you, just as I have commanded you, and you may eat within your gates as much as your heart desires. [22]Just as the gazelle and the deer are eaten, so you may eat them; the unclean and the clean alike may eat them. [23]Only be sure that you do not eat the blood, [x]for the blood *is* the life; you may not eat the life with the meat. [24]You shall not eat it; you shall pour it on the earth like water. [25]You shall not eat it, [y]that it may go well with you and your children after you, [z]when you do *what is* right in the sight of the LORD. [26]Only the [a]holy things which you have, and your vowed offerings, you shall take and go to the place which the LORD chooses. [27]And [b]you shall offer your burnt offerings, the meat and the blood, on the altar of the LORD your God; and the blood of your sacrifices shall be poured out on the altar of the LORD your God, and you shall eat the meat. [28]Observe and obey all these words which I command you, [c]that it may go well with you and your children after you forever, when you do *what is* good and right in the sight of the LORD your God.

Beware of False Gods

[29]"When [d]the LORD your God cuts off from before you the nations which you go to dispossess, and you displace them and dwell in their land, [30]take heed to yourself that you are not ensnared to follow them, after they are destroyed from before you, and that you do not inquire after their gods, saying, 'How did these nations serve their gods? I also will do likewise.' [31e]You shall not worship the LORD your God in that way; for every abomination to the LORD which He hates they have done to their gods; for [f]they burn even their sons and daughters in the fire to their gods.

[32]"Whatever I command you, be careful to observe it; [g]you shall not add to it nor take away from it.

Punishment of Apostates

13 "If there arises among you a prophet or a [a]dreamer of dreams, [b]and he gives you a sign or a wonder, [2]and [c]the sign or the wonder comes to pass, of which he spoke to you, saying, 'Let us go after other gods'—which you have not known—'and let us serve them,' [3]you shall not listen to the words of that prophet or that dreamer of dreams, for the LORD your God [d]is testing you to know whether you love the LORD your God with all your heart and with all your soul. [4]You shall [e]walk after the LORD your God and fear Him, and keep His commandments and obey His voice; you shall serve Him and [f]hold fast to Him. [5]But [g]that prophet or that dreamer of dreams shall be put to death, because he has spoken in order to turn *you* away from the LORD your God, who brought you out of the land of Egypt and redeemed you from the house of bondage, to entice you from the way in which the LORD your God commanded you to walk. [h]So you shall put away the evil from your midst.

[6i]"If your brother, the son of your mother, your son or your daughter, [j]the wife of your bosom, or your friend [k]who is as your own soul, secretly entices you, saying, 'Let us go and serve other gods,' which you have not known, neither you nor your fathers, [7]of the gods of the people which *are* all around you, near to you or far off from you, from *one* end of the earth to the *other*

12:30–31 take heed . . . that you are not ensnared. For forty years the basic sin which kept Israel out of Canaan was unbelief. However, once they settled in the Promised Land, the sin that eventually drove them out was idolatry. Idolatry is not only bowing down to a stone or wood image of a god; idolatry takes place every time our trust for our well-being is placed on something that is not the one true God. In the end, idolatry is the ultimate form of unbelief. It mocks God, because it imitates the dependence that people should have on Him, choosing a powerless placebo for the living God. The Lord would remove the temptation of the Canaanite nations, but the Israelites must not become curious and imitate the practices of the vanquished peoples. Calling it a snare was a warning that the temptation to copy them would be hidden, a trick, something that would catch them unaware.

13:1–2 a prophet or a dreamer. Both prophecy and dreams were legitimate forms of revelation.
13:3 testing you. The revelation of God through Moses was the test of any sign or message. When the message deviated from God's prior revelation, Israel had to discern false teaching.
13:5 put away the evil. Discipline, punishment, and testing were God's means of keeping His people pure.

12:20 [v]Ex. 34:24 **12:21** [w]Deut. 14:24 **12:23** [x]Gen. 9:4 **12:25** [y]Deut. 4:40; 6:18 [z]Ex. 15:26 **12:26** [a]Num. 5:9, 10; 18:19 **12:27** [b]Lev. 1:5, 9, 13, 17 **12:28** [c]Deut. 12:25 **12:29** [d]Ex. 23:23 **12:31** [e]Lev. 18:3, 26, 30; 20:1, 2 [f]Deut. 18:10 **12:32** [g]Rev. 22:18, 19 **13:1** [a]Zech. 10:2 [b]Matt. 24:24 **13:2** [c]Deut. 18:22 **13:3** [d]Deut. 8:2, 16 **13:4** [e]2 Kin. 23:3 [f]Deut. 30:20 **13:5** [g]Jer. 14:15 [h]Deut. 17:5, 7 **13:6** [i]Deut. 17:2 [j]Gen. 16:5 [k]1 Sam. 18:1, 3

end of the earth, **8**you shall *l*not consent to him or listen to him, nor shall your eye pity him, nor shall you spare him or conceal him; **9**but you shall surely kill him; your hand shall be first against him to put him to *m*death, and afterward the hand of all the people. **10**And you shall stone him with stones until he dies, because he sought to entice you away from the LORD your God, who brought you out of the land of Egypt, from the house of bondage. **11**So all Israel shall hear and *n*fear, and not again do such wickedness as this among you.

12o"If you hear someone in one of your cities, which the LORD your God gives you to dwell in, saying, **13**'Corrupt men have gone out from among you and enticed the inhabitants of their city, saying, "Let us go and serve other gods"'—which you have not known— **14**then you shall inquire, search out, and ask diligently. And *if it is* indeed true *and* certain *that* such an abomination was committed among you, **15**you shall surely strike the inhabitants of that city with the edge of the sword, utterly destroying it, all that is in it and its livestock—with the edge of the sword. **16**And you shall gather all its plunder into the middle of the street, and completely *p*burn with fire the city and all its plunder, for the LORD your God. It shall be *q*a heap forever; it shall not be built again. **17r**So none of the accursed things shall remain in your hand, that the LORD may *s*turn from the fierceness of His anger and show you mercy, have compassion on you and multiply you, just as He swore to your fathers, **18**because you have

listened to the voice of the LORD your God, *t*to keep all His commandments which I command you today, to do *what is* right in the eyes of the LORD your God.

Improper Mourning

14 "You *are* *a*the children of the LORD your God; *b*you shall not cut yourselves nor shave the front of your head for the dead. **2c**For you *are* a holy people to the LORD your God, and the LORD has chosen you to be a people for Himself, a special treasure above all the peoples who *are* on the face of the earth.

Clean and Unclean Meat

3d"You shall not eat any detestable thing. **4e**These *are* the animals which you may eat: the ox, the sheep, the goat, **5**the deer, the gazelle, the roe deer, the wild goat, the mountain goat,* the antelope, and the mountain sheep. **6**And you may eat every animal with cloven hooves, having the hoof split into two parts, *and that* chews the cud, among the animals. **7**Nevertheless, of those that chew the cud or have cloven hooves, you shall not eat, *such as* these: the camel, the hare, and the rock hyrax; for they chew the cud but do not have cloven hooves; they *are* unclean for you. **8**Also the swine is unclean for you, because it has cloven hooves, yet *does* not *chew* the cud; you shall not eat their flesh *or* touch their dead carcasses.

9g"These you may eat of all that *are* in the waters: you may eat all that have fins

---

* 14:5 Or addax

13:9 your hand shall be first. The relative or friend who brought the charge would lead in the capital punishment of the one who suggested idolatrous practices. With unforgettable words, Jesus emphasized the severity of this offense. Such a person should not have been born (Matt. 18:6–7).

13:13 serve other gods. Falling away from the truth is apostasy. Sometimes this can be fairly subtle, and that is why the word "enticed" is used with this concept. God clearly lays out a test that will always separate the truth from the lie. If someone says, "Let us go and serve other gods . . ." we know that the speaker is not from God. Our hope is in Christ alone. People do not recognize that they are going after "other gods" because they do not know the one true God. This is why it is so important to faithfully study the Bible, for in it all of the character and actions of God are revealed. We will not be fooled by the counterfeit if we are familiar with the genuine.

13:17–18 turn from the fierceness of His anger and show you mercy. This seemingly harsh judgment of evil was an act of obedience. God required the punishment of evildoers so that immoral practices would not spread throughout the land. God would bless the Israelites, and bless the land, but not while the evil practices were still going on.

14:2 God's Plan and Israel—The modern-day student of the Bible may well ask why so much of Scripture is taken up with the history of a single nation. Certainly many Christians wonder why one

nation should be called "God's chosen people." The answer to this question is bound up in God's purpose for Israel. When God promised Abraham that he would become the father of a great nation, He also promised that He would bless all peoples through that nation (Gen. 12:1–3). Therefore Israel was to be a channel of blessing as well as a recipient. Even their deliverance from Egypt was at least partially designed to show other nations that Israel's God was the only true God (Ex. 7:5; 14:18; Josh. 2:9–11). It was further prophesied by Isaiah that the Messiah would bring salvation to the Gentiles (Is. 49:6) The Psalms contain many invitations to other nations to come and worship the Lord in Israel (Ps. 2:10–12; 117:1). Ruth the Moabitess is an example of a foreigner who believed in Israel's God.

It is clear that God's promise to Abraham to bless the whole world through him is still being fulfilled. The life, ministry and death of Jesus Christ and the existence and influence of the church today, all came about through God's choice of Israel. All those the church wins to Christ, whether Jew or Gentile, enter into these great blessings channeled through Israel.

13:8 *l* Prov. 1:10 **13:9** *m* Deut. 17:7 **13:11** *n* Deut. 17:13 **13:12** *o* Judg. 20:1–48 **13:16** *p* Josh. 6:24 *q* Josh. 8:28 **13:17** *r* Josh. 6:18 *s* Josh. 7:26 **13:18** *t* Deut. 12:25, 28, 32 **14:1** *a* [Rom. 8:16] *b* Lev. 19:28; 21:1–5 **14:2** *c* Lev. 20:26 **14:3** *d* Ezek. 4:14 **14:4** *e* Lev. 11:2–45 **14:8** *f* Lev. 11:26, 27 **14:9** *g* Lev. 11:9

and scales. [10]And whatever does not have fins and scales you shall not eat; it *is* unclean for you.

[11]"All clean birds you may eat. [12h]But these you shall not eat: the eagle, the vulture, the buzzard, [13]the red kite, the falcon, and the kite after their kinds; [14]every raven after its kind; [15]the ostrich, the short-eared owl, the sea gull, and the hawk after their kinds; [16]the little owl, the screech owl, the white owl, [17]the jackdaw, the carrion vulture, the fisher owl, [18]the stork, the heron after its kind, and the hoopoe and the bat.

[19]"Also [i]every creeping thing that flies is unclean for you; [j]they shall not be eaten. [20]"You may eat all clean birds.

[21k]"You shall not eat anything that dies of itself; you may give it to the alien who *is* within your gates, that he may eat it, or you may sell it to a foreigner; [l]for you *are* a holy people to the LORD your God.

"[m]You shall not boil a young goat in its mother's milk.

Tithing Principles

[22n]"You shall truly tithe all the increase of your grain that the field produces year by year. [23o]And you shall eat before the LORD your God, in the place where He chooses to make His name abide, the tithe of your grain and your new wine and your oil, of [p]the firstborn of your herds and your flocks, that you may learn to fear the LORD your God always. [24]But if the journey is too long for you, so that you are not able to carry the tithe, or [q]if the place where the LORD your God chooses to put His name is too far from you, when the LORD your God has blessed you, [25]then you shall exchange *it* for money, take the money in your hand, and go to the place which the LORD your God chooses. [26]And you shall spend that money for whatever your heart desires: for oxen or sheep, for wine or similar drink, for whatever your heart desires; you shall eat there before the LORD your God, and you shall [r]rejoice, you and your household. [27]You shall not forsake the [s]Levite who *is*

within your gates, for he has no part nor inheritance with you.

[28t]"At the end of *every* third year you shall bring out the [u]tithe of your produce of that year and store *it* up within your gates. [29]And the Levite, because he has no portion nor inheritance with you, and the stranger and the fatherless and the widow who *are* within your gates, may come and eat and be satisfied, that the LORD your God may bless you in all the work of your hand which you do.

Debts Canceled Every Seven Years

15 "At the end of [a]every seven years you shall grant a release *of debts.* [2]And this *is* the form of the release: Every creditor who has lent *anything* to his neighbor shall release *it;* he shall not require *it* of his neighbor or his brother, because it is called the LORD's release. [3]Of a foreigner you may require *it;* but you shall give up your claim to what is owed by your brother, [4]except when there may be no poor among you; for the LORD will greatly [b]bless you in the land which the LORD your God is giving you to possess *as* an inheritance—[5]only if you carefully obey the voice of the LORD your God, to observe with care all these commandments which I command you today. [6]For the LORD your God will bless you just as He promised you; [c]you shall lend to many nations, but you shall not borrow; you shall reign over many nations, but they shall not reign over you.

Generosity to the Poor

[7]"If there is among you a poor man of your brethren, within any of the gates in your land which the LORD your God is giving you, [d]you shall not harden your heart nor shut your hand from your poor brother, [8]but [e]you shall open your hand wide to him and willingly lend him sufficient for his need, whatever he needs. [9]Beware lest there be a wicked thought in your heart, saying, 'The seventh year, the year of release, is at hand,' and your [f]eye be evil

---

14:21 not boil . . . in its mother's milk. Unlike the Canaanites who boiled young goats alive in the milk of their mothers as a sacrifice to fertility gods, Israel was to practice a more humane method of animal sacrifice.
14:22–29 tithe of your grain. The tithe was to be enjoyed in the presence of the Lord, unless the people had come from a great distance. Then they could exchange it for silver and purchase food and drink with it in Jerusalem.
14:25 money. Money refers to uncoined silver. Coins were not struck until the Persian era.
15:1 every seven years. God taught His people to think in cycles of holy time: six days of work, the seventh to rest; six years of business, the seventh of giving freedom to the poor; six years of agricultural cultivation, and the seventh to let the land lie fallow (Ex. 23:10–13; Lev. 25:1–7).
15:7–15 a poor man. Israel's uniqueness in the an-

cient world is seen in the laws which connect a right relationship with God and worship of Him with interpersonal relationships. If you love God, you will also treat others well. God is intensely interested in the poor, and it is the responsibility of His people to imitate His concern. The story of the Good Samaritan (Luke 10:30–37) is both the simplest and the most profound picture of how this concern works out in real life.
15:7 not harden. The people's attitude toward the

14:12 [h] Lev. 11:13   **14:19** [i] Lev. 11:20 [j] Lev. 11:23
14:21 [k] Lev. 17:15; 22:8 [l] Deut. 14:2 [m] Ex. 23:19; 34:26
14:22 [n] Lev. 27:30   **14:23** [o] Deut. 12:5–7 [p] Deut. 15:19, 20   **14:24** [q] Deut. 12:5, 21   **14:26** [r] Deut. 12:7
14:27 [s] Deut. 12:12   **14:28** [t] Deut. 26:12 [u] Num. 18:21–24
15:1 [a] Ex. 21:2; 23:10, 11   **15:4** [b] Deut. 7:13   **15:6** [c] Deut. 28:12, 44   **15:7** [d] Lev. 25:35–37   **15:8** [e] Matt. 5:42
15:9 [f] Deut. 28:54, 56

against your poor brother and you give him nothing, and [g]he cry out to the LORD against you, and [h]it become sin among you. 10You shall surely give to him, and [i]your heart should not be grieved when you give to him, because [j]for this thing the LORD your God will bless you in all your works and in all to which you put your hand. 11For [k]the poor will never cease from the land; therefore I command you, saying, 'You shall open your hand wide to your brother, to your poor and your needy, in your land.'

The Law Concerning Bondservants

12[l]"If your brother, a Hebrew man, or a Hebrew woman, is [m]sold to you and serves you six years, then in the seventh year you shall let him go free from you. 13And when you send him away free from you, you shall not let him go away empty-handed; 14you shall supply him liberally from your flock, from your threshing floor, and from your winepress. From what the LORD your God has [n]blessed you with, you shall give to him. 15oYou shall remember that you were a slave in the land of Egypt, and the LORD your God redeemed you; therefore I command you this thing today. 16pAnd if it happens that he says to you, 'I will not go away from you,' because he loves you and your house, since he prospers with you, 17then you shall take an awl and thrust it through his ear to the door, and he shall be your servant forever. Also to your female servant you shall do likewise. 18It shall not seem hard to you when you send him away free from you; for he has been worth [q]a double hired servant in serving you six years. Then the LORD your God will bless you in all that you do.

The Law Concerning Firstborn Animals

19r"All the firstborn males that come from your herd and your flock you shall sanctify to the LORD your God; you shall do no work with the firstborn of your herd, nor shear the firstborn of your flock. 20sYou and your household shall eat it before the LORD your God year by year in the place which the LORD chooses. 21tBut if there is a defect in it, if it is lame or blind or has any serious defect, you shall not

sacrifice it to the LORD your God. 22You may eat it within your gates; [u]the unclean and the clean person alike may eat it, as if it were a gazelle or a deer. 23Only you shall not eat its blood; you shall pour it on the ground like water.

The Passover Reviewed

16 "Observe the [a]month of Abib, and keep the Passover to the LORD your God, for [b]in the month of Abib the LORD your God brought you out of Egypt by night. 2Therefore you shall sacrifice the Passover to the LORD your God, from the flock and the herd, in the [d]place where the LORD chooses to put His name. 3You shall eat no leavened bread with it; [e]seven days you shall eat unleavened bread with it, that is, the bread of affliction (for you came out of the land of Egypt in haste), that you may [f]remember the day in which you came out of the land of Egypt all the days of your life. 4gAnd no leaven shall be seen among you in all your territory for seven days, nor shall any of the meat which you sacrifice the first day at twilight remain overnight until [h]morning.

5"You may not sacrifice the Passover within any of your gates which the LORD your God gives you; 6but at the place where the LORD your God chooses to make His name abide, there you shall sacrifice the Passover [i]at twilight, at the going down of the sun, at the time you came out of Egypt. 7And you shall roast and eat it in the place which the LORD your God chooses, and [j]in the morning you shall turn and go to your tents. 8Six days you shall eat unleavened bread, and [k]on the seventh day there shall be a sacred assembly to the LORD your God. You shall do no work on it.

The Feast of Weeks Reviewed

9"You shall count seven weeks for yourself; begin to count the seven weeks from the time you begin to put the sickle to the grain. 10Then you shall keep the [l]Feast of Weeks to the LORD your God with the tribute of a freewill offering from your hand, which you shall give [m]as the LORD your God blesses you. 11nYou shall rejoice before the LORD your God, you and your son and your daughter, your male servant and your female servant, the Levite who is within

---

poor should have been a reflection of their gratitude for God's gifts to them.

15:19 shall do no work . . . nor shear. The owners of firstborn male livestock could not profit from the firstborn because they belonged to the Lord.

16:1 Passover. Passover was observed on the fourteenth of Abib, or Nisan, which corresponds to our March-April (Ex. 12:1–21; Lev. 23:5–8; Num. 28:16–25).

16:6 going down of the sun. The twilight sacrifice was in commemoration of the Exodus, which occurred at night.

16:9 sickle to the grain. This took place on the second day of the Feast of the Passover.

15:9 g Deut. 24:15 h [Matt. 25:41, 42] **15:10** i 2 Cor. 9:5, 7 j Deut. 14:29 **15:11** k Matt. 26:11 **15:12** l Ex. 21:2–6 m Lev. 25:39–46 **15:14** n Prov. 10:22 **15:15** o Deut. 5:15 **15:16** p Ex. 21:5, 6 **15:18** q Is. 16:14 **15:19** r Ex. 13:2, 12 **15:20** s Deut. 12:5; 14:23 **15:21** t Lev. 22:19–25 **15:22** u Deut. 12:15, 16, 22 **16:1** a Ex. 12:2 b Ex. 13:4 **16:2** c Num. 28:19 d Deut. 12:5, 26; 15:20 **16:3** e Num. 29:12 f Ex. 13:3 **16:4** g Ex. 13:7 h Num. 9:12 **16:6** i Ex. 12:7–10 **16:7** j 2 Kin. 23:23 **16:8** k Lev. 23:8, 36 **16:10** l Ex. 34:22 m 1 Cor. 16:2 **16:11** n Deut. 16:14

your gates, the stranger and the fatherless and the widow who *are* among you, at the place where the LORD your God chooses to make His name abide. 12oAnd you shall remember that you were a slave in Egypt, and you shall be careful to observe these statutes.

The Feast of Tabernacles Reviewed

13p"You shall observe the Feast of Tabernacles seven days, when you have gathered from your threshing floor and from your winepress. 14And qyou shall rejoice in your feast, you and your son and your daughter, your male servant and your female servant and the Levite, the stranger and the fatherless and the widow, who *are* within your gates. 15rSeven days you shall keep a sacred feast to the LORD your God in the place which the LORD chooses, because the LORD your God will bless you in all your produce and in all the work of your hands, so that you surely rejoice.

16s"Three times a year all your males shall appear before the LORD your God in the place which He chooses: at the Feast of Unleavened Bread, at the Feast of Weeks, and at the Feast of Tabernacles; and tthey shall not appear before the LORD empty-handed. 17Every man *shall give* as he is able, uaccording to the blessing of the LORD your God which He has given you.

Justice Must Be Administered

18"You shall appoint vjudges and officers in all your gates, which the LORD your God gives you, according to your tribes, and they shall judge the people with just judgment. 19wYou shall not pervert justice; xyou shall not show partiality, ynor take a bribe, for a bribe blinds the eyes of the wise and twists the words of the righteous. 20You shall follow what is altogether just, that you may zlive and inherit the land which the LORD your God is giving you.

21a"You shall not plant for yourself any tree, as a wooden image, near the altar which you build for yourself to the LORD your God. 22bYou shall not set up a *sacred* pillar, which the LORD your God hates.

17 "You ashall not sacrifice to the LORD your God a bull or sheep which has any blemish *or* defect, for that *is* an abomination to the LORD your God.

2b"If there is found among you, within any of your gates which the LORD your God gives you, a man or a woman who has been wicked in the sight of the LORD your God, cin transgressing His covenant, 3who has gone and served other gods and worshiped them, either dthe sun or moon or any of the host of heaven, ewhich I have not commanded, 4fand it is told you, and you hear *of it*, then you shall inquire diligently. And if *it is* indeed true *and* certain that such an abomination has been committed in Israel, 5then you shall bring out to your gates that man or woman who has committed that wicked thing, and gshall stone hto death that man or woman with stones. 6Whoever is deserving of death shall be put to death on the testimony of two or three iwitnesses; he shall not be put to death on the testimony of one witness. 7The hands of the witnesses shall be the first against him to put him to death, and afterward the hands of all the people. So you shall put away the evil from among jyou.

8k"If a matter arises which is too hard for you to judge, between degrees of guilt for bloodshed, between one judgment or another, or between one punishment or another, matters of controversy within your gates, then you shall arise and go up to the lplace which the LORD your God chooses. 9And myou shall come to the priests, the Levites, and nto the judge *there* in those days, and inquire *of them*; othey shall pronounce upon you the sentence of judgment. 10You shall do according to the sentence which they pronounce

---

16:13–15 *Feast of Tabernacles.* The harvest festival was a time to celebrate God's goodness, and to remember how He cared for them when they lived in tents in the wilderness. Today this celebration is called Succoth, from the Hebrew word for booths.

16:19 *not pervert justice.* The foundation for a just and honest application of law in human society is God Himself. God entrusts rule to men who function in His place in dispensing justice. To pervert this justice with favoritism or bribes is to malign the character of God, and that is a sin that God always deals with sooner or later.

17:2 *transgressing.* The Hebrew verb for transgressing is used elsewhere to indicate the crossing of a border or stream. Here the word is used to indicate "crossing over" the boundaries that God had set for His people.

17:4–6 *inquire diligently.* An investigation, rather than gossip, determined the truth of any report of

idolatry. There must be two or three witnesses for a person to be condemned to death.

17:7 *hands of the witnesses . . . first.* The witnesses participated in the stoning of the guilty because they were responsible for the person's condemnation. Jesus' words about throwing the "first stone" referred to this practice (John 8:7).

17:8 *degrees of guilt.* This refers to cases of manslaughter or murder—that is, accidental or intentional homicide.

16:12 o Deut. 15:15 **16:13** p Ex. 23:16 **16:14** q Neh. 8:9 **16:15** r Lev. 23:39–41 **16:16** s Ex. 23:14–17; 34:22–24 t Ex. 23:15 **16:17** u Deut. 16:10 **16:18** v Deut. 1:16, 17 **16:19** w Ex. 23:2, 6 x Deut. 1:17 y Ex. 23:8 **16:20** z Ezek. 18:5–9 **16:21** a Ex. 34:13 **16:22** b Lev. 26:1 **17:1** a Deut. 15:21 **17:2** b Deut. 5:2 c Josh. 7:11 **17:3** d Deut. 4:19 e Jer. 7:22 **17:4** f Deut. 13:12, 14 **17:5** g Lev. 24:14–16 h Deut. 13:6–18 i Num. 35:30 **17:7** j Deut. 13:5; 19:19 **17:8** k Deut. 1:17 l Deut. 12:5; 16:2 **17:9** m Jer. 18:18 n Deut. 19:17–19 o Ezek. 44:24

upon you in that place which the LORD chooses. And you shall be careful to do according to all that they order you. 11According to the sentence of the law in which they instruct you, according to the judgment which they tell you, you shall do; you shall not turn aside *to* the right hand or *to* the left from the sentence which they pronounce upon you. 12Now *p*the man who acts presumptuously and will not heed the priest who stands to minister there before the LORD your God, or the judge, that man shall die. So you shall put away the evil from Israel. 13*q*And all the people shall hear and fear, and no longer act presumptuously.

Principles Governing Kings

14"When you come to the land which the LORD your God is giving you, and possess it and dwell in it, and say, *r*'I will set a king over me like all the nations that *are* around me,' 15you shall surely set a king over you *s*whom the LORD your God chooses; *one* *t*from among your brethren you shall set as king over you; you may not set a foreigner over you, who *is* not your brother. 16But he shall not multiply *u*horses for himself, nor cause the people *v*to return to Egypt to multiply horses, for *w*the LORD has said to you, *x*'You shall not return that way again.' 17Neither shall he multiply wives for himself, lest his heart turn away; nor shall he greatly multiply silver and *y*gold for himself.

18"Also it shall be, when he sits on the throne of his kingdom, that he shall write for himself a copy of this law in a book, from *the one* *z*before the priests, the Levites. 19And *a*it shall be with him, and he shall read it all the days of his life, that he may learn to fear the LORD his God and be careful to observe all the words of this law and these statutes, 20that his heart may not be lifted above his brethren, that he *b*may not turn aside from the commandment *to* the right hand or *to* the left, and that he may prolong *his* days in his kingdom, he and his children in the midst of Israel.

The Portion of the Priests and Levites

18 "The priests, the Levites—all the tribe of Levi—shall have no part nor *a*inheritance with Israel; they shall eat the offerings of the LORD made by fire, and His portion. 2Therefore they shall have no inheritance among their brethren; the LORD is their inheritance, as He said to them.

3"And this shall be the priest's *b*due from the people, from those who offer a sacrifice, whether *it is* bull or sheep: they shall give to the priest the shoulder, the cheeks, and the stomach. 4*c*The firstfruits of your grain and your new wine and your oil, and the first of the fleece of your sheep, you shall give him. 5For *d*the LORD your God has chosen him out of all your tribes *e*to stand to minister in the name of the LORD, him and his sons forever.

6"So if a Levite comes from any of your gates, from where he *f*dwells among all Israel, and comes with all the desire of his mind *g*to the place which the LORD chooses, 7then he may serve in the name of the LORD his God *h*as all his brethren the Levites *do,* who stand there before the LORD. 8They shall have equal *i*portions to eat, besides what comes from the sale of his inheritance.

Avoid Wicked Customs

9"When you come into the land which the LORD your God is giving you, *j*you shall not learn to follow the abominations of those nations. 10There shall not be found among you *anyone* who makes his son or his daughter *k*pass through the fire, *l*or one who practices witchcraft, *or* a soothsayer, or one who interprets omens, or a sorcerer, 11*m*or *n*one who conjures spells, or a medium, or a spiritist, or one who calls up the dead. 12For all who do these things *are* an abomination to the LORD, and *o*because of these abominations the LORD your God drives them out from before you. 13You shall be blameless before the LORD your God. 14For these nations which you will dispossess listened to soothsayers and diviners; but as for you, the LORD your God has not appointed such for you.

17:12 *acts presumptuously.* It is presumptuous to ask for judgment and then to refuse to follow the verdict of the priests. It is both asking them to take the weight of the decision and then willfully disregarding that decision.

17:13 *hear.* To hear is to respond and obey.

17:14 *a king.* The regulations that follow anticipate the request that the Israelites would make for a king. At the time of Moses the Israelites were unique among nations. God Himself ruled them through appointed leaders, but there was no king.

18:10–12 *pass through the fire . . . witchcraft.* Each of the activities that the Lord forbids in this passage come under the category of occult activities. Passing through the fire was sacrificing a son or daughter to learn about the future or seek favor with a supposed deity. Divination, witchcraft, sorcery, casting spells

and interpreting omens, mediums, spiritists, and necromancers (those who call up the dead) are all part of the demonic realm, an attempt to bypass God in foretelling and controlling the future. These activities are detestable to God and should be to His followers as well.

17:12 *p* Num. 15:30   **17:13** *q* Deut. 13:11   **17:14** *r* 1 Sam. 8:5, 19, 20; 10:19   **17:15** *s* 1 Sam. 9:15, 16; 10:24; 16:12, 13   *t* Jer. 30:21   **17:16** *u* 1 Kin. 4:26; 10:26–29   *v* Ezek. 17:15   *w* Ex. 13:17, 18   *x* Deut. 28:68   **17:17** *y* 1 Kin. 10:14   **17:18** *z* Deut. 31:24–26   **17:19** *a* Ps. 119:97, 98   **17:20** *b* Deut. 5:32   **18:1** *a* Deut. 10:9   **18:3** *b* Lev. 7:32–34; 1 Sam. 2:13–16, 29   **18:4** *c* Ex. 22:29   **18:5** *d* Ex. 28:1   *e* Deut. 10:8   **18:6** *f* Num. 35:2   *g* Deut. 12:5; 14:23   **18:7** *h* 2 Chr. 31:2   **18:8** *i* 2 Chr. 31:4   **18:9** *j* Deut. 12:29, 30; 20:16–18   **18:10** *k* Deut. 12:31   *l* Is. 8:19   **18:11** *m* Lev. 20:27   *n* 1 Sam. 28:7   **18:12** *o* Lev. 18:24

A New Prophet Like Moses

15p"The LORD your God will raise up for you a Prophet like me from your midst, from your brethren. Him you shall hear, 16according to all you desired of the LORD your God in Horeb qin the day of the assembly, saying, r'Let me not hear again the voice of the LORD my God, nor let me see this great fire anymore, lest I die.'

17"And the LORD said to me: s'What they have spoken is good. 18tI will raise up for them a Prophet like you from among their brethren, and uwill put My words in His mouth, vand He shall speak to them all that I command Him. 19wAnd it shall be that whoever will not hear My words, which He speaks in My name, I will require it of him. 20But xthe prophet who presumes to speak a word in My name, which I have not commanded him to speak, or ywho speaks in the name of other gods, that prophet shall die.' 21And if you say in your heart, 'How shall we know the word which the LORD has not spoken?'— 22zwhen a prophet speaks in the name of the LORD, qif the thing does not happen or come to pass, that is the thing which the LORD has not spoken; the prophet has spoken it bpresumptuously; you shall not be afraid of him.

Three Cities of Refuge

19 "When the LORD your God ahas cut off the nations whose land the LORD your God is giving you, and you dispossess them and dwell in their cities and in their houses, 2byou shall separate three cities for yourself in the midst of your land which the LORD your God is giving you to possess. 3You shall prepare roads for yourself, and divide into three parts the territory of your land which the LORD your God is giving you to inherit, that any manslayer may flee there. 4"And cthis is the case of the manslayer who flees there, that he may live: Whoever

kills his neighbor unintentionally, not having hated him in time past— 5as when a man goes to the woods with his neighbor to cut timber, and his hand swings a stroke with the ax to cut down the tree, and the head slips from the handle and strikes his neighbor so that he dies—he shall flee to one of these cities and live; 6dlest the avenger of blood, while his anger is hot, pursue the manslayer and overtake him, because the way is long, and kill him, though he was not deserving of death, since he had not hated the victim in time past. 7Therefore I command you, saying, 'You shall separate three cities for yourself.'

8"Now if the LORD your God eenlarges your territory, as He swore to fyour fathers, and gives you the land which He promised to give to your fathers, 9and if you keep all these commandments and do them, which I command you today, to love the LORD your God and to walk always in His ways, gthen you shall add three more cities for yourself besides these three, 10hlest innocent blood be shed in the midst of your land which the LORD your God is giving you as an inheritance, and thus guilt of bloodshed be upon you.

11"But iif anyone hates his neighbor, lies in wait for him, rises against him and strikes him mortally, so that he dies, and he flees to one of these cities, 12then the elders of his city shall send and bring him from there, and deliver him over to the hand of the avenger of blood, that he may die. 13jYour eye shall not pity him, kbut you shall put away the guilt of innocent blood from Israel, that it may go well with you.

Property Boundaries

14l"You shall not remove your neighbor's landmark, which the men of old have set, in your inheritance which you will inherit in the land that the LORD your God is giving you to possess.

18:15 raise up for you a Prophet. A true prophet came from the Lord; no one could become a true prophet by self-will or desire.

18:22 shall not be afraid of him. These words of warning for discerning a false prophet were also words of comfort. If the prophet did not come from God, there was no need to become anxious about whatever he might predict.

19:3–4 divide into three parts. The cities of refuge were intertribal cities. Anyone from any tribe could flee to the city that was closest to him.

19:6 avenger of blood. The avenger was possibly a relative commissioned by the elders of the city to execute justice. This Hebrew word is sometimes translated kinsman redeemer, and in this verse means "protector of family rights." This individual also stood up for the family to redeem property and persons. The glory of Israel was that its Avenger and Kinsman Redeemer was God Himself (Is. 41:14).

19:9–13 keep all these. The people of Israel were about to enter a land where they would be exposed to ideas and practices in the name of religion that God

says are an abomination. The temptation to imitate would be great, but they must not do so. The believer is not different from his world for the sake of difference, but because he must not imitate the things that are inconsistent with a life of fellowship with a holy and just God. Copying the ways of the ungodly not only grieves the Lord, but it mars the picture He is making of Himself in the lives of those who follow Him.

19:14 remove your neighbor's landmark. Removing a landmark was far more than moving a stone. It

18:15 p Matt. 21:11; Luke 1:76; 2:25–34; 7:16; 24:19; John 1:45; Acts 3:22 **18:16** q Deut. 5:23–27 r Ex. 20:18, 19 **18:17** s Deut. 5:28 **18:18** t John 1:45; 6:14; Acts 3:22 u Is. 49:2; 51:16; John 17:8 v [John 4:25; 8:28] **18:19** w Acts 3:23; [Heb. 12:25] **18:20** x Jer. 14:14, 15 y Jer. 2:8 **18:22** z Jer. 28:9 a Deut. 13:2 b Deut. 18:20 **19:1** a Deut. 12:29 **19:2** b Num. 35:10–15 **19:4** c Num. 35:9–34 **19:6** d Num. 35:12 **19:8** e Deut. 12:20 f Gen. 15:18–21 **19:9** g Josh. 20:7–9 **19:10** h Deut. 21:1–9 **19:11** i Num. 35:16, 24 **19:13** j Deut. 13:8 k 1 Kin. 2:31 **19:14** l Prov. 22:28

The Law Concerning Witnesses

15m"One witness shall not rise against a man concerning any iniquity or any sin that he commits; by the mouth of two or three witnesses the matter shall be established. 16If a false witness nrises against any man to testify against him of wrongdoing, 17then both men in the controversy shall stand before the LORD, obefore the priests and the judges who serve in those days. 18And the judges shall make careful inquiry, and indeed, if the witness is a false witness, who has testified falsely against his brother, 19pthen you shall do to him as he thought to have done to his brother; so qyou shall put away the evil from among you. 20rAnd those who remain shall hear and fear, and hereafter they shall not again commit such evil among you. 21sYour eye shall not pity: tlife shall be for life, eye for eye, tooth for tooth, hand for hand, foot for foot.

Principles Governing Warfare

20 "When you go out to battle against your enemies, and see ahorses and chariots and people more numerous than you, do not be bafraid of them; for the LORD your God is cwith you, who brought you up from the land of Egypt. 2So it shall be, when you are on the verge of battle, that the priest shall approach and speak to the people. 3And he shall say to them, 'Hear, O Israel: Today you are on the verge of battle with your enemies. Do not let your heart faint, do not be afraid, and do not tremble or be terrified because of them; 4for the LORD your God is He who goes with you, dto fight for you against your enemies, to save you.'

5"Then the officers shall speak to the people, saying: 'What man is there who has built a new house and has not ededicated it? Let him go and return to his house, lest he die in the battle and another man dedicate it. 6Also what man is there who has planted a vineyard and has not eaten of it? Let him go and return to his house, lest he die in the battle and another man eat of it. 7fAnd what

man is there who is betrothed to a woman and has not married her? Let him go and return to his house, lest he die in the battle and another man marry her.'

8"The officers shall speak further to the people, and say, g*'What man is there who is fearful and fainthearted? Let him go and return to his house, lest the heart of his brethren faint* like his heart.' 9And so it shall be, when the officers have finished speaking to the people, that they shall make captains of the armies to lead the people.

10"When you go near a city to fight against it, hthen proclaim an offer of peace to it. 11And it shall be that if they accept your offer of peace, and open to you, then all the people who are found in it shall be placed under tribute to you, and serve you. 12Now if the city will not make peace with you, but war against you, then you shall besiege it. 13And when the LORD your God delivers it into your hands, iyou shall strike every male in it with the edge of the sword. 14But the women, the little ones, jthe livestock, and all that is in the city, all its spoil, you shall plunder for yourself; and kyou shall eat the enemies' plunder which the LORD your God gives you. 15Thus you shall do to all the cities which are very far from you, which are not of the cities of these nations.

16"But lof the cities of these peoples which the LORD your God gives you as an inheritance, you shall let nothing that breathes remain alive, 17but you shall utterly destroy them: the Hittite and the Amorite and the Canaanite and the Perizzite and the Hivite and the Jebusite, just as the LORD your God has commanded you, 18lest mthey teach you to do according to all their abominations which they have done for their gods, and you nsin against the LORD your God.

19"When you besiege a city for a long time, while making war against it to take it,

* 20:8 Following Masoretic Text and Targum; Samaritan Pentateuch, Septuagint, Syriac, and Vulgate read lest he make his brother's heart faint.

was changing a property line and in effect cheating some family out of the inheritance of land that God had given them.

19:15 by the mouth of two or three witnesses. Requiring two or three witnesses was a safeguard against the dangerous lies of an individual.

19:21 life shall be for life, eye for eye. The law of retribution established the principle that the punishment should not exceed the crime.

20:5–7 built a new house . . . planted a vineyard . . . betrothed to a woman. Each of these activities represents a time of planning and preparation that has not yet been fulfilled. The Lord graciously acknowledges that it is right for people to have a chance to enjoy the fruits of their labor before they risk their lives for the nation.

20:8 fearful and fainthearted. Unlike the previous situations, the fearful and fainthearted endanger their fellow soldiers. The number of warriors was not

as important as the army's belief that God was fighting for them.

20:17 utterly destroy. This was not just a symbolic war; the entire Canaanite population was to be destroyed.

20:18 lest they teach you. The principal concern of the Lord was for the welfare of His people. The Canaanite population in the land was like a deadly tumor eating away at the body. If the tumor was cut

19:15 m Num. 35:30   **19:16** n Ex. 23:1   **19:17** o Deut. 17:8–11; 21:5   **19:19** p Prov. 9:5   q Deut. 13:5; 17:7; 21:21; 22:21   **19:20** r Deut. 17:13; 21:21   **19:21** s Deut. 19:13   t Ex. 21:23, 24   **20:1** a Ps. 20:7   b Deut. 7:18   c 2 Chr. 13:12; 32:7, 8   **20:4** d Josh. 23:10   **20:5** e Neh. 12:27   **20:7** f Deut. 24:5   **20:8** g Judg. 7:3   **20:10** h 2 Sam. 10:19   **20:13** i Num. 31:7   **20:14** j Josh. 8:2   k 1 Sam. 14:30   **20:16** l Deut. 7:1–5   **20:18** m Deut. 7:4; 12:30; 18:9   n Ex. 23:33

you shall not destroy its trees by wielding an ax against them; if you can eat of them, do not cut them down to use in the siege, for the tree of the field *is* man's *food.* 20Only the trees which you know *are* not trees for food you may destroy and cut down, to build siegeworks against the city that makes war with you, until it is subdued.

The Law Concerning Unsolved Murder

21 "If *anyone* is found slain, lying in the field in the land which the LORD your God is giving you to possess, *and* it is not known who killed him, 2then your elders and your judges shall go out and measure *the distance* from the slain man to the surrounding cities. 3And it shall be *that* the elders of the city nearest to the slain man will take a heifer which has not been worked *and* which has not pulled with a *a*yoke. 4The elders of that city shall bring the heifer down to a valley with flowing water, which is neither plowed nor sown, and they shall break the heifer's neck there in the valley. 5Then the priests, the sons of Levi, shall come near, for *b*the LORD your God has chosen them to minister to Him and to bless in the name of the LORD; *c*by their word every controversy and every assault shall be *settled.* 6And all the elders of that city nearest to the slain *man* *d*shall wash their hands over the heifer whose neck was broken in the valley. 7Then they shall answer and say, 'Our hands have not shed this blood, nor have our eyes seen *it.* 8Provide atonement, O LORD, for Your people Israel, whom You have redeemed, *e*and do not lay innocent blood to the charge of Your people Israel.' And atonement shall be provided on their behalf for the blood. 9So *f*you shall put away the *guilt of* innocent blood from among you when you do *what is* right in the sight of the LORD.

Female Captives

10"When you go out to war against your enemies, and the LORD your God delivers

them into your hand, and you take them captive, 11and you see among the captives a beautiful woman, and desire her and would take her for your *g*wife, 12then you shall bring her home to your house, and she shall *h*shave her head and trim her nails. 13She shall put off the clothes of her captivity, remain in your house, and *i*mourn her father and her mother a full month; after that you may go in to her and be her husband, and she shall be your wife. 14And it shall be, if you have no delight in her, then you shall set her free, but you certainly shall not sell her for money; you shall not treat her brutally, because you have *j*humbled her.

Firstborn Inheritance Rights

15"If a man has two wives, one loved *k*and the other unloved, and they have borne him children, *both* the loved and the unloved, and *if* the firstborn son is of her who is unloved, 16then it shall be, *l*on the day he bequeaths his possessions to his sons, *that* he must not bestow firstborn status on the son of the loved wife in preference to the son of the unloved, the *true* firstborn. 17But he shall acknowledge the son of the unloved wife *as* the firstborn *m*by giving him a double portion of all that he has, for he *n*is the beginning of his strength; *o*the right of the firstborn *is* his.

The Rebellious Son

18"If a man has a stubborn and rebellious son who will not obey the voice of his father or the voice of his mother, and *who,* when they have chastened him, will not heed them, 19then his father and his mother shall take hold of him and bring him out to the elders of his city, to the gate of his city. 20And they shall say to the elders of his city, 'This son of ours is stubborn and rebellious; he will not obey our voice; he is a glutton and a drunkard.' 21Then all the men of his city shall stone him to death with stones; *p*so you shall put away the evil from among you, *q*and all Israel shall hear and fear.

---

out, the body could live. No one could thrive in that land as a follower of God as long as the Canaanites were there.

21:1–9 *anyone is found slain.* Although the people were innocent of the act and of any knowledge of the actual death of this individual, the elders must still ask the Lord for forgiveness for the shedding of innocent blood. An honest attempt must be made to find justice and to say, "We know this was wrong." God is teaching His people about an active social conscience in this passage. When we know that an innocent party has been wronged we are not to turn our backs and say that we are not involved. Even the simple act of publicly saying that such action is not pleasing to God is effective in reminding those who hear that God sees all and will judge the perpetrators of sin at some point.

21:15 *two wives.* Polygamy was commonly practiced in the cultures of the ancient Middle East and was assumed in the law of Moses. It is apparently something that God allowed, as He did divorce (Matt. 19:3–9), but from the beginning it was not that way.

21:16 *firstborn.* A father was expected to show consideration for the firstborn child, regardless of his attitude toward the child's mother.

21:3 *a* Num. 19:2   **21:5** *b* 1 Chr. 23:13   *c* Deut. 17:8, 9
21:6 *d* Matt. 27:24   **21:8** *e* Jon. 1:14   **21:9** *f* Deut. 19:13
21:11 *g* Num. 31:18   **21:12** *h* Lev. 14:8, 9   **21:13** *i* Ps. 45:10   **21:14** *j* Judg. 19:24   **21:15** *k* Gen. 29:33
21:16 *l* 1 Chr. 5:2; 26:10   **21:17** *m* 2 Kin. 2:9   *n* Gen. 49:3
o Gen. 25:31, 33   **21:21** *p* Deut. 13:5; 19:19, 20; 22:21, 24
q Deut. 13:11

Miscellaneous Laws

22"If a man has committed a sin ʳdeserving of death, and he is put to death, and you hang him on a tree, 23ˢhis body shall not remain overnight on the tree, but you shall surely bury him that day, so that ᵗyou do not defile the land which the LORD your God is giving you *as* an inheritance; for ᵘhe who is hanged *is* accursed of God.

22 "You ᵃshall not see your brother's ox or his sheep going astray, and hide yourself from them; you shall certainly bring them back to your brother. ²And if your brother *is* not near you, or if you do not know him, then you shall bring it to your own house, and it shall remain with you until your brother seeks it; then you shall restore it to him. ³You shall do the same with his donkey, and so shall you do with his garment; with any lost thing of your brother's, which he has lost and you have found, you shall do likewise; you must not hide yourself.

4ᵇ"You shall not see your brother's donkey or his ox fall down along the road, and hide yourself from them; you shall surely help him lift *them* up again.

5"A woman shall not wear anything that pertains to a man, nor shall a man put on a woman's garment, for all who do so *are* an abomination to the LORD your God.

6"If a bird's nest happens to be before you along the way, in any tree or on the ground, with young ones or eggs, with the mother sitting on the young or on the eggs, ᶜyou shall not take the mother with the young; 7you shall surely let the mother go, and take the young for yourself, ᵈthat it may be well with you and *that* you may prolong *your* days.

8"When you build a new house, then you shall make a parapet for your roof, that you may not bring guilt of bloodshed on your household if anyone falls from it.

9ᵉ"You shall not sow your vineyard with different kinds of seed, lest the yield of the seed which you have sown and the fruit of your vineyard be defiled.

10ᶠ"You shall not plow with an ox and a donkey together.

11ᵍ"You shall not wear a garment of different sorts, *such as* wool and linen mixed together.

12"You shall make ʰtassels on the four corners of the clothing with which you cover *yourself.*

Laws of Sexual Morality

13"If any man takes a wife, and goes in to her, and ⁱdetests her, 14and charges her with shameful conduct, and brings a bad name on her, and says, 'I took this woman, and when I came to her I found she *was* not a virgin,' 15then the father and mother of the young woman shall take and bring out *the evidence of* the young woman's virginity to the elders of the city at the gate. 16And the young woman's father shall say to the elders, 'I gave my daughter to this man as wife, and he detests her. 17Now he has charged her with shameful conduct, saying, "I found your daughter *was* not a virgin," and yet these *are the evidences of* my daughter's virginity.' And they shall spread the cloth before the elders of the city. 18Then the elders of that city shall take that man and punish him; 19and they shall fine him one hundred *shekels* of silver and give *them* to the father of the young woman, because he has brought a bad name on a virgin of Israel. And she shall be his wife; he cannot divorce her all his days.

20"But if the thing is true, *and evidences of* virginity are not found for the young woman, 21then they shall bring out the young woman to the door of her father's house, and the men of her city shall stone her to death with ʲstones, because she has ᵏdone a disgraceful thing in Israel, to play the harlot in her father's house. ˡSo you shall put away the evil from among you.

22ᵐ"If a man is found lying with a woman married to a husband, then both of them shall die—the man that lay with the woman, and the woman; so you shall put away the evil from Israel.

23"If a young woman *who is* a virgin is

21:22 hang him. The guilty person was not executed by hanging, but after the person was stoned the corpse was impaled for public viewing as an example. **22:1–4 Kindness**—In the same way that God cares for us, we are to care for others. If we see a kindness that we can do for another, we are to do it cheerfully and willingly. Receiving an act of kindness is heartwarming; doing such an act is a great joy. **22:8 parapet.** The parapet was a low wall around the edge of the roof. The rooftop was used as an extra room, and if the home owner did not provide safety measures, he would be responsible for any accidents. **22:11 wool and linen . . . together.** These restrictions were a reminder that the Hebrews were not a mixed people. They were separated to God and they were not to mix with other nations, nor were they to mix two kinds of animals, grain, or fabric. It was part of the concept of purity that governed every aspect of life. **22:14 brings a bad name on her.** Charging her indicated a public accusation. Virginity was highly regarded, for if the legitimacy of children was disputable, inheritance rights and positions in family would also be disputed. It is easy to determine the mother of a child, for pregnancy is obvious, but determining the father of the child was a matter of trust that the wife was faithful to marriage vows.

21:22 ʳ Acts 23:29 **21:23** ˢ John 19:31 ᵗ Lev. 18:25 ᵘ Gal. 3:13 **22:1** ᵃ Ex. 23:4 **22:4** ᵇ Ex. 23:5 **22:6** ᶜ Lev. 22:28 **22:7** ᵈ Deut. 4:40 **22:9** ᵉ Lev. 19:19 **22:10** ᶠ [2 Cor. 6:14–16] **22:11** ᵍ Lev. 19:19 **22:12** ʰ Num. 15:37–41 **22:13** ⁱ Deut. 21:15; 24:3 **22:21** ʲ Deut. 21:21 ᵏ Gen. 34:7 ˡ Deut. 13:5 **22:22** ᵐ Lev. 20:10

betrothed to a husband, and a man finds her in the city and lies with her, 24then you shall bring them both out to the gate of that city, and you shall stone them to death with stones, the young woman because she did not cry out in the city, and the man because he ohumbled his neighbor's wife; pso you shall put away the evil from among you.

25"But if a man finds a betrothed young woman in the countryside, and the man forces her and lies with her, then only the man who lay with her shall die. 26But you shall do nothing to the young woman; *there is* in the young woman no sin *deserving* of death, for just as when a man rises against his neighbor and kills him, even so *is* this matter. 27For he found her in the countryside, *and* the betrothed young woman cried out, but *there was* no one to save her.

28q"If a man finds a young woman *who is* a virgin, who is not betrothed, and he seizes her and lies with her, and they are found out, 29then the man who lay with her shall give to the young woman's father rfifty *shekels* of silver, and she shall be his wife sbecause he has humbled her; he shall not be permitted to divorce her all his days.

30t"A man shall not take his father's wife, nor uuncover his father's bed.

Those Excluded from the Congregation

23 "He who is emasculated by crushing or mutilation shall anot enter the assembly of the LORD.

2"One of illegitimate birth shall not enter the assembly of the LORD; even to the tenth generation none of his *descendants* shall enter the assembly of the LORD.

3b"An Ammonite or Moabite shall not enter the assembly of the LORD; even to the tenth generation none of his *descendants* shall enter the assembly of the LORD forever, 4cbecause they did not meet you with bread and water on the road when you came out of Egypt, and dbecause they hired against you Balaam the son of Beor from Pethor of Mesopotamia,* to curse you. 5Nevertheless the LORD your God would not listen to Balaam, but the LORD your God turned the curse into a blessing

for you, because the LORD your God eloves you. 6fYou shall not seek their peace nor their prosperity all your days forever.

7"You shall not abhor an Edomite, gfor he *is* your brother. You shall not abhor an Egyptian, because hyou were an alien in his land. 8The children of the third generation born to them may enter the assembly of the LORD.

Cleanliness of the Campsite

9"When the army goes out against your enemies, then keep yourself from every wicked thing. 10iIf there is any man among you who becomes unclean by some occurrence in the night, then he shall go outside the camp; he shall not come inside the camp. 11But it shall be, when evening comes, that jhe shall wash with water; and when the sun sets, he may come into the camp.

12"Also you shall have a place outside the camp, where you may go out; 13and you shall have an implement among your equipment, and when you sit down outside, you shall dig with it and turn and cover your refuse. 14For the LORD your God kwalks in the midst of your camp, to deliver you and give your enemies over to you; therefore your camp shall be holy, that He may see no unclean thing among you, and turn away from you.

Miscellaneous Laws

15l"You shall not give back to his master the slave who has escaped from his master to you. 16He may dwell with you in your midst, in the place which he chooses within one of your gates, where it seems best to him; myou shall not oppress him.

17"There shall be no *ritual* harlot*n of the daughters of Israel, or a operverted* one of the sons of Israel. 18You shall not bring the wages of a harlot or the price of a dog to the house of the LORD your God for any vowed offering, for both of these *are* an abomination to the LORD your God.

---

* **23:4** Hebrew *Aram Naharaim* * **23:17** Hebrew *qedeshah*, feminine of *qadesh* (see next note) • Hebrew *qadesh*, that is, one practicing sodomy and prostitution in religious rituals

---

23:1 emasculated. An emasculated man had had all or part of the sexual organs removed. This was done to men who were put in charge of harems to prevent sexual relations with the women. It was also a pagan practice. Genital mutilation was prohibited in Israel.
23:17 harlot . . . perverted. The cult prostitute was used for the worship of the Canaanite gods and goddesses of fertility. They believed that having intimate relations with the cult prostitutes (either male or female) would bring fertility to their families, fields, and herds. This debased system of worship was one of the reasons God had decided to utterly destroy this group of people.
23:18 wages of a harlot . . . price of a dog. God did not need or want money earned by such practices

that He called abominations. "Dogs" does not refer to the animal. It is still insulting in the Middle East to call a person a dog, and "dogs" are listed with sorcerers, immoral persons, murderers, idolaters, and everyone who loves and practices lying, as those who are outside the heavenly city (Rev. 22:15).

22:23 n Matt. 1:18, 19   **22:24** o Deut. 21:14 p Deut. 22:21, 22   **22:28** q Ex. 22:16, 17   **22:29** r Ex. 22:16, 17 s Deut. 22:24   **22:30** t Deut. 27:20 u Ezek. 16:8   **23:1** a Lev. 21:20; 22:24   **23:3** b Neh. 13:1, 2   **23:4** c Deut. 2:27–30 d Num. 22:5, 6; 23:7   **23:5** e Deut. 4:37   **23:6** f Ezra 9:12   **23:7** g Obad. 10, 12 h Deut. 10:19   **23:10** i Lev. 15:16   **23:11** j Lev. 15:5   **23:14** k Lev. 26:12   **23:15** l 1 Sam. 30:15   **23:16** m Ex. 22:21   **23:17** n Lev. 19:29 o 2 Kin. 23:7

19p"You shall not charge interest to your brother—interest on money *or* food *or* anything that is lent out at interest. 20q"To a foreigner you may charge interest, but to your brother you shall not charge interest, rthat the LORD your God may bless you in all to which you set your hand in the land which you are entering to possess.

21s"When you make a vow to the LORD your God, you shall not delay to pay it; for the LORD your God will surely require it of you, and it would be sin to you. 22But if you abstain from vowing, it shall not be sin to you. 23tThat which has gone from your lips you shall keep and perform, for you voluntarily vowed to the LORD your God what you have promised with your mouth.

24"When you come into your neighbor's vineyard, you may eat your fill of grapes at your pleasure, but you shall not put *any* in your container. 25When you come into your neighbor's standing grain, uyou may pluck the heads with your hand, but you shall not use a sickle on your neighbor's standing grain.

Law Concerning Divorce

24 "When a aman takes a wife and marries her, and it happens that she finds no favor in his eyes because he has found some uncleanness in her, and he writes her a bcertificate of divorce, puts *it* in her hand, and sends her out of his house, 2when she has departed from his house, and goes and becomes another man's *wife,* 3if the latter husband detests her and writes her a certificate of divorce, puts *it* in her hand, and sends her out of his house, or if the latter husband dies who took her as his wife, 4c*then* her former husband who divorced her must not take her back to be his wife after she has been defiled; for that *is* an abomination before the LORD, and you shall not bring sin on the land which the LORD your God is giving you *as* an inheritance.

Miscellaneous Laws

5d"When a man has taken a new wife, he shall not go out to war or be charged with any business; he shall be free at home one year, and ebring happiness to his wife whom he has taken.

6"No man shall take the lower or the upper millstone in pledge, for he takes *one's* living in pledge.

7"If a man is ffound kidnapping any of his brethren of the children of Israel, and mistreats him or sells him, then that kidnapper shall die; gand you shall put away the evil from among you.

8"Take heed in han outbreak of leprosy, that you carefully observe and do according to all that the priests, the Levites, shall teach you; just as I commanded them, *so* you shall be careful to do. 9iRemember what the LORD your God did ito Miriam on the way when you came out of Egypt!

10"When you klend your brother anything, you shall not go into his house to get his pledge. 11You shall stand outside, and the man to whom you lend shall bring the pledge out to you. 12And if the man *is* poor, you shall not keep his pledge overnight. 13lYou shall in any case return the pledge to him again when the sun goes down, that he may sleep in his own garment and mbless you; and nit shall be righteousness to you before the LORD your God.

14"You shall not ooppress a hired servant *who is* poor and needy, *whether* one of your brethren or one of the aliens who *is* in your land within your gates. 15Each day pyou shall give *him* his wages, and not let the sun go down on it, for he *is* poor and has set his heart on it; qlest he cry out against you to the LORD, and it be sin to you.

16r"Fathers shall not be put to death for *their* children, nor shall children be put to death for *their* fathers; a person shall be put to death for his own sin.

17s"You shall not pervert justice due the stranger or the fatherless, tnor take a

---

23:21 *vow.* A vow was purely voluntary, and not necessary for the development of godliness. But if a vow was made, it must be kept.

24:1–4 *a certificate of divorce.* Marriage was instituted by God (Gen. 2:24). It was intended to be a union of one man and one woman for life. And yet, the Mosaic law allowed divorce, even though God said through His prophet Malachi (Mal. 2:16) that He hates divorce. When the Pharisees were asking Jesus about divorce, Jesus explained that it had not been so designed in the beginning, but "because of the hardness of your hearts" Moses had allowed it. Then Jesus raised the standard set by Moses, saying that those whom God had joined, no man should separate. With the death and resurrection of Christ, all believers receive the Holy Spirit, and it is at this point that hard hearts are changed.

24:4 *defiled.* Returning to her first husband after an intervening marriage might have placed the woman in the same position as an unfaithful wife.

24:6 *millstone.* A pair of millstones was used for grinding grain into flour. The flour was ground between two stones, and to deprive a household of the use of one of the stones was to deprive them of the necessities of daily life.

24:8 *leprosy.* Leprosy refers to a variety of infectious skin diseases. The disease known today as leprosy, Hansen's disease, is different from the diseases described here.

23:19p Ex. 22:25 **23:20**q Deut. 15:3 r Deut. 15:10 **23:21**s Eccl. 5:4, 5 **23:23**t Ps. 66:13, 14 **23:25**u Luke 6:1 **24:1**a [Matt. 5:31; 19:7] b [Jer. 3:8] **24:4**c [Jer. 3:1] **24:5**d Deut. 20:7 e Prov. 5:18 **24:7**f Ex. 21:16 g Deut. 19:19 **24:8**h Lev. 13:2; 14:2 **24:9**i [1 Cor. 10:6] j Num. 12:10 **24:10**k Matt. 5:42 **24:13**l Ex. 22:26 m 2 Tim. 1:18 n Deut. 6:25 **24:14**o [Mal. 3:5] **24:15**p Lev. 19:13 q James 5:4 **24:16**r Ezek. 18:20 **24:17**s Ex. 23:6 t Ex. 22:26

widow's garment as a pledge. [18]But [u]you shall remember that you were a slave in Egypt, and the LORD your God redeemed you from there; therefore I command you to do this thing.

[19v]"When you reap your harvest in your field, and forget a sheaf in the field, you shall not go back to get it; it shall be for the stranger, the fatherless, and the widow, that the LORD your God may [w]bless you in all the work of your hands. [20]When you beat your olive trees, you shall not go over the boughs again; it shall be for the stranger, the fatherless, and the widow. [21]When you gather the grapes of your vineyard, you shall not glean *it* afterward; it shall be for the stranger, the fatherless, and the widow. [22]And you shall remember that you were a slave in the land of Egypt; therefore I command you to do this thing.

25 "If there is a [a]dispute between men, and they come to court, that *the judges* may judge them, and they [b]justify the righteous and condemn the wicked, [2]then it shall be, if the wicked man [c]deserves to be beaten, that the judge will cause him to lie down [d]and be beaten in his presence, according to his guilt, with a certain number of blows. [3e]Forty blows he may give him *and* no more, lest he should exceed this and beat him with many blows above these, and your brother [f]be humiliated in your sight.

[4g]"You shall not muzzle an ox while it treads out *the grain*.

Marriage Duty of the Surviving Brother

[5h]"If brothers dwell together, and one of them dies and has no son, the widow of the dead man shall not be *married* to a stranger outside *the family;* her husband's brother shall go in to her, take her as his wife, and perform the duty of a husband's brother to her. [6]And it shall be *that* the firstborn son which she bears [i]will succeed to the name of his dead brother, that [j]his name may not be blotted out of Israel. [7]But if the man does

not want to take his brother's wife, then let his brother's wife go up to the [k]gate to the elders, and say, 'My husband's brother refuses to raise up a name to his brother in Israel; he will not perform the duty of my husband's brother.' [8]Then the elders of his city shall call him and speak to him. But if he stands firm and says, [l]'I do not want to take her,' [9]then his brother's wife shall come to him in the presence of the elders, [m]remove his sandal from his foot, spit in his face, and answer and say, 'So shall it be done to the man who will not [n]build up his brother's house.' [10]And his name shall be called in Israel, 'The house of him who had his sandal removed.'

Miscellaneous Laws

[11]"If *two* men fight together, and the wife of one draws near to rescue her husband from the hand of the one attacking him, and puts out her hand and seizes him by the genitals, [12]then you shall cut off her hand; [o]your eye shall not pity *her.*

[13p]"You shall not have in your bag differing weights, a heavy and a light. [14]You shall not have in your house differing measures, a large and a small. [15]You shall have a perfect and just weight, a perfect and just measure, [q]that your days may be lengthened in the land which the LORD your God is giving you. [16]For [r]all who do such things, all who behave unrighteously, *are* an abomination to the LORD your God.

Destroy the Amalekites

[17s]"Remember what Amalek did to you on the way as you were coming out of Egypt, [18]how he met you on the way and attacked your rear ranks, all the stragglers at your rear, when you *were* tired and weary; and he [t]did not fear God. [19]Therefore it shall be, [u]when the LORD your God has given you rest from your enemies all around, in the land which the LORD your God is giving you to possess *as* an inheritance, *that* you will [v]blot out the remembrance of Amalek from under heaven. You shall not forget.

25:3 Forty blows. Later Jewish law restricted the number to forty minus one (2 Cor. 11:24) to make sure that the authorities remained within the set limits.
25:4 not muzzle an ox. Muzzling kept the animal from eating while it worked. Later the apostle Paul used this law as a principle for providing a living for those who spend their lives preaching the gospel (1 Tim. 5:18).
25:5 dies and has no son. The firstborn son of the marriage would be acknowledged as the legal son of the dead brother. Taking a brother's widow as a second wife provided her with care, and preserved the name, position, and inheritance of the dead brother.
25:7–10 does not want to take. Legally the brother-in-law was bound to keep the family name alive. His unwillingness to do so was a public issue, involving the elders of the community. The removal of the

sandal was a sign of giving up of one's rights, and spitting was a strong act of public contempt.
25:19 blot out the remembrance. The Amalekites would in effect come under the same ban as the Canaanite nations. The fact that they did not fear God made them a stumbling block to any nation that was following God.

24:18 [u] Deut. 24:22   **24:19** [v] Lev. 19:9, 10   [w] Ps. 41:1
25:1 [a] Deut. 17:8–13; 19:17   [b] Prov. 17:15   **25:2** [c] Prov. 19:29   [d] Matt. 10:17   **25:3** [e] 2 Cor. 11:24   [f] Job 18:3
25:4 [g] [Prov. 12:10]   **25:5** [h] Matt. 22:24   **25:6** [i] Gen. 38:9   [j] Ruth 4:5, 10   **25:7** [k] Ruth 4:1, 2   **25:8** [l] Ruth 4:6
25:9 [m] Ruth 4:7, 8   [n] Ruth 4:11   **25:12** [o] Deut. 7:2; 19:13
25:13 [p] Mic. 6:11   **25:15** [q] Ex. 20:12   **25:16** [r] Prov. 11:1
25:17 [s] Ex. 17:8–16   **25:18** [t] Rom. 3:18   **25:19** [u] 1 Sam. 15:3   [v] Ex. 17:14

Offerings of Firstfruits and Tithes

26 "And it shall be, when you come into the land which the LORD your God is giving you *as* an inheritance, and you possess it and dwell in it, ²ᵃthat you shall take some of the first of all the produce of the ground, which you shall bring from your land that the LORD your God is giving you, and put *it* in a basket and ᵇgo to the place where the LORD your God chooses to make His name abide. ³And you shall go to the one who is priest in those days, and say to him, 'I declare today to the LORD your* God that I have come to the country which the LORD swore to our fathers to give us.'

⁴"Then the priest shall take the basket out of your hand and set it down before the altar of the LORD your God. ⁵And you shall answer and say before the LORD your God: 'My father *was* ᶜa Syrian,* ᵈabout to perish, and ᵉhe went down to Egypt and dwelt there, ᶠfew in number; and there he became a nation, ᵍgreat, mighty, and populous. ⁶But the ʰEgyptians mistreated us, afflicted us, and laid hard bondage on us. ⁷ⁱThen we cried out to the LORD God of our fathers, and the LORD heard our voice and looked on our affliction and our labor and our oppression. ⁸So ʲthe LORD brought us out of Egypt with a mighty hand and with an outstretched arm, ᵏwith great terror and with signs and wonders. ⁹He has brought us to this place and has given us this land, ˡ"a land flowing with milk and honey";* ¹⁰and now, behold, I have brought the firstfruits of the land which you, O LORD, have given me.'

"Then you shall set it before the LORD your God, and worship before the LORD your God. ¹¹So ᵐyou shall rejoice in every good *thing* which the LORD your God has given to you and your house, you and the Levite and the stranger who *is* among you.

¹²"When you have finished laying aside all the ⁿtithe of your increase in the third year—ᵒthe year of tithing—and have given *it* to the Levite, the stranger, the fatherless, and the widow, so that they may eat within your gates and be filled, ¹³then you shall say before the LORD your God: 'I have removed the holy *tithe* from *my* house, and also have given them to the Levite, the stranger, the fatherless, and the widow, according to all Your commandments which You have commanded me; I have not transgressed Your commandments, ᵖnor have I forgotten *them*. ¹⁴ᵠI have not eaten any of it when in mourning, nor have I removed *any* of it for an unclean *use*, nor given *any* of it for the dead. I have obeyed the voice of the LORD my God, and have done according to all that You have commanded me. ¹⁵ʳLook down from Your holy habitation, from heaven, and bless Your people Israel and the land which You have given us, just as You swore to our fathers, ˢ"a land flowing with milk and honey." '*

A Special People of God

¹⁶"This day the LORD your God commands you to observe these statutes and judgments; therefore you shall be careful to observe them with all your heart and with all your soul. ¹⁷Today you have ᵗproclaimed the LORD to be your God, and that you will walk in His ways and keep His statutes, His commandments, and His judgments, and that you will ᵘobey His voice. ¹⁸Also today ᵛthe LORD has proclaimed you to be His special people, just as He promised you, that *you* should keep all His commandments, ¹⁹and that He will set you ʷhigh above all nations which He has made, in praise, in name, and in honor, and that you may be ˣa holy people to the LORD your God, just as He has spoken."

The Law Inscribed on Stones

27 Now Moses, with the elders of Israel, commanded the people, saying: "Keep all the commandments which I command you today. ²And it shall be, on the day ᵃwhen you cross over the Jordan

---

*26:3 Septuagint reads *my*.   *26:5 Or *Aramean*
*26:9 Exodus 3:8   *26:15 Exodus 3:8

26:5 Syrian. This is a reference to Jacob, whose parents' ancestral home was in Syria (Gen. 24:1–10).

26:8 mighty hand . . . outstretched arm. God with His own hand demonstrated His power to the Egyptians and delivered the Israelites. The idea of God rescuing His people with His mighty arm is repeated in Isaiah 62 and 63.

26:10 I have brought. When the worshiper made a statement of what he was doing (see v. 13), he was taking responsibility for the items he was presenting to the Lord, not just blindly following a set form.

26:15 Your holy habitation. People direct their prayers to heaven, acknowledging at the same time that God is everywhere (Is. 66:1–2). Heaven most often refers to the dwelling place of God and the holy angels. Heaven is the place from which Christ came when He came to earth and He returned there after He was resurrected (Acts 1:11). One day He will come

from heaven back to earth (Matt. 24:30) and heaven will ultimately be the home of all believers (1 Pet. 1:4). Heaven is the place where the will of God is perfectly done, so it is a place of hope and inspiration.

26:16 with all your heart and with all your soul. This is a regular emphasis in Deuteronomy. God wants obedience, but He wants it to be the obedience of the engaged heart and mind.

26:2 ᵃ Ex. 22:29; 23:16, 19   ᵇ Deut. 12:5   **26:5** ᶜ Hos. 12:12
ᵈ Gen. 43:1, 2; 45:7, 11   ᵉ Acts 7:15   ᶠ Deut. 10:22   ᵍ Deut.
1:10   **26:6** ʰ Ex. 1:8–11, 14   **26:7** ⁱ Ex. 2:23–25; 3:9; 4:31
26:8 ʲ Deut. 5:15   ᵏ Deut. 4:34; 34:11, 12   **26:9** ˡ Ex. 3:8, 17
26:11 ᵐ Deut. 12:7; 16:11   **26:12** ⁿ Lev. 27:30   ᵒ Deut.
14:28, 29   **26:13** ᵖ Ps. 119:141, 153, 176   **26:14** ᵠ Hos.
9:4   **26:15** ʳ Is. 63:15   ˢ Ex. 3:8   **26:17** ᵗ Ex. 20:19   ᵘ Deut.
15:5   **26:18** ᵛ Ex. 6:7; 19:5   **26:19** ʷ Deut. 4:7, 8; 28:1
ˣ [1 Pet. 2:9]   **27:2** ᵃ Josh. 4:1

to the land which the LORD your God is giving you, that [b]you shall set up for yourselves large stones, and whitewash them with lime. [3] You shall write on them all the words of this law, when you have crossed over, that you may enter the land which the LORD your God is giving you, [c]'a land flowing with milk and honey,'* just as the LORD God of your fathers promised you. [4] Therefore it shall be, when you have crossed over the Jordan, that [d]on Mount Ebal you shall set up these stones, which I command you today, and you shall whitewash them with lime. [5] And there you shall build an altar to the LORD your God, an altar of stones; [e]you shall not use an iron tool on them. [6] You shall build with whole stones the altar of the LORD your God, and offer burnt offerings on it to the LORD your God. [7] You shall offer peace offerings, and shall eat there, and [f]rejoice before the LORD your God. [8] And you shall [g]write very plainly on the stones all the words of this law."

[9] Then Moses and the priests, the Levites, spoke to all Israel, saying, "Take heed and listen, O Israel: [h]This day you have become the people of the LORD your God. [10] Therefore you shall obey the voice of the LORD your God, and observe His commandments and His statutes which I command you today."

Curses Pronounced from Mount Ebal

[11] And Moses commanded the people on the same day, saying, [12] "These shall stand [i]on Mount Gerizim to bless the people, when you have crossed over the Jordan: Simeon, Levi, Judah, Issachar, Joseph, and Benjamin; [13] and [j]these shall stand on Mount Ebal to curse: Reuben, Gad, Asher, Zebulun, Dan, and Naphtali.

[14] "And [k]the Levites shall speak with a loud voice and say to all the men of Israel: [15] [l]'Cursed is the one who makes a carved or molded image, an abomination to the LORD, the work of the hands of the craftsman, and sets it up in secret.'

[m]"And all the people shall answer and say, 'Amen!'

[16] [n]'Cursed is the one who treats his father or his mother with contempt.'

"And all the people shall say, 'Amen!'

[17] [o]'Cursed is the one who moves his neighbor's landmark.'

"And all the people shall say, 'Amen!'

[18] [p]'Cursed is the one who makes the blind to wander off the road.'

"And all the people shall say, 'Amen!'

[19] [q]'Cursed is the one who perverts the justice due the stranger, the fatherless, and widow.'

"And all the people shall say, 'Amen!'

[20] [r]'Cursed is the one who lies with his father's wife, because he has uncovered his father's bed.'

"And all the people shall say, 'Amen!'

[21] [s]'Cursed is the one who lies with any kind of animal.'

"And all the people shall say, 'Amen!'

[22] [t]'Cursed is the one who lies with his sister, the daughter of his father or the daughter of his mother.'

"And all the people shall say, 'Amen!'

[23] [u]'Cursed is the one who lies with his mother-in-law.'

"And all the people shall say, 'Amen!'

[24] [v]'Cursed is the one who attacks his neighbor secretly.'

"And all the people shall say, 'Amen!'

[25] [w]'Cursed is the one who takes a bribe to slay an innocent person.'

"And all the people shall say, 'Amen!'

[26] [x]'Cursed is the one who does not confirm all the words of this law by observing them.'

"And all the people shall say, 'Amen!'"

Blessings on Obedience

28 "Now it shall come to pass, [a]if you diligently obey the voice of the LORD your God, to observe carefully all His commandments which I command you today, that the LORD your God [b]will set you high above all nations of the earth. [2] And all these blessings shall come upon you and [c]overtake you, because you obey the voice of the LORD your God:

* **27:3** Exodus 3:8

27:7 peace offerings. Many of the sacrifices had to do with sin, repentance, and making things right with God. This particular sacrifice was a time to be thankful and to rejoice in the good care of God.

27:11–13 Mount Gerizim . . . Mount Ebal. Mount Gerizim, the mountain of blessing, is usually covered with vegetation. Mount Ebal, the mountain of cursing, is a barren peak. The visual contrast made a memorable object lesson.

27:26 confirm all the words of this law by observing them. All of the actions listed in the curses are contrary to the law, as explained in the Book of Leviticus.

28:1–9 diligently obey. This passage repeatedly emphasizes the Israelites' responsibility to obey. God had already saved them from slavery, made them His people, promised to be their God, and to give them a

land to dwell in. But the blessings would only come with Israel's obedience. Sadly, Israel failed again and again to follow God. It was only after Christ that the followers of God could have the new Spirit which enabled them to obey from the heart (Rom. 7).

27:2 [b] Josh. 8:32   **27:3** [c] Ex. 3:8   **27:4** [d] Deut. 11:29
27:5 [e] Ex. 20:25   **27:7** [f] Deut. 26:11   **27:8** [g] Josh. 8:32
27:9 [h] Deut. 26:18   **27:12** [i] Josh. 8:33   **27:13** [j] Deut.
11:29   **27:14** [k] Deut. 33:10   **27:15** [l] Ex. 20:4, 23;
34:17   [m] Num. 5:22   **27:16** [n] Ezek. 22:7   **27:17** [o] Deut.
19:14   **27:18** [p] Lev. 19:14   **27:19** [q] Ex. 22:21, 22;
23:9   **27:20** [r] Deut. 22:30   **27:21** [s] Lev. 18:23; 20:15, 16
27:22 [t] Lev. 18:9   **27:23** [u] Lev. 18:17; 20:14   **27:24** [v] Ex.
20:13; 21:12   **27:25** [w] Ex. 23:7   **27:26** [x] Gal. 3:10
28:1 [a] Ex. 15:26   [b] Deut. 26:19   **28:2** [c] Deut. 28:15

3[d]"Blessed *shall* you *be* in the city, and
blessed *shall* you *be* [e]in the country.
4"Blessed *shall be* [f]the fruit of your
body, the produce of your ground and the
increase of your herds, the increase of your
cattle and the offspring of your flocks.
5"Blessed *shall be* your basket and your
kneading bowl.
6[g]"Blessed *shall* you *be* when you come
in, and blessed *shall* you *be* when you go
out.
7"The LORD [h]will cause your enemies
who rise against you to be defeated before
your face; they shall come out against you
one way and flee before you seven ways.
8"The LORD will [i]command the blessing on you in your storehouses and in all
to which you [j]set your hand, and He will
bless you in the land which the LORD your
God is giving you.
9[k]"The LORD will establish you as a
holy people to Himself, just as He has
sworn to you, if you keep the commandments of the LORD your God and walk in
His ways. 10Then all peoples of the earth
shall see that you are [l]called by the name
of the LORD, and they shall be [m]afraid of
you. 11And [n]the LORD will grant you plenty
of goods, in the fruit of your body, in the
increase of your livestock, and in the produce of your ground, in the land of which
the LORD swore to your fathers to give you.
12The LORD will open to you His good treasure, the heavens, [o]to give the rain to your
land in its season, and [p]to bless all the work
of your hand. [q]You shall lend to many nations, but you shall not borrow. 13And the
LORD will make [r]you the head and not the
tail; you shall be above only, and not be
beneath, if you heed the commandments
of the LORD your God, which I command
you today, and are careful to observe *them*.
14[s]So you shall not turn aside from any of
the words which I command you this day,
to the right or the left, to go after other
gods to serve them.

Curses on Disobedience

15"But it shall come to pass, [t]if you do
not obey the voice of the LORD your God, to
observe carefully all His commandments
and His statutes which I command you today, that all these curses will come upon
you and overtake you:
16"Cursed *shall* you *be* in the city, and
cursed *shall* you *be* in the country.
17"Cursed *shall be* your basket and your
kneading bowl.
18"Cursed *shall be* the fruit of your body
and the produce of your land, the increase
of your cattle and the offspring of your
flocks.
19"Cursed *shall* you *be* when you come
in, and cursed *shall* you *be* when you go
out.
20"The LORD will send on you [u]cursing,
[v]confusion, and [w]rebuke in all that you set
your hand to do, until you are destroyed
and until you perish quickly, because of the
wickedness of your doings in which you
have forsaken Me. 21The LORD will make
the plague cling to you until He has consumed you from the land which you are going to possess. 22[x]The LORD will strike you
with consumption, with fever, with inflammation, with severe burning fever, with the
sword, with [y]scorching, and with mildew;
they shall pursue you until you perish.
23And [z]your heavens which *are* over your
head shall be bronze, and the earth which
is under you *shall be* iron. 24The LORD will
change the rain of your land to powder and
dust; from the heaven it shall come down
on you until you are destroyed.
25[a]"The LORD will cause you to be defeated before your enemies; you shall go
out one way against them and flee seven
ways before them; and you shall become
troublesome to all the kingdoms of the
earth. 26[b]Your carcasses shall be food for
all the birds of the air and the beasts of
the earth, and no one shall frighten *them*
away. 27The LORD will strike you with [c]the
boils of Egypt, with [d]tumors, with the scab,
and with the itch, from which you cannot
be healed. 28The LORD will strike you with
madness and blindness and [e]confusion of
heart. 29And you shall [f]grope at noonday,
as a blind man gropes in darkness; you
shall not prosper in your ways; you shall be

28:15–19 Disobedience—The price of disobedience is always more than one can imagine in the beginning. It is not only the loss of peace or blessing, great as that may be, but there is also the loss of all that might have been. In God's plan the obedience is for the benefit of the follower of God, for the benefit of those who are watching and are influenced by this follower, and for the kingdom of God. If the follower disobeys, he may see how his actions affect himself, but he cannot know what other blessings are lost in the wider sphere of his own influence. It is a terrible thing to find oneself in the position of working against God.

28:20–57 *cursing, confusion, and rebuke.* Disobedience brings suffering, and this suffering often spills over onto other people, even into future generations. The suffering is a wake-up call, something that is meant to remind the disobedient that they are living against God, and that they need to repent, turn to God, and ask for help. The problem is, that often the disobedient have a skewed idea of who God is and what He desires, so they blame God and become more rebellious. There is another kind of suffering as well. This is the suffering of the innocent, as in the

28:3 [d]Ps. 128:1, 4 [e]Gen. 39:5 **28:4** [f]Gen. 22:17 **28:6** [g]Ps. 121:8 **28:7** [h]Lev. 26:7, 8 **28:8** [i]Lev. 25:21 [j]Deut. 15:10 **28:9** [k]Ex. 19:5, 6 **28:10** [l]Num. 6:27 [m]Deut. 11:25 **28:11** [n]Deut. 30:9 **28:12** [o]Lev. 26:4 [p]Deut. 14:29 [q]Deut. 15:6 **28:13** [r][Is. 9:14, 15] **28:14** [s]Deut. 5:32 **28:15** [t]Lev. 26:14–39 **28:20** [u]Mal. 2:2 [v]Is. 65:14 [w]Is. 30:17 **28:22** [x]Lev. 26:16 [y]Amos 4:9 **28:23** [z]Lev. 26:19 **28:25** [a]Deut. 32:30 **28:26** [b]1 Sam. 17:44 **28:27** [c]Ex. 15:26 [d]1 Sam. 5:6 **28:28** [e]Jer. 4:9 **28:29** [f]Job 5:14

only oppressed and plundered continually, and no one will save you. 30g"You shall betroth a wife, but another man shall lie with her; hyou shall build a house, but iyou shall not dwell in it; you shall plant a vineyard, but shall not gather its grapes. 31Your ox *shall be* slaughtered before your eyes, but you shall not eat of it; your donkey *shall be* violently taken away from before you, and shall not be restored to you; your sheep *shall be* given to your enemies, and you shall have no one to rescue *them.* 32Your sons and your daughters *shall be* given to janother people, and your eyes shall look and kfail *with longing* for them all day long; and *there shall be* no strength in your lhand. 33A nation whom you have not known shall eat mthe fruit of your land and the produce of your labor, and you shall be only oppressed and crushed continually. 34So you shall be driven mad because of the sight which your eyes see. 35The LORD will strike you in the knees and on the legs with severe boils which cannot be healed, and from the sole of your foot to the top of your head.

36"The LORD will nbring you and the king whom you set over you to a nation which neither you nor your fathers have known, and othere you shall serve other gods—wood and stone. 37And you shall become pan astonishment, a proverb, qand a byword among all nations where the LORD will drive you.

38r"You shall carry much seed out to the field but gather little in, for sthe locust shall consume it. 39You shall plant vineyards and tend *them,* but you shall neither drink *of* the twine nor gather the *grapes;* for the worms shall eat them. 40You shall have olive trees throughout all your territory, but you shall not anoint *yourself* with the oil; for your olives shall drop off. 41You shall beget sons and daughters, but they shall not be yours; for uthey shall go into captivity. 42Locusts shall consume all your trees and the produce of your land.

43"The alien who *is* among you shall rise higher and higher above you, and you shall come down lower and lower. 44He shall lend to you, but you shall not lend to him; he shall be the head, and you shall be the tail.

45"Moreover all these curses shall come upon you and pursue and overtake you,

until you are destroyed, because you did not obey the voice of the LORD your God, to keep His commandments and His statutes which He commanded you. 46And they shall be upon vyou for a sign and a wonder, and on your descendants forever.

47w"Because you did not serve the LORD your God with joy and gladness of heart, xfor the abundance of everything, 48therefore you shall serve your enemies, whom the LORD will send against you, in yhunger, in thirst, in nakedness, and in need of everything; and He zwill put a yoke of iron on your neck until He has destroyed you. 49aThe LORD will bring a nation against you from afar, from the end of the earth, bas swift as the eagle flies, a nation whose language you will not understand, 50a nation of fierce countenance, cwhich does not respect the elderly nor show favor to the young. 51And they shall eat the increase of your livestock and the produce of your land, until you are destroyed; they shall not leave you grain or new wine or oil, *or* the increase of your cattle or the offspring of your flocks, until they have destroyed you.

52"They shall dbesiege you at all your gates until your high and fortified walls, in which you trust, come down throughout all your land; and they shall besiege you at all your gates throughout all your land which the LORD your God has given you. 53eYou shall eat the fruit of your own body, the flesh of your sons and your daughters whom the LORD your God has given you, in the siege and desperate straits in which your enemy shall distress you. 54The sensitive and very refined man among you fwill be hostile toward his brother, toward gthe wife of his bosom, and toward the rest of his children whom he leaves behind, 55so that he will not give any of them the flesh of his children whom he will eat, because he has nothing left in the siege and desperate straits in which your enemy shall distress you at all your gates. 56The tender and delicate woman among you, who would not venture to set the sole of her foot on the ground because of her delicateness and sensitivity, will refuse* to the husband of her bosom, and to her son and her daughter, 57her placenta which

* 28:56 Literally *her eye shall be evil toward*

case of Job, where God allowed Satan to test him to show Satan that Job really loved God and was not merely faithful because God had blessed him.
28:30 betroth a wife . . . build a house . . . plant a vineyard. Each of these momentous events of life were reasons to be excused from service in the army (20:5–7), yet if the Israelites were disobedient, life itself would prevent them from realizing the fruits of their labors.
28:52–57 besiege you at all your gates. Moses forewarned the people of the terrible stresses of sieges (2 Kin. 6:24–31; Lam. 2:20; 4:10). The horrors of hunger

and deprivation would lead people to behave in ways that they otherwise could never imagine.

28:30 gJer. 8:10 hAmos 5:11 iDeut. 20:6 **28:32** j2 Chr. 29:9 kPs. 119:82 lNeh. 5:5 **28:33** mJer. 5:15, 17 **28:36** nJer. 39:1–9 oDeut. 4:28 **28:37** p 1 Kin. 9:7, 8 qPs. 44:14 **28:38** rMic. 6:15 sJoel 1:4 **28:39** tZeph. 1:13 **28:41** uDeut. 1:5 **28:46** vIs. 8:18 **28:47** wNeh. 9:35–37 xDeut. 32:15 **28:48** yLam. 4:4–6 zJer. 28:13, 14 **28:49** aJer. 5:15 bJer. 48:40; 49:22 **28:50** c2 Chr. 36:17 **28:52** d2 Kin. 25:1, 2, 4 **28:53** eLev. 26:29 **28:54** fDeut. 15:9 gDeut. 13:6

comes out *h*from between her feet and her children whom she bears; for she will eat them secretly for lack of everything in the siege and desperate straits in which your enemy shall distress you at all your gates.

⁵⁸"If you do not carefully observe all the words of this law that are written in this book, that you may fear *i*this glorious and awesome name, THE LORD YOUR GOD, ⁵⁹then the LORD will bring upon you and your descendants *j*extraordinary plagues—great and prolonged plagues— and serious and prolonged sicknesses. ⁶⁰Moreover He will bring back on you all *k*the diseases of Egypt, of which you were afraid, and they shall cling to you. ⁶¹Also every sickness and every plague, which *is* not written in this Book of the Law, will the LORD bring upon you until you are destroyed. ⁶²You *l*shall be left few in number, whereas you were *m*as the stars of heaven in multitude, because you would not obey the voice of the LORD your God. ⁶³And it shall be, *that* just as the LORD *n*rejoiced over you to do you good and multiply you, so the LORD *o*will rejoice over you to destroy you and bring you to nothing; and you shall be *p*plucked from off the land which you go to possess.

⁶⁴"Then the LORD *q*will scatter you among all peoples, from one end of the earth to the other, and *r*there you shall serve other gods, which neither you nor your fathers have known—wood and stone. ⁶⁵And *s*among those nations you shall find no rest, nor shall the sole of your foot have a resting place; *t*but there the LORD will give you a trembling heart, failing eyes, and *u*anguish of soul. ⁶⁶Your life shall hang in doubt before you; you shall fear day and night, and have no assurance of life. ⁶⁷*v*In the morning you shall say, 'Oh, that it were evening!' And at evening you shall say, 'Oh, that it were morning!' because of the fear which terrifies your heart, and *w*because of the sight which your eyes see.

⁶⁸"And the LORD *x*will take you back to Egypt in ships, by the way of which I said to you, *y*'You shall never see it again.' And there you shall be offered for sale to your enemies as male and female slaves, but no one will buy *you.*"

The Covenant Renewed in Moab

29 These *are* the words of the *a*covenant which the LORD commanded Moses to make with the children of Israel in the land of Moab, besides the covenant which He made with them in Horeb.

²Now Moses called all Israel and said to them: *b*"You have seen all that the LORD did before your eyes in the land of Egypt, to Pharaoh and to all his servants and to all his land— ³*c*the great trials which your eyes have seen, the signs, and those great wonders. ⁴Yet *d*the LORD has not given you a heart to perceive and eyes to see and ears to hear, to this *very* day. ⁵*e*And I have led you forty years in the wilderness. *f*Your clothes have not worn out on you, and your sandals have not worn out on your feet. ⁶*g*You have not eaten bread, nor have you drunk wine or *similar* drink, that you may know that I *am* the LORD your God. ⁷And when you came to this place, *h*Sihon king of Heshbon and Og king of Bashan came out against us to battle, and we conquered them. ⁸We took their land and *i*gave it as an inheritance to the Reubenites, to the Gadites, and to half the tribe of Manasseh. ⁹Therefore *j*keep the words of this covenant, and do them, that you may *k*prosper in all that you do.

¹⁰"All of you stand today before the LORD your God: your leaders and your tribes and your elders and your officers, all the men of Israel, ¹¹your little ones and your wives— also the stranger who *is* in your camp, from *l*the one who cuts your wood to the one who draws your water— ¹²that you may enter into covenant with the LORD your God, and *m*into His oath, which the LORD your God makes with you today, ¹³that He may *n*establish you today as a people for Himself, and *that* He may be God to you, *o*just as He has spoken to you, and *p*just as He has sworn to your fathers, to Abraham, Isaac, and Jacob.

¹⁴"I make this covenant and this oath, *q*not with you alone, ¹⁵but with *him* who stands here with us today before the LORD our God, *r*as well as with *him* who *is* not here with us today ¹⁶(for you know that we dwelt in the land of Egypt and that we came through the nations which you passed by, ¹⁷and you saw their abominations and their idols which *were* among them—wood and

---

29:9–13 *keep the words of this covenant.* The members of the covenant community included all adults, children, and strangers who had joined the Israelites, as well as those yet to be born.

29:10–15 The Covenant Renewed—As Israel reached the plains of Moab, anticipating their entrance into the Promised Land, it was important for the people to review and renew their covenantal relationship with God. So Moses summoned the people together and challenged them to keep the covenant that God had established with their forefathers. The essential terms of the covenant gave Israel the

28:57 *h* Gen. 49:10 **28:58** *i* Ex. 6:3 **28:59** *j* Dan. 9:12 **28:60** *k* Deut. 7:15 **28:62** *l* Deut. 4:27 *m* Neh. 9:23 **28:63** *n* Jer. 32:41 *o* Prov. 1:26 *p* Jer. 12:14; 45:4 **28:64** *q* Jer. 16:13 *r* Deut. 28:36 **28:65** *s* Amos 9:4 *t* Lev. 26:36 *u* Lev. 26:16 **28:67** *v* Job 7:4 *w* Deut. 28:34 **28:68** *x* Hos. 8:13 *y* Deut. 17:16 **29:1** *a* Deut. 5:2, 3 **29:2** *b* Ex. 19:4 **29:3** *c* Deut. 4:34; 7:19 **29:4** *d* [Acts 28:26, 27] **29:5** *e* Deut. 1:3; 8:2 *f* Deut. 8:4 **29:6** *g* Deut. 8:3 **29:7** *h* Num. 21:23, 24 **29:8** *i* Deut. 3:12, 13 **29:9** *j* Deut. 4:6 *k* Josh. 1:7 **29:11** *l* Josh. 9:21, 23, 27 **29:12** *m* Neh. 10:29 **29:13** *n* Deut. 28:9 *o* Ex. 6:7 *p* Gen. 17:7, 8 **29:14** *q* [Jer. 31:31] **29:15** *r* Acts 2:39

stone and silver and gold); [18]so that there may not be among you man or woman or family or tribe, *s*whose heart turns away today from the LORD our God, to go *and* serve the gods of these nations, *t*and that there may not be among you a root bearing *u*bitterness or wormwood; [19]and so it may not happen, when he hears the words of this curse, that he blesses himself in his heart, saying, 'I shall have peace, even though I follow the *v*dictates* of my heart'—*w*as though the drunkard could be included with the sober.

[20]*x*"The LORD would not spare him; for then *y*the anger of the LORD and *z*His jealousy would burn against that man, and every curse that is written in this book would settle on him, and the LORD *a*would blot out his name from under heaven. [21]And the LORD *b*would separate him from all the tribes of Israel for adversity, according to all the curses of the covenant that are written in this Book of the *c*Law, [22]so that the coming generation of your children who rise up after you, and the foreigner who comes from a far land, would say, when they *d*see the plagues of that land and the sicknesses which the LORD has laid on it:

[23]'The whole land *is* brimstone, *e*salt, and burning; it is not sown, nor does it bear, nor does any grass grow there, *f*like the overthrow of Sodom and Gomorrah, Admah, and Zeboiim, which the LORD overthrew in His anger and His wrath.' [24]All nations would say, *g*'Why has the LORD done so to this land? What does the heat of this great anger mean?' [25]Then *people* would say: 'Because they have forsaken the covenant of the LORD God of their fathers, which He made with them when He brought them out of the land of Egypt; [26]for they went and served other gods and worshiped them, gods that they did not know and that He had not given to them. [27]Then the anger of the LORD was aroused against this land, *h*to bring on it every curse that is written in this book. [28]And the LORD *i*uprooted them from their land in anger, in wrath, and in great indignation, and cast them into another land, as *it is* this day.'

[29]"The secret *things belong* to the LORD our God, but those *things which are* revealed *belong* to us and to our children forever, that *we* may do all the words of this law.

The Blessing of Returning to God

30 "Now *a*it shall come to pass, when *b*all these things come upon you, the blessing and the *c*curse which I have set before you, and *d*you call *them* to mind among all the nations where the LORD your God drives you, [2]and you *e*return to the LORD your God and obey His voice, according to all that I command you today, you and your children, with all your heart and with all your soul, [3]*f*that the LORD your God will bring you back from captivity,

---

* **29:19** Or *stubbornness*

Promised Land and prosperity in their possession of it, but only on the condition of their obedience and willingness to walk in God's ways.

29:18 heart turns away. To be in the position of once having known the way of the Lord, and then to have turned and followed a path of disobedience and rebellion is a miserable position. It is the cause of great heartache for the faithful ones who see it happening. The backslider becomes more and more hardened against God, and it will ultimately affect a wider and wider group of people. There is no security or safety while persisting in a course of flagrant and continuous rebellion. **root bearing bitterness or wormwood.** Tolerance for idolatry and pagan practices would always corrupt the community, and therefore the covenant relationship with God.

29:24–28 Why has the LORD done so. The lesson of faithless Israel would become known among the nations, even as the deliverance of Israel was to be known by them.

29:29 Revelation—Revelation may be defined as that process by which God gives to us truths that we would not otherwise know. The details of the creation story in Genesis 1 and 2 are an example of general revelation. In that man was not created until the sixth day, there was no human to even write about creation until after it happened. God revealed the creation facts to Moses. All created things have an innate knowledge of their Creator through creation itself.

We know God spoke to the human authors of our Bible. We are not sure exactly how it happened, but Scripture gives some examples of specific revelation. God's call to Samuel was in an audible voice he mistook for Eli's (1 Sam. 3). Often God spoke through angels such as when Gabriel was sent to tell Mary she would give birth to the Messiah (Luke 1:26–37). On other occasions it appears that God spoke directly to a man, as He did to Noah (Gen. 6) and Moses through the burning bush (Ex. 3). On still other occasions God communicated through dreams or visions as He did with the wise men (Matt. 2:12) and Peter (Acts 10).

One of the most important ways God reveals Himself to people in Scripture is through encounters where God takes on human form called a theophany or Christophany. In Genesis 32 Jacob wrestled with God, and in Joshua 5 Joshua encounters a commander of the Lord's that most Bible students take to be a preincarnate Christ.

30:1 when all these things come upon you. God had allowed Moses to foresee Israel's future apostasy and God's dispersal of the people among the nations. Hundreds of years later, these verses must have been both sad and encouraging to the Israelites as they saw the time of their dispersal.

29:18 *s* Deut. 11:16 *t* Heb. 12:15 *u* Deut. 32:32
29:19 *v* Jer. 3:17; 7:24 *w* Is. 30:1 **29:20** *x* Ezek. 14:7 *y* Ps. 74:1 *z* Ps. 79:5 *a* Deut. 9:14 **29:21** *b* [Matt. 24:51] *c* Deut. 30:10 **29:22** *d* Deut. 19:8; 49:17; 50:13 **29:23** *e* Zeph. 2:9 *f* Gen. 19:24, 25 **29:24** *g* 1 Kin. 9:8 **29:27** *h* Dan. 9:11 **29:28** *i* 1 Kin. 14:15 **30:1** *a* Lev. 26:40 *b* Deut. 28:2 *c* Deut. 28:15–45 *d* Deut. 4:29, 30 **30:2** *e* Neh. 1:9 **30:3** *f* Jer. 29:14

and have compassion on you, and ᵍgather you again from all the nations where the LORD your God has scattered you. ⁴ʰIf *any* of you are driven out to the farthest *parts* under heaven, from there the LORD your God will gather you, and from there He will bring you. ⁵Then the LORD your God will bring you to the land which your fathers possessed, and you shall possess it. He will prosper you and multiply you more than your fathers. ⁶And ⁱthe LORD your God will circumcise your heart and the heart of your descendants, to love the LORD your God with all your heart and with all your soul, that you may live.

⁷"Also the LORD your God will put all these ʲcurses on your enemies and on those who hate you, who persecuted you. ⁸And you will ᵏagain obey the voice of the LORD and do all His commandments which I command you today. ⁹ˡThe LORD your God will make you abound in all the work of your hand, in the fruit of your body, in the increase of your livestock, and in the produce of your land for good. For the LORD will again ᵐrejoice over you for good as He rejoiced over your fathers, ¹⁰if you obey the voice of the LORD your God, to keep His commandments and His statutes which are written in this Book of the Law, *and* if you turn to the LORD your God with all your heart and with all your soul.

The Choice of Life or Death

¹¹"For this commandment which I command you today ⁿis not *too* mysterious for you, nor *is* it far off. ¹²ᵒIt *is* not in heaven, that you should say, 'Who will ascend into heaven for us and bring it to us, that we may hear it and do it?' ¹³Nor *is* it beyond the sea, that you should say, 'Who will go over the sea for us and bring it to us, that we may hear it and do it?' ¹⁴But the word *is*

very near you, ᵖin your mouth and in your heart, that you may do it.

¹⁵"See, qI have set before you today life and good, death and evil, ¹⁶in that I command you today to love the LORD your God, to walk in His ways, and to keep His commandments, His statutes, and His judgments, that you may live and multiply; and the LORD your God will bless you in the land which you go to possess. ¹⁷But if your heart turns away so that you do not hear, and are drawn away, and worship other gods and serve them, ¹⁸ʳI announce to you today that you shall surely perish; you shall not prolong *your* days in the land which you cross over the Jordan to go in and possess. ¹⁹ˢI call heaven and earth as witnesses today against you, *that* ᵗI have set before you life and death, blessing and cursing; therefore choose life, that both you and your descendants may live; ²⁰that you may love the LORD your God, that you may obey His voice, and that you may cling to Him, for He *is* your ᵘlife and the length of your days; and that you may dwell in the land which the LORD swore to your fathers, to Abraham, Isaac, and Jacob, to give them."

Joshua the New Leader of Israel

31 Then Moses went and spoke these words to all Israel. ²And he said to them: "I ᵃam one hundred and twenty years old today. I can no longer ᵇgo out and come in. Also the LORD has said to me, ᶜ'You shall not cross over this Jordan.' ³The LORD your God ᵈHimself crosses over before you; He will destroy these nations from before you, and you shall dispossess them. ᵉJoshua himself crosses over before you, just ᶠas the LORD has said. ⁴gAnd the LORD will do to them ʰas He did to Sihon and Og, the kings of the Amorites and their land, when He destroyed them. ⁵ⁱThe LORD

30:6 *circumcise your heart.* God's intentions for His people have always been for the whole person to respond to Him. Outward symbols, such as circumcision, were always intended to be the mark of an inner reality, the heart that was tender to the Lord.
30:10 *this Book of the Law.* A reference to the Book of Deuteronomy. *all your heart . . . all your soul.* An open heart in the presence of God through the law creates a dynamic of "life" and "blessing" (v. 19).
30:11 *not too mysterious for you.* This is not a task that is hard to understand.
30:12–13 *not in heaven . . . beyond the sea.* Obeying God's law is entirely within the reach of the average person.
30:14 *very near you.* The revelation of God, unlike any other book, makes the truth of immediate importance to the reader.
30:18 *today.* Moses establishes here the best pattern for the preaching of the Word of God. Responses to God should not be delayed. Assuming that there will be a later day to respond to Him is dangerous thinking.
30:19 *life and death.* Biblical teaching is remarkable for the clarity with which it presents the great issues

that demand decision. Either we love the Lord and walk in His ways, or we turn from Him to worship idols. We can choose life or death, blessing or cursing. God takes no pleasure in the misery of sinners, but urges us to choose life for our good and the good of unborn generations. The Lord has spoken, and we cannot plead ignorance. *and your descendants.* The present generation's choice always determines the direction of future generations.
31:2–3 *You shall not cross over this Jordan.* Moses spoke regretfully of God's refusal to permit him to enter the Promised Land, yet he continued to make the most important point of all. The leadership of God Himself would not cease with Moses' death.

30:3 ᵍ Ezek. 34:13 **30:4** ʰ Neh. 1:9 **30:6** ⁱ Deut. 10:16 **30:7** ʲ Jer. 30:16, 20 **30:8** ᵏ Zeph. 3:20 **30:9** ˡ Deut. 28:11 ᵐ Jer. 32:41 **30:11** ⁿ Is. 45:19 **30:12** ᵒ Rom. 10:6–8 **30:14** ᵖ Rom. 10:8 **30:15** q Deut. 30:1, 19 **30:18** ʳ Deut. 4:26; 8:19 **30:19** ˢ Deut. 4:26 ᵗ Deut. 30:15 **30:20** ᵘ [John 11:25; 14:6] **31:2** ᵃ Deut. 34:7 ᵇ 1 Kin. 3:7 ᶜ Num. 20:12 **31:3** ᵈ Deut. 9:3 ᵉ Num. 27:18 ᶠ Num. 27:21 **31:4** g Deut. 3:21 ʰ Num. 21:24, 33 **31:5** ⁱ Deut. 7:2; 20:10–20

will give them over to you, that you may do
to them according to every commandment
which I have commanded you. 6 [j]Be strong
and of good courage, [k]do not fear nor be
afraid of them; for the LORD your God, [l]He
is the One who goes with you. [m]He will not
leave you nor forsake you."
7 Then Moses called Joshua and said to
him in the sight of all Israel, [n]"Be strong
and of good courage, for you must go with
this people to the land which the LORD has
sworn to their fathers to give them, and
you shall cause them to inherit it. 8 And
the LORD, [o]He *is* the One who goes before
you. [p]He will be with you, He will not leave
you nor forsake you; do not fear nor be dismayed."

The Law to Be Read Every Seven Years

9 So Moses wrote this law [q]and delivered
it to the priests, the sons of Levi, [r]who bore
the ark of the covenant of the LORD, and to
all the elders of Israel. 10 And Moses commanded them, saying: "At the end of *every*
seven years, at the appointed time in the
[s]year of release, [t]at the Feast of Tabernacles, 11 when all Israel comes to [u]appear
before the LORD your God in the [v]place
which He chooses, [w]you shall read this law
before all Israel in their hearing. 12 [x]Gather
the people together, men and women and
little ones, and the stranger who *is* within your gates, that they may hear and that
they may learn to fear the LORD your God
and carefully observe all the words of this
law, 13 and *that* their children, [y]who have
not known it, [z]may hear and learn to fear
the LORD your God as long as you live in
the land which you cross the Jordan to
possess."

Prediction of Israel's Rebellion

14 Then the LORD said to Moses, [a]"Behold, the days approach when you must
die; call Joshua, and present yourselves
in the tabernacle of meeting, that [b]I may
inaugurate him."
So Moses and Joshua went and presented themselves in the tabernacle of
meeting. 15 Now [c]the LORD appeared at
the tabernacle in a pillar of cloud, and the
pillar of cloud stood above the door of the
tabernacle.
16 And the LORD said to Moses: "Behold, you will rest with your fathers; and
this people will [d]rise and [e]play the harlot
with the gods of the foreigners of the land,
where they go *to be* among them, and they
will [f]forsake Me and [g]break My covenant
which I have made with them. 17 Then
My anger shall be [h]aroused against them
in that day, and [i]I will forsake them, and
I will [j]hide My face from them, and they
shall be devoured. And many evils and
troubles shall befall them, so that they will
say in that day, [k]'Have not these evils come
upon us because our God *is* [l]not among
us?' 18 And [m]I will surely hide My face in
that day because of all the evil which they
have done, in that they have turned to other
gods.
19 "Now therefore, write down this song
for yourselves, and teach it to the children
of Israel; put it in their mouths, that this
song may be [n]a witness for Me against the
children of Israel. 20 When I have brought
them to the land flowing with milk and
honey, of which I swore to their fathers,
and they have eaten and filled themselves
[o]and grown fat, [p]then they will turn to other gods and serve them; and they will provoke Me and break My covenant. 21 Then
it shall be, [q]when many evils and troubles
have come upon them, that this song will
testify against them as a witness; for it will
not be forgotten in the mouths of their descendants, for [r]I know the inclination [s]of
their behavior today, even before I have
brought them to the land of which I swore
to give them."
22 Therefore Moses wrote this song the
same day, and taught it to the children of
Israel. 23 [t]Then He inaugurated Joshua the
son of Nun, and said, [u]"Be strong and of
good courage; for you shall bring the children of Israel into the land of which I swore
to them, and I will be with you."
24 So it was, when Moses had completed
writing the words of this law in a book,
when they were finished, 25 that Moses

31:12–13 Obeying God—Because the Israelites had no Bibles, they had to come together to listen to God's word as read by a priest from a scroll. The laws were to be read to the whole assembly including women and children. No doubt memorization was important as a way of impressing the laws on the minds and hearts of the people. But it was not the end. The expected end result of hearing was obedience. Obedience to the Word of God is the only way that the child of God can please God in the new life. "But be doers of the word, and not hearers only, deceiving yourselves" (James 1:22).

31:16 *play the harlot.* This expression speaks both of spiritual adultery and physical acts of sexual immorality that were performed in association with the worship of Baal and Asherah, the gods of Canaan.

31:22 *Therefore Moses wrote.* Psalm 90 is also attributed to Moses, and perhaps Psalm 91. Both psalms are logical meditations for these last chapters of Deuteronomy.

31:6 [j] Josh. 10:25 [k] Deut. 1:29 [l] Deut. 20:4 [m] Heb. 13:5 **31:7** [n] Deut. 31:23 **31:8** [o] Ex. 13:21 [p] Josh. 1:5 **31:9** [q] Deut. 17:18; 31:25, 26 [r] Josh. 3:3 **31:10** [s] Deut. 15:1, 2 [t] Lev. 23:34 **31:11** [u] Deut. 16:16 [v] Deut. 12:5 [w] Josh. 8:34 **31:12** [x] Deut. 4:10 **31:13** [y] Deut. 11:2 [z] Ps. 78:6, 7 **31:14** [a] Num. 27:13 [b] Deut. 3:28 **31:15** [c] Ex. 33:9 **31:16** [d] Deut. 29:22 [e] Ex. 34:15 [f] Deut. 32:15 [g] Judg. 2:20 **31:17** [h] Judg. 2:14; 6:13 [i] 2 Chr. 15:2 [j] Deut. 32:20 [k] Judg. 6:13 [l] Num. 14:42 **31:18** [m] Deut. 31:17 **31:19** [n] Deut. 31:22, 26 **31:20** [o] Deut. 32:15–17 [p] Deut. 31:16 **31:21** [q] Deut. 31:17 [r] Hos. 5:3 [s] Amos 5:25, 26 **31:23** [t] Num. 27:23 [u] Deut. 31:7

commanded the Levites, who bore the ark of the covenant of the LORD, saying: 26"Take this Book of the Law, vand put it beside the ark of the covenant of the LORD your God, that it may be there was a witness against you; 27xfor I know your rebellion and your ystiff neck. If today, while I am yet alive with you, you have been rebellious against the LORD, then how much more after my death? 28Gather to me all the elders of your tribes, and your officers, that I may speak these words in their hearing zand call heaven and earth to witness against them. 29For I know that after my death you will abecome utterly corrupt, and turn aside from the way which I have commanded you. And bevil will befall you cin the latter days, because you will do evil in the sight of the LORD, to provoke Him to anger through the work of your hands."

The Song of Moses

30Then Moses spoke in the hearing of all the assembly of Israel the words of this song until they were ended:

32 "Give aear, O heavens, and I will speak;
And hear, O bearth, the words of my mouth.

2   Let cmy teaching drop as the rain,
My speech distill as the dew,
dAs raindrops on the tender herb,
And as showers on the grass.

3   For I proclaim the ename of the LORD:
fAscribe greatness to our God.

4   He is gthe Rock, hHis work is perfect;
For all His ways are justice,
iA God of truth and jwithout injustice;
Righteous and upright is He.

5   "Theyk have corrupted themselves;
They are not His children,

Because of their blemish:
A lperverse and crooked generation.

6   Do you thus mdeal with the LORD,
O foolish and unwise people?
Is He not nyour Father, who obought you?
Has He not pmade you and established you?

7   "Rememberq the days of old,
Consider the years of many generations.
rAsk your father, and he will show you;
Your elders, and they will tell you:

8   When the Most High sdivided their inheritance to the nations,
When He tseparated the sons of Adam,
He set the boundaries of the peoples
According to the number of the children of Israel.

9   For uthe LORD's portion is His people;
Jacob is the place of His inheritance.

10 "He found him vin a desert land
And in the wasteland, a howling wilderness;
He encircled him, He instructed him,
He wkept him as the apple of His eye.

11 xAs an eagle stirs up its nest,
Hovers over its young,
Spreading out its wings, taking them up,
Carrying them on its wings,

12 So the LORD alone led him,
And there was no foreign god with him.

13 "Hey made him ride in the heights of the earth,
That he might eat the produce of the fields;
He made him draw honey from the rock,
And oil from the flinty rock;

32:7 Remembering the Works of God—The Bible's revelation of God's work in the past provides an informative and exciting panorama of centuries of divine activity toward man.

First, it gives man an education in truths unknowable apart from divine revelation. For example, the creation of man described in Genesis 1 and 2 answers man's most basic questions: "Who am I?" and "Where did I come from?" The only way we can get this information is from God Himself.

Second, the Bible sets forth a significant body of historical evidence for the truth and validity of the Christian faith. These evidences include fulfilled prophecy, the miracles of Christ, and Christ's death and resurrection. The believer's faith is thus grounded in historical events and is much more than just "a leap in the dark."

Third, the Bible records examples to help present-day Christians. Israel's failures and the consequences that resulted are used by the New Testament writers as lessons. Believers are urged to avoid grumbling, as Israel did (1 Cor. 10:10–11), and the deviant behavior of Sodom and Gomorrah (2 Pet. 2: 4–9). Paul is said to be a living example for believers to follow

(1 Cor. 4:16; 11:1), as is Jesus' humility in the midst of suffering (1 Pet. 2:21).

Fourth, the Bible provides encouragement for Christians in their life and witness. If God could use an adulterer and murderer like David, then God can surely use a struggling Christian today if that person has David's passion for the Lord. Likewise, if God saved Saul of Tarsus, the chief enemy of the early church (Acts 9:1–31), He can certainly save the people with whom Christians daily share their faith.

32:12 the LORD alone. Deuteronomy is an extended argument against idolatry and paganism. Clearly the Israelites had no reason to abandon the God of grace and love, who had given them all they needed.

31:26 v 2 Kin. 22:8 w Deut. 31:19   **31:27** x Deut. 9:7, 24 y Ex. 32:9   **31:28** z Deut. 30:19   **31:29** a Judg. 2:19 b Deut. 28:15 c Gen. 49:1   **32:1** a Deut. 4:26 b Jer. 6:19   **32:2** c Is. 55:10, 11 d Ps. 72:6   **32:3** e Deut. 28:58 f 1 Chr. 29:11   **32:4** g Ps. 18:2 h 2 Sam. 22:31 i Is. 65:16 j Job 34:10   **32:5** k Deut. 4:25; 31:29 l Phil. 2:15   **32:6** m Ps. 116:12 n Is. 63:16 o Ps. 74:2 p Deut. 32:15   **32:7** q Ps. 44:1 r Ps. 78:5–8   **32:8** s Acts 17:26 t Gen. 11:8   **32:9** u Ex. 19:5   **32:10** v Jer. 2:6 w Ps. 17:8   **32:11** x Is. 31:5   **32:13** y Is. 58:14

14 Curds from the cattle, and milk of the
flock,
zWith fat of lambs;
And rams of the breed of Bashan, and
goats,
With the choicest wheat;
And you drank wine, the ablood of the
grapes.

15 "But Jeshurun grew fat and kicked;
bYou grew fat, you grew thick,
You are obese!
Then he cforsook God who dmade him,
And scornfully esteemed the eRock of
his salvation.

16 fThey provoked Him to jealousy with
foreign gods;
With abominations they provoked
Him to anger.

17 gThey sacrificed to demons, not to God,
To gods they did not know,
To new gods, new arrivals
That your fathers did not fear.

18 hOf the Rock who begot you, you are
unmindful,
And have iforgotten the God who
fathered you.

19 "Andj when the LORD saw it, He
spurned them,
Because of the provocation of His sons
and His daughters.

20 And He said: 'I will hide My face from
them,
I will see what their end will be,
For they are a perverse generation,
kChildren in whom is no faith.

21 lThey have provoked Me to jealousy by
what is not God;
They have moved Me to anger mby
their foolish idols.
But nI will provoke them to jealousy by
those who are not a nation;
I will move them to anger by a foolish
nation.

22 For oa fire is kindled in My anger,
And shall burn to the lowest hell;

It shall consume the earth with her
increase,
And set on fire the foundations of the
mountains.

23 'I will pheap disasters on them;
qI will spend My arrows on them.

24 They shall be wasted with hunger,
Devoured by pestilence and bitter
destruction;
I will also send against them the rteeth
of beasts,
With the poison of serpents of the dust.

25 The sword shall destroy outside;
There shall be terror within
For the young man and virgin,
The nursing child with the man of
gray hairs.

26 sI would have said, "I will dash them in
pieces,
I will make the memory of them to
cease from among men,"

27 Had I not feared the wrath of the
enemy,
Lest their adversaries should
misunderstand,
Lest they should say, t"Our hand is
high;
And it is not the LORD who has done
all this." '

28 "For they are a nation void of counsel,
Nor is there any understanding in
them.

29 uOh, that they were wise, that they
understood this,
That they would consider their vlatter
end!

30 How could one chase a thousand,
And two put ten thousand to flight,
Unless their Rock whad sold them,
And the LORD had surrendered them?

31 For their rock is not like our Rock,
xEven our enemies themselves being
judges.

32 For ytheir vine is of the vine of Sodom
And of the fields of Gomorrah;

32:15 Jeshurun. Jeshurun, a pet name for Israel, means "uprightness." This part of the song contrasts what Israel should have been (upright) and what they became (rebellious). **he forsook God.** A nation or a person who has forsaken God is godless. Because God is the source of blessing, peace, joy, wisdom, and comfort, they have also forsaken all of these attributes. One would think that that would be enough to drive people back to God. But persistence in willful disobedience and willful ignorance of God's ways creates a kind of blindness and deafness that makes people unwilling to turn back. At this point God sometimes hides His face, and they experience greater misfortunes.
32:17 demons. Scripture makes it clear that the false gods do not exist as such, and this passage identifies the power behind these gods: demons. It is important to remember this, especially in this era of multiculturalism, when many voices protest the exclusiveness of Christianity.
32:29 consider their latter end. In this great pro-

phetic song Moses longs for the nation of Israel to turn to God and repent of its wickedness. As history proved, there was continual need for Israel to repent and turn back to God. They did abandon their covenant with God, but God did not abandon them, although He let them reap the consequences of their disobedience. Moses was not the last prophet to long for their repentance, and we can only guess at the heavenly joy Moses felt on the Mount of Transfiguration, seeing Jesus the Christ, who would finally redeem the people (Mark 9).

32:14 z Ps. 81:16 a Gen. 49:11 **32:15** b Deut. 31:20 c Is. 1:4 d Is. 51:13 e Ps. 95:1 **32:16** f 1 Cor. 10:22 **32:17** g Rev. 9:20 **32:18** h Is. 17:10 i Jer. 2:32 **32:19** j Judg. 2:14 **32:20** k Matt. 17:17 **32:21** l Ps. 78:58 m Ps. 31:6 n Rom. 10:19 **32:22** o Lam. 4:11 **32:23** p Ex. 32:12 q Ps. 7:12, 13 **32:24** r Lev. 26:22 **32:26** s Ezek. 20:23 **32:27** t Is. 10:12–15 **32:29** u [Luke 19:42] v Deut. 31:29 **32:30** w Judg. 2:14 **32:31** x [1 Sam. 4:7, 8] **32:32** y Is. 1:8–10

Their grapes *are* grapes of gall,
Their clusters *are* bitter.
33 Their wine *is* [z]the poison of serpents,
And the cruel [a]venom of cobras.

34 '*Is* this not [b]laid up in store with Me,
Sealed up among My treasures?
35 [c]Vengeance is Mine, and recompense;
Their foot shall slip in *due* time;
[d]For the day of their calamity *is* at hand,
And the things to come hasten upon them.'

36 "For[e] the LORD will judge His people
[f]And have compassion on His servants,
When He sees that *their* power is gone,
And [g]*there is* no one *remaining*, bond or free.
37 He will say: [h]'Where *are* their gods,
The rock in which they sought refuge?
38 Who ate the fat of their sacrifices,
And drank the wine of their drink offering?
Let them rise and help you,
And be your refuge.

39 'Now see that [i]I, *even* I, *am* He,
And [j]*there is* no God besides Me;
[k]I kill and I make alive;
I wound and I heal;
Nor *is there any* who can deliver from My hand.
40 For I raise My hand to heaven,
And say, "As I live forever,
41 [l]If I whet My glittering sword,
And My hand takes hold on judgment,
I will render vengeance to My enemies,
And repay those who hate Me.
42 I will make My arrows drunk with blood,
And My sword shall devour flesh,
With the blood of the slain and the captives,
From the heads of the leaders of the enemy."'

43 "Rejoice,[m] O Gentiles, *with* His people;*
For He will [n]avenge the blood of His servants,
And render vengeance to His adversaries;
He [o]will provide atonement for His land *and* His people."

44 So Moses came with Joshua* the son of
Nun and spoke all the words of this song in
the hearing of the people. 45 Moses finished
speaking all these words to all Israel, 46 and
he said to them: [p]"Set your hearts on all the
words which I testify among you today,
which you shall command your [q]children
to be careful to observe—all the words of
this law. 47 For it *is* not a futile thing for you,
because it *is* your [r]life, and by this word you
shall prolong *your* days in the land which
you cross over the Jordan to possess."

Moses to Die on Mount Nebo

48 Then the LORD spoke to Moses that
very same day, saying: 49 [s]"Go up this mountain of the Abarim, Mount Nebo, which *is*
in the land of Moab, across from Jericho;
view the land of Canaan, which I give to
the children of Israel as a possession; 50 and
die on the mountain which you ascend, and
be gathered to your people, just as [t]Aaron
your brother died on Mount Hor and was
gathered to his people; 51 because [u]you trespassed against Me among the children of
Israel at the waters of Meribah Kadesh, in
the Wilderness of Zin, because you [v]did not
hallow Me in the midst of the children of Israel. 52 [w]Yet you shall see the land before *you*,
though you shall not go there, into the land
which I am giving to the children of Israel."

* **32:43** A Dead Sea Scroll fragment adds *And let all the gods (angels) worship Him* (compare Septuagint and Hebrews 1:6). * **32:44** Hebrew *Hoshea* (compare Numbers 13:8, 16)

32:35 *Vengeance is Mine.* Only God who is completely just can judge and make right all the wrongs committed (Rom. 12:19–20).

32:36 *have compassion on his servants.* God will discern between the righteous and the wicked (Mal. 3:16).

32:39 God's Sovereignty—In his final words to the Israelites, Moses reminds them where they came from. Their history could not be written without God being in the central position. Their future, likewise, was intimately tied to God. To think otherwise would be folly (Deut. 32:28–29). The basic point is that no matter how you want to look at it, God is in charge. That was the most basic fact in the Israelites' situation.

God's sovereignty is also the central fact in ours. It is not always easy to affirm it. We would much rather see *ourselves* as the central controlling force in our lives. Most of us simply don't like being told what to do or how to live. The problem is that the whole history of man teaches us that when God's laws are not followed, disaster ensues. When we put ourselves in charge, sooner or later we pay the price.

A whole generation of Israelites failed to understand God's sovereignty. As a result, they died in the desert, never having arrived at the Promised Land. While it is true that they lived out their lives, they surely missed out on what could have been. That fact is the basic backdrop for Moses' last words to the new generation, as they approached the Promised Land. We dare not ignore the lesson.

32:43 *Rejoice, O Gentiles.* The Gentiles are invited here to join in worship of the living God. All through history there have been a few who accepted this invitation (such as Ruth), and it was fulfilled in Christ (Rom. 15).

32:33 [z]Ps. 58:4 [a]Rom. 3:13 **32:34** [b][Jer. 2:22] **32:35** [c]Heb. 10:30 [d]2 Pet. 2:3 **32:36** [e]Ps. 135:14 [f]Jer. 31:20 [g]2 Kin. 14:26 **32:37** [h]Judg. 10:14 **32:39** [i]Is. 41:4; 43:10 [j]Is. 45:5 [k]1 Sam. 2:6 **32:41** [l]Is. 1:24; 66:16 **32:43** [m]Rom. 15:10 [n]Rev. 6:10; 19:2 [o]Ps. 65:3; 79:9; 85:1 **32:46** [p]Ezek. 40:4; 44:5 [q]Deut. 11:19 **32:47** [r]Deut. 8:3; 30:15–20 **32:49** [s]Num. 27:12–14 **32:50** [t]Num. 20:25, 28; 33:38 **32:51** [u]Num. 20:11–13 [v]Lev. 10:3 **32:52** [w]Deut. 34:1–5

Moses' Final Blessing on Israel

33 Now this *is* ᵃthe blessing with which Moses ᵇthe man of God blessed the children of Israel before his death. ²And he said:

ᶜ"The LORD came from Sinai,
And dawned on them from ᵈSeir;
He shone forth from ᵉMount Paran,
And He came with ᶠten thousands of
saints;
From His right hand
Came a fiery law for them.

³ Yes, ᵍHe loves the people;
ʰAll His saints *are* in Your hand;
They ⁱsit down at Your feet;
Everyone ʲreceives Your words.

⁴ ᵏMoses commanded a law for us,
ˡA heritage of the congregation of
Jacob.

⁵ And He was ᵐKing in ⁿJeshurun,
When the leaders of the people were
gathered,
All the tribes of Israel together.

⁶ "Let ᵒReuben live, and not die,
Nor let his men be few."

⁷And this he said of ᵖJudah:

"Hear, LORD, the voice of Judah,
And bring him to his people;
ᑫLet his hands be sufficient for him,
And may You be ʳa help against his
enemies."

⁸And of ˢLevi he said:

ᵗ"*Let* Your Thummim and Your Urim *be*
with Your holy one,
ᵘWhom You tested at Massah,
And with whom You contended at the
waters of Meribah,

⁹ ᵛWho says of his father and mother,
'I have not ʷseen them';
ˣNor did he acknowledge his brothers,
Or know his own children;
For ʸthey have observed Your word
And kept Your covenant.

¹⁰ ᶻThey shall teach Jacob Your judgments,
And Israel Your law.
They shall put incense before You,
ᵃAnd a whole burnt sacrifice on Your
altar.

¹¹ Bless his substance, LORD,
And ᵇaccept the work of his hands;
Strike the loins of those who rise
against him,
And of those who hate him, that they
rise not again."

¹²Of Benjamin he said:

"The beloved of the LORD shall dwell in
safety by Him,
Who shelters him all the day long;
And he shall dwell between His
shoulders."

¹³And of Joseph he said:

ᶜ"Blessed of the LORD *is* his land,
With the precious things of heaven,
with the ᵈdew,
And the deep lying beneath,

¹⁴ With the precious fruits of the sun,
With the precious produce of the
months,

¹⁵ With the best things of ᵉthe ancient
mountains,
With the precious things ᶠof the
everlasting hills,

¹⁶ With the precious things of the earth
and its fullness,
And the favor of ᵍHim who dwelt in
the bush.
Let *the blessing* come ʰ'on the head of
Joseph,
And on the crown of the head of
him *who was* separate from his
brothers.'*

¹⁷ His glory *is like* a ⁱfirstborn bull,
And his horns *like* the ʲhorns of the
wild ox;
Together with them
ᵏHe shall push the peoples
To the ends of the earth;
ˡThey *are* the ten thousands of Ephraim,
And they *are* the thousands of
Manasseh."

¹⁸And of Zebulun he said:

ᵐ"Rejoice, Zebulun, in your going out,
And Issachar in your tents!

¹⁹ They shall ⁿcall the peoples *to* the
mountain;

---

* **33:16** Genesis 49:26

33:1 Moses the man of God. In spite of his failure at the waters of Meribah Kadesh, Moses is noted here and throughout the Bible as "the man of God." **33:4 commanded a law for us.** God chose Israel alone to receive His instructions, yet the law was ultimately for His whole creation, as Jesus demonstrated when He broke down the wall between Jew and Gentile (Rom. 3–7). **33:9–10 they have observed Your word.** The Levites were keepers of God's word, even when it meant drawing their swords against their own brothers (Ex. 32:25–29). This is a degree of testing that most believers will never experience, but Jesus promised that the world would hate His followers, and they would experience opposition even from their own families (Matt. 10:22). It is not easy to be a follower of God in a world of sin and death, but the Christian may be assured that as he walks in obedience to God's truth, God "always leads us in triumph in Christ" (2 Cor. 2:14).

33:1 ᵃ Gen. 49:28 ᵇ Ps. 90 **33:2** ᶜ Ps. 68:8, 17 ᵈ Deut. 2:1, 4 ᵉ Num. 10:12 ᶠ Dan. 7:10 **33:3** ᵍ Hos. 11:1 ʰ 1 Sam. 2:9 ⁱ [Luke 10:39] ʲ Prov. 2:1 **33:4** ᵏ John 1:17; 7:19 ˡ Ps. 119:111 **33:5** ᵐ Ex. 15:18 ⁿ Deut. 32:15 **33:6** ᵒ Gen. 49:3, 4 **33:7** ᵖ Gen. 49:8–12 ᑫ Gen. 49:8 ʳ Ps. 146:5 **33:8** ˢ Gen. 49:5 ᵗ Ex. 28:30 ᵘ Ps. 81:7 **33:9** ᵛ [Num. 25:5–8] ʷ [Gen. 29:32] ˣ Ex. 32:26–28 ʸ Mal. 2:5, 6 **33:10** ᶻ Lev. 10:11 ᵃ Ps. 51:19 **33:11** ᵇ 2 Sam. 24:23 **33:13** ᶜ Gen. 49:22–26 ᵈ Gen. 27:28 **33:15** ᵉ Gen. 49:26 ᶠ Hab. 3:6 **33:16** ᵍ Ex. 3:2–4 ʰ Gen. 49:26 **33:17** ⁱ 1 Chr. 5:1 ʲ Num. 23:22 ᵏ Ps. 44:5 ˡ Gen. 48:19 **33:18** ᵐ Gen. 49:13–15 **33:19** ⁿ Is. 2:3

There °they shall offer sacrifices of
　　righteousness;
For they shall partake of the
　　abundance of the seas
And of treasures hidden in the sand."

20And of Gad he said:

"Blessed is he who Penlarges Gad;
He dwells as a lion,
And tears the arm and the crown of
　　his head.
21 qHe provided the first part for himself,
　　Because a lawgiver's portion was
　　　reserved there.
rHe came with the heads of the people;
He administered the justice of the LORD,
And His judgments with Israel."

22And of Dan he said:

"Dan is a lion's whelp;
sHe shall leap from Bashan."

23And of Naphtali he said:

"O Naphtali, tsatisfied with favor,
And full of the blessing of the LORD,
uPossess the west and the south."

24And of Asher he said:

v"Asher is most blessed of sons;
Let him be favored by his brothers,
And let him wdip his foot in oil.
25　Your sandals shall be xiron and
　　bronze;
　　As your days, so shall your
　　　strength be.

26 "There is yno one like the God of
　　zJeshurun,
aWho rides the heavens to help you,
And in His excellency on the clouds.
27　The eternal God is your brefuge,
　　And underneath are the everlasting
　　　arms;
cHe will thrust out the enemy from
　　before you,
And will say, 'Destroy!'
28　Then dIsrael shall dwell in safety,
　　eThe fountain of Jacob falone,
　　In a land of grain and new wine;
　　His gheavens shall also drop dew.
29 hHappy are you, O Israel!

iWho is like you, a people saved by the
　　LORD,
jThe shield of your help
And the sword of your majesty!
Your enemies kshall submit to you,
And lyou shall tread down their high
　　places."

Moses Dies on Mount Nebo

34 Then Moses went up from the plains
of Moab to aMount Nebo, to the top
of Pisgah, which is across from Jericho.
And the LORD showed him all the land of
Gilead as far as Dan, 2all Naphtali and the
land of Ephraim and Manasseh, all the
land of Judah as far as the Western Sea,*
3the South, and the plain of the Valley of
Jericho, bthe city of palm trees, as far as
Zoar. 4Then the LORD said to him, c"This
is the land of which I swore to give Abraham, Isaac, and Jacob, saying, 'I will give
it to your descendants.' dI have caused you
to see it with your eyes, but you shall not
cross over there."

5eSo Moses the servant of the LORD died
there in the land of Moab, according to the
word of the LORD. 6And He buried him in
a valley in the land of Moab, opposite Beth
Peor; but fno one knows his grave to this
day. 7gMoses was one hundred and twenty
years old when he died. hHis eyes were not
dim nor his natural vigor diminished. 8And
the children of Israel wept for Moses in the
plains of Moab ithirty days. So the days of
weeping and mourning for Moses ended.

9Now Joshua the son of Nun was full of
the jspirit of wisdom, for kMoses had laid
his hands on him; so the children of Israel
heeded him, and did as the LORD had commanded Moses.

10But since then there lhas not arisen in
Israel a prophet like Moses, mwhom the
LORD knew face to face, 11in all nthe signs
and wonders which the LORD sent him to
do in the land of Egypt, before Pharaoh,
before all his servants, and in all his land,
12and by all that mighty power and all the
great terror which Moses performed in the
sight of all Israel.

* **34:2** That is, the Mediterranean

33:22 lion's whelp. This may refer to the small size
of the tribe of Dan. Though Dan's land inheritance
was close to Judah by the coastal plains, the tribe
would not be able to keep their inheritance because
of the hostility of the Philistines. Therefore, the Danites
would one day migrate to the region of Bashan, south
of Mount Hermon (Judg. 18).

34:1–2 Moab . . . Jericho . . . Western Sea. Moab was
where Moses had given Israel an explanation of the
law and led them in a covenant renewal. Jericho was
the first city in Canaan to be conquered. The sea is the
Mediterranean.

34:6 no one knows his grave. If his burial place had
been known, some people would have been tempted
to make it a shrine and possibly have begun to worship
there.

34:9 Joshua . . . full of the spirit of wisdom. Joshua

was the leader chosen to succeed Moses, and God
filled him with the spirit of wisdom. But there was
another, a prophet like Moses, who would be greater
even than Moses. That other was the Lord Jesus Christ
(Acts 3:19–26).

33:19 o Ps. 4:5; 51:19　**33:20** P 1 Chr. 12:8　**33:21** q Num.
32:16, 17　r Josh. 4:12　**33:22** s Josh. 19:47　**33:23** r Gen.
49:21　u Josh. 19:32　**33:24** v Gen. 49:20　w Job 29:6
33:25 x Deut. 8:9　**33:26** y Ex. 15:11　z Deut. 32:15　a Ps.
68:3, 33, 34; 104:3　**33:27** b [Ps. 90:1; 91:2, 9]　c Deut.
9:3–5　**33:28** d Jer. 23:6; 33:16　e Deut. 8:7, 8　f Num.
23:9　g Gen. 27:28　**33:29** h Ps. 144:15　i 2 Sam. 7:23
j Ps. 115:9　k Ps. 18:44; 66:3　l Num. 33:52　**34:1** a Deut.
32:49　**34:3** b 2 Chr. 28:15　**34:4** c Gen. 12:7　d Deut.
3:27　**34:5** e Deut. 32:50; Josh. 1:1, 2　**34:6** f Jude 9
34:7 g Deut. 31:2　h Gen. 27:1; 48:10　**34:8** i Gen. 50:3, 10
34:9 j Is. 11:2　k Num. 27:18, 23　**34:10** l Deut. 18:15, 18
m Ex. 33:11　**34:11** n Deut. 7:19

THE BOOK OF
JOSHUA

▶ **AUTHOR:** Jewish tradition seems correct in assigning the authorship of this book to Joshua himself. The unity of style and organization suggest a single authorship for the majority of the book, with the exception of three small portions that may have been added after Joshua's death: Othniel's capture of Kirjath Sepher (15:13–19); Dan's migration to the north (19:47); and Joshua's death and burial (24:29–33). However, Joshua 24:26 makes this clear statement: "Then Joshua wrote these words in the Book of the Law of God."

▶ **TIME:** c. 1405–1398 B.C.   ▶ **KEY VERSE:** Josh. 11:23

▶ **THEME:** In the Book of Joshua, the Israelites are commanded to destroy everything and everybody so that they can take full possession of the land. The transition of leadership is from Moses to Joshua. A nomadic people attaches themselves to given tracts of land, and a nation is formed from a wandering tribe as the conquest is completed in 21:43–45. We also see how a failure to carry out God's plan completely lays a foundation for future problems.

God's Commission to Joshua

1 After the death of Moses the servant of the LORD, it came to pass that the LORD spoke to Joshua the son of Nun, Moses' *a*assistant, saying: 2*b*"Moses My servant is dead. Now therefore, arise, go over this Jordan, you and all this people, to the land which I am giving to them—the children of Israel. 3*c*Every place that the sole of your foot will tread upon I have given you, as I said to Moses. 4*d*From the wilderness and this Lebanon as far as the great river, the River Euphrates, all the land of the Hittites, and to the Great Sea toward the going down of the sun, shall be your territory. 5*e*No man shall *be able to* stand before you all the days of your life; *f*as I was with Moses, so *g*I will be with you. *h*I will not leave you nor forsake you. 6*i*Be strong and of good courage, for to this people you shall divide as an inheritance the land which I swore to their fathers to give them. 7Only be strong and very courageous, that you may observe to do according to all the law *j*which Moses My servant commanded you; *k*do not turn from it to the right hand or to the left, that you may prosper wherever you go. 8*l*This Book of the Law shall not depart from your mouth, but *m*you shall meditate in it day and night, that you may observe to do according to all that is written in it. For then you will make your way prosperous, and then you will have good success. 9*n*Have I not commanded you? Be strong

---

1:1 the servant of the LORD. In the Hebrew Scripture this is a special title given only to Moses, Joshua (24:29; Judg. 2:8), David (Ps. 18:title; 36:title), and the Messiah (Is. 42:19). **the LORD spoke to Joshua.** God spoke directly to Joshua encouraging him and urging him to obey all the law. True success cannot occur apart from knowing God personally and doing His will.

1:7–8 Perseverance—A successful mission in the service of the Lord is dependent upon courage, meditation and obedience. Keeping God's words in our hearts molds our character and guides our footsteps.

1:8 Meditating upon God's Word—Helping people become prosperous and successful is big business. Late night infomercials point to a plethora of techniques for getting rich. Everyone wants to be wealthy. Everyone wants to be successful. These kinds of feelings are particularly strong when starting a new endeavor as Joshua was. At the very beginning of Joshua's leadership of Israel, God lays out for

Joshua His key to success, meditating on God's word. Meditate upon the Word of God by rehearsing it in thought over and over in order to understand its implications for the situations of life. The meditation process results in changed thinking, because God's thoughts can literally become our thoughts. Then we are more likely to do what God wants of us. As we live in sync with God's plan for our lives, it follows that we will be more successful and prosperous than if we ignore His teachings.

People spend a large part of their lives in obtaining an education and working at a career in order to be prosperous and successful. Scripture points to itself as the primary means toward that end.

1:1 *a* Ex. 24:13   **1:2** *b* Deut. 34:5   **1:3** *c* Deut. 11:24
1:4 *d* Gen. 15:18   **1:5** *e* Deut. 7:24   *f* Ex. 3:12   *g* Deut. 31:8,
23   *h* Deut. 31:6, 7   **1:6** *i* Deut. 31:7, 23   **1:7** *j* Deut. 31:7
k Deut. 5:32   **1:8** *l* Josh. 8:34   *m* Ps. 1:1–3   **1:9** *n* Deut. 31:7

and of good courage; [o]do not be afraid, nor
be dismayed, for the LORD your God *is* with
you wherever you go."

The Order to Cross the Jordan

10 Then Joshua commanded the officers
of the people, saying, 11 "Pass through the
camp and command the people, saying,
'Prepare provisions for yourselves, for
[p]within three days you will cross over this
Jordan, to go in to possess the land which
the LORD your God is giving you to possess.'"
12 And to the Reubenites, the Gadites, and
half the tribe of Manasseh Joshua spoke,
saying, 13 "Remember [q]the word which Moses the servant of the LORD commanded
you, saying, 'The LORD your God is giving
you rest and is giving you this land.' 14 Your
wives, your little ones, and your livestock
shall remain in the land which Moses gave
you on this side of the Jordan. But you shall
pass before your brethren armed, all your
mighty men of valor, and help them, 15 until the LORD has given your brethren rest,
as He *gave* you, and they also have taken
possession of the land which the LORD your
God is giving them. [r]Then you shall return
to the land of your possession and enjoy
it, which Moses the LORD's servant gave
you on this side of the Jordan toward the
sunrise."
16 So they answered Joshua, saying, "All
that you command us we will do, and wherever you send us we will go. 17 Just as we
heeded Moses in all things, so we will heed
you. Only the LORD your God [s]be with you,
as He was with Moses. 18 Whoever rebels
against your command and does not heed
your words, in all that you command him,
shall be put to death. Only be strong and of
good courage."

Rahab Hides the Spies

2 Now Joshua the son of Nun sent out two
men [a]from Acacia Grove* to spy secretly, saying, "Go, view the land, especially
Jericho."
So they went, and [b]came to the house
of a harlot named [c]Rahab, and lodged
there. 2 And [d]it was told the king of Jericho,
saying, "Behold, men have come here tonight from the children of Israel to search
out the country."
3 So the king of Jericho sent to Rahab,
saying, "Bring out the men who have come
to you, who have entered your house, for
they have come to search out all the country."
4 [e]Then the woman took the two men
and hid them. So she said, "Yes, the men
came to me, but I did not know where they
were from. 5 And it happened as the gate
was being shut, when it was dark, that the
men went out. Where the men went I do not
know; pursue them quickly, for you may
overtake them." 6 (But [f]she had brought
them up to the roof and hidden them with
the stalks of flax, which she had laid in
order on the roof.) 7 Then the men pursued
them by the road to the Jordan, to the fords.
And as soon as those who pursued them
had gone out, they shut the gate.
8 Now before they lay down, she came up
to them on the roof, 9 and said to the men:
[g]"I know that the LORD has given you the
land, that [h]the terror of you has fallen on us,
and that all the inhabitants of the land [i]are
fainthearted because of you. 10 For we have
heard how the LORD [j]dried up the water of
the Red Sea for you when you came out of
Egypt, and [k]what you did to the two kings
of the Amorites who *were* on the other side
of the Jordan, Sihon and Og, whom you [l]ut-
terly destroyed. 11 And as soon as we [m]heard
these things, [n]our hearts melted; neither did
there remain any more courage in anyone
because of you, for [o]the LORD your God, He
is God in heaven above and on earth beneath. 12 Now therefore, I beg you, [p]swear
to me by the LORD, since I have shown you
kindness, that you also will show kindness
to [q]my father's house, and [r]give me a true
token, 13 and [s]spare my father, my mother,
my brothers, my sisters, and all that they
have, and deliver our lives from death."
14 So the men answered her, "Our lives
for yours, if none of you tell this business
of ours. And it shall be, when the LORD has
given us the land, that [t]we will deal kindly
and truly with you."

---

* **2:1** Hebrew *Shittim*

1:18 ***be strong and of good courage.*** Joshua's task was not an easy one, for not only must he deal with the ungodly inhabitants of the Promised Land, he must also provide leadership for his own fearful and complaining people.

2:1 ***Rahab.*** Rahab was a Canaanite prostitute, yet out of all the populace of Jericho, only she reached out to the living God, and He in turn saved her (6:25).

2:4–6 ***Where the men went I do not know.*** Rahab lied to the men searching for the Israelite spies, and Joshua praised her, as did the apostle James and the writer of Hebrews (Heb. 11:31; James 2:25). Throughout both the Old and the New Testament, the commands of God forbid lying, the prophets condemn it, and godly people avoid doing it. Scripture does not address Rahab's sin, but it does praise her for her faith in God. Christians have struggled for centuries over whether lying to save an innocent person's life is acceptable. There does not seem to be a clear-cut answer, but Rahab did her best with the knowledge she had to protect the Israelite men.

1:9 [o] Ps. 27:1 **1:11** [p] Deut. 9:1 **1:13** [q] Num. 32:20–28 **1:15** [r] Josh. 22:1–4 **1:17** [s] 1 Sam. 20:13 **2:1** [a] Num. 25:1 [b] James 2:25 [c] Matt. 1:5 **2:2** [d] Josh. 2:22 **2:4** [e] 2 Sam. 17:19, 20 **2:6** [f] Ex. 1:17 **2:9** [g] Deut. 1:8 [h] Deut. 2:25; 11:25 [i] Josh. 5:1 **2:10** [j] Ex. 14:21 [k] Num. 21:21–35 [l] Josh. 6:21 **2:11** [m] Ex. 15:14, 15 [n] Josh. 5:1; 7:5 [o] Deut. 4:39 **2:12** [p] 1 Sam. 20:14, 15, 17 [q] 1 Tim. 5:8 [r] Josh. 2:18 **2:13** [s] Josh. 6:23–25 **2:14** [t] Judg. 1:24

¹⁵Then she ᵘlet them down by a rope through the window, for her house *was* on the city wall; she dwelt on the wall. ¹⁶And she said to them, "Get to the mountain, lest the pursuers meet you. Hide there three days, until the pursuers have returned. Afterward you may go your way."

¹⁷So the men said to her: "We *will be* ᵛblameless of this oath of yours which you have made us swear, ¹⁸ᵂunless, *when* we come into the land, you bind this line of scarlet cord in the window through which you let us down, ˣand unless you bring your father, your mother, your brothers, and all your father's household to your own home. ¹⁹So it shall be *that* whoever goes outside the doors of your house into the street, his blood *shall be* on his own head, and we *will be* guiltless. And whoever is with you in the house, ʸhis blood *shall be* on our head if a hand is laid on him. ²⁰And if you tell this business of ours, then we will be free from your oath which you made us swear."

²¹Then she said, "According to your words, so *be* it." And she sent them away, and they departed. And she bound the scarlet cord in the window.

²²They departed and went to the mountain, and stayed there three days until the pursuers returned. The pursuers sought *them* all along the way, but did not find *them.* ²³So the two men returned, descended from the mountain, and crossed over; and they came to Joshua the son of Nun, and told him all that had befallen them. ²⁴And they said to Joshua, "Truly ᶻthe LORD has delivered all the land into our hands, for indeed all the inhabitants of the country are fainthearted because of us."

Israel Crosses the Jordan

3 Then Joshua rose early in the morning; and they set out ᵃfrom Acacia Grove* and came to the Jordan, he and all the children of Israel, and lodged there before they crossed over. ²So it was, ᵇafter three days, that the officers went through the camp; ³and they commanded the people, saying, ᶜ"When you see the ark of the covenant of the LORD your God, ᵈand the priests, the Levites, bearing it, then you shall set out from your place and go after it. ⁴ᵉYet there

shall be a space between you and it, about two thousand cubits by measure. Do not come near it, that you may know the way by which you must go, for you have not passed *this* way before."

⁵And Joshua said to the people, ᶠ"Sanctify yourselves, for tomorrow the LORD will do wonders among you." ⁶Then Joshua spoke to the priests, saying, ᵍ"Take up the ark of the covenant and cross over before the people."

So they took up the ark of the covenant and went before the people.

⁷And the LORD said to Joshua, "This day I will begin to ʰexalt you in the sight of all Israel, that they may know that, ⁱas I was with Moses, *so* I will be with you. ⁸You shall command ʲthe priests who bear the ark of the covenant, saying, 'When you have come to the edge of the water of the Jordan, ᵏyou shall stand in the Jordan.'"

⁹So Joshua said to the children of Israel, "Come here, and hear the words of the LORD your God." ¹⁰And Joshua said, "By this you shall know that ˡthe living God *is* among you, and *that* He will without fail ᵐdrive out from before you the ⁿCanaanites and the Hittites and the Hivites and the Perizzites and the Girgashites and the Amorites and the Jebusites: ¹¹Behold, the ark of the covenant of ᵒthe Lord of all the earth is crossing over before you into the Jordan. ¹²Now therefore, ᵖtake for yourselves twelve men from the tribes of Israel, one man from every tribe. ¹³And it shall come to pass, ᵟas soon as the soles of the feet of the priests who bear the ark of the LORD, ʳthe Lord of all the earth, shall rest in the waters of the Jordan, *that* the waters of the Jordan shall be cut off, the waters that come down from upstream, and they ˢshall stand as a heap."

¹⁴So it was, when the people set out from their camp to cross over the Jordan, with the priests bearing the ᵗark of the covenant before the people, ¹⁵and as those who bore the ark came to the Jordan, and the feet of the priests who bore the ark dipped in the edge of the water (for the ᵛJordan overflows all its banks ᵂduring the whole time

* 3:1 Hebrew *Shittim*

2:16 Get to the mountain. The pursuers had gone down to the Jordan River (v. 7), logically supposing that the spies would be returning to their camp on the eastern side of the river. The only hills near Jericho are to the west, in the opposite direction from the Israelite camp, and further into the land of Canaan.

3:4 two thousand cubits. Two thousand cubits was more than half a mile. God was serious about the people showing due respect for the ark of the covenant.

3:9 Inspiration—God conveyed His message by means of words spoken by a specific, chosen person. He descended to the human level and through humanity spoke His word of absolute truth.

3:13 Lord of all the earth. The term "Adonai," translated "Lord," means "master." It refers to the

fact that God is indeed the Sovereign of the entire universe.

3:15 Jordan overflows. God did not merely slow the great river to a trickle during a time of drought; He

2:15 ᵘ Acts 9:25   **2:17** ᵛ Ex. 20:7   **2:18** ᵂ Josh. 2:12   ˣ Josh. 6:23   **2:19** ʸ 1 Kin. 2:32   **2:24** ᶻ Ex. 23:31   **3:1** ᵃ Josh. 2:1   **3:2** ᵇ Josh. 1:10, 11   **3:3** ᶜ Num. 10:33   ᵈ Deut. 31:9, 25   **3:4** ᵉ Ex. 19:12   **3:5** ᶠ Josh. 7:13   **3:6** ᵍ Num. 4:15   **3:7** ʰ Josh. 4:14   ⁱ Josh. 1:5, 9   **3:8** ʲ Josh. 3:3   ᵏ Josh. 3:17   **3:10** ˡ 1 Thess. 1:9   ᵐ Ex. 33:2   ⁿ Acts 13:19   **3:11** ᵒ Zech. 4:14; 6:5   **3:12** ᵖ Josh. 4:2, 4   **3:13** ᵟ Josh. 3:15, 16   ʳ Josh. 3:11   ˢ Ps. 78:13; 114:3   **3:14** ᵗ Acts 7:44, 45   **3:15** ᵘ Josh. 3:13   ᵛ 1 Chr. 12:15   ᵂ Josh. 4:18; 5:10, 12

of harvest), [16]that the waters which came down from upstream stood *still, and* rose in a heap very far away at *Adam, the city that is beside* [x]Zaretan. So the waters that went down [y]into the Sea of the Arabah, [z]the Salt Sea, failed, *and* were cut off; and the people crossed over opposite Jericho. [17]Then the priests who bore the ark of the covenant of the LORD stood firm on dry ground in the midst of the Jordan; [q]and all Israel crossed over on dry ground, until all the people had crossed completely over the Jordan.

The Memorial Stones

4 And it came to pass, when all the people had completely crossed [a]over the Jordan, that the LORD spoke to Joshua, saying: [2b]"Take for yourselves twelve men from the people, one man from every tribe, [3]and command them, saying, 'Take for yourselves twelve stones from here, out of the midst of the Jordan, from the place where [c]the priests' feet stood firm. You shall carry them over with you and leave them in [d]the lodging place where you lodge tonight.'"

[4]Then Joshua called the twelve men whom he had appointed from the children of Israel, one man from every tribe; [5]and Joshua said to them: "Cross over before the ark of the LORD your God into the midst of the Jordan, and each one of you take up a stone on his shoulder, according to the number of the tribes of the children of Israel, [6]that this may be [e]a sign among you [f]when your children ask in time to come, saying, 'What do these stones *mean* to you?' [7]Then you shall answer them that [g]the waters of the Jordan were cut off before the ark of the covenant of the LORD; when it crossed over the Jordan, the waters of the Jordan were cut off. And these stones shall be for [h]a memorial to the children of Israel forever."

[8]And the children of Israel did so, just as Joshua commanded, and took up twelve stones from the midst of the Jordan, as the LORD had spoken to Joshua, according to

the number of the tribes of the children of Israel, and carried them over with them to the place where they lodged, and laid them down there. [9]Then Joshua set up twelve stones in the midst of the Jordan, in the place where the feet of the priests who bore the ark of the covenant stood; and they are there to this day.

[10]So the priests who bore the ark stood in the midst of the Jordan until everything was finished that the LORD had commanded Joshua to speak to the people, according to all that Moses had commanded Joshua; and the people hurried and crossed over. [11]Then it came to pass, when all the people had completely crossed over, that the [i]ark of the LORD and the priests crossed over in the presence of the people. [12]And [j]the men of Reuben, the men of Gad, and half the tribe of Manasseh crossed over armed before the children of Israel, as Moses had spoken to them. [13]About forty thousand prepared for war crossed over before the LORD for battle, to the plains of Jericho. [14]On that day the LORD [k]exalted Joshua in the sight of all Israel; and they feared him, as they had feared Moses, all the days of his life.

[15]Then the LORD spoke to Joshua, saying, [16]"Command the priests who bear [l]the ark of the Testimony to come up from the Jordan." [17]Joshua therefore commanded the priests, saying, "Come up from the Jordan." [18]And it came to pass, when the priests who bore the ark of the covenant of the LORD had come from the midst of the Jordan, *and* the soles of the priests' feet touched the dry land, that the waters of the Jordan returned to their place [m]and overflowed all its banks as before.

[19]Now the people came up from the Jordan on the tenth *day* of the first month, and they camped [n]in Gilgal on the east border of Jericho. [20]And [o]those twelve stones which they took out of the Jordan, Joshua set up in Gilgal. [21]Then he spoke to the children of Israel, saying: [p]"When your children ask their fathers in time to come, saying, 'What *are* these stones?' [22]then

---

stopped the waters when the river was high. This is significant because it makes the point that a great miracle was involved.

3:16 Adam. Adam was a city about 18 miles north of Jericho. The Sea of Arabah is another name for the Dead Sea, into which the Jordan flows from the north. The Dead Sea is the lowest place on earth, 1,286 feet below sea level. The phrase "Salt Sea" is added to the name because the sea has no outlet and loses its water by evaporation. The concentration of salt and other minerals is so high that nothing can live in it.

4:10 the people hurried and crossed over. This is a flashback; 3:17 and 4:1 have already told of the crossing over. The purpose is to look back and reflect upon the people's obedience.

4:14 the LORD exalted Joshua. God is once again proclaiming Joshua as the man He has chosen to take Moses' place as leader of His people.

4:16 Testimony. In this sense, a "testimony" is a reminder. The ark contained the two stone tablets on which the Ten Commandments were written, reminding people of God's covenant and His law.

4:21–24 Fear of God—The Scriptures are full of stories of the acts God performed that built up the respect of the people for Him. The awesome things God did were told to each new generation to develop respect for who God is. This miracle was performed

3:16 [x]1 Kin. 4:12; 7:46 [y]Deut. 3:17 [z]Gen. 14:3 **3:17** [a]Ex. 3:8; 6:1–8; 14:21, 22, 29; 33:1 **4:1** [a]Deut. 27:2 **4:2** [b]Josh. 3:12 **4:3** [c]Josh. 3:13 [d]Josh. 4:19, 20 **4:6** [e]Deut. 27:2 [f]Deut. 6:20 **4:7** [g]Josh. 3:13, 16 [h]Num. 16:40 **4:11** [i]Josh. 3:11; 6:11 **4:12** [j]Num. 32:17, 20, 27, 28 **4:14** [k]Josh. 3:7 **4:16** [l]Ex. 25:16, 22 **4:18** [m]Josh. 3:15 **4:19** [n]Josh. 5:9 **4:20** [o]Josh. 4:3; 5:9, 10 **4:21** [p]Josh. 4:6

you shall let your children know, saying, *a*'Israel crossed over this Jordan on *r*dry land'; [23]for the LORD your God dried up the waters of the Jordan before you until you had crossed over, as the LORD your God did to the Red Sea, *s*which He dried up before us until we had crossed over, [24]that all the peoples of the earth may know the hand of the LORD, that it *is* *u*mighty, that you may *v*fear the LORD your God forever."

The Second Generation Circumcised

5 So it was, when all the kings of the Amorites who *were* on the west side of the Jordan, and all the kings of the Canaanites *a*who *were* by the sea, *b*heard that the LORD had dried up the waters of the Jordan from before the children of Israel until we* had crossed over, that their heart melted; *c*and there was no spirit in them any longer because of the children of Israel.

[2]At that time the LORD said to Joshua, "Make *d*flint knives for yourself, and circumcise the sons of Israel again the second time." [3]So Joshua made flint knives for himself, and circumcised the sons of Israel at the hill of the foreskins.* [4]And this *is* the reason why Joshua circumcised them: *e*All the people who came out of Egypt *who were* males, all the men of war, had died in the wilderness on the way, after they had come out of Egypt. [5]For all the people who came out had been circumcised, but all the people born in the wilderness, on the way as they came out of Egypt, had not been circumcised. [6]For the children of Israel walked *f*forty years in the wilderness, till all the people *who were* men of war, who came out of Egypt, were consumed, because they did not obey the voice of the LORD—to whom the LORD swore that *g*He would not show them the land which the LORD had sworn to their fathers that He would give us, *h*"a land flowing with milk and honey."* [7]Then Joshua circumcised *i*their sons *whom* He raised up in their place; for they were uncircumcised, because they had not been circumcised on the way.

[8]So it was, when they had finished circumcising all the people, that they stayed in their places in the camp *j*till they were healed. [9]Then the LORD said to Joshua, "This day I have rolled away *k*the reproach of Egypt from you." Therefore the name of the place is called *l*Gilgal* to this day.

[10]Now the children of Israel camped in Gilgal, and kept the Passover *m*on the fourteenth day of the month at twilight on the plains of Jericho. [11]And they ate of the produce of the land on the day after the Passover, unleavened bread and parched grain, on the very same day. [12]Then *n*the manna ceased on the day after they had eaten the produce of the land; and the children of Israel no longer had manna, but they ate the food of the land of Canaan that year.

The Commander of the Army of the LORD

[13]And it came to pass, when Joshua was by Jericho, that he lifted his eyes and looked, and behold, *o*a Man stood opposite him *p*with His sword drawn in His hand. And Joshua went to Him and said to Him, "*Are* You for us or for our adversaries?"

[14]So He said, "No, but *as* Commander of the army of the LORD I have now come."

And Joshua *q*fell on his face to the earth and *r*worshiped, and said to Him, "What does my Lord say to His servant?"

[15]Then the Commander of the LORD's army said to Joshua, *s*"Take your sandal off your foot, for the place where you stand *is* holy." And Joshua did so.

The Destruction of Jericho

6 Now *a*Jericho was securely shut up because of the children of Israel; none went out, and none came in. [2]And the LORD said to Joshua: "See! *b*I have given Jericho into your hand, its *c*king, *and* the mighty men of valor. [3]You shall march around the city, all *you* men of war; you shall go all around the city once. This you shall do six days. [4]And seven priests shall

---

* **5:1** Following Kethib; Qere, some Hebrew manuscripts and editions, Septuagint, Syriac, Targum, and Vulgate read *they.*   * **5:3** Hebrew *Gibeath Haaraloth*   * **5:6** Exodus 3:8   * **5:9** Literally *Rolling*

---

not only for the purpose of getting the Israelites across the Jordan. It was also a sign to all peoples of the power of God.

5:2 the second time. The generation that left Egypt had been circumcised. However, that generation had died in the wilderness and for some reason they had neglected to circumcise their children, the generation which would enter the Promised Land.

5:6 milk and honey. The land God had promised to Israel was no wilderness, but a land that was fertile for both crops and cattle, and ready to provide for them and supply all their needs.

5:15 Take your sandal off. The command for Joshua to remove his sandal was practically identical to the command Moses received at the burning bush (Ex.

3:1–6). Joshua was confronted with the living God, just as Moses had been (Ex. 33:9–11).

6:3 all around the city once. The city of Jericho measured less than half a mile in circumference, so the march would have been completed quickly.

4:22 *q* Deut. 26:5–9 *r* Josh. 3:17   **4:23** *s* Ex. 14:21 **4:24** *t* 1 Kin. 8:42 *u* 1 Chr. 29:12 *v* Jer. 10:7   **5:1** *a* Num. 13:29 *b* Ex. 15:14, 15 *c* Josh. 2:10, 11; 9:9   **5:2** *d* Ex. 4:25 **5:4** *e* Deut. 2:14–16   **5:6** *f* Num. 14:33 *g* Heb. 3:11 *h* Ex. 3:8   **5:7** *i* Deut. 1:39   **5:8** *j* Gen. 34:25   **5:9** *k* Gen. 34:14 *l* Josh. 4:19   **5:10** *m* Ex. 12:6   **5:12** *n* Ex. 16:35 **5:13** *o* Gen. 18:1, 2; 32:24, 30 *p* Num. 22:23   **5:14** *q* Gen. 17:3 *r* Ex. 34:8   **5:15** *s* Ex. 3:5   **6:1** *a* Josh. 2:1 **6:2** *b* Josh. 2:9, 24; 8:1 *c* Deut. 7:24

bear seven [d]trumpets of rams' horns before the ark. But the seventh day you shall march around the city [e]seven times, and [f]the priests shall blow the trumpets. **5**It shall come to pass, when they make a long *blast* with the ram's horn, *and* when you hear the sound of the trumpet, that all the people shall shout with a great shout; then the wall of the city will fall down flat. And the people shall go up every man straight before him."

6Then Joshua the son of Nun called the priests and said to them, "Take up the ark of the covenant, and let seven priests bear seven trumpets of rams' horns before the ark of the LORD." **7**And he said to the people, "Proceed, and march around the city, and let him who is armed advance before the ark of the LORD."

8So it was, when Joshua had spoken to the people, that the seven priests bearing the seven trumpets of rams' horns before the LORD advanced and blew the trumpets, and the ark of the covenant of the LORD followed them. **9**The armed men went before the priests who blew the trumpets, [g]and the rear guard came after the ark, while *the priests* continued blowing the trumpets. **10**Now Joshua had commanded the people, saying, "You shall not shout or make any noise with your voice, nor shall a word proceed out of your mouth, until the day I say to you, 'Shout!' Then you shall shout." **11**So he had [h]the ark of the LORD circle the city, going around *it* once. Then they came into the camp and lodged in the camp.

12And Joshua rose early in the morning, [i]and the priests took up the ark of the LORD. **13**Then seven priests bearing seven trumpets of rams' horns before the ark of the LORD went on continually and blew with the trumpets. And the armed men went before them. But the rear guard came after the ark of the LORD, while *the priests* continued blowing the trumpets. **14**And the second day they marched around the city once and returned to the camp. So they did six days.

15But it came to pass on the seventh day that they rose early, about the dawning of the day, and marched around the city seven times in the same manner. On that day only they marched around the city seven times.

16And the seventh time it happened, when the priests blew the trumpets, that Joshua said to the people: "Shout, for the LORD has given you the city! **17**Now the city shall be [i]doomed by the LORD to destruction, it and all who *are* in it. Only [k]Rahab the harlot shall live, she and all who *are* with her in the house, because [l]she hid the messengers that we sent. **18**And you, [m]by all means abstain from the accursed things, lest you become accursed when you take of the accursed things, and make the camp of Israel a curse, [n]and trouble it. **19**But all the silver and gold, and vessels of bronze and iron, *are* consecrated to the LORD; they shall come into the treasury of the LORD."

20So the people shouted when *the priests* blew the trumpets. And it happened when the people heard the sound of the trumpet, and the people shouted with a great shout, that [o]the wall fell down flat. Then the people went up into the city, every man straight before him, and they took the city. **21**And they [p]utterly destroyed all that *was* in the city, both man and woman, young and old, ox and sheep and donkey, with the edge of the sword.

22But Joshua had said to the two men who had spied out the country, "Go into the harlot's house, and from there bring out the woman and all that she has, [q]as you swore to her." **23**And the young men who had been spies went in and brought out Rahab, [r]her father, her mother, her brothers, and all that she had. So they brought out all her relatives and left them outside the camp of Israel. **24**But they burned the city and all that *was* in it with fire. Only the silver and gold, and the vessels of bronze and iron, they put into the treasury of the house of the LORD. **25**And Joshua spared Rahab the harlot, her father's household, and all that she had. So [s]she dwells in Israel to this day, because she hid the messengers whom Joshua sent to spy out Jericho.

26Then Joshua charged *them* at that time, saying, [t]"Cursed *be* the man before the LORD who rises up and builds this city Jericho; he shall lay its foundation with his firstborn, and with his youngest he shall set up its gates."

27So the LORD was with Joshua, and his fame spread throughout all the country.

6:6–21 Zeal—Crossing the Jordan marked the beginning step in the fulfillment of God's promise to give His people the land of Canaan. Immediately the task of conquering Jericho loomed before them. The Lord appeared to Joshua reminding him that God Himself was in charge and the presence of the Holy One assured victory (v. 2). The plan for Jericho's capture was a test of Israel's zeal for the Lord and seems to have been designed to instill the lesson that submission to God's directives was key to victory. How different Israel's history would have been if they had continued to carry out God's plans fully and zealously! God calls us to the same level of obedience today.

6:26 Cursed . . . before the LORD. Joshua's curse found dramatic fulfillment many centuries later when Hiel of Bethel laid its foundation and rebuilt its gates at great personal cost (1 Kin. 16:34).

6:4 [d] Lev. 25:9 [e] 1 Kin. 18:43 [f] Num. 10:8 **6:9** [g] Num. 10:25 **6:11** [h] Josh. 4:11 **6:12** [i] Deut. 31:25 **6:17** [j] Deut. 13:17 [k] Matt. 1:5 [l] Josh. 2:4, 6 **6:18** [m] Deut. 7:26 [n] Josh. 7:1, 12, 25 **6:20** [o] Heb. 11:30 **6:21** [p] Deut. 7:2; 20:16, 17 **6:22** [q] Josh. 2:12–19 **6:23** [r] Josh. 2:13 **6:25** [s] [Matt. 1:5] **6:26** [t] 1 Kin. 16:34

Defeat at Ai

7 But the children of Israel committed a ᵃtrespass regarding the ᵇaccursed things, for ᶜAchan the son of Carmi, the son of Zabdi,* the son of Zerah, of the tribe of Judah, took of the accursed things; so the anger of the LORD burned against the children of Israel.

2Now Joshua sent men from Jericho to Ai, which is beside Beth Aven, on the east side of Bethel, and spoke to them, saying, "Go up and spy out the country." So the men went up and spied out Ai. 3And they returned to Joshua and said to him, "Do not let all the people go up, but let about two or three thousand men go up and attack Ai. Do not weary all the people there, for *the people of Ai are* few." 4So about three thousand men went up there from the people, ᵈbut they fled before the men of Ai. 5And the men of Ai struck down about thirty-six men, for they chased them *from* before the gate as far as Shebarim, and struck them down on the descent; therefore ᵉthe hearts of the people melted and became like water.

6Then Joshua ᶠtore his clothes, and fell to the earth on his face before the ark of the LORD until evening, he and the elders of Israel; and they ᵍput dust on their heads. 7And Joshua said, "Alas, Lord GOD, ʰwhy have You brought this people over the Jordan at all—to deliver us into the hand of the Amorites, to destroy us? Oh, that we had been content, and dwelt on the other side of the Jordan! 8O Lord, what shall I say when Israel turns its back before its enemies? 9For the Canaanites and all the inhabitants of the land will hear *it,* and surround us, and ⁱcut off our name from the earth. Then ʲwhat will You do for Your great name?"

The Sin of Achan

10So the LORD said to Joshua: "Get up! Why do you lie thus on your face? 11Israel has sinned, and they have also transgressed My covenant which I commanded them. ᵏFor they have even taken some of the accursed things, and have both stolen and ˡdeceived; and they have also put *it* among their own stuff. 12ᵐTherefore the children of Israel could not stand before their enemies, *but* turned *their* backs before their enemies, because ⁿthey have become doomed to destruction. Neither will I be with you anymore, unless you destroy the accursed from among you. 13Get up, ᵒsanctify the people, and say, ᵖ'Sanctify yourselves for tomorrow, because thus says the LORD God of Israel: "*There is* an accursed thing in your midst, O Israel; you cannot stand before your enemies until you take away the accursed thing from among you." 14In the morning therefore you shall be brought according to your tribes. And it shall be *that* the tribe which ᑫthe LORD takes shall come according to families; and the family which the LORD takes shall come by households; and the household which the LORD takes shall come man by man. 15ʳThen it shall be *that* he who is taken with the accursed thing shall be burned with fire, he and all that he has, because he has ˢtransgressed the covenant of the LORD, and because he ᵗhas done a disgraceful thing in Israel.'"

16So Joshua rose early in the morning and brought Israel by their tribes, and the tribe of Judah was taken. 17He brought the clan of Judah, and he took the family of the Zarhites; and he brought the family of the Zarhites man by man, and Zabdi was taken. 18Then he brought his household man by man, and Achan the son of Carmi, the son of Zabdi, the son of Zerah, of the tribe of Judah, ᵘwas taken.

19Now Joshua said to Achan, "My son, I beg you, ᵛgive glory to the LORD God of Israel, ʷand make confession to Him, and ˣtell me now what you have done; do not hide *it* from me."

20And Achan answered Joshua and said, "Indeed ʸI have sinned against the LORD God of Israel, and this is what I have done: 21When I saw among the spoils a beautiful Babylonian garment, two hundred shekels

---

* **7:1** Called *Zimri* in 1 Chronicles 2:6

7:6–9 Suffering—Joshua's prayer was one of despair. Why had God allowed their defeat? Whenever tragedy strikes it is hard to understand why God allowed it to happen to us. In this case it is clearly explained. Achan had greedily taken what was banned by God. Through his sin the whole camp was guilty of deception and thievery. There are other reasons, not related to sin, for God's permission of tragedy. Sometimes people suffer in order to fulfill a sovereign purpose not immediately apparent.
7:9 Your great name. Joshua is aware that there is an even larger issue at stake: God's reputation.
7:10–15 Israel has sinned. God had consistent standards for both Israel and the Canaanites. He had ordered Israel to destroy Canaan because of their sin. He could not allow Israel to accommodate sin and corruption, even that of only one man.

7:13 until you take away. The relationship between obedience and blessing is well illustrated here. Israel would have no further successes until the sin had been uncovered.
7:19 give glory to the LORD ... tell me now what you have done. We too dishonor the Lord when we hide our sins, and we honor Him when we confess them.

7:1 ᵃ Josh. 7:20, 21　ᵇ Josh. 6:17–19　ᶜ Josh. 22:20
7:4 ᵈ Lev. 26:17　**7:5** ᵉ Lev. 26:36　**7:6** ᶠ Gen. 37:29, 34
ᵍ 1 Sam. 4:12　**7:7** ʰ Ex. 17:3　**7:9** ⁱ Deut. 32:26　ʲ Ex.
32:12　**7:11** ᵏ Josh. 6:17–19　ˡ Acts 5:1, 2　**7:12** ᵐ Judg.
2:14　ⁿ [Hag. 2:13, 14]　**7:13** ᵒ Ex. 19:10　ᵖ Josh. 3:5
7:14 ᑫ [Prov. 16:33]　**7:15** ʳ 1 Sam. 14:38, 39　ˢ Josh.
7:11　ᵗ Gen. 34:7　**7:18** ᵘ 1 Sam. 14:42　**7:19** ᵛ Jer. 13:16
ʷ Num. 5:6, 7　ˣ 1 Sam. 14:43　**7:20** ʸ Num. 22:34

of silver, and a wedge of gold weighing fifty shekels, I coveted them and took them. And there they are, hidden in the earth in the midst of my tent, with the silver under it."

22So Joshua sent messengers, and they ran to the tent; and there it was, hidden in his tent, with the silver under it. 23And they took them from the midst of the tent, brought them to Joshua and to all the children of Israel, and laid them out before the LORD. 24Then Joshua, and all Israel with him, took Achan the son of Zerah, the silver, the garment, the wedge of gold, his sons, his daughters, his oxen, his donkeys, his sheep, his tent, and zall that he had, and they brought them to αthe Valley of Achor. 25And Joshua said, b"Why have you troubled us? The LORD will trouble you this day." cSo all Israel stoned him with stones; and they burned them with fire after they had stoned them with stones.

26Then they draised over him a great heap of stones, still there to this day. So ethe LORD turned from the fierceness of His anger. Therefore the name of that place has been called fthe Valley of Achor* to this day.

The Fall of Ai

8 Now the LORD said to Joshua: a"Do not be afraid, nor be dismayed; take all the people of war with you, and arise, go up to Ai. See, bI have given into your hand the king of Ai, his people, his city, and his land. 2And you shall do to Ai and its king as you did to cJericho and its king. Only dits spoil and its cattle you shall take as booty for yourselves. Lay an ambush for the city behind it."

3So Joshua arose, and all the people of war, to go up against Ai; and Joshua chose thirty thousand mighty men of valor and sent them away by night. 4And he commanded them, saying: "Behold, eyou shall lie in ambush against the city, behind the city. Do not go very far from the city, but all of you be ready. 5Then I and all the people who are with me will approach the city;

and it will come about, when they come out against us as at the first, that fwe shall flee before them. 6For they will come out after us till we have drawn them from the city, for they will say, 'They are fleeing before us as at the first.' Therefore we will flee before them. 7Then you shall rise from the ambush and seize the city, for the LORD your God will deliver it into your hand. 8And it will be, when you have taken the city, that you shall set the city on fire. According to the commandment of the LORD you shall do. gSee, I have commanded you."

9Joshua therefore sent them out; and they went to lie in ambush, and stayed between Bethel and Ai, on the west side of Ai; but Joshua lodged that night among the people. 10Then Joshua rose up early in the morning and mustered the people, and went up, he and the elders of Israel, before the people to Ai. 11hAnd all the people of war who were with him went up and drew near; and they came before the city and camped on the north side of Ai. Now a valley lay between them and Ai. 12So he took about five thousand men and set them in ambush between Bethel and Ai, on the west side of the city. 13And when they had set the people, all the army that was on the north of the city, and its rear guard on the west of the city, Joshua went that night into the midst of the valley.

14Now it happened, when the king of Ai saw it, that the men of the city hurried and rose early and went out against Israel to battle, he and all his people, at an appointed place before the plain. But he idid not know that there was an ambush against him behind the city. 15And Joshua and all Israel jmade as if they were beaten before them, and fled by the way of the wilderness. 16So all the people who were in Ai were called together to pursue them. And they pursued Joshua and were drawn away from the city. 17There was not a man left in Ai or Bethel who did not go out after Israel.

---

* 7:26 Literally Trouble

7:25 stoned him with stones. Achan and all that he had were brought out and stoned. This seems like a severe punishment and one that is hard to understand. But it illustrated God's firm insistence on holiness. God could not tolerate the sin Achan had committed and He had to deal with him. It is a sobering thought for us, to remember that often our sins do not affect only ourselves, they also cause others to stumble and fall. We deserve punishment as severe as Achan's, but Jesus Christ took over our penalty and through His blood we can be reconciled to God.

8:1 Do not be afraid, nor be dismayed. The sins of Achan had broken the special relationship God had established with His people, but God had not abandoned them.

8:7 the LORD your God will deliver it into your hand. Israel was completely dependent on God for their success.

8:12–17 Wisdom—The name Ai means "ruin" or "heap." Unlike Jericho, Ai was not a walled city, to Israel it was just a rubble heap. It looked so easy, especially after their resounding victory at Jericho, that they set out to attack without asking for the Lord's direction. In facing tasks that seem well within our powers, we also often forget to ask for the Lord's help. Wisdom in the believer's life demands persistence in depending on the Lord's strength and direction in little problems as well as the big ones.

7:24 z Num. 16:32, 33 a Josh. 7:26; 15:7 **7:25** b Josh. 6:18 c Deut. 17:5 **7:26** d 2 Sam. 18:17 e Deut. 13:17 f Is. 65:10 **8:1** a Josh. 1:9; 10:8 b Josh. 6:2 **8:2** c Josh. 6:21 d Deut. 20:14 **8:4** e Judg. 20:29 **8:5** f Judg. 20:32 **8:8** g 2 Sam. 13:28 **8:11** h Josh. 8:5 **8:14** i Judg. 20:34 **8:15** j Judg. 20:36

So they left the city open and pursued Israel.

[18] Then the LORD said to Joshua, "Stretch out the spear that *is* in your hand toward Ai, for I will give it into your hand." And Joshua stretched out the spear that *was* in his hand toward the city. [19] So *those in* ambush arose quickly out of their place; they ran as soon as he had stretched out his hand, and they entered the city and took it, and hurried to set the city on fire. [20] And when the men of Ai looked behind them, they saw, and behold, the smoke of the city ascended to heaven. So they had no power to flee this way or that way, and the people who had fled to the wilderness turned back on the pursuers. [21] Now when Joshua and all Israel saw that the ambush had taken the city and that the smoke of the city ascended, they turned back and struck down the men of Ai. [22] Then the others came out of the city against them; so they were *caught* in the midst of Israel, some on this side and some on that side. And they struck them down, so that they [k]let none of them remain or escape. [23] But the king of Ai they took alive, and brought him to Joshua.

[24] And it came to pass when Israel had made an end of slaying all the inhabitants of Ai in the field, in the wilderness where they pursued them, and when they all had fallen by the edge of the sword until they were consumed, that all the Israelites returned to Ai and struck it with the edge of the sword. [25] So it was *that* all who fell that day, both men and women, *were* twelve thousand—all the people of Ai. [26] For Joshua did not draw back his hand, with which he stretched out the spear, until he had [l]utterly destroyed all the inhabitants of Ai. [27] [m]Only the livestock and the spoil of that city Israel took as booty for themselves, according to the word of the LORD which He had [n]commanded Joshua. [28] So Joshua burned Ai and made it [o]a heap forever, a desolation to this day. [29] [p]And the king of Ai he hanged on a tree until evening. [q]And as soon as the sun was down, Joshua commanded that they should take his corpse down from the tree, cast it at the entrance of the gate of the city, and [r]raise over it a great heap of stones *that remains* to this day.

Joshua Renews the Covenant

[30] Now Joshua built an altar to the LORD God of Israel [s]in Mount Ebal, [31] as Moses the servant of the LORD had commanded the children of Israel, as it is written in the Book of the Law of Moses: [t]"an altar of whole stones over which no man has wielded an iron *tool*."* And [u]they offered on it burnt offerings to the LORD, and sacrificed peace offerings. [32] And there, in the presence of the children of Israel, [v]he wrote on the stones a copy of the law of Moses, which he had written. [33] Then all Israel, with their elders and officers and judges, stood on either side of the ark before the priests, the Levites, [w]who bore the ark of the covenant of the LORD, [x]the stranger as well as he who was born among them. Half of them *were* in front of Mount Gerizim and half of them in front of Mount Ebal, [y]as Moses the servant of the LORD had commanded before, that they should bless the people of Israel. [34] And afterward [z]he read all the words of the law, [a]the blessings and the cursings, according to all that is written in the [b]Book of the Law. [35] There was not a word of all that Moses had commanded which Joshua did not read before all the assembly of Israel, [c]with the women, the little ones, [d]and the strangers who were living among them.

The Treaty with the Gibeonites

9 And it came to pass when [a]all the kings who *were* on this side of the Jordan, in the hills and in the lowland and in all the coasts of [b]the Great Sea toward Lebanon—[c]the Hittite, the Amorite, the Canaanite, the Perizzite, the Hivite, and the Jebusite—heard *about it,* [2] that they [d]gathered together to fight with Joshua and Israel with one accord.

[3] But when the inhabitants of [e]Gibeon [f]heard what Joshua had done to Jericho and Ai, [4] they worked craftily, and went and pretended to be ambassadors. And they took old sacks on their donkeys, old wineskins torn and mended, [5] old and patched sandals on their feet, and old garments on themselves; and all the bread of their provision was dry *and* moldy. [6] And they went to Joshua, [g]to the camp at Gilgal, and said to him and to the men of Israel, "We have come from a far country; now therefore, make a covenant with us."

[7] Then the men of Israel said to the [h]Hivites, "Perhaps you dwell among us; so [i]how can we make a covenant with you?"

---

* 8:31 Deuteronomy 27:5, 6

9:3 Gibeon. Gibeon was relatively close to Ai, and about five miles northwest of Jerusalem.

9:6 We have come from a far country. Israel was allowed to make treaties with cities that were far away (Ex. 34:11–12; Deut. 20:10–18). If the Gibeonites had been telling the truth, a treaty with them would have been permissible.

8:22 [k] Deut. 7:2   **8:26** [l] Josh. 6:21   **8:27** [m] Num. 31:22, 26   [n] Josh. 8:2   **8:28** [o] Deut. 13:16   **8:29** [p] Josh. 10:26   [q] Deut. 21:22, 23   [r] Josh. 7:26; 10:27   **8:30** [s] Deut. 27:4–8   **8:31** [t] Ex. 20:25   [u] Ex. 20:24   **8:32** [v] Deut. 27:2, 3, 8   **8:33** [w] Deut. 31:9, 25   [x] Deut. 31:12   [y] Deut. 11:29; 27:12   **8:34** [z] Neh. 8:3   [a] Deut. 28:2, 15, 45; 29:20, 21; 30:19   [b] Josh. 1:8   **8:35** [c] Deut. 31:12   [d] Josh. 8:33   **9:1** [a] Josh. 3:10   [b] Num. 34:6   [c] Ex. 3:17; 23:23   **9:2** [d] Ps. 83:3, 5   **9:3** [e] Josh. 9:17, 22; 10:2; 21:17   [f] Josh. 6:27   **9:6** [g] Josh. 5:10   **9:7** [h] Josh. 9:1; 11:19   [i] Ex. 23:32

⁸But they said to Joshua, ʲ"We *are* your servants."

And Joshua said to them, "Who *are* you, and where do you come from?"

⁹So they said to him: ᵏ"From a very far country your servants have come, because of the name of the LORD your God; for we have ˡheard of His fame, and all that He did in Egypt, ¹⁰and ᵐall that He did to the two kings of the Amorites who *were* beyond the Jordan—to Sihon king of Heshbon, and Og king of Bashan, who was at Ashtaroth. ¹¹Therefore our elders and all the inhabitants of our country spoke to us, saying, 'Take provisions with you for the journey, and go to meet them, and say to them, "We *are* your servants; now therefore, make a covenant with us."' ¹²This bread of ours we took hot *for* our provision from our houses on the day we departed to come to you. But now look, it is dry and moldy. ¹³And these wineskins which we filled *were* new, and see, they are torn; and these our garments and our sandals have become old because of the very long journey."

¹⁴Then the men of Israel took some of their provisions; ⁿbut they did not ask counsel of the LORD. ¹⁵So Joshua ᵒmade peace with them, and made a covenant with them to let them live; and the rulers of the congregation swore to them.

¹⁶And it happened at the end of three days, after they had made a covenant with them, that they heard that they *were* their neighbors who dwelt near them. ¹⁷Then the children of Israel journeyed and came to their cities on the third day. Now their cities *were* ᵖGibeon, Chephirah, Beeroth, and Kirjath Jearim. ¹⁸But the children of Israel did not attack them, ᑫbecause the rulers of the congregation had sworn to them by the LORD God of Israel. And all the congregation complained against the rulers.

¹⁹Then all the rulers said to all the congregation, "We have sworn to them by the LORD God of Israel; now therefore, we may not touch them. ²⁰This we will do to them: We will let them live, lest ʳwrath be upon us because of the oath which we swore to them." ²¹And the rulers said to them, "Let them live, but let them be ˢwoodcutters and

water carriers for all the congregation, as the rulers had ᵗpromised them."

²²Then Joshua called for them, and he spoke to them, saying, "Why have you deceived us, saying, ᵘ'We *are* very far from you,' when ᵛyou dwell near us? ²³Now therefore, you *are* ʷcursed, and none of you shall be freed from being slaves—woodcutters and water carriers for the house of my God."

²⁴So they answered Joshua and said, "Because your servants were clearly told that the LORD your God ˣcommanded His servant Moses to give you all the land, and to destroy all the inhabitants of the land from before you; therefore ʸwe were very much afraid for our lives because of you, and have done this thing. ²⁵And now, here we are, ᶻin your hands; do with us as it seems good and right to do to us." ²⁶So he did to them, and delivered them out of the hand of the children of Israel, so that they did not kill them. ²⁷And that day Joshua made them ᵃwoodcutters and water carriers for the congregation and for the altar of the LORD, ᵇin the place which He would choose, even to this day.

The Sun Stands Still

10 Now it came to pass when Adoni-Zedek king of Jerusalem ᵃheard how Joshua had taken ᵇAi and had utterly destroyed it—ᶜas he had done to Jericho and its king, so he had done to ᵈAi and its king—and ᵉhow the inhabitants of Gibeon had made peace with Israel and were among them, ²that they ᶠfeared greatly, because Gibeon *was* a great city, like one of the royal cities, and because it *was* greater than Ai, and all its men *were* mighty. ³Therefore Adoni-Zedek king of Jerusalem sent to Hoham king of Hebron, Piram king of Jarmuth, Japhia king of Lachish, and Debir king of Eglon, saying, ⁴"Come up to me and help me, that we may attack Gibeon, for ᵍit has made peace with Joshua and with the children of Israel." ⁵Therefore the five kings of the ʰAmorites, the king of Jerusalem, the king of Hebron, the king of Jarmuth, the king of Lachish, *and* the king of Eglon, ⁱgathered together and went up,

---

9:14 did not ask counsel of the LORD. Significantly, the Israelites did not ask God's advice about making peace with the Gibeonites, contrary to God's explicit instructions to Joshua (Num. 27:21).

9:18 Questioning—The congregation rose up and complained to their leaders about making the treaty with Gibeon because they knew the leaders had not consulted the Lord. There is a time to confront leaders, specifically when they sin or when they act in their own wisdom without asking for God's direction. When the leaders appear to be traveling down the wrong path, the people can always ask respectfully, "Have you consulted the Lord about this? Did you get an answer?"

9:20 the oath which we swore. Oath taking and swearing was serious business. To take an oath was

to give a sacred and unbreakable promise to do a certain thing. Because of the unbreakable nature of an oath, the covenant the Israelites made with the Gibeonites could not be revoked, even though it was obtained under false pretenses.

9:8 ʲ Deut. 20:11   **9:9** ᵏ Deut. 20:15   ˡ Josh. 2:9, 10; 5:1   **9:10** ᵐ Num. 21:24, 33   **9:14** ⁿ Num. 27:21   **9:15** ᵒ 2 Sam. 21:2   **9:17** ᵖ Josh. 18:25   **9:18** ᑫ Ps. 15:4   **9:20** ʳ 2 Sam. 21:1, 2, 6   **9:21** ˢ Deut. 29:11   ᵗ Josh. 9:15   **9:22** ᵘ Josh. 9:6, 9   ᵛ Josh. 9:16   **9:23** ʷ Gen. 9:25   **9:24** ˣ Deut. 7:1, 2   ʸ Ex. 15:14   **9:25** ᶻ Gen. 16:6   **9:27** ᵃ Josh. 9:21, 23   ᵇ Deut. 12:5   **10:1** ᵃ Josh. 9:1   ᵇ Josh. 8:1   ᶜ Josh. 6:21   ᵈ Josh. 8:22, 26, 28   ᵉ Josh. 9:15   **10:2** ᶠ Ex. 15:14–16   **10:4** ᵍ Josh. 9:15; 10:1   **10:5** ʰ Num. 13:29   ⁱ Josh. 9:2

they and all their armies, and camped before Gibeon and made war against it.

6And the men of Gibeon sent to Joshua at the camp *j*at Gilgal, saying, "Do not forsake your servants; come up to us quickly, save us and help us, for all the kings of the Amorites who dwell in the mountains have gathered together against us."

7So Joshua ascended from Gilgal, he and *k*all the people of war with him, and all the mighty men of valor. **8**And the LORD said to Joshua, *l*"Do not fear them, for I have delivered *m*them into your hand; *m*not a man of them shall *n*stand before you." **9**Joshua therefore came upon them suddenly, having marched all night from Gilgal. **10**So the LORD *o*routed them before Israel, killed them with a great slaughter at Gibeon, chased them along the road that goes *p*to Beth Horon, and struck them down as far as *q*Azekah and Makkedah. **11**And it happened, as they fled before Israel *and* were on the descent of Beth Horon, *r*that the LORD cast down large hailstones from heaven on them as far as Azekah, and they died. *There were* more who died from the hailstones than the children of Israel killed with the sword.

12Then Joshua spoke to the LORD in the day when the LORD delivered up the Amorites before the children of Israel, and he said in the sight of Israel:

s"Sun, stand still over Gibeon;
And Moon, in the Valley of *t*Aijalon."
13 So the sun stood still,
And the moon stopped,
Till the people had revenge
Upon their enemies.

*u*Is this not written in the Book of Jasher? So the sun stood still in the midst of heaven, and did not hasten to go *down* for about a whole day. **14**And there has been *v*no day like that, before it or after it, that the LORD heeded the voice of a man; for *w*the LORD fought for Israel.

15*x*Then Joshua returned, and all Israel with him, to the camp at Gilgal.

The Amorite Kings Executed

16But these five kings had fled and hidden themselves in a cave at Makkedah. **17**And it was told Joshua, saying, "The five kings have been found hidden in the cave at Makkedah."

18So Joshua said, "Roll large stones against the mouth of the cave, and set men by it to guard them. **19**And do not stay *there* yourselves, *but* pursue your enemies, and attack their rear *guard*. Do not allow them to enter their cities, for the LORD your God has delivered them into your hand." **20**Then it happened, while Joshua and the children of Israel made an end of slaying them with a very great slaughter, till they had finished, that those who escaped entered fortified cities. **21**And all the people returned to the camp, to Joshua at Makkedah, in peace. *y*No one moved his tongue against any of the children of Israel.

22Then Joshua said, "Open the mouth of the cave, and bring out those five kings to me from the cave." **23**And they did so, and brought out those five kings to him from the cave: the king of Jerusalem, the king of Hebron, the king of Jarmuth, the king of Lachish, *and* the king of Eglon.

24So it was, when they brought out those kings to Joshua, that Joshua called for all the men of Israel, and said to the captains of the men of war who went with him, "Come near, put your feet on the necks of these kings." And they drew near and *z*put their feet on their necks. **25**Then Joshua said to them, *a*"Do not be afraid, nor be dismayed; be strong and of good courage, for *b*thus the LORD will do to all your enemies against whom you fight." **26**And afterward Joshua struck them and killed them, and hanged them on five trees; and they *c*were hanging on the trees until evening. **27**So it was at the time of the going down of the sun *that* Joshua commanded, and they *d*took them down from the trees, cast them into the cave where they had been hidden, and laid large stones against the cave's mouth, *which remain* until this very day.

10:10 *the LORD routed them.* Despite Joshua's presence with his warriors, it was God who gave the victory, and God who received the credit.

10:13 *the Book of Jasher.* This piece of literature is mentioned again in 2 Samuel 1:18, confirming what is said here. Nothing else is known of the Book of Jasher; it is not part of the Bible, and no known portion of it has survived.

10:14 *the LORD heeded the voice of a man.* Any person can gain God's attention in prayer. God may answer our pleas by saying no, but we can be certain that He always listens and answers. This incident was remembered as being like no other because God said yes to a request which He otherwise always answers no: He actually stopped time to allow the Israelites to finish the battle.

10:24 *put your feet on the necks of these kings.* Putting one's foot on a slain enemy was a declaration

of victory. In Psalm 110:1 the Lord said, "I [will] make Your enemies Your footstool" (see also Ps. 8:6). God also speaks of placing Jesus' enemies under His feet (1 Cor. 15:25–27). Ancient sculptures show Assyrian kings doing this to their vanquished enemies.

10:25 *be strong and of good courage.* Joshua encourages the people with the same words God used to encourage him (1:6,9; 10:8). God's words, written for us in the Bible, are the best form of encouragement we could have.

10:6 *j* Josh. 5:10; 9:6 **10:7** *k* Josh. 8:1 **10:8** *l* Josh. 11:6 *m* Josh. 1:5, 9 *n* Josh. 21:44 **10:10** *o* Is. 28:21 *p* Josh. 16:3, 5 *q* Josh. 15:35 **10:11** *r* Is. 30:30 **10:12** *s* Hab. 3:11 *t* Judg. 12:12 **10:13** *u* 2 Sam. 1:18 **10:14** *v* Is. 38:7, 8 *w* Deut. 1:30; 20:4 **10:15** *x* Josh. 10:43 **10:21** *y* Ex. 11:7 **10:24** *z* Mal. 4:3 **10:25** *a* Deut. 31:6–8 *b* Deut. 3:21; 7:19 **10:26** *c* Josh. 8:29 **10:27** *d* Deut. 21:22, 23

Conquest of the Southland

28On that day Joshua took Makkedah, and struck it and its king with the edge of the sword. He utterly *e*destroyed them*— all the people who *were* in it. He let none remain. He also did to the king of Makkedah *f*as he had done to the king of Jericho.

29Then Joshua passed from Makkedah, and all Israel with him, to *g*Libnah; and they fought against Libnah. 30And the LORD also delivered it and its king into the hand of Israel; he struck it and all the people who *were* in it with the edge of the sword. He let none remain in it, but did to its king as he had done to the king of Jericho.

31Then Joshua passed from Libnah, and all Israel with him, to Lachish; and they encamped against it and fought against it. 32And the LORD delivered Lachish into the hand of Israel, who took it on the second day, and struck it and all the people who *were* in it with the edge of the sword, according to all that he had done to Libnah.

33Then Horam king of Gezer came up to help Lachish; and Joshua struck him and his people, until he left him none remaining.

34From Lachish Joshua passed to Eglon, and all Israel with him; and they encamped against it and fought against it. 35They took it on that day and struck it with the edge of the sword; all the people who *were* in it he utterly destroyed that day, according to all that he had done to Lachish.

36So Joshua went up from Eglon, and all Israel with him, to *h*Hebron; and they fought against it. 37And they took it and struck it with the edge of the sword—its king, all its cities, and all the people who *were* in it; he left none remaining, according to all that he had done to Eglon, but utterly destroyed it and all the people who *were* in it.

38Then Joshua returned, and all Israel with him, to *i*Debir; and they fought

against it. 39And he took it and its king and all its cities; they struck them with the edge of the sword and utterly destroyed all the people who *were* in it. He left none remaining; as he had done to Hebron, so he did to Debir and its king, as he had done also to Libnah and its king.

40So Joshua conquered all the land: the *j*mountain country and the South* and the lowland and the wilderness slopes, and *k*all their kings; he left none remaining, but *l*utterly destroyed all that breathed, as the LORD God of Israel had commanded. 41And Joshua conquered them from *m*Kadesh Barnea as far as *n*Gaza, *o*and all the country of Goshen, even as far as Gibeon. 42All these kings and their land Joshua took at one time, *p*because the LORD God of Israel fought for Israel. 43Then Joshua returned, and all Israel with him, to the camp at Gilgal.

The Northern Conquest

11 And it came to pass, when Jabin king of Hazor heard *these things*, that he *a*sent to Jobab king of Madon, to the king *b*of Shimron, to the king of Achshaph, 2and to the kings who *were* from the north, in the mountains, in the plain south of *c*Chinneroth, in the lowland, and in the heights *d*of Dor on the west, 3to the Canaanites in the east and in the west, the *e*Amorite, the Hittite, the Perizzite, the Jebusite in the mountains, *f*and the Hivite below *g*Hermon *h*in the land of Mizpah. 4So they went out, they and all their armies with them, *as* many people *i*as the sand that *is* on the seashore in multitude, with very many horses and chariots. 5And when all these kings

* 10:28 Following Masoretic Text and most authorities; many Hebrew manuscripts, some manuscripts of the Septuagint, and some manuscripts of the Targum read *it*.   * 10:40 Hebrew *Negev*, and so throughout this book

---

10:30 the LORD. Here again we are reminded that the Lord was Israel's warrior. As He fought for them, we too can trust Him fully to fight for us. Indeed, He fought the ultimate fight for us on the cross, to set us free from death forever. We can also trust Him to be with us in the day-to-day fight against evil and sin.

10:28–43 Fervor—All of Israel was zealous to do just as the Lord commanded, and the success they experienced was attributed to the Lord. But how can such destruction be regarded as honoring to God? The Bible gives reasons for the wiping out of these peoples, and these reasons are in accord with the tenor of the whole Bible. The Canaanites were guilty of extreme wickedness (Deut. 7:2–11; 20:16–18). God is completely holy, and He therefore cannot tolerate sin. Sin must be judged. He is also patient. For many years the Canaanite sin did not justify annihilation. But that time did arrive, and it came in the time of Joshua. Israel was a tool in the hand of God to judge the wickedness of those nations. Leviticus 18 is a gruesome list of their evil actions, including incest, adultery, child sacrifice, homosexuality, and bestiality. The

Canaanites brought God's judgment on themselves by their own sins. Canaan was not destroyed without plenty of warning. God is never unjust. They were a thoroughly debased society, hostile to all God's ways (Deut. 9:4–5). The most sobering reflection is that now, today, many of those wicked sins listed in Leviticus 18 are present in our society. God's judgment in the last day will be complete indeed.

11:4 very many horses and chariots. In this time in history, horses were used for pulling chariots which accompanied the infantry and carried a rider with a bow or a supply of spears. The enemy of Israel came well armed and with many soldiers to fight—but it made no difference. Again God defeated Israel's

10:28 *e* Deut. 7:2, 16 *f* Josh. 6:21 **10:29** *g* Josh. 15:42; 21:13 **10:36** *h* Josh. 14:13–15; 15:13 **10:38** *i* Josh. 15:15 **10:40** *j* Deut. 1:7 *k* Deut. 7:24 *l* Deut. 20:16, 17 **10:41** *m* Deut. 9:23 *n* Gen. 10:19 *o* Josh. 11:16; 15:51 **10:42** *p* Josh. 10:14 **11:1** *a* Josh. 10:3 *b* Josh. 19:15 **11:2** *c* Num. 34:11 *d* Josh. 17:11 **11:3** *e* Josh. 9:1 *f* Judg. 3:3, 5 *g* Josh. 11:17; 13:5, 11 *h* Gen. 31:49 **11:4** *i* Judg. 7:12

had met together, they came and camped together at the waters of Merom to fight against Israel.

[6]But the LORD said to Joshua, [i]"Do not be afraid because of them, for tomorrow about this time I will deliver all of them slain before Israel. You shall [k]hamstring their horses and burn their chariots with fire." [7]So Joshua and all the people of war with him came against them suddenly by the waters of Merom, and they attacked them. [8]And the LORD delivered them into the hand of Israel, who defeated them and chased them to Greater [l]Sidon, to the Brook [m]Misrephoth,* and to the Valley of Mizpah eastward; they attacked them until they left none of them remaining. [9]So Joshua did to them as the LORD had told him: he hamstrung their horses and burned their chariots with fire.

[10]Joshua turned back at that time and took Hazor, and struck its king with the sword; for Hazor was formerly the head of all those kingdoms. [11]And they struck all the people who *were* in it with the edge of the sword, [n]utterly destroying *them*. There was none left [o]breathing. Then he burned Hazor with fire.

[12]So all the cities of those kings, and all their kings, Joshua took and struck with the edge of the sword. He utterly destroyed them, [p]as Moses the servant of the LORD had commanded. [13]But *as for* the cities that stood on their mounds,* Israel burned none of them, except Hazor only, *which* Joshua burned. [14]And all the [q]spoil of these cities and the livestock, the children of Israel took as booty for themselves; but they struck every man with the edge of the sword until they had destroyed them, and they left none breathing. [15r]As the LORD had commanded Moses His servant, [s]Moses commanded Joshua, and [t]so Joshua did. He left nothing undone of all that the LORD had commanded Moses.

Summary of Joshua's Conquests

[16]Thus Joshua took all this land: [u]the mountain country, all the South, [v]all the land of Goshen, the lowland, and the Jordan plain*—the mountains of Israel and its lowlands, [17w]from Mount Halak and the ascent to Seir, even as far as Baal Gad in the Valley of Lebanon below Mount Hermon. He captured [x]all their kings, and struck them down and killed them. [18]Joshua made war a long time with all those kings. [19]There was not a city that made peace with the children of Israel, except [y]the Hivites, the inhabitants of Gibeon. All *the others* they took in battle. [20]For [z]it was of the LORD to harden their hearts, that they should come against Israel in battle, that He might utterly destroy them, *and* that they might receive no mercy, but that He might destroy them, [a]as the LORD had commanded Moses.

[21]And at that time Joshua came and cut off [b]the Anakim from the mountains: from Hebron, from Debir, from Anab, from all the mountains of Judah, and from all the mountains of Israel; Joshua utterly destroyed them with their cities. [22]None of the Anakim were left in the land of the children of Israel; they remained only [c]in Gaza, in Gath, [d]and in Ashdod.

[23]So Joshua took the whole land, [e]according to all that the LORD had said to Moses; and Joshua gave it as an inheritance to Israel [f]according to their divisions by their tribes. Then the land [g]rested from war.

The Kings Conquered by Moses

12 These *are* the kings of the land whom the children of Israel defeated, and whose land they possessed on the other side of the Jordan toward the rising of the sun, [a]from the River Arnon [b]to Mount Hermon, and all the eastern Jordan plain: [2]*One king was* [c]Sihon king of the Amorites, who dwelt in Heshbon *and* ruled half of Gilead, from Aroer, which is on the bank of the River Arnon, from the middle of that river, even as far as the River Jabbok, *which is* the border of the Ammonites, [3]and [d]the eastern Jordan plain from the Sea of Chinneroth as far as the Sea of the Arabah (the

---

* **11:8** Hebrew *Misrephoth Maim*   * **11:13** Hebrew *tel*, a heap of successive city ruins
* **11:16** Hebrew *arabah*

---

enemy. God limited the size of the Israelite army so they would not be depending on military strength, but rather on Him.
11:8 *Greater Sidon, to the Brook Misrephoth.* Great Sidon was a Phoenician city on the Mediterranean coast, and Misrephoth was south of it. The defeat of the Canaanites described here shows them fleeing in all directions.
11:16—12:24 Zeal—Joshua and the people served as the instruments of divine justice and fulfilled the word spoken to Moses concerning the gift of the land of Canaan. The list of the defeated kings who had banded together against Israel bears testimony to the zeal of Israel for God and the obedience and faithfulness of Joshua. As Christians we can eagerly anticipate the final outcome of world history, when

the "kingdoms of this world have become the kingdoms of our Lord and of His Christ" (Rev. 11:15).
11:20 *to harden their hearts.* The people whose hearts God hardened were not good people, but people already committed to doing evil.

11:6 [i] Josh. 10:8 [k] 2 Sam. 8:4 **11:8** [l] Gen. 49:13 [m] Josh. 13:6 **11:11** [n] Deut. 20:16 [o] Josh. 10:40 **11:12** [p] Num. 33:50–56 **11:14** [q] Deut. 20:14–18 **11:15** [r] Ex. 34:10–17 [s] Deut. 31:7, 8 [t] Josh. 1:7 **11:16** [u] Josh. 12:8 [v] Josh. 10:40, 41 **11:17** [w] Josh. 12:7 [x] Deut. 7:24 **11:19** [y] Josh. 9:3–7 **11:20** [z] Deut. 2:30 [a] Deut. 20:16, 17 **11:21** [b] Num. 13:22, 33 **11:22** [c] 1 Sam. 17:4 [d] Josh. 15:46 **11:23** [e] Num. 34:2–15 [f] Num. 26:53 [g] Deut. 12:9, 10; 25:19 **12:1** [a] Num. 21:24 [b] Deut. 3:8 **12:2** [c] Deut. 2:24–27 **12:3** [d] Deut. 3:17

Salt Sea), ᵉthe road to Beth Jeshimoth, and southward below ᶠthe slopes of Pisgah. ⁴*The other king was* ᵍOg king of Bashan and his territory, *who was* of ʰthe remnant of the giants, ⁱwho dwelt at Ashtaroth and at Edrei, ⁵and reigned over ʲMount Hermon, ᵏover Salcah, over all Bashan, ˡas far as the border of the Geshurites and the Maachathites, and over half of Gilead *to* the border of Sihon king of Heshbon.

⁶ᵐThese Moses the servant of the LORD and the children of Israel had conquered; and ⁿMoses the servant of the LORD had given it *as* a possession to the Reubenites, the Gadites, and half the tribe of Manasseh.

The Kings Conquered by Joshua

⁷And these *are* the kings of the country ᵒwhich Joshua and the children of Israel conquered on this side of the Jordan, on the west, from Baal Gad in the Valley of Lebanon as far as Mount Halak and the ascent to ᵖSeir, which Joshua ᑫgave to the tribes of Israel *as* a possession according to their divisions, ⁸ʳin the mountain country, in the lowlands, in the *Jordan* plain, in the slopes, in the wilderness, and in the South—ˢthe Hittites, the Amorites, the Canaanites, the Perizzites, the Hivites, and the Jebusites: ⁹ᵗthe king of Jericho, one; ᵘthe king of Ai, which *is* beside Bethel, one; ¹⁰ᵛthe king of Jerusalem, one; the king of Hebron, one; ¹¹the king of Jarmuth, one; the king of Lachish, one; ¹²the king of Eglon, one; ʷthe king of Gezer, one; ¹³ˣthe king of Debir, one; the king of Geder, one; ¹⁴the king of Hormah, one; the king of Arad, one; ¹⁵ʸthe king of Libnah, one; the king of Adullam, one; ¹⁶ᶻthe king of Makkedah, one; ᵃthe king of Bethel, one; ¹⁷the king of Tappuah, one; ᵇthe king of Hepher, one; ¹⁸the king of Aphek, one; the king of Lasharon, one; ¹⁹the king of Madon, one; ᶜthe king of Hazor, one; ²⁰the king of ᵈShimron Meron, one; the king of Achshaph, one; ²¹the king of Taanach, one; the king of Megiddo, one; ²²ᵉthe king of Kedesh, one; the king of Jokneam in Carmel, one; ²³the king of Dor in the ᶠheights of Dor, one; the king of ᵍthe people of Gilgal, one; ²⁴the king of Tirzah, one—ʰall the kings, thirty-one.

Remaining Land to Be Conquered

13 Now Joshua ᵃwas old, advanced in years. And the LORD said to him: "You

are old, advanced in years, and there remains very much land yet to be possessed. ²ᵇThis is the land that yet remains: ᶜall the territory of the Philistines and all ᵈthat of the Geshurites, ³ᵉfrom Sihor, which *is* east of Egypt, as far as the border of Ekron northward (*which* is counted as Canaanite); the ᶠfive lords of the Philistines—the Gazites, the Ashdodites, the Ashkelonites, the Gittites, and the Ekronites; also ᵍthe Avites; ⁴from the south, all the land of the Canaanites, and Mearah that belongs to the Sidonians ʰas far as Aphek, to the border of ⁱthe Amorites; ⁵the land of ʲthe Gebalites,* and all Lebanon, toward the sunrise, ᵏfrom Baal Gad below Mount Hermon as far as the entrance to Hamath; ⁶all the inhabitants of the mountains from Lebanon as far as ˡthe Brook Misrephoth,* *and* all the Sidonians—them ᵐI will drive out from before the children of Israel; only ⁿdivide it by lot to Israel as an inheritance, as I have commanded you. ⁷Now therefore, divide this land as an inheritance to the nine tribes and half the tribe of Manasseh."

The Land Divided East of the Jordan

⁸With the other half-tribe the Reubenites and the Gadites received their inheritance, ᵒwhich Moses had given them, ᵖbeyond the Jordan eastward, as Moses the servant of the LORD had given them: ⁹from Aroer which *is* on the bank of the River Arnon, and the town that *is* in the midst of the ravine, ᑫand all the plain of Medeba as far as Dibon; ¹⁰ʳall the cities of Sihon king of the Amorites, who reigned in Heshbon, as far as the border of the children of Ammon; ¹¹ˢGilead, and the border of the Geshurites and Maachathites, all Mount Hermon, and all Bashan as far as Salcah; ¹²all the kingdom of Og in Bashan, who reigned in Ashtaroth and Edrei, who remained of ᵗthe remnant of the giants; ᵘfor Moses had defeated and cast out these.

¹³Nevertheless the children of Israel ᵛdid not drive out the Geshurites or the Maachathites, but the Geshurites and the Maachathites dwell among the Israelites until this day.

¹⁴ʷOnly to the tribe of Levi he had given

---

* **13:5** Or *Giblites* * **13:6** Hebrew *Misrephoth Maim*

13:14 *to the tribe of Levi he had given no inheritance.* Originally, the tribe of Levi was sentenced to be landless because of Levi's violent behavior (Gen.

12:3 ᵉ Josh. 13:20 ᶠ Deut. 3:17; 4:49 **12:4** ᵍ Num. 21:33 ʰ Deut. 3:11 ⁱ Deut. 1:4 **12:5** ʲ Deut. 3:8 ᵏ Deut. 3:10 ˡ Deut. 3:14 **12:6** ᵐ Num. 21:24, 35 ⁿ Num. 32:29–33 **12:7** ᵒ Josh. 11:17 ᵖ Gen. 14:6; 32:3 ᑫ Josh. 11:23 **12:8** ʳ Josh. 10:40; 11:16 ˢ Ex. 3:8; 23:23 **12:9** ᵗ Josh. 6:2 ᵘ Josh. 8:29 **12:10** ᵛ Josh. 10:23 **12:12** ʷ Josh. 10:33 **12:13** ˣ Josh. 10:38, 39 **12:15** ʸ Josh. 10:29, 30

12:16 ᶻ Josh. 10:28 ᵃ Judg. 1:22 **12:17** ᵇ 1 Kin. 4:10 **12:19** ᶜ Josh. 11:10 **12:20** ᵈ Josh. 11:1; 19:15 **12:22** ᵉ Josh. 19:37; 20:7; 21:32 **12:23** ᶠ Josh. 11:2 ᵍ Is. 9:1 **12:24** ʰ Deut. 7:24 **13:1** ᵃ Josh. 14:10; 23:1, 2 **13:2** ᵇ Judg. 3:1–3 ᶜ Joel 3:4 ᵈ 2 Sam. 3:3 **13:3** ᵉ Jer. 2:18 ᶠ Judg. 3:3 ᵍ Deut. 2:23 **13:4** ʰ Josh. 12:18; 19:30 ⁱ Judg. 1:34 **13:5** ʲ 1 Kin. 5:18; Ezek. 27:9 ᵏ Josh. 12:7 **13:6** ˡ Josh. 11:8 ᵐ Josh. 23:13 ⁿ Josh. 14:1, 2 **13:8** ᵒ Num. 32:33 ᵖ Josh. 12:1–6 **13:9** ᑫ Num. 21:30 **13:10** ʳ Num. 21:24, 25 **13:11** ˢ Josh. 12:5 **13:12** ᵗ Deut. 3:11 ᵘ Num. 21:24, 34, 35 **13:13** ᵛ Josh. 13:11 **13:14** ʷ Josh. 14:3, 4

no inheritance; the sacrifices of the LORD God of Israel made by fire *are* their inheritance, ˣas He said to them.

The Land of Reuben

¹⁵ʸAnd Moses had given to the tribe of the children of Reuben *an inheritance* according to their families. ¹⁶Their territory was ᶻfrom Aroer, which *is* on the bank of the River Arnon, ᵃand the city that *is* in the midst of the ravine, ᵇand all the plain by Medeba; ¹⁷ᶜHeshbon and all its cities that *are* in the plain: Dibon, Bamoth Baal, Beth Baal Meon, ¹⁸ᵈJahaza, Kedemoth, Mephaath, ¹⁹ᵉKirjathaim, ᶠSibmah, Zereth Shahar on the mountain of the valley, ²⁰Beth Peor, ᵍthe slopes of Pisgah, and Beth Jeshimoth— ²¹ʰall the cities of the plain and all the kingdom of Sihon king of the Amorites, who reigned in Heshbon, ⁱwhom Moses had struck ʲwith the princes of Midian: Evi, Rekem, Zur, Hur, and Reba, who *were* princes of Sihon dwelling in the country. ²²The children of Israel also killed with the sword ᵏBalaam the son of Beor, the soothsayer, among those who were killed by them. ²³And the border of the children of Reuben was the bank of the Jordan. This *was* the inheritance of the children of Reuben according to their families, the cities and their villages.

The Land of Gad

²⁴ˡMoses also had given *an inheritance* to the tribe of Gad, to the children of Gad according to their families. ²⁵ᵐTheir territory was Jazer, and all the cities of Gilead, ⁿand half the land of the Ammonites as far as Aroer, which *is* before ᵒRabbah, ²⁶and from Heshbon to Ramath Mizpah and Betonim, and from Mahanaim to the border of Debir, ²⁷and in the valley ᵖBeth Haram, Beth Nimrah, �q Succoth, and Zaphon, the rest of the kingdom of Sihon king of Heshbon, with the Jordan as *its* border, as far as the edge ʳof the Sea of Chinnereth, on the other side of the Jordan eastward. ²⁸This *is* the inheritance of the children of Gad according to their families, the cities and their villages.

Half the Tribe of Manasseh (East)

²⁹ˢMoses also had given *an inheritance* to half the tribe of Manasseh; it was for half the tribe of the children of Manasseh according to their families: ³⁰Their territory was from Mahanaim, all Bashan, all the kingdom of Og king of Bashan, and ᵗall the towns of Jair which are in Bashan, sixty cities; ³¹half of Gilead, and ᵘAshtaroth and Edrei, cities of the kingdom of Og in Bashan, *were* for the ᵛchildren of Machir the son of Manasseh, for half of the children of Machir according to their families.

³²These *are* the areas which Moses had distributed as an inheritance in the plains of Moab on the other side of the Jordan, by Jericho eastward. ³³ᵂBut to the tribe of Levi Moses had given no inheritance; the LORD God of Israel *was* their inheritance, ˣas He had said to them.

The Land Divided West of the Jordan

14 These *are the areas* which the children of Israel inherited in the land of Canaan, ᵃwhich Eleazar the priest, Joshua the son of Nun, and the heads of the fathers of the tribes of the children of Israel distributed as an inheritance to them. ²Their inheritance *was* ᵇby lot, as the LORD had commanded by the hand of Moses, for the nine tribes and the half-tribe. ³ᶜFor Moses had given the inheritance of the two tribes and the half-tribe on the other side of the Jordan; but to the Levites he had given no inheritance among them. ⁴For ᵈthe children of Joseph were two tribes: Manasseh and Ephraim. And they gave no part to the Levites in the land, except ᵉcities to dwell in, with their common-lands for their livestock and their property. ⁵ᶠAs the LORD had commanded Moses, so the children of Israel did; and they divided the land.

Caleb Inherits Hebron

⁶Then the children of Judah came to Joshua in Gilgal. And Caleb the son of Jephunneh the ᵍKenizzite said to him: "You know ʰthe word which the LORD said to Moses the man of God concerning ⁱyou

49:5–7). But later the Levites showed their faithfulness to the Lord (Ex. 32:25–28) and were promised a blessing (Deut. 33:8–11). Instead of land, the sacrifices of God would be their privileged inheritance.
13:22 Balaam the son of Beor. Balaam was a pagan fortune-teller who had been hired by Balak, king of Moab, to curse the Israelites in the wilderness (Num. 22–24).
14:6 Caleb . . . the Kenizzite. The Kenizzites were a non-Israelite group descended from Esau through Kenaz (Gen. 15:19; 36:11,15,42). It seems that Caleb, one of the most faithful to God of his time, was just a generation removed from a non-Israelite family. Although the Jews are indeed God's chosen people, He loves and honors anyone who obeys His commands.

13:14 ˣJosh. 13:33 **13:15** ʸNum. 34:14 **13:16** ᶻJosh. 12:2 ᵃNum. 21:28 ᵇNum. 21:30 **13:17** ᶜNum. 21:28, 30 **13:18** ᵈNum. 21:23 **13:19** ᵉNum. 32:37 ᶠNum. 32:38 **13:20** ᵍDeut. 3:17 **13:21** ʰDeut. 3:10 ⁱNum. 21:24 ʲNum. 31:8 **13:22** ᵏNum. 22:5; 31:8 **13:24** ˡNum. 34:14 **13:25** ᵐNum. 32:1, 35 ⁿJudg. 11:13, 15 ᵒDeut. 3:11 **13:27** ᵖNum. 32:36 qGen. 33:17 ʳNum. 34:11 **13:29** ˢNum. 34:14 **13:30** ᵗNum. 32:41 **13:31** ᵘJosh. 9:10; 12:4; 13:12 ᵛNum. 32:39, 40 **13:33** ᵂJosh. 13:14; 18:7 ˣNum. 18:20 **14:1** ᵃNum. 34:16–29 **14:2** ᵇNum. 26:55; 33:54; 34:13 **14:3** ᶜJosh. 13:8, 32, 33 **14:4** ᵈ2 Chr. 30:1 ᵉNum. 35:2–8 **14:5** ᶠJosh. 21:2 **14:6** ᵍNum. 32:11, 12 ʰNum. 14:24, 30 ⁱNum. 13:26

and me in Kadesh Barnea. 7I *was* forty
years old when Moses the servant of the
LORD [j]sent me from Kadesh Barnea to spy
out the land, and I brought back word to
him as *it was* in my heart. 8Nevertheless
[k]my brethren who went up with me made
the heart of the people melt, but I wholly
[l]followed the LORD my God. 9So Moses
swore on that day, saying, [m]'Surely the
land [n]where your foot has trodden shall
be your inheritance and your children's
forever, because you have wholly followed
the LORD my God.' 10And now, behold, the
LORD has kept me [o]alive, [p]as He said, these
forty-five years, ever since the LORD spoke
this word to Moses while Israel wandered
in the wilderness; and now, here I am this
day, eighty-five years old. 11[q]As yet I *am as*
strong this day as on the day that Moses
sent me; just as my strength *was* then, so
now *is* my strength for war, both [r]for going
out and for coming in. 12Now therefore,
give me this mountain of which the LORD
spoke in that day; for you heard in that day
how [s]the Anakim *were* there, and *that* the
cities *were* great *and* fortified. [t]It may be
that the LORD *will be* with me, and [u]I shall
be able to drive them out as the LORD said."
13And Joshua [v]blessed him, [w]and gave
Hebron to Caleb the son of Jephunneh as
an inheritance. 14[x]Hebron therefore became the inheritance of Caleb the son of
Jephunneh the Kenizzite to this day, because he [y]wholly followed the LORD God of
Israel. 15And [z]the name of Hebron formerly
was Kirjath Arba (*Arba was* the greatest
man among the Anakim).
[a]Then the land had rest from war.

The Land of Judah

15 So *this* was the lot of the tribe of the
children of Judah according to their
families:
[a]The border of Edom at the [b]Wilderness
of Zin southward *was* the extreme southern boundary. 2And their [c]southern border
began at the shore of the Salt Sea, from the
bay that faces southward. 3Then it went
out to the southern side of [d]the Ascent of
Akrabbim, passed along to Zin, ascended
on the south side of Kadesh Barnea, passed
along to Hezron, went up to Adar, and went
around to Karkaa. 4*From there* it passed
[e]toward Azmon and went out to the Brook
of Egypt; and the border ended at the sea.
This shall be your southern border.
5The east border *was* the Salt Sea as far
as the mouth of the Jordan.
And the [f]border on the northern quarter
began at the bay of the sea at the mouth
of the Jordan. 6The border went up to
[g]Beth Hoglah and passed north of Beth
Arabah; and the border went up [h]to the
stone of Bohan the son of Reuben. 7Then
the border went up toward [i]Debir from [j]the
Valley of Achor, and it turned northward
toward Gilgal, which *is* before the Ascent
of Adummim, which *is* on the south side
of the valley. The border continued toward
the waters of En Shemesh and ended at
[k]En Rogel. 8And the border went up [l]by the
Valley of the Son of Hinnom to the southern slope of the [m]Jebusite *city* (which *is*
Jerusalem). The border went up to the top
of the mountain that *lies* before the Valley
of Hinnom westward, which *is* at the end of
the Valley [n]of Rephaim* northward. 9Then
the border went around from the top of the
hill to [o]the fountain of the water of Nephtoah, and extended to the cities of Mount
Ephron. And the border went around [p]to
Baalah (which *is* [q]Kirjath Jearim). 10Then
the border turned westward from Baalah
to Mount Seir, passed along to the side
of Mount Jearim on the north (which *is*
Chesalon), went down to Beth Shemesh,
and passed on to [r]Timnah. 11And the border went out to the side of [s]Ekron northward. Then the border went around to
Shicron, passed along to Mount Baalah,
and extended to Jabneel; and the border
ended at the sea.
12The west border *was* [t]the coastline of
the Great Sea. This *is* the boundary of the
children of Judah all around according to
their families.

* **15:8** Literally *Giants*

14:10–11 Thankfulness—God's Word is as dependable as its author. His promise to Caleb waited forty-five years for fulfillment, but His blessing was sure. Caleb's view of all God's goodness to him resounded with thankfulness. Being silently thankful is important—God knows our hearts—but thankfulness should also be expressed with words of praise and glorification for the giver of all good things.

14:14 *he wholly followed the LORD God of Israel.* Caleb's wholehearted devotion to God was never a question, even in the wilderness. In the Bible, people are sometimes rewarded in this life for their faithfulness to God, but not always (Heb. 11:32–40). The believer's ultimate blessing will come in eternity. Those who set their hope on that promise will lose nothing, whatever they suffer in this life.

15:1–12 *the lot of the tribe.* The boundaries of Judah in southern Canaan are described in detail. These details may at first seem uninteresting, but they serve to underline the fact that this passage is talking about real people, in a real place, in a real time in history.

14:7 [j] Num. 13:6, 17; 14:6 **14:8** [k] Num. 13:31, 32 [l] Num. 14:24 **14:9** [m] Num. 14:23, 24 [n] Deut. 1:36 **14:10** [o] Num. 14:24, 30, 38 [p] Josh. 5:6 **14:11** [q] Deut. 34:7 [r] Deut. 31:2 **14:12** [s] Num. 13:28, 33 [t] Rom. 8:31 [u] Josh. 15:14 **14:13** [v] Josh. 22:6 [w] Josh. 10:37; 15:13 **14:14** [x] Josh. 21:12 [y] Josh. 14:8, 9 **14:15** [z] Gen. 23:2 [a] Josh. 11:23 **15:1** [a] Num. 34:3 [b] Num. 33:36 **15:2** [c] Num. 34:3, 4 **15:3** [d] Num. 34:4 **15:4** [e] Num. 34:5 **15:5** [f] Josh. 18:15–19 **15:6** [g] Josh. 18:19, 21 [h] Josh. 18:17 **15:7** [i] Josh. 13:26 [j] Josh. 7:26 [k] 2 Sam. 17:17 **15:8** [l] Josh. 18:16 [m] Judg. 1:21; 19:10 [n] Josh. 18:16 **15:9** [o] Josh. 18:15 [p] 1 Chr. 13:6 [q] Judg. 18:12 **15:10** [r] Gen. 38:13 **15:11** [s] Josh. 19:43 **15:12** [t] Num. 34:6, 7

Caleb Occupies Hebron and Debir

13uNow to Caleb the son of Jephunneh he gave a share among the children of vJudah, according to the commandment of the LORD to Joshua, namely, wKirjath Arba, which is Hebron (Arba was the father of Anak). 14Caleb drove out xthe three sons of Anak from there: ySheshai, Ahiman, and Talmai, the children of Anak. 15Then zhe went up from there to the inhabitants of Debir (formerly the name of Debir was Kirjath Sepher).

16aAnd Caleb said, "He who attacks Kirjath Sepher and takes it, to him I will give Achsah my daughter as wife." 17So bOthniel the cson of Kenaz, the brother of Caleb, took it; and he gave him dAchsah his daughter as wife. 18eNow it was so, when she came to him, that she persuaded him to ask her father for a field. So fshe dismounted from her donkey, and Caleb said to her, "What do you wish?" 19She answered, "Give me a gblessing; since you have given me land in the South, give me also springs of water." So he gave her the upper springs and the lower springs.

The Cities of Judah

20This was the inheritance of the tribe of the children of Judah according to their families:

21The cities at the limits of the tribe of the children of Judah, toward the border of Edom in the South, were Kabzeel, hEder, Jagur, 22Kinah, Dimonah, Adadah, 23Kedesh, Hazor, Ithnan, 24iZiph, Telem, Bealoth, 25Hazor, Hadattah, Kerioth, Hezron (which is Hazor), 26Amam, Shema, Moladah, 27Hazar Gaddah, Heshmon, Beth Pelet, 28Hazar Shual, jBeersheba, Bizjothjah, 29Baalah, Ijim, Ezem, 30Eltolad, Chesil, kHormah, 31lZiklag, Madmannah, Sansannah, 32Lebaoth, Shilhim, Ain, and mRimmon: all the cities are twenty-nine, with their villages.

33In the lowland: nEshtaol, Zorah, Ashnah, 34Zanoah, En Gannim, Tappuah, Enam, 35Jarmuth, oAdullam, Socoh, Azekah, 36Sharaim, Adithaim, Gederah, and Gederothaim: fourteen cities with their villages; 37Zenan, Hadashah, Migdal Gad,

38Dilean, Mizpah, pJoktheel, 39qLachish, Bozkath, rEglon, 40Cabbon, Lahmas,* Kithlish, 41Gederoth, Beth Dagon, Naamah, and Makkedah: sixteen cities with their villages; 42sLibnah, Ether, Ashan, 43Jiphtah, Ashnah, Nezib, 44Keilah, Achzib, and Mareshah: nine cities with their villages; 45Ekron, with its towns and villages; 46from Ekron to the sea, all that lay near tAshdod, with their villages; 47Ashdod with its towns and villages, Gaza with its towns and villages—as far as uthe Brook of Egypt and vthe Great Sea with its coastline.

48And in the mountain country: Shamir, Jattir, Sochoh, 49Dannah, Kirjath Sannah (which is Debir), 50Anab, Eshtemoh, Anim, 51wGoshen, Holon, and Giloh: eleven cities with their villages; 52Arab, Dumah, Eshean, 53Janum, Beth Tappuah, Aphekah, 54Humtah, xKirjath Arba (which is Hebron), and Zior: nine cities with their villages; 55yMaon, Carmel, Ziph, Juttah, 56Jezreel, Jokdeam, Zanoah, 57Kain, Gibeah, and Timnah: ten cities with their villages; 58Halhul, Beth Zur, Gedor, 59Maarath, Beth Anoth, and Eltekon: six cities with their villages; 60zKirjath Baal (which is Kirjath Jearim) and Rabbah: two cities with their villages.

61In the wilderness: Beth Arabah, Middin, Secacah, 62Nibshan, the City of Salt, and aEn Gedi: six cities with their villages.

63As for the Jebusites, the inhabitants of Jerusalem, bthe children of Judah could not drive them out; cbut the Jebusites dwell with the children of Judah at Jerusalem to this day.

Ephraim and West Manasseh

16 The lot fell to the children of Joseph from the Jordan, by Jericho, to the waters of Jericho on the east, to the awilderness that goes up from Jericho through the mountains to Bethel, 2then went out from bBethel to Luz,* passed along to the border of the Archites at Ataroth, 3and went down westward to the boundary of the Japhletites, cas far as the boundary of

---

* 15:40 Or Lahmam   * 16:2 Septuagint reads Bethel (that is, Luz).

15:13 Word of God—Caleb was not afraid to face the giants of Hebron because he knew God would be with him. In the same way, we as Christians need not fear the "giants" we face in spiritual battle. God will be with us also. His resources are more than sufficient to overcome the hosts of darkness which confront us in this world (1 John 4:4).

15:63 with the children of Judah. Judges 1:21 repeats this verse almost verbatim, except that it says Benjamin, not Judah, failed to drive the Jebusites out of Jerusalem. Jerusalem sat astride the boundary between Judah and Benjamin. In the early period, Jerusalem did not belong strictly to either tribe. The tribe of Judah later captured the city from the Jebusites (Judg. 1:8), and from then on it was considered a city of Judah.

15:13 u Josh. 14:13 v Num. 13:6 w Josh. 14:15
15:14 x Judg. 1:10, 20 y Num. 13:22 **15:15** z Judg. 1:11 **15:16** a Judg. 1:12 **15:17** b Judg. 1:13; 3:9 c Num. 32:12 d Judg. 1:12 **15:18** e Judg. 1:14 f Gen. 24:64 **15:19** g Gen. 33:11 **15:21** h Gen. 35:21 **15:24** i 1 Sam. 23:14 **15:28** i Gen. 21:31 **15:30** k Josh. 19:4 **15:31** l 1 Sam. 27:6; 30:1 **15:32** m Judg. 20:45, 47 **15:33** n Judg. 13:25; 16:31 **15:35** o 1 Sam. 22:1 **15:38** p 2 Kin. 14:7 **15:39** q 2 Kin. 14:19 r Josh. 10:3 **15:42** s Josh. 21:13 **15:46** t Josh. 11:22 **15:47** u Josh. 15:4 v Num. 34:6 **15:51** w Josh. 10:41; 11:16 **15:54** x Josh. 14:15 **15:55** y 1 Sam. 23:24, 25 **15:60** z Josh. 18:14 **15:62** a 1 Sam. 23:29 **15:63** b 2 Sam. 5:6 c Judg. 1:21 **16:1** a Josh. 8:15; 18:12 **16:2** b Josh. 18:13 **16:3** c 2 Chr. 8:5

Lower Beth Horon to dGezer; and it ended at the sea. 4eSo the children of Joseph, Manasseh and Ephraim, took their inheritance.

The Land of Ephraim

5fThe border of the children of Ephraim, according to their families, was *thus:* The border of their inheritance on the east side was gAtaroth Addar has far as Upper Beth Horon.

6And the border went out toward the sea on the north side of iMichmethath; then the border went around eastward to Taanath Shiloh, and passed by it on the east of Janohah. 7Then it went down from Janohah to Ataroth and Naarah,* reached to Jericho, and came out at the Jordan.

8The border went out from jTappuah westward to the kBrook Kanah, and it ended at the sea. This *was* the inheritance of the tribe of the children of Ephraim according to their families. 9lThe separate cities for the children of Ephraim *were* among the inheritance of the children of Manasseh, all the cities with their villages.

10mAnd they did not drive out the Canaanites who dwelt in Gezer; but the Canaanites dwell among the Ephraimites to this day and have become forced laborers.

The Other Half-Tribe of Manasseh (West)

17 There was also a lot for the tribe of Manasseh, for he *was* the afirstborn of Joseph: *namely* for bMachir the firstborn of Manasseh, the father of Gilead, because he was a man of war; therefore he was given cGilead and Bashan. 2And there was *a lot* for dthe rest of the children of Manasseh according to their families: efor the children of Abiezer,* the children of Helek, fthe children of Asriel, the children of Shechem, gthe children of Hepher, and the children of Shemida; these *were* the male children of Manasseh the son of Joseph according to their families.

3But hZelophehad the son of Hepher, the son of Gilead, the son of Machir, the son of Manasseh, had no sons, but only daughters. And these *are* the names of his daughters: Mahlah, Noah, Hoglah, Milcah, and Tirzah. 4And they came near before iEleazar the priest, before Joshua the son of Nun, and before the rulers, saying, j"The

LORD commanded Moses to give us an inheritance among our brothers." Therefore, according to the commandment of the LORD, he gave them an inheritance among their father's brothers. 5Ten shares fell to kManasseh, besides the land of Gilead and Bashan, which *were* on the other side of the Jordan, 6because the daughters of Manasseh received an inheritance among his sons; and the rest of Manasseh's sons had the land of Gilead.

7And the territory of Manasseh was from Asher to lMichmethath, that *lies* east of Shechem; and the border went along south to the inhabitants of En Tappuah. 8Manasseh had the land of Tappuah, but mTappuah on the border of Manasseh *belonged* to the children of Ephraim. 9And the border descended to the Brook Kanah, southward to the brook. nThese cities of Ephraim *are* among the cities of Manasseh. The border of Manasseh *was* on the north side of the brook; and it ended at the sea.

10Southward *it was* Ephraim's, northward *it was* Manasseh's, and the sea was its border. Manasseh's territory was adjoining Asher on the north and Issachar on the east. 11And in Issachar and in Asher, oManasseh had pBeth Shean and its towns, Ibleam and its towns, the inhabitants of Dor and its towns, the inhabitants of En Dor and its towns, the inhabitants of Taanach and its towns, and the inhabitants of Megiddo and its towns—three hilly regions. 12Yet qthe children of Manasseh could not drive out the *inhabitants of* those cities, but the Canaanites were determined to dwell in that land. 13And it happened, when the children of Israel grew strong, that they put the Canaanites to rforced labor, but did not utterly drive them out.

More Land for Ephraim and Manasseh

14sThen the children of Joseph spoke to Joshua, saying, "Why have you given us *only* tone lot and one share to inherit, since we *are* ua great people, inasmuch as the LORD has blessed us until now?"

15So Joshua answered them, "If you *are* a great people, *then* go up to the forest *country* and clear a place for yourself

---

* **16:7** Or *Naaran* (compare 1 Chronicles 7:28)
* **17:2** Called *Jeezer* in Numbers 26:30

17:3–6 *Zelophehad ... had no sons but only daughters.* This account serves to show again the theme of the Book of Joshua—that God is faithful to keep His promises. Joshua also was faithful to carry out the commands of God concerning His promise through Moses for the daughters of Zelophehad (Num. 26:33; 27:1–11).

16:3 d 1 Kin. 9:15   **16:4** e Josh. 17:14   **16:5** f Judg. 1:29
g Josh. 18:13   h 2 Chr. 8:5   **16:6** i Josh. 17:7   **16:8** j Josh.
17:8   k Josh. 17:9   **16:9** l Josh. 17:9   **16:10** m Judg.
1:29   **17:1** d Gen. 41:51; 46:20; 48:18   b Gen. 50:23
c Deut. 3:15   **17:2** d Num. 26:29–33   e 1 Chr. 7:18   f Num.
26:31   g Num. 26:32   **17:3** h Num. 26:33; 27:1; 36:2
17:4 i Josh. 14:1   j Num. 27:2–11   **17:5** k Josh. 22:7
17:7 l Josh. 16:6   **17:8** m Josh. 16:8   **17:9** n Josh. 16:9
17:11 o 1 Chr. 7:29   p 1 Kin. 4:12   **17:12** q Judg. 1:19, 27,
28   **17:13** r Josh. 16:10   **17:14** s Josh. 16:4   t Gen. 48:22
u Gen. 48:19

there in the land of the Perizzites and the
giants, since the mountains of Ephraim are
too confined for you."
16But the children of Joseph said, "The
mountain country is not enough for us; and
all the Canaanites who dwell in the land
of the valley have [v]chariots of iron, *both*
those who *are* of Beth Shean and its towns
and *those* who *are* [w]of the Valley of Jezreel."
17And Joshua spoke to the house of
Joseph—to Ephraim and Manasseh—
saying, "You *are* a great people and have
great power; you shall not have *only* one
lot, 18but the mountain country shall be
yours. Although it *is* wooded, you shall
cut it down, and its farthest extent shall be
yours; for you shall drive out the Canaanites, [x]though they have iron chariots *and*
are strong."

The Remainder of the Land Divided

18 Now the whole congregation of the
children of Israel assembled togeth-
er [a]at Shiloh, and [b]set up the tabernacle of
meeting there. And the land was subdued
before them. 2But there remained among
the children of Israel seven tribes which
had not yet received their inheritance.
3Then Joshua said to the children of Israel: [c]"How long will you neglect to go and
possess the land which the LORD God of
your fathers has given you? 4Pick out from
among you three men for *each* tribe, and
I will send them; they shall rise and go
through the land, survey it according to
their inheritance, and come *back* to me.
5And they shall divide it into seven parts.
[d]Judah shall remain in their territory on
the south, and the [e]house of Joseph shall
remain in their territory on the north. 6You
shall therefore survey the land in seven
parts and bring *the survey* here to me,
[f]that I may cast lots for you here before the
LORD our God. 7[g]But the Levites have no
part among you, for the priesthood of the
LORD *is* their inheritance. [h]And Gad, Reuben, and half the tribe of Manasseh have
received their inheritance beyond the Jordan on the east, which Moses the servant
of the LORD gave them."
8Then the men arose to go away; and
Joshua charged those who went to survey the land, saying, "Go, walk [i]through
the land, survey it, and come back to me,
that I may cast lots for you here before the
LORD in Shiloh." 9So the men went, passed
through the land, and wrote the survey in
a book in seven parts by cities; and they
came to Joshua at the camp in Shiloh.
10Then Joshua cast [j]lots for them in Shiloh
before the LORD, and there [k]Joshua divided
the land to the children of Israel according
to their divisions.

The Land of Benjamin

11[l]Now the lot of the tribe of the children of Benjamin came up according to
their families, and the territory of their lot
came out between the children of Judah
and the children of Joseph. 12[m]Their border on the north side began at the Jordan,
and the border went up to the side of Jericho on the north, and went up through the
mountains westward; it ended at the Wilderness of Beth Aven. 13The border went
over from there toward Luz, to the side of
Luz [n](which *is* Bethel) southward; and the
border descended to Ataroth Addar, near
the hill that *lies* on the south side [o]of Lower
Beth Horon.
14Then the border extended around the
west side to the south, from the hill that *lies*
before Beth Horon southward; and it ended
at [p]Kirjath Baal (which *is* Kirjath Jearim),
a city of the children of Judah. This *was*
the west side.
15The south side *began* at the end of
Kirjath Jearim, and the border extended
on the west and went out to [q]the spring of
the waters of Nephtoah. 16Then the border
came down to the end of the mountain that
lies before [r]the Valley of the Son of Hinnom, which *is* in the Valley of the Rephaim* on the north, descended to the Valley
of Hinnom, to the side of the Jebusite *city*
on the south, and descended to [s]En Rogel.
17And it went around from the north, went
out to En Shemesh, and extended toward
Geliloth, which is before the Ascent of
Adummim, and descended to [t]the stone of
Bohan the son of Reuben. 18Then it passed

* **18:16** Literally *Giants*

18:1 *Shiloh.* Shiloh was about 15 miles northwest of Jericho. Here the Israelites set up the tent of meeting (Ex. 26). This remained an important religious center for several hundred years (Judg. 18:31; 1 Sam. 1:9) until the taking of Jerusalem in David's day.

18:3 Unfaithfulness—The seven tribes yet to be settled seemed to have little desire to receive their inheritance and were rebuked for their half-heartedness. They had easily defeated the Canaanites, but they had not followed up on their victories and taken possession of all the land. This laziness was disobedience to God and showed lack of faith in His promises. In our own lives it is fatally easy to begin a work that God sets before us, and then slack off in our faithfulness before it is finished. The believer's inheritance is reserved in heaven, and cannot be bought by any work of our own. However, God requests holiness of living on our part, and His commands must be obeyed.

17:16 [v]Judg. 1:19; 4:3 [w]1 Kin. 4:12 **17:18** [x]Deut. 20:1 **18:1** [a]Jer. 7:12 [b]Judg. 18:31 **18:3** [c]Judg. 18:9 **18:5** [d]Josh. 15:1 [e]Josh. 16:1—17:18 **18:6** [f]Josh. 14:2; 18:10 **18:7** [g]Josh. 13:33 [h]Josh. 13:8 **18:8** [i]Gen. 13:17 **18:10** [j]Acts 13:19 [k]Num. 34:16–29 **18:11** [l]Judg. 1:21 **18:12** [m]Josh. 16:1 **18:13** [n]Gen. 28:19 [o]Josh. 16:3 **18:14** [p]Josh. 15:9 **18:15** [q]Josh. 15:9 **18:16** [r]Josh. 15:8 [s]Josh. 15:7 **18:17** [t]Josh. 15:6

along toward the north side of Arabah,*
and went down to Arabah. 19And the border passed along to the north side of Beth
Hoglah; then the border ended at the north
bay at the [u]Salt Sea, at the south end of the
Jordan. This *was* the southern boundary.
20The Jordan was its border on the east
side. This *was* the inheritance of the children of Benjamin, according to its boundaries all around, according to their families.
21Now the cities of the tribe of the children of Benjamin, according to their families, were Jericho, Beth Hoglah, Emek
Keziz, 22Beth Arabah, Zemaraim, Bethel,
23Avim, Parah, Ophrah, 24Chephar Haam-
moni, Ophni, and Gaba: twelve cities
with their villages; 25[v]Gibeon, [w]Ramah,
Beeroth, 26Mizpah, Chephirah, Mozah,
27Rekem, Irpeel, Taralah, 28Zelah, Eleph,
[x]Jebus (which *is* Jerusalem), Gibeath, *and*
Kirjath: fourteen cities with their villages.
This was the inheritance of the children of
Benjamin according to their families.

Simeon's Inheritance with Judah

19 The [a]second lot came out for Simeon,
for the tribe of the children of Simeon according to their families. [b]And their
inheritance was within the inheritance of
the children of Judah. 2[c]They had in their
inheritance Beersheba (Sheba), Moladah,
3Hazar Shual, Balah, Ezem, 4Eltolad,
Bethul, Hormah, 5Ziklag, Beth Marcaboth,
Hazar Susah, 6Beth Lebaoth, and Sha-
ruhen: thirteen cities and their villages;
7Ain, Rimmon, Ether, and Ashan: four cities and their villages; 8and all the villages
that *were* all around these cities as far as
Baalath Beer, [d]Ramah of the South. This
was the inheritance of the tribe of the children of Simeon according to their families.
9The inheritance of the children of Simeon *was included* in the share of the children
of Judah, for the share of the children of Judah was too much for them. [e]Therefore the
children of Simeon had *their* inheritance
within the inheritance of that people.

The Land of Zebulun

10The third lot came out for the children
of Zebulun according to their families, and
the border of their inheritance was as far
as Sarid. 11[f]Their border went toward the
west and to Maralah, went to Dabbasheth,
and extended along the brook that is [g]east
of Jokneam. 12Then from Sarid it went
eastward toward the sunrise along the border of Chisloth Tabor, and went out toward
[h]Daberath, bypassing Japhia. 13And from
there it passed along on the east of [i]Gath
Hepher, toward Eth Kazin, and extended to
Rimmon, which borders on Neah. 14Then
the border went around it on the north side
of Hannathon, and it ended in the Valley of
Jiphthah El. 15Included were Kattath, Na-
hallal, Shimron, Idalah, and Bethlehem:
twelve cities with their villages. 16This *was*
the inheritance of the children of Zebulun
according to their families, these cities
with their villages.

The Land of Issachar

17The fourth lot came out to Issachar,
for the children of Issachar according to
their families. 18And their territory went to
Jezreel, and *included* Chesulloth, Shunem,
19Haphraim, Shion, Anaharath, 20Rabbith,
Kishion, Abez, 21Remeth, En Gannim, En
Haddah, and Beth Pazzez. 22And the border reached to Tabor, Shahazimah, and
[j]Beth Shemesh; their border ended at the
Jordan: sixteen cities with their villages.
23This *was* the inheritance of the tribe of
the children of Issachar according to their
families, the cities and their villages.

The Land of Asher

24[k]The fifth lot came out for the tribe of
the children of Asher according to their
families. 25And their territory included
Helkath, Hali, Beten, Achshaph, 26Alam-
melech, Amad, and Mishal; it reached to
[l]Mount Carmel westward, along *the Brook*
Shihor Libnath. 27It turned toward the sunrise to Beth Dagon; and it reached to Zebulun and to the Valley of Jiphthah El, then
northward beyond Beth Emek and Neiel,
bypassing [m]Cabul *which was* on the left,
28including Ebron,* Rehob, Hammon, and
Kanah, [n]as far as Greater Sidon. 29And the
border turned to Ramah and to the fortified city of Tyre; then the border turned to
Hosah, and ended at the sea by the region
of [o]Achzib. 30Also Ummah, Aphek, and Rehob *were included:* twenty-two cities with
their villages. 31This *was* the inheritance
of the tribe of the children of Asher according to their families, these cities with their
villages.

The Land of Naphtali

32[p]The sixth lot came out to the children
of Naphtali, for the children of Naphtali
according to their families. 33And their
border began at Heleph, enclosing the territory from the terebinth tree in Zaanan-
nim, Adami Nekeb, and Jabneel, as far as
Lakkum; it ended at the Jordan. 34[q]From
Heleph the border extended westward to

* **18:18** Or *Beth Arabah* (compare 15:6 and 18:22)
* **19:28** Following Masoretic Text, Targum, and Vulgate; a few Hebrew manuscripts read *Abdon* (compare 21:30 and 1 Chronicles 6:74).

18:19 [u] Josh. 15:2, 5 **18:25** [v] 1 Kin. 3:4, 5 [w] Jer. 31:15 **18:28** [x] Josh. 15:8, 63 **19:1** [a] Judg. 1:3 [b] Josh. 19:9 **19:2** [c] 1 Chr. 4:28 **19:8** [d] 1 Sam. 30:27 **19:9** [e] Josh. 19:1 **19:11** [f] Gen. 49:13 [g] Josh. 12:22 **19:12** [h] 1 Chr. 6:72

19:13 [i] 2 Kin. 14:25 **19:22** [j] Josh. 15:10 **19:24** [k] Judg. 1:31, 32 **19:26** [l] Jer. 46:18 **19:27** [m] 1 Kin. 9:13 **19:28** [n] Judg. 1:31 **19:29** [o] Judg. 1:31 **19:32** [p] Judg. 1:33 **19:34** [q] Deut. 33:23

Aznoth Tabor, and went out from there toward Hukkok; it adjoined Zebulun on the south side and Asher on the west side, and ended at Judah by the Jordan toward the sunrise. ³⁵And the fortified cities *are* Ziddim, Zer, Hammath, Rakkath, Chinnereth, ³⁶Adamah, Ramah, Hazor, ³⁷ʳKedesh, Edrei, En Hazor, ³⁸Iron, Migdal El, Horem, Beth Anath, and Beth Shemesh: nineteen cities with their villages. ³⁹This *was* the inheritance of the tribe of the children of Naphtali according to their families, the cities and their villages.

The Land of Dan

⁴⁰ˢThe seventh lot came out for the tribe of the children of Dan according to their families. ⁴¹And the territory of their inheritance was Zorah, ᵗEshtaol, Ir Shemesh, ⁴²ᵘShaalabbin, ᵛAijalon, Jethlah, ⁴³Elon, Timnah, ʷEkron, ⁴⁴Eltekeh, Gibbethon, Baalath, ⁴⁵Jehud, Bene Berak, Gath Rimmon, ⁴⁶Me Jarkon, and Rakkon, with the region near Joppa. ⁴⁷And the ˣborder of the children of Dan went beyond these, because the children of Dan went up to fight against Leshem and took it; and they struck it with the edge of the sword, took possession of it, and dwelt in it. They called Leshem, ʸDan, after the name of Dan their father. ⁴⁸This *is* the inheritance of the tribe of the children of Dan according to their families, these cities with their villages.

Joshua's Inheritance

⁴⁹When they had made an end of dividing the land as an inheritance according to their borders, the children of Israel gave an inheritance among them to Joshua the son of Nun. ⁵⁰According to the word of the LORD they gave him the city which he asked for, ᶻTimnath ᵃSerah in the mountains of Ephraim; and he built the city and dwelt in it.

⁵¹ᵇThese *were* the inheritances which Eleazar the priest, Joshua the son of Nun, and the heads of the fathers of the tribes of the children of Israel divided as an inheritance by lot ᶜin Shiloh before the LORD, at the door of the tabernacle of meeting. So they made an end of dividing the country.

The Cities of Refuge

20 The LORD also spoke to Joshua, saying, ²"Speak to the children of Israel, saying: ᵃ'Appoint for yourselves cities of refuge, of which I spoke to you through Moses, ³that the slayer who kills a person accidentally *or* unintentionally may flee there; and they shall be your refuge from the avenger of blood. ⁴And when he flees to one of those cities, and stands at the entrance of the gate of the city, and declares his case in the hearing of the elders of that city, they shall take him into the city as one of them, and give him a place, that he may dwell among them. ⁵ᵇThen if the avenger of blood pursues him, they shall not deliver the slayer into his hand, because he struck his neighbor unintentionally, but did not hate him beforehand. ⁶And he shall dwell in that city ᶜuntil he stands before the congregation for judgment, *and* until the death of the one who is high priest in those days. Then the slayer may return and come to his own city and his own house, to the city from which he fled.'"

⁷So they appointed ᵈKedesh in Galilee, in the mountains of Naphtali, ᵉShechem in the mountains of Ephraim, and ᶠKirjath Arba (which *is* Hebron) in ᵍthe mountains of Judah. ⁸And on the other side of the Jordan, by Jericho eastward, they assigned ʰBezer in the wilderness on the plain, from the tribe of Reuben, ⁱRamoth in Gilead, from the tribe of Gad, and ʲGolan in Bashan, from the tribe of Manasseh. ⁹ᵏThese were the cities appointed for all the children of Israel and for the stranger who dwelt among them, that whoever killed a person accidentally might flee there, and not die by the hand of the avenger of blood ˡuntil he stood before the congregation.

Cities of the Levites

21 Then the heads of the fathers' *houses* of the ᵃLevites came near to ᵇEleazar the priest, to Joshua the son of Nun, and

---

19:50 Commandments—The account of the distribution of the land began with the recognition of Caleb's faithfulness to God. The conclusion recognizes Joshua as one who also believed God. Joshua's extreme service and faithfulness was rewarded by the Lord's command. When we delight to obey the word of the Lord, He also delights in giving us the desires of our hearts (Ps. 37:4).

20:3 accidentally. God's laws made allowance for motive and intent, just as modern criminal codes distinguish unintentional killing from murder. The avenger of blood was a close relative who was the "protector of family rights." (Ruth 3:13 and 4:1 translate the word used here for "avenger of blood" as "close relative.") God did not give license to take revenge however. He has clearly reserved that task for Himself alone (Deut. 32:35; Is. 34:8; Rom. 12:19). God's provision of these cities of refuge put a limit on private acts of vengeance.

20:7–8 appointed. The cities of refuge were evenly distributed so that none was more than a day's journey from any part of Israel's land.

19:37 ʳ Josh. 20:7 **19:40** ˢ Judg. 1:34–36 **19:41** ᵗ Josh. 15:33 **19:42** ᵘ Judg. 1:35 ᵛ Josh. 10:12; 21:24 **19:43** ʷ Judg. 1:18 **19:47** ˣ Judg. 18 ʸ Judg. 18:29 **19:50** ᶻ Josh. 24:30 ᵃ 1 Chr. 7:24 **19:51** ᵇ Num. 34:17 ᶜ Josh. 18:1, 10 **20:2** ᵃ Num. 35:6–34 **20:5** ᵇ Num. 35:12 **20:6** ᶜ Num. 35:12, 24, 25 **20:7** ᵈ 1 Chr. 6:76 ᵉ Josh. 21:21 ᶠ Josh. 14:15; 21:11, 13 ᵍ Luke 1:39 **20:8** ʰ Deut. 4:43 ⁱ Josh. 21:38 ʲ Josh. 21:27 **20:9** ᵏ Num. 35:15 ˡ Josh. 20:6 **21:1** ᵃ Num. 35:1–8 ᵇ Josh. 14:1; 17:4

to the heads of the fathers' *houses* of the tribes of the children of Israel. ²And they spoke to them at ᶜShiloh in the land of Canaan, saying, ᵈ"The LORD commanded through Moses to give us cities to dwell in, with their common-lands for our livestock." ³So the children of Israel gave to the Levites from their inheritance, at the commandment of the LORD, these cities and their common-lands:

⁴Now the lot came out for the families of the Kohathites. And ᵉthe children of Aaron the priest, *who were* of the Levites, ᶠhad thirteen cities by lot from the tribe of Judah, from the tribe of Simeon, and from the tribe of Benjamin. ⁵ᵍThe rest of the children of Kohath had ten cities by lot from the families of the tribe of Ephraim, from the tribe of Dan, and from the half-tribe of Manasseh.

⁶And ʰthe children of Gershon had thirteen cities by lot from the families of the tribe of Issachar, from the tribe of Asher, from the tribe of Naphtali, and from the half-tribe of Manasseh in Bashan.

⁷ⁱThe children of Merari according to their families had twelve cities from the tribe of Reuben, from the tribe of Gad, and from the tribe of Zebulun.

⁸ʲAnd the children of Israel gave these cities with their common-lands by lot to the Levites, ᵏas the LORD had commanded by the hand of Moses.

⁹So they gave from the tribe of the children of Judah and from the tribe of the children of Simeon these cities which are designated by name, ¹⁰which were for the children of Aaron, one of the families of the Kohathites, *who were* of the children of Levi; for the lot was theirs first. ¹¹ˡAnd they gave them Kirjath Arba (*Arba was* the father of ᵐAnak), ⁿwhich *is* Hebron, in the mountains of Judah, with the common-land surrounding it. ¹²But ᵒthe fields of the city and its villages they gave to Caleb the son of Jephunneh as his possession.

¹³Thus ᵖto the children of Aaron the priest they gave ᑫHebron with its common-land (a city of refuge for the slayer), ʳLibnah with its common-land, ¹⁴ˢJattir with its common-land, ᵗEshtemoa with its common-land, ¹⁵ᵘHolon with its common-land, ᵛDebir with its common-land, ¹⁶ʷAin with its common-land, ˣJuttah with its common-land, and ʸBeth Shemesh with its common-land: nine cities from those two tribes; ¹⁷and from the tribe of

Benjamin, ᶻGibeon with its common-land, ᵃGeba with its common-land, ¹⁸Anathoth with its common-land, and ᵇAlmon with its common-land: four cities. ¹⁹All the cities of the children of Aaron, the priests, *were* thirteen cities with their common-lands.

²⁰ᶜAnd the families of the children of Kohath, the Levites, the rest of the children of Kohath, even they had the cities of their lot from the tribe of Ephraim. ²¹For they gave them ᵈShechem with its common-land in the mountains of Ephraim (a city of refuge for the slayer), ᵉGezer with its common-land, ²²Kibzaim with its common-land, and Beth Horon with its common-land: four cities; ²³and from the tribe of Dan, Eltekeh with its common-land, Gibbethon with its common-land, ²⁴ᶠAijalon with its common-land, *and* Gath Rimmon with its common-land: four cities; ²⁵and from the half-tribe of Manasseh, Tanach with its common-land and Gath Rimmon with its common-land: two cities. ²⁶All the ten cities with their common-lands were for the rest of the families of the children of Kohath.

²⁷ᵍAlso to the children of Gershon, of the families of the Levites, from the *other* half-tribe of Manasseh, *they gave* ʰGolan in Bashan with its common-land (a city of refuge for the slayer), and Be Eshterah with its common-land: two cities; ²⁸and from the tribe of Issachar, Kishion with its common-land, Daberath with its common-land, ²⁹Jarmuth with its common-land, *and* En Gannim with its common-land: four cities; ³⁰and from the tribe of Asher, Mishal with its common-land, Abdon with its common-land, ³¹Helkath with its common-land, and Rehob with its common-land: four cities; ³²and from the tribe of Naphtali, ⁱKedesh in Galilee with its common-land (a city of refuge for the slayer), Hammoth Dor with its common-land, and Kartan with its common-land: three cities. ³³All the cities of the Gershonites according to their families *were* thirteen cities with their common-lands.

³⁴ʲAnd to the families of the children of Merari, the rest of the Levites, from the tribe of Zebulun, Jokneam with its common-land, Kartah with its common-land, ³⁵Dimnah with its common-land, *and* Nahalal with its common-land: four cities; ³⁶and from the tribe of Reuben, ᵏBezer with its common-land, Jahaz with its common-land, ³⁷Kedemoth with

---

21:4–8 by lot. Even though this seems as if it was done by chance, we know God was in control of every aspect of the inheritance process.

21:2 ᶜ Josh. 18:1 ᵈ Num. 35:2 21:4 ᵉ Josh. 21:8, 19 ᶠ Josh. 19:51 21:5 ᵍ Josh. 21:20 21:6 ʰ Josh. 21:27 21:7 ⁱ Josh. 21:34 21:8 ʲ Josh. 21:3 ᵏ Num. 35:2 21:11 ˡ 1 Chr. 6:55 ᵐ Josh. 14:15; 15:13, 14 ⁿ Josh. 20:7 21:12 ᵒ Josh.

14:14 21:13 ᵖ 1 Chr. 6:57 ᑫ Josh. 15:54; 20:2, 7 ʳ Josh. 15:42 21:14 ˢ Josh. 15:48 ᵗ Josh. 15:50 21:15 ᵘ 1 Chr. 6:58 ᵛ Josh. 15:49 21:16 ʷ 1 Chr. 6:59 ˣ Josh. 15:55 ʸ Josh. 15:10 21:17 ᶻ Josh. 18:25 ᵃ Josh. 18:24 21:18 ᵇ 1 Chr. 6:60 21:20 ᶜ 1 Chr. 6:66 21:21 ᵈ Josh. 20:7 ᵉ Judg. 1:29 21:24 ᶠ Josh. 10:12 21:27 ᵍ 1 Chr. 6:71 ʰ Josh. 20:8 21:32 ⁱ Josh. 20:7 21:34 ʲ 1 Chr. 6:77–81 21:36 ᵏ Josh. 20:8

its common-land, and Mephaath with its common-land: four cities;* ³⁸and from the tribe of Gad, *Ramoth in Gilead with its common-land (a city of refuge for the slayer), Mahanaim with its common-land, ³⁹Heshbon with its common-land, *and* Jazer with its common-land: four cities in all. ⁴⁰So all the cities for the children of Merari according to their families, the rest of the families of the Levites, were *by* their lot twelve cities. ⁴¹ᵐAll the cities of the Levites within the possession of the children of Israel *were* forty-eight cities with their common-lands. ⁴²Every one of these cities had its common-land surrounding it; thus *were* all these cities.

The Promise Fulfilled

⁴³So the LORD gave to Israel ⁿall the land of which He had sworn to give to their fathers, and they ᵒtook possession of it and dwelt in it. ⁴⁴ᵖThe LORD gave them ᑫrest all around, according to all that He had sworn to their fathers. And ʳnot a man of all their enemies stood against them; the LORD delivered all their enemies into their hand. ⁴⁵ˢNot a word failed of any good thing which the LORD had spoken to the house of Israel. All came to pass.

Eastern Tribes Return to Their Lands

22 Then Joshua called the Reubenites, the Gadites, and half the tribe of Manasseh, ²and said to them: "You have kept ᵃall that Moses the servant of the LORD commanded you, ᵇand have obeyed my voice in all that I commanded you. ³You have not left your brethren these many days, up to this day, but have kept the charge of the commandment of the LORD your God. ⁴And now the LORD your God has given ᶜrest to your brethren, as He promised them; now therefore, return and go to your tents *and* to the land of your possession, ᵈwhich the LORD gave you on the other side of the Jordan. ⁵But ᵉtake careful heed to do the commandment and the law which Moses

the servant of the LORD commanded you, ᶠto love the LORD your God, to walk in all His ways, to keep His commandments, to hold fast to Him, and to serve Him with all your heart and with all your soul." ⁶So Joshua ᵍblessed them and sent them away, and they went to their tents.

⁷Now to half the tribe of Manasseh Moses had given a possession in Bashan, ʰbut to the *other* half of it Joshua gave *a possession* among their brethren on this side of the Jordan, westward. And indeed, when Joshua sent them away to their tents, he blessed them, ⁸and spoke to them, saying, "Return with much riches to your tents, with very much livestock, with silver, with gold, with bronze, with iron, and with very much clothing. ⁱDivide the spoil of your enemies with your brethren."

⁹So the children of Reuben, the children of Gad, and half the tribe of Manasseh returned, and departed from the children of Israel at Shiloh, which *is* in the land of Canaan, to go to ʲthe country of Gilead, to the land of their possession, which they had obtained according to the word of the LORD by the hand of Moses.

An Altar by the Jordan

¹⁰And when they came to the region of the Jordan which *is* in the land of Canaan, the children of Reuben, the children of Gad, and half the tribe of Manasseh built an altar there by the Jordan—a great, impressive altar. ¹¹Now the children of Israel ᵏheard *someone* say, "Behold, the children of Reuben, the children of Gad, and half the tribe of Manasseh have built an altar on the frontier of the land of Canaan, in the region of the Jordan—on the children of Israel's side." ¹²And when the children of Israel heard *of it,* ˡthe whole congregation of the children of Israel gathered together at Shiloh to go to war against them. ¹³Then the children of Israel ᵐsent ⁿPhinehas the son of Eleazar the priest

* 21:37 Following Septuagint and Vulgate (compare 1 Chronicles 6:78, 79); Masoretic Text, Bomberg, and Targum omit verses 36 and 37.

21:43–45 which He had sworn. Again we see the nature of our God not only did He keep every promise, He also guaranteed that His people would have rest.

22:5 Perseverance—Past victories do not lessen the responsibility for present faithfulness. Joshua impressed upon the people, especially the tribes of Reuben, Gad, and Manasseh (because they would be living in isolation from the rest of Israel), the urgent need to continue to zealously serve God. Our zeal for the Lord cannot cease because a crisis has passed. There is no certificate of discharge from the army of Christ.

22:11–12 have built an altar. The Bible does not reveal why this altar was built until the events have developed into a full-blown crisis. God had

commanded Israel not to offer burnt offerings or sacrifices at any location except the tabernacle (Lev. 17:8–9) and not to worship other gods (Deut. 13:12–15). The punishment for violating both laws was death. This was why Israel gathered together to go to war against the three apparently erring tribes.

21:38 ʲJosh. 20:8　**21:41** ᵐNum. 35:7　**21:43** ⁿGen. 12:7; 26:3, 4; 28:4, 13, 14　ᵒNum. 33:53　**21:44** ᵖDeut. 7:23, 24　ᑫJosh. 1:13, 15; 11:23　ʳDeut. 7:24　**21:45** ˢJosh. 23:14　**22:2** ᵃNum. 32:20–22　ᵇJosh. 1:12–18　**22:4** ᶜJosh. 21:44　ᵈNum. 32:33　**22:5** ᵉDeut. 6:6, 17; 11:22　ᶠDeut. 10:12; 11:13, 22　**22:6** ᵍ2 Sam. 6:18　**22:7** ʰJosh. 17:1–13　**22:8** ⁱ1 Sam. 30:24　**22:9** ʲNum. 32:1, 26, 29　**22:11** ᵏJudg. 20:12, 13　**22:12** ˡJosh. 18:1　**22:13** ᵐDeut. 13:14　ⁿEx. 6:25

to the children of Reuben, to the children of Gad, and to half the tribe of Manasseh, into the land of Gilead, [14]and with him ten rulers, one ruler each from the chief house of every tribe of Israel; and [o]each one *was* the head of the house of his father among the divisions* of Israel. [15]Then they came to the children of Reuben, to the children of Gad, and to half the tribe of Manasseh, to the land of Gilead, and they spoke with them, saying, [16]"Thus says the whole congregation of the LORD: 'What [p]treachery *is* this that you have committed against the God of Israel, to turn away this day from following the LORD, in that you have built for yourselves an altar, [q]that you might rebel this day against the LORD? [17]*Is* the iniquity [r]of Peor not enough for us, from which we are not cleansed till this day, although there was a plague in the congregation of the LORD, [18]but that you must turn away this day from following the LORD? And it shall be, if you rebel today against the LORD, that tomorrow [s]He will be angry with the whole congregation of Israel. [19]Nevertheless, if the land of your possession *is* unclean, *then* cross over to the land of the possession of the LORD, [t]where the LORD's tabernacle stands, and take possession among us; but do not rebel against the LORD, nor rebel against us, by building yourselves an altar besides the altar of the LORD our God. [20u]Did not Achan the son of Zerah commit a trespass in the accursed thing, and wrath fell on all the congregation of Israel? And that man did not perish alone in his iniquity.'"

[21]Then the children of Reuben, the children of Gad, and half the tribe of Manasseh answered and said to the heads of the divisions* of Israel: [22]"The LORD [v]God of gods, the LORD God of gods, He [w]knows, and let Israel itself know—if *it is* in rebellion, or if in treachery against the LORD, do not save us this day. [23]If we have built ourselves an altar to turn from following the LORD, or if to offer on it burnt offerings or grain offerings, or if to offer peace offerings on it, let the LORD Himself [x]require *an account.* [24]But in fact we have done it for fear, for a reason, saying, 'In time to come your

descendants may speak to our descendants, saying, "What have you to do with the LORD God of Israel? [25]For the LORD has made the Jordan a border between you and us, you children of Reuben and children of Gad. You have no part in the LORD." So your descendants would make our descendants cease fearing the LORD.' [26]Therefore we said, 'Let us now prepare to build ourselves an altar, not for burnt offering nor for sacrifice, [27]but *that it may be* [y]a witness between you and us and our generations after us, that we may [z]perform the service of the LORD before Him with our burnt offerings, with our sacrifices, and with our peace offerings; that your descendants may not say to our descendants in time to come, "You have no part in the LORD."' [28]Therefore we said that it will be, when they say *this* to us or to our generations in time to come, that we may say, 'Here is the replica of the altar of the LORD which our fathers made, though not for burnt offerings nor for sacrifices; but it *is* a witness between you and us.' [29]Far be it from us that we should rebel against the LORD, and turn from following the LORD this day, [a]to build an altar for burnt offerings, for grain offerings, or for sacrifices, besides the altar of the LORD our God which *is* before His tabernacle."

[30]Now when Phinehas the priest and the rulers of the congregation, the heads of the divisions* of Israel who *were* with him, heard the words that the children of Reuben, the children of Gad, and the children of Manasseh spoke, it pleased them. [31]Then Phinehas the son of Eleazar the priest said to the children of Reuben, the children of Gad, and the children of Manasseh, "This day we perceive that the LORD *is* [b]among us, because you have not committed this treachery against the LORD. Now you have delivered the children of Israel out of the hand of the LORD."

[32]And Phinehas the son of Eleazar the priest, and the rulers, returned from the children of Reuben and the children of

---

* **22:14** Literally *thousands* * **22:21** Literally *thousands* * **22:30** Literally *thousands*

22:16–18 treachery. This is sometimes translated "trespass" and is the same word used to describe Achan's sin (7:1). No one can sin in isolation. If the tribes east of the Jordan were indeed sinning, then the entire nation would feel the effects, as in the case of Achan.

22:23–28 we have done it for fear. The tribes to the east of the Jordan were afraid that geographical distance would isolate them and in time cause the Israelites west of the Jordan to reject them. Thus they built the altar to help prevent the existing unity from being lost. The eastern tribes were careful to label the altar for what it really was—a replica to serve as a witness for future generations.

22:30–31 Prudence—Jumping to conclusions can bring one to the brink of disaster. While their motives

were good (maintaining purity), they did not stop to find out what was really going on. This incident provides us with a good example of the importance of communicating before we act. Even when we are dealing with a case of serious sin (as the western tribes thought they were), the first reaction should be to try and persuade the sinner to repent and return to the Lord.

22:14 [o] Num. 1:4 **22:16** [p] Deut. 12:5–14 [q] Lev. 17:8, 9 **22:17** [r] Num. 25:1–9 **22:18** [s] Num. 16:22 **22:19** [t] Josh. 18:1 **22:20** [u] Josh. 7:1–26 **22:22** [v] Deut. 4:35; 10:17 [w] [Jer. 12:3] **22:23** [x] 1 Sam. 20:16 **22:27** [y] Gen. 31:48 [z] Deut. 12:5, 14 **22:29** [a] Deut. 12:13, 14 **22:31** [b] Lev. 26:11, 12

Gad, from the land of Gilead to the land of Canaan, to the children of Israel, and brought back word to them. 33So the thing pleased the children of Israel, and the children of Israel cblessed God; they spoke no more of going against them in battle, to destroy the land where the children of Reuben and Gad dwelt.

34The children of Reuben and the children of Gad* called the altar, *Witness*, "For *it is* a witness between us that the LORD is God."

Joshua's Farewell Address

23 Now it came to pass, a long time after the LORD ahad given rest to Israel from all their enemies round about, that Joshua bwas old, advanced in age. 2And Joshua ccalled for all Israel, for their elders, for their heads, for their judges, and for their officers, and said to them:

"I am old, advanced in age. 3You have seen all that the dLORD your God has done to all these nations because of you, for the eLORD your God is He who has fought for you. 4See, fI have divided to you by lot these nations that remain, to be an inheritance for your tribes, from the Jordan, with all the nations that I have cut off, as far as the Great Sea westward. 5And the LORD your God gwill expel them from before you and drive them out of your sight. So you shall possess their land, has the LORD your God promised you. 6iTherefore be very courageous to keep and to do all that is written in the Book of the Law of Moses, jlest you turn aside from it to the right hand or to the left, 7and lest you kgo among these nations, these who remain among you. You shall not lmake mention of the name of their gods, nor cause *anyone* to mswear *by them*; you shall not nserve them nor bow down to them, 8but you shall ohold fast to the LORD your God, as you have done to this day. 9pFor the LORD has driven out from before you great and strong nations; but

as for you, no one has been able to stand against you to this day. 10qOne man of you shall chase a thousand, for the LORD your God *is* He who fights for you, ras He promised you. 11sTherefore take careful heed to yourselves, that you love the LORD your God. 12Or else, if indeed you do tgo back, and cling to the remnant of these nations—these that remain among you—and umake marriages with them, and go in to them and they to you, 13know for certain that vthe LORD your God will no longer drive out these nations from before you. wBut they shall be snares and traps to you, and scourges on your sides and thorns in your eyes, until you perish from this good land which the LORD your God has given you.

14"Behold, this day xI *am* going the way of all the earth. And you know in all your hearts and in all your souls that ynot one thing has failed of all the good things which the LORD your God spoke concerning you. All have come to pass for you; not one word of them has failed. 15zTherefore it shall come to pass, that as all the good things have come upon you which the LORD your God promised you, so the LORD will bring upon you aall harmful things, until He has destroyed you from this good land which the LORD your God has given you. 16When you have transgressed the covenant of the LORD your God, which He commanded you, and have gone and served other gods, and bowed down to them, then the banger of the LORD will burn against you, and you shall perish quickly from the good land which He has given you."

The Covenant at Shechem

24 Then Joshua gathered all the tribes of Israel to aShechem and bcalled for the elders of Israel, for their heads, for their judges, and for their officers; and they

---

* **22:34** Septuagint adds *and half the tribe of Manasseh.*

23:3 He who has fought for you. This is a reminder that the land belonged to the Lord and that He gave it to Israel.

23:10 One man of you shall chase. The power seen in God's people was so dramatic it had to be miraculous.

23:11 Duty—Certain outlines of duty are imposed on all mankind (Mic. 6:8). We know that one man's specific duty may differ from another's, but all share a single common requirement: all must give account before God of what they have done or left undone. The church cannot decide how well each person is performing; there is no "spiritual commitment meter" to give an exact rating of each person's fulfillment of duty. Each person is responsible to maintain his or her own spiritual life.

23:12–13 make marriages with them. Years later, Solomon ignored this command and proved how destructive the sin of being unequally yoked could be (1 Kin. 3:1; 11:1–8; 2 Cor. 6:14).

23:16 perish . . . from the good land. This warning

saw its most dramatic fulfillment when Judah was carried into Babylon because of its repeated rebellion against God (2 Kin. 25). The saddest thing is that Israel's rebellion began almost immediately. God lovingly gave them every good thing, but when they disobeyed, they had to be punished.

24:1 Shechem. Shechem was a site of ancient religious significance and covenant making going back to Abraham's day (Gen. 12:6; 33:18–20).

22:33 c 1 Chr. 29:20 **23:1** a Josh. 21:44; 22:4 b Josh. 13:1; 24:29 **23:2** c Deut. 31:28 **23:3** d Ps. 44:3 e Deut. 1:30 **23:4** f Josh. 13:2, 6; 18:10 **23:5** g Ex. 23:30; 33:2 h Num. 33:53 **23:6** i Josh. 1:7 j Deut. 5:32 **23:7** k Deut. 7:2, 3 l Ex. 23:13 m Deut. 6:13; 10:20 n Ex. 20:5 **23:8** o Deut. 10:20 **23:9** p Deut. 7:24; 11:23 **23:10** q Lev. 26:8 r Ex. 14:14 **23:11** s Josh. 22:5 **23:12** t [2 Pet. 2:20, 21] u Deut. 7:3, 4 **23:13** v Judg. 2:3 w Ex. 23:33; 34:12 **23:14** x 1 Kin. 2:2 y Josh. 21:45 **23:15** z Deut. 28:63 a Deut. 28:15–68 **23:16** b Deut. 4:24–28 **24:1** a Gen. 35:4 b Josh. 23:2

[c]presented themselves before God. 2And
Joshua said to all the people, "Thus says
the LORD God of Israel: [d]'Your fathers, *including* Terah, the father of Abraham and
the father of Nahor, dwelt on the other side
of the River* in old times; and [e]they served
other gods. 3[f]Then I took your father Abraham from the other side of the River, led
him throughout all the land of Canaan, and
multiplied his descendants and [g]gave him
Isaac. 4To Isaac I gave [h]Jacob and Esau.
To [i]Esau I gave the mountains of Seir to
possess, [j]but Jacob and his children went
down to Egypt. 5[k]Also I sent Moses and
Aaron, and [l]I plagued Egypt, according
to what I did among them. Afterward I
brought you out.
6'Then I [m]brought your fathers out of
Egypt, and you came to the sea; and the
Egyptians pursued your fathers with chariots and horsemen to the Red Sea. 7So they
cried out to the LORD; and He put [n]darkness
between you and the Egyptians, brought
the sea upon them, and covered them. And
[o]your eyes saw what I did in Egypt. Then
you dwelt in the wilderness [p]a long time.
8And I brought you into the land of the Amorites, who dwelt on the other side of the
Jordan, [q]and they fought with you. But I
gave them into your hand, that you might
possess their land, and I destroyed them
from before you. 9Then [r]Balak the son of
Zippor, king of Moab, arose to make war
against Israel, and [s]sent and called Balaam
the son of Beor to curse you. 10[t]But I would
not listen to Balaam; [u]therefore he continued to bless you. So I delivered you out of
his hand. 11Then [v]you went over the Jordan and came to Jericho. And [w]the men of
Jericho fought against you—*also* the Amorites, the Perizzites, the Canaanites, the
Hittites, the Girgashites, the Hivites, and
the Jebusites. But I delivered them into your
hand. 12[x]I sent the hornet before you which
drove them out from before you, *also* the
two kings of the Amorites, *but* [y]not with
your sword or with your bow. 13I have giv-
en you a land for which you did not labor,
and [z]cities which you did not build, and you
dwell in them; you eat of the vineyards and
olive groves which you did not plant.'
14[a]"Now therefore, fear the LORD, serve
Him in [b]sincerity and in truth, and [c]put
away the gods which your fathers served
on the other side of the River and [d]in Egypt.
Serve the LORD! 15And if it seems evil to you
to serve the LORD, [e]choose for yourselves
this day whom you will serve, whether [f]the
gods which your fathers served that *were*
on the other side of the River, or [g]the gods
of the Amorites, in whose land you dwell.
[h]But as for me and my house, we will serve
the LORD."
16So the people answered and said: "Far
be it from us that we should forsake the
LORD to serve other gods; 17for the LORD
our God *is* He who brought us and our
fathers up out of the land of Egypt, from
the house of bondage, who did those great
signs in our sight, and preserved us in all
the way that we went and among all the
people through whom we passed. 18And
the LORD drove out from before us all the
people, including the Amorites who dwelt
in the land. [i]We also will serve the LORD,
for He *is* our God."
19But Joshua said to the people, [j]"You
cannot serve the LORD, for He *is* a [k]holy
God. He *is* [l]a jealous God; [m]He will not
forgive your transgressions nor your sins.
20[n]If you forsake the LORD and serve foreign gods, [o]then He will turn and do you
harm and consume you, after He has done
you good."
21And the people said to Joshua, "No, but
we will serve the LORD!"
22So Joshua said to the people, "You *are*
witnesses against yourselves that [p]you
have chosen the LORD for yourselves, to
serve Him."
And they said, "*We are* witnesses!"
23"Now therefore," *he said,* [q]"put away
the foreign gods which *are* among you, and
[r]incline your heart to the LORD God of Israel."
24And the people [s]said to Joshua, "The
LORD our God we will serve, and His voice
we will obey!"
25So Joshua [t]made a covenant with the
people that day, and made for them a statute and an ordinance [u]in Shechem.
26Then Joshua [v]wrote these words in
the Book of the Law of God. And he took
[w]a large stone, and [x]set it up there [y]under

* **24:2** Hebrew *Nahar,* the Euphrates, and so in verses 3, 14, and 15

24:13 *a land for which you did not labor.* This fulfills the promise given to Moses in Deuteronomy 6:10–11. The land was a gift from God to His people. In a similar sense, He has given us another gift for which we did not labor. The gift of salvation, through Jesus Christ, cannot be bought or paid for; it is graciously given from a loving God to those who will accept it.

24:15 *as for me and my house.* Joshua's famous words show the stand we must take—on the side of the living God.

24:1 [c] 1 Sam. 10:19 **24:2** [d] Gen. 11:7–32 [e] Josh. 24:14 **24:3** [f] Gen. 12:1; Acts 7:2, 3 [g] [Ps. 127:3] **24:4** [h] Gen. 25:24–26 [i] Deut. 2:5 [j] Gen. 46:1, 3, 6 **24:5** [k] Ex. 3:10 [l] Ex. 7–10 **24:6** [m] Ex. 12:37, 51; 14:2–31 **24:7** [n] Ex. 14:20 [o] Deut. 4:34 [p] Josh. 5:6 **24:8** [q] Num. 21:21–35 **24:9** [r] Judg. 11:25 [s] Num. 22:2–14 **24:10** [t] Deut. 23:5 [u] Num. 23:11, 20; 24:10 **24:11** [v] Josh. 3:14, 17 [w] Josh. 6:1; 10:1 **24:12** [x] Ex. 23:28 [y] Ps. 44:3 **24:13** [z] Deut. 6:10, 11 **24:14** [a] 1 Sam. 12:24 [b] 2 Cor. 1:12 [c] Ezek. 20:18 [d] Ezek. 20:7, 8 **24:15** [e] 1 Kin. 18:21 [f] Josh. 24:2 [g] Ex. 23:24, 32 [h] Gen. 18:19 **24:18** [i] Ps. 116:16 **24:19** [j] Matt. 6:24 [k] 1 Sam. 6:20 [l] Ex. 20:5 [m] Ex. 23:21 **24:20** [n] Ezra 8:22 [o] Deut. 4:24–26 **24:22** [p] Ps. 119:173 **24:23** [q] Gen. 35:2 [r] 1 Kin. 8:57, 58 **24:24** [s] Deut. 5:24–27 **24:25** [t] Ex. 15:25 [u] Josh. 24:1 **24:26** [v] Deut. 31:24 [w] Judg. 9:6 [x] Gen. 28:18 [y] Gen. 35:4

the oak that *was* by the sanctuary of the LORD. 27And Joshua said to all the people, "Behold, this stone shall be ᶻa witness to us, for ᵃit has heard all the words of the LORD which He spoke to us. It shall therefore be a witness to you, lest you deny your God." 28So ᵇJoshua let the people depart, each to his own inheritance.

Death of Joshua and Eleazar

29cNow it came to pass after these things that Joshua the son of Nun, the servant of the LORD, died, *being* one hundred and ten years old. 30And they buried him within the border of his inheritance at ᵈTimnath Serah, which *is* in the mountains of Ephraim, on the north side of Mount Gaash.

31eIsrael served the LORD all the days of Joshua, and all the days of the elders who outlived Joshua, who had ᶠknown all the works of the LORD which He had done for Israel. 32gThe bones of Joseph, which the children of Israel had brought up out of Egypt, they buried at Shechem, in the plot of ground ʰwhich Jacob had bought from the sons of Hamor the father of Shechem for one hundred pieces of silver, and which had become an inheritance of the children of Joseph.

33And ⁱEleazar the son of Aaron died. They buried him in a hill *belonging to* ʲPhinehas his son, which was given to him in the mountains of Ephraim.

24:32 *The bones of Joseph.* The brief account of the transfer of Joseph's body to Canaan from Egypt notes the fulfillment of Joseph's prophecy hundreds of years before (Gen. 50:24–25).

24:27 ᶻGen. 31:48 ᵃDeut. 32:1 **24:28** ᵇJudg. 2:6, 7 **24:29** ᶜJudg. 2:8 **24:30** ᵈJosh. 19:50 **24:31** ᵉJudg. 2:7 ᶠDeut. 11:2 **24:32** gGen. 50:25 ʰGen. 33:19 **24:33** ⁱEx. 28:1 ʲEx. 6:25

THE BOOK OF
JUDGES

▶ **AUTHOR:** Although the author of Judges is anonymous, Jewish tradition contained in the Talmud attributes Judges to Samuel. Samuel lived during the time the book could have been written, and he was a principal character in the transition to the next phase. He would have been aware of the events that occur in the book. Samuel certainly was the crucial link between the period of the judges and the period of the kings. His prophetic ministry clearly fits the moral commentary of Judges, and the consistent style and orderly scheme of the book points to a single compiler.

▶ **TIME:** c. 1380–1045 B.C.   ▶ **KEY VERSES:** Judg. 2:20–21

▶ **THEME:** During the Book of Judges, the land wasn't fully conquered. There was political chaos. The Israelites appeared to live mostly in the land between the cities of the Philistines, who dominate them much of the time. Two common phrases occur in the book: The first is the Israelites "did evil in the sight of the LORD." The second is "everyone did what was right in his own eyes." In the midst of this situation God raises up judges, who in addition to playing the role of adjudicator, also provide leadership in pulling the tribes together to fight the unconquered nations. Most are reluctant. Nevertheless, God is able to use them and demonstrate His power through these individuals.

The Continuing Conquest of Canaan

1 Now after the ᵃdeath of Joshua it came to pass that the children of Israel ᵇasked the LORD, saying, "Who shall be first to go up for us against the ᶜCanaanites to fight against them?"

²And the LORD said, ᵈ"Judah shall go up. Indeed I have delivered the land into his hand."

³So Judah said to ᵉSimeon his brother, "Come up with me to my allotted territory, that we may fight against the Canaanites; and ᶠI will likewise go with you to your allotted territory." And Simeon went with him. ⁴Then Judah went up, and the LORD delivered the Canaanites and the Perizzites into their hand; and they killed ten thousand men at ᵍBezek. ⁵And they found Adoni-Bezek in Bezek, and fought against

him; and they defeated the Canaanites and the Perizzites. ⁶Then Adoni-Bezek fled, and they pursued him and caught him and cut off his thumbs and big toes. ⁷And Adoni-Bezek said, "Seventy kings with their thumbs and big toes cut off used to gather *scraps* under my table; ʰas I have done, so God has repaid me." Then they brought him to Jerusalem, and there he died.

⁸Now ⁱthe children of Judah fought against Jerusalem and took it; they struck it with the edge of the sword and set the city on fire. ⁹ʲAnd afterward the children of Judah went down to fight against the Canaanites who dwelt in the mountains, in the South,* and in the lowland. ¹⁰Then Judah went against the Canaanites who dwelt in ᵏHebron. (Now the name of Hebron *was*

---

* **1:9** Hebrew *Negev*, and so throughout this book

1:1 *Now after the death of Joshua.* Judges begins as the Book of Joshua does, with reference to the death of the previous leader. Yet no new leader was commissioned to lead Israel after Joshua. The tribe of Judah was designated to lead in the fight against the Canaanites, the first hint of the fulfillment of Jacob's prophecy (Gen. 49:8–12).
1:3 *Judah . . . Simeon.* History bound the tribes of Judah and Simeon together. They were descended from the same mother (Gen. 29:33–35), and Simeon had inherited land in Judah's territory (Josh. 19:1,9).
1:6–7 *thumbs and big toes.* To cut off a warrior's thumbs and big toes would prevent him from ever

engaging in battle again, besides subjecting him to pain and humiliation.
1:8 *Jerusalem.* Jerusalem was captured and burned, but not settled. The complete conquest and settlement of Jerusalem was not accomplished until David's day (2 Sam. 5:6–10).
1:10 *Hebron.* Hebron, about 20 miles southwest of

1:1 ᵃ Josh. 24:29 ᵇ Num. 27:21 ᶜ Josh. 17:12, 13
1:2 ᵈ Gen. 49:8, 9 **1:3** ᵉ Josh. 19:1 ᶠ Judg. 1:17
1:4 ᵍ 1 Sam. 11:8 **1:7** ʰ Lev. 24:19 **1:8** ⁱ Josh. 15:63
1:9 ʲ Josh. 10:36; 11:21; 15:13 **1:10** ᵏ Josh. 15:13–19

formerly *f*Kirjath Arba.) And they killed Sheshai, Ahiman, and Talmai.

¹¹*m*From there they went against the inhabitants of Debir. (The name of Debir *was* formerly Kirjath Sepher.)

¹²*n*Then Caleb said, "Whoever attacks Kirjath Sepher and takes it, to him I will give my daughter Achsah as wife." ¹³And Othniel the son of Kenaz, *o*Caleb's younger brother, took it; so he gave him his daughter Achsah as wife. ¹⁴*p*Now it happened, when she came *to him,* that she urged him* to ask her father for a field. And she dismounted from *her* donkey, and Caleb said to her, "What do you wish?" ¹⁵So she said to him, *q*"Give me a blessing; since you have given me land in the South, give me also springs of water."

And Caleb gave her the upper springs and the lower springs.

¹⁶*r*Now the children of the Kenite, Moses' father-in-law, went up *s*from the City of Palms with the children of Judah into the Wilderness of Judah, which *lies* in the South *near* *t*Arad; *u*and they went and dwelt among the people. ¹⁷*v*And Judah went with his brother Simeon, and they attacked the Canaanites who inhabited Zephath, and utterly destroyed it. So the name of the city was called *w*Hormah. ¹⁸Also Judah took *x*Gaza with its territory, Ashkelon with its territory, and Ekron with its territory. ¹⁹So the LORD was with Judah. And they drove out the mountaineers, but they could not drive out the inhabitants of the lowland, because they had *y*chariots of iron. ²⁰*z*And they gave Hebron to Caleb, as Moses had said. Then he expelled from there the *a*three sons of Anak. ²¹*b*But the children of Benjamin did not drive out the Jebusites who inhabited Jerusalem; so the Jebusites dwell with the children of Benjamin in Jerusalem to this day.

²²And the house of Joseph also went up against Bethel, *c*and the LORD *was* with them. ²³So the house of Joseph *d*sent men to spy out Bethel. (The name of the city *was* formerly *e*Luz.) ²⁴And when the spies saw a man coming out of the city, they said to

him, "Please show us the entrance to the city, and *f*we will show you mercy." ²⁵So he showed them the entrance to the city, and they struck the city with the edge of the sword; but they let the man and all his family go. ²⁶And the man went to the land of the Hittites, built a city, and called its name Luz, which *is* its name to this day.

Incomplete Conquest of the Land

²⁷*g*However, Manasseh did not drive out *the inhabitants of* Beth Shean and its villages, or *h*Taanach and its villages, or the inhabitants of *i*Dor and its villages, or the inhabitants of Ibleam and its villages, or the inhabitants of Megiddo and its villages; for the Canaanites were determined to dwell in that land. ²⁸And it came to pass, when Israel was strong, that they put the Canaanites under tribute, but did not completely drive them out.

²⁹*j*Nor did Ephraim drive out the Canaanites who dwelt in Gezer; so the Canaanites dwelt in Gezer among them.

³⁰Nor did *k*Zebulun drive out the inhabitants of Kitron or the inhabitants of Nahalol; so the Canaanites dwelt among them, and were put under tribute.

³¹*l*Nor did Asher drive out the inhabitants of Acco or the inhabitants of Sidon, or of Ahlab, Achzib, Helbah, Aphik, or Rehob. ³²So the Asherites *m*dwelt among the Canaanites, the inhabitants of the land; for they did not drive them out.

³³*n*Nor did Naphtali drive out the inhabitants of Beth Shemesh or the inhabitants of Beth Anath; but they dwelt among the Canaanites, the inhabitants of the land. Nevertheless the inhabitants of Beth Shemesh and Beth Anath were put under tribute to them.

³⁴And the Amorites forced the children of Dan into the mountains, for they would not allow them to come down to the valley; ³⁵and the Amorites were determined to dwell in Mount Heres, *o*in Aijalon, and in Shaalbim;* yet when the strength of the

---

* **1:14** Septuagint and Vulgate read *he urged her.*
* **1:35** Spelled *Shaalabbin* in Joshua 19:42

Jerusalem, was where Abraham settled and built an altar (Gen. 13:18).

1:16 the Kenite. The Kenites were Midianites, descendants of Abraham's son by Keturah (Gen. 25:1–4).

1:18 Gaza . . . Ashkelon . . . Ekron. Israel was not able to hold these cities for long. By Samson's day, all three were in Philistine hands again (14:19; 16:1; 1 Sam. 5:10).

1:21 Unfaithfulness—This verse duplicates Joshua 15:63 almost exactly, except that in Joshua the tribe of Judah is held responsible. Jerusalem lay on the border between Judah and Benjamin; either or both tribes were responsible for driving out the Canaanites. Their failure to do so was not because the task was too hard, but because they did not really take God's commands and promises seriously. Jerusalem was not claimed for Israel until David came, a man who trusted the Lord for his victories and obeyed

His word. Victories for the Lord are won only through faith.

1:22 Bethel. Bethel means "house of God." It was a site with an honored history, beginning with Abraham's first sacrifice to God (Gen. 13:3–4) and Jacob's revelation of God there (Gen. 31:13).

1:10 *l* Josh. 14:15   **1:11** *m* Josh. 15:15   **1:12** *n* Josh. 15:16, 17   **1:13** *o* Judg. 3:9   **1:14** *p* Josh. 15:18, 19   **1:15** *q* Gen. 33:11   **1:16** *r* Num. 10:29–32 *s* Deut. 34:3 *t* Josh. 12:14 *u* 1 Sam. 15:6   **1:17** *v* Judg. 1:3 *w* Num. 21:3   **1:18** *x* Josh. 11:22   **1:19** *y* Josh. 17:16, 18   **1:20** *z* Josh. 14:9, 14 *a* Josh. 15:14   **1:21** *b* Josh. 15:63   **1:22** *c* Judg. 1:19   **1:23** *d* Josh. 2:1; 7:2 *e* Gen. 28:19   **1:24** *f* Josh. 2:12, 14   **1:27** *g* Josh. 17:11–13 *h* Josh. 21:25 *i* Josh. 17:11   **1:29** *j* Josh. 16:10   **1:30** *k* Josh. 19:10–16   **1:31** *l* Josh. 19:24–31   **1:32** *m* Ps. 106:34, 35   **1:33** *n* Josh. 19:32–39   **1:35** *o* Josh. 19:42

house of Joseph became greater, they were put under tribute. [36]Now the boundary of the Amorites *was* [p]from the Ascent of Akrabbim, from Sela, and upward.

Israel's Disobedience

2 Then the Angel of the LORD came up from Gilgal to Bochim, and said: [a]"I led you up from Egypt and [b]brought you to the land of which I swore to your fathers; and [c]I said, 'I will never break My covenant with you. [2]And [d]you shall make no covenant with the inhabitants of this land; [e]you shall tear down their altars.' [f]But you have not obeyed My voice. Why have you done this? [3]Therefore I also said, 'I will not drive them out before you; but they shall be [g]thorns in your side,[*] and [h]their gods shall be a [i]snare to you.'" [4]So it was, when the Angel of the LORD spoke these words to all the children of Israel, that the people lifted up their voices and wept.

[5]Then they called the name of that place Bochim;[*] and they sacrificed there to the LORD. [6]And when [j]Joshua had dismissed the people, the children of Israel went each to his own inheritance to possess the land.

Death of Joshua

[7k]So the people served the LORD all the days of Joshua, and all the days of the elders who outlived Joshua, who had seen all the great works of the LORD which He had done for Israel. [8]Now [l]Joshua the son of Nun, the servant of the LORD, died *when he was* one hundred and ten years old. [9m]And they buried him within the border of his inheritance at [n]Timnath Heres, in the mountains of Ephraim, on the north side of Mount Gaash. [10]When all that generation had been gathered to their fathers, another generation arose after them who [o]did not know the LORD nor the work which He had done for Israel.

Israel's Unfaithfulness

[11]Then the children of Israel did [p]evil in the sight of the LORD, and served the Baals; [12]and they [q]forsook the LORD God of their fathers, who had brought them out of the land of Egypt; and they followed [r]other gods from *among* the gods of the people who *were* all around them, and they [s]bowed down to them; and they provoked the LORD to anger. [13]They forsook the LORD [t]and served Baal and the Ashtoreths.[*] [14u]And the anger of the LORD was hot against Israel. So He [v]delivered them into the hands of plunderers who despoiled them; and [w]He sold them into the hands of their enemies all around, so that they [x]could no longer stand before their enemies. [15]Wherever they went out, the hand of the LORD was against them for calamity, as the LORD had said, and as the LORD had [y]sworn to them. And they were greatly distressed.

[16]Nevertheless, [z]the LORD raised up judges who delivered them out of the hand of those who plundered them. [17]Yet they would not listen to their judges, but they [a]played the harlot with other gods, and bowed down to them. They turned quickly from the way in which their fathers walked, in obeying the commandments of the LORD; they did not do so. [18]And when the LORD raised up judges for them, [b]the LORD was with the judge and delivered them out of the hand of their enemies all the days of the judge; [c]for the LORD was moved to pity by their groaning because of those who oppressed them and harassed them. [19]And it came to pass, [d]when the judge was dead, that they reverted and behaved more corruptly than their fathers, by following other gods, to serve them and bow down to

---

* **2:3** Septuagint, Targum, and Vulgate read *enemies to you.*   * **2:5** Literally *Weeping*
* **2:13** Canaanite goddesses

2:1 *the Angel of the LORD.* The Angel of the Lord appears as God's representative here, speaking authoritatively to the people about their covenant disobedience.

2:2 *you shall make no covenant.* God's commands to make no covenants with pagan nations and to tear down their altars are found in Exodus 23:32; 34:13; Deuteronomy 12:3.

2:8–10 *Joshua . . . died.* Most likely the reference to Joshua's death in 1:1 is placed chronologically, and this subsequent passage has been inserted by the author out of sequence. It is a "flashback" that leads into the second major section of the book, emphasizing the spiritual downfall of the nation after their leader was gone.

2:13 *Ashtoreths.* Ashtoreth was a female fertility goddess and a goddess of love and war, closely associated with Baal (10:6; 1 Sam. 7:4; 12:10).

2:15 *as the LORD had sworn.* God had promised to deliver Israel into the hands of its enemies if the people forsook Him (Deut. 28:25; Josh. 23:13).

2:18 Pity—God is compassionate toward His people at all times. But God had given notice to His people

(Deut. 28) that if they disobeyed Him, and did not live according to the covenant, then He would have to discipline them. However, if they did live according to the covenant, then He would bless them as a nation. Throughout Judges the pattern occurred that when the people forgot God another nation would come down upon them as an act of judgment from God. When the nation turned to God, He also would turn and "hear" and "pity" them and bring deliverance. God had not forgotten them when they were in trouble, but He wanted that trouble to cause them to turn to Him.

1:36 [p] Josh. 15:3   **2:1** [a] Ex. 20:2 [b] Deut. 1:8 [c] Gen. 17:7, 8
2:2 [d] Deut. 7:2 [e] Deut. 12:3 [f] Ps. 106:34   **2:3** [g] Josh. 23:13 [h] Judg. 3:6 [i] Ps. 106:36   **2:6** [j] Josh. 22:6; 24:28–31
2:7 [k] Josh. 24:31   **2:8** [l] Josh. 24:29   **2:9** [m] Josh. 24:30
[n] Josh. 19:49, 50   **2:10** [o] 1 Sam. 2:12   **2:11** [p] Judg. 3:7, 12; 4:1; 6:1   **2:12** [q] Deut. 31:16 [r] Deut. 6:14 [s] Ex. 20:5   **2:13** [t] Judg. 10:6   **2:14** [u] Deut. 31:17 [v] 2 Kin. 17:20 [w] Is. 50:1 [x] Lev. 26:37   **2:15** [y] Lev. 26:14–26   **2:16** [z] Ps. 106:43–45   **2:17** [a] Ex. 34:15   **2:18** [b] Josh. 1:5 [c] Gen. 6:6
2:19 [d] Judg. 3:12

them. They did not cease from their own doings nor from their stubborn way.

20Then the anger of the LORD was hot against Israel; and He said, "Because this nation has ᵉtransgressed My covenant which I commanded their fathers, and has not heeded My voice, 21I also will no longer drive out before them any of the nations which Joshua ᶠleft when he died, 22so ᵍthat through them I may ʰtest Israel, whether they will keep the ways of the LORD, to walk in them as their fathers kept them, or not." 23Therefore the LORD left those nations, without driving them out immediately; nor did He deliver them into the hand of Joshua.

The Nations Remaining in the Land

3 Now these are ᵃthe nations which the LORD left, that He might test Israel by them, that is, all who had not known any of the wars in Canaan 2(this was only so that the generations of the children of Israel might be taught to know war, at least those who had not formerly known it), 3namely, ᵇfive lords of the Philistines, all the Canaanites, the Sidonians, and the Hivites who dwelt in Mount Lebanon, from Mount Baal Hermon to the entrance of Hamath. 4And they were left, that He might test Israel by them, to know whether they would obey the commandments of the LORD, which He had commanded their fathers by the hand of Moses.

5ᶜThus the children of Israel dwelt among the Canaanites, the Hittites, the Amorites, the Perizzites, the Hivites, and the Jebusites. 6And ᵈthey took their daughters to be their wives, and gave their daughters to their sons; and they served their gods.

Othniel

7So the children of Israel did ᵉevil in the sight of the LORD. They ᶠforgot the LORD their God, and served the Baals and Asherahs.* 8Therefore the anger of the LORD was hot against Israel, and He ᵍsold them

into the hand of ʰCushan-Rishathaim king of Mesopotamia; and the children of Israel served Cushan-Rishathaim eight years. 9When the children of Israel ⁱcried out to the LORD, the LORD ʲraised up a deliverer for the children of Israel, who delivered them: ᵏOthniel the son of Kenaz, Caleb's younger brother. 10ˡThe Spirit of the LORD came upon him, and he judged Israel. He went out to war, and the LORD delivered Cushan-Rishathaim king of Mesopotamia into his hand; and his hand prevailed over Cushan-Rishathaim. 11So the land had rest for forty years. Then Othniel the son of Kenaz died.

Ehud

12ᵐAnd the children of Israel again did evil in the sight of the LORD. So the LORD strengthened ⁿEglon king of Moab against Israel, because they had done evil in the sight of the LORD. 13Then he gathered to himself the people of Ammon and ᵒAmalek, went and defeated Israel, and took possession of ᵖthe City of Palms. 14So the children of Israel ᵠserved Eglon king of Moab eighteen years.

15But when the children of Israel ʳcried out to the LORD, the LORD raised up a deliverer for them: Ehud the son of Gera, the Benjamite, a ˢleft-handed man. By him the children of Israel sent tribute to Eglon king of Moab. 16Now Ehud made himself a dagger (it was double-edged and a cubit in length) and fastened it under his clothes on his right thigh. 17So he brought the tribute to Eglon king of Moab. (Now Eglon was a very fat man.) 18And when he had finished presenting the tribute, he sent away the people who had carried the tribute. 19But he himself turned back ᵗfrom the stone images that were at Gilgal, and said, "I have a secret message for you, O king."

He said, "Keep silence!" And all who attended him went out from him.

20So Ehud came to him (now he was

---

* 3:7 Name or symbol for Canaanite goddesses

3:1 test Israel. The idea of testing implies difficulty and adversity; elsewhere the same word refers to God's testing of Abraham (Gen. 22:1) and Hezekiah (2 Chr. 32:31). Here God was testing Israel to refine it.
3:8 Cushan-Rishathaim. This name means "Cushan of double wickedness." This may not have been his actual name, but instead a name pinned on him by the author of Judges for ridicule.
3:9 Othniel. Othniel was the hero who captured the city of Kirjath Sepher (1:13; Josh. 15:17). He was from Judah and was Caleb's near kinsman.
3:12 Moab. Moab was a plateau southeast of the Dead Sea. It was populated by nomadic herders and farmers in small agrarian settlements but had no large cities. It sat on either side of the King's Highway, an important north-south trade route. The ancestor of the Moabites was the offspring of Lot's incestuous relationship with his older daughter (Gen. 19:37), so

the Moabites and Israelites were distantly related. The Bible frequently mentions conflict between the two peoples, and particularly the trouble caused by the Israelite tendency to embrace Moab's false gods.
3:20 cool private chamber. In ancient cities, a small room was often built onto the flat roof of a house, providing a cool, private place away from the cooking fires and general living areas.

2:20 ᵉ [Josh. 23:16] **2:21** ᶠ Josh. 23:4, 5, 13
2:22 ᵍ Judg. 3:1, 4 ʰ Deut. 8:2, 16; 13:3 **3:1** ᵃ Judg. 1:1;
2:21, 22 **3:3** ᵇ Josh. 13:3 **3:5** ᶜ Ps. 106:35 **3:6** ᵈ Ex.
34:15, 16 **3:7** ᵉ Judg. 2:11 ᶠ Deut. 32:18 **3:8** ᵍ Judg.
2:14 ʰ Hab. 3:7 **3:9** ⁱ Judg. 3:15 ʲ Judg. 2:16 ᵏ Judg.
1:13 **3:10** ˡ Num. 27:18 **3:12** ᵐ Judg. 2:19 ⁿ 1 Sam.
12:9 **3:13** ᵒ Judg. 5:14 ᵖ Judg. 1:16 **3:14** ᵠ Deut. 28:48
3:15 ʳ Ps. 78:34 ˢ Judg. 20:16 **3:19** ᵗ Josh. 4:20

sitting upstairs in his cool private chamber). Then Ehud said, "I have a message
from God for you." So he arose from *his*
seat. 21 Then Ehud reached with his left
hand, took the dagger from his right thigh,
and thrust it into his belly. 22 Even the hilt
went in after the blade, and the fat closed
over the blade, for he did not draw the dagger out of his belly; and his entrails came
out. 23 Then Ehud went out through the
porch and shut the doors of the upper room
behind him and locked them.
24 When he had gone out, *Eglon's** servants came to look, and *to their* surprise,
the doors of the upper room were locked.
So they said, "He is probably [u]attending to
his needs in the cool chamber." 25 So they
waited till they were [v]embarrassed, and
still he had not opened the doors of the upper room. Therefore they took the key and
opened *them*. And there was their master,
fallen dead on the floor.
26 But Ehud had escaped while they delayed, and passed beyond the stone images
and escaped to Seirah. 27 And it happened,
when he arrived, that [w]he blew the trumpet
in the [x]mountains of Ephraim, and the children of Israel went down with him from
the mountains; and he led them. 28 Then he
said to them, "Follow *me*, for [y]the LORD has
delivered your enemies the Moabites into
your hand." So they went down after him,
seized the [z]fords of the Jordan leading to
Moab, and did not allow anyone to cross
over. 29 And at that time they killed about
ten thousand men of Moab, all stout men of
valor; not a man escaped. 30 So Moab was
subdued that day under the hand of Israel.
And [a]the land had rest for eighty years.

Shamgar

31 After him was [b]Shamgar the son of
Anath, who killed six hundred men of the
Philistines [c]with an ox goad; [d]and he also
delivered [e]Israel.

Deborah

4 When Ehud was dead, [a]the children
of Israel again did [b]evil in the sight of
the LORD. 2 So the LORD [c]sold them into
the hand of Jabin king of Canaan, who
reigned in [d]Hazor. The commander of his
army *was* [e]Sisera, who dwelt in [f]Harosheth
Hagoyim. 3 And the children of Israel cried
out to the LORD; for Jabin had nine hundred [g]chariots of iron, and for twenty years
[h]he had harshly oppressed the children of
Israel.
4 Now Deborah, a prophetess, the wife of
Lapidoth, was judging Israel at that time.
5 [i]And she would sit under the palm tree of
Deborah between Ramah and Bethel in the
mountains of Ephraim. And the children of
Israel came up to her for judgment. 6 Then
she sent and called for [j]Barak the son of
Abinoam from [k]Kedesh in Naphtali, and
said to him, "Has not the LORD God of Israel commanded, 'Go and deploy *troops* at
Mount [l]Tabor; take with you ten thousand
men of the sons of Naphtali and of the sons
of Zebulun; 7 and against you [m]I will deploy
Sisera, the commander of Jabin's army,
with his chariots and his multitude at the
[n]River Kishon; and I will deliver him into
your hand'?"
8 And Barak said to her, "If you will go
with me, then I will go; but if you will not
go with me, I will not go!"
9 So she said, "I will surely go with you;
nevertheless there will be no glory for you
in the journey you are taking, for the LORD
will [o]sell Sisera into the hand of a woman."
Then Deborah arose and went with Barak
to Kedesh. 10 And Barak called [p]Zebulun
and Naphtali to Kedesh; he went up with
ten thousand men [q]under his command,*
and Deborah went up with him.
11 Now Heber [r]the Kenite, of the children
of [s]Hobab the father-in-law of Moses, had
separated himself from the Kenites and
pitched his tent near the terebinth tree at
Zaanaim, [t]which *is* beside Kedesh.
12 And they reported to Sisera that Barak
the son of Abinoam had gone up to Mount
Tabor. 13 So Sisera gathered together all his
chariots, nine hundred chariots of iron,

* **3:24** Literally *his* * **4:10** Literally *at his feet*

4:2 *Jabin king of Canaan, who reigned in Hazor.* Years earlier, Joshua had defeated a king of Hazor named Jabin (Josh. 11:1–15). Probably Jabin was a title rather than a proper name.

4:4 *Deborah.* Deborah is shown in the best light of all the judges in the book. She is called a prophetess (v. 4), and many sought out her decisions (v. 5). For this reason, she is called "a mother in Israel" (5:7). She is probably included among the leaders in Israel (5:2), and she instructed Barak in the strategy of the battle (4:9,14). She was also a prominent author of the victory song (5:1) and gave her name to a place in Israel, the palm tree of Deborah (v. 5).

4:9 *no glory for you.* Barak clearly respected Deborah as the Lord's spokesperson, and wanted her to be nearby so that he could receive instructions from the Lord. It is not clear whether Deborah's response was a rebuke, or just a statement, but it seems that part of the reason Israel was judged by a woman was because the men were not listening that closely to God, or willing to take the responsibility. Whatever his stage of spiritual growth was at the time, Barak did obey the Lord and is listed in the Book of Hebrews as a man of great faith (Heb. 11:32).

3:24 [u] 1 Sam. 24:3 **3:25** [v] 2 Kin. 2:17; 8:11 **3:27** [w] 1 Sam. 13:3 [x] Josh. 17:15 **3:28** [y] Judg. 7:9, 15 [z] Josh. 2:7 **3:30** [a] Judg. 3:11 **3:31** [b] Judg. 5:6 [c] 1 Sam. 17:47 [d] Judg. 2:16 [e] 1 Sam. 4:1 **4:1** [a] Judg. 2:19 [b] Judg. 2:11 **4:2** [c] Judg. 2:14 [d] Josh. 11:1, 10 [e] 1 Sam. 12:9 [f] Judg. 4:13, 16 **4:3** [g] Judg. 1:19 [h] Ps. 106:42 **4:5** [i] Gen. 35:8 **4:6** [j] Heb. 11:32 [k] Josh. 19:37; 21:32 [l] Judg. 8:18 **4:7** [m] Ex. 14:4 [n] Ps. 83:9, 10 **4:9** [o] Judg. 2:14 **4:10** [p] Judg. 5:18 [q] 1 Kin. 20:10 **4:11** [r] Judg. 1:16 [s] Num. 10:29 [t] Judg. 4:6

and all the people who *were* with him, from Harosheth Hagoyim to the River Kishon.

¹⁴Then Deborah said to Barak, "Up! For this *is* the day in which the LORD has delivered Sisera into your hand. ᵘHas not the LORD gone out before you?" So Barak went down from Mount Tabor with ten thousand men following him. ¹⁵And the LORD routed Sisera and all *his* chariots and all *his* army with the edge of the sword before Barak; and Sisera alighted from *his* chariot and fled away on foot. ¹⁶But Barak pursued chariots and the army as far as Harosheth Hagoyim, and all the army of Sisera fell by the edge of the sword; not a man was ᵛleft.

¹⁷However, Sisera had fled away on foot to the tent of ʷJael, the wife of Heber the Kenite; for *there was* peace between Jabin king of Hazor and the house of Heber the Kenite. ¹⁸And Jael went out to meet Sisera, and said to him, "Turn aside, my lord, turn aside to me; do not fear." And when he had turned aside with her into the tent, she covered him with a blanket.

¹⁹Then he said to her, "Please give me a little water to drink, for I am thirsty." So she opened ˣa jug of milk, gave him a drink, and covered him. ²⁰And he said to her, "Stand at the door of the tent, and if any man comes and inquires of you, and says, 'Is there any man here?' you shall say, 'No.'"

²¹Then Jael, Heber's wife, ʸtook a tent peg and took a hammer in her hand, and went softly to him and drove the peg into his temple, and it went down into the ground; for he was fast asleep and weary. So he died. ²²And then, as Barak pursued Sisera, Jael came out to meet him, and said to him, "Come, I will show you the man whom you seek." And when he went into her *tent*, there lay Sisera, dead with the peg in his temple.

²³So on that day God subdued Jabin king of Canaan in the presence of the children of Israel. ²⁴And the hand of the children of Israel grew stronger and stronger against Jabin king of Canaan, until they had destroyed Jabin king of Canaan.

The Song of Deborah

5 Then Deborah and Barak the son of Abinoam ᵃsang on that day, saying:

2 "When leaders ᵇlead in Israel,
  ᶜWhen the people willingly offer
    themselves,
  Bless the LORD!

3 "Hear,ᵈ O kings! Give ear, O princes!
  I, *even* ᵉI, will sing to the LORD;
  I will sing praise to the LORD God of
    Israel.

4 "LORD, ᶠwhen You went out from Seir,
  When You marched from ᵍthe field of
    Edom,
  The earth trembled and the heavens
    poured,
  The clouds also poured water;

5 ʰThe mountains gushed before the
    LORD,
  ⁱThis Sinai, before the LORD God of
    Israel.

6 "In the days of ʲShamgar, son of Anath,
  In the days of ᵏJael,
  ˡThe highways were deserted,
  And the travelers walked along the
    byways.

7 Village life ceased, it ceased in Israel,
  Until I, Deborah, arose,
  Arose a mother in Israel.

8 They chose ᵐnew gods;
  Then *there was* war in the gates;
  Not a shield or spear was seen among
    forty thousand in Israel.

9 My heart *is* with the rulers of Israel
  Who offered themselves willingly with
    the people.
  Bless the LORD!

10 "Speak, you who ride on white
    ⁿdonkeys,
  Who sit in judges' attire,
  And who walk along the road.

11 Far from the noise of the archers,
    among the watering places,
  There they shall recount the righteous
    acts of the LORD,
  The righteous acts *for* His villagers in
    Israel;
  Then the people of the LORD shall go
    down to the gates.

12 "Awake,ᵒ awake, Deborah!
  Awake, awake, sing a song!
  Arise, Barak, and lead your captives
    away,
  O son of Abinoam!

5:2 when leaders lead in Israel. The phrase literally means "the long-haired ones who let their hair hang loose." The precise meaning of the phrase is obscure, but it may mean that loosed locks or flowing hair were signs of great strength or leadership.
5:2–3 Praise—Deborah did not attribute their success to herself or to Barak, or even to Jael, but to the Lord. He was the one to whom all praise and thanksgiving were directed in the celebration of their victory.
5:7 a mother in Israel. This phrase occurs twice in the Old Testament, here and in 2 Samuel 20:19. The title is given to Deborah as one of honor, respect, and prominence.

5:10 ride on white donkeys . . . walk along the road. This verse calls all classes of society to bear witness to the mighty acts of God, from the ruling classes, those riding on white donkeys, to the lowest classes, those who walk on the road.

4:14 ᵘDeut. 9:3; 31:3 4:16 ᵛEx. 14:28 4:17 ʷJudg. 5:6 4:19 ˣJudg. 5:24–27 4:21 ʸJudg. 5:24–27 5:1 ᵃJudg. 4:4 5:2 ᵇPs. 8:47 ᶜ2 Chr. 17:16 5:3 ᵈDeut. 32:1, 3 ᵉPs. 27:6 5:4 ᶠDeut. 33:2 ᵍPs. 68:8 5:5 ʰPs. 97:5 ⁱEx. 19:18 5:6 ʲJudg. 3:31 ᵏJudg. 4:17 ˡIs. 33:8 5:8 ᵐDeut. 32:17 5:10 ⁿJudg. 10:4; 12:14 5:12 ᵒPs. 57:8

13 "Then the survivors came down, the people against the nobles;
The LORD came down for me against the mighty.
14 From Ephraim *were* those whose roots were in [p]Amalek.
After you, Benjamin, with your peoples,
From Machir rulers came down,
And from Zebulun those who bear the recruiter's staff.
15 And the princes of Issachar* *were* with Deborah;
As Issachar, so *was* Barak
Sent into the valley under his command;*
Among the divisions of Reuben
There were great resolves of heart.
16 Why did you sit among the sheepfolds,
To hear the pipings for the flocks?
The divisions of Reuben have great searchings of heart.
17 [q]Gilead stayed beyond the Jordan,
And why did Dan remain on ships?*
[r]Asher continued at the seashore,
And stayed by his inlets.
18 [s]Zebulun *is* a people *who* jeopardized their lives to the point of death,
Naphtali also, on the heights of the battlefield.

19 "The kings came *and* fought,
Then the kings of Canaan fought
In [t]Taanach, by the waters of Megiddo;
They took no spoils of silver.
20 They fought from the heavens;
The stars from their courses fought against Sisera.
21 [u]The torrent of Kishon swept them away,
That ancient torrent, the torrent of Kishon.
O my soul, march on in strength!
22 Then the horses' hooves pounded,
The galloping, galloping of his steeds.
23 'Curse Meroz,' said the angel* of the LORD,
'Curse its inhabitants bitterly,
Because they did not come to the help of the LORD,
To the help of the LORD against the mighty.'

24 "Most blessed among women is Jael,
The wife of Heber the Kenite;
[v]Blessed is she among women in tents.
25 He asked for water, she gave milk;
She brought out cream in a lordly bowl.
26 She stretched her hand to the tent peg,
Her right hand to the workmen's hammer;
She pounded Sisera, she pierced his head,
She split and struck through his temple.
27 At her feet he sank, he fell, he lay still;
At her feet he sank, he fell;
Where he sank, there he fell [w]dead.

28 "The mother of Sisera looked through the window,
And cried out through the lattice,
'Why is his chariot *so* long in coming?
Why tarries the clatter of his chariots?'
29 Her wisest ladies answered her,
Yes, she answered herself,
30 'Are they not finding and dividing the spoil:
To every man a girl *or* two;
For Sisera, plunder of dyed garments,
Plunder of garments embroidered and dyed,
Two pieces of dyed embroidery for the neck of the looter?'

31 "Thus let all Your enemies [x]perish, O LORD!
But *let* those who love Him *be* [y]like the [z]sun
When it comes out in full [a]strength."
So the land had rest for forty years.

Midianites Oppress Israel

6 Then the children of Israel did [a]evil
in the sight of the LORD. So the LORD
delivered them into the hand of [b]Midian
for seven years, 2and the hand of Midian
prevailed against Israel. Because of the

* **5:15** Following Septuagint, Syriac, Targum, and Vulgate; Masoretic Text reads *And my princes in Issachar.* • Literally *at his feet* * **5:17** Or *at ease* * **5:23** Or *Angel*

5:17 remain on ships. The reference to Dan remaining "in ships" probably reflects the location of their original inheritance, which was along the south-central coastal plain where they would have had access to the sea (Josh. 19:40–46). Later they migrated northward, having been forced out of their territory (1:34; 18:1; Josh. 19:47).

5:26 *Sisera.* The poem describes Sisera's death using graphic, emotive language, which it repeats several times to make the point. Sisera's death was probably a bloodier affair than the prose account indicates.

6:1 *Midian.* Midian was located in the Arabian Peninsula, southeast of Israel and east of the Sinai Peninsula. The Midianites were descendants of Abraham through his wife Keturah (Gen. 25:1–2), so they were distantly related to the Israelites. Midianites bought Joseph from his brothers (Gen. 37:25–36), welcomed Moses in the wilderness (Ex. 2:15–21), and hired Balaam to curse Israel (Num. 22:7). Generally speaking, Israel counted Midian among its foes. In this account, the Midianites were menacing Israel, burning, looting, and leaving many near starvation (6:4–5).

5:14 [p] Judg. 3:13 **5:17** [q] Josh. 22:9 [r] Josh. 19:29, 31 **5:18** [s] Judg. 4:6, 10 **5:19** [t] Judg. 1:27 **5:21** [u] Judg. 4:7 **5:24** [v] [Luke 1:28] **5:27** [w] Judg. 4:18–21 **5:31** [x] Ps. 92:9 [y] 2 Sam. 23:4 [z] Ps. 37:6; 89:36, 37 [a] Ps. 19:5 **6:1** [a] Judg. 2:11 [b] Num. 22:4; 31:1–3

Midianites, the children of Israel made for themselves the dens, ^cthe caves, and the strongholds which *are* in the mountains. ³So it was, whenever Israel had sown, Midianites would come up; also Amalekites and the ^dpeople of the East would come up against them. ⁴Then they would encamp against them and ^edestroy the produce of the earth as far as Gaza, and leave no sustenance for Israel, neither sheep nor ox nor ^fdonkey. ⁵For they would come up with their livestock and their tents, coming in as numerous as locusts; both they and their camels were without number; and they would enter the land to destroy it. ⁶So Israel was greatly impoverished because of the Midianites, and the children of Israel ^gcried out to the LORD.

⁷And it came to pass, when the children of Israel cried out to the LORD because of the Midianites, ⁸that the LORD sent a prophet to the children of Israel, who said to them, "Thus says the LORD God of Israel: 'I brought you up from Egypt and brought you out of the ^hhouse of bondage; ⁹and I delivered you out of the hand of the Egyptians and out of the hand of all who oppressed you, and ⁱdrove them out before you and gave you their land. ¹⁰Also I said to you, "I *am* the LORD your God; ^jdo not fear the gods of the Amorites, in whose land you dwell." But you have not obeyed My ^kvoice.' "

Gideon

¹¹Now the Angel of the LORD came and sat under the terebinth tree which *was* in Ophrah, which *belonged* to Joash ^lthe Abiezrite, while his son ^mGideon threshed wheat in the winepress, in order to hide *it*

from the Midianites. ¹²And the ⁿAngel of the LORD appeared to him, and said to him, "The LORD *is* ^owith you, you mighty man of valor!"

¹³Gideon said to Him, "O my lord,* if the LORD is with us, why then has all this happened to us? And ^pwhere *are* all His miracles ^qwhich our fathers told us about, saying, 'Did not the LORD bring us up from Egypt?' But now the LORD has ^rforsaken us and delivered us into the hands of the Midianites."

¹⁴Then the LORD turned to him and said, ^s"Go in this might of yours, and you shall save Israel from the hand of the Midianites. ^tHave I not sent you?"

¹⁵So he said to Him, "O my Lord,* how can I save Israel? Indeed ^umy clan *is* the weakest in Manasseh, and I *am* the least in my father's house."

¹⁶And the LORD said to him, ^v"Surely I will be with you, and you shall defeat the Midianites as one man."

¹⁷Then he said to Him, "If now I have found favor in Your sight, then ^wshow me a sign that it is You who talk with me. ¹⁸^xDo not depart from here, I pray, until I come to You and bring out my offering and set *it* before You."

And He said, "I will wait until you come back."

¹⁹^ySo Gideon went in and prepared a young goat, and unleavened bread from an ephah of flour. The meat he put in a basket, and he put the broth in a pot; and he brought *them* out to Him under the terebinth tree and presented *them*. ²⁰The

---

* **6:13** Hebrew *adoni*, used of man   * **6:15** Hebrew *Adonai*, used of God

---

6:3 *Amalekites.* The Amalekites were a nomadic people who lived in the Sinai desert and the Negev, the desert south of Israel. They were descendants of Esau (Gen. 36:12) and they joined the Midianites against Israel.

6:11–16 Doubt—Doubt, at first thought, appears to be an innocuous sin, so harmless that it affects only the attitude of the one who doubts. But doubt is much more serious than this. Doubt of God's Word, planted by the arch deceiver, was at the root of that first sin committed in the garden of Eden. Doubt of God's goodness and truth arose before desire for the forbidden fruit led to disobedience. Doubt of God and doubt of God's Word cause men to make decisions based on human reckonings. Doubts undispelled lead to sin and defeat.

6:11 *terebinth.* The terebinth, sometimes called an oak, is a large tree with a thick trunk and heavy branches. Botanically speaking, it is not an oak tree, but it has a similar majestic appearance. ***winepress.*** A winepress was a square or circular pit carved into rock, in which grapes were crushed. Wheat was usually separated on open threshing floors so the wind could carry away the chaff in the winnowing process. The fact that Gideon was forced to thresh wheat hidden inside a winepress—despite the fact that he had access to a threshing floor (v. 37)—is yet

another illustration of the desperate state the Israelites were in.

6:13 *my lord . . . the LORD.* "My lord" was a polite form of address, but "the LORD" is the personal name of God (Yahweh).

6:15 *I am the least in my father's house.* Gideon's objection is reminiscent of the words spoken by Moses (Ex. 3:11) and Jeremiah (Jer. 1:6).

6:16 *I will be with you.* This was the same great promise that God had given to Moses and Joshua previously (Ex. 3:12; Josh. 1:5–9). This should have greatly encouraged Gideon, but he still had doubts. Often we are quick to judge those who doubt God even when they have firsthand evidence of His mighty works. But we all fail to trust God fully at times. God accomplished His will despite Gideon's weakness, and He can do the same through us.

6:2 ^c 1 Sam. 13:6   **6:3** ^d Judg. 7:12   **6:4** ^e Lev. 26:16 ^f Deut. 28:31   **6:6** ^g Hos. 5:15   **6:8** ^h Josh. 24:17   **6:9** ⁱ Ps. 44:2, 3   **6:10** ^j 2 Kin. 17:35, 37, 38   ^k Judg. 2:1, 2   **6:11** ^l Josh. 17:2 ^m Heb. 11:32   **6:12** ⁿ Judg. 13:3 ^o Josh. 1:5   **6:13** ^p [Is. 59:1] ^q Ps. 44:1 ^r Ps. 44:9–16   **6:14** ^s 1 Sam. 12:11 ^t Josh. 1:9   **6:15** ^u 1 Sam. 9:21   **6:16** ^v Ex. 3:12   **6:17** ^w Judg. 6:36, 37   **6:18** ^x Gen. 18:3, 5   **6:19** ^y Gen. 18:6–8

Angel of God said to him, "Take the meat and the unleavened bread and ᶻlay *them* on this rock, and ᵃpour out the broth." And he did so.

²¹Then the Angel of the LORD put out the end of the staff that *was* in His hand, and touched the meat and the unleavened bread; and ᵇfire rose out of the rock and consumed the meat and the unleavened bread. And the Angel of the LORD departed out of his sight.

²²Now Gideon ᶜperceived that He *was* the Angel of the LORD. So Gideon said, "Alas, O Lord GOD! ᵈFor I have seen the Angel of the LORD face to face."

²³Then the LORD said to him, ᵉ"Peace *be* with you; do not fear, you shall not die." ²⁴So Gideon built an altar there to the LORD, and called it The-LORD-Is-Peace.* To this day it *is* still ᶠin Ophrah of the Abiezrites.

²⁵Now it came to pass the same night that the LORD said to him, "Take your father's young bull, the second bull of seven years old, and ᵍtear down the altar of ʰBaal that your father has, and ⁱcut down the wooden image* that *is* beside it; ²⁶and build an altar to the LORD your God on top of this rock in the proper arrangement, and take the second bull and offer a burnt sacrifice with the wood of the image which you shall cut down." ²⁷So Gideon took ten men from among his servants and did as the LORD had said to him. But because he feared his father's household and the men of the city too much to do *it* by day, he did *it* by night.

Gideon Destroys the Altar of Baal

²⁸And when the men of the city arose early in the morning, there was the altar of Baal, torn down; and the wooden image that *was* beside it was cut down, and the second bull was being offered on the altar *which had been* built. ²⁹So they said to one another, "Who has done this thing?" And when they had inquired and asked, they said, "Gideon the son of Joash has done this thing." ³⁰Then the men of the city said to Joash, "Bring out your son, that he may die, because he has torn down the altar of Baal, and because he has cut down the wooden image that *was* beside it."

³¹But Joash said to all who stood against him, "Would you plead for Baal? Would you save him? Let the one who would plead for him be put to death by morning! If he *is* a god, let him plead for himself, because his altar has been torn down!" ³²Therefore on that day he called him ʲJerubbaal,* saying, "Let Baal plead against him, because he has torn down his altar."

³³Then all ᵏthe Midianites and Amalekites, the people of the East, gathered together; and they crossed over and encamped in ˡthe Valley of Jezreel. ³⁴But ᵐthe Spirit of the LORD came upon Gideon; then he ⁿblew the trumpet, and the Abiezrites gathered behind him. ³⁵And he sent messengers throughout all Manasseh, who also gathered behind him. He also sent messengers to ᵒAsher, ᵖZebulun, and Naphtali; and they came up to meet them.

The Sign of the Fleece

³⁶So Gideon said to God, "If You will save Israel by my hand as You have said— ³⁷ᵠlook, I shall put a fleece of wool on the threshing floor; if there is dew on the fleece only, and *it is* dry on all the ground, then I shall know that You will save Israel by my hand, as You have said." ³⁸And it was so. When he rose early the next morning and squeezed the fleece together, he wrung the dew out of the fleece, a bowlful of water. ³⁹Then Gideon said to God, ʳ"Do not be angry with me, but let me speak just once more: Let me test, I pray, just once more with the fleece; let it now be dry only on

---

* **6:24** Hebrew *YHWH Shalom*   * **6:25** Hebrew *Asherah*, a Canaanite goddess   * **6:32** Literally *Let Baal Plead*

===

6:22 *Gideon perceived.* When the Angel of the Lord vanished, then Gideon realized who it was and feared for his life. This reaction of fear appears to have been rooted in the knowledge that anyone who gazed upon God would die (Ex. 33:20).

6:24 *To this day.* This expression lends authenticity to the account. It is the author's way of declaring to later generations that they could verify the story by going and seeing this altar themselves.

6:25 *wooden image.* Asherah was the Canaanite fertility goddess. Sacred wooden poles or groves were erected at places where she was worshiped.

6:26 *the wood of the image.* Gideon's sacrifice was to be a bold statement of the superiority of the Lord over the false gods His people were worshiping.

6:36–40 *Prayer*—Gideon had already received an unmistakable message from God, and he had been assured that God would lead him to victory. His prayer and request for a sign were the result of his lack of faith, but in spite of Gideon's wavering, God kindly accommodated his requests. Many people

have relied on Gideon's example as a way of seeking guidance from the Lord. Occasionally God has chosen to answer such requests, even as He did for Gideon, because He is compassionate and makes allowances for our weakness, but putting out a fleece is not the action of faith. Isaiah modeled a proper response to God's clearly revealed will: he said, "Here am I; send me" (Is. 6:8). So too did the disciples, who dropped their nets immediately and followed Jesus (Mark 1:18).

6:39 *Let me test . . . just once more.* Gideon's desire to test God's sign could have been a violation of the law which prohibited people from testing God (Deut.

6:20 ᶻ Judg. 13:19   ᵃ 1 Kin. 18:33, 34   **6:21** ᵇ Lev. 9:24   **6:22** ᶜ Judg. 13:21, 22   ᵈ Gen. 16:13   **6:23** ᵉ Dan. 10:19   **6:24** ᶠ Judg. 8:32   **6:25** ᵍ Judg. 2:2   ʰ Judg. 3:7   ⁱ Ex. 34:13   **6:32** ʲ 1 Sam. 12:11   **6:33** ᵏ Judg. 6:3   ˡ Josh. 17:16   **6:34** ᵐ Judg. 3:10   ⁿ Judg. 3:27   **6:35** ᵒ Judg. 5:17; 7:23   ᵖ Judg. 4:6, 10; 5:18   **6:37** ᵠ [Ex. 4:3–7]   **6:39** ʳ Gen. 18:32

the fleece, but on all the ground let there be dew." 40And God did so that night. It was dry on the fleece only, but there was dew on all the ground.

Gideon's Valiant Three Hundred

7 Then *a*Jerubbaal (that *is*, Gideon) and all the people who *were* with him rose early and encamped beside the well of Harod, so that the camp of the Midianites was on the north side of them by the hill of Moreh in the valley.

2And the LORD said to Gideon, "The people who *are* with you *are* too many for Me to give the Midianites into their hands, lest Israel *b*claim glory for itself against Me, saying, 'My own hand has saved me.' 3Now therefore, proclaim in the hearing of the people, saying, *c*'Whoever *is* fearful and afraid, let him turn and depart at once from Mount Gilead.'" And twenty-two thousand of the people returned, and ten thousand remained.

4But the LORD said to Gideon, "The people *are* still *too* many; bring them down to the water, and I will test them for you there. Then it will be, *that* of whom I say to you, 'This one shall go with you,' the same shall go with you; and of whomever I say to you, 'This one shall not go with you,' the same shall not go." 5So he brought the people down to the water. And the LORD said to Gideon, "Everyone who laps from the water with his tongue, as a dog laps, you shall set apart by himself; likewise everyone who gets down on his knees to drink." 6And the number of those who lapped, *putting* their hand to their mouth, was three hundred men; but all the rest of the people got down on their knees to drink water. 7Then the LORD said to Gideon, *d*"By the three hundred men who lapped I will save you, and deliver the Midianites into your hand. Let all the *other* people go, every man to his place." 8So the people took provisions and their trumpets in their hands. And he sent away all *the rest of* Israel, every man to his tent, and retained those three hundred men. Now the camp of Midian was below him in the valley.

9It happened on the same *e*night that the LORD said to him, "Arise, go down against the camp, for I have delivered it into your hand. 10But if you are afraid to go down, go down to the camp with Purah your servant,

11and you shall *f*hear what they say; and afterward your hands shall be strengthened to go down against the camp." Then he went down with Purah his servant to the outpost of the armed men who *were* in the camp. 12Now the Midianites and Amalekites, *g*all the people of the East, were lying in the valley *h*as numerous as locusts; and their camels *were* without number, as the sand by the seashore in multitude.

13And when Gideon had come, there was a man telling a dream to his companion. He said, "I have had a dream: *To my* surprise, a loaf of barley bread tumbled into the camp of Midian; it came to a tent and struck it so that it fell and overturned, and the tent collapsed." 14Then his companion answered and said, "This *is* nothing else but the sword of Gideon the son of Joash, a man of Israel! Into his hand *i*God has delivered Midian and the whole camp."

15And so it was, when Gideon heard the telling of the dream and its interpretation, that he worshiped. He returned to the camp of Israel, and said, "Arise, for the LORD has delivered the camp of Midian into your hand." 16Then he divided the three hundred men *into* three companies, and he put a trumpet into every man's hand, with empty pitchers, and torches inside the pitchers. 17And he said to them, "Look at me and do likewise; watch, and when I come to the edge of the camp you shall do as I do: 18When I blow the trumpet, I and all who *are* with me, then you also blow the trumpets on every side of the whole camp, and say, 'The sword of the LORD and of Gideon!'"

19So Gideon and the hundred men who *were* with him came to the outpost of the camp at the beginning of the middle watch, just as they had posted the watch; and they blew the trumpets and broke the pitchers that *were* in their hands. 20Then the three companies blew the trumpets and broke the pitchers—they held the torches in their left hands and the trumpets in their right hands for blowing—and they cried, "The sword of the LORD and of Gideon!" 21And *j*every man stood in his place all around the camp; *k*and the whole army ran and cried out and fled. 22When the three hundred *l*blew the trumpets, *m*the LORD set *n*every man's sword against his companion throughout

---

6:16). Gideon himself was aware that he was doing something unwise, if not sinful, since he asked God not to be angry with him.
7:3 fearful and afraid. Mosaic law allowed military exemptions for several classes of people, including those who had just built a home, those who had just planted a vineyard, those engaged to be married, and those who were fearful (Deut. 20:5–8).
7:4–5 The people are still too many. God reduced Gideon's army to emphasize who was really bringing victory.

7:19 middle watch. According to Jewish tradition, the hours between sunset and sunrise were divided into three watches, which would put the time of this attack at roughly 10:00 P.M.

7:1 *a* Judg. 6:32   **7:2** *b* Deut. 8:17   **7:3** *c* Deut. 20:8   **7:7** *d* 1 Sam. 14:6   **7:9** *e* Judg. 6:25   **7:11** *f* 1 Sam. 14:9, 10   **7:12** *g* Judg. 6:3, 33; 8:10   *h* Judg. 6:5   **7:14** *i* Judg. 6:14, 16   **7:21** *j* 2 Chr. 20:17   *k* 2 Kin. 7:7   **7:22** *l* Josh. 6:4, 16, 20   *m* Is. 9:4   *n* 1 Sam. 14:20

the whole camp; and the army fled to Beth
Acacia,* toward Zererah, as far as the border of [o]Abel Meholah, by Tabbath.
23 And the men of Israel gathered together from [p]Naphtali, Asher, and all Manasseh, and pursued the Midianites.
24 Then Gideon sent messengers throughout all the [q]mountains of Ephraim, saying,
"Come down against the Midianites, and
seize from them the watering places as far
as Beth Barah and the Jordan." Then all
the men of Ephraim gathered together and
[r]seized the watering places as far as [s]Beth
Barah and the Jordan. 25 And they captured
[t]two princes of the Midianites, [u]Oreb and
Zeeb. They killed Oreb at the rock of Oreb,
and Zeeb they killed at the winepress of
Zeeb. They pursued Midian and brought
the heads of Oreb and Zeeb to Gideon on
the [v]other side of the Jordan.

Gideon Subdues the Midianites

8 Now [a]the men of Ephraim said to him,
"Why have you done this to us by not
calling us when you went to fight with the
Midianites?" And they reprimanded him
sharply.
2 So he said to them, "What have I done
now in comparison with you? *Is* not the
gleaning *of the grapes* of Ephraim better
than the vintage of [b]Abiezer? 3 [c]God has
delivered into your hands the princes of
Midian, Oreb and Zeeb. And what was I
able to do in comparison with you?" Then
their [d]anger toward him subsided when he
said that.
4 When Gideon came [e]to the Jordan,
he and [f]the three hundred men who *were*
with him crossed over, exhausted but
still in pursuit. 5 Then he said to the men
of [g]Succoth, "Please give loaves of bread
to the people who follow me, for they are
exhausted, and I am pursuing Zebah and
Zalmunna, kings of Midian."
6 And the leaders of Succoth said, [h]"*Are*
the hands of Zebah and Zalmunna now in
your hand, that [i]we should give bread to
your army?"
7 So Gideon said, "For this cause, when
the LORD has delivered Zebah and Zalmunna into my hand, [j]then I will tear your
flesh with the thorns of the wilderness and
with briers!" 8 Then he went up from there
[k]to Penuel and spoke to them in the same
way. And the men of Penuel answered him
as the men of Succoth had answered. 9 So
he also spoke to the men of Penuel, saying,
"When I [l]come back in peace, [m]I will tear
down this tower!"
10 Now Zebah and Zalmunna *were* at
Karkor, and their armies with them, about
fifteen thousand, all who were left of [n]all
the army of the people of the East; for [o]one
hundred and twenty thousand men who
drew the sword had fallen. 11 Then Gideon
went up by the road of those who dwell in
tents on the east of [p]Nobah and Jogbehah;
and he attacked the army while the camp
felt [q]secure. 12 When Zebah and Zalmunna
fled, he pursued them; and he [r]took the two
kings of Midian, Zebah and Zalmunna,
and routed the whole army.
13 Then Gideon the son of Joash returned
from battle, from the Ascent of Heres.
14 And he caught a young man of the men
of Succoth and interrogated him; and he
wrote down for him the leaders of Succoth
and its elders, seventy-seven men. 15 Then
he came to the men of Succoth and said,
"Here are Zebah and Zalmunna, about
whom you [s]ridiculed me, saying, '*Are* the
hands of Zebah and Zalmunna now in your
hand, that we should give bread to your
weary men?'" 16 [t]And he took the elders of
the city, and thorns of the wilderness and
briers, and with them he taught the men of
Succoth. 17 [u]Then he tore down the tower of
[v]Penuel and killed the men of the city.
18 And he said to Zebah and Zalmunna,
"What kind of men *were they* whom you
killed at [w]Tabor?"
So they answered, "As you *are*, so *were*
they; each one resembled the son of a king."
19 Then he said, "They *were* my brothers,
the sons of my mother. *As* the LORD lives, if
you had let them live, I would not kill you."
20 And he said to Jether his firstborn, "Rise,
kill them!" But the youth would not draw
his sword; for he was afraid, because he
was still a youth.
21 So Zebah and Zalmunna said, "Rise
yourself, and kill us; for as a man *is, so is*
his strength." So Gideon arose and [x]killed
Zebah and Zalmunna, and took the cres-
cent ornaments that *were* on their camels'
necks.

* **7:22** Hebrew *Beth Shittah*

8:5 ***Succoth.*** Succoth was east of the Jordan, near the Jabbok River.

8:14 ***he wrote down for him the leaders of Succoth.*** Literacy in early civilizations was at first limited to the educated elite, as in Mesopotamia and Egypt. Their writing systems were complex and only a tiny portion of the population could read and write. However, the spread of alphabetic systems vastly simplified the task of reading and writing. Hundreds of potsherds from throughout Palestine have simple inscriptions on them, indicating that some degree of literacy had become widely accessible by Gideon's day.

7:22 [o] 1 Kin. 4:12 **7:23** [p] Judg. 6:35 **7:24** [q] Judg. 3:27 [r] Judg. 3:28 [s] John 1:28 **7:25** [t] Judg. 8:3 [u] Ps. 83:11 [v] Judg. 8:4 **8:1** [a] Judg. 12:1 **8:2** [b] Judg. 6:11 **8:3** [c] Judg. 7:24, 25 [d] Prov. 15:1 **8:4** [e] Judg. 7:25 [f] Judg. 7:6 **8:5** [g] Gen. 33:17 **8:6** [h] Judg. 8:15 [i] 1 Sam. 25:11 **8:7** [j] Judg. 8:16 **8:8** [k] Gen. 32:30, 31 **8:9** [l] 1 Kin. 22:27 [m] Judg. 8:17 **8:10** [n] Judg. 7:12 [o] Judg. 6:5 **8:11** [p] Num. 32:35, 42 [q] Judg. 18:27 **8:12** [r] Ps. 83:11 **8:15** [s] Judg. 8:6 **8:16** [t] Judg. 8:7 **8:17** [u] Judg. 8:9 [v] 1 Kin. 12:25 **8:18** [w] Judg. 4:6 **8:21** [x] Ps. 83:11

Gideon's Ephod

²²Then the men of Israel said to Gideon, ^y"Rule over us, both you and your son, and your grandson also; for you have ^zdelivered us from the hand of Midian." ²³But Gideon said to them, "I will not rule over you, nor shall my son rule over you; ^athe LORD shall rule over you." ²⁴Then Gideon said to them, "I would like to make a request of you, that each of you would give me the earrings from his plunder." For they had golden earrings, ^bbecause they *were* Ishmaelites.

²⁵So they answered, "We will gladly give *them*." And they spread out a garment, and each man threw into it the earrings from his plunder. ²⁶Now the weight of the gold earrings that he requested was one thousand seven hundred *shekels* of gold, besides the crescent ornaments, pendants, and purple robes which *were* on the kings of Midian, and besides the chains that *were* around their camels' necks. ²⁷Then Gideon ^cmade it into an ephod and set it up in his city, ^dOphrah. And all Israel ^eplayed the harlot with it there. It became ^fa snare to Gideon and to his house.

²⁸Thus Midian was subdued before the children of Israel, so that they lifted their heads no more. ^gAnd the country was quiet for forty years in the days of Gideon.

Death of Gideon

²⁹Then ^hJerubbaal the son of Joash went and dwelt in his own house. ³⁰Gideon had ⁱseventy sons who were his own offspring, for he had many wives. ³¹j And his concubine who *was* in Shechem also bore him a son, whose name he called Abimelech. ³²Now Gideon the son of Joash died ^kat a good old age, and was buried in the tomb of Joash his father, ^lin Ophrah of the Abiezrites.

³³So it was, ^mas soon as Gideon was dead, that the children of Israel again ⁿplayed the harlot with the Baals, ^oand made Baal-Berith their god. ³⁴Thus the children of Israel ^pdid not remember the LORD their God, who had delivered them from the hands of all their enemies on every side; ³⁵nor did they show kindness to the house of Jerubbaal (Gideon) in accordance with the good he had done for Israel.

Abimelech's Conspiracy

9 Then Abimelech the son of Jerubbaal went to Shechem, to ^ahis mother's brothers, and spoke with them and with all the family of the house of his mother's father, saying, ²"Please speak in the hearing of all the men of Shechem: 'Which is better for you, that all ^bseventy of the sons of Jerubbaal reign over you, or that one reign over you?' Remember that I *am* your own flesh and ^cbone."

³And his mother's brothers spoke all these words concerning him in the hearing of all the men of Shechem; and their heart was inclined to follow Abimelech, for they said, "He is our ^dbrother." ⁴So they gave him seventy *shekels* of silver from the temple of ^eBaal-Berith, with which Abimelech hired ^fworthless and reckless men; and they followed him. ⁵Then he went to his father's house ^gat Ophrah and ^hkilled his brothers, the seventy sons of Jerubbaal, on one stone. But Jotham the youngest son of Jerubbaal was left, because he hid himself. ⁶And all the men of Shechem gathered together, all of Beth Millo, and they went and made Abimelech king beside the terebinth tree at the pillar that *was* in Shechem.

8:22–23 Self-Denial—In the initial flush of victory Gideon was offered hereditary rulership over Israel, which he wisely rejected. God the Lord was Judge with ultimate authority, and He would rule over the people. Gideon knew his place before God. In the same way, we are taught not to think more highly of ourselves than we ought, but "as God has dealt" (Rom. 12:3).

8:22 Rule over us. This request, while understandable from a human perspective, failed to acknowledge that it was God, not Gideon, who had delivered the people.

8:23 the LORD shall rule over you. The word order of the Hebrew makes it clear that God's claim was exclusive; it might be paraphrased, "It is the Lord, and no one else, who shall rule over you." This statement is widely assumed to indicate that God intended that Israel should never have a king, but that He would be their only King. However, God had promised Abraham that he would count kings among his descendants (Gen. 17:6). The problem was not in the concept of having a king, but in their motivation. They wanted to have a visible, human leader, rather than trusting in God's leadership. The role of a true king would be to lead the people in devotion to God's rule.

8:27 ephod. The original ephod was an ornate ceremonial garment worn by the high priest (Ex. 29:5).

Gideon's motivation for making this golden ephod is unclear, but his imitation of the sacred objects devoted to the worship of God ended up distracting the people and undermining the true worship of God.

8:31 Abimelech. This name means "my father is king." Some think that Gideon did become a king in practice if not in name, for he gave his son a royal name and acted as a leader of the people (vv. 24–27).

9:1–57 Conspiracy—The seeds of Abimelech's violent grab for power were sown in Israel's persistent infidelity to God, which led to another rejection of the Lord (8:22,24–27,33–35).

9:6 terebinth tree at the pillar. Sadly, this coronation took place at the same tree where Jacob had put away his foreign gods many years before (Gen. 35:4),

8:22^y [Judg. 9:8] ^z Judg. 3:9; 9:17　**8:23**^a 1 Sam. 8:7; 10:19; 12:12　**8:24**^b Gen. 37:25, 28　**8:27**^c Judg. 17:5　^d Judg. 6:11, 24　^e [Ps. 106:39]　^f Deut. 7:16　**8:28**^g Judg. 5:31　**8:29**^h Judg. 6:32; 7:1　**8:30**ⁱ Judg. 9:2, 5　**8:31**^j Judg. 9:1　**8:32**^k Gen. 25:8　^l Judg. 6:24; 8:27　**8:33**^m Judg. 2:19　ⁿ Judg. 2:17　^o Judg. 9:4, 46　**8:34**^p Deut. 4:9　**8:35**^q Judg. 9:16–18　**9:1**^a Judg. 8:31, 35　**9:2**^b Judg. 8:30; 9:5, 18　^c Gen. 29:14　**9:3**^d Gen. 29:15　**9:4**^e Judg. 8:33　^f Judg. 11:3　**9:5**^g Judg. 6:24　^h 2 Kin. 11:1, 2

The Parable of the Trees

7Now when they told Jotham, he went and stood on top of *i*Mount Gerizim, and lifted his voice and cried out. And he said to them:

"Listen to me, you men of Shechem,
That God may listen to you!

8 "The*j* trees once went forth to anoint a
king over them.
And they said to the olive tree,
k'Reign over us!'
9 But the olive tree said to them,
'Should I cease giving my oil,
*l*With which they honor God and men,
And go to sway over trees?'
10 "Then the trees said to the fig tree,
'You come *and* reign over us!'
11 But the fig tree said to them,
'Should I cease my sweetness and my
good fruit,
And go to sway over trees?'
12 "Then the trees said to the vine,
'You come *and* reign over us!'
13 But the vine said to them,
'Should I cease my new wine,
*m*Which cheers *both* God and men,
And go to sway over trees?'
14 "Then all the trees said to the bramble,
'You come *and* reign over us!'
15 And the bramble said to the trees,
'If in truth you anoint me as king over
you,
Then come *and* take shelter in my
*n*shade;
But if not, *o*let fire come out of the
bramble
And devour the *p*cedars of Lebanon!'

16"Now therefore, if you have acted in truth and sincerity in making Abimelech king, and if you have dealt well with Jerubbaal and his house, and have done to him *q*as he deserves— **17**for my *r*father fought for you, risked his life, and *s*delivered you out of the hand of Midian; **18***t*but you have risen up against my father's house this day, and killed his seventy sons on one stone, and made Abimelech, the son of his *u*female servant, king over the men of Shechem, because he is your brother— **19**if then you have acted in truth and sincerity with Jerubbaal

and with his house this day, *then* *v*rejoice in Abimelech, and let him also rejoice in you. **20**But if not, *w*let fire come from Abimelech and devour the men of Shechem and Beth Millo; and let fire come from the men of Shechem and from Beth Millo and devour Abimelech!" **21**And Jotham ran away and fled; and he went to *x*Beer and dwelt there, for fear of Abimelech his brother.

Downfall of Abimelech

22After Abimelech had reigned over Israel three years, **23***y*God sent a *z*spirit of ill will between Abimelech and the men of Shechem; and the men of Shechem *a*dealt treacherously with Abimelech, **24***b*that the crime *done* to the seventy sons of Jerubbaal might be settled and their *c*blood be laid on Abimelech their brother, who killed them, and on the men of Shechem, who aided them in the killing of his brothers. **25**And the men of Shechem set men in ambush against him on the tops of the mountains, and they robbed all who passed by them along that way; and it was told Abimelech.

26Now Gaal the son of Ebed came with his brothers and went over to Shechem; and the men of Shechem put their confidence in him. **27**So they went out into the fields, and gathered *grapes* from their vineyards, and trod *them*, and made merry. And they went into *d*the house of their god, and ate and drank, and cursed Abimelech. **28**Then Gaal the son of Ebed said, *e*"Who *is* Abimelech, and who *is* Shechem, that we should serve him? *Is he* not the son of Jerubbaal, and *is not* Zebul his officer? Serve the men of *f*Hamor the father of Shechem; but why should we serve him? **29***g*If only this people were under my authority!* Then I would remove Abimelech." So he* said to Abimelech, "Increase your army and come out!"

30When Zebul, the ruler of the city, heard the words of Gaal the son of Ebed, his anger was aroused. **31**And he sent messengers to Abimelech secretly, saying, "Take note! Gaal the son of Ebed and his brothers have come to Shechem; and here they are, fortifying the city against you.

---

* **9:29** Literally *hand* • Following Masoretic Text and Targum; Dead Sea Scrolls read *they*; Septuagint reads *I*.

---

and where Joshua had commemorated his covenant with God (Josh. 24:26).
9:14–15 Pride—The pomp and ceremony that goes with royalty is a source of pride not only for the king but also for his subjects. The idea of having a man from their own tribe ruling the entire nation appealed to the pride of the men of Shechem. Pride led them to surrender their freedom and submit to the rule of man rather than God. It is the cause of many kinds of injustice in society: social, economic, and political. It often leads to war and violence, as it did in this case. Within a brief period of time after Abimelech was anointed king they realized their mistake. The

prophecy of Jotham was fulfilled, since fire did come out of the bramble (from Abimelech) to consume the men of Shechem. Pride led to their destruction.

9:7 *i* Deut. 11:29; 27:12   **9:8** *j* 2 Kin. 14:9   *k* Judg. 8:22, 23   **9:9** *l* [John 5:23]   **9:13** *m* Ps. 104:15   **9:15** *n* Is. 30:2   *o* Num. 21:28   *p* 2 Kin. 14:9   **9:16** *q* Judg. 8:35   **9:17** *r* Judg. 7   *s* Judg. 8:22   **9:18** *t* Judg. 8:30, 35; 9:2, 5, 6   *u* Judg. 8:31   **9:19** *v* Is. 8:6   **9:20** *w* Judg. 9:15, 45, 56, 57   **9:21** *x* Num. 21:16   **9:23** *y* Is. 19:14   *z* 1 Sam. 16:14; 18:9, 10   *a* Is. 33:1   **9:24** *b* 1 Kin. 2:32   *c* Num. 35:33   **9:27** *d* Judg. 9:4   **9:28** *e* 1 Sam. 25:10   *f* Gen. 34:2, 6   **9:29** *g* 2 Sam. 15:4

³²Now therefore, get up by night, you and the people who *are* with you, and lie in wait in the field. ³³And it shall be, as soon as the sun is up in the morning, *that* you shall rise early and rush upon the city; and *when* he and the people who are with him come out against you, you may then do to them as you find opportunity."

³⁴So Abimelech and all the people who *were* with him rose by night, and lay in wait against Shechem in four companies. ³⁵When Gaal the son of Ebed went out and stood in the entrance to the city gate, Abimelech and the people who *were* with him rose from lying in wait. ³⁶And when Gaal saw the people, he said to Zebul, "Look, people are coming down from the tops of the mountains!"

But Zebul said to him, "You see the shadows of the mountains as *if they were* men."

³⁷So Gaal spoke again and said, "See, people are coming down from the center of the land, and another company is coming from the Diviners'* Terebinth Tree."

³⁸Then Zebul said to him, "Where indeed *is* your mouth now, with which you ʰsaid, 'Who is Abimelech, that we should serve him?' *Are* not these the people whom you despised? Go out, if you will, and fight with them now."

³⁹So Gaal went out, leading the men of Shechem, and fought with Abimelech. ⁴⁰And Abimelech chased him, and he fled from him; and many fell wounded, to the *very* entrance of the gate. ⁴¹Then Abimelech dwelt at Arumah, and Zebul drove out Gaal and his brothers, so that they would not dwell in Shechem.

⁴²And it came about on the next day that the people went out into the field, and they told Abimelech. ⁴³So he took his people, divided them into three companies, and lay in wait in the field. And he looked, and there were the people, coming out of the city; and he rose against them and attacked them. ⁴⁴Then Abimelech and the company that *was* with him rushed forward and stood at the entrance of the gate of the city; and the *other* two companies rushed upon all who *were* in the fields and killed them. ⁴⁵So Abimelech fought against the city all that day; ⁱhe took the city and killed the people who *were* in it; and he ʲdemolished the city and sowed it with salt.

⁴⁶Now when all the men of the tower of Shechem had heard *that,* they entered the stronghold of the temple ᵏof the god Berith. ⁴⁷And it was told Abimelech that all the men of the tower of Shechem were gathered together. ⁴⁸Then Abimelech went up to Mount ˡZalmon, he and all the people who *were* with him. And Abimelech took an ax in his hand and cut down a bough from the trees, and took it and laid *it* on his shoulder; then he said to the people who were with him, "What you have seen me do, make haste *and* do as I *have done.*" ⁴⁹So each of the people likewise cut down his own bough and followed Abimelech, put *them* against the stronghold, and set the stronghold on fire above them, so that all the people of the tower of Shechem died, about a thousand men and women.

⁵⁰Then Abimelech went to Thebez, and he encamped against Thebez and took it. ⁵¹But there was a strong tower in the city, and all the men and women—all the people of the city—fled there and shut themselves in; then they went up to the top of the tower. ⁵²So Abimelech came as far as the tower and fought against it; and he drew near the door of the tower to burn it with fire. ⁵³But a certain woman ᵐdropped an upper millstone on Abimelech's head and crushed his skull. ⁵⁴Then ⁿhe called quickly to the young man, his armorbearer, and said to him, "Draw your sword and kill me, lest men say of me, 'A woman killed him.'" So his young man thrust him through, and he died. ⁵⁵And when the men of Israel saw that Abimelech was dead, they departed, every man to his place.

⁵⁶ᵒThus God repaid the wickedness of Abimelech, which he had done to his father by killing his seventy brothers. ⁵⁷And all the evil of the men of Shechem God returned on their own heads, and on them came ᵖthe curse of Jotham the son of Jerubbaal.

Tola

10 After Abimelech there ᵃarose to save Israel Tola the son of Puah, the son of Dodo, a man of Issachar; and he dwelt in Shamir in the mountains of Ephraim. ²He judged Israel twenty-three years; and he died and was buried in Shamir.

Jair

³After him arose Jair, a Gileadite; and he judged Israel twenty-two years. ⁴Now he had thirty sons who ᵇrode on thirty donkeys; they also had thirty towns, ᶜwhich

---

* **9:37** Hebrew *Meonenim*

9:37 the Diviners' Terebinth Tree. This appears to have had some association with occult or magical practices, and this particular terebinth tree was certainly an important landmark (Gen. 35:4; Josh. 24:26).
9:45 sowed it with salt. Spreading salt on the land turned the area into a barren desert. Salt will kill most vegetation, and it takes a long time for the land to become good again.
9:56 God repaid the wickedness of Abimelech.

Abimelech was not a true king; he had established his reign through murder and in no way sought to lead the people to the Lord. God did not allow this kind of rebellion to pass unnoticed.

9:38 ʰ Judg. 9:28, 29   **9:45** ⁱ Judg. 9:20 ʲ 2 Kin. 3:25
9:46 ᵏ Judg. 8:33   **9:48** ˡ Ps. 68:14   **9:53** ᵐ 2 Sam. 11:21
9:54 ⁿ 1 Sam. 31:4   **9:56** ᵒ Job 31:3   **9:57** ᵖ Judg. 9:20
10:1 ᵃ Judg. 2:16   **10:4** ᵇ Judg. 5:10; 12:14 ᶜ Deut. 3:14

are called "Havoth Jair"* to this day, which *are* in the land of Gilead. 5And Jair died and was buried in Camon.

Israel Oppressed Again

6Then dthe children of Israel again did evil in the sight of the LORD, and eserved the Baals and the Ashtoreths, fthe gods of Syria, the gods of gSidon, the gods of Moab, the gods of the people of Ammon, and the gods of the Philistines; and they forsook the LORD and did not serve Him. 7So the anger of the LORD was hot against Israel; and He hsold them into the hands of the iPhilistines and into the hands of the people of jAmmon. 8From that year they harassed and oppressed the children of Israel for eighteen years—all the children of Israel who *were* on the other side of the Jordan in the kland of the Amorites, in Gilead. 9Moreover the people of Ammon crossed over the Jordan to fight against Judah also, against Benjamin, and against the house of Ephraim, so that Israel was severely distressed.

10lAnd the children of Israel cried out to the LORD, saying, "We have msinned against You, because we have both forsaken our God and served the Baals!" 11So the LORD said to the children of Israel, "*Did I* not *deliver you* nfrom the Egyptians and ofrom the Amorites and pfrom the people of Ammon and qfrom the Philistines? 12Also rthe Sidonians sand Amalekites and Maonites* toppressed you; and you cried out to Me, and I delivered you from their hand. 13uYet you have forsaken Me and served other gods. Therefore I will deliver you no more. 14"Go and vcry out to the gods which you have chosen; let them deliver you in your time of distress." 15And the children of Israel said to the LORD, "We have sinned! wDo to us whatever seems best to You; only deliver us this day, we pray." 16xSo they put away the

foreign gods from among them and served the LORD. And yHis soul could no longer endure the misery of Israel.

17Then the people of Ammon gathered together and encamped in Gilead. And the children of Israel assembled together and encamped in zMizpah. 18And the people, the leaders of Gilead, said to one another, "Who *is* the man who will begin the fight against the people of Ammon? He shall abe head over all the inhabitants of Gilead."

Jephthah

11 Now aJephthah the Gileadite was ba mighty man of valor, but he *was* the son of a harlot; and Gilead begot Jephthah. 2Gilead's wife bore sons; and when his wife's sons grew up, they drove Jephthah out, and said to him, "You shall have cno inheritance in our father's house, for you *are* the son of another woman." 3Then Jephthah fled from his brothers and dwelt in the land of dTob; and eworthless men banded together with Jephthah and went out *raiding* with him.

4It came to pass after a time that the fpeople of Ammon made war against Israel. 5And so it was, when the people of Ammon made war against Israel, that the elders of Gilead went to get Jephthah from the land of Tob. 6Then they said to Jephthah, "Come and be our commander, that we may fight against the people of Ammon."

7So Jephthah said to the elders of Gilead, g"Did you not hate me, and expel me from my father's house? Why have you come to me now when you are in distress?"

8hAnd the elders of Gilead said to Jephthah, "That is why we have iturned again to you now, that you may go with us

---

* **10:4** Literally *Towns of Jair* (compare Numbers 32:41 and Deuteronomy 3:14)   * **10:12** Some Septuagint manuscripts read *Midianites*.

10:6–18 Mercy—A lengthy introduction precedes the story of Jephthah. These verses repeat the themes of apostasy and God's unfailing mercy. A new theme here is the emphasis on Israel's confession and repentance (vv. 10,15–16).

10:6 Baals and the Ashtoreths, the gods of Syria... Sidon... Moab... Ammon. This list demonstrates the extent of Israel's idolatry. Not only did the people worship the major Canaanite gods (Baal and Asherah), but they also absorbed the religions of other groups.

10:7–8 Suffering—Here and elsewhere the Book of Judges underscores the consequences of disobedience. Those consequences are always tragic. The Israelites were never oppressed because they did not have a big enough military, or a strong enough leader, or because God could not protect them. They were oppressed by God's permission because of their disobedience and sin. Defeat and miserable suffering do loom large whenever believers retreat from their exclusive commitment to God. They become their own worst enemy.

10:14 the gods which you have chosen. This is a

response of confrontation. When Israel cried out to God, He reminded them again of their faithless ways.

10:16 His soul could no longer endure the misery. Not only is God a God of great justice, He is a God of great mercy and compassion. Despite their constant sinning and backsliding, God still loved the Israelites and shared their misery, much as parents are moved by their children's suffering.

11:8 you may go with us and fight. This is almost the same phrase that the Israelites used when they asked Samuel for a king (1 Sam. 8:20).

10:6 d Judg. 2:11; 3:7; 6:1; 13:1 e Judg. 2:13 f Judg. 2:12
g 1 Kin. 11:33 **10:7** h 1 Sam. 12:9 i Judg. 13:1 j Judg.
3:13 **10:8** k Num. 32:33 **10:10** l 1 Sam. 12:10 m Deut.
1:41 **10:11** n Ex. 14:30 o Num. 21:21, 24, 25 p Judg.
3:12, 13 q Judg. 3:31 **10:12** r Judg. 1:31; 5:19 s Judg. 6:3;
7:12 t Ps. 106:42, 43 **10:13** u [Jer. 2:13] **10:14** v Deut.
32:37, 38 **10:15** w 1 Sam. 3:18 **10:16** x Jer. 18:7, 8
y Is. 63:9 **10:17** z Judg. 11:11, 29 **10:18** a Judg. 11:8,
11 **11:1** a Heb. 11:32 b 2 Kin. 5:1 **11:2** c Gen. 21:10
11:3 d 2 Sam. 10:6, 8 e 1 Sam. 22:2 **11:4** f Judg. 10:9, 17
11:7 g Gen. 26:27 **11:8** h Judg. 10:18 i [Luke 17:4]

and fight against the people of Ammon, and be *j*our head over all the inhabitants of Gilead."

⁹So Jephthah said to the elders of Gilead, "If you take me back home to fight against the people of Ammon, and the LORD delivers them to me, shall I be your head?"

¹⁰And the elders of Gilead said to Jephthah, *k*"The LORD will be a witness between us, if we do not do according to your words." ¹¹Then Jephthah went with the elders of Gilead, and the people made him *l*head and commander over them; and Jephthah spoke all his words *m*before the LORD in Mizpah.

¹²Now Jephthah sent messengers to the king of the people of Ammon, saying, *n*"What do you have against me, that you have come to fight against me in my land?"

¹³And the king of the people of Ammon answered the messengers of Jephthah, *o*"Because Israel took away my land when they came up out of Egypt, from *p*the Arnon as far as *q*the Jabbok, and to the Jordan. Now therefore, restore those *lands* peaceably."

¹⁴So Jephthah again sent messengers to the king of the people of Ammon, ¹⁵and said to him, "Thus says Jephthah: *r*'Israel did not take away the land of Moab, nor the land of the people of Ammon; ¹⁶for when Israel came up from Egypt, they walked through the wilderness as far as the Red Sea and *s*came to Kadesh. ¹⁷Then *t*Israel sent messengers to the king of Edom, saying, "Please let me pass through your land." *u*But the king of Edom would not heed. And in like manner they sent to the *v*king of Moab, but he would not *consent*. So Israel *w*remained in Kadesh. ¹⁸And they

*x*went along through the wilderness and *y*bypassed the land of Edom and the land of Moab, came to the east side of the land of Moab, and encamped on the other side of the Arnon. But they did not enter the border of Moab, for the Arnon *was* the border of Moab. ¹⁹Then *z*Israel sent messengers to Sihon king of the Amorites, king of Heshbon; and Israel said to him, "Please *a*let us pass through your land into our place." ²⁰*b*But Sihon did not trust Israel to pass through his territory. So Sihon gathered all his people together, encamped in Jahaz, and fought against Israel. ²¹And the LORD God of Israel *c*delivered Sihon and all his people into the hand of Israel, and they *d*defeated them. Thus Israel gained possession of all the land of the Amorites, who inhabited that country. ²²They took possession of *e*all the territory of the Amorites, from the Arnon to the Jabbok and from the wilderness to the Jordan.

²³'And now the LORD God of Israel has dispossessed the Amorites from before His people Israel; should you then possess it? ²⁴Will you not possess whatever *f*Chemosh your god gives you to possess? So whatever *g*the LORD our God takes possession of before us, we will possess. ²⁵And now, *are* you any better than *h*Balak the son of Zippor, king of Moab? Did he ever strive against Israel? Did he ever fight against them? ²⁶While Israel dwelt in *i*Heshbon and its villages, in *j*Aroer and its villages, and in all the cities along the banks of the Arnon, for three hundred years, why did you not recover *them* within that time? ²⁷Therefore I have not sinned against you, but you wronged me by fighting against me. May the LORD, *k*the Judge, *l*render judgment this

---

11:11 words before the LORD. Jephthah's "words before the LORD" are a strange mixture of faith and foolishness. While Jephthah did acknowledge God, his self-interest and foolishness often overruled his faith. The Book of Hebrews has a more positive view of him. Jephthah is one of those listed "who through faith subdued kingdoms, worked righteousness, obtained promises . . ." (Heb. 11:32–33).

11:21 the LORD God of Israel. Israel was not merely an aggressor, but the recipient of the Lord's generosity. The Ammonites had brought their misfortune on themselves by hindering Israel's advance into the Promised Land. Israel would not have taken Ammonite land, since God had expressly commanded them not to (Deut. 2:19). The Ammonites were only indirectly affected by Israel's expansion (Num. 21:25–26). In addition, the Ammonites never really had true claim to the land to begin with; it was in fact the land of the Amorites (vv. 19–22). The limits of the Amorite land in verse 22 are precisely what the Ammonites claimed as theirs in v. 13 (Num. 21:24 also rebuts the Ammonites' claim). Israel had occupied the land in dispute for at least three hundred years, long enough to make a legitimate claim on it (v. 26).

11:24 whatever Chemosh your god gives you. Usually the worship of Chemosh is associated with Moab; elsewhere the Ammonites' god was called Molech.

However, Ammon and Moab lived side by side, and apparently shared culture and religion as well as their common descent from Lot (Gen. 19:37–38). Jephthah's comment was a derisive jab at the ineffectiveness of their gods.

11:27 the LORD, the Judge. God is the ultimate source of all justice. He has the right to judge every man and woman. With His divine authority and power, God always judges with justice, while at the same time He is loving, compassionate, and perfect.

11:27 Strife—Given the depravity of the human heart it is only expected that nation will declare war on nation. We also deal with "wars" and strife in our interpersonal relationships. When we are faced with unjust attacks, we can only do as Jephthah did and trust God to judge rightly between the two sides of the dispute.

11:8 *j* Judg. 10:18   **11:10** *k* Jer. 29:23; 42:5
11:11 *l* Judg. 11:8   *m* Judg. 10:17; 20:1   **11:12** *n* 2 Sam. 16:10   **11:13** *o* Num. 21:24–26   *p* Josh. 13:9   *q* Gen. 32:22   **11:15** *r* Deut. 2:9, 19   **11:16** *s* Num. 13:26; 20:1   **11:17** *t* Num. 20:14   *u* Num. 20:14–21   *v* Josh. 24:9   *w* Num. 20:1   **11:18** *x* Deut. 2:9, 18, 19   *y* Num. 21:4   **11:19** *z* Num. 21:21   **11:20** *b* Deut. 2:27   **11:21** *c* Josh. 24:8   *d* Num. 21:24, 25   **11:22** *e* Deut. 2:36, 37   **11:24** *f* Num. 21:29   *g* [Deut. 9:4, 5]   **11:25** *h* Num. 22:2   **11:26** *i* Num. 21:25, 26   *j* Deut. 2:36   **11:27** *k* Gen. 18:25   *l* Gen. 16:5; 31:53

day between the children of Israel and the
people of Ammon.'" 28However, the king
of the people of Ammon did not heed the
words which Jephthah sent him.

Jephthah's Vow and Victory

29Then [m]the Spirit of the LORD came
upon Jephthah, and he passed through
Gilead and Manasseh, and passed through
Mizpah of Gilead; and from Mizpah of
Gilead he advanced *toward* the people of
Ammon. 30And Jephthah [n]made a vow to
the LORD, and said, "If You will indeed deliver the people of Ammon into my hands,
31then it will be that whatever comes out of
the doors of my house to meet me, when I
return in peace from the people of Ammon,
[o]shall surely be the LORD's, [p]and I will offer
it up as a burnt offering."
32So Jephthah advanced toward the people of Ammon to fight against them, and
the LORD delivered them into his hands.
33And he defeated them from Aroer as far
as [q]Minnith—twenty cities—and to Abel
Keramim,* with a very great slaughter.
Thus the people of Ammon were subdued
before the children of Israel.

Jephthah's Daughter

34When Jephthah came to his house at
[r]Mizpah, there was [s]his daughter, coming
out to meet him with timbrels and dancing; and she *was his* only child. Besides her
he had neither son nor daughter. 35And it
came to pass, when he saw her, that he [t]tore
his clothes, and said, "Alas, my daughter!
You have brought me very low! You are
among those who trouble me! For I [u]have
given my word to the LORD, and [v]I cannot
go back on it."
36So she said to him, "My father, *if* you
have given your word to the LORD, [w]do to
me according to what has gone out of your
mouth, because [x]the LORD has avenged
you of your enemies, the people of Ammon." 37Then she said to her father, "Let
this thing be done for me: let me alone for
two months, that I may go and wander on
the mountains and bewail my virginity, my
friends and I."
38So he said, "Go." And he sent her away
for two months; and she went with her
friends, and bewailed her virginity on the
mountains. 39And it was so at the end of
two months that she returned to her father,
and he [y]carried out his vow with her which
he had vowed. She knew no man.
And it became a custom in Israel 40*that*
the daughters of Israel went four days each
year to lament the daughter of Jephthah
the Gileadite.

Jephthah's Conflict with Ephraim

12 Then [a]the men of Ephraim gathered together, crossed over toward
Zaphon, and said to Jephthah, "Why did
you cross over to fight against the people
of Ammon, and did not call us to go with
you? We will burn your house down on you
with fire!"
2And Jephthah said to them, "My people and I were in a great struggle with the

* **11:33** Literally *Plain of Vineyards*

11:31 *whatever comes out of the doors of my house.* Some have interpreted Jephthah's vow as a clear intention to offer a human sacrifice. The phrase "to meet me," coupled with coming out of the house seems to refer more appropriately to a human than an animal. Undoubtedly Jephthah knew that human sacrifice was strictly forbidden in Israel (Lev. 18:21; 20:2; Deut. 12:31; 18:10; Jer. 19:5; Ezek. 20:30–31; 23:37–39), but his foolishness and lack of faith impelled him to make a reckless vow in order to try to manipulate God.

11:35 *I have given my word . . . I cannot go back.* Did Jephthah have to follow through on his vow? Ordinarily the answer would be yes. Vows were made only to God, and they were solemn pledges that had to be kept (Deut. 23:21–23; Ps. 15:4; Eccl. 5:4–5). But if Jephthah intended his vow to include human sacrifice, he was vowing to sin, an action which could hardly please the Lord.

11:39 *he carried out his vow.* The text does not explicitly say that he killed his daughter, and some believe that instead he "sacrificed" her by dedicating her to a life of virginity. Human sacrifice was contrary to the law of Moses (Lev. 18:21; 20:2–5; Deut. 12:31; 18:10). Until the wicked reigns of Ahaz and Manasseh centuries later (2 Kin. 16:3; 21:6), there is no record of human sacrifice in Israel, even by those who followed Baal. The great respect that Jephthah had for God would surely have prevented him from making such a perverse offering. The several references to her virginity seem to support the idea of lifelong celibacy, and the Bible provides evidence that such devoted service for women did exist at the central sanctuary (Ex. 38:8; 1 Sam. 2:22; Luke 2:36–37). Jephthah's vow in verse 31 could be translated "shall be the LORD's, *or* I will offer it up as a burnt offering." Thus his vow could be interpreted that if a person came out first, he would dedicate that person to the Lord, or if an animal came out first, he would offer the animal as a burnt sacrifice. As is frequently the case in the Book of Judges, we are given the bare facts of a puzzling story and no comment about what God thought of it.

12:2 Strife—Gilead and Ephraim grew so hostile that they came to blows, brother fighting against brother. Instead of putting their energy into fighting their common enemy, they were fighting each other. In the same way today, Christians often react with hurt feelings, pride, and resentment, and prefer to fight against flesh and blood rather than against principalities and powers. The constant infighting Christians indulge in is often a reason for the rest of the world to pass the church off as much ado about nothing.

11:29 [m] Judg. 3:10 **11:30** [n] Gen. 28:20 **11:31** [o] Lev. 27:2, 3, 28 [p] Ps. 66:13 **11:33** [q] Ezek. 27:17 **11:34** [r] Judg. 10:17; 11:11 [s] Ex. 15:20 **11:35** [t] Gen. 37:29, 34 [u] Eccl. 5:2, 4, 5 [v] Num. 30:2 **11:36** [w] Num. 30:2 [x] 2 Sam. 18:19, 31 **11:39** [y] Judg. 11:31 **12:1** [a] Judg. 8:1

people of Ammon; and when I called you, you did not deliver me out of their hands. ³So when I saw that you would not deliver *me*, I ᵇtook my life in my hands and crossed over against the people of Ammon; and the LORD delivered them into my hand. Why then have you come up to me this day to fight against me?" ⁴Now Jephthah gathered together all the men of Gilead and fought against Ephraim. And the men of Gilead defeated Ephraim, because they said, "You Gileadites ᶜare fugitives of Ephraim among the Ephraimites *and* among the Manassites." ⁵The Gileadites seized the ᵈfords of the Jordan before the Ephraimites *arrived*. And when *any* Ephraimite who escaped said, "Let me cross over," the men of Gilead would say to him, "*Are* you an Ephraimite?" If he said, "No," ⁶then they would say to him, "Then say, ᵉ'Shibboleth'!" And he would say, "Sibboleth," for he could not pronounce *it* right. Then they would take him and kill him at the fords of the Jordan. There fell at that time forty-two thousand Ephraimites.

⁷And Jephthah judged Israel six years. Then Jephthah the Gileadite died and was buried among the cities of Gilead.

Ibzan, Elon, and Abdon

⁸After him, Ibzan of Bethlehem judged Israel. ⁹He had thirty sons. And he gave away thirty daughters in marriage, and brought in thirty daughters from elsewhere for his sons. He judged Israel seven years. ¹⁰Then Ibzan died and was buried at Bethlehem.

¹¹After him, Elon the Zebulunite judged Israel. He judged Israel ten years. ¹²And Elon the Zebulunite died and was buried at Aijalon in the country of Zebulun.

¹³After him, Abdon the son of Hillel the Pirathonite judged Israel. ¹⁴He had forty sons and thirty grandsons, who ᶠrode on seventy young donkeys. He judged Israel eight years. ¹⁵Then Abdon the son of Hillel the Pirathonite died and was buried in Pirathon in the land of Ephraim, ᵍin the mountains of the Amalekites.

The Birth of Samson

13 Again the children of Israel ᵃdid evil in the sight of the LORD, and the LORD delivered them ᵇinto the hand of the Philistines for forty years.

²Now there was a certain man from ᶜZorah, of the family of the Danites, whose name *was* Manoah; and his wife *was* barren and had no children. ³And the ᵈAngel of the LORD appeared to the woman and said to her, "Indeed now, you are barren and have borne no children, but you shall conceive and bear a son. ⁴Now therefore, please be careful ᵉnot to drink wine or *similar* drink, and not to eat anything unclean. ⁵For behold, you shall conceive and bear a son. And no ᶠrazor shall come upon his head, for the child shall be ᵍa Nazirite to God from the womb; and he shall ʰbegin to deliver Israel out of the hand of the Philistines."

⁶So the woman came and told her husband, saying, ⁱ"A Man of God came to me, and His ʲcountenance *was* like the countenance of the Angel of God, very awesome; but I ᵏdid not ask Him where He *was* from, and He did not tell me His name. ⁷And He said to me, 'Behold, you shall conceive and bear a son. Now drink no wine or *similar* drink, nor eat anything unclean, for the child shall be a Nazirite to God from the womb to the day of his death.'"

⁸Then Manoah prayed to the LORD, and said, "O my Lord, please let the Man of God

---

12:4 *You . . . are fugitives of Ephraim.* This insult may have its roots in the division of the nation into eastern and western groups (5:17; Josh. 1:12–15). Despite the emphasis in Joshua on the unity of all the tribes (Josh. 1:12–15; 22:1–34), the practical reality in the period of the judges was dramatically different.

12:6 *Shibboleth . . . Sibboleth.* This is the only significant reference to the linguistic differences which apparently existed between the tribes. Today the English word *shibboleth* means an otherwise minor difference that becomes a sticking point because it distinguishes one side from the other.

13:1—16:31 *Samson*—The last of the judges lived at the beginning of the eleventh century B.C. He was unusual among the judges in many ways. He did not lead an army, but carried on his campaign against the Philistines single-handed. He is mentioned in Hebrews 11:32 in the list of judges who accomplished great things through faith. The Book of Judges, in contrast, paints a darker picture. His checkered history of heroism and moral failure resembles Israel's troubles during the time of the judges.

13:3 *the Angel of the LORD.* The Angel of the Lord made a supernatural appearance, described here as "very awesome." Manoah's wife recognized him as

"a Man of God." The essential character of the angel, embodied in his name, was not revealed to them (vv. 17–18). It seems that the Angel of the Lord was God Himself, in a form they could perceive (13:21–22; Gen. 22:1; Ex. 3:14–15).

13:5 *Nazirite.* The regulations of the Nazirite vows are found in Numbers 6:1–21. Samson's Nazirite service was remarkable in three ways. First, he did not take his vow voluntarily; it was his before birth. Second, his service was to be lifelong, not temporary. Third, he eventually broke every one of its stipulations.

13:6 *Man of God.* This was a term used to describe the prophets (Deut. 33:1; 1 Kin. 17:18). At first Samson's mother may have thought she was talking to a prophet, but His radiant appearance convinced her otherwise.

12:3 ᵇ 1 Sam. 19:5; 28:21   **12:4** ᶜ 1 Sam. 25:10   **12:5** ᵈ Josh. 22:11   **12:6** ᵉ Ps. 69:2, 15   **12:14** ᶠ Judg. 5:10; 10:4   **12:15** ᵍ Judg. 3:13, 27; 5:14   **13:1** ᵃ Judg. 2:11   ᵇ 1 Sam. 12:9   **13:2** ᶜ Josh. 19:41   **13:3** ᵈ Judg. 6:12   **13:4** ᵉ Num. 6:2, 3, 20   **13:5** ᶠ Num. 6:5   ᵍ Num. 6:2   ʰ 1 Sam. 7:13   **13:6** ⁱ Gen. 32:24–30   ʲ Matt. 28:3   ᵏ Judg. 13:17, 18

whom You sent come to us again and teach us what we shall do for the child who will be born."

9And God listened to the voice of Manoah, and the Angel of God came to the woman again as she was sitting in the field; but Manoah her husband *was* not with her. 10Then the woman ran in haste and told her husband, and said to him, "Look, the Man who came to me the *other* day has just now appeared to me!"

11So Manoah arose and followed his wife. When he came to the Man, he said to Him, "Are You the Man who spoke to this woman?"

And He said, "I *am.*"

12Manoah said, "Now let Your words come *to pass!* What will be the boy's rule of life, and his work?"

13So the Angel of the LORD said to Manoah, "Of all that I said to the woman let her be careful. 14She may not eat anything that comes from the vine, *l*nor may she drink wine or *similar* drink, nor eat anything unclean. All that I commanded her let her observe."

15Then Manoah said to the Angel of the LORD, "Please *m*let us detain You, and we will prepare a young goat for You."

16And the Angel of the LORD said to Manoah, "Though you detain Me, I will not eat your food. But if you offer a burnt offering, you must offer it to the LORD." (For Manoah did not know He *was* the Angel of the LORD.)

17Then Manoah said to the Angel of the LORD, "What *is* Your name, that when Your words come *to pass* we may honor You?"

18And the Angel of the LORD said to him, *n*"Why do you ask My name, seeing it *is* wonderful?"

19So Manoah took the young goat with the grain offering, *o*and offered it upon the rock to the LORD. And He did a wondrous thing while Manoah and his wife looked on—20it happened as the flame went up toward heaven from the altar—the Angel of

the LORD ascended in the flame of the altar! When Manoah and his wife saw *this,* they *p*fell on their faces to the ground. 21When the Angel of the LORD appeared no more to Manoah and his wife, *q*then Manoah knew that He *was* the Angel of the LORD.

22And Manoah said to his wife, *r*"We shall surely die, because we have seen God!"

23But his wife said to him, "If the LORD had desired to kill us, He would not have accepted a burnt offering and a grain offering from our hands, nor would He have shown us all these *things,* nor would He have told us *such things* as these at this time."

24So the woman bore a son and called his name *s*Samson; and *t*the child grew, and the LORD blessed him. 25u*And the Spirit of the LORD began to move upon him at Mahaneh Dan* *v*between Zorah and *w*Eshtaol.

Samson's Philistine Wife

14 Now Samson went down *a*to Timnah, and *b*saw a woman in Timnah of the daughters of the Philistines. 2So he went up and told his father and mother, saying, "I have seen a woman in Timnah of the daughters of the Philistines; now therefore, *c*get her for me as a wife."

3Then his father and mother said to him, "*Is there* no woman among the daughters of *d*your brethren, or among all my people, that you must go and get a wife from the *e*uncircumcised Philistines?"

And Samson said to his father, "Get her for me, for she pleases me well."

4But his father and mother did not know that it was *f*of the LORD—that He was seeking an occasion to move against the Philistines. For at that time *g*the Philistines had dominion over Israel.

5So Samson went down to Timnah with his father and mother, and came to the vineyards of Timnah.

---

* **13:25** Literally *Camp of Dan* (compare 18:12)

13:21–22 the Angel of the LORD. Manoah's reaction is similar to the reaction Gideon had when he recognized the Angel of the Lord (6:22).

13:25 the Spirit of the LORD began to move upon him. The Hebrew word translated *move* can also mean *impel.* The Spirit of the Lord was pushing Samson toward doing the work that God wanted him to do.

14:2 get her for me as a wife. Such marriages with foreigners were prohibited for Israelites (Ex. 34:16; Deut. 7:3).

14:3 she pleases me well. Samson's words reveal his self-centered attitude. Instead of seeking to serve God, he was seeking to please himself. Samson's comment here foreshadows the author's summary of the entire period of the judges (17:6; 18:1; 19:1; 21:25).

14:3 Unfaithfulness—The beginning of Samson's downfall was his disobedience to the Lord in his marriage. The theme of marriage within the covenant is common in the Old Testament. From earliest times the people of God were told not to contract marriages

with unbelievers (Gen. 6:2). When the covenant was renewed prior to the people's entry into Canaanite territory, Joshua warned them not to intermarry; to do so would be evidence of their failure to cling to the Lord (Josh. 23:8,12). It is a tragic picture of the decadence of this period to see Samson's unfaithfulness to the Lord in taking a pagan wife. The New Covenant believer remains under the same divine command to marry only in the Lord (1 Cor. 7:39; 2 Cor. 6:14).

14:4 it was of the LORD. God would use Samson's defiant wish as a way of defeating the Philistines and providing relief for His people.

13:14 *l* Num. 6:3, 4   **13:15** *m* Gen. 18:5   **13:18** *n* Gen. 32:29   **13:19** *o* Judg. 6:19–21   **13:20** *p* Ezek. 1:28   **13:21** *q* Judg. 6:22   **13:22** *r* Deut. 5:26   **13:24** *s* Heb. 11:32   *t* 1 Sam. 3:19   **13:25** *u* Judg. 3:10   *v* Judg. 18:11   *w* Judg. 16:31   **14:1** *a* Josh. 15:10, 57   *b* Gen. 34:2   **14:2** *c* Gen. 21:21   **14:3** *d* Gen. 24:3, 4   *e* Gen. 34:14   **14:4** *f* Josh. 11:20   *g* Deut. 28:48

Now *to his* surprise, a young lion *came* roaring against him. [6]And [h]the Spirit of the LORD came mightily upon him, and he tore the lion apart as one would have torn apart a young goat, though *he had* nothing in his hand. But he did not tell his father or his mother what he had done. [7]Then he went down and talked with the woman; and she pleased Samson well. [8]After some time, when he returned to get her, he turned aside to see the carcass of the lion. And behold, a swarm of bees and honey *were* in the carcass of the lion. [9]He took some of it in his hands and went along, eating. When he came to his father and mother, he gave *some* to them, and they also ate. But he did not tell them that he had taken the honey out of the [i]carcass of the lion.

[10]So his father went down to the woman. And Samson gave a feast there, for young men used to do so. [11]And it happened, when they saw him, that they brought thirty companions to be with him.

[12]Then Samson said to them, "Let me [j]pose a riddle to you. If you can correctly solve and explain it to me [k]within the seven days of the feast, then I will give you thirty linen garments and thirty [l]changes of clothing. [13]But if you cannot explain *it* to me, then you shall give me thirty linen garments and thirty changes of clothing."

And they said to him, [m]"Pose your riddle, that we may hear it."

[14]So he said to them:

"Out of the eater came something to eat,
And out of the strong came something sweet."

Now for three days they could not explain the riddle.

[15]But it came to pass on the seventh* day that they said to Samson's wife, [n]"Entice your husband, that he may explain the riddle to us, [o]or else we will burn you and your father's house with fire. Have you invited us in order to take what is ours? *Is that* not *so?*"

[16]Then Samson's wife wept on him, and said, [p]"You only hate me! You do not love me! You have posed a riddle to the sons of my people, but you have not explained *it* to me."

And he said to her, "Look, I have not explained *it* to my father or my mother; so should I explain *it* to you?" [17]Now she had wept on him the seven days while their feast lasted. And it happened on the seventh day that he told her, because she pressed him so much. Then she explained the riddle to the sons of her people. [18]So the men of the city said to him on the seventh day before the sun went down:

"What *is* sweeter than honey?
And what *is* stronger than a lion?"

And he said to them:

"If you had not plowed with my heifer,
You would not have solved my riddle!"

[19]Then [q]the Spirit of the LORD came upon him mightily, and he went down to Ashkelon and killed thirty of their men, took their apparel, and gave the changes *of clothing* to those who had explained the riddle. So his anger was aroused, and he went back up to his father's house. [20]And Samson's wife [r]was *given* to his companion, who had been [s]his best man.

Samson Defeats the Philistines

15 After a while, in the time of wheat harvest, it happened that Samson visited his wife with a [a]young goat. And he said, "Let me go in to my wife, into *her* room." But her father would not permit him to go in.

[2]Her father said, "I really thought that you thoroughly [b]hated her; therefore I gave her to your companion. *Is* not her younger sister better than she? Please, take her instead."

[3]And Samson said to them, "This time I shall be blameless regarding the Philistines if I harm them!" [4]Then Samson went and caught three hundred foxes; and he took torches, turned *the foxes* tail to tail,

---

* **14:15** Following Masoretic Text, Targum, and Vulgate; Septuagint and Syriac read *fourth.*

14:6 *the Spirit of the LORD came mightily upon him.* The Old Testament speaks numerous times of God's Spirit coming mightily upon individuals, usually to empower them physically for great feats of strength (3:10; 6:34; 11:29). The Spirit empowered others for the important task of speaking God's word (Gen. 41:38; Num. 24:2; 1 Sam. 10:6; 19:20). It appears that the work of the Holy Spirit in the Old Testament was primarily a special anointing to accomplish a certain task, and was different from the indwelling Presence that believers enjoy today. Saul (1 Sam. 10:10; 16:23) and David (1 Sam. 16:13; Ps. 51:11) were both filled with the Holy Spirit when they were anointed as king, but this presence seems to have been directly linked to their obedience.

14:8–9 *carcass of the lion.* Touching the dead lion violated Samson's Nazirite vow (13:5).

14:10 *feast.* The word translated *feast* denotes a banquet with considerable drinking. The passage does not say so, but it is not unlikely that this occasioned another violation of Samson's Nazirite vow (13:5).

15:1 *the time of wheat harvest.* This would have been late May or early June. The wheat harvest was associated with the second of the three great feasts in Israel, the Feast of Weeks, also known as Pentecost (Lev. 23:15–22; Deut. 16:9–12).

14:6 [h] Judg. 3:10   **14:9** [i] Lev. 11:27   **14:12** [j] Ezek. 17:2   **14:12** [k] Gen. 29:27   [l] 2 Kin. 5:22   **14:13** [m] Ezek. 17:2
14:15 [n] Judg. 16:5   [o] Judg. 15:6   **14:16** [p] Judg. 16:15
14:19 [q] Judg. 3:10; 13:25   **14:20** [r] Judg. 15:2   [s] John 3:29
15:1 [a] Gen. 38:17   **15:2** [b] Judg. 14:20

and put a torch between each pair of tails.
⁵When he had set the torches on fire, he let
the foxes go into the standing grain of the
Philistines, and burned up both the shocks
and the standing grain, as well as the vineyards *and* olive groves.

⁶Then the Philistines said, "Who has
done this?"

And they answered, "Samson, the son-
in-law of the Timnite, because he has taken
his wife and given her to his companion."
ᶜSo the Philistines came up and burned her
and her father with fire.

⁷Samson said to them, "Since you would
do a thing like this, I will surely take revenge on you, and after that I will cease."
⁸So he attacked them hip and thigh with
a great slaughter; then he went down and
dwelt in the cleft of the rock of ᵈEtam.

⁹Now the Philistines went up, encamped in Judah, and deployed themselves
ᵉagainst Lehi. ¹⁰And the men of Judah said,
"Why have you come up against us?"

So they answered, "We have come up to
arrest Samson, to do to him as he has done
to us."

¹¹Then three thousand men of Judah
went down to the cleft of the rock of Etam,
and said to Samson, "Do you not know that
the Philistines ᶠrule over us? What *is* this
you have done to us?"

And he said to them, "As they did to me,
so I have done to them."

¹²But they said to him, "We have come
down to arrest you, that we may deliver
you into the hand of the Philistines."

Then Samson said to them, "Swear to me
that you will not kill me yourselves."

¹³So they spoke to him, saying, "No, but
we will tie you securely and deliver you
into their hand; but we will surely not kill
you." And they bound him with two ᵍnew
ropes and brought him up from the rock.

¹⁴When he came to Lehi, the Philistines
came shouting against him. Then ʰthe
Spirit of the LORD came mightily upon him;
and the ropes that *were* on his arms became like flax that is burned with fire, and
his bonds broke loose from his hands. ¹⁵He
found a fresh jawbone of a donkey, reached
out his hand and took it, and ⁱkilled a thousand men with it. ¹⁶Then Samson said:

"With the jawbone of a donkey,
Heaps upon heaps,

With the jawbone of a donkey
I have slain a thousand men!"

¹⁷And so it was, when he had finished
speaking, that he threw the jawbone from
his hand, and called that place Ramath
Lehi.*

¹⁸Then he became very thirsty; so he
cried out to the LORD and said, ʲ"You have
given this great deliverance by the hand
of Your servant; and now shall I die of
thirst and fall into the hand of the uncircumcised?" ¹⁹So God split the hollow place
that *is* in Lehi,* and water came out, and
he drank; and ᵏhis spirit returned, and he
revived. Therefore he called its name En
Hakkore,* which is in Lehi to this day.
²⁰And ˡhe judged Israel ᵐtwenty years ⁿin
the days of the Philistines.

Samson and Delilah

16 Now Samson went to ᵃGaza and saw
a harlot there, and went in to her.
²*When* the Gazites *were told,* "Samson
has come here!" they ᵇsurrounded *the
place* and lay in wait for him all night at
the gate of the city. They were quiet all
night, saying, "In the morning, when it is
daylight, we will kill him." ³And Samson
lay *low* till midnight; then he arose at midnight, took hold of the doors of the gate of
the city and the two gateposts, pulled them
up, bar and all, put *them* on his shoulders,
and carried them to the top of the hill that
faces Hebron.

⁴Afterward it happened that he loved
a woman in the Valley of Sorek, whose
name *was* Delilah. ⁵And the ᶜlords of the
Philistines came up to her and said to her,
ᵈ"Entice him, and find out where his great
strength *lies,* and by what *means* we may
overpower him, that we may bind him to
afflict him; and every one of us will give
you eleven hundred *pieces* of silver."

⁶So Delilah said to Samson, "Please tell
me where your great strength *lies,* and
with what you may be bound to afflict you."

⁷And Samson said to her, "If they bind
me with seven fresh bowstrings, not yet
dried, then I shall become weak, and be
like any *other* man."

---

* **15:17** Literally *Jawbone Height*   * **15:19** Literally
Jawbone (compare verse 14) • Literally *Spring of
the Caller*

15:13 *two new ropes.* Ropes were made of leather,
hair, or plant fibers; one common fiber was flax (Josh.
2:6). Being new, these ropes were the strongest possible.

15:15 *a fresh jawbone.* A fresh jawbone would have
been tough, resilient, and virtually unbreakable.

15:18 *cried out to the LORD.* This is the first record of
Samson calling on the Lord.

16:2 *at the gate.* The gates of this time in history
were at least two stories high, with guard rooms
on either side of a narrow opening. The Philistines
waited in the recesses of the gate, hoping to trap
Samson.

16:3 *carried them to the top of the hill.* Given the
large size of the doors of a city gate, Samson's feat
was astounding. Hebron is 40 miles east of Gaza.
Samson's trip would have taken the better part of a
day.

15:6 ᶜ Judg. 14:15   **15:8** ᵈ 2 Chr. 11:6   **15:9** ᵉ Judg.
15:19   **15:11** ᶠ Judg. 13:1; 14:4   **15:13** ᵍ Judg. 16:11, 12
15:14 ʰ Judg. 3:10; 14:6   **15:15** ⁱ Lev. 26:8   **15:18** ʲ Ps. 3:7
15:19 ᵏ Is. 40:29   **15:20** ˡ Judg. 10:2; 12:7–14   ᵐ Judg.
16:31   ⁿ Judg. 13:1   **16:1** ᵃ Josh. 15:47   **16:2** ᵇ 1 Sam.
23:26   **16:5** ᶜ Josh. 13:3   ᵈ Judg. 14:15

⁸So the lords of the Philistines brought up to her seven fresh bowstrings, not yet dried, and she bound him with them. ⁹Now *men were* lying in wait, staying with her in the room. And she said to him, "The Philistines *are* upon you, Samson!" But he broke the bowstrings as a strand of yarn breaks when it touches fire. So the secret of his strength was not known.

¹⁰Then Delilah said to Samson, "Look, you have mocked me and told me lies. Now, please tell me what you may be bound with."

¹¹So he said to her, "If they bind me securely with ᵉnew ropes that have never been used, then I shall become weak, and be like any *other* man."

¹²Therefore Delilah took new ropes and bound him with them, and said to him, "The Philistines *are* upon you, Samson!" And *men were* lying in wait, staying in the room. But he broke them off his arms like a thread.

¹³Delilah said to Samson, "Until now you have mocked me and told me lies. Tell me what you may be bound with."

And he said to her, "If you weave the seven locks of my head into the web of the loom"—

¹⁴So she wove *it* tightly with the batten of the loom, and said to him, "The Philistines *are* upon you, Samson!" But he awoke from his sleep, and pulled out the batten and the web from the loom.

¹⁵Then she said to him, ᶠ"How can you say, 'I love you,' when your heart *is* not with me? You have mocked me these three times, and have not told me where your great strength *lies*." ¹⁶And it came to pass, when she pestered him daily with her words and pressed him, *so* that his soul was vexed to death, ¹⁷that he ᵍtold her all his heart, and said to her, ʰ"No razor has ever come upon my head, for I *have been* a Nazirite to God from my mother's womb. If I am shaven, then my strength will leave me, and I shall become weak, and be like any *other* man."

¹⁸When Delilah saw that he had told her all his heart, she sent and called for the lords of the Philistines, saying, "Come up once more, for he has told me all his

heart." So the lords of the Philistines came up to her and brought the money in their hand. ¹⁹ⁱThen she lulled him to sleep on her knees, and called for a man and had him shave off the seven locks of his head. Then she began to torment him,* and his strength left him. ²⁰And she said, "The Philistines *are* upon you, Samson!" So he awoke from his sleep, and said, "I will go out as before, at other times, and shake myself free!" But he did not know that the LORD ʲhad departed from him.

²¹Then the Philistines took him and put out his ᵏeyes, and brought him down to Gaza. They bound him with bronze fetters, and he became a grinder in the prison. ²²However, the hair of his head began to grow again after it had been shaven.

Samson Dies with the Philistines

²³Now the lords of the Philistines gathered together to offer a great sacrifice to ˡDagon their god, and to rejoice. And they said:

"Our god has delivered into our hands
    Samson our enemy!"

²⁴When the people saw him, they ᵐpraised their god; for they said:

"Our god has delivered into our hands
        our enemy,
    The destroyer of our land,
    And the one who multiplied our dead."

²⁵So it happened, when their hearts were ⁿmerry, that they said, "Call for Samson, that he may perform for us." So they called for Samson from the prison, and he performed for them. And they stationed him between the pillars. ²⁶Then Samson said to the lad who held him by the hand, "Let me feel the pillars which support the temple, so that I can lean on them." ²⁷Now the temple was full of men and women. All the lords of the Philistines *were* there—about three thousand men and women on the ᵒroof watching while Samson performed.

²⁸Then Samson called to the LORD,

---

* **16:19** Following Masoretic Text, Targum, and Vulgate; Septuagint reads *he began to be weak.*

16:16 *pestered him.* Delilah pestered him just as his wife had done earlier (14:17). Samson's foolishness prevented him from learning the lesson of his earlier experience.

16:19 *and his strength left him.* When he broke the final stipulation of the Nazirite vow by allowing his hair to be cut, the Lord left him and he was captured.

16:20 *he did not know.* This is one of the few editorial comments by the author.

16:23 *Dagon.* Dagon was the principal Philistine god. A Philistine temple for Dagon was at Beth Shan, in northern Israel, in the days of Saul (1 Sam. 31:9–10; 1 Chr. 10:10), and it was in another such temple that the Philistines stored the ark of the covenant for a time (1 Sam. 5:1–7). Dagon was once commonly

thought to be a fish god, but modern excavations have shown that he was a god of grain. In fact, one of the Hebrew words for grain is *dagan.*

16:24 *Our god has delivered into our hands our enemy.* The Philistines viewed their success over Samson as a triumph for their god (Judg. 16:23–24). In reality it was the Lord who had delivered Samson into their hands, for "the LORD had departed from him" (v. 20).

16:11 ᵉ Judg. 15:13	**16:15** ᶠ Judg. 14:16	**16:17** ᵍ [Mic. 7:5]
ʰ Judg. 13:5	**16:19** ⁱ Prov. 7:26, 27	**16:20** ʲ [Josh. 7:12]
16:21 ᵏ 2 Kin. 25:7	**16:23** ˡ 1 Sam. 5:2	
16:24 ᵐ Dan. 5:4	**16:25** ⁿ Judg. 9:27	**16:27** ᵒ Deut. 22:8

saying, "O Lord GOD, *p*remember me, I pray! Strengthen me, I pray, just this once, O God, that I may with one *blow* take vengeance on the Philistines for my two eyes!" ²⁹And Samson took hold of the two middle pillars which supported the temple, and he braced himself against them, one on his right and the other on his left. ³⁰Then Samson said, "Let me die with the Philistines!" And he pushed with *all his* might, and the temple fell on the lords and all the people who *were* in it. So the dead that he killed at his death were more than he had killed in his life.

³¹And his brothers and all his father's household came down and took him, and brought *him* up and *q*buried him between Zorah and Eshtaol in the tomb of his father Manoah. He had judged Israel *r*twenty years.

Micah's Idolatry

17 Now there was a man from the mountains of Ephraim, whose name *was* *a*Micah. ²And he said to his mother, "The eleven hundred *shekels* of silver that were taken from you, and on which you *b*put a curse, even saying *it* in my ears—here *is* the silver with me; I took it."

And his mother said, *c*"*May you be* blessed by the LORD, my son!" ³So when he had returned the eleven hundred *shekels* of silver to his mother, his mother said, "I had wholly dedicated the silver from my hand

to the LORD for my son, to *d*make a carved image and a molded image; now therefore, I will return it to you." ⁴Thus he returned the silver to his mother. Then his mother *e*took two hundred *shekels* of silver and gave them to the silversmith, and he made it into a carved image and a molded image; and they were in the house of Micah.

⁵The man Micah had a *f*shrine, and made an *g*ephod and *h*household idols;* and he consecrated one of his sons, who became his priest. ⁶*i*In those days *there was* no king in Israel; *j*everyone did *what was* right in his own eyes.

⁷Now there was a young man from *k*Bethlehem in Judah, of the family of Judah; he *was* a Levite, and *l*was staying there. ⁸The man departed from the city of Bethlehem in Judah to stay wherever he could find *a place*. Then he came to the mountains of Ephraim, to the house of Micah, as he journeyed. ⁹And Micah said to him, "Where do you come from?"

So he said to him, "I *am* a Levite from Bethlehem in Judah, and I am on my way to find *a place* to stay."

¹⁰Micah said to him, "Dwell with me, and be a *m*father and a priest to me, and I will give you *n*ten *shekels* of silver per year, a suit of clothes, and your sustenance." So the Levite went in. ¹¹Then the Levite was content to dwell with the man; and the

---

* **17:5** Hebrew *teraphim*

16:30 Zeal—The famous lament of David over Saul and Jonathan, "How the mighty have fallen!" (2 Sam. 1:19,27), could also be applied to Samson. He came from a godly home, but often was overcome by evil passion, pride, and violence. Yet at death his zeal for the Lord brought about a great victory over the Philistines and their god Dagon, and he is listed in Hebrews as a man of faith (Heb. 11:32). The plan and purpose of God overruled Samson's folly and the Philistines' arrogance.

16:31 He had judged Israel twenty years. The story of the judges concludes with final editorial comments. Samson, the last judge, had been empowered by God's Spirit, just as the first had been. Despite the manifold failings of the judges themselves, God had delivered Israel and caused other nations to bow before Him. Samson's life is ultimately a story about God's faithfulness in spite of human weakness.

17:1—21:25 Conclusion—The Book of Judges closes with two appendices (chs. 17–18; 19–21). They seem to be unrelated to the material preceding them, and to each other. While chapters 2–16 describe foreign threats to Israel, these last chapters show an internal breakdown of Israel's worship and unity. Furthermore, the events of these chapters appear to have taken place early in the period of the judges. These chapters may have been written independently of the book's earlier chapters, but there is a certain logic to placing them at the end of the book. The structure highlights the theme of the disintegration of Israel, with the last chapters emphasizing that "everyone did what was right in his own eyes" (17:6; 21:25).

17:3 I had wholly dedicated the silver . . . to the

LORD. Micah's mother approved of his action, claiming that these images would be offered on the Lord's behalf. Today the temptation to mix elements of true worship of God with practices unacceptable to Him remains with us, even though it is in different ways.

17:5 shrine. This is literally "a house of God." This was a perversion of the true sanctuary where all worship was to take place. At this time the true "house of God" was at Shiloh (18:31). Micah further violated the law by appointing his own son as his private priest. Micah sinned because his son had not descended from Aaron, nor was he even a Levite (Ex. 28:1; 40:12–15; Num. 16:39–40; 17:8).

17:6 what was right in his own eyes. This editorial comment is echoed in the last verse of the book (21:25). The author suggests that times were so bad that people did whatever they wanted, not what was right in the Lord's eyes (14:3). We may infer that a king who focused Israel's attention on the Lord would have prevented the outbreaks of sin and oppression so prevalent during the time of the judges.

17:10 be a father and a priest to me. To be called father was a title of honor. Micah wanted the Levite to be his priest, since his background would lend legitimacy to his service. Micah thought this would bring him God's favor (v. 13).

16:28 *p* Jer. 15:15 **16:31** *q* Judg. 13:25 *r* Judg. 15:20 **17:1** *a* Judg. 18:2 **17:2** *b* Lev. 5:1 *c* Gen. 14:19 **17:3** *d* Ex. 20:4, 23; 34:17 **17:4** *e* Is. 46:6 **17:5** *f* Judg. 18:24 *g* Judg. 8:27; 18:14 *h* Gen. 31:19, 30 **17:6** *i* Judg. 18:1; 19:1 *j* Deut. 12:8 **17:7** *k* Matt. 2:1, 5, 6 *l* Deut. 18:6 **17:10** *m* Judg. 18:19 *n* Gen. 45:8

young man became like one of his sons to him. 12So Micah oconsecrated the Levite, and the young man pbecame his priest, and lived in the house of Micah. 13Then Micah said, "Now I know that the LORD will be good to me, since I have a Levite as qpriest!"

The Danites Adopt Micah's Idolatry

18 In athose days there was no king in Israel. And in those days bthe tribe of the Danites was seeking an inheritance for itself to dwell in; for until that day their inheritance among the tribes of Israel had not fallen to them. 2So the children of Dan sent five men of their family from their territory, men of valor from cZorah and Eshtaol, dto spy out the land and search it. They said to them, "Go, search the land." So they went to the mountains of Ephraim, to the ehouse of Micah, and lodged there. 3While they were at the house of Micah, they recognized the voice of the young Levite. They turned aside and said to him, "Who brought you here? What are you doing in this place? What do you have here?"

4He said to them, "Thus and so Micah did for me. He has fhired me, and I have become his priest."

5So they said to him, "Please ginquire of hGod, that we may know whether the journey on which we go will be prosperous."

6And the priest said to them, i"Go in peace. The presence of the LORD be with you on your way."

7So the five men departed and went to jLaish. They saw the people who were there, khow they dwelt safely, in the manner of the Sidonians, quiet and secure. There were no rulers in the land who might put them to shame for anything. They were far from the lSidonians, and they had no ties with anyone.*

8Then the spies came back to their brethren at mZorah and Eshtaol, and their brethren said to them, "What is your report?"

9So they said, n"Arise, let us go up against them. For we have seen the land, and indeed it is very good. Would you odo nothing? Do not hesitate to go, and enter to possess the land. 10When you go, you will come to a psecure people and a large land. For God has given it into your hands, qa place where there is no lack of anything that is on the earth."

11And six hundred men of the family of the Danites went from there, from Zorah and Eshtaol, armed with weapons of war. 12Then they went up and encamped in rKirjath Jearim in Judah. (Therefore they call that place sMahaneh Dan* to this day. There it is, west of Kirjath Jearim.) 13And they passed from there to the mountains of Ephraim, and came to tthe house of Micah.

14uThen the five men who had gone to spy out the country of Laish answered and said to their brethren, "Do you know that vthere are in these houses an ephod, household idols, a carved image, and a molded image? Now therefore, consider what you should do." 15So they turned aside there, and came to the house of the young Levite man—to the house of Micah—and greeted him. 16The wsix hundred men armed with their weapons of war, who were of the children of Dan, stood by the entrance of the gate. 17Then xthe five men who had gone to spy out the land went up. Entering there, they took ythe carved image, the ephod, the household idols, and the molded image. The priest stood at the entrance of the gate with the six hundred men who were armed with weapons of war.

18When these went into Micah's house and took the carved image, the ephod, the household idols, and the molded image, the priest said to them, "What are you doing?"

19And they said to him, "Be quiet, zput your hand over your mouth, and come with us; abe a father and a priest to us. Is it better for you to be a priest to the household of one man, or that you be a priest to a tribe and a family in Israel?" 20So the priest's heart was glad; and he took the ephod, the household idols, and the carved image, and took his place among the people.

21Then they turned and departed, and put the little ones, the livestock, and the goods in front of them. 22When they were

---

* **18:7** Following Masoretic Text, Targum, and Vulgate; Septuagint reads with Syria.   * **18:12** Literally Camp of Dan

---

18:1 Danites. The Danites were looking for a place to settle because they had been unable to settle effectively in their allotted territory. Compare their allotment in Joshua 19:41–47 and their failure to capture it all (1:34–35). It seems clear that this story is not placed chronologically, but refers back to the first chapters of Judges. The Danites' migration in search of new land probably would have come soon after the events of 1:34, not some three centuries or more later.

18:7 Sidonians. Sidon was a port city northwest of Israel, in what today is Lebanon.

18:19 be a father and a priest to us. The Levite's cynical acceptance of this opportunity for greater prestige indicates further how debased conditions had become. Those who had been divinely appointed to minister before the Lord were selling false spiritual services to the highest bidder.

17:12 o Judg. 17:5 p Judg. 18:30 **17:13** q Judg. 18:4 **18:1** a Judg. 17:6; 19:1; 21:25 b Josh. 19:40–48 **18:2** c Judg. 13:25 d Num. 13:17 e Judg. 17:1 **18:4** f Judg. 17:10, 12 **18:5** g Hos. 4:12 h Judg. 1:1; 17:5; 18:14 **18:6** i 1 Kin. 22:6 **18:7** j Josh. 19:47 k Judg. 18:27–29 l Judg. 10:12 **18:8** m Judg. 18:2 **18:9** n Num. 13:30 o 1 Kin. 22:3 **18:10** p Judg. 18:7, 27 q Deut. 8:9 **18:12** r Josh. 15:60 s Judg. 13:25 **18:13** t Judg. 18:2 **18:14** u 1 Sam. 14:28 v Judg. 17:5 **18:16** w Judg. 18:11 **18:17** x Judg. 18:2, 14 y Judg. 17:4, 5 **18:19** z Job 21:5; 29:9; 40:4 a Judg. 17:10

a good way from the house of Micah, the men who *were* in the houses near Micah's house gathered together and overtook the children of Dan. ²³And they called out to the children of Dan. So they turned around and said to Micah, *b*"What ails you, that you have gathered such a company?"

²⁴So he said, "You have *c*taken away my gods which I made, and the priest, and you have gone away. Now what more do I have? How can you say to me, 'What ails you?'"

²⁵And the children of Dan said to him, "Do not let your voice be heard among us, lest angry men fall upon you, and you lose your life, with the lives of your household!" ²⁶Then the children of Dan went their way. And when Micah saw that they *were* too strong for him, he turned and went back to his house.

Danites Settle in Laish

²⁷So they took *the things* Micah had made, and the priest who had belonged to him, and went to Laish, to a people quiet and secure; *d*and they struck them with the edge of the sword and burned the city with fire. ²⁸ *There was* no deliverer, because it *was* *e*far from Sidon, and they had no ties with anyone. It was in the valley that belongs *f*to Beth Rehob. So they rebuilt the city and dwelt there. ²⁹And *g*they called the name of the city *h*Dan, after the name of Dan their father, who was born to Israel. However, the name of the city formerly *was* Laish.

³⁰Then the children of Dan set up for themselves the carved image; and Jonathan the son of Gershom, the son of Manasseh,* and his sons were priests to the tribe of Dan *i*until the day of the captivity of the land. ³¹So they set up for themselves Micah's carved image which he made, *j*all the time that the house of God was in Shiloh.

The Levite's Concubine

19 And it came to pass in those days, *a*when *there was* no king in Israel, that there was a certain Levite staying in the remote mountains of Ephraim. He took for himself a concubine from *b*Bethlehem in Judah. ²But his concubine played the harlot against him, and went away from him to her father's house at Bethlehem in Judah, and was there four whole months. ³Then her husband arose and went after

her, to *c*speak kindly to her *and* bring her back, having his servant and a couple of donkeys with him. So she brought him into her father's house; and when the father of the young woman saw him, he was glad to meet him. ⁴Now his father-in-law, the young woman's father, detained him; and he stayed with him three days. So they ate and drank and lodged there.

⁵Then it came to pass on the fourth day that they arose early in the morning, and he stood to depart; but the young woman's father said to his son-in-law, *d*"Refresh your heart with a morsel of bread, and afterward go your way."

⁶So they sat down, and the two of them ate and drank together. Then the young woman's father said to the man, "Please be content to stay all night, and let your heart be merry." ⁷And when the man stood to depart, his father-in-law urged him; so he lodged there again. ⁸Then he arose early in the morning on the fifth day to depart, but the young woman's father said, "Please refresh your heart." So they delayed until afternoon; and both of them ate.

⁹And when the man stood to depart— he and his concubine and his servant—his father-in-law, the young woman's father, said to him, "Look, the day is now drawing toward evening; please spend the night. See, the day is coming to an end; lodge here, that your heart may be merry. Tomorrow go your way early, so that you may get home."

¹⁰However, the man was not willing to spend that night; so he rose and departed, and came opposite *e*Jebus (that *is*, Jerusalem). With him were the two saddled donkeys; his concubine *was* also with him. ¹¹They *were* near Jebus, and the day was far spent; and the servant said to his master, "Come, please, and let us turn aside into this city *f*of the Jebusites and lodge in it."

¹²But his master said to him, "We will not turn aside here into a city of foreigners, who *are* not of the children of Israel; we will go on *g*to Gibeah." ¹³So he said to his servant, "Come, let us draw near to one of these places, and spend the night in Gibeah or in *h*Ramah." ¹⁴And they passed by and went their way; and the sun went down on them near Gibeah, which belongs

---

* **18:30** Septuagint and Vulgate read *Moses.*

18:31 *all the time that the house of God was in Shiloh.* The true worship of God in the appointed place was available all this time—the Danites just did not want to bother with it.

19:1 *a concubine.* A concubine was a female servant regarded as a part of the family, often chosen to bear children. Several of the patriarchs had children with concubines: Abraham with Hagar (Gen. 16); Jacob with Bilhah and Zilpah (Gen. 30:4–13).

19:10 *Jebus (that is, Jerusalem).* The city of Jerusalem was at this time in the hands of the Jebusites, and

it is called a "city of foreigners" in verse 12 (see Josh. 15:63).

18:23 *b* 2 Kin. 6:28   **18:24** *c* Gen. 31:30   **18:27** *d* Josh. 19:47   **18:28** *e* Judg. 18:7 *f* 2 Sam. 10:6   **18:29** *g* Josh. 19:47 *h* Judg. 20:1   **18:30** *i* 2 Kin. 15:29   **18:31** *j* Josh. 18:1, 8   **19:1** *a* Judg. 17:6; 18:1; 21:25 *b* Judg. 17:7   **19:3** *c* Gen. 34:3; 50:21   **19:5** *d* Gen. 18:5   **19:10** *e* 1 Chr. 11:4, 5   **19:11** *f* Josh. 15:8, 63   **19:12** *g* Josh. 18:28   **19:13** *h* Josh. 18:25

to Benjamin. ¹⁵They turned aside there to go in to lodge in Gibeah. And when he went in, he sat down in the open square of the city, for no one would ⁱtake them into *his* house to spend the night.

¹⁶Just then an old man came in from ^jhis work in the field at evening, who also *was* from the mountains of Ephraim; he was staying in Gibeah, whereas the men of the place *were* Benjamites. ¹⁷And when he raised his eyes, he saw the traveler in the open square of the city; and the old man said, "Where are you going, and where do you come from?"

¹⁸So he said to him, "We *are* passing from Bethlehem in Judah toward the remote mountains of Ephraim; I *am* from there. I went to Bethlehem in Judah; *now* I am going to ^kthe house of the LORD. But there *is* no one who will take me into his house, ¹⁹although we have both straw and fodder for our donkeys, and bread and wine for myself, for your female servant, and for the young man *who is* with your servant; *there is* no lack of anything."

²⁰And the old man said, ^l"Peace *be* with you! However, *let* all your needs *be* my responsibility; ^monly do not spend the night in the open square." ²¹ⁿSo he brought him into his house, and gave fodder to the donkeys. ^oAnd they washed their feet, and ate and drank.

Gibeah's Crime

²²As they were ^penjoying themselves, suddenly ^qcertain men of the city, ^rperverted men,* surrounded the house *and* beat on the door. They spoke to the master of the house, the old man, saying, ^s"Bring out the man who came to your house, that we may know him *carnally!*"

²³But ^tthe man, the master of the house, went out to them and said to them, "No, my brethren! I beg you, do not act *so* wickedly!

Seeing this man has come into my house, ^udo not commit this outrage. ^{24v}Look, *here is* my virgin daughter and *the man's** concubine; let me bring them out now. ^wHumble them, and do with them as you please; but to this man do not do such a vile thing!" ²⁵But the men would not heed him. So the man took his concubine and brought *her* out to them. And they ^xknew her and abused her all night until morning; and when the day began to break, they let her go.

²⁶Then the woman came as the day was dawning, and fell down at the door of the man's house where her master *was*, till it was light.

²⁷When her master arose in the morning, and opened the doors of the house and went out to go his way, there was his concubine, fallen *at* the door of the house with her hands on the threshold. ²⁸And he said to her, "Get up and let us be going." But ^ythere was no answer. So the man lifted her onto the donkey; and the man got up and went to his place.

²⁹When he entered his house he took a knife, laid hold of his concubine, and ^zdivided her into twelve pieces, limb by limb,* and sent her throughout all the territory of Israel. ³⁰And so it was that all who saw it said, "No such deed has been done or seen from the day that the children of Israel came up from the land of Egypt until this day. Consider it, ^aconfer, and speak up!"

Israel's War with the Benjamites

20 So ^aall the children of Israel came out, from ^bDan to ^cBeersheba, as well as from the land of Gilead, and the congregation gathered together as one man before the LORD ^dat Mizpah. ²And the leaders of all the people, all the tribes of Israel,

* **19:22** Literally *sons of Belial*   * **19:24** Literally *his*   * **19:29** Literally *with her bones*

19:22–26 *men of the city.* This section closely resembles Genesis 19:4–9; indeed, the author may have written this story to make the comparison with Sodom unmistakable, as if to say, "Things were as bad as they were in the days of Sodom and Gomorrah."
19:22 *perverted men.* Literally "sons of Belial," this is a phrase describing wicked or worthless people. The name Belial came to designate Satan, as it is used in 2 Corinthians 6:15. *may know him.* This same expression is found in Genesis 19:5, where the men of Sodom wanted to force homosexual relations on Lot's guests.
19:22–30 Perversion—For a man to be raped by a group of town ruffians would be a terrible humiliation; the fact that offering the concubine and the virgin daughter could be considered a solution clearly illustrates the level of perversion and depravity to which the people had sunk. Women were no longer considered the companions and helpers that they were created to be (Gen. 2:22–24), but as property, to be enjoyed or disposed of at will. The author offers no comment upon the horror perpetrated here, merely stating the cold facts and leaving a strong

impression of the heartless and conscienceless state of the people.
19:30 *No such deed has been done or seen.* This phrase is ambiguous. It is uncertain whether they were horrified by discovering the dismembered body or by learning about the cruel rape and murder.
20:1 *from Dan to Beersheba.* This is a common expression for the full extent of the land of Israel from north to south.
20:1–2,8 Unity—Both individually and corporately the Israelites of this period were functioning as a law unto themselves. "Everyone did what was right in his own eyes" (21:25). One notable exception to this was the response to the loathsome rape and killing

19:15 ⁱ Matt. 25:43   **19:16** ^j Ps. 104:23   **19:18** ^k Josh. 18:1   **19:20** ^l Gen. 43:23   ^m Gen. 19:2   **19:21** ⁿ Gen. 24:32; 43:24   ^o John 13:5   **19:22** ^p Judg. 16:25; 19:6, 9   ^q Hos. 9:9; 10:9   ^r Deut. 13:13   ^s [Rom. 1:26, 27]   **19:23** ^t Gen. 19:6, 7   ^u 2 Sam. 13:12   **19:24** ^v Gen. 19:8   ^w Gen. 34:2   **19:25** ^x Gen. 4:1   **19:28** ^y Judg. 20:5   **19:29** ^z 1 Sam. 11:7   **19:30** ^a Judg. 20:7   **20:1** ^a Josh. 22:12   ^b 2 Sam. 3:10; 24:2   ^c Josh. 19:2   ^d 1 Sam. 7:5

presented themselves in the assembly of the people of God, four hundred thousand foot soldiers ᵉwho drew the sword. ³(Now the children of Benjamin heard that the children of Israel had gone up to Mizpah.) Then the children of Israel said, "Tell *us*, how did this wicked deed happen?"

⁴So the Levite, the husband of the woman who was murdered, answered and said, "My concubine and ᶠI went into Gibeah, which belongs to Benjamin, to spend the night. ⁵ᵍAnd the men of Gibeah rose against me, and surrounded the house at night because of me. They intended to kill me, ʰbut instead they ravished my concubine so that she died. ⁶So ⁱI took hold of my concubine, cut her in pieces, and sent her throughout all the territory of the inheritance of Israel, because they ʲcommitted lewdness and outrage in Israel. ⁷Look! All of you *are* children of Israel; ᵏgive your advice and counsel here and now!"

⁸So all the people arose as one man, saying, "None *of us* will go to his tent, nor will any turn back to his house; ⁹but now this *is* the thing which we will do to Gibeah: *We will go up* ˡagainst it by lot. ¹⁰We will take ten men out of *every* hundred throughout all the tribes of Israel, a hundred out of *every* thousand, and a thousand out of *every* ten thousand, to make provisions for the people, that when they come to Gibeah in Benjamin, they may repay all the vileness that they have done in Israel." ¹¹So all the men of Israel were gathered against the city, united together as one man.

¹²ᵐThen the tribes of Israel sent men through all the tribe of Benjamin, saying, "What *is* this wickedness that has occurred among you? ¹³Now therefore, deliver up the men, ⁿthe perverted men* who *are* in Gibeah, that we may put them to death and ᵒremove the evil from Israel!" But the children of Benjamin would not listen to the voice of their brethren, the children of Israel. ¹⁴Instead, the children of Benjamin gathered together from their cities to Gibeah, to go to battle against the children of Israel. ¹⁵And from their cities at that time ᵖthe children

of Benjamin numbered twenty-six thousand men who drew the sword, besides the inhabitants of Gibeah, who numbered seven hundred select men. ¹⁶Among all this people *were* seven hundred select men who were �q left-handed; every one could sling a stone at a hair's *breadth* and not miss. ¹⁷Now besides Benjamin, the men of Israel numbered four hundred thousand men who drew the sword; all of these *were* men of war.

¹⁸Then the children of Israel arose and ʳwent up to the house of God* to ˢinquire of God. They said, "Which of us shall go up first to battle against the children of Benjamin?"

The LORD said, ᵗ"Judah first!"

¹⁹So the children of Israel rose in the morning and encamped against Gibeah. ²⁰And the men of Israel went out to battle against Benjamin, and the men of Israel put themselves in battle array to fight against them at Gibeah. ²¹Then ᵘthe children of Benjamin came out of Gibeah, and on that day cut down to the ground twenty-two thousand men of the Israelites. ²²And the people, that is, the men of Israel, encouraged themselves and again formed the battle line at the place where they had put themselves in array on the first day. ²³ᵛThen the children of Israel went up and wept before the LORD until evening, and asked counsel of the LORD, saying, "Shall I again draw near for battle against the children of my brother Benjamin?"

And the LORD said, "Go up against him."

²⁴So the children of Israel approached the children of Benjamin on the second day. ²⁵And ʷBenjamin went out against them from Gibeah on the second day, and cut down to the ground eighteen thousand more of the children of Israel; all these drew the sword.

²⁶Then all the children of Israel, that is, all the people, ˣwent up and came to the house of God* and wept. They sat there

* **20:13** Literally *sons of Belial*   * **20:18** Or *Bethel*
* **20:26** Or *Bethel*

---

of a concubine in the Benjamite territory of Gibeah (19:11–30). The result of this outrageous covenant violation was that all Israel gathered together as one man, and decided that they would not rest until the crime was punished. The people were shocked into unity against sin. It is still true that crises in life often serve to bring people together to work for a common cause or fight against a common enemy. While this can be a good result of difficult times, it is important that God's people be united in serving Him in peace as well as crisis.

20:9 by lot. God's role is not mentioned here, but one can assume that the people were using lots to seek His will. To their credit, the Israelite tribes were united together as one man, a quality notably absent up to this point in the Book of Judges (v. 11).

20:18 Judah first. The book begins and ends with Judah in this prominent position (1:1–2). This is no

accident, since the end of the book points toward the monarchy, whose true expression would come out of Judah.

20:23 Go up against him. The Lord graciously answered the Israelites twice when they called upon Him (v. 18).

20:26 came to the house of God and wept. The Israelites suffered a second major defeat (v. 25). The

20:2 ᵉ Judg. 8:10   **20:4** ᶠ Judg. 19:15   **20:5** ᵍ Judg. 19:22   ʰ Judg. 19:25, 26   **20:6** ⁱ Judg. 19:29   ʲ Josh. 7:15   **20:7** ᵏ Judg. 19:30   **20:9** ˡ Judg. 1:3   **20:12** ᵐ Deut. 13:14   **20:13** ⁿ Deut. 13:13   ᵒ Deut. 17:12   **20:15** ᵖ Num. 1:36, 37; 2:23; 26:41   **20:16** q 1 Chr. 12:2   **20:18** ʳ Judg. 20:23, 26   ˢ Num. 27:21   ᵗ Judg. 1:1, 2   **20:21** ᵘ [Gen. 49:27]   **20:23** ᵛ Judg. 20:26, 27   **20:25** ʷ Judg. 20:21   **20:26** ˣ Judg. 20:18, 23; 21:2

before the LORD and fasted that day until evening; and they offered burnt offerings and peace offerings before the LORD. [27]So the children of Israel inquired of the LORD (ythe ark of the covenant of God *was* there in those days, [28]zand Phinehas the son of Eleazar, the son of Aaron, astood before it in those days), saying, "Shall I yet again go out to battle against the children of my brother Benjamin, or shall I cease?"

And the LORD said, "Go up, for tomorrow I will deliver them into your hand."

[29]Then Israel bset men in ambush all around Gibeah. [30]And the children of Israel went up against the children of Benjamin on the third day, and put themselves in battle array against Gibeah as at the other times. [31]So the children of Benjamin went out against the people, *and* were drawn away from the city. They began to strike down *and* kill some of the people, as at the other times, in the highways c(one of which goes up to Bethel and the other to Gibeah) and in the field, about thirty men of Israel. [32]And the children of Benjamin said, "They *are* defeated before us, as at first."

But the children of Israel said, "Let us flee and draw them away from the city to the highways." [33]So all the men of Israel rose from their place and put themselves in battle array at Baal Tamar. Then Israel's men in ambush burst forth from their position in the plain of Geba. [34]And ten thousand select men from all Israel came against Gibeah, and the battle was fierce. dBut *the Benjamites** did not know that disaster *was* upon them. [35]The LORD defeated Benjamin before Israel. And the children of Israel destroyed that day twenty-five thousand one hundred Benjamites; all these drew the sword.

[36]So the children of Benjamin saw that they were defeated. eThe men of Israel had given ground to the Benjamites, because they relied on the men in ambush whom they had set against Gibeah. [37]fAnd the men in ambush quickly rushed upon Gibeah; the men in ambush spread out and struck the whole city with the edge of the sword. [38]Now the appointed signal between the men of Israel and the men in ambush was that they would make a great cloud of gsmoke rise up from the city, [39]whereupon the men of Israel would turn in battle. Now Benjamin had begun to strike *and* kill about thirty of the men of Israel. For

they said, "Surely they are defeated before us, as *in* the first battle." [40]But when the cloud began to rise from the city in a column of smoke, the Benjamites hlooked behind them, and there was the whole city going up *in smoke* to heaven. [41]And when the men of Israel turned back, the men of Benjamin panicked, for they saw that disaster had come upon them. [42]Therefore they turned *their backs* before the men of Israel in the direction of the wilderness; but the battle overtook them, and whoever *came* out of the cities they destroyed in their midst. [43]They surrounded the Benjamites, chased them, *and* easily trampled them down as far as the front of Gibeah toward the east. [44]And eighteen thousand men of Benjamin fell; all these *were* men of valor. [45]Then they* turned and fled toward the wilderness to the rock of iRimmon; and they cut down five thousand of them on the highways. Then they pursued them relentlessly up to Gidom, and killed two thousand of them. [46]So all who fell of Benjamin that day were twenty-five thousand men who drew the sword; all these *were* men of valor.

[47]iBut six hundred men turned and fled toward the wilderness to the rock of Rimmon, and they stayed at the rock of Rimmon for four months. [48]And the men of Israel turned back against the children of Benjamin, and struck them down with the edge of the sword—from *every* city, men and beasts, all who were found. They also set fire to all the cities they came to.

Wives Provided for the Benjamites

21 Now athe men of Israel had sworn an oath at Mizpah, saying, "None of us shall give his daughter to Benjamin as a wife." [2]Then the people came bto the house of God,* and remained there before God till evening. They lifted up their voices and wept bitterly, [3]and said, "O LORD God of Israel, why has this come to pass in Israel, that today there should be one tribe *missing* in Israel?"

[4]So it was, on the next morning, that the people rose early and cbuilt an altar there, and offered burnt offerings and peace offerings. [5]The children of Israel said, "Who *is there* among all the tribes of Israel who

---

* **20:34** Literally *they*   * **20:45** Septuagint reads *the rest.*   * **21:2** Or *Bethel*

---

result drove them to fasting and sacrificing at Bethel, something done very rarely in this period.
20:28 Phinehas. Phinehas was the grandson of Aaron who had stopped the plague at Peor (Num. 25:6–11). The fact that he was still alive shows that the organization of the Book of Judges is not strictly chronological. The author may have placed this account at the end of the book to make the point even more strongly about the spiritual deterioration of the nation.
20:48 and struck them down with the edge of the

sword. The spiritual decay of Israel had resulted in the destruction of its own people with a vengeance once reserved for pagan nations.

20:27 y Josh. 18:1   **20:28** z Josh. 24:33   a Deut. 10:8; 18:5   **20:29** b Josh. 8:4   **20:31** c Judg. 20:19   **20:34** d Josh. 8:14   **20:36** e Josh. 8:15   **20:37** f Josh. 8:19   **20:38** g Josh. 8:20   **20:40** h Josh. 8:20   **20:45** i Josh. 15:32   **20:47** j Judg. 21:13   **21:1** a Judg. 20:1   **21:2** b Judg. 20:18, 26   **21:4** c 2 Sam. 24:25

did not come up with the assembly to the LORD?" [d]For they had made a great oath concerning anyone who had not come up to the LORD at Mizpah, saying, "He shall surely be put to death." [6]And the children of Israel grieved for Benjamin their brother, and said, "One tribe is cut off from Israel today. [7]What shall we do for wives for those who remain, seeing we have sworn by the LORD that we will not give them our daughters as wives?"

[8]And they said, "What one *is there* from the tribes of Israel who did not come up to Mizpah to the LORD?" And, in fact, no one had come to the camp from [e]Jabesh Gilead to the assembly. [9]For when the people were counted, indeed, not one of the inhabitants of Jabesh Gilead *was* there. [10]So the congregation sent out there twelve thousand of their most valiant men, and commanded them, saying, [f]"Go and strike the inhabitants of Jabesh Gilead with the edge of the sword, including the women and children. [11]And this *is* the thing that you shall do: [g]You shall utterly destroy every male, and every woman who has known a man intimately." [12]So they found among the inhabitants of Jabesh Gilead four hundred young virgins who had not known a man intimately; and they brought them to the camp at [h]Shiloh, which is in the land of Canaan.

[13]Then the whole congregation sent *word* to the children of Benjamin [i]who *were* at the rock of Rimmon, and announced peace to them. [14]So Benjamin came back at that time, and they gave them the women whom they had saved alive of the women of Jabesh Gilead; and yet they had not found enough for them.

[15]And the people [j]grieved for Benjamin, because the LORD had made a void in the tribes of Israel.

[16]Then the elders of the congregation said, "What shall we do for wives for those who remain, since the women of Benjamin have been destroyed?" [17]And they said, "*There must be* an inheritance for the survivors of Benjamin, that a tribe may not be destroyed from Israel. [18]However, we cannot give them wives from our daughters, [k]for the children of Israel have sworn an oath, saying, 'Cursed *be* the one who gives a wife to Benjamin.'" [19]Then they said, "In fact, *there is* a yearly [l]feast of the LORD in [m]Shiloh, which *is* north of Bethel, on the east side of the [n]highway that goes up from Bethel to Shechem, and south of Lebonah."

[20]Therefore they instructed the children of Benjamin, saying, "Go, lie in wait in the vineyards, [21]and watch; and just when the daughters of Shiloh come out [o]to perform their dances, then come out from the vineyards, and every man catch a wife for himself from the daughters of Shiloh; then go to the land of Benjamin. [22]Then it shall be, when their fathers or their brothers come to us to complain, that we will say to them, 'Be kind to them for our sakes, because we did not take a wife for any of them in the war; for *it is* not *as though* you have given the *women* to them at this time, making yourselves guilty of your oath.'"

[23]And the children of Benjamin did so; they took enough wives for their number from those who danced, whom they caught. Then they went and returned to their inheritance, and they [p]rebuilt the cities and dwelt in them. [24]So the children of Israel departed from there at that time, every man to his tribe and family; they went out from there, every man to his inheritance.

[25][q]In those days *there was* no king in Israel; [r]everyone did *what was* right in his own eyes.

21:6 Repentance—In the midst of this terrible account of great sin within the nation of Israel, we find that the people realized that it was important that none of the tribes should perish. The example set by the nation of Israel is important for believers today. The people of Israel felt sorry for their brothers after the brothers had been disciplined for their great sin. Restoration and continuance of fellowship are important for people who have fallen into sin (2 Cor. 2:6–8; Gal. 6:1–2).

21:11 *utterly destroy.* This phrase is found numerous times in the Book of Joshua in regard to the conquest of the Canaanites. However, there is no hint that God supported the bloodbath at Jabesh Gilead.

21:19 *feast of the LORD.* Because of the dancing association, some believe that the yearly feast mentioned here was the Passover. Others believe that it was the Feast of Tabernacles, celebrated in the fall, since vineyards are mentioned (vv. 20–21). The grape harvest came in the early fall.

21:23 *took enough wives for their number.* No justification is given for this peculiar abduction except for the supposed needs of the Benjamites. This interesting episode was a way for the rest of Israel to sidestep their oath (v. 1), and try to preserve the tribe of Benjamin.

21:25 *what was right in his own eyes.* This statement sums up the whole Book of Judges. What happened was governed by whatever people happened to feel like, rather than by listening to God, and the stories at the end of the book clearly illustrate the results of this mindset.

21:5 [d] Judg. 20:1–3   21:8 [e] 1 Sam. 11:1; 31:11
21:10 [f] Num. 31:17   21:11 [g] Num. 31:17   21:12 [h] Josh. 18:1   21:13 [i] Judg. 20:47   21:15 [j] Judg. 21:6
21:18 [k] Judg. 11:35; 21:1   21:19 [l] Lev. 23:2   [m] 1 Sam. 1:3
[n] Judg. 20:31   21:21 [o] Judg. 11:34   21:23 [p] Judg. 20:48
21:25 [q] Judg. 17:6; 18:1; 19:1   [r] Judg. 17:6

THE BOOK OF
RUTH

▶ **AUTHOR:** The Book of Ruth provides a cameo to the other side of the biblical story—the godly remnant who remain true to the laws of God. Although the author of Ruth is not given anywhere in the book, the anonymity should not detract from its spiritual value or literary beauty. Tradition has attributed the writing of Ruth to Samuel, but this is difficult to reconcile with the mention of David when Samuel died before David was installed as king.

▶ **TIME:** During the Judges   ▶ **KEY VERSE:** Ruth 1:16

▶ **THEME:** Ruth is a simple yet intriguing short story. Throughout the story, the characters develop and eventually exhibit wisdom, loyalty, and obedience to God and the customs of the day. We see an interesting romance bloom out of most unusual circumstances. It provides a platform for some profound understanding of God's covenant plans with His people, Israel. We see the details of His plan unfold in the lives of a widow, her foreign born daughter-in-law, and a distant relative. We also see the lineage of David and Christ established and blessed.

Elimelech's Family Goes to Moab

1 Now it came to pass, in the days when *a*the judges ruled, that there was *b*a famine in the land. And a certain man of *c*Bethlehem, Judah, went to dwell in the country of *d*Moab, he and his wife and his two sons. 2The name of the man *was* Elimelech, the name of his wife *was* Naomi, and the names of his two sons *were* Mahlon and Chilion—*e*Ephrathites of Bethlehem, Judah. And they went *f*to the country of Moab and remained there. 3Then Elimelech, Naomi's husband, died; and she was left, and her two sons. 4Now they took wives of the women of Moab: the name of the one *was* Orpah, and the name of the other Ruth. And they dwelt there about ten years. 5Then both Mahlon and Chilion also died; so the woman survived her two sons and her husband.

Naomi Returns with Ruth

6Then she arose with her daughters-in-law that she might return from the country of Moab, for she had heard in the country of Moab that the LORD had *g*visited His people by *h*giving them bread. 7Therefore she went out from the place where she was, and her two daughters-in-law with her; and they went on the way to return to the land of Judah. 8And Naomi said to her two daughters-in-law, *i*"Go, return each to her mother's house. *j*The LORD deal kindly with you, as you have dealt *k*with the dead and with me. 9The LORD grant that you may find *l*rest, each in the house of her husband."

So she kissed them, and they lifted up their voices and wept. 10And they said to her, "Surely we will return with you to your people."

11But Naomi said, "Turn back, my daughters; why will you go with me? *Are* there still sons in my womb, *m*that they may be your husbands? 12Turn back, my daughters, go—for I am too old to have a husband. If I should say I have hope, *if* I should have a husband tonight and should also bear sons, 13would you wait for them till they were grown? Would you restrain yourselves from having husbands? No, my daughters; for it grieves me very much for your sakes that *n*the hand of the LORD has gone out against me!"

14Then they lifted up their voices and

1:4 *Ruth*. The name Ruth means "friend" or "compassionate friend." Throughout the account of her life it is easy to see that this name fittingly described Ruth's character.

1:8 *kindly*. The Hebrew word translated "kindly" is often used to describe God. It can also be interpreted as "loyal love."

1:13 *gone out against me*. Naomi felt that the Lord was disciplining her. To be a widow in such a time and also without children was very difficult indeed.

1:14 Perseverance—When we sacrifice what would seem to be our best interest for another's welfare, God may unexpectedly use it to uplift and reward us. Ruth's desire to stay with Naomi not only lightened

1:1 *a* Judg. 2:16–18 *b* Gen. 12:10; 26:1 *c* Judg. 17:8 *d* Gen. 19:37 **1:2** *e* Gen. 35:19 *f* Judg. 3:30 **1:6** *g* Ex. 3:16; 4:31 *h* Matt. 6:11 **1:8** *i* Josh. 24:15 *j* 2 Tim. 1:16–18 *k* Ruth 2:20 **1:9** *l* Ruth 3:1 **1:11** *m* Deut. 25:5 **1:13** *n* Judg. 2:15

wept again; and Orpah kissed her mother-in-law, but Ruth ᵒclung to her.

¹⁵And she said, "Look, your sister-in-law has gone back to ᵖher people and to her gods; �qreturn after your sister-in-law."

¹⁶But Ruth said:

ʳ"Entreat me not to leave you,
    Or to turn back from following after
        you;
    For wherever you go, I will go;
    And wherever you lodge, I will lodge;
    ˢYour people *shall be* my people,
        And your God, my God.
¹⁷ Where you die, I will die,
    And there will I be buried.
    ᵗThe LORD do so to me, and more also,
    If *anything but* death parts you and
        me."

¹⁸ᵘWhen she saw that she was determined to go with her, she stopped speaking to her.

¹⁹Now the two of them went until they came to Bethlehem. And it happened, when they had come to Bethlehem, that ᵛall the city was excited because of them; and the women said, ʷ"*Is* this Naomi?"

²⁰But she said to them, "Do not call me Naomi;* call me Mara,* for the Almighty has dealt very bitterly with me. ²¹I went out full, ˣand the LORD has brought me home again empty. Why do you call me Naomi, since the LORD has testified against me, and the Almighty has afflicted me?"

²²So Naomi returned, and Ruth the Moabitess her daughter-in-law with her, who returned from the country of Moab. Now they came to Bethlehem ʸat the beginning of barley harvest.

Ruth Meets Boaz

2 There was a ᵃrelative of Naomi's husband, a man of great wealth, of the family of ᵇElimelech. His name *was* ᶜBoaz. ²So Ruth the Moabitess said to Naomi, "Please let me go to the ᵈfield, and glean heads of grain after *him* in whose sight I may find favor."

And she said to her, "Go, my daughter."

³Then she left, and went and gleaned in the field after the reapers. And she happened to come to the part of the field *belonging* to Boaz, who *was* of the family of Elimelech.

⁴Now behold, Boaz came from ᵉBethlehem, and said to the reapers, ᶠ"The LORD *be* with you!"

And they answered him, "The LORD bless you!"

⁵Then Boaz said to his servant who was in charge of the reapers, "Whose young woman *is* this?"

⁶So the servant who was in charge of the reapers answered and said, "It *is* the young Moabite woman ᵍwho came back with Naomi from the country of Moab. ⁷And she said, 'Please let me glean and gather after the reapers among the sheaves.' So she came and has continued from morning until now, though she rested a little in the house."

⁸Then Boaz said to Ruth, "You will listen, my daughter, will you not? Do not go to glean in another field, nor go from here, but stay close by my young women. ⁹*Let* your eyes *be* on the field which they reap, and go after them. Have I not commanded the young men not to touch you? And when you are thirsty, go to the vessels and drink from what the young men have drawn."

¹⁰So she ʰfell on her face, bowed down to the ground, and said to him, "Why have I found ⁱfavor in your eyes, that you should take notice of me, since I *am* a foreigner?"

¹¹And Boaz answered and said to her, "It has been fully reported to me, ʲall that you have done for your mother-in-law since the death of your husband, and *how* you have left your father and your mother and the land of your birth, and have come to a people whom you did not know before. ¹²ᵏThe LORD repay your work, and a full reward be given you by the LORD God of Israel, ˡunder whose wings you have come for refuge."

¹³Then she said, ᵐ"Let me find favor in your sight, my lord; for you have comforted me, and have spoken kindly to your maidservant, ⁿthough I am not like one of your maidservants."

¹⁴Now Boaz said to her at mealtime, "Come here, and eat of the bread, and dip your piece of bread in the vinegar." So

---

* **1:20** Literally *Pleasant* • Literally *Bitter*

Naomi's lot, but it also brought Ruth into the Messiah's ancestral line.

1:16–17 your God, my God. Ruth is casting her lot with Naomi, turning her back on all she has known. Most important she is turning away from the many gods of Moab to the One True God of Israel.

1:22 Moabitess. God extended His protection to Ruth even though she was a foreigner and a member of a nation which had been the enemy of God and Israel (Num. 22–25).

2:1 Boaz. As a relative of Naomi's husband Elimelech, as well as a man of both wealth and good character, Boaz was the ideal person to stand up for the rights of the two widows. In the ancient Middle East, a woman without a husband or father was a woman unprotected and with no way to make a living.

2:2 glean. The law of Moses allowed the poor to glean in the fields of the farmers (Lev. 23:22), picking up the loose grain that fell from the sheaves as the reapers gathered them up.

2:14–16 Come here, and eat of the bread. Boaz not only let Ruth glean, he also amply provided her with

---

1:14 ᵒ [Prov. 17:17] **1:15** ᵖ Judg. 11:24 �q Josh. 1:15
1:16 ʳ 2 Kin. 2:2, 4, 6 ˢ Ruth 2:11, 12 **1:17** ᵗ 1 Sam.
3:17 **1:18** ᵘ Acts 21:14 **1:19** ᵛ Matt. 21:10 ʷ Lam.
2:15 **1:21** ˣ Job 1:21 **1:22** ʸ 2 Sam. 21:9 **2:1** ᵃ Ruth
3:2, 12 ᵇ Ruth 1:2 ᶜ Ruth 4:21 **2:2** ᵈ Lev. 19:9, 10;
23:22 **2:4** ᵉ Ruth 1:1 ᶠ Ps. 129:7, 8 **2:6** ᵍ Ruth 1:22
2:10 ʰ 1 Sam. 25:23 ⁱ 1 Sam. 1:18 **2:11** ʲ Ruth 1:14–18
2:12 ᵏ 1 Sam. 24:19 ˡ Ruth 1:16 **2:13** ᵐ Gen. 33:15
ⁿ 1 Sam. 25:41

she sat beside the reapers, and he passed parched *grain* to her; and she ate and [o]was satisfied, and kept some back. [15]And when she rose up to glean, Boaz commanded his young men, saying, "Let her glean even among the sheaves, and do not reproach her. [16]Also let *grain* from the bundles fall purposely for her; leave *it* that she may glean, and do not rebuke her."

[17]So she gleaned in the field until evening, and beat out what she had gleaned, and it was about an ephah of [p]barley. [18]Then she took *it* up and went into the city, and her mother-in-law saw what she had gleaned. So she brought out and gave to her [q]what she had kept back after she had been satisfied.

[19]And her mother-in-law said to her, "Where have you gleaned today? And where did you work? Blessed be the one who [r]took notice of you."

So she told her mother-in-law with whom she had worked, and said, "The man's name with whom I worked today *is* Boaz."

[20]Then Naomi said to her daughter-in-law, [s]"Blessed *be* he of the LORD, who [t]has not forsaken His kindness to the living and the dead!" And Naomi said to her, "This man *is* a relation of ours, [u]one of our close relatives."

[21]Ruth the Moabitess said, "He also said to me, 'You shall stay close by my young men until they have finished all my harvest.' "

[22]And Naomi said to Ruth her daughter-in-law, "*It is* good, my daughter, that you go out with his young women, and that people do not meet you in any other field." [23]So she stayed close by the young women of Boaz, to glean until the end of barley harvest and wheat harvest; and she dwelt with her mother-in-law.

Ruth's Redemption Assured

3 Then Naomi her mother-in-law said to her, "My daughter, [a]shall I not seek [b]security for you, that it may be well with you? [2]Now Boaz, [c]whose young women you were with, *is he* not our relative? In fact, he is winnowing barley tonight at the

threshing floor. [3]Therefore wash yourself and [d]anoint yourself, put on your *best* garment and go down to the threshing floor; *but* do not make yourself known to the man until he has finished eating and drinking. [4]Then it shall be, when he lies down, that you shall notice the place where he lies; and you shall go in, uncover his feet, and lie down; and he will tell you what you should do."

[5]And she said to her, "All that you say to me I will do."

[6]So she went down to the threshing floor and did according to all that her mother-in-law instructed her. [7]And after Boaz had eaten and drunk, and [e]his heart was cheerful, he went to lie down at the end of the heap of grain; and she came softly, uncovered his feet, and lay down.

[8]Now it happened at midnight that the man was startled, and turned himself; and there, a woman was lying at his feet. [9]And he said, "Who *are* you?"

So she answered, "I *am* Ruth, your maidservant. [f]Take your maidservant under your wing,* for you are [g]a close relative."

[10]Then he said, [h]"Blessed *are* you of the LORD, my daughter! For you have shown more kindness at the end than [i]at the beginning, in that you did not go after young men, whether poor or rich. [11]And now, my daughter, do not fear. I will do for you all that you request, for all the people of my town know that you *are* a [j]virtuous woman. [12]Now it is true that I *am* a [k]close relative; however, [l]there is a relative closer than I. [13]Stay this night, and in the morning it shall be *that* if he will [m]perform the duty of a close relative for you—good; let him do it. But if he does not want to perform the duty for you, then I will perform the duty for you, [n]*as* the LORD lives! Lie down until morning."

[14]So she lay at his feet until morning, and she arose before one could recognize another. Then he said, [o]"Do not let it be known that the woman came to the

---

* **3:9** Or *Spread the corner of your garment over your maidservant*

---

food. He went beyond the letter of the law, demonstrating God's compassion and the concern that each believer ought to show for others.

3:4 *uncover his feet.* By uncovering Boaz's feet in this manner Ruth was showing her submission to him while also asking him to be her protector.

3:9 *close relative.* Ruth reminded Boaz that he was a close relative of her dead husband, and in keeping with the law a close relative was required to be a "kinsman redeemer." This meant that if a man was slain, his kinsman redeemer had to avenge his death. If a man was sold into slavery, his kinsman redeemer paid the price to release him. If a man died childless, his kinsman redeemer had the responsibility to marry his wife and father a child to bear his name (Deut.

15:5–10). Ruth was placing herself so that Boaz would know that she was willing for him to redeem her.

3:12 *closer than I.* Boaz remembers that there is yet a closer relative; that relative would have the responsibility and the right to redeem Ruth first. If, however, he did not wish to or was unable to, Boaz would be free to do it himself.

2:14 [o] Ruth 2:18   **2:17** [p] Ruth 1:22   **2:18** [q] Ruth 2:14   **2:19** [r] [Ps. 41:1]   **2:20** [s] 2 Sam. 2:5   [t] Prov. 17:17   [u] Ruth 3:9; 4:4, 6   **3:1** [a] 1 Tim. 5:8   [b] Ruth 1:9   **3:2** [c] Ruth 2:3, 8   **3:3** [d] 2 Sam. 14:2   **3:7** [e] Judg. 19:6, 9, 22   **3:9** [f] Ezek. 16:8   [g] Ruth 2:20; 3:12   **3:10** [h] Ruth 2:20   [i] Ruth 1:8   **3:11** [j] Prov. 12:4; 31:10–31   **3:12** [k] Ruth 3:9   [l] Ruth 4:1   **3:13** [m] Deut. 25:5–10   [n] Jer. 4:2; 12:16   **3:14** [o] [1 Cor. 10:32]

threshing floor." 15Also he said, "Bring the shawl that *is* on you and hold it." And when she held it, he measured six *ephahs* of barley, and laid *it* on her. Then she* went into the city.

16When she came to her mother-in-law, she said, "*Is* that you, my daughter?"

Then she told her all that the man had done for her. 17And she said, "These six *ephahs* of barley he gave me; for he said to me, 'Do not go empty-handed to your mother-in-law.'"

18Then she said, *p*"Sit still, my daughter, until you know how the matter will turn out; for the man will not rest until he has concluded the matter this day."

Boaz Redeems Ruth

4 Now Boaz went up to the gate and sat down there; and behold, *a*the close relative of whom Boaz had spoken came by. So Boaz said, "Come aside, friend,* sit down here." So he came aside and sat down. 2And he took ten men of *b*the elders of the city, and said, "Sit down here." So they sat down. 3Then he said to the close relative, "Naomi, who has come back from the country of Moab, sold the piece of land *c*which *belonged* to our brother Elimelech. 4And I thought to inform you, saying, *d*'Buy it back *e*in the presence of the inhabitants and the elders of my people. If you will redeem *it*, redeem *it*; but if you* will not redeem *it*, *then* tell me, that I may know; *f*for *there is* no one but you to redeem *it*, and I *am* next after you.'"

And he said, "I will redeem *it*."

5Then Boaz said, "On the day you buy the field from the hand of Naomi, you must also buy *it* from Ruth the Moabitess, the wife of the dead, *g*to perpetuate* the name of the dead through his inheritance."

6*h*And the close relative said, "I cannot redeem *it* for myself, lest I ruin my own inheritance. You redeem my right of redemption for yourself, for I cannot redeem *it*."

7*i*Now this *was the custom* in former times in Israel concerning redeeming

and exchanging, to confirm anything: one man took off his sandal and gave *it* to the other, and this *was* a confirmation in Israel.

8Therefore the close relative said to Boaz, "Buy *it* for yourself." So he took off his sandal. 9And Boaz said to the elders and all the people, "You *are* witnesses this day that I have bought all that was Elimelech's, and all that *was* Chilion's and Mahlon's, from the hand of Naomi. 10Moreover, Ruth the Moabitess, the widow of Mahlon, I have acquired as my wife, to perpetuate the name of the dead through his inheritance, *j*that the name of the dead may not be cut off from among his brethren and from his position at the gate.* You *are* witnesses this day."

11And all the people who *were* at the gate, and the elders, said, "*We are* witnesses. *k*The LORD make the woman who is coming to your house like Rachel and Leah, the two who *l*built the house of Israel; and may you prosper in *m*Ephrathah and be famous in *n*Bethlehem. 12May your house be like the house of *o*Perez, *p*whom Tamar bore to Judah, because of *q*the offspring which the LORD will give you from this young woman."

Descendants of Boaz and Ruth

13So Boaz *r*took Ruth and she became his wife; and when he went in to her, *s*the LORD gave her conception, and she bore a son. 14Then *t*the women said to Naomi, "Blessed *be* the LORD, who has not left you this day without a close relative; and may his name be famous in Israel! 15And may he be to you a restorer of life and a nourisher of your old age; for your daughter-in-law, who loves you, who is *u*better to you than seven sons, has borne him." 16Then Naomi

---

* **3:15** Many Hebrew manuscripts, Syriac, and Vulgate read *she;* Masoretic Text, Septuagint, and Targum read *he.* * **4:1** Hebrew *peloni almoni;* literally *so and so* * **4:4** Following many Hebrew manuscripts, Septuagint, Syriac, Targum, and Vulgate; Masoretic Text reads *he.* * **4:5** Literally *raise up* * **4:10** Probably his civic office

---

4:1–2 *the gate.* The gate of the city was the place where the men congregated and where the officials of a city were to be found. Legal business was typically carried on here where the elders of the city were present to be witnesses.

4:11 *like Rachel and Leah.* The people blessed Ruth and asked the Lord to bless her as He had the founding mothers of the twelve tribes of Israel. Even though she was a Moabitess, Ruth was accepted.

4:14–15 *who loves you . . . is better to you than seven sons.* Ruth, although not knowing the outcome, sowed kindness by staying with Naomi. Because of this she also reaped what she had sown: abundant blessing. She became the great-grandmother of King David, and had a place in the genealogy of Christ Jesus. Boaz, as the kinsman redeemer had to sacrifice his name—the son that was born

would bear the family name of Mahlon—but he was also abundantly blessed. Boaz received the admiration of the people (4:11), the beautiful and faithful Ruth became his wife, and together they became ancestors of the great Redeemer, Jesus Christ. This story of Boaz's redemption of the foreign woman points to the wonderful redemption of Jesus for all those who believe in Him.

3:18 *p* [Ps. 37:3, 5]   **4:1** *a* Ruth 3:12   **4:2** *b* 1 Kin. 21:8   **4:3** *c* Lev. 25:25   **4:4** *d* Jer. 32:7, 8 *e* Gen. 23:18 *f* Lev. 25:25   **4:5** *g* Matt. 22:24   **4:6** *h* Ruth 3:12, 13   **4:7** *i* Deut. 25:7–10   **4:10** *j* Deut. 25:6   **4:11** *k* Ps. 127:3; 128:3 *l* Gen. 29:25–30 *m* Gen. 35:16–18 *n* Mic. 5:2   **4:12** *o* Matt. 1:3 *p* Gen. 38:6–29 *q* 1 Sam. 2:20   **4:13** *r* Ruth 3:11 *s* Gen. 29:31; 33:5   **4:14** *t* Luke 1:58   **4:15** *u* 1 Sam. 1:8

took the child and laid him on her bosom, and became a nurse to him. [17v]Also the neighbor women gave him a name, saying, "There is a son born to Naomi." And they called his name Obed. He *is* the father of Jesse, the father of David.

[18w]Now this *is* the genealogy of Perez: [x]Perez begot Hezron; [19]Hezron begot Ram, and Ram begot Amminadab; [20]Amminadab begot [y]Nahshon, and Nahshon begot [z]Salmon;* [21]Salmon begot Boaz, and Boaz begot Obed; [22]Obed begot Jesse, and Jesse begot [a]David.

---

* **4:20** Hebrew *Salmah*

4:17 [v] Luke 1:58   **4:18** [w] 1 Chr. 2:4, 5   [x] Num. 26:20, 21 | **4:20** [y] Num. 1:7   [z] Matt. 1:4   **4:22** [a] Matt. 1:6

THE FIRST BOOK OF
SAMUEL

▶ **AUTHOR:** The author of 1 and 2 Samuel is anonymous. Samuel may have written the first portion of the book, but his death recorded in 1 Samuel 25:1 makes it clear that he did not write all of 1 or 2 Samuel. It is very possible that a single compiler, perhaps a member of the prophetic school mentioned in 1 Chronicles 29:29, used the various writings referenced as the chronicles of "Nathan the prophet," "Gad the seer," and "Samuel the seer."

▶ **TIME:** c. 1105–1011 B.C.   ▶ **KEY VERSE:** 1 Sam. 13:14

▶ **THEME:** First Samuel tells the story of three characters: Samuel, Saul, and David. Saul's story begins the line of Israel's monarchy. His story ends with the end of 1 Samuel. David's starts in 1 Samuel, goes through 2 Samuel and ends in the first few chapters of 1 Kings. All three of the main characters in this book make mistakes that cost them dearly. Samuel has problems with his own sons. The result is the end of the rule of judges. Saul seems to be a classic study in what a poor self-image can do to a person. David's early violence prevents him from being able to build the temple later on when he is king.

The Family of Elkanah

1 Now there was a certain man of Ramathaim Zophim, of the ^amountains of Ephraim, and his name *was* ^bElkanah the son of Jeroham, the son of Elihu,* the son of Tohu,* the son of Zuph, ^can Ephraimite. ²And he had ^dtwo wives: the name of one *was* Hannah, and the name of the other Peninnah. Peninnah had children, but Hannah had no children. ³This man went up from his city ^eyearly ^fto worship and sacrifice to the LORD of hosts in ^gShiloh. Also the two sons of Eli, Hophni and Phinehas, the priests of the LORD, *were* there. ⁴And whenever the time came for Elkanah to make an ^hoffering, he would give portions to Peninnah his wife and to all her sons and daughters. ⁵But to Hannah he would give a double portion, for he loved Hannah, ⁱalthough the LORD had closed her womb. ⁶And her rival also ^jprovoked her severely, to make her miserable, because the LORD had closed her womb. ⁷So it was, year by year, when she went up to the house of the LORD, that she provoked her; therefore she wept and did not eat.

Hannah's Vow

⁸Then Elkanah her husband said to her, "Hannah, why do you weep? Why do you not eat? And why is your heart grieved? *Am* I not ^kbetter to you than ten sons?"

⁹So Hannah arose after they had finished eating and drinking in Shiloh. Now Eli the priest was sitting on the seat by the doorpost of ^lthe tabernacle* of the LORD. ¹⁰^mAnd she *was* in bitterness of soul, and prayed to the LORD and wept in anguish. ¹¹Then she ⁿmade a vow and said, "O LORD of hosts, if You will indeed ^olook on the affliction of Your maidservant and ^premember me, and not forget Your maidservant,

---

* **1:1** Spelled *Eliel* in 1 Chronicles 6:34 • Spelled *Toah* in 1 Chronicles 6:34   * **1:9** Hebrew *heykal*, palace or temple

---

1:1 *Elkanah.* Elkanah was a Levite (1 Chr. 6:26) who lived in a village about five miles north of Jerusalem. He is referred to as an Ephraimite because he lived in the territory of Ephraim.
1:3 *LORD of hosts.* The term "LORD of hosts" refers to God as the One who commands the angelic armies of heaven (1 Kin. 22:19; Rev. 19:14) and the armies of Israel (17:45). ***Shiloh.*** Shiloh, located twenty miles north of Jerusalem, was the religious center for the nation at this time and the location of the tabernacle (Josh. 18:1).
1:9 *Eli.* Eli, Israel's high priest and judge, was from the family of Ithamar, Aaron's fourth son (1 Chr. 24:1–3).

The last high priest mentioned before him was Phinehas, the son of Eleazar (Judg. 20:28). It is not known why or how the office of high priest passed from the house of Eleazar to that of Ithamar.
1:11 *vow.* Hannah vowed that the child she would bear would be a servant to the Lord all of his life. Can a parent really make a vow that the child will carry

---

1:1 ^a Josh. 17:17, 18; 24:33   ^b 1 Chr. 6:27, 33–38   ^c Ruth 1:2   **1:2** ^d Deut. 21:15–17   **1:3** ^e Luke 2:41   ^f Deut. 12:5–7; 16:16   ^g Josh. 18:1   **1:4** ^h Deut. 12:17, 18   **1:5** ⁱ Gen. 16:1; 30:1, 2   **1:6** ^j Job 24:21   **1:8** ^k Ruth 4:15   **1:9** ^l 1 Sam. 3:3   **1:10** ^m Job 7:11   **1:11** ⁿ Num. 30:6–11   ^o Ps. 25:18   ^p Gen. 8:1

but will give Your maidservant a male child, then I will give him to the LORD all the days of his life, and ⁿno razor shall come upon his head."

¹²And it happened, as she continued praying before the LORD, that Eli watched her mouth. ¹³Now Hannah spoke in her heart; only her lips moved, but her voice was not heard. Therefore Eli thought she was drunk. ¹⁴So Eli said to her, "How long will you be drunk? Put your wine away from you!"

¹⁵But Hannah answered and said, "No, my lord, I *am* a woman of sorrowful spirit. I have drunk neither wine nor intoxicating drink, but have ʳpoured out my soul before the LORD. ¹⁶Do not consider your maidservant a ˢwicked woman,* for out of the abundance of my complaint and grief I have spoken until now."

¹⁷Then Eli answered and said, ᵗ"Go in peace, and ᵘthe God of Israel grant your petition which you have asked of Him."

¹⁸And she said, ᵛ"Let your maidservant find favor in your sight." So the woman ʷwent her way and ate, and her face was no longer *sad*.

Samuel Is Born and Dedicated

¹⁹Then they rose early in the morning and worshiped before the LORD, and returned and came to their house at Ramah. And Elkanah ˣknew Hannah his wife, and the LORD ʸremembered her. ²⁰So it came to pass in the process of time that Hannah conceived and bore a son, and called his name Samuel,* *saying*, "Because I have asked for him from the LORD."

²¹Now the man Elkanah and all his house ᶻwent up to offer to the LORD the yearly sacrifice and his vow. ²²But Hannah did not go up, for she said to her husband, "*Not* until the child is weaned; then I will ⁿtake him, that he may appear before the LORD and ᵇremain there ᶜforever."

²³So ᵈElkanah her husband said to her, "Do what seems best to you; wait until you have weaned him. Only let the LORD establish His* word." Then the woman stayed and nursed her son until she had weaned him.

²⁴Now when she had weaned *him*, she ᵉtook him up with her, with three bulls,* one ephah of flour, and a skin of wine, and brought him to ᶠthe house of the LORD in Shiloh. And the child *was* young. ²⁵Then they slaughtered a bull, and ᵍbrought the child to Eli. ²⁶And she said, "O my lord! ʰAs your soul lives, my lord, I *am* the woman who stood by you here, praying to the LORD. ²⁷ᶦFor this child I prayed, and the LORD has granted me my petition which I asked of Him. ²⁸Therefore I also have lent him to the LORD; as long as he lives he shall be lent to the LORD." So they ʲworshiped the LORD there.

Hannah's Prayer

2 And Hannah ⁿprayed and said:

ᵇ"My heart rejoices in the LORD;
ᶜMy horn* is exalted in the LORD.

* **1:16** Literally *daughter of Belial* * **1:20** Literally *Heard by God* * **1:23** Following Masoretic Text, Targum, and Vulgate; Dead Sea Scrolls, Septuagint, and Syriac read *your*. * **1:24** Dead Sea Scrolls, Septuagint, and Syriac read *a three-year-old bull.* * **2:1** That is, strength

---

out? Hannah surely both taught Samuel and prayed for him, but it was Samuel who said "yes" to the Lord and to the promise his mother had made. Every single relationship with the Lord is between that individual and the Lord. No one is a follower of God just because his parents are. But there is much that parents can do to encourage and teach their children about loving and serving the Lord, and a heartfelt enthusiastic example is the very best incentive that a parent can provide. **no razor shall come upon his head.** The Nazirite vow involved a designated period of time (usually a few weeks or months) during which there was a commitment to refrain completely from wine, from cutting the hair, and touching any dead body. Hannah promised that her son would be a Nazirite for life.

1:17 Petition—The Lord went to great lengths to ensure that Scripture records all the instances in which God heard and answered prayer; unlike the gods of Israel's surrounding nations. In the contest on Mount Carmel, Elijah's prayers were answered while the prayers of the prophets of Baal went nowhere (1 Kin. 18). The psalmist says "But certainly God has heard me; He has attended to the voice of my prayer" (Ps. 66:19).

Petitions are requests that we pray by faith (James 1:6), in the name of Jesus (John 14:13). If we pray in this manner, we are assured that God hears us (1 John 5:14–15). We should pray for cleansing (1 John 1:9), wisdom (James 1:5), spiritual leaders (Col. 4:3), sick believers (James 5:14), rulers (1 Tim. 2:1–3), and even for our enemies (Matt. 5:44).

1:22 *until the child is weaned.* Hebrew children were normally weaned when they were two or three years old.

1:23 *Do what seems best to you.* According to law, Elkanah could have declared Hannah's vow a rash promise and prohibited her from fulfilling it (Num. 30:10–15). When he told her to "do what seems best to you" he was validating her promise to God.

2:1–10 Prayer—Hannah's prayer is one of praise to God. We often think of prayer as supplication or intercession, but this is a prayer of rejoicing in the Lord, His salvation, His power to raise up and to shatter,

1:11 ⁿ Num. 6:5 **1:15** ʳ Ps. 42:4; 62:8 **1:16** ˢ Deut. 13:13 **1:17** ᵗ Mark 5:34 ᵘ Ps. 20:3–5 **1:18** ᵛ Ruth 2:13 ʷ Rom. 15:13 **1:19** ˣ Gen. 4:1 ʸ Gen. 21:1; 30:22 **1:21** ᶻ 1 Sam. 1:3 **1:22** ᵈ Luke 2:22 ᵇ 1 Sam. 1:11, 28 ᶜ Ex. 21:6 **1:23** ᵈ Num. 30:7, 10, 11 **1:24** ᵉ Num. 15:9, 10 ᶠ Josh. 18:1 **1:25** ᵍ Luke 2:22 **1:26** ʰ 2 Kin. 2:2, 4, 6; 4:30 **1:27** ᶦ [Matt. 7:7] **1:28** ʲ Gen. 24:26, 52 **2:1** ⁿ Phil. 4:6 ᵇ Luke 1:46–55 ᶜ Ps. 75:10; 89:17, 24; 92:10; 112:9

I smile at my enemies,
Because I [d]rejoice in Your salvation.

2 "No[e] one is holy like the LORD,
For *there is* [f]none besides You,
Nor *is there* any [g]rock like our God.

3 "Talk no more so very proudly;
[h]Let no arrogance come from your
mouth,
For the LORD *is* the God of [i]knowledge;
And by Him actions are weighed.

4 "The[j] bows of the mighty men *are*
broken,
And those who stumbled are girded
with strength.

5 *Those who were* full have hired
themselves out for bread,
And the hungry have ceased *to*
hunger.
Even [k]the barren has borne seven,
And [l]she who has many children has
become feeble.

6 "The[m] LORD kills and makes alive;
He brings down to the grave and
brings up.

7 The LORD [n]makes poor and makes
rich;
[o]He brings low and lifts up.

8 [p]He raises the poor from the dust
And lifts the beggar from the ash
heap,
[q]To set *them* among princes
And make them inherit the throne of
glory.

[r]"For the pillars of the earth *are* the
LORD's,
And He has set the world upon them.

9 [s]He will guard the feet of His saints,
But the [t]wicked shall be silent in
darkness.

"For by strength no man shall prevail.

10 The adversaries of the LORD shall be
[u]broken in pieces;
[v]From heaven He will thunder against
them.
[w]The LORD will judge the ends of the
earth.

[x]"He will give [y]strength to His king,
And [z]exalt the horn of His anointed."

[11]Then Elkanah went to his house at Ramah. But the child ministered to the LORD
before Eli the priest.

The Wicked Sons of Eli

[12]Now the sons of Eli *were* [a]corrupt;*
[b]they did not know the LORD. [13]And the
priests' custom with the people *was that*
when any man offered a sacrifice, the
priest's servant would come with a three-
pronged fleshhook in his hand while the
meat was boiling. [14]Then he would thrust
it into the pan, or kettle, or caldron, or pot;
and the priest would take for himself all
that the fleshhook brought up. So they did
in [c]Shiloh to all the Israelites who came
there. [15]Also, before they [d]burned the fat,
the priest's servant would come and say
to the man who sacrificed, "Give meat for
roasting to the priest, for he will not take
boiled meat from you, but raw."

[16]And *if* the man said to him, "They
should really burn the fat first; *then* you
may take *as much* as your heart desires,"
he would then answer him, "*No*, but you
must give *it* now; and if not, I will take *it*
by force."

[17]Therefore the sin of the young men
was very great [e]before the LORD, for men
[f]abhorred the offering of the LORD.

Samuel's Childhood Ministry

[18]But Samuel ministered before the
LORD, *even as* a child, [h]wearing a linen
ephod. [19]Moreover his mother used to
make him a little robe, and bring *it* to him
year by year when she [i]came up with her
husband to offer the yearly sacrifice. [20]And
Eli [j]would bless Elkanah and his wife, and
say, "The LORD give you descendants from
this woman for the loan that was [k]given to
the LORD." Then they would go to their own
home.

[21]And the LORD [l]visited Hannah, so that
she conceived and bore three sons and two
daughters. Meanwhile the child Samuel
[m]grew before the LORD.

Prophecy Against Eli's Household

[22]Now Eli was very old; and he heard
everything his sons did to all Israel,* and
how they lay with [n]the women who assembled at the door of the tabernacle of meeting. [23]So he said to them, "Why do you do
such things? For I hear of your evil dealings

---

* 2:12 Literally *sons of Belial*   * 2:22 Following
Masoretic Text, Targum, and Vulgate; Dead Sea
Scrolls and Septuagint omit the rest of this verse.

His justice, and His strength. To pray like this requires
focusing on who God is, thoughtful recollection of
His attributes, and thanksgiving for His work in our
lives.

2:13–15 take for himself. The priests' rightful share
of a sacrifice was the breast and the right thigh of the
animal (Lev. 7:34). Eli's sons sinned by taking any part
they wanted and demanding the meat immediately,
before the fat consecrated to God had been burned
on the altar.

2:1 [d] Ps. 9:14; 13:5; 35:9   2:2 [e] Ex. 15:11   [f] Deut. 4:35
[g] Deut. 32:4, 30, 31   2:3 [h] Ps. 94:4   [i] 1 Sam. 16:7
2:4 [j] Ps. 37:15; 46:9   2:5 [k] Ps. 113:9   [l] Is. 54:1   2:6 [m] Deut.
32:39   2:7 [n] Deut. 8:17, 18   [o] Ps. 75:7   2:8 [p] Luke
1:52   [q] Job 36:7   [r] Job 38:4–6   2:9 [s] [1 Pet. 1:5]   [t] [Rom.
3:19]   2:10 [u] Ps. 2:9   [v] Ps. 18:13, 14   [w] Ps. 96:13; 98:9
[x] [Matt. 28:18]   [y] Ps. 21:1, 7   [z] Ps. 89:24   2:12 [a] Deut.
13:13   [b] Judg. 2:10   2:14 [c] 1 Sam. 1:3   2:15 [d] Lev. 3:3–5,
16   2:17 [e] Gen. 6:11   [f] [Mal. 2:7–9]   2:18 [g] 1 Sam. 2:11;
3:1   [h] Ex. 28:4   2:19 [i] 1 Sam. 1:3, 21   2:20 [j] Gen. 14:19
[k] 1 Sam. 1:11, 27, 28   2:21 [l] Gen. 21:1   [m] 1 Sam. 2:26;
3:19–21   2:22 [n] Ex. 38:8

from all the people. 24No, my sons! For *it is* not a good report that I hear. You make the LORD's people transgress. 25If one man sins against another, *o*God will judge him. But if a man *p*sins against the LORD, who will intercede for him?" Nevertheless they did not heed the voice of their father, *q*because the LORD desired to kill them.

26And the child Samuel *r*grew in stature, and *s*in favor both with the LORD and men.

27Then a *t*man of God came to Eli and said to him, "Thus says the LORD: *u*'Did I not clearly reveal Myself to the house of your father when they were in Egypt in Pharaoh's house? 28Did I not *v*choose him out of all the tribes of Israel *to be* My priest, to offer upon My altar, to burn incense, and to wear an ephod before Me? And *w*did I not give to the house of your father all the offerings of the children of Israel made by fire? 29Why do you *x*kick at My sacrifice and My offering which I have commanded *in* My *y*dwelling place, and honor your sons more than *z*Me, to make yourselves fat with the best of all the offerings of Israel My people?' 30Therefore the LORD God of Israel says: *a*'I said indeed *that* your house and the house of your father would walk before Me forever.' But now the LORD says: *b*'Far be it from Me; for those who honor Me I will honor, and *c*those who despise Me shall be lightly esteemed. 31Behold, *d*the days are coming that I will cut off your arm and the arm of your father's house, so that there will not be an old man in your house. 32And you will see an enemy *in My* dwelling place, despite all the good which God does for Israel. And there shall not be *e*an old man in your house forever. 33But any of your men whom I do not cut off from My altar shall consume your eyes and grieve your heart. And all the descendants of your house shall die in the flower of their age. 34Now this *shall be f*a sign to you that will come

upon your two sons, on Hophni and Phinehas: *g*in one day they shall die, both of them. 35Then *h*I will raise up for Myself a faithful priest *who* shall do according to what *is* in My heart and in My mind. *i*I will build him a sure house, and he shall walk before *j*My anointed forever. 36*k*And it shall come to pass that everyone who is left in your house will come *and* bow down to him for a piece of silver and a morsel of bread, and say, "Please, put me in one of the priestly positions, that I may eat a piece of bread." ' "

Samuel's First Prophecy

3 Now *a*the boy Samuel ministered to the LORD before Eli. And *b*the word of the LORD was rare in those days; *there was* no widespread revelation. 2And it came to pass at that time, while Eli *was* lying down in his place, and when his eyes had begun to grow *c*so dim that he could not see, 3and before *d*the lamp of God went out in the tabernacle* of the LORD where the ark of God *was*, and while Samuel was lying down, 4that the LORD called Samuel. And he answered, "Here I am!" 5So he ran to Eli and said, "Here I am, for you called me."

And he said, "I did not call; lie down again." And he went and lay down.

6Then the LORD called yet again, "Samuel!"

So Samuel arose and went to Eli, and said, "Here I am, for you called me." He answered, "I did not call, my son; lie down again." 7(Now Samuel *e*did not yet know the LORD, nor was the word of the LORD yet revealed to him.)

8And the LORD called Samuel again the third time. So he arose and went to Eli, and said, "Here I am, for you did call me."

Then Eli perceived that the LORD had called the boy. 9Therefore Eli said to

---

* 3:3 Hebrew *heykal*, palace or temple

2:30 Godlessness—Whenever a priesthood or church or nation falls into apostasy, the people who should have been served suffer. Eli failed his people far more than his disgraceful sons did, because the Israelites trusted Eli's integrity and his discernment. He should have restrained his sons, and he did not. The price of disobedience is always high, and the spiritual cost to a community that has lost trust in one whom they thought was close to God is greater than most people are willing to calculate.

2:31–34 will not be an old man in your house. The judgment was partially fulfilled in the massacre of the priests of Nob (22:11–19), and was ultimately fulfilled when the priesthood was transferred to the family of Zadok in the time of Solomon (1 Kin. 2:26–27,35).

2:35 faithful priest. This term refers to Zadok, who was faithful to God and to the line of David (1 Kin. 1:7–8; 2:26–27,35).

3:1–19 Listening for God's Call—Samuel heard God's call in an audible voice. That experience is not a common one in the history of those who follow after God. While most of us get a sense of a call by some

other means, Samuel's experience does help us to understand what our attitude and response should be.

Samuel's attitude was one of readiness and eager response with a desire to listen. It is that attitude of listening that was foundational to Samuel's whole life and ministry. Throughout his life we see him listening to God's word and following God's direction. He listened for the general will of God and also had an ear for the more specific directions that God gave him. Sometimes he raised questions about why he was doing a particular thing, but the word from God was paramount. He listened for it and responded to it.

2:25 *o* Deut. 1:17; 25:1, 2 *p* Num. 15:30 *q* Josh. 11:20 **2:26** *r* 1 Sam. 2:21 *s* Prov. 3:4 **2:27** *t* 1 Kin. 13:1 *u* Ex. 4:14–16; 12:1 **2:28** *v* Ex. 28:1, 4 *w* Num. 5:9 **2:29** *x* Deut. 32:15 *y* Deut. 12:5 *z* Matt. 10:37 **2:30** *a* Ex. 29:9 *b* Jer. 18:9, 10 *c* Mal. 2:9–12 **2:31** *d* 1 Kin. 2:27, 35 **2:32** *e* Zech. 8:4 **2:34** *f* 1 Kin. 13:3 *g* 1 Sam. 4:11, 17 **2:35** *h* 1 Kin. 2:35 *i* 1 Kin. 11:38 *j* Ps. 18:50 **2:36** *k* 1 Kin. 2:27 **3:1** *a* 1 Sam. 2:11, 18 *b* Ps. 74:9 **3:2** *c* 1 Sam. 4:15 **3:3** *d* Ex. 27:20, 21 **3:7** *e* 1 Sam. 2:12

Samuel, "Go, lie down; and it shall be, if He calls you, that you must say, [f]'Speak, LORD, for Your servant hears.'" So Samuel went and lay down in his place.

10Now the LORD came and stood and called as at other times, "Samuel! Samuel!"

And Samuel answered, "Speak, for Your servant hears."

11Then the LORD said to Samuel: "Behold, I will do something in Israel [g]at which both ears of everyone who hears it will tingle. 12In that day I will perform against Eli [h]all that I have spoken concerning his house, from beginning to end. 13[i]For I have told him that I will [j]judge his house forever for the iniquity which he knows, because [k]his sons made themselves vile, and he [l]did not restrain them. 14And therefore I have sworn to the house of Eli that the iniquity of Eli's house [m]shall not be atoned for by sacrifice or offering forever."

15So Samuel lay down until morning,* and opened the doors of the house of the LORD. And Samuel was afraid to tell Eli the vision. 16Then Eli called Samuel and said, "Samuel, my son!"

He answered, "Here I am."

17And he said, "What is the word that the LORD spoke to you? Please do not hide it from me. [n]God do so to you, and more also, if you hide anything from me of all the things that He said to you." 18Then Samuel told him everything, and hid nothing from him. And he said, [o]"It is the LORD. Let Him do what seems good to Him."

19So Samuel [p]grew, and [q]the LORD was with him [r]and let none of his words fall to the ground. 20And all Israel [s]from Dan to Beersheba knew that Samuel had been established as a prophet of the LORD. 21Then the LORD appeared again in Shiloh. For the LORD revealed Himself to Samuel in Shiloh by [t]the word of the LORD.

4 And the word of Samuel came to all Israel.*

The Ark of God Captured

Now Israel went out to battle against the Philistines, and encamped beside [a]Ebenezer; and the Philistines encamped in Aphek. 2Then the [b]Philistines put themselves in battle array against Israel. And when they joined battle, Israel was defeated by the Philistines, who killed about four thousand men of the army in the field. 3And when the people had come into the camp, the elders of Israel said, "Why has the LORD defeated us today before the Philistines? [c]Let us bring the ark of the covenant of the LORD from Shiloh to us, that when it comes among us it may save us from the hand of our enemies." 4So the people sent to Shiloh, that they might bring from there the ark of the covenant of the LORD of hosts, [d]who dwells between [e]the cherubim. And the [f]two sons of Eli, Hophni and Phinehas, were there with the ark of the covenant of God.

5And when the ark of the covenant of the LORD came into the camp, all Israel shouted so loudly that the earth shook. 6Now when the Philistines heard the noise of the shout, they said, "What does the sound of this great shout in the camp of the Hebrews mean?" Then they understood that the ark of the LORD had come into the camp. 7So the Philistines were afraid, for they said, "God has come into the camp!" And they said, [g]"Woe to us! For such a thing has never happened before. 8Woe to us! Who will deliver us from the hand of these mighty gods? These are the gods who struck the Egyptians with all the plagues in the wilderness. 9[h]Be strong and conduct yourselves like men, you Philistines, that you do not become servants of the Hebrews, [i]as they have been to you. Conduct yourselves like men, and fight!"

10So the Philistines fought, and [j]Israel was defeated, and every man fled to his tent. There was a very great slaughter, and there fell of Israel thirty thousand foot soldiers. 11Also [k]the ark of God was captured; and [l]the two sons of Eli, Hophni and Phinehas, died.

---

* 3:15 Following Masoretic Text, Targum, and Vulgate; Septuagint adds and he arose in the morning.   * 4:1 Following Masoretic Text and Targum; Septuagint and Vulgate add And it came to pass in those days that the Philistines gathered themselves together to fight; Septuagint adds further against Israel.

3:14 shall not be atoned for. Eli and his sons were guilty of presumptuous sin (Num. 15:30–31). For such sin, there was no atoning sacrifice.

3:20 from Dan to Beersheba. This expression denotes the whole territory of Israel, from its most northern point to its most southern (Judg. 20:1).

4:1 the Philistines. Abraham and Isaac had contact with the Philistines as early as the twentieth century B.C. With their aggressive invasions and fortress cities, the Philistines established strong political and military control of the southern coastal plain of Palestine. They had iron weapons, and were a significant threat to the Israelites.

4:4 who dwells between the cherubim. Cherubim are angels generally regarded as guardians of God's holiness (Gen. 3:24; Ps. 80:1; Ezek. 10:9).

4:6–7 the ark of the LORD had come into the camp . . . the Philistines were afraid. Apparently the Philistines viewed the ark as some sort of idol.

4:11 the ark of God was captured. The loss of the ark, symbolic of God's presence among His people, was a great tragedy for Israel—even worse than

---

3:9 [f]1 Kin. 2:17   **3:11** [g]2 Kin. 21:12   **3:12** [h]1 Sam. 2:27–36   **3:13** [i]1 Sam. 2:29–31 / [j]1 Sam. 2:22 [k]1 Sam. 2:12, 17, 22 / [l]1 Sam. 2:23, 25   **3:14** [m]Num. 15:30, 31   **3:17** [n]Ruth 1:17   **3:18** [o]Is. 39:8   **3:19** [p]1 Sam. 2:21 [q]Gen. 21:22; 28:15; 39:2, 21, 23 / [r]1 Sam. 9:6   **3:20** [s]Judg. 20:1   **3:21** [t]1 Sam. 3:1, 4   **4:1** [a]1 Sam. 7:12   **4:2** [b]1 Sam. 12:9   **4:3** [c]Josh. 6:6–21   **4:4** [d]1 Sam. 6:2 [e]Num. 7:89 [f]1 Sam. 2:12   **4:7** [g]Ex. 15:14   **4:9** [h]1 Cor. 16:13 [i]Judg. 13:1   **4:10** [j]Deut. 28:15, 25   **4:11** [k]Ps. 78:60, 61 [l]1 Sam. 2:34

Death of Eli

[12] Then a man of Benjamin ran from the battle line the same day, and [m]came to Shiloh with his clothes torn and [n]dirt on his head. [13] Now when he came, there was Eli, sitting on [o]a seat by the wayside watching,* for his heart trembled for the ark of God. And when the man came into the city and told *it*, all the city cried out. [14] When Eli heard the noise of the outcry, he said, "What *does* the sound of this tumult *mean*?" And the man came quickly and told Eli. [15] Eli was ninety-eight years old, and [p]his eyes were so dim that he could not see.

[16] Then the man said to Eli, "I *am* he who came from the battle. And I fled today from the battle line."

And he said, [q]"What happened, my son?"

[17] So the messenger answered and said, "Israel has fled before the Philistines, and there has been a great slaughter among the people. Also your two sons, Hophni and Phinehas, are dead; and the ark of God has been captured."

[18] Then it happened, when he made mention of the ark of God, that Eli fell off the seat backward by the side of the gate; and his neck was broken and he died, for the man was old and heavy. And he had judged Israel forty years.

Ichabod

[19] Now his daughter-in-law, Phinehas' wife, was with child, *due* to be delivered; and when she heard the news that the ark of God was captured, and that her father-in-law and her husband were dead, she bowed herself and gave birth, for her labor pains came upon her. [20] And about the time of her death [r]the women who stood by her said to her, "Do not fear, for you have borne a son." But she did not answer, nor did she regard *it*. [21] Then she named the child [s]Ichabod,* saying, [t]"The glory has departed from Israel!" because the ark of God had been captured and because of her father-in-law and her husband. [22] And she said, "The glory has departed from Israel, for the ark of God has been captured."

The Philistines and the Ark

5 Then the Philistines took the ark of God and brought it [a]from Ebenezer to Ashdod. [2] When the Philistines took the ark of God, they brought it into the house of [b]Dagon* and set it by Dagon. [3] And when the people of Ashdod arose early in the morning, there was Dagon, [c]fallen on its face to the earth before the ark of the LORD. So they took Dagon and [d]set it in its place again. [4] And when they arose early the next morning, there was Dagon, fallen on its face to the ground before the ark of the LORD. [e]The head of Dagon and both the palms of its hands *were* broken off on the threshold; only Dagon's *torso** was left of it. [5] Therefore neither the priests of Dagon nor any who come into Dagon's house [f]tread on the threshold of Dagon in Ashdod to this day.

[6] But the [g]hand of the LORD was heavy on the people of Ashdod, and He [h]ravaged them and struck them with [i]tumors,* *both* Ashdod and its [j]territory. [7] And when the men of Ashdod saw how *it was*, they said, "The ark of the [k]God of Israel must not remain with us, for His hand is harsh toward us and Dagon our god." [8] Therefore they sent and gathered to themselves all the [l]lords of the Philistines, and said, "What shall we do with the ark of the God of Israel?"

And they answered, "Let the ark of the God of Israel be carried away to [m]Gath." So they carried the ark of the God of Israel away. [9] So it was, after they had carried it away, that [n]the hand of the LORD was against the city with a very great destruction; and He struck the men of the city, both small and great, and tumors broke out on them.

[10] Therefore they sent the ark of God to Ekron. So it was, as the ark of God came to Ekron, that the Ekronites cried out, saying,

---

* **4:13** Following Masoretic Text and Vulgate; Septuagint reads *beside the gate watching the road.*
* **4:21** Literally *Inglorious*   * **5:2** A Philistine idol
* **5:4** Following Septuagint, Syriac, Targum, and Vulgate; Masoretic Text reads *Dagon.*   * **5:6** Probably bubonic plague. Septuagint and Vulgate add here *And in the midst of their land rats sprang up, and there was a great death panic in the city.*

---

the loss of life. The ark probably never returned to Shiloh.

4:21 Ichabod. The name Ichabod, meaning "no glory," reflected Israel's circumstances. The loss of the ark meant the absence of God's glory in Israel.

5:2 Dagon. This god appears to be a Philistine adaptation of the Canaanite god Baal. Philistia was in an important grain producing area, and the worship of Dagon was thought to ensure a good crop.

5:6–7 Idolatry—The residents of Ashdod made one fatal mistake. They tried to place a false god alongside the true God. These ancient Philistines are not the only ones who have tried this sort of idolatry. People are quick to recognize that there is "something"

about the living God, and they want Him. But they want to have God with qualifiers—"God and my career track," "God and my dedication to entertainment," "God and my secret sin," "God and my own way." But God will not share the throne of any man's heart. It has to be God, and God alone.

4:12 [m] 2 Sam. 1:2   [n] Josh. 7:6   **4:13** [o] 1 Sam. 1:9; 4:18
4:15 [p] 1 Sam. 3:2   **4:16** [q] 2 Sam. 1:4   **4:20** [r] Gen. 35:16–19   **4:21** [s] 1 Sam. 14:3   [t] Ps. 26:8; 78:61   **5:1** [a] 1 Sam. 4:1; 7:12   **5:2** [b] 1 Chr. 10:8–10   **5:3** [c] Is. 19:1; 46:1, 2   [d] Is. 46:7
5:4 [e] Mic. 1:7   **5:5** [f] Zeph. 1:9   **5:6** [g] Ex. 9:3   [h] 1 Sam. 6:5   [i] Deut. 28:27; Ps. 78:66   [j] Josh. 15:46, 47   **5:7** [k] 1 Sam. 6:5
5:8 [l] 1 Sam. 6:4   [m] Josh. 11:22   **5:9** [n] Deut. 2:15

"They have brought the ark of the God of Israel to us, to kill us and our people!" [11]So they sent and gathered together all the lords of the Philistines, and said, "Send away the ark of the God of Israel, and let it go back to its own place, so that it does not kill us and our people." For there was a deadly destruction throughout all the city; the hand of God was very heavy there. [12]And the men who did not die were stricken with the tumors, and the [o]cry of the city went up to heaven.

The Ark Returned to Israel

6 Now the ark of the LORD was in the country of the Philistines seven months. [2]And the Philistines [a]called for the priests and the diviners, saying, "What shall we do with the ark of the LORD? Tell us how we should send it to its place."

[3]So they said, "If you send away the ark of the God of Israel, do not send it [b]empty; but by all means return it to Him with [c]a trespass offering. Then you will be healed, and it will be known to you why His hand is not removed from you."

[4]Then they said, "What is the trespass offering which we shall return to Him?"

They answered, [d]"Five golden tumors and five golden rats, according to the number of the lords of the Philistines. For the same plague was on all of you and on your lords. [5]Therefore you shall make images of your tumors and images of your rats that [e]ravage the land, and you shall [f]give glory to the God of Israel; perhaps He will [g]lighten His hand from you, from [h]your gods, and from your land. [6]Why then do you harden your hearts [i]as the Egyptians and Pharaoh hardened their hearts? When He did mighty things among them, [j]did they not let the people go, that they might depart? [7]Now therefore, make [k]a new cart, take two milk cows [l]which have never been yoked, and hitch the cows to the cart; and take their calves home, away from them. [8]Then take the ark of the LORD and set it on the cart; and put [m]the articles of gold which you are returning to Him as a trespass offering in a chest by its side. Then send it away, and let it go. [9]And watch: if it goes up the road to its own territory, to [n]Beth Shemesh, then He has done us this great evil. But if not, then [o]we shall know that it is not His hand that struck us—it happened to us by chance."

[10]Then the men did so; they took two milk cows and hitched them to the cart, and shut up their calves at home. [11]And they set the ark of the LORD on the cart, and the chest with the gold rats and the images of their tumors. [12]Then the cows headed straight for the road to Beth Shemesh, and went along the [p]highway, lowing as they went, and did not turn aside to the right hand or the left. And the lords of the Philistines went after them to the border of Beth Shemesh.

[13]Now the people of Beth Shemesh were reaping their [q]wheat harvest in the valley; and they lifted their eyes and saw the ark, and rejoiced to see it. [14]Then the cart came into the field of Joshua of Beth Shemesh, and stood there; a large stone was there. So they split the wood of the cart and offered the cows as a burnt offering to the LORD. [15]The Levites took down the ark of the LORD and the chest that was with it, in which were the articles of gold, and put them on the large stone. Then the men of Beth Shemesh offered burnt offerings and made sacrifices the same day to the LORD. [16]So when [r]the five lords of the Philistines had seen it, they returned to Ekron the same day.

[17][s]These are the golden tumors which the Philistines returned as a trespass offering to the LORD: one for Ashdod, one for Gaza, one for Ashkelon, one for [t]Gath, one for Ekron; [18]and the golden rats, according to the number of all the cities of the Philistines belonging to the five lords, both fortified cities and country villages, even as far as the large stone of Abel on which they set the ark of the LORD, which stone remains to this day in the field of Joshua of Beth Shemesh.

[19]Then [u]He struck the men of Beth Shemesh, because they had looked into the ark of the LORD. He [v]struck fifty thousand and seventy men* of the people, and the people lamented because the LORD had struck the people with a great slaughter.

* **6:19** Or He struck seventy men of the people and fifty oxen of a man

---

6:8 send it away, and let it go. This seemed like a good test to the Philistines. The natural inclination of the cows would be to return home to their calves. If the cows went against their normal instincts, it would show that God was causing them to walk away from their calves.

6:14 offered the cows as a burnt offering. The law required that sacrifices be offered only at the central sanctuary (Deut. 12:4–14). Apparently the people felt that special circumstances required an immediate offering of thanksgiving.

6:19 Presumption—The Israelites who looked into the ark were glad to have it back. Perhaps they thought that the Philistines had looked inside it, and certainly they had more right than the Philistines to gaze upon the holy objects contained in the ark. Their reasons may have seemed good at the moment, but they were ignoring God's specific commands and treating His holiness as unimportant. In the same way

5:12 [o] Jer. 14:2   **6:2** [a] Gen. 41:8   **6:3** [b] Deut. 16:16   [c] Lev. 5:15, 16   **6:4** [d] 1 Sam. 5:6, 9, 12; 6:17   **6:5** [e] 1 Sam. 5:6   [f] Josh. 7:19   [g] 1 Sam. 5:6, 11   [h] 1 Sam. 5:3, 4, 7   **6:6** [i] Ex. 7:13; 8:15; 9:34; 14:17   [j] Ex. 12:31   **6:7** [k] 2 Sam. 6:3   [l] Num. 19:2   **6:8** [m] 1 Sam. 6:4, 5   **6:9** [n] Josh. 15:10; 21:16   [o] 1 Sam. 6:3   **6:12** [p] Num. 20:19   **6:13** [q] 1 Sam. 12:17   **6:16** [r] Josh. 13:3   **6:17** [s] 1 Sam. 6:4   [t] 1 Sam. 5:8   **6:19** [u] Ex. 19:21   [v] 2 Sam. 6:7

The Ark at Kirjath Jearim

²⁰And the men of Beth Shemesh said, ᵂ"Who is able to stand before this holy LORD God? And to whom shall it go up from us?" ²¹So they sent messengers to the inhabitants of ˣKirjath Jearim, saying, "The Philistines have brought back the ark of the LORD; come down *and* take it up with you."

7 Then the men of ᵃKirjath Jearim came and took the ark of the LORD, and brought it into the house of ᵇAbinadab on the hill, and ᶜconsecrated Eleazar his son to keep the ark of the LORD.

Samuel Judges Israel

²So it was that the ark remained in Kirjath Jearim a long time; it was there twenty years. And all the house of Israel lamented after the LORD.

³Then Samuel spoke to all the house of Israel, saying, "If you ᵈreturn to the LORD with all your hearts, *then* ᵉput away the foreign gods, and the ᶠAshtoreths* from among you, and ᵍprepare your hearts for the LORD, and ʰserve Him only; and He will deliver you from the hand of the Philistines." ⁴So the children of Israel put away the ⁱBaals and the Ashtoreths,* and served the LORD only.

⁵And Samuel said, ʲ"Gather all Israel to Mizpah, and ᵏI will pray to the LORD for you." ⁶So they gathered together at Mizpah, ˡdrew water, and poured *it* out before the LORD. And they ᵐfasted that day, and said there, ⁿ"We have sinned against the LORD." And Samuel judged the children of Israel at Mizpah.

⁷Now when the Philistines heard that the children of Israel had gathered together at Mizpah, the lords of the Philistines went up against Israel. And when the children of Israel heard *of it*, they were afraid of the Philistines. ⁸So the children of Israel said to Samuel, ᵒ"Do not cease to cry out to the LORD our God for us, that He may save us from the hand of the Philistines."

⁹And Samuel took a ᵖsuckling lamb and offered *it as* a whole burnt offering to the LORD. Then ᵍSamuel cried out to the LORD for Israel, and the LORD answered him. ¹⁰Now as Samuel was offering up the burnt offering, the Philistines drew near to battle against Israel. ʳBut the LORD thundered with a loud thunder upon the Philistines that day, and so confused them that they were overcome before Israel. ¹¹And the men of Israel went out of Mizpah and pursued the Philistines, and drove them back as far as below Beth Car. ¹²Then Samuel ˢtook a stone and set *it* up between Mizpah and Shen, and called its name Ebenezer,* saying, "Thus far the LORD has helped us."

¹³ᵗSo the Philistines were subdued, and they ᵘdid not come anymore into the territory of Israel. And the hand of the LORD was against the Philistines all the days of Samuel. ¹⁴Then the cities which the Philistines had taken from Israel were restored to Israel, from Ekron to Gath; and Israel recovered its territory from the hands of the Philistines. Also there was peace between Israel and the Amorites.

¹⁵And Samuel ᵛjudged Israel all the days of his life. ¹⁶He went from year to year on a circuit to Bethel, Gilgal, and Mizpah, and judged Israel in all those places. ¹⁷But ʷhe always returned to Ramah, for his home *was* there. There he judged Israel, and there he ˣbuilt an altar to the LORD.

Israel Demands a King

8 Now it came to pass when Samuel was ᵃold that he ᵇmade his ᶜsons judges over Israel. ²The name of his firstborn was Joel, and the name of his second, Abijah; *they were* judges in Beersheba. ³But his sons ᵈdid not walk in his ways; they turned aside ᵉafter dishonest gain, ᶠtook bribes, and perverted justice.

⁴Then all the elders of Israel gathered together and came to Samuel at Ramah, ⁵and said to him, "Look, you are old, and your sons do not walk in your ways. Now ᵍmake us a king to judge us like all the nations."

*** 7:3** Canaanite goddesses   *** 7:4** Canaanite goddesses   *** 7:12** Literally *Stone of Help*

---

today, we can end up trivializing who God is. We can speak frivolously of the things of God, calling Him the "Man upstairs," or being "Sunday Christians." We can presume on our relationship with God without remembering what it cost Jesus to obtain it for us.

7:2 twenty years. It was probably twenty years before Samuel called the assembly at Mizpah (v. 5). The ark remained at Kirjath Jearim until David brought it to Jerusalem in the first year of his reign over all Israel.

7:6 poured it out. The pouring of water was symbolic of repentance (Lam. 2:19).

7:12 Ebenezer. The name Ebenezer means "stone of help." Samuel followed Joshua's practice of commemorating the victories of God for His people with stone markers. Some old gospel hymns refer to an "Ebenezer," meaning a particular notation of something special God has done.

7:14 Amorites. This name may refer to the original inhabitants of Canaan (Gen. 15:16).

7:17 Ramah. Samuel was back in the town where he was born.

8:5 make us a king. The reasons given for wanting a king were Samuel's age and his sons' unreliability. This is a sad commentary on Samuel's failure to raise

---

6:20 ʷ Mal. 3:2   **6:21** ˣ 1 Chr. 13:5, 6   **7:1** ᵃ 1 Sam. 6:21 ᵇ 2 Sam. 6:3, 4 ᶜ Lev. 21:8   **7:3** ᵈ Deut. 30:2–10 ᵉ Gen. 35:2 ᶠ Judg. 2:13 ᵍ Job 11:13 ʰ Luke 4:8   **7:4** ⁱ Judg. 2:11; 10:16   **7:5** ʲ Judg. 10:17; 20:1 ᵏ 1 Sam. 12:17–19   **7:6** ˡ 2 Sam. 14:14 ᵐ Neh. 9:1, 2 ⁿ 1 Sam. 12:10   **7:8** ᵒ Is. 37:4   **7:9** ᵖ Lev. 22:27 ᵍ 1 Sam. 12:18   **7:10** ʳ 2 Sam. 22:14, 15   **7:12** ˢ Josh. 4:9; 24:26   **7:13** ᵗ Judg. 13:1 ᵘ 1 Sam. 13:5   **7:15** ᵛ 1 Sam. 12:11   **7:17** ʷ 1 Sam. 8:4 ˣ Judg. 21:4   **8:1** ᵃ 1 Sam. 12:2 ᵇ Deut. 16:18, 19 ᶜ Judg. 10:4   **8:3** ᵈ Jer. 22:15–17 ᵉ Ex. 18:21 ᶠ Ex. 23:6–8 **8:5** ᵍ Deut. 17:14, 15

6But the thing [h]displeased Samuel when
they said, "Give us a king to judge us." So
Samuel [i]prayed to the LORD. 7And the LORD
said to Samuel, "Heed the voice of the people in all that they say to you; for [j]they have
not rejected you, but [k]they have rejected
Me, that I should not reign over them. 8Ac-
cording to all the works which they have
done since the day that I brought them up
out of Egypt, even to this day—with which
they have forsaken Me and served other
gods—so they are doing to you also. 9Now
therefore, heed their voice. However, you
shall solemnly forewarn them, and [l]show
them the behavior of the king who will
reign over them."

10So Samuel told all the words of the
LORD to the people who asked him for a
king. 11And he said, [m]"This will be the
behavior of the king who will reign over
you: He will take your [n]sons and appoint
them for his own [o]chariots and *to be* his
horsemen, and *some* will run before his
chariots. 12He will [p]appoint captains over
his thousands and captains over his fifties,
will set some to plow his ground and reap
his harvest, and *some* to make his weapons
of war and equipment for his chariots. 13He
will take your daughters *to be* perfumers,
cooks, and bakers. 14And [q]he will take the
best of your fields, your vineyards, and
your olive groves, and give *them* to his servants. 15He will take a tenth of your grain
and your vintage, and give it to his officers
and servants. 16And he will take your male
servants, your female servants, your finest
young men,* and your donkeys, and put
them to his work. 17He will take a tenth of
your sheep. And you will be his servants.
18And you will cry out in that day because
of your king whom you have chosen for
yourselves, and the LORD [r]will not hear
you in that day."

19Nevertheless the people [s]refused to
obey the voice of Samuel; and they said,
"No, but we will have a king over us, 20that
we also may be [t]like all the nations, and
that our king may judge us and go out before us and fight our battles."

21And Samuel heard all the words of
the people, and he repeated them in the
hearing of the LORD. 22So the LORD said to
Samuel, [u]"Heed their voice, and make them
a king."

And Samuel said to the men of Israel,
"Every man go to his city."

Saul Chosen to Be King

9 There was a man of Benjamin whose
name *was* [a]Kish the son of Abiel, the
son of Zeror, the son of Bechorath, the son
of Aphiah, a Benjamite, a mighty man of
power. 2And he had a choice and handsome
son whose name *was* Saul. *There was* not a
more handsome person than he among the
children of Israel. [b]From his shoulders upward *he was* taller than any of the people.

3Now the donkeys of Kish, Saul's father,
were lost. And Kish said to his son Saul,
"Please take one of the servants with you,
and arise, go and look for the donkeys."
4So he passed through the mountains of
Ephraim and through the land of [c]Sha-
lisha, but they did not find *them*. Then
they passed through the land of Shaalim,
and *they were* not *there*. Then he passed
through the land of the Benjamites, but
they did not find *them*.

5When they had come to the land of
[d]Zuph, Saul said to his servant who *was*
with him, "Come, let [e]us return, lest my father cease *caring* about the donkeys and
become worried about us."

6And he said to him, "Look now, *there is*
in this city [f]a man of God, and *he is* an honorable man; [g]all that he says surely comes
to pass. So let us go there; perhaps he can
show us the way that we should go."

7Then Saul said to his servant, "But look,
if we go, [h]what shall we bring the man? For
the bread in our vessels is all gone, and
there is no present to bring to the man of
God. What do we have?"

8And the servant answered Saul again
and said, "Look, I have here at hand one-
fourth of a shekel of silver. I will give *that*
to the man of God, to tell us our way."
9(Formerly in Israel, when a man [i]went to
inquire of God, he spoke thus: "Come, let us
go to the seer"; for *he who is* now *called* a
prophet was formerly called [j]a seer.)

10Then Saul said to his servant, "Well

* **8:16** Septuagint reads *cattle*.

his sons to honor and obey the Lord, particularly considering the example of Eli's sons. But this was not really a reason to ask for a king. The Israelite judges had always been appointed by God, rather than gaining their position by inheritance. There was no reason to think that God would not appoint someone to succeed Samuel.

8:7 *they have rejected Me.* This actually fulfilled the prophecy in Deuteronomy 17:14–20. God knew long ago that the Israelites would chose to be like the other nations and have a king, instead of being ruled more directly by God through judges. He warned them of the pitfalls of having a king, and set out some guidelines for the kings to follow.

8:20 *and fight our battles.* The Israelites were looking for human leadership on the battlefield, instead of recognizing that God would lead them in battle, and win (Ex. 15:3; Judg. 7).

8:6 [h] 1 Sam. 12:17 [i] 1 Sam. 7:9 **8:7** [j] Ex. 16:8 [k] 1 Sam. 10:19 **8:9** [l] 1 Sam. 8:11–18 **8:11** [m] Deut. 17:14–20 [n] 1 Sam. 14:52 [o] 2 Sam. 15:1 **8:12** [p] 1 Sam. 22:7 **8:14** [q] 1 Kin. 21:7 **8:18** [r] Is. 1:15 **8:19** [s] Jer. 44:16 **8:20** [t] 1 Sam. 8:5 **8:22** [u] Hos. 13:11 **9:1** [a] 1 Chr. 8:33; 9:36–39 **9:2** [b] 1 Sam. 10:23 **9:4** [c] 2 Kin. 4:42 **9:5** [d] 1 Sam. 1:1 [e] 1 Sam. 10:2 **9:6** [f] Deut. 33:1 [g] 1 Sam. 3:19 **9:7** [h] Judg. 6:18; 13:17 **9:9** [i] Gen. 25:22 [j] 2 Kin. 17:13

said; come, let us go." So they went to the city where the man of God *was.*

[11]As they went up the hill to the city, [k]they met some young women going out to draw water, and said to them, "Is the seer here?"

[12]And they answered them and said, "Yes, there he is, just ahead of you. Hurry now; for today he came to this city, because [l]there is a sacrifice of the people today [m]on the high place. [13]As soon as you come into the city, you will surely find him before he goes up to the high place to eat. For the people will not eat until he comes, because he must bless the sacrifice; afterward those who are invited will eat. Now therefore, go up, for about this time you will find him." [14]So they went up to the city. As they were coming into the city, there was Samuel, coming out toward them on his way up to the high place.

[15n]Now the LORD had told Samuel in his ear the day before Saul came, saying, [16]"Tomorrow about this time [o]I will send you a man from the land of Benjamin, [p]and you shall anoint him commander over My people Israel, that he may save My people from the hand of the Philistines; for I have [q]looked upon My people, because their cry has come to Me."

[17]So when Samuel saw Saul, the LORD said to him, [r]"There he is, the man of whom I spoke to you. This one shall reign over My people." [18]Then Saul drew near to Samuel in the gate, and said, "Please tell me, where *is* the seer's house?"

[19]Samuel answered Saul and said, "I *am* the seer. Go up before me to the high place, for you shall eat with me today; and tomorrow I will let you go and will tell you all that *is* in your heart. [20]But as for [s]your donkeys that were lost three days ago, do not be anxious about them, for they have been found. And on whom [t]is all the desire of Israel? *Is it* not on you and on all your father's house?"

[21]And Saul answered and said, [u]"Am I not a Benjamite, of the [v]smallest of the tribes of Israel, and [w]my family the least of all the families of the tribe* of Benjamin? Why then do you speak like this to me?"

[22]Now Samuel took Saul and his servant and brought them into the hall, and had them sit in the place of honor among those who were invited; there *were* about thirty persons. [23]And Samuel said to the cook, "Bring the portion which I gave you, of which I said to you, 'Set it apart.'" [24]So the cook took up [x]the thigh with its upper part and set *it* before Saul. And *Samuel* said, "Here it is, what was kept back. *It* was set apart for you. Eat; for until this time it has been kept for you, since I said I invited the people." So Saul ate with Samuel that day.

[25]When they had come down from the high place into the city, *Samuel* spoke with Saul on [y]the top of the house.* [26]They arose early; and it was about the dawning of the day that Samuel called to Saul on the top of the house, saying, "Get up, that I may send you on your way." And Saul arose, and both of them went outside, he and Samuel.

Saul Anointed King

[27]As they were going down to the outskirts of the city, Samuel said to Saul, "Tell the servant to go on ahead of us." And he went on. "But you stand here awhile, that I may announce to you the word of God."

10 Then [a]Samuel took a flask of oil and poured *it* on his head, [b]and kissed him and said: "*Is it* not because [c]the LORD has anointed you commander over [d]His inheritance?* [2]When you have departed from

---

* **9:21** Literally *tribes* * **9:25** Following Masoretic Text and Targum; Septuagint omits *He spoke with Saul on the top of the house;* Septuagint and Vulgate add *And he prepared a bed for Saul on the top of the house, and he slept.* * **10:1** Following Masoretic Text, Targum, and Vulgate; Septuagint reads *His people Israel; and you shall rule the people of the Lord;* Septuagint and Vulgate add *And you shall deliver His people from the hands of their enemies all around them. And this shall be a sign to you, that God has anointed you to be a prince.*

9:12 the high place. A hill that was used for worship was called "a high place." The Canaanites were known for building their places for worship on hills, and the Israelites apparently used similar sites for worship after the ark was taken from the tabernacle at Shiloh. They believed that the presence of the Lord had departed from the tabernacle, and it was apparently at that point that Shiloh ceased to be a gathering center for the nation.

9:20 Providence—God, in His providence, is directing our lives according to His plan and purpose. Hunting our livestock or having a vehicle break down are normal nuisances, something we can handle, but seldom think about as being the providence of God. Yet if we realize that God has His hand on all of our circumstances, everything that changes our plans puts us into a position to meet, pray for, help, or witness to someone else who would not normally come our way.

9:21 the smallest of the tribes. Benjamin was the second smallest tribe at the first census following the Exodus (Num. 1:36–37). The tribe was reduced to six hundred fighting men during the punishment of Benjamin for the atrocity at Gibeah (Judg. 19–20).

9:24 the thigh. Giving Saul the thigh was intended to honor him in the presence of the other guests.

10:1 the LORD has anointed you. The anointing of a ruler was a religious act. That is why David had such high regard for Saul, refusing to lift a hand against "the LORD's anointed." **His inheritance.** The land of Israel was God's gift to His people, but it would return

9:11 [k]Ex. 2:16 **9:12** [l]Gen. 31:54 [m]1 Kin. 3:2 **9:15** [n]1 Sam. 15:1 **9:16** [o]Deut. 17:15 [p]1 Sam. 10:1 [q]Ex. 2:23–25; 3:7, 9 **9:17** [r]1 Sam. 16:12 **9:20** [s]1 Sam. 9:3 [t]1 Sam. 8:5, 19; 12:13 **9:21** [u]1 Sam. 15:17 [v]Judg. 20:46–48 [w]Judg. 6:15 **9:24** [x]Lev. 7:32, 33 **9:25** [y]Deut. 22:8 **10:1** [a]2 Kin. 9:3, 6 [b]Ps. 2:12 [c]Acts 13:21 [d]Deut. 32:9

me today, you will find two men by [e]Ra-
chel's tomb in the territory of Benjamin [f]at
Zelzah; and they will say to you, 'The donkeys which you went to look for have been
found. And now your father has ceased
caring about the donkeys and is worrying
about [g]you, saying, "What shall I do about
my son?"' 3Then you shall go on forward
from there and come to the terebinth tree
of Tabor. There three men going up [h]to God
at Bethel will meet you, one carrying three
young goats, another carrying three loaves
of bread, and another carrying a skin of
wine. 4And they will greet you and give
you two *loaves* of bread, which you shall
receive from their hands. 5After that you
shall come to the hill of God [i]where the
Philistine garrison *is*. And it will happen,
when you have come there to the city, that
you will meet a group of prophets coming
down [j]from the high place with a stringed
instrument, a tambourine, a flute, and a
harp before them; [k]and they will be prophesying. 6Then [l]the Spirit of the LORD will
come upon you, and [m]you will prophesy
with them and be turned into another man.
7And let it be, when these [n]signs come to
you, *that* you do as the occasion demands;
for [o]God *is* with you. 8You shall go down
before me [p]to Gilgal; and surely I will come
down to you to offer burnt offerings *and*
make sacrifices of peace offerings. [q]Seven
days you shall wait, till I come to you and
show you what you should do."
9So it was, when he had turned his back
to go from Samuel, that God gave him another heart; and all those signs came to
pass that day. 10[r]When they came there
to the hill, there was [s]a group of prophets
to meet him; then the Spirit of God came
upon him, and he prophesied among them.
11And it happened, when all who knew
him formerly saw that he indeed prophesied among the prophets, that the people
said to one another, "What *is* this *that* has
come upon the son of Kish? [t]*Is* Saul also
among the prophets?" 12Then a man from
there answered and said, "But [u]who *is* their
father?" Therefore it became a proverb:
"*Is* Saul also among the prophets?" 13And
when he had finished prophesying, he
went to the high place.
14Then Saul's [v]uncle said to him and his
servant, "Where did you go?"
So he said, "To look for the donkeys.
When we saw that *they were* nowhere *to
be found*, we went to Samuel."
15And Saul's uncle said, "Tell me, please,
what Samuel said to you."
16So Saul said to his uncle, "He told us
plainly that the donkeys had been [w]found."
But about the matter of the kingdom, he did
not tell him what Samuel had said.

Saul Proclaimed King

17Then Samuel called the people together [x]to the LORD [y]at Mizpah, 18and said to
the children of Israel, [z]"Thus says the LORD
God of Israel: 'I brought up Israel out of
Egypt, and delivered you from the hand
of the Egyptians *and* from the hand of all
kingdoms and from those who oppressed
you.' 19[a]But you have today rejected your
God, who Himself saved you from all your
adversities and your tribulations; and you
have said to Him, 'No, set a king over us!'
Now therefore, present yourselves before
the LORD by your tribes and by your clans."*
20And when Samuel had [b]caused all
the tribes of Israel to come near, the tribe
of Benjamin was chosen. 21When he had
caused the tribe of Benjamin to come near
by their families, the family of Matri was
chosen. And Saul the son of Kish was chosen. But when they sought him, he could not
be found. 22Therefore they [c]inquired of the
LORD further, "Has the man come here yet?"

* **10:19** Literally *thousands*

---

to God's direct control if the people did not manage it according to God's laws (Deut. 27–30).

10:4 *two loaves of bread.* The bread that the strangers would offer to Saul would have been bread prepared for use in the worship of God. Giving the bread to Saul was a sacred act, as well as a sign for Saul.

10:9 *God gave him another heart.* God's Spirit prepared Saul for the kingship. It probably was not spiritual regeneration in the way it is understood in New Testament times. Saul wanted to worship God, but he continually struggled with wanting to do things his own way.

10:19 Unfaithfulness—This was not the first time that the Israelites had been unfaithful. Sometimes they could see what God was doing and respond with thanksgiving, and sometimes they seemed to forget everything about Him and go headlong into the very sins He had warned them would bring nothing but disaster. Believers today have the incredible gift of the Holy Spirit to direct them and remind them of the ways of God. It is hard to imagine what it would be like to follow God without the help of the Holy Spirit, the comforter, the helper (John 14:25–26). It is important to remember that for humanity, unfaithfulness is our middle name, and to thank God for His mercy and grace which provided a way for us to belong to Him.

10:20 *was chosen.* Even though Samuel already knew that Saul was to be the king, the designation of Saul as Israel's first monarch was made by casting lots. The lots were cast like dice, and God's will was determined by asking yes and no questions. They believed that God controlled all events, including the lots when they were used to seek God.

10:2 [e]Gen. 35:16–20; 48:7 [f]Josh. 18:28 [g]1 Sam. 9:3–5 **10:3** [h]Gen. 28:22; 35:1, 3, 7 **10:5** [i]1 Sam. 13:2, 3 [j]1 Sam. 19:12, 20 [k]2 Kin. 3:15 **10:6** [l]Num. 11:25, 29 [m]1 Sam. 10:10; 19:23, 24 **10:7** [n]Ex. 4:8 [o]Judg. 6:12 **10:8** [p]1 Sam. 11:14, 15; 13:8 [q]1 Sam. 13:8–10 **10:10** [r]1 Sam. 10:5 [s]1 Sam. 19:20 **10:11** [t]Matt. 13:54–57 **10:12** [u]John 5:30, 36 **10:14** [v]1 Sam. 14:50 **10:16** [w]1 Sam. 9:20 **10:17** [x]Judg. 20:1 [y]1 Sam. 7:5, 6 **10:18** [z]Judg. 6:8, 9 **10:19** [a]1 Sam. 8:7, 19; 12:12 **10:20** [b]Acts 1:24, 26 **10:22** [c]1 Sam. 23:2, 4, 10, 11

And the LORD answered, "There he is, hidden among the equipment."

²³So they ran and brought him from there; and when he stood among the people, ᵈhe was taller than any of the people from his shoulders upward. ²⁴And Samuel said to all the people, "Do you see him ᵉwhom the LORD has chosen, that *there is* no one like him among all the people?"

So all the people shouted and said, ᶠ"Long live the king!"

²⁵Then Samuel explained to the people ᵍthe behavior of royalty, and wrote *it* in a book and laid *it* up before the LORD. And Samuel sent all the people away, every man to his house. ²⁶And Saul also went home ʰto Gibeah; and valiant *men* went with him, whose hearts God had touched. ²⁷ⁱBut some ʲrebels said, "How can this man save us?" So they despised him, ᵏand brought him no presents. But he held his peace.

Saul Saves Jabesh Gilead

11 Then ᵃNahash the Ammonite came up and encamped against ᵇJabesh Gilead; and all the men of Jabesh said to Nahash, ᶜ"Make a covenant with us, and we will serve you."

²And Nahash the Ammonite answered them, "On this *condition* I will make *a covenant* with you, that I may put out all your right eyes, and bring ᵈreproach on all Israel."

³Then the elders of Jabesh said to him, "Hold off for seven days, that we may send messengers to all the territory of Israel. And then, if *there is* no one to save us, we will come out to you."

⁴So the messengers came ᵉto Gibeah of Saul and told the news in the hearing of the people. And ᶠall the people lifted up their voices and wept. ⁵Now there was Saul, coming behind the herd from the field; and Saul said, "What *troubles* the people, that they weep?" And they told him the words of the men of Jabesh. ⁶ᵍThen the Spirit of God came upon Saul when he heard this news, and his anger was greatly aroused. ⁷So he took a yoke of oxen and ʰcut them in pieces, and sent *them* throughout all the territory of Israel by the hands of messengers, saying, ⁱ"Whoever does not go out with Saul and Samuel to battle, so it shall be done to his oxen."

And the fear of the LORD fell on the people, and they came out with one consent. ⁸When he numbered them in ʲBezek, the children ᵏof Israel were three hundred thousand, and the men of Judah thirty thousand. ⁹And they said to the messengers who came, "Thus you shall say to the men of Jabesh Gilead: 'Tomorrow, by *the time* the sun is hot, you shall have help.'" Then the messengers came and reported *it* to the men of Jabesh, and they were glad. ¹⁰Therefore the men of Jabesh said, "Tomorrow we will come out to you, and you may do with us whatever seems good to you."

¹¹So it was, on the next day, that ˡSaul put the people ᵐin three companies; and they came into the midst of the camp in the morning watch, and killed Ammonites until the heat of the day. And it happened that those who survived were scattered, so that no two of them were left together.

¹²Then the people said to Samuel, ⁿ"Who *is* he who said, 'Shall Saul reign over us?' ᵒBring the men, that we may put them to death."

¹³But Saul said, ᵖ"Not a man shall be put to death this day, for today ᑫthe LORD has accomplished salvation in Israel."

¹⁴Then Samuel said to the people, "Come, let us go ʳto Gilgal and renew the kingdom there." ¹⁵So all the people went to Gilgal, and there they made Saul king ˢbefore the LORD in Gilgal. ᵗThere they made sacrifices of peace offerings before the LORD, and there Saul and all the men of Israel rejoiced greatly.

Samuel's Address at Saul's Coronation

12 Now Samuel said to all Israel: "Indeed I have heeded ᵃyour voice in all that you said to me, and ᵇhave made a king over you. ²And now here is the king, ᶜwalking before you; ᵈand I am old and grayheaded, and look, my sons *are* with you. I have walked before you from my childhood to this day. ³Here I am. Witness against me

---

10:24 *whom the LORD has chosen.* Long ago, before they crossed the Jordan, the Lord had told Moses that the Israelites would want a king. At that time the Lord laid out guidelines for the king, and one of them was that the king must be an Israelite chosen by the Lord (Deut. 17:14–20).

11:1 *Ammonite.* The Ammonites, who were descendants of Lot, occupied the fringes of the desert east of the territories of Gad and Manasseh.

11:5 *from the field.* Saul had been appointed king, but he did not assume governmental authority at once. He continued farming until he could answer Israel's expectations of him by delivering them from their enemies. This pattern was more in the style of the judges of Israel.

11:11 *morning watch.* The Israelites divided the night into three watches: nine to twelve, twelve to three, and three to six in the morning.

10:23 ᵈ1 Sam. 9:2   **10:24** ᵉ2 Sam. 21:6 ᶠ1 Kin. 1:25, 39   **10:25** ᵍ1 Sam. 8:11–18   **10:26** ʰJudg. 20:14   **10:27** ⁱ1 Sam. 11:12 ʲDeut. 13:13 ᵏ1 Kin. 4:21; 10:25   **11:1** ᵃ1 Sam. 12:12 ᵇJudg. 21:8 ᶜGen. 26:28   **11:2** ᵈGen. 34:14   **11:4** ᵉ1 Sam. 10:26; 15:34 ᶠJudg. 2:4; 20:23, 26; 21:2   **11:6** ᵍJudg. 3:10; 6:34; 11:29; 13:25; 14:6   **11:7** ʰJudg. 19:29 ⁱJudg. 21:5, 8, 10   **11:8** ʲJudg. 1:5 ᵏ2 Sam. 24:9   **11:11** ˡ1 Sam. 7:16, 20   **11:12** ⁿ1 Sam. 10:27 ᵒLuke 19:27   **11:13** ᵖ2 Sam. 19:22 ᑫEx. 14:13, 30   **11:14** ʳ1 Sam. 7:16; 10:8   **11:15** ˢ1 Sam. 10:17 ᵗ1 Sam. 10:8   **12:1** ᵃ1 Sam. 8:5, 7, 9, 20, 22 ᵇ1 Sam. 10:24; 11:14, 15   **12:2** ᶜNum. 27:17 ᵈ1 Sam. 8:1, 5

before the LORD and before [e]His anointed:
[f]Whose ox have I taken, or whose donkey
have I taken, or whom have I cheated?
Whom have I oppressed, or from whose
hand have I received *any* [g]bribe with which
to [h]blind my eyes? I will restore *it* to you."
4And they said, [i]"You have not cheated
us or oppressed us, nor have you taken
anything from any man's hand."
5Then he said to them, "The LORD *is*
witness against you, and His anointed *is*
witness this day, [j]that you have not found
anything [k]in my hand."
And they answered, "*He is* witness."
6Then Samuel said to the people, [l]"*It is*
the LORD who raised up Moses and Aaron,
and who brought your fathers up from the
land of Egypt. 7Now therefore, stand still,
that I may [m]reason with you before the
LORD concerning all the [n]righteous acts of
the LORD which He did to you and your fathers: 8[o]When Jacob had gone into Egypt,*
and your fathers [p]cried out to the LORD,
then the LORD [q]sent Moses and Aaron,
who brought your fathers out of Egypt and
made them dwell in this place. 9And when
they [r]forgot the LORD their God, He sold
them into the hand of [s]Sisera, commander
of the army of Hazor, into the hand of the
[t]Philistines, and into the hand of the king
of [u]Moab; and they fought against them.
10Then they cried out to the LORD, and
said, [v]'We have sinned, because we have
forsaken the LORD [w]and served the Baals
and Ashtoreths;* but now deliver us from
the hand of our enemies, and we will serve
You.' 11And the LORD sent Jerubbaal,* Be-
dan,* [x]Jephthah, and [y]Samuel,* and delivered you out of the hand of your enemies on
every side; and you dwelt in safety. 12And
when you saw that [z]Nahash king of the
Ammonites came against you, [a]you said
to me, 'No, but a king shall reign over us,'
when [b]the LORD your God *was* your king.
13"Now therefore, [c]here is the king
[d]whom you have chosen *and* whom you
have desired. And take note, [e]the LORD has
set a king over you. 14If you [f]fear the LORD
and serve Him and obey His voice, and
do not rebel against the commandment of
the LORD, then both you and the king who
reigns over you will continue following
the LORD your God. 15However, if you do
[g]not obey the voice of the LORD, but [h]re-
bel against the commandment of the LORD,
then the hand of the LORD will be against
you, as *it was* against your fathers.
16"Now therefore, [i]stand and see this
great thing which the LORD will do before your eyes: 17*Is* today not the [j]wheat
harvest? [k]I will call to the LORD, and He
will send thunder and [l]rain, that you may
perceive and see that [m]your wickedness *is*
great, which you have done in the sight of
the LORD, in asking a king for yourselves."
18So Samuel called to the LORD, and the
LORD sent thunder and rain that day; and
[n]all the people greatly feared the LORD and
Samuel.
19And all the people said to Samuel,
[o]"Pray for your servants to the LORD your
God, that we may not die; for we have added to all our sins the evil of asking a king
for ourselves."
20Then Samuel said to the people, "Do
not fear. You have done all this wickedness; [p]yet do not turn aside from following
the LORD, but serve the LORD with all your
heart. 21And [q]do not turn aside; [r]for *then
you would go* after empty things which
cannot profit or deliver, for they *are* nothing. 22For [s]the LORD will not forsake [t]His
people, [u]for His great name's sake, because
[v]it has pleased the LORD to make you His
people. 23Moreover, as for me, far be it from
me that I should sin against the LORD [w]in
ceasing to pray for you; but [x]I will teach
you the [y]good and the right way. 24[z]Only
fear the LORD, and serve Him in truth with

* **12:8** Following Masoretic Text, Targum, and Vulgate; Septuagint adds *and the Egyptians afflicted them.* * **12:10** Canaanite goddesses * **12:11** Syriac reads *Deborah;* Targum reads *Gideon.* • Septuagint and Syriac read *Barak;* Targum reads *Simson.* • Syriac reads *Simson.*

12:9 *they forgot the LORD their God.* Samuel recounted the nation's apostasy and subsequent divine discipline. Israel was having problems because they had stopped obeying God. It was not because either God or Samuel was inadequate.

12:17 *wheat harvest.* The season for harvesting wheat in Israel is the months of May and June. ***thunder and rain.*** The land of Israel receives its rainfall during the winter season. For rain to fall during the wheat harvest would be both unusual and detrimental to the harvest.

12:22 *His people.* God's desire to raise up a people for His great name's sake is not based on pride, but on love. He is pleased to show His goodness to the world, and He is willing to reach out to us in spite of our rebellion and foolishness. The whole history of the human race is littered with mankind's failure to acknowledge and follow the living God who created us. But even if we are faithless, God will remain faithful (2 Tim. 2:13), and that is our great comfort. We cannot even be faithful without His help, but "if God is for us, who can be against us?" (Rom. 8:31).

12:3 [e] 1 Sam. 10:1; 24:6 [f] Num. 16:15 [g] Ex. 23:8 [h] Deut. 16:19 **12:4** [i] Lev. 19:13 **12:5** [j] Acts 23:9; 24:20 [k] Ex. 22:4 **12:6** [l] Mic. 6:4 **12:7** [m] Is. 1:18 [n] Judg. 5:11 **12:8** [o] Gen. 46:5, 6 [p] Ex. 2:23–25 [q] Ex. 3:10; 4:14–16 **12:9** [r] Judg. 3:7 [s] Judg. 4:2 [t] Judg. 3:31; 10:7; 13:1 [u] Judg. 3:12–30 **12:10** [v] Judg. 10:10 [w] Judg. 2:13; 3:7 **12:11** [x] Judg. 11:1 [y] 1 Sam. 7:13 **12:12** [z] 1 Sam. 11:1, 2 [a] 1 Sam. 8:5, 19, 20 [b] Judg. 8:23 **12:13** [c] 1 Sam. 10:24 [d] 1 Sam. 8:5; 12:17, 19 [e] Hos. 13:11 **12:14** [f] Josh. 24:14 **12:15** [g] Deut. 28:15 [h] Is. 1:20 **12:16** [i] Ex. 14:13, 31 **12:17** [j] Gen. 30:14 [k] [James 5:16–18] [l] Ezra 10:9 [m] 1 Sam. 8:7 **12:18** [n] Ex. 14:31 **12:19** [o] Ex. 9:28 **12:20** [p] Deut. 11:16 **12:21** [q] 2 Chr. 25:15 [r] Is. 41:29 **12:22** [s] Deut. 31:6 [t] Is. 43:21 [u] Jer. 14:21 [v] Deut. 7:6–11 **12:23** [w] Rom. 1:9 [x] Ps. 34:11 [y] 1 Kin. 8:36 **12:24** [z] Eccl. 12:13

all your heart; for *a*consider what *b*great things He has done for you. 25But if you still do wickedly, *c*you shall be swept away, *d*both you and your king."

Saul's Unlawful Sacrifice

13 Saul reigned one year; and when he had reigned two years over Israel,* 2Saul chose for himself three thousand *men* of Israel. Two thousand were with Saul in *a*Michmash and in the mountains of Bethel, and a thousand were with *b*Jonathan in *c*Gibeah of Benjamin. The rest of the people he sent away, every man to his tent.

3And Jonathan attacked *d*the garrison of the Philistines that *was* in *e*Geba, and the Philistines heard *of it.* Then Saul blew the trumpet throughout all the land, saying, "Let the Hebrews hear!" 4Now all Israel heard it said *that* Saul had attacked a garrison of the Philistines, and *that* Israel had also become an abomination to the Philistines. And the people were called together to Saul at Gilgal.

5Then the Philistines gathered together to fight with Israel, thirty* thousand chariots and six thousand horsemen, and people *f*as the sand which *is* on the seashore in multitude. And they came up and encamped in Michmash, to the east of *g*Beth Aven. 6When the men of Israel saw that they were in danger (for the people were distressed), then the people *h*hid in caves, in thickets, in rocks, in holes, and in pits. 7And *some of* the Hebrews crossed over the Jordan to the *i*land of Gad and Gilead.

As for Saul, he *was* still in Gilgal, and all the people followed him trembling. 8*j*Then he waited seven days, according to the time set by Samuel. But Samuel did not come to Gilgal; and the people were scattered from him. 9So Saul said, "Bring a burnt offering and peace offerings here to me." And he offered the burnt offering. 10Now it happened, as soon as he had finished presenting the burnt offering, that Samuel came; and Saul went out to meet him, that he might greet him.

11And Samuel said, "What have you done?"

Saul said, "When I saw that the people were scattered from me, and *that* you did not come within the days appointed, and *that* the Philistines gathered together at Michmash, 12then I said, 'The Philistines will now come down on me at Gilgal, and I have not made supplication to the LORD.' Therefore I felt compelled, and offered a burnt offering."

13And Samuel said to Saul, *k*"You have done foolishly. *l*You have not kept the commandment of the LORD your God, which He commanded you. For now the LORD would have established your kingdom over Israel forever. 14*m*But now your kingdom shall not continue. *n*The LORD has sought for Himself a man *o*after His own heart, and the LORD has commanded him *to be* commander over His people, because you have *p*not kept what the LORD commanded you."

15Then Samuel arose and went up from Gilgal to Gibeah of Benjamin.* And Saul numbered the people present with him, *q*about six hundred men.

No Weapons for the Army

16Saul, Jonathan his son, and the people present with them remained in Gibeah of Benjamin. But the Philistines encamped in Michmash. 17Then raiders came out of the camp of the Philistines in three companies. One company turned onto the road to *r*Ophrah, to the land of Shual, 18another company turned to the road *to* *s*Beth Horon, and another company turned *to* the road of the border that overlooks the Valley of *t*Zeboim toward the wilderness.

19Now *u*there was no blacksmith to be found throughout all the land of Israel, for the Philistines said, "Lest the Hebrews make swords or spears." 20But all the Israelites would go down to the Philistines to sharpen each man's plowshare, his mattock, his ax, and his sickle; 21and the charge for a sharpening was a pim* for the

---

* **13:1** The Hebrew is difficult (compare 2 Samuel 5:4; 2 Kings 14:2; see also 2 Samuel 2:10; Acts 13:21). * **13:5** Following Masoretic Text, Septuagint, Targum, and Vulgate; Syriac and some manuscripts of the Septuagint read *three.* * **13:15** Following Masoretic Text and Targum; Septuagint and Vulgate add *And the rest of the people went up after Saul to meet the people who fought against them, going from Gilgal to Gibeah in the hill of Benjamin.* * **13:21** About two-thirds shekel weight

---

13:8–9 Presumption—We will never know what would have happened if Saul had waited for Samuel. Whenever we assume we "know better" and take action on our own authority, we cannot know what would have happened if we had followed God's way. Some of the snarls that are the result of stubborn rebellion are often too difficult for us to set right. This is why we must pay such careful attention not only to the direct commandments in the Bible, but to the spirit behind them.

13:19 no blacksmith. The Canaanites and Philistines learned how to forge iron from the Hittites. Although they were not great in numerical strength, the Philistines were able to dominate Israel because of their superior weaponry. By the end of David's reign, the Israelites had also acquired iron technology.

12:24 *a* Is. 5:12 *b* Deut. 10:21 **12:25** *c* Josh. 24:20 *d* Deut. 28:36 **13:2** *a* 1 Sam. 14:5, 31 *b* 1 Sam. 14:1 *c* 1 Sam. 10:26 **13:3** *d* 1 Sam. 10:5 *e* 2 Sam. 5:25 **13:5** *f* Judg. 7:12 *g* Josh. 7:2 **13:6** *h* Judg. 6:2 **13:7** *i* Num. 32:1–42 **13:8** *j* 1 Sam. 10:8 **13:13** *k* 2 Chr. 16:9 *l* 1 Sam. 15:11, 22, 28 **13:14** *m* 1 Sam. 15:28; 31:6 *n* 1 Sam. 16:1 *o* Acts 7:46; 13:22 *p* 1 Sam. 15:11, 19 **13:15** *q* 1 Sam. 13:2, 6, 7; 14:2 **13:17** *r* Josh. 18:23 **13:18** *s* Josh. 16:3; 18:13, 14 *t* Neh. 11:34 **13:19** *u* Judg. 5:8

plowshares, the mattocks, the forks, and the axes, and to set the points of the goads. [22]So it came about, on the day of battle, that [v]there was neither sword nor spear found in the hand of any of the people who *were* with Saul and Jonathan. But they were found with Saul and Jonathan his son.

[23][w]And the garrison of the Philistines went out to the pass of Michmash.

Jonathan Defeats the Philistines

14 Now it happened one day that Jonathan the son of Saul said to the young man who bore his armor, "Come, let us go over to the Philistines' garrison that *is* on the other side." But he did not tell his father. [2]And Saul was sitting in the outskirts of [a]Gibeah under a pomegranate tree which *is* in Migron. The people who *were* with him *were* about six hundred men. [3][b]Ahijah the son of Ahitub, [c]Ichabod's brother, the son of Phinehas, the son of Eli, the LORD's priest in Shiloh, was [d]wearing an ephod. But the people did not know that Jonathan had gone.

[4]Between the passes, by which Jonathan sought to go over [e]to the Philistines' garrison, *there was* a sharp rock on one side and a sharp rock on the other side. And the name of one *was* Bozez, and the name of the other Seneh. [5]The front of one faced northward opposite Michmash, and the other southward opposite Gibeah.

[6]Then Jonathan said to the young man who bore his armor, "Come, let us go over to the garrison of these [f]uncircumcised; it may be that the LORD will work for us. For nothing restrains the LORD [g]from saving by many or by few."

[7]So his armorbearer said to him, "Do all that is in your heart. Go then; here I am with you, according to your heart."

[8]Then Jonathan said, "Very well, let us cross over to *these* men, and we will show ourselves to them. [9]If they say thus to us, 'Wait until we come to you,' then we will stand still in our place and not go up to them. [10]But if they say thus, 'Come up to us,' then we will go up. For the LORD has delivered them into our hand, and [h]this *will be* a sign to us."

[11]So both of them showed themselves to the garrison of the Philistines. And the Philistines said, "Look, the Hebrews are coming out of the holes where they have [i]hidden." [12]Then the men of the garrison called to Jonathan and his armorbearer,

and said, "Come up to us, and we will show you something."

Jonathan said to his armorbearer, "Come up after me, for the LORD has delivered them into the hand of Israel." [13]And Jonathan climbed up on his hands and knees with his armorbearer after him; and they [j]fell before Jonathan. And as he came after him, his armorbearer killed them. [14]That first slaughter which Jonathan and his armorbearer made was about twenty men within about half an acre of land.*

[15]And [k]there was trembling in the camp, in the field, and among all the people. The garrison and [l]the raiders also trembled; and the earth quaked, so that it was [m]a very great trembling. [16]Now the watchmen of Saul in Gibeah of Benjamin looked, and *there* was the multitude, melting away; and they [n]went here and there. [17]Then Saul said to the people who *were* with him, "Now call the roll and see who has gone from us." And when they had called the roll, surprisingly, Jonathan and his armorbearer *were* not *there.* [18]And Saul said to Ahijah, "Bring the ark* of God here" (for at that time the ark* of God was with the children of Israel). [19]Now it happened, while Saul [o]talked to the priest, that the noise which *was* in the camp of the Philistines continued to increase; so Saul said to the priest, "Withdraw your hand." [20]Then Saul and all the people who *were* with him, assembled, and they went to the battle; and indeed [p]every man's sword was against his neighbor, *and there was* very great confusion. [21]Moreover the Hebrews *who* were with the Philistines before that time, who went up with them into the camp *from the* surrounding *country,* they also joined the Israelites who *were* with Saul and Jonathan. [22]Likewise all the men of Israel who [q]had hidden in the mountains of Ephraim, *when* they heard that the Philistines fled, they also followed hard after them in the battle. [23][r]So the LORD saved Israel that day, and the battle shifted [s]to Beth Aven.

Saul's Rash Oath

[24]And the men of Israel were distressed that day, for Saul had [t]placed the people under oath, saying, "Cursed *is* the man

---

* **14:14** Literally *half the area plowed by a yoke* (of oxen in a day) * **14:18** Following Masoretic Text, Targum, and Vulgate; Septuagint reads *ephod.* • Following Masoretic Text, Targum, and Vulgate; Septuagint reads *ephod.*

13:22 *neither sword nor spear.* The weapons available to the Israelite soldiers would have included slings, bows and arrows, and numerous instruments made of bronze.

14:14 *half an acre of land.* This can also be translated "half a yoke of land." A yoke of land was the area a pair of oxen could plow in one day.

14:24 *had placed the people under oath.* This was not only an oath, but an oath with a curse. Yet food

13:22 [v]Judg. 5:8   **13:23** [w]1 Sam. 14:1, 4   **14:2** [a]1 Sam. 13:15, 16   **14:3** [b]1 Sam. 22:9, 11, 20   [c]1 Sam. 4:21   [d]1 Sam. 2:28   **14:4** [e]1 Sam. 13:23   **14:6** [f]1 Sam. 17:26, 36   [g]Judg. 7:4, 7   **14:10** [h]Gen. 24:14   **14:11** [i]1 Sam. 13:6; 14:22   **14:13** [j]Lev. 26:8   **14:15** [k]Job 18:11   [l]1 Sam. 13:17   [m]Gen. 35:5   **14:16** [n]1 Sam. 14:20   **14:19** [o]Num. 27:21   **14:20** [p]Judg. 7:22   **14:22** [q]1 Sam. 13:6   **14:23** [r]Ex. 14:30   [s]1 Sam. 13:5   **14:24** [t]Josh. 6:26

who eats *any* food until evening, before I have taken vengeance on my enemies." So none of the people tasted food. ²⁵ᵘNow all *the people* of the land came to a forest; and there was ᵛhoney on the ground. ²⁶And when the people had come into the woods, there was the honey, dripping; but no one put his hand to his mouth, for the people feared the oath. ²⁷But Jonathan had not heard his father charge the people with the oath; therefore he stretched out the end of the rod that *was* in his hand and dipped it in a honeycomb, and put his hand to his mouth; and his countenance brightened. ²⁸Then one of the people said, "Your father strictly charged the people with an oath, saying, 'Cursed *is* the man who eats food this day.'" And the people were faint.

²⁹But Jonathan said, "My father has troubled the land. Look now, how my countenance has brightened because I tasted a little of this honey. ³⁰How much better if the people had eaten freely today of the spoil of their enemies which they found! For now would there not have been a much greater slaughter among the Philistines?"

³¹Now they had driven back the Philistines that day from Michmash to Aijalon. So the people were very faint. ³²And the people rushed on the spoil, and took sheep, oxen, and calves, and slaughtered *them* on the ground; and the people ate *them* ʷwith the blood. ³³Then they told Saul, saying, "Look, the people are sinning against the LORD by eating with the blood!"

So he said, "You have dealt treacherously; roll a large stone to me this day." ³⁴Then Saul said, "Disperse yourselves among the people, and say to them, 'Bring me here every man's ox and every man's sheep, slaughter *them* here, and eat; and do not sin against the LORD by eating with the blood.'" So every one of the people brought his ox with him that night, and slaughtered *it* there. ³⁵Then Saul ˣbuilt an altar to the

LORD. This was the first altar that he built to the LORD.

³⁶Now Saul said, "Let us go down after the Philistines by night, and plunder them until the morning light; and let us not leave a man of them."

And they said, "Do whatever seems good to you."

Then the priest said, "Let us draw near to God here."

³⁷So Saul ʸasked counsel of God, "Shall I go down after the Philistines? Will You deliver them into the hand of Israel?" But ᶻHe did not answer him that day. ³⁸And Saul said, ᵃ"Come over here, all you chiefs of the people, and know and see what this sin was today. ³⁹For ᵇas the LORD lives, who saves Israel, though it be in Jonathan my son, he shall surely die." But not a man among all the people answered him. ⁴⁰Then he said to all Israel, "You be on one side, and my son Jonathan and I will be on the other side."

And the people said to Saul, "Do what seems good to you."

⁴¹Therefore Saul said to the LORD God of Israel, ᶜ"Give a perfect *lot*."* ᵈSo Saul and Jonathan were taken, but the people escaped. ⁴²And Saul said, "Cast *lots* between my son Jonathan and me." So Jonathan was taken. ⁴³Then Saul said to Jonathan, ᵉ"Tell me what you have done."

And Jonathan told him, and said, ᶠ"I only tasted a little honey with the end of the rod that *was* in my hand. So now I must die!"

⁴⁴Saul answered, ᵍ"God do so and more also; ʰfor you shall surely die, Jonathan."

⁴⁵But the people said to Saul, "Shall Jonathan die, who has accomplished this great deliverance in Israel? Certainly not!

---

* 14:41 Following Masoretic Text and Targum; Septuagint and Vulgate read *Why do You not answer Your servant today? If the injustice is with me or Jonathan my son, O LORD God of Israel, give proof; and if You say it is with Your people Israel, give holiness.*

---

would have helped the soldiers fight with better stamina. Keeping the oath was a matter of loyalty to Saul as he avenged his enemies. But the enemies were not Saul's personal enemies, they were the enemies of the whole nation, and the power in the vengeance came from God, not Saul. Saul should have focused the faith of the people on God, not on himself. This oath is an example of poor leadership, foolish vows, and misplaced loyalties. It is easy to get into trouble with an impulsive vow. It may sound very noble and wise in the heat of the moment, but it doesn't turn out to be practical. The kinds of vows that will never get us in trouble are the vows that echo the things that Scripture teaches. Such vows as determining to raise our children for the Lord, promising to stay away from habits that control us, or commitment to pray for certain people will never leave us entangled in promises that we should not have made.

14:32 *rushed on.* If the soldiers had not been fasting as they fought, they might have had the self-control

to properly bleed the animals before they began eating.

14:37 *He did not answer him.* God's silence was taken by Saul as evidence of sin in the camp.

14:39 *he shall surely die.* This was Saul's second foolish oath. Saul is not the only one who bound himself in trouble because of an impulsive oath. Jephthah made a tragic vow (Judg. 11:29–40), John the Baptist was beheaded because of Herod's thoughtless oath (Matt. 14:7–9), and a group of Jews bound themselves together with a curse, promising not to eat or drink until they had killed Paul (Acts 23:12). Jesus taught His followers not to swear to foolish vows, but to let their yes be yes, and their no be no (Matt. 5:37; James 5:12).

14:25 ᵘDeut. 9:28 ᵛEx. 3:8 **14:32** ʷDeut. 12:16, 23, 24
14:35 ˣ1 Sam. 7:12, 17 **14:37** ʸJudg. 20:18 ᶻ1 Sam. 28:6
14:38 ᵃJosh. 7:14 **14:39** ᵇ2 Sam. 12:5 **14:41** ᶜActs
1:24–26 ᵈ1 Sam. 10:20, 21 **14:43** ᵉJosh. 7:19 ᶠ1 Sam.
14:27 **14:44** ᵍRuth 1:17 ʰ1 Sam. 14:39

*i*As the LORD lives, not one hair of his head shall fall to the ground, for he has worked *j*with God this day." So the people rescued Jonathan, and he did not die.

⁴⁶Then Saul returned from pursuing the Philistines, and the Philistines went to their own place.

Saul's Continuing Wars

⁴⁷So Saul established his sovereignty over Israel, and fought against all his enemies on every side, against Moab, against the people of *k*Ammon, against Edom, against the kings of *l*Zobah, and against the Philistines. Wherever he turned, he harassed *them.** ⁴⁸And he gathered an army and *m*attacked the Amalekites, and delivered Israel from the hands of those who plundered them.

⁴⁹*n*The sons of Saul were Jonathan, Jishui,* and Malchishua. And the names of his two daughters *were these:* the name of the firstborn Merab, and the name of the younger *o*Michal. ⁵⁰The name of Saul's wife *was* Ahinoam the daughter of Ahimaaz. And the name of the commander of his army *was* Abner the son of Ner, Saul's *p*uncle. ⁵¹*q*Kish *was* the father of Saul, and Ner the father of Abner *was* the son of Abiel.

⁵²Now there was fierce war with the Philistines all the days of Saul. And when Saul saw any strong man or any valiant man, *r*he took him for himself.

Saul Spares King Agag

15 Samuel also said to Saul, *a*"The LORD sent me to anoint you king over His people, over Israel. Now therefore, heed the voice of the words of the LORD. ²Thus says the LORD of hosts: 'I will punish Amalek *for* what he did to Israel, *b*how he ambushed him on the way when he came up from Egypt. ³Now go and *c*attack Amalek, and *d*utterly destroy all that they have, and do not spare them. But kill both man and woman, infant and nursing child, ox and sheep, camel and donkey.'"

⁴So Saul gathered the people together and numbered them in Telaim, two hundred thousand foot soldiers and ten thousand men of Judah. ⁵And Saul came to a city of Amalek, and lay in wait in the valley.

⁶Then Saul said to *e*the Kenites, *f*"Go, depart, get down from among the Amalekites, lest I destroy you with them. For *g*you showed kindness to all the children of Israel when they came up out of Egypt." So the Kenites departed from among the Amalekites. ⁷*h*And Saul attacked the Amalekites, from *i*Havilah all the way to *j*Shur, which is east of Egypt. ⁸*k*He also took Agag king of the Amalekites alive, and *l*utterly destroyed all the people with the edge of the sword. ⁹But Saul and the people *m*spared Agag and the best of the sheep, the oxen, the fatlings, the lambs, and all *that was* good, and were unwilling to utterly destroy them. But everything despised and worthless, that they utterly destroyed.

Saul Rejected as King

¹⁰Now the word of the LORD came to Samuel, saying, ¹¹*n*"I greatly regret that I have set up Saul *as* king, for he has *o*turned back from following Me, *p*and has not performed My commandments." And it *q*grieved Samuel, and he cried out to the LORD all night. ¹²So when Samuel rose early in the morning to meet Saul, it was told Samuel, saying, "Saul went to *r*Carmel, and indeed, he set up a monument for himself; and he has gone on around, passed by, and gone down to Gilgal." ¹³Then Samuel went to Saul, and Saul said to him, *s*"Blessed *are* you of the LORD! I have performed the commandment of the LORD."

¹⁴But Samuel said, "What then *is* this bleating of the sheep in my ears, and the lowing of the oxen which I hear?"

¹⁵And Saul said, "They have brought them from the Amalekites; *t*for the people spared the best of the sheep and the oxen, to sacrifice to the LORD your God; and the rest we have utterly destroyed."

¹⁶Then Samuel said to Saul, "Be quiet! And I will tell you what the LORD said to me last night."

And he said to him, "Speak on."

¹⁷So Samuel said, *u*"When you *were* little in your own eyes, *were* you not head of

---

* **14:47** Septuagint and Vulgate read *prospered.*
* **14:49** Called *Abinadab* in 1 Chronicles 8:33 and 9:39

14:47 Moab . . . Ammon. The Moabites and Ammonites were descendants of Lot (Gen. 19:30–38). They occupied regions east of the Jordan and Dead Sea. **Edom.** The Edomites were descendants of Esau (Gen. 36:8) who ruled over a region southeast of the Dead Sea. **Zobah.** This was the Aramean kingdom in the Bekaa valley. **Philistines.** The Philistines lived on the coastal plain west of the hill country.
14:48 Amalekites. These nomadic desert tribesmen lived south of the hill country.
15:6 Kenites. The Kenites were a nomadic offshoot of the Midianites (Num. 10:29). They had been loosely associated with the Israelites since Moses' marriage to the daughter of Jethro, a Kenite (Judg. 1:16; 4:11).

14:45 *i* 1 Kin. 1:52 *j* [2 Cor. 6:1]   **14:47** *k* 1 Sam. 11:1–13 *l* 2 Sam. 10:6   **14:48** *m* 1 Sam. 15:3–7   **14:49** *n* 1 Sam. 31:2 *o* 1 Sam. 18:17–20, 27; 19:12   **14:50** *p* 1 Sam. 10:14   **14:51** *q* 1 Sam. 9:1, 21   **14:52** *r* 1 Sam. 8:11   **15:1** *a* 1 Sam. 9:16; 10:1   **15:2** *b* Deut. 25:17–19   **15:3** *c* Deut. 25:19 *d* Num. 24:20   **15:6** *e* Num. 24:21 *f* Gen. 18:25; 19:12, 14 *g* Ex. 18:10, 19   **15:7** *h* 1 Sam. 14:48 *i* Gen. 2:11; 25:17, 18 *j* Gen. 16:7   **15:8** *k* 1 Sam. 15:32, 33 *l* 1 Sam. 27:8, 9   **15:9** *m* 1 Sam. 15:3, 15, 19   **15:11** *n* Gen. 6:6, 7 *o* 1 Kin. 9:6 *p* 1 Sam. 13:13; 15:3, 9 *q* 1 Sam. 15:35; 16:1   **15:12** *r* Josh. 15:55   **15:13** *s* Judg. 17:2   **15:15** *t* [Gen. 3:12, 13]; 1 Sam. 15:9, 21   **15:17** *u* 1 Sam. 9:21; 10:22

the tribes of Israel? And did not the LORD anoint you king over Israel? [18]Now the LORD sent you on a mission, and said, 'Go, and utterly destroy the sinners, the Amalekites, and fight against them until they are consumed.' [19]Why then did you not obey the voice of the LORD? Why did you swoop down on the spoil, and do evil in the sight of the LORD?"

[20]And Saul said to Samuel, v"But I have obeyed the voice of the LORD, and gone on the mission on which the LORD sent me, and brought back Agag king of Amalek; I have utterly destroyed the Amalekites. [21]wBut the people took of the plunder, sheep and oxen, the best of the things which should have been utterly destroyed, to sacrifice to the LORD your God in Gilgal."

[22]So Samuel said:

x"Has the LORD as great delight in burnt
offerings and sacrifices,
As in obeying the voice of the LORD?
Behold, yto obey is better than
sacrifice,
And to heed than the fat of rams.
[23] For rebellion is as the sin of witchcraft,
And stubbornness is as iniquity and
idolatry.
Because you have rejected the word of
the LORD,
zHe also has rejected you from being
king."

[24a]Then Saul said to Samuel, "I have sinned, for I have transgressed the commandment of the LORD and your words, because I bfeared the people and obeyed their voice. [25]Now therefore, please pardon my sin, and return with me, that I may worship the LORD."

[26]But Samuel said to Saul, "I will not return with you, cfor you have rejected the word of the LORD, and the LORD has rejected you from being king over Israel."

[27]And as Samuel turned around to go away, dSaul seized the edge of his robe, and it tore. [28]So Samuel said to him, e"The LORD has torn the kingdom of Israel from

you today, and has given it to a neighbor of yours, who is better than you. [29]And also the Strength of Israel fwill not lie nor relent. For He is not a man, that He should relent."

[30]Then he said, "I have sinned; yet ghonor me now, please, before the elders of my people and before Israel, and return with me, that I may worship the LORD your God." [31]So Samuel turned back after Saul, and Saul worshiped the LORD.

[32]Then Samuel said, "Bring Agag king of the Amalekites here to me." So Agag came to him cautiously.

And Agag said, "Surely the bitterness of death is past."

[33]But Samuel said, h"As your sword has made women childless, so shall your mother be childless among women." And Samuel hacked Agag in pieces before the LORD in Gilgal.

[34]Then Samuel went to iRamah, and Saul went up to his house at iGibeah of Saul. [35]And kSamuel went no more to see Saul until the day of his death. Nevertheless Samuel mourned for Saul, and the LORD regretted that He had made Saul king over Israel.

David Anointed King

16 Now the LORD said to Samuel, a"How long will you mourn for Saul, seeing I have rejected him from reigning over Israel? bFill your chorn with oil, and go; I am sending you to cJesse the Bethlehemite. For dI have provided Myself a king among his sons."

[2]And Samuel said, "How can I go? If Saul hears it, he will kill me."

But the LORD said, "Take a heifer with you, and say, e'I have come to sacrifice to the LORD.' [3]Then invite Jesse to the sacrifice, and I will show you what you shall do; you shall anoint for Me the one I name to you."

[4]So Samuel did what the LORD said, and went to Bethlehem. And the elders of the town ftrembled at his coming, and said, g"Do you come peaceably?"

15:22 Obedience—If we love God we are commanded to keep His commandments (John 14:15). The problem is, we sometimes fool ourselves. Saul thought he was doing something good for God. He was partially obeying. He killed a lot of the Amalekites, and instead of killing the animals, he sacrificed them. They would still be dead, and it would honor God, too. But He was not pleased. Saul did what was "right in his own eyes" but this was not obedience.

15:23 witchcraft. Witchcraft, divination, idolatry, and other occult activities are an attempt to manipulate spiritual powers for our own ends. In his rebellion Saul was treating God as if He were a moody, cranky pagan god, who could be thwarted, and then appeased by sacrifices. **He also has rejected you.** Saul was rejected because he was still treating God as a force to be used. He was sorry he got caught, but he still thought he was right and could give a quick sacrifice and go on with the plan.

15:35 see. God was through with Saul as king, and so was Samuel.

16:2 I have come to sacrifice to the LORD. At this time Shiloh was still the designated central location for sacrifices (Deut. 12:1–14). But with the disruptions of the priesthood, the ark located at Kirjath Jearim (7:2), and the general belief that God had removed His presence from Shiloh, it would not be surprising if the sacrificial system had been interrupted as well. In

15:20 v 1 Sam. 15:13   **15:21** w 1 Sam. 15:15   **15:22** x [Is. 1:11–17] y [Hos. 6:6]   **15:23** z 1 Sam. 13:14; 16:1   **15:24** a Josh. 7:20 b [Is. 51:12, 13]   **15:26** c 1 Sam. 2:30   **15:27** d 1 Kin. 11:30, 31   **15:28** e 1 Kin. 11:31   **15:29** f Num. 23:19   **15:30** g [John 5:44; 12:43]   **15:33** h [Gen. 9:6]   **15:34** i 1 Sam. 7:17 j 1 Sam. 11:4   **15:35** k 1 Sam. 19:24   **16:1** a 1 Sam. 15:23, 35 b 1 Sam. 9:16; 10:1 c Ruth 4:18–22 d Acts 13:22   **16:2** e 1 Sam. 9:12   **16:4** f 1 Sam. 21:1 g 1 Kin. 2:13

⁵And he said, "Peaceably; I have come to sacrifice to the LORD. ʰSanctify yourselves, and come with me to the sacrifice." Then he consecrated Jesse and his sons, and invited them to the sacrifice.

⁶So it was, when they came, that he looked at ⁱEliab and ʲsaid, "Surely the LORD's anointed *is* before Him!"

⁷But the LORD said to Samuel, ᵏ"Do not look at his appearance or at his physical stature, because I have refused him. ˡFor *the LORD does* not *see* as man sees;* for man ᵐlooks at the outward appearance, but the LORD looks at the ⁿheart."

⁸So Jesse called Abinadab, and made him pass before Samuel. And he said, "Neither has the LORD chosen this one." ⁹Then Jesse made Shammah pass by. And he said, "Neither has the LORD chosen this one." ¹⁰Thus Jesse made seven of his sons pass before Samuel. And Samuel said to Jesse, "The LORD has not chosen these." ¹¹And Samuel said to Jesse, "Are all the young men here?" Then he said, "There remains yet the youngest, and there he is, keeping the ᵒsheep."

And Samuel said to Jesse, "Send and bring him. For we will not sit down* till he comes here." ¹²So he sent and brought him in. Now he *was* ᵖruddy, ۹with bright eyes, and good-looking. ʳAnd the LORD said, "Arise, anoint him; for this *is* the one!" ¹³Then Samuel took the horn of oil and anointed him in the midst of his brothers; and ˢthe Spirit of the LORD came upon David from that day forward. So Samuel arose and went to Ramah.

A Distressing Spirit Troubles Saul

¹⁴ᵗBut the Spirit of the LORD departed from Saul, and ᵘa distressing spirit from the LORD troubled him. ¹⁵And Saul's servants said to him, "Surely, a distressing spirit from God is troubling you. ¹⁶Let our master now command your servants, *who are* before you, to seek out a man *who is* a skillful player on the harp. And it shall be that he will ᵛplay it with his hand when the distressing spirit from God is upon you, and you shall be well."

¹⁷So Saul said to his servants, "Provide me now a man who can play well, and bring *him* to me."

¹⁸Then one of the servants answered and said, "Look, I have seen a son of Jesse the Bethlehemite, *who is* skillful in playing, a mighty man of valor, a man of war, prudent in speech, and a handsome person; and ʷthe LORD *is* with him."

¹⁹Therefore Saul sent messengers to Jesse, and said, "Send me your son David, who *is* with the sheep." ²⁰And Jesse ˣtook a donkey *loaded with* bread, a skin of wine, and a young goat, and sent *them* by his son David to Saul. ²¹So David came to Saul and ʸstood before him. And he loved him greatly, and he became his armorbearer. ²²Then Saul sent to Jesse, saying, "Please let David stand before me, for he has found favor in my sight." ²³And so it was, whenever the spirit from God was upon Saul, that David would take a harp and play *it* with his hand. Then Saul would become refreshed and well, and the distressing spirit would depart from him.

David and Goliath

17 Now the Philistines gathered their armies together to battle, and were

* **16:7** Septuagint reads *For God does not see as man sees;* Targum reads *It is not by the appearance of a man;* Vulgate reads *Nor do I judge according to the looks of a man.* * **16:11** Following Septuagint and Vulgate; Masoretic Text reads *turn around;* Targum and Syriac read *turn away.*

any case, God did direct Samuel to make this sacrifice at Bethlehem.

16:7 God—Our Creator knows His human creatures intimately, and He is able to discern our thoughts and purposes before we ourselves are aware of them. He always looks beyond appearance and stature to the heart.

16:12 *anoint him.* David was anointed with olive oil. This religious ritual consecrated him to the kingship, although he did not take the role of king for many years. The heart God saw in David is the one He wants to see in all of us. It has purposefulness, intelligence, and willingness to obey. If our heart is centered on God, He can use us to extend His kingdom.

16:14 *departed from Saul.* After the Spirit of God came upon David, Saul was no longer empowered by the Spirit to serve as king. In Old Testament times the Holy Spirit came upon people selectively, usually a king, prophet, or judge. It was only after the resurrection of Jesus that the Holy Spirit came to indwell all believers (John 16:5–11; Acts 2:4).

16:15 *distressing spirit from God.* This affliction is understood in various ways. Perhaps the spirit was a demon that God allowed to harass Saul, in the same way that God allowed Satan to tempt Job (Job 1:8–12). Perhaps Saul had a spirit of discontent in his heart, caused by the absence of the Holy Spirit. Perhaps pride, that same sin that caused Satan to fall, was allowed to grow in Saul's heart and dominate his thoughts and actions. Scripture is clear that God is always holy, just, and righteous, so this spirit was something that God allowed to come upon Saul, but it was not a part of God.

16:21 *David came to Saul.* David played for Saul, and was his armorbearer. It is unclear exactly how much time David spent with Saul. Probably David at this time continued to come and go from Saul's household to his father's.

17:1 *the Philistines gathered their armies together to battle.* The Philistine and Israelite armies were

16:5 ʰ Ex. 19:10 **16:6** ⁱ 1 Sam. 17:13, 28 ʲ 1 Kin. 12:26 **16:7** ᵏ Ps. 147:10 ˡ Is. 55:8, 9 ᵐ 2 Cor. 10:7 ⁿ 1 Kin. 8:39 **16:11** ᵒ 2 Sam. 7:8 **16:12** ᵖ 1 Sam. 17:42 ۹ Gen. 39:6 ʳ 1 Sam. 9:17 **16:13** ˢ Num. 27:18 **16:14** ᵗ Judg. 16:20 ᵘ Judg. 9:23 **16:16** ᵛ 1 Sam. 18:10; 19:9 **16:18** ʷ 1 Sam. 3:19; 18:12, 14 **16:20** ˣ 1 Sam. 10:4, 27 **16:21** ʸ Gen. 41:46

gathered at ᵃSochoh, which *belongs* to Judah; they encamped between Sochoh and Azekah, in Ephes Dammim. ²And Saul and the men of Israel were gathered together, and they encamped in the Valley of Elah, and drew up in battle array against the Philistines. ³The Philistines stood on a mountain on one side, and Israel stood on a mountain on the other side, with a valley between them.

⁴And a champion went out from the camp of the Philistines, named ᵇGoliath, from ᶜGath, whose height *was* six cubits and a span. ⁵He had a bronze helmet on his head, and he *was* armed with a coat of mail, and the weight of the coat *was* five thousand shekels of bronze. ⁶And he had bronze armor on his legs and a bronze javelin between his shoulders. ⁷Now the staff of his spear *was* like a weaver's beam, and his iron spearhead *weighed* six hundred shekels; and a shield-bearer went before him. ⁸Then he stood and cried out to the armies of Israel, and said to them, "Why have you come out to line up for battle? *Am* I not a Philistine, and you the ᵈservants of Saul? Choose a man for yourselves, and let him come down to me. ⁹If he is able to fight with me and kill me, then we will be your servants. But if I prevail against him and kill him, then you shall be our servants and ᵉserve us." ¹⁰And the Philistine said, ᶠ"I defy the armies of Israel this day; give me a man, that we may fight together." ¹¹When Saul and all Israel heard these words of the Philistine, they were dismayed and greatly afraid.

¹²Now David *was* ᵍthe son of that ʰEphrathite of Bethlehem Judah, whose name *was* Jesse, and who had ⁱeight sons. And the man was old, advanced *in years*, in the days of Saul. ¹³The three oldest sons of Jesse had gone to follow Saul to the battle. The ʲnames of his three sons who went to the battle *were* Eliab the firstborn, next

to him Abinadab, and the third Shammah. ¹⁴David *was* the youngest. And the three oldest followed Saul. ¹⁵But David occasionally went and returned from Saul ᵏto feed his father's sheep at Bethlehem.

¹⁶And the Philistine drew near and presented himself forty days, morning and evening.

¹⁷Then Jesse said to his son David, "Take now for your brothers an ephah of this dried *grain* and these ten loaves, and run to your brothers at the camp. ¹⁸And carry these ten cheeses to the captain of *their* thousand, and ˡsee how your brothers fare, and bring back news of them." ¹⁹Now Saul and they and all the men of Israel *were* in the Valley of Elah, fighting with the Philistines.

²⁰So David rose early in the morning, left the sheep with a keeper, and took *the things* and went as Jesse had commanded him. And he came to the camp as the army was going out to the fight and shouting for the battle. ²¹For Israel and the Philistines had drawn up in battle array, army against army. ²²And David left his supplies in the hand of the supply keeper, ran to the army, and came and greeted his brothers. ²³Then as he talked with them, there was the champion, the Philistine of Gath, Goliath by name, coming up from the armies of the Philistines; and he spoke ᵐaccording to the same words. So David heard *them*. ²⁴And all the men of Israel, when they saw the man, fled from him and were dreadfully afraid. ²⁵So the men of Israel said, "Have you seen this man who has come up? Surely he has come up to defy Israel; and it shall be *that* the man who kills him the king will enrich with great riches, ⁿwill give him his daughter, and give his father's house exemption *from taxes* in Israel."

²⁶Then David spoke to the men who stood by him, saying, "What shall be done for the man who kills this Philistine and takes away ᵒthe reproach from Israel? For

---

gathered in the Elah valley, about 15 miles west of David's hometown of Bethlehem. The Philistines were camped on a hill, south of the valley, between the cities of Azekah and Sochoh.
17:2 *Valley of Elah.* The valley is an east-west valley, leading from the hill country of Judah toward the lowlands of the Philistines. It had a steep ravine that extended the length of the valley, making it unfit for the Philistines' chariots. Probably the ravine prevented a full-scale assault by the Philistines, causing the long delay before engaging in battle.
17:4 *champion.* The champion was a warrior who would fight in single combat as a stand-in for the entire army. The most likely person to take on this champion would be Saul, who, when he was chosen king, stood head and shoulders above his countrymen. *six cubits and a span.* The cubit was about 18 inches, and a span was 9 inches. Goliath stood approximately 9 feet, 9 inches tall.
17:5 *bronze helmet.* Ordinary troops had leather helmets. *coat of mail.* Goliath's coat of mail was made of overlapping plates of bronze sewn on leather. *five*

thousand shekels. The coat of armor weighed about 125 pounds.
17:7 *six hundred shekels.* The spear was a weapon designed for hand-to-hand combat, like a long sword. The head of Goliath's spear weighed about 17 pounds. *a shield-bearer.* The soldier carried a small round shield, usually worn on the left arm. The shield-carrier bore the much larger, oblong shield.
17:12 *Ephrathite.* Ephrath was the early name for Bethlehem.
17:17 *Take now for your brothers.* In ancient times, soldiers usually lived off the land they conquered or depended on personal supplies that they or someone else brought from home.

17:1 ᵃ Josh. 15:35   **17:4** ᵇ 2 Sam. 21:19 ᶜ Josh. 11:21, 22   **17:8** ᵈ 1 Sam. 8:17   **17:9** ᵉ 1 Sam. 11:1   **17:10** ᶠ 1 Sam. 17:26, 36, 45   **17:12** ᵍ Ruth 4:22 ʰ Gen. 35:19 ⁱ 1 Sam. 16:10, 11   **17:13** ʲ 1 Sam. 16:6, 8, 9   **17:15** ᵏ 1 Sam. 16:11, 19   **17:18** ˡ Gen. 37:13, 14   **17:23** ᵐ 1 Sam. 17:8–10   **17:25** ⁿ Josh. 15:16   **17:26** ᵒ 1 Sam. 11:2

who *is* this Puncircumcised Philistine, that he should qdefy the armies of rthe living God?"

27And the people answered him in this manner, saying, s"So shall it be done for the man who kills him."

28Now Eliab his oldest brother heard when he spoke to the men; and Eliab's tanger was aroused against David, and he said, "Why did you come down here? And with whom have you left those few sheep in the wilderness? I know your pride and the insolence of your heart, for you have come down to see the battle."

29And David said, "What have I done now? u*Is there* not a cause?" 30Then he turned from him toward another and vsaid the same thing; and these people answered him as the first ones *did.*

31Now when the words which David spoke were heard, they reported *them* to Saul; and he sent for him. 32Then David said to Saul, w"Let no man's heart fail because of him; xyour servant will go and fight with this Philistine."

33And Saul said to David, y"You are not able to go against this Philistine to fight with him; for you *are* a youth, and he a man of war from his youth."

34But David said to Saul, "Your servant used to keep his father's sheep, and when a zlion or a bear came and took a lamb out of the flock, 35I went out after it and struck it, and delivered *the lamb* from its mouth; and when it arose against me, I caught *it* by its beard, and struck and killed it. 36Your servant has killed both lion and bear; and this uncircumcised Philistine will be like one of them, seeing he has defied the armies of the living God." 37Moreover David said, a"The LORD, who delivered me from the paw of the lion and from the paw of the bear, He will deliver me from the hand of this Philistine."

And Saul said to David, b"Go, and the LORD be with you!"

38So Saul clothed David with his armor, and he put a bronze helmet on his head; he also clothed him with a coat of mail. 39David fastened his sword to his armor and tried to walk, for he had not tested *them.*

And David said to Saul, "I cannot walk with these, for I have not tested *them.*" So David took them off.

40Then he took his staff in his hand; and he chose for himself five smooth stones from the brook, and put them in a shepherd's bag, in a pouch which he had, and his sling was in his hand. And he drew near to the Philistine. 41So the Philistine came, and began drawing near to David, and the man who bore the shield *went* before him. 42And when the Philistine looked about and saw David, he cdisdained him; for he was *only* a youth, druddy and good-looking. 43So the Philistine esaid to David, "*Am* I a dog, that you come to me with sticks?" And the Philistine cursed David by his gods. 44And the Philistine fsaid to David, "Come to me, and I will give your flesh to the birds of the air and the beasts of the field!"

45Then David said to the Philistine, "You come to me with a sword, with a spear, and with a javelin. gBut I come to you in the name of the LORD of hosts, the God of the armies of Israel, whom you have hdefied. 46This day the LORD will deliver you into my hand, and I will strike you and take your head from you. And this day I will give ithe carcasses of the camp of the Philistines to the birds of the air and the wild beasts of the earth, jthat all the earth may know that there is a God in Israel. 47Then all this assembly shall know that the LORD kdoes not save with sword and spear; for lthe battle *is* the LORD's, and He will give you into our hands."

48So it was, when the Philistine arose and came and drew near to meet David, that David hurried and mran toward the army to meet the Philistine. 49Then David put his hand in his bag and took out a stone; and he slung *it* and struck the Philistine in his forehead, so that the stone sank into his forehead, and he fell on his face to the earth. 50So David prevailed over the Philistine with a nsling and a stone, and struck the Philistine and killed him. But *there was* no sword in the hand of David. 51Therefore David ran and stood over the Philistine, took his osword and drew it out

---

17:39–40 Wisdom—David had embarked on a risky venture. It might seem smart to meet Goliath with the best armor, but David had wisdom enough to know that if he was going to attack the giant, it would have to be on his own terms. The years of solitary shepherding had given David the time to practice with his sling, and the opportunity to know that it was the Lord who gave him the strength and the will to kill the predators that threatened his flock. The insight and practices gained through difficult experiences blossom as wisdom. We can look back on these times with thankfulness because that is how God has equipped us for the next task.

17:40 *sling.* A sling was the typical equipment of the shepherd. It was a hollow pocket of leather attached to two cords. Putting a stone in the pouch, the slinger

would whirl it around his head to build up momentum. Releasing one of the cords would hurl the stone at its target. It takes skill and practice to be expert with a sling. Slingers were a regular part of armies in the ancient Middle East.

17:26P 1 Sam. 14:6; 17:36 q 1 Sam. 17:10 rDeut. 5:26 **17:27**s 1 Sam. 17:25 **17:28**f [Matt. 10:36] **17:29**u 1 Sam. 17:17 **17:30**v 1 Sam. 17:26, 27 **17:32**w Deut. 20:1–4 x 1 Sam. 16:18 **17:33**y Num. 13:31 **17:34**z Judg. 14:5 **17:37**a [2 Cor. 1:10] b 1 Chr. 22:11, 16 **17:42**c [Ps. 123:4] d 1 Sam. 16:12 **17:43**e 2 Kin. 8:13 **17:44**f 1 Kin. 20:10, 11 **17:45**g Heb. 11:33, 34 h 1 Sam. 17:10 **17:46**i Deut. 28:26 j Josh. 4:24 **17:47**k Hos. 1:7 l 2 Chr. 20:15 **17:48**m Ps. 27:3 **17:50**n Judg. 3:31; 15:15; 20:16 **17:51**o 1 Sam. 21:9

of its sheath and killed him, and cut off his
head with it.
And when the Philistines saw that their
champion was dead, [p]they fled. 52 Now the
men of Israel and Judah arose and shouted,
and pursued the Philistines as far as the
entrance of the valley* and to the gates of
Ekron. And the wounded of the Philistines
fell along the road to [q]Shaaraim, even as
far as Gath and Ekron. 53 Then the children
of Israel returned from chasing the Philistines, and they plundered their tents. 54 And
David took the head of the Philistine and
brought it to Jerusalem, but he put his armor in his tent.
55 When Saul saw David going out
against the Philistine, he said to [r]Abner, the
commander of the army, "Abner, [s]whose
son *is* this youth?"
And Abner said, "As your soul lives, O
king, I do not know."
56 So the king said, "Inquire whose son
this young man *is*."
57 Then, as David returned from the
slaughter of the Philistine, Abner took him
and brought him before Saul [t]with the head
of the Philistine in his hand. 58 And Saul
said to him, "Whose son *are* you, young
man?"
So David answered, [u]"I *am* the son of
your servant Jesse the Bethlehemite."

Saul Resents David

18 Now when he had finished speaking
to Saul, [a]the soul of Jonathan was
knit to the soul of David, [b]and Jonathan
loved him as his own soul. 2 Saul took him
that day, [c]and would not let him go home
to his father's house anymore. 3 Then Jonathan and David made a [d]covenant, because
he loved him as his own soul. 4 And Jonathan took off the robe that *was* on him and
gave it to David, with his armor, even to his
sword and his bow and his belt.
5 So David went out wherever Saul sent
him, *and* behaved wisely. And Saul set him
over the men of war, and he was accepted
in the sight of all the people and also in the
sight of Saul's servants. 6 Now it had happened as they were coming *home*, when
David was returning from the slaughter of
the Philistine, that [e]the women had come
out of all the cities of Israel, singing and
dancing, to meet King Saul, with tambourines, with joy, and with musical instruments. 7 So the women [f]sang as they
danced, and said:

[g]"Saul has slain his thousands,
And David his ten thousands."

8 Then Saul was very angry, and the saying [h]displeased him; and he said, "They
have ascribed to David ten thousands, and
to me they have ascribed *only* thousands.
Now *what* more can he have but [i]the kingdom?" 9 So Saul eyed David from that day
forward.
10 And it happened on the next day that
[j]the distressing spirit from God came upon
Saul, [k]and he prophesied inside the house.
So David [l]played *music* with his hand, as
at other times; [m]but *there was* a spear in
Saul's hand. 11 And Saul [n]cast the spear, for
he said, "I will pin David to the wall!" But
David escaped his presence twice.
12 Now Saul was [o]afraid of David, because [p]the LORD was with him, but had
[q]departed from Saul. 13 Therefore Saul removed him from his presence, and made
him his captain over a thousand; and [r]he
went out and came in before the people.
14 And David behaved wisely in all his ways,
and [s]the LORD *was* with him. 15 Therefore,
when Saul saw that he behaved very wisely, he was afraid of him. 16 But [t]all Israel
and Judah loved David, because he went
out and came in before them.

David Marries Michal

17 Then Saul said to David, "Here is my
older daughter Merab; [u]I will give her to
you as a wife. Only be valiant for me, and
fight [v]the LORD's battles." For Saul thought,
[w]"Let my hand not be against him, but let
the hand of the Philistines be against him."
18 So David said to Saul, [x]"Who *am* I,
and what *is* my life *or* my father's family
in Israel, that I should be son-in-law to the
king?" 19 But it happened at the time when
Merab, Saul's daughter, should have been
given to David, that she was given to [y]Adri-
el the [z]Meholathite as a wife.
20 [a]Now Michal, Saul's daughter, loved

* **17:52** Following Masoretic Text, Syriac, Targum, and Vulgate; Septuagint reads *Gath*.

17:55 *whose son is this youth.* How does this question fit with the fact that David had been serving as a musician in Saul's court and as Saul's armorbearer, and that Saul "loved him greatly" (16:18–23)? Possibly in Saul's unstable mental condition he did not recall David, or perhaps he did not know his name, even if he did recognize him. David was not at court full time until after he had killed Goliath. It would not be unusual for the king to know nothing personal about a servant, even a servant he appreciated.
18:16 *he went out and came in before them.* David's military activities elevated him to prominence before the people.

17:51 [p] Heb. 11:34 **17:52** [q] Josh. 15:36 **17:55** [r] 1 Sam. 14:50 [s] 1 Sam. 16:21, 22 **17:57** [t] 1 Sam. 17:54 **17:58** [u] 1 Sam. 17:12 **18:1** [a] Gen. 44:30 [b] 1 Sam. 20:17 **18:2** [c] 1 Sam. 17:15 **18:3** [d] 1 Sam. 20:8–17 **18:6** [e] Ex. 15:20, 21 **18:7** [f] Ex. 15:21 [g] 1 Sam. 21:11; 29:5 **18:8** [h] Eccl. 4:4 [i] 1 Sam. 15:28 **18:10** [j] 1 Sam. 16:14 [k] 1 Sam. 19:24 [l] 1 Sam. 16:23 [m] 1 Sam. 19:9, 10 **18:11** [n] 1 Sam. 19:10; 20:33 **18:12** [o] 1 Sam. 18:15, 29 [p] 1 Sam. 16:13, 18 [q] 1 Sam. 16:14; 28:15 **18:13** [r] Num. 27:17 **18:14** [s] Josh. 6:27 **18:16** [t] 1 Sam. 18:5 **18:17** [u] 1 Sam. 14:49; 17:25 [v] Num. 32:20, 27, 29 [w] 1 Sam. 18:21, 25 **18:18** [x] 2 Sam. 7:18 **18:19** [y] 2 Sam. 21:8 [z] Judg. 7:22 **18:20** [a] 1 Sam. 18:28

David. And they told Saul, and the thing pleased him. [21]So Saul said, "I will give her to him, that she may be a snare to him, and that [b]the hand of the Philistines may be against him." Therefore Saul said to David a second time, [c]"You shall be my son-in-law today."

[22]And Saul commanded his servants, "Communicate with David secretly, and say, 'Look, the king has delight in you, and all his servants love you. Now therefore, become the king's son-in-law.'"

[23]So Saul's servants spoke those words in the hearing of David. And David said, "Does it seem to you a light *thing* to be a king's son-in-law, seeing I *am* a poor and lightly esteemed man?" [24]And the servants of Saul told him, saying, "In this manner David spoke."

[25]Then Saul said, "Thus you shall say to David: 'The king does not desire any [d]dowry but one hundred foreskins of the Philistines, to take [e]vengeance on the king's enemies.'" But Saul [f]thought to make David fall by the hand of the Philistines. [26]So when his servants told David these words, it pleased David well to become the king's son-in-law. Now [g]the days had not expired; [27]therefore David arose and went, he and [h]his men, and killed two hundred men of the Philistines. And [i]David brought their foreskins, and they gave them in full count to the king, that he might become the king's son-in-law. Then Saul gave him Michal his daughter as a wife.

[28]Thus Saul saw and knew that the Lord *was* with David, and *that* Michal, Saul's daughter, loved him; [29]and Saul was still more afraid of David. So Saul became David's enemy continually. [30]Then the princes of the Philistines [j]went out *to war.* And so it was, whenever they went out, *that* David [k]behaved more wisely than all the servants of Saul, so that his name became highly esteemed.

Saul Persecutes David

19 Now Saul spoke to Jonathan his son and to all his servants, that they should kill [a]David; but Jonathan, Saul's son, [b]delighted greatly in David. [2]So Jonathan told David, saying, "My father Saul seeks to kill you. Therefore please be on your guard until morning, and stay in a secret *place* and hide. [3]And I will go out and stand beside my father in the field where you *are*, and I will speak with my father about you. Then what I observe, I will tell [c]you."

[4]Thus Jonathan [d]spoke well of David to Saul his father, and said to him, "Let not the king [e]sin against his servant, against David, because he has not sinned against you, and because his works *have been* very good toward you. [5]For he took his [f]life in his hands, and [g]killed the Philistine, and [h]the Lord brought about a great deliverance for all Israel. You saw *it* and rejoiced. [i]Why then will you [j]sin against innocent blood, to kill David without a cause?"

[6]So Saul heeded the voice of Jonathan, and Saul swore, "*As* the Lord lives, he shall not be killed." [7]Then Jonathan called David, and Jonathan told him all these things. So Jonathan brought David to Saul, and he was in his presence [k]as in times past.

[8]And there was war again; and David went out and fought with the Philistines, [l]and struck them with a mighty blow, and they fled from him.

[9]Now [m]the distressing spirit from the Lord came upon Saul as he sat in his house with his spear in his hand. And David was playing *music* with *his* hand. [10]Then Saul sought to pin David to the wall with the spear, but he slipped away from Saul's presence; and he drove the spear into the wall. So David fled and escaped that night.

[11][n]Saul also sent messengers to David's house to watch him and to kill him in the morning. And Michal, David's wife, told him, saying, "If you do not save your life tonight, tomorrow you will be killed." [12]So Michal [o]let David down through a window. And he went and fled and escaped. [13]And Michal took an image and laid *it* in the bed, put a cover of goats' *hair* for his head, and covered *it* with clothes. [14]So when Saul

---

18:25 *dowry.* A sum of money, about fifty shekels (Deut. 22:29), was paid by the bridegroom to the father of the bride as economic compensation for the loss of a daughter.

18:30 *more wisely than all.* David's wise actions contrast significantly with Saul's foolish actions (13:13).

18:30 Wisdom—David was popular, he had even been privately anointed to be the next king, and Saul had just thrown a spear at him. Yet David did nothing to take justice in his own hands. He remained calm and loyal. It is clear that David decided very early in the time after he was anointed that if he became king, it would have to be totally by the hand of God. He would do nothing to destroy the man that God had previously anointed king. Historically we can see what a very wise choice this was, but it must have been very difficult for David to choose the path of

wisdom when he could have raised the power of the people to his side so easily.

19:11 *tomorrow you will be killed.* The story of David's escape is alluded to in the title of Psalm 59.

19:12 *Michal let David down through a window.* Saul had imagined that Michal would be loyal to him and a snare to David. But she loved David, and her loyalty was to her husband.

18:21 [b] 1 Sam. 18:17 [c] 1 Sam. 18:26   **18:25** [d] Ex. 22:17
[e] 1 Sam. 14:24 [f] 1 Sam. 18:17   **18:26** [g] 1 Sam. 18:21
18:27 [h] 1 Sam. 18:13 [i] 2 Sam. 3:14   **18:30** [j] 2 Sam.
11:1 [k] 1 Sam. 18:5   **19:1** [a] 1 Sam. 8:8, 9 [b] 1 Sam.
18:1   **19:3** [c] 1 Sam. 20:8–13   **19:4** [d] [Prov. 31:8, 9]
[e] [Prov. 17:13]   **19:5** [f] Judg. 9:17; 12:3 [g] 1 Sam. 17:49,
50 [h] 1 Sam. 11:13 [i] 1 Sam. 20:32 [j] [Deut. 19:10–13]
19:7 [k] 1 Sam. 16:21; 18:2, 10, 13   **19:8** [l] 1 Sam. 18:27;
23:5 **19:9** [m] 1 Sam. 16:14; 18:10, 11   **19:11** [n] Ps. 59:title
19:12 [o] Josh. 2:15

sent messengers to take David, she said, "He *is* sick."

15 Then Saul sent the messengers *back* to see David, saying, "Bring him up to me in the bed, that I may kill him." 16 And when the messengers had come in, there was the image in the bed, with a cover of goats' *hair* for his head. 17 Then Saul said to Michal, "Why have you deceived me like this, and sent my enemy away, so that he has escaped?"

And Michal answered Saul, "He said to me, 'Let me go! *p*Why should I kill you?'"

18 So David fled and escaped, and went to *q*Samuel at *r*Ramah, and told him all that Saul had done to him. And he and Samuel went and stayed in Naioth. 19 Now it was told Saul, saying, "Take note, David *is* at Naioth in Ramah!" 20 Then *s*Saul sent messengers to take David. *t*And when they saw the group of prophets prophesying, and Samuel standing *as* leader over them, the Spirit of God came upon the messengers of Saul, and they also *u*prophesied. 21 And when Saul was told, he sent other messengers, and they prophesied likewise. Then Saul sent messengers again the third time, and they prophesied also. 22 Then he also went to Ramah, and came to the great well that *is* at Sechu. So he asked, and said, "Where *are* Samuel and David?"

And *someone* said, "Indeed *they are* at Naioth in Ramah." 23 So he went there to Naioth in Ramah. Then *v*the Spirit of God was upon him also, and he went on and prophesied until he came to Naioth in Ramah. 24*w*And he also stripped off his clothes and prophesied before Samuel in like manner, and lay down *x*naked all that day and all that night. Therefore they say, *y*"*Is* Saul also among the prophets?"*

Jonathan's Loyalty to David

20 Then David fled from Naioth in Ramah, and went and said to Jonathan, "What have I done? What *is* my iniquity, and what *is* my sin before your father, that he seeks my life?"

2 So Jonathan said to him, "By no means! You shall not die! Indeed, my father will do nothing either great or small without first telling me. And why should my father hide this thing from me? It *is* not *so!*"

3 Then David took an oath again, and said, "Your father certainly knows that I

have found favor in your eyes, and he has said, 'Do not let Jonathan know this, lest he be grieved.' But *a*truly, *as* the LORD lives and *as* your soul lives, *there is* but a step between me and death."

4 So Jonathan said to David, "Whatever you yourself desire, I will do *it* for you."

5 And David said to Jonathan, "Indeed tomorrow *is* the *b*New Moon, and I should not fail to sit with the king to eat. But let me go, that I may *c*hide in the field until the third *day* at evening. 6 If your father misses me at all, then say, 'David earnestly asked *permission* of me that he might run over *d*to Bethlehem, his city, for *there is* a yearly sacrifice there for all the family.' 7*e*If he says thus: '*It is* well,' your servant will be safe. But if he is very angry, be sure that *f*evil is determined by him. 8 Therefore you shall *g*deal kindly with your servant, for *h*you have brought your servant into a covenant of the LORD with you. Nevertheless, *i*if there is iniquity in me, kill me yourself, for why should you bring me to your father?"

9 But Jonathan said, "Far be it from you! For if I knew certainly that evil was determined by my father to come upon you, then would I not tell you?"

10 Then David said to Jonathan, "Who will tell me, or what *if* your father answers you roughly?"

11 And Jonathan said to David, "Come, let us go out into the field." So both of them went out into the field. 12 Then Jonathan said to David: "The LORD God of Israel *is* witness! When I have sounded out my father sometime tomorrow, *or* the third *day*, and indeed *there is* good toward David, and I do not send to you and tell you, 13 may *i*the LORD do so and much more to Jonathan. But if it pleases my father to *do* you evil, then I will report it to you and send you away, that you may go in safety. And *k*the LORD be with you as He has *l*been with my father. 14 And you shall not only show me the kindness of the LORD while I still live, that I may not die; 15 but *m*you shall not cut off your kindness from my house forever, no, not when the LORD has cut off every one of the enemies of David from the face of the earth." 16 So Jonathan made *a* covenant with the house of David, *saying,*

---

* **19:24** Compare 1 Samuel 10:12

20:5 *tomorrow is the New Moon.* The first day of the month, the New Moon, was observed as a religious festival (Num. 10:10; 28:11–15). It was celebrated with a sacrificial meal and rest from work.

20:6 *yearly sacrifice.* Apparently Jesse's family gathered for a special time of worship during the New Moon celebration.

20:16–17 *Love*—The love and loyalty displayed by Jonathan to David is unparalleled among human relationships in the Bible. He was a living example of the New Testament phrase, "does not seek its own"

(1 Cor. 13:5). In protecting David from the murderous plots of Saul, Jonathan was in reality closing the door

19:17 *p* 2 Sam. 2:22 **19:18** *q* 1 Sam. 16:13 *r* 1 Sam. 7:17 **19:20** *s* John 7:32 *t* 1 Sam. 10:5, 6, 10 *u* Joel 2:28 **19:23** *v* 1 Sam. 10:10 **19:24** *w* Is. 20:2 *x* Mic. 1:8 *y* 1 Sam. 10:10–12 **20:3** *a* 1 Sam. 27:1 **20:5** *b* Num. 10:10; 28:11–15 *c* 1 Sam. 19:2, 3 **20:6** *d* 1 Sam. 16:4; 17:12 **20:7** *e* 2 Sam. 17:4 *f* 1 Sam. 25:17 **20:8** *g* Josh. 2:14 *h* 1 Sam. 18:3; 20:16; 23:18 *i* 2 Sam. 14:32 **20:13** *j* Ruth 1:17 *k* Josh. 1:5 *l* 1 Sam. 10:7 **20:15** *m* 2 Sam. 9:1, 3, 7; 21:7

[n]"Let the LORD require *it* at the hand of David's enemies."

¹⁷Now Jonathan again caused David to vow, because he loved him; [o]for he loved him as he loved his own soul. ¹⁸Then Jonathan said to David, [p]"Tomorrow *is* the New Moon; and you will be missed, because your seat will be empty. ¹⁹And *when* you have stayed three days, go down quickly and come to [q]the place where you hid on the day of the deed; and remain by the stone Ezel. ²⁰Then I will shoot three arrows to the side, as though I shot at a target; ²¹and there I will send a lad, *saying,* 'Go, find the arrows.' If I expressly say to the lad, 'Look, the arrows *are* on this side of you; get them and come'— then, [r]as the LORD lives, *there is* safety for you and no harm. ²²But if I say thus to the young man, 'Look, the arrows *are* beyond you'—go your way, for the LORD has sent you away. ²³And as for [s]the matter which you and I have spoken of, indeed the LORD *be* between you and me forever."

²⁴Then David hid in the field. And when the New Moon had come, the king sat down to eat the feast. ²⁵Now the king sat on his seat, as at other times, on a seat by the wall. And Jonathan arose,* and Abner sat by Saul's side, but David's place was empty. ²⁶Nevertheless Saul did not say anything that day, for he thought, "Something has happened to him; he *is* unclean, surely he *is* [t]unclean." ²⁷And it happened the next day, the second *day* of the month, that David's place was empty. And Saul said to Jonathan his son, "Why has the son of Jesse not come to eat, either yesterday or today?"

²⁸So Jonathan [u]answered Saul, "David earnestly asked *permission* of me *to go* to Bethlehem. ²⁹And he said, 'Please let me go, for our family has a sacrifice in the city, and my brother has commanded me *to be there.* And now, if I have found favor in your eyes, please let me get away and see my brothers.' Therefore he has not come to the king's table."

³⁰Then Saul's anger was aroused against Jonathan, and he said to him, "You son of a perverse, rebellious *woman!* Do I not know that you have chosen the son of Jesse to your own shame and to the shame of your mother's nakedness? ³¹For as long as the son of Jesse lives on the earth, you shall not be established, nor your kingdom. Now therefore, send and bring him to me, for he shall surely die."

³²And Jonathan answered Saul his father, and said to him, [v]"Why should he be killed? What has he done?" ³³Then Saul [w]cast a spear at him to kill him, [x]by which Jonathan knew that it was determined by his father to kill David.

³⁴So Jonathan arose from the table in fierce anger, and ate no food the second day of the month, for he was grieved for David, because his father had treated him shamefully.

³⁵And so it was, in the morning, that Jonathan went out into the field at the time appointed with David, and a little lad *was* with him. ³⁶Then he said to his lad, "Now run, find the arrows which I shoot." As the lad ran, he shot an arrow beyond him. ³⁷When the lad had come to the place where the arrow was which Jonathan had shot, Jonathan cried out after the lad and said, "*Is* not the arrow beyond you?" ³⁸And Jonathan cried out after the lad, "Make haste, hurry, do not delay!" So Jonathan's lad gathered up the arrows and came back to his master. ³⁹But the lad did not know anything. Only Jonathan and David knew of the matter. ⁴⁰Then Jonathan gave his weapons to his lad, and said to him, "Go, carry *them* to the city."

⁴¹As soon as the lad had gone, David arose from *a place* toward the south, fell on his face to the ground, and bowed down three times. And they kissed one another; and they wept together, but David more so. ⁴²Then Jonathan said to David, [y]"Go in peace, since we have both sworn in the name of the LORD, saying, 'May the LORD be between you and me, and between your descendants and my descendants, forever.'" So he arose and departed, and Jonathan went into the city.

---

* **20:25** Following Masoretic Text, Syriac, Targum, and Vulgate; Septuagint reads *he sat across from Jonathan.*

---

to his own possible reign over Israel after his father's death. Jonathan knew this, but his faithfulness to David continued until his death on a battlefield (1 Sam. 31:2).

20:16 Let the LORD require it. Jonathan prayed that the Lord would hold David accountable to the obligations of the covenant.

20:30 to the shame of your mother's nakedness. This was a way of saying that Jonathan shamed his mother who conceived him by maintaining loyalty to David. It was a slur on Jonathan, and a slur on his mother.

20:31 Justice—If David had been taking matters into his own hands, and making moves to secure the kingdom for himself, perhaps Saul would have been justified in seeking David's life. But Saul could charge David with no wrongdoing. Saul was enraged at David, at Jonathan, and in rebellion against God. Because he was driven by anger, Saul could no longer see the injustice in his own thinking.

20:16 [n] 1 Sam. 25:22; 31:2 **20:17** [o] 1 Sam. 18:1 **20:18** [p] 1 Sam. 20:5, 24 **20:19** [q] 1 Sam. 19:2 **20:21** [r] Jer. 4:2 **20:23** [s] 1 Sam. 20:14, 15 **20:26** [t] Lev. 7:20, 21; 15:5 **20:28** [u] 1 Sam. 20:6 **20:32** [v] Gen. 31:36 **20:33** [w] 1 Sam. 18:11; 19:10 [x] 1 Sam. 20:7 **20:42** [y] 1 Sam. 1:17

David and the Holy Bread

21 Now David came to Nob, to Ahim-elech the priest. And ^aAhimelech was ^bafraid when he met David, and said to him, "Why *are* you alone, and no one is with you?"

²So David said to Ahimelech the priest, "The king has ordered me on some busi-ness, and said to me, 'Do not let anyone know anything about the business on which I send you, or what I have command-ed you.' And I have directed *my* young men to such and such a place. ³Now therefore, what have you on hand? Give *me* five *loaves of* bread in my hand, or whatever can be found."

⁴And the priest answered David and said, "*There is* no common bread on hand; but there is ^choly bread, ^dif the young men have at least kept themselves from women."

⁵Then David answered the priest, and said to him, "Truly, women *have been* kept from us about three days since I came out. And the ^evessels of the young men are holy, and *the bread is* in effect common, even though it was consecrated ^fin the vessel this day."

⁶So the priest ^ggave him holy *bread;* for there was no bread there but the show-bread ^hwhich had been taken from before the LORD, in order to put hot bread *in its place* on the day when it was taken away.

⁷Now a certain man of the servants of Saul *was* there that day, detained before the LORD. And his name *was* ⁱDoeg, an Edomite, the chief of the herdsmen who *belonged* to Saul.

⁸And David said to Ahimelech, "Is there not here on hand a spear or a sword? For I have brought neither my sword nor my weapons with me, because the king's busi-ness required haste."

⁹So the priest said, "The sword of Goliath the Philistine, whom you killed in ^jthe Valley of Elah, ^kthere it is, wrapped in a cloth behind the ephod. If you will take that, take *it.* For *there is* no other except that one here."

And David said, "*There is* none like it; give it to me."

David Flees to Gath

¹⁰Then David arose and fled that day from before Saul, and went to Achish the king of Gath. ¹¹And ^lthe servants of Achish said to him, "*Is* this not David the king of the land? Did they not sing of him to one another in dances, saying:

^m'Saul has slain his thousands,
And David his ten thousands'?"*

¹²Now David ⁿtook these words to heart, and was very much afraid of Achish the king of Gath. ¹³So ^ohe changed his be-havior before them, pretended madness in their hands, scratched on the doors of the gate, and let his saliva fall down on his beard. ¹⁴Then Achish said to his servants, "Look, you see the man is insane. Why have you brought him to me? ¹⁵Have I need of madmen, that you have brought this *fel-low* to play the madman in my presence? Shall this *fellow* come into my house?"

David's Four Hundred Men

22 David therefore departed from there and ^aescaped ^bto the cave of Adul-lam. So when his brothers and all his father's house heard *it,* they went down there to him. ²^cAnd everyone *who was* in distress, everyone who *was* in debt, and everyone *who was* discontented gathered to him. So he became captain over them.

---

* **21:11** Compare 1 Samuel 18:7

21:1 *Nob.* Nob was a Levitical community in Benja-min where the tabernacle was located after it was in Shiloh. ***Ahimelech.*** Ahimelech, the great-grandson of Eli, was serving as high priest.
21:4 *no common bread.* Ahimelech explained that the only bread available was holy bread, sometimes called the "showbread," which had been displayed before the Lord in the tabernacle (Ex. 25:30; Lev. 24:5–9). According to God's law, this bread could be eaten only by priests.
21:6 *gave him holy bread.* This was the bread that had been displayed before the Lord for a week, and was removed for fresh bread. In giving the bread to David, Ahimelech broke the law, yet in his compas-sion he kept the spirit of the law. Jesus referred to this incident when He explained to the Pharisees that it was all right to pick grain to eat on the Sabbath (Matt. 12:2–4).
21:7 *detained before the LORD.* Apparently Doeg, although he was not an Israelite, was at the taberna-cle under a spiritual vow.
21:10 *Gath.* Gath was one of the five major cities of the Philistines (6:17).
21:12–13 *Achish the king of Gath.* These verses

provide the background for Psalms 34 and 56. In Psalm 34 Achish is referred to as Abimelech, which was apparently a dynastic title used by the Philistine rulers (Gen. 26:1).
22:1 *cave of Adullam.* The cave near the city of Adul-lam was about ten miles southeast of Gath and six-teen miles southwest of Jerusalem. It was here that David composed Psalm 142, and possibly Psalm 57.
22:2 *everyone who was in distress . . . debt.* The men who gathered around David were not so much taking sides with him as escaping Saul. The sense of desolation in Psalm 142:4 reflects David's feeling of being all alone. ***became captain over them.*** Never-theless, David organized them, governed them, and made them into a loyal and obedient unit.

21:1 ^a 1 Sam. 14:3 ^b 1 Sam. 16:4 **21:4** ^c Lev. 24:5–9 ^d Ex. 19:15 **21:5** ^e 1 Thess. 4:4 ^f Lev. 8:26 **21:6** ^g Luke 6:3, 4 ^h Lev. 24:8, 9 **21:7** ⁱ 1 Sam. 14:47; 22:9 **21:9** ^j 1 Sam. 17:2, 50 ^k 1 Sam. 31:10 **21:11** ^l Ps. 56:title ^m 1 Sam. 18:6–8; 29:5 **21:12** ⁿ Luke 2:19 **21:13** ^o Ps. 34:title **22:1** ^a Ps. 57:title; 142:title ^b 2 Sam. 23:13 **22:2** ^c Judg. 11:3

And there were about ᵈfour hundred men with him.

³Then David went from there to Mizpah of ᵉMoab; and he said to the king of Moab, "Please let my father and mother come here with you, till I know what God will do for me." ⁴So he brought them before the king of Moab, and they dwelt with him all the time that David was in the stronghold.

⁵Now the prophet ᶠGad said to David, "Do not stay in the stronghold; depart, and go to the land of Judah." So David departed and went into the forest of Hereth.

Saul Murders the Priests

⁶When Saul heard that David and the men who *were* with him had been discovered—now Saul was staying in ᵍGibeah under a tamarisk tree in Ramah, with his spear in his hand, and all his servants standing about him—⁷then Saul said to his servants who stood about him, "Hear now, you Benjamites! Will the son of Jesse ʰgive every one of you fields and vineyards, *and* make you all captains of thousands and captains of hundreds? ⁸All of you have conspired against me, and *there is* no one who reveals to me that ⁱmy son has made a covenant with the son of Jesse; and *there is* not one of you who is sorry for me or reveals to me that my son has stirred up my servant against me, to lie in wait, as *it is* this day."

⁹Then answered ʲDoeg the Edomite, who was set over the servants of Saul, and said, "I saw the son of Jesse going to Nob, to ᵏAhimelech the son of ˡAhitub. ¹⁰ᵐAnd he inquired of the LORD for him, ⁿgave him provisions, and gave him the sword of Goliath the Philistine."

¹¹So the king sent to call Ahimelech the priest, the son of Ahitub, and all his father's house, the priests who *were* in Nob. And they all came to the king. ¹²And Saul said, "Hear now, son of Ahitub!"

He answered, "Here I am, my lord."

¹³Then Saul said to him, "Why have you conspired against me, you and the son of Jesse, in that you have given him bread and a sword, and have inquired of God for him, that he should rise against me, to lie in wait, as it is this day?"

¹⁴So Ahimelech answered the king and said, "And who among all your servants *is as* ᵒfaithful as David, who is the king's son-in-law, who goes at your bidding, and is honorable in your house? ¹⁵Did I then begin to inquire of God for him? Far be it from me! Let not the king impute anything to his servant, *or* to any in the house of my father. For your servant knew nothing of all this, little or much."

¹⁶And the king said, "You shall surely die, Ahimelech, you and all ᵖyour father's house!" ¹⁷Then the king said to the guards who stood about him, "Turn and kill the priests of the LORD, because their hand also *is* with David, and because they knew when he fled and did not tell it to me." But the servants of the king �q would not lift their hands to strike the priests of the LORD. ¹⁸And the king said to Doeg, "You turn and kill the priests!" So Doeg the Edomite turned and struck the priests, and ʳkilled on that day eighty-five men who wore a linen ephod. ¹⁹ˢAlso Nob, the city of the priests, he struck with the edge of the sword, both men and women, children and nursing infants, oxen and donkeys and sheep—with the edge of the sword.

²⁰ᵗNow one of the sons of Ahimelech the son of Ahitub, named Abiathar, ᵘescaped and fled after David. ²¹And Abiathar told David that Saul had killed the LORD's priests. ²²So David said to Abiathar, "I knew that day, when Doeg the Edomite *was* there, that he would surely tell Saul. I have caused *the death* of all the persons of your father's house. ²³Stay with me; do not fear. ᵛFor he who seeks my life seeks your life, but with me you *shall be* safe."

David Saves the City of Keilah

23 Then they told David, saying, "Look, the Philistines are fighting against ᵃKeilah, and they are robbing the threshing floors."

²Therefore David ᵇinquired of the LORD, saying, "Shall I go and attack these Philistines?"

And the LORD said to David, "Go and attack the Philistines, and save Keilah."

³But David's men said to him, "Look, we are afraid here in Judah. How much more then if we go to Keilah against the armies of the Philistines?" ⁴Then David inquired of the LORD once again.

And the LORD answered him and said, "Arise, go down to Keilah. For I will deliver the Philistines into your hand." ⁵And David and his men went to Keilah and ᶜfought with the Philistines, struck them with a mighty blow, and took away their livestock. So David saved the inhabitants of Keilah.

⁶Now it happened, when Abiathar the

22:18 Doeg. Only Doeg, who was a descendant of Esau, but not an Israelite, was willing to kill the priests of the living God.

22:22 I have caused the death. David felt responsible for the death of the priests and their families because he knew that he was jeopardizing them by receiving help from them. He knew Doeg would betray him, and he felt that he should have done something to prevent this or to warn the priests.

22:2 ᵈ 1 Sam. 25:13 **22:3** ᵉ 2 Sam. 8:2 **22:5** ᶠ 2 Sam. 24:11 **22:6** ᵍ 1 Sam. 15:34 **22:7** ʰ 1 Sam. 8:14 **22:8** ⁱ 1 Sam. 18:3; 20:16, 30 **22:9** ʲ 1 Sam. 21:7; 22:22 ᵏ 1 Sam. 21:1 ˡ 1 Sam. 14:3 **22:10** ᵐ Num. 27:21 ⁿ 1 Sam. 21:6, 9 **22:14** ᵒ 1 Sam. 19:4, 5; 20:32; 24:11 **22:16** ᵖ Deut. 24:16 **22:17** �q Ex. 1:17 **22:18** ʳ 1 Sam. 2:31 **22:19** ˢ 1 Sam. 22:9, 11 **22:20** ᵗ 1 Sam. 23:6, 9; 30:7 ᵘ 1 Sam. 2:33 **22:23** ᵛ 1 Kin. 2:26 **23:1** ᵃ Josh. 15:44 **23:2** ᵇ 2 Sam. 5:19, 23 **23:5** ᶜ 1 Sam. 19:8

son of Ahimelech ^dfled to David at Keilah, *that* he went down *with* an ephod in his hand.

7And Saul was told that David had gone to Keilah. So Saul said, "God has delivered him into my hand, for he has shut himself in by entering a town that has gates and bars." 8Then Saul called all the people together for war, to go down to Keilah to besiege David and his men.

9When David knew that Saul plotted evil against him, ^ehe said to Abiathar the priest, "Bring the ephod here." 10Then David said, "O LORD God of Israel, Your servant has certainly heard that Saul seeks to come to Keilah ^fto destroy the city for my sake. 11Will the men of Keilah deliver me into his hand? Will Saul come down, as Your servant has heard? O LORD God of Israel, I pray, tell Your servant."

And the LORD said, "He will come down."

12Then David said, "Will the men of Keilah deliver me and my men into the hand of Saul?"

And the LORD said, "They will deliver *you.*"

13So David and his men, ^gabout six hundred, arose and departed from Keilah and went wherever they could go. Then it was told Saul that David had escaped from Keilah; so he halted the expedition.

David in Wilderness Strongholds

14And David stayed in strongholds in the wilderness, and remained in ^hthe mountains in the Wilderness of ⁱZiph. Saul ^jsought him every day, but God did not deliver him into his hand. 15So David saw that Saul had come out to seek his life. And David *was* in the Wilderness of Ziph in a forest.* 16Then Jonathan, Saul's son, arose and went to David in the woods and strengthened his hand in God. 17And he said to him, ^k"Do not fear, for the hand of Saul my father shall not find you. You shall be king over Israel, and I shall be next to you. ^lEven my father Saul knows that." 18So

the two of them ^mmade a covenant before the LORD. And David stayed in the woods, and Jonathan went to his own house.

19Then the Ziphites ⁿcame up to Saul at Gibeah, saying, "Is David not hiding with us in strongholds in the woods, in the hill of Hachilah, which *is* on the south of Jeshimon? 20Now therefore, O king, come down according to all the desire of your soul to come down; and ^oour part *shall be* to deliver him into the king's hand."

21And Saul said, "Blessed *are* you of the LORD, for you have compassion on me. 22Please go and find out for sure, and see the place where his hideout is, *and* who has seen him there. For I am told he is very crafty. 23See therefore, and take knowledge of all the lurking places where he hides; and come back to me with certainty, and I will go with you. And it shall be, if he is in the land, that I will search for him throughout all the clans* of Judah."

24So they arose and went to Ziph before Saul. But David and his men *were* in the Wilderness ^pof Maon, in the plain on the south of Jeshimon. 25When Saul and his men went to seek *him,* they told David. Therefore he went down to the rock, and stayed in the Wilderness of Maon. And when Saul heard *that,* he pursued David in the Wilderness of Maon. 26Then Saul went on one side of the mountain, and David and his men on the other side of the mountain. ^qSo David made haste to get away from Saul, for Saul and his men ^rwere encircling David and his men to take them.

27sBut a messenger came to Saul, saying, "Hurry and come, for the Philistines have invaded the land!" 28Therefore Saul returned from pursuing David, and went against the Philistines; so they called that place the Rock of Escape.* 29Then David went up from there and dwelt in strongholds at ^tEn Gedi.

---

* 23:15 Or *in Horesh*   * 23:23 Literally *thousands*
* 23:28 Hebrew *Sela Hammahlekoth*

23:14 *Wilderness of Ziph.* This barren region about four miles southeast of Hebron had many caves and ravines in which David and his men could hide.

23:16–18 *strengthened his hand in God.* Visiting David was risky, for Saul considered David his enemy. Jonathan was treading a narrow line between following his own convictions and obeying his father. He had a fervent love for God, and encouraged David to continue in his obedient walk with the Lord at a time when David must have been feeling very discouraged and alone.

23:17–18 *Love*—Love "rejoices in the truth" (1 Cor. 13:6). Jonathan had the happy faculty of delighting in the Lord's plan. He is never seen comparing his role with David's role, but he continually encouraged David to live up to the great responsibility that God had given him. Jonathan was the kind of friend that we all need and seldom find. If we want to put love

into action, we can look at Jonathan and rejoice with our friends over the great favor God has shown them, encourage them to remain faithful to their calling, and remind them that we will be "next to them," if not in fact, then in prayer.

23:19 *Jeshimon.* Jeshimon is the barren wilderness of Judah.

23:19–29 *Is David not hiding with us.* The background for Psalm 54 is David's narrow escape from being captured by Saul.

23:6 ^d 1 Sam. 22:20   **23:9** ^e 1 Sam. 23:6; 30:7   **23:10** ^f 1 Sam. 22:19   **23:13** ^g 1 Sam. 22:2; 25:13   **23:14** ^h Ps. 11:1 ⁱ Josh. 15:55 ^j Ps. 32:7; 54:3, 4   **23:17** ^k [Heb. 13:6] ^l 1 Sam. 20:31; 24:20   **23:18** ^m 2 Sam. 9:1; 21:7   **23:19** ⁿ 1 Sam. 26:1   **23:20** ^o Ps. 54:3   **23:24** ^p 1 Sam. 25:2   **23:26** ^q Ps. 31:22 ^r Ps. 17:9   **23:27** ^s 2 Kin. 19:9   **23:29** ^t 2 Chr. 20:2

David Spares Saul

24 Now it happened, *a*when Saul had returned from following the Philistines, that it was told him, saying, "Take note! David *is* in the Wilderness of En Gedi." ²Then Saul took three thousand chosen men from all Israel, and *b*went to seek David and his men on the Rocks of the Wild Goats. ³So he came to the sheepfolds by the road, where there *was* a cave; and *c*Saul went in to *d*attend to his needs. (*e*David and his men were staying in the recesses of the cave.) *4f*Then the men of David said to him, "This is the day of which the LORD said to you, 'Behold, I will deliver your enemy into your hand, that you may do to him as it seems good to you.'" And David arose and secretly cut off a corner of Saul's robe. ⁵Now it happened afterward that *g*David's heart troubled him because he had cut Saul's robe. ⁶And he said to his men, *h*"The LORD forbid that I should do this thing to my master, the LORD's anointed, to stretch out my hand against him, seeing he *is* the anointed of the LORD." ⁷So David *i*restrained his servants with *these* words, and did not allow them to rise against Saul. And Saul got up from the cave and went on *his* way.

⁸David also arose afterward, went out of the cave, and called out to Saul, saying, "My lord the king!" And when Saul looked behind him, David stooped with his face to the earth, and bowed down. ⁹And David said to Saul: *j*"Why do you listen to the words of men who say, 'Indeed David seeks your harm'? ¹⁰Look, this day your eyes have seen that the LORD delivered you today into my hand in the cave, and *someone* urged *me* to kill you. But *my eye* spared you, and I said, 'I will not stretch out my hand against my lord, for he *is* the LORD's anointed.' ¹¹Moreover, my father, see! Yes, see the corner of your robe in my hand! For in that I cut off the corner of your robe, and did not kill you, know and see that *there is* *k*neither evil nor rebellion in my hand, and I have not sinned

against you. Yet you *l*hunt my life to take it. ¹²*m*Let the LORD judge between you and me, and let the LORD avenge me on you. But my hand shall not be against you. ¹³As the proverb of the ancients says, *n*'Wickedness proceeds from the wicked.' But my hand shall not be against you. ¹⁴After whom has the king of Israel come out? Whom do you pursue? *o*A dead dog? *p*A flea? ¹⁵*q*Therefore let the LORD be judge, and judge between you and me, and *r*see and *s*plead my case, and deliver me out of your hand."

¹⁶So it was, when David had finished speaking these words to Saul, that Saul said, *t*"Is this your voice, my son David?" And Saul lifted up his voice and wept. ¹⁷*u*Then he said to David: "You *are* *v*more righteous than I; for *w*you have rewarded me with good, whereas I have rewarded you with evil. ¹⁸And you have shown this day how you have dealt well with me; for when *x*the LORD delivered me into your hand, you did not kill me. ¹⁹For if a man finds his enemy, will he let him get away safely? Therefore may the LORD reward you with good for what you have done to me this day. ²⁰And now *y*I know indeed that you shall surely be king, and that the kingdom of Israel shall be established in your hand. ²¹*z*Therefore swear now to me by the LORD *a*that you will not cut off my descendants after me, and that you will not destroy my name from my father's house."

²²So David swore to Saul. And Saul went home, but David and his men went up to *b*the stronghold.

Death of Samuel

25 Then *a*Samuel died; and the Israelites gathered together and *b*lamented for him, and buried him at his home in Ramah. And David arose and went down *c*to the Wilderness of Paran.*

---

* **25:1** Following Masoretic Text, Syriac, Targum, and Vulgate; Septuagint reads *Maon.*

24:3 *sheepfolds.* At night shepherds in the wild area would gather their sheep into a protective rock enclosure. A low stone wall would keep the sheep from wandering, and the shepherd would position himself at the entrance to keep guard. Often a cave with a wall built across its mouth served as a sheepcote.

24:10–12 *Mercy*—David does not say the words, "I forgive you," in this passage, but he speaks as one who has forgiven Saul for his foolish and violent acts against himself. A big part of forgiving an unrepentant individual is deliberately putting the whole situation in God's hands, knowing that it is only God who can judge rightly. God will vindicate the innocent, and punish the guilty, if necessary.

24:12 *my hand shall not be against you.* David knew that the Lord had anointed him to be the king to succeed Saul, and Saul knew it too. Saul, probably thinking of how he himself would have responded, was sure that David would seize power and oust him with trickery and violence. David had to prove to Saul

that he was not going to harm him, and the only way to do this was to turn down every opportunity he had to kill the king. It was God's job, and His alone, to arrange the transfer of power from Saul to David.

24:22 *David swore to Saul.* David agreed to Saul's requests, and he kept his promise (2 Sam. 9:1–13; 21:1–14), as Saul knew he would. However, David had no great confidence in the lasting value of Saul's expressions of remorse, so David remained in hiding.

24:1 *a* 1 Sam. 23:19, 28, 29   **24:2** *b* 1 Sam. 26:2   **24:3** *c* 1 Sam. 24:10   *d* Judg. 3:24   *e* Ps. 57:title; 142:title   **24:4** *f* 1 Sam. 26:8–11   **24:5** *g* 2 Sam. 24:10   **24:6** *h* 1 Sam. 26:11   **24:7** *i* [Matt. 5:44]   **24:9** *j* Ps. 141:6   **24:11** *k* Ps. 7:3; 35:7   *l* 1 Sam. 26:20   **24:12** *m* 1 Sam. 26:10–23   **24:13** *n* [Matt. 7:16–20]   **24:14** *o* 2 Sam. 9:8   *p* 1 Sam. 26:20   **24:15** *q* 1 Sam. 24:12   *r* 2 Chr. 24:22   *s* Ps. 35:1; 43:1; 119:154   **24:16** *t* 1 Sam. 26:17   **24:17** *u* 1 Sam. 26:21   *v* Gen. 38:26   *w* [Matt. 5:44]   **24:18** *x* 1 Sam. 26:23   **24:20** *y* 1 Sam. 23:17   **24:21** *z* Gen. 21:23   *a* 2 Sam. 21:6–8   **24:22** *b* 1 Sam. 23:29   **25:1** *a* 1 Sam. 28:3   *b* Deut. 34:8   *c* Gen. 21:21

David and the Wife of Nabal

2Now *there was* a man *d*in Maon whose business *was* in *e*Carmel, and the man *was* very rich. He had three thousand sheep and a thousand goats. And he was shearing his sheep in Carmel. 3The name of the man *was* Nabal, and the name of his wife Abigail. And *she was* a woman of good understanding and beautiful appearance; but the man *was* harsh and evil in *his* doings. He *was of the house of* *f*Caleb.

4When David heard in the wilderness that Nabal was *g*shearing his sheep, 5David sent ten young men; and David said to the young men, "Go up to Carmel, go to Nabal, and greet him in my name. 6And thus you shall say to him who lives in prosperity: *h*'Peace *be* to you, peace to your house, and peace to all that you have! 7Now I have heard that you have shearers. Your shepherds were with us, and we did not hurt them, *i*nor was there anything missing from them all the while they were in Carmel. 8Ask your young men, and they will tell you. Therefore let *my* young men find favor in your eyes, for we come on *j*a feast day. Please give whatever comes to your hand to your servants and to your son David.'"

9So when David's young men came, they spoke to Nabal according to all these words in the name of David, and waited. 10Then Nabal answered David's servants, and said, *k*"Who *is* David, and who *is* the son of Jesse? There are many servants nowadays who break away each one from his master. 11*l*Shall I then take my bread and my water and my meat that I have killed for my shearers, and give *it* to men when I do not know where they *are* from?"

12So David's young men turned on their heels and went back; and they came and told him all these words. 13Then David said to his men, "Every man gird on his sword." So every man girded on his sword, and David also girded on his sword. And about four hundred men went with David, and two hundred *m*stayed with the supplies.

14Now one of the young men told Abigail, Nabal's wife, saying, "Look, David sent messengers from the wilderness to greet our master; and he reviled them. 15But the men *were* very good to us, and *n*we were not hurt, nor did we miss anything as long as we accompanied them, when we were

in the fields. 16They were *o*a wall to us both by night and day, all the time we were with them keeping the sheep. 17Now therefore, know and consider what you will do, for *p*harm is determined against our master and against all his household. For he *is* such a *q*scoundrel* that *one* cannot speak to him."

18Then Abigail made haste and *r*took two hundred *loaves* of bread, two skins of wine, five sheep already dressed, five seahs of roasted *grain*, one hundred clusters of raisins, and two hundred cakes of figs, and loaded *them* on donkeys. 19And she said to her servants, *s*"Go on before me; see, I am coming after you." But she did not tell her husband Nabal.

20So it was, *as* she rode on the donkey, that she went down under cover of the hill; and there were David and his men, coming down toward her, and she met them. 21Now David had said, "Surely in vain I have protected all that this *fellow* has in the wilderness, so that nothing was missed of all that *belongs* to him. And he has *t*repaid me evil for good. 22*u*May God do so, and more also, to the enemies of David, if I *v*leave *w*one male of all who *belong* to him by morning light."

23Now when Abigail saw David, she *x*dismounted quickly from the donkey, fell on her face before David, and bowed down to the ground. 24So she fell at his feet and said: "On me, my lord, *on me let* this iniquity *be!* And please let your maidservant speak in your ears, and hear the words of your maidservant. 25Please, let not my lord regard this scoundrel Nabal. For as his name *is*, so *is* he: Nabal* *is* his name, and folly *is* with him! But I, your maidservant, did not see the young men of my lord whom you sent. 26Now therefore, my lord, *y*as the LORD lives and *as* your soul lives, since the LORD has *z*held you back from coming to bloodshed and from *a*avenging yourself with your own hand, now then, *b*let your enemies and those who seek harm for my lord be as Nabal. 27And now *c*this present which your maidservant has brought to my lord, let it be given to the young men who follow my lord. 28Please forgive the trespass of your maidservant. For *d*the

---

* **25:17** Literally *son of Belial*　* **25:25** Literally *Fool*

25:2 *Maon.* Located in the Judean hill country, Maon was about eight miles south of Hebron. ***Carmel.*** Carmel was located on the edge of the Judean wilderness, about a mile north of Maon. ***shearing his sheep.*** Like the times of harvest, sheep shearing was a festive occasion.

25:21 *repaid me evil for good.* Saul had returned David evil for good, and David refrained from retaliation. But Nabal's insult did not meet with such forbearance. David's fierce response is actually a response of the natural man, and as such gives an

25:2 *d* 1 Sam. 23:24 *e* Josh. 15:55　**25:3** *f* Josh. 15:13 **25:4** *g* Gen. 38:13　**25:6** *h* 1 Chr. 12:18　**25:7** *i* 1 Sam. 25:15, 21　**25:8** *j* Esth. 8:17; 9:19, 22　**25:10** *k* Judg. 9:28　**25:11** *l* Judg. 8:6, 15　**25:13** *m* 1 Sam. 30:24　**25:15** *n* 1 Sam. 25:7, 21　**25:16** *o* Ex. 14:22 **25:17** *p* 1 Sam. 20:7　*q* Deut. 13:13　**25:18** *r* Gen. 32:13　**25:19** *s* Gen. 32:16, 20　**25:21** *t* Ps. 109:5 **25:22** *u* 1 Sam. 3:17; 20:13, 16　*v* 1 Sam. 25:34　*w* 1 Kin. 14:10; 21:21　**25:23** *x* Judg. 1:14　**25:26** *y* 2 Kin. 2:2 *z* Gen. 20:6　*a* [Rom. 12:19]　*b* 2 Sam. 18:32　**25:27** *c* Gen. 33:11　**25:28** *d* 2 Sam. 7:11–16, 27

Lord will certainly make for my lord an enduring house, because my lord [e]fights the battles of the Lord, [f]and evil is not found in you throughout your days. 29Yet a man has risen to pursue you and seek your life, but the life of my lord shall be [g]bound in the bundle of the living with the Lord your God; and the lives of your enemies He shall [h]sling out, *as from* the pocket of a sling. 30And it shall come to pass, when the Lord has done for my lord according to all the good that He has spoken concerning you, and has appointed you [i]ruler over Israel, 31that this will be no grief to you, nor offense of heart to my lord, either that you have shed blood without cause, or that my lord has avenged himself. But when the Lord has dealt well with my lord, then remember your maidservant."

32Then David said to Abigail: [j]"Blessed *is* the Lord God of Israel, who sent you this day to meet me! 33And blessed *is* your advice and blessed *are* you, because you have [k]kept me this day from coming to bloodshed and from avenging myself with my own hand. 34For indeed, *as* the Lord God of Israel lives, who has [l]kept me back from hurting you, unless you had hurried and come to meet me, surely [m]by morning light no males would have been left to Nabal!" 35So David received from her hand what she had brought him, and said to her, [n]"Go up in peace to your house. See, I have heeded your voice and [o]respected your person."

36Now Abigail went to Nabal, and there he was, [p]holding a feast in his house, like the feast of a king. And Nabal's heart *was* merry within him, for he *was* very drunk; therefore she told him nothing, little or much, until morning light. 37So it was, in the morning, when the wine had gone from Nabal, and his wife had told him these things, that his heart died within him, and he became *like* a stone. 38Then it happened,

after about ten days, that the Lord [q]struck Nabal, and he died.

39So when David heard that Nabal was dead, he said, [r]"Blessed *be* the Lord, who has [s]pleaded the cause of my reproach from the hand of Nabal, and has [t]kept His servant from evil! For the Lord has [u]returned the wickedness of Nabal on his own head."

And David sent and proposed to Abigail, to take her as his wife. 40When the servants of David had come to Abigail at Carmel, they spoke to her saying, "David sent us to you, to ask you to become his wife."

41Then she arose, bowed her face to the earth, and said, "Here is your maidservant, a servant to [v]wash the feet of the servants of my lord." 42So Abigail rose in haste and rode on a donkey, attended by five of her maidens; and she followed the messengers of David, and became his wife. 43David also took Ahinoam [w]of Jezreel, [x]and so both of them were his wives.

44But Saul had given [y]Michal his daughter, David's wife, to Palti* the son of Laish, who *was* from [z]Gallim.

David Spares Saul a Second Time

26 Now the Ziphites came to Saul at Gibeah, saying, [a]"Is David not hiding in the hill of Hachilah, opposite Jeshimon?" 2Then Saul arose and went down to the Wilderness of Ziph, having [b]three thousand chosen men of Israel with him, to seek David in the Wilderness of Ziph. 3And Saul encamped in the hill of Hachilah, which *is* opposite Jeshimon, by the road. But David stayed in the wilderness, and he saw that Saul came after him into the wilderness. 4David therefore sent out spies, and understood that Saul had indeed come.

5So David arose and came to the place

---

* **25:44** Spelled *Paltiel* in 2 Samuel 3:15

---

even better understanding of the force of David's commitment to restrain his natural response to Saul for the sake of his Lord.
25:29 bound in the bundle of the living with the Lord your God. This metaphor reflects the custom of binding valuables in a bundle to protect them from injury. The point here is that God cares for His own as a man cares for his valuable treasure.
25:30–31 Prudence—Abigail's courageous and gracious intervention saved not only her own household, but all that David had worked so hard to maintain during the years he was a fugitive. It takes more strength of character to restrain oneself than to lash out and return sting for sting. But the bitterness of grief that follows a vicious tongue or a vicious deed is a far heavier burden than suffering an injustice.
25:33 blessed is your advice and blessed are you. David responds to the wisdom of Abigail's entreaty, and he also shows that he knows she came to him without regard to personal risk. Abigail laid out the facts and David responded to her godly counsel because he was accustomed to listening to the Lord, and recognized that she was representing God's point of view.

25:39 the Lord has returned the wickedness. David was very thankful that the Lord had kept him from taking revenge on Nabal, for that would have been evil. But David was also thankful that the Lord, in His justice, had seen fit to punish Nabal. For David this would have been a reminder of his situation with Saul. David was not to touch the Lord's anointed, and the Lord would indeed at some point deal with Saul for trying to take David's life.
26:2 Ziph. Ziph was 4 miles southeast of Hebron, which would have been about 4 or 5 miles from Maon, where Nabal lived.

25:28 [e]1 Sam. 18:17 [f]1 Sam. 24:11 **25:29**[g][Col. 3:3] [h]Jer. 10:18 **25:30**[i]1 Sam. 13:14; 15:28 **25:32**[j]Luke 1:68 **25:33**[k]1 Sam. 25:26 **25:34**[l]1 Sam. 25:26 [m]1 Sam. 25:22 **25:35**[n]2 Kin. 5:19 [o]Gen. 19:21 **25:36**[p]2 Sam. 13:28 **25:38**[q]1 Sam. 26:10 **25:39**[r]1 Sam. 25:32 [s]Prov. 22:23 [t]1 Sam. 25:26, 34 [u]1 Kin. 2:44 **25:41**[v]Luke 7:38, 44 **25:43**[w]Josh. 15:56 [x]1 Sam. 27:3; 30:5 **25:44**[y]2 Sam. 3:14 [z]Is. 10:30 **26:1**[a]1 Sam. 23:19 **26:2**[b]1 Sam. 13:2; 24:2

where Saul had encamped. And David saw the place where Saul lay, and ^cAbner the son of Ner, the commander of his army. Now Saul lay within the camp, with the people encamped all around him. ⁶Then David answered, and said to Ahimelech the Hittite and to Abishai ^dthe son of Zeruiah, brother of ^eJoab, saying, "Who will ^fgo down with me to Saul in the camp?"

And ^gAbishai said, "I will go down with you."

⁷So David and Abishai came to the people by night; and there Saul lay sleeping within the camp, with his spear stuck in the ground by his head. And Abner and the people lay all around him. ⁸Then Abishai said to David, ^h"God has delivered your enemy into your hand this day. Now therefore, please, let me strike him at once with the spear, right to the earth; and I will not have to strike him a second time!"

⁹But David said to Abishai, "Do not destroy him; ⁱfor who can stretch out his hand against the LORD's anointed, and be guiltless?" ¹⁰David said furthermore, "As the LORD lives, ^jthe LORD shall strike him, or ^khis day shall come to die, or he shall ^lgo out to battle and perish. ¹¹^mThe LORD forbid that I should stretch out my hand against the LORD's anointed. But please, take now the spear and the jug of water that are by his head, and let us go." ¹²So David took the spear and the jug of water by Saul's head, and they got away; and no man saw or knew it or awoke. For they were all asleep, because ⁿa deep sleep from the LORD had fallen on them.

¹³Now David went over to the other side, and stood on the top of a hill afar off, a great distance being between them. ¹⁴And David called out to the people and to Abner the son of Ner, saying, "Do you not answer, Abner?"

Then Abner answered and said, "Who are you, calling out to the king?"

¹⁵So David said to Abner, "Are you not a man? And who is like you in Israel? Why then have you not guarded your lord the king? For one of the people came in to destroy your lord the king. ¹⁶This thing that you have done is not good. As the LORD lives, you deserve to die, because you have not guarded your master, the LORD's anointed. And now see where the king's spear is, and the jug of water that was by his head."

¹⁷Then Saul knew David's voice, and said, ^o"Is that your voice, my son David?"

David said, "It is my voice, my lord, O king." ¹⁸And he said, ^p"Why does my lord thus pursue his servant? For what have I done, or what evil is in my hand? ¹⁹Now therefore, please, let my lord the king hear the words of his servant: If the LORD has ^qstirred you up against me, let Him accept an offering. But if it is the children of men, may they be cursed before the LORD, ^rfor they have driven me out this day from sharing in the ^sinheritance of the LORD, saying, 'Go, serve other gods.' ²⁰So now, do not let my blood fall to the earth before the face of the LORD. For the king of Israel has come out to seek ^ta flea, as when one hunts a partridge in the mountains."

²¹Then Saul said, ^u"I have sinned. Return, my son David. For I will harm you no more, because my life was precious in your eyes this day. Indeed I have played the fool and erred exceedingly."

²²And David answered and said, "Here is the king's spear. Let one of the young men come over and get it. ²³^vMay the LORD ^wrepay every man for his righteousness and his faithfulness; for the LORD delivered you into my hand today, but I would not stretch out my hand against the LORD's anointed.

26:6 Abishai. Abishai was David's nephew (1 Chr. 2:16).

26:10 the LORD shall strike him, or . . . to die. David had just been reminded that the Lord could and would deal with his enemies, which strengthened him for his next encounter with Saul. David had not trusted in the value of Saul's expressions of remorse, but it must have been discouraging even so, to be faced with the same relentless pursuit, the same dogged determination to kill him, even though David repeatedly said he would not stretch out his hand against Saul, the king who had been anointed by God.

26:19 If the LORD has stirred you up. David knew that God could bring adverse events into someone's life to turn him to the Lord. If Saul was pursuing David because God wanted him to, God would accept a sin offering from David. But if men had stirred up Saul to kill David, that would be wicked injustice. In that case, David had no hesitation in asking God to curse them. For in driving David out of his homeland, he was effectively cut off from the inheritance of the Lord, which would include the land, the blessings on

the land and people, and the special ways God had ordained for worship and sacrifice.

26:20 partridge. A partridge was known to flee for safety by running rather than fighting. David was reminding Saul that he was not fighting against the king.

26:23 Righteousness—One mark of a righteous person is that he can walk away from a situation where he has a golden chance to get in the last kick. And as he walks away, he says, "Father, forgive him, for he does not know what he is doing." David never lost sight of the fact that this business of being king was God's plan, not his own.

26:5 ^c 1 Sam. 14:50, 51; 17:55 **26:6** ^d 1 Chr. 2:16 ^e 2 Sam. 2:13 ^f Judg. 7:10, 11 ^g 2 Sam. 2:18, 24 **26:8** ^h 1 Sam. 24:4 **26:9** ⁱ 1 Sam. 24:6, 7 **26:10** ^j 1 Sam. 25:26, 38 ^k [Job 7:1; 14:5] ^l 1 Sam. 31:6 **26:11** ^m 1 Sam. 24:6–12 **26:12** ⁿ Gen. 2:21; 15:12 **26:17** ^o 1 Sam. 24:16 **26:18** ^p 1 Sam. 24:9, 11–14 **26:19** ^q 2 Sam. 16:11; 24:1 ^r Deut. 4:27, 28 ^s 2 Sam. 14:16; 20:19 **26:20** ^t 1 Sam. 24:14 **26:21** ^u 1 Sam. 15:24, 30; 24:17 **26:23** ^v Ps. 7:8; 18:20; 62:12 ^w 2 Sam. 22:21

²⁴And indeed, as your life was valued much this day in my eyes, so let my life be valued much in the eyes of the LORD, and let Him deliver me out of all tribulation."

²⁵Then Saul said to David, "*May you be* blessed, my son David! You shall both do great things and also still ˣprevail."

So David went on his way, and Saul returned to his place.

David Allied with the Philistines

27 And David said in his heart, "Now I shall perish someday by the hand of Saul. *There is* nothing better for me than that I should speedily escape to the land of the Philistines; and Saul will despair of me, to seek me anymore in any part of Israel. So I shall escape out of his hand." ²Then David arose ᵃand went over with the six hundred men who *were* with him ᵇto Achish the son of Maoch, king of Gath. ³So David dwelt with Achish at Gath, he and his men, each man with his household, *and* David ᶜwith his two wives, Ahinoam the Jezreelitess, and Abigail the Carmelitess, Nabal's widow. ⁴And it was told Saul that David had fled to Gath; so he sought him no more.

⁵Then David said to Achish, "If I have now found favor in your eyes, let them give me a place in some town in the country, that I may dwell there. For why should your servant dwell in the royal city with you?" ⁶So Achish gave him Ziklag that day. Therefore ᵈZiklag has belonged to the kings of Judah to this day. ⁷Now the time that David ᵉdwelt in the country of the Philistines was one full year and four months.

⁸And David and his men went up and raided ᶠthe Geshurites, ᵍthe Girzites,* and the ʰAmalekites. For those *nations* were the inhabitants of the land from of old, ⁱas you go to Shur, even as far as the land of Egypt. ⁹Whenever David attacked the land, he left neither man nor woman alive, but took away the sheep, the oxen, the donkeys, the camels, and the apparel, and returned and came to Achish. ¹⁰Then Achish would say, "Where have you made a raid today?" And David would say, "Against the southern *area* of Judah, or against the southern *area* of ʲthe Jerahmeelites, or against the southern *area* of ᵏthe Kenites." ¹¹David would save neither man nor woman alive, to bring *news* to Gath, saying, "Lest they should inform on us, saying, 'Thus David did.'" And thus *was* his behavior all the time he dwelt in the country of the Philistines. ¹²So Achish believed David, saying, "He has made his people Israel utterly abhor him; therefore he will be my servant forever."

28 Now ᵃit happened in those days that the Philistines gathered their armies together for war, to fight with Israel. And Achish said to David, "You assuredly know that you will go out with me to battle, you and your men."

²So David said to Achish, "Surely you know what your servant can do."

And Achish said to David, "Therefore I will make you one of my chief guardians forever."

Saul Consults a Medium

³Now ᵇSamuel had died, and all Israel had lamented for him and buried him in ᶜRamah, in his own city. And Saul had put ᵈthe mediums and the spiritists out of the land.

⁴Then the Philistines gathered together, and came and encamped at ᵉShunem. So Saul gathered all Israel together, and they encamped at ᶠGilboa. ⁵When Saul saw the army of the Philistines, he was ᵍafraid, and

* **27:8** Or *Gezrites*

27:5 give me a place in some town. David was probably wanting more independence of movement in his own city and freedom from daily involvement with Achish's household and religious practices. This request was also a good way to find out how much Achish trusted him. If Achish was willing for David to live independently, he was not likely to be treating David as a spy or enemy.
27:10 the southern area of Judah. The Negev was a dry pastoral region, south of Hebron.
27:12 he will be my servant forever. It seems that David was double dealing with Achish in a way that was dishonest, and indeed he was. But Achish was not David's friend. He was the sworn enemy of David's people and all that David held dear. Achish intended to use David's military expertise for his own ends. This account does not say what God, whose very character is truth, thought about David's strategy. It is clear that God continued to protect and bless David during this very vulnerable time, and the raiding that David had done was continuing the commission the Lord had given the Israelites when they first came into the land.

28:2 you know what your servant can do. In this case, David is purposely ambiguous. He states that his prowess is well known, without saying that he commits this skill to Achish. David could not refuse Achish's offer without risking his life. He trusted the Lord to rescue him from this compromising situation.
28:3 Samuel had died. No one could go to Samuel for advice or direction from the Lord. **mediums and the spiritists.** The term *mediums* refers to necromancers, those who presume to communicate with the dead. *Spiritists* is a general term for those who have contact with spirits. In keeping with God's law, persons associated with necromancy and spiritism had been expelled from the land (Ex. 22:18; Lev. 19:31; Deut. 18:9–14).

26:25 ˣGen. 32:28   **27:2** ᵃ1 Sam. 25:13   ᵇ1 Sam. 21:10   **27:3** ᶜ1 Sam. 25:42, 43   **27:6** ᵈJosh. 15:31; 19:5   **27:7** ᵉ1 Sam. 29:3   **27:8** ᶠJosh. 13:2, 13   ᵍJudg. 1:29   ʰEx. 17:8, 16   ⁱGen. 25:18   **27:10** ʲ1 Chr. 2:9, 25   ᵏJudg. 1:16   **28:1** ᵃ1 Sam. 29:1, 2   **28:3** ᵇ1 Sam. 25:1   ᶜ1 Sam. 1:19   ᵈDeut. 18:10, 11   **28:4** ᵉJosh. 19:18   ᶠ1 Sam. 31:1   **28:5** ᵍJob 18:11

his heart trembled greatly. 6 And when Saul
inquired of the LORD, [h]the LORD did not answer him, either by [i]dreams or [j]by Urim or
by the prophets.
7 Then Saul said to his servants, "Find
me a woman who is a medium, [k]that I may
go to her and inquire of her."
And his servants said to him, "In fact,
there is a woman who is a medium at En
Dor."
8 So Saul disguised himself and put on
other clothes, and he went, and two men
with him; and they came to the woman
by night. And [l]he said, "Please conduct a
séance for me, and bring up for me the one
I shall name to you."
9 Then the woman said to him, "Look,
you know what Saul has done, how he has
[m]cut off the mediums and the spiritists
from the land. Why then do you lay a snare
for my life, to cause me to die?"
10 And Saul swore to her by the LORD,
saying, "*As* the LORD lives, no punishment
shall come upon you for this thing."
11 Then the woman said, "Whom shall I
bring up for you?"
And he said, "Bring up Samuel for me."
12 When the woman saw Samuel, she
cried out with a loud voice. And the woman spoke to Saul, saying, "Why have you
deceived me? For you *are* Saul!"
13 And the king said to her, "Do not be
afraid. What did you see?"
And the woman said to Saul, "I saw [n]a
spirit* ascending out of the earth."
14 So he said to her, "What *is* his form?"
And she said, "An old man is coming
up, and he *is* covered with [o]a mantle." And
Saul perceived that it *was* Samuel, and he
stooped with *his* face to the ground and
bowed down.
15 Now Samuel said to Saul, "Why have
you [p]disturbed me by bringing me up?"
And Saul answered, "I am deeply distressed; for the Philistines make war
against me, and [q]God has departed from
me and [r]does not answer me anymore, neither by prophets nor by dreams. Therefore
I have called you, that you may reveal to me
what I should do."
16 Then Samuel said: "So why do you ask
me, seeing the LORD has departed from you
and has become your enemy? 17 And the
LORD has done for Himself* [s]as He spoke
by me. For the LORD has torn the kingdom
out of your hand and given it to your neighbor, David. 18 [t]Because you did not obey the
voice of the LORD nor execute His fierce
wrath upon [u]Amalek, therefore the LORD
has done this thing to you this day. 19 Moreover the LORD will also deliver Israel with
you into the hand of the Philistines. And
tomorrow you and your sons *will be* with
[v]me. The LORD will also deliver the army
of Israel into the hand of the Philistines."
20 Immediately Saul fell full length on the
ground, and was dreadfully afraid because
of the words of Samuel. And there was no
strength in him, for he had eaten no food
all day or all night.
21 And the woman came to Saul and saw
that he was severely troubled, and said to
him, "Look, your maidservant has obeyed
your voice, and I have [w]put my life in my
hands and heeded the words which you
spoke to me. 22 Now therefore, please, heed
also the voice of your maidservant, and let
me set a piece of bread before you; and eat,
that you may have strength when you go
on *your* way."

* **28:13** Hebrew *elohim* * **28:17** Or *him*, that is, David

---

28:6 *when Saul inquired of the LORD.* It sounds as if Saul was desperate to hear from the Lord. But he had never said, "Whatever You want, Lord, I will do it." Saul knew that he had been rejected by God as king, and if he wanted to repent, Saul could have admitted to God that he was not fit to be king, and asked God to turn the kingdom over to the man of His choice. But Saul wanted to be king, and to hear from God, and have David ejected, and have the Philistines leave him alone, none of which was possible for a man who had decided to deliberately disobey the Lord.

28:7–11 Unfaithfulness—It started with disobeying God's directions about fighting with the Amalekites, and it ended with a medium. Saul apparently never saw himself as a rebel. He knew that the Lord had rejected him, but he thought that it was unjust. Rejecting God is the beginning of a downward spiral, and finally the man who had hounded the mediums from the land, was asking one for guidance because he had no hope of hearing from God.

28:10 *Saul swore to her by the LORD.* While engaging in a practice that was essentially a denial of God's control of everything, Saul swore in God's name that he would protect the woman.

28:12 *When the woman saw Samuel.* The appearance of Samuel has been interpreted in various ways. Some think that a demon impersonated Samuel, and others think that Saul was tricked into believing it was Samuel. It seems best to follow the early view that this was a genuine appearance of Samuel, which God Himself brought about. Several points favor this interpretation. The medium herself was surprised and frightened by his appearance. Saul identified the figure as Samuel. The message Samuel spoke was clearly from God. The text says the figure was Samuel. There is no inherent difficulty with God bringing back the spirit of Samuel from heaven and allowing him to appear to Saul—in spite of the woman's evil profession.

28:19 *with me.* The words "with me" refer to the grave. This text is not intended to provide a final answer concerning Saul's spiritual status. At the very least, it does indicate the reality of life after death.

28:6 [h] 1 Sam. 14:37 [i] Num. 12:6 [j] Ex. 28:30 **28:7** [k] 1 Chr. 10:13 **28:8** [l] Deut. 18:10, 11 **28:9** [m] 1 Sam. 28:3 **28:13** [n] Ex. 22:28 **28:14** [o] 1 Sam. 15:27 **28:15** [p] Is. 14:9 [q] 1 Sam. 16:14; 18:12 [r] 1 Sam. 28:6 **28:17** [s] 1 Sam. 15:28 **28:18** [t] 1 Chr. 10:13 [u] 1 Sam. 15:3–9 **28:19** [v] Job 3:17–19 **28:21** [w] Job 13:14

²³But he refused and said, "I will not eat." So his servants, together with the woman, urged him; and he heeded their voice. Then he arose from the ground and sat on the bed. ²⁴Now the woman had a fatted calf in the house, and she hastened to kill it. And she took flour and kneaded *it*, and baked unleavened bread from it. ²⁵So she brought *it* before Saul and his servants, and they ate. Then they rose and went away that night.

The Philistines Reject David

29 Then ᵃthe Philistines gathered together all their armies ᵇat Aphek, and the Israelites encamped by a fountain which *is* in Jezreel. ²And the ᶜlords of the Philistines passed in review by hundreds and by thousands, but ᵈDavid and his men passed in review at the rear with Achish. ³Then the princes of the Philistines said, "What *are* these Hebrews *doing here*?"

And Achish said to the princes of the Philistines, "*Is* this not David, the servant of Saul king of Israel, who has been with me ᵉthese days, or these years? And to this day I have ᶠfound no fault in him since he defected *to me*."

⁴But the princes of the Philistines were angry with him; so the princes of the Philistines said to him, ᵍ"Make this fellow return, that he may go back to the place which you have appointed for him, and do not let him go down with us to ʰbattle, lest ⁱin the battle he become our adversary. For with what could he reconcile himself to his master, if not with the heads of these ʲmen? ⁵*Is* this not David, ᵏof whom they sang to one another in dances, saying:

ˡ'Saul has slain his thousands,
And David his ten thousands'?"*

⁶Then Achish called David and said to him, "Surely, *as* the Lᴏʀᴅ lives, you have been upright, and ᵐyour going out and your coming in with me in the army *is* good in my sight. For to this day ⁿI have not found evil in you since the day of your coming to me. Nevertheless the lords do not favor you. ⁷Therefore return now, and go in peace, that you may not displease the lords of the Philistines."

⁸So David said to Achish, "But what have I done? And to this day what have you found in your servant as long as I have been with you, that I may not go and fight against the enemies of my lord the king?"

⁹Then Achish answered and said to David, "I know that you *are* as good in my sight ᵒas an angel of God; nevertheless ᵖthe princes of the Philistines have said, 'He shall not go up with us to the battle.' ¹⁰Now therefore, rise early in the morning with your master's servants ᵠwho have come with you.* And as soon as you are up early in the morning and have light, depart."

¹¹So David and his men rose early to depart in the morning, to return to the land of the Philistines. ʳAnd the Philistines went up to Jezreel.

David's Conflict with the Amalekites

30 Now it happened, when David and his men came to ᵃZiklag, on the third day, that the ᵇAmalekites had invaded the South and Ziklag, attacked Ziklag and burned it with fire, ²and had taken captive the ᶜwomen and those who *were* there, from small to great; they did not kill anyone, but carried *them* away and went their way. ³So David and his men came to the city, and there it was, burned with fire; and their wives, their sons, and their daughters had been taken captive. ⁴Then David and the people who *were* with him lifted up their voices and wept, until they had no more power to weep. ⁵And David's two ᵈwives, Ahinoam the Jezreelitess, and Abigail the widow of Nabal the Carmelite, had been taken captive. ⁶Now David was greatly distressed, for ᵉthe people spoke

* **29:5** Compare 1 Samuel 18:7 * **29:10** Following Masoretic Text, Targum, and Vulgate; Septuagint adds *and go to the place which I have selected for you there; and set no bothersome word in your heart, for you are good before me. And rise on your way.*

29:6 you have been upright. David had not been honest with Achish, but he had not turned his hand against Achish personally.
29:7 return. This was the God-orchestrated escape from a compromising situation that David was confident God would provide. **go in peace.** This farewell was more than a courtesy. Achish was releasing David from any further obligation that he had incurred when Achish had made David his vassal in Ziklag.
29:9–10 Prudence—Achish saw David as an angel of God. There must have been something in the way that David conducted himself that showed even a pagan Philistine that David belonged to the God of Israel, and that this was a good place to be. David was being very careful in how he dealt with the Philistine. He could not endanger the people who depended on him, nor be unfaithful to his Lord. Only

God can help us when we have to live in such a difficult situation.
30:1 Amalekites. The Amalekites were a nomadic people who roamed the dry land south of the hill country. For their attack on the Israelites after the exodus from Egypt (Ex. 17:8–13), they were placed under divine judgment (Deut. 25:19).

29:1 ᵃ 1 Sam. 28:1 ᵇ 1 Sam. 4:1 **29:2** ᶜ 1 Sam. 6:4; 7:7 ᵈ 1 Sam. 28:1, 2 **29:3** ᵉ 1 Sam. 27:7 ᶠ Dan. 6:5 **29:4** ᵍ 1 Sam. 27:6 ʰ 1 Sam. 14:21 ⁱ 1 Sam. 29:9 ʲ 1 Chr. 12:19, 20 **29:5** ᵏ 1 Sam. 21:11 ˡ 1 Sam. 18:7 **29:6** ᵐ 2 Sam. 3:25 ⁿ 1 Sam. 29:3 **29:9** ᵒ 2 Sam. 14:17, 20; 19:27 ᵖ 1 Sam. 29:4 **29:10** ᵠ 1 Chr. 12:19, 22 **29:11** ʳ 2 Sam. 4:4 **30:1** ᵃ 1 Sam. 27:6 ᵇ 1 Sam. 15:7; 27:8 **30:2** ᶜ 1 Sam. 27:2, 3 **30:5** ᵈ 1 Sam. 25:42, 43 **30:6** ᵉ Ex. 17:4

of stoning him, because the soul of all the people was grieved, every man for his sons and his daughters. [f]But David strengthened himself in the LORD his God.

7 [g]Then David said to Abiathar the priest, Ahimelech's son, "Please bring the ephod here to me." And [h]Abiathar brought the ephod to David. 8 [i]So David inquired of the LORD, saying, "Shall I pursue this troop? Shall I overtake them?"

And He answered him, "Pursue, for you shall surely overtake *them* and without fail recover *all*."

9 So David went, he and the six hundred men who *were* with him, and came to the Brook Besor, where those stayed who were left behind. 10 But David pursued, he and four hundred men; [j]for two hundred stayed *behind*, who were so weary that they could not cross the Brook Besor.

11 Then they found an Egyptian in the field, and brought him to David; and they gave him bread and he ate, and they let him drink water. 12 And they gave him a piece of [k]a cake of figs and two clusters of raisins. So [l]when he had eaten, his strength came back to him; for he had eaten no bread nor drunk water for three days and three nights. 13 Then David said to him, "To whom do you *belong*, and where *are* you from?"

And he said, "I *am* a young man from Egypt, servant of an Amalekite; and my master left me behind, because three days ago I fell sick. 14 We made an invasion of the southern *area* of [m]the Cherethites, in the *territory* which *belongs* to Judah, and of the southern *area* [n]of Caleb; and we burned Ziklag with fire."

15 And David said to him, "Can you take me down to this troop?"

So he said, "Swear to me by God that you will neither kill me nor deliver me into the hands of my [o]master, and I will take you down to this troop."

16 And when he had brought him down, there they were, spread out over all the land, [p]eating and drinking and dancing, because of all the great spoil which they had taken from the land of the Philistines and from the land of Judah. 17 Then David attacked them from twilight until the evening of the next day. Not a man of them escaped, except four hundred young men who rode on camels and fled. 18 So David recovered all that the Amalekites had carried away, and David rescued his two wives. 19 And nothing of theirs was lacking, either small or great, sons or daughters, spoil or anything which they had taken from them; [q]David recovered all. 20 Then David took all the flocks and herds they had driven before those *other* livestock, and said, "This *is* David's spoil."

21 Now David came to the [r]two hundred men who had been so weary that they could not follow David, whom they also had made to stay at the Brook Besor. So they went out to meet David and to meet the people who *were* with him. And when David came near the people, he greeted them. 22 Then all the wicked and [s]worthless men* of those who went with David answered and said, "Because they did not go with us, we will not give them *any* of the spoil that we have recovered, except for every man's wife and children, that they may lead *them* away and depart."

23 But David said, "My brethren, you shall not do so with what the LORD has given us, who has preserved us and delivered into our hand the troop that came against us. 24 For who will heed you in this matter? But [t]as his part *is* who goes down to the battle, so *shall* his part *be* who stays by the supplies; they shall share alike." 25 So it was, from that day forward; he made it a statute and an ordinance for Israel to this day.

26 Now when David came to Ziklag, he sent *some* of the spoil to the elders of Judah, to his friends, saying, "Here is a present for you from the spoil of the enemies of the LORD"— 27 to *those* who *were* in Bethel, *those* who *were* in [u]Ramoth of the South, *those* who *were* in [v]Jattir, 28 *those* who *were* in [w]Aroer, *those* who *were* in [x]Siphmoth, *those* who *were* in [y]Eshtemoa, 29 *those* who *were* in Rachal, *those* who *were* in the cities of [z]the Jerahmeelites, *those* who *were* in the cities of the [a]Kenites, 30 *those* who *were* in [b]Hormah, *those* who *were* in Chorashan,* *those* who *were* in Athach, 31 *those* who *were* in [c]Hebron, and to all the places where David himself and his men were accustomed to [d]rove.

* **30:22** Literally *men of Belial* * **30:30** Or *Borashan*

30:7 *ephod.* The Urim and Thumim were attached to the ephod. The Lord could be consulted by the means of the Urim and Thummim, but the Bible does not say how this worked.

30:10 *so weary.* The weariness of David's men was due to the fact that they had traveled about 80 miles from Aphek to Ziklag (29:1; 30:1), only to set off immediately in pursuit of the Amalekites.

30:26 *sent some of the spoil to the elders of Judah.* This goodwill gesture helped David reestablish his relationships among the leaders of Judah after his stay in Philistine territory.

30:31 *Hebron.* Hebron was a Levitical city, and a city of refuge, and it was soon to become David's capital (2 Sam. 5:3).

30:6 [f] Hab. 3:17–19 **30:7** [g] 1 Sam. 23:2–9 [h] 1 Sam. 23:6 **30:8** [i] 1 Sam. 23:2, 4 **30:10** [j] 1 Sam. 30:9, 21 **30:12** [k] 1 Sam. 25:18 [l] Judg. 15:19 **30:14** [m] 2 Sam. 8:18 [n] Josh. 14:13; 15:13 **30:15** [o] Deut. 23:15 **30:16** [p] 1 Thess. 5:3 **30:19** [q] 1 Sam. 30:8 **30:21** [r] 1 Sam. 30:10 **30:22** [s] Deut. 13:13 **30:24** [t] Josh. 22:8 **30:27** [u] Josh. 19:8 [v] Josh. 15:48; 21:14 **30:28** [w] Josh. 13:16 [x] 1 Chr. 27:27 [y] Josh. 15:50 **30:29** [z] 1 Sam. 27:10 [a] Judg. 1:16 **30:30** [b] Judg. 1:17 **30:31** [c] 2 Sam. 2:1 [d] 1 Sam. 23:22

The Tragic End of Saul and His Sons

31 Now *a*the Philistines fought against Israel; and the men of Israel fled from before the Philistines, and fell slain on Mount *b*Gilboa. 2Then the Philistines followed hard after Saul and his sons. And the Philistines killed *c*Jonathan, Abinadab, and Malchishua, Saul's sons. 3*d*The battle became fierce against Saul. The archers hit him, and he was severely wounded by the archers.

4*e*Then Saul said to his armorbearer, "Draw your sword, and thrust me through with it, lest *f*these uncircumcised men come and thrust me through and abuse me."

But his armorbearer would not, *g*for he was greatly afraid. Therefore Saul took a sword and *h*fell on it. 5And when his armorbearer saw that Saul was dead, he also fell on his sword, and died with him. 6So Saul, his three sons, his armorbearer, and all his men died together that same day.

7And when the men of Israel who *were* on the other side of the valley, and *those* who *were* on the other side of the Jordan, saw that the men of Israel had fled and that Saul and his sons were dead, they forsook the cities and fled; and the Philistines came and dwelt in them. 8So it happened the next day, when the Philistines came to strip the slain, that they found Saul and his three sons fallen on Mount Gilboa. 9And they cut off his head and stripped off his armor, and sent *word* throughout the land of the Philistines, to *i*proclaim *it in* the temple of their idols and among the people. 10*j*Then they put his armor in the temple of the *k*Ashtoreths, and *l*they fastened his body to the wall of *m*Beth Shan.*

11*n*Now when the inhabitants of Jabesh Gilead heard what the Philistines had done to Saul, 12*o*all the valiant men arose and traveled all night, and took the body of Saul and the bodies of his sons from the wall of Beth Shan; and they came to Jabesh and *p*burned them there. 13Then they took their bones and *q*buried *them* under the tamarisk tree at *r*Jabesh, and fasted seven days.

---

* **31:10** Spelled *Beth Shean* in Joshua 17:11 and elsewhere

---

31:2 *Saul and his sons.* Saul's fourth son, Ishbosheth, was apparently not present at this battle, since Abner promoted him to king after Saul's death (2 Sam. 2:8–10).

31:6 *all his men.* This does not refer to the whole army, but rather to men who were particularly associated with Saul, such as his royal body guards.

31:11 *inhabitants of Jabesh Gilead.* The inhabitants of this town had been delivered from the threats of Nahash the Ammonite by Saul in his first military campaign as king of Israel (11:1–11).

31:13 *and fasted seven days.* In ancient Israel, fasting was a way of expressing sorrow in mourning. With their fasting, the men of Jabesh showed their respect for Israel's first king.

31:1 *a* 1 Chr. 10:1–12 *b* 1 Sam. 28:4   **31:2** *c* 1 Sam. 14:49   **31:3** *d* 2 Sam. 1:6   **31:4** *e* Judg. 9:54 *f* 1 Sam. 14:6; 17:26, 36 *g* 2 Sam. 1:14 *h* 2 Sam. 1:6, 10   **31:9** *i* 2 Sam. 1:20   **31:10** *j* 1 Sam. 21:9 *k* Judg. 2:13 *l* 2 Sam. 21:12 *m* Judg. 1:27   **31:11** *n* 1 Sam. 11:1–13   **31:12** *o* 2 Sam. 2:4–7 *p* 2 Chr. 16:14   **31:13** *q* 2 Sam. 2:4, 5; 21:12–14 *r* Gen. 50:10

THE SECOND BOOK OF
SAMUEL

▶ **AUTHOR:** No author is mentioned anywhere in this book. Although the tradition-al view is that Samuel wrote 2 Samuel, it was probably compiled by one man who combined the written chronicles of "Nathan the prophet" and "Gad the seer" (1 Chr. 29:29). In addition to these written sources, the compiler evidently used another source called the "Book of Jasher" (1:18).

▶ **TIME:** c. 1011–971 B.C.   ▶ **KEY VERSES:** 2 Sam. 7:12–13

▶ **THEME:** Second Samuel begins with Saul's death and David's ascension to the throne of Judah. A few years later he becomes the king of all of Israel. During his reign there were many problems, most of which can be traced back to David's own behavior. He abuses power and plays favorites with his sons. The result is much per-sonal sorrow and the seeds of discord that follow in succeeding generations. Sec-ond Samuel gives us a full picture of a king, a poet, a soldier, and a sinner who yearns after God's own heart and follows where He leads.

The Report of Saul's Death

1 Now it came to pass after the ᵃdeath of Saul, when David had returned from ᵇthe slaughter of the Amalekites, and Da-vid had stayed two days in Ziklag, ²on the third day, behold, it happened that ᶜa man came from Saul's camp ᵈwith his clothes torn and dust on his head. So it was, when he came to David, that he ᵉfell to the ground and prostrated himself.

³And David said to him, "Where have you come from?"

So he said to him, "I have escaped from the camp of Israel."

⁴Then David said to him, ᶠ"How did the matter go? Please tell me."

And he answered, "The people have fled from the battle, many of the people are fall-en and dead, and Saul and ᵍJonathan his son are dead also."

⁵So David said to the young man who told him, "How do you know that Saul and Jonathan his son are dead?"

⁶Then the young man who told him said, "As I happened by chance to be on ʰMount Gilboa, there was ⁱSaul, leaning on his spear; and indeed the chariots and horsemen followed hard after him. ⁷Now when he looked behind him, he saw me and called to me. And I answered, 'Here I am.' ⁸And he said to me, 'Who are you?' So I answered him, 'I am an Amalekite.' ⁹He said to me again, 'Please stand over me and kill me, for anguish has come upon me, but my life still remains in me.' ¹⁰So I stood over him and ʲkilled him, because I was sure that he could not live after he had fallen. And I took the crown that was on his head and the bracelet that was on his arm, and have brought them here to my lord."

¹¹Therefore David took hold of his own clothes and ᵏtore them, and so did all the men who were with him. ¹²And they ˡmourned and wept and ᵐfasted until eve-ning for Saul and for Jonathan his son, for the ⁿpeople of the LORD and for the house of Israel, because they had fallen by the sword.

¹³Then David said to the young man who told him, "Where are you from?"

And he answered, "I am the son of an alien, an Amalekite."

1:2 clothes torn and dust on his head. Dust or ashes on the head, torn clothing, and sackcloth were all signs of mourning.

1:12 fasted. Spiritual fasting is abstaining from food to devote time and energy to prayer. Sometimes people plan a time of fasting, and sometimes it just comes upon them because overwhelming spiritual needs supersede all thought of food. This was a time of true calamity for Israel, even though it solved a problem for David. He was personally very grieved, for he had known the man Saul as he could have been, and he had lost Jonathan, the best friend he would ever have. His future as king seemed assured, but the task of uniting the nation would be very dif-ficult.

1:1 ᵃ 1 Sam. 31:6 ᵇ 1 Sam. 30:1, 17, 26   **1:2** ᶜ 2 Sam. 4:10 ᵈ 1 Sam. 4:12 ᵉ 1 Sam. 25:23   **1:4** ᶠ 1 Sam. 4:16; 31:3 ᵍ 1 Sam. 31:2   **1:6** ʰ 1 Sam. 31:1 ⁱ 1 Sam. 31:2–4   **1:10** ʲ Judg. 9:54   **1:11** ᵏ 2 Sam. 3:31; 13:31   **1:12** ˡ 2 Sam. 3:31 ᵐ 1 Sam. 31:13 ⁿ 2 Sam. 6:21

14 So David said to him, "How [o]was it you
were not [p]afraid to [q]put forth your hand to
destroy the LORD's anointed?" 15 Then [r]Da-
vid called one of the young men and said,
"Go near, *and* execute him!" And he struck
him so that he died. 16 So David said to him,
[s]"Your blood *is* on your own head, for [t]your
own mouth has testified against you, saying, 'I have killed the LORD's anointed.'"

The Song of the Bow

17 Then David lamented with this lamentation over Saul and over Jonathan his son,
18 [u]and he told *them* to teach the children
of Judah *the Song of* the Bow; indeed *it is*
written [v]in the Book of Jasher:

19 "The beauty of Israel is slain on your
high places!
[w]How the mighty have fallen!
20 [x]Tell *it* not in Gath,
Proclaim *it* not in the streets of
[y]Ashkelon—
Lest [z]the daughters of the Philistines
rejoice,
Lest the daughters of [a]the
uncircumcised triumph.

21 "O [b]mountains of Gilboa,
[c]*Let there be* no dew nor rain upon
you,
Nor fields of offerings.
For the shield of the mighty is cast
away there!
The shield of Saul, not [d]anointed with
oil.
22 From the blood of the slain,
From the fat of the mighty,
[e]The bow of Jonathan did not turn
back,
And the sword of Saul did not return
empty.

23 "Saul and Jonathan *were* beloved and
pleasant in their lives,
And in their [f]death they were not
divided;
They were swifter than eagles,
They were [g]stronger than lions.

24 "O daughters of Israel, weep over Saul,
Who clothed you in scarlet, with
luxury;
Who put ornaments of gold on your
apparel.

25 "How the mighty have fallen in the
midst of the battle!
Jonathan *was* slain in your high
places.
26 I am distressed for you, my brother
Jonathan;
You have been very pleasant to me;
[h]Your love to me was wonderful,
Surpassing the love of women.

27 "How[i] the mighty have fallen,
And the weapons of war perished!"

David Anointed King of Judah

2 It happened after this that David [a]in-
quired of the LORD, saying, "Shall I go
up to any of the cities of Judah?"
And the LORD said to him, "Go up."
David said, "Where shall I go up?"
And He said, "To [b]Hebron."
2 So David went up there, and his [c]two
wives also, Ahinoam the Jezreelitess, and
Abigail the widow of Nabal the Carmelite.
3 And David brought up [d]the men who *were*
with him, every man with his household.
So they dwelt in the cities of Hebron.
4 [e]Then the men of Judah came, and there
they [f]anointed David king over the house of
Judah. And they told David, saying, [g]"The
men of Jabesh Gilead *were the ones* who
buried Saul." 5 So David sent messengers to
the men of Jabesh Gilead, and said to them,
[h]"You *are* blessed of the LORD, for you have
shown this kindness to your lord, to Saul,
and have buried him. 6 And now may [i]the
LORD show kindness and truth to you. I
also will repay you this kindness, because
you have done this thing. 7 Now therefore,
let your hands be strengthened, and be valiant; for your master Saul is dead, and also
the house of Judah has anointed me king
over them."

Ishbosheth Made King of Israel

8 But [j]Abner the son of Ner, commander
of Saul's army, took Ishbosheth* the son of
Saul and brought him over to [k]Mahanaim;

*2:8 Called *Esh-Baal* in 1 Chronicles 8:33 and 9:39

1:14 *the LORD's anointed.* David's use of the phrase "the LORD's anointed" indicates that even though Saul was his enemy, David honored the position that Saul had as God's representative. David repeatedly refused to harm Saul because of this (1 Sam. 24:6; 26:9).

1:15 *struck him.* The Amalekite had probably been hoping for a reward from David. His story was a lie (1 Sam. 31), and this lie cost him his life. David's execution of the Amalekite was a strong testimony to those under his command that he had no part in Saul's death and did not reward it in any way.

2:5 *kindness.* David was grateful to the men who had shown kindness to Saul. This acknowledgment was not an act of politeness, but came from David's own heart of compassion. Saul repeatedly demonstrated that he considered himself above correction, but David was careful to maintain an attitude of kindness and humility.

1:14 [o] Num. 12:8 [p] 1 Sam. 31:4 [q] 1 Sam. 24:6; 26:9 **1:15** [r] 2 Sam. 4:10, 12 **1:16** [s] 1 Kin. 2:32–37 [t] Luke 19:22 **1:18** [u] 1 Sam. 31:3 [v] Josh. 10:13 **1:19** [w] 2 Sam. 1:27 **1:20** [x] Mic. 1:10 [y] Jer. 25:20 [z] Ex. 15:20 [a] 1 Sam. 31:4 **1:21** [b] 1 Sam. 31:1 [c] Ezek. 31:15 [d] 1 Sam. 10:1 **1:22** [e] 1 Sam. 18:4 **1:23** [f] 1 Sam. 31:2–4 [g] Judg. 14:18 **1:26** [h] 1 Sam. 18:1–4; 19:2; 20:17 **1:27** [i] 2 Sam. 1:19, 25 **2:1** [a] Judg. 1:1 [b] 1 Sam. 30:31 **2:2** [c] 1 Sam. 25:42, 43; 30:5 **2:3** [d] 1 Chr. 12:1 **2:4** [e] 1 Sam. 30:26 [f] 1 Sam. 16:13 [g] 1 Sam. 31:11–13 **2:5** [h] Ruth 2:20; 3:10 **2:6** [i] 2 Tim. 1:16, 18 **2:8** [j] 1 Sam. 14:50 [k] 2 Sam. 17:24

9 and he made him king over [l]Gilead,
over the [m]Ashurites, over [n]Jezreel, over
Ephraim, over Benjamin, and over all Israel. 10 Ishbosheth, Saul's son, *was* forty
years old when he began to reign over Israel, and he reigned two years. Only the
house of Judah followed David. 11 And [o]the
time that David was king in Hebron over
the house of Judah was seven years and
six months.

Israel and Judah at War

12 Now Abner the son of Ner, and the servants of Ishbosheth the son of Saul, went
out from Mahanaim to [p]Gibeon. 13 And
[q]Joab the son of Zeruiah, and the servants
of David, went out and met them by [r]the
pool of Gibeon. So they sat down, one on
one side of the pool and the other on the
other side of the pool. 14 Then Abner said
to Joab, "Let the young men now arise and
compete before us."

And Joab said, "Let them arise."

15 So they arose and went over by number, twelve from Benjamin, *followers* of
Ishbosheth the son of Saul, and twelve
from the servants of David. 16 And each
one grasped his opponent by the head
and *thrust* his sword in his opponent's
side; so they fell down together. Therefore
that place was called the Field of Sharp
Swords,* which *is* in Gibeon. 17 So there
was a very fierce battle that day, and Abner
and the men of Israel were beaten before
the servants of David.

18 Now the [s]three sons of Zeruiah were
there: Joab and Abishai and Asahel. And
Asahel *was* [t]*as* fleet of foot [u]as a wild gazelle. 19 So Asahel pursued Abner, and in
going he did not turn to the right hand or
to the left from following Abner.

20 Then Abner looked behind him and
said, "*Are* you Asahel?"

He answered, "I *am*."

21 And Abner said to him, "Turn aside
to your right hand or to your left, and lay
hold on one of the young men and take his
armor for yourself." But Asahel would not
turn aside from following him. 22 So Abner
said again to Asahel, "Turn aside from following me. Why should I strike you to the
ground? How then could I face your brother
Joab?" 23 However, he refused to turn aside.
Therefore Abner struck him [v]in the stomach with the blunt end of the spear, so that
the spear came out of his back; and he fell
down there and died on the spot. So it was
that as many as came to the place where
Asahel fell down and died, stood [w]still.

24 Joab and Abishai also pursued Abner. And the sun was going down when
they came to the hill of Ammah, which *is*
before Giah by the road to the Wilderness
of Gibeon. 25 Now the children of Benjamin
gathered together behind Abner and became a unit, and took their stand on top of
a hill. 26 Then Abner called to Joab and said,
"Shall the sword devour forever? Do you not
know that it will be bitter in the latter end?
How long will it be then until you tell the people to return from pursuing their brethren?"

27 And Joab said, "*As* God lives, unless
[x]you had spoken, surely then by morning
all the people would have given up pursuing their brethren." 28 So Joab blew a trumpet; and all the people stood still and did
not pursue Israel anymore, nor did they
fight anymore. 29 Then Abner and his men
went on all that night through the plain,
crossed over the Jordan, and went through
all Bithron; and they came to Mahanaim.

30 So Joab returned from pursuing Abner. And when he had gathered all the people together, there were missing of David's
servants nineteen men and Asahel. 31 But
the servants of David had struck down, of
Benjamin and Abner's men, three hundred
and sixty men who died. 32 Then they took
up Asahel and buried him in his father's
tomb, which *was in* [y]Bethlehem. And Joab
and his men went all night, and they came
to Hebron at daybreak.

3 Now there was a long [a]war between the
house of Saul and the house of David.
But David grew stronger and stronger, and
the house of Saul grew weaker and weaker.

Sons of David

2 Sons were born [b]to David in Hebron:
His firstborn was Amnon [c]by Ahinoam

* **2:16** Hebrew *Helkath Hazzurim*

2:18 ***Joab and Abishai and Asahel.*** The three brothers were David's nephews, children of his sister Zeruiah (1 Chr. 2:13–16).

2:19 ***Asahel pursued Abner.*** Asahel did not have a personal grudge against Abner. This was a military move. If Abner, the chief military leader, was dead, Ishbosheth's power base would dissolve.

3:1 Strife—Finally David was in a position to push to establish his kingdom. It was still a contest of power and loyalty. An important question had to be settled: Is the king chosen by God? Or is the one who seizes the power the king? David knew he had to establish himself both politically and militarily, but he wanted to show, even in battle, that he trusted God to establish his kingdom.

3:2 ***Sons were born to David.*** David began his reign in Judah with two wives, Ahinoam and Abigail. His wife Michal, the daughter of Saul, had been given to another when David fled from Saul. In Hebron David married four more wives, in spite of the warning from Moses that a king should not "multiply wives for himself" (Deut. 17:17).

2:9 [l] Josh. 22:9 [m] Judg. 1:32 [n] 1 Sam. 29:1 **2:11** [o] 2 Sam. 5:5 **2:12** [p] Josh. 10:2–12; 18:25 **2:13** [q] 1 Chr. 2:16; 11:6 [r] Jer. 41:12 **2:18** [s] 1 Chr. 2:16 [t] 1 Chr. 12:8 [u] Ps. 18:33 **2:23** [v] 2 Sam. 3:27; 4:6; 20:10 [w] 2 Sam. 20:12 **2:27** [x] 2 Sam. 2:14 **2:32** [y] 1 Sam. 20:6 **3:1** [a] 1 Kin. 14:30 **3:2** [b] 1 Chr. 3:1–4 [c] 1 Sam. 25:42, 43

the Jezreelitess; 3his second, Chileab, by
Abigail the widow of Nabal the Carmelite;
the third, [d]Absalom the son of Maacah, the
daughter of Talmai, king [e]of Geshur; 4the
fourth, [f]Adonijah the son of Haggith; the
fifth, Shephatiah the son of Abital; 5and
the sixth, Ithream, by David's wife Eglah.
These were born to David in Hebron.

Abner Joins Forces with David

6Now it was so, while there was war between the house of Saul and the house of
David, that Abner was strengthening *his
hold* on the house of Saul.
7And Saul had a concubine, whose name
was [g]Rizpah, the daughter of Aiah. So *Ishbosheth* said to Abner, "Why have you
[h]gone in to my father's concubine?"
8Then Abner became very angry at the
words of Ishbosheth, and said, "*Am* I [i]a
dog's head that belongs to Judah? Today
I show loyalty to the house of Saul your
father, to his brothers, and to his friends,
and have not delivered you into the hand
of David; and you charge me today with a
fault concerning this woman? 9[j]May God
do so to Abner, and more also, if I do not do
for David [k]as the LORD has sworn to him—
10to transfer the kingdom from the house
of Saul, and set up the throne of David over
Israel and over Judah, [l]from Dan to Beersheba." 11And he could not answer Abner
another word, because he feared him.
12Then Abner sent messengers on his
behalf to David, saying, "Whose *is* the
land?" saying *also*, "Make your covenant
with me, and indeed my hand *shall be* with
you to bring all Israel to you."
13And *David* said, "Good, I will make a
covenant with you. But one thing I require
of you: [m]you shall not see my face unless
you first bring [n]Michal, Saul's daughter,
when you come to see my face." 14So David
sent messengers to [o]Ishbosheth, Saul's son,
saying, "Give *me* my wife Michal, whom
I betrothed to myself [p]for a hundred foreskins of the Philistines." 15And Ishbosheth
sent and took her from *her* husband, from
Paltiel* the son of Laish. 16Then her husband went along with her to [q]Bahurim,
weeping behind her. So Abner said to him,
"Go, return!" And he returned.
17Now Abner had communicated with
the elders of Israel, saying, "In time past
you were seeking for David *to be* king over
you. 18Now then, do *it!* [r]For the LORD has
spoken of David, saying, 'By the hand of
My servant David, I* will save My people
Israel from the hand of the Philistines
and the hand of all their enemies.'" 19And
Abner also spoke in the hearing of [s]Ben-
jamin. Then Abner also went to speak in
the hearing of David in Hebron all that
seemed good to Israel and the whole house
of Benjamin.
20So Abner and twenty men with him
came to David at Hebron. And David made
a feast for Abner and the men who *were*
with him. 21Then Abner said to David, "I
will arise and go, and [t]gather all Israel
to my lord the king, that they may make
a covenant with you, and that you may
[u]reign over all that your heart desires."
So David sent Abner away, and he went in
peace.

Joab Murders Abner

22At that moment the servants of David
and Joab came from a raid and brought
much spoil with them. But Abner *was* not
with David in Hebron, for he had sent him
away, and he had gone in peace. 23When
Joab and all the troops that *were* with him
had come, they told Joab, saying, "Abner
the son of Ner came to the king, and he
sent him away, and he has gone in peace."

* **3:15** Spelled *Palti* in 1 Samuel 25:44 * **3:18** Following many Hebrew manuscripts, Septuagint, Syriac, and Targum; Masoretic Text reads *he.*

3:3 *Chileab.* Chileab is also called Daniel (1 Chr. 3:1).
3:5 *born to David in Hebron.* These six sons, each from a different mother, constituted the royal family during David's reign over the house of Judah. The dynastic lists in Chronicles include four sons of David by Bathsheba (1 Chr. 3:5) and nine other sons whose mothers are not named (1 Chr. 3:6–8).
3:7 *gone in to my father's concubine.* The royal harem was the property of the king's successor. Taking a king's concubine was tantamount to claiming the throne.
3:8 *dog's head.* In the ancient Middle East dogs were scavengers, living off dead animals and garbage, and were viewed with contempt. ***Judah.*** The tribe of Judah was the enemy of Ishbosheth. In essence Abner was saying, "Do you think I am the scum of the enemy?"
3:13 *Michal.* David's first wife, Michal (1 Sam. 18:17–27) was left in Gibeah when David fled from Saul's court (1 Sam. 19:11–27). Saul then gave his daughter Michal, perhaps out of spite, to a man named Palti (1 Sam. 25:44). This request of David's was certainly in line with his rights as a husband who had given a proper dowry for his bride, and it was also a political statement. He was asserting his power over the house of Saul. (See note at 3:7.)
3:16 *her husband went along with her.* Michal's husband wept. Nothing is said of Michal's feelings, or of David's. A king did not leave his wife with another man, for that was in the same category as another man taking the king's concubines. How he, or anyone else felt about it, had no bearing on the situation. (See note at 3:7.)
3:22 *gone in peace.* The words "gone in peace" are repeated (v. 21), to emphasize that the hostilities between David and Abner had been resolved.

3:3 [d] 2 Sam. 15:1–10 [e] Josh. 13:13 **3:4** [f] 1 Kin. 1:5 **3:7** [g] 2 Sam. 21:8–11 [h] 2 Sam. 16:21 **3:8** [i] 1 Sam. 24:14 **3:9** [j] 1 Kin. 19:2 [k] 1 Chr. 12:23 **3:10** [l] 1 Sam. 3:20 **3:13** [m] Gen. 43:3 [n] 1 Sam. 18:20; 19:11; 25:44 **3:14** [o] 2 Sam. 2:10 [p] 1 Sam. 18:25–27 **3:16** [q] 2 Sam. 16:5; 19:16 **3:18** [r] 2 Sam. 3:9 **3:19** [s] 1 Chr. 12:29 **3:21** [t] 2 Sam. 3:10, 12 [u] 1 Kin. 11:37

²⁴Then Joab came to the king and said, "What have you done? Look, Abner came to you; why *is it that* you sent him away, and he has already gone? ²⁵Surely you realize that Abner the son of Ner came to deceive you, to know ᵛyour going out and your coming in, and to know all that you are doing."

²⁶And when Joab had gone from David's presence, he sent messengers after Abner, who brought him back from the well of Sirah. But David did not know *it.* ²⁷Now when Abner had returned to Hebron, Joab ʷtook him aside in the gate to speak with him privately, and there stabbed him ˣin the stomach, so that he died for the blood of ʸAsahel his brother.

²⁸Afterward, when David heard *it,* he said, "My kingdom and I *are* guiltless before the LORD forever of the blood of Abner the son of Ner. ²⁹ᶻLet it rest on the head of Joab and on all his father's house; and let there never fail to be in the house of Joab one ᵃwho has a discharge or is a leper, who leans on a staff or falls by the sword, or who lacks bread." ³⁰So Joab and Abishai his brother killed Abner, because he had killed their brother ᵇAsahel at Gibeon in the battle.

David's Mourning for Abner

³¹Then David said to Joab and to all the people who were with him, ᶜ"Tear your clothes, ᵈgird yourselves with sackcloth, and mourn for Abner." And King David followed the coffin. ³²So they buried Abner in Hebron; and the king lifted up his voice and wept at the grave of Abner, and all the people wept. ³³And the king sang *a lament* over Abner and said:

"Should Abner die as a ᵉfool dies?
³⁴ Your hands were not bound
 Nor your feet put into fetters;
 As a man falls before wicked men, *so* you fell."

Then all the people wept over him again.

³⁵And when all the people came ᶠto persuade David to eat food while it was still day, David took an oath, saying, ᵍ"God do so to me, and more also, if I taste bread or anything else ʰtill the sun goes down!"

³⁶Now all the people took note *of it,* and it pleased them, since whatever the king did pleased all the people. ³⁷For all the people and all Israel understood that day that it had not been the king's *intent* to kill Abner the son of Ner. ³⁸Then the king said to his servants, "Do you not know that a prince and a great man has fallen this day in Israel? ³⁹And I *am* weak today, though anointed king; and these men, the sons of Zeruiah, ⁱare too harsh for me. ʲThe LORD shall repay the evildoer according to his wickedness."

Ishbosheth Is Murdered

4 When Saul's son* heard that Abner had died in Hebron, ᵃhe lost heart, and all Israel was ᵇtroubled. ²Now Saul's son *had* two men *who were* captains of troops. The name of one *was* Baanah and the name of the other Rechab, the sons of Rimmon the Beerothite, of the children of Benjamin. (For ᶜBeeroth also was *part* of Benjamin, ³because the Beerothites fled to ᵈGittaim and have been sojourners there until this day.)

⁴ᵉJonathan, Saul's son, had a son *who was* lame in *his* feet. He was five years old when the news about Saul and Jonathan came ᶠfrom Jezreel; and his nurse took him up and fled. And it happened, as she made haste to flee, that he fell and became lame. His name *was* ᵍMephibosheth.*

⁵Then the sons of Rimmon the Beerothite, Rechab and Baanah, set out and came at about the heat of the day to the ʰhouse of Ishbosheth, who was lying on his bed at noon. ⁶And they came there, all the way into the house, *as though* to get wheat, and they stabbed him ⁱin the stomach. Then Rechab and Baanah his brother escaped. ⁷For when they came into the house, he was lying on his bed in his bedroom; then they struck him and killed him, beheaded him and took his head, and were all night escaping through the plain. ⁸And they brought the head of Ishbosheth to David at Hebron, and said to the king, "Here is the head of Ishbosheth, the son of Saul your enemy, ʲwho sought your life; and the LORD

---

* **4:1** That is, Ishbosheth   * **4:4** Called *Merib-Baal* in 1 Chronicles 8:34 and 9:40

4:8–10 brought the head of Ishbosheth to David. Ishbosheth was Jonathan's friend. Whether or not they looked alike, David had no desire to have the head of his beloved friend's brother brought to him as a prize. Once again, greed for a reward overcame prudence, and the plotters lost their lives on their own testimony.

4:9–12 Strife—Once again David was faced with the question: Who was going to establish his kingdom? In David's mind the answer could only be "God." David wanted to meet his adversary honestly on the field of battle or over a flag of truce, but he would have nothing to do with murder. There was another compelling reason for David to conduct himself honorably. David

was closely associated with Ishbosheth as the brother of his wife and of his best friend, and he did not find it easy to be at war with him.

3:25 ᵛ 1 Sam. 29:6   **3:27** ʷ 1 Kin. 2:5 ˣ 2 Sam. 4:6
ʸ 2 Sam. 2:23   **3:29** ᶻ 1 Kin. 2:32, 33 ᵃ Lev. 15:2
3:30 ᵇ 2 Sam. 2:23   **3:31** ᶜ Josh. 7:6 ᵈ Gen. 37:34
3:33 ᵉ 2 Sam. 13:12, 13   **3:35** ᶠ 2 Sam. 12:17 ᵍ Ruth 1:17
ʰ 2 Sam. 1:12   **3:39** ⁱ 2 Sam. 19:5–7 ʲ 1 Kin. 2:5, 6, 32–34
4:1 ᵃ Ezra 4:4 ᵇ Matt. 2:3   **4:2** ᶜ Josh. 18:25   **4:3** ᵈ Neh.
11:33   **4:4** ᵉ 2 Sam. 9:3 ᶠ 1 Sam. 29:1, 11 ᵍ 2 Sam. 9:6
4:5 ʰ 2 Sam. 2:8, 9   **4:6** ⁱ 2 Sam. 2:23; 20:10   **4:8** ʲ 1 Sam.
19:2, 10, 11; 23:15; 25:29

has avenged my lord the king this day of Saul and his descendants."

⁹But David answered Rechab and Baanah his brother, the sons of Rimmon the Beerothite, and said to them, "As the LORD lives, ᵏwho has redeemed my life from all adversity, ¹⁰when ˡsomeone told me, saying, 'Look, Saul is dead,' thinking to have brought good news, I arrested him and had him executed in Ziklag—the one who *thought* I would give him a reward for *his* news. ¹¹How much more, when wicked men have killed a righteous person in his own house on his bed? Therefore, shall I not now ᵐrequire his blood at your hand and remove you from the earth?" ¹²So David ⁿcommanded his young men, and they executed them, cut off their hands and feet, and hanged *them* by the pool in Hebron. But they took the head of Ishbosheth and buried *it* in the ᵒtomb of Abner in Hebron.

David Reigns over All Israel

5 Then all the tribes of Israel ᵃcame to David at Hebron and spoke, saying, "Indeed ᵇwe *are* your bone and your flesh. ²Also, in time past, when Saul was king over us, ᶜyou were the one who led Israel out and brought them in; and the LORD said to you, ᵈ'You shall shepherd My people Israel, and be ruler over Israel.'" ³ᵉTherefore all the elders of Israel came to the king at Hebron, ᶠand King David made a covenant with them at Hebron ᵍbefore the LORD. And they anointed David king over Israel. ⁴David *was* ʰthirty years old when he began to reign, *and* ⁱhe reigned forty years. ⁵In Hebron he reigned over Judah ʲseven years and six months, and in Jerusalem he reigned thirty-three years over all Israel and Judah.

The Conquest of Jerusalem

⁶ᵏAnd the king and his men went to Jerusalem against ˡthe Jebusites, the inhabitants of the land, who spoke to David, saying, "You shall not come in here; but the blind and the lame will repel you," thinking, "David cannot come in here." ⁷Nevertheless David took the stronghold of Zion ᵐ(that *is*, the City of David).

⁸Now David said on that day, "Whoever climbs up by way of the water shaft and defeats the Jebusites (the lame and the blind, *who are* hated by David's soul), ⁿhe shall be chief and captain."* Therefore they say, "The blind and the lame shall not come into the house."

⁹Then David dwelt in the stronghold, and called it ᵒthe City of David. And David built all around from the Millo* and inward. ¹⁰So David went on and became great, and ᵖthe LORD God of hosts *was* with �q him. ¹¹Then ʳHiram ˢking of Tyre sent messengers to David, and cedar trees, and carpenters and masons. And they built David a house. ¹²So David knew that the LORD had established him as king over Israel, and that He had ᵗexalted His kingdom ᵘfor the sake of His people Israel.

¹³And ᵛDavid took more concubines and wives from Jerusalem, after he had come from Hebron. Also more sons and daughters were born to David. ¹⁴Now ʷthese *are*

* **5:8** Compare 1 Chronicles 11:6 * **5:9** Literally *The Landfill*

4:11 *righteous person.* Ishbosheth had accepted what he considered to be his rightful role as the next king after his father, Saul. Apparently, even in David's mind, Ishbosheth's supposition was reasonable.

5:3 *anointed David king over Israel.* This was the third time that David was anointed as king. The first time was in anticipation of his rule (1 Sam. 16:13), the second time was acknowledgment of his rule over Judah (2:4), and the third time acknowledged his rule over the entire nation.

5:6 *went to Jerusalem.* The city of Jerusalem was strategically located on a hill, just south of Mount Moriah, with steep cliffs on all sides except the north, making it a natural fortress. It was near the border of Judah and Benjamin. Jerusalem became the site of the temple, and the place, more than any other place on earth, which was identified with the Jewish people. It was there that Jesus was crucified, and it is there that He will come again (Zech. 14:4). **the blind and the lame.** Jerusalem was so strategically situated that the blind and the lame would be enough to defeat David.

5:7 *Zion.* The word Zion originally applied to the Jebusite stronghold, which became the City of David after its capture. As the city expanded to the north, encompassing Mount Moriah, the temple mount came to be called Zion (Ps. 78:68–69). Eventually the term was used as a synonym for Jerusalem (Is. 40:9).

5:8 *water shaft.* The water tunnel extended about 230 feet up from the Gihon spring to the top of the hill where the Jebusite fortress was situated (2 Chr. 32:30). The tunnel gave the city a secure water supply in the event of a siege.

5:11 *cedar trees.* Most buildings in Israel were made of stone. The use of cedar added elegance to David's palace.

5:13 *took more concubines and wives.* These marriages probably reflect David's involvement in international treaties and alliances which were sealed with the marriage of a king's daughter to the other participant in the treaty. Concubines, wives who did not have the legal rights of a true marriage, were a part of a royal harem. The status of kings in ancient times was often measured in part by the size of their harem. But Israel's kings had been warned not to acquire many wives (Deut. 17:17).

4:9 ᵏ Gen. 48:16 **4:10** ˡ 2 Sam. 1:2–16 **4:11** ᵐ [Gen. 9:5, 6] **4:12** ⁿ 2 Sam. 1:15 ᵒ 2 Sam. 3:32 **5:1** ᵃ 1 Chr. 11:1–3 ᵇ 2 Sam. 19:12, 13 **5:2** ᶜ 1 Sam. 18:5, 13, 16 ᵈ 1 Sam. 16:1 **5:3** ᵉ 2 Sam. 3:17 ᶠ 2 Kin. 11:17 ᵍ 1 Sam. 23:18 **5:4** ʰ Gen. 41:46 ⁱ 1 Chr. 26:31; 29:27 **5:5** ʲ 2 Sam. 2:11 **5:6** ᵏ Judg. 1:21 ˡ Josh. 15:63 **5:7** ᵐ 1 Kin. 2:10; 8:1; 9:24 **5:8** ⁿ 1 Chr. 11:6–9 **5:9** ᵒ 2 Sam. 5:7 **5:10** ᵖ 1 Sam. 17:45 �q 1 Sam. 18:12, 28 **5:11** ʳ 1 Kin. 5:1–18 ˢ 1 Chr. 14:1 **5:12** ᵗ Num. 24:7 ᵘ Is. 45:4 **5:13** ᵛ [Deut. 17:17] **5:14** ʷ 1 Chr. 3:5–8

the names of those who were born to him in Jerusalem: Shammua,* Shobab, Nathan, *Solomon, ¹⁵Ibhar, Elishua,* Nepheg, Japhia, ¹⁶Elishama, Eliada, and Eliphelet.

The Philistines Defeated

¹⁷ʸNow when the Philistines heard that they had anointed David king over Israel, all the Philistines went up to search for David. And David heard of it ᶻand went down to the stronghold. ¹⁸The Philistines also went and deployed themselves in ᵃthe Valley of Rephaim. ¹⁹So David ᵇinquired of the LORD, saying, "Shall I go up against the Philistines? Will You deliver them into my hand?"

And the LORD said to David, "Go up, for I will doubtless deliver the Philistines into your hand."

²⁰So David went to ᶜBaal Perazim, and David defeated them there; and he said, "The LORD has broken through my enemies before me, like a breakthrough of water." Therefore he called the name of that place Baal Perazim.* ²¹And they left their images there, and David and his men ᵈcarried them away.

²²ᵉThen the Philistines went up once again and deployed themselves in the Valley of Rephaim. ²³Therefore ᶠDavid inquired of the LORD, and He said, "You shall not go up; circle around behind them, and come upon them in front of the mulberry trees. ²⁴And it shall be, when you ᵍhear the sound of marching in the tops of the mulberry trees, then you shall advance quickly. For then ʰthe LORD will go out before you to strike the camp of the Philistines." ²⁵And David did so, as the LORD commanded him; and he drove

back the Philistines from ⁱGeba* as far as ʲGezer.

The Ark Brought to Jerusalem

6 Again David gathered all the choice men of Israel, thirty thousand. ²And ᵃDavid arose and went with all the people who were with him from Baale Judah to bring up from there the ark of God, whose name is called by the Name,* the LORD of Hosts, ᵇwho dwells between the cherubim. ³So they set the ark of God on a new cart, and brought it out of the house of Abinadab, which was on ᶜthe hill; and Uzzah and Ahio, the sons of Abinadab, drove the new cart.* ⁴And they brought it out of ᵈthe house of Abinadab, which was on the hill, accompanying the ark of God; and Ahio went before the ark. ⁵Then David and all the house of Israel ᵉplayed music before the LORD on all kinds of instruments of fir wood, on harps, on stringed instruments, on tambourines, on sistrums, and on cymbals.

⁶And when they came to ᶠNachon's threshing floor, Uzzah put out his ᵍhand to the ark of God and took hold of it, for the oxen stumbled. ⁷Then the anger of the LORD was aroused against Uzzah, and God struck him there for his error; and he died there by the ark of God. ⁸And David became angry because of the

---

* **5:14** Spelled *Shimea* in 1 Chronicles 3:5
* **5:15** Spelled *Elishama* in 1 Chronicles 3:6
* **5:20** Literally *Master of Breakthroughs*
* **5:25** Following Masoretic Text, Targum, and Vulgate; Septuagint reads *Gibeon.* * **6:2** Septuagint, Targum, and Vulgate omit *by the Name*; many Hebrew manuscripts and Syriac read *there.*
* **6:3** Septuagint adds *with the ark.*

5:18 *Valley of Rephaim.* This valley extends southwest from Jerusalem toward the coastal plain, and is a strategic approach to the city.
5:21 *left their images.* The Philistines would have regarded their gods as being defeated by the God of Israel.
6:2 *Baale Judah.* The name means "masters of Judah," and the city was also called Baalah and Kirjath Jearim. It was here that the ark had been left after it was returned by the Philistines in the days when Samuel was a young man and there was no king (1 Sam. 7:1–2). *cherubim.* Cherubim are angelic beings generally regarded as guardians of God's holiness (Ex. 25:22).
6:3 *set the ark of God on a new cart.* The law was specific that the ark was to be carried by the sons of Kohath, not by a cart or any other vehicle (Ex. 25:14–15; Num. 7:8–9).
6:6–8 *Respect for the Ark*—It is easy to understand David's anger at God. Uzzah's death seems quite unnecessary. It looks like his motives were in fact good ones. Reading about this event elicits fear and questioning. Why? We can't see how the punishment fits the crime. This seems incredibly arbitrary. How can we possibly understand the mystery that's involved here? Why such tragedy in the midst of this celebration?

The instructions on handling the ark are found in Numbers 4:15,19–20. There it says if you touch the holy things you die. We still don't understand why, but obviously there was more to the ark than anybody could imagine and no human could control it or use it. It was God's, made to be representative of His holiness and glory. God placed such power in the ark that a human would be overwhelmed by it.

We have such a poor sense of the holiness of God that we only see this event from our perspective. Fear and awe must be a part of a healthy relationship with God. While God is love, He is also to be feared.
6:6 *threshing floor.* A threshing floor was a place for processing grain, separating kernels from the chaff (Ruth 3:2).
6:7 *for his error.* God had warned His people that not even the Kohathites of the tribe of Levi could touch the holy objects of the tabernacle. All of the holy objects were to be covered by the priests before the

5:14ˣ 2 Sam. 12:24 **5:17**ʸ 1 Chr. 11:16 ᶻ 2 Sam. 23:14 **5:18**ᵃ 1 Chr. 11:15 **5:19**ᵇ 1 Sam. 23:2 **5:20**ᶜ Is. 28:21 **5:21**ᵈ Deut. 7:5, 25 **5:22**ᵉ 1 Chr. 14:13 **5:23**ᶠ 2 Sam. 5:19 **5:24**ᵍ 1 Chr. 14:15 ʰ Judg. 4:14 **5:25**ⁱ 1 Chr. 14:16 ʲ Josh. 16:10 **6:2**ᵃ 1 Chr. 13:5, 6 ᵇ Ps. 80:1 **6:3**ᶜ 1 Sam. 26:1 **6:4**ᵈ 1 Sam. 7:1 **6:5**ᵉ 1 Sam. 18:6, 7 **6:6**ᶠ 1 Chr. 13:9 ᵍ Num. 4:15, 19, 20

LORD's outbreak against Uzzah; and he called the name of the place Perez Uzzah* to this day.

9hDavid was afraid of the LORD that day; and he said, "How can the ark of the LORD come to me?" 10So David would not move the ark of the LORD with him into the iCity of David; but David took it aside into the house of Obed-Edom the jGittite. 11kThe ark of the LORD remained in the house of Obed-Edom the Gittite three months. And the LORD lblessed Obed-Edom and all his household.

12Now it was told King David, saying, "The LORD has blessed the house of Obed-Edom and all that *belongs* to him, because of the ark of God." mSo David went and brought up the ark of God from the house of Obed-Edom to the City of David with gladness. 13And so it was, when nthose bearing the ark of the LORD had gone six paces, that he sacrificed ooxen and fatted sheep. 14Then David pdanced before the LORD with all *his* might; and David *was* wearing qa linen ephod. 15rSo David and all the house of Israel brought up the ark of the LORD with shouting and with the sound of the trumpet.

16Now as the ark of the LORD came into the City of David, sMichal, Saul's daughter, looked through a window and saw King David leaping and whirling before the LORD; and she despised him in her heart. 17So tthey brought the ark of the LORD, and set it in uits place in the midst of the tabernacle that David had erected for it. Then David voffered burnt offerings and peace offerings before the LORD. 18And when David had finished offering burnt offerings and peace offerings, whe blessed the people in the name of the LORD of hosts.

19xThen he distributed among all the people, among the whole multitude of Israel, both the women and the men, to everyone a loaf of bread, a piece *of meat*, and a cake of raisins. So all the people departed, everyone to his house.

20yThen David returned to bless his household. And Michal the daughter of Saul came out to meet David, and said, "How glorious was the king of Israel today, zuncovering himself today in the eyes of the maids of his servants, as one of the abase fellows shamelessly uncovers himself!"

21So David said to Michal, "It *was* before the LORD, bwho chose me instead of your father and all his house, to appoint me ruler over the cpeople of the LORD, over Israel. Therefore I will play *music* before the LORD. 22And I will be even more undignified than this, and will be humble in my own sight. But as for the maidservants of whom you have spoken, by them I will be held in honor."

23Therefore Michal the daughter of Saul had no children dto the day of her death.

God's Covenant with David

7 Now it came to pass awhen the king was dwelling in his house, and the LORD had given him rest from all his enemies all around, 2that the king said to Nathan the prophet, "See now, I dwell in ba house of cedar, cbut the ark of God dwells inside tent dcurtains."

3Then Nathan said to the king, "Go, do all that *is* in your eheart, for the LORD *is* with you."

---

* 6:8 Literally *Outburst Against Uzzah*

---

sons of Kohath came to carry them so they would not "touch any holy thing, lest they die" (Num. 4:15).

6:10 *Obed-Edom.* Obed-Edom was a Levite of the family of Korah, and later one of the doorkeepers for the tabernacle (1 Chr. 15:18,24; 26:4–8). **the Gittite.** He was called the Gittite because he was from the Levitical city of Gath Rimmon (Josh. 21:24).

6:14 *linen ephod.* The linen ephod was a short sleeveless garment worn by priests (1 Sam. 2:18). David wore it to honor the Lord because of his worshipful activities that day (v. 13).

6:17 *the tabernacle that David had erected for it.* There are no descriptive details of this tent. It is not clear exactly what happened to the tabernacle after it was moved from Shiloh to Nob (1 Sam. 5; 21:1–5). At the time that David bought the threshing floor from Araunah (2 Sam. 24:21–25), the tabernacle of the Lord, which Moses had made in the wilderness, and the altar of burnt offering were in the high place of Gibeon (1 Chr. 21:29), which was about six miles northwest of Jerusalem.

6:18–19 *peace offerings.* A distinctive feature of the peace offering was that a portion of it would be eaten by the worshiper as a fellowship meal before the Lord.

6:20–23 *uncovering himself.* The love and respect that Michal once had for David was gone. She ridiculed his enthusiasm as he worshiped the Lord, and for David that was not an attitude he could overlook. It is difficult to comprehend the complexities of a marriage where multiple wives and concubines are a part of the picture, and the wife is viewed as chattel before she is viewed as a person. As in so many places in the Bible, the picture is drawn, but without comment on what God thought. Jesus clarifies this a little when He comments on the hardness of hearts, and says, "from the beginning it was not so" (Matt. 19:8).

7:2 *Nathan.* Nathan was a personal advisor to David. As a prophet, he spoke for God, advising David on religious matters. He also chronicled the reigns of David and Solomon (1 Chr. 29:29).

6:9 h Ps. 119:120   **6:10** i 2 Sam. 5:7 j 1 Chr. 13:13; 26:4–8   **6:11** k 1 Chr. 13:14 l Gen. 30:27; 39:5   **6:12** m 1 Chr. 15:25—16:3   **6:13** n Josh. 3:3 o 1 Kin. 8:5   **6:14** p Ps. 30:11; 149:3 q 1 Sam. 2:18, 28   **6:15** r 1 Chr. 15:28   **6:16** s 2 Sam. 3:14   **6:17** t 1 Chr. 16:1 u 1 Chr. 15:1 v 1 Kin. 8:5, 62, 63   **6:18** w 1 Kin. 8:14, 15, 55   **6:19** x 1 Chr. 16:3   **6:20** y Ps. 30:title z 2 Sam. 6:14, 16 a Judg. 9:4   **6:21** b 1 Sam. 13:14; 15:28 c 2 Kin. 11:17   **6:23** d Is. 22:14   **7:1** a 1 Chr. 17:1–27   **7:2** b 2 Sam. 5:11 c Acts 7:46 d Ex. 26:1   **7:3** e 1 Kin. 8:17, 18

4But it happened that night that the word of the LORD came to Nathan, saying, 5"Go and tell My servant David, 'Thus says the LORD: [f]"Would you build a house for Me to dwell in? 6For I have not dwelt in a house [g]since the time that I brought the children of Israel up from Egypt, even to this day, but have moved about in [h]a tent and in a tabernacle. 7Wherever I have [i]moved about with all the children of Israel, have I ever spoken a word to anyone from the tribes of Israel, whom I commanded [j]to shepherd My people Israel, saying, 'Why have you not built Me a house of cedar?'"' 8Now therefore, thus shall you say to My servant David, 'Thus says the LORD of hosts: [k]"I took you from the sheepfold, from following the sheep, to be ruler over My people, over Israel. 9And [l]I have been with you wherever you have gone, [m]and have cut off all your enemies from before you, and have made you a great name, like the name of the great men who *are* on the earth. 10Moreover I will appoint a place for My people Israel, and will [n]plant them, that they may dwell in a place of their own and move no more; [o]nor shall the sons of wickedness oppress them anymore, as previously, 11[p]since the time that I commanded judges *to be* over My people Israel, and have caused you to rest from all your enemies. Also the LORD tells you [q]that He will make you a house.*

12[r]"When your days are fulfilled and you [s]rest with your fathers, [t]I will set up your seed after you, who will come from your body, and I will establish his kingdom. 13[u]He shall build a house for My name, and I will [v]establish the throne of his kingdom forever. 14[w]I will be his Father, and he shall be [x]My son. If he commits iniquity, I will chasten him with the rod of men and with the blows of the sons of men. 15But My mercy shall not depart from him, [y]as I took *it* from Saul, whom I removed from before you. 16And [z]your house and your kingdom shall be established forever before you.* Your throne shall be established forever."'"

17According to all these words and according to all this vision, so Nathan spoke to David.

David's Thanksgiving to God

18Then King David went in and sat before the LORD; and he said: [a]"Who *am* I, O Lord GOD? And what is my house, that You have brought me this far? 19And yet this was a small thing in Your sight, O Lord GOD; and You have also spoken of Your servant's house for a great while to come. [b]*Is* this the manner of man, O Lord GOD? 20Now what more can David say to You? For You, Lord GOD, [c]know Your servant. 21For Your word's sake, and according to Your own heart, You have done all these great things, to make Your servant know *them*. 22Therefore [d]You are great, O Lord GOD.* For [e]*there is* none like You, nor *is there any* God besides You, according to all that we have heard with our [f]ears. 23And who *is* like Your people, like Israel, [g]the one nation on the earth whom God went to redeem for Himself as a people, to make for Himself a name—and to do for Yourself great and awesome deeds for Your land—before [h]Your people whom You redeemed for Yourself from Egypt, the nations, and their gods? 24For [i]You have made Your people Israel Your very own people forever; [j]and You, LORD, have become their God.

25"Now, O LORD God, the word which You have spoken concerning Your servant and concerning his house, establish *it* forever and do as You have said. 26So let Your name be magnified forever, saying, 'The LORD of hosts *is* the God over Israel.' And let the house of Your servant David be established before You. 27For You, O LORD of hosts, God of Israel, have revealed *this* to Your servant, saying, 'I will build you a house.' Therefore Your servant has found it in his heart to pray this prayer to You.

* **7:11** That is, a royal dynasty * **7:16** Septuagint reads *Me*. * **7:22** Targum and Syriac read *O LORD God*.

7:4–17 The Covenant with David—The Davidic covenant contains God's promise to Israel and to David. God promised Israel that Palestine would always be their place (v. 10). He also promised that David would have an unending dynasty and an everlasting kingdom. This promise is fulfilled in Christ. Both Matthew and Luke, in their Gospels, trace Jesus' ancestry back to David.

7:13 ***the throne of his kingdom forever.*** This is not to say that Solomon would rule forever. Rather, the right to rule, represented by the image of the throne, would always belong to his descendants. Further, there would always be a male heir who would be able to rule. Ultimately this promise is fulfilled in Christ (Matt. 1).

7:19 ***for a great while to come.*** God extended the promise concerning David's dynasty far into the future. All of human history leads inevitably to the rule of Christ on earth. This is its destiny, its prophetic fulfillment, the final meaning of all history.

7:27 ***prayer.*** David was a king for God, not for himself. It is not likely that he was totally without pride in his position, but he did not seem to be a man who was full of himself. His purpose in wanting to build the temple was to glorify God whom he loved, not to glorify himself. David's prayer of worship and thanksgiving is an intimate key that shows how he was able

7:5 [f] 1 Kin. 5:3, 4; 8:19 **7:6** [g] 1 Kin. 8:16 [h] Ex. 40:18, 34 **7:7** [i] Lev. 26:11, 12 [j] 2 Sam. 5:2 **7:8** [k] 1 Sam. 16:11, 12 **7:9** [l] 2 Sam. 5:10 [m] 1 Sam. 31:6 **7:10** [n] Ps. 44:2; 80:8 [o] Ps. 89:22, 23 **7:11** [p] Judg. 2:14–16 [q] 2 Sam. 7:27 **7:12** [r] 1 Kin. 2:1 [s] Deut. 31:16 [t] Ps. 132:11 **7:13** [u] 1 Kin. 5:5; 8:19 [v] [Is. 9:7; 49:8] **7:14** [w] [Heb. 1:5] [x] [Ps. 2:7; 89:26, 27, 30] **7:15** [y] 1 Sam. 15:23, 28; 16:14 **7:16** [z] 2 Sam. 7:13 **7:18** [a] Ex. 3:11 **7:19** [b] [Is. 55:8, 9] **7:20** [c] John 21:17 **7:22** [d] Deut. 10:17 [e] Ex. 15:11 [f] Ex. 10:2 **7:23** [g] Ps. 147:20 [h] Deut. 9:26; 33:29 **7:24** [i] [Deut. 26:18] [j] Ps. 48:14

28"And now, O Lord God, You are God, and *k*Your words are true, and You have promised this goodness to Your servant. 29Now therefore, let it please You to bless the house of Your servant, that it may continue before You forever; for You, O Lord God, have spoken *it,* and with Your blessing let the house of Your servant be blessed *l*forever."

David's Further Conquests

8 After this it came to pass that David attacked the Philistines and subdued them. And David took Metheg Ammah from the hand of the Philistines.

2Then *a*he defeated Moab. Forcing them down to the ground, he measured them off with a line. With two lines he measured off those to be put to death, and with one full line those to be kept alive. So the Moabites became David's *b*servants, *and* *c*brought tribute.

3David also defeated Hadadezer the son of Rehob, king of *d*Zobah, as he went to recover *e*his territory at the River Euphrates. 4David took from him one thousand *chari*ots, seven hundred* horsemen, and twenty thousand foot soldiers. Also David *f*hamstrung all the chariot *horses,* except that he spared *enough* of them for one hundred chariots.

5gWhen the Syrians of Damascus came to help Hadadezer king of Zobah, David killed twenty-two thousand of the Syrians. 6Then David put garrisons in Syria of Damascus; and the Syrians became David's servants, *and* brought tribute. So *h*the Lord preserved David wherever he went. 7And David took *i*the shields of gold that had belonged to the servants of Hadadezer, and brought them to Jerusalem. 8Also from Betah* and from *j*Berothai, cities of Hadadezer, King David took a large amount of bronze.

9When Toi* king of *k*Hamath heard that David had defeated all the army of Hadadezer, 10then Toi sent Joram* his son to King David, to greet him and bless him,

because he had fought against Hadadezer and defeated him (for Hadadezer had been at war with Toi); and *Joram* brought with him articles of silver, articles of gold, and articles of bronze. 11King David also *l*dedicated these to the Lord, along with the silver and gold that he had dedicated from all the nations which he had subdued— 12from Syria,* from Moab, from the people of Ammon, from the *m*Philistines, from Amalek, and from the spoil of Hadadezer the son of Rehob, king of Zobah.

13And David made *himself* a *n*name when he returned from killing *o*eighteen thousand Syrians* in *p*the Valley of Salt. 14He also put garrisons in Edom; throughout all Edom he put garrisons, and *q*all the Edomites became David's servants. And the Lord preserved David wherever he went.

David's Administration

15So David reigned over all Israel; and David administered judgment and justice to all his people. 16rJoab the son of Zeruiah *was* over the army; *s*Jehoshaphat the son of Ahilud *was* recorder; 17tZadok the son of Ahitub and Ahimelech the son of Abiathar *were* the priests; Seraiah* *was* the scribe; 18uBenaiah the son of Jehoiada *was* over both the *v*Cherethites and the Pelethites; and David's sons were chief ministers.

David's Kindness to Mephibosheth

9 Now David said, "Is there still anyone who is left of the house of Saul, that I may *a*show him kindness for Jonathan's sake?"

2And *there was* a servant of the house of

---

* **8:4** Or *seven thousand* (compare 1 Chronicles 18:4) * **8:8** Spelled *Tibhath* in 1 Chronicles 18:8 * **8:9** Spelled *Tou* in 1 Chronicles 18:9 * **8:10** Spelled *Hadoram* in 1 Chronicles 18:10 * **8:12** Septuagint, Syriac, and some Hebrew manuscripts read *Edom.* * **8:13** Septuagint, Syriac, and some Hebrew manuscripts read *Edomites* (compare 1 Chronicles 18:12). * **8:17** Spelled *Shavsha* in 1 Chronicles 18:16

---

to keep himself both willing and trusting as he followed God.

7:28 You are God, and Your words are true. This is David's theme, throughout his life, and this is why he was a man after God's heart (1 Sam. 13:14).

8:2 Moabites. The Moabites were descendants of the incestuous relationship between Lot and his older daughter (Gen. 19:36–37).

8:4 hamstrung. David disabled the horses by cutting the back sinews of the hind legs to prevent them from being used for military activity (Josh. 11:6,9).

8:5 Damascus. Damascus was located at an oasis near the foot of the Anti-Lebanon mountains and was one of the most strategically located cities of the ancient world. Damascus lay at the crossroads of the two main international highways: the Via Maris, leading south and west to Egypt, and the King's Highway, leading from the east side of the Jordan south to Arabia.

8:8 Berothai. This city was about 30 miles northwest of Damascus.

8:15 David reigned over all Israel. As a result of David's conquests, the sovereignty of Israel extended from the Gulf of Aqaba and the River of Egypt to the Euphrates River—the very region God had promised Abraham (Gen. 15:18).

9:1–13 kindness. David wrote in Psalm 23:5, "You prepare a table before me in the presence of my enemies." And that is just what David did for Mephibosheth, for the sake of his father Jonathan. Jonathan and David had been separated by the hostility that

---

7:28 *k* John 17:17   **7:29** *l* 2 Sam. 22:51   **8:2** *a* Num. 24:17   *b* 2 Sam. 12:31 *c* 1 Kin. 4:21   *d* 1 Sam. 14:47 *e* 2 Sam. 10:15–19   **8:4** *f* Josh. 11:6, 9   **8:5** *g* 1 Kin. 11:23–25   **8:6** *h* 2 Sam. 7:9; 8:14   **8:7** *i* 1 Kin. 10:16   **8:8** *j* Ezek. 47:16   **8:9** *k* 1 Kin. 8:65   **8:11** *l* 1 Kin. 7:51   **8:12** *m* 2 Sam. 5:17–25   **8:13** *n* 2 Sam. 7:9   *o* 2 Kin. 14:7   *p* 1 Chr. 18:12   **8:14** *q* Gen. 27:29, 37–40   **8:16** *r* 2 Sam. 19:13; 20:23   *s* 1 Kin. 4:3   **8:17** *t* 1 Chr. 6:4–8; 24:3   **8:18** *u* 1 Chr. 18:17   *v* 1 Sam. 30:14   **9:1** *a* 1 Sam. 18:3; 20:14–16

Saul whose name *was* ᵇZiba. So when they had called him to David, the king said to him, "*Are* you Ziba?"

He said, "At your service!"

³Then the king said, "*Is* there not still someone of the house of Saul, to whom I may show ᶜthe kindness of God?"

And Ziba said to the king, "There is still a son of Jonathan *who is* ᵈlame in *his* feet."

⁴So the king said to him, "Where *is* he?"

And Ziba said to the king, "Indeed he *is* in the house of ᵉMachir the son of Ammiel, in Lo Debar."

⁵Then King David sent and brought him out of the house of Machir the son of Ammiel, from Lo Debar.

⁶Now when ᶠMephibosheth the son of Jonathan, the son of Saul, had come to David, he fell on his face and prostrated himself. Then David said, "Mephibosheth?"

And he answered, "Here is your servant!"

⁷So David said to him, "Do not fear, for I will surely show you kindness for Jonathan your father's sake, and will restore to you all the land of Saul your grandfather; and you shall eat bread at my table continually."

⁸Then he bowed himself, and said, "What *is* your servant, that you should look upon such ᵍa dead dog as I?"

⁹And the king called to Ziba, Saul's servant, and said to him, ʰ"I have given to your master's son all that belonged to Saul and to all his house. ¹⁰You therefore, and your sons and your servants, shall work the land for him, and you shall bring in *the harvest,* that your master's son may have food to eat. But Mephibosheth your master's son ⁱshall eat bread at my table always." Now Ziba had ʲfifteen sons and twenty servants.

¹¹Then Ziba said to the king, "According to all that my lord the king has commanded his servant, so will your servant do."

"As for Mephibosheth," *said the king,*

"he shall eat at my table* like one of the king's sons." ¹²Mephibosheth had a young son ᵏwhose name *was* Micha. And all who dwelt in the house of Ziba *were* servants of Mephibosheth. ¹³So Mephibosheth dwelt in Jerusalem, ˡfor he ate continually at the king's table. And he ᵐwas lame in both his feet.

The Ammonites and Syrians Defeated

10 It happened after this that the ᵃking of the people of Ammon died, and Hanun his son reigned in his place. ²Then David said, "I will show ᵇkindness to Hanun the son of ᶜNahash, as his father showed kindness to me."

So David sent by the hand of his servants to comfort him concerning his father. And David's servants came into the land of the people of Ammon. ³And the princes of the people of Ammon said to Hanun their lord, "Do you think that David really honors your father because he has sent comforters to you? Has David not *rather* sent his servants to you to search the city, to spy it out, and to overthrow it?"

⁴Therefore Hanun took David's servants, shaved off half of their beards, cut off their garments in the middle, ᵈat their buttocks, and sent them away. ⁵When they told David, he sent to meet them, because the men were greatly ashamed. And the king said, "Wait at Jericho until your beards have grown, and *then* return."

⁶When the people of Ammon saw that they ᵉhad made themselves repulsive to David, the people of Ammon sent and hired ᶠthe Syrians of ᵍBeth Rehob and the Syrians of Zoba, twenty thousand foot soldiers; and from the king of ʰMaacah one thousand men, and from ⁱIsh-Tob twelve

---

* **9:11** Septuagint reads *David's table.*

Saul had for David, and as far as Mephibosheth would have understood, David was an enemy to the house of Saul. But the bond of love and friendship that David and Jonathan had was greater than the hostility of Saul, and David was faithful to honor those bonds.

9:4 *Machir the son of Ammiel.* Machir was a man, apparently of wealth and position, who extended hospitality to David during Absalom's revolt (17:27–29). He showed himself to be a man of kindness who was willing to help someone in need, even if it might not be politically expedient.

9:11 *like one of the king's sons.* David kept his promise to Jonathan. The two young men had vowed that the Lord would be between them, and between their descendants forever (1 Sam. 20:42). It was a way of saying that the Lord would always be in their relationships with each other, keeping them loyal, kind, honest, and willing to bear each other's burdens. Now Jonathan's son was provided for as one of David's sons.

10:1 *the king of the people of Ammon.* The king

of Ammon was probably the same Nahash who was defeated by Saul at Jabesh Gilead (1 Sam. 11:1–11).

10:2 *as his father showed kindness to me.* The occasion of Nahash's kindness is not recorded. One possibility is that Nahash, an enemy of Saul, had given aid to David during his war with Ishbosheth (2:8—4:12).

10:6 *Beth Rehob and . . . Zoba.* These two Aramean city-states were located north of Israel. **Maacah.** The small Aramean kingdom east of the Jordan was part of the territory assigned to the half-tribe of Manasseh (Josh. 12:5; 13:11) **Ish-Tob.** Tob was also an area east of the Jordan, but not a part of Israel. (Judg. 11:3).

9:2 ᵇ 2 Sam. 16:1–4; 19:17, 29   **9:3** ᶜ 1 Sam. 20:14   ᵈ 2 Sam. 4:4   **9:4** ᵉ 2 Sam. 17:27–29   **9:6** ᶠ 2 Sam. 16:4; 19:24–30   **9:8** ᵍ 2 Sam. 16:9   **9:9** ʰ 2 Sam. 16:4; 19:29   **9:10** ⁱ 2 Sam. 9:7, 11, 13; 19:28   ʲ 2 Sam. 19:17   **9:12** ᵏ 1 Chr. 8:34   **9:13** ˡ 2 Sam. 9:7, 10, 11   ᵐ 2 Sam. 9:3   **10:1** ᵃ 1 Chr. 19:1   **10:2** ᵇ 2 Sam. 9:1   ᶜ 1 Sam. 11:1   **10:4** ᵈ Is. 20:4; 47:2   **10:6** ᵉ Gen. 34:30   ᶠ 2 Sam. 8:3, 5   ᵍ Judg. 18:28   ʰ Deut. 3:14   ⁱ Judg. 11:3, 5

thousand men. 7Now when David heard
of it, he sent Joab and all the army of [j]the
mighty men. 8Then the people of Ammon
came out and put themselves in battle array at the entrance of the gate. And [k]the
Syrians of Zoba, Beth Rehob, Ish-Tob, and
Maacah *were* by themselves in the field.
9When Joab saw that the battle line was
against him before and behind, he chose
some of Israel's best and put *them* in battle
array against the Syrians. 10And the rest
of the people he put under the command of
[l]Abishai his brother, that he might set *them*
in battle array against the people of Ammon. 11Then he said, "If the Syrians are too
strong for me, then you shall help me; but if
the people of Ammon are too strong for you,
then I will come and help you. 12[m]Be of good
courage, and let us [n]be strong for our people and for the cities of our God. And may
[o]the LORD do *what is* good in His sight."
13So Joab and the people who *were* with
him drew near for the battle against the
Syrians, and they fled before him. 14When
the people of Ammon saw that the Syrians
were fleeing, they also fled before Abishai,
and entered the city. So Joab returned from
the people of Ammon and went to [p]Jeru-
salem.
15When the Syrians saw that they had
been defeated by Israel, they gathered
together. 16Then Hadadezer* sent and
brought out the Syrians who *were* beyond
the River,* and they came to Helam. And
Shobach the commander of Hadadezer's
army *went* before them. 17When it was
told David, he gathered all Israel, crossed
over the Jordan, and came to Helam. And
the Syrians set themselves in battle array
against David and fought with him. 18Then
the Syrians fled before Israel; and David
killed seven hundred charioteers and forty thousand [q]horsemen of the Syrians, and
struck Shobach the commander of their
army, who died there. 19And when all the
kings *who were* servants to Hadadezer*
saw that they were defeated by Israel, they
made peace with Israel and [r]served them.
So the Syrians were afraid to help the people of Ammon anymore.

David, Bathsheba, and Uriah

11 It happened in the spring of the year,
at the [a]time when kings go out *to battle,* that [b]David sent Joab and his servants
with him, and all Israel; and they destroyed
the people of Ammon and besieged [c]Rab-
bah. But David remained at Jerusalem.
2Then it happened one evening that David arose from his bed [d]and walked on the
roof of the king's house. And from the roof
he [e]saw a woman bathing, and the woman
was very beautiful to behold. 3So David
sent and inquired about the woman. And
someone said, "*Is* this not Bathsheba, the
daughter of Eliam, the wife [f]of Uriah the
[g]Hittite?" 4Then David sent messengers,
and took her; and she came to him, and [h]he
lay with her, for she was [i]cleansed from her
impurity; and she returned to her house.
5And the woman conceived; so she sent
and told David, and said, "I *am* with child."
6Then David sent to Joab, *saying,* "Send
me Uriah the Hittite." And Joab sent Uriah
to David. 7When Uriah had come to him,
David asked how Joab was doing, and how
the people were doing, and how the war
prospered. 8And David said to Uriah, "Go
down to your house and [j]wash your feet."
So Uriah departed from the king's house,
and a gift *of food* from the king followed
him. 9But Uriah slept at the [k]door of the
king's house with all the servants of his
lord, and did not go down to his house. 10So
when they told David, saying, "Uriah did
not go down to his house," David said to
Uriah, "Did you not come from a journey?
Why did you not go down to your house?"
11And Uriah said to David, [l]"The ark and
Israel and Judah are dwelling in tents, and
[m]my lord Joab and the servants of my lord
are encamped in the open fields. Shall I
then go to my house to eat and drink, and to
lie with my wife? *As* you live, and *as* your
soul lives, I will not do this thing."
12Then David said to Uriah, "Wait here
today also, and tomorrow I will let you
depart." So Uriah remained in Jerusalem

---

* **10:16** Hebrew *Hadarezer* • That is, *the Euphrates* * **10:19** Hebrew *Hadarezer*

10:8 *entrance of the gate.* Some cities had multiple gates. If attackers broke through one gate, they would find another gate in front of them. The Ammonites fought near the entrance of the city so they could retreat behind the city gates if the battle turned against them. The mercenary soldiers were in more exposed positions in the field.

10:10 *Abishai.* Abishai was one of David's mighty men (23:18). He was a brave warrior (1 Sam. 26:6–9) and a successful commander (1 Chr. 18:12–13), but was impetuous and perhaps even bloodthirsty (16:9; 19:21). He had played a part in the murder of Abner.

11:1 *in the spring of the year, at the time when kings go out to battle.* Spring was a good time to mount a campaign. They could be assured of good weather and an abundance of food along the way.

11:2 *from the roof he saw a woman bathing.* She was probably in the enclosed courtyard of her home, a place of privacy, not visible from the street.

11:5 *the woman conceived.* The law commanded both parties in an adulterous relationship to be put to death (Lev. 20:10). In practice, a woman who became pregnant might be forced to bear the shame and guilt alone (John 8:1–11).

10:7 [j] 2 Sam. 23:8 **10:8** [k] 2 Sam. 10:6 **10:10** [l] 2 Sam. 3:30 **10:12** [m] Deut. 31:6 [n] 1 Cor. 16:13 [o] 1 Sam. 3:18 **10:14** [p] 2 Sam. 11:1 **10:18** [q] 1 Chr. 19:18 **10:19** [r] 2 Sam. 8:6 **11:1** [a] 1 Kin. 20:22–26 [b] 1 Chr. 20:1 [c] 2 Sam. 12:26 **11:2** [d] Deut. 22:8 [e] Gen. 34:2 **11:3** [f] 2 Sam. 23:39 [g] 1 Sam. 26:6 **11:4** [h] [James 1:14, 15] [i] Lev. 15:19, 28 **11:8** [j] Gen. 18:4; 19:2 **11:9** [k] 1 Kin. 14:27, 28 **11:11** [l] 2 Sam. 7:2, 6 [m] 2 Sam. 20:6–22

that day and the next. 13Now when David
called him, he ate and drank before him;
and he made him [n]drunk. And at evening
he went out to lie on his bed [o]with the servants of his lord, but he did not go down to
his house.
14In the morning it happened that David
[p]wrote a letter to Joab and sent *it* by the
hand of Uriah. 15And he wrote in the letter,
saying, "Set Uriah in the forefront of the
hottest battle, and retreat from him, that
he may [q]be struck down and die." 16So it
was, while Joab besieged the city, that he
assigned Uriah to a place where he knew
there *were* valiant men. 17Then the men
of the city came out and fought with Joab.
And *some* of the people of the servants of
David fell; and Uriah the Hittite died also.
18Then Joab sent and told David all the
things concerning the war, 19and charged
the messenger, saying, "When you have
finished telling the matters of the war to
the king, 20if it happens that the king's
wrath rises, and he says to you: 'Why did
you approach so near to the city when you
fought? Did you not know that they would
shoot from the wall? 21Who struck [r]Abi-
melech the son of Jerubbesheth?* Was it
not a woman who cast a piece of a millstone on him from the wall, so that he
died in Thebez? Why did you go near the
wall?'—then you shall say, 'Your servant
Uriah the Hittite is dead also.'"
22So the messenger went, and came and
told David all that Joab had sent by him.
23And the messenger said to David, "Surely
the men prevailed against us and came out
to us in the field; then we drove them back
as far as the entrance of the gate. 24The archers shot from the wall at your servants;
and *some* of the king's servants are dead,
and your servant Uriah the Hittite is dead
also."
25Then David said to the messenger,
"Thus you shall say to Joab: 'Do not let this
thing displease you, for the sword devours
one as well as another. Strengthen your attack against the city, and overthrow it.' So
encourage him."
26When the wife of Uriah heard that
Uriah her husband was dead, she mourned
for her husband. 27And when her mourning
was over, David sent and brought her to his
house, and she [s]became his wife and bore
him a son. But the thing that David had
done [t]displeased the LORD.

Nathan's Parable and David's Confession

12 Then the LORD sent Nathan to David. And [a]he came to him, and [b]said
to him: "There were two men in one city,
one rich and the other poor. 2The rich *man*
had exceedingly many flocks and herds.
3But the poor *man* had nothing, except one
little ewe lamb which he had bought and
nourished; and it grew up together with
him and with his children. It ate of his own
food and drank from his own cup and lay
in his bosom; and it was like a daughter to
him. 4And a traveler came to the rich man,
who refused to take from his own flock and
from his own herd to prepare one for the
wayfaring man who had come to him; but
he took the poor man's lamb and prepared
it for the man who had come to him."
5So David's anger was greatly aroused
against the man, and he said to Nathan,
"*As* the LORD lives, the man who has done
this shall surely die! 6And he shall restore
[c]fourfold for the lamb, because he did this
thing and because he had no pity."
7Then Nathan said to David, "You *are*
the man! Thus says the LORD God of Israel:
'I [d]anointed you king over Israel, and I delivered you from the hand of Saul. 8I gave
you your master's house and your master's
wives into your keeping, and gave you the
house of Israel and Judah. And if *that had
been* too little, I also would have given you
much more! 9[e]Why have you [f]despised the
commandment of the LORD, to do evil in
His sight? [g]You have killed Uriah the Hittite with the sword; you have taken his wife
to be your wife, and have killed him with
the sword of the people of Ammon. 10Now
therefore, [h]the sword shall never depart
from your house, because you have despised Me, and have taken the wife of Uriah the Hittite to be your wife.' 11Thus says
the LORD: 'Behold, I will raise up adversity
against you from your own house; and I
will [i]take your wives before your eyes and
give *them* to your neighbor, and he shall
lie with your wives in the sight of this sun.

* **11:21** Same as *Jerubbaal* (Gideon), Judges 6:32ff

11:21 *Was it not a woman.* The story referred to here is recorded in Judges 9:50–55. For a soldier to die at the hand of a woman was at best shameful, if not a point of ridicule (Judg. 4:17–24). It seems that Joab was letting David know that he knew David's real reasons for wanting Uriah dead.

12:7 *You are the man.* It took courage and a strong commitment to the Lord for Nathan to speak these words to the king. Nathan's rebuke was centered on who the Lord is, and what the Lord expects of His servants. It was the word of the Lord that convicted David, not the force of Nathan's character or rhetoric.

12:9 *despised the commandment of the LORD.* David had broken the commandments about coveting, adultery, and murder (Ex. 20:13–17). The word despised means "to think lightly of."

11:13 [n] Gen. 19:33, 35 [o] 2 Sam. 11:9 **11:14** [p] 1 Kin. 21:8, 9 **11:15** [q] 2 Sam. 12:9 **11:21** [r] Judg. 9:50–54 **11:27** [s] 2 Sam. 12:9 [t] 1 Chr. 21:7 **12:1** [a] Ps. 51:title [b] 1 Kin. 20:35–41 **12:6** [c] [Ex. 22:1] **12:7** [d] 1 Sam. 16:13 **12:9** [e] 1 Sam. 15:19 [f] Num. 15:31 [g] 2 Sam. 11:14–17, 27 **12:10** [h] [Amos 7:9] **12:11** [i] 2 Sam. 16:21, 22

12For you did *it* secretly, *j*but I will do this thing before all Israel, before the sun.'"

13*k*So David said to Nathan, *l*"I have sinned against the LORD."

And Nathan said to David, "The LORD also has *m*put away your sin; you shall not die. 14However, because by this deed you have given great occasion to the enemies of the LORD *n*to blaspheme, the child also *who is* born to you shall surely die." 15Then Nathan departed to his house.

The Death of David's Son

And the *o*LORD struck the child that Uriah's wife bore to David, and it became ill. 16David therefore pleaded with God for the child, and David fasted and went in and *p*lay all night on the ground. 17So the elders of his house arose *and went* to him, to raise him up from the ground. But he would not, nor did he eat food with them. 18Then on the seventh day it came to pass that the child died. And the servants of David were afraid to tell him that the child was dead. For they said, "Indeed, while the child was alive, we spoke to him, and he would not heed our voice. How can we tell him that the child is dead? He may do some harm!"

19When David saw that his servants were whispering, David perceived that the child was dead. Therefore David said to his servants, "Is the child dead?"

And they said, "He is dead."

20So David arose from the ground, washed and *q*anointed himself, and changed his clothes; and he went into the house of the LORD and *r*worshiped. Then he went to his own house; and when he requested, they set food before him, and he ate. 21Then his servants said to him, "What *is* this that you have done? You fasted and wept for the child *while he was* alive, but when the child died, you arose and ate food."

22And he said, "While the child was alive, I fasted and wept; *s*for I said, 'Who can tell *whether* the LORD* will be gracious to me, that the child may live?' 23But now he

is dead; why should I fast? Can I bring him back again? I shall go *t*to him, but *u*he shall not return to me."

Solomon Is Born

24Then David comforted Bathsheba his wife, and went in to her and lay with her. So *v*she bore a son, and *w*he* called his name Solomon. Now the LORD loved him, 25and He sent *word* by the hand of Nathan the prophet: So he* called his name Jedidiah,* because of the LORD.

Rabbah Is Captured

26Now *x*Joab fought against *y*Rabbah of the people of Ammon, and took the royal city. 27And Joab sent messengers to David, and said, "I have fought against Rabbah, and I have taken the city's water *supply.* 28Now therefore, gather the rest of the people together and encamp against the city and take it, lest I take the city and it be called after my name." 29So David gathered all the people together and went to Rabbah, fought against it, and took it. 30*z*Then he took their king's crown from his head. Its weight *was* a talent of gold, with precious stones. And it was *set* on David's head. Also he brought out the spoil of the city in great abundance. 31And he brought out the people who *were* in it, and put *them to work* with saws and iron picks and iron axes, and made them cross over to the brick works. So he did to all the cities of the people of Ammon. Then David and all the people returned to Jerusalem.

Amnon and Tamar

13 After this *a*Absalom the son of David had a lovely sister, whose name *was* *b*Tamar; and *c*Amnon the son of David

---

* **12:22** A few Hebrew manuscripts and Syriac read *God.*   * **12:24** Following Kethib, Septuagint, and Vulgate; Qere, a few Hebrew manuscripts, Syriac, and Targum read *she.*   * **12:25** Qere, some Hebrew manuscripts, Syriac, and Targum read *she.*   • Literally *Beloved of the LORD*

12:13 *I have sinned against the LORD.* David did not attempt to rationalize his sin or make an excuse for himself. A fuller expression of David's confession is found in Psalm 51. ***you shall not die.*** David deserved death (Lev. 20:10; Num. 35:31–33), but God's grace is able to circumvent His own plan for punishment.
12:14 Adultery—Adultery is forbidden in the Ten Commandments (Ex. 20:14), and it is not difficult to think of a long list of the messy problems that accompany adultery. But adultery is not just a problem involving other people. It is also a problem with God. It is a direct and deliberate disobedience of a nonnegotiable command. This kind of disobedience is also a choice to stop listening to God in other areas—not because He won't communicate, but because we won't. We don't want to ask for help because we don't want to hear Him say, "And what about the affair with ____?" Adultery is more expensive than we can calculate.

12:24 *Solomon.* The name Solomon is related to the Hebrew word for *peace.*
12:25 *Jedidiah.* The name Jedidiah means "beloved of the Lord." The Hebrew name is related to David's name, meaning "beloved." This name, coming from the prophet Nathan, surely must have comforted David and Bathsheba with assurance of God's forgiveness.
12:30 *a talent of gold.* The crown weighed about 75 pounds.
13:1 Temptation—Not all temptation is equal. Some kinds of temptations are easily squelched,

12:12 *j* 2 Sam. 16:22   **12:13** *k* 1 Sam. 15:24   *l* 2 Sam. 24:10   *m* [Mic. 7:18]   **12:14** *n* Is. 52:5   **12:15** *o* 1 Sam. 25:38   **12:16** *p* 2 Sam. 13:31   **12:20** *q* Ruth 3:3   *r* Job 1:20   **12:22** *s* Jon. 3:9   **12:23** *t* Gen. 37:35   *u* Job 7:8–10   **12:24** *v* Matt. 1:6   *w* 1 Chr. 22:9   **12:26** *x* 1 Chr. 20:1   *y* Deut. 3:11   **12:30** *z* 1 Chr. 20:2   **13:1** *a* 2 Sam. 3:2, 3   *b* 1 Chr. 3:9   *c* 2 Sam. 3:2

loved her. [2]Amnon was so distressed over his sister Tamar that he became sick; for she *was* a virgin. And it was improper for Amnon to do anything to her. [3]But Amnon had a friend whose name *was* Jonadab [d]the son of Shimeah, David's brother. Now Jonadab *was* a very crafty man. [4]And he said to him, "Why *are* you, the king's son, becoming thinner day after day? Will you not tell me?"

Amnon said to him, "I love Tamar, my brother Absalom's sister."

[5]So Jonadab said to him, "Lie down on your bed and pretend to be ill. And when your father comes to see you, say to him, 'Please let my sister Tamar come and give me food, and prepare the food in my sight, that I may see *it* and eat it from her hand.'"

[6]Then Amnon lay down and pretended to be ill; and when the king came to see him, Amnon said to the king, "Please let Tamar my sister come and [e]make a couple of cakes for me in my sight, that I may eat from her hand."

[7]And David sent home to Tamar, saying, "Now go to your brother Amnon's house, and prepare food for him." [8]So Tamar went to her brother Amnon's house; and he was lying down. Then she took flour and kneaded *it*, made cakes in his sight, and baked the cakes. [9]And she took the pan and placed *them* out before him, but he refused to eat. Then Amnon said, [f]"Have everyone go out from me." And they all went out from him. [10]Then Amnon said to Tamar, "Bring the food into the bedroom, that I may eat from your hand." And Tamar took the cakes which she had made, and brought *them* to Amnon her brother in the bedroom. [11]Now when she had brought *them* to him to eat, [g]he took hold of her and said to her, "Come, lie with me, my sister."

[12]But she answered him, "No, my brother, do not force me, for [h]no such thing should be done in Israel. Do not do this [i]disgraceful thing! [13]And I, where could I take my shame? And as for you, you would be like one of the fools in Israel. Now therefore, please speak to the king; [j]for he will not withhold me from you." [14]However, he would not heed her voice; and being stronger than she, he [k]forced her and lay with her.

[15]Then Amnon hated her exceedingly, so that the hatred with which he hated her *was* greater than the love with which he had loved her. And Amnon said to her, "Arise, be gone!"

[16]So she said to him, "No, indeed! This evil of sending me away *is* worse than the other that you did to me."

But he would not listen to her. [17]Then he called his servant who attended him, and said, "Here! Put this *woman* out, away from me, and bolt the door behind her." [18]Now she had on [l]a robe of many colors, for the king's virgin daughters wore such apparel. And his servant put her out and bolted the door behind her.

[19]Then Tamar put [m]ashes on her head, and tore her robe of many colors that *was* on her, and [n]laid her hand on her head and went away crying bitterly. [20]And Absalom her brother said to her, "Has Amnon your brother been with you? But now hold your peace, my sister. He *is* your brother; do not take this thing to heart." So Tamar remained desolate in her brother Absalom's house.

[21]But when King David heard of all these things, he was very angry. [22]And Absalom spoke to his brother Amnon [o]neither good nor bad. For Absalom [p]hated Amnon, because he had forced his sister Tamar.

---

and others must be fought with vigilance and every ounce of energy that we have. The battle begins in the mind, and one of the first steps in combating temptation is to make up one's mind that the answer must be "no." Once we begin thinking of how nice it would be to give in, the temptation has a foothold that can grow into full blown sin. God always provides a way out, but we have to want to take that way (1 Cor. 10:13).

13:4 *I love . . . my brother Absalom's sister.* Such relationships are clearly forbidden in the law (Lev. 18:9,29; 20:17). The lust which he conceived in his heart gave birth to sin, and that sin, when accomplished, brought death (James 1:15). Amnon did die, but even worse, his heart was hardened so that he did not care what he had done to Tamar. For her, the price of his wickedness was very high.

13:17 *Put this woman out.* It is difficult to translate the contempt which Amnon had for Tamar. His order to his servant suggests the words and tone used when asking a servant to dump trash. If he had not been his sister, Amnon would have been forced to marry her (Deut. 22:28–29).

13:19 *ashes on her head . . . tore her robe . . . laid her hand on her head.* All of these gestures, as

well as her public weeping, were traditional signs of mourning. Amnon had wantonly destroyed her, and there was nothing anyone could do to set her life right. Women who have been raped often feel abandoned by society, and the very people who should have protected them are oblivious to their need for comfort. Rape is a private crime, and yet it is also a very public menace. It is difficult to redress the wrongs caused by rape without subjecting the victim to more publicity than is comfortable for someone who has already been severely traumatized.

13:21 *very angry.* David was angry, but he took no steps to discipline his son. Perhaps he felt he could not enforce exile on his son (Lev. 18:9,29; 20:17), when the Lord had forgiven him in a similar circumstance. The big difference between David and Amnon was that David acknowledged his sin and was remorseful and repentant.

13:3 [d] 1 Sam. 16:9 **13:6** [e] Gen. 18:6 **13:9** [f] Gen. 45:1 **13:11** [g] Gen. 39:12 **13:12** [h] [Lev. 18:9–11; 20:17] [i] Judg. 19:23; 20:6 **13:13** [j] Gen. 20:12 **13:14** [k] 2 Sam. 12:11 **13:18** [l] Gen. 37:3 **13:19** [m] Josh. 7:6 [n] Jer. 2:37 **13:22** [o] Gen. 24:50; 31:24 [p] [Lev. 19:17, 18]

Absalom Murders Amnon

23And it came to pass, after two full years, that Absalom qhad sheepshearers in Baal Hazor, which *is* near Ephraim; so Absalom invited all the king's sons. 24Then Absalom came to the king and said, "Kindly note, your servant has sheepshearers; please, let the king and his servants go with your servant."

25But the king said to Absalom, "No, my son, let us not all go now, lest we be a burden to you." Then he urged him, but he would not go; and he blessed him.

26Then Absalom said, "If not, please let my brother Amnon go with us."

And the king said to him, "Why should he go with you?" 27But Absalom urged him; so he let Amnon and all the king's sons go with him.

28Now Absalom had commanded his servants, saying, "Watch now, when Amnon's rheart is merry with wine, and when I say to you, 'Strike Amnon!' then kill him. Do not be afraid. Have I not commanded you? Be courageous and valiant." 29So the servants of Absalom sdid to Amnon as Absalom had commanded. Then all the king's sons arose, and each one got on this mule and fled.

30And it came to pass, while they were on the way, that news came to David, saying, "Absalom has killed all the king's sons, and not one of them is left!" 31So the king arose and utore his garments and vlay on the ground, and all his servants stood by with their clothes torn. 32Then wJonadab the son of Shimeah, David's brother, answered and said, "Let not my lord suppose they have killed all the young men, the king's sons, for only Amnon is dead. For by the command of Absalom this has been determined from the day that he forced his sister Tamar. 33Now therefore, xlet not my lord the king take the thing to his heart, to think that all the king's sons are dead. For only Amnon is dead."

Absalom Flees to Geshur

34yThen Absalom fled. And the young man who was keeping watch lifted his eyes and looked, and there, many people were coming from the road on the hillside behind him.* 35And Jonadab said to the king,

"Look, the king's sons are coming; as your servant said, so it is." 36So it was, as soon as he had finished speaking, that the king's sons indeed came, and they lifted up their voice and wept. Also the king and all his servants wept very bitterly.

37But Absalom fled and went to zTalmai the son of Ammihud, king of Geshur. And *David* mourned for his son every day. 38So Absalom fled and went to aGeshur, and was there three years. 39And King David* longed to go to* Absalom. For he had been bcomforted concerning Amnon, because he was dead.

Absalom Returns to Jerusalem

14 So Joab the son of Zeruiah perceived that the king's heart *was* concerned aabout Absalom. 2And Joab sent to bTekoa and brought from there a wise woman, and said to her, "Please pretend to be a mourner, cand put on mourning apparel; do not anoint yourself with oil, but act like a woman who has been mourning a long time for the dead. 3Go to the king and speak to him in this manner." So Joab dput the words in her mouth.

4And when the woman of Tekoa spoke* to the king, she efell on her face to the ground and prostrated herself, and said, f"Help, O king!"

5Then the king said to her, "What troubles you?"

And she answered, g"Indeed I *am* a widow, my husband is dead. 6Now your maidservant had two sons; and the two fought with each other in the field, and *there was* no one to part them, but the one struck the other and killed him. 7And now the whole family has risen up against your maidservant, and they said, 'Deliver him who struck his brother, that we may execute him hfor the life of his brother whom he

---

* **13:34** Septuagint adds *And the watchman went and told the king, and said, "I see men from the way of Horonaim, from the regions of the mountains."* * **13:39** Following Masoretic Text, Syriac, and Vulgate; Septuagint reads *the spirit of the king;* Targum reads *the soul of King David.* • Following Masoretic Text and Targum; Septuagint and Vulgate read *ceased to pursue after.* * **14:4** Many Hebrew manuscripts, Septuagint, Syriac, and Vulgate read *came.*

13:23 Ephraim. This does not refer to the tribal area, but to a city about 13 miles north of Jerusalem (John 11:54).

13:29 mule. The mule, the offspring of a donkey and a horse, combines the size and strength of a donkey with the surefootedness and endurance of a donkey. Although the Israelites were forbidden to breed such hybrids (Lev. 19:19), mules were imported into Israel. They were the preferred mount of royalty during this period. (18:9; 1 Kin. 1:33).

13:37 Talmai. Talmai was Absalom's grandfather, the father of David's wife Maacah (3:3). He ruled as king of the territory of Geshur, northeast of the Sea of Galilee.

14:7 extinguish my ember which is left. The woman used a graphic picture of the extinction of her family. The demise of a family name and the end of a surviving remnant or family line were crucial matters to the Hebrew people.

13:23 q 1 Sam. 25:4 **13:28** r 1 Sam. 25:36 **13:29** s 2 Sam. 12:10 t 2 Sam. 18:9 **13:31** u 2 Sam. 1:11 v 2 Sam. 12:16 **13:32** w 2 Sam. 13:3–5 **13:33** x 2 Sam. 19:19 **13:34** y 2 Sam. 13:37, 38 **13:37** z 2 Sam. 3:3 **13:38** a 2 Sam. 14:23, 32; 15:8 **13:39** b 2 Sam. 12:19, 23 **14:1** a 2 Sam. 13:39 **14:2** b 2 Chr. 11:6 c Ruth 3:3 **14:3** d 2 Sam. 14:19 **14:4** e 1 Sam. 20:41; 25:23 f 2 Kin. 6:26, 28 **14:5** g [Zech. 7:10] **14:7** h Deut. 19:12, 13

killed; and we will destroy the heir also.'
So they would extinguish my ember that is
left, and leave to my husband *neither* name
nor remnant on the earth."
8 Then the king said to the woman, "Go
to your house, and I will give orders concerning you."
9 And the woman of Tekoa said to the
king, "My lord, O king, *let* [i]the iniquity *be*
on me and on my father's house, [j]and the
king and his throne *be* guiltless."
10 So the king said, "Whoever says *anything* to you, bring him to me, and he shall
not touch you anymore."
11 Then she said, "Please let the king remember the LORD your God, and do not
permit [k]the avenger of blood to destroy
anymore, lest they destroy my son."
And he said, [l]"*As* the LORD lives, not one
hair of your son shall fall to the ground."
12 Therefore the woman said, "Please, let
your maidservant speak *another* word to
my lord the king."
And he said, "Say on."
13 So the woman said: "Why then have
you schemed such a thing against [m]the
people of God? For the king speaks this
thing as one who is guilty, *in that* the
king does not bring [n]his banished one
home again. 14 For we [o]will surely die and
become like water spilled on the ground,
which cannot be gathered up again. Yet
God does not [p]take away a life; but He
[q]devises means, so that His banished ones
are not expelled from Him. 15 Now therefore, I have come to speak of this thing to
my lord the king because the people have
made me afraid. And your maidservant
said, 'I will now speak to the king; it may
be that the king will perform the request of
his maidservant. 16 For the king will hear
and deliver his maidservant from the hand
of the man *who would* destroy me and my
son together from the [r]inheritance of God.'
17 Your maidservant said, 'The word of my
lord the king will now be comforting; for
[s]as the angel of God, so *is* my lord the king
in [t]discerning good and evil. And may the
LORD your God be with you.'"
18 Then the king answered and said to
the woman, "Please do not hide from me
anything that I ask you."
And the woman said, "Please, let my lord
the king speak."
19 So the king said, "*Is* the hand of Joab
with you in all this?" And the woman answered and said, "*As* you live, my lord the
king, no one can turn to the right hand or
to the left from anything that my lord the
king has spoken. For your servant Joab
commanded me, and [u]he put all these
words in the mouth of your maidservant.
20 To bring about this change of affairs
your servant Joab has done this thing; but
my lord *is* wise, [v]according to the wisdom
of the angel of God, to know everything
that *is* in the earth."
21 And the king said to Joab, "All right,
I have granted this thing. Go therefore,
bring back the young man Absalom."
22 Then Joab fell to the ground on his
face and bowed himself, and thanked the
king. And Joab said, "Today your servant
knows that I have found favor in your sight,
my lord, O king, in that the king has fulfilled the request of his servant." 23 So Joab
arose [w]and went to Geshur, and brought
Absalom to Jerusalem. 24 And the king
said, "Let him return to his own house, but
[x]do not let him see my face." So Absalom
returned to his own house, but did not see
the king's face.

14:11 ***avenger of blood.*** The Hebrew phrase, "avenger of blood" or "redeemer of blood" is closely related to the term "kinsman redeemer." The kinsman redeemer is the protector of family rights. Here, the protector of the family would be expected to bring vengeance on one who had taken the life of a family member. Cities of refuge had been established under Moses for protection from a blood avenger in cases where the killing was accidental (Num. 35:9–34).

14:14 Restoration—The wise woman from Tekoa spoke compellingly of Absalom's (the banished one's) need to make things right with God. David, whose heart was leaning toward his son, was touched, and he brought Absalom back. But no restoration took place. Neither Absalom nor David discussed how they had failed to seek justice according to law in the case of Amnon and Tamar. Restoration is only possible if we are willing to look sin in the face and acknowledge the need to repent before God and turn to new and righteous ways.

It is difficult to know exactly what the woman is saying to David, because she is speaking with double meanings. On the surface is her made-up story, which is supposed to speak allegorically to David. In this instance she is referring to the fact that because "her son" did not kill "his brother" in premeditated murder, he should have found safety in a city of refuge. Absalom, however, did kill his brother in premeditated murder. The mitigating factor is that Amnon should have been banished for his rape of Tamar, and the king, Tamar's first protector, had done nothing. Absalom was the next in line as near relative of Tamar, so there was some justice in his desire to bring Amnon to account.

14:19 ***hand of Joab.*** The exact extent of the game Joab was playing is not explained. Joab had been a difficult force in David's life (13:37–39). Joab had killed Abner in a way that David considered unjust, and it was Joab who arranged Uriah's death for David. These factors, and the fact that Joab was in some way sponsoring Absalom's return, made the relationship between David and Joab uneasy. The old trust was gone.

14:24 ***do not let him see my face.*** Absalom was allowed to return, but his position was not restored.

14:9 [i] 1 Sam. 25:24 [j] 1 Kin. 2:33 **14:11** [k] Num. 35:19, 21 [l] 1 Sam. 14:45 **14:13** [m] Judg. 20:2 [n] 2 Sam. 13:37, 38 **14:14** [o] [Heb. 9:27] [p] Job 34:19 [q] Num. 35:15 **14:16** [r] Deut. 32:9 **14:17** [s] 2 Sam. 19:27 [t] 1 Kin. 3:9 **14:19** [u] 2 Sam. 14:3 **14:20** [v] 2 Sam. 14:17; 19:27 **14:23** [w] 2 Sam. 13:37, 38 **14:24** [x] 2 Sam. 3:13

David Forgives Absalom

25Now in all Israel there was no one who was praised as much as Absalom for his good looks. yFrom the sole of his foot to the crown of his head there was no blemish in him. 26And when he cut the hair of his head—at the end of every year he cut it because it was heavy on him—when he cut it, he weighed the hair of his head at two hundred shekels according to the king's standard. 27zTo Absalom were born three sons, and one daughter whose name was Tamar. She was a woman of beautiful appearance.

28And Absalom dwelt two full years in Jerusalem, abut did not see the king's face. 29Therefore Absalom sent for Joab, to send him to the king, but he would not come to him. And when he sent again the second time, he would not come. 30So he said to his servants, "See, Joab's field is near mine, and he has barley there; go and set it on fire." And Absalom's servants set the field on fire.

31Then Joab arose and came to Absalom's house, and said to him, "Why have your servants set my field on fire?"

32And Absalom answered Joab, "Look, I sent to you, saying, 'Come here, so that I may send you to the king, to say, "Why have I come from Geshur? It would be better for me to be there still."' Now therefore, let me see the king's face; but bif there is iniquity in me, let him execute me."

33So Joab went to the king and told him. And when he had called for Absalom, he came to the king and bowed himself on his face to the ground before the king. Then the king ckissed Absalom.

Absalom's Treason

15 After this ait happened that Absalom bprovided himself with chariots and horses, and fifty men to run before him. 2Now Absalom would rise early and stand beside the way to the gate. So it was, whenever anyone who had a clawsuit came to the king for a decision, that Absalom would call to him and say, "What city are you from?" And he would say, "Your servant is from such and such a tribe of Israel." 3Then Absalom would say to him, "Look, your case is good and right; but there is no deputy of the king to hear you." 4Moreover Absalom would say, d"Oh, that I were made judge in the land, and everyone who has any suit or cause would come to me; then I would give him justice." 5And so it was, whenever anyone came near to bow down to him, that he would put out his hand and take him and ekiss him. 6In this manner Absalom acted toward all Israel who came to the king for judgment. fSo Absalom stole the hearts of the men of Israel.

7Now it came to pass gafter forty* years that Absalom said to the king, "Please, let me go to hHebron and pay the vow which I made to the LORD. 8iFor your servant jtook a vow kwhile I dwelt at Geshur in Syria, saying, 'If the LORD indeed brings me back to Jerusalem, then I will serve the LORD.'"

9And the king said to him, "Go in peace." So he arose and went to Hebron.

10Then Absalom sent spies throughout all the tribes of Israel, saying, "As soon as you hear the sound of the trumpet, then you shall say, 'Absalom lreigns in Hebron!'" 11And with Absalom went two hundred men minvited from Jerusalem, and they nwent along innocently and did not know anything. 12Then Absalom sent for Ahithophel the Gilonite, oDavid's counselor, from his city—from pGiloh—while he offered sacrifices. And the conspiracy grew strong, for the people with Absalom qcontinually increased in number.

---

* 15:7 Septuagint manuscripts, Syriac, and Josephus read four.

There were issues of justice that had not been settled. One was David's apparent indifference to the sin of Amnon, and the other was whether Amnon's death was an act of justice or an act of murder. It never pays to let matters of justice remain undecided for a long period of time. It creates bitterness and disrespect for the authorities whose job it is to decide matters of justice, and the people involved become set in their attitudes in a way that makes repentance and restitution virtually impossible.

14:26 two hundred shekels. The weight of Absalom's hair was about 5 pounds.

14:27 three sons. Apparently Absalom's sons did not live to maturity. When he set up a pillar in Jerusalem to memorialize his name, he said it was because he had no son.

14:32 Come here. Apparently Joab did not sponsor Absalom to the extent of acting as a go-between with his father. Absalom responded with the attitude of a superior to an inferior, not what one might expect from the king's son to his father's highest ranking officer. It seems from the fearless and high handed way in which he answered Joab that Absalom was already seeing himself as his father's successor.

15:4 I would give him justice. Administration of justice, the proper relationship between people in society according to God's standard of righteousness, was a major concern of the Old Testament rulers and prophets (8:15; 1 Kin. 3:28; Is. 1:17; Amos 5:24). Absalom is playing on the people's emotions, and perhaps justifying himself in his actions against Amnon as well.

14:25 y Is. 1:6 **14:27** z 2 Sam. 13:1; 18:18 **14:28** a 2 Sam. 14:24 **14:32** b 1 Sam. 20:8 **14:33** c Luke 15:20 **15:1** a 2 Sam. 12:11 b 1 Kin. 1:5 **15:2** c Deut. 19:17 **15:4** d Judg. 9:29 **15:5** e 2 Sam. 14:33; 20:9 **15:6** f [Rom. 16:18] **15:7** g [Deut. 23:21] h 2 Sam. 3:2, 3 **15:8** i 1 Sam. 16:2 j Gen. 28:20, 21 k 2 Sam. 13:38 **15:10** l 1 Kin. 1:34 **15:11** m 1 Sam. 16:3, 5 n Gen. 20:5 **15:12** o 1 Chr. 27:33 p Josh. 15:51 q Ps. 3:1

David Escapes from Jerusalem

¹³Now a messenger came to David, saying, ʳ"The hearts of the men of Israel are with Absalom."

¹⁴So David said to all his servants who *were* with him at Jerusalem, "Arise, and let us ˢflee, or we shall not escape from Absalom. Make haste to depart, lest he overtake us suddenly and bring disaster upon us, and strike the city with the edge of the sword."

¹⁵And the king's servants said to the king, "We *are* your servants, *ready to do* whatever my lord the king commands."

¹⁶Then ᵗthe king went out with all his household after him. But the king left ᵘten women, concubines, to keep the house.

¹⁷And the king went out with all the people after him, and stopped at the outskirts.

¹⁸Then all his servants passed before him; ᵛand all the Cherethites, all the Pelethites, and all the Gittites, ʷsix hundred men who had followed him from Gath, passed before the king.

¹⁹Then the king said to ˣIttai the Gittite, "Why are you also going with us? Return and remain with the king. For you *are* a foreigner and also an exile from your own place. ²⁰In fact, you came *only* yesterday. Should I make you wander up and down with us today, since I go ʸI know not where? Return, and take your brethren back. Mercy and truth *be* with you."

²¹But Ittai answered the king and said, ᶻ"As the LORD lives, and *as* my lord the king lives, surely in whatever place my lord the king shall be, whether in death or life, even there also your servant will be."

²²So David said to Ittai, "Go, and cross over." Then Ittai the Gittite and all his men and all the little ones who *were* with him crossed over. ²³And all the country wept with a loud voice, and all the people crossed over. The king himself also crossed over the Brook Kidron, and all the people crossed over toward the way of the ᵃwilderness.

²⁴There was ᵇZadok also, and all the Levites with him, bearing the ᶜark of the covenant of God. And they set down the ark of God, and ᵈAbiathar went up until all the people had finished crossing over from the city. ²⁵Then the king said to Zadok, "Carry the ark of God back into the city. If I find favor in the eyes of the LORD, He ᵉwill bring me back and show me *both* it and ᶠHis dwelling place. ²⁶But if He says thus: 'I have no ᵍdelight in you,' here I am, ʰlet Him do to me as seems good to Him." ²⁷The king also said to Zadok the priest, "*Are* you *not* a ⁱseer? Return to the city in peace, and ʲyour two sons with you, Ahimaaz your son, and Jonathan the son of Abiathar. ²⁸See, ᵏI will wait in the plains of the wilderness until word comes from you to inform me." ²⁹Therefore Zadok and Abiathar carried the ark of God back to Jerusalem. And they remained there.

³⁰So David went up by the Ascent of the *Mount of* Olives, and wept as he went up; and he ˡhad his head covered and went ᵐbarefoot. And all the people who *were* with him ⁿcovered their heads and went up, ᵒweeping as they went up. ³¹Then someone told David, saying, ᵖ"Ahithophel *is* among the conspirators with Absalom." And David said, "O LORD, I pray, �qturn the counsel of Ahithophel into foolishness!"

15:13 *The hearts of the men of Israel.* When David's power in Judah was confined to Hebron (ch. 2) he was resented by the supporters of Saul in the rest of the country. Old suspicions and resentments can be stoked again by a person who knows how to use people to his own advantage—a disreputable quality in which Absalom excelled.

15:15 *We are your servants.* The loyalty of David's servants must have been a real encouragement in a time of such disloyalty from David's own family.

15:18 *Cherethites . . . Pelethites.* The Cherethites and Pelethites were elite units of David's army. These trusted troops of David were not Israelites, but mercenaries from a variety of nations, possibly Crete and Philistia. They had been with David for years, owed him their loyalty, and would defend him and his family to the death. ***Gittites.*** The Gittites were probably Philistine mercenary soldiers who were among David's original followers from Gath (1 Sam. 22:1–2).

15:19–21 Righteousness—Making the choice to stand with the right man, even when it looked like he might spend the rest of his life in exile was not practical, but it was right. We will all have to make choices to tell the truth, stand up for honorable actions, or support someone who is right but not powerful. Taking the right path does not mean it will be easy, but when we are on the right path, God is with us, "Yea . . . through the valley of the shadow of death" (Ps. 23:4)

15:21 *whether in death or life.* David rewarded Ittai's loyalty when he made Ittai commander of a third of the army (18:2).

15:23 *Brook Kidron.* The Brook Kidron is a small stream that flows through the valley separating Jerusalem and the Mount of Olives during the rainy season (October through March). ***way of the wilderness.*** The way of the wilderness refers to the road leading through the wilderness of Judah to Jericho and down to the fords of the Jordan.

15:25 *He will bring me back.* David committed the entire situation to the care and will of the Lord.

15:31 *Ahithophel.* Ahithophel was Bathsheba's grandfather (11:3; 23:34). A wise counselor (16:23), he had been in David's service (v. 12) but had switched

15:13 ʳ Judg. 9:3   **15:14** ˢ Ps. 3:title   **15:16** ᵗ Ps. 3:title   ᵘ 2 Sam. 12:11; 16:21, 22   **15:18** ᵛ 2 Sam. 8:18   ʷ 1 Sam. 23:13; 25:13; 30:1, 9   **15:19** ˣ 2 Sam. 18:2   **15:20** ʸ 1 Sam. 23:13   **15:21** ᶻ Ruth 1:16, 17   **15:23** ᵃ 2 Sam. 15:28; 16:2   **15:24** ᵇ 2 Sam. 8:17   ᶜ Num. 4:15   ᵈ 1 Sam. 22:20   **15:25** ᵉ [Ps. 43:3]   ᶠ Ex. 15:13   **15:26** ᵍ Num. 14:8   ʰ 1 Sam. 3:18   **15:27** ⁱ 1 Sam. 9:6–9   ʲ 2 Sam. 17:17–20   **15:28** ᵏ 2 Sam. 17:16   **15:30** ˡ Esth. 6:12   ᵐ Is. 20:2–4   ⁿ Jer. 14:3, 4   ᵒ [Ps. 126:6]   **15:31** ᵖ Ps. 3:1, 2; 55:12   q 2 Sam. 16:23; 17:14, 23

³²Now it happened when David had come to the top *of the mountain*, where he worshiped God—there was Hushai the ʳArchite coming to meet him ˢwith his robe torn and dust on his head. ³³David said to him, "If you go on with me, then you will become ᵗa burden to me. ³⁴But if you return to the city, and say to Absalom, ᵘ'I will be your servant, O king; *as I was* your father's servant previously, so I *will* now also *be* your servant,' then you may defeat the counsel of Ahithophel for me. ³⁵And *do* you not *have* Zadok and Abiathar the priests with you there? Therefore it will be *that* whatever you hear from the king's house, you shall tell to ᵛZadok and Abiathar the priests. ³⁶Indeed *they have* there ʷwith them their two sons, Ahimaaz, Zadok's *son*, and Jonathan, Abiathar's *son*; and by them you shall send me everything you hear."

³⁷So Hushai, ˣDavid's friend, went into the city. ʸAnd Absalom came into Jerusalem.

Mephibosheth's Servant

16 Whenª David was a little past the top *of the mountain*, there was ᵇZiba the servant of Mephibosheth, who met him with a couple of saddled donkeys, and on them two hundred *loaves* of bread, one hundred clusters of raisins, one hundred summer fruits, and a skin of wine. ²And the king said to Ziba, "What do you mean to do with these?"

So Ziba said, "The donkeys *are* for the king's household to ride on, the bread and summer fruit for the young men to eat, and the wine for ᶜthose who are faint in the wilderness to drink."

³Then the king said, "And where *is* your ᵈmaster's son?"

ᵉAnd Ziba said to the king, "Indeed he is staying in Jerusalem, for he said, 'Today the house of Israel will restore the kingdom of my father to me.'"

⁴So the king said to Ziba, "Here, all that *belongs* to Mephibosheth *is* yours."

And Ziba said, "I humbly bow before you, *that* I may find favor in your sight, my lord, O king!"

Shimei Curses David

⁵Now when King David came to ᶠBahurim, there was a man from the family of the house of Saul, whose name *was* ᵍShimei the son of Gera, coming from there. He came out, cursing continuously as he came. ⁶And he threw stones at David and at all the servants of King David. And all the people and all the mighty men *were* on his right hand and on his left. ⁷Also Shimei said thus when he cursed: "Come out! Come out! You bloodthirsty man, ʰyou rogue! ⁸The LORD has ⁱbrought upon you all ʲthe blood of the house of Saul, in whose place you have reigned; and the LORD has delivered the kingdom into the hand of Absalom your son. So now you *are caught* in your own evil, because you are a bloodthirsty man!"

⁹Then Abishai the son of Zeruiah said to the king, "Why should this ᵏdead dog ˡcurse my lord the king? Please, let me go over and take off his head!"

¹⁰But the king said, ᵐ"What have I to do with you, you sons of Zeruiah? So let him curse, because ⁿthe LORD has said to him, 'Curse David.' ᵒWho then shall say, 'Why have you done so?'"

¹¹And David said to Abishai and all his servants, "See how ᵖmy son who �q came from my own body seeks my life. How much more now *may this* Benjamite? Let him alone, and let him curse; for so the LORD has ordered him. ¹²It may be that the LORD will look on my affliction,* and that the LORD will ʳrepay me with ˢgood for

---

* **16:12** Following Kethib, Septuagint, Syriac, and Vulgate; Qere reads *my eyes;* Targum reads *tears of my eyes.*

---

his allegiance to Absalom. David's prayer was for his enemy to be confused. The name Ahithophel may mean "Brother of Folly."

15:34 *defeat the counsel.* David had committed the entire situation to the care and will of the Lord, but he was acting wisely to protect himself and to provide a source of information as well as an inside confederate to confound the enemy.

16:1 *Ziba.* A longtime servant of both Saul and Mephibosheth, Ziba was expressing his loyalty to King David.

16:5 *Bahurim.* Bahurim was near Jerusalem, east of the Mount of Olives (3:16). ***cursing continuously.*** These were not simple insults or the words of someone with a foul mouth. Shimei was asking God to destroy David (Num. 22:6).

16:6 *threw stones.* Throwing stones is a gesture of contempt, as if the fleeing king were merely a stray dog. Stones can also be deadly, as is shown by the fact that stoning was a normal means of capital punishment among the Hebrews (1 Kin. 21:13).

16:9–13 Forbearance—David was more aware of his failure as a father than his dignity as a king. David knew that both Moses and Saul had been disciplined by God, and he certainly did not rule out the idea that both Absalom's rebellion and Shimei's cursing might be part of a lesson that God had for him. He was willing to endure both while he waited to see how God would work things out.

16:10 *What have I to do with you.* This idiom means that David did not share the feelings and views of Abishai.

15:32 ʳJosh. 16:2 ˢ2 Sam. 1:2 **15:33** ᵗ2 Sam. 19:35 **15:34** ᵘ2 Sam. 16:19 **15:35** ᵛ2 Sam. 17:15, 16 **15:36** ʷ2 Sam. 15:27 **15:37** ˣ1 Chr. 27:33 ʸ2 Sam. 16:15 **16:1** ª2 Sam. 15:30, 32 ᵇ2 Sam. 9:2; 19:17, 29 **16:2** ᶜ2 Sam. 15:23; 17:29 **16:3** ᵈ2 Sam. 9:9, 10 ᵉ2 Sam. 19:27 **16:5** ᶠ2 Sam. 3:16 ᵍ2 Sam. 19:21 **16:7** ʰDeut. 13:13 **16:8** ⁱJudg. 9:24, 56, 57 ʲ2 Sam. 1:16; 3:28, 29; 4:11, 12 **16:9** ᵏ2 Sam. 9:8 ˡEx. 22:28 **16:10** ᵐ2 Sam. 3:39; 19:22 ⁿ[Lam. 3:38] ᵒ[Rom. 9:20] **16:11** ᵖ2 Sam. 12:11 qGen. 15:4 **16:12** ʳProv. 20:22 ˢ[Rom. 8:28]

his cursing this day." ¹³And as David and his men went along the road, Shimei went along the hillside opposite him and cursed as he went, threw stones at him and kicked up dust. ¹⁴Now the king and all the people who *were* with him became weary; so they refreshed themselves there.

The Advice of Ahithophel

¹⁵Meanwhile ᵗAbsalom and all the people, the men of Israel, came to Jerusalem; and Ahithophel *was* with him. ¹⁶And so it was, when Hushai the Archite, ᵘDavid's friend, came to Absalom, that ᵛHushai said to Absalom, "Long live the king! Long live the king!"

¹⁷So Absalom said to Hushai, "Is this your loyalty to your friend? ʷWhy did you not go with your friend?"

¹⁸And Hushai said to Absalom, "No, but whom the LORD and this people and all the men of Israel choose, his I will be, and with him I will remain. ¹⁹Furthermore, ˣwhom should I serve? *Should I* not *serve* in the presence of his son? As I have served in your father's presence, so will I be in your presence."

²⁰Then Absalom said to ʸAhithophel, "Give advice as to what we should do."

²¹And Ahithophel said to Absalom, "Go in to your father's ᶻconcubines, whom he has left to keep the house; and all Israel will hear that you ᵃare abhorred by your father. Then ᵇthe hands of all who are with you will be strong." ²²So they pitched a tent for Absalom on the top of the house, and Absalom went in to his father's concubines ᶜin the sight of all Israel.

²³Now the advice of Ahithophel, which he gave in those days, *was* as if one had inquired at the oracle of God. So *was* all the advice of Ahithophel ᵈboth with David and with Absalom.

17 Moreover Ahithophel said to Absalom, "Now let me choose twelve thousand men, and I will arise and pursue David tonight. ²I will come upon him while he *is* ᵃweary and weak, and make him afraid. And all the people who *are* with him will flee, and I will ᵇstrike only the king. ³Then I will bring back all the people to you. When all return except the man whom you seek, all the people will be at peace." ⁴And the saying pleased Absalom and all the ᶜelders of Israel.

The Advice of Hushai

⁵Then Absalom said, "Now call Hushai the Archite also, and let us hear what he ᵈsays too." ⁶And when Hushai came to Absalom, Absalom spoke to him, saying, "Ahithophel has spoken in this manner. Shall we do as he says? If not, speak up."

⁷So Hushai said to Absalom: "The advice that Ahithophel has given *is* not good at this time. ⁸For," said Hushai, "you know your father and his men, that they *are* mighty men, and they *are* enraged in their minds, like ᵉa bear robbed of her cubs in the field; and your father *is* a man of war, and will not camp with the people. ⁹Surely by now he is hidden in some pit, or in some *other* place. And it will be, when some of them are overthrown at the first, that whoever hears *it* will say, 'There is a slaughter among the people who follow Absalom.' ¹⁰And even he *who is* valiant, whose heart *is* like the heart of a lion, will ᶠmelt completely. For all Israel knows that your father *is* a mighty man, and *those* who *are* with him *are* valiant men. ¹¹Therefore I advise that all Israel be fully gathered to you, ᵍfrom Dan to Beersheba, ʰlike the sand that *is* by the sea for multitude, and that you go to battle in person. ¹²So we will come upon him in some place where he may be found, and we will fall on him as the dew falls on the ground. And of him and all the men who *are* with him there shall not be left so much as one. ¹³Moreover, if he has withdrawn into a city, then all Israel shall bring ropes to that city; and we will ᶦpull it into the river, until there is not one small stone found there."

¹⁴So Absalom and all the men of Israel said, "The advice of Hushai the Archite *is* better than the advice of Ahithophel." For ʲthe LORD had purposed to defeat the good advice of Ahithophel, to the intent that the LORD might bring disaster on Absalom.

Hushai Warns David to Escape

¹⁵ᵏThen Hushai said to Zadok and Abiathar the priests, "Thus and so Ahithophel advised Absalom and the elders of Israel, and thus and so I have advised. ¹⁶Now therefore, send quickly and tell David, saying, 'Do not spend this night ᶥin the plains of the wilderness, but speedily cross over, lest the king and all the people who *are*

16:21–22 concubines. In ancient times taking over a king's harem was a recognized means of claiming the throne. Once Absalom violated David's concubines, he was set on a course of sure and final alienation from his father. Putting his tent on the roof was a public and insolent act.

17:2 I will strike only the king. In a battle, it is a little rash to promise to kill only one person. Ahithophel was suggesting that David's companions and troops would switch their loyalty to Absalom if David were killed.

17:8 bear robbed of her cubs. There is no more

dangerous foe in the woods than a mother bear who believes her cubs to be in danger.

16:15 ᵗ 2 Sam. 15:12, 37   **16:16** ᵘ 2 Sam. 15:37 ᵛ 2 Sam. 15:34   **16:17** ʷ 2 Sam. 19:25   **16:19** ˣ 2 Sam. 15:34   **16:20** ʸ 2 Sam. 15:12   **16:21** ᶻ 2 Sam. 15:16; 20:3 ᵃ Gen. 34:30 ᵇ 2 Sam. 2:7   **16:22** ᶜ 2 Sam. 12:11, 12   **16:23** ᵈ 2 Sam. 15:12   **17:2** ᵃ 2 Sam. 16:14 ᵇ Zech. 13:7   **17:4** ᶜ 2 Sam. 5:3; 9:11   **17:5** ᵈ 2 Sam. 15:32–34   **17:8** ᵉ Hos. 13:8   **17:10** ᶠ Josh. 2:11   **17:11** ᵍ 2 Sam. 3:10 ʰ Gen. 22:17   **17:13** ᶦ Mic. 1:6   **17:14** ʲ 2 Sam. 15:31, 34   **17:15** ᵏ 2 Sam. 15:35, 36   **17:16** ᶥ 2 Sam. 15:28

with him be swallowed up.'" [17m]Now Jonathan and Ahimaaz [n]stayed at [o]En Rogel, for they dared not be seen coming into the city; so a female servant would come and tell them, and they would go and tell King David. [18]Nevertheless a lad saw them, and told Absalom. But both of them went away quickly and came to a man's house [p]in Bahurim, who had a well in his court; and they went down into it. [19q]Then the woman took and spread a covering over the well's mouth, and spread ground grain on it; and the thing was not known. [20]And when Absalom's servants came to the woman at the house, they said, "Where are Ahimaaz and Jonathan?"

So [r]the woman said to them, "They have gone over the water brook."

And when they had searched and could not find them, they returned to Jerusalem. [21]Now it came to pass, after they had departed, that they came up out of the well and went and told King David, and said to David, [s]"Arise and cross over the water quickly. For thus has Ahithophel advised against you." [22]So David and all the people who were with him arose and crossed over the Jordan. By morning light not one of them was left who had not gone over the Jordan.

[23]Now when Ahithophel saw that his advice was not followed, he saddled a donkey, and arose and went home to [t]his house, to his city. Then he put his [u]household in order, and [v]hanged himself, and died; and he was buried in his father's tomb.

[24]Then David went to [w]Mahanaim. And Absalom crossed over the Jordan, he and all the men of Israel with him. [25]And Absalom made [x]Amasa captain of the army instead of Joab. This Amasa was the son of a man whose name was Jithra,* an Israelite,* who had gone in to [y]Abigail the daughter of Nahash, sister of Zeruiah, Joab's mother. [26]So Israel and Absalom encamped in the land of Gilead.

[27]Now it happened, when David had come to Mahanaim, that [z]Shobi the son of Nahash from Rabbah of the people of Ammon, [a]Machir the son of Ammiel from Lo Debar, and [b]Barzillai the Gileadite

from Rogelim, [28]brought beds and basins, earthen vessels and wheat, barley and flour, parched grain and beans, lentils and parched seeds, [29]honey and curds, sheep and cheese of the herd, for David and the people who were with him to eat. For they said, "The people are hungry and weary and thirsty [c]in the wilderness."

Absalom's Defeat and Death

18 And David numbered the people who were with him, and [a]set captains of thousands and captains of hundreds over them. [2]Then David sent out one third of the people under the hand of Joab, [b]one third under the hand of Abishai the son of Zeruiah, Joab's brother, and one third under the hand of [c]Ittai the Gittite. And the king said to the people, "I also will surely go out with you myself."

[3]But the people answered, "You shall not go out! For if we flee away, they will not care about us; nor if half of us die, will they care about us. But you are worth ten thousand of us now. For you are now more help to us in the city."

[4]Then the king said to them, "Whatever seems best to you I will do." So the king stood beside the gate, and all the people went out by hundreds and by thousands. [5]Now the king had commanded Joab, Abishai, and Ittai, saying, "Deal gently for my sake with the young man Absalom." [e]And all the people heard when the king gave all the captains orders concerning Absalom.

[6]So the people went out into the field of battle against Israel. And the battle was in the [f]woods of Ephraim. [7]The people of Israel were overthrown there before the servants of David, and a great slaughter of twenty thousand took place there that day. [8]For the battle there was scattered over the face of the whole countryside, and the

---

* **17:25** Spelled *Jether* in 1 Chronicles 2:17 and elsewhere • Following Masoretic Text, some manuscripts of the Septuagint, and Targum; some manuscripts of the Septuagint read *Ishmaelite* (compare 1 Chronicles 2:17); Vulgate reads *of Jezrael*.

17:22 crossed over the Jordan. Although the Jordan was not a large river, crossing it provided a barrier between him and his enemies. The tribal allotments included land on both sides of the Jordan, but there was always an emotional understanding that the "real" land of Israel was west of the Jordan. David was truly an exile.

17:27 Shobi . . . Barzillai. The gifts of these three men showed a real understanding of the material needs of the exiles, and this act of kindness must have been very encouraging to them. **Machir.** Jonathan's son Mephibosheth was living with Machir when David found him (9:4).

18:3–4 Wisdom—One facet of good leadership is the ability to delegate authority to others and leave the results in the hands of God. Waiting in safety

was not David's idea, but it seemed best to others, so David agreed. David's strength as a leader lay in having the hearts of his followers, and they in turn put his safety as a high priority. These loyal men did not think that God was done with David as king, and David needed their wisdom.

17:17 [m] 2 Sam. 15:27, 36 [n] Josh. 2:4–6 [o] Josh. 15:7;
18:16 **17:18** [p] 2 Sam. 3:16; 16:5 **17:19** [q] Josh.
2:4–6 **17:20** [r] Josh. 2:3–5 **17:21** [s] 2 Sam. 17:15,
16 **17:23** [t] 2 Sam. 15:12 [u] 2 Kin. 20:1 [v] Matt. 27:5
17:24 [w] 2 Sam. 2:8; 19:32 **17:25** [x] 1 Kin. 2:5, 32 [y] 1 Chr.
2:16 **17:27** [z] 2 Sam. 10:1; 12:29 [a] 2 Sam. 9:4 [b] 2 Sam.
19:31, 32 **17:29** [c] 2 Sam. 16:2, 14 **18:1** [a] Ex. 18:25
18:2 [b] Judg. 7:16 [c] 2 Sam. 15:19–22 **18:3** [d] 2 Sam. 21:17
18:5 [e] 2 Sam. 18:12 **18:6** [f] Josh. 17:15, 18

woods devoured more people that day than the sword devoured.

9Then Absalom met the servants of David. Absalom rode on a mule. The mule went under the thick boughs of a great terebinth tree, and *g*his head caught in the terebinth; so he was left hanging between heaven and earth. And the mule which *was* under him went on. 10Now a certain man saw *it* and told Joab, and said, "I just saw Absalom hanging in a terebinth tree!"

11So Joab said to the man who told him, "You just saw *him!* And why did you not strike him there to the ground? I would have given you ten *shekels* of silver and a belt."

12But the man said to Joab, "Though I were to receive a thousand *shekels* of silver in my hand, I would not raise my hand against the king's son. *h*For in our hearing the king commanded you and Abishai and Ittai, saying, 'Beware lest anyone *touch* the young man Absalom!'* 13Otherwise I would have dealt falsely against my own life. For there is nothing hidden from the king, and you yourself would have set yourself against *me*."

14Then Joab said, "I cannot linger with you." And he took three spears in his hand and thrust them through Absalom's heart, while he was *still* alive in the midst of the terebinth tree. 15And ten young men who bore Joab's armor surrounded Absalom, and struck and killed him.

16So Joab blew the trumpet, and the people returned from pursuing Israel. For Joab held back the people. 17And they took Absalom and cast him into a large pit in the woods, and *i*laid a very large heap of stones over him. Then all Israel *j*fled, everyone to his tent.

18Now Absalom in his lifetime had taken and set up a pillar for himself, which *is* in *k*the King's Valley. For he said, *l*"I have no son to keep my name in remembrance." He called the pillar after his own name. And to this day it is called Absalom's Monument.

David Hears of Absalom's Death

19Then *m*Ahimaaz the son of Zadok said, "Let me run now and take the news to the king, how the LORD has avenged him of his enemies."

20And Joab said to him, "You shall not take the news this day, for you shall take the news another day. But today you shall take no news, because the king's son is dead." 21Then Joab said to the Cushite, "Go, tell the king what you have seen." So the Cushite bowed himself to Joab and ran.

22And Ahimaaz the son of Zadok said again to Joab, "But whatever happens, please let me also run after the Cushite."

So Joab said, "Why will you run, my son, since you have no news ready?"

23"But whatever happens," *he said*, "let me run."

So he said to him, "Run." Then Ahimaaz ran by way of the plain, and outran the Cushite.

24Now David was sitting between the *n*two gates. And the watchman went up to the roof over the gate, to the wall, lifted his eyes and looked, and there was a man, running alone. 25Then the watchman cried out and told the king. And the king said, "If he *is* alone, *there is* news in his mouth." And he came rapidly and drew near.

26Then the watchman saw *another* man running, and the watchman called to the gatekeeper and said, "There is *another* man, running alone!"

And the king said, "He also brings news."

27So the watchman said, "I think the running of the first is like the running of Ahimaaz the son of Zadok."

And the king said, "He *is* a good man, and comes with *o*good news."

28So Ahimaaz called out and said to the king, "All is well!" Then he bowed down with his face to the earth before the king, and said, *p*"Blessed *be* the LORD your God, who has delivered up the men who raised their hand against my lord the king!"

29The king said, "Is the young man Absalom safe?"

Ahimaaz answered, "When Joab sent the king's servant and *me* your servant, I saw a great tumult, but I did not know what *it was about*."

30And the king said, "Turn aside *and* stand here." So he turned aside and stood still.

31Just then the Cushite came, and the Cushite said, "There is good news, my lord the king! For the LORD has avenged you this day of all those who rose against you."

32And the king said to the Cushite, "Is the young man Absalom safe?"

So the Cushite answered, "May the enemies of my lord the king, and all who rise against you to do harm, be like *that* young man!"

---

* **18:12** The ancient versions read 'Protect the young man Absalom for me!'

18:9 terebinth. The terebinth, sometimes called an oak, was native to the land of Israel and was a strong tree that grew to a height of about 35 feet.

18:23 by way of the plain. The plain was the floor of the Jordan valley. Ahimaaz took a longer route, but avoided the hilly terrain on the road taken by the Cushite.

18:9 *g* 2 Sam. 14:26   **18:12** *h* 2 Sam. 18:5   **18:17** *i* Josh. 7:26; 8:29   *j* 2 Sam. 19:8; 20:1, 22   **18:18** *k* Gen. 14:17   *l* 2 Sam. 14:27   **18:19** *m* 2 Sam. 15:36; 17:17   **18:24** *n* 2 Kin. 9:17   **18:27** *o* 1 Kin. 1:42   **18:28** *p* 2 Sam. 16:12

David's Mourning for Absalom

33 Then the king was deeply moved, and went up to the chamber over the gate, and wept. And as he went, he said thus: *q*"O my son Absalom—my son, my son Absalom—if only I had died in your place! O Absalom my son, *r*my son!"

19 And Joab was told, "Behold, the king is weeping and *a*mourning for Absalom." 2 So the victory that day was *turned* into *b*mourning for all the people. For the people heard it said that day, "The king is grieved for his son." 3 And the people stole back *c*into the city that day, as people who are ashamed steal away when they flee in battle. 4 But the king *d*covered his face, and the king cried out with a loud voice, *e*"O my son Absalom! O Absalom, my son, my son!"

5 Then *f*Joab came into the house to the king, and said, "Today you have disgraced all your servants who today have saved your life, the lives of your sons and daughters, the lives of your wives and the lives of your concubines, 6 in that you love your enemies and hate your friends. For you have declared today that you regard neither princes nor servants; for today I perceive that if Absalom had lived and all of us had died today, then it would have pleased you well. 7 Now therefore, arise, go out and speak comfort to your servants. For I swear by the LORD, if you do not go out, not one will stay with you this night. And that will be worse for you than all the evil that has befallen you from your youth until now." 8 Then the king arose and sat in the *g*gate. And they told all the people, saying, "There is the king, sitting in the gate." So all the people came before the king.

For everyone of Israel had *h*fled to his tent.

David Returns to Jerusalem

9 Now all the people were in a dispute throughout all the tribes of Israel, saying, "The king saved us from the hand of our *i*enemies, he delivered us from the hand of the *j*Philistines, and now he has *k*fled from the land because of Absalom. 10 But Absalom, whom we anointed over us, has died in battle. Now therefore, why do you say nothing about bringing back the king?"

11 So King David sent to *l*Zadok and Abiathar the priests, saying, "Speak to the elders of Judah, saying, 'Why are you the last to bring the king back to his house, since the words of all Israel have come to the king, to his *very* house? 12 You *are* my brethren, you *are* *m*my bone and my flesh. Why then are you the last to bring back the king?' 13 *n*And say to Amasa, '*Are* you not my bone and my flesh? *o*God do so to me, and more also, if you are not commander of the army before me continually in place of Joab.'" 14 So he swayed the hearts of all the men of Judah, *p*just as *the heart of* one man, so that they sent *this word* to the king: "Return, you and all your servants!"

15 Then the king returned and came to the Jordan. And Judah came to *q*Gilgal, to go to meet the king, to escort the king *r*across the Jordan. 16 And *s*Shimei the son of Gera, a Benjamite, who *was* from Bahurim, hurried and came down with the men of Judah to meet King David. 17 *There were* a thousand men of *t*Benjamin with him, and *u*Ziba the servant of the house of Saul, and his fifteen sons and his twenty servants with him; and they went over the Jordan before the king. 18 Then a ferryboat went across to carry over the king's household, and to do what he thought good.

David's Mercy to Shimei

Now Shimei the son of Gera fell down before the king when he had crossed the Jordan. 19 Then he said to the king, *v*"Do not let my lord impute iniquity to me, or remember what *w*wrong your servant did on the day that my lord the king left Jerusalem, that the king should *x*take *it* to heart. 20 For I, your servant, know that I have sinned. Therefore here I am, the first

---

18:33 *O my son Absalom.* David's grief can be understood by any parent who has lost a child to vice or crime. Absalom was a rebel, but he had been a little boy born to David in the early years as king in Hebron, and for David he would always be that beloved son. Absalom deserved to die, and David knew it, but he still longed for things to have turned out differently. In a few short years the repercussions of his sin with Bathsheba had destroyed the lives of Amnon, Tamar, and Absalom.

18:33 Despondency—In many ways mental suffering is more intense and devastating than physical suffering. It was hard for David to even imagine taking up life again and going back to Jerusalem as king. It is only the Lord who can give courage in such moments, and He often does it by reminding us of who He is, what He has done in the past, and what He promises to do in the future. Sandwiched in these certainties, we can begin to see that His hand is on us even in our grief. **19:11** *elders of Judah.* David asked his friends the

priests, to begin the movement to invite David back to his throne. Apparently he did not want to come into Jerusalem without public support for his rule.
19:13 *Amasa.* David's nephew Amasa had commanded the army of Absalom (17:25). When David offered him the position of commander it was probably intended to secure Amasa's allegiance as well as discipline Joab for killing Absalom against David's orders.

18:33 *q* 2 Sam. 12:10 *r* 2 Sam. 19:4 **19:1** *a* Jer. 14:2 **19:2** *b* Esth. 4:3 **19:3** *c* 2 Sam. 17:24, 27; 19:32 **19:4** *d* 2 Sam. 15:30 *e* 2 Sam. 18:33 **19:5** *f* 2 Sam. 18:14 **19:8** *g* 2 Sam. 15:2; 18:24 *h* 2 Sam. 18:17 **19:9** *i* 2 Sam. 8:1–14 *j* 2 Sam. 3:18 *k* 2 Sam. 15:14 **19:11** *l* 2 Sam. 15:24 **19:12** *m* 2 Sam. 5:1 **19:13** *n* 2 Sam. 17:25 *o* Ruth 1:17 **19:14** *p* Judg. 20:1 **19:15** *q* Josh. 5:9 *r* 2 Sam. 17:22 **19:16** *s* 2 Sam. 16:5 **19:17** *t* 1 Kin. 12:21 *u* 2 Sam. 9:2, 10; 16:1, 2 **19:19** *v* 1 Sam. 22:15 *w* 2 Sam. 16:5, 6 *x* 2 Sam. 13:33

to come today of all ʸthe house of Joseph to go down to meet my lord the king."

²¹But Abishai the son of Zeruiah answered and said, "Shall not Shimei be put to death for this, ᶻbecause he ᵃcursed the LORD's anointed?"

²²And David said, ᵇ"What have I to do with you, you sons of Zeruiah, that you should be adversaries to me today? ᶜShall any man be put to death today in Israel? For do I not know that today I *am* king over Israel?" ²³Therefore ᵈthe king said to Shimei, "You shall not die." And the king swore to him.

David and Mephibosheth Meet

²⁴Now ᵉMephibosheth the son of Saul came down to meet the king. And he had not cared for his feet, nor trimmed his mustache, nor washed his clothes, from the day the king departed until the day he returned in peace. ²⁵So it was, when he had come to Jerusalem to meet the king, that the king said to him, ᶠ"Why did you not go with me, Mephibosheth?"

²⁶And he answered, "My lord, O king, my servant deceived me. For your servant said, 'I will saddle a donkey for myself, that I may ride on it and go to the king,' because your servant *is* lame. ²⁷And ᵍhe has slandered your servant to my lord the king, ʰbut my lord the king *is* like the angel of God. Therefore do *what is* good in your eyes. ²⁸For all my father's house were but dead men before my lord the king. ⁱYet you set your servant among those who eat at your own table. Therefore what right have I still to cry out anymore to the king?"

²⁹So the king said to him, "Why do you speak anymore of your matters? I have said, 'You and Ziba divide the land.'"

³⁰Then Mephibosheth said to the king, "Rather, let him take it all, inasmuch as my lord the king has come back in peace to his own house."

David's Kindness to Barzillai

³¹And ʲBarzillai the Gileadite came down from Rogelim and went across the Jordan with the king, to escort him across the Jordan. ³²Now Barzillai was a very aged man, eighty years old. And ᵏhe had provided the

king with supplies while he stayed at Mahanaim, for he *was* a very rich man. ³³And the king said to Barzillai, "Come across with me, and I will provide for you while you are with me in Jerusalem."

³⁴But Barzillai said to the king, "How long have I to live, that I should go up with the king to Jerusalem? ³⁵I *am* today ˡeighty years old. Can I discern between the good and bad? Can your servant taste what I eat or what I drink? Can I hear any longer the voice of singing men and singing women? Why then should your servant be a further burden to my lord the king? ³⁶Your servant will go a little way across the Jordan with the king. And why should the king repay me *with* such a reward? ³⁷Please let your servant turn back again, that I may die in my own city, near the grave of my father and mother. But here is your servant ᵐChimham; let him cross over with my lord the king, and do for him what seems good to you."

³⁸And the king answered, "Chimham shall cross over with me, and I will do for him what seems good to you. Now whatever you request of me, I will do for you." ³⁹Then all the people went over the Jordan. And when the king had crossed over, the king ⁿkissed Barzillai and blessed him, and he returned to his own place.

The Quarrel About the King

⁴⁰Now the king went on to Gilgal, and Chimham* went on with him. And all the people of Judah escorted the king, and also half the people of Israel. ⁴¹Just then all the men of Israel came to the king, and said to the king, "Why have our brethren, the men of Judah, stolen you away and ᵒbrought the king, his household, and all David's men with him across the Jordan?"

⁴²So all the men of Judah answered the men of Israel, "Because the king *is* ᵖa close relative of ours. Why then are you angry over this matter? Have we ever eaten at the king's *expense?* Or has he given us any gift?"

⁴³And the men of Israel answered the men of Judah, and said, �q"We have ten shares in the king; therefore we also have

---

* **19:40** Masoretic Text reads *Chimham*.

19:23 the king swore to him. The king was willing to accept Shimei as a loyal subject if he continued in his loyalty, and he swore that he would not kill Shimei. Apparently David did not trust Shimei, for he later directed Solomon to kill him (1 Kin. 2:8) along with others that he considered dangerous to Solomon's reign. David could not put Shimei to death himself because of his oath, but his son could do it if there was just cause.

19:27 do what is good in your eyes. David did not try to decide whether it was Ziba or Mephibosheth who was telling the truth. He commanded that they divide the land. Each was provided for; neither was validated in his claims.

19:36 Love—Barzillai's acts of hospitality were acts of love: love for the Lord, and love for his king (Mark 9:41). Such true acts of kindness may bring a reward, but the real reward is the pleasure that comes with giving.

19:20 ʸ Judg. 1:22   **19:21** ᶻ [Ex. 22:28]   ᵃ [1 Sam. 26:9]   **19:22** ᵇ 2 Sam. 3:39; 16:10   ᶜ 1 Sam. 11:13
19:23 ᵈ 1 Kin. 2:8, 9, 37, 46   **19:24** ᵉ 2 Sam. 9:6; 21:7
19:25 ᶠ 2 Sam. 16:17   **19:27** ᵍ 2 Sam. 16:3, 4   ʰ 2 Sam. 14:17, 20   **19:28** ⁱ 2 Sam. 9:7–13   **19:31** ʲ 1 Kin. 2:7
19:32 ᵏ 2 Sam. 17:27–29   **19:35** ˡ Ps. 90:10   **19:37** ᵐ Jer. 41:17   **19:39** ⁿ Gen. 31:55   **19:41** ᵒ 2 Sam. 19:15
19:42 ᵖ 2 Sam. 19:12   **19:43** q 1 Kin. 11:30, 31

more *right* to David than you. Why then do you despise us—were we not the first to advise bringing back our king?"

Yet *r*the words of the men of Judah were fiercer than the words of the men of Israel.

The Rebellion of Sheba

20 And there happened to be there a rebel,* whose name *was* Sheba the son of Bichri, a Benjamite. And he blew a trumpet, and said:

a"We have no share in David,
Nor do we have inheritance in the son of Jesse;
*b*Every man to his tents, O Israel!"

²So every man of Israel deserted David, *and* followed Sheba the son of Bichri. But the *c*men of Judah, from the Jordan as far as Jerusalem, remained loyal to their king.

³Now David came to his house at Jerusalem. And the king took the ten women, *d*his concubines whom he had left to keep the house, and put them in seclusion and supported them, but did not go in to them. So they were shut up to the day of their death, living in widowhood.

⁴And the king said to Amasa, *e*"Assemble the men of Judah for me within three days, and be present here yourself." ⁵So Amasa went to assemble *the men of* Judah. But he delayed longer than the set time which David had appointed him. ⁶And David said to *f*Abishai, "Now Sheba the son of Bichri will do us more harm than Absalom. Take *g*your lord's servants and pursue him, lest he find for himself fortified cities, and escape us." ⁷So Joab's men, with the *h*Cherethites, the Pelethites, and *i*all the mighty men, went out after him. And they went out of Jerusalem to pursue Sheba the son of Bichri. ⁸When they *were* at the large stone which *is* in Gibeon, Amasa came before them. Now Joab was dressed in battle armor; on it was a belt *with* a sword fastened in its sheath at his hips; and as he was going forward, it fell out. ⁹Then Joab said to Amasa, "*Are* you in health, my brother?" *j*And Joab took Amasa by the beard with his right hand to kiss him. ¹⁰But Amasa did not notice the sword that *was* in Joab's hand. And *k*he struck him with it *l*in the stomach, and his entrails poured out on the ground; and he did not *strike* him again. Thus he died.

Then Joab and Abishai his brother pursued Sheba the son of Bichri. ¹¹Meanwhile one of Joab's men stood near Amasa, and said, "Whoever favors Joab and whoever *is* for David—follow Joab!" ¹²But Amasa wallowed in *his* blood in the middle of the highway. And when the man saw that all the people stood still, he moved Amasa from the highway to the field and threw a garment over him, when he saw that everyone who came upon him halted. ¹³When he was removed from the highway, all the people went on after Joab to pursue Sheba the son of Bichri.

¹⁴And he went through all the tribes of Israel to *m*Abel and Beth Maachah and all the Berites. So they were gathered together and also went after *Sheba.** ¹⁵Then they came and besieged him in Abel of Beth Maachah; and they *n*cast up a siege mound against the city, and it stood by the rampart. And all the people who *were* with Joab battered the wall to throw it down.

¹⁶Then a wise woman cried out from the city, "Hear, hear! Please say to Joab, 'Come nearby, that I may speak with you.'"

¹⁷When he had come near to her, the woman said, "*Are* you Joab?"

He answered, "I *am.*"

Then she said to him, "Hear the words of your maidservant."

And he answered, "I am listening."

¹⁸So she spoke, saying, "They used to talk in former times, saying, 'They shall surely seek *guidance* at Abel,' and so they would end *disputes.* ¹⁹I *am among the* peaceable *and* faithful in Israel. You seek to destroy a city and a mother in Israel. Why would you swallow up *o*the inheritance of the LORD?"

²⁰And Joab answered and said, "Far be it, far be it from me, that I should swallow up or destroy! ²¹That *is* not so. But a man from the mountains of Ephraim, Sheba the son of Bichri by name, has raised his hand against the king, against David. Deliver him only, and I will depart from the city."

So the woman said to Joab, "Watch, his head will be thrown to you over the wall." ²²Then the woman *p*in her wisdom went to all the people. And they cut off the head of

* **20:1** Literally *man of Belial*   * **20:14** Literally *him*

20:6 *do us more harm.* Sheba's revolt had more potential for destroying David's reign than Absalom's revolt because it was based on long-standing tribal animosity between Judah and the tribe of Benjamin.
20:9 *my brother.* This was not the first time Joab had killed a man while pretending to have a friendly word with him (3:27). The text does not say whether he suspected Amasa of treachery in his delay, or if Joab was acting out of jealousy, protecting his own long-standing position of leader of David's army.
20:13–22 Strife—Once again David had an opportunity to demonstrate that it was God who had

chosen him to be king. If a leader has to contend for his position he is sure to leave rebellion and destruction in his wake.

19:43 *r* Judg. 8:1; 12:1   **20:1** *a* 1 Kin. 12:16   *b* 2 Sam. 18:17   **20:2** *c* 2 Sam. 19:14   **20:3** *d* 2 Sam. 15:16; 16:21, 22   **20:4** *e* 2 Sam. 17:25; 19:13   **20:6** *f* 2 Sam. 2:17   *g* 2 Sam. 11:11   **20:7** *h* 1 Kin. 1:38, 44   *i* 2 Sam. 15:18   **20:9** *j* Matt. 26:49   **20:10** *k* 1 Kin. 2:5   *l* 2 Sam. 2:23   **20:14** *m* 2 Kin. 15:29   **20:15** *n* 2 Kin. 19:32   **20:19** *o* 1 Sam. 26:19   **20:22** *p* [Eccl. 9:13–16]

Sheba the son of Bichri, and threw *it* out to Joab. Then he blew a trumpet, and they withdrew from the city, every man to his tent. So Joab returned to the king at Jerusalem.

David's Government Officers

23And qJoab *was* over all the army of Israel; Benaiah the son of Jehoiada *was* over the Cherethites and the Pelethites; 24Adoram *was* rin charge of revenue; sJehoshaphat the son of Ahilud *was* recorder; 25Sheva *was* scribe; tZadok and Abiathar *were* the priests; 26uand Ira the Jairite *was* a chief minister under David.

David Avenges the Gibeonites

21 Now there was a famine in the days of David for three years, year after year; and David qinquired of the LORD. And the LORD answered, "*It is* because of Saul and *his* bloodthirsty house, because he killed the Gibeonites." 2So the king called the Gibeonites and spoke to them. Now the Gibeonites *were* not of the children of Israel, but bof the remnant of the Amorites; the children of Israel had sworn protection to them, but Saul had sought to kill them cin his zeal for the children of Israel and Judah.

3Therefore David said to the Gibeonites, "What shall I do for you? And with what shall I make atonement, that you may bless dthe inheritance of the LORD?"

4And the Gibeonites said to him, "We will have no silver or gold from Saul or from his house, nor shall you kill any man in Israel for us."

So he said, "Whatever you say, I will do for you."

5Then they answered the king, "As for the man who consumed us and plotted against us, *that* we should be destroyed from remaining in any of the territories of Israel, 6let seven men of his descendants be delivered eto us, and we will hang them before the LORD fin Gibeah of Saul, gwhom the LORD chose."

And the king said, "I will give *them*."

7But the king spared hMephibosheth the son of Jonathan, the son of Saul, because of ithe LORD's oath that *was* between them, between David and Jonathan the son of Saul. 8So the king took Armoni and Mephibosheth, the two sons of jRizpah the daughter of Aiah, whom she bore to Saul, and the five sons of Michal* the daughter of Saul, whom she brought up for Adriel the son of Barzillai the Meholathite; 9and he delivered them into the hands of the Gibeonites, and they hanged them on the hill kbefore the LORD. So they fell, *all* seven together, and were put to death in the days of harvest, in the first *days*, in the beginning of barley harvest.

10Now lRizpah the daughter of Aiah took sackcloth and spread it for herself on the rock, mfrom the beginning of harvest until the late rains poured on them from heaven. And she did not allow the birds of the air to rest on them by day nor the beasts of the field by night.

11And David was told what Rizpah the daughter of Aiah, the concubine of Saul, had done. 12Then David went and took the bones of Saul, and the bones of Jonathan his son, from the men of nJabesh Gilead who had stolen them from the street of Beth Shan,* where the oPhilistines had hung them up, after the Philistines had struck down Saul in Gilboa. 13So he brought up the bones of Saul and the bones of Jonathan his son from there; and they gathered the bones of those who had been hanged. 14They buried the bones of Saul and Jonathan his son in the country of Benjamin in pZelah, in the tomb of Kish his father. So they performed all that the king commanded. And after that qGod heeded the prayer for the land.

Philistine Giants Destroyed

15When the Philistines were at war again with Israel, David and his servants went down and fought against the Philistines; and David grew faint. 16Then Ishbi-Benob, who *was* one of the sons of the rgiant, the weight of whose

* 21:8 Or *Merab* (compare 1 Samuel 18:19 and 25:44; 2 Samuel 3:14 and 6:23)   * 21:12 Spelled *Beth Shean* in Joshua 17:11 and elsewhere

---

21:1 *because he killed the Gibeonites.* When the Israelites first came into the Promised Land under the leadership of Joshua, the Gibeonites had deceived them into making a treaty that guaranteed their protection and security (Josh. 9:3–27). Saul had broken that agreement.

21:10 *Rizpah.* Rizpah remained near the bodies, protecting them from scavengers, from the barley harvest to the early rains (late April to October). This heartbreaking devotion from the mother of two of the slain men commended her to David, and finally the bones of Saul and all of his sons were buried in the family grave site.

21:14 *God heeded the prayer for the land.* It is hard to understand why the death of the descendants of Saul as payment for his treachery was something that would be connected to God hearing prayers for

famine. Saul was described as rebellious, and apparently his disobedience was more far reaching than is recorded in Scripture. Possibly the men who were killed had been implicated in killing the Gibeonites. Even if we do not understand, we can always be sure that God is just and God is righteous.

21:16 *giant.* The giants were the Rephaim, a people living in Canaan who were noted for their large size.

20:23 q 2 Sam. 8:16–18   20:24 r 1 Kin. 4:6   s 2 Sam. 8:16
20:25 t 1 Kin. 4:4   20:26 u 2 Sam. 8:18   21:1 a Num. 27:21
21:2 b Josh. 9:3, 15–20   c [Ex. 34:11–16]   21:3 d 2 Sam.
20:19   21:6 e Num. 25:4   f 1 Sam. 10:26   g 1 Sam. 10:24
21:7 h 2 Sam. 4:4; 9:10   i 2 Sam. 9:1–7   21:8 j 2 Sam. 3:7
21:9 k 2 Sam. 6:17   21:10 l 2 Sam. 3:7; 21:8   m Deut. 21:23
21:12 n 1 Sam. 31:11–13   o 1 Sam. 31:8   21:14 p Josh. 18:28
q 2 Sam. 24:25   21:16 r 2 Sam. 21:18–22

bronze spear *was* three hundred *shekels*, who was bearing a new *sword*, thought he could kill David. ¹⁷But ^sAbishai the son of Zeruiah came to his aid, and struck the Philistine and killed him. Then the men of David swore to him, saying, ^t"You shall go out no more with us to battle, lest you quench the ^ulamp of Israel."

¹⁸^vNow it happened afterward that there was again a battle with the Philistines at Gob. Then ^wSibbechai the Hushathite killed Saph,* who *was* one of the sons of the giant. ¹⁹Again there was war at Gob with the Philistines, where ^xElhanan the son of Jaare-Oregim* the Bethlehemite killed ^y*the brother of* Goliath the Gittite, the shaft of whose spear *was* like a weaver's beam.

²⁰Yet again ^zthere was war at Gath, where there was a man of *great* stature, who had six fingers on each hand and six toes on each foot, twenty-four in number; and he also was born to the giant. ²¹So when he ^adefied Israel, Jonathan the son of Shimea,* David's brother, killed him.

²²^bThese four were born to the giant in Gath, and fell by the hand of David and by the hand of his servants.

Praise for God's Deliverance

22 Then David ^aspoke to the LORD the words of this song, on the day when the LORD had ^bdelivered him from the hand of all his enemies, and from the hand of Saul. ²And he ^csaid:*

^d"The LORD *is* my rock and my ^efortress and my deliverer;
³ The God of my strength, ^fin whom I will trust;
My ^gshield and the ^hhorn of my salvation,
My ⁱstronghold and my ^jrefuge;
My Savior, You save me from violence.
⁴ I will call upon the LORD, *who is worthy* to be praised;
So shall I be saved from my enemies.

⁵ "When the waves of death surrounded me,
The floods of ungodliness made me afraid.
⁶ The ^ksorrows of Sheol surrounded me;
The snares of death confronted me.

⁷ In my distress ^lI called upon the LORD,
And cried out to my God;
He ^mheard my voice from His temple,
And my cry *entered* His ears.

⁸ "Then ⁿthe earth shook and trembled;
^oThe foundations of heaven* quaked and were shaken,
Because He was angry.
⁹ Smoke went up from His nostrils,
And devouring ^pfire from His mouth;
Coals were kindled by it.
¹⁰ He ^qbowed the heavens also, and came down
With ^rdarkness under His feet.
¹¹ He rode upon a cherub, and flew;
And He was seen* ^supon the wings of the wind.
¹² He made ^tdarkness canopies around Him,
Dark waters *and* thick clouds of the skies.
¹³ From the brightness before Him
Coals of fire were kindled.

¹⁴ "The LORD ^uthundered from heaven,
And the Most High uttered His voice.
¹⁵ He sent out ^varrows and scattered them;
Lightning bolts, and He vanquished them.
¹⁶ Then the channels of the sea ^wwere seen,
The foundations of the world were uncovered,
At the ^xrebuke of the LORD,
At the blast of the breath of His nostrils.

¹⁷ "He^y sent from above, He took me,
He drew me out of many waters.
¹⁸ He delivered me from my strong enemy,
From those who hated me;
For they were too strong for me.

---

* **21:18** Spelled *Sippai* in 1 Chronicles 20:4
* **21:19** Spelled *Jair* in 1 Chronicles 20:5
* **21:21** Spelled *Shammah* in 1 Samuel 16:9 and elsewhere * **22:2** Compare Psalm 18 * **22:8** Following Masoretic Text, Septuagint, and Targum; Syriac and Vulgate read *hills* (compare Psalm 18:7). * **22:11** Following Masoretic Text and Septuagint; many Hebrew manuscripts, Syriac, and Vulgate read *He flew* (compare Psalm 18:10); Targum reads *He spoke with power.*

---

three hundred shekels. The spear weighed approximately seven and a half pounds.
22:1 words of this song. This psalm later became part of the congregational worship of Israel (Ps. 18), but it began as David's personal and earnest expression of praise to the Lord.
22:3 the horn of my salvation. The horn of an animal is used for protection and defense, so it is a good word picture for a sign of might and power.
22:6 Sheol. This word is used in Hebrew poetry as a synonym for death. In the Old Testament, Sheol is described as a place of dust, referring to death (Job 17:16), a place of decay (Ps. 16:10), and as a pit (Is. 14:15).

21:17 ^s 2 Sam. 20:6–10 ^t 2 Sam. 18:3 ^u 1 Kin. 11:36 **21:18** ^v 1 Chr. 20:4–8 ^w 1 Chr. 11:29; 27:11 **21:19** ^x 2 Sam. 23:24 ^y 1 Chr. 20:5 **21:20** ^z 1 Chr. 20:6 **21:21** ^a 1 Sam. 17:10 **21:22** ^b 1 Chr. 20:8 **22:1** ^a Ex. 15:1 ^b Ps. 18:title; 34:19 **22:2** ^c Ps. 18 ^d Deut. 32:4 ^e Ps. 91:2 **22:3** ^f Heb. 2:13 ^g Gen. 15:1 ^h Luke 1:69 ⁱ Prov. 18:10 ^j Ps. 9:9; 46:1, 7, 11 **22:6** ^k Ps. 116:3 **22:7** ^l Ps. 116:4; 120:1 ^m Ex. 3:7 **22:8** ⁿ Judg. 5:4 ^o Job 26:11 **22:9** ^p Heb. 12:29 **22:10** ^q Is. 64:1 ^r Ex. 20:21 **22:11** ^s Ps. 104:3 **22:12** ^t Job 36:29 **22:14** ^u Job 37:2–5 **22:15** ^v Deut. 32:23 **22:16** ^w Nah. 1:4 ^x Ex. 15:8 **22:17** ^y Ps. 144:7

19 They confronted me in the day of my
calamity,
But the LORD was my [z]support.
20 [a]He also brought me out into a broad
place;
He delivered me because He [b]delighted
in me.

21 "The[c] LORD rewarded me according to
my righteousness;
According to the [d]cleanness of my
hands
He has recompensed me.
22 For I have [e]kept the ways of the
LORD,
And have not wickedly departed from
my God.
23 For all His [f]judgments *were* before me;
And *as for* His statutes, I did not
depart from them.
24 I was also [g]blameless before Him,
And I kept myself from my iniquity.
25 Therefore [h]the LORD has recompensed
me according to my
righteousness,
According to my cleanness in His
eyes.*

26 "With [i]the merciful You will show
Yourself merciful;
With a blameless man You will show
Yourself blameless;
27 With the pure You will show Yourself
pure;
And [j]with the devious You will show
Yourself shrewd.
28 You will save the [k]humble people;
But Your eyes *are* on [l]the haughty,
that You may bring *them*
down.

29 "For You *are* my [m]lamp, O LORD;
The LORD shall enlighten my
darkness.
30 For by You I can run against a
troop;
By my God I can leap over a [n]wall.
31 *As for* God, [o]His way *is* perfect;
[p]The word of the LORD *is* proven;
He *is* a shield to all who trust in
Him.

32 "For [q]who *is* God, except the LORD?
And who *is* a rock, except our God?
33 God *is* my [r]strength *and* power,*
And He [s]makes my* way [t]perfect.
34 He makes my* feet [u]like the *feet* of
deer,
And [v]sets me on my high places.
35 He teaches my hands to make
war,
So that my arms can bend a bow of
bronze.

36 "You have also given me the shield of
Your salvation;
Your gentleness has made me great.
37 You [w]enlarged my path under me;
So my feet did not slip.

38 "I have pursued my enemies and
destroyed them;
Neither did I turn back again till they
were destroyed.
39 And I have destroyed them and
wounded them,
So that they could not rise;
They have fallen [x]under my feet.
40 For You have [y]armed me with strength
for the battle;
You have subdued under me [z]those
who rose against me.
41 You have also given me the [a]necks of
my enemies,
So that I destroyed those who
hated me.
42 They looked, but *there was* none to
save;
Even [b]to the LORD, but He did not
answer them.
43 Then I beat them as fine [c]as the dust of
the earth;
I trod them [d]like dirt in the streets,
And I spread them out.

44 "You[e] have also delivered me from the
strivings of my people;
You have kept me as the [f]head of the
nations.
[g]A people I have not known shall
serve me.

---

* **22:25** Septuagint, Syriac, and Vulgate read *the cleanness of my hands in His sight* (compare Psalm 18:24); Targum reads *my cleanness before His word.* * **22:33** Dead Sea Scrolls, Septuagint, Syriac, and Vulgate read *It is God who arms me with strength* (compare Psalm 18:32); Targum reads *It is God who sustains me with strength.* • Following Qere, Septuagint, Syriac, Targum, and Vulgate (compare Psalm 18:32); Kethib reads *His.* * **22:34** Following Qere, Septuagint, Syriac, Targum, and Vulgate (compare Psalm 18:33); Kethib reads *His.*

22:22 *I have kept the ways of the LORD.* David did not keep the ways of the Lord perfectly. His sins have been written down for the whole world to know throughout the ages. But he never forgot the Lord, always knew that what he did mattered to God, and always turned his steps back to the Lord when he went astray. Like Paul, David ran the race in such a way as to get the prize (1 Cor. 9:24).
22:34 *the feet of deer.* The deer or hind is noted for its swiftness, agility, and surefootedness.
22:35 *can bend a bow of bronze.* It would take unusual strength to bend a steel bow (Job 20:24).

22:19 [z] Is. 10:20 **22:20** [a] Ps. 31:8; 118:5 [b] 2 Sam. 15:26 **22:21** [c] 1 Sam. 26:23 [d] Ps. 24:4 **22:22** [e] Ps. 119:3 **22:23** [f] [Deut. 6:6–9; 7:12] **22:24** [g] [Eph. 1:4] **22:25** [h] 2 Sam. 22:21 **22:26** [i] [Matt. 5:7] **22:27** [j] [Lev. 26:23, 24] **22:28** [k] Ps. 72:12 [l] Job 40:11 **22:29** [m] Ps. 119:105; 132:17 **22:30** [n] 2 Sam. 5:6–8 **22:31** [o] [Matt. 5:48] [p] Ps. 12:6 **22:32** [q] Is. 45:5, 6 **22:33** [r] Ps. 27:1 [s] [Heb. 13:21] [t] Ps. 101:2, 6 **22:34** [u] 2 Sam. 2:18 [v] Is. 33:16 **22:37** [w] Prov. 4:12 **22:39** [x] Mal. 4:3 **22:40** [y] [Ps. 18:32] [z] [Ps. 44:5] **22:41** [a] Gen. 49:8 **22:42** [b] 1 Sam. 28:6 **22:43** [c] Ps. 18:42 [d] Is. 10:6 **22:44** [e] 2 Sam. 3:1 [f] Deut. 28:13 [g] [Is. 55:5]

45 The foreigners submit to me;
　　As soon as they hear, they
　　　obey me.
46 The foreigners fade away,
　　And come frightened* *h*from their
　　　hideouts.

47 "The LORD lives!
　　Blessed *be* my Rock!
　　Let God be exalted,
　　The *i*Rock of my salvation!
48 *It is* God who avenges me,
　　And *j*subdues the peoples under me;
49 He delivers me from my enemies.
　　You also lift me up above those who
　　　rise against me;
　　You have delivered me from the
　　　*k*violent man.
50 Therefore I will give thanks to You,
　　O LORD, among *l*the Gentiles,
　　And sing praises to Your *m*name.

51 "*He*n *is* the tower of salvation to His
　　　king,
　　And shows mercy to His *o*anointed,
　　To David and *p*his descendants
　　　forevermore."

David's Last Words

23 Now these *are* the last words of
David.

　　Thus says David the son of Jesse;
　　Thus says *a*the man raised up on
　　　high,
　　*b*The anointed of the God of Jacob,
　　And the sweet psalmist of Israel:

2 "The*c* Spirit of the LORD spoke by me,
　　And His word *was* on my tongue.
3 The God of Israel said,
　　*d*The Rock of Israel spoke to me:
　　'He who rules over men *must be*
　　　just,

Ruling *e*in the fear of God.
4 And *f*he shall be* like the light
　　　of the morning *when* the sun
　　　rises,
　　A morning without clouds,
　　Like the tender grass *springing* out of
　　　the earth,
　　By clear shining after rain.'

5 "Although my house *is* not so with
　　　God,
　　*g*Yet He has made with me an
　　　everlasting covenant,
　　Ordered in all *things* and secure.
　　For *this is* all my salvation and all *my*
　　　desire;
　　Will He not make *it* increase?
6 But *the sons* of rebellion *shall* all *be* as
　　　thorns thrust away,
　　Because they cannot be taken with
　　　hands.
7 But the man *who* touches them
　　Must be armed with iron and the shaft
　　　of a spear,
　　And they shall be utterly burned with
　　　fire in *their* place."

David's Mighty Men

8 These *are* the names of the mighty men
whom David had: Josheb-Basshebeth* the
Tachmonite, chief among the captains.*
He was called Adino the Eznite, because
he had killed eight hundred men at one
time. 9 And after him *was* *h*Eleazar the
son of Dodo,* the Ahohite, *one* of the

---

* **22:46** Following Septuagint, Targum, and Vulgate (compare Psalm 18:45); Masoretic Text reads *gird themselves.*　*　**23:8** Literally *One Who Sits in the Seat* (compare 1 Chronicles 11:11) • Following Masoretic Text and Targum; Septuagint and Vulgate read *the three.*　*　**23:9** Spelled *Dodai* in 1 Chronicles 27:4

22:47 The LORD lives. This shout of exaltation is the heart cry of every follower of God. The difference between the Living God and the dead idols that entrapped so many in the countries around him stood out very strongly to David.
22:51 His anointed. David was anointed by God to be king of Israel. He was set aside for a certain job. Jesus is the ultimate Anointed One, which is the meaning of the Hebrew name Messiah and the Greek name Christ.
23:1 sweet psalmist of Israel. Of the 150 psalms in the Book of Psalms, 73 are attributed to David by the text. No person in Scriptures is more closely associated with music in the worship of the Lord than King David. He left behind a beautiful record of his heartfelt love of the Lord, his struggles, and his victories.
23:3–4 Fear of God—For centuries certain dynasties of rulers in Europe claimed the divine right to rule. Certainly the Bible teaches that government is ordained of God (Rom. 13). But it also teaches that rulers have a deep stewardship responsibility. They are to rule men in the fear of God. Over and over again it is shown that God sets rulers in place, and also deposes those who consistently rebel against Him.

23:5 everlasting covenant. David celebrates his everlasting covenant (7:12–16) here and in Psalm 89.
23:6–7 the sons of rebellion. The worthless, rebellious, or literally "the sons of Belial." This is a term of contempt and scorn, the word that Shimei hurled at David when David was fleeing from the rebellion of his son Absalom (16:7). The word was also used to describe Sheba, the scoundrel from the tribe of Benjamin (20:1). David anticipated God's judgment on the ungodly, who are likened to thorns fit only to be burned.
23:8 mighty men. The term "mighty men" suggests that these were the elite of David's troops, possibly his personal bodyguards. These men were heroes in the full sense of the word. Their listing must have inspired others to attain such accomplishments.

22:46 *h* [Mic. 7:17]　**22:47** *i* Ps. 89:26　**22:48** *j* Ps. 144:2　**22:49** *k* Ps. 140:1, 4, 11　**22:50** *l* 2 Sam. 8:1–14　*m* Rom. 15:9　**22:51** *n* Ps. 144:10　*o* Ps. 89:20　*p* 2 Sam. 7:12–16　**23:1** *a* 2 Sam. 7:8, 9　*b* 1 Sam. 16:12, 13　**23:2** *c* [2 Pet. 1:21]　**23:3** *d* [Deut. 32:4]　*e* Ex. 18:21　**23:4** *h* Ps. 89:36　**23:5** *g* Ps. 89:29　**23:9** *h* 1 Chr. 11:12; 27:4

three mighty men with David when they defied the Philistines *who* were gathered there for battle, and the men of Israel had retreated. [10]He arose and attacked the Philistines until his hand was [i]weary, and his hand stuck to the sword. The LORD brought about a great victory that day; and the people returned after him only to [j]plunder. [11]And after him *was* [k]Shammah the son of Agee the Hararite. [l]The Philistines had gathered together into a troop where there was a piece of ground full of lentils. So the people fled from the Philistines. [12]But he stationed himself in the middle of the field, defended it, and killed the Philistines. So the LORD brought about a great victory.

[13]Then [m]three of the thirty chief men went down at harvest time and came to David at [n]the cave of Adullam. And the troop of Philistines encamped in [o]the Valley of Rephaim. [14]David *was* then in [p]the stronghold, and the garrison of the Philistines *was* then *in* Bethlehem. [15]And David said with longing, "Oh, that someone would give me a drink of the water from the well of Bethlehem, which *is* by the gate!" [16]So the three mighty men broke through the camp of the Philistines, drew water from the well of Bethlehem that *was* by the gate, and took it and brought *it* to David. Nevertheless he would not drink it, but poured it out to the LORD. [17]And he said, "Far be it from me, O LORD, that I should do this! Is *this not* [q]the blood of the men who went in *jeopardy of* their lives?" Therefore he would not drink it.

These things were done by the three mighty men.

[18]Now [r]Abishai the brother of Joab, the son of Zeruiah, was chief of *another* three.* He lifted his spear against three hundred *men,* killed *them,* and won a name among *these* three. [19]Was he not the most honored of three? Therefore he became their captain. However, he did not attain to the *first* three.

[20]Benaiah *was* the son of Jehoiada, the son of a valiant man from [s]Kabzeel, who had done many deeds. [t]He had killed two lion-like heroes of Moab. He also had gone down and killed a lion in the midst of a pit on a snowy day. [21]And he killed an Egyptian, a spectacular man. The Egyptian *had* a spear in his hand; so he went down to him with a staff, wrested the spear out of the Egyptian's hand, and killed him with his own spear. [22]These *things* Benaiah the son of Jehoiada did, and won a name among three mighty men. [23]He was more honored than the thirty, but he did not attain to the *first* three. And David appointed him [u]over his guard.

[24][v]Asahel the brother of Joab *was* one of the thirty; Elhanan the son of Dodo of Bethlehem, [25][w]Shammah the Harodite, Elika the Harodite, [26]Helez the Paltite, Ira the son of Ikkesh the Tekoite, [27]Abiezer the Anathothite, Mebunnai the Hushathite, [28]Zalmon the Ahohite, Maharai the Netophathite, [29]Heleb the son of Baanah (the Netophathite), Ittai the son of Ribai from Gibeah of the children of Benjamin, [30]Benaiah a Pirathonite, Hiddai from the brooks of [x]Gaash, [31]Abi-Albon the Arbathite, Azmaveth the Barhumite, [32]Eliahba the Shaalbonite (of the sons of Jashen), Jonathan, [33][y]Shammah the Hararite, Ahiam the son of Sharar the Hararite, [34]Eliphelet the son of Ahasbai, the son of the Maachathite, Eliam the son of [z]Ahithophel the Gilonite, [35]Hezrai* the Carmelite, Paarai the Arbite, [36]Igal the son of Nathan of [a]Zobah, Bani the Gadite, [37]Zelek the Ammonite, Naharai the Beerothite (armorbearer of Joab the son of Zeruiah), [38][b]Ira the Ithrite, Gareb the Ithrite, [39]*and* [c]Uriah the Hittite: thirty-seven in all.

David's Census of Israel and Judah

24 Again [a]the anger of the LORD was aroused against Israel, and He moved David against them to say, [b]"Go, number Israel and Judah."

[2]So the king said to Joab the commander of the army who *was* with him, "Now go throughout all the tribes of Israel, [c]from Dan to Beersheba, and count the people, that [d]I may know the number of the people."

* 23:18 Following Masoretic Text, Septuagint, and Vulgate; some Hebrew manuscripts and Syriac read *thirty*; Targum reads *the mighty men.*
* 23:35 Spelled *Hezro* in 1 Chronicles 11:37

23:13–14 *Valley of Rephaim.* This valley was a route to Jerusalem. *Bethlehem.* David's hometown (1 Sam. 16:1–3) was about six miles south of Jerusalem.
23:15 *give me drink of the water from the well of Bethlehem.* Anyone who has grown up with an especially good well for drinking water can identify with David's craving. The taste of the water from the well at "home" seems more thirst-quenching, more heartening, than any other.
23:16 *poured it out to the LORD.* David was deeply moved by this act of loyalty. He could have let it make him feel important, but instead he dedicated the water to the Lord, knowing that no man's craving should be satisfied at the risk of another man's life.

23:10 [i] Judg. 8:4 [j] 1 Sam. 30:24, 25 **23:11** [k] 1 Chr. 11:27 [l] 1 Chr. 11:13, 14 **23:13** [m] 1 Chr. 11:15 [n] 1 Sam. 22:1 [o] 2 Sam. 5:18 **23:14** [p] 1 Sam. 22:4, 5 **23:17** [q] [Lev. 17:10] **23:18** [r] 1 Chr. 11:20 **23:20** [s] Josh. 15:21 [t] Ex. 15:15 **23:23** [u] 2 Sam. 8:18; 20:23 **23:24** [v] 2 Samv. 2:18 **23:25** [w] 1 Chr. 11:27 **23:30** [x] Judg. 2:9 **23:33** [y] 2 Sam. 23:11 **23:34** [z] 2 Sam. 15:12 **23:36** [a] 2 Sam. 8:3 **23:38** [b] 1 Chr. 2:53 **23:39** [c] 2 Sam. 11:3, 6 **24:1** [a] 2 Sam. 21:1, 2 [b] 1 Chr. 27:23, 24 **24:2** [c] Judg. 20:1 [d] [Jer. 17:5]

³And Joab said to the king, "Now may the LORD your God ᵉadd to the people a hundred times more than there are, and may the eyes of my lord the king see *it*. But why does my lord the king desire this thing?" ⁴Nevertheless the king's word prevailed against Joab and against the captains of the army. Therefore Joab and the captains of the army went out from the presence of the king to count the people of Israel.

⁵And they crossed over the Jordan and camped in ᶠAroer, on the right side of the town which *is* in the midst of the ravine of Gad, and toward ᵍJazer. ⁶Then they came to Gilead and to the land of Tahtim Hodshi; they came to ʰDan Jaan and around to ⁱSidon; ⁷and they came to the stronghold of ʲTyre and to all the cities of the ᵏHivites and the Canaanites. Then they went out to South Judah *as far as* Beersheba. ⁸So when they had gone through all the land, they came to Jerusalem at the end of nine months and twenty days. ⁹Then Joab gave the sum of the number of the people to the king. ˡAnd there were in Israel eight hundred thousand valiant men who drew the sword, and the men of Judah were five hundred thousand men.

The Judgment on David's Sin

¹⁰And ᵐDavid's heart condemned him after he had numbered the people. So ⁿDavid said to the LORD, ᵒ"I have sinned greatly in what I have done; but now, I pray, O LORD, take away the iniquity of Your servant, for I have ᵖdone very foolishly."

¹¹Now when David arose in the morning, the word of the LORD came to the prophet ᑫGad, David's ʳseer, saying, ¹²"Go and tell David, 'Thus says the LORD: "I offer you three *things*; choose one of them for yourself, that I may do *it* to you."'" ¹³So Gad came to David and told him; and he said to him, "Shall ˢseven* years of famine come to you in your land? Or shall you flee three months before your enemies, while they pursue you? Or shall there be three days' plague in your land? Now consider and see what answer I should take back to Him who sent me."

¹⁴And David said to Gad, "I am in great distress. Please let us fall into the hand of the LORD, ᵗfor His mercies *are* great; but ᵘdo not let me fall into the hand of man."

¹⁵So ᵛthe LORD sent a plague upon Israel from the morning till the appointed time. From Dan to Beersheba seventy thousand men of the people died. ¹⁶ʷAnd when the angel* stretched out His hand over Jerusalem to destroy it, ˣthe LORD relented from the destruction, and said to the angel who was destroying the people, "It is enough; now restrain your hand." And the angel of the LORD was by the threshing floor of Araunah* the Jebusite.

¹⁷Then David spoke to the LORD when he saw the angel who was striking the people, and said, "Surely ʸI have sinned, and I have done wickedly; but these sheep, what have they done? Let Your hand, I pray, be against me and against my father's house."

The Altar on the Threshing Floor

¹⁸And Gad came that day to David and said to him, ᶻ"Go up, erect an altar to the LORD on the threshing floor of Araunah the Jebusite." ¹⁹So David, according to the word of Gad, went up as the LORD commanded. ²⁰Now Araunah looked, and saw the king and his servants coming toward him. So Araunah went out and bowed before the king with his face to the ground.

²¹Then Araunah said, "Why has my lord the king come to his servant?"

ᵃAnd David said, "To buy the threshing floor from you, to build an altar to the LORD, that ᵇthe plague may be withdrawn from the people."

²²Now Araunah said to David, "Let my lord the king take and offer up whatever *seems* good to him. ᶜLook, *here are* oxen for burnt sacrifice, and threshing

---

* **24:13** Following Masoretic Text, Syriac, Targum, and Vulgate; Septuagint reads *three* (compare 1 Chronicles 21:12). * **24:16** Or *Angel* • Spelled *Ornan* in 1 Chronicles 21:15

24:3 *why does my lord the king desire this thing.* God was angry with Israel, and the numbering and resulting pestilence were a part of His plan to deal with Israel in such a way that they did not become complacent. This incident is not well explained in Scripture. Joab knew that David was acting presumptuously, but at this point David could not see it. Perhaps the census showed a lack of trust in the Lord, and a sense that the might of the nation rested in its armed men.
24:9 *men who drew the sword.* The numbers given refer only to men of military age. It is impressive that the division of Israel and Judah was so well established. This division would in the end result in a divided kingdom.

24:10 *David's heart condemned him.* The text does not state precisely what David's sin was. His heart was always sensitive to God's will, and he quickly confessed his sin and sought restoration with the Lord.

24:3 ᵉDeut. 1:11 **24:5** ᶠDeut. 2:36 ᵍNum. 32:1, 3 **24:6** ʰJudg. 18:29 ⁱJosh. 19:28 **24:7** ʲJosh. 19:29 ᵏJosh. 11:3 **24:9** ˡ1 Chr. 21:5 **24:10** ᵐ1 Sam. 24:5 ⁿ2 Sam. 23:1 ᵒ2 Sam. 12:13 ᵖ1 Sam. 13:13 **24:11** ᑫ1 Sam. 22:5 ʳ1 Sam. 9:9 **24:13** ˢEzek. 14:21 **24:14** ᵗ[Ps. 51:1; 103:8, 13, 14; 119:156; 130:4, 7] ᵘ[Is. 47:6] **24:15** ᵛ1 Chr. 21:14 **24:16** ʷEx. 12:23 ˣGen. 6:6 **24:17** ʸPs. 74:1 **24:18** ᶻ1 Chr. 21:18 **24:21** ᵃGen. 23:8–16 ᵇNum. 16:48, 50 **24:22** ᶜ1 Kin. 19:21

implements and the yokes of the oxen for wood. 23All these, O king, Araunah has given to the king."

And Araunah said to the king, "May the LORD your God daccept you."

24Then the king said to Araunah, "No, but I will surely buy it from you for a price; nor will I offer burnt offerings to the LORD my God with that which costs me nothing." So eDavid bought the threshing floor and the oxen for fifty shekels of silver. 25And David built there an altar to the LORD, and offered burnt offerings and peace offerings. fSo the LORD heeded the prayers for the land, and gthe plague was withdrawn from Israel.

24:24 threshing floor. The threshing floor was located on Mount Moriah, where Abraham had bound Isaac (Gen. 22:2). Later, Solomon would build the temple at this site (1 Kin. 6:1; 1 Chr. 21:27—22:1; 2 Chr. 3:1). **fifty shekels of silver.** The fifty shekels of silver paid only for the threshing floor, the oxen, and the implements. The land that surrounded the threshing floor would cost considerably more—six hundred shekels, or 15 pounds of gold (1 Chr. 21:25).
24:25 burnt offerings and peace offerings. The burnt offering was the principal atoning sacrifice for unintentional sins (Lev. 1:1–17; 6:8–13). It was completely consumed on the altar, except for the hide, which was given to the officiating priest. The peace offering was an optional sacrifice, which did not form any part of the regular offerings required in the tabernacle or temple. It was a voluntary expression of thanksgiving or worship (Lev. 3:1–17; 7:11–34).

24:23 d [Ezek. 20:40, 41]   **24:24** e 1 Chr. 21:24, 25
24:25 f 2 Sam. 21:14   g 2 Sam. 24:21

THE FIRST BOOK OF THE
KINGS

▶ **AUTHOR:** Both 1 and 2 Kings emphasize God's righteous judgment on idolatry and immorality. The style of these books is similar to that found in Jeremiah. The author of 1 Kings is unknown, but evidence supports the Talmudic tradition that Kings was written by Jeremiah. Clearly, the author was a prophet/historian as evidenced in the prophetic exposé of apostasy.

▶ **TIME:** c. 971–851 B.C.   ▶ **KEY VERSES:** 1 Kin. 9:4–5

▶ **THEME:** First Kings continues the saga of the kings of Israel after David. Solomon's reign and the details of the building of the temple take up a major portion of 1 Kings. After Solomon, the kingdom divides, and we have parallel narratives of the northern kingdom, Israel, and the southern kingdom, Judah. The book covers a span of about 120 years. During these years, idolatry becomes the norm, and God is largely forgotten. After Solomon, the main character of the book is Elijah the prophet.

Adonijah Presumes to Be King

1 Now King David was ᵃold, advanced in years; and they put covers on him, but he could not get warm. ²Therefore his servants said to him, "Let a young woman, a virgin, be sought for our lord the king, and let her stand before the king, and let her care for him; and let her lie in your bosom, that our lord the king may be warm." ³So they sought for a lovely young woman throughout all the territory of Israel, and found ᵇAbishag the ᶜShunammite, and brought her to the king. ⁴The young woman *was* very lovely; and she cared for the king, and served him; but the king did not know her.

⁵Then ᵈAdonijah the son of Haggith exalted himself, saying, "I will be king"; and ᵉhe prepared for himself chariots and horsemen, and fifty men to run before him. ⁶(And his father had not rebuked him at any time by saying, "Why have you done so?" He *was* also very good-looking. ᶠHis

mother had borne him after Absalom.) ⁷Then he conferred with ᵍJoab the son of Zeruiah and with ʰAbiathar the priest, and ⁱthey followed and helped Adonijah. ⁸But ʲZadok the priest, ᵏBenaiah the son of Jehoiada, ˡNathan the prophet, ᵐShimei, Rei, and ⁿthe mighty men who *belonged* to David were not with Adonijah.

⁹And Adonijah sacrificed sheep and oxen and fattened cattle by the stone of Zoheleth, which *is* by ᵒEn Rogel; he also invited all his brothers, the king's sons, and all the men of Judah, the king's servants. ¹⁰But he did not invite Nathan the prophet, Benaiah, the mighty men, or ᵖSolomon his brother.

¹¹So Nathan spoke to Bathsheba the mother of Solomon, saying, "Have you not heard that Adonijah the son of �q Haggith has become king, and David our lord does not know *it*? ¹²Come, please, let me now give you advice, that you may save your own life and the life of your son Solomon.

1:1 King David was old. David was about seventy years old at the time of his death (2 Sam. 5:4; 1 Chr. 29:26–28), and the long years of warfare had doubtlessly taken their physical toll.

1:5 Adonijah. The name Adonijah means "the LORD is my Lord." Amnon and Absalom both experienced violent deaths (2 Sam. 13:28–29; 18:14). Chiliab, his second son, apparently died at an early age. Adonijah was David's oldest surviving son.

1:6 had not rebuked him. While David had been a most capable leader and a man of deep spiritual sensitivity, he had not exercised proper parental discipline of his children (2 Sam. 13:21–39; 14:18–24).

1:11 Nathan. It is a mark of David's integrity that Nathan, who had confronted him with his terrible sin

with Bathsheba, was still welcome in the royal household (2 Sam. 12:1–15).

1:11–14 Wisdom—In Old Testament times, messages from God were often given through personal prophecy. Today, believers do not often receive messages through prophecy. God has given the higher privilege of direct access to His wisdom through the ministry of the indwelling Holy Spirit in all who

---

1:1 ᵃ 1 Chr. 23:1   **1:3** ᵇ 1 Kin. 2:17   ᶜ Josh. 19:18   **1:5** ᵈ 2 Sam. 3:4   ᵉ 2 Sam. 15:1   **1:6** ᶠ 2 Sam. 3:3, 4   **1:7** ᵍ 1 Chr. 11:6   ʰ 2 Sam. 20:25   ⁱ 1 Kin. 2:22, 28   **1:8** ʲ 1 Kin. 2:35   ᵏ 1 Kin. 2:25   ˡ 2 Sam. 12:1   ᵐ 1 Kin. 4:18   ⁿ 2 Sam. 23:8   **1:9** ᵒ Josh. 15:7; 18:16   **1:10** ᵖ 2 Sam. 12:24   **1:11** �q 2 Sam. 3:4

¹³Go immediately to King David and say to him, 'Did you not, my lord, O king, swear to your maidservant, saying, ᴿ"Assuredly your son Solomon shall reign after me, and he shall sit on my throne"? Why then has Adonijah become king?' ¹⁴Then, while you are still talking there with the king, I also will come in after you and confirm your words."

¹⁵So Bathsheba went into the chamber to the king. (Now the king was very old, and Abishag the Shunammite was serving the king.) ¹⁶And Bathsheba bowed and did homage to the king. Then the king said, "What is your wish?"

¹⁷Then she said to him, "My lord, ˢyou swore by the LORD your God to your maidservant, *saying,* 'Assuredly Solomon your son shall reign after me, and he shall sit on my throne.' ¹⁸So now, look! Adonijah has become king; and now, my lord the king, you do not know about *it.* ¹⁹ᵗHe has sacrificed oxen and fattened cattle and sheep in abundance, and has invited all the sons of the king, Abiathar the priest, and Joab the commander of the army; but Solomon your servant he has not invited. ²⁰And as for you, my lord, O king, the eyes of all Israel *are* on you, that you should tell them who will sit on the throne of my lord the king after him. ²¹Otherwise it will happen, when my lord the king ᵘrests with his fathers, that I and my son Solomon will be counted as offenders."

²²And just then, while she was still talking with the king, Nathan the prophet also came in. ²³So they told the king, saying, "Here is Nathan the prophet." And when he came in before the king, he bowed down before the king with his face to the ground. ²⁴And Nathan said, "My lord, O king, have you said, 'Adonijah shall reign after me, and he shall sit on my throne'? ²⁵ᵛFor he has gone down today, and has sacrificed oxen and fattened cattle and sheep in abundance, and has invited all the king's sons, and the commanders of the army, and Abiathar the priest; and look! They are eating and drinking before him; and they say, ʷ'Long live King Adonijah!' ²⁶But he has not invited me—me your servant—nor Zadok the priest, nor Benaiah the son of Jehoiada, nor your servant Solomon. ²⁷Has this thing been done by my lord the king, and you have not told your servant who should sit on the throne of my lord the king after him?"

David Proclaims Solomon King

²⁸Then King David answered and said, "Call Bathsheba to me." So she came into the king's presence and stood before the king. ²⁹And the king took an oath and said, ˣ"As the LORD lives, who has redeemed my life from every distress, ³⁰ʸjust as I swore to you by the LORD God of Israel, saying, 'Assuredly Solomon your son shall be king after me, and he shall sit on my throne in my place,' so I certainly will do this day."

³¹Then Bathsheba bowed with *her* face to the earth, and paid homage to the king, and said, ᶻ"Let my lord King David live forever!"

³²And King David said, "Call to me Zadok the priest, Nathan the prophet, and Benaiah the son of Jehoiada." So they came before the king. ³³The king also said to them, ᵃ"Take with you the servants of your lord, and have Solomon my son ride on my own ᵇmule, and take him down to ᶜGihon. ³⁴There let Zadok the priest and Nathan the prophet ᵈanoint him king over Israel; and ᵉblow the horn, and say, '*Long* live King Solomon!' ³⁵Then you shall come up after him, and he shall come and sit on my throne, and he shall be king in my place. For I have appointed him to be ruler over Israel and Judah."

³⁶Benaiah the son of Jehoiada answered the king and said, ᶠ"Amen! May the LORD God of my lord the king say so *too.* ³⁷ᵍAs the LORD has been with my lord the king, even so may He be with Solomon, and ʰmake his throne greater than the throne of my lord King David."

³⁸So Zadok the priest, Nathan the prophet, ⁱBenaiah the son of Jehoiada, the ʲCherethites, and the Pelethites went down and had Solomon ride on King David's mule, and took him to Gihon. ³⁹Then Zadok the priest took a horn of ᵏoil from the tabernacle and ˡanointed Solomon. And they blew the horn, ᵐand all the people said, "*Long* live King Solomon!" ⁴⁰And all the people went

---

believe. Today believers have access to God's wisdom through His Word, His indwelling Spirit, and counsel from mature Christians.

1:29 who has redeemed my life. In these words of praise, David celebrated the innumerable times that the Lord had acted on his behalf, to deliver him from his enemies and from his own sins. Some of David's psalms were written in connection with those times of God's deliverance (Ps. 40; 142).

1:38 the Cherethites, and the Pelethites. These two groups were part of David's bodyguard (2 Sam. 8:18; 15:18; 20:7). Their association with David stretched back to his days among the Philistines, with whom the Cherethites are usually identified (1 Sam. 30:13–14; Ezek. 25:16; Zeph. 2:5).

1:39 Zadok . . . anointed Solomon. Every priestly anointing would recall the words of Psalm 2, in accordance with the words of the Davidic covenant of 2 Samuel 7. The anointing announced that the anointed one was now the adopted son of the living God.

1:13 ʳ 1 Chr. 22:9–13 **1:17** ˢ 1 Kin. 1:13, 30 **1:19** ᵗ 1 Kin. 1:7–9, 25 **1:21** ᵘ Deut. 31:16 **1:25** ᵛ 1 Kin. 1:9, 19 ʷ 1 Sam. 10:24 **1:29** ˣ 2 Sam. 4:9; 12:5 **1:30** ʸ 1 Kin. 1:13, 17 **1:31** ᶻ Dan. 2:4; 3:9 **1:33** ᵃ 2 Sam. 20:6 ᵇ Esth. 6:8 ᶜ 2 Chr. 32:30; 33:14 **1:34** ᵈ 1 Sam. 10:1; 16:3, 12 ᵉ 2 Sam. 15:10 **1:36** ᶠ Jer. 28:6 **1:37** ᵍ 1 Sam. 20:13 ʰ 1 Kin. 1:47 **1:38** ⁱ 2 Sam. 8:18; 23:20–23 ʲ 2 Sam. 20:7 **1:39** ᵏ Ps. 89:20 ˡ 1 Chr. 29:22 ᵐ 1 Sam. 10:24

up after him; and the people played the flutes and rejoiced with great joy, so that the earth *seemed to* split with their sound.

41Now Adonijah and all the guests who *were* with him heard *it* as they finished eating. And when Joab heard the sound of the horn, he said, "Why *is* the city in such a noisy uproar?" 42While he was still speaking, there came ⁿJonathan, the son of Abiathar the priest. And Adonijah said to him, "Come in, for ᵒyou *are* a prominent man, and bring good news."

43Then Jonathan answered and said to Adonijah, "No! Our lord King David has made Solomon king. 44The king has sent with him Zadok the priest, Nathan the prophet, Benaiah the son of Jehoiada, the Cherethites, and the Pelethites; and they have made him ride on the king's mule. 45So Zadok the priest and Nathan the prophet have anointed him king at Gihon; and they have gone up from there rejoicing, so that the city is in an uproar. This *is* the noise that you have heard. 46Also Solomon ᵖsits on the throne of the kingdom. 47And moreover the king's servants have gone to bless our lord King David, saying, ᑫ'May God make the name of Solomon better than your name, and may He make his throne greater than your throne.' ʳThen the king bowed himself on the bed. 48Also the king said thus, 'Blessed *be* the LORD God of Israel, who has ˢgiven *one* to sit on my throne this day, while my eyes see ᵗit!'"

49So all the guests who were with Adonijah were afraid, and arose, and each one went his way.

50Now Adonijah was afraid of Solomon; so he arose, and went and ᵘtook hold of the horns of the altar. 51And it was told Solomon, saying, "Indeed Adonijah is afraid of King Solomon; for look, he has taken hold of the horns of the altar, saying, 'Let King Solomon swear to me today that he will not put his servant to death with the sword.'"

52Then Solomon said, "If he proves himself a worthy man, ᵛnot one hair of him shall fall to the earth; but if wickedness is found in him, he shall die." 53So King Solomon sent them to bring him down from the altar. And he came and fell down before King Solomon; and Solomon said to him, "Go to your house."

David's Instructions to Solomon

2 Now ᵃthe days of David drew near that he should die, and he charged Solomon his son, saying: 2ᵇ"I go the way of all the earth; ᶜbe strong, therefore, and prove yourself a man. 3And keep the charge of the LORD your God: to walk in His ways, to keep His statutes, His commandments, His judgments, and His testimonies, as it is written in the Law of Moses, that you may ᵈprosper in all that you do and wherever you turn; 4that the LORD may ᵉfulfill His word which He spoke concerning me, saying, ᶠ'If your sons take heed to their way, to ᵍwalk before Me in truth with all their heart and with all their soul,' He said, ʰ'you shall not lack a man on the throne of Israel.'

5"Moreover you know also what Joab the son of Zeruiah ⁱdid to me, *and* what he did to the two commanders of the armies of Israel, to ʲAbner the son of Ner and ᵏAmasa the son of Jether, whom he killed. And he shed the blood of war in peacetime, and put the blood of war on his belt that *was* around his waist, and on his sandals that *were* on his feet. 6Therefore do ˡaccording to your wisdom, and do not let his gray hair go down to the grave in peace.

7"But show kindness to the sons of ᵐBarzillai the Gileadite, and let them be among those who ⁿeat at your table, for so ᵒthey came to me when I fled from Absalom your brother.

8"And see, *you have* with you ᵖShimei the son of Gera, a Benjamite from Bahurim, who cursed me with a malicious

---

1:50 *took hold of the horns of the altar.* This action was in keeping with the traditional function of the altar as a haven of refuge for those who had committed unintentional crimes (Ex. 21:12–14).

1:53 Forgiveness—Solomon chose to forgive Adonijah for his attempted usurpation of the throne, realizing that Adonijah had legitimate reason to think that he should be the next king. Wiser than his years, young Solomon overlooked the offense of his brother rather than bring any reproach on his reign at this early stage. Sadly, Adonijah proved himself unworthy of his pardon, making another attempt to take the throne after his father David was dead.

2:4 *shall not lack a man on the throne.* God had made an unconditional covenant with David (2 Sam. 7:12–16; 1 Chr. 17:11–14; Ps. 89), granting him a continual posterity and a royal dynasty. Although the Davidic covenant was an everlasting sacred promise, individual kings through their evil behavior could fail to receive the benefits of the covenant. The line of promise would be preserved, but the time would come when the promised Ruler would not be on

an earthly throne (Hos. 3:4). God's prophets predict that the heir to the throne of David will yet reign over a repentant, regathered, and restored Israel (Jer. 33:19–26; Ezek. 34:22–31) in fulfillment of the promises of the covenants (Ezek. 37:21–28; Mic. 7:18–20). The New Testament reveals that all this will be realized in Jesus Christ, the Savior King (Acts 3:25–26; 15:16–17; Gal. 3:26–29; Rev. 3:21), who is David's Heir in the ultimate sense (Acts 2:22–36).

2:5–8 Joab . . . Shimei. David knew that these two men would cause trouble for Solomon if they were not dealt with. Joab had murdered two generals (2 Sam.

1:42 ⁿ 2 Sam. 17:17, 20 ᵒ 2 Sam. 18:27   **1:46** ᵖ 1 Chr. 29:23   **1:47** ᑫ 1 Kin. 1:37 ʳ Gen. 47:31   **1:48** ˢ 1 Kin. 3:6 ᵗ 2 Sam. 7:12   **1:50** ᵘ 1 Kin. 2:28   **1:52** ᵛ 1 Sam. 14:45   **2:1** ᵃ Gen. 47:29   **2:2** ᵇ Josh. 23:14 ᶜ Deut. 31:7, 23   **2:3** ᵈ [Deut. 29:9]   **2:4** ᵉ 2 Sam. 7:25 ᶠ [Ps. 132:12] ᵍ 2 Kin. 20:3 ʰ 2 Sam. 7:12, 13   **2:5** ⁱ 2 Sam. 3:39; 18:5, 12, 14 ʲ 2 Sam. 3:27 ᵏ 2 Sam. 20:10   **2:6** ˡ 1 Kin. 2:9   **2:7** ᵐ 2 Sam. 19:31–39 ⁿ 2 Sam. 9:7, 10; 19:28 ᵒ 2 Sam. 17:17–29   **2:8** ᵖ 2 Sam. 16:5–13

curse in the day when I went to Mahanaim. But *q*he came down to meet me at the Jordan, and *r*I swore to him by the LORD, saying, 'I will not put you to death with the sword.' ⁹Now therefore, *s*do not hold him guiltless, for you *are* a wise man and know what you ought to do to him; but *t*bring his gray hair down to the grave with blood."

Death of David

¹⁰So *u*David rested with his fathers, and was buried in *v*the City of David. ¹¹The period that David *w*reigned over Israel *was* forty years; seven years he reigned in Hebron, and in Jerusalem he reigned thirty-three years. ¹²*x*Then Solomon sat on the throne of his father David; and his kingdom was *y*firmly established.

Solomon Executes Adonijah

¹³Now Adonijah the son of Haggith came to Bathsheba the mother of Solomon. So she said, *z*"Do you come peaceably?"

And he said, "Peaceably." ¹⁴Moreover he said, "I have something *to say* to you."

And she said, "Say it." ¹⁵Then he said, "You know that the kingdom was *a*mine, and all Israel had set their expectations on me, that I should reign. However, the kingdom has been turned over, and has become my brother's; for *b*it was his from the LORD. ¹⁶Now I ask one petition of you; do not deny me."

And she said to him, "Say it." ¹⁷Then he said, "Please speak to King Solomon, for he will not refuse you, that he may give me *c*Abishag the Shunammite as wife."

¹⁸So Bathsheba said, "Very well, I will speak for you to the king."

¹⁹Bathsheba therefore went to King Solomon, to speak to him for Adonijah. And the king rose up to meet her and *d*bowed down to her, and sat down on his throne and a throne set for the king's mother; *e*so she sat at his right hand. ²⁰Then she said, "I desire one small petition of you; do not refuse me."

And the king said to her, "Ask it, my mother, for I will not refuse you." ²¹So she said, "Let Abishag the Shunammite be given to Adonijah your brother as wife."

²²And King Solomon answered and said to his mother, "Now why do you ask Abishag the Shunammite for Adonijah? Ask for him the kingdom also—for he *is* my *f*older brother—for him, and for *g*Abiathar the priest, and for Joab the son of Zeruiah." ²³Then King Solomon swore by the LORD, saying, *h*"May God do so to me, and more also, if Adonijah has not spoken this word against his own life! ²⁴Now therefore, *as* the LORD lives, who has confirmed me and set me on the throne of David my father, and who has established a house* for me, as He *i*promised, Adonijah shall be put to death today!"

²⁵So King Solomon sent by the hand of *j*Benaiah the son of Jehoiada; and he struck him down, and he died.

Abiathar Exiled, Joab Executed

²⁶And to Abiathar the priest the king said, "Go to *k*Anathoth, to your own fields, for you *are* deserving of death; but I will not put you to death at this time, *l*because you carried the ark of the Lord GOD before my father David, and because you were afflicted every time my father was afflicted." ²⁷So Solomon removed Abiathar from being priest to the LORD, that he might *m*fulfill the word of the LORD which He spoke concerning the house of Eli at Shiloh.

²⁸Then news came to Joab, for Joab *n*had defected to Adonijah, though he had not defected to Absalom. So Joab fled to the tabernacle of the LORD, and *o*took hold of the horns of the altar. ²⁹And King Solomon was told, "Joab has fled to the tabernacle of the LORD; there *he is*, by the altar." Then Solomon sent Benaiah the son of Jehoiada, saying, "Go, *p*strike him down." ³⁰So Benaiah went to the tabernacle of the LORD, and said to him, "Thus says the king, *q*'Come out!'"

And he said, "No, but I will die here." And Benaiah brought back word to the king, saying, "Thus said Joab, and thus he answered me."

³¹Then the king said to him, *r*"Do as he has said, and strike him down and bury him, *s*that you may take away from me and from the house of my father the innocent

---

* 2:24 That is, a royal dynasty

3:27; 20:10), killed David's son Absalom (2 Sam. 18:14), and joined Adonijah's conspiracy (1:7,19). Shimei had cursed the king and treated him shamefully as he was fleeing from Absalom (2 Sam. 16:5–13; 19:16–23).

2:27 Abiathar. This act fulfilled God's word to Eli, removing the last of his descendants from serving before the Lord (1 Sam. 2:30–33). When Abiathar was removed from office, his influence was greatly restricted. Solomon spared his life in recognition of his past service to God and David (2 Sam. 15:24,29; 1 Chr. 15:11–15).

2:28 horns of the altar. Because Joab was a murderer (2 Sam. 3:27; 18:14; 20:10), he could not claim

the protective sanctity of the horns of the altar, and could not escape execution.

2:8 *q* 2 Sam. 19:18 *r* 2 Sam. 19:23   **2:9** *s* Ex. 20:7 *t* Gen. 42:38; 44:31   **2:10** *u* Acts 2:29; 13:36 *v* 2 Sam. 5:7   **2:11** *w* 2 Sam. 5:4, 5   **2:12** *x* 1 Chr. 29:23 *y* 2 Chr. 1:1   **2:13** *z* 1 Sam. 16:4, 5   **2:15** *a* 1 Kin. 1:11, 18 *b* [Dan. 2:21]   **2:17** *c* 1 Kin. 1:3, 4   **2:19** *d* [Ex. 20:12] *e* Ps. 45:9   **2:22** *f* 1 Chr. 3:2, 5 *g* 1 Kin. 1:7   **2:23** *h* Ruth 1:17   **2:24** *i* 2 Sam. 7:11, 13   **2:25** *j* 2 Sam. 8:18   **2:26** *k* Josh. 21:18 *l* 2 Sam. 15:14, 29   **2:27** *m* 1 Sam. 2:31–35   **2:28** *n* 1 Kin. 1:7 *o* 1 Kin. 1:50   **2:29** *p* 1 Kin. 2:5, 6   **2:30** *q* [Ex. 21:14]   **2:31** *r* [Ex. 21:14] *s* [Num. 35:33]

blood which Joab shed. [32]So the LORD [t]will return his blood on his head, because he struck down two men more righteous [u]and better than he, and killed them with the sword—[v]Abner the son of Ner, the commander of the army of Israel, and [w]Amasa the son of Jether, the commander of the army of Judah—though my father David did not know *it*. [33]Their blood shall therefore return upon the head of Joab and [x]upon the head of his descendants forever. [y]But upon David and his descendants, upon his house and his throne, there shall be peace forever from the LORD."

[34]So Benaiah the son of Jehoiada went up and struck and killed him; and he was buried in his own house in the wilderness. [35]The king put Benaiah the son of Jehoiada in his place over the army, and the king put [z]Zadok the priest in the place of [a]Abiathar.

Shimei Executed

[36]Then the king sent and called for [b]Shimei, and said to him, "Build yourself a house in Jerusalem and dwell there, and do not go out from there anywhere. [37]For it shall be, on the day you go out and cross [c]the Brook Kidron, know for certain you shall surely die; [d]your blood shall be on your own head."

[38]And Shimei said to the king, "The saying *is* good. As my lord the king has said, so your servant will do." So Shimei dwelt in Jerusalem many days.

[39]Now it happened at the end of three years, that two slaves of Shimei ran away to [e]Achish the son of Maachah, king of Gath. And they told Shimei, saying, "Look, your slaves *are* in Gath!" [40]So Shimei arose, saddled his donkey, and went to Achish at Gath to seek his slaves. And Shimei went and brought his slaves from Gath. [41]And Solomon was told that Shimei had gone from Jerusalem to Gath and had come back. [42]Then the king sent and called for Shimei, and said to him, "Did I not make you swear by the LORD, and warn you, saying, 'Know for certain that on the day you go out and travel anywhere, you shall surely die'? And you said to me, 'The word I have heard *is* good.' [43]Why then have you not kept the oath of the LORD and the commandment that I gave you?" [44]The king said moreover

to Shimei, "You know, as your heart acknowledges, [f]all the wickedness that you did to my father David; therefore the LORD will [g]return your wickedness on your own head. [45]But King Solomon *shall be* blessed, and [h]the throne of David shall be established before the LORD forever."

[46]So the king commanded Benaiah the son of Jehoiada; and he went out and struck him down, and he died. Thus the [i]kingdom was established in the hand of Solomon.

Solomon Requests Wisdom

3 Now [a]Solomon made a treaty with Pharaoh king of Egypt, and married Pharaoh's daughter; then he brought her [b]to the City of David until he had finished building his [c]own house, and [d]the house of the LORD, and [e]the wall all around Jerusalem. [2][f]Meanwhile the people sacrificed at the high places, because there was no house built for the name of the LORD until those days. [3]And Solomon [g]loved the LORD, [h]walking in the statutes of his father David, except that he sacrificed and burned incense at the high places.

[4]Now [i]the king went to Gibeon to sacrifice there, [j]for that *was* the great high place: Solomon offered a thousand burnt offerings on that altar. [5][k]At Gibeon the LORD appeared to Solomon [l]in a dream by night; and God said, "Ask! What shall I give you?"

[6][m]And Solomon said: "You have shown great mercy to Your servant David my father, because he [n]walked before You in truth, in righteousness, and in uprightness of heart with You; You have continued this great kindness for him, and You [o]have given him a son to sit on his throne, as *it is* this day. [7]Now, O LORD my God, You have made Your servant king instead of my father David, but I *am* a [p]little child; I do not know *how* [q]to go out or come in. [8]And Your servant *is* in the midst of Your people whom You [r]have chosen, a great people, too [s]numerous to be numbered or counted. [9][t]Therefore give to Your servant an understanding heart [u]to judge Your people, that I may [v]discern between good and evil. For who is able to judge this great people of Yours?"

2:35 *Zadok*. Zadok was a descendant of Eleazar, the son of Aaron (1 Chr. 6:4–8).

3:1 *made a treaty*. In the ancient Middle East, political alliances were often ratified by the marriage of the son of one king to the daughter of another. Except in unusual circumstances, the pharaohs of Egypt did not observe this custom. Therefore, the giving of Pharaoh's daughter to Solomon attested to the Israelite king's growing prestige and importance to the Egyptians.

3:7 *but I am a little child*. The term "child" often refers to a servant or to an inexperienced person still in training for a profession. With proper humility, Solomon stressed his relative youth and inexperience.

2:32 [f] Judg. 9:24, 57 [u] 2 Chr. 21:13, 14 [v] 2 Sam. 3:27 [w] 2 Sam. 20:9, 10 **2:33** [x] 2 Sam. 3:29 [y] [Prov. 25:5] **2:35** [z] 1 Sam. 2:35 [a] 1 Kin. 2:27 **2:36** [b] 1 Kin. 2:8 **2:37** [c] 2 Sam. 15:23 [d] Josh. 2:19 **2:39** [e] 1 Sam. 27:2 **2:44** [f] 2 Sam. 16:5–13 [g] 1 Sam. 25:39 **2:45** [h] [Prov. 25:5] **2:46** [i] 2 Chr. 1:1 **3:1** [a] 1 Kin. 7:8; 9:24 [b] 2 Sam. 5:7 [c] 1 Kin. 7:1 [d] 1 Kin. 6 [e] 1 Kin. 9:15, 19 **3:2** [f] [Deut. 12:2–5, 13, 14] **3:3** [g] [Rom. 8:28] [h] [1 Kin. 3:6, 14] **3:4** [i] 2 Chr. 1:3 [j] 1 Chr. 16:39; 21:29 **3:5** [k] 1 Kin. 9:2; 11:9 [l] Num. 12:6 **3:6** [m] 2 Chr. 1:8 [n] 1 Kin. 2:4; 9:4 [o] 1 Kin. 1:48 **3:7** [p] Jer. 1:6, 7 [q] Num. 27:17 **3:8** [r] [Deut. 7:6] [s] Gen. 13:6; 15:5; 22:17 **3:9** [t] 2 Chr. 1:10 [u] Ps. 72:1, 2 [v] [Heb. 5:14]

¹⁰The speech pleased the Lord, that Solomon had asked this thing. ¹¹Then God said to him: "Because you have asked this thing, and have ʷnot asked long life for yourself, nor have asked riches for yourself, nor have asked the life of your enemies, but have asked for yourself understanding to discern justice, ¹²ˣbehold, I have done according to your words; ʸsee, I have given you a wise and understanding heart, so that there has not been anyone like you before you, nor shall any like you arise after you. ¹³And I have also ᶻgiven you what you have not asked: both ᵃriches and honor, so that there shall not be anyone like you among the kings all your days. ¹⁴So ᵇif you walk in My ways, to keep My statutes and My commandments, ᶜas your father David walked, then I will ᵈlengthen your days."

¹⁵Then Solomon ᵉawoke; and indeed it had been a dream. And he came to Jerusalem and stood before the ark of the covenant of the LORD, offered up burnt offerings, offered peace offerings, and ᶠmade a feast for all his servants.

Solomon's Wise Judgment

¹⁶Now two women *who were* harlots came to the king, and ᵍstood before him. ¹⁷And one woman said, "O my lord, this woman and I dwell in the same house; and I gave birth while she *was* in the house. ¹⁸Then it happened, the third day after I had given birth, that this woman also gave birth. And we *were* together; no one *was* with us in the house, except the two of us in the house. ¹⁹And this woman's son died in the night, because she lay on him. ²⁰So she arose in the middle of the night and took my son from my side, while your maidservant slept, and laid him in her bosom, and laid her dead child in my bosom. ²¹And when I rose in the morning to nurse my son, there he was, dead. But when I had examined him in the morning, indeed, he was not my son whom I had borne."

²²Then the other woman said, "No! But the living one *is* my son, and the dead one *is* your son."

And the first woman said, "No! But the dead one *is* your son, and the living one *is* my son."

Thus they spoke before the king.

²³And the king said, "The one says, 'This *is* my son, who lives, and your son *is* the dead one'; and the other says, 'No! But your son *is* the dead one, and my son *is* the living one.'" ²⁴Then the king said, "Bring me a sword." So they brought a sword before the king. ²⁵And the king said, "Divide the living child in two, and give half to one, and half to the other."

²⁶Then the woman whose son *was* living spoke to the king, for ʰshe yearned with compassion for her son; and she said, "O my lord, give her the living child, and by no means kill him!"

But the other said, "Let him be neither mine nor yours, *but* divide *him*."

²⁷So the king answered and said, "Give the first woman the living child, and by no means kill him; she *is* his mother."

²⁸And all Israel heard of the judgment which the king had rendered; and they feared the king, for they saw that the ⁱwisdom of God *was* in him to administer justice.

Solomon's Administration

4 So King Solomon was king over all Israel. ²And these *were* his officials: Azariah the son of Zadok, the priest; ³Elihoreph and Ahijah, the sons of Shisha, scribes; ᵃJehoshaphat the son of Ahilud, the recorder; ⁴ᵇBenaiah the son of Jehoiada, over the army; Zadok and ᶜAbiathar, the priests; ⁵Azariah the son of Nathan, over ᵈthe officers; Zabud the son of Nathan, ᵉa priest *and* ᶠthe king's friend; ⁶Ahishar, over the household; and ᵍAdoniram the son of Abda, over the labor force.

3:14 Obedience—Because he loved God above all at this time of his life (v. 3), and chose wisdom and discernment for his office, Solomon received even more—riches and honor and distinction. Obedient in many ways, he was accordingly blessed by God. When commands are given by a loving, caring person, obedience must result in blessing. God repeatedly stated this principle (Deut. 5:29—6:24). Saul, David, and Solomon all lost blessing because of disobedience. This was not because of narrowness or rigidity on God's part. He does not give us commands to make our lives harder, or to be harsh and demanding. His commands have blessings built in—He is showing us the best way to live.

3:15 *ark of the covenant.* Although David had brought the ark of the covenant to Jerusalem (2 Sam. 6) the tabernacle and its furnishings remained in Gibeon, which served as an important worship center (v. 4; 2 Chr. 1:3–5). After its capture by the Philistines (1 Sam. 5–6), the ark never returned to the tabernacle.

The ark was not in the Most Holy Place again until it was placed in Solomon's temple.
3:28 *wisdom . . . justice.* These important qualities which marked Solomon's reign would characterize the rule of Israel's Messiah in a far greater way (Is. 11.1–5). David's final words to Solomon were, "do according to your wisdom" (2:6). Wisdom does not dwell as a recluse among books in the study. Rather, wisdom stands with confidence at the crossroads of life. Solomon's wisdom was decisive. Through God he was able to observe the actions of others and in this way have a revelation of the truth.

3:11 ʷ [James 4:3]   **3:12** ˣ [1 John 5:14, 15]   ʸ Eccl. 1:16   **3:13** ᶻ [Matt. 6:33]   ᵃ 1 Kin. 4:21, 24; 10:23   **3:14** ᵇ [1 Kin. 6:12]   ᶜ 1 Kin. 15:5   ᵈ Ps. 91:16   **3:15** ᵉ Gen. 41:7   ᶠ 1 Kin. 8:65   **3:16** ᵍ Num. 27:2   **3:26** ʰ Jer. 31:20   **3:28** ⁱ 1 Kin. 3:9, 11, 12   **4:3** ᵃ 2 Sam. 8:16; 20:24   **4:4** ᵇ 1 Kin. 2:35   ᶜ 1 Kin. 2:27   **4:5** ᵈ 1 Kin. 4:7   ᵉ 2 Sam. 8:18; 20:26   ᶠ 2 Sam. 15:37; 16:16   **4:6** ᵍ 1 Kin. 5:14

⁷And Solomon had twelve governors over all Israel, who provided food for the king and his household; each one made provision for one month of the year. ⁸These *are* their names: Ben-Hur,* in the mountains of Ephraim; ⁹Ben-Deker,* in Makaz, Shaalbim, Beth Shemesh, and Elon Beth Hanan; ¹⁰Ben-Hesed,* in Arubboth; to him *belonged* Sochoh and all the land of Hepher; ¹¹Ben-Abinadab,* *in* all the regions of Dor; he had Taphath the daughter of Solomon as wife; ¹²Baana the son of Ahilud, *in* Taanach, Megiddo, and all Beth Shean, which *is* beside Zaretan below Jezreel, from Beth Shean to Abel Meholah, as far as the other side of Jokneam; ¹³Ben-Geber,* in Ramoth Gilead; to him *belonged* ʰthe towns of Jair the son of Manasseh, in Gilead; to him *also belonged* ⁱthe region of Argob in Bashan—sixty large cities with walls and bronze gatebars; ¹⁴Ahinadab the son of Iddo, *in* Mahanaim; ¹⁵ʲAhimaaz, in Naphtali; he also took Basemath the daughter of Solomon as wife; ¹⁶Baanah the son of ᵏHushai, in Asher and Aloth; ¹⁷Jehoshaphat the son of Paruah, in Issachar; ¹⁸ˡShimei the son of Elah, in Benjamin; ¹⁹Geber the son of Uri, in the country of Sihon king of the Amorites, and of Og king of Bashan. *He was* the only governor who *was* in the land.

Prosperity and Wisdom of Solomon's Reign

²⁰Judah and Israel *were* as numerous ⁿas the sand by the sea in multitude, ᵒeating and drinking and rejoicing. ²¹So ᵖSolomon reigned over all kingdoms from ᵠthe River* *to* the land of the Philistines, as far as the border of Egypt. ʳThey brought tribute and served Solomon all the days of his life.

²²ˢNow Solomon's provision for one day was thirty kors of fine flour, sixty kors of meal, ²³ten fatted oxen, twenty oxen from the pastures, and one hundred sheep, besides deer, gazelles, roebucks, and fatted fowl.

²⁴For he had dominion over all *the region* on this side of the River* from Tiphsah even to Gaza, namely over ᵗall the kings on this side of the River; and ᵘhe had peace on every side all around him. ²⁵And Judah and Israel ᵛdwelt safely, ʷeach man under his vine and his fig tree, ˣfrom Dan as far as Beersheba, all the days of Solomon.

²⁶ʸSolomon had forty* thousand stalls of ᶻhorses for his chariots, and twelve thousand horsemen. ²⁷And ᵃthese governors, each man in his month, provided food for King Solomon and for all who came to King Solomon's table. There was no lack in their supply. ²⁸They also brought barley and straw to the proper place, for the horses and steeds, each man according to his charge.

²⁹And ᵇGod gave Solomon wisdom and exceedingly great understanding, and largeness of heart like the sand on the seashore. ³⁰Thus Solomon's wisdom excelled the wisdom of all the men ᶜof the East and all ᵈthe wisdom of Egypt. ³¹For he was ᵉwiser than all men—ᶠthan Ethan the Ezrahite, ᵍand Heman, Chalcol, and Darda, the sons of Mahol; and his fame was in all the surrounding nations. ³²ʰHe spoke three thousand proverbs, and his ⁱsongs were one thousand and five. ³³Also he spoke of trees, from the cedar tree of Lebanon even to the hyssop that springs out of the wall; he spoke also of animals, of birds, of creeping things, and of fish. ³⁴And men of all nations, from all the kings of the earth who had heard of his wisdom, ʲcame to hear the wisdom of Solomon.

---

* **4:8** Literally *Son of Hur*   * **4:9** Literally *Son of Deker*   * **4:10** Literally *Son of Hesed*   * **4:11** Literally *Son of Abinadab*   * **4:13** Literally *Son of Geber*   * **4:21** That is, the Euphrates   * **4:24** That is, the Euphrates   * **4:26** Following Masoretic Text and most other authorities; some manuscripts of the Septuagint read *four* (compare 2 Chronicles 9:25).

4:7–19 twelve governors. These men were responsible for handling lesser administrative tasks and raising revenue for the crown. The districts did not follow tribal boundaries.

4:18 Shimei. This is not the same Shimei who cursed David (2 Sam. 16:5–13), but probably the man mentioned in 1:8 as a supporter of Solomon.

4:20 numerous as the sand. God fulfilled His promise to make Abraham's descendants numerous (Gen. 15:5,18). Solomon's empire extended far beyond the traditional boundaries of Israel. Through this greatly expanded empire, Hebrew people not only traveled to far-flung regions, but they took with them knowledge of the living God.

4:21 from the River. This refers to the Euphrates.

4:22 kors. A kor was the same size as a homer (Ezek. 45:14); at between six and seven bushels, it was the normal load for a donkey.

4:29 wisdom. The three terms used in this verse underscore Solomon's depth of understanding. He was not merely intelligent, able to understand facts and logic; he was also given the ability to apply his intelligence to problems which defy logic, possessing a rare understanding of human beings with all their emotional and spiritual complexities.

4:32–34 proverbs . . . songs. Solomon was the author of a large part of the Book of Proverbs. He is also traditionally assigned the authorship of the Song of Solomon, Psalms 72 and 127, and Ecclesiastes.

4:13 ʰ Num. 32:41   ⁱ Deut. 3:4   **4:15** ʲ 2 Sam. 15:27   **4:16** ᵏ 1 Chr. 27:33   **4:18** ˡ 1 Kin. 1:8   **4:19** ᵐ Deut. 3:8–10   **4:20** ⁿ Gen. 22:17; 32:12   ᵒ Mic. 4:4   **4:21** ᵖ Ps. 72:8   ᵠ Gen. 15:18   ʳ Ps. 68:29   **4:22** ˢ Neh. 5:18   **4:24** ᵗ Ps. 72:11   ᵘ 1 Chr. 22:9   **4:25** ᵛ [Jer. 23:6]   ʷ [Mic. 4:4]   ˣ Judg. 20:1   **4:26** ʸ 1 Kin. 10:26   ᶻ [Deut. 17:16]   **4:27** ᵃ 1 Kin. 4:7   **4:29** ᵇ 1 Kin. 3:12   **4:30** ᶜ Gen. 25:6   ᵈ Is. 19:11, 12   **4:31** ᵉ 1 Kin. 3:12   ᶠ 1 Chr. 15:19   ᵍ 1 Chr. 2:6   **4:32** ʰ Eccl. 12:9   ⁱ Song 1:1   **4:34** ʲ 1 Kin. 10:1

Solomon Prepares to Build the Temple

5 Now ªHiram king of Tyre sent his servants to Solomon, because he heard that they had anointed him king in place of his father, ᵇfor Hiram had always loved David. ²Then ᶜSolomon sent to Hiram, saying:

3 ᵈYou know how my father David could not build a house for the name of the LORD his God ᵉbecause of the wars which were fought against him on every side, until the LORD put *his foes** under the soles of his feet.

4 But now the LORD my God has given me ᶠrest on every side; *there is* neither adversary nor evil occurrence.

5 ᵍAnd behold, I propose to build a house for the name of the LORD my God, ʰas the LORD spoke to my father David, saying, "Your son, whom I will set on your throne in your place, he shall build the house for My name."

6 Now therefore, command that they cut down ⁱcedars for me from Lebanon; and my servants will be with your servants, and I will pay you wages for your servants according to whatever you say. For you know *there is* none among us who has skill to cut timber like the Sidonians.

⁷So it was, when Hiram heard the words of Solomon, that he rejoiced greatly and said,

Blessed *be* the LORD this day, for He has given David a wise son over this great people!

⁸Then Hiram sent to Solomon, saying:

I have considered *the message* which you sent me, *and* I will do all you desire concerning the cedar and cypress logs.

9 My servants shall bring *them* down ʲfrom Lebanon to the sea; I will float them in rafts by sea to the place you indicate to me, and will have them broken apart there; then you can take *them* away. And you shall fulfill my desire ᵏby giving food for my household.

¹⁰Then Hiram gave Solomon cedar and cypress logs *according to* all his desire. ¹¹ˡAnd Solomon gave Hiram twenty thousand kors of wheat *as* food for his household, and twenty* kors of pressed oil. Thus Solomon gave to Hiram year by year.

¹²So the LORD gave Solomon wisdom, ᵐas He had promised him; and there was peace between Hiram and Solomon, and the two of them made a treaty together.

¹³Then King Solomon raised up a labor force out of all Israel; and the labor force was thirty thousand men. ¹⁴And he sent them to Lebanon, ten thousand a month in shifts: they were one month in Lebanon *and* two months at home; ⁿAdoniram *was* in charge of the labor force. ¹⁵ºSolomon had seventy thousand who carried burdens, and eighty thousand who quarried *stone* in the mountains, ¹⁶besides three thousand three hundred* from the ᵖchiefs of Solomon's deputies, who supervised the people who labored in the work. ¹⁷And the king commanded them to quarry large stones, costly stones, *and* ᑫhewn stones, to lay the foundation of the temple.* ¹⁸So Solomon's builders, Hiram's builders, and the Gebalites quarried *them*; and they prepared timber and stones to build the temple.

Solomon Builds the Temple

6 And ªit came to pass in the four hundred and eightieth* year after the children of Israel had come out of the land of Egypt, in the fourth year of Solomon's reign over Israel, in the month of Ziv, which *is* the second month, ᵇthat he began to build the house of the LORD. ²Now ᶜthe house which King Solomon built for the LORD, its length *was* sixty cubits, its width twenty, and its height thirty cubits. ³The vestibule in front

---

* **5:3** Literally *them*   * **5:11** Following Masoretic Text, Targum, and Vulgate; Septuagint and Syriac read *twenty thousand.*   * **5:16** Following Masoretic Text, Targum, and Vulgate; Septuagint reads *three thousand six hundred.*   * **5:17** Literally *house*, and so frequently throughout this book   * **6:1** Following Masoretic Text, Targum, and Vulgate; Septuagint reads *fortieth.*

5:1 Hiram. This Phoenician king ruled over Tyre for 34 years (978–944 B.C.).
5:7 Blessed be the LORD. Acknowledging the deities of another people is well known in the Bible (Dan. 3:28) and other ancient Middle Eastern literature. It does not necessarily imply that Hiram was expressing faith in God.
5:13 raised up a labor force . . . thirty thousand men. Solomon's long and extensive use of this type of social conscription to accomplish his vast building projects became a source of considerable difficulty for his successor, Rehoboam (12:4).
6:1 four hundred and eightieth year. Many scholars take this date as the key date for establishing the time of the Exodus. The division of the kingdom at the death of Solomon can be dated at 930 B.C. (11:41–43). Allowing forty years for Solomon's rule (11:42), the fourth year of his reign would be 966 B.C.

If the Exodus took place 480 years before 966 B.C., its date was 1446 B.C.
6:2 house . . . for the LORD. Solomon followed the floor plan of the tabernacle, but doubled its dimensions. Solomon's temple was constructed on Mount Moriah, the mountain where Abraham was told to offer Isaac as a sacrifice (Gen. 22:2; 2 Chr. 3:1), on the site of the threshing floor of Araunah where God had spoken to David (2 Sam. 24:24). **cubits.** The standard cubit was about 18 inches.

5:1 ª 2 Chr. 2:3   ᵇ 2 Sam. 5:11   **5:2** ᶜ 2 Chr. 2:3
5:3 ᵈ 1 Chr. 28:2, 3   ᵉ 1 Chr. 22:8; 28:3   **5:4** ᶠ 1 Kin. 4:24   **5:5** ᵍ 2 Chr. 2:4   ʰ 2 Sam. 7:12, 13   **5:6** ⁱ 2 Chr. 2:8, 10   **5:9** ʲ Ezra 3:7   ᵏ Ezek. 27:17   **5:11** ˡ 2 Chr. 2:10   **5:12** ᵐ 1 Kin. 3:12   **5:14** ⁿ 1 Kin. 12:18   **5:15** º 2 Chr. 2:17, 18   **5:16** ᵖ 1 Kin. 9:23   **5:17** ᑫ 1 Kin. 6:7   **6:1** ª 2 Chr. 3:1, 2   ᵇ Acts 7:47   **6:2** ᶜ Ezek. 41:1

of the sanctuary* of the house *was* twenty cubits long across the width of the house, *and* the width of *the vestibule* extended ten cubits from the front of the house. [4]And he made for the house [d]windows with beveled frames.

[5]Against the wall of the temple he built [e]chambers all around, *against* the walls of the temple, all around the sanctuary [f]and the inner sanctuary.* Thus he made side chambers all around it. [6]The lowest chamber *was* five cubits wide, the middle *was* six cubits wide, and the third *was* seven cubits wide; for he made narrow ledges around the outside of the temple, so that *the support beams* would not be fastened into the walls of the temple. [7]And [g]the temple, when it was being built, was built with stone finished at the quarry, so that no hammer or chisel *or* any iron tool was heard in the temple while it was being built. [8]The doorway for the middle story* *was* on the right side of the temple. They went up by stairs to the middle *story,* and from the middle to the third.

[9h]So he built the temple and finished it, and he paneled the temple with beams and boards of cedar. [10]And he built side chambers against the entire temple, each five cubits high; they were attached to the temple with cedar beams.

[11]Then the word of the LORD came to Solomon, saying: [12]"Concerning this temple which you are building, [i]if you walk in My statutes, execute My judgments, keep all My commandments, and walk in them, then I will perform My word with you, [j]which I spoke to your father David. [13]And [k]I will dwell among the children of Israel, and will not [l]forsake My people Israel."

[14]So Solomon built the temple and finished it. [15]And he built the inside walls of the temple with cedar boards; from the floor of the temple to the ceiling he paneled the inside with wood; and he covered the floor of the temple with planks of cypress. [16]Then he built the twenty-cubit room at the rear of the temple, from floor to ceiling, with cedar boards; he built *it* inside as the inner sanctuary, as the [m]Most Holy *Place.* [17]And in front of it the temple sanctuary was forty cubits *long.* [18]The inside of the

temple was cedar, carved with ornamental buds and open flowers. All *was* cedar; there was no stone *to be* seen.

[19]And he prepared the inner sanctuary inside the temple, to set the ark of the covenant of the LORD there. [20]The inner sanctuary *was* twenty cubits long, twenty cubits wide, and twenty cubits high. He overlaid it with pure gold, and overlaid the altar of cedar. [21]So Solomon overlaid the inside of the temple with pure gold. He stretched gold chains across the front of the inner sanctuary, and overlaid it with gold. [22]The whole temple he overlaid with gold, until he had finished all the temple; also he overlaid with gold [n]the entire altar that *was* by the inner sanctuary.

[23]Inside the inner sanctuary [o]he made two cherubim *of* olive wood, *each* ten cubits high. [24]One wing of the cherub *was* five cubits, and the other wing of the cherub five cubits: ten cubits from the tip of one wing to the tip of the other. [25]And the other cherub *was* ten cubits; both cherubim *were* of the same size and shape. [26]The height of one cherub *was* ten cubits, and so *was* the other cherub. [27]Then he set the cherubim inside the inner room;* and [p]they stretched out the wings of the cherubim so that the wing of the one touched *one* wall, and the wing of the other cherub touched the other wall. And their wings touched each other in the middle of the room. [28]Also he overlaid the cherubim with gold.

[29]Then he carved all the walls of the temple all around, both the inner and outer *sanctuaries,* with carved [q]figures of cherubim, palm trees, and open flowers. [30]And the floor of the temple he overlaid with gold, both the inner and outer *sanctuaries.*

[31]For the entrance of the inner sanctuary he made doors *of* olive wood; the lintel *and* doorposts *were* one-fifth *of the wall.*

---

* **6:3** Hebrew *heykal;* here the main room of the temple, elsewhere called the holy place (compare Exodus 26:33 and Ezekiel 41:1) • Literally *it* * **6:5** Hebrew *debir;* here the inner room of the temple, elsewhere called the Most Holy Place (compare verse 16) * **6:8** Following Masoretic Text and Vulgate; Septuagint reads *upper story;* Targum reads *ground story.* * **6:27** Literally *house*

6:11 word of the LORD. This message to Solomon might have come by means of a prophet. On other occasions, Solomon had more personal encounters with the Lord (3:5; 9:2; 11:11).

6:19 ark of the covenant. The ark of the covenant (Deut. 10:8) was so named because it housed the two stone tablets of the covenant—the Ten Commandments (Deut. 10:1–5). The ark symbolized the presence of the sovereign God in the midst of His people (8:10–11; Josh. 3:13).

6:20 inner sanctuary. The Most Holy Place was a cube of thirty feet. **gold.** The amount of gold used in this room was about 21 tons or 600 talents (2 Chr. 3:8).

6:23 cherubim. Cherubim are mighty angelic beings, they were often depicted in the furnishings of the

tabernacle and temple. Not a great deal is known about their nature. Cherubim were set to guard the entrance to the garden of Eden (Gen. 3:24). The only extensive description of their appearance is in the Book of Ezekiel (Ezek. 1:5–14; 10:1).

6:31 doors of olive wood. A veil or curtain was hung here as well (Ex. 26:31–36; 2 Chr. 3:14).

6:4 [d]Ezek. 40:16; 41:16   **6:5** [e]Ezek. 41:6   [f]1 Kin. 6:16, 19–21, 31   **6:7** [g]Deut. 27:5, 6   **6:9** [h]1 Kin. 6:14, 38   **6:12** [i]1 Kin. 2:4; 9:4   [j]2 Sam. 7:13]   **6:13** [k]Ex. 25:8   [l][Deut. 31:6]   **6:16** [m]Ex. 26:33   **6:22** [n]Ex. 30:1, 3, 6   **6:23** [o]2 Chr. 3:10–12   **6:27** [p]2 Chr. 5:8   **6:29** [q]Ex. 36:8, 35

32 The two doors *were of* olive wood; and he carved on them figures of cherubim, palm trees, and open flowers, and overlaid *them* with gold; and he spread gold on the cherubim and on the palm trees. 33 So for the door of the sanctuary he also made doorposts *of* olive wood, one-fourth of *the wall.* 34 And the two doors *were of* cypress wood; *r*two panels *comprised* one folding door, and two panels *comprised* the other folding door. 35 Then he carved cherubim, palm trees, and open flowers *on them,* and overlaid *them* with gold applied evenly on the carved work.

36 And he built the *s*inner court with three rows of hewn stone and a row of cedar beams.

37 *t*In the fourth year the foundation of the house of the LORD was laid, in the month of Ziv. 38 And in the eleventh year, in the month of Bul, which is the eighth month, the house was finished in all its details and according to all its plans. So he was *u*seven years in building it.

Solomon's Other Buildings

7 But Solomon took *a*thirteen years to build his own house; so he finished all his house.

2 He also built the *b*House of the Forest of Lebanon; its length *was* one hundred cubits, its width fifty cubits, and its height thirty cubits, with four rows of cedar pillars, and cedar beams on the pillars. 3 And it was paneled with cedar above the beams that *were* on forty-five pillars, fifteen *to* a row. 4 *There were* windows *with* beveled frames *in* three rows, and window *was* opposite window *in* three tiers. 5 And all the doorways and doorposts *had* rectangular frames; and window *was* opposite window *in* three tiers.

6 He also made the Hall of Pillars: its length *was* fifty cubits, and its width thirty cubits; and in front of them *was* a portico with pillars, and a canopy *was* in front of them.

7 Then he made a hall for the throne, the Hall of Judgment, where he might judge; and *it was* paneled with cedar from floor to ceiling.*

8 And the house where he dwelt *had*

another court inside the hall, of like workmanship. Solomon also made a house like this hall for Pharaoh's daughter, *c*whom he had taken *as wife.*

9 All these *were of* costly stones cut to size, trimmed with saws, inside and out, from the foundation to the eaves, and also on the outside to the great court. 10 The foundation *was of* costly stones, large stones, some ten cubits and some eight cubits. 11 And above *were* costly stones, hewn to size, and cedar wood. 12 The great court *was* enclosed with three rows of hewn stones and a row of cedar beams. So were the *d*inner court of the house of the LORD *e*and the vestibule of the temple.

Hiram the Craftsman

13 Now King Solomon sent and brought Huram* from Tyre. 14 *f*He *was* the son of a widow from the tribe of Naphtali, and *g*his father *was* a man of Tyre, a bronze worker; *h*he was filled with wisdom and understanding and skill in working with all kinds of bronze work. So he came to King Solomon and did all his work.

The Bronze Pillars for the Temple

15 And he cast *i*two pillars of bronze, each one eighteen cubits high, and a line of twelve cubits measured the circumference of each. 16 Then he made two capitals *of* cast bronze, to set on the tops of the pillars. The height of one capital *was* five cubits, and the height of the other capital *was* five cubits. 17 *He* made a lattice network, with wreaths of chainwork, for the capitals which *were* on top of the pillars: seven chains for one capital and seven for the other capital. 18 So he made the pillars, and two rows of pomegranates above the network all around to cover the capitals that *were* on top; and thus he did for the other capital.

19 The capitals which *were* on top of the pillars in the hall *were* in the shape of lilies, four cubits. 20 The capitals on the two pillars also *had pomegranates* above, by

---

* 7:7 Literally *floor,* that is, of the upper level
* 7:13 Hebrew *Hiram* (compare 2 Chronicles 2:13, 14)

6:38 Worship in the midst of Solomon's building project he received a prophetic revelation from the Lord (vv. 11–14) in which a promise and a condition were prominent: the Lord would fulfill His promise to David if Solomon obeyed His laws. The temple was the external sign that the Lord would keep His covenant of grace and dwell among the people. Worship can never be divorced from obedience to God's laws in everyday life.

7:1–2 *House of the Forest of Lebanon.* This building was also apparently used as an armory (10:16–17; Is. 22:8).

7:13–14 *Huram.* Huram (also called Hiram) was of mixed parentage. His father was a Phoenician artisan who had married a widow from the tribe of Naphtali

(2 Chr. 2:14). Like his father, Huram had become a master craftsman; his contributions to the work on the temple were extensive.

7:16 five cubits. Jeremiah 52:22 agrees with this measurement, but 2 Kings 25:17 records the height as three cubits. This apparent discrepancy may just be a difference in whether the capitals of the pillars were included in the measurement height.

6:34 *r* Ezek. 41:23–25 **6:36** *s* 1 Kin. 7:12 **6:37** *t* 1 Kin. 6:1 **6:38** *u* 1 Kin. 5:5; 6:1; 8:19 **7:1** *a* 2 Chr. 8:1 **7:2** *b* 2 Chr. 9:16 **7:8** *c* 2 Chr. 8:11 **7:12** *d* 1 Kin. 6:36 *e* John 10:23 **7:14** *f* 2 Chr. 2:14 *g* 2 Chr. 4:16 *h* Ex. 31:3; 36:1 **7:15** *i* Jer. 52:21

the convex surface which *was* next to the network; and there *were* *i*two hundred such pomegranates in rows on each of the capitals all around.

21*k*Then he set up the pillars by the vestibule of the temple; he set up the pillar on the right and called its name Jachin, and he set up the pillar on the left and called its name Boaz. 22The tops of the pillars were in the shape of lilies. So the work of the pillars was finished.

The Sea and the Oxen

23And he made *l*the Sea of cast bronze, ten cubits from one brim to the other; *it was* completely round. Its height *was* five cubits, and a line of thirty cubits measured its circumference.

24Below its brim *were* ornamental buds encircling it all around, ten to a cubit, *m*all the way around the Sea. The ornamental buds *were* cast in two rows when it was cast. 25It stood on *n*twelve oxen: three looking toward the north, three looking toward the west, three looking toward the south, and three looking toward the east; the Sea *was set* upon them, and all their back parts *pointed* inward. 26It *was* a handbreadth thick; and its brim was shaped like the brim of a cup, *like* a lily blossom. It contained two thousand* baths.

The Carts and the Lavers

27He also made ten carts of bronze; four cubits *was* the length of each cart, four cubits its width, and three cubits its height. 28And this *was* the design of the carts: They had panels, and the panels *were* between frames; 29on the panels that *were* between the frames *were* lions, oxen, and cherubim. And on the frames *was* a pedestal on top. Below the lions and oxen *were* wreaths of plaited work. 30Every cart had four bronze wheels and axles of bronze, and its four feet had supports. Under the laver *were* supports of cast *bronze* beside each wreath. 31Its opening inside the crown at the top *was* one cubit in diameter; and the opening *was* round, shaped *like* a pedestal, one and a half cubits in outside diameter; and also on the opening *were* engravings, but the panels were square, not round. 32Under the panels *were* the four wheels, and the axles of the wheels *were joined* to the cart. The height of a wheel *was* one and a half

cubits. 33The workmanship of the wheels *was* like the workmanship of a chariot wheel; their axle pins, their rims, their spokes, and their hubs *were* all of cast *bronze.* 34And *there were* four supports at the four corners of each cart; its supports *were* part of the cart itself. 35On the top of the cart, at the height of half a cubit, *it was* perfectly round. And on the top of the cart, its flanges and its panels *were* of the same casting. 36On the plates of its flanges and on its panels he engraved cherubim, lions, and palm trees, wherever there was a clear space on each, with wreaths all around. 37Thus he made the ten carts. All of them were of the same mold, one measure, *and* one shape.

38Then *o*he made ten lavers of bronze; each laver contained forty baths, *and* each laver *was* four cubits. On each of the ten carts *was* a laver. 39And he put five carts on the right side of the house, and five on the left side of the house. He set the Sea on the right side of the house, toward the southeast.

Furnishings of the Temple

40*p*Huram* made the lavers and the shovels and the bowls. So Huram finished doing all the work that he was to do for King Solomon *for* the house of the LORD: 41the two pillars, the *two* bowl-shaped capitals that *were* on top of the two pillars; the two *q*networks covering the two bowl-shaped capitals which *were* on top of the pillars; 42*r*four hundred pomegranates for the two networks (two rows of pomegranates for each network, to cover the two bowl-shaped capitals that *were* on top of the pillars); 43the ten carts, and ten lavers on the carts; 44one Sea, and twelve oxen under the Sea; 45*s*the pots, the shovels, and the bowls.

All these articles which Huram* made for King Solomon *for* the house of the LORD *were* of burnished bronze. 46*t*In the plain of Jordan the king had them cast in clay molds, between *u*Succoth and *v*Zaretan. 47And Solomon did not weigh all the articles, because *there were* so many; the weight of the bronze was not *w*determined.

---

* **7:26** Or *three thousand* (compare 2 Chronicles 4:5)   * **7:40** Hebrew *Hiram* (compare 2 Chronicles 2:13, 14)   * **7:45** Hebrew *Hiram* (compare 2 Chronicles 2:13, 14)

7:21 Jachin . . . Boaz. Jachin means "He will establish." Boaz may mean "in Him is strength." Another possible meaning is "He is quick." These two pillars were placed near the porch in front of the temple (2 Chr. 3:17).

7:40–47 Service—When talents and skills are used in God's service, no work is insignificant. All is deserving of our best because it is done for God (Matt. 10:42). For this task Huram was filled with wisdom, understanding, and skill (v. 14). This description is

similar to the description of Bezalel's work on the tabernacle (Ex. 31:2–6). The Holy Spirit is the source of natural gifts as well as the supernatural gifts used in the service of the Lord.

7:20 *j* Jer. 52:23	**7:21** *k* 2 Chr. 3:17	**7:23** *l* 2 Chr. 4:2
7:24 *m* 2 Chr. 4:3	**7:25** *n* Jer. 52:20	**7:38** *o* 2 Chr. 4:6
7:40 *p* 2 Chr. 4:11—5:1	**7:41** *q* 1 Kin. 7:17, 18	
7:42 *r* 1 Kin. 7:20	**7:45** *s* Ex. 27:3	**7:46** *t* 2 Chr. 4:17
u Gen. 33:17	*v* Josh. 3:16	**7:47** *w* 1 Chr. 22:3, 14

48Thus Solomon had all the furnishings made for the house of the LORD: xthe altar of gold, and ythe table of gold on which *was* zthe showbread; 49the lampstands of pure gold, five on the right *side* and five on the left in front of the inner sanctuary, with the flowers and the lamps and the wicktrimmers of gold; 50the basins, the trimmers, the bowls, the ladles, and the censers of pure gold; and the hinges of gold, *both* for the doors of the inner room (the Most Holy *Place*) *and* for the doors of the main hall of the temple.

51So all the work that King Solomon had done for the house of the LORD was finished; and Solomon brought in the things awhich his father David had dedicated: the silver and the gold and the furnishings. He put them in the treasuries of the house of the LORD.

The Ark Brought into the Temple

8 Now aSolomon assembled the elders of Israel and all the heads of the tribes, the chief fathers of the children of Israel, to King Solomon in Jerusalem, bthat they might bring cup the ark of the covenant of the LORD from the City of David, which *is* Zion. 2Therefore all the men of Israel assembled with King Solomon at the dfeast in the month of Ethanim, which *is* the seventh month. 3So all the elders of Israel came, eand the priests took up the ark. 4Then they brought up the ark of the LORD, fthe tabernacle of meeting, and all the holy furnishings that *were* in the tabernacle. The priests and the Levites brought them up. 5Also King Solomon, and all the congregation of Israel who were assembled with him, *were* with him before the ark, gsacrificing sheep and oxen that could not be counted or numbered for multitude. 6Then the priests hbrought in the ark of the covenant of the LORD to iits place, into the inner sanctuary of the temple, to the Most Holy *Place*, junder the wings of the cherubim. 7For the cherubim spread *their*

two wings over the place of the ark, and the cherubim overshadowed the ark and its poles. 8The poles kextended so that the ends of the poles could be seen from the holy *place*, in front of the inner sanctuary; but they could not be seen from outside. And they are there to this day. 9lNothing *was* in the ark mexcept the two tablets of stone which Moses nput there at Horeb, owhen the LORD made *a covenant* with the children of Israel, when they came out of the land of Egypt.

10And it came to pass, when the priests came out of the holy *place*, that the cloud pfilled the house of the LORD, 11so that the priests could not continue ministering because of the cloud; for the qglory of the LORD filled the house of the LORD.

12rThen Solomon spoke:

"The LORD said He would dwell sin the dark cloud.
13 tI have surely built You an exalted house,
uAnd a place for You to dwell in forever."

Solomon's Speech at Completion of the Work

14Then the king turned around and vblessed the whole assembly of Israel, while all the assembly of Israel was standing. 15And he said: w"Blessed *be* the LORD God of Israel, who xspoke with His mouth to my father David, and with His hand has fulfilled *it*, saying, 16'Since the day that I brought My people Israel out of Egypt, I have chosen no city from any tribe of Israel *in which* to build a house, that yMy name might be there; but I chose zDavid to be over My people Israel.' 17Now ait was in the heart of my father David to build a temple* for the name of the LORD God of Israel. 18bBut the LORD said to my father David, 'Whereas it was in your heart to build

---

* **8:17** Literally *house*, and so in verses 18–20

7:48 furnishings. The furnishings of the temple were designed to correspond with similar furnishings in the tabernacle (Ex. 25; 30). Although Solomon made ten tables and lampstands instead of one, their functions remained the same, all ten being considered one unit (2 Chr. 29:18).
7:51 David. David's personal example of giving (1 Chr. 29:1–9) provided a high model of godly concern in leadership.
8:1 ark of the covenant. The ark had been in Jerusalem for some time (2 Sam. 6), and now it was finally in its proper setting. With the erection of the temple and the placement of the ark, the division of spiritual activities between Gibeon, the location of the tabernacle, and Jerusalem, where the ark had resided in a temporary shelter, was now at an end. The pattern of central worship set up in the wilderness could once again be observed (Deut. 12:1–4).
8:9 two tablets of stone. The two tablets upon which the Ten Commandments were inscribed were

known as the "tablets of the covenant" (Deut. 9:9) and were kept in the ark (Deut. 10:1–5,8) along with the jar of manna (Ex. 16:33–34) and Aaron's rod that budded (Num. 17:10).
8:10–11 the cloud. This visible presence of God's dwelling with His people sometimes called the "shekinah glory"—had also covered the tabernacle when it was inaugurated (Ex. 40:34–35).

7:48 x Ex. 37:25, 26; 2 Chr. 4:8 y Ex. 37:10, 11 z Lev. 24:5–8 **7:51** a 2 Sam. 8:11 **8:1** a 2 Chr. 5:2–14 b 2 Sam. 6:12–17 c 2 Sam. 5:7; 6:12, 16 **8:2** d Lev. 23:34 **8:3** e Num. 4:15; 7:9 **8:4** f 2 Chr. 1:3 **8:5** g 2 Sam. 6:13 **8:6** h 2 Sam. 6:17 i 1 Kin. 6:19 j 1 Kin. 6:27 **8:8** k Ex. 25:13–15; 37:4, 5 **8:9** l Ex. 25:21 m Deut. 10:5 n Ex. 24:7, 8; 40:20 o Ex. 34:27, 28 **8:10** p Ex. 40:34, 35 **8:11** q 2 Chr. 7:1, 2 **8:12** r 2 Chr. 6:1 s Ps. 18:11; 97:2 **8:13** t 2 Sam. 7:13 u Ps. 132:14 **8:14** v 2 Sam. 6:18 **8:15** w Luke 1:68 x 2 Sam. 7:2, 12, 13, 25 **8:16** y 1 Kin. 8:29 z 2 Sam. 7:8 **8:17** a 2 Sam. 7:2, 3 **8:18** b 2 Chr. 6:8, 9

a temple for My name, you did well that it was in your heart. [19]Nevertheless [c]you shall not build the temple, but your son who will come from your body, he shall build the temple for My name.' [20]So the LORD has fulfilled His word which He spoke; and I have filled the position of my father David, and sit on the throne of Israel, [d]as the LORD promised; and I have built a temple for the name of the LORD God of Israel. [21]And there I have made a place for the ark, in which is [e]the covenant of the LORD which He made with our fathers, when He brought them out of the land of Egypt."

Solomon's Prayer of Dedication

[22]Then Solomon stood before [f]the altar of the LORD in the presence of all the assembly of Israel, and [g]spread out his hands toward heaven; [23]and he said: "LORD God of Israel, [h]there is no God in heaven above or on earth below like You, [i]who keep Your covenant and mercy with Your servants who [j]walk before You with all their hearts. [24]You have kept what You promised Your servant David my father; You have both spoken with Your mouth and fulfilled it with Your hand, as it is this day. [25]Therefore, LORD God of Israel, now keep what You promised Your servant David my father, saying, [k]'You shall not fail to have a man sit before Me on the throne of Israel, only if your sons take heed to their way, that they walk before Me as you have walked before Me.' [26l]And now I pray, O God of Israel, let Your word come true, which You have spoken to Your servant David my father.

[27]"But [m]will God indeed dwell on the earth? Behold, heaven and the [n]heaven of heavens cannot contain You. How much less this temple which I have built! [28]Yet regard the prayer of Your servant and his supplication, O LORD my God, and listen to the cry and the prayer which Your servant is praying before You today: [29]that Your eyes may be open toward this temple night and day, toward the place of which You said, [o]'My name shall be [p]there,' that You may hear the prayer which Your servant makes [q]toward this place. [30]And may You hear the supplication of Your servant and of Your people Israel, when they pray toward this place. Hear in heaven Your dwelling place; and when You hear, forgive.

[31]"When anyone sins against his neighbor, and is forced to take [s]an oath, and comes and takes an oath before Your altar in this temple, [32]then hear in heaven, and act, and judge Your servants, [t]condemning the wicked, bringing his way on his head, and justifying the righteous by giving him according to his righteousness.

[33u]"When Your people Israel are defeated before an enemy because they have sinned against You, and [v]when they turn back to You and confess Your name, and pray and make supplication to You in this temple, [34]then hear in heaven, and forgive the sin of Your people Israel, and bring them back to the land which You gave to their [w]fathers.

[35x]"When the heavens are shut up and there is no rain because they have sinned against You, when they pray toward this place and confess Your name, and turn from their sin because You afflict them, [36]then hear in heaven, and forgive the sin of Your servants, Your people Israel, that

---

8:20 the LORD has fulfilled. Israel's God is a keeper of promises. His promise to give Abraham's descendants a land (Gen. 15:13–14,18–21; Josh. 14:12–15) had been provisionally realized (Josh. 21:43–45). Solomon also appropriated God's promise to David (2 Sam. 7:12–18). Subsequent kings in the Davidic line could likewise by faith enjoy the blessings of God promised in the Davidic covenant (Ps. 89:3–4,19–24,27–37).

8:27 God. God is infinite; no mere building, no matter how wonderful, can contain Him. God rules from heaven in a realm far superior to anything that man can imagine. Unlike the pagan gods who were thought to actually live in the temples built for them, He is not limited by time or space (Acts 7:48; 17:24). Yet God has committed Himself to fellowship with men, walking among them on the earth and being their God. Incredibly, He has chosen to dwell in the hearts of human beings. The true believer is the temple that God desires (1 Cor. 3:16–19).

8:29–30 The Temple in the Life of Israel—Once Solomon built the temple, it became the primary location for the ceremonial worship of Israel. But it was also to be a house of prayer (Is. 56:7), a special place where God's people could rightly maintain their individual relationships with God. The temple was a place for repentance and forgiveness (Luke

18:10–14). It was a place for petitions to be brought to God. The temple was the central point of worship and life for Israel. Even today in many European towns, beautiful church buildings stand in the town square as a testament to the centrality that the church once had in the life of the community.

Too often we fall into a practice that makes ceremony itself the central thing or in some cases the only thing. Here, we can see what mattered most was not the ritualistic practices but communication with God. This passage and others like it give clarity to many of the claims of the prophets mentioned later in Scripture. If the people had been praying and listening to God as a part of the act of worship, surely they would have been more obedient to His commands, especially in view of the fact that prophets continually rebuked them.

8:19 [c]2 Sam. 7:5, 12, 13   **8:20** [d]1 Chr. 28:5, 6
8:21 [e]Deut. 31:26   **8:22** [f]2 Chr. 6:12   [g]Ezra 9:5
8:23 [h]Ex. 15:11   [i][Neh. 1:5]   [j][Gen. 17:1]   **8:25** [k]1 Kin.
2:4; 9:5   **8:26** [l]2 Sam. 7:25   **8:27** [m][Acts 7:49; 17:24]
[n]2 Cor. 12:2   **8:29** [o]Deut. 12:11   [p]1 Kin. 9:3   [q]Dan.
6:10   **8:30** [r]Neh. 1:6   **8:31** [s]Ex. 22:8–11   **8:32** [t]Deut.
25:1   **8:33** [u]Deut. 28:25   [v]Lev. 26:39, 40   **8:34** [w][Lev.
26:40–42]   **8:35** [x]Deut. 28:23

You may [y]teach them [z]the good way in
which they should walk; and send rain on
Your land which You have given to Your
people as an inheritance.
37 [a]"When there is famine in the land,
pestilence *or* blight *or* mildew, locusts *or*
grasshoppers; when their enemy besieges
them in the land of their cities; whatever plague or whatever sickness *there is;*
38 whatever prayer, whatever supplication
is made by anyone, *or* by all Your people
Israel, when each one knows the plague of
his own heart, and spreads out his hands
toward this temple: 39 then hear in heav-
en Your dwelling place, and forgive, and
act, and give to everyone according to all
his ways, whose heart You know (for You
alone [b]know the hearts of all the sons of
men), 40 [c]that they may fear You all the days
that they live in the land which You gave to
our fathers.
41 "Moreover, concerning a foreigner,
who *is* not of Your people Israel, but has
come from a far country for Your name's
sake 42 (for they will hear of Your great
name and Your [d]strong hand and Your outstretched arm), when he comes and prays
toward this temple, 43 hear in heaven Your
dwelling place, and do according to all for
which the foreigner calls to You, [e]that all
peoples of the earth may know Your name
and [f]fear You, as *do* Your people Israel, and
that they may know that this temple which
I have built is called by Your name.
44 "When Your people go out to battle
against their enemy, wherever You send
them, and when they pray to the LORD
toward the city which You have chosen
and the temple which I have built for Your
name, 45 then hear in heaven their prayer
and their supplication, and maintain their
cause.
46 "When they sin against You [g](for *there*
is no one who does not sin), and You become angry with them and deliver them
to the enemy, and they take them captive
[h]to the land of the enemy, far or near; 47 [i]*yet*
when they come to themselves in the land
where they were carried captive, and repent, and make supplication to You in the
land of those who took them captive, [j]say-
ing, 'We have sinned and done wrong, we
have committed wickedness'; 48 and *when*
they [k]return to You with all their heart
and with all their soul in the land of their
enemies who led them away captive, and
[l]pray to You toward their land which You
gave to their fathers, the city which You
have chosen and the temple which I have
built for Your name: 49 then hear in heaven
Your dwelling place their prayer and their
supplication, and maintain their cause,
50 and forgive Your people who have sinned
against You, and all their transgressions
which they have transgressed against You;
and [m]grant them compassion before those
who took them captive, that they may have
compassion on them 51 (for [n]they *are* Your
people and Your inheritance, whom You
brought out of Egypt, [o]out of the iron furnace), 52 [p]that Your eyes may be open to the
supplication of Your servant and the supplication of Your people Israel, to listen to
them whenever they call to You. 53 For You
separated them from among all the peoples
of the earth *to be* Your inheritance, [q]as You
spoke by Your servant Moses, when You
brought our fathers out of Egypt, O Lord
GOD."

Solomon Blesses the Assembly

54 [r]And so it was, when Solomon had finished praying all this prayer and supplication to the LORD, that he arose from before
the altar of the LORD, from kneeling on his
knees with his hands spread up to heav-
en. 55 Then he stood [s]and blessed all the
assembly of Israel with a loud voice, saying: 56 "Blessed *be* the LORD, who has given
[t]rest to His people Israel, according to all
that He promised. [u]There has not failed
one word of all His good promise, which
He promised through His servant Moses.
57 May the LORD our God be with us, as He
was with our fathers. [v]May He not leave us
nor forsake us, 58 that He may [w]incline our
hearts to Himself, to walk in all His ways,
and to keep His commandments and His
statutes and His judgments, which He
commanded our fathers. 59 And may these

8:41 *foreigner.* Unlike God's people or resident aliens within the commonwealth of Israel (Deut. 10:18–19), foreigners had no particular claim on the ear of God. But the Israelites expected foreigners to be drawn to God by the way His people worshiped Him.

8:54 *arose . . . from kneeling.* Chronicles adds that Solomon's prayer and blessing were accompanied by heavenly fire that consumed the sacrifice on the altar (2 Chr. 7:1–3).

8:58 Regeneration—Solomon prayed for an ability given by God that would allow the people to live according to the covenant which had been given at the time of Moses. Solomon was aware that the nation's history was full of examples of the people turning away from God and from His written revelation. Ultimately, the promise of God to the nation of Israel was that there would be a new covenant given to them which would be internalized and which would be brought about by the Holy Spirit (Jer. 31)—the new covenant which was ratified in Jesus' blood (1 Cor. 11:25). Believers today have a power which enables us to live according to God's word—the Holy Spirit who is the agent of our regeneration.

8:36 [y] Ps. 25:4; 27:11; 94:12 [z] 1 Sam. 12:23 **8:37** [a] Lev. 26:16, 25, 26 **8:39** [b] [1 Sam. 16:7] **8:40** [c] [Ps. 130:4] **8:42** [d] Deut. 3:24 **8:43** [e] [1 Sam. 17:46] [f] Ps. 102:15 **8:46** [g] Ps. 130:3 [h] Lev. 26:34, 44 **8:47** [i] [Lev. 26:40–42] [j] Dan. 9:5 **8:48** [k] Jer. 29:12–14 [l] Dan. 6:10 **8:50** [m] Ps. 106:46 **8:51** [n] Deut. 9:26–29 [o] Jer. 11:4 **8:52** [p] 1 Kin. 8:29 **8:53** [q] Ex. 19:5, 6 **8:54** [r] 2 Chr. 7:1 **8:55** [s] 2 Sam. 6:18 **8:56** [t] 1 Chr. 22:18 [u] Deut. 12:10 **8:57** [v] Deut. 31:6 **8:58** [w] Ps. 119:36

words of mine, with which I have made supplication before the LORD, be near the LORD our God day and night, that He may maintain the cause of His servant and the cause of His people Israel, as each day may require, [60]xthat all the peoples of the earth may know that the LORD is God; *there is* no other. [61]Let your zheart therefore be loyal to the LORD our God, to walk in His statutes and keep His commandments, as at this day."

Solomon Dedicates the Temple

[62]Then athe king and all Israel with him offered sacrifices before the LORD. [63]And Solomon offered a sacrifice of peace offerings, which he offered to the LORD, twenty-two thousand bulls and one hundred and twenty thousand sheep. So the king and all the children of Israel dedicated the house of the LORD. [64]On bthe same day the king consecrated the middle of the court that *was* in front of the house of the LORD; for there he offered burnt offerings, grain offerings, and the fat of the peace offerings, because the cbronze altar that *was* before the LORD *was* too small to receive the burnt offerings, the grain offerings, and the fat of the peace offerings.

[65]At that time Solomon held da feast, and all Israel with him, a great assembly from ethe entrance of Hamath to fthe Brook of Egypt, before the LORD our God, gseven days and seven *more* days—fourteen days. [66]hOn the eighth day he sent the people away; and they blessed the king, and went to their tents joyful and glad of heart for all the good that the LORD had done for His servant David, and for Israel His people.

God's Second Appearance to Solomon

9 And ait came to pass, when Solomon had finished building the house of the LORD band the king's house, and call Solomon's desire which he wanted to do, [2]that the LORD appeared to Solomon the second time, das He had appeared to him at Gibeon. [3]And the LORD said to him: e"I have heard your prayer and your supplication that you have made before Me; I have consecrated this house which you

have built fto put My name there forever, and gMy eyes and My heart will be there perpetually. [4]Now if you hwalk before Me ias your father David walked, in integrity of heart and in uprightness, to do according to all that I have commanded you, *and* if you jkeep My statutes and My judgments, [5]then I will establish the throne of your kingdom over Israel forever, kas I promised David your father, saying, 'You shall not fail to have a man on the throne of Israel.' [6]lBut if you or your sons at all turn from following Me, and do not keep My commandments *and* My statutes which I have set before you, but go and serve other gods and worship them, [7]mthen I will cut off Israel from the land which I have given them; and this house which I have consecrated nfor My name I will cast out of My sight. oIsrael will be a proverb and a byword among all peoples. [8]And *as for* pthis house, *which* is exalted, everyone who passes by it will be astonished and will hiss, and say, q'Why has the LORD done thus to this land and to this house?' [9]Then they will answer, 'Because they forsook the LORD their God, who brought their fathers out of the land of Egypt, and have embraced other gods, and worshiped them and served them; therefore the LORD has brought all this rcalamity on them.'"

Solomon and Hiram Exchange Gifts

[10]Now sit happened at the end of twenty years, when Solomon had built the two houses, the house of the LORD and the king's house, [11]t(Hiram the king of Tyre had supplied Solomon with cedar and cypress and gold, as much as he desired), *that* King Solomon then gave Hiram twenty cities in the land of Galilee. [12]Then Hiram went from Tyre to see the cities which Solomon had given him, but they did not please him. [13]So he said, "What *kind of* cities *are* these which you have given me, my brother?" uAnd he called them the land of Cabul,* as they are to this day. [14]Then Hiram sent the king one hundred and twenty talents of gold.

* **9:13** Literally *Good for Nothing*

8:60 *all the peoples of the earth.* This verse does not limit God to the Jews but includes the Gentiles as well.

9:2 *second time.* God had appeared previously to Solomon in Gibeon (3:4–15). The Lord's warning was a necessary reminder for Solomon, who eventually did compromise the conditions required for enjoying God's blessing (11:1–11).

9:12 *they did not please him.* Hiram's displeasure with Solomon's gift would later result in Solomon's redeeming the towns by repaying the debt in another manner (2 Chr. 8:1–2).

9:14 *one hundred and twenty talents.* A talent was

said to be the full load one man could easily carry. It was equal to three thousand shekels, or about 70 pounds.

8:60x 1 Sam. 17:46 y Deut. 4:35, 39 **8:61**z Deut. 18:13 **8:62**a 2 Chr. 7:4–10 **8:64**b 2 Chr. 7:7 c 2 Chr. 4:1 **8:65**d Lev. 23:34 e Num. 34:8 f Gen. 15:18 g 2 Chr. 7:8 **8:66**h 2 Chr. 7:9 **9:1**a 2 Chr. 7:11 b 1 Kin. 7:1 c 2 Chr. 8:6 **9:2**d 1 Kin. 3:5; 11:9 **9:3**e Ps. 10:17 f 1 Kin. 8:29 g Deut. 11:12 **9:4**h Gen. 17:1 i 1 Kin. 11:4, 6; 15:5 j 1 Kin. 8:61 **9:5**k 2 Sam. 7:12, 16 **9:6**l 2 Sam. 7:14–16 **9:7**m [Lev. 18:24–29] n [Jer. 7:4–14] o Ps. 44:14 **9:8**p 2 Chr. 7:21 q [Deut. 29:24–26] **9:9**r [Deut. 29:25–28] **9:10**s 2 Chr. 8:1 **9:11**t 1 Kin. 5:1 **9:13**u Josh. 19:27

Solomon's Additional Achievements

15And this *is* the reason for ᵛthe labor force which King Solomon raised: to build the house of the LORD, his own house, ʷMillo,* the wall of Jerusalem, ˣHazor, ʸMegiddo, and ᶻGezer. 16(Pharaoh king of Egypt had gone up and taken Gezer and burned it with fire, ᵃhad killed the Canaanites who dwelt in the city, and had given it *as* a dowry to his daughter, Solomon's wife.) 17Solomon built Gezer, Lower ᵇBeth Horon, 18cBaalath, and Tadmor in the wilderness, in the land of *Judah*, 19all the storage cities that Solomon had, cities for ᵈhis chariots and cities for his ᵉcavalry, and whatever Solomon ᶠdesired to build in Jerusalem, in Lebanon, and in all the land of his dominion.

20ᵍAll the people *who were* left of the Amorites, Hittites, Perizzites, Hivites, and Jebusites, who *were* not of the children of Israel— 21that is, their descendants ʰwho were left in the land after them, ⁱwhom the children of Israel had not been able to destroy completely—ʲfrom these Solomon raised ᵏforced labor, as it is to this day. 22But of the children of Israel Solomon ˡmade no forced laborers, because they *were* men of war and his servants: his officers, his captains, commanders of his chariots, and his cavalry.

23Others *were* chiefs of the officials who *were* over Solomon's work: ᵐfive hundred and fifty, who ruled over the people who did the work.

24But ⁿPharaoh's daughter came up from the City of David to ᵒher house which *Solomon** had built for her. ᵖThen he built the Millo.

25ᵃNow three times a year Solomon offered burnt offerings and peace offerings on the altar which he had built for the LORD, and he burned incense with them *on the altar* that *was* before the LORD. So he finished the temple.

26ʳKing Solomon also built a fleet of ships at ˢEzion Geber, which *is* near Elath* on the shore of the Red Sea, in the land of Edom. 27ᵗThen Hiram sent his servants with the fleet, seamen who knew the sea, to work with the servants of Solomon. 28And they went to ᵘOphir, and acquired four hundred and twenty talents of gold from there, and brought *it* to King Solomon.

The Queen of Sheba's Praise of Solomon

10 Now when the ᵃqueen of Sheba heard of the fame of Solomon concerning the name of the LORD, she came ᵇto test him with hard questions. 2She came to Jerusalem with a very great retinue, with camels that bore spices, very much gold, and precious stones; and when she came to Solomon, she spoke with him about all that was in her heart. 3So Solomon answered all her questions; there was nothing so difficult for the king that he could not explain *it* to her. 4And when the queen of Sheba had seen all the wisdom of Solomon, the house that he had built, 5the food on his table, the seating of his servants, the service of his waiters and their apparel, his cupbearers, ᶜand his entryway by which he went up to the house of the LORD, there was no more spirit in her. 6Then she said to the king: "It was a true report which I heard in my own land about your words and your wisdom. 7However I did not believe the words until I came and saw with my own eyes; and indeed the half was not told me. Your wisdom and prosperity exceed the fame of which I heard. 8ᵈHappy *are* your men and happy *are* these your servants, who stand continually before you *and* hear your wisdom! 9eBlessed be the LORD your God, who ᶠdelighted in you, setting you on the throne of Israel! Because the LORD has loved Israel forever, therefore He made you king, ᵍto do justice and righteousness."

---

* **9:15** Literally *The Landfill*   * **9:24** Literally *he*
(compare 2 Chronicles 8:11)   * **9:26** Hebrew *Eloth*
(compare 2 Kings 14:22)

9:16 *Gezer.* Gezer had been a strong Canaanite city, a part of Ephraim's territorial assignment. Ephraim had never taken Gezer; however, Egypt had conquered the city. Its key location on the edge of the lowlands west of Jerusalem made it a splendid gift for Pharaoh to give on the occasion of his daughter's marriage to Solomon.
9:26 *Ezion Geber.* Ezion Geber was at the head of the modern Gulf of Aqaba. Its key location as an outlet to the Red Sea and the regions beyond made it commercially important to Solomon and to Hiram, his Phoenician trading partner (2 Chr. 8:17–18).
9:28 *Ophir.* The exact location of Ophir is a mystery. Some have speculated that it may have been in Africa, since it was reached by sea (1 Kin. 22:48). It was certainly a celebrated gold area, the source of much of the wealth David and Solomon used to pay for their vast building projects (1 Chr. 29:4).
10:1 *Sheba.* Located in southwestern Arabia

(present-day Yemen), Sheba was the homeland of the Sabeans, a people whose far-flung commercial enterprises stretched from Syria to east Africa to distant India. The Sabeans dealt in such precious commodities as gold, gemstones, perfumes, and rare spices.
10:9 *Blessed be the LORD your God.* The queen's acknowledgment of Solomon's God and the Lord's

9:15 ᵛ 1 Kin. 5:13   ʷ 2 Sam. 5:9   ˣ Josh. 11:1; 19:36   ʸ Josh. 17:11   ᶻ Josh. 16:10   **9:16** ᵃ Josh. 16:10   **9:17** ᵇ 2 Chr. 8:5   **9:18** ᶜ Josh. 19:44   **9:19** ᵈ 1 Kin. 10:26   ᵉ 1 Kin. 4:26   ᶠ 1 Kin. 9:1   **9:20** ᵍ 2 Chr. 8:7   **9:21** ʰ Judg. 1:21–36; 3:1   ⁱ Josh. 15:63; 17:12, 13   ʲ Judg. 1:28, 35   ᵏ Ezra 2:55, 58   **9:22** ˡ [Lev. 25:39]   **9:23** ᵐ 2 Chr. 8:10   **9:24** ⁿ 1 Kin. 3:1   ᵒ 1 Kin. 7:8   ᵖ 2 Sam. 5:9   **9:25** ᵃ Ex. 23:14–17   **9:26** ʳ 2 Chr. 8:17, 18   ˢ Num. 33:35   **9:27** ᵗ 1 Kin. 5:6, 9; 10:11   **9:28** ᵘ Job 22:24   **10:1** ᵃ Matt. 12:42   ᵇ Judg. 14:12   **10:5** ᶜ 1 Chr. 26:16   **10:8** ᵈ Prov. 8:34   **10:9** ᵉ 1 Kin. 5:7   ᶠ 2 Sam. 22:20   ᵍ Ps. 72:2

[10]Then she [h]gave the king one hundred and twenty talents of gold, spices in great quantity, and precious stones. There never again came such abundance of spices as the queen of Sheba gave to King Solomon. [11i]Also, the ships of Hiram, which brought gold from Ophir, brought great quantities of almug* wood and precious stones from Ophir. [12j]And the king made steps of the almug wood for the house of the LORD and for the king's house, also harps and stringed instruments for singers. There never again came such [k]almug wood, nor has the like been seen to this day.

[13]Now King Solomon gave the queen of Sheba all she desired, whatever she asked, besides what Solomon had given her according to the royal generosity. So she turned and went to her own country, she and her servants.

Solomon's Great Wealth

[14]The weight of gold that came to Solomon yearly was six hundred and sixty-six talents of gold, [15]besides that from the [l]traveling merchants, from the income of traders, [m]from all the kings of Arabia, and from the governors of the country.

[16]And King Solomon made two hundred large shields of hammered gold; six hundred shekels of gold went into each shield. [17]He also made [n]three hundred shields of hammered gold; three minas of gold went into each shield. The king put them in the [o]House of the Forest of Lebanon.

[18p]Moreover the king made a great throne of ivory, and overlaid it with pure gold. [19]The throne had six steps, and the top of the throne was round at the back; there were armrests on either side of the place of the seat, and two lions stood beside the armrests. [20]Twelve lions stood there, one on each side of the six steps; nothing like this had been made for any other kingdom.

[21a]All King Solomon's drinking vessels were gold, and all the vessels of the House of the Forest of Lebanon were pure gold. Not one was silver, for this was accounted as nothing in the days of Solomon. [22]For the king had [r]merchant ships* at sea with the fleet of Hiram. Once every three years the merchant [s]ships came bringing gold, silver, ivory, apes, and monkeys.* [23]So [t]King Solomon surpassed all the kings of the earth in riches and wisdom.

[24]Now all the earth sought the presence of Solomon to hear his wisdom, which God had put in his heart. [25]Each man brought his present: articles of silver and gold, garments, armor, spices, horses, and mules, at a set year by year.

[26u]And Solomon [v]gathered chariots and horsemen; he had one thousand four hundred chariots and twelve thousand horsemen, whom he stationed* in the chariot cities and with the king at Jerusalem. [27w]The king made silver as common in Jerusalem as stones, and he made cedar trees as abundant as the sycamores which are in the lowland. [28x]Also Solomon had horses imported from Egypt and Keveh; the king's merchants bought them in Keveh at the current price. [29]Now a chariot that was imported from Egypt cost six hundred shekels of silver, and a horse one hundred and fifty; [y]and thus, through their agents,* they exported them to all the kings of the Hittites and the kings of Syria.

Solomon's Heart Turns from the LORD

11 But [a]King Solomon loved [b]many foreign women, as well as the daughter of Pharaoh: women of the Moabites,

---

* **10:11** Or algum (compare 2 Chronicles 9:10, 11) * **10:22** Literally ships of Tarshish, deep-sea vessels • Or peacocks * **10:26** Following Septuagint, Syriac, Targum, and Vulgate (compare 2 Chronicles 9:25); Masoretic Text reads led.
* **10:29** Literally by their hands

---

covenant faithfulness towards Israel does not necessarily mean that she made a commitment of personal faith in the Lord. She may simply have been expressing respect for Solomon's God (see 5:7).
10:26 one thousand four hundred chariots. Shalmaneser III of Assyria reported that at the battle of Qarqar (853 B.C.) he faced a combined enemy chariot force of 3,900, some two thousand of which were supplied by Israel.
10:27 silver . . . cedar trees. Under Solomon, Israel enjoyed its greatest period of prosperity. This time of prosperity and peace also must have allowed for the growth of scholarship and for arts and music.
11:1 many foreign women. Taking foreign wives violated the Lord's prohibitions against marrying Canaanite women (v. 2; Ex. 34:12–17; Deut. 7:1–3); taking many wives violated the standard of monogamy established at the beginning (Gen. 2:24–25), and resulted in rampant polygamy, something God had also forbidden to Israel's future kings (Deut. 17:17).
11:1–2 Materialism—Even before Israel crossed

over the Jordan and entered the Promised Land, God had given special instructions for the nation's future kings, warning them against materialism: they were not to collect horses, women, or gold for themselves (Deut. 17:16–17). However, King Solomon did all three, resulting in his downfall. He owned many horses (4:26); he gathered hundreds of wives and concubines (v. 3); and he possessed much gold and silver (10:14–27). The gathering of material wealth, when gained honestly, is not prohibited in the Bible. Improper love of possessions, however, is idolatry. We can own things, but things must not own us.

10:10 [h] Ps. 72:10, 15   **10:11** [i] 1 Kin. 9:27, 28
10:12 [j] 2 Chr. 9:11 [k] 2 Chr. 9:10   **10:15** [l] 2 Chr. 1:16 [m] Ps. 72:10   **10:17** [n] 1 Kin. 14:26 [o] 1 Kin. 7:2   **10:18** [p] 2 Chr. 9:17   **10:21** [q] 2 Chr. 9:20   **10:22** [r] Gen. 10:4 [s] 1 Kin. 9:26–28; 22:48   **10:23** [t] 1 Kin. 3:12, 13; 4:30   **10:26** [u] 1 Kin. 4:26 [v] 1 Kin. 9:19   **10:27** [w] 2 Chr. 1:15–17   **10:28** [x] [Deut. 17:16]   **10:29** [y] 2 Kin. 7:6, 7   **11:1** [a] [Neh. 13:26] [b] [Deut. 17:17]

Ammonites, Edomites, Sidonians, *and* Hittites— ²from the nations of whom the LORD had said to the children of Israel, ᶜ"You shall not intermarry with them, nor they with you. Surely they will turn away your hearts after their gods." Solomon clung to these in love. ³And he had seven hundred wives, princesses, and three hundred concubines; and his wives turned away his heart. ⁴For it was so, when Solomon was old, ᵈthat his wives turned his heart after other gods; and his ᵉheart was not loyal to the LORD his God, ᶠas *was* the heart of his father David. ⁵For Solomon went after ᵍAshtoreth the goddess of the Sidonians, and after ʰMilcom the abomination of the ⁱAmmonites. ⁶Solomon did evil in the sight of the LORD, and did not fully follow the LORD, as *did* his father David. ⁷ʲThen Solomon built a high place for ᵏChemosh the abomination of Moab, on ˡthe hill that *is* east of Jerusalem, and for Molech the abomination of the people of Ammon. ⁸And he did likewise for all his foreign wives, who burned incense and sacrificed to their gods.

⁹So the LORD became angry with Solomon, because his heart had turned from the LORD God of Israel, ᵐwho had appeared to him twice, ¹⁰and ⁿhad commanded him concerning this thing, that he should not go after other gods; but he did not keep what the LORD had commanded. ¹¹Therefore the LORD said to Solomon, "Because you have done this, and have not kept My covenant and My statutes, which I have commanded you, ᵒI will surely tear the kingdom away from you and give it to your ᵖservant. ¹²Nevertheless I will not do it in your days, for the sake of your father David; I will tear it out of the hand of your son. ¹³ᵠHowever I will not tear away the whole kingdom; I will give ʳone tribe to your son ˢfor the sake of My servant David, and for the sake of Jerusalem ᵗwhich I have chosen."

Adversaries of Solomon

¹⁴Now the LORD ᵘraised up an adversary against Solomon, Hadad the Edomite; he *was* a descendant of the king in Edom. ¹⁵ᵛFor it happened, when David was in Edom, and Joab the commander of the army had gone up to bury the slain, ʷafter he had killed every male in Edom ¹⁶(because for six months Joab remained there with all Israel, until he had cut down every male in Edom), ¹⁷that Hadad fled to go to Egypt, he and certain Edomites of his father's servants with him. Hadad *was* still a little child. ¹⁸Then they arose from Midian and came to Paran; and they took men with them from Paran and came to Egypt, to Pharaoh king of Egypt, who gave him a house, apportioned food for him, and gave him land. ¹⁹And Hadad found great favor in the sight of Pharaoh, so that he gave him as wife the sister of his own wife, that is, the sister of Queen Tahpenes. ²⁰Then the sister of Tahpenes bore him Genubath his son, whom Tahpenes weaned in Pharaoh's house. And Genubath was in Pharaoh's household among the sons of Pharaoh.

²¹ˣSo when Hadad heard in Egypt that David rested with his fathers, and that Joab the commander of the army was dead, Hadad said to Pharaoh, "Let me depart, that I may go to my own country."

²²Then Pharaoh said to him, "But what have you lacked with me, that suddenly you seek to go to your own country?"

So he answered, "Nothing, but do let me go anyway."

²³And God raised up *another* adversary against him, Rezon the son of Eliadah, who had fled from his lord, ʸHadadezer king of Zobah. ²⁴So he gathered men to him and became captain over a band *of raiders,* ᶻwhen David killed those *of Zobah.* And they went to Damascus and dwelt there, and reigned in Damascus. ²⁵He was an

---

11:1–4 Unfaithfulness—Solomon was affected by the contemporary practices of the surrounding culture. Entering into a political marriage was a means to consolidate a relationship with a neighboring monarch, and Solomon followed this custom at the expense of obedience to God. Unfaithfulness creeps into our lives when our hearts are more closely attuned to contemporary culture and peer pressure than to the voice of God. The heinousness of Solomon's unfaithfulness stands in contrast with the abundance of God's favor and the plainness of His commands (vv. 9–10).

11:3 seven hundred . . . three hundred. If the reference to 60 queens and 80 concubines in Song of Solomon 6:8 is to Solomon's wives, it represents a much earlier period in Solomon's reign.

11:4 not loyal. Although it is true that David did not always live up to God's standards, he was loyal to God and trusted Him implicitly, even when he was rebuked for his sins (2 Sam. 12:13; Ps. 32:1–5; 53:1–5).

11:7 high place. The use of high places in association with the worship of foreign gods shows the terrible danger that the high places presented to

Israel (3:2–4; 14:23; Mic. 1:3). **Molech.** The worship of Molech was associated with Baal worship and with human sacrifice (Jer. 7:31–32; 19:5–6; 32:35).

11:13 one tribe. The one tribe left to the house of David was Judah, the principal tribe of the southern kingdom. By this time, Simeon had assimilated with Judah (12:17–21).

11:14 Hadad the Edomite. Hadad was one of the survivors who had escaped when David defeated the Edomite army (2 Sam. 8:13–14). Pharaoh's ready reception and favorable treatment of Hadad probably had political ramifications, the pharaoh seeing him as a potential future ally on Israel's border.

11:2 ᶜ [Deut. 7:3, 4] **11:4** ᵈ [Deut. 17:17] ᵉ 1 Kin. 8:61 ᶠ 1 Kin. 9:4 **11:5** ᵍ Judg. 2:13 ʰ [Lev. 20:2–5] ⁱ 2 Kin. 23:13 **11:7** ʲ Num. 33:52 ᵏ Judg. 11:24 ˡ 2 Kin. 23:13 **11:9** ᵐ 1 Kin. 3:5; 9:2 **11:10** ⁿ 1 Kin. 6:12; 9:6, 7 **11:11** ᵒ 1 Kin. 11:31; 12:15, 16 ᵖ 1 Kin. 11:31, 37 **11:13** ᵠ 2 Sam. 7:15 ʳ 1 Kin. 12:20 ˢ 2 Sam. 7:15, 16 ᵗ Deut. 12:11 **11:14** ᵘ 1 Chr. 5:26 **11:15** ᵛ 2 Sam. 8:14 ʷ Num. 24:18, 19 **11:21** ˣ 1 Kin. 2:10, 34 **11:23** ʸ 2 Sam. 8:3; 10:16 **11:24** ᶻ 2 Sam. 8:3; 10:8, 18

adversary of Israel all the days of Solomon (besides the trouble that Hadad *caused*); and he abhorred Israel, and reigned over Syria.

Jeroboam's Rebellion

26Then Solomon's servant, aJeroboam the son of Nebat, an Ephraimite from Zereda, whose mother's name *was* Zeruah, a widow, balso crebelled against the king.

27And this *is* what caused him to rebel against the king: dSolomon had built the Millo *and* repaired the damages to the City of David his father. 28The man Jeroboam *was* a mighty man of valor; and Solomon, seeing that the young man was eindustrious, made him the officer over all the labor force of the house of Joseph.

29Now it happened at that time, when Jeroboam went out of Jerusalem, that the prophet fAhijah the Shilonite met him on the way; and he had clothed himself with a new garment, and the two *were* alone in the field. 30Then Ahijah took hold of the new garment that *was* on him, and gtore it *into* twelve pieces. 31And he said to Jeroboam, "Take for yourself ten pieces, for hthus says the LORD, the God of Israel: 'Behold, I will tear the kingdom out of the hand of Solomon and will give ten tribes to you 32(but he shall have one tribe for the sake of My servant David, and for the sake of Jerusalem, the city which I have chosen out of all the tribes of Israel), 33ibecause they have* forsaken Me, and worshiped Ashtoreth the goddess of the Sidonians, Chemosh the god of the Moabites, and Milcom the god of the people of Ammon, and have not walked in My ways to do *what is* right in My eyes and *keep* My statutes and My judgments, as *did* his father David. 34However I will not take the whole kingdom out of his hand, because I have made him ruler all the days of his life for the sake of My servant David, whom I chose

because he kept My commandments and My statutes. 35But jI will take the kingdom out of his son's hand and give it to you— ten tribes. 36And to his son I will give one tribe, that kMy servant David may always have a lamp before Me in Jerusalem, the city which I have chosen for Myself, to put My name there. 37So I will take you, and you shall reign over all your heart desires, and you shall be king over Israel. 38Then it shall be, if you heed all that I command you, walk in My ways, and do *what is* right in My sight, to keep My statutes and My commandments, as My servant David did, then lI will be with you and mbuild for you an enduring house, as I built for David, and will give Israel to you. 39And I will afflict the descendants of David because of this, but not forever.'"

40Solomon therefore sought to kill Jeroboam. But Jeroboam arose and fled to Egypt, to nShishak king of Egypt, and was in Egypt until the death of Solomon.

Death of Solomon

41Now othe rest of the acts of Solomon, all that he did, and his wisdom, *are* they not written in the book of the acts of Solomon? 42pAnd the period that Solomon reigned in Jerusalem over all Israel *was* forty years. 43qThen Solomon rested with his fathers, and was buried in the City of David his father. And Rehoboam his son reigned in his rplace.

The Revolt Against Rehoboam

12 And aRehoboam went to bShechem, for all Israel had gone to Shechem to make him king. 2So it happened, when cJeroboam the son of Nebat heard *it* (he was still in dEgypt, for he had fled from

---

* **11:33** Following Masoretic Text and Targum; Septuagint, Syriac, and Vulgate read *he has.*

11:26 *Jeroboam.* At first a trusted official for Solomon (v. 28), Jeroboam came under his wrath and fled to Egypt. Eventually, Jeroboam was instrumental in bringing about the prophesied schism of the country (12:2–19). He became the first king of the northern kingdom (12:20).

11:31–32 *ten tribes . . . one tribe.* The twelfth tribe might be Simeon, which was absorbed by Judah; it is also possible that Benjamin existed for some time as a "buffer state" between Israel and Judah, linked at times with the southern kingdom (2 Chr. 11:3).

11:36 *a lamp.* This is an image of one of the divinely intended functions of the kings of ancient Israel. In the midst of the darkness of a pagan world, the Davidic kings were to be a lamp to the nations, in anticipation of the coming Messiah who would be the Light of the World (John 1:1–9; 2 Sam. 21:17; 2 Kin. 8:19; 2 Chr. 21:7).

11:40 *Shishak.* Shishak (or Sheshonq I, 945–924 B.C.) was the first pharaoh of Egypt's strong twenty-second dynasty. Ironically, this future destroyer of Israel appears here as a protector of one of its future kings.

11:41 *the book of the acts of Solomon.* This book is mentioned only here; compare the references to the Book of the Chronicles of the Kings of Israel (14:19) and the Book of the Chronicles of the Kings of Judah (14:29). It is likely that the author of the books of Kings drew on these sources.

12:1 *Shechem.* Shechem was an important center of Israelite activity. It was the first place mentioned in Canaan with reference to Abraham (Gen. 12:6). It was also one of the Levitical cities of refuge (Num. 35:6). By going for his coronation to a place with ancient ties to the history of his people, and which was situated in

11:26 a 1 Kin. 12:2   b 2 Kin. 13:6   c 2 Sam. 20:21   **11:27** d 1 Kin. 9:15, 24   **11:28** e [Prov. 22:29]   **11:29** f 2 Chr. 9:29   **11:30** g 1 Sam. 15:27, 28; 24:5   **11:31** h 1 Kin. 11:11, 13   **11:33** i 1 Kin. 11:5–8   **11:35** j 1 Kin. 12:16, 17   **11:36** k [1 Kin. 15:4]   **11:38** l Josh. 1:5   m 2 Sam. 7:11, 27   **11:40** n 2 Chr. 12:2–9   **11:41** o 2 Chr. 9:29   **11:42** p 2 Chr. 9:30   **11:43** q 2 Chr. 9:31   r 2 Chr. 10:1   **12:1** o 2 Chr. 10:1   b Judg. 9:6   **12:2** c 1 Kin. 11:26   d 1 Kin. 11:40

the presence of King Solomon and had been dwelling in Egypt), ³that they sent and called him. Then Jeroboam and the whole assembly of Israel came and spoke to Rehoboam, saying, ⁴"Your father made our ᵉyoke heavy; now therefore, lighten the burdensome service of your father, and his heavy yoke which he put on us, and we will serve you."

⁵So he said to them, "Depart *for* three days, then come back to me." And the people departed.

⁶Then King Rehoboam consulted the elders who stood before his father Solomon while he still lived, and he said, "How do you advise *me* to answer these people?"

⁷And they spoke to him, saying, ᶠ"If you will be a servant to these people today, and serve them, and answer them, and speak good words to them, then they will be your servants forever."

⁸But he rejected the advice which the elders had given him, and consulted the young men who had grown up with him, who stood before him. ⁹And he said to them, "What advice do you give? How should we answer this people who have spoken to me, saying, 'Lighten the yoke which your father put on us'?"

¹⁰Then the young men who had grown up with him spoke to him, saying, "Thus you should speak to this people who have spoken to you, saying, 'Your father made our yoke heavy, but you make *it* lighter on us'—thus you shall say to them: 'My little *finger* shall be thicker than my father's waist! ¹¹And now, whereas my father put a heavy yoke on you, I will add to your yoke; my father chastised you with whips, but I will chastise you with scourges!'"*

¹²So Jeroboam and all the people came to Rehoboam the third day, as the king had directed, saying, "Come back to me the third day." ¹³Then the king answered the people roughly, and rejected the advice

which the elders had given him; ¹⁴and he spoke to them according to the advice of the young men, saying, "My father made your yoke heavy, but I will add to your yoke; my father chastised you with whips, but I will chastise you with scourges!"*

¹⁵So the king did not listen to the people; for ᵍthe turn *of events* was from the LORD, that He might fulfill His word, which the LORD had ʰspoken by Ahijah the Shilonite to Jeroboam the son of Nebat.

¹⁶Now when all Israel saw that the king did not listen to them, the people answered the king, saying:

ᶦ"What share have we in David?
  We have no inheritance in the son of Jesse.
To your tents, O Israel!
Now, see to your own house, O David!"

So Israel departed to their tents. ¹⁷But Rehoboam reigned over ʲthe children of Israel who dwelt in the cities of Judah.

¹⁸Then King Rehoboam ᵏsent Adoram, who *was* in charge of the revenue; but all Israel stoned him with stones, and he died. Therefore King Rehoboam mounted his chariot in haste to flee to Jerusalem. ¹⁹So ˡIsrael has been in rebellion against the house of David to this day.

²⁰Now it came to pass when all Israel heard that Jeroboam had come back, they sent for him and called him to the congregation, and made him king over all ᵐIsrael. There was none who followed the house of David, but the tribe of Judah ⁿonly.

²¹And when ᵒRehoboam came to Jerusalem, he assembled all the house of Judah with the tribe of ᵖBenjamin, one hundred and eighty thousand chosen *men* who were warriors, to fight against the house of Israel, that he might restore the kingdom to

---

* **12:11** Literally *scorpions*   * **12:14** Literally *scorpions*

---

the region of the northern tribes, Rehoboam doubtless believed that he was making a strategic move.
12:15 *from the LORD.* Even at this crucial time of national schism, God was sovereignly working through human events to accomplish His will, which had been made known through earlier prophecy (11:29–39). *might fulfill His word.* All things derive their origin and destiny from God. They are determined, controlled, and directed from beginning to end by His wise and sovereign counsel. His plan encompasses everything that comes to pass, including all ends and all the ways and means to those ends. His plan also incorporates the folly of men in their deliberations, advice, and decisions, without compelling them to it by external constraint. In fact, God's Word reveals the solemn truth that His plan encompasses even the sin, ungodliness, and evil of men in their motivations and aspirations, their thoughts, words, and deeds, without eliminating their full responsibility for it (Acts 2:22–23; 4:27–28).
12:16 *What share have we in David?* The ancient rivalry felt by the northern tribes now came to a peak

in resentment against the tribe of Judah and the house of David
12:17 *cities of Judah.* The southern section of the land also included the tribal allotment of Simeon. But Simeon by this time had been absorbed by Judah, their allotment was "within the inheritance of the children of Judah" (Josh. 19:1).
12:20 *made him king.* The coronation of Jeroboam had been prophesied by Ahijah the prophet of the Lord (11:29–31). Nonetheless, the actual coronation apparently was done apart from priest or prophet of the Lord; there was no divine anointing, no true religious ceremony. Only the kings of the southern kingdom would have the sanction of the Davidic covenant (2 Sam. 7).

12:4 ᵉ 1 Sam. 8:11–18   **12:7** ᶠ 2 Chr. 10:7   **12:15** ᵍ Judg. 14:4 ʰ 1 Kin. 11:11, 29, 31   **12:16** ʲ 2 Sam. 20:1   **12:17** ʲ 1 Kin. 11:13, 36   **12:18** ᵏ 1 Kin. 4:6; 5:14   **12:19** ˡ 2 Kin. 17:21   **12:20** ᵐ 2 Kin. 17:21 ⁿ 1 Kin. 11:13, 32, 36   **12:21** ᵒ 2 Chr. 11:1–4 ᵖ 2 Sam. 19:17

Rehoboam the son of Solomon. ²²But ᵠthe word of God came to Shemaiah the man of God, saying, ²³"Speak to Rehoboam the son of Solomon, king of Judah, to all the house of Judah and Benjamin, and to the rest of the people, saying, ²⁴'Thus says the LORD: "You shall not go up nor fight against your brethren the children of Israel. Let every man return to his house, ʳfor this thing is from Me."'" Therefore they obeyed the word of the LORD, and turned back, according to the word of the LORD.

Jeroboam's Gold Calves

²⁵Then Jeroboam ˢbuilt Shechem in the mountains of Ephraim, and dwelt there. Also he went out from there and built ᵗPenuel. ²⁶And Jeroboam said in his heart, "Now the kingdom may return to the house of David: ²⁷If these people ᵘgo up to offer sacrifices in the house of the LORD at Jerusalem, then the heart of this people will turn back to their lord, Rehoboam king of Judah, and they will kill me and go back to Rehoboam king of Judah."

²⁸Therefore the king asked advice, ᵛmade two calves of gold, and said to the people, "It is too much for you to go up to Jerusalem. ʷHere are your gods, O Israel, which brought you up from the land of Egypt!" ²⁹And he set up one in ˣBethel, and the other he put in ʸDan. ³⁰Now this thing became ᶻa sin, for the people went *to worship* before the one as far as Dan. ³¹He made shrines* on the high places, ᵃand made priests from every class of people, who were not of the sons of Levi.

³²Jeroboam ordained a feast on the fifteenth day of the eighth month, like ᵇthe feast that *was* in Judah, and offered sacrifices on the altar. So he did at Bethel, sacrificing to the calves that he had made. ᶜAnd at Bethel he installed the priests of the high places which he had made. ³³So he made offerings on the altar which he had made at Bethel on the fifteenth day of the eighth month, in the month which he had ᵈdevised in his own heart. And he ordained a feast for the children of Israel, and offered sacrifices on the altar and ᵉburned incense.

The Message of the Man of God

13 And behold, ᵃa man of God went from Judah to Bethel by the word of the LORD, ᵇand Jeroboam stood by the altar to burn incense. ²Then he cried out against the altar by the word of the LORD, and said, "O altar, altar! Thus says the LORD: 'Behold, a child, ᶜJosiah by name, shall be born to the house of David; and on you he shall sacrifice the priests of the high places who burn incense on you, and men's bones shall be ᵈburned on you.'" ³And he gave ᵉa sign the same day, saying, "This *is* the sign which the LORD has spoken: Surely the altar shall split apart, and the ashes on it shall be poured out."

⁴So it came to pass when King Jeroboam heard the saying of the man of God, who cried out against the altar in Bethel, that he stretched out his hand from the altar, saying, "Arrest him!" Then his hand, which he stretched out toward him, withered, so that he could not pull it back to himself. ⁵The altar also was split apart, and the ashes poured out from the altar, according to the sign which the man of God had given by the word of the LORD.

---

* **12:31** Literally *a house*

12:22 Shemaiah. According to 2 Chronicles 12:15, Iddo the prophet and Shemaiah together wrote a history of Rehoboam's reign.
12:28 two calves of gold. Not only would they strike a familiar chord from Israel's history, but the two calves would arouse the interest of the remaining Canaanites in the northern kingdom. The result of Jeroboam's action was religious confusion and apostasy; this was the first time that a deliberate attempt had been made to establish a heterodox doctrine, an unauthorized variation of the true religion. It appears that Jeroboam was doing the same thing that Aaron did, presenting the calves as representations of God, and thus luring people away from true worship.
12:29 Bethel. Bethel was north of Jerusalem in Benjamite territory, it had enjoyed a prominent place in Israelite history throughout the earlier patriarchal period (Gen. 28:10–21). Dan was in the north; before its capture by the Danites it had a reputation as a center for pagan worship (Judg. 18:30). Jeroboam's choice of these two sites was a brilliant move. He had one site in the northernmost part of his kingdom and another in the southernmost part; both had long ties to Israel's past, and eliminated the need for long, tedious treks to Jerusalem.
12:31 not of the sons of Levi. Jeroboam's new

religious institutions included starting a new religious order that did not include the Levites; setting up shrines at high places (3:2–3); and replacing the Feast of Tabernacles with a fall festival of the eighth month. His various attempts at religious innovation would quickly incur God's wrath and earn him a reputation that would live in infamy (13:33–34; 22:52).
13:4–5 Arrest him. The life and character of Jeroboam stands in stark contrast to that of King David. When David was told that he would become king, he never forgot that it was God who gave him the position, and God who would maintain it. Jeroboam, however, seemed to think that he would only stay in office by his own efforts. When David was confronted with his sin by Nathan the prophet, he humbly confessed (2 Sam. 12:13). The wicked Jeroboam sought to arrest his accuser.

12:22 ᵠ 2 Chr. 11:2; 12:5–7 **12:24** ʳ 1 Kin. 12:15
12:25 ˢ Judg. 9:45–49 ᵗ Judg. 8:8, 17 **12:27** ᵘ [Deut. 12:5–7, 14] **12:28** ᵛ 2 Kin. 10:29; 17:16 ʷ Ex. 32:4, 8
12:29 ˣ Gen. 28:19 ʸ Judg. 18:26–31 **12:30** ᶻ 1 Kin. 13:34
12:31 ᵈ 2 Kin. 17:32 **12:32** ᵇ Lev. 23:33, 34 ᶜ Amos 7:10–13 **12:33** ᵈ Num. 15:39 ᵉ 1 Kin. 13:1 **13:1** ᵃ 2 Kin. 23:17 ᵇ 1 Kin. 12:32, 33 **13:2** ᶜ 2 Kin. 23:15, 16 ᵈ [Lev. 26:30] **13:3** ᵉ Is. 7:14; 38:7

⁶Then the king answered and said to the man of God, "Please ⁱentreat the favor of the LORD your God, and pray for me, that my hand may be restored to me."

So the man of God entreated the LORD, and the king's hand was restored to him, and became as before. ⁷Then the king said to the man of God, "Come home with me and refresh yourself, and ᵍI will give you a reward."

⁸But the man of God said to the king, ʰ"If you were to give me half your house, I would not go in with you; nor would I eat bread or drink water in this place. ⁹For so it was commanded me by the word of the LORD, saying, ⁱ'You shall not eat bread, nor drink water, nor return by the same way you came.'" ¹⁰So he went another way and did not return by the way he came to Bethel.

Death of the Man of God

¹¹Now an ʲold prophet dwelt in Bethel, and his sons came and told him all the works that the man of God had done that day in Bethel; they also told their father the words which he had spoken to the king. ¹²And their father said to them, "Which way did he go?" For his sons had seen* which way the man of God went who came from Judah. ¹³Then he said to his sons, "Saddle the donkey for me." So they saddled the donkey for him; and he rode on it, ¹⁴and went after the man of God, and found him sitting under an oak. Then he said to him, "Are you the man of God who came from Judah?"

And he said, "I am."

¹⁵Then he said to him, "Come home with me and eat bread."

¹⁶And he said, ᵏ"I cannot return with you nor go in with you; neither can I eat bread nor drink water with you in this place. ¹⁷For I have been told ˡby the word of the LORD, 'You shall not eat bread nor drink water there, nor return by going the way you came.'"

¹⁸He said to him, "I too am a prophet as you are, and an angel spoke to me by the word of the LORD, saying, 'Bring him back with you to your house, that he may eat bread and drink water.'" (He was lying to him.)

¹⁹So he went back with him, and ate bread in his house, and drank water.

²⁰Now it happened, as they sat at the table, that the word of the LORD came to the prophet who had brought him back; ²¹and he cried out to the man of God who came from Judah, saying, "Thus says the LORD: 'Because you have disobeyed the word of the LORD, and have not kept the commandment which the LORD your God commanded you, ²²but you came back, ate bread, and drank water in the ᵐplace of which the LORD said to you, "Eat no bread and drink no water," your corpse shall not come to the tomb of your fathers.'"

²³So it was, after he had eaten bread and after he had drunk, that he saddled the donkey for him, the prophet whom he had brought back. ²⁴When he was gone, ⁿa lion met him on the road and killed him. And his corpse was thrown on the road, and the donkey stood by it. The lion also stood by the corpse. ²⁵And there, men passed by and saw the corpse thrown on the road, and the lion standing by the corpse. Then they went and told it in the city where the old prophet dwelt.

²⁶Now when the prophet who had brought him back from the way heard it, he said, "It is the man of God who was disobedient to the word of the LORD. Therefore the LORD has delivered him to the lion, which has torn him and killed him, according to the word of the LORD which He spoke to him." ²⁷And he spoke to his sons, saying, "Saddle the donkey for me." So they saddled it. ²⁸Then he went and found his corpse thrown on the road, and the donkey and the lion standing by the corpse. The lion had not eaten

* **13:12** Septuagint, Syriac, Targum, and Vulgate read *showed him.*

13:6 *the LORD your God.* This language may be simply deferential to the prophet, but here it may indicate recognition by Jeroboam that he was no longer really serving the living God.
13:7–8 *reward.* The prophet was not just being ungracious, he was following a direct command from God. In biblical times, sharing a meal was more than just a social custom. It implied an intimate fellowship. Great religious ceremonies from the Passover to the Lord's Table center on people eating together. The prophet did not want his act of mercy to suggest that God accepted Jeroboam's deviant worship, or leave the impression that a touch from God could be bought and paid for. Giving a gift can be an easy way to avoid the really important matter of changing lives and lifestyles. If a person is convinced that by his giving he is rewarding a church or a pastor, then it becomes impossible for that church or pastor to have any kind of prophetic ministry to that individual. Instead, they become his debtor.

13:11 *an old prophet.* This prophet was clearly an apostate. He had not spoken against Jeroboam; instead, he boldly lied to the Lord's true prophet.
13:19 *went back with him.* The man of God had withstood Jeroboam's persuasions; he probably came expecting just such pressure. Sadly, he made the mistake of letting down his guard when he had passed the test he was expecting. There is never any excuse for violating God's clear instructions, and he paid a terrible price for his disobedience.
13:24 *a lion.* The way the lion stood by both the man of God and his donkey shows that the lion did not kill for food but was God's executioner (vv. 25–26,28).

13:6 ⁱ[James 5:16] **13:7** ᵍ1 Sam. 9:7 **13:8** ʰNum. 22:18; 24:13 **13:9** ⁱ[1 Cor. 5:11] **13:11** ʲ1 Kin. 13:25 **13:16** ᵏ1 Kin. 13:8, 9 **13:17** ˡ1 Kin. 20:35 **13:22** ᵐ1 Kin. 13:9 **13:24** ⁿ1 Kin. 20:36

the corpse nor torn the donkey. ²⁹And the prophet took up the corpse of the man of God, laid it on the donkey, and brought it back. So the old prophet came to the city to mourn, and to bury him. ³⁰Then he laid the corpse in his own tomb; and they mourned over him, *saying*, ᵒ"Alas, my brother!" ³¹So it was, after he had buried him, that he spoke to his sons, saying, "When I am dead, then bury me in the tomb where the man of God *is* buried; ᵖlay my bones beside his bones. ³²ᵠFor the saying which he cried out by the word of the LORD against the altar in Bethel, and against all the shrines* on the high places which *are* in the cities of ʳSamaria, will surely come to pass."

³³ˢAfter this event Jeroboam did not turn from his evil way, but again he made priests from every class of people for the high places; whoever wished, he consecrated him, and he became *one* of the priests of the high places. ³⁴ᵗAnd this thing was the sin of the house of Jeroboam, so as ᵘto exterminate and destroy *it* from the face of the earth.

Judgment on the House of Jeroboam

14 At that time Abijah the son of Jeroboam became sick. ²And Jeroboam said to his wife, "Please arise, and disguise yourself, that they may not recognize you as the wife of Jeroboam, and go to Shiloh. Indeed, Ahijah the prophet *is* there, who told me that ᵃI *would be* king over this people. ³ᵇAlso take with you ten loaves, *some* cakes, and a jar of honey, and go to him; he will tell you what will become of the child." ⁴And Jeroboam's wife did so; she arose ᶜand went to Shiloh, and came to the house of Ahijah. But Ahijah could not see, for his eyes were glazed by reason of his age.

⁵Now the LORD had said to Ahijah, "Here is the wife of Jeroboam, coming to ask you something about her son, for he *is* sick. Thus and thus you shall say to her; for it will be, when she comes in, that she will pretend *to be* another *woman*."

⁶And so it was, when Ahijah heard the sound of her footsteps as she came through the door, he said, "Come in, wife of Jeroboam. Why do you pretend *to be* another *person?* For I *have been* sent to you *with* bad *news*. ⁷Go, tell Jeroboam, 'Thus says the LORD God of Israel: ᵈ"Because I exalted you from among the people, and made you ruler over My people Israel, ⁸and ᵉtore the kingdom away from the house of David, and gave it to you; and *yet* you have not been as My servant David, ᶠwho kept My commandments and who followed Me with all his heart, to do only *what was* right in My eyes; ⁹but you have done more evil than all who were before you, ᵍfor you have gone and made for yourself other gods and molded images to provoke Me to anger, and ʰhave cast Me behind your back— ¹⁰therefore behold! ⁱI will bring disaster on the house of Jeroboam, and ʲwill cut off from Jeroboam every male in Israel, ᵏbond and free; I will take away the remnant of the house of Jeroboam, as one takes away refuse until it is all gone. ¹¹The dogs shall eat ˡwhoever belongs to Jeroboam and dies in the city, and the birds of the air shall eat whoever dies in the field; for the LORD has spoken!' " ¹²Arise therefore, go to your own house. ᵐWhen your feet enter the city, the child shall die. ¹³And all Israel shall mourn for him and bury him, for he is the only one of Jeroboam who shall come to the grave, because in him ⁿthere is found something good toward the LORD God of Israel in the house of Jeroboam.

¹⁴ᵒ"Moreover the LORD will raise up for Himself a king over Israel who shall cut off the house of Jeroboam; this is the day. What? Even now! ¹⁵For the LORD will strike Israel, as a reed is shaken in the water. He will ᵖuproot Israel from this ᵠgood land which He gave to their fathers, and will scatter them ʳbeyond the River,* ˢbecause they have made their wooden images,*

---

* **13:32** Literally *houses*   * **14:15** That is, the Euphrates • Hebrew *Asherim*, Canaanite deities

---

13:32 *cities of Samaria.* The city of Samaria did not, in fact, come into being for nearly half a century (16:24), but the author mentions it here from his own later perspective.

13:33 *evil way.* Rather than learning from the report of this incident, Jeroboam was even more set in his evil ways. His apostasy would earn for him his reputation as the one who "made Israel to sin" (16:26).

14:4 *Shiloh.* Located about twenty miles north of Jerusalem, Shiloh had been the religious center for the nation during the time of the judges and was the location of the tabernacle (Josh. 18:1; 1 Sam. 1:3). The city was destroyed by the Philistines after the loss of the ark (1 Sam. 4:1–11; Jer. 7:12–15). *could not see.* Although he was blind, Ahijah could "see" by means of the revelation of the living God.

14:11 *dogs.* Dogs were scavengers, and in the Middle East they came to symbolize the dregs of society (2 Kin. 8:13).

14:14 *cut off the house.* As prophesied here, the end of Jeroboam's reign would soon be accomplished (15:27—16:7).

14:15 *wooden images.* This refers to the wooden poles or images associated with the worship of the goddess Asherah (Judg. 3:7; 2 Kin. 23:4). Her worship would become one of the sins that would bring about the downfall of the northern kingdom (2 Kin. 17:9–11).

13:30 ᵒ Jer. 22:18   **13:31** ᵖ 2 Kin. 23:17, 18   **13:32** ᵠ 2 Kin. 23:16, 19   ʳ 1 Kin. 16:24   **13:33** ˢ 1 Kin. 12:31, 32   **13:34** ᵗ 1 Kin. 12:30   ᵘ [1 Kin. 14:10; 15:29, 30]   **14:2** ᵃ 1 Kin. 11:29–31   **14:3** ᵇ 1 Sam. 9:7, 8   **14:4** ᶜ 1 Kin. 11:29   **14:7** ᵈ 1 Kin. 16:2   **14:8** ᵉ 1 Kin. 11:31   ᶠ 1 Kin. 11:33, 38; 15:5   **14:9** ᵍ 1 Kin. 12:28   ʰ Ps. 50:17   **14:10** ⁱ 1 Kin. 15:29   ʲ 1 Kin. 21:21   ᵏ Deut. 32:36   **14:11** ˡ 1 Kin. 16:4; 21:24   **14:12** ᵐ 1 Kin. 14:17   **14:13** ⁿ 2 Chr. 12:12; 19:3   **14:14** ᵒ 1 Kin. 15:27–29   **14:15** ᵖ 2 Kin. 17:6   ᵠ [Josh. 23:15, 16]   ʳ 2 Kin. 15:29   ˢ [Ex. 34:13, 14]

provoking the LORD to anger. [16]And He will give Israel up because of the sins of Jeroboam, [t]who sinned and who made Israel sin." [17]Then Jeroboam's wife arose and departed, and came to [u]Tirzah. [v]When she came to the threshold of the house, the child died. [18]And they buried him; and all Israel mourned for him, [w]according to the word of the LORD which He spoke through His servant Ahijah the prophet.

Death of Jeroboam

[19]Now the rest of the acts of Jeroboam, how he [x]made war and how he reigned, indeed they *are* written in the book of the chronicles of the kings of Israel. [20]The period that Jeroboam reigned *was* twenty-two years. So he rested with his fathers. [y]Then Nadab his son reigned in his place.

Rehoboam Reigns in Judah

[21]And Rehoboam the son of Solomon reigned in Judah. [z]Rehoboam *was* forty-one years old when he became king. He reigned seventeen years in Jerusalem, the city [a]which the LORD had chosen out of all the tribes of Israel, to put His name there. [b]His mother's name *was* Naamah, an Ammonitess. [22c]Now Judah did evil in the sight of the LORD, and they [d]provoked Him to jealousy with their sins which they committed, more than all that their fathers had done. [23]For they also built for themselves [e]high places, [f]*sacred* pillars, and [g]wooden images on every high hill and [h]under every green tree. [24i]And there were also perverted persons* in the land. They did according to all the [j]abominations of the nations which the LORD had cast out before the children of [k]Israel.

[25l]It happened in the fifth year of King Rehoboam *that* Shishak king of Egypt came up against Jerusalem. [26m]And he took away the treasures of the house of the LORD and the treasures of the king's house; he took away everything. He also took away all the gold shields [n]which Solomon had made. [27]Then King Rehoboam made bronze shields in their place, and committed *them* to the hands of the captains of the guard, who guarded the doorway of the king's house. [28]And whenever the king entered the house of the LORD, the guards carried them, then brought them back into the guardroom. [29o]Now the rest of the acts of Rehoboam, and all that he did, *are* they not written in the book of the chronicles of the kings of Judah? [30]And there was [p]war between Rehoboam and Jeroboam all *their* days. [31q]So Rehoboam rested with his fathers, and was buried with his fathers in the City of David. [r]His mother's name *was* Naamah, an Ammonitess. Then [s]Abijam* his son reigned in his place.

Abijam Reigns in Judah

15 [a]In the eighteenth year of King Jeroboam the son of Nebat, Abijam became king over Judah. [2]He reigned three years in Jerusalem. [b]His mother's name *was* [c]Maachah the granddaughter of [d]Abishalom. [3]And he walked in all the sins of his father, which he had done before him; [e]his heart was not loyal to the LORD his God, as was the heart of his father David. [4]Nevertheless [f]for David's sake

---

14:17 *Tirzah.* Famed for its beauty (Song 6:4), Tirzah was a royal retreat and the capital of the northern kingdom's first two dynasties (15:33).

14:19 *the book of the chronicles of the kings of Israel.* This book is mentioned 15 times in Kings. Apparently it was an official record of events in the southern kingdom down to the days of Jehoiakim. This work should not be confused with the biblical books of Chronicles, which were written much later, after the exile.

14:20 *Jeroboam.* Each of the subsequent kings of Israel was judged against the example of the wickedness of Jeroboam (15:34). Only with Ahab was a worse pattern set (16:31).

14:23 *high places.* The high places were a problem throughout the history of Judah and Israel (Mic. 1:3). At times, the worship offered on them may have been done sincerely, in true worship of God (3:2–4; 2 Kin. 12:3). But these were also the places in which Canaanite worship rites were practiced, and images set up to honor Baal and Asherah. Even when the worship on the high places was not mixed with pagan rituals, it was not in accord with the law of Moses (see 2 Chr. 1:3).

14:24 *abominations.* This is an exceedingly strong term; it describes perverted activities that impelled

God to dispossess the Canaanite peoples from their land (Deut. 18:9–12).

14:26 *treasures of the house of the LORD.* The sacking of the temple is particularly shocking when we think of the long and detailed description of Solomon's building and furnishing the house of the Lord.

15:2 *Maachah.* Elsewhere she is described as "the daughter of Uriel of Gibeah" (2 Chr. 13:2), and "the daughter of Absalom" (2 Chr. 11:21). It is thought that she was the granddaughter of Absalom, the daughter of Uriel of Gibeah and Absalom's daughter Tamar (2 Sam. 14:27). She was the favorite of Rehoboam's many wives. The fact that she is mentioned in

14:16 [r] 1 Kin. 12:30; 13:34; 15:30, 34; 16:2 **14:17** [u] Song 6:4 [v] 1 Kin. 14:12 **14:18** [w] 1 Kin. 14:13 **14:19** [x] 2 Chr. 13:2–20 **14:20** [y] 1 Kin. 15:25 **14:21** [z] 2 Chr. 12:13 [a] 1 Kin. 11:32, 36 [b] 1 Kin. 14:31 **14:22** [c] 2 Chr. 12:1, 14 [d] Deut. 32:21 **14:23** [e] Deut. 12:2 [f] [Deut. 16:22] [g] [2 Kin. 17:9, 10] [h] Is. 57:5 **14:24** [i] Deut. 23:17 [j] Deut. 20:18 [k] [Deut. 9:4, 5] **14:25** [l] 1 Kin. 11:40 **14:26** [m] 2 Chr. 12:9–11 [n] 1 Kin. 10:17 **14:29** [o] 2 Chr. 12:15, 16 **14:30** [p] 1 Kin. 12:21–24; 15:6 **14:31** [q] 2 Chr. 12:16 [r] 1 Kin. 14:21 [s] 2 Chr. 12:16 **15:1** [a] 2 Chr. 13:1 **15:2** [b] 2 Chr. 11:20–22 [c] 2 Chr. 13:2 [d] 2 Chr. 11:21 **15:3** [e] Ps. 119:80 **15:4** [f] 2 Sam. 21:17

the LORD his God gave him a lamp in Jerusalem, by setting up his son after him and by establishing Jerusalem; ⁵because David ᵍdid what was right in the eyes of the LORD, and had not turned aside from anything that He commanded him all the days of his life, ʰexcept in the matter of Uriah the Hittite. ⁶ⁱAnd there was war between Rehoboam* and Jeroboam all the days of his life. ⁷ʲNow the rest of the acts of Abijam, and all that he did, are they not written in the book of the chronicles of the kings of Judah? And there was war between Abijam and Jeroboam.

⁸ᵏSo Abijam rested with his fathers, and they buried him in the City of David. Then Asa his son reigned in his place.

Asa Reigns in Judah

⁹In the twentieth year of Jeroboam king of Israel, Asa became king over Judah. ¹⁰And he reigned forty-one years in Jerusalem. His grandmother's name was Maachah the granddaughter of Abishalom. ¹¹ˡAsa did what was right in the eyes of the LORD, as did his father David. ¹²ᵐAnd he banished the perverted persons* from the land, and removed all the idols that his fathers had made. ¹³Also he removed ⁿMaachah his grandmother from being queen mother, because she had made an obscene image of Asherah.* And Asa cut down her obscene image and ᵒburned it by the Brook Kidron. ¹⁴ᵖBut the high places were not removed. Nevertheless Asa's ᵍheart was loyal to the LORD all his days. ¹⁵He also brought into the house of the LORD the things which his father ʳhad dedicated, and the things which he himself had dedicated: silver and gold and utensils.

¹⁶Now there was war between Asa and Baasha king of Israel all their days. ¹⁷And ˢBaasha king of Israel came up against Judah, and built ᵗRamah, ᵘthat he might let none go out or come in to Asa king of Judah. ¹⁸Then Asa took all the silver and gold that was left in the treasuries of the house of the LORD and the treasuries of the king's house, and delivered them into the hand of his servants. And King Asa sent them to ᵛBen-Hadad the son of Tabrimmon, the son of Hezion, king of Syria, who dwelt in ʷDamascus, saying, ¹⁹"Let there be a treaty between you and me, as there was between my father and your father. See, I have sent you a present of silver and gold. Come and break your treaty with Baasha king of Israel, so that he will withdraw from me."

* 15:6 Following Masoretic Text, Septuagint, Targum, and Vulgate; some Hebrew manuscripts and Syriac read Abijam.   * 15:12 Hebrew qedeshim, that is, those practicing sodomy and prostitution in religious rituals   * 15:13 A Canaanite goddess

---

connection with both her son Abijam and her grandson Asa (vv. 10,12) makes it appear that she was an important figure, probably wielding a good deal of influence.
15:4 for David's sake. That is, because of God's love for David and the promise He had made to him (2 Sam. 7). **lamp.** This is one of the lovely images of God's intended blessing on the Davidic house.
15:5 Perseverance—The lamp of God was still shining in Jerusalem during the reign of Abijam, even though he was not wholly devoted to the Lord, nor was his father who reigned before him. In spite of the sins of Abijam and his father, God continued to let His light shine in Jerusalem for the sake of David, whose heart was all for the Lord. In a similar way, our actions will affect the generations which follow us. If we are committed to God's ways, and willing to stand for what is right, our children will benefit; if we selfishly follow our own pleasures, our children often are left picking up the pieces.
15:10 His grandmother's name was Maachah. Literally "mother's." It is apparent from verse 2 that Maachah was Asa's grandmother. It is important to remember that many times the Hebrews used the terms "father, mother, son, daughter" loosely, to indicate ancestry rather than exact generation (v. 3).
15:13 he removed. Asa's many spiritual activities (2 Chr. 14:2–5; 15:1–18) are telescoped into a few statements here. Although the reforms mentioned took place early in Asa's reign (2 Chr. 14:2–5), the chronicler indicates that the deposing of Maachah took place in the fifteenth year of his rule (895 B.C.). Maachah's removal came as a result of a time of covenant renewal (2 Chr. 15:1–16) and a consequent reaction against her vile idolatry.

15:14 high places. In some instances, the high places were places where the Lord was worshiped (1 Sam. 9:12); in other cases they were used for pagan purposes (2 Chr. 14:2–3).
15:17 Ramah. Ramah was about five and a half miles north of Jerusalem on the main north-south commercial route through the land, and it was therefore of great importance to both kingdoms. It gave east-west access to both the foothills of Ephraim and the Mediterranean coast, so it was of strategic military importance as well. Baasha was striking a blow for control of the center of the land.
15:18–19 Unfaithfulness—Asa's life was a mixture of good and evil, faithfulness and faithlessness. He took a stand against the rampant idolatry, removing male cult prostitutes and idolatrous worship, and even demoting his own grandmother to reduce her evil influence (v. 13). Yet later in his life, he signally failed to trust God for either safety or health. When Baasha, king of Israel, attacked him, he sought help from the Syrians (vv. 17–18) rather than from God, and resented and rejected the prophetic rebuke he received (2 Chr. 16:7–10). Near the end of his life, Asa suffered a crippling disease in his feet; yet even in this "he did not seek the LORD, but the physicians" (2 Chr. 16:12).

15:5 ᵍ 1 Kin. 9:4; 14:8 ʰ 2 Sam. 11:3, 15–17; 12:9, 10
15:6 ⁱ 1 Kin. 14:30   **15:7** ʲ 2 Chr. 13:2–22   **15:8** ᵏ 2 Chr. 14:1   **15:11** ˡ 2 Chr. 14:2   **15:12** ᵐ 1 Kin. 14:24; 22:46
15:13 ⁿ 2 Chr. 15:16–18 ᵒ Ex. 32:20   **15:14** ᵖ 1 Kin. 3:2; 22:43 ᵍ 1 Kin. 8:61; 15:3   **15:15** ʳ 1 Kin. 7:51
15:17 ˢ 2 Chr. 16:1–6 ᵗ Josh. 18:25 ᵘ 1 Kin. 12:26–29
15:18 ᵛ 2 Chr. 16:2 ʷ 1 Kin. 11:23, 24

20So Ben-Hadad heeded King Asa, and ˣsent the captains of his armies against the cities of Israel. He attacked ʸIjon, ᶻDan, ᵃAbel Beth Maachah, and all Chinneroth, with all the land of Naphtali. 21Now it happened, when Baasha heard *it*, that he stopped building Ramah, and remained in ᵇTirzah.

22ᶜThen King Asa made a proclamation throughout all Judah; none *was* exempted. And they took away the stones and timber of Ramah, which Baasha had used for building; and with them King Asa built ᵈGeba of Benjamin, and ᵉMizpah.

23The rest of all the acts of Asa, all his might, all that he did, and the cities which he built, *are* they not written in the book of the chronicles of the kings of Judah? But ᶠin the time of his old age he was diseased in his feet. 24So Asa rested with his fathers, and was buried with his fathers in the City of David his father. ᵍThen ʰJehoshaphat his son reigned in his place.

Nadab Reigns in Israel

25Now ⁱNadab the son of Jeroboam became king over Israel in the second year of Asa king of Judah, and he reigned over Israel two years. 26And he did evil in the sight of the LORD, and walked in the way of his father, and in ʲhis sin by which he had made Israel sin.

27ᵏThen Baasha the son of Ahijah, of the house of Issachar, conspired against him. And Baasha killed him at ˡGibbethon, which *belonged* to the Philistines, while Nadab and all Israel laid siege to Gibbethon. 28Baasha killed him in the third year of Asa king of Judah, and reigned in his place. 29And it was so, when he became king, *that* he killed all the house of Jeroboam. He did not leave to Jeroboam anyone that breathed, until he had destroyed him, according to ᵐthe word of the LORD which He had spoken by His servant Ahijah the Shilonite, 30ⁿbecause of the sins of Jeroboam, which he had sinned and by which he had made Israel sin, because of his provocation with which he had provoked the LORD God of Israel to anger.

31Now the rest of the acts of Nadab, and

all that he did, *are* they not written in the book of the chronicles of the kings of Israel? 32ᵒAnd there was war between Asa and Baasha king of Israel all their days.

Baasha Reigns in Israel

33In the third year of Asa king of Judah, Baasha the son of Ahijah became king over all Israel in Tirzah, and *reigned* twenty-four years. 34He did evil in the sight of the LORD, and walked in ᵖthe way of Jeroboam, and in his sin by which he had made Israel sin.

16 Then the word of the LORD came to ᵃJehu the son of ᵇHanani, against ᶜBaasha, saying: 2ᵈ"Inasmuch as I lifted you out of the dust and made you ruler over My people Israel, and ᵉyou have walked in the way of Jeroboam, and have made My people Israel sin, to provoke Me to anger with their sins, 3surely I will ᶠtake away the posterity of Baasha and the posterity of his house, and I will make your house like ᵍthe house of Jeroboam the son of Nebat. 4The dogs shall eat ʰwhoever belongs to Baasha and dies in the city, and the birds of the air shall eat whoever dies in the fields."

5Now the rest of the acts of Baasha, what he did, and his might, ⁱare they not written in the book of the chronicles of the kings of Israel? 6So Baasha rested with his fathers and was buried in ʲTirzah. Then Elah his son reigned in his place.

7And also the word of the LORD came by the prophet ᵏJehu the son of Hanani against Baasha and his house, because of all the evil that he did in the sight of the LORD in provoking Him to anger with the work of his hands, in being like the house of Jeroboam, and because ˡhe killed them.

Elah Reigns in Israel

8In the twenty-sixth year of Asa king of Judah, Elah the son of Baasha became king over Israel, *and reigned* two years in Tirzah. 9ᵐNow his servant Zimri, commander of half *his* chariots, conspired against him as he was in Tirzah drinking himself drunk in the house of Arza, ⁿsteward of *his* house in Tirzah. 10And Zimri went in and struck him and killed him in

---

15:25 Nadab. His name means "generous" or "noble," but he did not live up to his name.
15:29 according to the word of the LORD. The death of Nadab was in line with the prophetic fulfillment of God's judgment on the house of Jeroboam (14:9,16). Nonetheless, the manner of his death was condemned by God through His prophet Jehu (16:7).
16:1–7 Jehu. This Jehu is not to be confused with Jehu the king of Israel (2 Kin. 9:2). Jehu the prophet came from the southern kingdom; his long prophetic ministry lasted into the days of Jehoshaphat. Like his father before him, he confronted sin fearlessly, even in the royal house (2 Chr. 16:7–10).
16:10 Zimri. Zimri's treacherous act was the prophesied judgment on Baasha and Elah for their wickedness.

15:20 ˣ1 Kin. 20:1 ʸ2 Kin. 15:29 ᶻJudg. 18:29 ᵘ2 Sam. 20:14, 15 **15:21** ᵇ1 Kin. 14:17; 16:15–18 **15:22** ᶜ2 Chr. 16:6 ᵈJosh. 21:17 ᵉJosh. 18:26 **15:23** ᶠ2 Chr. 16:11–14 **15:24** ᵍ2 Chr. 17:1 ʰMatt. 1:8 **15:25** ⁱ1 Kin. 14:20 **15:26** ʲ1 Kin. 12:28–33; 14:16 **15:27** ᵏ1 Kin. 14:14 ˡJosh. 19:44; 21:23 **15:29** ᵐ1 Kin. 14:10–14 **15:30** ⁿ1 Kin. 14:9, 16 **15:32** ᵒ1 Kin. 15:16 **15:34** ᵖ1 Kin. 13:33; 14:16 **16:1** ᵃ2 Chr. 19:2; 20:34 ᵇ2 Chr. 16:7–10 ᶜ1 Kin. 15:27 **16:2** ᵈ1 Kin. 14:7 ᵉ1 Kin. 12:25–33; 15:34 **16:3** ᶠ1 Kin. 16:11; 21:21 ᵍ1 Kin. 14:10; 15:29 **16:4** ʰ1 Kin. 14:11; 21:24 **16:5** ⁱ2 Chr. 16:11 **16:6** ʲ1 Kin. 14:17; 15:21 **16:7** ᵏ1 Kin. 16:1 ˡ1 Kin. 15:27, 29 **16:9** ᵐ2 Kin. 9:30–33 ⁿ1 Kin. 18:3

the twenty-seventh year of Asa king of Judah, and reigned in his place.

[11] Then it came to pass, when he began to reign, as soon as he was seated on his throne, *that* he killed all the household of Baasha; he [o]did not leave him one male, neither of his relatives nor of his friends. [12] Thus Zimri destroyed all the household of Baasha, [p]according to the word of the LORD, which He spoke against Baasha by Jehu the prophet, [13] for all the sins of Baasha and the sins of Elah his son, by which they had sinned and by which they had made Israel sin, in provoking the LORD God of Israel to anger [q]with their idols.

[14] Now the rest of the acts of Elah, and all that he did, *are* they not written in the book of the chronicles of the kings of Israel?

Zimri Reigns in Israel

[15] In the twenty-seventh year of Asa king of Judah, Zimri had reigned in Tirzah seven days. And the people *were* encamped [r]against Gibbethon, which *belonged* to the Philistines. [16] Now the people *who were* encamped heard it said, "Zimri has conspired and also has killed the king." So all Israel made Omri, the commander of the army, king over Israel that day in the camp. [17] Then Omri and all Israel with him went up from Gibbethon, and they besieged Tirzah. [18] And it happened, when Zimri saw that the city was taken, that he went into the citadel of the king's house and burned the king's house down upon himself with fire, and died, [19] because of the sins which he had committed in doing evil in the sight of the LORD, [s]in walking in the [t]way of Jeroboam, and in his sin which he had committed to make Israel sin.

[20] Now the rest of the acts of Zimri, and the treason he committed, *are* they not written in the book of the chronicles of the kings of Israel?

Omri Reigns in Israel

[21] Then the people of Israel were divided into two parts: half of the people followed Tibni the son of Ginath, to make him king, and half followed Omri. [22] But the people

who followed Omri prevailed over the people who followed Tibni the son of Ginath. So Tibni died and Omri reigned. [23] In the thirty-first year of Asa king of Judah, Omri became king over Israel, *and reigned* twelve years. Six years he reigned in [u]Tirzah. [24] And he bought the hill of Samaria from Shemer for two talents of silver; then he built on the hill, and called the name of the city which he built, [v]Samaria, after the name of Shemer, owner of the hill. [25w]Omri did evil in the eyes of the LORD, and did worse than all who *were* before him. [26] For he [x]walked in all the ways of Jeroboam the son of Nebat, and in his sin by which he had made Israel sin, provoking the LORD God of Israel to anger with their [y]idols.

[27] Now the rest of the acts of Omri which he did, and the might that he showed, *are* they not written in the book of the chronicles of the kings of Israel?

[28] So Omri rested with his fathers and was buried in Samaria. Then Ahab his son reigned in his place.

Ahab Reigns in Israel

[29] In the thirty-eighth year of Asa king of Judah, Ahab the son of Omri became king over Israel; and Ahab the son of Omri reigned over Israel in Samaria twenty-two years. [30] Now Ahab the son of Omri did evil in the sight of the LORD, more than all who *were* before him. [31] And it came to pass, as though it had been a trivial thing for him to walk in the sins of Jeroboam the son of Nebat, [z]that he took as wife Jezebel the daughter of Ethbaal, king of the [a]Sidonians; [b]and he went and served Baal and worshiped him. [32] Then he set up an altar for Baal in [c]the temple of Baal, which he had built in Samaria. [33d]And Ahab made a wooden image.* Ahab [e]did more to provoke the LORD God of Israel to anger than all the kings of Israel who were before him. [34] In his days Hiel of Bethel built Jericho. He laid its foundation with Abiram his firstborn, and with his youngest *son* Segub he set up its gates, [f]according to the word of

---

* **16:33** Hebrew *Asherah*, a Canaanite goddess

16:23 Omri. Omri's exploits are commemorated in the Moabite Stone and the Assyrian annals. Indeed, he was so important to the Assyrians that they called Israel "the House of Omri" long after his death. Yet the author of Kings describes little of Omri's achievements, because he did evil in the eyes of the Lord.

16:30 Ahab. In Ahab we come to the very lowest point in the degeneration of the spiritual life of the kings of Israel. Each of the kings of the northern kingdom had been guilty of walking in the steps of Jeroboam, but Ahab's sins made Jeroboam's look trivial. His greatest crime was his promotion of Baal worship as the state religion.

16:31 Jezebel. Ahab's marriage to Jezebel was politically important and demonstrated the rising prominence of Israel's third dynasty. Her father was both king and priest of Baal in Sidon; similarly, Jezebel was

princess and priestess of Baal. Her Phoenician name was Abizebel, meaning "my father [Baal] is noble." The Hebrew scribes purposely dropped a letter from her name, calling her Jezebel, "lacking honor." **went and served Baal and worshiped him.** Ahab completely abandoned even a skewed worship of God, and became a full-fledged worshiper of Baal.

16:34 built Jericho. Jericho had been semi-occupied at various times (Judg. 3:13), but not as a permanently

16:11 [o] 1 Sam. 25:22   **16:12** [p] 1 Kin. 16:3   **16:13** [q] Deut. 32:21   **16:15** [r] 1 Kin. 15:27   **16:19** [s] 1 Kin. 15:26, 34 [t] 1 Kin. 12:25–33   **16:23** [u] 1 Kin. 15:21   **16:24** [v] 1 Kin. 13:32   **16:25** [w] Mic. 6:16   **16:26** [x] 1 Kin. 16:19 [y] 1 Kin. 16:13   **16:31** [z] Deut. 7:3   [a] Judg. 18:7   [b] 1 Kin. 21:25, 26 **16:32** [c] 2 Kin. 10:21, 26, 27   **16:33** [d] 2 Kin. 13:6   [e] 1 Kin. 14:9; 16:29, 30; 21:25   **16:34** [f] Josh. 6:26

the Lord, which He had spoken through Joshua the son of Nun.*

Elijah Proclaims a Drought

17 And Elijah the Tishbite, of the ᵃinhabitants of Gilead, said to Ahab, ᵇ"As the Lord God of Israel lives, ᶜbefore whom I stand, ᵈthere shall not be dew nor rain ᵉthese years, except at my word."

²Then the word of the Lord came to him, saying, ³"Get away from here and turn eastward, and hide by the Brook Cherith, which flows into the Jordan. ⁴And it will be *that* you shall drink from the brook, and I have commanded the ᶠravens to feed you there."

⁵So he went and did according to the word of the Lord, for he went and stayed by the Brook Cherith, which flows into the Jordan. ⁶The ravens brought him bread and meat in the morning, and bread and meat in the evening; and he drank from the brook. ⁷And it happened after a while that the brook dried up, because there had been no rain in the land.

Elijah and the Widow

⁸Then the word of the Lord came to him, saying, ⁹"Arise, go to ᵍZarephath, which *belongs* to ʰSidon, and dwell there. See, I have commanded a widow there to provide for you." ¹⁰So he arose and went to Zarephath. And when he came to the gate of the city, indeed a widow *was* there gathering sticks. And he called to her and said, "Please bring me a little water in a cup, that I may drink." ¹¹And as she was going to get *it*, he called to her and said, "Please bring me a morsel of bread in your hand."

¹²So she said, "As the Lord your God lives, I do not have bread, only a handful of flour in a bin, and a little oil in a jar; and see, I *am* gathering a couple of sticks that I may go in and prepare it for myself and my son, that we may eat it, and ⁱdie."

¹³And Elijah said to her, "Do not fear; go *and* do as you have said, but make me a small cake from it first, and bring *it* to me; and afterward make *some* for yourself and your son. ¹⁴For thus says the Lord God of Israel: 'The bin of flour shall not be used up, nor shall the jar of oil run dry, until the day the Lord sends rain on the earth.'"

¹⁵So she went away and did according to the word of Elijah; and she and he and her household ate for *many* days. ¹⁶The bin of flour was not used up, nor did the jar of oil run dry, according to the word of the Lord which He spoke by Elijah.

Elijah Revives the Widow's Son

¹⁷Now it happened after these things *that* the son of the woman who owned the house became sick. And his sickness was so serious that there was no breath left in him. ¹⁸So she said to Elijah, ʲ"What have I to do with you, O man of God? Have you come to me to bring my sin to remembrance, and to kill my son?"

¹⁹And he said to her, "Give me your son." So he took him out of her arms and carried him to the upper room where he was staying, and laid him on his own bed. ²⁰Then he cried out to the Lord and said, "O Lord my God, have You also brought tragedy on the widow with whom I lodge, by killing her son?" ²¹ᵏAnd he stretched himself out on the child three times, and cried out to the Lord and said, "O Lord my God, I pray, let this child's soul come back to him." ²²Then the Lord heard the voice of Elijah; and the soul of the child came back to him, and he ˡrevived.

²³And Elijah took the child and brought him down from the upper room into the house, and gave him to his mother. And Elijah said, "See, your son lives!"

²⁴Then the woman said to Elijah, "Now by this ᵐI know that you *are* a man of God, *and* that the word of the Lord in your mouth *is* the truth."

* **16:34** Compare Joshua 6:26

---

occupied fortified city. Either Hiel offered his sons as foundation sacrifices, or they died in some mishap. However it happened, Joshua's curse was carried out. **17:1 Elijah.** No prophet had arisen since Moses who was like Elijah. His name means "the Lord is God," a statement which was the core of his message to the unbelieving nation. **dew nor rain.** Elijah's pronouncement was an immediate challenge: Baal was supposed to govern the weather, but Elijah was declaring him powerless before the living God. **17:6 ravens.** It is interesting to note that ravens were considered unclean birds (Lev. 11:15). **17:9 Zarephath.** Zarephath was in Phoenician territory, seven miles south of Sidon, the stronghold of Baal. The Lord's sustaining Elijah first by a raven and then by a widow provided the prophet with a dramatic test of faith at the outset of his ministry. The widow, too, would be taught the value of trusting in God alone. **17:14 shall not be used up.** While an apostate Israelite nation suffered because of the drought, God

supplied the daily necessities to a non-Israelite who willingly took Him at His word. Both the prophet and the widow were reminded of the value of personal trust in Him who alone is sufficient to meet every need (Phil. 4:19). **17:17–23 Resurrection**—Resurrection from the dead was not a miracle ordinary people expected to see, even from a prophet of God. This widow, however, would have had reason to hope for God's help. She had opened her home to Elijah, and she had seen firsthand His power and the results of complete trust in Him. Yet it was not until she had seen the miracle of her son brought back to life that she expressed faith in God.

17:1 ᵃ Judg. 12:4 ᵇ 2 Kin. 3:14; 5:20 ᶜ Deut. 10:8 ᵈ James 5:17 ᵉ Luke 4:25 **17:4** ᶠ Job 38:41 **17:9** ᵍ Obad. 20 ʰ 2 Sam. 24:6 **17:12** ⁱ Deut. 28:23, 24 **17:18** ʲ Luke 5:8 **17:21** ᵏ 2 Kin. 4:34, 35 **17:22** ˡ Heb. 11:35 **17:24** ᵐ John 2:11; 3:2; 16:30

Elijah's Message to Ahab

18 And it came to pass *after* ᵃmany days that the word of the LORD came to Elijah, in the third year, saying, "Go, present yourself to Ahab, and ᵇI will send rain on the earth."

²So Elijah went to present himself to Ahab; and *there was* a severe famine in Samaria. ³And Ahab had called Obadiah, who *was* in charge of *his* house. (Now Obadiah feared the LORD greatly. ⁴For so it was, while Jezebel massacred the prophets of the LORD, that Obadiah had taken one hundred prophets and hidden them, fifty to a cave, and had fed them with bread and water.) ⁵And Ahab had said to Obadiah, "Go into the land to all the springs of water and to all the brooks; perhaps we may find grass to keep the horses and mules alive, so that we will not have to kill any livestock." ⁶So they divided the land between them to explore it; Ahab went one way by himself, and Obadiah went another way by himself.

⁷Now as Obadiah was on his way, suddenly Elijah met him; and he ᶜrecognized him, and fell on his face, and said, "*Is that* you, my lord Elijah?"

⁸And he answered him, "*It is* I. Go, tell your master, 'Elijah *is here*.'"

⁹So he said, "How have I sinned, that you are delivering your servant into the hand of Ahab, to kill me? ¹⁰*As* the LORD your God lives, there is no nation or kingdom where my master has not sent someone to hunt for you; and when they said, '*He is not here*,' he took an oath from the kingdom or nation that they could not find you. ¹¹And now you say, 'Go, tell your master, "Elijah *is here*"'! ¹²And it shall come to pass, *as soon as* I am gone from you, that ᵈthe Spirit of the LORD will carry you to a place I do not know; so when I go and tell Ahab, and he cannot find you, he will kill me. But I your servant have feared the LORD from my youth. ¹³Was it not reported to my lord what I did when Jezebel killed the prophets of the LORD, how I hid one hundred men of the LORD's prophets, fifty to a cave, and fed them with bread and water? ¹⁴And now you say, 'Go, tell your master, "Elijah *is here*."' He will kill me!"

¹⁵Then Elijah said, "*As* the LORD of hosts lives, before whom I stand, I will surely present myself to him today."

¹⁶So Obadiah went to meet Ahab, and told him; and Ahab went to meet Elijah.

¹⁷Then it happened, when Ahab saw Elijah, that Ahab said to him, ᵉ"*Is that* you, O ᶠtroubler of Israel?"

¹⁸And he answered, "I have not troubled Israel, but you and your father's house *have*, ᵍin that you have forsaken the commandments of the LORD and have followed the Baals. ¹⁹Now therefore, send *and* gather all Israel to me on ʰMount Carmel, the four hundred and fifty prophets of Baal, ⁱand the four hundred prophets of Asherah,* who eat at Jezebel's table."

Elijah's Mount Carmel Victory

²⁰So Ahab sent for all the children of Israel, and ʲgathered the prophets together on Mount Carmel. ²¹And Elijah came to all the people, and said, ᵏ"How long will you falter between two opinions? If the LORD *is* God, follow Him; but if Baal, ˡfollow him." But the people answered him not a word. ²²Then Elijah said to the people, ᵐ"I alone am left a prophet of the LORD; ⁿbut Baal's prophets *are* four hundred and fifty men. ²³Therefore let them give us two bulls; and let them choose one bull for themselves, cut it in pieces, and lay *it* on the wood, but put no fire *under it*; and I will prepare the other bull, and lay *it* on the wood, but put no fire *under it*. ²⁴Then you call on the name of your gods, and I will call on the name of the LORD; and the God who ᵒanswers by fire, He is God."

So all the people answered and said, "It is well spoken."

²⁵Now Elijah said to the prophets of Baal, "Choose one bull for yourselves and prepare *it* first, for you *are* many; and call on the name of your god, but put no fire *under it*."

²⁶So they took the bull which was given them, and they prepared *it*, and called on the name of Baal from morning even till noon, saying, "O Baal, hear us!" But *there*

---

* 18:19 A Canaanite goddess

18:3 Obadiah. Although tradition has sometimes identified them, this Obadiah is probably not the author of the prophetic book of that name. It is clear that this Obadiah was a man of great faith, whose heroic actions give us a more balanced picture of the situation people of faith endured in Israel at this time.
18:18 Baals. The wording indicates that Ahab had a practice of attending services at various local shrines where this deity was worshiped.
18:19 Baal . . . Asherah. The worship of Baal and Asherah held a constant fascination for Israel from earliest times (Ex. 34:13; Num. 25; Judg. 2:13) and eventually caused Israel's demise (2 Kin. 17:16–18).
18:21 two opinions. We are confronted today with a choice no less momentous than the Israelites' choice

between the Lord and Baal. Here is a broad road that leads down to destruction; there, a way narrow and difficult that leads upward to life (Matt. 7:13–14). God doesn't share devotion with anything or anyone. We have to make the choice to be on God's side—we cannot serve two masters. We will either gratify self, conforming to the corrupt pattern of this present age, or glorify Him who alone is worthy of worship.

18:1 ᵃ Luke 4:25 ᵇ Deut. 28:12 **18:7** ᶜ 2 Kin. 1:6–8
18:12 ᵈ Acts 8:39 **18:17** ᵉ 1 Kin. 21:20 ᶠ Josh. 7:25
18:18 ᵍ [2 Chr. 15:2] **18:19** ʰ Josh. 19:26 ⁱ 1 Kin. 16:33
18:20 ʲ 1 Kin. 22:6 **18:21** ᵏ [Matt. 6:24] ˡ Josh. 24:15
18:22 ᵐ 1 Kin. 19:10, 14 ⁿ 1 Kin. 18:19 **18:24** ᵒ 1 Chr. 21:26

was ᵖno voice; no one answered. Then they leaped about the altar which they had made.

²⁷And so it was, at noon, that Elijah mocked them and said, "Cry aloud, for he *is* a god; either he is meditating, or he is busy, or he is on a journey, *or* perhaps he is sleeping and must be awakened." ²⁸So they cried aloud, and ᑫcut themselves, as was their custom, with knives and lances, until the blood gushed out on them. ²⁹And when midday was past, ʳthey prophesied until the *time* of the offering of the *evening* sacrifice. But *there was* ˢno voice; no one answered, no one paid attention.

³⁰Then Elijah said to all the people, "Come near to me." So all the people came near to him. ᵗAnd he repaired the altar of the Lᴏʀᴅ *that was* broken down. ³¹And Elijah took twelve stones, according to the number of the tribes of the sons of Jacob, to whom the word of the Lᴏʀᴅ had come, saying, ᵘ"Israel shall be your name."* ³²Then with the stones he built an altar ᵛin the name of the Lᴏʀᴅ; and he made a trench around the altar large enough to hold two seahs of seed. ³³And he ʷput the wood in order, cut the bull in pieces, and laid *it* on the wood, and said, "Fill four waterpots with water, and ˣpour *it* on the burnt sacrifice and on the wood." ³⁴Then he said, "Do *it* a second time," and they did *it* a second time; and he said, "Do *it* a third time," and they did *it* a third time. ³⁵So the water ran all around the altar; and he also filled ʸthe trench with water.

³⁶And it came to pass, at *the time of* the offering of the *evening* sacrifice, that Elijah the prophet came near and said, "Lᴏʀᴅ ᶻGod of Abraham, Isaac, and Israel, ᵃlet it be known this day that You *are* God in Israel and I *am* Your servant, and that ᵇI have done all these things at Your word. ³⁷Hear me, O Lᴏʀᴅ, hear me, that this people may know that You *are* the Lᴏʀᴅ God, and *that* You have turned their hearts back to You again."

³⁸Then ᶜthe fire of the Lᴏʀᴅ fell and consumed the burnt sacrifice, and the wood and the stones and the dust, and it

licked up the water that *was* in the trench. ³⁹Now when all the people saw *it*, they fell on their faces; and they said, ᵈ"The Lᴏʀᴅ, He *is* God! The Lᴏʀᴅ, He *is* God!"

⁴⁰And Elijah said to them, ᵉ"Seize the prophets of Baal! Do not let one of them escape!" So they seized them; and Elijah brought them down to the Brook ᶠKishon and ᵍexecuted them there.

The Drought Ends

⁴¹Then Elijah said to Ahab, "Go up, eat and drink; for *there is* the sound of abundance of rain." ⁴²So Ahab went up to eat and drink. And Elijah went up to the top of Carmel; ʰthen he bowed down on the ground, and put his face between his knees, ⁴³and said to his servant, "Go up now, look toward the sea."

So he went up and looked, and said, "*There is* nothing." And seven times he said, "Go again."

⁴⁴Then it came to pass the seventh *time*, that he said, "There is a cloud, as small as a man's hand, rising out of the sea!" So he said, "Go up, say to Ahab, 'Prepare *your* chariot, and go down before the rain stops you.'"

⁴⁵Now it happened in the meantime that the sky became black with clouds and wind, and there was a heavy rain. So Ahab rode away and went to Jezreel. ⁴⁶Then the ⁱhand of the Lᴏʀᴅ came upon Elijah; and he ʲgirded up his loins and ran ahead of Ahab to the entrance of Jezreel.

Elijah Escapes from Jezebel

19 And Ahab told Jezebel all that Elijah had done, also how he had ᵃexecuted all the prophets with the sword. ²Then Jezebel sent a messenger to Elijah, saying, ᵇ"So let the gods do *to me*, and more also, if I do not make your life as the life of one of them by tomorrow about this time." ³And when he saw *that*, he arose and ran for his life, and went to Beersheba, which *belongs* to Judah, and left his servant there.

---

* **18:31** Genesis 32:28

18:27 *busy, or he is on a journey.* "On a journey" is a euphemism with the same meaning as our euphemism "on a comfort break." Elijah was piling on the sarcasm—a god is not supposed to have embarrassing bodily functions.

18:30 *repaired the altar.* This was an earlier altar that had been used by the true people of God. Elijah avoided all contact with the altar that was associated with Baal.

18:36 *Lᴏʀᴅ God of Abraham, Isaac and Israel.* This phrase, so characteristic of worship in the early period (Gen. 50:24; Ex. 3:6), reminded Elijah's hearers that the God who made the covenant with Abraham was still the God of the northern kingdom, and the nation's only hope of life, protection, and blessing (Deut. 30:20).

18:46 *girded up his loins.* Elijah tucked his garment

into his sash, enabling him to run freely the 13 miles to Jezreel.

19:3 *ran for his life.* One may ask why a man who had seen God's mighty power should give way to fear, but we must realize that God did not criticize Elijah for his reaction. Elijah was not a superhero but a man with a nature like ours (James 5:17). He had seen a great

18:26 ᵖ Jer. 10:5   **18:28** ᑫ [Deut. 14:1]   **18:29** ʳ Ex. 29:39, 41   ˢ 1 Kin. 18:26   **18:30** ᵗ 2 Chr. 33:16   **18:31** ᵘ Gen. 32:28; 35:10   **18:32** ᵛ [Col. 3:17]   **18:33** ʷ Lev. 1:6–8   ˣ Judg. 6:20   **18:35** ʸ 1 Kin. 18:32, 38   **18:36** ᶻ Ex. 3:6; 4:5   ᵃ 1 Kin. 8:43   ᵇ Num. 16:28   **18:38** ᶜ 1 Chr. 21:26   **18:39** ᵈ 1 Kin. 18:21, 24   **18:40** ᵉ 2 Kin. 10:25   ᶠ Judg. 4:7; 5:21   ᵍ [Deut. 13:5; 18:20]   **18:42** ʰ James 5:17, 18   **18:46** ⁱ 2 Kin. 3:15   ʲ 2 Kin. 4:29; 9:1   **19:1** ᵃ 1 Kin. 18:40   **19:2** ᵇ Ruth 1:17

4But he himself went a day's journey into the wilderness, and came and sat down under a broom tree. And he cprayed that he might die, and said, "It is enough! Now, LORD, take my life, for I *am* no better than my fathers!"

5Then as he lay and slept under a broom tree, suddenly an angel* touched him, and said to him, "Arise *and* eat." 6Then he looked, and there by his head *was* a cake baked on coals, and a jar of water. So he ate and drank, and lay down again. 7And the angel* of the LORD came back the second time, and touched him, and said, "Arise *and* eat, because the journey *is* too great for you." 8So he arose, and ate and drank; and he went in the strength of that food forty days and dforty nights as far as eHoreb, the mountain of God.

9And there he went into a cave, and spent the night in that place; and behold, the word of the LORD *came* to him, and He said to him, "What are you doing here, Elijah?"

10So he said, f"I have been very gzealous for the LORD God of hosts; for the children of Israel have forsaken Your covenant, torn down Your altars, and hkilled Your prophets with the sword. iI alone am left; and they seek to take my life."

God's Revelation to Elijah

11Then He said, "Go out, and stand jon the mountain before the LORD." And behold, the LORD kpassed by, and la great and strong wind tore into the mountains and broke the rocks in pieces before the LORD, *but* the LORD *was* not in the wind; and after the wind an earthquake, *but* the LORD *was* not in the earthquake; 12and after the earthquake a fire, *but* the LORD *was* not in the fire; and after the fire a still small voice.

13So it was, when Elijah heard *it*, that he mwrapped his face in his mantle and went out and stood in the entrance of the cave. nSuddenly a voice *came* to him, and said, "What are you doing here, Elijah?"

14oAnd he said, "I have been very zealous for the LORD God of hosts; because the children of Israel have forsaken Your covenant, torn down Your altars, and killed Your prophets with the sword. I alone am left; and they seek to take my life."

15Then the LORD said to him: "Go, return on your way to the Wilderness of Damascus; pand when you arrive, anoint Hazael *as* king over Syria. 16Also you shall anoint qJehu the son of Nimshi *as* king over Israel. And rElisha the son of Shaphat of Abel Meholah you shall anoint *as* prophet in your place. 17sIt shall be *that* whoever escapes the sword of Hazael, Jehu will tkill; and whoever escapes the sword of Jehu, uElisha will kill. 18vYet I have reserved seven thousand in Israel, all whose knees have not bowed to Baal, wand every mouth that has not kissed him."

Elisha Follows Elijah

19So he departed from there, and found Elisha the son of Shaphat, who *was* plowing *with* twelve yoke *of* oxen before him, and he was with the twelfth. Then Elijah passed by him and threw his xmantle on him. 20And he left the oxen and ran after Elijah, and said, y"Please let me kiss my father and my mother, and *then* I will follow you."

And he said to him, "Go back again, for what have I done to you?"

21So *Elisha* turned back from him, and took a yoke of oxen and slaughtered them and zboiled their flesh, using the oxen's equipment, and gave it to the people, and they ate. Then he arose and followed Elijah, and became his servant.

---

* **19:5** Or *Angel*   * **19:7** Or *Angel*

---

victory on Mount Carmel, but he also knew that Jezebel was still in power, the faith of the people was still weak, at best, and his life truly was in danger. To run for his life did not necessarily indicate lack of trust; running is sometimes just the act of prudence.

19:5 Arise and eat. God's response to Elijah's fear and discouragement was to give him the very tangible, physical encouragement of food and rest.

19:7 the angel of the LORD. This term sometimes refers to God Himself (Ex. 3:2–6), and other times it seems to refer simply to a heavenly messenger (2 Kin. 1:3; 19:35).

19:8 Horeb. The name Horeb refers to Mount Sinai itself, "the mountain of God" (Ex. 3:1).

19:11 the LORD was not in the earthquake. Although each of the things mentioned in these verses could signal God's presence (Ex. 40:38; Zech. 14:4–5; Acts 2:2–3), Elijah learned that God is not just the God of the spectacular.

19:12 still small voice. Elijah had called for fire and national revival. What Elijah did not see was that God was already quietly at work in the lives of many people (v. 18).

19:18 have not bowed. In times of widespread drift and deliberate deviation from biblical standards of doctrine and ethics, it is easy to suffer from an "Elijah complex." We think that we alone have been on fire for God when everyone else has rejected His covenant, profaned His altars, and persecuted His prophets. Whenever we are tempted to imagine that we are the only ones left to represent the cause of the gospel, we are also open to the dangers of self-pity and self-righteousness. But we are not alone when we belong to the family of God. In every age, God has preserved faithful people who rejoice in Him and are on fire for the truth.

19:4 c Num. 11:15   **19:8** d Matt. 4:2 e Ex. 3:1; 4:27
19:10 f Rom. 11:3 g Ps. 69:9 h 1 Kin. 18:4 i 1 Kin. 18:22
19:11 j Ex. 19:20; 24:12, 18 k Ex. 33:21, 22 l Ezek. 1:4;
37:7   **19:13** m Ex. 3:6 n 1 Kin. 19:9   **19:14** o 1 Kin.
19:10   **19:15** p 2 Kin. 8:8–15   **19:16** q 2 Kin. 9:1–10
r 2 Kin. 2:9–15   **19:17** s 2 Kin. 8:12; 13:3, 22 t 2 Kin.
9:14—10:28 u [Hos. 6:5]   **19:18** v Rom. 11:4 w Hos.
13:2   **19:19** x 2 Kin. 2:8, 13, 14   **19:20** y [Matt. 8:21, 22]
19:21 z 2 Sam. 24:22

Ahab Defeats the Syrians

20 Now ^aBen-Hadad the king of Syria gathered all his forces together; thirty-two kings *were* with him, with horses and chariots. And he went up and besieged ^bSamaria, and made war against it. ²Then he sent messengers into the city to Ahab king of Israel, and said to him, "Thus says Ben-Hadad: ³'Your silver and your gold *are* mine; your loveliest wives and children are mine.'"

⁴And the king of Israel answered and said, "My lord, O king, just as you say, I and all that I have *are* yours."

⁵Then the messengers came back and said, "Thus speaks Ben-Hadad, saying, 'Indeed I have sent to you, saying, "You shall deliver to me your silver and your gold, your wives and your children"; ⁶but I will send my servants to you tomorrow about this time, and they shall search your house and the houses of your servants. And it shall be, *that* whatever is pleasant in your eyes, they will put *it* in their hands and take *it*.'"

⁷So the king of Israel called all the elders of the land, and said, "Notice, please, and see how this *man* seeks trouble, for he sent to me for my wives, my children, my silver, and my gold; and I did not deny him."

⁸And all the elders and all the people said to him, "Do not listen or consent."

⁹Therefore he said to the messengers of Ben-Hadad, "Tell my lord the king, 'All that you sent for to your servant the first time I will do, but this thing I cannot do.'"

And the messengers departed and brought back word to him.

¹⁰Then Ben-Hadad sent to him and said, ^c"The gods do so to me, and more also, if enough dust is left of Samaria for a handful for each of the people who follow me."

¹¹So the king of Israel answered and said, "Tell *him*, 'Let not the one who puts on *his* armor ^dboast like the one who takes *it* off.'"

¹²And it happened when *Ben-Hadad* heard this message, as he and the kings *were* ^edrinking at the command post, that he said to his servants, "Get ready." And they got ready to attack the city.

¹³Suddenly a prophet approached Ahab king of Israel, saying, "Thus says the LORD: 'Have you seen all this great multitude? Behold, ^fI will deliver it into your hand today, and you shall know that I *am* the LORD.'"

¹⁴So Ahab said, "By whom?"

And he said, "Thus says the LORD: 'By the young leaders of the provinces.'"

Then he said, "Who will set the battle in order?"

And he answered, "You."

¹⁵Then he mustered the young leaders of the provinces, and there were two hundred and thirty-two; and after them he mustered all the people, all the children of Israel—seven thousand.

¹⁶So they went out at noon. Meanwhile Ben-Hadad and the thirty-two kings helping him were ^ggetting drunk at the command post. ¹⁷The young leaders of the provinces went out first. And Ben-Hadad sent out *a patrol*, and they told him, saying, "Men are coming out of Samaria!" ¹⁸So he said, "If they have come out for peace, take them alive; and if they have come out for war, take them alive."

¹⁹Then these young leaders of the provinces went out of the city with the army which followed them. ²⁰And each one killed his man; so the Syrians fled, and Israel pursued them; and Ben-Hadad the king of Syria escaped on a horse with the cavalry. ²¹Then the king of Israel went out and attacked the horses and chariots, and killed the Syrians with a great slaughter.

²²And the prophet came to the king of Israel and said to him, "Go, strengthen yourself; take note, and see what you should do, ^hfor in the spring of the year the king of Syria will come up against you."

The Syrians Again Defeated

²³Then the servants of the king of Syria said to him, "Their gods *are* gods of the hills. Therefore they were stronger than we; but if we fight against them in the plain, surely we will be stronger than they. ²⁴So do this thing: Dismiss the kings, each from his position, and put captains in their places; ²⁵and you shall muster an army like the army that you have lost, horse for horse and chariot for chariot. Then we will fight against them in the plain; surely we will be stronger than they."

And he listened to their voice and did so.

²⁶So it was, in the spring of the year, that Ben-Hadad mustered the Syrians and went up to ⁱAphek to fight against Israel. ²⁷And the children of Israel were mustered and given provisions, and they went against

---

20:1 Ben-Hadad. Ben-Hadad II (860–842 B.C.) was king of Aram, the ancient name for the area which is Syria today.
20:2 Ahab. When he is associated with his wicked wife Jezebel, Ahab appears as thoroughly evil. But in this chapter he appears as a capable leader in a time of international turmoil, and as a person who had some sense of the power and presence of God (vv. 13–14).
20:13 a prophet. This prophet was not named, but his true message reminds us that there were still many prophets who were faithful to the Lord (18:13; 20:35).

20:23 gods of the hills. The Aramean advisors reflected traditional ancient Middle Eastern theological concepts. Their gods were limited to certain geographical locations.
20:26 Aphek. This is not the Philistine city where the ark was lost (1 Sam. 4:1), but another location just east

20:1 ^a 2 Kin. 6:24 ^b 1 Kin. 16:24 **20:10** ^c 1 Kin. 19:2 **20:11** ^d Prov. 27:1 **20:12** ^e 1 Kin. 20:16 **20:13** ^f 1 Kin. 20:28 **20:16** ^g 1 Kin. 16:9; 20:12 **20:22** ^h 2 Sam. 11:1 **20:26** ⁱ Josh. 13:4

them. Now the children of Israel encamped before them like two little flocks of goats, while the Syrians filled the [j]countryside.

28Then a [k]man of God came and spoke to the king of Israel, and said, "Thus says the LORD: 'Because the Syrians have said, "The LORD is God of the hills, but He is not God of the valleys," therefore [l]I will deliver all this great multitude into your hand, and you shall know that I am the LORD.'" 29And they encamped opposite each other for seven days. So it was that on the seventh day the battle was joined; and the children of Israel killed one hundred thousand foot soldiers of the Syrians in one day. 30But the rest fled to Aphek, into the city; then a wall fell on twenty-seven thousand of the men who were left.

And Ben-Hadad fled and went into the city, into an inner chamber.

Ahab's Treaty with Ben-Hadad

31Then his servants said to him, "Look now, we have heard that the kings of the house of Israel are merciful kings. Please, let us [m]put sackcloth around our waists and ropes around our heads, and go out to the king of Israel; perhaps he will spare your life." 32So they wore sackcloth around their waists and put ropes around their heads, and came to the king of Israel and said, "Your servant Ben-Hadad says, 'Please let me live.'"

And he said, "Is he still alive? He is my brother."

33Now the men were watching closely to see whether any sign of mercy would come from him; and they quickly grasped at this word and said, "Your brother Ben-Hadad."

So he said, "Go, bring him." Then Ben-Hadad came out to him; and he had him come up into the chariot.

34So Ben-Hadad said to him, [n]"The cities which my father took from your father I will restore; and you may set up marketplaces for yourself in Damascus, as my father did in Samaria."

Then Ahab said, "I will send you away with this treaty." So he made a treaty with him and sent him away.

Ahab Condemned

35Now a certain man of [o]the sons of the prophets said to his neighbor [p]by the word of the LORD, "Strike me, please." And the man refused to strike him. 36Then he said to him, "Because you have not obeyed the voice of the LORD, surely, as soon as you depart from me, a lion shall kill you." And as soon as he left him, [q]a lion found him and killed him.

37And he found another man, and said, "Strike me, please." So the man struck him, inflicting a wound. 38Then the prophet departed and waited for the king by the road, and disguised himself with a bandage over his eyes. 39Now [r]as the king passed by, he cried out to the king and said, "Your servant went out into the midst of the battle; and there, a man came over and brought a man to me, and said, 'Guard this man; if by any means he is missing, [s]your life shall be for his life, or else you shall pay a talent of silver.' 40While your servant was busy here and there, he was gone."

Then the king of Israel said to him, "So shall your judgment be; you yourself have decided it."

41And he hastened to take the bandage away from his eyes; and the king of Israel recognized him as one of the prophets. 42Then he said to him, "Thus says the LORD: [t]'Because you have let slip out of your hand a man whom I appointed to utter destruction, therefore your life shall go for his life, and your people for his people.'"

43So the king of Israel [u]went to his house sullen and displeased, and came to Samaria.

Naboth Is Murdered for His Vineyard

21 And it came to pass after these things that Naboth the Jezreelite had a vineyard which was in [a]Jezreel, next to the palace of Ahab king of Samaria. 2So Ahab spoke to Naboth, saying, "Give me your [b]vineyard, that I may have it for a vegetable garden, because it is near, next to my house; and for it I will give you a vineyard

---

of the Jordan in northern Gilead. They were launching their second campaign in the Jordan valley, but they would learn that the power of the living God is not limited to the mountains as they had hoped.
20:28 not God of the valleys. The God of Israel is Lord of the universe, and there is no limit to His power and authority. Not only are we responsible to Him as individuals, but so are the social, economic, and political institutions of the world. Just as it was presumption for the Arameans to think that God was bound by geography, it is also presumption to think that if we follow the laws of morality in our private lives, we can violate them in our social, economic, and political relationships. Separation of church and state should not mean separation of God and state. The nation that violates the moral laws of God will eventually suffer defeat.

20:43 sullen and displeased. Rather than repenting of his sin, Ahab felt ill used by God and resented his punishment, adamantly refusing to change his ways.
21:1 Samaria. Samaria was Ahab's capital city; sometimes its name is used to represent all Israel (2 Kin. 1:3; 2 Chr. 24:23; Jon. 3:6).
21:2 Give me your vineyard. All the land was the Lord's, who granted it to each Israelite tribe and family, and provisions were made so that the land could

20:27 [j] Judg. 6:3–5   **20:28** [k] 1 Kin. 17:18   [l] 1 Kin. 20:13   **20:31** [m] Gen. 37:34   **20:34** [n] 1 Kin. 15:20   **20:35** [o] 2 Kin. 2:3, 5, 7, 15   [p] 1 Kin. 13:17, 18   **20:36** [q] 1 Kin. 13:24   **20:39** [r] 2 Sam. 12:1   [s] 2 Kin. 10:24   **20:42** [t] 1 Kin. 22:31–37   **20:43** [u] 1 Kin. 21:4   **21:1** [a] 1 Kin. 18:45, 46   **21:2** [b] 1 Sam. 8:14

better than it. *Or,* if it seems good to you, I
will give you its worth in money."
3But Naboth said to Ahab, "The LORD
forbid [c]that I should give the inheritance
of my fathers to you!"
4So Ahab went into his house sullen
and displeased because of the word which
Naboth the Jezreelite had spoken to him;
for he had said, "I will not give you the inheritance of my fathers." And he lay down
on his bed, and turned away his face, and
would eat no food. 5But [d]Jezebel his wife
came to him, and said to him, "Why is your
spirit so sullen that you eat no food?"
6He said to her, "Because I spoke to
Naboth the Jezreelite, and said to him,
'Give me your vineyard for money; or else,
if it pleases you, I will give you *another*
vineyard for it.' And he answered, 'I will
not give you my vineyard.'"
7Then Jezebel his wife said to him, "You
now exercise authority over Israel! Arise,
eat food, and let your heart be cheerful; I
will give you the vineyard of Naboth the
Jezreelite."
8And she wrote letters in Ahab's name,
sealed *them* with his seal, and sent the letters to the elders and the nobles who *were*
dwelling in the city with Naboth. 9She
wrote in the letters, saying,

> Proclaim a fast, and seat Naboth with
> high honor among the people; 10and
> seat two men, scoundrels, before him to
> bear witness against him, saying, "You
> have [e]blasphemed God and the king."
> *Then* take him out, and [f]stone him, that
> he may die.

11So the men of his city, the elders and
nobles who were inhabitants of his city,
did as Jezebel had sent to them, as it *was*
written in the letters which she had sent
to them. 12[g]They proclaimed a fast, and
seated Naboth with high honor among the
people. 13And two men, scoundrels, came
in and sat before him; and the scoundrels
[h]witnessed against him, against Naboth, in
the presence of the people, saying, "Naboth
has blasphemed God and the king!" [i]Then
they took him outside the city and stoned
him with stones, so that he died. 14Then
they sent to Jezebel, saying, "Naboth has
been stoned and is dead."
15And it came to pass, when Jezebel
heard that Naboth had been stoned and
was dead, that Jezebel said to Ahab, "Arise,
take possession of the vineyard of Naboth
the Jezreelite, which he refused to give
you for money; for Naboth is not alive, but
dead." 16So it was, when Ahab heard that
Naboth was dead, that Ahab got up and
went down to take possession of the vineyard of Naboth the Jezreelite.

The LORD Condemns Ahab

17[j]Then the word of the LORD came to
[k]Elijah the Tishbite, saying, 18"Arise, go
down to meet Ahab king of Israel, [l]who
lives in Samaria. There *he is,* in the vineyard of Naboth, where he has gone down
to take possession of it. 19You shall speak
to him, saying, 'Thus says the LORD: "Have
you murdered and also taken possession?"'
And you shall speak to him, saying, 'Thus
says the LORD: [m]"In the place where dogs
licked the blood of Naboth, dogs shall lick
your blood, even yours."'"
20So Ahab said to Elijah, [n]"Have you
found me, O my enemy?"
And he answered, "I have found *you,*
because [o]you have sold yourself to do evil
in the sight of the LORD: 21'Behold, [p]I will
bring calamity on you. I will take away
your [q]posterity, and will cut off from Ahab
[r]every male in Israel, both [s]bond and free.
22I will make your house like the house of
[t]Jeroboam the son of Nebat, and like the
house of [u]Baasha the son of Ahijah, because of the provocation with which you
have provoked *Me* to anger, and made Israel sin.' 23And [v]concerning Jezebel the
LORD also spoke, saying, 'The dogs shall
eat Jezebel by the wall* of Jezreel.' 24The
dogs shall eat [w]whoever belongs to Ahab
and dies in the city, and the birds of the air
shall eat whoever dies in the field."

---

* **21:23** Following Masoretic Text and Septuagint; some Hebrew manuscripts, Syriac, Targum, and Vulgate read *plot of ground* (compare 2 Kings 9:36).

---

not be permanently sold out of the family to whom it had been given (Lev. 25:23–28; Num. 36:2–9). In this sense, the vineyard was not Naboth's to dispose of. It belonged to his descendants as much as it did to him.

21:13 *outside the city.* God's law was followed in the manner and place of his death (Lev. 24:14–16,23), although his execution was an outrage, based on false testimony, lies, greed, and refusal to honor the laws concerning the land.

21:19 *Have you murdered.* In Genesis 9:6 the principle was established that those who shed human blood must have their blood shed by other humans. Ahab had previously allowed his wicked wife Jezebel to plot the murder of an innocent landowner in order to obtain his vineyard. As a result, God determined that both Ahab and Jezebel would die bloody deaths, and this is exactly what happened (22:34–38; 2 Kin. 9:30–37). How tragic that these two brilliant, capable, and talented members of royalty, whose lives could have brought so much blessing to Israel, would instead bring about their own downfall by choosing the path of wickedness rather than the path of life.

21:3 [c] [Num. 36:7] **21:5** [d] 1 Kin. 19:1, 2 **21:10** [e] [Ex. 22:28] [f] [Lev. 24:14] **21:12** [g] Is. 58:4 **21:13** [h] [Ex. 20:16; 23:1, 7] [i] 2 Kin. 9:26 **21:17** [j] [Ps. 9:12] [k] 1 Kin. 19:1 **21:18** [l] 2 Chr. 22:9 **21:19** [m] 1 Kin. 22:38 **21:20** [n] 1 Kin. 18:17 [o] [Rom. 7:14] **21:21** [p] 1 Kin. 14:10 [q] 2 Kin. 10:10 [r] 1 Sam. 25:22 [s] 1 Kin. 14:10 **21:22** [t] 1 Kin. 15:29 [u] 1 Kin. 16:3, 11 **21:23** [v] 2 Kin. 9:10, 30–37 **21:24** [w] 1 Kin. 14:11; 16:4

25But *there was no one like Ahab who sold himself to do wickedness in the sight of the LORD, ʸbecause Jezebel his wife stirred him up. 26And he behaved very abominably in following idols, according to all ᶻthat the Amorites had done, whom the LORD had cast out before the children of Israel.

27So it was, when Ahab heard those words, that he tore his clothes and ᵃput sackcloth on his body, and fasted and lay in sackcloth, and went about mourning.

28And the word of the LORD came to Elijah the Tishbite, saying, 29"See how Ahab has humbled himself before Me? Because he ᵇhas humbled himself before Me, I will not bring the calamity in his days. ᶜIn the days of his son I will bring the calamity on his house."

Micaiah Warns Ahab

22 Now three years passed without war between Syria and Israel. 2Then it came to pass, in the third year, that ᵃJehoshaphat the king of Judah went down to visit the king of Israel.

3And the king of Israel said to his servants, "Do you know that ᵇRamoth in Gilead is ours, but we hesitate to take it out of the hand of the king of Syria?" 4So he said to Jehoshaphat, "Will you go with me to fight at Ramoth Gilead?"

Jehoshaphat said to the king of Israel, ᶜ"I am as you are, my people as your people, my horses as your horses." 5Also Jehoshaphat said to the king of Israel, ᵈ"Please inquire for the word of the LORD today."

6Then the king of Israel ᵉgathered the prophets together, about four hundred men, and said to them, "Shall I go against Ramoth Gilead to fight, or shall I refrain?"

So they said, "Go up, for the Lord will deliver it into the hand of the king."

7And ᶠJehoshaphat said, "Is there not still a prophet of the LORD here, that we may inquire of Him?"*

8So the king of Israel said to Jehoshaphat, "There is still one man, Micaiah the son of Imlah, by whom we may inquire of the LORD; but I hate him, because he does not prophesy good concerning me, but evil."

And Jehoshaphat said, "Let not the king say such things!"

9Then the king of Israel called an officer and said, "Bring Micaiah the son of Imlah quickly!"

10The king of Israel and Jehoshaphat the king of Judah, having put on their robes, sat each on his throne, at a threshing floor at the entrance of the gate of Samaria; and all the prophets prophesied before them. 11Now Zedekiah the son of Chenaanah had made ᵍhorns of iron for himself; and he said, "Thus says the LORD: 'With these you shall ʰgore the Syrians until they are destroyed.'" 12And all the prophets prophesied so, saying, "Go up to Ramoth Gilead and prosper, for the LORD will deliver it into the king's hand."

13Then the messenger who had gone to call Micaiah spoke to him, saying, "Now listen, the words of the prophets with one accord encourage the king. Please, let your word be like the word of one of them, and speak encouragement."

14And Micaiah said, "As the LORD lives, ⁱwhatever the LORD says to me, that I will speak."

15Then he came to the king; and the king said to him, "Micaiah, shall we go to war against Ramoth Gilead, or shall we refrain?"

And he answered him, "Go and prosper, for the LORD will deliver it into the hand of the king!"

16So the king said to him, "How many times shall I make you swear that you tell me nothing but the truth in the name of the LORD?"

17Then he said, "I saw all Israel ⱼscattered

---

* **22:7** Or him

21:27 when Ahab heard those words. The vacillating nature of Ahab's conduct is seen clearly in verses 25–29. He did great evil, under the influence of his evil wife. Nevertheless, he could at times display real courage (22:34–35) and even real humility before God (v. 29). His life is a sad picture of what happens when we are ruled by our own passions rather than by God.

22:4 Jehoshaphat. Jehoshaphat was the fourth king of the southern kingdom. He was related to Ahab through the marriage of his son Jehoram to Ahab's daughter Athaliah (2 Kin. 8:18–27).

22:9 Micaiah. The prophet Micaiah is not known except in connection with this incident (2 Chr. 18:8–27).

22:14 whatever the LORD says to me, that I will speak. Unless a prophecy is truly directed by God, it is valueless. Micaiah's response was what one would expect from a godly man, but his first statement to

Ahab (v. 15) is a little puzzling. It seems that Micaiah was playing with Ahab a little, pointing out to him the futility of asking for favorable prophecy rather than true prophecy. It seems obvious that Micaiah (or God through Micaiah), was in no way deceiving Ahab, since Ahab was instantly aware that he had not been given a real prophecy.

22:16–17 truth. All of us wish to hear good news, not bad. We want to hear the favorable, the acceptable, the words that bring us happiness and do not condemn. It can be tempting to speak only what will

21:25 ˣ 1 Kin. 16:30–33; 21:20 ʸ 1 Kin. 16:31
21:26 ᶻ 2 Kin. 21:11   **21:27** ᵃ Gen. 37:34   **21:29** ᵇ [2 Kin. 22:19] ᶜ 2 Kin. 9:25; 10:11, 17   **22:2** ᵃ 2 Chr. 18:2
22:3 ᵇ Deut. 4:43   **22:4** ᶜ 2 Kin. 3:7   **22:5** ᵈ 2 Kin. 3:11
22:6 ᵉ 1 Kin. 18:19   **22:7** ᶠ 2 Kin. 3:11   **22:11** ᵍ Zech. 1:18–21 ʰ Deut. 33:17   **22:14** ⁱ Num. 22:38; 24:13
22:17 ⱼ Matt. 9:36

on the mountains, as sheep that have no shepherd. And the LORD said, 'These have no master. Let each return to his house in peace.'"

18And the king of Israel said to Jehoshaphat, "Did I not tell you he would not prophesy good concerning me, but evil?"

19Then *Micaiah* said, "Therefore hear the word of the LORD: *k*I saw the LORD sitting on His throne, *l*and all the host of heaven standing by, on His right hand and on His left. 20And the LORD said, 'Who will persuade Ahab to go up, that he may fall at Ramoth Gilead?' So one spoke in this manner, and another spoke in that manner. 21Then a spirit came forward and stood before the LORD, and said, 'I will persuade him.' 22The LORD said to him, 'In what way?' So he said, 'I will go out and be a lying spirit in the mouth of all his prophets.' And the LORD said, *m*'You shall persuade *him*, and also prevail. Go out and do so.' 23*n*Therefore look! The LORD has put a lying spirit in the mouth of all these prophets of yours, and the LORD has declared disaster against you."

24Now Zedekiah the son of Chenaanah went near and *o*struck Micaiah on the cheek, and said, *p*"Which way did the spirit from the LORD go from me to speak to you?"

25And Micaiah said, "Indeed, you shall see on that day when you go into an *q*inner chamber to hide!"

26So the king of Israel said, "Take Micaiah, and return him to Amon the governor of the city and to Joash the king's son; 27and say, 'Thus says the king: "Put this *fellow* in *r*prison, and feed him with bread of affliction and water of affliction, until I come in peace."'"

28But Micaiah said, "If you ever return in peace, *s*the LORD has not spoken by me." And he said, "Take heed, all you people!"

Ahab Dies in Battle

29So the king of Israel and Jehoshaphat the king of Judah went up to Ramoth Gilead. 30And the king of Israel said to Jehoshaphat, "I will disguise myself and go into battle; but you put on your robes." So the king of Israel *t*disguised himself and went into battle.

31Now the *u*king of Syria had commanded the thirty-two *v*captains of his chariots,

saying, "Fight with no one small or great, but only with the king of Israel." 32So it was, when the captains of the chariots saw Jehoshaphat, that they said, "Surely it *is* the king of Israel!" Therefore they turned aside to fight against him, and Jehoshaphat *w*cried out. 33And it happened, when the captains of the chariots saw that it *was* not the king of Israel, that they turned back from pursuing him. 34Now a *certain* man drew a bow at random, and struck the king of Israel between the joints of his armor. So he said to the driver of his chariot, "Turn around and take me out of the battle, for I am wounded."

35The battle increased that day; and the king was propped up in his chariot, facing the Syrians, and died at evening. The blood ran out from the wound onto the floor of the chariot. 36Then, as the sun was going down, a shout went throughout the army, saying, "Every man to his city, and every man to his own country!"

37So the king died, and was brought to Samaria. And they buried the king in Samaria. 38Then *someone* washed the chariot at a pool in Samaria, and the dogs licked up his blood while the harlots bathed,* according *x*to the word of the LORD which He had spoken.

39Now the rest of the acts of Ahab, and all that he did, *y*the ivory house which he built and all the cities that he built, *are* they not written in the book of the chronicles of the kings of Israel? 40So Ahab rested with his fathers. Then *z*Ahaziah his son reigned in his place.

Jehoshaphat Reigns in Judah

41*a*Jehoshaphat the son of Asa had become king over Judah in the fourth year of Ahab king of Israel. 42Jehoshaphat *was* thirty-five years old when he became king, and he reigned twenty-five years in Jerusalem. His mother's name *was* Azubah the daughter of Shilhi. 43And *b*he walked in all the ways of his father Asa. He did not turn aside from them, doing *what was* right in the eyes of the LORD. Nevertheless *c*the high places were not taken away, *for* the people offered sacrifices and burned incense on

---

* **22:38** Syriac and Targum read *they washed his armor.*

---

be well-received even if it is not true, but neither God nor man is served by untruth. While the truth should always be spoken in love (Eph. 4:15), it must be the sole content of what we say. The prophet had to speak only the truth, or he would no longer have been a prophet—his words were the words of the Lord spoken in His name. Our words should be true because, if we are His people, we speak in His name.
22:38 the dogs licked up his blood. Elijah's grisly prophecy concerning the house of Ahab came to pass here (21:19–24).

22:39 ivory house. Archaeological excavations at Samaria have illustrated the nature of Ahab's palace, a house with luxurious decorations made of ivory.

22:19 *k* Is. 6:1 *l* Dan. 7:10 **22:22** *m* Judg. 9:23 **22:23** *n* [Ezek. 14:9] **22:24** *o* Jer. 20:2 *p* 2 Chr. 18:23 **22:25** *q* 1 Kin. 20:30 **22:27** *r* 2 Chr. 16:10; 18:25–27 **22:28** *s* Num. 16:29 **22:30** *t* 2 Chr. 35:22 **22:31** *u* 1 Kin. 20:1 *v* 1 Kin. 20:24 **22:32** *w* 2 Chr. 18:31 **22:38** *x* 1 Kin. 21:19 **22:39** *y* Amos 3:15 **22:40** *z* 2 Kin. 1:2, 18 **22:41** *a* 2 Chr. 20:31 **22:43** *b* 2 Chr. 17:3; 20:32, 33 *c* 2 Kin. 12:3

the high places. ⁴⁴Also ᵈJehoshaphat made ᵉpeace with the king of Israel.

⁴⁵Now the rest of the acts of Jehoshaphat, the might that he showed, and how he made war, *are* they not written ᶠin the book of the chronicles of the kings of Judah? ⁴⁶ᵍAnd the rest of the perverted persons,* who remained in the days of his father Asa, he banished from the land. ⁴⁷ʰThere *was* then no king in Edom, only a deputy of the king.

⁴⁸ⁱJehoshaphat ʲmade merchant ships* to go to ᵏOphir for gold; ˡbut they never sailed, for the ships were wrecked at ᵐEzion Geber. ⁴⁹Then Ahaziah the son of Ahab said to Jehoshaphat, "Let my servants go with your servants in the ships." But Jehoshaphat would not.

⁵⁰And ⁿJehoshaphat rested with his fathers, and was buried with his fathers in the City of David his father. Then Jehoram his son reigned in his place.

Ahaziah Reigns in Israel

⁵¹ᵒAhaziah the son of Ahab became king over Israel in Samaria in the seventeenth year of Jehoshaphat king of Judah, and reigned two years over Israel. ⁵²He did evil in the sight of the LORD, and ᵖwalked in the way of his father and in the way of his mother and in the way of Jeroboam the son of Nebat, who had made Israel sin; ⁵³for ᵠhe served Baal and worshiped him, and provoked the LORD God of Israel to anger, ʳaccording to all that his father had done.

---

* **22:46** Hebrew *qadesh,* that is, one practicing sodomy and prostitution in religious rituals
* **22:48** Or *ships of Tarshish*

22:46 *perverted persons.* Apparently male prostitution was a part of the debased religious practices of Baal worship (14:24).
22:53 Conclusion—The story does not end here but is continued in 2 Kings. The division of the Book of Kings is not original, but was done for convenience when the Bible was translated into Greek in the second century B.C.

22:44 ᵈ 2 Chr. 19:2 ᵉ 2 Chr. 18:1 **22:45** ᶠ 2 Chr. 20:34 **22:46** ᵍ 1 Kin. 14:24; 15:12 **22:47** ʰ 2 Sam. 8:14 **22:48** ⁱ 2 Chr. 20:35–37 ʲ 1 Kin. 10:22 ᵏ 1 Kin. 9:28 ˡ 2 Chr. 20:37 ᵐ 1 Kin. 9:26 **22:50** ⁿ 2 Chr. 21:1 **22:51** ᵒ 1 Kin. 22:40 **22:52** ᵖ 1 Kin. 15:26; 21:25 **22:53** ᵠ Judg. 2:11 ʳ 1 Kin. 16:30–32

THE SECOND BOOK OF THE

KINGS

▶ **AUTHOR:** This book, thought to originally be part of 1 Kings, is similar to the Book of Jeremiah. It has been observed that the omission of Jeremiah's ministry in the account of King Josiah and his successors may indicate that Jeremiah himself was the recorder of the events. The last two chapters were evidently added to the book after the Babylonian captivity and written by someone other than Jeremiah.

▶ **TIME:** 853–560 B.C.   ▶ **KEY VERSES:** 2 Kin. 17:22–23

▶ **THEME:** Both Elijah in 1 Kings and Elisha in 2 Kings are prime examples of how prophets functioned in Israel. They fearlessly confronted kings. They were involved in miracles. Both seemed to always be involved in the middle of some political controversy. Most importantly, they called on God and got results. In 2 Kings, Israel's story begins with the reign of Ahab's son, Ahaziah, continues with the capture and deportation of Israel to Assyria in 722 B.C., and ends with Judah's fall in 587 B.C., when Nebuchadnezzar burns the temple and palace in Jerusalem and deports many people back to Babylon.

God Judges Ahaziah

1 Moab ^arebelled against Israel ^bafter the death of Ahab.

²Now ^cAhaziah fell through the lattice of his upper room in Samaria, and was injured; so he sent messengers and said to them, "Go, inquire of ^dBaal-Zebub, the god of ^eEkron, whether I shall recover from this injury." ³But the angel* of the LORD said to Elijah the Tishbite, "Arise, go up to meet the messengers of the king of Samaria, and say to them, 'Is it because there is no God in Israel that you are going to inquire of Baal-Zebub, the god of Ekron?' ⁴Now therefore, thus says the LORD: 'You shall not come down from the bed to which you have gone up, but you shall surely die.'" So Elijah departed.

⁵And when the messengers returned to him, he said to them, "Why have you come back?"

⁶So they said to him, "A man came up to meet us, and said to us, 'Go, return to the king who sent you, and say to him, "Thus says the LORD: 'Is it because there is no God in Israel that you are sending to inquire of Baal-Zebub, the god of Ekron? Therefore you shall not come down from the bed to which you have gone up, but you shall surely die.'"'"

⁷Then he said to them, "What kind of man was it who came up to meet you and told you these words?"

⁸So they answered him, ^f"A hairy man wearing a leather belt around his waist."

And he said, ^g"It is Elijah the Tishbite."

⁹Then the king sent to him a captain of fifty with his fifty men. So he went up to him; and there he was, sitting on the top of a hill. And he spoke to him: "Man of God, the king has said, 'Come down!'"

¹⁰So Elijah answered and said to the captain of fifty, "If I *am* a man of God, then ^hlet fire come down from heaven and

* **1:3** Or *Angel*

1:2 Ahaziah. The account of his brief, wicked reign begins in 1 Kings 22:51. The division of the Book of Kings into two parts was for the convenience of the translators, as is indicated by the fact that Ahaziah's reign carries over from one book to the other without a break.

1:6 Unbelief—Just as in the days of Ahaziah, men and women today often will turn to everything but the one genuine source of truth. But because there is no help or life or power in man's gods, man's ideas and philosophies, belief in them will end only in wasted, ineffective lives, and eventually in eternal death. True joy and meaning in life can only be found through trust in God.

1:8 A hairy man. This may refer to Elijah's garments, but the usual translation of "hairy man" is supported by the ancient versions.

1:10 fire . . . from heaven. Heavenly fire could signal divine judgment (Gen. 19:24). Elijah had already called down such fire in his contest with the prophets of Baal (1 Kin. 18:36–38). If this fire was lightning, the episode would have been a particularly significant slap in the face of their religion, showing that Baal

1:1 ^a 2 Sam. 8:2 ^b 2 Kin. 3:5   **1:2** ^c 1 Kin. 22:40 ^d Matt. 10:25 ^e 1 Sam. 5:10   **1:8** ^f Zech. 13:4 ^g 1 Kin. 18:7 **1:10** ^h Luke 9:54

consume you and your fifty men." And fire came down from heaven and consumed him and his fifty. ¹¹Then he sent to him another captain of fifty with his fifty men.

And he answered and said to him: "Man of God, thus has the king said, 'Come down quickly!'"

¹²So Elijah answered and said to them, "If I *am* a man of God, let fire come down from heaven and consume you and your fifty men." And the fire of God came down from heaven and consumed him and his fifty.

¹³Again, he sent a third captain of fifty with his fifty men. And the third captain of fifty went up, and came and fell on his knees before Elijah, and pleaded with him, and said to him: "Man of God, please let my life and the life of these fifty servants of yours ᶠbe precious in your sight. ¹⁴Look, fire has come down from heaven and burned up the first two captains of fifties with their fifties. But let my life now be precious in your sight."

¹⁵And the angel* of the LORD said to Elijah, "Go down with him; do not be afraid of him." So he arose and went down with him to the king. ¹⁶Then he said to him, "Thus says the LORD: 'Because you have sent messengers to inquire of Baal-Zebub, the god of Ekron, *is it* because *there is* no God in Israel to inquire of His word? Therefore you shall not come down from the bed to which you have gone up, but you shall surely die.'"

¹⁷So *Ahaziah* died according to the word of the LORD which Elijah had spoken. Because he had no son, ʲJehoram* became king in his place, in the second year of Jehoram the son of Jehoshaphat, king of Judah.

¹⁸Now the rest of the acts of Ahaziah which he did, *are* they not written in the book of the chronicles of the kings of Israel?

Elijah Ascends to Heaven

2 And it came to pass, when the LORD was about to ᵃtake up Elijah into heaven by a whirlwind, that Elijah went with ᵇElisha from Gilgal. ²Then Elijah said to Elisha, ᶜ"Stay here, please, for the LORD has sent me on to Bethel."

But Elisha said, "*As* the LORD lives, and ᵈ*as* your soul lives, I will not leave you!" So they went down to Bethel.

³Now ᵉthe sons of the prophets who *were* at Bethel came out to Elisha, and said to him, "Do you know that the LORD will take away your master from over you today?"

And he said, "Yes, I know; keep silent!"

⁴Then Elijah said to him, "Elisha, stay here, please, for the LORD has sent me on to Jericho."

But he said, "*As* the LORD lives, and *as* your soul lives, I will not leave you!" So they came to Jericho.

⁵Now the sons of the prophets who *were* at Jericho came to Elisha and said to him, "Do you know that the LORD will take away your master from over you today?"

So he answered, "Yes, I know; keep silent!"

⁶Then Elijah said to him, "Stay here, please, for the LORD has sent me on to the Jordan."

But he said, "*As* the LORD lives, and *as* your soul lives, I will not leave you!" So the two of them went on. ⁷And fifty men of the sons of the prophets went and stood facing *them* at a distance, while the two of them stood by the Jordan. ⁸Now Elijah took his mantle, rolled *it* up, and struck the water; and ᶠit was divided this way and that, so that the two of them crossed over on dry ᵍground.

⁹And so it was, when they had crossed over, that Elijah said to Elisha, "Ask! What may I do for you, before I am taken away from you?"

Elisha said, "Please let a double portion of your spirit be upon me."

¹⁰So he said, "You have asked a hard thing. *Nevertheless*, if you see me *when I am* taken from you, it shall be so for you; but if not, it shall not be *so*." ¹¹Then it happened, as they continued on and talked, that suddenly ʰa chariot of fire *appeared* with horses of fire, and separated the two of them; and Elijah ⁱwent up by a whirlwind into heaven.

¹²And Elisha saw *it*, and he cried out,

---

* **1:15** Or *Angel*   * **1:17** The son of Ahab king of Israel (compare 3:1)

---

was not the god of the storm he was reputed to be. The God of Israel was—and is—the Lord of creation. **2:3 take away.** The same Hebrew word is used for Enoch's entrance to heaven (Gen. 5:24). The work that God was about to do had been divinely revealed to many of God's servants (vv. 3,5). This widespread knowledge of God's purpose would protect against later denials by cynical persons that the event had ever taken place.
2:9 double portion. In material things, the principal heir received a double portion of his father's goods. Elisha wanted the principle of primary inheritance to apply to spiritual things. Far from being a self-ish request, Elisha's petition reflects his humble

acknowledgment that if Elijah's ministry were to continue through him, it would take special God-given spiritual power.
2:11 heaven. The Bible does not give very much information about exactly what happens to the believer after death. Elijah is described as being "caught up to heaven," and it is assumed that he went to the same place to which Enoch had been taken up (Heb. 11:5).

1:13 ⁱ 1 Sam. 26:21   **1:17** ʲ 1 Kin. 22:50   **2:1** ᵃ Gen. 5:24   ᵇ 1 Kin. 19:16–21   **2:2** ᶜ Ruth 1:15, 16   ᵈ 1 Sam. 1:26   **2:3** ᵉ 1 Kin. 20:35   **2:8** ᶠ Ex. 14:21, 22   ᵍ Josh. 3:17   **2:11** ʰ 2 Kin. 6:17   ⁱ Heb. 11:5

j"My father, my father, the chariot of Israel and its horsemen!" So he saw him no more. And he took hold of his own clothes and tore them into two pieces. ¹³He also took up the mantle of Elijah that had fallen from him, and went back and stood by the bank of the Jordan. ¹⁴Then he took the mantle of Elijah that had fallen from him, and struck the water, and said, "Where *is* the LORD God of Elijah?" And when he also had struck the water, *k*it was divided this way and that; and Elisha crossed over.

¹⁵Now when the sons of the prophets who *were l*from Jericho saw him, they said, "The spirit of Elijah rests on Elisha." And they came to meet him, and bowed to the ground before him. ¹⁶Then they said to him, "Look now, there are fifty strong men with your servants. Please let them go and search for your master, *m*lest perhaps the Spirit of the LORD has taken him up and cast him upon some mountain or into some valley."

And he said, "You shall not send anyone."

¹⁷But when they urged him till he was *n*ashamed, he said, "Send *them!*" Therefore they sent fifty men, and they searched for three days but did not find him. ¹⁸And when they came back to him, for he had stayed in Jericho, he said to them, "Did I not say to you, 'Do not go'?"

Elisha Performs Miracles

¹⁹Then the men of the city said to Elisha, "Please notice, the situation of this city *is* pleasant, as my lord sees; but the water *is* bad, and the ground barren."

²⁰And he said, "Bring me a new bowl, and put salt in it." So they brought *it* to him. ²¹Then he went out to the source of the water, and *o*cast in the salt there, and said, "Thus says the LORD: 'I have healed this water; from it there shall be no more death or barrenness.'" ²²So the water remains *p*healed to this day, according to the word of Elisha which he spoke.

²³Then he went up from there to Bethel; and as he was going up the road, some youths came from the city and mocked him, and said to him, "Go up, you baldhead! Go up, you baldhead!"

²⁴So he turned around and looked at them, and *q*pronounced a curse on them in the name of the LORD. And two female bears came out of the woods and mauled forty-two of the youths.

²⁵Then he went from there to *r*Mount Carmel, and from there he returned to Samaria.

Moab Rebels Against Israel

3 Now *a*Jehoram the son of Ahab became king over Israel at Samaria in the eighteenth year of Jehoshaphat king of Judah, and reigned twelve years. ²And he did evil in the sight of the LORD, but not like his father and mother; for he put away the *sacred* pillar of Baal *b*that his father had made. ³Nevertheless he persisted in *c*the sins of Jeroboam the son of Nebat, who had made Israel sin; he did not depart from them.

⁴Now Mesha king of Moab was a sheepbreeder, and he *d*regularly paid the king of Israel one hundred thousand *e*lambs and the wool of one hundred thousand rams. ⁵But it happened, when *f*Ahab died, that the king of Moab rebelled against the king of Israel.

⁶So King Jehoram went out of Samaria at that time and mustered all Israel. ⁷Then he went and sent to Jehoshaphat king of Judah, saying, "The king of Moab has rebelled against me. Will you go with me to fight against Moab?"

Jesus assured the thief on the cross that he would be in "paradise" with Him (Luke 23:43), a place of which Paul also had a brief glimpse (2 Cor. 12:1–4). While we do not have a clear picture of what it is like, we know that God will provide a place of beauty and rest for all His children.
2:15 The spirit of Elijah. The prophets witnessed both the miracle of Elijah (v. 8) and the similar miracle of Elisha. In this way there would be common agreement that Elisha was the successor of Elijah. They bowed, not in worship, but in respect and submission to the will of God.
2:17 he was ashamed. Although these words may indicate Elisha's sense of shame on behalf of his disciples for their disbelief, the use of the phrase elsewhere indicates that it means Elisha was worn out, no longer willing to resist (8:11). He came to the point where he gave in to their request.
2:23 Go up, you baldhead. The words of these youths indicate their disbelief of Elijah's "going up" into heaven and their disrespect for God's prophet. God did not tolerate blasphemy against Himself by the demeaning of Elijah's departure, or the abuse of His prophet, whom He had called for an important task at a critical period in Israel's history.

3:2 sacred pillar of Baal. Probably this was a stone pillar or statue erected by Ahab and bearing an inscription and image of the god Baal. Although it was put away temporarily, it apparently was not destroyed, because it later became one of the objects of Jehu's purge (10:26–27).
3:4 Mesha king of Moab. The existence of this Moabite king is confirmed by an inscription on a pillar known as the Moabite Stone. The inscription indicates that Omri had conquered the plains of Moab north of the Arnon River, and that the area remained under Israelite control throughout Ahab's reign. Thus the events of this chapter probably took place after Jehoram's accession and shortly before Jehoshaphat's death in 847 B.C. **sheepbreeder.** This Hebrew word is used only of Mesha and of Amos, the prophet (Amos 1:1).
3:7 Will you go with me. Because Jehoshaphat

2:12 *j* 2 Kin. 13:14 **2:14** *k* 2 Kin. 2:8 **2:15** *l* 2 Kin. 2:7 **2:16** *m* 1 Kin. 18:12 **2:17** *n* 2 Kin. 8:11 **2:21** *o* Ex. 15:25, 26 **2:22** *p* Ezek. 47:8, 9 **2:24** *q* Deut. 27:13–26 **2:25** *r* 2 Kin. 4:25 **3:1** *a* 2 Kin. 1:17 **3:2** *b* 1 Kin. 16:31, 32 **3:3** *c* 1 Kin. 12:28–32 **3:4** *d* 2 Sam. 8:2 *e* Is. 16:1, 2 **3:5** *f* 2 Kin. 1:1

And he said, "I will go up; gI *am* as you *are*, my people as your people, my horses as your horses." 8Then he said, "Which way shall we go up?"

And he answered, "By way of the Wilderness of Edom."

9So the king of Israel went with the king of Judah and the king of Edom, and they marched on that roundabout route seven days; and there was no water for the army, nor for the animals that followed them. 10And the king of Israel said, "Alas! For the LORD has called these three kings together to deliver them into the hand of Moab."

11But hJehoshaphat said, "*Is there* no prophet of the LORD here, that we may inquire of the LORD by him?"

So one of the servants of the king of Israel answered and said, "Elisha the son of Shaphat *is* here, who ipoured water on the hands of Elijah."

12And Jehoshaphat said, "The word of the LORD is with him." So the king of Israel and Jehoshaphat and the king of Edom jwent down to him.

13Then Elisha said to the king of Israel, k"What have I to do with you? lGo to mthe prophets of your father and the nprophets of your mother."

But the king of Israel said to him, "No, for the LORD has called these three kings *together* to deliver them into the hand of Moab."

14And Elisha said, o"As the LORD of hosts lives, before whom I stand, surely were it not that I regard the presence of Jehoshaphat king of Judah, I would not look at you, nor see you. 15But now bring me pa musician."

Then it happened, when the musician qplayed, that rthe hand of the LORD came upon him. 16And he said, "Thus says the LORD: s'Make this valley full of ditches.' 17For thus says the LORD: 'You shall not see wind, nor shall you see rain; yet that valley shall be filled with water, so that you, your cattle, and your animals may drink.' 18And this is a simple matter in the sight of the LORD; He will also deliver the Moabites into your hand. 19Also you shall attack every fortified city and every choice city, and shall cut down every good tree, and stop up every spring of water,

and ruin every good piece of land with stones."

20Now it happened in the morning, when tthe grain offering was offered, that suddenly water came by way of Edom, and the land was filled with water.

21And when all the Moabites heard that the kings had come up to fight against them, all who were able to bear arms and older were gathered; and they stood at the border. 22Then they rose up early in the morning, and the sun was shining on the water; and the Moabites saw the water on the other side *as* red as blood. 23And they said, "This is blood; the kings have surely struck swords and have killed one another; now therefore, Moab, to the spoil!"

24So when they came to the camp of Israel, Israel rose up and attacked the Moabites, so that they fled before them; and they entered *their* land, killing the Moabites. 25Then they destroyed the cities, and each man threw a stone on every good piece of land and filled it; and they stopped up all the springs of water and cut down all the good trees. But they left the stones of uKir Haraseth *intact*. However the slingers surrounded and attacked it.

26And when the king of Moab saw that the battle was too fierce for him, he took with him seven hundred men who drew swords, to break through to the king of Edom, but they could not. 27Then vhe took his eldest son who would have reigned in his place, and offered him *as* a burnt offering upon the wall; and there was great indignation against Israel. wSo they departed from him and returned to *their own* land.

Elisha and the Widow's Oil

4 A certain woman of the wives of athe sons of the prophets cried out to Elisha, saying, "Your servant my husband is dead, and you know that your servant feared the LORD. And the creditor is coming bto take my two sons to be his slaves."

2So Elisha said to her, "What shall I do for you? Tell me, what do you have in the house?" And she said, "Your maidservant has nothing in the house but a jar of oil."

3Then he said, "Go, borrow vessels from everywhere, from all your neighbors— empty vessels; cdo not gather just a few.

---

was related to the throne of the northern kingdom through the marriage of his son Jehoram to Ahab's daughter Athaliah, it could be presumed that he would be available as an ally.

3:14 *I would not look at you.* As a devotee of Baal, Jehoram had no claim on the favor of God. Nevertheless, he would enjoy the benefits of God's grace toward Jehoshaphat.

3:20 *filled with water.* The dry stream beds can easily overflow their banks in downpours of rain. Even distant areas can be flooded by water from faraway mountain streams swelled by heavy rains.

4:1 *A certain woman.* The fate of widows was perilous in the ancient Middle East. A practical test of biblical piety was to observe how those in power treated widows and orphans (Job 24:21; Ps. 146:9).

3:7 g 1 Kin. 22:4   **3:11** h 1 Kin. 22:7   i 1 Kin. 19:21
3:12 j 2 Kin. 2:25   **3:13** k [Ezek. 14:3]   l Judg. 10:14
m 1 Kin. 22:6–11   n 1 Kin. 18:19   **3:14** o 1 Kin. 17:1
3:15 p 1 Sam. 10:5   q 1 Sam. 16:16, 23   r Ezek. 1:3; 3:14, 22;
8:1   **3:16** s Jer. 14:3   **3:20** t Ex. 29:39, 40   **3:25** u Is.
16:7, 11   **3:27** v [Amos 2:1]   w 2 Kin. 8:20   **4:1** a 1 Kin.
20:35   b [Lev. 25:39–41, 48]   **4:3** c 2 Kin. 3:16

⁴And when you have come in, you shall shut the door behind you and your sons; then pour it into all those vessels, and set aside the full ones."

⁵So she went from him and shut the door behind her and her sons, who brought *the vessels* to her; and she poured *it* out. ⁶Now it came to pass, when the vessels were full, that she said to her son, "Bring me another vessel."

And he said to her, "*There is* not another vessel." So the oil ceased. ⁷Then she came and told the man of God. And he said, "Go, sell the oil and pay your debt; and you *and* your sons live on the rest."

Elisha Raises the Shunammite's Son

⁸Now it happened one day that Elisha went to ᵈShunem, where there *was* a notable woman, and she persuaded him to eat some food. So it was, as often as he passed by, he would turn in there to eat some food. ⁹And she said to her husband, "Look now, I know that this *is* a holy man of God, who passes by us regularly. ¹⁰Please, let us make a small upper room on the wall; and let us put a bed for him there, and a table and a chair and a lampstand; so it will be, whenever he comes to us, he can turn in there."

¹¹And it happened one day that he came there, and he turned in to the upper room and lay down there. ¹²Then he said to ᵉGehazi his servant, "Call this Shunammite woman." When he had called her, she stood before him. ¹³And he said to him, "Say now to her, 'Look, you have been concerned for us with all this care. What *can I* do for you? Do you want me to speak on your behalf to the king or to the commander of the army?'" She answered, "I dwell among my own people."

¹⁴So he said, "What then *is* to be done for her?"

And Gehazi answered, "Actually, she has no son, and her husband is old."

¹⁵So he said, "Call her." When he had called her, she stood in the doorway. ¹⁶Then he said, "About this time next year you shall embrace a son."

And she said, "No, my lord. Man of God, ᶠdo not lie to your maidservant!"

¹⁷But the woman conceived, and bore a son when the appointed time had come, of which Elisha had told her.

¹⁸And the child grew. Now it happened one day that he went out to his father, to the reapers. ¹⁹And he said to his father, "My head, my head!"

So he said to a servant, "Carry him to his mother." ²⁰When he had taken him and brought him to his mother, he sat on her knees till noon, and *then* died. ²¹And she went up and laid him on the bed of the man of God, shut *the door* upon him, and went out. ²²Then she called to her husband, and said, "Please send me one of the young men and one of the donkeys, that I may run to the man of God and come back."

²³So he said, "Why are you going to him today? *It is* neither the ᵍNew Moon nor the Sabbath."

And she said, "*It is* well." ²⁴Then she saddled a donkey, and said to her servant, "Drive, and go forward; do not slacken the pace for me unless I tell you." ²⁵And so she departed, and went to the man of God ʰat Mount Carmel.

So it was, when the man of God saw her afar off, that he said to his servant Gehazi, "Look, the Shunammite woman! ²⁶Please run now to meet her, and say to her, 'Is it well with you? *Is it* well with your husband? *Is it* well with the child?'"

And she answered, "*It is* well." ²⁷Now when she came to the man of God at the hill, she caught him by the feet, but Gehazi came near to push her away. But the man of God said, "Let her alone; for her soul *is* in deep distress, and the LORD has hidden *it* from me, and has not told me."

²⁸So she said, "Did I ask a son of my lord? ⁱDid I not say, 'Do not deceive me'?"

²⁹Then he said to Gehazi, ʲ"Get yourself ready, and take my staff in your hand, and be on your way. If you meet anyone, ᵏdo not greet him; and if anyone greets you, do not answer him; but ˡlay my staff on the face of the child."

³⁰And the mother of the child said, ᵐ"As the LORD lives, and *as* your soul lives, ⁿI will not leave you." So he arose and followed her. ³¹Now Gehazi went on ahead of them, and laid the staff on the face of the child; but *there was* neither voice nor

---

4:10 *small upper room.* The flat roofs of houses in this time were used as extra living space, and often a small room would be built on the roof which could be reached from outside. This accommodated a guest while providing privacy. Recognizing Elisha as one of God's chosen servants, the Shunammite woman was especially concerned that the normal measures of hospitality be applied even more fully.

4:12–13 Thankfulness—Both Elijah and the Shunammite woman illustrate the vitally important teaching of Scripture: Be thankful; be ready both to receive and to give; express your thankfulness always with words and deeds. Too many blessings, kind words, and thoughtful actions go thankless until it is too late. The kindness and love expressed to Elijah

registered in his heart and mind. His loving question should be our question in response to kindness: "What can I do for you?"

4:23 *New Moon . . . Sabbath.* There was no work on these days, so they would be more suitable for going to see the prophet (Ex. 20:9–12; Amos 8:5).

4:27 *the LORD has hidden it.* The prophets did not know everything, but only what God made known to them (5:26).

4:8 ᵈ Josh. 19:18   **4:12** ᵉ 2 Kin. 4:29–31; 5:20–27; 8:4, 5   **4:16** ᶠ 2 Kin. 4:28   **4:23** ᵍ 1 Chr. 23:31   **4:25** ʰ 2 Kin. 2:25   **4:28** ⁱ 2 Kin. 4:16   **4:29** ʲ 1 Kin. 18:46   ᵏ Luke 10:4   ˡ Ex. 7:19; 14:16   **4:30** ᵐ 2 Kin. 2:2   ⁿ 2 Kin. 2:4

hearing. Therefore he went back to meet
him, and told him, saying, "The child has
[o]not awakened."
32 When Elisha came into the house, there
was the child, lying dead on his bed. 33 He
[p]went in therefore, shut the door behind
the two of them, [q]and prayed to the LORD.
34 And he went up and lay on the child, and
put his mouth on his mouth, his eyes on
his eyes, and his hands on his hands; and
[r]he stretched himself out on the child, and
the flesh of the child became warm. 35 He
returned and walked back and forth in the
house, and again went up [s]and stretched
himself out on him; then [t]the child sneezed
seven times, and the child opened his eyes.
36 And he called Gehazi and said, "Call this
Shunammite woman." So he called her.
And when she came in to him, he said,
"Pick up your son." 37 So she went in, fell at
his feet, and bowed to the ground; then she
[u]picked up her son and went out.

Elisha Purifies the Pot of Stew

38 And Elisha returned to [v]Gilgal, and
there was a [w]famine in the land. Now the
sons of the prophets *were* [x]sitting before
him; and he said to his servant, "Put on the
large pot, and boil stew for the sons of the
prophets." 39 So one went out into the field
to gather herbs, and found a wild vine, and
gathered from it a lapful of wild gourds,
and came and sliced *them* into the pot of
stew, though they did not know *what they
were*. 40 Then they served it to the men to
eat. Now it happened, as they were eating
the stew, that they cried out and said, "Man
of God, *there is* [y]death in the pot!" And they
could not eat *it*.
41 So he said, "Then bring some flour."
And [z]he put *it* into the pot, and said, "Serve
it to the people, that they may eat." And
there was nothing harmful in the pot.

Elisha Feeds One Hundred Men

42 Then a man came from [a]Baal Shalisha,
[b]and brought the man of God bread of the
firstfruits, twenty loaves of barley bread,
and newly ripened grain in his knapsack.
And he said, "Give *it* to the people, that
they may eat."
43 But his servant said, [c]"What? Shall I
set this before one hundred men?"
He said again, "Give it to the people,
that they may eat; for thus says the LORD:
[d]'They shall eat and have *some* left over.'"
44 So he set *it* before them; and they ate [e]and
had *some* left over, according to the word
of the LORD.

Naaman's Leprosy Healed

5 Now [a]Naaman, commander of the army
of the king of Syria, was [b]a great and
honorable man in the eyes of his master,
because by him the LORD had given victory to Syria. He was also a mighty man
of valor, *but* a leper. 2 And the Syrians had
gone out [c]on raids, and had brought back
captive a young girl from the land of Israel.
She waited on Naaman's wife. 3 Then she
said to her mistress, "If only my master
were with the prophet who *is* in Samaria!
For he would heal him of his leprosy." 4 And
Naaman went in and told his master, saying, "Thus and thus said the girl who *is*
from the land of Israel."
5 Then the king of Syria said, "Go now,
and I will send a letter to the king of Israel."
So he departed and [d]took with him ten
talents of silver, six thousand *shekels* of
gold, and ten changes of clothing. 6 Then
he brought the letter to the king of Israel,
which said,

> Now be advised, when this letter comes
> to you, that I have sent Naaman my
> servant to you, that you may heal him
> of his leprosy.

7 And it happened, when the king of Israel
read the letter, that he tore his clothes and
said, "*Am* I [e]God, to kill and make alive,
that this man sends a man to me to heal him
of his leprosy? Therefore please consider,
and see how he seeks a quarrel with me."

4:33 *prayed to the LORD.* Elisha's actions demonstrate that his faith was in the person and power of God alone, and not in the staff that symbolized his prophetic office. The restoration of the boy's life is a demonstration that life itself is in the hands of God.

4:36 Resurrection—When the writer of Hebrews tells us about those "women [who] received their dead raised to life again" (Heb. 11:35), he is probably referring to the two women about whom we read in 1 Kings 17:8–24 and 2 Kings 4:8–37. Many similarities can be seen between these two resurrection miracles, but it is clear that neither prophet followed a "resurrection formula." God is not bound to follow certain procedures or respond to incantations. Instead, He heals whom He will, in what way He wills.

4:41 *flour.* The meal or flour had no magical properties. Elisha's faith in the living God effected the miraculous cure.

5:1 *king of Syria.* The king of Aram (or Syria) was Ben-Hadad II (860–842 B.C.). He was a constant threat against the northern kingdom and would lead an invasion against it later (6:24—7:20).

5:3 *the prophet who is in Samaria.* Although Elisha traveled frequently and may sometimes have lived at Mount Carmel (4:25), he apparently maintained a residence in the capital city of Samaria (2:25; 6:9—7:20).

5:7 *tore his clothes.* While such letters of introduction were common in the ancient Middle East, Ben-Hadad's frequent forays against Israel made the king suspicious that the Arameans were seeking a pretext for another attack. Tearing one's robes was a sign of grief or agitation.

4:31 [o]John 11:11 **4:33** [p][Matt. 6:6] [q]1 Kin. 17:20 **4:34** [r]1 Kin. 17:21–23 **4:35** [s]1 Kin. 17:21 [t]2 Kin. 8:1, 5 **4:37** [u][Heb. 11:35] **4:38** [v]2 Kin. 2:1 [w]2 Kin. 8:1 [x]Acts 22:3 **4:40** [y]Ex. 10:17 **4:41** [z]Ex. 15:25 **4:42** [a]1 Sam. 9:4 [b][1 Cor. 9:11] **4:43** [c]John 6:9 [d]Luke 9:17 **4:44** [e]John 6:13 **5:1** [a]Luke 4:27 [b]Ex. 11:3 **5:2** [c]2 Kin. 6:23; 13:20 **5:5** [d]1 Sam. 9:8 **5:7** [e][Gen. 30:2]

8So it was, when Elisha the man of God heard that the king of Israel had torn his clothes, that he sent to the king, saying, "Why have you torn your clothes? Please let him come to me, and he shall know that there is a prophet in Israel."

9Then Naaman went with his horses and chariot, and he stood at the door of Elisha's house. 10And Elisha sent a messenger to him, saying, "Go and fwash in the Jordan seven times, and your flesh shall be restored to you, and you shall be clean." 11But Naaman became furious, and went away and said, "Indeed, I said to myself, 'He will surely come out to me, and stand and call on the name of the LORD his God, and wave his hand over the place, and heal the leprosy.' 12Are not the Abanah* and the Pharpar, the rivers of Damascus, better than all the waters of Israel? Could I not wash in them and be clean?" So he turned and went away in a rage. 13And his gservants came near and spoke to him, and said, "My father, if the prophet had told you to do something great, would you not have done it? How much more then, when he says to you, 'Wash, and be clean'?" 14So he went down and dipped seven times in the Jordan, according to the saying of the man of God; and his hflesh was restored like the flesh of a little child, and ihe was clean.

15And he returned to the man of God, he and all his aides, and came and stood before him; and he said, "Indeed, now I know that there is jno God in all the earth, except in Israel; now therefore, please take ka gift from your servant."

16But he said, l"As the LORD lives, before whom I stand, mI will receive nothing." And he urged him to take it, but he refused.

17So Naaman said, "Then, if not, please let your servant be given two mule-loads of earth; for your servant will no longer offer either burnt offering or sacrifice to other gods, but to the LORD. 18Yet in this thing may the LORD pardon your servant: when my master goes into the temple of Rimmon to worship there, and nhe leans on my hand, and I bow down in the temple of Rimmon—when I bow down in the temple of Rimmon, may the LORD please pardon your servant in this thing."

19Then he said to him, "Go in peace." So he departed from him a short distance.

Gehazi's Greed

20But oGehazi, the servant of Elisha the man of God, said, "Look, my master has spared Naaman this Syrian, while not receiving from his hands what he brought; but as the LORD lives, I will run after him and take something from him." 21So Gehazi pursued Naaman. When Naaman saw him running after him, he got down from the chariot to meet him, and said, "Is all well?"

22And he said, "All is pwell. My master has sent me, saying, 'Indeed, just now two young men of the sons of the prophets have come to me from the mountains of Ephraim. Please give them a talent of silver and two changes of garments.' "

23So Naaman said, "Please, take two talents." And he urged him, and bound two talents of silver in two bags, with two changes of garments, and handed them to two of his servants; and they carried them on ahead of him. 24When he came to the citadel, he took them from their hand, and stored them away in the house; then he let the men go, and they departed. 25Now he went in and stood before his master. Elisha said to him, "Where did you go, Gehazi?"

And he said, "Your servant did not go anywhere."

26Then he said to him, "Did not my heart go with you when the man turned back from his chariot to meet you? Is it qtime to receive money and to receive clothing, olive groves and vineyards, sheep and oxen, male and female servants? 27Therefore the leprosy of Naaman rshall cling to you and your descendants forever." And he went out from his presence sleprous, as white as snow.

---

* 5:12 Following Kethib, Septuagint, and Vulgate; Qere, Syriac, and Targum read Amanah.

5:10 wash in the Jordan. Elisha's instructions illustrate the fact that simple obedience to God's will, even if it is not what we imagined, is the only road to receiving God's blessings.

5:15 no God ... except in Israel. Naaman is an unusual example of a foreigner who came to faith in God.

5:17 earth. Naaman's unusual request may refer back to God's instructions to the Israelites in the desert (Ex. 20:24). Altars built for the worship of the Lord were to be made of earth or undressed stones, perhaps to avoid the possibility of the altar itself becoming an object of veneration.

5:23 talents. A talent was an enormous amount of silver—equal to 3,000 shekels, or about 75 pounds.

5:26 my heart go with you. The use of the term heart suggests not only Elisha's knowledge but also his strong feelings for Gehazi.

5:26–27 Worldliness—Naaman, in gratitude, urged Elisha to receive a gift, but Elisha steadfastly refused. The prophet wanted the new convert to understand clearly that the God of Israel cannot be bribed. His gifts are bestowed because of His gracious heart. Gehazi's sin was serious—it involved covetousness, lying, misrepresentation of the prophet and, more importantly, brought disgrace on the name of the God of Israel. Gehazi was acting in his own self-interest rather than for the cause of God. When we choose according to the values of unregenerate men, we are worldly and damage the interests of God's kingdom.

5:10 f John 9:7   **5:13** g 1 Sam. 28:23   **5:14** h Job 33:25   i Luke 4:27; 5:13   **5:15** j Dan. 2:47; 3:29; 6:26, 27   k Gen. 33:11   **5:16** l 2 Kin. 3:14   m Gen. 14:22, 23   **5:18** n 2 Kin. 7:2, 17   **5:20** o 2 Kin. 4:12; 8:4, 5   **5:22** p 2 Kin. 4:26   **5:26** q [Eccl. 3:1, 6]   **5:27** r [1 Tim. 6:10]   s Ex. 4:6

The Floating Ax Head

6 And ᵃthe sons of the prophets said to Elisha, "See now, the place where we dwell with you is too small for us. ²Please, let us go to the Jordan, and let every man take a beam from there, and let us make there a place where we may dwell."

So he answered, "Go."

³Then one said, ᵇ"Please consent to go with your servants."

And he answered, "I will go." ⁴So he went with them. And when they came to the Jordan, they cut down trees. ⁵But as one was cutting down a tree, the iron *ax head* fell into the water; and he cried out and said, "Alas, master! For it was ᶜborrowed."

⁶So the man of God said, "Where did it fall?" And he showed him the place. So ᵈhe cut off a stick, and threw *it* in there; and he made the iron float. ⁷Therefore he said, "Pick *it* up for yourself." So he reached out his hand and took it.

The Blinded Syrians Captured

⁸Now the ᵉking of Syria was making war against Israel; and he consulted with his servants, saying, "My camp *will be* in such and such a place." ⁹And the man of God sent to the king of Israel, saying, "Beware that you do not pass this place, for the Syrians are coming down there." ¹⁰Then the king of Israel sent *someone* to the place of which the man of God had told him. Thus he warned him, and he was watchful there, not just once or twice.

¹¹Therefore the heart of the king of Syria was greatly troubled by this thing; and he called his servants and said to them, "Will you not show me which of us *is* for the king of Israel?"

¹²And one of his servants said, "None, my lord, O king; but Elisha, the prophet who *is* in Israel, tells the king of Israel the words that you speak in your bedroom."

¹³So he said, "Go and see where he *is*, that I may send and get him."

And it was told him, saying, "Surely he *is* in ᶠDothan."

¹⁴Therefore he sent horses and chariots and a great army there, and they came by night and surrounded the city. ¹⁵And when the servant of the man of God arose early and went out, there was an army, surrounding the city with horses and chariots. And his servant said to him, "Alas, my master! What shall we do?"

¹⁶So he answered, ᵍ"Do not fear, for ʰthose who *are* with us *are* more than those who *are* with them." ¹⁷And Elisha prayed, and said, "LORD, I pray, open his eyes that he may see." Then the LORD ⁱopened the eyes of the young man, and he saw. And behold, the mountain *was* full of ʲhorses and chariots of fire all around Elisha. ¹⁸So when *the Syrians* came down to him, Elisha prayed to the LORD, and said, "Strike this people, I pray, with blindness." And ᵏHe struck them with blindness according to the word of Elisha.

¹⁹Now Elisha said to them, "This *is* not the way, nor *is* this the city. Follow me, and I will bring you to the man whom you seek." But he led them to Samaria.

²⁰So it was, when they had come to Samaria, that Elisha said, "LORD, open the eyes of these *men*, that they may see." And the LORD opened their eyes, and they saw; and there *they were*, inside Samaria!

²¹Now when the king of Israel saw them, he said to Elisha, "My ˡfather, shall I kill *them*? Shall I kill *them*?"

²²But he answered, "You shall not kill *them*. Would you kill those whom you have taken captive with your sword and your bow? ᵐSet food and water before them, that they may eat and drink and go to their master." ²³Then he prepared a great feast for them; and after they ate and drank, he sent them away and they went to their

---

6:6 made the iron float. At a time when most tools were still made of bronze, an iron blade was valuable.

6:13 Dothan. Dothan was in the central highlands of Israel. It is mentioned only here and in Genesis 37:17, when Joseph was sold to the Midianites.

6:15 servant of the man of God. Since Gehazi had become a leper (5:27), this is probably another servant. However, Gehazi is mentioned again in 8:4 as one who was still faithfully representing the miracles done through Elisha.

6:16–17 Understanding the Big Picture—Spiritually, we don't often make the personal progress we should. We fall back into old patterns of behavior too easily. We feel like God has left us out there alone to fight with our internal weaknesses as well as external forces that often seem to overpower us.

We're like Elisha's servant who couldn't see the full reality. We don't have a big enough vision to see what God is doing around us and in us. We're too wrapped up in our own physical and emotional reality. We're so full of ourselves that there's no room for God and the new vision He can bring to our lives.

Curiously, this story doesn't contain any record of the servant's response to what he saw. Did that new vision dramatically change his life? Did he forever understand the extent of God's protective care? Maybe that happened, or maybe like most of us, he was only able to catch a glimpse. We must live by faith that the full reality is represented by those brief and beautiful glimpses of the bigger picture.

6:19 I will bring you. Elisha's words are technically true, although he was undoubtedly misleading and deceiving the Arameans. The fact that he did not use his unfair advantage to kill Israel's enemies is worthy of notice.

6:1 ᵃ 2 Kin. 4:38 **6:3** ᵇ 2 Kin. 5:23 **6:5** ᶜ [Ex. 22:14] **6:6** ᵈ 2 Kin. 2:21; 4:41 **6:8** ᵉ 2 Kin. 8:28, 29 **6:13** ᶠ Gen. 37:17 **6:16** ᵍ Ex. 14:13 ʰ [Rom. 8:31] **6:17** ⁱ Num. 22:31 ʲ 2 Kin. 2:11 **6:18** ᵏ Gen. 19:11 **6:21** ˡ 2 Kin. 2:12; 5:13; 8:9 **6:22** ᵐ [Rom. 12:20]

master. So [n]the bands of Syrian *raiders*
came no more into the land of Israel.

Syria Besieges Samaria in Famine

24 And it happened after this that [o]Ben-
Hadad king of Syria gathered all his army,
and went up and besieged Samaria. 25 And
there was a great [p]famine in Samaria; and
indeed they besieged it until a donkey's
head was *sold* for eighty *shekels* of silver,
and one-fourth of a kab of dove droppings
for five *shekels* of silver.

26 Then, as the king of Israel was passing
by on the wall, a woman cried out to him,
saying, "Help, my lord, O king!"

27 And he said, "If the LORD does not help
you, where can I find help for you? From
the threshing floor or from the winepress?"
28 Then the king said to her, "What is troubling you?"

And she answered, "This woman said to
me, 'Give your son, that we may eat him
today, and we will eat my son tomorrow.'
29 So [q]we boiled my son, and ate him. And I
said to her on the next day, 'Give your son,
that we may eat him'; but she has hidden
her son."

30 Now it happened, when the king heard
the words of the woman, that he [r]tore his
clothes; and as he passed by on the wall,
the people looked, and there underneath *he
had* sackcloth on his body. 31 Then he said,
[s]"God do so to me and more also, if the
head of Elisha the son of Shaphat remains
on him today!"

32 But Elisha was sitting in his house,
and [t]the elders were sitting with him. And
the king sent a man ahead of him, but before the messenger came to him, he said
to the elders, [u]"Do you see how this son
of [v]a murderer has sent someone to take
away my head? Look, when the messenger
comes, shut the door, and hold him fast at
the door. *Is* not the sound of his master's
feet behind him?" 33 And while he was still
talking with them, there was the messenger, coming down to him; and then *the
king* said, "Surely this calamity *is* from the
LORD; [w]why should I wait for the LORD any
longer?"

7 Then Elisha said, "Hear the word of the
LORD. Thus says the LORD: [a]'Tomorrow
about this time a seah of fine flour *shall be
sold* for a shekel, and two seahs of barley
for a shekel, at the gate of Samaria.'"

2 [b]So an officer on whose hand the king
leaned answered the man of God and said,
"Look, [c]*if* the LORD would make windows
in heaven, could this thing be?"

And he said, "In fact, you shall see *it*
with your eyes, but you shall not eat of it."

The Syrians Flee

3 Now there were four leprous men [d]at
the entrance of the gate; and they said
to one another, "Why are we sitting here
until we die? 4 If we say, 'We will enter the
city,' the famine *is* in the city, and we shall
die there. And if we sit here, we die also.
Now therefore, come, let us surrender to
the [e]army of the Syrians. If they keep us
alive, we shall live; and if they kill us, we
shall only die." 5 And they rose at twilight
to go to the camp of the Syrians; and when
they had come to the outskirts of the Syrian camp, to their surprise no one *was*
there. 6 For the Lord had caused the army
of the Syrians [f]to hear the noise of chariots and the noise of horses—the noise of
a great army; so they said to one another,
"Look, the king of Israel has hired against
us [g]the kings of the Hittites and the kings
of the Egyptians to attack us!" 7 Therefore
they [h]arose and fled at twilight, and left
the camp intact—their tents, their horses,
and their donkeys—and they fled for their
lives. 8 And when these lepers came to the
outskirts of the camp, they went into one
tent and ate and drank, and carried from it
silver and gold and clothing, and went and
hid *them;* then they came back and entered
another tent, and carried *some* from there
also, and went and hid *it.*

9 Then they said to one another, "We are
not doing right. This day *is* a day of good
news, and we remain silent. If we wait until morning light, some punishment will
come upon us. Now therefore, come, let us
go and tell the king's household." 10 So they
went and called to the gatekeepers of the
city, and told them, saying, "We went to
the Syrian camp, and surprisingly no one
was there, not a human sound—only horses and donkeys tied, and the tents intact."

6:25 ***donkey's head.*** Donkeys were unclean for food (Lev. 11:3). ***dove droppings.*** It is not known whether this term is meant to refer to the actual manure of doves or pigeons, or whether it is a slang term for some kind of bean or seed (some translations say "seed pods" or "locust beans").

6:28 ***eat him.*** Israel had been warned that national disobedience could reduce the people to such a loathsome deed (Lev. 26:29; Deut. 28:53–57).

7:3 ***leprous men.*** Because lepers were excluded from the city (Lev. 13:4–6; Num. 5:2–3), and avoided by all, they probably were ignored by the invaders and had been left to their fate. If the ordinary people of the city were suffering from hunger, these men must have been in even worse plight. They concluded that they had nothing to lose by going to the other side.

7:9 ***good news.*** Good news and good fortune had to be shared (Prov. 15:27; 21:17), and the men feared that failure to do so might merit divine punishment.

6:23 [n] 2 Kin. 5:2; 6:8, 9 **6:24** [o] 1 Kin. 20:1 **6:25** [p] 2 Kin. 4:38; 8:1 **6:29** [q] Lev. 26:27–29 **6:30** [r] 1 Kin. 21:27 **6:31** [s] Ruth 1:17 **6:32** [t] Ezek. 8:1; 14:1; 20:1 [u] Luke 13:32 [v] 1 Kin. 18:4, 13, 14; 21:10, 13 **6:33** [w] Job 2:9 **7:1** [a] 2 Kin. 7:18, 19 **7:2** [b] 2 Kin. 5:18; 7:17, 19, 20 [c] Mal. 3:10 **7:3** [d] [Num. 5:2–4; 12:10–14] **7:4** [e] 2 Kin. 6:24 **7:6** [f] 2 Sam. 5:24 [g] 1 Kin. 10:29 **7:7** [h] Ps. 48:4–6

¹¹And the gatekeepers called out, and they told *it* to the king's household inside.

¹²So the king arose in the night and said to his servants, "Let me now tell you what the Syrians have done to us. They know that we *are* ⁱhungry; therefore they have gone out of the camp to hide themselves in the field, saying, 'When they come out of the city, we shall catch them alive, and get into the city.'"

¹³And one of his servants answered and said, "Please, let several *men* take five of the remaining horses which are left in the city. Look, they *may either become* like all the multitude of Israel that are left in it; or indeed, *I say*, they *may become* like all the multitude of Israel left from those who are consumed; so let us send them and see."

¹⁴Therefore they took two chariots with horses; and the king sent them in the direction of the Syrian army, saying, "Go and see." ¹⁵And they went after them to the Jordan; and indeed all the road *was* full of garments and weapons which the Syrians had thrown away in their haste. So the messengers returned and told the king. ¹⁶Then the people went out and plundered the tents of the Syrians. So a seah of fine flour was *sold* for a shekel, and two seahs of barley for a shekel, ʲaccording to the word of the LORD.

¹⁷Now the king had appointed the officer on whose hand he leaned to have charge of the gate. But the people trampled him in the gate, and he died, just ᵏas the man of God had said, who spoke when the king came down to him. ¹⁸So it happened just as the man of God had spoken to the king, saying, ˡ"Two seahs of barley for a shekel, and a seah of fine flour for a shekel, shall be *sold* tomorrow about this time in the gate of Samaria."

¹⁹Then that officer had answered the man of God, and said, "Now look, *if* the LORD would make windows in heaven, could such a thing be?"

And he had said, "In fact, you shall see *it* with your eyes, but you shall not eat of it." ²⁰And so it happened to him, for the people trampled him in the gate, and he died.

The King Restores the Shunammite's Land

8 Then Elisha spoke to the woman ᵃwhose son he had restored to life, saying, "Arise and go, you and your household, and stay wherever you can; for the LORD ᵇhas called for a ᶜfamine, and furthermore, it will come upon the land for seven years." ²So the woman arose and did according to the saying of the man of God, and she went with her household and dwelt in the land of the Philistines seven years.

³It came to pass, at the end of seven years, that the woman returned from the land of the Philistines; and she went to make an appeal to the king for her house and for her land. ⁴Then the king talked with ᵈGehazi, the servant of the man of God, saying, "Tell me, please, all the great things Elisha has done." ⁵Now it happened, as he was telling the king how he had restored the dead to life, that there was the woman whose son he had ᵉrestored to life, appealing to the king for her house and for her land. And Gehazi said, "My lord, O king, this *is* the woman, and this *is* her son whom Elisha restored to life." ⁶And when the king asked the woman, she told him.

So the king appointed a certain officer for her, saying, "Restore all that *was* hers, and all the proceeds of the field from the day that she left the land until now."

Death of Ben-Hadad

⁷Then Elisha went to Damascus, and ᶠBen-Hadad king of Syria was sick; and it was told him, saying, "The man of God has come here." ⁸And the king said to ᵍHazael, ʰ"Take a present in your hand, and go to meet the man of God, and go to ⁱinquire of the LORD by him, saying, 'Shall I recover from this disease?'" ⁹So ʲHazael went to meet him and took a present with him, of every good thing of Damascus, forty camel-loads; and he came and stood before him, and said, "Your son Ben-Hadad king of Syria has sent me to you, saying, 'Shall I recover from this disease?'"

¹⁰And Elisha said to him, "Go, say to

8:1 Kindness—Performing an act of kindness can be compared to throwing sand in the wind. You can be sure some of it will come back to you. The woman mentioned here could give glowing testimony to this. She had been led to feed and house the prophet Elisha (4:8–10), and this act of kindness produced good fruit. Through Elisha's prayers, her child was born and restored (ch. 4), and now Elisha warned her of the coming famine. God always remembers our acts of kindness (Mal. 3:16). In fact, the only thing God "forgets" about us is our confessed sins (Jer. 31:34).

8:3 *she went to make an appeal.* The Shunammite woman had not renounced or sold her property, nor merely had left during the previous famine. Moreover, she had returned within seven years (Deut. 15:1–6; Ruth 4:3–4). Since the property was still legally hers, she pressed her claim to the king himself.

8:4 *Gehazi.* At this point, Gehazi was still faithful to the ministry of Elisha.

8:6 *Restore all.* We get a complex picture of King Jehoram. At times he was so angry with Elisha that he wished him dead (6:31), yet even then he was in mourning for his people. In this section, his righteous judgment should be contrasted with the wretched behavior of the wicked Ahab (1 Kin. 21:1–16).

8:10 *You shall certainly recover.* Elisha was answering Ben-Hadad's exact question: his illness was not deadly, in the natural course of things he would have

---

7:12 ⁱ 2 Kin. 6:24–29 **7:16** ʲ 2 Kin. 7:1 **7:17** ᵏ 2 Kin. 6:32; 7:2 **7:18** ˡ 2 Kin. 7:1 **8:1** ᵃ 2 Kin. 4:18, 31–35 ᵇ Hag. 1:11 ᶜ 2 Sam. 21:1 **8:4** ᵈ 2 Kin. 4:12; 5:20–27 **8:5** ᵉ 2 Kin. 4:35 **8:7** ᶠ 2 Kin. 6:24 **8:8** ᵍ 1 Kin. 19:15 ʰ 1 Sam. 9:7 ⁱ 2 Kin. 1:2 **8:9** ʲ 1 Kin. 19:15

him, 'You shall certainly recover.' However the LORD has shown me that ^{k}he will really die." ^{11}Then he set his countenance in a stare until he was ashamed; and the man of God ^{l}wept. ^{12}And Hazael said, "Why is my lord weeping?"

He answered, "Because I know ^{m}the evil that you will do to the children of Israel: Their strongholds you will set on fire, and their young men you will kill with the sword; and you ^{n}will dash their children, and rip open their women with child."

^{13}So Hazael said, "But what ^{o}is your servant—a dog, that he should do this gross thing?"

And Elisha answered, ^{p}"The LORD has shown me that you will become king over Syria."

^{14}Then he departed from Elisha, and came to his master, who said to him, "What did Elisha say to you?" And he answered, "He told me you would surely recover." ^{15}But it happened on the next day that he took a thick cloth and dipped it in water, and spread it over his face so that he died; and Hazael reigned in his place.

Jehoram Reigns in Judah

^{16}Now ^{q}in the fifth year of Joram the son of Ahab, king of Israel, Jehoshaphat having been king of Judah, ^{r}Jehoram the son of Jehoshaphat began to reign as king of Judah. ^{17}He was ^{s}thirty-two years old when he became king, and he reigned eight years in Jerusalem. ^{18}And he walked in the way of the kings of Israel, just as the house of Ahab had done, for ^{t}the daughter of Ahab was his wife; and he did evil in the sight of the LORD. ^{19}Yet the LORD would not destroy Judah, for the sake of His servant David, ^{u}as He promised him to give a lamp to him and his sons forever.

^{20}In his days ^{v}Edom revolted against Judah's authority, ^{w}and made a king over themselves. ^{21}So Joram* went to Zair, and all his chariots with him. Then he rose by

night and attacked the Edomites who had surrounded him and the captains of the chariots; and the troops fled to their tents. ^{22}Thus Edom has been in revolt against Judah's authority to this day. ^{x}And Libnah revolted at that time.

^{23}Now the rest of the acts of Joram, and all that he did, are they not written in the book of the chronicles of the kings of Judah? ^{24}So Joram rested with his fathers, and was buried with his fathers in the City of David. Then ^{y}Ahaziah his son reigned in his place.

Ahaziah Reigns in Judah

^{25}In the twelfth year of Joram the son of Ahab, king of Israel, Ahaziah the son of Jehoram, king of Judah, began to reign. ^{26}Ahaziah was ^{z}twenty-two years old when he became king, and he reigned one year in Jerusalem. His mother's name was Athaliah the granddaughter of Omri, king of Israel. ^{27a}And he walked in the way of the house of Ahab, and did evil in the sight of the LORD, like the house of Ahab, for he was the son-in-law of the house of Ahab.

^{28}Now he went ^{b}with Joram the son of Ahab to war against Hazael king of Syria at ^{c}Ramoth Gilead; and the Syrians wounded Joram. ^{29}Then ^{d}King Joram went back to Jezreel to recover from the wounds which the Syrians had inflicted on him at Ramah, when he fought against Hazael king of Syria. ^{e}And Ahaziah the son of Jehoram, king of Judah, went down to see Joram the son of Ahab in Jezreel, because he was sick.

Jehu Anointed King of Israel

9 And Elisha the prophet called one of ^{a}the sons of the prophets, and said to him, ^{b}"Get yourself ready, take this flask of oil in your hand, ^{c}and go to Ramoth Gilead. ^{2}Now when you arrive at that place, look there for Jehu the son of Jehoshaphat,

* **8:21** Spelled Jehoram in verse 16

---

recovered. However, Elisha also knew that Ben-Hadad's life would be taken by his servant Hazael.

8:11 ashamed. Elisha had reached the end of his ability to resist his emotions and wept over the suffering that Hazael would bring.

8:13 dog. In the ancient Middle East, dogs were despised as scavengers and unclean animals. Shalmaneser III of Assyria noted Hazael's accession to the throne with the words: "Hazael, son of nobody, seizes the throne."

8:16 Joram . . . Jehoram. These are variant spellings of the same name; the two kings were brothers-in-law since Jehoram of Judah had married the sister of Joram of Israel.

8:16–19 Apostasy—The complete picture of Jehoram's shameful apostasy is presented by the chronicler (2 Chr. 21:2–26). There were two powerful influences in Jehoram's life, one good and one evil; sadly, the evil influence prevailed. His father, Jehoshaphat, was one of the few godly kings of Judah, but Jehoram's wife was Athaliah, daughter of

Jezebel, who influenced him to worship Baal (v. 18). Jehoram's life of unfaithfulness earned God's judgment, and he died a lonely and miserable death. Nevertheless, the Lord remained committed to His covenant promise (v. 19). Human unfaithfulness cannot destroy God's purpose of salvation.

8:27 the way of the house of Ahab. The lowest point of Israel's religious apostasy was reached in the reign of Ahab and his wicked wife Jezebel (1 Kin. 16:31).

9:2 Jehu. The name Jehu means "the Lord is He."

8:10 ^{k} 2 Kin. 8:15 **8:11** ^{l} Luke 19:41 **8:12** ^{m} Amos 1:3, 4 ^{n} Hos. 13:16 **8:13** ^{o} 1 Sam. 17:43 ^{p} 1 Kin. 19:15 **8:16** ^{q} 2 Kin. 1:17; 3:1 ^{r} 2 Chr. 21:3 **8:17** ^{s} 2 Chr. 21:5–10 **8:18** ^{t} 2 Kin. 8:26, 27 **8:19** ^{u} 2 Sam. 7:13 **8:20** ^{v} Gen. 27:40 ^{w} 1 Kin. 22:47 **8:22** ^{x} Josh. 21:13 **8:24** ^{y} 2 Kin. 22:1, 7 **8:26** ^{z} 2 Chr. 22:2 **8:27** ^{a} 2 Chr. 22:3, 4 **8:28** ^{b} 2 Chr. 22:5 ^{c} 1 Kin. 22:3, 29 **8:29** ^{d} 2 Kin. 9:15 ^{e} 2 Chr. 22:6, 7 **9:1** ^{a} 1 Kin. 20:35 ^{b} 2 Kin. 4:29 ^{c} 2 Kin. 8:28, 29

the son of Nimshi, and go in and make him
rise up from among [d]his associates, and
take him to an inner room. 3Then [e]take the
flask of oil, and pour *it* on his head, and
say, 'Thus says the LORD: "I have anointed
you king over Israel."' Then open the door
and flee, and do not delay."
4So the young man, the servant of the
prophet, went to Ramoth Gilead. 5And
when he arrived, there *were* the captains
of the army sitting; and he said, "I have a
message for you, Commander."
Jehu said, "For which *one* of us?"
And he said, "For you, Commander."
6Then he arose and went into the house.
And he poured the oil on his head, and said
to him, [f]"Thus says the LORD God of Israel:
'I have anointed you king over the people
of the LORD, over Israel. 7You shall strike
down the house of Ahab your master, that
I may [g]avenge the blood of My servants
the prophets, and the blood of all the servants of the LORD, [h]at the hand of Jezebel.
8For the whole house of Ahab shall perish;
and [i]I will cut off from Ahab all [j]the males
in Israel, both [k]bond and free. 9So I will
make the house of Ahab like the house of
[l]Jeroboam the son of Nebat, and like the
house of [m]Baasha the son of Ahijah. 10[n]The
dogs shall eat Jezebel on the plot *of ground*
at Jezreel, and *there shall be* none to bury
her.'" And he opened the door and fled.
11Then Jehu came out to the servants of
his master, and *one* said to him, "*Is* all well?
Why did [o]this madman come to you?"
And he said to them, "You know the man
and his babble."
12And they said, "A lie! Tell us now."
So he said, "Thus and thus he spoke to
me, saying, 'Thus says the LORD: "I have
anointed you king over Israel."'"
13Then each man hastened [p]to take his
garment and put *it* under him on the top of
the steps; and they blew trumpets, saying,
"Jehu is king!"

Joram of Israel Killed

14So Jehu the son of Jehoshaphat, the son
of Nimshi, conspired against [q]Joram. (Now
Joram had been defending Ramoth Gilead,
he and all Israel, against Hazael king of
Syria. 15But [r]King Joram had returned to
Jezreel to recover from the wounds which
the Syrians had inflicted on him when he
fought with Hazael king of Syria.) And
Jehu said, "If you are so minded, let no one
leave *or* escape from the city to go and tell
it in Jezreel." 16So Jehu rode in a chariot
and went to Jezreel, for Joram was laid
up there; [s]and Ahaziah king of Judah had
come down to see Joram.
17Now a watchman stood on the tower in
Jezreel, and he saw the company of Jehu
as he came, and said, "I see a company of
men."
And Joram said, "Get a horseman and
send him to meet them, and let him say, '*Is
it* peace?'"
18So the horseman went to meet him,
and said, "Thus says the king: '*Is it* peace?'"
And Jehu said, "What have you to do
with peace? Turn around and follow me."
So the watchman reported, saying, "The
messenger went to them, but is not coming
back."
19Then he sent out a second horseman
who came to them, and said, "Thus says the
king: '*Is it* peace?'"
And Jehu answered, "What have you
to do with peace? Turn around and follow
me."
20So the watchman reported, saying,
"He went up to them and is not coming
back; and the driving *is* like the driving of
Jehu the son of Nimshi, for he drives furiously!"
21Then Joram said, "Make ready." And
his chariot was made ready. Then [t]Joram
king of Israel and Ahaziah king of Judah
went out, each in his chariot; and they went
out to meet Jehu, and met him [u]on the property of Naboth the Jezreelite. 22Now it happened, when Joram saw Jehu, that he said,
"*Is it* peace, Jehu?"
So he answered, "What peace, as long as
the harlotries of your mother Jezebel and
her witchcraft *are so* many?"
23Then Joram turned around and fled,
and said to Ahaziah, "Treachery, Ahaziah!" 24Now Jehu drew his bow with full
strength and shot Jehoram between his
arms; and the arrow came out at his heart,

9:6 *poured the oil.* The last part of the Lord's threefold command to Elijah had been carried out (1 Kin. 19:15–21; 2 Kin. 8:7–13). In the Old Testament, anointing was customarily reserved for a king (2 Sam. 2:4) or the high priest (Ex. 40:13).

9:13 *garment.* This action was a mark of homage fit for a king (Matt. 21:8). This scene is reminiscent of the anointing of King Solomon (1 Kin. 1:34).

9:21 *the property of Naboth.* Ahab's dynasty ended on the very stolen property that occasioned the divine sentence of judgment (1 Kin. 21:17–24). Ahab's unlawful seizure of the land of Naboth was regarded as one of his most heinous crimes.

9:22 *harlotries of . . . Jezebel.* Jezebel's spiritual adultery had brought vile demonic practices into the kingdom and sealed its doom (1 Kin. 21:25–26). As God had said, such activities would surely bring about the nation's demise (Deut. 28:25–26). Jehu justified his actions as a judgment on Jezebel's sins.

9:23 *Treachery.* In reality, Joram and Ahaziah were the true traitors, the ones who had led the people in

9:2 [d] 2 Kin. 9:5, 11 **9:3** [e] 1 Kin. 19:16 **9:6** [f] 2 Chr. 22:7 **9:7** [g] [Deut. 32:35, 41] [h] 1 Kin. 18:4; 21:15 **9:8** [i] 2 Kin. 10:17 [j] 1 Sam. 25:22 [k] Deut. 32:36 **9:9** [l] 1 Kin. 14:10; 15:29; 21:22 [m] 1 Kin. 16:3, 11 **9:10** [n] 1 Kin. 21:23 **9:11** [o] Jer. 29:26 **9:13** [p] Matt. 21:7, 8 **9:14** [q] 2 Kin. 8:28 **9:15** [r] 2 Kin. 8:29 **9:16** [s] 2 Kin. 8:29 **9:21** [t] 1 Kin. 19:17 [u] 1 Kin. 21:1–14

and he sank down in his chariot. ²⁵Then *Jehu* said to Bidkar his captain, "Pick *him* up, *and* throw him into the tract of the field of Naboth the Jezreelite; for remember, when you and I were riding together behind Ahab his father, that ^vthe LORD laid this ^wburden upon him: ²⁶'Surely I saw yesterday the blood of Naboth and the blood of his sons,' says the LORD, ^x'and I will repay you in this plot,' says the LORD. Now therefore, take *and* throw him on the plot *of ground*, according to the word of the LORD."

Ahaziah of Judah Killed

²⁷But when Ahaziah king of Judah saw *this*, he fled by the road to Beth Haggan.* So Jehu pursued him, and said, "Shoot him also in the chariot." *And they shot him* at the Ascent of Gur, which is by Ibleam. Then he fled to ^yMegiddo, and died there. ²⁸And his servants carried him in the chariot to Jerusalem, and buried him in his tomb with his fathers in the City of David. ²⁹In the eleventh year of Joram the son of Ahab, Ahaziah had become king over Judah.

Jezebel's Violent Death

³⁰Now when Jehu had come to Jezreel, Jezebel heard *of it*; ^zand she put paint on her eyes and adorned her head, and looked through a window. ³¹Then, as Jehu entered at the gate, she said, ^a"*Is it* peace, Zimri, murderer of your master?"

³²And he looked up at the window, and said, "Who *is* on my side? Who?" So two *or* three eunuchs looked out at him. ³³Then he said, "Throw her down." So they threw her down, and *some* of her blood spattered on the wall and on the horses; and he trampled her underfoot. ³⁴And when he had gone in, he ate and drank. Then he said, "Go now, see to this accursed *woman*, and bury her, for ^bshe was a king's daughter." ³⁵So they went to bury her, but they found no more of her than the skull and the feet and the palms of *her* hands. ³⁶Therefore they came back and told him. And he said, "This *is* the word of the LORD, which He spoke by His servant Elijah the Tishbite, saying, ^c'On the plot *of ground* at Jezreel dogs shall eat the flesh of Jezebel;* ³⁷and the corpse of Jezebel shall be ^das refuse on the surface of the field, in the plot at Jezreel, so that they shall not say, "Here *lies* Jezebel."'"

Ahab's Seventy Sons Killed

10 Now Ahab had seventy sons in Samaria. And Jehu wrote and sent letters to Samaria, to the rulers of Jezreel,* to the elders, and to those who reared Ahab's *sons*, saying:

² Now as soon as this letter comes to you, since your master's sons *are* with you, and you have chariots and horses, a fortified city also, and weapons, ³choose the best qualified of your master's sons, set *him* on his father's throne, and fight for your master's house.

⁴But they were exceedingly afraid, and said, "Look, ^atwo kings could not stand up to him; how then can we stand?" ⁵And he who *was* in charge of the house, and he who *was* in charge of the city, the elders also, and those who reared *the sons*, sent to Jehu, saying, "We *are* your servants, we will do all you tell us; but we will not make anyone king. Do *what is* good in your sight." ⁶Then he wrote a second letter to them, saying:

If you *are* for me and will obey my voice, take the heads of the men, your master's sons, and come to me at Jezreel by this time tomorrow.

Now the king's sons, seventy persons, *were* with the great men of the city, who were rearing them. ⁷So it was, when the letter came to them, that they took the king's sons and ^bslaughtered seventy persons, put their heads in baskets and sent *them* to him at Jezreel.

⁸Then a messenger came and told him, saying, "They have brought the heads of the king's sons."

And he said, "Lay them in two heaps at the entrance of the gate until morning." ⁹So it was, in the morning, that he went out and stood, and said to all the people,

---

---

rebellion against God and sealed their own doom by their disobedience.

10:1 *seventy sons.* Ahab's "seventy sons" probably included the children of his concubines, as well as grandchildren.

10:9 Righteousness—Jehu declared Ahab's "great men" (v. 6) innocent of the death of Ahab's seventy sons. The Hebrew word translates literally as "just" or "righteous." They were righteous in the same sense that Jehu himself was (v. 30), in that God had ordered the death of Ahab's family and they were actually carrying out God's orders. However, this did not mean that these men could be considered righteous in any other sense. They had already thrown in their lot with Ahab and his wicked ways, they were his "great men," and as such, they had to meet the same fate as the rest of his family (v. 11). They had almost accidentally been obedient to God's will, but their hearts were still for the enemy.

9:25 ^v 1 Kin. 21:19, 24–29   ^w Is. 13:1   **9:26** ^x 1 Kin. 21:13, 19   **9:27** ^y 2 Chr. 22:7, 9   **9:30** ^z Ezek. 23:40   **9:31** ^a 1 Kin. 16:9–20   **9:34** ^b 1 Kin. 16:31   **9:36** ^c 1 Kin. 21:23   **9:37** ^d Ps. 83:10   **10:4** ^a 2 Kin. 9:24, 27   **10:7** ^b 1 Kin. 21:21

"You *are* righteous. Indeed ᶜI conspired against my master and killed him; but who killed all these? ¹⁰Know now that nothing shall ᵈfall to the earth of the word of the LORD which the LORD spoke concerning the house of Ahab; for the LORD has done what He spoke ᵉby His servant Elijah." ¹¹So Jehu killed all who remained of the house of Ahab in Jezreel, and all his great men and his close acquaintances and his priests, until he left him none remaining.

Ahaziah's Forty-two Brothers Killed

¹²And he arose and departed and went to Samaria. On the way, at Beth Eked* of the Shepherds, ¹³ᶠJehu met with the brothers of Ahaziah king of Judah, and said, "Who *are* you?"

So they answered, "We *are* the brothers of Ahaziah; we have come down to greet the sons of the king and the sons of the queen mother."

¹⁴And he said, "Take them alive!" So they took them alive, and ᵍkilled them at the well of Beth Eked, forty-two men; and he left none of them.

The Rest of Ahab's Family Killed

¹⁵Now when he departed from there, he met ʰJehonadab the son of ⁱRechab, *coming* to meet him; and he greeted him and said to him, "Is your heart right, as my heart *is* toward your heart?"

And Jehonadab answered, "It is."

Jehu said, "If it is, ʲgive *me* your hand." So he gave *him* his hand, and he took him up to him into the chariot. ¹⁶Then he said, "Come with me, and see my ᵏzeal for the LORD." So they had him ride in his chariot. ¹⁷And when he came to Samaria, ˡhe killed all who remained to Ahab in Samaria, till he had destroyed them, according to the word of the LORD ᵐwhich He spoke to Elijah.

Worshipers of Baal Killed

¹⁸Then Jehu gathered all the people together, and said to them, ⁿ"Ahab served Baal a little, Jehu will serve him much.

¹⁹Now therefore, call to me all the ᵒprophets of Baal, all his servants, and all his priests. Let no one be missing, for I have a great sacrifice for Baal. Whoever is missing shall not live." But Jehu acted deceptively, with the intent of destroying the worshipers of Baal. ²⁰And Jehu said, "Proclaim a solemn assembly for Baal." So they proclaimed *it.* ²¹Then Jehu sent throughout all Israel; and all the worshipers of Baal came, so that there was not a man left who did not come. So they came into the temple* of Baal, and the ᵖtemple of Baal was full from one end to the other. ²²And he said to the one in charge of the wardrobe, "Bring out vestments for all the worshipers of Baal." So he brought out vestments for them. ²³Then Jehu and Jehonadab the son of Rechab went into the temple of Baal, and said to the worshipers of Baal, "Search and see that no servants of the LORD are here with you, but only the worshipers of Baal." ²⁴So they went in to offer sacrifices and burnt offerings. Now Jehu had appointed for himself eighty men on the outside, and had said, "If any of the men whom I have brought into your hands escapes, *whoever lets him escape, it shall be* ᑫhis life for the life of the other."

²⁵Now it happened, as soon as he had made an end of offering the burnt offering, that Jehu said to the guard and to the captains, "Go in *and* kill them; let no one come out!" And they killed them with the edge of the sword; then the guards and the officers threw *them* out, and went into the inner room of the temple of Baal. ²⁶And they brought the ʳsacred pillars out of the temple of Baal and burned them. ²⁷Then they broke down the *sacred* pillar of Baal, and tore down the temple of Baal and ˢmade it a refuse dump to this day. ²⁸Thus Jehu destroyed Baal from Israel.

²⁹However Jehu did not turn away from the sins of Jeroboam the son of Nebat, who had made Israel sin, *that is,* from ᵗthe golden calves that *were* at Bethel and Dan.

---

* **10:12** Or *The Shearing House*   * **10:21** Literally *house,* and so elsewhere in this chapter

---

10:10 the LORD has done what He spoke. Evaluating Jehu is difficult. His praise for the ministry of the prophets of God and his stated respect for the word of God commend him to us, but later he did not exhibit faithfulness to the Lord (10:31).

10:15 Jehonadab. The name Jehonadab means "the LORD is noble." He was an ascetic, nomadic Rechabite. These people were known for their faithfulness to God and the austere regulations laid down by Jehonadab (Jer. 35:1–16).

10:21 temple of Baal. This was the temple constructed by Ahab (1 Kin. 16:32).

10:21–24 Worship—At times Israel imported pagan ideas and practices into their worship and attempted to mix them with the worship of the Lord. The extremity of this apostasy was reached when Ahab erected an altar for Baal, the fertility god of the Canaanites,

in a temple built for Baal in Samaria (1 Kin. 16:32). The participants in Baal worship engaged not only in immoral sexual orgies but in the detestable practice of child sacrifice (Num. 25:1–8; Jer. 19:5). God could not tolerate such behavior and Jehu's purge was the punishment that He had promised for disobedience.

10:29 the golden calves. Jehu's destruction of Baal worship was a political act. His continuing of the state

10:9 ᶜ 2 Kin. 9:14–24   **10:10** ᵈ 1 Sam. 3:19   ᵉ 1 Kin. 21:17–24, 29   **10:13** ᶠ 2 Chr. 22:8   **10:14** ᵍ 2 Chr. 22:8   **10:15** ʰ Jer. 35:6   ⁱ 1 Chr. 2:55   ʲ Ezra 10:19   **10:16** ᵏ 1 Kin. 19:10   **10:17** ˡ 2 Kin. 9:8   ᵐ 1 Kin. 21:21, 29   **10:18** ⁿ 1 Kin. 16:31, 32   **10:19** ᵒ 1 Kin. 18:19; 22:6   **10:21** ᵖ 1 Kin. 16:32   **10:24** ᑫ 1 Kin. 20:39   **10:26** ʳ [Deut. 7:5, 25]   **10:27** ˢ Ezra 6:11   **10:29** ᵗ 1 Kin. 12:28–30; 13:33, 34

³⁰And the L ORD ᵘsaid to Jehu, "Because you have done well in doing *what is* right in My sight, *and* have done to the house of Ahab all that *was* in My heart, ᵛyour sons shall sit on the throne of Israel to the fourth *generation*." ³¹But Jehu took no heed to walk in the law of the L ORD God of Israel with all his heart; for he did not depart from ʷthe sins of Jeroboam, who had made Israel sin.

Death of Jehu

³²In those days the L ORD began to cut off *parts* of Israel; and ˣHazael conquered them in all the territory of Israel ³³from the Jordan eastward: all the land of Gilead— Gad, Reuben, and Manasseh—from ʸAroer, which *is* by the River Arnon, including ᶻGilead and Bashan.

³⁴Now the rest of the acts of Jehu, all that he did, and all his might, *are* they not written in the book of the chronicles of the kings of Israel? ³⁵So Jehu rested with his fathers, and they buried him in Samaria. Then ᵃJehoahaz his son reigned in his place. ³⁶And the period that Jehu reigned over Israel in Samaria *was* twenty-eight years.

Athaliah Reigns in Judah

11 When ᵃAthaliah ᵇthe mother of Ahaziah saw that her son was ᶜdead, she arose and destroyed all the royal heirs. ²But Jehosheba, the daughter of King Joram, sister of ᵈAhaziah, took Joash the son of Ahaziah, and stole him away from among the king's sons *who were* being murdered; and they hid him and his nurse in the bedroom, from Athaliah, so that he was not killed. ³So he was hidden with her in the house of the L ORD for six years, while Athaliah reigned over the land.

Joash Crowned King of Judah

⁴In ᵉthe seventh year Jehoiada sent and brought the captains of hundreds— of the bodyguards and the escorts—and

brought them into the house of the L ORD to him. And he made a covenant with them and took an oath from them in the house of the L ORD, and showed them the king's son. ⁵Then he commanded them, saying, "This *is* what you shall do: One-third of you who come on duty ᶠon the Sabbath shall be keeping watch over the king's house, ⁶one-third *shall be* at the gate of Sur, and one-third at the gate behind the escorts. You shall keep the watch of the house, lest it be broken down. ⁷The two contingents of you who go off duty on the Sabbath shall keep the watch of the house of the L ORD for the king. ⁸But you shall surround the king on all sides, every man with his weapons in his hand; and whoever comes within range, let him be put to death. You are to be with the king as he goes out and as he comes in."

⁹ᵍSo the captains of the hundreds did according to all that Jehoiada the priest commanded. Each of them took his men who were to be on duty on the Sabbath, with those who were going off duty on the Sabbath, and came to Jehoiada the priest. ¹⁰And the priest gave the captains of hundreds the spears and shields which *had belonged* to King David, ʰthat were in the temple of the L ORD. ¹¹Then the escorts stood, every man with his weapons in his hand, all around the king, from the right side of the temple to the left side of the temple, by the altar and the house. ¹²And he brought out the king's son, put the crown on him, and *gave him* the ⁱTestimony;* they made him king and anointed him, and they clapped their hands and said, ʲ"Long live the king!"

Death of Athaliah

¹³ᵏNow when Athaliah heard the noise of the escorts *and* the people, she came to the people *in* the temple of the L ORD.

* **11:12** That is, the Law (compare Exodus 25:16, 21 and Deuteronomy 31:9)

---

worship policies established by Jeroboam clearly shows his disregard for true spiritual revival in Israel.
10:32 *the L ORD began to cut off parts of Israel.* The attacks of Hazael were part of God's judgment on Israel.
11:1 *Athaliah.* This name means "the L ORD is exalted." Sadly, she did not live up to her name, and instead exalted herself.
11:2 *Jehosheba.* Josephus says that Jehosheba was Ahaziah's half sister. As the wife of the high priest Jehoiada, her marriage and her relation to the royal house made it possible for her to rescue and hide her nephew Joash.
11:3 *hidden . . . in the house of the L ORD.* Joash was to inherit the promises of the Davidic covenant. His righteous reign may be attributed in part to his early years spent in the house of the Lord and to the godly instruction and protection of his aunt Jehosheba and her husband.
11:9 *did according to all . . . the priest commanded.*

The remarkably willing obedience of the royal guard would seem to indicate that even her own followers were disgusted by Athaliah's wickedness.
11:12 *gave him the Testimony.* Deuteronomy prescribed the duties of the king with regard to the preservation of God's law (Deut. 17:18). By putting a copy of the Law in Joash's hand and the crown on his head, Jehoiada presented him as the rightful heir to the throne. The term "Testimony" recalls the covenant, emphasizing that Joash's coronation was given both its scriptural warrant and its rightful connection to the Davidic covenant.

10:30 ᵘ 2 Kin. 9:6, 7	ᵛ 2 Kin. 13:1, 10; 14:23; 15:8,
12 **10:31** ʷ 1 Kin. 14:16	**10:32** ˣ 2 Kin. 8:12; 13:22
10:33 ʸ Deut. 2:36	ᶻ Amos 1:3–5 **10:35** ᵃ 2 Kin.
13:1 **11:1** ᵃ 2 Chr. 22:10	ᵇ 2 Kin. 8:26 ᶜ 2 Kin. 9:27
11:2 ᵈ 2 Kin. 8:25 **11:4** ᵉ 2 Chr. 23:1	**11:5** ᶠ 1 Chr. 9:25
11:9 ᵍ 2 Chr. 23:8 **11:10** ʰ 2 Sam. 8:7	**11:12** ⁱ Ex. 25:16;
31:18 ʲ 1 Sam. 10:24 **11:13** ᵏ 2 Chr. 23:12	

14When she looked, there was the king standing by *l*a pillar according to custom; and the leaders and the trumpeters were by the king. All the people of the land were rejoicing and blowing trumpets. So Athaliah tore her clothes and cried out, "Treason! Treason!"

15And Jehoiada the priest commanded the captains of the hundreds, the officers of the army, and said to them, "Take her outside under guard, and slay with the sword whoever follows her." For the priest had said, "Do not let her be killed in the house of the LORD." 16So they seized her; and she went by way of the horses' entrance *into* the king's house, and there she was killed.

17*m*Then Jehoiada *n*made a covenant between the LORD, the king, and the people, that they should be the LORD's people, and *also* obetween the king and the people. 18And all the people of the land went to the *p*temple of Baal, and tore it down. They thoroughly *q*broke in pieces its altars and images, and *r*killed Mattan the priest of Baal before the altars. And *s*the priest appointed officers over the house of the LORD. 19Then he took the captains of hundreds, the bodyguards, the escorts, and all the people of the land; and they brought the king down from the house of the LORD, and went by way of the gate of the escorts to the king's house. Then he sat on the throne of the kings. 20So all the people of the land rejoiced; and the city was quiet, for they had slain Athaliah with the sword *in* the king's house. 21Jehoash *was* *t*seven years old when he became king.

Jehoash Repairs the Temple

12 In the seventh year of Jehu, *a*Jehoash* became king, and he reigned forty years in Jerusalem. His mother's name *was* Zibiah of Beersheba. 2Jehoash did *what was* right in the sight of the LORD all the days in which *b*Jehoiada the priest instructed him. 3But *c*the high places were not taken away; the people still sacrificed and burned incense on the high places.

4And Jehoash said to the priests, *d*"All the money of the dedicated gifts that are brought into the house of the LORD— each man's *e*census money, each man's

*f*assessment money*—*and* all the money that a man *g*purposes in his heart to bring into the house of the LORD, 5let the priests take *it* themselves, each from his constituency; and let them repair the damages of the temple, wherever any dilapidation is found."

6Now it was so, by the twenty-third year of King Jehoash, *h*that the priests had not repaired the damages of the temple. 7*i*So King Jehoash called Jehoiada the priest and the *other* priests, and said to them, "Why have you not repaired the damages of the temple? Now therefore, do not take *more* money from your constituency, but deliver it for repairing the damages of the temple." 8And the priests agreed that they would neither receive *more* money from the people, nor repair the damages of the temple.

9Then Jehoiada the priest took *j*a chest, bored a hole in its lid, and set it beside the altar, on the right side as one comes into the house of the LORD; and the priests who kept the door put *k*there all the money brought into the house of the LORD. 10So it was, whenever they saw that *there was* much money in the chest, that the king's *l*scribe and the high priest came up and put it in bags, and counted the money that was found in the house of the LORD. 11Then they gave the money, which had been apportioned, into the hands of those who did the work, who had the oversight of the house of the LORD; and they paid it out to the carpenters and builders who worked on the house of the LORD, 12and to masons and stonecutters, and for buying timber and hewn stone, to *m*repair the damage of the house of the LORD, and for all that was paid out to repair the temple. 13However *n*there were not made for the house of the LORD basins of silver, trimmers, sprinkling-bowls, trumpets, any articles of gold or articles of silver, from the money brought into the house of the LORD. 14But they gave that to the workmen, and they repaired the house of the LORD with it. 15Moreover *o*they did not require an account from the men

---

* **12:1** Spelled *Joash* in 11:2ff   * **12:4** Compare Leviticus 27:2ff

---

11:17 covenant. Covenant renewal was particularly necessary after the usurpation by the wicked Athaliah.
11:20 rejoiced . . . quiet. The joy of the people and the peacefulness of the land were marks of God's blessing to the restored Davidic dynasty.
11:21 Jehoash. This variant spelling is used interchangeably with Joash.
12:2 all the days in which Jehoiada the priest instructed him. Sadly, after Jehoiada's death Joash's reign took a different turn; nonetheless, he was one of the few kings of Judah who showed some signs of righteousness.
12:3 high places. Although the high places seem to

have been used at times for the worship of the true God, they were also strongly associated with Canaanite religious rites (1 Kin. 3:2–4; 14:23). Apostasy would become a besetting sin later in Joash's reign (2 Chr. 24:17–19,24).

11:14 *l* 2 Chr. 34:31   **11:17** *m* 2 Chr. 23:16   *n* Josh. 24:24, 25   *o* 2 Sam. 5:3   **11:18** *p* 2 Kin. 10:26, 27   *q* [Deut. 12:3]   *r* 1 Kin. 18:40   *s* 2 Chr. 23:18   **11:21** *t* 2 Chr. 24:1–14   **12:1** *a* 2 Chr. 24:1   **12:2** *b* 2 Kin. 11:4   **12:3** *c* 2 Kin. 14:4; 15:35   **12:4** *d* 2 Kin. 22:4   *e* Ex. 30:13–16   *f* Lev. 27:2–28   *g* Ex. 35:5   **12:6** *h* 2 Chr. 24:5   **12:7** *i* 2 Chr. 24:6   **12:9** *j* 2 Chr. 23:1; 24:8   *k* Mark 12:41   **12:10** *l* 2 Sam. 8:17   **12:12** *m* 2 Kin. 22:5, 6   **12:13** *n* 2 Chr. 24:14   **12:15** *o* 2 Kin. 22:7

into whose hand they delivered the money to be paid to workmen, for they dealt faithfully. [16]pThe money from the trespass offerings and the money from the sin offerings was not brought into the house of the LORD. qIt belonged to the priests.

Hazael Threatens Jerusalem

[17]rHazael king of Syria went up and fought against Gath, and took it; then sHazael set his face to go up to Jerusalem. [18]And Jehoash king of Judah ttook all the sacred things that his fathers, Jehoshaphat and Jehoram and Ahaziah, kings of Judah, had dedicated, and his own sacred things, and all the gold found in the treasuries of the house of the LORD and in the king's house, and sent them to Hazael king of Syria. Then he went away from Jerusalem.

Death of Joash

[19]Now the rest of the acts of Joash,* and all that he did, are they not written in the book of the chronicles of the kings of Judah?

[20]And uhis servants arose and formed a conspiracy, and killed Joash in the house of the Millo,* which goes down to Silla. [21]For Jozachar* the son of Shimeath and Jehozabad the son of Shomer,* his servants, struck him. So he died, and they buried him with his fathers in the City of David. Then vAmaziah his son reigned in his place.

Jehoahaz Reigns in Israel

13 In the twenty-third year of aJoash* the son of Ahaziah, king of Judah, bJehoahaz the son of Jehu became king over Israel in Samaria, and reigned seventeen years. [2]And he did evil in the sight of the LORD, and followed the csins of Jeroboam the son of Nebat, who had made Israel sin. He did not depart from them.

[3]Then dthe anger of the LORD was aroused against Israel, and He delivered them into the hand of eHazael king of Syria, and into the hand of fBen-Hadad the son of Hazael, all their days. [4]So Jehoahaz gpleaded with the LORD, and the LORD listened to him; for hHe saw the oppression of Israel, because the king of Syria oppressed them. [5]iThen the LORD gave Israel a deliverer, so that they escaped from under the hand of the Syrians; and the children of Israel dwelt in their tents as before. [6]Nevertheless they did not depart from the sins of the house of Jeroboam, who had made Israel sin, but walked in them; jand the wooden image* also remained in Samaria. [7]For He left of the army of Jehoahaz only fifty horsemen, ten chariots, and ten thousand foot soldiers; for the king of Syria had destroyed them kand made them like the dust at threshing.

[8]Now the rest of the acts of Jehoahaz, all that he did, and his might, are they not written in the book of the chronicles of the kings of Israel? [9]So Jehoahaz rested with his fathers, and they buried him in Samaria. Then Joash his son reigned in his place.

Jehoash Reigns in Israel

[10]In the thirty-seventh year of Joash king of Judah, Jehoash* the son of Jehoahaz became king over Israel in Samaria, and reigned sixteen years. [11]And he did evil in the sight of the LORD. He did not depart from all the sins of Jeroboam the son of Nebat, who made Israel sin, but walked in them.

[12]mNow the rest of the acts of Joash, nall that he did, and ohis might with which he

* **12:19** Spelled Jehoash in 12:1ff   * **12:20** Literally The Landfill   * **12:21** Called Zabad in 2 Chronicles 24:26   • Called Shimrith in 2 Chronicles 24:26   * **13:1** Spelled Jehoash in 12:1   * **13:6** Hebrew Asherah, a Canaanite goddess   * **13:10** Spelled Joash in verse 9

12:17 Hazael king of Syria. The Aramean invasion recorded here took place late in Joash's reign. The king fell into apostasy and this invasion came as a judgment of his wickedness.

12:20 killed Joash. Joash had been severely wounded in Hazael's invasion (2 Chr. 24:24–25), and then fell victim to dissent and unpopularity that culminated in his assassination. Because of Joash's apostasy and murder of Zechariah, Jehoiada's son (2 Chr. 24:17–22), the king was not laid to rest in the royal tombs (2 Chr. 24:25).

13:2 evil . . . the sins of Jeroboam. After the end of the house of Omri in Jehu's purge, the kings of Israel reverted to the level of syncretism that had been established by Jeroboam I, indulging in a skewed religion in which worship of the Lord was mixed with idolatry.

13:4 pleaded with the LORD. Although Jehoahaz did not follow the Lord exclusively, God graciously heard his genuine plea for help. In His longsuffering mercy, God often deals patiently with people and

blesses them in spite of their failures (1 Kin. 21:25–29; 2 Pet. 3:9).

13:6 Unbelief—No one is bound to continue following a path of sin. We always have the option of turning to God. However, the tendency to maintain things as they are and have been, to resist change no matter how urgently needed or how right it may be, or how much good it promises, is powerful. We cling to the known, the familiar, no matter how unsatisfying and ineffective it may be or how unhappy it may make us. Changing direction is not easy or painless, but the good news is that it really can be done. God is loving

12:16 p [Lev. 5:15, 18]   q [Num. 18:9]   **12:17** r 2 Kin. 8:12   s 2 Chr. 24:23   **12:18** t 1 Kin. 15:18   **12:20** u 2 Kin. 14:5   **12:21** v 2 Chr. 24:27   **13:1** a 2 Kin. 12:1   b 2 Kin. 10:35   **13:2** c 1 Kin. 12:26–33   **13:3** d Judg. 2:14   e 2 Kin. 8:12   f Amos 1:4   **13:4** g [Ps. 78:34]   h [Ex. 3:7, 9]   **13:5** i 2 Kin. 13:25; 14:25, 27   **13:6** j 1 Kin. 16:33   **13:7** k 2 Kin. 10:32   l [Amos 1:3]   **13:12** m 2 Kin. 14:8–15   n 2 Kin. 13:14–19, 25   o 2 Kin. 14:9

fought against Amaziah king of Judah, *are*
they not written in the book of the chronicles of the kings of Israel? 13So Joash [p]rest-
ed with his fathers. Then Jeroboam sat on
his throne. And Joash was buried in Samaria with the kings of Israel.

Death of Elisha

14Elisha had become sick with the illness of which he would die. Then Joash
the king of Israel came down to him, and
wept over his face, and said, "O my father,
my father, [q]the chariots of Israel and their
horsemen!"
15And Elisha said to him, "Take a bow
and some arrows." So he took himself a
bow and some arrows. 16Then he said to
the king of Israel, "Put your hand on the
bow." So he put his hand *on it,* and Elisha
put his hands on the king's hands. 17And
he said, "Open the east window"; and he
opened *it.* Then Elisha said, "Shoot"; and
he shot. And he said, "The arrow of the
LORD's deliverance and the arrow of deliverance from Syria; for you must strike the
Syrians at [r]Aphek till you have destroyed
them." 18Then he said, "Take the arrows";
so he took *them.* And he said to the king
of Israel, "Strike the ground"; so he struck
three times, and stopped. 19And the man of
God was angry with him, and said, "You
should have struck five or six times; then
you would have struck Syria till you had
destroyed *it!* [s]But now you will strike Syria
only three times."
20Then Elisha died, and they buried him.
And the [t]*raiding* bands from Moab invaded the land in the spring of the year. 21So
it was, as they were burying a man, that
suddenly they spied a band *of raiders;* and
they put the man in the tomb of Elisha; and
when the man was let down and touched
the bones of Elisha, he revived and stood
on his feet.

Israel Recaptures Cities from Syria

22And [u]Hazael king of Syria oppressed
Israel all the days of Jehoahaz. 23But the
LORD was [v]gracious to them, had compassion on them, and [w]regarded them,
[x]because of His covenant with Abraham,
Isaac, and Jacob, and would not yet destroy
them or cast them from His presence.
24Now Hazael king of Syria died. Then
Ben-Hadad his son reigned in his place.
25And Jehoash* the son of Jehoahaz recaptured from the hand of Ben-Hadad, the son
of Hazael, the cities which he had taken
out of the hand of Jehoahaz his father by
war. [y]Three times Joash defeated him and
recaptured the cities of Israel.

Amaziah Reigns in Judah

14 In [a]the second year of Joash the son
of Jehoahaz, king of Israel, [b]Amazi-
ah the son of Joash, king of Judah, became
king. 2He was twenty-five years old when
he became king, and he reigned twenty-
nine years in Jerusalem. His mother's
name was Jehoaddan of Jerusalem. 3And
he did *what was* right in the sight of the
LORD, yet not like his father David; he did
everything [c]as his father Joash had done.
4[d]However the high places were not taken
away, and the people still sacrificed and
burned incense on the high places.
5Now it happened, as soon as the kingdom was established in his hand, that he
executed his servants [e]who had murdered
his father the king. 6But the children of the
murderers he did not execute, according
to what is written in the Book of the Law
of Moses, in which the LORD commanded,
saying, [f]"Fathers shall not be put to death
for their children, nor shall children be put
to death for their fathers; but a person shall
be put to death for his own sin."*
7[g]He killed ten thousand Edomites in
[h]the Valley of Salt, and took Sela by war,
[i]and called its name Joktheel to this day.
8[j]Then Amaziah sent messengers to Jehoash* the son of Jehoahaz, the son of Jehu,
king of Israel, saying, "Come, let us face one

* **13:25** Spelled *Joash* in verses 12–14, 25
* **14:6** Deuteronomy 24:16 * **14:8** Spelled *Joash* in 13:12ff and 2 Chronicles 25:17ff

and forgiving, and when we repent of sin, He gives us the power to overcome it.

13:14 *O my father.* The grief of Jehoash at the impending death of Elisha shows that, like his father Jehoahaz, this Israelite king possessed some genuine spirituality. The line of Jehu had its good moments and received some reward from the Lord (10:30). However, none of this line or any other of the kings of Israel served God with all their hearts.

13:18 *he struck three times, and stopped.* Jehoash's half-hearted compliance with Elisha's instructions exposed his weak faith and illustrated God's unfavorable evaluation of his character (v. 11).

13:21 *he revived.* There was no magic in Elisha's bones; this was a demonstration of the power of God associated with His servant.

13:23 *had compassion on them.* This glimpse of the wonderful mercy of the living God is like a drink of fresh water in the midst of the sad tale of the northern kingdom.

14:1 *Amaziah.* The name Amaziah means "the LORD is mighty." He was one of the few godly kings in the kingdom of Judah.

14:4 *high places.* Like his father Joash before him (12:3), Amaziah allowed worship at the high places to continue. This practice blossomed into open idolatry in the reigns of subsequent kings (16:4; 21:3).

13:13 [p] 2 Kin. 14:16 **13:14** [q] 2 Kin. 2:12 **13:17** [r] 1 Kin. 20:26 **13:19** [s] 2 Kin. 13:25 **13:20** [t] 2 Kin. 3:5; 24:2 **13:22** [u] 2 Kin. 8:12, 13 **13:23** [v] 2 Kin. 14:27 [w] [Ex. 2:24, 25] [x] Ex. 32:13 **13:25** [y] 2 Kin. 13:18, 19 **14:1** [a] 2 Kin. 13:10 [b] 2 Chr. 25:1, 2 **14:3** [c] 2 Kin. 12:2 **14:4** [d] 2 Kin. 12:3 **14:5** [e] 2 Kin. 12:20 **14:6** [f] [Ezek. 18:4, 20] **14:7** [g] 2 Chr. 25:5–16 [h] 2 Sam. 8:13 [i] Josh. 15:38 **14:8** [j] 2 Chr. 25:17, 18

another *in battle.*" 9 And Jehoash king of Israel sent to Amaziah king of Judah, saying,
[k]"The thistle that *was* in Lebanon sent to
the [l]cedar that *was* in Lebanon, saying,
'Give your daughter to my son as wife'; and
a wild beast that *was* in Lebanon passed by
and trampled the thistle. 10 You have indeed
defeated Edom, and [m]your heart has lifted
you up. Glory *in that,* and stay at home; for
why should you meddle with trouble so that
you fall—you and Judah with you?"
11 But Amaziah would not heed. Therefore Jehoash king of Israel went out; so he
and Amaziah king of Judah faced one another at [n]Beth Shemesh, which *belongs* to
Judah. 12 And Judah was defeated by Israel,
and every man fled to his tent. 13 Then Jehoash king of Israel captured Amaziah king of
Judah, the son of Jehoash, the son of Ahaziah, at Beth Shemesh; and he went to Jerusalem, and broke down the wall of Jerusalem
from [o]the Gate of Ephraim to [p]the Corner
Gate—four hundred cubits. 14 And he took
all [q]the gold and silver, all the articles
that were found in the house of the LORD
and in the treasuries of the king's house,
and hostages, and returned to Samaria.
15 [r]Now the rest of the acts of Jehoash
which he did—his might, and how he
fought with Amaziah king of Judah—*are*
they not written in the book of the chronicles of the kings of Israel? 16 So Jehoash
rested with his fathers, and was buried in
Samaria with the kings of Israel. Then Jeroboam his son reigned in his place.
17 [s]Amaziah the son of Joash, king of Judah, lived fifteen years after the death of
Jehoash the son of Jehoahaz, king of Israel.
18 Now the rest of the acts of Amaziah, *are*
they not written in the book of the chronicles of the kings of Judah? 19 And [t]they
formed a conspiracy against him in Jerusalem, and he fled to [u]Lachish; but they
sent after him to Lachish and killed him
there. 20 Then they brought him on horses,
and he was buried at Jerusalem with his
fathers in the City of David.
21 And all the people of Judah took [v]Aza-
riah,* who *was* sixteen years old, and made
him king instead of his father Amaziah.
22 He built [w]Elath and restored it to Judah,
after the king rested with his fathers.

Jeroboam II Reigns in Israel

23 In the fifteenth year of Amaziah the
son of Joash, king of Judah, Jeroboam the
son of Joash, king of Israel, became king
in Samaria, *and reigned* forty-one years.
24 And he did evil in the sight of the LORD;
he did not depart from all the [x]sins of Jeroboam the son of Nebat, who had made
Israel sin. 25 He [y]restored the territory of Israel [z]from the entrance of Hamath to [a]the
Sea of the Arabah, according to the word
of the LORD God of Israel, which He had
spoken through His servant [b]Jonah the
son of Amittai, the prophet who *was* from
[c]Gath Hepher. 26 For the LORD [d]saw *that*
the affliction of Israel *was* very bitter; and
whether bond or free, [e]there was no helper
for Israel. 27 [f]And the LORD did not say that
He would blot out the name of Israel from
under heaven; but He saved them by the
hand of Jeroboam the son of Joash.
28 Now the rest of the acts of Jeroboam,
and all that he did—his might, how he
made war, and how he recaptured for Israel, from [g]Damascus and Hamath, [h]*what
had belonged* to Judah—*are* they not written in the book of the chronicles of the
kings of Israel? 29 So Jeroboam rested with
his fathers, the kings of Israel. Then [i]Zech-
ariah his son reigned in his place.

* **14:21** Called *Uzziah* in 2 Chronicles 26:1ff, Isaiah 6:1, and elsewhere

14:9–10 Pride—Amaziah's conquest of the formidable city of Sela atop the seemingly unapproachable cliffs of the Wadi Musa was a monumental accomplishment. Rather than recognize God's hand in this feat, Amaziah became proud and fell into spiritual compromise (2 Chr. 25:5–16). A little success can sometimes be a dangerous thing. Failure to acknowledge God's power leads to personal pride, and such pride leads inevitably to downfall. God will not share His glory.

14:11 *Beth Shemesh.* The name of the city means "house of the sun," indicating that there had once been a temple to the sun god there in Canaanite times. Beth Shemesh was in the Valley of Sorek, about 15 miles west of Jerusalem. This was the town where the holy ark was taken after its "wanderings" among the Philistines.

14:17 *fifteen years.* The notice of fifteen years of life for Amaziah suggests he was released after the death of Jehoash for an additional period (782–767 B.C.). If so, he reigned alongside his son Azariah (or Uzziah), whose 52-year reign began in 792 B.C. (15:2).

14:23 *forty-one years.* Jeroboam II had a very long reign. His 41 years included 10 years as coregent with his father Jehoash (792–782 B.C.).

14:25 *Jonah.* Once again a prophet of God gave direction to a king. The reference to Jonah here provides the historical setting for the famous prophet (Jon. 1:1)

14:28 *his might.* The Scriptures emphasize Jeroboam's military prowess. Yet Jeroboam's might may have also been economic. The well-known Samaritan Ostraca, which may date from this period, record the delivery to Samaria of fine oil and barley produced on the royal estates.

14:29 *Zechariah.* The brief reign of Zechariah is noted in 15:8–12. He was the fourth in the line of Jehu to reign in Israel, in fulfillment of God's gracious promise to Jehu (10:30).

14:9 [k] Judg. 9:8–15 [l] 1 Kin. 4:33 **14:10** [m] Deut. 8:14 **14:11** [n] Josh. 19:38; 21:16 **14:13** [o] Neh. 8:16; 12:39 [p] Jer. 31:38 **14:14** [q] 1 Kin. 7:51 **14:15** [r] 2 Kin. 13:12, 13 **14:17** [s] 2 Chr. 25:25–28 **14:19** [t] 2 Chr. 25:27 [u] Josh. 10:31 **14:21** [v] 2 Kin. 15:13 **14:22** [w] 2 Kin. 16:6 **14:24** [x] 1 Kin. 12:26–33 **14:25** [y] 2 Kin. 10:32; 13:5, 25 [z] 1 Kin. 8:65 [a] Deut. 3:17 [b] Jon. 1:1 [c] Josh. 19:13 **14:26** [d] 2 Kin. 13:4 [e] Deut. 32:36 **14:27** [f] [2 Kin. 13:5, 23] **14:28** [g] 1 Kin. 11:24 [h] 2 Chr. 8:3 **14:29** [i] 2 Kin. 15:8

Azariah Reigns in Judah

15 In the twenty-seventh year of Jeroboam king of Israel, ^aAzariah the son of Amaziah, king of Judah, ^bbecame king. ²He was sixteen years old when he became king, and he reigned fifty-two years in Jerusalem. His mother's name *was* Jecholiah of Jerusalem. ³And he did *what was* right in the sight of the LORD, according to all that his father Amaziah had done, ^{4c}except that the high places were not removed; the people still sacrificed and burned incense on the high places. ⁵Then the LORD ^dstruck the king, so that he was a leper until the day of his ^edeath; so he ^fdwelt in an isolated house. And Jotham the king's son *was* over the *royal* house, judging the people of the land.

⁶Now the rest of the acts of Azariah, and all that he did, *are* they not written in the book of the chronicles of the kings of Judah? ⁷So Azariah rested with his fathers, and ^gthey buried him with his fathers in the City of David. Then Jotham his son reigned in his place.

Zechariah Reigns in Israel

⁸In the thirty-eighth year of Azariah king of Judah, ^hZechariah the son of Jeroboam reigned over Israel in Samaria six months. ⁹And he did evil in the sight of the LORD, ⁱas his fathers had done; he did not depart from the sins of Jeroboam the son of Nebat, who had made Israel sin. ¹⁰Then Shallum the son of Jabesh conspired against him, and ^jstruck and killed him in front of the people; and he reigned in his place.

¹¹Now the rest of the acts of Zechariah, indeed they *are* written in the book of the chronicles of the kings of Israel. ¹²This *was* the word of the LORD which He spoke to Jehu, saying, ^k"Your sons shall sit on the throne of Israel to the fourth *generation.*"* And so it was.

Shallum Reigns in Israel

¹³Shallum the son of Jabesh became king in the thirty-ninth year of Uzziah* king of Judah; and he reigned a full month in Samaria. ¹⁴For Menahem the son of Gadi went up from ^lTirzah, came to Samaria, and struck Shallum the son of Jabesh in Samaria and killed him; and he reigned in his place.

¹⁵Now the rest of the acts of Shallum, and the conspiracy which he led, indeed they *are* written in the book of the chronicles of the kings of Israel. ¹⁶Then from Tirzah, Menahem attacked ^mTiphsah, all who *were* there, and its territory. Because they did not surrender, therefore he attacked *it.* All ⁿthe women there who were with child he ripped open.

Menahem Reigns in Israel

¹⁷In the thirty-ninth year of Azariah king of Judah, Menahem the son of Gadi became king over Israel, *and reigned* ten years in Samaria. ¹⁸And he did evil in the sight of the LORD; he did not depart all his days from the sins of Jeroboam the son of Nebat, who had made Israel sin. ¹⁹oPul* king of Assyria came against the land; and Menahem gave Pul a thousand talents of silver, that his hand might be with him to ^pstrengthen the kingdom under his control. ²⁰And Menahem ^qexacted the money from Israel, from all the very wealthy, from each man fifty shekels of silver, to give to the king of Assyria. So the king of Assyria turned back, and did not stay there in the land.

²¹Now the rest of the acts of Menahem, and all that he did, *are* they not written in the book of the chronicles of the kings of Israel? ²²So Menahem rested with his

* **15:12** 2 Kings 10:30   * **15:13** Called *Azariah* in 14:21ff and 15:1ff   * **15:19** That is, Tiglath-Pileser III (compare verse 29)

15:1 Azariah. Also called Uzziah (2 Chr. 26:1), this king is credited with 52 years of reign. This figure includes 10 years during which his father Amaziah was held captive (792–782 B.C.). The latter part of Azariah's reign was tainted by his intrusion into the priestly office (2 Chr. 26:16–19), an act that resulted in his being stricken with leprosy (v. 5). This condition put his son Jotham on the throne to rule with him and handle public matters relative to the royal office. The nature of Jotham's duties (v. 5), the assigning of a full 52 years of reign to Azariah, and Isaiah's dating of his call to the year of Azariah's (or Uzziah's) death (Is. 6:1) may indicate that Azariah retained the power of the throne until the end.
15:5 leper. The events that brought about this affliction are described in 2 Chr. 26:16–21.
15:12 fourth generation. Jehu had been promised a continuing posterity into the fourth generation as a reward for carrying out his divine commission (10:30), but after the death of Zechariah in 752 B.C., Israel plunged into a period of degeneracy, bloody

conspiracies and international intrigue that would bring about its demise in 722 B.C.
15:17 Menahem. This wicked king came into power by assassination and established his authority by brutal acts against humanity. Ironically, his name means "comforter."
15:19 Pul. Pul is a second Babylonian name for the Assyrian king Tiglath-Pileser III (745–727 B.C.; 1 Chr. 5:26). Although he came to the throne as a usurper from the ranks of the military, he would prove a competent king. Under Tiglath-Pileser III and his successors, Assyria became the dominant power in the Middle East for well over a century (747–612 B.C.).

15:1 ^a 2 Kin. 15:13, 30 ^b 2 Kin. 14:21   **15:4** ^c 2 Kin. 12:3; 14:4; 15:35   **15:5** ^d 2 Chr. 26:19–23 ^e Is. 6:1 ^f [Lev. 13:46]   **15:7** ^g 2 Chr. 26:23   **15:8** ^h 2 Kin. 14:29   **15:9** ⁱ 2 Kin. 14:24   **15:10** ^j Amos 7:9   **15:12** ^k 2 Kin. 10:30   **15:14** ^l 1 Kin. 14:17   **15:16** ^m 1 Kin. 4:24 ⁿ 2 Kin. 8:12   **15:19** ^o Hos. 8:9 ^p 2 Kin. 14:5   **15:20** ^q 2 Kin. 23:35

fathers. Then Pekahiah his son reigned in his place.

Pekahiah Reigns in Israel

23In the fiftieth year of Azariah king of Judah, Pekahiah the son of Menahem became king over Israel in Samaria, *and reigned* two years. 24And he did evil in the sight of the LORD; he did not depart from the sins of Jeroboam the son of Nebat, who had made Israel sin. 25Then Pekah the son of Remaliah, an officer of his, conspired against him and killed him in Samaria, in the ʳcitadel of the king's house, along with Argob and Arieh; and with him were fifty men of Gilead. He killed him and reigned in his place.

26Now the rest of the acts of Pekahiah, and all that he did, indeed they *are* written in the book of the chronicles of the kings of Israel.

Pekah Reigns in Israel

27In the fifty-second year of Azariah king of Judah, ˢPekah the son of Remaliah became king over Israel in Samaria, *and reigned* twenty years. 28And he did evil in the sight of the LORD; he did not depart from the sins of Jeroboam the son of Nebat, who had made Israel sin. 29In the days of Pekah king of Israel, Tiglath-Pileser king of Assyria ᵗcame and took ᵘIjon, Abel Beth Maachah, Janoah, Kedesh, Hazor, Gilead, and Galilee, all the land of Naphtali; and he ᵛcarried them captive to Assyria. 30Then Hoshea the son of Elah led a conspiracy against Pekah the son of Remaliah, and struck and killed him; so he ʷreigned in his place in the twentieth year of Jotham the son of Uzziah.

31Now the rest of the acts of Pekah, and all that he did, indeed they *are* written in the book of the chronicles of the kings of Israel.

Jotham Reigns in Judah

32In the second year of Pekah the son of Remaliah, king of Israel, ˣJotham the son of Uzziah, king of Judah, began to reign. 33He was twenty-five years old when he became king, and he reigned sixteen years in Jerusalem. His mother's name *was* Jerusha* the daughter of Zadok. 34And he did *what was* right in the sight of the LORD; he did ʸaccording to all that his father Uzziah had done. 35zHowever the high places were not removed; the people still sacrificed and burned incense on the high places. ᵃHe built the Upper Gate of the house of the LORD.

36Now the rest of the acts of Jotham, and all that he did, *are* they not written in the book of the chronicles of the kings of Judah? 37In those days the LORD began to send ᵇRezin king of Syria and ᶜPekah the son of Remaliah against Judah. 38So Jotham rested with his fathers, and was buried with his fathers in the City of David his father. Then Ahaz his son reigned in his place.

Ahaz Reigns in Judah

16 In the seventeenth year of Pekah the son of Remaliah, Ahaz the son of Jotham, king of Judah, began to reign. 2Ahaz *was* twenty years old when he became king, and he reigned sixteen years in Jerusalem; and he did not do *what was* right in the sight of the LORD his God, as his father David *had done.* 3But he walked in the way of the kings of Israel; indeed ᵃhe made his son pass through the

---

* 15:33 Spelled *Jerushah* in 2 Chronicles 27:1

15:23 *Pekahiah.* Pekahiah means "the Lord has opened the eyes." After an evil reign of two years, a usurper "closed his eyes" for him.

15:25 Murder—Sometimes a corrupt leader needs to be taken out of power, but when this is done by coup and murder, the new leader ends up being just as bad as the old one. He lives in fear that someone will do the same thing to him; in an attempt to keep his position, he will exercise the same control and perpetrate the same kind of abuses as the leader he deposed. A vicious cycle is begun, as we can see from the succession of murders and new kings in Israel. Anytime leadership changes through conniving and coup, even if actual murder is not part of the picture, problems in trust and confidence will result.

15:27 *Pekah.* Because Hoshea's nine-year reign (17:1) began in 732 B.C., Pekah's twenty years must have included a time of kingship in his own district during the unsettled days of Shallum, Menahem, and Pekahiah (752–740 B.C.). Apparently Pekah rode the crest of anti-Assyrian sentiment.

15:30 *Hoshea . . . led a conspiracy.* The annals of Tiglath-Pileser III record Hoshea's heavy tribute and the Assyrian king's claim that he himself set the new Israelite king in office.

15:32 *Jotham.* Jotham's reign was partly righteous. After the purge of Ahaziah and Athaliah (9:27–29; 11:13–16), the kings of Judah who reigned in relative righteousness were Joash (12:2–3), Amaziah (14:3–4), and Azariah (15:3–4). A positive righteousness would be modeled by Hezekiah (18:3–6) and again by Josiah (22:2).

16:1 *Ahaz . . . began to reign.* The seventeenth year of Pekah was 736–735 B.C. Ahaz's 16-year reign apparently ended in 720 B.C. If so, like Jotham before him, Ahaz must have lived on another four years after giving up his rule. Hezekiah's first year of independent rule began in 715 B.C., 14 years before Sennacherib's invasion of Judah and his siege of Jerusalem in 701 B.C.

16:3 *made his son pass through the fire.* According to the author of Chronicles, this rite was connected with the Baal worship practiced in the valley of the

---

15:25 ʳ 1 Kin. 16:18   **15:27** ˢ Is. 7:1   **15:29** ᵗ 1 Chr. 5:26 ᵘ 1 Kin. 15:20 ᵛ 2 Kin. 17:6   **15:30** ʷ [Hos. 10:3, 7, 15] **15:32** ˣ 2 Chr. 27:1   **15:34** ʸ 2 Kin. 15:3, 4   **15:35** ᶻ 2 Kin. 15:4 ᵃ 2 Chr. 23:20; 27:3   **15:37** ᵇ 2 Kin. 16:5–9 ᶜ 2 Kin. 15:26, 27   **16:3** ᵃ [Lev. 18:21]

fire, according to the [b]abominations of the nations whom the LORD had cast out from before the children of Israel. [4]And he sacrificed and burned incense on the [c]high places, [d]on the hills, and under every green tree.

[5e]Then Rezin king of Syria and Pekah the son of Remaliah, king of Israel, came up to Jerusalem to *make* war; and they besieged Ahaz but could not overcome *him.* [6]At that time Rezin king of Syria [f]captured Elath for Syria, and drove the men of Judah from Elath. Then the Edomites* went to Elath, and dwell there to this day.

[7]So Ahaz sent messengers to [g]Tiglath-Pileser king of Assyria, saying, "I *am* your servant and your son. Come up and save me from the hand of the king of Syria and from the hand of the king of Israel, who rise up against me." [8]And Ahaz [h]took the silver and gold that was found in the house of the LORD, and in the treasuries of the king's house, and sent *it as* a present to the king of Assyria. [9]So the king of Assyria heeded him; for the king of Assyria went up against [i]Damascus and [j]took it, carried *its people* captive to [k]Kir, and killed Rezin.

[10]Now King Ahaz went to Damascus to meet Tiglath-Pileser king of Assyria, and saw an altar that *was* at Damascus; and King Ahaz sent to Urijah the priest the design of the altar and its pattern, according to all its workmanship. [11]Then [l]Urijah the priest built an altar according to all that King Ahaz had sent from Damascus. So Urijah the priest made *it* before King Ahaz came back from Damascus. [12]And when the king came back from Damascus, the king saw the altar; and [m]the king approached the altar and made offerings on it. [13]So he burned his burnt offering and his grain offering; and he poured his drink offering and sprinkled the blood of his peace offerings on the altar. [14]He also brought [n]the bronze altar which *was* before the LORD, from the front of the temple—from between the *new* altar and the house of the LORD—and put it on the north side of the *new* altar. [15]Then King Ahaz commanded Urijah the priest, saying, "On the great *new* altar burn [o]the morning burnt offering, the evening grain offering, the king's burnt sacrifice, and his grain offering, with the burnt offering of all the people of the land, their grain offering, and their drink offerings; and sprinkle on it all the blood of the burnt offering and all the blood of the sacrifice. And the bronze altar shall be for me to inquire *by.*" [16]Thus did Urijah the priest, according to all that King Ahaz commanded.

[17p]And King Ahaz cut off [q]the panels of the carts, and removed the lavers from them; and he took down [r]the Sea from the bronze oxen that *were* under it, and put it on a pavement of stones. [18]Also he removed the Sabbath pavilion which they had built in the temple, and he removed the king's outer entrance from the house of the LORD, on account of the king of Assyria.

[19]Now the rest of the acts of Ahaz which he did, *are* they not written in the book of the chronicles of the kings of Judah? [20]So Ahaz rested with his fathers, and [s]was buried with his fathers in the City of David. Then Hezekiah his son reigned in his place.

Hoshea Reigns in Israel

17 In the twelfth year of Ahaz king of Judah, [a]Hoshea the son of Elah became king of Israel in Samaria, *and he reigned* nine years. [2]And he did evil in the sight of the LORD, but not as the kings of Israel who were before him. [3b]Shalmaneser king of Assyria came up against him; and Hoshea [c]became his vassal, and paid him tribute money. [4]And the king of Assyria uncovered a conspiracy by Hoshea; for he had sent messengers to So, king of Egypt, and brought no tribute to the king of Assyria, as *he had done* year by year. Therefore the king of Assyria shut him up, and bound him in prison.

---

* **16:6** Some ancient authorities read *Syrians.*

---

son of Hinnom (2 Chr. 28:2–3). Ahaz was an apostate who personally led his people in the religious worship practices of Canaan.

16:7 sent messengers . . . king of Assyria. Tiglath-Pileser's records list the tribute of both Hoshea and Ahaz.

16:10–16 Vanity—The king of Israel was commanded to pattern his reign according to God's Word, but Ahaz apparently thought his own ideas were better. Once the Word of God has been set aside, there is no stopping point for presumptuous spirituality and immoral activities. Such practices may be aesthetically and humanly pleasing, but Jesus designated them as vain worship because they are based upon precepts and traditions of men, rather than on God's holy and sufficient Word (Matt. 15:7–9).

16:18 the king of Assyria. Ahaz was more interested in imitating the foreign king than in following God. His use of the altar to make sacrifices to God and his many other religious innovations underscored Ahaz's essential paganism (2 Chr. 28:2–4,22–25). He went so far in his apostasy as to shut the doors of the temple (2 Chr. 28:24).

17:1 twelfth year. Hoshea became king in 732 B.C., so the twelve years of Ahaz indicate a period of coregency with his father Jotham.

17:3 Shalmaneser. Shalmaneser V succeeded Tiglath-Pileser III as king of Assyria in 727 B.C.

16:3 [b] [Deut. 12:31]   **16:4** [c] 2 Kin. 15:34, 35   [d] [Deut. 12:2]   **16:5** [e] Is. 7:1, 4   **16:6** [f] 2 Kin. 14:22   **16:7** [g] 1 Chr. 5:26   **16:8** [h] 2 Kin. 12:17, 18   **16:9** [i] 2 Kin. 14:28   [j] Amos 1:5   [k] Amos 9:7   **16:11** [l] Is. 8:2   **16:12** [m] 2 Chr. 26:16, 19   **16:14** [n] 2 Chr. 4:1   **16:15** [o] Ex. 29:39–41   **16:17** [p] 2 Chr. 28:24   [q] 1 Kin. 7:27–29   [r] 1 Kin. 7:23–25   **16:20** [s] 2 Chr. 28:27   **17:1** [a] 2 Kin. 15:30   **17:3** [b] 2 Kin. 18:9–12   [c] 2 Kin. 24:1

Israel Carried Captive to Assyria

5Now dthe king of Assyria went throughout all the land, and went up to Samaria
and besieged it for three years. 6eIn the
ninth year of Hoshea, the king of Assyria
took Samaria and fcarried Israel away to
Assyria, gand placed them in Halah and by
the Habor, the River of Gozan, and in the
cities of the Medes.

7For hso it was that the children of Israel
had sinned against the LORD their God,
who had brought them up out of the land
of Egypt, from under the hand of Pharaoh
king of Egypt; and they had ifeared other
gods, 8and jhad walked in the statutes of
the nations whom the LORD had cast out
from before the children of Israel, and of
the kings of Israel, which they had made.
9Also the children of Israel secretly did
against the LORD their God things that
were not right, and they built for themselves high places in all their cities, kfrom
watchtower to fortified city. 10lThey set up
for themselves sacred pillars and mwood-
en images* non every high hill and under
every green tree. 11There they burned incense on all the high places, like the nations whom the LORD had carried away
before them; and they did wicked things
to provoke the LORD to anger, 12for they
served idols, oof which the LORD had said
to them, p"You shall not do this thing."

13Yet the LORD testified against Israel
and against Judah, by all of His qprophets,
revery seer, saying, s"Turn from your evil
ways, and keep My commandments and
My statutes, according to all the law which
I commanded your fathers, and which I
sent to you by My servants the prophets."
14Nevertheless they would not hear, but
tstiffened their necks, like the necks of their
fathers, who udid not believe in the LORD
their God. 15And they vrejected His statutes
wand His covenant that He had made with
their fathers, and His testimonies which He
had testified against them; they followed
xidols, ybecame idolaters, and went after
the nations who were all around them,
concerning whom the LORD had charged
them that they should znot do like them.
16So they left all the commandments of
the LORD their God, amade for themselves
a molded image and two calves, bmade a
wooden image and worshiped all the chost
of heaven, dand served Baal. 17eAnd they
caused their sons and daughters to pass
through the fire, fpracticed witchcraft and
soothsaying, and gsold themselves to do
evil in the sight of the LORD, to provoke
Him to anger. 18Therefore the LORD was
very angry with Israel, and removed them
from His sight; there was none left hbut the
tribe of Judah alone.

19Also iJudah did not keep the commandments of the LORD their God, but
walked in the statutes of Israel which they
made. 20And the LORD rejected all the descendants of Israel, afflicted them, and jde-
livered them into the hand of plunderers,
until He had cast them from His ksight.
21For lHe tore Israel from the house of David, and mthey made Jeroboam the son of
Nebat king. Then Jeroboam drove Israel
from following the LORD, and made them
commit a great sin. 22For the children of
Israel walked in all the sins of Jeroboam
which he did; they did not depart from
them, 23until the LORD removed Israel out
of His sight, nas He had said by all His servants the prophets. oSo Israel was carried

---

* **17:10** Hebrew Asherim, Canaanite deities

17:7 Israel had sinned. The reason for the fall of
Samaria and the end of the northern kingdom was
clearly its spiritual failure; they had turned away from
the living God.
17:14–18 Israel's Disobedience—These verses
are a good summary of the spiritual departure from
God that led to Israel's eventual downfall. The people of Israel didn't listen and three specific results are
recorded:

1. The Israelites refused to believe. All the fulfilled
promises, all the history of God's saving acts
were simply ignored. It didn't matter what God
had done. They had ears to hear and eyes to see,
yet failed to do so.

2. They rejected God's laws and covenant. They willfully turned their backs on the way of living that
God had directed them toward.

3. They worshiped idols. They actually worshiped
anything and everything but what they were
instructed to worship. In spite of God's clear
mandate to them to have no other gods before
Him, the Israelites were easily influenced by any
culture they came in contact with.

The common denominator here is the will. This
was willful rebellion. We are no different. Every day
each of us, by an act of our own will, does something
disobedient. We worry unnecessarily, we have fears for
aspects of our lives that we know God has promised
to protect and care for. Sometimes we simply don't
care what God has said. We'd rather do what we want
because it feels good or because His way is too difficult. We are truly sinners in need of a forgiving God.
**17:21 Jeroboam drove Israel from following the
LORD.** Jeroboam had initiated the false worship that
set the standard for all of Israel's idolatrous activities.
The worship of the calves at Dan and Bethel, and Israel's fascination with Baal worship (1 Kin. 12:28–29;
16:32–33), are repeatedly cited as the chief causes of
Israel's spiritual defeat and political collapse.

17:5 d Hos. 13:16   **17:6** e Hos. 1:4; 13:16   f [Deut. 28:36,
64; 29:27, 28]   g 1 Chr. 5:26   **17:7** h [Josh. 23:16]   i Judg.
6:10   **17:8** j [Lev. 18:3]   **17:9** k 2 Kin. 18:8   **17:10** l Is.
57:5   m [Ex. 34:12–14]   n [Deut. 12:2]   **17:12** o [Ex. 20:3–5]
p [Deut. 4:19]   **17:13** q Neh. 9:29, 30   r 1 Sam. 9:9   s [Jer.
18:11; 25:5; 35:15]   **17:14** t [Acts 7:51]   u Deut. 9:23
17:15 v Jer. 44:3   w Deut. 29:25   x Deut. 32:21   y [Rom.
1:21–23]   z [Deut. 12:30, 31]   **17:16** a 1 Kin. 12:28   b [1 Kin.
14:15]   c [Deut. 4:19]   d 1 Kin. 16:31; 22:53   **17:17** e 2 Kin.
16:3   f [Deut. 18:10–12]   g 1 Kin. 21:20   **17:18** h 1 Kin.
11:13, 32   **17:19** i Jer. 3:8   **17:20** j 2 Kin. 13:3; 15:29
k 2 Kin. 24:20   **17:21** l 1 Kin. 11:11, 31   m 1 Kin. 12:20, 28
17:23 n 1 Kin. 14:16   o 2 Kin. 17:6

away from their own land to Assyria, *as it is* to this day.

Assyria Resettles Samaria

24pThen the king of Assyria brought *people* from Babylon, Cuthah, qAva, Hamath, and from Sepharvaim, and placed *them* in the cities of Samaria instead of the children of Israel; and they took possession of Samaria and dwelt in its cities. 25And it was so, at the beginning of their dwelling there, *that* they did not fear the LORD; therefore the LORD sent lions among them, which killed *some* of them. 26So they spoke to the king of Assyria, saying, "The nations whom you have removed and placed in the cities of Samaria do not know the rituals of the God of the land; therefore He has sent lions among them, and indeed, they are killing them because they do not know the rituals of the God of the land." 27Then the king of Assyria commanded, saying, "Send there one of the priests whom you brought from there; let him go and dwell there, and let him teach them the rituals of the God of the land." 28Then one of the priests whom they had carried away from Samaria came and dwelt in Bethel, and taught them how they should fear the LORD.

29However every nation continued to make gods of its own, and put *them* rin the shrines on the high places which the Samaritans had made, *every* nation in the cities where they dwelt. 30The men of sBabylon made Succoth Benoth, the men of Cuth made Nergal, the men of Hamath made Ashima, 31tand the Avites made Nibhaz and Tartak; and the Sepharvites uburned their children in fire to Adrammelech and Anammelech, the gods of Sepharvaim. 32So they feared the LORD, vand from every class they appointed for themselves priests of the high places, who sacrificed for them in the shrines of the high places. 33wThey feared the LORD, yet served their own gods— according to the rituals of the nations from among whom they were carried away.

34To this day they continue practicing the former rituals; they do not fear the LORD, nor do they follow their statutes or their ordinances, or the law and commandment which the LORD had commanded the children of Jacob, xwhom He named Israel, 35with whom the LORD had made a covenant and charged them, saying: y"You shall not fear other gods, nor zbow down to them nor serve them nor sacrifice to them; 36but the LORD, who abrought you up from the land of Egypt with great power and ban outstretched arm, cHim you shall fear, Him you shall worship, and to Him you shall offer sacrifice. 37And the statutes, the ordinances, the law, and the commandment which He wrote for you, dyou shall be careful to observe forever; you shall not fear other gods. 38And the covenant that I have made with you, eyou shall not forget, nor shall you fear other gods. 39But the LORD your God you shall fear; and He will deliver you from the hand of all your enemies." 40However they did not obey, but they followed their former rituals. 41So these nations feared the LORD, yet served their carved images; also their children and their children's children have continued doing as their fathers did, even to this day.

Hezekiah Reigns in Judah

18 Now it came to pass in the third year of aHoshea the son of Elah, king of Israel, *that* bHezekiah the son of Ahaz, king of Judah, began to reign. 2He was twenty-five years old when he became king, and he reigned twenty-nine years in Jerusalem. His mother's name *was* cAbi* the daughter of Zechariah. 3And he did *what was* right in the sight of the LORD, according to all that his father David had done.

4dHe removed the high places and broke the *sacred* pillars, cut down the wooden image* and broke in pieces the ebronze

* 18:2 Called *Abijah* in 2 Chronicles 29:1ff
* 18:4 Hebrew *Asherah*, a Canaanite goddess

17:24 king of Assyria. This was probably Sargon II (722–705 B.C.), although the practice described here was continued by later kings as well. Such a mixing of populations was designed to break down ethnic distinctions and weaken the loyalties that the people had. It would also help create a sense of empire. **Samaria.** This was the whole region where the repopulation took place; eventually the inhabitants would be called Samaritans.
17:33 feared the LORD, yet served their own gods. This is the classic example of syncretism, the attempt to mix the worship of the true God with other religious traditions and beliefs. The apostate religion of the people of Samaria caused them to be rejected by the faithful Jews who returned from the exile (Ezra 4:1–5), and by the time of the New Testament, hostility was very strong between the two groups (John 4:9; 8:48).
18:1 the third year of Hoshea. The 29 years of

Hezekiah's reign thus included a period of coregency with his father Ahaz before he ruled independently (715–699 B.C.). The name Hezekiah means "the LORD has strengthened."
18:3 he did what was right in the sight of the LORD. Hezekiah was the first king since David who served the Lord with all his heart.
18:4 high places. Consistently, the kings who preceded Hezekiah are criticized by the author for not destroying the high places (15:34–35). While there

---

17:24 PEzra 4:2, 10 q2 Kin. 18:34   17:29 r1 Kin. 12:31; 13:32   17:30 s2 Kin. 17:24   17:31 tEzra 4:9 u[Deut. 12:31]   17:32 v1 Kin. 12:31; 13:33   17:33 wZeph. 1:5   17:34 xGen. 32:28; 35:10   17:35 yJudg. 6:10   z[Ex. 20:5]   17:36 dEx. 14:15–30 bEx. 6:6; 9:15 c[Deut. 10:20]   17:37 dDeut. 5:32   17:38 eDeut. 4:23; 6:12   17:41 f2 Kin. 17:32, 33   18:1 a2 Kin. 17:1 b2 Chr. 28:27; 29:1   18:2 cIs. 38:5   18:4 d2 Chr. 31:1 eNum. 21:5–9

serpent that Moses had made; for until those days the children of Israel burned incense to it, and called it Nehushtan.* [5]He [f]trusted in the LORD God of Israel, [g]so that after him was none like him among all the kings of Judah, nor who were before him. [6]For he [h]held fast to the LORD; he did not depart from following Him, but kept His commandments, which the LORD had commanded Moses. [7]The LORD [i]was with him; he [j]prospered wherever he went. And he [k]rebelled against the king of Assyria and did not serve him. [8]He subdued the Philistines, as far as Gaza and its territory, [m]from watchtower to fortified city.

[9]Now [n]it came to pass in the fourth year of King Hezekiah, which was the seventh year of Hoshea the son of Elah, king of Israel, that Shalmaneser king of Assyria came up against Samaria and besieged it. [10]And at the end of three years they took it. In the sixth year of Hezekiah, that is, [o]the ninth year of Hoshea king of Israel, Samaria was taken. [11][p]Then the king of Assyria carried Israel away captive to Assyria, and put them [q]in Halah and by the Habor, the River of Gozan, and in the cities of the Medes, [12]because they [r]did not obey the voice of the LORD their God, but transgressed His covenant and all that Moses the servant of the LORD had commanded; and they would neither hear nor do them.

[13]And [s]in the fourteenth year of King Hezekiah, Sennacherib king of Assyria came up against all the fortified cities of Judah and took them. [14]Then Hezekiah king of Judah sent to the king of Assyria at Lachish, saying, "I have done wrong; turn away from me; whatever you impose on me I will pay." And the king of Assyria assessed Hezekiah king of Judah three hundred talents of silver and thirty talents of gold. [15]So Hezekiah [t]gave him all the silver that was found in the house of the LORD and in the treasuries of the king's house. [16]At that time Hezekiah stripped the gold from the doors of the temple of the LORD, and from the pillars which Hezekiah king of Judah had overlaid, and gave it to the king of Assyria.

Sennacherib Boasts Against the LORD

[17]Then the king of Assyria sent the Tartan,* the Rabsaris,* and the Rabshakeh* from Lachish, with a great army against Jerusalem, to King Hezekiah. And they went up and came to Jerusalem. When they had come up, they went and stood by the [u]aqueduct from the upper pool, [v]which was on the highway to the Fuller's Field. [18]And when they had called to the king, [w]Eliakim the son of Hilkiah, who was over the household, Shebna the scribe, and Joah the son of Asaph, the recorder, came out to them. [19]Then the Rabshakeh said to them, "Say now to Hezekiah, 'Thus says the great king, the king of Assyria: [x]"What confidence is this in which you trust? [20]You speak of having plans and power for war; but they are mere words. And in whom do you trust, that you rebel against me? [21][y]Now look! You are trusting in the staff of this broken reed, Egypt, on which if a man leans, it will go into his hand and pierce it. So is Pharaoh king of Egypt to all who trust in him. [22]But if you say to me, 'We trust in the LORD our God,' is it not He [z]whose high places and whose altars Hezekiah has taken away, and said to Judah and Jerusalem, 'You shall worship before this

---

* 18:4 Literally Bronze Thing　* 18:17 A title, probably Commander in Chief ● A title, probably Chief Officer ● A title, probably Chief of Staff or Governor

---

were traditions of worship of the true God at these locations, far too often they became sites for the licentious worship of Baal and Asherah. Hezekiah's reforms included not only the destruction of the pagan cult objects introduced in the days of his apostate father Ahaz, but the bronze serpent that had been preserved since the days of Moses (2 Chr. 29–31). Symbols all too easily can be made into objects of veneration.

18:5 none like him. Hezekiah's faith was unparalleled by any other king who had preceded him after the time of David; Josiah's adherence to the law would be extolled in a similar manner (23:25).

18:6 Obedience—The obedience of Hezekiah provides a powerful lesson for all of God's people. He "clung" to the Lord, staying true to God and His commandments. He must have faced strong opposition as he eliminated practices which had been going on for generations, and destroyed objects which had long been considered sacred, but he knew that God's approval was more important than human approbation. In the same way, we must be willing to serve God before we please those around us.

18:13 fourteenth year. Hezekiah's fourteenth year of

sole rule was 701 B.C. The details of the generally rebellious situation that provoked Sennacherib to invade the western portion of his empire are recounted in his annals, where Hezekiah is particularly mentioned for his involvement in the whole affair.

18:17 Tartan . . . Rabsaris . . . Rabshakeh. These titles suggest persons of high station in Assyria.

18:20 in whom do you trust. Perhaps Hezekiah's reputation for trusting in God was already widely known (v. 5). Trusting became the focal point of the Assyrian's psychological warfare (vv. 19–22,24–30).

18:21 broken reed. Actually, Sennacherib's warning against confidence in Egypt was well taken, the point having been made previously by Isaiah (Is. 30:3–5; 31:1–3).

18:5 [f] 2 Kin. 19:10　[g] 2 Kin. 23:25　18:6 [h] Deut. 10:20　18:7 [i] [2 Chr. 15:2]　[j] 1 Sam. 18:5, 14　[k] 2 Kin. 16:7　18:8 [l] Is. 14:29　[m] 2 Kin. 17:9　18:9 [n] 2 Kin. 17:3　18:10 [o] 2 Kin. 17:6　18:11 [p] 2 Kin. 17:6　[q] 1 Chr. 5:26　18:12 [r] 2 Kin. 17:7–18　18:13 [s] 2 Chr. 32:1　18:15 [t] 2 Kin. 12:18; 16:8　18:17 [u] 2 Kin. 20:20　[v] Is. 7:3　18:18 [w] Is. 22:20　18:19 [x] 2 Chr. 32:10　18:21 [y] Ezek. 29:6, 7　18:22 [z] 2 Kin. 18:4

altar in Jerusalem'?"' ²³Now therefore, I urge you, give a pledge to my master the king of Assyria, and I will give you two thousand horses—if you are able on your part to put riders on them! ²⁴How then will you repel one captain of the least of my master's servants, and put your trust in Egypt for chariots and horsemen? ²⁵Have I now come up without the LORD against this place to destroy it? The LORD said to me, 'Go up against this land, and destroy it.'"

²⁶ᵃThen Eliakim the son of Hilkiah, Shebna, and Joah said to *the* Rabshakeh, "Please speak to your servants in ᵇAramaic, for we understand *it*; and do not speak to us in Hebrew* in the hearing of the people who *are* on the wall."

²⁷But *the* Rabshakeh said to them, "Has my master sent me to your master and to you to speak these words, and not to the men who sit on the wall, who will eat and drink their own waste with you?"

²⁸Then *the* Rabshakeh stood and called out with a loud voice in Hebrew, and spoke, saying, "Hear the word of the great king, the king of Assyria! ²⁹Thus says the king: ᶜ"Do not let Hezekiah deceive you, for he shall not be able to deliver you from his hand; ³⁰nor let Hezekiah make you trust in the LORD, saying, "The LORD will surely deliver us; this city shall not be given into the hand of the king of Assyria."' ³¹Do not listen to Hezekiah; for thus says the king of Assyria: 'Make *peace* with me by a present and come out to me; and every one of you eat from his own ᵈvine and every one from his own fig tree, and every one of you drink the waters of his own cistern; ³²until I come and take you away to a land like your own land, ᵉa land of grain and new wine, a land of bread and vineyards, a land of olive groves and honey, that you may live and not die. But do not listen to Hezekiah, lest he persuade you, saying, "The LORD will deliver us." ³³ᶠHas any of the gods of the nations at all delivered its land from the hand of the king of Assyria? ³⁴Where *are* the gods of ᵍHamath and Arpad? Where *are* the gods of Sepharvaim and Hena and ʰIvah? Indeed, have they delivered Samaria from my hand? ³⁵Who among all the gods of the lands have delivered their countries from my hand, ⁱthat the LORD should deliver Jerusalem from my hand?'"

³⁶But the people held their peace and answered him not a word; for the king's commandment was, "Do not answer him." ³⁷Then Eliakim the son of Hilkiah, who *was* over the household, Shebna the scribe, and Joah the son of Asaph, the recorder, came to Hezekiah ʲwith *their* clothes torn, and told him the words of *the* Rabshakeh.

Isaiah Assures Deliverance

19 And ᵃso it was, when King Hezekiah heard *it*, that he tore his clothes, covered himself with ᵇsackcloth, and went into the house of the LORD. ²Then he sent Eliakim, who *was* over the household, Shebna the scribe, and the elders of the priests, covered with sackcloth, to Isaiah the prophet, the son of Amoz. ³And they said to him, "Thus says Hezekiah: 'This day *is* a day of trouble, and rebuke, and blasphemy; for the children have come to birth, but *there is* no strength to bring them forth. ⁴ᶜIt may be that the LORD your God will hear all the words of *the* Rabshakeh, whom his master the king of Assyria has sent to ᵈreproach the living God, and will ᵉrebuke the words which the LORD your God has heard. Therefore lift up *your* prayer for the remnant that is left.'"

⁵So the servants of King Hezekiah came to Isaiah. ⁶ᶠAnd Isaiah said to them, "Thus you shall say to your master, 'Thus says the LORD: "Do not be ᵍafraid of the words which you have heard, with which

---

* **18:26** Literally *Judean*

18:25 The LORD said to me. The Assyrians may have been aware of prophecies concerning the judgment of Judah and Jerusalem and Assyria's own role as God's avengers (Is. 10:5–11). The remark was intended to introduce stark terror into the hearts of the people of Jerusalem (2 Chr. 32:18) by pointing out that now even their God was against them.

18:25 Self-Righteousness—The Assyrians were God's instrument for punishing Israel (Is. 10:5–10), but this fact was not due to any righteousness or virtue on Assyria's part. Rather, their attitude was blasphemous and proud (19:22). The lesson for the powerful king of Assyria is the lesson for kings, nations, and all individuals: no one may boast before the Lord (1 Cor. 1:29).

18:33 the gods of the nations. Rabshakeh's assertion that none of the gods of the nations who had opposed Assyria had withstood the Assyrian king is another aspect of the continued psychological warfare and evidence of the Rabshakeh's awareness of Isaiah's prophetic words (Is. 10:7–11).

19:2 Isaiah. The ministry of the great prophet Isaiah

had begun in the year that Uzziah (or Azariah) died (Is. 6:1), nearly four decades earlier (740 B.C.). Once Isaiah had sought out Judah's godless King Ahaz to minister to him (Is. 7:3); now the prophet was being sought by the godly Hezekiah (the details of 18:13—20:19 are also recorded in Is. 36–39).

19:4 hear . . . reproach. The first verb does not suggest that God is unaware of the words of Rabshakeh. Rather, the words describe God as determining to redress the wrong.

19:6 Do not be afraid. Isaiah's prophecy was one of comfort. Not only would Sennacherib fail to conquer Jerusalem, but he would face a violent death upon his return home. Both points of this prophetic message would come true, although Sennacherib was

---

18:26 ᵃ Is. 36:11—39:8 ᵇ Ezra 4:7 **18:29** ᶜ 2 Chr. 32:15 **18:31** ᵈ 1 Kin. 4:20, 25 **18:32** ᵉ Deut. 8:7–9; 11:12 **18:33** ᶠ 2 Kin. 19:12 **18:34** ᵍ 2 Kin. 19:13 ʰ 2 Kin. 17:24 **18:35** ⁱ Dan. 3:15 **18:37** ʲ Is. 33:7 **19:1** ᵃ Is. 37:1 ᵇ Ps. 69:11 **19:4** ᶜ 2 Sam. 16:12 ᵈ 2 Kin. 18:35 ᵉ Ps. 50:21 **19:6** ᶠ Is. 37:6 ᵍ [Ps. 112:7]

the [h]servants of the king of Assyria have blasphemed Me. [7]Surely I will send [i]a spirit upon him, and he shall hear a rumor and return to his own land; and I will cause him to fall by the sword in his own land.'"'"

Sennacherib's Threat and Hezekiah's Prayer

[8]Then *the* Rabshakeh returned and found the king of Assyria warring against Libnah, for he heard that he had departed [j]from Lachish. [9]And [k]the king heard concerning Tirhakah king of Ethiopia, "Look, he has come out to make war with you." So he again sent messengers to Hezekiah, saying, [10]"Thus you shall speak to Hezekiah king of Judah, saying: 'Do not let your God [l]in whom you trust deceive you, saying, "Jerusalem shall not be given into the hand of the king of Assyria." [11]Look! You have heard what the kings of Assyria have done to all lands by utterly destroying them; and shall you be delivered? [12m]Have the gods of the nations delivered those whom my fathers have destroyed, Gozan and Haran and Rezeph, and the people of [n]Eden who *were* in Telassar? [13o]Where *is* the king of Hamath, the king of Arpad, and the king of the city of Sepharvaim, Hena, and Ivah?'"

[14p]And Hezekiah received the letter from the hand of the messengers, and read it; and Hezekiah went up to the house of the LORD, and spread it before the LORD. [15]Then Hezekiah prayed before the LORD, and said: "O LORD God of Israel, *the One* [q]who dwells *between* the cherubim, [r]You are God, You alone, of all the kingdoms of the earth. You have made heaven and earth. [16s]Incline Your ear, O LORD, and hear; [t]open Your eyes, O LORD, and see; and hear the words of Sennacherib, [u]which he has sent to reproach the living God. [17]Truly, LORD, the kings of Assyria have laid waste the nations and their lands, [18]and have cast

their gods into the fire; for they *were* [v]not gods, but [w]the work of men's hands—wood and stone. Therefore they destroyed them. [19]Now therefore, O LORD our God, I pray, save us from his hand, [x]that all the kingdoms of the earth may [y]know that You *are* the LORD God, You alone."

The Word of the LORD Concerning Sennacherib

[20]Then Isaiah the son of Amoz sent to Hezekiah, saying, "Thus says the LORD God of Israel: [z]'Because you have prayed to Me against Sennacherib king of Assyria, [a]I have heard.' [21]This *is* the word which the LORD has spoken concerning him:

'The virgin, [b]the daughter of Zion,
    Has despised you, laughed you to
        scorn;
The daughter of Jerusalem
[c]Has shaken *her* head behind your
        back!
[22] 'Whom have you reproached and
        blasphemed?
    Against whom have you raised *your*
        voice,
    And lifted up your eyes on high?
    Against [d]the Holy *One* of Israel.
[23] [e]By your messengers you have
        reproached the Lord,
    And said: [f]"By the multitude of my
        chariots
    I have come up to the height of the
        mountains,
    To the limits of Lebanon;
    I will cut down its tall cedars
    And its choice cypress trees;
    I will enter the extremity of its
        borders,
    To its fruitful forest.
[24] I have dug and drunk strange water,
    And with the soles of my feet I have
        [g]dried up
    All the brooks of defense."

---

not assassinated until 20 years later (c. 681 B.C.). In his annals Sennacherib boasts of five more campaigns; however, he makes no mention of any other invasions of Judah.

19:9 Tirhakah king of Ethiopia. Since Tirhakah did not become king until 690 B.C., there is an apparent problem with the chronology of this verse. However, it is possible that the biblical author merely calls Tirhakah by the title he was best known by at the time of writing.

19:12 Eden. This is not the Eden of Genesis, but an area known today as Bit-Adini, south of Haran (Ezek. 27:23; Amos 1:5).

19:15 You have made heaven and earth. The conflict mentioned in this chapter involves far more than the kings of Egypt, Assyria, or Judah. The warfare is one in which the gods of the pagan world would dishonor the true and living God of Israel. Hezekiah's prayer was addressed to the God who alone is sovereign over all the kingdoms of the world. His sovereignty is related to the fact of creation; He is the God

who made heaven and earth. The heathen gods are born in corrupted human imaginations, and backed by a rebellious angel (Satan), but God is the one who owns and controls the universe.

19:21 daughter of Zion. As elsewhere in the Old Testament (Zeph. 3:14), this phrase should be written "daughter Zion," without the "of." Zion (Jerusalem) is like a daughter to God, whom He will protect and guard as only a father would.

19:22 Holy One of Israel. This title is characteristic of Isaiah's own manner of referring to God. He uses the

19:6 [h] 2 Kin. 18:17   **19:7** [i] 2 Kin. 19:35–37   **19:8** [j] 2 Kin. 18:14, 17   **19:9** [k] 1 Sam. 23:27   **19:10** [l] 2 Kin. 18:5   **19:12** [m] 2 Kin. 18:33, 34   [n] Ezek. 27:23   **19:13** [o] 2 Kin. 18:34   **19:14** [p] Is. 37:14   **19:15** [q] Ex. 25:22   [r] [Is. 44:6]   **19:16** [s] Ps. 31:2   [t] 2 Chr. 6:40   [u] 2 Kin. 19:4   **19:18** [v] [Jer. 10:3–5]   [w] [Acts 17:29]   **19:19** [x] Ps. 83:18   [y] 1 Kin. 8:42, 43   **19:20** [z] Is. 37:21   [a] 2 Kin. 20:5   **19:21** [b] Lam. 2:13   [c] Ps. 22:7, 8   **19:22** [d] Jer. 51:5   **19:23** [e] 2 Kin. 18:17   [f] Ps. 20:7   **19:24** [g] Is. 19:6

25 'Did you not hear long ago
   How ʰI made it,
   From ancient times that I formed it?
   Now I have brought it to pass,
   That ⁱyou should be
   For crushing fortified cities *into* heaps
      of ruins.
26 Therefore their inhabitants had little
      power;
   They were dismayed and confounded;
   They were *as* the grass of the field
   And the green herb,
   As ʲthe grass on the housetops
   And *grain* blighted before it is grown.

27 'But ᵏI know your dwelling place,
   Your going out and your coming in,
   And your rage against Me.
28 Because your rage against Me and
      your tumult
   Have come up to My ears,
   Therefore ˡI will put My hook in your
      nose
   And My bridle in your lips,
   And I will turn you back
   ᵐBy the way which you came.

29'This *shall be* a ⁿsign to you:

   You shall eat this year such as grows
      of itself,
   And in the second year what springs
      from the same;
   Also in the third year sow and reap,
   Plant vineyards and eat the fruit of
      them.
30 ᵒAnd the remnant who have escaped of
      the house of Judah
   Shall again take root downward,
   And bear fruit upward.
31 For out of Jerusalem shall go a
      remnant,
   And those who escape from Mount
      Zion.
   ᵖThe zeal of the LORD of hosts* will do
      this.'

32"Therefore thus says the LORD concerning the king of Assyria:

   'He shall ᑫnot come into this city,
   Nor shoot an arrow there,

Nor come before it with shield,
   Nor build a siege mound against it.
33 By the way that he came,
   By the same shall he return;
   And he shall not come into this city,'
   Says the LORD.
34 'For ʳI will ˢdefend this city, to save it
   For My own sake and ᵗfor My servant
      David's sake.'"

Sennacherib's Defeat and Death

35And ᵘit came to pass on a certain night
that the angel* of the LORD went out, and
killed in the camp of the Assyrians one
hundred and eighty-five thousand; and
when *people* arose early in the morning,
there were the corpses—all dead. 36So
Sennacherib king of Assyria departed and
went away, returned *home*, and remained at
ᵛNineveh. 37Now it came to pass, as he was
worshiping in the temple of Nisroch his god,
that his sons ʷAdrammelech and Sharezer
ˣstruck him down with the sword; and
they escaped into the land of Ararat. Then
ʸEsarhaddon his son reigned in his place.

Hezekiah's Life Extended

20 In ᵃthose days Hezekiah was sick and
near death. And Isaiah the prophet,
the son of Amoz, went to him and said to
him, "Thus says the LORD: 'Set your house
in order, for you shall die, and not live.'"

2Then he turned his face toward the
wall, and prayed to the LORD, saying,
3ᵇ"Remember now, O LORD, I pray, how I
have walked before You in truth and with a
loyal heart, and have done *what was* good
in Your sight." And Hezekiah wept bitterly.

4And it happened, before Isaiah had gone
out into the middle court, that the word of
the LORD came to him, saying, 5"Return
and tell Hezekiah ᶜthe leader of My people,
'Thus says the LORD, the God of David your
father: ᵈ"I have heard your prayer, I have
seen ᵉyour tears; surely I will heal you. On

---

* **19:31** Following many Hebrew manuscripts and
ancient versions (compare Isaiah 37:32); Masoretic
Text omits *of hosts*.   * **19:35** Or *Angel*

---

phrase 26 times (Is. 6:3). Sennacherib needed to know
that his boastful pride blasphemed the sovereign and
holy God of all nations.
19:30 remnant . . . Shall again take root. The promises in these verses were both for the immediate
situation and ultimately for the final regathering of
the Jewish people into their land in the time of the
coming Messiah.
19:32 not come into this city. While Sennacherib
later boasted of taking some 46 Judean cities, with
reference to Jerusalem he could only report that he
made Hezekiah "prisoner in Jerusalem, his royal residence, like a bird in a cage." God's defense and deliverance of Jerusalem demonstrated His faithfulness to
the Davidic covenant.
19:37 struck him down with the sword. The events
depicted here took place 20 years after God's deliver-

ance of Jerusalem. When his father was assassinated,
Esarhaddon took the throne and ruled from 681 to
668 B.C.
20:3 I have walked before You. Hezekiah's prayer
recognized that although all of life is in God's hands,
God is also a rewarder of those who faithfully serve
Him (Deut. 5:30–33; 30:15–16).

19:25 ʰ [Is. 45:7] ⁱ Is. 10:5, 6   **19:26** ʲ Ps. 129:6
19:27 ᵏ Ps. 139:1–3   **19:28** ˡ Ezek. 29:4; 38:4 ᵐ 2 Kin.
19:33, 36   **19:29** ⁿ 2 Kin. 20:8, 9   **19:30** ᵒ 2 Chr. 32:22,
23   **19:31** ᵖ Is. 9:7   **19:32** ᑫ Is. 8:7–10   **19:34** ʳ 2 Kin.
20:6 ˢ Is. 31:5 ᵗ 1 Kin. 11:12, 13   **19:35** ᵘ Is. 10:12–19;
37:36   **19:36** ᵛ Gen. 10:11   **19:37** ʷ 2 Kin. 17:31 ˣ 2 Kin.
19:7 ʸ Ezra 4:2   **20:1** ᵃ Is. 38:1–22   **20:3** ᵇ Neh. 13:22
20:5 ᶜ 1 Sam. 9:16; 10:1 ᵈ Ps. 65:2 ᵉ Ps. 39:12; 56:8

the third day you shall go up to the house of the LORD. 6And I will add to your days fifteen years. I will deliver you and this city from the hand of the king of Assyria; and *f*I will defend this city for My own sake, and for the sake of My servant David.'"'

7Then *g*Isaiah said, "Take a lump of figs." So they took and laid *it* on the boil, and he recovered.

8And Hezekiah said to Isaiah, *h*"What *is* the sign that the LORD will heal me, and that I shall go up to the house of the LORD the third day?"

9Then Isaiah said, *i*"This is the sign to you from the LORD, that the LORD will do the thing which He has spoken: *shall* the shadow go forward ten degrees or go backward ten degrees?"

10And Hezekiah answered, "It is an easy thing for the shadow to go down ten degrees; no, but let the shadow go backward ten degrees."

11So Isaiah the prophet cried out to the LORD, and *j*He brought the shadow ten degrees backward, by which it had gone down on the sundial of Ahaz.

The Babylonian Envoys

12*k*At that time Berodach-Baladan* the son of Baladan, king of Babylon, sent letters and a present to Hezekiah, for he heard that Hezekiah had been sick. 13And *l*Hezekiah was attentive to them, and showed them all the house of his treasures—the silver and gold, the spices and precious ointment, and all* his armory—all that was found among his treasures. There was nothing in his house or in all his dominion that Hezekiah did not show them.

14Then Isaiah the prophet went to King Hezekiah, and said to him, "What did these men say, and from where did they come to you?"

So Hezekiah said, "They came from a far country, from Babylon."

15And he said, "What have they seen in your house?"

So Hezekiah answered, *m*"They have seen all that *is* in my house; there is nothing among my treasures that I have not shown them."

16Then Isaiah said to Hezekiah, "Hear the word of the LORD: 17'Behold, the days are coming when all that *is* in your house, and what your fathers have accumulated until this day, *n*shall be carried to Babylon; nothing shall be left,' says the LORD. 18'And *o*they shall take away some of your sons who will descend from you, whom you will beget; *p*and they shall be *q*eunuchs in the palace of the king of Babylon.'"

19So Hezekiah said to Isaiah, *r*"The word of the LORD which you have spoken *is* good!" For he said, "Will there not be peace and truth at least in my days?"

Death of Hezekiah

20*s*Now the rest of the acts of Hezekiah—all his might, and how he *t*made a *u*pool and a tunnel and *v*brought water into the city—*are* they not written in the book of the chronicles of the kings of Judah? 21So *w*Hezekiah rested with his fathers. Then Manasseh his son reigned in his place.

Manasseh Reigns in Judah

21 Manasseh *a*was twelve years old when he became king, and he reigned fifty-five years in Jerusalem. His mother's name *was* Hephzibah. 2And he did evil in the sight of the LORD, *b*according to the abominations of the nations whom the LORD had

---

* **20:12** Spelled *Merodach-Baladan* in Isaiah 39:1
* **20:13** Following many Hebrew manuscripts, Syriac, and Targum; Masoretic Text omits *all*.

20:7 lump of figs. The practice of applying figs to an ulcerated sore is well attested in the records of the ancient Middle East, being mentioned as early as 2000 B.C.

20:12 Berodach-Baladan. This was a Chaldean king who twice ruled in Babylon (721–710, 703 B.C.). A perennial enemy of Assyria, he was twice defeated by them and cast out from Babylon. His search for allies in his resistance to Assyria may have occasioned the embassy to Hezekiah, especially because he had heard of Hezekiah's miraculous deliverance from the Assyrian army (2 Chr. 32:31).

20:13 showed them all the house of his treasures. One of the remarkable features of the Bible is the fact that it does not gloss over the faults of its best heroes and heroines. This account of the foolishness of Hezekiah follows immediately on the narrative of his great trust in the Lord (vv. 1–11).

20:16–18 Vanity—How much better for Israel's welfare if Hezekiah had been interested in introducing the Babylonian envoys to his God rather than to the treasures of the nation. The prophet's rebuke confirms that Hezekiah's action arose from a vain desire to impress the Babylonians with the externals of his

kingdom. Human pride, and the vain hope that deliverance will come from man, must be forsaken if God's blessing is to be experienced.

20:19 The word of the LORD . . . is good. Hezekiah's response seems a little heartless. He did verbally acknowledge God's right to decide, but it does not appear that he had any real sense of the trouble his folly would bring on the people.

20:20 a pool and a tunnel. Hezekiah dug a tunnel between the spring of Gihon and the Pool of Siloam to bring a ready supply of water within the eastern wall of Jerusalem. This tunnel is still in existence, a crooked shaft 1,750 feet long.

21:1 Manasseh. This wicked king's fifty-five year reign was the longest of any of the kings of the divided kingdom. Externally, the period was one of

---

20:6 *f* 2 Kin. 19:34   **20:7** *g* Is. 38:21   **20:8** *h* Judg. 6:17, 37, 39   **20:9** *i* Is. 38:7, 8   **20:11** *j* Is. 38:8   **20:12** *k* Is. 39:1–8   **20:13** *l* 2 Chr. 32:27, 31   **20:15** *m* 2 Kin. 20:13   **20:17** *n* Jer. 27:21, 22; 52:17   **20:18** *o* 2 Kin. 24:12   *p* Dan. 1:3–7   *q* Dan. 1:11, 18   **20:19** *r* 1 Sam. 3:18   **20:20** *s* 2 Chr. 32:32   *t* Neh. 3:16   *u* Is. 7:3   *v* 2 Chr. 32:3, 30   **20:21** *w* 2 Chr. 32:33   **21:1** *a* 2 Chr. 33:1–9   **21:2** *b* 2 Kin. 16:3

cast out before the children of Israel. 3For he rebuilt the high places cwhich Hezekiah his father had destroyed; he raised up altars for Baal, and made a wooden image,* das Ahab king of Israel had done; and he eworshiped all the host of heaven* and served them. 4fHe also built altars in the house of the LORD, of which the LORD had said, g"In Jerusalem I will put My name." 5And he built altars for all the host of heaven in the htwo courts of the house of the LORD. 6iAlso he made his son pass through the fire, practiced jsoothsaying, used witchcraft, and consulted spiritists and mediums. He did much evil in the sight of the LORD, to provoke Him to anger. 7He even set a carved image of Asherah* that he had made, in the house of which the LORD had said to David and to Solomon his son, k"In this house and in Jerusalem, which I have chosen out of all the tribes of Israel, I will put My name forever; 8land I will not make the feet of Israel wander anymore from the land which I gave their fathers—only if they are careful to do according to all that I have commanded them, and according to all the law that My servant Moses commanded them." 9But they paid no attention, and Manasseh mseduced them to do more evil than the nations whom the LORD had destroyed before the children of Israel.

10And the LORD spoke nby His servants the prophets, saying, 11o"Because Manasseh king of Judah has done these abominations (phe has acted more wickedly than all the qAmorites who were before him, and rhas also made Judah sin with his idols), 12therefore thus says the LORD God of Israel: 'Behold, I am bringing such calamity upon Jerusalem and Judah, that whoever hears of it, both shis ears will tingle. 13And I will stretch over Jerusalem tthe measuring line of Samaria and the plummet of the house of Ahab; uI will wipe Jerusalem as one wipes a dish, wiping it and turning it upside down. 14So I will forsake the vremnant of My inheritance and deliver them into the hand of their enemies; and they

shall become victims of plunder to all their enemies, 15because they have done evil in My sight, and have provoked Me to anger since the day their fathers came out of Egypt, even to this day.'"

16wMoreover Manasseh shed very much innocent blood, till he had filled Jerusalem from one end to another, besides his sin by which he made Judah sin, in doing evil in the sight of the LORD.

17Now xthe rest of the acts of yManasseh—all that he did, and the sin that he committed—are they not written in the book of the chronicles of the kings of Judah? 18So zManasseh rested with his fathers, and was buried in the garden of his own house, in the garden of Uzza. Then his son Amon reigned in his place.

Amon's Reign and Death

19aAmon was twenty-two years old when he became king, and he reigned two years in Jerusalem. His mother's name was Meshullemeth the daughter of Haruz of Jotbah. 20And he did evil in the sight of the LORD, bas his father Manasseh had done. 21So he walked in all the ways that his father had walked; and he served the idols that his father had served, and worshiped them. 22He cforsook the LORD God of his fathers, and did not walk in the way of the LORD.

23dThen the servants of Amon econspired against him, and killed the king in his own house. 24But the people of the land fexecuted all those who had conspired against King Amon. Then the people of the land made his son Josiah king in his place.

25Now the rest of the acts of Amon which he did, are they not written in the book of the chronicles of the kings of Judah? 26And he was buried in his tomb in the garden of Uzza. Then Josiah his son reigned in his place.

---

* 21:3 Hebrew Asherah, a Canaanite goddess • The gods of the Assyrians
* 21:7 A Canaanite goddess

---

political stability. It is known as the Assyrian Peace, an era in which the kings Esarhaddon (681–668 B.C.) and Ashurbanipal (668–626 B.C.) reigned and brought the Assyrian Empire to its zenith. However, the length of Manasseh's reign does not indicate a good rule, but rather God's persevering mercy and faithfulness to the Davidic covenant (2 Chr. 33:10–13).
21:3 host of heaven. Worship of heavenly bodies was strictly forbidden (Deut. 4:19; 17:2–7) and was condemned strongly by Israel's prophets (Is. 47:13; Amos 5:26). Yet Manasseh paid no attention to either the law or the prophets (2 Chr. 33:2–10).
21:4 altars in the house of the LORD. All that had been accomplished by the godly kings of Judah was undone by this reprobate. But wicked as Manasseh was, God heard his prayer when he repented (2 Chr. 33:12–16).
21:15 since the day. The story of the Old Testament is not a record of God's anger, but of His mercy and the delay of His just wrath.

21:23 conspired against him. No reason is assigned for the conspiracy that brought about Amon's assassination. While it may have had some connection with the international crisis that precipitated Ashurbanipal's renewed attention to the west, Amon's own wickedness may have provided sufficient cause.

21:3 c 2 Kin. 18:4, 22 d 1 Kin. 16:31–33 e [Deut. 4:19; 17:2–5] **21:4** f Jer. 7:30; 32:34 g 1 Kin. 11:13 **21:5** h 1 Kin. 6:36; 7:12 **21:6** i [Lev. 18:21; 20:2] j [Deut. 18:10–14] **21:7** k 1 Kin. 8:29; 9:3 **21:8** l 2 Sam. 7:10 **21:9** m [Prov. 29:12] **21:10** n 2 Kin. 17:13 **21:11** o 2 Kin. 23:26, 27; 24:3, 4 p 1 Kin. 21:26 q Gen. 15:16 r 2 Kin. 21:9 **21:12** s Jer. 19:3 **21:13** t Amos 7:7, 8 u 2 Kin. 22:16–19; 25:4–11 **21:14** v Jer. 6:9 **21:16** w 2 Kin. 24:4 **21:17** x 2 Chr. 33:11–19 y 2 Kin. 20:21 **21:18** z 2 Chr. 33:20 **21:19** d 2 Chr. 33:21–23 **21:20** b 2 Kin. 21:2–6, 11, 16 **21:22** c 1 Kin. 11:33 **21:23** d 2 Chr. 33:24, 25 e 2 Kin. 12:20; 14:19 **21:24** f 2 Kin. 14:5

Josiah Reigns in Judah

22 Josiah [a]*was* eight years old when he
became king, and he reigned thirty-
one years in Jerusalem. His mother's name
was Jedidah the daughter of Adaiah of
[b]Bozkath. 2And he did *what was* right in
the sight of the LORD, and walked in all the
ways of his father David; he [c]did not turn
aside to the right hand or to the left.

Hilkiah Finds the Book of the Law

3[d]Now it came to pass, in the eighteenth
year of King Josiah, *that* the king sent
Shaphan the scribe, the son of Azaliah,
the son of Meshullam, to the house of the
LORD, saying: 4"Go up to Hilkiah the high
priest, that he may count the money which
has been [e]brought into the house of the
LORD, which [f]the doorkeepers have gathered from the people. 5And let them [g]deliv-
er it into the hand of those doing the work,
who are the overseers in the house of the
LORD; let them give it to those who *are* in
the house of the LORD doing the work, to
repair the damages of the house— 6to carpenters and builders and masons—and to
buy timber and hewn stone to repair the
house. 7However [h]there need be no accounting made with them of the money delivered into their hand, because they deal
faithfully."
8Then Hilkiah the high priest said to
Shaphan the scribe, [i]"I have found the
Book of the Law in the house of the LORD."
And Hilkiah gave the book to Shaphan,
and he read it. 9So Shaphan the scribe
went to the king, bringing the king word,
saying, "Your servants have gathered the
money that was found in the house, and
have delivered it into the hand of those who
do the work, who oversee the house of the
LORD." 10Then Shaphan the scribe showed
the king, saying, "Hilkiah the priest has
given me a book." And Shaphan read it before the king.
11Now it happened, when the king heard
the words of the Book of the Law, that he
tore his clothes. 12Then the king commanded Hilkiah the priest, [j]Ahikam the son of
Shaphan, Achbor* the son of Michaiah,
Shaphan the scribe, and Asaiah a servant
of the king, saying, 13"Go, inquire of the
LORD for me, for the people and for all
Judah, concerning the words of this book
that has been found; for great *is* [k]the wrath
of the LORD that is aroused against us,
because our fathers have not obeyed the
words of this book, to do according to all
that is written concerning us."
14So Hilkiah the priest, Ahikam, Achbor, Shaphan, and Asaiah went to Huldah
the prophetess, the wife of Shallum the
son of [l]Tikvah, the son of Harhas, keeper
of the wardrobe. (She dwelt in Jerusalem
in the Second Quarter.) And they spoke
with her. 15Then she said to them, "Thus
says the LORD God of Israel, 'Tell the man
who sent you to Me, 16"Thus says the
LORD: 'Behold, [m]I will bring calamity on
this place and on its inhabitants—all the
words of the book which the king of Judah
has read— 17[n]because they have forsaken
Me and burned incense to other gods, that
they might provoke Me to anger with all
the works of their hands. Therefore My
wrath shall be aroused against this place
and shall not be quenched.' " ' 18But as for
[o]the king of Judah, who sent you to inquire
of the LORD, in this manner you shall speak
to him, 'Thus says the LORD God of Israel:
"*Concerning* the words which you have
heard— 19because your [p]heart was tender, and you [q]humbled yourself before the
LORD when you heard what I spoke against
this place and against its inhabitants, that
they would become [r]a desolation and [s]a
curse, and you tore your clothes and wept
before Me, I also have heard *you*," says the

* **22:12** *Abdon the son of Micah* in 2 Chronicles 34:20

22:1 *Josiah.* The name Josiah means "the Lord supports." Like the name of Cyrus (Is. 44:28; 45:1) and of the city of Bethlehem (Mic. 5:2), the name Josiah was announced by a prophet long before the time of his birth (1 Kin. 13:1–2).

22:2 *did not turn aside.* Not many rulers can rival Josiah's thirty-eight years of perseverance in righteousness. Some begin with high ideals and a commitment to do what is right in the sight of the Lord, but they soon learn that compromise is the art of politics. Compromise can be right and good. We ought to think more highly of others than ourselves and be willing to let go of our own preferences and opinions for the good of others. However, good can never result from compromising God's revealed ethics, morality, and justice. We must learn to live like Josiah, putting obedience to God before comfort and popular acceptance.

22:4 *Hilkiah the high priest.* This man was a major figure in the revival of true religion that young Josiah accomplished. The work of restoring the temple was under his direction.

22:8 *the Book of the Law.* This may mean either parts or all of the Pentateuch. Although it was placed by the side of the ark of the covenant (Deut. 31:26), it may have been lost, set aside, or hidden during the wicked reigns of Manasseh and Amon.

22:14 *Huldah the prophetess.* Huldah is one of only a few women mentioned in Scripture as a prophetess. She served at the same time as other godly prophets, such as Jeremiah and Zephaniah, and some have suggested that her husband Shallum was a relative of Jeremiah (Jer. 32:7–12).

22:1 [a] 2 Chr. 34:1 [b] Josh. 15:39 **22:2** [c] Deut. 5:32 **22:3** [d] 2 Chr. 34:8 **22:4** [e] 2 Kin. 12:4 [f] 2 Kin. 12:9, 10 **22:5** [g] 2 Kin. 12:11–14 **22:7** [h] 2 Kin. 12:15 **22:8** [i] Deut. 31:24–26 **22:12** [j] Jer. 26:24 **22:13** [k] [Deut. 29:23–28; 31:17, 18] **22:14** [l] 2 Chr. 34:22 **22:16** [m] Deut. 29:27 **22:17** [n] Deut. 29:25–27 **22:18** [o] 2 Chr. 34:26 **22:19** [p] [Ps. 51:17] [q] 1 Kin. 21:29 [r] Lev. 26:31, 32 [s] Jer. 26:6; 44:22

LORD. **20**"Surely, therefore, I will gather you to your fathers, and you ^tshall be gathered to your grave in peace; and your eyes shall not see all the calamity which I will bring on this place."'" So they brought back word to the king.

Josiah Restores True Worship

23 Now ^athe king sent them to gather all the elders of Judah and Jerusalem to him. **2**The king went up to the house of the LORD with all the men of Judah, and with him all the inhabitants of Jerusalem—the priests and the prophets and all the people, both small and great. And he ^bread in their hearing all the words of the Book of the Covenant ^cwhich had been found in the house of the LORD.

3Then the king ^dstood by a pillar and made a ^ecovenant before the LORD, to follow the LORD and to keep His commandments and His testimonies and His statutes, with all *his* heart and all *his* soul, to perform the words of this covenant that were written in this book. And all the people took a stand for the covenant. **4**And the king commanded Hilkiah the high priest, the ^fpriests of the second order, and the doorkeepers, to bring ^gout of the temple of the LORD all the articles that were made for Baal, for Asherah,* and for all the host of heaven;* and he burned them outside Jerusalem in the fields of Kidron, and carried their ashes to Bethel. **5**Then he removed the idolatrous priests whom the kings of Judah had ordained to burn incense on the high places in the cities of Judah and in the places all around Jerusalem, and those who burned incense to Baal, to the sun, to the moon, to the constellations, and to ^hall the host of heaven. **6**And he brought out the ⁱwooden image* from the house of the LORD, to the Brook Kidron outside Jerusalem, burned it at the Brook Kidron and ground *it* to ^jashes, and threw its ashes on ^kthe graves of the common

people. **7**Then he tore down the *ritual* booths ^lof the perverted persons* that *were* in the house of the LORD, ^mwhere the ⁿwomen wove hangings for the wooden image. **8**And he brought all the priests from the cities of Judah, and defiled the high places where the priests had burned incense, from ^oGeba to Beersheba; also he broke down the high places at the gates which *were* at the entrance of the Gate of Joshua the governor of the city, which *were* to the left of the city gate. **9**^pNevertheless the priests of the high places did not come up to the altar of the LORD in Jerusalem, ^qbut they ate unleavened bread among their brethren.

10And he defiled ^rTopheth, which *is* in ^sthe Valley of the Son* of Hinnom, ^tthat no man might make his son or his daughter ^upass through the fire to Molech. **11**Then he removed the horses that the kings of Judah had dedicated to the sun, at the entrance to the house of the LORD, by the chamber of Nathan-Melech, the officer who *was* in the court; and he burned the chariots of the sun with fire. **12**The altars that *were* ^von the roof, the upper chamber of Ahaz, which the kings of Judah had made, and the altars which ^wManasseh had made in the two courts of the house of the LORD, the king broke down and pulverized there, and threw their dust into the Brook Kidron. **13**Then the king defiled the high places that *were* east of Jerusalem, which *were* on the south of the Mount of Corruption, which ^xSolomon king of Israel had built for Ashtoreth the abomination of the Sidonians, for Chemosh the abomination of the Moabites, and for Milcom the abomination of the people of Ammon. **14**And he ^ybroke

---

* **23:4** A Canaanite goddess • The gods of the Assyrians   * **23:6** Hebrew *Asherah,* a Canaanite goddess   * **23:7** Hebrew *qedeshim,* that is, those practicing sodomy and prostitution in religious rituals   * **23:10** Kethib reads Sons.

23:2 *he read . . . the words of the Book.* Like Moses (Ex. 24:3–8) and Joshua (Josh. 8:34–35) before him, Josiah followed the ancient standard for godly leadership (Deut. 17:18–20; 31:9–13) and assembled the people to renew the covenant.

23:3 Knowing the Will of God—Christians often act as if learning the will of God is some mysterious process fraught with the danger of making all kinds of mistakes. This passage points to the fact that most of what we need to know about the will of God is contained in the Scriptures. The best place to *learn* the will of God is from reading the Bible. The only way to *do* the will of God is to obey the teaching of the Bible. God may have more specific plans for each of us, but His basic plan for all of us is to do what He says as revealed in His written word.

23:5 *idolatrous priests.* This term is also used by Zephaniah to describe the priests who led the rites associated with Baal and with star worship of various kinds (Zeph. 1:4). These priests had been appointed by Judah's past kings but functioned outside the divinely established priesthood.

23:6 *wooden image.* Although they had been destroyed by Hezekiah, these wooden images had been reintroduced by Manasseh (21:7) and also by Amon (21:21).

23:10 Topheth. This appears to have been a place in the valley of Hinnom where human sacrifices were made to Molech (Jer. 7:31–32; 32:35). *pass through the fire to Molech.* Some think that Molech was a god of the Ammonites (1 Kin. 11:5), or that Molech was the name of a type of child sacrifice associated with Baal worship (Jer. 19:5–6). Evidence of such child sacrifice has been found in the excavations at the Phoenician city of Carthage.

22:20 ^t [Is. 57:1, 2]   **23:1** ^a 2 Chr. 34:29, 30   **23:2** ^b Deut. 31:10–13   ^c 2 Kin. 22:8   **23:3** ^d 2 Kin. 11:14   ^e 2 Kin. 11:17   **23:4** ^f 2 Kin. 25:18   ^g 2 Kin. 21:3–7   **23:5** ^h 2 Kin. 21:3   **23:6** ⁱ 2 Kin. 21:7 / Ex. 32:20   ^k 2 Chr. 34:4   **23:7** ^l 1 Kin. 14:24; 15:12   ^m Ezek. 16:16   ⁿ Ex. 38:8   **23:8** ^o Josh. 21:17   **23:9** ^p [Ezek. 44:10–14]   ^q 1 Sam. 2:36   **23:10** ^r Is. 30:33   ^s Josh. 15:8   ^t [Lev. 18:21]   ^u 2 Kin. 21:6   **23:12** ^v Jer. 19:13   ^w 2 Kin. 21:5   **23:13** ^x 1 Kin. 11:5–7   **23:14** ^y [Ex. 23:24]

in pieces the *sacred* pillars and cut down the wooden images, and filled their places with the bones of men.

15Moreover the altar that *was* at Bethel, *and* the high place ᶻwhich Jeroboam the son of Nebat, who made Israel sin, had made, both that altar and the high place he broke down; and he burned the high place *and* crushed *it* to powder, and burned the wooden image. 16As Josiah turned, he saw the tombs that *were* there on the mountain. And he sent and took the bones out of the tombs and burned *them* on the altar, and defiled it according to the ᵃword of the LORD which the man of God proclaimed, who proclaimed these words. 17Then he said, "What gravestone *is* this that I see?"

So the men of the city told him, "*It is* ᵇthe tomb of the man of God who came from Judah and proclaimed these things which you have done against the altar of Bethel."

18And he said, "Let him alone; let no one move his bones." So they let his bones alone, with the bones of ᶜthe prophet who came from Samaria.

19Now Josiah also took away all the shrines of the high places that *were* ᵈin the cities of Samaria, which the kings of Israel had made to provoke the LORD* to anger; and he did to them according to all the deeds he had done in Bethel. 20ᵉHe ᶠexecuted all the priests of the high places who *were* there, on the altars, and ᵍburned men's bones on them; and he returned to Jerusalem.

21Then the king commanded all the people, saying, ʰ"Keep the Passover to the LORD your God, ⁱas *it is* written in this Book of the Covenant." 22ʲSuch a Passover surely had never been held since the days of the judges who judged Israel, nor in all the days of the kings of Israel and the kings of Judah. 23But in the eighteenth year of King Josiah this Passover was held before the LORD in Jerusalem. 24Moreover Josiah put away those who consulted mediums and spiritists, the household gods and idols, all the abominations that were seen in the land of Judah and in Jerusalem, that he might perform the words of ᵏthe law which were written in the book ˡthat Hilkiah the priest found in the house of the LORD. 25ᵐNow before him there was no king like him, who turned to the LORD with all his heart, with all his soul, and with all his might, according to all the Law of Moses; nor after him did *any* arise like him.

Impending Judgment on Judah

26Nevertheless the LORD did not turn from the fierceness of His great wrath, with which His anger was aroused against Judah, ⁿbecause of all the provocations with which Manasseh had provoked Him. 27And the LORD said, "I will also remove Judah from My sight, as ᵒI have removed Israel, and will cast off this city Jerusalem which I have chosen, and the house of which I said, ᵖ'My name shall be there.' "*

Josiah Dies in Battle

28Now the rest of the acts of Josiah, and all that he did, *are* they not written in the book of the chronicles of the kings of Judah? 29ᑫIn his days Pharaoh Necho king of Egypt went to the aid of the king of Assyria, to the River Euphrates; and King Josiah went against him. And *Pharaoh Necho*

* **23:19** Following Septuagint, Syriac, and Vulgate; Masoretic Text and Targum omit *the LORD.*
* **23:27** 1 Kings 8:29

23:18 the prophet . . . from Samaria. The prophet from Samaria was the old prophet of Bethel (1 Kin. 13:11). Samaria is the name for an entire area, not just the city that was later the capital of the northern kingdom (1 Kin. 13:32; 16:23–24). After the death of the man of God who had denounced Jeroboam's altar at Bethel, the aged prophet of Bethel requested that at his death he should be buried in Bethel beside that prophet of Judah.

23:22 Such a Passover. The restoration of religious places was part of the revival of spiritual worship. Although Hezekiah had held a Passover (2 Chr. 30), he had done so with some modification of the law (2 Chr. 30:13–20). Accordingly, Josiah's meeting of the strict requirements of the law (2 Chr. 35:1–19) was truly unparalleled since the days of the judges.

23:25 no king like him. Like his grandfather Hezekiah, who was famed for being without equal in his trust of the Lord (18:5), Josiah was truly a righteous king. Because of their outstanding examples of godliness, the authors of Kings and Chronicles devote considerable space to their reigns.

23:26–27 Unfaithfulness—The revival under Josiah, recorded in chapters 22 and 23, was like a stay of execution. It gave Judah some additional time but it was too little, too late. The die had been cast in

Manasseh's reign as God threatened to wipe out Jerusalem as one wipes a dish (21:13) because Manasseh did more evil than the other nations whom the Lord had destroyed. In the light of Jeremiah 18:7–8 we must assume that Josiah's people responded only externally to God's principles and not from the heart. Unfaithfulness was deeply rooted, and professions of religion could not change them from the inside.

23:29 Pharaoh Necho. During the long years of Josiah's reign (640–609 B.C.), Assyrian power had steadily crumbled until, as Nahum had predicted, Nineveh itself had fallen (612 B.C.). The surviving Assyrian forces had regrouped at Haran. Because Egypt was a long-standing ally of Assyria, Necho journeyed northward to help the beleaguered Assyrians. Josiah's deployment of his forces to the valley of Megiddo was an attempt to prevent the Egyptians

23:15 ᶻ 1 Kin. 12:28–33   **23:16** ᵃ 1 Kin. 13:2   **23:17** ᵇ 1 Kin. 13:1, 30, 31   **23:18** ᶜ 1 Kin. 13:11, 31   **23:19** ᵈ 2 Chr. 34:6, 7   **23:20** ᵉ 1 Kin. 13:2 ᶠ 2 Kin. 10:25; 11:18 ᵍ 2 Kin. 34:5   **23:21** ʰ 2 Chr. 35:1 ⁱ Deut. 16:2–8   **23:22** ʲ 2 Chr. 35:18, 19   **23:24** ᵏ [Lev. 19:31; 20:27] ˡ 2 Kin. 22:8   **23:25** ᵐ 2 Kin. 18:5   **23:26** ⁿ Jer. 15:4   **23:27** ᵒ 2 Kin. 17:18, 20; 18:11; 21:13 ᵖ 1 Kin. 8:29; 9:3   **23:29** ᑫ Jer. 2:16; 46:2

killed him at [r]Megiddo when he [s]confronted him. [30t]Then his servants moved his body in a chariot from Megiddo, brought him to Jerusalem, and buried him in his own tomb. And [u]the people of the land took Jehoahaz the son of Josiah, anointed him, and made him king in his father's place.

The Reign and Captivity of Jehoahaz

[31v]Jehoahaz *was* twenty-three years old when he became king, and he reigned three months in Jerusalem. His mother's name *was* [w]Hamutal the daughter of Jeremiah of Libnah. [32]And he did evil in the sight of the LORD, according to all that his fathers had done. [33]Now Pharaoh Necho put him in prison [x]at Riblah in the land of Hamath, that he might not reign in Jerusalem; and he imposed on the land a tribute of one hundred talents of silver and a talent of gold. [34]Then [y]Pharaoh Necho made Eliakim the son of Josiah king in place of his father Josiah, and [z]changed his name to [a]Jehoiakim. And *Pharaoh* took Jehoahaz [b]and went to Egypt, and he* died there.

Jehoiakim Reigns in Judah

[35]So Jehoiakim gave [c]the silver and gold to Pharaoh; but he taxed the land to give money according to the command of Pharaoh; he exacted the silver and gold from the people of the land, from every one according to his assessment, to give *it* to Pharaoh Necho. [36d]Jehoiakim *was* twenty-five years old when he became king, and he reigned eleven years in Jerusalem. His mother's name *was* Zebudah the daughter of Pedaiah of Rumah. [37]And he did evil in the sight of the LORD, according to all that his fathers had done.

Judah Overrun by Enemies

24 In [a]his days Nebuchadnezzar king of [b]Babylon came up, and Jehoiakim

became his vassal *for* three years. Then he turned and rebelled against him. [2c]And the LORD sent against him *raiding* bands of Chaldeans, bands of Syrians, bands of Moabites, and bands of the people of Ammon; He sent them against Judah to destroy it, [d]according to the word of the LORD which He had spoken by His servants the prophets. [3]Surely at the commandment of the LORD *this* came upon Judah, to remove *them* from His sight [e]because of the sins of Manasseh, according to all that he had done, [4f]and also because of the innocent blood that he had shed; for he had filled Jerusalem with innocent blood, which the LORD would not pardon.

[5]Now the rest of the acts of Jehoiakim, and all that he did, *are* they not written in the book of the chronicles of the kings of Judah? [6g]So Jehoiakim rested with his fathers. Then Jehoiachin his son reigned in his place.

[7]And [h]the king of Egypt did not come out of his land anymore, for [i]the king of Babylon had taken all that belonged to the king of Egypt from the Brook of Egypt to the River Euphrates.

The Reign and Captivity of Jehoiachin

[8j]Jehoiachin *was* eighteen years old when he became king, and he reigned in Jerusalem three months. His mother's name *was* Nehushta the daughter of Elnathan of Jerusalem. [9]And he did evil in the sight of the LORD, according to all that his father had done.

[10k]At that time the servants of Nebuchadnezzar king of Babylon came up against Jerusalem, and the city was besieged. [11]And Nebuchadnezzar king of Babylon came against the city, as his servants were besieging it. [12l]Then Jehoiachin king of

* **23:34** That is, Jehoahaz

from aiding the Assyrian forces at Haran. Although Pharaoh Necho was delayed sufficiently so that Haran was lost to the Assyrians, Josiah's action ultimately cost him his life (2 Chr. 35:20–25).

23:31 Jehoahaz. Jehoahaz, also called Shallum (Jer. 22:11), was Josiah's third son (24:18; 1 Chr. 3:15).

23:34 went to Egypt, and he died there. The curse for Judah's disobedience was beginning to fall (Deut. 28:64–68).

23:37 he did evil. Jehoiakim's short reign was noted for its extreme wickedness (2 Chr. 36:5–8). Jeremiah depicts him as a despicable monster who took advantage of his people (Jer. 22:13–14,17), filled the land with every sort of vice and violence (Jer. 18:18–20), and opposed all that was holy (Jer. 25:1–7). Unlike his father Josiah, who led the nation in reformation at the hearing of the Word of God (22:11; 23:1–25), Jehoiakim went so far as to cut up and burn a scroll of Scripture (Jer. 36:21–24) and to kill Urijah, a true prophet of God (Jer. 26:20–23).

24:2 Chaldeans. This name originally applied to

certain inhabitants of southern Mesopotamia, but by this time the term had come to be identified with the Babylonians, and Babylonia was called Chaldea. After the fall of the Babylonian Empire, the term Chaldean came to mean "soothsayer" (Dan. 2:2).

24:8 Jehoiachin. Because the scriptural description of Jehoiachin seems to represent him as a mature young man (Jer. 22:24–30; Ezek. 19:6), Jehoiachin's age at accession was probably eighteen rather than eight, as given elsewhere in some manuscripts (compare 2 Chr. 36:9).

23:29 [r] Zech. 12:11 [s] 2 Kin. 14:8   **23:30** [t] 2 Chr. 35:24 [u] 2 Chr. 36:1–4   **23:31** [v] Jer. 22:11 [w] 2 Kin. 24:18   **23:33** [x] 2 Kin. 25:6   **23:34** [y] 2 Chr. 36:4 [z] Dan. 1:7 [a] Matt. 1:11 [b] Ezek. 19:3, 4   **23:35** [c] 2 Kin. 23:33   **23:36** [d] 2 Chr. 36:5   **24:1** [a] Dan. 1:1 [b] 2 Kin. 20:14   **24:2** [c] Jer. 25:9; 32:28; 35:11 [d] 2 Kin. 20:17; 21:12–14; 23:27   **24:3** [e] 2 Kin. 21:2, 11; 23:26   **24:4** [f] 2 Kin. 21:16   **24:6** [g] Jer. 22:18, 19   **24:7** [h] Jer. 37:5–7 [i] Jer. 46:2   **24:8** [j] 2 Chr. 36:9   **24:10** [k] Dan. 1:1   **24:12** [l] Jer. 22:24–30; 24:1; 29:1, 2

Judah, his mother, his servants, his princes, and his officers went out to the king of Babylon; and the king of Babylon, *m*in the eighth year of his reign, took him prisoner.

The Captivity of Jerusalem

13*n*And he carried out from there all the treasures of the house of the LORD and the treasures of the king's house, and he *o*cut in pieces all the articles of gold which Solomon king of Israel had made in the temple of the LORD, *p*as the LORD had said. 14Also *q*he carried into captivity all Jerusalem: all the captains and all the mighty men of valor, *r*ten thousand captives, and *s*all the craftsmen and smiths. None remained except *t*the poorest people of the land. 15And *u*he carried Jehoiachin captive to Babylon. The king's mother, the king's wives, his officers, and the mighty of the land he carried into captivity from Jerusalem to Babylon. 16*v*All the valiant men, seven thousand, and craftsmen and smiths, one thousand, all *who were* strong *and* fit for war, these the king of Babylon brought captive to Babylon.

Zedekiah Reigns in Judah

17Then *w*the king of Babylon made Mattaniah, *x*Jehoiachin's* uncle, king in his place, and *y*changed his name to Zedekiah.

18*z*Zedekiah *was* twenty-one years old when he became king, and he reigned eleven years in Jerusalem. His mother's name *was* *a*Hamutal the daughter of Jeremiah of Libnah. 19*b*He also did evil in the sight of the LORD, according to all that Jehoiakim had done. 20For because of the anger of the LORD *this* happened in Jerusalem and Judah, that He finally cast them out from His presence. *c*Then Zedekiah rebelled against the king of Babylon.

The Fall and Captivity of Judah

25 Now it came to pass *a*in the ninth year of his reign, in the tenth month, on the tenth *day* of the month, *that*

Nebuchadnezzar king of Babylon and all his army came against Jerusalem and encamped against it; and they built a siege wall against it all around. 2So the city was besieged until the eleventh year of King Zedekiah. 3By the ninth *day* of the *b*fourth month the famine had become so severe in the city that there was no food for the people of the land.

4Then *c*the city wall was broken through, and all the men of war *fled* at night by way of the gate between two walls, which was by the king's garden, even though the Chaldeans *were* still encamped all around against the city. And *d*the king* went by way of the plain.* 5But the army of the Chaldeans pursued the king, and they overtook him in the plains of Jericho. All his army was scattered from him. 6So they took the king and brought him up to the king of Babylon *e*at Riblah, and they pronounced judgment on him. 7Then they killed the sons of Zedekiah before his eyes, *f*put out the eyes of Zedekiah, bound him with bronze fetters, and took him to Babylon.

8And in the fifth month, *g*on the seventh *day* of the month (which *was* *h*the nineteenth year of King Nebuchadnezzar king of Babylon), *i*Nebuzaradan the captain of the guard, a servant of the king of Babylon, came to Jerusalem. 9*j*He burned the house of the LORD *k*and the king's house; all the houses of Jerusalem, that is, all the houses of the great, *l*he burned with fire. 10And all the army of the Chaldeans who *were with* the captain of the guard *m*broke down the walls of Jerusalem all around.

11Then Nebuzaradan the captain of the guard carried away captive *n*the rest of the people *who* remained in the city and the defectors who had deserted to the king of Babylon, with the rest of the multitude. 12But the captain of the guard *o*left *some*

---

* **24:17** Literally *his* * **25:4** Literally *he* • Or *Arabah*, that is, the Jordan Valley

---

24:12 Jehoiachin. Jehoiakim apparently had died before Nebuchadnezzar arrived at Jerusalem, because it was Jehoiachin who was carried off captive with other leaders of Judah (such as Ezekiel; Ezek. 1:1). Jeremiah called him "Jeconiah" and "Coniah" (Jer. 22:24–28).
24:14–16 carried. The people of Israel lost their freedom and independence because of their own perpetually iniquitous ways. To be exiled is to be torn away from everything familiar, from everything traditional, from all identifiable scenery, and forced to live in a place where one has no identity and no roots. The people's whole sense of national identity was bound to their land, the place God had given them, and to be torn from that land was the ultimate evidence that God had rejected them.
24:15 carried Jehoiachin captive. Jehoiachin's captivity was prophesied in Jeremiah 22:24–27. Jehoiachin's eventual release is recorded in 25:27–30 and Jeremiah 52:31–34.
24:17 Mattaniah. This was Josiah's youngest son

(1 Chr. 3:15). He reigned until the fall of Jerusalem in 586 B.C.
25:7 put out the eyes. The last thing Zedekiah saw was the reward of his sinful folly—the horrible spectacle of his own loved ones being put to death. He would carry this picture with him until his own death in a Babylonian prison (Jer. 52:11).
25:10 broke down the walls. These walls would lie in ruins for a century and a half (Neh. 2:11—6:16).

24:12 *m* 2 Chr. 36:10   **24:13** *n* Is. 39:6   *o* Dan. 5:2, 3   *p* Jer. 20:5   **24:14** *q* Jer. 24:1   *r* 2 Kin. 24:16   *s* 1 Sam. 13:19   *t* 2 Kin. 25:12   **24:15** *u* Jer. 22:24–28   **24:16** *v* Jer. 52:28   **24:17** *w* Jer. 37:1   *x* 2 Chr. 36:10   *y* 2 Chr. 36:4   **24:18** *z* Jer. 52:1   *a* 2 Kin. 23:31   **24:19** *b* 2 Chr. 36:12   **24:20** *c* Ezek. 17:15   **25:1** *a* Jer. 6:6; 34:2   **25:3** *b* Lam. 4:9, 10   **25:4** *c* Jer. 39:2   *d* Ezek. 12:12   **25:6** *e* Jer. 52:9   **25:7** *f* Jer. 39:7   **25:8** *g* Jer. 52:12   *h* 2 Kin. 24:12   *i* Jer. 39:9   **25:9** *j* 2 Chr. 36:19   *k* Jer. 39:8   *l* Jer. 17:27   **25:10** *m* Neh. 1:3   **25:11** *n* Jer. 5:19; 39:9   **25:12** *o* Jer. 39:10; 40:7; 52:16

of the poor of the land as vinedressers and farmers. ¹³ᵖThe bronze ᵃpillars that *were* in the house of the LORD, and ʳthe carts and ˢthe bronze Sea that *were* in the house of the LORD, the Chaldeans broke in pieces, and ᵗcarried their bronze to Babylon. ¹⁴They also took away ᵘthe pots, the shovels, the trimmers, the spoons, and all the bronze utensils with which the priests ministered. ¹⁵The firepans and the basins, the things of solid gold and solid silver, the captain of the guard took away. ¹⁶The two pillars, one Sea, and the carts, which Solomon had made for the house of the LORD, ᵛthe bronze of all these articles was beyond measure. ¹⁷ʷThe height of one pillar *was* eighteen cubits, and the capital on it *was* of bronze. The height of the capital was three cubits, and the network and pomegranates all around the capital were all of bronze. The second pillar was the same, with a network.

¹⁸ˣAnd the captain of the guard took ʸSeraiah the chief priest, ᶻZephaniah the second priest, and the three doorkeepers. ¹⁹He also took out of the city an officer who had charge of the men of war, ᵃfive men of the king's close associates who were found in the city, the chief recruiting officer of the army, who mustered the people of the land, and sixty men of the people of the land *who were* found in the city. ²⁰So Nebuzaradan, captain of the guard, took these and brought them to the king of Babylon at Riblah. ²¹Then the king of Babylon struck them and put them to death at Riblah in the land of Hamath. ᵇThus Judah was carried away captive from its own land.

Gedaliah Made Governor of Judah

²²Then he made Gedaliah the son of ᶜAhikam, the son of Shaphan, governor over ᵈthe people who remained in the land of Judah, whom Nebuchadnezzar king of

Babylon had left. ²³Now when all the ᵉcaptains of the armies, they and *their* men, heard that the king of Babylon had made Gedaliah governor, they came to Gedaliah at Mizpah—Ishmael the son of Nethaniah, Johanan the son of Careah, Seraiah the son of Tanhumeth the Netophathite, and Jaazaniah* the son of a Maachathite, they and their men. ²⁴And Gedaliah took an oath before them and their men, and said to them, "Do not be afraid of the servants of the Chaldeans. Dwell in the land and serve the king of Babylon, and it shall be well with you."

²⁵But ᶠit happened in the seventh month that Ishmael the son of Nethaniah, the son of Elishama, of the royal family, came with ten men and struck and killed Gedaliah, the Jews, as well as the Chaldeans who were with him at Mizpah. ²⁶And all the people, small and great, and the captains of the armies, arose ᵍand went to Egypt; for they were afraid of the Chaldeans.

Jehoiachin Released from Prison

²⁷ʰNow it came to pass in the thirty-seventh year of the captivity of Jehoiachin king of Judah, in the twelfth month, on the twenty-seventh *day* of the month, *that* Evil-Merodach* king of Babylon, in the year that he began to reign, ⁱreleased Jehoiachin king of Judah from prison. ²⁸He spoke kindly to him, and gave him a more prominent seat than those of the kings who *were* with him in Babylon. ²⁹So Jehoiachin changed from his prison garments, and he ʲate bread regularly before the king all the days of his life. ³⁰And as for his provisions, *there was* a regular ration given him by the king, a portion for each day, all the days of his life.

---

* 25:23 Spelled *Jezaniah* in Jeremiah 40:8
* 25:27 Literally *Man of Marduk*

25:17 three cubits. This may be the height of the capitals not including the ornamental work; 1 Kings 7:16 and Jeremiah 52:22 say five cubits.
25:18 Seraiah. Although Seraiah was executed (v. 21), his son Jehozadak was deported (1 Chr. 6:15). Through Jehozadak's line would come Ezra, the priest and great reformer, who one day would return to Jerusalem and take up Seraiah's work (Ezra 7:1).
25:22 Gedaliah. Gedaliah's father Ahikam had supported Jeremiah in his struggles with the apostate officials of Judah (Jer. 26:24). The prophet Jeremiah was allowed to stay and assist Gedaliah in the process of reconstruction (Jer. 39:11–14; 40:1–6).
25:27 Evil-Merodach. This king succeeded Nebuchadnezzar and reigned a short time (561–560 B.C.).

Tablets from the reign of Nabonidus (555–539 B.C.) record the daily rations of Jehoiachin who is called "Yaukin, king of the land of Yahud (Judah)."
25:28 spoke kindly. Evil-Merodach's kindness toward Jehoiachin brings the books of Kings to an end on a ray of hope. Exile was neither the end of Israel nor of the Davidic line.

25:13 ᵖ Jer. 52:17 ᵍ 1 Kin. 7:15 ʳ 1 Kin. 7:27 ˢ 1 Kin. 7:23 ᵗ Jer. 27:19–22 **25:14** ᵘ Ex. 27:3 **25:16** ᵛ 1 Kin. 7:47 **25:17** ʷ 1 Kin. 7:15–22 **25:18** ˣ Jer. 39:9–13; 52:12–16, 24 ʸ Ezra 7:1 ᶻ Jer. 21:1; 29:25, 29 **25:19** ᵃ Jer. 52:25 **25:21** ᵇ Deut. 28:36, 64 **25:22** ᶜ 2 Kin. 22:12 ᵈ Is. 1:9; Jer. 40:5 **25:23** ᵉ Jer. 40:7–9 **25:25** ᶠ Jer. 41:1–3 **25:26** ᵍ Jer. 43:4–7 **25:27** ʰ Jer. 52:31–34 ⁱ Gen. 40:13, 20 **25:29** ʲ 2 Sam. 9:7

THE FIRST BOOK OF THE
CHRONICLES

▶ **AUTHOR:** Tradition in the Jewish Talmud supports Ezra the priest as the author of 1 Chronicles. The content points to priestly authorship because of the emphasis on the temple, the priesthood, and the theocratic line of David in the southern kingdom of Judah. Ezra was an educated scribe (Ezra 7:6), and according to the apocryphal book of 2 Maccabees 2:13–15, Nehemiah collected an extensive library which was available to Ezra for his use in compiling Chronicles.

▶ **TIME:** c. 1004–971 B.C.   ▶ **KEY VERSES:** 1 Chr. 7:11–14

▶ **THEME:** First Chronicles is largely a retelling of the texts of 1 and 2 Samuel with administrative details and the roles that the various tribes and alliances played in the events of the nation. We don't see the family conflict with Michal when the ark is brought to Jerusalem or the affair with Bathsheba and its fallout. When it comes to succession, all we are told is that David chose Solomon to succeed him. This is a primary document of the history of Israel.

The Family of Adam— Seth to Abraham

1 Adam,*a b*Seth, Enosh, **2**Cainan,* Mahalalel, Jared, **3**Enoch, Methuselah, Lamech, **4c**Noah,* Shem, Ham, and Japheth.

5dThe sons of Japheth *were* Gomer, Magog, Madai, Javan, Tubal, Meshech, and Tiras. **6**The sons of Gomer *were* Ashkenaz, Diphath,* and Togarmah. **7**The sons of Javan *were* Elishah, Tarshishah,* Kittim, and Rodanim.*

8eThe sons of Ham *were* Cush, Mizraim, Put, and Canaan. **9**The sons of Cush *were* Seba, Havilah, Sabta,* Raama,* and Sabtecha. The sons of Raama *were* Sheba and Dedan. **10**Cush *f*begot Nimrod; he began to be a mighty one on the earth. **11**Mizraim begot Ludim, Anamim, Lehabim, Naphtuhim, **12**Pathrusim, Casluhim (from whom came the Philistines and the *g*Caphtorim). **13h**Canaan begot Sidon, his firstborn, and Heth; **14**the Jebusite, the Amorite, and the Girgashite; **15**the Hivite, the Arkite, and the Sinite; **16**the Arvadite, the Zemarite, and the Hamathite.

17The sons of *i*Shem *were* Elam, Asshur, *j*Arphaxad, Lud, Aram, Uz, Hul, Gether, and Meshech.* **18**Arphaxad begot Shelah, and Shelah begot Eber. **19**To Eber were born two sons: the name of one *was* Peleg,* for in his days the earth was divided; and his brother's name *was* Joktan. **20k**Joktan begot Almodad, Sheleph, Hazarmaveth, Jerah, **21**Hadoram, Uzal, Diklah, **22**Ebal,* Abimael, Sheba, **23**Ophir, Havilah, and Jobab. All these *were* the sons of Joktan.

24l Shem, Arphaxad, Shelah, **25m**Eber, Peleg, Reu, **26**Serug, Nahor, Terah, **27**and *n*Abram, who *is* Abraham. **28o**The sons of Abraham *were* *p*Isaac and *q*Ishmael.

The Family of Ishmael

29These *are* their genealogies: The *r*firstborn of Ishmael *was* Nebajoth; then Kedar, Adbeel, Mibsam, **30**Mishma, Dumah,

* **1:2** Hebrew *Qenan*   * **1:4** Following Masoretic Text and Vulgate; Septuagint adds *the sons of Noah*.   * **1:6** Spelled *Riphath* in Genesis 10:3   * **1:7** Spelled *Tarshish* in Genesis 10:4 • Spelled *Dodanim* in Genesis 10:4   * **1:9** Spelled *Sabtah* in Genesis 10:7 • Spelled *Raamah* in Genesis 10:7   * **1:17** Spelled *Mash* in Genesis 10:23   * **1:19** Literally *Division*   * **1:22** Spelled *Obal* in Genesis 10:28

1:1 *Adam, Seth, Enosh.* Including the names of these pre-flood people along with the rest of the genealogical record indicates that the chronicler had no question of their historical identity.
1:18 *Eber.* Eber was the ancestor of Abraham, Isaac, and Jacob. The name Hebrew, a derivative of Eber's name, was applied to the Israelites.
1:19 *the earth was divided.* This refers to the division of the earth's population by the scattering of the human race following the judgment of God on the tower of Babel.

1:1 *a* Gen. 1:27; 2:7; 5:1, 2, 5   *b* Gen. 4:25, 26; 5:3–9
1:4 *c* Gen. 5:28—10:1   **1:5** *d* Gen. 10:2–4   **1:8** *e* Gen. 10:6   **1:10** *f* Gen. 10:8–10, 13   **1:12** *g* Deut. 2:23
1:13 *h* Gen. 9:18, 25–27; 10:15   **1:17** *i* Gen. 10:22–29; 11:10   *j* Luke 3:36   **1:20** *k* Gen. 10:26   **1:24** *l* Luke 3:34–36   **1:25** *m* Gen. 11:15   **1:27** *n* Gen. 17:5
1:28 *o* Gen. 21:2, 3   *p* Gen. 21:2   *q* Gen. 16:11, 15
1:29 *r* Gen. 25:13–16

Massa, Hadad,* Tema, ³¹Jetur, Naphish, and Kedemah. These *were* the sons of Ishmael.

The Family of Keturah

³²Now ˢthe sons born to Keturah, Abraham's concubine, *were* Zimran, Jokshan, Medan, Midian, Ishbak, and Shuah. The sons of Jokshan *were* Sheba and Dedan. ³³The sons of Midian *were* Ephah, Epher, Hanoch, Abida, and Eldaah. All these were the children of Keturah.

The Family of Isaac

³⁴And ᵗAbraham begot Isaac. ᵘThe sons of Isaac *were* Esau and Israel. ³⁵The sons of ᵛEsau *were* Eliphaz, Reuel, Jeush, Jaalam, and Korah. ³⁶And the sons of Eliphaz *were* Teman, Omar, Zephi,* Gatam, *and* Kenaz; and *by* ʷTimna,* Amalek. ³⁷The sons of Reuel *were* Nahath, Zerah, Shammah, and Mizzah.

The Family of Seir

³⁸ˣThe sons of Seir *were* Lotan, Shobal, Zibeon, Anah, Dishon, Ezer, and Dishan. ³⁹And the sons of Lotan *were* Hori and Homam; Lotan's sister *was* Timna. ⁴⁰The sons of Shobal *were* Alian,* Manahath, Ebal, Shephi,* and Onam. The sons of Zibeon *were* Ajah and Anah. ⁴¹The son of Anah *was* ʸDishon. The sons of Dishon *were* Hamran,* Eshban, Ithran, and Cheran. ⁴²The sons of Ezer *were* Bilhan, Zaavan, *and* Jaakan.* The sons of Dishan *were* Uz and Aran.

The Kings of Edom

⁴³Now these *were* the ᶻkings who reigned in the land of Edom before a king reigned over the children of Israel: Bela the son of Beor, and the name of his city was Dinhabah. ⁴⁴And when Bela died, Jobab the son of Zerah of Bozrah reigned in his place. ⁴⁵When Jobab died, Husham of the land of the Temanites reigned in his place. ⁴⁶And when Husham died, Hadad the son of Bedad, who attacked Midian in the field of Moab, reigned in his place. The name of his city *was* Avith. ⁴⁷When Hadad

died, Samlah of Masrekah reigned in his place. ⁴⁸ᵃAnd when Samlah died, Saul of Rehoboth-by-the-River reigned in his place. ⁴⁹When Saul died, Baal-Hanan the son of Achbor reigned in his place. ⁵⁰And when Baal-Hanan died, Hadad* reigned in his place; and the name of his city was Pai.* His wife's name was Mehetabel the daughter of Matred, the daughter of Mezahab. ⁵¹Hadad died also. And the chiefs of Edom were Chief Timnah, Chief Aliah,* Chief Jetheth, ⁵²Chief Aholibamah, Chief Elah, Chief Pinon, ⁵³Chief Kenaz, Chief Teman, Chief Mibzar, ⁵⁴Chief Magdiel, and Chief Iram. These *were* the chiefs of Edom.

The Family of Israel

2 These *were* the ᵃsons of Israel: ᵇReuben, Simeon, Levi, Judah, Issachar, Zebulun, ²Dan, Joseph, Benjamin, Naphtali, Gad, and Asher.

From Judah to David

³The sons of ᶜJudah *were* Er, Onan, and Shelah. *These* three were born to him by the daughter of ᵈShua, the Canaanitess. ᵉEr, the firstborn of Judah, was wicked in the sight of the LORD; so He killed him. ⁴And ᶠTamar, his daughter-in-law, ᵍbore him Perez and Zerah. All the sons of Judah *were* five.

⁵The sons of ʰPerez *were* Hezron and Hamul. ⁶The sons of Zerah *were* Zimri, ⁱEthan, Heman, Calcol, and Dara—five of them in all.

⁷The son of ʲCarmi *was* Achar,* the troubler of Israel, who transgressed in the ᵏaccursed thing.

⁸The son of Ethan *was* Azariah.

⁹Also the sons of Hezron who were

---

* **1:30** Spelled *Hadar* in Genesis 25:15
* **1:36** Spelled *Zepho* in Genesis 36:11 • Compare Genesis 36:12 * **1:40** Spelled *Alvan* in Genesis 36:23 • Spelled *Shepho* in Genesis 36:23 * **1:41** Spelled *Hemdan* in Genesis 36:26 * **1:42** Spelled *Akan* in Genesis 36:27 * **1:50** Spelled *Hadar* in Genesis 36:39 • Spelled *Pau* in Genesis 36:39 * **1:51** Spelled *Alvah* in Genesis 36:40 * **2:7** Spelled *Achan* in Joshua 7:1 and elsewhere

---

1:36 Timna. Timna was Eliphaz's concubine (Gen. 36:12). Her son Amalek was the founder of the Amalekites, a people that became one of Israel's most persistent enemies (Ex. 17:8–16; Deut. 25:17–19; 1 Sam. 15:1–3).

1:38 Seir. Seir was the patriarchal name of the pre-Edomite population in the region east and south of the Dead Sea (Gen. 36:20–30). **Lotan.** Lotan was Timna's brother, and Timna was the concubine of Esau's son. This is how the people of Seir and the descendants of Esau were related, and together these two people groups became the kingdom of Edom.

1:43 the kings . . . of Edom. Although the kings of Edom ruled in succession, they were not part of a dynasty. Apparently Edom did not have a capital, and its kings ruled from their own cities.

1:51 chiefs. The word "chiefs" usually referred to military leaders (Gen. 36:40–43).

2:1–55 Family—The Hebrew nation, descended through Abraham, kept one of the most carefully preserved family records of all time. To be associated with the family of Israel was to be identified with the God of Israel, and the history of this people is closely associated with the things that God taught each of these ancestors.

1:32 ˢGen. 25:1–4 **1:34** ᵗGen. 21:2 ᵘGen. 25:9, 25, 26, 29; 32:28 **1:35** ᵛGen. 36:10–19 **1:36** ʷGen. 36:12 **1:38** ˣGen. 36:20–28 **1:41** ʸGen. 36:25 **1:43** ᶻGen. 36:31–43 **1:48** ᵃGen. 36:37 **2:1** ᵃGen. 29:32–35; 35:23, 26; 46:8–27 ᵇGen. 29:32; 35:22 **2:3** ᶜNum. 26:19 ᵈGen. 38:2 ᵉGen. 38:7 **2:4** ᶠGen. 38:6 ᵍMatt. 1:3 **2:5** ʰRuth 4:18 **2:6** ⁱ1 Kin. 4:31 **2:7** ʲ1 Chr. 4:1 ᵏJosh. 6:18

born to him *were* Jerahmeel, Ram, and Chelubai.* [10]Ram *b*begot Amminadab, and Amminadab begot Nahshon, *m*leader of the children of Judah; [11]Nahshon begot Salma,* and Salma begot Boaz; [12]Boaz begot Obed, and Obed begot Jesse; [13]*n*Jesse begot Eliab his firstborn, Abinadab the second, Shimea* the third, [14]Nethanel the fourth, Raddai the fifth, [15]Ozem the sixth, *and* David the *o*seventh.

[16]Now their sisters *were* Zeruiah and Abigail. *p*And the sons of Zeruiah *were* Abishai, Joab, and Asahel—three. [17]Abigail bore Amasa; and the father of Amasa *was* Jether the Ishmaelite.*

The Family of Hezron

[18]Caleb the son of Hezron had children by Azubah, *his* wife, and by Jerioth. Now these were her sons: Jesher, Shobab, and Ardon. [19]When Azubah died, Caleb took *q*Ephrath* as his wife, who bore him Hur. [20]And Hur begot Uri, and Uri begot *r*Bezalel.

[21]Now afterward Hezron went in to the daughter of *s*Machir the father of Gilead, whom he married when he *was* sixty years old; and she bore him Segub. [22]Segub begot *t*Jair, who had twenty-three cities in the land of Gilead. [23]*u*(Geshur and Syria took from them the towns of Jair, with Kenath and its towns—sixty towns.) All these *belonged to* the sons of Machir the father of Gilead. [24]After Hezron died in Caleb Ephrathah, Hezron's wife Abijah bore him *v*Ashhur the father of Tekoa.

The Family of Jerahmeel

[25]The sons of Jerahmeel, the firstborn of Hezron, *were* Ram, the firstborn, and Bunah, Oren, Ozem, *and* Ahijah. [26]Jerahmeel had another wife, whose name was Atarah; she was the mother of Onam. [27]The sons of Ram, the firstborn of Jerahmeel, were Maaz, Jamin, and Eker. [28]The sons of Onam were Shammai and Jada. The sons of Shammai *were* Nadab and Abishur.

[29]And the name of the wife of Abishur *was* Abihail, and she bore him Ahban and Molid. [30]The sons of Nadab *were* Seled and Appaim; Seled died without children. [31]The son of Appaim *was* Ishi, the son of Ishi *was* Sheshan, and *w*Sheshan's son *was* Ahlai. [32]The sons of Jada, the brother of Shammai, *were* Jether and Jonathan; Jether died without children. [33]The sons of Jonathan *were* Peleth and Zaza. These were the sons of Jerahmeel.

[34]Now Sheshan had no sons, only daughters. And Sheshan had an Egyptian servant whose name *was* Jarha. [35]Sheshan gave his daughter to Jarha his servant as wife, and she bore him Attai. [36]Attai begot Nathan, and Nathan begot *x*Zabad; [37]Zabad begot Ephlal, and Ephlal begot *y*Obed; [38]Obed begot Jehu, and Jehu begot Azariah; [39]Azariah begot Helez, and Helez begot Eleasah; [40]Eleasah begot Sismai, and Sismai begot Shallum; [41]Shallum begot Jekamiah, and Jekamiah begot Elishama.

The Family of Caleb

[42]The descendants of Caleb the brother of Jerahmeel *were* Mesha, his firstborn, who was the father of Ziph, and the sons of Mareshah the father of Hebron. [43]The sons of Hebron *were* Korah, Tappuah, Rekem, and Shema. [44]Shema begot Raham the father of Jorkoam, and Rekem begot Shammai. [45]And the son of Shammai *was* Maon, and Maon *was* the father of Beth Zur.

[46]Ephah, Caleb's concubine, bore Haran, Moza, and Gazez; and Haran begot Gazez. [47]And the sons of Jahdai *were* Regem, Jotham, Geshan, Pelet, Ephah, and Shaaph.

[48]Maachah, Caleb's concubine, bore Sheber and Tirhanah. [49]She also bore Shaaph the father of Madmannah, Sheva the father of Machbenah and the father of Gibea. And the daughter of Caleb *was* *z*Achsah.

[50]These were the descendants of Caleb: The sons of *a*Hur, the firstborn of Ephrathah, *were* Shobal the father of *b*Kirjath Jearim, [51]Salma the father of Bethlehem, *and* Hareph the father of Beth Gader.

[52]And Shobal the father of Kirjath Jearim had descendants: Haroeh, *and* half

---

* **2:9** Spelled *Caleb* in 2:18, 42   * **2:11** Spelled *Salmon* in Ruth 4:21 and Luke 3:32   * **2:13** Spelled *Shammah* in 1 Samuel 16:9 and elsewhere
* **2:17** Compare 2 Samuel 17:25   * **2:19** Spelled *Ephrathah* elsewhere

---

2:10 Nahshon. This genealogy is selective, focusing on the members important to the lineage of David. Nahshon was head of the tribe of Judah at the time of the wilderness march from Sinai to Kadesh Barnea (Num. 1:7; 2:3; 7:12). He was more than five generations removed from Judah.

2:16 sisters. Sisters are not usually mentioned in ancient genealogies. However this genealogy pays particular attention to the family of David, and as his sister's sons were important members of his military units, the sisters are listed.

2:18 Caleb. This Caleb is not the famous companion of Joshua (Num. 13:6; Josh. 14:6–7), who lived several centuries later during the conquest of Canaan.

2:51 father of Bethlehem. The chronicler recorded Caleb's genealogy because of the significance of Bethlehem, the birthplace of King David. One of Caleb's descendants, Salma, was the founder of Bethlehem.

2:10 *l*Matt. 1:4 *m*Num. 1:7; 2:3	**2:13** *n*1 Sam. 16:6
2:15 *o*1 Sam. 16:10, 11; 17:12	**2:16** *p*2 Sam. 2:18
2:19 *q*1 Chr. 2:50	**2:20** *r*Ex. 31:2; 38:22
2:21 *s*Num. 27:1	**2:22** *t*Judg. 10:3 **2:23** *u*Deut. 3:14
2:24 *v*1 Chr. 4:5	**2:31** *w*1 Chr. 2:34, 35
2:36 *x*1 Chr. 11:41	**2:37** *y*2 Chr. 23:1 **2:49** *z*Josh. 15:17
2:50 *a*1 Chr. 4:4 *b*Josh. 9:17; 18:14	

of the *families of* Manuhoth.* ⁵³The families of Kirjath Jearim *were* the Ithrites, the Puthites, the Shumathites, and the Mishraites. From these came the Zorathites and the Eshtaolites.

⁵⁴The sons of Salma *were* Bethlehem, the Netophathites, Atroth Beth Joab, half of the Manahethites, and the Zorites.

⁵⁵And the families of the scribes who dwelt at Jabez *were* the Tirathites, the Shimeathites, *and* the Suchathites. These *were* the ᶜKenites who came from Hammath, the father of the house of ᵈRechab.

The Family of David

3 Now these were the sons of David who were born to him in Hebron: The firstborn *was* ᵃAmnon, by ᵇAhinoam the ᶜJezreelitess; the second, Daniel,* by ᵈAbigail the Carmelitess; ²the third, ᵉAbsalom the son of Maacah, the daughter of Talmai, king of Geshur; the fourth, ᶠAdonijah the son of Haggith; ³the fifth, Shephatiah, by Abital; the sixth, Ithream, by his wife ᵍEglah.

⁴*These* six were born to him in Hebron. ʰThere he reigned seven years and six months, and ⁱin Jerusalem he reigned thirty-three years. ⁵ʲAnd these were born to him in Jerusalem: Shimea,* Shobab, Nathan, and ᵏSolomon—four by Bathshua* the daughter of Ammiel.* ⁶Also *there* were Ibhar, Elishama,* Eliphelet,* ⁷Nogah, Nepheg, Japhia, ⁸Elishama, Eliada,* and Eliphelet—ˡnine *in all.* ⁹*These were* all the sons of David, besides the sons of the concubines, and ᵐTamar their sister.

The Family of Solomon

¹⁰Solomon's son *was* ⁿRehoboam; Abijah* *was* his son, Asa his son, Jehoshaphat his son, ¹¹Joram* his son, Ahaziah his son, Joash* his son, ¹²Amaziah his son, Azariah* his son, Jotham his son, ¹³Ahaz his son, Hezekiah his son, Manasseh his son, ¹⁴Amon his son, *and* Josiah his son. ¹⁵The sons of Josiah *were* Johanan the firstborn, the second Jehoiakim, the third Zedekiah, and the fourth Shallum.* ¹⁶The sons

of ᵒJehoiakim *were* Jeconiah his son *and* Zedekiah* his son.

The Family of Jeconiah

¹⁷And the sons of Jeconiah* *were* Assir,* Shealtiel ᵖhis son, ¹⁸*and* Malchiram, Pedaiah, Shenazzar, Jecamiah, Hoshama, and Nedabiah. ¹⁹The sons of Pedaiah *were* Zerubbabel and Shimei. The sons of Zerubbabel *were* Meshullam, Hananiah, Shelomith their sister, ²⁰and Hashubah, Ohel, Berechiah, Hasadiah, and Jushab-Hesed—five *in all.*

²¹The sons of Hananiah *were* Pelatiah and Jeshaiah, the sons of Rephaiah, the sons of Arnan, the sons of Obadiah, and the sons of Shechaniah. ²²The son of Shechaniah *was* Shemaiah. The sons of Shemaiah *were* ᵠHattush, Igal, Bariah, Neariah, and Shaphat—six *in all.* ²³The sons of Neariah *were* Elioenai, Hezekiah, and Azrikam—three *in all.* ²⁴The sons of Elioenai *were* Hodaviah, Eliashib, Pelaiah, Akkub, Johanan, Delaiah, and Anani—seven *in all.*

The Family of Judah

4 The sons of Judah *were* ᵃPerez, Hezron, Carmi, Hur, and Shobal. ²And Reaiah the son of Shobal begot Jahath, and Jahath begot Ahumai and Lahad. These *were* the families of the Zorathites. ³These *were the* sons *of* the father of Etam: Jezreel, Ishma, and Idbash; and the name of their sister *was* Hazelelponi; ⁴and Penuel *was* the father of Gedor, and Ezer *was the* father of Hushah.

---

* **2:52** Same as *the Manahethites*, verse 54
* **3:1** Called *Chileab* in 2 Samuel 3:3 * **3:5** Spelled *Shammua* in 14:4 and 2 Samuel 5:14 • Spelled *Bathsheba* in 2 Samuel 11:3 • Called *Eliam* in 2 Samuel 11:3 * **3:6** Spelled *Elishua* in 14:5 and 2 Samuel 5:15 • Spelled *Elpelet* in 14:5 * **3:8** Spelled *Beeliada* in 14:7 * **3:10** Spelled *Abijam* in 1 Kings 15:1 * **3:11** Spelled *Jehoram* in 2 Kings 1:17 and 8:16 • Spelled *Jehoash* in 2 Kings 12:1 * **3:12** Called *Uzziah* in Isaiah 6:1 * **3:15** Called *Jehoahaz* in 2 Kings 23:31 * **3:16** Compare 2 Kings 24:17 * **3:17** Also called *Coniah* in Jeremiah 22:24 and *Jehoiachin* in 2 Kings 24:8 • Or *Jeconiah the captive were*

3:1–5 *sons of David.* The fact that David had six sons by six wives in Hebron does not condone polygamy. David had apparently followed the custom of marrying the daughters of neighboring kings to create allies, in spite of the warning Moses gave for the kings to avoid accumulating many wives (Deut. 17:17). Jesus refers back to creation when He addresses the concept of single partners for life (Matt. 19:1–12), so it is clear that even though some polygamy was practiced, it has never been God's plan for marriage.

3:19 *Pedaiah.* Zerubbabel here is designated as a son of Pedaiah, but elsewhere (Ezra 3:2,8; 5:2; Neh. 12:1; Hag. 1:12,14; 2:2,23) as a son of Pedaiah's brother Salathiel (v. 17). It is likely that Salathiel had died while Zerubbabel was young, and that the youth was raised by his uncle Pedaiah. This relationship may explain Luke's statement that Zerubbabel was "the son of

Salathiel" (Luke 3:27), who was a descendant of David through his son Nathan.

4:1 *sons of Judah.* The chronicler here refers to other persons and events relative to Judah's genealogy (2:3–17). In the list in this verse Perez is Judah's son, Hezron is his grandson, Carmi his nephew, Hur the grandson of Hezron, and Shobal the grandson of Hur. **4:4 *Ephrathah.*** Ephrathah is the wife of the early Caleb (2:19) and the mother of Hur, whose son Salma was the "father of Bethlehem." The names of

---

2:55 ᶜ Judg. 1:16 ᵈ Jer. 35:2 **3:1** ᵃ 2 Sam. 3:2–5 ᵇ 1 Sam. 25:43 ᶜ Josh. 15:56 ᵈ 1 Sam. 25:39–42 **3:2** ᵉ 2 Sam. 13:37; 15:1 ᶠ 1 Kin. 1:5 **3:3** ᵍ 2 Sam. 3:5 **3:4** ʰ 2 Sam. 2:11 ⁱ 2 Sam. 5:5 **3:5** ʲ 1 Chr. 14:4–7 ᵏ 2 Sam. 12:24, 25 **3:8** ˡ 2 Sam. 5:14–16 **3:9** ᵐ 2 Sam. 13:1 **3:10** ⁿ 1 Kin. 11:43 **3:16** ᵒ Matt. 1:11 **3:17** ᵖ Matt. 1:12 **3:22** ᵠ Ezra 8:2 **4:1** ᵃ Gen. 38:29; 46:12

These *were* the sons of [b]Hur, the firstborn of Ephrathah the father of Bethlehem.

[5]And [c]Ashhur the father of Tekoa had two wives, Helah and Naarah. [6]Naarah bore him Ahuzzam, Hepher, Temeni, and Haahashtari. These *were* the sons of Naarah. [7]The sons of Helah *were* Zereth, Zohar, and Ethnan; [8]and Koz begot Anub, Zobebah, and the families of Aharhel the son of Harum.

[9]Now Jabez was [d]more honorable than his brothers, and his mother called his name Jabez,* saying, "Because I bore *him* in pain." [10]And Jabez called on the God of Israel saying, "Oh, that You would bless me indeed, and enlarge my territory, that Your hand would be with me, and that You would keep *me* from evil, that I may not cause pain!" So God granted him what he requested.

[11]Chelub the brother of [e]Shuhah begot Mehir, who *was* the father of Eshton. [12]And Eshton begot Beth-Rapha, Paseah, and Tehinnah the father of Ir-Nahash. These *were* the men of Rechah.

[13]The sons of Kenaz *were* [f]Othniel and Seraiah. The sons of Othniel *were* Hathath,* [14]and Meonothai *who* begot Ophrah. Seraiah begot Joab the father of [g]Ge Harashim,* for they were craftsmen. [15]The sons of [h]Caleb the son of Jephunneh *were* Iru, Elah, and Naam. The son of Elah *was* Kenaz. [16]The sons of Jehallelel *were* Ziph, Ziphah, Tiria, and Asarel. [17]The sons of Ezrah *were* Jether, Mered, Epher, and Jalon. And *Mered's wife** bore Miriam, Shammai, and Ishbah the father of Eshtemoa. [18](His wife Jehudijah* bore Jered the father of Gedor, Heber the father of Sochoh, and Jekuthiel the father of Zanoah.) And these were the sons of Bithiah the daughter of Pharaoh, whom Mered took.

[19]The sons of Hodiah's wife, the sister of Naham, *were* the fathers of Keilah the Garmite and of Eshtemoa the [i]Maachathite. [20]And the sons of Shimon *were* Amnon, Rinnah, Ben-Hanan, and Tilon. And the sons of Ishi *were* Zoheth and Ben-Zoheth.

[21]The sons of [j]Shelah [k]the son of Judah *were* Er the father of Lecah, Laadah the

father of Mareshah, and the families of the house of the linen workers of the house of Ashbea; [22]also Jokim, the men of Chozeba, and Joash; Saraph, who ruled in Moab, and Jashubi-Lehem. Now the records are ancient. [23]These *were* the potters and those who dwell at Netaim* and Gederah;* there they dwelt with the king for his work.

The Family of Simeon

[24]The [l]sons of Simeon *were* Nemuel, Jamin, Jarib,* Zerah,* *and* Shaul, [25]Shallum his son, Mibsam his son, and Mishma his son. [26]And the sons of Mishma *were* Hamuel his son, Zacchur his son, and Shimei his son. [27]Shimei had sixteen sons and six daughters; but his brothers did not have many children, [m]nor did any of their families multiply as much as the children of Judah.

[28]They dwelt at Beersheba, Moladah, Hazar Shual, [29]Bilhah, Ezem, Tolad, [30]Bethuel, Hormah, Ziklag, [31]Beth Marcaboth, Hazar Susim, Beth Biri, and at Shaaraim. These *were* their cities until the reign of David. [32]And their villages *were* Etam, Ain, Rimmon, Tochen, and Ashan—five cities— [33]and all the villages that *were* around these cities as far as Baal.* These *were* their dwelling places, and they maintained their genealogy: [34]Meshobab, Jamlech, and Joshah the son of Amaziah; [35]Joel, and Jehu the son of Joshibiah, the son of Seraiah, the son of Asiel; [36]Elioenai, Jaakobah, Jeshohaiah, Asaiah, Adiel, Jesimiel, and Benaiah; [37]Ziza the son of Shiphi, the son of Allon, the son of Jedaiah, the son of Shimri, the son of Shemaiah— [38]these mentioned by name were leaders in their families, and their father's house increased greatly.

[39]So they went to the entrance of Gedor, as far as the east side of the valley, to seek pasture for their flocks. [40]And they found rich, good pasture, and the land *was* broad,

---

* 4:9 Literally *He Will Cause Pain*   * 4:13 Septuagint and Vulgate add *and Meonothai.*   * 4:14 Literally *Valley of Craftsmen*   * 4:17 Literally *she*   * 4:18 Or *His Judean wife*   * 4:23 Literally *Plants* • Literally *Hedges*   * 4:24 Called *Jachin* in Genesis 46:10 • Called *Zohar* in Genesis 46:10   * 4:33 Or *Baalath Beer* (compare Joshua 19:8)

Bethlehem and Ephrath are closely connected (Gen. 35:19; Ruth 4:11), and the birthplace of the anticipated Messiah is called Bethlehem Ephrathah (Mic. 5:2).

4:9–10 Providence—This passage does not say why or how Jabez was more honorable than his brothers. At the least, he recognized that God is the source of all blessings, and Jabez asked God to bless him. James said that we have not because we ask not (James 4:2–3), and then goes on to address the issue of selfish motives in prayer. Paul encourages believers not to be anxious, but to make our requests to God, with prayer and thanksgiving (Phil. 4:6). It is clear that it is right to ask God for the things that we believe are good, to thank Him for them, and to keep in mind that we can trust Him to meet all of our needs.

4:15 Caleb. This is the Caleb who was the friend and colleague of Joshua (Josh. 14:6–7).

4:21 Er. The fact the Shelah named his son "Er" indicates that he followed the levirate custom of raising up a child in the name of a deceased brother (Gen. 38:6–11).

4:24 Simeon. The tribe of Simeon had no land allotted to them (Josh. 19:1–9) because they were a small tribe. They settled in the territory of Judah.

4:4 [b]1 Chr. 2:50   4:5 [c]1 Chr. 2:24   4:9 [d]Gen. 34:19
4:11 [e]Job 8:1   4:13 [f]Josh. 15:17   4:14 [g]Neh. 11:35
4:15 [h]1 Chr. 6:56   4:19 [i]2 Kin. 25:23   4:21 [j]Gen. 38:11, 14   [k]Gen. 38:1–5; 46:12   4:24 [l]Num. 26:12–14
4:27 [m]Num. 2:9

quiet, and peaceful; for some Hamites formerly lived there. 41These recorded by name came in the days of Hezekiah king of Judah; and they nattacked their tents and the Meunites who were found there, and outterly destroyed them, as it is to this day. So they dwelt in their place, because there was pasture for their flocks there. 42Now some of them, five hundred men of the sons of Simeon, went to Mount Seir, having as their captains Pelatiah, Neariah, Rephaiah, and Uzziel, the sons of Ishi. 43And they defeated pthe rest of the Amalekites who had escaped. They have dwelt there to this day.

The Family of Reuben

5 Now the sons of Reuben the firstborn of Israel—ahe was indeed the firstborn, but because he bdefiled his father's bed, chis birthright was given to the sons of Joseph, the son of Israel, so that the genealogy is not listed according to the birthright; 2yet dJudah prevailed over his brothers, and from him came a eruler, although the birthright was Joseph's—3the sons of fReuben the firstborn of Israel were Hanoch, Pallu, Hezron, and Carmi.

4The sons of Joel were Shemaiah his son, Gog his son, Shimei his son, 5Micah his son, Reaiah his son, Baal his son, 6and Beerah his son, whom Tiglath-Pileser* king of Assyria gcarried into captivity. He was leader of the Reubenites. 7And his brethren by their families, hwhen the genealogy of their generations was registered: the chief, Jeiel, and Zechariah, 8and Bela the son of Azaz, the son of Shema, the son of Joel, who dwelt in iAroer, as far as Nebo and Baal Meon. 9Eastward they settled as far as the entrance of the wilderness this side of the River Euphrates, because their cattle had multiplied jin the land of Gilead.

10Now in the days of Saul they made war kwith the Hagrites, who fell by their hand; and they dwelt in their tents throughout the entire area east of Gilead.

The Family of Gad

11And the lchildren of Gad dwelt next to them in the land of mBashan as far as nSalcah: 12Joel was the chief, Shapham the next, then Jaanai and Shaphat in Bashan,

13and their brethren of their father's house: Michael, Meshullam, Sheba, Jorai, Jachan, Zia, and Eber—seven in all. 14These were the children of Abihail the son of Huri, son of Jaroah, the son of Gilead, the son of Michael, the son of Jeshishai, the son of Jahdo, the son of Buz; 15Ahi the son of Abdiel, the son of Guni, was chief of their father's house. 16And the Gadites dwelt in Gilead, in Bashan and in its villages, and in all the common-lands of oSharon within their borders. 17All these were registered by genealogies in the days of pJotham king of Judah, and in the days of qJeroboam king of Israel.

18The sons of Reuben, the Gadites, and half the tribe of Manasseh had forty-four thousand seven hundred and sixty valiant men, men able to bear shield and sword, to shoot with the bow, and skillful in war, who went to war. 19They made war with the Hagrites, rJetur, Naphish, and Nodab. 20And sthey were helped against them, and the Hagrites were delivered into their hand, and all who were with them, for they tcried out to God in the battle. He heeded their prayer, because they uput their trust in Him. 21Then they took away their livestock—fifty thousand of their camels, two hundred and fifty thousand of their sheep, and two thousand of their donkeys—also one hundred thousand of their men; 22for many fell dead, because the war vwas God's. And they dwelt in their place until wthe captivity.

The Family of Manasseh (East)

23So the children of the half-tribe of Manasseh dwelt in the land. Their numbers increased from Bashan to Baal Hermon, that is, to xSenir, or Mount Hermon. 24These were the heads of their fathers' houses: Epher, Ishi, Eliel, Azriel, Jeremiah, Hodaviah, and Jahdiel. They were mighty men of valor, famous men, and heads of their fathers' houses.

25And they were unfaithful to the God of their fathers, and yplayed the harlot after the gods of the peoples of the land, whom God had destroyed before them. 26So the God of Israel stirred up the spirit of zPul king of Assyria, that is, aTiglath-Pileser*

---

* 5:6 Hebrew Tilgath-Pilneser   * 5:26 Hebrew Tilgath-Pilneser

---

5:9 entrance . . . the River Euphrates. The Reubenites had pushed east into the wilderness, so they were the first to be deported by the Assyrians (v. 6).

5:25 Unbelief—In marriage, adultery is the ultimate breach of trust, breaking a solemn promise of faithfulness and commitment. These tribes of Israel acted just like adulterers when they chose idols instead of the living God. Like a prostitute who has chosen crudity, vulgarity, and cheap finery instead of the steady faithful love and fine clothing from her husband, so Israel had believed a lie and abandoned their covenant with the living God.

5:26 Tiglath Pileser. The famous king Tiglath Pileser, who reigned around 745–727 B.C., has gone down in

4:41 n 2 Kin. 18:8 o 2 Kin. 19:11   **4:43** p 1 Sam. 15:8; 30:17   **5:1** a Gen. 29:32; 49:3 b Gen. 35:22; 49:4 c Gen. 48:15, 22   **5:2** d Gen. 49:8, 10 e Mic. 5:2   **5:3** f Ex. 6:14   **5:6** g 2 Kin. 18:11   **5:7** h 1 Chr. 5:17   **5:8** i Josh. 12:2; 13:15, 16   **5:9** j Josh. 22:8, 9   **5:10** k Gen. 25:12   **5:11** l Num. 26:15–18 m Josh. 13:11, 24–28 n Deut. 3:10   **5:16** o 1 Chr. 2:29   **5:17** p 2 Kin. 15:5, 32 q 2 Kin. 14:16, 28   **5:19** r Gen. 25:15   **5:20** s [1 Chr. 5:22] t 2 Chr. 14:11–13 u Ps. 9:10; 20:7, 8; 22:4, 5   **5:22** v [Josh. 23:10] w 2 Kin. 15:29; 17:6   **5:23** x Deut. 3:9   **5:25** y 2 Kin. 17:7   **5:26** z 2 Kin. 15:19 a 2 Kin. 15:29

king of Assyria. He carried the Reubenites, the Gadites, and the half-tribe of Manasseh into captivity. He took them to [b]Halah, Habor, Hara, and the river of Gozan to this day.

The Family of Levi

6 The sons of Levi were [a]Gershon, Kohath, and Merari. [2]The sons of Kohath were Amram, [b]Izhar, Hebron, and Uzziel. [3]The children of Amram were Aaron, Moses, and Miriam. And the sons of Aaron were [c]Nadab, Abihu, Eleazar, and Ithamar. [4]Eleazar begot Phinehas, and Phinehas begot Abishua; [5]Abishua begot Bukki, and Bukki begot Uzzi; [6]Uzzi begot Zerahiah, and Zerahiah begot Meraioth; [7]Meraioth begot Amariah, and Amariah begot Ahitub; [8][d]Ahitub begot [e]Zadok, and Zadok begot Ahimaaz; [9]Ahimaaz begot Azariah, and Azariah begot Johanan; [10]Johanan begot Azariah (it was he [f]who ministered as priest in the [g]temple that Solomon built in Jerusalem); [11][h]Azariah begot [i]Amariah, and Amariah begot Ahitub; [12]Ahitub begot Zadok, and Zadok begot Shallum; [13]Shallum begot Hilkiah, and Hilkiah begot Azariah; [14]Azariah begot [j]Seraiah, and Seraiah begot Jehozadak. [15]Jehozadak went into captivity [k]when the LORD carried Judah and Jerusalem into captivity by the hand of Nebuchadnezzar.

[16]The sons of Levi were [l]Gershon,* Kohath, and Merari. [17]These are the names of the sons of Gershon: Libni and Shimei. [18]The sons of Kohath were Amram, Izhar,

Hebron, and Uzziel. [19]The sons of Merari were Mahli and Mushi. Now these are the families of the Levites according to their fathers: [20]Of Gershon were Libni his son, Jahath his son, [m]Zimmah his son, [21]Joah his son, Iddo his son, Zerah his son, and Jeatherai his son. [22]The sons of Kohath were Amminadab his son, [n]Korah his son, Assir his son, [23]Elkanah his son, Ebiasaph his son, Assir his son, [24]Tahath his son, Uriel his son, Uzziah his son, and Shaul his son. [25]The sons of Elkanah were [o]Amasai and Ahimoth. [26]As for Elkanah,* the sons of Elkanah were Zophai* his son, Nahath* his son, [27]Eliab* his son, Jeroham his son, and Elkanah his son. [28]The sons of Samuel were Joel* the firstborn, and Abijah the second.* [29]The sons of Merari were Mahli, Libni his son, Shimei his son, Uzzah his son, [30]Shimea his son, Haggiah his son, and Asaiah his son.

Musicians in the House of the LORD

[31]Now these are [p]the men whom David appointed over the service of song in the house of the LORD, after the [q]ark came to rest. [32]They were ministering with music before the dwelling place of the tabernacle of

---

* **6:16** Hebrew *Gershom* (alternate spelling of *Gershon,* as in verses 1, 17, 20, 43, 62, and 71)　* **6:26** Compare verse 35　* Spelled *Zuph* in verse 35 and 1 Samuel 1:1　* Compare verse 34　* **6:27** Compare verse 34　* **6:28** Following Septuagint, Syriac, and Arabic (compare verse 33 and 1 Samuel 8:2)　* Hebrew *Vasheni*

Assyrian annals as one of the most powerful rulers of the neo-Assyrian period (v. 6).

6:1–60 Family—Families are usually marked by certain traits or characteristics. Because the Levites were the designated priests, they had a special responsibility to have a reputation for uprightness and faithfulness, but all Israelites were a representation of God to the nations around them. If we are a part of the family of God, we should ask ourselves if we look like God. When people see us, do they see His characteristics?

6:1 Levi. All religious personnel involved in tabernacle or temple ministry had to be members of the tribe of Levi. Aaron himself was a Levite, and from the beginning of the priesthood his descendants were designated as the only ones who could serve as high priests (6:16–25; Ex. 28:1).

6:2–4 Kohath. This son of Levi was the one to whom the office of priest became exclusively connected. Every priest had to be a Levite, but not every Levite could become a priest. The high priests were descended from Aaron, Kohath's grandson. *Eleazar.* Beginning with Eleazar, the genealogy traces the line of high priests through Jehozadak, the priest who went into Babylonian exile with his people (v. 15). *Ithamar.* Another line of high priests began with Ithamar, including such persons as Eli, Ahimelech, and Abiathar. In the days of David the priestly service was divided between the Eleazar and the Ithamar priests. Solomon rejected the Ithamar priesthood, and accepted only the priests descended from Eleazar (1 Kin. 2:26–27). From Eleazar to Jehozadak, there were at least 22 high priests in unbroken succession.

6:8 Zadok. This priest, not the same person as the Zadok of verse 12, was the one selected by David to serve along with Ahimelech the son of Abiathar as high priest (2 Sam. 8:17).

6:14 Jehozadak. The last priest in the list was carried into Babylon (v. 15). He was the father of Joshua, the priest who returned from Babylon with Zerubbabel to rebuild the temple and reestablish the Jewish community (Hag. 1:12,14).

6:17 Gershon. The purpose of this genealogy is to list the principal offspring of the sons of Levi who were not priests, but servants in the temple.

6:22 Amminadab. Amminadab is another name for Ishar (v. 18) who otherwise appears as the father of Korah (6:37–38; Ex. 6:21; Num. 16:1).

6:28 Samuel. Samuel's ancestors were described as Ephraimites (1 Sam. 1:1). Although Samuel was an Ephraimite because he lived in a city in the tribal territory of Ephraim, this genealogy makes it clear that he was a Levite. Levites lived in their own cities among all the tribes, because they did not receive a land inheritance. As a Levite, he could be trained under Eli (1 Sam. 2:11), and later officiate at public services that included sacrifices (1 Sam. 9:13; 10:8).

5:26 [b] 2 Kin. 17:6; 18:11　**6:1** [a] Ex. 6:16　**6:2** [b] 1 Chr. 6:18, 22　**6:3** [c] Lev. 10:1, 2　**6:8** [d] 2 Sam. 8:17　[e] 2 Sam. 15:27　**6:10** [f] 2 Chr. 26:17, 18　[g] 1 Kin. 6:1　**6:11** [h] Ezra 7:3　[i] 2 Chr. 19:11　**6:14** [j] Neh. 11:11　**6:15** [k] 2 Kin. 25:21　**6:16** [l] Ex. 6:16　**6:20** [m] 1 Chr. 6:42　**6:22** [n] Num. 16:1　**6:25** [o] 1 Chr. 6:35, 36　**6:31** [p] 1 Chr. 15:16–22, 27; 16:4–6　[q] 1 Chr. 15:25—16:1

meeting, until Solomon had built the house of the LORD in Jerusalem, and they served in their office according to their order.

33And these *are* the ones who ministered with their sons: Of the sons of the ʳKohathites *were* Heman the singer, the son of Joel, the son of Samuel, 34the son of Elkanah, the son of Jeroham, the son of Eliel,* the son of Toah,* 35the son of Zuph, the son of Elkanah, the son of Mahath, the son of Amasai, 36the son of Elkanah, the son of Joel, the son of Azariah, the son of Zephaniah, 37the son of Tahath, the son of Assir, the son of ˢEbiasaph, the son of Korah, 38the son of Izhar, the son of Kohath, the son of Levi, the son of Israel. 39And his brother ᵗAsaph, who stood at his right hand, *was* Asaph the son of Berachiah, the son of Shimea, 40the son of Michael, the son of Baaseiah, the son of Malchijah, 41the son of ᵘEthni, the son of Zerah, the son of Adaiah, 42the son of Ethan, the son of Zimmah, the son of Shimei, 43the son of Jahath, the son of Gershon, the son of Levi.

44Their brethren, the sons of Merari, on the left hand, *were* Ethan the son of Kishi, the son of Abdi, the son of Malluch, 45the son of Hashabiah, the son of Amaziah, the son of Hilkiah, 46the son of Amzi, the son of Bani, the son of Shamer, 47the son of Mahli, the son of Mushi, the son of Merari, the son of Levi.

48And their brethren, the Levites, *were* appointed to every ᵛkind of service of the tabernacle of the house of God.

The Family of Aaron

49ʷBut Aaron and his sons offered sacrifices ˣon the altar of burnt offering and ʸon the altar of incense, for all the work of the Most Holy *Place*, and to make atonement for Israel, according to all that Moses the servant of God had commanded. 50Now these *are* the ᶻsons of Aaron: Eleazar his son, Phinehas his son, Abishua his son, 51Bukki his son, Uzzi his son, Zerahiah his son, 52Meraioth his son, Amariah his son, Ahitub his son, 53Zadok his son, *and* Ahimaaz his son.

Dwelling Places of the Levites

54aNow these *are* their dwelling places throughout their settlements in their territory, for they were *given* by lot to the sons of Aaron, of the family of the Kohathites: 55bThey gave them Hebron in the land of Judah, with its surrounding commonlands. 56cBut the fields of the city and its villages they gave to Caleb the son of Jephunneh. 57And ᵈto the sons of Aaron they gave *one of* the cities of refuge, Hebron; also Libnah with its common-lands, Jattir, Eshtemoa with its common-lands, 58Hilen* with its common-lands, Debir with its common-lands, 59Ashan* with its common-lands, and Beth Shemesh with its common-lands. 60And from the tribe of Benjamin: Geba with its common-lands, Alemeth* with its common-lands, and Anathoth with its common-lands. All their cities among their families *were* thirteen.

61eTo the rest of the family of the tribe of the Kohathites they gave ᶠby lot ten cities from half the tribe of Manasseh. 62And to the sons of Gershon, throughout their families, *they gave* thirteen cities from the tribe of Issachar, from the tribe of Asher, from the tribe of Naphtali, and from the tribe of Manasseh in Bashan. 63To the sons of Merari, throughout their families, *they gave* ᵍtwelve cities from the tribe of Reuben, from the tribe of Gad, and from the tribe of Zebulun. 64So the children of Israel gave *these* cities with their common-lands to the Levites. 65And they gave by lot from the tribe of the children of Judah, from the tribe of the children of Simeon, and from the tribe of the children of Benjamin these cities which are called by *their* names.

66Now ʰsome of the families of the sons of Kohath *were* given cities as their territory from the tribe of Ephraim. 67ⁱAnd they gave them *one of* the cities of refuge, Shechem with its common-lands, in the mountains of Ephraim, also Gezer with its common-lands, 68ʲJokmeam with its common-lands, Beth Horon with its common-lands, 69Aijalon with its common-lands, and Gath Rimmon with its common-lands. 70And from the half-tribe of Manasseh: Aner with its common-lands and Bileam with its

---

* **6:34** Spelled *Elihu* in 1 Samuel 1:1 • Spelled *Tohu* in 1 Samuel 1:1 * **6:58** Spelled *Holon* in Joshua 21:15 * **6:59** Spelled *Ain* in Joshua 21:16 * **6:60** Spelled *Almon* in Joshua 21:18

6:57 Hebron. The law specified that if a person killed another unintentionally he could find sanctuary in one of six specified cities, and there wait in safety for the trial (Num. 35:6–27). No one could take revenge as long as he was in the city of refuge. These six cities were included among the 48 Levitical cities, and Hebron, located in Judah, was one of them.

6:61—7:27 Family—In any family record, some of the names have strong memories associated with them. The reputations may be good or bad, but they are all a part of the family reputation. It is comforting to know that the family that produced Saul, the unfaithful king, is the same line that produced Saul, who became the faithful apostle Paul.

6:67 Shechem. Shechem was both a Levitical city and a city of refuge. Shechem was especially significant in Israel. It was the site of Abraham's first altar in Canaan (Gen. 12:6–7), the place where Jacob bought a piece of land (Gen. 33:19), and the location of the first capital of the northern kingdom (1 Kin. 12:25).

6:33 ʳNum. 26:57　**6:37** ˢEx. 6:24　**6:39** ᵗ2 Chr. 5:12　**6:41** ᵘ1 Chr. 6:21　**6:48** ᵛ1 Chr. 9:14–34　**6:49** ʷ[Num. 18:1–8] ˣLev. 1:8, 9 ʸEx. 30:7　**6:50** ᶻ1 Chr. 6:4–8　**6:54** ᵃJosh. 21　**6:55** ᵇJosh. 14:13; 21:11, 12　**6:56** ᶜJosh. 14:13; 15:13　**6:57** ᵈJosh. 21:13, 19　**6:61** ᵉ1 Chr. 6:66–70　ᶠJosh. 21:5　**6:63** ᵍJosh. 21:7, 34–40　**6:66** ʰ1 Chr. 6:61　**6:67** ⁱJosh. 21:21　**6:68** ʲJosh. 21:22

common-lands, for the rest of the family of the sons of Kohath.

71From the family of the half-tribe of Manasseh the sons of Gershon *were given* Golan in Bashan with its common-lands and Ashtaroth with its common-lands. 72And from the tribe of Issachar: Kedesh with its common-lands, Daberath with its common-lands, 73Ramoth with its common-lands, and Anem with its common-lands. 74And from the tribe of Asher: Mashal with its common-lands, Abdon with its common-lands, 75Hukok with its common-lands, and Rehob with its common-lands. 76And from the tribe of Naphtali: Kedesh in Galilee with its common-lands, Hammon with its common-lands, and Kirjathaim with its common-lands.

77From the tribe of Zebulun the rest of the children of Merari *were given* Rimmon* with its common-lands and Tabor with its common-lands. 78And on the other side of the Jordan, across from Jericho, on the east side of the Jordan, *they were given* from the tribe of Reuben: Bezer in the wilderness with its common-lands, Jahzah with its common-lands, 79Kedemoth with its common-lands, and Mephaath with its common-lands. 80And from the tribe of Gad: Ramoth in Gilead with its common-lands, Mahanaim with its common-lands, 81Heshbon with its common-lands, and Jazer with its common-lands.

The Family of Issachar

7 The sons of Issachar *were* aTola, Puah,* Jashub, and Shimron—four *in all*. 2The sons of Tola *were* Uzzi, Rephaiah, Jeriel, Jahmai, Jibsam, and Shemuel, heads of their father's house. *The sons* of Tola *were* mighty men of valor in their generations; btheir number in the days of David *was* twenty-two thousand six hundred. 3The son of Uzzi *was* Izrahiah, and the sons of Izrahiah *were* Michael, Obadiah, Joel, and Ishiah. All five of them *were* chief men. 4And with them, by their generations, according to their fathers' houses, *were* thirty-six thousand troops ready for war; for they had many wives and sons. 5Now their brethren among all the families of Issachar *were* mighty men of valor, listed by their genealogies, eighty-seven thousand in all.

The Family of Benjamin

6*The sons* of cBenjamin *were* Bela, Becher, and Jediael—three *in all*. 7The sons of Bela were Ezbon, Uzzi, Uzziel, Jerimoth, and Iri—five *in all*. They *were* heads of *their* fathers' houses, and they were listed by their genealogies, twenty-two thousand and thirty-four mighty men of valor.

8The sons of Becher *were* Zemirah, Joash, Eliezer, Elioenai, Omri, Jerimoth, Abijah, Anathoth, and Alemeth. All these *are* the sons of Becher. 9And they were recorded by genealogy according to their generations, heads of their fathers' houses, twenty thousand two hundred mighty men of valor. 10The son of Jediael *was* Bilhan, and the sons of Bilhan *were* Jeush, Benjamin, Ehud, Chenaanah, Zethan, Tharshish, and Ahishahar.

11All these sons of Jediael *were* heads of their fathers' houses; *there were* seventeen thousand two hundred mighty men of valor fit to go out for war *and* battle. 12Shuppim and Huppim* *were* the sons of Ir, *and* Hushim *was* the son of Aher.

The Family of Naphtali

13The dsons of Naphtali *were* Jahziel,* Guni, Jezer, and Shallum,* the sons of Bilhah.

The Family of Manasseh (West)

14The edescendants of Manasseh: his Syrian concubine bore him fMachir the father of Gilead, the father of Asriel.* 15Machir took as his wife *the sister* of Huppim and Shuppim,* whose name *was* Maachah. The name of *Gilead's* grandson* *was* gZelophehad,* but Zelophehad begot only daughters. 16(Maachah the wife of Machir bore a son, and she called his name Peresh. The name of his brother *was* Sheresh, and his sons *were* Ulam and Rakem. 17The son of Ulam *was* hBedan.) These *were* the descendants of Gilead the son of Machir, the son of Manasseh.

---

* **6:77** Hebrew *Rimmono*, alternate spelling of *Rimmon*; see 4:32 * **7:1** Spelled *Puvah* in Genesis 46:13 * **7:12** Called *Hupham* in Numbers 26:39 * **7:13** Spelled *Jahzeel* in Genesis 46:24 • Spelled *Shillem* in Genesis 46:24 * **7:14** The son of Gilead (compare Numbers 26:30, 31) * **7:15** Compare verse 12 • Literally *the second* • Compare Numbers 26:30–33

6:76 Kedesh. Kedesh was another of the six cities of refuge. It was the most northern of the three west of the Jordan.

6:78 Bezer. Bezer was also a city of refuge, the farthest south of those east of the Jordan.

6:80 Ramoth in Gilead. Another city of refuge, Ramoth, was directly east of the Jordan. In this way the cities of refuge were distributed throughout the land so that any Israelite could be within a few miles of one of them. All six cities were assigned to the Levites, with Hebron designated for the priests (Deut. 17:8–13; 19:17–21).

7:14 Manasseh . . . Machir. Manasseh was the son of Joseph, and his son was Machir. Machir's daughter became the wife of Judah's grandson Hezron (2:2), which joined the two tribes of Judah and Manasseh.

7:15 Zelophehad begot only daughters. This man had no sons, so Moses made provision for inheritance rights for daughters in such cases (Num. 36:1–9).

7:1 d Num. 26:23–25 **7:2** b 2 Sam. 24:1–9 **7:6** c Gen. 46:21 **7:13** d Num. 26:48–50 **7:14** e Num. 26:29–34 f 1 Chr. 2:21 **7:15** g Num. 26:30–33; 27:1 **7:17** h 1 Sam. 12:11

18His sister Hammoleketh bore Ishhod, Abiezer, and Mahlah.

19And the sons of Shemida were Ahian, Shechem, Likhi, and Aniam.

The Family of Ephraim

20iThe sons of Ephraim were Shuthelah, Bered his son, Tahath his son, Eladah his son, Tahath his son, 21Zabad his son, Shuthelah his son, and Ezer and Elead. The men of Gath who were born in that land killed them because they came down to take away their cattle. 22Then Ephraim their father mourned many days, and his brethren came to comfort him.

23And when he went in to his wife, she conceived and bore a son; and he called his name Beriah,* because tragedy had come upon his house. 24Now his daughter was Sheerah, who built Lower and Upper jBeth Horon and Uzzen Sheerah; 25and Rephah was his son, as well as Resheph, and Telah his son, Tahan his son, 26Laadan his son, Ammihud his son, kElishama his son, 27Nun* his son, and lJoshua his son.

28Now their mpossessions and dwelling places were Bethel and its towns: to the east Naaran, to the west Gezer and its towns, and Shechem and its towns, as far as Ayyah* and its towns; 29and by the borders of the children of nManasseh were Beth Shean and its towns, Taanach and its towns, oMegiddo and its towns, Dor and its towns. In these dwelt the children of Joseph, the son of Israel.

The Family of Asher

30pThe sons of Asher were Imnah, Ishvah, Ishvi, Beriah, and their sister Serah. 31The sons of Beriah were Heber and Malchiel, who was the father of Birzaith.* 32And Heber begot Japhlet, Shomer,* Hotham,* and their sister Shua. 33The sons of Japhlet were Pasach, Bimhal, and Ashvath. These were the children of Japhlet. 34The sons of qShemer were Ahi, Rohgah, Jehubbah, and Aram. 35And the sons of his brother Helem were Zophah, Imna, Shelesh, and Amal. 36The sons of Zophah were Suah, Harnepher, Shual, Beri, Imrah, 37Bezer, Hod, Shamma, Shilshah, Jithran,* and Beera. 38The sons of Jether were Jephunneh, Pispah, and Ara. 39The sons of Ulla were Arah, Haniel, and Rizia.

40All these were the children of Asher, heads of their fathers' houses, choice men, mighty men of valor, chief leaders. And they were recorded by genealogies among the army fit for battle; their number was twenty-six thousand.

The Family Tree of King Saul of Benjamin

8 Now Benjamin begot aBela his firstborn, Ashbel the second, Aharah* the third, 2Nohah the fourth, and Rapha the fifth. 3The sons of Bela were Addar,* Gera, Abihud, 4Abishua, Naaman, Ahoah, 5Gera, Shephuphan, and Huram.

6These are the sons of Ehud, who were the heads of the fathers' houses of the inhabitants of bGeba, and who forced them to move to cManahath: 7Naaman, Ahijah, and Gera who forced them to move. He begot Uzza and Ahihud.

8Also Shaharaim had children in the country of Moab, after he had sent away Hushim and Baara his wives. 9By Hodesh his wife he begot Jobab, Zibia, Mesha, Malcam, 10Jeuz, Sachiah, and Mirmah. These were his sons, heads of their fathers' houses.

11And by Hushim he begot Abitub and Elpaal. 12The sons of Elpaal were Eber, Misham, and Shemed, who built Ono and Lod with its towns; 13and Beriah and dShema, who were heads of their fathers' houses of the inhabitants of Aijalon, who drove out the inhabitants of Gath. 14Ahio, Shashak, Jeremoth, 15Zebadiah, Arad, Eder, 16Michael, Ispah, and Joha were the sons of Beriah. 17Zebadiah, Meshullam, Hizki, Heber, 18Ishmerai, Jizliah, and Jobab were the sons of Elpaal. 19Jakim, Zichri, Zabdi, 20Elienai, Zillethai, Eliel, 21Adaiah, Beraiah, and Shimrath were the sons of Shimei. 22Ishpan, Eber, Eliel, 23Abdon, Zichri, Hanan, 24Hananiah, Elam, Antothijah, 25Iphdeiah, and Penuel were the sons of Shashak. 26Shamsherai, Shehariah, Athaliah, 27Jaareshiah, Elijah, and Zichri were the sons of Jeroham.

28These were heads of the fathers' houses by their generations, chief men. These dwelt in Jerusalem.

---

* **7:23** Literally In Tragedy * **7:27** Hebrew Non
* **7:28** Many Hebrew manuscripts, Bomberg, Septuagint, Targum, and Vulgate read Gazza.
* **7:31** Or Birzavith or Birzoth * **7:32** Spelled Shemer in verse 34 • Spelled Helem in verse 35
* **7:37** Spelled Jether in verse 38 * **8:1** Spelled Ahiram in Numbers 26:38 * **8:3** Called Ard in Numbers 26:40

7:20–21 Tahath...Shuthelah. The repetition of these two names illustrates the custom of sons being named for their grandfathers or more remote ancestors.

8:1 Benjamin. The reason for this second and much more detailed genealogy of Benjamin is its focus on the genealogy of King Saul (vv. 29–40).

8:9 Mesha. There was a well-known Moabite king named Mesha. Both the Scriptures (2 Kin. 3:4) and the Moabite Stone attest to this fact. The reference here to Mesha as a son of Shaharaim and Hodesh, his Moabite wife (v. 8), suggests the illustrious Moabite king may have had a Benjamite father, but the evidence is not conclusive.

8:28 chief men...dwelt in Jerusalem. This city was not taken by David until approximately 1004 B.C., so the line of Benjamin was traced to at least that time.

7:20 i Num. 26:35–37	**7:24** j Josh. 16:3, 5	**7:26** k Num. 10:22
7:27 l Ex. 17:9, 14; 24:13; 33:11		**7:28** m Josh. 16:1–10
7:29 n Josh. 17:7	o Josh. 17:11	**7:30** p Num. 26:44–47
7:34 q 1 Chr. 7:32	**8:1** a Gen. 46:21	
8:6 b 1 Chr. 6:60	c 1 Chr. 2:52	**8:13** d 1 Chr. 8:21

²⁹Now the father of Gibeon, whose *e*wife's name *was* Maacah, dwelt at Gibeon. ³⁰And his firstborn son *was* Abdon, then Zur, Kish, Baal, Nadab, ³¹Gedor, Ahio, Zecher, ³²and Mikloth, *who* begot Shimeah.* They also dwelt alongside their relatives in Jerusalem, with their brethren. ³³*f*Ner* begot Kish, Kish begot Saul, and Saul begot Jonathan, Malchishua, Abinadab,* and Esh-Baal.* ³⁴The son of Jonathan *was* Merib-Baal,* and Merib-Baal begot *g*Micah. ³⁵The sons of Micah *were* Pithon, Melech, Tarea, and Ahaz. ³⁶And Ahaz begot Jehoaddah;* Jehoaddah begot Alemeth, Azmaveth, and Zimri; and Zimri begot Moza. ³⁷Moza begot Binea, Raphah* his son, Eleasah his son, *and* Azel his son.

³⁸Azel had six sons whose names *were* these: Azrikam, Bocheru, Ishmael, Sheariah, Obadiah, and Hanan. All these *were* the sons of Azel. ³⁹And the sons of Eshek his brother *were* Ulam his firstborn, Jeush the second, and Eliphelet the third.

⁴⁰The sons of Ulam were mighty men of valor—archers. *They* had many sons and grandsons, one hundred and fifty *in all.* These *were* all sons of Benjamin.

9 So *a*all Israel was recorded by genealogies, and indeed, they *were* inscribed in the book of the kings of Israel. But Judah was carried away captive to Babylon because of their unfaithfulness. ²*b*And the first inhabitants who *dwelt* in their possessions in their cities *were* Israelites, priests, Levites, and *c*the Nethinim.

Dwellers in Jerusalem

³Now in *d*Jerusalem the children of Judah dwelt, and some of the children of Benjamin, and of the children of Ephraim and Manasseh: ⁴Uthai the son of Ammihud, the son of Omri, the son of Imri, the son of Bani, of the descendants of Perez, the son of Judah. ⁵Of the Shilonites: Asaiah the firstborn and his sons. ⁶Of the sons of Zerah: Jeuel, and their brethren—six hundred and ninety. ⁷Of the sons of Benjamin: Sallu the son of Meshullam, the son of Hodaviah, the son of Hassenuah; ⁸Ibneiah the son of Jeroham; Elah the son of Uzzi, the son of Michri; Meshullam the son of Shephatiah, the son of Reuel, the son of Ibnijah; ⁹and their brethren, according to their generations—nine hundred and fifty-six. All these men *were* heads of a father's *house* in their fathers' houses.

The Priests at Jerusalem

¹⁰*e*Of the priests: Jedaiah, Jehoiarib, and Jachin; ¹¹Azariah the son of Hilkiah, the son of Meshullam, the son of Zadok, the son of Meraioth, the son of Ahitub, the *f*officer over the house of God; ¹²Adaiah the son of Jeroham, the son of Pashur, the son of Malchijah; Maasai the son of Adiel, the son of Jahzerah, the son of Meshullam, the son of Meshillemith, the son of Immer; ¹³and their brethren, heads of their fathers' houses—one thousand seven hundred and sixty. *They were* very able men for the work of the service of the house of God.

The Levites at Jerusalem

¹⁴Of the Levites: Shemaiah the son of Hasshub, the son of Azrikam, the son of Hashabiah, of the sons of Merari; ¹⁵Bakbakkar, Heresh, Galal, and Mattaniah the son of Micah, the son of *g*Zichri, the son of Asaph; ¹⁶*h*Obadiah the son of *i*Shemaiah,

---

* **8:32** Spelled *Shimeam* in 9:38 * **8:33** Also the son of Gibeon (compare 9:36, 39) • Called *Jishui* in 1 Samuel 14:49 • Called *Ishbosheth* in 2 Samuel 2:8 and elsewhere * **8:34** Called *Mephibosheth* in 2 Samuel 4:4 * **8:36** Spelled *Jarah* in 9:42 * **8:37** Spelled *Rephaiah* in 9:43

Even after David took the city, there may have been Benjamites who still lived there, for David gave Benjamites positions of responsibility in his government (11:31; 12:1–7,29).

8:30 Kish. Kish was the father of Saul (v. 33; 9:39). In this passage the relationship between Jeiel and Kish is unclear because Kish is also named as the son of Ner (v. 33). However, in 9:35–39 the lineage is clearly traced from Jeiel to Ner to Kish and finally to Saul.

8:32 Jerusalem. Jerusalem remained under Jebusite control until David conquered it (2 Sam. 5:6–19). Perhaps at this time the Benjamites lived among the Jebusites.

8:33 Esh-Baal. Esh-Baal was evidently Saul's youngest son, since he was not named in the genealogies of the beginning of Saul's reign (1 Sam. 14:49). Usually called Ishbosheth, which means "man of shame," he reigned for a short time after his father's death (2 Sam. 2:10).

9:1 Unfaithfulness—Blatant disobedience always leads to disaster. God is serious about working righteousness in our lives, and He knows the changes that both trials and blessings can bring to our hearts. He will not leave us in a state of lethargy and peace if we

need to be ignited. Sometimes He will test us to see if we are serious about walking with Him. Like the Israelites, we need to ask ourselves if we are obedient or compromising.

9:2 Israelites. The deportation of Israel by the Assyrians from 734 to 722 B.C. resulted in Israel's dispersion throughout the eastern Mediterranean world. However, it is apparent from this verse that some of them joined their Judean brethren in the return from Babylon after 539 B.C.

9:3 Ephraim and Manasseh. Both of these tribes were from the northern kingdom, or Israel. This is another confirmation that the returning community included Israelites as well as Judeans. It is very possible that some of those in the northern tribes, who had remained faithful to the Lord, may have migrated into Judah before Assyria took Israel captive.

8:29 *e* 1 Chr. 9:35–38   **8:33** *f* 1 Sam. 14:51
8:34 *g* 2 Sam. 9:12   **9:1** *a* Ezra 2:59   **9:2** *b* Neh. 7:73
c Ezra 2:43; 8:20   **9:3** *d* Neh. 11:1, 2   **9:10** *e* Neh. 11:10–14   **9:11** *f* Jer. 20:1   **9:15** *g* Neh. 11:17   **9:16** *h* Neh. 11:17   *i* Neh. 11:17

the son of Galal, the son of Jeduthun; and Berechiah the son of Asa, the son of Elkanah, who lived in the villages of the Netophathites.

The Levite Gatekeepers

17And the gatekeepers were Shallum, Akkub, Talmon, Ahiman, and their brethren. Shallum was the chief. 18Until then they had been gatekeepers for the camps of the children of Levi at the King's Gate on the east.

19Shallum the son of Kore, the son of Ebiasaph, the son of Korah, and his brethren, from his father's house, the Korahites, were in charge of the work of the service, gatekeepers of the tabernacle. Their fathers had been keepers of the entrance to the camp of the LORD. 20And iPhinehas the son of Eleazar had been the officer over them in time past; the LORD was with him. 21kZechariah the son of Meshelemiah was keeper of the door of the tabernacle of meeting.

22All those chosen as gatekeepers were two hundred and twelve. lThey were recorded by their genealogy, in their villages. David and Samuel mthe seer had appointed them to their trusted office. 23So they and their children were in charge of the gates of the house of the LORD, the house of the tabernacle, by assignment. 24The gatekeepers were assigned to the four directions: the east, west, north, and south. 25And their brethren in their villages had to come with them from time to time nfor seven days. 26For in this trusted office were four chief gatekeepers; they were Levites. And they had charge over the chambers and treasuries of the house of God. 27And they lodged all around the house of God because they had the oresponsibility, and they were in charge of opening it every morning.

Other Levite Responsibilities

28Now some of them were in charge of the serving vessels, for they brought them in and took them out by count. 29Some of them were appointed over the furnishings and over all the implements of the sanctuary, and over the pfine flour and the wine and the oil and the incense and the spices. 30And some of the sons of the priests made qthe ointment of the spices.

31Mattithiah of the Levites, the firstborn of Shallum the Korahite, had the trusted office rover the things that were baked in the pans. 32And some of their brethren of

the sons of the Kohathites swere in charge of preparing the showbread for every Sabbath.

33These are tthe singers, heads of the fathers' houses of the Levites, who lodged in the chambers, and were free from other duties; for they were employed in that work day and night. 34These heads of the fathers' houses of the Levites were heads throughout their generations. They dwelt at Jerusalem.

The Family of King Saul

35Jeiel the father of Gibeon, whose wife's name was uMaacah, dwelt at Gibeon. 36His firstborn son was Abdon, then Zur, Kish, Baal, Ner, Nadab, 37Gedor, Ahio, Zechariah,* and Mikloth. 38And Mikloth begot Shimeam.* They also dwelt alongside their relatives in Jerusalem, with their brethren. 39vNer begot Kish, Kish begot Saul, and Saul begot Jonathan, Malchishua, Abinadab, and Esh-Baal. 40The son of Jonathan was Merib-Baal, and Merib-Baal begot Micah. 41The sons of Micah were Pithon, Melech, Tahrea,*w and Ahaz.* 42And Ahaz begot Jarah;* Jarah begot Alemeth, Azmaveth, and Zimri; and Zimri begot Moza; 43Moza begot Binea, Rephaiah* his son, Eleasah his son, and Azel his son.

44And Azel had six sons whose names were these: Azrikam, Bocheru, Ishmael, Sheariah, Obadiah, and Hanan; these were the sons of Azel.

Tragic End of Saul and His Sons

10 Now athe Philistines fought against Israel; and the men of Israel fled from before the Philistines, and fell slain on Mount Gilboa. 2Then the Philistines followed hard after Saul and his sons. And the Philistines killed Jonathan, Abinadab, and Malchishua, Saul's sons. 3The battle became fierce against Saul. The archers hit him, and he was wounded by the archers. 4Then Saul said to his armorbearer, "Draw your sword, and thrust me through with it, lest these uncircumcised men come and abuse me." But his armorbearer would not, for he was greatly afraid. Therefore Saul took a sword and fell on it. 5And when his armorbearer saw that Saul was dead,

---

* **9:37** Called Zecher in 8:31 * **9:38** Spelled Shimeah in 8:32 * **9:41** Spelled Tarea in 8:35 • Following Arabic, Syriac, Targum, and Vulgate (compare 8:35); Masoretic Text and Septuagint omit and Ahaz. * **9:42** Spelled Jehoaddah in 8:36 * **9:43** Spelled Raphah in 8:37

9:19 Korah. As descendants of Kohath (Ex. 6:18) Korah and his line had close connections with the priesthood. They could not be priests, but they ministered closely with the temple, first as carriers of the holy objects (Num. 4:5–15), and later as gatekeepers. **10:4 uncircumcised.** For the Hebrew, circumcision was a sign of God's promise through Abraham to them. The uncircumcised were those outside the

9:20 j Num. 25:6–13; 31:6 **9:21** k 1 Chr. 26:2, 14 **9:22** l 1 Chr. 26:1, 2 m 1 Sam. 9:9 **9:25** n 2 Kin. 11:4–7 **9:27** o 1 Chr. 23:30–32 **9:29** p 1 Chr. 23:29 **9:30** q Ex. 30:22–25 **9:31** r Lev. 2:5; 6:21 **9:32** s Lev. 24:5–8 **9:33** t 1 Chr. 6:31; 25:1 **9:35** u 1 Chr. 8:29–32 **9:39** v 1 Chr. 8:33–38 **9:41** w 1 Chr. 8:35 **10:1** a 1 Sam. 31:1, 2

he also fell on his sword and died. **6**So Saul and his three sons died, and all his house died together. **7**And when all the men of Israel who *were* in the valley saw that they had fled and that Saul and his sons were dead, they forsook their cities and fled; then the Philistines came and dwelt in them.

8So it happened the next day, when the Philistines came to strip the slain, that they found Saul and his sons fallen on Mount Gilboa. **9**And they stripped him and took his head and his armor, and sent word throughout the land of the Philistines to proclaim the news *in the temple* of their idols and among the people. **10b**Then they put his armor in the temple of their gods, and fastened his head in the temple of Dagon.

11And when all Jabesh Gilead heard all that the Philistines had done to Saul, **12**all the ᶜvaliant men arose and took the body of Saul and the bodies of his sons; and they brought them to ᵈJabesh, and buried their bones under the tamarisk tree at Jabesh, and fasted seven days.

13So Saul died for his unfaithfulness which he had committed against the LORD, ᵉbecause he did not keep the word of the LORD, and also because ᶠhe consulted a medium for guidance. **14**But *he* did not inquire of the LORD; therefore He killed him, and ᵍturned the kingdom over to David the son of Jesse.

David Made King over All Israel

11 Then ᵃall Israel came together to David at Hebron, saying, "Indeed we *are* your bone and your flesh. **2**Also, in time past, even when Saul was king, you *were* the one who led Israel out and brought them in; and the LORD your ᵇGod said to you, 'You shall ᶜshepherd My people Israel, and be ruler over My people Israel.'" **3**Therefore

all the elders of Israel came to the king at Hebron, and David made a covenant with them at Hebron before the LORD. And ᵈthey anointed David king over Israel, according to the word of the LORD by ᵉSamuel.

The City of David

4And David and all Israel ᶠwent to Jerusalem, which is Jebus, ᵍwhere the Jebusites *were*, the inhabitants of the land. **5**But the inhabitants of Jebus said to David, "You shall not come in here!" Nevertheless David took the stronghold of Zion (that is, the City of David). **6**Now David said, "Whoever attacks the Jebusites first shall be chief and captain." And Joab the son of Zeruiah went up first, and became chief. **7**Then David dwelt in the stronghold; therefore they called it the City of David. **8**And he built the city around it, from the Millo* to the surrounding area. Joab repaired the rest of the city. **9**So David ʰwent on and became great, and the LORD of hosts *was* with ⁱhim.

The Mighty Men of David

10Now ʲthese *were* the heads of the mighty men whom David had, who strengthened themselves with him in his kingdom, with all Israel, to make him king, according to ᵏthe word of the LORD concerning Israel.

11And this *is* the number of the mighty men whom David had: ˡJashobeam the son of a Hachmonite, ᵐchief of the captains;* he had lifted up his spear against three hundred, killed *by him* at one time.

12After him *was* Eleazar the son of ⁿDodo, the Ahohite, who *was* one of the

* **11:8** Literally *The Landfill*   * **11:11** Following Qere; Kethib, Septuagint, and Vulgate read *the thirty* (compare 2 Samuel 23:8).

---

promise, often their enemies. **abuse.** The abuse of the Philistines might take the form of cutting off Saul's thumbs and big toes, which would leave him crippled and humiliated (Judg. 1:6–7). Whatever they did would have been meant to belittle Saul, his kingdom, and his God. **was greatly afraid.** The armorbearer was not afraid of Saul. He was afraid of God. He was afraid of killing one who had been anointed king over Israel and who belonged to God who had set him apart. **sword and fell on it.** Suicide was very rare among Hebrews of Old Testament times.

10:10 Dagon. Dagon was worshiped by the Philistines and other peoples in Syria and northwest Mesopotamia as the god of grain. Apparently the Philistines celebrated military victory by bringing a trophy of their success back to their temple where it could be displayed as a tribute to the might of their god.

10:14 He killed him. This statement is shocking in its bluntness. In the final analysis, Saul's death was not by his own hand, but by the hand of God. The Lord let Saul pursue a course that led to death.

11:1–2 Unity—The history of events between the death of Saul and the beginning of David's reign over all Israel is omitted by the chronicler, but is narrated in 2 Samuel 2–4. The fighting between the house of

David and the house of Saul continued until Saul's son Ishbosheth was killed. Israel could not be unified as long as some were trying to be loyal to Saul. God had already rejected Saul and chosen David, but until Saul's house was gone, the people could not focus on God's choice for king. We as believers often find ourselves in a state of disunity because we are mixed up with our own agendas instead of seeing God's plan.

11:8 he built the city. Once David occupied Mount Ophel, the original and very small area of Jerusalem, he greatly enlarged it by building retaining walls along the Kidron valley to the east and south and the Tyropoeon valley to the west. Between these walls and the top of the hill he built terraces, so that various buildings could be constructed there.

10:10 ᵇ 1 Sam. 31:10   **10:12** ᶜ 1 Sam. 14:52 ᵈ 2 Sam. 21:12   **10:13** ᵉ 1 Sam. 13:13, 14; 15:22–26 ᶠ 1 Sam. 28:7   **10:14** ᵍ 1 Sam. 15:28   **11:1** ᵃ 2 Sam. 5:1   **11:2** ᵇ Ps. 78:70–72 ᶜ 2 Sam. 7:7   **11:3** ᵈ 2 Sam. 5:3 ᵉ 1 Sam. 16:1, 4, 12, 13   **11:4** ᶠ 2 Sam. 5:6 ᵍ Judg. 1:21; 19:10, 11   **11:9** ʰ 2 Sam. 3:1 ⁱ 1 Sam. 16:18   **11:10** ʲ 2 Sam. 23:8 ᵏ 1 Sam. 16:1, 12   **11:11** ˡ 1 Chr. 27:2 ᵐ 1 Chr. 12:18   **11:12** ⁿ 1 Chr. 27:4

three mighty men. ¹³He was with David at Pasdammim. Now there the Philistines were gathered for battle, and there was a piece of ground full of barley. So the people fled from the Philistines. ¹⁴But they stationed themselves in the middle of *that* field, defended it, and killed the Philistines. So the LORD brought about a great victory.

¹⁵Now three of the thirty chief men ᵒwent down to the rock to David, into the cave of Adullam; and the army of the Philistines encamped ᵖin the Valley of Rephaim. ¹⁶David *was* then in the stronghold, and the garrison of the Philistines *was* then in Bethlehem. ¹⁷And David said with longing, "Oh, that someone would give me a drink of water from the well of Bethlehem, which is by the gate!" ¹⁸So the three broke through the camp of the Philistines, drew water from the well of Bethlehem that *was* by the gate, and took *it* and brought *it* to David. Nevertheless David would not drink it, but poured it out to the LORD. ¹⁹And he said, "Far be it from me, O my God, that I should do this! Shall I drink the blood of these men *who have put* their lives *in jeopardy?* For at the risk of their lives they brought it." Therefore he would not drink it. These things were done by the three mighty men.

²⁰Abishai the brother of Joab was chief of *another* three.* He had lifted up his spear against three hundred *men,* killed *them,* and won a name among *these* three. ²¹ʳOf the three he was more honored than the other two men. Therefore he became their captain. However he did not attain to the *first* three.

²²Benaiah was the son of Jehoiada, the son of a valiant man from Kabzeel, who had done many deeds. ˢHe had killed two lion-like heroes of Moab. He also had gone down and killed a lion in the midst of a pit on a snowy day. ²³And he killed an Egyptian, a man of *great* height, five cubits tall. In the Egyptian's hand *there was* a spear like a weaver's beam; and he went down to him with a staff, wrested the spear out of the Egyptian's hand, and killed him with his own spear. ²⁴These *things* Benaiah the son of Jehoiada did, and won a name among three mighty men. ²⁵Indeed he was more honored than the thirty, but he did

not attain to the *first* three. And David appointed him over his guard.

²⁶Also the mighty warriors *were* ᵗAsahel the brother of Joab, Elhanan the son of Dodo of Bethlehem, ²⁷Shammoth the Harorite,* ᵘHelez the Pelonite,* ²⁸ᵛIra the son of Ikkesh the Tekoite, ʷAbiezer the Anathothite, ²⁹Sibbechai the Hushathite, Ilai the Ahohite, ³⁰ˣMaharai the Netophathite, Heled* the son of Baanah the Netophathite, ³¹Ithai* the son of Ribai of Gibeah, of the sons of Benjamin, ʸBenaiah the Pirathonite, ³²Hurai* of the brooks of Gaash, Abiel* the Arbathite, ³³Azmaveth the Baharumite,* Eliahba the Shaalbonite, ³⁴the sons of Hashem the Gizonite, Jonathan the son of Shageh the Hararite, ³⁵Ahiam the son of Sacar the Hararite, Eliphal the son of Ur, ³⁶Hepher the Mecherathite, Ahijah the Pelonite, ³⁷Hezro the Carmelite, Naarai the son of Ezbai, ³⁸Joel the brother of Nathan, Mibhar the son of Hagri, ³⁹Zelek the Ammonite, Naharai the Berothite* (the armorbearer of Joab the son of Zeruiah), ⁴⁰Ira the Ithrite, Gareb the Ithrite, ⁴¹ᶻUriah the Hittite, Zabad the son of Ahlai, ⁴²Adina the son of Shiza the Reubenite (a chief of the Reubenites) and thirty with him, ⁴³Hanan the son of Maachah, Joshaphat the Mithnite, ⁴⁴Uzzia the Ashterathite, Shama and Jeiel the sons of Hotham the Aroerite, ⁴⁵Jediael the son of Shimri, and Joha his brother, the Tizite, ⁴⁶Eliel the Mahavite, Jeribai and Joshaviah the sons of Elnaam, Ithmah the Moabite, ⁴⁷Eliel, Obed, and Jaasiel the Mezobaite.

The Growth of David's Army

12 Now ᵃthese *were* the men who came to David at ᵇZiklag while he was still a fugitive from Saul the son of Kish; and they *were* among the mighty men, helpers in the war, ²armed with bows, using

---

* **11:20** Following Masoretic Text, Septuagint, and Vulgate; Syriac reads *thirty.* * **11:27** Spelled *Harodite* in 2 Samuel 23:25 • Called *Paltite* in 2 Samuel 23:26 * **11:30** Spelled *Heleb* in 2 Samuel 23:29 and *Heldai* in 1 Chronicles 27:15 * **11:31** Spelled *Ittai* in 2 Samuel 23:29 * **11:32** Spelled *Hiddai* in 2 Samuel 23:30 • Spelled *Abi-Albon* in 2 Samuel 23:31 * **11:33** Spelled *Barhumite* in 2 Samuel 23:31 * **11:39** Spelled *Beerothite* in 2 Samuel 23:37

11:18 *poured it out to the LORD.* Even though he had been longing for a drink from his "home well," David never considered sending any of his brave supporters to get it for him. When they risked their lives to bring it to him, David responded by pouring it on the ground, as if it had been a blood offering for God. The Israelites were strictly forbidden to eat blood (Lev. 3:17; Deut. 12:23), and David considered this water to be in the same category. Only God should receive such a sacrifice (Gen. 35:14).

11:23 *five cubits.* The Egyptian was about seven and a half feet tall.

11:41 *Uriah.* This is the same Uriah who was the husband of Bathsheba. The fact that Uriah was one of the

mighty men of valor, who did so much to establish David as king, makes David's betrayal of Uriah doubly tragic (2 Sam. 11).

12:2 *of Benjamin, Saul's brethren.* There is a curious little play on words here. Benjamin means "son of the right hand." These Benjamites could shoot and sling with either the right hand or the left hand, which

---

11:15 ᵒ2 Sam. 23:13 ᵖ2 Sam. 5:18 **11:20** ᵠ2 Sam. 23:18 **11:21** ʳ2 Sam. 23:19 **11:22** ˢ2 Sam. 23:20 **11:26** ᵗ2 Sam. 23:24 **11:27** ᵘ1 Chr. 27:10 **11:28** ᵛ1 Chr. 27:9 ʷ1 Chr. 27:12 **11:30** ˣ1 Chr. 27:13 **11:31** ʸ1 Chr. 27:14 **11:41** ᶻ2 Sam. 11 **12:1** ᵃ1 Sam. 27:2 ᵇ1 Sam. 27:6

both the right hand and ᶜthe left in *hurling* stones and *shooting* arrows with the bow. *They were* of Benjamin, Saul's brethren.

³The chief *was* Ahiezer, then Joash, the sons of Shemaah the Gibeathite; Jeziel and Pelet the sons of Azmaveth; Berachah, and Jehu the Anathothite; ⁴Ishmaiah the Gibeonite, a mighty man among the thirty, and over the thirty; Jeremiah, Jahaziel, Johanan, and Jozabad the Gederathite; ⁵Eluzai, Jerimoth, Bealiah, Shemariah, and Shephatiah the Haruphite; ⁶Elkanah, Jisshiah, Azarel, Joezer, and Jashobeam, the Korahites; ⁷and Joelah and Zebadiah the sons of Jeroham of Gedor.

⁸*Some* Gadites joined David at the stronghold in the wilderness, mighty men of valor, men trained for battle, who could handle shield and spear, whose faces *were like* the faces of lions, and *were* ᵈas swift as gazelles on the mountains: ⁹Ezer the first, Obadiah the second, Eliab the third, ¹⁰Mishmannah the fourth, Jeremiah the fifth, ¹¹Attai the sixth, Eliel the seventh, ¹²Johanan the eighth, Elzabad the ninth, ¹³Jeremiah the tenth, and Machbanai the eleventh. ¹⁴These *were* from the sons of Gad, captains of the army; the least was over a hundred, and the greatest was over a ᵉthousand. ¹⁵These *are* the ones who crossed the Jordan in the first month, when it had overflowed all its ᶠbanks; and they put to flight all *those* in the valleys, to the east and to the west.

¹⁶Then some of the sons of Benjamin and Judah came to David at the stronghold. ¹⁷And David went out to meet them, and answered and said to them, "If you have come peaceably to me to help me, my heart will be united with you; but if to betray me to my enemies, since *there is* no wrong in my hands, may the God of our fathers look and bring judgment." ¹⁸Then the Spirit came upon ᵍAmasai, chief of the captains, *and he said:*

"*We are* yours, O David;
 We *are* on your side, O son of Jesse!
 Peace, peace to you,
 And peace to your helpers!
 For your God helps you."

So David received them, and made them captains of the troop.

¹⁹And *some* from Manasseh defected to David ʰwhen he was going with the Philistines to battle against Saul; but they did not help them, for the lords of the Philistines sent him away by agreement, saying, ⁱ"He may defect to his master Saul *and endanger* our heads." ²⁰When he went to Ziklag, those of Manasseh who defected to him were Adnah, Jozabad, Jediael, Michael, Jozabad, Elihu, and Zillethai, captains of the thousands who *were* from Manasseh. ²¹And they helped David against ʲthe bands *of raiders*, for they *were* all mighty men of valor, and they were captains in the army. ²²For at *that* time they came to David day by day to help him, until *it was* a great army, ᵏlike the army of God.

David's Army at Hebron

²³Now these *were* the numbers of the divisions *that were* equipped for war, *and* ˡcame to David at ᵐHebron to ⁿturn over the kingdom of Saul to him, ᵒaccording to the word of the LORD: ²⁴of the sons of Judah bearing shield and spear, six thousand eight hundred armed for war; ²⁵of the sons of Simeon, mighty men of valor fit for war, seven thousand one hundred; ²⁶of the sons of Levi four thousand six hundred; ²⁷Jehoiada, the leader of the Aaronites, and with him three thousand seven hundred; ²⁸ᵖZadok, a young man, a valiant warrior, and from his father's house twenty-two captains; ²⁹of the sons of Benjamin, relatives of Saul, three thousand (until then ۹the greatest part of them had remained loyal to the house of Saul); ³⁰of the sons of Ephraim twenty thousand eight hundred, mighty men of valor, famous men throughout their father's house; ³¹of the half-tribe of Manasseh eighteen thousand, who were designated by name to come and make David king; ³²of the sons of Issachar ʳwho had understanding of the times, to know what Israel ought to do, their chiefs were two hundred; and all their brethren were at their command; ³³of Zebulun there were fifty thousand who

---

made them particularly versatile in battle. They were more than "sons of the right hand" to David. They were "sons of the left hand" as well.

12:15 *in the first month.* The first month was Nisan, corresponding approximately to April, the time of spring rains. Ordinarily a person could not cross the Jordan at flood stage, but the fact that the Gadites were not stopped by the floods is a testimony of their unusual courage.

12:28 *Zadok.* This Zadok was probably the same Zadok who was first appointed by David as priest at Gibeon (16:39). The office of priest was not incompatible with that of warrior, as Phinehas showed (Num. 25:6–9; Josh. 22:13–30).

12:32 *Wisdom*—The men of Issachar were dealing with the issue of "the Lord's anointed." There was no longer any question that David was the Lord's choice,

and that Saul had been replaced, but the timing was crucial. It would do no good to anoint David if it took rebellion and treason to place him on the throne. Men who gain power by trickery usually assume that others will be ready to do likewise, and dishonesty and intrigue are not a good foundation for a God-honoring nation. It is sometimes hard to wait for God's timing, or even hard to tell just what His timing is, but if we ask for wisdom, He will give it to us (James 1:5).

12:2 ᶜ Judg. 3:15; 20:16   **12:8** ᵈ 2 Sam. 2:18
12:14 ᵉ 1 Sam. 18:13   **12:15** ᶠ Josh. 3:15; 4:18, 19
12:19 ᵍ 2 Sam. 17:25   **12:19** ʰ 1 Sam. 29:2   ⁱ 1 Sam. 29:4   **12:21** ʲ 1 Sam. 30:1, 9, 10   **12:22** ᵏ Josh. 5:13–15
12:23 ˡ 2 Sam. 2:1–4 ᵐ 1 Chr. 11:1 ⁿ 1 Chr. 10:14 ᵒ 1 Sam. 16:1–4   **12:28** ᵖ 2 Sam. 8:17   **12:29** ۹ 2 Sam. 2:8, 9
12:32 ʳ Esth. 1:13

went out to battle, expert in war with all weapons of war, ˢstouthearted men who could keep ranks; ³⁴of Naphtali one thousand captains, and with them thirty-seven thousand with shield and spear; ³⁵of the Danites who could keep battle formation, twenty-eight thousand six hundred; ³⁶of Asher, those who could go out to war, able to keep battle formation, forty thousand; ³⁷of the Reubenites and the Gadites and the half-tribe of Manasseh, from the other side of the Jordan, one hundred and twenty thousand armed for battle with every *kind* of weapon of war.

³⁸All these men of war, who could keep ranks, came to Hebron with a loyal heart, to make David king over all Israel; and all the rest of Israel *were* of ᵗone mind to make David king. ³⁹And they were there with David three days, eating and drinking, for their brethren had prepared for them. ⁴⁰Moreover those who were near to them, from as far away as Issachar and Zebulun and Naphtali, were bringing food on donkeys and camels, on mules and oxen—provisions of flour and cakes of figs and cakes of raisins, wine and oil and oxen and sheep abundantly, for *there was* joy in Israel.

The Ark Brought from Kirjath Jearim

13 Then David consulted with the ᵃcaptains of thousands and hundreds, *and* with every leader. ²And David said to all the assembly of Israel, "If *it seems* good to you, and if it is of the LORD our God, let us send out to our brethren everywhere *who are* ᵇleft in all the land of Israel, and with them to the priests and Levites *who are* in their cities *and* their common-lands, that they may gather together to us; ³and let us bring the ark of our God back to us, ᶜfor we have not inquired at it since the days of Saul." ⁴Then all the assembly said that they would do so, for the thing was right in the eyes of all the people.

⁵So ᵈDavid gathered all Israel together, from ᵉShihor in Egypt to as far as the entrance of Hamath, to bring the ark of God ᶠfrom Kirjath Jearim. ⁶And David and all Israel went up to ᵍBaalah,* to Kirjath Jearim, which belonged to Judah, to bring up from there the ark of God the LORD, ʰwho dwells *between* the cherubim, where *His* name is proclaimed. ⁷So they carried the ark of God ⁱon a new cart ʲfrom the house of Abinadab, and Uzza and Ahio drove the cart. ⁸Then ᵏDavid and all Israel played *music* before God with all *their* might, with singing, on harps, on stringed instruments, on tambourines, on cymbals, and with trumpets.

⁹And when they came to Chidon's* threshing floor, Uzza put out his hand to hold the ark, for the oxen stumbled. ¹⁰Then the anger of the LORD was aroused against Uzza, and He struck him ˡbecause he put his hand to the ark; and he ᵐdied there before God. ¹¹And David became angry because of the LORD's outbreak against Uzza; therefore that place is called Perez Uzza* to this day. ¹²David was afraid of God that day, saying, "How can I bring the ark of God to me?"

¹³So David would not move the ark with him into the City of David, but took it aside into the house of Obed-Edom the Gittite. ¹⁴ⁿThe ark of God remained in the family of Obed-Edom in his house three months. And the LORD blessed ᵒthe house of Obed-Edom and all that he had.

David Established at Jerusalem

14 Now ᵃHiram king of Tyre sent messengers to David, and cedar trees, with masons and carpenters, to build him a house. ²So David knew that the LORD had established him as king over Israel, for his

---

* **13:6** Called *Baale Judah* in 2 Samuel 6:2
* **13:9** Called *Nachon* in 2 Samuel 6:6   * **13:11** Literally *Outburst Against Uzza*

13:3 the ark of our God. This was the ark of the covenant that contained a copy of the Ten Commandments (Ex. 25:10–22). Besides holding the stone tablets, the ark represented the presence of the living God among the Israelites.

13:5 Commitment—One of David's first official actions upon becoming king was to bring the ark of God to Jerusalem. The ark had been in Kirjath Jearim since the time it was returned by the Philistines when Samuel was a boy (1 Sam. 6:20—7:1). Moving the ark to Jerusalem was a sign of David's commitment to place the Lord first in his reign.

13:6 the LORD, who dwells between the cherubim. On each side of the ark of the covenant were two cherubim. They extended their wings over the cover, also called the mercy seat (Ex. 25:17–22), and the glory of God was perceived as sitting on top of the ark, as a King sits on a throne. **Where His name is proclaimed.** In Deuteronomy, the presence of God is often spoken of as the presence of His name (Deut. 12:1–14).

13:9 Chidon's threshing floor. Also called "Nachon's threshing floor" (2 Sam. 6:6), this hard flat surface was used for separating the grain kernels from the straw and husks.

13:11 Perez Uzza. Perez Uzza means "outbreak against Uzza." The ark should have been carried on poles by Levites (Num. 4:14–15). This direction for transporting the holy things was very clear, and should have been remembered.

14:1–2 Hiram king of Tyre. A powerful ruler of the Phoenician city-state of Tyre, Hiram is mentioned in the Scriptures and in other sources. He was a

---

12:33 ˢPs. 12:2   **12:38** ᵗ2 Chr. 30:12   **13:1** ᵃ1 Chr. 11:15; 12:34   **13:2** ᵇIs. 37:4   **13:3** ᶜ1 Sam. 7:1, 2   **13:5** ᵈ1 Sam. 7:5 ᵉJosh. 13:3 ᶠ1 Sam. 6:21; 7:1, 2   **13:6** ᵍJosh. 15:9, 60 ʰEx. 25:22   **13:7** ⁱ1 Sam. 6:7 ʲ1 Sam. 7:1   **13:8** ᵏ2 Sam. 6:5   **13:10** ˡ[Num. 4:15] ᵐLev. 10:2   **13:14** ⁿ2 Sam. 6:11 ᵒ1 Chr. 26:4–8   **14:1** ᵃ2 Sam. 5:11

kingdom was [b]highly exalted for the sake of His people Israel.

[3]Then David took more wives in Jerusalem, and David begot more sons and daughters. [4]And [c]these are the names of his children whom he had in Jerusalem: Shammua,* Shobab, Nathan, Solomon, [5]Ibhar, Elishua,* Elpelet,* [6]Nogah, Nepheg, Japhia, [7]Elishama, Beeliada,* and Eliphelet.

The Philistines Defeated

[8]Now when the Philistines heard that [d]David had been anointed king over all Israel, all the Philistines went up to search for David. And David heard of it and went out against them. [9]Then the Philistines went and made a raid [e]on the Valley of Rephaim. [10]And David [f]inquired of God, saying, "Shall I go up against the Philistines? Will You deliver them into my hand?"

The LORD said to him, "Go up, for I will deliver them into your hand."

[11]So they went up to Baal Perazim, and David defeated them there. Then David said, "God has broken through my enemies by my hand like a breakthrough of water." Therefore they called the name of that place Baal Perazim.* [12]And when they left their gods there, David gave a commandment, and they were burned with fire.

[13g]Then the Philistines once again made a raid on the valley. [14]Therefore David inquired again of God, and God said to him, "You shall not go up after them; circle around them, [h]and come upon them in front of the mulberry trees. [15]And it shall be, when you hear a sound of marching in the tops of the mulberry trees, then you shall go out to battle, for God has gone out before you to strike the camp of the Philistines." [16]So David did as God commanded him, and they drove back the army of the Philistines from Gibeon as far as Gezer. [17]Then [i]the fame of David went out into all lands, and the LORD [j]brought the fear of him upon all nations.

The Ark Brought to Jerusalem

15 David built houses for himself in the City of David; and he prepared a place for the ark of God, [a]and pitched a tent for it. [2]Then David said, "No one may carry the [b]ark of God but the Levites, for [c]the LORD has chosen them to carry the ark of God and to minister before Him forever." [3]And David [d]gathered all Israel together at Jerusalem, to bring up the ark of the LORD to its place, which he had prepared for it. [4]Then David assembled the children of Aaron and the Levites: [5]of the sons of Kohath, Uriel the chief, and one hundred and twenty of his brethren; [6]of the sons of Merari, Asaiah the chief, and two hundred and twenty of his brethren; [7]of the sons of Gershom, Joel the chief, and one hundred and thirty of his brethren; [8]of the sons of [e]Elizaphan, Shemaiah the chief, and two hundred of his brethren; [9]of the sons of [f]Hebron, Eliel the chief, and eighty of his brethren; [10]of the sons of Uzziel, Amminadab the chief, and one hundred and twelve of his brethren.

[11]And David called for [g]Zadok and [h]Abiathar the priests, and for the Levites: for Uriel, Asaiah, Joel, Shemaiah, Eliel, and

* **14:4** Spelled *Shimea* in 3:5　* **14:5** Spelled *Elishama* in 3:6 • Spelled *Eliphelet* in 3:6　* **14:7** Spelled *Eliada* in 3:8　* **14:11** Literally *Master of Breakthroughs*

---

contemporary of both David and Solomon. He helped build David's house, and he also supplied material for the temple and other building projects in Solomon's reign (1 Kin. 9:10).
14:3 took more wives. See the note at 3:1–5.
14:4 children. The first four listed here are all sons of Bathsheba (3:5).
15:1 place for the ark. The place for the ark was in the tent in the City of David. The original tabernacle built in Moses' day had been placed at Shiloh (Josh. 18:1). It remained there until the capture of the ark by the Philistines (1 Sam. 4;1–11), when it was evidently moved to Nob, just two miles from Jerusalem (1 Sam. 21:1–6). Then it was moved to a high place at Gibeon (2 Chr. 1:3), about two miles north of Saul's city Gibeah. When David became king, he left the Mosaic tabernacle at Gibeon and appointed the priest Zadok to attend to its ministry (16:39). Even after he had built a new tabernacle on Mount Zion and brought the ark into it, the original tent remained at Gibeon. Solomon brought the ark from Mount Zion and the tabernacle of Moses from Gibeon and placed them in the new temple he had built on Mount Moriah (2 Chr. 5:4–5).
15:2 No one . . . but the Levites. According to the provisions of the Law, the ark was to be carried only by the Levites, by means of poles inserted through corner rings (Num. 4:14–15).

15:11 Zadok. The other line of the priesthood descended from Aaron's son Eleazar, and included Zadok (6:8). During David's time representatives of both Ithamar and Eleazar served. Zadok served at the tabernacle at Gibeon, and Abiathar served as chief priest at Jerusalem. When Solomon became king, Abiathar was deposed and Zadok ministered as high priest at the temple (1 Kin. 2:26–27,35). The dismissal of Abiathar as priest was in accordance with the Lord's word to Eli because of the unfaithfulness of Eli's sons (1 Sam. 2:27–36). **Abiathar.** The transition from the rule of Saul to David involved a transition from the old Mosaic tabernacle to the new place David had established on Mount Zion in preparation for the temple (v. 1). Abiathar's father, the priest Ahimelech, was in charge of the old tabernacle when it left Shiloh and was moved to Nob (1 Sam. 21:1). Ahimelech was Eli's great-grandson (1 Sam. 14:3; 22:9). Eli is considered to have been a descendant of Aaron's son Ithamar.

14:2 [b] Num. 24:7　**14:4** [c] 1 Chr. 3:5–8　**14:8** [d] 2 Sam. 5:17–21　**14:9** [e] 1 Chr. 11:15; 14:13　**14:10** [f] 1 Sam. 23:2, 4; 30:8　**14:13** [g] 2 Sam. 5:22–25　**14:14** [h] 2 Sam. 5:23　**14:17** [i] Josh. 6:27　[j] [Deut. 2:25; 11:25]　**15:1** [a] 1 Chr. 16:1　**15:2** [b] [Num. 4:15]　[c] Deut. 10:8; 31:9　**15:3** [d] 1 Kin. 8:1　**15:8** [e] Ex. 6:22　**15:9** [f] Ex. 6:18　**15:11** [g] 1 Chr. 12:28　[h] 1 Kin. 2:22, 26, 27

Amminadab. [12]He said to them, "You *are* the heads of the fathers' *houses* of the Levites; sanctify yourselves, you and your brethren, that you may bring up the ark of the LORD God of Israel to *the place* I have prepared for it. [13]For *i*because you *did* not *do it* the first *time*, *j*the LORD our God broke out against us, because we did not consult Him about the proper order."

[14]So the priests and the Levites sanctified themselves to bring up the ark of the LORD God of Israel. [15]And the children of the Levites bore the ark of God on their shoulders, by its poles, as *k*Moses had commanded according to the word of the LORD.

[16]Then David spoke to the leaders of the Levites to appoint their brethren *to be* the singers accompanied by instruments of music, stringed instruments, harps, and cymbals, by raising the voice with resounding joy. [17]So the Levites appointed *l*Heman the son of Joel; and of his brethren, *m*Asaph the son of Berechiah; and of their brethren, the sons of Merari, *n*Ethan the son of Kushaiah; [18]and with them their brethren of the second *rank*: Zechariah, Ben,* Jaaziel, Shemiramoth, Jehiel, Unni, Eliab, Benaiah, Maaseiah, Mattithiah, Elipheleh, Mikneiah, Obed-Edom, and Jeiel, the gatekeepers; [19]the singers, Heman, Asaph, and Ethan, *were* to sound the cymbals of bronze; [20]Zechariah, Aziel, Shemiramoth, Jehiel, Unni, Eliab, Maaseiah, and Benaiah, with strings according to *o*Alamoth; [21]Mattithiah, Elipheleh, Mikneiah, Obed-Edom, Jeiel, and Azaziah, to direct with harps on the *p*Sheminith; [22]Chenaniah, leader of the Levites, was instructor *in charge of* the music, because he *was* skillful; [23]Berechiah and Elkanah *were* doorkeepers for the ark; [24]Shebaniah, Joshaphat, Nethanel, Amasai, Zechariah, Benaiah, and Eliezer,

the priests, *q*were to blow the trumpets before the ark of God; and *r*Obed-Edom and Jehiah, doorkeepers for the ark.

[25]So *s*David, the elders of Israel, and the captains over thousands went to bring up the ark of the covenant of the LORD from the house of Obed-Edom with joy. [26]And so it was, when God helped the Levites who bore the ark of the covenant of the LORD, that they offered seven bulls and seven rams. [27]David was clothed with a robe of fine *t*linen, as were all the Levites who bore the ark, the singers, and Chenaniah the music master *with* the singers. David also wore a linen ephod. [28]*u*Thus all Israel brought up the ark of the covenant of the LORD with shouting and with the sound of the horn, with trumpets and with cymbals, making music with stringed instruments and harps.

[29]And it happened, *v*as the ark of the covenant of the LORD came to the City of David, that Michal, Saul's daughter, looked through a window and saw King David whirling and playing music; and she despised him in her heart.

The Ark Placed in the Tabernacle

16 So *a*they brought the ark of God, and set it in the midst of the tabernacle that David had erected for it. Then they offered burnt offerings and peace offerings before God. [2]And when David had finished offering the burnt offerings and the peace offerings, *b*he blessed the people in the name of the LORD. [3]Then he distributed to everyone of Israel, both man and woman, to everyone a loaf of bread, a piece *of meat*, and a cake of raisins.

---

* **15:18** Following Masoretic Text and Vulgate; Septuagint omits *Ben*.

15:17 Heman. The musician Heman was the grandson of the prophet Samuel (6:33). He is probably the same Heman who appears in the superscription of Psalm 88. **Asaph.** Asaph was leader of the Gershonite Levites (6:39–43). Asaph and his sons ministered primarily as singers (25:1–2; 2 Chr. 20:14) and composers, as their superscriptions suggest (Ps. 50; 73–83). **Ethan.** Ethan was the head of the Merarite division of musicians (6:44). He may be the composer of Psalm 89. **15:20 with strings according to Alamoth.** The meaning of "alamoth" is uncertain. It may mean a soprano voice. **15:21 harps on the Sheminith.** The meaning of "sheminith" is uncertain, but it is apparently a musical term, perhaps derived from the Hebrew word for eighth, referring to musical scales. **15:24 Obed-Edom.** It is likely that Obed-Edom in this verse was the same person who had custody of the ark in the months before it was brought to Jerusalem (13:13–14). He apparently was a Levite and certainly a righteous man. **15:29 Michal, Saul's daughter.** Michal was David's first wife, whom he married before Saul started pursuing him (1 Sam. 18:27; 19:11–17). When David was hiding from Saul, Michal was given in marriage

to another (1 Sam. 25:44). One of the conditions of David's peace agreement with Abner was that Michal be returned to him (2 Sam. 3:13–16). The Bible does not say why Michal despised David, but it seems probable that the real source of her attitude was bitterness about her life. If she had no understanding of God's hand in her life and the life of the nation, seeing David's joyful abandonment before the Lord would have been galling. **16:3 he distributed.** David's distribution of food was in line with the nature of the peace offerings. Such offerings often accompanied occasions of praise and thanksgiving such as this one. They were unique in that they provided a common meal in which all participated before God—the offerer, his family and friends, and the priests (Lev. 7:11–14; 28–34; Deut. 12:17–19).

15:13 *i* 2 Sam. 6:3 *j* 1 Chr. 13:7–11 **15:15** *k* Ex. 25:14 **15:17** *l* 1 Chr. 6:33; 25:1 *m* 1 Chr. 6:39 *n* 1 Chr. 6:44 **15:20** *o* Ps. 46:title **15:21** *p* Ps. 6:title **15:24** *q* [Num. 10:8] *r* 1 Chr. 13:13, 14 **15:25** *s* 1 Kin. 8:1 **15:27** *t* 1 Sam. 2:18, 28 **15:28** *u* 1 Chr. 13:8 **15:29** *v* 2 Sam. 3:13, 14; 6:16, 20–23 **16:1** *a* 2 Sam. 6:17 **16:2** *b* 1 Kin. 8:14

4And he appointed some of the Levites to minister before the ark of the LORD, to ccommemorate, to thank, and to praise the LORD God of Israel: 5Asaph the chief, and next to him Zechariah, then dJeiel, Shemiramoth, Jehiel, Mattithiah, Eliab, Benaiah, and Obed-Edom: Jeiel with stringed instruments and harps, but Asaph made music with cymbals; 6Benaiah and Jahaziel the priests regularly *blew* the trumpets before the ark of the covenant of God.

David's Song of Thanksgiving

7On that day eDavid ffirst delivered *this psalm* into the hand of Asaph and his brethren, to thank the LORD:

8 gOh, give thanks to the LORD!
Call upon His name;
Make known His deeds among the peoples!
9 Sing to Him, sing psalms to Him;
Talk of all His wondrous works!
10 Glory in His holy name;
Let the hearts of those rejoice who seek the LORD!
11 Seek the LORD and His strength;
Seek His face evermore!
12 Remember His marvelous works which He has done,
His wonders, and the judgments of His mouth,
13 O seed of Israel His servant,
You children of Jacob, His chosen ones!
14 He *is* the LORD our God;
His hjudgments *are* in all the earth.
15 Remember His covenant forever,
The word which He commanded, for a thousand generations,
16 *The* icovenant *which* He made with Abraham,
And His oath to Isaac,

17 And iconfirmed it to kJacob for a statute,
To Israel *for* an everlasting covenant,
18 Saying, "To you I will give the land of Canaan
As the allotment of your inheritance,"
19 When you were lfew in number,
Indeed very few, and strangers in it.
20 When they went from one nation to another,
And from *one* kingdom to another people,
21 He permitted no man to do them wrong;
Yes, He mrebuked kings for their sakes,
22 *Saying,* n"Do not touch My anointed ones,
And do My prophets no harm."*
23 oSing to the LORD, all the earth;
Proclaim the good news of His salvation from day to day.
24 Declare His glory among the nations,
His wonders among all peoples.
25 For the LORD *is* great and greatly to be praised;
He *is* also to be feared above all gods.
26 For all the gods pof the peoples *are* idols,
But the LORD made the heavens.
27 Honor and majesty *are* before Him;
Strength and gladness are in His place.
28 Give to the LORD, O families of the peoples,
Give to the LORD glory and strength.
29 Give to the LORD the glory *due* His name;

---

* **16:22** Compare verses 8–22 with Psalm 105:1–15

16:4 *Levites.* The appointment of Levites described here was of a more permanent nature than that of 15:1–24, which concerned the immediate task of moving the ark into Jerusalem. Some of the same persons were involved, as verses 5 and 6 make clear.

16:7 *to thank the LORD.* David's musical abilities are well-known, both as a harpist (1 Sam. 16:18) and as the writer of many of the psalms. This psalm consists of three different parts. Each portion correlates with part of another psalm. Verses 8–22 correspond with Psalm 105:1–15; verses 23–33 with Psalm 96:1–13; and verses 34–36 with Psalm 106:1,47–48.

16:12–16 *Obedience*—"Remember His marvelous works . . . Remember His covenant forever . . ." and for those of us who are believers, "proclaim the Lord's death till He comes" (1 Cor. 11:23–26). Remembering is connected to obedience, only when we remember His commands can we obey Him.

16:22 *anointed.* In this context "anointed ones" means those set apart for God's service, not necessarily literally anointed with oil.

16:29 *The Meaning of Worship*—Worship refers to the honor and praise given in thought or deed to a person or thing. The Bible teaches that God alone

is worthy of worship (Ps. 29:2). But it also records accounts of those who worshiped inappropriately: people (Acts 14:8–18); false gods (2 Kin. 10:19); images and idols (Is. 2:8); heavenly bodies (2 Kin. 21:3); Satan (Rev. 13:4); and demons (Rev. 9:20).

True worship involves at least three important elements:

1. *Reverence.* This includes the honor and respect directed toward the Lord in thought and feeling. Jesus said that those who worship God must do so "in spirit and truth" (John 4:24). The term *spirit* speaks of the personal nature of worship. It is from my person to God's person and involves the intellect, emotions, and will. The word *truth* speaks of the content of worship. God is pleased when we worship Him, understanding His true character.

16:4 cPs. 38:title; 70:title   **16:5** d1 Chr. 15:18
16:7 e2 Sam. 22:1; 23:1   fPs. 105:1–15   **16:8** gPs. 105:1–15
16:14 h[Is. 26:9]   **16:16** iGen. 17:2; 26:3; 28:13; 35:11
16:17 jGen. 35:11, 12   kGen. 28:10–15   **16:19** lGen. 34:30
16:21 mGen. 12:17; 20:3   **16:22** nGen. 20:7   **16:23** oPs. 96:1–13   **16:26** pLev. 19:4

Bring an offering, and come before
Him.
Oh, worship the LORD in the beauty of
holiness!
30 Tremble before Him, all the earth.
The world also is firmly established,
It shall not be moved.

31 Let the heavens rejoice, and let the
earth be glad;
And let them say among the nations,
"The LORD reigns."
32 Let the sea roar, and all its fullness;
Let the field rejoice, and all that *is* in it.
33 Then the [q]trees of the woods shall
rejoice before the LORD,
For He is [r]coming to judge the earth.*

34 [s]Oh, give thanks to the LORD, for *He is*
good!
For His mercy *endures* forever.*
35 [t]And say, "Save us, O God of our
salvation;
Gather us together, and deliver us
from the Gentiles,
To give thanks to Your holy name,
To triumph in Your praise."

36 [u]Blessed *be* the LORD God of Israel
From everlasting to everlasting!*

And all [v]the people said, "Amen!" and
praised the LORD.

Regular Worship Maintained

37 So he left [w]Asaph and his brothers
there before the ark of the covenant of the
LORD to minister before the ark regularly,
as every day's work [x]required; 38 and
[y]Obed-Edom with his sixty-eight brethren,
including Obed-Edom the son of Jeduthun,
and Hosah, *to be* gatekeepers; 39 and Zadok
the priest and his brethren the priests, [z]be-
fore the tabernacle of the LORD [a]at the high
place that *was* at Gibeon, 40 to offer burnt
offerings to the LORD on the altar of burnt
offering regularly [b]morning and evening,
and *to do* according to all that is written in
the Law of the LORD which He commanded
Israel; 41 and with them Heman and Jeduthun and the rest who were chosen, who
were designated by name, to give thanks
to the LORD, [c]because His mercy *endures*
forever; 42 and with them Heman and Jeduthun, to sound aloud with trumpets and
cymbals and the musical instruments of
God. Now the sons of Jeduthun *were* gatekeepers.
43 [d]Then all the people departed, every
man to his house; and David returned to
bless his house.

God's Covenant with David

17 Now [a]it came to pass, when David was
dwelling in his house, that David said
to Nathan the prophet, "See now, I dwell
in a house of cedar, but the ark of the covenant of the LORD *is* under tent curtains."
2 Then Nathan said to David, "Do all that
is in your heart, for God *is* with you."

* **16:33** Compare verses 23–33 with Psalm 96:1–13 * **16:34** Compare verse 34 with Psalm 106:1 * **16:36** Compare verses 35, 36 with Psalm 106:47, 48

2. *Public expression.* This was particularly prevalent in the Old Testament because of the sacrificial system. For example, when a believer received a particular blessing for which he wanted to thank God, it was not sufficient to say it privately; he expressed his thanks publicly with a thank offering (Lev. 7:12).
3. *Service.* The words for worship in both Testaments originally referred to the labor of slaves for the master. Worship especially includes the joyful service which Christians render to Christ their Master. The concept of worship involves much more than church attendance once or twice a week. It involves an entire life of obedience, service, and praise to God.

16:33 ***trees . . . rejoice.*** This is a figure of speech called personification, in which inanimate things are spoken of as if they had human characteristics. Because the whole creation was negatively affected by the fall of humanity into sin, it could not be restored to perfection and could not truly rejoice until humanity was redeemed. ***He is coming.*** When the Lord returns to the earth, all creation will burst out in praise.

16:38 ***Obed-Edom.*** There are two men by this name in this verse. The first is the Obed-Edom whose house sheltered the ark for three months (13:14) and who was a doorkeeper (15:24). The second was also a gatekeeper, a son of Jeduthun.

16:39 ***Zadok.*** Until the temple of Solomon was completed, there were two legitimate places for community worship—the Mosaic tabernacle at Gibeon, and David's tabernacle on Mount Zion. Zadok, a descendant of Eleazar, served at Gibeon, while Abiathar, a descendant of Ithamar, served at Jerusalem (see note at 15:11).

16:41 ***Jeduthun.*** This was probably another name for the musician Ethan, who is usually named together with Asaph and Heman (15:17,19; 6:33,39,44).

16:42 ***musical instruments of God.*** It is difficult to overemphasize the importance of music in Old Testament worship. The Book of Psalms in itself, and constant references to choral and orchestral ministry demonstrate the significance of music as the people worshiped their Creator (9:33; 15:16–24; 16:4–6; 25:1–31).

17:1 ***Nathan the prophet.*** Nathan was a prophet at the time of both David and Solomon. He was closely connected with both kings, and was trusted as a faithful spokesman of God (2 Sam. 7:2–3; 12:1–15; 1 Kin. 1:8–38; 45; 2 Chr. 29:25). The "book of Nathan the prophet" provided a source for the composition of the books of Chronicles (29:29; 2 Chr. 9:29). ***a house of cedar.*** Cedar paneling was too expensive to be used in an ordinary home.

16:33 [q] Is. 55:12, 13 [r] [Matt. 25:31–46] **16:34** [s] Ps. 106:1; 107:1; 118:1; 136:1 **16:35** [t] Ps. 106:47, 48 **16:36** [u] 1 Kin. 8:15, 56 [v] Deut. 27:15 **16:37** [w] 1 Chr. 16:4, 5 [x] Ezra 3:4 **16:38** [y] 1 Chr. 13:14 **16:39** [z] 2 Chr. 1:3 [a] 1 Kin. 3:4 **16:40** [b] [Ex. 29:38–42] **16:41** [c] 2 Chr. 5:13; 7:3 **16:43** [d] 2 Sam. 6:18–20 **17:1** [a] 2 Sam. 7:1

3But it happened that night that the word of God came to Nathan, saying, 4"Go and tell My servant David, 'Thus says the LORD: "You shall bnot build Me a house to dwell in. 5For I have not dwelt in a house since the time that I brought up Israel, even to this day, but have gone from tent to tent, and from one tabernacle to another. 6Wherever I have moved about with all Israel, have I ever spoken a word to any of the judges of Israel, whom I commanded to shepherd My people, saying, 'Why have you not built Me a house of cedar?'"' 7Now therefore, thus shall you say to My servant David, 'Thus says the LORD of hosts: "I took you cfrom the sheepfold, from following the sheep, to be ruler over My people Israel. 8And I have been with you wherever you have gone, and have cut off all your enemies from before you, and have made you a name like the name of the great men who are on the earth. 9Moreover I will appoint a place for My people Israel, and will dplant them, that they may dwell in a place of their own and move no more; nor shall the sons of wickedness oppress them anymore, as previously, 10since the time that I commanded judges to be over My people Israel. Also I will subdue all your enemies. Furthermore I tell you that the LORD will build you a house.* 11And it shall be, when your days are efulfilled, when you must go to be with your fathers, that I will set up your fseed after you, who will be of your sons; and I will establish his kingdom. 12gHe shall build Me a house, and I will establish his throne forever. 13hI will be his Father, and he shall be My son; and I will not take My mercy away from him, ias I took it from him who was before you. 14And jI will establish him in My house and in My kingdom forever; and his throne shall be established forever."'"

15According to all these words and according to all this vision, so Nathan spoke to David.

16kThen King David went in and sat before the LORD; and he said: "Who am I, O LORD God? And what is my house, that You have brought me this far? 17And yet this was a small thing in Your sight, O God; and You have also spoken of Your servant's house for a great while to come, and have regarded me according to the rank of a man of high degree, O LORD God. 18What more can David say to You for the honor of Your servant? For You know Your servant. 19O LORD, for Your servant's sake, and according to Your own heart, You have done all this greatness, in making known all these great things. 20O LORD, there is none like You, nor is there any God besides You, according to all that we have heard with our ears. 21lAnd who is like Your people Israel, the one nation on the earth whom God went to redeem for Himself as a people— to make for Yourself a name by great and awesome deeds, by driving out nations from before Your people whom You redeemed from Egypt? 22For You have made Your people Israel Your very own people forever; and You, LORD, have become their God.

23"And now, O LORD, the word which You have spoken concerning Your servant and concerning his house, let it be established forever, and do as You have said. 24So let it be established, that Your name may be magnified forever, saying, 'The LORD of hosts, the God of Israel, is Israel's God.' And let the house of Your servant David be established before You. 25For You, O my God, have revealed to Your servant that You will build him a house. Therefore Your servant has found it in his heart to pray before You. 26And now, LORD, You are God, and have promised this goodness to Your servant. 27Now You have been pleased to bless the house of Your servant, that it may continue before You forever; for You have blessed it, O LORD, and it shall be blessed forever."

David's Further Conquests

18 After this ait came to pass that David attacked the Philistines, subdued them, and took Gath and its towns from the hand of the Philistines. 2Then he defeated bMoab, and the Moabites became David's cservants, and brought tribute.

---

* 17:10 That is, a royal dynasty

17:9 I will appoint a place. This did not mean that Israel would move to another land, but it was a restating of God's promise that they were meant to inherit the land (Gen. 13:14–17; 15:18–21; 17:8; Ex. 3:16–17; 6:8; Deut. 1:8; Josh. 1:2–5).

17:16–18 Thankfulness—As with David, God's willingness to bless us is not because we are great but because He is good. His purpose is for us to be like Him, and to bless us and establish us forever with Him through Christ (John 14).

17:20 any God besides You. This is a clear assertion of the uniqueness of Israel's God. Statements such as "all gods" and "the gods of the peoples" in David's song of thanksgiving (16:25–26) must be understood in the light of this clear confession that there is only one living God.

18:1 took Gath. This is the only record of David taking a Philistine city, although he had defeated the Philistines many times in battle. Gath was the Philistine city closest to Israelite territory, so it posed the greatest threat to Israel.

18:2 Moab. David's great-grandmother Ruth was a Moabitess (Ruth 4:13–17), and David had sent his own family to Moab for protection when he was

17:4 b [1 Chr. 28:2, 3]   **17:7** c 1 Sam. 16:11–13
17:9 d Amos 9:14   **17:11** e 1 Kin. 2:10   f [1 Chr. 22:9–13; 28:20]; Matt. 1:6; Luke 3:31   **17:12** g [Ps. 89:20–37; Luke 1:33]   **17:13** h Heb. 1:5   i [1 Sam. 15:23–28]   **17:14** j Matt. 19:28; 25:31; [Luke 1:31–33]; Acts 2:30   **17:16** k 2 Sam. 7:18   **17:21** l Ps. 147:20   **18:1** a 2 Sam. 8:1–18   **18:2** b 2 Sam. 8:2   c Ps. 60:8

³And ᵈDavid defeated Hadadezer* king of Zobah *as far as* Hamath, as he went to establish his power by the River Euphrates. ⁴David took from him one thousand chariots, seven thousand* horsemen, and twenty thousand foot soldiers. Also David hamstrung all the chariot *horses*, except that he spared enough of them for one hundred chariots.

⁵When the ᵉSyrians of Damascus came to help Hadadezer king of Zobah, David killed twenty-two thousand of the Syrians. ⁶Then David put *garrisons* in Syria of Damascus; and the Syrians became David's servants, *and* brought tribute. So the LORD preserved David wherever he went. ⁷And David took the shields of gold that were on the servants of Hadadezer, and brought them to Jerusalem. ⁸Also from Tibhath* and from Chun, cities of Hadadezer, David brought a large amount of ᶠbronze, with which ᵍSolomon made the bronze Sea, the pillars, and the articles of bronze.

⁹Now when Tou* king of Hamath heard that David had defeated all the army of Hadadezer king of Zobah, ¹⁰he sent Hadoram* his son to King David, to greet him and bless him, because he had fought against Hadadezer and defeated him (for Hadadezer had been at war with Tou); and *Hadoram brought with him* all kinds of ʰarticles of gold, silver, and bronze. ¹¹King David also dedicated these to the LORD, along with the silver and gold that he had brought from all *these* nations—from Edom, from Moab, from the ⁱpeople of Ammon, from the ʲPhilistines, and from ᵏAmalek.

¹²Moreover ˡAbishai the son of Zeruiah killed ᵐeighteen thousand Edomites* in the Valley of Salt. ¹³ⁿHe also put garrisons in Edom, and all the Edomites became David's servants. And the LORD preserved David wherever he went.

David's Administration

¹⁴So David reigned over all Israel, and administered judgment and justice to all his people. ¹⁵Joab the son of Zeruiah *was* over the army; Jehoshaphat the son of Ahilud *was* recorder; ¹⁶Zadok the son of

Ahitub and Abimelech the son of Abiathar *were* the priests; Shavsha* *was* the scribe; ¹⁷ᵒBenaiah the son of Jehoiada *was* over the Cherethites and the Pelethites; and David's sons *were* chief ministers at the king's side.

The Ammonites and Syrians Defeated

19 Itᵃ happened after this that Nahash the king of the people of Ammon died, and his son reigned in his place. ²Then David said, "I will show kindness to Hanun the son of Nahash, because his father showed kindness to me." So David sent messengers to comfort him concerning his father. And David's servants came to Hanun in the land of the people of Ammon to comfort him.

³And the princes of the people of Ammon said to Hanun, "Do you think that David really honors your father because he has sent comforters to you? Did his servants not come to you to search and to overthrow and to spy out the land?" ⁴Therefore Hanun took David's servants, shaved them, and cut off their garments in the middle, at their ᵇbuttocks, and sent them away. ⁵Then *some* went and told David about the men; and he sent to meet them, because the men were greatly ashamed. And the king said, "Wait at Jericho until your beards have grown, and *then* return."

⁶When the people of Ammon saw that they had made themselves repulsive to David, Hanun and the people of Ammon sent a thousand talents of silver to hire for themselves chariots and horsemen from Mesopotamia,* from Syrian Maach, ᶜand from Zobah.* ⁷So they hired for themselves thirty-two thousand chariots, with the king of Maacah and his people, who came and encamped before Medeba. Also the

---

* **18:3** Hebrew *Hadarezer*, and so throughout chapters 18 and 19   * **18:4** Or *seven hundred* (compare 2 Samuel 8:4)   * **18:8** Spelled *Betah* in 2 Samuel 8:8   * **18:9** Spelled *Toi* in 2 Samuel 8:9, 10   * **18:10** Spelled *Joram* in 2 Samuel 8:10   * **18:12** Or *Syrians* (compare 2 Samuel 8:13)   * **18:16** Spelled *Seraiah* in 2 Samuel 8:17   * **19:6** Hebrew *Aram Naharaim* • Spelled *Zoba* in 2 Samuel 10:6

---

hiding from Saul (1 Sam. 22:3–4). Yet Moab had been an enemy of Israel (Num. 23), and would be again (Ezek. 25:9).

18:11 dedicated . . . to the LORD. The fact that David dedicated all the spoils of war to God suggests that he viewed the battles as campaigns initiated and led by God. When Solomon built the temple, he brought all the dedicated things into the temple treasuries (2 Chr. 5:1).

18:17 Cherethites . . . Pelethites. These were companies of soldiers, probably mercenaries from Philistia (Ezek. 25:16; 1 Sam. 30:14; 2 Sam. 15:18).

19:1 Nahash. Nahash was reigning in Saul's earliest years (1 Sam. 11:1); the present incident must have occurred early in David's reign at Jerusalem.

19:3 Slander—The delegation was treated scandalously, and David's motives were slanderously

attacked. Of course there were no grounds for such suspicions. Men who themselves act basely toward their neighbors are most likely to suspect such behavior in others. One of the marks of a godly person is that he does not slander with his tongue (Ps. 15:3).

19:4 shaved . . . cut off. Hebrew men were proud of their beards and scrupulously modest in their attire. The Ammonites had humiliated David's men in the most offensive way possible.

19:6 a thousand talents. A talent is about 75 pounds.

18:3 ᵈ 2 Sam. 8:3	**18:5** ᵉ 2 Sam. 8:5, 6	**18:8** ᶠ 2 Sam. 8:8
ᵍ 1 Kin. 7:15, 23	**18:10** ʰ 2 Sam. 8:10–12	**18:11** ⁱ 2 Sam. 10:14 ʲ 2 Sam. 5:17–25 ᵏ 2 Sam. 1:1	**18:12** ˡ 2 Sam. 23:18
ᵐ 2 Sam. 8:13	**18:13** ⁿ 2 Sam. 8:14	**18:17** ᵒ 2 Sam. 8:18
19:1 ᵃ 2 Sam. 10:1–19	**19:4** ᵇ Is. 20:4	**19:6** ᶜ 1 Chr. 18:5, 9

people of Ammon gathered together from their cities, and came to battle.

8Now when David heard *of it*, he sent Joab and all the army of the mighty men. 9Then the people of Ammon came out and put themselves in battle array before the gate of the city, and the kings who had come *were* by themselves in the field.

10When Joab saw that the battle line was against him before and behind, he chose some of Israel's best and put *them* in battle array against the Syrians. 11And the rest of the people he put under the command of Abishai his brother, and they set *themselves* in battle array against the people of Ammon. 12Then he said, "If the Syrians are too strong for me, then you shall help me; but if the people of Ammon are too strong for you, then I will help you. 13Be of good courage, and let us be strong for our people and for the cities of our God. And may the LORD do *what is* good in His sight."

14So Joab and the people who *were* with him drew near for the battle against the Syrians, and they fled before him. 15When the people of Ammon saw that the Syrians were fleeing, they also fled before Abishai his brother, and entered the city. So Joab went to Jerusalem.

16Now when the Syrians saw that they had been defeated by Israel, they sent messengers and brought the Syrians who were beyond the River,* and Shophach* the commander of Hadadezer's army *went* before them. 17When it was told David, he gathered all Israel, crossed over the Jordan and came upon them, and set up in *battle* array against them. So when David had set up in battle array against the Syrians, they fought with him. 18Then the Syrians fled before Israel; and David killed seven thousand* charioteers and forty thousand foot soldiers* of the Syrians, and killed Shophach the commander of the army. 19And when the servants of Hadadezer saw that they were defeated by Israel, they made peace with David and became his servants. So the Syrians were not willing to help the people of Ammon anymore.

Rabbah Is Conquered

20 It*a* happened in the spring of the year, at the time kings go out *to battle*,

that Joab led out the armed forces and ravaged the country of the people of Ammon, and came and besieged Rabbah. But *b*David stayed at Jerusalem. And *c*Joab defeated Rabbah and overthrew it. 2Then David *d*took their king's crown from his head, and found it to weigh a talent of gold, and *there were* precious stones in it. And it was set on David's head. Also he brought out the spoil of the city in great abundance. 3And he brought out the people who *were* in it, and put *them* to work* with saws, with iron picks, and with axes. So David did to all the cities of the people of Ammon. Then David and all the people returned *to* Jerusalem.

Philistine Giants Destroyed

4Now it happened afterward *e*that war broke out at Gezer with the Philistines, at which time *f*Sibbechai the Hushathite killed Sippai,* *who was one* of the sons of the giant. And they were subdued.

5Again there was war with the Philistines, and Elhanan the son of Jair* killed Lahmi the brother of Goliath the Gittite, the shaft of whose spear *was* like a weaver's *g*beam.

6Yet again *h*there was war at Gath, where there was a man of *great* stature, with twenty-four fingers and toes, six *on each hand* and six *on each foot*; and he also was born to the giant. 7So when he defied Israel, Jonathan the son of Shimea,* David's brother, killed him.

8These were born to the giant in Gath, and they fell by the hand of David and by the hand of his servants.

The Census of Israel and Judah

21 Now *a*Satan stood up against Israel, and moved David to number Israel. 2So David said to Joab and to the leaders of the people, "Go, number Israel from Beersheba to Dan, *b*and bring the number of them to me that I may know *it*."

---

* **19:16** That is, the Euphrates • Spelled *Shobach* in 2 Samuel 10:16 * **19:18** Or *seven hundred* (compare 2 Samuel 10:18) • Or *horsemen* (compare 2 Samuel 10:18) * **20:3** Septuagint reads *cut them.* * **20:4** Spelled *Saph* in 2 Samuel 21:18 * **20:5** Spelled *Jaare-Oregim* in 2 Samuel 21:19 * **20:7** Spelled *Shimeah* in 2 Samuel 21:21 and *Shammah* in 1 Samuel 16:9

19:19 servants. "Servants" did not signify household slaves, but national subservience to a greater power, in this case, Israel.

20:1 David stayed at Jerusalem. This is the time that David committed adultery with Bathsheba (2 Sam. 11). The chronicler omits this story, not because it is unsavory, but because it has no bearing on his theme. He is showing how the Davidic dynasty was the fulfillment of God's promises.

20:2 crown. The crown David took was ceremonial and not for wearing, since it weighed about 75 pounds. David put the crown on his head to demonstrate that he had vanquished the Ammonites and now reigned over them as well.

20:7 Shimea. This was David's older brother, the third son of Jesse (2:13).

20:8 the giant in Gath. Goliath was from Gath (1 Sam. 17:4).

21:1 Temptation by Satan—The role of Satan as the Christian's opponent is well summed up by the meaning of the name Satan, which means "adversary." He is also called "the devil," meaning "accuser." He can

---

20:1 *a* 2 Sam. 11:1 *b* 2 Sam. 11:2—12:25 *c* 2 Sam. 12:26 **20:2** *d* 2 Sam. 12:30, 31 **20:4** *e* 2 Sam. 21:18 *f* 1 Chr. 11:29 **20:5** *g* 1 Sam. 17:7 **20:6** *h* 2 Sam. 21:20 **21:1** *a* 2 Sam. 24:1–25 **21:2** *b* 1 Chr. 27:23, 24

3And Joab answered, "May the LORD make His people a hundred times more than they are. But, my lord the king, *are* they not all my lord's servants? Why then does my lord require this thing? Why should he be a cause of guilt in Israel?"

4Nevertheless the king's word prevailed against Joab. Therefore Joab departed and went throughout all Israel and came to Jerusalem. 5Then Joab gave the sum of the number of the people to David. All Israel *had* one million one hundred thousand men who drew the sword, and Judah *had* four hundred and seventy thousand men who drew the sword. 6cBut he did not count Levi and Benjamin among them, for the king's word was abominable to Joab.

7And God was displeased with this thing; therefore He struck Israel. 8So David said to God, d"I have sinned greatly, because I have done this thing; ebut now, I pray, take away the iniquity of Your servant, for I have done very foolishly."

9Then the LORD spoke to Gad, David's fseer, saying, 10"Go and tell David, gsaying, 'Thus says the LORD: "I offer you three *things;* choose one of them for yourself, that I may do *it* to you."'"

11So Gad came to David and said to him, "Thus says the LORD: 'Choose for yourself, 12heither three* years of famine, or three months to be defeated by your foes with the sword of your enemies overtaking *you,* or else for three days the sword of the LORD— the plague in the land, with the angel* of the LORD destroying throughout all the territory of Israel.' Now consider what answer I should take back to Him who sent me."

13And David said to Gad, "I am in great distress. Please let me fall into the hand of the LORD, for His imercies *are* very great; but do not let me fall into the hand of man."

14So the LORD sent a jplague upon Israel, and seventy thousand men of Israel fell. 15And God sent an kangel to Jerusalem to destroy it. As he* was destroying, the LORD looked and lrelented of the disaster, and said to the angel who was destroying, "It is enough; now restrain your* hand." And the angel of the LORD stood by the mthreshing floor of Ornan* the Jebusite.

* **21:12** Or *seven* (compare 2 Samuel 24:13) • Or *Angel,* and so elsewhere in this chapter
* **21:15** Or *He* • Or *Your* • Spelled *Araunah* in 2 Samuel 24:16

---

appear as a dragon (Rev. 12:3–4,9) or as a beautifully deceptive "angel of light" (2 Cor. 11:14). He stands hatefully opposed to all the work of God and promotes defiance among men (Job 2:4–5). When Satan sinned he was expelled from heaven (Luke 10:18), although apparently he still had some access to God (Job 2:4–5). A multitude of angels joined him in his rebellion and subsequently became the demons mentioned often in the biblical record (Matt. 12:24; Rev. 12:7). Although Satan's doom was secured by Jesus' death on the cross (John 16:11), he will continue to hinder God's program until he and his angels are destroyed (Matt. 25:41).

The terrifying work of Satan in the unbeliever is described in Scripture as follows: he blinds their minds (2 Cor. 4:4); he takes the Word of God from their hearts (Luke 8:12); and he controls them (Acts 13:8). In regard to Christians, Satan may accuse them (Rev. 12:10), devour their testimony for Christ (1 Pet. 5:8–9), deceive them (Col. 2:8), hinder their work (1 Thess. 2:18), tempt them to immorality (1 Cor. 7:5), and even be used by God to discipline Christians (1 Cor. 5:5; 2 Cor. 12:7).

The Christian's response to Satan is to recognize his power and deception (2 Cor. 2:11; Eph. 6:11), to adhere steadfastly to the faith (1 Pet. 5:9) to resist him openly (James 4:7), and not to give him opportunities. In practice, the best way to oppose him is to be a growing Christian. Believers can respond to temptation by Satan with confidence. We know that nothing can separate us from the love of God (Rom. 8:38–39). Also in light of Satan's tremendous power to blind men to the gospel, Christians must always be aggressively and compassionately witnessing to the lost in order to snatch them from his control.

21:2 David said. Samuel attributed David's impulse to number the people to God Himself (2 Sam. 24:1) while here it is attributed to Satan (v. 1). The apparent contradiction can be resolved by recognizing that though Satan is the author of all evil, he cannot

exercise his evil intentions apart from the permission of God. Moreover, God could use Satan to accomplish His own purposes of judgment (1 Kin. 22:19–23; Job 1) or discipline (as here with David). **Go, number.** David's plan to take a census was not evil in itself, for the Lord Himself at other times had commanded the Israelites to be counted (Num. 1). The problem seems to have been David's presumptuous attitude. He apparently wanted to have a number to look at, instead of remembering that no matter how many or few were the Israelites, their strength was always in the Lord. **Beersheba to Dan.** This was the traditional way of describing all of Israel from south to north. The distance is about 150 miles.

21:3 a cause of guilt. Joab's warning was David's chance to repent of his intention to number the people for his own purposes. God does not entice us to evil (James 1:13–15; 4:7–8), and even though God was using Satan in this situation, David was still the one who decided to sin (v. 17). God knew what was in David's heart, and either through Joab's rebuke or through David carrying out his sinful thoughts, God intended to deal with David's attitude.

21:9 seer. Gad was a prophet, one who received revelations from the Lord (1 Sam. 22:5).

21:15 Jerusalem to destroy it. When God saw David's repentance and heard his intercessory prayer (v. 17), He relented and stopped the destroying angel. God responded to David's heartfelt prayer. One of the most important aspects of intercessory prayer is how it turns the heart of the one praying toward God, and aligns the intercessor with God's attitudes and purposes.

21:6 c 1 Chr. 27:24 **21:8** d 2 Sam. 24:10 e 2 Sam. 12:13 **21:9** f 1 Sam. 9:9 **21:10** g 2 Sam. 24:12–14 **21:12** h 2 Sam. 24:13 **21:13** i Ps. 51:1; 130:4, 7 **21:14** j 1 Chr. 27:24 **21:15** k 2 Sam. 24:16 l Gen. 6:6 m 2 Chr. 3:1

[16]Then David lifted his eyes and [n]saw the angel of the LORD standing between earth and heaven, having in his hand a drawn sword stretched out over Jerusalem. So David and the elders, clothed in sackcloth, fell on their faces. [17]And David said to God, "Was it not I who commanded the people to be numbered? I am the one who has sinned and done evil indeed; but these [o]sheep, what have they done? Let Your hand, I pray, O LORD my God, be against me and my father's house, but not against Your people that they should be plagued."

[18]Therefore, the [p]angel of the LORD commanded Gad to say to David that David should go and erect an altar to the LORD on the threshing floor of Ornan the Jebusite. [19]So David went up at the word of Gad, which he had spoken in the name of the LORD. [20]Now Ornan turned and saw the angel; and his four sons who were with him hid themselves, but Ornan continued threshing wheat. [21]So David came to Ornan, and Ornan looked and saw David. And he went out from the threshing floor, and bowed before David with his face to the ground. [22]Then David said to Ornan, "Grant me the place of this threshing floor, that I may build an altar on it to the LORD. You shall grant it to me at the full price, that the plague may be withdrawn from the people."

[23]But Ornan said to David, "Take it to yourself, and let my lord the king do what is good in his eyes. Look, I also give you the oxen for burnt offerings, the threshing implements for wood, and the wheat for the grain offering; I give it all."

[24]Then King David said to Ornan, "No, but I will surely buy it for the full price, for I will not take what is yours for the LORD, nor offer burnt offerings with that which costs me nothing." [25]So [q]David gave Ornan six hundred shekels of gold by weight for the place. [26]And David built there an altar to the LORD, and offered burnt offerings and peace offerings, and called on the LORD; and [r]He answered him from heaven by fire on the altar of burnt offering.

[27]So the LORD commanded the angel, and he returned his sword to its sheath.

[28]At that time, when David saw that the LORD had answered him on the threshing floor of Ornan the Jebusite, he sacrificed there. [29]For the tabernacle of the LORD and the altar of the burnt offering, which Moses had made in the wilderness, were at that time at the high place in [t]Gibeon. [30]But David could not go before it to inquire of God, for he was afraid of the sword of the angel of the LORD.

David Prepares to Build the Temple

22 Then David said, [a]"This is the house of the LORD God, and this is the altar of burnt offering for Israel." [2]So David commanded to gather the [b]aliens who were in the land of Israel; and he appointed masons to [c]cut hewn stones to build the house of God. [3]And David prepared iron in abundance for the nails of the doors of the gates and for the joints, and bronze in abundance [d]beyond measure, [4]and cedar trees in abundance; for the [e]Sidonians and those from Tyre brought much cedar wood to David.

[5]Now David said, [f]"Solomon my son is young and inexperienced, and the house to be built for the LORD must be exceedingly magnificent, famous and glorious throughout all countries. I will now make preparation for it." So David made abundant preparations before his death.

[6]Then he called for his son Solomon, and charged him to build a house for the LORD God of Israel. [7]And David said to Solomon: "My son, as for me, [g]it was in my mind to build a house [h]to the name of the LORD my God; [8]but the word of the LORD came to me, saying, [i]'You have shed much blood and have made great wars; you shall not build a house for My name, because you have shed much blood on the earth in My sight. [9]Behold, a son shall be born to you, who shall be a man of rest; and I will give him [k]rest from all his enemies all around. His name shall be Solomon,* for I will give peace and quietness to Israel in his days. [10][l]He shall build a house for My name, and [m]he shall be My son, and I will be his Father; and I will establish the throne of his kingdom over Israel forever.' [11]Now,

---

* **22:9** Literally *Peaceful*

21:24 costs me nothing. David showed a clear perception of the essence of sacrifice. Every prayer, every sacrifice must come from the heart and labor of the one who offers these things to God. No one can have a relationship with God for or on the behalf of someone else.

21:29 tabernacle . . . which Moses had made. The Old Testament account does not fully trace the movement of the tabernacle after Shiloh, but it did end up first at Nob and finally at Gibeon (15:1).

22:1 This is the house of the LORD God. As long as the ark remained at Kirjath Jearim and the tabernacle of Moses was at Nob and Gibeon, it was impossible for worship to be carried out in the manner originally intended. When the house of God was built, the ark and the altar would be together once again.

22:5 young and inexperienced. Solomon was born about halfway through David's reign. At the time that David began to gather building materials, Solomon was probably not over 18 years old.

21:16 [n] 2 Chr. 3:1   **21:17** [o] 2 Sam. 7:8   **21:18** [p] 2 Chr. 3:1
21:25 [q] 2 Sam. 24:24   **21:26** [r] Lev. 9:24   **21:29** [s] 1 Kin. 3:4
[t] 1 Chr. 16:39   **22:1** [a] Deut. 12:5   **22:2** [b] 1 Kin. 9:20, 21
[c] 1 Chr. 5:17, 18   **22:3** [d] 1 Kin. 7:47   **22:4** [e] 1 Kin. 5:6–10
22:5 [f] 1 Chr. 29:1, 2   **22:7** [g] 2 Sam. 7:1, 2   [h] Deut. 12:5, 11
22:8 [i] 1 Chr. 28:3   **22:9** [j] 1 Chr. 28:5   [k] 1 Kin. 4:20, 25; 5:4
22:10 [l] 1 Chr. 17:12, 13; 28:6   [m] Matt. 1:6; Heb. 1:5

my son, may [n]the LORD be with you; and may you prosper, and build the house of the LORD your God, as He has said to you. [12]Only may the LORD [o]give you wisdom and understanding, and give you charge concerning Israel, that you may keep the law of the LORD your God. [13p]Then you will prosper, if you take care to fulfill the statutes and judgments with which the LORD charged Moses concerning Israel. [q]Be strong and of good courage; do not fear nor be dismayed. [14]Indeed I have taken much trouble to prepare for the house of the LORD one hundred thousand talents of gold and one million talents of silver, and bronze and iron [r]beyond measure, for it is so abundant. I have prepared timber and stone also, and you may add to them. [15]Moreover there are workmen with you in abundance: woodsmen and stonecutters, and all types of skillful men for every kind of work. [16]Of gold and silver and bronze and iron there is no limit. Arise and begin working, and [s]the LORD be with you."

[17]David also commanded all the [t]leaders of Israel to help Solomon his son, saying, [18]"Is not the LORD your God with you? [u]And has He not given you rest on every side? For He has given the inhabitants of the land into my hand, and the land is subdued before the LORD and before His people. [19]Now set your heart and your soul to seek the LORD your God. Therefore arise and build the sanctuary of the LORD God, to [v]bring the ark of the covenant of the LORD and the holy articles of God into the house that is to be built [w]for the name of the LORD."

The Divisions of the Levites

23 So when David was old and full of days, he made his son [a]Solomon king over Israel.

[2]And he gathered together all the leaders of Israel, with the priests and the Levites. [3]Now the Levites were numbered from the age of [b]thirty years and above; and the number of individual males was thirty-eight thousand. [4]Of these, twenty-four thousand were to [c]look after the work of the house of the LORD, six thousand

were [d]officers and judges, [5]four thousand were gatekeepers, and four thousand [e]praised the LORD with musical instruments, [f]"which I made," said David, "for giving praise."

[6]Also [g]David separated them into divisions among the sons of Levi: Gershon, Kohath, and Merari.

[7]Of the [h]Gershonites: Laadan* and Shimei. [8]The sons of Laadan: the first Jehiel, then Zetham and Joel—three in all. [9]The sons of Shimei: Shelomith, Haziel, and Haran—three in all. These were the heads of the fathers' houses of Laadan. [10]And the sons of Shimei: Jahath, Zina,* Jeush, and Beriah. These were the four sons of Shimei. [11]Jahath was the first and Zizah the second. But Jeush and Beriah did not have many sons; therefore they were assigned as one father's house.

[12i]The sons of Kohath: Amram, Izhar, Hebron, and Uzziel—four in all. [13]The sons of [j]Amram: Aaron and Moses; and [k]Aaron was set apart, he and his sons forever, that he should sanctify the most holy things, [l]to burn incense before the LORD, [m]to minister to Him, and [n]to give the blessing in His name forever. [14]Now [o]the sons of Moses the man of God were reckoned to the tribe of Levi. [15p]The sons of Moses were Gershon* and Eliezer. [16]Of the sons of Gershon, [q]Shebuel* was the first. [17]Of the descendants of Eliezer, [r]Rehabiah was the first. And Eliezer had no other sons, but the sons of Rehabiah were very many. [18]Of the sons of Izhar, [s]Shelomith was the first. [19t]Of the sons of Hebron, Jeriah was the first, Amariah the second, Jahaziel the third, and Jekameam the fourth. [20]Of the sons of Uzziel, Michah was the first and Jesshiah the second.

[21u]The sons of Merari were Mahli and Mushi. The sons of Mahli were Eleazar and [v]Kish. [22]And Eleazar died, and [w]had no sons, but only daughters; and their brethren, the sons of Kish, [x]took them as wives.

* **23:7** Spelled Libni in Exodus 6:17 * **23:10** Septuagint and Vulgate read Zizah (compare verse 11). * **23:15** Hebrew Gershom (compare 6:16) * **23:16** Spelled Shubael in 24:20

22:13 Zeal—David says in Psalm 71, "O God, You have taught me from my youth: and to this day I declare Your wondrous works" (v. 17). Wherever he went, David proclaimed the goodness and majesty of God, and now he saw the temple and the centrality of worship as the pinnacle of his service for God. He could encourage Solomon to proceed with confidence because he knew he was doing God's will.

22:18 subdued before the LORD. The conquest of the land began in Joshua's time and was completed under David. It had been a long process, including times of great disobedience and others of great faith. There is an element of submission in this statement, relating both to the Israelites and the land itself.

23:1 his son Solomon king. This phrasing suggests

that this is an official appointment, perhaps in the role of coregent with David. It was later ratified by the whole nation (29:22).

22:11 [n] 1 Chr. 22:16   **22:12** [o] 1 Kin. 3:9–12
22:13 [p] 1 Chr. 28:7 [q] [Josh. 1:6, 7, 9]   **22:14** [r] 1 Chr. 22:3
22:16 [s] 1 Chr. 22:11   **22:17** [t] 1 Chr. 28:1–6   **22:18** [u] Josh. 22:4   **22:19** [v] 2 Chr. 5:2–14 [w] 1 Kin. 5:3   **23:1** [a] 1 Kin. 1:33–40   **23:3** [b] Num. 4:1–3   **23:4** [c] Ezra 3:8, 9 [d] Deut. 16:18–20   **23:5** [e] 1 Chr. 15:16 [f] 2 Chr. 29:25–27   **23:6** [g] Ex. 6:16   **23:7** [h] 1 Chr. 26:21   **23:12** [i] Ex. 6:18   **23:13** [j] Ex. 6:20 [k] Heb. 5:4 [l] 1 Sam. 2:28 [m] [Deut. 21:5] [n] Num. 6:23   **23:14** [o] 1 Chr. 26:20–24   **23:15** [p] Ex. 18:3, 4   **23:16** [q] 1 Chr. 26:24   **23:17** [r] 1 Chr. 26:25   **23:18** [s] 1 Chr. 24:22   **23:19** [t] 1 Chr. 24:23   **23:21** [u] 1 Chr. 24:26 [v] 1 Chr. 24:29   **23:22** [w] 1 Chr. 24:28 [x] Num. 36:6

23yThe sons of Mushi *were* Mahli, Eder, and Jeremoth—three *in all.*

24These *were* the sons of zLevi by their fathers' houses—the heads of the fathers' *houses* as they were counted individually by the number of their names, who did the work for the service of the house of the LORD, from the age of atwenty years and above.

25For David said, "The LORD God of Israel bhas given rest to His people, that they may dwell in Jerusalem forever"; 26and also to the Levites, "They shall no longer ccarry the tabernacle, or any of the articles for its service." 27For by the dlast words of David the Levites *were* numbered from twenty years old and above; 28because their duty *was* to help the sons of Aaron in the service of the house of the LORD, in the courts and in the chambers, in the purifying of all holy things and the work of the service of the house of God, 29both with ethe showbread and fthe fine flour for the grain offering, with gthe unleavened cakes and hwhat is *baked in* the pan, with what is mixed and with all kinds of imeasures and sizes; 30to stand every morning to thank and praise the LORD, and likewise at evening; 31and at every presentation of a burnt offering to the LORD jon the Sabbaths and on the New Moons and on the kset feasts, by number according to the ordinance governing them, regularly before the LORD; 32and that they should lattend to the mneeds of the tabernacle of meeting, the needs of the holy *place,* and the nneeds of the sons of Aaron their brethren in the work of the house of the LORD.

The Divisions of the Priests

24 Now *these are* the divisions of the sons of Aaron. aThe sons of Aaron *were* Nadab, Abihu, Eleazar, and Ithamar. 2And bNadab and Abihu died before their father, and had no children; therefore Eleazar and Ithamar ministered as priests. 3Then David with Zadok of the sons of Eleazar, and cAhimelech of the sons of Ithamar,

divided them according to the schedule of their service.

4There were more leaders found of the sons of Eleazar than of the sons of Ithamar, and *thus* they were divided. Among the sons of Eleazar *were* sixteen heads of *their* fathers' houses, and eight heads of their fathers' houses among the sons of Ithamar. 5Thus they were divided by lot, one group as another, for there were officials of the sanctuary and officials *of the house* of God, from the sons of Eleazar and from the sons of Ithamar. 6And the scribe, Shemaiah the son of Nethanel, *one of* the Levites, wrote them down before the king, the leaders, Zadok the priest, Ahimelech the son of Abiathar, and the heads of the fathers' *houses* of the priests and Levites, one father's house taken for Eleazar and *one* for Ithamar.

7Now the first lot fell to Jehoiarib, the second to Jedaiah, 8the third to Harim, the fourth to Seorim, 9the fifth to Malchijah, the sixth to Mijamin, 10the seventh to Hakkoz, the eighth to dAbijah, 11the ninth to Jeshua, the tenth to Shecaniah, 12the eleventh to Eliashib, the twelfth to Jakim, 13the thirteenth to Huppah, the fourteenth to Jeshebeab, 14the fifteenth to Bilgah, the sixteenth to Immer, 15the seventeenth to Hezir, the eighteenth to Happizzez,* 16the nineteenth to Pethahiah, the twentieth to Jehezekel,* 17the twenty-first to Jachin, the twenty-second to Gamul, 18the twenty-third to Delaiah, the twenty-fourth to Maaziah.

19This *was* the schedule of their service efor coming into the house of the LORD according to their ordinance by the hand of Aaron their father, as the LORD God of Israel had commanded him.

Other Levites

20And the rest of the sons of Levi: of the sons of Amram, Shubael;* of the sons of Shubael, Jehdeiah. 21Concerning fRehabiah, of the sons of Rehabiah, the first *was*

---

* **24:15** Septuagint and Vulgate read *Aphses.*
* **24:16** Masoretic Text reads *Jehezkel.*
* **24:20** Spelled *Shebuel* in 23:16

23:26 no longer carry. When the tabernacle was replaced by a permanent building, the role of the Levites changed. This is another aspect of the subdued land. The Israelites were there to stay.

23:30 Praise—This is a beautiful picture of daily praise, thanking the Lord for the day that begins and the day that ends. As believers, we don't need someone else to thank the Lord on our behalf. We need to praise Him. The value of praise is that it lifts our hearts to God's heart. It keeps us thinking about Him and worshiping Him. Life can be almost overwhelming at times, and a habit of praising God lifts our thoughts above our troubles and focuses on who He is and what He has done.

23:32 holy place. This referred to the outer room of the tabernacle. The Most Holy Place was only approached by the high priest.

24:1 sons of Aaron. See notes at 6:2–4; 15:11.

24:10 Abijah. This Abijah may be the ancestor of Zacharias, father of John the Baptist, who is named in Luke 1:5.

24:20–21 sons of Levi. The nonpriestly Levites also were divided by clan to determine their service rotation.

23:23y 1 Chr. 24:30 **23:24**z Num. 10:17, 21 aEzra 3:8 **23:25**b 1 Chr. 22:18 **23:26**c Num. 4:5, 15; 7:9 **23:27**d 2 Sam. 23:1 **23:29**e Ex. 25:30 fLev. 6:20 gLev. 2:1, 4 hLev. 2:5, 7 iLev. 19:35 **23:31**j Num. 10:10 kLev. 23:2–4 **23:32**l 2 Chr. 13:10, 11 m[Num. 1:53] nNum. 3:6–9, 38 **24:1**a Lev. 10:1–6 **24:2**b Num. 3:1–4; 26:61 **24:3**c 1 Chr. 18:16 **24:10**d Luke 1:5 **24:19**e 1 Chr. 9:25 **24:21**f 1 Chr. 23:17

Isshiah. [22]Of the Izharites, Shelomoth;* of the sons of Shelomoth, Jahath. [23]Of the sons of ᵍHebron,* Jeriah was the first,* Amariah the second, Jahaziel the third, and Jekameam the fourth. [24]Of the sons of Uzziel, Michah; of the sons of Michah, Shamir. [25]The brother of Michah, Isshiah; of the sons of Isshiah, Zechariah. [26]ʰThe sons of Merari were Mahli and Mushi; the son of Jaaziah, Beno. [27]The sons of Merari by Jaaziah were Beno, Shoham, Zaccur, and Ibri. [28]Of Mahli: Eleazar, ⁱwho had no sons. [29]Of Kish: the son of Kish, Jerahmeel.

[30]Also ʲthe sons of Mushi were Mahli, Eder, and Jerimoth. These were the sons of the Levites according to their fathers' houses.

[31]These also cast lots just as their brothers the sons of Aaron did, in the presence of King David, Zadok, Ahimelech, and the heads of the fathers' houses of the priests and Levites. The chief fathers did just as their younger brethren.

The Musicians

25 Moreover David and the captains of the army separated for the service some of the sons of ᵃAsaph, of Heman, and of Jeduthun, who should prophesy with harps, stringed instruments, and cymbals. And the number of the skilled men performing their service was: [2]Of the sons of Asaph: Zaccur, Joseph, Nethaniah, and Asharelah;* the sons of Asaph were under the direction of Asaph, who prophesied according to the order of the king. [3]Of ᵇJeduthun, the sons of Jeduthun: Gedaliah, Zeri,* Jeshaiah, Shimei, Hashabiah, and Mattithiah, six,* under the direction of their father Jeduthun, who prophesied with a harp to give thanks and to praise the LORD. [4]Of Heman, the sons of Heman: Bukkiah, Mattaniah, Uzziel,* Shebuel,* Jerimoth,* Hananiah, Hanani, Eliathah, Giddalti, Romamti-Ezer, Joshbekashah, Mallothi, Hothir, and Mahazioth. [5]All these were the sons of Heman the king's seer in the words of God, to exalt his ᶜhorn.* For God gave Heman fourteen sons and three daughters.

[6]All these were under the direction of their father for the music in the house of the LORD, with cymbals, stringed instruments, and ᵈharps, for the service of the house of God. Asaph, Jeduthun, and Heman were ᵉunder the authority of the king. [7]So the ᶠnumber of them, with their brethren who were instructed in the songs of the LORD, all who were skillful, was two hundred and eighty-eight.

[8]And they cast lots for their duty, the small as well as the great, ᵍthe teacher with the student.

[9]Now the first lot for Asaph came out for Joseph; the second for Gedaliah, him with his brethren and sons, twelve; [10]the third for Zaccur, his sons and his brethren, twelve; [11]the fourth for Jizri,* his sons and his brethren, twelve; [12]the fifth for Nethaniah, his sons and his brethren, twelve; [13]the sixth for Bukkiah, his sons and his brethren, twelve; [14]the seventh for Jesharelah,* his sons and his brethren, twelve; [15]the eighth for Jeshaiah, his sons and his brethren, twelve; [16]the ninth for Mattaniah, his sons and his brethren, twelve; [17]the tenth for Shimei, his sons and his brethren, twelve; [18]the eleventh for Azarel,* his sons and his brethren, twelve; [19]the twelfth for Hashabiah, his sons and his brethren, twelve; [20]the thirteenth for Shubael,* his sons and his brethren, twelve; [21]the fourteenth for Mattithiah, his sons and his brethren, twelve; [22]the fifteenth for Jeremoth,* his sons and his brethren, twelve; [23]the sixteenth for Hananiah, his sons and his brethren, twelve; [24]the seventeenth for Joshbekashah, his sons and his brethren, twelve; [25]the eighteenth for Hanani, his sons and his brethren, twelve; [26]the nineteenth for Mallothi, his sons and his brethren, twelve; [27]the twentieth for Eliathah, his sons and his brethren, twelve; [28]the twenty-first for Hothir, his sons and his brethren, twelve; [29]the twenty-second for Giddalti, his sons and his brethren, twelve; [30]the twenty-third for Mahazioth, his sons and his brethren, twelve; [31]the twenty-fourth for Romamti-Ezer, his sons and his brethren, twelve.

---

* **24:22** Spelled Shelomith in 23:18 • * **24:23** Supplied from 23:19 (following some Hebrew manuscripts and Septuagint manuscripts) • Supplied from 23:19 (following some Hebrew manuscripts and Septuagint manuscripts) • * **25:2** Spelled Jesharelah in verse 14 • * **25:3** Spelled Jizri in verse 11 • Shimei, appearing in one Hebrew and several Septuagint manuscripts, completes the total of six sons (compare verse 17). * **25:4** Spelled Azarel in verse 18 • Spelled Shubael in verse 20 • Spelled Jeremoth in verse 22 * **25:5** That is, to increase his power or influence * **25:11** Spelled Zeri in verse 3 • * **25:14** Spelled Asharelah in verse 2 • * **25:18** Spelled Uzziel in verse 4 • * **25:20** Spelled Shebuel in verse 4 * **25:22** Spelled Jerimoth in verse 4

25:1 *prophesy with harps, stringed instruments, and cymbals.* The role of prophet was not limited to a prediction or proclamation in words. Vocal and instrumental music could be a kind of prophetic message, usually in the form of praise (1 Sam. 10:5–6).

25:2 *according to the order of the king.* This underscored the leading role that David took in the religious life of the nation.

24:23 ᵍ 1 Chr. 23:19; 26:31   **24:26** ʰ Ex. 6:19
24:28 ⁱ 1 Chr. 23:22   **24:30** ʲ 1 Chr. 23:23   **25:1** ᵃ 1 Chr. 6:30, 33, 39, 44   **25:3** ᵇ 1 Chr. 16:41, 42   **25:5** ᶜ 1 Chr. 16:42   **25:6** ᵈ 1 Chr. 15:16 ᵉ 1 Chr. 15:19; 25:2
25:7 ᶠ 1 Chr. 23:5   **25:8** ᵍ 2 Chr. 23:13

The Gatekeepers

26 Concerning the divisions of the gatekeepers: of the Korahites, Meshelemiah the son of ªKore, of the sons of Asaph. ²And the sons of Meshelemiah *were* ᵇZechariah the firstborn, Jediael the second, Zebadiah the third, Jathniel the fourth, ³Elam the fifth, Jehohanan the sixth, Eliehoenai the seventh.

⁴Moreover the sons of ᶜObed-Edom *were* Shemaiah the firstborn, Jehozabad the second, Joah the third, Sacar the fourth, Nethanel the fifth, ⁵Ammiel the sixth, Issachar the seventh, Peulthai the eighth; for God blessed him.

⁶Also to Shemaiah his son were sons born who governed their fathers' houses, because they *were* men of great ability. ⁷The sons of Shemaiah *were* Othni, Rephael, Obed, and Elzabad, whose brothers Elihu and Semachiah *were* able men.

⁸All these *were* of the sons of Obed-Edom, they and their sons and their brethren, ᵈable men with strength for the work: sixty-two of Obed-Edom.

⁹And Meshelemiah had sons and brethren, eighteen able men.

¹⁰Also ᵉHosah, of the children of Merari, had sons: Shimri the first (for *though* he was not the firstborn, his father made him the first), ¹¹Hilkiah the second, Tebaliah the third, Zechariah the fourth; all the sons and brethren of Hosah *were* thirteen.

¹²Among these *were* the divisions of the gatekeepers, among the chief men, *having* duties just like their brethren, to serve in the house of the LORD. ¹³And they ᶠcast lots for each gate, the small as well as the great, according to their father's house. ¹⁴The lot for the East *Gate* fell to Shelemiah. Then they cast lots *for* his son Zechariah, a wise counselor, and his lot came out for the North Gate; ¹⁵to Obed-Edom the South Gate, and to his sons the storehouse.* ¹⁶To Shuppim and Hosah *the lot came out for* the West Gate, with the Shallecheth Gate on the ᵍascending highway—watchman opposite watchman. ¹⁷On the east *were* six Levites, on the north four each day, on the south four each day, and for the storehouse* two by two. ¹⁸As for the Parbar* on the west, *there were* four on the highway *and* two at the Parbar. ¹⁹These were the divisions of the gatekeepers among the sons of Korah and among the sons of Merari.

The Treasuries and Other Duties

²⁰Of the Levites, Ahijah *was* ʰover the treasuries of the house of God and over the treasuries of the ⁱdedicated things. ²¹The sons of Laadan, the descendants of the Gershonites of Laadan, heads of their fathers' *houses*, of Laadan the Gershonite: Jehieli. ²²The sons of Jehieli, Zetham and Joel his brother, *were* over the treasuries of the house of the LORD. ²³Of the ʲAmramites, the Izharites, the Hebronites, and the Uzzielites: ²⁴ᵏShebuel the son of Gershom, the son of Moses, *was* overseer of the treasuries. ²⁵And his brethren by Eliezer *were* Rehabiah his son, Jeshaiah his son, Joram his son, Zichri his son, and ˡShelomith his son.

²⁶This Shelomith and his brethren *were* over all the treasuries of the dedicated things ᵐwhich King David and the heads of fathers' *houses*, the captains over thousands and hundreds, and the captains of the army, had dedicated. ²⁷Some of the spoils won in battles they dedicated to maintain the house of the LORD. ²⁸And all that Samuel ⁿthe seer, Saul the son of Kish, Abner the son of Ner, and Joab the son of Zeruiah had dedicated, every dedicated *thing*, was under the hand of Shelomith and his brethren.

²⁹Of the Izharites, Chenaniah and his sons ᵒperformed duties as ᵖofficials and judges over Israel outside Jerusalem.

³⁰Of the Hebronites, ᵠHashabiah and his brethren, one thousand seven hundred able men, had the oversight of Israel on the west side of the Jordan for all the business of the LORD, and in the service of the king. ³¹Among the Hebronites, ʳJerijah *was* head of the Hebronites according to his genealogy of the fathers. In the fortieth year of the reign of David they were sought, and there were found among them capable men ˢat Jazer of Gilead. ³²And his brethren *were* two thousand seven hundred able men, heads of fathers' *houses*, whom King David made officials over the Reubenites, the Gadites, and the half-tribe of Manasseh, for every matter pertaining to God and the ᵗaffairs of the king.

* **26:15** Hebrew *asuppim*   * **26:17** Hebrew *asuppim*   * **26:18** Probably a court or colonnade extending west of the temple

---

26:1–32 Duty—Our duties include all of the activities required to fulfill an assigned service. We are not praised for doing these jobs, and sometimes only the Lord sees what we have done. The temple servants knew that their jobs were "for" the Lord, but they were not personally very visible among the hundreds who did similar tasks. From the gatekeepers to the guardians of the treasures, faithfulness was the moral obligation, or duty, of each officer. For us as believers, the moral obligation is the same. We are never off duty.

26:14 lot for the East Gate. The East Gate was the most important because it led straight into the main entrance of the temple.

26:1 ª Ps. 42:title   **26:2** ᵇ 1 Chr. 9:21   **26:4** ᶜ 1 Chr. 15:18, 21   **26:8** ᵈ 1 Chr. 9:13   **26:10** ᵉ 1 Chr. 16:38   **26:13** ᶠ 1 Chr. 24:5, 31; 25:8   **26:16** ᵍ 1 Kin. 10:5   **26:20** ʰ 1 Chr. 9:26   ⁱ 1 Chr. 26:22, 24, 26; 28:12   **26:23** ʲ Ex. 6:18   **26:24** ᵏ 1 Chr. 23:16   **26:25** ˡ 1 Chr. 23:18   **26:26** ᵐ 2 Sam. 8:11   **26:28** ⁿ 1 Sam. 9:9   **26:29** ᵒ Neh. 11:16   ᵖ 1 Chr. 23:4   **26:30** ᵠ 1 Chr. 27:17   **26:31** ʳ 1 Chr. 23:19   ˢ Josh. 21:39   **26:32** ᵗ 2 Chr. 19:11

The Military Divisions

27 And the children of Israel, according to their number, the heads of fathers' *houses*, the captains of thousands and hundreds and their officers, served the king in every matter of the *military* divisions. *These divisions* came in and went out month by month throughout all the months of the year, each division *having* twenty-four thousand. ²Over the first division for the first month *was* ªJashobeam the son of Zabdiel, and in his division *were* twenty-four thousand; ³*he was* of the children of Perez, and the chief of all the captains of the army for the first month. ⁴Over the division of the second month *was* Dodai* an Ahohite, and of his division Mikloth also *was* the leader; in his division *were* twenty-four thousand. ⁵The third captain of the army for the third month *was* ᵇBenaiah, the son of Jehoiada the priest, who was chief; in his division *were* twenty-four thousand. ⁶This was the Benaiah *who was* ᶜmighty *among* the thirty, and was over the thirty; in his division *was* Ammizabad his son. ⁷The fourth *captain* for the fourth month *was* ᵈAsahel the brother of Joab, and Zebadiah his son after him; in his division *were* twenty-four thousand. ⁸The fifth captain for the fifth month *was* Shamhuth* the Izrahite; in his division were twenty-four thousand. ⁹The sixth *captain* for the sixth month *was* ᵉIra the son of Ikkesh the Tekoite; in his division *were* twenty-four thousand. ¹⁰The seventh *captain* for the seventh month *was* ᶠHelez the Pelonite, of the children of Ephraim; in his division *were* twenty-four thousand. ¹¹The eighth *captain* for the eighth month *was* ᵍSibbechai the Hushathite, of the Zarhites; in his division *were* twenty-four thousand. ¹²The ninth *captain* for the ninth month *was* ʰAbiezer the Anathothite, of the Benjamites; in his division *were* twenty-four thousand. ¹³The tenth *captain* for the tenth month *was* ⁱMaharai the Netophathite, of the Zarhites; in his division *were* twenty-four thousand. ¹⁴The eleventh *captain* for the eleventh

month *was* ʲBenaiah the Pirathonite, of the children of Ephraim; in his division *were* twenty-four thousand. ¹⁵The twelfth *captain* for the twelfth month *was* Heldai* the Netophathite, of Othniel; in his division *were* twenty-four thousand.

Leaders of Tribes

¹⁶Furthermore, over the tribes of Israel: the officer over the Reubenites *was* Eliezer the son of Zichri; over the Simeonites, Shephatiah the son of Maachah; ¹⁷over the Levites, ᵏHashabiah the son of Kemuel; over the Aaronites, Zadok; ¹⁸over Judah, ˡElihu, *one* of David's brothers; over Issachar, Omri the son of Michael; ¹⁹over Zebulun, Ishmaiah the son of Obadiah; over Naphtali, Jerimoth the son of Azriel; ²⁰over the children of Ephraim, Hoshea the son of Azaziah; over the half-tribe of Manasseh, Joel the son of Pedaiah; ²¹over the half-*tribe* of Manasseh in Gilead, Iddo the son of Zechariah; over Benjamin, Jaasiel the son of Abner; ²²over Dan, Azarel the son of Jeroham. These *were* the leaders of the tribes of Israel.

²³But David did not take the number of those twenty years old and under, because ᵐthe LORD had said He would multiply Israel like the ⁿstars of the heavens. ²⁴Joab the son of Zeruiah began a census, but he did not finish, for ᵒwrath came upon Israel because of this census; nor was the number recorded in the account of the chronicles of King David.

Other State Officials

²⁵And Azmaveth the son of Adiel *was* over the king's treasuries; and Jehonathan the son of Uzziah was over the storehouses in the field, in the cities, in the villages, and in the fortresses. ²⁶Ezri the son of Chelub was over those who did the work of the field for tilling the ground. ²⁷And

---

* **27:4** Hebrew *Dodai,* usually spelled *Dodo* (compare 2 Samuel 23:9)   * **27:8** Spelled *Shammoth* in 11:27 and *Shammah* in 2 Samuel 23:11   * **27:15** Spelled *Heled* in 11:30 and *Heleb* in 2 Samuel 23:29

27:1 heads of fathers' houses, the captains. Apparently a professional standing army is being described here, one that was divided into twelve corps.
27:2 Jashobeam. A connection can be made here to the list of David's mighty men, which is also headed by Jashobeam (11:11–12). He was one of "the three," which meant that he was regarded as unusually heroic.
27:4 Dodai. David's son Eleazar was the second of the mighty men included in the first trio along with Jashobeam (11:12).
27:5 Benaiah. As the son of a priest, Benaiah was from the tribe of Levi. In the earlier list of mighty men he was celebrated for killing a lion and a gigantic Egyptian (11:22–23). Because of this kind of courage, he was honored among the thirty mighty men, though he was not one of "the three" (11:24). Later he was named as commander of the entire Israelite army (2 Kin. 4:4).

27:7 Asahel. David's nephew Asahel (2:15–16) was among the thirty mighty men, but did not achieve a position among "the three" (11:26).
27:11–12 Sibbechai . . . Abiezer. These two men were also members of the elite thirty mighty men. (11:28–29).
27:18 Elihu. This brother of David is usually called Eliab (1 Sam. 16:6).

27:2 ª 1 Chr. 11:11   **27:5** ᵇ 1 Chr. 18:17   **27:6** ᶜ 2 Sam. 23:20–23   **27:7** ᵈ 1 Chr. 11:26   **27:9** ᵉ 1 Chr. 11:28   **27:10** ᶠ 1 Chr. 11:27   **27:11** ᵍ 2 Sam. 21:18   **27:12** ʰ 1 Chr. 11:28   **27:13** ⁱ 1 Chr. 11:30   **27:14** ʲ 1 Chr. 11:31   **27:17** ᵏ 1 Chr. 26:30   **27:18** ˡ 1 Sam. 16:6   **27:23** ᵐ [Deut. 6:3]   ⁿ Gen. 15:5; 22:17; 26:4   **27:24** ᵒ 1 Chr. 21:1–7

Shimei the Ramathite *was* over the vineyards, and Zabdi the Shiphmite was over the produce of the vineyards for the supply of wine. ²⁸Baal-Hanan the Gederite *was* over the olive trees and the sycamore trees that *were* in the lowlands, and Joash *was* over the store of oil. ²⁹And Shitrai the Sharonite *was* over the herds that fed in Sharon, and Shaphat the son of Adlai was over the herds *that were* in the valleys. ³⁰Obil the Ishmaelite *was* over the camels, Jehdeiah the Meronothite *was* over the donkeys, ³¹and Jaziz the ᵖHagrite *was* over the flocks. All these *were* the officials over King David's property.

³²Also Jehonathan, David's uncle, *was* a counselor, a wise man, and a scribe; and Jehiel the son of Hachmoni *was* with the king's sons. ³³ᵠAhithophel *was* the king's counselor, and ʳHushai the Archite *was* the king's companion. ³⁴After Ahithophel *was* Jehoiada the son of Benaiah, then ˢAbiathar. And the general of the king's army *was* ᵗJoab.

Solomon Instructed to Build the Temple

28 Now David assembled at Jerusalem all ᵃthe leaders of Israel: the officers of the tribes and ᵇthe captains of the divisions who served the king, the captains over thousands and captains over hundreds, and ᶜthe stewards over all the substance and possessions of the king and of his sons, with the officials, the valiant men, and all ᵈthe mighty men of valor.

²Then King David rose to his feet and said, "Hear me, my brethren and my people: ᵉI had it in my heart to build a house of rest for the ark of the covenant of the LORD, and for ᶠthe footstool of our God, and had made preparations to build it. ³But God said to me, ᵍ'You shall not build a house for My name, because you *have been* a man of war and have shed ʰblood.' ⁴However the LORD God of Israel ⁱchose me above all the house of my father to be king over Israel forever, for He has chosen ʲJudah *to be* the ruler. And of the house of Judah, ᵏthe house of my father, and ˡamong the sons of my father, He was pleased with me to make *me* king over all Israel. ⁵ᵐAnd of all my sons (for the LORD has given me many sons) ⁿHe has chosen my son Solomon to sit on the throne of the kingdom of the LORD over Israel. ⁶Now He said to me, 'It is ᵒyour son Solomon *who* shall build My house and My courts; for I have chosen him *to be* My son, and I will be his Father. ⁷Moreover I will establish his kingdom forever, ᵖif he is steadfast to observe My commandments and My judgments, as it is this day.' ⁸Now therefore, in the sight of all Israel, the assembly of the LORD, and in the hearing of our God, be careful to seek out all the commandments of the LORD your God, that you may possess this good land, and leave *it* as an inheritance for your children after you forever.

⁹"As for you, my son Solomon, ᵠknow the

27:29 Sharonite. A fertile plain between Israelite and Philistine territory, Sharon was ideal for grazing cattle and sheep. It is appropriate that someone from Sharon, who knew the land and all its seasonal changes, should be in charge of the livestock.
27:30 Ishmaelite. As inhabitants of the desert, the Ishmaelites were at home with the breeding and use of camels.
28:2 footstool. The word "footstool" is a metaphor describing either the ark of the covenant or the tabernacle as the earthly base of God's activity. The words make a little picture of God on His throne in heaven, resting His feet on the earth.
28:4–6 Government of Israel—The government of Israel was under two important headings; the laws, and the leaders. *The laws*—The "commandments," especially the Ten Commandments, revealed God's holiness and set up a divine standard of righteousness for the people to follow (Ex. 20:1–17). The judgments governed the social life of the people (Ex. 21). The ordinances included the sacrifices that showed that blood must be shed for the forgiveness of sins (Lev. 1–17). *The leaders*—At first Moses was the primary leader; then he was replaced by Joshua. After Joshua's death the nation was governed for many years by judges who were usually raised up by God to oppose a specific enemy. Finally, at the people's request, God granted them a king, thus establishing the monarchy (1 Sam. 8:6–17).

Through most of Israel's history four leadership roles can be seen:

1. *The king* was the Lord's representative who ruled the people, but only as the Lord's servant. He led in war (1 Sam. 8:20) and made judicial decisions (2 Sam. 15:2), but could not make law, since he himself was under the law (Deut. 17:14–20).
2. *The priest* taught the Lord's laws and officiated at the offering of sacrifices (Lev. 1:5).
3. *The prophet* was the man of God who spoke for God and gave divine pronouncements for the present or the future.
4. *The wise man* produced literary works stressing practical wisdom (Prov. 1:1), taught discipline of character to the young (Prov. 22:17), and gave counsel to the king (2 Sam. 16:20).

28:6 be My son . . . I will be his Father. This remarkable statement not only shows that the Davidic kings enjoyed unparalleled access to the Lord as His adopted sons (17:3; Ps. 2:7), but it anticipates the absolute sonship of the Son of David, Jesus Christ (Acts 13:33; Heb. 1:5).

27:31 ᵖ 1 Chr. 5:10   **27:33** ᵠ 2 Sam. 15:12   ʳ 2 Sam. 15:32–37   **27:34** ˢ 1 Kin. 1:7   ᵗ 1 Chr. 11:6   **28:1** ᵃ 1 Chr. 27:16   ᵇ 1 Chr. 27:1, 2   ᶜ 1 Chr. 27:25   ᵈ 1 Chr. 11:10–47   **28:2** ᵉ 2 Sam. 7:2   ᶠ Ps. 99:5; 132:7   **28:3** ᵍ 2 Sam. 7:5, 13   ʰ [1 Chr. 17:4; 22:8]   **28:4** ⁱ 1 Sam. 16:6–13   ʲ Gen. 49:8–10   ᵏ 1 Sam. 16:1   ˡ 1 Sam. 13:14; 16:12, 13   **28:5** ᵐ 1 Chr. 3:1–9; 14:3–7; 23:1   ⁿ 1 Chr. 22:9; 29:1   **28:6** ᵒ 2 Sam. 7:13, 14   **28:7** ᵖ 1 Chr. 22:13   **28:9** ᵠ [John 17:3]

God of your father, and serve Him ʳwith a loyal heart and with a willing mind; for ˢthe LORD searches all hearts and understands all the intent of the thoughts. ᵗIf you seek Him, He will be found by you; but if you forsake Him, He will ᵘcast you off forever. ¹⁰Consider now, ᵛfor the LORD has chosen you to build a house for the sanctuary; be strong, and do it."

¹¹Then David gave his son Solomon ʷthe plans for the vestibule, its houses, its treasuries, its upper chambers, its inner chambers, and the place of the mercy seat; ¹²and the ˣplans for all that he had by the Spirit, of the courts of the house of the LORD, of all the chambers all around, ʸof the treasuries of the house of God, and of the treasuries for the dedicated things; ¹³also for the division of the priests and the ᶻLevites, for all the work of the service of the house of the LORD, and for all the articles of service in the house of the LORD. ¹⁴He gave gold by weight for things of gold, for all articles used in every kind of service; also silver for all articles of silver by weight, for all articles used in every kind of service; ¹⁵the weight for the ᵃlampstands of gold, and their lamps of gold, by weight for each lampstand and its lamps; for the lampstands of silver by weight, for the lampstand and its lamps, according to the use of each lampstand. ¹⁶And by weight he gave gold for the tables of the showbread, for each ᵇtable, and silver for the tables of silver; ¹⁷also pure gold for the forks, the basins, the pitchers of pure gold, and the golden bowls—he gave gold by weight for every bowl; and for the silver bowls, silver by weight for every bowl; ¹⁸and refined gold by weight for the ᶜaltar of incense, and for the construction of the chariot, that is, the gold ᵈcherubim that spread their wings and overshadowed the ark of the covenant of the LORD. ¹⁹"All this," said David, ᵉ"the LORD made me understand in writing, by His hand upon me, all the works of these plans."

²⁰And David said to his son Solomon, ᶠ"Be strong and of good courage, and do it;

do not fear nor be dismayed, for the LORD God—my God—will be with you. ᵍHe will not leave you nor forsake you, until you have finished all the work for the service of the house of the LORD. ²¹Here are ʰthe divisions of the priests and the Levites for all the service of the house of God; and ⁱevery willing craftsman will be with you for all manner of workmanship, for every kind of service; also the leaders and all the people will be completely at your command."

Offerings for Building the Temple

29 Furthermore King David said to all the assembly: "My son Solomon, whom alone God has ᵃchosen, is ᵇyoung and inexperienced; and the work is great, because the temple* is not for man but for the LORD God. ²Now for the house of my God I have prepared with all my might: gold for things to be made of gold, silver for things of silver, bronze for things of bronze, iron for things of iron, wood for things of wood, ᶜonyx stones, stones to be set, glistening stones of various colors, all kinds of precious stones, and marble slabs in abundance. ³Moreover, because I have set my affection on the house of my God, I have given to the house of my God, over and above all that I have prepared for the holy house, my own special treasure of gold and silver: ⁴three thousand talents of gold, of the gold of ᵈOphir, and seven thousand talents of refined silver, to overlay the walls of the houses; ⁵the gold for things of gold and the silver for things of silver, and for all kinds of work to be done by the hands of craftsmen. Who then is ᵉwilling to consecrate himself this day to the LORD?"

⁶Then ᶠthe leaders of the fathers' houses, leaders of the tribes of Israel, the captains of thousands and of hundreds, with ᵍthe officers over the king's work, ʰoffered willingly. ⁷They gave for the work of the house of God five thousand talents and ten

---

* **29:1** Literally palace

28:19 by His hand upon me. The plans for the temple were from God, just as the plans of the tabernacle of Moses were. This was extremely important, for God had stressed the necessity of making the tabernacle exactly according to His instructions (Ex. 38:22; 39:5–7,42–43). The Israelites would need to know that this permanent building was God's plan, not just David's.

28:20 Be strong and of good courage. David's charge to Solomon is very similar to the charge given to Joshua when Moses handed over the leadership of Israel to him (Josh. 1:6–9).

29:4 Generosity—It is extremely difficult to assign a modern monetary value to ancient goods and services, but we might compare David's gift for the temple to approximately one billion, eight hundred thousand dollars in gold, and eighty-four million in silver. This kind of personal wealth is astounding, but

for David, its value was significant only as provision for the temple for the Lord. He never lost sight of the fact that both honor and riches come from God. They are His to give, His to use, and His to remove.

29:7 five thousand talents. This represents about 190 tons of gold. **ten thousand darics.** This is about 185 pounds of gold. **eighteen thousand talents.**

28:9 ʳ 2 Kin. 20:3 ˢ [1 Sam. 16:7] ᵗ 2 Chr. 15:2 ᵘ Deut. 31:17 **28:10** ᵛ 1 Chr. 22:13; 28:6 **28:11** ʷ 1 Chr. 28:19 **28:12** ˣ Heb. 8:5 ʸ 1 Chr. 26:20, 28 **28:13** ᶻ 1 Chr. 23:6 **28:15** ᵃ Ex. 25:31–39 **28:16** ᵇ 1 Kin. 7:48 **28:18** ᶜ Ex. 30:1–10 ᵈ Ex. 25:18–22 **28:19** ᵉ Ex. 25:40 **28:20** ᶠ 1 Chr. 22:13 ᵍ Josh. 1:5 **28:21** ʰ 1 Chr. 24–26 ⁱ Ex. 35:25–35; 36:1, 2 **29:1** ᵃ 1 Chr. 28:5 ᵇ 1 Kin. 3:7 **29:2** ᶜ Is. 54:11, 12 **29:4** ᵈ 1 Kin. 9:28 **29:5** ᵉ [2 Cor. 8:5, 12] **29:6** ᶠ 1 Chr. 27:1; 28:1 ᵍ 1 Chr. 27:25–31 ʰ Ex. 35:21–35

thousand darics of gold, ten thousand talents of silver, eighteen thousand talents of bronze, and one hundred thousand talents of iron. ⁸And whoever had *precious* stones gave *them* to the treasury of the house of the LORD, into the hand of ʲJehiel* the Gershonite. ⁹Then the people rejoiced, for they had offered willingly, because with a loyal heart they had ʲoffered willingly to the LORD; and King David also rejoiced greatly.

David's Praise to God

¹⁰Therefore David blessed the LORD before all the assembly; and David said:

"Blessed are You, LORD God of
    Israel, our Father, forever and
    ever.
¹¹ ᵏYours, O LORD, *is* the greatness,
    The power and the glory,
    The victory and the majesty;
    For all *that is* in heaven and in earth
        is Yours;
    Yours *is* the kingdom, O LORD,
    And You are exalted as head
        over all.
¹² ˡBoth riches and honor *come* from
        You,
    And You reign over all.
    In Your hand *is* power and might;
    In Your hand *it is* to make great
    And to give strength to all.
¹³ "Now therefore, our God,
    We thank You
    And praise Your glorious name.
¹⁴ But who *am* I, and who *are* my people,
    That we should be able to offer so
        willingly as this?
    For all things *come* from You,
    And of Your own we have given You.
¹⁵ For ᵐwe *are* aliens and pilgrims before
        You,
    As *were* all our fathers;

ⁿOur days on earth *are* as a
    shadow,
    And without hope.

¹⁶"O LORD our God, all this abundance that we have prepared to build You a house for Your holy name is from Your hand, and *is* all Your own. ¹⁷I know also, my God, that You ᵒtest the heart and ᵖhave pleasure in uprightness. As for me, in the uprightness of my heart I have willingly offered all these *things;* and now with joy I have seen Your people, who are present here to offer willingly to You. ¹⁸O LORD God of Abraham, Isaac, and Israel, our fathers, keep this forever in the intent of the thoughts of the heart of Your people, and fix their heart toward You. ¹⁹And ᵍgive my son Solomon a loyal heart to keep Your commandments and Your testimonies and Your statutes, to do all *these things*, and to build the temple* for which ʳI have made provision.

²⁰Then David said to all the assembly, "Now bless the LORD your God." So all the assembly blessed the LORD God of their fathers, and bowed their heads and prostrated themselves before the LORD and the king.

Solomon Anointed King

²¹And they made sacrifices to the LORD and offered burnt offerings to the LORD on the next day: a thousand bulls, a thousand rams, a thousand lambs, with their drink offerings, and ˢsacrifices in abundance for all Israel. ²²So they ate and drank before the LORD with great gladness on that day. And they made Solomon the son of David king the second time, and ᵗanointed *him* before the LORD *to be* the leader, and Zadok to

---

* **29:8** Possibly the same as *Jehieli* (compare 26:21, 22)   * **29:19** Literally *palace*

This was equivalent to about 675 tons. **one hundred thousand talents.** This was approximately 3,750 tons.
29:10 blessed the LORD. David modeled before the people the worship of the living God. He started with praise for God's goodness, greatness, and glory, and then acknowledged his place under the care and blessing of God.
29:14–15 All That We Have—Even though David was king and could accumulate whatever he wanted, he was more conscious of the need to give, particularly to God. How can anyone strive to accumulate, if you know in the long run that none of what you've gathered is really yours? Generosity is the natural outcome of a right perspective on possessions.
    Verse 15 points to two other elements that indicate a basis for generosity. David understood where his real home was, namely with God. If a king regards himself as an alien in his own land, how much more should we? Somehow he resisted the temptation to regard the land as his to do with as he wished. He understood the brevity of life. Why spend time

accumulating when we can't take it with us? Living with this perspective allows us to be transparent before God. We can be in sync with God because we're keeping nothing from Him. What we have has value only as it furthers the kingdom, and God is quite capable of supplying everything we need to be able to live.
    It also means we're functioning clearly in the context of the biblical mandate of stewardship. We're here to have dominion (Gen. 1:28) but with the end that God is honored by what we do.
29:18 God of Abraham, Isaac, and Israel. These familiar words identify the Israelites with the promises of God to their forefathers, and to the God of those promises.
29:22 king the second time. This refers to the ratification of Solomon's kingship (see note at 23:1).

29:8 ʲ 1 Chr. 23:8   **29:9** ʲ 2 Cor. 9:7   **29:11** ᵏ 1 Tim. 1:17
29:12 ˡ Rom. 11:36   **29:15** ᵐ Heb. 11:13, 14 ⁿ Job 14:2
29:17 ᵒ [1 Chr. 28:9] ᵖ Prov. 11:20   **29:19** ᵍ [1 Chr. 28:9]
ʳ 1 Chr. 29:1, 2   **29:21** ˢ 1 Kin. 8:62, 63   **29:22** ᵗ 1 Kin.
1:32–35, 39

be priest. 23Then Solomon sat on the throne of the LORD as king instead of David his father, and prospered; and all Israel obeyed him. 24All the leaders and the mighty men, and also all the sons of King David, usubmitted themselves to King Solomon. 25So the LORD exalted Solomon exceedingly in the sight of all Israel, and vbestowed on him *such* royal majesty as had not been on any king before him in Israel.

The Close of David's Reign

26Thus David the son of Jesse reigned over all Israel. 27wAnd the period that he reigned over Israel *was* forty years; xseven years he reigned in Hebron, and thirty-three *years* he reigned in Jerusalem. 28So he ydied in a good old age, zfull of days and riches and honor; and Solomon his son reigned in his place. 29Now the acts of King David, first and last, indeed they *are* written in the book of Samuel the seer, in the book of Nathan the prophet, and in the book of Gad the seer, 30with all his reign and his might, aand the events that happened to him, to Israel, and to all the kingdoms of the lands.

29:23 *throne of the LORD.* The position of king may have passed from David to Solomon, but the throne was the Lord's. Eventually Jesus the Son of David and the Son of God would sit on that throne and reign forever (Luke 1:32).

29:24 u Eccl. 8:2   **29:25** v 1 Kin. 3:13   **29:27** w 1 Kin. 2:11   x 2 Sam. 5:5   **29:28** y Gen. 25:8   z 1 Chr. 23:1 **29:30** a Dan. 2:21; 4:23, 25

THE SECOND BOOK OF THE
CHRONICLES

▶ **AUTHOR:** The sources of 1 and 2 Chronicles include multiple official and prophetic records. In addition to these, the author-compiler had access to genealogical lists and documents, such as the message and letters of Sennacherib (2 Chr. 32:10–17). It seems likely that Ezra was the author as Jewish tradition suggests.

▶ **TIME:** c. 991–538 B.C.   ▶ **KEY VERSE:** 2 Chr. 7:14

▶ **THEME:** Second Chronicles begins with Solomon's reign and ends with the fall of Jerusalem. It covers more extensively the details involved in the building and dedication of the temple. The kings of Judah are detailed down through the last king, Zedekiah, who is exiled to Babylon in 587 B.C. It largely ignores what happens in the northern kingdom after the split into two nations.

Solomon Requests Wisdom

1 Now ªSolomon the son of David was strengthened in his kingdom, and ᵇthe LORD his God *was* with him and ᶜexalted him exceedingly.

²And Solomon spoke to all Israel, to ᵈthe captains of thousands and of hundreds, to the judges, and to every leader in all Israel, the heads of the fathers' *houses.* ³Then Solomon, and all the assembly with him, went to the high place that *was* at ᵉGibeon; for the tabernacle of meeting with God was there, which Moses the servant of the LORD had ᶠmade in the wilderness. ⁴ᵍBut David had brought up the ark of God from Kirjath Jearim to *the place* David had prepared for it, for he had pitched a tent for it at Jerusalem. ⁵Now ʰthe bronze altar that ⁱBezalel the son of Uri, the son of Hur, had made, he put* before the tabernacle of the LORD; Solomon and the assembly sought Him *there.* ⁶And Solomon went up there to the bronze altar before the LORD, which *was* at the tabernacle of meeting, and ʲoffered a thousand burnt offerings on it.

⁷ᵏOn that night God appeared to Solomon, and said to him, "Ask! What shall I give you?"

⁸And Solomon said to God: "You have shown great ˡmercy to David my father, and have made me ᵐking in his place. ⁹Now, O LORD God, let Your promise to David my father be established, ⁿfor You have made me king over a people like the ᵒdust of the earth in multitude. ¹⁰ᵖNow give me wisdom and knowledge, that I may ᵍgo out and come in before this people; for who can judge this great people of Yours?"

¹¹ʳThen God said to Solomon: "Because this was in your heart, and you have not asked riches or wealth or honor or the life of your enemies, nor have you asked long life—but have asked wisdom and knowledge for yourself, that you may judge My people over whom I have made you king— ¹²wisdom and knowledge *are* granted to you; and I will give you riches and wealth and honor, such as ˢnone of the kings have

* **1:5** Some authorities read *it was there.*

1:3 high place. In the Old Testament the high places were usually associated with pagan worship (Num. 22:41). The Israelites were specifically charged to destroy these places of worship so that they would not become a snare and lead them into idol worship (Num. 33:53; Deut. 33:59). Nevertheless, Israelites often chose the high places to worship (1 Sam. 9:12). The high place at Gibeon was the location of the Mosaic tabernacle and the great bronze altar throughout David's reign (see note at 1 Kin. 14:23).
1:10 go out and come in. This figure of speech refers to the totality of Solomon's life. As king he would lead by example as well as by edict.
1:11–12 Wisdom—There's significance here in what Solomon didn't ask for. He didn't ask for honor, money, a long life, or the death of his enemies. He

didn't ask for the things that would be on the top of most people's lists. He didn't ask for what would make life comfortable and easy. He asked for what would make life good. He asked for wisdom with an eye toward how he would rule, knowing that the quality of his reign largely depended on the quality of his judgments in dealing with people and issues. His priority was his service to others rather than doing

1:1 ª 1 Kin. 2:46 ᵇ Gen. 39:2 ᶜ 1 Chr. 29:25 **1:2** ᵈ 1 Chr. 27:1–34 **1:3** ᵉ 1 Kin. 3:4 ᶠ Ex. 25–27; 35:4—36:38 **1:4** ᵍ 2 Sam. 6:2–17 **1:5** ʰ Ex. 27:1, 2; 38:1, 2 ⁱ Ex. 31:2 **1:6** ʲ 1 Kin. 3:4 **1:7** ᵏ 1 Kin. 3:5–14; 9:2 **1:8** ˡ Ps. 18:50 ᵐ 1 Chr. 28:5 **1:9** ⁿ 2 Sam. 7:8–16 ᵒ Gen. 13:16 **1:10** ᵖ 1 Kin. 3:9 ᵍ Deut. 31:2 **1:11** ʳ 1 Kin. 3:11–13 **1:12** ˢ 2 Chr. 9:22

had who *were* before you, nor shall any after you have the like."

Solomon's Military and Economic Power

¹³So Solomon came to Jerusalem from the high place that *was* at Gibeon, from before the tabernacle of meeting, and reigned over Israel. ¹⁴ᵗAnd Solomon gathered chariots and horsemen; he had one thousand four hundred chariots and twelve thousand horsemen, whom he stationed in the chariot cities and with the king in Jerusalem. ¹⁵ᵘAlso the king made silver and gold as common in Jerusalem as stones, and he made cedars as abundant as the sycamores which *are* in the lowland. ¹⁶ᵛAnd Solomon had horses imported from Egypt and Keveh; the king's merchants bought them in Keveh at the *current* price. ¹⁷They also acquired and imported from Egypt a chariot for six hundred *shekels* of silver, and a horse for one hundred and fifty; thus, through their agents,* they exported them to all the kings of the Hittites and the kings of Syria.

Solomon Prepares to Build the Temple

2 Then Solomon ᵃdetermined to build a temple for the name of the LORD, and a royal house for himself. ²ᵇSolomon selected seventy thousand men to bear burdens, eighty thousand to quarry *stone* in the mountains, and three thousand six hundred to oversee them.

³Then Solomon sent to Hiram* king of Tyre, saying:

ᶜAs you have dealt with David my father, and sent him cedars to build himself a house to dwell in, *so deal with me.* ⁴Behold, ᵈI am building a temple for the name of the LORD my God, to dedicate *it* to Him, ᵉto burn before Him sweet incense, for ᶠthe continual showbread, for ᵍthe burnt offerings morning and evening, on the ʰSabbaths, on the New Moons, and on the set feasts of the LORD our God. This *is an ordinance* forever to Israel.

⁵ And the temple which I build *will be* great, for ⁱour God is greater than all gods. ⁶ʲBut who is able to build Him a temple, since heaven and the heaven of heavens cannot contain Him? Who *am* I then, that I should build Him a temple, except to burn sacrifice before Him?

⁷ Therefore send me at once a man skillful to work in gold and silver, in bronze and iron, in purple and crimson and blue, who has skill to engrave with the skillful men who are with me in Judah and Jerusalem, ᵏwhom David my father provided. ⁸ˡAlso send me cedar and cypress and algum logs from Lebanon, for I know that your servants have skill to cut timber in Lebanon; and indeed my servants *will be* with your servants, ⁹to prepare timber for me in abundance, for the temple which I am about to build *shall be* great and wonderful.

¹⁰ ᵐAnd indeed I will give to your servants, the woodsmen who cut timber,

* 1:17 Literally *by their hands*   * 2:3 Hebrew *Huram* (compare 1 Kings 5:1)

---

what was supposedly best for his personal well-being.
What would be an equivalent today? A corporate executive wanting to know how to make his company contribute for the good of society as opposed to focusing exclusively on profit? A manager being more interested in seeing his staff happy and functioning well rather than getting ahead himself? A father making personal sacrifices for the health of his family?

1:14 *chariots.* A chariot force of 1,400 units was a significant achievement for Israel, a nation located primarily in hilly terrain where chariots were of limited value. ***horsemen.*** Moses warned the future kings not to multiply horses for themselves, nor were they to send people back to Egypt to multiply horses (Deut. 17:16). The number of horses that Solomon had for his 1,400 chariots was probably about 4,000.

1:17 *six hundred shekels of silver.* It is often difficult to assign a price in modern currency to the goods and services of the ancient world. This verse suggests that a chariot cost as much as four horses. ***exported.*** Solomon had a thriving business in horses and chariots. Because Israel was on the route between Asia and Africa, such goods would go through Israel and become subject to Solomon's heavy import and export taxes.

2:3 *Hiram the king of Tyre.* Also called Huram, he

was the same Phoenician ruler who had provided men and materials for David's palace.

2:5 *our God is greater than all gods.* Solomon's statement means that God is the only true God, not that He is the greatest among many lesser ones. All pagan "gods" are not gods at all (1 Cor. 8:4–5; 10:20).

2:6 Heaven—God is omnipresent. This means that He is everywhere present at all times. There are no bounds or limitations to His presence. But in a special sense, God does have a center for His existence. This is described by Solomon as the "heaven of heavens," an expression also used by Moses (Deut. 10:14). The "LORD of hosts" (1 Sam. 1:3) suggests that the dwelling of God is populated by angels and other heavenly beings. It is here that His throne is situated (Is. 6:1). In this sphere His will is done perfectly (Dan. 4:35).

2:10 *wheat . . . barley.* The amount of wheat and barley was about 125,000 bushels, or 3,750 tons of each. ***wine . . . oil.*** Twenty thousand baths of wine and oil was approximately 115,000 gallons of each.

1:14 ᵗ1 Kin. 10:26   **1:15** ᵘ2 Chr. 9:27   **1:16** ᵛ1 Kin. 10:28; 22:36   **2:1** ᵃ1 Kin. 5:5   **2:2** ᵇ2 Chr. 2:18   **2:3** ᶜ1 Chr. 14:1   **2:4** ᵈ2 Chr. 2:1 ᵉEx. 30:7 ᶠEx. 25:30 ᵍEx. 29:38–42 ʰNum. 28:3, 9–11   **2:5** ⁱPs. 135:5   **2:6** ʲ1 Kin. 8:27   **2:7** ᵏ1 Chr. 22:15   **2:8** ˡ1 Kin. 5:6   **2:10** ᵐ1 Kin. 5:11

twenty thousand kors of ground wheat, twenty thousand kors of barley, twenty thousand baths of wine, and twenty thousand baths of oil.

[11]Then Hiram king of Tyre answered in writing, which he sent to Solomon:

[n]Because the LORD loves His people, He has made you king over them.

[12]Hiram* also said:

[o]Blessed be the LORD God of Israel, [p]who made heaven and earth, for He has given King David a wise son, endowed with prudence and understanding, who will build a temple for the LORD and a royal house for himself!

[13] And now I have sent a skillful man, endowed with understanding, Huram* my master* craftsman [14a](the son of a woman of the daughters of Dan, and his father was a man of Tyre), skilled to work in gold and silver, bronze and iron, stone and wood, purple and blue, fine linen and crimson, and to make any engraving and to accomplish any plan which may be given to him, with your skillful men and with the skillful men of my lord David your father.

[15] Now therefore, the wheat, the barley, the oil, and the wine which [r]my lord has spoken of, let him send to his servants. [16s]And we will cut wood from Lebanon, as much as you need; we will bring it to you in rafts by sea to Joppa, and you will carry it up to Jerusalem.

[17t]Then Solomon numbered all the aliens who were in the land of Israel, after the census in which [u]David his father had numbered them; and there were found to be one hundred and fifty-three thousand six hundred. [18]And he made [v]seventy thousand of them bearers of burdens, eighty thousand stonecutters in the mountain,

and three thousand six hundred overseers to make the people work.

Solomon Builds the Temple

3 Now [a]Solomon began to build the house of the LORD at [b]Jerusalem on Mount Moriah, where the LORD* had appeared to his father David, at the place that David had prepared on the threshing floor of [c]Ornan* the Jebusite. [2]And he began to build on the second day of the second month in the fourth year of his reign.

[3]This is the foundation [d]which Solomon laid for building the house of God: The length was sixty cubits (by cubits according to the former measure) and the width twenty cubits. [4]And the [e]vestibule that was in front of the sanctuary* was twenty cubits long across the width of the house, and the height was one hundred and* twenty. He overlaid the inside with pure gold. [5f]The larger room* he [g]paneled with cypress which he overlaid with fine gold, and he carved palm trees and chainwork on it. [6]And he decorated the house with precious stones for beauty, and the gold was gold from Parvaim. [7]He also overlaid the house—the beams and doorposts, its walls and doors—with gold; and he carved cherubim on the walls.

[8]And he made the [h]Most Holy Place. Its length was according to the width of the house, twenty cubits, and its width twenty cubits. He overlaid it with six hundred

---

* **2:12** Hebrew Huram (compare 1 Kings 5:1)
* **2:13** Spelled Hiram in 1 Kings 7:13 • Literally father (compare 1 Kings 7:13, 14)   * **3:1** Literally He, following Masoretic Text and Vulgate; Septuagint reads the LORD; Targum reads the Angel of the LORD. • Spelled Araunah in 2 Samuel 24:16ff
* **3:4** The main room of the temple; elsewhere called the holy place (compare 1 Kings 6:3) • Following Masoretic Text, Septuagint, and Vulgate; Arabic, some manuscripts of the Septuagint, and Syriac omit one hundred and.   * **3:5** Literally house

---

2:12 Prudence—The wisdom and generosity of King Hiram toward Solomon showed him to be a prudent king. He wanted things to go well for Solomon because he liked and respected his father David, and good neighbors created stability for both nations.

2:14 woman of the daughters of Dan. His mother was an Israelite from the tribe of Dan.

3:1 Mount Moriah. This was the mountain where Abraham brought his son Isaac to sacrifice him (Gen. 22) and where the Lord provided a ram instead. It was suitable that this place where Abraham showed such incredible obedience should be the site of the temple that dealt with the issues of sacrifice and sin. **threshing floor of Ornan.** It was here that David saw the angel of death and prayed for the people (2 Sam. 24).

3:2 second day of the second month. The second month fell in our month of April.

3:3 cubits according to the former measure. The Israelites had two standard cubits, one about 17 inches and the other about 20 inches. The temple

was probably made on the cubit that measured a little over 17 inches, which means that its foundation was approximately 90 feet long and 30 feet wide. The tabernacle that Moses made in the wilderness was about 45 feet long and 15 feet wide (Ex. 26:15–37). More details of the temple are in 1 Kings 5–7.

3:5 larger room. This room was the holy place, or sanctuary (1 Kin. 6:17).

3:8 Most Holy Place. The "holy of holies," or Most Holy Place, was the inner sanctuary where the ark of the covenant was kept. This room was cubical, 30 feet on a side. **six hundred talents.** The room was overlaid with about 23 tons of gold.

2:11 [n] 2 Chr. 9:8   **2:12** [o] 1 Kin. 5:7   [p] Rev. 10:6
2:14 [q] 1 Kin. 7:13, 14   **2:15** [r] 2 Chr. 2:10   **2:16** [s] 1 Kin. 5:8, 9   **2:17** [t] 1 Kin. 5:13; 2 Chr. 8:7, 8   [u] 1 Chr. 22:2
2:18 [v] 2 Chr. 2:2   **3:1** [a] 1 Kin. 6:1   [b] Gen. 22:2–14
[c] 1 Chr. 21:18; 22:1   **3:3** [d] 1 Kin. 6:2   **3:4** [e] 1 Kin. 6:3
3:5 [f] 1 Kin. 6:17   [g] 1 Kin. 6:15   **3:8** [h] Ex. 26:33

talents of fine gold. 9The weight of the nails *was* fifty shekels of gold; and he overlaid the upper *i*area with gold. 10*j*In the Most Holy Place he made two cherubim, fashioned by carving, and overlaid them with gold. 11The wings of the cherubim *were* twenty cubits in *overall* length: one wing *of the one cherub was* five cubits, touching the wall of the room, and the other wing *was* five cubits, touching the wing of the other cherub; 12*one* wing of the other cherub *was* five cubits, touching the wall of the room, and the other wing *also was* five cubits, touching the wing of the other cherub. 13The wings of these cherubim spanned twenty cubits overall. They stood on their feet, and they faced inward. 14And he made the *k*veil of blue, purple, crimson, and fine linen, and wove cherubim into it.

15Also he made in front of the temple* *l*two pillars thirty-five* cubits high, and the capital that *was* on the top of each of *them* was five cubits. 16He made wreaths of chainwork, as in the inner sanctuary, and put *them* on top of the pillars; and he made *m*one hundred pomegranates, and put *them* on the wreaths of chainwork. 17Then he *n*set up the pillars before the temple, one on the right hand and the other on the left; he called the name of the one on the right hand Jachin, and the name of the one on the left Boaz.

Furnishings of the Temple

4 Moreover he made *a*a bronze altar: twenty cubits was its length, twenty cubits its width, and ten cubits its height. 2*b*Then he made the Sea of cast *bronze*,

ten cubits from one brim to the other; *it was* completely round. Its height *was* five cubits, and a line of thirty cubits measured its circumference. 3*c*And under it *was* the likeness of oxen encircling it all around, ten to a cubit, all the way around the Sea. The oxen *were* cast in two rows, when it was cast. 4It stood on twelve *d*oxen: three looking toward the north, three looking toward the west, three looking toward the south, and three looking toward the east; the Sea *was set* upon them, and all their back parts *pointed* inward. 5It *was* a handbreadth thick; and its brim was shaped like the brim of a cup, *like* a lily blossom. It contained three thousand* baths.

6He also made *e*ten lavers, and put five on the right side and five on the left, to wash in them; such things as they offered for the burnt offering they would wash in them, but the Sea *was* for the *f*priests to wash in. 7*g*And he made ten lampstands of gold *h*according to their design, and set *them* in the temple, five on the right side and five on the left. 8*i*He also made ten tables, and placed *them* in the temple, five on the right side and five on the left. And he made one hundred *j*bowls of gold.

9Furthermore *k*he made the court of the priests, and the *l*great court and doors for the court; and he overlaid these doors with bronze. 10*m*He set the Sea on the right side, toward the southeast.

11Then *n*Huram made the pots and the

---

* 3:15 Literally *house* • Or *eighteen* (compare 1 Kings 7:15; 2 Kings 25:17; and Jeremiah 52:21)
* 4:5 Or *two thousand* (compare 1 Kings 7:26)

3:9 nails . . . gold. Gold by itself is too soft to use for nails, so the nails mentioned here must have been plated with gold, as the weight would indicate.

3:13 twenty cubits. The wings of the cherubim spanned the entire width of the room.

3:14 the veil. The veil was a heavy curtain between the holy place and the Most Holy Place. It shielded the ark and cherubim from view, and as God was visualized as sitting on the mercy seat under the wings of the cherubim (see note at 1 Chr. 13:6), it also shielded even the priests from the most intimate presence of God. The veil between the holy place and the Most Holy Place was ripped in two when Jesus died on the cross (Matt. 27:51). The tearing of the temple curtain is seen as a symbol that through Jesus, believers have direct access to God (Heb. 6:19; 9:1—10:20).

3:15 thirty-five cubits . . . five cubits. The pillars were about 53 feet tall with a 7 foot capital on top.

3:17 Jachin . . . Boaz. The names of the two pillars mean "He establishes" and "in Him is strength."

4:2 Sea of cast bronze. The Sea was a receptacle for water corresponding to the much smaller bronze basin of the Mosaic tabernacle (Ex. 30:17–21). The basin provided water for the priests to wash their hands and feet in preparation for ministering at the altar. The Sea served the same purpose. It was huge—15 feet in diameter and 45 feet in circumference.

4:5 three thousand baths. When filled with about

27,000 gallons of water the sea would have weighed about 108 tons.

4:6 ten lavers. Each laver held 40 baths, or about 230 gallons (1 Kin. 7:38). They could accommodate large animals, such as oxen. The law of burnt offerings required certain parts of the animal to be washed in water before it was placed on the altar (Lev. 1:9,13).

4:7 ten lampstands. The wilderness tabernacle had only one lampstand (Ex. 25:31), but the temple had ten.

4:8 ten tables. There had been only one table in the tabernacle (Ex. 25:23). The increase reflects the grandeur of the temple, as well as the large number of people to be served.

4:9 court of the priests. There were areas in and about the temple that only the priests could enter. One of these was the area immediately surrounding it and enclosed by a separating wall, the "court of the priests." **great court.** The great court was an outer area where the people in general could go.

3:9 *i* 1 Chr. 28:11   **3:10** *j* 1 Kin. 6:23–28   **3:14** *k* Ex. 26:31   **3:15** *l* 1 Kin. 7:15–20   **3:16** *m* 1 Kin. 7:20   **3:17** *n* 1 Kin. 7:21   **4:1** *a* Ex. 27:1, 2   **4:2** *b* 1 Kin. 7:23–26   **4:3** *c* 1 Kin. 7:24–26   **4:4** *d* 1 Kin. 7:25   **4:6** *e* 1 Kin. 7:38, 40   *f* Ex. 30:19–21   **4:7** *g* 1 Kin. 7:49   *h* Ex. 25:31   **4:8** *i* 1 Kin. 7:48   *j* 1 Chr. 28:17   **4:9** *k* 1 Kin. 6:36   *l* 2 Kin. 21:5   **4:10** *m* 1 Kin. 7:39   **4:11** *n* 1 Kin. 7:40–51

shovels and the bowls. So Huram finished doing the work that he was to do for King Solomon for the house of God: 12the two pillars and °the bowl-shaped capitals *that were* on top of the two pillars; the two networks covering the two bowl-shaped capitals which *were* on top of the pillars; 13pfour hundred pomegranates for the two networks (two rows of pomegranates for each network, to cover the two bowl-shaped capitals that *were* on the pillars); 14he also made qcarts and the lavers on the carts; 15one Sea and twelve oxen under it; 16also the pots, the shovels, the forks—and all their articles rHuram his master* *craftsman* made of burnished bronze for King Solomon for the house of the LORD.

17In the plain of Jordan the king had them cast in clay molds, between Succoth and Zeredah.* 18sAnd Solomon had all these articles made in such great abundance that the weight of the bronze was not determined.

19Thus tSolomon had all the furnishings made for the house of God: the altar of gold and the tables on which *was* uthe showbread; 20the lampstands with their lamps of pure gold, to burn vin the prescribed manner in front of the inner sanctuary, 21with wthe flowers and the lamps and the wick-trimmers of gold, of purest gold; 22the trimmers, the bowls, the ladles, and the censers of pure gold. As for the entry of the sanctuary, its inner doors to the Most Holy *Place,* and the doors of the main hall of the temple, *were* gold.

5 So ªall the work that Solomon had done for the house of the LORD was finished; and Solomon brought in the things which his father David had dedicated: the silver and the gold and all the furnishings. And he put *them* in the treasuries of the house of God.

The Ark Brought into the Temple

2bNow Solomon assembled the elders of Israel and all the heads of the tribes, the chief fathers of the children of Israel, in Jerusalem, that they might bring the ark of the covenant of the LORD up cfrom the City of David, which *is* Zion. 3dTherefore all the men of Israel assembled with the king eat the feast, which *was* in the seventh month. 4So all the elders of Israel came, and the fLevites took up the ark. 5Then they brought up the ark, the tabernacle of meeting, and all the holy furnishings that *were* in the tabernacle. The priests and the Levites brought them up. 6Also King Solomon, and all the congregation of Israel who were assembled with him before the ark, were sacrificing sheep and oxen that could not be counted or numbered for multitude. 7Then the priests brought in the ark of the covenant of the LORD to its place, into the ginner sanctuary of the temple,* to the Most Holy *Place,* under the wings of the cherubim. 8For the cherubim spread *their* wings over the place of the ark, and the cherubim overshadowed the ark and its poles. 9The poles extended so that the ends of the hpoles of the ark could be seen from *the holy place,* in front of the inner sanctuary; but they could not be seen from outside. And they are there to this day. 10Nothing was in the ark except the two tablets which Moses iput *there* at Horeb, when the LORD made *a covenant* with the children of Israel, when they had come out of Egypt.

11And it came to pass when the priests came out of the *Most Holy Place* (for all the priests who *were* present had sanctified themselves, without keeping to their

---

* **4:16** Literally *father*   * **4:17** Spelled *Zaretan* in 1 Kings 7:46   * **5:7** Literally *house*

4:14 carts. The carts had four bronze wheels (1 Kin. 7:27–37).

4:17 cast in clay molds. Many bronze products were made at a place in the Jordan valley about 35 miles north of the Dead Sea. Archaeologists have uncovered evidence of this work in an area where the clay is suitable for bronze casting.

4:19 altar of gold. This altar was used for offering incense (Ex. 30:1–10; 1 Kin. 7:48). It was in the holy place just in front of the veil.

4:22 inner doors. The tabernacle had a veil between the Most Holy Place, where the ark was, and the "house," or holy place. Solomon's temple had a set of doors there as well.

5:2 ark of the covenant. Though David had built a tabernacle, or tent, on Mount Zion to house the ark (1 Chr. 15:1), it was still separate from the original tabernacle and bronze altar at Gibeon. Completing Solomon's temple made it possible for the ark and the altar to be in the same place for the first time since the Israelites lost the ark to the Philistines during the days when the tabernacle was at Shiloh and Samuel was a little boy (1 Sam. 4–6).

5:3 feast. Since this was the seventh month, the feast was the Feast of Tabernacles. This was an appropriate occasion for moving the ark to a permanent location because the feast commemorated Israel's wandering in the wilderness when the ark had no permanent place (Lev. 23:39–43).

5:5 tabernacle. This tent was the Mosaic tabernacle. Solomon ended worship at the high place at Gibeon by dismantling the tabernacle and bringing it and all its furnishings to Jerusalem.

5:9 to this day. The ark was supposed to remain safely in the temple forever. At the time of the writing of this book (probably between 460 and 430 B.C.), the temple had been destroyed and the ark was gone. No one knows what happened to the ark after Nebuchadnezzar destroyed Jerusalem in 586 B.C.

4:12 ° 1 Kin. 7:41   **4:13** P 1 Kin. 7:20   **4:14** q 1 Kin. 7:27, 43   **4:16** r 1 Kin. 7:45   **4:18** s 1 Kin. 7:47   **4:19** t 1 Kin. 7:48–50   u Ex. 25:30   **4:20** v Ex. 27:20, 21   **4:21** w Ex. 25:31   **5:1** ª 1 Kin. 7:51   **5:2** b 1 Kin. 8:1–9   c 2 Sam. 6:12   **5:3** d 1 Kin. 8:2   e 2 Chr. 7:8–10   **5:4** f 1 Chr. 15:2, 15   **5:7** g 2 Chr. 4:20   **5:9** h Ex. 25:13–15   **5:10** i Deut. 10:2, 5

ʲdivisions), ¹²ᵏand the Levites *who were* the singers, all those of Asaph and Heman and Jeduthun, with their sons and their brethren, stood at the east end of the altar, clothed in white linen, having cymbals, stringed instruments and harps, ˡand with them one hundred and twenty priests sounding with trumpets— ¹³indeed it came to pass, when the trumpeters and singers *were* as one, to make one sound to be heard in praising and thanking the LORD, and when they lifted up their voice with the trumpets and cymbals and instruments of music, and praised the LORD, *saying:*

ᵐ"For He is good,
  For His mercy *endures* forever,"*

that the house, the house of the LORD, was filled with a cloud, ¹⁴so that the priests could not continue ministering because of the cloud; ⁿfor the glory of the LORD filled the house of God.

6 Then ᵃSolomon spoke:

"The LORD said He would dwell in the ᵇdark cloud.
2 I have surely built You an exalted house,
   And ᶜa place for You to dwell in forever."

Solomon's Speech upon Completion of the Work

³Then the king turned around and ᵈblessed the whole assembly of Israel, while all the assembly of Israel was standing. ⁴And he said: "Blessed *be* the LORD God of Israel, who has fulfilled with His hands *what* He spoke with His mouth to my father David, ᵉsaying, ⁵'Since the day that I brought My people out of the land of Egypt, I have chosen no city from any tribe of Israel *in which* to build a house, that My name might be there, nor did I choose any man to be a ruler over My people Israel. ⁶ᶠYet I have chosen Jerusalem, that My name may be there, and I ᵍhave chosen David to be over My people Israel.' ⁷Now ʰit

was in the heart of my father David to build a temple* for the name of the LORD God of Israel. ⁸But the LORD said to my father David, 'Whereas it was in your heart to build a temple for My name, you did well in that it was in your heart. ⁹Nevertheless you shall not build the temple, but your son who will come from your body, he shall build the temple for My ⁱname.' ¹⁰So the LORD has fulfilled His word which He spoke, and I have filled the position of my father David, and ʲsit on the throne of Israel, as the LORD promised; and I have built the temple for the name of the LORD God of Israel. ¹¹And there I have put the ark, ᵏin which *is* the covenant of the LORD which He made with the children of Israel."

Solomon's Prayer of Dedication

¹²ˡThen *Solomon** stood before the altar of the LORD in the presence of all the assembly of Israel, and spread out his hands ¹³(for Solomon had made a bronze platform five cubits long, five cubits wide, and three cubits high, and had set it in the midst of the court; and he stood on it, knelt down on his knees before all the assembly of Israel, and spread out his hands toward heaven); ¹⁴and he said: "LORD God of Israel, ᵐthere *is* no God in heaven or on earth like You, who keep *Your* ⁿcovenant and mercy with Your servants who walk before You with all their hearts. ¹⁵ᵒYou have kept what You promised Your servant David my father; You have both spoken with Your mouth and fulfilled *it* with Your hand, as *it is* this day. ¹⁶Therefore, LORD God of Israel, now keep what You promised Your servant David my father, saying, ᵖ'You shall not fail to have a man sit before Me on the throne of Israel, ᵠonly if your sons take heed to their way, that they walk in My law as you have walked before Me.' ¹⁷And now, O LORD God of Israel, let Your word come true, which You have spoken to Your servant David.

---

* **5:13** Compare Psalm 106:1   * **6:7** Literally *house*, and so in verses 8–10   * **6:12** Literally *he* (compare 1 Kings 8:22)

5:12 Asaph . . . Heman . . . Jeduthun. These men were the heads of the divisions of Levitical musicians (1 Chr. 6:33,39; 25:1).
5:13 Praise—Praise and worship are simply recognizing the perfections and worthiness of the Lord. His lovingkindness never runs out or diminishes. Every day His mercy and grace exist in perfection on our behalf. A time for daily praise is one of the best ways to grow closer to God.
6:2 to dwell in forever. It did not occur to Solomon that one day the glory of the Lord would depart from this temple and it would be destroyed (Ezek. 10:18).
6:14 there is no God . . . like You. Solomon's acclamation is echoed by every child of God who reflects on God's faithfulness and mercy to those who "walk before Him" with "all their hearts." It is not that Solomon considered other gods to be valid, but he was in a position to see the kind of trust that pagans put

in their gods, and how whimsical and unfaithful these "gods" were.
6:16 only if your sons take heed. Solomon was recognizing that the covenant was dependent on the people remaining faithful to God, and he wanted his line to walk with God as David had. Even though future generations did not imitate David, God's faithfulness was carried out through Jesus, the Son of David (Matt. 9:27; 15:22; 22:41–45).

5:11 ʲ 1 Chr. 24:1–5   **5:12** ᵏ 1 Chr. 25:1–7 ˡ 1 Chr. 13:8; 15:16, 24   **5:13** ᵐ 1 Chr. 16:34, 41; Ps. 100:5; 106:1; 136   **5:14** ⁿ Ex. 40:35   **6:1** ᵃ 1 Kin. 8:12–21 ᵇ [Lev. 16:2]   **6:2** ᶜ 2 Chr. 7:12   **6:3** ᵈ 2 Sam. 6:18   **6:4** ᵉ 1 Chr. 17:5   **6:6** ᶠ Deut. 12:5–7 ᵍ 1 Chr. 28:4   **6:7** ʰ 2 Sam. 7:2   **6:9** ⁱ 1 Chr. 28:3–6   **6:10** ʲ 1 Kin. 2:12; 10:9   **6:11** ᵏ 2 Chr. 5:7–10   **6:12** ˡ 1 Kin. 8:22   **6:14** ᵐ [Ex. 15:11] ⁿ [Deut. 7:9]   **6:15** ᵒ 1 Chr. 22:9, 10   **6:16** ᵖ 2 Chr. 7:18 ᵠ Ps. 132:12

18"But will God indeed dwell with men on the earth? 'Behold, heaven and the heaven of heavens cannot contain You. How much less this temple* which I have built! 19Yet regard the prayer of Your servant and his supplication, O LORD my God, and listen to the cry and the prayer which Your servant is praying before You: 20that Your eyes may be *open toward this temple day and night, toward the place where You said You would put Your name, that You may hear the prayer which Your servant makes 'toward this place. 21And may You hear the supplications of Your servant and of Your people Israel, when they pray toward this place. Hear from heaven Your dwelling place, and when You hear, "forgive.

22"If anyone sins against his neighbor, and is forced to take an 'oath, and comes and takes an oath before Your altar in this temple, 23then hear from heaven, and act, and judge Your servants, bringing retribution on the wicked by bringing his way on his own head, and justifying the righteous by giving him according to his "righteousness.

24"Or if Your people Israel are defeated before an *enemy because they have sinned against You, and return and confess Your name, and pray and make supplication before You in this temple, 25then hear from heaven and forgive the sin of Your people Israel, and bring them back to the land which You gave to them and their fathers.

26"When the *heavens are shut up and there is no rain because they have sinned against You, when they pray toward this place and confess Your name, and turn from their sin because You afflict them, 27then hear in heaven, and forgive the sin of Your servants, Your people Israel, that You may teach them the good way in which they should walk; and send rain on Your land which You have given to Your people as an inheritance.

28"When there *is famine in the land, pestilence or blight or mildew, locusts or grasshoppers; when their enemies besiege them in the land of their cities; whatever plague or whatever *sickness there is; 29whatever prayer, whatever supplication is made by anyone, or by all Your people Israel, when each one knows his own burden and his own grief, and spreads out his hands to this temple: 30then hear from heaven Your dwelling place, and forgive, and give to everyone according to all his ways, whose heart You know (for You alone *know the *hearts of the sons of men), 31that they may fear You, to walk in Your ways as long as they live in the land which You gave to our fathers.

32"Moreover, concerning a foreigner, *who is not of Your people Israel, but has come from a far country for the sake of Your great name and Your mighty hand and Your outstretched arm, when they come and pray in this temple; 33then hear from heaven Your dwelling place, and do according to all for which the foreigner calls to You, that all peoples of the earth may know Your name and fear You, as do Your people Israel, and that they may know that this temple which I have built is called by Your name.

34"When Your people go out to battle against their enemies, wherever You send them, and when they pray to You toward this city which You have chosen and the temple which I have built for Your name, 35then hear from heaven their prayer and their supplication, and maintain their cause.

36"When they sin against You (for there is *no one who does not sin), and You become angry with them and deliver them to the enemy, and they take them *captive to a land far or near; 37yet when they come to themselves in the land where they were carried captive, and repent, and make supplication to You in the land of their captivity, saying, 'We have sinned, we have done wrong, and have committed wickedness'; 38and when they return to You with all their heart and with all their soul in the land of their captivity, where they have been carried captive, and pray toward their land which You

---

* **6:18** Literally *house*

6:23 *hear from heaven.* Solomon's request that God hear from heaven underscored God's transcendence. Although God had chosen to be present on earth at the temple, He is also beyond the limits of the temple building.
6:25 *bring them back.* This statement is a hint of the future captivity and deportation of God's disobedient people (Deut. 28:29–30). When the exile to Babylon became a reality, the temple was destroyed and no one could pray at that place as before. But even in those days, God's people directed their prayer toward Jerusalem (Dan. 6:10).
6:32–33 *concerning a foreigner.* God made His covenant exclusively with Israel, the nation descended from Abraham, but He did so for the purpose of attracting the nations to Himself, the Creator of all

people. A foreigner who embraced the Lord as God would be numbered among God's people.
6:36 *there is no one who does not sin.* This statement is repeated in the New Testament (Rom. 3:23; 1 John 1:8–10). **take them captive.** Solomon's speech anticipated the possibility of exile (v. 25), something that had already taken place by the time Chronicles was written.

6:18 *r* [2 Chr. 2:6]   **6:20** *s* 2 Chr. 7:15   *t* Dan. 6:10
6:21 *u* [Mic. 7:18]   **6:22** *v* Ex. 22:8–11   **6:23** *w* [Job 34:11]
6:24 *x* 2 Kin. 21:14, 15   **6:26** *y* 1 Kin. 17:1   **6:28** *z* 2 Chr.
20:9 *a* [Mic. 6:13]   **6:30** *b* [1 Chr. 28:9] *c* [1 Sam. 16:7]
6:32 *d* John 12:20   **6:36** *e* [Rom. 3:9, 19; 5:12] *f* Deut.
28:63–68

gave to their fathers, the ᵍcity which You have chosen, and toward the temple which I have built for Your name: ³⁹then hear from heaven Your dwelling place their prayer and their supplications, and maintain their cause, and forgive Your people who have sinned against You. ⁴⁰Now, my God, I pray, let Your eyes be ʰopen and *let* Your ears *be* attentive to the prayer *made* in this place.

⁴¹ⁱ"Now therefore,
Arise, O LORD God, to Your ʲresting place,
You and the ark of Your strength.
Let Your priests, O LORD God, be clothed with salvation,
And let Your saints ᵏrejoice in goodness.

⁴² "O LORD God, do not turn away the face of Your Anointed;
ˡRemember the mercies of Your servant David."*

Solomon Dedicates the Temple

7 When ᵃSolomon had finished praying, ᵇfire came down from heaven and consumed the burnt offering and the sacrifices; and ᶜthe glory of the LORD filled the temple.* ²ᵈAnd the priests could not enter the house of the LORD, because the glory of the LORD had filled the LORD's house. ³When all the children of Israel saw how the fire came down, and the glory of the LORD on the temple, they bowed their faces to the ground on the pavement, and worshiped and praised the LORD, *saying:*

ᵉ"For *He is* good,
ᶠFor His mercy *endures* forever."*

⁴ᵍThen the king and all the people offered sacrifices before the LORD. ⁵King Solomon offered a sacrifice of twenty-two thousand bulls and one hundred and twenty thousand sheep. So the king and all the people dedicated the house of God. ⁶ʰAnd the priests attended to their services; the Levites also with instruments of the music of the LORD, which King David had made to praise the LORD, saying, "For His mercy *endures* forever,"* whenever David offered praise by their ministry. ⁱThe priests sounded trumpets opposite them, while all Israel stood.

⁷Furthermore ʲSolomon consecrated the middle of the court that *was* in front of the house of the LORD; for there he offered burnt offerings and the fat of the peace offerings, because the bronze altar which Solomon had made was not able to receive the burnt offerings, the grain offerings, and the fat.

⁸ᵏAt that time Solomon kept the feast seven days, and all Israel with him, a very great assembly ˡfrom the entrance of Hamath to ᵐthe Brook of Egypt.* ⁹And on the eighth day they held a ⁿsacred assembly, for they observed the dedication of the altar seven days, and the feast seven days.

---

*6:42 Compare Psalm 132:8–10 *7:1 Literally *house* *7:3 Compare Psalm 106:1 *7:6 Compare Psalm 106:1 *7:8 That is, the Shihor (compare 1 Chronicles 13:5)

7:1 Miracles—This event marks the third of four events when supernatural fire fell from heaven. The first occurred during the dedication of the tabernacle in the days of Moses (Lev. 9:24). The second happened when David dedicated a piece of ground to the Lord that later became the site of Solomon's temple (1 Chr. 21:26). The final occurrence transpired on Mount Carmel when Elijah prayed for fire to consume his offering (1 Kin. 18:38). We often think that a miracle will convince an unbeliever of the reality of the living God, and sometimes it does. But sensing the presence of God, or seeing His work, does not equal believing. The Israelites often backslid, even after miraculous events, and even the miracles of Jesus did not convince all that He was the Messiah (Matt. 11:20–24).

7:3 Need for Worship—The first reason for worship is simply that God commands it (1 Chr. 16:29; Matt. 4:10). The first four of the Ten Commandments charge men and women to worship the one true God and Him alone (Ex. 20:3–10). To allow anything or anyone other than God to have a position of lordship over us constitutes gross disobedience to the will of God and incurs His terrible wrath (Ex. 20:5; Deut. 27:15). Eventually all peoples will bow to God anyway, even if they do so unwillingly (Phil. 2:10).

An equally important reason for worship is that God is worthy of our worship. He designed us for worship. He alone possesses the attributes that merit our worship and service. Among these are goodness (Ps. 100:5), mercy (Ex. 4:31), holiness (Ps. 99:5,9), and creative

power (Rev. 4:11). When men of biblical times clearly saw the unveiled glory of God, they could not help but fall prostrate in worship. Examples of this response can be seen in the actions of Moses (Ex. 34:5–8), Isaiah (Is. 6), Paul (Acts 9:3–6), and John (Rev. 1:9–17).

A final reason for worship is that men and women need to give it. People cannot find personal fulfillment apart from the glad submission of themselves in worshipful obedience to God. He is the Creator and they are the creatures (Rev. 4:11). We are made to worship God. If we do anything less, we fail to be who God created us to be. One who worships God not only participates in the occupation of heaven (Rev. 7:9–12), but also finds joyful satisfaction in the present time (Rom. 12:2; Col. 3:24).

7:8 feast. The feast was the Feast of Tabernacles, which began on the fifteenth day of the seventh month and continued through the twenty-second day (see note at 5:3). **Hamath . . . Brook of Egypt.** These geographical locations specify the extent of Solomon's early kingdom from north to south.

7:9 dedication of the altar. This is the same dedication referred to in 5:3.

6:38 ᵍDan. 6:10 6:40 ʰ2 Chr. 6:20 6:41 ⁱPs. 132:8–10, 16 ʲ1 Chr. 28:2 ᵏNeh. 9:25 6:42 ˡPs. 89:49; 132:1, 8–10 7:1 ᵃ1 Kin. 8:54 ᵇLev. 9:24 ᶜ1 Kin. 8:10, 11 7:2 ᵈ2 Chr. 5:14 7:3 ᵉPs. 106:1; 136:1 ᶠ2 Chr. 20:21 7:4 ᵍ1 Kin. 8:62, 63 7:6 ʰ1 Chr. 15:16 ⁱ2 Chr. 5:12 7:7 ʲ1 Kin. 8:64–66; 9:3 7:8 ᵏ1 Kin. 8:65 ˡ1 Kin. 4:21, 24 ᵐJosh. 13:3 7:9 ⁿLev. 23:36

¹⁰oOn the twenty-third day of the seventh month he sent the people away to their tents, joyful and glad of heart for the good that the Lord had done for David, for Solomon, and for His people Israel. ¹¹Thus pSolomon finished the house of the Lord and the king's house; and Solomon successfully accomplished all that came into his heart to make in the house of the Lord and in his own house.

God's Second Appearance to Solomon

¹²Then the Lord qappeared to Solomon by night, and said to him: "I have heard your prayer, rand have chosen this splace for Myself as a house of sacrifice. ¹³tWhen I shut up heaven and there is no rain, or command the locusts to devour the land, or send pestilence among My people, ¹⁴if My people who are ucalled by My name will vhumble themselves, and pray and seek My face, and turn from their wicked ways, wthen I will hear from heaven, and will forgive their sin and heal their land. ¹⁵Now xMy eyes will be open and My ears attentive to prayer made in this place. ¹⁶For now yI have chosen and sanctified this house, that My name may be there forever; and My eyes and My heart will be there perpetually. ¹⁷zAs for you, if you walk before Me as your father David walked, and according to all that I have commanded you, and if you keep My statutes and My judgments, ¹⁸then I will establish the throne of your kingdom, as I covenanted with David your father, saying, a'You shall not fail to have a man as ruler in Israel.'

¹⁹b"But if you turn away and forsake My statutes and My commandments which I have set before you, and go and serve other gods, and worship them, ²⁰cthen I will uproot them from My land which I have given them; and this house which I have sanctified for My name I will cast out of My sight, and will make it a proverb and a dbyword among all peoples.

²¹"And as for ethis house, which is exalted, everyone who passes by it will be fastonished and say, g'Why has the Lord done thus to this land and this house?' ²²Then they will answer, 'Because they forsook the Lord God of their fathers, who brought them out of the land of Egypt, and embraced other gods, and worshiped them and served them; therefore He has brought all this calamity on them.'"

Solomon's Additional Achievements

8 It acame to pass at the end of btwenty years, when Solomon had built the house of the Lord and his own house, ²that the cities which Hiram* had given to Solomon, Solomon built them; and he settled the children of Israel there. ³And Solomon went to Hamath Zobah and seized it. ⁴cHe also built Tadmor in the wilderness, and all the storage cities which he built in dHamath. ⁵He built Upper Beth Horon and eLower Beth Horon, fortified cities with walls, gates, and bars, ⁶also Baalath and all the storage cities that Solomon had, and all the chariot cities and the cities of the cavalry, and all that Solomon fdesired to build in Jerusalem, in Lebanon, and in all the land of his dominion.

⁷gAll the people who were left of the Hittites, Amorites, Perizzites, Hivites, and Jebusites, who were not of Israel— ⁸that is, their descendants who were left in the land after them, whom the children of Israel did not destroy—from these Solomon raised forced labor, as it is to this day. ⁹But Solomon did not make the children of Israel servants for his work. Some were men of

---

* **8:2** Hebrew *Huram* (compare 2 Chronicles 2:3)

7:10 *sent the people away to their tents.* The people returned to their huts, or booths, where they stayed as a part of the Feast of Tabernacles. Few if any Israelites used tents for their housing at this time.
7:11 *house of the Lord ... king's house.* Since it took Solomon 13 years to build his palace and 20 years in all to build both it and the temple, these events are halfway through Solomon's 40-year reign.
7:14 Prayer—This promise to hear, if the people will pray, is directly linked to the covenant promises that God made with the Israelites (Deut. 28–30). Blessings were linked to obedience, curses linked to rebellion, and the promise that God would hear if they repented was the reminder that God had eternal commitment to them. Even nations outside this covenant have taken great comfort in remembering this promise. God always hears the sincere prayers of His people, and Christians are directed to pray for the leaders of the nations (1 Tim. 2:1–2).
8:4 *Tadmor.* Solomon built and fortified cities such as Tadmor because they were on vital caravan routes.

These fortified cities provided protection to his caravans and became the customs points at which Solomon collected taxes. *storage cities.* Facilities were scattered throughout Solomon's outlying provinces to provide warehouses for his armies and merchantmen, as well as to store produce and other tributes paid by the vassal states (1 Kin. 9:19).
8:5 *Upper Beth Horon and Lower Beth Horon.* These cities were strategically located near the border between Judah and the northern tribal districts, along a major mountain pass to the Mediterranean (Josh. 10:10; 1 Sam. 13:18).

7:10 o 1 Kin. 8:66 **7:11** p 1 Kin. 9:1 **7:12** q 1 Kin. 3:5; 11:9 r Deut. 12:5, 11 s 2 Chr. 6:20 **7:13** t 2 Chr. 6:26–28 **7:14** u [Is. 43:7] v [James 4:10] w 2 Chr. 6:27, 30 **7:15** x 2 Chr. 6:20, 40 **7:16** y 2 Chr. 6:6 **7:17** z 1 Kin. 9:4 **7:18** a 2 Chr. 6:16 **7:19** b Lev. 26:14, 33 **7:20** c Deut. 28:63–68 d Ps. 44:14 **7:21** e 2 Kin. 25:9 f 2 Chr. 29:8 g [Deut. 29:24, 25] **8:1** a 1 Kin. 9:10–14 b 1 Kin. 6:38—7:1 **8:4** c 1 Kin. 9:17, 18 d 1 Chr. 18:3, 9 **8:5** e 1 Chr. 7:24 **8:6** f 2 Chr. 7:11 **8:7** g 1 Kin. 9:20

war, captains of his officers, captains of his chariots, and his cavalry. [10]And others *were* chiefs of the officials of King Solomon: [h]two hundred and fifty, who ruled over the people.

[11]Now Solomon [i]brought the daughter of Pharaoh up from the City of David to the house he had built for her, for he said, "My wife shall not dwell in the house of David king of Israel, because *the places* to which the ark of the LORD has come are holy."

[12]Then Solomon offered burnt offerings to the LORD on the altar of the LORD which he had built before the vestibule, [13]according to the [j]daily rate, offering according to the commandment of Moses, for the Sabbaths, the New Moons, and the [k]three appointed yearly [l]feasts—the Feast of Unleavened Bread, the Feast of Weeks, and the Feast of Tabernacles. [14]And, according to the order of David his father, he appointed the [m]divisions of the priests for their service, [n]the Levites for their duties (to praise and serve before the priests) as the duty of each day required, and the [o]gatekeepers by their divisions at each gate; for so David the man of God had commanded. [15]They did not depart from the command of the king to the priests and Levites concerning any matter or concerning the [p]treasuries.

[16]Now all the work of Solomon was well-ordered from* the day of the foundation of the house of the LORD until it was finished. So the house of the LORD was completed.

[17]Then Solomon went to [q]Ezion Geber and Elath* on the seacoast, in the land of Edom. [18r]And Hiram sent him ships by the hand of his servants, and servants who knew the sea. They went with the servants of Solomon to [s]Ophir, and acquired four hundred and fifty talents of gold from there, and brought it to King Solomon.

The Queen of Sheba's Praise of Solomon

9 Now [a]when the queen of Sheba heard of the fame of Solomon, she came to Jerusalem to test Solomon with hard questions, *having* a very great retinue, camels that bore spices, gold in abundance, and precious stones; and when she came to Solomon, she spoke with him about all that was in her heart. [2]So Solomon answered all her questions; there was nothing so

difficult for Solomon that he could not explain it to her. [3]And when the queen of Sheba had seen the wisdom of Solomon, the house that he had built, [4]the food on his table, the seating of his servants, the service of his waiters and their apparel, his [b]cupbearers and their apparel, and his entryway by which he went up to the house of the LORD, there was no more spirit in her.

[5]Then she said to the king: "*It was* a true report which I heard in my own land about your words and your wisdom. [6]However I did not believe their words until I came and saw with my own eyes; and indeed the half of the greatness of your wisdom was not told me. You exceed the fame of which I heard. [7]Happy *are* your men and happy *are* these your servants, who stand continually before you and hear your wisdom! [8]Blessed be the LORD your God, who delighted in you, setting you on His throne *to be* king for the LORD your God! Because your God has [c]loved Israel, to establish them forever, therefore He made you king over them, to do justice and righteousness."

[9]And she gave the king one hundred and twenty talents of gold, spices in great abundance, and precious stones; there never were any spices such as those the queen of Sheba gave to King Solomon.

[10]Also, the servants of Hiram and the servants of Solomon, [d]who brought gold from Ophir, brought algum* wood and precious stones. [11]And the king made walkways *of* the algum* wood for the house of the LORD and for the king's house, also harps and stringed instruments for singers; and there were none such *as these* seen before in the land of Judah.

[12]Now King Solomon gave to the queen of Sheba all she desired, whatever she asked, *much more* than she had brought to the king. So she turned and went to her own country, she and her servants.

Solomon's Great Wealth

[13e]The weight of gold that came to Solomon yearly was six hundred and sixty-six

---

* **8:16** Following Septuagint, Syriac, and Vulgate; Masoretic Text reads *as far as*.   * **8:17** Hebrew *Eloth* (compare 2 Kings 14:22)   * **9:10** Or *almug* (compare 1 Kings 10:11, 12)   * **9:11** Or *almug* (compare 1 Kings 10:11, 12)

8:18 Hiram. The Phoenicians were world famous mariners, so when Solomon undertook a merchant marine enterprise he called once more on his good friend Hiram, king of Tyre. **Ophir.** A source of finest gold (1 Chr. 29:4); the location of Ophir is not known, except that it was reached by sea. People have speculated that it may have been in South Arabia, India, or Africa.

9:1 Sheba. Sheba was more than a thousand miles south of Israel, at the southern end of the Arabian peninsula.

9:8 Blessed be the LORD your God. The language of politeness in the ancient world does not necessarily

suggest that the queen of Sheba was converted. Visiting dignitaries customarily praised the god of the host nation.

9:13 six hundred and sixty-six talents of gold. Solomon's annual income in gold amounted to 25 tons.

8:10 [h] 1 Kin. 9:23   **8:11** [i] 1 Kin. 3:1; 7:8; 9:24; 11:1
8:13 [j] Num. 28:3, 9, 11, 26; 29:1   [k] Ex. 23:14–17; 34:22, 23
[l] Lev. 23:1–44   **8:14** [m] 1 Chr. 24:3   [n] 1 Chr. 25:1   [o] 1 Chr.
9:17; 26:1   **8:15** [p] 1 Chr. 26:20–28   **8:17** [q] 1 Kin. 9:26
8:18 [r] 2 Chr. 9:10, 13   [s] 1 Chr. 29:4   **9:1** [a] [Matt. 12:42]
9:4 [b] Neh. 1:11   **9:8** [c] Deut. 7:8   **9:10** [d] 2 Chr. 8:18
9:13 [e] 1 Kin. 10:14–29

talents of gold, ¹⁴besides *what* the traveling merchants and traders brought. And all the kings of Arabia and governors of the country brought gold and silver to Solomon. ¹⁵And King Solomon made two hundred large shields of hammered gold; six hundred *shekels* of hammered gold went into each shield. ¹⁶*He* also *made* three hundred shields of hammered gold; three hundred *shekels** of gold went into each shield. The king put them in the ᶠHouse of the Forest of Lebanon.

¹⁷Moreover the king made a great throne of ivory, and overlaid it with pure gold. ¹⁸The throne *had* six steps, with a footstool of gold, *which were* fastened to the throne; there were armrests on either side of the place of the seat, and two lions stood beside the armrests. ¹⁹Twelve lions stood there, one on each side of the six steps; nothing like *this* had been made for any *other* kingdom.

²⁰All King Solomon's drinking vessels *were* gold, and all the vessels of the House of the Forest of Lebanon *were* pure gold. Not *one was* silver, for this was accounted as nothing in the days of Solomon. ²¹For the king's ships went to ᵍTarshish with the servants of Hiram.* Once every three years the merchant ships* came, bringing gold, silver, ivory, apes, and monkeys.*

²²So King Solomon surpassed all the kings of the earth in riches and wisdom. ²³And all the kings of the earth sought the presence of Solomon to hear his wisdom, which God had put in his heart. ²⁴Each man brought his present: articles of silver and gold, garments, ʰarmor, spices, horses, and mules, at a set rate year by year.

²⁵Solomon ⁱhad four thousand stalls for horses and chariots, and twelve thousand horsemen whom he stationed in the chariot cities and with the king at Jerusalem.

²⁶ʲSo he reigned over all the kings ᵏfrom the River* to the land of the Philistines, as far as the border of Egypt. ²⁷ˡThe king made silver *as common* in Jerusalem as stones, and he made cedar trees ᵐas abundant as the sycamores which *are* in the lowland. ²⁸ⁿAnd they brought horses to Solomon from Egypt and from all lands.

Death of Solomon

²⁹ᵒNow the rest of the acts of Solomon, first and last, *are* they not written in the book of Nathan the prophet, in the prophecy of ᵖAhijah the Shilonite, and in the visions of ᑫIddo the seer concerning Jeroboam the son of Nebat? ³⁰ʳSolomon reigned in Jerusalem over all Israel forty years. ³¹Then Solomon rested with his fathers, and was buried in the City of David his father. And Rehoboam his son reigned in his place.

The Revolt Against Rehoboam

10 And ᵃRehoboam went to Shechem, for all Israel had gone to Shechem to make him king. ²So it happened, when Jeroboam the son of Nebat heard (he was in Egypt, ᵇwhere he had fled from the presence of King Solomon), that Jeroboam returned from Egypt. ³Then they sent for him and called him. And Jeroboam and all Israel came and spoke to Rehoboam, saying, ⁴"Your father made our yoke heavy; now therefore, lighten the burdensome service of your father and his heavy yoke which he put on us, and we will serve you."

---

* **9:16** Or *three minas* (compare 1 Kings 10:17) * **9:21** Hebrew *Huram* (compare 1 Kings 10:22) • Literally *ships of Tarshish* (deep-sea vessels) • Or *peacocks* * **9:26** That is, the Euphrates

---

This figure probably reflects the annual revenues of the entire nation through taxes.
9:14 kings . . . governors . . . brought. The gold and silver that the kings and governors brought to Solomon was tribute, a form of taxation on vassal states, not a voluntary gift.
9:15 shields of hammered gold. The targets or shields of beaten gold were for decorative or ceremonial purpose, not the armory. Gold was too expensive, too heavy, and too soft to use in battle.
9:26 to the land of the Philistines. Most of the kings of Israel had continuing trouble with the Philistines, even though they were able to subdue every other surrounding neighbor. David had some success against the Philistines (1 Chr. 18:1), and later Jehoshaphat managed to exact tribute from some of them (17:11).
9:29 Nathan the prophet. This is the same Nathan that rebuked David for his adultery and murder (2 Sam. 12:1–15). He was a confidant and counselor to both David and Solomon (1 Kin. 1:8–11). **Ahijah . . . Iddo.** Ahijah and Iddo were contemporaries who compiled the accounts of both Jeroboam and Rehoboam (12:15).
9:31 Rehoboam. Rehoboam was a son of Solomon by his wife Naamah of Ammon (12:13). He was 41

when he began to rule, so he must have been born during the period when Solomon ruled alongside David (1 Chr. 29:22–23).
10:1 Shechem. Rehoboam probably chose Shechem as the place to be crowned because a rift had begun to develop between the northern and southern tribes (1 Kin. 11:26–40).
10:4 Wisdom—Bravado is different than wisdom. Saying that one is going to be tough is different than being wise. Short of despotic force, no king can rule a people who do not trust him, and even if there is not outright rebellion, the resistance makes an unhappy nation. Like many other people, Rehoboam mistook conciliation for weakness, and lost his chance to have influence with most of the nation. It is important to remember that the outcome of this encounter was just what God wanted. Rehoboam was reaping the fruits of his father's (and his own) indifference to God.

9:16 ᶠ1 Kin. 7:2 **9:21** ᵍ2 Chr. 20:36, 37 **9:24** ʰ1 Kin. 20:11 **9:25** ⁱ1 Kin. 4:26; 10:26 **9:26** ʲ1 Kin. 4:21 ᵏGen. 15:18 **9:27** ˡ1 Kin. 10:27 ᵐ2 Chr. 1:15–17 **9:28** ⁿ2 Chr. 1:16 **9:29** ᵒ1 Kin. 11:41 ᵖ1 Kin. 11:29 ᑫ2 Chr. 12:15; 13:22 **9:30** ʳ1 Kin. 4:21; 11:42, 43 **10:1** ᵃ1 Kin. 12:1–20 **10:2** ᵇ1 Kin. 11:40

⁵So he said to them, "Come back to me after three days." And the people departed.

⁶Then King Rehoboam consulted the elders who stood before his father Solomon while he still lived, saying, "How do you advise me to answer these people?"

⁷And they spoke to him, saying, "If you are kind to these people, and please them, and speak good words to them, they will be your servants forever."

⁸ᶜBut he rejected the advice which the elders had given him, and consulted the young men who had grown up with him, who stood before him. ⁹And he said to them, "What advice do you give? How should we answer this people who have spoken to me, saying, 'Lighten the yoke which your father put on us'?"

¹⁰Then the young men who had grown up with him spoke to him, saying, "Thus you should speak to the people who have spoken to you, saying, 'Your father made our yoke heavy, but you make it lighter on us'—thus you shall say to them: 'My little finger shall be thicker than my father's waist! ¹¹And now, whereas my father put a heavy yoke on you, I will add to your yoke; my father chastised you with whips, but I will chastise you with scourges!'"*

¹²So ᵈJeroboam and all the people came to Rehoboam on the third day, as the king had directed, saying, "Come back to me the third day." ¹³Then the king answered them roughly. King Rehoboam rejected the advice of the elders, ¹⁴and he spoke to them according to the advice of the young men, saying, "My father* made your yoke heavy, but I will add to it; my father chastised you with whips, but I will chastise you with scourges!"* ¹⁵So the king did not listen to the people; ᵉfor the turn of events was from God, that the LORD might fulfill His ᶠword, which He had spoken by the hand of Ahijah the Shilonite to Jeroboam the son of Nebat.

¹⁶Now when all Israel saw that the king did not listen to them, the people answered the king, saying:

"What share have we in David?
We have no inheritance in the son of Jesse.
Every man to your tents, O Israel!
Now see to your own house, O David!"

So all Israel departed to their tents. ¹⁷But Rehoboam reigned over the children of Israel who dwelt in the cities of Judah.

¹⁸Then King Rehoboam sent Hadoram, who was in charge of revenue; but the children of Israel stoned him with stones, and he died. Therefore King Rehoboam mounted his chariot in haste to flee to Jerusalem. ¹⁹ᵍSo Israel has been in rebellion against the house of David to this day.

11 Now ᵃwhen Rehoboam came to Jerusalem, he assembled from the house of Judah and Benjamin one hundred and eighty thousand chosen men who were warriors, to fight against Israel, that he might restore the kingdom to Rehoboam.

²But the word of the LORD came ᵇto Shemaiah the man of God, saying, ³"Speak to Rehoboam the son of Solomon, king of Judah, and to all Israel in Judah and Benjamin, saying, ⁴'Thus says the LORD: "You shall not go up or fight against your brethren! Let every man return to his house, for this thing is from Me."'" Therefore they obeyed the words of the LORD, and turned back from attacking Jeroboam.

Rehoboam Fortifies the Cities

⁵So Rehoboam dwelt in Jerusalem, and built cities for defense in Judah. ⁶And he built Bethlehem, Etam, Tekoa, ⁷Beth Zur, Sochoh, Adullam, ⁸Gath, Mareshah, Ziph, ⁹Adoraim, Lachish, Azekah, ¹⁰Zorah, Aijalon, and Hebron, which are in Judah and Benjamin, fortified cities. ¹¹And he fortified the strongholds, and put captains in them, and stores of food, oil, and wine. ¹²Also in every city he put shields and spears, and made them very strong, having Judah and Benjamin on his side.

Priests and Levites Move to Judah

¹³And from all their territories the priests and the Levites who were in all Israel took their stand with him. ¹⁴For the Levites left ᶜtheir common-lands and their possessions and came to Judah and Jerusalem, for ᵈJeroboam and his sons had rejected them from serving as priests to the LORD. ¹⁵ᵉThen he appointed for himself priests for the high places, for ᶠthe demons, and ᵍthe calf idols which he had made. ¹⁶ʰAnd after the Levites left,* those from all the tribes

---

* **10:11** Literally scorpions   * **10:14** Following many Hebrew manuscripts, Septuagint, Syriac, and Vulgate (compare verse 10 and 1 Kings 12:14); Masoretic Text reads I. • Literally scorpions
* **11:16** Literally after them

10:15 the turn of events was from God. Human foolishness and decisions often achieve God's purposes. Solomon's defection from God late in his reign had already disqualified his descendants from ruling over all Israel (1 Kin. 11:9–13). Rehoboam initiated the split with his own foolish actions.

11:13 all their territories. Though Israel and Judah had split into two kingdoms, the priests and Levites of Israel sided with Judah. One reason for this was that they knew that Rehoboam was of the lineage of David, and therefore part of God's covenant promise to David. Another reason was that Jeroboam had

established his own religious cult, which had no need for the true priests of God (1 Kin. 12:24–33).

11:16 came to Jerusalem. Once the legitimate religious leaders had left Israel, the worshipers of God in the northern kingdom could no longer worship in

---

10:8 ᶜ 1 Kin. 12:8–11   **10:12** ᵈ 1 Kin. 12:12–14
10:15 ᵉ 1 Chr. 5:22 ᶠ 1 Kin. 11:29–39   **10:19** ᵍ 1 Kin. 12:19
11:1 ᵃ 1 Kin. 12:21–24   **11:2** ᵇ 1 Kin. 12:5   **11:14** ᶜ Num. 35:2–5 ᵈ 2 Chr. 13:9   **11:15** ᵉ 1 Kin. 12:31; 13:33; 14:9
ᶠ [Lev. 17:7] ᵍ 1 Kin. 12:28   **11:16** ʰ 2 Chr. 14:7

of Israel, such as set their heart to seek the Lord God of Israel, *i*came to Jerusalem to sacrifice to the Lord God of their fathers. ¹⁷So they *j*strengthened the kingdom of Judah, and made Rehoboam the son of Solomon strong for three years, because they walked in the way of David and Solomon for three years.

The Family of Rehoboam

¹⁸Then Rehoboam took for himself as wife Mahalath the daughter of Jerimoth the son of David, *and of* Abihail the daughter of *k*Eliah the son of Jesse. ¹⁹And she bore him children: Jeush, Shamariah, and Zaham. ²⁰After her he took *l*Maachah the granddaughter* of *m*Absalom; and she bore him *n*Abijah, Attai, Ziza, and Shelomith. ²¹Now Rehoboam loved Maachah the granddaughter of Absalom more than all his *o*wives and his concubines; for he took eighteen wives and sixty concubines, and begot twenty-eight sons and sixty daughters. ²²And Rehoboam *p*appointed *q*Abijah the son of Maachah as chief, *to be* leader among his brothers; for he *intended* to make him king. ²³He dealt wisely, and dispersed some of his sons throughout all the territories of Judah and Benjamin, to every *r*fortified city; and he gave them provisions in abundance. He also sought many wives *for them.*

Egypt Attacks Judah

12 Now *a*it came to pass, when Rehoboam had established the kingdom and had strengthened himself, that *b*he forsook the law of the Lord, and all Israel along with him. ²*c*And it happened in the fifth year of King Rehoboam *that* Shishak king of Egypt came up against Jerusalem, because they had transgressed against the Lord, ³with twelve hundred chariots, sixty thousand horsemen, and people without

number who came with him out of Egypt—*d*the Lubim and the Sukkiim and the Ethiopians. ⁴And he took the fortified cities of Judah and came to Jerusalem.

⁵Then *e*Shemaiah the prophet came to Rehoboam and the leaders of Judah, who were gathered together in Jerusalem because of Shishak, and said to them, "Thus says the Lord: 'You have forsaken Me, and therefore I also have left you in the hand of Shishak.'"

⁶So the leaders of Israel and the king *f*humbled themselves; and they said, *g*"The Lord *is* righteous."

⁷Now when the Lord saw that they humbled themselves, *h*the word of the Lord came to Shemaiah, saying, "They have humbled themselves; *therefore* I will not destroy them, but I will grant them some deliverance. My wrath shall not be poured out on Jerusalem by the hand of Shishak. ⁸Nevertheless *i*they will be his servants, that they may distinguish *j*My service from the service of the kingdoms of the nations."

⁹*k*So Shishak king of Egypt came up against Jerusalem, and took away the treasures of the house of the Lord and the treasures of the king's house; he took everything. He also carried away the gold shields which Solomon had *l*made. ¹⁰Then King Rehoboam made bronze shields in their place, and committed *them* *m*to the hands of the captains of the guard, who guarded the doorway of the king's house. ¹¹And whenever the king entered the house of the Lord, the guard would go and bring them out; then they would take them back into the guardroom. ¹²When he humbled himself, the wrath of the Lord turned from him, so as not to destroy *him* completely; and things also went well in Judah.

---

* **11:20** Literally *daughter,* but in the broader sense of granddaughter (compare 2 Chronicles 13:2)

---

good conscience, so they either made pilgrimages to Jerusalem, or moved there (1 Kin. 12:25–33). At the time of the Babylonian captivity (36:10) the northern kingdom was already captured by Assyria (2 Kin. 17), but there were many representatives from the northern tribes living in Judah.

11:22 Abijah. Rehoboam named his son Abijah as the next king to ensure a smooth succession following his death. Abijah probably served under or alongside Rehoboam, just as Solomon had served under David (1 Chr. 23:1).

12:2 Egypt. Egypt was beginning to recover from a long period of decline and wanted to reestablish control over Israel. God used their ambitions to discipline Rehoboam for abandoning the Lord.

12:3 Lubim . . . Sukkiim. The Lubim were the Libyans, and the Sukkiim were other desert tribes, probably from western Libya. **Ethiopians.** These famous warriors, sometimes referred to as Cushites, originated in the lands south of Egypt.

12:6 Righteousness—The king and princes of Judah recognized that the Lord was righteous, even

in leaving them in the hands of Shishak. What they did not know, was the difference between being the "vassal" of the righteous Lord, and the vassal of the unrighteous Shishak. Like the Israelites, we count on the righteousness and graciousness of the Lord toward us. It is good to know that He is unfailing in His lovingkindness, but it is not something to presume upon, as if our conforming to His image does not really matter.

12:9 took away the treasures. Judah was now a vassal state of Egypt.

11:16 *i* 2 Chr. 15:9, 10; 30:11, 18   **11:17** *j* 2 Chr. 12:1, 13   **11:18** *k* 1 Sam. 16:6   **11:20** *l* 2 Chr. 13:2 *m* 1 Kin. 15:2   *n* 1 Kin. 14:31   **11:21** *o* Deut. 17:17   **11:22** *p* Deut. 21:15–17 *q* 2 Chr. 13:1   **11:23** *r* 2 Chr. 11:5   **12:1** *a* 2 Chr. 11:17 *b* 1 Kin. 14:22–24   **12:2** *c* 1 Kin. 11:40; 14:25   **12:3** *d* 2 Chr. 16:8   **12:5** *e* 2 Chr. 11:2   **12:6** *f* [James 4:10] *g* Ex. 9:27   **12:7** *h* 1 Kin. 21:28, 29   **12:8** *i* Is. 26:13 *j* [Deut. 28:47, 48]   **12:9** *k* 1 Kin. 14:25, 26 *l* 2 Chr. 9:15, 16   **12:10** *m* 1 Kin. 14:27

The End of Rehoboam's Reign

13Thus King Rehoboam strengthened
himself in Jerusalem and reigned. Now
[n]Rehoboam *was* forty-one years old when
he became king; and he reigned seventeen years in Jerusalem, [o]the city which
the LORD had chosen out of all the tribes
of Israel, to put His name there. His mother's name *was* Naamah, an [p]Ammonitess.
14And he did evil, because he did not prepare his heart to seek the LORD.
15The acts of Rehoboam, first and last,
are they not written in the book of Shemaiah the prophet, [q]and of Iddo the seer
concerning genealogies? [r]And *there were*
wars between Rehoboam and Jeroboam
all their days. 16So Rehoboam rested with
his fathers, and was buried in the City of
David. Then [s]Abijah* his son reigned in
his place.

Abijah Reigns in Judah

13 In [a]the eighteenth year of King Jeroboam, Abijah became king over
[b]Judah. 2He reigned three years in Jerusalem. His mother's name *was* Michaiah* the
daughter of Uriel of Gibeah.
And there was war between Abijah and
Jeroboam. 3Abijah set the battle in order
with an army of valiant warriors, four hundred thousand choice men. Jeroboam also
drew up in battle formation against him
with eight hundred thousand choice men,
mighty men of valor.
4Then Abijah stood on Mount [c]Zemara-
im, which *is* in the mountains of Ephraim,
and said, "Hear me, Jeroboam and all Israel: 5Should you not know that the LORD
God of Israel [d]gave the dominion over Israel to David forever, to him and his sons,
[e]by a covenant of salt? 6Yet Jeroboam the
son of Nebat, the servant of Solomon the
son of David, rose up and [f]rebelled against
his lord. 7Then [g]worthless rogues gathered to him, and strengthened themselves
against Rehoboam the son of Solomon,
when Rehoboam was [h]young and inexperienced and could not withstand them. 8And
now you think to withstand the kingdom of
the LORD, which is in the hand of the sons
of David; and you *are* a great multitude,
and with you are the gold calves which Jeroboam [i]made for you as gods. 9[j]Have you
not cast out the priests of the LORD, the
sons of Aaron, and the Levites, and made
for yourselves priests, like the peoples of
other lands, [k]so that whoever comes to
consecrate himself with a young bull and
seven rams may be a priest of [l]*things that
are* not gods? 10But as for us, the LORD *is*
our [m]God, and we have not forsaken Him;
and the priests who minister to the LORD
are the sons of Aaron, and the Levites *attend* to *their* duties. 11[n]And they burn to
the LORD every morning and every evening burnt sacrifices and sweet incense;
they also *set* the [o]showbread *in order on*
the pure *gold* table, and the lampstand of
gold with its lamps [p]to burn every evening;
for we keep the command of the LORD our
God, but you have forsaken Him. 12Now
look, God Himself is with us as *our* [q]head,
[r]and His priests with sounding trumpets to
sound the alarm against you. O children of
Israel, do not fight against the LORD God
of your fathers, for you shall not prosper!"
13But Jeroboam caused an ambush to go
around behind them; so they were in front
of Judah, and the ambush *was* behind
them. 14And when Judah looked around,
to their surprise the battle line *was* at
both front and rear; and they [s]cried out
to the LORD, and the priests sounded the

* **12:16** Spelled *Abijam* in 1 Kings 14:31
* **13:2** Spelled *Maachah* in 11:20, 21 and 1 Kings 15:2

13:2 *His mother's name was Michaiah.* Michaiah is a variation of "Maachah." She is the daughter of "Uriel of Gibeah" in this passage, as well as the "daughter of Absalom" (11:21). It is thought that she was the granddaughter of Absalom, the daughter of Uriel of Gibeah and Absalom's daughter Tamar (2 Sam. 14:27). The terms "father, mother, son, daughter" were often used in talking of ancestors instead of generations. Jesus is referred to as the "Son of David" (Matt. 9:27; 15:22; 22:42), which is clearly a reference to His ancestry.

13:5 *covenant of salt.* Salt was a preservative and symbolized durability, so a covenant of salt was one that would not be broken. Sometimes covenant makers each took a pinch of salt and mixed it, to show that just as the salt could not be separated, so the promise could not be set aside.

13:6 *Yet Jeroboam.* The throne had been promised to David's line forever, yet the promise was contingent on the faithfulness of his descendants (7:18–19). Because Solomon had turned from God, part of the kingdom was taken from him, and Jeroboam was chosen by God through the prophet Ahijah to rule over the part of the kingdom that was taken from Solomon (10:2). So far this story mirrors the events in the lives of Saul and David. But unlike David, Jeroboam did not wait for the Lord to deliver the promised kingdom to him. Jeroboam took his place by force, and immediately turned from God. His name became a byword, synonymous with "bad king." (See also 1 Kin. 11–14.)

13:7 *when Rehoboam was young and inexperienced.* Abijah's version of the nation's division put his father in a relatively good light. Rehoboam was 41 years old when he became king (12:13).

12:13 [n] 1 Kin. 14:21 [o] 2 Chr. 6:6 [p] 1 Kin. 11:1, 5 **12:15** [q] 2 Chr. 9:29; 13:22 [r] 1 Kin. 14:30 **12:16** [s] 2 Chr. 11:20–22 **13:1** [a] 1 Kin. 15:1 [b] 1 Kin. 12:17 **13:4** [c] Josh. 18:22 **13:5** [d] 2 Sam. 7:8–16 [e] Num. 18:19 **13:6** [f] 1 Kin. 11:28; 12:20 **13:7** [g] Judg. 9:4 [h] 2 Chr. 12:13 **13:8** [i] 1 Kin. 12:28; 14:9 **13:9** [j] 2 Chr. 11:13–15 [k] Ex. 29:29–33 [l] Jer. 2:11; 5:7 **13:10** [m] Josh. 24:15 **13:11** [n] 2 Chr. 2:4 [o] Lev. 24:5–9 [p] Ex. 27:20, 21 **13:12** [q] [Heb. 2:10] [r] [Num. 10:8–10] **13:14** [s] 2 Chr. 6:34, 35; 14:11

trumpets. 15Then the men of Judah gave a shout; and as the men of Judah shouted, it happened that God tstruck Jeroboam and all Israel before Abijah and Judah. 16And the children of Israel fled before Judah, and God delivered them into their hand. 17Then Abijah and his people struck them with a great slaughter; so five hundred thousand choice men of Israel fell slain. 18Thus the children of Israel were subdued at that time; and the children of Judah prevailed, ubecause they relied on the LORD God of their fathers.

19And Abijah pursued Jeroboam and took cities from him: Bethel with its villages, Jeshanah with its villages, and vEphrain* with its villages. 20So Jeroboam did not recover strength again in the days of Abijah; and the LORD wstruck him, and xhe died.

21But Abijah grew mighty, married fourteen wives, and begot twenty-two sons and sixteen daughters. 22Now the rest of the acts of Abijah, his ways, and his sayings are written in ythe annals of the prophet Iddo.

14 So Abijah rested with his fathers, and they buried him in the City of David. Then aAsa his son reigned in his place. In his days the land was quiet for ten years.

Asa Reigns in Judah

2Asa did what was good and right in the eyes of the LORD his God, 3for he removed the altars of the foreign gods and bthe high places, and cbroke down the sacred pillars dand cut down the wooden images. 4He commanded Judah to eseek the LORD God of their fathers, and to observe the law and the commandment. 5He also removed the high places and the incense altars from all the cities of Judah, and the kingdom was quiet under him. 6And he built fortified cities in Judah, for the land had rest; he had no war in those years, because the LORD had given him frest. 7Therefore he said to Judah, "Let us build these cities and make walls around them, and towers, gates, and

bars, while the land is yet before us, because we have sought the LORD our God; we have sought Him, and He has given us rest on every side." So they built and prospered. 8And Asa had an army of three hundred thousand from Judah who carried shields and spears, and from Benjamin two hundred and eighty thousand men who carried shields and drew gbows; all these were mighty men of hvalor.

9iThen Zerah the Ethiopian came out against them with an army of a million men and three hundred chariots, and he came to jMareshah. 10So Asa went out against him, and they set the troops in battle array in the Valley of Zephathah at Mareshah. 11And Asa kcried out to the LORD his God, and said, "LORD, it is lnothing for You to help, whether with many or with those who have no power; help us, O LORD our God, for we rest on You, and min Your name we go against this multitude. O LORD, You are our God; do not let man prevail against You!"

12So the LORD nstruck the Ethiopians before Asa and Judah, and the Ethiopians fled. 13And Asa and the people who were with him pursued them to oGerar. So the Ethiopians were overthrown, and they could not recover, for they were broken before the LORD and His army. And they carried away very much spoil. 14Then they defeated all the cities around Gerar, for pthe fear of the LORD came upon them; and they plundered all the cities, for there was exceedingly much spoil in them. 15They also attacked the livestock enclosures, and carried off sheep and camels in abundance, and returned to Jerusalem.

The Reforms of Asa

15 Now athe Spirit of God came upon Azariah the son of Oded. 2And he went out to meet Asa, and said to him:

---

* **13:19** Or Ephron

14:2–4 Faithfulness—King Asa chose to be faithful to God as he began his reign. His people enjoyed ten years of peace because of Asa's obedience. For each one of us there is a peace that comes with faithfulness to God. This does not necessarily mean that outer circumstances are uncomplicated, but in our hearts the peace of God can still reign. Like Asa, our actions affect the lives of those around us. We are created to have an eternal relationship with God, and that begins in the life of faith, believing that He is who He says He is and that we need Him. "Now faith is the substance of things hoped for, the evidence of things not seen" (Heb. 11:1).

14:3 pillars . . . images. Sacred pillars were stone posts associated with Canaanite fertility rites. Asherah was a Canaanite goddess associated with Baal worship. Asherim were the poles, trees, or groves that were symbolic parts of Asherah worship.

14:9 Zerah the Ethiopian. Since Egypt was strong at this time (12:3) and fully in control of its own territory, it is likely that Zerah and his large army were mercenaries of the Egyptian king Osorkon I (914–874 B.C.), successor of Shishak. **Mareshah.** Mareshah was one of Asa's important fortified cities, about 25 miles southwest of Jerusalem (11:8). It was near the Via Maris, the coastal highway connecting Egypt and Canaan, making it strategically important.

14:13 Gerar. Gerar was at the frontier between Egypt and Canaan and might have been in Egyptian territory at this time.

13:15 t 2 Chr. 14:12   **13:18** u 2 Chr. 14:11   **13:19** v Josh. 15:9   **13:20** w 1 Sam. 2:6; 25:38   x 1 Kin. 14:20   **13:22** y 2 Chr. 9:29   **14:1** a 1 Kin. 15:8   **14:3** b 1 Kin. 15:14   c [Ex. 34:13]   d 1 Kin. 11:7   **14:4** e [2 Chr. 7:14]   **14:6** f 2 Chr. 15:15   **14:8** g 1 Chr. 12:2   h 2 Chr. 13:3   **14:9** i 2 Chr. 12:2, 3; 16:8   j Josh. 15:44   **14:11** k Ex. 14:10   l [1 Sam. 14:6]   m 1 Sam. 17:45   **14:12** n 2 Chr. 13:15   **14:13** o Gen. 10:19; 20:1   **14:14** p 2 Chr. 17:10   **15:1** a 2 Chr. 20:14; 24:20

"Hear me, Asa, and all Judah and Benjamin. [b]The LORD is with you while you are with Him. [c]If you seek Him, He will be found by you; but if [d]you forsake Him, He will forsake you. 3[e]For a long time Israel *has been* without the true God, without a [f]teaching priest, and without [g]law; 4but [h]when in their trouble they turned to the LORD God of Israel, and sought Him, He was found by them. 5And in those times *there was* no peace to the one who went out, nor to the one who came in, but great turmoil *was* on all the inhabitants of the lands. 6[i]So nation was destroyed by nation, and city by city, for God troubled them with every adversity. 7But you, be strong and do not let your hands be weak, for your work shall be rewarded!"

8And when Asa heard these words and the prophecy of Oded* the prophet, he took courage, and removed the abominable idols from all the land of Judah and Benjamin and from the cities [j]which he had taken in the mountains of Ephraim; and he restored the altar of the LORD that *was* before the vestibule of the LORD. 9Then he gathered all Judah and Benjamin, and [k]those who dwelt with them from Ephraim, Manasseh, and Simeon, for they came over to him in great numbers from Israel when they saw that the LORD his God was with him.

10So they gathered together at Jerusalem in the third month, in the fifteenth year of the reign of Asa. 11[l]And they offered to the LORD at that time seven hundred bulls and seven thousand sheep from the spoil they had brought. 12Then they [m]entered into a covenant to seek the LORD God of their fathers with all their heart and with all their soul; 13[n]and whoever would not seek the LORD God of Israel [o]was to be put to death, whether small or great, whether man or woman. 14Then they took an oath before the LORD with a loud voice, with shouting and trumpets and rams' horns. 15And all Judah rejoiced at the oath, for they had sworn with all their heart and [p]sought Him with all their soul; and He was found by them, and the LORD gave them [q]rest all around.

16Also he removed [r]Maachah, the mother

of Asa the king, from *being* queen mother, because she had made an obscene image of Asherah;* and Asa cut down her obscene image, then crushed and burned *it* by the Brook Kidron. 17But [s]the high places were not removed from Israel. Nevertheless the heart of Asa was loyal all his days.

18He also brought into the house of God the things that his father had dedicated and that he himself had dedicated: silver and gold and utensils. 19And there was no war until the thirty-fifth year of the reign of Asa.

Asa's Treaty with Syria

16 In the thirty-sixth year of the reign of Asa, [a]Baasha king of Israel came up against Judah and built Ramah, [b]that he might let none go out or come in to Asa king of Judah. 2Then Asa brought silver and gold from the treasuries of the house of the LORD and of the king's house, and sent to Ben-Hadad king of Syria, who dwelt in Damascus, saying, 3"*Let there be* a treaty between you and me, as there was between my father and your father. See, I have sent you silver and gold; come, break your treaty with Baasha king of Israel, so that he will withdraw from me."

4So Ben-Hadad heeded King Asa, and sent the captains of his armies against the cities of Israel. They attacked Ijon, Dan, Abel Maim, and all the storage cities of Naphtali. 5Now it happened, when Baasha heard *it*, that he stopped building Ramah and ceased his work. 6Then King Asa took all Judah, and they carried away the stones and timber of Ramah, which Baasha had used for building; and with them he built Geba and Mizpah.

Hanani's Message to Asa

7And at that time [c]Hanani the seer came to Asa king of Judah, and said to him: [d]"Because you have relied on the king of Syria, and have not relied on the LORD your God,

---

* **15:8** Following Masoretic Text and Septuagint; Syriac and Vulgate read *Azariah the son of Oded* (compare verse 1). * **15:16** A Canaanite deity

---

15:10 third month. This quite likely locates this festival at the time of the firstfruits, the Feast of Pentecost (Lev. 23:15–21; Num. 28:26–31).

15:16 Maachah. It appears that "mother" is used in the sense of ancestress; Maachah was the mother of Asa's father, Abijah (13:2). Still, Asa demoted her from her position as queen mother because she set up pagan idols—a courageous and delicate task for anyone, even a king.

15:17 Perseverance—Asa started his reign with a determination to serve the Lord and to abolish idol worship. Oded the prophet spurred him on to finish the job, to get rid of idols in his land and the land just captured. Paul talks about fighting the good fight, finishing the course, keeping the faith (2 Tim. 4:7). We all need people like Oded in our lives, who encourage us to keep on being faithful. In the same

manner, we need to encourage others to persevere to the end.

16:6 Geba and Mizpah. Geba was just east of Ramah, and Mizpah was between Ramah and Bethel. Fortifying these two cities effectively stopped Israel from rebuilding Ramah because it was now between two of Asa's fortresses.

16:7–9 Hanani the seer. Hanani was probably the

15:2 [b] [James 4:8] [c] [1 Chr. 28:9] [d] 2 Chr. 24:20 **15:3** [e] Hos. 3:4 [f] 2 Kin. 12:2 [g] Lev. 10:11 **15:4** [h] [Deut. 4:29] **15:6** [i] Matt. 24:7 **15:8** [j] 2 Chr. 13:19 **15:9** [k] 2 Chr. 11:16 **15:11** [l] 2 Chr. 14:13–15 **15:12** [m] 2 Chr. 23:3 **15:13** [n] Ex. 22:20 [o] Deut. 13:5–15 **15:15** [p] 2 Chr. 15:2 [q] 2 Chr. 14:7 **15:16** [r] 1 Kin. 15:2, 10, 13 **15:17** [s] 1 Kin. 15:14 **16:1** [a] 1 Kin. 15:17–22 [b] 2 Chr. 15:9 **16:7** [c] 2 Chr. 19:2 [d] [Jer. 17:5]

therefore the army of the king of Syria has escaped from your hand. 8Were ethe Ethiopians and fthe Lubim not a huge army with very many chariots and horsemen? Yet, because you relied on the LORD, He delivered them into your ghand. 9hFor the eyes of the LORD run to and fro throughout the whole earth, to show Himself strong on behalf of *those* whose heart *is* loyal to Him. In this iyou have done foolishly; therefore from now on iyou shall have wars." 10Then Asa was angry with the seer, and kput him in prison, for *he was* enraged at him because of this. And Asa oppressed *some* of the people at that time.

Illness and Death of Asa

11lNote that the acts of Asa, first and last, are indeed written in the book of the kings of Judah and Israel. 12And in the thirty-ninth year of his reign, Asa became diseased in his feet, and his malady was severe; yet in his disease he mdid not seek the LORD, but the physicians.

13nSo Asa rested with his fathers; he died in the forty-first year of his reign. 14They buried him in his own tomb, which he had made for himself in the City of David; and they laid him in the bed which was filled owith spices and various ingredients prepared in a mixture of ointments. They made pa very great burning for him.

Jehoshaphat Reigns in Judah

17 Then aJehoshaphat his son reigned in his place, and strengthened himself against Israel. 2And he placed troops in all the fortified cities of Judah, and set garrisons in the land of bJudah and in the cities of Ephraim cwhich Asa his father had taken. 3Now the LORD was with Jehoshaphat, because he walked in the former ways of his father David; he did not seek the Baals, 4but sought the God* of his father, and walked in His commandments and not according to dthe acts of Israel. 5Therefore the LORD established the kingdom in his hand; and all Judah egave presents to Jehoshaphat, fand he had riches and honor in abundance. 6And his heart took delight in the ways of the LORD; moreover ghe removed the high places and wooden images from Judah.

7Also in the third year of his reign he sent his leaders, Ben-Hail, Obadiah, Zechariah, Nethanel, and Michaiah, hto teach in the cities of Judah. 8And with them *he sent* Levites: Shemaiah, Nethaniah, Zebadiah, Asahel, Shemiramoth, Jehonathan, Adonijah, Tobijah, and Tobadonijah—the Levites; and with them Elishama and Jehoram, the priests. 9iSo they taught in Judah, and *had* the Book of the Law of the LORD with them; they went throughout all the cities of Judah and taught the people.

10And ithe fear of the LORD fell on all the kingdoms of the lands that *were* around Judah, so that they did not make war against Jehoshaphat. 11Also *some* of the Philistines kbrought Jehoshaphat presents and silver as tribute; and the Arabians brought him flocks, seven thousand seven hundred rams and seven thousand seven hundred male goats.

12So Jehoshaphat became increasingly powerful, and he built fortresses and storage cities in Judah. 13He had much property in the cities of Judah; and the men of war, mighty men of valor, *were* in Jerusalem.

14These *are* their numbers, according to their fathers' houses. Of Judah, the captains of thousands: Adnah the captain, and with him three hundred thousand mighty men of valor; 15and next to him *was* Jehohanan the captain, and with him two hundred and eighty thousand; 16and next to him *was* Amasiah the son of Zichri, lwho willingly offered himself to the LORD, and with him two hundred thousand mighty men of valor. 17Of Benjamin: Eliada a mighty man of valor, and with him two hundred thousand armed with bow and shield; 18and next to him *was* Jehozabad, and with him one hundred and eighty thousand prepared for war. 19These served the king, besides mthose the king put in the fortified cities throughout all Judah.

Micaiah Warns Ahab

18 Jehoshaphat ahad riches and honor in abundance; and by marriage he ballied himself with cAhab. 2dAfter some years he went down to *visit* Ahab in

---

* **17:4** Septuagint reads LORD God.

---

father of another prophet, Jehu, who once challenged King Jehoshaphat of Judah (19:2; 20:34).

17:2 *cities of Ephraim.* Ephraim is a synonym for Israel. The cities referred to here are mentioned also in 15:8.

17:13–18 *men of war, mighty men of valor.* Jehoshaphat's men were grouped into three divisions of Judeans with a total number of 780,000 and two divisions of Benjamites numbering 380,000. The Hebrew word for thousand can mean family, or clan, (Judg. 6:15; 1 Sam. 10:19; Mic. 5:2). In that case, the 780,000 would be 780 companies, and the 380,000 would be 380 companies, and the total warriors would be nearer to 78,000 and 38,000.

18:2 *Ramoth Gilead.* This important city was some 35 miles east of Beth Shan, and was controlled by the

16:8 e 2 Chr. 14:9 f 2 Chr. 12:3 g 2 Chr. 13:16, 18
16:9 h Zech. 4:10 i 1 Sam. 13:13 j 1 Kin. 15:32 **16:10** k Jer. 20:2 **16:11** l 1 Kin. 15:23, 24 **16:12** m [Jer. 17:5]
16:13 n 1 Kin. 15:24 **16:14** o John 19:39, 40 p 2 Chr. 21:19 **17:1** a 1 Kin. 15:24 **17:2** b 2 Chr. 11:5 c 2 Chr. 15:8 **17:4** d 1 Kin. 12:28 **17:5** e 1 Kin. 10:25 f 2 Chr. 18:1
17:6 g 1 Kin. 22:43 **17:7** h 2 Chr. 15:3; 35:3 **17:9** i Neh. 8:3, 7 **17:10** j 2 Chr. 14:14 **17:11** k 2 Chr. 9:14; 26:8
17:16 l Judg. 5:2, 9 **17:19** m 2 Chr. 17:2 **18:1** a 2 Chr. 17:5 b 2 Kin. 8:18 c 1 Kin. 22:40 **18:2** d 1 Kin. 22:2

Samaria; and Ahab killed sheep and oxen in abundance for him and the people who were with him, and persuaded him to go up *with him* to Ramoth Gilead. ³So Ahab king of Israel said to Jehoshaphat king of Judah, "Will you go with me *against* Ramoth Gilead?"

And he answered him, "I *am* as you *are*, and my people as your people; *we will be* with you in the war."

⁴Also Jehoshaphat said to the king of Israel, ᵉ"Please inquire for the word of the LORD today."

⁵Then the king of Israel gathered the prophets together, four hundred men, and said to them, "Shall we go to war against Ramoth Gilead, or shall I refrain?"

So they said, "Go up, for God will deliver it into the king's hand."

⁶But Jehoshaphat said, "*Is there* not still a prophet of the LORD here, that we may inquire of ᶠHim?"*

⁷So the king of Israel said to Jehoshaphat, "*There is* still one man by whom we may inquire of the LORD; but I hate him, because he never prophesies good concerning me, but always evil. He *is* Micaiah the son of Imla."

And Jehoshaphat said, "Let not the king say such things!"

⁸Then the king of Israel called one *of his* officers and said, "Bring Micaiah the son of Imla quickly!"

⁹The king of Israel and Jehoshaphat king of Judah, clothed in *their* robes, sat each on his throne; and they sat at a threshing floor at the entrance of the gate of Samaria; and all the prophets prophesied before them. ¹⁰Now Zedekiah the son of Chenaanah had made ᵍhorns of iron for himself; and he said, "Thus says the LORD: 'With these you shall gore the Syrians until they are destroyed.'"

¹¹And all the prophets prophesied so, saying, "Go up to Ramoth Gilead and prosper, for the LORD will deliver *it* into the king's hand."

¹²Then the messenger who had gone to call Micaiah spoke to him, saying, "Now listen, the words of the prophets with one accord encourage the king.

Therefore please let your word be like *the word of* one of them, and speak encouragement."

¹³And Micaiah said, "*As* the LORD lives, ʰwhatever my God says, that I will speak."

¹⁴Then he came to the king; and the king said to him, "Micaiah, shall we go to war against Ramoth Gilead, or shall I refrain?"

And he said, "Go and prosper, and they shall be delivered into your hand!"

¹⁵So the king said to him, "How many times shall I make you swear that you tell me nothing but the truth in the name of the LORD?"

¹⁶Then he said, "I saw all Israel ⁱscattered on the mountains, as sheep that have no ʲshepherd. And the LORD said, 'These have no master. Let each return to his house in peace.'"

¹⁷And the king of Israel said to Jehoshaphat, "Did I not tell you he would not prophesy good concerning me, but evil?"

¹⁸Then *Micaiah* said, "Therefore hear the word of the LORD: I saw the LORD sitting on His ᵏthrone, and all the host of heaven standing on His right hand and His left. ¹⁹And the LORD said, 'Who will persuade Ahab king of Israel to go up, that he may fall at Ramoth Gilead?' So one spoke in this manner, and another spoke in that manner. ²⁰Then a ˡspirit came forward and stood before the LORD, and said, 'I will persuade him.' The LORD said to him, 'In what way?' ²¹So he said, 'I will go out and be a lying spirit in the mouth of all his prophets.' And *the* LORD said, 'You shall persuade *him* and also prevail; go out and do so.' ²²Therefore look! ᵐThe LORD has put a lying spirit in the mouth of these prophets of yours, and the LORD has declared disaster against you."

²³Then Zedekiah the son of Chenaanah went near and ⁿstruck Micaiah on the cheek, and said, "Which way did the spirit from the LORD go from me to speak to you?"

²⁴And Micaiah said, "Indeed you shall see on that day when you go into an inner chamber to hide!"

* 18:6 Or *him*

Arameans. It was also one of the Israelite cities of refuge (Josh. 20:8; 1 Chr. 6:80).
18:5 prophets. These prophets were probably prophets of Baal or Ashera (1 Kin. 18:19), the Canaanite gods worshiped by Ahab's wife Jezebel.
18:11 prophesied. The true prophet's words come directly from God, and they show God's thoughts, and sometimes His plans. These false prophets were speaking authoritatively, probably accompanied with such ravings and demonstrations as would show their power and ability to see the future (1 Kin. 18:26–29).
18:15 nothing but the truth. Ahab knew from experience that his prophets told him what they thought he wanted to hear, not the truth. Because their

prophecies agreed with Micaiah's he knew that Micaiah must have been mocking when he prophesied success.
18:22 lying spirit. The spirits who stood before the Lord were both angels and demons, none of whom could act without God's permission. God allowed this spirit to work in the mouths of the false prophets to accomplish His own purposes of judgment (1 Chr. 21:1; Job 1).

18:4 ᵉ 2 Sam. 2:1   **18:6** ᶠ 2 Kin. 3:11   **18:10** ᵍ Zech. 1:18–21   **18:13** ʰ Num. 22:18–20, 35; 23:12, 26   **18:16** ⁱ [Jer. 23:1–8; 31:10] / Matt. 9:36   **18:18** ᵏ Is. 6:1–5   **18:20** ˡ Job 1:6   **18:22** ᵐ Ezek. 14:9   **18:23** ⁿ Jer. 20:2

25Then the king of Israel said, "Take Micaiah, and return him to Amon the governor of the city and to Joash the king's son; 26and say, 'Thus says the king: o"Put this *fellow* in prison, and feed him with bread of affliction and water of affliction, until I return in peace."'"

27But Micaiah said, "If you ever return in peace, the LORD has not spoken by pme." And he said, "Take heed, all you people!"

Ahab Dies in Battle

28So the king of Israel and Jehoshaphat the king of Judah went up to Ramoth Gilead. 29And the king of Israel said to Jehoshaphat, "I will qdisguise myself and go into battle; but you put on your robes." So the king of Israel disguised himself, and they went into battle.

30Now the king of Syria had commanded the captains of the chariots who *were* with him, saying, "Fight with no one small or great, but only with the king of Israel." 31So it was, when the captains of the chariots saw Jehoshaphat, that they said, "It *is* the king of Israel!" Therefore they surrounded him to attack; but Jehoshaphat rcried out, and the LORD helped him, and God diverted them from him. 32For so it was, when the captains of the chariots saw that it was not the king of Israel, that they turned back from pursuing him. 33Now a certain man drew a bow at random, and struck the king of Israel between the joints of his armor. So he said to the driver of his chariot, "Turn around and take me out of the battle, for I am wounded." 34The battle increased that day, and the king of Israel propped *himself* up in *his* chariot facing the Syrians until evening; and about the time of sunset he died.

19 Then Jehoshaphat the king of Judah returned safely to his house in Jerusalem. 2And Jehu the son of Hanani athe seer went out to meet him, and said to King Jehoshaphat, "Should you help the wicked and blove those who hate the LORD? Therefore the cwrath of the LORD *is* upon you. 3Nevertheless dgood things are found in you, in that you have removed the wooden images from the land, and have eprepared your heart to seek God."

The Reforms of Jehoshaphat

4So Jehoshaphat dwelt at Jerusalem; and he went out again among the people from Beersheba to the mountains of Ephraim, and brought them back to the LORD God of their ffathers. 5Then he set gjudges in the land throughout all the fortified cities of Judah, city by city, 6and said to the judges, "Take heed to what you are doing, for hyou do not judge for man but for the LORD, iwho *is* with you in the judgment. 7Now therefore, let the fear of the LORD be upon you; take care and do *it*, for jthere *is* no iniquity with the LORD our God, no kpartiality, nor taking of bribes."

8Moreover in Jerusalem, for the judgment of the LORD and for controversies, Jehoshaphat lappointed some of the Levites and priests, and some of the chief fathers of Israel, when they returned to Jerusalem.* 9And he commanded them, saying, "Thus you shall act min the fear of the LORD, faithfully and with a loyal heart: 10nWhatever case comes to you from your brethren who dwell in their cities, whether of bloodshed or offenses against law or commandment, against statutes or ordinances, you shall warn them, lest they trespass against the LORD and owrath come upon pyou and your brethren. Do this, and you will not be guilty. 11And take notice: qAmariah the chief priest *is* over you rin all matters of the LORD; and Zebadiah the son of Ishmael, the ruler of the house of Judah, for all the king's matters; also the Levites *will be* officials before you. Behave courageously, and the LORD will be swith the good."

Ammon, Moab, and Mount Seir Defeated

20 It happened after this *that* the people of aMoab with the people of bAmmon, and *others* with them besides the cAmmonites,* came to battle against Jehoshaphat. 2Then some came and told Jehoshaphat, saying, "A great multitude is coming against you from beyond the

---

* **19:8** Septuagint and Vulgate read *for the inhabitants of Jerusalem.* * **20:1** Following Masoretic Text and Vulgate; Septuagint reads *Meunites* (compare 26:7).

18:33 *at random.* From the human perspective, this was a chance shot. From God's perspective, chance had no part in it. Ahab's disguise could not foil God's plan.

19:3 **Repentance**—Repentance is never by word only. It is always followed by actions which show that the attitude of repentance is really present. Part of repentance is acknowledging that God is right and that He knows how we should live. It was the change in Jehoshaphat's actions that proved his change of heart.

19:4 *mountains of Ephraim.* The mountains of Ephraim became the northern border of Judah after

the division into two kingdoms. This is another way of saying that the whole country was brought back to the Lord.

18:26 o 2 Chr. 16:10 **18:27** p Deut. 18:22 **18:29** q 2 Chr. 35:22 **18:31** r 2 Chr. 13:14, 15 **19:2** a 1 Kin. 16:1 b Ps. 139:21 c 2 Chr. 32:25 **19:3** d 2 Chr. 17:4, 6 e 2 Chr. 30:19 **19:4** f 2 Chr. 15:8–13 **19:5** g [Deut. 16:18–20] **19:6** h [Deut. 1:17] i Ps. 82:1 **19:7** j [Deut. 32:4] k [Deut. 10:17, 18] **19:8** l 2 Chr. 17:8 **19:9** m [2 Sam. 23:3] **19:10** n Deut. 17:8 o Num. 16:46 p [Ezek. 3:18] **19:11** q Ezra 7:3 r 1 Chr. 26:30 s [2 Chr. 15:2; 20:17] **20:1** a 1 Chr. 18:2 b 1 Chr. 19:15 c 2 Chr. 26:7

sea, from Syria;* and they are ᵈin Haza-zon Tamar" (which is ᵉEn Gedi). ³And Je-hoshaphat feared, and set himself to ᶠseek the LORD, and ᵍproclaimed a fast through-out all Judah. ⁴So Judah gathered together to ask ʰhelp from the LORD; and from all the cities of Judah they came to seek the LORD.

⁵Then Jehoshaphat stood in the assem-bly of Judah and Jerusalem, in the house of the LORD, before the new court, ⁶and said: "O LORD God of our fathers, are You not ⁱGod in heaven, and ʲdo You not rule over all the kingdoms of the nations, and ᵏin Your hand is there not power and might, so that no one is able to withstand You? ⁷Are You not ˡour God, who ᵐdrove out the inhabi-tants of this land before Your people Israel, and gave it to the descendants of Abraham ⁿYour friend forever? ⁸And they dwell in it, and have built You a sanctuary in it for Your name, saying, ⁹o'If disaster comes upon us—sword, judgment, pestilence, or famine—we will stand before this temple and in Your presence (for Your ᵖname is in this temple), and cry out to You in our af-fliction, and You will hear and save.' ¹⁰And now, here are the people of Ammon, Moab, and Mount Seir—whom You ᵠwould not let Israel invade when they came out of the land of Egypt, but ʳthey turned from them and did not destroy them— ¹¹here they are, rewarding us ˢby coming to throw us out of Your possession which You have given us to inherit. ¹²O our God, will You not ᵗjudge them? For we have no power against this great multitude that is coming against us; nor do we know what to do, but ᵘour eyes are upon You."

¹³Now all Judah, with their little ones, their wives, and their children, stood be-fore the LORD.

¹⁴Then ᵛthe Spirit of the LORD came upon Jahaziel the son of Zechariah, the son of Benaiah, the son of Jeiel, the son of Mat-taniah, a Levite of the sons of Asaph, in the midst of the assembly. ¹⁵And he said, "Lis-ten, all you of Judah and you inhabitants of Jerusalem, and you, King Jehoshaphat! Thus says the LORD to you: ʷ'Do not be afraid nor dismayed because of this great multitude, ˣfor the battle is not yours, but

God's. ¹⁶Tomorrow go down against them. They will surely come up by the Ascent of Ziz, and you will find them at the end of the brook before the Wilderness of Jeruel. ¹⁷ʸYou will not need to fight in this battle. Position yourselves, stand still and see the salvation of the LORD, who is with you, O Judah and Jerusalem!' Do not fear or be dismayed; tomorrow go out against them, ᶻfor the LORD is with you."

¹⁸And Jehoshaphat ᵃbowed his head with his face to the ground, and all Judah and the inhabitants of Jerusalem bowed before the LORD, worshiping the LORD. ¹⁹Then the Levites of the children of the Kohathites and of the children of the Kora-hites stood up to praise the LORD God of Israel with voices loud and high.

²⁰So they rose early in the morning and went out into the Wilderness of Tekoa; and as they went out, Jehoshaphat stood and said, "Hear me, O Judah and you inhabi-tants of Jerusalem: ᵇBelieve in the LORD your God, and you shall be established; believe His prophets, and you shall pros-per." ²¹And when he had consulted with the people, he appointed those who should sing to the LORD, ᶜand who should praise the beauty of holiness, as they went out before the army and were saying:

ᵈ"Praise the LORD,
ᵉFor His mercy endures forever."*

²²Now when they began to sing and to praise, ᶠthe LORD set ambushes against the people of Ammon, Moab, and Mount Seir, who had come against Judah; and they were defeated. ²³For the people of Ammon and Moab stood up against the inhabitants of Mount Seir to utterly kill and destroy them. And when they had made an end of the inhabitants of Seir, ᵍthey helped to de-stroy one another.

²⁴So when Judah came to a place over-looking the wilderness, they looked toward the multitude; and there were their dead bodies, fallen on the earth. No one had es-caped.

²⁵When Jehoshaphat and his people

---

* **20:2** Following Masoretic Text, Septuagint, and Vulgate; some Hebrew manuscripts and Old Latin read Edom.   * **20:21** Compare Psalm 106:1

20:14 Jahaziel. As a member of the Asaph division of the Levites (1 Chr. 6:39; 15:17–19; 16:7) Jahaziel was probably a musician. The spiritual work of the musi-cians was closely linked with prophecy (1 Chr. 25:1).
20:19 Kohathites . . . Korahites. The Kohathites were members of the Levitical division of Heman the singer (1 Chr. 6:33). The Korahites were a subdivision of the Kohathites (1 Chr. 6:37,39) who were employed as gatekeepers to the temple.
20:21 Thankfulness—More necessary than guns for soldiers, more important than strategy, is the giv-ing of thanks to God. Judah faced a literal, physical battle involving great odds. They sent their singers out first, singing praises to God and thanking Him

for His everlasting lovingkindness. Is this the way we face battles in our lives? Do we first thank God for who He is, what He has done, and for His faithfulness to us?

20:2 ᵈGen. 14:7 ᵉJosh. 15:62 **20:3** ᶠ2 Chr. 15:3 ᵍEzra 8:21 **20:4** ʰ2 Chr. 14:11 **20:6** ⁱDeut. 4:39 ʲDan. 4:17, 25, 32 ᵏ1 Chr. 29:12 **20:7** ˡEx. 6:7 ᵐPs. 44:2 ⁿIs. 41:8 **20:9** ᵒ2 Chr. 6:28–30 ᵖ2 Chr. 6:20 **20:10** ᵠDeut. 2:4, 9, 19 ʳNum. 20:21 **20:11** ˢPs. 83:1–18 **20:12** ᵗJudg. 11:27 ᵘPs. 25:15; 121:1, 2; 123:1, 2; 141:8 **20:14** ᵛ2 Chr. 15:1; 24:20 **20:15** ʷ[Deut. 1:29, 30; 31:6, 8] ˣ1 Sam. 17:47 **20:17** ʸEx. 14:13, 14 ᶻNum. 14:9 **20:18** ᵃEx. 4:31 **20:20** ᵇIs. 7:9 **20:21** ᶜ1 Chr. 16:29 ᵈPs. 106:1; 136:1 ᵉ2 Chr. 5:13 **20:22** ᶠJudg. 7:22 **20:23** ᵍ1 Sam. 14:20

came to take away their spoil, they found among them an abundance of valuables on the dead bodies,* and precious jewelry, which they stripped off for themselves, more than they could carry away; and they were three days gathering the spoil because there was so much. 26And on the fourth day they assembled in the Valley of Berachah, for there they blessed the LORD; therefore the name of that place was called The Valley of Berachah* until this day. 27Then they returned, every man of Judah and Jerusalem, with Jehoshaphat in front of them, to go back to Jerusalem with joy, for the LORD had hmade them rejoice over their enemies. 28So they came to Jerusalem, with stringed instruments and harps and trumpets, to the house of the LORD. 29And the fear of God was on all the kingdoms of those countries when they heard that the LORD had fought against the enemies of Israel. 30Then the realm of Jehoshaphat was quiet, for his iGod gave him rest all around.

The End of Jehoshaphat's Reign

31kSo Jehoshaphat was king over Judah. He was thirty-five years old when he became king, and he reigned twenty-five years in Jerusalem. His mother's name was Azubah the daughter of Shilhi. 32And he walked in the way of his father lAsa, and did not turn aside from it, doing what was right in the sight of the LORD. 33Nevertheless mthe high places were not taken away, for as yet the people had not ndirected their hearts to the God of their fathers. 34Now the rest of the acts of Jehoshaphat, first and last, indeed they are written in the book of Jehu the son of Hanani, owhich is mentioned in the book of the kings of Israel.

35After this pJehoshaphat king of Judah allied himself with Ahaziah king of Israel, qwho acted very rwickedly. 36And he allied himself with him sto make ships to go to Tarshish, and they made the ships in Ezion Geber. 37But Eliezer the son of Dodavah of Mareshah prophesied against Jehoshaphat, saying, "Because you have allied yourself with Ahaziah, the LORD

has destroyed your works." tThen the ships were wrecked, so that they were not able to go uto Tarshish.

Jehoram Reigns in Judah

21 And aJehoshaphat rested with his fathers, and was buried with his fathers in the City of David. Then Jehoram his son reigned in his place. 2He had brothers, the sons of Jehoshaphat: Azariah, Jehiel, Zechariah, Azaryahu, Michael, and Shephatiah; all these were the sons of Jehoshaphat king of Israel. 3Their father gave them great gifts of silver and gold and precious things, with fortified cities in Judah; but he gave the kingdom to Jehoram, because he was the firstborn.

4Now when Jehoram was established over the kingdom of his father, he strengthened himself and killed all his brothers with the sword, and also others of the princes of Israel.

5bJehoram was thirty-two years old when he became king, and he reigned eight years in Jerusalem. 6And he walked in the way of the kings of Israel, just as the house of Ahab had done, for he had the daughter of cAhab as a wife; and he did evil in the sight of the LORD. 7Yet the LORD would not destroy the house of David, because of the dcovenant that He had made with David, and since He had promised to give a lamp to him and to his esons forever.

8fIn his days Edom revolted against Judah's authority, and made a king over themselves. 9So Jehoram went out with his officers, and all his chariots with him. And he rose by night and attacked the Edomites who had surrounded him and the captains of the chariots. 10Thus Edom has been in revolt against Judah's authority to this day. At that time Libnah revolted against his rule, because he had forsaken the LORD God of his fathers. 11Moreover he made high places in the mountains of Judah, and caused the inhabitants of Jerusalem to gcommit harlotry, and led Judah astray.

---

* **20:25** A few Hebrew manuscripts, Old Latin, and Vulgate read garments; Septuagint reads armor.
* **20:26** Literally Blessing

20:26 Valley of Berachah. The Judeans renamed Ziz "the Valley of Berachah," meaning "blessing," to remind themselves of God's goodness.
20:34 Jehu. The son of the prophet Hanani, Jehu was a prophet himself (19:2). He is mentioned in 1 Kings in connection with the kings of Israel, and was therefore a good source of information about both the northern and southern kingdoms.
20:35 Ahaziah. Ahaziah was the son of Ahab. He succeeded his father and reigned for two years (1 Kin. 22:51). Ahaziah was injured in a fall and turned to the Philistine gods rather than to the Lord for healing (2 Kin. 1:2).
21:11 commit harlotry. Israel's relationship with God was like a marriage relationship. Worship of other

gods was a violation in the same way that prostitution violates a marriage. It not only says that the true husband is not worthy of respect, it is a rejection of the whole idea of the faithfulness and care of the true husband.

20:27 h Neh. 12:43   **20:29** i 2 Chr. 14:14; 17:10   **20:30** j Job 34:29   **20:31** k [1 Kin. 22:41–43]   **20:32** l 2 Chr. 14:2   **20:33** m 2 Chr. 15:17; 17:6   n 2 Chr. 12:14; 19:3   **20:34** o 1 Kin. 16:1, 7   **20:35** p 2 Chr. 18:1   q 1 Kin. 22:48–53   r [2 Chr. 19:2]   **20:36** s 1 Kin. 9:26; 10:22   **20:37** t 1 Kin. 22:48   u 2 Chr. 9:21   **21:1** a 1 Kin. 22:50   **21:5** b 2 Kin. 8:17–22   **21:6** c 2 Chr. 18:1   **21:7** d 2 Sam. 7:8–17   e 1 Kin. 11:36   **21:8** f 2 Kin. 8:20; 14:7, 10   **21:11** g [Lev. 20:5]

¹²And a letter came to him from Elijah the prophet, saying,

Thus says the LORD God of your father David:
Because you have not walked in the ways of Jehoshaphat your father, or in the ways of Asa king of Judah, ¹³but have walked in the way of the kings of Israel, and have ʰmade Judah and the inhabitants of Jerusalem to ⁱplay the harlot like the ʲharlotry of the house of Ahab, and also have ᵏkilled your brothers, those of your father's household, *who were* better than yourself, ¹⁴behold, the LORD will strike your people with a serious affliction—your children, your wives, and all your possessions; ¹⁵and you *will become* very sick with a ˡdisease of your intestines, until your intestines come out by reason of the sickness, day by day.

¹⁶Moreover the ᵐLORD ⁿstirred up against Jehoram the spirit of the Philistines and the ᵒArabians who *were* near the Ethiopians. ¹⁷And they came up into Judah and invaded it, and carried away all the possessions that were found in the king's house, and also ᵖhis sons and his wives, so that there was not a son left to him except Jehoahaz,* the youngest of his sons.

¹⁸After all this the LORD struck him �q in his intestines with an incurable disease. ¹⁹Then it happened in the course of time, after the end of two years, that his intestines came out because of his sickness; so he died in severe pain. And his people made no burning for him, like ʳthe burning for his fathers.

²⁰He was thirty-two years old when he became king. He reigned in Jerusalem eight years and, to no one's sorrow, departed. However they buried him in the City of David, but not in the tombs of the kings.

Ahaziah Reigns in Judah

22 Then the inhabitants of Jerusalem made ᵃAhaziah his youngest son king in his place, for the raiders who came with the ᵇArabians into the camp had killed all the ᶜolder *sons.* So Ahaziah the son of Jehoram, king of Judah, reigned. ²Ahaziah *was* forty-two* years old when he became king, and he reigned one year in Jerusalem. His mother's name *was* ᵈAthaliah the granddaughter of Omri. ³He also walked in the ways of the house of Ahab, for his mother advised him to do wickedly. ⁴Therefore he did evil in the sight of the LORD, like the house of Ahab; for they were his counselors after the death of his father, to his destruction. ⁵He also followed their advice, and went with Jehoram* the son of Ahab king of Israel to war against Hazael king of Syria at Ramoth Gilead; and the Syrians wounded Joram. ⁶ᵉThen he returned to Jezreel to recover from the wounds which he had received at Ramah, when he fought against Hazael king of Syria. And Azariah* the son of Jehoram, king of Judah, went down to see Jehoram the son of Ahab in Jezreel, because he was sick.

⁷His going to Joram ᶠwas God's occasion for Ahaziah's downfall; for when he arrived, ᵍhe went out with Jehoram against Jehu the son of Nimshi, ʰwhom the LORD had anointed to cut off the house of Ahab. ⁸And it happened, when Jehu was ⁱexecuting judgment on the house of Ahab, and ʲfound the princes of Judah and the sons of Ahaziah's brothers who served Ahaziah, that he killed them. ⁹ᵏThen he searched for Ahaziah; and they caught him (he was hiding in Samaria), and brought him to Jehu. When they had killed him, they buried him, "because," they said, "he is the son of ˡJehoshaphat, who ᵐsought the LORD with all his heart."

So the house of Ahaziah had no one to assume power over the kingdom.

---

* **21:17** Elsewhere called *Ahaziah* (compare 2 Chronicles 22:1)   * **22:2** Or *twenty-two* (compare 2 Kings 8:26)   * **22:5** Also spelled *Joram* (compare verses 5 and 7; 2 Kings 8:28; and elsewhere)
* **22:6** Some Hebrew manuscripts, Septuagint, Syriac, Vulgate, and 2 Kings 8:29 read *Ahaziah.*

21:12 *Elijah the prophet.* Though 1 and 2 Kings pay considerable attention to Elijah (1 Kin. 17:1—2 Kin. 2:18), the books of Chronicles mention him only here. He had been taken up into heaven after King Ahaziah's death (2 Kin. 1:17; 2:1).

21:20 *tombs of the kings.* These tombs were a royal cemetery in Jerusalem where most of the kings of David's dynasty were buried. (Asa was an exception, 16:14.)

22:1 *Ahaziah.* Ahaziah of Judah was the namesake of his uncle from Israel. His father Jehoram had married a sister of Ahab's son Ahaziah (1 Kin. 22:40; 2 Kin. 8:18).

22:5 *Jehoram the son of Ahab.* Jehoram succeeded his brother Ahaziah because Ahaziah had no son of his own (2 Kin. 1:17). He is also called Joram, a short form of Jehoram, to distinguish him from his brother-in-law Jehoram who was king of Judah. ***Hazael.*** Hazael was the king of Damascus who came to power

after assassinating Ben-Hadad (2 Kin. 8:7–15). Elijah had prophesied that this would come about and had even commissioned Elisha to anoint Hazael to his new position (1 Kin. 19:15). Elisha wept after he had anointed Hazael, for he knew that Hazael would cruelly kill many Israelites. ***Ramoth-Gilead.*** Ahab and Jehoshaphat had tried to recover this city from Aramean domination 12 years earlier (18:3).

21:13 ʰ 2 Chr. 21:11   ⁱ Deut. 31:16   ʲ 2 Kin. 9:22   ᵏ 2 Chr. 21:4   **21:15** ˡ 2 Chr. 21:18, 19   **21:16** ᵐ 2 Chr. 33:11   ⁿ 1 Kin. 11:14, 23   ᵒ 2 Chr. 17:11   **21:17** ᵖ 2 Chr. 24:7   **21:18** �q 2 Chr. 13:20; 21:15   **21:19** ʳ 2 Chr. 16:14   **22:1** ᵃ 2 Chr. 21:17; 22:6   ᵇ 2 Chr. 21:16   ᶜ 2 Chr. 21:17   **22:2** ᵈ 2 Chr. 21:6   **22:6** ᵉ 2 Kin. 9:15   **22:7** ᶠ 2 Chr. 10:15   ᵍ 2 Kin. 9:21–24   ʰ 2 Kin. 9:6, 7   **22:8** ⁱ 2 Kin. 9:22–24   ʲ 2 Kin. 10:10–14   **22:9** ᵏ [2 Kin. 9:27]   ˡ 1 Kin. 15:24   ᵐ 2 Chr. 17:4; 20:3, 4

Athaliah Reigns in Judah

10nNow when Athaliah the mother of Ahaziah saw that her son was dead, she arose and destroyed all the royal heirs of the house of Judah. 11But Jehoshabeath,* the daughter of the king, took oJoash the son of Ahaziah, and stole him away from among the king's sons who were being murdered, and put him and his nurse in a bedroom. So Jehoshabeath, the daughter of King Jehoram, the wife of Jehoiada the priest (for she was the sister of Ahaziah), hid him from Athaliah so that she did not kill him. 12And he was hidden with them in the house of God for six years, while Athaliah reigned over the land.

Joash Crowned King of Judah

23 In athe seventh year bJehoiada strengthened himself, and made a covenant with the captains of hundreds: Azariah the son of Jeroham, Ishmael the son of Jehohanan, Azariah the son of cObed, Maaseiah the son of Adaiah, and Elishaphat the son of Zichri. 2And they went throughout Judah and gathered the Levites from all the cities of Judah, and the dchief fathers of Israel, and they came to Jerusalem.

3Then all the assembly made a covenant with the king in the house of God. And he said to them, "Behold, the king's son shall reign, as the LORD has esaid of the sons of David. 4This is what you shall do: One-third of you fentering on the Sabbath, of the priests and the Levites, shall be keeping watch over the doors; 5one-third shall be at the king's house; and one-third at the Gate of the Foundation. All the people shall be in the courts of the house of the LORD. 6But let no one come into the house of the LORD except the priests and gthose of the Levites who serve. They may go in, for they are holy; but all the people shall keep the watch of the LORD. 7And the Levites shall surround the king on all sides, every man with his weapons in his hand; and whoever comes into the house, let him be put to death. You are to be with the king when he comes in and when he goes out."

8So the Levites and all Judah did according to all that Jehoiada the priest

commanded. And each man took his men who were to be on duty on the Sabbath, with those who were going off duty on the Sabbath; for Jehoiada the priest had not dismissed hthe divisions. 9And Jehoiada the priest gave to the captains of hundreds the spears and the large and small ishields which had belonged to King David, that were in the temple of God. 10Then he set all the people, every man with his weapon in his hand, from the right side of the temple to the left side of the temple, along by the altar and by the temple, all around the king. 11And they brought out the king's son, put the crown on him, jgave him the Testimony,* and made him king. Then Jehoiada and his sons anointed him, and said, "Long live the king!"

Death of Athaliah

12Now when kAthaliah heard the noise of the people running and praising the king, she came to the people in the temple of the LORD. 13When she looked, there was the king standing by his pillar at the entrance; and the leaders and the trumpeters were by the king. All the people of the land were rejoicing and blowing trumpets, also the singers with musical instruments, and lthose who led in praise. So Athaliah tore her clothes and said, m"Treason! Treason!"

14And Jehoiada the priest brought out the captains of hundreds who were set over the army, and said to them, "Take her outside under guard, and slay with the sword whoever follows her." For the priest had said, "Do not kill her in the house of the LORD."

15So they seized her; and she went by way of the entrance nof the Horse Gate into the king's house, and they killed her there.

16Then Jehoiada made a ocovenant between himself, the people, and the king, that they should be the LORD's people. 17And all the people went to the temple* of Baal, and tore it down. They broke in pieces its altars and images, and pkilled Mattan the priest of Baal before the altars. 18Also Jehoiada

---

* **22:11** Spelled Jehosheba in 2 Kings 11:2
* **23:11** That is, the Law (compare Exodus 25:16, 21; 31:18) * **23:17** Literally house

---

22:10 the royal heirs. Most of the royal heirs that Athaliah murdered were her own grandchildren. She wanted to stamp out the Davidic dynasty and bring Judah back under Israelite control. Satan had been diligent in his attempts to thwart the plans of God, and because the Davidic line was directly linked to the Messiah, this would have been a strategic move. It is not unlike the murder of the baby boys by Herod at the time of Jesus' birth (Matt. 2:10–18).

23:3 Unity—Unity is only unity when we are "the same" on issues of the truth. The removal of Athaliah could not have occurred without the cooperation and teamwork of everyone. Knowing that they were doing God's will gave them great courage.

23:11 the Testimony. The Testimony was a copy of the law of Moses, part of which outlined the king's covenant privileges and duties (Deut. 17:18–20; 1 Chr. 29:19). **anointed him.** Anointing was a sign and seal of the king's appointment by God (1 Sam. 16:3; 1 Kin. 1:39).

22:10 n 2 Kin. 11:1–3   **22:11** o 2 Kin. 12:18   **23:1** a 2 Kin. 11:4 b 2 Kin. 12:2 c 1 Chr. 2:37, 38   **23:2** d Ezra 1:5   **23:3** e 2 Sam. 7:12   **23:4** f 1 Chr. 9:25   **23:6** g 1 Chr. 23:28–32   **23:8** h 1 Chr. 24:1–31   **23:9** i 2 Sam. 8:7   **23:11** j Deut. 17:18   **23:12** k 2 Chr. 22:10   **23:13** l 1 Chr. 25:6–8   m 2 Kin. 9:23   **23:15** n Neh. 3:28   **23:16** o Josh. 24:24, 25   **23:17** p Deut. 13:6–9

appointed the oversight of the house of the LORD to the hand of the priests, the Levites, whom David had *q*assigned in the house of the LORD, to offer the burnt offerings of the LORD, as *it is* written in the *r*Law of Moses, with rejoicing and with singing, *as it was established* by David. 19And he set the *s*gatekeepers at the gates of the house of the LORD, so that no one *who was* in any way unclean should enter.

20tThen he took the captains of hundreds, the nobles, the governors of the people, and all the people of the land, and brought the king down from the house of the LORD; and they went through the Upper Gate to the king's house, and set the king on the throne of the kingdom. 21So all the people of the land rejoiced; and the city was quiet, for they had slain Athaliah with the sword.

Joash Repairs the Temple

24 Joash *a*was seven years old when he became king, and he reigned forty years in Jerusalem. His mother's name *was* Zibiah of Beersheba. 2Joash *b*did *what was* right in the sight of the LORD all the days of Jehoiada the priest. 3And Jehoiada took for him two wives; and he had sons and daughters.

4Now it happened after this *that* Joash set his heart on repairing the house of the LORD. 5Then he gathered the priests and the Levites, and said to them, "Go out to the cities of Judah, and *c*gather from all Israel money to repair the house of your God from year to year, and see that you do it quickly."

However the Levites did not do it quickly. 6dSo the king called Jehoiada the chief *priest*, and said to him, "Why have you not required the Levites to bring in from Judah and from Jerusalem the collection, *according to the commandment* of *e*Moses the servant of the LORD and of the assembly of Israel, for the *f*tabernacle of witness?" 7For *g*the sons of Athaliah, that wicked woman, had broken into the house of God, and had also presented all the *h*dedicated things of the house of the LORD to the Baals.

8Then at the king's command *i*they made a chest, and set it outside at the gate of the

house of the LORD. 9And they made a proclamation throughout Judah and Jerusalem to bring to the LORD *j*the collection *that* Moses the servant of God *had imposed* on Israel in the wilderness. 10Then all the leaders and all the people rejoiced, brought their contributions, and put *them* into the chest until all had given. 11So it was, at that time, when the chest was brought to the king's official by the hand of the Levites, and *k*when they saw that *there was* much money, that the king's scribe and the high priest's officer came and emptied the chest, and took it and returned it to its place. Thus they did day by day, and gathered money in abundance.

12The king and Jehoiada gave it to those who did the work of the service of the house of the LORD; and they hired masons and carpenters to *l*repair the house of the LORD, and also those who worked in iron and bronze to restore the house of the LORD. 13So the workmen labored, and the work was completed by them; they restored the house of God to its original condition and reinforced it. 14When they had finished, they brought the rest of the money before the king and Jehoiada; *m*they made from it articles for the house of the LORD, articles for serving and offering, spoons and vessels of gold and silver. And they offered burnt offerings in the house of the LORD continually all the days of Jehoiada.

Apostasy of Joash

15But Jehoiada grew old and was full of days, and he died; he *was* one hundred and thirty years old when he died. 16And they buried him in the City of David among the kings, because he had done good in Israel, both toward God and His house.

17Now after the death of Jehoiada the leaders of Judah came and bowed down to the king. And the king listened to them. 18Therefore they left the house of the LORD God of their fathers, and served *n*wooden images and idols; and *o*wrath came upon Judah and Jerusalem because of their trespass. 19Yet He *p*sent prophets to them, to bring them back to the LORD; and they testified against them, but they would not listen. 20Then the Spirit of God came upon

---

24:7 dedicated things. The dedicated things included gold, silver, and other valuables collected as tribute from defeated enemies and presented to God as spoils of war, acknowledging that the victory was His and for His purposes (2 Sam. 8:10–11).

24:14 all the days of Jehoiada. As long as Jehoiada remained alive, Judah enjoyed a revival of the true worship of God.

24:20–21 Zechariah the son of Jehoiada. This priest is not the prophet of the same name who wrote the Book of Zechariah, nor is he the Zechariah mentioned by Jesus (Matt. 23:35). Zechariah, whose father rescued the young Joash, may even have been raised like a brother to King Joash. The "Zechariah son

of Berechiah," that Jesus refers to was probably the prophet who wrote the Book of Zechariah (Zech. 1:7), although the reference to his death is found only in the Gospels.

23:18 *q* 1 Chr. 23:6, 30, 31; 24:1 *r* Num. 28:2
23:19 *s* 1 Chr. 26:1–19 **23:20** *t* 2 Kin. 11:19 **24:1** *a* 2 Kin. 11:21; 12:1–15 **24:2** *b* 2 Chr. 26:4, 5 **24:5** *c* 2 Kin. 12:4 **24:6** *d* 2 Kin. 12:7 *e* Ex. 30:12–16 *f* Num. 1:50 **24:7** *g* 2 Chr. 21:17 *h* 2 Kin. 12:4 **24:8** *i* 2 Kin. 12:9 **24:9** *j* 2 Chr. 24:6 **24:11** *k* 2 Kin. 12:10 **24:12** *l* 2 Chr. 30:12 **24:14** *m* 2 Kin. 12:13 **24:18** *n* 1 Kin. 14:23 *o* [Ex. 34:12–14] **24:19** *p* 2 Chr. 36:15, 16

*q*Zechariah the son of Jehoiada the priest, who stood above the people, and said to them, "Thus says God: *r*'Why do you transgress the commandments of the LORD, so that you cannot prosper? *s*Because you have forsaken the LORD, He also has forsaken you.'" ²¹So they conspired against him, and at the command of the king they *t*stoned him with stones in the court of the house of the LORD. ²²Thus Joash the king did not remember the kindness which Jehoiada his father had done to him, but killed his son; and as he died, he said, "The LORD look on *it*, and *u*repay!"

Death of Joash

²³So it happened in the spring of the year that *v*the army of Syria came up against him; and they came to Judah and Jerusalem, and destroyed all the leaders of the people from among the people, and sent all their spoil to the king of Damascus. ²⁴For the army of the Syrians *w*came with a small company of men; but the LORD *x*delivered a very great army into their hand, because they had forsaken the LORD God of their fathers. So they *y*executed judgment against Joash. ²⁵And when they had withdrawn from him (for they left him severely wounded), *z*his own servants conspired against him because of the blood of the sons* of Jehoiada the priest, and killed him on his bed. So he died. And they buried him in the City of David, but they did not bury him in the tombs of the kings. ²⁶These are the ones who conspired against him: Zabad* the son of Shimeath the Ammonitess, and Jehozabad the son of Shimrith* the Moabitess. ²⁷Now *concerning* his sons, and *a*the many oracles about him, and the repairing of the house of God, indeed they *are* written in the annals of the book of the kings. *b*Then Amaziah his son reigned in his place.

Amaziah Reigns in Judah

25 Amaziah *a*was twenty-five years old *when* he became king, and he reigned twenty-nine years in Jerusalem. His mother's name *was* Jehoaddan of Jerusalem. ²And he did *what was* right in the sight of the LORD, *b*but not with a loyal heart.

³*c*Now it happened, as soon as the kingdom was established for him, that he executed his servants who had murdered his father the king. ⁴However he did not execute their children, but *did* as *it is* written in the Law in the Book of Moses, where the LORD commanded, saying, *d*"The fathers shall not be put to death for their children, nor shall the children be put to death for their fathers; but a person shall die for his own sin."*

The War Against Edom

⁵Moreover Amaziah gathered Judah together and set over them captains of thousands and captains of hundreds, according to *their* fathers' houses, throughout all Judah and Benjamin; and he numbered them *e*from twenty years old and above, and found them to be three hundred thousand choice *men, able* to go to war, who could handle spear and shield. ⁶He also hired one hundred thousand mighty men of valor from Israel for one hundred talents of silver. ⁷But a *f*man of God came to him, saying, "O king, do not let the army of Israel go with you, for the LORD *is* not with Israel— *not with* any of the children of Ephraim. ⁸But if you go, be gone! Be strong in battle! *Even so*, God shall make you fall before the enemy; for God has *g*power to help and to overthrow."

⁹Then Amaziah said to the man of God, "But what *shall* we do about the hundred talents which I have given to the troops of Israel?"

And the man of God answered, *h*"The LORD is able to give you much more than this." ¹⁰So Amaziah discharged the troops that had come to him from Ephraim, to go back home. Therefore their anger was greatly aroused against Judah, and they returned home in great anger.

---

* **24:25** Septuagint and Vulgate read *son* (compare verses 20–22). * **24:26** Or *Jozachar* (compare 2 Kings 12:21) • Or *Shomer* (compare 2 Kings 12:21) * **25:4** Deuteronomy 24:16

24:22 Martyrs—Zechariah is one of the pre-Christian martyrs who gave his life for his faith in God. Some of these faithful ones are listed in Hebrews 11; some are known only to God. Jesus predicted that those killed for their faith would actually increase in the last days (Matt. 10:21; 24:9) and during the coming great tribulation, the ranks of the martyrs will swell to unprecedented size (Rev. 7:14). The "offense" of martyrs is their relationship with God; their comfort is that God knows, and He keeps them faithful to the end (2 Tim. 4:8).

24:24 executed judgment. God arranged for Israel's defeat and Joash's death in fulfillment of Zechariah's dying cry for justice (v. 22). Judgment for evil does not always come so quickly, but it is just as inevitable, no matter how long it is delayed.

25:7 do not let the army of Israel go with you. As long as Israel was in rebellion against God, He would not bless any alliance with them. **Ephraim.** Ephraim was the dominant tribe in Israel, so the whole kingdom was sometimes referred to as Ephraim (Hos. 4:15–19).

24:20 *q* Matt. 23:35 *r* Num. 14:41 *s* [2 Chr. 15:2]
24:21 *t* [Neh. 9:26] **24:22** *u* [Gen. 9:5] **24:23** *v* 2 Kin. 12:17 **24:24** *w* Lev. 26:8; Is. 30:17 *x* Lev. 26:25 *y* 2 Chr. 22:8 **24:25** *z* 2 Kin. 12:20, 21 **24:27** *a* 2 Kin. 12:18 *b* 2 Kin. 12:21 **25:1** *a* 2 Kin. 14:1–6 **25:2** *b* 2 Chr. 25:14 **25:3** *c* 2 Kin. 14:5 **25:4** *d* Deut. 24:16 **25:5** *e* Num. 1:3 **25:7** *f* 2 Kin. 11:2 **25:8** *g* 2 Chr. 14:11; 20:6 **25:9** *h* [Deut. 8:18]

11 Then Amaziah strengthened himself,
and leading his people, he went to [i]the Valley of Salt and killed ten thousand of the
people of Seir. 12 Also the children of Judah
took captive ten thousand alive, brought
them to the top of the rock, and cast them
down from the top of the rock, so that they
all were dashed in pieces.
13 But as for the soldiers of the army
which Amaziah had discharged, so that
they would not go with him to battle, they
raided the cities of Judah from Samaria to
Beth Horon, killed three thousand in them,
and took much spoil.
14 Now it was so, after Amaziah came
from the slaughter of the Edomites, that
[j]he brought the gods of the people of Seir,
set them up *to be* [k]his gods, and bowed
down before them and burned incense to
them. 15 Therefore the anger of the LORD
was aroused against Amaziah, and He sent
him a prophet who said to him, "Why have
you sought [l]the gods of the people, which
[m]could not rescue their own people from
your hand?"
16 So it was, as he talked with him, that
the king said to him, "Have we made you
the king's counselor? Cease! Why should
you be killed?"
Then the prophet ceased, and said, "I
know that God has [n]determined to destroy
you, because you have done this and have
not heeded my advice."

Israel Defeats Judah

17 Now [o]Amaziah king of Judah asked
advice and sent to Joash* the son of Jehoahaz, the son of Jehu, king of Israel, saying,
"Come, let us face one another *in battle*."
18 And Joash king of Israel sent to Amaziah king of Judah, saying, "The thistle
that *was* in Lebanon sent to the cedar that
was in Lebanon, saying, 'Give your daughter to my son as wife'; and a wild beast that
was in Lebanon passed by and trampled
the thistle. 19 Indeed you say that you have
defeated the Edomites, and your heart is
lifted up to [p]boast. Stay at home now; why
should you meddle with trouble, that you
should fall—you and Judah with you?"
20 But Amaziah would not heed, for [q]it
came from God, that He might give them
into the hand *of their enemies*, because
they [r]sought the gods of Edom. 21 So Joash
king of Israel went out; and he and Amaziah king of Judah faced one another at
[s]Beth Shemesh, which *belongs* to Judah.
22 And Judah was defeated by Israel, and
every man fled to his tent. 23 Then Joash
the king of Israel captured Amaziah king
of Judah, the son of Joash, the son of [t]Je-
hoahaz, at Beth Shemesh; and he brought
him to Jerusalem, and broke down the wall
of Jerusalem from the Gate of Ephraim to
the Corner Gate—four hundred cubits.
24 And *he took* all the gold and silver, all
the articles that were found in the house of
God with [u]Obed-Edom, the treasures of the
king's house, and hostages, and returned
to Samaria.

Death of Amaziah

25 [v]Amaziah the son of Joash, king of Judah, lived fifteen years after the death of
Joash the son of Jehoahaz, king of Israel.
26 Now the rest of the acts of Amaziah, from
first to last, indeed *are* they not written in
the book of the kings of Judah and Israel?
27 After the time that Amaziah turned away
from following the LORD, they made a conspiracy against him in Jerusalem, and he
fled to Lachish; but they sent after him to
Lachish and killed him there. 28 Then they
brought him on horses and buried him
with his fathers in the City of Judah.

Uzziah Reigns in Judah

26 Now all the people of Judah took Uzziah,* who *was* sixteen years old, and
made him king instead of his father Amaziah. 2 He built Elath* and restored it to Judah, after the king rested with his fathers.
3 Uzziah *was* sixteen years old when
he became king, and he reigned fifty-two
years in Jerusalem. His mother's name was
Jecholiah of Jerusalem. 4 And he did *what*

* **25:17** Spelled *Jehoash* in 2 Kings 14:8ff
* **26:1** Called *Azariah* in 2 Kings 14:21ff
* **26:2** Hebrew *Eloth*

25:11 ***Valley of Salt.*** This valley was probably in the desert south of the Dead Sea. ***people of Seir.*** These people were Edomites, descendants of Esau.
25:18 ***thistle . . . cedar.*** The thistle represents Amaziah, and the cedar, Joash. It was arrogant for the weak, insignificant Amaziah to suppose that he could defeat Joash. ***wild beast.*** The wild beast that tramples the thistle represents the war that Amaziah was so eager to pursue.
25:19 Vanity—Those who reject God's counsel in favor of their own way are taking counsel against Him; their devisings are in vain and will come to nothing (Ps. 2:12). Refusing God's counsel, though seeking counsel from others, Amaziah decided to challenge the king of Israel to war (v. 17). It is hard to imagine how he thought he could succeed under such circumstances. One of the delusions that goes with rejection of God is a false confidence in ones' own powers of understanding.
25:27 ***Lachish.*** The fact that Amaziah reached the city of Lachish on the border with Philistia, some 25 miles from Jerusalem, suggests that he may have been seeking sanctuary among the Philistines.
26:2 ***Elath.*** On the eastern arm of the Red Sea, Elath was technically in Edomite territory (8:17), but it was regularly under Israel or Judah throughout Old Testament times (21:8–10).

25:11 [i] 2 Kin. 14:7 **25:14** [j] 2 Chr. 28:23 [k] [Ex. 20:3, 5] **25:15** [l] [Ps. 96:5] [m] 2 Chr. 25:11 **25:16** [n] [1 Sam. 2:25] **25:17** [o] 2 Kin. 14:8–14 **25:19** [p] 2 Chr. 26:16; 32:25 **25:20** [q] 1 Kin. 12:15 [r] 2 Chr. 25:14 **25:21** [s] Josh. 19:38 **25:23** [t] 2 Chr. 21:17; 22:1, 6 **25:24** [u] 1 Chr. 26:15 **25:25** [v] 2 Kin. 14:17–22

was ᵃright in the sight of the LORD, according to all that his father Amaziah had done. ⁵ᵇHe sought God in the days of Zechariah, who ᶜhad understanding in the visions* of God; and as long as he sought the LORD, God made him ᵈprosper.

⁶Now he went out and ᵉmade war against the Philistines, and broke down the wall of Gath, the wall of Jabneh, and the wall of Ashdod; and he built cities *around* Ashdod and among the Philistines. ⁷God helped him against ᶠthe Philistines, against the Arabians who lived in Gur Baal, and against the Meunites. ⁸Also the Ammonites ᵍbrought tribute to Uzziah. His fame spread as far as the entrance of Egypt, for he became exceedingly strong.

⁹And Uzziah built towers in Jerusalem at the ʰCorner Gate, at the Valley Gate, and at the corner buttress of the wall; then he fortified them. ¹⁰Also he built towers in the desert. He dug many wells, for he had much livestock, both in the lowlands and in the plains; *he also had* farmers and vinedressers in the mountains and in Carmel, for he loved the soil.

¹¹Moreover Uzziah had an army of fighting men who went out to war by companies, according to the number on their roll as prepared by Jeiel the scribe and Maaseiah the officer, under the hand of Hananiah, *one* of the king's captains. ¹²The total number of chief officers* of the mighty men of valor *was* two thousand six hundred. ¹³And under their authority *was* an army of three hundred and seven thousand five hundred, that made war with mighty power, to help the king against the enemy. ¹⁴Then Uzziah prepared for them, for the entire army, shields, spears, helmets, body armor, bows, and slings *to cast* stones. ¹⁵And he made devices in Jerusalem, invented by ⁱskillful men, to be on the towers and the corners, to shoot arrows and large stones. So his fame spread far and wide, for he was marvelously helped till he became strong.

The Penalty for Uzziah's Pride

¹⁶But ʲwhen he was strong his heart was ᵏlifted up, to *his* destruction, for he transgressed against the LORD his God ˡby entering the temple of the LORD to burn incense on the altar of incense. ¹⁷So ᵐAzariah the priest went in after him, and with him were eighty priests of the LORD— valiant men. ¹⁸And they withstood King Uzziah, and said to him, "*It* ⁿis not for you, Uzziah, to burn incense to the LORD, but for the ᵒpriests, the sons of Aaron, who are consecrated to burn incense. Get out of the sanctuary, for you have trespassed! You *shall have* no honor from the LORD God."

¹⁹Then Uzziah became furious; and he *had* a censer in his hand to burn incense. And while he was angry with the priests, ᵖleprosy broke out on his forehead, before the priests in the house of the LORD, beside the incense altar. ²⁰And Azariah the chief priest and all the priests looked at him, and there, on his forehead, he *was* leprous; so they thrust him out of that place. Indeed he also ᵠhurried to get out, because the LORD had struck him.

²¹ʳKing Uzziah was a leper until the day of his death. He dwelt in an ˢisolated house, because he was a leper; for he was cut off from the house of the LORD. Then Jotham his son *was* over the king's house, judging the people of the land.

²²Now the rest of the acts of Uzziah, from first to last, ᵗthe prophet Isaiah the son of Amoz wrote. ²³ᵘSo Uzziah rested with his fathers, and they buried him with his fathers in the field of burial which *belonged* to the kings, for they said, "He is a leper." Then Jotham his son reigned in his place.

Jotham Reigns in Judah

27 Jotham ᵃwas twenty-five years old when he became king, and he reigned sixteen years in Jerusalem. His mother's name *was* Jerushah* the daughter of Zadok. ²And he did *what was* right in the sight of the LORD, according to all that his father Uzziah had done (although he did not enter the temple of the LORD). But still ᵇthe people acted corruptly.

* **26:5** Several Hebrew manuscripts, Septuagint, Syriac, Targum, and Arabic read *fear.*
* **26:12** Literally *chief fathers* * **27:1** Spelled *Jerusha* in 2 Kings 15:33

26:15 *devices.* This is one of the earliest references to catapults, which seem to have been defensive weapons, since their users were on the towers and in the corners.

26:19 *leprosy.* Leprosy was any kind of serious skin condition (Lev. 13:1—14:32). Today the term "leprosy" refers technically only to Hansen's disease. The law viewed leprosy as a breach of God's own holiness; it was a graphic symbol of defilement.

26:22 *Isaiah.* Isaiah the prophet witnessed the last years of Uzziah, but very little about Uzziah is included in the Book of Isaiah. The books of Kings and Chronicles frequently refer to further details written about the kings, but they were not part of the Scripture, so we know very little about these records.

27:1 *sixteen years.* Jotham's sixteen years began eleven years before Uzziah died. This suggests that Uzziah had leprosy for more than a decade before he died.

26:4 ᵈ 2 Chr. 24:2 **26:5** ᵇ 2 Chr. 24:2 ᶜ Dan. 1:17; 10:1 ᵈ [2 Chr. 15:2; 20:20; 31:21] **26:6** ᵉ Is. 14:29 **26:7** ᶠ 2 Chr. 21:16 **26:8** ᵍ 2 Chr. 17:11 **26:9** ʰ Neh. 3:13, 19, 32 **26:15** ⁱ Ex. 39:3, 8 **26:16** ʲ [Deut. 32:15] ᵏ 2 Chr. 25:19 ˡ 2 Kin. 16:12, 13 **26:17** ᵐ 1 Chr. 6:10 **26:18** ⁿ [Num. 3:10; 16:39, 40; 18:7] ᵒ Ex. 30:7, 8 **26:19** ᵖ 2 Kin. 5:25–27 **26:20** ᵠ Ex. 6:12 **26:21** ʳ 2 Kin. 15:5 ˢ [Lev. 13:46] **26:22** ᵗ Is. 1:1 **26:23** ᵘ Is. 6:1 **27:1** ᵃ 2 Kin. 15:32–35 **27:2** ᵇ 2 Kin. 15:35

³He built the Upper Gate of the house of the LORD, and he built extensively on the wall of cOphel. ⁴Moreover he built cities in the mountains of Judah, and in the forests he built fortresses and towers. ⁵He also fought with the king of the dAmmonites and defeated them. And the people of Ammon gave him in that year one hundred talents of silver, ten thousand kors of wheat, and ten thousand of barley. The people of Ammon paid this to him in the second and third years also. ⁶So Jotham became mighty, ebecause he prepared his ways before the LORD his God.

⁷Now the rest of the acts of Jotham, and all his wars and his ways, indeed they *are* written in the book of the kings of Israel and Judah. ⁸He was twenty-five years old when he became king, and he reigned sixteen years in Jerusalem. ⁹fSo Jotham rested with his fathers, and they buried him in the City of David. Then gAhaz his son reigned in his place.

Ahaz Reigns in Judah

28 Ahaz ªwas twenty years old when he became king, and he reigned sixteen years in Jerusalem; and he did not do *what was* right in the sight of the LORD, as his father David *had done.* ²For he walked in the ways of the kings of Israel, and made bmolded images for cthe Baals. ³He burned incense in dthe Valley of the Son of Hinnom, and burned ehis children in the ffire, according to the abominations of the nations whom the LORD had gcast out before the children of Israel. ⁴And he sacrificed and burned incense on the high places, on the hills, and under every green tree.

Syria and Israel Defeat Judah

⁵Therefore hthe LORD his God delivered him into the hand of the king of Syria.

They idefeated him, and carried away a great multitude of them as captives, and brought *them* to Damascus. Then he was also delivered into the hand of the king of Israel, who defeated him with a great slaughter. ⁶For jPekah the son of Remaliah killed one hundred and twenty thousand in Judah in one day, all valiant men, kbecause they had forsaken the LORD God of their fathers. ⁷Zichri, a mighty man of Ephraim, killed Maaseiah the king's son, Azrikam the officer over the house, and Elkanah *who was* second to the king. ⁸And the children of Israel carried away captive of their lbrethren two hundred thousand women, sons, and daughters; and they also took away much spoil from them, and brought the spoil to Samaria.

Israel Returns the Captives

⁹But a mprophet of the LORD was there, whose name *was* Oded; and he went out before the army that came to Samaria, and said to them: "Look, nbecause the LORD God of your fathers was angry with Judah, He has delivered them into your hand; but you have killed them in a rage *that* oreaches up to heaven. ¹⁰And now you propose to force the children of Judah and Jerusalem to be your pmale and female slaves; *but are* you not also guilty before the LORD your God? ¹¹Now hear me, therefore, and return the captives, whom you have taken captive from your brethren, qfor the fierce wrath of the LORD *is* upon you."

¹²Then some of the heads of the children of Ephraim, Azariah the son of Johanan, Berechiah the son of Meshillemoth, Jehizkiah the son of Shallum, and Amasa the son of Hadlai, stood up against those who came from the war, ¹³and said to them, "You shall not bring the captives here, for we *already* have offended the LORD. You

---

27:3 *Upper Gate.* This gate connected the temple and the royal palace. ***wall of Ophel.*** Ophel was the original Jebusite area of Jerusalem. Its walls dated back hundreds of years and must have required regular maintenance.
27:6 Truth—In the face of deep moral corruption among his people, Jotham set his course to act on God's truth. There is always blessing in obedience, even if the blessing is not the sort that the rest of the world can see.
28:1 *did not do what was right in the sight of the LORD.* During Ahaz's reign Isaiah and Micah prophesied in Judah, and Hosea prophesied in Israel.
28:3 *Valley of the Son of Hinnom.* This valley, also called the Valley of Ben-Hinnom, was just outside the western wall of Jerusalem. It was a dumping ground for all kinds of refuse, much of which was burned. The valley itself became a symbol of impurity. It was used as a site of pagan worship, including human sacrifice (2 Kin. 23:10; Jer. 7:31–32; 19:2–6; 32:35). ***abominations of the nations.*** Worshipers of the Ammonite god Molech practiced human and child sacrifice (Lev. 18:21; 20:2–5; Deut. 12:31).
28:4 *every green tree.* Canaanite nature cults focused

on evergreens, probably as symbols of perpetual fertility (see note at 14:3).
28:6 Pekah. Pekah, who assassinated Pekahiah son of Menahem so that he could become king of Israel (2 Kin. 15:23–27), reigned for 20 years. He was murdered in a plot headed by Hoshea, the last king of Israel. ***because they had forsaken the LORD God.*** Pekah was not offended by Judah's godlessness and did not himself initiate this purge. God used Pekah to carry out His judgment.
28:9 Oded. The prophet Oded is mentioned only here. ***killed them in a rage.*** God used the Israelite armies to carry out His judgment on Judah (v. 6), but He never intended for the Israelites to enjoy it.
28:13 *our guilt is great.* Within ten years the Assyrians would capture Samaria and deport all of the

---

27:3 c 2 Chr. 33:14 **27:5** d 2 Chr. 26:8 **27:6** e 2 Chr. 26:5 **27:9** f 2 Kin. 15:38 g Is. 1:1 **28:1** a 2 Kin. 16:2–4 **28:2** b Ex. 34:17 c Judg. 2:11 **28:3** d Josh. 15:8 e 2 Kin. 23:10 f [Lev. 18:21] g [Lev. 18:24–30] **28:5** h [Is. 10:5] i Is. 7:1, 17 **28:6** j 2 Kin. 15:27 k [2 Chr. 29:8] **28:8** l Deut. 28:25, 41 **28:9** m 2 Chr. 25:15 n [Is. 10:5; 47:6] o Rev. 18:5 **28:10** p [Lev. 25:39, 42, 43, 46] **28:11** q James 2:13

intend to add to our sins and to our guilt; for our guilt is great, and *there is* fierce wrath against Israel." [14]So the armed men left the captives and the spoil before the leaders and all the assembly. [15]Then the men rwho were designated by name rose up and took the captives, and from the spoil they clothed all who were naked among them, dressed them and gave them sandals, sgave them food and drink, and anointed them; and they let all the feeble ones ride on donkeys. So they brought them to their brethren at Jericho, tthe city of palm trees. Then they returned to Samaria.

Assyria Refuses to Help Judah

[16]uAt the same time King Ahaz sent to the kings* of Assyria to help him. [17]For again the vEdomites had come, attacked Judah, and carried away captives. [18]wThe Philistines also had invaded the cities of the lowland and of the South of Judah, and had taken Beth Shemesh, Aijalon, Gederoth, Sochoh with its villages, Timnah with its villages, and Gimzo with its villages; and they dwelt there. [19]For the LORD brought Judah low because of Ahaz king of xIsrael, for he had yencouraged moral decline in Judah and had been continually unfaithful to the LORD. [20]Also zTiglath-Pileser* king of Assyria came to him and distressed him, and did not assist him. [21]For Ahaz took part *of the treasures* from the house of the LORD, from the house of the king, and from the leaders, and he gave *it* to the king of Assyria; but he did not help him.

Apostasy and Death of Ahaz

[22]Now in the time of his distress King Ahaz became increasingly unfaithful to the LORD. This *is that* King Ahaz. [23]For qhe sacrificed to the gods of Damascus which had defeated him, saying, "Because the gods of the kings of Syria help them, I will

sacrifice to them bthat they may help me." But they were the ruin of him and of all Israel. [24]So Ahaz gathered the articles of the house of God, cut in pieces the articles of the house of God, cshut up the doors of the house of the LORD, and made for himself altars in every corner of Jerusalem. [25]And in every single city of Judah he made high places to burn incense to other gods, and provoked to anger the LORD God of his fathers.

[26]dNow the rest of his acts and all his ways, from first to last, indeed they *are* written in the book of the kings of Judah and Israel. [27]So Ahaz rested with his fathers, and they buried him in the city, in Jerusalem; but they edid not bring him into the tombs of the kings of Israel. Then Hezekiah his son reigned in his place.

Hezekiah Reigns in Judah

29 Hezekiah abecame king *when he was* twenty-five years old, and he reigned twenty-nine years in Jerusalem. His mother's name *was* Abijah* the daughter of Zechariah. [2]And he did *what was* right in the sight of the LORD, according to all that his father David had done.

Hezekiah Cleanses the Temple

[3]In the first year of his reign, in the first month, he bopened the doors of the house of the LORD and repaired them. [4]Then he brought in the priests and the Levites, and gathered them in the East Square, [5]and said to them: "Hear me, Levites! Now sanctify yourselves, csanctify the house of the LORD God of your fathers, and carry out the rubbish from the holy *place.* [6]For our fathers have trespassed and done evil in the eyes of

---

* **28:16** Septuagint, Syriac, and Vulgate read *king* (compare verse 20).   * **28:20** Hebrew *Tilgath-Pilneser*   * **29:1** Spelled *Abi* in 2 Kings 18:2

Israelites, treating them far more cruelly than they were treating the Judeans. The Israelites brought this judgment on themselves not only by this incident, but by the whole course of the history of their unfaithfulness to God.

28:16 kings of Assyria. The kings of Assyria were Tiglath-Pileser III, Shalamaneser V, and Sargon II.

28:18 Beth Shemesh . . . Gimzo. All these places were near valleys that led up to central Judah from the surrounding plains. Control of them meant control of Judah itself. Because Ahaz understood this, he appealed to Assyria.

28:20 Tiglath-Pileser. Tiglath-Pileser brought the Mesopotamian influence over the countries of the eastern Mediterranean to its highest point. He undertook a campaign against Arpad in Syria and terrorized Menahem of Israel so much that Menahem paid him a huge bribe to be left alone (2 Kin. 15:19). Tiglath returned to the west again, and Ahaz scrambled for protection against Syria and Israel (2 Kin. 16:5–7; Is. 7:1–2). The Assyrians overran Damascus and replaced the assassinated Pekah of Israel with Hoshea (2 Kin. 15:30), but they did not assist Ahaz. The king of

Judah's troubles with the Edomites, Philistines, Arameans, and even the Israelites (Is. 7:1) were over for the time being, but at great cost.

28:23 Unbelief—Looking to the gods of his enemies, foolishly believing that the gods had aided his enemies in their victory, Ahaz went farther from God into unbelief. Ahaz committed two grievous sins. He ascribed to another source what was God's doing, and he placed his faith in what was imagined, to bring success to himself. There is never a time when God is out of control. Even if things do not turn out the way we wish they would, we can be sure that if we keep our minds and attitudes in line with God's ways, we will eventually see these events from His perspective.

28:15 r 2 Chr. 28:12   s [Prov. 25:21, 22]   t Deut. 34:3
28:16 u 2 Kin. 16:7   **28:17** v Obad. 10–14   **28:18** w Ezek. 16:27, 57   x 2 Chr. 21:2   y Ex. 32:25   **28:20** z 1 Chr. 5:26   **28:23** a 2 Chr. 25:14   b Jer. 44:17, 18   **28:24** c 2 Chr. 29:3, 7   **28:26** d 2 Kin. 16:19, 20   **28:27** e 2 Chr. 21:20; 24:25   **29:1** a 2 Kin. 18:1   **29:3** b 2 Chr. 28:24; 29:7
29:5 c 2 Chr. 29:15, 34; 35:6

the LORD our God; they have forsaken Him, have ᵈturned their faces away from the dwelling place of the LORD, and turned *their* backs *on Him.* ⁷ᵉThey have also shut up the doors of the vestibule, put out the lamps, and have not burned incense or offered burnt offerings in the holy *place* to the God of Israel. ⁸Therefore the ᶠwrath of the LORD fell upon Judah and Jerusalem, and He has ᵍgiven them up to trouble, to desolation, and to ʰjeering, as you see with your ᶦeyes. ⁹For indeed, because of this ʲour fathers have fallen by the sword; and our sons, our daughters, and our wives *are* in captivity.

¹⁰"Now *it is* in my heart to make ᵏa covenant with the LORD God of Israel, that His fierce wrath may turn away from us. ¹¹My sons, do not be negligent now, for the LORD has ᶦchosen you to stand before Him, to serve Him, and that you should minister to Him and burn incense."

¹²Then these Levites arose: ᵐMahath the son of Amasai and Joel the son of Azariah, of the sons of the ⁿKohathites; of the sons of Merari, Kish the son of Abdi and Azariah the son of Jehallelel; of the Gershonites, Joah the son of Zimmah and Eden the son of Joah; ¹³of the sons of Elizaphan, Shimri and Jeiel; of the sons of Asaph, Zechariah and Mattaniah; ¹⁴of the sons of Heman, Jehiel and Shimei; and of the sons of Jeduthun, Shemaiah and Uzziel.

¹⁵And they gathered their brethren, ᵒsanctified themselves, and went according to the commandment of the king, at the words of the LORD, ᵖto cleanse the house of the LORD. ¹⁶Then the priests went into the inner part of the house of the LORD to cleanse *it*, and brought out all the debris that they found in the temple of the LORD to the court of the house of the LORD. And the Levites took *it* out and carried *it* to the Brook �qKidron.

¹⁷Now they began to sanctify on the first *day* of the first month, and on the eighth day of the month they came to the vestibule of the LORD. So they sanctified the house of the LORD in eight days, and on the sixteenth day of the first month they finished. ¹⁸Then they went in to King Hezekiah and said, "We have cleansed all the house

of the LORD, the altar of burnt offerings with all its articles, and the table of the showbread with all its articles. ¹⁹Moreover all the articles which King Ahaz in his reign had ʳcast aside in his transgression we have prepared and sanctified; and there they *are*, before the altar of the LORD."

Hezekiah Restores Temple Worship

²⁰Then King Hezekiah rose early, gathered the rulers of the city, and went up to the house of the LORD. ²¹And they brought seven bulls, seven rams, seven lambs, and seven male goats for a ˢsin offering for the kingdom, for the sanctuary, and for Judah. Then he commanded the priests, the sons of Aaron, to offer *them* on the altar of the LORD. ²²So they killed the bulls, and the priests received the blood and ᵗsprinkled *it* on the altar. Likewise they killed the rams and sprinkled the blood on the altar. They also killed the lambs and sprinkled the blood on the altar. ²³Then they brought out the male goats *for* the sin offering before the king and the assembly, and they laid their ᵘhands on them. ²⁴And the priests killed them; and they presented their blood on the altar as a sin offering ᵛto make an atonement for all Israel, for the king commanded *that* the burnt offering and the sin offering *be made* for all Israel.

²⁵ʷAnd he stationed the Levites in the house of the LORD with cymbals, with stringed instruments, and with harps, ˣaccording to the commandment of David, of ʸGad the king's seer, and of Nathan the prophet; ᶻfor thus *was* the commandment of the LORD by His prophets. ²⁶The Levites stood with the instruments ᵃof David, and the priests with ᵇthe trumpets. ²⁷Then Hezekiah commanded *them* to offer the burnt offering on the altar. And when the burnt offering began, ᶜthe song of the LORD *also* began, with the trumpets and with the instruments of David king of Israel. ²⁸So all the assembly worshiped, the singers sang, and the trumpeters sounded; all *this* *continued* until the burnt offering was finished. ²⁹And when they had finished offering, ᵈthe king and all who were present with him bowed and worshiped. ³⁰Moreover

---

29:9 *in captivity.* Under the wicked leadership of Ahaz, many of the people of Judah had been taken captive by Rezin of Damascus and Pekah of Israel (28:5–8). **29:12 *Kohathites . . . Merari . . . Gershonites.*** Hezekiah summoned the leaders of the three major Levitical clans, two leaders from each clan.
29:21 *bulls . . . rams . . . lambs . . . goats.* The law required the sacrifice of these animals for atonement of sin in general (Lev. 1:3–13). On the other hand, the sacrifice of goats atoned for specific sins (Lev. 4:1—5:13). Here the priests offered seven of each kind to signify the wholeness of their repentance.
29:24 *all Israel.* The repetition of "all Israel" here suggests that Hezekiah meant to include all twelve tribes, including the northern kingdom (30:1–9).
29:30 *the words of David and of Asaph.* This refers

to the psalms of David and Asaph (1 Chr. 6:39; 15:17; 16:5; 25:1), many of them in the Book of Psalms. The people of Judah used these psalms for community worship and private meditation.

29:6 ᵈEzek. 8:16 **29:7** ᵉ2 Chr. 28:24 **29:8** ᶠ2 Chr. 24:18 ᵍ2 Chr. 28:5 ʰ1 Kin. 9:8 ᶦDeut. 28:32 **29:9** ʲ2 Chr. 28:5–8, 17 **29:10** ᵏ2 Chr. 15:12; 23:16 **29:11** ᶦNum. 3:6; 8:14; 18:2, 6 **29:12** ᵐ2 Chr. 31:13 ⁿNum. 3:19, 20 **29:15** ᵒ2 Chr. 29:5 ᵖ1 Chr. 23:28 **29:16** �q2 Chr. 15:16; 30:14 **29:19** ʳ2 Chr. 28:24 **29:21** ˢLev. 4:3–14 **29:22** ᵗLev. 8:14, 15, 19, 24 **29:23** ᵘLev. 4:15, 24; 8:14 **29:24** ᵛLev. 14:20 **29:25** ʷ1 Chr. 16:4; 25:6 ˣ2 Chr. 8:14 ʸ2 Sam. 24:11 ᶻ2 Chr. 30:12 **29:26** ᵃ1 Chr. 23:5 ᵇ2 Chr. 5:12 **29:27** ᶜ2 Chr. 23:18 **29:29** ᵈ2 Chr. 20:18

King Hezekiah and the leaders commanded the Levites to sing praise to the LORD with the words of David and of Asaph the seer. So they sang praises with gladness, and they bowed their heads and worshiped. 31Then Hezekiah answered and said, "Now *that* you have consecrated yourselves to the LORD, come near, and bring sacrifices and *e*thank offerings into the house of the LORD." So the assembly brought in sacrifices and thank offerings, and as many as were of a *f*willing heart *brought* burnt offerings. 32And the number of the burnt offerings which the assembly brought was seventy bulls, one hundred rams, *and* two hundred lambs; all these *were* for a burnt offering to the LORD. 33The consecrated things *were* six hundred bulls and three thousand sheep. 34But the priests were too few, so that they could not skin all the burnt offerings; therefore *g*their brethren the Levites helped them until the work was ended and until the *other* priests had sanctified themselves, *h*for the Levites were *i*more diligent in *j*sanctifying themselves than the priests. 35Also the burnt offerings *were* in abundance, with *k*the fat of the peace offerings and *with l*the drink offerings for *every* burnt offering.

So the service of the house of the LORD was set in order. 36Then Hezekiah and all the people rejoiced that God had prepared the people, since the events took place so suddenly.

Hezekiah Keeps the Passover

30 And Hezekiah sent to all Israel and Judah, and also wrote letters to Ephraim and Manasseh, that they should come to the house of the LORD at Jerusalem, to keep the Passover to the LORD God of Israel. 2For the king and his leaders and all the assembly in Jerusalem had agreed to keep the Passover in the second *a*month. 3For they could not keep it *b*at the regular time,* *c*because a sufficient number of priests had not consecrated themselves, nor had the people gathered together at Jerusalem. 4And the matter pleased the king and all the assembly. 5So they resolved to make a proclamation throughout all Israel, from Beersheba to Dan, that they should come to keep the Passover to the LORD God of Israel at Jerusalem, since they had not done *it* for a long *time* in the *prescribed* manner.

6Then the *d*runners went throughout all Israel and Judah with the letters from the king and his leaders, and spoke according to the command of the king: "Children of Israel, *e*return to the LORD God of Abraham, Isaac, and Israel; then He will return to the remnant of you who have escaped from the hand of *f*the kings of *g*Assyria. 7And do not be *h*like your fathers and your brethren, who trespassed against the LORD God of their fathers, so that He *i*gave them up to *j*desolation, as you see. 8Now do not be *k*stiff-necked, as your fathers *were*, but yield yourselves to the LORD; and enter His sanctuary, which He has sanctified forever, and serve the LORD your God, *l*that the fierceness of His wrath may turn away from you. 9For if you return to the LORD, your brethren and your children *will be treated* with *m*compassion by those who lead them captive, so that they may come back to this land; for the LORD your God *is n*gracious and merciful, and will not turn *His* face from you if you *o*return to Him."

10So the runners passed from city to city through the country of Ephraim and Manasseh, as far as Zebulun; but *p*they laughed at them and mocked them. 11Nevertheless *q*some from Asher, Manasseh, and Zebulun humbled themselves and came to Jerusalem. 12Also *r*the hand of God was on Judah to give them singleness of heart to obey the command of the king and the leaders, *s*at the word of the LORD.

13Now many people, a very great assembly, gathered at Jerusalem to keep the Feast

---

* **30:3** That is, the first month (compare Leviticus 23:5); literally *at that time*

29:31 thank offerings. Sometimes called "peace" or "fellowship" offerings, thank offerings celebrated the relationship gained by the offerings of atonement (vv. 21–24; Lev. 3:1–17; 7:11–36). The thank offerings included people and priests in a great banquet together, all in fellowship with God.

29:34 priests were too few. Under Ahaz the priests and Levites had been stripped of their duties. Now, 20 years later, there were not enough priests.

30:1 sent to all Israel. Though the kingdom of Israel had split more than two centuries before, Hezekiah never lost sight of the fact that God's covenant was made with all twelve tribes and that His promises included them all (Ezek. 37:15–28).

30:8 enter His sanctuary. People who were not priests were not allowed to enter the temple. This phrase is a figure of speech for serving the Lord.

30:9 if you return to the LORD. Hezekiah was referring to the covenant (Deut. 28–30) which promised that obedience would lead to blessing in the land, and disobedience would result in exile.

30:10 as far as Zebulun. Zebulun was probably the northernmost territory of Israel at this time because Naphtali had been taken by Tiglath-Pileser III (2 Kin. 15:29).

29:31 *e* Lev. 7:12 *f* Ex. 35:5, 22 **29:34** *g* 2 Chr. 35:11 *h* 2 Chr. 30:3 *i* Ps. 7:10 *j* 2 Chr. 29:5 **29:35** *k* Lev. 3:15, 16 *l* Num. 15:5–10 **30:2** *a* Num. 9:10, 11 **30:3** *b* Ex. 12:6, 18 *c* 2 Chr. 29:17, 34 **30:6** *d* Esth. 8:14 *e* [Jer. 4:1] *f* 2 Kin. 15:19, 29 *g* 2 Chr. 28:20 **30:7** *h* Ezek. 20:18 *i* Is. 1:9 *j* 2 Chr. 29:8 **30:8** *k* Ex. 32:9 *l* 2 Chr. 29:10 **30:9** *m* Ps. 106:46 *n* [Ex. 34:6] *o* [Is. 55:7] **30:10** *p* 2 Chr. 36:16 **30:11** *q* 2 Chr. 11:16; 30:18, 21 **30:12** *r* [Phil. 2:13] *s* 2 Chr. 29:25

of ᵗUnleavened Bread in the second month. ¹⁴They arose and took away the ᵘaltars that *were* in Jerusalem, and they took away all the incense altars and cast *them* into the Brook ᵛKidron. ¹⁵Then they slaughtered the Passover *lambs* on the fourteenth *day* of the second month. The priests and the Levites were ʷashamed, and sanctified themselves, and brought the burnt offerings to the house of the LORD. ¹⁶They stood in their ˣplace according to their custom, according to the Law of Moses the man of God; the priests sprinkled the blood *received* from the hand of the Levites. ¹⁷For *there were* many in the assembly who had not sanctified themselves; ʸtherefore the Levites had charge of the slaughter of the Passover *lambs* for everyone *who was* not clean, to sanctify *them* to the LORD. ¹⁸For a multitude of the people, ᶻmany from Ephraim, Manasseh, Issachar, and Zebulun, had not cleansed themselves, ᵃyet they ate the Passover contrary to what was written. But Hezekiah prayed for them, saying, "May the good LORD provide atonement for everyone ¹⁹*who* ᵇprepares his heart to seek God, the LORD God of his fathers, though *he is* not *cleansed* according to the purification of the sanctuary." ²⁰And the LORD listened to Hezekiah and healed the people.

²¹So the children of Israel who were present at Jerusalem kept ᶜthe Feast of Unleavened Bread seven days with great gladness; and the Levites and the priests praised the LORD day by day, *singing* to the LORD, accompanied by loud instruments. ²²And Hezekiah gave encouragement to all the Levites ᵈwho taught the good knowledge of the LORD; and they ate throughout the feast seven days, offering peace offerings and ᵉmaking confession to the LORD God of their fathers.

²³Then the whole assembly agreed to keep *the feast* ᶠanother seven days, and they kept it *another* seven days with

gladness. ²⁴For Hezekiah king of Judah ᵍgave to the assembly a thousand bulls and seven thousand sheep, and the leaders gave to the assembly a thousand bulls and ten thousand sheep; and a great number of priests ʰsanctified themselves. ²⁵The whole assembly of Judah rejoiced, also the priests and Levites, all the assembly that came from Israel, the sojourners ⁱwho came from the land of Israel, and those who dwelt in Judah. ²⁶So there was great joy in Jerusalem, for since the time of ʲSolomon the son of David, king of Israel, *there had* been nothing like this in Jerusalem. ²⁷Then the priests, the Levites, arose and ᵏblessed the people, and their voice was heard; and their prayer came *up* to ˡHis holy dwelling place, to heaven.

The Reforms of Hezekiah

31 Now when all this was finished, all Israel who were present went out to the cities of Judah and ᵃbroke the *sacred* pillars in pieces, cut down the wooden images, and threw down the high places and the altars—from all Judah, Benjamin, Ephraim, and Manasseh—until they had utterly destroyed them all. Then all the children of Israel returned to their own cities, every man to his possession.

²And Hezekiah appointed ᵇthe divisions of the priests and the Levites according to their divisions, each man according to his service, the priests and Levites ᶜfor burnt offerings and peace offerings, to serve, to give thanks, and to praise in the gates of the camp* of the LORD. ³The king also *appointed* a portion of his ᵈpossessions for the burnt offerings: for the morning and evening burnt offerings, the burnt offerings for the Sabbaths and the New Moons and the set feasts, as *it is* written in the ᵉLaw of the LORD.

---

* **31:2** That is, the temple

30:17 Levites had charge of the slaughter. Traditionally the slaughter of the Passover lamb was performed by the head of the family (Ex. 12:3–6). But on this occasion many were not ritually purified, and the Levites acted on their behalf.
30:22 who taught the good knowledge. The Levites' ministry included teaching (17:8–10). The people of Israel had had virtually no consistent teaching of God's revelation for 200 years, apart from the witness of the prophets such as Elijah, Elisha, Hosea, and Amos.
30:25 sojourners. The strangers were aliens who lived in Israel and Judah and who could come to the festivals because they adhered to God and the law (Deut. 16:11; 26:11; 29:11; 31:12).
30:26 Heaven—Solomon asked God to hear the prayers of the people as they directed their prayers toward the temple in Jerusalem, and to respond from His dwelling in heaven (2 Chr. 6:21). The people, nearly 200 years after Solomon made this prayer, sought the Lord, and He heard them. There is great joy among the people when they realize that God hears them

from heaven, and there is great joy in heaven when one sinner repents (Luke 15:7).
31:2 Hezekiah appointed. The long interruption (28:24) of Judah's official worship in the time of Ahaz brought chaos to their religious life. David had originally organized the Levitical system, but because of the years of neglect, Hezekiah had to reorganize it.
31:3 New Moons. The new moon celebrations came at the appearance of the new moon, the beginning of another month (Num. 28:11–15). **set feasts.** The fixed festivals were the Passover and Feast of Unleavened Bread (Lev. 23:4–8); Feast of Firstfruits or Pentecost

30:13 ᶠLev. 23:6   **30:14** ᵘ2 Chr. 28:24 ᵛ2 Chr. 29:16   **30:15** ʷ2 Chr. 29:34   **30:16** ˣ2 Chr. 35:10, 15   **30:17** ʸ2 Chr. 29:34   **30:18** ᶻ2 Chr. 30:1, 11, 25 ᵃ[Num. 9:10]   **30:19** ᵇ2 Chr. 19:3   **30:21** ᶜEx. 12:15; 13:6   **30:22** ᵈ2 Chr. 17:9; 35:3 ᵉEzra 10:11   **30:23** ᶠ1 Kin. 8:65   **30:24** ᵍ2 Chr. 35:7, 8 ʰ2 Chr. 29:34   **30:25** ⁱ2 Chr. 30:11, 18   **30:26** ʲ2 Chr. 7:8–10   **30:27** ᵏNum. 6:23 ˡDeut. 26:15   **31:1** ᵃ2 Kin. 18:4   **31:2** ᵇ1 Chr. 23:6; 24:1 ᶜ1 Chr. 23:30, 31   **31:3** ᵈ2 Chr. 35:7 ᵉNum. 28:1—29:40

4Moreover he commanded the people who dwelt in Jerusalem to contribute fsupport for the priests and the Levites, that they might devote themselves to gthe Law of the LORD.

5As soon as the commandment was circulated, the children of Israel brought in abundance hthe firstfruits of grain and wine, oil and honey, and of all the produce of the field; and they brought in abundantly the itithe of everything. 6And the children of Israel and Judah, who dwelt in the cities of Judah, brought the tithe of oxen and sheep; also the jtithe of holy things which were consecrated to the LORD their God they laid in heaps.

7In the third month they began laying them in heaps, and they finished in the seventh month. 8And when Hezekiah and the leaders came and saw the heaps, they blessed the LORD and His people Israel. 9Then Hezekiah questioned the priests and the Levites concerning the heaps. 10And Azariah the chief priest, from the khouse of Zadok, answered him and said, l"Since the people began to bring the offerings into the house of the LORD, we have had enough to eat and have plenty left, for the LORD has blessed His people; and what is left is this great mabundance."

11Now Hezekiah commanded them to nprepare rooms in the house of the LORD, and they prepared them. 12Then they faithfully brought in the offerings, the tithes, and the dedicated things; oCononiah the Levite had charge of them, and Shimei his brother was the next. 13Jehiel, Azaziah, Nahath, Asahel, Jerimoth, Jozabad, Eliel, Ismachiah, Mahath, and Benaiah were overseers under the hand of Cononiah and Shimei his brother, at the commandment of Hezekiah the king and Azariah the pruler of the house of God. 14Kore the son of Imnah the Levite, the keeper of the East Gate, was over the qfreewill offerings to God, to distribute the offerings of the LORD and the most holy things. 15And under him were rEden, Miniamin, Jeshua, Shemaiah, Amariah, and Shecaniah, his faithful assistants in sthe cities of the priests, to distribute tallotments to their brethren by divisions, to the great as well as the small.

16Besides those males from three years old and up who were written in the genealogy, they distributed to everyone who entered the house of the LORD his daily portion for the work of his service, by his division, 17and to the priests who were written in the genealogy according to their father's house, and to the Levites ufrom twenty years and up according to their work, by their divisions, 18and to all who were written in the genealogy—their little ones and their wives, their sons and daughters, the whole company of them—for in their faithfulness they sanctified themselves in holiness.

19Also for the sons of Aaron the priests, who were in vthe fields of the commonlands of their cities, in every single city, there were men who were wdesignated by name to distribute portions to all the males among the priests and to all who were listed by genealogies among the Levites.

20Thus Hezekiah did throughout all Judah, and he xdid what was good and right and true before the LORD his God. 21And in every work that he began in the service of the house of God, in the law and in the commandment, to seek his God, he did it with all his heart. So he yprospered.

Sennacherib Boasts Against the LORD

32 After athese deeds of faithfulness, Sennacherib king of Assyria came and entered Judah; he encamped against the fortified cities, thinking to win them over to himself. 2And when Hezekiah saw that Sennacherib had come, and that his purpose was to make war against Jerusalem, 3he consulted with his leaders and commanders* to stop the water from the springs which were outside the city; and they helped him. 4Thus many people gathered together

---

* **32:3** Literally *mighty men*

(Lev. 23:15–22); and the Feast of Tabernacles (Lev. 23:33–43).
31:5 firstfruits. The early harvests of grain, particularly barley, were being reaped at this time. The Passover had been held a month late (30:2) and it was now the third month. The first fruits began appearing at the time of the late Passover, and the harvests were fully gathered in some 50 days later, at the time of Pentecost (Lev. 23:9–22). **the tithe.** A tenth of the harvest belonged to the Levites (Num. 18:21–24).
31:17 genealogy . . . by their divisions. All temple servants had to descend from Levi, but the priests had to trace their genealogy specifically to Aaron (1 Chr. 6:49–53).
32:1 Sennacherib. In Hezekiah's fourteenth year, Sennacherib invaded Judah and eventually laid siege to Jerusalem (2 Kin. 18:13–17). One of the most imperialistic of Assyria's kings, Sennacherib

undertook many military campaigns to the west. In his own inscriptions he boasts of having taken many of Judah's cities, a claim supported by the parallel account in 2 Kings.
32:3 stop the water. Hezekiah managed to stop the water by concealing the springs outside the city and then digging a tunnel to bring them to the Pool of Siloam inside the city walls. Hezekiah hid the source of water and made it unavailable to the enemy (2 Kin. 20:20). The Siloam Inscription describes how

---

31:4 fNum. 18:8 gMal. 2:7 **31:5** hEx. 22:29 i[Lev. 27:30]
31:6 jDeut. 14:28 **31:10** k1 Chr. 6:8, 9 l[Mal. 3:10]
mEx. 36:5 **31:11** n1 Kin. 6:5–8 **31:12** o2 Chr. 35:9
31:13 pJer. 20:1 **31:14** qDeut. 23:23 **31:15** r2 Chr.
29:12 sJosh. 21:1–3, 9 t1 Chr. 9:26 **31:17** u1 Chr. 23:24,
27 **31:19** vLev. 25:34 w2 Chr. 31:12–15 **31:20** x2 Kin.
20:3; 22:2 **31:21** yPs. 1:3 **32:1** a2 Kin. 18:13—19:37

who stopped all the [b]springs and the brook that ran through the land, saying, "Why should the kings* of Assyria come and find much water?" [5]And [c]he strengthened himself, [d]built up all the wall that was broken, raised *it* up to the towers, and *built* another wall outside; also he repaired the [e]Millo* *in* the City of David, and made weapons and shields in abundance. [6]Then he set military captains over the people, gathered them together to him in the open square of the city gate, and [f]gave them encouragement, saying, [7g]"Be strong and courageous; [h]do not be afraid nor dismayed before the king of Assyria, nor before all the multitude that *is* with him; for [i]there are more with us than with him. [8]With him *is* an [j]arm of flesh; but [k]with us *is* the LORD our God, to help us and to fight our battles." And the people were strengthened by the words of Hezekiah king of Judah.

[9l]After this Sennacherib king of Assyria sent his servants to Jerusalem (but he and all the forces with him *laid siege* against Lachish), to Hezekiah king of Judah, and to all Judah who *were* in Jerusalem, saying, [10m]"Thus says Sennacherib king of Assyria: 'In what do you trust, that you remain under siege in Jerusalem? [11]Does not Hezekiah persuade you to give yourselves over to die by famine and by thirst, saying, [n]"The LORD our God will deliver us from the hand of the king of Assyria"? [12o]Has not the same Hezekiah taken away His high places and His altars, and commanded Judah and Jerusalem, saying, "You shall worship before one altar and burn incense on [p]it"? [13]Do you not know what I and my fathers have done to all the peoples of *other* lands? [q]Were the gods of the nations of those lands in any way able to deliver their lands out of my hand? [14]Who *was there* among all the gods of those nations that my fathers utterly destroyed that could deliver his people from my hand, that your God should be able to deliver you from my [r]hand? [15]Now therefore, [s]do not let Hezekiah deceive you or persuade you like this, and do not believe him; for no god of any nation or kingdom

was able to deliver his people from my hand or the hand of my fathers. How much less will your God deliver you from my hand?' "

[16]Furthermore, his servants spoke against the LORD God and against His servant Hezekiah.

[17]He also wrote letters to revile the LORD God of Israel, and to speak against Him, saying, [t]"As the gods of the nations of *other* lands have not delivered their people from my hand, so the God of Hezekiah will not deliver His people from my [u]hand." [18v]Then they called out with a loud voice in Hebrew* to the people of Jerusalem who *were* on the wall, to frighten them and trouble them, that they might take the city. [19]And they spoke against the God of Jerusalem, as against the gods of the people of the earth—[w]the work of men's hands.

Sennacherib's Defeat and Death

[20x]Now because of this King Hezekiah and [y]the prophet Isaiah, the son of Amoz, prayed and cried out to heaven. [21z]Then the LORD sent an angel who cut down every mighty man of valor, leader, and captain in the camp of the king of Assyria. So he returned [a]shamefaced to his own land. And when he had gone into the temple of his god, some of his own offspring struck him down with the sword there.

[22]Thus the LORD saved Hezekiah and the inhabitants of Jerusalem from the hand of Sennacherib the king of Assyria, and from the hand of all *others*, and guided them* on every side. [23]And many brought gifts to the LORD at Jerusalem, and [b]presents to Hezekiah king of Judah, so that he was [c]exalted in the sight of all nations thereafter.

Hezekiah Humbles Himself

[24d]In those days Hezekiah was sick and near death, and he prayed to the LORD;

---

* **32:4** Following Masoretic Text and Vulgate; Arabic, Septuagint, and Syriac read *king.*   * **32:5** Literally *The Landfill*   * **32:18** Literally *Judean*
* **32:22** Septuagint reads *gave them rest;* Vulgate reads *gave them treasures.*

---

workmen constructed the 1,800 foot tunnel connecting the springs of Gihon to the Pool of Siloam.
32:5 repaired the Millo. Millo means "landfill" and refers to extensive terracing that surrounded the ancient hills of Ophel and Mount Zion. The work of extending the hills of Jerusalem was first undertaken by David (1 Chr. 11:7–8) and continued by Solomon (1 Kin. 9:15).
32:9 laid siege against Lachish. Both the Old Testament and Assyrian inscriptions document the siege against Lachish, an important fortified city west of Jerusalem and near the great coastal route (11:9). Its capture by Assyria would cut off access to Jerusalem from the west and would give Assyria control of the coast.
32:18 in Hebrew. Aramaic had become the language of international communication and diplomacy and there was no reason to continue the dialogue in Hebrew except to traumatize the people.

32:20 the prophet Isaiah. By now the prophet Isaiah had been involved in public ministry to the kings of Judah for nearly 40 years (26:22; Is. 6:1). He had considerable prestige and was especially important as a counselor of young Hezekiah (Is. 37:1–7).

32:4 [b] 2 Kin. 20:20   **32:5** [c] Is. 22:9, 10   [d] 2 Chr. 25:23   [e] 2 Kin. 5:9   **32:6** [f] 2 Chr. 30:22   **32:7** [g] [Deut. 31:6]   [h] 2 Chr. 20:15   [i] 2 Kin. 6:16   **32:8** [j] [Jer. 17:5]   [k] [Rom. 8:31]   **32:9** [l] 2 Kin. 18:17   **32:10** [m] 2 Kin. 18:19   **32:11** [n] 2 Kin. 18:30   **32:12** [o] 2 Kin. 18:22   [p] 2 Chr. 31:1, 2   **32:13** [q] 2 Kin. 18:33–35   **32:14** [r] [Is. 10:5–12]   **32:15** [s] 2 Kin. 18:29   **32:17** [t] 2 Kin. 19:9   [u] 2 Kin. 19:12   **32:18** [v] 2 Kin. 18:28   **32:19** [w] [Ps. 96:5; 115:4–8]   **32:20** [x] 2 Kin. 19:15   [y] 2 Kin. 19:2   **32:21** [z] Zech. 14:3   [a] Ps. 44:7   **32:23** [b] 2 Sam. 8:10   [c] 2 Chr. 1:1   **32:24** [d] Is. 38:1–8

and He spoke to him and gave him a sign. ²⁵But Hezekiah ^edid not repay according to the favor *shown* him, for ^fhis heart was lifted up; ^gtherefore wrath was looming over him and over Judah and Jerusalem. ²⁶^hThen Hezekiah humbled himself for the pride of his heart, he and the inhabitants of Jerusalem, so that the wrath of the LORD did not come upon them ⁱin the days of Hezekiah.

Hezekiah's Wealth and Honor

²⁷Hezekiah had very great riches and honor. And he made himself treasuries for silver, for gold, for precious stones, for spices, for shields, and for all kinds of desirable items; ²⁸storehouses for the harvest of grain, wine, and oil; and stalls for all kinds of livestock, and folds for flocks.* ²⁹Moreover he provided cities for himself, and possessions of flocks and herds in abundance; for ^jGod had given him very much property. ³⁰^kThis same Hezekiah also stopped the water outlet of Upper Gihon, and brought the water by tunnel* to the west side of the City of David. Hezekiah ^lprospered in all his works.

³¹However, *regarding* the ambassadors of the princes of Babylon, whom they ^msent to him to inquire about the wonder that was *done* in the land, God withdrew from him, in order to ⁿtest him, that He might know all *that was* in his heart.

Death of Hezekiah

³²Now the rest of the acts of Hezekiah, and his goodness, indeed they *are* written in ^othe vision of Isaiah the prophet, the son of Amoz, *and* in the ^pbook of the kings of Judah and Israel. ³³^qSo Hezekiah rested with his fathers, and they buried him in the upper tombs of the sons of David; and all Judah and the inhabitants of Jerusalem ^rhonored him at his death. Then Manasseh his son reigned in his place.

Manasseh Reigns in Judah

33 Manasseh ^a*was* twelve years old when he became king, and he reigned fifty-five years in Jerusalem. ²But he did evil in the sight of the LORD, according to the ^babominations of the nations whom the LORD had cast out before the children of Israel. ³For he rebuilt the high places which Hezekiah his father had ^cbroken down; he raised up altars for the Baals, and ^dmade wooden images; and he worshiped ^eall the host of heaven* and served them. ⁴He also built altars in the house of the LORD, of which the LORD had said, ^f"In Jerusalem shall My name be forever." ⁵And he built altars for all the host of heaven ^gin the two courts of the house of the LORD. ⁶^hAlso he caused his sons to pass through the fire in the Valley of the Son of Hinnom; he practiced ⁱsoothsaying, used witchcraft and sorcery, and ^jconsulted mediums and spiritists. He did much evil in the sight of the LORD, to provoke Him to anger. ⁷^kHe even set a carved image, the idol which he had made, in the house of God, of which God had said to David and to Solomon his son, ^l"In this house and in Jerusalem, which I have chosen out of all the tribes of Israel, I will put My name forever; ⁸^mand I will not again remove the foot of Israel from the land which I have appointed for your fathers—only if they are careful to do all that I have commanded them, according to the whole law and the statutes and the ordinances by the hand of Moses." ⁹So Manasseh seduced Judah and the inhabitants of Jerusalem to do more evil than the nations whom the LORD had destroyed before the children of Israel.

---

* **32:28** Following Septuagint and Vulgate; Arabic and Syriac omit *folds for flocks;* Masoretic Text reads *flocks for sheepfolds.*   * **32:30** Literally *brought it straight* (compare 2 Kings 20:20)
* **33:3** The gods of the Assyrians

32:25 his heart was lifted up. Hezekiah had received Babylonian envoys who had come to congratulate him on his recovery, and probably to enlist his support in their struggle against Assyria (2 Kin. 20:12–19). Their visit ignited his desire to show off the treasures of his kingdom, and this treasure was eventually seized by the same Babylonians (2 Kin. 20:16–18; Is. 39:6–7).
32:31 test. This test was not for God's benefit, but for Hezekiah's.
33:4 In Jerusalem shall My name be. The point was that God had the exclusive right to inhabit the temple, as opposed to the deities Manasseh introduced (v. 5).
33:6 pass through the fire. Like Ahaz, Manasseh practiced human sacrifice, going so far as to offer up his own children (28:3). **practiced soothsaying.** Soothsaying is an attempt to determine the plans and purposes of the gods so that one can avoid their hostility or take advantage of their favors (Is. 2:6; Jer. 27:9). **witchcraft . . . sorcery.** Witchcraft and sorcery

attempt to bring about desired results by employing magical or mystical rituals. **mediums . . . spiritists.** Mediums are those who claim to contact and consult with the dead. Spiritists are the "knowing ones" whose specialty is also communication with the dead in the hope of acquiring information inaccessible to the living. All such practices were common among Canaanite and other pagan religions and were to be strictly avoided by God's people (Deut. 13:1–6; 18:9–14).

32:25 ^ePs. 116:12 ^f[Hab. 2:4] ^g2 Chr. 24:18   **32:26** ^hJer. 26:18, 19 ⁱ2 Kin. 20:19   **32:29** ^j1 Chr. 29:12   **32:30** ^kIs. 22:9–11 ^l2 Chr. 31:21   **32:31** ^mIs. 39:1 ⁿ[Deut. 8:2, 16]   **32:32** ^oIs. 36–39 ^p2 Kin. 18–20   **32:33** ^q2 Kin. 20:21   ^rProv. 10:7   **33:1** ^a2 Kin. 21:1–9   **33:2** ^b2 Chr. 28:3   **33:3** ^c2 Kin. 18:4 ^dDeut. 16:21 ^eDeut. 17:3   **33:4** ^f2 Chr. 6:6; 7:16   **33:5** ^g2 Chr. 4:9   **33:6** ^h[Lev. 18:21] ⁱDeut. 18:11 ^j2 Kin. 21:6   **33:7** ^k2 Chr. 25:14 ^lPs. 132:14   **33:8** ^m2 Sam. 7:10

Manasseh Restored After Repentance

[10]And the LORD spoke to Manasseh and his people, but they would not listen. [11]n Therefore the LORD brought upon them the captains of the army of the king of Assyria, who took Manasseh with hooks,* [o]bound him with bronze *fetters*, and carried him off to Babylon. [12]Now when he was in affliction, he implored the LORD his God, and [p]humbled himself greatly before the God of his fathers, [13]and prayed to Him; and He [q]received his entreaty, heard his supplication, and brought him back to Jerusalem into his kingdom. Then Manasseh [r]knew that the LORD *was* God.

[14]After this he built a wall outside the City of David on the west side of [s]Gihon, in the valley, as far as the entrance of the Fish Gate; and *it* [t]enclosed Ophel, and he raised it to a very great height. Then he put military captains in all the fortified cities of Judah. [15]He took away [u]the foreign gods and the idol from the house of the LORD, and all the altars that he had built in the mount of the house of the LORD and in Jerusalem; and he cast *them* out of the city. [16]He also repaired the altar of the LORD, sacrificed peace offerings and [v]thank offerings on it, and commanded Judah to serve the LORD God of Israel. [17]w Nevertheless the people still sacrificed on the high places, *but* only to the LORD their God.

Death of Manasseh

[18]Now the rest of the acts of Manasseh, his prayer to his God, and the words of [x]the seers who spoke to him in the name of the LORD God of Israel, indeed they *are* written in the book* of the kings of Israel. [19]Also his prayer and *how God* received his entreaty, and all his sin and trespass, and the sites where he built high places and set up wooden images and carved images, before he was humbled, indeed they *are* written among the sayings of Hozai.* [20]y So Manasseh rested with his fathers, and they

buried him in his own house. Then his son Amon reigned in his place.

Amon's Reign and Death

[21]z Amon *was* twenty-two years old when he became king, and he reigned two years in Jerusalem. [22]But he did evil in the sight of the LORD, as his father Manasseh had done; for Amon sacrificed to all the carved images which his father Manasseh had made, and served them. [23]And he did not humble himself before the LORD, [a]as his father Manasseh had humbled himself; but Amon trespassed more and more. [24]b Then his servants conspired against him, and [c]killed him in his own house. [25]But the people of the land executed all those who had conspired against King Amon. Then the people of the land made his son Josiah king in his place.

Josiah Reigns in Judah

34 Josiah [a]*was* eight years old when he became king, and he reigned thirty-one years in Jerusalem. [2]And he did *what was* right in the sight of the LORD, and walked in the ways of his father David; *he* did *not* turn aside to the right hand or to the left.

[3]For in the eighth year of his reign, while he was still [b]young, he began to [c]seek the God of his father David; and in the twelfth year he began [d]to purge Judah and Jerusalem [e]of the high places, the wooden images, the carved images, and the molded images. [4]f They broke down the altars of the Baals in his presence, and the incense altars which *were* above them he cut down; and the wooden images, the carved images, and the molded images he broke in pieces, and made dust of them [g]and scattered *it* on the graves of those who had sacrificed to them. [5]He also [h]burned the bones of the priests on their [i]altars, and cleansed Judah

---

* **33:11** That is, nose hooks (compare 2 Kings 19:28)   * **33:18** Literally *words*   * **33:19** Septuagint reads *the seers*.

33:11 Babylon. For some time Babylon had been part of the Assyrian Empire, though it had broken free on occasion, especially under the leadership of Berodach-Baladan, Hezekiah's contemporary (2 Kin. 20:12). Ashurbanipal brought Babylon back under Assyrian domination. He was the king who took Manasseh to Babylon as a prisoner.
33:14 wall outside the city of David. The term "city of David" originally referred to Mount Zion alone (1 Chr. 11:5) but eventually designated the entire city, including Mount Zion, the original Jebusite settlement. **Gihon.** Gihon was the spring that was the main source of water for Jerusalem (33:2,4,30). It was in the Kidron valley near the northeastern brow of Mount Zion. **Fish Gate.** The Fish Gate was in the center of the wall north of the temple. Manasseh's construction was a total distance of about 750 yards.
33:20 buried him in his own house. Manasseh had truly converted (v. 13), but his prior sin had been so

heinous that he was denied burial in the royal cemetery.
34:3 carved images. See note at 14:3.
34:5 burned the bones of the priests. This act of Josiah, which took place at Bethel, fulfilled the words of the prophet of Judah in the days of Jeroboam I, king of Israel (1 Kin. 13:1–2; 2 Kin. 23:15–16). The prophet had mentioned Josiah by name three hundred years before.

33:11 [n] Deut. 28:36 [o] 2 Chr. 36:6   **33:12** [p] 2 Chr. 7:14; 32:26   **33:13** [q] Ezra 8:23 [r] Dan. 4:25   **33:14** [s] 1 Kin. 1:33 [t] 2 Chr. 27:3   **33:15** [u] 2 Chr. 33:3, 5, 7   **33:16** [v] Lev. 7:12   **33:17** [w] 2 Chr. 32:12   **33:18** [x] 1 Sam. 9:9   **33:20** [y] 2 Kin. 21:18   **33:21** [z] 2 Kin. 21:19–24   **33:23** [a] 2 Chr. 33:12, 19   **33:24** [b] 2 Chr. 24:25 [c] 2 Chr. 25:27   **34:1** [a] 2 Kin. 22:1, 2   **34:3** [b] Eccl. 12:1 [c] 2 Chr. 15:2 [d] 1 Kin. 13:2 [e] 2 Chr. 33:17–19, 22   **34:4** [f] Lev. 26:30 [g] 2 Kin. 23:6   **34:5** [h] 1 Kin. 13:2 [i] 2 Kin. 23:20

and Jerusalem. [6]And *so he did* in the cities of Manasseh, Ephraim, and Simeon, as far as Naphtali and all around, with axes.* [7]When he had broken down the altars and the wooden images, had *j*beaten the carved images into powder, and cut down all the incense altars throughout all the land of Israel, he returned to Jerusalem.

Hilkiah Finds the Book of the Law

[8k]In the eighteenth year of his reign, when he had purged the land and the temple,* he sent *l*Shaphan the son of Azaliah, Maaseiah the *m*governor of the city, and Joah the son of Joahaz the recorder, to repair the house of the LORD his God. [9]When they came to Hilkiah the high priest, they delivered *n*the money that was brought into the house of God, which the Levites who kept the doors had gathered from the hand of Manasseh and Ephraim, from all the *o*remnant of Israel, from all Judah and Benjamin, and *which* they had brought back to Jerusalem. [10]Then they put *it* in the hand of the foremen who had the oversight of the house of the LORD; and they gave it to the workmen who worked in the house of the LORD, to repair and restore the house. [11]They gave *it* to the craftsmen and builders to buy hewn stone and timber for beams, and to floor the houses which the kings of Judah had destroyed. [12]And the men did the work faithfully. Their overseers *were* Jahath and Obadiah the Levites, of the sons of Merari, and Zechariah and Meshullam, of the sons of the Kohathites, to supervise. *Others of* the Levites, all of whom were skillful with instruments of music, [13]*were* *p*over the burden bearers and *were* overseers of all who did work in any kind of service. *q*And *some* of the Levites *were* scribes, officers, and gatekeepers.

[14]Now when they brought out the money that was brought into the house of the LORD, Hilkiah the priest *r*found the Book of the Law of the LORD *given* by Moses. [15]Then Hilkiah answered and said to Shaphan the scribe, "I have found the Book of the Law in the house of the LORD." And Hilkiah gave the *s*book to Shaphan.

[16]So Shaphan carried the book to the king, bringing the king word, saying, "All that was committed to your servants they are doing. [17]And they have gathered the money that was found in the house of the LORD, and have delivered it into the hand of the overseers and the workmen." [18]Then Shaphan the scribe told the king, saying, "Hilkiah the priest has given me a book." And Shaphan read it before the king.

[19]Thus it happened, when the king heard the words of the Law, that he tore his clothes. [20]Then the king commanded Hilkiah, *t*Ahikam the son of Shaphan, Abdon* the son of Micah, Shaphan the scribe, and Asaiah a servant of the king, saying, [21]"Go, inquire of the LORD for me, and for those who are left in Israel and Judah, concerning the words of the book that is found; for great *is* the wrath of the LORD that is poured out on us, because our fathers have not *u*kept the word of the LORD, to do according to all that is written in this book."

[22]So Hilkiah and those the king *had appointed* went to Huldah the prophetess, the wife of Shallum the son of Tokhath,* the son of Hasrah,* keeper of the wardrobe. (She dwelt in Jerusalem in the Second Quarter.) And they spoke to her to that *effect*.

[23]Then she answered them, "Thus says the LORD God of Israel, 'Tell the man who sent you to Me, [24]"Thus says the LORD: 'Behold, I will *v*bring calamity on this place and on its inhabitants, all the curses that are written in the *w*book which they have read before the king of Judah, [25]because they have forsaken Me and burned incense to other gods, that they might provoke Me to anger with all the works of their hands. Therefore My wrath will be poured out on this place, and not be quenched.' " ' [26]But as for the king of Judah, who sent you to inquire of the LORD, in this manner you shall speak to him, 'Thus says the LORD God of Israel: "Concerning the words which you have heard— [27]because your heart was

---

* **34:6** Literally *swords* * **34:8** Literally *house* * **34:20** *Achbor the son of Michaiah* in 2 Kings 22:12 * **34:22** Spelled *Tikvah* in 2 Kings 22:14 • Spelled *Harhas* in 2 Kings 22:14

34:8 Shaphan. Shaphan was a scribe or secretary of the king (v. 15). He was responsible for state records that must have included the original temple plans and specifications. The temple was repaired strictly according to its original pattern. **Joahaz the recorder.** The recorder kept the royal diaries. Official happenings were duly noted and recorded for posterity. The work of men like Joahaz provided sources for later historians such as the author of Chronicles (1 Chr. 18:15).
34:22 Huldah the prophetess. Huldah is one of four female prophets named in the Old Testament. The other three are Miriam (Ex. 15:20), Deborah (Judg. 4:4), and Noadiah (Neh. 6:14).
34:24 all the curses that are written in the book. Both Deuteronomy and Leviticus had long lists of

blessings for obedience and curses for rebellion, which were part of the conditions attached to the covenant with Israel (Deut. 28–30).
34:25 Apostasy—In all of life, no greater sin, no more serious or sadder error could be made than to forsake God and believe other gods. Such an act cuts one off from all of the loving care, wisdom, and discipline of the Creator God. Apostasy grieves God, and it grieves those who love God.

34:7 *j* Deut. 9:21	**34:8** *k* 2 Kin. 22:3–20 *l* 2 Kin. 25:22 *m* 2 Chr. 18:25	**34:9** *n* 2 Kin. 12:4 *o* 2 Chr. 30:6	**34:13** *p* 2 Chr. 8:10 *q* 1 Chr. 23:4, 5	**34:14** *r* 2 Kin. 22:8	**34:15** *s* Deut. 31:24, 26	**34:20** *t* Jer. 26:24 **34:21** *u* 2 Kin. 17:15–19	**34:24** *v* 2 Chr. 36:14–20 *w* Deut. 28:15–68

tender, and you humbled yourself before God when you heard His words against this place and against its inhabitants, and you humbled yourself before Me, and you tore your clothes and wept before Me, I also have heard *you*," says the ˣLORD. ²⁸"Surely I will gather you to your fathers, and you shall be gathered to your grave in peace; and your eyes shall not see all the calamity which I will bring on this place and its inhabitants."' " So they brought back word to the king.

Josiah Restores True Worship

²⁹ʸThen the king sent and gathered all the elders of Judah and Jerusalem. ³⁰The king went up to the house of the LORD, with all the men of Judah and the inhabitants of Jerusalem—the priests and the Levites, and all the people, great and small. And he ᶻread in their hearing all the words of the Book of the Covenant which had been found in the house of the LORD. ³¹Then the king ᵃstood in ᵇhis place and made a ᶜcovenant before the LORD, to follow the LORD, and to keep His commandments and His testimonies and His statutes with all his heart and all his soul, to perform the words of the covenant that were written in this book. ³²And he made all who were present in Jerusalem and Benjamin take a stand. So the inhabitants of Jerusalem did according to the covenant of God, the God of their fathers. ³³Thus Josiah removed all the ᵈabominations from all the country that *belonged* to the children of Israel, and made all who were present in Israel diligently serve the LORD their God. ᵉAll his days they did not depart from following the LORD God of their fathers.

Josiah Keeps the Passover

35 Now ᵃJosiah kept a Passover to the LORD in Jerusalem, and they slaughtered the Passover *lambs* on the ᵇfourteenth *day* of the first month. ²And he set the priests in their ᶜduties and ᵈencouraged them for the service of the house of the LORD. ³Then he said to the Levites ᵉwho taught all Israel, who were holy to

the LORD: ᶠ"Put the holy ark ᵍin the house which Solomon the son of David, king of Israel, built. ʰ*It shall* no longer *be* a burden on *your* shoulders. Now serve the LORD your God and His people Israel. ⁴Prepare *yourselves* ⁱaccording to your fathers' houses, according to your divisions, following the ʲwritten instruction of David king of Israel and the ᵏwritten instruction of Solomon his son. ⁵And ˡstand in the holy *place* according to the divisions of the fathers' houses of your brethren the *lay* people, and *according to* the division of the father's house of the Levites. ⁶So slaughter the Passover *offerings*, ᵐconsecrate yourselves, and prepare *them* for your brethren, that *they* may do according to the word of the LORD by the hand of Moses."

⁷Then Josiah ⁿgave the *lay* people lambs and young goats from the flock, all for Passover *offerings* for all who were present, to the number of thirty thousand, as well as three thousand cattle; these *were* from the king's ᵒpossessions. ⁸And his ᵖleaders gave willingly to the people, to the priests, and to the Levites. Hilkiah, Zechariah, and Jehiel, rulers of the house of God, gave to the priests for the Passover *offerings* two thousand six hundred *from the flock*, and three hundred cattle. ⁹Also �q Conaniah, his brothers Shemaiah and Nethanel, and Hashabiah and Jeiel and Jozabad, chief of the Levites, gave to the Levites for Passover *offerings* five thousand *from the flock* and five hundred cattle.

¹⁰So the service was prepared, and the priests ʳstood in their places, and the ˢLevites in their divisions, according to the king's command. ¹¹And they slaughtered the Passover *offerings*; and the priests ᵗsprinkled *the blood* with their hands, while the Levites ᵘskinned *the animals*. ¹²Then they removed the burnt offerings that *they* might give them to the divisions of the fathers' houses of the *lay* people, to offer to the LORD, as *it is* written ᵛin the Book of Moses. And so *they* did with the cattle. ¹³Also they ʷroasted the Passover *offerings* with fire according to the ordinance; but the *other* holy *offerings* they ˣboiled in

---

34:31 *a covenant . . . to follow the LORD.* Very few of the kings of Judah promised to follow the Lord as Josiah did. After David, only Joash, Hezekiah, and Josiah made such public commitments (23:3; 29:10; 1 Chr. 17:7–14).

35:3 *Put the holy ark in the house . . . It shall no longer be a burden on your shoulders.* The ark had apparently been removed from the temple. Who removed it and when or why is not known, but plenty of wicked kings could have done it. Manasseh's vehement opposition to God must have kept the ark in constant jeopardy, so perhaps it had been removed for protection. The only proper way to carry the ark was on the shoulders of the priests (Num. 4:5; 6:1).

35:6 *slaughter the Passover offerings.* The Levites were standing in for the people in the sacrifice of the

Passover lambs. This became the tradition from that time on, with the result that the priests gained influence and power.

35:13 *holy offerings.* The other holy offerings, distinguished from the Passover offering, were

34:27 ˣ 2 Chr. 12:7; 30:6; 33:12, 13 **34:29** ʸ 2 Kin. 23:1–3 **34:30** ᶻ Neh. 8:1–3 **34:31** ᵃ 2 Chr. 6:13 ᵇ 2 Kin. 11:14; 23:3 ᶜ 2 Chr. 23:16; 29:10 **34:33** ᵈ 1 Kin. 11:5 ᵉ Jer. 3:10 **35:1** ᵃ 2 Kin. 23:21, 22 ᵇ Ex. 12:6 **35:2** ᶜ 2 Chr. 23:18 ᵈ 2 Chr. 29:5–15 **35:3** ᵉ Deut. 33:10 ᶠ 2 Chr. 34:14 ᵍ 2 Chr. 5:7 ʰ 1 Chr. 23:26 **35:4** ⁱ 1 Chr. 9:10–13 ʲ 1 Chr. 23–26 ᵏ 2 Chr. 8:14 **35:5** ˡ Ps. 134:1 **35:6** ᵐ 2 Chr. 29:5, 15 **35:7** ⁿ 2 Chr. 30:24 ᵒ 2 Chr. 31:3 **35:8** ᵖ Num. 7:2 **35:9** q 2 Chr. 31:12 **35:10** ʳ Ezra 6:18 ˢ 2 Chr. 5:12; 7:6; 8:14, 15; 13:10; 29:25–34 **35:11** ᵗ 2 Chr. 29:22 ᵘ 2 Chr. 29:34 **35:12** ᵛ Ezra 6:18 **35:13** ʷ Ex. 12:8, 9 ˣ 1 Sam. 2:13–15

pots, in caldrons, and in pans, and divided *them* quickly among all the *lay* people. 14Then afterward they prepared portions for themselves and for the priests, because the priests, the sons of Aaron, *were busy* in offering burnt offerings and fat until night; therefore the Levites prepared portions for themselves and for the priests, the sons of Aaron. 15And the singers, the sons of Asaph, *were* in their places, according to the *y*command of David, Asaph, Heman, and Jeduthun the king's seer. Also the gatekeepers *z*were at each gate; they did not have to leave their position, because their brethren the Levites prepared portions for them.

16So all the service of the LORD was prepared the same day, to keep the Passover and to offer burnt offerings on the altar of the LORD, according to the command of King Josiah. 17And the children of Israel who were present kept the Passover at that time, and the Feast of *a*Unleavened Bread for seven days. 18*b*There had been no Passover kept in Israel like that since the days of Samuel the prophet; and none of the kings of Israel had kept such a Passover as Josiah kept, with the priests and the Levites, all Judah and Israel who were present, and the inhabitants of Jerusalem. 19In the eighteenth year of the reign of Josiah this Passover was kept.

Josiah Dies in Battle

20*c*After all this, when Josiah had prepared the temple, Necho king of Egypt came up to fight against *d*Carchemish by the Euphrates; and Josiah went out against him. 21But he sent messengers to him, saying, "What have I to do with you, king of Judah? *I have* not *come* against you this day, but against the house with which I have war; for God commanded me to make haste. Refrain *from meddling with* God, who *is* with me, lest He destroy you." 22Nevertheless Josiah would not turn his

face from him, but *e*disguised himself so that he might fight with him, and did not heed the words of Necho from the mouth of God. So he came to fight in the Valley of Megiddo.

23And the archers shot King Josiah; and the king said to his servants, "Take me away, for I am severely wounded." 24*f*His servants therefore took him out of that chariot and put him in the second chariot that he had, and they brought him to Jerusalem. So he died, and was buried in *one of* the tombs of his fathers. And *g*all Judah and Jerusalem mourned for Josiah.

25Jeremiah also *h*lamented for *i*Josiah. And to this day *j*all the singing men and the singing women speak of Josiah in their lamentations. *k*They made it a custom in Israel; and indeed they *are* written in the Laments. 26Now the rest of the acts of Josiah and his goodness, according to *what was* written in the Law of the LORD, 27and his deeds from first to last, indeed they *are* written in the book of the kings of Israel and Judah.

The Reign and Captivity of Jehoahaz

36 Then *a*the people of the land took Jehoahaz the son of Josiah, and made him king in his father's place in Jerusalem. 2Jehoahaz* *was* twenty-three years old when he became king, and he reigned three months in Jerusalem. 3Now the king of Egypt deposed him at Jerusalem; and he imposed on the land a tribute of one hundred talents of silver and a talent of gold. 4Then the king of Egypt made *Jehoahaz's** brother Eliakim king over Judah and Jerusalem, and changed his name to Jehoiakim. And Necho took Jehoahaz* his brother and carried him off to Egypt.

---

* **36:2** Masoretic Text reads *Joahaz.*   * **36:4** Literally *his* • Masoretic Text reads *Joahaz.*

---

the cattle slaughtered for thank, or peace offerings (v. 7).

35:18 *since the days of Samuel the prophet.* It had been almost four hundred years since the days of Samuel.

35:20 *to fight against Carchemish.* Carchemish was one of the last strongholds of Assyria to resist the onslaught of the rising neo-Babylonian kingdom. The Babylonians and Medes were on their way to subdue Haran and Carchemish. Necho, more afraid of the Babylonians than the Assyrians, was hoping to get to Carchemish in time to assist his Assyrian allies in their time of need. Josiah was an ally of Babylon, so he went to Megiddo to intercept the Egyptians.

35:21 *God commanded me.* God sometimes spoke to pagan rulers about a course of action He wanted them to take (36:22; Gen. 20:6; 41:25; Dan. 2:28). Necho did not know the source of his divine leading, but God did direct him, displaying His sovereignty over even the wicked and unbelieving powers of this world (Is. 44:28–45).

35:22 *Megiddo.* The major route from Egypt to the upper Euphrates was the Via Maris, or Way of the Sea. This route went up the coast of Israel before turning inland through the mountain pass at Megiddo. It crossed the plain of Jezreel, crossed the Jordan near the Sea of Galilee, and went on through Damascus where it joined the north-south route to upper Syria. If Josiah could control the pass at Megiddo, he could control the movement of traffic on that vital route.

36:3 *king of Egypt.* After Assyria's defeat at Haran and Carchemish, the Egyptian army withdrew south of the Euphrates, dominating Syria and Judah. Judah became an Egyptian vassal state, which explains why Necho could depose Jehoahaz and require tribute.

35:15 *y* 1 Chr. 25:1–6 *z* 1 Chr. 9:17, 18   **35:17** *d* Ex. 12:15; 13:6   **35:18** *b* 2 Kin. 23:22, 23   **35:20** *c* 2 Kin. 23:29 *d* Jer. 46:2   **35:22** *e* 2 Chr. 18:29   **35:24** *f* 2 Kin. 23:30 *g* Zech. 12:11   **35:25** *h* Lam. 4:20 *i* Jer. 22:10, 11 *j* Matt. 9:23 *k* Jer. 22:20   **36:1** *a* 2 Kin. 23:30–34

The Reign and Captivity of Jehoiakim

⁵ᵇJehoiakim *was* twenty-five years old when he became king, and he reigned eleven years in Jerusalem. And he did ᶜevil in the sight of the LORD his God. ⁶ᵈNebuchadnezzar king of Babylon came up against him, and bound him in bronze *fetters* to ᵉcarry him off to Babylon. ⁷ᶠNebuchadnezzar also carried off *some* of the articles from the house of the LORD to Babylon, and put them in his temple at Babylon. ⁸Now the rest of the acts of Jehoiakim, the abominations which he did, and what was found against him, indeed they *are* written in the book of the kings of Israel and Judah. Then Jehoiachin his son reigned in his place.

The Reign and Captivity of Jehoiachin

⁹ᵍJehoiachin *was* eight* years old when he became king, and he reigned in Jerusalem three months and ten days. And he did evil in the sight of the LORD. ¹⁰At the turn of the year ʰKing Nebuchadnezzar summoned *him* and took him to Babylon, ⁱwith the costly articles from the house of the LORD, and made ʲZedekiah, *Jehoiakim's** brother, king over Judah and Jerusalem.

Zedekiah Reigns in Judah

¹¹ᵏZedekiah *was* twenty-one years old when he became king, and he reigned eleven years in Jerusalem. ¹²He did evil in the sight of the LORD his God, *and* ˡdid not humble himself before Jeremiah the prophet, *who spoke* from the mouth of the LORD.

¹³And he also ᵐrebelled against King Nebuchadnezzar, who had made him swear *an oath* by God; but he ⁿstiffened his neck and hardened his heart against turning to the LORD God of Israel. ¹⁴Moreover all the leaders of the priests and the people transgressed more and more, *according* to all the abominations of the nations, and defiled the house of the LORD which He had consecrated in Jerusalem.

The Fall of Jerusalem

¹⁵ᵒAnd the LORD God of their fathers sent *warnings* to them by His messengers, rising up early and sending *them*, because He had compassion on His people and on His dwelling place. ¹⁶But ᵖthey mocked the messengers of God, qdespised His words, and ʳscoffed at His prophets, until the ˢwrath of the LORD arose against His people, till *there was* no remedy.

¹⁷ᵗTherefore He brought against them the king of the Chaldeans, who ᵘkilled their young men with the sword in the house of their sanctuary, and had no compassion on young man or virgin, on the aged or the weak; He gave *them* all into his hand. ¹⁸ᵛAnd all the articles from the house of God, great and small, the treasures of the house of the LORD, and the treasures of the king and of his leaders, all *these* he took to Babylon. ¹⁹ʷThen they burned the house of God, broke down the wall of Jerusalem, burned all its palaces with fire,

---

* **36:9** Some Hebrew manuscripts, Septuagint, Syriac, and 2 Kings 24:8 read *eighteen.*   * **36:10** Literally *his* (compare 2 Kings 24:17)

36:6 Nebuchadnezzar. Nebuchadnezzar was leading a campaign against Carchemish when he succeeded his father. He drove Egypt out of Syria and Judah and took some Jewish captives, including Daniel, back to Babylon (Dan. 1:1). At the same time, Jehoiakim changed his loyalty from Necho to Nebuchadnezzar and remained a trusted vassal for three years (2 Kin. 24:1). But then Jehoiakim rebelled against Babylon, and in about 602 B.C. Nebuchadnezzar returned to Jerusalem to punish him. **to carry him off to Babylon.** Jehoiakim was not actually taken to Babylon since he reigned until 598 B.C. and died of natural causes in Jerusalem (2 Kin. 26:6; Jer. 22:18).

36:7 carried off some of the articles from the house of the LORD. The Babylonian king looted the temple of much of its treasure, fulfilling the prophecy made to Hezekiah a century earlier (32:31). **his temple.** His temple was the temple of the Babylonians' patron god Marduk.

36:10 Zedekiah. Zedekiah was the youngest of the four sons of Josiah, and the third to rule over Judah (v. 1). He became king by Nebuchadnezzar's appointment, showing Judah's status as a Babylonian vassal (v. 3).

36:12 Jeremiah. Jeremiah was the famous prophet who composed the Book of Jeremiah, which included his words to Zedekiah (Jer. 21:3–7; 32:5).

36:14 all the abominations of the nations. This statement refers primarily to idolatry and all the immorality and perversity that went with it. God's covenant with Israel required them to be different from the nations in this key respect (Ex. 23:24; Lev. 26:1; Deut. 4:15–20, 25–28; 18:9–14; 27:14–15).

36:16 Unbelief—There is a line of divine patience that a nation can cross, bringing doom upon that country. In 586 B.C. Judah stepped over that mark. Prior to this God had graciously given His people many opportunities to repent of their unbelief. When we earnestly pray for our country as commanded by God (1 Tim. 2:1–2) we are asking to be kept from overstepping the limit of God's patience. About three thousand years ago, Solomon succinctly said, "Righteousness exalts a nation, but sin is a reproach to any people" (Prov. 14:34).

36:17 king of the Chaldeans. The Chaldean, or Babylonian, king was Nebuchadnezzar, who reigned from 605 to 562 B.C. He became an instrument of God's judgment all through Judah's last years and well into the exile (Dan. 2:37–38; 5:18–19).

36:5 ᵇ 2 Kin. 23:36, 37 ᶜ [Jer. 22:13–19]   **36:6** ᵈ 2 Kin. 24:1 ᵉ Jer. 36:30   **36:7** ᶠ Dan. 1:1, 2   **36:9** ᵍ 2 Kin. 24:8–17   **36:10** ʰ 2 Kin. 24:10–17 ⁱ Dan. 1:1, 2 ʲ Jer. 37:1   **36:11** ᵏ Jer. 52:1   **36:12** ˡ Jer. 21:3–7; 44:10   **36:13** ᵐ Ezek. 17:15 ⁿ 2 Kin. 17:14   **36:15** ᵒ Jer. 7:13; 25:3, 4   **36:16** ᵖ Jer. 5:12, 13 q [Prov. 1:24–32] ʳ Jer. 38:6 ˢ Ps. 79:5   **36:17** ᵗ 2 Kin. 25:1 ᵘ Ps. 74:20   **36:18** ᵛ 2 Kin. 25:13–15   **36:19** ʷ 2 Kin. 25:9

and destroyed all its precious possessions. [20]And [x]those who escaped from the sword he carried away to Babylon, [y]where they became servants to him and his sons until the rule of the kingdom of Persia, [21]to fulfill the word of the LORD by the mouth of [z]Jeremiah, until the land [a]had enjoyed her Sabbaths. As long as she lay desolate [b]she kept Sabbath, to fulfill seventy years.

The Proclamation of Cyrus

[22c]Now in the first year of Cyrus king of Persia, that the word of the LORD by the mouth of [d]Jeremiah might be fulfilled, the LORD stirred up the spirit of [e]Cyrus king of Persia, so that he made a proclamation throughout all his kingdom, and also *put it* in writing, saying,

23 [f]Thus says Cyrus king of Persia:

All the kingdoms of the earth the LORD God of heaven has given me. And He has commanded me to build Him a house at Jerusalem which is in Judah. Who *is* among you of all His people? May the LORD his God *be* with him, and let him go up!

36:20 *until the rule of the kingdom of Persia.* Cyrus conquered Babylon in 539 B.C. and allowed the Jews to return to Jerusalem the following year.

36:21 *Jeremiah.* In two places (Jer. 25:12; 29:10) Jeremiah predicted the exile and its length (Dan. 9:2). *Sabbath.* According to the law of Moses, the land was to lie fallow every seventh year (Lev. 25:4). Judah's exile in Babylon allowed the land to enjoy the sabbaths it had missed because of disobedience (Lev. 26:33–35).

36:22 *the first year of Cyrus.* The first year refers to the first year of Cyrus' rule over Babylon, not his first year over Media and Persia. He began to rule Media and Persia in 550 B.C. Twelve years later he brought Babylon under his control and issued his famous decree, known from the Old Testament (Ezra 1:2–4) and from his own records, the Cylinder of Cyrus. Jeremiah's seventy years were from about 609 to 539 B.C. *the LORD stirred up.* Cyrus was both a mighty monarch and the instrument by whom God delivered His people from exile, returned them to their land, and rebuilt the temple (Is. 44:28–45). Like many rulers

who encountered the living God, Cyrus recognized and even extolled His power as the God of Israel, but this was not the same as abandoning all other gods and following the Lord alone.

36:23 Providence—God is the Lord of the universe. He not only rules over those who are called by His name, but He also moves upon the hearts and minds of others whom He chooses to use in the fulfillment of His purpose. It was part of God's plan for the Jews to be taken captive by Babylon, and for Babylon to be taken by Persia. Cyrus had been chosen and ordained for his role in returning the Jews to their own land, and was even called by name by Isaiah the prophet (Is. 44:28; 45:1). It is not always possible to understand the things that the Lord is doing, but we can still rejoice in His providence, confident that the Judge of all the earth will do right (Gen. 18:25).

36:20 [x] 2 Kin. 25:11 [y] Jer. 17:4; 27:7 **36:21** [z] Jer. 25:9–12; 27:6–8; 29:10 [a] Lev. 26:34–43 [b] Lev. 25:4, 5 **36:22** [c] Ezra 1:1–3 [d] Jer. 29:10 [e] Is. 44:28; 45:1 **36:23** [f] Ezra 1:2, 3

THE BOOK OF
EZRA

▶ **AUTHOR:** Although Ezra is not specifically named as the author, Jewish tradition attributes the book to him. This seems appropriate as portions of the book are written in the first person, from Ezra's point of view (7:28—9:15). Similar to Chronicles, this book has a strong priestly emphasis. Ezra was a direct descendant of Aaron through Eleazar, Phinehas, and Zadok, and so came from a long and illustrious priestly line. It is believed that Ezra had access to the extensive library of written documents gathered by Nehemiah and that this was one of the sources used in writing this book as well as Chronicles.

▶ **TIME:** c. 538–457 B.C.   ▶ **KEY VERSE:** Ezra 1:3

▶ **THEME:** Many scholars think Ezra and Nehemiah belong together as one book. Together they tell parts of the same story. The exile is over and the temple is to be rebuilt along with the wall of Jerusalem despite considerable opposition. While Nehemiah's perspective is that of a civil servant and building contractor, Ezra is a teacher of the law and a priest, and as such, provides leadership by bringing God's Word to the people and by restoring proper worship. When the people respond to the Word and reestablish their relationship with God through worship, the building process is renewed and completed.

End of the Babylonian Captivity

1 Now in the first year of Cyrus king of Persia, that the word of the LORD ᵃby the mouth of Jeremiah might be fulfilled, the LORD stirred up the spirit of Cyrus king of Persia, ᵇso that he made a proclamation throughout all his kingdom, and also *put it* in writing, saying,

2 Thus says Cyrus king of Persia:
All the kingdoms of the earth the LORD God of heaven has given me. And He has ᶜcommanded me to build Him a house at Jerusalem which *is* in Judah. ³Who *is* among you of all His people? May his God be with him, and let him go up to Jerusalem which *is* in Judah, and build the house of the LORD God of Israel ᵈ(He *is* God), which *is* in Jerusalem. ⁴And whoever is left in any place where he dwells, let the men of his place help him with silver and gold, with goods and livestock, besides the freewill offerings for the house of God which *is* in Jerusalem.

⁵Then the heads of the fathers' *houses* of Judah and Benjamin, and the priests and the Levites, with all whose spirits ᵉGod had moved, arose to go up and build the house of the LORD which *is* in Jerusalem. ⁶And all those who *were* around them encouraged them with articles of silver and gold, with goods and livestock, and with precious things, besides all *that* was ᶠwillingly offered.

⁷ᵍKing Cyrus also brought out the articles of the house of the LORD, ʰwhich

---

1:1 *first year of Cyrus.* This refers to the first year of Cyrus' reign over Babylon. Cyrus the Great, the founder of the Persian Empire and the Achaemenid dynasty, conquered Babylon in 539 B.C. The events in the Book of Ezra were taking place at the same time as the latter part of the Book of Daniel, after the overthrow of Belshazzar by the Medes and Persians, and the absorption of Babylon into the Persian Empire (Dan. 5:28,30–31; 6:28). ***Jeremiah.*** Jeremiah had prophesied that the Babylonian captivity would last 70 years (Jer. 25:11; 29:10) after which the Lord would judge Babylon (Jer. 25:12–14). ***he made a proclamation.*** One hundred and forty years before Cyrus the Great was even born, Isaiah the prophet called him by name, foretelling the decree he would issue allowing the Israelites to return to their homeland (Is. 44:28; 45:14).

1:4 *let the men of his place help him.* The assistance that the Israelites were to receive from their non-Jewish neighbors in rebuilding the temple was similar to the help an earlier generation received from the Egyptians before the Exodus (Ex. 12:33–36). In a sense, the return to Jerusalem to rebuild the temple was a second exodus (Is. 43:14–21; 48:20–21).

1:7 *which Nebuchadnezzar had taken.* See 2 Kings

1:1 ᵃ 2 Chr. 36:22, 23   ᵇ Ezra 5:13, 14   **1:2** ᶜ Is. 44:28; 45:1, 13   **1:3** ᵈ Dan. 6:26   **1:5** ᵉ [Phil. 2:13]   **1:6** ᶠ Ezra 2:68
1:7 ᵍ Ezra 5:14; 6:5 ʰ 2 Kin. 24:13

Nebuchadnezzar had taken from Jerusalem and put in the temple of his gods; [8]and Cyrus king of Persia brought them out by the hand of Mithredath the treasurer, and counted them out to *i*Sheshbazzar the prince of Judah. [9]This *is* the number of them: thirty gold platters, one thousand silver platters, twenty-nine knives, [10]thirty gold basins, four hundred and ten silver basins of a similar *kind, and* one thousand other articles. [11]All the articles of gold and silver *were* five thousand four hundred. All *these* Sheshbazzar took with the captives who were brought from Babylon to Jerusalem.

The Captives Who Returned to Jerusalem

2 Now* *a*these *are* the people of the province who came back from the captivity, of those who had been carried away, *b*whom Nebuchadnezzar the king of Babylon had carried away to Babylon, and who returned to Jerusalem and Judah, everyone to his *own* city.

[2]*Those* who came with Zerubbabel *were* Jeshua, Nehemiah, Seraiah, Reelaiah, Mordecai, Bilshan, Mispar,* Bigvai, Rehum,* *and* Baanah. The number of the men of the people of Israel: [3]the people of Parosh, two thousand one hundred and seventy-two; [4]the people of Shephatiah, three hundred and seventy-two; [5]the people of Arah, *c*seven hundred and seventy-five; [6]the people of *d*Pahath-Moab, of the people of Jeshua *and* Joab, two thousand eight hundred and twelve; [7]the people of Elam, one thousand two hundred and fifty-four; [8]the people of Zattu, nine hundred and forty-five; [9]the people of Zaccai, seven hundred and sixty; [10]the people of Bani,* six hundred and forty-two; [11]the people of Bebai, six hundred and twenty-three; [12]the people of Azgad, one thousand two hundred and twenty-two; [13]the people of Adonikam, six hundred and sixty-six; [14]the people of Bigvai, two thousand and fifty-six; [15]the people of Adin, four hundred and fifty-four; [16]the people of Ater of Hezekiah, ninety-eight; [17]the people of Bezai, three hundred and twenty-three;

[18]the people of Jorah,* one hundred and twelve; [19]the people of Hashum, two hundred and twenty-three; [20]the people of Gibbar,* ninety-five; [21]the people of Bethlehem, one hundred and twenty-three; [22]the men of Netophah, fifty-six; [23]the men of Anathoth, one hundred and twenty-eight; [24]the people of Azmaveth,* forty-two; [25]the people of Kirjath Arim,* Chephirah, and Beeroth, seven hundred and forty-three; [26]the people of Ramah and Geba, six hundred and twenty-one; [27]the men of Michmas, one hundred and twenty-two; [28]the men of Bethel and Ai, two hundred and twenty-three; [29]the people of Nebo, fifty-two; [30]the people of Magbish, one hundred and fifty-six; [31]the people of the other *e*Elam, one thousand two hundred and fifty-four; [32]the people of Harim, three hundred and twenty; [33]the people of Lod, Hadid, and Ono, seven hundred and twenty-five; [34]the people of Jericho, three hundred and forty-five; [35]the people of Senaah, three thousand six hundred and thirty.

[36]The priests: the sons of *f*Jedaiah, of the house of Jeshua, nine hundred and seventy-three; [37]the sons of *g*Immer, one thousand and fifty-two; [38]the sons of *h*Pashhur, one thousand two hundred and forty-seven; [39]the sons of *i*Harim, one thousand and seventeen.

[40]The Levites: the sons of Jeshua and Kadmiel, of the sons of Hodaviah,* seventy-four.

[41]The singers: the sons of Asaph, one hundred and twenty-eight.

[42]The sons of the gatekeepers: the sons of Shallum, the sons of Ater, the sons of Talmon, the sons of Akkub, the sons of Hatita, and the sons of Shobai, one hundred and thirty-nine *in* all.

[43]*j*The Nethinim: the sons of Ziha, the sons of Hasupha, the sons of Tabbaoth,

---

* **2:1** Compare this chapter with Nehemiah 7:6–73.
* **2:2** Spelled *Mispereth* in Nehemiah 7:7 • Spelled *Nehum* in Nehemiah 7:7   * **2:10** Spelled *Binnui* in Nehemiah 7:15   * **2:18** Called *Hariph* in Nehemiah 7:24   * **2:20** Called *Gibeon* in Nehemiah 7:25 * **2:24** Called *Beth Azmaveth* in Nehemiah 7:28 * **2:25** Called *Kirjath Jearim* in Nehemiah 7:29 * **2:40** Spelled *Hodevah* in Nehemiah 7:43

24:1–7,11–13; 25:8–17; 2 Chronicles 36:5–19; and Daniel 1:2.

1:8 Sheshbazzar. Ezra 5:2 and 5:16 appear to identify Sheshbazzar and Zerubbabel as one and the same person. The name Sheshbazzar occurs in only two passages (vv. 8–11; 5:14–16) and both times are related to official Persian actions. It is possible, and considered likely, that Sheshbazzar was the Persian name for Zerubbabel.

2:2 Nehemiah . . . Mordecai. The Nehemiah mentioned here is not the same man who rebuilt the walls of Jerusalem 90 years later. The Mordecai in this verse is also considered to be a different man than the one who figured so prominently in the Book of Esther.

2:40–42 The Levites . . . The singers . . . The sons of the gatekeepers. The Levites assisted the priests in

the temple and in teaching the people the law. The singers were also Levites and had the responsibility of praising God with music (1 Chr. 15:16). Although only 128 singers returned to Jerusalem, at one time there had been as many as four thousand who praised the Lord with musical instruments in Solomon's temple (1 Chr. 23:5). The gatekeepers were another set of Levites who prevented unauthorized people from entering the restricted area of the temple.

2:43 The Nethinim. *Nethinim* means "given ones"

1:8 *i* Ezra 5:14, 16   **2:1** *a* Neh. 7:6–73   *b* 2 Kin. 24:14–16; 25:11   **2:5** *c* Neh. 7:10   **2:6** *d* Neh. 7:11   **2:31** *e* Ezra 2:7 **2:36** *f* 1 Chr. 24:7–18   **2:37** *g* 1 Chr. 24:14   **2:38** *h* 1 Chr. 9:12   **2:39** *i* 1 Chr. 24:8   **2:43** *j* 1 Chr. 9:2

44the sons of Keros, the sons of Siaha,* the sons of Padon, 45the sons of Lebanah, the sons of Hagabah, the sons of Akkub, 46the sons of Hagab, the sons of Shalmai, the sons of Hanan, 47the sons of Giddel, the sons of Gahar, the sons of Reaiah, 48the sons of Rezin, the sons of Nekoda, the sons of Gazzam, 49the sons of Uzza, the sons of Paseah, the sons of Besai, 50the sons of Asnah, the sons of Meunim, the sons of Nephusim,* 51the sons of Bakbuk, the sons of Hakupha, the sons of Harhur, 52the sons of Bazluth,* the sons of Mehida, the sons of Harsha, 53the sons of Barkos, the sons of Sisera, the sons of Tamah, 54the sons of Neziah, and the sons of Hatipha.

55The sons of kSolomon's servants: the sons of Sotai, the sons of lSophereth, the sons of Peruda,* 56the sons of Jaala, the sons of Darkon, the sons of Giddel, 57the sons of Shephatiah, the sons of Hattil, the sons of Pochereth of Zebaim, and the sons of Ami.* 58All the mNethinim and the children of nSolomon's servants were three hundred and ninety-two.

59And these were the ones who came up from Tel Melah, Tel Harsha, Cherub, Addan,* and Immer; but they could not identify their father's house or their genealogy,* whether they were of Israel: 60the sons of Delaiah, the sons of Tobiah, and the sons of Nekoda, six hundred and fifty-two; 61and of the sons of the priests: the sons of oHabaiah, the sons of Koz,* and the sons of pBarzillai, who took a wife of the daughters of Barzillai the Gileadite, and was called by their name. 62These sought their listing among those who were registered by genealogy, but they were not found; qtherefore they were excluded from the priesthood as defiled. 63And the governor* said to them that they rshould not eat of the most holy things till a priest could consult with the sUrim and Thummim.

64tThe whole assembly together was forty-two thousand three hundred and

sixty, 65besides their male and female servants, of whom there were seven thousand three hundred and thirty-seven; and they had two hundred men and women singers. 66Their horses were seven hundred and thirty-six, their mules two hundred and forty-five, 67their camels four hundred and thirty-five, and their donkeys six thousand seven hundred and twenty.

68uSome of the heads of the fathers' houses, when they came to the house of the LORD which is in Jerusalem, offered freely for the house of God, to erect it in its place: 69According to their ability, they gave to the vtreasury for the work sixty-one thousand gold drachmas, five thousand minas of silver, and one hundred priestly garments.

70wSo the priests and the Levites, some of the people, the singers, the gatekeepers, and the Nethinim, dwelt in their cities, and all Israel in their cities.

Worship Restored at Jerusalem

3 And when the aseventh month had come, and the children of Israel were in the cities, the people gathered together as one man to Jerusalem. 2Then Jeshua the son of bJozadak* and his brethren the priests, cand Zerubbabel the son of dShealtiel and his brethren, arose and built the altar of the God of Israel, to offer burnt offerings on it, as it is ewritten in the Law of Moses the man of God. 3Though fear had come upon them because of the people of those countries, they set the altar on its bases; and they offered fburnt offerings on it to the LORD, both the morning and evening burnt offerings. 4gThey also kept the Feast of

---

* **2:44** Spelled Sia in Nehemiah 7:47
* **2:50** Spelled Nephishesim in Nehemiah 7:52
* **2:52** Spelled Bazlith in Nehemiah 7:54
* **2:55** Spelled Perida in Nehemiah 7:57
* **2:57** Spelled Amon in Nehemiah 7:59
* **2:59** Spelled Addon in Nehemiah 7:61 • Literally seed * **2:61** Or Hakkoz * **2:63** Hebrew Tirshatha * **3:2** Spelled Jehozadak in 1 Chronicles 6:14

---

or "dedicated ones." In 1 Chronicles 9:2, the Nethinim are distinguished from the priests and the Levites. Jewish tradition identifies the Nethinim with the Gibeonites who had been assigned by Joshua to assist the Levites in more menial tasks (Josh. 9:27).
2:63 Urim and Thummim. The Urim and Thummim were somehow used to determine God's will (Ex. 28:30). It is not known exactly what they were, but it has been speculated that they were special sacred stones, used for casting lots.
2:64 forty-two thousand three hundred and sixty. The individual numbers listed in chapter 2 add up to only 29,818. The difference is accounted for because the larger total includes women, who are not named in the lists.
2:65 men and women singers. These men and women are thought to be other than the choir of the temple (v. 41). They were probably professional singers employed for banquets and feasts (2 Chr. 35:25; Eccl. 2:7–8). It could be that some of the Jews achieved prosperity and a degree of luxury in

Babylon. They had not, after all, been enslaved in exile, but only restricted from returning to their land.
3:1 seventh month. The seventh month was a sacred month to the Jewish people. The first day of the month was the Feast of Trumpets (Num. 29:1–6), the tenth day was the Day of Atonement (Num. 29:7–11), and the fifteenth day was the Feast of Tabernacles (Num. 29:12–38).
3:2–3 Jeshua. This is believed to be the same person as the priest Joshua mentioned by the prophets Haggai and Zechariah (Hag. 1:1; Zech. 3:1).
3:4 Feast of Tabernacles. The Feast of Booths, or Tabernacles, was a feast instituted as a remembrance

---

2:55 k 1 Kin. 9:21 l Neh. 7:57–60   **2:58** m 1 Chr. 9:2 n 1 Kin. 9:21   **2:61** o Neh. 7:63 p 2 Sam. 17:27 **2:62** q Num. 3:10   **2:63** r Lev. 22:2, 10, 15, 16 s Ex. 28:30 **2:64** t Neh. 7:66   **2:68** u Neh. 7:70   **2:69** v Ezra 8:25–35 **2:70** w Neh. 7:73   **3:1** a Neh. 7:73; 8:1, 2   **3:2** b Neh. 12:1, 8 c Ezra 2:2; 4:2, 3; 5:2 d 1 Chr. 3:17 e Deut. 12:5, 6 **3:3** f Num. 28:3   **3:4** g Neh. 8:14–18

Tabernacles, *h*as *it is* written, and *i*offered the daily burnt offerings in the number required by ordinance for each day. ⁵Afterwards *they offered* the *j*regular burnt offering, and *those* for New Moons and for all the appointed feasts of the LORD that were consecrated, and *those* of everyone who willingly offered a freewill offering to the LORD. ⁶From the first day of the seventh month they began to offer burnt offerings to the LORD, although the foundation of the temple of the LORD had not been laid. ⁷They also gave money to the masons and the carpenters, and *k*food, drink, and oil to the people of Sidon and Tyre to bring cedar logs from Lebanon to the sea, to *l*Joppa, *m*according to the permission which they had from Cyrus king of Persia.

Restoration of the Temple Begins

⁸Now in the second month of the second year of their coming to the house of God at Jerusalem, *n*Zerubbabel the son of Shealtiel, Jeshua the son of Jozadak,* and the rest of their brethren the priests and the Levites, and all those who had come out of the captivity to Jerusalem, began *work* *o*and appointed the Levites from twenty years old and above to oversee the work of the house of the LORD. ⁹Then Jeshua *with* his sons and brothers, Kadmiel *with* his sons, and the sons of Judah,* arose as one to oversee those working on the house of God: the sons of Henadad *with* their sons and their brethren the Levites.

¹⁰When the builders laid the foundation of the temple of the LORD, *p*the priests stood* in their apparel with trumpets, and the Levites, the sons of Asaph, with cymbals, to praise the LORD, according to the *q*ordinance of David king of Israel. ¹¹*r*And they sang responsively, praising and giving thanks to the LORD:

s"For *He is* good,
*t*For His mercy *endures* forever toward Israel."*

Then all the people shouted with a great shout, when they praised the LORD, because the foundation of the house of the LORD was laid.

¹²But many of the priests and Levites and *u*heads of the fathers' *houses,* old men who had seen the first temple, wept with a loud voice when the foundation of this temple was laid before their eyes. Yet many shouted aloud for joy, ¹³so that the people could not discern the noise of the shout of joy from the noise of the weeping of the people, for the people shouted with a loud shout, and the sound was heard afar off.

Resistance to Rebuilding the Temple

4 Now when *a*the adversaries of Judah and Benjamin heard that the descendants of the captivity were building the temple of the LORD God of Israel, ²they came to Zerubbabel and the heads of the fathers' *houses,* and said to them, "Let us build with you, for we seek your God as you *do;* and we have sacrificed to Him *b*since the days of Esarhaddon king of Assyria, who brought us here." ³But Zerubbabel and Jeshua and the rest of the heads of the fathers' *houses* of Israel said to them, *c*"You may do nothing with us to build a house for our God; but we alone will build to the LORD God of Israel, as *d*King Cyrus the king of Persia has commanded us." ⁴Then *e*the people of the land tried to discourage the people of Judah. They troubled them in building, ⁵and hired counselors against them to frustrate their purpose all the days of Cyrus king of Persia, even until the reign of *f*Darius king of Persia.

* **3:8** Spelled *Jehozadak* in 1 Chronicles 6:14
* **3:9** Or *Hodaviah* (compare 2:40) * **3:10** Following Septuagint, Syriac, and Vulgate; Masoretic Text reads *they stationed the priests.*
* **3:11** Compare Psalm 136:1

---

of the earlier generations' wanderings in the wilderness (Num. 29:13–38).

3:11 Patience—In spite of Israel's history of sin, leading to the broken empire, captivity, exile, the destruction of the temple and walls of Jerusalem, God still had not forgotten His people. Joy filled the hearts of the Israelites, for God's love had endured. Patiently, faithfully, He was keeping every promise. He is equally faithful and patient to each of us, even though we so often miss the mark. He does not give us up, but showers us with benefits and never ceases to show us His unchanging persistent love.

4:1 the adversaries of Judah. The enemies of Judah were the Samaritans. Esarhaddon (v. 2), who ruled Assyria from 681–669 B.C., had transported the conquered people of the northern kingdom to other lands. He then brought people from elsewhere into Palestine. These foreigners intermarried with the Hebrews who were left in the land. Their offspring became the Samaritans mentioned in the New Testament.

4:4–5 Persecution—Israel encountered hostility when they returned to their land. At first glance it might seem that Israel was at fault for turning down help. These people said they had been offering sacrifices to Jehovah. This did not mean, however, that they had ceased to serve their idols (2 Kin. 17:29–35). Whatever their hidden reasons for offering help, it would not have been in favor of the Israelites. Their underlying hostility became obvious as they succeeded in hindering the work on the temple.

3:4 *h* Ex. 23:16 *i* Num. 29:12, 13 **3:5** *j* Ex. 29:38
3:7 *k* Acts 12:20 *l* 2 Chr. 2:16 *m* Ezra 1:2; 6:3 **3:8** *n* Ezra 3:2; 4:3 *o* 1 Chr. 23:4, 24 **3:10** *p* 1 Chr. 16:5, 6 *q* 1 Chr. 6:31; 16:4; 25:1 **3:11** *r* Neh. 12:24 *s* Ps. 136:1 *t* Jer. 33:11 **3:12** *u* Ezra 2:68 **4:1** *a* Ezra 4:7–9 **4:2** *b* 2 Kin. 17:24; 19:37 **4:3** *c* Neh. 2:20 *d* Ezra 1:1–4 **4:4** *e* Ezra 3:3 **4:5** *f* Ezra 5:5; 6:1

Rebuilding of Jerusalem Opposed

[6]In the reign of Ahasuerus, in the beginning of his reign, they wrote an accusation against the inhabitants of Judah and Jerusalem.

[7]In the days of [g]Artaxerxes also, Bishlam, Mithredath, Tabel, and the rest of their companions wrote to Artaxerxes king of Persia; and the letter *was* written in [h]Aramaic script, and translated into the Aramaic language. [8]Rehum* the commander and Shimshai the scribe wrote a letter against Jerusalem to King Artaxerxes in this fashion:

[9] From* Rehum the commander, Shimshai the scribe, and the rest of their companions—*representatives* of [i]the Dinaites, the Apharsathchites, the Tarpelites, the people of Persia and Erech and Babylon and Shushan,* the Dehavites, the Elamites, [10][j]and the rest of the nations whom the great and noble Osnapper took captive and settled in the cities of Samaria and the remainder beyond the River*—[k]and so forth.*

[11](This *is* a copy of the letter that they sent him)

To King Artaxerxes from your servants, the men *of the region* beyond the River, and so forth:*

[12] Let it be known to the king that the Jews who came up from you have come to us at Jerusalem, and are building the [l]rebellious and evil city, and are finishing *its* [m]walls and repairing the foundations. [13]Let it now be known to the king that, if this city is built and the walls completed, they will not pay [n]tax, tribute, or custom, and the king's treasury will be diminished.[14]Now because we receive support from the palace, and it was not proper for us to see the king's dishonor; therefore we have sent and informed the king,[15]that search may be made in the book of the records of your fathers. And you will find in the book of the records and know that this city *is* a rebellious city, harmful to kings and provinces, and that they have incited sedition within the city in former times, for which cause this city was destroyed.

[16] We inform the king that if this city is rebuilt and its walls are completed, the result will be that you will have no dominion beyond the River.

[17]The king sent an answer:

To Rehum the commander, *to* Shimshai the scribe, *to* the rest of their companions who dwell in Samaria, and *to* the remainder beyond the River:

Peace, and so forth.*

[18] The letter which you sent to us has been clearly read before me. [19]And I gave the command, and a search has been made, and it was found that this city in former times has revolted against kings, and rebellion and sedition have been fostered in it. [20]There have also been mighty kings over Jerusalem, who have [o]ruled over all *the region* [p]beyond the River; and tax, tribute, and custom were paid to them. [21]Now give the command to make these men cease, that this city may not be built until the command is given by me.

[22] Take heed now that you do not fail to do this. Why should damage increase to the hurt of the kings?

[23]Now when the copy of King Artaxerxes' letter *was* read before Rehum, Shimshai the scribe, and their companions, they went up in haste to Jerusalem against the Jews, and by force of arms made them cease. [24]Thus the work of the house of God which *is* at Jerusalem ceased, and it was discontinued until the second year of the reign of Darius king of Persia.

Restoration of the Temple Resumed

5 Then the prophet [a]Haggai and [b]Zechariah the son of Iddo, prophets, prophesied to the Jews who *were* in Judah and Jerusalem, in the name of the God of Israel, *who was* over them. [2]So [c]Zerubbabel the son of Shealtiel and Jeshua the son of Jozadak* rose up and began to build the house of God which *is* in Jerusalem; and [d]the prophets of God *were* with them, helping them.

[3]At the same time [e]Tattenai the governor of *the region* beyond the River* and Shethar-Boznai and their companions

---

* **4:8** The original language of Ezra 4:8 through 6:18 is Aramaic.   * **4:9** Literally *Then* • Or *Susa*
* **4:10** That is, the Euphrates • Literally *and now*
* **4:11** Literally *and now*   * **4:17** Literally *and now*   * **5:2** Spelled *Jehozadak* in 1 Chronicles 6:14
* **5:3** That is, the Euphrates

4:6 *Ahasuerus.* When Darius I died (486 B.C.) his son Ahasuerus reigned (485–465 B.C.). Ahasuerus's Greek name was Xerxes. This is the same king who appears in the Book of Esther.

4:10 *the River.* This reference to simply "the River" means the River Euphrates.

4:21 *this city may not be built.* The Persian king Artaxerxes ordered the Jewish people to cease their work on the temple. Years later at the request of Nehemiah the decision was reviewed (Neh. 2:1–8).

4:24 *Darius king of Persia.* This is not the same Darius as the Darius of Daniel 5 and 6.

4:7 [g] Ezra 7:1, 21   [h] 2 Kin. 18:26   **4:9** [i] 2 Kin. 17:30, 31
4:10 [j] 2 Kin. 17:24   [k] Ezra 4:11, 17; 7:12   **4:12** [l] 2 Chr. 36:13
[m] Ezra 5:3, 9   **4:13** [n] Ezra 4:20; 7:24   **4:20** [o] Ps. 72:8
[p] Gen. 15:18   **5:1** [a] Hag. 1:1   [b] Zech. 1:1   **5:2** [c] Ezra 3:2
[d] Hag. 2:4   **5:3** [e] Ezra 5:6; 6:6

came to them and spoke thus to them: *f*"Who has commanded you to build this temple and finish this wall?" 4*g*Then, accordingly, we told them the names of the men who were constructing this building. 5But *h*the eye of their God was upon the elders of the Jews, so that they could not make them cease till a report could go to Darius. Then a *i*written answer was returned concerning this *matter.* 6This is a copy of the letter that Tattenai sent:

The governor of *the region* beyond the River, and Shethar-Boznai, *j*and his companions, the Persians who *were in the region* beyond the River, to Darius the king.

7(They sent a letter to him, in which was written thus)

To Darius the king:

All peace.

8 Let it be known to the king that we went into the province of Judea, to the temple of the great God, which is being built with heavy stones, and timber is being laid in the walls; and this work goes on diligently and prospers in their hands.

9 Then we asked those elders, *and* spoke thus to them: *k*"Who commanded you to build this temple and to finish these walls?" 10We also asked them their names to inform you, that we might write the names of the men who *were* chief among them.

11 And thus they returned us an answer, saying: "We are the servants of the God of heaven and earth, and we are rebuilding the temple that was built many years ago, which a great king of Israel built *l*and completed. 12But *m*because our fathers provoked the God of heaven to wrath, He gave them into the hand of *n*Nebuchadnezzar king of Babylon, the Chaldean, *who* destroyed this temple and *o*carried the people away to Babylon. 13However, in the first year of *p*Cyrus king of Babylon, King Cyrus issued a decree to build this house of God. 14Also, *q*the gold and silver articles of the house of God, which Nebuchadnezzar had taken from

the temple that *was* in Jerusalem and carried into the temple of Babylon— those King Cyrus took from the temple of Babylon, and they were given to *r*one named Sheshbazzar, whom he had made governor. 15And he said to him, 'Take these articles; go, carry them to the temple *site* that *is* in Jerusalem, and let the house of God be rebuilt on its former site.' 16Then the same Sheshbazzar came *and s*laid the foundation of the house of God which *is* in Jerusalem; but from that time even until now it has been under construction, and *t*it is not finished."

17 Now therefore, if *it seems* good to the king, *u*let a search be made in the king's treasure house, which *is* there in Babylon, whether it is *so* that a decree was issued by King Cyrus to build this house of God at Jerusalem, and let the king send us his pleasure concerning this *matter.*

The Decree of Darius

6 Then King Darius issued a decree, *a*and a search was made in the archives,* where the treasures were stored in Babylon. 2And at Achmetha,* in the palace that *is* in the province of *b*Media, a scroll was found, and in it a record *was* written thus:

3 In the first year of King Cyrus, King Cyrus issued a *c*decree *concerning* the house of God at Jerusalem: "Let the house be rebuilt, the place where they offered sacrifices; and let the foundations of it be firmly laid, its height sixty cubits *and* its width sixty cubits, 4*d*with three rows of heavy stones and one row of new timber. Let the *e*expenses be paid from the king's treasury. 5Also let *f*the gold and silver articles of the house of God, which Nebuchadnezzar took from the temple which *is* in Jerusalem and brought to Babylon, be restored and taken back to the temple which *is* in Jerusalem, *each* to its place; and deposit *them* in the house of God"—

6 *g*Now *therefore,* Tattenai, governor of *the region* beyond the River, and

---

* **6:1** Literally *house of the scrolls* * **6:2** Probably *Echatana,* the ancient capital of Media

---

5:12 *our fathers provoked the God of heaven.* Although the Jewish people acknowledged that Nebuchadnezzar destroyed the first temple, they traced the cause not to his power, but to their sin and God's judgment.

6:2 *Achmetha.* This city, also called "Ecbatana," was the summer residence of the Persian kings.

6:3 *its height sixty cubits and its width sixty cubits.* Though the complete dimensions are not given, it is likely that the second temple was built on the foundation stones that were still in place from the time of Solomon (1 Kin. 6:2).

5:3 *f* Ezra 1:3; 5:9 **5:4** *g* Ezra 5:10 **5:5** *h* Ps. 33:18 *i* Ezra 6:6 **5:6** *j* Ezra 4:7–10 **5:9** *k* Ezra 5:3, 4 **5:11** *l* 1 Kin. 6:1, 38 **5:12** *m* 2 Chr. 34:25; 36:16, 17 *n* 2 Kin. 24:2; 25:8–11 *o* Jer. 13:19 **5:13** *p* Ezra 1:1 **5:14** *q* Ezra 1:7, 8; 6:5 *r* Hag. 1:14; 2:2, 21 **5:16** *s* Ezra 3:8–10 *t* Ezra 6:15 **5:17** *u* Ezra 6:1, 2 **6:1** *a* Ezra 5:17 **6:2** *b* 2 Kin. 17:6 **6:3** *c* Ezra 1:1; 5:13 **6:4** *d* 1 Kin. 6:36 *e* Ezra 3:7 **6:5** *f* Ezra 1:7, 8; 5:14 **6:6** *g* Ezra 5:3, 6

Shethar-Boznai, and your companions the Persians who *are* beyond the River, keep yourselves far from there. 7Let the work of this house of God alone; let the governor of the Jews and the elders of the Jews build this house of God on its site.

8 Moreover I issue a decree *as to* what you shall do for the elders of these Jews, for the building of this house of God: Let the cost be paid at the king's expense from taxes *on the region* beyond the River; this is to be given immediately to these men, so that they are not hindered. 9And whatever they need—young bulls, rams, and lambs for the burnt offerings of the God of heaven, wheat, salt, wine, and oil, according to the request of the priests who *are* in Jerusalem—let it be given them day by day without fail, 10*h*that they may offer sacrifices of sweet aroma to the God of heaven, and pray for the life of the king and his sons.

11 Also I issue a decree that whoever alters this edict, let a timber be pulled from his house and erected, and let him be hanged on it; *i*and let his house be made a refuse heap because of this. 12And may the God who causes His *j*name to dwell there destroy any king or people who put their hand to alter it, or to destroy this house of God which is in Jerusalem. I Darius issue a decree; let it be done diligently.

The Temple Completed and Dedicated

13Then Tattenai, governor of *the region* beyond the River, Shethar-Boznai, and their companions diligently did according to what King Darius had sent. 14*k*So the elders of the Jews built, and they prospered through the prophesying of Haggai the prophet and Zechariah the son of Iddo. And they built and finished *it*, according

to the commandment of the God of Israel, and according to the command of *l*Cyrus, *m*Darius, and *n*Artaxerxes king of Persia. 15Now the temple was finished on the third day of the month of Adar, which was in the sixth year of the reign of King Darius. 16Then the children of Israel, the priests and the Levites and the rest of the descendants of the captivity, celebrated *o*the dedication of this house of God with joy. 17And they *p*offered sacrifices at the dedication of this house of God, one hundred bulls, two hundred rams, four hundred lambs, and as a sin offering for all Israel twelve male goats, according to the number of the tribes of Israel. 18They assigned the priests to their *q*divisions and the Levites to their *r*divisions, over the service of God in Jerusalem, *s*as it is written in the Book of Moses.

The Passover Celebrated

19And the descendants of the captivity kept the Passover *t*on the fourteenth *day* of the first month. 20For the priests and the Levites had *u*purified themselves; all of them *were ritually* clean. And they *v*slaughtered the Passover *lambs* for all the descendants of the captivity, for their brethren the priests, and for themselves. 21Then the children of Israel who had returned from the captivity ate together with all who had separated themselves from the *w*filth of the nations of the land in order to seek the LORD God of Israel. 22And they kept the *x*Feast of Unleavened Bread seven days with joy; for the LORD made them joyful, and *y*turned the heart *z*of the king of Assyria toward them, to strengthen their hands in the work of the house of God, the God of Israel.

The Arrival of Ezra

7 Now after these things, in the reign of *a*Artaxerxes king of Persia, Ezra the *b*son of Seraiah, *c*the son of Azariah, the son of *d*Hilkiah, 2the son of Shallum, the

---

6:8–10 *Moreover.* Not only could Tattenai not stop reconstruction of the temple, he also had to fund its completion.

6:16 *celebrated the dedication . . . with joy.* Some have suggested that Psalms 145–148 were used to celebrate the completion of the rebuilding of the temple.

6:19 *kept the Passover.* This celebration must have been exceptionally memorable; it was the first time since the captivity that the people were able to celebrate according to the law, with sacrifices offered in the temple (v. 20).

6:21 *the nations of the land.* The term probably refers to the people who had been transplanted into Palestine by the Assyrians.

6:22 *Providence*—The situation the Jews faced seemed hopeless. But God in His providence caused Cyrus to look favorably upon the Jews and allow them to return to their homeland. What seemed impossible

became possible through God. Sometimes it is easy for us to forget that even in the worst of times and circumstances God is still on His throne.

7:1–5 *after these things.* The events of chapter 6 took place during the reign of King Darius. The temple was completed and dedicated in 515 B.C. Chapter 7 jumps forward many years to the reign of Artaxerxes (464–424 B.C.). Thus, between chapters 6 and 7 there is a gap of approximately 60 years. During this period the events of the Book of Esther took place.

6:10 *h* Ezra 7:23 **6:11** *i* Dan. 2:5; 3:29 **6:12** *j* 1 Kin. 9:3 **6:14** *k* Ezra 5:1, 2 *l* Ezra 1:1; 5:13; 6:3 *m* Ezra 4:24; 6:12 *n* Ezra 7:1, 11 **6:16** *o* 1 Kin. 8:63 **6:17** *p* Ezra 8:35 **6:18** *q* 1 Chr. 24:1 *r* 1 Chr. 23:6 *s* Num. 3:6; 8:9 **6:19** *t* Ex. 12:6 **6:20** *u* 2 Chr. 29:34; 30:15 *v* 2 Chr. 35:11 **6:21** *w* Ezra 9:11 **6:22** *x* Ex. 12:15; 13:6, 7 *y* [Prov. 21:1] *z* Ezra 1:1; 6:1 **7:1** *a* Neh. 2:1 *b* 1 Chr. 6:14 *c* Jer. 52:24 *d* 2 Chr. 35:8

son of Zadok, the son of Ahitub, ³the son of Amariah, the son of Azariah, the son of Meraioth, ⁴the son of Zerahiah, the son of Uzzi, the son of Bukki, ⁵the son of Abishua, the son of Phinehas, the son of Eleazar, the son of Aaron the chief priest— ⁶this Ezra came up from Babylon; and he *was* ᵉa skilled scribe in the Law of Moses, which the LORD God of Israel had given. The king granted him all his request, ᶠaccording to the hand of the LORD his God upon him. ⁷ᵍ*Some* of the children of Israel, the priests, ʰthe Levites, the singers, the gatekeepers, and ⁱthe Nethinim came up to Jerusalem in the seventh year of King Artaxerxes. ⁸And Ezra came to Jerusalem in the fifth month, which *was* in the seventh year of the king. ⁹On the first *day* of the first month he began *his* journey from Babylon, and on the first *day* of the fifth month he came to Jerusalem, ʲaccording to the good hand of his God upon him. ¹⁰For Ezra had prepared his heart to ᵏseek the Law of the LORD, and to do *it*, and to ˡteach statutes and ordinances in Israel.

The Letter of Artaxerxes to Ezra

¹¹This *is* a copy of the letter that King Artaxerxes gave Ezra the priest, the scribe, expert in the words of the commandments of the LORD, and of His statutes to Israel:

¹² Artaxerxes,* ᵐking of kings,

To Ezra the priest, a scribe of the Law of the God of heaven:

Perfect *peace,* ⁿand so forth.*

¹³ I issue a decree that all those of the people of Israel and the priests and Levites in my realm, who volunteer to go up to Jerusalem, may go with you. ¹⁴And whereas you are being sent by the king and his ᵒseven counselors to inquire concerning Judah and Jerusalem, with regard to the Law of your God which *is* in your hand; ¹⁵and *whereas you are* to carry the silver and gold which the king and his counselors have freely offered to the God of Israel, ᵖwhose dwelling *is* in Jerusalem; ¹⁶ᑫand *whereas* all the silver and gold that you may find in all

the province of Babylon, along with the freewill offering of the people and the priests, *are to be* ʳfreely offered for the house of their God in Jerusalem— ¹⁷now therefore, be careful to buy with this money bulls, rams, and lambs, with their ˢgrain offerings and their drink offerings, and ᵗoffer them on the altar of the house of your God in Jerusalem.

¹⁸ And whatever seems good to you and your brethren to do with the rest of the silver and the gold, do it according to the will of your God. ¹⁹Also the articles that are given to you for the service of the house of your God, deliver in full before the God of Jerusalem. ²⁰And whatever more may be needed for the house of your God, which you may have occasion to provide, pay *for it* from the king's treasury.

²¹ And I, *even* I, Artaxerxes the king, issue a decree to all the treasurers who *are in the region* beyond the River, that whatever Ezra the priest, the scribe of the Law of the God of heaven, may require of you, let it be done diligently, ²²up to one hundred talents of silver, one hundred kors of wheat, one hundred baths of wine, one hundred baths of oil, and salt without prescribed limit. ²³Whatever is commanded by the God of heaven, let it diligently be done for the house of the God of heaven. For why should there be wrath against the realm of the king and his sons?

²⁴ Also we inform you that it shall not be lawful to impose tax, tribute, or custom on any of the priests, Levites, singers, gatekeepers, Nethinim, or servants of this house of God. ²⁵And you, Ezra, according to your God-given wisdom, ᵘset magistrates and judges who may judge all the people who *are in the region* beyond the River, all such as know the laws of your God; and ᵛteach those

---

* **7:12** The original language of Ezra 7:12–26 is Aramaic. • Literally *and now*

7:6 *a skilled scribe in the Law of Moses.* A scribe was one who copied and studied the law. After the exile, the office of scribe came into prominence, in some ways replacing the prophet in importance, and eventually eclipsing the role of the priest. In the Gospels, numerous references are made to the scribes as ones who were considered spiritual leaders of the people. **7:9 *first month . . . fifth month.*** The first month corresponds to March-April, the fifth month to July-August. ***the good hand of his God.*** Ezra was grateful for God's protection even more since the route he traveled was dangerous because of rebellion in Egypt and the fact that spring was the time armies began their campaigns. **7:9–10 Obedience**—Ezra followed God's command and made his paramount exercise the study, practice, and teaching of God's law. The "good hand of his

God" was upon Ezra, for he "had prepared his heart to seek the Law of the LORD." That same command is for us also. We don't always know when we as Christians are being watched by others, but if we are diligent to obey, our lives will point to Christ. **7:22 *one hundred talents of silver.*** One hundred talents of silver weighed nearly four tons. One hundred kors of wheat amounted to about 625 bushels; one hundred baths of wine or oil equaled about six hundred gallons each.

7:6 ᵉ Ezra 7:11, 12, 21 ᶠ Ezra 7:9, 28; 8:22 **7:7** ᵍ Ezra 8:1–14 ʰ Ezra 8:15 ⁱ Ezra 2:43; 8:20 **7:9** ʲ Neh. 2:8, 18 **7:10** ᵏ Ps. 119:45 ˡ Deut. 33:10 **7:12** ᵐ Dan. 2:37 ⁿ Ezra 4:10 **7:14** ᵒ Esth. 1:14 **7:15** ᵖ Ezra 6:12 **7:16** ᑫ Ezra 8:25 ʳ 1 Chr. 29:6, 9 **7:17** ˢ Num. 15:4–13 ᵗ Deut. 12:5–11 **7:25** ᵘ Ex. 18:21, 22 ᵛ [Mal. 2:7]

who do not know *them*. 26Whoever will not observe the law of your God and the law of the king, let judgment be executed speedily on him, whether *it be* death, or banishment, or confiscation of goods, or imprisonment.

27wBlessed *be* the LORD God of our fathers, xwho has put *such a thing* as this in the king's heart, to beautify the house of the LORD which *is* in Jerusalem, 28and yhas extended mercy to me before the king and his counselors, and before all the king's mighty princes.

So I was encouraged, as zthe hand of the LORD my God *was* upon me; and I gathered leading men of Israel to go up with me.

Heads of Families Who Returned with Ezra

8 These *are* the heads of their fathers' houses, and *this is* the genealogy of those who went up with me from Babylon, in the reign of King Artaxerxes: 2of the sons of Phinehas, Gershom; of the sons of Ithamar, Daniel; of the sons of David, aHattush; 3of the sons of Shecaniah, of the sons of bParosh, Zechariah; and registered with him *were* one hundred and fifty males; 4of the sons of cPahath-Moab, Eliehoenai the son of Zerahiah, and with him two hundred males; 5of the sons of Shechaniah,* Ben-Jahaziel, and with him three hundred males; 6of the sons of Adin, Ebed the son of Jonathan, and with him fifty males; 7of the sons of Elam, Jeshaiah the son of Athaliah, and with him seventy males; 8of the sons of Shephatiah, Zebadiah the son of Michael, and with him eighty males; 9of the sons of Joab, Obadiah the son of Jehiel, and with him two hundred and eighteen males; 10of the sons of Shelomith,* Ben-Josiphiah, and with him one hundred and sixty males; 11of the sons of dBebai, Zechariah the son of Bebai, and with him twenty-eight males; 12of the sons of Azgad, Johanan the son of Hakkatan, and with him one hundred and ten males; 13of the last sons of Adonikam, whose names *are* these—Eliphelet, Jeiel, and Shemaiah—and with them sixty males; 14also of the sons of Bigvai, Uthai and Zabbud, and with them seventy males.

Servants for the Temple

15Now I gathered them by the river that flows to Ahava, and we camped there three days. And I looked among the people and the priests, and found none of the esons of Levi there. 16Then I sent for Eliezer, Ariel, Shemaiah, Elnathan, Jarib, Elnathan, Nathan, Zechariah, and fMeshullam, leaders; also for Joiarib and Elnathan, men of understanding. 17And I gave them a command for Iddo the chief man at the place Casiphia, and I told them what they should say to Iddo *and* his brethren* the Nethinim at the place Casiphia—that they should bring us servants for the house of our God. 18Then, by the good hand of our God upon us, they gbrought us a man of understanding, of the sons of Mahli the son of Levi, the son of Israel, namely Sherebiah, with his sons and brothers, eighteen men; 19and hHashabiah, and with him Jeshaiah of the sons of Merari, his brothers and their sons, twenty men; 20ialso of the Nethinim, whom David and the leaders had appointed for the service of the Levites, two hundred and twenty Nethinim. All of them were designated by name.

Fasting and Prayer for Protection

21Then I jproclaimed a fast there at the river of Ahava, that we might khumble ourselves before our God, to seek from Him the lright way for us and our little ones and all our possessions. 22For mI was ashamed to request of the king an escort of soldiers and horsemen to help us against the enemy on the road, because we had spoken to the king, saying, n"The hand of our God *is* upon all those for ogood who seek Him, but His power and His wrath *are* pagainst all those who qforsake Him." 23So we fasted and entreated our God for this, and He ranswered our prayer.

Gifts for the Temple

24And I separated twelve of the leaders of the priests—Sherebiah, Hashabiah, and ten of their brethren with them—25and weighed out to them sthe silver, the gold, and the articles, the offering for the house of our God which the king and his counselors and his princes, and all Israel *who were* present, had offered. 26I weighed into their hand six hundred and fifty talents of silver, silver

---

* **8:5** Following Masoretic Text and Vulgate; Septuagint reads *the sons of Zatho, Shechaniah.*
* **8:10** Following Masoretic Text and Vulgate; Septuagint reads *the sons of Banni, Shelomith.*
* **8:17** Following Vulgate; Masoretic Text reads *to Iddo his brother;* Septuagint reads *to their brethren.*

8:17 Casiphia. The significance of Casiphia is uncertain, but it is thought that there may have been a Jewish sanctuary or temple there.

8:22 seek Him. Ezra knew that God would protect him; he wasn't afraid to "stick his neck out" even though it might have been more comfortable to have the security of soldiers as escorts. In our own lives, it is the same. Our responsibility is obedience, no matter what. Our safety is God's responsibility.

7:27 w 1 Chr. 29:10 x Ezra 6:22 **7:28** y Ezra 9:9 z Ezra 5:5; 7:6, 9; 8:18 **8:2** a 1 Chr. 3:22 **8:3** b Ezra 2:3 **8:4** c Ezra 10:30 **8:11** d Ezra 10:28 **8:15** e Ezra 7:7; 8:2 **8:16** f Ezra 10:15 **8:18** g Neh. 8:7 **8:19** h Neh. 12:24 **8:20** i Ezra 2:43; 7:7 **8:21** j 1 Sam. 7:6 k Is. 58:3, 5 l Ps. 5:8 **8:22** m 1 Cor. 9:15 n Ezra 7:6, 9, 28 o [Rom. 8:28] p [Ps. 34:16] q [2 Chr. 15:2] **8:23** r 2 Chr. 33:13 **8:25** s Ezra 7:15, 16

articles *weighing* one hundred talents, one hundred talents of gold, [27]twenty gold basins *worth* a thousand drachmas, and two vessels of fine polished bronze, precious as gold. [28]And I said to them, "You *are* [t]holy to the LORD; the articles *are* [u]holy also; and the silver and the gold *are* a freewill offering to the LORD God of your fathers. [29]Watch and keep *them* until you weigh *them* before the leaders of the priests and the Levites and [v]heads of the fathers' *houses* of Israel in Jerusalem, *in* the chambers of the house of the LORD." [30]So the priests and the Levites received the silver and the gold and the articles by weight, to bring *them* to Jerusalem to the house of our God.

The Return to Jerusalem

[31]Then we departed from the river of Ahava on the twelfth *day* of the first month, to go to Jerusalem. And [w]the hand of our God was upon us, and He delivered us from the hand of the enemy and from ambush along the road. [32]So we [x]came to Jerusalem, and stayed there three days.

[33]Now on the fourth day the silver and the gold and the articles were [y]weighed in the house of our God by the hand of Meremoth the son of Uriah the priest, and with him *was* Eleazar the son of Phinehas; with them *were* the Levites, [z]Jozabad the son of Jeshua and Noadiah the son of Binnui, [34]with the number *and* weight of everything. All the weight was written down at that time.

[35]The children of those who had been [a]carried away captive, who had come from the captivity, [b]offered burnt offerings to the God of Israel: twelve bulls for all Israel, ninety-six rams, seventy-seven lambs, and twelve male goats *as* a sin offering. All *this was* a burnt offering to the LORD.

[36]And they delivered the king's [c]orders to the king's satraps and the governors *in the region* beyond the River. So they gave support to the people and the house of God.

Intermarriage with Pagans

9 When these things were done, the leaders came to me, saying, "The people of Israel and the priests and the Levites have not [a]separated themselves from the peoples of the lands, [b]with respect to the abominations of the Canaanites, the Hittites, the Perizzites, the Jebusites, the Ammonites, the Moabites, the Egyptians, and the Amorites. [2]For they have [c]taken some

of their daughters *as wives* for themselves and their sons, so that the [d]holy seed is [e]mixed with the peoples of *those* lands. Indeed, the hand of the leaders and rulers has been foremost in this trespass." [3]So when I heard this thing, [f]I tore my garment and my robe, and plucked out some of the hair of my head and beard, and sat down [g]astonished. [4]Then everyone who [h]trembled at the words of the God of Israel assembled to me, because of the transgression of those who had been carried away captive, and I sat astonished until the [i]evening sacrifice.

[5]At the evening sacrifice I arose from my fasting; and having torn my garment and my robe, I fell on my knees and [j]spread out my hands to the LORD my God. [6]And I said: "O my God, I am too [k]ashamed and humiliated to lift up my face to You, my God; for [l]our iniquities have risen higher than *our* heads, and our guilt has [m]grown up to the heavens. [7]Since the days of our fathers to this day [n]we *have been* very guilty, and for our iniquities [o]we, our kings, *and* our priests have been delivered into the hand of the kings of the lands, to the [p]sword, to captivity, to plunder, and to [q]humiliation, as *it is* this day. [8]And now for a little while grace has been *shown* from the LORD our God, to leave us a remnant to escape, and to give us a peg in His holy place, that our God may [r]enlighten our eyes and give us a measure of revival in our bondage. [9s]For we *were* slaves. [t]Yet our God did not forsake us in our bondage; but [u]He extended mercy to us in the sight of the kings of Persia, to revive us, to repair the house of our God, to rebuild its ruins, and to give us [v]a wall in Judah and Jerusalem. [10]And now, O our God, what shall we say after this? For we have forsaken Your commandments, [11]which You commanded by Your servants the prophets, saying, 'The land which you are entering to possess is an unclean land, with the [w]uncleanness of the peoples of the lands, with their abominations which have filled it from one end to another with their impurity. [12]Now therefore, [x]do not give your daughters as wives for their sons, nor take their daughters to your sons; and [y]never seek their peace or prosperity, that you may be strong and eat the good of the land, and [z]leave *it* as an inheritance to your children forever.' [13]And after all that has come upon us for our evil deeds and for our great guilt, since You our God [a]have punished us

---

9:2 *taken some of their daughters as wives for themselves.* Intermarrying with people who did not worship the One True God was expressly forbidden (Ex. 34:16; Deut. 7:3). While there are instances of marriages to non-Israelites being blessed (Rahab, Ruth), these were cases where the woman had clearly taken a stand as a believer in Yahweh, renouncing her old religion.

9:13–14 *punished us less than our iniquities deserve.* Israel was guilty and deserved whatever punishment God gave them. God would have been

8:28 [t]Lev. 21:6–9 [u]Lev. 22:2, 3 **8:29** [v]Ezra 4:3 **8:31** [w]Ezra 7:6, 9, 28 **8:32** [x]Neh. 2:11 **8:33** [y]Ezra 8:26, 30 [z]Neh. 11:16 **8:35** [a]Ezra 2:1 [b]Ezra 6:17 **8:36** [c]Ezra 7:21–24 **9:1** [a]Neh. 9:2 [b]Deut. 12:30, 31 **9:2** [c][Deut. 7:3] [d]Ex. 22:31 [e][2 Cor. 6:14] **9:3** [f]Job 1:20 [g]Ps. 143:4 **9:4** [h]Ezra 10:3 [i]Ex. 29:39 **9:5** [j]Ex. 9:29 **9:6** [k]Dan. 9:7, 8 [l]Ps. 38:4 [m]Rev. 18:5 **9:7** [n]Dan. 9:5, 6 [o]Deut. 28:36 [p]Deut. 32:25 [q]Dan. 9:7, 8 **9:8** [r]Ps. 34:5 **9:9** [s]Neh. 9:36 [t]Ps. 136:23 [u]Ezra 7:28 [v]Is. 5:2 **9:11** [w]Ezra 6:21 **9:12** [x][Deut. 7:3, 4] [y]Deut. 23:6 [z][Prov. 13:22; 20:7] **9:13** [a][Ps. 103:10]

less than our iniquities *deserve*, and have given us *such* deliverance as this, [14]should we [b]again break Your commandments, and [c]join in marriage with the people *committing* these abominations? Would You not be [d]angry with us until You had consumed *us*, so that *there would be* no remnant or survivor? [15]O LORD God of Israel, [e]You *are* righteous, for we are left as a remnant, as *it is* this day. [f]Here we *are* before You, [g]in our guilt, though no one can stand before You because of this!"

Confession of Improper Marriages

10 Now [a]while Ezra was praying, and while he was confessing, weeping, and bowing down [b]before the house of God, a very large assembly of men, women, and children gathered to him from Israel; for the people wept very [c]bitterly. [2]And Shechaniah the son of Jehiel, *one* of the sons of Elam, spoke up and said to Ezra, "We have [d]trespassed against our God, and have taken pagan wives from the peoples of the land; yet now there is hope in Israel in spite of this. [3]Now therefore, let us make [e]a covenant with our God to put away all these wives and those who have been born to them, according to the advice of my master and of those who [f]tremble at [g]the commandment of our God; and let it be done according to the [h]law. [4]Arise, for *this* matter *is* your *responsibility*. We also *are* with you. [i]Be of good courage, and do *it*."

[5]Then Ezra arose, and made the leaders of the priests, the Levites, and all Israel [j]swear an oath that they would do according to this word. So they swore an oath. [6]Then Ezra rose up from before the house of God, and went into the chamber of Jehohanan the son of Eliashib; and *when* he came there, he [k]ate no bread and drank no water, for he mourned because of the guilt of those from the captivity.

[7]And they issued a proclamation throughout Judah and Jerusalem to all the descendants of the captivity, that they must gather at Jerusalem, [8]and that whoever would not come within three days, according to the instructions of the leaders and elders, all his property would be confiscated, and he himself would be separated from the assembly of those from the captivity.

[9]So all the men of Judah and Benjamin gathered at Jerusalem within three days. It *was* the ninth month, on the twentieth of the month; and [l]all the people sat in the open square of the house of God, trembling because of *this* matter and because of heavy rain. [10]Then Ezra the priest stood up and said to them, "You have transgressed and have taken pagan wives, adding to the guilt of Israel. [11]Now therefore, [m]make confession to the LORD God of your fathers, and do His will; [n]separate yourselves from the peoples of the land, and from the pagan wives."

[12]Then all the assembly answered and said with a loud voice, "Yes! As you have said, so we must do. [13]But *there are* many people; *it is* the season for heavy rain, and we are not able to stand outside. Nor *is this* the work of one or two days, for *there are* many of us who have transgressed in this matter. [14]Please, let the leaders of our entire assembly stand; and let all those in our cities who have taken pagan wives come at appointed times, together with the elders and judges of their cities, until [o]the fierce wrath of our God is turned away from us in this matter." [15]Only Jonathan the son of Asahel and Jahaziah the son of Tikvah opposed this, and [p]Meshullam and Shabbethai the Levite gave them support.

[16]Then the descendants of the captivity

---

just in consuming them, even to the point of leaving no remnant or survivor. But in His great mercy, God provided a way out for Israel. In an even greater way, He provided a way out for all mankind. Sin is always sin, no matter how small it may seem to us. God would be justified in destroying us all for only one sin. God is just. This means that He cannot tolerate sin even a little bit. But He is also more loving, kind, and compassionate than we can comprehend. In His mercy, He provided the way out. He sent His son to pay the price of our sin for us. In this way His justice was satisfied, and at the same time His love provided a way to save us.

9:15 *we are left as a remnant.* It is true that Israel was rebellious and evil at times in her history. Kings and Chronicles record how wicked they had become. But the people who returned to rebuild the temple were a chastened and different generation from the one taken into captivity. The men and women who went back were determined to obey God's laws and would not tolerate idolatry. While the returning Jews succeeded in ridding themselves of heathen idol worship, they created another problem. They set in motion a legalistic system that culminated with a

people who valued their interpretation of the law over the Scriptures. The condition progressed until Jesus spoke out against their extremism and their lack of mercy and compassion (Matt. 23:1–36).

10:3 Fear of God—When one thinks of fear, usually what comes to mind is dread and alarm—an unpleasant emotion caused by the anticipation of danger or a threat. But the fear of God is another thing. We tremble and obey Him, not out of dread but out of deep reverence for an almighty God. The covenant the men of Israel made with God was the most binding form of covenant a person could make. They were pledging "in the fear of God" to do as they promised.

10:9 the ninth month. The ninth month, Chislev, corresponds to November-December.

9:14[b] [John 5:14] [c] Neh. 13:23 [d] Deut. 9:8 **9:15**[e] Dan. 9:14
[f] [Rom. 3:19] [g] 1 Cor. 15:17 **10:1**[a] Dan. 9:4, 20 [b] 2 Chr. 20:9
[c] Neh. 8:1–9 **10:2**[d] Neh. 13:23–27 **10:3**[e] 2 Chr. 34:31
[f] Ezra 9:4 [g] Deut. 7:2, 3 [h] Deut. 24:1, 2 **10:4**[i] 1 Chr. 28:10
10:5[j] Neh. 5:12; 13:25 **10:6**[k] Deut. 9:18 **10:9**[l] 1 Sam.
12:18 **10:11**[m] [Prov. 28:13] [n] Ezra 10:3 **10:14**[o] 2 Chr.
28:11–13; 29:10; 30:8 **10:15**[p] Neh. 3:4

did so. And Ezra the priest, *with* certain ᵍheads of the fathers' *households*, were set apart by the fathers' households, each of them by name; and they sat down on the first day of the tenth month to examine the matter. ¹⁷By the first day of the first month they finished *questioning* all the men who had taken pagan wives.

Pagan Wives Put Away

¹⁸And among the sons of the priests who had taken pagan wives *the following* were found of the sons of ʳJeshua the son of Jozadak,* and his brothers: Maaseiah, Eliezer, Jarib, and Gedaliah. ¹⁹And they ˢgave their promise that they would put away their wives; and *being* ᵗguilty, *they presented* a ram of the flock as their ᵘtrespass offering.

²⁰Also of the sons of Immer: Hanani and Zebadiah; ²¹of the sons of Harim: Maaseiah, Elijah, Shemaiah, Jehiel, and Uzziah; ²²of the sons of Pashhur: Elioenai, Maaseiah, Ishmael, Nethanel, Jozabad, and Elasah.

²³Also of the Levites: Jozabad, Shimei, Kelaiah (the same *is* Kelita), Pethahiah, Judah, and Eliezer.

²⁴Also of the singers: Eliashib; and of the gatekeepers: Shallum, Telem, and Uri.

²⁵And others of Israel: of the ᵛsons of Parosh: Ramiah, Jeziah, Malchiah, Mijamin, Eleazar, Malchijah, and Benaiah; ²⁶of the sons of Elam: Mattaniah, Zechariah, Jehiel, Abdi, Jeremoth, and Eliah; ²⁷of the sons of Zattu: Elioenai, Eliashib, Mattaniah, Jeremoth, Zabad, and Aziza; ²⁸of the ʷsons of Bebai: Jehohanan, Hananiah, Zabbai, *and* Athlai; ²⁹of the sons of Bani: Meshullam, Malluch, Adaiah, Jashub, Sheal, *and* Ramoth;* ³⁰of the ˣsons of Pahath-Moab: Adna, Chelal, Benaiah, Maaseiah, Mattaniah, Bezalel, Binnui, and Manasseh; ³¹*of* the sons of Harim: Eliezer, Ishijah, Malchijah, Shemaiah, Shimeon, ³²Benjamin, Malluch, *and* Shemariah; ³³of the sons of Hashum: Mattenai, Mattattah, Zabad, Eliphelet, Jeremai, Manasseh, *and* Shimei; ³⁴of the sons of Bani: Maadai, Amram, Uel, ³⁵Benaiah, Bedeiah, Cheluh,* ³⁶Vaniah, Meremoth, Eliashib, ³⁷Mattaniah, Mattenai, Jaasai,* ³⁸Bani, Binnui, Shimei, ³⁹Shelemiah, Nathan, Adaiah, ⁴⁰Machnadebai, Shashai, Sharai, ⁴¹Azarel, Shelemiah, Shemariah, ⁴²Shallum, Amariah, *and* Joseph; ⁴³of the sons of Nebo: Jeiel, Mattithiah, Zabad, Zebina, Jaddai,* Joel, *and* Benaiah.

⁴⁴All these had taken pagan wives, and *some* of them had wives *by whom* they had children.

---

* **10:18** Spelled *Jehozadak* in 1 Chronicles 6:14
* **10:29** Or *Jeremoth*   * **10:35** Or *Cheluhi*, or *Cheluhu*   * **10:37** Or *Jaasu*   * **10:43** Or *Jaddu*

10:16 ᵍEzra 4:3   **10:18** ʳEzra 5:2   **10:19** ˢ2 Kin.
10:15   ᵗLev. 6:4, 6   ᵘLev. 5:6, 15   **10:25** ᵛEzra 2:3; 8:3

10:28 ʷEzra 8:11   **10:30** ˣEzra 8:4

THE BOOK OF
NEHEMIAH

▶ **AUTHOR:** It is apparent that much of this book came from Nehemiah's personal memoirs. The account is extremely vivid and frank. Obviously, 1:1—7:5; 12:27–43; and 13:4–31 are the "words of Nehemiah." Some scholars state that Nehemiah composed the above portions and compiled the rest. Others feel that Ezra wrote 7:6—12:26 and 12:44—13:3, then put together the rest using Nehemiah's diary. Nehemiah 7:5–73 and Ezra 2:1–70 are almost identical, but both lists may have been pulled from an existing record of the same period.

▶ **TIME:** 444–425 B.C.   ▶ **KEY VERSE:** Neh. 6:15

▶ **THEME:** Nehemiah's role in rebuilding the temple and the walls of Jerusalem is more political than physical, as he deals with the new political situation arising in Persia and in Jerusalem. He also serves as the general contractor who pulls together the raw materials and the workers while orchestrating the rebuilding process. Within all his work, there is an underlying understanding that he has been called by God to do this work and is fulfilling God's purposes. When the people don't follow through with adhering to the law, Nehemiah is just as forceful as Ezra in calling the people back to repentance and obedience.

Nehemiah Prays for His People

1 The words of ᵃNehemiah the son of Hachaliah.

It came to pass in the month of Chislev, *in* the ᵇtwentieth year, as I was in ᶜShushan* the citadel, ²that ᵈHanani one of my brethren came with men from Judah; and I asked them concerning the Jews who had escaped, who had survived the captivity, and concerning Jerusalem. ³And they said to me, "The survivors who are left from the captivity in the ᵉprovince *are* there in great distress and ᶠreproach. ᵍThe wall of Jerusalem ʰ*is* also broken down, and its gates are burned with fire."

⁴So it was, when I heard these words, that I sat down and wept, and mourned *for many* days; I was fasting and praying before the God of heaven.

⁵And I said: "I pray, ⁱLᴏʀᴅ God of heaven, O great and ʲawesome God, ᵏ*You* who keep *Your* covenant and mercy with those who love You* and observe Your* commandments, ⁶please let Your ear be attentive and ˡYour eyes open, that You may hear the prayer of Your servant which I pray before You now, day and night, for the children of Israel Your servants, and ᵐconfess the sins of the children of Israel which we have sinned against You. Both my father's house and I have sinned. ⁷ⁿWe have acted very corruptly against You, and have ᵒnot kept the commandments, the statutes, nor the ordinances which You commanded Your servant Moses. ⁸Remember, I pray, the word that You commanded Your

---

* **1:1** Or *Susa*   * **1:5** Literally *Him* • Literally *His*

1:1 Nehemiah. Nehemiah, whose name means "the Lord comforts," was a highly placed statesman associated with Ezra in the work of reestablishing the people of Judah in the Promised Land. *the twentieth year.* This is a reference to the twentieth year of rule of Artaxerxes I Longimanus (456–424 B.C.). It was he who had commissioned Ezra to return to Jerusalem (Ezra 7:1). *Shushan the citadel.* The capital, or fortified royal palace, was built on an acropolis about 150 miles north of the Persian Gulf, in present day Iran. This is the city where Daniel received his vision about the rams and goats (Dan. 8:2) and the home of Mordecai and Esther (Esth. 1:2).
1:2 men from Judah . . . Jerusalem. The journey from Susa to Jerusalem, which covered nearly one thousand miles, probably took about four months.

1:5 Obedience—The covenant of God with the Israelites had been made with the understanding that obedience would bring God's great blessings, and the result of rebellion would be curses, one of which was captivity (Deut. 28–30). God had been patient for a long time, but eventually the nation was overpowered, and many of the people taken into captivity. Nehemiah acknowledged not only the necessity of obedience, but the confidence that he had that God would answer his prayer because God said He would hear and bless the obedient.

1:1 ᵃNeh. 10:1 ᵇNeh. 2:1 ᶜEsth. 1:1, 2, 5   **1:2** ᵈNeh. 7:2   **1:3** ᵉNeh. 7:6 ᶠNeh. 2:17 ᵍNeh. 2:17 ʰ2 Kin. 25:10   **1:5** ⁱDan. 9:4 ʲNeh. 4:14 ᵏ[Ex. 20:6; 34:6, 7]   **1:6** ˡ2 Chr. 6:40 ᵐDan. 9:20   **1:7** ⁿDan. 9:5 ᵒDeut. 28:15

servant Moses, saying, *p'If* you are unfaithful, I will scatter you among the nations;* *9q*but *if* you return to Me, and keep My commandments and do them, *r*though some of you were cast out to the farthest part of the heavens, *yet* I will gather them from there, and bring them to the place which I have chosen as a dwelling for My name.'* *10s*Now these *are* Your servants and Your people, whom You have redeemed by Your great power, and by Your strong hand. *11*O Lord, I pray, please *t*let Your ear be attentive to the prayer of Your servant, and to the prayer of Your servants who *u*desire to fear Your name; and let Your servant prosper this day, I pray, and grant him mercy in the sight of this man."

For I was the king's *v*cupbearer.

Nehemiah Sent to Judah

2 And it came to pass in the month of Nisan, in the twentieth year of *a*King Artaxerxes, *when* wine *was* before him, that *b*I took the wine and gave it to the king. Now I had never been sad in his presence before. *2*Therefore the king said to me, "Why *is* your face sad, since you *are* not sick? This *is* nothing but *c*sorrow of heart."

So I became dreadfully afraid, *3*and said to the king, *d*"May the king live forever! Why should my face not be sad, when *e*the city, the place of my fathers' tombs, *lies* waste, and its gates are burned with *f*fire?" *4*Then the king said to me, "What do you request?"

So I *g*prayed to the God of heaven. *5*And I said to the king, "If it pleases the king, and if your servant has found favor in your sight, I ask that you send me to Judah, to the city of my fathers' tombs, that I may rebuild it." *6*Then the king said to me (the queen also sitting beside him), "How long will your journey be? And when will you return?" So it pleased the king to send me; and I set him *h*a time. *7*Furthermore I said to the king, "If it pleases the king, let letters be given to me for the *i*governors *of the region* beyond the River,* that they must permit me to pass through till I come to Judah, *8*and a letter to Asaph the keeper of the king's forest, that he must give me timber to make beams for the gates of the citadel which *pertains* *j*to the temple,* for the city wall, and for the house that I will occupy." And the king granted *them* to me *k*according to the good hand of my God upon me.

*9*Then I went to the governors *in the region* beyond the River, and gave them the king's letters. Now the king had sent captains of the army and horsemen with me. *10*When *l*Sanballat the Horonite and Tobiah the Ammonite official* heard *of it*, they were deeply disturbed that a man had come to seek the well-being of the children of Israel.

Nehemiah Views the Wall of Jerusalem

*11*So I *m*came to Jerusalem and was there three days. *12*Then I arose in the night, I and a few men with me; I told no one what my God had put in my heart to do at Jerusalem; nor was there any animal with me, except the one on which I rode. *13*And I went out by night *n*through the Valley Gate to the Serpent Well and the Refuse Gate, and viewed the walls of Jerusalem which were *o*broken down and its gates which were burned with fire. *14*Then I went on to the *p*Fountain Gate and to the *q*King's Pool, but *there was* no room for the animal under me to pass. *15*So I went up in the night by the *r*valley, and viewed the wall; then I turned back and entered by the Valley Gate, and so returned. *16*And the officials did not know where I had gone or what I had done; I had not yet told the Jews, the priests, the nobles, the officials, or the others who did the work.

*17*Then I said to them, "You see the distress that we *are* in, how Jerusalem *lies*

---

* **1:8** Leviticus 26:33   * **1:9** Deuteronomy 30:2–5
* **2:7** That is, the Euphrates, and so elsewhere in this book   * **2:8** Literally *house*   * **2:10** Literally *servant*, and so elsewhere in this book.

1:11 the king's cupbearer. As the king's cupbearer, Nehemiah held an honored position. His constant proximity to the king of Persia made him privy to the state secrets and personal affairs of the king.
2:2 face sad. Persian monarchs believed that just being in their presence would make any person happy. Yet, Nehemiah was about to request the emperor's permission to go to Jerusalem, suggesting that he would rather be somewhere other than in the emperor's presence. In addition to this, it was Artaxerxes himself who had ordered the work on the wall to be stopped (Ezra 4:21–23). Nehemiah had reason to be afraid.
2:4 I prayed. Even though Nehemiah had come into the presence of the king, he never left the presence of God.
2:8 the king's forest . . . timber. Jerusalem had plenty of limestone for building projects, but timber was scarce.
2:10 the Ammonite. At the time of Nehemiah, the Ammonites (Gen. 19:38) had pushed west into the land vacated by Judah. The prospect of a strong Jewish community in newly fortified Jerusalem would have seemed threatening.

1:8 *p* Lev. 26:33   **1:9** *q* [Deut. 4:29–31; 30:2–5]   *r* Deut. 30:4   **1:10** *s* Deut. 9:29   **1:11** *t* Neh. 1:6   *u* Is. 26:8   *v* Neh. 2:1   **2:1** *a* Ezra 7:1   *b* Neh. 1:11   **2:2** *c* Prov. 15:13   **2:3** *d* Dan. 2:4; 5:10; 6:6, 21   *e* 2 Chr. 36:19   *f* Neh. 1:3   **2:4** *g* Neh. 1:4   **2:6** *h* Neh. 5:14; 13:6   **2:7** *i* Ezra 7:21; 8:36   **2:8** *j* Neh. 3:7   *k* Ezra 5:5; 7:6, 9, 28   **2:10** *l* Neh. 2:19; 4:1   **2:11** *m* Ezra 8:32   **2:13** *n* Neh. 3:13   *o* Neh. 1:3; 2:17   **2:14** *p* Neh. 3:15   *q* 2 Kin. 20:20   **2:15** *r* 2 Sam. 15:23

waste, and its gates are burned with fire. Come and let us build the wall of Jerusalem, that we may no longer be ᵃa reproach." ¹⁸And I told them of ᵗthe hand of my God which had been good upon me, and also of the king's words that he had spoken to me.

So they said, "Let us rise up and build." Then they ᵘset their hands to *this* good *work.*

¹⁹But when Sanballat the Horonite, Tobiah the Ammonite official, and Geshem the Arab heard *of it,* they laughed at us and despised us, and said, "What *is* this thing that you are doing? ᵛWill you rebel against the king?"

²⁰So I answered them, and said to them, "The God of heaven Himself will prosper us; therefore we His servants will arise and build, ʷbut you have no heritage or right or memorial in Jerusalem."

Rebuilding the Wall

3 Then ᵃEliashib the high priest rose up with his brethren the priests ᵇand built the Sheep Gate; they consecrated it and hung its doors. They built ᶜas far as the Tower of the Hundred,* *and* consecrated it, then as far as the Tower of ᵈHananel. ²Next to *Eliashib* ᵉthe men of Jericho built. And next to them Zaccur the son of Imri built.

³Also the sons of Hassenaah built ᶠthe Fish Gate; they laid its beams and ᵍhung its doors with its bolts and bars. ⁴And next to them ʰMeremoth the son of Urijah, the son of Koz,* made repairs. Next to them ⁱMeshullam the son of Berechiah, the son of Meshezabel, made repairs. Next to them Zadok the son of Baana made repairs. ⁵Next to them the Tekoites made repairs; but their nobles did not put their shoulders* to ʲthe work of their Lord.

⁶Moreover Jehoiada the son of Paseah and Meshullam the son of Besodeiah repaired ᵏthe Old Gate; they laid its beams and hung its doors, with its bolts and bars. ⁷And next to them Melatiah the Gibeonite, Jadon the Meronothite, the ˡmen of Gibeon and Mizpah, repaired the ᵐresidence* of the governor *of the region* beyond the River. ⁸Next to him Uzziel the son of Harhaiah, one of the goldsmiths, made repairs. Also next to him Hananiah, one* of the perfumers, made repairs; and they fortified Jerusalem as far as the ⁿBroad Wall. ⁹And next to them Rephaiah the son of Hur, leader of half the district of Jerusalem, made

repairs. ¹⁰Next to them Jedaiah the son of Harumaph made repairs in front of his house. And next to him Hattush the son of Hashabniah made repairs.

¹¹Malchijah the son of Harim and Hashub the son of Pahath-Moab repaired another section, ᵒas well as the Tower of the Ovens. ¹²And next to him was Shallum the son of Hallohesh, leader of half the district of Jerusalem; he and his daughters made repairs.

¹³Hanun and the inhabitants of Zanoah repaired ᵖthe Valley Gate. They built it, hung its doors with its bolts and bars, and *repaired* a thousand cubits of the wall as far as ᑫthe Refuse Gate.

¹⁴Malchijah the son of Rechab, leader of the district of ʳBeth Haccerem, repaired the Refuse Gate; he built it and hung its doors with its bolts and bars.

¹⁵Shallun the son of Col-Hozeh, leader of the district of Mizpah, repaired ˢthe Fountain Gate; he built it, covered it, hung its doors with its bolts and bars, and repaired the wall of the Pool of ᵗShelah by the ᵘKing's Garden, as far as the stairs that go down from the City of David. ¹⁶After him Nehemiah the son of Azbuk, leader of half the district of Beth Zur, made repairs as far as *the place* in front of the tombs* of David, to the ᵛman-made pool, and as far as the House of the Mighty.

¹⁷After him the Levites, *under* Rehum the son of Bani, made repairs. Next to him Hashabiah, leader of half the district of Keilah, made repairs for his district. ¹⁸After him their brethren, *under* Bavai* the son of Henadad, leader of the *other* half of the district of Keilah, made repairs. ¹⁹And next to him Ezer the son of Jeshua, the leader of Mizpah, repaired another section in front of the Ascent to the Armory at the ʷbuttress. ²⁰After him Baruch the son of Zabbai* carefully repaired the other section, from the buttress to the door of the house of Eliashib the high priest. ²¹After him Meremoth the son of Urijah, the son of Koz,* repaired another section, from the

---

* **3:1** Hebrew *Hammeah,* also at 12:39 * **3:2** Literally *On his hand* * **3:4** Or *Hakkoz* * **3:5** Literally *necks* * **3:7** Literally *throne* * **3:8** Literally *the son* * **3:16** Septuagint, Syriac, and Vulgate read *tomb.* * **3:18** Following Masoretic Text and Vulgate; some Hebrew manuscripts, Septuagint, and Syriac read *Binnui* (compare verse 24). * **3:20** A few Hebrew manuscripts, Syriac, and Vulgate read *Zaccai.* * **3:21** Or *Hakkoz*

2:18 *God which had been good.* Nehemiah emphasized that it was not just his own idea to rebuild the wall of Jerusalem. The idea had come to him from the Lord (vv. 8,12).

3:8 *the Broad Wall.* The Broad Wall was probably built in the seventh century B.C. by Hezekiah to accommodate the influx of refugees from the fall of Samaria in 722 B.C. (2 Chr. 32:5).

3:15 *Pool of Shelah.* This pool is also known as the Pool of Siloam.

2:17 ˢ Neh. 1:3 **2:18** ᵗ Neh. 2:8 ᵘ 2 Sam. 2:7 **2:19** ᵛ Neh. 6:6 **2:20** ʷ Ezra 4:3 **3:1** ᵃ Neh. 3:20; 12:10; 13:4, 7, 28 ᵇ John 5:2 ᶜ Neh. 12:39 ᵈ Jer. 31:38 **3:2** ᵉ Neh. 7:36 **3:3** ᶠ Zeph. 1:10 ᵍ Neh. 6:1; 7:1 **3:4** ʰ Ezra 8:33 ⁱ Ezra 10:15 **3:5** ʲ [Judg. 5:23] **3:6** ᵏ Neh. 12:39 **3:7** ˡ Neh. 7:25 ᵐ Neh. 2:7–9 **3:8** ⁿ Neh. 12:38 **3:11** ᵒ Neh. 12:38 **3:13** ᵖ Neh. 2:13, 15 ᑫ Neh. 2:13 **3:14** ʳ Jer. 6:1 **3:15** ˢ Neh. 2:14 ᵗ Is. 8:6 ᵘ 2 Kin. 25:4 **3:16** ᵛ 2 Kin. 20:20 **3:19** ʷ 2 Chr. 26:9

door of the house of Eliashib to the end of the house of Eliashib.

22And after him the priests, the men of the plain, made repairs. 23After him Benjamin and Hasshub made repairs opposite their house. After them Azariah the son of Maaseiah, the son of Ananiah, made repairs by his house. 24After him xBinnui the son of Henadad repaired another section, from the house of Azariah to ythe buttress, even as far as the corner. 25Palal the son of Uzai *made repairs* opposite the buttress, and on the tower which projects from the king's upper house that *was* by the zcourt of the prison. After him Pedaiah the son of Parosh *made repairs.*

26Moreover athe Nethinim who dwelt in bOphel *made repairs* as far as *the place* in front of cthe Water Gate toward the east, and on the projecting tower. 27After them the Tekoites repaired another section, next to the great projecting tower, and as far as the wall of Ophel.

28Beyond the dHorse Gate the priests made repairs, each in front of his *own* house. 29After them Zadok the son of Immer made repairs in front of his *own* house. After him Shemaiah the son of Shechaniah, the keeper of the East Gate, made repairs. 30After him Hananiah the son of Shelemiah, and Hanun, the sixth son of Zalaph, repaired another section. After him Meshullam the son of Berechiah made repairs in front of his dwelling. 31After him Malchijah, one of the goldsmiths, made repairs as far as the house of the Nethinim and of the merchants, in front of the Miphkad* Gate, and as far as the upper room at the corner. 32And between the upper room at the corner, as far as the eSheep Gate, the goldsmiths and the merchants made repairs.

The Wall Defended Against Enemies

4 But it so happened, awhen Sanballat heard that we were rebuilding the wall, that he was furious and very indignant, and mocked the Jews. 2And he spoke before his brethren and the army of Samaria, and said, "What are these feeble Jews doing? Will they fortify themselves? Will they offer sacrifices? Will they complete it in a day? Will they revive the stones from the heaps of rubbish—*stones* that are burned?"

3Now bTobiah the Ammonite *was* beside him, and he said, "Whatever they build, if even a fox goes up *on it,* he will break down their stone wall."

4cHear, O our God, for we are despised; dturn their reproach on their own heads, and give them as plunder to a land of captivity! 5eDo not cover their iniquity, and do not let their sin be blotted out from before You; for they have provoked *You* to anger before the builders.

6So we built the wall, and the entire wall was joined together up to half its *height,* for the people had a mind to work.

7Now it happened, fwhen Sanballat, Tobiah, gthe Arabs, the Ammonites, and the Ashdodites heard that the walls of Jerusalem were being restored and the gaps were beginning to be closed, that they became very angry, 8and all of them hconspired together to come *and* attack Jerusalem and create confusion. 9Nevertheless iwe made our prayer to our God, and because of them we set a watch against them day and night.

10Then Judah said, "The strength of the laborers is failing, and *there is* so much rubbish that we are not able to build the wall."

11And our adversaries said, "They will neither know nor see anything, till we come into their midst and kill them and cause the work to cease."

12So it was, when the Jews who dwelt near them came, that they told us ten times, "From whatever place you turn, *they will be* upon us."

13Therefore I positioned *men* behind the lower parts of the wall, at the openings; and I set the people according to their families, with their swords, their spears, and their bows. 14And I looked, and arose and said to the nobles, to the leaders, and to the rest of the people, j"Do not be afraid of them. Remember the Lord, kgreat and awesome, and lfight for your brethren, your sons, your daughters, your wives, and your houses."

15And it happened, when our enemies heard that it was known to us, and mthat God had brought their plot to nothing, that all of us returned to the wall, everyone to his work. 16So it was, from that time on, *that* half of my servants worked at construction, while the other half held the

---

* 3:31 Literally *Inspection* or *Recruiting*

4:2 revive the stones. When limestone is subjected to intense heat, it becomes unsuitable for building. The stones from the burned wall would not be useable.

4:9 Prayer—It is difficult to work in a hostile environment. Ambition, courage, and preparation are important in a situation like this, and so is prayer. If we are not careful to ask God to protect us, our fear can cripple us as much as the animosity of our enemies. No matter how prepared we may be for a crisis, the power of God is the ultimate factor in determining whether we win or lose.

3:24 x Ezra 8:33 y Neh. 3:19 **3:25** z Jer. 32:2; 33:1; 37:21 **3:26** a Neh. 11:21 b 2 Chr. 27:3 c Neh. 8:1, 3; 12:37 **3:28** d 2 Chr. 23:15 **3:32** e Neh. 3:1; 12:39 **4:1** a Neh. 2:10, 19 **4:3** b Neh. 2:10, 19 **4:4** c Ps. 123:3, 4 d Ps. 79:12 **4:5** e Jer. 18:23 **4:7** f Neh. 4:1 g Neh. 2:19 **4:8** h Ps. 83:3–5 **4:9** i [Ps. 50:15] **4:14** j Deut. 1:29 k [Deut. 10:17] l 2 Sam. 10:12 **4:15** m Job 5:12

spears, the shields, the bows, and *wore* armor; and the leaders *were* behind all the house of Judah. ¹⁷Those who built on the wall, and those who carried burdens, loaded themselves so that with one hand they worked at construction, and with the other held a weapon. ¹⁸Every one of the builders had his sword girded at his side as he built. And the one who sounded the trumpet *was* beside me.

¹⁹Then I said to the nobles, the rulers, and the rest of the people, "The work *is* great and extensive, and we are separated far from one another on the wall. ²⁰Wherever you hear the sound of the trumpet, rally to us there. ⁿOur God will fight for us."

²¹So we labored in the work, and half of *the men** held the spears from daybreak until the stars appeared. ²²At the same time I also said to the people, "Let each man and his servant stay at night in Jerusalem, that they may be our guard by night and a working party by day." ²³So neither I, my brethren, my servants, nor the men of the guard who followed me took off our clothes, *except* that everyone took them off for washing.

Nehemiah Deals with Oppression

5 And there was a great ᵃoutcry of the people and their wives against their ᵇJewish brethren. ²For there were those who said, "We, our sons, and our daughters *are* many; therefore let us get grain, that we may eat and live."

³There were also *some* who said, "We have mortgaged our lands and vineyards and houses, that we might buy grain because of the famine."

⁴There were also those who said, "We have borrowed money for the king's tax *on* our lands and vineyards. ⁵Yet now ᶜour flesh *is* as the flesh of our brethren, our children as their children; and indeed we ᵈare forcing our sons and our daughters to be slaves, and *some* of our daughters have been brought into slavery. *It is* not in our power *to redeem them*, for other men have our lands and vineyards."

⁶And I became very angry when I heard their outcry and these words. ⁷After serious thought, I rebuked the nobles and rulers, and said to them, ᵉ"Each of you is exacting usury from his brother." So I called a great assembly against them. ⁸And I said to them, "According to our ability we have ᶠredeemed our Jewish brethren who were sold to the nations. Now indeed, will you even sell your brethren? Or should they be sold to us?" Then they were silenced and found nothing *to say.* ⁹Then I said, "What you are doing *is* not good. Should you not walk ᵍin the fear of our God ʰbecause of the reproach of the nations, our enemies? ¹⁰I also, *with* my brethren and my servants, am lending them money and grain. Please, let us stop this usury! ¹¹Restore now to them, even this day, their lands, their vineyards, their olive groves, and their houses, also a hundredth of the money and the grain, the new wine and the oil, that you have charged them."

¹²So they said, "We will restore *it*, and will require nothing from them; we will do as you say."

Then I called the priests, ⁱand required an oath from them that they would do according to this promise. ¹³Then ʲI shook out the fold of my garment* and said, "So may God shake out each man from his house, and from his property, who does not perform this promise. Even thus may he be shaken out and emptied."

And all the assembly said, "Amen!" and praised the LORD. ᵏThen the people did according to this promise.

The Generosity of Nehemiah

¹⁴Moreover, from the time that I was appointed to be their governor in the land of Judah, from the twentieth year ˡuntil the thirty-second year of King Artaxerxes, twelve years, neither I nor my brothers ᵐate the governor's provisions. ¹⁵But the former governors who *were* before me laid burdens on the people, and took from them bread and wine, besides forty shekels of silver. Yes, even their servants bore rule over the people, but ⁿI did not do so,

---

* **4:21** Literally *them*   * **5:13** Literally *my lap*

5:7 *exacting usury.* It was not wrong to lend money to a fellow Jew, or even to lend money at interest to a non-Jewish person, but it was forbidden to charge interest to a fellow Jew (Ex. 22:25; Deut. 23:19–20). The people had already fallen back into disobedience.

5:9 Fear of God—Fear of God is the knowledge that God has the right to judge our actions for good or evil. It is the basis for keeping the commandments which concern other men. We do not murder because it is taking the life of one who bears the image and likeness of God. We deal honestly with one another, we do not covet our neighbor's possessions, or abridge any of his rights, because those things are given to him by God, and our neighbor belongs to God who created him. If we do not walk in the fear of the Lord,

we demonstrate our pride and presumption to those who are watching us.

5:11 hundredth. This is probably a reference to the interest the nobles and rulers had been charging.

5:15 former governors. Several former governors had paid their own expenses with the people's taxes. During his twelve year administration (444–432 B.C.), Nehemiah did not collect taxes from the people, although as the governor he had the right to.

4:20 ⁿ Ex. 14:14, 25   **5:1** ᵃ Neh. 5:7, 8 ᵇ Deut. 15:7
5:5 ᶜ Is. 58:7 ᵈ Ex. 21:7   **5:7** ᵉ [Ex. 22:25]   **5:8** ᶠ Lev. 25:48   **5:9** ᵍ Lev. 25:36 ʰ 2 Sam. 12:14   **5:12** ⁱ Ezra 10:5
5:13 ʲ Acts 13:51; 18:6 ᵏ 2 Kin. 23:3   **5:14** ˡ Neh. 2:1; 13:6
ᵐ [1 Cor. 9:4–15]   **5:15** ⁿ 2 Cor. 11:9; 12:13

because of the ᵒfear of God. ¹⁶Indeed, I also continued the ᵖwork on this wall, and we* did not buy any land. All my servants *were* gathered there for the work.

¹⁷And �qat my table *were* one hundred and fifty Jews and rulers, besides those who came to us from the nations around us. ¹⁸Now *that* ʳwhich was prepared daily *was* one ox *and* six choice sheep. Also fowl were prepared for me, and once every ten days an abundance of all kinds of wine. Yet in spite of this I ˢdid not demand the governor's provisions, because the bondage was heavy on this people.

¹⁹ᵗRemember me, my God, for good, *according to* all that I have done for this people.

Conspiracy Against Nehemiah

6 Now it happened ªwhen Sanballat, Tobiah, Geshem the Arab, and the rest of our enemies heard that I had rebuilt the wall, and *that* there were no breaks left in it ᵇ(though at that time I had not hung the doors in the gates), ²that Sanballat and Geshem ᶜsent to me, saying, "Come, let us meet together among the villages in the plain of ᵈOno." But they ᵉthought to do me harm.

³So I sent messengers to them, saying, "I *am* doing a great work, so that I cannot come down. Why should the work cease while I leave it and go down to you?"

⁴But they sent me this message four times, and I answered them in the same manner.

⁵Then Sanballat sent his servant to me as before, the fifth time, with an open letter in his hand. ⁶In it *was* written:

It is reported among the nations, and Geshem* says, *that* you and the Jews plan to rebel; therefore, according to these rumors, you are rebuilding the wall, ᶠthat you may be their king. ⁷And you have also appointed prophets to proclaim concerning you at Jerusalem, saying, "*There is* a king in Judah!" Now these matters will be reported to the king. So come, therefore, and let us consult together.

⁸Then I sent to him, saying, "No such things as you say are being done, but you invent them in your own heart."

⁹For they all *were trying to* make us afraid, saying, "Their hands will be weakened in the work, and it will not be done." Now therefore, *O God,* strengthen my hands.

¹⁰Afterward I came to the house of Shemaiah the son of Delaiah, the son of Mehetabel, who *was* a secret informer; and he said, "Let us meet together in the house of God, within the temple, and let us close the doors of the temple, for they are coming to kill you; indeed, at night they will come to kill you."

¹¹And I said, "Should such a man as I flee? And who *is there* such as I who would go into the temple to save his life? I will not go in!" ¹²Then I perceived that God had not sent him at all, but that ᵍhe pronounced *this* prophecy against me because Tobiah and Sanballat had hired him. ¹³For this reason he *was* hired, that I should be afraid and act that way and sin, so *that* they might have *cause* for an evil report, that they might reproach me.

¹⁴ʰMy God, remember Tobiah and Sanballat, according to these their works, and the ⁱprophetess Noadiah and the rest of the prophets who would have made me afraid.

The Wall Completed

¹⁵So the wall was finished on the twenty-fifth *day* of Elul, in fifty-two days. ¹⁶And it happened, ʲwhen all our enemies heard *of it,* and all the nations around us saw *these things,* that they were very disheartened in their own eyes; for ᵏthey perceived that this work was done by our God.

¹⁷Also in those days the nobles of Judah sent many letters to Tobiah, and *the letters of* Tobiah came to them. ¹⁸For many in Judah were pledged to him, because he was the ˡson-in-law of Shechaniah the son of Arah, and his son Jehohanan had married the daughter of ᵐMeshullam the son of Berechiah. ¹⁹Also they reported his good deeds before me, and reported my words to him. Tobiah sent letters to frighten me.

7 Then it was, when the wall was built and I had ªhung the doors, when the gatekeepers, the singers, and the Levites

---

* **5:16** Following Masoretic Text; Septuagint, Syriac, and Vulgate read *I.* * **6:6** Hebrew *Gashmu*

6:2 the plain of Ono. The plain of Ono was about twenty miles northwest of Jerusalem.
6:10 Shemaiah. Shemaiah was a false prophet, not the Levite of the same name who helped build the wall (3:29) or the priest who sealed the covenant with Nehemiah (10:8). Whether he was pretending to represent God, or was speaking with "authority" because he claimed that he had inside information, Shemaiah's strategy was to get Nehemiah sidetracked.
6:16 Providence—The fact that the Jews were able to finish the wall so quickly and with such singleness of purpose said even to their enemies that it was God who had helped them. God always provides everything we need to do His work. It is when we get off on our own

agendas that we are short of energy and resources. Like Nehemiah, we need to pray for God's direct guidance, and then pray to keep our focus on His plan.
7:1 gatekeepers . . . singers . . . Levites. The Levites were assistants to the priests (Num. 18:1–4) who guarded and cleaned the sanctuary. The gatekeepers

5:15 ᵒNeh. 5:9 **5:16** ᵖNeh. 4:1; 6:1 **5:17** q1 Kin. 18:19 **5:18** ʳ1 Kin. 4:22 ˢNeh. 5:14, 15 **5:19** ᵗNeh. 13:14, 22, 31 **6:1** ªNeh. 2:10, 19; 4:1, 7; 13:28 ᵇNeh. 3:1, 3 **6:2** ᶜProv. 26:24, 25 ᵈ1 Chr. 8:12 ᵉPs. 37:12, 32 **6:6** ᶠNeh. 2:19 **6:12** ᵍEzek. 13:22 **6:14** ʰNeh. 13:29 ⁱEzek. 13:17 **6:16** ʲNeh. 2:10, 20; 4:1, 7; 6:1 ᵏPs. 126:2 **6:18** ˡNeh. 13:4, 28 ᵐEzra 10:15 **7:1** ªNeh. 6:1, 15

had been appointed, ²that I gave the charge of Jerusalem to my brother ᵇHanani, and Hananiah the leader ᶜof the citadel, for he *was* a faithful man and ᵈfeared God more than many.

³And I said to them, "Do not let the gates of Jerusalem be opened until the sun is hot; and while they stand *guard*, let them shut and bar the doors; and appoint guards from among the inhabitants of Jerusalem, one at his watch station and another in front of his own house."

The Captives Who Returned to Jerusalem

⁴Now the city *was* large and spacious, but the people in it *were* ᵉfew, and the houses *were* not rebuilt. ⁵Then my God put it into my heart to gather the nobles, the rulers, and the people, that they might be registered by genealogy. And I found a register of the genealogy of those who had come up in the first *return*, and found written in it:

6 ᶠThese* *are* the people of the province who came back from the captivity, of those who had been carried away, whom Nebuchadnezzar the king of Babylon had carried away, and who returned to Jerusalem and Judah, everyone to his city.

7 Those who came with ᵍZerubbabel *were* Jeshua, Nehemiah, Azariah, Raamiah, Nahamani, Mordecai, Bilshan, Mispereth,* Bigvai, Nehum, and Baanah.

The number of the men of the people of Israel: ⁸the sons of Parosh, two thousand one hundred and seventy-two;
⁹the sons of Shephatiah, three hundred and seventy-two;
¹⁰the sons of Arah, six hundred and fifty-two;
¹¹the sons of Pahath-Moab, of the sons of Jeshua and Joab, two thousand eight hundred and eighteen;
¹²the sons of Elam, one thousand two hundred and fifty-four;
¹³the sons of Zattu, eight hundred and forty-five;
¹⁴the sons of Zaccai, seven hundred and sixty;
¹⁵the sons of Binnui,* six hundred and forty-eight;

¹⁶the sons of Bebai, six hundred and twenty-eight;
¹⁷the sons of Azgad, two thousand three hundred and twenty-two;
¹⁸the sons of Adonikam, six hundred and sixty-seven;
¹⁹the sons of Bigvai, two thousand and sixty-seven;
²⁰the sons of Adin, six hundred and fifty-five;
²¹the sons of Ater of Hezekiah, ninety-eight;
²²the sons of Hashum, three hundred and twenty-eight;
²³the sons of Bezai, three hundred and twenty-four;
²⁴the sons of Hariph,* one hundred and twelve;
²⁵the sons of Gibeon,* ninety-five;
²⁶the men of Bethlehem and Netophah, one hundred and eighty-eight;
²⁷the men of Anathoth, one hundred and twenty-eight;
²⁸the men of Beth Azmaveth,* forty-two;
²⁹the men of Kirjath Jearim, Chephirah, and Beeroth, seven hundred and forty-three;
³⁰the men of Ramah and Geba, six hundred and twenty-one;
³¹the men of Michmas, one hundred and twenty-two;
³²the men of Bethel and Ai, one hundred and twenty-three;
³³the men of the other Nebo, fifty-two;
³⁴the sons of the other ʰElam, one thousand two hundred and fifty-four;
³⁵the sons of Harim, three hundred and twenty;
³⁶the sons of Jericho, three hundred and forty-five;
³⁷the sons of Lod, Hadid, and Ono, seven hundred and twenty-one;
³⁸the sons of Senaah, three thousand nine hundred and thirty.

39 The priests: the sons of ⁱJedaiah, of the house of Jeshua, nine hundred and seventy-three;

---

* **7:6** Compare verses 6–72 with Ezra 2:1–70
* **7:7** Spelled *Mispar* in Ezra 2:2   * **7:15** Spelled *Bani* in Ezra 2:10   * **7:24** Called *Jorah* in Ezra 2:18   * **7:25** Called *Gibbar* in Ezra 2:20   * **7:28** Called *Azmaveth* in Ezra 2:24

---

and singers were also Levites (1 Chr. 9:17–19; 26:12–19).

7:3 gates. The gates of a city normally opened at sunrise. If an enemy mounted a surprise attack at sunrise, he would find a city just beginning to wake up. By keeping the gates closed a little longer, the city was safer.

7:4 people . . . were few. For the size of the city, Jerusalem was underpopulated. Even though it had been 90 years since people had returned under Zerubbabel to live there, Jerusalem still had a lot of undeveloped space within the walls renewed by Nehemiah.

7:5 my God put it into my heart. Nehemiah attributed to the Lord the idea of a census that would show the distribution of the population. If he knew the population pattern in the capital and the countryside, he could then determine which districts could best afford to lose a portion of their inhabitants to Jerusalem.

7:2 ᵇ Neh. 1:2 ᶜ Neh. 2:8; 10:23 ᵈ Ex. 18:21 **7:4** ᵉ Deut. 4:27 **7:6** ᶠ Ezra 2:1–70 **7:7** ᵍ Ezra 5:2 **7:34** ʰ Neh. 7:12 **7:39** ⁱ 1 Chr. 24:7

[40]the sons of [j]Immer, one thousand and fifty-two;
[41]the sons of [k]Pashhur, one thousand two hundred and forty-seven;
[42]the sons of [l]Harim, one thousand and seventeen.

[43] The Levites: the sons of Jeshua, of Kadmiel,
and of the sons of Hodevah,* seventy-four.

[44] The singers: the sons of Asaph, one hundred and forty-eight.

[45] The gatekeepers: the sons of Shallum, the sons of Ater,
the sons of Talmon,
the sons of Akkub,
the sons of Hatita,
the sons of Shobai, one hundred and thirty-eight.

[46] The Nethinim: the sons of Ziha, the sons of Hasupha,
the sons of Tabbaoth,
[47]the sons of Keros,
the sons of Sia,*
the sons of Padon,
[48]the sons of Lebana,*
the sons of Hagaba,*
the sons of Salmai,*
[49]the sons of Hanan,
the sons of Giddel,
the sons of Gahar,
[50]the sons of Reaiah,
the sons of Rezin,
the sons of Nekoda,
[51]the sons of Gazzam,
the sons of Uzza,
the sons of Paseah,
[52]the sons of Besai,
the sons of Meunim,
the sons of Nephishesim,*
[53]the sons of Bakbuk,
the sons of Hakupha,
the sons of Harhur,
[54]the sons of Bazlith,*
the sons of Mehida,
the sons of Harsha,
[55]the sons of Barkos,
the sons of Sisera,
the sons of Tamah,
[56]the sons of Neziah,
and the sons of Hatipha.

[57] The sons of Solomon's servants: the sons of Sotai,
the sons of Sophereth,
the sons of Perida,*
[58]the sons of Jaala,
the sons of Darkon,
the sons of Giddel,
[59]the sons of Shephatiah,
the sons of Hattil,

the sons of Pochereth of Zebaim, and the sons of Amon.*
[60]All the Nethinim, and the sons of Solomon's servants, *were* three hundred and ninety-two.

[61] And these *were* the ones who came up from Tel Melah, Tel Harsha, Cherub, Addon,* and Immer, but they could not identify their father's house nor their lineage, whether they *were* of Israel:
[62]the sons of Delaiah,
the sons of Tobiah,
the sons of Nekoda, six hundred and forty-two;
[63]and of the priests: the sons of Habaiah,
the sons of Koz,*
the sons of Barzillai, who took a wife of the daughters of Barzillai the Gileadite, and was called by their name.
[64]These sought their listing *among* those who were registered by genealogy, but it was not found; therefore they were excluded from the priesthood as defiled. [65]And the governor* said to them that they should not eat of the most holy things till a priest could consult with the Urim and Thummim.

[66] Altogether the whole assembly *was* forty-two thousand three hundred and sixty, [67]besides their male and female servants, of whom *there were* seven thousand three hundred and thirty-seven; and they had two hundred and forty-five men and women singers.
[68]Their horses were seven hundred and thirty-six, their mules two hundred and forty-five, [69]*their* camels four hundred and thirty-five, *and* donkeys six thousand seven hundred and twenty.

[70] And some of the heads of the fathers' *houses* gave to the work. [m]The governor* gave to the treasury one thousand gold drachmas, fifty basins, and five hundred and thirty priestly garments. [71]Some of the heads of the fathers' *houses* gave to the treasury of the work [n]twenty thousand gold drachmas, and two thousand two hundred silver minas. [72]And that which the rest of the people gave *was* twenty thousand gold drachmas, two thousand silver minas, and sixty-seven priestly garments.

---

* **7:43** Spelled *Hodaviah* in Ezra 2:40
* **7:47** Spelled *Siaha* in Ezra 2:44   * **7:48** Masoretic Text reads *Lebanah*. • Masoretic Text reads *Hogabah*. • Or *Shalmai*, or *Shamlai*
* **7:52** Spelled *Nephusim* in Ezra 2:50
* **7:54** Spelled *Bazluth* in Ezra 2:52   * **7:57** Spelled *Peruda* in Ezra 2:55   * **7:59** Spelled *Ami* in Ezra 2:57   * **7:61** Spelled *Addon* in Ezra 2:59
* **7:63** Or *Hakkoz*   * **7:65** Hebrew *Tirshatha*
* **7:70** Hebrew *Tirshatha*

7:70 drachmas. One thousand gold drachmas would weigh about nine pounds.

7:40 [j] 1 Chr. 9:12   **7:41** [k] Ezra 2:38; 10:22   **7:42** [l] 1 Chr. 24:8   **7:70** [m] Neh. 8:9   **7:71** [n] Ezra 2:69

⁷³So the priests, the Levites, the gatekeepers, the singers, *some* of the people, the Nethinim, and all Israel dwelt in their cities.

Ezra Reads the Law

⁰When the seventh month came, the children of Israel *were* in their cities.

8 Now all ᵃthe people gathered together as one man in the open square that *was* ᵇin front of the Water Gate; and they told Ezra the ᶜscribe to bring the Book of the Law of Moses, which the LORD had commanded Israel. ²So Ezra the priest brought ᵈthe Law before the assembly of men and women and all who *could* hear with understanding ᵉon the first day of the seventh month. ³Then he ᶠread from it in the open square that *was* in front of the Water Gate from morning until midday, before the men and women and those who could understand; and the ears of all the people *were* attentive to the Book of the Law.

⁴So Ezra the scribe stood on a platform of wood which they had made for the purpose; and beside him, at his right hand, stood Mattithiah, Shema, Anaiah, Urijah, Hilkiah, and Maaseiah; and at his left hand Pedaiah, Mishael, Malchijah, Hashum, Hashbadana, Zechariah, *and* Meshullam. ⁵And Ezra opened the book in the sight of all the people, for he was *standing* above all the people; and when he opened it, all the people ᵍstood up. ⁶And Ezra blessed the LORD, the great God.

Then all the people ʰanswered, "Amen, Amen!" while ⁱlifting up their hands. And they ʲbowed their heads and worshiped the LORD with *their* faces to the ground.

⁷Also Jeshua, Bani, Sherebiah, Jamin, Akkub, Shabbethai, Hodijah, Maaseiah, Kelita, Azariah, Jozabad, Hanan, Pelaiah, and the Levites, ᵏhelped the people to understand the Law; and the people ˡstood in their place. ⁸So they read distinctly from the book, in the Law of God; and they gave the sense, and helped *them* to understand the reading.

⁹ᵐAnd Nehemiah, who *was* the governor,* Ezra the priest *and* scribe, and the

* **8:9** Hebrew *Tirshatha*

8:2 men and women, and all who could hear with understanding. This is a more specific list of those gathered than is usual. "All who could hear" includes older children, as well as adults. **first day of the seventh month.** The wall had been completed on the twenty-fifth day of the sixth month (6:15) so this event took place just a few days after the completion of the wall.

8:3 Reading God's Word—There are many parts of the world today that still have limited access to the Bible and below-average literacy rates. Even if they could obtain a Bible they might not be able to read it. Other areas of the world have a well-educated population and freedom to pursue any religion they choose. Throughout much of history, the only access to Scripture was through someone who read it in a public or church setting. Today most of the western world has access to audio recordings of the Bible or to numerous printed versions. Here are some suggestions to aid you in receiving the greatest benefit from reading or listening to the Bible:

- *Read the Bible prayerfully.* Ask the Spirit of God to meet your heart's need as you read (Ps. 119:18).
- *Read the Bible thoughtfully.* Think about the meaning and implications of what you are reading.
- *Read the Bible carefully.* Take careful note not only of the words that are used but also of how they relate to one another.
- *Read the Bible repeatedly.* It may be of great help to read the same portion over and over again each day for a month's time. This is a good way for the words to take root in your heart. If you are reading a short book, read it every day. Divide longer books up into manageable portions of two or three chapters and read that portion through every day.
- *Read the Bible extensively.* Sometimes it is of great help to read large portions of the Word of God through at one sitting. If you do this, do it at a time when you are alert and not likely to be disturbed during your reading.
- *Read the Bible regularly.* It is good to have a

particular time every day when you habitually give yourself to the reading of the Word of God.
- *Read the Bible faithfully.* Inevitably there will be days when you will fail to read the Bible. Do not let your momentary lapse discourage you. Faithfully resume your practice of reading God's Word.
- *Read the Bible obediently.* Because the Bible is God's Word written to you, it is essential to obey it (Ex. 42:3).
- *Read the Bible thankfully.* Thank God for the gift He has given us in Scripture. Thank Him that you have the freedom or the opportunity to read the Bible at all.

8:5 all the people stood up. Standing signified their reverence for the Word. This gesture later became characteristic of the Jewish people in synagogue services.

8:6 lifting up their hands. The people answered "Amen" and lifted their hands, indicating their participation with Ezra in prayer.

8:9 God's Word Convicts—One of the great proofs that the Bible is really God's inspired Word is its unique ability to convict men and women of their sins. There are many biblical stories that point to this phenomenon where people realize the extent of their sin and the need to repent of it.

Under Josiah's rule a copy of God's Word is found in the temple. When it is read both the king and the people are convicted of their sins in not keeping God's law. Afterwards a great revival occurs (2 Chr. 34:14–28).

When Nehemiah returns to Israel to help the returning Jews rebuild the gates of Jerusalem, he assembles the people and has the Scriptures read to them for three hours a day. This soon causes them to confess their sin (Neh. 9:3).

In the New Testament we see many instances where the Holy Spirit uses God's Word to convict

---

7:73 ⁰ Ezra 3:1   **8:1** ᵃ Ezra 3:1   ᵇ Neh. 3:26   ᶜ Ezra 7:6
8:2 ᵈ [Deut. 31:11, 12]   ᵉ Lev. 23:24   **8:3** ᶠ 2 Kin. 23:2
8:5 ᵍ Judg. 3:20   **8:6** ʰ Neh. 5:13   ⁱ Ps. 28:2   ʲ 2 Chr. 20:18
8:7 ᵏ [Mal. 2:7]   ˡ Neh. 9:3   **8:9** ᵐ Neh. 7:65, 70; 10:1

Levites who taught the people said to all the people, [n]"This day *is* holy to the LORD your God; [o]do not mourn nor weep." For all the people wept, when they heard the words of the Law.

[10]Then he said to them, "Go your way, eat the fat, drink the sweet, [p]and send portions to those for whom nothing is prepared; for *this* day *is* holy to our Lord. Do not sorrow, for the joy of the LORD is your strength."

[11]So the Levites quieted all the people, saying, "Be still, for the day *is* holy; do not be grieved." [12]And all the people went their way to eat and drink, to [q]send portions and rejoice greatly, because they [r]understood the words that were declared to them.

The Feast of Tabernacles

[13]Now on the second day the heads of the fathers' *houses* of all the people, with the priests and Levites, were gathered to Ezra the scribe, in order to understand the words of the Law. [14]And they found written in the Law, which the LORD had commanded by Moses, that the children of Israel should dwell in [s]booths during the feast of the seventh month, [15]and [t]that they should announce and proclaim in all their cities and [u]in Jerusalem, saying, "Go out to the mountain, and [v]bring olive branches, branches of oil trees, myrtle branches, palm branches, and branches of leafy trees, to make booths, as *it is* written."

[16]Then the people went out and brought *them* and made themselves booths, each one on the [w]roof of his house, or in their courtyards or the courts of the house of God, and in the open square of the [x]Water Gate [y]and in the open square of the Gate of Ephraim. [17]So the whole assembly of those who had returned from the captivity made booths and sat under the booths; for since the days of Joshua the son of Nun until that day the children of Israel had not done so. And there was very [z]great gladness. [18]Also [a]day by day, from the first day until the last day, he read from the Book of the Law of God. And they kept the feast [b]seven days; and on the [c]eighth day *there was* a sacred assembly, according to the *prescribed* manner.

The People Confess Their Sins

9 Now on the twenty-fourth day of [a]this month the children of Israel were assembled with fasting, in sackcloth, [b]and with dust on their heads.* [2]Then [c]those of Israelite lineage separated themselves from all foreigners; and they stood and [d]confessed their sins and the iniquities of their fathers. [3]And they stood up in their place and [e]read from the Book of the Law of the LORD their God *for one*-fourth of the day; and *for another* fourth they confessed and worshiped the LORD their God.

[4]Then Jeshua, Bani, Kadmiel, Shebaniah, Bunni, Sherebiah, Bani, *and* Chenani stood on the stairs of the Levites and cried out with a loud voice to the LORD their God. [5]And the Levites, Jeshua, Kadmiel, Bani, Hashabniah, Sherebiah, Hodijah, Shebaniah, *and* Pethahiah, said:

"Stand up *and* bless the LORD your God
Forever and ever!

"Blessed be [f]Your glorious name,
Which is exalted above all blessing
     and praise!
6 [g]You alone *are* the LORD;
   [h]You have made heaven,
   [i]The heaven of heavens, with [j]all their
     host,
   The earth and everything on it,
   The seas and all that is in them,
   And You [k]preserve them all.
   The host of heaven worships You.

---

* **9:1** Literally *earth on them*

---

people of their sin. At Pentecost Peter uses the Scriptures to rebuke Israel for crucifying its Messiah. The result of his sermon is three thousand souls being convicted and accepting Christ (Acts 2:37,41).

8:9–10 Repentance—Once the people understood the Word of God, they wept. They had heard the high standard of the law, recognized their low standing before the Lord, and were convicted. Weeping and sorrow for sin are part of repentance. But the other part of repentance is change. With change comes joy. The joy of the Lord is the joy that springs up in our hearts because of our relationship to the Lord. It is a God-given gladness found when we are in communion with God. When our goal is to know more about the Lord, the byproduct is this joy.

8:17 since the days of Joshua. The reference here is to the construction of booths. The people of Israel had celebrated the Feast of Tabernacles since the days of Joshua (1 Kin. 8:65; 2 Chr. 7:9; Ezra 3:4).

9:1 the twenty-fourth day of this month. The people's public worship had begun on the first day of the seventh month (8:2). More than three weeks later, the people were still engaged in public worship. **fasting,**

in sackcloth, and with dust. These are all traditional signs of mourning.

9:2 separated . . . from all foreigners. The separation was a sacred separation from foreign persons who worshiped other gods and whose practices might have brought harm to the integrity of the worship of the Lord.

9:3 confessed. When this word is used with God as its object, as in this verse, it refers to the praise of God. They were acknowledging His attributes and worthiness of praise.

9:6 You alone are the LORD. One of the fundamental teachings of Scripture is that God is not one among many. He alone is the living God (Deut. 6:4).

8:9 [n] Num. 29:1 [o] Deut. 16:14 **8:10** [p] Rev. 11:10
8:12 [q] Neh. 8:10 [r] Neh. 8:7, 8 **8:14** [s] Lev. 23:34, 40, 42
8:15 [t] Lev. 23:4 [u] Deut. 16:16 [v] Lev. 23:40 **8:16** [w] Deut. 22:8 [x] Neh. 12:37 [y] 2 Kin. 14:13 **8:17** [z] 2 Chr. 30:21
8:18 [a] Deut. 31:11 [b] Lev. 23:36 [c] Num. 29:35 **9:1** [a] Neh. 8:2 [b] 1 Sam. 4:12 **9:2** [c] Neh. 13:3, 30 [d] Neh. 1:6
9:3 [e] Neh. 8:7, 8 **9:5** [f] 1 Chr. 29:13 **9:6** [g] 2 Kin. 19:15, 19 [h] Rev. 14:7 [i] [Deut. 10:14] [j] Gen. 2:1 [k] [Ps. 36:6]

7 "You *are* the LORD God,
Who chose ʲAbram,
And brought him out of Ur of the
  Chaldeans,
And gave him the name ᵐAbraham;
8 You found his heart ⁿfaithful before
  You,
And made a ᵒcovenant with him
To give the land of the Canaanites,
The Hittites, the Amorites,
The Perizzites, the Jebusites,
And the Girgashites—
To give *it* to his descendants.
You ᵖhave performed Your words,
For You *are* righteous.

9 "You⁹ saw the affliction of our fathers
  in Egypt,
And ʳheard their cry by the Red Sea.
10 You ˢshowed signs and wonders
  against Pharaoh,
Against all his servants,
And against all the people of his land.
For You knew that they ᵗacted proudly
  against them.
So You ᵘmade a name for Yourself, as
  it is this day.
11 ᵛAnd You divided the sea before them,
So that they went through the midst of
  the sea on the dry land;
And their persecutors You threw into
  the deep,
ʷAs a stone into the mighty waters.
12 Moreover You ˣled them by day with a
  cloudy pillar,
And by night with a pillar of fire,
To give them light on the road
Which they should travel.
13 "Youʸ came down also on Mount Sinai,
And spoke with them from heaven,
And gave them ᶻjust ordinances and
  true laws,
Good statutes and commandments.
14 You made known to them Your ᵃholy
  Sabbath,
And commanded them precepts,
  statutes and laws,
By the hand of Moses Your servant.
15 You ᵇgave them bread from heaven for
  their hunger,

And ᶜbrought them water out of the
  rock for their thirst,
And told them to ᵈgo in to possess the
  land
Which You had sworn to give them.

16 "Butᵉ they and our fathers acted
  proudly,
ᶠHardened their necks,
And did not heed Your
  commandments.
17 They refused to obey,
And ᵍthey were not mindful of Your
  wonders
That You did among them.
But they hardened their necks,
And in their rebellion*
They appointed ʰa leader
To return to their bondage.
But You *are* God,
Ready to pardon,
ⁱGracious and merciful,
Slow to anger,
Abundant in kindness,
And did not forsake them.
18 "Even ʲwhen they made a molded calf
  for themselves,
And said, 'This *is* your god
That brought you up out of Egypt,'
And worked great provocations,
19 Yet in Your ᵏmanifold mercies
You did not forsake them in the
  wilderness.
The ˡpillar of the cloud did not depart
  from them by day,
To lead them on the road;
Nor the pillar of fire by night,
To show them light,
And the way they should go.
20 You also gave Your ᵐgood Spirit to
  instruct them,
And did not withhold Your ⁿmanna
  from their mouth,
And gave them ᵒwater for their thirst.
21 ᵖForty years You sustained them in the
  wilderness;
They lacked nothing;

---

* 9:17 Following Masoretic Text and Vulgate;
Septuagint reads *in Egypt.*

9:7 You are the LORD God. The word order of the
Hebrew text is striking: "You are He, Yahweh (the)
God." The use of the definite article marks Him as
"the true God."
9:9 affliction of our fathers in Egypt. The Book of
Exodus tells about the plight of the Israelites in Egypt
and their complaint to the Lord for deliverance. It
then speaks of God's mercy in His response to the
people's need. This verse suggests that before the
people expressed their hurt, the Lord was already
aware of their troubles.
9:11 Persecution—No one asks for or welcomes
persecution. But history has borne out the fact that
when believers are persecuted they draw close to the
Lord. They are keenly aware that they are dependent
on Him for strength, endurance, and even sustenance.

Some of the sweetest times with the Lord are the times
when unbelievers pity us for our tribulation. Times of
rest bring independence of spirit. This is when it helps
to go back and remember the things the Lord has
done in the past and rejoice, and to remember that He
is sufficient for future persecution as well.

9:7 ʲGen. 11:31 ᵐGen. 17:5 **9:8** ⁿGen. 15:6; 22:1–3
ᵒGen. 15:18 ᵖJosh. 23:14 **9:9** ⁹Ex. 2:25; 3:7 ʳEx. 14:10
9:10 ˢEx. 7–14 ᵗEx. 18:11 ᵘJer. 32:20 **9:11** ᵛEx. 14:20–
28 ʷEx. 15:1, 5 **9:12** ˣEx. 13:21, 22 **9:13** ʸEx. 20:1–18
ᶻ[Rom. 7:12] **9:14** ᵃGen. 2:3 **9:15** ᵇEx. 16:14–17 ᶜEx.
17:6 ᵈDeut. 1:8 **9:16** ᵉPs. 106:6 ᶠDeut. 1:26–33; 31:27
9:17 ᵍPs. 78:11, 42–45 ʰNum. 14:4 ⁱJoel 2:13 **9:18** ʲEx.
32:4–8, 31 **9:19** ᵏPs. 106:45 ˡ1 Cor. 10:1 **9:20** ᵐNum.
11:17 ⁿEx. 16:14–16 ᵒEx. 17:6 **9:21** ᵖDeut. 2:7

Their ᵃclothes did not wear out*
And their feet did not swell.

22 "Moreover You gave them kingdoms
and nations,
And divided them into districts.*
So they took possession of the land of
ʳSihon,
The land of* the king of Heshbon,
And the land of Og king of Bashan.

23 You also multiplied ˢtheir children as
the stars of heaven,
And brought them into the land
Which You had told their fathers
To go in and possess.

24 So ᵗthe people went in
And possessed the land;
ᵘYou subdued before them the
inhabitants of the land,
The Canaanites,
And gave them into their hands,
With their kings
And the people of the land,
That they might do with them as they
wished.

25 And they took strong cities and a ᵛrich
land,
And possessed ʷhouses full of all
goods,
Cisterns *already* dug, vineyards, olive
groves,
And fruit trees in abundance.
So they ate and were filled and ˣgrew
fat,
And delighted themselves in Your
great ʸgoodness.

26 "Nevertheless they ᶻwere disobedient
And rebelled against You,
ᵃCast Your law behind their backs
And killed Your ᵇprophets, who
testified against them
To turn them to Yourself;
And they worked great provocations.

27 ᶜTherefore You delivered them into the
hand of their enemies,
Who oppressed them;
And in the time of their trouble,
When they cried to You,
You ᵈheard from heaven;
And according to Your abundant
mercies
ᵉYou gave them deliverers who saved
them
From the hand of their enemies.

28 "But after they had rest,
ᶠThey again did evil before You.
Therefore You left them in the hand of
their enemies,
So that they had dominion over
them;
Yet when they returned and cried out
to You,
You heard from heaven;
And ᵍmany times You delivered them
according to Your mercies;

29 And testified against them,
That You might bring them back to
Your law.
Yet they acted proudly,
And did not heed Your
commandments,
But sinned against Your judgments,
ʰ'Which if a man does, he shall live by
them.'*
And they shrugged their shoulders,
Stiffened their necks,
And would not hear.

30 Yet for many years You had patience
with them,
And testified ⁱagainst them by Your
Spirit ʲin Your prophets.
Yet they would not listen;
ᵏTherefore You gave them into the
hand of the peoples of the lands.

31 Nevertheless in Your great mercy
ˡYou did not utterly consume them nor
forsake them;
For You *are* God, gracious and
merciful.

32 "Now therefore, our God,
The great, the ᵐmighty, and awesome
God,
Who keeps covenant and mercy:
Do not let all the trouble seem small
before You
That has come upon us,
Our kings and our princes,
Our priests and our prophets,
Our fathers and on all Your people,
ⁿFrom the days of the kings of Assyria
until this day.

---

* **9:21** Compare Deuteronomy 29:5   * **9:22** Literally *corners* • Following Masoretic Text
and Vulgate; Septuagint omits *The land of.*
* **9:29** Leviticus 18:5

9:26 *killed Your prophets.* Jesus also directed this
charge against the rebellious people of His time
(Matt. 23:31).
9:30–31 **Patience**—Nehemiah writes, "You had
patience with them." This is the same eternal God who
still patiently bears with His people. Even as born-again
believers we struggle with sin, and we are thankful
that He is patient with us as we grow in the grace and
knowledge of our Lord and Savior, Jesus Christ (2 Pet.
3:18). This patience does not mean that He is tolerant
of sin, but that He knows that it takes perseverance to
walk as a Christian. He gives us time to grow. Indeed,
God is patient to the whole world, not wishing for any
to perish, but for all to come to repentance (2 Pet. 3:9).

9:32 *covenant.* God's covenant and loyalty are
unbreakable (2 Tim. 2:11–13). *this day.* "This day"
refers to the time of the great revival under Ezra
(8:1–2).

9:21 ᵃ Deut. 8:4; 29:5   **9:22** ʳ Num. 21:21–35
9:23 ˢ Gen. 15:5; 22:17   **9:24** ᵗ Josh. 1:2–4 ᵘ [Ps. 44:2, 3]
9:25 ᵛ Num. 13:27 ʷ Deut. 6:11 ˣ [Deut. 32:15] ʸ Hos.
3:5   **9:26** ᶻ Judg. 2:11 ᵃ 1 Kin. 14:9 ᵇ 1 Kin. 18:4; 19:10
9:27 ᶜ Judg. 2:14 ᵈ Ps. 106:44 ᵉ Judg. 2:18   **9:28** ᶠ Judg.
3:12 ᵍ Ps. 106:43   **9:29** ʰ Lev. 18:5   **9:30** ⁱ Jer. 7:25
ʲ [Acts 7:51] ᵏ Is. 5:5   **9:31** ˡ Jer. 4:27   **9:32** ᵐ [Ex. 34:6, 7]
ⁿ 2 Kin. 15:19; 17:3–6

33 However [o]You *are* just in all that has
befallen us;
For You have dealt faithfully,
But [p]we have done wickedly.
34 Neither our kings nor our princes,
Our priests nor our fathers,
Have kept Your law,
Nor heeded Your commandments and
Your testimonies,
With which You testified against them.
35 For they have [q]not served You in their
kingdom,
Or in the many good *things* that You
gave them,
Or in the large and rich land which
You set before them;
Nor did they turn from their wicked
works.

36 "Here [r]we *are,* servants today!
And the land that You gave to our
fathers,
To eat its fruit and its bounty,
Here we *are,* servants in it!
37 And [s]it yields much increase to the
kings
You have set over us,
Because of our sins;
Also they have [t]dominion over our
bodies and our cattle
At their pleasure;
And we *are* in great distress.
38 "And because of all this,
We [u]make a sure *covenant* and write
it;
Our leaders, our Levites, *and* our
priests [v]seal *it.*"

The People Who Sealed the Covenant

10 Now those who placed *their* seal on
the document were:
Nehemiah the governor, [a]the son of Hac-
aliah, and Zedekiah, 2 [b]Seraiah, Azariah,
Jeremiah, 3 Pashhur, Amariah, Malchijah,
4 Hattush, Shebaniah, Malluch, 5 Harim,
Meremoth, Obadiah, 6 Daniel, Ginnethon,
Baruch, 7 Meshullam, Abijah, Mijamin,
8 Maaziah, Bilgai, *and* Shemaiah. These
were the priests.
9 The Levites: Jeshua the son of Azaniah,
Binnui of the sons of Henadad, *and* Kadmiel.
10 Their brethren: Shebaniah, Hodijah,
Kelita, Pelaiah, Hanan, 11 Micha, Rehob,
Hashabiah, 12 Zaccur, Sherebiah, Shebaniah, 13 Hodijah, Bani, *and* Beninu.
14 The leaders of the people: [c]Parosh,
Pahath-Moab, Elam, Zattu, Bani, 15 Bunni, Azgad, Bebai, 16 Adonijah, Bigvai,
Adin, 17 Ater, Hezekiah, Azzur, 18 Hodijah, Hashum, Bezai, 19 Hariph, Anathoth,
Nebai, 20 Magpiash, Meshullam, Hezir,
21 Meshezabel, Zadok, Jaddua, 22 Pelatiah, Hanan, Anaiah, 23 Hoshea, Hananiah, Hasshub, 24 Hallohesh, Pilha, Shobek,
25 Rehum, Hashabnah, Maaseiah, 26 Ahijah, Hanan, Anan, 27 Malluch, Harim, *and*
Baanah.

The Covenant That Was Sealed

28 [d]Now the rest of the people—the
priests, the Levites, the gatekeepers, the
singers, the Nethinim, [e]and all those who
had separated themselves from the peoples
of the lands to the Law of God, their wives,
their sons, and their daughters, everyone
who had knowledge and understanding—
29 these joined with their brethren, their nobles, [f]and entered into a curse and an oath
[g]to walk in God's Law, which was given by
Moses the servant of God, and to observe
and do all the commandments of the LORD
our Lord, and His ordinances and His statutes: 30 We would not give [h]our daughters
as wives to the peoples of the land, nor
take their daughters for our sons; 31 [i]*if* the
peoples of the land brought wares or any
grain to sell on the Sabbath day, we would
not buy it from them on the Sabbath, or on
a holy day; and we would forego the [j]sev-
enth year's *produce* and the [k]exacting of
every debt.
32 Also we made ordinances for ourselves, to exact from ourselves yearly
[l]one-third of a shekel for the service of
the house of our God: 33 for [m]the showbread, for the regular grain offering, for
the [n]regular burnt offering of the Sabbaths, the New Moons, and the set feasts;
for the holy things, for the sin offerings
to make atonement for Israel, and all the
work of the house of our God. 34 We cast
lots among the priests, the Levites, and the
people, [o]for bringing the wood offering
into the house of our God, according to our

9:38 *because of all this.* The psalm ends in action, not just sentiment. The intent was to bring the participants in this time of worship and remembrance to a commitment to change behavior and to pledge to mirror God's faithfulness.

10:1 *those who placed their seal.* The way a person in official capacity "signed" a document in the ancient world was similar to the use of a wax seal. A personally distinctive seal was pressed into soft clay. The pattern of the seal identified the official who had issued the document.

10:30 *would not give our daughters.* Marriage with non-Jewish people was strictly forbidden in Scriptures (Ex. 34:12–16; Deut. 7:3; Josh. 23:12–13; Judg. 3:6). Ezra had dealt very decisively with those who had married foreign wives, and this was still in their memory (Ezra 9–10).

9:33 [o][Dan. 9:14] [p][Dan. 9:5, 6, 8] **9:35** [q]Deut. 28:47 **9:36** [r]Deut. 28:48 **9:37** [s]Deut. 28:33, 51 [t]Deut. 28:48 **9:38** [u]2 Kin. 23:3 [v]Neh. 10:1 **10:1** [a]Neh. 1:1 **10:2** [b]Neh. 12:1–21 **10:14** [c]Ezra 2:3 **10:28** [d]Ezra 2:36–43 [e]Neh. 13:3 **10:29** [f]Deut. 29:12 [g]2 Kin. 23:3 **10:30** [h]Ex. 34:16 **10:31** [i]Ex. 20:10 [j]Lev. 25:4 [k][Deut. 15:1, 2] **10:32** [l]Matt. 17:24 **10:33** [m]Lev. 24:5 [n]Num. 28; 29 **10:34** [o]Neh. 13:31

fathers' houses, at the appointed times year
by year, to burn on the altar of the LORD
our God [p]as *it is* written in the Law.
35And *we made ordinances* [q]to bring the
firstfruits of our ground and the firstfruits
of all fruit of all trees, year by year, to the
house of the LORD; 36to bring the [r]firstborn
of our sons and our cattle, as *it is* written
in the Law, and the firstborn of our herds
and our flocks, to the house of our God, to
the priests who minister in the house of our
God; 37[s]to bring the firstfruits of our dough,
our offerings, the fruit from all kinds of
trees, *the* new wine and oil, to the priests,
to the storerooms of the house of our God;
and to bring [t]the tithes of our land to the
Levites, for the Levites should receive the
tithes in all our farming communities.
38And the priest, the descendant of Aaron,
shall be with the Levites [u]when the Levites
receive tithes; and the Levites shall bring
up a tenth of the tithes to the house of our
God, to [v]the rooms of the storehouse.
39For the children of Israel and the children of Levi [w]shall bring the offering of the
grain, of the new wine and the oil, to the
storerooms where the articles of the sanctuary *are, where* the priests who minister
and the gatekeepers [x]and the singers *are;*
and we will not [y]neglect the house of our
God.

The People Dwelling in Jerusalem

11 Now the leaders of the people dwelt at
Jerusalem; the rest of the people cast
lots to bring one out of ten to dwell in Jerusalem, [a]the holy city, and nine-tenths *were
to dwell* in *other* cities. 2And the people
blessed all the men who [b]willingly offered
themselves to dwell at Jerusalem.
3[c]These *are* the heads of the province
who dwelt in Jerusalem. (But in the cities
of Judah everyone dwelt in his own possession in their cities—Israelites, priests,
Levites, [d]Nethinim, and [e]descendants of
Solomon's servants.) 4Also [f]in Jerusalem
dwelt *some* of the children of Judah and of
the children of Benjamin.
The children of Judah: Athaiah the son
of Uzziah, the son of Zechariah, the son of
Amariah, the son of Shephatiah, the son of
Mahalalel, of the children of [g]Perez; 5and
Maaseiah the son of Baruch, the son of
Col-Hozeh, the son of Hazaiah, the son of
Adaiah, the son of Joiarib, the son of Zechariah, the son of Shiloni. 6All the sons of
Perez who dwelt at Jerusalem *were* four
hundred and sixty-eight valiant men.
7And these are the sons of Benjamin:
Sallu the son of Meshullam, the son of
Joed, the son of Pedaiah, the son of Kolaiah, the son of Maaseiah, the son of Ithiel,
the son of Jeshaiah; 8and after him Gabbai
and Sallai, nine hundred and twenty-eight.
9Joel the son of Zichri *was* their overseer,
and Judah the son of Senuah* *was* second
over the city.
10[h]Of the priests: Jedaiah the son of Joiarib, and Jachin; 11Seraiah the son of Hilkiah, the son of Meshullam, the son of Zadok,
the son of Meraioth, the son of Ahitub,
was the leader of the house of God. 12Their
brethren who did the work of the house
were eight hundred and twenty-two; and
Adaiah the son of Jeroham, the son of Pela-
liah, the son of Amzi, the son of Zechariah,
the son of Pashhur, the son of Malchijah,
13and his brethren, heads of the fathers'
houses, were two hundred and forty-two;
and Amashai the son of Azarel, the son of
Ahzai, the son of Meshillemoth, the son of
Immer, 14and their brethren, mighty men of
valor, *were* one hundred and twenty-eight.
Their overseer *was* Zabdiel the son of *one
of* the great men.*
15Also of the Levites: Shemaiah the son
of Hasshub, the son of Azrikam, the son of
Hashabiah, the son of Bunni; 16[i]Shabbethai
and [j]Jozabad, of the heads of the Levites,
had the oversight of [k]the business outside
of the house of God; 17Mattaniah the son of
Micha,* the son of Zabdi, the son of Asaph,
the leader *who* began the thanksgiving
with prayer; Bakbukiah, the second among
his brethren; and Abda the son of Shammua, the son of Galal, the son of Jeduthun.
18All the Levites in [l]the holy city *were* two
hundred and eighty-four.
19Moreover the gatekeepers, Akkub,
Talmon, and their brethren who kept
the gates, *were* one hundred and seventy-
two.
20And the rest of Israel, of the priests
and Levites, *were* in all the cities of Judah,
everyone in his inheritance. 21[m]But the
Nethinim dwelt in Ophel. And Ziha and
Gishpa *were* over the Nethinim.
22Also the overseer of the Levites at
Jerusalem *was* Uzzi the son of Bani, the
son of Hashabiah, the son of Mattaniah,
the son of Micha, of the sons of Asaph,
the singers in charge of the service of
the house of God. 23For [n]*it was* the king's
command concerning them that a certain

* **11:9** Or *Hassenuah* * **11:14** Or *the son of Haggedolim* * **11:17** Or *Michah*

11:1 *cast lots.* Casting lots was considered a good way to determine God's will when there was no other clear direction. Solomon wrote, "The lot is cast into the lap, but its every decision is from the LORD" (Prov. 16:33). ***one out of ten.*** This was the proportion determined in order to bring the population of Jerusalem to the level deemed necessary for its strength and viability.

10:34 [p] Lev. 6:12 **10:35** [q] Ex. 23:19; 34:26 **10:36** [r] Ex. 13:2, 12, 13 **10:37** [s] Lev. 23:17 [t] Lev. 27:30 **10:38** [u] Num. 18:26 [v] 1 Chr. 9:26 **10:39** [w] Deut. 12:6, 11 [x] Neh. 13:10, 11 [y] [Heb. 10:25] **11:1** [a] Matt. 4:5; 5:35; 27:53 **11:2** [b] Judg. 5:9 **11:3** [c] 1 Chr. 9:2, 3 [d] Ezra 2:43 [e] Ezra 2:55 **11:4** [f] 1 Chr. 9:3 [g] Gen. 38:29 **11:10** [h] 1 Chr. 9:10 **11:16** [i] Ezra 10:15 [j] Ezra 8:33 [k] 1 Chr. 26:29 **11:18** [l] Neh. 11:1 **11:21** [m] Neh. 3:26 **11:23** [n] Ezra 6:8, 9; 7:20

portion should be for the singers, a quota day by day. [24]Pethahiah the son of Meshezabel, of the children of [o]Zerah the son of Judah, *was* [p]the king's deputy* in all matters concerning the people.

The People Dwelling Outside Jerusalem

[25]And as for the villages with their fields, *some* of the children of Judah dwelt in [q]Kirjath Arba and its villages, Dibon and its villages, Jekabzeel and its villages; [26]in Jeshua, Moladah, Beth Pelet, [27]Hazar Shual, and Beersheba and its villages; [28]in Ziklag and Meconah and its villages; [29]in En Rimmon, Zorah, Jarmuth, [30]Zanoah, Adullam, and their villages; in Lachish and its fields; in Azekah and its villages. They dwelt from Beersheba to the Valley of Hinnom.

[31]Also the children of Benjamin from Geba *dwelt* in Michmash, Aija, and Bethel, and their villages; [32]in Anathoth, Nob, Ananiah; [33]in Hazor, Ramah, Gittaim; [34]in Hadid, Zeboim, Neballat; [35]in Lod, Ono, *and* [r]the Valley of Craftsmen. [36]Some of the Judean divisions of Levites *were* in Benjamin.

The Priests and Levites

12 Now these *are* the [a]priests and the Levites who came up with [b]Zerubbabel the son of Shealtiel, and Jeshua: [c]Seraiah, Jeremiah, Ezra, [2]Amariah, Malluch, Hattush, [3]Shechaniah, Rehum, Meremoth, [4]Iddo, Ginnethoi,* [d]Abijah, [5]Mijamin, Maadiah, Bilgah, [6]Shemaiah, Joiarib, Jedaiah, [7]Sallu, Amok, Hilkiah, *and* Jedaiah.

These *were* the heads of the priests and their brethren in the days of [e]Jeshua.

[8]Moreover the Levites *were* Jeshua, Binnui, Kadmiel, Sherebiah, Judah, *and* Mattaniah [f]*who led* the thanksgiving *psalms*, he and his brethren. [9]Also Bakbukiah and Unni, their brethren, *stood* across from them in *their* duties.

[10]Jeshua begot Joiakim, Joiakim begot Eliashib, Eliashib begot Joiada, [11]Joiada begot Jonathan, and Jonathan begot Jaddua.

[12]Now in the days of Joiakim, the priests, the [g]heads of the fathers' *houses were*: of Seraiah, Meraiah; of Jeremiah, Hananiah; [13]of Ezra, Meshullam; of Amariah,

Jehohanan; [14]of Melichu,* Jonathan; of Shebaniah,* Joseph; [15]of Harim,* Adna; of Meraioth,* Helkai; [16]of Iddo, Zechariah; of Ginnethon, Meshullam; [17]of Abijah, Zichri; *the son* of Minjamin;* of Moadiah,* Piltai; [18]of Bilgah, Shammua; of Shemaiah, Jehonathan; [19]of Joiarib, Mattenai; of Jedaiah, Uzzi; [20]of Sallai,* Kallai; of Amok, Eber; [21]of Hilkiah, Hashabiah; *and* of Jedaiah, Nethanel.

[22]During the reign of Darius the Persian, a record *was also kept* of the Levites and priests *who had been* [h]heads of their fathers' *houses* in the days of Eliashib, Joiada, Johanan, and Jaddua. [23]The sons of Levi, the heads of the fathers' *houses* until the days of Johanan the son of Eliashib, *were* written in the book of the [i]chronicles.

[24]And the heads of the Levites *were* Hashabiah, Sherebiah, and Jeshua the son of Kadmiel, with their brothers across from them, to [j]praise *and* give thanks, [k]group alternating with group, [l]according to the command of David the man of God. [25]Mattaniah, Bakbukiah, Obadiah, Meshullam, Talmon, and Akkub *were* gatekeepers keeping the watch at the storerooms of the gates. [26]These *lived* in the days of Joiakim the son of Jeshua, the son of Jozadak,* and in the days of Nehemiah [m]the governor, and of Ezra the priest, [n]the scribe.

Nehemiah Dedicates the Wall

[27]Now at [o]the dedication of the wall of Jerusalem they sought out the Levites in all their places, to bring them to Jerusalem to celebrate the dedication with gladness, [p]both with thanksgivings and singing, *with* cymbals and stringed instruments and harps. [28]And the sons of the singers gathered together from the countryside around Jerusalem, from the [q]villages of the Netophathites, [29]from the house of Gilgal, and from the fields of Geba and Azmaveth;

* 11:24 Literally *at the king's hand* * 12:4 Or *Ginnethon* (compare verse 16) * 12:14 Or *Malluch* (compare verse 2) • Or *Shechaniah* (compare verse 3) * 12:15 Or *Rehum* (compare verse 3) • Or *Meremoth* (compare verse 3) * 12:17 Or *Mijamin* (compare verse 5) • Or *Maadiah* (compare verse 5) * 12:20 Or *Sallu* (compare verse 7) * 12:26 Spelled *Jehozadak* in 1 Chronicles 6:14

11:25 *Kirjath Arba*. Kirjath Arba is another name for Hebron.
12:1 *Zerubbabel*. The return of Zerubbabel is recorded in Ezra 1–6. *Jeshua*. Jeshua is Joshua the priest. *Ezra*. This is not the priest who wrote the book of the same name.
12:22 *Darius*. Darius refers to Darius II (Nothus), who ruled Persia from 423 to 405 B.C.
12:23 *the book of the chronicles*. The book of the chronicles was not the biblical book, but an official record of the heads of the fathers' houses.
12:27 *dedication of the wall*. After the completion

of Jerusalem's wall (ch. 6), the people repented and renewed their commitment to the Lord (chs. 8–10). The repopulation of Jerusalem was ordered, so the dedication was delayed.

11:24 [o]Gen. 38:30 [p]1 Chr. 18:17   **11:25** [q]Josh. 14:15
11:35 [r]1 Chr. 4:14   **12:1** [a]Ezra 2:1, 2; 7:7 [b]Neh. 7:7 [c]Neh. 10:2–8   **12:4** [d]Luke 1:5   **12:7** [e]Zech. 3:1   **12:8** [f]Neh. 11:17   **12:12** [g]Neh. 7:70, 71; 8:13; 11:13   **12:22** [h]1 Chr. 24:6   **12:23** [i]1 Chr. 9:14–22   **12:24** [j]Neh. 11:17 [k]Ezra 3:11 [l]1 Chr. 23–26   **12:26** [m]Neh. 8:9 [n]Ezra 7:6, 11   **12:27** [o]Deut. 20:5 [p]1 Chr. 25:6   **12:28** [q]1 Chr. 9:16

for the singers had built themselves villages all around Jerusalem. 30Then the priests and Levites 'purified themselves, and purified the people, the gates, and the wall.

31So I brought the leaders of Judah up on the wall, and appointed two large thanksgiving choirs. sOne went to the right hand on the wall 'toward the Refuse Gate. 32After them went Hoshaiah and half of the leaders of Judah, 33and Azariah, Ezra, Meshullam, 34Judah, Benjamin, Shemaiah, Jeremiah, 35and some of the priests' sons uwith trumpets—Zechariah the son of Jonathan, the son of Shemaiah, the son of Mattaniah, the son of Michaiah, the son of Zaccur, the son of Asaph, 36and his brethren, Shemaiah, Azarel, Milalai, Gilalai, Maai, Nethanel, Judah, and Hanani, with vthe musical winstruments of David the man of God. And Ezra the scribe went before them. 37xBy the Fountain Gate, in front of them, they went up ythe stairs of the zCity of David, on the stairway of the wall, beyond the house of David, as far as athe Water Gate eastward.

38bThe other thanksgiving choir went the opposite way, and I was behind them with half of the people on the wall, going past the cTower of the Ovens as far as dthe Broad Wall, 39eand above the Gate of Ephraim, above fthe Old Gate, above gthe Fish Gate, hthe Tower of Hananel, the Tower of the Hundred, as far as ithe Sheep Gate; and they stopped by jthe Gate of the Prison.

40So the two thanksgiving choirs stood in the house of God, likewise I and the half of the rulers with me; 41and the priests, Eliakim, Maaseiah, Minjamin,* Michaiah, Elioenai, Zechariah, and Hananiah, with trumpets; 42also Maaseiah, Shemaiah, Eleazar, Uzzi, Jehohanan, Malchijah, Elam, and Ezer. The singers sang loudly with Jezrahiah the director.

43Also that day they offered great sacrifices, and rejoiced, for God had made them rejoice with great joy; the women and the children also rejoiced, so that the joy of Jerusalem was heard kafar off.

Temple Responsibilities

44lAnd at the same time some were appointed over the rooms of the storehouse for the offerings, the firstfruits, and the mtithes, to gather into them from the fields of the cities the portions specified by the Law for the priests and Levites; for Judah rejoiced over the priests and Levites who ministered. 45Both the singers and the gatekeepers kept the charge of their God and the charge of the purification, naccording to the command of David and Solomon his son. 46For in the days of David oand Asaph of old there were chiefs of the singers, and songs of praise and thanksgiving to God. 47In the days of Zerubbabel and in the days of Nehemiah all Israel gave the portions for the singers and the gatekeepers, a portion for peach day. qThey also consecrated holy things for the Levites, rand the Levites consecrated them for the children of Aaron.

Principles of Separation

13 On that day athey read from the Book of Moses in the hearing of the people, and in it was found written bthat no Ammonite or Moabite should ever come into the assembly of God, 2because they had not met the children of Israel with bread and water, but chired Balaam against them to curse them. dHowever, our God turned the curse into a blessing. 3So it was, when they had heard the Law, ethat they separated all the mixed multitude from Israel.

The Reforms of Nehemiah

4Now before this, fEliashib the priest, having authority over the storerooms of the house of our God, was allied with gTobiah. 5And he had prepared for him a large room, hwhere previously they had stored the grain offerings, the frankincense, the articles, the tithes of grain, the new wine and oil, iwhich were commanded to be given to the Levites and singers and gatekeepers, and the offerings for the priests. 6But during all this I was not in Jerusalem, jfor in the thirty-second year of Artaxerxes king of Babylon I had returned to the king.

* 12:41 Or Mijamin (compare verse 5)

12:31–46 Praise—Nehemiah choreographed a dramatic demonstration of praise, thanksgiving, and celebration on top of the wall. It was a wholehearted celebration to the Lord, and a visible victory dance before Israel's enemies. This time of praise had been preceded by repentance and reorganization of their duties to the temple and the city of Jerusalem. Praise that rises deep in the heart is always praise that comes from knowing that we are in good standing with God. We have repented of our sins and set our hearts and minds on obedience. God is good, His ways are infinitely right, and He is worthy of all of our enthusiastic worship.

12:43 sacrifices. The sacrifices offered at the dedication of the wall probably were not burnt offerings, but peace offerings in which the people shared a common meal. The dedication was an occasion for great rejoicing, and men, women, and children took part.

13:4–9 Tobiah. Tobiah was an Ammonite (2:10).

12:30 rNeh. 13:22, 30   12:31 sNeh. 12:38 tNeh. 2:13; 3:13   12:35 uNum. 10:2, 8   12:36 v1 Chr. 23:5 w2 Chr. 29:26, 27   12:37 xNeh. 2:14; 3:15 yNeh. 3:15 z2 Sam. 5:7–9 aNeh. 3:26; 8:1, 3, 16   12:38 bNeh. 12:31 cNeh. 3:11 dNeh. 3:8   12:39 e2 Kin. 14:13 fNeh. 3:6 gNeh. 3:3 hNeh. 3:1 iNeh. 3:32 jJer. 32:2   12:43 kEzra 3:13   12:44 lNeh. 13:5, 12, 13 mNeh. 10:37–39   12:45 n1 Chr. 25, 26   12:46 o2 Chr. 29:30   12:47 pNeh. 11:23 qNum. 18:21, 24 rNum. 18:26   13:1 aNeh. 8:3, 6; 9:3 bDeut. 23:3, 4   13:2 cNum. 22:5 dNum. 23:1; 24:10   13:3 eNeh. 9:2; 10:28   13:4 fNeh. 12:10 gNeh. 2:10; 4:3; 6:1   13:5 hNeh. 12:44 iNum. 18:21, 24   13:6 jNeh. 5:14–16

Then after certain days I obtained leave from the king, [7]and I came to Jerusalem and discovered the evil that Eliashib had done for Tobiah, in [k]preparing a room for him in the courts of the house of God. [8]And it grieved me bitterly; therefore I threw all the household goods of Tobiah out of the room. [9]Then I commanded them to [l]cleanse the rooms; and I brought back into them the articles of the house of God, with the grain offering and the frankincense.

[10]I also realized that the portions for the Levites had [m]not been given *them;* for each of the Levites and the singers who did the work had gone back to [n]his field. [11]So [o]I contended with the rulers, and said, [p]"Why is the house of God forsaken?" And I gathered them together and set them in their place. [12][q]Then all Judah brought the tithe of the grain and the new wine and the oil to the storehouse. [13][r]And I appointed as treasurers over the storehouse Shelemiah the priest and Zadok the scribe, and of the Levites, Pedaiah; and next to them *was* Hanan the son of Zaccur, the son of Mattaniah; for they were considered [s]faithful, and their task *was* to distribute to their brethren.

[14][t]Remember me, O my God, concerning this, and do not wipe out my good deeds that I have done for the house of my God, and for its services!

[15]In those days I saw *people* in Judah treading winepresses [u]on the Sabbath, and bringing in sheaves, and loading donkeys with wine, grapes, figs, and all *kinds of* burdens, [v]which they brought into Jerusalem on the Sabbath day. And I warned *them* about the day on which they were selling provisions. [16]Men of Tyre dwelt there also, who brought in fish and all kinds of goods, and sold *them* on the Sabbath to the children of Judah, and in Jerusalem.

[17]Then I contended with the nobles of Judah, and said to them, "What evil thing *is* this that you do, by which you profane the Sabbath day? [18][w]Did not your fathers do thus, and did not our God bring all this disaster on us and on this city? Yet you bring added wrath on Israel by profaning the Sabbath."

[19]So it was, at the gates of Jerusalem, as it [x]began to be dark before the Sabbath, that I commanded the gates to be shut, and charged that they must not be opened till after the Sabbath. [y]Then I posted *some* of my servants at the gates, *so that* no burdens would be brought in on the Sabbath day. [20]Now the merchants and sellers of all kinds of wares lodged outside Jerusalem once or twice.

[21]Then I warned them, and said to them, "Why do you spend the night around the wall? If you do *so* again, I will lay hands on you!" From that time on they came no *more* on the Sabbath. [22]And I commanded the Levites that [z]they should cleanse themselves, and that they should go and guard the gates, to sanctify the Sabbath day.

Remember me, O my God, *concerning* this also, and spare me according to the greatness of Your mercy!

[23]In those days I also saw Jews *who* [a]had married women of [b]Ashdod, Ammon, *and* Moab. [24]And half of their children spoke the language of Ashdod, and could not speak the language of Judah, but spoke according to the language of one or the other people.

[25]So I [c]contended with them and cursed them, struck some of them and pulled out their hair, and made them [d]swear by God, *saying,* "You shall not give your daughters as wives to their sons, nor take their daughters for your sons or yourselves. [26][e]Did not Solomon king of Israel sin by these things? Yet among many nations there was no king like him, [f]who was beloved of his God; and God made him king over all Israel. [g]Nevertheless pagan women caused even him to sin. [27]Should we then hear of your doing all this great evil, [h]transgressing against our God by marrying pagan women?"

[28]And *one* of the sons [i]of Joiada, the son of Eliashib the high priest, *was* a son-in-law of [j]Sanballat the Horonite; therefore I drove him from me.

[29][k]Remember them, O my God, because they have defiled the priesthood and [l]the covenant of the priesthood and the Levites.

[30][m]Thus I cleansed them of everything pagan. I also [n]assigned duties to the priests and the Levites, each to his service, [31]and *to bringing* [o]the wood offering and the firstfruits at appointed times.

[p]Remember me, O my God, for good!

13:23–24 *Jews that had married wives of Ashdod, Ammon, and Moab.* The problem of Jews marrying foreigners had been dealt with thirty years before by Ezra (Ezra 9–10).

13:25 *cursed them . . . struck . . . them . . . pulled out their hair.* It is unnerving to read this list of verbs and imagine the scene. These were not the dispassionate remarks of someone giving a seminar. Nehemiah forced them to comply to the will of God in this matter. After all, this was the principal issue that had led to Israel's captivity in the beginning.

13:28 *son-in-law of Sanballat.* The marriage was particularly offensive because it formed a treasonable alliance with Israel's enemies and compromised the purity of the high priesthood.

13:7 [k] Neh. 13:1, 5   **13:9** [l] 2 Chr. 29:5, 15, 16   **13:10** [m] Neh. 10:37   [n] Num. 35:2   **13:11** [o] Neh. 13:17, 25   [p] Neh. 10:39   **13:12** [q] Neh. 10:38; 12:44   **13:13** [r] 2 Chr. 31:12   [s] 1 Cor. 4:2   **13:14** [t] Neh. 5:19; 13:22, 31   **13:15** [u] [Ex. 20:10]   [v] [Jer. 17:21]   **13:18** [w] [Jer. 17:21]   **13:19** [x] Lev. 23:32   [y] Neh. 17:21, 22   **13:22** [z] Neh. 12:30   **13:23** [a] Ezra 9:2   [b] Neh. 4:7   **13:25** [c] Prov. 28:4   [d] Neh. 10:29, 30   **13:26** [e] 1 Kin. 11:1, 2   [f] 2 Sam. 12:24, 25   [g] 1 Kin. 11:4–8   **13:27** [h] [Ezra 10:2]   **13:28** [i] Neh. 12:10, 12   [j] Neh. 4:1, 7; 6:1, 2   **13:29** [k] Neh. 6:14   [l] Mal. 2:4, 11, 12   **13:30** [m] Neh. 10:30   [n] Neh. 12:1   **13:31** [o] Neh. 10:34   [p] Neh. 13:14, 22

THE BOOK OF
ESTHER

▶ **AUTHOR:** Even though the author's identity is not given in the text, it is obvious from the intimate knowledge of Persian customs and etiquette, the palace in Susa, and the details of the reign of King Ahasuerus, that the author lived in Persia during this period. The love expressed here for the Jewish people and the author's knowledge of Jewish customs further suggest Jewish authorship. It is also thought that this Persian Jew was either an eyewitness to the events or knew an eyewitness. It may be that this author had access to the detailed records kept by Mordecai.

▶ **TIME:** c. 483–473 B.C.   ▶ **KEY VERSE:** Esth. 4:14

▶ **THEME:** Esther is unique among the Scriptures for two reasons: God is not mentioned by name once, and the heroine is a woman who is part of the harem of a foreign king. The events of the book take place about 30 years before Nehemiah, after the temple in Jerusalem was rebuilt but before the walls were refinished. Esther probably helped to pave the way for Nehemiah's work. The book fits well within the tapestry of the Old Testament. Just as in so many other Old Testament narratives, God provides the means to preserve His people in the face of a severe crisis. It is still read aloud as part of the Purim celebration by Jewish people.

The King Dethrones Queen Vashti

1 Now it came to pass in the days of ^aAhasuerus* (this *was* the Ahasuerus who reigned ^bover one hundred and twenty-seven provinces, ^cfrom India to Ethiopia), ²in those days when King Ahasuerus ^dsat on the throne of his kingdom, which *was* in ^eShushan* the citadel, ³*that* in the third year of his reign he ^fmade a feast for all his officials and servants— the powers of Persia and Media, the nobles, and the princes of the provinces *being* before him— ⁴when he showed the riches of his glorious kingdom and the splendor of his excellent majesty for many days, one hundred and eighty days *in all.*

⁵And when these days were completed, the king made a feast lasting seven days for all the people who were present in Shushan the citadel, from great to small, in the court of the garden of the king's palace. ⁶*There were* white and blue linen *curtains* fastened with cords of fine linen and purple on silver rods and marble pillars; *and the*

^gcouches *were* of gold and silver on a mosaic pavement of alabaster, turquoise, and white and black marble. ⁷And they served drinks in golden vessels, each vessel being different from the other, with royal wine in abundance, ^haccording to the generosity of the king. ⁸In accordance with the law, the drinking was not compulsory; for so the king had ordered all the officers of his household, that they should do according to each man's pleasure.

⁹Queen Vashti also made a feast for the women *in* the royal palace which *belonged* to King Ahasuerus.

¹⁰On the seventh day, when the heart of the king was merry with wine, he commanded Mehuman, Biztha, ⁱHarbona, Bigtha, Abagtha, Zethar, and Carcas, seven eunuchs who served in the presence of King Ahasuerus, ¹¹to bring Queen Vashti before the king, *wearing* her royal crown, in order to show her beauty to the people

---

* **1:1** Generally identified with Xerxes I (485–464 B.C.)   * **1:2** Or *Susa,* and so throughout this book

---

1:1 *Ahasuerus.* The kingdom of Ahasuerus extended from India (the region drained by the Indus River) to Ethiopia (northern Sudan). The Persian Kingdom under Ahasuerus was divided into smaller areas called provinces and larger divisions called satrapies.
1:6 *white . . . blue . . . and purple.* These were the royal colors of the Persians.
1:8 *not compulsory.* The usual Persian custom was that guests at a banquet were required to drink each time the king raised his cup.

1:10 *eunuchs.* These were eunuchs who were castrated for the purpose of acting as harem attendants. They would have had the physical strength and stamina of any man, but not be a sexual threat to the king's women.

1:1 ^a Ezra 4:6 ^b Esth. 8:9 ^c Dan. 6:1 **1:2** ^d 1 Kin. 1:46 ^e Neh. 1:1 **1:3** ^f Gen. 40:20 **1:6** ^g Amos 2:8; 6:4 **1:7** ^h Esth. 2:18 **1:10** ⁱ Esth. 7:9

and the officials, for she *was* beautiful to
behold. 12But Queen Vashti refused to come
at the king's command *brought* by *his* eunuchs; therefore the king was furious, and
his anger burned within him.
13Then the king said to the [j]wise men
[k]who understood the times (for this *was*
the king's manner toward all who knew
law and justice, 14those closest to him
being Carshena, Shethar, Admatha, Tarshish, Meres, Marsena, and Memucan, the
[l]seven princes of Persia and Media, [m]who
had access to the king's presence, *and* who
ranked highest in the kingdom): 15"What
shall we do to Queen Vashti, according
to law, because she did not obey the command of King Ahasuerus *brought to her* by
the eunuchs?"
16And Memucan answered before the
king and the princes: "Queen Vashti has
not only wronged the king, but also all the
princes, and all the people who *are* in all
the provinces of King Ahasuerus. 17For
the queen's behavior will become known
to all women, so that they will [n]despise
their husbands in their eyes, when they report, 'King Ahasuerus commanded Queen
Vashti to be brought in before him, but she
did not come.' 18This very day the *noble*
ladies of Persia and Media will say to all
the king's officials that they have heard of
the behavior of the queen. Thus *there will
be* excessive contempt and wrath. 19If it
pleases the king, let a royal decree go out
from him, and let it be recorded in the laws
of the Persians and the Medes, so that it
will [o]not be altered, that Vashti shall come
no more before King Ahasuerus; and let
the king give her royal position to another
who is better than she. 20When the king's
decree which he will make is proclaimed
throughout all his empire (for it is great),
all wives will [p]honor their husbands, both
great and small."
21And the reply pleased the king and the
princes, and the king did according to the
word of Memucan. 22Then he sent letters to
all the king's provinces, [q]to each province
in its own script, and to every people in
their own language, that each man should
[r]be master in his own house, and speak in
the language of his own people.

Esther Becomes Queen

2 After these things, when the wrath of
King Ahasuerus subsided, he remembered Vashti, [a]what she had done, and
what had been decreed against her. 2Then
the king's servants who attended him said:
"Let beautiful young virgins be sought for
the king; 3and let the king appoint officers
in all the provinces of his kingdom, that
they may gather all the beautiful young
virgins to Shushan the citadel, into the
women's quarters, under the custody of
Hegai* the king's eunuch, custodian of the
women. And let beauty preparations be
given *them*. 4Then let the young woman
who pleases the king be queen instead of
Vashti."
This thing pleased the king, and he
did so.
5In Shushan the citadel there was a
certain Jew whose name *was* Mordecai
the son of Jair, the son of Shimei, the son
of [b]Kish, a Benjamite. 6[c]*Kish** had been
carried away from Jerusalem with the
captives who had been captured with Jeconiah* king of Judah, whom Nebuchadnezzar the king of Babylon had carried away.
7And *Mordecai* had brought up Hadassah,
that *is*, Esther, [d]his uncle's daughter, for she
had neither father nor mother. The young
woman *was* lovely and beautiful. When
her father and mother died, Mordecai took
her as his own daughter.
8So it was, when the king's command
and decree were heard, and when many
young women were [e]gathered at Shushan
the citadel, *under* the custody of Hegai, that
Esther also was taken to the king's palace,
into the care of Hegai the custodian of the
women. 9Now the young woman pleased

*2:3 Hebrew *Hege* *2:6 Literally *Who* • Same as *Jehoiachin*, 2 Kings 24:6 and elsewhere

1:16–18 *Memucan.* Acting as spokesman for the others, Memucan responded shrewdly by enlarging the offense beyond a personal affront to the king. The Hebrew word used for *despise* occurs only here in the Old Testament.

2:5 *Kish.* Some think this may have been the Kish who was the father of King Saul (1 Sam. 9:1–2). It was not uncommon to refer to someone as "the son of" a more distant ancestor (Matt. 15:22).

2:6 *had been carried away.* This verse is a little confusing, as the Hebrew text does not indicate the subject of the verb "had been carried away." It seems highly unlikely that it could be Mordecai, because if he had been among those carried to Babylon, he would probably not be alive in the time of Ahasuerus. If the name Kish does not refer to a more distant ancestor, he may have been the one taken into captivity. Whatever the case, it is obvious that Mordecai and his family were among those descended from the captives taken to Babylon in the days of Nebuchadnezzar.

2:7 *Hadassah.* Hadassah is a Hebrew name that means "myrtle." Esther is a Persian name meaning "star." Jewish people in that time customarily had two names when they lived in places other than Israel. One would be their secular name, which was understood by their adopted culture, and the other would be their sacred name, given in Hebrew.

2:8 *Esther also was taken.* We cannot determine whether Esther went willingly or reluctantly to the

1:13 [j] Dan. 2:12 [k] 1 Chr. 12:32 **1:14** [l] Ezra 7:14 [m] 2 Kin. 25:19 **1:17** [n] [Eph. 5:33] **1:19** [o] Esth. 8:8 **1:20** [p] [Col. 3:18] **1:22** [q] Esth. 3:12; 8:9 [r] [Eph. 5:22–24] **2:1** [a] Esth. 1:19, 20 **2:5** [b] 1 Sam. 9:1 **2:6** [c] 2 Kin. 24:14, 15 **2:7** [d] Esth. 2:15 **2:8** [e] Esth. 2:3

him, and she obtained his favor; so he readily gave *f*beauty preparations to her, besides her allowance. Then seven choice maidservants were provided for her from the king's palace, and he moved her and her maidservants to the best *place* in the house of the women.

10*g*Esther had not revealed her people or family, for Mordecai had charged her not to reveal *it.* 11And every day Mordecai paced in front of the court of the women's quarters, to learn of Esther's welfare and what was happening to her.

12Each young woman's turn came to go in to King Ahasuerus after she had completed twelve months' preparation, according to the regulations for the women, for thus were the days of their preparation apportioned: six months with oil of myrrh, and six months with perfumes and preparations for beautifying women. 13Thus *prepared, each* young woman went to the king, and she was given whatever she desired to take with her from the women's quarters to the king's palace. 14In the evening she went, and in the morning she returned to the second house of the women, to the custody of Shaashgaz, the king's eunuch who kept the concubines. She would not go in to the king again unless the king delighted in her and called for her by name.

15Now when the turn came for Esther *h*the daughter of Abihail the uncle of Mordecai, who had taken her as his daughter, to go in to the king, she requested nothing but what Hegai the king's eunuch, the custodian of the women, advised. And Esther *i*obtained favor in the sight of all who saw her. 16So Esther was taken to King Ahasuerus, into his royal palace, in the tenth month, which *is* the month of Tebeth, in the seventh year of his reign. 17The king loved Esther more than all the *other* women, and she obtained grace and favor in his sight more than all the virgins; so he set the royal *j*crown upon her head and made her queen instead of Vashti. 18Then the king *k*made a great feast, the Feast of Esther,

for all his officials and servants; and he proclaimed a holiday in the provinces and gave gifts according to the generosity of a king.

Mordecai Discovers a Plot

19When virgins were gathered together a second time, Mordecai sat within the king's gate. 20*l*Now Esther had not revealed her family and her people, just as Mordecai had charged her, for Esther obeyed the command of Mordecai as when she was brought up by him.

21In those days, while Mordecai sat within the king's gate, two of the king's eunuchs, Bigthan and Teresh, doorkeepers, became furious and sought to lay hands on King Ahasuerus. 22So the matter became known to Mordecai, *m*who told Queen Esther, and Esther informed the king in Mordecai's name. 23And when an inquiry was made into the matter, it was confirmed, and both were hanged on a gallows; and it was written in *n*the book of the chronicles in the presence of the king.

Haman's Conspiracy Against the Jews

3 After these things King Ahasuerus promoted Haman, the son of Hammedatha the *a*Agagite, and *b*advanced him and set his seat above all the princes who *were* with him. 2And all the king's servants who *were* *c*within the king's gate bowed and paid homage to Haman, for so the king had commanded concerning him. But Mordecai *d*would not bow or pay homage. 3Then the king's servants who *were* within the king's gate said to Mordecai, "Why do you transgress the *e*king's command?" 4Now it happened, when they spoke to him daily and he would not listen to them, that they told *it* to Haman, to see whether Mordecai's words would stand; for *Mordecai* had told them that he *was* a Jew. 5When Haman saw that Mordecai *f*did not bow or pay him homage, Haman was *g*filled with wrath.

palace complex. But perhaps God was already preparing her for the work he had for her to do.
2:14 concubines. These women lived unfortunate, though highly pampered lives. If the king never called them again, they were destined to remain secluded in the harem for the rest of their lives.
2:21 sat within the king's gate. In ancient cities, the gates were the "courthouse" of the town, where official business was carried out (Deut. 22:13–15). The "king's gate" may have served a similar purpose.
3:1 the Agagite. Some believe Agagite is a reference to the historical district of Agag within the Persian Empire. Others believe this term more likely links Haman's descent to the Amalekites. These descendants of Esau (Gen. 36:12) were ancient enemies of the Hebrews (Ex. 17:8). Agag, a king of the Amalekites, was captured by King Saul (1 Sam. 15:8). If Haman was descended from the Amalekites, and Mordecai from the family of Saul (v. 5), then the irritation Haman

had for Mordecai could have been a symptom of a long-standing family hostility.
3:2 bowed and paid homage. It is not known whether the bowing was required as an act of worship to the king's man, or merely as an overt sign of deep respect. If such obeisance indicated worship, Mordecai's reason for refusal is obvious. If it was merely a sign of respect, he may not have been able to bring himself to show such honor to one who was an ancestral enemy.
3:5–6 filled with wrath. If Haman was of Amalekite ancestry, it could be that this was the cause of his deep hatred. Also, it is possible that Haman simply

2:9 *f* Esth. 2:3, 12   2:10 *g* Esth. 2:20   2:15 *h* Esth. 2:7; 9:29   *i* Esth. 5:2, 8   2:17 *j* Esth. 1:11   2:18 *k* Esth. 1:3   2:20 *l* Esth. 2:10   2:22 *m* Esth. 6:1, 2   2:23 *n* Esth. 6:1   3:1 *a* Num. 24:7   *b* Esth. 5:11   3:2 *c* Esth. 2:19, 21; 5:9   *d* Ps. 15:4   3:3 *e* Esth. 3:2   3:5 *f* Esth. 3:2; 5:9   *g* Dan. 3:19

6But he disdained to lay hands on Mordecai alone, for they had told him of the people of Mordecai. Instead, Haman hsought to destroy all the Jews who were throughout the whole kingdom of Ahasuerus—the people of Mordecai.

7In the first month, which is the month of Nisan, in the twelfth year of King Ahasuerus, ithey cast Pur (that is, the lot), before Haman to determine the day and the month,* until it fell on the twelfth month,* which is the month of Adar.

8Then Haman said to King Ahasuerus, "There is a certain people scattered and dispersed among the people in all the provinces of your kingdom; jtheir laws are different from all other people's, and they do not keep the king's laws. Therefore it is not fitting for the king to let them remain. 9If it pleases the king, let a decree be written that they be destroyed, and I will pay ten thousand talents of silver into the hands of those who do the work, to bring it into the king's treasuries."

10So the king htook lhis signet ring from his hand and gave it to Haman, the son of Hammedatha the Agagite, the menemy of the Jews. 11And the king said to Haman, "The money and the people are given to you, to do with them as seems good to you."

12nThen the king's scribes were called on the thirteenth day of the first month, and a decree was written according to all that Haman commanded—to the king's satraps, to the governors who were over each province, to the officials of all people, to every province oaccording to its script, and to every people in their language. pIn the name of King Ahasuerus it was written, and sealed with the king's signet ring. 13And the letters were qsent by couriers into all the king's provinces, to destroy, to kill, and to annihilate all the Jews, both young and old, little children and women, rin one

day, on the thirteenth day of the twelfth month, which is the month of Adar, and sto plunder their possessions.* 14tA copy of the document was to be issued as law in every province, being published for all people, that they should be ready for that day. 15The couriers went out, hastened by the king's command; and the decree was proclaimed in Shushan the citadel. So the king and Haman sat down to drink, but uthe city of Shushan was perplexed.

Esther Agrees to Help the Jews

4 When Mordecai learned all that had happened, he atore his clothes and put on sackcloth band ashes, and went out into the midst of the city. He ccried out with a loud and bitter cry. 2He went as far as the front of the king's gate, for no one might enter the king's gate clothed with sackcloth. 3And in every province where the king's command and decree arrived, there was great mourning among the Jews, with fasting, weeping, and wailing; and many lay in sackcloth and ashes.

4So Esther's maids and eunuchs came and told her, and the queen was deeply distressed. Then she sent garments to clothe Mordecai and take his sackcloth away from him, but he would not accept them. 5Then Esther called Hathach, one of the king's eunuchs whom he had appointed to attend her, and she gave him a command concerning Mordecai, to learn what and why this was. 6So Hathach went out to Mordecai in the city square that was in front of the king's gate. 7And Mordecai told

---

* 3:7 Septuagint adds to destroy the people of Mordecai in one day; Vulgate adds the nation of the Jews should be destroyed. • Following Masoretic Text and Vulgate; Septuagint reads and the lot fell on the fourteenth of the month.   * 3:13 Septuagint adds the text of the letter here.

---

could not stand to see anyone who did not properly respect his position.

3:7 Pur (that is, the lot). The casting of lots was common in ancient times. Haman's casting a lot at the beginning of the year to determine the best time to destroy the Jewish people fits in with the culture of the day, as the Babylonians believed that the gods gathered at the beginning of each year to establish the destiny of human beings. The word *pur* is the basis for the name of the new feast in chapter 9.

3:8 Slander—Haman was sly. He devised an accusation to convince the king that the Jews were a dangerous and treasonous people. His accusation contained a clever mixture of truth and falsehood. The laws of the Jewish people were admittedly different, but this was not unusual, nor was it a threat to Persia, which contained many minorities. Not only was accusing the whole Jewish nation of civil disobedience a lie, it was also intended to lead to something much worse: murder.

3:10 ring. The king's signet ring symbolized his authority. He would have used this signet as a stamp to authorize official documents.

3:15 Haman sat down to drink. Haman was so unconcerned about the death sentence he was placing on the Jewish people that he sat down comfortably to relax while the city was in confusion.

4:1–2 sackcloth and ashes. Sackcloth and ashes were used as a visible sign of mourning, indicating a sense of desolation.

4:3 fasting. It is interesting to note that throughout the entire Book of Esther, God is not mentioned by name even once. One assumes that Esther's fasting was accompanied by prayer, but it is never mentioned. Fasting was a religious custom, and we know the Jews relied on God for their safety. Many think the author of Esther was writing the story to a secular audience, and this is the reason for God's actual name being left out.

3:6 h Ps. 83:4   3:7 i Esth. 9:24–26   3:8 j Acts 16:20, 21   3:10 k Gen. 41:42   l Esth. 8:2, 8   m Esth. 7:6   3:12 n Esth. 8:9   o Esth. 1:22   p Esth. 8:8–10   3:13 q Esth. 8:10, 14   r Esth. 8:12   s Esth. 8:11; 9:10   3:14 t Esth. 8:13, 14   3:15 u Esth. 8:15   4:1 a 2 Sam. 1:11   b Josh. 7:6   c Gen. 27:34

him all that had happened to him, and ᵈthe sum of money that Haman had promised to pay into the king's treasuries to destroy the Jews. ⁸He also gave him ᵉa copy of the written decree for their destruction, which was given at Shushan, that he might show it to Esther and explain it to her, and that he might command her to go in to the king to make supplication to him and plead before him for her people. ⁹So Hathach returned and told Esther the words of Mordecai.

¹⁰Then Esther spoke to Hathach, and gave him a command for Mordecai: ¹¹"All the king's servants and the people of the king's provinces know that any man or woman who goes into ᶠthe inner court to the king, who has not been called, ᵍhe has but one law: put *all* to death, except the one ʰto whom the king holds out the golden scepter, that he may live. Yet I myself have not been ⁱcalled to go in to the king these thirty days." ¹²So they told Mordecai Esther's words.

¹³And Mordecai told *them* to answer Esther: "Do not think in your heart that you will escape in the king's palace any more than all the other Jews. ¹⁴For if you remain completely silent at this time, relief and deliverance will arise for the Jews from another place, but you and your father's house will perish. Yet who knows whether you have come to the kingdom for *such a time as this?*"

¹⁵Then Esther told *them* to reply to Mordecai: ¹⁶"Go, gather all the Jews who are present in Shushan, and fast for me; neither eat nor drink for ʲthree days, night or day. My maids and I will fast likewise. And so I will go to the king, which *is* against the law; ᵏand if I perish, I perish!" ¹⁷So Mordecai went his way and did according to all that Esther commanded him.*

Esther's Banquet

5 Now it happened ᵃon the third day that Esther put on *her* royal *robes* and stood in ᵇthe inner court of the king's palace,

across from the king's house, while the king sat on his royal throne in the royal house, facing the entrance of the house.* ²So it was, when the king saw Queen Esther standing in the court, *that* ᶜshe found favor in his sight, and ᵈthe king held out to Esther the golden scepter that *was* in his hand. Then Esther went near and touched the top of the scepter.

³And the king said to her, "What do you wish, Queen Esther? What *is* your request? ᵉIt shall be given to you—up to half the kingdom!"

⁴So Esther answered, "If it pleases the king, let the king and Haman come today to the banquet that I have prepared for him."

⁵Then the king said, "Bring Haman quickly, that he may do as Esther has said." So the king and Haman went to the banquet that Esther had prepared.

⁶At the banquet of wine ᶠthe king said to Esther, ᵍ"What *is* your petition? It shall be granted you. What *is* your request, up to half the kingdom? It shall be done!"

⁷Then Esther answered and said, "My petition and request *is this:* ⁸If I have found favor in the sight of the king, and if it pleases the king to grant my petition and fulfill my request, then let the king and Haman come to the ʰbanquet which I will prepare for them, and tomorrow I will do as the king has said."

Haman's Plot Against Mordecai

⁹So Haman went out that day ⁱjoyful and with a glad heart; but when Haman saw Mordecai in the king's gate, and ʲthat he did not stand or tremble before him, he was filled with indignation against Mordecai. ¹⁰Nevertheless Haman ᵏrestrained himself and went home, and he sent and called for his friends and his wife Zeresh. ¹¹Then Haman told them of his great riches, ˡthe multitude of his children, everything in which the king had promoted him, and how he

---

* 4:17 Septuagint adds a prayer of Mordecai here.
* 5:1 Septuagint adds many extra details in verses 1 and 2.

4:11 not been called. Esther understood that Mordecai was asking her to risk her life. She would be taking her life into her hands to go uncalled to the king in any circumstances; the fact that she had not been called for a month probably meant that she was even more unsure of her reception.

4:14 for such a time as this. Even though this verse does not directly mention God, Mordecai obviously believed that Esther was made queen through God's design, and she should be acting as God's agent to deliver His people.

4:16 Self-Denial—Even though Esther must have been afraid, knowing that she was breaking the law, she decided to trust God. Her statement "if I perish, I perish," was not despair, but willingness to act however God willed, recognizing that the consequences were in His hands. Self-denial is not easy, but God never fails His children.

5:2 she found favor in his sight. When Esther illegally entered the king's court, he was pleased by her appearance and decided to overlook her offense. In this scene we again see the hand of God.

5:8 tomorrow I will do as the king has said. Why did Esther delay in telling the king her real request? Perhaps she was afraid, and used the intervening time to strengthen her courage. But it seems that here also is God's hand, for the delay provided time for the king's sleepless night and the events that followed.

4:7 ᵈ Esth. 3:9   **4:8** ᵉ Esth. 3:14, 15   **4:11** ᶠ Esth. 5:1; 6:4   ᵍ Dan. 2:9   ʰ Esth. 5:2; 8:4   ⁱ Esth. 2:14   **4:16** ʲ Esth. 5:1   ᵏ Gen. 43:14   **5:1** ᵃ Esth. 4:16   ᵇ Esth. 4:11; 6:4   **5:2** ᶜ [Prov. 21:1]   ᵈ Esth. 4:11; 8:4   **5:3** ᵉ Mark 6:23   **5:6** ᶠ Esth. 7:2   ᵍ Esth. 9:12   **5:8** ʰ Esth. 6:14   **5:9** ⁱ [Job 20:5]   ʲ Esth. 3:5   **5:10** ᵏ 2 Sam. 13:22   **5:11** ˡ Esth. 9:7–10

had *m*advanced him above the officials and servants of the king.

¹²Moreover Haman said, "Besides, Queen Esther invited no one but me to come in with the king to the banquet that she prepared; and tomorrow I am again invited by her, along with the king. ¹³Yet all this avails me nothing, so long as I see Mordecai the Jew sitting at the king's gate."

¹⁴Then his wife Zeresh and all his friends said to him, "Let a *n*gallows be made, fifty cubits high, and in the morning *o*suggest to the king that Mordecai be hanged on it; then go merrily with the king to the banquet."

And the thing pleased Haman; so he had *p*the gallows made.

The King Honors Mordecai

6 That night the king could not sleep. So one was commanded to bring *a*the book of the records of the chronicles; and they were read before the king. ²And it was found written that Mordecai had told of Bigthana and Teresh, two of the king's eunuchs, the doorkeepers who had sought to lay hands on King Ahasuerus. ³Then the king said, "What honor or dignity has been bestowed on Mordecai for this?"

And the king's servants who attended him said, "Nothing has been done for him."

⁴So the king said, "Who *is* in the court?" Now Haman had *just* entered *b*the outer court of the king's palace *c*to suggest that the king hang Mordecai on the gallows that he had prepared for him.

⁵The king's servants said to him, "Haman is there, standing in the court."

And the king said, "Let him come in."

⁶So Haman came in, and the king asked him, "What shall be done for the man whom the king delights to honor?"

Now Haman thought in his heart, "Whom would the king delight to honor more than *d*me?" ⁷And Haman answered the king, "*For* the man whom the king delights to honor, ⁸let a royal robe be brought which the king has worn, and *e*a horse on which the king has ridden, which has a royal crest placed on its head. ⁹Then let this robe and horse be delivered to the hand of one of the king's most noble princes, that he may array the man whom the king delights to honor. Then parade

him on horseback through the city square, *f*and proclaim before him: 'Thus shall it be done to the man whom the king delights to honor!'"

¹⁰Then the king said to Haman, "Hurry, take the robe and the horse, as you have suggested, and do so for Mordecai the Jew who sits within the king's gate! Leave nothing undone of all that you have spoken."

¹¹So Haman took the robe and the horse, arrayed Mordecai and led him on horseback through the city square, and proclaimed before him, "Thus shall it be done to the man whom the king delights to honor!"

¹²Afterward Mordecai went back to the king's gate. But Haman *g*hurried to his house, mourning *h*and with his head covered. ¹³When Haman told his wife Zeresh and all his friends everything that had happened to him, his wise men and his wife Zeresh said to him, "If Mordecai, before whom you have begun to fall, is of Jewish descent, you will not prevail against *i*him but will surely fall before him."

¹⁴While they *were* still talking with him, the king's eunuchs came, and hastened to bring Haman to *j*the banquet which Esther had prepared.

Haman Hanged Instead of Mordecai

7 So the king and Haman went to dine with Queen Esther. ²And on the second day, *a*at the banquet of wine, the king again said to Esther, "What *is* your petition, Queen Esther? It shall be granted you. And what *is* your request, up to half the kingdom? It shall be done!"

³Then Queen Esther answered and said, "If I have found favor in your sight, O king, and if it pleases the king, let my life be given me at my petition, and my people at my request. ⁴For we have been *b*sold, my people and I, to be destroyed, to be killed, and to be annihilated. Had we been sold as *c*male and female slaves, I would have held my tongue, although the enemy could never compensate for the king's loss."

⁵So King Ahasuerus answered and said to Queen Esther, "Who is he, and where is he, who would dare presume in his heart to do such a thing?"

5:14 gallows. The gallows height, 50 cubits, was about 75 feet.

6:1 the king could not sleep. Within this chapter we observe a series of events that point unmistakably to God's sovereign hand. Only because of the "chance happening" of his sleepless night did the king learn of Mordecai's past loyalty.

6:4 had just entered the outer court. Here again is the Lord's hand at work on behalf of His people. No sooner had Mordecai's reward been discussed than Haman appeared in the court.

6:10 Jew. The term "Jew," derived from Judah, came

into use during the exile because the people were primarily from the southern kingdom of Judah.

7:3 my people at my request. Esther disclosed her real identity to the king in her plea for the lives of her people.

5:11 *m* Esth. 3:1 **5:14** *n* Esth. 7:9 *o* Esth. 6:4 *p* Esth. 7:10 **6:1** *a* Esth. 2:23; 10:2 **6:4** *b* Esth. 5:1 *c* Esth. 5:14 **6:6** *d* [Prov. 16:18; 18:12] **6:8** *e* 1 Kin. 1:33 **6:9** *f* Gen. 41:43 **6:12** *g* 2 Chr. 26:20 *h* 2 Sam. 15:30 **6:13** *i* Zech. 2:8 **6:14** *j* Esth. 5:8 **7:2** *a* Esth. 5:6 **7:4** *b* Esth. 3:9; 4:7 *c* Deut. 28:68

⁶And Esther said, "The adversary and ᵈenemy *is* this wicked Haman!"

So Haman was terrified before the king and queen.

⁷Then the king arose in his wrath from the banquet of wine *and went* into the palace garden; but Haman stood before Queen Esther, pleading for his life, for he saw that evil was determined against him by the king. ⁸When the king returned from the palace garden to the place of the banquet of wine, Haman had fallen across ᵉthe couch where Esther *was.* Then the king said, "Will he also assault the queen while I *am* in the house?"

As the word left the king's mouth, they ᶠcovered Haman's face. ⁹Now ᵍHarbonah, one of the eunuchs, said to the king, "Look! ʰThe gallows, fifty cubits high, which Haman made for Mordecai, who spoke ⁱgood on the king's behalf, is standing at the house of Haman."

Then the king said, "Hang him on it!"

¹⁰So ʲthey ᵏhanged Haman on the gallows that he had prepared for Mordecai. Then the king's wrath subsided.

Esther Saves the Jews

8 On that day King Ahasuerus gave Queen Esther the house of Haman, the ᵃenemy of the Jews. And Mordecai came before the king, for Esther had told ᵇhow he *was related* to her. ²So the king took off ᶜhis signet ring, which he had taken from Haman, and gave it to Mordecai; and Esther appointed Mordecai over the house of Haman.

³Now Esther spoke again to the king, fell down at his feet, and implored him with tears to counteract the evil of Haman the Agagite, and the scheme which he had devised against the Jews. ⁴And ᵈthe king held out the golden scepter toward Esther. So Esther arose and stood before the king, ⁵and said, "If it pleases the king, and if I have found favor in his sight and the thing *seems* right to the king and I am pleasing in his eyes, let it be written to revoke the ᵉletters devised by Haman, the son of Hammedatha the Agagite, which he wrote to annihilate the Jews who *are* in all the king's provinces. ⁶For how can I endure to see ᶠthe evil that will come to my people? Or how can I endure to see the destruction of my countrymen?"

⁷Then King Ahasuerus said to Queen Esther and Mordecai the Jew, "Indeed, ᵍI have given Esther the house of Haman, and they have hanged him on the gallows because he *tried to* lay his hand on the Jews. ⁸You yourselves write *a decree* concerning the Jews, as you please, in the king's name, and seal *it* with the king's signet ring; for whatever is written in the king's name and sealed with the king's signet ring ʰno one can revoke.

⁹ⁱSo the king's scribes were called at that time, in the third month, which *is* the month of Sivan, on the twenty-third *day;* and it was written, according to all that Mordecai commanded, to the Jews, the satraps, the governors, and the princes of the provinces ʲfrom India to Ethiopia, one hundred and twenty-seven provinces *in all,* to every province ᵏin its own script, to every people in their own language, and to the Jews in their own script and language. ¹⁰ˡAnd he wrote in the name of King Ahasuerus, sealed *it* with the king's signet ring, and sent letters by couriers on horseback, riding on royal horses bred from swift steeds.*

¹¹By these letters the king permitted the Jews who *were* in every city to ᵐgather together and protect their lives—to ⁿdestroy, kill, and annihilate all the forces of any people or province that would assault them, *both* little children and women, and to plunder their possessions, ¹²ᵒon one day in all the provinces of King Ahasuerus, on the thirteenth *day* of the twelfth month, which *is* the month of Adar.* ¹³ᵖA copy of the document was to be issued as a decree in every province and published for all people, so that the Jews would be ready on that day to avenge themselves on their enemies. ¹⁴The couriers who rode on royal horses went out, hastened and pressed on by the king's command. And the decree was issued in Shushan the citadel.

¹⁵So Mordecai went out from the presence of the king in royal apparel of blue and white, with a great crown of gold and a garment of fine linen and purple; and ᵠthe city of Shushan rejoiced and was glad. ¹⁶The Jews had ʳlight and gladness, joy and honor. ¹⁷And in every province and

---

* **8:10** Literally *sons of the swift horses*
* **8:12** Septuagint adds the text of the letter here.

7:6 *this wicked Haman.* In Haman's evil plan to kill his enemy he had unwittingly threatened the queen's life.

7:8 *covered Haman's face.* The covering of his face signified that he was condemned to death.

8:2 *he had taken from Haman.* Mordecai was given Haman's position as prime minister.

8:8 *no one can revoke.* In the Persian Empire, a royal decree could not be altered, but a second one could be written that effectively invalidated the first.

8:17 *became Jews.* This is the only place in the Old Testament that refers to conversion to Judaism. Before, a person was a Jew if he or she was born so, and now it appears as a religion to which one could convert.

7:6 ᵈ Esth. 3:10   **7:8** ᵉ Esth. 1:6 ᶠ Job 9:24   **7:9** ᵍ Esth. 1:10 ʰ Esth. 5:14 ⁱ Esth. 6:2   **7:10** ʲ [Ps. 7:16; 94:23] ᵏ Dan. 6:24   **8:1** ᵃ Esth. 7:6 ᵇ Esth. 2:7, 15   **8:2** ᶜ Esth. 3:10   **8:4** ᵈ Esth. 4:11; 5:2   **8:5** ᵉ Esth. 3:13   **8:6** ᶠ Neh. 2:3   **8:7** ᵍ Prov. 13:22   **8:8** ʰ Dan. 6:8, 12, 15   **8:9** ⁱ Esth. 3:12 ʲ Esth. 1:1 ᵏ Esth. 1:22; 3:12   **8:10** ˡ 1 Kin. 21:8   **8:11** ᵐ Esth. 9:2 ⁿ Esth. 9:10, 15, 16   **8:12** ᵒ Esth. 3:13; 9:1   **8:13** ᵖ Esth. 3:14, 15   **8:15** ᵠ Prov. 29:2   **8:16** ʳ Ps. 97:11; 112:4

city, wherever the king's command and decree came, the Jews had joy and gladness, a feast ^{s}and a holiday. Then many of the people of the land ^{t}became Jews, because ^{u}fear of the Jews fell upon them.

The Jews Destroy Their Tormentors

9 Now ^{a}in the twelfth month, that *is*, the month of Adar, on the thirteenth day, ^{b}*the time* came for the king's command and his decree to be executed. On the day that the enemies of the Jews had hoped to overpower them, the opposite occurred, in that the Jews themselves ^{c}overpowered those who hated them. ^{2}The Jews ^{d}gathered together in their cities throughout all the provinces of King Ahasuerus to lay hands on those who ^{e}sought their harm. And no one could withstand them, ^{f}because fear of them fell upon all people. ^{3}And all the officials of the provinces, the satraps, the governors, and all those doing the king's work, helped the Jews, because the fear of Mordecai fell upon them. ^{4}For Mordecai *was* great in the king's palace, and his fame spread throughout all the provinces; for this man Mordecai ^{g}became increasingly prominent. ^{5}Thus the Jews defeated all their enemies with the stroke of the sword, with slaughter and destruction, and did what they pleased with those who hated them.

^{6}And in ^{h}Shushan the citadel the Jews killed and destroyed five hundred men. ^{7}Also Parshandatha, Dalphon, Aspatha, ^{8}Poratha, Adalia, Aridatha, ^{9}Parmashta, Arisai, Aridai, and Vajezatha— ^{10}^{i}the ten sons of Haman the son of Hammedatha, the enemy of the Jews—they killed; ^{j}but they did not lay a hand on the plunder.

^{11}On that day the number of those who were killed in Shushan the citadel was brought to the king. ^{12}And the king said to Queen Esther, "The Jews have killed and destroyed five hundred men in Shushan the citadel, and the ten sons of Haman. What have they done in the rest of the king's provinces? Now ^{k}what *is* your petition? It shall be granted to you. Or what *is* your further request? It shall be done."

^{13}Then Esther said, "If it pleases the king, let it be granted to the Jews who *are* in Shushan to do again tomorrow ^{l}according to today's decree, and let Haman's ten sons ^{m}be hanged on the gallows."

^{14}So the king commanded this to be done; the decree was issued in Shushan, and they hanged Haman's ten sons.

^{15}And the Jews who *were* in Shushan ^{n}gathered together again on the fourteenth day of the month of Adar and killed three hundred men at Shushan; ^{o}but they did not lay a hand on the plunder.

^{16}The remainder of the Jews in the king's provinces ^{p}gathered together and protected their lives, had rest from their enemies, and killed seventy-five thousand of their enemies; ^{q}but they did not lay a hand on the plunder. ^{17}*This was* on the thirteenth day of the month of Adar. And on the fourteenth of *the month*[*] they rested and made it a day of feasting and gladness.

The Feast of Purim

^{18}But the Jews who *were* at Shushan assembled together ^{r}on the thirteenth *day*, as well as on the fourteenth; and on the fifteenth of *the month*[*] they rested, and made it a day of feasting and gladness. ^{19}Therefore the Jews of the villages who dwelt in the unwalled towns celebrated the fourteenth day of the month of Adar ^{s}*with* gladness and feasting, ^{t}as a holiday, and for ^{u}sending presents to one another.

^{20}And Mordecai wrote these things and sent letters to all the Jews, near and far, who *were* in all the provinces of King Ahasuerus, ^{21}to establish among them that they should celebrate yearly the fourteenth and fifteenth days of the month of Adar, ^{22}as the days on which the Jews had rest from their enemies, as the month which was turned from sorrow to joy for them, and from mourning to a holiday; that they should make them days of feasting and joy, of ^{v}sending presents to one another and gifts to the ^{w}poor. ^{23}So the Jews accepted the custom which they had begun, as Mordecai had written to them, ^{24}because Haman, the son of Hammedatha the Agagite, the enemy of all the Jews, ^{x}had plotted against the Jews to annihilate them, and had cast Pur (that *is*, the lot), to consume them and destroy them; ^{25}but ^{y}when *Esther*[*] came before the king, he commanded by letter that this[*] wicked plot which *Haman* had devised against the Jews should ^{z}return on his own head, and that he and his sons should be hanged on the gallows.

^{26}So they called these days Purim, after the name Pur. Therefore, because of all the words of ^{a}this letter, what they had

*9:17 Literally *it* • *9:18 Literally *it* • *9:25 Literally *she* or *it* • Literally *his*

9:7–10 ten sons of Haman. The patterns of reprisal and revenge were so deeply ingrained in the culture of the ancient Middle East that the survival of even one of these sons might mean trouble for the next generation of Jews.

9:26–28 Purim. Purim (from the word *pur,* referring to the lots Haman cast to determine the best day for destroying the Jews; 3:7) reminds the Jews of God's deliverance from their day of destruction.

8:17 ^{s} Esth. 9:19 ^{t} Ps. 18:43 ^{u} Gen. 35:5   **9:1** ^{a} Esth. 8:12 ^{b} Esth. 3:13 ^{c} 2 Sam. 22:41   **9:2** ^{d} Esth. 8:11; 9:15–18 ^{e} Ps. 71:13, 14 ^{f} Esth. 8:17   **9:4** ^{g} 2 Sam. 3:1   **9:6** ^{h} Esth. 1:2; 3:15; 4:16   **9:10** ^{i} Esth. 5:11; 9:7–10 ^{j} Esth. 8:11 **9:12** ^{k} Esth. 5:6; 7:2   **9:13** ^{l} Esth. 8:11; 9:15 ^{m} 2 Sam. 21:6, 9   **9:15** ^{n} Esth. 8:11; 9:2 ^{o} Esth. 9:10   **9:16** ^{p} Esth. 9:2 ^{q} Esth. 8:11   **9:18** ^{r} Esth. 9:11, 15   **9:19** ^{s} Deut. 16:11, 14 ^{t} Esth. 8:16, 17 ^{u} Neh. 8:10, 12   **9:22** ^{v} Neh. 8:10 ^{w} [Deut. 15:7–11]   **9:24** ^{x} Esth. 3:6, 7; 9:26   **9:25** ^{y} Esth. 7:4–10; 8:3; 9:13, 14 ^{z} Esth. 7:10   **9:26** ^{a} Esth. 9:20

seen concerning this matter, and what had happened to them, [27]the Jews established and imposed it upon themselves and their descendants and all who would [b]join them, that without fail they should celebrate these two days every year, according to the written *instructions* and according to the *prescribed* time, [28]*that* these days *should be* remembered and kept throughout every generation, every family, every province, and every city, that these days of Purim should not fail *to be observed* among the Jews, and *that* the memory of them should not perish among their descendants.

[29]Then Queen Esther, [c]the daughter of Abihail, with Mordecai the Jew, wrote with full authority to confirm this [d]second letter about Purim. [30]And *Mordecai* sent letters to all the Jews, to [e]the one hundred and twenty-seven provinces of the kingdom of Ahasuerus, *with* words of peace and truth, [31]to confirm these days of Purim at their *appointed* time, as Mordecai the Jew and Queen Esther had prescribed for them,

and as they had decreed for themselves and their descendants concerning matters of their [f]fasting and lamenting. [32]So the decree of Esther confirmed these matters of Purim, and it was written in the book.

Mordecai's Advancement

10 And King Ahasuerus imposed tribute on the land and *on* [a]the islands of the sea. [2]Now all the acts of his power and his might, and the account of the greatness of Mordecai, [b]to which the king advanced him, *are* they not written in the book of the [c]chronicles of the kings of Media and Persia? [3]For Mordecai the Jew *was* [d]second to King Ahasuerus, and was great among the Jews and well received by the multitude of his brethren, [e]seeking the good of his people and speaking peace to all his countrymen.*

---

* **10:3** Literally *seed.* Septuagint and Vulgate add a dream of Mordecai here; Vulgate adds six more chapters.

9:27 [b] Esth. 8:17 **9:29** [c] Esth. 2:15 [d]Esth. 8:10; 9:20, 21 **9:30** [e] Esth. 1:1 **9:31** [f] Esth. 4:3, 16 **10:1** [a]Is. 11:11;

24:15 **10:2** [b] Esth. 8:15; 9:4 [c] Esth. 6:1 **10:3** [d]Gen. 41:40, 43, 44 [e]Neh. 2:10

THE BOOK OF
JOB

▶ **AUTHOR:** The author of Job is unknown and there are no textual hints as to his identity. The non-Hebraic cultural background may point to a Gentile authorship, but an interesting school of thought maintains that Moses may have written this book. The land of Uz (1:1) is directly adjacent to Midian, where Moses lived for 40 years. Perhaps the oldest book of the Bible, set in the time of the patriarchs (Abraham, Isaac, Jacob, and Joseph), it is conceivable that Moses obtained a record of the dialogue left by Job or Elihu.

▶ **TIME:** Unknown   ▶ **KEY VERSE:** Job 13:15

▶ **THEME:** There are many things that set Job apart from the rest of Scripture. Its dramatic format is unique. It is a story that is not part of the flow of the history of Israel. And the thematic focus is narrower than other books of its size. A classic work of literature, its primary subject matter is the most basic question man has of God: Why do we suffer? The Book of Job is the biblical text that addresses this issue head-on, and the dramatic nature of the story intensifies the conflict of ideas and understanding between God and man.

Job and His Family in Uz

1 There was a man *a*in the land of Uz, whose name *was* *b*Job; and that man was *c*blameless and upright, and one who *d*feared God and shunned evil. 2And seven sons and three daughters were born to him. 3Also, his possessions were seven thousand sheep, three thousand camels, five hundred yoke of oxen, and five hundred female donkeys, and a very large household, so that this man was the greatest of all the people of the East.

4And his sons would go and feast *in their* houses, each on his *appointed* day, and would send and invite their three sisters to eat and drink with them. 5So it was, when the days of feasting had run their course, that Job would send and sanctify them, and he would rise early in the morning *e*and offer burnt offerings *according to* the number of them all. For Job said, "It may be that my sons have sinned and *f*cursed* God in their hearts." Thus Job did regularly.

Satan Attacks Job's Character

6Now *g*there was a day when the sons of God came to present themselves before the LORD, and Satan* also came among them. 7And the LORD said to Satan, "From where do you come?"

---

* **1:5** Literally *blessed*, but used here in the evil sense, and so in verse 11 and 2:5, 9   * **1:6** Literally *the Adversary*, and so throughout this book

---

1:1 Uz. The precise location of Uz is unknown, but it may have been near Edom. Some of the other towns and peoples mentioned in this book are known to have been located near Edom, so it is logical to assume that Uz was in the same area.

1:2 Why Do We Suffer?—Scripture points us to multiple reasons for suffering. Here, as in Job's case, suffering somehow is involved in God's purposes, and we are to learn from it. The New Testament echoes this teaching in James 1 where it says to "count it all joy when you fall into various trials, knowing that the testing of your faith produces patience" (James 1:2–3). Suffering also happens as a result of our own sin. David suffered many family trials because of his sin with Bathsheba. Other times we suffer directly because of our faith, as martyrs have done for centuries. Sometimes living out our faith comes in direct conflict with the ruling powers, and we suffer because of it. Still other times we suffer because we

live in a fallen world where things go wrong or natural disasters occur.

Both Peter and Paul advise us to commit our pain and suffering to God, realizing He is faithful to work out all things for our good and God's glory (Rom. 8:28; 1 Pet. 4:9). This lesson is often learned over a whole lifetime as we see in numerous psalms and in the lives of many biblical characters.

1:6 the sons of God. Celestial beings or angels are called "sons of God" because they had no parents. They were created by God to serve Him (2:1; 4:18; Ps. 103:20). This can also mean a group of saints (Gen. 6:2). Adam was also called "the son of God" (Luke 3:38) because God was his Creator rather than having a human father and mother. Here Satan is said

---

1:1 *a* 1 Chr. 1:17 *b* Ezek. 14:14, 20 *c* Gen. 6:9; 17:1 *d* [Prov. 16:6]   **1:5** *e* [Job 42:8] *f* 1 Kin. 21:10, 13   **1:6** *g* Job 2:1

So Satan answered the LORD and said, "From [h]going to and fro on the earth, and from walking back and forth on it."

8 Then the LORD said to Satan, "Have you considered My servant Job, that *there is* none like him on the earth, a blameless and upright man, one who fears God and shuns evil?"

9 So Satan answered the LORD and said, "Does Job fear God for nothing? 10[i]Have You not made a hedge around him, around his household, and around all that he has on every side? [j]You have blessed the work of his hands, and his possessions have increased in the land. 11[k]But now, stretch out Your hand and touch all that he has, and he will surely [l]curse You to Your face!"

12 And the LORD said to Satan, "Behold, all that he has *is* in your power; only do not lay a hand on his *person.*"

So Satan went out from the presence of the LORD.

Job Loses His Property and Children

13 Now there was a day [m]when his sons and daughters *were* eating and drinking wine in their oldest brother's house; 14 and a messenger came to Job and said, "The oxen were plowing and the donkeys feeding beside them, 15 when the Sabeans* raided *them* and took them away—indeed they have killed the servants with the edge of the sword; and I alone have escaped to tell you!"

16 While he *was* still speaking, another also came and said, "The fire of God fell from heaven and burned up the sheep and the servants, and consumed them; and I alone have escaped to tell you!"

17 While he *was* still speaking, another also came and said, "The Chaldeans formed three bands, raided the camels and took them away, yes, and killed the servants with the edge of the sword; and I alone have escaped to tell you!"

18 While he *was* still speaking, another also came and said, [n]"Your sons and daughters *were* eating and drinking wine in their oldest brother's house, 19 and suddenly a great wind came from across* the wilderness and struck the four corners of the house, and it fell on the young people, and they are dead; and I alone have escaped to tell you!"

20 Then Job arose, [o]tore his robe, and shaved his head; and he [p]fell to the ground and worshiped. 21 And he said:

[q]"Naked I came from my mother's womb,
   And naked shall I return there.
The LORD [r]gave, and the LORD has
   [s]taken away;
[t]Blessed be the name of the LORD."

22[u]In all this Job did not sin nor charge God with wrong.

Satan Attacks Job's Health

2 Again [a]there was a day when the sons of God came to present themselves before the LORD, and Satan came also among them to present himself before the LORD. 2 And the LORD said to Satan, "From where do you come?"

* **1:15** Literally *Sheba* (compare 6:19) * **1:19** Septuagint omits *across.*

---

to be among them. **Satan.** At some point after creation, Satan, who was the highest created angel (Ezek. 28:12–15), aspired to be as God Himself (Is. 14:13–14). As a result, he was barred from his heavenly position (Ezek. 28:16) and took a large number of angels with him in his rebellion, over whom he rules (Matt. 12:24). Jesus said that He saw Satan fall from heaven (Luke 10:18), but this chapter in Job, and the incident of the lying spirit with the false prophets of Ahab (2 Chr. 18:8–22), indicate that Satan still has access to heaven and heavenly counsels. God can and does limit Satan (1:12). The cross defeated Satan (John 12:31), but the final judgment will not occur until the end of the millennium (Rev. 20:10). In the meantime, Satan tries to thwart and defeat the work of God. God sometimes uses Satan to teach a lesson (1 Chr. 21; 2 Cor. 12:7–10), but it is still God who is in control.
1:7 the LORD. The Hebrew word Yahweh, usually translated "the LORD," is the personal name of the true God of the Old Testament (Ex. 3:14–15). It is the particular name of God in covenantal relations with His people Israel (Ex. 6:1–6; 19:3–8).
1:8 *a blameless and upright man.* The Lord was not saying that Job was sinless, but He was saying that Job had his priorities right. Job feared the Lord and it showed in his life.
1:10 hedge. No harm could come to Job unless the

Lord permitted it (v. 12). Believers today should take great comfort from the biblical teaching that the Lord protects His people—whether by a cloud (Ex. 14:19–20), or by a wall of fiery chariots (2 Kin. 6:17), or through guardian angels (Heb. 1:14).
1:11 curse. The sin of cursing God is a pivotal issue for the Book of Job. Job feared that his children might think or speak irreverently of God (v. 5). But Satan asserted that Job would surely curse God if his prosperity and blessings were removed. Even Job's wife urged him to "curse God and die" (2:9).
1:15 Sabeans. The Sabeans were nomadic raiders from Sheba, probably located in southwestern Arabia, in present-day Yemen.
1:17 Chaldeans. The Chaldeans were part of various west Semitic marauding tribes active in the middle Euphrates from the twelfth to the ninth centuries B.C. They migrated eastward into Assyria and then Babylonia, and were the forerunners of the Chaldean or neo-Babylonian dynasty established by Nebuchadnezzar's father.

1:7 [h] [1 Pet. 5:8] **1:10** [i] Ps. 34:7 [j] [Prov. 10:22]
1:11 [k] Job 2:5; 19:21 [l] Is. 8:21 **1:13** [m] [Eccl. 9:12]
1:18 [n] Job 1:4, 13 **1:20** [o] Gen. 37:29, 34 [p] [1 Pet. 5:6]
1:21 [q] [Eccl. 5:15] [r] [James 1:17] [s] Gen. 31:16 [t] Eph. 5:20
1:22 [u] Job 2:10 **2:1** [a] Job 1:6–8

[b]Satan answered the LORD and said, "From going to and fro on the earth, and from walking back and forth on it."

3Then the LORD said to Satan, "Have you considered My servant Job, that *there is* none like him on the earth, [c]a blameless and upright man, one who fears God and shuns evil? And still he [d]holds fast to his integrity, although you incited Me against him, [e]to destroy him without cause."

4So Satan answered the LORD and said, "Skin for skin! Yes, all that a man has he will give for his life. 5But stretch out Your hand now, and touch his [g]bone and his flesh, and he will surely curse You to Your face!"

6[h]And the LORD said to Satan, "Behold, he *is* in your hand, but spare his life."

7So Satan went out from the presence of the LORD, and struck Job with painful boils [i]from the sole of his foot to the crown of his head. 8And he took for himself a potsherd with which to scrape himself [j]while he sat in the midst of the ashes.

9Then his wife said to him, "Do you still hold fast to your integrity? Curse God and die!"

10But he said to her, "You speak as one of the foolish women speaks. [k]Shall we indeed accept good from God, and shall we not accept adversity?" [l]In all this Job did not [m]sin with his lips.

Job's Three Friends

11Now when Job's three friends heard of all this adversity that had come upon him, each one came from his own place—Eliphaz the [n]Temanite, Bildad the [o]Shuhite, and Zophar the Naamathite. For they had made an appointment together to come [p]and mourn with him, and to comfort him. 12And when they raised their eyes from afar, and did not recognize him, they lifted their voices and wept; and each one tore his robe and [q]sprinkled dust on his head toward heaven. 13So they sat down with him on the ground [r]seven days and seven nights, and no one spoke a word

to him, for they saw that *his* grief was very great.

Job Deplores His Birth

3 After this Job opened his mouth and cursed the day of his *birth*. 2And Job spoke, and said:

3 "May[a] the day perish on which I was born,
   And the night *in which* it was said,
   'A male child is conceived.'
4 May that day be darkness;
   May God above not seek it,
   Nor the light shine upon it.
5 May darkness and [b]the shadow of death claim it;
   May a cloud settle on it;
   May the blackness of the day terrify it.
6 *As for* that night, may darkness seize it;
   May it not rejoice* among the days of the year,
   May it not come into the number of the months.
7 Oh, may that night be barren!
   May no joyful shout come into it!
8 May those curse it who curse the day,
   Those [c]who are ready to arouse Leviathan.
9 May the stars of its morning be dark;
   May it look for light, but *have* none,
   And not see the dawning of the day;
10 Because it did not shut up the doors of my *mother's* womb,
   Nor hide sorrow from my eyes.

11 "Why[d] did I not die at birth?
   Why did I *not* perish when I came from the womb?
12 [e]Why did the knees receive me?
   Or why the breasts, that I should nurse?
13 For now I would have lain still and been quiet,
   I would have been asleep;
   Then I would have been at rest

---

* 3:6 Septuagint, Syriac, Targum, and Vulgate read *be joined.*

2:10 *good … adversity.* This comment of Job's is one of the central themes of the whole book. A person of faith will trust in God through prosperity or adversity, even if they are unable to understand why bad things happen (Hab. 3:17–19).

2:11 *Temanite . . . Shuhite . . . Naamathite.* A Temanite was probably an Edomite from Teman in northern Edom, and a Naamathite probably came from Naameh, a mountainous area in northwestern Arabia. From this context, it can be assumed that a Shuhite was also a person from a certain town, unknown in modern times.

3:1 *cursed the day.* The Hebrew word for "cursed," meaning "to hold in contempt," is elsewhere employed of cursing God (Ex. 22:28; Lev. 24:15) or cursing one's parents (Ex. 21:17). Job expressed a strong malediction against the day of his birth and the night of his conception, but he did not

commit blasphemy. He did not curse the Chaldeans, or Sabeans, much less God. Neither did he express thoughts of suicide.

3:8 *curse.* Job employed two separate Hebrew words translated "curse," different from the term in verse 1. He wished that the popular magicians who cast spells on the day for their clients could have cast a spell on his day so that he never could have been born. He was not endorsing pagan magic, but was speaking vividly and forcefully to express his agony and despair.

2:2 [b] Job 1:7   **2:3** [c] Job 1:1, 8 [d] Job 27:5, 6 [e] Job 9:17
2:5 [f] Job 1:11 [g] Job 19:20   **2:6** [h] Job 1:12   **2:7** [i] Is. 1:6
2:8 [j] Ezek. 27:30   **2:10** [k] Job 1:21, 22 [l] Job 1:22 [m] Ps. 39:1
2:11 [n] Gen. 36:11 [o] Gen. 25:2 [p] Rom. 12:15   **2:12** [q] Neh. 9:1
2:13 [r] Gen. 50:10   **3:3** [a] Jer. 20:14–18   **3:5** [b] Jer. 13:16
3:8 [c] Jer. 9:17   **3:11** [d] Job 10:18, 19   **3:12** [e] Gen. 30:3

14 With kings and counselors of the
earth,
Who *f*built ruins for themselves,
15 Or with princes who had gold,
Who filled their houses *with* silver;
16 Or *why* was I not hidden *g*like a
stillborn child,
Like infants who never saw light?
17 There the wicked cease *from*
troubling,
And there the weary are at *h*rest.
18 *There* the prisoners rest together;
*i*They do not hear the voice of the
oppressor.
19 The small and great are there,
And the servant *is* free from his
master.

20 "Why*j* is light given to him who is in
misery,
And life to the *k*bitter of soul,
21 Who *l*long for death, but it does not
come,
And search for it more than *m*hidden
treasures;
22 Who rejoice exceedingly,
And are glad when they can find the
*n*grave?
23 *Why is light given* to a man whose
way is hidden,
*o*And whom God has hedged in?
24 For my sighing comes before I eat,*
And my groanings pour out like water.
25 For the thing I greatly *p*feared has
come upon me,
And what I dreaded has happened
to me.
26 I am not at ease, nor am I quiet;
I have no rest, for trouble comes."

Eliphaz: Job Has Sinned

4 Then Eliphaz the Temanite answered
and said:

2 "*If* one attempts a word with you, will
you become weary?
But who can withhold himself from
speaking?
3 Surely you have instructed many,
And you *a*have strengthened weak
hands.

4 Your words have upheld him who was
stumbling,
And you *b*have strengthened the feeble
knees;
5 But now it comes upon you, and you
are weary;
It touches you, and you are troubled.
6 *Is* not *c*your reverence *d*your
confidence?
And the integrity of your ways your
hope?

7 "Remember now, *e*who *ever* perished
being innocent?
Or where were the upright *ever* cut
off?
8 Even as I have seen,
*f*Those who plow iniquity
And sow trouble reap the same.
9 By the blast of God they perish,
And by the breath of His anger they
are consumed.
10 The roaring of the lion,
The voice of the fierce lion,
And *g*the teeth of the young lions are
broken.
11 *h*The old lion perishes for lack of prey,
And the cubs of the lioness are
scattered.

12 "Now a word was secretly brought to
me,
And my ear received a whisper of it.
13 *i*In disquieting thoughts from the
visions of the night,
When deep sleep falls on men,
14 Fear came upon me, and *j*trembling,
Which made all my bones shake.
15 Then a spirit passed before my face;
The hair on my body stood up.
16 It stood still,
But I could not discern its appearance.
A form *was* before my eyes;
There was silence;
Then I heard a voice *saying:*
17 'Can a mortal be more righteous than
God?
Can a man be more pure than his
Maker?

---

* **3:24** Literally *my bread*

3:20–22 long for death. Even though Job longed for
death, he was not considering suicide. The context of
the other passages indicates that Job merely wished
that the Lord would let him die (7:15–21; 10:18–22).
3:23 whom God has hedged in. The irony is that Job
perceived God's hedge as keeping him from a desirable
death instead of seeing it as God's protection of his life.
4:7 who ever perished being innocent. Eliphaz concluded that since Job was suffering, he must have
sin in his life. Eliphaz supported the retribution doctrine: God supports the righteous but abandons the
wicked.
4:8 sow trouble reap the same. It can be true that
planting wicked actions will yield a crop of trauma,
but the converse is not necessarily true. Hard times
can come to anyone, and the crop that is harvested in

hard times depends on whether or not we continue
to follow God in times of trouble.
4:13 visions of the night. Eliphaz appealed to a
vision to authenticate his theology, but all dreams
do not come from God. The reader of this book has
different information, for God pulled aside the curtain of heaven to reveal the true background for Job's
troubles.

3:14 *f* Job 15:28 **3:16** *g* Ps. 58:8 **3:17** *h* Job 17:16
3:18 *i* Job 39:7 **3:20** *j* Jer. 20:18 *k* 2 Kin. 4:27 **3:21** *l* Rev.
9:6 *m* Prov. 2:4 **3:22** *n* Job 7:15, 16 **3:23** *o* Job 19:8
3:25 *p* [Job 9:28; 30:15] **4:3** *a* Is. 35:3 **4:4** *b* Is. 35:3
4:6 *c* Job 1:1 *d* Prov. 3:26 **4:7** *e* [Ps. 37:25] **4:8** *f* [Prov.
22:8] **4:10** *g* Ps. 58:6 **4:11** *h* Ps. 34:10 **4:13** *i* Job
33:15 **4:14** *j* Hab. 3:16

18 If He ᵏputs no trust in His servants,
If He charges His angels with error,
19 How much more those who dwell in
houses of clay,
Whose foundation is in the dust,
Who are crushed before a moth?
20 ˡThey are broken in pieces from
morning till evening;
They perish forever, with no one
regarding.
21 Does not their own excellence go
away?
They die, even without wisdom.'

Eliphaz: Job Is Chastened by God

5 "Call out now;
Is there anyone who will answer you?
And to which of the holy ones will
you turn?
2 For wrath kills a foolish man,
And envy slays a simple one.
3 ᵃI have seen the foolish taking root,
But suddenly I cursed his dwelling
place.
4 His sons are ᵇfar from safety,
They are crushed in the gate,
And ᶜ*there is* no deliverer.
5 Because the hungry eat up his harvest,
Taking it even from the thorns,*
And a snare snatches their substance.*
6 For affliction does not come from the
dust,
Nor does trouble spring from the
ground;
7 Yet man is ᵈborn to trouble,
As the sparks fly upward.
8 "But as for me, I would seek God,
And to God I would commit my
cause—
9 Who does great things, and
unsearchable,
Marvelous things without number.
10 ᵉHe gives rain on the earth,
And sends waters on the fields.
11 ᶠHe sets on high those who are lowly,
And those who mourn are lifted to
safety.

12 ᵍHe frustrates the devices of the crafty,
So that their hands cannot carry out
their plans.
13 He catches the ʰwise in their own
craftiness,
And the counsel of the cunning comes
quickly upon them.
14 They meet with darkness in the
daytime,
And grope at noontime as in the night.
15 But ⁱHe saves the needy from the
sword,
From the mouth of the mighty,
And from their hand.
16 ʲSo the poor have hope,
And injustice shuts her mouth.
17 "Behold,ᵏ happy *is* the man whom God
corrects;
Therefore do not despise the
chastening of the Almighty.
18 ˡFor He bruises, but He binds up;
He wounds, but His hands make
whole.
19 ᵐHe shall deliver you in six troubles,
Yes, in seven ⁿno evil shall touch you.
20 ᵒIn famine He shall redeem you from
death,
And in war from the power of the
sword.
21 ᵖYou shall be hidden from the scourge
of the tongue,
And you shall not be afraid of
destruction when it comes.
22 You shall laugh at destruction and
famine,
And ᑫyou shall not be afraid of the
ʳbeasts of the earth.
23 ˢFor you shall have a covenant with the
stones of the field,
And the beasts of the field shall be at
peace with you.

---

*5:5 Septuagint reads *They shall not be taken
from evil men;* Vulgate reads *And the armed man
shall take him by violence.* • Septuagint reads
The might shall draw them off; Vulgate reads *And
the thirsty shall drink up their riches.*

4:19 Death—We live in houses of clay, and our foundations are in the dust. We may presume upon tomorrow, having illusions of permanence, but suddenly the cords of our tent are pulled up and our existence collapses. We perish, more readily than a moth encircling a flame. Surely the transience of life, the reality of death, and the certainty of judgment should move us to pray that the Eternal God will teach us to number our days so we can use them wisely (Ps. 90:12). This awareness gives us a sense of urgency in turning from sin and serving our Savior.

5:17 chastening. Eliphaz insinuated that since Job's suffering was a result of God's discipline for his sin, Job should not reject what God was trying to teach him. While it is true that God sometimes disciplines people for their own good (Prov. 3:11–12; Heb. 12:7), Eliphaz was suggesting that trouble in one's life necessarily means that one is being disciplined. Once again, the reader of this book has insight that the

participants in the story do not have. Job's troubles do indeed teach him more about God, but the troubles originated because God was showing Satan that His followers are not following Him for what they get, but because of who He is.

5:23 covenant with the stones of the field. Stones in the field are a significant hindrance to farming, just as wild animals or lack of rain are a hindrance. Eliphaz was saying that one who accepts the discipline of the Almighty will not find himself fighting the

---

4:18 ᵏ Job 15:15   4:20 ˡ Ps. 90:5, 6   5:3 ᵃ Jer.
12:1–3   5:4 ᵇ Ps. 119:155   ᶜ Ps. 109:12   5:7 ᵈ Job 14:1
5:10 ᵉ [Job 36:27–29; 37:6–11; 38:26]   5:11 ᶠ Ps. 113:7
5:12 ᵍ Neh. 4:15   5:13 ʰ [1 Cor. 3:19]   5:15 ⁱ Ps. 35:10
5:16 ʲ 1 Sam. 2:8   5:17 ᵏ Ps. 94:12   5:18 ˡ [1 Sam. 2:6,
7]   5:19 ᵐ Ps. 34:19; 91:3   ⁿ Ps. 91:10   5:20 ᵒ Ps. 33:19,
20; 37:19   5:21 ᵖ Ps. 31:20   5:22 ᑫ Ezek. 34:25   ʳ Hos.
2:18   5:23 ˢ Ps. 91:12

24 You shall know that your tent *is* in peace;
   You shall visit your dwelling and find nothing amiss.
25 You shall also know that ᵗyour descendants *shall be* many,
   And your offspring ᵘlike the grass of the earth.
26 ᵛYou shall come to the grave at a full age,
   As a sheaf of grain ripens in its season.
27 Behold, this we have ʷsearched out;
   It *is* true.
   Hear it, and know for yourself."

Job: My Complaint Is Just

6 Then Job answered and said:

2 "Oh, that my grief were fully weighed,
   And my calamity laid with it on the scales!
3 For then it would be heavier than the sand of the sea—
   Therefore my words have been rash.
4 ᵃFor the arrows of the Almighty *are* within me;
   My spirit drinks in their poison;
   ᵇThe terrors of God are arrayed ᶜagainst me.
5 Does the ᵈwild donkey bray when it has grass,
   Or does the ox low over its fodder?
6 Can flavorless food be eaten without salt?
   Or is there *any* taste in the white of an egg?
7 My soul refuses to touch them;
   They *are* as loathsome food to me.
8 "Oh, that I might have my request,
   That God would grant *me* the thing that I long for!
9 That it would please God to crush me,
   That He would loose His hand and ᵉcut me off!
10 Then I would still have comfort;
   Though in anguish I would exult,

He will not spare;
   For ᶠI have not concealed the words of ᵍthe Holy One.
11 "What strength do I have, that I should hope?
   And what *is* my end, that I should prolong my life?
12 *Is* my strength the strength of stones?
   Or is my flesh bronze?
13 *Is* my help not within me?
   And is success driven from me?
14 "To ʰ him who is afflicted, kindness *should be shown* by his friend,
   Even though he forsakes the fear of the Almighty.
15 ⁱMy brothers have dealt deceitfully like a brook,
   ʲLike the streams of the brooks that pass away,
16 Which are dark because of the ice,
   And into which the snow vanishes.
17 When it is warm, they cease to flow;
   When it is hot, they vanish from their place.
18 The paths of their way turn aside,
   They go nowhere and perish.
19 The caravans of ᵏTema look,
   The travelers of ˡSheba hope for them.
20 They are ᵐdisappointed because they were confident;
   They come there and are confused.
21 For now ⁿyou are nothing,
   You see terror and ᵒare afraid.
22 Did I ever say, 'Bring *something* to me'?
   Or, 'Offer a bribe for me from your wealth'?
23 Or, 'Deliver me from the enemy's hand'?
   Or, 'Redeem me from the hand of oppressors'?
24 "Teach me, and I will hold my tongue;
   Cause me to understand wherein I have erred.
25 How forceful are right words!
   But what does your arguing prove?

---

elements of nature. It is true that God is a deliverer, a healer, and one who disciplines His followers. We can safely trust Him to care for us. But having disaster, wounds, or failure is not necessarily a sign of God's discipline.

6:9 Prayer—Job thought it would be better to die than to endure all the pain and suffering that resulted from the tragedies he had experienced. He could not know that the fact that he was alive was actually because God had protected him. This prayer should be a great comfort to believers. We cannot always see God's hedge of protection in a traumatic situation. We can cry out for relief, when God wants us to endure. He knows far more about our situation than we do, and we can trust Him, even as we anguish over unanswered prayer.

6:10 *still have comfort.* Job's single comfort was that he had not denied God, even though he believed that God was the one who had wounded him.

6:15 *streams of the brooks that pass away.* A brook is a stream that only carries water during the rainy season. Other times of the year it is a dry path. Job was likening his friends to a dry stream.

6:24 *Cause me to understand wherein.* If Job's friends could show him error in his ways, Job was willing to listen. The problem was that Job's friends were reasoning backwards. They were assuming that they knew his error, based on the extent of Job's suffering. But they had their formula wrong. Sinners may suffer, but suffering does not equal sin or the Lord's discipline.

5:25 ᵗ Ps. 112:2 ᵘ Ps. 72:16 **5:26** ᵛ [Prov. 9:11; 10:27] **5:27** ʷ Ps. 111:2 **6:4** ᵃ Ps. 38:2 ᵇ Ps. 88:15, 16 ᶜ Job 30:15 **6:5** ᵈ Job 39:5–8 **6:9** ᵉ Job 7:16; 9:21; 10:1 **6:10** ᶠ Acts 20:20 ᵍ [Is. 57:15] **6:14** ʰ [Prov. 17:17] **6:15** ⁱ Ps. 38:11 ʲ Jer. 15:18 **6:19** ᵏ Gen. 25:15 ˡ 1 Kin. 10:1 **6:20** ᵐ Jer. 14:3 **6:21** ⁿ Job 13:4 ᵒ Ps. 38:11

26 Do you intend to rebuke *my* words,
 And the speeches of a desperate one,
 which are as wind?
27 Yes, you overwhelm the fatherless,
 And you ᵖundermine your friend.
28 Now therefore, be pleased to look at
 me;
 For I would never lie to your face.
29 ᵃYield now, let there be no injustice!
 Yes, concede, my ʳrighteousness still
 stands!
30 Is there injustice on my tongue?
 Cannot my taste discern the
 unsavory?

Job: My Suffering Is Comfortless

7 "*Is there* not ᵃa time of hard service for
 man on earth?
 Are not his days also like the days of a
 hired man?
2 Like a servant who earnestly desires
 the shade,
 And like a hired man who eagerly
 looks for his wages,
3 So I have been allotted ᵇmonths of
 futility,
 And wearisome nights have been
 appointed to me.
4 ᶜWhen I lie down, I say, 'When shall I
 arise,
 And the night be ended?'
 For I have had my fill of tossing till
 dawn.
5 My flesh is ᵈcaked with worms and
 dust,
 My skin is cracked and breaks out
 afresh.
6 "Myᵉ days are swifter than a weaver's
 shuttle,
 And are spent without hope.
7 Oh, remember that ᶠmy life *is* a
 breath!
 My eye will never again see good.
8 ᵍThe eye of him who sees me will see
 me no *more*;
 While your eyes *are* upon me, I shall
 no longer *be*.
9 *As* the cloud disappears and vanishes
 away,
 So ʰhe who goes down to the grave
 does not come up.
10 He shall never return to his house,
 ⁱNor shall his place know him
 anymore.

11 "Therefore I will ʲnot restrain my
 mouth;
 I will speak in the anguish of my spirit;
 I will ᵏcomplain in the bitterness of
 my soul.
12 *Am* I a sea, or a sea serpent,
 That You set a guard over me?
13 ˡWhen I say, 'My bed will comfort me,
 My couch will ease my complaint,'
14 Then You scare me with dreams
 And terrify me with visions,
15 So that my soul chooses strangling
 And death rather than my body.*
16 ᵐI loathe *my* life;
 I would not live forever.
 ⁿLet me alone,
 For ᵒmy days *are but* a breath.

17 "Whatᵖ *is* man, that You should exalt
 him,
 That You should set Your heart on
 him,
18 That You should visit him every
 morning,
 And test him every moment?
19 How long?
 Will You not look away from me,
 And let me alone till I swallow my
 saliva?
20 Have I sinned?
 What have I done to You, ᵠO watcher
 of men?
 Why ʳhave You set me as Your target,
 So that I am a burden to myself?*
21 Why then do You not pardon my
 transgression,
 And take away my iniquity?
 For now I will lie down in the dust,
 And You will seek me diligently,
 But I *will* no longer *be*."

Bildad: Job Should Repent

8 Then Bildad the Shuhite answered and
 said:

2 "How long will you speak these *things*,
 And the words of your mouth *be like* a
 strong wind?
3 ᵃDoes God subvert judgment?
 Or does the Almighty pervert justice?
4 If ᵇyour sons have sinned against
 Him,

---

* **7:15** Literally *my bones*   * **7:20** Following Masoretic Text, Targum, and Vulgate; Septuagint and Jewish tradition read *to You.*

7:6 hope. Job's choice of the word "hope" in the context of the weaver's shuttle may convey a double meaning. The Hebrew word for "hope" sounds like the Hebrew word that means "thread" or "cord."

7:20 What have I done to You. Job, too, was assuming that his troubles came from God. Job did not believe that he had sinned in a way that would cause God to bring trouble on him. This may sound presumptuous, as if Job thought he was without any sin at all. But we remember that God Himself referred to Job as upright and blameless. God was not finding fault with the way that Job was living out his life of faith in God.

8:3 Does God subvert judgment? Bildad was saying that Job and his children received what they deserved.

6:27 ᵖ Ps. 57:6   **6:29** ᵠ Job 17:10   ʳ Job 27:5, 6; 34:5
7:1 ᵃ [Job 14:5, 13, 14]   **7:3** ᵇ [Job 15:31]   **7:4** ᶜ Deut.
28:67   **7:5** ᵈ Is. 14:11   **7:6** ᵉ Job 9:25; 16:22; 17:11
7:7 ᶠ Ps. 78:39; 89:47   **7:8** ᵍ Job 8:18; 20:9   **7:9** ʰ 2 Sam.
12:23   **7:10** ⁱ Ps. 103:16   **7:11** ʲ Ps. 39:1, 9   ᵏ 1 Sam.
1:10   **7:13** ˡ Job 9:27   **7:16** ᵐ Job 10:1   ⁿ Job 14:6   ᵒ Ps.
62:9   **7:17** ᵖ Ps. 8:4; 144:3   **7:20** ᵠ Ps. 36:6   ʳ Ps. 21:12
8:3 ᵃ [Deut. 32:4]   **8:4** ᵇ Job 1:5, 18, 19

He has cast them away for their
  transgression.
5 cIf you would earnestly seek God
  And make your supplication to the
    Almighty,
6 If you *were* pure and upright,
  Surely now He would awake for you,
  And prosper your rightful dwelling
    place.
7 Though your beginning was small,
  Yet your latter end would dincrease
    abundantly.

8 "Fore inquire, please, of the former age,
  And consider the things discovered by
    their fathers;
9 For fwe *were* born yesterday, and
    know nothing,
  Because our days on earth *are* a
    shadow.
10 Will they not teach you and tell you,
   And utter words from their heart?

11 "Can the papyrus grow up without a
     marsh?
   Can the reeds flourish without water?
12 gWhile it *is* yet green *and* not cut down,
   It withers before any *other* plant.
13 So *are* the paths of all who hforget
     God;
   And the hope of the ihypocrite shall
     perish,
14 Whose confidence shall be cut off,
   And whose trust *is* a spider's web.
15 jHe leans on his house, but it does not
     stand.
   He holds it fast, but it does not endure.
16 He grows green in the sun,
   And his branches spread out in his
     garden.
17 His roots wrap around the rock heap,
   And look for a place in the stones.
18 kIf he is destroyed from his place,
   Then *it* will deny him, *saying*, 'I have
     not seen you.'

19 "Behold, this is the joy of His way,
   And lout of the earth others will grow.
20 Behold, mGod will not cast away the
     blameless,
   Nor will He uphold the evildoers.
21 He will yet fill your mouth with
     laughing,
   And your lips with rejoicing.
22 Those who hate you will be nclothed
     with shame,

And the dwelling place of the wicked
  will come to nothing."*

Job: There Is No Mediator

9 Then Job answered and said:

2 "Truly I know *it is* so,
  But how can a aman be brighteous
    before God?
3 If one wished to contend with Him,
  He could not answer Him one time out
    of a thousand.
4 cGod *is* wise in heart and mighty in
    strength.
  Who has hardened *himself* against
    Him and prospered?
5 He removes the mountains, and they
    do not know
  When He overturns them in His
    anger;
6 He dshakes the earth out of its place,
  And its epillars tremble;
7 He commands the sun, and it does not
    rise;
  He seals off the stars;
8 fHe alone spreads out the heavens,
  And treads on the waves of the sea;
9 gHe made the Bear, Orion, and the
    Pleiades,
  And the chambers of the south;
10 hHe does great things past finding
     out,
   Yes, wonders without number.
11 iIf He goes by me, I do not see *Him*;
   If He moves past, I do not perceive
     Him;
12 jIf He takes away, who can hinder
     Him?
   Who can say to Him, 'What are You
     doing?'
13 God will not withdraw His anger,
   kThe allies of the proud* lie prostrate
     beneath Him.

14 "How then can I answer Him,
   And choose my words *to reason* with
     Him?
15 lFor though I were righteous, I could
     not answer Him;
   I would beg mercy of my Judge.
16 If I called and He answered me,
   I would not believe that He was
     listening to my voice.

---

* **8:22** Literally *will not be* * **9:13** Hebrew *rahab*

8:6 *If you were pure and upright.* This was actually
the way God described Job (1:8; 2:3). Bildad's concept
that one must "get right with God" was not erroneous. But his error was his assumption that loss of possessions was equal with loss of God's favor.
8:13 *So are the paths of all who forget God.* Bildad
falsely deduced that one can always determine the
cause by looking at the effect. We can know that the
people around us suffer, but it is not given to us to
know the spiritual causes, if any, behind this suffering.
9:3 *If one wished to contend with Him.* The word
"contend" indicates a legal argument, not a quarrel.

Job was seeking justice. He did not think he had
sinned (as his friends indicated) so that God would
punish him.

8:5 c [Job 5:17–27; 11:13] **8:7** d Job 42:12 **8:8** e Deut. 4:32;
32:7 **8:9** f Gen. 47:9 **8:12** g Ps. 129:6 **8:13** h Ps. 9:17
i Job 11:20; 18:14; 27:8 **8:15** j Job 8:22; 27:18 **8:18** k Job
7:10 **8:19** l Ps. 113:7 **8:20** m Job 4:7 **8:22** n Ps. 35:26;
109:29 **9:2** a [Job 4:17; 15:14–16] b [Hab. 2:4] **9:4** c Job
36:5 **9:6** d Heb. 12:26 e Job 26:11 **9:8** f Ps. 104:2, 3
9:9 g Amos 5:8 **9:10** h Job 5:9 **9:11** i [Job 23:8, 9; 35:14]
9:12 j [Is. 45:9] **9:13** k Job 26:12 **9:15** l Job 10:15; 23:1–7

17 For He crushes me with a tempest,
And multiplies my wounds [m]without cause.
18 He will not allow me to catch my breath,
But fills me with bitterness.
19 If *it is a matter* of strength, indeed *He is* strong;
And if of justice, who will appoint my day *in court?*
20 Though I were righteous, my own mouth would condemn me;
Though I *were* blameless, it would prove me perverse.

21 "I am blameless, yet I do not know myself;
I despise my life.
22 It *is* all one *thing;*
Therefore I say, [n]'He destroys the blameless and the wicked.'
23 If the scourge slays suddenly,
He laughs at the plight of the innocent.
24 The earth is given into the hand of the wicked.
He covers the faces of its judges.
If it is not *He*, who else could it be?

25 "Now [o]my days are swifter than a runner;
They flee away, they see no good.
26 They pass by like swift ships,
[p]Like an eagle swooping on its prey.
27 [q]If I say, 'I will forget my complaint,
I will put off my sad face and wear a smile,'
28 [r]I am afraid of all my sufferings;
I know that You [s]will not hold me innocent.
29 *If* I am condemned,
Why then do I labor in vain?
30 [t]If I wash myself with snow water,
And cleanse my hands with soap,
31 Yet You will plunge me into the pit,
And my own clothes will abhor me.

32 "For [u]*He is* not a man, as I *am*,
That I may answer Him,
And that we should go to court together.
33 [v]Nor is there any mediator between us,
Who may lay his hand on us both.
34 [w]Let Him take His rod away from me,
And do not let dread of Him terrify me.
35 *Then* I would speak and not fear Him,
But it is not so with me.

Job: I Would Plead with God

10 "My [a]soul loathes my life;
I will give free course to my complaint,
[b]I will speak in the bitterness of my soul.
2 I will say to God, 'Do not condemn me;
Show me why You contend with me.
3 *Does it* seem good to You that You should oppress,
That You should despise the work of Your hands,
And smile on the counsel of the wicked?
4 Do You have eyes of flesh?
Or [c]do You see as man sees?
5 *Are* Your days like the days of a mortal man?
Are Your years like the days of a mighty man,
6 That You should seek for my iniquity
And search out my sin,
7 Although You know that I am not wicked,
And *there is* no one who can deliver from Your hand?

8 'Your[d] hands have made me and fashioned me,
An intricate unity;
Yet You would [e]destroy me.
9 Remember, I pray, [f]that You have made me like clay.
And will You turn me into dust again?
10 [g]Did You not pour me out like milk,
And curdle me like cheese,
11 Clothe me with skin and flesh,
And knit me together with bones and sinews?
12 You have granted me life and favor,
And Your care has preserved my spirit.

13 'And these *things* You have hidden in Your heart;
I know that this *was* with You:

9:17 *crushes me with a tempest.* Job saw God as Lord of the heavens (vv. 7–8) and assumed that it was God who sent the tempest that destroyed his children. Job did not know that it was Satan who sought to destroy him, and that God drew a line of protection around him.

10:1–3 Affliction—In the face of his adversities, Job despaired of life, but he continued to plead with God in prayer for an answer. Job's friends saw all suffering in a mathematical equation with sin. If these friends were right, that would reduce our relationship with God to a formula that says, "If you are good, God will rescue you, and if you are bad, God will abandon you to suffering." The converse of that statement says, "If you are suffering, you are bad, and because I am not suffering, I am good." It is often in the converse that a formula is shown to be faulty. Who can really claim to be good? We are all sinners in need of a savior.

10:7 *I am not wicked . . . there is no one who can deliver.* Job thought that God was unjust in oppressing him, yet he realized that there is no one higher than God to deliver him from God. Job's thinking was twisted in much the same way that his friends' was. He was equating innocence with peace, and he could not imagine any reason why God would not rescue him.

9:17 [m] Job 2:3 **9:22** [n] Ezek. 21:3 **9:25** [o] Job 7:6, 7 **9:26** [p] Hab. 1:8 **9:27** [q] Job 7:13 **9:28** [r] Ps. 119:120 [s] Ex. 20:7 **9:30** [t] [Jer. 2:22] **9:32** [u] [Is. 45:9] **9:33** [v] [1 Sam. 2:25] **9:34** [w] Job 13:20, 21 **10:1** [a] Job 7:16 [b] Job 7:11 **10:4** [c] [1 Sam. 16:7] **10:8** [d] Ps. 119:73 [e] [Job 9:22] **10:9** [f] Gen. 2:7 **10:10** [g] [Ps. 139:14–16]

14 If I sin, then [h]You mark me,
And will not acquit me of my iniquity.
15 If I am wicked, [i]woe to me;
[j]Even *if* I am righteous, I cannot lift up
my head.
I am full of disgrace;
[k]See my misery!
16 If *my head* is exalted,
[l]You hunt me like a fierce lion,
And again You show Yourself
awesome against me.
17 You renew Your witnesses against me,
And increase Your indignation toward
me;
Changes and war are *ever* with me.
18 'Why[m] then have You brought me out
of the womb?
Oh, that I had perished and no eye had
seen me!
19 I would have been as though I had not
been.
I would have been carried from the
womb to the grave.
20 [n]Are not my days few?
Cease! [o]Leave me alone, that I may
take a little comfort,
21 Before I go *to the place from which* I
shall not return,
[p]To the land of darkness [q]and the
shadow of death,
22 A land as dark as darkness *itself,*
As the shadow of death, without any
order,
Where even the light *is* like darkness.'"

Zophar Urges Job to Repent

11 Then Zophar the Naamathite answered and said:

2 "Should not the multitude of words be
answered?
And should a man full of talk be
vindicated?
3 Should your empty talk make men
hold their peace?
And when you mock, should no one
rebuke you?
4 For you have said,
[a]'My doctrine *is* pure,

And I am clean in your eyes.'
5 But oh, that God would speak,
And open His lips against you,
6 That He would show you the secrets of
wisdom!
For *they would* double *your* prudence.
Know therefore that [b]God exacts from
you
Less than your iniquity *deserves.*

7 "Can[c] you search out the deep things of
God?
Can you find out the limits of the
Almighty?
8 *They are* higher than heaven—what
can you do?
Deeper than Sheol—what can you
know?
9 Their measure *is* longer than the earth
And broader than the sea.

10 "If[d] He passes by, imprisons, and
gathers *to judgment,*
Then who can hinder Him?
11 For [e]He knows deceitful men;
He sees wickedness also.
Will He not then consider *it?*
12 For an [f]empty-headed man will be
wise,
When a wild donkey's colt is born a
man.

13 "If you would [g]prepare your heart,
And [h]stretch out your hands toward
Him;
14 If iniquity *were* in your hand, *and you*
put it far away,
And [i]would not let wickedness dwell
in your tents;
15 [j]Then surely you could lift up your face
without spot;
Yes, you could be steadfast, and not
fear;
16 Because you would [k]forget *your*
misery,
And remember *it* as waters *that have*
passed away,
17 And *your* life [l]would be brighter than
noonday.
Though you were dark, you would be
like the morning.

10:18 brought me out of the womb. Job wondered
how the God who so carefully fashioned him in the
womb (vv. 9–11) could turn against him. This was the
desperate cry of a sufferer blind to the fact that God
was working good out of all the tragic events of his
life.
11:4 My doctrine is pure. Zophar exaggerated what
Job had said about his innocence (9:14–21) to make
Job look foolish.
11:7 Can you search out the deep things of God?
Zophar was correct in saying that understanding the
depths of God is beyond man. But the fact that we
cannot know everything about God does not mean
that we cannot know anything about Him, nor that it
is wrong to try to know and understand Him better.
11:13 stretch out your hands toward Him. Stretching out the hands was a posture of prayer as well as

of praise (Ps. 134:2). Assuming that Job was suffering
because of his iniquity, this was not bad advice.
11:15 steadfast, and not fear. There is peace and
comfort for those who have repented of their sin and
turned to God. This is true and important to remember. But Zophar's presupposition that iniquity causes
suffering kept him from understanding what Job's
struggle was.

10:14 [h] Ps. 139:1   **10:15** [i] Is. 3:11   [j] [Job 9:12,
15]   [k] Ps. 25:18   **10:16** [l] Is. 38:13   **10:18** [m] Job
3:11–13   **10:20** [n] Ps. 39:5   [o] Job 7:16, 19   **10:21** [p] Ps.
88:12   [q] Ps. 23:4   **11:4** [a] Job 6:30   **11:6** [b] [Ezra 9:13]
11:7 [c] [Eccl. 3:11]   **11:10** [d] [Rev. 3:7]   **11:11** [e] [Ps.
10:14]   **11:12** [f] Rom. 1:22   **11:13** [g] [1 Sam. 7:3]   [h] Ps.
88:9   **11:14** [i] Ps. 101:3   **11:15** [j] Ps. 119:6   **11:16** [k] Is.
65:16   **11:17** [l] Is. 58:8, 10

18 And you would be secure, because
    there is hope;
    Yes, you would dig *around you, and*
    ^mtake your rest in safety.
19 You would also lie down, and no one
    would make *you* afraid;
    Yes, many would court your favor.
20 But ⁿthe eyes of the wicked will fail,
    And they shall not escape,
    And ^otheir hope—loss of life!"

Job Answers His Critics

12 Then Job answered and said:

2 "No doubt you *are* the people,
    And wisdom will die with you!
3 But I have understanding as well as
    you;
    I *am* not ^ainferior to you.
    Indeed, who does not *know* such
    things as these?

4 "I^b am one mocked by his friends,
    Who ^ccalled on God, and He answered
    him,
    The just and blameless *who is*
    ridiculed.
5 A lamp* is despised in the thought of
    one who is at ease;
    It is made ready for ^dthose whose feet
    slip.
6 ^eThe tents of robbers prosper,
    And those who provoke God are
    secure—
    In what God provides by His hand.

7 "But now ask the beasts, and they will
    teach you;
    And the birds of the air, and they will
    tell you;
8 Or speak to the earth, and it will teach
    you;
    And the fish of the sea will explain to
    you.
9 Who among all these does not know
    That the hand of the LORD has done
    this,
10 ^fIn whose hand *is* the life of every
    living thing,
    And the ^gbreath of all mankind?
11 Does not the ear test words
    And the mouth taste its food?
12 Wisdom *is* with aged men,
    And with length of days, understanding.

13 "With Him *are* ^hwisdom and strength,
    He has counsel and understanding.
14 If ⁱHe breaks *a thing* down, it cannot
    be rebuilt;

If He imprisons a man, there can be no
    release.
15 If He ^jwithholds the waters, they dry up;
    If He ^ksends them out, they overwhelm
    the earth.
16 With Him *are* strength and prudence.
    The deceived and the deceiver *are* His.
17 He leads counselors away plundered,
    And makes fools of the judges.
18 He loosens the bonds of kings,
    And binds their waist with a belt.
19 He leads princes* away plundered,
    And overthrows the mighty.
20 ^lHe deprives the trusted ones of speech,
    And takes away the discernment of
    the elders.
21 ^mHe pours contempt on princes,
    And disarms the mighty.
22 He ⁿuncovers deep things out of
    darkness,
    And brings the shadow of death to
    light.
23 ^oHe makes nations great, and destroys
    them;
    He enlarges nations, and guides them.
24 He takes away the understanding*
    of the chiefs of the people of the
    earth,
    And ^pmakes them wander in a
    pathless wilderness.
25 ^qThey grope in the dark without light,
    And He makes them ^rstagger like a
    drunken *man.*

13 "Behold, my eye has seen all *this,*
    My ear has heard and understood it.
2 ^aWhat you know, I also know;
    I *am* not inferior to you.
3 ^bBut I would speak to the Almighty,
    And I desire to reason with God.
4 But you forgers of lies,
    ^cYou *are* all worthless physicians.
5 Oh, that you would be silent,
    And ^dit would be your wisdom!
6 Now hear my reasoning,
    And heed the pleadings of my lips.
7 ^eWill you speak wickedly for God,
    And talk deceitfully for Him?
8 Will you show partiality for Him?
    Will you contend for God?
9 Will it be well when He searches you
    out?
    Or can you mock Him as one mocks
    a man?

* **12:5** Or *disaster*   * **12:19** Literally *priests,* but
not in a technical sense   * **12:24** Literally *heart*

12:13 *He has counsel and understanding.* Job was
sure that he did not understand what was happening
to him, but he knew that God did know the answer.
13:4 *forgers of lies.* Job's friends were accusing him
of hidden sin, offering a false formula for peace with
God, and assuming that they had a greater understanding both of Job and of God's ways than they
really did. False doctrine, even if held with sincerity,
is still a lie.

11:18 ^m Lev. 26:5, 6   **11:20** ⁿ Deut. 28:65   ^o [Prov. 11:7]
12:3 ^a Job 13:2   **12:4** ^b Job 21:3   ^c Ps. 91:15   **12:5** ^d Prov.
14:2   **12:6** ^e [Job 9:24; 21:6–16]   **12:10** ^f [Acts 17:28]
^g Job 27:3; 33:4   **12:13** ^h Job 9:4; 36:5   **12:14** ⁱ Job 11:10
12:15 ^j [1 Kin. 8:35, 36]   ^k Gen. 7:11–24   **12:20** ^l Job 32:9
12:21 ^m Ps. 107:40   **12:22** ⁿ [1 Cor. 4:5]   **12:23** ^o Is. 9:3;
26:15   **12:24** ^p Ps. 107:4   **12:25** ^q Job 5:14; 15:30; 18:18
^r Ps. 107:27   **13:2** ^a Job 12:3   **13:3** ^b Job 23:3; 31:35
13:4 ^c Job 6:21   **13:5** ^d Prov. 17:28   **13:7** ^e Job 27:4; 36:4

10 He will surely rebuke you
If you secretly show partiality.
11 Will not His excellence make you afraid,
And the dread of Him fall upon you?
12 Your platitudes *are* proverbs of ashes,
Your defenses are defenses of clay.

13 "Hold your peace with me, and let me speak,
Then let come on me what *may!*
14 Why *f*do I take my flesh in my teeth,
And put my life in my hands?
15 *g*Though He slay me, yet will I trust Him.
*h*Even so, I will defend my own ways before Him.
16 He also *shall* be my salvation,
For a *i*hypocrite could not come before Him.
17 Listen carefully to my speech,
And to my declaration with your ears.
18 See now, I have prepared *my* case,
I know that I shall be *j*vindicated.
19 *k*Who *is* he *who* will contend with me?
If now I hold my tongue, I perish.

Job's Despondent Prayer

20 "Only*l* two *things* do not do to me,
Then I will not hide myself from You:
21 *m*Withdraw Your hand far from me,
And let not the dread of You make me afraid.
22 Then call, and I will *n*answer;
Or let me speak, then You respond to me.
23 How many *are* my iniquities and sins?
Make me know my transgression and my sin.
24 *o*Why do You hide Your face,
And *p*regard me as Your enemy?
25 *q*Will You frighten a leaf driven to and fro?
And will You pursue dry stubble?
26 For You write bitter things against me,
And *r*make me inherit the iniquities of my youth.
27 *s*You put my feet in the stocks,
And watch closely all my paths.
You set a limit* for the soles of my feet.

28 "Man* decays like a rotten thing,
Like a garment that is moth-eaten.

14 "Man *who is* born of woman
Is of few days and *a*full of trouble.
2 *b*He comes forth like a flower and fades away;
He flees like a shadow and does not continue.
3 And *c*do You open Your eyes on such a one,
And *d*bring me* to judgment with Yourself?
4 Who *e*can bring a clean *thing* out of an unclean?
No one!
5 *f*Since his days *are* determined,
The number of his months *is* with You;
You have appointed his limits, so that he cannot pass.
6 *g*Look away from him that he may rest,
Till *h*like a hired man he finishes his day.

7 "For there is hope for a tree,
If it is cut down, that it will sprout again,
And that its tender shoots will not cease.
8 Though its root may grow old in the earth,
And its stump may die in the ground,
9 Yet at the scent of water it will bud
And bring forth branches like a plant.
10 But man dies and is laid away;
Indeed he breathes his last
And where *is* *i*he?
11 *As* water disappears from the sea,
And a river becomes parched and dries up,
12 So man lies down and does not rise.
*j*Till the heavens *are* no more,
They will not awake
Nor be roused from their sleep.

13 "Oh, that You would hide me in the grave,
That You would conceal me until Your wrath is past,
That You would appoint me a set time, and remember me!

* **13:27** Literally *inscribe a print*   * **13:28** Literally *He*   * **14:3** Septuagint, Syriac, and Vulgate read *him.*

13:12 platitudes ... defenses. The quickest way to make ourselves look silly is to try to explain something that we don't understand. Prayer is far more helpful than worthless counsel.

13:21 Withdraw Your hand ... make me afraid. Job was not cocky as he turned to plead his case before God. His requests were safe and wise for any believer who struggles with what life has handed him. Job asked God not to give up on him, and he asked God to keep him from being overpowered by the terror and majesty of God. Job knew very well that he was far below God, and that all that God is and does could be totally overwhelming to him.

14:13 hide me ... until Your wrath is past. Job's wish for the grave to be a temporary hiding place from God's wrath differed dramatically from his earlier

remarks concerning the grave (7:9–10; 10:18–22). He attributed the cause of his suffering to God's wrath because he assumed the retribution dogma that the righteous are always blessed and the wicked will eventually experience God's judgment. It did not occur to Job that he was being tested.

13:14 *f* Job 18:4   **13:15** *g* Ps. 23:4   *h* Job 27:5   **13:16** *i* Job 8:13   **13:18** *j* [Rom. 8:34]   **13:19** *k* Is. 50:8   **13:20** *l* Job 9:34   **13:21** *m* Ps. 39:10   **13:22** *n* Job 9:16; 14:15   **13:24** *o* [Deut. 32:20]   *p* Lam. 2:5   **13:25** *q* Is. 42:3   **13:26** *r* Job 20:11   **13:27** *s* Job 33:11   **14:1** *a* Eccl. 2:23   **14:2** *b* Job 8:9   **14:3** *c* Ps. 8:4; 144:3   *d* [Ps. 143:2]   **14:4** *e* [Ps. 51:2, 5, 10]   **14:5** *f* Job 7:1; 21:21   **14:6** *g* Ps. 39:13   *h* Job 7:1   **14:10** *i* Job 10:21, 22   **14:12** *j* [Is. 51:6; 65:17; 66:22]

14 If a man dies, shall he live *again?*
  All the days of my hard service ᵏI will
    wait,
  Till my change comes.
15 ˡYou shall call, and I will answer You;
  You shall desire the work of Your
    hands.
16 For now ᵐYou number my steps,
  But do not watch over my sin.
17 ⁿMy transgression *is* sealed up in a
    bag,
  And You cover* my iniquity.
18 "But *as* a mountain falls *and* crumbles
    away,
  And *as* a rock is moved from its place;
19 *As* water wears away stones,
  And as torrents wash away the soil of
    the earth;
  So You destroy the hope of man.
20 You prevail forever against him, and
    he passes on;
  You change his countenance and send
    him away.
21 His sons come to honor, and ᵒhe does
    not know *it;*
  They are brought low, and he does not
    perceive *it.*
22 But his flesh will be in pain over it,
  And his soul will mourn over it."

Eliphaz Accuses Job of Folly

15 Then ᵃEliphaz the Temanite answered and said:

2 "Should a wise man answer with empty
    knowledge,
  And fill himself with the east wind?
3 Should he reason with unprofitable
    talk,
  Or by speeches with which he can do
    no good?
4 Yes, you cast off fear,
  And restrain prayer before God.
5 For your iniquity teaches your mouth,
  And you choose the tongue of the
    crafty.
6 ᵇYour own mouth condemns you, and
    not I;
  Yes, your own lips testify against you.

7 "*Are* you the first man *who* was born?
  ᶜOr were you made before the hills?

8 ᵈHave you heard the counsel of God?
  Do you limit wisdom to yourself?
9 ᵉWhat do you know that we do not
    know?
  What do you understand that *is* not
    in us?
10 ᶠBoth the gray-haired and the aged *are*
    among us,
  Much older than your father.
11 *Are* the consolations of God too small
    for you,
  And the word *spoken* gently* with you?
12 Why does your heart carry you away,
  And what do your eyes wink at,
13 That you turn your spirit against God,
  And let *such* words go out of your
    mouth?

14 "Whatᵍ *is* man, that he could be pure?
  And *he who is* born of a woman, that
    he could be righteous?
15 ʰIf *God* puts no trust in His saints,
  And the heavens are not pure in His
    sight,
16 ⁱHow much less man, *who is*
    abominable and filthy,
  ʲWho drinks iniquity like water!

17 "I will tell you, hear me;
  What I have seen I will declare,
18 What wise men have told,
  Not hiding *anything received* ᵏfrom
    their fathers,
19 To whom alone the land was given,
  And ˡno alien passed among them:
20 The wicked man writhes with pain all
    his days,
  ᵐAnd the number of years is hidden
    from the oppressor.
21 Dreadful sounds *are* in his ears;
  ⁿIn prosperity the destroyer comes
    upon him.
22 He does not believe that he will ᵒreturn
    from darkness,
  For a sword is waiting for him.
23 He ᵖwanders about for bread, *saying,*
    'Where *is* it?'
  He knows ᑫthat a day of darkness is
    ready at his hand.
24 Trouble and anguish make him afraid;

---

* **14:17** Literally *plaster over*   * **15:11** Septuagint
reads *a secret thing.*

14:14 live again. Job had some understanding of man's potential for immortality. The answer to his question comes in the New Testament with an emphatic "Yes!" by Jesus (John 11:23–26; 1 Cor. 15:3–57).

15:21 Dreadful sounds. Eliphaz began his subtle argument to prove that Job was a wicked man. He alluded to Job's dread, the same word translated *feared* in 3:25, as an implicit indicator that Job was wicked.

15:24 Trouble . . . afraid. In contrast to 14:20 where Job complained to God that He overpowered people, Eliphaz said that the wicked man's (by implication, Job's) own fears overpower him. Eliphaz's statement may have been true, but that did not mean it applied to Job. Job did not understand God's ways correctly,

but neither did Eliphaz. Job was overpowered by Satan's attacks, and he could not see what God was doing. Eliphaz assumed that because Job was overpowered, it was because he had behaved arrogantly towards God.

14:14 ᵏ Job 13:15   **14:15** ˡ Job 13:22   **14:16** ᵐ Prov. 5:21
14:17 ⁿ Deut. 32:32–34   **14:21** ᵒ Eccl. 9:5   **15:1** ᵃ Job 4:1
15:6 ᵇ [Luke 19:22]   **15:7** ᶜ Prov. 8:25   **15:8** ᵈ Rom.
11:34   **15:9** ᵉ Job 12:3; 13:2   **15:10** ᶠ Job 8:8–10; 12:12;
32:6, 7   **15:14** ᵍ Prov. 20:9   **15:15** ʰ Job 4:18; 25:5
15:16 ⁱ Ps. 14:3; 53:3 ʲ Prov. 19:28   **15:18** ᵏ Job 8:8; 20:4
15:19 ˡ Joel 3:17   **15:20** ᵐ Ps. 90:12   **15:21** ⁿ 1 Thess.
5:3   **15:22** ᵒ Job 14:10–12   **15:23** ᵖ Ps. 59:15; 109:10
ᑫ Job 18:12

They overpower him, like a king ready for battle.

25 For he stretches out his hand against God,
And acts defiantly against the Almighty,

26 Running stubbornly against Him
With his strong, embossed shield.

27 "Though[r] he has covered his face with his fatness,
And made *his* waist heavy with fat,

28 He dwells in desolate cities,
In houses which no one inhabits,
Which are destined to become ruins.

29 He will not be rich,
Nor will his wealth [s]continue,
Nor will his possessions overspread the earth.

30 He will not depart from darkness;
The flame will dry out his branches,
And [t]by the breath of His mouth he will go away.

31 Let him not [u]trust in futile *things*, deceiving himself,
For futility will be his reward.

32 It will be accomplished [v]before his time,
And his branch will not be green.

33 He will shake off his unripe grape like a vine,
And cast off his blossom like an olive tree.

34 For the company of hypocrites *will be* barren,
And fire will consume the tents of bribery.

35 [w]They conceive trouble and bring forth futility;
Their womb prepares deceit."

Job Reproaches His Pitiless Friends

16 Then Job answered and said:

2 "I have heard many such things;
[a]Miserable comforters *are* you all!

3 Shall words of wind have an end?
Or what provokes you that you answer?

4 I also could speak as you *do*,
If your soul were in my soul's place.
I could heap up words against you,
And [b]shake my head at you;

5 *But* I would strengthen you with my mouth,
And the comfort of my lips would relieve *your* grief.

6 "Though I speak, my grief is not relieved;
And *if* I remain silent, how am I eased?

7 But now He has [c]worn me out;
You [d]have made desolate all my company.

8 You have shriveled me up,
And it is a [e]witness *against me*;
My leanness rises up against me
And bears witness to my face.

9 [f]He tears *me* in His wrath, and hates me;
He gnashes at me with His teeth;
[g]My adversary sharpens His gaze on me.

10 They [h]gape at me with their mouth,
They [i]strike me reproachfully on the cheek,
They gather together against me.

11 God [j]has delivered me to the ungodly,
And turned me over to the hands of the wicked.

12 I was at ease, but He has [k]shattered me;
He also has taken *me* by my neck, and shaken me to pieces;
He has [l]set me up for His target,

13 His archers surround me.
He pierces my heart* and does not pity;
He pours out my gall on the ground.

14 He breaks me with wound upon wound;
He runs at me like a warrior.*

15 "I have sewn sackcloth over my skin,
And [m]laid my head* in the dust.

16 My face is flushed from weeping,
And on my eyelids *is* the shadow of death;

---

* **16:13** Literally *kidneys*   * **16:14** Vulgate reads *giant*.   * **16:15** Literally *horn*

15:31 *trust in futile things.* Eliphaz was entirely right in his comments about the fruitlessness of a wicked life, and that the Lord will bring the wicked into judgment. But Eliphaz did not have the concept that in this life the wicked can appear to prosper, and the righteous can appear to struggle. Judgment may not fall in this life.

15:34 *fire will consume.* In mentioning the fire that consumes the tents of the wicked, Eliphaz implied that the fire of God that destroyed Job's sheep and servants (1:16) was a direct result of Job's corruption.

16:7–17 Afflictions—One of the clear lessons of the Book of Job is that it is possible to give false and insensitive counsel to one who is experiencing affliction and testing. When we suffer, some of the lessons learned are for us, some of the lessons are for others who are watching, and some are for the kingdom of God. We may not know in this life what all of the implications are. Our afflictions are designed by God to drive us out of ourselves to the Eternal God who is our refuge and who supports us with His everlasting arms (Deut. 33:27). As friends of the afflicted, we must be sympathetic, loving, and kind, remembering that often only God has the answers. If we have suffered similarly, we have comfort to offer (2 Cor. 1:6–7), and if we have not suffered similarly, we can support our friends in prayer and practical service.

15:27 [r] Ps. 17:10; 73:7; 119:70   **15:29** [s] Job 20:28; 27:16, 17   **15:30** [t] Job 4:9   **15:31** [u] Is. 59:4   **15:32** [v] Job 22:16   **15:35** [w] Is. 59:4   **16:2** [a] Job 13:4; 21:34   **16:4** [b] Ps. 22:7; 109:25   **16:7** [c] Job 7:3   [d] Job 16:20; 19:13–15   **16:8** [e] Job 10:17   **16:9** [f] Hos. 6:1   [g] Job 13:24; 33:10   **16:10** [h] Ps. 22:13; 35:21   [i] Lam. 3:30   **16:11** [j] Job 1:15, 17   **16:12** [k] Job 9:17   [l] Job 7:20   **16:15** [m] Ps. 7:5

17 Although no violence *is* in my hands,
And my prayer *is* pure.

18 "O earth, do not cover my blood,
And *n*let my cry have no *resting* place!
19 Surely even now *o*my witness *is* in
heaven,
And my evidence *is* on high.
20 My friends scorn me;
My eyes pour out *tears* to God.
21 *p*Oh, that one might plead for a man
with God,
As a man *pleads* for his neighbor!
22 For when a few years are finished,
I shall *q*go the way of no return.

Job Prays for Relief

17 "My spirit is broken,
My days are extinguished,
*a*The grave *is* ready for me.
2 *Are* not mockers with me?
And does not my eye dwell on their
*b*provocation?

3 "Now put down a pledge for me with
Yourself.
Who *is* he *who* *c*will shake hands with
me?
4 For You have hidden their heart from
*d*understanding;
Therefore You will not exalt *them.*
5 He who speaks flattery to *his* friends,
Even the eyes of his children will *e*fail.

6 "But He has made me *f*a byword of the
people,
And I have become one in whose face
men spit.
7 *g*My eye has also grown dim because of
sorrow,
And all my members *are* like shadows.
8 Upright *men* are astonished at this,
And the innocent stirs himself up
against the hypocrite.
9 Yet the righteous will hold to his *h*way,
And he who has *i*clean hands will be
stronger and stronger.

10 "But please, *j*come back again, all of
you,*

For I shall not find *one* wise *man*
among you.
11 *k*My days are past,
My purposes are broken off,
Even the thoughts of my heart.
12 They change the night into day;
'The light *is* near,' *they say,* in the face
of darkness.
13 If I wait *for* the grave *as* my house,
If I make my bed in the darkness,
14 If I say to corruption, 'You *are* my
father,'
And to the worm, 'You *are* my mother
and my sister,'
15 Where then *is* my *l*hope?
As for my hope, who can see it?
16 *Will* they go down *m*to the gates of
Sheol?
Shall *we have* *n*rest together in the
dust?"

Bildad: The Wicked Are Punished

18 Then *a*Bildad the Shuhite answered
and said:

2 "How long *till* you put an end to words?
Gain understanding, and afterward
we will speak.
3 Why are we counted *b*as beasts,
And regarded as stupid in your sight?
4 *c*You who tear yourself in anger,
Shall the earth be forsaken for you?
Or shall the rock be removed from its
place?

5 "The*d* light of the wicked indeed goes
out,
And the flame of his fire does not shine.
6 The light is dark in his tent,
*e*And his lamp beside him is put out.
7 The steps of his strength are shortened,
And *f*his own counsel casts him down.
8 For *g*he is cast into a net by his own
feet,
And he walks into a snare.

* **17:10** Following some Hebrew manuscripts, Septuagint, Syriac, and Vulgate; Masoretic Text and Targum read *all of them.*

16:21 *one might plead.* Job was expressing the need for an intercessor. This need anticipated Jesus Christ, who is our Intercessor (Heb. 7:25) and Advocate (1 John 2:1).

17:3 *pledge.* In another legal metaphor, Job appealed to God by laying down a pledge, that is, by providing bail. The use of the same metaphor in Psalm 119:121–122 to indicate the psalmist's request for relief from his oppressors may suggest that Job was pleading for God to demonstrate confidence in his innocence.

17:9 *the righteous will hold to his way.* Job seems to be entertaining a little sarcasm here. He had referred to himself as a byword, one at whom men spit. Then he said that the righteous will grow stronger, which was not a reference to himself, even though he still did not think he deserved the trouble that had fallen upon him. He was probably referring to his friends, who considered themselves righteous, with clean

hands, and who repeatedly strengthened their position and arguments.

18:4 *who tear yourself in anger.* This may be Bildad's response to Job's allegation that God had torn Job in His anger (16:13).

18:8–10 *net . . . snare.* Six different Hebrew synonyms for various types of nets and snares emphasize the many imminent dangers that God has designed

16:18 *n* [Ps. 66:18]   **16:19** *o* Rom. 1:9   **16:21** *p* Job 31:35   **16:22** *q* Eccl. 12:5   **17:1** *a* Ps. 88:3, 4   **17:2** *b* Job 12:4; 17:6; 30:1, 9; 34:7   **17:3** *c* Prov. 6:1; 17:18; 22:26   **17:4** *d* Job 12:20; 32:9   **17:5** *e* Job 11:20   **17:6** *f* Job 30:9   **17:7** *g* Ps. 6:7; 31:9   **17:9** *h* Prov. 4:18   *i* Ps. 24:4   **17:10** *j* Job 6:29   **17:11** *k* Job 7:6   **17:15** *l* Job 7:6; 13:15; 14:19; 19:10   **17:16** *m* Jon. 2:6   *n* Job 3:17–19; 21:33   **18:1** *a* Job 8:1   **18:3** *b* Ps. 73:22   **18:4** *c* Job 13:14   **18:5** *d* Prov. 13:9; 20:20; 24:20   **18:6** *e* Job 21:17   **18:7** *f* Job 5:12, 13; 15:6   **18:8** *g* Job 22:10

9 The net takes *him* by the heel,
   And ᵸa snare lays hold of him.
10 A noose *is* hidden for him on the
   ground,
   And a trap for him in the road.
11 ⁱTerrors frighten him on every side,
   And drive him to his feet.
12 His strength is starved,
   And ʲdestruction *is* ready at his side.
13 It devours patches of his skin;
   The firstborn of death devours his
   limbs.
14 He is uprooted from ᵏthe shelter of his
   tent,
   And they parade him before the king
   of terrors.
15 They dwell in his tent *who are* none of
   his;
   Brimstone is scattered on his
   dwelling.
16 ˡHis roots are dried out below,
   And his branch withers above.
17 ᵐThe memory of him perishes from the
   earth,
   And he has no name among the
   renowned.*
18 He is driven from light into darkness,
   And chased out of the world.
19 ⁿHe has neither son nor posterity
   among his people,
   Nor any remaining in his dwellings.
20 Those in the west are astonished ᵒat
   his day,
   As those in the east are frightened.
21 Surely such *are* the dwellings of the
   wicked,
   And this *is* the place *of him who* ᵖdoes
   not know God.”

Job Trusts in His Redeemer

19 Then Job answered and said:

2 “How long will you torment my soul,
   And break me in pieces with words?
3 These ten times you have reproached
   me;
   You are not ashamed *that* you have
   wronged me.*

4 And if indeed I have erred,
   My error remains with me.
5 If indeed you ᵃexalt *yourselves* against
   me,
   And plead my disgrace against me,
6 Know then that ᵇGod has wronged me,
   And has surrounded me with His net.
7 “If I cry out concerning wrong, I am not
   heard.
   If I cry aloud, *there is* no justice.
8 ᶜHe has fenced up my way, so that I
   cannot pass;
   And He has set darkness in my paths.
9 ᵈHe has stripped me of my glory,
   And taken the crown *from* my head.
10 He breaks me down on every side,
   And I am gone;
   My ᵉhope He has uprooted like a tree.
11 He has also kindled His wrath against
   me,
   And ᶠHe counts me as *one of* His
   enemies.
12 His troops come together
   And build up their road against me;
   They encamp all around my tent.
13 “Heᵍ has removed my brothers far from
   me,
   And my acquaintances are completely
   estranged from me.
14 My relatives have failed,
   And my close friends have
   forgotten me.
15 Those who dwell in my house, and my
   maidservants,
   Count me as a stranger;
   I am an alien in their sight.
16 I call my servant, but he gives no
   answer;
   I beg him with my mouth.
17 My breath is offensive to my wife,
   And I am repulsive to the children of
   my own body.
18 Even ʰyoung children despise me;
   I arise, and they speak against me.

---

* **18:17** Literally *before the outside*, meaning
distinguished, famous   * **19:3** A Jewish tradition
reads *make yourselves strange to me.*

---

for the wicked to ensure that they will be caught in
their wickedness.
18:21 wicked. Bildad believed that the evidence he
had exhibited in verses 5–20 implicated Job himself
as the wicked one. Bildad was right that, in the end,
the wicked will perish dramatically. But in this life they
are not necessarily judged. If it were that simple, that
the wicked never prospered and the righteous always
thrived, people might try to be followers of God just
for the blessings. The whole thrust of the Book of Job
is that God Himself is reason enough to follow God,
whether or not there is prosperity (1:9–11).
19:7 Despondency—The despondency of Job was
a swollen river into which many streams had poured.
He had experienced the loss of family, property, and
health. Wife and friends had misunderstood him. The
suffering saint felt tormented, crushed with the irrelevant words of critics who should have comforted

instead of corrected him. Crying out for help, Job
received none and came to the conclusion that there
is no justice anywhere. The interesting thing about
Job is that while he may have despaired of hearing
from God, he never doubted that God was there and
knew what was going on.
19:8 He has fenced up my way. Job felt fenced in by
God, when it was really Satan who had been mistreating him (1:10; 3:23). The only fence from God was a
hedge of protection.

18:9 ʰ Job 5:5   **18:11** ⁱ Jer. 6:25   **18:12** ʲ Job 15:23
18:14 ᵏ Job 11:20   **18:16** ˡ Job 29:19   **18:17** ᵐ [Ps. 34:16]
18:19 ⁿ Is. 14:22   **18:20** ᵒ Ps. 37:13   **18:21** ᵖ Jer.
9:3   **19:5** ᵃ Ps. 35:26; 38:16; 55:12, 13   **19:6** ᵇ Job 6:11
19:8 ᶜ Job 3:23   **19:9** ᵈ Ps. 89:44   **19:10** ᵉ Job 17:14–16
19:11 ᶠ Job 13:24; 33:10   **19:13** ᵍ Ps. 31:11; 38:11; 69:8;
88:8, 18   **19:18** ʰ 2 Kin. 2:23

19 *i*All my close friends abhor me,
And those whom I love have turned against me.
20 *j*My bone clings to my skin and to my flesh,
And I have escaped by the skin of my teeth.
21 "Have pity on me, have pity on me,
O you my friends,
For the hand of God has struck me!
22 Why do you *k*persecute me as God *does*,
And are not satisfied with my flesh?
23 "Oh, that my words were written!
Oh, that they were inscribed in a book!
24 That they were engraved on a rock
With an iron pen and lead, forever!
25 For I know that my *l*Redeemer lives,
And He shall stand at last on the earth;
26 And after my skin is destroyed, this *I know*,
That *m*in my flesh I shall see God,
27 Whom I shall see for myself,
And my eyes shall behold, and not another.
How my heart yearns within me!
28 If you should say, 'How shall we persecute him?'—
Since the root of the matter is found in me,
29 Be afraid of the sword for yourselves;
For wrath *brings* the punishment of the sword,
That you may know *there is* a judgment."

Zophar's Sermon on the Wicked Man

20 Then *a*Zophar the Naamathite answered and said:

2 "Therefore my anxious thoughts make me answer,
Because of the turmoil within me.
3 I have heard the rebuke that reproaches me,
And the spirit of my understanding causes me to answer.
4 "Do you *not* know this of *b*old,
Since man was placed on earth,

5 *c*That the triumphing of the wicked is short,
And the joy of the hypocrite is *but* for a *d*moment?
6 *e*Though his haughtiness mounts up to the heavens,
And his head reaches to the clouds,
7 *Yet* he will perish forever like his own refuse;
Those who have seen him will say, 'Where is he?'
8 He will fly away *f*like a dream, and not be found;
Yes, he *g*will be chased away like a vision of the night.
9 The eye *that* saw him will *see him* no more,
Nor will his place behold him anymore.
10 His children will seek the favor of the poor,
And his hands will restore his wealth.
11 His bones are full of *h*his youthful vigor,
*i*But it will lie down with him in the dust.
12 "Though evil is sweet in his mouth,
And he hides it under his tongue,
13 *Though* he spares it and does not forsake it,
But still keeps it in his mouth,
14 *Yet* his food in his stomach turns sour;
It becomes cobra venom within him.
15 He swallows down riches
And vomits them up again;
God casts them out of his belly.
16 He will suck the poison of cobras;
The viper's tongue will slay him.
17 He will not see *j*the streams,
The rivers flowing with honey and cream.
18 He will restore that for which he labored,
And will not swallow *it* down;
From the proceeds of business He will get no enjoyment.
19 For he has oppressed *and* forsaken the poor,
He has violently seized a house which he did not build.

19:25 I know that my Redeemer lives. Job's longing for a mediator (9:33) and his desire for someone to plead on his behalf with God (16:19–21) may suggest that he was thinking of someone other than God. Here was a strong, resolute hope for a mediator between God and humanity. Ultimately Job's longing for a vindicator or mediator was fulfilled in Jesus Christ (1 Tim. 2:5).
19:26 in my flesh I shall see God. Job was stating his strong belief in the eternality of the soul, and even of the resurrected body, although it was not until Christ's resurrection that followers of the Living God understood all the implications of this belief (1 Cor. 15:12–19).

19:29 Be afraid of the sword. Job anticipated the reaction of his friends to his stated confidence that some day he would see God face-to-face.
20:7 refuse. The word "refuse" may also be translated *dung*. This was a scathing comment.

19:19 *i* Ps. 38:11; 55:12, 13   **19:20** *j* Ps. 102:5   **19:22** *k* Ps. 69:26   **19:25** *l* 1 Cor. 1:31; Gal. 3:13; Heb. 9:12   **19:26** *m* [Ps. 17:15]   **20:1** *a* Job 11:1   **20:4** *b* Job 8:8; 15:10   **20:5** *c* Ps. 37:35, 36   *d* [Job 8:13; 13:16; 15:34; 27:8]   **20:6** *e* Is. 14:13, 14   **20:8** *f* Ps. 73:20; 90:5   *g* Job 18:18; 27:21–23   **20:11** *h* Job 33:26   *i* Job 21:26   **20:17** *j* Jer. 17:8

20 "Because[k] he knows no quietness in his heart,*
He will not save anything he desires.
21 Nothing is left for him to eat;
Therefore his well-being will not last.
22 In his self-sufficiency he will be in distress;
Every hand of misery will come against him.
23 *When* he is about to fill his stomach,
God will cast on him the fury of His wrath,
And will rain *it* on him while he is eating.
24 [l]He will flee from the iron weapon;
A bronze bow will pierce him through.
25 It is drawn, and comes out of the body;
Yes, [m]the glittering *point comes* out of his gall.
[n]Terrors *come* upon him;
26 Total darkness *is* reserved for his treasures.
[o]An unfanned fire will consume him;
It shall go ill with him who is left in his tent.
27 The heavens will reveal his iniquity,
And the earth will rise up against him.
28 The increase of his house will depart,
And his goods will flow away in the day of His [p]wrath.
29 [q]This *is* the portion from God for a wicked man,
The heritage appointed to him by God."

Job's Discourse on the Wicked

21 Then Job answered and said:

2 "Listen carefully to my speech,
And let this be your consolation.
3 Bear with me that I may speak,
And after I have spoken, keep [a]mocking.

4 "As for me, *is* my complaint against man?

And if *it were*, why should I not be impatient?
5 Look at me and be astonished;
[b]Put *your* hand over *your* mouth.
6 Even when I remember I am terrified,
And trembling takes hold of my flesh.
7 [c]Why do the wicked live *and* become old,
Yes, become mighty in power?
8 Their descendants are established with them in their sight,
And their offspring before their eyes.
9 Their houses *are* safe from fear,
[d]Neither *is* the rod of God upon them.
10 Their bull breeds without failure;
Their cow calves [e]without miscarriage.
11 They send forth their little ones like a flock,
And their children dance.
12 They sing to the tambourine and harp,
And rejoice to the sound of the flute.
13 They [f]spend their days in wealth,
And in a moment go down to the grave.*
14 [g]Yet they say to God, 'Depart from us,
For we do not desire the knowledge of Your ways.
15 [h]Who *is* the Almighty, that we should serve Him?
And [i]what profit do we have if we pray to Him?'
16 Indeed their prosperity *is* not in their hand;
[j]The counsel of the wicked is far from me.

17 "How often is the lamp of the wicked put out?
How often does their destruction come upon them,
The sorrows *God* [k]distributes in His anger?
18 [l]They are like straw before the wind,
And like chaff that a storm carries away.

---

* **20:20** Literally *belly*   * **21:13** Or *Sheol*

20:20 no quietness. In stating that the wicked person knows no quietness, Zophar implied that Job had received what he deserved.
20:27 heavens will reveal his iniquity. Zophar apparently reversed Job's appeal to the earth and heavens (16:18–19) for vindication. He argued that the heavens and earth would bear witness not to Job's innocence, but to his iniquity.
20:29 heritage appointed to him by God. In contrast to his previous words (11:13–20) Zophar seemed to be suggesting that it was too late for Job to repent. It is true, as Zophar says (v. 5) that the wicked and godless will be judged. But that does not mean either that Job was one of the wicked, or that the judgment of the wicked would be in this life (Luke 16:19–25).
21:7 wicked live. With a rhetorical question, Job began exposing the loopholes in the retribution dogma—the belief that suffering always indicates God's punishment of a person. Other biblical writers also agonized over the prosperity of the wicked (Ps.

37; 73; Jer. 12:1–4), but Scriptures affirm that God is controlling everything to accomplish His good purpose (Rom. 8:28).
21:9 safe from fear. Job reacted to Eliphaz's argument (15:21–24) that although the wicked live peacefully for a while, they live in terror of inevitable destruction.
21:17 lamp of the wicked put out. The rhetorical questions introduced by "how often" expected the answer, "not very often." Job challenged Bildad's belief that the wicked person's light does go out (18:5–6).

20:20 [k] Eccl. 5:13–15   **20:24** [l] Amos 5:19   **20:25** [m] Job 16:13 [n] Job 18:11, 14   **20:26** [o] Ps. 21:9   **20:28** [p] Job 20:15; 21:30   **20:29** [q] Job 27:13; 31:2, 3   **21:3** [a] Job 16:10   **21:5** [b] Judg. 18:19   **21:7** [c] [Jer. 12:1]   **21:9** [d] Ps. 73:5   **21:10** [e] Ex. 23:26   **21:13** [f] Job 21:23; 36:11   **21:14** [g] Job 22:17   **21:15** [h] Ex. 5:2   [i] Mal. 3:14   **21:16** [j] Prov. 1:10   **21:17** [k] [Luke 12:46]   **21:18** [l] Ps. 1:4; 35:5

19 *They say,* 'God lays up one's* iniquity
[m]for his children';
Let Him recompense him, that he may
know *it.*
20 Let his eyes see his destruction,
And [n]let him drink of the wrath of the
Almighty.
21 For what does he care about his
household after him,
When the number of his months is cut
in half?

22 "Can[o] *anyone* teach God knowledge,
Since He judges those on high?
23 One dies in his full strength,
Being wholly at ease and secure;
24 His pails* are full of milk,
And the marrow of his bones is
moist.
25 Another man dies in the bitterness of
his soul,
Never having eaten with pleasure.
26 They [p]lie down alike in the dust,
And worms cover them.

27 "Look, I know your thoughts,
And the schemes *with which* you
would wrong me.
28 For you say,
'Where *is* the house of the prince?
And where *is* the tent,*
The dwelling place of the wicked?'
29 Have you not asked those who travel
the road?
And do you not know their signs?
30 [q]For the wicked are reserved for the
day of doom;
They shall be brought out on the day
of wrath.
31 Who condemns his way to his face?
And who repays him *for what* he has
done?
32 Yet he shall be brought to the grave,
And a vigil kept over the tomb.
33 The clods of the valley shall be sweet
to him;
[r]Everyone shall follow him,
As countless *have gone* before him.
34 How then can you comfort me with
empty words,
Since falsehood remains in your
answers?"

Eliphaz Accuses Job of Wickedness

22 Then [a]Eliphaz the Temanite answered and said:

2 "Can[b] a man be profitable to God,
Though he who is wise may be
profitable to himself?
3 *Is it* any pleasure to the Almighty that
you are righteous?
Or *is it* gain *to Him* that you make
your ways blameless?

4 "Is it because of your fear of Him that
He corrects you,
And enters into judgment with you?
5 *Is* not your wickedness great,
And your iniquity without end?
6 For you have [c]taken pledges from your
brother for no reason,
And stripped the naked of their
clothing.
7 You have not given the weary water to
drink,
And you [d]have withheld bread from
the hungry.
8 But the mighty man possessed the
land,
And the honorable man dwelt in it.
9 You have sent widows away empty,
And the strength of the fatherless was
crushed.
10 Therefore snares *are* all around you,
And sudden fear troubles you,
11 Or darkness *so that* you cannot see;
And an abundance of [e]water covers
you.

12 "Is not God in the height of heaven?
And see the highest stars, how lofty
they are!
13 And you say, [f]'What does God know?
Can He judge through the deep
darkness?
14 [g]Thick clouds cover Him, so that He
cannot see,
And He walks above the circle of
heaven.'
15 Will you keep to the old way
Which wicked men have trod,

***21:19** Literally *his* ***21:24** Septuagint and Vulgate read *bowels;* Syriac reads *sides;* Targum reads *breasts.* ***21:28** Vulgate omits *the tent.*

21:19 *iniquity for his children.* Job denied the dogma that even if a wicked person prospers temporarily, his children will be punished. Job's position is sustained by other passages in the Bible (Deut. 24:16; Ezek. 18:1–28; John 9:1–3).

22:2 *man be profitable to God.* The implication of Eliphaz's rhetorical question—that man cannot put God under any obligation that God must repay—was a valid theological principle that the Lord Himself corroborates in 41:11. However, his application of that principle to Job's circumstances (vv. 3–5) was invalid, for it was based on the faulty assumption that the righteous are always blessed and the wicked always experience God's judgment on earth.

22:3–4 *blameless . . . fear.* The same Hebrew root words ("reverence" and "integrity") had earlier been used by Eliphaz in his courteous remarks about Job (4:6). In these verses Eliphaz is being sarcastic.

22:6–9 *naked . . . weary . . . widows.* These trumped up charges were categorically denied by Job (29:11–17; 31:13–22), and God's own witness to Satan revealed to the reader that the charges were false (1:8).

21:19 [m] [Ex. 20:5] **21:20** [n] Is. 51:17 **21:22** [o] [Is. 40:13; 45:9] **21:26** [p] Eccl. 9:2 **21:30** [q] [Prov. 16:4] **21:33** [r] Heb. 9:27 **22:1** [a] Job 4:1; 15:1; 42:9 **22:2** [b] [Luke 17:10] **22:6** [c] [Ex. 22:26, 27] **22:7** [d] Deut. 15:7 **22:11** [e] Ps. 69:1, 2; 124:5 **22:13** [f] Ps. 73:11 **22:14** [g] Ps. 139:11, 12

16 Who ^hwere cut down before their time,
Whose foundations were swept away
by a flood?
17 ⁱThey said to God, 'Depart from us!
What can the Almighty do to them?'*
18 Yet He filled their houses with good
things;
But the counsel of the wicked is far
from me.

19 "The^j righteous see *it* and are glad,
And the innocent laugh at them:
20 'Surely our adversaries* are cut down,
And the fire consumes their remnant.'

21 "Now acquaint yourself with Him, and
^kbe at peace;
Thereby good will come to you.
22 Receive, please, ^linstruction from His
mouth,
And ^mlay up His words in your heart.
23 If you return to the Almighty, you will
be built up;
You will remove iniquity far from your
tents.
24 Then you will ⁿlay your gold in the
dust,
And the *gold* of Ophir among the
stones of the brooks.
25 Yes, the Almighty will be your gold*
And your precious silver;
26 For then you will have your ^odelight in
the Almighty,
And lift up your face to God.
27 ^pYou will make your prayer to Him,
He will hear you,
And you will pay your vows.
28 You will also declare a thing,
And it will be established for you;
So light will shine on your ways.
29 When they cast *you* down, and you
say, 'Exaltation *will come!*'
Then ^qHe will save the humble *person.*
30 He will *even* deliver one who is not
innocent;
Yes, he will be delivered by the purity
of your hands."

Job Proclaims God's Righteous Judgments

23 Then Job answered and said:

2 "Even today my ^acomplaint is bitter;
My* hand is listless because of my
groaning.
3 ^bOh, that I knew where I might find
Him,
That I might come to His seat!

4 I would present *my* case before Him,
And fill my mouth with arguments.
5 I would know the words *which* He
would answer me,
And understand what He would say
to me.
6 ^cWould He contend with me in His
great power?
No! But He would take *note* of me.
7 There the upright could reason with
Him,
And I would be delivered forever from
my Judge.

8 "Look,^d I go forward, but He is not
there,
And backward, but I cannot perceive
Him;
9 When He works on the left hand, I
cannot behold *Him;*
When He turns to the right hand, I
cannot see *Him.*
10 But ^eHe knows the way that I take;
When ^fHe has tested me, I shall come
forth as gold.
11 ^gMy foot has held fast to His steps;
I have kept His way and not turned
aside.
12 I have not departed from the
^hcommandment of His lips;
ⁱI have treasured the words of His
mouth
More than my necessary *food.*

13 "But He *is* unique, and who can make
Him change?
And *whatever* ^jHis soul desires, *that*
He does.
14 For He performs *what is* ^kappointed
for me,
And many such *things are* with
Him.
15 Therefore I am terrified at His
presence;
When I consider *this*, I am afraid of
Him.
16 For God ^lmade my heart weak,
And the Almighty terrifies me;
17 Because I was not ^mcut off from the
presence of darkness,
And He did *not* hide deep darkness
from my face.

* **22:17** Septuagint and Syriac read *us.*
* **22:20** Septuagint reads *substance.* * **22:25** The
ancient versions suggest *defense;* Hebrew reads
gold as in verse 24. * **23:2** Following Masoretic
Text, Targum, and Vulgate; Septuagint and Syriac
read *His.*

22:18 the counsel of the wicked is far from me. Eliphaz was repeating Job (21:16).
22:30 purity of your hands. This was actually fulfilled through Job's prayer for the three friends (42:8–10).
23:13 unique. When Job contemplated the unique power and sovereign freedom of God, he was terrified (13:21).

22:16 ^h Job 14:19; 15:32 **22:17** ⁱ Job 21:14, 15 **22:19** ^j Ps. 52:6; 58:10; 107:42 **22:21** ^k Is. 27:5 **22:22** ^l Prov. 2:6 ^m [Ps. 119:11] **22:24** ⁿ 2 Chr. 1:15 **22:26** ^o Job 27:10; Ps. 37:4; Is. 58:14 **22:27** ^p [Is. 58:9–11] **22:29** ^q [1 Pet. 5:5] **23:2** ^a Job 7:11 **23:3** ^b Job 13:3, 18; 16:21; 31:35 **23:6** ^c Is. 57:16 **23:8** ^d Job 9:11; 35:14 **23:10** ^e [Ps. 1:6; 139:1–3] ^f [James 1:12] **23:11** ^g Ps. 17:5 **23:12** ^h Job 6:10; 22:22 ⁱ Ps. 44:18 **23:13** ^j [Ps. 115:3] **23:14** ^k [1 Thess. 3:2–4] **23:16** ^l Ps. 22:14 **23:17** ^m Job 10:18, 19

Job Complains of Violence on the Earth

24 "Since ªtimes are not hidden from the Almighty,
Why do those who know Him see not His ᵇdays?

2 "Some remove ᶜlandmarks;
They seize flocks violently and feed *on them*;

3 They drive away the donkey of the fatherless;
They ᵈtake the widow's ox as a pledge.

4 They push the needy off the road;
All the ᵉpoor of the land are forced to hide.

5 Indeed, *like* wild donkeys in the desert,
They go out to their work, searching for food.
The wilderness yields food for them *and* for *their* children.

6 They gather their fodder in the field
And glean in the vineyard of the wicked.

7 They ᶠspend the night naked, without clothing,
And have no covering in the cold.

8 They are wet with the showers of the mountains,
And ᵍhuddle around the rock for want of shelter.

9 "Some snatch the fatherless from the breast,
And take a pledge from the poor.

10 They cause *the poor* to go naked, without ʰclothing;
And they take away the sheaves from the hungry.

11 They press out oil within their walls,
And tread winepresses, yet suffer thirst.

12 The dying groan in the city,
And the souls of the wounded cry out;
Yet God does not charge *them* with wrong.

13 "There are those who rebel against the light;
They do not know its ways
Nor abide in its paths.

14 ⁱThe murderer rises with the light;
He kills the poor and needy;
And in the night he is like a thief.

15 ʲThe eye of the adulterer waits for the twilight,
ᵏSaying, 'No eye will see me';
And he disguises *his* face.

16 In the dark they break into houses
Which they marked for themselves in the daytime;
ˡThey do not know the light.

17 For the morning is the same to them as the shadow of death;
If *someone* recognizes *them*,
They are in the terrors of the shadow of death.

18 "They *should be* swift on the face of the waters,
Their portion *should be* cursed in the earth,
So that no *one would* turn into the way of their vineyards.

19 As drought and heat consume the snow waters,
So the grave* *consumes those who* have sinned.

20 The womb *should* forget him,
The worm *should* feed sweetly on him;
ᵐHe *should* be remembered no more,
And wickedness *should* be broken like a tree.

21 For he preys on the barren *who* do not bear,
And does no good for the widow.

22 "But *God* draws the mighty away with His power;
He rises up, but no *man* is sure of life.

23 He gives them security, and they rely on *it*;
Yet ⁿHis eyes *are* on their ways.

24 They are exalted for a little while,
Then they are gone.
They are brought low;
They are taken out of the way like all *others*;
They dry out like the heads of grain.

25 "Now if *it is* not *so*, who will prove me a liar,
And make my speech worth nothing?"

Bildad: How Can Man Be Righteous?

25 Then ªBildad the Shuhite answered and said:

2 "Dominion and fear *belong* to Him;
He makes peace in His high places.

3 Is there any number to His armies?
Upon whom does ᵇHis light not rise?

4 ᶜHow then can man be righteous before God?

* 24:19 Or *Sheol*

24:2 remove landmarks. Removing landmarks was tantamount to stealing land. The landmarks set boundaries, and moving them would have been like moving surveyor's stakes (Deut. 27:17).
24:16 break into houses. The walls of houses were built of mud bricks, through which thieves could dig.
24:24 brought low. Job was not so much arguing that the wicked would not prosper (vv. 18–25), as he was saying that everyone is brought low.

24:1 ª [Acts 1:7] ᵇ [Is. 2:12]   **24:2** ᶜ [Deut. 19:14; 27:17]
24:3 ᵈ [Deut. 24:6, 10, 12, 17]   **24:4** ᵉ Prov. 28:28
24:7 ᶠ Ex. 22:26, 27   **24:8** ᵍ Lam. 4:5   **24:10** ʰ Job
31:19   **24:14** ⁱ Ps. 10:8   **24:15** ʲ Prov. 7:7–10   ᵏ Ps. 10:11
24:16 ˡ [John 3:20]   **24:20** ᵐ Prov. 10:7   **24:23** ⁿ [Prov.
15:3]   **25:1** ª Job 8:1; 18:1   **25:3** ᵇ James 1:17
25:4 ᶜ Job 4:17; 15:14

Or how can he be ᵈpure *who is* born of
a woman?
5 If even the moon does not shine,
And the stars are not pure in His
ᵉsight,
6 How much less man, *who is* ᶠa maggot,
And a son of man, *who is* a worm?"

Job: Man's Frailty and God's Majesty

26 But Job answered and said:

2 "How have you helped *him who is*
without power?
How have you saved the arm *that has*
no strength?
3 How have you counseled *one who has*
no wisdom?
And *how* have you declared sound
advice to many?
4 To whom have you uttered words?
And whose spirit came from you?

5 "The dead tremble,
Those under the waters and those
inhabiting them.
6 ᵃSheol *is* naked before Him,
And Destruction has no covering.
7 ᵇHe stretches out the north over empty
space;
He hangs the earth on nothing.
8 ᶜHe binds up the water in His thick
clouds,
Yet the clouds are not broken under it.
9 He covers the face of *His* throne,
And spreads His cloud over it.
10 ᵈHe drew a circular horizon on the face
of the waters,
At the boundary of light and darkness.
11 The pillars of heaven tremble,
And are astonished at His rebuke.
12 ᵉHe stirs up the sea with His power,
And by His understanding He breaks
up the storm.
13 ᶠBy His Spirit He adorned the heavens;
His hand pierced ᵍthe fleeing serpent.

14 Indeed these *are* the mere edges of His
ways,
And how small a whisper we hear of
Him!
But the thunder of His power who can
understand?"

Job Maintains His Integrity

27 Moreover Job continued his discourse, and said:

2 "As God lives, ᵃwho has taken away my
justice,
And the Almighty, *who* has made my
soul bitter,
3 As long as my breath *is* in me,
And the breath of God in my
nostrils,
4 My lips will not speak wickedness,
Nor my tongue utter deceit.
5 Far be it from me
That I should say you are right;
Till I die ᵇI will not put away my
integrity from me.
6 My righteousness I ᶜhold fast, and will
not let it go;
ᵈMy heart shall not reproach *me* as
long as I live.

7 "May my enemy be like the wicked,
And he who rises up against me like
the unrighteous.
8 ᵉFor what is the hope of the hypocrite,
Though he may gain *much*,
If God takes away his life?
9 ᶠWill God hear his cry
When trouble comes upon him?
10 ᵍWill he delight himself in the
Almighty?
Will he always call on God?

11 "I will teach you about the hand of
God;
What *is* with the Almighty I will not
conceal.
12 Surely all of you have seen *it*;
Why then do you behave with
complete nonsense?

25:6 worm. What a contrast to the words of God (Gen. 1:26–31) when He made humans in His own image and declared them "very good." Bildad was conscious of the great gap between God and man, but unlike Job, he did not feel that he could make the connection of communication that Job was striving for.

26:4 whose spirit came from you. The contrast between Bildad's comments about God (ch. 25) and Job's worshipful declaration of God's majesty (vv. 7–14) indicate the difference in the level of their understanding of who God is.

26:6 Sheol is naked. This is the place of the dead and "destruction," which were fearful hidden concepts to Job and his contemporaries, but they held no secrets for the all-knowing God.

26:7 hangs the earth on nothing. Job's comments on the suspension of the earth, the manner of clouds (v. 8) and the horizon (v. 10) speak much for his powers of observation as well as the inspiration of Scripture.

27:2 who has made my soul bitter. Though Job repeatedly complained of a bitter spirit (7:11; 10:1), the Lord did not cause him to respond that way. Job's responses only exposed the attitude that lay deep within his being. The message of the Lord for Job was that no matter what the circumstances, one should resolutely trust in God (40:8; 42:1–6).

27:5 say you are right. Job maintained that his friends were erroneous in their reasoning, and to agree with them would be to compromise his integrity.

27:12 complete nonsense. Job maintained that the actions of his friends were foolish, considering the knowledge of God that they should have had.

25:4 ᵈ [Job 14:4] **25:5** ᵉ Job 15:15 **25:6** ᶠ Ps. 22:6 **26:6** ᵃ Prov. 15:11 **26:7** ᵇ Job 9:8 **26:8** ᶜ Prov. 30:4 **26:10** ᵈ Prov. 8:29 **26:12** ᵉ Is. 51:15 **26:13** ᶠ Ps. 33:6 ᵍ Is. 27:1 **27:2** ᵃ Job 34:5 **27:5** ᵇ Job 2:9; 13:15 **27:6** ᶜ Job 2:3; 33:9 ᵈ Acts 24:16 **27:8** ᵉ Matt. 16:26 **27:9** ᶠ Jer. 14:12 **27:10** ᵍ Job 22:26, 27

13 "This[h] is the portion of a wicked man
with God,
And the heritage of oppressors,
received from the Almighty:
14 [i]If his children are multiplied, it is for
the sword;
And his offspring shall not be satisfied
with bread.
15 Those who survive him shall be buried
in death,
And [j]their* widows shall not weep,
16 Though he heaps up silver like dust,
And piles up clothing like clay—
17 He may pile it up, but [k]the just will
wear it,
And the innocent will divide the silver.
18 He builds his house like a moth,*
[l]Like a booth which a watchman
makes.
19 The rich man will lie down,
But not be gathered up;*
He opens his eyes,
And he is [m]no more.
20 [n]Terrors overtake him like a flood;
A tempest steals him away in the
night.
21 The east wind carries him away, and
he is gone;
It sweeps him out of his place.
22 It hurls against him and does not
[o]spare;
He flees desperately from its power.
23 Men shall clap their hands at him,
And shall hiss him out of his place.

Job's Discourse on Wisdom

28 "Surely there is a mine for silver,
And a place where gold is refined.
2 Iron is taken from the earth,
And copper is smelted from ore.
3 Man puts an end to darkness,
And searches every recess
For ore in the darkness and the
shadow of death.
4 He breaks open a shaft away from
people;
In places forgotten by feet
They hang far away from men;
They swing to and fro.
5 As for the earth, from it comes bread,
But underneath it is turned up as by fire;
6 Its stones are the source of sapphires,
And it contains gold dust.
7 That path no bird knows,
Nor has the falcon's eye seen it.

8 The proud lions* have not trodden it,
Nor has the fierce lion passed over it.
9 He puts his hand on the flint;
He overturns the mountains at the
roots.
10 He cuts out channels in the rocks,
And his eye sees every precious thing.
11 He dams up the streams from
trickling;
What is hidden he brings forth to
light.
12 "But[a] where can wisdom be found?
And where is the place of
understanding?
13 Man does not know its [b]value,
Nor is it found in the land of the living.
14 [c]The deep says, 'It is not in me';
And the sea says, 'It is not with me.'
15 It [d]cannot be purchased for gold,
Nor can silver be weighed for its
price.
16 It cannot be valued in the gold of
Ophir,
In precious onyx or sapphire.
17 Neither [e]gold nor crystal can equal it,
Nor can it be exchanged for jewelry of
fine gold.
18 No mention shall be made of coral or
quartz,
For the price of wisdom is above
[f]rubies.
19 The topaz of Ethiopia cannot equal it,
Nor can it be valued in pure [g]gold.
20 "From[h] where then does wisdom come?
And where is the place of
understanding?
21 It is hidden from the eyes of all living,
And concealed from the birds of the
air.
22 [i]Destruction and Death say,
'We have heard a report about it with
our ears.'
23 God understands its way,
And He knows its place.
24 For He looks to the ends of the earth,
And [j]sees under the whole heavens,

---

* **27:15** Literally his   * **27:18** Following Masoretic Text and Vulgate; Septuagint and Syriac
read spider (compare 8:14); Targum reads decay.
* **27:19** Following Masoretic Text and Targum;
Septuagint and Syriac read But shall not add
(that is, do it again); Vulgate reads But take away
nothing.   * **28:8** Literally sons of pride, figurative
of the great lions

27:13 portion of a wicked man. Job likened the
foolishness of his friends to wickedness, and indeed
it is wicked to knowingly misrepresent God. The rest
of the chapter is a satirical paraphrase of the friends'
teaching about the fate of the wicked (24:18–25),
which Job has thrown back in his friends' faces.
28:13–19 not. Every verse in this whole stanza has
the Hebrew word for "not" at least once, stressing the
absence of wisdom or even the desire for wisdom.
The rhetorical questions concerning the whereabouts of wisdom and understanding (v. 12) receive

an emphatic answer: not anywhere in the land of the
living or dead.

27:13 [h] Job 20:29   **27:14** [i] Deut. 28:41   **27:15** [j] Ps.
78:64   **27:17** [k] Prov. 28:8   **27:18** [l] Is. 1:8   **27:19** [m] Job
7:8, 21; 20:7   **27:20** [n] Job 18:11   **27:22** [o] Jer. 13:14
28:12 [a] Eccl. 7:24   **28:13** [b] Prov. 3:15   **28:14** [c] Job
28:22   **28:15** [d] Prov. 3:13–15; 8:10, 11, 19   **28:17** [e] Prov.
8:10; 16:16   **28:18** [f] Prov. 3:15; 8:11   **28:19** [g] Prov. 8:19
28:20 [h] Job 28:12   **28:22** [i] Job 28:14   **28:24** [j] [Prov.
15:3]

25 kTo establish a weight for the wind,
And apportion the waters by measure.
26 When He lmade a law for the rain,
And a path for the thunderbolt,
27 Then He saw *wisdom** and declared it;
He prepared it, indeed, He searched
it out.
28 And to man He said,
'Behold, mthe fear of the Lord, that *is*
wisdom,
And to depart from evil *is*
understanding.'"

Job's Summary Defense

29 Job further continued his discourse,
and said:

2 "Oh, that I were as *in* months *a*past,
As *in* the days *when* God *b*watched
over me;
3 *c*When His lamp shone upon my head,
And when by His light I walked
through darkness;
4 Just as I was in the days of my prime,
When *d*the friendly counsel of God
was over my tent;
5 When the Almighty *was* yet with me,
When my children *were* around me;
6 When *e*my steps were bathed with
cream,*
And *f*the rock poured out rivers of oil
for me!

7 "When I went out to the gate by the city,
When I took my seat in the open
square,
8 The young men saw me and hid,
And the aged arose *and* stood;
9 The princes refrained from talking,
And *g*put *their* hand on their mouth;
10 The voice of nobles was hushed,
And their *h*tongue stuck to the roof of
their mouth.
11 When the ear heard, then it blessed
me,
And when the eye saw, then it
approved me;
12 Because *i*I delivered the poor who
cried out,
The fatherless and *the one who* had no
helper.
13 The blessing of a perishing *man* came
upon me,
And I caused the widow's heart to sing
for joy.

14 *i*I put on righteousness, and it clothed
me;
My justice *was* like a robe and a
turban.
15 I *was* *k*eyes to the blind,
And I *was* feet to the lame.
16 I *was* a father to the poor,
And *l*I searched out the case *that* I did
not know.
17 I broke *m*the fangs of the wicked,
And plucked the victim from his teeth.

18 "Then I said, *n*'I shall die in my nest,
And multiply *my* days as the sand.
19 *o*My root *is* spread out *p*to the waters,
And the dew lies all night on my
branch.
20 My glory *is* fresh within me,
And my *q*bow is renewed in my hand.'

21 "*Men* listened to me and waited,
And kept silence for my counsel.
22 After my words they did not speak
again,
And my speech settled on them *as*
dew.
23 They waited for me *as* for the rain,
And they opened their mouth wide *as*
for *r*the spring rain.
24 *If* I mocked at them, they did not
believe *it*,
And the light of my countenance they
did not cast down.
25 I chose the way for them, and sat as
chief;
So I dwelt as a king in the army,
As one *who* comforts mourners.

30 "But now they mock at me, *men*
younger than I,
Whose fathers I disdained to put with
the dogs of my flock.
2 Indeed, what *profit* is the strength of
their hands to me?
Their vigor has perished.
3 *They are* gaunt from want and famine,
Fleeing late to the wilderness, desolate
and waste,
4 Who pluck mallow by the bushes,
And broom tree roots *for* their food.
5 They were driven out from among
men,
They shouted at them as *at* a thief.

---

* **28:27** Literally *it*   * **29:6** Masoretic Text reads
wrath; ancient versions and some Hebrew manuscripts read *cream* (compare 20:17).

28:28 fear of the Lord. To fear God is to acknowledge
that God has the right to judge our actions for good
or evil. Job had talked a lot about injustice and his
innocence, but he was solidly aware that only God
has wisdom, and in the end, his fear of the Lord was
greater than his protestations of blamelessness.
29:12 delivered the poor. Considering Job's account
of his life when he was prosperous, Eliphaz's accusations of Job sending the widows away empty and
crushing the orphans (22:9) was a calculated insult.
29:14 put on righteousness . . . a turban. This vivid

portrait of Job was a stark contrast to his present condition, with his flesh being "clothed" in worms and dust.

28:25 *k* Ps. 135:7   **28:26** *l* Job 37:3; 38:25
28:28 *m* [Prov. 1:7; 9:10]   **29:2** *a* Job 1:1–5   *b* Job 1:10
29:3 *c* Job 18:6   **29:4** *d* [Ps. 25:14]   **29:6** *e* Deut. 32:14;
Job 20:17   *f* Ps. 81:16   **29:9** *g* Job 21:5   **29:10** *h* Ps.
137:6   **29:12** *i* [Ps. 72:12]   **29:14** *j* [Is. 59:17; 61:10]
29:15 *k* Num. 10:31   **29:16** *l* Prov. 29:7   **29:17** *m* Prov.
30:14   **29:18** *n* Ps. 30:6   **29:19** *o* Job 18:16   *P* Ps. 1:3
29:20 *q* Gen. 49:24   **29:23** *r* [Zech. 10:1]

6 *They had* to live in the clefts of the
valleys,
In caves of the earth and the rocks.
7 Among the bushes they brayed,
Under the nettles they nestled.
8 *They were* sons of fools,
Yes, sons of vile men;
They were scourged from the land.

9 "And*ᵃ* now I am their taunting song;
Yes, I am their byword.
10 They abhor me, they keep far from me;
They do not hesitate *ᵇ*to spit in my
face.
11 Because *ᶜ*He has loosed my* bowstring
and afflicted me,
They have cast off restraint before me.
12 At *my* right *hand* the rabble arises;
They push away my feet,
And *ᵈ*they raise against me their ways
of destruction.
13 They break up my path,
They promote my calamity;
They have no helper.
14 They come as broad breakers;
Under the ruinous storm they roll
along.
15 Terrors are turned upon me;
They pursue my honor as the wind,
And my prosperity has passed like a
cloud.

16 "And*ᵉ* now my soul is *ᶠ*poured out
because of my *plight;*
The days of affliction take hold of me.
17 My bones are pierced in me at night,
And my gnawing pains take no rest.
18 By great force my garment is
disfigured;
It binds me about as the collar of my
coat.
19 He has cast me into the mire,
And I have become like dust and
ashes.
20 "I *ᵍ*cry out to You, but You do not
answer me;
I stand up, and You regard me.
21 *But* You have become cruel to me;
With the strength of Your hand You
*ʰ*oppose me.
22 You lift me up to the wind and cause
me to ride *on it;*
You spoil my success.

23 For I know *that* You will bring me *to*
death,
And *to* the house *ⁱ*appointed for all
living.

24 "Surely He would not stretch out *His*
hand against a heap of ruins,
If they cry out when He destroys *it.*
25 *ʲ*Have I not wept for him who was in
trouble?
Has *not* my soul grieved for the poor?
26 *ᵏ*But when I looked for good, evil came
to me;
And when I waited for light, then came
darkness.
27 My heart is in turmoil and cannot rest;
Days of affliction confront me.
28 *ˡ*I go about mourning, but not in the
sun;
I stand up in the assembly *and* cry out
for help.
29 *ᵐ*I am a brother of jackals,
And a companion of ostriches.
30 *ⁿ*My skin grows black and falls from
me;
*ᵒ*My bones burn with fever.
31 My harp is *turned* to mourning,
And my flute to the voice of those who
weep.

31 "I have made a covenant with my
eyes;
Why then should I look upon a *ᵃ*young
woman?
2 For what *is* the *ᵇ*allotment of God from
above,
And the inheritance of the Almighty
from on high?
3 *Is* it not destruction for the wicked,
And disaster for the workers of
iniquity?
4 *ᶜ*Does He not see my ways,
And count all my steps?

5 "If I have walked with falsehood,
Or if my foot has hastened to deceit,
6 Let me be weighed on honest scales,
That God may know my *ᵈ*integrity.
7 If my step has turned from the way,
Or *ᵉ*my heart walked after my eyes,
Or if any spot adheres to my hands,

---

* **30:11** Following Masoretic Text, Syriac, and
Targum; Septuagint and Vulgate read *His.*

30:11 *loosed my bowstring.* A bow that is not strung
up is not ready for use. This was a terrible contrast to
his former life, described in 29:20, where Job referred
to himself as having his bowstring renewed. A bow
that is being used has its string replaced regularly so
that the bow can operate at its maximum strength.
30:21 *strength of Your hand.* Job blamed God's
strong hand, which Satan could not move, for calamities that were actually caused by the hand of Satan
(1:11–12,18–19).
31:5 *If.* The word "if" was a part of a formula used
by accused persons to swear their innocence. The
full oath formula was, in effect, "If I am guilty of
this crime, may God impose that curse." Because of

hesitation about speaking a curse, the person swearing the oath would normally use an abbreviated version. By contrast, Job used the full formula four times,
which demonstrated his confidence that he would be
acquitted.

30:9 *ᵃ* Job 17:6 **30:10** *ᵇ* Is. 50:6 **31:11** *ᶜ* Job
12:18 **30:12** *ᵈ* Job 19:12 **30:16** *ᵉ* Ps. 42:4 *ᶠ* Ps. 22:14
30:20 *ᵍ* Job 19:7 **30:21** *ʰ* Job 10:3; 16:9, 14; 19:6, 22
30:23 *ⁱ* [Heb. 9:27] **30:25** *ʲ* Ps. 35:13, 14 **30:26** *ᵏ* Jer.
8:15 **30:28** *ˡ* Ps. 38:6; 42:9; 43:2 **30:29** *ᵐ* Mic.
1:8 **30:30** *ⁿ* Ps. 119:83 *ᵒ* Ps. 102:3 **31:1** *ᵃ* [Matt. 5:28]
31:2 *ᵇ* Job 20:29 **31:4** *ᶜ* [2 Chr. 16:9] **31:6** *ᵈ* Job 23:10;
27:5, 6 **31:7** *ᵉ* Ezek. 6:9

8   *Then* [f]let me sow, and another eat;
    Yes, let my harvest be rooted out.

9   "If my heart has been enticed by a
    woman,
    Or *if* I have lurked at my neighbor's
    door,

10 *Then* let my wife grind for [g]another,
    And let others bow down over her.

11 For that *would be* wickedness;
    Yes, [h]it *would be* iniquity *deserving of*
    judgment.

12 For that *would be* a fire *that* consumes
    to destruction,
    And would root out all my increase.

13 "If I have [i]despised the cause of my
    male or female servant
    When they complained against me,

14 What then shall I do when [j]God rises
    up?
    When He punishes, how shall I answer
    Him?

15 [k]Did not He who made me in the womb
    make them?
    Did not the same One fashion us in the
    womb?

16 "If I have kept the poor from *their*
    desire,
    Or caused the eyes of the widow to
    [l]fail,

17 Or eaten my morsel by myself,
    So that the fatherless could not eat
    of it

18 (But from my youth I reared him as a
    father,
    And from my mother's womb I guided
    the widow*);

19 If I have seen anyone perish for lack of
    clothing,
    Or any poor *man* without covering;

20 If his heart* has not [m]blessed me,
    And *if* he was *not* warmed with the
    fleece of my sheep;

21 If I have raised my hand [n]against the
    fatherless,
    When I saw I had help in the gate;

22 *Then* let my arm fall from my
    shoulder,
    Let my arm be torn from the socket.

23 For [o]destruction *from* God *is* a terror
    to me,
    And because of His magnificence I
    cannot endure.

24 "If[p] I have made gold my hope,
    Or said to fine gold, '*You are* my
    confidence';

25 [q]If I have rejoiced because my wealth
    was great,

    And because my hand had gained
    much;

26 [r]If I have observed the sun* when it
    shines,
    Or the moon moving *in* brightness,

27 So that my heart has been secretly
    enticed,
    And my mouth has kissed my hand;

28 This also *would be* an iniquity
    deserving of judgment,
    For I would have denied God *who is*
    above.

29 "If[s] I have rejoiced at the destruction of
    him who hated me,
    Or lifted myself up when evil found
    him

30 [t](Indeed I have not allowed my mouth
    to sin
    By asking for a curse on his soul);

31 If the men of my tent have not said,
    'Who is there that has not been
    satisfied with his meat?'

32 [u](But no sojourner had to lodge in the
    street,
    For I have opened my doors to the
    traveler*);

33 If I have covered my transgressions
    [v]as Adam,
    By hiding my iniquity in my bosom,

34 Because I feared the great [w]multitude,
    And dreaded the contempt of families,
    So that I kept silence
    And did not go out of the door—

35 [x]Oh, that I had one to hear me!
    Here is my mark.
    Oh, [y]*that* the Almighty would answer
    me,
    That my Prosecutor had written a book!

36 Surely I would carry it on my shoulder,
    And bind it on me *like* a crown;

37 I would declare to Him the number of
    my steps;
    Like a prince I would approach Him.

38 "If my land cries out against me,
    And its furrows weep together;

39 If [z]I have eaten its fruit* without
    money,
    Or [a]caused its owners to lose their
    lives;

40 *Then* let [b]thistles grow instead of wheat,
    And weeds instead of barley."

The words of Job are ended.

---

* **31:18** Literally *her* (compare verse 16)
* **31:20** Literally *loins*   * **31:26** Literally *light*
* **31:32** Following Septuagint, Syriac, Targum, and
Vulgate; Masoretic Text reads *road*.   * **31:39** Literally *its strength*

31:27 mouth has kissed my hand. This phrase refers
to the apparent ancient custom of kissing the hand
as a prelude to the superstitious and idolatrous act of
throwing a kiss to the heavenly bodies.

31:8 [f]Lev. 26:16   **31:10** [g]Jer. 8:10   **31:11** [h]Gen. 38:24
31:13 [i][Deut. 24:14, 15]   **31:14** [j][Ps. 44:21]   **31:15** [k]Job

34:19   **31:16** [l]Job 29:12   **31:20** [m][Deut. 24:13]
31:21 [n]Job 22:9   **31:23** [o]Is. 13:6   **31:24** [p][Mark
10:23–25]   **31:25** [q]Ps. 62:10   **31:26** [r]Ezek.
8:16   **31:29** [s][Prov. 17:5; 24:17]   **31:30** [t][Matt.
5:44]   **31:32** [u]Gen. 19:2, 3   **31:33** [v][Prov. 28:13]
31:34 [w]Ex. 23:2   **31:35** [x]Job 19:7; 30:20, 24, 28 [y]Job
13:22, 24; 33:10   **31:39** [z]Job 24:6, 10–12 [a]1 Kin. 21:19
31:40 [b]Gen. 3:18

Elihu Contradicts Job's Friends

32 So these three men ceased answering Job, because he *was* ^arighteous in his own eyes. ²Then the wrath of Elihu, the son of Barachel the ^bBuzite, of the family of Ram, was aroused against Job; his wrath was aroused because he ^cjustified himself rather than God. ³Also against his three friends his wrath was aroused, because they had found no answer, and *yet* had condemned Job.

⁴Now because they *were* years older than he, Elihu had waited to speak to Job.*
⁵When Elihu saw that *there was* no answer in the mouth of these three men, his wrath was aroused.

⁶So Elihu, the son of Barachel the Buzite, answered and said:

"I *am* ^dyoung in years, and you *are* very old;
Therefore I was afraid,
And dared not declare my opinion to you.
⁷ I said, 'Age* should speak,
And multitude of years should teach wisdom.'
⁸ But *there is* a spirit in man,
And ^ethe breath of the Almighty gives him understanding.
⁹ ^fGreat men* are not *always* wise,
Nor do the aged *always* understand justice.

¹⁰ "Therefore I say, 'Listen to me,
I also will declare my opinion.'
¹¹ Indeed I waited for your words,
I listened to your reasonings, while you searched out what to say.
¹² I paid close attention to you;
And surely not one of you convinced Job,
Or answered his words—
¹³ ^gLest you say,
'We have found wisdom';
God will vanquish him, not man.
¹⁴ Now he has not directed *his* words against me;
So I will not answer him with your words.

¹⁵ "They are dismayed and answer no more;
Words escape them.
¹⁶ And I have waited, because they did not speak,
Because they stood still *and* answered no more.
¹⁷ I also will answer my part,
I too will declare my opinion.
¹⁸ For I am full of words;
The spirit within me compels me.
¹⁹ Indeed my belly *is* like wine *that* has no vent;
It is ready to burst like new wineskins.
²⁰ I will speak, that I may find relief;
I must open my lips and answer.
²¹ Let me not, I pray, show partiality to anyone;
Nor let me flatter any man.
²² For I do not know how to flatter,
Else my Maker would soon take me ^haway.

Elihu Contradicts Job

33 "But please, Job, hear my speech,
And listen to all my words.
² Now, I open my mouth;
My tongue speaks in my mouth.
³ My words *come* from my upright heart;
My lips utter pure knowledge.
⁴ ^aThe Spirit of God has made me,
And the breath of the Almighty gives me life.
⁵ If you can answer me,
Set *your words* in order before me;
Take your stand.
⁶ ^bTruly I *am* as your spokesman* before God;
I also have been formed out of clay.
⁷ ^cSurely no fear of me will terrify you,
Nor will my hand be heavy on you.
⁸ "Surely you have spoken in my hearing,
And I have heard the sound of *your* words, *saying,*
⁹ 'I^d *am* pure, without transgression;
I *am* innocent, and *there is* no iniquity in me.
¹⁰ Yet He finds occasions against me,
^eHe counts me as His enemy;
¹¹ ^fHe puts my feet in the stocks,
He watches all my paths.'
¹² "Look, *in* this you are not righteous.
I will answer you,
For God is greater than man.

---

* **32:4** Vulgate reads *till Job had spoken.*
* **32:7** Literally *Days,* that is, years   * **32:9** Or *Men of many years*   * **33:6** Literally *as your mouth*

32:1 *righteous in his own eyes.* Job's friends accused him of self-righteousness because of his denial of the sins they ascribed to him. Job considered himself blameless (and so did God), but he was not without sin. Job needed to see how he compared to God's utter holiness, in spite of the fact that he had none of the unconfessed sins that his friends accused him of. **32:2 *wrath was aroused.*** Elihu's first mistake was in dealing with a delicate situation while he was angry. He did use the same arguments as the three friends, but he did not understand the whole situation any

better than they did. Only the reader is aware of the counsel that took place in heaven (ch. 1). **33:12 *in this you are not righteous.*** Elihu was correct in saying that God was not answerable to Job. God does not ever have to explain Himself to us,

---

32:1 ^a Job 6:29; 31:6; 33:9   **32:2** ^b Gen. 22:21   ^c Job 27:5, 6
32:6 ^d Lev. 19:32   **32:8** ^e [Prov. 2:6]   **32:9** ^f [1 Cor. 1:26]
32:13 ^g [Jer. 9:23]   **32:22** ^h Job 27:8   **33:4** ^a [Gen. 2:7]   **33:6** ^b Job 4:19   **33:7** ^c Job 9:34   **33:9** ^d Job 10:7
33:10 ^e Job 13:24; 16:9   **33:11** ^f Job 13:27; 19:8

13 Why do you [g]contend with Him?
For He does not give an accounting of any of His words.
14 [h]For God may speak in one way, or in another,
Yet man does not perceive it.
15 [i]In a dream, in a vision of the night,
When deep sleep falls upon men,
While slumbering on their beds,
16 [j]Then He opens the ears of men,
And seals their instruction.
17 In order to turn man *from his* deed,
And conceal pride from man,
18 He keeps back his soul from the Pit,
And his life from perishing by the sword.

19 "*Man* is also chastened with pain on his [k]bed,
And with strong *pain* in many of his bones,
20 [l]So that his life abhors [m]bread,
And his soul succulent food.
21 His flesh wastes away from sight,
And his bones stick out *which once* were not seen.
22 Yes, his soul draws near the Pit,
And his life to the executioners.

23 "If there is a messenger for him,
A mediator, one among a thousand,
To show man His uprightness,
24 Then He is gracious to him, and says,
'Deliver him from going down to the Pit;
I have found a ransom';
25 His flesh shall be young like a child's,
He shall return to the days of his youth.
26 He shall pray to God, and He will delight in him,
He shall see His face with joy,
For He restores to man His righteousness.
27 Then he looks at men and [n]says,
'I have sinned, and perverted *what was* right,
And it [o]did not profit me.'
28 He will [p]redeem his* soul from going down to the Pit,
And his* life shall see the light.

29 "Behold, God works all these *things*,
Twice, *in fact*, three *times* with a man,
30 [q]To bring back his soul from the Pit,
That he may be enlightened with the light of life.

31 "Give ear, Job, listen to me;
Hold your peace, and I will speak.
32 If you have anything to say, answer me;
Speak, for I desire to justify you.
33 If not, [r]listen to me;
Hold your peace, and I will teach you wisdom."

Elihu Proclaims God's Justice

34 Elihu further answered and said:

2 "Hear my words, you wise *men;*
Give ear to me, you who have knowledge.
3 [a]For the ear tests words
As the palate tastes food.
4 Let us choose justice for ourselves;
Let us know among ourselves what *is* good.

5 "For Job has said, [b]'I am righteous,
But [c]God has taken away my justice;
6 [d]Should I lie concerning my right?
My wound *is* incurable, *though I am* without transgression.'
7 What man *is* like Job,
[e]*Who* drinks scorn like water,
8 Who goes in company with the workers of iniquity,
And walks with wicked men?
9 For [f]he has said, 'It profits a man nothing
That he should delight in God.'

10 "Therefore listen to me, you men of understanding:
[g]Far be it from God *to do* wickedness,
And *from* the Almighty *to commit* iniquity.
11 [h]For He repays man *according to* his work,
And makes man to find a reward according to *his* way.
12 Surely God will never do wickedly,
Nor will the Almighty [i]pervert justice.

* **33:28** Or *my* (Kethib) • Or *my* (Kethib)

even though He often graciously does so. Job had great respect for God, and understood the fear of the Lord (28:28). He was persistent in asking God for an answer, and in the end, God did reply.

33:29–30 ***To bring back his soul from the Pit.*** Again, one of Job's advisors had some correct understanding of God, but he mistakenly applied it to Job. It is true that the chastening of pain or trouble sometimes causes men to turn to God and repent of wickedness. But Job's problem was not perverting what was right (v. 27). For him, the answer for the purpose of his pain could not be "to bring back his soul from the Pit." Without claiming that Job was sin free, God had called him blameless and upright (1:8).

34:8 ***walks with wicked men.*** There was no justice in this charge against Job.

34:12 ***do wickedly . . . pervert justice.*** Elihu was unhappy with Job's persistent charges that God was unjust (9:22–24; 24:1–25), and this was a proper concern. The judge of all the earth will always do right (Rev. 15:3).

33:13 [g] [Is. 45:9] **33:14** [h] Ps. 62:11 **33:15** [i] [Num. 12:6] **33:16** [j] [Job 36:10, 15] **33:19** [k] Job 30:17 **33:20** [l] Ps. 107:18 [m] Job 3:24; 6:7 **33:27** [n] [Luke 15:21] [o] [Rom. 6:21] **33:28** [p] Is. 38:17 **33:30** [q] Ps. 56:13 **33:33** [r] Ps. 34:11 **34:3** [a] Job 6:30; 12:11 **34:5** [b] Job 13:18; 33:9 [c] Job 27:2 **34:6** [d] Job 6:4; 9:17 **34:7** [e] Job 15:16 **34:9** [f] Mal. 3:14 **34:10** [g] Job 8:3; 36:23 **34:11** [h] Ps. 62:12 **34:12** [i] Job 8:3

13 Who gave Him charge over the earth?
Or who appointed *Him over* the whole
world?
14 If He should set His heart on it,
If He should *j*gather to Himself His
Spirit and His breath,
15 *k*All flesh would perish together,
And man would return to dust.

16 "If *you have* understanding, hear this;
Listen to the sound of my words:
17 *l*Should one who hates justice govern?
Will you *m*condemn *Him who is* most
just?
18 *n*Is it fitting to say to a king, 'You are
worthless,'
And to nobles, '*You are* wicked'?
19 Yet He *o*is not partial to princes,
Nor does He regard the rich more than
the poor;
For *p*they *are* all the work of His
hands.
20 In a moment they die, *q*in the middle of
the night;
The people are shaken and pass away;
The mighty are taken away without
a hand.

21 "For*r* His eyes *are* on the ways of man,
And He sees all his steps.
22 *s*There is no darkness nor shadow of
death
Where the workers of iniquity may
hide themselves.
23 For He need not further consider a
man,
That he should go before God in
judgment.
24 *t*He breaks in pieces mighty men
without inquiry,
And sets others in their place.
25 Therefore He knows their works;
He overthrows *them* in the night,
And they are crushed.
26 He strikes them as wicked *men*
In the open sight of others,
27 Because they *u*turned back from Him,
And *v*would not consider any of His
ways,
28 So that they *w*caused the cry of the
poor to come to Him;
For He *x*hears the cry of the afflicted.
29 When He gives quietness, who then
can make trouble?

And when He hides *His* face, who then
can see Him,
Whether *it is* against a nation or a
man alone?—
30 That the hypocrite should not reign,
Lest the people be ensnared.

31 "For has *anyone* said to God,
'I have borne *chastening*;
I will offend no more;
32 Teach me *what* I do not see;
If I have done iniquity, I will do no
more'?
33 Should He repay *it* according to your
terms,
Just because you disavow it?
You must choose, and not I;
Therefore speak what you know.

34 "Men of understanding say to me,
Wise men who listen to me:
35 'Job*y* speaks without knowledge,
His words *are* without wisdom.'
36 Oh, that Job were tried to the utmost,
Because *his* answers *are like* those of
wicked men!
37 For he adds *z*rebellion to his sin;
He claps *his hands* among us,
And multiplies his words against
God."

Elihu Condemns Self-Righteousness

35 Moreover Elihu answered and said:

2 "Do you think this is right?
Do you say,
'My righteousness is more than God's'?
3 For *a*you say,
'What advantage will it be to You?
What profit shall I have, more than *if* I
had sinned?'

4 "I will answer you,
And *b*your companions with you.
5 *c*Look to the heavens and see;
And behold the clouds—
They are higher than you.
6 If you sin, what do you accomplish
*d*against Him?
Or, *if* your transgressions are
multiplied, what do you do to
Him?

34:16 hear this. As indicated by the singular Hebrew verb translated "hear," Elihu was addressing Job directly in verses 16–33.
34:24 breaks in pieces mighty men. Job was a mighty man who was broken. Elihu's implication is that Job was a worker of iniquity (v. 22).
34:37 adds rebellion to his sin. Job was stubborn, but he was not rebellious. He was willing to accept punishment if he deserved it (31:5–6).
35:6 If you sin. This is the same argument used by Eliphaz (22:2). The point that Elihu was making here and through verse 8, is that God's stature is not affected either by the sinfulness or righteousness of man. He cannot be diminished by sin nor made greater by

righteousness. This is a true and important point. But it leaves out the understanding that God created man to be in His image, and He does care about the actions of man. God wants men to live blamelessly (ch. 1), and it is good to want to please God.

34:14/Ps. 104:29　**34:15**k [Gen. 3:19]　**34:17**l 2 Sam. 23:3　m Job 40:8　**34:18**n Ex. 22:28　**34:19**o [Deut. 10:17]　p Job 31:15　**34:20**q Ex. 12:29　**34:21**r Job 31:4　**34:22**s [Amos 9:2, 3]　**34:24**t [Dan. 2:21]　**34:27**u 1 Sam. 15:11　v Is. 5:12　**34:28**w Job 35:9　x [Ex. 22:23]　**34:35**y Job 35:16; 38:2　**34:37**z Job 7:11; 10:1　**35:3**a Job 21:15; 34:9　**35:4**b Job 34:8　**35:5**c [Job 22:12]　**35:6**d [Jer. 7:19]

7 eIf you are righteous, what do you give
Him?
Or what does He receive from your
hand?
8 Your wickedness affects a man such
as you,
And your righteousness a son of man.
9 "Becausef of the multitude of
oppressions they cry out;
They cry out for help because of the
arm of the mighty.
10 But no one says, g'Where is God my
Maker,
hWho gives songs in the night,
11 Who iteaches us more than the beasts
of the earth,
And makes us wiser than the birds of
heaven?'
12 jThere they cry out, but He does not
answer,
Because of the pride of evil men.
13 kSurely God will not listen to empty
talk,
Nor will the Almighty regard it.
14 lAlthough you say you do not see Him,
Yet justice is before Him, and myou
must wait for Him.
15 And now, because He has not
npunished in His anger,
Nor taken much notice of folly,
16 oTherefore Job opens his mouth in
vain;
He multiplies words without
knowledge."

Elihu Proclaims God's Goodness

36 Elihu also proceeded and said:

2 "Bear with me a little, and I will show
you
That there are yet words to speak on
God's behalf.
3 I will fetch my knowledge from afar;
I will ascribe righteousness to my
Maker.
4 For truly my words are not false;
One who is perfect in knowledge is
with you.

5 "Behold, God is mighty, but despises no
one;

aHe is mighty in strength of
understanding.
6 He does not preserve the life of the
wicked,
But gives justice to the boppressed.
7 cHe does not withdraw His eyes from
the righteous;
But dthey are on the throne with kings,
For He has seated them forever,
And they are exalted.
8 And eif they are bound in fetters,
Held in the cords of affliction,
9 Then He tells them their work and
their transgressions—
That they have acted defiantly.
10 fHe also opens their ear to instruction,
And commands that they turn from
iniquity.
11 If they obey and serve Him,
They shall gspend their days in
prosperity,
And their years in pleasures.
12 But if they do not obey,
They shall perish by the sword,
And they shall die without
hknowledge.*

13 "But the hypocrites in heart istore up
wrath;
They do not cry for help when He
binds them.
14 jThey die in youth,
And their life ends among the
perverted persons.*
15 He delivers the poor in their affliction,
And opens their ears in oppression.

16 "Indeed He would have brought you out
of dire distress,
kInto a broad place where there is no
restraint;
And lwhat is set on your table would
be full of mrichness.
17 But you are filled with the judgment
due the nwicked;
Judgment and justice take hold of you.

---

* **36:12** Masoretic Text reads as one without
knowledge.   * **36:14** Hebrew qedeshim, that
is, those practicing sodomy and prostitution in
religious rituals

35:12 Pride—Elihu accused Job of pride because Job had declared his own righteousness (32:1). But Elihu's presumption and self-righteousness became even more excessive than Job's as he developed his pompous speech against Job (36:4). Later Elihu would understand that God had accepted Job, while his "friends" were condemned. Even knowledge about God and commitment to God can become a source of pride that blinds us to other things that God is doing, both in ourselves and in others.

35:13 empty talk. Elihu was assuming that Job had no answer from God because God knew that Job's cry was empty.

36:2 speak on God's behalf. Elihu believed that he was speaking for God and that he was setting Job straight. It is interesting to note that God asked Job

to pray for the other three friends (42:7–10), but no word, either of censure or praise, was said about Elihu.

36:6–14 does not preserve the life of the wicked. Elihu repeats the concept that the wicked are judged by being cut off and the repentant are rewarded.

35:7 e Prov. 9:12   **35:9** f Job 34:28   **35:10** g Is. 51:13   h Acts 16:25   **35:11** i Ps. 94:12   **35:12** j Prov. 1:28   **35:13** k [Is. 1:15]   **35:14** l Job 9:11   m [Ps. 37:5, 6]   **35:15** n Ps. 89:32   **35:16** o Job 34:35; 38:2   **36:5** a Job 12:13, 16; 37:23   **36:6** b Job 5:15   **36:7** c [Ps. 33:18; 34:15]   d Ps. 113:8   **36:8** e Ps. 107:10   **36:10** f Job 33:16; 36:15   **36:11** g [Is. 1:19, 20]   **36:12** h Job 4:21   **36:13** i [Rom. 2:5]   **36:14** j Ps. 55:23   **36:16** k Ps. 18:19; 31:8; 118:5   l Ps. 23:5   m Ps. 36:8   **36:17** n Job 22:5, 10, 11

18 Because *there is* wrath, *beware* lest He
take you away with *one* blow;
For [o]a large ransom would not help
you avoid *it.*
19 [p]Will your riches,
Or all the mighty forces,
Keep you from distress?
20 Do not desire the night,
When people are cut off in their place.
21 Take heed, [q]do not turn to iniquity,
For [r]you have chosen this rather than
affliction.

22 "Behold, God is exalted by His power;
Who teaches like Him?
23 [s]Who has assigned Him His way,
Or who has said, 'You have done
[t]wrong'?

Elihu Proclaims God's Majesty

24 "Remember to [u]magnify His work,
Of which men have sung.
25 Everyone has seen it;
Man looks on *it* from afar.

26 "Behold, God *is* great, and we [v]do not
know *Him;*
[w]Nor can the number of His years *be*
discovered.
27 For He [x]draws up drops of water,
Which distill as rain from the mist,
28 [y]Which the clouds drop down
And pour abundantly on man.
29 Indeed, can *anyone* understand the
spreading of clouds,
The thunder from His canopy?
30 Look, He [z]scatters His light upon it,
And covers the depths of the sea.
31 For [a]by these He judges the peoples;
He [b]gives food in abundance.
32 [c]He covers *His* hands with lightning,
And commands it to strike.
33 [d]His thunder declares it,
The cattle also, concerning the rising
storm.

37 "At this also my heart trembles,
And leaps from its place.
2 Hear attentively the thunder of His
voice,
And the rumbling *that* comes from
His mouth.
3 He sends it forth under the whole
heaven,
His lightning to the ends of the earth.
4 After it [a]a voice roars;
He thunders with His majestic voice,
And He does not restrain them when
His voice is heard.
5 God thunders marvelously with His
voice;
[b]He does great things which we cannot
comprehend.
6 For [c]He says to the snow, 'Fall *on* the
earth';
Likewise to the gentle rain and the
heavy rain of His strength.
7 He seals the hand of every man,
[d]That [e]all men may know His work.
8 The beasts [f]go into dens,
And remain in their lairs.
9 From the chamber *of the south* comes
the whirlwind,
And cold from the scattering winds *of
the north.*
10 [g]By the breath of God ice is given,
And the broad waters are frozen.
11 Also with moisture He saturates the
thick clouds;
He scatters His bright clouds.
12 And they swirl about, being turned by
His guidance,
That they may [h]do whatever He
commands them
On the face of the whole earth.*
13 [i]He causes it to come,
Whether for correction,
Or [j]for His land,
Or [k]for mercy.

14 "Listen to this, O Job;
Stand still and [l]consider the wondrous
works of God.

* **37:12** Literally *the world of the earth*

36:23 *You have done wrong.* This is probably the most accurate warning that Elihu gives to Job. Even though Job was sure that God would vindicate his actions (and the reader knows that God saw Job as blameless and upright), he could not defend his position without telling God that He had done wrong. God cannot sin, nor will He tempt people to sin.
36:24 *magnify His work.* This is the best advice that Elihu gave Job, and indeed, it was something that Job had already done (26:5–14; 28:1–28). Exalting God for who He is and what He has done is one of the best ways to gain perspective when we are in trouble or despair.
36:26 *Behold, God is great.* As Elihu begins to praise God, his anger with Job disappears, and he speaks accurately and joyfully of the things that he knows about God. From here to the end of chapter 37 Elihu is praising God. The speeches of Elihu are the most difficult of the friends' admonitions to analyze, and scholars are not in total agreement about which charges by Elihu are discerning and which charges are misapplied "conventional wisdom." Like all mixtures of truth and misunderstanding, Elihu's discourse needs careful sorting.
37:7 *seals the hand of every man.* God uses the winter storm to stop man so that he cannot work, but instead may recognize the work of God.
37:12 *guidance.* This is a nautical term which literally means "steerings" or "rope-pullings" (Prov. 15) and portrays God as the wise Captain who skillfully charts

36:18 [o] Ps. 49:7 **36:19** [p] [Prov. 11:4] **36:21** [q] [Ps. 31:6; 66:18] [r] [Heb. 11:25] **36:23** [s] Job 34:13; [Is. 40:13, 14] [t] Job 8:3 **36:24** [u] [Rev. 15:3] **36:26** [v] [1 Cor. 13:12] [w] Heb. 1:12 **36:27** [x] Ps. 147:8 **36:28** [y] [Prov. 3:20] **36:30** [z] Job 37:3 **36:31** [a] [Acts 14:17] [b] Ps. 104:14, 15 **36:32** [c] Ps. 147:8 **36:33** [d] 1 Kin. 18:41 **37:4** [a] Ps. 29:3 **37:5** [b] Job 5:9; 9:10; 36:26 **37:6** [c] Ps. 147:16, 17 **37:7** [d] Ps. 109:27 [e] Ps. 19:3, 4 **37:8** [f] Ps. 104:21, 22 **37:10** [g] Ps. 147:17, 18 **37:12** [h] Job 36:32 **37:13** [i] Ex. 9:18, 23 [j] Job 38:26, 27 [k] 1 Kin. 18:41–46 **37:14** [l] Ps. 111:2

15 Do you know when God dispatches
　　them,
　　And causes the light of His cloud to
　　　shine?
16 ᵐDo you know how the clouds are
　　balanced,
　　Those wondrous works of ⁿHim who is
　　　perfect in knowledge?
17 Why *are* your garments hot,
　　When He quiets the earth by the south
　　　wind?
18 With Him, have you ᵒspread out the
　　ᵖskies,
　　Strong as a cast metal mirror?

19 "Teach us what we should say to Him,
　　For we can prepare nothing because of
　　　the darkness.
20 Should He be told that I *wish to* speak?
　　If a man were to speak, surely he
　　　would be swallowed up.
21 Even now *men* cannot look at the light
　　when it is bright in the skies,
　　When the wind has passed and
　　　cleared them.
22 He comes from the north *as* golden
　　splendor;
　　With God *is* awesome majesty.
23 *As for* the Almighty, ᵖwe cannot find
　　Him;
　　ʳ*He is* excellent in power,
　　In judgment and abundant justice;
　　He does not oppress.
24 Therefore men ˢfear Him;
　　He shows no partiality to any *who are*
　　　ᵗwise of heart."

The Lord Reveals His Omnipotence to Job

38 Then the Lord answered Job ᵃout of
　　the whirlwind, and said:

2 "Whoᵇ is this who darkens counsel
　　By ᶜwords without knowledge?
3 ᵈNow prepare yourself like a man;
　　I will question you, and you shall
　　　answer Me.

4 "Whereᵉ were you when I laid the
　　foundations of the earth?
　　Tell *Me*, if you have understanding.

5 Who determined its measurements?
　　Surely you know!
　　Or who stretched the line upon it?
6 To what were its foundations fastened?
　　Or who laid its cornerstone,
7 When the morning stars sang together,
　　And all ᶠthe sons of God shouted for
　　　joy?

8 "Orᵍ *who* shut in the sea with doors,
　　When it burst forth *and* issued from
　　　the womb;
9 When I made the clouds its garment,
　　And thick darkness its swaddling
　　　band;
10 When ʰI fixed My limit for it,
　　And set bars and doors;
11 When I said,
　　'This far you may come, but no farther,
　　And here your proud waves ⁱmust stop!'

12 "Have you ʲcommanded the morning
　　　since your days *began*,
　　And caused the dawn to know its
　　　place,
13 That it might take hold of the ends of
　　　the earth,
　　And ᵏthe wicked be shaken out of it?
14 It takes on form like clay *under* a seal,
　　And stands out like a garment.
15 From the wicked their ˡlight is
　　　withheld,
　　And ᵐthe upraised arm is broken.

16 "Have you ⁿentered the springs of the
　　　sea?
　　Or have you walked in search of the
　　　depths?
17 Have ᵒthe gates of death been revealed
　　　to you?
　　Or have you seen the doors of the
　　　shadow of death?
18 Have you comprehended the breadth
　　　of the earth?
　　Tell *Me*, if you know all this.

19 "Where *is* the way *to* the dwelling of
　　　light?
　　And darkness, where *is* its place,
20 That you may take it to its territory,
　　That you may know the paths *to* its
　　　home?

---

the course for the clouds, which respond obediently
to His hand at the helm.
37:18 Strong . . . cast metal mirror. Ancient mirrors
were firm and unbreakable because they were made
of polished bronze.
37:24 partiality . . . wise of heart. Even though
Elihu had claimed earlier to be one who "is perfect in
knowledge" (36:4), he knew that God does not give
preferential treatment, even to the wise.
38:2 words without knowledge. The theme of the
first speech of the Lord is given here. Job did not
know what he was talking about. God quite quickly
points out that there is a wide gap in understanding
between God and man. God was not saying that Job
had sinned in the way that his friends had accused
him, but He was saying that Job had been presumptuous with his superficial knowledge of divine things.

Job, along with his friends, had to learn that suffering
may serve a purpose known only to God. In that case,
a follower of God will submit even to loss and trauma,
without complaint, for the glory of God.
38:10 My limit. If God controls the sea and places
boundaries on it, He can place boundaries on anything else that will affect mankind.

37:16 ᵐ Job 36:29 ⁿ Job 36:4 **37:18** ᵒ [Is. 44:24]
ᵖ Ps. 104:2 **37:23** ᵖ [1 Tim. 6:16] ʳ [Job 9:4; 36:5]
37:24 ˢ [Matt. 10:28] ᵗ [Matt. 11:25] **38:1** ᵃ Ex.
19:16 **38:2** ᵇ Job 34:35; 42:3 ᶜ 1 Tim. 1:7 **38:3** ᵈ Job
40:7 **38:4** ᵉ Ps. 104:5 **38:7** ᶠ Job 1:6 **38:8** ᵍ Gen. 1:9
38:10 ʰ Job 26:10 **38:11** ⁱ [Ps. 89:9; 93:4] **38:12** ʲ [Ps.
74:16; 148:5] **38:13** ᵏ Ps. 104:35 **38:15** ˡ Job 18:5 ᵐ Ps.
10:15; 37:17 **38:16** ⁿ [Ps. 77:19] **38:17** ᵒ Ps. 9:13

21 Do you know *it*, because you were
  born then,
  Or *because* the number of your days
    is great?

22 "Have you entered pthe treasury of
    snow,
  Or have you seen the treasury of hail,
23 qWhich I have reserved for the time of
    trouble,
  For the day of battle and war?
24 By what way is light diffused,
  Or the east wind scattered over the
    earth?

25 "Who rhas divided a channel for the
    overflowing *water*,
  Or a path for the thunderbolt,
26 To cause it to rain on a land *where
    there is* no one,
  A wilderness in which *there is* no man;
27 sTo satisfy the desolate waste,
  And cause to spring forth the growth
    of tender grass?
28 tHas the rain a father?
  Or who has begotten the drops of dew?
29 From whose womb comes the ice?
  And the ufrost of heaven, who gives it
    birth?
30 The waters harden like stone,
  And the surface of the deep is vfrozen.

31 "Can you bind the cluster of the wPleiades,
  Or loose the belt of Orion?
32 Can you bring out Mazzaroth* in its
    season?
  Or can you guide the Great Bear with
    its cubs?
33 Do you know xthe ordinances of the
    heavens?
  Can you set their dominion over the
    earth?

34 "Can you lift up your voice to the
    clouds,
  That an abundance of water may cover
    you?
35 Can you send out lightnings, that they
    may go,
  And say to you, 'Here we *are!*'?
36 yWho has put wisdom in the mind?*
  Or who has given understanding to
    the heart?
37 Who can number the clouds by
    wisdom?
  Or who can pour out the bottles of
    heaven,

38 When the dust hardens in clumps,
  And the clods cling together?
39 "Canz you hunt the prey for the lion,
  Or satisfy the appetite of the young
    lions,
40 When they crouch in *their* dens,
  Or lurk in their lairs to lie in wait?
41 aWho provides food for the raven,
  When its young ones cry to God,
  And wander about for lack of food?

39 "Do you know the time when the
  wild amountain goats bear
  young?
  Or can you mark when bthe deer gives
    birth?
2 Can you number the months *that* they
    fulfill?
  Or do you know the time when they
    bear young?
3 They bow down,
  They bring forth their young,
  They deliver their offspring.*
4 Their young ones are healthy,
  They grow strong with grain;
  They depart and do not return to them.

5 "Who set the wild donkey free?
  Who loosed the bonds of the onager,
6 cWhose home I have made the
    wilderness,
  And the barren land his dwelling?
7 He scorns the tumult of the city;
  He does not heed the shouts of the
    driver.
8 The range of the mountains *is* his
    pasture,
  And he searches after devery green
    thing.

9 "Will the ewild ox be willing to serve
    you?
  Will he bed by your manger?
10 Can you bind the wild ox in the furrow
    with ropes?
  Or will he plow the valleys behind you?
11 Will you trust him because his
    strength *is* great?
  Or will you leave your labor to him?
12 Will you trust him to bring home your
    grain,
  And gather it to your threshing floor?

---

* **38:32** Literally *Constellations*   * **38:36** Literally
inward parts   * **39:3** Literally *pangs*, figurative
of offspring

38:26 *where there is no one.* Though God utilizes
meteorological elements to intervene in human
affairs, He also uses them in areas that lie outside the
human realm, for the sake of the land itself.
38:32 *Great Bear.* This is a reference to the constellation
known as Ursa Major, also called the Big Dipper.
39:1 *Do you know.* God continues His probing of Job.
He has shown His control of the earth and seas, the
elements and the heavens, and now He shows the
splendor and mysteries of the wild forces of nature,
which are also all in God's control.

39:5 *loosed the bands of the onager.* God shows His
compassion even for beasts of burden. This contrasts
sharply with Job's complaints about God not noticing
the oppression by the wicked (24:1–12).

38:22 pPs. 135:7   **38:23** qIs. 30:30   **38:25** rJob 28:26
38:27 sPs. 104:13, 14; 107:35   **38:28** tJob 36:27, 28
38:29 uPs. 147:16, 17   **38:30** vJob 37:10]   **38:31** wAmos
5:8   **38:33** xJer. 31:35, 36   **38:36** y[Ps. 51:6]   **38:39** zPs.
104:21   **38:41** a[Matt. 6:26]   **39:1** aPs. 104:18   bPs. 29:9
39:6 cJer. 2:24   **39:8** dGen. 1:29   **39:9** eNum. 23:22

13 "The wings of the ostrich wave proudly,
  But are her wings and pinions *like the*
    kindly stork's?
14 For she leaves her eggs on the ground,
  And warms them in the dust;
15 She forgets that a foot may crush them,
  Or that a wild beast may break them.
16 She *f*treats her young harshly, as
    though *they were* not hers;
  Her labor is in vain, without concern,
17 Because God deprived her of wisdom,
  And did not *g*endow her with
    understanding.
18 When she lifts herself on high,
  She scorns the horse and its rider.

19 "Have you given the horse strength?
  Have you clothed his neck with thunder?*
20 Can you frighten him like a locust?
  His majestic snorting strikes terror.
21 He paws in the valley, and rejoices in
    his strength;
  *h*He gallops into the clash of arms.
22 He mocks at fear, and is not
    frightened;
  Nor does he turn back from the sword.
23 The quiver rattles against him,
  The glittering spear and javelin.
24 He devours the distance with
    fierceness and rage;
  Nor does he come to a halt because the
    trumpet *has* sounded.
25 At *the blast of* the trumpet he says,
    'Aha!'
  He smells the battle from afar,
  The thunder of captains and shouting.

26 "Does the hawk fly by your wisdom,
  And spread its wings toward the
    south?
27 Does the *i*eagle mount up at your
    command,
  And *j*make its nest on high?
28 On the rock it dwells and resides,
  On the crag of the rock and the
    stronghold.
29 From there it spies out the prey;
  Its eyes observe from afar.
30 Its young ones suck up blood;
  And *k*where the slain *are*, there it *is*."

40 Moreover the LORD *a*answered Job,
    and said:

2 "Shall *b*the one who contends with the
    Almighty correct *Him*?
  He who *c*rebukes God, let him answer it."

Job's Response to God

3 Then Job answered the LORD and said:

4 "Behold,*d* I am vile;
  What shall I answer You?
  *e*I lay my hand over my mouth.
5 Once I have spoken, but I will not
    answer;
  Yes, twice, but I will proceed no
    further."

God's Challenge to Job

6 *f*Then the LORD answered Job out of the
whirlwind, and said:

7 "Now*g* prepare yourself like a man;
  *h*I will question you, and you shall
    answer Me:
8 "Would*i* you indeed annul My judgment?
  Would you condemn Me that you may
    be justified?
9 Have you an arm like God?
  Or can you thunder with *j*a voice like
    His?
10 *k*Then adorn yourself *with* majesty and
    splendor,
  And array yourself with glory and
    beauty.
11 Disperse the rage of your wrath;
  Look on everyone *who is* proud, and
    humble him.
12 Look on everyone *who is l*proud, *and*
    bring him low;
  Tread down the wicked in their place.
13 Hide them in the dust together,
  Bind their faces in hidden *darkness*.
14 Then I will also confess to you
  That your own right hand can save you.

15 "Look now at the behemoth,* which I
    made *along* with you;
  He eats grass like an ox.
16 See now, his strength *is* in his hips,
  And his power *is* in his stomach
    muscles.
17 He moves his tail like a cedar;
  The sinews of his thighs are tightly
    knit.
18 His bones *are like* beams of bronze,
  His ribs like bars of iron.
19 He *is* the first of the *m*ways of God;
  Only He who made him can bring near
    His sword.

---

* **39:19** Or *a mane*   * **40:15** A large animal, exact
identity unknown

39:30 *where the slain are, there it is.* The animals
that feed on the blood of the slain prevent the spread
of disease. This too is part of God's intricate plan.
40:8 *condemn Me that You may be justified.*
Because Job had been arguing against the inflexible
retribution dogma, which views suffering as God's
punishment for sin, Job had to condemn God in order
to maintain his own innocence.
40:15 *behemoth.* Suggestions for the identity of
this beast include the elephant, the hippopota-
mus, or a dinosaur. The name means "great beast,"

and the description most nearly fits a dinosaur, as
neither the elephant nor the hippo has a tail like a
cedar.

39:16 *f*Lam. 4:3   **39:17** *g*Job 35:11   **39:21** *h*Jer.
8:6   **39:27** *i*Prov. 30:18, 19   *j*Jer. 49:16   **39:30** *k*Matt.
24:28   **40:1** *a*Job 38:1   **40:2** *b*Job 9:3; 10:2; 33:13   *c*Job
13:3; 23:4   **40:4** *d*Ezra 9:6   *e*Job 29:9   **40:6** *f*Job 38:1
40:7 *g*Job 38:3   *h*Job 42:4   **40:8** *i*[Rom. 3:4]   **40:9** *j*[Ps.
29:3, 4]   **40:10** *k*Ps. 93:1; 104:1   **40:12** *l*Dan. 4:37
40:19 *m*Job 26:14

20 Surely the mountains [n]yield food for
him,
And all the beasts of the field play
there.
21 He lies under the lotus trees,
In a covert of reeds and marsh.
22 The lotus trees cover him *with* their
shade;
The willows by the brook surround him.
23 Indeed the river may rage,
Yet he is not disturbed;
He is confident, though the Jordan
gushes into his mouth,
24 *Though* he takes it in his eyes,
Or one pierces *his* nose with a snare.

41 "Can you draw out [a]Leviathan* with
a hook,
Or *snare* his tongue with a line *which*
you lower?
2 Can you [b]put a reed through his nose,
Or pierce his jaw with a hook?
3 Will he make many supplications to
you?
Will he speak softly to you?
4 Will he make a covenant with you?
Will you take him as a servant forever?
5 Will you play with him as *with* a bird,
Or will you leash him for your
maidens?
6 Will *your* companions make a
banquet* of him?
Will they apportion him among the
merchants?
7 Can you fill his skin with harpoons,
Or his head with fishing spears?
8 Lay your hand on him;
Remember the battle—
Never do it again!
9 Indeed, *any* hope of *overcoming* him is
false;
Shall *one not* be overwhelmed at the
sight of him?
10 No one *is* so fierce that he would dare
stir him up.
Who then is able to stand against Me?
11 [c]Who has preceded Me, that I should
pay *him*?
[d]Everything under heaven is Mine.

12 "I will not conceal* his limbs,
His mighty power, or his graceful
proportions.
13 Who can remove his outer coat?
Who can approach *him* with a double
bridle?
14 Who can open the doors of his face,
With his terrible teeth all around?
15 *His* rows of scales are *his* pride,
Shut up tightly *as with* a seal;
16 One is so near another
That no air can come between them;

17 They are joined one to another,
They stick together and cannot be
parted.
18 His sneezings flash forth light,
And his eyes *are* like the eyelids of the
morning.
19 Out of his mouth go burning lights;
Sparks of fire shoot out.
20 Smoke goes out of his nostrils,
As *from* a boiling pot and burning
rushes.
21 His breath kindles coals,
And a flame goes out of his mouth.
22 Strength dwells in his neck,
And sorrow dances before him.
23 The folds of his flesh are joined
together;
They are firm on him and cannot be
moved.
24 His heart is as hard as stone,
Even as hard as the lower *millstone.*
25 When he raises himself up, the mighty
are afraid;
Because of his crashings they are
beside* themselves.
26 *Though* the sword reaches him, it
cannot avail;
Nor does spear, dart, or javelin.
27 He regards iron as straw,
And bronze as rotten wood.
28 The arrow cannot make him flee;
Slingstones become like stubble to
him.
29 Darts are regarded as straw;
He laughs at the threat of javelins.
30 His undersides *are* like sharp
potsherds;
He spreads pointed *marks* in the mire.
31 He makes the deep boil like a pot;
He makes the sea like a pot of
ointment.
32 He leaves a shining wake behind him;
One would think the deep had white
hair.
33 On earth there is nothing like him,
Which is made without fear.
34 He beholds every high *thing*;
He *is* king over all the children of
pride."

Job's Repentance and Restoration

42 Then Job answered the LORD and
said:

2 "I know that You [a]can do everything,
And that no purpose *of Yours* can be
withheld from You.

* 41:1 A large sea creature, exact identity unknown   * 41:6 Or *bargain over him*
* 41:12 Literally *keep silent about*   * 41:25 Or
purify themselves

41:1 Leviathan. The identity of Leviathan, which is a
transliteration for the Hebrew word "sea monster," or
"sea serpent," is disputed. His description (vv. 12–18)
sounds like the traditional dragon. He is a sea animal,
an uncontrollable giant.

40:20 [n] Ps. 104:14   **41:1** [a] Is. 27:1   **41:2** [b] Is. 37:29
41:11 [c] [Rom. 11:35]   [d] Ps. 24:1; 50:12   **42:2** [a] [Matt. 19:26]

3 You asked, *b*'Who is this who hides
  counsel without knowledge?'
  Therefore I have uttered what I did not
  understand,
  *c*Things too wonderful for me, which I
  did not know.
4 Listen, please, and let me speak;
  You said, *d*'I will question you, and you
  shall answer Me.'
5 "I have *e*heard of You by the hearing of
  the ear,
  But now my eye sees You.
6 Therefore I *f*abhor *myself*,
  And repent in dust and ashes."

7And so it was, after the LORD had spoken these words to Job, that the LORD said to Eliphaz the Temanite, "My wrath is aroused against you and your two friends, for you have not spoken of Me *what is* right, as My servant Job *has*. 8Now therefore, take for yourselves *g*seven bulls and seven rams, *h*go to My servant Job, and offer up for yourselves a burnt offering; and My servant Job shall *i*pray for you. For I will accept him, lest I deal with you *according to your* folly; because you have not spoken of Me *what is* right, as My servant Job *has*."

9So Eliphaz the Temanite and Bildad the Shuhite *and* Zophar the Naamathite went and did as the LORD commanded them;

for the LORD had accepted Job. 10*j*And the LORD restored Job's losses* when he prayed for his friends. Indeed the LORD gave Job *k*twice as much as he had before. 11Then *l*all his brothers, all his sisters, and all those who had been his acquaintances before, came to him and ate food with him in his house; and they consoled him and comforted him for all the adversity that the LORD had brought upon him. Each one gave him a piece of silver and each a ring of gold.

12Now the LORD blessed *m*the latter *days* of Job more than his beginning; for he had *n*fourteen thousand sheep, six thousand camels, one thousand yoke of oxen, and one thousand female donkeys. 13*o*He also had seven sons and three daughters. 14And he called the name of the first Jemimah, the name of the second Keziah, and the name of the third Keren-Happuch. 15In all the land were found no women *so* beautiful as the daughters of Job; and their father gave them an inheritance among their brothers.

16After this Job *p*lived one hundred and forty years, and saw his children and grandchildren *for* four generations. 17So Job died, old and *q*full of days.

---

* 42:10 Literally *Job's captivity*, that is, what was captured from Job

---

42:4 you shall answer Me. Job was completely done with his complaints of injustice. He knew that his presuppositions were wrong, and that he needed God's wisdom.
42:5 Conviction—Job was not convicted of a particular sin, but of too small a view of God. In the Bible, the revelation of the character and person of God is the criterion for proper self-evaluation (Is. 6:5). Job regretted that his trust in God had been so imperfect, for he now understood God in a new way.
42:6 repent in dust and ashes. Dust and ashes were a sign of mourning. Job could not retract more fully.
42:7 spoken of Me ... as My servant Job has. Even though God had just shown Job his presumption, God still validated Job's doggedly held position that

God had not brought suffering on him because of sin in his life.
42:10 restored Job's losses when he prayed. Not only did God deal with Job's presumption and the wrong ideas of his friends, but He provided the perfect way to restore their relationship with each other, as well as with God.

42:3 *b* Job 38:2 *c* Ps. 40:5; 131:1; 139:6 42:4 *d* Job 38:3; 40:7 42:5 *e* Job 26:14 42:6 *f* Ezra 9:6 42:8 *g* Num. 23:1 *h* [Matt. 5:24] *i* Gen. 20:17 42:10 *j* Deut. 30:3 *k* Is. 40:2 42:11 *l* Job 19:13 42:12 *m* James 5:11 *n* Job 1:3 42:13 *o* Job 1:2 42:16 *p* Job 5:26; Prov. 3:16 42:17 *q* Gen. 15:15; 25:8

THE BOOK OF
PSALMS

▶ **AUTHOR:** Seventy-five of the psalms in the book are designated as Davidic: 3–9; 11–32; 34–41; 51–65; 68–70; 86; 101; 103; 108–110; 122; 124; 131; 133; and 138–145. The New Testament tells us that the "anonymous" Psalms 2 and 95 were also written by David. In addition to these, twelve are by Asaph, a priest who headed the service of music; ten are by the sons of Korah, a guild of singers and composers; two are by Solomon, Israel's most powerful king; one is by Moses; one by Heman, a wise man; and one is by Ethan, another wise man. The remaining fifty psalms are anonymous, but tradition attributes them to Ezra.

▶ **TIME:** c. 1410–430 B.C.   ▶ **KEY VERSE:** Ps. 19:14

▶ **THEME:** A collection of songs that literally covers hundreds of years of Jewish history from the patriarchs down through the postexilic period, the Book of Psalms is practical and personal as well as scenic and magnificently beautiful. The Psalms teach us how to pray, how to grieve, how to rejoice, and how to worship. Any Christian who makes building a relationship with God a priority in his or her life will find great spiritual nourishment in the Psalms. It is the prayer book for all who believe in the God of the universe. Jesus used it as such, and so should we.

BOOK ONE

Psalms 1–41

Psalm 1

The Way of the Righteous and the End of the Ungodly

1   Blessed *a*is the man
    Who walks not in the counsel of the
        ungodly,
    Nor stands in the path of sinners,
    *b*Nor sits in the seat of the scornful;

2   But *c*his delight *is* in the law of the LORD,
    *d*And in His law he meditates day
        and night.
3   He shall be like a tree
    *e*Planted by the rivers of water,
    That brings forth its fruit in its
        season,
    Whose leaf also shall not wither;
    And whatever he does shall *f*prosper.
4   The ungodly *are* not so,
    But *are* *g*like the chaff which the wind
        drives away.
5   Therefore the ungodly shall not stand
        in the judgment,
    Nor sinners in the congregation of the
        righteous.

1:1 Success—Psalm 1 sets the tone for the whole Book of Psalms. It contrasts the ways of life of the blessed man and the wicked man. Being blessed or successful is not a once for all time, dramatic event, but rather a lifetime of choosing to follow God and His commandments. Success happens when we move from grudging acceptance to enthusiastic delight in absorbing and then following God's laws and mandates. Nothing provides more resources. No motivational speakers will set us on a better course. No degrees will give us more of a life-changing education.

At first glance this kind of lifestyle may not look like the most exciting way to live. We can go through life, plodding along this way, without anybody even noticing. It's a lifestyle that doesn't fill up trophy cases or result in monuments being created. It can, however, end with "Well done, good and faithful servant" from our Lord. The excitement is in the results of being in a position to help family and friends grow.

Success comes from being in a relationship with God that means fruitfulness by His definition.
1:1 Blessed is the man. Hebrew wisdom literature and poetry is filled with descriptions of two favorite characters: "the righteous man" and "wisdom" (often personified as "she"). In this context, "the righteous man" is a literary tool used to represent those who love and desire to please God, rather than an actual individual.
1:2 meditates. Biblical meditation is focusing the mind on Scripture or the attributes and actions of God.
1:3 shall prosper. This is not a guarantee of the future financial worth of the righteous; rather, the righteous person is always useful and productive to the Lord.

1:1 *a*Prov. 4:14 *b* Jer. 15:17   **1:2** *c*Ps. 119:14, 16, 35 *d* [Josh. 1:8]   **1:3** *e* Jer. 17:8 *f*Gen. 39:2, 3, 23   **1:4** *g* Job 21:18

6 For ʰthe Lᴏʀᴅ knows the way of the
righteous,
But the way of the ungodly shall
perish.

When ʰHis wrath is kindled but a
little.
ⁱBlessed *are* all those who put their
trust in Him.

Psalm 2

The Messiah's Triumph and Kingdom

1 Why ᵃdo the nations rage,
And the people plot a vain thing?
2 The kings of the earth set themselves,
And the ᵇrulers take counsel together,
Against the Lᴏʀᴅ and against His
ᶜAnointed, *saying,*
3 "Let ᵈus break Their bonds in pieces
And cast away Their cords from us."

4 He who sits in the heavens ᵉshall
laugh;
The Lord shall hold them in derision.
5 Then He shall speak to them in His
wrath,
And distress them in His deep
displeasure:
6 "Yet I have set My King
On My holy hill of Zion."

7 "I will declare the decree:
The Lᴏʀᴅ has said to Me,
ᶠ'You *are* My Son,
Today I have begotten You.
8 Ask of Me, and I will give *You*
The nations *for* Your inheritance,
And the ends of the earth *for* Your
possession.
9 ᵍYou shall break* them with a rod of
iron;
You shall dash them to pieces like a
potter's vessel.'"

10 Now therefore, be wise, O kings;
Be instructed, you judges of the earth.
11 Serve the Lᴏʀᴅ with fear,
And rejoice with trembling.
12 Kiss the Son,* lest He* be angry,
And you perish *in* the way,

Psalm 3

The Lᴏʀᴅ Helps His Troubled People

A Psalm of David ᵃwhen he fled from
Absalom his son.

1 Lᴏʀᴅ, how they have increased who
trouble me!
Many *are* they who rise up
against me.
2 Many *are* they who say of me,
"*There is* no help for him in God." *Selah*

3 But You, O Lᴏʀᴅ, *are* ᵇa shield for me,
My glory and ᶜthe One who lifts up
my head.
4 I cried to the Lᴏʀᴅ with my voice,
And ᵈHe heard me from His ᵉholy hill.
Selah

5 ᶠI lay down and slept;
I awoke, for the Lᴏʀᴅ sustained me.
6 ᵍI will not be afraid of ten thousands of
people
Who have set *themselves* against me
all around.

7 Arise, O Lᴏʀᴅ;
Save me, O my God!
ʰFor You have struck all my enemies on
the cheekbone;
You have broken the teeth of the
ungodly.
8 ⁱSalvation *belongs* to the Lᴏʀᴅ.
Your blessing *is* upon Your people.
Selah

---

* **2:9** Following Masoretic Text and Targum; Septuagint, Syriac, and Vulgate read *rule* (compare
Revelation 2:27).   * **2:12** Septuagint and Vulgate
read *Embrace discipline;* Targum reads *Receive
instruction.* • Septuagint reads *the Lᴏʀᴅ.*

1:6 *knows the way.* The verb "knows" in this context
refers not just to God's awareness, but to an intimate, personal knowledge (101:4). God is intimately
involved with the way of the righteous, but has no
connection with the way of the ungodly, except in
judgment (146:9).
2:1 *Why do the nations rage.* David, the human
author of this psalm (Acts 4:24–26), was probably referring to the nations that confronted him and his legitimate heirs to the throne of Israel. But the Davidic kings
were mere shadows of the coming great King, the
Savior Jesus. Consequently, in a larger sense, this verse
refers to any attack on Jesus and His divine kingdom.
This assault occurred in its most dramatic form at the
cross, but resistance to God's kingdom has continued.
2:12 *Kiss the Son.* All peoples are presented with
a clear choice. They can either love and respect the
Lord's anointed, and so experience His great blessing,
or they can refuse to submit, and incur God's wrath.

3:title *when he fled from Absalom.* The history
behind this psalm is recorded in 1 Samuel 15.
3:2 *Selah.* This is probably a literary or musical term,
perhaps indicating a pause in the lyrics for a musical
interlude.
3:7 *struck . . . on the cheekbone.* In the poetic imagery that David uses, his enemies are like powerful
beasts whose strength is in their jaws and whose terror is in their teeth. God's strike at the source of their
strength means that they are no longer a threat.

1:6 ʰ Ps. 37:18   **2:1** ᵈ Acts 4:25, 26   **2:2** ᵇ [Matt.
12:14; 26:3, 4, 59–66; 27:1, 2; Mark 3:6; 11:18]; Acts
4:25–28 ᶜ [John 1:41]   **2:3** ᵈ Luke 19:14   **2:4** ᵉ Ps.
37:13   **2:7** ᶠ [Heb. 1:5; 5:5]   **2:9** ᵍ Ps. 89:23; 110:5, 6
2:12 ʰ [Rev. 6:16, 17] ⁱ [Ps. 5:11; 34:22]   **3:title** ᵃ 2 Sam.
15:13–17   **3:3** ᵇ Ps. 5:12; 28:7 ᶜ Ps. 9:13; 27:6   **3:4** ᵈ Ps.
4:3; 34:4 ᵉ Ps. 2:6; 15:1; 43:3   **3:5** ᶠ Lev. 26:6   **3:6** ᵍ Ps.
23:4; 27:3   **3:7** ʰ Job 16:10   **3:8** ⁱ [Is. 43:11]

Psalm 4

The Safety of the Faithful

To the Chief Musician. With stringed instruments. A Psalm of David.

1 Hear me when I call, O God of my
righteousness!
You have relieved me in *my* distress;
Have mercy on me, and hear my
prayer.

2 How long, O you sons of men,
Will you turn my glory to shame?
How long will you love worthlessness
And seek falsehood?   *Selah*

3 But know that ªthe LORD has set
apart* for Himself him who is
godly;
The LORD will hear when I call to Him.

4 ᵇBe angry, and do not sin.
ᶜMeditate within your heart on your
bed, and be still.   *Selah*

5 Offer ᵈthe sacrifices of righteousness,
And ᵉput your trust in the LORD.

6 *There are* many who say,
"Who will show us *any* good?"
ᶠLORD, lift up the light of Your
countenance upon us.

7 You have put ᵍgladness in my heart,
More than in the season that their
grain and wine increased.

8 ʰI will both lie down in peace, and
sleep;
ⁱFor You alone, O LORD, make me dwell
in safety.

Psalm 5

A Prayer for Guidance

To the Chief Musician. With flutes.*
A Psalm of David.

1 Give ªear to my words, O LORD,
Consider my meditation.

2 Give heed to the voice of my cry,
My King and my God,
For to You I will pray.

3 My voice You shall hear in the
morning, O LORD;
ᵇIn the morning I will direct *it* to You,
And I will look up.

4 For You *are* not a God who takes
pleasure in wickedness,
Nor shall evil dwell with You.

5 The ᶜboastful shall not ᵈstand in Your
sight;
You hate all workers of iniquity.

6 You shall destroy those who speak
falsehood;
The LORD abhors the ᵉbloodthirsty
and deceitful man.

7 But as for me, I will come into Your
house in the multitude of Your
mercy;
In fear of You I will worship toward
Your holy temple.

8 ᶠLead me, O LORD, in Your
righteousness because of my
enemies;
Make Your way straight before my
face.

9 For *there is* no faithfulness in their
mouth;
Their inward part *is* destruction;
ᵍTheir throat *is* an open tomb;
They flatter with their tongue.

10 Pronounce them guilty, O God!
Let them fall by their own counsels;
Cast them out in the multitude of their
transgressions,
For they have rebelled against You.

11 But let all those rejoice who put their
trust in You;
Let them ever shout for joy, because
You defend them;
Let those also who love Your name
Be joyful in You.

12 For You, O LORD, will bless the
righteous;
With favor You will surround him as
with a shield.

---

* 4:3 Many Hebrew manuscripts, Septuagint, Targum, and Vulgate read *made wonderful.*
* 5:title Hebrew *nehiloth*

4:1 *O God of my righteousness.* This phrase can also be translated "O my righteous God." It has two meanings: only God is righteous, and all of a person's righteousness is found in Him alone.

4:4 *Be angry, and do not sin.* These words are cited by Paul in the New Testament (Eph. 4:26). This is a good description of what righteous indignation should look like.

4:7 *their grain and wine.* The joy God gives transcends the joy of the harvest. Agricultural produce, the result of abundant rain on fertile soil, was a blessing of God on His people. But there is something greater than full barns and overflowing cisterns—the joy of God's presence.

5:7 *Your holy temple.* David was a leader in reforming the worship of God in Jerusalem, and he established a structure for the worship that would take place in the temple to be built by Solomon. David uses the word "temple" in anticipation of the future glorious building; all later generations of Hebrew worshipers would understand their own worship better because of the use of this word in these psalms.

5:9 *Their throat is an open tomb.* Paul echoed the words of these verses in describing the depravity of all people (Rom. 3:13).

4:3 ª [2 Tim. 2:19]   4:4 ᵇ [Eph. 4:26] ᶜ Ps. 77:6
4:5 ᵈ Deut. 33:19 ᵉ Ps. 37:3, 5; 62:8   4:6 ᶠ Num. 6:26
4:7 ᵍ Is. 9:3   4:8 ʰ Ps. 3:5 ⁱ [Lev. 25:18]   5:1 ª Ps. 4:1
5:3 ᵇ Ps. 55:17; 88:13   5:5 ᶜ [Hab. 1:13] ᵈ Ps. 1:5   5:6 ᵉ Ps. 55:23   5:8 ᶠ Ps. 25:4, 5; 27:11; 31:3   5:9 ᵍ Rom. 3:13

Psalm 6

A Prayer of Faith in Time of Distress

To the Chief Musician. With stringed instruments. [a]On an eight-stringed harp.* A Psalm of David.

1 O LORD, [b]do not rebuke me in Your anger,
Nor chasten me in Your hot displeasure.
2 Have mercy on me, O LORD, for I *am* weak;
O LORD, [c]heal me, for my bones are troubled.
3 My soul also is greatly [d]troubled;
But You, O LORD—how long?
4 Return, O LORD, deliver me!
Oh, save me for Your mercies' sake!
5 [e]For in death *there is* no remembrance of You;
In the grave who will give You thanks?
6 I am weary with my groaning;
All night I make my bed swim;
I drench my couch with my tears.
7 [f]My eye wastes away because of grief;
It grows old because of all my enemies.
8 [g]Depart from me, all you workers of iniquity;
For the LORD has [h]heard the voice of my weeping.
9 The LORD has heard my supplication;
The LORD will receive my prayer.
10 Let all my enemies be ashamed and greatly troubled;
Let them turn back *and* be ashamed suddenly.

Psalm 7

Prayer and Praise for Deliverance from Enemies

A [a]Meditation* of David, which he sang to the LORD [b]concerning the words of Cush, a Benjamite.

1 O LORD my God, in You I put my trust;
[c]Save me from all those who persecute me;
And deliver me,

2 [d]Lest they tear me like a lion,
[e]Rending *me* in pieces, while *there is* none to deliver.
3 O LORD my God, [f]if I have done this:
If there is [g]iniquity in my hands,
4 If I have repaid evil to him who was at peace with me,
Or [h]have plundered my enemy without cause,
5 Let the enemy pursue me and overtake *me*;
Yes, let him trample my life to the earth,
And lay my honor in the dust.   *Selah*

6 Arise, O LORD, in Your anger;
[i]Lift Yourself up because of the rage of my enemies;
[j]Rise up for me* *to* the judgment You have commanded!
7 So the congregation of the peoples shall surround You;
For their sakes, therefore, return on high.
8 The LORD shall judge the peoples;
[k]Judge me, O LORD, [l]according to my righteousness,
And according to my integrity within me.
9 Oh, let the wickedness of the wicked come to an end,
But establish the just;
[m]For the righteous God tests the hearts and minds.
10 My defense *is* of God,
Who saves the [n]upright in heart.
11 God *is* a just judge,
And God is angry *with the wicked* every day.
12 If he does not turn back,
He will [o]sharpen His sword;
He bends His bow and makes it ready.
13 He also prepares for Himself instruments of death;
He makes His arrows into fiery shafts.

* **6:title** Hebrew *sheminith*   * **7:title** Hebrew *Shiggaion*   * **7:6** Following Masoretic Text, Targum, and Vulgate; Septuagint reads O LORD *my God.*

6:4 for Your mercies' sake. Perhaps the most significant single term in the Hebrew text regarding the character of God is the word rendered "mercies" here. The Hebrew word describes what some prefer to call the "loyal love" or "lovingkindness" of God.

6:6–7 grief. The sighing and tears of this psalm are to be understood as responses to the psalmist's physical afflictions experienced at the hands of his enemies, and also to reflect the seriousness with which he felt the weight and burden of his own sinfulness. All affliction is not directly related to sin; however, it is an occasion when a spiritual accounting with God should be taken and in which the believer should be inclined to strengthen himself in God.

7:1 in You I put my trust. The dominant message in the Book of Psalms is twofold: (1) God is good, and (2) life is difficult. The life of faith is lived between these two realities.

7:12 If he does not turn back. God abhors sin, but He is also merciful, giving people the opportunity to repent before they are punished for their wickedness.

6:title [a] Ps. 12:title   **6:1** [b] Ps. 38:1; 118:18   **6:2** [c] [Hos. 6:1]   **6:3** [d] Ps. 88:3   **6:5** [e] [Eccl. 9:10]   **6:7** [f] Job 17:7   **6:8** [g] [Matt. 25:41]   [h] Ps. 3:4; 28:6   **7:title** [a] Hab. 3:1   [b] 2 Sam. 16   **7:1** [c] Ps. 31:15   **7:2** [d] Is. 38:13   [e] Ps. 50:22   **7:3** [f] 2 Sam. 16:7   [g] 1 Sam. 24:11   **7:4** [h] 1 Sam. 24:7; 26:9   **7:6** [i] Ps. 94:2   [j] Ps. 35:23; 44:23   **7:8** [k] Ps. 26:1; 35:24; 43:1   [l] Ps. 18:20; 35:24   **7:9** [m] [1 Sam. 16:7]   **7:10** [n] Ps. 97:10, 11; 125:4   **7:12** [o] Deut. 32:41

14 [p]Behold, *the wicked* brings forth
iniquity;
Yes, he conceives trouble and brings
forth falsehood.
15 He made a pit and dug it out,
[q]And has fallen into the ditch *which* he
made.
16 [r]His trouble shall return upon his own
head,
And his violent dealing shall come
down on his own crown.

17 I will praise the LORD according to His
righteousness,
And will sing praise to the name of the
LORD Most High.

Psalm 8

The Glory of the LORD in Creation

To the Chief Musician. On the
instrument of Gath.* A Psalm of David.

1 O LORD, our Lord,
How [a]excellent *is* Your name in all the
earth,
Who have [b]set Your glory above the
heavens!

2 [c]Out of the mouth of babes and nursing
infants
You have ordained strength,
Because of Your enemies,
That You may silence [d]the enemy and
the avenger.

3 When I [e]consider Your heavens, the
work of Your fingers,
The moon and the stars, which You
have ordained,
4 [f]What is man that You are mindful of
him,
And the son of man that You [g]visit
him?
5 For You have made him a little lower
than the angels,*
And You have crowned him with glory
and honor.
6 [h]You have made him to have dominion
over the works of Your hands;
[i]You have put all *things* under his feet,
7 All sheep and oxen—
Even the beasts of the field,
8 The birds of the air,
And the fish of the sea
That pass through the paths of the seas.

9 [j]O LORD, our Lord,
How excellent *is* Your name in all the
earth!

Psalm 9

Prayer and Thanksgiving for the LORD's Righteous Judgments

To the Chief Musician. To *the tune of*
"Death of the Son."* A Psalm of David.

1 I will praise *You*, O LORD, with my
whole heart;
I will tell of all Your marvelous works.
2 I will be glad and [a]rejoice in You;
I will sing praise to Your name,
[b]O Most High.

3 When my enemies turn back,
They shall fall and perish at Your
presence.
4 For You have maintained my right and
my cause;
You sat on the throne judging in
righteousness.
5 You have rebuked the nations,
You have destroyed the wicked;
You have [c]blotted out their name
forever and ever.

6 O enemy, destructions are finished
forever!
And you have destroyed cities;
Even their memory has [d]perished.

---

* **8:title** Hebrew *Al Gittith* * **8:5** Hebrew *Elohim, God;* Septuagint, Syriac, Targum, and Jewish tradition translate as *angels.* * **9:title** Hebrew *Muth Labben*

7:14 *he conceives trouble.* These words are echoed in the apostle James' description of the progress of sin (James 1:14–15).

8:5 *a little lower than the angels.* Mankind stands at the summit of God's creation. The Septuagint, an ancient Greek translation of the Old Testament, translates the Hebrew word meaning "God" (*elohim*) as "angels." The author of Hebrews bases his argument in 2:5–9 on this translation, and both readings are true. God made man (human beings) in His own image, just a little lower than angels. God created human beings as majestic creatures who were to rule over His creation. In our fallen state, we are profoundly disfigured, a perversion of the majesty God intended. However, Jesus restores those who put their trust in Him. In Christ, we recover majesty; in Him, we become the people that God wants us to be. Whenever we feel worthless, the words of this psalm should encourage us. We and all other human beings are valuable because God Himself created us in His own glorious image.

8:9 *O LORD, our Lord.* The first word is the divine name Yahweh. The second Hebrew word translated "our Lord" speaks of the One in control: "our Sovereign."

9:1 *with my whole heart.* Real praise is not halfhearted; it involves one's whole being (146:2). The words of these two verses are characteristic of the praise of God in the Psalms. He is to be praised for His works and His name. His name represents who He is; His works represent what He does.

7:14 [p] Is. 59:4 **7:15** [q] [Job 4:8] **7:16** [r] Esth. 9:25 **8:1** [a] Ps. 148:13 [b] Ps. 113:4 **8:2** [c] [1 Cor. 1:27] [d] Ps. 44:16 **8:3** [e] Ps. 111:2 **8:4** [f] Job 7:17, 18 [g] [Job 10:12] **8:6** [h] [Gen. 1:26, 28] [i] [Heb. 2:8] **8:9** [j] Ps. 8:1 **9:2** [a] Ps. 5:11; 104:34 [b] [Ps. 83:18; 92:1] **9:5** [c] Prov. 10:7 **9:6** [d] [Ps. 34:16]

7 eBut the LORD shall endure forever;
He has prepared His throne for
judgment.
8 fHe shall judge the world in
righteousness,
And He shall administer judgment for
the peoples in uprightness.
9 The LORD also will be a grefuge for the
oppressed,
A refuge in times of trouble.
10 And those who hknow Your name will
put their trust in You;
For You, LORD, have not forsaken
those who seek You.
11 Sing praises to the LORD, who dwells
in Zion!
iDeclare His deeds among the people.
12 jWhen He avenges blood, He
remembers them;
He does not forget the cry of the
humble.
13 Have mercy on me, O LORD!
Consider my trouble from those who
hate me,
You who lift me up from the gates of
death,
14 That I may tell of all Your praise
In the gates of the daughter of Zion.
I will krejoice in Your salvation.
15 lThe nations have sunk down in the pit
which they made;
In the net which they hid, their own
foot is caught.
16 The LORD is mknown by the judgment
He executes;
The wicked is snared in the work of
his own hands.
nMeditation.*   Selah
17 The wicked shall be turned into hell,
And all the nations othat forget God.
18 pFor the needy shall not always be
forgotten;
qThe expectation of the poor shall not
perish forever.
19 Arise, O LORD,
Do not let man prevail;
Let the nations be judged in Your
sight.
20 Put them in fear, O LORD,

That the nations may know
themselves to be but men.   Selah

Psalm 10

A Song of Confidence in God's
Triumph over Evil

1 Why do You stand afar off, O LORD?
Why do You hide in times of trouble?
2 The wicked in his pride persecutes the
poor;
aLet them be caught in the plots which
they have devised.
3 For the wicked bboasts of his heart's
desire;
He cblesses the greedy and renounces
the LORD.
4 The wicked in his proud countenance
does not seek God;
God is in none of his dthoughts.
5 His ways are always prospering;
Your judgments are far above, out of
his sight;
As for all his enemies, he sneers at
them.
6 eHe has said in his heart, "I shall not be
moved;
fI shall never be in adversity."
7 gHis mouth is full of cursing and hdeceit
and oppression;
Under his tongue is trouble and
iniquity.
8 He sits in the lurking places of the
villages;
In the secret places he murders the
innocent;
His eyes are secretly fixed on the
helpless.
9 He lies in wait secretly, as a lion in his
den;
He lies in wait to catch the poor;
He catches the poor when he draws
him into his net.
10 So he crouches, he lies low,
That the helpless may fall by his
strength.

* 9:16 Hebrew Higgaion

9:10 those who know Your name. Those in Old Testament times who "knew the name of the Lord" were those who looked forward with saving faith to God's promised redemption, just as we look back with saving faith to the redemption accomplished.
9:14 the daughter of Zion. This endearing term for Jerusalem indicated the close relationship and nurturing care God had for His people.
10:1 Why. Psalm 10 is found as the second half of Psalm 9 in the Septuagint, the ancient Greek translation of the Hebrew Scripture.
10:3 the greedy. The verb "to boast," as translated here, is most commonly rendered "praise." The wicked offer praise, but not to the Lord. Rather, their

hearts offer praise and worship to their own greedy desires. Their desires know no divinely set limits, since the wicked do not seek Him, but live with the conscious thought that there is no God (v. 4).

9:7 e Heb. 1:11   **9:8** f [Ps. 96:13; 98:9]   **9:9** g Ps. 32:7;
46:1; 91:2   **9:10** h Ps. 91:14   **9:11** i Ps. 66:16; 107:22
9:12 j [Ps. 72:14]   **9:14** k Ps. 13:5; 20:5; 35:9   **9:15** l Ps.
7:15, 16   **9:16** m Ex. 7:5   n Ps. 92:3   **9:17** o Job 8:13
9:18 p Ps. 9:12; 12:5   q Prov. 23:18   **10:2** a Ps. 7:16; 9:16
10:3 b Ps. 49:6; 94:3, 4   c Prov. 28:4   **10:4** d Ps. 14:1; 36:1
10:6 e [Eccl. 8:11]   f Rev. 18:7   **10:7** g [Rom. 3:14]   h Ps.
55:10, 11

11 He has said in his heart,
"God has forgotten;
He hides His face;
He will never see."

12 Arise, O LORD!
O God, ʲlift up Your hand!
Do not forget the ʲhumble.

13 Why do the wicked renounce God?
He has said in his heart,
"You will not require *an account*."

14 But You have ᵏseen, for You observe
trouble and grief,
To repay *it* by Your hand.
The helpless ˡcommits himself to You;
ᵐYou are the helper of the fatherless.

15 Break the arm of the wicked and the
evil *man*;
Seek out his wickedness *until* You find
none.

16 ⁿThe LORD *is* King forever and ever;
The nations have perished out of His
land.

17 LORD, You have heard the desire of the
humble;
You will prepare their heart;
You will cause Your ear to hear,

18 To do justice to the fatherless and the
oppressed,
That the man of the earth may oppress
no more.

Psalm 11

Faith in the LORD's Righteousness

To the Chief Musician. *A Psalm of
David.*

1 In ᵃthe LORD I put my trust;
How can you say to my soul,
"Flee *as* a bird to your mountain"?

2 For look! ᵇThe wicked bend *their* bow,
They make ready their arrow on the
string,
That they may shoot secretly at the
upright in heart.

3 ᶜIf the foundations are destroyed,
What can the righteous do?

4 The LORD *is* in His holy temple,
The LORD's ᵈthrone *is* in heaven;
ᵉHis eyes behold,
His eyelids test the sons of men.

5 The LORD ᶠtests the righteous,
But the wicked and the one who loves
violence His soul hates.

6 Upon the wicked He will rain coals;
Fire and brimstone and a burning wind
ᵍShall be the portion of their cup.

7 For the LORD *is* righteous,
He ʰloves righteousness;
His countenance beholds the upright.*

Psalm 12

Man's Treachery and God's Constancy

To the Chief Musician. ᵃOn an eight-
stringed harp.* A Psalm of David.

1 Help, LORD, for the godly man ᵇceases!
For the faithful disappear from among
the sons of men.

2 ᶜThey speak idly everyone with his
neighbor;
With flattering lips *and* a double heart
they speak.

3 May the LORD cut off all flattering lips,
And the tongue that speaks proud
things,

4 Who have said,
"With our tongue we will prevail;
Our lips *are* our own;
Who *is* lord over us?"

5 "For the oppression of the poor, for the
sighing of the needy,
Now I will arise," says the LORD;
"I will set *him* in the safety for which he
yearns."

6 The words of the LORD *are* ᵈpure words,
Like silver tried in a furnace of earth,
Purified seven times.

* **11:7** Or *The upright beholds His countenance*
* **12:title** Hebrew *sheminith*

10:11 God has forgotten. The wicked behave the way they do because they doubt that the Lord knows, cares, or will act. They want to believe that there will be no final judgment, so they feel free to do as they please. But the truth is that God will establish justice.
11:1 In the LORD I put my trust. In contrast to the surrounding psalms of lament (9; 10; 12), this psalm expresses great trust in the Almighty Lord.
11:3 If the foundations are destroyed. The wicked may taunt, but in fact the foundations are not destroyed and will never be.
11:5 The LORD tests. Undergoing trials and suffering is not necessarily a mark of sin or of God's disfavor. Such tests will show the true allegiance of our hearts.
12:2 idly. The very foundation of a nation is undermined when falsehood prevails. Every aspect of

life—home, business, social life—is based on truth. Falsehood breeds suspicion and distrust, which will destroy the very fabric of society and civilization.
12:6 pure words. In contrast to the idle words of the wicked, the words of God are altogether trustworthy. The eternal and steadfast nature of the Lord Himself stands behind His words. He will establish justice just as He has promised to David (v. 5).

10:12 ⁱ Mic. 5:9 ʲ Ps. 9:12 **10:14** ᵏ [Ps. 11:4] ˡ [2 Tim. 1:12] ᵐ Ps. 68:5 **10:16** ⁿ Ps. 29:10 **11:1** ᵃ Ps. 56:11 **11:2** ᵇ Ps. 64:3, 4 **11:3** ᶜ Ps. 82:5; 87:1; 119:152 **11:4** ᵈ [Is. 66:1] ᵉ [Ps. 33:18; 34:15, 16] **11:5** ᶠ Gen. 22:1 **11:6** ᵍ Ps. 75:8 **11:7** ʰ Ps. 33:5; 45:7 **12:title** ᵃ Ps. 6:title **12:1** ᵇ [Is. 57:1] **12:2** ᶜ Ps. 10:7; 41:6 **12:6** ᵈ 2 Sam. 22:31; Ps. 18:30; 119:140

7 You shall keep them, O Lord,
   You shall preserve them from this
      generation forever.
8 The wicked prowl on every side,
   When vileness is exalted among the
      sons of men.

Psalm 13

Trust in the Salvation of the Lord

To the Chief Musician. A Psalm of
David.

1 How long, O Lord? Will You forget me
      forever?
   aHow long will You hide Your face from
      me?
2 How long shall I take counsel in my
      soul,
   Having sorrow in my heart daily?
   How long will my enemy be exalted
      over me?
3 Consider *and* hear me, O Lord my
      God;
   bEnlighten my eyes,
   cLest I sleep the *sleep of* death;
4 Lest my enemy say,
   "I have prevailed against him";
   Lest those who trouble me rejoice
      when I am moved.

5 But I have trusted in Your mercy;
   My heart shall rejoice in Your salvation.
6 I will sing to the Lord,
   Because He has dealt bountifully
      with me.

Psalm 14

Folly of the Godless, and God's Final Triumph

To the Chief Musician. *A Psalm* of
David.

1 The afool has said in his heart,
   "*There is* no God."

They are corrupt,
   They have done abominable
      works,
   There is none who does good.
2 bThe Lord looks down from heaven
      upon the children of men,
   To see if there are any who
      understand, who seek God.
3 cThey have all turned aside,
   They have together become corrupt;
   There is none who does good,
   No, not one.
4 Have all the workers of iniquity no
      knowledge,
   Who eat up my people *as* they eat
      bread,
   And ddo not call on the Lord?
5 There they are in great fear,
   For God *is* with the generation of the
      righteous.
6 You shame the counsel of the poor,
   But the Lord *is* his erefuge.
7 fOh, that the salvation of Israel *would*
      come out of Zion!
   gWhen the Lord brings back the
      captivity of His people,
   Let Jacob rejoice *and* Israel be glad.

Psalm 15

The Character of Those Who May Dwell with the Lord

A Psalm of David.

1 Lord, awho may abide in Your
      tabernacle?
   Who may dwell in Your holy hill?
2 He who walks uprightly,
   And works righteousness,
   And speaks the btruth in his heart;
3 He *who* cdoes not backbite with his
      tongue,
   Nor does evil to his neighbor,
   dNor does he take up a reproach
      against his friend;

13:1 *How long, O Lord?* The Lord allows David to pour out his anxiety before Him. But by the end of David's prayer, the Lord has granted him a correct perspective on his situation. David's only option is to trust in the sovereign mercy of his loving God.
13:5 *Your mercy.* This word refers to God's loyal love or lovingkindness, His faithfulness to His commitment to take care of His people.
14:1 *fool.* This word does not refer to mental inability, but to moral and spiritual insensitivity. A fool is one who lives a life of "practical atheism," the view that even if there is a God, it really does not matter to one's life.
14:4 *no knowledge.* The wicked lack knowledge of God's truth. Although people may be brilliant in their chosen fields, they can still be morally insensitive and spiritually closed to the issues that have eternal consequences.

15:1 *who may abide in Your tabernacle.* No one except Jesus the Messiah is righteous enough to approach God. But there have always been those who stand before God as forgiven sinners, whose righteousness comes as a gift from God. We may come boldly into God's presence because our sins have been covered by Christ's blood.
15:2 *He who walks uprightly, And works righteousness.* The Lord commands us to be holy (1 Pet. 1:15–16), and He also gives us the power to become holy (2 Thess. 2:16–17).

13:1 a Job 13:24   13:3 b Ezra 9:8 c Jer. 51:39   14:1 a Ps. 10:4; 53:1   14:2 b Ps. 33:13, 14; 102:19   14:3 c Rom. 3:12   14:4 d Is. 64:7   14:6 e Ps. 9:9; 40:17; 46:1; 142:5   14:7 f Ps. 53:6 g Job 42:10   15:1 a Ps. 24:3–5   15:2 b [Eph. 4:25]   15:3 c [Lev. 19:16–18] d Ex. 23:1

4 ᵉIn whose eyes a vile person is despised,
But he honors those who fear the
LORD;
He *who* ᶠswears to his own hurt and
does not change;
5 He *who* does not put out his money at
usury,
Nor does he take a bribe against the
innocent.

He who does these *things* ᵍshall never
be moved.

Psalm 16

The Hope of the Faithful, and the Messiah's Victory

A ᵃMichtam of David.

1 Preserve me, O God, for in You I put
my trust.

2 *O my soul,* you have said to the LORD,
"You *are* my Lord,
ᵇMy goodness is nothing apart from
You."

3 As for the saints who *are* on the earth,
"They are the excellent ones, in ᶜwhom
is all my delight."

4 Their sorrows shall be multiplied who
hasten *after* another *god;*
Their drink offerings of ᵈblood I will
not offer,
ᵉNor take up their names on my lips.

5 O LORD, *You are* the portion of my
inheritance and my cup;
You maintain my lot.

6 The lines have fallen to me in pleasant
places;
Yes, I have a good inheritance.

7 I will bless the LORD who has given me
counsel;

My heart also instructs me in the night
seasons.

8 ᶠI have set the LORD always before me;
Because *He is* at my right hand I shall
not be moved.

9 Therefore my heart is glad, and my
glory rejoices;
My flesh also will rest in hope.

10 ᵍFor You will not leave my soul in
Sheol,
Nor will You allow Your Holy One to
see corruption.

11 You will show me me the ʰpath of life;
In Your presence *is* fullness of joy;
At Your right hand *are* pleasures
forevermore.

Psalm 17

Prayer with Confidence in Final Salvation

A Prayer of David.

1 Hear a just cause, O LORD,
Attend to my cry;
Give ear to my prayer *which is* not
from deceitful lips.

2 Let my vindication come from Your
presence;
Let Your eyes look on the things that
are upright.

3 You have tested my heart;
You have visited *me* in the night;
ᵃYou have tried me and have found
nothing;
I have purposed that my mouth shall
not ᵇtransgress.

4 Concerning the works of men,
By the word of Your lips,
I have kept away from the paths of the
destroyer.

16:5 my inheritance. This phrase refers to the Promised Land. God had given this inheritance to His people (Deut. 6:1–3). However, there was a greater inheritance for the Levites, who did not receive a share in the land (Num. 26:62); their share of the inheritance was in the Lord. David had an ancestral inheritance in the land. As king, he also had extensive royal holdings. But he realized that no inheritance was greater than his relationship with Almighty God.

16:10 Sheol. Sheol is "the grave," or the realm of the dead. Not much is known of the ancient Hebrew's concept of life after death. Sheol seems to be a dreaded place, shrouded in mystery.

17:3 tested my heart. David knew that God had done what he was requesting even before he asked. That is, God knew David's needs and what was in his heart. David's prayer helped him to focus on the source of his strength and to reaffirm his determination to live a pure life.

17:4 God's Word Corrects—There are many symbols for God's word that can be found in the Bible itself. It can be thought of as a mirror (James 1:23–25),

a seed (1 Pet. 1:23), a lamp (Ps. 119:105), a sword (Eph. 6:17), and even food (Heb. 5:12–14). But the Bible also serves as a measuring rod that can be used as a standard against which to measure our beliefs.

God Himself sometimes uses His word to correct us as He did with David. "You have dealt well with Your servant, O LORD, according to Your word . . . Before I was afflicted I went astray, but now I keep Your word" (Ps. 119:65,67).

There are times when God's word can correct believers when they are in honest and unintentional error. Aquila and Priscilla, a godly Christian couple, used the Scriptures to help a young preacher named Apollos (Acts 18:24–28). Paul does the same thing for some former disciples of John the Baptist that he met in the city of Ephesus (Acts 19:1–7).

15:4 ᵉ Esth. 3:2 ᶠLev. 5:4 **15:5** ᵍ 2 Pet. 1:10
16:title ᵃPs. 56–60 **16:2** ᵇ Job 35:7 **16:3** ᶜ Ps. 119:63
16:4 ᵈPs. 106:37, 38 ᵉ[Ex. 23:13] **16:8** ᶠ[Acts 2:25–28]
16:10 ᵍ Ps. 49:15; 86:13 **16:11** ʰ [Matt. 7:14] **17:3** ᵃ Job 23:10 ᵇ Ps. 39:1

5 cUphold my steps in Your paths,
That my footsteps may not slip.
6 dI have called upon You, for You will
hear me, O God;
Incline Your ear to me, *and* hear my
speech.
7 Show Your marvelous lovingkindness
by Your right hand,
O You who save those who trust *in You*
From those who rise up *against them.*
8 Keep me as the apple of Your eye;
Hide me under the shadow of Your
wings,
9 From the wicked who oppress me,
From my deadly enemies who
surround me.
10 They have closed up their efat *hearts;*
With their mouths they fspeak
proudly.
11 They have now surrounded us in our
steps;
They have set their eyes, crouching
down to the earth,
12 As a lion is eager to tear his prey,
And like a young lion lurking in secret
places.
13 Arise, O LORD,
Confront him, cast him down;
Deliver my life from the wicked with
Your sword,
14 With Your hand from men, O LORD,
From men of the world *who have* their
portion in *this* life,
And whose belly You fill with Your
hidden treasure.
They are satisfied with children,
And leave the rest of their *possession*
for their babes.
15 As for me, gI will see Your face in
righteousness;
hI shall be satisfied when I iawake in
Your likeness.

Psalm 18

God the Sovereign Savior

To the Chief Musician. *A Psalm* of
David athe servant of the LORD,
who spoke to the LORD the words of
bthis song on the day that the LORD
delivered him from the hand of all his
enemies and from the hand of Saul.
And he said:

1 I cwill love You, O LORD, my strength.
2 The LORD is my rock and my fortress
and my deliverer;
My God, my strength, din whom I will
trust;
My shield and the horn of my
salvation, my stronghold.
3 I will call upon the LORD, ewho is
worthy to be praised;
So shall I be saved from my enemies.

4 fThe pangs of death surrounded me,
And the floods of ungodliness made
me afraid.
5 The sorrows of Sheol surrounded me;
The snares of death confronted me.
6 In my distress I called upon the
LORD,
And cried out to my God;
He heard my voice from His temple,
And my cry came before Him, *even* to
His ears.

7 gThen the earth shook and trembled;
The foundations of the hills also
quaked and were shaken,
Because He was angry.
8 Smoke went up from His nostrils,
And devouring fire from His mouth;
Coals were kindled by it.
9 hHe bowed the heavens also, and came
down
With darkness under His feet.

17:14 *who have their portion in this life.* The wicked
live their lives with only the pursuit of the pleasures
of this world in mind. The righteous should not try to
obtain what this life can offer, but instead pursue God
and His ways.
17:15 *I will see Your face.* In the Old Testament there
is no well-developed theology of heaven, yet there
are times when the faith of the writer rises to utter
statements of hope of resurrection and of life eternal
with God. It would appear that such a view was always
a part of godly faith, even though dim in comparison
with the later revelation through Christ. Both Psalms
16 and 17 are testimonies to a growing faith that
entrance into God's presence would be the fruit of
a relationship with God in this life. The afflictions on
earth cause faith to look forward to a time after this
life when one will behold God's face in righteousness,
and faith in God will be vindicated by seeing God.
18:1 *I will love You, O LORD.* Twice in the Psalms the
poet declares a love for God (116:1). Here an unusual
word for love is used, referring to compassion as
deep as a mother's love. The text for this psalm is also
found in 2 Samuel 22.

18:2 *The LORD is my rock.* This is a particularly apt
image for David, who many times had to hide in the
mountains for security (1 Sam. 26:1,20).
18:5-6 *distress.* As the title of Psalm 18 indicates,
this poem of praise was composed in the midst of
very trying times (2 Sam. 22:1). Once again, David had
become the object of Saul's uncontrollable rage; in
his bouts of paranoia, Saul mistakenly suspected that
David was laying the foundation of a revolt against
his own royal position. How foolish David would have
been had he said, "In my distress I took the matter
into my own hands." Rather he said, "In my distress I
called upon the LORD." We have no other option when
caught in our distressing situations. Otherwise we
compound the suffering.

17:5 c Ps. 44:18; 119:133   **17:6** d Ps. 86:7; 116:2
17:10 e Ezek. 16:49 f [1 Sam. 2:3]   **17:15** g [1 John 3:2] h Ps.
4:6, 7; 16:11 i [Is. 26:19]   **18:title** a Ps. 36:title b 2 Sam.
22   **18:1** c Ps. 144:1   **18:2** d Heb. 2:13   **18:3** e Rev. 5:12
18:4 f Ps. 116:3   **18:7** g Acts 4:31   **18:9** h Ps. 144:5

10 [i]And He rode upon a cherub, and flew;
[j]He flew upon the wings of the wind.
11 He made darkness His secret place;
[k]His canopy around Him *was* dark waters
And thick clouds of the skies.
12 [l]From the brightness before Him,
His thick clouds passed with hailstones and coals of fire.

13 The LORD thundered from heaven,
And the Most High uttered [m]His voice,
Hailstones and coals of fire.*
14 [n]He sent out His arrows and scattered the foe,
Lightnings in abundance, and He vanquished them.
15 Then the channels of the sea were seen,
The foundations of the world were uncovered
At Your rebuke, O LORD,
At the blast of the breath of Your nostrils.

16 [o]He sent from above, He took me;
He drew me out of many waters.
17 He delivered me from my strong enemy,
From those who hated me,
For they were too strong for me.
18 They confronted me in the day of my calamity,
But the LORD was my support.
19 [p]He also brought me out into a broad place;
He delivered me because He delighted in me.

20 [q]The LORD rewarded me according to my righteousness;
According to the cleanness of my hands
He has recompensed me.
21 For I have kept the ways of the LORD,
And have not wickedly departed from my God.
22 For all His judgments *were* before me,
And I did not put away His statutes from me.
23 I was also blameless before Him,
And I kept myself from my iniquity.
24 [r]Therefore the LORD has recompensed me according to my righteousness,
According to the cleanness of my hands in His sight.

25 [s]With the merciful You will show Yourself merciful;
With a blameless man You will show Yourself blameless;
26 With the pure You will show Yourself pure;
And [t]with the devious You will show Yourself shrewd.
27 For You will save the humble people,
But will bring down [u]haughty looks.
28 [v]For You will light my lamp;
The LORD my God will enlighten my darkness.
29 For by You I can run against a troop,
By my God I can leap over a wall.
30 *As for* God, [w]His way *is* perfect;
[x]The word of the LORD is proven;
He *is* a shield [y]to all who trust in Him.

31 [z]For who *is* God, except the LORD?
And who *is* a rock, except our God?
32 *It is* God who [a]arms me with strength,
And makes my way perfect.
33 [b]He makes my feet like the *feet of* deer,
And [c]sets me on my high places.
34 [d]He teaches my hands to make war,
So that my arms can bend a bow of bronze.

35 You have also given me the shield of Your salvation;
Your right hand has held me up,
Your gentleness has made me great.
36 You enlarged my path under me,
[e]So my feet did not slip.

37 I have pursued my enemies and overtaken them;
Neither did I turn back again till they were destroyed.
38 I have wounded them,
So that they could not rise;
They have fallen under my feet.
39 For You have armed me with strength for the battle;
You have subdued under me those who rose up against me.
40 You have also given me the necks of my enemies,
So that I destroyed those who hated me.
41 They cried out, but *there was* none to save;

---

* **18:13** Following Masoretic Text, Targum, and Vulgate; a few Hebrew manuscripts and Septuagint omit *Hailstones and coals of fire.*

18:11–12 *darkness . . . brightness.* The references to darkness speak of the hiddenness of God. He cannot be completely understood by those whom He has created. The references to brightness speak of God's holiness.

18:35 *the shield of Your salvation.* The use of battle armor as an image of God's provision for the righteous is found in both the Old and New Testaments (Eph. 6:10–20).

18:41 *They cried out . . . to the LORD.* Apparently, in the extremes of battle, the enemies of David found no help from their gods, so they screamed aloud to David's God for deliverance. But God would not answer them.

18:10 [i]Ps. 80:1; 99:1 [j][Ps. 104:3] **18:11** [k]Ps. 97:2 **18:12** [l]Ps. 97:3; 140:10 **18:13** [m][Ps. 29:3–9; 104:7] **18:14** [n]Ps. 144:6 **18:16** [o]Ps. 144:7 **18:19** [p]Ps. 4:1; 31:8; 118:5 **18:20** [q]1 Sam. 24:19 **18:24** [r]1 Sam. 26:23 **18:25** [s][1 Kin. 8:32] **18:26** [t][Lev. 26:23–28] **18:27** [u][Ps. 101:5] **18:28** [v]Job 18:6 **18:30** [w]Rev. 15:3 [x]Ps. 12:6; 119:140 [y][Ps. 17:7] **18:31** [z][1 Sam. 2:2] **18:32** [a][Ps. 91:2] **18:33** [b]Hab. 3:19 [c]Deut. 32:13; 33:29 **18:34** [d]Ps. 144:1 **18:36** [e]Prov. 4:12

*f*Even to the LORD, but He did not
answer them.
42 Then I beat them as fine as the dust
before the wind;
I *g*cast them out like dirt in the streets.

43 You have delivered me from the
strivings of the people;
*h*You have made me the head of the
nations;
*i*A people I have not known shall
serve me.
44 As soon as they hear of me they obey me;
The foreigners submit to me.
45 *j*The foreigners fade away,
And come frightened from their
hideouts.

46 The LORD lives!
Blessed *be* my Rock!
Let the God of my salvation be exalted.
47 *It is* God who avenges me,
*k*And subdues the peoples under me;
48 He delivers me from my enemies.
*l*You also lift me up above those who
rise against me;
You have delivered me from the
violent man.
49*m*Therefore I will give thanks to You,
O LORD, among the Gentiles,
And sing praises to Your name.

50 *n*Great deliverance He gives to His king,
And shows mercy to His anointed,
To David and his descendants
forevermore.

Psalm 19

The Perfect Revelation of the LORD

To the Chief Musician. A Psalm of
David.

1 The *a*heavens declare the glory of God;
And the *b*firmament shows His
handiwork.

2 Day unto day utters speech,
And night unto night reveals
knowledge.
3 *There is* no speech nor language
Where their voice is not heard.
4 *c*Their line* has gone out through all
the earth,
And their words to the end of the
world.

In them He has set a tabernacle for
the sun,
5 Which *is* like a bridegroom coming
out of his chamber,
*d*And rejoices like a strong man to run
its race.
6 Its rising *is* from one end of heaven,
And its circuit to the other end;
And there is nothing hidden from its
heat.

7 *e*The law of the LORD *is* perfect,
converting the soul;
The testimony of the LORD *is* sure,
making *f*wise the simple;
8 The statutes of the LORD *are* right,
rejoicing the heart;
The commandment of the LORD *is*
pure, enlightening the eyes;
9 The fear of the LORD *is* clean,
enduring forever;
The judgments of the LORD *are* true
and righteous altogether.
10 More to be desired *are they* than *g*gold,
Yea, than much fine gold;
Sweeter also than honey and the
honeycomb.
11 Moreover by them Your servant is
warned,
And in keeping them *there is* great
reward.

12 Who can understand *his* errors?
*h*Cleanse me from secret *faults*.

---

* 19:4 Septuagint, Syriac, and Vulgate read *sound;*
Targum reads *business.*

There is only one prayer from the wicked to which He
gladly listens—the prayer of repentance.
18:43 *head of the nations.* David gained his empire
by the work of the Lord on his behalf. But David's
empire was only a picture of the kingdom of God that
will one day be governed by David's greater Son, the
Lord Jesus.
18:49 *among the Gentiles.* By proclaiming the victories of God to the Gentiles, David was calling for
the nations to respond in faith. How fitting that Paul
would cite this verse (or its parallel in 2 Sam. 22:50) in
Romans 15:9 as an indicator of God's ongoing intention to bring His salvation to all people.
19:1 *The heavens declare.* All of creation reveals
God's glory and majesty (Rom. 1:18–20).
19:4 *a tabernacle for the sun.* In the ancient Middle
East, the sun was often thought of as a god. In this
poem, the sun was but the stunning workmanship of
the Creator, glorifying the God who made it.
19:7–8 *The law of the LORD.* The world reveals God's
glory, and the Word reveals His saving grace. God's

law (or teaching) described as "perfect," which is
best understood here as "complete." This law needs
no alteration in part or in whole. It has power to bring
deep and radical change in the inner life or soul. It
is God's great instrument in conversion (James 1:18;
1 Pet. 1:23). The Word of God is spoken of as God's
"testimony" because it is His own instruction concerning His person and purpose. In Scripture, God
testifies concerning Himself, His Son, and sinners.
God's Word is sure (2 Pet. 1:19), and may be trusted
because He is faithful (1 Tim. 1:15). To those wise
in their own eyes, the truth of God is hidden (Matt.
11:25), but to the simple the Scriptures give wisdom
that leads to salvation (2 Tim. 3:15).

18:41 *f* Job 27:9   **18:42** *g* Zech. 10:5   **18:43** *h* 2 Sam. 8
i Is. 52:15   **18:45** *j* Mic. 7:17   **18:47** *k* Ps. 47:3
18:48 *l* Ps. 27:6; 59:1   **18:49** *m* Rom. 15:9   **18:50** *n* Ps.
21:1; 144:10   **19:1** *a* Is. 40:22   *b* Gen. 1:6, 7   **19:4** *c* Rom.
10:18   **19:5** *d* Eccl. 1:5   **19:7** *e* Ps. 111:7   *f* Ps. 119:130
19:10 *g* Ps. 119:72, 127   **19:12** *h* [Ps. 51:1, 2]

13 Keep back Your servant also from
   *i*presumptuous *sins;*
   Let them not have *j*dominion over me.
   Then I shall be blameless,
   And I shall be innocent of great
      transgression.

14 *k*Let the words of my mouth and the
      meditation of my heart
   Be acceptable in Your sight,
   O LORD, my strength and my
      *l*Redeemer.

Psalm 20

The Assurance of God's Saving Work

To the Chief Musician. A Psalm of
David.

1 May the LORD answer you in the day
      of trouble;
   May the name of the God of Jacob
      defend you;
2 May He send you help from the
      sanctuary,
   And strengthen you out of Zion;
3 May He remember all your offerings,
   And accept your burnt sacrifice. *Selah*

4 May He grant you according to your
      heart's *desire,*
   And *a*fulfill all your purpose.
5 We will rejoice in your salvation,
   And in the name of our God we will
      set up *our* banners!
   May the LORD fulfill all your
      petitions.

6 Now I know that the LORD saves His
      anointed;
   He will answer him from His holy
      heaven
   With the saving strength of His right
      hand.
7 Some *trust* in chariots, and some in
      *b*horses;
   But we will remember the name of the
      LORD our God.
8 They have bowed down and fallen;
   But we have risen and stand upright.

9 Save, LORD!
   May the King answer us when we call.

Psalm 21

Joy in the Salvation of the LORD

To the Chief Musician. A Psalm of
David.

1 The king shall have joy in Your
      strength, O LORD;
   And in Your salvation how greatly
      shall he rejoice!
2 You have given him his heart's desire,
   And have not withheld the *a*request of
      his lips.   *Selah*

3 For You meet him with the blessings of
      goodness;
   You set a crown of pure gold upon his
      head.
4 *b*He asked life from You, *and* You gave
      it to him—
   Length of days forever and ever.
5 His glory *is* great in Your salvation;
   Honor and majesty You have placed
      upon him.
6 For You have made him most blessed
      forever;
   *c*You have made him exceedingly glad
      with Your presence.
7 For the king trusts in the LORD,
   And through the mercy of the Most
      High he shall not be moved.

8 Your hand will find all Your enemies;
   Your right hand will find those who
      hate You.
9 You shall make them as a fiery oven in
      the time of Your anger;
   The LORD shall swallow them up in
      His wrath,
   And the fire shall devour them.
10 Their offspring You shall destroy from
      the earth,
   And their descendants from among
      the sons of men.
11 For they intended evil against You;
   They devised a plot *which* they are not
      able *to* *d*perform.
12 Therefore You will make them turn
      their back;
   You will make ready *Your arrows* on
      Your string toward their faces.

13 Be exalted, O LORD, in Your own
      strength!
   We will sing and praise Your power.

19:14 *my Redeemer.* God is the One who purchases our freedom from any bondage or slavery. The principal meaning of the word is "defender of family rights."

20:5 *salvation.* In the immediate context, salvation is used to describe daily deliverance from the rigors of the battle and the victory over the enemy. But the Lord's deliverance of us from our spiritual troubles should prompt the same type of praise.

20:6 *His right hand.* This is a slogan that describes God's powerful deliverance of the Israelites from Egypt (17:7; 44:3; 118:16; Ex. 15:6).

21:2 *his heart's desire.* The Lord gives people their aspirations when they are derived from a fundamental desire for God's honor and glory (20:4; 37:4; 145:19).

21:9 *the time of Your anger.* This may refer to any period of God's judgment, but compare to "the day of the LORD" (Joel 2:1; Zeph. 1:14).

19:13 *i* Num. 15:30 *j* Ps. 119:133   **19:14** *k* Ps. 51:15 *l* Is. 47:4   **20:4** *a* Ps. 21:2   **20:7** *b* Ps. 33:16, 17   **21:2** *a* 2 Sam. 7:26–29   **21:4** *b* Ps. 61:5, 6; 133:3   **21:6** *c* Ps. 16:11; 45:7   **21:11** *d* Ps. 2:1–4

Psalm 22

The Suffering, Praise, and Posterity of the Messiah

To the Chief Musician. Set to "The Deer of the Dawn."* A Psalm of David.

1 My [a]God, My God, why have You
forsaken Me?
Why are You so far from helping Me,
And from the words of My groaning?
2 O My God, I cry in the daytime, but
You do not hear;
And in the night season, and am not
silent.

3 But You *are* holy,
Enthroned in the [b]praises of Israel.
4 Our fathers trusted in You;
They trusted, and You delivered
them.
5 They cried to You, and were delivered;
[c]They trusted in You, and were not
ashamed.

6 But I *am* [d]a worm, and no man;
[e]A reproach of men, and despised by
the people.
7 [f]All those who see Me ridicule Me;
They shoot out the lip, they shake the
head, *saying*,
8 "He[g] trusted* in the LORD, let Him
rescue Him;
[h]Let Him deliver Him, since He delights
in Him!"

9 [i]But You *are* He who took Me out of the
womb;
You made Me trust *while* on My
mother's breasts.
10 I was cast upon You from birth.
From My mother's womb
[j]You *have been* My God.
11 Be not far from Me,
For trouble *is* near;
For *there is* none to help.

12 [k]Many bulls have surrounded Me;
Strong *bulls* of [l]Bashan have
encircled Me.
13 [m]They gape at Me *with* their mouths,
Like a raging and roaring lion.

14 I am poured out like water,
[n]And all My bones are out of joint;
My heart is like wax;
It has melted within Me.
15 [o]My strength is dried up like a
potsherd,
And [p]My tongue clings to My jaws;
You have brought Me to the dust of
death.

16 For dogs have surrounded Me;
The congregation of the wicked has
enclosed Me.
[q]They pierced* My hands and My feet;
17 I can count all My bones.
[r]They look *and* stare at Me.
18 [s]They divide My garments among
them,
And for My clothing they cast lots.

19 But You, O LORD, do not be far from
Me;
O My Strength, hasten to help Me!
20 Deliver Me from the sword,
[t]My precious *life* from the power of the
dog.
21 [u]Save Me from the lion's mouth
And from the horns of the wild oxen!

[v]You have answered Me.

22 [w]I will declare Your name to [x]My
brethren;
In the midst of the assembly I will
praise You.
23 [y]You who fear the LORD, praise Him!
All you descendants of Jacob, glorify
Him,
And fear Him, all you offspring of
Israel!
24 For He has not despised nor abhorred
the affliction of the afflicted;
Nor has He hidden His face from Him;
But [z]when He cried to Him, He heard.

25 [a]My praise *shall be* of You in the great
assembly;
[b]I will pay My vows before those who
fear Him.

---

*22:title Hebrew *Aijeleth Hashahar* *22:8 Septuagint, Syriac, and Vulgate read *hoped;* Targum reads *praised.* *22:16 Following some Hebrew manuscripts, Septuagint, Syriac, Vulgate; Masoretic Text reads *Like a lion.*

22:1 ***My God, My God, why have You forsaken Me?*** David used these words to express a painful sense of separation from God at a time of great trouble (38:21). These were the very words used by Christ while in agony on the cross (Matt. 27:46; Mark 15:34).

22:6 ***despised by the people.*** When David was at his lowest, his enemies ridiculed his faith in the Lord. These words also describe the experience of the Savior who endured the verbal abuse of His tormentors (Matt. 27:27–31,39–44).

22:15 ***My tongue clings to My jaws.*** Jesus' words "I thirst" (John 19:28) also expressed the pain of terrible thirst.

22:16 ***they pierced My hands and My feet.*** This verse explicitly predicts the crucifixion of the Lord Jesus Christ. The words were a figure of speech for David, but they were literally true for Jesus.

22:18 ***for My clothing they cast lots.*** This text was directly fulfilled by the soldiers who gambled at the

22:1 [a] [Mark 15:34] **22:3** [b] Deut. 10:21 **22:5** [c] Is. 49:23 **22:6** [d] Is. 41:14 [e] [Is. 53:3] **22:7** [f] Matt. 27:39 **22:8** [g] Matt. 27:43 [h] Ps. 91:14 **22:9** [i] [Ps. 71:5, 6] **22:10** [j] [Is. 46:3; 49:1] **22:12** [k] Ps. 22:21; 68:30 [l] Deut. 32:14 **22:13** [m] Job 16:10 **22:14** [n] Dan. 5:6 **22:15** [o] Prov. 17:22 [p] John 19:28 **22:16** [q] Matt. 27:35 **22:17** [r] Luke 23:27, 35 **22:18** [s] Matt. 27:35 **22:20** [t] Ps. 35:17 **22:21** [u] 2 Tim. 4:17 [v] Is. 34:7 **22:22** [w] Heb. 2:12 [x] [Rom. 8:29] **22:23** [y] Ps. 135:19, 20 **22:24** [z] Heb. 5:7 **22:25** [a] Ps. 35:18; 40:9, 10 [b] Eccl. 5:4

26 The poor shall eat and be satisfied;
   Those who seek Him will praise the
   LORD.
   Let your heart live forever!

27 All the ends of the world
   Shall remember and turn to the LORD,
   And all the families of the nations
   Shall worship before You.*

28 cFor the kingdom is the LORD's,
   And He rules over the nations.

29 dAll the prosperous of the earth
   Shall eat and worship;
   eAll those who go down to the dust
   Shall bow before Him,
   Even he who cannot keep himself alive.

30 A posterity shall serve Him.
   It will be recounted of the Lord to the
      next generation,

31 They will come and declare His
      righteousness to a people who
      will be born,
   That He has done this.

Psalm 23

The LORD the Shepherd
of His People

A Psalm of David.

1 The LORD is amy shepherd;
  bI shall not want.

2 cHe makes me to lie down in green
      pastures;
  dHe leads me beside the still waters.

3 He restores my soul;
  eHe leads me in the paths of
      righteousness
  For His name's sake.

4 Yea, though I walk through the valley
      of fthe shadow of death,
  gI will fear no evil;
  hFor You are with me;
  Your rod and Your staff, they
      comfort me.

5 You iprepare a table before me in the
      presence of my enemies;
  You janoint my head with oil;
  My cup runs over.

6 Surely goodness and mercy shall
      follow me
  All the days of my life;
  And I will dwell* in the house of the
      LORD
  Forever.

Psalm 24

The King of Glory and His Kingdom

A Psalm of David.

1 The aearth is the LORD's, and all its
      fullness,
  The world and those who dwell
      therein.

2 For He has bfounded it upon the
      seas,
  And established it upon the waters.

3 cWho may ascend into the hill of the
      LORD?
  Or who may stand in His holy
      place?

4 He who has dclean hands and ea pure
      heart,

---

* 22:27 Following Masoretic Text, Septuagint, and Targum; Arabic, Syriac, and Vulgate read Him.
* 23:6 Following Septuagint, Syriac, Targum, and Vulgate; Masoretic Text reads return.

---

foot of the cross for the possession of Jesus' robe (Matt. 27:35).

22:27 all the families of the nations. This is speaking of the eventual spread of the gospel of redemption to the whole world, fulfilling God's promise to bless all nations through Abraham's descendants (Gen. 12:3).

23:1 The LORD is my shepherd. Even though the word "king" does not appear in it, this psalm is a description of what it means to be a good ruler. Moreover, the psalm prophetically speaks of Jesus. He is the Good Shepherd whose flock trusts in Him (John 10:1–18) and the King whose perfect rule will be established (Luke 23:2–3).

23:4 the valley of the shadow of death. The awareness of our own mortality often comes with sickness, trials, and hardship. But the Lord our protector can lead us through these dark and difficult valleys to eternal life with Him. There is no need to fear death's power (1 Cor. 15:25–27). Our Lord has already traveled this road and come through the valley of darkness. Because He lives, we too shall live. Death is not our final destiny.

23:6 the house of the LORD forever. God's promise for the Israelites was not just for the enjoyment of this life in the land of promise; it was also for the

full enjoyment of the life to come in His presence (16:9–11; 17:15; 49:15).

24:1 Affirming God's Ownership of the World— Whose world is this anyway? David, of course, who lived in the hills with the animals, had a firm answer. It is God's world. This statement should shape our thinking about a great deal of life. We should have a heightened sense of stewardship to care for God's creation. We should look to God more to understand what is important and what is not important. Seeing God's creation every day should help make praise and thanksgiving a way of life. It should also help us desire to understand God's redemptive acts in history and in our lives.

24:4 clean hands and a pure heart. God looks at a person's actions and also at the attitudes of the heart.

22:28 c Matt. 6:13 22:29 d Ps. 17:10; 45:12 e [Is. 26:19]
23:1 a [Is. 40:11] b [Phil. 4:19] 23:2 c Ezek. 34:14 d [Rev. 7:17] 23:3 e Ps. 5:8; 31:3 23:4 f Job 3:5; 10:21, 22; 24:17
g [Ps. 3:6; 27:1] h [Is. 43:2] 23:5 i Ps. 104:15 j Ps. 92:10
24:1 a 1 Cor. 10:26, 28 24:2 b Ps. 89:11 24:3 c Ps. 15:1–5 24:4 d [Job 17:9] e [Matt. 5:8]

Who has not lifted up his soul to an idol,
Nor *f*sworn deceitfully.
5 He shall receive blessing from the LORD,
And righteousness from the God of his salvation.
6 This *is* Jacob, the generation of those who *g*seek Him,
Who seek Your face. *Selah*

7 *h*Lift up your heads, O you gates!
And be lifted up, you everlasting doors!
*i*And the King of glory shall come in.
8 Who *is* this King of glory?
The LORD strong and mighty,
The LORD mighty in *j*battle.
9 Lift up your heads, O you gates!
Lift up, you everlasting doors!
And the King of glory shall come in.
10 Who is this King of glory?
The LORD of hosts,
He *is* the King of glory. *Selah*

Psalm 25

A Plea for Deliverance and Forgiveness

A Psalm of David.

1 To *a*You, O LORD, I lift up my soul.
2 O my God, I *b*trust in You;
Let me not be ashamed;
*c*Let not my enemies triumph over me.
3 Indeed, let no one who waits on You be ashamed;
Let those be ashamed who deal treacherously without cause.
4 *d*Show me Your ways, O LORD;
Teach me Your paths.
5 Lead me in Your truth and teach me,
For You *are* the God of my salvation;
On You I wait all the day.
6 Remember, O LORD, *e*Your tender mercies and Your lovingkindnesses,
For they *are* from of old.

7 Do not remember *f*the sins of my youth, nor my transgressions;
*g*According to Your mercy remember me,
For Your goodness' sake, O LORD.
8 Good and upright *is* the LORD;
Therefore He teaches sinners in the way.
9 The humble He guides in justice,
And the humble He teaches His way.
10 All the paths of the LORD *are* mercy and truth,
To such as keep His covenant and His testimonies.
11 *h*For Your name's sake, O LORD,
Pardon my iniquity, for it *is* great.
12 Who *is* the man that fears the LORD?
*i*Him shall He* teach in the way He* chooses.
13 *j*He himself shall dwell in prosperity,
And *k*his descendants shall inherit the earth.
14 *l*The secret of the LORD *is* with those who fear Him,
And He will show them His covenant.
15 *m*My eyes *are* ever toward the LORD,
For He shall pluck my feet out of the net.
16 *n*Turn Yourself to me, and have mercy on me,
For I *am* desolate and afflicted.
17 The troubles of my heart have enlarged;
Bring me out of my distresses!
18 *o*Look on my affliction and my pain,
And forgive all my sins.
19 Consider my enemies, for they are many;
And they hate me with cruel hatred.
20 Keep my soul, and deliver me;
Let me not be ashamed, for I put my trust in You.
21 Let integrity and uprightness preserve me,
For I wait for You.

22 *p*Redeem Israel, O God,
Out of all their troubles!

* 25:12 Or *he* • Or *he*

24:9 And the King of glory shall come in. When Jesus came, the meaning of this ancient poem became clear (Matt. 21:1–10; Rev. 19:11–16).
25:3 who waits on You. Waiting on the Lord is the equivalent of hoping in Him (25:5; 40:1).
25:7 sins of my youth. Both the sins of immaturity and the transgressions of adulthood need forgiveness (1 John 1:9).
25:14 with those who fear Him. Those who fear the Lord pay attention to His instructions and thus learn the secrets of God's wisdom (111:10; Prov. 1:7; 3:32).
25:19 they hate me. This psalm is a prayer for forgiveness, instruction, and protection from the forces of darkness which are oppressing the writer. His most prominent trial is hostility from enemies. The

animosity which the psalmist encountered was not primarily personal, but was the result of his identification with God's cause. Therefore, he could ask the Lord to look upon him and vindicate him in the face of his afflictions. The writer's suffering had its roots in the origins of redemptive history (Gen. 3:15)—there

24:4 *f* Ps. 15:4 **24:6** *g* Ps. 27:4, 8 **24:7** *h* Is. 26:2 *i* Ps. 29:2, 9; 97:6 **24:8** *j* Rev. 19:13–16 **25:1** *a* Ps. 86:4; 143:8 **25:2** *b* Ps. 34:8 *c* Ps. 13:4; 41:11 **25:4** *d* Ex. 33:13 **25:6** *e* Ps. 103:17; 106:1 **25:7** *f* [Jer. 3:25] *g* Ps. 51:1 **25:11** *h* Ps. 31:3; 79:9; 109:21; 143:11 **25:12** *i* [Ps. 25:8; 37:23] **25:13** *j* [Prov. 19:23] *k* Matt. 5:5 **25:14** *l* [John 7:17] **25:15** *m* [Ps. 123:2; 141:8] **25:16** *n* Ps. 69:16 **25:18** *o* 2 Sam. 16:12 **25:22** *p* [Ps. 130:8]

Psalm 26

A Prayer for Divine Scrutiny and Redemption

A Psalm of David.

1 Vindicate *a*me, O LORD,
For I have *b*walked in my integrity.
*c*I have also trusted in the LORD;
I shall not slip.

2 *d*Examine me, O LORD, and prove me;
Try my mind and my heart.

3 For Your lovingkindness *is* before my eyes,
And *e*I have walked in Your truth.

4 I have not *f*sat with idolatrous mortals,
Nor will I go in with hypocrites.

5 I have *g*hated the assembly of evildoers,
And will not sit with the wicked.

6 I will wash my hands in innocence;
So I will go about Your altar, O LORD,

7 That I may proclaim with the voice of thanksgiving,
And tell of all Your wondrous works.

8 LORD, *h*I have loved the habitation of Your house,
And the place where Your glory dwells.

9 *i*Do not gather my soul with sinners,
Nor my life with bloodthirsty men,

10 In whose hands *is* a sinister scheme,
And whose right hand is full of *j*bribes.

11 But as for me, I will walk in my integrity;
Redeem me and be merciful to me.

12 *k*My foot stands in an even place;
In the congregations I will bless the LORD.

Psalm 27

An Exuberant Declaration of Faith

A Psalm of David.

1 The LORD *is* my *a*light and my salvation;
Whom shall I fear?
The *b*LORD *is* the strength of my life;
Of whom shall I be afraid?

2 When the wicked came against me
To *c*eat up my flesh,
My enemies and foes,
They stumbled and fell.

3 *d*Though an army may encamp against me,
My heart shall not fear;
Though war may rise against me,
In this I *will be* confident.

4 *e*One *thing* I have desired of the LORD,
That will I seek:
That I may *f*dwell in the house of the LORD
All the days of my life,
To behold the beauty of the LORD,
And to inquire in His temple.

5 For *g*in the time of trouble
He shall hide me in His pavilion;
In the secret place of His tabernacle
He shall hide me;
He shall *h*set me high upon a rock.

6 And now *i*my head shall be lifted up above my enemies all around me;
Therefore I will offer sacrifices of joy in His tabernacle;
I will sing, yes, I will sing praises to the LORD.

7 Hear, O LORD, *when* I cry with my voice!
Have mercy also upon me, and answer me.

8 *When You said,* "Seek My face,"
My heart said to You, "Your face, LORD, I will seek."

9 *i*Do not hide Your face from me;
Do not turn Your servant away in anger;
You have been my help;
Do not leave me nor forsake me,
O God of my salvation.

10 *k*When my father and my mother forsake me,
Then the LORD will take care of me.

11 *l*Teach me Your way, O LORD,
And lead me in a smooth path,
because of my enemies.

12 Do not deliver me to the will of my adversaries;
For *m*false witnesses have risen against me,
And such as breathe out violence.

---

would be enmity between the seed of the woman and the seed of the serpent, between the godly and the ungodly. Jesus also reminded His disciples that hatred directed against His servants on His account was to be expected (John 15:18–20).

26:3 *Your lovingkindness.* The loyal love (13:5) of God is the recurring focus of the Book of Psalms.

26:9 *Do not gather my soul.* On the basis of his protests of integrity (vv. 1–2), David prays for divine discrimination (4:3). God distinguishes those who have responded to His grace from those who have not.

27:6 *sacrifices of joy.* These are praise offerings that

the believers bring to God to celebrate the blessings He gives them (Heb. 13:15).

26:1 *a*Ps. 7:8 *b*2 Kin. 20:3 *c*[Ps. 13:5; 28:7] **26:2** *d*Ps. 17:3; 139:23 **26:3** *e*2 Kin. 20:3 **26:4** *f*Ps. 1:1 **26:5** *g*Ps. 31:6; 139:21 **26:8** *h*Ps. 27:4; 84:1–4, 10 **26:9** *i*Ps. 28:3 **26:10** *j*1 Sam. 8:3 **26:12** *k*Ps. 40:2 **27:1** *a*[Mic. 7:8] *b*Ps. 62:7; 118:14 **27:2** *c*Ps. 14:4 **27:3** *d*Ps. 3:6 **27:4** *e*Ps. 26:8; 65:4 *f*Luke 2:37 **27:5** *g*Ps. 31:20; 91:1 *h*Ps. 40:2 **27:6** *i*Ps. 3:3 **27:9** *j*Ps. 69:17; 143:7 **27:10** *k*Is. 49:15 **27:11** *l*Ps. 25:4; 86:11; 119:33 **27:12** *m*Ps. 35:11

13 *I would have lost heart*, unless I had
believed
That I would see the goodness of the
LORD
ⁿIn the land of the living.

14 ᵒWait on the LORD;
Be of good courage,
And He shall strengthen your heart;
Wait, I say, on the LORD!

Psalm 28

Rejoicing in Answered Prayer

A Psalm of David.

1 To You I will cry, O LORD my Rock:
ᵃDo not be silent to me,
ᵇLest, if You *are* silent to me,
I become like those who go down to
the pit.

2 Hear the voice of my supplications
When I cry to You,
ᶜWhen I lift up my hands ᵈtoward Your
holy sanctuary.

3 Do not take me away with the wicked
And with the workers of iniquity,
ᵉWho speak peace to their neighbors,
But evil *is* in their hearts.

4 ᶠGive them according to their deeds,
And according to the wickedness of
their endeavors;
Give them according to the work of
their hands;
Render to them what they deserve.

5 Because ᵍthey do not regard the works
of the LORD,
Nor the operation of His hands,
He shall destroy them
And not build them up.

6 Blessed *be* the LORD,
Because He has heard the voice of my
supplications.

7 The LORD *is* ʰmy strength and my
shield;
My heart ⁱtrusted in Him, and I am
helped;
Therefore my heart greatly rejoices,
And with my song I will praise Him.

8 The LORD *is* their strength,*
And He *is* the ʲsaving refuge of His
anointed.

9 Save Your people,
And bless ᵏYour inheritance;
Shepherd them also,
ˡAnd bear them up forever.

Psalm 29

Praise to God in His Holiness and Majesty

A Psalm of David.

1 Give ᵃunto the LORD, O you mighty
ones,
Give unto the LORD glory and
strength.

2 Give unto the LORD the glory due to
His name;
Worship the LORD in ᵇthe beauty of
holiness.

3 The voice of the LORD *is* over the
waters;
ᶜThe God of glory thunders;
The LORD *is* over many waters.

---

* **28:8** Following Masoretic Text and Targum;
Septuagint, Syriac, and Vulgate read *the strength
of His people.*

27:14 *Wait on the LORD.* To wait for the Lord is to demonstrate confident expectation. The Hebrew word for "wait" may also be translated "hope." To hope in God is to wait for His timing and His action (40:1; Is. 40:31).

28:1 *the pit.* This is one of the terms for death in the Psalms (55:23; 143:7).

28:5 *they do not regard.* The language here is similar to that of Paul in Romans 1:18–32. One day even the wicked will have to acknowledge God as their Creator and give Him the glory He deserves.

28:8 *His anointed.* This term acknowledges God's covenant with David, His promise that He would be David's God and David would be His representative. This passage became a heritage of the monarchy, a treasure for each godly king in the Davidic line to go back to for strength and encouragement.

29:1 *O you mighty ones.* This means "O sons of gods." This Hebrew phrase refers to spiritual beings who are in the presence of God (see Job 1:6).

29:2 Worship by Israel—The central aspect of Israel's worship was the object of their worship, the Lord. While other nations paid homage to many gods, including inanimate objects such as trees and stones, Israel worshiped the one true God. This

worship could be private, as a family, or corporate as a congregation.

Israel's worship occurred in many different contexts and many different elements. It included offering sacrifices (1 Sam. 1:3), adopting a reverent posture (2 Chr. 7:6), verbal praise—either spoken (1 Chr. 16:7) or sung (Ps. 57:7), instrumental praise (Ps. 150:3–5), prayer (2 Chr. 6:14–42), and the great feasts (Lev. 23; 25).

The first place of worship for the people of Israel was the tabernacle constructed by Moses (Ex. 25; 27; 30–31; 35; 40). Solomon's temple in Jerusalem became the permanent place for the central worship of the whole nation when it was completed. The New Testament teaching is that there is no limitation on location for worship. Access to God is direct and immediate (1 Cor. 6:19).

27:13 ⁿ Ezek. 26:20 **27:14** ᵒ Is. 25:9 **28:1** ᵃ Ps. 35:22; 39:12; 83:1 ᵇ Ps. 88:4; 143:7 **28:2** ᶜ Ps. 5:7 ᵈ Ps. 138:2 **28:3** ᵉ Ps. 12:2; 55:21; 62:4 **28:4** ᶠ [Rev. 18:6; 22:12] **28:5** ᵍ Is. 5:12 **28:7** ʰ Ps. 18:2; 59:17 ⁱ Ps. 13:5; 112:7 **28:8** ʲ Ps. 20:6 **28:9** ᵏ [Deut. 9:29; 32:9] ˡ Deut. 1:31 **29:1** ᵃ 1 Chr. 16:28, 29 **29:2** ᵇ 2 Chr. 20:21 **29:3** ᶜ [Job 37:4, 5]

4 The voice of the LORD *is* powerful;
The voice of the LORD *is* full of majesty.

5 The voice of the LORD breaks *d*the
cedars,
Yes, the LORD splinters the cedars of
Lebanon.

6 *e*He makes them also skip like a calf,
Lebanon and *f*Sirion like a young
wild ox.

7 The voice of the LORD divides the
flames of fire.

8 The voice of the LORD shakes the
wilderness;
The LORD shakes the Wilderness of
*g*Kadesh.

9 The voice of the LORD makes the *h*deer
give birth,
And strips the forests bare;
And in His temple everyone says,
"Glory!"

10 The *i*LORD sat *enthroned* at the
Flood,
And *j*the LORD sits as King forever.

11 *k*The LORD will give strength to His
people;
The LORD will bless His people with
peace.

Psalm 30

The Blessedness of Answered Prayer

A Psalm. A Song *a*at the dedication of
the house of David.

1 I will extol You, O LORD, for You have
*b*lifted me up,
And have not let my foes *c*rejoice
over me.

2 O LORD my God, I cried out to You,
And You *d*healed me.

3 O LORD, *e*You brought my soul up
from the grave;
You have kept me alive, that I should
not go down to the pit.*

4 *f*Sing praise to the LORD, you saints of
His,
And give thanks at the remembrance
of His holy name.*

5 For *g*His anger *is but for* a moment,
*h*His favor *is for* life;
Weeping may endure for a night,
But joy *comes* in the morning.

6 Now in my prosperity I said,
"I shall never be moved."

7 LORD, by Your favor You have made
my mountain stand strong;
*i*You hid Your face, *and* I was troubled.

8 I cried out to You, O LORD;
And to the LORD I made supplication:

9 "What profit *is there* in my blood,
When I go down to the pit?
*j*Will the dust praise You?
Will it declare Your truth?

10 Hear, O LORD, and have mercy on me;
LORD, be my helper!"

11 *k*You have turned for me my mourning
into dancing;
You have put off my sackcloth and
clothed me with gladness,

12 To the end that *my* glory may sing
praise to You and not be silent.
O LORD my God, I will give thanks to
You forever.

Psalm 31

The LORD a Fortress in Adversity

To the Chief Musician. A Psalm of
David.

1 In *a*You, O LORD, I put my trust;
Let me never be ashamed;
Deliver me in Your righteousness.

2 *b*Bow down Your ear to me,
Deliver me speedily;
Be my rock of refuge,
A fortress of defense to save me.

3 *c*For You *are* my rock and my fortress;
Therefore, *d*for Your name's sake,
Lead me and guide me.

4 Pull me out of the net which they have
secretly laid for me,
For You *are* my strength.

---

* **30:3** Following Qere and Targum; Kethib, Septuagint, Syriac, and Vulgate read *from those who
descend to the pit.* * **30:4** Or *His holiness*

29:6 *Sirion.* This was an ancient name for Mount Hermon (Deut. 3:9).
29:10 *at the Flood.* God is the true victor over all.
He even controlled the waters at the height of their
destructive power during the flood.
30:3 *from the grave.* David is not reporting a resurrection, but a deliverance from a nearly fatal illness.
As in 28:1, the psalmist describes death as a great pit
into which a person drops into the enveloping darkness of the unknown.
30:10 *my helper.* "Helper" can also be translated
"power" or "strength" (33:20). Jesus promised His
disciples that the Holy Spirit would be their Helper
(John 14:16).

31:1 *I put my trust.* This is a psalm of lament, yet
David expresses deep trust in God in spite of his
afflictions.

29:5 *d* Is. 2:13; 14:8   **29:6** *e* Ps. 114:4 *f* Deut. 3:9
29:8 *g* Num. 13:26   **29:9** *h* Job 39:1   **29:10** *i* Gen. 6:17
j Ps. 10:16   **29:11** *k* Ps. 28:8; 68:35   **30:title** *a* Deut.
20:5   **30:1** *b* Ps. 28:9 *c* Ps. 25:2   **30:2** *d* Ps. 6:2; 103:3
30:3 *e* Ps. 86:13   **30:4** *f* Ps. 97:12   **30:5** *g* Ps. 103:9
h Ps. 63:3   **30:7** *i* [Ps. 104:29; 143:7]   **30:9** *j* [Ps. 6:5]
30:11 *k* Jer. 31:4   **31:1** *a* Ps. 22:5   **31:2** *b* Ps. 17:6; 71:2;
86:1; 102:2   **31:3** *c* [Ps. 18:2] *d* Ps. 23:3; 25:11

5 eInto Your hand I commit my spirit;
  You have redeemed me, O LORD God
    of ftruth.
6 I have hated those gwho regard useless
    idols;
  But I trust in the LORD.
7 I will be glad and rejoice in Your
    mercy,
  For You have considered my trouble;
  You have hknown my soul in
    adversities,
8 And have not ishut me up into the
    hand of the enemy;
  jYou have set my feet in a wide place.

9 Have mercy on me, O LORD, for I am in
    trouble;
  kMy eye wastes away with grief,
  Yes, my soul and my body!
10 For my life is spent with grief,
  And my years with sighing;
  My strength fails because of my iniquity,
  And my bones waste away.
11 lI am a reproach among all my
    enemies,
  But mespecially among my neighbors,
  And am repulsive to my
    acquaintances;
  nThose who see me outside flee from me.
12 oI am forgotten like a dead man, out of
    mind;
  I am like a broken vessel.
13 pFor I hear the slander of many;
  qFear is on every side;
  While they rtake counsel together
    against me,
  They scheme to take away my life.

14 But as for me, I trust in You, O LORD;
  I say, "You are my God."
15 My times are in Your shand;
  Deliver me from the hand of my
    enemies,
  And from those who persecute me.
16 tMake Your face shine upon Your
    servant;
  Save me for Your mercies' sake.
17 uDo not let me be ashamed, O LORD, for
    I have called upon You;
  Let the wicked be ashamed;
  vLet them be silent in the grave.

18 wLet the lying lips be put to silence,
  Which xspeak insolent things proudly
    and contemptuously against the
    righteous.

19 yOh, how great is Your goodness,
  Which You have laid up for those who
    fear You,
  Which You have prepared for those
    who trust in You
  In the presence of the sons of men!
20 zYou shall hide them in the secret place
    of Your presence
  From the plots of man;
  aYou shall keep them secretly in a
    pavilion
  From the strife of tongues.

21 Blessed be the LORD,
  For bHe has shown me His marvelous
    kindness in a strong city!
22 For I said in my haste,
  "I am cut off from before Your eyes";
  Nevertheless You heard the voice of
    my supplications
  When I cried out to You.

23 Oh, love the LORD, all you His saints!
  For the LORD preserves the faithful,
  And fully repays the proud person.
24 cBe of good courage,
  And He shall strengthen your heart,
  All you who hope in the LORD.

Psalm 32

The Joy of Forgiveness

A Psalm of David. A Contemplation.*

1 Blessed is he whose atransgression is
    forgiven,
  Whose sin is covered.
2 Blessed is the man to whom the LORD
    bdoes not impute iniquity,
  And cin whose spirit there is no
    deceit.

3 When I kept silent, my bones grew old
  Through my groaning all the day long.

---

* 32:title Hebrew Maschil

31:5 Into Your hand I commit my spirit. With these words, David expressed his complete dependence on God. These very words were spoken by Jesus on the cross shortly before His death (Luke 23:46), and by Stephen when he was stoned (Acts 7:59).
31:15 My times are in Your hand. Even when we cannot understand the "why," we can trust that God is in control of when each life begins and ends, and also of our times of suffering.
31:22 I said in my haste. The psalmist's emotional response was to accuse God of abandoning him instead of asking for help, yet God still answered his true need.
32:1 Blessed. "Blessed" means "happy." It is appropriate that this word is used both of the righteous (1:1) and of the forgiven.

32:3 kept silent. When we refuse to admit our sin, we will suffer. David realized that it was not just his feelings that were assaulting him, but the heavy hand of God (38:1,6–8). No matter who else is hurt, the principal offense of any sin is always against the Lord.

31:5 e Luke 23:46 f [Deut. 32:4] **31:6** g Jon. 2:8
31:7 h [John 10:27] **31:8** i [Deut. 32:30] j [Ps. 4:1;
18:19] **31:9** k Ps. 6:7 **31:11** l [Is. 53:4] m Job 19:13 n Ps.
64:8 **31:12** o Ps. 88:4, 5 **31:13** p Jer. 20:10 q Lam. 2:22
r Matt. 27:1 **31:15** s [Job 14:5; 24:1] **31:16** t Ps. 4:6; 80:3
31:17 u Ps. 25:2, 20 v Ps. 94:17; 115:17 **31:18** w Ps. 109:2;
120:2 x Ps. 94:4 **31:19** y [Rom. 2:4; 11:22] **31:20** z [Ps.
27:5; 32:7] a Job 5:21 **31:21** b [Ps. 17:7] **31:24** c [Ps.
27:14] **32:1** a [Ps. 85:2; 103:3] **32:2** b [2 Cor. 5:19]
c John 1:47

4 For day and night Your ᵈhand was
    heavy upon me;
My vitality was turned into the
    drought of summer.   *Selah*
5 I acknowledged my sin to You,
And my iniquity I have not hidden.
ᵉI said, "I will confess my
    transgressions to the LORD,"
And You forgave the iniquity of my
    sin.   *Selah*

6 ᶠFor this cause everyone who is godly
    shall ᵍpray to You
In a time when You may be found;
Surely in a flood of great waters
They shall not come near him.
7 ʰYou *are* my hiding place;
You shall preserve me from trouble;
You shall surround me with ⁱsongs of
    deliverance.   *Selah*

8 I will instruct you and teach you in the
    way you should go;
I will guide you with My eye.
9 Do not be like the ʲhorse *or* like the
    mule,
Which have no understanding,
Which must be harnessed with bit and
    bridle,
Else they will not come near you.

10 ᵏMany sorrows *shall be* to the wicked;
But ˡhe who trusts in the LORD, mercy
    shall surround him.
11 ᵐBe glad in the LORD and rejoice, you
    righteous;
And shout for joy, all *you* upright in
    heart!

Psalm 33

The Sovereignty of the LORD in Creation and History

1 Rejoice ᵃin the LORD, O you righteous!
For praise from the upright is
    beautiful.

2 Praise the LORD with the harp;
Make melody to Him with an
    instrument of ten strings.
3 Sing to Him a new song;
Play skillfully with a shout of joy.

4 For the word of the LORD *is* right,
And all His work *is done* in truth.
5 He loves righteousness and justice;
The earth is full of the goodness of the
    LORD.

6 ᵇBy the word of the LORD the heavens
    were made,
And all the ᶜhost of them ᵈby the
    breath of His mouth.
7 ᵉHe gathers the waters of the sea
    together as a heap;*
He lays up the deep in storehouses.

8 Let all the earth fear the LORD;
Let all the inhabitants of the world
    stand in awe of Him.
9 For ᶠHe spoke, and it was *done;*
He commanded, and it stood fast.

10 ᵍThe LORD brings the counsel of the
    nations to nothing;
He makes the plans of the peoples of
    no effect.
11 ʰThe counsel of the LORD stands
    forever,
The plans of His heart to all
    generations.
12 Blessed *is* the nation whose God *is* the
    LORD,
The people He has ⁱchosen as His own
    inheritance.

13 ʲThe LORD looks from heaven;
He sees all the sons of men.
14 From the place of His dwelling He
    looks
On all the inhabitants of the earth;
15 He fashions their hearts individually;
ᵏHe considers all their works.

* **33:7** Septuagint, Targum, and Vulgate read *in a vessel.*

32:5 What Should Be Done About Sin—There are only two things that the believer should do about his sin: confess it and forsake it. He should never condone or attempt to excuse his sin. Here David confesses his sin and experiences forgiveness. Similarly 1 John 1:9 makes the same point. When the believer confesses his sin, he has the assurance that God "is faithful" (He can be counted on to keep His word) and "just" (He is just in dealing with our sins because He paid the price for them) "to forgive us our sins and to cleanse us from all unrighteousness." God is able to cleanse us completely from anything that is inconsistent with His own moral character. Having received forgiveness and cleansing, the believer is to forsake his sin and yield himself completely to God. In so doing, the believer is restored to full fellowship with God.

32:9 *bit and bridle, else they will not come near you.* God does not want to drive His people with rules and regulations, the "bit and bridle" of righteousness. Rather, He wants His people to follow Him willingly,

that they desire above all to please Him, not just to appease Him.

33:5 *the earth is full.* In spite of the fallen nature of our world, much of the creation remains as it was in the beginning: "very good" (Gen. 1:31). We do have to deal with evil, but every time we see the goodness of God's creation we should rejoice.

33:9 *He spoke, and it was done.* The creation account in Genesis 1 describes God's spoken word as the controlling element in creation; John 1 shows that Word to be Jesus Christ, God's Son.

33:15 *He fashions their hearts . . . He considers.*

32:4 ᵈ 1 Sam. 5:6   **32:5** ᵉ [Prov. 28:13]   **32:6** ᶠ [1 Tim. 1:16] ᵍ Is. 55:6   **32:7** ʰ Ps. 9:9 ⁱ Ex. 15:1   **32:9** ʲ Prov. 26:3   **32:10** ᵏ [Rom. 2:9] ˡ Prov. 16:20   **32:11** ᵐ Ps. 64:10; 68:3; 97:12   **33:1** ᵃ Ps. 32:11; 97:12   **33:6** ᵇ [Heb. 11:3] ᶜ Gen. 2:1 ᵈ [Job 26:13]   **33:7** ᵉ Job 26:10; 38:8   **33:9** ᶠ Gen. 1:3   **33:10** ᵍ Is. 8:10; 19:3   **33:11** ʰ [Job 23:13]   **33:12** ⁱ [Ex. 19:5]   **33:13** ʲ Job 28:24   **33:15** ᵏ [Jer. 32:19]

16 *l*No king *is* saved by the multitude of an army;
A mighty man is not delivered by great strength.
17 *m*A horse *is* a vain hope for safety;
Neither shall it deliver *any* by its great strength.
18 *n*Behold, the eye of the LORD *is* on those who fear Him,
On those who hope in His mercy,
19 To deliver their soul from death,
And *o*to keep them alive in famine.
20 Our soul waits for the LORD;
He *is* our help and our shield.
21 For our heart shall rejoice in Him,
Because we have trusted in His holy name.
22 Let Your mercy, O LORD, be upon us,
Just as we hope in You.

Psalm 34

The Happiness of Those Who Trust in God

A Psalm of David *a*when he pretended madness before Abimelech, who drove him away, and he departed.

1 I will *b*bless the LORD at all times;
His praise *shall* continually *be* in my mouth.
2 My soul shall make its boast in the LORD;
The humble shall hear *of it* and be glad.
3 Oh, magnify the LORD with me,
And let us exalt His name together.
4 I *c*sought the LORD, and He heard me,
And delivered me from all my fears.
5 They looked to Him and were radiant,
And their faces were not ashamed.
6 This poor man cried out, and the LORD heard *him*,
And saved him out of all his troubles.

7 *d*The angel* of the LORD *e*encamps all around those who fear Him,
And delivers them.
8 Oh, *f*taste and see that the LORD *is* good;
*g*Blessed *is* the man *who* trusts in Him!
9 Oh, fear the LORD, you His saints!
There is no want to those who fear Him.
10 The young lions lack and suffer hunger;
*h*But those who seek the LORD shall not lack any good *thing*.
11 Come, you children, listen to me;
*i*I will teach you the fear of the LORD.
12 *j*Who *is* the man *who* desires life,
And loves *many* days, that he may see good?
13 Keep your tongue from evil,
And your lips from speaking *k*deceit.
14 *l*Depart from evil and do good;
*m*Seek peace and pursue it.
15 *n*The eyes of the LORD *are* on the righteous,
And His ears *are open* to their cry.
16 *o*The face of the LORD *is* against those who do evil,
*p*To cut off the remembrance of them from the earth.
17 *The righteous* cry out, and *q*the LORD hears,
And delivers them out of all their troubles.
18 *r*The LORD *is* near *s*to those who have a broken heart,
And saves such as have a contrite spirit.
19 *t*Many *are* the afflictions of the righteous,
*u*But the LORD delivers him out of them all.
20 He guards all his bones;
*v*Not one of them is broken.

---

* **34:7** Or *Angel*

When we are troubled and weary and suffering, we can never say that God does not notice or understand. He made us carefully, and He continues to watch over all that we do.
33:18 hope. Those who hoped for the Lord's lovingkindness were looking forward in faith to the promised redemption, the ultimate fulfillment of the covenants, just as believers today who have the same hope, based on faith in Christ's finished work of redemption.
34:1 at all times. The determination of David to praise God is similar to the words of Paul in 1 Thessalonians 5:18. The story behind this psalm may be found in 1 Samuel 21:10–15.
34:7 The angel of the LORD. This term is often used interchangeably with the name of God (Ex. 3). When we realize that God Himself is watching over us, there is no need to fear.

34:9 Oh, fear the LORD. This is a call to awe, wonder, worship, and reverence (Prov. 1:7). To fear God is to respond to Him in obedience.
34:20 guards all his bones. John 19:33–36 shows that the words of this verse were fulfilled in detail in the death of Jesus. Despite the terrible suffering that the Savior endured, none of His bones were broken.

33:16 *j* Ps. 44:6; 60:11   **33:17** *m* [Prov. 21:31]
33:18 *n* [Job 36:7]   **33:19** *o* Job 5:20   **34:title** *a* 1 Sam. 21:10–15   **34:1** *b* [Eph. 5:20]   **34:4** *c* [Matt. 7:7]
34:7 *d* Dan. 6:22   *e* 2 Kin. 6:17   **34:8** *f* 1 Pet. 2:3   *g* Ps. 2:12
34:10 *h* [Ps. 84:11]   **34:11** *i* Ps. 32:8   **34:12** *j* [1 Pet. 3:10–12]   **34:13** *k* [Eph. 4:25]   **34:14** *l* Ps. 37:27
m [Rom. 14:19]   **34:15** *n* Job 36:7   **34:16** *o* Lev. 17:10
p [Prov. 10:7]   **34:17** *q* Ps. 34:6; 145:19   **34:18** *r* [Ps. 145:18]   *s* [Is. 57:15]   **34:19** *t* Prov. 24:16   *u* Ps. 34:4, 6, 17
34:20 *v* John 19:33, 36

21 ʷEvil shall slay the wicked,
  And those who hate the righteous
    shall be condemned.
22 The LORD ˣredeems the soul of His
    servants,
  And none of those who trust in Him
    shall be condemned.

Psalm 35

The LORD the Avenger of His People

A Psalm of David.

1 Plead *my cause*, O LORD, with those
    who strive with me;
  Fight against those who fight
    against me.
2 Take hold of shield and buckler,
  And stand up for my help.
3 Also draw out the spear,
  And stop those who pursue me.
  Say to my soul,
  "I *am* your salvation."

4 ᵃLet those be put to shame and brought
    to dishonor
  Who seek after my life;
  Let those be ᵇturned back and brought
    to confusion
  Who plot my hurt.
5 ᶜLet them be like chaff before the wind,
  And let the angel* of the LORD chase
    them.
6 Let their way be ᵈdark and slippery,
  And let the angel of the LORD pursue
    them.
7 For without cause they have ᵉhidden
    their net for me *in* a pit,
  Which they have dug without cause
    for my life.
8 Let ᶠdestruction come upon him
    unexpectedly,
  And let his net that he has hidden
    catch himself;
  Into very destruction let him fall.

9 And my soul shall be joyful in the LORD;
  It shall rejoice in His salvation.
10 ᵍAll my bones shall say,
  "LORD, ʰwho *is* like You,

Delivering the poor from him who is
    too strong for him,
  Yes, the poor and the needy from him
    who plunders him?"
11 Fierce ⁱwitnesses rise up;
  They ask me *things* that I do not know.
12 ʲThey reward me evil for good,
  To the sorrow of my soul.
13 But as for me, ᵏwhen they were sick,
  My clothing *was* sackcloth;
  I humbled myself with fasting;
  And my prayer would return to my
    own heart.
14 I paced about as though *he were* my
    friend *or* brother;
  I bowed down heavily, as one who
    mourns *for his* mother.
15 But in my adversity they rejoiced
  And gathered together;
  Attackers gathered against me,
  And I did not know *it*;
  They tore *at me* and did not cease;
16 With ungodly mockers at feasts
  They gnashed at me with their teeth.

17 Lord, how long will You ˡlook on?
  Rescue me from their destructions,
  My precious *life* from the lions.
18 I will give You thanks in the great
    assembly;
  I will praise You among many people.
19 ᵐLet them not rejoice over me who are
    wrongfully my enemies;
  Nor let them wink with the eye who
    hate me without a cause.
20 For they do not speak peace,
  But they devise deceitful matters
  Against *the* quiet ones in the land.
21 They also opened their mouth wide
    against me,
  And said, "Aha, aha!
  Our eyes have seen *it*."
22 *This* You have seen, O LORD;
  Do not keep silence.
  O Lord, do not be far from me.
23 Stir up Yourself, and awake to my
    vindication,
  To my cause, my God and my Lord.

---

* **35:5** Or *Angel*

35:2 stand up for my help. David did not hesitate to call upon God for vindication, comfort, and justice. He placed complete dependence on the Lord.

35:8 Let destruction come upon him. David's response is certainly not an example of turning the other cheek or loving his enemies (Matt. 5:39,44), but it shows David's keen awareness of the battle between good and evil, the reality of wickedness, and his understanding that wickedness is an abomination to the Lord.

35:18 assembly. Three times a year, at three of the great annual feasts, all males were required to appear before the Lord in Jerusalem. Each brought his offering to the Lord on these occasions. When they came accompanied by their families, as was often the case, Jerusalem was flooded by a vast horde of people

intent upon worshiping God. David viewed speaking before this "great assembly" or the congregation of Israel as the ultimate opportunity for testimony. A constant testimony is given to the world by believers as they give voice to praise Him for His watchful care over them.

35:19 hate me without a cause. This passage was fulfilled in the suffering of Jesus, the Savior (John 15:23–25).

34:21 ʷ Ps. 94:23; 140:11　**34:22** ˣ 1 Kin. 1:29　**35:4** ᵃ Ps. 40:14, 15; 70:2, 3　ᵇ Ps. 129:5　**35:5** ᶜ Job 21:18　**35:6** ᵈ Ps. 73:18　**35:7** ᵉ Ps. 9:15　**35:8** ᶠ [1 Thess. 5:3]　**35:10** ᵍ Ps. 51:8　ʰ [Ex. 15:11]　**35:11** ⁱ Matt. 26:3–4, 59–66; 27:1–2　**35:12** ʲ John 10:32　**35:13** ᵏ Job 30:25　**35:17** ˡ [Hab. 1:13]　**35:19** ᵐ Ps. 69:4; 109:3

24 Vindicate me, O LORD my God,
　　according to Your righteousness;
　And let them not rejoice over me.
25 Let them not say in their hearts, "Ah,
　　so we would have it!"
　Let them not say, "We have swallowed
　　him up."
26 Let them be ashamed and brought to
　　mutual confusion
　Who rejoice at my hurt;
　Let them be ⁿclothed with shame and
　　dishonor
　Who exalt themselves against me.
27 ᵒLet them shout for joy and be glad,
　Who favor my righteous cause;
　And let them say continually,
　"Let the LORD be magnified,
　Who has pleasure in the prosperity of
　　His servant."
28 And my tongue shall speak of Your
　　righteousness
　And of Your praise all the day long.

Psalm 36

Man's Wickedness and God's Perfections

To the Chief Musician. A Psalm of
David the servant of the LORD.

1 An oracle within my heart concerning
　　the transgression of the wicked:
　ᵃThere is no fear of God before his eyes.
2 For he flatters himself in his own eyes,
　When he finds out his iniquity and
　　when he hates.
3 The words of his mouth are
　　wickedness and deceit;
　ᵇHe has ceased to be wise and to do
　　good.
4 ᶜHe devises wickedness on his bed;
　He sets himself ᵈin a way that is not
　　good;
　He does not abhor ᵉevil.
5 Your mercy, O LORD, is in the heavens;
　Your faithfulness reaches to the
　　clouds.
6 Your righteousness is like the great
　　mountains;

ᶠYour judgments are a great deep;
　O LORD, You preserve man and
　　beast.
7 How precious is Your lovingkindness,
　　O God!
　Therefore the children of men ᵍput
　　their trust under the shadow of
　　Your wings.
8 ʰThey are abundantly satisfied with the
　　fullness of Your house,
　And You give them drink from ⁱthe
　　river of Your pleasures.
9 ʲFor with You is the fountain of life;
　ᵏIn Your light we see light.
10 Oh, continue Your lovingkindness to
　　those who know You,
　And Your righteousness to the upright
　　in heart.
11 Let not the foot of pride come against
　　me,
　And let not the hand of the wicked
　　drive me away.
12 There the workers of iniquity have
　　fallen;
　They have been cast down and are not
　　able to rise.

Psalm 37

The Heritage of the Righteous and the Calamity of the Wicked

A Psalm of David.

1 Doᵃ not fret because of evildoers,
　Nor be envious of the workers of
　　iniquity.
2 For they shall soon be cut down ᵇlike
　　the grass,
　And wither as the green herb.
3 Trust in the LORD, and do good;
　Dwell in the land, and feed on His
　　faithfulness.
4 ᶜDelight yourself also in the LORD,
　And He shall give you the desires of
　　your ᵈheart.
5 ᵉCommit your way to the LORD,
　Trust also in Him,
　And He shall bring it to pass.

35:26 ashamed. The phrase "be ashamed" does not refer just to simple embarrassment, but to the revelation of the complete emptiness of wickedness before the judgment seat of God.
36:1 no fear of God. Underlying wickedness is a complete disregard for the reality of God in a person's life and in the world.
36:9 fountain of life. God's salvation and continuing mercy to His people are often described in terms of life-giving water (Is. 12:3; Jer. 2:13; John 4:1–14).
37:1 Do not fret. When the wicked seem to prosper, the psalmist calls for patience, a renewed sense of dependence on the Lord, and a new sense of pleasure in knowing Him.

37:4 the desires of your heart. Many times, we read this verse as a promise that God will give us anything that we want because He wants us to be happy. In reality, this verse goes much deeper. When we truly delight in God, He plants in our hearts godly desires that He delights to fulfill.

35:26 ⁿ Ps. 109:29　**35:27** ᵒ Rom. 12:15　**36:1** ᵃ Rom. 3:18　**36:3** ᵇ Jer. 4:22　**36:4** ᶜ Prov. 4:16 ᵈ Is. 65:2 ᵉ [Rom. 12:9]　**36:6** ᶠ [Rom. 11:33]　**36:7** ᵍ Ps. 17:8; 57:1; 91:4　**36:8** ʰ Ps. 63:5; 65:4 ⁱ Rev. 22:1　**36:9** ʲ [Jer. 2:13] ᵏ [1 Pet. 2:9]　**37:1** ᵃ Ps. 73:3　**37:2** ᵇ Ps. 90:5, 6; 92:7 **37:4** ᶜ Is. 58:14 ᵈ Ps. 21:2; 145:19　**37:5** ᵉ [Ps. 55:22]

6 *f*He shall bring forth your
   righteousness as the light,
   And your justice as the noonday.

7 Rest in the LORD, *g*and wait patiently
   for Him;
   Do not fret because of him who
   *h*prospers in his way,
   Because of the man who brings
   wicked schemes to pass.

8 *i*Cease from anger, and forsake wrath;
   *j*Do not fret—*it* only *causes* harm.

9 For evildoers shall be cut off;
   But those who wait on the LORD,
   They shall *k*inherit the earth.

10 For *l*yet a little while and the wicked
   shall be no *more;*
   Indeed, *m*you will look carefully for
   his place,
   But it *shall be* no *more.*

11 *n*But the meek shall inherit the earth,
   And shall delight themselves in the
   abundance of peace.

12 The wicked plots against the just,
   *o*And gnashes at him with his teeth.

13 *p*The Lord laughs at him,
   For He sees that *q*his day is coming.

14 The wicked have drawn the sword
   And have bent their bow,
   To cast down the poor and needy,
   To slay those who are of upright
   conduct.

15 Their sword shall enter their own heart,
   And their bows shall be broken.

16 *r*A little that a righteous man has
   Is better than the riches of many
   wicked.

17 For the arms of the wicked shall be
   broken,
   But the LORD upholds the righteous.

18 The LORD knows the days of the
   upright,
   And their inheritance shall be forever.

19 They shall not be ashamed in the evil
   time,
   And in the days of famine they shall
   be satisfied.

20 But the wicked shall perish;
   And the enemies of the LORD,

Like the splendor of the meadows,
   shall vanish.
Into smoke they shall vanish away.

21 The wicked borrows and does not
   repay,
   But *s*the righteous shows mercy and
   gives.

22 *t*For *those* blessed by Him shall inherit
   the earth,
   But *those* cursed by Him shall be cut
   off.

23 *u*The steps of a *good* man are ordered
   by the LORD,
   And He delights in his way.

24 *v*Though he fall, he shall not be utterly
   cast down;
   For the LORD upholds *him with* His
   hand.

25 I have been young, and *now* am old;
   Yet I have not seen the righteous
   forsaken,
   Nor his descendants begging bread.

26 *w*He *is* ever merciful, and lends;
   And his descendants *are* blessed.

27 Depart from evil, and do good;
   And dwell forevermore.

28 For the LORD loves justice,
   And does not forsake His saints;
   They are preserved forever,
   But the descendants of the wicked
   shall be cut off.

29 *x*The righteous shall inherit the
   land,
   And dwell in it forever.

30 *y*The mouth of the righteous speaks
   wisdom,
   And his tongue talks of justice.

31 The law of his God *is* in his heart;
   None of his steps shall slide.

32 The wicked *z*watches the righteous,
   And seeks to slay him.

33 The LORD *a*will not leave him in his
   hand,
   Nor condemn him when he is
   judged.

34 *b*Wait on the LORD,
   And keep His way,

37:7 Rest in the LORD . . . do not fret. This is not a call to stop caring and go to sleep, but to depend actively on the living Lord, leaving our lives and times in His hands.
37:13 He sees that his day is coming. The wicked sometimes appear to prosper, but from God's perspective, the flourishing of the wicked is short (Eccl. 3:16–17).
37:21 the righteous shows mercy and gives. There are many contrasts between the wicked and the righteous in the wisdom psalms; this one is based on contrasting attitudes toward possessions (15:5; 112:5). Jesus said that such generous givers would be rewarded with "good measure, pressed down, shaken together, and running over" (Luke 6:38).
37:25 begging bread. Some interpret these words as referring to spiritual famine—the righteous will

never be deprived of the Lord's presence (John 6:35). However, many have taken these words literally and experienced God's miraculous provision for their material needs.
37:27 Depart from evil. In this life people must choose either to cling to God and righteousness or to pursue evil.

37:6 *f* Job 11:17   37:7 *g* [Lam. 3:26]   *h* [Ps. 73:3–12]
37:8 *i* [Eph. 4:26]   *j* Ps. 73:3   37:9 *k* [Is. 57:13; 60:21]
37:10 *l* [Heb. 10:37]   *m* Job 7:10   37:11 *n* [Matt.
5:5]   37:12 *o* Ps. 35:16   37:13 *p* Ps. 2:4; 59:8   *q* 1 Sam.
26:10   37:16 *r* Prov. 15:16; 16:8   37:21 *s* Ps. 112:5, 9
37:22 *t* [Prov. 3:33]   37:23 *u* [1 Sam. 2:9]   37:24 *v* Prov.
24:16   37:26 *w* [Deut. 15:8]   37:29 *x* Prov.
2:21   37:30 *y* [Matt. 12:35]   37:32 *z* Ps. 10:8; 17:11
37:33 *a* [2 Pet. 2:9]   37:34 *b* Ps. 27:14; 37:9

And He shall exalt you to inherit the
land;
When the wicked are cut off, you shall
see *it.*
35 I have seen the wicked in great power,
And spreading himself like a native
green tree.
36 Yet he passed away,* and behold, he
was no *more;*
Indeed I sought him, but he could not
be found.
37 Mark the blameless *man,* and observe
the upright;
For the future of *that* man *is* peace.
38 cBut the transgressors shall be
destroyed together;
The future of the wicked shall be cut
off.
39 But the salvation of the righteous *is*
from the LORD;
He is their strength din the time of
trouble.
40 And ethe LORD shall help them and
deliver them;
He shall deliver them from the wicked,
And save them,
fBecause they trust in Him.

Psalm 38

Prayer in Time of Chastening

A Psalm of David. aTo bring to
remembrance.

1 O LORD, do not brebuke me in Your
wrath,
Nor chasten me in Your hot
displeasure!
2 For Your arrows pierce me deeply,
And Your hand presses me down.
3 *There is* no soundness in my flesh
Because of Your anger,
Nor *any* health in my bones
Because of my sin.
4 For my iniquities have gone over my
head;
Like a heavy burden they are too
heavy for me.
5 My wounds are foul *and* festering
Because of my foolishness.
6 I am troubled, I am bowed down
greatly;
I go mourning all the day long.

7 For my loins are full of inflammation,
And *there is* no soundness in my
flesh.
8 I am feeble and severely broken;
I groan because of the turmoil of my
heart.
9 Lord, all my desire *is* before You;
And my sighing is not hidden from
You.
10 My heart pants, my strength
fails me;
As for the light of my eyes, it also has
gone from me.
11 My loved ones and my friends cstand
aloof from my plague,
And my relatives stand afar off.
12 Those also who seek my life lay snares
for me;
Those who seek my hurt speak of
destruction,
And plan deception all the day long.
13 But I, like a deaf *man,* do not hear;
And *I am* like a mute *who* does not
open his mouth.
14 Thus I am like a man who does not
hear,
And in whose mouth *is* no response.
15 For in You, O LORD, dI hope;
You will hear, O Lord my God.
16 For I said, "*Hear me,* lest they rejoice
over me,
Lest, when my foot slips, they exalt
themselves against me."
17 eFor I *am* ready to fall,
And my sorrow *is* continually
before me.
18 For I will fdeclare my iniquity;
I will be gin anguish over my sin.
19 But my enemies *are* vigorous, *and* they
are strong;
And those who hate me wrongfully
have multiplied.
20 Those also hwho render evil for
good,
They are my adversaries, because I
follow *what is* good.
21 Do not forsake me, O LORD;
O my God, ibe not far from me!
22 Make haste to help me,
O Lord, my salvation!

---

* **37:36** Following Masoretic Text, Septuagint, and
Targum; Syriac and Vulgate read *I passed by.*

37:39 *salvation.* The principal issue here is not
regeneration, but sanctification—the daily deliverance of God's people from temptation and evil.
38:1 *do not rebuke me.* David is not saying, "Don't
tell me I'm wrong," but "Have mercy on my sinfulness." David's penitent psalms can serve as a model
for our own prayers of confession.
38:14 *a man who does not hear.* David was determined not to present an opportunity for his enemies to condemn the name of the Lord. His silence

foreshadowed the silence of Jesus before His accusers (Mark 14:61).
38:18 *I will declare.* David's silence was only before
his enemies; to the Lord he willingly confessed his sins.

37:38 c [Ps. 1:4–6; 37:20, 28]   **37:39** d Ps. 9:9; 37:19
37:40 e Is. 31:5   f 1 Chr. 5:20   **38:title** a Ps. 70:title
38:1 b Ps. 6:1   **38:11** c Ps. 31:11; 88:18   **38:15** d [Ps.
39:7]   **38:17** e Ps. 51:3   **38:18** f Ps. 32:5   g [2 Cor.
7:9, 10]   **38:20** h Ps. 35:12   **38:21** i Ps. 22:19; 35:22

Psalm 39

Prayer for Wisdom and Forgiveness

To the Chief Musician. To Jeduthun.
A Psalm of David.

1 I said, "I will guard my ways,
   Lest I sin with my ^atongue;
   I will restrain my mouth with a
      muzzle,
   While the wicked are before me."
2 ^bI was mute with silence,
   I held my peace *even* from good;
   And my sorrow was stirred up.
3 My heart was hot within me;
   While I was musing, the fire burned.
   Then I spoke with my tongue:

4 "LORD, ^cmake me to know my end,
   And what *is* the measure of my days,
   That I may know how frail I *am*.
5 Indeed, You have made my days *as*
      handbreadths,
   And my age *is* as nothing before You;
   Certainly every man at his best state *is*
   but ^dvapor.   *Selah*
6 Surely every man walks about like a
      shadow;
   Surely they busy themselves in vain;
   He heaps up *riches,*
   And does not know who will gather
      them.

7 "And now, Lord, what do I wait for?
   My ^ehope *is* in You.
8 Deliver me from all my transgressions;
   Do not make me ^fthe reproach of the
      foolish.
9 ^gI was mute, I did not open my mouth,
   Because it was ^hYou who did *it*.
10 ⁱRemove Your plague from me;
   I am consumed by the blow of Your
      hand.
11 When with rebukes You correct man
      for iniquity,
   You make his beauty ^jmelt away like
      a moth;
   Surely every man *is* vapor.   *Selah*

12 "Hear my prayer, O LORD,
   And give ear to my cry;

Do not be silent at my tears;
   For I *am* a stranger with You,
   A sojourner, ^kas all my fathers *were.*
13 ^lRemove Your gaze from me, that I may
      regain strength,
   Before I go away and ^mam no more."

Psalm 40

Faith Persevering in Trial

To the Chief Musician. A Psalm of
David.

1 I ^awaited patiently for the LORD;
   And He inclined to me,
   And heard my cry.
2 He also brought me up out of a
      horrible pit,
   Out of ^bthe miry clay,
   And ^cset my feet upon a rock,
   And established my steps.
3 ^dHe has put a new song in my mouth—
   Praise to our God;
   Many will see *it* and fear,
   And will trust in the LORD.

4 ^eBlessed *is* that man who makes the
      LORD his trust,
   And does not respect the proud, nor
      such as turn aside to lies.
5 ^fMany, O LORD my God, *are* Your
      wonderful works
   Which You have done;
   ^gAnd Your thoughts toward us
   Cannot be recounted to You in
      order;
   If I would declare and speak *of*
      them,
   They are more than can be
      numbered.

6 ^hSacrifice and offering You did not
      desire;
   My ears You have opened.
   Burnt offering and sin offering You
      did not require.
7 Then I said, "Behold, I come;
   In the scroll of the book *it is* written
   of me.

39:1 *I will guard my ways.* David determined to be silent in suffering so that he would not speak out foolishly.

39:9 *It was You who did it.* David knows that his only chance of deliverance is in God. But he also believes that his trouble has come from God. He is in a quandary. Should he ask for God's help, or should he ask for God to leave him alone?

39:13 *Remove Your gaze from me.* If God is not going to deliver him, the despondent psalmist asks God to leave him alone. It is rare outside the Book of Job to find language such as this (Job 7:19). The pain of the psalmist was so far from being resolved that he remained in despair until the last verse. Yet the fact that God saves those who call upon Him is described again and again in the Book of Psalms (22:31; 118:21).

40:1 *I waited patiently.* The verb "to wait" expresses

a confident trust or faith in the Lord (130:5). David knows that salvation comes only from the Almighty (3:8).

40:6 *My ears You have opened.* God allows us to hear His words, and He also gives us understanding and wisdom to internalize and apply them.

40:7 *Behold, I come.* According to Hebrews 10:4–7, Jesus spoke these words to the Father.

39:1 ^a [James 3:5–12]   **39:2** ^b Ps. 38:13   **39:4** ^c Ps. 90:12; 119:84   **39:5** ^d Ps. 62:9   **39:7** ^e Ps. 38:15   **39:8** ^f Ps. 44:13; 79:4; 119:22   **39:9** ^g Ps. 39:2   ^h Job 2:10   **39:10** ⁱ Job 9:34; 13:21   **39:11** ^j Job 13:28   **39:12** ^k Gen. 47:9   **39:13** ^l Job 7:19; 10:20, 21; 14:6   ^m [Job 14:10]   **40:1** ^a Ps. 25:5; 27:14; 37:7   **40:2** ^b Ps. 69:2, 14   ^c Ps. 27:5   **40:3** ^d Ps. 32:7; 33:3   **40:4** ^e Ps. 34:8; 84:12   **40:5** ^f Job 9:10   ^g [Is. 55:8]   **40:6** ^h [Heb. 10:5–9]

8 *i*I delight to do Your will, O my God,
　　And Your law *is* *j*within my heart."

9 *k*I have proclaimed the good news of
　　righteousness
　　In the great assembly;
　　Indeed, *l*I do not restrain my lips,
　　O Lord, You Yourself know.

10 *m*I have not hidden Your righteousness
　　within my heart;
　　I have declared Your faithfulness and
　　Your salvation;
　　I have not concealed Your
　　lovingkindness and Your truth
　　From the great assembly.

11 Do not withhold Your tender mercies
　　from me, O Lord;
　　*n*Let Your lovingkindness and Your
　　truth continually preserve me.

12 For innumerable evils have
　　surrounded me;
　　*o*My iniquities have overtaken me, so
　　that I am not able to look up;
　　They are more than the hairs of my
　　head;
　　Therefore my heart fails me.

13 *p*Be pleased, O Lord, to deliver me;
　　O Lord, make haste to help me!

14 *q*Let them be ashamed and brought to
　　mutual confusion
　　Who seek to destroy my life;
　　Let them be driven backward and
　　brought to dishonor
　　Who wish me evil.

15 Let them be *r*confounded because of
　　their shame,
　　Who say to me, "Aha, aha!"

16 *s*Let all those who seek You rejoice and
　　be glad in You;

Let such as love Your salvation *t*say
　　continually,
"The Lord be magnified!"

17 *u*But I *am* poor and needy;
　　*v*Yet the Lord thinks upon me.
　　You *are* my help and my deliverer;
　　Do not delay, O my God.

Psalm 41

The Blessing and Suffering of the Godly

*To the Chief Musician. A Psalm of
David.*

1 Blessed *is* he who considers the
　　poor;
　　The Lord will deliver him in time of
　　trouble.

2 The Lord will preserve him and keep
　　him alive,
　　And he will be blessed on the earth;
　　*a*You will not deliver him to the will of
　　his enemies.

3 The Lord will strengthen him on his
　　bed of illness;
　　You will sustain him on his sickbed.

4 I said, "Lord, be merciful to me;
　　*b*Heal my soul, for I have sinned against
　　You."

5 My enemies speak evil of me:
　　"When will he die, and his name
　　perish?"

6 And if he comes to see *me*, he speaks
　　lies;
　　His heart gathers iniquity to itself;
　　When he goes out, he tells *it*.

40:8 To Know God's Will—Knowing the will of God is not simply a vehicle for finding the right vocation for a life's work. While vocation is important, it is only a small part of God's will. The will of God must be thought of in more comprehensive terms. The will of God is for everyone to live in such a way as to bring honor and glory to God. For different people God may have very different things in mind. We must continually stay in God's Word so that He can make clear to us what His will is for us. We must also be still, listen, and know that He is God.

The first step towards understanding God's will is believing in Christ (John 3:14–16). If we do not accept this gift from God, we will not be saved from judgment (Matt. 7:21). Second, Scripture teaches us that it is God's will for every believer to be sanctified (2 Thess. 2:13–17). Third, the Bible declares God's will as it must be applied to our lives (Deut. 29:29). This fact involves commands to be obeyed, principles to be followed, prohibitions of things to be avoided and living examples to be imitated or shunned. God takes great joy in those who cheerfully do His will.

Although the Bible is a comprehensive revelation of God's will, there are always decisions we make that Scripture does not directly address. In order to know God's will in these situations we need to be in fellowship with the Lord (1 John 1:6–7), seek principles from

the Word (1 Cor. 10:6), obtain advice from godly counselors (Prov. 11:14), use common sense, and remember that God works through our own minds and He desires for us to do His will (Phil. 2:13).

40:9 assembly. In Psalm 35 David prayed for deliverance from his enemies and promised to give God praise before "the great assembly," the congregation of Israel, for that deliverance. Psalm 40 is a joyful account of his deliverance from trouble, and his witness of God's righteousness before the people. The believer is obligated to speak of God's righteous acts toward him, so that others may hear of the goodness and glory of God.

40:11 tender mercies. This term refers to God's affection for us. David is asking God to surround him with warmth and comfort that is practically maternal.

41:4 for I have sinned. In the context of this psalm, this is a general acknowledgment of sin and the need for God's forgiveness and restoration (1 John 1:9).

40:8 *i* [John 4:34; 6:38] *j* [Jer. 31:33]　**40:9** *k* Ps. 22:22, 25　*l* Ps. 119:13　**40:10** *m* Acts 20:20, 27　**40:11** *n* Ps. 61:7　**40:12** *o* Ps. 38:4; 65:3　**40:13** *p* Ps. 70:1　**40:14** *q* Ps. 35:4, 26; 70:2; 71:13　**40:15** *r* Ps. 73:19　**40:16** *s* Ps. 70:4　*t* Ps. 35:27　**40:17** *u* Ps. 70:5; 86:1; 109:22　*v* 1 Pet. 5:7　**41:2** *a* Ps. 27:12　**41:4** *b* Ps. 6:2; 103:3; 147:3

7 All who hate me whisper together
   against me;
   Against me they devise my hurt.
8 "An evil disease," *they say,* "clings to
   him.
   And *now* that he lies down, he will rise
   up no more."
9 *c*Even my own familiar friend in whom
   I trusted,
   *d*Who ate my bread,
   Has lifted up *his* heel against me.

10 But You, O LORD, be merciful to me,
   and raise me up,
   That I may repay them.
11 By this I know that You are well
   pleased with me,
   Because my enemy does not triumph
   over me.
12 As for me, You uphold me in my
   integrity,
   And *e*set me before Your face forever.

13 *f*Blessed *be* the LORD God of Israel
   From everlasting to everlasting!
   Amen and Amen.

BOOK TWO

Psalms 42–72

Psalm 42

Yearning for God in the Midst of Distresses

To the Chief Musician.
A Contemplation* of the sons of Korah.

1 As the deer pants for the water brooks,
   So pants my soul for You, O God.
2 *a*My soul thirsts for God, for the *b*living
   God.
   When shall I come and appear before
   God?*
3 *c*My tears have been my food day and
   night,
   While they continually say to me,
   d"Where *is* your God?"
4 When I remember these *things,*
   *e*I pour out my soul within me.

For I used to go with the multitude;
*f*I went with them to the house of God,
With the voice of joy and praise,
With a multitude that kept a pilgrim
   feast.

5 *g*Why are you cast down, O my soul?
   And *why* are you disquieted within
   me?
   *h*Hope in God, for I shall yet praise
   Him
   For the help of His countenance.*

6 O my God,* my soul is cast down
   within me;
   Therefore I will remember You from
   the land of the Jordan,
   And from the heights of Hermon,
   From the Hill Mizar.
7 Deep calls unto deep at the noise of
   Your waterfalls;
   *i*All Your waves and billows have gone
   over me.
8 The LORD will *j*command His
   lovingkindness in the daytime,
   And *k*in the night His song *shall be*
   with me—
   A prayer to the God of my life.

9 I will say to God my Rock,
   l"Why have You forgotten me?
   Why do I go mourning because of the
   oppression of the enemy?"
10 *As* with a breaking of my bones,
   My enemies reproach me,
   *m*While they say to me all day long,
   "Where *is* your God?"

11 *n*Why are you cast down, O my soul?
   And why are you disquieted within
   me?
   Hope in God;
   For I shall yet praise Him,
   The help of my countenance and my
   God.

---

* **42:title** Hebrew *Maschil* * **42:2** Following
Masoretic Text and Vulgate; some Hebrew manuscripts, Septuagint, Syriac, and Targum read *I
see the face of God.* * **42:5** Following Masoretic
Text and Targum; a few Hebrew manuscripts, Septuagint, Syriac, and Vulgate read *The help of my
countenance, my God.* * **42:6** Following Masoretic Text and Targum; a few Hebrew manuscripts,
Septuagint, Syriac, and Vulgate put *my God* at the
end of verse 5.

41:9 my own familiar friend. Jesus quoted this
verse, noting its fulfillment in Judas (John 13:18).
41:13 Blessed. This psalm begins with a blessing
of God on the righteous; it ends with the righteous
blessing their Lord. This word "blessed" is different
from the word in verse 1. Here the word identifies the
Lord as the source of our blessing.
**42:4 I used to go with the multitude . . . to the house
of God.** This psalm was written in exile. The psalmist is remembering with longing and tears the times
when he was able to worship God in Jerusalem.
42:5 I shall yet praise Him. As is common in the
Psalms, the poet is not describing an act of private
devotion, but of public praise of the goodness of

God. This is praise in words and songs that would
be repeated in the midst of the congregation (22:22;
Eph. 5:19; Heb. 13:15).
42:6 the land of the Jordan . . . of Hermon. These
are references to the Promised Land, from which the
people were exiled.

41:9 *c* 2 Sam. 15:12 *d* John 13:18, 21–30 **41:12** *e* [Job
36:7] **41:13** *f* Ps. 72:18, 19; 89:52; 106:48; 150:6
42:2 *a* Ps. 63:1; 84:2; 143:6 *b* 1 Thess. 1:9 **42:3** *c* Ps.
80:5; 102:9 *d* Ps. 79:10; 115:2 **42:4** *e* Job 30:16 *f* Is.
30:29 **42:5** *g* Ps. 42:11; 43:5 *h* Lam. 3:24 **42:7** *i* Ps. 69:1,
2; 88:7 **42:8** *j* Deut. 28:8 *k* Job 35:10 **42:9** *l* Ps. 38:6
42:10 *m* Joel 2:17 **42:11** *n* Ps. 43:5

Psalm 43

Prayer to God in Time of Trouble

1 Vindicate *a*me, O God,
And *b*plead my cause against an
ungodly nation;
Oh, deliver me from the deceitful and
unjust man!

2 For You *are* the God of my strength;
Why do You cast me off?
*c*Why do I go mourning because of the
oppression of the enemy?

3 *d*Oh, send out Your light and Your
truth!
Let them lead me;
Let them bring me to *e*Your holy hill
And to Your tabernacle.

4 Then I will go to the altar of God,
To God my exceeding joy;
And on the harp I will praise You,
O God, my God.

5 *f*Why are you cast down, O my soul?
And why are you disquieted within
me?
Hope in God;
For I shall yet praise Him,
The help of my countenance and my
God.

Psalm 44

Redemption Remembered in Present Dishonor

To the Chief Musician.
A *a*Contemplation* of the sons of Korah.

1 We have heard with our ears,
O God,
*b*Our fathers have told us,
The deeds You did in their days,
In days of old:

2 *c*You drove out the nations with Your
hand,
But them You planted;
You afflicted the peoples, and cast
them out.

3 For *d*they did not gain possession of
the land by their own sword,
Nor did their own arm save them;
But it was Your right hand, Your
arm, and the light of Your
countenance,
*e*Because You favored them.

4 *f*You are my King, O God;*
Command* victories for Jacob.

5 Through You *g*we will push down our
enemies;
Through Your name we will
trample those who rise up
against us.

6 For *h*I will not trust in my bow,
Nor shall my sword save me.

7 But You have saved us from our
enemies,
And have put to shame those who
hated us.

8 *i*In God we boast all day long,
And praise Your name forever.   *Selah*

9 But *j*You have cast *us* off and put us to
shame,
And You do not go out with our
armies.

10 You make us *k*turn back from the
enemy,
And those who hate us have taken
spoil for themselves.

11 *l*You have given us up like sheep
intended for food,
And have *m*scattered us among the
nations.

12 *n*You sell Your people for *next to*
nothing,
And are not enriched by selling
them.

13 *o*You make us a reproach to our
neighbors,
A scorn and a derision to those all
around us.

14 *p*You make us a byword among the
nations,

---

* **44:title** Hebrew *Maschil*   * **44:4** Following Masoretic Text and Targum; Septuagint and Vulgate read *and my God.* • Following Masoretic Text and Targum; Septuagint, Syriac, and Vulgate read *Who commands.*

43:1 *Vindicate me.* It is believed that Psalm 43 is a continuation of Psalm 42.

43:5 *cast down.* Psalms 42 and 43 reflect a uniform feeling of being cut off from God, rejected and forsaken by Him. There is a common refrain in both psalms in which the author reasons with himself in order to surmount his feelings of depression and loneliness. Prayer is still possible when God seems to be absent, and we can hope in God in the face of present affliction because faith enables the believer to give thanks before the answer is experienced.

44:4 *You are my King.* In this community lament, it is striking that here the speaker is singular. It may be that these words are spoken by Israel's king to the King of glory. As the king of the nation, it was appropriate for him to lead the people in asking for God's renewed favor.

44:9 *You have cast us off.* The army of Israel was not just a group of soldiers. They were the warriors of the Almighty; their victories were the victories of God, and their defeats were losses that He allowed them to endure. If He ceased accompanying them to battle, they were doomed to failure.

43:1 *a* [Ps. 26:1; 35:24] *b* Ps. 35:1   **43:2** *c* Ps. 42:9
43:3 *d* [Ps. 40:11] *e* Ps. 3:4   **43:5** *f* Ps. 42:5, 11
44:title *a* Ps. 42:title   **44:1** *b* [Ex. 12:26, 27]   **44:2** *c* Ex. 15:17   *d* [Deut. 8:17, 18] *e* [Deut. 4:37; 7:7, 8]
44:4 *f* [Ps. 74:12]   **44:5** *g* [Dan. 8:4]   **44:6** *h* Ps. 33:16
44:8 *i* Ps. 34:2   **44:9** *j* Ps. 60:1   **44:10** *k* Lev. 26:17
44:11 *l* Rom. 8:36 *m* Deut. 4:27; 28:64   **44:12** *n* Is. 52:3, 4
44:13 *o* Jer. 24:9   **44:14** *p* Deut. 28:37

qA shaking of the head among the
peoples.
15 My dishonor *is* continually before
me,
And the shame of my face has covered
me,
16 Because of the voice of him who
reproaches and reviles,
rBecause of the enemy and the
avenger.

17 sAll this has come upon us;
But we have not forgotten You,
Nor have we dealt falsely with Your
covenant.
18 Our heart has not turned back,
tNor have our steps departed from
Your way;
19 But You have severely broken us in
uthe place of jackals,
And covered us vwith the shadow of
death.

20 If we had forgotten the name of our
God,
Or wstretched out our hands to a
foreign god,
21 xWould not God search this out?
For He knows the secrets of the
heart.
22 yYet for Your sake we are killed all day
long;
We are accounted as sheep for the
slaughter.

23 zAwake! Why do You sleep,
O Lord?
Arise! Do not cast *us* off forever.
24 aWhy do You hide Your face,
And forget our affliction and our
oppression?
25 For bour soul is bowed down to the
dust;
Our body clings to the ground.
26 Arise for our help,
And redeem us for Your mercies'
sake.

Psalm 45

The Glories of the Messiah and
His Bride

To the Chief Musician. aSet to "The
Lilies."* A Contemplation* of the sons
of Korah. A Song of Love.

1 My heart is overflowing with a good
theme;
I recite my composition concerning
the King;
My tongue *is* the pen of a ready writer.

2 You are fairer than the sons of men;
bGrace is poured upon Your lips;
Therefore God has blessed You
forever.
3 Gird Your csword upon *Your* thigh,
dO Mighty One,
With Your eglory and Your majesty.
4 fAnd in Your majesty ride prosperously
because of truth, humility, *and*
righteousness;
And Your right hand shall teach You
awesome things.
5 Your arrows *are* sharp in the heart of
the King's enemies;
The peoples fall under You.
6 gYour throne, O God, *is* forever and
ever;
A hscepter of righteousness *is* the
scepter of Your kingdom.
7 You love righteousness and hate
wickedness;
Therefore God, Your God, has
ianointed You
With the oil of jgladness more than
Your companions.
8 All Your garments *are* kscented with
myrrh and aloes *and* cassia,
Out of the ivory palaces, by which they
have made You glad.

---

* **45:title** Hebrew *Shoshannim* • Hebrew *Maschil*

44:17 we have not forgotten You. The faithful remnant had to bear the punishment of exile as well as the wicked. Human beings are so interwoven that it is impossible to sin alone. Inevitably others will have to share the burden of our just punishment.
44:22 as sheep. These words predict another beloved Son of the Most High who would also feel cast off by the Lord (Is. 53:7; Rom. 8:36).
45:3 O Mighty One. In the ancient Middle East the king was supposed to be a great warrior. The model in Israel was David, the celebrated champion who defeated the giant Goliath (1 Sam. 17). The term "most mighty" is also a messianic title.
45:6–7 O God . . . God, Your God. The words "Your throne" indicate the messianic direction of the psalm. Here the King is addressed as God, yet it is "God, Your God" who anointed Him. The writer to the Hebrews used these verses to assert Jesus' deity (Heb. 1:8–9).
45:7 righteousness. A person is known by his loves and his hates. If a person "loves" something, he will "hate" its opposite. One who loves justice will hate

oppression. One who loves truth will hate falsehood. One who loves kindness will hate cruelty. The psalm deliberately uses very strong verbs: *love* righteousness, *hate* wickedness. We might prefer to be a bit more moderate and tone down the language, but the Scripture calls us to disengage ourselves radically from wickedness, for it is both a virus and a vice. **anointed You.** Anointing set aside a particular person for special service to God. In Old Testament times, those who were anointed for special service foreshadowed the Anointed One, the Messiah.

44:14 q Job 16:4 **44:16** r Ps. 8:2 **44:17** s Dan.
9:13 **44:18** t Job 23:11 **44:19** u Is. 34:13 v [Ps.
23:4] **44:20** w [Deut. 6:14] **44:21** x [Ps. 139:1, 2]
44:22 y Rom. 8:36 **44:23** z Ps. 7:6 **44:24** a Job 13:24
44:25 b Ps. 119:25 **45:title** a Ps. 69:title **45:2** b Luke
4:22 **45:3** c [Heb. 4:12] d [Is. 9:6] e Jude 25 **45:4** f Rev.
6:2 **45:6** g [Ps. 93:2] h [Num. 24:17] **45:7** i Ps. 2:2 j Ps.
21:6 **45:8** k Song 1:12, 13

9 ᶦKings' daughters *are* among Your
  honorable women;
  ᵐAt Your right hand stands the queen in
  gold from Ophir.

10 Listen, O daughter,
   Consider and incline your ear;
   ⁿForget your own people also, and your
   father's house;
11 So the King will greatly desire your
   beauty;
   ᵒBecause He *is* your Lord, worship
   Him.
12 And the daughter of Tyre *will come*
   with a gift;
   ᵖThe rich among the people will seek
   your favor.

13 The royal daughter *is* all glorious
   within *the palace;*
   Her clothing *is* woven with gold.
14 ᵃShe shall be brought to the King in
   robes of many colors;
   The virgins, her companions who
   follow her, shall be brought to
   You.
15 With gladness and rejoicing they shall
   be brought;
   They shall enter the King's palace.

16 Instead of Your fathers shall be Your
   sons,
   ʳWhom You shall make princes in all
   the earth.
17 ˢI will make Your name to be
   remembered in all generations;
   Therefore the people shall praise You
   forever and ever.

Psalm 46

God the Refuge of His People and Conqueror of the Nations

To the Chief Musician. *A Psalm* of the
sons of Korah. A Song ᵃfor Alamoth.

1 God *is* our ᵇrefuge and strength,
  ᶜA very present help in trouble.
2 Therefore we will not fear,
  Even though the earth be removed,
  And though the mountains be carried
  into the midst of the sea;

3 ᵈThough its waters roar *and* be
  troubled,
  Though the mountains shake with its
  swelling.   *Selah*

4 *There is* a ᵉriver whose streams shall
  make glad the ᶠcity of God,
  The holy *place* of the tabernacle of the
  Most High.
5 God *is* ᵍin the midst of her, she shall
  not be moved;
  God shall help her, just at the break of
  dawn.
6 ʰThe nations raged, the kingdoms were
  moved;
  He uttered His voice, the earth melted.

7 The ᶦLORD of hosts *is* with us;
  The God of Jacob *is* our refuge.   *Selah*

8 Come, behold the works of the LORD,
  Who has made desolations in the
  earth.
9 ʲHe makes wars cease to the end of the
  earth;
  ᵏHe breaks the bow and cuts the spear
  in two;
  ᶦHe burns the chariot in the fire.

10 Be still, and know that I *am* God;
   ᵐI will be exalted among the nations,
   I will be exalted in the earth!
11 The LORD of hosts *is* with us;
   The God of Jacob *is* our refuge.   *Selah*

Psalm 47

Praise to God, the Ruler of the Earth

To the Chief Musician. A Psalm of the
sons of Korah.

1 Oh, clap your hands, all you peoples!
  Shout to God with the voice of
  triumph!
2 For the LORD Most High *is* awesome;
  He is a great ᵃKing over all the earth.
3 ᵇHe will subdue the peoples under us,
  And the nations under our feet.
4 He will choose our ᶜinheritance for us,
  The excellence of Jacob whom He
  loves.   *Selah*

45:9 Ophir. Possibly located in southern Arabia or in Africa (2 Chr. 8:17–18), this place was known in the Old Testament world as a source of fine gold.
45:14 robes of many colors. In the ancient world, the beauty of the bride's gowns might be an expression of her family's wealth, their pride in her, and their love for her.
46:2 though the earth be removed. God is a refuge for His people against everything actual or imagined.
46:5 God is in the midst of her. We do not have an absentee deliverer, a defense that is only sometimes present. The Lord lives with His people and His protection can be counted on.
46:10 Be still, and know that I am God. This call for

stillness before the Lord is not preparation for worship, but for impending judgment (Hab. 2:20; Zeph. 1:7; Zech. 2:13).
47:4 whom He loves. To love means "to make one's choice in." God had chosen the Israelites to be His

45:9 ᶦSong 6:8 ᵐ1 Kin. 2:19   **45:10** ⁿDeut. 21:13
45:11 ᵒ[Is. 54:5]   **45:12** ᵖIs. 49:23   **45:14** ᵃSong 1:4
45:16 ʳ[1 Pet. 2:9]   **45:17** ˢMal. 1:11   **46:title** ᵃ1 Chr. 15:20   **46:1** ᵇPs. 62:7, 8 ᶜ[Deut. 4:7]   **46:3** ᵈ[Ps. 93:3, 4]
46:4 ᵉ[Ezek. 47:1–12] ᶠIs. 60:14   **46:5** ᵍ[Zeph. 3:15]
46:6 ʰPs. 2:1, 2   **46:7** ᶦNum. 14:9   **46:9** ʲIs. 2:4 ᵏPs. 76:3 ᶦEzek. 39:9   **46:10** ᵐ[Is. 2:11, 17]   **47:2** ᵃNeh. 1:5
47:3 ᵇPs. 18:47   **47:4** ᶜ[1 Pet. 1:4]

5 ^dGod has gone up with a shout,
 The LORD with the sound of a trumpet.
6 Sing praises to God, sing praises!
 Sing praises to our King, sing praises!
7 ^eFor God *is* the King of all the earth;
 ^fSing praises with understanding.

8 ^gGod reigns over the nations;
 God ^hsits on His ⁱholy throne.
9 The princes of the people have
  gathered together,
 ^jThe people of the God of Abraham.
 ^kFor the shields of the earth *belong* to
  God;
 He is greatly exalted.

Psalm 48

The Glory of God in Zion

A Song. A Psalm of the sons of Korah.

1 Great *is* the LORD, and greatly to be
  praised
 In the ^acity of our God,
 In His holy mountain.
2 ^bBeautiful in elevation,
 The joy of the whole earth,
 Is Mount Zion *on* the sides of the
  north,
 The city of the great King.
3 God *is* in her palaces;
 He is known as her refuge.

4 For behold, ^cthe kings assembled,
 They passed by together.
5 They saw *it,* so they marveled;
 They were troubled, they hastened
  away.
6 Fear ^dtook hold of them there,
 And pain, as of a woman in birth
  pangs,
7 As *when* You break the ^eships of
  Tarshish
 With an east wind.

8 As we have heard,
 So we have seen

In the city of the LORD of hosts,
 In the city of our God:
 God will ^festablish it forever.   *Selah*

9 We have thought, O God, on ^gYour
   lovingkindness,
 In the midst of Your temple.
10 According to ^hYour name, O God,
 So *is* Your praise to the ends of the
   earth;
 Your right hand is full of
   righteousness.
11 Let Mount Zion rejoice,
 Let the daughters of Judah be glad,
 Because of Your judgments.

12 Walk about Zion,
 And go all around her.
 Count her towers;
13 Mark well her bulwarks;
 Consider her palaces;
 That you may ⁱtell *it* to the generation
   following.
14 For this *is* God,
 Our God forever and ever;
 ^jHe will be our guide
 Even to death.*

Psalm 49

The Confidence of the Foolish

To the Chief Musician. A Psalm of the
 sons of Korah.

1 Hear this, all peoples;
 Give ear, all inhabitants of the world,
2 Both low and high,
 Rich and poor together.
3 My mouth shall speak wisdom,
 And the meditation of my heart *shall
  give* understanding.
4 I will incline my ear to a proverb;
 I will disclose my dark saying on the
  harp.

---

* **48:14** Following Masoretic Text and Syriac;
Septuagint and Vulgate read *Forever.*

---

holy people and, in that way, He loved them. In His
dialogue with Nicodemus, Jesus explained that God's
love extended to all the nations as well as to Israel
(John 3:16).
47:9 The people of the God of Abraham. This is the
prophetic picture of the ultimate fulfillment of the
Abrahamic covenant (Gen. 12:1–3). One day all the
peoples of the earth who have come to faith in God
through Jesus will discover that they are one people.
They are all the true seed of Abraham because they,
like Abraham, believed in God (Gen. 15:6; Gal. 3:5–8).
48:1 Great is the LORD. Psalm 48 unites with Psalms 46
and 47 to form three great psalms of praise to God for
His kingship and His love for the holy city of Jerusalem.
This emphasis on Jerusalem has led many scholars to
speak of these psalms as "Songs of Zion." **the city of
our God.** The city of Jerusalem had a particularly dear
place in the heart of God's people (1 Kin. 14:21). The city
was holy because of the presence of God in the temple.

48:2 The joy of the whole earth. As is strongly established in the Book of Psalms, the purpose of God's
work in Israel was to draw all nations to Himself. **city
of the great King.** Jesus quoted these words in Matthew 5:35, speaking of Jerusalem.
48:12 Walk about Zion. Praising the city of Zion was
another way of praising God, whose dwelling was
there.
49:4 dark saying. Also translated "riddle," this word
refers to a perplexing moral problem. How do the
righteous come to terms with oppressive rich people
who seem to have no thought for God?

47:5 ^dPs. 68:24, 25   **47:7** ^eZech. 14:9 ^f1 Cor. 14:15
47:8 ^g1 Chr. 16:31 ^hPs. 97:2 ⁱPs. 48:1   **47:9** ^j[Rom. 4:11,
12] ^k[Ps. 89:18]   **48:1** ^aPs. 46:4; 87:3   **48:2** ^bPs. 50:2
48:4 ^c2 Sam. 10:6, 14   **48:6** ^dEx. 15:15   **48:7** ^eEzek.
27:25   **48:8** ^f[Ps. 87:5]   **48:9** ^gPs. 26:3   **48:10** ^hMal.
1:11   **48:13** ⁱ[Ps. 78:5–7]   **48:14** ^jIs. 58:11

5 Why should I fear in the days of evil,
  When the iniquity at my heels
    surrounds me?
6 Those who ᵃtrust in their wealth
  And boast in the multitude of their
    riches,
7 None *of them* can by any means
    redeem *his* brother,
  Nor ᵇgive to God a ransom for him—
8 For ᶜthe redemption of their souls *is*
    costly,
  And it shall cease forever—
9 That he should continue to live
    eternally,
  And ᵈnot see the Pit.

10 For he sees wise men die;
   Likewise the fool and the senseless
     person perish,
   And leave their wealth to others.
11 Their inner thought *is that* their
     houses *will last* forever,*
   Their dwelling places to all
     generations;
   They ᵉcall *their* lands after their own
     names.
12 Nevertheless man, *though* in honor,
     does not remain;*
   He is like the beasts *that* perish.

13 This is the way of those who *are*
     ᶠfoolish,
   And of their posterity who approve
     their sayings.   *Selah*
14 Like sheep they are laid in the grave;
   Death shall feed on them;
   ᵍThe upright shall have dominion over
     them in the morning;
   ʰAnd their beauty shall be consumed in
     the grave, far from their dwelling.
15 But God ⁱwill redeem my soul from the
     power of the grave,
   For He shall ʲreceive me.   *Selah*

16 Do not be afraid when one becomes
     rich,
   When the glory of his house is
     increased;
17 For when he dies he shall carry
     nothing away;
   His glory shall not descend after him.

18 Though while he lives ᵏhe blesses
     himself
   (For *men* will praise you when you do
     well for yourself),
19 He shall go to the generation of his
     fathers;
   They shall never see ˡlight.
20 A man *who is* in honor, yet does not
     understand,
   ᵐIs like the beasts *that* perish.

Psalm 50

God the Righteous Judge

A Psalm of Asaph.

1 The ᵃMighty One, God the LORD,
  Has spoken and called the earth
  From the rising of the sun to its going
    down.
2 Out of Zion, the perfection of beauty,
  ᵇGod will shine forth.
3 Our God shall come, and shall not
    keep silent;
  ᶜA fire shall devour before Him,
  And it shall be very tempestuous all
    around Him.

4 ᵈHe shall call to the heavens from
    above,
  And to the earth, that He may judge
    His people:
5 "Gather ᵉMy saints together to Me,
  ᶠThose who have made a covenant with
    Me by sacrifice."
6 Let the ᵍheavens declare His
    righteousness,
  For ʰGod Himself *is* Judge.   *Selah*

7 "Hear, O My people, and I will speak,
  O Israel, and I will testify against you;
  ⁱI *am* God, your God!
8 ʲI will not rebuke you ᵏfor your
    sacrifices

---

* **49:11** Septuagint, Syriac, Targum, and Vulgate
read *Their graves shall be their houses forever.*
* **49:12** Following Masoretic Text and Targum;
Septuagint, Syriac, and Vulgate read *understand*
(compare verse 20).

49:6 *Those who trust in their wealth.* The accumulation of material wealth is of no value in the life to come (Mark 10:23). Money can never buy redemption. Only God has the power to deliver us from death and hell.
49:14 *Death shall feed on them.* Death is the great leveler. People who have beauty, riches (vv. 16–17), and power in this world will lose them all at death. They will be stripped of everything except their character or soul. This is why the Scriptures exhort us to pursue character development—God's law, holiness, wisdom, and knowledge—more than anything else.
50:1 *The Mighty One, God the LORD.* These three titles give a stunning introduction to the poem, a grand display of God Himself in the midst of His people.

50:8 *rebuke you for your sacrifices.* The sacrifices were commanded by God in Leviticus, but the people had difficulty keeping a godly perspective on the nature of sacrifices. God did not need their offerings—He is already the owner of all the earth. The sacrifices were for their sakes, so that they would understand that sin equals death, and atonement comes by blood.

49:6 ᵃ [Mark 10:23, 24]   **49:7** ᵇ Job 36:18, 19
49:8 ᶜ [Matt. 16:26]   **49:9** ᵈ Ps. 89:48   **49:11** ᵉ Gen.
4:17   **49:13** ᶠ [Luke 12:20]   **49:14** ᵍ [Dan. 7:18]   ʰ Job
4:21   **49:15** ⁱ [Hos. 13:4] ʲ Ps. 73:24   **49:18** ᵏ Deut.
29:19   **49:19** ˡ Job 33:30   **49:20** ᵐ Eccl. 3:19   **50:1** ᵃ Is.
9:6   **50:2** ᵇ Ps. 80:1   **50:3** ᶜ [Ps. 97:3]   **50:4** ᵈ Is.
1:2   **50:5** ᵉ Deut. 33:3 ᶠ Ex. 24:7   **50:6** ᵍ [Ps. 97:6]
ʰ Ps. 75:7   **50:7** ⁱ Ex. 20:2   **50:8** ʲ Jer. 7:22 ᵏ [Hos. 6:6]

Or your burnt offerings,
Which are continually before Me.
9 [l]I will not take a bull from your house,
Nor goats out of your folds.
10 For every beast of the forest *is* Mine,
And the cattle on a thousand hills.
11 I know all the birds of the mountains,
And the wild beasts of the field *are* Mine.

12 "If I were hungry, I would not tell you;
[m]For the world *is* Mine, and all its fullness.
13 [n]Will I eat the flesh of bulls,
Or drink the blood of goats?
14 [o]Offer to God thanksgiving,
And [p]pay your vows to the Most High.
15 [q]Call upon Me in the day of trouble;
I will deliver you, and you shall glorify Me."

16 But to the wicked God says:
"What *right* have you to declare My statutes,
Or take My covenant in your mouth,
17 [r]Seeing you hate instruction
And cast My words behind you?
18 When you saw a thief, you [s]consented* with him,
And have been a [t]partaker with adulterers.
19 You give your mouth to evil,
And [u]your tongue frames deceit.
20 You sit *and* speak against your brother;
You slander your own mother's son.
21 These *things* you have done, and I kept silent;
[v]You thought that I was altogether like you;
But I will rebuke you,
And [w]set *them* in order before your eyes.

22 "Now consider this, you who [x]forget God,
Lest I tear *you* in pieces,
And *there be* none to deliver:
23 Whoever offers praise glorifies Me;
And [y]to him who orders *his* conduct *aright*
I will show the salvation of God."

Psalm 51

A Prayer of Repentance

To the Chief Musician. A Psalm of David [a]when Nathan the prophet went to him, after he had gone in to Bathsheba.

1 Have mercy upon me, O God,
According to Your lovingkindness;
According to the multitude of Your tender mercies,
[b]Blot out my transgressions.
2 [c]Wash me thoroughly from my iniquity,
And cleanse me from my sin.

3 For I acknowledge my transgressions,
And my sin *is* always before me.
4 [d]Against You, You only, have I sinned,
And done *this* evil [e]in Your sight—
[f]That You may be found just when You speak,*
And blameless when You judge.

5 [g]Behold, I was brought forth in iniquity,
And in sin my mother conceived me.
6 Behold, You desire truth in the inward parts,
And in the hidden *part* You will make me to know wisdom.

7 [h]Purge me with hyssop, and I shall be clean;

*__50:18__ Septuagint, Syriac, Targum, and Vulgate read *ran.* *__51:4__ Septuagint, Targum, and Vulgate read *in Your words.*

50:12 ***If I were hungry, I would not tell you.*** God doesn't hunger for food—and even if He did, He would not need His people to bring it to Him. He hungers for the righteousness of His people.

50:18 ***have been a partaker with adulterers.*** In this psalm the Lord brings a legal case against His people for violations of the covenant (v. 4). Verses 7–15 address the formalists, whose major emphasis is on the outward and external observances of the ceremonial law. Verses 16–23 are spoken to wicked members of the community who do not put God's commandments into practice in everyday life. The believer's attitude toward evil is to be one of total rejection: "Do not love the world or the things in the world" (1 John 2:15). There is no neutrality in regard to the moral law, and no approval can be given to those who disobey God's law (Rom. 1:32).

51:1 ***Have mercy upon me.*** This psalm is associated with one of the hardest experiences of David's life, the aftermath of his affair with Bathsheba. For the account of David's sin and the prophet Nathan's rebuke, see 2 Samuel 11:1—12:15. ***the multitude of Your tender mercies.*** David's call for mercy is the only appropriate request for a confessing sinner. No sinner should ask for justice, for that would mean judgment and ruin.

51:4 ***Against You.*** David had sinned against Bathsheba, Uriah, and the nation he was called to rule. But none of these indictments were as serious as David's offense against God.

51:5 ***iniquity.*** The psalmist should not be misunderstood as teaching that the pollution of human nature results from anything inherently corrupt in sexual relations between husband and wife. We are male and female by the sovereign will and creative power of God (Gen. 1:27). What David confesses, however, is the reality of human depravity (Rom. 5:12). We are inclined to gratify the cravings of our sinful nature, following its desires and thoughts,

50:9 [l]Ps. 69:31 **50:12** [m]Ex. 19:5 **50:13** [n][Ps. 51:15–17] **50:14** [o]Heb. 13:15 [p]Deut. 23:21 **50:15** [q][Zech. 13:9] **50:17** [r]Rom. 2:21 **50:18** [s][Rom. 1:32] [t]1 Tim. 5:22 **50:19** [u]Ps. 52:2 **50:21** [v][Rom. 2:4] [w][Ps. 90:8] **50:22** [x][Job 8:13] **50:23** [y]Gal. 6:16 **51:title** [a]2 Sam. 12:1 **51:1** [b][Is. 43:25; 44:22] **51:2** [c][Heb. 9:14] **51:4** [d]2 Sam. 12:13 [e][Luke 5:21] [f]Rom. 3:4 **51:5** [g][Job 14:4] **51:7** [h]Heb. 9:19

Wash me, and I shall be *f*whiter than
  snow.
8 Make me hear joy and gladness,
  That the bones You have broken *j*may
  rejoice.
9 Hide Your face from my sins,
  And blot out all my iniquities.

10 *k*Create in me a clean heart, O God,
  And renew a steadfast spirit
  within me.
11 Do not cast me away from Your
  presence,
  And do not take Your *l*Holy Spirit
  from me.
12 Restore to me the joy of Your salvation,
  And uphold me *by Your* *m*generous
  Spirit.
13 *Then* I will teach transgressors Your
  ways,
  And sinners shall be converted to You.

14 Deliver me from the guilt of
  bloodshed, O God,
  The God of my salvation,
  And my tongue shall sing aloud of
  Your righteousness.
15 O Lord, open my lips,
  And my mouth shall show forth Your
  praise.
16 For *n*You do not desire sacrifice, or else
  I would give *it;*
  You do not delight in burnt offering.
17 *o*The sacrifices of God *are* a broken
  spirit,
  A broken and a contrite heart—
  These, O God, You will not despise.

18 Do good in Your good pleasure to Zion;
  Build the walls of Jerusalem.
19 Then You shall be pleased with *p*the
  sacrifices of righteousness,
  With burnt offering and whole burnt
  offering;
  Then they shall offer bulls on Your
  altar.

Psalm 52

The End of the Wicked and the Peace of the Godly

To the Chief Musician.
A Contemplation* of David *a*when
Doeg the Edomite went and *b*told Saul,
and said to him, "David has gone to the
house of Ahimelech."

1 Why do you boast in evil, O mighty man?
  The goodness of God *endures*
  continually.
2 Your tongue devises destruction,
  Like a sharp razor, working deceitfully.
3 You love evil more than good,
  Lying rather than speaking
  righteousness.   *Selah*
4 You love all devouring words,
  You deceitful tongue.

5 God shall likewise destroy you forever;
  He shall take you away, and pluck you
  out of *your* dwelling place,
  And uproot you from the land of the
  living.   *Selah*
6 The righteous also shall see and fear,
  And shall laugh at him, *saying,*
7 "Here is the man *who* did not make God
  his strength,
  But trusted in the abundance of his
  riches,
  And strengthened himself in his
  wickedness."

8 But I *am* *c*like a green olive tree in the
  house of God;
  I trust in the mercy of God forever and
  ever.
9 I will praise You forever,
  Because You have done *it;*
  And in the presence of Your saints
  I will wait on Your name, for *it is* good.

---

* **52:title** Hebrew *Maschil*

---

contradicting God's commands. This is why we must experience radical regeneration by the supernatural power of the Holy Spirit. Apart from that rebirth, we can neither see nor enter the kingdom of God (John 3:3–5).
51:7 hyssop. Here David refers to the ritual acts of cleansing described in the law of Moses (Lev. 14:4; Num. 19:6).
51:10–13 Confession—Confession leads to forgiveness, but what does that look like? Psalm 51 gives us a picture. The results of forgiveness are a clean heart, a renewed spirit, a restored relationship with God, and a joyful experience of God's salvation. God cleans us up. He makes us presentable. He reorients us towards Himself, helping us to focus on what it is right. By forgiving us, God crosses over the canyon of sin that separates us from Him. When you put all this together there is great cause for joy on our part. Forgiveness is more than a theological abstract. It makes the salvation experience deeply personal and emotional in every sense. It takes that which is wrong in our life and makes it right.

51:16 You do not desire sacrifice. God's pleasure is not in the sacrificed animal, but in the willing obedience of His people (Gen. 4:1–7; John 4:21–24; Rom. 12:1–2). The motions of sacrifice not accompanied by a contrite heart are not acceptable to God (Is. 1:12–20).
52:2 Your tongue. This phrase refers to more than just words. These people used language as a weapon, for they believed that the gods could empower their words to a devastating effect.
52:6 see and fear. This fear is a deepened respect for God and a sense of awe before His throne.
52:8 a green olive tree. An olive tree was a symbol of beauty. In Romans 11:16–24, the olive tree is used as a symbol of the Gentiles who are grafted into the root—the people of God or the church.

51:7 *i* [Is. 1:18]   **51:8** *j* [Matt. 5:4]   **51:10** *k* [Ezek. 18:31]   **51:11** *l* [Luke 11:13]   **51:12** *m* [2 Cor. 3:17]   **51:16** *n* [1 Sam. 15:22]   **51:17** *o* Ps. 34:18   **51:19** *p* Ps. 4:5   **52:title** *a* 1 Sam. 22:9   *b* Ezek. 22:9   **52:8** *c* Jer. 11:16

Psalm 53

Folly of the Godless, and the Restoration of Israel

To the Chief Musician. Set to "Mahalath." A Contemplation* of David.

1 The ᵃfool has said in his heart,
"*There is* no God."
They are corrupt, and have done
abominable iniquity;
ᵇ*There is* none who does good.

2 God looks down from heaven upon the
children of men,
To see if there are *any* who
understand, who ᶜseek God.

3 Every one of them has turned aside;
They have together become corrupt;
There is none who does good,
No, not one.

4 Have the workers of iniquity ᵈno
knowledge,
Who eat up my people *as* they eat bread,
And do not call upon God?

5 ᵉThere they are in great fear
Where no fear was,
For God has scattered the bones of
him who encamps against you;
You have put *them* to shame,
Because God has despised them.

6 ᶠOh, that the salvation of Israel would
come out of Zion!
When God brings back the captivity of
His people,
Let Jacob rejoice *and* Israel be glad.

Psalm 54

Answered Prayer for Deliverance from Adversaries

To the Chief Musician. With stringed instruments.* A Contemplation* of David ᵃwhen the Ziphites went and said to Saul, "Is David not hiding with us?"

1 Save me, O God, by Your name,
And vindicate me by Your strength.

2 Hear my prayer, O God;
Give ear to the words of my mouth.

3 For strangers have risen up against me,
And oppressors have sought after my
life;
They have not set God before them.
Selah

4 Behold, God *is* my helper;
The Lord *is* with those who uphold
my life.

5 He will repay my enemies for their evil.
Cut them off in Your truth.

6 I will freely sacrifice to You;
I will praise Your name, O LORD, for *it
is* good.

7 For He has delivered me out of all
trouble;
ᵇAnd my eye has seen *its desire* upon
my enemies.

Psalm 55

Trust in God Concerning the Treachery of Friends

To the Chief Musician. With stringed instruments.* A Contemplation* of David.

1 Give ear to my prayer, O God,
And do not hide Yourself from my
supplication.

2 Attend to me, and hear me;
I ᵃam restless in my complaint, and
moan noisily,

3 Because of the voice of the enemy,
Because of the oppression of the
wicked;
ᵇFor they bring down trouble upon me,
And in wrath they hate me.

4 ᶜMy heart is severely pained within me,
And the terrors of death have fallen
upon me.

---

* **53:title** Hebrew *Maschil*   * **54:title** Hebrew *neginoth* • Hebrew *Maschil*   * **55:title** Hebrew *neginoth* • Hebrew *Maschil*

53:1 The fool. In the Bible, the term "fool" does not indicate mental incompetence, but moral and spiritual insensitivity.
53:5 scattered the bones. This is a prophetic pronouncement of the final judgment on the wicked.
54:3 They have not set God before them. In one of the dark moments of David's life, when the insanely jealous King Saul was bent on destroying him, David was able to lift his heart in supplication, trust, and praise to God. He had been hiding with his men in the hill country south of Jeshimon, but his location was betrayed to Saul by the people of Ziph (1 Sam. 23:19; 26:1). These were the "strangers" who doubtless stood to profit from David's death. They had no regard for covenant law, which bade the Israelites to love their neighbors as themselves (Lev. 19:18). Nor did they love the Lord their God wholeheartedly

(Deut. 6:5), but instead turned their hands against His anointed. Betrayal is a supreme act of treachery, whether in terms of a human being such as David, or of Jesus (Luke 22:48), the anointed Son of God. As such, it merits the most severe punishment from God (Mark 14:21).
54:5 He will repay. David did not take vengeance into his own hands. Only the Lord can take revenge.
55:4 terrors of death. David's intense pain can be felt in his strong language. The phrase "terrors of death" is unusual. The Hebrew word for "terror" or "dread"

53:1 ᵃPs. 10:4 ᵇRom. 3:10–12   **53:2** ᶜ[2 Chr. 15:2]
53:4 ᵈJer. 4:22   **53:5** ᵉProv. 28:1   **53:6** ᶠPs. 14:7
54:title ᵃ1 Sam. 23:19   **54:7** ᵇPs. 59:10   **55:2** ᵃIs. 38:14; 59:11   **55:3** ᵇ2 Sam. 16:7, 8   **55:4** ᶜPs. 116:3

5 Fearfulness and trembling have come
　　upon me,
　And horror has overwhelmed me.
6 So I said, "Oh, that I had wings like a
　　dove!
　I would fly away and be at rest.
7 Indeed, I would wander far off,
　　And remain in the wilderness. 　*Selah*
8 I would hasten my escape
　From the windy storm *and* tempest."

9 Destroy, O Lord, *and* divide their
　　tongues,
　For I have seen ᵈviolence and strife in
　　the city.
10 Day and night they go around it on its
　　walls;
　ᵉIniquity and trouble *are* also in the
　　midst of it.
11 Destruction *is* in its midst;
　ᶠOppression and deceit do not depart
　　from its streets.

12 ᵍFor *it is* not an enemy *who* reproaches
　　me;
　Then I could bear *it*.
　Nor *is it* one *who* hates me who has
　　ʰexalted *himself* against me;
　Then I could hide from him.
13 But *it was* you, a man my equal,
　ⁱMy companion and my acquaintance.
14 We took sweet counsel together,
　And ʲwalked to the house of God in the
　　throng.

15 Let death seize them;
　Let them ᵏgo down alive into hell,
　For wickedness *is* in their dwellings
　　and among them.

16 As for me, I will call upon God,
　And the Lord shall save me.
17 ˡEvening and morning and at noon
　I will pray, and cry aloud,
　And He shall hear my voice.
18 He has redeemed my soul in peace
　　from the battle *that was* against
　　me,
　For ᵐthere were many against me.
19 God will hear, and afflict them,
　ⁿEven He who abides from of old. *Selah*
　Because they do not change,
　Therefore they do not fear God.

20 He has ᵒput forth his hands against
　　those who ᵖwere at peace with him;

He has broken his covenant.
21 ᑫ*The words* of his mouth were
　　smoother than butter,
　But war *was* in his heart;
　His words were softer than oil,
　Yet they *were* drawn swords.

22 ʳCast your burden on the Lord,
　And ˢHe shall sustain you;
　He shall never permit the righteous to
　　be moved.

23 But You, O God, shall bring them
　　down to the pit of destruction;
　ᵗBloodthirsty and deceitful men ᵘshall
　　not live out half their days;
　But I will trust in You.

Psalm 56

Prayer for Relief from Tormentors

To the Chief Musician. Set to "The
Silent Dove in Distant Lands."*
A Michtam of David when the
ᵃPhilistines captured him in Gath.

1 Be ᵇmerciful to me, O God, for man
　　would swallow me up;
　Fighting all day he oppresses me.
2 My enemies would ᶜhound *me* all day,
　For *there are* many who fight against
　　me, O Most High.

3 Whenever I am afraid,
　I will trust in You.
4 In God (I will praise His word),
　In God I have put my trust;
　ᵈI will not fear.
　What can flesh do to me?

5 All day they twist my words;
　All their thoughts *are* against me for
　　evil.
6 They gather together,
　They hide, they mark my steps,
　When they lie in wait for my life.
7 Shall they escape by iniquity?
　In anger cast down the peoples, O God!

8 You number my wanderings;
　Put my tears into Your bottle;
　ᵉ*Are they* not in Your book?

---

* **56:title** Hebrew *Jonath Elem Rechokim*

---

is first used in Scripture to describe the horror that
Abraham felt in the unnatural darkness that seized
him as God was about to come near (Gen. 15:12). The
word also described the horrors that would fall on the
people of Canaan when the Lord gave the land to the
Israelites (Ex. 15:16). To strengthen this feeling, David
speaks of fear and trembling and an overwhelming
horror (Ezek. 7:18).
55:15 *Let them go down alive into hell.* David could
express his emotions to God in prayer, but judgment
or revenge was in God's hands (Rom. 12:19).
55:22 *Cast your burden on the Lord.* The Lord is the
one constant in life, and the one true Friend.

56:1 *Be merciful to me.* David cried out to God
because of his overwhelming sense of loss during his
time as a fugitive in a foreign land (1 Sam. 21:10–15).
56:8 *Put my tears into Your bottle.* Nothing that

55:9 ᵈ Jer. 6:7　**55:10** ᵉ Ps. 10:7　**55:11** ᶠ Ps. 10:7
55:12 ᵍ Ps. 41:9　ʰ Ps. 35:26; 38:16　**55:13** ⁱ 2 Sam. 15:12
55:14 ʲ Ps. 42:4　**55:15** ᵏ Num. 16:30, 33　**55:17** ˡ Dan.
6:10　**55:18** ᵐ 2 Chr. 32:7, 8　**55:19** ⁿ [Deut. 33:27]
55:20 ᵒ Acts 12:1　ᵖ Ps. 7:4　**55:21** ᑫ Ps. 28:3; 57:4
55:22 ʳ [Ps. 37:5]　ˢ Ps. 37:24　**55:23** ᵗ Ps. 5:6　ᵘ Prov. 10:27
56:title ᵃ 1 Sam. 21:11　**56:1** ᵇ Ps. 57:1　**56:2** ᶜ Ps. 57:3
56:4 ᵈ Ps. 118:6　**56:8** ᵉ [Mal. 3:16]

9 When I cry out *to You,*
Then my enemies will turn back;
This I know, because *f*God *is* for me.
10 In God (I will praise *His* word),
In the LORD (I will praise *His* word),
11 In God I have put my trust;
I will not be afraid.
What can man do to me?

12 Vows *made* to You *are binding* upon
me, O God;
I will render praises to You,
13 *g*For You have delivered my soul from
death.
Have You not *kept* my feet from
falling,
That I may walk before God
In the *h*light of the living?

Psalm 57

Prayer for Safety from Enemies

To the Chief Musician. Set to "Do Not
Destroy."* A Michtam of David *a*when
he fled from Saul into the cave.

1 Be merciful to me, O God, be merciful
to me!
For my soul trusts in You;
*b*And in the shadow of Your wings I will
make my refuge,
*c*Until *these* calamities have passed by.
2 I will cry out to God Most High,
To God *d*who performs *all things*
for me.
3 *e*He shall send from heaven and save
me;
He reproaches the one who would
swallow me up. *Selah*
God *f*shall send forth His mercy and
His truth.
4 My soul *is* among lions;
I lie *among* the sons of men
Who are set on fire,
*g*Whose teeth *are* spears and arrows,
And their tongue a sharp sword.

5 *h*Be exalted, O God, above the heavens;
Let Your glory *be* above all the earth.

6 *i*They have prepared a net for my steps;
My soul is bowed down;
They have dug a pit before me;
Into the midst of it they *themselves*
have fallen. *Selah*

7 *j*My heart is steadfast, O God, my heart
is steadfast;
I will sing and give praise.
8 Awake, *k*my glory!
Awake, lute and harp!
I will awaken the dawn.

9 *l*I will praise You, O Lord, among the
peoples;
I will sing to You among the nations.
10 *m*For Your mercy reaches unto the
heavens,
And Your truth unto the clouds.

11 *n*Be exalted, O God, above the heavens;
Let Your glory *be* above all the earth.

Psalm 58

The Just Judgment of the Wicked

To the Chief Musician. Set to "Do Not
Destroy."* A Michtam of David.

1 Do you indeed speak righteousness,
you silent ones?
Do you judge uprightly, you sons of
men?
2 No, in heart you work wickedness;
You weigh out the violence of your
hands in the earth.

3 *a*The wicked are estranged from the
womb;
They go astray as soon as they are
born, speaking lies.
4 *b*Their poison *is* like the poison of a
serpent;

---

* **57:title** Hebrew *Al Tashcheth*   * **58:title** Hebrew
Al Tashcheth

---

happens to us escapes God's notice and care; not a
tear falls to the ground that He does not remember.
When we suffer, it is a great comfort to know that God
is *for* us—everything that we live through will be put
to use for our good.
57:title *Saul into the cave.* The narrative of David's
life indicates that he twice hid in caves—once in
Adullam (1 Sam. 22:1–5) which was the setting of
Psalm 142, and once in En Gedi (1 Sam. 24:1–7), the
setting of this poem. In En Gedi, David spared Saul's
life even though he had a perfect chance to put Saul
out of the way and claim the kingship for himself.
57:1–3 *I will cry out to God.* Although he had lived
a righteous life, David still realized that he did not
deserve the protection of God and that if his life was
saved it would be by the grace of God. He trusted
God to care for him just as a mother hen protects her
young by covering them with her wings.

57:5 *Be exalted.* One of the ways in which God exalts
Himself is by graciously delivering the needy.
57:7 *My heart is steadfast.* Just as Paul was
able to say that he had kept the faith (2 Tim. 4:7),
David rejoiced that his trust in God had remained
strong.
58:1 *silent ones.* This may also be translated "mighty
ones" or "judges." Although they were merely
humans, the wicked judges were behaving as though
they claimed divine authority.

56:9 *f* [Rom. 8:31]   **56:13** *g* Ps. 116:8, 9 *h* Job 33:30
57:title *a* 1 Sam. 22:1   **57:1** *b* Ps. 17:8; 63:7 *c* Is.
26:20   **57:2** *d* [Ps. 138:8]   **57:3** *e* Ps. 144:5, 7 *f* Ps.
43:3   **57:4** *g* Prov. 30:14   **57:5** *h* Ps. 108:5   **57:6** *i* Ps.
9:15   **57:7** *j* Ps. 108:1–5   **57:8** *k* Ps. 16:9   **57:9** *l* Ps.
108:3   **57:10** *m* Ps. 103:11   **57:11** *n* Ps. 57:5   **58:3** *a* [Is.
48:8]   **58:4** *b* Eccl. 10:11

They *are* like the deaf cobra *that* stops
    its ear,
5 Which will not ᶜheed the voice of
    charmers,
    Charming ever so skillfully.

6 ᵈBreak their teeth in their mouth,
    O God!
    Break out the fangs of the young lions,
    O LORD!
7 ᵉLet them flow away as waters *which*
    run continually;
    When he bends *his bow,*
    Let his arrows be as if cut in pieces.
8 *Let them be* like a snail which melts
    away as it goes,
    ᶠLike a stillborn child of a woman, that
    they may not see the sun.

9 Before your ᵍpots can feel *the burning*
    thorns,
    He shall take them away ʰas with a
    whirlwind,
    As in His living and burning wrath.
10 The righteous shall rejoice when he
    sees the ⁱvengeance;
    ʲHe shall wash his feet in the blood of
    the wicked,
11 ᵏSo that men will say,
    "Surely *there is* a reward for the
    righteous;
    Surely He is God who ˡjudges in the
    earth."

Psalm 59

The Assured Judgment of the Wicked

To the Chief Musician. Set to "Do Not
Destroy."* A Michtam of David ᵃwhen
Saul sent men, and they watched the
house in order to kill him.

1 Deliver me from my enemies, O my
    God;
    Defend me from those who rise up
    against me.

2 Deliver me from the workers of
    iniquity,
    And save me from bloodthirsty men.
3 For look, they lie in wait for my life;
    ᵇThe mighty gather against me,
    Not *for* my transgression nor *for* my
    sin, O LORD.
4 They run and prepare themselves
    through no fault *of mine.*

    ᶜAwake to help me, and behold!
5 You therefore, O LORD God of hosts,
    the God of Israel,
    Awake to punish all the nations;
    Do not be merciful to any wicked
    transgressors.   *Selah*

6 ᵈAt evening they return,
    They growl like a dog,
    And go all around the city.
7 Indeed, they belch with their mouth;
    ᵉSwords *are* in their lips;
    For *they say,* ᶠ"Who hears?"

8 But ᵍYou, O LORD, shall laugh at
    them;
    You shall have all the nations in
    derision.
9 I will wait for You, O You his
    Strength;*
    ʰFor God *is* my defense.
10 My God of mercy* shall ⁱcome to meet
    me;
    God shall let ʲme see *my desire* on my
    enemies.

11 Do not slay them, lest my people
    forget;
    Scatter them by Your power,
    And bring them down,
    O Lord our shield.

---

* **59:title** Hebrew *Al Tashcheth*   * **59:9** Following
Masoretic Text and Syriac; some Hebrew manuscripts, Septuagint, Targum, and Vulgate read *my
Strength.*   * **59:10** Following Qere; some Hebrew
manuscripts, Septuagint, and Vulgate read *My
God, His mercy*; Kethib, some Hebrew manuscripts and Targum read *O God, my mercy*; Syriac
reads *O God, Your mercy.*

58:6 *Break their teeth.* The wicked are pictured as
having powerful teeth, as though they were carni-
vores, eating the righteous alive. Here David asks God
to shatter their teeth, symbolizing the destruction of
the power of the wicked over the poor and defenseless.
58:10 *wash his feet in the blood of the wicked.* We
know that it is wrong to rejoice in the downfall of
another human being; the picture of the righteous
wading in the blood of their fallen enemies is hard
for modern Western Christians to understand. Jesus
clearly taught that our attitude towards our enemies
should be one of compassion and forgiveness (Matt.
5:43–48; Luke 23:34), but this does not mean that we
should take a soft attitude towards sin. Wickedness
grieves and angers God, and when wickedness has
finally been dealt with, we will rejoice.
59:1 *Deliver me from my enemies.* The story behind
this psalm of lament is found in 1 Samuel 19:9–17.

59:3 *Not for my transgression.* There were times
in David's life when he knew that he was suffering
because of sin in his life (32:1–7), but at other times
he was hounded by wicked persons even though he
was innocent.
59:6 *a dog.* Dogs were unclean animals, semi-wild
scavengers rather than the beloved pets of our own
day. To call someone a dog or compare him to a dog
was a profound insult.
59:11 *Do not slay them . . . scatter.* The imprecation or curse in this verse is unusual. Instead of asking
for the destruction of the wicked, the psalmist asks

58:5 ᶜ Jer. 8:17   **58:6** ᵈ Job 4:10   **58:7** ᵉ Josh. 2:11; 7:5
58:8 ᶠ Job 3:16   **58:9** ᵍ Eccl. 7:6 ʰ Prov. 10:25   **58:10** ⁱ Jer.
11:20 ʲ Ps. 68:23   **58:11** ᵏ Ps. 92:15 ˡ Ps. 50:6; 75:7
59:title ᵃ 1 Sam. 19:11   **59:3** ᵇ Ps. 56:6   **59:4** ᶜ Ps. 35:23
59:6 ᵈ Ps. 59:14   **59:7** ᵉ Prov. 12:18 ᶠ Ps. 10:11   **59:8** ᵍ Prov.
1:26   **59:9** ʰ [Ps. 62:2]   **59:10** ⁱ Ps. 21:3 ʲ Ps. 54:7

¹² ᵏFor the sin of their mouth *and* the
  words of their lips,
  Let them even be taken in their pride,
  And for the cursing and lying *which*
  they speak.
¹³ ˡConsume *them* in wrath, consume *them*,
  That they *may* not *be;*
  And ᵐlet them know that God rules in
  Jacob
  To the ends of the earth. *Selah*
¹⁴ And ⁿat evening they return,
  They growl like a dog,
  And go all around the city.
¹⁵ They ᵒwander up and down for food,
  And howl* if they are not satisfied.
¹⁶ But I will sing of Your power;
  Yes, I will sing aloud of Your mercy in
  the morning;
  For You have been my defense
  And refuge in the day of my trouble.
¹⁷ To You, ᵖO my Strength, I will sing
  praises;
  For God *is* my defense,
  My God of mercy.

Psalm 60

Urgent Prayer for the Restored Favor of God

To the Chief Musician. ᵃSet to "Lily of
the Testimony."* A Michtam of David.
For teaching. ᵇWhen he fought against
Mesopotamia and Syria of Zobah,
and Joab returned and killed twelve
thousand Edomites in the Valley of Salt.

¹ O God, ᶜYou have cast us off;
  You have broken us down;
  You have been displeased;
  Oh, restore us again!
² You have made the earth tremble;
  You have broken it;
  ᵈHeal its breaches, for it is shaking.
³ ᵉYou have shown Your people hard
  things;

ᶠYou have made us drink the wine of
  confusion.
⁴ ᵍYou have given a banner to those who
  fear You,
  That it may be displayed because of
  the truth. *Selah*
⁵ ʰThat Your beloved may be delivered,
  Save *with* Your right hand, and
  hear me.
⁶ God has ⁱspoken in His holiness:
  "I will rejoice;
  I will ʲdivide ᵏShechem
  And measure out ˡthe Valley of Succoth.
⁷ Gilead *is* Mine, and Manasseh *is* Mine;
  ᵐEphraim also *is* the helmet for My head;
  ⁿJudah *is* My lawgiver.
⁸ ᵒMoab *is* My washpot;
  ᵖOver Edom I will cast My shoe;
  ᵠPhilistia, shout in triumph because of
  Me."
⁹ Who will bring me *to* the strong city?
  Who will lead me to Edom?
¹⁰ *Is it* not You, O God, ʳwho cast us off?
  And You, O God, *who* did ˢnot go out
  with our armies?
¹¹ Give us help from trouble,
  ᵗFor the help of man *is* useless.
¹² Through God ᵘwe will do valiantly,
  For *it is* He *who* shall tread down our
  enemies.*

Psalm 61

Assurance of God's Eternal Protection

To the Chief Musician. On a stringed
instrument.* A *Psalm* of David.

¹ Hear my cry, O God;
  Attend to my prayer.

---

* **59:15** Following Septuagint and Vulgate;
Masoretic Text, Syriac, and Targum read *spend
the night.*   * **60:title** Hebrew *Shushan Eduth*
* **60:12** Compare verses 5–12 with 108:6–13
* **61:title** Hebrew *neginah*

---

for them to be scattered, to be made fugitives. This
would be a constant reminder of the consequences
of evil.
59:16–17 I will sing. David knew that King Saul had
sent a murder squad to track him down and kill him.
Yet he arose in the morning with joy in his heart and
a song on his lips. This was in contrast to his enemies,
who would return to the city each evening after a
long, fruitless search for David. They were nervous,
irritable, and arrogant.
60:1 You have broken us down. This is a poetic
description of an otherwise unknown defeat of the
armies of Israel in a battle that was part of the campaign against Aram of Zobah and his Mesopotamian
allies (2 Sam. 8). The defeat was so startling that it
caused the people of Israel to feel as though God had
made the earth tremble.
60:5 Your beloved. This term is particularly endearing (Is. 5:1; Jer. 11:15). God did not merely act for His
people out of duty, He loved them.

60:8 Moab . . . Edom . . . Philistia. These traditional
enemies of Israel were also enemies of God. The Lord
would not allow them to disturb His people.
60:12 we will do valiantly. As the title records, this
was what happened. David's general Joab led the
battle, and under God's hand Israel's enemies were
soundly defeated. When the help of man proves useless, often God dramatically provides strength and
power so that our boast is solely in Him.

59:12 ᵏProv. 12:13   **59:13** ˡPs. 104:35   ᵐPs. 83:18
59:14 ⁿPs. 59:6   **59:15** ᵒJob 15:23   **59:17** ᵖPs.
18:1   **60:title** ᵃPs. 80   ᵇ2 Sam. 8:3, 13   **60:1** ᶜPs.
44:9   **60:2** ᵈ[2 Chr. 7:14]   **60:3** ᵉPs. 71:20   ᶠJer. 25:15
60:4 ᵍPs. 20:5   **60:5** ʰPs. 108:6–13   **60:6** ⁱPs. 89:35
ʲJosh. 1:6   ᵏGen. 12:6   ˡJosh. 13:27   **60:7** ᵐDeut. 33:17
ⁿ[Gen. 49:10]   **60:8** ᵒ2 Sam. 8:2   ᵖ2 Sam. 8:14   ᵠ2 Sam.
8:1   **60:10** ʳPs. 108:11   ˢJosh. 7:12   **60:11** ᵗPs. 118:8;
146:3   **60:12** ᵘNum. 24:18

2 From the end of the earth I will cry to
You,
When my heart is overwhelmed;
Lead me to the rock that is higher than I.
3 For You have been a shelter for me,
ᵃA strong tower from the enemy.
4 I will abide in Your tabernacle forever;
ᵇI will trust in the shelter of Your wings.
Selah
5 For You, O God, have heard my vows;
You have given *me* the heritage of
those who fear Your name.
6 You will prolong the king's life,
His years as many generations.
7 He shall abide before God forever.
Oh, prepare mercy ᶜand truth, *which*
may preserve him!
8 So I will sing praise to Your name
forever,
That I may daily perform my vows.

Psalm 62

A Calm Resolve to Wait for the Salvation of God

To the Chief Musician. To ᵃJeduthun.
A Psalm of David.

1 Truly ᵇmy soul silently *waits* for God;
From Him *comes* my salvation.
2 He only *is* my rock and my salvation;
He is my defense;
I shall not be greatly ᶜmoved.
3 How long will you attack a man?
You shall be slain, all of you,
ᵈLike a leaning wall and a tottering
fence.
4 They only consult to cast *him* down
from his high position;
They ᵉdelight in lies;
They bless with their mouth,
But they curse inwardly. *Selah*
5 My soul, wait silently for God alone,
For my expectation *is* from Him.

6 He only *is* my rock and my salvation;
He is my defense;
I shall not be moved.
7 ᶠIn God *is* my salvation and my glory;
The rock of my strength,
And my refuge, *is* in God.
8 Trust in Him at all times, you people;
ᵍPour out your heart before Him;
God *is* a refuge for us. *Selah*
9 ʰSurely men of low degree *are* a vapor,
Men of high degree *are* a lie;
If they are weighed on the scales,
They *are* altogether *lighter* than
vapor.
10 Do not trust in oppression,
Nor vainly hope in robbery;
ⁱIf riches increase,
Do not set *your* heart *on them.*
11 God has spoken once,
Twice I have heard this:
That power *belongs* to God.
12 Also to You, O Lord, *belongs* mercy;
For ʲYou render to each one according
to his work.

Psalm 63

Joy in the Fellowship of God

A Psalm of David ᵃwhen he was in the
wilderness of Judah.

1 O God, You *are* my God;
Early will I seek You;
ᵇMy soul thirsts for You
My flesh longs for You
In a dry and thirsty land
Where there is no water.
2 So I have looked for You in the
sanctuary,
To see ᶜYour power and Your glory.
3 ᵈBecause Your lovingkindness *is* better
than life,
My lips shall praise You.
4 Thus I will bless You while I live;
I will ᵉlift up my hands in Your name.

61:2 *the rock that is higher than I.* The imagery of God as a Rock for the believer was introduced by Moses (Deut. 32:4) and is developed elsewhere in the Psalms (62:2; 71:3; 144:1).
61:6 *as many generations.* This phrase refers to David's long rule, but more literally prophesies the eternal rule of Jesus, the King of kings.
62:title *Jeduthun.* Jeduthun was appointed by David as one of those in charge of the music associated with worship (1 Chr. 16:41–42).
62:8 *Trust . . . you people.* David addresses the righteous with his lesson of reliance on God. What is true for David is extended to all in the believing community.
62:11 *spoken once, Twice.* It is a convention of wisdom literature to use a number and then raise it by one (Prov. 30:15–31), emphasizing the certainty of the point made.

63:title *in the wilderness of Judah.* This possibly refers to an incident during the period when Saul was chasing David (1 Sam. 22–24).
63:2 *in the sanctuary.* The sanctuary had been at Nob (1 Sam. 21:1), and it was there that David had sought the presence of the Lord. Later it was moved to Jerusalem (76:1–2).
63:4 *lift up my hands.* To lift the hands to the Lord expresses dependence on Him, coupled with an acknowledgment of His power, wonder, and majesty.

61:3 ᵃProv. 18:10   61:4 ᵇPs. 91:4   61:7 ᶜPs. 40:11
62:title ᵃ1 Chr. 25:1   62:1 ᵇPs. 33:20   62:2 ᶜPs. 55:22
62:3 ᵈIs. 30:13   62:4 ᵉPs. 28:3   62:7 ᶠ[Jer. 3:23]
62:8 ᵍ1 Sam. 1:15   62:9 ʰIs. 40:17   62:10 ⁱ[Luke 12:15]
62:12 ʲ[Matt. 16:27]   63:title ᵃ1 Sam. 22:5   63:1 ᵇPs. 42:2   63:2 ᶜPs. 27:4   63:3 ᵈPs. 138:2   63:4 ᵉPs. 28:2; 143:6

5 My soul shall be satisfied as with
  marrow and fatness,
  And my mouth shall praise *You* with
  joyful lips.
6 When *f*I remember You on my bed,
  I meditate on You in the *night*
  watches.
7 Because You have been my help,
  Therefore in the shadow of Your wings
  I will rejoice.
8 My soul follows close behind You;
  Your right hand upholds me.

9 But those *who* seek my life, to destroy
  it,
  Shall go into the lower parts of the
  earth.
10 They shall fall by the sword;
  They shall be a portion for jackals.

11 But the king shall rejoice in God;
  *g*Everyone who swears by Him shall
  glory;
  But the mouth of those who speak lies
  shall be stopped.

Psalm 64

Oppressed by the Wicked but Rejoicing in the LORD

To the Chief Musician. A Psalm of
David.

1 Hear my voice, O God, in my
  meditation;
  Preserve my life from fear of the
  enemy.
2 Hide me from the secret plots of the
  wicked,
  From the rebellion of the workers of
  iniquity,
3 Who sharpen their tongue like a
  sword,
  *a*And bend *their bows to shoot* their
  arrows—bitter words,
4 That they may shoot in secret at the
  blameless;
  Suddenly they shoot at him and do not
  fear.
5 They encourage themselves *in* an evil
  matter;
  They talk of laying snares secretly;
  *b*They say, "Who will see them?"
6 They devise iniquities:
  "We have perfected a shrewd scheme."

Both the inward thought and the heart
  of man are deep.
7 But God shall shoot at them *with* an
  arrow;
  Suddenly they shall be wounded.
8 So He will make them stumble over
  their own tongue;
  *c*All who see them shall flee away.
9 All men shall fear,
  And shall *d*declare the work of God;
  For they shall wisely consider His
  doing.

10 *e*The righteous shall be glad in the
  LORD, and trust in Him.
  And all the upright in heart shall
  glory.

Psalm 65

Praise to God for His Salvation and Providence

To the Chief Musician. A Psalm of
David. A Song.

1 Praise is awaiting You, O God, in
  Zion;
  And to You the vow shall be
  performed.
2 O You who hear prayer,
  *a*To You all flesh will come.
3 Iniquities prevail against me;
  As for our transgressions,
  You will *b*provide atonement for
  them.
4 *c*Blessed *is the man* You *d*choose,
  And cause to approach *You*,
  That he may dwell in Your courts.
  *e*We shall be satisfied with the
  goodness of Your house,
  Of Your holy temple.
5 *By* awesome deeds in righteousness
  You will answer us,
  O God of our salvation,
  You who are the confidence of all the
  ends of the earth,
  And of the far-off seas;
6 Who established the mountains by His
  strength,
  *f*Being clothed with power;
7 *g*You who still the noise of the seas,
  The noise of their waves,
  *h*And the tumult of the peoples.

63:8 Your right hand. The same power of God that delivered Israel from Egypt (Ex. 15:6) would support David—and all other believers in their daily lives.
64:10 trust in Him. By placing our problems into God's hands, we can rest in His sovereign will for our lives. Concerns about the future can be cast aside, for the Lord controls our future and has good plans for us (Rom. 8:28).
65:3 provide atonement for them. David speaks of

a coming day when sin will be dealt with fully, when redemption will be completely paid. This took place in the death and resurrection of Jesus Christ (Eph. 1:7).

63:6 *f* Ps. 42:8   **63:11** *g* Deut. 6:13   **64:3** *a* Ps. 58:7
64:5 *b* Ps. 10:11; 59:7   **64:8** *c* Ps. 31:11   **64:9** *d* Jer.
50:28; 51:10   **64:10** *e* Ps. 32:11   **65:2** *a* [Is. 66:23]
65:3 *b* [Heb. 9:14]   **65:4** *c* Ps. 33:12 *d* Ps. 4:3 *e* Ps. 36:8
65:6 *f* Ps. 93:1   **65:7** *g* Matt. 8:26 *h* Is. 17:12, 13

8 They also who dwell in the farthest
parts are afraid of Your signs;
You make the outgoings of the
morning and evening rejoice.

9 You visit the earth and *i*water it,
You greatly enrich it;
*j*The river of God is full of water;
You provide their grain,
For so You have prepared it.

10 You water its ridges abundantly,
You settle its furrows;
You make it soft with showers,
You bless its growth.

11 You crown the year with Your
goodness,
And Your paths drip *with*
abundance.

12 They drop *on* the pastures of the
wilderness,
And the little hills rejoice on every
side.

13 The pastures are clothed with flocks;
*k*The valleys also are covered with
grain;
They shout for joy, they also sing.

Psalm 66

Praise to God for His
Awesome Works

To the Chief Musician. A Song.
A Psalm.

1 Make *a*a joyful shout to God, all the
earth!

2 Sing out the honor of His name;
Make His praise glorious.

3 Say to God,
"How *b*awesome are Your works!
*c*Through the greatness of Your power
Your enemies shall submit themselves
to You.

4 *d*All the earth shall worship You
And sing praises to You;
They shall sing praises *to* Your name."
Selah

5 Come and see the works of God;
He is awesome *in His* doing toward the
sons of men.

6 *e*He turned the sea into dry *land*;
*f*They went through the river on foot.
There we will rejoice in Him.

7 He rules by His power forever;
His eyes observe the nations;
Do not let the rebellious exalt
themselves. *Selah*

8 Oh, bless our God, you peoples!
And make the voice of His praise to be
heard,

9 Who keeps our soul among the
living,
And does not allow our feet to be
moved.

10 For *g*You, O God, have tested us;
*h*You have refined us as silver is
refined.

11 *i*You brought us into the net;
You laid affliction on our backs.

12 *j*You have caused men to ride over our
heads;
*k*We went through fire and through
water;
But You brought us out to rich
fulfillment.

13 *l*I will go into Your house with burnt
offerings;
*m*I will pay You my vows,

14 Which my lips have uttered
And my mouth has spoken when I was
in trouble.

15 I will offer You burnt sacrifices of fat
animals,
With the sweet aroma of rams;
I will offer bulls with goats. *Selah*

16 Come *and* hear, all you who fear
God,
And I will declare what He has done
for my soul.

17 I cried to Him with my mouth,
And He was extolled with my
tongue.

18 *n*If I regard iniquity in my heart,
The Lord will not hear.

19 *But* certainly God *o*has heard *me*;
He has attended to the voice of my
prayer.

20 Blessed *be* God,
Who has not turned away my prayer,
Nor His mercy from me!

65:9 You visit the earth. Rainfall is seen here as a gracious visitation of God. This is in keeping with the provisions of God's covenant with Israel (Deut. 28:12). These words have some fulfillment every time the rains bring productivity to the earth.
66:1 all the earth. As in Psalm 100:1, the call is not only for the people of Israel, but for the peoples of all the earth to join in the praises of the living God, the Most High (87:7; 96:1–6; 117:1).
66:2 the honor of His name. The Lord's name describes His character, so honoring God's name is honoring God Himself (Ex. 3:14–15).
66:8 O bless our God. To bless God is to identify Him as the source of our blessing.

66:13 Your house. This term refers to the temple in Jerusalem where God lived among His people.
66:16 all you who fear God. Those who fear God are those who respond in awe and wonder to Him.
66:18 regard iniquity. Ongoing sin tolerated in a believer's life is one of the main things that blocks effective prayer and hinders growth.

65:9 *i* Jer. 5:24 *j* Ps. 46:4; 104:13; 147:8 **65:13** *k* Is. 44:23; 55:12 **66:1** *a* Ps. 100:1 **66:3** *b* Ps. 65:5 *c* Ps. 18:44 **66:4** *d* Ps. 117:1 **66:6** *e* Ex. 14:21 *f* Josh. 3:14–16 **66:10** *g* Ps. 17:3 *h* [1 Pet. 1:7] **66:11** *i* Lam. 1:13 **66:12** *j* Is. 51:23 *k* Is. 43:2 **66:13** *l* Ps. 100:4; 116:14, 17–19 *m* [Eccl. 5:4] **66:18** *n* Is. 1:15 **66:19** *o* Ps. 116:1, 2

Psalm 67

An Invocation and a Doxology

To the Chief Musician. On stringed
instruments.* A Psalm. A Song.

1 God be merciful to us and bless us,
And [a]cause His face to shine upon us,
Selah

2 That [b]Your way may be known on
earth,
[c]Your salvation among all nations.

3 Let the peoples praise You, O God;
Let all the peoples praise You.

4 Oh, let the nations be glad and sing for
joy!
For [d]You shall judge the people
righteously,
And govern the nations on earth.
Selah

5 Let the peoples praise You, O God;
Let all the peoples praise You.

6 [e]Then the earth shall yield her
increase;
God, our own God, shall bless us.

7 God shall bless us,
And all the ends of the earth shall fear
Him.

Psalm 68

The Glory of God in His Goodness to Israel

To the Chief Musician. A Psalm of
David. A Song.

1 Let [a]God arise,
Let His enemies be scattered;
Let those also who hate Him flee
before Him.

2 [b]As smoke is driven away,
So drive *them* away;
[c]As wax melts before the fire,
So let the wicked perish at the
presence of God.

3 But [d]let the righteous be glad;
Let them rejoice before God;
Yes, let them rejoice exceedingly.

4 Sing to God, sing praises to His
name;
[e]Extol Him who rides on the clouds,*
[f]By His name YAH,
And rejoice before Him.

5 [g]A father of the fatherless, a defender of
widows,
Is God in His holy habitation.

6 [h]God sets the solitary in families;
[i]He brings out those who are bound
into prosperity;
But [j]the rebellious dwell in a dry *land*.

7 O God, [k]when You went out before
Your people,
When You marched through the
wilderness, *Selah*

8 The earth shook;
The heavens also dropped *rain* at the
presence of God;
Sinai itself *was moved* at the presence
of God, the God of Israel.

9 [l]You, O God, sent a plentiful rain,
Whereby You confirmed Your
inheritance,
When it was weary.

10 Your congregation dwelt in it;
[m]You, O God, provided from Your
goodness for the poor.

11 The Lord gave the word;
Great *was* the company of those who
proclaimed *it:*

12 "Kings[n] of armies flee, they flee,
And she who remains at home divides
the spoil.

13 [o]Though you lie down among the
sheepfolds,
[p]*You will be* like the wings of a dove
covered with silver,
And her feathers with yellow gold."

---

* **67:title** Hebrew *neginoth*   * **68:4** Masoretic Text
reads *deserts;* Targum reads *heavens* (compare
verse 34 and Isaiah 19:1).

67:1 *His face to shine.* In the language of Aaron's
benediction (Num. 6:24–26), the psalmist calls for
God to smile on His people.

67:2 *known on earth.* From the beginning God
had intended to bring His blessing to all nations, in
fulfillment of the provisions of the Abrahamic covenant (Gen. 12:3). This passage anticipates the thrust
of world mission that is found in the New Testament
(Matt. 28:18–20; Acts 1:8).

67:6 *yield her increase.* The coming of God's kingdom on earth will be marked by a magnificent
increase in production. The curse on the land (Gen.
3:17–19; Rom. 8:22) will be lifted at that time.

68:1 *Let God arise.* This psalm is based in part on
the Song of Deborah in Judges 5. The presence of
the wicked on the earth is an assault on God's holiness and a constant threat to the righteous. Only
God's mercy compels Him to delay His judgment
(75:2).

68:5–6 *father.* The view of God as Father is not as
fully developed in the Old Testament as it is in the
New Testament. This passage affords some insight
into the character of God as Father. He is not seen in
these verses as the Almighty God destroying His foes.
He is pictured rather as the Father helping His children in need. He delights in kindly works which bring
a happy existence to His children.

68:11 *the company of those who proclaimed.* This
may refer to the women who gave praise to God
under the direction of Miriam (Ex. 15:20–21).

67:1 [a] Num. 6:25   **67:2** [b] Acts 18:25   [c] Titus
2:11   **67:4** [d] [Ps. 96:10, 13; 98:9]   **67:6** [e] Lev. 26:4
68:1 [a] Num. 10:35   **68:2** [b] [Is. 9:18]   [c] Mic. 1:4   **68:3** [d] Ps.
32:11   **68:4** [e] Deut. 33:26   [f] [Ex. 6:3]   **68:5** [g] [Ps. 10:14,
18; 146:9]   **68:6** [h] Ps. 107:4–7   [i] Acts 12:6–11   [j] Ps. 107:34
68:7 [k] Ex. 13:21   **68:9** [l] Deut. 11:11   **68:10** [m] Deut. 26:5
68:12 [n] Josh. 10:16   **68:13** [o] Ps. 81:6   [p] Ps. 105:37

14 ᵃWhen the Almighty scattered kings in
it,
It was *white* as snow in Zalmon.

15 A mountain of God *is* the mountain of
Bashan;
A mountain *of many* peaks *is* the
mountain of Bashan.

16 Why do you fume with envy, you
mountains of *many* peaks?
ʳThis *is* the mountain *which* God
desires to dwell in;
Yes, the LORD will dwell *in it* forever.

17 ˢThe chariots of God *are* twenty
thousand,
Even thousands of thousands;
The Lord is among them *as in* Sinai, in
the Holy *Place.*

18 ᵗYou have ascended on high,
ᵘYou have led captivity captive;
ᵛYou have received gifts among men,
Even *from* ʷthe rebellious,
ˣThat the LORD God might dwell *there.*

19 Blessed *be* the Lord,
Who daily loads us *with benefits,*
The God of our salvation! *Selah*

20 Our God *is* the God of salvation;
And ʸto GOD the Lord *belong* escapes
from death.

21 But ᶻGod will wound the head of His
enemies,
ᵃThe hairy scalp of the one who still
goes on in his trespasses.

22 The Lord said, "I will bring ᵇback from
Bashan,
I will bring *them* back ᶜfrom the
depths of the sea,

23 ᵈThat your foot may crush *them**in
blood,
ᵉAnd the tongues of your dogs *may have*
their portion from *your* enemies."

24 They have seen Your procession,
O God,
The procession of my God, my King,
into the sanctuary.

25 ᶠThe singers went before, the players
on instruments *followed* after;
Among *them were* the maidens
playing timbrels.

26 Bless God in the congregations,
The Lord, from ᵍthe fountain of Israel.

27 ʰThere *is* little Benjamin, their leader,
The princes of Judah *and* their
company,
The princes of Zebulun *and* the
princes of Naphtali.

28 Your God has ⁱcommanded* your
strength;
Strengthen, O God, what You have
done for us.

29 Because of Your temple at Jerusalem,
ʲKings will bring presents to You.

30 Rebuke the beasts of the reeds,
ᵏThe herd of bulls with the calves of the
peoples,
Till everyone ˡsubmits himself with
pieces of silver.
Scatter the peoples *who* delight in war.

31 ᵐEnvoys will come out of Egypt;
ⁿEthiopia will quickly ᵒstretch out her
hands to God.

32 Sing to God, you ᵖkingdoms of the
earth;
Oh, sing praises to the Lord,   *Selah*

33 To Him ᑫwho rides on the heaven of
heavens, *which were* of old!
Indeed, He sends out His voice, a
ʳmighty voice.

34 ˢAscribe strength to God;
His excellence *is* over Israel,
And His strength *is* in the clouds.

35 O God, ᵗ*You are* more awesome than
Your holy places.
The God of Israel *is* He who gives
strength and power to *His* people.

Blessed *be* God!

Psalm 69

An Urgent Plea for Help in Trouble

To the Chief Musician. Set to "The
Lilies."* A *Psalm* of David.

1 Save me, O God!
For ᵃthe waters have come up to *my*
neck.

---

* **68:23** Septuagint, Syriac, Targum, and Vulgate
read *you may dip your foot.*   * **68:28** Septuagint,
Syriac, Targum, and Vulgate read *Command,*
O God.   * **69:title** Hebrew *Shoshannim*

68:14 the Almighty. This translates the name
"Shaddai," a title that refers to the majesty and
strength of the Lord (91:1).
68:18 You have led captivity captive. Paul quotes
this verse in Ephesians 4:8, applying it to Jesus Christ.
received gifts. When God delivered His people from
Egypt, He brought them out with great treasures
from the Egyptians (Ex. 12:35–36). These gifts were
used by the people of Israel to build the tabernacle
(Ex. 35:20–29), where the Lord promised to dwell.
68:29 Kings will bring presents to You. Royal guests
came to Solomon with gifts (1 Kin. 10:1–10); but the
ultimate prophetic fulfillment of this verse was in the
kings who came to Jerusalem to bring gifts to the
infant Jesus (Matt. 2:1–12). One day all kings will show

their obedience and humility before Jesus, the great
King (2:10–12; 76:11).
69:1 the waters have come up to my neck. This highly
messianic psalm presents a remarkable description of

68:14 ᑫ Josh. 10:10   **68:16** ʳ [Deut. 12:5]   **68:17** ˢ Deut.
33:2   **68:18** ᵗ Eph. 4:8   ᵘ Judg. 5:12   ᵛ Acts 2:4, 33; 10:44–
46   ʷ [1 Tim. 1:13]   ˣ Ps. 78:60   **68:20** ʸ [Deut. 32:39]
68:21 ᶻ Hab. 3:13   ᵃ Ps. 55:23   **68:22** ᵇ Num. 21:33   ᶜ Ex.
14:22   **68:23** ᵈ Ps. 58:10   ᵉ 1 Kin. 21:19   **68:25** ᶠ 1 Chr.
13:8   **68:26** ᵍ Deut. 33:28   **68:27** ʰ 1 Sam. 9:21
68:28 ⁱ Is. 26:12   **68:29** ʲ Ps. 45:12; 72:10   **68:30** ᵏ Ps.
22:12   ˡ 2 Sam. 8:2   **68:31** ᵐ Is. 19:19–23   ⁿ Is. 45:14   ᵒ Ps.
44:20   **68:32** ᵖ [Ps. 67:3, 4]   **68:33** ᑫ Ps. 18:10   ʳ Ps. 46:6
68:34 ˢ Ps. 29:1   **68:35** ᵗ Ps. 76:12   **69:1** ᵃ Jon. 2:5

2 bI sink in deep mire,
Where *there is* no standing;
I have come into deep waters,
Where the floods overflow me.
3 cI am weary with my crying;
My throat is dry;
dMy eyes fail while I wait for my God.

4 Those who ehate me without a cause
Are more than the hairs of my head;
They are mighty who would destroy me,
Being my enemies wrongfully;
Though I have stolen nothing,
I *still* must restore *it.*

5 O God, You know my foolishness;
And my sins are not hidden from You.
6 Let not those who wait for You,
O Lord GOD of hosts, be ashamed
because of me;
Let not those who seek You be
confounded because of me,
O God of Israel.

7 Because for Your sake I have borne
reproach;
Shame has covered my face.
8 fI have become a stranger to my
brothers,
And an alien to my mother's children;
9 gBecause zeal for Your house has eaten
me up,
hAnd the reproaches of those who
reproach You have fallen on me.
10 When I wept *and chastened* my soul
with fasting,
That became my reproach.
11 I also made sackcloth my garment;
I became a byword to them.
12 Those who sit in the gate speak
against me,
And I *am* the song of the idrunkards.

13 But as for me, my prayer *is* to You,
O LORD, *in* the acceptable time;
O God, in the multitude of Your mercy,
Hear me in the truth of Your salvation.

14 Deliver me out of the mire,
And let me not sink;
Let me be delivered from those who
hate me,
And out of the deep waters.
15 Let not the floodwater overflow me,
Nor let the deep swallow me up;
And let not the pit shut its mouth on me.

16 Hear me, O LORD, for Your
lovingkindness *is* good;
Turn to me according to the multitude
of Your tender mercies.
17 And do not hide Your face from Your
servant,
For I am in trouble;
Hear me speedily.
18 Draw near to my soul, *and* redeem it;
Deliver me because of my enemies.

19 You know jmy reproach, my shame,
and my dishonor;
My adversaries *are* all before You.
20 Reproach has broken my heart,
And I am full of heaviness;
kI looked *for someone* to take pity, but
there was none;
And for lcomforters, but I found none.
21 They also gave me gall for my food,
mAnd for my thirst they gave me
vinegar to drink.

22 nLet their table become a snare before
them,
And their well-being a trap.
23 oLet their eyes be darkened, so that
they do not see;
And make their loins shake
continually.
24 pPour out Your indignation upon them,
And let Your wrathful anger take hold
of them.
25 qLet their dwelling place be desolate;
Let no one live in their tents.
26 For they persecute the *ones* rYou have
struck,

---

the suffering of Jesus Christ. Psalm 22 describes Jesus' physical sufferings, while Psalm 69 focuses more on His emotional and spiritual suffering. Yet, like Psalm 22, this psalm was written by David approximately a thousand years before the events it describes. Both psalms begin with the sufferings of David but have their full meaning in the sufferings of Jesus. For these reasons, the apostles in the New Testament acknowledge that David was a prophet of God (Acts 2:30).
69:4 *without a cause.* The Savior suffered affliction even though He was holy, harmless, and undefiled, and so no amount of holiness in His followers can prevent the enmity of a wicked world (John 15:19). In the Sermon on the Mount, Jesus promised blessing and a great reward to His followers who suffered for the sake of righteousness, a cause which is identified with Christ's own person (Matt. 5:10–11). Peter must have taken seriously Jesus' words on this subject, for he reminds believers that if they are reviled for the name of Christ, it is a blessing which indicates that the Spirit of God is resting upon them (1 Pet. 4:14).

69:9 *zeal for Your house has eaten me up.* Like Phinehas in Numbers 25, David describes himself as a zealot for the house of the Lord. Jesus' cleansing of the temple was a fulfillment of these words (John 2:17).
69:21 *gall.* "Gall" is commonly employed in Scripture as a synonym for poison, or bitterness. When Jesus hung on the cross, He actually was offered some sour wine mixed with gall (probably the bitter herb myrrh), a drink given occasionally to relieve the crucified person's thirst and pain (Matt. 27:34).
69:25 *Let their dwelling place be desolate.* These words were fulfilled in Judas Iscariot. See Acts 1:20, in which the words of this verse are joined to the words of 109:8.

69:2 b Ps. 40:2 **69:3** c Ps. 6:6 d Ps. 119:82, 123
69:4 e John 15:25 **69:8** f Is. 53:3 **69:9** g John 2:17 h Rom.
15:3 **69:12** i Job 30:9 **69:19** j Ps. 22:6, 7 **69:20** k Is.
63:5 l Job 16:2 **69:21** m Matt. 27:34, 48 **69:22** n Rom.
11:9, 10 **69:23** o Is. 6:9, 10 **69:24** p [1 Thess. 2:16]
69:25 q Matt. 23:38 **69:26** r [Is. 53:4]

And talk of the grief of those You have
wounded.
27 sAdd iniquity to their iniquity,
tAnd let them not come into Your
righteousness.
28 Let them ube blotted out of the book of
the living,
vAnd not be written with the
righteous.

29 But I *am* poor and sorrowful;
Let Your salvation, O God, set me up
on high.
30 wI will praise the name of God with a
song,
And will magnify Him with
thanksgiving.
31 xThis also shall please the LORD better
than an ox *or* bull,
Which has horns and hooves.
32 yThe humble shall see *this and* be
glad;
And you who seek God, zyour hearts
shall live.
33 For the LORD hears the poor,
And does not despise aHis prisoners.

34 bLet heaven and earth praise Him,
The seas cand everything that moves
in them.
35 dFor God will save Zion
And build the cities of Judah,
That they may dwell there and
possess it.
36 Also, ethe descendants of His servants
shall inherit it,
And those who love His name shall
dwell in it.

Psalm 70

Prayer for Relief from Adversaries

To the Chief Musician. *A Psalm* of
David. aTo bring to remembrance.

1 *Make haste,* bO God, to deliver me!
Make haste to help me, O LORD!
2 cLet them be ashamed and confounded
Who seek my life;
Let them be turned back* and
confused
Who desire my hurt.

3 dLet them be turned back because of
their shame,
Who say, "Aha, aha!"

4 Let all those who seek You rejoice and
be glad in You;
And let those who love Your salvation
say continually,
"Let God be magnified!"

5 eBut I *am* poor and needy;
fMake haste to me, O God!
You *are* my help and my deliverer;
O LORD, do not delay.

Psalm 71

God the Rock of Salvation

1 In aYou, O LORD, I put my trust;
Let me never be put to shame.
2 bDeliver me in Your righteousness, and
cause me to escape;
cIncline Your ear to me, and save me.
3 dBe my strong refuge,
To which I may resort continually;
You have given the ecommandment to
save me,
For You *are* my rock and my fortress.

4 fDeliver me, O my God, out of the hand
of the wicked,
Out of the hand of the unrighteous and
cruel man.
5 For You are gmy hope, O Lord GOD;
You are my trust from my youth.
6 hBy You I have been upheld from birth;
You are He who took me out of my
mother's womb.
My praise *shall be* continually of You.

7 iI have become as a wonder to many,
But You *are* my strong refuge.
8 Let jmy mouth be filled *with* Your
praise
And with Your glory all the day.

9 Do not cast me off in the time of old
age;
Do not forsake me when my strength
fails.

---

* **70:2** Following Masoretic Text, Septuagint, Targum, and Vulgate; some Hebrew manuscripts and
Syriac read *be appalled* (compare 40:15).

70:2 *be ashamed and confounded.* David prays that
those who rejoice in his misery will be proven wrong
in their assumption that the Lord is unable to help His
people. In this way, the Lord's deliverance of David
will result in God's name being glorified—both by
the joy of God's people and the shame of His enemies.
71:2 *Your righteousness.* The psalmist is concerned
with his own plight and also with the character of
God. The psalmist's point is that God could display His
righteousness by answering the needs of the psalmist, whose life had been lived in constant trust in God.
71:7 *a wonder.* The poet declares that the work of
God in his life has made him a special sign to the

people, similar to the great miracles of God through
Moses and Aaron in Egypt (Ex. 7:3; 11:9).

69:27 s [Rom. 1:28] t [Is. 26:10] **69:28** u [Ex. 32:32]
v Ezek. 13:9 **69:30** w [Ps. 28:7] **69:31** x Ps. 50:13, 14,
23; 51:16 **69:32** y Ps. 34:2 z Ps. 22:26 **69:33** a Eph.
3:1 **69:34** b Ps. 96:11 c Is. 55:12 **69:35** d Is.
44:26 **69:36** e Ps. 102:28 **70:title** a Ps. 38:title
70:1 b Ps. 40:13–17 **70:2** c Ps. 35:4, 26 **70:3** d Ps.
40:15 **70:5** e Ps. 72:12, 13 f Ps. 141:1 **71:1** a Ps. 25:2, 3
71:2 b Ps. 31:1 c Ps. 17:6 **71:3** d Ps. 31:2, 3 e Ps. 44:4
71:4 f Ps. 140:1, 3 **71:5** g Jer. 14:8; 17:7, 13, 17; 50:7
71:6 h Ps. 22:9, 10 **71:7** i Is. 8:18 **71:8** j Ps. 35:28

10 For my enemies speak against me;
And those who lie in wait for my life
    *k*take counsel together,
11 Saying, "God has forsaken him;
Pursue and take him, for *there is* none
    to deliver *him.*"
12 *l*O God, do not be far from me;
O my God, *m*make haste to help me!
13 Let them be confounded *and*
    consumed
Who are adversaries of my life;
Let them be covered *with* reproach
    and dishonor
Who seek my hurt.

14 But I will hope continually,
And will praise You yet more and
    more.
15 My mouth shall tell of Your
    righteousness
And Your salvation all the day,
For I do not know *their* limits.
16 I will go in the strength of the Lord
    GOD;
I will make mention of Your
    righteousness, of Yours only.

17 O God, You have taught me from my
    *n*youth;
And to this *day* I declare Your
    wondrous works.
18 Now also *o*when *I am* old and
    grayheaded,
O God, do not forsake me,
Until I declare Your strength to *this*
    generation,
Your power to everyone *who* is to
    come.

19 Also *p*Your righteousness, O God, *is*
    very high,
You who have done great things;
*q*O God, who *is* like You?
20 *r*You, who have shown me great and
    severe troubles,
*s*Shall revive me again,
And bring me up again from the
    depths of the earth.
21 You shall increase my greatness,
And comfort me on every side.

22 Also *t*with the lute I will praise You—
And Your faithfulness, O my God!
To You I will sing with the harp,
O *u*Holy One of Israel.

23 My lips shall greatly rejoice when I
    sing to You,
And *v*my soul, which You have
    redeemed.
24 My tongue also shall talk of Your
    righteousness all the day long;
For they are confounded,
For they are brought to shame
Who seek my hurt.

Psalm 72

Glory and Universality of the Messiah's Reign

A Psalm *a*of Solomon.

1 Give the king Your judgments,
    O God,
And Your righteousness to the king's
    Son.
2 *b*He will judge Your people with
    righteousness,
And Your poor with justice.
3 *c*The mountains will bring peace to the
    people,
And the little hills, by righteousness.
4 *d*He will bring justice to the poor of the
    people;
He will save the children of the needy,
And will break in pieces the
    oppressor.

5 They shall fear You*
*e*As long as the sun and moon endure,
Throughout all generations.
6 *f*He shall come down like rain upon the
    grass before mowing,
Like showers *that* water the earth.
7 In His days the righteous shall
    flourish,
*g*And abundance of peace,
Until the moon is no more.

8 *h*He shall have dominion also from sea
    to sea,
And from the River to the ends of the
    earth.
9 *i*Those who dwell in the wilderness
    will bow before Him,
*j*And His enemies will lick the dust.

---

* **72:5** Following Masoretic Text and Targum; Septuagint and Vulgate read *They shall continue.*

71:22 the lute . . . the harp. The psalmist praised God with music, both vocal and instrumental. His worship came from his inner being ("my soul," v. 23) which was filled with praises to the living God. No matter what form our worship takes, it is worthless unless it comes from the heart.

72:1 Give the king Your judgments. Solomon's prayer for his own godly reign is an intensely messianic poem, speaking in ideal terms of the coming of the great King. The psalm calls for a good king to govern Israel under God's blessing. Ultimately this king is the Savior Jesus.

72:8 He shall have dominion also from sea to sea.

The promises of God to Abraham included a promise that his descendants would have dominion over the land of Canaan (Gen. 15:18–21). These verses expand the geographical dimensions to include the entire earth. **the River.** This refers to the Euphrates.

71:10 *k* 2 Sam. 17:1   **71:12** *l* Ps. 35:22   *m* Ps. 70:1
71:17 *n* Deut. 4:5; 6:7   **71:18** *o* [Is. 46:4]   **71:19** *p* Ps. 57:10
q Ps. 35:10   **71:20** *r* Ps. 60:3   *s* Hos. 6:1, 2   **71:22** *t* Ps.
92:1–3   *u* 2 Kin. 19:22   **71:23** *v* Ps. 103:4   **72:title** *a* Ps.
127:title   **72:2** *b* [Is. 9:7; 11:2–5; 32:1]   **72:3** *c* Ps. 85:10
72:4 *d* Is. 11:4   **72:5** *e* Ps. 72:7, 17; 89:36   **72:6** *f* Hos. 6:3
72:7 *g* Is. 2:4   **72:8** *h* Ex. 23:31   **72:9** *i* Is. 23:13   *j* Is. 49:23

10 ᵏThe kings of Tarshish and of the
    isles
    Will bring presents;
    The kings of Sheba and Seba
    Will offer gifts.
11 ˡYes, all kings shall fall down before
    Him;
    All nations shall serve Him.
12 For He ᵐwill deliver the needy when
    he cries,
    The poor also, and him who has no
    helper.
13 He will spare the poor and needy,
    And will save the souls of the
    needy.
14 He will redeem their life from
    oppression and violence;
    And ⁿprecious shall be their blood in
    His sight.
15 And He shall live;
    And the gold of ᵒSheba will be given
    to Him;
    Prayer also will be made for Him
    continually,
    And daily He shall be praised.
16 There will be an abundance of grain
    in the earth,
    On the top of the mountains;
    Its fruit shall wave like Lebanon;
    ᵖAnd those of the city shall flourish
    like grass of the earth.
17 ᵠHis name shall endure forever;
    His name shall continue as long as
    the sun.
    And ʳmen shall be blessed in Him;
    ˢAll nations shall call Him blessed.
18 ᵗBlessed be the LORD God, the God of
    Israel,
    ᵘWho only does wondrous things!
19 And ᵛblessed be His glorious name
    forever!

ʷAnd let the whole earth be filled with
    His glory.
    Amen and Amen.
20 The prayers of David the son of Jesse
    are ended.

BOOK THREE

Psalms 73–89

Psalm 73

The Tragedy of the Wicked, and the Blessedness of Trust in God

A Psalm of ᵃAsaph.

1 Truly God is good to Israel,
    To such as are pure in heart.
2 But as for me, my feet had almost
    stumbled;
    My steps had nearly ᵇslipped.
3 ᶜFor I was envious of the boastful,
    When I saw the prosperity of the
    ᵈwicked.
4 For there are no pangs in their death,
    But their strength is firm.
5 ᵉThey are not in trouble as other
    men,
    Nor are they plagued like other
    men.
6 Therefore pride serves as their
    necklace;
    Violence covers them ᶠlike a garment.
7 ᵍTheir eyes bulge* with abundance;
    They have more than heart could
    wish.

---

* **73:7** Targum reads face bulges; Septuagint,
Syriac, and Vulgate read iniquity bulges.

72:14 He will redeem their life. This verse points to
Jesus' death on the cross, when He paid the price to
redeem us from the oppression of sin.
72:17 His name shall endure forever. The name of
the great King will be regarded as the greatest in the
universe. Paul speaks this way of Jesus' name in Philippians 2:9–11.
72:20 The prayers of David . . . are ended. The
superscription of this psalm attributes it to Solomon.
It is possible that Solomon wrote this poem as the
close of a collection of his father's psalms. Other
psalms were later added to this original collection.
73:1 Walking in the Spirit—An important prerequisite to walking in the Spirit is the confession of sin.
Sin must be confessed in order to restore fellowship
and to continue receiving God's forgiveness (1 John
1:5–10). Confession means that we agree with God
about our sin. That involves much more than simply
acknowledging the sin. Confession requires an attitude of sorrow for the sin and a willingness to turn
from it. It does not mean that we will never commit
the same sin again, but it does mean that the attitude
of repentance towards the sin is present.
Confession should be made at the moment the

Christian becomes aware of sin. The Scriptures actually mention two specific times for confession: before
the close of the day (Eph. 4:26) and before the Lord's
Supper (1 Cor. 11:27–32). Failure to do the latter is a
special cause for discipline from the Lord.
Confession of sin should involve only those who
have knowledge of the sin. This means that private
sins should be confessed privately, sins between
individuals confessed between those involved (Matt.
5:23–24), and public sins confessed publicly (Matt.
18:17). Public confession is normally made for the edification of the church (1 Cor. 14:26).
73:3 For I was envious. This psalmist is open with the
readers concerning his own weakness and doubts; he
also shows that he came to the right conclusion in the
end: to trust God.

72:10 ᵏ 2 Chr. 9:21   **72:11** ˡ Is. 49:23   **72:12** ᵐ Job 29:12
72:14 ⁿ [Ps. 116:15]   **72:15** ᵒ Is. 60:6   **72:16** ᵖ 1 Kin.
4:20   **72:17** ᵠ [Ps. 89:36]   ʳ [Gen. 12:3]   ˢ Luke 1:48
72:18 ᵗ 1 Chr. 29:10   ᵘ Ex. 15:11   **72:19** ᵛ [Neh. 9:5]
ʷ Num. 14:21   **73:title** ᵃ Ps. 50:title   **73:2** ᵇ Job
12:5   **73:3** ᶜ Ps. 37:1, 7   ᵈ Job 21:5–16   **73:5** ᵉ Job 21:9
73:6 ᶠ Ps. 109:18   **73:7** ᵍ Jer. 5:28

8 [h]They scoff and speak wickedly
concerning oppression;
They [i]speak loftily.
9 They set their mouth [j]against the
heavens,
And their tongue walks through the
earth.

10 Therefore his people return here,
[k]And waters of a full *cup* are drained
by them.
11 And they say, [l]"How does God know?
And is there knowledge in the Most
High?"
12 Behold, these *are* the ungodly,
Who are always at ease;
They increase *in* riches.
13 Surely I have cleansed my heart *in*
[m]vain,
And washed my hands in innocence.
14 For all day long I have been plagued,
And chastened every morning.

15 If I had said, "I will speak thus,"
Behold, I would have been untrue to
the generation of Your children.
16 When I thought *how* to understand
this,
It *was* too painful for me—
17 Until I went into the sanctuary of God;
Then I understood their [n]end.

18 Surely [o]You set them in slippery
places;
You cast them down to destruction.
19 Oh, how they are *brought* to
desolation, as in a moment!
They are utterly consumed with
terrors.
20 As a dream when *one* awakes,
So, Lord, when You awake,
You shall despise their image.

21 Thus my heart was grieved,
And I was vexed in my mind.
22 [p]I *was* so foolish and ignorant;
I was *like* a beast before You.

23 Nevertheless I *am* continually with You;
You hold *me* by my right hand.
24 [q]You will guide me with Your counsel,
And afterward receive me *to* glory.

25 [r]Whom have I in heaven *but You?*
And *there is* none upon earth *that* I
desire besides You.
26 [s]My flesh and my heart fail;
But God *is* the strength of my heart
and my [t]portion forever.

27 For indeed, [u]those who are far from
You shall perish;
You have destroyed all those who
desert You for harlotry.
28 But *it is* good for me to [v]draw near to
God;
I have put my trust in the Lord GOD,
That I may [w]declare all Your works.

Psalm 74

A Plea for Relief from Oppressors

A Contemplation* of Asaph.

1 O God, why have You cast *us* off
forever?
Why does Your anger smoke against
the sheep of Your pasture?
2 Remember Your congregation, *which*
You have purchased of old,
The tribe of Your inheritance, *which*
You have redeemed—
This Mount Zion where You have dwelt.
3 Lift up Your feet to the perpetual
desolations.
The enemy has damaged everything
in the sanctuary.
4 [a]Your enemies roar in the midst of Your
meeting place;
[b]They set up their banners *for* signs.

* **74:title** Hebrew *Maschil*

73:12 ***always at ease.*** It often does appear that ungodly people get away with everything, ending up on the top of the heap and leaving the godly wondering whether their own acts of righteous living are without meaning or purpose.

73:15 ***would have been untrue.*** Even as he struggled with the apparent lack of reward for righteousness, Asaph knew in his heart that such thoughts were wrong. Even when we can't understand the surface facts, God's witness in our spirits lets us know when we are moving down the wrong track.

73:22 ***like a beast before You.*** An animal has no sense of eternity or divine perspective. When the psalmist wondered about the value of righteousness, his thinking was based only on the present, like an animal, rather than understanding the bigger picture as a being with an eternal soul.

73:28 ***it is good for me to draw near to God.*** There are those who may enjoy great wealth and notoriety today, but nothing they have or do will last forever. Compared to a relationship with the living God, nothing else matters.

74:1 ***anger.*** The Babylonian destruction of the temple in 586 B.C. occasioned a crisis of faith among the ancient covenant people. Since the temple served as the external sign of God's covenant with Israel, its destruction may have caused the impression that God's promise to David had been canceled (2 Sam. 7:12–14). The psalmist is deeply conscious that God is angry with the nation, and the reason for His anger is unmistakably clear. The people had forsaken the covenant, and worshiped and served other gods (Deut. 29:25–26). God's anger reminds us of His eternal hatred of all unrighteousness. It is the holiness of God stirred into an appropriate response to sin.

73:8 [h] Ps. 53:1 [i] 2 Pet. 2:18 **73:9** [j] Rev. 13:6 **73:10** [k] [Ps. 75:8] **73:11** [l] Job 22:13 **73:13** [m] Job 21:15; 35:3 **73:17** [n] [Ps. 37:38; 55:23] **73:18** [o] Ps. 35:6 **73:22** [p] Ps. 92:6 **73:24** [q] Ps. 32:8; 48:14 **73:25** [r] [Phil. 3:8] **73:26** [s] Ps. 84:2 [t] Ps. 16:5 **73:27** [u] [Ps. 119:155] **73:28** [v] [Heb. 10:22] [w] 2 Cor. 4:13 **74:4** [a] Lam. 2:7 [b] Num. 2:2

5 They seem like men who lift up
    Axes among the thick trees.
6 And now they break down its carved
      work, all at once,
    With axes and hammers.
7 They have set fire to Your sanctuary;
    They have defiled the dwelling place
      of Your name to the ground.
8 cThey said in their hearts,
    "Let us destroy them altogether."
    They have burned up all the meeting
      places of God in the land.

9 We do not see our signs;
    dThere is no longer any prophet;
    Nor is there any among us who knows
      how long.
10 O God, how long will the adversary
      reproach?
    Will the enemy blaspheme Your name
      forever?
11 eWhy do You withdraw Your hand,
      even Your right hand?
    Take it out of Your bosom and destroy
      them.
12 For fGod is my King from of old,
    Working salvation in the midst of the
      earth.
13 gYou divided the sea by Your strength;
    You broke the heads of the sea
      serpents in the waters.
14 You broke the heads of Leviathan in
      pieces,
    And gave him as food to the people
      inhabiting the wilderness.
15 hYou broke open the fountain and the
      flood;
    iYou dried up mighty rivers.
16 The day is Yours, the night also is
      jYours;
    kYou have prepared the light and the sun.
17 You have lset all the borders of the
      earth;
    mYou have made summer and winter.

18 Remember this, that the enemy has
      reproached, O LORD,
    And that a foolish people has
      blasphemed Your name.
19 Oh, do not deliver the life of Your
      turtledove to the wild beast!
    Do not forget the life of Your poor
      forever.

20 nHave respect to the covenant;
    For the dark places of the earth are
      full of the haunts of cruelty.
21 Oh, do not let the oppressed return
      ashamed!
    Let the poor and needy praise Your
      name.

22 Arise, O God, plead Your own cause;
    Remember how the foolish man
      reproaches You daily.
23 Do not forget the voice of Your
      enemies;
    The tumult of those who rise up
      against You increases continually.

Psalm 75

Thanksgiving for God's Righteous Judgment

To the Chief Musician. Set to a"Do Not
Destroy."* A Psalm of Asaph. A Song.

1 We give thanks to You, O God, we give
      thanks!
    For Your wondrous works declare that
      Your name is near.

2 "When I choose the proper time,
    I will judge uprightly.
3 The earth and all its inhabitants are
      dissolved;
    I set up its pillars firmly.   Selah
4 "I said to the boastful, 'Do not deal
      boastfully,'
    And to the wicked, b'Do not lift up the
      horn.
5 Do not lift up your horn on high;
    Do not speak with a stiff neck.' "

6 For exaltation comes neither from the
      east
    Nor from the west nor from the south.
7 But cGod is the Judge:
    dHe puts down one,
    And exalts another.
8 For ein the hand of the LORD there is a
      cup,
    And the wine is red;

---

* 75:title Hebrew Al Tashcheth

74:12 my King from of old. The Lord is King by virtue
of His creation of the earth (Ps. 93). He is King because
of His special relationship with Israel (44:4; 99:1–3).
And He is the coming King who will reign over all
(96:13; 97:1–6; 98:6–9).
74:14 Leviathan. This creature was used to poetically describe various evil forces over which God
has ultimate control and victory. Eventually the Leviathan (Job 41:1–10) became a symbol for Satan (Is.
27:1) who is "the dragon, that serpent of old" (Rev.
20:2).
74:15 dried up mighty rivers. God enabled His people to cross over the Red Sea (Ex. 14) and the River
Jordan (Josh. 3).
75:2 When I choose the proper time. God will not

be rushed, even by His devoted followers. When we
grow impatient to see justice done, we must remember that God has a better sense of time than we do.
75:8 a cup. This is not a cup of blessing, but of the
Lord's wrath. The biblical image of wine and judgment goes back to Jacob's blessing on Judah (Gen.
49:11) and is referred to in Christ's judgment as
depicted in Revelation 19:13–15.

74:8 c Ps. 83:4   **74:9** d Amos 8:11   **74:11** e Lam. 2:3
74:12 f Ps. 44:4   **74:13** g Ex. 14:21   **74:15** h Ex. 17:5, 6
i Josh. 2:10; 3:13   **74:16** j Job 38:12   k Gen. 1:14–18
74:17 l Acts 17:26   m Gen. 8:22   **74:20** n Lev. 26:44, 45
75:title a Ps. 57:title   **75:4** b [1 Sam. 2:3]   **75:7** c Ps.
50:6   d 1 Sam. 2:7   **75:8** e Jer. 25:15

It is fully mixed, and He pours it out;
Surely its dregs shall all the wicked of
the earth
Drain *and* drink down.

9 But I will declare forever,
I will sing praises to the God of Jacob.

10 "All*f* the horns of the wicked I will also
cut off,
But *g*the horns of the righteous shall
be *h*exalted."

Psalm 76

The Majesty of God in Judgment

To the Chief Musician. On stringed
instruments.* A Psalm of Asaph.
A Song.

1 In *a*Judah God *is* known;
His name *is* great in Israel.
2 In Salem* also is His tabernacle,
And His dwelling place in Zion.
3 There He broke the arrows of the bow,
The shield and sword of battle.   *Selah*

4 You *are* more glorious and excellent
*b*Than the mountains of prey.
5 *c*The stouthearted were plundered;
*d*They have sunk into their sleep;
And none of the mighty men have
found the use of their hands.
6 *e*At Your rebuke, O God of Jacob,
Both the chariot and horse were cast
into a dead sleep.

7 You, Yourself, *are* to be feared;
And *f*who may stand in Your presence
When once You are angry?
8 *g*You caused judgment to be heard from
heaven;
*h*The earth feared and was still,
9 When God *i*arose to judgment,
To deliver all the oppressed of the
earth.   *Selah*

10 *i*Surely the wrath of man shall praise
You;
With the remainder of wrath You shall
gird Yourself.

11 *k*Make vows to the LORD your God, and
pay *them;*
*l*Let all who are around Him bring
presents to Him who ought to be
feared.
12 He shall cut off the spirit of princes;
*m*He is awesome to the kings of the earth.

Psalm 77

The Consoling Memory of God's Redemptive Works

To the Chief Musician. *a*To Jeduthun.
A Psalm of Asaph.

1 I cried out to God with my voice—
To God with my voice;
And He gave ear to me.
2 In the day of my trouble I sought the
Lord;
My hand was stretched out in the
night without ceasing;
My soul refused to be comforted.
3 I remembered God, and was troubled;
I complained, and my spirit was
overwhelmed.   *Selah*

4 You hold my eyelids *open;*
I am so troubled that I cannot speak.
5 I have considered the days of old,
The years of ancient times.
6 I call to remembrance my song in the
night;
I meditate within my heart,
And my spirit makes diligent search.

7 Will the Lord cast off forever?
And will He be favorable no more?
8 Has His mercy ceased forever?
Has *His* *b*promise failed forevermore?
9 Has God forgotten to be gracious?
Has He in anger shut up His tender
mercies?   *Selah*

10 And I said, "This *is* my anguish;
But *I will remember* the years of the
right hand of the Most High."

* **76:title** Hebrew *neginoth*   * **76:2** That is,
Jerusalem

76:2 *Salem.* Salem is the shortened form of the name
Jerusalem.
76:6 *chariot and horse.* This verse is referring to the
defeat of the army of Pharaoh (Ex. 14:13–29; 15).
76:7 *to be feared.* For the righteous, the fear of God
is a response of awe, wonder, adoration, and worship.
For the wicked, the fear of God is terror, for there is no
escape from Him (14:5).
76:11 *bring presents.* As one might bring gifts to
a king, so the righteous should bring their gifts to
God—the ultimate gift being the dedication of their
lives to the service of God (Rom. 12:1).
77:3 *remembered . . . troubled.* What he knew of
God contrasted with what he was experiencing. The
more the psalmist thought about these things, the
more troubled he became.

77:7–8 *Will the Lord cast off forever?* Even though
we have put our faith in Christ and committed ourselves to obeying His will, this doesn't automatically
guarantee total and perpetual immunity from trouble. There will be seasons when God seems remote
and we begin to wonder about God's unfailing love.
It is in these times that we must hold most firmly to
what we know about God, rather than what we feel.

75:10 *f* Jer. 48:25 *g* Ps. 89:17; 148:14 *h* 1 Sam. 2:1
76:1 *a* Ps. 48:1, 3 **76:4** *b* Ezek. 38:12 **76:5** *c* Is. 10:12;
46:12 *d* Ps. 13:3 **76:6** *e* Ex. 15:1–21 **76:7** *f* [Nah.
1:6] **76:8** *g* Ex. 19:9 *h* 2 Chr. 20:29 **76:9** *i* [Ps. 9:7–9]
76:10 *j* Rom. 9:17 **76:11** *k* [Eccl. 5:4–6] *l* 2 Chr. 32:22, 23
76:12 *m* Ps. 68:35 **77:title** *a* Ps. 39:title **77:8** *b* [2 Pet.
3:8, 9]

11 I will remember the works of the
   LORD;
   Surely I will remember Your wonders
      of old.
12 I will also meditate on all Your work,
   And talk of Your deeds.
13 Your way, O God, *is* in the ᶜsanctuary;
   Who *is* so great a God as *our* God?
14 You *are* the God who does wonders;
   You have declared Your strength
      among the peoples.
15 You have with *Your* arm redeemed
      Your people,
   The sons of Jacob and Joseph.   *Selah*

16 The waters saw You, O God;
   The waters saw You, they were
      ᵈafraid;
   The depths also trembled.
17 The clouds poured out water;
   The skies sent out a sound;
   Your arrows also flashed about.
18 The voice of Your thunder *was* in the
      whirlwind;
   The lightnings lit up the world;
   The earth trembled and shook.
19 Your way *was* in the sea,
   Your path in the great waters,
   And Your footsteps were not known.
20 You led Your people like a flock
   By the hand of Moses and Aaron.

Psalm 78

God's Kindness to Rebellious Israel

A ᵃContemplation* of Asaph.

1 Give ear, O my people, *to* my law;
   Incline your ears to the words of my
      mouth.
2 I will open my mouth in a ᵇparable;
   I will utter dark sayings of old,
3 Which we have heard and known,
   And our fathers have told us.
4 ᶜWe will not hide *them* from their
      children,
   ᵈTelling to the generation to come the
      praises of the LORD,
   And His strength and His wonderful
      works that He has done.

5 For ᵉHe established a testimony in
      Jacob,
   And appointed a law in Israel,
   Which He commanded our fathers,
   That ᶠthey should make them known
      to their children;
6 ᵍThat the generation to come might
      know *them*,
   The children *who* would be born,

---

* **78:title** Hebrew *Maschil*

God has neither forgotten to show mercy nor stifled His compassion.
77:11 *I will remember.* Asaph did not *feel* any more at peace, but he made a conscious decision to turn from his pain and focus his thoughts on the person, works, and wonders of God. When we are in distress, we often feel that it is our right to vent our frustrations and complaints as long as we still feel them, but God doesn't call us to be driven by feelings. Instead, we have to consciously decide to praise God, trusting that the feelings will follow.
77:20 *You led Your people like a flock.* Lost in contemplation of the greatness of God, the poet seems thoroughly distracted from his pain. He does not mention it again, not daring to compare it to the greatness of the Almighty.
78:1 *my law.* The psalmist uses the vocabulary of the wisdom school to establish himself. "My law" is the familiar word *Torah*. The wisdom writers used this word to indicate insight; their instruction is always in accord with the law of Moses (Prov. 1:8; 3:1; 4:2).
78:2 *dark sayings.* These are riddles, or instructions with a deeper meaning beyond the surface.
78:4 Israel's History—The biblical history of Israel covers 1,800 years and represents a marvelous panorama of God's gracious working through promise, miracle, blessing, and judgment. Israel begins as only a promise to Abraham (Gen. 12:2). For over four hundred years the people of Israel maintain their belief in that promise while in bondage in Egypt. Finally, in God's perfect timing, He brings the nation out of Egypt with the greatest series of miracles recorded in the Old Testament (Ex. 7–15). This event is called the Exodus, meaning a *going out*. It is the formative event in the history of the nation. It was a great act of redemption and in the Old Testament is the foremost

example of God's care for His people (Ps. 77:14–20; 78:12–55; Hos. 11:1).
   Once God had redeemed Israel He established His covenant with them at Mount Sinai (Ex. 19:5–8). From that point on He has been their God and they His people. The covenant foretells gracious blessings for obedience and severe judgments for disobedience. The rest of Israel's history demonstrates the certainty of that prophecy. Throughout periods of conquest, judges, monarchy, exile, restoration and Gentile domination, Israel was blessed when she obeyed and judged when she disobeyed. The nation is finally destroyed in A.D. 70, although this event is not described in the New Testament. Many prophecies appear to promise a future redemption (Rom. 11:26).
   There are at least three good reasons to study the history of Israel:
   1. It sets forth examples to be followed or avoided (1 Cor. 10:6).
   2. It shows God's control of historical events (Ps. 78).
   3. It serves as a model for all ages of God's kindness and mercy towards His people (Ps. 78).
78:5–7 *testimony.* The history of Israel is told in a series of cycles with steps in each cycle ranging from a firm, dependent hope in God to deep apostasy. One generation would seek the works of God, hope in Him, and follow Him. The next generation would forget the mighty works of God and depart from reliance and confidence in Him. To avert this endless round of making the same mistakes, God

---

77:13 ᶜPs. 73:17 **77:16** ᵈEx. 14:21 **78:title** ᵃPs. 74:title
78:2 ᵇMatt. 13:34, 35 **78:4** ᶜDeut. 4:9; 6:7 ᵈEx. 13:8, 14
78:5 ᵉPs. 147:19 ᶠDeut. 4:9; 11:19 **78:6** ᵍPs. 102:18

That they may arise and declare *them*
to their children,
7 That they may set their hope in God,
And not forget the works of God,
But keep His commandments;
8 And [h]may not be like their fathers,
[i]A stubborn and rebellious generation,
A generation [j]*that* did not set its heart
aright,
And whose spirit was not faithful to
God.

9 The children of Ephraim, *being* armed
and carrying bows,
Turned back in the day of battle.
10 [k]They did not keep the covenant of
God;
They refused to walk in His law,
11 And [l]forgot His works
And His wonders that He had shown
them.

12 [m]Marvelous things He did in the sight of
their fathers,
In the land of Egypt, [n]*in* the field of
Zoan.
13 [o]He divided the sea and caused them to
pass through;
And [p]He made the waters stand up like
a heap.
14 [q]In the daytime also He led them with
the cloud,
And all the night with a light of fire.
15 [r]He split the rocks in the wilderness,
And gave *them* drink in abundance
like the depths.
16 He also brought [s]streams out of the
rock,
And caused waters to run down like
rivers.

17 But they sinned even more against
Him
By [t]rebelling against the Most High in
the wilderness.
18 And [u]they tested God in their heart
By asking for the food of their fancy.
19 [v]Yes, they spoke against God:
They said, "Can God prepare a table in
the wilderness?
20 [w]Behold, He struck the rock,
So that the waters gushed out,
And the streams overflowed.
Can He give bread also?
Can He provide meat for His people?"

21 Therefore the LORD heard *this* and
[x]was furious;
So a fire was kindled against Jacob,
And anger also came up against
Israel,
22 Because they [y]did not believe in God,
And did not trust in His salvation.
23 Yet He had commanded the clouds
above,
[z]And opened the doors of heaven,
24 [a]Had rained down manna on them to
eat,
And given them of the bread of
[b]heaven.
25 Men ate angels' food;
He sent them food to the full.

26 [c]He caused an east wind to blow in the
heavens;
And by His power He brought in the
south wind.
27 He also rained meat on them like the
dust,
Feathered fowl like the sand of the
seas;
28 And He let *them* fall in the midst of
their camp,
All around their dwellings.
29 [d]So they ate and were well filled,
For He gave them their own desire.
30 They were not deprived of their
craving;
But [e]while their food *was* still in their
mouths,
31 The wrath of God came against them,
And slew the stoutest of them,
And struck down the choice *men* of
Israel.

32 In spite of this [f]they still sinned,
And [g]did not believe in His wondrous
works.
33 [h]Therefore their days He consumed in
futility,
And their years in fear.

34 [i]When He slew them, then they sought
Him;
And they returned and sought
earnestly for God.
35 Then they remembered that [j]God *was*
their rock,
And the Most High God [k]their
Redeemer.
36 Nevertheless they [l]flattered Him with
their mouth,

---

commanded His people to make His laws a regular part of their everyday lives (Deut. 6:4–9), so that they could not forget.

78:9 *Ephraim . . . Turned back.* The poet may be referring to Ephraim's conflict with Jephthah (Judg. 12:1–7).

78:29 *He gave them their own desire.* When we turn our hearts toward the Lord, our desires will change to match His will. Then He delights to give us our desires because they are right things which will lead to wholeness and goodness (37:4). Without God, we don't have the wisdom to know what we should long for.

78:8 [h] 2 Kin. 17:14 [i] Ex. 32:9 [j] Ps. 78:37 **78:10** [k] 2 Kin. 17:15 **78:11** [l] Ps. 106:13 **78:12** [m] Ex. 7–12 [n] Num. 13:22 **78:13** [o] Ex. 14:21 [p] Ex. 15:8 **78:14** [q] Ex. 13:21 **78:15** [r] Num. 20:11 **78:16** [s] Num. 20:8, 10, 11 **78:17** [t] Heb. 3:16 **78:18** [u] Ex. 16:2 **78:19** [v] Num. 11:4; 20:3; 21:5 **78:20** [w] Num. 20:11 **78:21** [x] Num. 11:1 **78:22** [y] [Heb. 3:18] **78:23** [z] [Mal. 3:10] **78:24** [a] Ex. 16:4 [b] John 6:31 **78:26** [c] Num. 11:31 **78:29** [d] Num. 11:19, 20 **78:30** [e] Num. 11:33 **78:32** [f] Num. 14:16, 17 [g] Num. 14:11 **78:33** [h] Num. 14:29, 35 **78:34** [i] [Hos. 5:15] **78:35** [j] [Deut. 32:4, 15] [k] Is. 41:14; 44:6; 63:9 **78:36** [l] Ezek. 33:31

And they lied to Him with their
   tongue;
37 For their heart was not steadfast with
   Him,
   Nor were they faithful in His
   covenant.
38 *m*But He, *being* full of *n*compassion,
   forgave *their* iniquity,
   And did not destroy *them*.
   Yes, many a time *o*He turned His
   anger away,
   And *p*did not stir up all His wrath;
39 For *q*He remembered *r*that they *were*
   but flesh,
   *s*A breath that passes away and does
   not come again.
40 How often they *t*provoked Him in the
   wilderness,
   And grieved Him in the desert!
41 Yes, *u*again and again they tempted
   God,
   And limited the Holy One of Israel.
42 They did not remember His power:
   The day when He redeemed them from
   the enemy,
43 When He worked His signs in Egypt,
   And His wonders in the field of Zoan;
44 *v*Turned their rivers into blood,
   And their streams, that they could not
   drink.
45 *w*He sent swarms of flies among them,
   which devoured them,
   And *x*frogs, which destroyed them.
46 He also gave their crops to the
   caterpillar,
   And their labor to the *y*locust.
47 *z*He destroyed their vines with hail,
   And their sycamore trees with frost.
48 He also gave up their *a*cattle to the
   hail,
   And their flocks to fiery lightning.
49 He cast on them the fierceness of His
   anger,
   Wrath, indignation, and trouble,
   By sending angels of destruction
   among them.
50 He made a path for His anger;
   He did not spare their soul from death,
   But gave their life over to the plague,
51 And destroyed all the *b*firstborn in
   Egypt,

The first of *their* strength in the tents
   of Ham.
52 But He *c*made His own people go forth
   like sheep,
   And guided them in the wilderness
   like a flock;
53 And He *d*led them on safely, so that
   they did not fear;
   But the sea *e*overwhelmed their
   enemies.
54 And He brought them to His *f*holy
   border,
   This mountain *g*which His right hand
   had acquired.
55 *h*He also drove out the nations before
   them,
   *i*Allotted them an inheritance by survey,
   And made the tribes of Israel dwell in
   their tents.
56 *j*Yet they tested and provoked the Most
   High God,
   And did not keep His testimonies,
57 But *k*turned back and acted
   unfaithfully like their fathers;
   They were turned aside *l*like a
   deceitful bow.
58 *m*For they provoked Him to anger with
   their *n*high places,
   And moved Him to jealousy with their
   carved images.
59 When God heard *this*, He was furious,
   And greatly abhorred Israel,
60 *o*So that He forsook the tabernacle of
   Shiloh,
   The tent He had placed among men,
61 *p*And delivered His strength into
   captivity,
   And His glory into the enemy's hand.
62 *q*He also gave His people over to the
   sword,
   And was furious with His inheritance.
63 The fire consumed their young men,
   And *r*their maidens were not given in
   marriage.
64 *s*Their priests fell by the sword,
   And *t*their widows made no
   lamentation.

65 Then the Lord awoke as *from* sleep,
   *u*Like a mighty man who shouts
   because of wine.

78:38 full of compassion. The awesome transcendence of the Lord is complemented in this section (v.
35) by an emphasis on His compassionate mercy.
78:58 high places. These places of worship were
associated with the Canaanite worship of Baal and
other fertility gods.
78:60 the tabernacle of Shiloh. This reference to
Shiloh, the place where the tabernacle was set up
in the time of Eli, places the time of disobedience
described here in the latter period of the judges
(1 Sam. 1:3).
78:61 delivered His strength into captivity. This
term is an unusual way of speaking of the ark of the
covenant which was lost to the Philistines during
the battle of Aphek (1 Sam. 4:1–11). At this time the

suffering of the people was acute, including even the
deaths of priests (1 Sam. 4:17–18).

78:38 *m* [Num. 14:18–20] *n* Ex. 34:6 *o* [Is. 48:9] *p* 1 Kin.
21:29 **78:39** *q* Job 10:9 *r* John 3:6 *s* [Job 7:7, 16]
78:40 *t* Heb. 3:16 **78:41** *u* Num. 14:22 **78:44** *v* Ex.
7:20 **78:45** *w* Ex. 8:24 *x* Ex. 8:6 **78:46** *y* Ex. 10:14
78:47 *z* Ex. 9:23–25 **78:48** *a* Ex. 9:19 **78:51** *b* Ex.
12:29, 30 **78:52** *c* Ps. 77:20 **78:53** *d* Ex. 14:19, 20 *e* Ex.
14:27, 28 **78:54** *f* Ex. 15:17 *g* Ps. 44:3 **78:55** *h* Ps.
44:2 *i* Josh. 13:7; 19:51; 23:4 **78:56** *j* Judg. 2:11–13
78:57 *k* Ezek. 20:27, 28 *l* Hos. 7:16 **78:58** *m* Judg.
2:12 *n* Deut. 12:2 **78:60** *o* 1 Sam. 4:11 **78:61** *p* Judg.
18:30 **78:62** *q* 1 Sam. 4:10 **78:63** *r* Jer. 7:34; 16:9;
25:10 **78:64** *s* 1 Sam. 4:17; 22:18 *t* Job 27:15; Ezek. 24:23
78:65 *u* Is. 42:13

66 And *v*He beat back His enemies;
He put them to a perpetual reproach.
67 Moreover He rejected the tent of
Joseph,
And did not choose the tribe of
Ephraim,
68 But chose the tribe of Judah,
Mount Zion *w*which He loved.
69 And He built His *x*sanctuary like the
heights,
Like the earth which He has
established forever.
70 *y*He also chose David His servant,
And took him from the sheepfolds;
71 From following *z*the ewes that had
young He brought him,
*a*To shepherd Jacob His people,
And Israel His inheritance.
72 So he shepherded them according to
the *b*integrity of his heart,
And guided them by the skillfulness of
his hands.

Psalm 79

A Dirge and a Prayer for Israel, Destroyed by Enemies

A Psalm of Asaph.

1 O God, the nations have come into
*a*Your inheritance;
Your holy temple they have defiled;
*b*They have laid Jerusalem in heaps.
2 *c*The dead bodies of Your servants
They have given *as* food for the birds
of the heavens,
The flesh of Your saints to the beasts
of the earth.
3 Their blood they have shed like water
all around Jerusalem,
And *there was* no one to bury *them.*
4 We have become a reproach to our
*d*neighbors,
A scorn and derision to those who are
around us.
5 *e*How long, LORD?
Will You be angry forever?
Will Your *f*jealousy burn like fire?

6 *g*Pour out Your wrath on the nations
that *h*do not know You,
And on the kingdoms that *i*do not call
on Your name.
7 For they have devoured Jacob,
And laid waste his dwelling place.
8 *j*Oh, do not remember former iniquities
against us!
Let Your tender mercies come speedily
to meet us,
For we have been brought very low.
9 Help us, O God of our salvation,
For the glory of Your name;
And deliver us, and provide atonement
for our sins,
*k*For Your name's sake!
10 *l*Why should the nations say,
"Where *is* their God?"
Let there be known among the nations
in our sight
The avenging of the blood of Your
servants *which has been* shed.
11 Let *m*the groaning of the prisoner
come before You;
According to the greatness of Your
power
Preserve those who are appointed to die;
12 And return to our neighbors
*n*sevenfold into their bosom
*o*Their reproach with which they have
reproached You, O Lord.
13 So *p*we, Your people and sheep of Your
pasture,
Will give You thanks forever;
*q*We will show forth Your praise to all
generations.

Psalm 80

Prayer for Israel's Restoration

To the Chief Musician. *a*Set to "The
Lilies."* A Testimony* of Asaph.
A Psalm.

1 Give ear, O Shepherd of Israel,
*b*You who lead Joseph *c*like a flock;

---

* 80:title Hebrew *Shoshannim* • Hebrew *Eduth*

78:68 *Mount Zion which He loved.* The description of the sanctuary in verses 68–69 suggests that this psalm was written after Solomon's temple was built.
78:71 *To shepherd Jacob His people.* The shepherding attributed to David is an ideal; it will be fully realized in the Savior King, Jesus, the true Good Shepherd (Matt. 2:6; John 10:1–18).
79:1 *Your holy temple.* The destruction described in this verse may be what the Babylonians did in 586 B.C.
79:6 *Pour out Your wrath.* An imprecation or curse on one's enemies is often found in the psalms of lament (137:7–9). Vengeance is left to the Lord, but such a call for vengeance is based in part on the covenant provisions that God established with Abraham. God had promised to curse those who cursed Abraham's descendants (Gen. 12:2–3).
79:12 *return to our neighbors sevenfold . . . Their*

reproach.* While the Israelites' cries for vengeance seem to be missing the concept of "love your neighbor," it is clear that they understand both the seriousness of the offense against God and also the fact that it is God, not they, who must avenge.
80:1 *Shepherd of Israel.* The concept of God as the Good Shepherd who cares for His people is clearly

78:66 *v* 1 Sam. 5:6   **78:68** *w* [Ps. 87:2]   **78:69** *x* 1 Kin. 6:1–38   **78:70** *y* 1 Sam. 16:11, 12   **78:71** *z* [Is. 40:11] *a* 2 Sam. 5:2   **78:72** *b* 1 Kin. 9:4   **79:1** *a* Ps. 74:2 *b* Mic. 3:12   **79:2** *c* Jer. 7:33; 19:7; 34:20   **79:4** *d* Ps. 44:13   **79:5** *e* Ps. 74:1, 9 *f* [Zeph. 3:8]   **79:6** *g* Jer. 10:25 *h* Is. 45:4, 5 *i* Ps. 53:4   **79:8** *j* Is. 64:9   **79:9** *k* Jer. 14:7, 21   **79:10** *l* Ps. 42:10   **79:11** *m* Ps. 102:20   **79:12** *n* Gen. 4:15 *o* Ps. 74:10, 18, 22   **79:13** *p* Ps. 74:1; 95:7 *q* Is. 43:21   **80:title** *a* Ps. 45:title   **80:1** *b* [Ex. 25:20–22] *c* Ps. 77:20

You who dwell *between* the cherubim,
dShine forth!
2 Before eEphraim, Benjamin, and
Manasseh,
Stir up Your strength,
And come *and* save us!

3 fRestore us, O God;
gCause Your face to shine,
And we shall be saved!

4 O LORD God of hosts,
hHow long will You be angry
Against the prayer of Your people?
5 iYou have fed them with the bread of
tears,
And given them tears to drink in great
measure.
6 You have made us a strife to our
neighbors,
And our enemies laugh among
themselves.

7 Restore us, O God of hosts;
Cause Your face to shine,
And we shall be saved!

8 You have brought ja vine out of Egypt;
kYou have cast out the nations, and
planted it.
9 You prepared *room* for it,
And caused it to take deep root,
And it filled the land.
10 The hills were covered with its
shadow,
And the mighty cedars with its
lboughs.
11 She sent out her boughs to the Sea,*
And her branches to the River.*
12 Why have You mbroken down her
hedges,
So that all who pass by the way pluck
her *fruit*?
13 The boar out of the woods uproots it,
And the wild beast of the field
devours it.

14 Return, we beseech You, O God of
hosts;
nLook down from heaven and see,
And visit this vine
15 And the vineyard which Your right
hand has planted,

And the branch *that* You made strong
oFor Yourself.
16 *It is* burned with fire, *it is* cut down;
pThey perish at the rebuke of Your
countenance.
17 qLet Your hand be upon the man of
Your right hand,
Upon the son of man *whom* You made
strong for Yourself.
18 Then we will not turn back from You;
Revive us, and we will call upon Your
name.

19 Restore us, O LORD God of hosts;
Cause Your face to shine,
And we shall be saved!

Psalm 81

An Appeal for Israel's Repentance

To the Chief Musician. aOn an
instrument of Gath.* *A Psalm* of
Asaph.

1 Sing aloud to God our strength;
Make a joyful shout to the God of
Jacob.
2 Raise a song and strike the timbrel,
The pleasant harp with the lute.
3 Blow the trumpet at the time of the
New Moon,
At the full moon, on our solemn feast
day.
4 For bthis *is* a statute for Israel,
A law of the God of Jacob.
5 This He established in Joseph *as* a
testimony,
When He went throughout the land of
Egypt,
cWhere I heard a language I did not
understand.

6 "I removed his shoulder from the
burden;
His hands were freed from the baskets.
7 dYou called in trouble, and I delivered
you;

---

* **80:11** That is, the Mediterranean • That is, the
Euphrates   * **81:title** Hebrew *Al Gittith*

---

shown by Jesus In John 10.1–18. **dwell between the
cherubim.** In the Most Holy Place, the ark of the covenant was topped by the mercy seat on which were
two cherubim, heavenly symbols of the throne of
God (Ex. 25:22).
80:8 You have brought a vine out of Egypt. The
picture of Israel as God's vine recurs other places
in Scripture (see, for example, Is. 5:1–25). In the
New Testament, Jesus used the same metaphor to
describe the relationship of God with all who trust in
Him (John 15:1–8).
81:3 the New Moon. The New Moon festival is mentioned in association with the Feast of Trumpets
(Num. 29:6). Regulations for this festival can be found
in the instructions to the Levites during the time of

David (1 Chr. 23:31) and Solomon (2 Chr. 2:4). This
psalm seems to be a basic instruction on the festival.
The language and regulations are as solemn as any
in the Torah.
81:7 I answered you. The Lord's appearance to
Moses on Mount Sinai was God's great revelation of
Himself (Ex. 19:20).

80:1 dDeut. 33:2   **80:2** ePs. 78:9, 67   **80:3** fLam.
5:21   gNum. 6:25   **80:4** hPs. 79:5   **80:5** iIs.
30:20   **80:8** j[Is. 5:1, 7]   kPs. 44:2   **80:10** lLev. 23:40
80:12 mIs. 5:5   **80:14** nIs. 63:15   **80:15** o[Is. 49:5]
80:16 p[Ps. 39:11]   **80:17** qPs. 89:21   **81:title** aPs.
8:title   **81:4** bNum. 10:10   **81:5** cPs. 114:1   **81:7** dEx.
2:23; 14:10

*e*I answered you in the secret place of
thunder;
I *f*tested you at the waters of Meribah.
Selah

8 "Hear,*g* O My people, and I will
admonish you!
O Israel, if you will listen to Me!
9 There shall be no *h*foreign god among
you;
Nor shall you worship any foreign god.
10 *i*I *am* the LORD your God,
Who brought you out of the land of
Egypt;
*j*Open your mouth wide, and I will
fill it.

11 "But My people would not heed My
voice,
And Israel would *have* *k*none of Me.
12 *l*So I gave them over to their own
stubborn heart,
To walk in their own counsels.

13 "Oh,*m* that My people would listen to
Me,
That Israel would walk in My ways!
14 I would soon subdue their enemies,
And turn My hand against their
adversaries.
15 *n*The haters of the LORD would pretend
submission to Him,
But their fate would endure forever.
16 He would *o*have fed them also with the
finest of wheat;
And with honey *p*from the rock I
would have satisfied you."

Psalm 82

A Plea for Justice

A Psalm of Asaph.

1 God *a*stands in the congregation of the
mighty;
He judges among *b*the gods.*
2 How long will you judge unjustly,
And *c*show partiality to the wicked?
Selah
3 Defend the poor and fatherless;
Do justice to the afflicted and *d*needy.

4 Deliver the poor and needy;
Free *them* from the hand of the
wicked.
5 They do not know, nor do they
understand;
They walk about in darkness;
All the *e*foundations of the earth are
unstable.

6 I said, *f*"You *are* gods,*
And all of you *are* children of the Most
High.
7 But you shall die like men,
And fall like one of the princes."

8 Arise, O God, judge the earth;
*g*For You shall inherit all nations.

Psalm 83

Prayer to Frustrate Conspiracy Against Israel

A Song. A Psalm of Asaph.

1 Do*a* not keep silent, O God!
Do not hold Your peace,
And do not be still, O God!
2 For behold, *b*Your enemies make a
tumult;
And those who hate You have lifted up
their head.
3 They have taken crafty counsel
against Your people,
And consulted together *c*against Your
sheltered ones.
4 They have said, "Come, and *d*let us cut
them off from *being* a nation,
That the name of Israel may be
remembered no more."

5 For they have consulted together with
one consent;
They form a confederacy against You:
6 *e*The tents of Edom and the Ishmaelites;
Moab and the Hagrites;
7 Gebal, Ammon, and Amalek;
Philistia with the inhabitants of Tyre;

---

* **82:1** Hebrew *elohim, mighty ones;* that is, the
judges   * **82:6** Hebrew *elohim, mighty ones;* that
is, the judges

81:9 no foreign god. Asaph, the chief musician
during David's reign, reviews the goodness of God
and His marvelous deliverance of Israel from the land
of bondage (Ex. 7–12). The plagues sent upon Egypt
were meant to accomplish a purpose: first, to show to
God's people the power of the true God; and second,
to demonstrate to the Egyptians the total inability of
their false gods. In spite of these dramatic object lessons against idolatry, Israel began worshiping pagan
images almost as soon as they left Egypt.
82:6 You are gods. Jesus quoted this verse in His
exchange with the religious authorities who wanted
to stone Him for declaring Himself to be the Son of
God (John 10:31–35). The word translated "gods" here
is the same word translated such in verse 1. This word

(*elohim*) is used to refer to the one God, to false gods,
to angels, or to "mighty ones" (that is, the judges).
83:6 tents of Edom. The place names in this passage
refer to nations on the borders of Israel and Judah.
The Hagrites may have come from Arabia (1 Chr.
5:10,19–20).

81:7 *e* Ex. 19:19; 20:18   *f* Ex. 17:6, 7   **81:8** *g* [Ps.
50:7]   **81:9** *h* [Is. 43:12]   **81:10** *i* Ex. 20:2 *j* Ps. 103:5
81:11 *k* Deut. 32:15   **81:12** *l* [Acts 7:42]   **81:13** *m* [Is.
48:18]   **81:15** *n* Rom. 1:30   **81:16** *o* Deut. 32:14 *p* Job
w29:6   **82:1** *a* [2 Chr. 19:6] *b* Ps. 82:6   **82:2** *c* [Deut.
1:17]   **82:3** *d* [Deut. 24:17]   **82:5** *e* Ps. 11:3   **82:6** *f* John
10:34   **82:8** *g* [Rev. 11:15]   **83:1** *a* Ps. 28:1   **83:2** *b* Ps.
81:15   **83:3** *c* [Ps. 27:5]   **83:4** *d* Jer. 11:19; 31:36
83:6 *e* 2 Chr. 20:1, 10, 11

8 Assyria also has joined with them;
  They have helped the children of Lot.
                                    Selah

9 Deal with them as *with* fMidian,
  As *with* gSisera,
  As *with* Jabin at the Brook Kishon,
10 Who perished at En Dor,
  h Who became *as* refuse on the earth.
11 Make their nobles like iOreb and like
       Zeeb,
  Yes, all their princes like jZebah and
       Zalmunna,
12 Who said, "Let us take for ourselves
  The pastures of God for a possession."

13 kO my God, make them like the
       whirling dust,
  lLike the chaff before the wind!
14 As the fire burns the woods,
  And as the flame msets the mountains
       on fire,
15 So pursue them with Your tempest,
  And frighten them with Your storm.
16 Fill their faces with shame,
  That they may seek Your name,
       O LORD.
17 Let them be confounded and dismayed
       forever;
  Yes, let them be put to shame and
       perish,
18 nThat they may know that You, whose
       oname alone *is* the LORD,
  Are pthe Most High over all the earth.

Psalm 84

The Blessedness of Dwelling in the House of God

To the Chief Musician. aOn an
instrument of Gath.* A Psalm of the
sons of Korah.

1 How blovely *is* Your tabernacle,
  O LORD of hosts!

2 cMy soul longs, yes, even faints
  For the courts of the LORD;
  My heart and my flesh cry out for the
       living God.

3 Even the sparrow has found a home,
  And the swallow a nest for herself,
  Where she may lay her young—
  Even Your altars, O LORD of hosts,
  My King and my God.

4 Blessed *are* those who dwell in Your
       dhouse;
  They will still be praising You.   *Selah*

5 Blessed *is* the man whose strength *is*
       in You,
  Whose heart *is* set on pilgrimage.

6 *As they* pass through the Valley eof
       Baca,
  They make it a spring;
  The rain also covers it with pools.

7 They go ffrom strength to strength;
  Each one gappears before God in
       Zion.*

8 O LORD God of hosts, hear my
       prayer;
  Give ear, O God of Jacob!   *Selah*

9 hO God, behold our shield,
  And look upon the face of Your
       anointed.

10 For a day in Your courts *is* better than
       a thousand.
  I would rather be a doorkeeper in the
       house of my God
  Than dwell in the tents of wickedness.

11 For the LORD God *is* ia sun and jshield;
  The LORD will give grace and glory;
  kNo good *thing* will He withhold
  From those who walk uprightly.

12 O LORD of hosts,
  lBlessed *is* the man who trusts in You!

* 84:title Hebrew *Al Gittith*   * 84:7 Septuagint,
Syriac, and Vulgate read *The God of gods shall
be seen.*

83:9 *Sisera.* God's victory over Sisera was accomplished through Deborah and Barak (Judg. 4–5). The same God who had battled Israel's enemies in the past would fight all those who might oppose His people in the future.

83:16 *That they may seek Your name.* Asaph's first call for God to shame Israel's enemies is redemptive—that the nations might hear, feel shame, repent, and seek the Lord. Yet, if they continued in their wicked path, they would be further confounded and would one day face God in judgment.

84:1 *How lovely is Your tabernacle.* This psalm celebrates God's presence in Jerusalem, the city where His temple was built. Today it is not necessary to go to Jerusalem to draw near to God, for God is near to those who trust in His Son (Matt. 28:18–20).

84:6 *the Valley of Baca.* The Valley of Baca, or "Valley of Weeping," refers to the various difficulties that one might face on a pilgrimage. With God, even times of hardship and sorrow can become times of great joy and blessing.

84:9 *Your anointed.* The two phrases "our shield" and "Your anointed" both point to the same person, the king of Israel (89:3–4). These anointed kings foreshadowed the coming Messiah—the Anointed One.

84:11 *No good thing will He withhold.* When we go through times of darkness and difficulty, it sometimes seems that God is not giving us what we need. However, God is far wiser than we can ever be, and He never withholds what is good from us. When it seems that He does, we must assume that what we want would not actually be a good thing for us to have.

83:9 f Judg. 7:22 g Judg. 4:15–24; 5:20, 21   83:10 h Zeph.
1:17   83:11 i Judg. 7:25 j Judg. 8:12–21   83:13 k Is.
17:13 l Ps. 35:5   83:14 m Deut. 32:22   83:18 n Ps. 59:13
o Ex. 6:3 p [Ps. 92:8]   84:title a Ps. 8:title   84:1 b Ps.
27:4; 46:4, 5   84:2 c Ps. 42:1, 2   84:4 d [Ps. 65:4]
84:6 e 2 Sam. 5:22–25   84:7 f Prov. 4:18 g Deut. 16:16
84:9 h Gen. 15:1   84:11 i Is. 60:19, 20 j Gen. 15:1   k Ps.
34:9, 10   84:12 l [Ps. 2:12; 40:4]

Psalm 85

Prayer that the LORD Will Restore Favor to the Land

To the Chief Musician. A Psalm ^aof the sons of Korah.

1 LORD, You have been favorable to Your
land;
You have ^bbrought back the captivity
of Jacob.
2 You have forgiven the iniquity of Your
people;
You have covered all their sin. *Selah*
3 You have taken away all Your wrath;
You have turned from the fierceness of
Your anger.

4 ^cRestore us, O God of our salvation,
And cause Your anger toward us to
cease.
5 ^dWill You be angry with us forever?
Will You prolong Your anger to all
generations?
6 Will You not ^erevive us again,
That Your people may rejoice in You?
7 Show us Your mercy, LORD,
And grant us Your salvation.

8 I will hear what God the LORD will
speak,
For He will speak peace
To His people and to His saints;
But let them not turn back to folly.
9 Surely ^fHis salvation *is* near to those
who fear Him,
^gThat glory may dwell in our land.

10 Mercy and truth have met together;
^hRighteousness and peace have kissed.
11 Truth shall spring out of the earth,
And righteousness shall look down
from heaven.
12 ⁱYes, the LORD will give *what is* good;
And our land will yield its increase.
13 Righteousness will go before Him,
And shall make His footsteps *our*
pathway.

Psalm 86

Prayer for Mercy, with Meditation on the Excellencies of the LORD

A Prayer of David.

1 Bow down Your ear, O LORD, hear me;
For I *am* poor and needy.
2 Preserve my life, for I *am* holy;
You are my God;
Save Your servant who trusts in You!
3 Be merciful to me, O Lord,
For I cry to You all day long.
4 Rejoice the soul of Your servant,
^aFor to You, O Lord, I lift up my soul.
5 For ^bYou, Lord, *are* good, and ready to
forgive,
And abundant in mercy to all those
who call upon You.

6 Give ear, O LORD, to my prayer;
And attend to the voice of my
supplications.
7 In the day of my trouble I will call
upon You,
For You will answer me.

8 ^cAmong the gods *there is* none like
You, O Lord;
Nor *are there any works* like Your
works.
9 All nations whom You have made
Shall come and worship before You,
O Lord,
And shall glorify Your name.
10 For You *are* great, and ^ddo wondrous
things;
^eYou alone *are* God.

11 ^fTeach me Your way, O LORD;
I will walk in Your truth;
Unite my heart to fear Your name.
12 I will praise You, O Lord my God, with
all my heart,
And I will glorify Your name
forevermore.
13 For great *is* Your mercy toward me,
And You have delivered my soul from
the depths of Sheol.

85:1 *You have brought back the captivity.* The setting for this psalm appears to be the restoration of the people of God following a great catastrophe—perhaps the Babylonian captivity.
85:2–3 *You have forgiven.* In all its forms, from hideous to petty, sin alienates people from God and is deserving of His punishment. The wonderful message of the Bible is that God will forgive even the most despicable sinner if that sinner repents and turns from wickedness. God's forgiveness is not just an arbitrary overlooking of our sin, but a judicial act whereby He applies the penalty paid by His son to our account. Our sins are thus covered by Jesus' blood, and God considers us righteous.
85:10 *Mercy and truth have met together.* Kindness without truth is hypocrisy, while truth without love and mercy is cruel. Only when the two meet can we experience wholeness and healing.
86:1 *Bow down Your ear.* David's dramatic phrase

captures the grandeur of God on high and his own humble position on the earth below.
86:8 *Among the gods.* The ancient nations took their sense of identity in part from their ties to their supposed gods. When the nations found out that their "gods" did not exist, they would have to acknowledge that the Lord alone is God. Here David envisions other nations worshiping the true God and thus anticipates the missionary thrust of the New Testament (Ps. 117:1; Matt. 28:18–20).
86:13 *You have delivered my soul.* The cold hand of death knocks at everyone's door, whether we dwell in a luxury condominium with security guards or a

85:title ^a Ps. 42:title   85:1 ^b Joel 3:1   85:4 ^c Ps. 80:3, 7
85:5 ^d Ps. 79:5   85:6 ^e Hab. 3:2   85:9 ^f Is. 46:13 ^g Zech.
2:5   85:10 ^h Ps. 72:3   85:12 ⁱ [Ps. 84:11]   86:4 ^a Ps.
25:1; 143:8   86:5 ^b [Joel 2:13]   86:8 ^c [Ex. 15:11]
86:10 ^d [Ex. 15:11] ^e Deut. 6:4   86:11 ^f Ps. 27:11; 143:8

¹⁴ O God, the proud have risen against me,
And a mob of violent *men* have sought
my life,
And have not set You before them.
¹⁵ But ^gYou, O Lord, *are* a God full of
compassion, and gracious,
Longsuffering and abundant in mercy
and truth.
¹⁶ Oh, turn to me, and have mercy on me!
Give Your strength to Your servant,
And save the son of Your maidservant.
¹⁷ Show me a sign for good,
That those who hate me may see *it* and
be ashamed,
Because You, LORD, have helped me
and comforted me.

Psalm 87

The Glories of the City of God

A Psalm of the sons of Korah. A Song.

¹ His foundation *is* in the holy
mountains.
² ^aThe LORD loves the gates of Zion
More than all the dwellings of Jacob.
³ ^bGlorious things are spoken of you,
O city of God! *Selah*

⁴ "I will make mention of Rahab and
Babylon to those who know Me;
Behold, O Philistia and Tyre, with
Ethiopia:
'This *one* was born there.'"

⁵ And of Zion it will be said,
"This *one* and that *one* were born in
her;
And the Most High Himself shall
establish her."
⁶ The LORD will record,
When He ^cregisters the peoples:
"This *one* was born there." *Selah*

⁷ Both the singers and the players on
instruments *say,*
"All my springs *are* in you."

Psalm 88

A Prayer for Help in Despondency

A Song. A Psalm of the sons of
Korah. To the Chief Musician.
Set to "Mahalath Leannoth."
A Contemplation* of ^aHeman the
Ezrahite.

¹ O LORD, ^bGod of my salvation,
I have cried out day and night before
You.
² Let my prayer come before You;
Incline Your ear to my cry.

³ For my soul is full of troubles,
And my life ^cdraws near to the grave.
⁴ I am counted with those who ^dgo down
to the pit;
^eI am like a man *who has* no strength,
⁵ Adrift among the dead,
Like the slain who lie in the grave,
Whom You remember no more,
And who are cut off from Your hand.

⁶ You have laid me in the lowest pit,
In darkness, in the depths.
⁷ Your wrath lies heavy upon me,
And You have afflicted *me* with all
^fYour waves. *Selah*
⁸ ^gYou have put away my acquaintances
far from me;
You have made me an abomination to
them;
^hI *am* shut up, and I cannot get out;
⁹ My eye wastes away because of
affliction.

---

* **88:title** Hebrew *Maschil*

---

tenement surrounded by urban blight. The good news, however, is that the Lord has not left us at the mercy of death, but has provided for the deliverance of our souls from the depths of the grave. We can face the future confidently, knowing that, when our bodies die, our spirits will be with Christ, and that one day we shall also experience the resurrection of the body by His mighty power (Phil. 3:20–21).
87:1 *His foundation.* God Himself established Zion (or Jerusalem) as the center of true worship. He ordained Solomon to build a temple there so that He could live among the Israelites (1 Kin. 6:13). Zion is holy because of God's declaration (1 Kin. 11:13), His promise, the worship given Him there (1 Kin. 8:14–66), the future work of the Savior there (Matt. 21:4–11), and the future rule of the King there (Rev. 21).
87:4 *Rahab.* Rahab is a symbolic name for Egypt (Is. 30:7) that has negative connotations, alluding to the arrogance of the Egyptians. ***Babylon.*** Babylon was the proverbial seat of apostasy and idolatry (Gen. 10:10).
87:5 *born in her.* Despite their foreign heritage, the

people who worshiped God were considered to have been born in Zion. It appears that this is referring to a spiritual birth, foreshadowing Jesus' teaching about being born again (John 3:1–8).
88:title *Heman.* Heman is identified in 1 Kings 4:31 as a gifted wise man, and in 1 Chronicles 15:16–19 as one of the musically gifted Levites who ministered in worship during the time of David.
88:1 *God of my salvation.* Even in the midst of despair, Heman confesses his faith in God's saving goodness.
88:3 *grave.* This is also translated "Sheol," which is the Hebrew word for "hell." It is often linked with the term "pit" as a symbol of the end of earthly existence. The Old Testament has very little to say about what happens to a soul after death, but it is clear that to go to Sheol is the end of all we know.

86:15 ^g Ex. 34:6   **87:2** ^a Ps. 78:67, 68   **87:3** ^b Is. 60:1
87:6 ^c Is. 4:3   **88:title** ^a 1 Kin. 4:31   **88:1** ^b Ps. 27:9
88:3 ^c Ps. 107:18   **88:4** ^d [Ps. 28:1]   ^e Ps. 31:12   **88:7** ^f Ps. 42:7   **88:8** ^g Job 19:13, 19   ^h Lam. 3:7

[i]LORD, I have called daily upon You;
I have stretched out my hands to You.
10 Will You work wonders for the dead?
Shall the dead arise *and* praise You?
                                    Selah
11 Shall Your lovingkindness be declared
in the grave?
Or Your faithfulness in the place of
destruction?
12 Shall Your wonders be known in the
dark?
And Your righteousness in the land of
forgetfulness?
13 But to You I have cried out, O LORD,
And in the morning my prayer comes
before You.
14 LORD, why do You cast off my soul?
Why do You hide Your face from me?
15 I *have been* afflicted and ready to die
from *my* youth;
I suffer Your terrors;
I am distraught.
16 Your fierce wrath has gone over me;
Your terrors have cut me off.
17 They came around me all day long like
water;
They engulfed me altogether.
18 [j]Loved one and friend You have put far
from me,
And my acquaintances into darkness.

Psalm 89

Remembering the Covenant with David, and Sorrow for Lost Blessings

A Contemplation* of [a]Ethan the
Ezrahite.

1 I will sing of the mercies of the LORD
forever;
With my mouth will I make known
Your faithfulness to all
generations.
2 For I have said, "Mercy shall be built
up forever;
[b]Your faithfulness You shall establish
in the very heavens."
3 "I[c] have made a covenant with My
chosen,
I have [d]sworn to My servant David:

4 'Your seed I will establish forever,
And build up your throne [e]to all
generations.'"   *Selah*
5 And [f]the heavens will praise Your
wonders, O LORD;
Your faithfulness also in the assembly
of the saints.
6 [g]For who in the heavens can be
compared to the LORD?
Who among the sons of the mighty
can be likened to the LORD?
7 [h]God is greatly to be feared in the
assembly of the saints,
And to be held in reverence by all
those around Him.
8 O LORD God of hosts,
Who *is* mighty like You, O LORD?
Your faithfulness also surrounds You.
9 [i]You rule the raging of the sea;
When its waves rise, You still them.
10 [j]You have broken Rahab in pieces, as
one who is slain;
You have scattered Your enemies with
Your mighty arm.
11 [k]The heavens *are* Yours, the earth also
is Yours;
The world and all its fullness, You
have founded them.
12 The north and the south, You have
created them;
[l]Tabor and [m]Hermon rejoice in Your
name.
13 You have a mighty arm;
Strong is Your hand, *and* high is Your
right hand.
14 Righteousness and justice *are* the
foundation of Your throne;
Mercy and truth go before Your face.
15 Blessed *are* the people who know the
[n]joyful sound!
They walk, O LORD, in the light of
Your countenance.
16 In Your name they rejoice all day
long,
And in Your righteousness they are
exalted.
17 For You *are* the glory of their strength,
And in Your favor our horn is [o]exalted.
18 For our shield *belongs* to the LORD,
And our king to the Holy One of Israel.

---

* **89:title** Hebrew *Maschil*

88:11 destruction. This word is also translated "Abaddon."
89:1 the mercies of the LORD. The lovingkindness of the Lord in this psalm centers on the covenant that He made with David, promising him an eternal dynasty (2 Sam. 7).
89:6 sons of the mighty. This phrase may mean "sons of gods" or "heavenly beings." The reference could be to other supposed gods or to angels, members of the heavenly court (Job 1:6).
89:10 Rahab. Rahab is a title for Egypt (87:4).
89:13 a mighty arm. God is the great Deliverer; He brandished His arm and hand in delivering His people from Egypt (Ex. 6:6; 15:6).

89:18 the Holy One of Israel. This is the title that Isaiah used to describe God, following his experience of God's holiness in his memorable vision of God's throne (Is. 6:1–5).

88:9 [i]Ps. 86:3   **88:18** [j]Ps. 31:11; 38:11   **89:title** [a]1 Kin. 4:31   **89:2** [b][Ps. 119:89, 90]   **89:3** [c]1 Kin. 8:16 [d]2 Sam. 7:11   **89:4** [e][Luke 1:33]   **89:5** [f][Ps. 19:1]   **89:6** [g]Ps. 86:8; 113:5   **89:7** [h]Ps. 76:7, 11   **89:9** [i]Ps. 65:7; 93:3, 4; 107:29   **89:10** [j]Ps. 87:4   **89:11** [k][Gen. 1:1]   **89:12** [l]Josh. 19:22 [m]Josh. 11:17; 12:1   **89:15** [n]Ps. 98:6   **89:17** [o]Ps. 75:10; 92:10; 132:17

19 Then You spoke in a vision to Your
   holy one,*
   And said: "I have given help to *one
   who is* mighty;
   I have exalted one *p*chosen from the
   people.
20 *q*I have found My servant David;
   With My holy oil I have anointed him,
21 *r*With whom My hand shall be
   established;
   Also My arm shall strengthen him.
22 The enemy shall not outwit him,
   Nor the son of wickedness afflict him.
23 I will beat down his foes before his face,
   And plague those who hate him.

24 "But My faithfulness and My mercy
   shall be with him,
   And in My name his horn shall be
   exalted.
25 Also I will *s*set his hand over the sea,
   And his right hand over the rivers.
26 He shall cry to Me, 'You *are* *t*my Father,
   My God, and *u*the rock of my
   salvation.'
27 Also I will make him *v*My firstborn,
   *w*The highest of the kings of the earth.
28 *x*My mercy I will keep for him forever,
   And My covenant shall stand firm
   with him.
29 His seed also I will make *to endure*
   forever,
   *y*And his throne *z*as the days of heaven.

30 "If*a* his sons *b*forsake My law
   And do not walk in My judgments,
31 If they break My statutes
   And do not keep My commandments,
32 Then I will punish their transgression
   with the rod,
   And their iniquity with stripes.
33 *c*Nevertheless My lovingkindness I will
   not utterly take from him,
   Nor allow My faithfulness to fail.
34 My covenant I will not break,
   Nor *d*alter the word that has gone out
   of My lips.
35 Once I have sworn *e*by My holiness;
   I will not lie to David:
36 *f*His seed shall endure forever,
   And his throne *g*as the sun before Me;
37 It shall be established forever like the
   moon,
   Even *like* the faithful witness in the
   sky."   *Selah*

38 But You have *h*cast off and *i*abhorred,
   You have been furious with Your
   anointed.
39 You have renounced the covenant of
   Your servant;
   *j*You have profaned his crown *by
   casting it* to the ground.
40 You have broken down all his hedges;
   You have brought his strongholds to
   ruin.
41 All who pass by the way *k*plunder him;
   He is a reproach to his neighbors.
42 You have exalted the right hand of his
   adversaries;
   You have made all his enemies rejoice.
43 You have also turned back the edge of
   his sword,
   And have not sustained him in the
   battle.
44 You have made his glory cease,
   And cast his throne down to the
   ground.
45 The days of his youth You have
   shortened;
   You have covered him with shame.
                                      Selah

46 How long, LORD?
   Will You hide Yourself forever?
   Will Your wrath burn like fire?
47 Remember how short my time *l*is;
   For what *m*futility have You created all
   the children of men?
48 What man can live and not see *n*death?
   Can he deliver his life from the power
   of the grave?   *Selah*

49 Lord, where *are* Your former
   lovingkindnesses,
   Which You *o*swore to David *p*in Your
   truth?
50 Remember, Lord, the reproach of Your
   servants—
   *q*How I bear in my bosom *the reproach
   of* all the many peoples,
51 *r*With which Your enemies have
   reproached, O LORD,
   With which they have reproached the
   footsteps of Your anointed.

52 *s*Blessed *be* the LORD forevermore!
   Amen and Amen.

---

* **89:19** Following many Hebrew manuscripts;
Masoretic Text, Septuagint, Targum, and Vulgate
read *holy ones.*

89:29 seed . . . throne. These words echo the covenant God made with David (2 Sam. 7:8–17).
89:34 My covenant I will not break. God is determined to complete, fulfill, and accomplish His grand plan for David's dynasty (2 Sam. 7:1–24).
89:49–51 Which You swore to David. The writer complains that God has not been keeping His promises to David (2 Sam. 7:1–24). As a result, His people are experiencing harsh treatment from their enemies. There is no resolution to this psalm; it ends with the people, the king, and the psalmist in distress. Yet the inclusion of this psalm among the praises of Israel suggests that God did answer this prayer of His people, just as He did in the case of Psalm 60.

89:19 *p* 1 Kin. 11:34   **89:20** *q* 1 Sam. 13:14; 16:1–12
89:21 *r* Ps. 80:17   **89:25** *s* Ps. 72:8   **89:26** *t* [1 Chr.
22:10] *u* 2 Sam. 22:47   **89:27** *v* [Col. 1:15, 18] *w* Rev.
19:16   **89:28** *x* Is. 55:3   **89:29** *y* Jer. 33:17 *z* Deut. 11:21
89:30 *a* [2 Sam. 7:14] *b* Ps. 119:53   **89:33** *c* 2 Sam. 7:14, 15
89:34 *d* Jer. 33:20–22   **89:35** *e* Amos 4:2   **89:36** *f* [Luke
1:33] *g* Ps. 72:17   **89:38** *h* [1 Chr. 28:9] *i* Deut. 32:19
89:39 *j* Lam. 5:16   **89:41** *k* Ps. 80:12   **89:47** *l* Ps. 90:9
m Ps. 62:9   **89:48** *n* [Eccl. 3:19]   **89:49** *o* [2 Sam. 7:15]
p Ps. 54:5   **89:50** *q* Ps. 69:9, 19   **89:51** *r* Ps. 74:10, 18, 22
89:52 *s* Ps. 41:13

BOOK FOUR

Psalms 90–106

Psalm 90

The Eternity of God, and Man's Frailty

A Prayer *a*of Moses the man of God.

1 Lord, *b*You have been our dwelling
place* in all generations.
2 *c*Before the mountains were brought
forth,
Or ever You had formed the earth and
the world,
Even from everlasting to everlasting,
You *are* God.

3 You turn man to destruction,
And say, *d*"Return, O children of men."
4 *e*For a thousand years in Your sight
Are like yesterday when it is past,
And *like* a watch in the night.
5 You carry them away *like* a flood;
*f*They *are* like a sleep.
In the morning *g*they are like grass
which grows up:
6 In the morning it flourishes and grows
up;
In the evening it is cut down and
withers.

7 For we have been consumed by Your
anger,
And by Your wrath we are terrified.
8 *h*You have set our iniquities before
You,
Our *i*secret *sins* in the light of Your
countenance.
9 For all our days have passed away in
Your wrath;
We finish our years like a sigh.

10 The days of our lives *are* seventy years;
And if by reason of strength *they are*
eighty years,
Yet their boast *is* only labor and
sorrow;
For it is soon cut off, and we fly away.
11 Who knows the power of Your anger?
For as the fear of You, *so is* Your
wrath.
12 *i*So teach *us* to number our days,
That we may gain a heart of wisdom.

13 Return, O LORD!
How long?
And *k*have compassion on Your
servants.
14 Oh, satisfy us early with Your mercy,
*l*That we may rejoice and be glad all
our days!
15 Make us glad according to the days *in
which* You have afflicted us,
The years *in which* we have seen evil.
16 Let *m*Your work appear to Your
servants,
And Your glory to their children.
17 *n*And let the beauty of the LORD our
God be upon us,
And *o*establish the work of our hands
for us;
Yes, establish the work of our hands.

Psalm 91

Safety of Abiding in the Presence of God

1 He *a*who dwells in the secret place of
the Most High
Shall abide *b*under the shadow of the
Almighty.

---

* **90:1** Septuagint, Targum, and Vulgate read *refuge.*

90:1 Lord. This is not God's personal name (Ex. 3:14–15), but a Hebrew word celebrating His majestic authority.
90:4 a thousand years . . . like yesterday. A thousand years may seem long at the time, but in comparison with God's eternal existence, they are nothing.
90:7 Your anger. The unbelieving Israelites in the wilderness experienced God's anger (Num. 13–14). An entire generation spent their lives wandering because of their unbelief and rebellion.
90:10 seventy years . . . eighty years. The point here is not to set a maximum, but to present a context for the brevity of human life. No matter how long people live, death is inevitable.
90:12 Counting Our Days—This prayer of Moses, probably written near the end of his life, gives us some excellent insight into living. We need to seek wisdom, be sober-minded and diligent, and seek to use our time wisely, living in light of the Lord's commands.
• Life is often painful, sometimes very painful, but survivable.

• We perpetually fall short of God's plan for us.
• We are loved by an all-powerful yet merciful God who knows all about us.
• The only true satisfaction is in knowing and obeying God.
• Serve God to your fullest because your time here on earth is short.
90:17 establish the work of our hands. We need to have a sense of lasting meaning in our lives, something that will continue to the next generation.
91:1 in the secret place. The person who trusts in God is the one who lives close to Him. **Most High.** This title emphasizes God's majesty and is parallel to the term "Almighty." Together, the terms "Most High" and "Almighty" speak of God as a mountain-like majesty.

90:title *a* Deut. 33:1   **90:1** *b* [Ezek. 11:16]   **90:2** *c* [Prov. 8:25, 26]   **90:3** *d* Gen. 3:19   **90:4** *e* 2 Pet. 3:8
90:5 *f* Ps. 73:20 *g* Is. 40:6   **90:8** *h* Ps. 50:21 *i* Ps. 19:12
90:12 *j* Ps. 39:4   **90:13** *k* Deut. 32:36   **90:14** *l* Ps. 85:6
90:16 *m* Hab. 3:2   **90:17** *n* Ps. 27:4 *o* Is. 26:12   **91:1** *a* Ps. 27:5; 31:20; 32:7 *b* Ps. 17:8

2 cI will say of the LORD, "He is my refuge
       and my fortress;
   My God, in Him I will trust."

3 Surely dHe shall deliver you from the
       snare of the fowler*
   And from the perilous pestilence.
4 eHe shall cover you with His feathers,
   And under His wings you shall take
       refuge;
   His truth *shall be your* shield and
       buckler.
5 fYou shall not be afraid of the terror by
       night,
   Nor of the arrow *that* flies by day,
6 Nor of the pestilence *that* walks in
       darkness,
   Nor of the destruction *that* lays waste
       at noonday.

7 A thousand may fall at your side,
   And ten thousand at your right hand;
   But it shall not come near you.
8 Only gwith your eyes shall you look,
   And see the reward of the wicked.

9 Because you have made the LORD, *who
       is* hmy refuge,
   Even the Most High, iyour dwelling
       place,
10 jNo evil shall befall you,
   Nor shall any plague come near your
       dwelling;
11 kFor He shall give His angels charge
       over you,
   To keep you in all your ways.
12 In *their* hands they shall bear you up,
   lLest you dash your foot against a
       stone.
13 You shall tread upon the lion and the
       cobra,
   The young lion and the serpent you
       shall trample underfoot.

14 "Because he has set his love upon Me,
       therefore I will deliver him;
   I will set him on high, because he has
       mknown My name.
15 He shall ncall upon Me, and I will
       answer him;
   I *will be* owith him in trouble;
   I will deliver him and honor him.

16 With long life I will satisfy him,
   And show him My salvation."

Psalm 92

Praise to the LORD for His Love and Faithfulness

A Psalm. A Song for the Sabbath day.

1 *It is* agood to give thanks to the LORD,
   And to sing praises to Your name,
       O Most High;
2 To bdeclare Your lovingkindness in the
       morning,
   And Your faithfulness every night,
3 cOn an instrument of ten strings,
   On the lute,
   And on the harp,
   With harmonious sound.
4 For You, LORD, have made me glad
       through Your work;
   I will triumph in the works of Your
       hands.

5 dO LORD, how great are Your works!
   eYour thoughts are very deep.
6 fA senseless man does not know,
   Nor does a fool understand this.
7 When gthe wicked spring up like grass,
   And when all the workers of iniquity
       flourish,
   It is that they may be destroyed
       forever.

8 hBut You, LORD, *are* on high forevermore.
9 For behold, Your enemies, O LORD,
   For behold, Your enemies shall perish;
   All the workers of iniquity shall ibe
       scattered.
10 But jmy horn You have exalted like a
       wild ox;
   I have been kanointed with fresh oil.
11 lMy eye also has seen *my desire* on my
       enemies;
   My ears hear *my desire* on the wicked
   Who rise up against me.

---

* **91:3** That is, one who catches birds in a trap or snare

91:4 feathers . . . wings. Just as chicks take refuge under the wings of the mother hen, so we can take refuge in God's enveloping care.
91:7 A thousand may fall at your side. The Israelites in Egypt were spared the danger that touched their neighbors (Ex. 9:26; 10:23; 11:7); similarly, believers in the Lord are protected from Satan's attacks.
91:11 give His angels charge over you. These words were used by Satan to tempt the Savior (Matt. 4:5–6).
91:13 lion and the cobra. The animal and snake imagery in this verse pictures all kinds of evil that might threaten believers.
91:14 he has set his love upon Me. The word used here is not the usual Hebrew word for love. It has the idea of "holding close to," or even "hugging tightly in love" (Deut. 7:8; 10:15).

92:6 A senseless man . . . a fool. A foolish or senseless person is not someone with intelligence, but rather a person who is spiritually obtuse—someone who ignores God and refuses to accept responsibility.
92:10 my horn You have exalted. This is a figure of speech for the psalmist's eventual triumph, the celebration of the psalmist's strength.

91:2 c Ps. 142:5 **91:3** d Ps. 124:7 **91:4** e Ps. 17:8 **91:5** f [Job 5:19] **91:8** g Mal. 1:5 **91:9** h Ps. 91:2 i Ps. 90:1 **91:10** j [Prov. 12:21] **91:11** k [Heb. 1:14] **91:12** l Matt. 4:6 **91:14** m [Ps. 9:10] **91:15** n Ps. 50:15 o Is. 43:2 **92:1** a Ps. 147:1 **92:2** b Ps. 89:1 **92:3** c 1 Chr. 23:5 **92:5** d Ps. 40:5 e [Is. 28:29] **92:6** f Ps. 73:22 **92:7** g Job 12:6 **92:8** h [Ps. 83:18] **92:9** i Ps. 68:1 **92:10** j Ps. 89:17 k Ps. 23:5 **92:11** l Ps. 54:7

12 *m*The righteous shall flourish like a
palm tree,
He shall grow like a cedar in Lebanon.
13 Those who are planted in the house of
the LORD
Shall flourish in the courts of our God.
14 They shall still bear fruit in old age;
They shall be fresh and flourishing,
15 To declare that the LORD is upright;
*n*He is my rock, and *o*there is no
unrighteousness in Him.

Psalm 93

The Eternal Reign of the LORD

1 The *a*LORD reigns, He is clothed with
majesty;
The LORD is clothed,
*b*He has girded Himself with strength.
Surely the world is established, so that
it cannot be moved.
2 *c*Your throne *is* established from of old;
You *are* from everlasting.

3 The floods have lifted up, O LORD,
The floods have lifted up their voice;
The floods lift up their waves.
4 *d*The LORD on high *is* mightier
Than the noise of many waters,
Than the mighty waves of the sea.

5 Your testimonies are very sure;
Holiness adorns Your house,
O LORD, forever.

Psalm 94

God the Refuge of the Righteous

1 O LORD God, *a*to whom vengeance
belongs—
O God, to whom vengeance belongs,
shine forth!
2 Rise up, O *b*Judge of the earth;

Render punishment to the proud.
3 LORD, *c*how long will the wicked,
How long will the wicked triumph?

4 They *d*utter speech, *and* speak insolent
things;
All the workers of iniquity boast in
themselves.
5 They break in pieces Your people,
O LORD,
And afflict Your heritage.
6 They slay the widow and the stranger,
And murder the fatherless.
7 *e*Yet they say, "The LORD does not see,
Nor does the God of Jacob
understand."

8 Understand, you senseless among the
people;
And *you* fools, when will you be wise?
9 *f*He who planted the ear, shall He not
hear?
He who formed the eye, shall He not
see?
10 He who instructs the nations, shall He
not correct,
He who teaches man knowledge?
11 The LORD *g*knows the thoughts of
man,
That they *are* futile.

12 Blessed *is* the man whom You
*h*instruct, O LORD,
And teach out of Your law,
13 That You may give him rest from the
days of adversity,
Until the pit is dug for the wicked.
14 For the LORD will not cast off His
people,
Nor will He forsake His inheritance.
15 But judgment will return to
righteousness,
And all the upright in heart will
follow it.

16 Who will rise up for me against the
evildoers?
Who will stand up for me against the
workers of iniquity?

92:12 flourish like a palm tree. This promise does
not refer to success as the world counts it—the righteous are not often wealthy or powerful—but rather
to spiritual success. Those who are committed to
following God's ways will be so alive spiritually that
even in old age they will appear young and vibrant.
93:1 is clothed with majesty. This language
describes the victor of one-on-one combat. God is
dressed in the garments of victory.
93:4 The LORD on high is mightier. The Creator King
is infinite in power; no force in the universe competes
with Him.
94:2 Judge of the earth. Even when the poets call
out for divine vengeance, they recognize that God
decides when to exercise His wrath and judgment.
God's law clearly states that vengeance belongs to
Him (Deut. 32:35).
94:6 slay the widow and the stranger. The Israelites had been commanded to comfort widows
and orphans and to welcome strangers, as long

as those strangers obeyed the law of God (Ex.
22:21–22).
94:12 Blessed is the man whom You instruct. The
word "blessed" means "happy." Instruction, even if
accompanied by chastening, is always for our ultimate good, and thus shows the depth of God's love
for us (Heb. 12:7–11).
94:13 the pit is dug for the wicked. "Pit" is one of the
words used as a synonym for Sheol (16:10). Digging
the "pit" is a way of describing the preparations for
the final judgment of the wicked (Rev. 20:11–15).
94:14 the LORD will not cast off His people. God will
not forget His people any more than He will forget or
deny Himself (2 Tim. 2:13).

92:12 *m* Ps. 52:8 **92:15** *n* [Deut. 32:4] *o* [Rom. 9:14]
93:1 *a* Ps. 96:10 *b* Ps. 65:6 **93:2** *c* Ps. 45:6 **93:4** *d* Ps.
65:7 **94:1** *a* [Nah. 1:2] **94:2** *b* [Gen. 18:25] **94:3** *c* [Job
20:5] **94:4** *d* Ps. 31:18 **94:7** *e* Ps. 10:11 **94:9** *f* [Ex.
4:11] **94:11** *g* 1 Cor. 3:20 **94:12** *h* [Heb. 12:5, 6]

17 Unless the LORD *had been* my help,
   My soul would soon have settled in
      silence.
18 If I say, "My foot slips,"
   Your mercy, O LORD, will hold me up.
19 In the multitude of my anxieties
      within me,
   Your comforts delight my soul.

20 Shall *i*the throne of iniquity, which
      devises evil by law,
   Have fellowship with You?
21 They gather together against the life of
      the righteous,
   And condemn *j*innocent blood.
22 But the LORD has been my defense,
   And my God the rock of my refuge.
23 He has brought on them their own
      iniquity,
   And shall cut them off in their own
      wickedness;
   The LORD our God shall cut them off.

Psalm 95

A Call to Worship and Obedience

1 Oh come, let us sing to the LORD!
   Let us shout joyfully to the Rock of our
      salvation.
2 Let us come before His presence with
      thanksgiving;
   Let us shout joyfully to Him with
      *a*psalms.
3 For *b*the LORD *is* the great God,
   And the great King above all gods.
4 In His hand *are* the deep places of the
      earth;
   The heights of the hills *are* His also.
5 *c*The sea *is* His, for He made it;
   And His hands formed the dry *land.*

6 Oh come, let us worship and bow
      down;
   Let *d*us kneel before the LORD our
      Maker.

7 For He *is* our God,
   And *e*we *are* the people of His pasture,
   And the sheep of His hand.

   *f*Today, if you will hear His voice:
8 "Do not harden your hearts, as in the
      rebellion,*
   *g*As *in* the day of trial* in the wilderness,
9 When *h*your fathers tested Me;
   They tried Me, though they *i*saw My
      work.
10 *j*For forty years I was grieved with *that*
      generation,
   And said, 'It *is* a people who go astray
      in their hearts,
   And they do not know My ways.'
11 So *k*I swore in My wrath,
   'They shall not enter My rest.'"

Psalm 96

A Song of Praise to God Coming in Judgment

1 Oh, *a*sing to the LORD a new song!
   Sing to the LORD, all the earth.
2 Sing to the LORD, bless His name;
   Proclaim the good news of His
      salvation from day to day.
3 Declare His glory among the nations,
   His wonders among all peoples.

4 For *b*the LORD *is* great and *c*greatly to
      be praised;
   *d*He *is* to be feared above all gods.
5 For *e*all the gods of the peoples *are* idols,
   *f*But the LORD made the heavens.
6 Honor and majesty *are* before Him;
   Strength and *g*beauty *are* in His
      sanctuary.

7 *h*Give to the LORD, O families of the
      peoples,
   Give to the LORD glory and strength.

* **95:8** Or *Meribah* • Or *Massah*

94:18 Your mercy. God's "mercy" or "lovingkindness" refers to His loyal, covenant love.
95:1–7 Let us shout joyfully. Along with others (Ps. 96–100), this song was probably sung at the dedication of the temple after it was restored by Ezra and Nehemiah. It was a time of great celebration. The hearts of the people were filled with joy as they sang and shouted to God, whom they declared to be the great King above all gods.
95:6 worship . . . bow down . . . kneel. These words amplify each other and call for a reflective, humble approach to God. Worship is joyful and can be done with abandon (vv. 1–5); but at other times worship may be quiet reverence of the Almighty (Ps. 134).
95:7–11 For He is our God. This whole section is quoted in Hebrews 3:7–11, with a notable introduction: "Therefore, as the Holy Spirit says . . . ." This phrase reminds us that the words of the Psalms, which are the response of the worshiping Israelite community, are also the oracles of God.

95:8 rebellion. Also translated "Meribah," this word would remind the Israelites of a time when they had doubted the Lord's provision (Ex. 17:7; Num. 20:13).
96:3 all peoples. This is a bold declaration that one day the message of God's mercy will be known the world over, the fulfillment of God's covenant promise to Abraham that through his descendants all nations of the earth would be blessed (Gen. 12:1–3).
96:7 O families of the peoples. The allusion to the Abrahamic covenant continues (vv. 2–3; Gen. 12:1–3).

94:20 *i* Amos 6:3   **94:21** *j* [Ex. 23:7]   **95:2** *a* James 5:13
95:3 *b* [Ps. 96:4]   **95:5** *c* Gen. 1:9, 10   **95:6** *d* [Phil. 2:10]
95:7 *e* Ps. 79:13   *f* Heb. 3:7–11, 15; 4:7   **95:8** *g* Ex. 17:2–7
95:9 *h* Ps. 78:18   *i* Num. 14:22   **95:10** *j* Heb. 3:10, 17
95:11 *k* Heb. 4:3, 5   **96:1** *a* 1 Chr. 16:23–33   **96:4** *b* Ps.
145:3   *c* Ps. 18:3   *d* Ps. 95:3   **96:5** *e* [Jer. 10:11]   *f* Is. 42:5
96:6 *g* Ps. 29:2   **96:7** *h* Ps. 29:1, 2

8 Give to the LORD the glory *due* His
name;
Bring an offering, and come into His
courts.
9 Oh, worship the LORD *i*in the beauty of
holiness!
Tremble before Him, all the earth.
10 Say among the nations, *j*"The LORD
reigns;
The world also is firmly established,
It shall not be moved;
*k*He shall judge the peoples
righteously."
11 *l*Let the heavens rejoice, and let the
earth be glad;
*m*Let the sea roar, and all its fullness;
12 Let the field be joyful, and all that *is*
in it.
Then all the trees of the woods will
rejoice
13 before the LORD.
For He is coming, for He is coming to
judge the earth.
*n*He shall judge the world with
righteousness,
And the peoples with His truth.

5 *f*The mountains melt like wax at the
presence of the LORD,
At the presence of the Lord of the
whole earth.
6 *g*The heavens declare His righteousness,
And all the peoples see His glory.
7 *h*Let all be put to shame who serve
carved images,
Who boast of idols.
*i*Worship Him, all *you* gods.
8 Zion hears and is glad,
And the daughters of Judah rejoice
Because of Your judgments, O LORD.
9 For You, LORD, *are* *j*most high above
all the earth;
*k*You are exalted far above all gods.
10 You who love the LORD, *l*hate evil!
*m*He preserves the souls of His saints;
*n*He delivers them out of the hand of the
wicked.
11 *o*Light is sown for the righteous,
And gladness for the upright in heart.
12 *p*Rejoice in the LORD, you righteous,
*q*And give thanks at the remembrance
of His holy name.*

Psalm 97

A Song of Praise to the
Sovereign LORD

1 The LORD *a*reigns;
Let the earth rejoice;
Let the multitude of isles be glad!
2 *b*Clouds and darkness surround Him;
*c*Righteousness and justice *are* the
foundation of His throne.
3 *d*A fire goes before Him,
And burns up His enemies round
about.
4 *e*His lightnings light the world;
The earth sees and trembles.

Psalm 98

A Song of Praise to the LORD for His
Salvation and Judgment

A Psalm.

1 Oh, *a*sing to the LORD a new song!
For He has *b*done marvelous things;
His right hand and His holy arm have
gained Him the victory.
2 *c*The LORD has made known His
salvation;
*d*His righteousness He has revealed in
the sight of the nations.

---

* 97:12 Or *His holiness*

96:10 The LORD reigns. This key phrase was the countercultural cry of ancient Israelites in a world that believed that gods could rise and fall. In contrast, the living God remains Ruler for all eternity.
96:11–13 Let the heavens rejoice . . . for He is coming. All creation groans under the curse, but when Christ returns, "the creation itself also will be delivered from the bondage of corruption into the glorious liberty of the children of God" (Rom. 8:21).
97:2 Clouds and darkness. These words may be rephrased as "impenetrable clouds," an indicator of the final judgment and God's awesome power (Joel 2:2; Zeph. 1:15).
97:7 Worship Him, all you gods. One day, people will be forced to acknowledge that God is the only one worthy of worship, as they see that the very things they devoted themselves to in rejection of God must bow down to the Creator as Lord.
97:10 hate. The righteousness of God evokes a response either of delight or of shame because of sin (Is. 6:5). The subjects of the kingdom, the lovers of God,

follow Him by loving what He loves and hating what He hates. "The fear of the LORD is to hate evil" (Prov. 8:13). Sin is portrayed in Scripture as an active and powerful force in unrelenting pursuit of its victims (Gen. 4:7; 1 Pet. 5:8), and the believer is called to total war against it.
98:1 His right hand. The "right hand" of the Lord is a way of referring to His great salvation of Israel from Egypt (Ex. 15:6; Deut. 4:34). The phrase is like a slogan for the Lord's redemption.
98:2 revealed in the sight of the nations. God's salvation was designed to be a witness to the nations (Deut. 4:6).

96:9 *i* Ps. 29:2   96:10 *j* Ps. 93:1; 97:1   *k* Ps. 67:4   96:11 *l* Ps. 69:34   *m* Ps. 98:7   96:13 *n* [Rev. 19:11]   97:1 *a* [Ps. 96:10]   97:2 *b* Ps. 18:11   *c* [Ps. 89:14]   97:3 *d* Ps. 18:8   97:4 *e* Ex. 19:18   97:5 *f* Mic. 1:4   97:6 *g* Ps. 19:1   97:7 *h* [Ex. 20:4]   *i* [Heb. 1:6]   97:9 *j* Ps. 83:18   *k* Ex. 18:11   97:10 *l* [Ps. 34:14]   *m* Prov. 2:8   *n* Ps. 37:40   97:11 *o* Job 22:28   97:12 *p* Ps. 33:1   *q* Ps. 30:4   98:1 *a* Is. 42:10   *b* Ex. 15:11   98:2 *c* Is. 52:10   *d* Is. 62:2

3 He has remembered His mercy and
His faithfulness to the house of
Israel;
  eAll the ends of the earth have seen the
salvation of our God.

4 Shout joyfully to the LORD, all the
earth;
Break forth in song, rejoice, and sing
praises.

5 Sing to the LORD with the harp,
With the harp and the sound of a
psalm,

6 With trumpets and the sound of a
horn;
Shout joyfully before the LORD, the
King.

7 Let the sea roar, and all its fullness,
The world and those who dwell in it;

8 Let the rivers clap *their* hands;
Let the hills be joyful together

9 before the LORD.
fFor He is coming to judge the earth.
With righteousness He shall judge the
world,
And the peoples with equity.

Psalm 99

Praise to the LORD for His Holiness

1 The LORD reigns;
Let the peoples tremble!
aHe dwells *between* the cherubim;
Let the earth be moved!

2 The LORD *is* great in Zion,
And He *is* high above all the peoples.

3 Let them praise Your great and
awesome name—
He *is* holy.

4 The King's strength also loves justice;
You have established equity;
You have executed justice and
righteousness in Jacob.

5 Exalt the LORD our God,
And worship at His footstool—
He *is* holy.

6 Moses and Aaron were among His
priests,
And Samuel was among those who
bcalled upon His name;
They called upon the LORD, and He
answered them.

7 He spoke to them in the cloudy pillar;
They kept His testimonies and the
ordinance He gave them.

8 You answered them, O LORD our God;
You were to them God-Who-Forgives,
Though You took vengeance on their
deeds.

9 Exalt the LORD our God,
And worship at His holy hill;
For the LORD our God *is* holy.

Psalm 100

A Song of Praise for the LORD's Faithfulness to His People

aA Psalm of Thanksgiving.

1 Make ba joyful shout to the LORD, all
you lands!

2 Serve the LORD with gladness;
Come before His presence with
singing.

3 Know that the LORD, He *is* God;
cIt is He *who* has made us, and not we
ourselves;*
dWe *are* His people and the sheep of
His pasture.

4 eEnter into His gates with thanksgiving,
And into His courts with praise.
Be thankful to Him, *and* bless His
name.

5 For the LORD *is* good;
fHis mercy *is* everlasting,
And His truth *endures* to all
generations.

---

* **100:3** Following Kethib, Septuagint, and Vulgate;
Qere, many Hebrew manuscripts, and Targum
read *we are His.*

98:9 For He is coming. Creation rejoices at the coming of the Lord because when He establishes His kingdom, the curse will be lifted, and all creation will be freed from its slavery to corruption (Rom. 8:21–22).
99:1 cherubim. Cherubim are the angels most closely related to the glory of God. Two gold cherubim graced the mercy seat of the ark of the covenant (Ex. 25:18–22).
99:3 name . . . He is holy. To be holy is to be "distinct from," "separated," "set apart." This is the principal Hebrew word used to describe the transcendence of God (113:4–6).
99:5 His footstool. The footstool of the Lord is sometimes said to be the earth (Is. 66:1); but more specifically, Zion is the Lord's footstool (132:7; Is. 60:13). When the Israelites came to the temple in Jerusalem to worship, they pictured themselves as being at the feet of the Creator.

100:1 Make a joyful shout. This command is addressed not just to Israel but to all the earth. The Israelites were to be a people who would attract the nations to worship God.
100:3 the LORD, He is God. These words reflect the great confession of faith in Deuteronomy 6:4–9.
100:5 the LORD is good. The shout of the goodness of God in this verse is buttressed by an appeal to His lovingkindness and faithfulness. The Hebrew root for the word for "truth" comes from the word meaning "to be established" or "to be confirmed." From this word also comes the word "amen," meaning "surely" or "truly." God's goodness is based on His loyal love and His truth.

98:3 e Luke 3:6   **98:9** f [Ps. 96:10, 13]   **99:1** a Ex.
25:22   **99:6** b 1 Sam. 7:9; 12:18   **100:title** a Ps. 145:title
100:1 b Ps. 95:1   **100:3** c [Eph. 2:10] d Ezek. 34:30, 31
100:4 e Ps. 66:13; 116:17–19   **100:5** f Ps. 136:1

Psalm 101

Promised Faithfulness to the LORD

A Psalm of David.

1 I will sing of mercy and justice;
To You, O LORD, I will sing praises.

2 I will behave wisely in a perfect way.
Oh, when will You come to me?
I will *a*walk within my house with a
perfect heart.

3 I will set nothing wicked before my
eyes;
*b*I hate the work of those *c*who fall
away;
It shall not cling to me.

4 A perverse heart shall depart from me;
I will not *d*know wickedness.

5 Whoever secretly slanders his neighbor,
Him I will destroy;
*e*The one who has a haughty look and a
proud heart,
Him I will not endure.

6 My eyes *shall be* on the faithful of the
land,
That they may dwell with me;
He who walks in a perfect way,
He shall serve me.

7 He who works deceit shall not dwell
within my house;
He who tells lies shall not continue in
my presence.

8 *f*Early I will destroy all the wicked of
the land,
That I may cut off all the evildoers
*g*from the city of the LORD.

Psalm 102

The LORD's Eternal Love

A Prayer of the afflicted, *a*when he
is overwhelmed and pours out his
complaint before the LORD.

1 Hear my prayer, O LORD,
And let my cry come to You.

2 *b*Do not hide Your face from me in the
day of my trouble;
Incline Your ear to me;
In the day that I call, answer me
speedily.

3 For my days are *c*consumed like smoke,
And my bones are burned like a
hearth.

4 My heart is stricken and withered like
grass,
So that I forget to eat my bread.

5 Because of the sound of my groaning
My bones cling to my skin.

6 I am like a pelican of the wilderness;
I am like an owl of the desert.

7 I lie awake,
And am like a sparrow alone on the
housetop.

8 My enemies reproach me all day long;
Those who deride me swear an oath
against me.

9 For I have eaten ashes like bread,
And mingled my drink with weeping,

10 Because of Your indignation and Your
wrath;
For You have lifted me up and cast me
away.

11 My days *are* like a shadow that
lengthens,
And I wither away like grass.

12 But You, O LORD, shall endure forever,
And the remembrance of Your name to
all generations.

13 You will arise *and* have mercy on
Zion;
For the time to favor her,
Yes, the set time, has come.

14 For Your servants take pleasure in her
stones,
And show favor to her dust.

15 So the nations shall *d*fear the name of
the LORD,
And all the kings of the earth Your
glory.

16 For the LORD shall build up Zion;
*e*He shall appear in His glory.

17 *f*He shall regard the prayer of the
destitute,
And shall not despise their prayer.

18 This will be *g*written for the generation
to come,
That *h*a people yet to be created may
praise the LORD.

19 For He *i*looked down from the height
of His sanctuary;
From heaven the LORD viewed the
earth,

20 *j*To hear the groaning of the prisoner,
To release those appointed to death,

101:1 *mercy and justice.* God's loyal love is coupled with justice. He does not allow sin to go unnoticed or unpunished, either in His children or in those who oppress them.
101:4 *not know wickedness.* The verb "to know" here has the idea of experience or intimate relationship with something or someone.
101:6 *My eyes shall be on the faithful.* David made a covenant with his eyes (Job 31:1) to observe the righteous and sustain them in their walk.
102:12 *endure forever.* Our days may be just a passing shadow, but God is King forever. He is gracious, loves His people, and promises to favor them.
102:15 *the nations shall fear.* A time will come when the Lord will rule over all the earth.

101:2 *a* 1 Kin. 11:4   **101:3** *b* Ps. 97:10   *c* Josh. 23:6
101:4 *d* [Ps. 119:115]   **101:5** *e* Prov. 6:17   **101:8** *f* Jer. 21:12
g Ps. 48:2, 8   **102:title** *a* Ps. 61:2   **102:2** *b* Ps. 27:9; 69:17
102:3 *c* James 4:14   **102:15** *d* 1 Kin. 8:43   **102:16** *e* [Is.
60:1, 2]   **102:17** *f* Neh. 1:6   **102:18** *g* [Rom. 15:4]   *h* Ps.
22:31   **102:19** *i* Deut. 26:15   **102:20** *j* Ps. 79:11

21 To ^{k}declare the name of the LORD in
  Zion,
  And His praise in Jerusalem,
22 ^{l}When the peoples are gathered
    together,
  And the kingdoms, to serve the LORD.
23 He weakened my strength in the
    way;
  He ^{m}shortened my days.
24 ^{n}I said, "O my God,
  Do not take me away in the midst of
    my days;
  ^{o}Your years are throughout all
    generations.
25 ^{p}Of old You laid the foundation of the
    earth,
  And the heavens are the work of Your
    hands.
26 ^{q}They will perish, but You will endure;
  Yes, they will all grow old like a
    garment;
  Like a cloak You will change them,
  And they will be changed.
27 But ^{r}You are the same,
  And Your years will have no end.
28 ^{s}The children of Your servants will
    continue,
  And their descendants will be
    established before You."

Psalm 103

Praise for the LORD's Mercies

A Psalm of David.

1 Bless ^{a}the LORD, O my soul;
  And all that is within me, bless His
    holy name!
2 Bless the LORD, O my soul,
  And forget not all His benefits:
3 ^{b}Who forgives all your iniquities,
  Who ^{c}heals all your diseases,
4 Who redeems your life from
    destruction,
  ^{d}Who crowns you with lovingkindness
    and tender mercies,

5 Who satisfies your mouth with good
    things,
  So that ^{e}your youth is renewed like
    the eagle's.
6 The LORD executes righteousness
  And justice for all who are oppressed.
7 ^{f}He made known His ways to Moses,
  His acts to the children of Israel.
8 ^{g}The LORD is merciful and gracious,
  Slow to anger, and abounding in
    mercy.
9 ^{h}He will not always strive with us,
  Nor will He keep His anger forever.
10 ^{i}He has not dealt with us according to
    our sins,
  Nor punished us according to our
    iniquities.
11 For as the heavens are high above the
    earth,
  So great is His mercy toward those
    who fear Him;
12 As far as the east is from the west,
  So far has He ^{j}removed our
    transgressions from us.
13 ^{k}As a father pities his children,
  So the LORD pities those who fear Him.
14 For He knows our frame;
  He remembers that we are dust.
15 As for man, ^{l}his days are like grass;
  As a flower of the field, so he flourishes.
16 ^{m}For the wind passes over it, and it is
    gone,
  And ^{n}its place remembers it no more.*
17 But the mercy of the LORD is from
    everlasting to everlasting
  On those who fear Him,
  And His righteousness to children's
    children,
18 ^{o}To such as keep His covenant,
  And to those who remember His
    commandments to do them.
19 The LORD has established His throne
    in heaven,
  And ^{p}His kingdom rules over all.

---

* **103:16** Compare Job 7:10

102:25 Of old. God is eternal and His works are from ancient times. The writer of the Book of Hebrews applies these words of creation and eternality to the Son (vv. 25–27; Heb. 1:10 12).
103:1 Bless the LORD. To bless the Lord is to remember that He is the source of all our blessings. The psalmist blesses the Lord with his entire being (146:2).
103:3 heals all your diseases. This cannot be seen as a promise that the godly will never suffer from disease. Many believers have suffered and died of illnesses, despite repeated prayers for healing. Even though He does not always choose to heal, God is the source of all healing. This verse could also be seen as a parallel construction, coupling pardon from iniquity with healing from the disease of sin.
103:8 merciful and gracious. This is a basic description of God in the Old Testament (86:15; Ex. 34:6–7). If

God dealt with us according to our sins, no one could stand before Him (130:3).
103:11 as the heavens are high above the earth. There is no way to compare the divine with the mortal; the mercy of God is greater than the heavens.
103:17 the mercy of the LORD. God's loyal love is forever.

102:21 ^{k}Ps. 22:22 **102:22** ^{l}[Is. 2:2, 3; 49:22, 23; 60:3] **102:23** ^{m}Job 21:21 **102:24** ^{n}Is. 38:10 ^{o}[Ps. 90:2] **102:25** ^{p}[Heb. 1:10–12] **102:26** ^{q}Is. 34:4; 51:6 **102:27** ^{r}[Mal. 3:6] **102:28** ^{s}Ps. 69:36 **103:1** ^{a}Ps. 104:1, 35 **103:3** ^{b}Ps. 130:8 ^{c}[Ex. 15:26] **103:4** ^{d}[Ps. 5:12] **103:5** ^{e}[Is. 40:31] **103:7** ^{f}Ps. 147:19 **103:8** ^{g}[Ex. 34:6, 7] **103:9** ^{h}[Ps. 30:5] **103:10** ^{i}[Ezra 9:13] **103:12** ^{j}[Is. 38:17; 43:25] **103:13** ^{k}Mal. 3:17 **103:15** ^{l}1 Pet. 1:24 **103:16** ^{m}[Is. 40:7] ^{n}Job 7:10 **103:18** ^{o}[Deut. 7:9] **103:19** ^{p}[Dan. 4:17, 25]

20 ᵃBless the LORD, you His angels,
  Who excel in strength, who ʳdo His
    word,
  Heeding the voice of His word.
21 Bless the LORD, all you His hosts,
  ˢYou ministers of His, who do His
    pleasure.
22 Bless the LORD, all His works,
  In all places of His dominion.

  Bless the LORD, O my soul!

Psalm 104

Praise to the Sovereign LORD for His Creation and Providence

1 Bless ᵃthe LORD, O my soul!

  O LORD my God, You are very great:
  You are clothed with honor and
    majesty,
2 Who cover *Yourself* with light as *with*
    a garment,
  Who stretch out the heavens like a
    curtain.

3 ᵇHe lays the beams of His upper
    chambers in the waters,
  Who makes the clouds His chariot,
  Who walks on the wings of the wind,
4 Who makes His angels spirits,
  His ministers a flame of fire.

5 *You who* laid the foundations of the
    earth,
  So *that* it should not be moved forever,
6 You ᶜcovered it with the deep as *with* a
    garment;
  The waters stood above the
    mountains.
7 At Your rebuke they fled;
  At the voice of Your thunder they
    hastened away.
8 They went up over the mountains;
  They went down into the valleys,
  To the place which You founded for
    them.

9 You have ᵈset a boundary that they
    may not pass over,
  ᵉThat they may not return to cover the
    earth.

10 He sends the springs into the valleys;
  They flow among the hills.
11 They give drink to every beast of the
    field;
  The wild donkeys quench their thirst.
12 By them the birds of the heavens have
    their home;
  They sing among the branches.
13 ᶠHe waters the hills from His upper
    chambers;
  The earth is satisfied with ᵍthe fruit of
    Your works.

14 ʰHe causes the grass to grow for the
    cattle,
  And vegetation for the service of man,
  That he may bring forth ᶦfood from the
    earth,
15 And ʲwine *that* makes glad the heart
    of man,
  Oil to make *his* face shine,
  And bread *which* strengthens man's
    heart.
16 The trees of the LORD are full *of sap*,
  The cedars of Lebanon which He
    planted,
17 Where the birds make their nests;
  The stork has her home in the fir trees.
18 The high hills *are* for the wild goats;
  The cliffs are a refuge for the ᵏrock
    badgers.*
19 ˡHe appointed the moon for seasons;
  The ᵐsun knows its going down.
20 ⁿYou make darkness, and it is night,
  In which all the beasts of the forest
    creep about.
21 ᵒThe young lions roar after their prey,
  And seek their food from God.
22 *When* the sun rises, they gather
    together
  And lie down in their dens.
23 Man goes out to ᵖhis work
  And to his labor until the evening.

* **104:18** Or *rock hyrax* (compare Leviticus 11:5)

103:20–22 Bless the LORD. The poet began the psalm with a call to his own inner being to respond with praise to God (v. 1); he concludes the psalm with a call to heaven and earth to join him.
104:2 cover Yourself with light. God is Spirit (John 4:24), and descriptions of Him vary throughout the Bible. One strong description of Him is "light" (1 John 1:5). Here, light is described as the garment that enfolds His wonder. The first act of God in Genesis was the command for light (Gen. 1:3).
104:5 laid the foundations of the earth. The poet retells the story of creation from Genesis 1.
104:6 covered it with the deep. The term "deep" is the same word used in Genesis 1:2.
104:9 set a boundary. God promised that never again would the entire earth be covered as in the flood (Gen. 8:21–22).
104:15 wine . . . Oil . . . bread. It is clear that the earth

was created for human beings and filled with good things for our sake.
104:19 He appointed the moon for seasons. In the ancient world, the heavenly bodies (sun, moon, and stars) were often worshiped as gods. God makes it clear that, far from being objects of worship, these things were created and set in place specifically for humans. The moon is not our god but our servant, set in place to keep track of times and seasons.

103:20 ᵍ Ps. 148:2 ʳ [Matt. 6:10] **103:21** ˢ [Heb. 1:14]
104:1 ᵃ Ps. 103:1 **104:3** ᵇ [Amos 9:6] **104:6** ᶜ Gen.
1:6 **104:9** ᵈ [Jer. 5:22] ᵉ Gen. 9:11–15 **104:13** ᶠ Ps.
147:8 ᵍ Jer. 10:13 **104:14** ʰ Gen. 1:29 ᶦ Job 28:5
104:15 ʲ Judg. 9:13 **104:18** ᵏ Lev. 11:5 **104:19** ˡ Gen.
1:14 ᵐ Ps. 19:6 **104:20** ⁿ [Is. 45:7] **104:21** ᵒ Job 38:39
104:23 ᵖ Gen. 3:19

24 ^qO Lord, how manifold are Your works!
   In wisdom You have made them all.
   The earth is full of Your ^rpossessions—
25 This great and wide sea,
   In which *are* innumerable teeming
      things,
   Living things both small and great.
26 There the ships sail about;
   There is that ^sLeviathan
   Which You have made to play there.

27 ^tThese all wait for You,
   That You may give *them* their food in
      due season.
28 *What* You give them they gather in;
   You open Your hand, they are filled
      with good.
29 You hide Your face, they are troubled;
   ^uYou take away their breath, they die
      and return to their dust.
30 ^vYou send forth Your Spirit, they are
      created;
   And You renew the face of the earth.

31 May the glory of the Lord endure
      forever;
   May the Lord ^wrejoice in His works.
32 He looks on the earth, and it ^xtrembles;
   ^yHe touches the hills, and they smoke.

33 ^zI will sing to the Lord as long as I live;
   I will sing praise to my God while I
      have my being.
34 May my ^ameditation be sweet to Him;
   I will be glad in the Lord.
35 May ^bsinners be consumed from the
      earth,
   And the wicked be no more.

   Bless the Lord, O my soul!
   Praise the Lord!

Psalm 105

The Eternal Faithfulness of the Lord

1 Oh, ^agive thanks to the Lord!
   Call upon His name;

^bMake known His deeds among the
      peoples!
2 Sing to Him, sing psalms to Him;
   ^cTalk of all His wondrous works!
3 Glory in His holy name;
   Let the hearts of those rejoice who
      seek the Lord!
4 Seek the Lord and His strength;
   ^dSeek His face evermore!
5 ^eRemember His marvelous works
      which He has done,
   His wonders, and the judgments of His
      mouth,
6 O seed of Abraham His servant,
   You children of Jacob, His chosen
      ones!

7 He *is* the Lord our God;
   ^fHis judgments *are* in all the earth.
8 He ^gremembers His covenant forever,
   The word *which* He commanded, for a
      thousand generations,
9 ^h*The covenant* which He made with
      Abraham,
   And His oath to Isaac,
10 And confirmed it to Jacob for a statute,
   To Israel *as* an everlasting covenant,
11 Saying, ⁱ"To you I will give the land of
      Canaan
   As the allotment of your inheritance,"
12 ^jWhen they were few in number,
   Indeed very few, ^kand strangers in it.
13 When they went from one nation to
      another,
   From *one* kingdom to another people,
14 ^lHe permitted no one to do them
      wrong;
   Yes, ^mHe rebuked kings for their sakes,
15 *Saying*, "Do not touch My anointed
      ones,
   And do My prophets no harm."

16 Moreover ⁿHe called for a famine in
      the land;
   He destroyed all the ^oprovision of
      bread.
17 ^pHe sent a man before them—
   Joseph—*who* ^qwas sold as a slave.

104:27 *These all wait for You.* All creation depends on the Creator for birth, life, and sustenance. Even death is controlled by the Sovereign One.
104:31 *May the Lord rejoice in His works.* The Lord considered His creation "good" from the beginning (Gen. 1:31), and His pleasure in it remains (Prov. 8:30–31).
105:5 *Remember His marvelous works.* The psalmist calls to memory what God did for His people in fulfillment of the covenant with Abraham (Gen. 12:1–3; 22:16–18).
105:8 *He remembers.* The words of the original promise to Abraham set out the Lord's obligation in strong terms (Gen. 12:1–3).
105:13–15 *went . . . rebuked kings for their sakes.* The descendants of Abraham have more than once been strangers in a foreign land, but each time the Lord has preserved their identity as a people and has rescued them from destruction. He saved them from

the hand of Pharaoh (Exodus), and from the Persians (Esther). Today, the Jews are again scattered, but even though many have forgotten their God, they still do not forget that they are Jews. God's miraculous preservation of the identity of His people indicates that He is not yet finished with them.
105:17 *Joseph.* The story of Joseph's life is told in Genesis 37–50.

104:24 ^q Prov. 3:19 ^r Ps. 65:9 **104:26** ^s Job 41:1
104:27 ^t Ps. 136:25 **104:29** ^u Job 34:15 **104:30** ^v Is. 32:15 **104:31** ^w Gen. 1:31 **104:32** ^x Hab. 3:10
^y Ps. 144:5 **104:33** ^z Ps. 63:4 **104:34** ^a Ps. 19:14
104:35 ^b Ps. 37:38 **105:1** ^a Is. 12:4 ^b Ps. 145:12
105:2 ^c Ps. 119:27 **105:4** ^d Ps. 27:8 **105:5** ^e Ps. 77:11
105:7 ^f [Is. 26:9] **105:8** ^g Luke 1:72 **105:9** ^h Gen. 17:2
105:11 ⁱ Gen. 13:15; 15:18 **105:12** ^j [Deut. 7:7] ^k Heb. 11:9 **105:14** ^l Gen. 35:5 ^m Gen. 12:17 **105:16** ⁿ Gen. 41:54 ^o Lev. 26:26 **105:17** ^p [Gen. 45:5] ^q Gen. 37:28, 36

18 [r]They hurt his feet with fetters,
He was laid in irons.
19 Until the time that his word came to pass,
[s]The word of the LORD tested him.
20 [t]The king sent and released him,
The ruler of the people let him go free.
21 [u]He made him lord of his house,
And ruler of all his possessions,
22 To bind his princes at his pleasure,
And teach his elders wisdom.

23 [v]Israel also came into Egypt,
And Jacob dwelt [w]in the land of Ham.
24 [x]He increased His people greatly,
And made them stronger than their enemies.
25 [y]He turned their heart to hate His people,
To deal craftily with His servants.

26 [z]He sent Moses His servant,
And Aaron whom He had chosen.
27 They [a]performed His signs among them,
And wonders in the land of Ham.
28 He sent darkness, and made *it* dark;
And they did not rebel against His word.
29 [b]He turned their waters into blood,
And killed their fish.
30 [c]Their land abounded with frogs,
Even in the chambers of their kings.
31 [d]He spoke, and there came swarms of flies,
And lice in all their territory.
32 [e]He gave them hail for rain,
And flaming fire in their land.
33 [f]He struck their vines also, and their fig trees,
And splintered the trees of their territory.
34 [g]He spoke, and locusts came,
Young locusts without number,
35 And ate up all the vegetation in their land,
And devoured the fruit of their ground.
36 [h]He also destroyed all the firstborn in their land,
[i]The first of all their strength.

37 [j]He also brought them out with silver and gold,
And *there was* none feeble among His tribes.
38 [k]Egypt was glad when they departed,
For the fear of them had fallen upon them.
39 [l]He spread a cloud for a covering,
And fire to give light in the night.
40 [m]*The people* asked, and He brought quail,
And [n]satisfied them with the bread of heaven.
41 [o]He opened the rock, and water gushed out;
It ran in the dry places *like* a river.

42 For He remembered [p]His holy promise,
And Abraham His servant.
43 He brought out His people with joy,
His chosen ones with gladness.
44 [q]He gave them the lands of the Gentiles,
And they inherited the labor of the nations,
45 [r]That they might observe His statutes
And keep His laws.

Praise the LORD!

Psalm 106

Joy in Forgiveness of Israel's Sins

1 Praise the LORD!

[a]Oh, give thanks to the LORD, for *He is* good!
For His mercy *endures* forever.
2 Who can utter the mighty acts of the LORD?
Who can declare all His praise?
3 Blessed *are* those who keep justice,
And he who [b]does* righteousness at [c]all times!

4 [d]Remember me, O LORD, with the favor
You have toward Your people.
Oh, visit me with Your salvation,
5 That I may see the benefit of Your chosen ones,
That I may rejoice in the gladness of Your nation,
That I may glory with Your inheritance.

6 [e]We have sinned with our fathers,
We have committed iniquity,
We have done wickedly.

* **106:3** Septuagint, Syriac, Targum, and Vulgate read *those who do*.

105:26–36 *He sent Moses.* The full story of the Israelites' slavery in Egypt and the plagues God sent upon the Egyptians is told in Exodus 1–11.
105:44 *gave them the lands of the Gentiles.* It is believed that this psalm may have been composed after the return from exile in Babylon. A celebration of God's gift of land would have been a tremendous source of encouragement to the people who had just returned to Israel.
106:6 *sinned with our fathers.* It is easy to point out the places where people have gone wrong in the past and to marvel at their stupidity and rebellion, but we have to point the finger at ourselves as well.

105:18 [r]Gen. 40:15 **105:19** [s]Gen. 39:11–21; 41:25, 42, 43 **105:20** [t]Gen. 41:14 **105:21** [u]Gen. 41:40–44 **105:23** [v]Gen. 46:6 [w]Ps. 78:51 **105:24** [x]Ex. 1:7, 9 **105:25** [y]Ex. 1:8–10; 4:21 **105:26** [z]Ex. 3:10; 4:12–15 **105:27** [a]Ps. 78:43 **105:29** [b]Ex. 7:20, 21 **105:30** [c]Ex. 8:6 **105:31** [d]Ex. 8:16, 17 **105:32** [e]Ex. 9:23–25 **105:33** [f]Ps. 78:47 **105:34** [g]Ex. 10:4 **105:36** [h]Ex. 12:29; 13:15 [i]Gen. 49:3 **105:37** [j]Ex. 12:35, 36 **105:38** [k]Ex. 12:33 **105:39** [l]Ex. 13:21 **105:40** [m]Ex. 16:12 [n]Ps. 78:24 **105:41** [o]Ex. 17:6 **105:42** [p]Gen. 15:13, 14 **105:44** [q]Josh. 11:16–23; 13:7 **105:45** [r][Deut. 4:1, 40] **106:1** [a]1 Chr. 16:34, 41 **106:3** [b]Ps. 15:2 [c][Gal. 6:9] **106:4** [d]Ps. 119:132 **106:6** [e][Dan. 9:5]

7 Our fathers in Egypt did not
understand Your wonders;
They did not remember the multitude
of Your mercies,
fBut rebelled by the sea—the Red Sea.

8 Nevertheless He saved them for His
name's sake,
gThat He might make His mighty
power known.

9 hHe rebuked the Red Sea also, and it
dried up;
So iHe led them through the depths,
As through the wilderness.

10 He jsaved them from the hand of him
who hated them,
And redeemed them from the hand of
the enemy.

11 kThe waters covered their enemies;
There was not one of them left.

12 lThen they believed His words;
They sang His praise.

13 mThey soon forgot His works;
They did not wait for His counsel,

14 nBut lusted exceedingly in the
wilderness,
And tested God in the desert.

15 oAnd He gave them their request,
But psent leanness into their soul.

16 When qthey envied Moses in the camp,
And Aaron the saint of the LORD,

17 rThe earth opened up and swallowed
Dathan,
And covered the faction of Abiram.

18 sA fire was kindled in their company;
The flame burned up the wicked.

19 tThey made a calf in Horeb,
And worshiped the molded image.

20 Thus uthey changed their glory
Into the image of an ox that eats
grass.

21 They forgot God their Savior,
Who had done great things in Egypt,

22 Wondrous works in the land of Ham,
Awesome things by the Red Sea.

23 vTherefore He said that He would
destroy them,
Had not Moses His chosen one wstood
before Him in the breach,
To turn away His wrath, lest He
destroy them.

24 Then they despised xthe pleasant
land;
They ydid not believe His word,

25 zBut complained in their tents,
And did not heed the voice of the
LORD.

26 aTherefore He raised His hand in an
oath against them,
bTo overthrow them in the wilderness,

27 cTo overthrow their descendants
among the nations,
And to scatter them in the lands.

28 dThey joined themselves also to Baal of
Peor,
And ate sacrifices made to the dead.

29 Thus they provoked Him to anger with
their deeds,
And the plague broke out among
them.

30 eThen Phinehas stood up and
intervened,
And the plague was stopped.

31 And that was accounted to him ffor
righteousness
To all generations forevermore.

32 gThey angered Him also at the waters
of strife,*
hSo that it went ill with Moses on
account of them;

33 iBecause they rebelled against His
Spirit,
So that he spoke rashly with his lips.

---

* 106:32 Or Meribah

106:12 Then they believed. The people had faith-
lessly rebelled, but God graciously rescued them
anyway, proving that His word is true and worth
believing.
106:13 They soon forgot. Faith which is only active
in the face of abundant proof is weak and short-lived.
106:15 He gave them their request. When the people rebelliously kept asking for their own desires, God
finally let them have their own way—and also let
them take the consequences. We don't have to fear
that we might accidentally pray for something wrong
and then receive a bad gift from the Lord. Even when
we pray wrongly, if our hearts are turned towards
God, He will redirect our desires and teach us the
better way (37:4). However, it is sin if we keep praying
for something when we already know that He said
no, and we may have to bear consequences that we
never dreamed of.
106:20 changed their glory. These words are
echoed by Paul in Romans 1:22–23.
106:24–25 They did not believe. The Old Testament
books of Exodus and Joshua illustrate God's plan of
salvation. The first relates how Israel was brought

out of the land of bondage, and the second describes
how they were brought into the land of blessing. The
wilderness route they traveled was of His choosing,
but not the aimless wandering which followed. That
sad 40-year episode was a direct result of their sin of
unbelief.
106:28 Baal of Peor. After Balaam was prevented
from cursing the Israelites, he suggested that the
Moabites could destroy the Israelites in another way,
by leading them into sin against their God (Num. 25).

106:7 f Ex. 14:11, 12   **106:8** g Ex. 9:16   **106:9** h Ex.
14:21   i Is. 63:11–13   **106:10** j Ex. 14:30   **106:11** k Ex.
14:27, 28; 15:5   **106:12** l Ex. 15:1–21   **106:13** m Ex.
15:24; 16:2; 17:2   **106:14** n 1 Cor. 10:6   **106:15** o Num.
11:31   p Is. 10:16   **106:16** q Num. 16:1–3   **106:17** r Deut.
11:6   **106:18** s Num. 16:35, 46   **106:19** t Ex. 32:1–4
106:20 u Rom. 1:23   **106:23** v Ex. 32:10   w Ezek. 22:30
106:24 x Deut. 8:7   y [Heb. 3:18, 19]   **106:25** z Num.
14:2, 27   **106:26** a Ezek. 20:15, 16   b Num. 14:28–30
106:27 c Lev. 26:33   **106:28** d Hos. 9:10   **106:30** e Num.
25:7, 8   **106:31** f Num. 25:11–13   **106:32** g Num.
20:3–13   h Deut. 1:37; 3:26   **106:33** i Num. 20:3, 10

34 [j]They did not destroy the peoples,
[k]Concerning whom the LORD had commanded them,
35 [l]But they mingled with the Gentiles
And learned their works;
36 [m]They served their idols,
[n]Which became a snare to them.
37 [o]They even sacrificed their sons
And their daughters to [p]demons,
38 And shed innocent blood,
The blood of their sons and daughters,
Whom they sacrificed to the idols of Canaan;
And [q]the land was polluted with blood.
39 Thus they were [r]defiled by their own works,
And [s]played the harlot by their own deeds.

40 Therefore [t]the wrath of the LORD was kindled against His people,
So that He abhorred [u]His own inheritance.
41 And [v]He gave them into the hand of the Gentiles,
And those who hated them ruled over them.
42 Their enemies also oppressed them,
And they were brought into subjection under their hand.
43 [w]Many times He delivered them;
But they rebelled in their counsel,
And were brought low for their iniquity.

44 Nevertheless He regarded their affliction,
When [x]He heard their cry;
45 [y]And for their sake He remembered His covenant,
And [z]relented [a]according to the multitude of His mercies.
46 [b]He also made them to be pitied
By all those who carried them away captive.

47 [c]Save us, O LORD our God,
And gather us from among the Gentiles,
To give thanks to Your holy name,
To triumph in Your praise.

48 [d]Blessed *be* the LORD God of Israel
From everlasting to everlasting!
And let all the people say, "Amen!"

Praise the LORD!

BOOK FIVE

Psalms 107–150

Psalm 107

Thanksgiving to the LORD for His Great Works of Deliverance

1 Oh, [a]give thanks to the LORD, for *He is* good!
For His mercy *endures* forever.
2 Let the redeemed of the LORD say *so*,
Whom He has redeemed from the hand of the enemy,
3 And [b]gathered out of the lands,
From the east and from the west,
From the north and from the south.

4 They wandered in [c]the wilderness in a desolate way;
They found no city to dwell in.
5 Hungry and thirsty,
Their soul fainted in them.
6 [d]Then they cried out to the LORD in their trouble,
And He delivered them out of their distresses.
7 And He led them forth by the [e]right way,
That they might go to a city for a dwelling place.
8 [f]Oh, that *men* would give thanks to the LORD *for* His goodness,
And *for* His wonderful works to the children of men!
9 For [g]He satisfies the longing soul,
And fills the hungry soul with goodness.

10 Those who [h]sat in darkness and in the shadow of death,
[i]Bound in affliction and irons—
11 Because they [j]rebelled against the words of God,
And despised [k]the counsel of the Most High,
12 Therefore He brought down their heart with labor;
They fell down, and *there was* [l]none to help.

106:34 *destroy the peoples.* If Israel had obeyed and the Canaanites had been driven out, the people might never have succumbed to the idolatry that marked their existence for hundreds of years.
106:45 *He remembered His covenant.* God's wrath must always be seen in the context of His loyal love and His long forbearance. Even when the people brought down His wrath by their sins, He remained faithful to the covenant.
107:1 *His mercy endures forever.* God's "loyal love" or "mercies" will never end. He is always willing to restore those who call on Him.
107:9 *He satisfies the longing soul.* Only God can fulfill the spiritual longings of the human soul.

106:34 [j] Judg. 1:21 [k] [Deut. 7:2, 16] **106:35** [l] Judg. 3:5, 6 **106:36** [m] Judg. 2:12 [n] Deut. 7:16 **106:37** [o] 2 Kin. 16:3; 17:17 [p] [Lev. 17:7] **106:38** [q] [Num. 35:33] **106:39** [r] Ezek. 20:18 [s] [Lev. 17:7] **106:40** [t] Judg. 2:14 [u] [Deut. 9:29; 32:9] **106:41** [v] Judg. 2:14 **106:43** [w] Judg. 2:16 **106:44** [x] Judg. 3:9; 6:7; 10:10 **106:45** [y] [Lev. 26:41, 42] [z] Judg. 2:18 [a] Ps. 69:16 **106:46** [b] Ezra 9:9 **106:47** [c] 1 Chr. 16:35, 36 **106:48** [d] Ps. 41:13 **107:1** [a] Ps. 106:1 **107:3** [b] Is. 43:5, 6 **107:4** [c] [Deut. 2:7; 32:10] **107:6** [d] Ps. 50:15 **107:7** [e] Ezra 8:21 **107:8** [f] Ps. 107:15, 21 **107:9** [g] [Ps. 34:10] **107:10** [h] [Luke 1:79] [i] Job 36:8 **107:11** [j] Lam. 3:42 [k] [Ps. 73:24] **107:12** [l] Ps. 22:11

13 Then they cried out to the LORD in
their trouble,
And He saved them out of their
distresses.
14 mHe brought them out of darkness and
the shadow of death,
And broke their chains in pieces.
15 Oh, that *men* would give thanks to the
LORD *for* His goodness,
And *for* His wonderful works to the
children of men!
16 For He has nbroken the gates of bronze,
And cut the bars of iron in two.
17 Fools, obecause of their transgression,
And because of their iniquities, were
afflicted.
18 pTheir soul abhorred all manner of food,
And they qdrew near to the gates of
death.
19 Then they cried out to the LORD in
their trouble,
And He saved them out of their
distresses.
20 rHe sent His word and shealed them,
And tdelivered *them* from their
destructions.
21 Oh, that *men* would give thanks to the
LORD *for* His goodness,
And *for* His wonderful works to the
children of men!
22 uLet them sacrifice the sacrifices of
thanksgiving,
And vdeclare His works with rejoicing.

23 Those who go down to the sea in ships,
Who do business on great waters,
24 They see the works of the LORD,
And His wonders in the deep.
25 For He commands and wraises the
stormy wind,
Which lifts up the waves of the sea.
26 They mount up to the heavens,
They go down again to the depths;
xTheir soul melts because of trouble.
27 They reel to and fro, and stagger like a
drunken man,
And are at their wits' end.
28 Then they cry out to the LORD in their
trouble,
And He brings them out of their
distresses.
29 yHe calms the storm,
So that its waves are still.
30 Then they are glad because they are
quiet;

So He guides them to their desired
haven.
31 zOh, that *men* would give thanks to the
LORD *for* His goodness,
And *for* His wonderful works to the
children of men!
32 Let them exalt Him also ain the
assembly of the people,
And praise Him in the company of the
elders.
33 He bturns rivers into a wilderness,
And the watersprings into dry ground;
34 A cfruitful land into barrenness,
For the wickedness of those who dwell
in it.
35 dHe turns a wilderness into pools of
water,
And dry land into watersprings.
36 There He makes the hungry dwell,
That they may establish a city for a
dwelling place,
37 And sow fields and plant vineyards,
That they may yield a fruitful harvest.
38 eHe also blesses them, and they
multiply greatly;
And He does not let their cattle
fdecrease.
39 When they are gdiminished and
brought low
Through oppression, affliction, and
sorrow,
40 hHe pours contempt on princes,
And causes them to wander in the
wilderness *where there is* no way;
41 iYet He sets the poor on high, far from
affliction,
And jmakes *their* families like a flock.
42 kThe righteous see *it* and rejoice,
And all liniquity stops its mouth.
43 mWhoever *is* wise will observe these
things,
And they will understand the
lovingkindness of the LORD.

Psalm 108

Assurance of God's Victory
over Enemies

A Song. A Psalm of David.

1 O aGod, my heart is steadfast;
I will sing and give praise, even with
my glory.

107:17 *Fools.* This harsh word emphasizes moral failure (Prov. 1:7; 15:5). These people deserved the trouble they suffered, yet they too may call upon the Lord, and He will deliver and restore them.
107:33 *He turns rivers into a wilderness.* During the reign of King Ahab of the northern kingdom of Israel, God sentenced the land to three years of drought because of their Baal worship (1 Kin. 17:1–7).
107:43 *Whoever is wise.* There is no wisdom apart from centering in on and responding to the love of God. The psalmist exhorts the readers to review God's history of delivering those in trouble and to praise His great love.

108:title *A Song.* This psalm is actually a medley of two other psalms of David. Verses 1–5 are from

107:14 m Ps. 68:6   **107:16** n Is. 45:1, 2   **107:17** o Lam. 3:39   **107:18** p Job 33:20   q Job 33:22   **107:20** r Matt. 8:8   s Ps. 30:2   t Job 33:28, 30   **107:22** u Lev. 7:12   v Ps. 9:11   **107:25** w Jon. 1:4   **107:26** x Ps. 22:14   **107:29** y Ps. 89:9   **107:31** z Ps. 107:8, 15, 21   **107:32** a Ps. 22:22, 25   **107:33** b 1 Kin. 17:1, 7   **107:34** c Gen. 13:10   **107:35** d Ps. 114:8   **107:38** e Gen. 12:2; 17:16, 20   f [Deut. 7:14]   **107:39** g 2 Kin. 10:32   **107:40** h Job 12:21, 24   **107:41** i 1 Sam. 2:8   j Ps. 78:52   **107:42** k Job 5:15, 16   l [Rom. 3:19]   **107:43** m Jer. 9:12   **108:1** a Ps. 57:7–11

2 *b*Awake, lute and harp!
I will awaken the dawn.
3 I will praise You, O LORD, among the
peoples,
And I will sing praises to You among
the nations.
4 For Your mercy *is* great above the
heavens,
And Your truth *reaches* to the clouds.

5 *c*Be exalted, O God, above the heavens,
And Your glory above all the earth;
6 *d*That Your beloved may be delivered,
Save *with* Your right hand, and
hear me.

7 God has spoken in His holiness:
"I will rejoice;
I will divide Shechem
And measure out the Valley of
Succoth.
8 Gilead *is* Mine; Manasseh *is* Mine;
Ephraim also *is* the helmet for My
head;
*e*Judah *is* My lawgiver.
9 Moab *is* My washpot;
Over Edom I will cast My shoe;
Over Philistia I will triumph."

10 *f*Who will bring me *into* the strong
city?
Who will lead me to Edom?
11 *Is* it not *You,* O God, *who* cast us off?
And *You,* O God, *who* did not go out
with our armies?
12 Give us help from trouble,
For the help of man is useless.
13 *g*Through God we will do valiantly,
For *it is* He *who* shall tread down our
enemies.*

Psalm 109

Plea for Judgment of False Accusers

To the Chief Musician. A Psalm
of David.

1 Do*a* not keep silent,
O God of my praise!

2 For the mouth of the wicked and the
mouth of the deceitful
Have opened against me;
They have spoken against me with a
*b*lying tongue.
3 They have also surrounded me with
words of hatred,
And fought against me *c*without a
cause.
4 In return for my love they are my
accusers,
But I *give myself to* prayer.
5 Thus *d*they have rewarded me evil for
good,
And hatred for my love.

6 Set a wicked man over him,
And let *e*an accuser* stand at his right
hand.
7 When he is judged, let him be found
guilty,
And *f*let his prayer become sin.
8 Let his days be *g*few,
And *h*let another take his office.
9 *i*Let his children be fatherless,
And his wife a widow.
10 Let his children continually be
vagabonds, and beg;
Let them seek *their bread** also from
their desolate places.
11 *j*Let the creditor seize all that he has,
And let strangers plunder his labor.
12 Let there be none to extend mercy to
him,
Nor let there be any to favor his
fatherless children.
13 *k*Let his posterity be cut off,
And in the generation following let
their *l*name be blotted out.

14 *m*Let the iniquity of his fathers be
remembered before the LORD,
And let not the sin of his mother *n*be
blotted out.
15 Let them be continually before the
LORD,

---

* **108:13** Compare verses 6–13 with 60:5–12
* **109:6** Hebrew *satan*   * **109:10** Following Masoretic Text and Targum; Septuagint and Vulgate read *be cast out.*

57:7–11, and verses 6–13 are from 60:5–12. David is the author of both of these psalms, and 108 is attributed to him as well, even though the arrangement may have been someone else's.
108:7 I will rejoice. The remarkable fact about these words is that they are spoken by God. The Lord has pleasure in delivering His people and giving them victory. He celebrates His deliverance of them.
109:8 let another take his office. These words (along with 69:25) are quoted in Acts 1:20 as having been fulfilled in the replacement of Judas Iscariot.
109:9 fatherless . . . a widow. The curses that the psalmist wants to call down on his enemies seem very harsh and unforgiving. It is hard to understand how we should take this kind of language, in the face of Christ's teaching about loving our enemies and doing good to those who hurt us. However, two important

points are clear: the psalmist left vengeance in the hands of the Lord, and he also clearly understood the reality of wickedness. We must remember that forgiveness is not saying, "It wasn't really bad." True forgiveness does not pretend that sin did not happen; it recognizes evil, and then releases the desire for vengeance into God's hands. God has promised that He will judge the wicked in the end.

108:2 *b* Ps. 57:8–11   **108:5** *c* Ps. 57:5, 11   **108:6** *d* Ps. 60:5–12   **108:8** *e* [Gen. 49:10]   **108:10** *f* Ps. 60:9   **108:13** *g* Ps. 60:12   **109:1** *a* Ps. 83:1   **109:2** *b* Ps. 27:12   **109:3** *c* John 15:25   **109:5** *d* Ps. 35:7, 12; 38:20   **109:6** *e* Zech. 3:1   **109:7** *f* [Prov. 28:9]   **109:8** *g* [Ps. 55:23]   *h* Acts 1:20   **109:9** *i* Ex. 22:24   **109:11** *j* Job 5:5; 18:9   **109:13** *k* Job 18:19   *l* Prov. 10:7   **109:14** *m* [Ex. 20:5]   *n* Neh. 4:5

That He may [o]cut off the memory of
them from the earth;
16 Because he did not remember to show
mercy,
But persecuted the poor and needy
man,
That he might even slay the [p]broken
in heart.
17 [q]As he loved cursing, so let it come to
him;
As he did not delight in blessing, so let
it be far from him.
18 As he clothed himself with cursing as
with his garment,
So let it [r]enter his body like water,
And like oil into his bones.
19 Let it be to him like the garment which
covers him,
And for a belt with which he girds
himself continually.
20 *Let* this *be* the LORD's reward to my
accusers,
And to those who speak evil against
my person.

21 But You, O GOD the Lord,
Deal with me for Your name's sake;
Because Your mercy *is* good,
deliver me.
22 For I *am* poor and needy,
And my heart is wounded within me.
23 I am gone [s]like a shadow when it
lengthens;
I am shaken off like a locust.
24 My [t]knees are weak through fasting,
And my flesh is feeble from lack of
fatness.
25 I also have become [u]a reproach to
them;
When they look at me, [v]they shake
their heads.

26 Help me, O LORD my God!
Oh, save me according to Your mercy,
27 [w]That they may know that this *is* Your
hand—
That You, LORD, have done it!
28 [x]Let them curse, but You bless;
When they arise, let them be
ashamed,
But let [y]Your servant rejoice.
29 [z]Let my accusers be clothed with
shame,
And let them cover themselves with
their own disgrace as with a
mantle.

30 I will greatly praise the LORD with my
mouth;
Yes, [a]I will praise Him among the
multitude.
31 For [b]He shall stand at the right hand of
the poor,
To save *him* from those who condemn
him.

Psalm 110

Announcement of the Messiah's Reign

A Psalm of David.

1 The [a]LORD said to my Lord,
"Sit at My right hand,
Till I make Your enemies Your
[b]footstool."
2 The LORD shall send the rod of Your
strength [c]out of Zion.
[d]Rule in the midst of Your enemies!

3 [e]Your people *shall be* volunteers
In the day of Your power;
[f]In the beauties of holiness, from the
womb of the morning,
You have the dew of Your youth.
4 The LORD has sworn
And [g]will not relent,
"You *are* a [h]priest forever
According to the order of
[i]Melchizedek."

109:27 *That they may know.* Even in the psalmist's intense emotional state, he wants to see the name of God defended, proclaimed, and honored.

110:1 *The LORD.* "LORD" is the translation of the Hebrew name Yahweh (I AM) and refers to God the Father. According to Jesus' interpretation of the passage (Matt. 22:41–45; Mark 12:35–37; Luke 20:41–44), the second "Lord" is a reference to the Son of God in heaven in the presence of the Father. David himself confesses the Son to be his Lord—that is, his master or sovereign. ***at My right hand.*** This position of high honor beside the Father was given to the Savior upon His resurrection and ascension (Acts 2:33–36; 1 Cor. 15:20–28; Col. 3:1; Heb. 1:13). The Savior placing His feet on His foes depicts the utter defeat of the enemies of Christ (1 Cor. 15:25–26; Eph. 1:22–23).

110:3 *In the beauties of holiness.* This description of the people who join the King in His great battle fits with Revelation 19:14.

110:4 *a priest.* God is seen appointing the coming Messiah to be a priest (Heb. 7). This was a source of confusion for Jews, as demonstrated by the questions that the New Testament Jews had about the Messiah. Some Dead Sea Scrolls give evidence that more than one Messiah was anticipated. According to Scripture, the Messiah would be a descendant of David (Is. 9:7), but this prophecy presents Him as a priest. This might seem to be a contradiction because true priests had to be descendants of Aaron, but the Messiah is presented as a priest by divine declaration rather than human descent. ***Melchizedek.*** Melchizedek is first mentioned in Genesis 14:18–20. He was a true priest of the Most High God, unrelated to Abraham and living hundreds of years before Aaron. He became a

109:15 [o] Job 18:17 **109:16** [p] [Ps. 34:18] **109:17** [q] Prov. 14:14 **109:18** [r] Num. 5:22 **109:23** [s] Ps. 102:11 **109:24** [t] Heb. 12:12 **109:25** [u] Ps. 22:7 [v] Matt. 27:39 **109:27** [w] Job 37:7 **109:28** [x] 2 Sam. 6:11, 12 [y] Is. 65:14 **109:29** [z] Ps. 35:26 **109:30** [a] Ps. 35:18; 111:1 **109:31** [b] [Ps. 16:8] **110:1** [a] Matt. 22:44 [b] [1 Cor. 15:25] **110:2** [c] [Rom. 11:26, 27] [d] [Dan. 7:13, 14] **110:3** [e] Judg. 5:2 [f] Ps. 96:9 **110:4** [g] [Num. 23:19] [h] [Zech. 6:13] [i] [Heb. 5:6, 10; 6:20]

5 The Lord *is* [i]at Your right hand;
He shall execute kings [k]in the day of
His wrath.
6 He shall judge among the nations,
He shall fill *the places* with dead
bodies,
[l]He shall execute the heads of many
countries.
7 He shall drink of the brook by the
wayside;
[m]Therefore He shall lift up the head.

Psalm 111

Praise to God for His Faithfulness and Justice

1 Praise the LORD!

[a]I will praise the LORD with *my* whole
heart,
In the assembly of the upright and *in*
the congregation.

2 [b]The works of the LORD *are* great,
[c]Studied by all who have pleasure in
them.
3 His work *is* [d]honorable and glorious,
And His righteousness endures
forever.
4 He has made His wonderful works to
be remembered;
[e]The LORD *is* gracious and full of
compassion.
5 He has given food to those who fear
Him;
He will ever be mindful of His
covenant.
6 He has declared to His people the
power of His works,
In giving them the heritage of the
nations.
7 The works of His hands *are* [f]verity and
justice;
All His precepts *are* sure.
8 [g]They stand fast forever and ever,
And are [h]done in truth and
uprightness.
9 [i]He has sent redemption to His people;

He has commanded His covenant
forever:
[j]Holy and awesome *is* His name.

10 [k]The fear of the LORD *is* the beginning
of wisdom;
A good understanding have all those
who do *His commandments.*
His praise endures forever.

Psalm 112

The Blessed State of the Righteous

1 Praise the LORD!

Blessed *is* the man *who* fears the
LORD,
Who [a]delights greatly in His
commandments.
2 [b]His descendants will be mighty on
earth;
The generation of the upright will be
blessed.
3 [c]Wealth and riches *will be* in his house,
And his righteousness endures
forever.
4 [d]Unto the upright there arises light in
the darkness;
He is gracious, and full of compassion,
and righteous.
5 [e]A good man deals graciously and
lends;
He will guide his affairs [f]with
discretion.
6 Surely he will never be shaken;
[g]The righteous will be in everlasting
remembrance.
7 [h]He will not be afraid of evil tidings;
His heart is steadfast, trusting in the
LORD.
8 His [i]heart *is* established;
[j]He will not be afraid,
Until he [k]sees *his desire* upon his
enemies.
9 He has dispersed abroad,
He has given to the poor;
His righteousness endures forever;
His horn will be exalted with honor.

---

prototype of the Messiah, whose priesthood was not based on connection with the line of Aaron but was by divine decree (Heb. 5:5–11; 6:20; 7:1–28).
111:1 *Praise the LORD.* This translates the Hebrew word *hallelujah.*
111:9 *redemption.* The psalmists constantly look back to the Exodus, but they also speak of that which was still to come—the redemption of mankind through the Messiah.
111:10 *fear of the LORD.* The fear of the Lord describes an obedient response of wonder and awe before the Most High God.
112:1 *Praise the LORD.* Like Psalm 111, this psalm begins with the Hebrew word "hallelujah." It then picks up where Psalm 111 left off. ***Blessed.*** This word, meaning "manifestly happy," is the same word which begins the Book of Psalms.

112:2 *His descendants will be mighty.* Compare the blessings of this psalm with the curses placed on the wicked in 109:6–13.
112:9 *given to the poor.* The gracious and compassionate nature of God is also seen in His people, especially in their acts of benevolence toward the poor. The poor are the materially destitute and

110:5 [i] [Ps. 16:8] [k] Ps. 2:5, 12 **110:6** [l] Ps. 68:21 **110:7** [m] [Is. 53:12] **111:1** [a] Ps. 35:18 **111:2** [b] Ps. 92:5 [c] Ps. 143:5 **111:3** [d] Ps. 145:4, 5 **111:4** [e] [Ps. 86:5] **111:7** [f] [Rev. 15:3] **111:8** [g] Is. 40:8 [h] [Rev. 15:3] **111:9** [i] Luke 1:68 [j] Luke 1:49 **111:10** [k] Eccl. 12:13 **112:1** [a] Ps. 128:1 **112:2** [b] [Ps. 102:28] **112:3** [c] [Matt. 6:33] **112:4** [d] Job 11:17 **112:5** [e] [Luke 6:35] [f] [Eph. 5:15] **112:6** [g] Prov. 10:7 **112:7** [h] [Prov. 1:33] **112:8** [i] Heb. 13:9 [j] Prov. 1:33; 3:24 [k] Ps. 59:10

10 The wicked will see *it* and be
grieved;
He will gnash his teeth and melt
away;
The desire of the wicked shall
perish.

Psalm 113

The Majesty and Condescension of God

1 Praise the LORD!

   ᵃPraise, O servants of the LORD,
   Praise the name of the LORD!
2 ᵇBlessed be the name of the LORD
   From this time forth and forevermore!
3 ᶜFrom the rising of the sun to its going
   down
   The LORD's name *is* to be praised.

4 The LORD *is* ᵈhigh above all nations,
   ᵉHis glory above the heavens.
5 ᶠWho *is* like the LORD our God,
   Who dwells on high,
6 ᵍWho humbles Himself to behold
   The things that are in the heavens and
   in the earth?

7 ʰHe raises the poor out of the dust,
   And lifts the ⁱneedy out of the ash
   heap,
8 That He may ʲseat *him* with
   princes—
   With the princes of His people.
9 ᵏHe grants the barren woman a home,
   Like a joyful mother of children.

   Praise the LORD!

Psalm 114

The Power of God in His Deliverance of Israel

1 When ᵃIsrael went out of Egypt,
   The house of Jacob ᵇfrom a people of
   strange language,
2 ᶜJudah became His sanctuary,
   And Israel His dominion.

3 ᵈThe sea saw *it* and fled;
   ᵉJordan turned back.
4 ᶠThe mountains skipped like rams,
   The little hills like lambs.
5 ᵍWhat ails you, O sea, that you
   fled?
   O Jordan, *that* you turned back?
6 O mountains, *that* you skipped like
   rams?
   O little hills, like lambs?

7 Tremble, O earth, at the presence of
   the Lord,
   At the presence of the God of
   Jacob,
8 ʰWho turned the rock *into* a pool of
   water,
   The flint into a fountain of waters.

Psalm 115

The Futility of Idols and the Trustworthiness of God

1 Not ᵃunto us, O LORD, not unto us,
   But to Your name give glory,
   Because of Your mercy,
   Because of Your truth.

---

helpless segments of society—widows, orphans, and aliens—whose rights are more easily violated. Scripture tells us that giving to the poor is lending to the Lord and will be repaid by the Lord (Prov. 19:17). To give freely to the poor literally means "to scatter" God's gifts, which suggests that the poor will be provided for and that abundance will come to the giver as well (2 Cor. 9:8–9). **His horn.** The horn is a symbol of power. When used for a righteous person, it speaks of prominence and a lasting sense of worth in his or her life.

113:1 *Praise the LORD.* This psalm of descriptive praise begins and ends with the Hebrew word "hallelujah." This psalm, along with Psalm 114, is traditionally read before the Passover meal.

113:2 *the name of the LORD.* In biblical times there was a close association between a person's name and identity. Praising the name of God centers one's thoughts on His character.

113:4 *high above all nations.* Unlike the manmade gods of the ancient Middle East, the Lord is not limited to a certain tribe or territory. Not only is He supreme over all nations, but His glory cannot be contained in the universe.

113:6 *humbles Himself.* God is not some far distant deity who set the world in motion and then went about His business. Instead, He is deeply involved

in the lives of the people He created and loves us so much that He came down from His high position to save us (Phil. 2:5–9).

113:9 *barren woman.* In that time and culture, a barren woman was without significance and without joy. The joy of a barren woman who has been given children is a picture of the joy we receive when God stoops down to touch us.

114:1 *out of Egypt.* This psalm recalling the salvation of Israel from Egypt is traditionally read along with Psalm 113 before the Passover meal.

114:2 *Judah became His sanctuary.* This verse anticipates the New Testament sense of God living among His people (Ezek. 37:26–27; 2 Cor. 6:16–18).

115:1 *to Your name give glory.* This community psalm of praise focuses on the glory of the Lord in the salvation of His people. It is one of the Passover psalms (115–118; 136), traditionally read or sung after the Passover meal.

113:1 ᵃPs. 135:1   113:2 ᵇ[Dan. 2:20]   113:3 ᶜIs.
59:19   113:4 ᵈPs. 97:9; 99:2 ᵉ[Ps. 8:1]   113:5 ᶠ[Is.
57:15]   113:6 ᵍ[Ps. 11:4]   113:7 ʰ1 Sam. 2:8 ⁱPs. 72:12
113:8 ʲ[Job 36:7]   113:9 ᵏ1 Sam. 2:5   114:1 ᵃEx.
12:51; 13:3 ᵇPs. 81:5   114:2 ᶜEx. 6:7; 19:6; 25:8; 29:45,
46   114:3 ᵈEx. 14:21 ᵉJosh. 3:13–16   114:4 ᶠPs. 29:6
114:5 ᵍHab. 3:8   114:8 ʰEx. 17:6   115:1 ᵃ[Is. 48:11]

2 Why should the Gentiles say,
b"So where *is* their God?"

3 cBut our God *is* in heaven;
He does whatever He pleases.
4 dTheir idols *are* silver and gold,
The work of men's hands.
5 They have mouths, but they do not
speak;
Eyes they have, but they do not see;
6 They have ears, but they do not hear;
Noses they have, but they do not
smell;
7 They have hands, but they do not
handle;
Feet they have, but they do not walk;
Nor do they mutter through their
throat.
8 eThose who make them are like them;
So is everyone who trusts in them.

9 fO Israel, trust in the LORD;
gHe *is* their help and their shield.
10 O house of Aaron, trust in the LORD;
He *is* their help and their shield.
11 You who fear the LORD, trust in the
LORD;
He *is* their help and their shield.

12 The LORD has been mindful of *us;*
He will bless *us;*
He will bless the house of Israel;
He will bless the house of Aaron.
13 hHe will bless those who fear the LORD,
Both small and great.

14 May the LORD give you increase more
and more,
You and your children.
15 *May* you *be* iblessed by the LORD,
jWho made heaven and earth.

16 The heaven, *even* the heavens, *are* the
LORD's;
But the earth He has given to the
children of men.
17 kThe dead do not praise the LORD,
Nor any who go down into silence.
18 lBut we will bless the LORD
From this time forth and
forevermore.

Praise the LORD!

Psalm 116

Thanksgiving for Deliverance from Death

1 I alove the LORD, because He has
heard
My voice *and* my supplications.
2 Because He has inclined His ear
to me,
Therefore I will call *upon Him* as long
as I live.

3 bThe pains of death surrounded me,
And the pangs of Sheol laid hold of
me;
I found trouble and sorrow.
4 Then I called upon the name of the
LORD:
"O LORD, I implore You, deliver my
soul!"

5 cGracious *is* the LORD, and drighteous;
Yes, our God *is* merciful.
6 The LORD preserves the simple;
I was brought low, and He saved me.
7 Return to your erest, O my soul,
For fthe LORD has dealt bountifully
with you.

8 gFor You have delivered my soul from
death,
My eyes from tears,
And my feet from falling.
9 I will walk before the LORD
hIn the land of the living.
10 iI believed, therefore I spoke,
"I am greatly afflicted."
11 jI said in my haste,
k"All men *are* liars."

12 What shall I render to the LORD
For all His benefits toward me?
13 I will take up the cup of salvation,
And call upon the name of the
LORD.
14 lI will pay my vows to the LORD
Now in the presence of all His
people.

15 mPrecious in the sight of the LORD
Is the death of His saints.

115:4–8 idols. Like the prophets (Is. 40:18–20; Jer. 10:1–10), the psalms are derisive toward the idols of the nations.
115:18 Praise the LORD. Many of the Passover psalms (115–117) conclude with the Hebrew word "hallelujah."
116:1 I love the LORD. This messianic psalm is one of the Passover psalms (113–118). It was probably recited by Jesus on the night of His arrest, the night He celebrated the Passover with His disciples (Luke 22:15).
116:3 pains of death. These words point prophetically to the Savior's anguish on the cross (Matt. 27:27–35).
116:10 I believed, therefore I spoke. This belief is the hope of eternal life articulated in verse 9. Paul quotes this verse (translated "I believed, and

therefore I spoke") as proof of the scriptural hope of the resurrection (2 Cor. 4:13).
116:13 the cup of salvation. This psalm is traditionally read after the Passover meal, following the third cup of wine, called the cup of salvation. How appropriate that this Passover psalm would call to mind God's cup of salvation the very night that the Savior was betrayed (Matt. 26:27; Luke 22:14–22).

115:2 b Ps. 42:3, 10   **115:3** c [1 Chr. 16:26]   **115:4** d Jer. 10:3   **115:8** e Is. 44:9–11   **115:9** f Ps. 118:2, 3   g Ps. 33:20   **115:13** h Ps. 128:1, 4   **115:15** i [Gen. 14:19]   j Gen. 1:1   **115:17** k [Is. 38:18]   **115:18** l Dan. 2:20   **116:1** a Ps. 18:1   **116:3** b Ps. 18:4–6   **116:5** c [Ps. 103:8]   d [Ezra 9:15]   **116:7** e [Jer. 6:16]   f Ps. 13:6   **116:8** g Ps. 56:13   **116:9** h Ps. 27:13   **116:10** i 2 Cor. 4:13   **116:11** j Ps. 31:22   k Rom. 3:4   **116:14** l Ps. 116:18   **116:15** m Ps. 72:14

16 O LORD, truly ⁿI *am* Your servant;
  I *am* Your servant, ᵒthe son of Your
      maidservant;
  You have loosed my bonds.
17 I will offer to You ᵖthe sacrifice of
      thanksgiving,
  And will call upon the name of the
      LORD.
18 I will pay my vows to the LORD
  Now in the presence of all His
      people,
19 In the ᑫcourts of the LORD's house,
  In the midst of you, O Jerusalem.

  Praise the LORD!

Psalm 117

Let All Peoples Praise the LORD

1 Praise ᵃthe LORD, all you Gentiles!
  Laud Him, all you peoples!
2 For His merciful kindness is great
      toward us,
  And ᵇthe truth of the LORD *endures*
      forever.

  Praise the LORD!

Psalm 118

Praise to God for His Everlasting Mercy

1 Oh, ᵃgive thanks to the LORD, for *He is*
      good!
  ᵇFor His mercy *endures* forever.

2 ᶜLet Israel now say,
  "His mercy *endures* forever."
3 Let the house of Aaron now say,
  "His mercy *endures* forever."
4 Let those who fear the LORD now
      say,
  "His mercy *endures* forever."

5 ᵈI called on the LORD in distress;
  The LORD answered me *and* ᵉset *me* in
      a broad place.

6 ᶠThe LORD *is* on my side;
  I will not fear.
  What can man do to me?
7 ᵍThe LORD is for me among those who
      help me;
  Therefore ʰI shall see *my desire* on
      those who hate me.
8 ⁱ*It is* better to trust in the LORD
  Than to put confidence in man.
9 ʲ*It is* better to trust in the LORD
  Than to put confidence in princes.
10 All nations surrounded me,
  But in the name of the LORD I will
      destroy them.
11 They ᵏsurrounded me,
  Yes, they surrounded me;
  But in the name of the LORD I will
      destroy them.
12 They surrounded me ˡlike bees;
  They were quenched ᵐlike a fire of
      thorns;
  For in the name of the LORD I will
      destroy them.
13 You pushed me violently, that I might
      fall,
  But the LORD helped me.
14 ⁿThe LORD *is* my strength and
      song,
  And He has become my salvation.*
15 The voice of rejoicing and
      salvation
  Is in the tents of the righteous;
  The right hand of the LORD does
      valiantly.
16 ᵒThe right hand of the LORD is
      exalted;
  The right hand of the LORD does
      valiantly.
17 ᵖI shall not die, but live,
  And ᑫdeclare the works of the
      LORD.
18 The LORD has ʳchastened me
      severely,
  But He has not given me over to
      death.
19 ˢOpen to me the gates of
      righteousness;

---

* **118:14** Compare Exodus 15:2

118:1 *give thanks.* This is the climax of the group of psalms called the Passover psalms. These psalms were probably sung by Jesus on the night before His death. **118:2 *His mercy endures forever.*** This refrain praises God's loyal, merciful, covenant love throughout the psalm.
118:9 *put confidence in princes.* Although relying on other people is part of living, our ultimate trust can only be placed in the Lord God. Even powerful rulers are limited by their own mortality (146:3).
118:13 *the LORD helped me.* Compare this to Paul's words in 2 Timothy 4:17–18. Deliverance always comes from God.
118:14 *my strength and song.* These words are a quotation from "the Song of Moses" (Ex. 15:2); they are also quoted in Isaiah 12:2. The God who delivered

the Israelites by dividing the waters of the Red Sea was ready to deliver the psalmist from trouble.
118:19 *Open to me the gates of righteousness.* The poet draws on the wording and imagery of Psalm 24. There is only One who can enter the gates of the Lord of His own accord—Jesus, the perfect King of glory.

116:16 ⁿPs. 119:125; 143:12 ᵒPs. 86:16   **116:17** ᵖLev. 7:12   **116:19** ᑫPs. 96:8   **117:1** ᵃRom. 15:11   **117:2** ᵇ[Ps. 100:5]   **118:1** ᵃ1 Chr. 16:8, 34   ᵇ[Ps. 136:1–26]   **118:2** ᶜ[Ps. 115:9]   **118:5** ᵈPs. 120:1   ᵉPs. 18:19   **118:6** ᶠPs. 27:1; 56:9   **118:7** ᵍPs. 54:4   ʰPs. 59:10   **118:8** ⁱPs. 40:4   **118:9** ʲPs. 146:3   **118:11** ᵏPs. 88:17   **118:12** ˡDeut. 1:44   ᵐNah. 1:10   **118:14** ⁿIs. 12:2   **118:16** ᵒEx. 15:6   **118:17** ᵖHab. 1:12   ᑫPs. 73:28   **118:18** ʳ2 Cor. 6:9   **118:19** ˢIs. 26:2

I will go through them,
And I will praise the LORD.
20 *t*This is the gate of the LORD,
*u*Through which the righteous shall
enter.

21 I will praise You,
For You have *v*answered me,
And have become my salvation.

22 *w*The stone *which* the builders
rejected
Has become the chief cornerstone.
23 This was the LORD's doing;
It *is* marvelous in our eyes.
24 This *is* the day the LORD has made;
We will rejoice and be glad in it.

25 Save now, I pray, O LORD;
O LORD, I pray, send now
prosperity.
26 *x*Blessed *is* he who comes in the name
of the LORD!
We have blessed you from the house of
the LORD.
27 God *is* the LORD,
And He has given us *y*light;
Bind the sacrifice with cords to the
horns of the altar.
28 You *are* my God, and I will praise
You;
*z*You *are* my God, I will exalt You.

29 Oh, give thanks to the LORD, for *He is*
good!
For His mercy *endures* forever.

Psalm 119

Meditations on the Excellencies of the Word of God

א ALEPH
1 Blessed *are* the undefiled in the way,
*a*Who walk in the law of the LORD!
2 Blessed *are* those who keep His
testimonies,
Who seek Him with the *b*whole heart!
3 *c*They also do no iniquity;
They walk in His ways.
4 You have commanded *us*
To keep Your precepts diligently.
5 Oh, that my ways were directed
To keep Your statutes!
6 *d*Then I would not be ashamed,
When I look into all Your
commandments.
7 I will praise You with uprightness of
heart,
When I learn Your righteous
judgments.
8 I will keep Your statutes;
Oh, do not forsake me utterly!

ב BETH
9 How can a young man cleanse his
way?
By taking heed according to Your
word.

118:20 *gate of the LORD.* The literal reference may be to the gate of Jerusalem, the city of God—or even to a gate of the temple. Jesus declared that He was the gate or door leading to salvation (John 10:9).

118:22 *the chief cornerstone.* The potent imagery of this verse depicts Jesus' rejection by many (Is. 53:3; Mark 8:31; Luke 9:22; 17:25). Jesus elaborated on this prophetic verse with the parable of the vineyard owner. In this parable, the rejection included the murder of the owner's son—a reference to God's only Son (Mark 12:1–12). But, even though the Savior was rejected, He was elevated to the right hand of God (Acts 7:56). The cross, the symbol of Jesus' rejection, has become the symbol of our salvation (1 Cor. 1:18; Heb. 12:2).

118:25 *Save now.* These words are familiar to us in the transliteration of the Hebrew word "hosanna." The words are so significant that, if the people had not shouted them aloud (Matt. 21:16) when Jesus entered Jerusalem, the stones would have had to shout them (Luke 19:40).

118:26 *Blessed is he who comes.* These are the very words that the people used to bless Jesus as He rode into Jerusalem the week before the Passover (Matt. 21:9; Mark 11:9; Luke 19:38).

119:1 *Blessed are the undefiled.* This very lengthy poem is an acrostic. For each of the 22 consonants in the Hebrew alphabet, there are eight verses beginning with that letter. Within the psalm, eight words for God's law occur again and again: law, testimonies, promise, precepts, statutes, judgments, word. These words elaborate the application of the law of God to daily life and to Israel's destiny.

the law of the LORD. The Hebrew word *torah*, translated "law," basically means "instruction" or "direction." Broadly, it refers to all God's instructions from Moses to the prophets. More strictly, it refers to the first five books of the Old Testament. The law was never designed as a means of salvation; no one could be saved by keeping it. Instead, the law was the means for the Israelites to learn how to live as God's holy people. The psalmists consistently describe the law of God as a great blessing, for it was God's gracious revelation to His people for their own good (Deut. 6:1–3). In the law, God mercifully pointed out the right path to follow. Only mistaken legalistic interpretations of the law prompted the negative statements in the New Testament.

119:9–11 *Your word.* The Lord designs that His Word should bring purity (v. 9), security (v. 23), freedom (v. 45), hope (v. 49), life (v. 50), light (v. 105), and peace (v. 165).

119:9 God's Word Cleanses—One of the pieces of furniture in the Old Testament tabernacle was called the bronze laver (Ex. 38:8). It was a huge upright bronze bowl filled with water, resting upon a pedestal. The priests would often stop at this laver to perform their ritualistic cleansings. The Word of God is like this laver. Only the Word can remove the

118:20 *t* Ps. 24:7 *u* Is. 35:8 118:21 *v* Ps. 116:1 118:22 *w* Matt. 21:42 118:26 *x* Mark 11:9 118:27 *y* [1 Pet. 2:9] 118:28 *z* Is. 25:1 119:1 *a* Ps. 128:1 119:2 *b* Deut. 6:5; 10:12; 11:13; 13:3 119:3 *c* [1 John 3:9; 5:18] 119:6 *d* Job 22:26

10 With my whole heart I have *e*sought
    You;
  Oh, let me not wander from Your
    commandments!
11 *f*Your word I have hidden in my
    heart,
  That I might not sin against You.
12 Blessed *are* You, O LORD!
  Teach me Your statutes.
13 With my lips I have *g*declared
  All the judgments of Your mouth.
14 I have rejoiced in the way of Your
    testimonies,
  As *much as* in all riches.
15 I will meditate on Your precepts,
  And contemplate Your ways.
16 I will *h*delight myself in Your
    statutes;
  I will not forget Your word.

ג GIMEL

17 *i*Deal bountifully with Your servant,
  That I may live and keep Your word.
18 Open my eyes, that I may see
  Wondrous things from Your law.
19 *j*I *am* a stranger in the earth;
  Do not hide Your commandments
    from me.
20 *k*My soul breaks with longing
  For Your judgments at all times.
21 You rebuke the proud—the cursed,
  Who stray from Your
    commandments.
22 *l*Remove from me reproach and
    contempt,
  For I have kept Your testimonies.
23 Princes also sit *and* speak against
    me,
  But Your servant meditates on Your
    statutes.
24 Your testimonies also *are* my
    delight
  And my counselors.

ד DALETH

25 *m*My soul clings to the dust;
  *n*Revive me according to Your word.
26 I have declared my ways, and You
    answered me;
  *o*Teach me Your statutes.
27 Make me understand the way of Your
    precepts;
  So *p*shall I meditate on Your
    wonderful works.
28 *q*My soul melts from heaviness;
  Strengthen me according to Your
    word.
29 Remove from me the way of lying,
  And grant me Your law graciously.
30 I have chosen the way of truth;
  Your judgments I have laid
    before me.
31 I cling to Your testimonies;
  O LORD, do not put me to shame!
32 I will run the course of Your
    commandments,
  For You shall *r*enlarge my heart.

ה HE

33 *s*Teach me, O LORD, the way of Your
    statutes,
  And I shall keep it *to* the end.
34 *t*Give me understanding, and I shall
    keep Your law;
  Indeed, I shall observe it with *my*
    whole heart.
35 Make me walk in the path of Your
    commandments,
  For I delight in it.
36 Incline my heart to Your testimonies,
  And not to *u*covetousness.
37 *v*Turn away my eyes from *w*looking at
    worthless things,
  And revive me in Your way.*

* **119:37** Following Masoretic Text, Septuagint, and Vulgate; Targum reads *Your words.*

---

filth and dirt from our hearts (1 Pet. 1:22) just as the bronze laver removed the physical impurities from the priests.

How can the Bible cleanse us? It can cleanse us from wrong thoughts (Ps. 19:12; 51:10; Phil. 4:8–9). It can help eliminate fear (Judg. 1:9). It can cleanse us from wrong actions (1 John 1:9). Jesus directly promises all this: "You are already clean because of the word which I have spoken to you" (John 15:3).

119:11 Memorizing Scripture—The Bible recognizes the importance of Scripture memorization. By memorizing the Word, we have access to it no matter where we are or what our circumstances. The following benefits can be cited:

• It keeps us from sinning (Ps. 119:11).
• It provides comfort in times of trouble (Ps. 119:52,92).
• It provides daily sustenance for the spiritual life (Deut. 8:3).
• It provides continual and ready guidance in all the situations of life (Prov. 6:20–23).
• It provides the basis for formal and informal instruction of children (Deut. 6:6–7).

119:16 statutes. The Hebrew word translated "statutes" refers to something marked out as a boundary, something inscribed or engraved. Hence the word speaks of the permanence of the law, which God Himself had engraved in stone (Ex. 24:12). The same word is often translated "decree" (2:7).

119:22 testimonies. The Hebrew word translated "testimonies" is derived from the verb meaning "to witness" or "to testify." It refers to the Ten Commandments, called the "two tablets of the Testimony" (Ex. 31:18). The commandments were a testimony because they were a witness to the Israelites of their faithfulness or unfaithfulness to the covenant (Deut. 31:26).

119:37 Your way. The will of God is like a path leading to life; His ways are a reflection of His good character.

119:10 *e* 2 Chr. 15:15 **119:11** *f* Luke 2:19 **119:13** *g* Ps. 34:11 **119:16** *h* Ps. 1:2 **119:17** *i* Ps. 116:7 **119:19** *j* Heb. 11:13 **119:20** *k* Ps. 42:1, 2; 63:1; 84:2 **119:22** *l* Ps. 39:8 **119:25** *m* Ps. 44:25 *n* Ps. 143:11 **119:26** *o* Ps. 25:4; 27:11; 86:11 **119:27** *p* Ps. 145:5, 6 **119:28** *q* Ps. 107:26 **119:32** *r* Is. 60:5 **119:33** *s* [Rev. 2:26] **119:34** *t* [Prov. 2:6] **119:36** *u* Ezek. 33:31 **119:37** *v* Is. 33:15 *w* Prov. 23:5

38 ˣEstablish Your word to Your servant,
Who *is devoted* to fearing You.
39 Turn away my reproach which I
dread,
For Your judgments *are* good.
40 Behold, I long for Your precepts;
Revive me in Your righteousness.

ו WAW

41 Let Your mercies come also to me,
O LORD—
Your salvation according to Your
word.
42 So shall I have an answer for him
who reproaches me,
For I trust in Your word.
43 And take not the word of truth
utterly out of my mouth,
For I have hoped in Your ordinances.
44 So shall I keep Your law continually,
Forever and ever.
45 And I will walk at ʸliberty,
For I seek Your precepts.
46 ᶻI will speak of Your testimonies also
before kings,
And will not be ashamed.
47 And I will delight myself in Your
commandments,
Which I love.
48 My hands also I will lift up to Your
commandments,
Which I love,
And I will meditate on Your statutes.

ז ZAYIN

49 Remember the word to Your servant,
Upon which You have caused me to
hope.
50 This *is* my ᵃcomfort in my affliction,
For Your word has given me life.
51 The proud have me in great derision,
Yet I do not turn aside from Your law.
52 I remembered Your judgments of old,
O LORD,
And have comforted myself.
53 ᵇIndignation has taken hold of me
Because of the wicked, who forsake
Your law.
54 Your statutes have been my songs
In the house of my pilgrimage.
55 ᶜI remember Your name in the night,
O LORD,
And I keep Your law.
56 This has become mine,
Because I kept Your precepts.

ח HETH

57 ᵈ*You are* my portion, O LORD;
I have said that I would keep Your
words.
58 I entreated Your favor with *my* whole
heart;
Be merciful to me according to Your
word.
59 I ᵉthought about my ways,
And turned my feet to Your
testimonies.
60 I made haste, and did not delay
To keep Your commandments.
61 The cords of the wicked have bound
me,
But I have not forgotten Your law.
62 ᶠAt midnight I will rise to give thanks
to You,
Because of Your righteous
judgments.
63 I *am* a companion of all who fear
You,
And of those who keep Your
precepts.
64 ᵍThe earth, O LORD, is full of Your
mercy;
Teach me Your statutes.

ט TETH

65 You have dealt well with Your
servant,
O LORD, according to Your word.
66 Teach me good judgment and
ʰknowledge,
For I believe Your commandments.
67 Before I was ⁱafflicted I went astray,
But now I keep Your word.
68 You *are* ʲgood, and do good;
Teach me Your statutes.
69 The proud have ᵏforged a lie against
me,
But I will keep Your precepts with
my whole heart.
70 ˡTheir heart is as fat as grease,
But I delight in Your law.
71 *It is* good for me that I have been
afflicted,
That I may learn Your statutes.
72 ᵐThe law of Your mouth *is* better to me
Than thousands of *coins of* gold and
silver.

י YOD

73 ⁿYour hands have made me and
fashioned me;

119:45 at liberty. Many think of laws, instructions, and commandments as limiting and restricting, but the law of God paradoxically frees us. It frees us from sin (v. 133) and gives us the peace that comes from following the Lord's instructions (v. 165).

119:56 precepts. This Hebrew word means "an appointed thing," "something for which one is given charge." The word has the same idea as "commandment" for both words assume that the One who commands has the authority to take charge or appoint (v. 4).

119:70 delight. This is not the delight of a passive observer, but the delight of a disciple who has staked his life and security on a cause or principle.

119:38 ˣ 2 Sam. 7:25   119:45 ʸ Prov. 4:12
119:46 ᶻ Matt. 10:18   119:50 ᵃ [Rom. 15:4]
119:53 ᵇ Ezra 9:3   119:55 ᶜ Ps. 63:6   119:57 ᵈ Jer. 10:16
119:59 ᵉ Luke 15:17   119:62 ᶠ Acts 16:25   119:64 ᵍ Ps.
33:5   119:66 ʰ Phil. 1:9   119:67 ⁱ [Heb. 12:5–11]
119:68 ʲ [Matt. 19:17]   119:69 ᵏ Job 13:4   119:70 ˡ Acts
28:27   119:72 ᵐ Ps. 19:10   119:73 ⁿ Job 10:8; 31:15

Give me understanding, that I may
learn Your commandments.
74 oThose who fear You will be glad
when they see me,
Because I have hoped in Your word.
75 I know, O LORD, pthat Your
judgments are right,
And that in faithfulness You have
afflicted me.
76 Let, I pray, Your merciful kindness
be for my comfort,
According to Your word to Your
servant.
77 Let Your tender mercies come to me,
that I may live;
For Your law is my delight.
78 Let the proud qbe ashamed,
For they treated me wrongfully with
falsehood;
But I will meditate on Your
precepts.
79 Let those who fear You turn to me,
Those who know Your testimonies.
80 Let my heart be blameless regarding
Your statutes,
That I may not be ashamed.

 כ KAPH
81 rMy soul faints for Your salvation,
But I hope in Your word.
82 My eyes fail from searching Your
word,
Saying, "When will You comfort
me?"
83 For sI have become like a wineskin in
smoke,
Yet I do not forget Your statutes.
84 tHow many are the days of Your
servant?
uWhen will You execute judgment on
those who persecute me?
85 vThe proud have dug pits for me,
Which is not according to Your law.
86 All Your commandments are faithful;
They persecute me wwrongfully;
Help me!
87 They almost made an end of me on
earth,
But I did not forsake Your precepts.
88 Revive me according to Your
lovingkindness,
So that I may keep the testimony of
Your mouth.

ל LAMED
89 xForever, O LORD,
Your word is settled in heaven.

90 Your faithfulness endures to all
generations;
You established the earth, and it
abides.
91 They continue this day according to
yYour ordinances,
For all are Your servants.
92 Unless Your law had been my
delight,
I would then have perished in my
affliction.
93 I will never forget Your precepts,
For by them You have given me life.
94 I am Yours, save me;
For I have sought Your precepts.
95 The wicked wait for me to destroy me,
But I will consider Your testimonies.
96 zI have seen the consummation of all
perfection,
But Your commandment is
exceedingly broad.

מ MEM
97 Oh, how I love Your law!
aIt is my meditation all the day.
98 You, through Your commandments,
make me bwiser than my
enemies;
For they are ever with me.
99 I have more understanding than all
my teachers,
cFor Your testimonies are my
meditation.
100 dI understand more than the ancients,
Because I keep Your precepts.
101 I have restrained my feet from every
evil way,
That I may keep Your word.
102 I have not departed from Your
judgments,
For You Yourself have taught me.
103 eHow sweet are Your words to my
taste,
Sweeter than honey to my mouth!
104 Through Your precepts I get
understanding;
Therefore I hate every false way.

נ NUN
105 fYour word is a lamp to my feet
And a light to my path.
106 gI have sworn and confirmed
That I will keep Your righteous
judgments.
107 I am afflicted very much;
Revive me, O LORD, according to
Your word.

119:82 Your word. The Hebrew term for "word" is
derived from the verb "to say." The term is a general
word for God's law, encompassing everything that
the Lord has promised and spoken.
119:97 how I love Your law. Fundamentally, the
psalmist's attraction to the law is the result of his love
for God Himself, his Teacher (vv. 102,132).
119:105 a light to my path. God's word is a guide for
everyday living.

119:74 o Ps. 34:2   **119:75** p [Heb. 12:10]   **119:78** q Ps.
25:3   **119:81** r Ps. 73:26; 84:2   **119:83** s Job
30:30   **119:84** t Ps. 39:4   u Rev. 6:10   **119:85** v Ps.
35:7   **119:86** w Ps. 35:19   **119:89** x Matt. 24:35
119:91 y Jer. 33:25   **119:96** z Matt. 5:18   **119:97** a Ps.
1:2   **119:98** b Deut. 4:6   **119:99** c [2 Tim.
3:15]   **119:100** d [Job 32:7–9]   **119:103** e Prov. 8:11
119:105 f Prov. 6:23   **119:106** g Neh. 10:29

108 Accept, I pray, *h*the freewill offerings
of my mouth, O LORD,
And teach me Your judgments.
109 *i*My life *is* continually in my hand,
Yet I do not forget Your law.
110 *j*The wicked have laid a snare for me,
Yet I have not strayed from Your
precepts.
111 *k*Your testimonies I have taken as a
heritage forever,
For they *are* the rejoicing of my
heart.
112 I have inclined my heart to perform
Your statutes
Forever, to the very end.

ⲇ SAMEK
113 I hate the double-minded,
But I love Your law.
114 *l*You *are* my hiding place and my
shield;
I hope in Your word.
115 *m*Depart from me, you evildoers,
For I will keep the commandments of
my God!
116 Uphold me according to Your word,
that I may live;
And do not let me *n*be ashamed of my
hope.
117 Hold me up, and I shall be safe,
And I shall observe Your statutes
continually.
118 You reject all those who stray from
Your statutes,
For their deceit *is* falsehood.
119 You put away all the wicked of the
earth *o*like dross;
Therefore I love Your testimonies.
120 *p*My flesh trembles for fear of You,
And I am afraid of Your judgments.

ⲩ AYIN
121 I have done justice and
righteousness;
Do not leave me to my oppressors.
122 Be *q*surety for Your servant for good;
Do not let the proud oppress me.
123 My eyes fail *from seeking* Your
salvation
And Your righteous word.
124 Deal with Your servant according to
Your mercy,
And teach me Your statutes.
125 *r*I *am* Your servant;
Give me understanding,
That I may know Your testimonies.

126 *It is* time for *You* to act, O LORD,
For they have regarded Your law as
void.
127 *s*Therefore I love Your
commandments
More than gold, yes, than fine gold!
128 Therefore all *Your* precepts
concerning all *things*
I consider *to be* right;
I hate every false way.

ⲫ PE
129 Your testimonies are wonderful;
Therefore my soul keeps them.
130 The entrance of Your words gives
light;
*t*It gives understanding to the *u*simple.
131 I opened my mouth and *v*panted,
For I longed for Your
commandments.
132 *w*Look upon me and be *x*merciful to me,
As Your custom *is* toward those who
love Your name.
133 *y*Direct my steps by Your word,
And *z*let no iniquity have dominion
over me.
134 *a*Redeem me from the oppression of
man,
That I may keep Your precepts.
135 *b*Make Your face shine upon Your
servant,
And teach me Your statutes.
136 *c*Rivers of water run down from my
eyes,
Because *men* do not keep Your law.

ⲭ TSADDE
137 *d*Righteous *are* You, O LORD,
And upright *are* Your judgments.
138 *e*Your testimonies, *which* You have
commanded,
Are righteous and very faithful.
139 *f*My zeal has consumed me,
Because my enemies have forgotten
Your words.
140 *g*Your word *is* very pure;
Therefore Your servant loves it.
141 I *am* small and despised,
Yet I do not forget Your precepts.
142 Your righteousness *is* an everlasting
righteousness,
And Your law *is* *h*truth.
143 Trouble and anguish have overtaken
me,
Yet Your commandments *are* my
delights.

119:127 commandments. This word alludes to God's
authority to govern His people. The commandments
of God help believers to find their way in a world that
is filled with confusion, sin, and error.

119:136 Rivers of water. One of the earmarks of a
true believer is the remorse and sorrow that is felt
when the person sins and fails to keep God's law.

119:108 *h* Hos. 14:2 **119:109** *i* Job 13:14 **119:110** *j* Ps.
140:5 **119:111** *k* Deut. 33:4 **119:114** *l* [Ps. 32:7]
119:115 *m* Matt. 7:23 **119:116** *n* [Rom. 5:5; 9:33;
10:11] **119:119** *o* Ezek. 22:18, 19 **119:120** *p* Hab. 3:16
119:122 *q* Heb. 7:22 **119:125** *r* Ps. 116:16 **119:127** *s* Ps.
19:10 **119:130** *t* Prov. 6:23 *u* [Ps. 19:7] **119:131** *v* Ps.
42:1 **119:132** *w* Ps. 106:4 *x* [2 Thess. 1:6] **119:133** *y* Ps.
17:5 *z* [Rom. 6:12] **119:134** *a* Luke 1:74 **119:135** *b* Ps.
4:6 **119:136** *c* Jer. 9:1, 18; 14:17 **119:137** *d* Neh.
9:33 **119:138** *e* [Ps. 19:7–9] **119:139** *f* John 2:17
119:140 *g* Ps. 12:6 **119:142** *h* [John 17:17]

144 The righteousness of Your
testimonies *is* everlasting;
Give me understanding, and I shall
live.

ק QOPH

145 I cry out with *my* whole heart;
Hear me, O Lord!
I will keep Your statutes.
146 I cry out to You;
Save me, and I will keep Your
testimonies.
147 *i*I rise before the dawning of the
morning,
And cry for help;
I hope in Your word.
148 *j*My eyes are awake through the *night*
watches,
That I may meditate on Your word.
149 Hear my voice according to Your
lovingkindness;
O Lord, revive me according to Your
justice.
150 They draw near who follow after
wickedness;
They are far from Your law.
151 You *are* *k*near, O Lord,
And all Your commandments *are*
truth.
152 Concerning Your testimonies,
I have known of old that You have
founded them *l*forever.

ר RESH

153 *m*Consider my affliction and deliver
me,
For I do not forget Your law.
154 *n*Plead my cause and redeem me;
Revive me according to Your word.
155 Salvation *is* far from the wicked,
For they do not seek Your statutes.
156 Great *are* Your tender mercies,
O Lord;
Revive me according to Your
judgments.
157 Many *are* my persecutors and my
enemies,
Yet I do not *o*turn from Your
testimonies.
158 I see the treacherous, and *p*am
disgusted,
Because they do not keep Your word.

159 Consider how I love Your precepts;
Revive me, O Lord, according to
Your lovingkindness.
160 The entirety of Your word *is* truth,
And every one of Your righteous
judgments *endures* forever.

ש SHIN

161 *q*Princes persecute me without a
cause,
But my heart stands in awe of Your
word.
162 I rejoice at Your word
As one who finds great treasure.
163 I hate and abhor lying,
But I love Your law.
164 Seven times a day I praise You,
Because of Your righteous
judgments.
165 *r*Great peace have those who love
Your law,
And nothing causes them to stumble.
166 *s*Lord, I hope for Your salvation,
And I do Your commandments.
167 My soul keeps Your testimonies,
And I love them exceedingly.
168 I keep Your precepts and Your
testimonies,
*t*For all my ways *are* before You.

ת TAU

169 Let my cry come before You, O Lord;
*u*Give me understanding according to
Your word.
170 Let my supplication come before You;
Deliver me according to Your word.
171 *v*My lips shall utter praise,
For You teach me Your statutes.
172 My tongue shall speak of Your word,
For all Your commandments *are*
righteousness.
173 Let Your hand become my help,
For *w*I have chosen Your precepts.
174 *x*I long for Your salvation, O Lord,
And *y*Your law *is* my delight.
175 Let my soul live, and it shall praise
You;
And let Your judgments help me.
176 *z*I have gone astray like a lost sheep;
Seek Your servant,
For I do not forget Your
commandments.

119:149 *revive*. With this word, the psalmist begs God to transform him, to breathe new life back into his soul. The psalmist does not want his obedience to be mechanical; he asks for a renewed spirit. The basis for his plea is God's covenantal love and His just nature.
119:159 *lovingkindness*. The lovingkindness of God is a recurring theme in the Book of Psalms, describing His loyal, covenant love and merciful care of His people.
119:162 *rejoice*. Jesus also described the "kingdom of God" as a great treasure, one so valuable that it would be worth selling everything one had in order to possess it (Matt. 13:44–46).
119:176 *like a lost sheep*. Jesus, the Messiah,

described Himself as the Good Shepherd who would lay down His own life in order to protect and rescue His sheep (John 10:11). He affirmed that God does indeed seek lost sinners in order to bring them to Himself (Luke 15:3–7).

119:147 *i* Ps. 5:3   **119:148** *j* Ps. 63:1, 6   **119:151** *k* [Ps. 145:18]   **119:152** *l* Luke 21:33   **119:153** *m* Lam. 5:1   **119:154** *n* 1 Sam. 24:15   **119:157** *o* Ps. 44:18   **119:158** *p* Ezek. 9:4   **119:161** *q* 1 Sam. 24:11; 26:18   **119:165** *r* Prov. 3:2   **119:166** *s* Gen. 49:18   **119:168** *t* Prov. 5:21   **119:169** *u* Ps. 119:27, 144   **119:171** *v* Ps. 119:7   **119:173** *w* Josh. 24:22   **119:174** *x* Ps. 119:166   *y* Ps. 119:16, 24   **119:176** *z* [Is. 53:6]

Psalm 120

Plea for Relief from Bitter Foes

A Song of Ascents.

1 In ^amy distress I cried to the LORD,
  And He heard me.
2 Deliver my soul, O LORD, from lying lips
  And from a deceitful tongue.

3 What shall be given to you,
  Or what shall be done to you,
  You false tongue?
4 Sharp arrows of the warrior,
  With coals of the broom tree!

5 Woe is me, that I dwell in ^bMeshech,
  ^c*That* I dwell among the tents of Kedar!
6 My soul has dwelt too long
  With one who hates peace.
7 I *am for* peace;
  But when I speak, they *are* for war.

Psalm 121

God the Help of Those Who Seek Him

A Song of Ascents.

1 I ^awill lift up my eyes to the hills—
  From whence comes my help?
2 ^bMy help *comes* from the LORD,
  Who made heaven and earth.

3 ^cHe will not allow your foot to be moved;
  ^dHe who keeps you will not slumber.
4 Behold, He who keeps Israel
  Shall neither slumber nor sleep.

5 The LORD *is* your keeper;
  The LORD *is* ^eyour shade ^fat your right hand.

6 ^gThe sun shall not strike you by day,
  Nor the moon by night.

7 The LORD shall preserve you from all evil;
  He shall ^hpreserve your soul.
8 The LORD shall ⁱpreserve your going out and your coming in
  From this time forth, and even forevermore.

Psalm 122

The Joy of Going to the House of the LORD

A Song of Ascents. Of David.

1 I was glad when they said to me,
  ^a"Let us go into the house of the LORD."
2 Our feet have been standing
  Within your gates, O Jerusalem!

3 Jerusalem is built
  As a city that is ^bcompact together,
4 ^cWhere the tribes go up,
  The tribes of the LORD,
  To ^dthe Testimony of Israel,
  To give thanks to the name of the LORD.
5 ^eFor thrones are set there for judgment,
  The thrones of the house of David.

6 ^fPray for the peace of Jerusalem:
  "May they prosper who love you.
7 Peace be within your walls,
  Prosperity within your palaces."
8 For the sake of my brethren and companions,
  I will now say, "Peace *be* within you."
9 Because of the house of the LORD our God
  I will ^gseek your good.

120:1 *In my distress I cried.* This psalm is the first of a group of psalms called the Songs of Ascent (120–134). This group of hymns was probably used by pilgrims making their way to Jerusalem to worship the Lord during the three annual feasts—Passover, Pentecost, and Tabernacles (Lev. 23). Since Jerusalem is on a high hill, a traveler always goes "up" to Jerusalem; hence the term "songs of ascent."

120:5 *Meshech . . . Kedar.* These seem to be examples of the pagan peoples among whom the psalmist had to live.

121:1 *my eyes to the hills.* This Song of Ascent (see Ps. 120) dramatically pictures a traveler approaching the city of Jerusalem.

121:2 *from the LORD.* As comforting as the sight of the holy city would be to a pilgrim, the psalmist emphasizes the real reason for rejoicing: God's tender care for His people. *Who made.* We might have expected the psalmist to emphasize God as a loving heavenly Father or a tender and compassionate Savior, but instead he ascribes our everlasting safety to the God of creation. God owns the world because He made it; nothing that happens is beyond Him.

121:6 *Nor the moon by night.* There is never a time when the Lord is "off duty" and does not see what is happening to His people.

122:1 *I was glad.* This third Song of Ascent (see Ps. 120) describes the joy of the pilgrim on arriving at Jerusalem to worship God.

122:4 *the tribes go up.* This refers to the three annual feasts of ancient Israel (Lev. 23), as well as to any time that an individual or family needed to worship the Lord in the holy city.

122:5 *thrones . . . for judgment.* Jerusalem was not only the central place for worship, it was also the site where civil judgments and decisions were made. Religious and civil issues were closely intertwined in the law of God.

122:6 *the peace of Jerusalem.* True peace will only come when the Prince of Peace returns to establish His rule (Ps. 98:5–6; Rev. 21:9–27).

120:1 ^aJon. 2:2   **120:5** ^bGen. 10:2   ^cGen. 25:13
121:1 ^a[Jer. 3:23]   **121:2** ^b[Ps. 124:8]   **121:3** ^c1 Sam. 2:9   ^dIs. 27:3   **121:5** ^eIs. 25:4   ^fPs. 16:8   **121:6** ^gIs. 49:10   **121:7** ^hPs. 41:2   **121:8** ⁱDeut. 28:6   **122:1** ^a[Is. 2:3]   **122:3** ^b2 Sam. 5:9   **122:4** ^cDeut. 16:16   ^dEx. 16:34   **122:5** ^eDeut. 17:8   **122:6** ^fPs. 51:18   **122:9** ^gNeh. 2:10

Psalm 123

Prayer for Relief from Contempt

A Song of Ascents.

1 Unto You *a*I lift up my eyes,
O You *b*who dwell in the heavens.
2 Behold, as the eyes of servants *look* to
the hand of their masters,
As the eyes of a maid to the hand of
her mistress,
*c*So our eyes *look* to the LORD our God,
Until He has mercy on us.
3 Have mercy on us, O LORD, have
mercy on us!
For we are exceedingly filled with
contempt.
4 Our soul is exceedingly filled
With the scorn of those who are at ease,
With the contempt of the proud.

Psalm 124

The LORD the Defense of His People

A Song of Ascents. Of David.

1 "If it had not been the LORD who was on
our *a*side,"
*b*Let Israel now say—
2 "If it had not been the LORD who was on
our side,
When men rose up against us,
3 Then they would have *c*swallowed us
alive,
When their wrath was kindled against
us;
4 Then the waters would have
overwhelmed us,
The stream would have gone over our
soul;
5 Then the swollen waters
Would have gone over our soul."
6 Blessed *be* the LORD,
Who has not given us *as* prey to their
teeth.
7 *d*Our soul has escaped *e*as a bird from
the snare of the fowlers;*
The snare is broken, and we have
escaped.
8 *f*Our help *is* in the name of the LORD,
*g*Who made heaven and earth.

Psalm 125

The LORD the Strength of His People

A Song of Ascents.

1 Those who trust in the LORD
Are like Mount Zion,
Which cannot be moved, *but* abides
forever.
2 As the mountains surround
Jerusalem,
So the LORD surrounds His people
From this time forth and forever.
3 For *a*the scepter of wickedness shall
not rest
On the land allotted to the righteous,
Lest the righteous reach out their
hands to iniquity.
4 Do good, O LORD, to *those who are*
good,
And to *those who are* upright in their
hearts.
5 As for such as turn aside to their
*b*crooked ways,
The LORD shall lead them away
With the workers of iniquity.

*c*Peace *be* upon Israel!

Psalm 126

A Joyful Return to Zion

A Song of Ascents.

1 When *a*the LORD brought back the
captivity of Zion,
*b*We were like those who dream.
2 Then *c*our mouth was filled with
laughter,
And our tongue with singing.
Then they said among the nations,
"The LORD has done great things for
them."
3 The LORD has done great things
for us,
And we are glad.

---

* **124:7** That is, persons who catch birds in a trap
or snare

123:2 *as the eyes of servants.* Good servants keep
watch over their masters, anticipating their wants
and keeping themselves in constant readiness to
obey orders. In the same way, we should keep ourselves focused on pleasing God. The more we look at
Him, the more we become like Him (2 Cor. 3:18).
124:1 *the LORD who was on our side.* It is because
God is "on our side" that He sent His Son to save the
world (John 3:16).
124:6 *Blessed be the LORD.* To bless God is to identify
Him as the source of our blessings (103:2).
125:2 *the mountains surround Jerusalem.* Jerusalem is built on one of seven mountain peaks in the

region. The mountains provided some protection
for the city, since any invading army would have to
march through difficult terrain to reach the city.
126:1 *brought back the captivity.* This seventh Song
of Ascent (see Ps. 120) comes from the time of the
restoration of Jerusalem, following the Babylonian
captivity.

123:1 *a* Ps. 121:1; 141:8 *b* Ps. 2:4; 11:4; 115:3 **123:2** *c* Ps.
25:15 **124:1** *a* [Rom. 8:31] *b* Ps. 129:1 **124:3** *c* Prov.
1:12 **124:7** *d* Ps. 91:3 *e* Prov. 6:5 **124:8** *f* [Ps. 121:2]
g Gen. 1:1 **125:3** *a* Prov. 22:8 **125:5** *b* Prov. 2:15 *c* [Gal.
6:16] **126:1** *a* Hos. 6:11 *b* Acts 12:9 **126:2** *c* Job 8:21

4 Bring back our captivity, O LORD,
As the streams in the South.

5 ^dThose who sow in tears
Shall reap in joy.

6 He who continually goes forth weeping,
Bearing seed for sowing,
Shall doubtless come again with
^erejoicing,
Bringing his sheaves *with him.*

Psalm 127

Laboring and Prospering
with the LORD

A Song of Ascents. Of Solomon.

1 Unless the LORD builds the house,
They labor in vain who build it;
Unless ^athe LORD guards the city,
The watchman stays awake in vain.

2 *It is* vain for you to rise up early,
To sit up late,
To ^beat the bread of sorrows;
For so He gives His beloved sleep.

3 Behold, ^cchildren *are* a heritage from
the LORD,
^dThe fruit of the womb *is* a ^ereward.

4 Like arrows in the hand of a warrior,
So *are* the children of one's youth.

5 ^fHappy *is* the man who has his quiver
full of them;
^gThey shall not be ashamed,
But shall speak with their enemies in
the gate.

Psalm 128

Blessings of Those Who Fear
the LORD

A Song of Ascents.

1 Blessed ^a*is* every one who fears the LORD,
Who walks in His ways.

2 ^bWhen you eat the labor of your
hands,
You *shall be* happy, and *it shall be*
^cwell with you.

3 Your wife *shall be* ^dlike a fruitful
vine
In the very heart of your house,
Your ^echildren ^flike olive plants
All around your table.

4 Behold, thus shall the man be
blessed
Who fears the LORD.

5 ^gThe LORD bless you out of Zion,
And may you see the good of
Jerusalem
All the days of your life.

6 Yes, may you ^hsee your children's
children.

ⁱPeace *be* upon Israel!

Psalm 129

Song of Victory over Zion's Enemies

A Song of Ascents.

1 "Many a time they have ^aafflicted me
from ^bmy youth,"
^cLet Israel now say—

2 "Many a time they have afflicted me
from my youth;
Yet they have not prevailed
against me.

3 The plowers plowed on my back;
They made their furrows long."

4 The LORD *is* righteous;
He has cut in pieces the cords of the
wicked.

5 Let all those who hate Zion
Be put to shame and turned back.

6 Let them be as the ^dgrass *on* the
housetops,
Which withers before it grows up,

7 With which the reaper does not fill his
hand,

126:4 Bring back. The people who returned were a small percentage of those who had been exiled; the people still prayed that God would complete the restoration of His people to their land.

127:1 Unless the LORD. This psalm, the eighth Song of Ascent (see Ps. 120), is one of only two psalms attributed to Solomon (see Ps. 72).

127:2 bread of sorrows. This phrase captures the essence of those removed from a sense of the Lord in their lives. The food that should give them strength for life and a zest for living only maintains their miserable state.

127:5 in the gate. The gate was the place where the elders of the city met and where citizens would convene (Ruth 4:1–12).

128:1 Blessed. This word describes the happiness of those who trust in the Lord and do His will (127:5).
fears. The fear of God is an attitude of respect, a response of reverence and wonder. It is the only appropriate response to our Creator and Redeemer.

128:2 the labor of your hands. There is a reward in work and a satisfaction in labor that is a blessing of God (Eccl. 3:9–13).

129:1–4 Many a time. The psalm begins with a litany of suffering, as the people of God acknowledge that throughout their history in the land they have been under constant assault by various peoples.

129:6 grass on the housetops. Sod was sometimes used on the roofs of the houses. After a spring rain, there might be grass growing on the housetop, but

---

126:5 ^d Jer. 31:9   **126:6** ^e Is. 61:3   **127:1** ^a [Ps. 121:3–5]   **127:2** ^b [Gen. 3:17, 19]   **127:3** ^c [Josh. 24:3, 4]   ^d Deut. 7:13; 28:4   ^e [Ps. 113:9]   **127:5** ^f Ps. 128:2, 3   ^g Prov. 27:11   **128:1** ^a Ps. 119:1   **128:2** ^b Is. 3:10   ^c Deut. 4:40   **128:3** ^d Ezek. 19:10   ^e Ps. 127:3–5   ^f Ps. 52:8; 144:12   **128:5** ^g Ps. 134:3   **128:6** ^h Job 42:16   ⁱ Ps. 125:5   **129:1** ^a [Jer. 1:19; 15:20]   ^b Ezek. 23:3   ^c Ps. 124:1   **129:6** ^d Ps. 37:2

Nor he who binds sheaves, his
    arms.
8 Neither let those who pass by them
    say,
  e"The blessing of the LORD *be* upon
    you;
  We bless you in the name of the
    LORD!"

Psalm 130

Waiting for the Redemption of the LORD

A Song of Ascents.

1 Out aof the depths I have cried to You,
    O LORD;
2 Lord, hear my voice!
  Let Your ears be attentive
  To the voice of my supplications.

3 bIf You, LORD, should mark
    iniquities,
  O Lord, who could cstand?
4 But *there is* dforgiveness with You,
  That eYou may be feared.

5 fI wait for the LORD, my soul waits,
  And gin His word I do hope.
6 hMy soul *waits* for the Lord
  More than those who watch for the
    morning—
  Yes, more than those who watch for
    the morning.

7 iO Israel, hope in the LORD;
  For jwith the LORD *there is* mercy,
  And with Him *is* abundant
    redemption.

8 And kHe shall redeem Israel
  From all his iniquities.

Psalm 131

Simple Trust in the LORD

A Song of Ascents. Of David.

1 LORD, my heart is not haughty,
  Nor my eyes lofty.
  aNeither do I concern myself with great
    matters,
  Nor with things too profound for me.
2 Surely I have calmed and quieted my
    soul,
  bLike a weaned child with his mother;
  Like a weaned child *is* my soul
    within me.
3 cO Israel, hope in the LORD
  From this time forth and forever.

Psalm 132

The Eternal Dwelling of God in Zion

A Song of Ascents.

1 LORD, remember David
  And all his afflictions;
2 How he swore to the LORD,
  a*And* vowed to bthe Mighty One of Jacob:
3 "Surely I will not go into the chamber of
    my house,
  Or go up to the comfort of my bed;
4 I will cnot give sleep to my eyes
  Or slumber to my eyelids,

---

this was not grass that flourished; it lacked roots and soon withered under the summer heat.
130:1 *Out of the depths.* The placement of this penitential psalm is fitting. We must not be so interested in the destruction of the wicked (Ps. 129) that we fail to understand our own heart before the Lord.
130:3 *iniquities.* Does the Lord keep a record of our sins? The answer is both yes and no. At the end of all things, Christ will sit on the judgment seat, the books will be opened, and everyone will be judged according to the actual record (Rev. 20:11–15). However, if we cry to Him for mercy now in this life, we shall find forgiveness. Then the record of our sins will be cast away into the depth of God's forgetfulness. They are covered by the blood of Jesus.
130:4 *forgiveness . . . that You may be feared.* God's provision for forgiveness is not to be taken lightly (Rom. 6:1–2). The truly forgiven sinner realizes the magnitude of God's grace, remains grateful for Jesus' sacrifice for sins, and lives in the fear or awe of God (Ps. 128).
130:8 *He shall redeem.* God had redeemed the people from slavery in Egypt; the psalmist also looked forward to the time when He would redeem the people from slavery to their own sinful natures, through the death and resurrection of Jesus Christ (Gal. 3:13).

131:1 *my heart is not haughty.* David presents himself with genuine humility, a delicate balance between self-abasement and arrogant pride. From the life of David, we know that he was not always able to keep this balance. But it was his desire, and at times—by God's grace—a reality in his life.
131:1 *Like a weaned child.* A weaned child is comforted just by the presence of his mother, without crying for the more tangible comfort of milk as a younger baby does.
132:1 *remember.* This psalm was one of the 15 Songs of Ascent sung by pilgrims as they approached the holy city to worship. Each year, as they marched and sang, they anticipated that perhaps this was the year that this prophecy would be fulfilled. ***David . . . his afflictions.*** If this psalm was written during the period after the exile, these words have a significant meaning. During the years between the return of the people to Jerusalem and the birth of Jesus, there would have been a growing desire on the part of

129:8 e Ruth 2:4   **130:1** a Lam. 3:55   **130:3** b [Ps.
143:2] c [Nah. 1:6]   **130:4** d [Ex. 34:7] e [1 Kin. 8:39,
40]   **130:5** f [Ps. 27:14] g Ps. 119:81   **130:6** h Ps. 119:147
130:7 i Ps. 131:3 j [Is. 55:7]   **130:8** k [Ps. 103:3, 4]
131:1 a [Rom. 12:16]   **131:2** b [Matt. 18:3]   **131:3** c [Ps.
130:7]   **132:2** a Ps. 65:1 b Gen. 49:24   **132:4** c Prov. 6:4

5 Until I [d]find a place for the LORD,
A dwelling place for the Mighty One of Jacob."

6 Behold, we heard of it [e]in Ephrathah;
[f]We found it [g]in the fields of the woods.*
7 Let us go into His tabernacle;
[h]Let us worship at His footstool.
8 [i]Arise, O LORD, to Your resting place,
You and [j]the ark of Your strength.
9 Let Your priests [k]be clothed with righteousness,
And let Your saints shout for joy.

10 For Your servant David's sake,
Do not turn away the face of Your Anointed.

11 [l]The LORD has sworn *in* truth to David;
He will not turn from it:
"I will set upon your throne [m]the fruit of your body.
12 If your sons will keep My covenant
And My testimony which I shall teach them,
Their sons also shall sit upon your throne forevermore."

13 [n]For the LORD has chosen Zion;
He has desired *it* for His dwelling place:
14 "This[o] *is* My resting place forever;
Here I will dwell, for I have desired it.
15 [p]I will abundantly bless her provision;
I will satisfy her poor with bread.
16 [q]I will also clothe her priests with salvation,
[r]And her saints shall shout aloud for joy.
17 [s]There I will make the horn of David grow;
[t]I will prepare a lamp for My Anointed.
18 His enemies I will [u]clothe with shame,
But upon Himself His crown shall flourish."

Psalm 133

Blessed Unity of the People of God

A Song of Ascents. Of David.

1 Behold, how good and how pleasant *it is*
For [a]brethren to dwell together in unity!

2 *It is* like the precious oil upon the head,
Running down on the beard,
The beard of Aaron,
Running down on the edge of his garments.
3 *It is* like the dew of [b]Hermon,
Descending upon the mountains of Zion;
For [c]there the LORD commanded the blessing—
Life forevermore.

Psalm 134

Praising the LORD in His House at Night

A Song of Ascents.

1 Behold, bless the LORD,
All *you* servants of the LORD,
Who by night stand in the house of the LORD!
2 [a]Lift up your hands *in* the sanctuary,
And bless the LORD.

3 The LORD who made heaven and earth
Bless you from Zion!

Psalm 135

Praise to God in Creation and Redemption

1 Praise the LORD!

Praise the name of the LORD;
[a]Praise *Him*, O you servants of the LORD!

* 132:6 Hebrew *Jaar*

godly people for the Lord to restore David's kingdom in fulfillment of His promise.

132:6 *Ephrathah.* This name refers to the region of Bethlehem (Ruth 1:2).

132:12 *sit upon your throne forevermore.* The ultimate fulfillment of God's covenant with David (2 Sam. 7:8–16) is in Jesus Christ, the Son of David (Luke 1:32–33; Acts 2:30).

132:16 *joy.* God's presence is a source of joy to the upright. God had chosen Zion as His resting place, and His godly ones shouted "aloud for joy." When God rules on the throne of the human spirit, joy reigns within.

132:17 *horn . . . lamp.* The words "horn" and "lamp" speak of the Messiah's authority and righteousness (Is. 11:1–5).

133:3 *the dew of Hermon.* This high mountain to the north of Israel received such large amounts of water that it seemed to be a source of moisture for the lands below.

134:1 *All you servants of the LORD.* This psalm concludes the Songs of Ascent. The people who had come to worship at the temple were getting ready to go home, but the priests would remain at the holy temple, continuing to lift up worship to the Lord.

132:5 [d] Acts 7:46 **132:6** [e] 1 Sam. 17:12 [f] 1 Sam. 7:1 [g] 1 Chr. 13:5 **132:7** [h] Ps. 5:7; 99:5 **132:8** [i] Num. 10:35 [j] Ps. 78:61 **132:9** [k] Job 29:14 **132:11** [l] [Ps. 89:3, 4, 33; 110:4] [m] 2 Sam. 7:12 **132:13** [n] [Ps. 48:1, 2] **132:14** [o] Ps. 68:16 **132:15** [p] Ps. 147:14 **132:16** [q] 2 Chr. 6:41 [r] 1 Sam. 4:5 **132:17** [s] Ezek. 29:21 [t] 1 Kin. 11:36; 15:4 **132:18** [u] Ps. 35:26 **133:1** [a] Gen. 13:8 **133:3** [b] Deut. 4:48 [c] Lev. 25:21 **134:2** [a] [1 Tim. 2:8] **135:1** [a] Ps. 113:1

2 [b]You who stand in the house of the LORD,
In [c]the courts of the house of our God,
3 Praise the LORD, for [d]the LORD *is* good;
Sing praises to His name, [e]for *it is* pleasant.
4 For [f]the LORD has chosen Jacob for Himself,
Israel for His special treasure.

5 For I know that [g]the LORD *is* great,
And our Lord *is* above all gods.
6 [h]Whatever the LORD pleases He does,
In heaven and in earth,
In the seas and in all deep places.
7 [i]He causes the vapors to ascend from the ends of the earth;
[j]He makes lightning for the rain;
He brings the wind out of His [k]treasuries.

8 [l]He destroyed the firstborn of Egypt,
Both of man and beast.
9 [m]He sent signs and wonders into the midst of you, O Egypt,
[n]Upon Pharaoh and all his servants.
10 [o]He defeated many nations
And slew mighty kings—
11 Sihon king of the Amorites,
Og king of Bashan,
And [p]all the kingdoms of Canaan—
12 [q]And gave their land *as* a heritage,
A heritage to Israel His people.

13 [r]Your name, O LORD, *endures* forever,
Your fame, O LORD, throughout all generations.
14 [s]For the LORD will judge His people,
And He will have compassion on His servants.

15 [t]The idols of the nations *are* silver and gold,
The work of men's hands.
16 They have mouths, but they do not speak;
Eyes they have, but they do not see;
17 They have ears, but they do not hear;
Nor is there *any* breath in their mouths.
18 Those who make them are like them;
So is everyone who trusts in them.

19 [u]Bless the LORD, O house of Israel!
Bless the LORD, O house of Aaron!
20 Bless the LORD, O house of Levi!
You who fear the LORD, bless the LORD!
21 Blessed be the LORD [v]out of Zion,
Who dwells in Jerusalem!

Praise the LORD!

Psalm 136

Thanksgiving to God for His Enduring Mercy

1 Oh, [a]give thanks to the LORD, for *He is* good!
[b]For His mercy *endures* forever.
2 Oh, give thanks to [c]the God of gods!
For His mercy *endures* forever.
3 Oh, give thanks to the Lord of lords!
For His mercy *endures* forever:

4 To Him [d]who alone does great wonders,
For His mercy *endures* forever;
5 [e]To Him who by wisdom made the heavens,
For His mercy *endures* forever;
6 [f]To Him who laid out the earth above the waters,
For His mercy *endures* forever;
7 [g]To Him who made great lights,
For His mercy *endures* forever—
8 [h]The sun to rule by day,
For His mercy *endures* forever;
9 The moon and stars to rule by night,
For His mercy *endures* forever.

10 [i]To Him who struck Egypt in their firstborn,
For His mercy *endures* forever;
11 [j]And brought out Israel from among them,
For His mercy *endures* forever;
12 [k]With a strong hand, and with an outstretched arm,
For His mercy *endures* forever;
13 [l]To Him who divided the Red Sea in two,
For His mercy *endures* forever;

135:8 *the firstborn of Egypt.* The defeat of Egypt was solely the work of the Lord. Israel was merely His instrument; the battle belonged to Him (Ex. 12:12; 15:3).
135:15 *idols of the nations.* The people who returned from Babylon had had their fill of the worship of idols; at long last, the people of Israel were ready to worship the only true God.
135:19 *Bless the LORD.* To bless the Lord is to identify Him as the source of all blessings and to be grateful for all that He has given.
136:1 *mercy.* This word, also translated "lovingkindness" or "loyal love," is the most significant term used in the Psalms to describe the character of God. His love is forever; it is part of His eternal character.
136:4–9 *great wonders.* God's creation of the universe is the grand display of His wisdom. The heavens give a clear presentation of the glory of God (19:1–6). Romans 1:20 teaches that God's "invisible attributes" are clearly seen through the things He has made.

135:2 [b] Luke 2:37 [c] Ps. 116:19 **135:3** [d] [Ps. 119:68] [e] Ps. 147:1 **135:4** [f] [Ex. 19:5] **135:5** [g] Ps. 95:3; 97:9 **135:6** [h] Ps. 115:3 **135:7** [i] Jer. 10:13 [j] Job 28:25, 26; 38:24–28 [k] Jer. 51:16 **135:8** [l] Ex. 12:12 **135:9** [m] Ex. 7:10 [n] Ps. 136:15 **135:10** [o] Num. 21:24 **135:11** [p] Josh. 12:7–24 **135:12** [q] Ps. 78:55; 136:21, 22 **135:13** [r] [Ex. 3:15] **135:14** [s] Deut. 32:36 **135:15** [t] [Ps. 115:4–8] **135:19** [u] [Ps. 115:9] **135:21** [v] Ps. 134:3 **136:1** [a] Ps. 106:1 [b] 1 Chr. 16:34 **136:2** [c] [Deut. 10:17] **136:4** [d] Ps. 72:18 **136:5** [e] Jer. 51:15 **136:6** [f] Jer. 10:12 **136:7** [g] Gen. 1:14–18 **136:8** [h] Gen. 1:16 **136:10** [i] Ex. 12:29 **136:11** [j] Ex. 12:51; 13:3, 16 **136:12** [k] Ex. 6:6 **136:13** [l] Ex. 14:21

14 And made Israel pass through the
 midst of it,
 For His mercy *endures* forever;
15 *m*But overthrew Pharaoh and his army
 in the Red Sea,
 For His mercy *endures* forever;
16 *n*To Him who led His people through
 the wilderness,
 For His mercy *endures* forever;
17 *o*To Him who struck down great kings,
 For His mercy *endures* forever;
18 *p*And slew famous kings,
 For His mercy *endures* forever—
19 *q*Sihon king of the Amorites,
 For His mercy *endures* forever;
20 *r*And Og king of Bashan,
 For His mercy *endures* forever—
21 *s*And gave their land as a heritage,
 For His mercy *endures* forever;
22 A heritage to Israel His servant,
 For His mercy *endures* forever.
23 Who *t*remembered us in our lowly state,
 For His mercy *endures* forever;
24 And *u*rescued us from our enemies,
 For His mercy *endures* forever;
25 *v*Who gives food to all flesh,
 For His mercy *endures* forever.
26 Oh, give thanks to the God of heaven!
 For His mercy *endures* forever.

Psalm 137

Longing for Zion in a Foreign Land

1 By the rivers of Babylon,
 There we sat down, yea, we wept
 When we remembered Zion.
2 We hung our harps
 Upon the willows in the midst of it.
3 For there those who carried us away
 captive asked of us a song,
 And those who *a*plundered us
 requested mirth,

Saying, "Sing us *one* of the songs of
 Zion!"

4 How shall we sing the LORD's song
 In a foreign land?
5 If I forget you, O Jerusalem,
 Let my right hand forget *its skill!*
6 If I do not remember you,
 Let my *b*tongue cling to the roof of my
 mouth—
 If I do not exalt Jerusalem
 Above my chief joy.

7 Remember, O LORD, against *c*the sons
 of Edom
 The day of Jerusalem,
 Who said, "Raze *it,* raze *it,*
 To its very foundation!"

8 O daughter of Babylon, *d*who are to be
 destroyed,
 Happy the one *e*who repays you as you
 have served us!
9 Happy the one who takes and *f*dashes
 Your little ones against the rock!

Psalm 138

The LORD's Goodness to the Faithful

A Psalm of David.

1 I will praise You with my whole heart;
 *a*Before the gods I will sing praises to
 You.
2 *b*I will worship *c*toward Your holy
 temple,
 And praise Your name
 For Your lovingkindness and Your
 truth;
 For You have *d*magnified Your word
 above all Your name.
3 In the day when I cried out, You
 answered me,
 And made me bold *with* strength in
 my soul.

136:23 *remembered us.* It is possible that these words suggest the return of the people of Judah and Jerusalem to their land following the Babylonian captivity.
137:1 *Babylon.* Babylon was one of the great empires in world history. When this psalm was written, the Jews were living there in exile.
137:5 *If I forget you.* The love of the people for Jerusalem was not just for the place, but for its function in their lives. The place was holy because it was the dwelling place of God and the place of worship and sacrifice for sins.
137:9 *Happy the one.* The idea of rejoicing and happiness at the violence depicted here is hard to swallow. Like some of the other difficult stories recorded in Scripture (see the Book of Judges), this imprecatory psalm is included with no comments about how God viewed the psalmist's emotion. Elsewhere in Scripture, we receive strict commands condemning taking vengeance into our own hands (Rom. 12:19–21), rejoicing when others suffer (Obad. 12), and refusing to forgive (Matt. 5:43–45; 6:14–15). However, none

of these passages are saying that we should pretend that evil doesn't exist. This psalmist's violent reaction to evil should remind us of how seriously God takes sin. He will not allow wickedness to go unpunished.
138:1 *Before the gods.* David is so confident in his faith in the Lord that he is determined to take the name of God into foreign territory.
138:2 *Your holy temple.* The use of the word "temple" does not rule out David as the author of this or similar poems (15:1). The Hebrew term is a general one that would fit whatever building was in use in David's day.

136:15 *m* Ex. 14:27 **136:16** *n* Ex. 13:18;
15:22 **136:17** *o* Ps. 135:10–12 **136:18** *p* Deut.
29:7 **136:19** *q* Num. 21:21 **136:20** *r* Num. 21:33
136:21 *s* Josh. 12:1 **136:23** *t* Gen. 8:1 **136:24** *u* Ps.
44:7 **136:25** *v* Ps. 104:27; 145:15 **137:3** *a* Ps. 79:1
137:6 *b* Ezek. 3:26 **137:7** *c* Jer. 49:7–22 **137:8** *d* Is.
13:1–6; 47:1 *e* Jer. 50:15 **137:9** *f* Is. 13:16 **138:1** *a* Ps.
119:46 **138:2** *b* Ps. 28:2 *c* 1 Kin. 8:29 *d* Is. 42:21

4 ^eAll the kings of the earth shall praise
You, O LORD,
When they hear the words of Your
mouth.
5 Yes, they shall sing of the ways of the
LORD,
For great *is* the glory of the LORD.
6 ^fThough the LORD *is* on high,
Yet ^gHe regards the lowly;
But the proud He knows from afar.

7 ^hThough I walk in the midst of trouble,
You will revive me;
You will stretch out Your hand
Against the wrath of my enemies,
And Your right hand will save me.
8 ⁱThe LORD will perfect *that which*
concerns me;
Your mercy, O LORD, *endures* forever;
^jDo not forsake the works of Your hands.

Psalm 139

God's Perfect Knowledge of Man

For the Chief Musician. A Psalm of
David.

1 O LORD, ^aYou have searched me and
known *me.*
2 ^bYou know my sitting down and my
rising up;
You ^cunderstand my thought afar off.
3 ^dYou comprehend my path and my
lying down,
And are acquainted with all my ways.
4 For *there is* not a word on my tongue,
But behold, O LORD, ^eYou know it
altogether.
5 You have hedged me behind and
before,
And laid Your hand upon me.

6 ^fSuch knowledge *is* too wonderful
for me;
It is high, I cannot *attain* it.

7 ^gWhere can I go from Your Spirit?
Or where can I flee from Your presence?
8 ^hIf I ascend into heaven, You *are* there;
ⁱIf I make my bed in hell, behold, You
are there.
9 *If* I take the wings of the morning,
And dwell in the uttermost parts of
the sea,
10 Even there Your hand shall lead me,
And Your right hand shall hold me.
11 If I say, "Surely the darkness shall fall*
on me,"
Even the night shall be light about me;
12 Indeed, ⁱthe darkness shall not hide
from You,
But the night shines as the day;
The darkness and the light *are* both
alike *to* You.

13 For You formed my inward parts;
You covered me in my mother's womb.
14 I will praise You, for I am fearfully *and*
wonderfully made;*
Marvelous are Your works,
And *that* my soul knows very well.
15 ^kMy frame was not hidden from You,
When I was made in secret,
And skillfully wrought in the lowest
parts of the earth.
16 Your eyes saw my substance, being yet
unformed.
And in Your book they all were written,
The days fashioned for me,
When *as yet there were* none of them.

---

* **139:11** Vulgate and Symmachus read *cover.*
* **139:14** Following Masoretic Text and Targum;
Septuagint, Syriac, and Vulgate read *You are
fearfully wonderful.*

138:6 *the lowly.* When man is boastful and conceited before God, he separates himself from God. Yet God bends with a special concern toward those who are humble before Him.
138:8 *mercy . . . endures forever.* God's loyal covenant love will never be rescinded or forgotten.
139:5 *You have hedged me behind and before.* The purpose of God's intimate knowledge of His servants is protective and helpful, not judgmental and condemning.
139:7–12 *You are there.* The believer can rejoice and rest in the knowledge that God is present in every place and every situation in life.
139:12 *the darkness and the light are both alike to You.* God can see what is happening to us even under cover of darkness. Nothing can conceal His people from Him.
139:14 God's Omniscience—He is the God who knows. He knows everything that has happened and will happen. He understands all of nature perfectly. In fact He knows everything there is to know. God knows so much that it would be impossible to overstate what He knows. The proper theological term for this attribute of God is: *omniscience.*
God knows all of our thoughts, motives, and

deeds. God knows us better than we know ourselves. We are all uneasy with the fact that God knows us so well. Like Adam and Eve, we fear the exposure of our sin.
There is, however, great reason to rejoice in the fact that God knows us so well. He loves us in spite of what He knows about us; in the midst of our sin He still loves us. He knows the worst things there are to know about us and still wants to save us. He also knows the best things about us. When everyone else misunderstands us, He understands us fully. Finally, God knows what we will be. He has a marvelous end in mind that should give us great comfort no matter what our present state.
139:16 *in Your book.* The idea is that all human beings, and the structure and meaning of each person's life, are all established from the beginning by God.

138:4 ^e Ps. 102:15 **138:6** ^f [Ps. 113:4–7] ^g [James
4:6] **138:7** ^h [Ps. 23:3, 4] **138:8** ⁱ Ps. 57:2 ^j Job 10:3, 8
139:1 ^a Ps. 17:3 **139:2** ^b 2 Kin. 19:27 ^c Matt. 9:4
139:3 ^d Job 14:16; 31:4 **139:4** ^e [Heb. 4:13] **139:6** ^f Job
42:3 **139:7** ^g [Jer. 23:24] **139:8** ^h [Amos 9:2–4] ⁱ [Job
26:6] **139:12** ^j Job 26:6; 34:22 **139:15** ^k Job 10:8, 9

17 ^lHow precious also are Your thoughts
to me, O God!
How great is the sum of them!
18 *If* I should count them, they would be
more in number than the sand;
When I awake, I am still with You.
19 Oh, that You would ^mslay the wicked,
O God!
ⁿDepart from me, therefore, you
bloodthirsty men.
20 For they ^ospeak against You wickedly;
Your enemies take *Your name* in
vain.*
21 ^pDo I not hate them, O LORD, who hate
You?
And do I not loathe those who rise up
against You?
22 I hate them with perfect hatred;
I count them my enemies.

23 ^qSearch me, O God, and know my heart;
Try me, and know my anxieties;
24 And see if *there is any* wicked way in
me,
And ^rlead me in the way everlasting.

Psalm 140

Prayer for Deliverance from Evil Men

To the Chief Musician. A Psalm
of David.

1 Deliver me, O LORD, from evil men;
Preserve me from violent men,
2 Who plan evil things in *their* hearts;
^aThey continually gather together *for*
war.
3 They sharpen their tongues like a
serpent;
The ^bpoison of asps *is* under their lips.
Selah

4 ^cKeep me, O LORD, from the hands of
the wicked;
Preserve me from violent men,
Who have purposed to make my steps
stumble.
5 The proud have hidden a ^dsnare for
me, and cords;
They have spread a net by the wayside;
They have set traps for me. *Selah*

6 I said to the LORD: "You *are* my God;
Hear the voice of my supplications,
O LORD.
7 O GOD the Lord, the strength of my
salvation,
You have covered my head in the day
of battle.
8 Do not grant, O LORD, the desires of
the wicked;
Do not further his *wicked* scheme,
^eLest they be exalted. *Selah*
9 "*As for* the head of those who surround
me,
Let the evil of their lips cover them;
10 ^fLet burning coals fall upon them;
Let them be cast into the fire,
Into deep pits, that they rise not up
again.
11 Let not a slanderer be established in
the earth;
Let evil hunt the violent man to
overthrow *him.*"

12 I know that the LORD will ^gmaintain
The cause of the afflicted,
And justice for the poor.
13 Surely the righteous shall give thanks
to Your name;
The upright shall dwell in Your
presence.

Psalm 141

Prayer for Safekeeping from Wickedness

A Psalm of David.

1 LORD, I cry out to You;
Make haste to me!
Give ear to my voice when I cry out
to You.
2 Let my prayer be set before You ^a*as*
incense,
^bThe lifting up of my hands *as* ^cthe
evening sacrifice.

3 Set a guard, O LORD, over my
^dmouth;
Keep watch over the door of my lips.

---

* **139:20** Septuagint and Vulgate read *They take*
Your cities in vain.

139:23 *Search me, O God.* It is only when we are aware
of our sins that we can repent of them and be healed.
140:6 *You are my God.* David confessed his complete
trust in the Lord even though he was surrounded by
people plotting his destruction. On the basis of his
trust, he pled with the Lord to deliver him.
140:10 *Let burning coals fall.* David recalls the judgment of Sodom and Gomorrah (Gen. 19:12–29) and asks
God to once again judge the enemies of the righteous.
140:12 *justice for the poor.* The cause of the poor
and afflicted is of special interest to the Lord. He
promises to uphold and comfort them (41:1; 72:4;
109:31; Luke 4:18; 6:20).

141:2 *as incense.* The prayers of God's people are
also compared to incense in Revelation 8:3–4.
141:3 *Set a guard . . . over my mouth.* David recognized how terribly easy it is to sin in what we say
(Prov. 30:32–33; James 3:1–12).

139:17 ^l [Ps. 40:5]   **139:19** ^m [Is. 11:4]   ⁿ Ps. 119:115
139:20 ^o Jude 15   **139:21** ^p 2 Chr. 19:2   **139:23** ^q Job
31:6   **139:24** ^r Ps. 5:8; 143:10   **140:2** ^a Ps. 56:6
140:3 ^b Ps. 58:4   **140:4** ^c Ps. 71:4   **140:5** ^d Jer. 18:22
140:8 ^e Deut. 32:27   **140:10** ^f Ps. 11:6   **140:12** ^g 1 Kin.
8:45   **141:2** ^a [Rev. 5:8; 8:3, 4]   ^b [1 Tim. 2:8]   ^c Ex. 29:39,
41   **141:3** ^d [Prov. 13:3; 21:23]

4 Do not incline my heart to any evil
thing,
To practice wicked works
With men who work iniquity;
eAnd do not let me eat of their
delicacies.

5 fLet the righteous strike me;
It shall be a kindness.
And let him rebuke me;
It shall be as excellent oil;
Let my head not refuse it.

For still my prayer *is* against the deeds
of the wicked.
6 Their judges are overthrown by the
sides of the cliff,
And they hear my words, for they are
sweet.
7 Our bones are scattered at the mouth
of the grave,
As when one plows and breaks up the
earth.

8 But gmy eyes *are* upon You, O GOD the
Lord;
In You I take refuge;
Do not leave my soul destitute.
9 Keep me from hthe snares they have
laid for me,
And from the traps of the workers of
iniquity.
10 iLet the wicked fall into their own nets,
While I escape safely.

Psalm 142

A Plea for Relief from Persecutors

A aContemplation* of David. A Prayer
bwhen he was in the cave.

1 I cry out to the LORD with my voice;
With my voice to the LORD I make my
supplication.
2 I pour out my complaint before Him;
I declare before Him my trouble.

3 When my spirit was coverwhelmed
within me,
Then You knew my path.
In the way in which I walk

They have secretly dset a snare for me.
4 Look on *my* right hand and see,
For *there is* no one who acknowledges
me;
Refuge has failed me;
No one cares for my soul.

5 I cried out to You, O LORD:
I said, "You *are* my refuge,
My portion in the land of the living.
6 Attend to my cry,
For I am brought very low;
Deliver me from my persecutors,
For they are stronger than I.
7 Bring my soul out of prison,
That I may epraise Your name;
The righteous shall surround me,
For You shall deal bountifully with me."

Psalm 143

An Earnest Appeal for Guidance and Deliverance

A Psalm of David.

1 Hear my prayer, O LORD,
Give ear to my supplications!
In Your faithfulness answer me,
And in Your righteousness.
2 Do not enter into judgment with Your
servant,
aFor in Your sight no one living is
righteous.

3 For the enemy has persecuted my soul;
He has crushed my life to the ground;
He has made me dwell in darkness,
Like those who have long been dead.
4 bTherefore my spirit is overwhelmed
within me;
My heart within me is distressed.

5 cI remember the days of old;
I meditate on all Your works;
I muse on the work of Your hands.
6 I spread out my hands to You;
dMy soul *longs* for You like a thirsty
land. *Selah*

---

* 142:title Hebrew *Maschil*

141:5 *Let the righteous strike me; it shall be a kindness.* The rebuke of a righteous person, even if it is painful at the time, is designed to bring about good. Sometimes being "nice" isn't really the kindest thing we can do for someone.
141:8 *my eyes are upon You.* If we focus on the strength of wickedness, we will be overcome with fear. If we focus on ourselves, we will become absorbed in our difficulties or exalt ourselves in our victories. Only when we focus on God can we achieve balance and health.
142:title *when he was in the cave.* This may refer to one of two occasions when David hid from King Saul in a cave: at En Gedi (Ps. 57; 1 Sam. 24), and at Adullam (1 Sam. 22:1).
142:5 *You are my refuge.* Sometimes God allows

us to go through times when we have no one at our right hand, "no one cares," just so that we will be very aware of our need for God.
143:2 *no one living is righteous.* This is not so much a confession as an observation that everyone is sinful.
143:3 *in darkness.* To live in darkness is similar to being in the pit (v. 7); this is the reason for the parallel to those who are already dead (Job 10:21–22).

141:4 e Prov. 23:6   **141:5** f [Prov. 9:8]   **141:8** g Ps. 25:15
141:9 h Ps. 119:110   **141:10** i Ps. 35:8   **142:title** a Ps.
32:title   b 1 Sam. 22:1   **142:3** c Ps. 77:3   d Ps. 141:9
142:7 e Ps. 34:1, 2   **143:2** a [Gal. 2:16]   **143:4** b Ps. 77:3
143:5 c Ps. 77:5, 10, 11   **143:6** d Ps. 63:1

7 Answer me speedily, O LORD;
My spirit fails!
Do not hide Your face from me,
ᵉLest I be like those who go down into
the pit.
8 Cause me to hear Your lovingkindness
ᶠin the morning,
For in You do I trust;
ᵍCause me to know the way in which I
should walk,
For ʰI lift up my soul to You.

9 Deliver me, O LORD, from my
enemies;
In You I take shelter.*
10 ⁱTeach me to do Your will,
For You *are* my God;
ʲYour Spirit *is* good.
Lead me in ᵏthe land of uprightness.

11 ˡRevive me, O LORD, for Your name's
sake!
For Your righteousness' sake bring my
soul out of trouble.
12 In Your mercy ᵐcut off my enemies,
And destroy all those who afflict my
soul;
For I *am* Your servant.

Psalm 144

A Song to the LORD Who Preserves
and Prospers His People

A Psalm of David.

1 Blessed *be* the LORD my Rock,
ᵃWho trains my hands for war,
And my fingers for battle—
2 My lovingkindness and my
fortress,
My high tower and my deliverer,
My shield and *the One* in whom I take
refuge,
Who subdues my people* under me.

3 ᵇLORD, what *is* man, that You take
knowledge of him?
Or the son of man, that You are
mindful of him?
4 ᶜMan is like a breath;
ᵈHis days *are* like a passing shadow.

5 ᵉBow down Your heavens, O LORD, and
come down;
ᶠTouch the mountains, and they shall
smoke.
6 ᵍFlash forth lightning and scatter
them;
Shoot out Your arrows and destroy
them.
7 Stretch out Your hand from above;
Rescue me and deliver me out of great
waters,
From the hand of foreigners,
8 Whose mouth ʰspeaks lying words,
And whose right hand *is* a right hand
of falsehood.

9 I will ⁱsing a new song to You, O God;
On a harp of ten strings I will sing
praises to You,
10 *The One* who gives salvation to
kings,
ʲWho delivers David His servant
From the deadly sword.

11 Rescue me and deliver me from the
hand of foreigners,
Whose mouth speaks lying words,
And whose right hand *is* a right hand
of falsehood—
12 That our sons *may be* ᵏas plants
grown up in their youth;
That our daughters *may be* as
pillars,
Sculptured in palace style;
13 *That* our barns *may be* full,
Supplying all kinds of produce;
That our sheep may bring forth
thousands
And ten thousands in our fields;
14 *That* our oxen *may be* well laden;
That there be no breaking in or going
out;
That there be no outcry in our
streets.
15 ˡHappy *are* the people who are in such
a state;
Happy *are* the people whose God *is* the
LORD!

---

* **143:9** Septuagint and Vulgate read *To You I flee.*
* **144:2** Following Masoretic Text, Septuagint,
and Vulgate; Syriac and Targum read *the peoples*
(compare 18:47).

143:11 *for Your name's sake.* The requests of the
psalmists are often tied to various character traits of
God. When we pray "in Jesus' name," we pray both
in the authority of His name and in the character it
represents.

144:4 *like a passing shadow.* Human life apart from
God is presented in the darkest terms by the Word of
God. Briefly stated, it is short and full of trouble (Job
14:1), uncertain (Luke 12:16–20), and empty (Eccl. 1:2).
In contrast, Paul the apostle describes the life of the
redeemed as being like a victorious soldier, a winning
athlete, a successful farmer, a diligent student, and a
useable vessel (2 Tim. 2). The redeemed life is marked
by peace and purpose now, and eternity with Christ
later.

144:11 *hand of falsehood.* The principal lie of the
enemy was that the Lord could not save His people
(Is. 36:18–20).

144:15 *Happy.* This word could also be translated
"Blessed." The happiness that David describes refers
both to external well-being and to internal peace.

143:7 ᵉ Ps. 28:1 **143:8** ᶠ Ps. 46:5 ᵍ Ps. 5:8 ʰ Ps. 25:1
143:10 ⁱ Ps. 25:4, 5 ʲ Neh. 9:20 ᵏ Is. 26:10 **143:11** ˡ Ps.
119:25 **143:12** ᵐ Ps. 54:5 **144:1** ᵃ 2 Sam. 22:35
144:3 ᵇ Heb. 2:6 **144:4** ᶜ Ps. 39:11 ᵈ Job 8:9; 14:2
144:5 ᵉ Ps. 18:9 ᶠ Ps. 104:32 **144:6** ᵍ Ps. 18:13, 14
144:8 ʰ Ps. 12:2 **144:9** ⁱ Ps. 33:2, 3; 40:3 **144:10** ʲ Ps.
18:50 **144:12** ᵏ Ps. 128:3 **144:15** ˡ [Ps. 33:12]

Psalm 145

A Song of God's Majesty and Love

*a*A Praise of David.

1 I will extol You, my God, O King;
And I will bless Your name forever
and ever.
2 Every day I will bless You,
And I will praise Your name forever
and ever.
3 *b*Great *is* the LORD, and greatly to be
praised;
And *c*His greatness *is* unsearchable.
4 *d*One generation shall praise Your
works to another,
And shall declare Your mighty acts.
5 I* will meditate on the glorious
splendor of Your majesty,
And on Your wondrous works.*
6 *Men* shall speak of the might of Your
awesome acts,
And I will declare Your greatness.
7 They shall utter the memory of Your
great goodness,
And shall sing of Your
righteousness.
8 *e*The LORD *is* gracious and full of
compassion,
Slow to anger and great in mercy.
9 *f*The LORD *is* good to all,
And His tender mercies *are* over all
His works.
10 *g*All Your works shall praise You,
O LORD,
And Your saints shall bless You.
11 They shall speak of the glory of Your
kingdom,
And talk of Your power,
12 To make known to the sons of men His
mighty acts,
And the glorious majesty of His
kingdom.
13 *h*Your kingdom *is* an everlasting
kingdom,
And Your dominion *endures*
throughout all generations.*
14 The LORD upholds all who fall,
And *i*raises up all *who are* bowed
down.
15 *j*The eyes of all look expectantly to
You,

And *k*You give them their food in due
season.
16 You open Your hand
*l*And satisfy the desire of every living
thing.
17 The LORD *is* righteous in all His ways,
Gracious in all His works.
18 *m*The LORD *is* near to all who call upon
Him,
To all who call upon Him *n*in truth.
19 He will fulfill the desire of those who
fear Him;
He also will hear their cry and save
them.
20 *o*The LORD preserves all who love Him,
But all the wicked He will destroy.
21 My mouth shall speak the praise of the
LORD,
And all flesh shall bless His holy name
Forever and ever.

Psalm 146

The Happiness of Those Whose Help Is the LORD

1 Praise the LORD!

*a*Praise the LORD, O my soul!
2 *b*While I live I will praise the LORD;
I will sing praises to my God while I
have my being.

3 *c*Do not put your trust in princes,
Nor in a son of man, in whom *there is*
no help.
4 *d*His spirit departs, he returns to his
earth;
In that very day *e*his plans perish.
5 *f*Happy *is* he who *has* the God of Jacob
for his help,
Whose hope *is* in the LORD his God,
6 *g*Who made heaven and earth,
The sea, and all that *is* in them;
Who keeps truth forever,

---

* **145:5** Following Masoretic Text and Targum;
Dead Sea Scrolls, Septuagint, Syriac, and Vulgate
read *They*. • Literally *on the words of Your wondrous works*   * **145:13** Following Masoretic Text
and Targum; Dead Sea Scrolls, Septuagint, Syriac,
and Vulgate add *The LORD is faithful in all His
words, And holy in all His works.*

145:8 gracious and full of compassion. In contrast
to the popular image of God as stern and critical, God
is full of compassion for erring humans—so much so
that He sent His own Son to redeem them (John 3:16).
145:13 an everlasting kingdom. The rule of God is
eternal, and the message of His wonders needs to be
delivered to all people in the present time.
145:17 righteous . . . Gracious. The pairing of these
two terms is a powerful description of the character of
God. Righteousness alone would lead to our destruction because of our sin, but God is also kind and gracious and has arranged a way for us to be saved.

146:3 in princes. Even the best of people are not
adequate help in times of terrible stress.
146:5 hope. Most people are aware that there is

145:title *a* Ps. 100:title   **145:3** *b* [Ps. 147:5]   *c* [Rom.
11:33]   **145:4** *d* Is. 38:19   **145:8** *e* [Num. 14:18]
145:9 *f* Nah. 1:7   **145:10** *g* Ps. 19:1   **145:13** *h* [1 Tim.
1:17]   **145:14** *i* Ps. 146:8   **145:15** *j* Ps. 104:27   *k* Ps.
136:25   **145:16** *l* Ps. 104:21, 28   **145:18** *m* [Deut. 4:7]
n [John 4:24]   **145:20** *o* [Ps. 31:23]   **146:1** *a* Ps. 103:1
146:2 *b* Ps. 104:33   **146:3** *c* [Is. 2:22]   **146:4** *d* [Eccl.
12:7]   *e* [1 Cor. 2:6]   **146:5** *f* Jer. 17:7   **146:6** *g* Rev. 14:7

7 ^hWho executes justice for the
oppressed,
ⁱWho gives food to the hungry.
^jThe LORD gives freedom to the
prisoners.

8 ^kThe LORD opens *the eyes of* the
blind;
^lThe LORD raises those who are bowed
down;
The LORD loves the righteous.
9 ^mThe LORD watches over the
strangers;
He relieves the fatherless and
widow;
ⁿBut the way of the wicked He turns
upside down.

10 ^oThe LORD shall reign forever—
Your God, O Zion, to all generations.

Praise the LORD!

Psalm 147

Praise to God for His Word and Providence

1 Praise the LORD!
For ^a*it is* good to sing praises to our
God;
^bFor *it is* pleasant, *and* ^cpraise is
beautiful.
2 The LORD ^dbuilds up Jerusalem;
^eHe gathers together the outcasts of
Israel.
3 ^fHe heals the brokenhearted
And binds up their wounds.
4 ^gHe counts the number of the stars;
He calls them all by name.
5 ^hGreat *is* our Lord, and ⁱmighty in
power;
^jHis understanding *is* infinite.
6 ^kThe LORD lifts up the humble;
He casts the wicked down to the
ground.

7 Sing to the LORD with thanksgiving;
Sing praises on the harp to our
God,
8 ^lWho covers the heavens with
clouds,
Who prepares rain for the earth,
Who makes grass to grow on the
mountains.
9 ^mHe gives to the beast its food,
And ⁿto the young ravens that cry.
10 ^oHe does not delight in the strength of
the horse;
He takes no pleasure in the legs of a
man.
11 The LORD takes pleasure in those who
fear Him,
In those who hope in His mercy.
12 Praise the LORD, O Jerusalem!
Praise your God, O Zion!
13 For He has strengthened the bars of
your gates;
He has blessed your children within
you.
14 ^pHe makes peace *in* your borders,
And ^qfills you with the finest wheat.
15 ^rHe sends out His command *to the*
earth;
His word runs very swiftly.
16 ^sHe gives snow like wool;
He scatters the frost like ashes;
17 He casts out His hail like morsels;
Who can stand before His cold?
18 ^tHe sends out His word and melts
them;
He causes His wind to blow, *and* the
waters flow.
19 ^uHe declares His word to Jacob,
^vHis statutes and His judgments to
Israel.
20 ^wHe has not dealt thus with any
nation;
And *as for His* judgments, they have
not known them.

Praise the LORD!

---

more in life than they are getting out of it. They try many things to satisfy their desire for a fuller life. But like Solomon, who gives his testimony in the Book of Ecclesiastes, they find that "things" do not satisfy. Blessedness, or fullness of life, comes to those who have a relationship with God and hope of eternal life with Him.
146:10 *reign forever.* God's reign is both present and eternal.
147:2 *builds up Jerusalem.* The few people who had returned from captivity faced an immense task. They needed to remember that the work was God's and He would see that it was accomplished.
147:3 *heals the brokenhearted.* God's principal work is always within the human heart (51:10–12).
147:6 *lifts up the humble.* God's greatness may be approached only by the humble (James 4:6).
147:9 *beast its food.* Jesus describes God's care as extending even to sparrows (Matt. 10:29).
147:10 *He does not delight.* The joy that God finds

in His "very good" creation (Gen. 1) does not compare with the delight that He takes in humans whose hearts are turned to Him.
147:19 *His word.* God's word goes throughout His creation, causing snow, frost, hail, wind, and every other aspect of weather to obey His command. He has also given His Word to His people. Will we obey as the wind does, or will we be the only element of creation that is unresponsive to Him?

146:7 ^h Ps. 103:6 ⁱ Ps. 107:9 ^j Ps. 107:10 **146:8** ^k Matt. 9:30 ^l Luke 13:13 **146:9** ^m Deut. 10:18 ⁿ Ps. 147:6 **146:10** ^o Ex. 15:18 **147:1** ^a Ps. 92:1 ^b Ps. 135:3 ^c Ps. 33:1 **147:2** ^d Ps. 102:16 ^e Deut. 30:3 **147:3** ^f [Ps. 51:17] **147:4** ^g Is. 40:26 **147:5** ^h Ps. 48:1 ⁱ Nah. 1:3 ^j Is. 40:28 **147:6** ^k Ps. 146:8, 9 **147:8** ^l Job 38:26 **147:9** ^m Job 38:41 ⁿ [Matt. 6:26] **147:10** ^o Ps. 33:16, 17 **147:14** ^p Is. 54:13; 60:17, 18 ^q Ps. 132:15 **147:15** ^r [Ps. 107:20] **147:16** ^s Job 37:6 **147:18** ^t Job 37:10 **147:19** ^u Deut. 33:4 ^v Mal. 4:4 **147:20** ^w [Rom. 3:1, 2]

Psalm 148

Praise to the LORD from Creation

1 Praise the LORD!

Praise the LORD from the heavens;
Praise Him in the heights!
2 Praise Him, all His angels;
Praise Him, all His hosts!
3 Praise Him, sun and moon;
Praise Him, all you stars of light!
4 Praise Him, [a]you heavens of
heavens,
And [b]you waters above the heavens!

5 Let them praise the name of the LORD,
For [c]He commanded and they were
created.
6 [d]He also established them forever and
ever;
He made a decree which shall not pass
away.

7 Praise the LORD from the earth,
[e]You great sea creatures and all the
depths;
8 Fire and hail, snow and clouds;
Stormy wind, fulfilling His word;
9 [f]Mountains and all hills;
Fruitful trees and all cedars;
10 Beasts and all cattle;
Creeping things and flying fowl;
11 Kings of the earth and all peoples;
Princes and all judges of the earth;
12 Both young men and maidens;
Old men and children.

13 Let them praise the name of the
LORD,
For His [g]name alone is exalted;
His glory is above the earth and
heaven.
14 And He [h]has exalted the horn of His
people,
The praise of [i]all His saints—
Of the children of Israel,
[j]A people near to Him.

Praise the LORD!

Psalm 149

Praise to God for His Salvation and Judgment

1 Praise the LORD!

[a]Sing to the LORD a new song,
And His praise in the assembly of
saints.

2 Let Israel rejoice in their Maker;
Let the children of Zion be joyful in
their [b]King.
3 [c]Let them praise His name with the
dance;
Let them sing praises to Him with the
timbrel and harp.
4 For [d]the LORD takes pleasure in His
people;
[e]He will beautify the humble with
salvation.

5 Let the saints be joyful in glory;
Let them [f]sing aloud on their beds.
6 Let the high praises of God be in their
mouth,
And [g]a two-edged sword in their
hand,
7 To execute vengeance on the nations,
And punishments on the peoples;
8 To bind their kings with chains,
And their nobles with fetters of iron;
9 [h]To execute on them the written
judgment—
[i]This honor have all His saints.

Praise the LORD!

Psalm 150

Let All Things Praise the LORD

1 Praise[a] the LORD!

Praise God in His sanctuary;
Praise Him in His mighty firmament!

148:5 He commanded and they were created. The reality of God as Creator of the universe is the basis of His claim on our lives.
148:14 A people near to Him. When we consider the meaning of God's holiness (99:1; Is. 6:3) and the reality of His power, the marvel that He approaches us to mercifully provide for us becomes overwhelming.
149:1 in the assembly. One of the primary emphases in the Book of Psalms is that the praise of God is to take place in the center of the worshiping community. Praise unites the people of God (33:1–3).
149:5 the saints. This term (also translated "godly ones") refers to those who demonstrate in their lives the characteristics of the God whom they serve.
149:6 two-edged sword. The focus of the psalm switches from the congregation at worship to the army in training. Israel's army was to be the vanguard for the battle of the Lord. Their training was to have a strong component of praise and worship to God.

150:1 Praise the LORD. This psalm is a development of the Hebrew word "hallelujah," meaning "praise the Lord."
150:1 Praise—To praise God is to acknowledge who He is in all His glory. While thanksgiving is given to acknowledge what God has done, praise is given to declare who God is. Here are some facts about praise:
• God alone is worthy of our praise (Ps. 18:3; 113:3).
• It is His will for us to praise Him (Ps. 50:23).

148:4 [a] 1 Kin. 8:27 [b] Gen. 1:7 **148:5** [c] Gen. 1:1, 6
148:6 [d] Ps. 89:37 **148:7** [e] Is. 43:20 **149:8** [f] Is. 44:23;
49:13 **148:13** [g] Ps. 8:1 **148:14** [h] Ps. 75:10 [i] Ps.
149:7 [j] Eph. 2:17 **149:1** [a] Ps. 33:3 **149:2** [b] Zech.
9:9 **149:3** [c] Ps. 81:2 **149:4** [d] Ps. 35:27 [e] Ps. 132:16
149:5 [f] Job 35:10 **149:6** [g] Heb. 4:12 **149:9** [h] Deut.
7:1, 2 [i] 1 Cor. 6:2 **150:1** [a] Ps. 145:5, 6

2 Praise Him for His mighty acts;
  Praise Him according to His excellent
    [b]greatness!

3 Praise Him with the sound of the
    trumpet;
  Praise Him with the lute and harp!
4 Praise Him with the timbrel and
    dance;

Praise Him with stringed instruments
    and flutes!
5 Praise Him with loud cymbals;
  Praise Him with clashing cymbals!

6 Let everything that has breath praise
    the LORD.

Praise the LORD!

• Praise should be continuous (Ps. 34:1; 71:6) and also public (Ps. 22:25).
• We are to praise God for His holiness (2 Chr. 20:21), grace (Eph. 1:6), goodness (Ps. 135:3), and kindness (Ps. 138:2).
• All nature praises God (Ps. 148).
• The sun, moon, and stars praise Him (Ps. 19:1).
• The angels praise Him (Ps. 148:2).
150:6 *everything that has breath.* The very breath that God gives us should be used to praise Him. As long as we live we should praise our Creator (146:1–2). By His breath God created all things (33:6), and by our breath we should adore Him. The Book of Psalms begins with God's blessing on the righteous (1:1) and concludes with all of creation blessing its loving Creator.

150:2 [b] Deut. 3:24

THE BOOK OF
PROVERBS

▶ **AUTHOR:** Solomon's name appears at the beginning of the three sections that he wrote: 1–9; 10:1—22:16; and 25–29. Only about 800 of the more than 3,000 proverbs attributed to Solomon are recorded here. It is likely that Solomon collected and edited proverbs other than his own. The collection of Solomonic proverbs in chapters 25–29 was assembled by the scribes of King Hezekiah. Some of the sayings in Proverbs are quite similar to those found in *The Wisdom of Amenemope*, a document of teachings on civil service by an Egyptian who probably lived between 1000 B.C. and 600 B.C.

▶ **TIME:** c. 950–700 B.C.   ▶ **KEY VERSES:** Prov. 3:5–6

▶ **THEME:** The Proverbs are part of what is commonly called the wisdom literature of the Bible. Each society needs a way to pass on what it understands to be the best way to live to succeeding generations. Biblical wisdom literature provided that means for the Jewish community. The Proverbs contain nuggets of truth that endure not only in the Jewish culture, but also make sense today. It contains basic wisdom on how to deal with the most common everyday issues that we face. Transcending personality and culture, the simple truth is that if people followed the advice of Proverbs, many of their problems would be reduced dramatically.

The Beginning of Knowledge

1 The ᵃproverbs of Solomon the son of David, king of Israel:

2 To know wisdom and instruction,
To perceive the words of understanding,
3 To receive the instruction of wisdom,
Justice, judgment, and equity;
4 To give prudence to the ᵇsimple,
To the young man knowledge and
discretion—
5 ᶜA wise *man* will hear and increase
learning,
And a man of understanding will
attain wise counsel,
6 To understand a proverb and an
enigma,
The words of the wise and their
ᵈriddles.

7 ᵉThe fear of the LORD *is* the beginning
of knowledge,
But fools despise wisdom and
instruction.

Shun Evil Counsel

8 ᶠMy son, hear the instruction of your
father,
And do not forsake the law of your
mother;

1:2–3 To know . . . To perceive . . . To receive. These verbs refer to the ways we acquire wisdom. *Wisdom* refers to skill. *Instruction* could also be translated discipline; it refers to the process of receiving knowledge and applying it to daily life.
1:3 Justice, judgment, and equity. Biblical wisdom also has a moral context. It involves all of life and may often involve a change of behavior and a commitment to justice.
1:4 To the young man knowledge and discretion. The young have little experience and are more likely to make mistakes. A wise person has learned by experience how to distinguish what is true, praiseworthy, and good from what is false, shameful, and bad (Rom. 12:1–2).
1:7 The fear of the LORD. This concept is the most basic ingredient in wisdom. Fools have rejected the fear of the Lord. The term "despise" is strongly

negative. Not fearing God is the same as rejecting wisdom outright (Dan. 11:32; John 17:3).
1:8 My son, hear. The opening words of wisdom's instruction come as an appeal from parent to son (a generic term for child)—a theme that continues throughout the book. Both the Old and New Testaments have one central teaching for children to understand—obey your parents. The Fifth Commandment makes honoring parents the foundational teaching in human relationships. It is also the only Commandment that comes with a promise, "that your days may be long" (Deut. 5:16). Paul's teaching in Ephesians 6:1 echoes what we see here in Proverbs. Obeying parents is the right thing to do.

1:1 ᵃ 1 Kin. 4:32   **1:4** ᵇ Prov. 9:4   **1:5** ᶜ Prov. 9:9
1:6 ᵈ Ps. 78:2   **1:7** ᵉ Job 28:28   **1:8** ᶠ Prov. 4:1

9 For they *will be* a ᵍgraceful ornament
on your head,
And chains about your neck.

10 My son, if sinners entice you,
ʰDo not consent.
11 If they say, "Come with us,
Let us ⁱlie in wait to *shed* blood;
Let us lurk secretly for the innocent
without cause;
12 Let us swallow them alive like Sheol,*
And whole, ʲlike those who go down to
the Pit;
13 We shall find all *kinds* of precious
possessions,
We shall fill our houses with spoil;
14 Cast in your lot among us,
Let us all have one purse"—
15 My son, ᵏdo not walk in the way with
them,
ˡKeep your foot from their path;
16 ᵐFor their feet run to evil,
And they make haste to shed blood.
17 Surely, in vain the net is spread
In the sight of any bird;
18 But they lie in wait for their *own* blood,
They lurk secretly for their *own* lives.
19 ⁿSo *are* the ways of everyone who is
greedy for gain;
It takes away the life of its owners.

The Call of Wisdom

20 ᵒWisdom calls aloud outside;
She raises her voice in the open
squares.
21 She cries out in the chief concourses,*
At the openings of the gates in the city
She speaks her words:
22 "How long, you simple ones, will you
love simplicity?
For scorners delight in their scorning,
And fools hate knowledge.
23 Turn at my rebuke;
Surely ᵖI will pour out my spirit on you;
I will make my words known to you.

24 ᵅBecause I have called and you refused,
I have stretched out my hand and no
one regarded,
25 Because you ʳdisdained all my counsel,
And would have none of my rebuke;
26 ˢI also will laugh at your calamity;
I will mock when your terror comes,
27 When ᵗyour terror comes like a storm,
And your destruction comes like a
whirlwind,
When distress and anguish come upon
you.

28 "Thenᵘ they will call on me, but I will
not answer;
They will seek me diligently, but they
will not find me.
29 Because they ᵛhated knowledge
And did not ʷchoose the fear of the
Lord,
30 ˣThey would have none of my counsel
And despised my every rebuke.
31 Therefore ʸthey shall eat the fruit of
their own way,
And be filled to the full with their own
fancies.
32 For the turning away of the simple will
slay them,
And the complacency of fools will
destroy them;
33 But whoever listens to me will dwell
ᶻsafely,
And ᵅwill be secure, without fear of
evil."

The Value of Wisdom

2 My son, if you receive my words,
And ᵅtreasure my commands within
you,
2 So that you incline your ear to wisdom,
And apply your heart to understanding;

* 1:12 Or *the grave*   * 1:21 Septuagint, Syriac,
and Targum read *top of the walls*; Vulgate reads
the head of multitudes.

From obedience springs the ability to deal with all the other important issues of life. The child who has not learned to obey his parents, who are God's representatives in the family, will probably not learn to obey God.

Christ's obedience is the perfect illustration. He was obedient to God the Father even though that obedience resulted in His death (Phil. 2:6–8). Being obedient for Christ meant no qualifications or limitations on that obedience.
1:15–18 *My son, do not walk in the way with them.* The parents speak words of caution. One step on the precipitous path is a step toward destruction. Spreading a net in the sight of the bird one wishes to trap would be a fruitless task. Yet the fool is less sensible than the bird; he will watch the trap being set and get caught in it anyway.
1:19 *takes away the life.* The study of wisdom is a matter of life and death.
1:20–21 *Wisdom calls aloud outside.* The word *wisdom* is plural and intensive. This fact calls attention to the word and heightens its meaning.
1:22–27 *How long, you simple ones, will you love*

simplicity? Wisdom addresses the *simple ones*. These are young people who have not yet made up their minds about life or the direction they will take. Wisdom ridicules those who reject her when they come to face the inevitable judgment of their foolishness (Ps. 2:4). Yet wisdom also laughs with joy at God's work and has delight in the people of God (8:30–31).
1:28–33 *I will not answer.* When fools despise wisdom, they must face the results of their choice. Their hatred for wisdom arises out of refusal to fear God (v. 29). Fools bring about their own destruction. In contrast, those who listen to her will find security.
2:1–5 *My son.* These verses begin the second of the

1:9 ᵍ Prov. 3:22   **1:10** ʰ Gen. 39:7–10   **1:11** ⁱ Jer.
5:26   **1:12** ʲ Ps. 28:1   **1:15** ᵏ Ps. 1:1   ˡ Ps. 119:101
1:16 ᵐ Is. 59:7]   **1:19** ⁿ [1 Tim. 6:10]   **1:20** ᵒ [John
7:37]   **1:23** ᵖ Joel 2:28   **1:24** ᵠ Jer. 7:13   **1:25** ʳ Luke
7:30   **1:26** ˢ Ps. 2:4   **1:27** ᵗ [Prov. 10:24, 25]   **1:28** ᵘ Is.
1:15   **1:29** ᵛ Job 21:14   ʷ Ps. 119:173   **1:30** ˣ Ps.
81:11   **1:31** ʸ Job 4:8   **1:33** ᶻ Prov. 3:24–26   ᵅ Ps. 112:7
2:1 ᵅ [Prov. 4:21]

3   Yes, if you cry out for discernment,
    And lift up your voice for
    understanding,
4   *b*If you seek her as silver,
    And search for her as *for* hidden
    treasures;
5   *c*Then you will understand the fear of
    the Lord,
    And find the knowledge of God.
6   *d*For the Lord gives wisdom;
    From His mouth *come* knowledge and
    understanding;
7   He stores up sound wisdom for the
    upright;
    eHe is a shield to those who walk
    uprightly;
8   He guards the paths of justice,
    And *f*preserves the way of His saints.
9   Then you will understand
    righteousness and justice,
    Equity *and* every good path.

10   When wisdom enters your heart,
    And knowledge is pleasant to your
    soul,
11   Discretion will preserve you;
    *g*Understanding will keep you,
12   To deliver you from the way of evil,
    From the man who speaks perverse
    things,
13   From those who leave the paths of
    uprightness
    To *h*walk in the ways of darkness;
14   *i*Who rejoice in doing evil,
    And delight in the perversity of the
    wicked;
15   *j*Whose ways *are* crooked,
    And *who are* devious in their paths;
16   To deliver you from *k*the immoral
    woman,
    *l*From the seductress *who* flatters with
    her words,
17   Who forsakes the companion of her
    youth,
    And forgets the covenant of her God.

18   For *m*her house leads down to death,
    And her paths to the dead;
19   None who go to her return,
    Nor do they regain the paths of life—
20   So you may walk in the way of
    goodness,
    And keep *to* the paths of
    righteousness.
21   For the upright will dwell in the *n*land,
    And the blameless will remain in it;
22   But the wicked will be cut off from the
    earth,
    And the unfaithful will be uprooted
    from it.

Guidance for the Young

3   My son, do not forget my law,
    *a*But let your heart keep my
    commands;
2   For length of days and long life
    And *b*peace they will add to you.

3   Let not mercy and truth forsake you;
    *c*Bind them around your neck,
    *d*Write them on the tablet of your heart,
4   *e*And so find favor and high esteem
    In the sight of God and man.

5   *f*Trust in the Lord with all your heart,
    *g*And lean not on your own
    understanding;
6   *h*In all your ways acknowledge Him,
    And He shall direct* your paths.

7   Do not be wise in your own *i*eyes;
    Fear the Lord and depart from evil.
8   It will be health to your flesh,*
    And *i*strength* to your bones.

9   *k*Honor the Lord with your
    possessions,
    And with the firstfruits of all your
    increase;

---

* **3:6** Or *make smooth* or *straight*   * **3:8** Literally *navel*, figurative of the body • Literally *drink* or *refreshment*

"my son" passages and tie the concepts of wisdom and the knowledge of God more closely together. Wisdom is near but not always easy to embrace.
2:5–8 the fear of the Lord . . . the knowledge of God. When a person seeks wisdom, he or she finds it. Those who know God fear or revere Him. **sound wisdom.** This is another word for wisdom that can also mean "abiding success" or "victory."
2:10–11 wisdom enters your heart. This phrase stresses the internalization of wisdom. The proverbs do not merely provide knowledge; they provide insight into practical living.
2:12–15 the way of evil. Evil is directly contrasted with wisdom. It is characterized by perverse things such as lies, deceptions, and deviousness.
2:16–19 the immoral woman. The adulteress is described as a flatterer, and flattery is the method used by the adulteress, not only in trapping her victims, but in excusing her sin (30:20). She is unfaithful to her husband and prefers to forget the covenant of her God (2:17).
3:3–4 mercy and truth. These words describe God's

character (Ps. 100:5). The apostle John used the Greek equivalent of these words, "grace and truth," to describe Jesus' character in John 1:14.
3:5–6 Trust in the Lord. The verb "trust" is complemented by the verb "lean." Trusting in God is a conscious dependence on God, much like leaning on a tree for support. The command to acknowledge Him means to observe Him and get to know Him in the process of living. These are the vital elements of faith that should fill every area of life.
3:9 the firstfruits of all your increase. God expects that out of the blessings we receive we should readily give. One aspect of worship is giving. These verses

---

2:4 *b* [Prov. 3:14]   **2:5** *c* [James 1:5, 6]   **2:6** *d* 1 Kin. 3:9, 12   **2:7** *e* [Ps. 84:11]   **2:8** *f* [1 Sam. 2:9]   **2:11** *g* Prov. 4:6; 6:22   **2:13** *h* [John 3:19, 20]   **2:14** *i* [Rom. 1:32]   **2:15** *j* Ps. 125:5   **2:16** *k* Prov. 5:20; 6:24; 7:5   *l* Prov. 5:3   **2:18** *m* Prov. 7:27   **2:21** *n* Ps. 37:3   **3:1** *a* Deut. 8:1   **3:2** *b* Ps. 119:165   **3:3** *c* Prov. 6:21   *d* [2 Cor. 3:3]   **3:4** *e* Rom. 14:18   **3:5** *f* [Ps. 37:3, 5]   *g* [Jer. 9:23, 24]   **3:6** *h* [1 Chr. 28:9]   **3:7** *i* Rom. 12:16   **3:8** *j* Job 21:24   **3:9** *k* Ex. 22:29

10 *l*So your barns will be filled with
plenty,
And your vats will overflow with new
wine.

11 *m*My son, do not despise the chastening
of the LORD,
Nor detest His correction;
12 For whom the LORD loves He corrects,
*n*Just as a father the son *in whom* he
delights.

13 *o*Happy *is* the man *who* finds wisdom,
And the man *who* gains
understanding;
14 *p*For her proceeds *are* better than the
profits of silver,
And her gain than fine gold.
15 She *is* more precious than rubies,
And *q*all the things you may desire
cannot compare with her.
16 *r*Length of days *is* in her right hand,
In her left hand riches and honor.
17 *s*Her ways *are* ways of pleasantness,
And all her paths *are* peace.
18 She *is* *t*a tree of life to those who take
hold of her,
And happy *are* all who retain her.

19 *u*The LORD by wisdom founded the
earth;
By understanding He established the
heavens;
20 By His knowledge the depths were
*v*broken up,
And clouds drop down the dew.

21 My son, let them not depart from your
eyes—
Keep sound wisdom and discretion;
22 So they will be life to your soul
And grace to your neck.
23 *w*Then you will walk safely in your way,
And your foot will not stumble.
24 When you lie down, you will not be
afraid;
Yes, you will lie down and your sleep
will be sweet.
25 *x*Do not be afraid of sudden terror,
Nor of trouble from the wicked when
it comes;

26 For the LORD will be your confidence,
And will keep your foot from being
caught.

27 *y*Do not withhold good from those to
whom it is due,
When it is in the power of your hand
to do *so*.
28 *z*Do not say to your neighbor,
"Go, and come back,
And tomorrow I will give *it*,"
When you have it with you.
29 Do not devise evil against your
neighbor,
For he dwells by you for safety's sake.
30 *a*Do not strive with a man without
cause,
If he has done you no harm.

31 *b*Do not envy the oppressor,
And choose none of his ways;
32 For the perverse *person is* an
abomination to the LORD,
*c*But His secret counsel *is* with the
upright.
33 *d*The curse of the LORD *is* on the house
of the wicked,
But *e*He blesses the home of the just.
34 *f*Surely He scorns the scornful,
But gives grace to the humble.
35 The wise shall inherit glory,
But shame shall be the legacy of fools.

Security in Wisdom

4 Hear, *a*my children, the instruction of
a father,
And give attention to know
understanding;
2 For I give you good doctrine:
Do not forsake my law.
3 When I was my father's son,
*b*Tender and the only one in the sight of
my mother,
4 *c*He also taught me, and said to me:
"Let your heart retain my words;
*d*Keep my commands, and live.
5 *e*Get wisdom! Get understanding!
Do not forget, nor turn away from the
words of my mouth.

---

should not be taken as a formula for getting rich.
They point to what is the proper response to God's
gifts to us, not a return we get for investing.
3:11–12 *the chastening of the LORD.* Discipline is the
other side of God's grace. We should cherish God's
correction in our lives, because God disciplines those
He loves (Heb. 2:7–10).
3:13–18 *Happy.* The Beatitudes of Jesus in the Sermon on the Mount (Matt. 5:3–12) work much the way
these verses do. God is pleased with people who discover that wisdom is a priceless treasure.
3:19 *by wisdom founded the earth.* One of the central themes in Proverbs is the association of wisdom
with creation (8:1–36).
3:21 *let them not depart.* This verse encourages the
son to keep faith with wisdom. The intent is much like
that of the Shema (Deut. 6:4–9).
4:1–4 *I was my father's son.* In Israel training in

wisdom happened in the home. As his father had
taught him, so the son now teaches his own sons, one
generation instructing another. The call for parents to
teach the things of God to their children is based on
Deuteronomy 6:7.
4:5–7 *Get wisdom.* Verses 5–9 present an impas-
sioned plea from the father to his sons to acquire
wisdom whatever the cost. The presentation follows

3:10 *l* Deut. 28:8 **3:11** *m* Job 5:17 **3:12** *n* Deut.
8:5 **3:13** *o* Prov. 8:32, 34, 35 **3:14** *p* Job 28:13
3:15 *q* Matt. 13:44 **3:16** *r* [1 Tim. 4:8] **3:17** *s* [Matt.
11:29] **3:18** *t* Gen. 2:9 **3:19** *u* Ps. 104:24 **3:20** *v* Gen.
7:11 **3:23** *w* Prov. 10:9 **3:25** *x* Ps. 91:5 **3:27** *y* Rom.
13:7 **3:28** *z* Lev. 19:13 **3:30** *a* [Rom. 12:18] **3:31** *b* Ps.
37:1 **3:32** *c* Ps. 25:14 **3:33** *d* Zech. 5:3, 4 *e* Ps. 1:3
3:34 *f* James 4:6 **4:1** *a* Ps. 34:11 **4:3** *b* 1 Chr. 29:1
4:4 *c* 1 Chr. 28:9 *d* Prov. 7:2 **4:5** *e* Prov. 2:2, 3

6 Do not forsake her, and she will
preserve you;
*f*Love her, and she will keep you.
7 *g*Wisdom *is* the principal thing;
Therefore get wisdom.
And in all your getting, get
understanding.
8 *h*Exalt her, and she will promote you;
She will bring you honor, when you
embrace her.
9 She will place on your head *i*an
ornament of grace;
A crown of glory she will deliver to
you."

10 Hear, my son, and receive my sayings,
*j*And the years of your life will be many.
11 I have *k*taught you in the way of
wisdom;
I have led you in right paths.
12 When you walk, *l*your steps will not be
hindered,
*m*And when you run, you will not
stumble.
13 Take firm hold of instruction, do not
let go;
Keep her, for she *is* your life.

14 *n*Do not enter the path of the wicked,
And do not walk in the way of evil.
15 Avoid it, do not travel on it;
Turn away from it and pass on.
16 *o*For they do not sleep unless they have
done evil;
And their sleep is taken away unless
they make *someone* fall.
17 For they eat the bread of wickedness,
And drink the wine of violence.
18 *p*But the path of the just *q*is like the
shining sun,*
That shines ever brighter unto the
perfect day.
19 *r*The way of the wicked *is* like
darkness;
They do not know what makes them
stumble.

20 My son, give attention to my words;
Incline your ear to my sayings.
21 Do not let them depart from your eyes;
Keep them in the midst of your heart;

22 For they *are* life to those who find
them,
And health to all their flesh.
23 Keep your heart with all diligence,
For out of it *spring* the issues of *s*life.
24 Put away from you a deceitful mouth,
And put perverse lips far from you.
25 Let your eyes look straight ahead,
And your eyelids look right before you.
26 Ponder the path of your *t*feet,
And let all your ways be established.
27 Do not turn to the right or the left;
Remove your foot from evil.

The Peril of Adultery

5 My son, pay attention to my wisdom;
Lend your ear to my understanding,
2 That you may preserve discretion,
And your lips *a*may keep knowledge.
3 *b*For the lips of an immoral woman drip
honey,
And her mouth *is* *c*smoother than oil;
4 But in the end she is bitter as
wormwood,
Sharp as a two-edged sword.
5 Her feet go down to death,
*d*Her steps lay hold of hell.*
6 Lest you ponder *her* path of life—
Her ways are unstable;
You do not know *them*.

7 Therefore hear me now, *my* children,
And do not depart from the words of
my mouth.
8 Remove your way far from her,
And do not go near the door of her
house,
9 Lest you give your honor to others,
And your years to the cruel *one*;
10 Lest aliens be filled with your wealth,
And your labors *go* to the house of a
foreigner;
11 And you mourn at last,
When your flesh and your body are
consumed,
12 And say:
"How I have hated instruction,
And my heart despised correction!

---

* 4:18 Literally *light*   * 5:5 Or *Sheol*

---

a pattern: statement, restatement, embellishment.
By making creative use of creative restatement, the
ideas come through strongly.
4:9 ornament of grace . . . crown of glory. These
phrases emphasize the supreme value of wisdom.
The person who holds wisdom in highest esteem and
embraces it will be exalted and honored.
4:20–27 Keep your heart with all diligence. This
section demands constancy of heart and purpose,
honesty in speech, steadiness of gaze, and a right
goal in walk and life. Setting off on the path of wisdom is no casual thing.
5:1–6 the lips of an immoral woman drip honey.
Chapter 5 returns to the theme of the immoral
woman (2:16–19). This passage speaks strongly for
marital fidelity against all pressure to the contrary.
5:5 Her feet go down to death. This verse warns

us of the deadly effects of immorality. Fornication,
adultery, and prostitution lead to personality decay,
venereal disease, abortion, separation, and divorce.
5:8–10 Remove your way far from her. Some
temptations should be avoided at all cost. A wise
son knows this and will not go near an immoral
woman. The apostle Paul's instruction to Timothy
to flee youthful lusts (2 Tim. 2:22) teaches the same
theme.

4:6 *f* 2 Thess. 2:10   **4:7** *g* Matt. 13:44   **4:8** *h* 1 Sam. 2:30
4:9 *i* Prov. 3:22   **4:10** *j* Prov. 3:2   **4:11** *k* 1 Sam. 12:23
4:12 *l* Ps. 18:36   *m* [Ps. 91:11]   **4:14** *n* Ps. 1:1   **4:16** *o* Ps.
36:4   **4:18** *p* Matt. 5:14, 45   *q* 2 Sam. 23:4   **4:19** *r* [Is.
59:9, 10]   **4:23** *s* [Matt. 12:34; 15:18, 19]   **4:26** *t* Heb.
12:13   **5:2** *a* Mal. 2:7   **5:3** *b* Prov. 2:16   *c* Ps. 55:21
5:5 *d* Prov. 7:27

13 I have not obeyed the voice of my
teachers,
Nor inclined my ear to those who
instructed me!
14 I was on the verge of total ruin,
In the midst of the assembly and
congregation."

15 Drink water from your own cistern,
And running water from your own
well.
16 Should your fountains be dispersed
abroad,
Streams of water in the streets?
17 Let them be only your own,
And not for strangers with you.
18 Let your fountain be blessed,
And rejoice with *e*the wife of your
youth.
19 *fAs a* loving deer and a graceful doe,
Let her breasts satisfy you at all times;
And always be enraptured with her
love.
20 For why should you, my son, be
enraptured by *g*an immoral
woman,
And be embraced in the arms of a
seductress?

21 *h*For the ways of man *are* before the
eyes of the LORD,
And He ponders all his paths.
22 *i*His own iniquities entrap the wicked
man,
And he is caught in the cords of his
sin.
23 *j*He shall die for lack of instruction,
And in the greatness of his folly he
shall go astray.

Dangerous Promises

6 My son, *a*if you become surety for your
friend,
If you have shaken hands in pledge for
a stranger,
2 You are snared by the words of your
mouth;
You are taken by the words of your
mouth.
3 So do this, my son, and deliver
yourself;

For you have come into the hand of
your friend:
Go and humble yourself;
Plead with your friend.
4 *b*Give no sleep to your eyes,
Nor slumber to your eyelids.
5 Deliver yourself like a gazelle from the
hand of *the hunter*,
And like a bird from the hand of the
fowler.*

The Folly of Indolence

6 *c*Go to the ant, you sluggard!
Consider her ways and be wise,
7 Which, having no captain,
Overseer or ruler,
8 Provides her supplies in the summer,
And gathers her food in the harvest.
9 *d*How long will you slumber,
O sluggard?
When will you rise from your sleep?
10 A little sleep, a little slumber,
A little folding of the hands to sleep—
11 *e*So shall your poverty come on you like
a prowler,
And your need like an armed man.

The Wicked Man

12 A worthless person, a wicked man,
Walks with a perverse mouth;
13 *f*He winks with his eyes,
He shuffles his feet,
He points with his fingers;
14 Perversity *is* in his heart,
*g*He devises evil continually,
*h*He sows discord.
15 Therefore his calamity shall come
*i*suddenly;
Suddenly he shall *j*be broken *k*without
remedy.

16 These six *things* the LORD hates,
Yes, seven *are* an abomination to Him:
17 *l*A proud look,
*m*A lying tongue,
*n*Hands that shed innocent blood,
18 *o*A heart that devises wicked plans,
*p*Feet that are swift in running to evil,

---

* **6:5** That is, one who catches birds in a trap or
snare

5:15 *Drink water from your own cistern.* This image
is a clear call to marital fidelity.
5:18 *and rejoice with the wife of your youth.* We are
encouraged to find mutual joy and pleasure in the
marriage bed. It is in fact blessed by God.
6:1 *if you become surety for your friend.* This phrase
refers to responsibility for someone else's debt as in
cosigning a loan. This does not mean we should never
be generous, only that we should not promise what
we cannot deliver.
6:6 *Go to the ant, you sluggard.* This passage is a
warning about laziness. The sluggard is a lazy person
who is captive to leisure. He can learn all he needs to
know by studying the work habits of the ant.
6:12 *a wicked man.* He is a troublemaker. Unlike
the sluggard, whose only desire is to take a nap, the

troublemaker cannot wait to cause more problems.
He delights in creating dissension.
6:16 *Yes, seven are an abomination to Him.* The
use of numerical progression—six, even seven—in
these proverbs is a rhetorical device that embellishes
the poetry and serves as a memory aid. It gives the
impression that there is more to be said about the

5:18 *e* Mal. 2:14   **5:19** *f* Song 2:9   **5:20** *g* Prov.
2:16   **5:21** *h* Hos. 7:2   **5:22** *i* Num. 32:23   **5:23** *j* Job
4:21   **6:1** *a* Prov. 11:15   **6:4** *b* Ps. 132:4   **6:6** *c* Job 12:7
6:9 *d* Prov. 24:33, 34   **6:11** *e* Prov. 10:4   **6:13** *f* Job
15:12   **6:14** *g* Mic. 2:1   *h* Prov. 6:19   **6:15** *i* Is. 30:13   *j* Jer.
19:11   *k* 2 Chr. 36:16   **6:17** *l* Ps. 101:5   *m* Ps. 120:2   *n* Is. 1:15
6:18 *o* Gen. 6:5   *p* Is. 59:7

19 ᵃA false witness *who* speaks lies,
And one who ʳsows discord among
brethren.

Beware of Adultery

20 ˢMy son, keep your father's command,
And do not forsake the law of your
mother.
21 ᵗBind them continually upon your
heart;
Tie them around your neck.
22 ᵘWhen you roam, they* will lead you;
When you sleep, ᵛthey will keep you;
And *when* you awake, they will speak
with you.
23 ʷFor the commandment *is* a lamp,
And the law a light;
Reproofs of instruction *are* the way
of life,
24 ˣTo keep you from the evil woman,
From the flattering tongue of a
seductress.
25 ʸDo not lust after her beauty in your
heart,
Nor let her allure you with her
eyelids.
26 For ᶻby means of a harlot
A man is reduced to a crust of bread;
ᵃAnd an adulteress* will ᵇprey upon his
precious life.
27 Can a man take fire to his bosom,
And his clothes not be burned?
28 Can one walk on hot coals,
And his feet not be seared?
29 So *is* he who goes in to his neighbor's
wife;
Whoever touches her shall not be
innocent.
30 *People* do not despise a thief
If he steals to satisfy himself when he
is starving.
31 Yet *when* he is found, ᶜhe must restore
sevenfold;
He may have to give up all the
substance of his house.

32 Whoever commits adultery with a
woman ᵈlacks understanding;
He *who* does so destroys his own soul.
33 Wounds and dishonor he will get,
And his reproach will not be wiped
away.
34 For ᵉjealousy *is* a husband's fury;
Therefore he will not spare in the day
of vengeance.
35 He will accept no recompense,
Nor will he be appeased though you
give many gifts.

7 My son, keep my words,
And ᵃtreasure my commands within
you.
2 ᵇKeep my commands and live,
ᶜAnd my law as the apple of your eye.
3 ᵈBind them on your fingers;
Write them on the tablet of your heart.
4 Say to wisdom, "You *are* my sister,"
And call understanding *your* nearest
kin,
5 ᵉThat they may keep you from the
immoral woman,
From the seductress *who* flatters with
her words.

The Crafty Harlot

6 For at the window of my house
I looked through my lattice,
7 And saw among the simple,
I perceived among the youths,
A young man ᶠdevoid of understanding,
8 Passing along the street near her
corner;
And he took the path to her house
9 ᵍIn the twilight, in the evening,
In the black and dark night.
10 And there a woman met him,
With the attire of a harlot, and a crafty
heart.

---

* **6:22** Literally *it* * **6:26** Literally *a man's wife,*
that is, of another

---

topic. The word "abomination" is the Bible's strongest expression of hatred for wickedness.
6:23 Illumination of God's Word—Illumination is the last of three important steps that God takes to communicate with us. The first step is revelation which occurred when God spoke to the authors of the Bible. The second step was inspiration, which is the process God used to guide them in correctly writing down His message. The third step provides understanding as men and women hear and see God's message. It is a divine process whereby God causes the written revelation to be understood by the human heart.
Christians need this illumination because we are blinded by our fallen fleshly natures (1 Cor. 2:14) and by Satan himself (2 Cor. 4:3–4). The Holy Spirit is the one who illumines us (John 14:26). We see this illumination process at work in Acts 2 when over 3,000 people respond to Peter's message and become followers of Christ.
Christians also need this illumination on a day-to-

day basis to help them fully grasp the marvelous message in God's Word. Paul tells us that the Holy Spirit will show these tremendous truths to us as we read the Scriptures (1 Cor. 2:10; 2 Cor. 4:6).
6:30 if he steals to satisfy himself . . . starving. This passage is not condoning theft. It merely contrasts theft with adultery, which never makes sense. For ancient Israelites, marital fidelity was a mark of one's fidelity to God.
7:1–5 as the apple of your eye. People should guard wise words as instinctively as they protect the pupil of the eye.

6:19 ᵍPs. 27:12 ʳProv. 6:14   **6:20** ˢEph. 6:1   **6:21** ᵗProv. 3:3   **6:22** ᵘ[Prov. 3:23] ᵛProv. 2:11   **6:23** ʷPs. 19:8   **6:24** ˣProv. 2:16`   **6:25** ʸMatt. 5:28   **6:26** ᶻProv. 29:3 ᵃGen. 39:14 ᵇEzek. 13:18   **6:31** ᶜEx. 22:1–4   **6:32** ᵈProv. 7:7   **6:34** ᵉSong 8:6   **7:1** ᵃProv. 2:1   **7:2** ᵇLev. 18:5 ᶜDeut. 32:10   **7:3** ᵈDeut. 6:8   **7:5** ᵉProv. 2:16; 5:3   **7:7** ᶠ[Prov. 6:32; 9:4, 16]   **7:9** ᵍJob 24:15

11 *h*She *was* loud and rebellious,
  *i*Her feet would not stay at home.
12 At times *she was* outside, at times in
    the open square,
  Lurking at every corner.
13 So she caught him and kissed him;
  With an impudent face she said to
    him:
14 "I *have* peace offerings with me;
  Today I have paid my vows.
15 So I came out to meet you,
  Diligently to seek your face,
  And I have found you.
16 I have spread my bed with tapestry,
  Colored coverings of *j*Egyptian linen.
17 I have perfumed my bed
  With myrrh, aloes, and cinnamon.
18 Come, let us take our fill of love until
    morning;
  Let us delight ourselves with love.
19 For my husband *is* not at home;
  He has gone on a long journey;
20 He has taken a bag of money with
    him,
  And will come home on the appointed
    day."

21 With *k*her enticing speech she caused
    him to yield,
  *l*With her flattering lips she seduced
    him.
22 Immediately he went after her, as an
    ox goes to the slaughter,
  Or as a fool to the correction of the
    stocks,*
23 Till an arrow struck his liver.
  *m*As a bird hastens to the snare,
  He did not know it *would cost* his life.

24 Now therefore, listen to me, *my*
    children;
  Pay attention to the words of my
    mouth:
25 Do not let your heart turn aside to her
    ways,
  Do not stray into her paths;
26 For she has cast down many wounded,
  And *n*all who were slain by her were
    strong *men.*
27 *o*Her house *is* the way to hell,*
  Descending to the chambers of death.

The Excellence of Wisdom

8 Does not *a*wisdom cry out,
  And understanding lift up her voice?
2 She takes her stand on the top of the
    high hill,
  Beside the way, where the paths meet.
3 She cries out by the gates, at the entry
    of the city,
  At the entrance of the doors:
4 "To you, O men, I call,
  And my voice *is* to the sons of men.
5 O you simple ones, understand
    prudence,
  And you fools, be of an understanding
    heart.
6 Listen, for I will speak of *b*excellent
    things,
  And from the opening of my lips *will
    come* right things;
7 For my mouth will speak truth;
  Wickedness *is* an abomination to my
    lips.
8 All the words of my mouth *are* with
    righteousness;
  Nothing crooked or perverse *is* in
    them.
9 They *are* all plain to him who
    understands,
  And right to those who find
    knowledge.
10 Receive my instruction, and not silver,
  And knowledge rather than choice
    gold;
11 *c*For wisdom *is* better than rubies,
  And all the things one may desire
    cannot be compared with her.

12 "I, wisdom, dwell with prudence,
  And find out knowledge *and*
    discretion.
13 *d*The fear of the LORD *is* to hate evil;
  *e*Pride and arrogance and the evil way
  And *f*the perverse mouth I hate.
14 Counsel *is* mine, and sound wisdom;
  I *am* understanding, *g*I have strength.
15 *h*By me kings reign,
  And rulers decree justice.

---

* 7:22 Septuagint, Syriac, and Targum read *as a
dog to bonds*; Vulgate reads *as a lamb … to bonds.*
* 7:27 Or *Sheol*

7:15 I came out to meet you. All the adulteress does
is perverse. Here she presents an offering as a feast for
the young man she plans to entrap. She overcomes
her target's fear by assuring him that her husband will
not come home and discover them together.
7:22 as a fool to the correction of the stocks. This
passage uses several unflattering metaphors to
describe how a young fool falls into immorality.
8:1 Does not wisdom cry out? Wisdom, in contrast
to foolishness, wants to reach everyone and therefore
broadcasts her message publicly, unlike the immoral
woman, who uses privacy and deception to achieve
her goals. Wisdom is open to all. Her location is at the
place of decision, the place of authority, the place of
beginnings. She speaks loudly, but only those who

adjust their lives to God's truth actually enjoy the
spoils of wisdom.
8:13 The fear of the LORD is to hate evil. The offer
of wisdom is held out only to those who fear God.
Coming to wisdom requires coming to God, and
coming to God means turning away from all that God
hates—evil, pride, and arrogance.
8:15 By me kings reign, and rulers. Power and
authority require the use of wisdom.

7:11 *h* Prov. 9:13 *i* Titus 2:5 **7:16** *i* Is. 19:9 **7:21** *k* Prov.
5:3 *l* Ps. 12:2 **7:23** *m* Eccl. 9:12 **7:26** *n* Neh. 13:26
7:27 *o* Prov. 2:18; 5:5; 9:18 **8:1** *a* Prov. 1:20, 21; 9:3
8:6 *b* Prov. 22:20 **8:11** *c* Job 28:15 **8:13** *d* Prov. 3:7;
16:6 *e* [Prov. 16:17, 18] *f* Prov. 4:24 **8:14** *g* Eccl. 7:19; 9:16
8:15 *h* Rom. 13:1

16 By me princes rule, and nobles,
All the judges of the earth.*
17 [i]I love those who love me,
And [j]those who seek me diligently will find me.
18 [k]Riches and honor *are* with me,
Enduring riches and righteousness.
19 My fruit *is* better than gold, yes, than fine gold,
And my revenue than choice silver.
20 I traverse the way of righteousness,
In the midst of the paths of justice,
21 That I may cause those who love me to inherit wealth,
That I may fill their treasuries.

22 "The[l] LORD possessed me at the beginning of His way,
Before His works of old.
23 [m]I have been established from everlasting,
From the beginning, before there was ever an earth.
24 When *there were* no depths I was brought forth,
When *there were* no fountains abounding with water.
25 [n]Before the mountains were settled,
Before the hills, I was brought forth;
26 While as yet He had not made the earth or the fields,
Or the primal dust of the world.
27 When He prepared the heavens, I *was* there,
When He drew a circle on the face of the deep,
28 When He established the clouds above,
When He strengthened the fountains of the deep,
29 [o]When He assigned to the sea its limit,
So that the waters would not transgress His command,
When [p]He marked out the foundations of the earth,
30 [q]Then I was beside Him *as* a master craftsman;*
[r]And I was daily *His* delight,
Rejoicing always before Him,
31 Rejoicing in His inhabited world,
And [s]my delight *was* with the sons of men.

32 "Now therefore, listen to me, *my* children,
For [t]blessed *are those who* keep my ways.
33 Hear instruction and be wise,
And do not disdain *it*.
34 [u]Blessed is the man who listens to me,
Watching daily at my gates,
Waiting at the posts of my doors.
35 For whoever finds me finds life,
And [v]obtains favor from the LORD;
36 But he who sins against me [w]wrongs his own soul;
All those who hate me love death."

The Way of Wisdom

9 Wisdom has [a]built her house,
She has hewn out her seven pillars;
2 [b]She has slaughtered her meat,
[c]She has mixed her wine,
She has also furnished her table.
3 She has sent out her maidens,
She cries out from the highest places of the city,
4 "Whoever[d] *is* simple, let him turn in here!"
As for him who lacks understanding, she says to him,
5 "Come,[e] eat of my bread
And drink of the wine I have mixed.
6 Forsake foolishness and live,
And go in the way of understanding.

7 "He who corrects a scoffer gets shame for himself,
And he who rebukes a wicked *man only* harms himself.
8 [f]Do not correct a scoffer, lest he hate you;
[g]Rebuke a wise *man*, and he will love you.

* **8:16** Masoretic Text, Syriac, Targum, and Vulgate read *righteousness;* Septuagint, Bomberg, and some manuscripts and editions read *earth.*
* **8:30** A Jewish tradition reads *one brought up.*

8:30–31 *as a master craftsman.* With wisdom's skill, God created the universe. A proper study of the universe is a progressive study of God's wisdom. Her greatest joy comes in the finest of the work of God—the sons of men—that is, humankind.
9:1 *seven pillars.* The number seven represents completeness, as it often does in Semitic poetry. That is, it is not that there were precisely seven pillars so much as that the house of wisdom was solidly built and substantial in character.
9:2 *mixed her wine.* Wine was a staple in ancient Israel; but when a feast was special, a homemaker would add aromatic spices to the wine, enlivening the bouquet and improving the taste (Song 8:2). This idea sets up a contrast with the foolish woman. While wisdom is busy, attending to every detail like a gracious hostess, the foolish woman sits at the entrance of her house with very little to do (9:14).
9:4 *Whoever is simple.* Wisdom makes a point of inviting the naive, meaning those who have not yet made up their minds about their course in life. The person who comes to wisdom has nothing to lose but naiveté. Hebrews 5:14 speaks of a mature person as one who is able to eat and enjoy solid food, in contrast to the naive, who is able only to drink milk.
9:7 *He who corrects a scoffer.* This personality is thoroughly set against wisdom (1:22) and scoffs at the things of God (Ps. 1:1). By contrast a wise man accepts correction and responds with gratitude to the one who points out his error.

8:17 [i][John 14:21] [j]James 1:5 **8:18** [k]Prov. 3:16 **8:22** [l]Prov. 3:19 **8:23** [m][Ps. 2:6] **8:25** [n]Job 15:7, 8 **8:29** [o]Gen. 1:9, 10 [p]Job 28:4, 6 **8:30** [q][John 1:1–3, 18] [r][Matt. 3:17] **8:31** [s]Ps. 16:3 **8:32** [t]Luke 11:28 **8:34** [u]Prov. 3:13, 18 **8:35** [v][John 17:3] **8:36** [w]Prov. 20:2 **9:1** [a][Matt. 16:18] **9:2** [b]Matt. 22:4 [c]Prov. 23:30 **9:4** [d]Ps. 19:7 **9:5** [e]Is. 55:1 **9:8** [f]Matt. 7:6 [g]Ps. 141:5

9 Give *instruction* to a wise *man*, and he
will be still wiser;
Teach a just *man*, [h]and he will
increase in learning.
10 "The[i] fear of the LORD *is* the beginning
of wisdom,
And the knowledge of the Holy One *is*
understanding.
11 [j]For by me your days will be multiplied,
And years of life will be added to you.
12 [k]If you are wise, you are wise for
yourself,
And *if* you scoff, you will bear *it* alone."

The Way of Folly

13 [l]A foolish woman is clamorous;
She is simple, and knows nothing.
14 For she sits at the door of her house,
On a seat [m]by the highest places of
the city,
15 To call to those who pass by,
Who go straight on their way:
16 "Whoever[n] *is* simple, let him turn in
here";
And *as for* him who lacks
understanding, she says to him,
17 "Stolen[o] water is sweet,
And bread *eaten* in secret is pleasant."
18 But he does not know that [p]the dead
are there,
That her guests *are* in the depths of
hell.*

Wise Sayings of Solomon

10 The proverbs of [a]Solomon:

[b]A wise son makes a glad father,
But a foolish son *is* the grief of his
mother.
2 [c]Treasures of wickedness profit
nothing,
[d]But righteousness delivers from death.

3 [e]The LORD will not allow the righteous
soul to famish,
But He casts away the desire of the
wicked.
4 [f]He who has a slack hand becomes poor,
But [g]the hand of the diligent makes
rich.
5 He who gathers in [h]summer *is* a wise
son;
He who sleeps in harvest *is* [i]a son who
causes shame.
6 Blessings *are* on the head of the
righteous,
But violence covers the mouth of the
wicked.
7 [j]The memory of the righteous *is* blessed,
But the name of the wicked will rot.
8 The wise in heart will receive
commands,
[k]But a prating fool will fall.
9 [l]He who walks with integrity walks
securely,
But he who perverts his ways will
become known.
10 He who winks with the eye causes
trouble,
But a prating fool will fall.
11 The mouth of the righteous *is* a well of
life,
But violence covers the mouth of the
wicked.
12 Hatred stirs up strife,
But [m]love covers all sins.
13 Wisdom is found on the lips of him
who has understanding,
But [n]a rod *is* for the back of him who is
devoid of understanding.

---

* 9:18 Or *Sheol*

9:13–18 *A foolish woman is clamorous.* This section is a parody of 9:1–6. Like personified wisdom, the woman of folly calls out an invitation. But she is brash, loud, undisciplined, and knows nothing (7:10–12). She cries out in the same words that wisdom has used, but she has no marvelous banquet for her guests, only shabby food, stolen and meager.
9:18 *the dead are there.* Fools cast away all restraint and express their freedom in direct defiance of heaven's moral law for the ordering of our conduct on earth. But they do not know that the end of such perverse behavior is death. The way of wisdom is to turn from such a disastrous course while there is time.
10:1 *The proverbs of Solomon.* This section focuses on the wise son in contrast with the foolish son. *Son* is used generically for son and daughter.
10:4 *slack hand.* Proverbs often links laziness with poverty, and hard work with riches.
10:7 *But the name of the wicked.* In biblical times a person's name was most significant. When a person's name was remembered by future generations for good, that person's life was believed to have been of great value. But when the memory of a name rotted away, it was as though that person had never lived.

10:9 *walks with integrity.* Many of the proverbs contrast two paths of life. This phrase means conforming to God's law as a course of life. Choosing crooked paths is willfully to disdain the guidance God so graciously provided.
10:12 *Hatred . . . love.* This verse describes interpersonal relationships, not salvation. When people respond in love to each other, they cover over the sins or offenses that would otherwise come between them.
10:13 *But a rod is for the back of him.* Rod refers to punishment, in this case deserved. The phrase "devoid of understanding" comes from the Hebrew idiom "lack heart." The one who "lacks heart" is contrasted with the one who is "wise in heart" (10:8).

9:9 [h] [Matt. 13:12]   **9:10** [i] Job 28:28   **9:11** [j] Prov. 3:2, 16
9:12 [k] Job 35:6, 7   **9:13** [l] Prov. 7:11   **9:14** [m] Prov. 9:3
9:16 [n] Prov. 7:7, 8   **9:17** [o] Prov. 20:17   **9:18** [p] Prov. 2:18;
7:27   **10:1** [a] Prov. 1:1; 25:1   [b] Prov. 15:20; 17:21, 25; 19:13;
29:3, 15   **10:2** [c] [Luke 12:19, 20]   [d] Dan. 4:27   **10:3** [e] Ps.
34:9, 10; 37:25   **10:4** [f] Prov. 19:15   [g] Prov. 12:24; 13:4;
21:5   **10:5** [h] Prov. 6:8   [i] Prov. 19:26   **10:7** [j] Eccl. 8:10
10:8 [k] Prov. 10:10   **10:9** [l] [Ps. 23:4]   **10:12** [m] [1 Cor.
13:4–7]   **10:13** [n] Prov. 26:3

14 Wise *people* store up knowledge,
But [o]the mouth of the foolish *is* near destruction.

15 The [p]rich man's wealth *is* his strong city;
The destruction of the poor *is* their poverty.

16 The labor of the righteous *leads* to [q]life,
The wages of the wicked to sin.

17 He who keeps instruction *is in* the way of life,
But he who refuses correction goes astray.

18 Whoever [r]hides hatred *has* lying lips,
And [s]whoever spreads slander *is* a fool.

19 [t]In the multitude of words sin is not lacking,
But [u]he who restrains his lips *is* wise.
20 The tongue of the righteous *is* choice silver;
The heart of the wicked *is worth* little.
21 The lips of the righteous feed many,
But fools die for lack of wisdom.*

22 [v]The blessing of the LORD makes *one* rich,
And He adds no sorrow with it.

23 [w]To do evil *is* like sport to a fool,
But a man of understanding has wisdom.
24 [x]The fear of the wicked will come upon him,
And [y]the desire of the righteous will be granted.
25 When the whirlwind passes by, [z]the wicked *is* no *more*,
But [a]the righteous *has* an everlasting foundation.

26 As vinegar to the teeth and smoke to the eyes,
So *is* the lazy *man* to those who send him.

27 [b]The fear of the LORD prolongs days,
But [c]the years of the wicked will be shortened.
28 The hope of the righteous *will be* gladness,
But the [d]expectation of the wicked will perish.
29 The way of the LORD *is* strength for the upright,
But [e]destruction *will come* to the workers of iniquity.

30 [f]The righteous will never be removed,
But the wicked will not inhabit the earth.
31 [g]The mouth of the righteous brings forth wisdom,
But the perverse tongue will be cut out.
32 The lips of the righteous know what is acceptable,
But the mouth of the wicked *what is* perverse.

11 [a]Dishonest scales *are* an abomination to the LORD,
But a just weight *is* His delight.

2 When pride comes, then comes [b]shame;
But with the humble *is* wisdom.

* **10:21** Literally *heart*

10:14–15 *store up knowledge.* This set of verses contrasts the wise person's pursuit of knowledge with the empty talk of a fool. Wealth is like a fortress. In biblical times only walled cities had any defense against enemy armies.
10:16–17 *The labor of the righteous leads to life.* These verses present the doctrine of the two ways. The righteous are on the way of life but the wicked wander from it.
10:23 *like sport to a fool.* Sport here usually means "joyous laughter." Here the proverb uses the word in a completely negative sense. For the fool, wickedness is only a game. He makes up the rules as he goes along; for losing is only in getting caught. But a person who has understanding takes a longer-term perspective.
10:25 *the righteous has an everlasting foundation.* The short-lived nature of the wicked is contrasted with the stability of the righteous. The foundation of righteousness is faith in God, much like the waters that nourish the tree of Psalm 1:3.
10:28 *hope . . . expectation.* The righteous have something to look forward to; the wicked do not.
10:29 *The way of the LORD is strength for the upright.* Different people see the way of the Lord differently. Those who are innocent see it as a shelter from the storm. Those who practice iniquity see it only as a source of condemnation and wrath. The viewer's perspective makes all the difference.
10:31–32 *The mouth of the righteous brings forth wisdom.* These verses form another pair of sentences about true and false speech. This repetition with variation indicates the significance of truth and falsehood.
11:1 *Dishonest scales are abomination to the LORD.* Dealing fairly with one another is an outgrowth of the command to love one's neighbor as oneself (Lev. 19:18), which in turn is an outgrowth of the central command given to Israel, to love God above all else (Deut. 6:4–9). That is why dishonest scales are an abomination to God.
11:2 *When pride comes.* Many proverbs contrast the arrogant with the humble, as this one does. The Hebrew word for pride comes from a root that means "to boil up"; it refers to a raging arrogance or insolence.

10:14 [o] Prov. 18:7 **10:15** [p] Job 31:24 **10:16** [q] Prov. 6:23 **10:18** [r] Prov. 26:24 [s] Ps. 15:3; 101:5 **10:19** [t] Eccl. 5:3 [u] [James 1:19; 3:2] **10:22** [v] Gen. 24:35; 26:12 **10:23** [w] Prov. 2:14; 15:21 **10:24** [x] Job 15:21 [y] Ps. 145:19 **10:25** [z] Ps. 37:9, 10 [a] Ps. 15:5 **10:27** [b] Prov. 9:11 [c] Job 15:32 **10:28** [d] Job 8:13 **10:29** [e] Ps. 1:6 **10:30** [f] Ps. 37:22 **10:31** [g] Ps. 37:30 **11:1** [a] Lev. 19:35, 36 **11:2** [b] Prov. 16:18; 18:12; 29:23

3 The integrity of the upright will guide
     cthem,
   But the perversity of the unfaithful
     will destroy them.
4 dRiches do not profit in the day of
     wrath,
   But erighteousness delivers from
     death.
5 The righteousness of the blameless
     will direct* his way aright,
   But the wicked will fall by his own
     fwickedness.
6 The righteousness of the upright will
     deliver them,
   But the unfaithful will be caught by
     their lust.

7 When a wicked man dies, his
     expectation will gperish,
   And the hope of the unjust perishes.
8 hThe righteous is delivered from
     trouble,
   And it comes to the wicked instead.
9 The hypocrite with his mouth destroys
     his neighbor,
   But through knowledge the righteous
     will be delivered.
10 iWhen it goes well with the righteous,
     the city rejoices;
   And when the wicked perish, there is
     jubilation.
11 By the blessing of the upright the city
     is jexalted,
   But it is overthrown by the mouth of
     the wicked.
12 He who is devoid of wisdom despises
     his neighbor,
   But a man of understanding holds his
     peace.
13 kA talebearer reveals secrets,
   But he who is of a faithful spirit
     lconceals a matter.
14 mWhere there is no counsel, the people
     fall;
   But in the multitude of counselors
     there is safety.

15 He who is nsurety for a stranger will
     suffer,
   But one who hates being surety is
     secure.
16 A gracious woman retains honor,
   But ruthless men retain riches.
17 oThe merciful man does good for his
     own soul,
   But he who is cruel troubles his own
     flesh.
18 The wicked man does deceptive work,
   But phe who sows righteousness will
     have a sure reward.
19 As righteousness leads to qlife,
   So he who pursues evil pursues it to
     his own rdeath.
20 Those who are of a perverse heart are
     an abomination to the LORD,
   But the blameless in their ways are
     His delight.
21 sThough they join forces,* the wicked
     will not go unpunished;
   But tthe posterity of the righteous will
     be delivered.

22 As a ring of gold in a swine's snout,
   So is a lovely woman who lacks
     discretion.

23 The desire of the righteous is only
     good,
   But the expectation of the wicked uis
     wrath.

24 There is one who vscatters, yet
     increases more;
   And there is one who withholds more
     than is right,
   But it leads to poverty.
25 wThe generous soul will be made rich,
   xAnd he who waters will also be
     watered himself.
26 The people will curse yhim who
     withholds grain,
   But zblessing will be on the head of
     him who sells it.

---

* 11:5 Or make smooth or straight   * 11:21 Literally hand to hand

---

11:10 When it goes well with the righteous. Truly righteous people bring justice to all the inhabitants of a city, and the city experiences true peace. Many of the psalm writers cried for vindication of the righteous and for a cessation of evil (Ps. 69:22–28).

11:13 A talebearer reveals secrets. A faithful friend conceals delicate matters that an unfaithful person reveals.

11:14 in the multitude of counselors. In modern times, as in the past, leaders of nations need adequate counsel. We all need to seek advice from wise and trustworthy people.

11:17 The merciful man does good for his own soul. Throughout the Bible, God promises that good actions will return to you in benefits. Behavior that hurts others will hurt you as well.

11:19 leads to life. Proverbs such as this remind us that the pursuit of righteousness is a matter of life and death.

11:22 ring of gold. A golden ring would be ludicrous on a pig's snout. To the ancient Israelites, pigs were unclean and repellent. The immoral person is compared to such an animal, no matter what the outward appearance might be.

11:24–26 There is one who scatters. These proverbs should shape our attitudes toward wealth: We should share it. Stinginess may lead to poverty. Generosity has the opposite effect. Selfishness is foolish because it only creates enemies and dishonors God.

11:3 c Prov. 13:6   **11:4** d Ezek. 7:19   e Gen. 7:1   **11:5** f Prov. 5:22   **11:7** g Prov. 10:28   **11:8** h Prov. 21:18   **11:10** i Prov. 28:12   **11:11** j Prov. 14:34   **11:13** k Lev. 19:16   l Prov. 19:11   **11:14** m 1 Kin. 12:1   **11:15** n Prov. 6:1, 2   **11:17** o [Matt. 5:7; 25:34–36]   **11:18** p Hos. 10:12   **11:19** q Prov. 10:16; 12:28   r [Rom. 6:23]   **11:21** s Prov. 16:5   t Ps. 112:2   **11:23** u Rom. 2:8, 9   **11:24** v Ps. 112:9   **11:25** w [2 Cor. 9:6, 7]   x [Matt. 5:7]   **11:26** y Amos 8:5, 6   z Job 29:13

27 He who earnestly seeks good finds
favor,
  aBut trouble will come to him who
  seeks *evil.*

28 bHe who trusts in his riches will fall,
But cthe righteous will flourish like
foliage.

29 He who troubles his own house dwill
inherit the wind,
And the fool *will be* eservant to the
wise of heart.

30 The fruit of the righteous *is a* tree of
life,
And fhe who wins souls *is* wise.

31 gIf the righteous will be recompensed
on the earth,
How much more the ungodly and the
sinner.

12 Whoever loves instruction loves
knowledge,
But he who hates correction *is* stupid.

2 A good *man* obtains favor from the
LORD,
But a man of wicked intentions He will
condemn.

3 A man is not established by
wickedness,
But the aroot of the righteous cannot
be moved.

4 bAn excellent* wife *is* the crown of her
husband,
But she who causes shame *is* clike
rottenness in his bones.

5 The thoughts of the righteous *are*
right,
But the counsels of the wicked *are*
deceitful.

6 dThe words of the wicked *are,* "Lie in
wait for blood,"
eBut the mouth of the upright will
deliver them.

7 fThe wicked are overthrown and *are* no
more,

But the house of the righteous will
stand.

8 A man will be commended according
to his wisdom,
gBut he who is of a perverse heart will
be despised.

9 hBetter *is the one* who is slighted but
has a servant,
Than he who honors himself but lacks
bread.

10 iA righteous *man* regards the life of his
animal,
But the tender mercies of the wicked
are cruel.

11 jHe who tills his land will be satisfied
with kbread,
But he who follows frivolity lis devoid
of understanding.*

12 The wicked covet the catch of evil *men,*
But the root of the righteous yields
fruit.

13 mThe wicked is ensnared by the
transgression of *his* lips,
nBut the righteous will come through
trouble.

14 oA man will be satisfied with good by
the fruit of *his* mouth,
pAnd the recompense of a man's hands
will be rendered to him.

15 qThe way of a fool *is* right in his own
eyes,
But he who heeds counsel *is* wise.

16 rA fool's wrath is known at once,
But a prudent *man* covers shame.

17 sHe *who* speaks truth declares
righteousness,
But a false witness, deceit.

18 tThere is one who speaks like the
piercings of a sword,
But the tongue of the wise *promotes*
health.

* **12:4** Literally *A wife of valor*   * **12:11** Literally
heart

11:31 much more. This proverb argues from a premise to a conclusion. Since the righteous will finally find their reward, it follows that the wicked, who are defiant toward God and in conflict with His works, will certainly receive judgment.
12:1 But he who hates correction is stupid. Literally "stupid as a cow."
12:4 An excellent wife. A husband should rejoice in such a woman because her noble character brings him honor.
12:5–6 The thoughts of the righteous. A person's thoughts are the foundation of his or her words and deeds. The words of wicked persons can be like a deadly ambush.
12:9 he who honors himself. This verse contrasts a person who is a "nobody" but has a servant with a person who makes a great display but does not even have food on the table. Pretension destroys those who indulge in it.

12:16 known at once. Careless words can make a fool out of us, so we are wise to think before we speak. Whereas the wise man restrains his anger and turns it away, the fool constantly loses his temper (29:11).
12:18–19 the tongue of the wise promotes health. Many proverbs praise people who speak carefully and truthfully. Speech reflects a person's character. The words of a righteous person soothe the listener.

11:27 a Esth. 7:10   **11:28** b Job 31:24 c Ps. 1:3
11:29 d Eccl. 5:16 e Prov. 14:19   **11:30** f [Dan. 12:3]
11:31 g Jer. 25:29   **12:3** a [Prov. 10:25]   **12:4** b 1 Cor.
11:7 c Prov. 14:30   **12:6** d Prov. 1:11, 18 e Prov.
14:3   **12:7** f Matt. 7:24–27   **12:8** g 1 Sam. 25:17
12:9 h Prov. 13:7   **12:10** i Deut. 25:4   **12:11** j Gen.
3:19 k Prov. 28:19 l Prov. 6:32   **12:13** m Prov. 18:7
n [2 Pet. 2:9]   **12:14** o Prov. 13:2; 15:23; 18:20 p [Is. 3:10,
11]   **12:15** q Luke 18:11   **12:16** r Prov. 11:13; 29:11
12:17 s Prov. 14:5   **12:18** t Ps. 57:4

19 The truthful lip shall be established forever,
   ^{u}But a lying tongue *is* but for a moment.
20 Deceit is in the heart of those who devise evil,
   But counselors of peace have joy.
21 ^{v}No grave trouble will overtake the righteous,
   But the wicked shall be filled with evil.
22 ^{w}Lying lips *are* an abomination to the LORD,
   But those who deal truthfully *are* His delight.
23 ^{x}A prudent man conceals knowledge,
   But the heart of fools proclaims foolishness.
24 ^{y}The hand of the diligent will rule,
   But the lazy *man* will be put to forced labor.
25 ^{z}Anxiety in the heart of man causes depression,
   But ^{a}a good word makes it glad.
26 The righteous should choose his friends carefully,
   For the way of the wicked leads them astray.
27 The lazy *man* does not roast what he took in hunting,
   But diligence *is* man's precious possession.
28 In the way of righteousness *is* life,
   And in *its* pathway *there is* no death.

13 A wise son *heeds* his father's instruction,
   ^{a}But a scoffer does not listen to rebuke.
2 ^{b}A man shall eat well by the fruit of *his* mouth,
   But the soul of the unfaithful feeds on violence.

3 ^{c}He who guards his mouth preserves his life,
   But he who opens wide his lips shall have destruction.
4 ^{d}The soul of a lazy *man* desires, and *has* nothing;
   But the soul of the diligent shall be made rich.
5 A righteous *man* hates lying,
   But a wicked *man* is loathsome and comes to shame.
6 ^{e}Righteousness guards *him whose* way is blameless,
   But wickedness overthrows the sinner.
7 ^{f}There is one who makes himself rich, yet *has* nothing;
   And one who makes himself poor, yet *has* great riches.
8 The ransom of a man's life *is* his riches,
   But the poor does not hear rebuke.
9 The light of the righteous rejoices,
   ^{g}But the lamp of the wicked will be put out.
10 By pride comes nothing but ^{h}strife,
   But with the well-advised *is* wisdom.
11 ^{i}Wealth *gained by* dishonesty will be diminished,
   But he who gathers by labor will increase.
12 Hope deferred makes the heart sick,
   But ^{j}when the desire comes, *it is* a tree of life.
13 He who ^{k}despises the word will be destroyed,
   But he who fears the commandment will be rewarded.
14 ^{l}The law of the wise *is* a fountain of life,
   To turn *one* away from ^{m}the snares of death.

12:22 Lying lips are an abomination. Abomination is something that "nauseates" God (11:20). The term conveys extreme hatred.
12:25 Anxiety in the heart of man. Anxiety loses some of its force in the face of a positive, encouraging word. Barnabas is an example of an encourager in the early church (Acts 4:36).
12:26 The righteous should choose his friends carefully. Our friends help to determine who we will become, and an excellent example inspires us to copy.
12:27 The lazy man. Lazy people do work, they just don't always finish what they start. The cure for their laziness is diligence—to follow through to the end.
13:5 A righteous man hates lying. The person who hates lying does not merely feel bad about it; he avoids it like the plague.
13:7 rich, yet has nothing. The paradox of greed causing poverty, and of generosity causing wealth, is a recurring theme in Scripture (Matt. 6:19–21). The point is not how much money you have, but what you do with it.
13:9 The light of the righteous rejoices. For an ancient Israelite, an oil lamp would be the only source

of light at night. Without it, a person had no way of seeing the path in front of him.
13:10 By pride. It is self-centeredness and having to push one's own ideas that bring quarrels. The wise know when to speak and when to keep still.
13:11 Wealth gained by dishonesty will be diminished. This proverb describes the natural long-term consequences of cheating. People who compromise their honesty to get rich merely postpone the inevitable need to earn their keep. The day comes when their cheating catches up with them, but by then their honest colleagues have become far better at obtaining wealth.
13:14 fountain of life. In an arid land such as ancient Judah, a fountain provided water for oneself and for

12:19 ^{u} Prov. 19:9   **12:21** ^{v} 1 Pet. 3:13   **12:22** ^{w} Rev. 22:15   **12:23** ^{x} Prov. 13:16   **12:24** ^{y} Prov. 10:4   **12:25** ^{z} Prov. 15:13 ^{a} Is. 50:4   **13:1** ^{a} Is. 28:14, 15   **13:2** ^{b} Prov. 12:14   **13:3** ^{c} Prov. 21:23   **13:4** ^{d} Prov. 10:4   **13:6** ^{e} Prov. 11:3, 5, 6   **13:7** ^{f} [Prov. 11:24; 12:9]   **13:9** ^{g} Prov. 24:20   **13:10** ^{h} Prov. 10:12   **13:11** ^{i} Prov. 10:2; 20:21   **13:12** ^{j} Prov. 13:19   **13:13** ^{k} Num. 15:31   **13:14** ^{l} Prov. 6:22; 10:11; 14:27 ^{m} 2 Sam. 22:6

15 Good understanding gains ⁿfavor,
But the way of the unfaithful *is* hard.
16 ᵒEvery prudent *man* acts with
knowledge,
But a fool lays open *his* folly.
17 A wicked messenger falls into
trouble,
But ᵖa faithful ambassador *brings*
health.
18 Poverty and shame *will come* to him
who disdains correction,
But qhe who regards a rebuke will be
honored.
19 A desire accomplished is sweet to the
soul,
But *it is* an abomination to fools to
depart from evil.
20 He who walks with wise *men* will be
wise,
But the companion of fools will be
destroyed.
21 ʳEvil pursues sinners,
But to the righteous, good shall be
repaid.
22 A good *man* leaves an inheritance to
his children's children,
But ˢthe wealth of the sinner is stored
up for the righteous.
23 ᵗMuch food *is in* the fallow *ground* of
the poor,
And for lack of justice there is waste.*
24 ᵘHe who spares his rod hates his son,
But he who loves him disciplines him
promptly.
25 ᵛThe righteous eats to the satisfying of
his soul,
But the stomach of the wicked shall be
in want.

14 The wise woman builds her house,
But the foolish pulls it down with her
hands.

2 He who walks in his uprightness
fears the LORD,
ᵃBut *he who is* perverse in his ways
despises Him.
3 In the mouth of a fool *is* a rod of
pride,
ᵇBut the lips of the wise will preserve
them.
4 Where no oxen *are*, the trough *is*
clean;
But much increase *comes* by the
strength of an ox.
5 A ᶜfaithful witness does not lie,
But a false witness will utter ᵈlies.
6 A scoffer seeks wisdom and does not
find it,
But ᵉknowledge *is* easy to him who
understands.
7 Go from the presence of a foolish
man,
When you do not perceive *in him* the
lips of ᶠknowledge.
8 The wisdom of the prudent *is* to
understand his way,
But the folly of fools *is* deceit.
9 ᵍFools mock at sin,
But among the upright *there is*
favor.
10 The heart knows its own
bitterness,
And a stranger does not share its
joy.
11 ʰThe house of the wicked will be
overthrown,
But the tent of the upright will
flourish.
12 ⁱThere is a way *that seems* right to a
man,
But ʲits end *is* the way of ᵏdeath.

---

* **13:23** Literally *what is swept away*

---

one's flocks. It was a necessity—a source of life. A
fountain is also a picture for salvation (Is. 12:1–3).
13:15 God understanding gains favor. Favor with
God and other people—a good reputation is highly
desirable because it ensures that you won't be alone
in life. A good reputation was the first qualification
listed by the apostles for deacons in the early church
(Acts 6:3).
13:20 *He who walks with wise men.* Our selection of
friends (12:26) is extremely important. Pressure from
peers is much stronger than many people realize.
13:24 *hates . . . loves.* This is the first of several proverbs on parental discipline. A parent's loving discipline
is modeled after God's loving correction (3:11–12).
14:1 *wise woman builds her house.* She develops a
peaceful setting for family nurture.
14:2 *fears the Lord.* This phrase contrasts starkly
with "despises him." Love for uprightness will naturally coincide with love and respect for the most
upright One of all, God Himself. Love for perversity
will likewise result in hatred for Him. Fear of the Lord

as the beginning of wisdom is the central theme of
Proverbs (1:7).
14:4 *the trough is clean.* A farmer has to put up with
some messes in the barn if he wants the help of an ox.
This is not an excuse to be slovenly, but an encouragement to work hard.
14:12 *There is a way that seems right to a man.*
Only when it is too late does the deluded person
discover that he is on the crowded highway to death.
The implication is not that he was tricked, but that he
relied too heavily on his own "wisdom" rather than
turning in humility to God.

13:15 ⁿ Prov. 3:4 **13:16** ᵒ Prov. 12:23 **13:17** ᵖ Prov.
25:13 **13:18** q Prov. 15:5, 31, 32 **13:21** ʳ Ps. 32:10
13:22 ˢ [Eccl. 2:26] **13:23** ᵗ Prov. 12:11 **13:24** ᵘ Prov.
19:18 **13:25** ᵛ Ps. 34:10 **14:2** ᵃ [Rom. 2:4]
14:3 ᵇ Prov. 12:6 **14:5** ᶜ Rev. 1:5; 3:14 ᵈ Prov. 6:19; 12:17
14:6 ᵉ Prov. 8:9; 17:24 **14:7** ᶠ Prov. 23:9 **14:9** ᵍ Prov.
10:23 **14:11** ʰ Job 8:15 **14:12** ⁱ Prov. 16:25 ʲ Rom. 6:21
ᵏ Prov. 12:15

13 Even in laughter the heart may sorrow,
And ᴵthe end of mirth *may be* grief.

14 The backslider in heart will be ᵐfilled
with his own ways,
But a good man *will be satisfied* from
ⁿabove.*

15 The simple believes every word,
But the prudent considers well his
steps.

16 ᵒA wise *man* fears and departs from
evil,
But a fool rages and is self-confident.

17 A quick-tempered *man* acts foolishly,
And a man of wicked intentions is
hated.

18 The simple inherit folly,
But the prudent are crowned with
knowledge.

19 The evil will bow before the good,
And the wicked at the gates of the
righteous.

20 ᵖThe poor *man* is hated even by his
own neighbor,
But the rich *has* many ᑫfriends.

21 He who despises his neighbor sins;
ʳBut he who has mercy on the poor,
happy *is* he.

22 Do they not go astray who devise
evil?
But mercy and truth *belong* to those
who devise good.

23 In all labor there is profit,
But idle chatter* *leads* only to poverty.

24 The crown of the wise is their riches,
But the foolishness of fools *is* folly.

25 A true witness delivers ˢsouls,
But a deceitful *witness* speaks lies.

26 In the fear of the LORD *there is* strong
confidence,
And His children will have a place of
refuge.

27 ᵗThe fear of the LORD *is* a fountain of
life,
To turn *one* away from the snares of
death.

28 In a multitude of people *is* a king's
honor,
But in the lack of people *is* the
downfall of a prince.

29 ᵘHe who is slow to wrath has great
understanding,
But *he who is* impulsive* exalts folly.

30 A sound heart *is* life to the body,
But ᵛenvy *is* ʷrottenness to the bones.

31 ˣHe who oppresses the poor reproaches
ʸhis Maker,
But he who honors Him has mercy on
the needy.

32 The wicked is banished in his
wickedness,
But ᶻthe righteous has a refuge in his
death.

33 Wisdom rests in the heart of him who
has understanding,
But ᵃ*what is* in the heart of fools is
made known.

34 Righteousness exalts a ᵇnation,
But sin *is* a reproach to *any* people.

35 ᶜThe king's favor *is* toward a wise
servant,
But his wrath *is against* him who
causes shame.

15 A ᵃsoft answer turns away wrath,
But ᵇa harsh word stirs up anger.
2 The tongue of the wise uses
knowledge rightly,
ᶜBut the mouth of fools pours forth
foolishness.

3 ᵈThe eyes of the LORD *are* in every
place,
Keeping watch on the evil and the
good.

4 A wholesome tongue *is* a tree of life,
But perverseness in it breaks the
spirit.

* **14:14** Literally *from above himself*   * **14:23** Literally *talk of the lips*   * **14:29** Literally *short of spirit*

14:19 *at the gates of the righteous.* In an ancient walled city, the gate area would normally be the weakest section of the wall. The city engineers of ancient Canaan developed complex structures to fortify this point. Controlling the gate of a city meant controlling the city.

14:31 *oppresses . . . honors.* The theme of "as you treat people, so you treat God" is central to Scripture (Ex. 22:22–24; Matt. 25:31–46).

14:32 *The wicked is banished in his wickedness.* Some of the proverbs describe deliverance from death itself (11:4). The teaching of life after death is not a major teaching in the Old Testament, but neither is it altogether neglected.

14:34 *Righteousness exalts a nation.* Although each individual is responsible for his or her actions, the effects extend to the whole community.

15:1 *A soft answer turns away wrath.* Often it is not so much what we say but the way we say it that prompts such varied responses as acceptance and anger. For Abigail's gentle words to David when he was angry, see 1 Samuel 25:12–34. Words can have either life-giving or death-producing results.

15:3 *The eyes of the LORD.* That they are in every place watching everything chills those who do evil and comforts those who submit to Him (Eccl. 12:12).

14:13 ᴵEccl. 2:1, 2   **14:14** ᵐProv. 1:31; 12:15   ⁿProv. 13:2; 18:20   **14:16** ᵒProv. 22:3   **14:20** ᵖProv. 19:7   ᑫProv. 19:4   **14:21** ʳPs. 112:9   **14:25** ˢ[Ezek. 3:18–21]   **14:27** ᵗProv. 13:14   **14:29** ᵘJames 1:19   **14:30** ᵛPs. 112:10   ʷProv. 12:4   **14:31** ˣMatt. 25:40   ʸ[Prov. 22:2]   **14:32** ᶻJob 13:15   **14:33** ᵃProv. 12:16   **14:34** ᵇProv. 11:11   **14:35** ᶜMatt. 24:45–47   **15:1** ᵃProv. 25:15   ᵇ1 Sam. 25:10   **15:2** ᶜProv. 12:23   **15:3** ᵈJob 34:21

5 eA fool despises his father's instruction,
fBut he who receives correction is
prudent.

6 In the house of the righteous there is
much treasure,
But in the revenue of the wicked is
trouble.

7 The lips of the wise disperse knowledge,
But the heart of the fool does not do so.

8 gThe sacrifice of the wicked is an
abomination to the LORD,
But the prayer of the upright is His
delight.

9 The way of the wicked is an
abomination to the LORD,
But He loves him who hfollows
righteousness.

10 iHarsh discipline is for him who
forsakes the way,
And jhe who hates correction will die.

11 kHell* and Destruction* are before the
LORD;
So how much more lthe hearts of the
sons of men.

12 mA scoffer does not love one who
corrects him,
Nor will he go to the wise.

13 nA merry heart makes a cheerful
countenance,
But oby sorrow of the heart the spirit
is broken.

14 The heart of him who has
understanding seeks knowledge,
But the mouth of fools feeds on
foolishness.

15 All the days of the afflicted are evil,
pBut he who is of a merry heart has a
continual feast.

16 qBetter is a little with the fear of the
LORD,
Than great treasure with trouble.

17 rBetter is a dinner of herbs* where love
is,
Than a fatted calf with hatred.

18 sA wrathful man stirs up strife,
But he who is slow to anger allays
contention.

19 tThe way of the lazy man is like a
hedge of thorns,
But the way of the upright is a
highway.

20 uA wise son makes a father glad,
But a foolish man despises his
mother.

21 vFolly is joy to him who is destitute of
discernment,
wBut a man of understanding walks
uprightly.

22 xWithout counsel, plans go awry,
But in the multitude of counselors they
are established.

23 A man has joy by the answer of his
mouth,
And ya word spoken in due season,
how good it is!

24 zThe way of life winds upward for the
wise,
That he may aturn away from hell*
below.

25 bThe LORD will destroy the house of the
proud,
But cHe will establish the boundary of
the widow.

---

* 15:11 Or Sheol • Hebrew Abaddon   * 15:17 Or
vegetables   * 15:24 Or Sheol

15:6 the house of the righteous. One house is a blessing and the other is ruinous; the reason for this lies in how the house was acquired and how it is being used. The house of the righteous contains great wealth because it is founded on wisdom and a proper response to God. On the other hand, the wicked never gain enough to suit them, and lose what they have because of their deceptive ways.

15:10 Harsh discipline. There is a consequence for those who forsake God's way. This discipline comes as a means of correction. Only the person who hates this correction will die.

15:11 how much more the hearts. This is a "how much more" proverb, which impresses on the reader the clarity with which the Lord sees people's hearts. The Hebrew word sheol, or "hell," connotes the fear of the unknown. The word actually means "the mysterious realm of death." Yet death is no mystery to the Lord. And if the mysterious realm of the dead is known to Him, then surely a person's heart is transparent to Him. This technique of arguing from the greater to the lesser appears in both Testaments.

15:12 A scoffer does not love. The scorner (14:6) is used as a foil or comparison in Proverbs to expose more sharply the character of the wise. Whereas the sluggard is a comic figure in Proverbs, the scorner is a villain. His basic problem is displayed in his response to correction. He does not learn from it nor does he seek it. The scorner is adamant in his folly.

15:14 The heart of him who has understanding. The person with an understanding heart, another description of the wise, is never satisfied with what he or she knows. The pursuit of wisdom and knowledge are lifelong occupations—never fully realized in this lifetime. But fools, not knowing the extent of their ignorance, continue to pursue folly.

15:18 A wrathful man stirs up strife. A hot-tempered person can stir up strife where there is none; but a person who has a slow fuse—who is slow to anger—soothes contention (15:1).

15:25 The LORD will destroy the house of the proud. God will bring about justice in the end. To the

---

15:5 eProv. 10:1 fProv. 13:18 15:8 gIs. 1:11 15:9 hProv. 21:21 15:10 i1 Kin. 22:8 jProv. 5:12 15:11 kJob 26:6 l2 Chr. 6:30 15:12 mAmos 5:10 15:13 nProv. 12:25 oProv. 17:22 15:15 pProv. 17:22 15:16 qPs. 37:16 15:17 rProv. 17:1 15:18 sProv. 26:21 15:19 tProv. 22:5 15:20 uProv. 10:1 15:21 vProv. 10:23 wEph. 5:15 15:22 xProv. 11:14 15:23 yProv. 25:11 15:24 zPhil. 3:20 aProv. 14:16 15:25 bProv. 12:7 cPs. 68:5, 6

26 dThe thoughts of the wicked *are* an
    abomination to the LORD,
  eBut the words of the pure *are* pleasant.

27 fHe who is greedy for gain troubles his
    own house,
  But he who hates bribes will live.

28 The heart of the righteous gstudies
    how to answer,
  But the mouth of the wicked pours
    forth evil.

29 hThe LORD *is* far from the wicked,
  But iHe hears the prayer of the
    righteous.

30 The light of the eyes rejoices the heart,
  And a good report makes the bones
    healthy.*

31 The ear that hears the rebukes of life
  Will abide among the wise.

32 He who disdains instruction despises
    his own soul,
  But he who heeds rebuke gets
    understanding.

33 jThe fear of the LORD *is* the instruction
    of wisdom,
  And kbefore honor *is* humility.

16 The apreparations of the heart
    belong to man,
  bBut the answer of the tongue *is* from
    the LORD.

2 All the ways of a man *are* pure in his
    own ceyes,
  But the LORD weighs the spirits.

3 dCommit your works to the LORD,
  And your thoughts will be established.

4 The eLORD has made all for Himself,
  fYes, even the wicked for the day of
    doom.

5 gEveryone proud in heart *is* an
    abomination to the LORD;
  Though they join forces,* none will go
    unpunished.

6 hIn mercy and truth
  Atonement is provided for iniquity;
  And iby the fear of the LORD *one*
    departs from evil.

7 When a man's ways please the
    LORD,
  He makes even his enemies to be at
    peace with him.

8 jBetter *is* a little with righteousness,
  Than vast revenues without justice.

9 kA man's heart plans his way,
  lBut the LORD directs his steps.

10 Divination *is* on the lips of the king;
  His mouth must not transgress in
    judgment.

11 mHonest weights and scales *are* the
    LORD'S;
  All the weights in the bag *are* His
    work.

12 *It is* an abomination for kings to
    commit wickedness,
  For na throne is established by
    righteousness.

13 oRighteous lips *are* the delight of kings,
  And they love him who speaks *what
    is* right.

---

* **15:30** Literally *fat*   * **16:5** Literally *hand to hand*

---

haughty, God will give a dose of humility. But for the widow, a completely defenseless person in ancient times, God will provide protection.

15:32 *despises his own soul.* The natural instinct for self-preservation is dangerous when it is time to listen to a necessary rebuke.

15:33 *The fear of the LORD . . . instruction.* Knowledge alone does not make a person wiser; the fear of the Lord must accompany it. The same is true of honor.

16:1–2 *The preparations of the heart.* These verses contrast human limitations with the sovereignty of God. Man can plan, dream, and hope, but the final outcome is from the Lord. Rather than "resign ourselves to fate," we should trust in God.

16:3 *Commit your works to the LORD.* The verb "commit to" is from a word meaning "to roll." The idea is to "roll your cares onto the Lord." Trusting the Lord with our decisions frees us from preoccupation with our problems (3:5–6).

Dedication is the foundation of commitment. Without it the believer is unable to offer God anything else. Paul explains this dedication process in Romans 12:1–2. He emphasizes three things. First, it is our body which is to be dedicated as a living sacrifice to God. Second, we are to avoid being conformed to this world, but should strive to be transformed by the Word. Finally, by doing this we can discover God's perfect will for our lives.

After the dedication of our bodies, what are we to commit? We are to commit our salvation to God (2 Tim. 1:12). We are to commit our works (Prov. 16:3). Then our goals in life are to be given to Him (Job 5:8; Ps. 37:5). It is difficult but vital to commit our suffering experiences to God (1 Pet. 4:19). Our Lord Jesus did this very thing when He was on earth (1 Pet. 2:23). Finally, in the hour of death, we can with confidence commit our very souls to God (Ps. 31:5). Paul the apostle assures us that any and all such commitments to the Lord will be accepted and honored (1 Cor. 15:58).

16:6 *In mercy and truth.* These words can also be translated "by genuine piety." "Atonement" probably alludes to a sacrificial offering, but not apart from a contrite heart.

16:10 *Divination.* This refers to judicial decisions made by the king. Because the nation rested in the king's hands, his first responsibility was to obey God (King Josiah's reform of Israel, 2 Kin. 22). Even the king had to submit to the dictates of justice.

15:26 dProv. 6:16, 18 ePs. 37:30 **15:27** fIs. 5:8
15:28 g1 Pet. 3:15 **15:29** hPs. 10:1; 34:16 iPs. 145:18
15:33 jProv. 1:7 kProv. 18:12 **16:1** aJer. 10:23 bMatt.
10:19 **16:2** cProv. 21:2 **16:3** dPs. 37:5 **16:4** eIs. 43:7
f[Rom. 9:22] **16:5** gProv. 6:17; 8:13 **16:6** hDan. 4:27
iProv. 8:13; 14:16 **16:8** jPs. 37:16 **16:9** kProv. 19:21
lJer. 10:23 **16:11** mLev. 19:36 **16:12** nProv. 25:5
16:13 oProv. 14:35

14 As messengers of death *is* the king's
wrath,
But a wise man will [p]appease it.
15 In the light of the king's face *is* life,
And his favor *is* like a [q]cloud of the
latter rain.

16 [r]How much better to get wisdom than
gold!
And to get understanding is to be
chosen rather than silver.

17 The highway of the upright *is* to
depart from evil;
He who keeps his way preserves his
soul.

18 Pride *goes* before destruction,
And a haughty spirit before a fall.
19 Better *to be* of a humble spirit with the
lowly,
Than to divide the spoil with the
proud.

20 He who heeds the word wisely will
find good,
And whoever [s]trusts in the LORD,
happy *is* he.

21 The wise in heart will be called
prudent,
And sweetness of the lips increases
learning.

22 Understanding *is* a wellspring of life to
him who has it.
But the correction of fools *is* folly.

23 The heart of the wise teaches his
mouth,
And adds learning to his lips.

24 Pleasant words *are like* a honeycomb,
Sweetness to the soul and health to the
bones.

25 There is a way *that seems* right to a
man,
But its end *is* the way of [t]death.

26 The person who labors, labors for
himself,
For his *hungry* mouth drives [u]him *on.*

27 An ungodly man digs up evil,
And *it is* on his lips like a burning [v]fire.
28 A perverse man sows strife,
And [w]a whisperer separates the best
of friends.
29 A violent man entices his neighbor,
And leads him in a way *that is* not
good.
30 He winks his eye to devise perverse
things;
He purses his lips *and* brings about
evil.

31 [x]The silver-haired head *is* a crown of
glory,
If it is found in the way of
righteousness.

32 [y]*He who is* slow to anger *is* better than
the mighty,
And he who rules his spirit than he
who takes a city.

33 The lot is cast into the lap,
But its every decision *is* from the LORD.

17 Better *is* [a]a dry morsel with
quietness,
Than a house full of feasting* *with*
strife.

2 A wise servant will rule over [b]a son
who causes shame,
And will share an inheritance among
the brothers.

---

* **17:1** Or *sacrificial meals*

16:15 *life . . . his favor.* Successfully courting a powerful person's favor is like seeing rain clouds in a dry land. The phrase about the light of the face in this proverb helps us understand Aaron's benediction in Numbers 6:24–26.

16:17 *The highway of the upright.* This phrase is a metaphor for the way a person lives habitually. An *upright* person's highway or habit is to *depart from evil.* He does not compromise; he consistently strives to do good.

16:24 *Pleasant words are like a honeycomb.* The Hebrew word for honeycomb is also used in Psalm 19:10–11 with regard to the Word of God. The Israelites saw honey as a healthy food as well as a sweetener. Any comparison to it would connote positive, healthful effects.

16:27–29 *ungodly . . . perverse . . . violent man.* These verses all begin in a similar way describing three different types of wicked people. The word "ungodly" means a man of Belial; this person is a muckraker who uses bad information for evil purposes; he destroys people on purpose. The "perverse" person starts fights between friends. The "violent man" uses his power of persuasion to recruit others to join in his attacks.

16:32 *better than the mighty.* Even though one of the most favored persons in the ancient Middle East was the military hero, this proverb suggests that one who is "slow to anger" or who "rules his spirit" is a greater hero than a returning warrior.

16:33 *The lot is cast into the lap.* The use of lots in ancient Israel (16:10) could easily be confused with luck. But when a *lot* was cast as a means of determining God's will, the people knew it did not fall indiscriminately. God exercises sovereignty over human affairs (16:4).

17:1 *Better is a dry morsel.* This expression means "very little" especially in comparison to feasting. But the feasting in this verse is tainted by contention. Feasting could also be part of a sacrifice to God, but even such a feast could be ruined by angry disputes between believers.

17:2 *A wise servant.* Reversals of fortune could happen if the wise servant was sufficiently skillful and the son and his brothers were undeserving. Much of

16:14 [p] Prov. 25:15 **16:15** [q] Zech. 10:1 **16:16** [r] Prov. 8:10, 11, 19 **16:20** [s] Ps. 34:8 **16:25** [t] Prov. 14:12 **16:26** [u] [Eccl. 6:7] **16:27** [v] [James 3:6] **16:28** [w] Prov. 17:9 **16:31** [x] Prov. 20:29 **16:32** [y] Prov. 14:29; 19:11 **17:1** [a] Prov. 15:17 **17:2** [b] Prov. 10:5

3 The refining pot *is* for silver and the furnace for gold,
  cBut the LORD tests the hearts.

4 An evildoer gives heed to false lips;
  A liar listens eagerly to a spiteful tongue.

5 dHe who mocks the poor reproaches his Maker;
  eHe who is glad at calamity will not go unpunished.

6 fChildren's children *are* the crown of old men,
  And the glory of children *is* their father.

7 Excellent speech is not becoming to a fool,
  Much less lying lips to a prince.

8 A present *is* a precious stone in the eyes of its possessor;
  Wherever he turns, he prospers.

9 gHe who covers a transgression seeks love,
  But hhe who repeats a matter separates friends.

10 iRebuke is more effective for a wise *man*
  Than a hundred blows on a fool.

11 An evil *man* seeks only rebellion;
  Therefore a cruel messenger will be sent against him.

12 Let a man meet ja bear robbed of her cubs,
  Rather than a fool in his folly.

13 Whoever krewards evil for good,
  Evil will not depart from his house.

14 The beginning of strife *is like* releasing water;
  Therefore lstop contention before a quarrel starts.

15 mHe who justifies the wicked, and he who condemns the just,
  Both of them alike *are* an abomination to the LORD.

16 Why *is there* in the hand of a fool the purchase price of wisdom,
  Since *he has* no heart *for it?*

17 nA friend loves at all times,
  And a brother is born for adversity.

18 oA man devoid of understanding shakes hands in a pledge,
  And becomes surety for his friend.

19 He who loves transgression loves strife,
  And phe who exalts his gate seeks destruction.

20 He who has a deceitful heart finds no good,
  And he who has qa perverse tongue falls into evil.

21 He who begets a scoffer *does so* to his sorrow,
  And the father of a fool has no joy.

22 A rmerry heart does good, *like* medicine,*
  But a broken spirit dries the bones.

23 A wicked *man* accepts a bribe behind the back*
  To pervert the ways of justice.

24 sWisdom *is* in the sight of him who has understanding,
  But the eyes of a fool *are* on the ends of the earth.

25 A tfoolish son *is* a grief to his father,
  And bitterness to her who bore him.

26 Also, to punish the righteous *is* not good,
  Nor to strike princes for *their* uprightness.

27 uHe who has knowledge spares his words,
  And a man of understanding is of a calm spirit.

28 vEven a fool is counted wise when he holds his peace;
  When he shuts his lips, *he is considered* perceptive.

18 A man who isolates himself seeks his own desire;
  He rages against all wise judgment.

---

* **17:22** Or *makes medicine even better*
* **17:23** Literally *from the bosom*

Genesis describes the unexpected rise of a younger son over his older brother (Gen. 25:23–34).
17:4 *A evildoer gives heed to false lips.* This proverb presents the "evildoer" and the "liar" as a parody of the wise. As the righteous person listens with care to the instruction of a teacher, so the wicked person listens with care to the ruinous speech of the unrighteous.
17:7 Excellent speech. It is a contradiction in terms for a fool to speak well or for a prince to be a liar.
17:12 *a bear robbed of her cubs.* Nothing matches the rage of a mother bear who has been separated from her cubs; yet there is nothing in life more dangerous than the fool in the midst of his folly.
17:15 *abomination to the LORD.* Since God is a God of justice, He detests those who pervert justice—both those who declare the innocent guilty and those who declare the guilty innocent.
18:1 *isolates himself.* When a person is seeking his own desires, he separates himself from wisdom. His

---

17:3 c Jer. 17:10   17:5 d Prov. 14:31   e Job 31:29
17:6 f [Ps. 127:3; 128:3]   17:9 g [Prov. 10:12]   h Prov. 16:28
17:10 i [Mic. 7:9]   17:12 j Hos. 13:8   17:13 k Ps. 109:4, 5
17:14 l [Prov. 20:3]   17:15 m Ex. 23:7   17:17 n Ruth 1:16
17:18 o Prov. 6:1   17:19 p Prov. 16:18   17:20 q James
3:8   17:22 r Prov. 12:25; 15:13, 15   17:24 s Eccl. 2:14
17:25 t Prov. 10:1; 15:20; 19:13   17:27 u James 1:19
17:28 v Job 13:5

2 A fool has no delight in understanding,
But in expressing his ^aown heart.

3 When the wicked comes, contempt
comes also;
And with dishonor *comes* reproach.

4 ^bThe words of a man's mouth *are* deep
waters;
^cThe wellspring of wisdom *is* a flowing
brook.

5 *It is* not good to show partiality to the
wicked,
Or to overthrow the righteous in
^djudgment.

6 A fool's lips enter into contention,
And his mouth calls for blows.

7 ^eA fool's mouth *is* his destruction,
And his lips *are* the snare of his ^fsoul.

8 ^gThe words of a talebearer *are* like
tasty trifles,*
And they go down into the inmost
body.

9 He who is slothful in his work
Is a brother to him who is a great
destroyer.

10 The name of the LORD *is* a strong
^htower;
The righteous run to it and are safe.

11 The rich man's wealth *is* his strong
city,
And like a high wall in his own
esteem.

12 ⁱBefore destruction the heart of a man
is haughty,
And before honor *is* humility.

13 He who answers a matter before he
hears *it,*
It *is* folly and shame to him.

14 The spirit of a man will sustain him in
sickness,
But who can bear a broken spirit?

15 The heart of the prudent acquires
knowledge,
And the ear of the wise seeks
knowledge.

16 ^jA man's gift makes room for him,
And brings him before great men.

17 The first *one* to plead his cause *seems*
right,
Until his neighbor comes and
examines him.

18 Casting ^klots causes contentions to
cease,
And keeps the mighty apart.

19 A brother offended *is harder to win*
than a strong city,
And contentions *are* like the bars of a
castle.

20 ^lA man's stomach shall be satisfied
from the fruit of his mouth;
From the produce of his lips he shall
be filled.

21 ^mDeath and life *are* in the power of the
tongue,
And those who love it will eat its fruit.

22 ⁿHe who finds a wife finds a good
thing,
And obtains favor from the LORD.

23 The poor *man* uses entreaties,
But the rich answers ^oroughly.

24 A man *who has* friends must himself
be friendly,*
^pBut there is a friend *who* sticks closer
than a brother.

19 Better ^a*is* the poor who walks in his
integrity
Than *one who is* perverse in his lips,
and is a fool.

2 Also it is not good *for* a soul *to be*
without knowledge,
And he sins who hastens with *his* feet.

3 The foolishness of a man twists his way,
And his heart frets against the LORD.

---

* **18:8** A Jewish tradition reads *wounds.*
* **18:24** Following Greek manuscripts, Syriac,
Targum, and Vulgate; Masoretic Text reads *may
come to ruin.*

---

selfishness puts him at odds with sound understanding.
18:2 *A fool has no delight in understanding.* A compulsive talker never listens, only pausing to plan what he will say next. Every speech confirms what a fool he is.
18:8 *The words of a talebearer.* These words are like delicious sweets. Although they are fun to eat, they ruin the person's health. Gossip is fun to listen to, but it damages the listener's innermost parts.
18:10–11 *The name of the LORD is a strong tower.* The phrase *name of the LORD* is a way of speaking of God's person. The righteous turn to God for security. Rich people, by contrast, tend to trust in their wealth.
18:12 *the heart of a man is haughty.* The Hebrew word for haughty, ordinarily negative, can also be used positively to mean courage and daring (2 Chr. 17:6). The path to honor, which the proud so covet, is humility.

18:14 *The spirit of a man will sustain him in sickness.* This proverb affirms the value of coping skills. Sickness can be overcome, but there is no medicine for a broken spirit.
18:20 *stomach . . . mouth.* Inner satisfaction comes from true and good speech.
18:22 *favor from the LORD.* Problems in marriage arise from breakdowns in communication or mutual respect, not from some flaw in marriage itself (12:4).

18:2 ^aEccl. 10:3   **18:4** ^bProv. 10:11   ^c[James 3:17]
18:5 ^dProv. 17:15   **18:7** ^eProv. 10:14   ^fEccl. 10:12
18:8 ^gProv. 12:18   **18:10** ^h2 Sam. 22:2, 3, 33   **18:12** ⁱProv.
15:33; 16:18   **18:16** ^jGen. 32:20, 21   **18:18** ^k[Prov.
16:33]   **18:20** ^lProv. 12:14; 14:14   **18:21** ^mMatt.
12:37   **18:22** ⁿ[Prov. 12:4; 19:14]   **18:23** ^oJames 2:3, 6
18:24 ^pProv. 17:17   **19:1** ^aProv. 28:6

4 [b]Wealth makes many friends,
But the poor is separated from his friend.
5 A [c]false witness will not go unpunished,
And *he who* speaks lies will not escape.
6 Many entreat the favor of the nobility,
And every man *is* a friend to one who gives gifts.
7 [d]All the brothers of the poor hate him;
How much more do his friends go [e]far from him!
He may pursue *them with* words, *yet* they abandon *him.*
8 He who gets wisdom loves his own soul;
He who keeps understanding [f]will find good.
9 A false witness will not go unpunished,
And *he who* speaks lies shall perish.
10 Luxury is not fitting for a fool,
Much less [g]for a servant to rule over princes.
11 [h]The discretion of a man makes him slow to anger,
[i]And his glory *is* to overlook a transgression.
12 [j]The king's wrath *is* like the roaring of a lion,
But his favor *is* [k]like dew on the grass.
13 [l]A foolish son *is* the ruin of his father,
[m]And the contentions of a wife *are* a continual dripping.
14 [n]Houses and riches *are* an inheritance from fathers,
But [o]a prudent wife *is* from the LORD.
15 [p]Laziness casts *one* into a deep sleep,
And an idle person will [q]suffer hunger.
16 [r]He who keeps the commandment keeps his soul,
But he who is careless* of his ways will die.
17 [s]He who has pity on the poor lends to the LORD,
And He will pay back what he has given.
18 [t]Chasten your son while there is hope,
And do not set your heart on his destruction.*
19 *A man of* great wrath will suffer punishment;
For if you rescue *him,* you will have to do it again.
20 Listen to counsel and receive instruction,
That you may be wise [u]in your latter days.
21 There are many plans in a man's heart,
[v]Nevertheless the LORD's counsel—that will stand.
22 What is desired in a man is kindness,
And a poor man is better than a liar.
23 [w]The fear of the LORD *leads* to life,
And *he who has it* will abide in satisfaction;
He will not be visited with evil.
24 [x]A lazy *man* buries his hand in the bowl,*
And will not so much as bring it to his mouth again.
25 Strike a scoffer, and the simple [y]will become wary;
[z]Rebuke one who has understanding, *and* he will discern knowledge.
26 He who mistreats *his* father *and* chases away *his* mother
Is [a]a son who causes shame and brings reproach.

* **19:16** Literally *despises,* figurative of recklessness or carelessness * **19:18** Literally *to put him to death;* a Jewish tradition reads *on his crying.* * **19:24** Septuagint and Syriac read *bosom;* Targum and Vulgate read *armpit.*

19:4 *Wealth makes many friends.* This proverb speaks of the effects of wealth and poverty on friendship. It does not describe how friends ought to behave, but how many friends actually do. Like a faithful spouse, a faithful friend is priceless (14:20).
19:8 *he who keeps understanding will find good.* Ultimately to "find good" means to find the Lord in His Word (16:20).
19:10 *is not fitting.* This phrase might also be rendered "is not a pretty sight" (compare 17:7). For the wrong people to rule is an outrage.
19:12 *roaring of a lion . . . dew on the grass.* These metaphors are especially fitting when a monarch has all power. His rage may be violent and unpredictable, his pleasure gracious and restorative. A good king will display rage and spread favor for the right reasons.
19:13 *A foolish son . . . the contentions of a wife.* The family exists as the basic unit of a godly society. Two threats against the family are pictured in this proverb. One is the wayward son. The second is an emotionally unstable wife.
19:21 *many plans in a man's heart.* A wise person commits his or her plans to the Lord (16:3). A person whose plans oppose the Lord (as in Ps. 2:1–3) may actually become God's enemy. But the person whose ways are from God will certainly succeed (16:1,9).
19:22 *kindness.* Kindness may also mean "beauty." Faithfulness is beautiful, whereas deception is a disfigurement of character (3:14; 31:18).
19:26–27 *son.* The desire for a good son—or daughter—is the subject of a significant portion of Proverbs (chs. 1–9). A child who is abusive to his parents shames them and violates God's command (20:20; Ex. 20:12; Deut. 5:16). As an abusive son is shameful, so an obedient son is faithful.

19:4 [b] Prov. 14:20 **19:5** [c] Ex. 23:1 **19:7** [d] Prov. 14:20 [e] Ps. 38:11 **19:8** [f] Prov. 16:20 **19:10** [g] Prov. 30:21, 22 **19:11** [h] James 1:19 [i] Eph. 4:32 **19:12** [j] Prov. 16:14 [k] Hos. 14:5 **19:13** [l] Prov. 10:1 [m] Prov. 21:9, 19 **19:14** [n] 2 Cor. 12:14 [o] Prov. 18:22 **19:15** [p] Prov. 6:9 [q] Prov. 10:4 **19:16** [r] Luke 10:28; 11:28 **19:17** [s] [2 Cor. 9:6–8] **19:18** [t] Prov. 13:24 **19:20** [u] Ps. 37:37 **19:21** [v] Heb. 6:17 **19:23** [w] [1 Tim. 4:8] **19:24** [x] Prov. 15:19 **19:25** [y] Deut. 13:11 [z] Prov. 9:8 **19:26** [a] Prov. 17:2

27 Cease listening to instruction, my son,
And you will stray from the words of
knowledge.

28 A disreputable witness scorns justice,
And *b*the mouth of the wicked devours
iniquity.

29 Judgments are prepared for scoffers,
*c*And beatings for the backs of fools.

20 Wine *a*is a mocker,
Strong drink *is* a brawler,
And whoever is led astray by it is not
wise.

2 The wrath* of a king *is* like the
roaring of a lion;
Whoever provokes him to anger sins
against his own life.

3 *b*It is honorable for a man to stop
striving,
Since any fool can start a quarrel.

4 *c*The lazy *man* will not plow because of
winter;
*d*He will beg during harvest and *have*
nothing.

5 Counsel in the heart of man *is like*
deep water,
But a man of understanding will draw
it out.

6 Most men will proclaim each his own
goodness,
But who can find a faithful man?

7 *e*The righteous *man* walks in his
integrity;
*f*His children *are* blessed after him.

8 A king who sits on the throne of
judgment
Scatters all evil with his eyes.

9 *g*Who can say, "I have made my heart
clean,
I am pure from my sin"?

10 *h*Diverse weights *and* diverse measures,
They *are* both alike, an abomination to
the LORD.

11 Even a child is *i*known by his deeds,
Whether what he does *is* pure and
right.

12 *j*The hearing ear and the seeing eye,
The LORD has made them both.

13 *k*Do not love sleep, lest you come to
poverty;
Open your eyes, *and* you will be
satisfied with bread.

14 "It is good for nothing,"* cries the
buyer;
But when he has gone his way, then he
boasts.

15 There is gold and a multitude of rubies,
But *l*the lips of knowledge *are* a
precious jewel.

16 *m*Take the garment of one who is surety
for a stranger,
And hold it as a pledge *when it* is for a
seductress.

17 *n*Bread gained by deceit *is* sweet to a
man,
But afterward his mouth will be filled
with gravel.

18 *o*Plans are established by counsel;
*p*By wise counsel wage war.

19 *q*He who goes about *as* a talebearer
reveals secrets;
Therefore do not associate with one
*r*who flatters with his lips.

20 *s*Whoever curses his father or his
mother,
*t*His lamp will be put out in deep
darkness.

---

* **20:2** Literally *fear* or *terror* which is produced by
the king's wrath   * **20:14** Literally *evil, evil*

20:1 Wine is a mocker. This chapter begins with a
warning against the abuse of wine, or excessive drinking (see this theme more extensively in 23:29–35). A
wise person takes the danger seriously.
20:5 draw it out. Motivation for behavior is complex.
A gifted counselor is able to draw out from a person
genuine feelings and motivations, just as someone
draws water from a deep well.
20:9 Who can say. This proverb is a rhetorical question. Everyone sins, a theme that Paul addresses at
length in Romans 3:10–23. Anyone who claims never
to sin is a liar (1 John 1:8–9). But those who confess
their sin obtain forgiveness (Rom. 4:7).
20:11 by his deeds. A pattern established early in life
may continue to mark a person for his or her lifetime.
Even at a very early age, a person's moral character
may be revealed.
20:13 sleep. While sleep is a gift from God, it can also
be a matter of excess and laziness. Hard work is necessary to make a living; laziness leads only to poverty
(6:6–9).
20:16 Take the garment. Clothing could be taken

as collateral for a debt (Deut. 24:10–13). If someone
assumes responsibility for the debt of an unknown
stranger, he or she should be held accountable even
to the point of taking his or her clothing as a pledge.
20:17 But afterward. The Scriptures do not say that
there is no pleasure in sinning, only that the reward
does not last (9:17–18).
20:20 Whoever curses. This proverb is about breaking the Fifth Commandment, "Honor your father
and your mother" (Ex. 20:12). The term for "curses"
is based on a word that means "to treat lightly, to
regard as insignificant." The statement "his lamp will
be put out in deep darkness," is a symbol of eternal
damnation.

19:28 *b* Job 15:16   **19:29** *c* Prov. 26:3   **20:1** *a* Gen.
9:21   **20:3** *b* Prov. 17:14   **20:4** *c* Prov. 10:4   *d* Prov.
19:15   **20:7** *e* 2 Cor. 1:12   *f* Ps. 37:26   **20:9** *g* [1 Kin. 8:46]
20:10 *h* Deut. 25:13   **20:11** *i* Matt. 7:16   **20:12** *j* Ex.
4:11   **20:13** *k* Rom. 12:11   **20:15** *l* [Prov. 3:13–15]
20:16 *m* Prov. 22:26   **20:17** *n* Prov. 9:17   **20:18** *o* Prov.
24:6   *p* Luke 14:31   **20:19** *q* Prov. 11:13   *r* Rom. 16:18
20:20 *s* Matt. 15:4   *t* Job 18:5, 6

21 ^uAn inheritance gained hastily at the beginning
^vWill not be blessed at the end.

22 ^wDo not say, "I will recompense evil";
^xWait for the LORD, and He will save you.

23 Diverse weights *are* an abomination to the LORD,
And dishonest scales *are* not good.

24 A man's steps *are* of the LORD;
How then can a man understand his own way?

25 *It is* a snare for a man to devote rashly *something* as holy,
And afterward to reconsider *his* vows.

26 ^yA wise king sifts out the wicked,
And brings the threshing wheel over them.

27 ^zThe spirit of a man *is* the lamp of the LORD,
Searching all the inner depths of his heart.*

28 ^aMercy and truth preserve the king,
And by lovingkindness he upholds his throne.

29 The glory of young men *is* their strength,
And ^bthe splendor of old men *is* their gray head.

30 Blows that hurt cleanse away evil,
As *do* stripes the inner depths of the heart.*

21 The king's heart *is* in the hand of the LORD,
Like the rivers of water;
He turns it wherever He wishes.

2 ^aEvery way of a man *is* right in his own eyes,
^bBut the LORD weighs the hearts.

3 ^cTo do righteousness and justice
Is more acceptable to the LORD than sacrifice.

4 ^dA haughty look, a proud heart,
And the plowing* of the wicked *are* sin.

5 ^eThe plans of the diligent *lead* surely to plenty,
But *those of* everyone *who is* hasty, surely to poverty.

6 ^fGetting treasures by a lying tongue
Is the fleeting fantasy of those who seek death.*

7 The violence of the wicked will destroy them,*
Because they refuse to do justice.

8 The way of a guilty man *is* perverse;*
But *as for* the pure, his work *is* right.

9 Better to dwell in a corner of a housetop,
Than in a house shared with ^ga contentious woman.

10 ^hThe soul of the wicked desires evil;
His neighbor finds no favor in his eyes.

11 When the scoffer is punished, the simple is made wise;
But when the ⁱwise is instructed, he receives knowledge.

12 The righteous *God* wisely considers the house of the wicked,
Overthrowing the wicked for *their* wickedness.

---

* **20:27** Literally *the rooms of the belly*
* **20:30** Literally *the rooms of the belly* * **21:4** Or *lamp* * **21:6** Septuagint reads *Pursue vanity on the snares of death;* Vulgate reads *Is vain and foolish, and shall stumble on the snares of death;* Targum reads *They shall be destroyed, and they shall fall who seek death.* * **21:7** Literally *drag them away* * **21:8** Or *The way of a man is perverse and strange*

20:25 *something as holy.* Several proverbs warn against making rash promises about holy things, then withdrawing the promises later (Eccl. 5:1–7). It is better never to vow than to vow and then change one's mind.

20:26 *A wise king sifts out the wicked.* This royal proverb presents discipline as a merciful act. To punish wickedness is entirely appropriate. When the wicked are separated and punished with the severity that their crimes demand, all of society benefits. Ideally, the king in Israel mirrored God's character.

20:30 *Blows that hurt cleanse away evil.* Suffering cleanses. No one wants to be hurt, but God can bring good out of any evil and make us better through hardship.

21:1 *The king's heart . . . rivers of water.* A person can look at a river and think that it is following a random pattern, but the water is following the direction of God's hand. So is the king.

21:3 *To do righteousness and justice.* This proverb affirms, as do Psalm 40:6–8; Micah 6:8, and numerous other passages in the Bible, that righteous living is more important than sacrifice (1 Sam. 15:22).

21:6 *Getting treasures by a lying tongue.* If you have to lie to gain your "treasure," you are ultimately choosing death to your dreams. There is no stability in anything gained by a lie.

21:9 *a corner of a housetop.* Ancient Israelite roofs were flat and could be used as a deck or terrace. On occasion people would build a temporary shelter on a part of the roof. Here, the harried husband finds he prefers to live on the housetop rather than below with the nagging words of his wife.

21:10 *The soul of the wicked desires evil.* Wicked persons typically refuse to think of anyone but themselves.

20:21 ^u Prov. 28:20 ^v Hab. 2:6 **20:22** ^w [Rom. 12:17–19] ^x 2 Sam. 16:12 **20:26** ^y Ps. 101:8 **20:27** ^z 1 Cor. 2:11 **20:28** ^a Prov. 21:21 **20:29** ^b Prov. 16:31 **21:2** ^a Prov. 16:2 ^b Prov. 24:12 **21:3** ^c 1 Sam. 15:22 **21:4** ^d Prov. 6:17 **21:5** ^e Prov. 10:4 **21:6** ^f 2 Pet. 2:3 **21:9** ^g Prov. 19:13 **21:10** ^h James 4:5 **21:11** ⁱ Prov. 19:25

13 [j]Whoever shuts his ears to the cry of the poor
Will also cry himself and not be heard.

14 A gift in secret pacifies anger,
And a bribe behind the back,* strong wrath.

15 *It is* a joy for the just to do justice,
But destruction *will come* to the workers of iniquity.

16 A man who wanders from the way of understanding
Will rest in the assembly of the [k]dead.

17 He who loves pleasure *will be* a poor man;
He who loves wine and oil will not be rich.

18 The wicked *shall be* a ransom for the righteous,
And the unfaithful for the upright.

19 Better to dwell in the wilderness,
Than with a contentious and angry woman.

20 [l]*There is* desirable treasure,
And oil in the dwelling of the wise,
But a foolish man squanders it.

21 [m]He who follows righteousness and mercy
Finds life, righteousness, and honor.

22 A [n]wise *man* scales the city of the mighty,
And brings down the trusted stronghold.

23 [o]Whoever guards his mouth and tongue
Keeps his soul from troubles.

24 A proud *and* haughty *man*—"Scoffer" *is* his name;
He acts with arrogant pride.

25 The [p]desire of the lazy *man* kills him,
For his hands refuse to labor.

26 He covets greedily all day long,
But the righteous [q]gives and does not spare.

27 [r]The sacrifice of the wicked *is* an abomination;
How much more *when* he brings it with wicked intent!

28 A false witness shall perish,
But the man who hears *him* will speak endlessly.

29 A wicked man hardens his face,
But *as for* the upright, he establishes* his way.

30 [s]*There is* no wisdom or understanding
Or counsel against the LORD.

31 The horse *is* prepared for the day of battle,
But [t]deliverance *is* of the LORD.

22 A [a]*good* name is to be chosen rather than great riches,
Loving favor rather than silver and gold.

2 The [b]rich and the poor have this in common,
The [c]LORD *is* the maker of them all.

3 A prudent *man* foresees evil and hides himself,
But the simple pass on and are [d]punished.

4 By humility *and* the fear of the LORD
Are riches and honor and life.

5 Thorns *and* snares *are* in the way of the perverse;
He who guards his soul will be far from them.

6 [e]Train up a child in the way he should go,
And when he is old he will not depart from it.

---

* **21:14** Literally *in the bosom* * **21:29** Qere and Septuagint read *understands.*

21:15 *joy . . . to do justice.* Doing justice is not a heavy obligation that weighs a person down. For the righteous, promoting justice is a joy.
21:16 *the assembly of the dead.* The term *dead* is a frightful one, meaning "shades" (9:18). Death in these verses may speak of physical death rather than spiritual death (as is the case in James 1).
21:21 *life, righteousness, and honor.* It is possible that these three ideas go together to mean "a more abundant life." The pursuit of righteousness is its own reward. But added rewards are found in fullness of life, achieving righteousness, and receiving honor. All these things are gifts from the Lord (15:9).
21:28 *A false witness shall perish.* A large number of proverbs focus on bearing false witness (19:28). The problem with a false witness is that his lies pervert justice for others.
22:2 *The LORD is the maker of them all.* This sentence repeats the theme of riches (v. 1). God makes both the rich and the poor. This means that those who favor the rich over the poor (James 2) have not only missed the point of creation, they have insulted the Creator (14:31).
22:4 *By humility and the fear of the LORD.* The writer of this proverb makes humility synonymous with the fear of the Lord. True humility begins with a proper attitude toward God. In such a spirit of submission to God, true fear of God is exhibited.
22:6 *Train up a child.* This verse, like the other proverbs, contains a wise statement that is usually true. Who your child turns out to be is a reflection of your parenting. As God has taught elsewhere in His word, parents are to teach their children the way of the Lord. Not only are they to teach it purposefully, but they are to do it constantly—when they talk and sit and walk

21:13 [j] [Matt. 7:2; 18:30–34] **21:16** [k] Ps. 49:14 **21:20** [l] Ps. 112:3 **21:21** [m] Matt. 5:6 **21:22** [n] Prov. 24:5 **21:23** [o] [James 3:2] **21:25** [p] Prov. 13:4 **21:26** [q] [Prov. 22:9] **21:27** [r] Jer. 6:20 **21:30** [s] [Jer. 9:23, 24] **21:31** [t] Ps. 3:8 **22:1** [a] Eccl. 7:1 **22:2** [b] Prov. 29:13 [c] Job 31:15 **22:3** [d] Prov. 27:12 **22:6** [e] Eph. 6:4

7 The [f]rich rules over the poor,
And the borrower *is* servant to the lender.

8 He who sows iniquity will reap [g]sorrow,
And the rod of his anger will fail.

9 [h]He who has a generous eye will be [i]blessed,
For he gives of his bread to the poor.

10 [j]Cast out the scoffer, and contention will leave;
Yes, strife and reproach will cease.

11 [k]He who loves purity of heart
And has grace on his lips,
The king *will be* his friend.

12 The eyes of the LORD preserve knowledge,
But He overthrows the words of the faithless.

13 [l]The lazy *man* says, "*There is* a lion outside!
I shall be slain in the streets!"

14 [m]The mouth of an immoral woman *is* a deep pit;
[n]He who is abhorred by the LORD will fall there.

15 Foolishness *is* bound up in the heart of a child;
[o]The rod of correction will drive it far from him.

16 He who oppresses the poor to increase his *riches*,
And he who gives to the rich, *will* surely *come* to poverty.

Sayings of the Wise

17 Incline your ear and hear the words of the wise,
And apply your heart to my knowledge;
18 For *it is* a pleasant thing if you keep them within you;
Let them all be fixed upon your lips,
19 So that your trust may be in the LORD;
I have instructed you today, even you.
20 Have I not written to you excellent things
Of counsels and knowledge,
21 [p]That I may make you know the certainty of the words of truth,
[q]That you may answer words of truth
To those who send to you?

22 Do not rob the [r]poor because he *is* poor,
Nor oppress the afflicted at the gate;
23 [s]For the LORD will plead their cause,
And plunder the soul of those who plunder them.

24 Make no friendship with an angry man,
And with a [t]furious man do not go,
25 Lest you learn his ways
And set a snare for your soul.

26 [u]Do not be one of those who shakes hands in a pledge,
One of those who is surety for debts;
27 If you have nothing *with which* to pay,
Why should he take away your bed from under you?

28 [v]Do not remove the ancient landmark
Which your fathers have set.

29 Do you see a man *who* excels in his work?
He will stand before kings;
He will not stand before unknown *men*.

23 When you sit down to eat with a ruler,
Consider carefully what *is* before you;
2 And put a knife to your throat
If you *are* a man given to appetite.

---

and lie down and get up (Deut. 6:7–8). If children see their parents speaking kindly, being forgiving and gracious, gentle and understanding, children will want these character attributes too. But even more important, if the parents teach that they depend upon God to build kindly habits in themselves, children will know that it is to the Lord that one turns for help in every part of life. Training children undoubtedly involves everything from wiping feet and closing doors to saying "please" and "thank you," and "I am sorry." But the most important training that a child receives is the continual teaching and daily example of their parents' dependence on the Lord.

22:10 *the scoffer.* This kind of person should be expelled from the community because his influence is harmful to everyone. The wise know that the scorner is not a laughing matter, because he is laughing at holy things, at God Himself.

22:12 *The eyes of the LORD.* God is the final arbiter of knowledge and justice. The eyes of human beings are simply not trustworthy.

22:13 *There is a lion outside.* This proverb about lazy people pokes fun at how the lazy invent all sorts of excuses for avoiding work and risk.

22:17—24:22 Proverbs Concerning Various Situations—Verse 17 marks a new section of Proverbs. Three elements distinguish this section: (1) the change from one-verse units to multiple-verse units; (2) section headings that are embedded in the text; and (3) the affinity of this section for ancient Egyptian wisdom texts.

22:17–21 *Incline your ear.* These introductory words call the reader to pay attention and to prepare to learn about and worship God. The advice emphasizes strongly that a person's trust must be in the Lord.

22:28 *Do not remove the ancient landmark.* The ancient Israelites regarded respect for the posted landmark as more than a question of private property. They saw it as a basic part of civil life. People

22:7 [f] James 2:6 **22:8** [g] Job 4:8 **22:9** [h] 2 Cor. 9:6 [i] [Prov. 19:17] **22:10** [j] Ps. 101:5 **22:11** [k] Ps. 101:6 **22:13** [l] Prov. 26:13 **22:14** [m] Prov. 2:16; 5:3; 7:5 [n] Eccl. 7:26 **22:15** [o] Prov. 13:24; 23:13, 14 **22:21** [p] Luke 1:3, 4 [q] 1 Pet. 3:15 **22:22** [r] Ex. 23:6 **22:23** [s] 1 Sam. 24:12 **22:24** [t] Prov. 29:22 **22:26** [u] Prov. 11:15 **22:28** [v] Deut. 19:14; 27:17

3 Do not desire his delicacies,
For they *are* deceptive food.

4 ^aDo not overwork to be rich;
^bBecause of your own understanding,
cease!

5 Will you set your eyes on that which is
not?
For *riches* certainly make themselves
wings;
They fly away like an eagle *toward*
heaven.

6 Do not eat the bread of ^ca miser,*
Nor desire his delicacies;

7 For as he thinks in his heart, so *is* he.
"Eat and drink!" ^dhe says to you,
But his heart is not with you.

8 The morsel you have eaten, you will
vomit up,
And waste your pleasant words.

9 ^eDo not speak in the hearing of a fool,
For he will despise the wisdom of your
words.

10 Do not remove the ancient landmark,
Nor enter the fields of the fatherless;

11 ^fFor their Redeemer *is* mighty;
He will plead their cause against you.

12 Apply your heart to instruction,
And your ears to words of knowledge.

13 ^gDo not withhold correction from a
child,
For *if* you beat him with a rod, he will
not die.

14 You shall beat him with a rod,
And deliver his soul from hell.*

15 My son, if your heart is wise,
My heart will rejoice—indeed, I myself;

16 Yes, my inmost being will rejoice
When your lips speak right things.

17 ^hDo not let your heart envy sinners,
But ⁱbe zealous for the fear of the
LORD all the day;

18 ^jFor surely there is a hereafter,
And your hope will not be cut off.

19 Hear, my son, and be wise;
And guide your heart in the way.

20 ^kDo not mix with winebibbers,
Or with gluttonous eaters of meat;

21 For the drunkard and the glutton will
come to poverty,
And drowsiness will clothe *a man*
with rags.

22 ^lListen to your father who begot you,
And do not despise your mother when
she is old.

23 ^mBuy the truth, and do not sell *it*,
Also wisdom and instruction and
understanding.

24 ⁿThe father of the righteous will greatly
rejoice,
And he who begets a wise *child* will
delight in him.

25 Let your father and your mother be
glad,
And let her who bore you rejoice.

26 My son, give me your heart,
And let your eyes observe my ways.

27 ^oFor a harlot *is* a deep pit,
And a seductress *is* a narrow well.

28 ^pShe also lies in wait as *for* a victim,
And increases the unfaithful among
men.

29 ^qWho has woe?
Who has sorrow?
Who has contentions?
Who has complaints?
Who has wounds without cause?
Who ^rhas redness of eyes?

30 ^sThose who linger long at the wine,
Those who go in search of ^tmixed wine.

31 Do not look on the wine when it is red,
When it sparkles in the cup,
When it swirls around smoothly;

32 At the last it bites like a serpent,
And stings like a viper.

33 Your eyes will see strange things,
And your heart will utter perverse
things.

34 Yes, you will be like one who lies
down in the midst of the sea,

---

* **23:6** Literally *one who has an evil eye*
* **23:14** Or *Sheol*

---

must feel a certain sense of public trust and fairness
for society to function.
23:4–5 *Do not overwork to be rich.* These verses
call for moderation in work. Although the proverbs
discourage laziness (22:13), they also discourage any
overworking whose purpose is greater wealth.
23:13–14 *if you beat him with a rod.* This language
was designed to motivate overly permissive parents,
who were afraid of damaging children with any kind
of discipline, or of making rules and enforcing them.
There is no call here for abuse. Loving discipline does
not destroy rebellious children; it does them a big favor.
23:15 *if your heart is wise.* Wisdom is an outgrowth
of a proper response to discipline. That wisdom in
turn is immediately discernible to the father and
brings joy that must be expressed.
23:21 *For the drunkard and the glutton.* These

kinds of people have no self-control, and this fact
plagues them. Hebrew culture gave a prominent
place to eating and drinking, but it had little tolerance for drunkenness and gluttony.
23:29–35 *Who has woe?* Along with Isaiah's celebrated description of debauchery (Is. 19:11–15), this
section is one of the sharpest attacks on drunkenness
in the Bible (vv. 19–21). The satire is razor sharp and
the imagery vivid.

23:4 ^a[1 Tim. 6:9, 10] ^bRom. 12:16 **23:6** ^cDeut.
15:9 **23:7** ^dProv. 12:2 **23:9** ^eMatt. 7:6 **23:11** ^fProv.
22:23 **23:13** ^gProv. 13:24 **23:17** ^hPs. 37:1 ⁱProv. 28:14
23:18 ^j[Ps. 37:37] **23:20** ^kIs. 5:22 **23:22** ^lProv. 1:8
23:23 ^m[Matt. 13:44] **23:24** ⁿProv. 10:1 **23:27** ^oProv.
22:14 **23:28** ^pProv. 7:12 **23:29** ^qIs. 5:11, 22 ^rGen.
49:12 **23:30** ^s[Eph. 5:18] ^tPs. 75:8

Or like one who lies at the top of the
mast, *saying:*
35 "They*u* have struck me, *but* I was not
hurt;
They have beaten me, but I did not
feel *it.*
When shall *v*I awake, that I may seek
another *drink?"*

24 Do not be *a*envious of evil men,
Nor desire to be with them;
2 For their heart devises violence,
And their lips talk of troublemaking.

3 Through wisdom a house is built,
And by understanding it is
established;
4 By knowledge the rooms are filled
With all precious and pleasant riches.

5 *b*A wise man *is* strong,
Yes, a man of knowledge increases
strength;
6 *c*For by wise counsel you will wage
your own war,
And in a multitude of counselors *there
is* safety.

7 *d*Wisdom *is* too lofty for a fool;
He does not open his mouth in the
gate.

8 He who *e*plots to do evil
Will be called a schemer.
9 The devising of foolishness *is* sin,
And the scoffer *is* an abomination to
men.

10 *If* you *f*faint in the day of adversity,
Your strength *is* small.

11 *g*Deliver *those who* are drawn toward
death,
And hold back *those* stumbling to the
slaughter.
12 If you say, "Surely we did not know
this,"
Does not *h*He who weighs the hearts
consider *it?*
He who keeps your soul, does He *not*
know *it?*
And will He *not* render to *each* man
*i*according to his deeds?

13 My son, *j*eat honey because *it is* good,
And the honeycomb *which is* sweet to
your taste;
14 *k*So *shall* the knowledge of wisdom *be*
to your soul;
If you have found *it,* there is a prospect,
And your hope will not be cut off.

15 Do not lie in wait, O wicked *man,*
against the dwelling of the
righteous;
Do not plunder his resting place;
16 *l*For a righteous *man* may fall seven
times
And rise again,
*m*But the wicked shall fall by calamity.

17 *n*Do not rejoice when your enemy
falls,
And do not let your heart be glad when
he stumbles;
18 Lest the LORD see *it,* and it displease
Him,
And He turn away His wrath from
him.

19 *o*Do not fret because of evildoers,
Nor be envious of the wicked;
20 For there will be no prospect for the
evil *man;*
The lamp of the wicked will be put out.

21 My son, *p*fear the LORD and the king;
Do not associate with those given to
change;
22 For their calamity will rise suddenly,
And who knows the ruin those two
can bring?

Further Sayings of the Wise
23These *things* also *belong* to the wise:

*q*It *is* not good to show partiality in
judgment.
24 *r*He who says to the wicked, "You *are*
righteous,"
Him the people will curse;
Nations will abhor him.
25 But those who rebuke *the wicked* will
have *s*delight,
And a good blessing will come upon
them.

24:6 The Will of God—Common sense tells us that
God often works through circumstances and through
wise counsel to reveal His will for us. A number of biblical examples illustrate this principle:
• God directed Abraham to substitute a ram, whose
horns had become entangled in a thicket, for the
life of Isaac (Gen. 22:13).
• God arranged for Pharaoh's daughter to be
bathing in the river Nile at the exact time the
baby Moses floated by in an ark of bulrushes (Ex.
2:1–10).
• Paul's young nephew happened to overhear a
plot to kill his uncle. He then reported it to the
authorities who saved Paul's life (Acts 23:11–35).
In light of the above, the Christian should ask
himself, "Is the Lord showing me something through
these circumstances?" We can also take great comfort

in Paul's reminder to the Romans that God causes all
things to "work together for good to those who love
God, to those who are the called according to His purpose" (Rom. 8:28).
24:21–22 *fear the LORD and the king.* This proverb
relates most fully to the Davidic kings, who were
God's regents on earth; one way the ancient Israelites could show respect for God was to respect the
king.

23:35 *u* Jer. 5:3 *v* Eph. 4:19   **24:1** *a* Ps. 1:1; 37:1
24:5 *b* Prov. 21:22   **24:6** *c* Luke 14:31   **24:7** *d* Ps.
10:5   **24:8** *e* Rom. 1:30   **24:10** *f* Heb. 12:3   **24:11** *g* Ps.
82:4   **24:12** *h* Prov. 21:2   *i* Ps. 62:12   **24:13** *j* Song 5:1
24:14 *k* Ps. 19:10; 58:11   **24:16** *l* [Mic. 7:8] *m* Esth. 7:10
24:17 *n* Obad. 12   **24:19** *o* Ps. 37:1   **24:21** *p* [1 Pet. 2:17]
24:23 *q* Lev. 19:15   **24:24** *r* Is. 5:23   **24:25** *s* Prov. 28:23

26 He who gives a right answer kisses the
lips.

27 ᵗPrepare your outside work,
Make it fit for yourself in the field;
And afterward build your house.

28 ᵘDo not be a witness against your
neighbor without cause,
For would you deceive* with your
lips?

29 ᵛDo not say, "I will do to him just as he
has done to me;
I will render to the man according to
his work."

30 I went by the field of the lazy *man*,
And by the vineyard of the man devoid
of understanding;

31 And there it was, ʷall overgrown with
thorns;
Its surface was covered with nettles;
Its stone wall was broken down.

32 When I saw *it*, I considered *it* well;
I looked on *it and* received
instruction:

33 ˣA little sleep, a little slumber,
A little folding of the hands to rest;

34 ʸSo shall your poverty come *like* a
prowler,
And your need like an armed man.

Further Wise Sayings of Solomon

25 Theseᵃ also *are* proverbs of Solomon
which the men of Hezekiah king of
Judah copied:

2 ᵇ*It is* the glory of God to conceal a
matter,
But the glory of kings *is* to search out
a matter.

3 As the heavens for height and the
earth for depth,
So the heart of kings *is*
unsearchable.

4 ᶜTake away the dross from silver,
And it will go to the silversmith *for*
jewelry.

5 Take away the wicked from before the
king,

And his throne will be established in
ᵈrighteousness.

6 Do not exalt yourself in the presence
of the king,
And do not stand in the place of the
great;

7 ᵉFor *it is* better that he say to you,
"Come up here,"
Than that you should be put lower in
the presence of the prince,
Whom your eyes have seen.

8 ᶠDo not go hastily to court;
For what will you do in the end,
When your neighbor has put you to
shame?

9 ᵍDebate your case with your neighbor,
And do not disclose the secret to
another;

10 Lest he who hears *it* expose your shame,
And your reputation be ruined.

11 A word fitly ʰspoken *is like* apples of
gold
In settings of silver.

12 *Like* an earring of gold and an
ornament of fine gold
Is a wise rebuker to an obedient ear.

13 ⁱLike the cold of snow in time of
harvest
Is a faithful messenger to those who
send him,
For he refreshes the soul of his masters.

14 ʲWhoever falsely boasts of giving
Is like ᵏclouds and wind without rain.

15 ˡBy long forbearance a ruler is
persuaded,
And a gentle tongue breaks a bone.

16 Have you found honey?
Eat only as much as you need,
Lest you be filled with it and vomit.

17 Seldom set foot in your neighbor's
house,
Lest he become weary of you and hate
you.

---

* **24:28** Septuagint and Vulgate read *Do not
deceive.*

25:1 *These also are proverbs of Solomon.* After
the first collection of proverbs from Solomon
(10:1—22:16) and proverbs from foreign sources
(22:17—24:22; 24:23–34) comes a collection of
proverbs attributed to Solomon, but which were not
compiled until the time of Hezekiah. The following
observations can be made: (1) The wisdom tradition
concerning Solomon was prodigious; (2) Israel's
interest in wisdom was particularly centered in times
of relative peace; (3) Hezekiah's involvement in this
activity was a mark of the strength of his rule and the
sense he had of restoring Solomon's glory.
25:6 *Do not exalt yourself.* Knowing your place
is a recurring theme in the Bible. It is humiliating
to be told to remove yourself from a seat of honor.
Jesus spoke of the same need for deference (Luke
14:11).

25:7 *Whom your eyes have seen.* This phrase
reflects the custom in the ancient world of never
looking directly in the eyes of a superior until told to
do so (Is. 6:5).
25:15 *By long forbearance a ruler is persuaded.* In
this passage the general rule that a gentle answer
turns away wrath is applied to a particular and most
difficult situation.

24:27 ᵗ Prov. 27:23–27 **24:28** ᵘ Eph. 4:25
24:29 ᵛ [Prov. 20:22] **24:31** ʷ Gen. 3:18 **24:33** ˣ Prov.
6:9, 10 **24:34** ʸ Prov. 6:9–11 **25:1** ᵃ 1 Kin. 4:32
25:2 ᵇ Deut. 29:23 **25:4** ᶜ 2 Tim. 2:21 **25:5** ᵈ Prov.
16:12; 20:8 **25:7** ᵉ Luke 14:7–11 **25:8** ᶠ Matt. 5:25
25:9 ᵍ [Matt. 18:15] **25:11** ʰ Prov. 15:23 **25:13** ⁱ Prov.
13:17 **25:14** ʲ Prov. 20:6 ᵏ Jude 12 **25:15** ˡ Prov. 15:1

18 *m*A man who bears false witness
   against his neighbor
   Is like a club, a sword, and a sharp
   arrow.
19 Confidence in an unfaithful *man* in
   time of trouble
   Is like a bad tooth and a foot out of joint.
20 *Like* one who takes away a garment in
   cold weather,
   And like vinegar on soda,
   Is one who *n*sings songs to a heavy
   heart.
21 *o*If your enemy is hungry, give him
   bread to eat;
   And if he is thirsty, give him water to
   drink;
22 For *so* you will heap coals of fire on
   his head,
   *p*And the LORD will reward you.
23 The north wind brings forth rain,
   And *q*a backbiting tongue an angry
   countenance.
24 *r*It is* better to dwell in a corner of a
   housetop,
   Than in a house shared with a
   contentious woman.
25 *As* cold water to a weary soul,
   So *is* *s*good news from a far country.
26 A righteous *man* who falters before
   the wicked
   Is like a murky spring and a polluted
   well.
27 *It is* not good to eat much honey;
   So *t*to seek one's own glory *is not* glory.
28 *u*Whoever *has* no rule over his own
   spirit
   Is like a city broken down, without
   walls.

26

As snow in summer *a*and rain in
harvest,
So honor is not fitting for a fool.
2 Like a flitting sparrow, like a flying
   swallow,
   So *b*a curse without cause shall not
   alight.
3 *c*A whip for the horse,
   A bridle for the donkey,
   And a rod for the fool's back.

4 Do not answer a fool according to his
   folly,
   Lest you also be like him.
5 *d*Answer a fool according to his folly,
   Lest he be wise in his own eyes.
6 He who sends a message by the hand
   of a fool
   Cuts off *his own* feet *and* drinks
   violence.
7 *Like* the legs of the lame that hang
   limp
   Is a proverb in the mouth of fools.
8 Like one who binds a stone in a sling
   Is he who gives honor to a fool.
9 *Like* a thorn *that* goes into the hand of
   a drunkard
   Is a proverb in the mouth of fools.
10 The great *God* who formed everything
   Gives the fool *his* hire and the
   transgressor *his* wages.*
11 *e*As a dog returns to his own vomit,
   *f*So a fool repeats his folly.
12 *g*Do you see a man wise in his own
   eyes?
   There is more hope for a fool than for
   him.
13 The lazy *man* says, "*There is* a lion in
   the road!
   A fierce lion *is* in the streets!"
14 *As* a door turns on its hinges,
   So *does* the lazy *man* on his bed.
15 The *h*lazy *man* buries his hand in the
   bowl;*
   It wearies him to bring it back to his
   mouth.
16 The lazy *man is* wiser in his own eyes
   Than seven men who can answer
   sensibly.
17 He who passes by *and* meddles in a
   quarrel not his own
   Is like one who takes a dog by the ears.
18 Like a madman who throws
   firebrands, arrows, and death,
19 *Is* the man *who* deceives his neighbor,
   And says, *i*"I was only joking!"
20 Where *there is* no wood, the fire goes
   out;
   And where *there is* no talebearer,
   strife ceases.

---

* **26:10** The Hebrew is difficult; ancient and modern translators differ greatly.   * **26:15** Compare 19:24

25:21–22 coals of fire. The words of Jesus in Matthew 5:43–48 have direct ties to these verses. They speak of God's judgment (Ps. 120:4; 140:10); the idea is that an act of kindness to your enemy may cause him or her to feel ashamed. This is just one way to overcome evil with good (Rom. 12:20).

26:4–5 according to his folly. Some people have called the two proverbs here contradictory, but that is not necessarily true. The phrase appears twice as a play on words with two shades of meaning. On the one hand, it means "avoid the temptation to stoop to his level"; that is do not use his methods, "lest you also be like him." On the other hand, it means "avoid the temptation to ignore him altogether"; that is respond in some way, or else he will become wise in his own eyes and his folly will get worse.

25:18 *m* Ps. 57:4   **25:20** *n* Dan. 6:18   **25:21** *o* Rom. 12:20   **25:22** *p* 2 Sam. 16:12   **25:23** *q* Ps. 101:5   **25:24** *r* Prov. 19:13   **25:25** *s* Prov. 15:30   **25:27** *t* Prov. 27:2   **25:28** *u* Prov. 16:32   **26:1** *a* 1 Sam. 12:17   **26:2** *b* Deut. 23:5   **26:3** *c* Ps. 32:9   **26:5** *d* Matt. 16:1–4   **26:11** *e* 2 Pet. 2:22   *f* Ex. 8:15   **26:12** *g* [Rev. 3:17]   **26:15** *h* Prov. 19:24   **26:19** *i* Eph. 5:4

21 *As charcoal *is* to burning coals, and
wood to fire,
So *is* a contentious man to kindle
strife.

22 The words of a talebearer *are* like
tasty trifles,
And they go down into the inmost
body.

23 Fervent lips with a wicked heart
Are like earthenware covered with
silver dross.

24 He who hates, disguises *it* with his
lips,
And lays up deceit within himself;

25 *k*When he speaks kindly, do not believe
him,
For *there are* seven abominations in
his heart;

26 *Though his* hatred is covered by
deceit,
His wickedness will be revealed before
the assembly.

27 *l*Whoever digs a pit will fall into it,
And he who rolls a stone will have it
roll back on him.

28 A lying tongue hates *those who are*
crushed by it,
And a flattering mouth works *m*ruin.

27 Do*a* not boast about tomorrow,
For you do not know what a day
may bring forth.

2 *b*Let another man praise you, and not
your own mouth;
A stranger, and not your own lips.

3 A stone *is* heavy and sand *is*
weighty,
But a fool's wrath *is* heavier than both
of them.

4 Wrath *is* cruel and anger a torrent,
But *c*who *is* able to stand before
jealousy?

5 *d*Open rebuke *is* better
Than love carefully concealed.

6 Faithful *are* the wounds of a friend,
But the kisses of an enemy *are*
*e*deceitful.

7 A satisfied soul loathes the
honeycomb,
But to a hungry soul every bitter thing
is sweet.

8 Like a bird that wanders from its nest
Is a man who wanders from his place.

9 Ointment and perfume delight the
heart,
And the sweetness of a man's friend
gives delight by hearty counsel.

10 Do not forsake your own friend or
your father's friend,
Nor go to your brother's house in the
day of your calamity;
*f*Better *is* a neighbor nearby than a
brother far away.

11 My son, be wise, and make my heart
glad,
*g*That I may answer him who
reproaches me.

12 A prudent *man* foresees evil *and* hides
himself;
The simple pass on *and* are *h*punished.

13 Take the garment of him who is surety
for a stranger,
And hold it in pledge *when* he is surety
for a seductress.

14 He who blesses his friend with a loud
voice, rising early in the morning,
It will be counted a curse to him.

15 A *i*continual dripping on a very rainy
day
And a contentious woman are alike;

16 Whoever restrains her restrains the
wind,
And grasps oil with his right hand.

17 *As* iron sharpens iron,
So a man sharpens the countenance of
his friend.

18 *j*Whoever keeps the fig tree will eat its
fruit;
So he who waits on his master will be
honored.

19 As in water face *reflects* face,
So a man's heart *reveals* the man.

20 *k*Hell* and Destruction* are never full;
So *l*the eyes of man are never satisfied.

* **27:20** Or *Sheol* • Hebrew *Abaddon*

26:23 earthenware covered with silver dross. The
meaning of this proverb is similar to Jesus' remarks to
His enemies that they were like whitewashed tombs
(Matt. 23:27). No amount of painting on the outside
changes the value of the rotten interior.
26:24–26 revealed before the assembly. A person
who hates says one thing but stores up anger within.
He may find that his hatred hurts him, when in his life
there is so much falsehood that no one believes him no
matter how gracious and truthful he might be at times.
27:7 to a hungry soul. Those who are full do not
appreciate what they have, while to those who are
hungry anything tastes good.

27:17 iron sharpens iron. This may also be translated
as applying to the will; "let iron sharpen iron, and so
let a person sharpen his friend." The idea is that people grow from interaction with one another.

26:21 *l* Prov. 15:18   **26:25** *k* Ps. 28:3   **26:27** *l* Ps.
7:15   **26:28** *m* Prov. 29:5   **27:1** *a* James 4:13–16
27:2 *b* Prov. 25:27   **27:4** *c* 1 John 3:12   **27:5** *d* [Prov.
28:23]   **27:6** *e* Matt. 26:49   **27:10** *f* Prov. 17:17;
18:24   **27:11** *g* Prov. 10:1; 23:15–26   **27:12** *h* Prov.
22:3   **27:15** *i* Prov. 19:13   **27:18** *j* [1 Cor. 3:8; 9:7–13]
27:20 *k* Hab. 2:5   *l* Eccl. 1:8; 4:8

21 *m*The refining pot *is* for silver and the furnace for gold,
And a man *is valued* by what others say of him.

22 *n*Though you grind a fool in a mortar with a pestle along with crushed grain,
Yet his foolishness will not depart from him.

23 Be diligent to know the state of your *o*flocks,
And attend to your herds;

24 For riches *are* not forever,
Nor does a crown *endure* to all generations.

25 *p*When the hay is removed, and the tender grass shows itself,
And the herbs of the mountains are gathered in,

26 The lambs *will provide* your clothing,
And the goats the price of a field;

27 *You shall have* enough goats' milk for your food,
For the food of your household,
And the nourishment of your maidservants.

28

The *a*wicked flee when no one pursues,
But the righteous are bold as a lion.

2 Because of the transgression of a land, many *are* its princes;
But by a man of understanding *and* knowledge
Right will be prolonged.

3 *b*A poor man who oppresses the poor
Is like a driving rain which leaves no food.

4 *c*Those who forsake the law praise the wicked,
*d*But such as keep the law contend with them.

5 *e*Evil men do not understand justice,
But *f*those who seek the LORD understand all.

6 Better *is* the poor who walks in his integrity
Than one perverse *in his* ways, though he *be* rich.

7 Whoever keeps the law *is* a discerning son,
But a companion of gluttons shames his father.

8 One who increases his possessions by usury and extortion
Gathers it for him who will pity the poor.

9 One who turns away his ear from hearing the law,
*g*Even his prayer *is* an abomination.

10 *h*Whoever causes the upright to go astray in an evil way,
He himself will fall into his own pit;
*i*But the blameless will inherit good.

11 The rich man *is* wise in his own eyes,
But the poor who has understanding searches him out.

12 When the righteous rejoice, *there is* great *j*glory;
But when the wicked arise, men hide themselves.

13 *k*He who covers his sins will not prosper,
But whoever confesses and forsakes *them* will have mercy.

14 Happy *is* the man who is always reverent,
But he who hardens his heart will fall into calamity.

15 *l*Like a roaring lion and a charging bear
*m*Is a wicked ruler over poor people.

16 A ruler who lacks understanding *is* a great *n*oppressor,
But he who hates covetousness will prolong *his* days.

17 *o*A man burdened with bloodshed will flee into a pit;
Let no one help him.

18 Whoever walks blamelessly will be saved,
But *he who is* perverse *in his* ways will suddenly fall.

19 *p*He who tills his land will have plenty of bread,

28:4–5 *Those who forsake the law.* When a person abandons God's law, he or she loses all sense of right and praise the wicked (Rom. 1:28–32). Since true justice is from God, the ungodly have trouble understanding it. This is why the fear of the Lord is the beginning of wisdom (1:7).
28:7 *a companion of gluttons.* One way of breaking God's law is to be a companion of gluttons (23:20–21). This is why Jesus' enemies charged Him with associating with gluttons and winebibbers. Such accusations were attacks on His faithfulness to God (Matt. 11:19).
28:8 *usury and extortion.* Profit gained by charging interest or high "profit margins" is unjust. God will help the poor eventually at their exploiters' expense.
28:14 *Happy is the man.* This is a repeat of Psalm 1:1 about a person who is in awe of God. The person who never thinks of God faces calamity.

27:21 *m* Prov. 17:3   **27:22** *n* Jer. 5:3   **27:23** *o* Prov. 24:27
27:25 *p* Ps. 104:14   **28:1** *a* Ps. 53:5   **28:3** *b* Matt. 18:28
28:4 *c* Ps. 49:18   *d* 1 Kin. 18:18   **28:5** *e* Ps. 92:6   *f* John 17:17   **28:9** *g* Prov. 15:8   **28:10** *h* Prov. 26:27   *i* [Matt. 6:33]   **28:12** *j* Prov. 11:10; 29:2   **28:13** *k* Ps. 32:3–5
28:15 *l* 1 Pet. 5:8   *m* Matt. 2:16   **28:16** *n* Eccl. 10:16
28:17 *o* Gen. 9:6   **28:19** *p* Prov. 12:11; 20:13

But he who follows frivolity will have
　　poverty enough!

20　A faithful man will abound with
　　　blessings,
　　ᵃBut he who hastens to be rich will not
　　　go unpunished.

21　ʳTo show partiality *is* not good,
　　ˢBecause for a piece of bread a man
　　　will transgress.

22　A man with an evil eye hastens after
　　　riches,
　　And does not consider that ᵗpoverty
　　　will come upon him.

23　ᵘHe who rebukes a man will find more
　　　favor afterward
　　Than he who flatters with the tongue.

24　Whoever robs his father or his mother,
　　And says, "*It is* no transgression,"
　　The same ᵛ*is* companion to a destroyer.

25　ʷHe who is of a proud heart stirs up
　　　strife,
　　ˣBut he who trusts in the Lᴏʀᴅ will be
　　　prospered.

26　He who ʸtrusts in his own heart is a
　　　fool,
　　But whoever walks wisely will be
　　　delivered.

27　ᶻHe who gives to the poor will not lack,
　　But he who hides his eyes will have
　　　many curses.

28　When the wicked arise, ᵃmen hide
　　　themselves;
　　But when they perish, the righteous
　　　increase.

29 Heᵃ who is often rebuked, *and*
　　　hardens *his* neck,
　　Will suddenly be destroyed, and that
　　　without remedy.

2　When the righteous are in authority,
　　　the ᵇpeople rejoice;
　　But when a wicked *man* rules, ᶜthe
　　　people groan.

3　Whoever loves wisdom makes his
　　　father rejoice,
　　But a companion of harlots wastes *his*
　　　wealth.

4　The king establishes the land by
　　　justice,

But he who receives bribes
　　overthrows it.

5　A man who ᵈflatters his neighbor
　　Spreads a net for his feet.

6　By transgression an evil man is
　　　snared,
　　But the righteous sings and rejoices.

7　The righteous ᵉconsiders the cause of
　　　the poor,
　　But the wicked does not understand
　　　such knowledge.

8　Scoffers ᶠset a city aflame,
　　But wise *men* turn away wrath.

9　*If* a wise man contends with a foolish
　　　man,
　　ᵍWhether *the fool* rages or laughs,
　　　there is no peace.

10　ʰThe bloodthirsty hate the blameless,
　　But the upright seek his well-being.*

11　A fool vents all his ⁱfeelings,*
　　But a wise *man* holds them back.

12　If a ruler pays attention to lies,
　　All his servants *become* wicked.

13　The poor *man* and the oppressor have
　　　this in common:
　　ʲThe Lᴏʀᴅ gives light to the eyes of
　　　both.

14　The king who judges the ᵏpoor with
　　　truth,
　　His throne will be established
　　　forever.

15　The rod and rebuke give ˡwisdom,
　　But a child left *to himself* brings
　　　shame to his mother.

16　When the wicked are multiplied,
　　　transgression increases;
　　But the righteous will see their ᵐfall.

17　Correct your son, and he will give you
　　　rest;
　　Yes, he will give delight to your soul.

18　ⁿWhere *there is* no revelation,* the
　　　people cast off restraint;
　　But ᵒhappy *is* he who keeps the law.

---

* **29:10** Literally *soul*　　* **29:11** Literally *spirit*
* **29:18** Or *prophetic vision*

28:23 *He who rebukes a man.* Constructive criticism
has more value than flattery, which aims only to win
people's affection.
28:25–26 *He who is . . . proud.* One of the main
causes of strife is pride; trust in God leads to blessing.
29:5 *Spreads a net.* Flattery is a lie. If you flatter your
neighbor you are making a trap of some kind for
him. God never lies. He always tells the truth and so
should we.
29:13 *The poor man and the oppressor.* God is
responsible for giving life to both. Jesus attested
that God causes rain to fall on the just and the unjust
(Matt. 5:45).

29:18 *Where there is no revelation.* Without God's
revelation of the law, the people flounder. True happiness is discovered within the constraints of revelation, in the counsel of the Savior.

28:20 ᵍ 1 Tim. 6:9　**28:21** ʳ Prov. 18:5　ˢ Ezek. 13:19
28:22 ᵗ Prov. 21:5　**28:23** ᵘ Prov. 27:5, 6　**28:24** ᵛ Prov.
18:9　**28:25** ʷ Prov. 13:10　ˣ 1 Tim. 6:6　**28:26** ʸ Prov. 3:5
28:27 ᶻ Deut. 15:7　**28:28** ᵃ Job 24:4　**29:1** ᵃ 2 Chr.
36:16　**29:2** ᵇ Prov. 28:12　ᶜ Esth. 4:3　**29:5** ᵈ Prov. 26:28
29:7 ᵉ Job 29:16　**29:8** ᶠ Prov. 11:11　**29:9** ᵍ Matt. 11:17
29:10 ʰ 1 John 3:12　**29:11** ⁱ Prov. 14:33　**29:13** ʲ [Matt.
5:45]　**29:14** ᵏ Is. 11:4　**29:15** ˡ Prov. 22:15　**29:16** ᵐ Ps.
37:34　**29:18** ⁿ 1 Sam. 3:1　ᵒ John 13:17

19 A servant will not be corrected by mere words;
For though he understands, he will not respond.

20 Do you see a man hasty in his words?
[p]*There is* more hope for a fool than for him.

21 He who pampers his servant from childhood
Will have him as a son in the end.

22 [q]An angry man stirs up strife,
And a furious man abounds in transgression.

23 [r]A man's pride will bring him low,
But the humble in spirit will retain honor.

24 Whoever is a partner with a thief hates his own life;
[s]He swears to tell the truth,* but reveals nothing.

25 [t]The fear of man brings a snare,
But whoever trusts in the LORD shall be safe.

26 [u]Many seek the ruler's favor,
But justice for man *comes* from the LORD.

27 An unjust man *is* an abomination to the righteous,
And *he who is* upright in the way *is* an abomination to the wicked.

The Wisdom of Agur

30 The words of Agur the son of Jakeh, *his* utterance. This man declared to Ithiel—to Ithiel and Ucal:

2 [a]Surely I *am* more stupid than *any* man,
And do not have the understanding of a man.
3 I neither learned wisdom
Nor have [b]knowledge of the Holy One.

4 [c]Who has ascended into heaven, or descended?
[d]Who has gathered the wind in His fists?
Who has bound the waters in a garment?
Who has established all the ends of the earth?
What *is* His name, and what *is* His Son's name,
If you know?

5 [e]Every word of God *is* pure;
[f]He *is* a shield to those who put their trust in Him.
6 [g]Do not add to His words,
Lest He rebuke you, and you be found a liar.

7 Two *things* I request of You
(Deprive me not before I die):
8 Remove falsehood and lies far from me;
Give me neither poverty nor riches—
[h]Feed me with the food allotted to me;
9 [i]Lest I be full and deny *You*,
And say, "Who *is* the LORD?"
Or lest I be poor and steal,
And profane the name of my God.

10 Do not malign a servant to his master,
Lest he curse you, and you be found guilty.

11 *There is* a generation *that* curses its [j]father,
And does not bless its mother.
12 *There is* a generation [k]*that is* pure in its own eyes,
Yet is not washed from its filthiness.
13 *There is* a generation—oh, how [l]lofty are their eyes!
And their eyelids are lifted up.
14 [m]*There is* a generation whose teeth *are like* swords,
And whose fangs *are like* knives,
[n]To devour the poor from off the earth,
And the needy from *among* men.

15 The leech has two daughters—
Give *and* Give!

There are three *things that* are never satisfied,
Four never say, "Enough!":
16 [o]The grave,*
The barren womb,

* **29:24** Literally *hears the adjuration*
* **30:16** Or *Sheol*

29:23 *A man's pride will bring him low.* Pride, inordinate self-esteem, causes others to lose respect for the conceited egotist. In contrast to this, humility draws honor from others. However, pride takes many forms and is not always the adornment of just the conceited egotist.
29:26 *but justice for man comes from the LORD.* God controls human affairs. Therefore it makes more sense to seek the Lord first before stooping to seek the favor of human rulers.
30:1 *The words of Agur.* This verse starts an entirely new section of Proverbs. Like Lemuel (31:1–9), Agur was a non-Hebrew contributor to the Book of Proverbs. He came to faith in the God of Israel in a foreign land.
30:4 *what is His name?* This verse gives the riddle that perplexed Agur. The questions all culminate in the last two lines. The Old Testament would answer that "His name" is the Lord God, but did not have a name for His Son. This riddle was to remain unsolved until Jesus answered it for Nicodemus (John 3:13). These verses form one of the most straightforward messianic texts in the Bible.

29:20[p] Prov. 26:12 **29:22**[q] Prov. 26:21 **29:23**[r] Is. 66:2 **29:24**[s] Lev. 5:1 **29:25**[t] Gen. 12:12; 20:2 **29:26**[u] Ps. 20:9 **30:2**[a] Ps. 73:22 **30:3**[b] [Prov. 9:10] **30:4**[c] [John 3:13] [d] Job 38:4 **30:5**[e] Ps. 12:6; 19:8; 119:140 [f] Ps. 18:30; 84:11; 115:9–11 **30:6**[g] Deut. 4:2; 12:32 **30:8**[h] Matt. 6:11 **30:9**[i] Deut. 8:12–14 **30:11**[j] Ex. 21:17 **30:12**[k] Luke 18:11 **30:13**[l] Prov. 6:17 **30:14**[m] Job 29:17 [n] Amos 8:4 **30:16**[o] Prov. 27:20

The earth *that* is not satisfied with
    water—
And the fire never says, "Enough!"

17 ᴾThe eye *that* mocks *his* father,
    And scorns obedience to *his* mother,
    The ravens of the valley will pick it out,
    And the young eagles will eat it.

18 There are three *things which* are too
    wonderful for me,
    Yes, four *which* I do not understand:
19 The way of an eagle in the air,
    The way of a serpent on a rock,
    The way of a ship in the midst of the
    sea,
    And the way of a man with a virgin.

20 This *is* the way of an adulterous
    woman:
    She eats and wipes her mouth,
    And says, "I have done no wickedness."

21 For three *things* the earth is
    perturbed,
    Yes, for four it cannot bear up:
22 ᵃFor a servant when he reigns,
    A fool when he is filled with food,
23 A hateful *woman* when she is married,
    And a maidservant who succeeds her
    mistress.

24 There are four *things which* are little
    on the earth,
    But they *are* exceedingly wise:
25 ʳThe ants *are* a people not strong,
    Yet they prepare their food in the
    summer;
26 ˢThe rock badgers* are a feeble folk,
    Yet they make their homes in the
    crags;
27 The locusts have no king,
    Yet they all advance in ranks;
28 The spider* skillfully grasps with its
    hands,
    And it is in kings' palaces.

29 There are three *things which* are
    majestic in pace,
    Yes, four *which* are stately in walk:
30 A lion, *which is* mighty among beasts
    And does not turn away from any;
31 A greyhound,*
    A male goat also,

And a king *whose* troops *are* with
    him.*
32 If you have been foolish in exalting
    yourself,
    Or if you have devised evil, ᵗput *your*
    hand on *your* mouth.
33 For *as* the churning of milk produces
    butter,
    And wringing the nose produces blood,
    So the forcing of wrath produces strife.

The Words of King Lemuel's Mother

31 The words of King Lemuel, the utter-
    ance which his mother taught him:

2 What, my son?
    And what, son of my womb?
    And what, ᵃson of my vows?
3 ᵇDo not give your strength to women,
    Nor your ways ᶜto that which destroys
    kings.

4 ᵈ*It is* not for kings, O Lemuel,
    It is not for kings to drink wine,
    Nor for princes intoxicating drink;
5 ᵉLest they drink and forget the law,
    And pervert the justice of all the
    afflicted.
6 ᶠGive strong drink to him who is
    perishing,
    And wine to those who are bitter of
    heart.
7 Let him drink and forget his poverty,
    And remember his misery no more.

8 ᵍOpen your mouth for the speechless,
    In the cause of all *who are* appointed
    to die.*
9 Open your mouth, ʰjudge righteously,
    And ᵢplead the cause of the poor and
    needy.

The Virtuous Wife

10 ʲWho* can find a virtuous* wife?
    For her worth *is* far above rubies.

---

* **30:26** Or *hyraxes*   * **30:28** Or *lizard*
* **30:31** Exact identity unknown • A Jewish
tradition reads a *king against whom there is no
uprising.*   * **31:8** Literally *sons of passing away*
* **31:10** Verses 10 through 31 are an alphabetic
acrostic in Hebrew (compare Psalm 119). • Literally *a wife of valor,* in the sense of all forms of
excellence

30:19 virgin. This term could also read *maid or young*
woman in this context.
30:20 This is the way. This verse contrasts with the
way of verse 19; this way is awful whereas the former
is wonderful. The *adulterous woman* regards her illicit
sexual relations without remorse.
30:24–28 four things which are little on the earth.
This numerical proverb speaks of four creatures
that are small in size but amazing in behavior. Each
of these small creatures has a behavioral trait from
which wise people can learn.
30:32–33 put your hand on your mouth. This
phrase means "stop it." The idea is if you are in the
middle of making trouble and suddenly realize your
foolishness, stop right then before things get worse.

31:1 The words of King Lemuel. This verse begins a
new section of material from a non-Israelite source.
31:4–5 Lest they drink and forget the law. In this
passage the consumption of strong drink is linked to
injustice.
31:10 a virtuous wife. Proverbs 31:10–31 is an
acrostic poem; each verse begins with a successive
letter to the Hebrew alphabet. As the Book of Proverbs begins with a Prologue (1:1–7), which gives the

30:17 ᵖ Gen. 9:22   **30:22** ᵠ Prov. 19:10   **30:25** ʳ Prov.
6:6   **30:26** ˢ Ps. 104:18   **30:32** ᵗ Mic. 7:16   **31:2** ᵃ Is.
49:15   **31:3** ᵇ Prov. 5:9   ᶜ Deut. 17:17   **31:4** ᵈ Eccl. 10:17
31:5 ᵉ Hos. 4:11   **31:6** ᶠ Ps. 104:15   **31:8** ᵍ Job 29:15, 16
31:9 ʰ Lev. 19:15   ᵢ Jer. 22:16   **31:10** ʲ Prov. 12:4; 19:14

11 The heart of her husband safely trusts
her;
So he will have no lack of gain.
12 She does him good and not evil
All the days of her life.
13 She seeks wool and flax,
And willingly works with her hands.
14 She is like the merchant ships,
She brings her food from afar.
15 kShe also rises while it is yet night,
And lprovides food for her household,
And a portion for her maidservants.
16 She considers a field and buys it;
From her profits she plants a vineyard.
17 She girds herself with strength,
And strengthens her arms.
18 She perceives that her merchandise is
good,
And her lamp does not go out by night.
19 She stretches out her hands to the
distaff,
And her hand holds the spindle.
20 mShe extends her hand to the poor,
Yes, she reaches out her hands to the
needy.
21 She is not afraid of snow for her
household,
For all her household is clothed with
scarlet.

22 She makes tapestry for herself;
Her clothing is fine linen and purple.
23 nHer husband is known in the gates,
When he sits among the elders of the
land.
24 She makes linen garments and sells
them,
And supplies sashes for the
merchants.
25 Strength and honor are her clothing;
She shall rejoice in time to come.
26 She opens her mouth with wisdom,
And on her tongue is the law of
kindness.
27 She watches over the ways of her
household,
And does not eat the bread of idleness.
28 Her children rise up and call her
blessed;
Her husband also, and he praises her:
29 "Many daughters have done well,
But you excel them all."
30 Charm is deceitful and beauty is
passing,
But a woman who fears the LORD, she
shall be praised.
31 Give her of the fruit of her hands,
And let her own works praise her in
the gates.

---

goals of wisdom in general terms, so now it concludes with this Epilogue, which presents them in a case study.
31:20–22 to the poor. The excellent woman works not to get rich, but to give to the poor. She can be concerned for others because she has provided for her own family.
31:26 on her tongue is the law of kindness. This attribute of kindness in a woman is valued far above physical charm in God's sight. Peter describes real beauty as a product of the heart and not the combination of certain physical features (1 Pet. 3:1–5).
31:30–31 Charm. Charm, which could be translated "graciousness," like beauty, can deceive us about the true nature of someone's character. But if a woman fears the Lord, that is trustworthy and more worthy of praise than physical comeliness.

31:15 k Rom. 12:11 l Luke 12:42   **31:20** m Eph. 4:28
31:23 n Prov. 12:4

THE BOOK OF
ECCLESIASTES

▶ **AUTHOR:** The author calls himself "the son of David, king in Jerusalem" in 1:1. Solomonic authorship is the standard Christian position, although some scholars, along with the Talmud, believe the work was later edited during the time of Hezekiah or possibly Ezra. The proverbs in this book are similar to those in the Book of Proverbs (Eccl. 7; 10). According to 12:9, the Preacher collected and arranged many proverbs, perhaps referring to the two Solomonic collections in Proverbs.

▶ **TIME:** c. 935 B.C.   ▶ **KEY VERSE:** Eccl. 2:24

▶ **THEME:** Ecclesiastes is a Greek word that is usually translated "the preacher" or "the teacher." The book was likely written late in Solomon's life, when he could see that the glorious era of his kingdom was beginning to decline. He had it all—power, prestige, pleasure—but none of that provides ultimate satisfaction. That fulfillment comes only through a relationship with God and obedience to His word. It is important to note that the arguments of the book are more thematic than linear. The same topics are addressed in different ways at different points within the work.

The Vanity of Life

1 The words of the Preacher, the son of David, ᵃking in Jerusalem.

2 "Vanityᵇ* of vanities," says the Preacher;
"Vanity of vanities, ᶜall *is* vanity."

3 ᵈWhat profit has a man from all his labor
In which he toils under the sun?

4 *One* generation passes away, and
another generation comes;
ᵉBut the earth abides forever.

5 ᶠThe sun also rises, and the sun goes down,
And hastens to the place where it arose.

6 ᵍThe wind goes toward the south,
And turns around to the north;
The wind whirls about continually,
And comes again on its circuit.

7 ʰAll the rivers run into the sea,
Yet the sea *is* not full;
To the place from which the rivers come,
There they return again.

8 All things *are* full of labor;
Man cannot express *it.*
ⁱThe eye is not satisfied with seeing,
Nor the ear filled with hearing.

9 ʲThat which has been *is* what will be,
That which *is* done is what will be done,
And *there is* nothing new under the sun.

10 Is there anything of which it may be said,
"See, this *is* new"?

---

* **1:2** Or *Absurdity, Frustration, Futility, Nonsense;* and so throughout this book

---

1:1 the Preacher. This word denotes a function or a profession. It literally means "one who assembles or gathers people together." Thus the word refers to Solomon as a person who convened an assembly of the wise in order to explore in a formal manner the meaning of life.
1:2 Vanity of vanities. This phrase translates the Hebrew superlative, familiar from such phrases as "Song of Songs" and "holy of holies." Here it might express "the ultimate absurdity" or "utter emptiness." The word vanity means "breath" or "vapor" and thus speaks of life as "quickly passing." Life is like a vapor; indeed, it is like the thinnest of vapors. Wherever we read the word *vanity* in Ecclesiastes, we should think not of what is "meaningless," but of what is "quickly passing" (v. 14; 6:12). This is one of the key terms in the Book of Ecclesiastes, for it is found 38 times here,

but only 34 times throughout the rest of the Old Testament. The teaching of the Preacher is to realize that life is a fleeting thing that needs to be savored and enjoyed as a gift from God.
1:4 One generation. This term suggests both the human actors and the natural phenomena as well. With the verb "passes" we have the first of a series of antitheses in Ecclesiastes. **the earth abides forever.** Only God is eternal and everlasting in the fullest sense. But compared to the lives of humankind, the earth abides with little change.

1:1 ᵃProv. 1:1   **1:2** ᵇPs. 39:5, 6; 62:9; 144:4   ᶜ[Rom. 8:20, 21]   **1:3** ᵈEccl. 2:22; 3:9   **1:4** ᵉPs. 104:5; 119:90   **1:5** ᶠPs. 19:4–6   **1:6** ᵍJohn 3:8   **1:7** ʰ[Jer. 5:22]   **1:8** ⁱProv. 27:20   **1:9** ʲEccl. 3:15

It has already been in ancient times
before us.
11 *There is* [k]no remembrance of former
things,
Nor will there be any remembrance of
things that are to come
By *those* who will come after.

The Grief of Wisdom

12 I, the Preacher, was king over Israel in
Jerusalem. 13 And I set my heart to seek and
[l]search out by wisdom concerning all that
is done under heaven; [m]this burdensome
task God has given to the sons of man, by
which they may be exercised. 14 I have seen
all the works that are done under the sun;
and indeed, all *is* vanity and grasping for
the wind.

15 [n]*What is* crooked cannot be made
straight,
And what is lacking cannot be
numbered.

16 I communed with my heart, saying,
"Look, I have attained greatness, and have
gained [o]more wisdom than all who were
before me in Jerusalem. My heart has
understood great wisdom and knowledge."
17 [p]And I set my heart to know wisdom and
to know madness and folly. I perceived that
this also is grasping for the wind.

18 For [q]in much wisdom *is* much grief,
And he who increases knowledge
increases sorrow.

The Vanity of Pleasure

2 I said [a]in my heart, "Come now, I will
test you with [b]mirth; therefore enjoy
pleasure"; but surely, [c]this also *was* vanity. 2 I said of laughter—"Madness!"; and
of mirth, "What does it accomplish?" 3 [d]I
searched in my heart *how* to gratify my
flesh with wine, while guiding my heart
with wisdom, and how to lay hold on folly,
till I might see what *was* [e]good for the sons
of men to do under heaven all the days of
their lives.
4 I made my works great, I built myself
[f]houses, and planted myself vineyards. 5 I
made myself gardens and orchards, and
I planted all *kinds* of fruit trees in them.
6 I made myself water pools from which
to water the growing trees of the grove. 7 I
acquired male and female servants, and
had servants born in my house. Yes, I had
greater possessions of herds and flocks
than all who were in Jerusalem before me.
8 [g]I also gathered for myself silver and gold
and the special treasures of kings and of
the provinces. I acquired male and female
singers, the delights of the sons of men,
and musical instruments* of all kinds.
9 [h]So I became great and excelled [i]more
than all who were before me in Jerusalem.
Also my wisdom remained with me.

10 Whatever my eyes desired I did not
keep from them.
I did not withhold my heart from any
pleasure,
For my heart rejoiced in all my labor;
And [j]this was my reward from all my
labor.
11 Then I looked on all the works that my
hands had done
And on the labor in which I had toiled;
And indeed all *was* [k]vanity and
grasping for the wind.
There was no profit under the sun.

The End of the Wise and the Fool

12 Then I turned myself to consider
wisdom [l]and madness and folly;
For what *can* the man *do* who
succeeds the king?—
Only what he has already [m]done.
13 Then I saw that wisdom [n]excels folly
As light excels darkness.
14 [o]The wise man's eyes *are* in his head,
But the fool walks in darkness.
Yet I myself perceived
That [p]the same event happens to them
all.
15 So I said in my heart,
"As it happens to the fool,
It also happens to me,

*2:8 Exact meaning unknown

1:13 *under heaven.* This is a synonymous expression for "under the sun" (vv. 3,9); it refers to life as it is lived by people on earth.
1:14 *grasping for the wind.* This phrase does not occur in the Hebrew Bible outside of Ecclesiastes. Seven of its nine occurrences (v. 14; 2:11,17,26; 4:4,6; 6:9) follow "vanity" statements. The phrase explains the nature of life according to the Preacher. Life is real, but quickly passing; any attempt to slow it is futile.
2:1 *Come now, I will test you with mirth.* The Preacher uses a literary device of conversing with himself as a way of describing his thought processes. ***pleasure.*** A new test is proposed, following the test of wisdom. It is the test of "joy."
2:2 *Madness.* Solomon labels the lighter side of pleasure and joy as sheer madness, but even the weightier aspects of laughter cause Solomon to ask if anything substantial is really achieved. As Solomon writes in Proverbs 14:13, "Even in laughter the heart may sorrow, and the end of mirth may be grief."
2:10 *my eyes desired.* Solomon had limitless ability to fulfill any and all of his desires.
2:11 *indeed all was vanity.* At the end of his grand quest for possessions and experiences, Solomon

1:11 [k]Eccl. 2:16 **1:13** [l][Eccl. 7:25; 8:16, 17] [m]Eccl. 3:10 **1:15** [n]Eccl. 7:13 **1:16** [o]1 Kin. 3:12, 13 **1:17** [p]Eccl. 2:3, 12; 7:23, 25 **1:18** [q]Eccl. 12:12 **2:1** [a]Luke 12:19 [b][Eccl. 7:4; 8:15] [c]Eccl. 1:2 **2:3** [d]Eccl. 1:17 [e][Eccl. 3:12, 13; 5:18; 6:12] **2:4** [f]1 Kin. 7:1–12 **2:8** [g]1 Kin. 9:28; 10:10, 14, 21 **2:9** [h]Eccl. 1:16 [i]2 Chr. 9:22 **2:10** [j]Eccl. 3:22; 5:18; 9:9 **2:11** [k]Eccl. 1:3, 14 **2:12** [l]Eccl. 1:17; 7:25 [m]Eccl. 1:9 **2:13** [n]Eccl. 7:11, 14, 19; 9:18; 10:10 **2:14** [o]Prov. 17:24 [p]Ps. 49:10

And why was I then more wise?"
Then I said in my heart,
"This also is vanity."
16 For there is qno more remembrance
of the wise than of the fool
forever,
Since all that now is will be forgotten
in the days to come.
And how does a wise man die?
As the fool!

17Therefore I hated life because the work that was done under the sun was distressing to me, for all is vanity and grasping for the wind. 18Then I hated all my labor in which I had toiled under the sun, because rI must leave it to the man who will come after me. 19And who knows whether he will be wise or a fool? Yet he will rule over all my labor in which I toiled and in which I have shown myself wise under the sun. This also is vanity. 20Therefore I turned my heart and despaired of all the labor in which I had toiled under the sun. 21For there is a man whose labor is with wisdom, knowledge, and skill; yet he must leave his heritage to a man who has not labored for it. This also is vanity and a great evil. 22sFor what has man for all his labor, and for the striving of his heart with which he has toiled under the sun? 23For all his days are tsorrowful, and his work burdensome; even in the night his heart takes no rest. This also is vanity.

24uNothing is better for a man than that he should eat and drink, and that his soul should enjoy good in his labor. This also, I saw, was from the hand of God. 25For who can eat, or who can have enjoyment, more than I?* 26For God gives vwisdom and

knowledge and joy to a man who is good in His sight; but to the sinner He gives the work of gathering and collecting, that whe may give to him who is good before God. This also is vanity and grasping for the wind.

Everything Has Its Time

3 To everything there is a season,
A atime for every purpose under
heaven:

2   A time to be born,
   And ba time to die;
   A time to plant,
   And a time to pluck what is planted;
3   A time to kill,
   And a time to heal;
   A time to break down,
   And a time to build up;
4   A time to cweep,
   And a time to laugh;
   A time to mourn,
   And a time to dance;
5   A time to cast away stones,
   And a time to gather stones;
   dA time to embrace,
   And a time to refrain from embracing;
6   A time to gain,
   And a time to lose;
   A time to keep,
   And a time to throw away;
7   A time to tear,
   And a time to sew;
   eA time to keep silence,
   And a time to fspeak;

* 2:25 Following Masoretic Text, Targum, and Vulgate; some Hebrew manuscripts, Septuagint, and Syriac read without Him.

concluded that it was "vanity" or a "vapor," a striving after the wind. That is, even with all he had done and experienced, there was still a sense that nothing lasting or enduring had been achieved.
2:17 Therefore I hated life. Such hatred of life is astonishing since the one who finds wisdom also finds life, according to Proverbs 3:16. But the Preacher's dissatisfaction was related to the quickly passing nature of everything (1:2), including the good things.
2:21 This also is vanity and a great evil. The term evil often has a sense of moral evil; here, however, it may mean "calamity" or "ruin." There is a sense of sadness that runs through this section. Nothing that we gain in this life can be carried on into the life to come.
2:24 eat and drink. The Preacher concludes that all good is located only in God. This phrase marks one of the central affirmations of the book (3:12,22; 8:15; 9:7); in the midst of a world of trouble, a believer is able to seize the moment in joy from God. Only God supplies the key to the meaning of life. Without Him, genuine meaning, satisfaction, and enjoyment in life are ultimately elusive.
2:26 God gives wisdom, and knowledge, and joy. One of the words used most frequently in Ecclesiastes to describe God's relationship to individuals is a verb "to give." It appears 11 times with God as the subject.

Joy is God's gift to the man who is good in His sight. God has designed us so that true joy is possible only through Him.
3:1–15 To everything there is a season. Some regard the Book of Ecclesiastes as describing life apart from God. But clearly this text describes life that is lived in relationship with God. Through these words, the Preacher is not saying that everything has an opportune time according to which one should choose one action or the other. Rather, he teaches that all events are in the hand of God, who makes everything happen in the time He judges appropriate.
3:5 A time to cast away stones. In times of peace, stones were cleared from the fields allowing for cultivation. In wartime, the rocks were thrown on the fields to make them unusable (2 Kin. 3:19,25).
3:7 A time to tear, And a time to sew. When bad news came, it was customary to rip one's garments to show grief (2 Sam. 13:31). When the problem passed, it was just as well to sew the garment back together.

2:16 q Eccl. 1:11; 4:16   2:18 r Ps. 49:10   2:22 s Eccl. 1:3; 3:9   2:23 t Job 5:7; 14:1   2:24 u Eccl. 3:12, 13, 22   2:26 v Prov. 2:6   w Prov. 28:8   3:1 a Eccl. 3:17; 8:6   3:2 b Heb. 9:27   3:4 c Rom. 12:15   3:5 d Joel 2:16   3:7 e Amos 5:13   f Prov. 25:11

8 A time to love,
  And a time to ᵍhate;
  A time of war,
  And a time of peace.

The God-Given Task

⁹ʰWhat profit has the worker from that in which he labors? ¹⁰ⁱI have seen the God-given task with which the sons of men are to be occupied. ¹¹He has made everything beautiful in its time. Also He has put eternity in their hearts, except that ʲno one can find out the work that God does from beginning to end.

¹²I know that nothing *is* ᵏbetter for them than to rejoice, and to do good in their lives, ¹³and also that ˡevery man should eat and drink and enjoy the good of all his labor—it *is* the gift of God.

14 I know that whatever God does,
     It shall be forever.
  ᵐNothing can be added to it,
     And nothing taken from it.
  God does *it*, that men should fear
     before Him.
15 ⁿThat which is has already been,
     And what is to be has already been;
  And God requires an account of what
     is past.

Injustice Seems to Prevail

¹⁶Moreover ᵒI saw under the sun:

  In the place of judgment,
     Wickedness *was* there;
  And *in* the place of righteousness,
     Iniquity *was* there.

¹⁷I said in my heart,

  ᵖ"God shall judge the righteous and the
     wicked,
  For *there is* a time there for every
     purpose and for every work."

¹⁸I said in my heart, "Concerning the condition of the sons of men, God tests them,

that they may see that they themselves are *like* animals." ¹⁹qFor what happens to the sons of men also happens to animals; one thing befalls them: as one dies, so dies the other. Surely, they all have one breath; man has no advantage over animals, for all *is* vanity. ²⁰All go to one place: ʳall are from the dust, and all return to dust. ²¹ˢWho knows the spirit of the sons of men, which goes upward, and the spirit of the animal, which goes down to the earth?* ²²ᵗSo I perceived that nothing *is* better than that a man should rejoice in his own works, for ᵘthat *is* his heritage. ᵛFor who can bring him to see what will happen after him?

4 Then I returned and considered all the ᵃoppression that is done under the sun:

  And look! The tears of the oppressed,
     But they have no comforter—
  On the side of their oppressors *there*
     is power,
  But they have no comforter.
2 ᵇTherefore I praised the dead who were
     already dead,
  More than the living who are still
     alive.
3 ᶜYet, better than both *is* he who has
     never existed,
  Who has not seen the evil work that is
     done under the sun.

The Vanity of Selfish Toil

⁴Again, I saw that for all toil and every skillful work a man is envied by his neighbor. This also *is* vanity and grasping for the wind.

5 ᵈThe fool folds his hands
     And consumes his own flesh.

---

* **3:21** Septuagint, Syriac, Targum, and Vulgate read *Who knows whether the spirit ... goes upward, and whether ... goes downward to the earth?*

3:9 *What profit has the worker.* This is the same question posed in 1:3. The answer here is that all of life unfolds at the appointment of God. All the toiling of man cannot change the time, circumstances, and control of events that God has reserved for Himself.
3:11 *put eternity in their hearts.* This phrase refers to a deep-seated, compulsive drive to transcend our mortality by knowing the meaning and destiny of the world. Because we are made in the image of God, we have an inborn inquisitiveness about eternal realities. We can find peace only when we come to know our eternal Creator. Even then, we know God only in part (1 Cor. 13:12).
3:12–13 *nothing is better . . . to rejoice.* As in 2:24, the advice of the Preacher is to seize the day in the joy of God. Biblical faith is a call for joy, even when we live in a wicked world and under terrible stress; this is because we find true joy in the living God.
3:16–17 *Wickedness was there.* It was outrageous that in the very establishments where people should expect justice, they could find only wickedness. The Preacher warns the wicked judges that God, the final

Judge, will come to rectify all wrongdoing and bring true justice.
3:20 *All go to one place.* Both humans and beasts die and go to the grave. But this is not the end for human beings—they will face eternal life or death.
4:1 *they have no comforter.* So much pain can come to the downtrodden that they may even despair of life (1 Kin. 19:4). Only when the oppressed go into the house of God will they gain perspective (5:1–6; Ps. 73:17).
4:3 *who has never existed.* So powerfully wrong and so lonely is the suffering of the oppressed, that Solomon, with a good deal of poetic license similar to Job 3:3–10, argues that nonexistence could be preferred over existence.

3:8 ᵍ Luke 14:26   **3:9** ʰ Eccl. 1:3   **3:10** ⁱ Eccl. 1:13
3:11 ʲ Rom. 11:33   **3:12** ᵏ Eccl. 2:3, 24   **3:13** ˡ Eccl. 2:24
3:14 ᵐ James 1:17   **3:15** ⁿ Eccl. 1:9   **3:16** ᵒ Eccl. 5:8
3:17 ᵖ [Rom. 2:6–10]   **3:19** q [Eccl. 2:16]   **3:20** ʳ Gen.
3:19   **3:21** ˢ Eccl. 12:7   **3:22** ᵗ Eccl. 2:24; 5:18 ᵘ Eccl. 2:10
ᵛ Eccl. 6:12; 8:7   **4:1** ᵃ Eccl. 3:16; 5:8   **4:2** ᵇ Job 3:17, 18
4:3 ᶜ Job 3:11–22   **4:5** ᵈ Prov. 6:10; 24:33

6 ^eBetter a handful *with* quietness
Than both hands full, *together with*
toil and grasping for the wind.

7Then I returned, and I saw vanity under the sun:

8 There is one alone, without
companion:
He has neither son nor brother.
Yet *there is* no end to all his labors,
Nor is his ^feye satisfied with riches.
But ^g*he never asks*,
"For whom do I toil and deprive myself of ^hgood?"
This also *is* vanity and a grave
misfortune.

The Value of a Friend

9 Two *are* better than one,
Because they have a good reward for
their labor.
10 For if they fall, one will lift up his
companion.
But woe to him *who is* alone when he
falls,
For *he has* no one to help him up.
11 Again, if two lie down together, they
will keep warm;
But how can one be warm *alone*?
12 Though one may be overpowered by
another, two can withstand him.
And a threefold cord is not quickly
broken.

Popularity Passes Away

13 Better a poor and wise youth
Than an old and foolish king who will
be admonished no more.
14 For he comes out of prison to be
king,
Although he was born poor in his
kingdom.
15 I saw all the living who walk under the
sun;
They were with the second youth who
stands in his place.
16 *There was* no end of all the people
over whom he was made king;
Yet those who come afterward will not
rejoice in him.

Surely this also *is* vanity and grasping
for the wind.

Fear God, Keep Your Vows

5 Walk ^aprudently when you go to the
house of God; and draw near to hear
rather ^bthan to give the sacrifice of fools,
for they do not know that they do evil.

2 Do not be ^crash with your mouth,
And let not your heart utter anything
hastily before God.
For God *is* in heaven, and you on
earth;
Therefore let your words ^dbe few.
3 For a dream comes through much
activity,
And ^ea fool's voice *is known* by *his*
many words.

4 ^fWhen you make a vow to God, do not
delay to ^gpay it;
For *He has* no pleasure in fools.
Pay what you have vowed—
5 ^hBetter not to vow than to vow and not
pay.

6Do not let your ⁱmouth cause your flesh
to sin, ^jnor say before the messenger *of*
God that it *was* an error. Why should God
be angry at your excuse* and destroy the
work of your hands? 7For in the multitude
of dreams and many words *there is* also
vanity. But ^kfear God.

The Vanity of Gain and Honor

8If you ^lsee the oppression of the poor,
and the violent perversion of justice and
righteousness in a province, do not marvel
at the matter; for ^mhigh official watches
over high official, and higher officials are
over them.
9Moreover the profit of the land is for all;
even the king is served from the field.

10 He who loves silver will not be
satisfied with silver;
Nor he who loves abundance, with
increase.
This also *is* vanity.

* **5:6** Literally *voice*

4:8 *Nor is his eye satisfied.* Man is in love with what is vanishing. The antidote for covetousness is to replace sinful desire for increase in wealth, with a strong passion for doing the will of God (1 John 2:17).
4:9–12 *Two are better than one.* Throughout this section there is an emphasis on the obvious benefits of companions. The intimacy and sharing of life brings relief for the problem of isolation and loneliness. A companion can offer assistance, comfort, and defense—a threefold cord.
5:1 *Walk prudently.* This means behave yourself. The idea of righteous behavior is rephrased at the end of the section in the words: "fear God" (5:7).
5:4–5 *When you make a vow to God.* One should not attempt to bribe God with a hasty vow. The first part of this verse is almost identical to Deuteronomy

23:21. See the later example of the lie of Ananias and Sapphira (Acts 5:1–11).
5:7 *fear God.* This is a central theme of the Book of Ecclesiastes. It does not mean to be afraid of God (Ex. 20:2). It means to have reverence, awe, and wonder in response to His glory.
5:10 *will not be satisfied.* Desire always outruns possessions, no matter how vast acquisitions may grow.

4:6 ^e Prov. 15:16, 17; 16:8　**4:8** ^f [1 John 2:16]　^g Ps. 39:6　^h Eccl. 2:18–21　**5:1** ^a Ex. 3:5　^b [1 Sam. 15:22]　**5:2** ^c Prov. 20:25　^d Matt. 6:7　**5:3** ^e Prov. 10:19　**5:4** ^f Num. 30:2　^g Ps. 66:13, 14　**5:5** ^h Acts 5:4　**5:6** ⁱ Prov. 6:2　^j 1 Cor. 11:10　**5:7** ^k [Eccl. 12:13]　**5:8** ^l Eccl. 3:16　^m [Ps. 12:5; 58:11; 82:1]

11 When goods increase,
They increase who eat them;
So what profit have the owners
Except to see *them* with their eyes?

12 The sleep of a laboring man *is* sweet,
Whether he eats little or much;
But the abundance of the rich will not
permit him to sleep.

13 *n*There is a severe evil *which* I have
seen under the sun:
Riches kept for their owner to his hurt.

14 But those riches perish through
misfortune;
When he begets a son, *there is* nothing
in his hand.

15 *o*As he came from his mother's womb,
naked shall he return,
To go as he came;
And he shall take nothing from his
labor
Which he may carry away in his hand.

16 And this also *is* a severe evil—
Just exactly as he came, so shall he go.
And *p*what profit has he *q*who has
labored for the wind?

17 All his days *r*he also eats in darkness,
And *he has* much sorrow and sickness
and anger.

18Here is what I have seen: *s*It *is* good
and fitting *for one* to eat and drink, and to
enjoy the good of all his labor in which he
toils under the sun all the days of his life
which God gives him; *t*for it *is* his heritage.
19As for *u*every man to whom God has giv-
en riches and wealth, and given him power
to eat of it, to receive his heritage and rejoice in his labor—this *is* the *v*gift of God.
20For he will not dwell unduly on the days
of his life, because God keeps *him* busy
with the joy of his heart.

6 There*a* is an evil which I have seen under the sun, and it *is* common among
men: 2A man to whom God has given riches and wealth and honor, *b*so that he lacks
nothing for himself of all he desires; *c*yet
God does not give him power to eat of it,
but a foreigner consumes it. This *is* vanity,
and it *is* an evil affliction.

3If a man begets a hundred *children* and
lives many years, so that the days of his
years are many, but his soul is not satisfied
with goodness, or *d*indeed he has no burial,
I say *that* *e*a stillborn child *is* better than
he— 4for it comes in vanity and departs
in darkness, and its name is covered with
darkness. 5Though it has not seen the sun
or known *anything*, this has more rest than
that man, 6even if he lives a thousand years
twice—but has not seen goodness. Do not
all go to one *f*place?

7 *g*All the labor of man *is* for his mouth,
And yet the soul is not satisfied.

8 For what more has the wise *man* than
the fool?
What does the poor man have,
Who knows *how* to walk before the
living?

9 Better *is* the *h*sight of the eyes than the
wandering of desire.
This also *is* vanity and grasping for
the wind.

10 Whatever one is, he has been named
*i*already,
For it is known that he *is* man;
*j*And he cannot contend with Him who
is mightier than he.

11 Since there are many things that
increase vanity,
How *is* man the better?

12For who knows what *is* good for man
in life, all the days of his vain life which he
passes like *k*a shadow? *l*Who can tell a man
what will happen after him under the sun?

The Value of Practical Wisdom

7 A *a*good name *is* better than precious
ointment,
And the day of death than the day of
one's *b*birth;

2 Better to go to the house of mourning
Than to the house of feasting,
For that *is* the end of all men;
And the living will take *it* to *c*heart.

3 Sorrow *is* better than laughter,
*d*For by a sad countenance the heart is
made better.

5:15 As he came . . . naked. The maxim that "you
can't take it with you" is affirmed here (2:21).
5:19 this is the gift of God. God has separated the
gift of enjoying something from the gift of the object
itself so that we might be driven back to the Giver.
6:2 God does not give him power. Prosperity without the divine gift of enjoyment amounts to nothing
(5:19).
6:6 Do not all go to one place? That *one place* is the
grave (3:20). If a long life terminates in death with no
prospect of anything else, will that life have been
worthwhile? Long life without knowing God and
without the power to enjoy it is indeed frustrating
and useless.
6:12 like a shadow. This phrase is a confirmation
of the meaning of the Hebrew word translated *vanity*. Life passes away quickly, like a vapor. **what will**

happen after him. The implied answer is that only
God knows what will happen to us after death. Rather
than imply that nothing exists beyond the grave, this
book teaches that each person's life will be reviewed
by God after death.
7:2–4 house of mourning. We may learn more about
the meaning of life in the house of mourning than in
the house of mirth.

5:13 *n* Eccl. 6:1, 2　**5:15** *o* 1 Tim. 6:7　**5:16** *p* Eccl. 1:3
q Prov. 11:29　**5:17** *r* Ps. 127:2　**5:18** *s* [1 Tim. 6:17]
t Eccl. 2:10; 3:22　**5:19** *u* [Eccl. 6:2]　*v* Eccl. 2:24; 3:13
6:1 *a* Eccl. 5:13　**6:2** *b* Job 21:10　*c* Luke 12:20　**6:3** *d* Is.
14:19, 20　*e* Job 3:16　**6:6** *f* Eccl. 2:14, 15　**6:7** *g* Prov.
16:26　**6:9** *h* Eccl. 11:9　**6:10** *i* Eccl. 1:9; 3:15　*j* Job 9:32
6:12 *k* James 4:14　*l* Eccl. 3:22　**7:1** *a* Prov. 22:1　*b* Eccl. 4:2
7:2 *c* [Ps. 90:12]　**7:3** *d* [2 Cor. 7:10]

4 The heart of the wise *is* in the house of mourning,
But the heart of fools *is* in the house of mirth.

5 [e]*It is* better to hear the rebuke of the wise
Than for a man to hear the song of fools.
6 [f]For like the crackling of thorns under a pot,
So *is* the laughter of the fool.
This also is vanity.
7 Surely oppression destroys a wise *man's* reason,
[g]And a bribe debases the heart.

8 The end of a thing *is* better than its beginning;
[h]The patient in spirit *is* better than the proud in spirit.
9 [i]Do not hasten in your spirit to be angry,
For anger rests in the bosom of fools.
10 Do not say,
"Why were the former days better than these?"
For you do not inquire wisely concerning this.

11 Wisdom *is* good with an inheritance,
And profitable [j]to those who see the sun.
12 For wisdom *is* a [k]defense *as* money *is* a defense,
But the excellence of knowledge *is that* wisdom gives [l]life to those who have it.

13 Consider the work of God;
For [m]who can make straight what He has made crooked?
14 [n]In the day of prosperity be joyful,
But in the day of adversity consider:
Surely God has appointed the one as well as the other,
So that man can find out nothing *that will come* after him.

15 I have seen everything in my days of vanity:

[o]There is a just *man* who perishes in his righteousness,
And there is a wicked *man* who prolongs *life* in his wickedness.

16 [p]Do not be overly righteous,
[q]Nor be overly wise:
Why should you destroy yourself?
17 Do not be overly wicked,
Nor be foolish:
[r]Why should you die before your time?
18 *It is* good that you grasp this,
And also not remove your hand from the other;
For he who [s]fears God will escape them all.

19 [t]Wisdom strengthens the wise
More than ten rulers of the city.

20 [u]For *there is* not a just man on earth who does good
And does not sin.

21 Also do not take to heart everything people say,
Lest you hear your servant cursing you.
22 For many times, also, your own heart has known
That even you have cursed others.

23 All this I have proved by wisdom.
[v]I said, "I will be wise";
But it *was* far from me.
24 [w]As for that which is far off and [x]exceedingly deep,
Who can find it out?
25 [y]I applied my heart to know,
To search and seek out wisdom and the reason *of things*,
To know the wickedness of folly,
Even of foolishness *and* madness.

7:9 *anger rests in the bosom of fools.* Anger is a destructive flood, working all kinds of havoc in our lives. It often leads to protracted and bitter strife (Prov. 30:33). It disrupts and disunites families (1 Sam. 20:30) and may lead to murder (Gen. 4:4–5; 49:6).

7:13 *straight what He has made crooked.* The bend that needs straightening is the presence of afflictions and adversities in life. Both prosperity and adversity come from the hand of God. For prosperity give thanks, but in adversity reflect on the goodness and the comprehensiveness of the plan of God.

7:15 *There is a just man.* There are inequities in life that will always be a mystery (3:16—4:3; 8:14).

7:16–18 *Be not be overly righteous.* Few verses in Ecclesiastes are more susceptible to incorrect interpretation than these. This one is not the so-called golden mean that advises: "Don't be too holy and don't be too wicked; sin to a moderate degree." The Preacher was warning instead about pseudo-religiosity and showy forms of worship as well as self-righteousness and judgmental legalism.

7:20 Individual Sin—The depravity of man is verifiable. In Romans 3:23, Paul echoes this when he says, "for all have sinned and fall short of the glory of God." All we have to do is watch the news or check the headlines and we are forced to deal with this reality. Each individual man, woman, and child needs the righteousness of God. Without God's righteousness no one can ever enter or stand in God's presence. We all need new life in Christ because we are all sinners.

7:24 *Who can find it out?* The theme of wisdom's inaccessibility also appears in Job 28. The answer to this search for wisdom is that God can find wisdom (Job 28:23–28).

7:5 [e] Ps. 141:5 **7:6** [f] Eccl. 2:2 **7:7** [g] Ex. 23:8 **7:8** [h] Prov. 14:29 **7:9** [i] James 1:19 **7:11** [j] Eccl. 11:7 **7:12** [k] Eccl. 9:18 [l] Prov. 3:18 **7:13** [m] Job 12:14 **7:14** [n] Deut. 28:47 **7:15** [o] Eccl. 8:12–14 **7:16** [p] Prov. 25:16 [q] Rom. 12:3 **7:17** [r] Job 15:32 **7:18** [s] Eccl. 3:14; 5:7; 8:12, 13 **7:19** [t] Prov. 21:22 **7:20** [u] 1 John 1:8 **7:23** [v] Rom. 1:22 **7:24** [w] 1 Tim. 6:16 [x] Rom. 11:33 **7:25** [y] Eccl. 1:17

26 [z]And I find more bitter than death
The woman whose heart *is* snares and nets,
Whose hands *are* fetters.
He who pleases God shall escape from her,
But the sinner shall be trapped by her.

27 "Here is what I have found," says [a]the Preacher,
"*Adding* one thing to the other to find out the reason,
28 Which my soul still seeks but I cannot find:
[b]One man among a thousand I have found,
But a woman among all these I have not found.
29 Truly, this only I have found:
[c]That God made man upright,
But [d]they have sought out many schemes."

8 Who *is* like a wise *man?*
And who knows the interpretation of a thing?
[a]A man's wisdom makes his face shine,
And [b]the sternness of his face is changed.

Obey Authorities for God's Sake

2 I *say*, "Keep the king's commandment
[c]for the sake of your oath to God. 3 [d]Do not
be hasty to go from his presence. Do not
take your stand for an evil thing, for he
does whatever pleases him."

4 Where the word of a king *is, there is* power;
And [e]who may say to him, "What are you doing?"
5 He who keeps his command will experience nothing harmful;
And a wise man's heart discerns both time and judgment,
6 Because [f]for every matter there is a time and judgment,
Though the misery of man increases greatly.
7 [g]For he does not know what will happen;
So who can tell him when it will occur?
8 [h]No one has power over the spirit to retain the spirit,
And no one has power in the day of death.
There is [i]no release from that war,
And wickedness will not deliver those who are given to it.

9 All this I have seen, and applied my
heart to every work that is done under the
sun: *There is* a time in which one man rules
over another to his own hurt.

Death Comes to All

10 Then I saw the wicked buried, who had
come and gone from the place of holiness,
and they were [j]forgotten* in the city where
they had so done. This also *is* vanity. 11 [k]Be-
cause the sentence against an evil work is
not executed speedily, therefore the heart
of the sons of men is fully set in them to
do evil. 12 [l]Though a sinner does evil a hundred *times*, and his *days* are prolonged,
yet I surely know that [m]it will be well with
those who fear God, who fear before Him.
13 But it will not be well with the wicked;
nor will he prolong *his* days, *which are* as
a shadow, because he does not fear before
God.

14 There is a vanity which occurs on
earth, that there are just *men* to whom it
[n]happens according to the work of the
wicked; again, there are wicked *men* to
whom it happens according to the work of
the [o]righteous. I said that this also *is* vanity.

15 [p]So I commended enjoyment, because
a man has nothing better under the sun
than to eat, drink, and be merry; for this
will remain with him in his labor *all* the
days of his life which God gives him under
the sun.

16 When I applied my heart to know wisdom and to see the business that is done on
earth, even though one sees no sleep day
or night, 17 then I saw all the work of God,
that [q]a man cannot find out the work that

*8:10 Some Hebrew manuscripts, Septuagint, and Vulgate read *praised*.

7:29 *God made man upright.* God created men to do right. They have preferred to search out their own path.

8:1 *makes his face shine . . . sternness of his face is changed.* This idiom is an image of a person who is stable. Out of the depths of experience and understanding, that person is able to enjoy life and build up others.

8:8 *power over the spirit to retain the spirit.* In this context *spirit* could mean "life force" (3:19). God is in charge.

8:15 *eat, drink, and be merry.* In contrast to the search for the meaning of all things is the contentment that a wise, loving God gives to those who will receive His gifts. Here is one of the central themes of Ecclesiastes. The Preacher marks the end of the third major section of his book with this refrain. The wicked person (the fool) decides that the best thing to do is "to eat, drink, and be merry" with no thought given to the living God. But the righteous person (the wise) can enjoy life while thinking of God and His good gifts.

7:26 [z]Prov. 5:3, 4 **7:27** [a]Eccl. 1:1, 2 **7:28** [b]Job 33:23 **7:29** [c]Gen. 1:27 [d]Gen. 3:6, 7 **8:1** [a]Acts 6:15 [b]Deut. 28:50 **8:2** [c]1 Chr. 29:24 **8:3** [d]Eccl. 10:4 **8:4** [e]Job 34:18 **8:6** [f]Eccl. 3:1, 17 **8:7** [g]Eccl. 6:12 **8:8** [h]Ps. 49:6, 7 [i]Deut. 20:5–8 **8:10** [j]Eccl. 2:16; 9:5 **8:11** [k]Is. 26:10 **8:12** [l]Is. 65:20 [m][Is. 3:10] **8:14** [n]Ps. 73:14 [o]Eccl. 2:14; 7:15; 9:1–3 **8:15** [p]Eccl. 2:24 **8:17** [q]Rom. 11:33

is done under the sun. For though a man labors to discover *it*, yet he will not find *it*; moreover, though a wise *man* attempts to know *it*, he will not be able to find *it*.

9 For I considered all this in my heart, so that I could declare it all: *a*that the righteous and the wise and their works *are* in the hand of God. People know neither love nor hatred *by* anything *they see* before them. ²*b*All things *come* alike to all:

One event *happens* to the righteous
　and the wicked;
To the good,* the clean, and the
　unclean;
To him who sacrifices and him who
　does not sacrifice.
As is the good, so *is* the sinner;
He who takes an oath as *he* who fears
　an oath.

³This *is* an evil in all that is done under the sun: that one thing *happens* to all. Truly the hearts of the sons of men are full of evil; madness *is* in their hearts while they live, and after that *they* go to the dead. ⁴But for him who is joined to all the living there is hope, for a living dog is better than a dead lion.

5　For the living know that they will
　　die;
　But *c*the dead know nothing,
　And they have no more reward,
　For *d*the memory of them is
　　forgotten.
6　Also their love, their hatred, and their
　　envy have now perished;
　Nevermore will they have a share
　In anything done under the sun.
7　Go, *e*eat your bread with joy,
　And drink your wine with a merry
　　heart;
　For God has already accepted your
　　works.
8　Let your garments always be white,
　And let your head lack no oil.

⁹Live joyfully with the wife whom you love all the days of your vain life which He has given you under the sun, all your days of vanity; *f*for that *is* your portion in life,

and in the labor which you perform under the sun. ¹⁰*g*Whatever your hand finds to do, do *it* with your *h*might; for *there is* no work or device or knowledge or wisdom in the grave where you are going.

¹¹I returned *i*and saw under the sun that—

The race *is* not to the swift,
Nor the battle to the strong,
Nor bread to the wise,
Nor riches to men of understanding,
Nor favor to men of skill;
But time and *j*chance happen to them
　all.
12　For *k*man also does not know his
　　time:
　Like fish taken in a cruel net,
　Like birds caught in a snare,
　So the sons of men *are* *l*snared in an
　　evil time,
　When it falls suddenly upon them.

Wisdom Superior to Folly

¹³This wisdom I have also seen under the sun, and it *seemed* great to me: ¹⁴*m*There *was* a little city with few men in it; and a great king came against it, besieged it, and built great snares* around it. ¹⁵Now there was found in it a poor wise man, and he by his wisdom delivered the city. Yet no one remembered that same poor man. ¹⁶Then I said:

"Wisdom *is* better than *n*strength.
Nevertheless *o*the poor man's wisdom
　is despised,
And his words are not heard.
17　Words of the wise, *spoken* quietly,
　　should be heard
　Rather than the shout of a ruler of
　　fools.
18　Wisdom *is* better than weapons of
　　war;
　But *p*one sinner destroys much
　　good."

---

* 9:2 Septuagint, Syriac, and Vulgate read *good and bad.*　* 9:14 Septuagint, Syriac, and Vulgate read *bulwarks.*

9:1 *neither love nor hatred.* Sometimes in Hebrew two opposites together are a way of saying "everything." Love and hate are best viewed as words for God's favor and disfavor.
9:5 *the dead know nothing.* This is not a flat denial of any hope beyond the grave. The point of view is limited to what can be known strictly from the human point of view, "under the sun."
9:8 *Let your garments always be white.* It was difficult in ancient times to keep white clothing clean (see analogy in Is. 1:18). White clothing and ointments—oil—were symbols of joy and purity.
9:11 *not to the swift . . . to the strong . . . wise . . . understanding . . . men of skill.* We would like to think that the best always win, that the deserving are always rewarded. But our experience shows that

these expectations are not always realized. These five assets were enjoyed by individuals. But while some planned and counted on their assets, God in the end determined their lot.
9:14–18 *There was a little city.* Here is a parable about how an unstoppable military operation against a small city was prevented by the wisdom of one poor but wise man. The conclusion is that wisdom is preferable to strength, and should be heeded.

9:1 *a*Eccl. 8:14　**9:2** *b*Mal. 3:15　**9:5** *c*Is. 63:16　*d*Is. 26:14　**9:7** *e*Eccl. 8:15　**9:9** *f*Eccl. 2:10　**9:10** *g*[Col. 3:17]　*h*Rom. 12:11　**9:11** *i*Amos 2:14, 15　*j*1 Sam. 6:9　**9:12** *k*Eccl. 8:7　*l*Prov. 29:6　**9:14** *m*2 Sam. 20:16–22　**9:16** *n*Eccl. 7:12, 19　*o*Mark 6:2, 3　**9:18** *p*Josh. 7:1–26

10 Dead flies putrefy* the perfumer's ointment,
And cause it to give off a foul odor;
So does a little folly to one respected for wisdom *and* honor.

2 A wise man's heart *is* at his right hand,
But a fool's heart to his left.

3 Even when a fool walks along the way,
He lacks wisdom,
aAnd he shows everyone *that* he *is* a fool.

4 If the spirit of the ruler rises against you,
bDo not leave your post;
For cconciliation pacifies great offenses.

5 There is an evil I have seen under the sun,
As an error proceeding from the ruler:

6 dFolly is set in great dignity,
While the rich sit in a lowly place.

7 I have seen servants eon horses,
While princes walk on the ground like servants.

8 fHe who digs a pit will fall into it,
And whoever breaks through a wall will be bitten by a serpent.

9 He who quarries stones may be hurt by them,
And he who splits wood may be endangered by it.

10 If the ax is dull,
And one does not sharpen the edge,
Then he must use more strength;
But wisdom brings success.

11 A serpent may bite gwhen *it is* not charmed;
The babbler is no different.

12 hThe words of a wise man's mouth *are* gracious,
But ithe lips of a fool shall swallow him up;

13 The words of his mouth begin with foolishness,
And the end of his talk *is* raving madness.

14 jA fool also multiplies words.
No man knows what is to be;

Who can tell him kwhat will be after him?

15 The labor of fools wearies them,
For they do not even know how to go to the city!

16 lWoe to you, O land, when your king *is* a child,
And your princes feast in the morning!

17 Blessed *are* you, O land, when your king *is* the son of nobles,
And your mprinces feast at the proper time—
For strength and not for drunkenness!

18 Because of laziness the building decays,
And nthrough idleness of hands the house leaks.

19 A feast is made for laughter,
And owine makes merry;
But money answers everything.

20 pDo not curse the king, even in your thought;
Do not curse the rich, even in your bedroom;
For a bird of the air may carry your voice,
And a bird in flight may tell the matter.

The Value of Diligence

11 Cast your bread aupon the waters,
bFor you will find it after many days.

2 cGive a serving dto seven, and also to eight,
eFor you do not know what evil will be on the earth.

3 If the clouds are full of rain,
They empty *themselves* upon the earth;
And if a tree falls to the south or the north,
In the place where the tree falls, there it shall lie.

4 He who observes the wind will not sow,
And he who regards the clouds will not reap.

---

* **10:1** Targum and Vulgate omit *putrefy*.

10:1 Dead flies putrefy the perfumer's ointment. Just as one fly can ruin a whole batch of ointment, so an ounce of folly will spoil a pound of wisdom.
10:2 A wise man's heart is at his right hand. In ancient thought, the right hand was the place of honor and favor, while the left hand was the reverse.
10:10 If the ax is dull. The wise person will sharpen the ax. A person of limited training will have to work harder, as though with a dull ax, than someone wiser whose tools are maintained.
10:17 Blessed are you, O land. Useful nobility expresses itself in a sense of responsibility and deference to social order. This verse is an argument for propriety.
11:1 Cast your bread upon the waters. Verses 1–6 emphasize the element of risk and uncertainty in commercial and agricultural enterprises. Thus if the preceding proverbs in chapter 10 deal with royalty and leaders, then verses 1–6 deal with common people. Men and women must venture forth judiciously if they are ever to realize a gain, even though there is always a certain amount of risk.
11:2 to seven, and also to eight. This urges us to be generous to as many as possible—and then some.
11:4 will not sow . . . will not reap. The person who

10:3 a Prov. 13:16; 18:2   **10:4** b Eccl. 8:3   c 1 Sam. 25:24–33   **10:6** d Esth. 3:1   **10:7** e Prov. 19:10; 30:22   **10:8** f Prov. 26:27   **10:11** g Jer. 8:17   **10:12** h Prov. 10:32   i Prov. 10:14   j [Prov. 15:2]   k Eccl. 3:22; 8:7   **10:16** l Is. 3:4, 5; 5:11   **10:17** m Prov. 31:4   **10:18** n Prov. 24:30–34   **10:19** o Ps. 104:15   **10:20** p Acts 23:5   **11:1** a Is. 32:20   b [Deut. 15:10]   **11:2** c [1 Tim. 6:18, 19]   d Mic. 5:5   e Eph. 5:16

5 As ᶠyou do not know what *is* the way
  of the wind,*
  ᵍOr how the bones *grow* in the womb of
  her who is with child,
  So you do not know the works of God
  who makes everything.
6 In the morning sow your seed,
  And in the evening do not withhold
  your hand;
  For you do not know which will
  prosper,
  Either this or that,
  Or whether both alike *will be* good.
7 Truly the light is sweet,
  And *it is* pleasant for the eyes ʰto
  behold the sun;
8 But if a man lives many years
  And ⁱrejoices in them all,
  Yet let him ʲremember the days of
  darkness,
  For they will be many.
  All that is coming *is* vanity.

Seek God in Early Life

9 Rejoice, O young man, in your
  youth,
  And let your heart cheer you in the
  days of your youth;
  ᵏWalk in the ways of your heart,
  And in the sight of your eyes;
  But know that for all these
  ˡGod will bring you into judgment.
10 Therefore remove sorrow from your
  heart,
  And ᵐput away evil from your
  flesh,
  ⁿFor childhood and youth *are*
  vanity.

12 Rememberᵃ now your Creator in the
  days of your youth,
  Before the difficult days come,
  And the years draw near ᵇwhen you
  say,
  "I have no pleasure in them":
2 While the sun and the light,
  The moon and the stars,
  Are not darkened,
  And the clouds do not return after the
  rain;

3 In the day when the keepers of the
  house tremble,
  And the strong men bow down;
  When the grinders cease because they
  are few,
  And those that look through the
  windows grow dim;
4 When the doors are shut in the
  streets,
  And the sound of grinding is low;
  When one rises up at the sound of a
  bird,
  And all ᶜthe daughters of music are
  brought low.
5 Also they are afraid of height,
  And of terrors in the way;
  When the almond tree blossoms,
  The grasshopper is a burden,
  And desire fails.
  For man goes to ᵈhis eternal home,
  And ᵉthe mourners go about the
  streets.
6 *Remember your Creator* before the
  silver cord is loosed,*
  Or the golden bowl is broken,
  Or the pitcher shattered at the
  fountain,
  Or the wheel broken at the well.
7 ᶠThen the dust will return to the earth
  as it was,
  ᵍAnd the spirit will return to God ʰwho
  gave it.
8 "Vanityⁱ of vanities," says the
  Preacher,
  "All *is* vanity."

The Whole Duty of Man

9And moreover, because the Preacher
was wise, he still taught the people knowledge; yes, he pondered and sought out
and ʲset in order many proverbs. 10The
Preacher sought to find acceptable words;
and *what was* written *was* upright—words
of truth. 11The words of the wise are like
goads, and the words of scholars* are like

---

* **11:5** Or *spirit*   * **12:6** Following Qere and
Targum; Kethib reads *removed;* Septuagint and
Vulgate read *broken.*   * **12:11** Literally *masters of
the assemblies*

---

is so cautious that he must wait for the ideal time
before he makes a move is doomed to fail.
11:9 *Walk in the ways of your heart.* This verse is
not an invitation to live sinfully in sensual pleasure
(as Num. 15:39 describes). Instead, it urges young
people to enjoy themselves completely while not
forgetting that God will review the quality of their life
(3:17; 12:14).
12:1–8 *Remember now your Creator.* Most interpreters have argued that this poem is an allegory of
old age.
12:2 *Are not darkened.* The person is losing his sight.
12:4 *sound of grinding is low.* A depiction of tooth-
less old age when eating only soft foods makes little
or no noise.
12:6 *the wheel broken at the well.* The system of

veins and arteries radiating out from the heart might
have appeared to the ancients like the spokes on a
wheel.
12:11 *The words of the wise are like goads.* Just as
an ox goad prods an animal in the right direction, so
will the words of this book, when they are properly
understood. ***well-driven nails.*** The nails or "pegs"
referred to here are the same as in 2 Chronicles 3:9
and Jeremiah 10:4. These are hooks in tents where

11:5 ᶠJohn 3:8 ᵍPs. 139:14   **11:7** ʰEccl. 7:11   **11:8** ⁱEccl.
9:7 ʲEccl. 12:1   **11:9** ᵏNum. 15:39 ˡEccl. 3:17; 12:14
11:10 ᵐ2 Cor. 7:1 ⁿPs. 39:5   **12:1** ᵃLam. 3:27 ᵇ2 Sam.
19:35   **12:4** ᶜ2 Sam. 19:35   **12:5** ᵈJob 17:13 ᵉJer. 9:17
12:7 ᶠGen. 3:19 ᵍEccl. 3:21 ʰJob 34:14   **12:8** ⁱPs. 62:9
12:9 ʲ1 Kin. 4:32

well-driven nails, given by one Shepherd. [12]And further, my son, be admonished by these. Of making many books *there is* no end, and [k]much study *is* wearisome to the flesh.

[13]Let us hear the conclusion of the whole matter:

[l]Fear God and keep His
    commandments,
For this is man's all.
[14] For [m]God will bring every work into
    judgment,
Including every secret thing,
Whether good or evil.

---

families hung the clothes and pots needed for everyday life. Here they refer to mental hooks giving stability and perspective to life.

12:13 *keep His commandments.* The commandments of the law are in view here. Jesus summed them up as to "love the Lord your God" and "your neighbor as yourself" (Matt. 22:34–40). We are whole or complete only when we fear God and obey His

commandments. What profit is there in living? If we follow what this book has said, we will have a relationship with God and find life in Him.

12:12 [k] Eccl. 1:18   **12:13** [l] [Deut. 6:2; 10:12]
12:14 [m] Matt. 12:36

THE
SONG OF SOLOMON

▶ **AUTHOR:** According to 1 Kings 4:32, Solomon wrote 1,005 songs, but this eulogy of love stood out among them as the "song of songs." Tradition strongly favors Solomon as the author of this book. Solomon is specifically mentioned seven times, and he is identified as the groom. There is also evidence in the book of incredible royal luxury and expensive imported goods, things that characterized Solomon's reign.

▶ **TIME:** c. 965 B.C.   ▶ **KEY VERSE:** Song 7:10

▶ **THEME:** Song of Solomon, or Song of Songs as it is sometimes known, is a one-of-a-kind love poem that concentrates on elements of the physical attraction between the sexes. It is possible that the Shulamite maiden was Abishag, who attended to David in his last days. Like Jesus' presence at a wedding, Song of Solomon is an indication of God's blessing on the physical union of man and woman. God created us for each other, and we should delight in physical intimacy within the context of marriage that God has sanctioned for us.

---

1 The *a*song of songs, which *is* Solomon's.

The Banquet

THE SHULAMITE*
2 Let him kiss me with the kisses of his
     mouth—
   *b*For your* love *is* better than wine.
3 Because of the fragrance of your good
     ointments,
   Your name *is* ointment poured forth;
   Therefore the virgins love you.
4 *c*Draw me away!

THE DAUGHTERS OF JERUSALEM
   *d*We will run after you.*

THE SHULAMITE
   The king *e*has brought me into his
     chambers.

THE DAUGHTERS OF JERUSALEM
   We will be glad and rejoice in you.*

We will remember your* love more
     than wine.

THE SHULAMITE
   Rightly do they love you.*

5 I *am* dark, but lovely,
   O daughters of Jerusalem,
   Like the tents of Kedar,
   Like the curtains of Solomon.
6 Do not look upon me, because I *am*
     dark,
   Because the sun has tanned me.
   My mother's sons were angry with me;

---

* **1:2** A young woman from the town of Shulam or Shunem (compare 6:13). The speaker and audience are identified according to the number, gender, and person of the Hebrew words. Occasionally the identity is not certain.   * **1:2** Masculine singular, that is, the Beloved   * **1:4** Masculine singular, that is, the Beloved • Feminine singular, that is, the Shulamite • Masculine singular, that is, the Beloved • Masculine singular, that is, the Beloved

---

1:1 *song of songs.* Like the superlative expressions "holy of holies" or "King of kings," *song of songs* means "the loveliest of songs." There are two principal speakers in this book, the woman (the Shulamite) and the man (Solomon).

1:2 *for your love is better than wine.* The Hebrew noun used here means sexual love, as it clearly does in Ezekiel 16:8. This is the Hebrew word that most approximates the Greek word *eros.* In the Song of Solomon, this plural word (a mark of intensity) speaks of divinely blessed lovemaking.

1:3 *your good ointments.* It was customary in biblical times to rub the body with fragrant oils

after a bath in preparation for a festive occasion (Ruth 3:3).

1:5 *I am dark, but lovely.* The Shulamite compares her dark coloring acquired from long hours working in the vineyards (v. 6) with the lighter complexion of the city maidens. The point here is her class and station in life. Unlike the young women of the court in Jerusalem who had been raised in comfort and conditions of ease, this woman had worked as a field

---

1:1 *a* 1 Kin. 4:32   **1:2** *b* Song 4:10   **1:4** *c* Hos. 11:4   *d* Phil. 3:12–14   *e* Ps. 45:14, 15

They made me the keeper of the
vineyards,
But my own *f*vineyard I have not kept.

(To Her Beloved)
7 Tell me, O you whom I love,
Where you feed *your flock,*
Where you make *it* rest at noon.
For why should I be as one who veils
herself*
By the flocks of your companions?

The Beloved
8 If you do not know, *g*O fairest among
women,
Follow in the footsteps of the flock,
And feed your little goats
Beside the shepherds' tents.
9 I have compared you, *h*my love,
*i*To my filly among Pharaoh's chariots.
10 *j*Your cheeks are lovely with
ornaments,
Your neck with chains *of gold.*

The Daughters of Jerusalem
11 We will make you* ornaments of gold
With studs of silver.

The Shulamite
12 While the king *is* at his table,
My spikenard sends forth its
fragrance.
13 A bundle of myrrh *is* my beloved to
me,
That lies all night between my
breasts.
14 My beloved *is* to me a cluster of henna
blooms
In the vineyards of En Gedi.

The Beloved
15 *k*Behold, you *are* fair, my love!
Behold, you *are* fair!
You *have* dove's eyes.

The Shulamite
16 Behold, you *are* *l*handsome, my
beloved!

Yes, pleasant!
Also our bed *is* green.
17 The beams of our houses *are* cedar,
And our rafters of fir.

2 I *am* the rose of Sharon,
And the lily of the valleys.

The Beloved
2 Like a lily among thorns,
So is my love among the daughters.

The Shulamite
3 Like an apple tree among the trees of
the woods,
So *is* my beloved among the sons.
I sat down in his shade with great
delight,
And *a*his fruit *was* sweet to my taste.

**The Shulamite to the Daughters
of Jerusalem**
4 He brought me to the banqueting
house,
And his banner over me *was* love.
5 Sustain me with cakes of raisins,
Refresh me with apples,
For I *am* lovesick.

6 *b*His left hand *is* under my head,
And his right hand embraces me.
7 *c*I charge you, O daughters of Jerusalem,
By the gazelles or by the does of the
field,
Do not stir up nor awaken love
Until it pleases.

The Beloved's Request

The Shulamite
8 The voice of my beloved!
Behold, he comes
Leaping upon the mountains,
Skipping upon the hills.

---

* **1:7** Septuagint, Syriac, and Vulgate read
wanders.   * **1:11** Feminine singular, that is, the
Shulamite

---

hand in the sun. She knows her beauty is not diminished by her more rugged manner of living.
1:7 *O you whom I love.* Here the woman mentally addresses Solomon, her husband. She pictures him as the shepherd of Israel.
1:8 *Follow in the footsteps of the flock.* It would be better if she returned to the borders of Lebanon and the life of the farm rather than live alone and anxious in Solomon's palace. The point of this verse is that one should always count the cost of marriage to a particular person before the marriage.
1:13 *A bundle of myrrh is my beloved to me.* This verse refers to an oriental custom for a woman to wear a small bag of myrrh, a perfumed ointment, around her neck at night. All the next day a lovely fragrance would linger about her.
1:17 *The beams of our houses are cedar.* As the Shulamite lies on their wedding bed (v. 16), she observes the marvelous cedar beams above her

head. The opulence of Solomon's personal and public buildings in Jerusalem is well documented (1 Kin. 7:1–12).
2:3 *Like an apple tree.* Raisin cakes (v. 5) and apples are symbols for sexual passion in ancient love songs.
2:4 *to the banqueting house.* The literal meaning of the phrase is "the house of wine," used because of the role that wine plays not only in feasting, but especially in weddings in biblical cultures (1:2). In the Bible, wine is a symbol of joy (Ps. 104:15).
2:8 *Skipping upon the hills.* This is the young bride's imaginative way of recalling the joy she experienced at her husband's arrival.

1:6 *f* Song 8:11, 12   **1:8** *g* Song 5:9   **1:9** *h* Song 2:2, 10,
13; 4:1, 7 *i* 2 Chr. 1:16   **1:10** *j* Ezek. 16:11   **1:15** *k* Song
4:1; 5:12   **1:16** *l* Song 5:10–16   **2:3** *a* Rev. 22:1, 2
2:6 *b* Song 8:3   **2:7** *c* Song 3:5; 8:4

9 dMy beloved is like a gazelle or a young
    stag.
  Behold, he stands behind our wall;
  He is looking through the windows,
  Gazing through the lattice.

10 My beloved spoke, and said to me:
  "Rise up, my love, my fair one,
  And come away.
11 For lo, the winter is past,
  The rain is over *and* gone.
12 The flowers appear on the earth;
  The time of singing has come,
  And the voice of the turtledove
  Is heard in our land.
13 The fig tree puts forth her green
    figs,
  And the vines *with* the tender grapes
  Give a *good* smell.
  Rise up, my love, my fair one,
  And come away!

14 "O my edove, in the clefts of the rock,
  In the secret *places* of the cliff,
  Let me see your face,
  fLet me hear your voice;
  For your voice *is* sweet,
  And your face *is* lovely."

HER BROTHERS
15 Catch us gthe foxes,
  The little foxes that spoil the vines,
  For our vines *have* tender grapes.

THE SHULAMITE
16 hMy beloved *is* mine, and I *am* his.
  He feeds *his flock* among the lilies.

(TO HER BELOVED)
17 iUntil the day breaks
  And the shadows flee away,
  Turn, my beloved,
  And be jlike a gazelle
  Or a young stag
  Upon the mountains of Bether.*

A Troubled Night

THE SHULAMITE
3 By anight on my bed I sought the one
    I love;

I sought him, but I did not find him.
2 "I will rise now," *I said,*
  "And go about the city;
  In the streets and in the squares
  I will seek the one I love."
  I sought him, but I did not find him.
3 bThe watchmen who go about the city
    found me;
  I said,
  "Have you seen the one I love?"

4 Scarcely had I passed by them,
  When I found the one I love.
  I held him and would not let him go,
  Until I had brought him to the chouse
    of my mother,
  And into the chamber of her who
    conceived me.

5 dI charge you, O daughters of Jerusalem,
  By the gazelles or by the does of the
    field,
  Do not stir up nor awaken love
  Until it pleases.

The Coming of Solomon

THE SHULAMITE
6 eWho *is* this coming out of the
    wilderness
  Like pillars of smoke,
  Perfumed with myrrh and
    frankincense,
  With all the merchant's fragrant
    powders?
7 Behold, it *is* Solomon's couch,
  With sixty valiant men around it,
  Of the valiant of Israel.
8 They all hold swords,
  Being expert in war.
  Every man *has* his sword on his thigh
  Because of fear in the night.

9 Of the wood of Lebanon
  Solomon the King
  Made himself a palanquin:*
10 He made its pillars *of* silver,
  Its support *of* gold,

---

* **2:17** Literally *Separation* * **3:9** A portable
enclosed chair

2:11–13 *the winter is past.* By this Solomon means that the time of joy has come; it is the summer of their love. Solomon may have come at a time of great beauty in the fields and forests where the young woman lived; he uses the beauty of creation to describe the ripeness of time for their love.
2:15 *Catch us the foxes.* The Shulamite's brothers called on Solomon to catch them the foxes. Many times they had seen little foxes creep into the vineyards they tended and destroy the roots by gnawing on them.
3:1 *on my bed.* This is a dream that took place before they were married. The young woman was becoming concerned about what she would be getting into in the royal marriage.
3:3 *Have you seen.* Her frantic search for her beloved is initially unsuccessful.

3:4 *the one I love.* At last she finds him and in her dream takes him to her mother's house. The worry of his absence is intolerable to her; she wants him to move back with her to her familiar home and lifestyle.
3:7 *Solomon's couch.* This was a sedan chair with poles projecting from the front and back so that a person could be carried by several bearers. (vv. 9–10). The Shulamite was being carried to the wedding and to her groom on Solomon's own couch.

2:9 d Song 2:17 **2:14** e Song 5:2 f Song 8:13
2:15 g Ezek. 13:4 **2:16** h Song 6:3 **2:17** i Song 4:6
j Song 8:14 **3:1** a Is. 26:9 **3:3** b Song 5:7 **3:4** c Song
8:2 **3:5** d Song 2:7; 8:4 **3:6** e Song 8:5

Its seat *of* purple,
Its interior paved *with* love
By the daughters of Jerusalem.
11 Go forth, O daughters of Zion,
And see King Solomon with the crown
With which his mother crowned him
On the day of his wedding,
The day of the gladness of his heart.

The Bridegroom Praises the Bride

THE BELOVED

4 Behold, *a*you *are* fair, my love!
Behold, you *are* fair!
You *have* dove's eyes behind your veil.
Your hair *is* like a *b*flock of goats,
Going down from Mount Gilead.
2 *c*Your teeth *are* like a flock of shorn
sheep
Which have come up from the washing,
Every one of which bears twins,
And none *is* barren among them.
3 Your lips *are* like a strand of scarlet,
And your mouth is lovely.
*d*Your temples behind your veil
Are like a piece of pomegranate.
4 *e*Your neck *is* like the tower of David,
Built *f*for an armory,
On which hang a thousand bucklers,
All shields of mighty men.
5 *g*Your two breasts *are* like two fawns,
Twins of a gazelle,
Which feed among the lilies.

6 *h*Until the day breaks
And the shadows flee away,
I will go my way to the mountain of
myrrh
And to the hill of frankincense.
7 *i*You *are* all fair, my love,
And *there is* no spot in you.
8 Come with me from Lebanon, *my*
spouse,
With me from Lebanon.
Look from the top of Amana,
From the top of Senir *j*and Hermon,
From the lions' dens,
From the mountains of the leopards.

9 You have ravished my heart,
My sister, *my* spouse;
You have ravished my heart
With one *look* of your eyes,
With one link of your necklace.
10 How fair is your love,
My sister, *my* spouse!
*k*How much better than wine is your love,
And the scent of your perfumes
Than all spices!
11 Your lips, O *my* spouse,
Drip as the honeycomb;
*l*Honey and milk *are* under your tongue;
And the fragrance of your garments
Is *m*like the fragrance of Lebanon.

12 A garden enclosed
Is my sister, *my* spouse,
A spring shut up,
A fountain sealed.
13 Your plants *are* an orchard of
pomegranates
With pleasant fruits,
Fragrant henna with spikenard,
14 Spikenard and saffron,
Calamus and cinnamon,
With all trees of frankincense,
Myrrh and aloes,
With all the chief spices—
15 A fountain of gardens,
A well of *n*living waters,
And streams from Lebanon.

THE SHULAMITE
16 Awake, O north *wind*,
And come, O south!
Blow upon my garden,
That its spices may flow out.
*o*Let my beloved come to his garden
And eat its pleasant *p*fruits.

THE BELOVED

5 I *a*have come to my garden, my *b*sister,
my spouse;
I have gathered my myrrh with my spice;
*c*I have eaten my honeycomb with my
honey;
I have drunk my wine with my milk.

4:1 Behold, you are fair. Solomon lavishly praises his bride's great beauty. He uses verbal symbols of loveliness to paint a picture of the breathtaking charm of the Shulamite. Dove's eyes are a picture of purity, innocence, and beauty. The king compared the movement of her flowing hair to the graceful movement of a flock of goats in their descent down from Mount Gilead.
4:2–5 teeth ... lips ... neck ... breasts. The king rhapsodizes of the perfection of her physical features. Her beauty is exquisite.
4:9 My sister, my spouse. This strange pairing of words was based on the idea that in marriage a couple became "related." The woman was dignified as a member of the king's family.
4:11 lips ... Honey and milk. The sweetness of his bride's kisses are like food to him (5:1; compare 1:2).
4:12 A garden enclosed ... A spring shut up. Solomon evokes thoughts of refreshment and delight.

His use of the words "shut up" and "sealed" indicate, in a poetic manner, his wife's virginity on their wedding night. This was the treasure she brought to him, and which she charged the other young women in the court to maintain for their wedding nights as well (2:7).
4:16 Let my beloved come to his garden. The bride is now ready to accept her lover for the first time to her "garden." She calls on the wind to blow through. That is, she is ready to make love to her husband for the first time.
5:1 I have drunk my wine with my milk. At the

4:1 *a* Song 1:15; 5:12 *b* Song 6:5   **4:2** *c* Song 6:6
4:3 *d* Song 6:7   **4:4** *e* Song 7:4 *f* Neh. 3:19   **4:5** *g* Song
7:3   **4:6** *h* Song 2:17   **4:7** *i* Eph. 5:27   **4:8** *j* Deut.
3:9   **4:10** *k* Song 1:2, 4   **4:11** *l* Prov. 24:13, 14 *m* Hos.
14:6, 7   **4:15** *n* Zech. 14:8   **4:16** *o* Song 5:1 *p* Song 7:13
5:1 *a* Song 4:16 *b* Song 4:9 *c* Song 4:11

(TO HIS FRIENDS)

Eat, O ᵈfriends!
Drink, yes, drink deeply,
O beloved ones!

The Shulamite's Troubled Evening

THE SHULAMITE

2 I sleep, but my heart is awake;
It is the voice of my beloved!
ᵉHe knocks, *saying,*
"Open for me, my sister, my love,
My dove, my perfect one;
For my head is covered with dew,
My locks with the drops of the night."

3 I have taken off my robe;
How can I put it on *again?*
I have washed my feet;
How can I defile them?

4 My beloved put his hand
By the latch *of the door,*
And my heart yearned for him.

5 I arose to open for my beloved,
And my hands dripped *with* myrrh,
My fingers with liquid myrrh,
On the handles of the lock.

6 I opened for my beloved,
But my beloved had turned away *and*
was gone.
My heart leaped up when he spoke.
ᶠI sought him, but I could not find him;
I called him, but he gave me no
answer.

7 ᵍThe watchmen who went about the
city found me.
They struck me, they wounded me;
The keepers of the walls
Took my veil away from me.

8 I charge you, O daughters of
Jerusalem,
If you find my beloved,
That you tell him I *am* lovesick!

THE DAUGHTERS OF JERUSALEM

9 What *is* your beloved
More than *another* beloved,
ʰO fairest among women?
What *is* your beloved
More than *another* beloved,
That you so charge us?

THE SHULAMITE

10 My beloved *is* white and ruddy,
Chief among ten thousand.

11 His head *is like* the finest gold;
His locks *are* wavy,
And black as a raven.

12 ⁱHis eyes *are* like doves
By the rivers of waters,
Washed with milk,
And fitly set.

13 His cheeks *are* like a bed of spices,
Banks of scented herbs.
His lips *are* lilies,
Dripping liquid myrrh.

14 His hands *are* rods of gold
Set with beryl.
His body *is* carved ivory
Inlaid *with* sapphires.

15 His legs *are* pillars of marble
Set on bases of fine gold.
His countenance *is* like Lebanon,
Excellent as the cedars.

16 His mouth *is* most sweet,
Yes, he *is* altogether lovely.
This *is* my beloved,
And this *is* my friend,
O daughters of Jerusalem!

THE DAUGHTERS OF JERUSALEM

6 Where has your beloved gone,
ᵃO fairest among women?
Where has your beloved turned
aside,
That we may seek him with you?

THE SHULAMITE

2 My beloved has gone to his ᵇgarden,
To the beds of spices,
To feed *his flock* in the gardens,
And to gather lilies.

3 ᶜI *am* my beloved's,
And my beloved *is* mine.
He feeds *his flock* among the lilies.

Praise of the Shulamite's Beauty

THE BELOVED

4 O my love, you *are as* beautiful as
Tirzah,
Lovely as Jerusalem,
Awesome as *an army* with banners!

---

conclusion of their lovemaking, the groom speaks of his complete satisfaction in his beautiful bride.

5:2–7 I sleep. These words begin a section (vv. 2–8) that most likely is another dream sequence (3:1–5). The bride dreams that her lover is coming to her, but she has already washed, removed her robe, and gotten into bed. (v. 3). She finally goes to the door to let him in, but he is gone. Her sorrow at this drives her into the city to search for him.

5:8–9 O daughters of Jerusalem. She asks for help in her search, but the daughters question what is so special about the one for whom she seeks.

6:1 that we may seek him with you. The chorus members now join in the search. In the dream sequence, we suspect that the chorus is well aware of

his location. It is only the bride who needs to discover his whereabouts.

6:3 I am my beloved's, and my beloved is mine. These words are an inversion of the words of 2:16; compare also 7:10. **he feeds his flock among the lilies.** With these words the bride comes to terms with the reality that, as much as she and the king are in love, he still has other responsibilities and so does she. His work as king makes him the shepherd of

5:1 ᵈLuke 15:7, 10   **5:2** ᵉRev. 3:20   **5:6** ᶠSong 3:1
5:7 ᵍSong 3:3   **5:9** ʰSong 1:8; 6:1   **5:12** ⁱSong 1:15; 4:1
6:1 ᵃSong 1:8; 5:9   **6:2** ᵇSong 4:16; 5:1   **6:3** ᶜSong
2:16; 7:10

5 Turn your eyes away from me,
   For they have overcome me.
   Your hair is ᵈlike a flock of goats
   Going down from Gilead.
6 ᵉYour teeth are like a flock of sheep
   Which have come up from the
      washing;
   Every one bears twins,
   And none is barren among them.
7 ᶠLike a piece of pomegranate
   Are your temples behind your veil.

8 There are sixty queens
   And eighty concubines,
   And ᵍvirgins without number.
9 My dove, my ʰperfect one,
   Is the only one,
   The only one of her mother,
   The favorite of the one who bore her.
   The daughters saw her
   And called her blessed,
   The queens and the concubines,
   And they praised her.

10 Who is she who looks forth as the
      morning,
   Fair as the moon,
   Clear as the sun,
   ⁱAwesome as an army with banners?

THE SHULAMITE

11 I went down to the garden of nuts
   To see the verdure of the valley,
   ʲTo see whether the vine had budded
   And the pomegranates had bloomed.
12 Before I was even aware,
   My soul had made me
   As the chariots of my noble people.*

THE BELOVED AND HIS FRIENDS

13 Return, return, O Shulamite;
   Return, return, that we may look upon
      you!

THE SHULAMITE

   What would you see in the
      Shulamite—
   As it were, the dance of the two
      camps?*

Expressions of Praise

THE BELOVED

7 How beautiful are your feet in sandals,
   ᵃO prince's daughter!

   The curves of your thighs are like
      jewels,
   The work of the hands of a skillful
      workman.
2 Your navel is a rounded goblet;
   It lacks no blended beverage.
   Your waist is a heap of wheat
   Set about with lilies.
3 ᵇYour two breasts are like two fawns,
   Twins of a gazelle.
4 ᶜYour neck is like an ivory tower,
   Your eyes like the pools in Heshbon
   By the gate of Bath Rabbim.
   Your nose is like the tower of
      Lebanon
   Which looks toward Damascus.
5 Your head crowns you like Mount
      Carmel,
   And the hair of your head is like
      purple;
   A king is held captive by your tresses.

6 How fair and how pleasant you are,
   O love, with your delights!
7 This stature of yours is like a palm
      tree,
   And your breasts like its clusters.
8 I said, "I will go up to the palm tree,
   I will take hold of its branches."
   Let now your breasts be like clusters
      of the vine,
   The fragrance of your breath like
      apples,
9 And the roof of your mouth like the
      best wine.

THE SHULAMITE

   The wine goes down smoothly for my
      beloved,
   Moving gently the lips of sleepers.*
10 ᵈI am my beloved's,
   And ᵉhis desire is toward me.

11 Come, my beloved,
   Let us go forth to the field;
   Let us lodge in the villages.
12 Let us get up early to the vineyards;
   Let us ᶠsee if the vine has budded,
   Whether the grape blossoms are
      open,
   And the pomegranates are in bloom.
   There I will give you my love.

---

* 6:12 Hebrew *Ammi Nadib*   * 6:13 Hebrew *Mahanaim*   * 7:9 Septuagint, Syriac, and Vulgate
read *lips and teeth.*

---

his people, yet his love for her does not necessarily
diminish because of his devotion to his work.
6:8–9 sixty . . . eighty. This use of numbers is a rhetorical device to emphasize that the bride alone is
Solomon's love.
6:13 Return, return, O Shulamite. The chorus calls
the bride back from her daydreams and reminds her
that she is Solomon's queen.
7:1 The curves of your thighs. The Hebrew wording
suggests not only her form but also the fluid motion
of her dance (6:13).
7:7–8 like a palm tree. This is a sexual image that has

its basis in the pollination of palm trees. To fertilize
a female palm tree, the gardener climbs the male
tree and takes some of its flowers. Then he climbs
the female tree and ties the pollen-bearing flowers
among its branches.

6:5 ᵈSong 4:1   **6:6** ᵉSong 4:2   **6:7** ᶠSong 4:3
6:8 ᵍSong 1:3   **6:9** ʰSong 2:14; 5:2   **6:10** ⁱSong
6:4   **6:11** ʲSong 7:12   **7:1** ᵃPs. 45:13   **7:3** ᵇSong
4:5   **7:4** ᶜSong 4:4   **7:10** ᵈSong 2:16; 6:3   ᵉPs. 45:11
7:12 ᶠSong 6:11

13 The ᵍmandrakes give off a fragrance,
And at our gates ʰare pleasant *fruits*,
All manner, new and old,
Which I have laid up for you, my
beloved.

8 Oh, that you were like my brother,
Who nursed at my mother's breasts!
If I should find you outside,
I would kiss you;
I would not be despised.
2 I would lead you *and* bring you
Into the ᵃhouse of my mother,
She *who* used to instruct me.
I would cause you to drink of ᵇspiced
wine,
Of the juice of my pomegranate.

(TO THE DAUGHTERS OF JERUSALEM)
3 ᶜHis left hand *is* under my head,
And his right hand embraces me.
4 ᵈI charge you, O daughters of
Jerusalem,
Do not stir up nor awaken love
Until it pleases.

Love Renewed in Lebanon

A RELATIVE
5 ᵉWho *is* this coming up from the
wilderness,
Leaning upon her beloved?

I awakened you under the apple tree.
There your mother brought you forth;
There she *who* bore you brought *you*
forth.

THE SHULAMITE TO HER BELOVED
6 ᶠSet me as a seal upon your heart,
As a seal upon your arm;
For love *is as* strong as death,
ᵍJealousy *as* cruel as the grave;*
Its flames *are* flames of fire,
A most vehement flame.*
7 Many waters cannot quench love,
Nor can the floods drown it.
ʰIf a man would give for love

All the wealth of his house,
It would be utterly despised.

THE SHULAMITE'S BROTHERS
8 ⁱWe have a little sister,
And she has no breasts.
What shall we do for our sister
In the day when she is spoken for?
9 If she *is* a wall,
We will build upon her
A battlement of silver;
And if she *is* a door,
We will enclose her
With boards of cedar.

THE SHULAMITE
10 I *am* a wall,
And my breasts like towers;
Then I became in his eyes
As one who found peace.
11 Solomon had a vineyard at Baal
Hamon;
ʲHe leased the vineyard to keepers;
Everyone was to bring for its fruit
A thousand silver *coins*.

(TO SOLOMON)
12 My own vineyard *is* before me.
You, O Solomon, *may have* a
thousand,
And those who tend its fruit two
hundred.

THE BELOVED
13 You who dwell in the gardens,
The companions listen for your voice—
ᵏLet me hear it!

THE SHULAMITE
14 ˡMake haste, my beloved,
And ᵐbe like a gazelle
Or a young stag
On the mountains of spices.

---

* **8:6** Or *Sheol* • Literally *A flame of YAH* (a poetic
form of *YHWH, the* LORD)

7:13 The mandrakes. The yellow fruit of the man-
drake was small, sweet-tasting, and fragrant. It was
considered a love potion (Gen. 30:16).
8:3 left . . . right. The repetition of 2:6–7 punctu-
ates both the joy of sexual intimacy with marriage
and the warnings against sexual activity before marriage.
8:6 as a seal. This is a symbol of possession or ownership. The Shulamite wants the king to feel a total
ownership of her in his heart. She is committed only
to him; and she wants him to be completely committed to her. As long as she resides in his heart, she feels
secure.

8:7 quench . . . despised. The point of this verse is
that true love cannot be destroyed or purchased.
8:10 I am a wall . . . towers. The woman explains
that she has been virtuous in youth and that she will
remain faithful in her adulthood.
8:14 *mountains of spices*. That is, she wants him to
return to her loving embrace (1:13).

7:13 ᵍGen. 30:14 ʰMatt. 13:52 **8:2** ᵃSong 3:4 ᵇProv.
9:2 **8:3** ᶜSong 2:6 **8:4** ᵈSong 2:7; 3:5 **8:5** ᵉSong
3:6 **8:6** ᶠJer. 22:24 ᵍProv. 6:34, 35 **8:7** ʰProv. 6:35
8:8 ⁱEzek. 23:33 **8:11** ʲMatt. 21:33 **8:13** ᵏSong 2:14
8:14 ˡRev. 22:17, 20 ᵐSong 2:7, 9, 17

THE BOOK OF
ISAIAH

▶ **AUTHOR:** Although there is much argument regarding the unity of the work, Isaiah is the commonly accepted author of this book. He was from a distinguished Jewish family and his education is evident in his impressive vocabulary and style. The New Testament writers John, Paul, Matthew, and Luke, as well as Jesus Himself, all quote from the Book of Isaiah and credit him with its authorship. This great poet was uncompromising, sincere, and compassionate. Isaiah maintained close contact with the royal court, but his exhortations against alliances with foreign powers were not always well received.

▶ **TIME:** c. 740–680 B.C.   ▶ **KEY VERSES:** Is. 9:6–7

▶ **THEME:** Because of the length of the book and Isaiah's interactions with the politics of the time, we probably get a better picture of Isaiah's ministry than we do of any of the other prophets. It also contains more of the well-known, classic prophecy texts than any other book. One commentator calls Isaiah "the Romans of the Old Testament," as in Isaiah we get a broad perspective on how and why God is working in history. Both God's holiness and grace come clearly into perspective through a careful study of this book.

---

1 The ᵃvision of Isaiah the son of Amoz, which he saw concerning Judah and Jerusalem in the ᵇdays of Uzziah, Jotham, Ahaz, *and* Hezekiah, kings of Judah.

The Wickedness of Judah

2 ᶜHear, O heavens, and give ear, O earth!
  For the LORD has spoken:
  "I have nourished and brought up
      children,
  And they have rebelled against Me;
3 ᵈThe ox knows its owner
  And the donkey its master's crib;
  But Israel ᵉdoes not know,
  My people do not consider."

4 Alas, sinful nation,
  A people laden with iniquity,
  ᶠA brood of evildoers,
  Children who are corrupters!
  They have forsaken the LORD,
  They have provoked to anger
  The Holy One of Israel,
  They have turned away backward.

5 ᵍWhy should you be stricken
      again?
  You will revolt more and more.
  The whole head is sick,
  And the whole heart faints.
6 From the sole of the foot even to the
      head,
  There is no soundness in it,
  But wounds and bruises and
      putrefying sores;
  They have not been closed or bound
      up,
  Or soothed with ointment.

7 ʰYour country *is* desolate,
  Your cities *are* burned with fire;
  Strangers devour your land in your
      presence;
  And *it is* desolate, as overthrown by
      strangers.
8 So the daughter of Zion is left ⁱas a
      booth in a vineyard,
  As a hut in a garden of cucumbers,
  ʲAs a besieged city.

1:1 *Isaiah the son of Amoz.* God sent His message through Isaiah to Judah, the people of the southern kingdom—specifically to their magistrates, priests, and prophets in Jerusalem. The nation had been divided into two parts: Judah (the southern kingdom) and Israel (the northern kingdom). While Isaiah's message was primarily for the southern kingdom, it was also for the northern kingdom. The entire nation was heading down a path of sin and idolatry that would end in destruction. Isaiah lived to see the nation of Assyria take the northern kingdom into captivity in 722 B.C. The record of Isaiah's visions contains the revelations that God gave during the reigns of Uzziah (792–740 B.C.), Jotham (752–736 B.C.), Ahaz (736–720 B.C.), and Hezekiah (729–699 B.C.). God never changes, and this revelation is still relevant for His people today.

1:1 ᵃ Num. 12:6 ᵇ 2 Chr. 26–32   **1:2** ᶜ Jer. 2:12
1:3 ᵈ Jer. 8:7 ᵉ Jer. 9:3, 6   **1:4** ᶠ Matt. 3:7   **1:5** ᵍ Jer. 5:3
1:7 ʰ Deut. 28:51, 52   **1:8** ⁱ Job 27:18 ʲ Jer. 4:17

9 ᵏUnless the LORD of hosts
  Had left to us a very small remnant,
  We would have become like ˡSodom,
  We would have been made like
    Gomorrah.

10 Hear the word of the LORD,
  You rulers ᵐof Sodom;
  Give ear to the law of our God,
  You people of Gomorrah:

11 "To what purpose is the multitude of
    your ⁿsacrifices to Me?"
  Says the LORD.
  "I have had enough of burnt offerings
    of rams
  And the fat of fed cattle.
  I do not delight in the blood of bulls,
  Or of lambs or goats.

12 "When you come ᵒto appear before Me,
  Who has required this from your hand,
  To trample My courts?

13 Bring no more ᵖfutile sacrifices;
  Incense is an abomination to Me.
  The New Moons, the Sabbaths, and
    ᑫthe calling of assemblies—
  I cannot endure iniquity and the
    sacred meeting.

14 Your ʳNew Moons and your ˢappointed
    feasts
  My soul hates;
  They are a trouble to Me,
  I am weary of bearing them.

15 ᵗWhen you spread out your hands,
  I will hide My eyes from you;
  ᵘEven though you make many prayers,
  I will not hear.
  Your hands are full of blood.

16 "Washᵛ yourselves, make yourselves
    clean;
  Put away the evil of your doings from
    before My eyes.
  ʷCease to do evil,

17 Learn to do good;
  Seek justice,
  Rebuke the oppressor;*
  Defend the fatherless,
  Plead for the widow.

18 "Come now, and let us ˣreason together,"
  Says the LORD,
  "Though your sins are like scarlet,
  ʸThey shall be as white as snow;
  Though they are red like crimson,
  They shall be as wool.

19 If you are willing and obedient,
  You shall eat the good of the land;

20 But if you refuse and rebel,
  You shall be devoured by the sword";
  ᶻFor the mouth of the LORD has spoken.

The Degenerate City

21 ᵃHow the faithful city has become a
    harlot!
  It was full of justice;
  Righteousness lodged in it,
  But now ᵇmurderers.

22 ᶜYour silver has become dross,
  Your wine mixed with water.

23 ᵈYour princes are rebellious,
  And ᵉcompanions of thieves;
  ᶠEveryone loves bribes,
  And follows after rewards.
  They ᵍdo not defend the fatherless,
  Nor does the cause of the widow come
    before them.

24 Therefore the Lord says,
  The LORD of hosts, the Mighty One of
    Israel,
  "Ah, ʰI will rid Myself of My
    adversaries,
  And take vengeance on My
    enemies.

---

* **1:17** Some ancient versions read *the oppressed.*

1:9 LORD of hosts. Isaiah describes God as ruler over all powers in heaven and earth through His command of His angelic armies. **remnant.** Though God punished His sinful people, He always preserved a remnant, or survivor (Gen. 22:16–17; Ex. 34:6–7; Mic. 7:19–20; Rom. 9:29; 11:15). **Sodom . . . Gomorrah.** These two cities were regarded as the epitome of sinfulness. It was a scathing condemnation to say that Jerusalem had become like those cities.
1:18–20 The Message of the Prophets—These verses contain the essence of the prophet's message to Israel, which is also meant for us today. We need to recognize the reality of our condition. We are a stiff-necked and rebellious people, who would rather do what we want, when we want. Even today, we want the benefits of God's grace without accepting any accountability to God.
  Just as in the days of Isaiah, God's people attempt to replace obedience with ceremony. We ignore God's commands to care for the destitute, and we lose sight of God's requirements for justice and righteousness. Each of us stands before God dirty and bloody, saying we are still His people, when we are clearly not ready to fellowship with a holy God. We need to be cleaned up first.

Our God is a redeeming God who knows how to deal with sin. Although there is no rebellion that goes beyond His reach, the remedy has to be His. The first step in obedience is repentance—turning away from the direction we are going in order to see God.
1:18 reason together. This term means "to come to a legal decision." It is not an invitation to negotiate or compromise. The people were to come to an agreement with God concerning the enormous gravity of their sin. God was not declaring His people innocent of wickedness, but He was prepared to pardon their sins if they would repent and turn to Him.
1:20 has spoken. The verb "has spoken" indicates finality (contrast the verb "says" in v. 18). God had graciously extended His offer of mercy over a significant period of time, but this was the only offer He made. They could not "cut another deal" with Him (40:5; 55:11).

1:9 ᵏ Lam. 3:22 ˡ Gen. 19:24 **1:10** ᵐ Deut. 32:32 **1:11** ⁿ [1 Sam. 15:22] **1:12** ᵒ Ex. 23:17 **1:13** ᵖ Matt. 15:9 ᑫ Joel 1:14 **1:14** ʳ Num. 28:11 ˢ Lam. 2:6 **1:15** ᵗ Prov. 1:28 ᵘ Mic. 3:4 **1:16** ᵛ Jer. 4:14 ʷ Rom. 12:9 **1:18** ˣ Is. 43:26 ʸ Ps. 51:7 **1:20** ᶻ [Titus 1:2] **1:21** ᵃ Jer. 2:20 ᵇ Mic. 3:1–3 **1:22** ᶜ Jer. 6:28 **1:23** ᵈ Hos. 9:15 ᵉ Prov. 29:24 ᶠ Jer. 22:17 ᵍ Jer. 5:28 **1:24** ʰ Deut. 28:63

25 I will turn My hand against you,
    And [i]thoroughly purge away your
       dross,
    And take away all your alloy.
26 I will restore your judges [j]as at the first,
    And your counselors as at the
       beginning.
    Afterward [k]you shall be called the
       city of righteousness, the faithful
       city."

27 Zion shall be redeemed with justice,
    And her penitents with righteousness.
28 The [l]destruction of transgressors and
       of sinners *shall be* together,
    And those who forsake the LORD shall
       be consumed.
29 For they* shall be ashamed of the
       terebinth trees
    Which you have desired;
    And you shall be embarrassed
       because of the gardens
    Which you have chosen.
30 For you shall be as a terebinth whose
       leaf fades,
    And as a garden that has no water.
31 [m]The strong shall be as tinder,
    And the work of it as a spark;
    Both will burn together,
    And no one shall [n]quench *them.*

The Future House of God

2 The word that Isaiah the son of Amoz
    saw concerning Judah and Jerusalem.

2 Now [a]it shall come to pass [b]in the
       latter days
    [c]*That* the mountain of the LORD's house
    Shall be established on the top of the
       mountains,

And shall be exalted above the hills;
    And all nations shall flow to it.
3   Many people shall come and say,
    [d]"Come, and let us go up to the mountain
       of the LORD,
    To the house of the God of Jacob;
    He will teach us His ways,
    And we shall walk in His paths."
    [e]For out of Zion shall go forth the law,
    And the word of the LORD from
       Jerusalem.
4   He shall judge between the nations,
    And rebuke many people;
    They shall beat their swords into
       plowshares,
    And their spears into pruning hooks;
    Nation shall not lift up sword against
       nation,
    Neither shall they learn war anymore.

The Day of the LORD
5   O house of Jacob, come and let us [f]walk
    In the light of the LORD.

6   For You have forsaken Your people,
       the house of Jacob,
    Because they are filled [g]with eastern
       ways;
    They *are* [h]soothsayers like the
       Philistines,
    [i]And they are pleased with the children
       of foreigners.
7   [j]Their land is also full of silver and gold,
    And there is no end to their treasures;
    Their land is also full of horses,
    And there is no end to their chariots.

---

* **1:29** Following Masoretic Text, Septuagint, and
Vulgate; some Hebrew manuscripts and Targum
read *you.*

1:27 redeemed. The Hebrew word for "redeemed"
means "ransomed" or "freed" from another's ownership through the payment of a price. **penitents.**
Zion's penitents, those who turned their backs on
idolatry and injustice, found freedom from sin and
judgment. **1:29 terebinth trees . . . gardens.** The terebinth was
a sacred tree, and the gardens with sacred groves
for fertility rites were part of idol worship, which the
people had chosen instead of worshiping only the
living God. **2:2 in the latter days.** The latter days refer to the
conditions in Christ's (the Messiah's) future kingdom.
At the time of the writing of the Book of Isaiah, no
one had a clear idea of what the coming of the Messiah would mean. They believed that, under His rule,
earthly kingdoms and authorities would vanish, and
everything would at last be the way God originally
planned before the fall (Gen. 3:1–22). But they did
not yet have an understanding of Christ dying on the
cross for the sins of the whole world, or of the church
age. Isaiah was looking forward to what Christians
are still looking forward to—what we call the second
coming, or return of Christ (Acts 1:11; Rev. 21–22).
2:4 Neither shall they learn war anymore. The Old
Testament term for "peace" meant soundness or
completeness. Just as man can never be truly at peace
apart from his Creator, so a nation of sinful humanity

cannot truly achieve peace apart from God. Men or
nations will be rebellious, self-centered, and at odds
with each other unless their harmony with God is
restored. This can only happen when, person by person, peace is provided by the Prince of Peace, Jesus
Christ. To look forward to the day when there will be
this peace for the whole world is to understand the
magnitude of God's promise in this passage.
2:6 You have forsaken. This was a present condition—but not a permanent condition—for the Israelites. God's covenant with Israel had always been
based on their obedience, and the Israelites (or house
of Jacob) were finally going to experience the results
of their disobedience (Deut. 27–30). **filled with eastern ways . . . soothsayers.** Copying other religions
and participating in the occult practices of peoples
of Canaan were strictly forbidden (Deut. 18:9–14).
Whoever did these things was detestable to the Lord.
2:7 full of silver and gold . . . full of horses. The king
was not to multiply horses, wives, or gold and silver
for himself, for this would cause his heart to turn away
from the Lord (Deut. 17:14–17).

1:25 [i] Mal. 3:3   **1:26** [j] Jer. 33:7–11   [k] Zech. 8:3
1:28 [l] [2 Thess. 1:8, 9]   **1:31** [m] Ezek. 32:21   [n] Mark 9:43
2:2 [a] Mic. 4:1   [b] Gen. 49:1   [c] Ps. 68:15   **2:3** [d] Jer. 50:5
[e] Luke 24:47   **2:5** [f] Eph. 5:8   **2:6** [g] Num. 23:7   [h] Deut.
18:14   [i] Ps. 106:35   **2:7** [j] Deut. 17:16

8 ^kTheir land is also full of idols;
They worship the work of their own
hands,
That which their own fingers have
made.
9 People bow down,
And each man humbles himself;
Therefore do not forgive them.
10 ^lEnter into the rock, and hide in the
dust,
From the terror of the LORD
And the glory of His majesty.
11 The lofty looks of man shall be
^mhumbled,
The haughtiness of men shall be
bowed down,
And the LORD alone shall be exalted
ⁿin that day.

12 For the day of the LORD of hosts
Shall come upon everything proud
and lofty,
Upon everything lifted up—
And it shall be brought low—
13 Upon all ^othe cedars of Lebanon *that
are* high and lifted up,
And upon all the oaks of Bashan;
14 ^pUpon all the high mountains,
And upon all the hills *that are* lifted up;
15 Upon every high tower,
And upon every fortified wall;
16 ^qUpon all the ships of Tarshish,
And upon all the beautiful sloops.
17 The loftiness of man shall be bowed
down,
And the haughtiness of men shall be
brought low;
The LORD alone will be exalted in that
day,
18 But the idols He shall utterly abolish.

19 They shall go into the ^rholes of the
rocks,
And into the caves of the earth,
^sFrom the terror of the LORD
And the glory of His majesty,
When He arises ^tto shake the earth
mightily.

20 In that day a man will cast away his
idols of silver
And his idols of gold,
Which they made, *each* for himself to
worship,
To the moles and bats,

21 To go into the clefts of the rocks,
And into the crags of the rugged rocks,
From the terror of the LORD
And the glory of His majesty,
When He arises to shake the earth
mightily.

22 ^uSever yourselves from such a man,
Whose ^vbreath *is* in his nostrils;
For of what account is he?

Judgment on Judah and Jerusalem

3 For behold, the Lord, the LORD of hosts,
^aTakes away from Jerusalem and from
Judah
^bThe stock and the store,
The whole supply of bread and the
whole supply of water;
2 ^cThe mighty man and the man of war,
The judge and the prophet,
And the diviner and the elder;
3 The captain of fifty and the honorable
man,
The counselor and the skillful artisan,
And the expert enchanter.

4 "I will give ^dchildren *to be* their
princes,
And babes shall rule over them.
5 The people will be oppressed,
Every one by another and every one
by his neighbor;
The child will be insolent toward the
elder,
And the base toward the honorable."

6 When a man takes hold of his brother
In the house of his father, *saying,*
"You have clothing;
You be our ruler,
And *let* these ruins *be* under your
power,"*
7 In that day he will protest, saying,
"I cannot cure *your* ills,
For in my house *is* neither food nor
clothing;
Do not make me a ruler of the people."

8 For ^eJerusalem stumbled,
And Judah is fallen,
Because their tongue and their doings
Are against the LORD,
To provoke the eyes of His glory.

---

* **3:6** Literally *hand*

2:8 *full of idols.* Idolatry was forbidden in the Ten Commandments (Ex. 20:4; Deut. 13), and it was a flagrant rebellion against the Lord who had rescued them from the land of Egypt and redeemed them from slavery. It was a seduction to unfaithfulness and was to be punished with death.
2:19 *caves of the earth . . . terror of the LORD.* Men will want to hide from the Lord whom they have not been willing to obey (Rev. 6:15–17).
3:4 *children . . . babes.* The rulers would be incompetent and inexperienced.
3:8 *against the LORD.* Prior to entering Canaan, Moses had the blessings and the curses of the law of

God recited to the people, warning of the serious consequences of unbelief. Unfaithfulness would result in captivity, worldwide dispersion, and aimless wandering among the Gentile nations (Deut. 28). Joshua gave the same warning after bringing them into the land (Josh. 24). Both warnings went unheeded. From

2:8 ^k Jer. 2:28   **2:10** ^l Rev. 6:15, 16   **2:11** ^m Prov. 16:5 ⁿ Hos. 2:16   **2:13** ^o Zech. 11:1, 2   **2:14** ^p Is. 30:25   **2:16** ^q 1 Kin. 10:22   **2:19** ^r Hos. 10:8 ^s [2 Thess. 1:9] ^t Hag. 2:6, 7   **2:22** ^u Jer. 17:5 ^v Job 27:3   **3:1** ^a Jer. 37:21 ^b Lev. 26:26   **3:2** ^c 2 Kin. 24:14   **3:4** ^d Eccl. 10:16   **3:8** ^e Mic. 3:12

9 The look on their countenance
witnesses against them,
And they declare their sin as ᶠSodom;
They do not hide *it*.
Woe to their soul!
For they have brought evil upon
themselves.

10 "Say to the righteous ᵍthat *it shall be*
well *with them*,
ʰFor they shall eat the fruit of their
doings.

11 Woe to the wicked! ᶦ*It shall be* ill *with
him*,
For the reward of his hands shall be
given him.

12 *As for* My people, children *are* their
oppressors,
And women rule over them.
O My people! ʲThose who lead you
cause *you* to err,
And destroy the way of your
paths."

Oppression and Luxury Condemned

13 The Lᴏʀᴅ stands up ᵏto plead,
And stands to judge the people.

14 The Lᴏʀᴅ will enter into judgment
With the elders of His people
And His princes:
"For you have eaten up ˡthe vineyard;
The plunder of the poor *is* in your
houses.

15 What do you mean by ᵐcrushing My
people
And grinding the faces of the poor?"
Says the Lord Gᴏᴅ of hosts.

16Moreover the Lᴏʀᴅ says:

"Because the daughters of Zion are
haughty,
And walk with outstretched necks
And wanton eyes,
Walking and mincing *as* they go,
Making a jingling with their feet,

17 Therefore the Lord will strike with ⁿa
scab
The crown of the head of the
daughters of Zion,
And the Lᴏʀᴅ will ᵒuncover their
secret parts."

18 In that day the Lord will take away the
finery:
The jingling anklets, the scarves, and
the ᵖcrescents;

19 The pendants, the bracelets, and the
veils;

20 The headdresses, the leg ornaments,
and the headbands;
The perfume boxes, the charms,

21 and the rings;
The nose jewels,

22 the festal apparel, and the mantles;
The outer garments, the purses,

23 and the mirrors;
The fine linen, the turbans, and the
robes.

24And so it shall be:

Instead of a sweet smell there will be
a stench;
Instead of a sash, a rope;
Instead of well-set hair, ᑫbaldness;
Instead of a rich robe, a girding of
sackcloth;
And branding instead of beauty.

25 Your men shall fall by the sword,
And your mighty in the war.

26 ʳHer gates shall lament and mourn,
And she *being* desolate ˢshall sit on the
ground.

4 And ᵃin that day seven women shall
take hold of one man, saying,
"We will ᵇeat our own food and wear
our own apparel;
Only let us be called by your name,
To take away ᶜour reproach."

The Renewal of Zion

2 In that day ᵈthe Branch of the Lᴏʀᴅ
shall be beautiful and glorious;
And the fruit of the earth *shall be*
excellent and appealing
For those of Israel who have escaped.

3And it shall come to pass that *he who is*
left in Zion and remains in Jerusalem ᵉwill
be called holy—everyone who is ᶠrecord-
ed among the living in Jerusalem. 4When
ᵍthe Lord has washed away the filth of the
daughters of Zion, and purged the blood of

---

a historical perspective, it is easy to be appalled at the people's heedlessness. They ignored specific and direct commands, apparently knowing well that they were courting disaster. But, if we as believers examine ourselves carefully, we might be appalled at our own unfaithfulness in certain areas. God's directives are always there for a reason, and unfaithfulness, even in little things, causes a rift in our relationship with God.
3:16 daughters of Zion. The plural "daughters" suggests the women of the city as well as a person-ification of Jerusalem. The list of finery (vv. 18–23), whether applied figuratively to the city of Jerusalem or to specific women, indicated a preoccupation with frivolity and wealth.
4:1 take away our reproach. It was considered a sign of inadequacy to have no children.

4:2 In that day. Isaiah is speaking of the future rev-elation of the glory of the Lord on earth (2:2–4). **the Branch of the Lᴏʀᴅ.** Jesus Christ is the fruitful Branch (Jer. 23:5; Zech. 3:8). The reign of Jesus, the King of Creation, will be marked by plenty. The earth will be released from its curse, producing all that God intended it to produce in the beginning.

3:9 ᶠGen. 13:13   **3:10** ᵍ[Eccl. 8:12] ʰPs. 128:2
3:11 ᶦ[Ps. 11:6]   **3:12** ʲIs. 9:16   **3:13** ᵏMic. 6:2
3:14 ˡMatt. 21:33   **3:15** ᵐMic. 3:2, 3   **3:17** ⁿDeut.
28:27 ᵒJer. 13:22   **3:18** ᵖJudg. 8:21, 26   **3:24** ᑫIs. 22:12
3:26 ʳJer. 14:2 ˢLam. 2:10   **4:1** ᵃIs. 2:11, 17 ᵇ2 Thess.
3:12 ᶜLuke 1:25   **4:2** ᵈ[Jer. 23:5]   **4:3** ᵉIs. 60:21 ᶠPhil.
4:3   **4:4** ᵍMal. 3:2, 3

Jerusalem from her midst, by the spirit of judgment and by the spirit of burning, 5then the LORD will create above every dwelling place of Mount Zion, and above her assemblies, *h*a cloud and smoke by day and *i*the shining of a flaming fire by night. For over all the glory there *will be* a covering. 6And there will be a tabernacle for shade in the daytime from the heat, *j*for a place of refuge, and for a shelter from storm and rain.

God's Disappointing Vineyard

5 Now let me sing to my Well-beloved
A song of my Beloved *a*regarding His
vineyard:

My Well-beloved has a vineyard
On a very fruitful hill.
2 He dug it up and cleared out its stones,
And planted it with the choicest vine.
He built a tower in its midst,
And also made a winepress in it;
*b*So He expected *it* to bring forth *good*
grapes,
But it brought forth wild grapes.

3 "And now, O inhabitants of Jerusalem
and men of Judah,
*c*Judge, please, between Me and My
vineyard.
4 What more could have been done to
My vineyard
That I have not done in *d*it?
Why then, when I expected *it* to bring
forth *good* grapes,
Did it bring forth wild grapes?
5 And now, please let Me tell you what I
will do to My vineyard:
*e*I will take away its hedge, and it shall
be burned;
And break down its wall, and it shall
be trampled down.
6 I will lay it *f*waste;
It shall not be pruned or dug,
But there shall come up briers and
*g*thorns.
I will also command the clouds
That they rain no rain on it."

7 For the vineyard of the LORD of hosts
is the house of Israel,
And the men of Judah are His pleasant
plant.
He looked for justice, but behold,
oppression;
For righteousness, but behold, a cry
for help.

Impending Judgment on Excesses

8 Woe to those who join *h*house to
house;
They add field to field,
Till *there is* no place
Where they may dwell alone in the
midst of the land!

9 *i*In my hearing the LORD of hosts *said,*
"Truly, many houses shall be
desolate,
Great and beautiful ones, without
inhabitant.
10 For ten acres of vineyard shall yield
one *j*bath,
And a homer of seed shall yield one
ephah."

11 *k*Woe to those who rise early in the
morning,
That they may follow intoxicating
drink;
Who continue until night, *till* wine
inflames them!
12 *l*The harp and the strings,
The tambourine and flute,
And wine are in their feasts;
But *m*they do not regard the work of
the LORD,
Nor consider the operation of His
hands.

13 *n*Therefore my people have gone into
captivity,
Because *they have* no *o*knowledge;
Their honorable men *are* famished,
And their multitude dried up with
thirst.
14 Therefore Sheol has enlarged itself
And opened its mouth beyond measure;
Their glory and their multitude and
their pomp,
And he who is jubilant, shall descend
into it.
15 People shall be brought down,
*p*Each man shall be humbled,
And the eyes of the lofty shall be
humbled.
16 But the LORD of hosts shall be *q*exalted
in judgment,
And God who is holy shall be hallowed
in righteousness.
17 Then the lambs shall feed in their
pasture,
And in the waste places of *r*the fat ones
strangers shall eat.

5:4 What more could have been done to My vineyard. This is a rhetorical question. There was nothing more that God could or should have done to bring forth good fruit from His vineyard. The failure was on the part of the people, not God (John 15:1).
5:6 briers and thorns. Briers and thorns symbolize the anarchy that will take over the land after the exile (3:4–5). **no rain.** As God promised in His covenant on Mount Sinai, sufficient rainfall would come to the people who were faithful to His commands, but the rain would be withheld if the people were rebellious (Deut. 28:12,23–24).

5:14 Sheol. This word is used for the grave or the place where the body goes after death. Its meaning is not precise, but this word is sometimes translated

4:5 *h* Ex. 13:21, 22 *i* Zech. 2:5 **4:6** *j* Is. 25:4 **5:1** *a* Matt. 21:33 **5:2** *b* Deut. 32:6 **5:3** *c* [Rom. 3:4] **5:4** *d* 2 Chr. 36:15, 16 **5:5** *e* Ps. 80:12; 89:40, 41 **5:6** *f* 2 Chr. 36:19–21 *g* Is. 7:19–25 **5:8** *h* Mic. 2:2 **5:9** *i* Is. 22:14 **5:10** *j* Ezek. 45:11 **5:11** *k* Prov. 23:29, 30 **5:12** *l* Amos 6:5 *m* Job 34:27 **5:13** *n* 2 Kin. 24:14–16 *o* Hos. 4:6 **5:15** *p* Is. 2:9, 11 **5:16** *q* Is. 2:11 **5:17** *r* Is. 10:16

18 Woe to those who draw iniquity with
cords of vanity,
And sin as if with a cart rope;
19 sThat say, "Let Him make speed *and*
hasten His work,
That we may see *it;*
And let the counsel of the Holy One of
Israel draw near and come,
That we may know *it.*"
20 Woe to those who call evil good, and
good evil;
Who put darkness for light, and light
for darkness;
Who put bitter for sweet, and sweet
for bitter!
21 Woe to *those who are* twise in their
own eyes,
And prudent in their own sight!
22 Woe to men mighty at drinking wine,
Woe to men valiant for mixing
intoxicating drink,
23 Who ujustify the wicked for a bribe,
And take away justice from the
righteous man!
24 Therefore, vas the fire devours the
stubble,
And the flame consumes the chaff,
So wtheir root will be as rottenness,
And their blossom will ascend like
dust;
Because they have rejected the law of
the LORD of hosts,
And despised the word of the Holy
One of Israel.
25 xTherefore the anger of the LORD is
aroused against His people;
He has stretched out His hand against
them
And stricken them,
And ythe hills trembled.
Their carcasses *were* as refuse in the
midst of the streets.

zFor all this His anger is not turned
away,
But His hand *is* stretched out still.

26 aHe will lift up a banner to the nations
from afar,
And will bwhistle to them from cthe
end of the earth;
Surely dthey shall come with speed,
swiftly.
27 No one will be weary or stumble
among them,
No one will slumber or sleep;
Nor ewill the belt on their loins be
loosed,
Nor the strap of their sandals be
broken;
28 fWhose arrows *are* sharp,
And all their bows bent;
Their horses' hooves will seem like
flint,
And their wheels like a whirlwind.
29 Their roaring *will be* like a lion,
They will roar like young lions;
Yes, they will roar
And lay hold of the prey;
They will carry *it* away safely,
And no one will deliver.
30 In that day they will roar against them
Like the roaring of the sea.
And if *one* glooks to the land,
Behold, darkness *and* sorrow;
And the light is darkened by the
clouds.

Isaiah Called to Be a Prophet

6 In the year that aKing Uzziah died, I
bsaw the Lord sitting on a throne, high
and lifted up, and the train of His *robe*
filled the temple. 2Above it stood seraphim; each one had six wings: with two he
covered his face, cwith two he covered his
feet, and with two he flew. 3And one cried
to another and said:

"hell" where the context considers the "grave" in a
negative sense.
5:18 vanity. A falsehood is a lie. Those who "draw
iniquity with cords of vanity" are those who are dragging sin behind them with ropes of lies. Essentially,
these lies are the various ways people have of justifying sin. They are not ashamed of their sin, but are
quite openly attached to it, carrying it wherever they
go. Of course, the big lie is the lie that sin does not
matter, that judgment will not come. The truth is that
the fruits of sin always catch up with us, and, unless
we make peace with God through Christ, the judgment for sin will follow.
6:1 King Uzziah died. King Uzziah died in 740 B.C.,
signaling the end of an age. He is described as a good
king (2 Chr. 26:1–15), but in his pride he was unfaithful to God (2 Chr. 26:16–23), and he died a leper. He
was succeeded by his son Jotham, who did right, and
then by wicked Ahaz (7:1). The relative prosperity
of the first half of the eighth century was replaced
by the Syro-Ephraimite wars and the Assyrian campaigns into Israel.
6:3 Holy, holy, holy. To say the word "holy" twice

in Hebrew is to describe someone as "most holy." To
say the word three times intensifies the idea to the
highest level. **The whole earth is full of His glory.**
We know that the glory of God transcends the universe, yet this phrase emphasizes God's closeness to
His creation—His involvement with the earth and its
people.
We know that our greatest failing is not realizing who God is nor what His character is like. This is
particularly true in the case of God's holiness. To be
holy means "to be set apart." God is set apart from the
power, practice, and presence of sin, and is set apart to
absolute righteousness and goodness. There is no sin
in God and God can have nothing to do with sin. If we
are to approach God, we must do so on God's terms.
We must be made holy by God's action in Christ.
Most of our lives are so caught up in the mundane

5:19 s Jer. 17:15   **5:21** t Rom. 1:22; 12:16   **5:23** u Prov. 17:15
5:24 v Ex. 15:7   w Job 18:16   **5:25** x 2 Kin. 22:13, 17   y Jer.
4:24   z Is. 9:12, 17   **5:26** a Is. 11:10, 12   b Is. 7:18   c Mal. 1:11
d Joel 2:7   **5:27** e Dan. 5:6   **5:28** f Jer. 5:16   **5:30** g Is.
8:22   **6:1** a 2 Kin. 15:7   b John 12:41   **6:2** c Ezek. 1:11

d"Holy, holy, holy *is* the LORD of hosts;
*e*The whole earth *is* full of His glory!"

4And the posts of the door were shaken by the voice of him who cried out, and the house was filled with smoke.
5So I said:

"Woe *is* me, for I am undone!
Because I *am* a man of *f*unclean lips,
And I dwell in the midst of a people of
unclean lips;
For my eyes have seen the King,
The LORD of hosts."

6Then one of the seraphim flew to me, having in his hand a live coal *which* he had taken with the tongs from *g*the altar. 7And he *h*touched my mouth *with it*, and said:

"Behold, this has touched your lips;
Your iniquity is taken away,
And your sin purged."

8Also I heard the voice of the Lord, saying:

"Whom shall I send,
And who will go for *i*Us?"

Then I said, "Here *am* I! Send me."
9And He said, "Go, and *j*tell this people:

'Keep on hearing, but do not
understand;
Keep on seeing, but do not perceive.'

10 "Make *k*the heart of this people dull,
And their ears heavy,
And shut their eyes;
*l*Lest they see with their eyes,
And hear with their ears,
And understand with their heart,
And return and be healed."

11Then I said, "Lord, how long?"
And He answered:

m"Until the cities are laid waste and
without inhabitant,
The houses are without a man,
The land is utterly desolate,
12 *n*The LORD has removed men far
away,
And the forsaken places *are* many in
the midst of the land.
13 But yet a tenth *will be* in it,
And will return and be for consuming,
As a terebinth tree or as an oak,
Whose stump *remains* when it is cut
down.
So *o*the holy seed *shall be* its stump."

Isaiah Sent to King Ahaz

7 Now it came to pass in the days of *a*Ahaz the son of Jotham, the son of Uzziah, king of Judah, *that* Rezin king of Syria and Pekah the son of Remaliah, king of Israel, went up to Jerusalem to *make* war against *b*it, but could not prevail against it. 2And it was told to the house of David, saying, "Syria's forces are deployed in Ephraim." So his heart and the heart of his people were moved as the trees of the woods are moved with the wind.
3Then the LORD said to Isaiah, "Go out now to meet Ahaz, you and Shear-Jashub* your son, at the end of the aqueduct from the upper pool, on the highway to the Fuller's Field, 4and say to him: 'Take heed, and be *c*quiet; do not fear or be fainthearted for these two stubs of smoking firebrands, for

* **7:3** Literally *A Remnant Shall Return*

that we don't understand and experience God's holiness as we should. There is little appreciation or understanding of the sacred "otherness" of God. We have too often reduced Him to only friend and advisor. We do so at our own peril; for it is that sacred "otherness" that brings us to our knees. That is where the relationship needs to begin. Isaiah received God's call in that position. He recognized God's holiness and his own uncleanness and the need for God to purify him before he would be fit to serve as a prophet.
The experience of coming to understand God's holiness is simultaneously humbling, challenging, and exhilarating. We touch the fullness of our potential as we are touched and purified by God in Christ's sacrifice for us.
6:6 live coal . . . from the altar. Brought face to face with the holiness of the Lord, Isaiah was stunned by his own uncleanness. Without taking any action on his own, Isaiah was offered forgiveness and cleansing. This was a unique event, especially for Isaiah, but not the last time that the Lord reached out to man to offer forgiveness and cleansing. Salvation through Christ is a gift, not received through works (Eph. 2:8–9).
6:10 heart . . . dull. Isaiah's call was to a very discouraging ministry. People with "fat" hearts were insensitive. They were "padded" with self-satisfaction so they could not feel the prick of the Lord's words. The more Isaiah proclaimed the Word of God, the less

response he received from the people. In truth, the call of God was for faithfulness to God, to His word, and to the call itself.
6:13 tenth. A "tenth" is one of Isaiah's expressions for the "remnant."
7:1 it came to pass. The next five chapters contain a series of prophecies related specifically to the Syro-Ephraimite wars—the invasion of Judah by Rezin and Pekah (2 Kin. 16). These prophecies aimed to call Judah back to faith in God.
7:2 house of David. The king was descended from David and was referred to as "from the house of David." **Ephraim.** The word Ephraim represents the northern kingdom of Israel.
7:3 Shear-Jashub. The name of Isaiah's son meant "a remnant will return." This name referred to a coming exile and the salvation of the remaining faithful, although all of those events occurred long after Isaiah's lifetime.
7:4 son of Remaliah. The son of Remaliah is Pekah, king of Israel.

6:3 *d* Rev. 4:8 *e* Num. 14:21 **6:5** *f* Ex. 6:12, 30 **6:6** *g* Rev. 8:3 **6:7** *h* Jer. 1:9 **6:8** *i* Gen. 1:26 **6:9** *j* Matt. 13:14 **6:10** *k* Ps. 119:70 *l* Jer. 5:21 **6:11** *m* Mic. 3:12 **6:12** *n* 2 Kin. 25:21 **6:13** *o* Ezra 9:2 **7:1** *a* 2 Chr. 28 *b* 2 Kin. 16:5, 9 **7:4** *c* Is. 30:15

the fierce anger of Rezin and Syria, and the son of Remaliah. ⁵Because Syria, Ephraim, and the son of Remaliah have plotted evil against you, saying, ⁶"Let us go up against Judah and trouble it, and let us make a gap in its wall for ourselves, and set a king over them, the son of Tabel"— ⁷thus says the Lord GOD:

ᵈ"It shall not stand,
Nor shall it come to pass.
⁸ ᵉFor the head of Syria *is* Damascus,
And the head of Damascus *is* Rezin.
Within sixty-five years Ephraim will
be broken,
So that it will not *be* a people.
⁹ The head of Ephraim *is* Samaria,
And the head of Samaria *is* Remaliah's
son.
ᶠIf you will not believe,
Surely you shall not be established."' "

The Immanuel Prophecy

¹⁰Moreover the LORD spoke again to Ahaz, saying, ¹¹ᵍ"Ask a sign for yourself from the LORD your God; ask it either in the depth or in the height above." ¹²But Ahaz said, "I will not ask, nor will I test the LORD!" ¹³Then he said, "Hear now, O house of David! *Is it* a small thing for you to weary men, but will you weary my God also? ¹⁴Therefore the Lord Himself will give you a sign: ʰBehold, the virgin shall conceive and bear ⁱa Son, and shall call His name ʲImmanuel.* ¹⁵Curds and honey He shall eat, that He may know to refuse the evil and choose the good. ¹⁶ᵏFor before the Child shall know to refuse the evil and choose the good, the land that you dread will be forsaken by ˡboth her kings. ¹⁷ᵐThe LORD will bring the king of Assyria upon you and your people and your father's house—days that have not come since the day that ⁿEphraim departed from Judah."

¹⁸ And it shall come to pass in that day
That the LORD ᵒwill whistle for
the fly
That *is* in the farthest part of the rivers
of Egypt,
And for the bee that *is* in the land of
Assyria.
¹⁹ They will come, and all of them will
rest
In the desolate valleys and in ᵖthe
clefts of the rocks,
And on all thorns and in all pastures.
²⁰ In the same day the Lord will shave
with a ᑫhired ʳrazor,
With those from beyond the River,*
with the king of Assyria,
The head and the hair of the legs,
And will also remove the beard.
²¹ It shall be in that day
That a man will keep alive a young
cow and two sheep;
²² So it shall be, from the abundance of
milk they give,
That he will eat curds;
For curds and honey everyone will eat
who is left in the land.
²³ It shall happen in that day,
That wherever there could be a
thousand vines
Worth a thousand *shekels* of silver,
ˢIt will be for briers and thorns.
²⁴ With arrows and bows *men* will come
there,
Because all the land will become
briers and thorns.
²⁵ And to any hill which could be dug
with the hoe,
You will not go there for fear of briers
and thorns;
But it will become a range for oxen
And a place for sheep to roam.

---

* 7:14 Literally *God-With-Us*   * 7:20 That is, the Euphrates

---

7:6 son of Tabel. Tabel means "good for nothing." Syria and Israel wanted to place an incompetent puppet king over Judah.

7:12 not ask, nor will I test. In the mouth of the wicked Ahaz, these words rang hollow. Ahaz was continually testing the Lord's patience by his disobedience.

7:14 Immanuel. The Christian church traditionally has seen this verse as a prophecy of the Christ child, in whose incarnation God became present in physical form with mankind. The name "Immanuel" means "God with us." Christ, as a descendant of the house of David, fulfills the requirements of the sign and reinforces Isaiah's message that the nation's destiny does not rest with a foreign people, but with the God of Sinai.

7:15 Curds and honey. Curds and honey contrast with "bread and wine" from cultivated lands and symbolically represent the Judean's simple diet after the Assyrian invasion. Thus, the Child, similar to Isaiah's son Shear-Jashub (v. 3), would be identified with the remnant.

7:16 For before. Similar prophecies were spoken of the child's birth and Isaiah's other son, Maher-Shalal-Hash-Baz (8:3). Israel and Syria would be destroyed before the child and Isaiah's son would reach maturity (see 8:4, where Syria is referred to as Damascus and Israel as Samaria). It is not uncommon for biblical prophecies to have one level of fulfillment in the immediate future and a final fulfillment many years later in the person and work of the Savior, Jesus. Thus, the birth of Isaiah's son could have been a sign to King Ahaz. However, this would have been an early fulfillment, not the ultimate fulfillment. It was the coming of Jesus, God's only Son, which was the complete fulfillment.

7:20 shave . . . beard. This was a symbol of humiliation.

7:7 ᵈIs. 8:10   7:8 ᵉ2 Sam. 8:6   7:9 ᶠ2 Chr. 20:20   7:11 ᵍMatt. 12:38   7:14 ʰMatt. 1:23   ⁱ[Is. 9:6] ʲIs. 8:8, 10   7:16 ᵏIs. 8:4 ˡ2 Kin. 15:30   7:17 ᵐ2 Chr. 28:19, 20 ⁿ1 Kin. 12:16   7:18 ᵒIs. 5:26   7:19 ᵖJer. 16:16   7:20 ᑫIs. 10:5, 15 ʳ2 Kin. 16:7   7:23 ˢIs. 5:6

Assyria Will Invade the Land

8 Moreover the LORD said to me, "Take
a large scroll, and [a]write on it with a
man's pen concerning Maher-Shalal-Hash-
Baz.* 2And I will take for Myself faithful
witnesses to record, [b]Uriah the priest and
Zechariah the son of Jeberechiah."
3Then I went to the prophetess, and she
conceived and bore a son. Then the LORD
said to me, "Call his name Maher-Shalal-
Hash-Baz; 4[c]for before the child shall have
knowledge to cry 'My father' and 'My
mother,' [d]the riches of Damascus and the
spoil of Samaria will be taken away before
the king of Assyria."
5The LORD also spoke to me again, saying:

6 "Inasmuch as these people refused
The waters of [e]Shiloah that flow softly,
And rejoice [f]in Rezin and in
Remaliah's son;
7 Now therefore, behold, the Lord brings
up over them
The waters of the River,* strong and
mighty—
The king of Assyria and all his glory;
He will go up over all his channels
And go over all his banks.
8 He will pass through Judah,
He will overflow and pass over,
[g]He will reach up to the neck;
And the stretching out of his
wings
Will fill the breadth of Your land,
O [h]Immanuel.*

9 "Be[i] shattered, O you peoples, and be
broken in pieces!
Give ear, all you from far countries.
Gird yourselves, but be broken in
pieces;
Gird yourselves, but be broken in
pieces.
10 [j]Take counsel together, but it will come
to nothing;
Speak the word, [k]but it will not stand,
[l]For God *is* with us."*

Fear God, Heed His Word

11For the LORD spoke thus to me with
a strong hand, and instructed me that I
should not walk in the way of this people,
saying:

12 "Do not say, 'A conspiracy,'
Concerning all that this people call a
conspiracy,
Nor be afraid of their threats, nor be
troubled.
13 The LORD of hosts, Him you shall
hallow;
Let Him *be* your fear,
And *let* Him *be* your dread.
14 [m]He will be as a sanctuary,
But [n]a stone of stumbling and a rock
of offense
To both the houses of Israel,
As a trap and a snare to the
inhabitants of Jerusalem.
15 And many among them shall [o]stumble;
They shall fall and be broken,
Be snared and taken."

16 Bind up the testimony,
Seal the law among my disciples.
17 And I will wait on the LORD,
Who [p]hides His face from the house
of Jacob;
And I [q]will hope in Him.
18 [r]Here am I and the children whom the
LORD has given me!
We [s]are for signs and wonders in Israel
From the LORD of hosts,
Who dwells in Mount Zion.

19And when they say to you, [t]"Seek those
who are mediums and wizards, [u]who whisper and mutter," should not a people seek
their God? *Should they* [v]*seek* the dead on
behalf of the living? 20[w]To the law and to
the testimony! If they do not speak according to this word, *it is* because [x]*there is* no
light in them.

* **8:1** Literally *Speed the Spoil, Hasten the Booty*
* **8:7** That is, the Euphrates * **8:8** Literally *God-With-Us* * **8:10** Hebrew *Immanuel*

8:2 ***Zechariah the son of Jeberechiah.*** This was not the Zechariah who wrote the Book of Zechariah.
8:3 ***the prophetess.*** Isaiah's wife was a prophetess in her own right. It is possible that this was a new wife, following the death of the mother of Shear-Jashub (7:3). ***Maher-Shalal-Hash-Baz.*** The child's name means "speed the spoil, hasten the booty."
8:4 ***spoil of Samaria . . . king of Assyria.*** This was a specific prediction of the fall of Samaria to the Assyrians in 722 B.C. This prophecy must have been written shortly before that time, as the fulfillment would come before the new child would be able to speak.
8:8 ***O Immanuel.*** Isaiah bestowed on Judah the name of the promised Child, Immanuel, which means "God with us" (7:14), because it would be preserved only because God was with that nation.
8:14 ***a stone of stumbling and a rock of offense.*** God is a stone of stumbling for unbelievers (Ps. 118:22; Luke 20:17–18; Rom. 9:33; 1 Pet. 2:6–8).
8:16 ***testimony . . . law.*** The testimony refers to a legal transaction. The law refers to God's instruction revealed through Isaiah. Isaiah's disciples put his prophecies in the form of a legal transaction, probably to prove their authenticity when they were fulfilled (see vv. 1–2; compare Jer. 28:9; 32:12–14).
8:18 ***children.*** Isaiah's name means "Jehovah has saved," and his two sons' names speak of the impending judgment of God (7:3; 8:3). They were symbols of God's intentions for the nation.
8:19 ***Seek those who are mediums and wizards.*** This indicates that the people were involved in necromancy, the practice of conjuring up the spirits of

8:1 [a] Hab. 2:2 **8:2** [b] 2 Kin. 16:10 **8:4** [c] 2 Kin. 17:6; Is. 7:16 [d] 2 Kin. 15:29 **8:6** [e] John 9:7 [f] Is. 7:1, 2 **8:8** [g] Is. 30:28 [h] Is. 7:14 **8:9** [i] Joel 3:9 **8:10** [j] Is. 7:7 [k] Is. 7:14 [l] Rom. 8:31 **8:14** [m] Ezek. 11:16 [n] Luke 2:34; 20:17 **8:15** [o] Matt. 21:44 **8:17** [p] Is. 54:8 [q] Hab. 2:3 **8:18** [r] Heb. 2:13 [s] Ps. 71:7 **8:19** [t] 1 Sam. 28:8 [u] Is. 29:4 [v] Ps. 106:28 **8:20** [w] Luke 16:29 [x] Mic. 3:6

²¹They will pass through it hard-pressed and hungry; and it shall happen, when they are hungry, that they will be enraged and ʸcurse their king and their God, and look upward. ²²Then they will look to the earth, and see trouble and darkness, gloom of anguish; and *they will be* driven into darkness.

The Government of the Promised Son

9 Nevertheless ᵃthe gloom *will* not *be* upon her who *is* distressed,
As when at ᵇfirst He lightly esteemed
The land of Zebulun and the land of Naphtali,
And ᶜafterward more heavily oppressed *her,*
By the way of the sea, beyond the Jordan,
In Galilee of the Gentiles.

2 ᵈThe people who walked in darkness
Have seen a great light;
Those who dwelt in the land of the shadow of death,
Upon them a light has shined.

3 You have multiplied the nation
And increased its joy;*
They rejoice before You
According to the joy of harvest,
As *men* rejoice ᵉwhen they divide the spoil.

4 For You have broken the yoke of his burden
And the staff of his shoulder,
The rod of his oppressor,
As in the day of ᶠMidian.

5 For every warrior's sandal from the noisy battle,
And garments rolled in blood,
ᵍWill be used for burning *and* fuel of fire.

6 ʰFor unto us a Child is born,
Unto us a ⁱSon is given;
And ʲthe government will be upon His shoulder,
And His name will be called
ᵏWonderful, Counselor, ˡMighty God,
Everlasting Father, ᵐPrince of Peace.

7 Of the increase of *His* government and peace
ⁿ*There will be* no end,
Upon the throne of David and over His kingdom,
To order it and establish it with judgment and justice
From that time forward, even forever.
The ᵒzeal of the LORD of hosts will perform this.

---

* **9:3** Following Qere and Targum; Kethib and Vulgate read *not increased joy;* Septuagint reads *Most of the people You brought down in Your joy.*

---

the dead in order to influence events. This practice, as well as the use of any mediums or spiritists, was strictly forbidden (Deut. 18:9–14).
9:1 *lightly esteemed.* The ancient tribal allotments of Zebulun and Naphtali (Josh. 19:10–16,32–39), which included Galilee, were the first to feel the brunt of the Assyrian invasions (2 Kin. 15:29). ***the way of the sea, beyond the Jordan, in Galilee of the Gentiles.*** These three phrases indicate administrative districts of the Assyrian conqueror Tiglath-Pileser III as a result of the three campaigns he waged in the west around 733 B.C. The city of Capernaum is "by the way of the sea," (Galilee) in the region of Zebulun and Naphtali. This is where Jesus began His ministry, in fulfillment of the prophecy of Isaiah 9:1–2 (Matt. 4:15–16).
9:2 *Have seen a great light.* The light stands for God's blessings, presence, and revelation, fulfilled in Jesus who came in the flesh (Matt. 4:15–16). The coming of Jesus revealed the mercy and grace of God in the same way that the rising sun reveals the nature of the land it shines upon. All history is labeled from that definitive moment: before the Light, or after the Light (John 1:9).
9:6–7 *a Child.* In this triumphant song Isaiah rejoices as though the promised Child of the house of David has already been born. The Child's birthright involves authority and rule, while His character is depicted with descriptive names. As "Wonderful" and "Counselor," He represents the sum of wisdom and knowledge, and His divinity is established clearly by the title "Mighty God." The Fatherhood of the Messiah is eternal, which again demonstrates His identity with God (John 10:30). Finally, as the "Prince of Peace" He brings peace into the world by His atoning death on the cross, paying the price of human sin and

reconciling us to God. The line of David will be the human line for the source of these blessings (2 Sam. 7:8–16; Luke 1:32–33), and the divine nature of the Messiah will guarantee their permanence.
9:7 The Son of God—In Luke 24:25–27 Jesus goes to great lengths to help two of His disciples understand what the Jewish Scriptures (the Old Testament) said about Him. Throughout the Old Testament there are numerous passages that point towards Jesus Christ in several ways. This prophecy in Isaiah is one of the most important of these passages. Here He is spoken of as a son before He became a man (see also Gal. 4:4). Micah prophesies His birth, but also states that His "goings forth are from of old, from everlasting" (Mic. 5:2). John says that He existed "in the beginning" before anything was created (John 1:1–3).
Even before He was born of Mary, He appeared to men in the Old Testament as the "Angel of the LORD." It is clear that this is no ordinary angel because He is identified as God (Ex. 3:2). He pardons sin (Ex. 23:20–21), and He is worshiped (Josh. 5:13–15). While these passages do not say that this member of the Godhead was the preincarnate Christ, we may conclude that they are the same person since their work is the same.
While Christ occasionally appeared to men in the Old Testament, He took on a physical, human body when He was conceived in Mary's womb. This incomparable event of God's becoming man in Jesus Christ

---

8:21 ʸRev. 16:11 **9:1** ᵃIs. 8:22 ᵇ2 Kin. 15:29 ᶜMatt. 4:13–16 **9:2** ᵈMatt. 4:16 **9:3** ᵉJudg. 5:30 **9:4** ᶠJudg. 7:22 **9:5** ᵍIs. 66:15 **9:6** ʰ[Luke 2:11] ⁱ[John 3:16] ʲ[Matt. 28:18] ᵏJudg. 13:18 ˡTitus 2:13 ᵐEph. 2:14 **9:7** ⁿDan. 2:44 ᵒIs. 37:32

The Punishment of Samaria

8 The Lord sent a word against pJacob,
And it has fallen on Israel.
9 All the people will know—
Ephraim and the inhabitant of
Samaria—
Who say in pride and arrogance of
heart:
10 "The bricks have fallen down,
But we will rebuild with hewn
stones;
The sycamores are cut down,
But we will replace *them* with cedars."
11 Therefore the LORD shall set up
The adversaries of Rezin against him,
And spur his enemies on,
12 The Syrians before and the Philistines
behind;
And they shall devour Israel with an
open mouth.

For all this His anger is not turned
away,
But His hand *is* stretched out still.

13 For the people do not turn to Him who
strikes them,
Nor do they seek the LORD of hosts.
14 Therefore the LORD will cut off head
and tail from Israel,
Palm branch and bulrush qin one day.
15 The elder and honorable, he *is* the head;
The prophet who teaches lies, he *is*
the tail.
16 For rthe leaders of this people cause
them to err,
And *those who are* led by them are
destroyed.
17 Therefore the Lord swill have no joy in
their young men,
Nor have mercy on their fatherless and
widows;
For everyone *is* a hypocrite and an
evildoer,
And every mouth speaks folly.

tFor all this His anger is not turned
away,
But His hand *is* stretched out still.

18 For wickedness uburns as the fire;
It shall devour the briers and thorns,
And kindle in the thickets of the
forest;
They shall mount up *like* rising smoke.
19 Through the wrath of the LORD of
hosts
vThe land is burned up,
And the people shall be as fuel for the
fire;
wNo man shall spare his brother.
20 And he shall snatch on the right
hand
And be hungry;
He shall devour on the left hand
xAnd not be satisfied;
yEvery man shall eat the flesh of his
own arm.
21 Manasseh *shall devour* Ephraim, and
Ephraim Manasseh;
Together they *shall be* zagainst Judah.

aFor all this His anger is not turned
away,
But His hand *is* stretched out still.

10 "Woe to those who adecree
unrighteous decrees,
Who write misfortune,
Which they have prescribed
2 To rob the needy of justice,
And to take what is right from the
poor of My people,
That widows may be their prey,
And *that* they may rob the fatherless.
3 bWhat will you do in cthe day of
punishment,
And in the desolation *which* will come
from dafar?
To whom will you flee for help?
And where will you leave your
glory?

---

is called the incarnation. This miracle was prophesied hundreds of years previously (7:14) and was fulfilled historically when Christ was born (Luke 2:7). Thus Christ, the sinless God-man, was qualified to become our Redeemer (2 Cor. 5:21).

As a man, Christ experienced normal physical, mental, social, and spiritual growth as others did (Luke 2:52). He had pain, hunger, thirst, fatigue, temptation, pleasure, rest, and even lack of knowledge (Mark 13:32). Because of His complete humanity He can be sympathetic and compassionate toward us (Heb. 4:15).

While Christ was fully man He was also fully God, as these facts indicate: He is called God (John 1:1; Heb. 1:8); He did works that only God could do, such as forgive sins (Mark 2:7) and create (Col. 1:16); He had attributes that only God could have, such as truth (John 14:6) and omniscience (John 2:24–25); and He claimed equality with God (John 10:30).

The question may be raised as to whether Christ lost anything of deity when He became a man (Phil. 2:6–8). While there is an inscrutable mystery involved in this unparalleled act of condescension, one can be

certain that He lost none of God's attributes, because He was still God (John 20:28). He is fully God and fully man united in one person forever. Even now, at the right hand of God, He is the God-man (1 Tim. 2:5). The great condescension of the Son of God in becoming a man serves eternally as a perfect model of humility and self-giving love (Phil. 2:8).

9:8 word against Jacob. The message was a judgment against the northern kingdom. The Lord would destroy it and its capital, Samaria.

10:1 Woe. Woe is a chilling word when spoken by God (5:8–23; 10:5). The leaders who make laws that affect a community for good or evil bear a fearful responsibility before God, whether they acknowledge it or not.

10:3 from afar. The Assyrians were the devastation that came from afar.

9:8 pGen. 32:28   **9:14** qRev. 18:8   **9:16** rIs. 3:12
9:17 sPs. 147:10   tIs. 5:25   **9:18** uMal. 4:1   **9:19** vIs. 8:22
wMic. 7:2, 6   **9:20** xLev. 26:26   yJer. 19:9   **9:21** z2 Chr.
28:6, 8   aIs. 9:12, 17   **10:1** aPs. 58:2   **10:3** bJob 31:14
cHos. 9:7   dIs. 5:26

4 Without Me they shall bow down
among the [e]prisoners,
And they shall fall among the slain."

[f]For all this His anger is not turned
away,
But His hand *is* stretched out still.

Arrogant Assyria Also Judged

5 "Woe to Assyria, [g]the rod of My anger
And the staff in whose hand is My
indignation.
6 I will send him against [h]an ungodly
nation,
And against the people of My wrath
I will [i]give him charge,
To seize the spoil, to take the prey,
And to tread them down like the mire
of the streets.
7 [j]Yet he does not mean so,
Nor does his heart think so;
But *it is* in his heart to destroy,
And cut off not a few nations.
8 [k]For he says,
'*Are* not my princes altogether kings?
9 *Is* not [l]Calno [m]like Carchemish?
Is not Hamath like Arpad?
Is not Samaria [n]like Damascus?
10 As my hand has found the kingdoms
of the idols,
Whose carved images excelled those
of Jerusalem and Samaria,
11 As I have done to Samaria and her
idols,
Shall I not do also to Jerusalem and
her idols?'"

12 Therefore it shall come to pass, when
the Lord has performed all His work [o]on
Mount Zion and on Jerusalem, *that He will
say,* [p]"I will punish the fruit of the arrogant
heart of the king of Assyria, and the glory
of his haughty looks."
13 [q]For he says:

"By the strength of my hand I have
done *it,*
And by my wisdom, for I am
prudent;
Also I have removed the boundaries of
the people,
And have robbed their treasuries;
So I have put down the inhabitants
like a valiant *man.*
14 [r]My hand has found like a nest the
riches of the people,
And as one gathers eggs *that are* left,
I have gathered all the earth;
And there was no one who moved *his*
wing,
Nor opened *his* mouth with even a peep."

15 Shall [s]the ax boast itself against him
who chops with it?
Or shall the saw exalt itself against
him who saws with it?
As if a rod could wield *itself* against
those who lift it up,
Or as if a staff could lift up, *as if it
were* not wood!
16 Therefore the Lord, the Lord* of hosts,
Will send leanness among his fat ones;
And under his glory
He will kindle a burning
Like the burning of a fire.
17 So the Light of Israel will be for a fire,
And his Holy One for a flame;
[t]It will burn and devour
His thorns and his briers in one day.
18 And it will consume the glory of his
forest and of [u]his fruitful field,
Both soul and body;
And they will be as when a sick man
wastes away.
19 Then the rest of the trees of his forest
Will be so few in number
That a child may write them.

The Returning Remnant of Israel

20 And it shall come to pass in that day
That the remnant of Israel,
And such as have escaped of the house
of Jacob,
[v]Will never again depend on him who
defeated them,
But will depend on the LORD, the Holy
One of Israel, in truth.
21 The remnant will return, the remnant
of Jacob,
To the [w]Mighty God.

* **10:16** Following Bomberg; Masoretic Text and Dead Sea Scrolls read *YHWH (the* LORD).

10:5 *Assyria.* Though God uses sinners as instruments of His will (7:17; 13:5), they will still be held accountable for their own wickedness. In this, God shows that He is just in all His ways (Hab. 1–3).
10:6 *an ungodly nation.* The ungodly nation is Judah (vv. 11–12).
10:9 *Calno . . . Damascus.* This is a list of cities that had already fallen to Assyria.
10:10 *idols . . . images.* The Assyrians had conquered the nations who had false gods. Surely, they believed, they would also have an easy time against "Jerusalem and her idols." Only the living God was to be worshiped by the Israelites, but they had repeatedly broken that command (Ex. 20:4–6; Judg. 2:19).
10:15 *Shall the ax boast.* The ax that boasted was the Assyrian army. They were an instrument in the hands of God.
10:16 *his fat ones.* The fat warriors who come under judgment are the Assyrians.
10:20 *remnant.* The Hebrew word used here for "remnant" is different than the word used in 1:9. The difference may be considered slight; it is the difference between those who were left, or remained (10:20,22), and those who survived (1:9).

10:4 [e] Is. 24:22 [f] Is. 5:25 **10:5** [g] Jer. 51:20 **10:6** [h] Is. 9:17 [i] Jer. 34:22 **10:7** [j] Gen. 50:20 **10:8** [k] 2 Kin. 19:10 **10:9** [l] Amos 6:2 [m] 2 Chr. 35:20 [n] 2 Kin. 16:9 **10:12** [o] 2 Kin. 19:31 [p] Jer. 50:18 **10:13** [q] Is. 37:24–27 **10:14** [r] Job 31:25 **10:15** [s] Jer. 51:20 **10:17** [t] Is. 9:18 **10:18** [u] 2 Kin. 19:23 **10:20** [v] 2 Kin. 16:7 **10:21** [w] [Is. 9:6]

22 ˣFor though your people, O Israel, be as
the sand of the sea,
ʸA remnant of them will return;
The destruction decreed shall
overflow with righteousness.
23 ᶻFor the Lord GOD of hosts
Will make a determined end
In the midst of all the land.

24Therefore thus says the Lord GOD of
hosts: "O My people, who dwell in Zion,
ᵃdo not be afraid of the Assyrian. He shall
strike you with a rod and lift up his staff
against you, in the manner of ᵇEgypt. 25For
yet a very little while ᶜand the indignation
will cease, as will My anger in their destruction." 26And the LORD of hosts will
stir up ᵈa scourge for him like the slaughter
of ᵉMidian at the rock of Oreb; ᶠas His rod
was on the sea, so will He lift it up in the
manner of Egypt.

27 It shall come to pass in that day
That his burden will be taken away
from your shoulder,
And his yoke from your neck,
And the yoke will be destroyed
because of ᵍthe anointing oil.

28 He has come to Aiath,
He has passed Migron;
At Michmash he has attended to his
equipment.
29 They have gone along ʰthe ridge,
They have taken up lodging at Geba.
Ramah is afraid,
ⁱGibeah of Saul has fled.
30 Lift up your voice,
O daughter ʲof Gallim!
Cause it to be heard as far as ᵏLaish—
O poor Anathoth!*
31 ˡMadmenah has fled,
The inhabitants of Gebim seek refuge.

32 As yet he will remain ᵐat Nob that
day;
He will ⁿshake his fist at the mount of
ᵒthe daughter of Zion,
The hill of Jerusalem.

33 Behold, the Lord,
The LORD of hosts,
Will lop off the bough with terror;
ᵖThose of high stature *will be* hewn
down,
And the haughty will be humbled.
34 He will cut down the thickets of the
forest with iron,
And Lebanon will fall by the Mighty
One.

The Reign of Jesse's Offspring

11 There ᵃshall come forth a Rod from
the stem of ᵇJesse,
And ᶜa Branch shall grow out of his
roots.
2 ᵈThe Spirit of the LORD shall rest upon
Him,
The Spirit of wisdom and
understanding,
The Spirit of counsel and might,
The Spirit of knowledge and of the
fear of the LORD.

3 His delight *is* in the fear of the LORD,
And He shall not judge by the sight of
His eyes,
Nor decide by the hearing of His ears;
4 But ᵉwith righteousness He shall judge
the poor,
And decide with equity for the meek of
the earth;

* **10:30** Following Masoretic Text, Targum, and
Vulgate; Septuagint and Syriac read *Listen to her,
O Anathoth.*

10:22 A remnant. Most of the people of the northern kingdom were carried off into captivity. But some
Israelites made their way to Judah and became part
of the southern kingdom. These people and their
descendants would act as a remnant by preserving
the names of the northern tribes among the people
of God.
10:28–32 Aiath . . . Jerusalem. These verses depict
Isaiah's vision of the king of Assyria's relentless march
south over difficult terrain from Aiath (or Ai), which
was ten miles north of Jerusalem on a point over-
looking the city. The cities as listed in these verses are
closer and closer to the capital at Jerusalem.
10:32 he. "He" refers to Assyria, the enemy.
10:33–34 bough . . . thickets. The bough and the
thickets are the Assyrian leaders and the Assyrian
army. The point is that God will bring judgment on
the instruments He used to judge Israel.
11:1 a Rod from the stem of Jesse. Jesse was King
David's father (1 Sam. 16:10–13). As David inaugurated a kingdom of righteousness and peace, the
new David—the "rod" or "root" (53:2) from David's
line—will establish an incomparably greater kingdom. The words "rod" and "root" are messianic terms.
They are figurative words for the great descendant
of the household of David, the Seed of the woman

promised in Genesis 3:15, Jesus Christ Himself (Matt.
1:17).
11:2 Spirit. As in the case of David (1 Sam. 16:13), the
Messiah would be empowered by the Holy Spirit (4:4;
42:1; 48:16; 59:21; 61:1; Luke 3:22), who was the Agent
for establishing God's kingdom (Gen. 1:1–2; Judg.
3:10; 6:34; 1 Sam. 10:6). **wisdom and understanding.**
The Messiah will be the ideal king. He will embody
the administrative skill to govern with righteousness
and justice far more than even Solomon (1 Kin. 3:9),
who asked for those gifts when he became king.
counsel. The Holy Spirit's "counsel" is not advice, but
authoritative plans and decisions. **fear of the LORD.**
The Messiah would demonstrate in all His life the correct response to God; He would honor and obey Him
(Ex. 20:20).
11:4 judge. In this context, judge does not mean to

10:22 ˣ Rom. 9:27, 28 ʸ Is. 6:13 **10:23** ᶻ Dan.
9:27 **10:24** ᵃ Is. 7:4; 12:2 ᵇ Ex. 14 **10:25** ᶜ Dan.
11:36 **10:26** ᵈ 2 Kin. 19:35 ᵉ Is. 9:4 ᶠ Ex. 14:26,
27 **10:27** ᵍ Ps. 105:15 **10:29** ʰ 1 Sam. 13:23 ⁱ 1 Sam.
11:4 **10:30** ʲ 1 Sam. 25:44 ᵏ Judg. 18:7 **10:31** ˡ Josh.
15:31 **10:32** ᵐ 1 Sam. 21:1 ⁿ Is. 13:2 ᵒ Is. 37:22
10:33 ᵖ Amos 2:9 **11:1** ᵃ [Zech. 6:12] ᵇ [Acts 13:23] ᶜ Is.
4:2 **11:2** ᵈ [John 1:32] **11:4** ᵉ Rev. 19:11

He shall [f]strike the earth with the rod of His mouth,
And with the breath of His lips He shall slay the wicked.

5 Righteousness shall be the belt of His loins,
And faithfulness the belt of His waist.

6 "The[g] wolf also shall dwell with the lamb,
The leopard shall lie down with the young goat,
The calf and the young lion and the fatling together;
And a little child shall lead them.

7 The cow and the bear shall graze;
Their young ones shall lie down together;
And the lion shall eat straw like the ox.

8 The nursing child shall play by the cobra's hole,
And the weaned child shall put his hand in the viper's den.

9 [h]They shall not hurt nor destroy in all My holy mountain,
For [i]the earth shall be full of the knowledge of the LORD
As the waters cover the sea.

10 "And[j] in that day [k]there shall be a Root of Jesse,
Who shall stand as a [l]banner to the people;
For the [m]Gentiles shall seek Him,
And His resting place shall be glorious."

11 It shall come to pass in that day
That the Lord shall set His hand again the second time
To recover the remnant of His people who are left,
[n]From Assyria and Egypt,
From Pathros and Cush,
From Elam and Shinar,
From Hamath and the islands of the sea.

12 He will set up a banner for the nations,
And will assemble the outcasts of Israel,
And gather together [o]the dispersed of Judah
From the four corners of the earth.

13 Also [p]the envy of Ephraim shall depart,
And the adversaries of Judah shall be cut off;
Ephraim shall not envy Judah,
And Judah shall not harass Ephraim.

14 But they shall fly down upon the shoulder of the Philistines toward the west;
Together they shall plunder the people of the East;
[q]They shall lay their hand on Edom and Moab;
And the people of Ammon shall obey them.

15 The LORD [r]will utterly destroy* the tongue of the Sea of Egypt;
With His mighty wind He will shake His fist over the River,*
And strike it in the seven streams,
And make *men* cross over dry-shod.

16 [s]There will be a highway for the remnant of His people
Who will be left from Assyria,
[t]As it was for Israel
In the day that he came up from the land of Egypt.

A Hymn of Praise

12 And [a]in that day you will say:

"O LORD, I will praise You;
Though You were angry with me,
Your anger is turned away, and You comfort me.

2 Behold, God *is* my salvation,
I will trust and not be afraid;
[b]'For [c]YAH, the LORD, *is* my strength and song;
He also has become my salvation.' "*

---

* **11:15** Following Masoretic Text and Vulgate; Septuagint, Syriac, and Targum read *dry up.* • That is, the Euphrates   * **12:2** Exodus 15:2

---

bring people to account, but to act on their behalf. As the Judge of His people, God sentences the wicked and offers protection and defense for the innocent and oppressed. **rod of His mouth . . . breath of His lips.** This concept is repeated in Revelation 19:15, when the Lord Jesus returns with power and great glory.
11:6–9 wolf also shall dwell with the lamb . . . shall not hurt nor destroy. This picture of cruel beasts regenerated with a new nature that makes them protect their natural prey portrays a reign of peace and security. This can only be realized in the return of the Messiah to establish the kingdom of God (65:17–25; Rev. 21:1–8).
11:10 the Gentiles. The revelation of the Messiah is for people of all nations.
11:11 the second time. The "second time" may refer to the remnant coming back to the land in 538 B.C., in

contrast to the first exodus from Egypt. Beyond that, it could also refer to the remnant's coming to Christ in the present age (Rom. 11:5) or to its future return to Christ (Rom. 11:11–27; Rev. 7:4–8).
12:1 in that day. The day refers to the day that the Lord rescues His people, whether it was the return of the remnant or the future return of Christ as portrayed in the Book of Revelation.
12:2 my strength and song. This psalm of redemption is based on the first psalm of redemption in Exodus (Ex. 15:2; Ps. 118:14).

11:4 [f] Job 4:9   **11:6** [g] Hos. 2:18   **11:9** [h] Job 5:23 [i] Hab. 2:14   **11:10** [j] Is. 2:11 [k] Rom. 15:12 [l] Is. 27:12, 13 [m] Rom. 15:10   **11:11** [n] Zech. 10:10   **11:12** [o] John 7:35 **11:13** [p] Jer. 3:18   **11:14** [q] Dan. 11:41   **11:15** [r] Zech. 10:10, 11   **11:16** [s] Is. 19:23 [t] Ex. 14:29   **12:1** [a] Is. 2:11 **12:2** [b] Ps. 83:18 [c] Ex. 15:2

3 Therefore with joy you will draw ᵈwater
From the wells of salvation.

⁴And in that day you will say:

ᵉ"Praise the LORD, call upon His name;
ᶠDeclare His deeds among the peoples,
Make mention that His ᵍname is
exalted.
5 ʰSing to the LORD,
For He has done excellent things;
This is known in all the earth.
6 ⁱCry out and shout, O inhabitant of
Zion,
For great is ʲthe Holy One of Israel in
your midst!"

Proclamation Against Babylon

13 The ᵃburden against Babylon which
Isaiah the son of Amoz saw.

2 "Liftᵇ up a banner ᶜon the high
mountain,
Raise your voice to them;
ᵈWave your hand, that they may enter
the gates of the nobles.
3 I have commanded My sanctified ones;
I have also called ᵉMy mighty ones for
My anger—
Those who ᶠrejoice in My exaltation."

4 The ᵍnoise of a multitude in the
mountains,
Like that of many people!
A tumultuous noise of the kingdoms of
nations gathered together!
The LORD of hosts musters
The army for battle.
5 They come from a far country,
From the end of heaven—
The ʰLORD and His weapons of
indignation,
To destroy the whole ⁱland.
6 Wail, ʲfor the day of the LORD is at hand!
ᵏIt will come as destruction from the
Almighty.
7 Therefore all hands will be limp,
Every man's heart will melt,

8 And they will be afraid.
ˡPangs and sorrows will take hold of
them;
They will be in pain as a woman in
childbirth;
They will be amazed at one another;
Their faces will be like flames.

9 Behold, ᵐthe day of the LORD comes,
Cruel, with both wrath and fierce
anger,
To lay the land desolate;
And He will destroy ⁿits sinners from it.
10 For the stars of heaven and their
constellations
Will not give their light;
The sun will be ᵒdarkened in its going
forth,
And the moon will not cause its light
to shine.

11 "I will ᵖpunish the world for its evil,
And the wicked for their iniquity;
qI will halt the arrogance of the proud,
And will lay low the haughtiness of
the terrible.
12 I will make a mortal more rare than
fine gold,
A man more than the golden wedge of
Ophir.
13 ʳTherefore I will shake the heavens,
And the earth will move out of her
place,
In the wrath of the LORD of hosts
And in ˢthe day of His fierce anger.
14 It shall be as the hunted gazelle,
And as a sheep that no man takes up;
ᵗEvery man will turn to his own people,
And everyone will flee to his own
land.
15 Everyone who is found will be thrust
through,
And everyone who is captured will fall
by the sword.
16 Their children also will be ᵘdashed to
pieces before their eyes;
Their houses will be plundered
And their wives ᵛravished.

12:3 wells of salvation. In an arid land, the provision of wells and springs was regarded as a divine gift. Hebrew poets often associate water with salvation (Ex. 17:1–7).

13:1 burden . . . which Isaiah . . . saw. The Book of Isaiah takes a major turn at chapter 13, which continues through chapter 27. The focus in this extended section is first on the Lord's judgments against the nations, through chapter 23, followed by an end-time prophecy in chapters 24–27. **Babylon.** Babylon was the crown jewel of the Assyrian Empire. This burden may refer to its destruction around 689 B.C. when Sennacherib quelled a rebellion there. Yet the Lord's overthrow of Babylon, the "glory of kingdoms" (v. 19), symbolizes His triumph over the world (v. 11). Babylon is the epitome of religion and culture in the ancient Middle East. Thus the burden is aimed against all nations, especially Assyria (14:24–27). Peter uses the term Babylon symbolically in the New Testament (1 Pet. 5:13), as does John (Rev. 14:8; 18:2,10–21).

13:6 the day of the LORD. This designated "day" refers to a time of unusual activity of God in the lives of people, for judgment or for mercy. **is at hand.** The basic idea of this term is not that of approaching a fixed date, but that the day of the Lord is about to burst into one's world. The day of the Lord is imminent—able to happen at any time—not because people have almost reached it as a destination, but because it may burst in upon people without further warning.

12:3 ᵈ [John 4:10, 14; 7:37, 38]   **12:4** ᵉ 1 Chr. 16:8   ᶠ Ps. 145:4–6   ᵍ Ps. 34:3   **12:5** ʰ Ex. 15:1   **12:6** ⁱ Zeph. 3:14, 15   ʲ Ps. 89:18   **13:1** ᵃ Jer. 50; 51   **13:2** ᵇ Is. 18:3   ᶜ Jer. 51:25   ᵈ Is. 10:32   **13:3** ᵉ Joel 3:11   ᶠ Ps. 149:2   **13:4** ᵍ Is. 17:12   **13:5** ʰ Is. 42:13   ⁱ Is. 24:1; 34:2   **13:6** ʲ Zeph. 1:7   ᵏ Joel 1:15   **13:8** ˡ Ps. 48:6   **13:9** ᵐ Mal. 4:1   ⁿ Prov. 2:22   **13:10** ᵒ Joel 2:31   **13:11** ᵖ Is. 26:21   q [Is. 2:17]   **13:13** ʳ Hag. 2:6   ˢ Lam. 1:12   **13:14** ᵗ Jer. 50:16; 51:9   **13:16** ᵘ Nah. 3:10   ᵛ Zech. 14:2

17 "Behold,ʷ I will stir up the Medes
against them,
Who will not regard silver;
And *as for* gold, they will not delight
in it.
18 Also *their* bows will dash the young
men to pieces,
And they will have no pity on the fruit
of the womb;
Their eye will not spare children.
19 ˣAnd Babylon, the glory of kingdoms,
The beauty of the Chaldeans' pride,
Will be as when God overthrew
ʸSodom and Gomorrah.
20 ᶻIt will never be inhabited,
Nor will it be settled from generation
to generation;
Nor will the Arabian pitch tents there,
Nor will the shepherds make their
sheepfolds there.
21 ᵃBut wild beasts of the desert will lie
there,
And their houses will be full of owls;
Ostriches will dwell there,
And wild goats will caper there.
22 The hyenas will howl in their citadels,
And jackals in their pleasant palaces.
ᵇHer time *is* near to come,
And her days will not be prolonged."

Mercy on Jacob

14 For the LORD ᵃwill have mercy on Jacob, and ᵇwill still choose Israel, and
settle them in their own land. ᶜThe strangers will be joined with them, and they will
cling to the house of Jacob. 2Then people
will take them ᵈand bring them to their
place, and the house of Israel will possess
them for servants and maids in the land
of the LORD; they will take them captive
whose captives they were, ᵉand rule over
their oppressors.

Fall of the King of Babylon

3It shall come to pass in the day the LORD
gives you rest from your sorrow, and from
your fear and the hard bondage in which

you were made to serve, 4that you ᶠwill take
up this proverb against the king of Babylon, and say:

"How the oppressor has ceased,
The ᵍgolden* city ceased!
5 The LORD has broken ʰthe staff of the
wicked,
The scepter of the rulers;
6 He who struck the people in wrath
with a continual stroke,
He who ruled the nations in anger,
Is persecuted *and* no one hinders.
7 The whole earth is at rest *and* quiet;
They break forth into singing.
8 ᶦIndeed the cypress trees rejoice over
you,
And the cedars of Lebanon,
Saying, 'Since you were cut down,
No woodsman has come up against us.'

9 "Hellʲ from beneath is excited about you,
To meet *you* at your coming;
It stirs up the dead for you,
All the chief ones of the earth;
It has raised up from their thrones
All the kings of the nations.
10 They all shall ᵏspeak and say to you:
'Have you also become as weak as we?
Have you become like us?'
11 Your pomp is brought down to Sheol,
And the sound of your stringed
instruments;
The maggot is spread under you,
And worms cover you.'

The Fall of Lucifer

12 "Howˡ you are fallen from heaven,
O Lucifer,* son of the morning!
How you are cut down to the ground,
You who weakened the nations!
13 For you have said in your heart:
ᵐ'I will ascend into heaven,
ⁿI will exalt my throne above the stars
of God;

---

* 14:4 Or *insolent*   * 14:12 Literally *Day Star*

13:21–22 owls...jackals. With the exception of the goat, all of the animals mentioned in these verses are unclean. This image created a clear message to the people of Israel of a place that was desolate and unfit to inhabit.
14:4 Babylon. Babylon is often used in Scripture for Satan's kingdom. This passage can be read with a double point of view. One, as if it were talking about an unnamed political king; and two, as a reference to and description of Satan's career. Both views are sobering and worth taking note of.
14:8 the cypress trees rejoice. The trees will no longer be cut down to construct machines of war.
14:9 Hell from beneath is excited. The commotion in the "grave" when the king of Babylon (or Satan; see Rev. 20:1–3) arrives contrasts sharply with the rest on earth when he is gone (v. 7).
14:12 fallen from heaven. This is a figure of speech meaning cast down from an exalted political position. Jesus said, "And you, Capernaum, who are

exalted to heaven, will be brought down to Hades" (Luke 10:15); and, apparently with the same meaning, "I saw Satan fall like lightning from heaven" (Luke 10:18). The "son of the morning," called Lucifer or Day Star in Hebrew, is the planet Venus. The poetic language of this verse describes the aspiration of this brightest star to climb to the zenith of the heavens and its extinction before the rising sun. This is an apt summary of the failed goal of Satan (or the king of Babylon, v. 4), who wanted to grasp universal and eternal domination (Ezek. 28:14–16; Rev. 12:12–13; 20:2).

13:17 ʷ Dan. 5:28, 31   **13:19** ˣ Is. 14:4 ʸ Gen. 19:24
13:20 ᶻ Jer. 50:3   **13:21** ᵃ Is. 34:11–15   **13:22** ᵇ Jer.
51:33   **14:1** ᵃ Ps. 102:13 ᵇ Zech. 1:17; 2:12 ᶜ Is. 60:4, 5,
10   **14:2** ᵈ Is. 49:22; 60:9; 66:20 ᵉ Is. 60:14   **14:4** ᶠ Hab.
2:6 ᵍ Rev. 18:16   **14:5** ʰ Ps. 125:3   **14:8** ᶦ Ezek. 31:16
14:9 ʲ Ezek. 32:21   **14:10** ᵏ Ezek. 32:21   **14:12** ˡ Is. 34:4
14:13 ᵐ Ezek. 28:2 ⁿ Dan. 8:10

I will also sit on the [o]mount of the congregation
[p]On the farthest sides of the north;
14 I will ascend above the heights of the clouds,
[q]I will be like the Most High.'
15 Yet you [r]shall be brought down to Sheol,
To the lowest depths of the Pit.

16 "Those who see you will gaze at you,
And consider you, *saying:*
'*Is* this the man who made the earth tremble,
Who shook kingdoms,
17 Who made the world as a wilderness
And destroyed its cities,
Who did not open the house of his prisoners?'

18 "All the kings of the nations,
All of them, sleep in glory,
Everyone in his own house;
19 But you are cast out of your grave
Like an abominable branch,
Like the garment of those who are slain,
Thrust through with a sword,
Who go down to the stones of the pit,
Like a corpse trodden underfoot.
20 You will not be joined with them in burial,
Because you have destroyed your land
And slain your people.
[s]The brood of evildoers shall never be named.
21 Prepare slaughter for his children
[t]Because of the iniquity of their fathers,
Lest they rise up and possess the land,
And fill the face of the world with cities."

Babylon Destroyed

22 "For I will rise up against them," says the LORD of hosts,
"And cut off from Babylon [u]the name and [v]remnant,
[w]And offspring and posterity," says the LORD.
23 "I will also make it a possession for the [x]porcupine,
And marshes of muddy water;
I will sweep it with the broom of destruction," says the LORD of hosts.

Assyria Destroyed

24 The LORD of hosts has sworn, saying,
"Surely, as I have thought, so it shall come to pass,
And as I have purposed, *so* it shall [y]stand:
25 That I will break the [z]Assyrian in My land,
And on My mountains tread him underfoot.
Then [a]his yoke shall be removed from them,
And his burden removed from their shoulders.
26 This *is* the [b]purpose that is purposed against the whole earth,
And this *is* the hand that is stretched out over all the nations.
27 For the LORD of hosts has [c]purposed,
And who will annul *it?*
His hand *is* stretched out,
And who will turn it back?"

Philistia Destroyed

28 This is the burden which came in the year that [d]King Ahaz died.

29 "Do not rejoice, all you of Philistia,
[e]Because the rod that struck you is broken;
For out of the serpent's roots will come forth a viper,
[f]And its offspring *will be* a fiery flying serpent.
30 The firstborn of the poor will feed,
And the needy will lie down in safety;
I will kill your roots with famine,
And it will slay your remnant.
31 Wail, O gate! Cry, O city!
All you of Philistia *are* dissolved;
For smoke will come from the north,
And no one *will be* alone in his appointed times."

32 What will they answer the messengers of the nation?
That [g]the LORD has founded Zion,
And [h]the poor of His people shall take refuge in it.

14:14 *I will be like the Most High.* This is the most outrageous of the arrogant desires of Satan (or of this unnamed king). He wanted to surpass the Most High, a term for the Lord that is often used in connection with the nations of the world (Ps. 87:5; 91:1; 92:1). This statement strongly speaks of Satan (v. 12), who purposes to work against God in every possible way. Satan's sin is centered in pride, the desire to be in submission to no one, not even God (1 Tim. 3:6). Ezekiel saw Satan's work in the king of Tyre (Ezek. 28), and Isaiah sees the parallel between the character and goals of Satan and this unnamed Babylonian king.

14:28 *Ahaz.* King Ahaz died in 720 B.C.

14:29 *rod.* The rod is probably a metaphor for the Assyrian king (10:5).

14:31 *gate.* The gate of a walled city was its weakest point. When the gate fell, the city could be taken. ***from the north.*** The Assyrian army would come from the north.

14:13 [o] Ezek. 28:14 [p] Ps. 48:2 **14:14** [q] 2 Thess. 2:4 **14:15** [r] Matt. 11:23 **14:20** [s] Ps. 21:10; 109:13 **14:21** [t] Ex. 20:5 **14:22** [u] Prov. 10:7 [v] 1 Kin. 14:10 [w] Job 18:19 **14:23** [x] Zeph. 2:14 **14:24** [y] Is. 43:13 **14:25** [z] Mic. 5:5, 6 [a] Is. 10:27 **14:26** [b] Is. 23:9 **14:27** [c] Dan. 4:31, 35 **14:28** [d] 2 Kin. 16:20 **14:29** [e] 2 Chr. 26:6 [f] 2 Kin. 18:8 **14:32** [g] Ps. 87:1, 5 [h] Zech. 11:11

Proclamation Against Moab

15 The ^aburden against Moab.

Because in the night ^bAr of ^cMoab is
laid waste
And destroyed,
Because in the night Kir of Moab is
laid waste
And destroyed,

2 He has gone up to the temple* and
Dibon,
To the high places to weep.
Moab will wail over Nebo and over
Medeba;
^dOn all their heads *will be* baldness,
And every beard cut off.

3 In their streets they will clothe
themselves with sackcloth;
On the tops of their houses
And in their streets
Everyone will wail, ^eweeping bitterly.

4 Heshbon and Elealeh will cry out,
Their voice shall be heard as far as
^fJahaz;
Therefore the armed soldiers* of Moab
will cry out;
His life will be burdensome to him.

5 "My^g heart will cry out for Moab;
His fugitives *shall flee* to Zoar,
Like a three-year-old heifer.*
For ^hby the Ascent of Luhith
They will go up with weeping;
For in the way of Horonaim
They will raise up a cry of destruction,

6 For the waters ⁱof Nimrim will be
desolate,
For the green grass has withered away;
The grass fails, there is nothing green.

7 Therefore the abundance they have
gained,
And what they have laid up,
They will carry away to the Brook of
the Willows.

8 For the cry has gone all around the
borders of Moab,
Its wailing to Eglaim
And its wailing to Beer Elim.

9 For the waters of Dimon* will be full of
blood;
Because I will bring more upon Dimon,*

^jLions upon him who escapes from
Moab,
And on the remnant of the land."

Moab Destroyed

16 Send ^athe lamb to the ruler of the
land,
^bFrom Sela to the wilderness,
To the mount of the daughter of Zion.

2 For it shall be as a ^cwandering bird
thrown out of the nest;
So shall be the daughters of Moab at
the fords of the ^dArnon.

3 "Take counsel, execute judgment;
Make your shadow like the night in
the middle of the day;
Hide the outcasts,
Do not betray him who escapes.

4 Let My outcasts dwell with you,
O Moab;
Be a shelter to them from the face of
the spoiler.
For the extortioner is at an end,
Devastation ceases,
The oppressors are consumed out of
the land.

5 In mercy ^ethe throne will be established;
And One will sit on it in truth, in the
tabernacle of David,
^fJudging and seeking justice and
hastening ^grighteousness."

6 We have heard of the ^hpride of Moab—
He is very proud—
Of his haughtiness and his pride and
his wrath;
ⁱBut his lies *shall* not *be* so.

7 Therefore Moab shall ^jwail for Moab;
Everyone shall wail.
For the foundations ^kof Kir Hareseth
you shall mourn;
Surely *they are* stricken.

---

* **15:2** Hebrew *bayith*, literally *house* * **15:4** Following Masoretic Text, Targum, and Vulgate; Septuagint and Syriac read *loins*. * **15:5** Or *The Third Eglath*, an unknown city (compare Jeremiah 48:34) * **15:9** Following Masoretic Text and Targum; Dead Sea Scrolls and Vulgate read *Dibon*; Septuagint reads *Rimon*. • Following Masoretic Text and Targum; Dead Sea Scrolls and Vulgate read *Dibon*; Septuagint reads *Rimon*.

15:1 Moab. For the origin of the people of Moab, see the story of Lot and his daughters in Genesis 19:30–38 (also Num. 22–25; Deut. 1:5).

15:2 high places. High places were sites of pagan worship (16:12).

15:5 heart will cry out. Isaiah does not rejoice in the downfall of Moab. He knew that the judgment from God was righteous, and he remembered that Moab had been a treacherous enemy to his nation, yet his heart cried out in pity. It is the mark of God's people that they do not rejoice in the downfall of the wicked, even though they may be glad to be free from oppression.

15:9 Dimon. The term Dimon sounds like "blood" in Hebrew. **Lions.** Fleeing from one tragedy after another in their flight southward, the refugees

turned to Judah in the west for asylum (16:1–5). A remnant would survive in Moab, as would be the case with Israel (1:9; 6:13; 10:20; 11:16)—but not with Assyria (14:22) and Philistia (14:30).

16:5 the throne will be established. Moab's salvation ultimately lies in the coming one, Jesus the Messiah, whose throne will be established (9:1–7; 11:1–5; Amos 9:11–12; Acts 15:16–17).

16:6 pride. In the end, it was the pride and the

15:1 ^a2 Kin. 3:4 ^bDeut. 2:9 ^cAmos 2:1–3 **15:2** ^dLev. 21:5 **15:3** ^eJer. 48:38 **15:4** ^fJer. 48:34 **15:5** ^gJer. 48:31 ^hJer. 48:5 **15:6** ⁱNum. 32:36 **15:9** ^j2 Kin. 17:25 **16:1** ^a2 Kin. 3:4 ^b2 Kin. 14:7 **16:2** ^cProv. 27:8 ^dNum. 21:13 **16:5** ^e[Dan. 7:14] ^fPs. 72:2 ^gIs. 9:7 **16:6** ^hJer. 48:29 ⁱIs. 28:15 **16:7** ^jJer. 48:20 ^k2 Kin. 3:25

8 For [l]the fields of Heshbon
languish,
And [m]the vine of Sibmah;
The lords of the nations have broken
down its choice plants,
Which have reached to Jazer
And wandered through the
wilderness.
Her branches are stretched out,
They are gone over the [n]sea.
9 Therefore I will bewail the vine of
Sibmah,
With the weeping of Jazer;
I will drench you with my
tears,
[o]O Heshbon and Elealeh;
For battle cries have fallen
Over your summer fruits and your
harvest.

10 [p]Gladness is taken away,
And joy from the plentiful field;
In the vineyards there will be no
singing,
Nor will there be shouting;
No treaders will tread out wine in the
presses;
I have made their shouting
cease.
11 Therefore [q]my heart shall resound like
a harp for Moab,
And my inner being for Kir Heres.

12 And it shall come to pass,
When it is seen that Moab is weary on
[r]the high place,
That he will come to his sanctuary to
pray;
But he will not prevail.

13 This *is* the word which the LORD has
spoken concerning Moab since that time.
14 But now the LORD has spoken, saying,
"Within three years, [s]as the years of a
hired man, the glory of Moab will be
despised with all that great multitude,
and the remnant *will be* very small *and*
feeble."

Proclamation Against Syria and Israel

17 The [a]burden against Damascus.

"Behold, Damascus will cease from
being a city,
And it will be a ruinous heap.
2 The cities of [b]Aroer *are* forsaken;*
They will be for flocks
Which lie down, and [c]no one will
make *them* afraid.
3 [d]The fortress also will cease from
Ephraim,
The kingdom from Damascus,
And the remnant of Syria;
They will be as the glory of the
children of Israel,"
Says the LORD of hosts.

4 "In that day it shall come to pass
That the glory of Jacob will
wane,
And [e]the fatness of his flesh grow
lean.
5 [f]It shall be as when the harvester
gathers the grain,
And reaps the heads with his arm;
It shall be as he who gathers heads of
grain
In the Valley of Rephaim.
6 [g]Yet gleaning grapes will be left
in it,
Like the shaking of an olive tree,
Two *or* three olives at the top of the
uppermost bough,
Four *or* five in its most fruitful
branches,"
Says the LORD God of Israel.

7 In that day a man will [h]look to his
Maker,
And his eyes will have respect for the
Holy One of Israel.

---

* **17:2** Following Masoretic Text and Vulgate; Septuagint reads *It shall be forsaken forever;* Targum reads *Its cities shall be forsaken and desolate.*

---

haughtiness and the wrath of Moab that brought the nation into judgment. The pride of Moab is not the honest pride in a difficult task well done, but the pride of a haughty, disdainful people who considered themselves above remonstrance. The third element of Moab's downfall, wrath, is closely linked with pride. A people who consider themselves the center of interest and importance lose their natural inhibition. They feel free to indulge in wrath because they are convinced that whatever they do is right.

16:8 ***vine.*** The vine refers to Moab.

16:9 ***Heshbon and Elealeh.*** These cities were among the principal settlements in ancient Moab (15:4).

16:12 ***high place . . . sanctuary.*** As long as people worship false gods, they will be doomed to pain, judgment, and recurring trouble (15:2–4). Even when the people weary of the false gods and try to pray to the one true God, they will not be able to communicate with Him because they have not repented and renounced the false gods.

16:14 ***Within three years.*** A former prophecy against Moab (15:2) would be realized within three years, perhaps referring to the quelling of a rebellion against Sargon in 715 B.C. However, a remnant would remain (15:9). Moab had far more hope for salvation than did either Babylon or Philistia.

17:3 ***fortress.*** This city may be Samaria, the capital city. ***Ephraim.*** Ephraim designates northern Israel.

17:5 ***Rephaim.*** The word "Rephaim" is the Hebrew word for "shades" or "ghosts." The "Valley of Rephaim" is the valley of death.

17:6 ***left.*** A remnant would be left (10:20) even though it would be pitifully small.

16:8 [l] Is. 24:7 [m] Is. 16:9 [n] Jer. 48:32 **16:9** [o] Is. 15:4 **16:10** [p] Is. 24:8 **16:11** [q] Jer. 48:36 **16:12** [r] Is. 15:2 **16:14** [s] Is. 21:16 **17:1** [a] Zech. 9:1 **17:2** [b] Num. 32:34 [c] Jer. 7:33 **17:3** [d] Is. 7:16; 8:4 **17:4** [e] Is. 10:16 **17:5** [f] Jer. 51:33 **17:6** [g] Is. 24:13 **17:7** [h] Mic. 7:7

8 He will not look to the altars,
The work of his hands;
He will not respect what his ᶦfingers
have made,
Nor the wooden images* nor the
incense altars.

9 In that day his strong cities will be as
a forsaken bough*
And an uppermost branch,*
Which they left because of the
children of Israel;
And there will be desolation.

10 Because you have forgotten ʲthe God
of your salvation,
And have not been mindful of the
Rock of your stronghold,
Therefore you will plant pleasant plants
And set out foreign seedlings;

11 In the day you will make your plant to
grow,
And in the morning you will make
your seed to flourish;
But the harvest *will be* a heap of ruins
In the day of grief and desperate sorrow.

12 Woe to the multitude of many people
Who make a noise ᵏlike the roar of the
seas,
And to the rushing of nations
That make a rushing like the rushing
of mighty waters!

13 The nations will rush like the rushing
of many waters;
But *God* will ᶫrebuke them and they
will flee far away,
And ᵐbe chased like the chaff of the
mountains before the wind,
Like a rolling thing before the
whirlwind.

14 Then behold, at eventide, trouble!
And before the morning, he *is* no more.
This *is* the portion of those who
plunder us,
And the lot of those who rob us.

Proclamation Against Ethiopia

18 Woe ᵃto the land shadowed with
buzzing wings,

Which *is* beyond the rivers of Ethiopia,

2 Which sends ambassadors by sea,
Even in vessels of reed on the waters,
saying,
"Go, swift messengers, to a nation tall
and smooth *of skin,*
To a people terrible from their
beginning onward,
A nation powerful and treading down,
Whose land the rivers divide."

3 All inhabitants of the world and
dwellers on the earth:
ᵇWhen he lifts up a banner on the
mountains, you see *it;*
And when he blows a trumpet, you
hear *it.*

4 For so the LORD said to me,
"I will take My rest,
And I will look from My dwelling place
Like clear heat in sunshine,
Like a cloud of dew in the heat of
harvest."

5 For before the harvest, when the bud is
perfect
And the sour grape is ripening in the
flower,
He will both cut off the sprigs with
pruning hooks
And take away *and* cut down the
branches.

6 They will be left together for the
mountain birds of prey
And for the beasts of the earth;
The birds of prey will summer on them,
And all the beasts of the earth will
winter on them.

7 In that time ᶜa present will be brought
to the LORD of hosts
From* a people tall and smooth *of skin,*

---

* **17:8** Hebrew *Asherim,* Canaanite deities
* **17:9** Septuagint reads *Hivites;* Targum reads *laid
waste;* Vulgate reads *as the plows.* • Septuagint
reads *Amorites;* Targum reads *in ruins;* Vulgate
reads *corn.*   * **18:7** Following Dead Sea Scrolls,
Septuagint, and Vulgate; Masoretic Text omits
From; Targum reads *To.*

17:10 forgotten. Forgetting God is letting the truth
of God fade by ignoring Him. In the end, such neglect
is unbelief, refusing to believe in God and refusing to
believe His Word. The safe caring place, the Refuge
from storms, is forgotten. God becomes like a friend
whom you never visit any more or think much about
and finally do not remember at all. This slippery slope
takes us far from the Rock of our refuge, the God of
our Salvation.
17:11 make your seed to flourish. This phrase may
allude to the ancient practice of force-blooming pot-
ted plants and allowing them to die. Pagans believed
that this reenactment of the life cycle would secure
fertile fields. But even after performing this rite, the
harvest would be in ruin. Just as the choice vines of the
Lord's vineyard disappointed Him (5:1–7), so His errant
people would find their harvest hopes shattered.
17:12 many people. The many people are the nations
that plunder Israel (v. 14).

17:14 before the morning. Sennacherib's army
would be destroyed between evening time and
morning (37:36–38). **us.** Isaiah identified himself with
his plundered people.
18:1 Ethiopia. Also called Cush in the Bible, Ethiopia
was at the southern end of Isaiah's world. A Cushite
dynasty took over Egypt in 715 B.C. and probably sent
ambassadors to Jerusalem.
18:5 before the harvest . . . cut off. This is another
example of a bad harvest (17:10–11).
18:7 place of the name. Note how closely the Lord
identifies with Mount Zion. This was the one place for
the true worship of God.

17:8 ᶦ Is. 2:8; 31:7   **17:10** ʲ Ps. 68:19   **17:12** ᵏ Jer. 6:23
17:13 ᶫ Ps. 9:5 ᵐ Hos. 13:3   **18:1** ᵃ Zeph. 2:12; 3:10
18:3 ᵇ Is. 5:26   **18:7** ᶜ Zeph. 3:10

And from a people terrible from their
    beginning onward,
A nation powerful and treading down,
Whose land the rivers divide—
To the place of the name of the LORD
    of hosts,
To Mount Zion.

Proclamation Against Egypt

19 The ªburden against Egypt.

Behold, the LORD ᵇrides on a swift
    cloud,
And will come into Egypt;
ᶜThe idols of Egypt will totter at His
    presence,
And the heart of Egypt will melt in its
    midst.

2 "I will ᵈset Egyptians against
    Egyptians;
Everyone will fight against his brother,
And everyone against his neighbor,
City against city, kingdom against
    kingdom.
3 The spirit of Egypt will fail in its
    midst;
I will destroy their counsel,
And they will ᵉconsult the idols and
    the charmers,
The mediums and the sorcerers.
4 And the Egyptians I will give
    ᶠInto the hand of a cruel master,
And a fierce king will rule over them,"
Says the Lord, the LORD of hosts.

5 ᵍThe waters will fail from the sea,
And the river will be wasted and
    dried up.
6 The rivers will turn foul;
The brooks ʰof defense will be emptied
    and dried up;
The reeds and rushes will wither.
7 The papyrus reeds by the River,* by
    the mouth of the River,
And everything sown by the River,
Will wither, be driven away, and be no
    more.
8 The fishermen also will mourn;
All those who cast hooks
    into the River,
And they will languish who spread
    nets on the waters.
9 Moreover those who work in ⁱfine flax
And those who weave fine fabric will
    be ashamed;

10 And its foundations will be broken.
All who make wages *will be* troubled
    of soul.

11 Surely the princes of ʲZoan *are* fools;
Pharaoh's wise counselors give foolish
    counsel.
    ᵏHow do you say to Pharaoh, "I *am* the
    son of the wise,
The son of ancient kings?"
12 ˡWhere *are* they?
Where are your wise men?
Let them tell you now,
And let them know what the LORD
    of hosts has ᵐpurposed against
    Egypt.
13 The princes of Zoan have become fools;
ⁿThe princes of Noph* are deceived;
They have also deluded Egypt,
Those who are the mainstay of its
    tribes.
14 The LORD has mingled ᵒa perverse
    spirit in her midst;
And they have caused Egypt to err in
    all her work,
As a drunken man staggers in his
    vomit.
15 Neither will there be *any* work for
    Egypt,
Which ᵖthe head or tail,
Palm branch or bulrush, may do.*

¹⁶In that day Egypt will ᑫbe like women,
and will be afraid and fear because of the
waving of the hand of the LORD of hosts,
ʳwhich He waves over it. ¹⁷And the land
of Judah will be a terror to Egypt; everyone who makes mention of it will be afraid
in himself, because of the counsel of the
LORD of hosts which He has ˢdetermined
against it.

Egypt, Assyria, and Israel Blessed

¹⁸In that day five cities in the land of
Egypt will ᵗspeak the language of Canaan
and ᵘswear by the LORD of hosts; one will
be called the City of Destruction.*

¹⁹In that day ᵛthere will be an altar to the
LORD in the midst of the land of Egypt, and
a pillar to the ʷLORD at its border. ²⁰And

---

* **19:7** That is, the Nile   * **19:13** That is, ancient
Memphis   * **19:15** Compare Isaiah 9:14–16
* **19:18** Some Hebrew manuscripts, Arabic, Dead
Sea Scrolls, Targum, and Vulgate read *Sun*; Septuagint reads *A sedek* (literally *Righteousness*).

19:2 *Egyptians against Egyptians.* The political
anarchy of the Egyptians has religious roots: their
many gods failed them.
19:3 *spirit of Egypt.* The principal key for understanding the world of ancient Egypt is the concept of
order, or *ma'at*. When the spirit of the Egyptians was
demoralized, they lost their sense of order and purpose. This would completely confuse and disarm any
aggression and would cause economic and political
upheaval.
19:13 *Noph.* This was Memphis, Egypt's ancient capital.

19:19–21 Worship—The prophets spoke of the
future when the Gentile nations would come to know
God and worship Him. Egypt is one of these nations

19:1 ª Joel 3:19 ᵇ Ps. 18:10; 104:3 ᶜ Jer. 43:12
19:2 ᵈ Judg. 7:22 **19:3** ᵉ Is. 8:19; 47:12 **19:4** ᶠ Ezek.
29:19 **19:5** ᵍ Jer. 51:36 **19:6** ʰ 2 Kin. 19:24
19:9 ⁱ Prov. 7:16 **19:11** ʲ Num. 13:22 ᵏ 1 Kin. 4:29,
30 **19:12** ˡ 1 Cor. 1:20 ᵐ Ps. 33:11 **19:13** ⁿ Jer. 2:16
19:14 ᵒ Is. 29:10 **19:15** ᵖ Is. 9:14–16 **19:16** ᑫ Nah. 3:13
ʳ Is. 11:15 **19:17** ˢ Dan. 4:35 **19:18** ᵗ Zeph. 3:9 ᵘ Is.
45:23 **19:19** ᵛ Ex. 24:4 ʷ Ps. 68:31

ˣit will be for a sign and for a witness to the LORD of hosts in the land of Egypt; for they will cry to the LORD because of the oppressors, and He will send them a ʸSavior and a Mighty One, and He will deliver them. ²¹Then the LORD will be known to Egypt, and the Egyptians will ᶻknow the LORD in that day, and ᵃwill make sacrifice and offering; yes, they will make a vow to the LORD and perform it. ²²And the LORD will strike Egypt, He will strike and ᵇheal it; they will return to the LORD, and He will be entreated by them and heal them.

²³In that day ᶜthere will be a highway from Egypt to Assyria, and the Assyrian will come into Egypt and the Egyptian into Assyria, and the Egyptians will ᵈserve with the Assyrians.

²⁴In that day Israel will be one of three with Egypt and Assyria—a blessing in the midst of the land, ²⁵whom the LORD of hosts shall bless, saying, "Blessed is Egypt My people, and Assyria ᵉthe work of My hands, and Israel My inheritance."

The Sign Against Egypt and Ethiopia

20 In the year that ᵃTartan* came to Ashdod, when Sargon the king of Assyria sent him, and he fought against Ashdod and took it, ²at the same time the LORD spoke by Isaiah the son of Amoz, saying, "Go, and remove ᵇthe sackcloth from your body, and take your sandals off your feet." And he did so, ᶜwalking naked and barefoot.

³Then the LORD said, "Just as My servant Isaiah has walked naked and barefoot three years ᵈfor a sign and a wonder against Egypt and Ethiopia, ⁴so shall the ᵉking of Assyria lead away the Egyptians as prisoners and the Ethiopians as captives, young and old, naked and barefoot, ᶠwith their buttocks uncovered, to the shame of Egypt. ⁵ᵍThen they shall be afraid and ashamed of Ethiopia their expectation and Egypt their glory. ⁶And the inhabitant of

this territory will say in that day, 'Surely such is our expectation, wherever we flee for ʰhelp to be delivered from the king of Assyria; and how shall we escape?'"

The Fall of Babylon Proclaimed

21 The burden against the Wilderness of the Sea.

As ᵃwhirlwinds in the South pass
    through,
So it comes from the desert, from a
    terrible land.
2 A distressing vision is declared to me;
ᵇThe treacherous dealer deals
    treacherously,
And the plunderer plunders.
ᶜGo up, O Elam!
Besiege, O Media!
All its sighing I have made to cease.
3 Therefore ᵈmy loins are filled with pain;
ᵉPangs have taken hold of me, like the
    pangs of a woman in labor.
I was distressed when I heard it;
I was dismayed when I saw it.
4 My heart wavered, fearfulness
    frightened me;
ᶠThe night for which I longed He turned
    into fear for me.
5 ᵍPrepare the table,
Set a watchman in the tower,
Eat and drink.
Arise, you princes,
Anoint the shield!
6 For thus has the Lord said to me:
"Go, set a watchman,
Let him declare what he sees."
7 And he saw a chariot with a pair of
    horsemen,
A chariot of donkeys, and a chariot of
    camels,
And he listened earnestly with great
    care.
8 Then he cried, "A lion,* my Lord!

---

* **20:1** Or the Commander in Chief   * **21:8** Dead Sea Scrolls read Then the observer cried.

---

for which there is a future mercy. The Egyptians will swear allegiance to the true God, institute extensive public worship of God, and become equal partners in the community of believers. This is a remarkable promise from our God, and one that is worth remembering in troubling political times.

19:25 My people . . . the work of My hands. Historically, Egypt and Assyria were enemies. When they change and turn to the Lord (symbolic of all converted Gentiles), they will be healed (v. 22) and blessed by God.

20:2 sackcloth. Isaiah replaced the garb of spiritual mourning with the signs of being exiled into captivity.

20:3 three years. Three years means "involving three years," a minimum of 14 months, but possibly more.

20:6 inhabitant of this territory. This probably refers to the nations, including Judah, bordering on the eastern shore of the Mediterranean Sea, who looked to Egypt to save them from Assyria.

21:2 Elam . . . Media. Elam, a major part of Persia, and

Media were allied in 700 B.C. Perhaps as a part of the Assyrian army (5:26), they helped to bring about the fall of Babylon in 689 B.C., since they certainly did so in 539 B.C. (11:11; 13:17).

21:4 heart wavered. Isaiah saw that even a longed-for event can have terrible consequences in its wake. The judgment of God on Babylon would not be easy to look at.

21:7 donkeys . . . camels. The Persians, who overthrew Babylon in 539 B.C., used donkeys and camels in their army.

19:20 ˣ Josh. 4:20; 22:27 ʸ Is. 43:11 **19:21** ᶻ [Is. 2:3, 4; 11:9] ᵃ Mal. 1:11 **19:22** ᵇ Deut. 32:39 **19:23** ᶜ Is. 11:16; 35:8; 49:11; 62:10 ᵈ Is. 27:13 **19:25** ᵉ Is. 29:23 **20:1** ᵃ 2 Kin. 18:17 **20:2** ᵇ Zech. 13:4 ᶜ 1 Sam. 19:24 **20:3** ᵈ Is. 8:18 **20:4** ᵉ Is. 19:4 ᶠ Jer. 13:22 **20:5** ᵍ 2 Kin. 18:21 **20:6** ʰ Is. 30:5, 7 **21:1** ᵃ Zech. 9:14 **21:2** ᵇ Is. 33:1 ᶜ Jer. 49:34 **21:3** ᵈ Is. 15:5; 16:11 ᵉ Is. 13:8 **21:4** ᶠ Deut. 28:67 **21:5** ᵍ Dan. 5:5

I stand continually on the [h]watchtower
  in the daytime;
I have sat at my post every night.
9 And look, here comes a chariot of men
  with a pair of horsemen!"
Then he answered and said,
[i]"Babylon is fallen, is fallen!
And [j]all the carved images of her gods
  He has broken to the ground."

10 [k]Oh, my threshing and the grain of my
  floor!
That which I have heard from the
  LORD of hosts,
The God of Israel,
I have declared to you.

Proclamation Against Edom

11[l]The burden against Dumah.

He calls to me out of [m]Seir,
"Watchman, what of the night?
Watchman, what of the night?"
12 The watchman said,
"The morning comes, and also the
  night.
If you will inquire, inquire;
Return! Come back!"

Proclamation Against Arabia

13[n]The burden against Arabia.

In the forest in Arabia you will
  lodge,
O you traveling companies [o]of
  Dedanites.
14 O inhabitants of the land of Tema,
Bring water to him who is thirsty;
With their bread they met him who
  fled.
15 For they fled from the swords, from
  the drawn sword,
From the bent bow, and from the
  distress of war.

16For thus the LORD has said to me:
"Within a year, [p]according to the year of
a hired man, all the glory of [q]Kedar will
fail; 17and the remainder of the number of
archers, the mighty men of the people of
Kedar, will be diminished; for the LORD
God of Israel has spoken *it.*"

Proclamation Against Jerusalem

22 The burden against the Valley of Vision.

What ails you now, that you have all
  gone up to the housetops,
2 You who are full of noise,
A tumultuous city, [a]a joyous city?
Your slain *men are* not slain with the
  sword,
Nor dead in battle.
3 All your rulers have fled together;
They are captured by the archers.
All who are found in you are bound
  together;
They have fled from afar.
4 Therefore I said, "Look away from me,
[b]I will weep bitterly;
Do not labor to comfort me
Because of the plundering of the
  daughter of my people."

5 [c]For *it is* a day of trouble and treading
  down and perplexity
[d]By the Lord GOD of hosts
In the Valley of Vision—
Breaking down the walls
And of crying to the mountain.
6 [e]Elam bore the quiver
With chariots of men *and* horsemen,
And [f]Kir uncovered the shield.
7 It shall come to pass *that* your choicest
  valleys
Shall be full of chariots,
And the horsemen shall set themselves
  in array at the gate.

8 [g]He removed the protection of Judah.
You looked in that day to the armor [h]of
  the House of the Forest;
9 [i]You also saw the damage to the city of
  David,
That it was great;
And you gathered together the waters
  of the lower pool.
10 You numbered the houses of
  Jerusalem,
And the houses you broke down
To fortify the wall.
11 [j]You also made a reservoir between the
  two walls
For the water of the old [k]pool.
But you did not look to its Maker,
Nor did you have respect for Him who
  fashioned it long ago.

12 And in that day the Lord GOD of
  hosts
[l]Called for weeping and for mourning,
[m]For baldness and for girding with
  sackcloth.

21:11 *Watchman.* The watchman was the night
patrol who kept watch on the city. The metaphor
refers to the prophet Isaiah, who, as a guard on the
walls, could see the dawn—the light of salvation—in
the east before the others.
21:13 *companies of Dedanites.* The Dedanites may
refer to the refugees (v. 15) from Dedan, which was
about 90 miles southeast of Tema (v. 14).
22:11 *reservoir between the two walls.* The defense
of the city depended upon the availability of water
within its walls. Hezekiah addressed this need by
digging a tunnel beneath the city, connecting the
lower pool in Jerusalem's southwestern valley with
the old pool, the source of water in the eastern valley.

21:8 [h] Hab. 2:1   **21:9** [i] Jer. 51:8 [j] Is. 46:1   **21:10** [k] Jer.
51:33   **21:11** [l] Gen. 25:14 [m] Gen. 32:3   **21:13** [n] Jer.
25:24; 49:28 [o] 1 Chr. 1:9, 32   **21:16** [p] Is. 16:14 [q] Ps. 120:5
22:2 [a] Is. 32:13   **22:4** [b] Jer. 4:19   **22:5** [c] Is. 37:3 [d] Lam.
1:5; 2:2   **22:6** [e] Jer. 49:35 [f] Is. 15:1   **22:8** [g] 2 Kin. 18:15,
16 [h] 1 Kin. 7:2; 10:17   **22:9** [i] 2 Kin. 20:20   **22:11** [j] Neh.
3:16 [k] 2 Chr. 32:3, 4   **22:12** [l] Joel 1:13; 2:17 [m] Mic. 1:16

13 But instead, joy and gladness,
Slaying oxen and killing sheep,
Eating meat and ⁿdrinking wine:
^o"Let us eat and drink, for tomorrow we
die!"

14 ^pThen it was revealed in my hearing by
the LORD of hosts,
"Surely for this iniquity there ^qwill be
no atonement for you,
Even to your death," says the Lord
GOD of hosts.

The Judgment on Shebna

15Thus says the Lord GOD of hosts:

"Go, proceed to this steward,
To ^rShebna, who *is* over the house,
and say:
16 'What have you here, and whom have
you here,
That you have hewn a sepulcher here,
As he ^swho hews himself a sepulcher
on high,
Who carves a tomb for himself in a
rock?
17 Indeed, the LORD will throw you away
violently,
O mighty man,
^tAnd will surely seize you.
18 He will surely turn violently and toss
you like a ball
Into a large country;
There you shall die, and there ^uyour
glorious chariots
Shall be the shame of your master's
house.
19 So I will drive you out of your office,
And from your position he will pull
you down.*
20 'Then it shall be in that day,
That I will call My servant ^vEliakim
the son of Hilkiah;
21 I will clothe him with your robe
And strengthen him with your belt;
I will commit your responsibility into
his hand.
He shall be a father to the inhabitants
of Jerusalem
And to the house of Judah.
22 The key of the house of David
I will lay on his ^wshoulder;
So he shall ^xopen, and no one shall shut;
And he shall shut, and no one shall
open.
23 I will fasten him *as* ^ya peg in a secure
place,
And he will become a glorious throne
to his father's house.

24'They will hang on him all the glory
of his father's house, the offspring and
the posterity, all vessels of small quantity,
from the cups to all the pitchers. 25In that
day,' says the LORD of hosts, 'the peg that
is fastened in the secure place will be removed and be cut down and fall, and the
burden that *was* on it will be cut off; for the
LORD has spoken.'"

Proclamation Against Tyre

23 The ^aburden against Tyre.

Wail, you ships of Tarshish!
For it is laid waste,
So that there is no house, no harbor;
From the land of Cyprus* it is revealed
to them.

2 Be still, you inhabitants of the
coastland,
You merchants of Sidon,
Whom those who cross the sea have
filled.*
3 And on great waters the grain of
Shihor,
The harvest of the River,* *is* her
revenue;
And ^bshe is a marketplace for the
nations.

4 Be ashamed, O Sidon;
For the sea has spoken,
The strength of the sea, saying,
"I do not labor, nor bring forth children;
Neither do I rear young men,
Nor bring up virgins."
5 ^cWhen the report *reaches* Egypt,
They also will be in agony at the
report of Tyre.

6 Cross over to Tarshish;
Wail, you inhabitants of the coastland!
7 *Is* this your ^djoyous *city,*
Whose antiquity *is* from ancient days,
Whose feet carried her far off to
dwell?
8 Who has taken this counsel against
Tyre, ^ethe crowning *city,*
Whose merchants *are* princes,
Whose traders *are* the honorable of
the earth?

* **22:19** Septuagint omits *he will pull you down;*
Syriac, Targum, and Vulgate read *I will pull you
down.*   * **23:1** Hebrew *Kittim,* western lands,
especially Cyprus   * **23:2** Following Masoretic Text and Vulgate; Septuagint and Targum
read *Passing over the water;* Dead Sea Scrolls
read *Your messengers passing over the sea.*
* **23:3** That is, the Nile

22:25 *peg . . . be cut off.* Even the firmly reliable
Eliakim could not sustain the burden of government.
Only Immanuel could do that (9:6–7).
23:1 *Tyre.* Tyre was besieged several times over a
period of about 400 years before it was finally laid
waste by Alexander the Great in 332 B.C.
23:6 *Tarshish.* Tarshish is Tartessus in Spain and represents the most distant place to the ancient Israelites.

22:13 ⁿ Luke 17:26–29 ^o 1 Cor. 15:32 **22:14** ^p Is. 5:9
^q Ezek. 24:13 **22:15** ^r Is. 36:3 **22:16** ^s Matt. 27:60
22:17 ^t Esth. 7:8 **22:18** ^u Is. 2:7 **22:20** ^v 2 Kin. 18:18
22:22 ^w Is. 9:6 ^x Job 12:14; Rev. 3:7 **22:23** ^y Ezra 9:8
23:1 ^a Zech. 9:2, 4 **23:3** ^b Ezek. 27:3–23 **23:5** ^c Is.
19:16 **23:7** ^d Is. 22:2; 32:13 **23:8** ^e Ezek. 28:2, 12

9 The LORD of hosts has ᶠpurposed it,
To bring to dishonor the ᵍpride of all
glory,
To bring into contempt all the
honorable of the earth.
10 Overflow through your land like the
River,*
O daughter of Tarshish;
There is no more strength.
11 He stretched out His hand over the
sea,
He shook the kingdoms;
The LORD has given a commandment
ʰagainst Canaan
To destroy its strongholds.
12 And He said, "You will rejoice no
more,
O you oppressed virgin daughter of
Sidon.
Arise, ⁱcross over to Cyprus;
There also you will have no rest."

13 Behold, the land of the ʲChaldeans,
This people *which* was not;
Assyria founded it for ᵏwild beasts of
the desert.
They set up its towers,
They raised up its palaces,
And brought it to ruin.

14 ˡWail, you ships of Tarshish!
For your strength is laid waste.

15Now it shall come to pass in that day
that Tyre will be forgotten seventy years,
according to the days of one king. At the
end of seventy years it will happen to Tyre
as *in* the song of the harlot:

16 "Take a harp, go about the city,
You forgotten harlot;
Make sweet melody, sing many songs,
That you may be remembered."

17And it shall be, at the end of seventy
years, that the LORD will deal with Tyre. She
will return to her hire, and ᵐcommit fornication with all the kingdoms of the world on
the face of the earth. 18Her gain and her pay
ⁿwill be set apart for the LORD; it will not be
treasured nor laid up, for her gain will be
for those who dwell before the LORD, to eat
sufficiently, and for fine clothing.

Impending Judgment on the Earth

24 Behold, the LORD makes the earth
empty and makes it waste,
Distorts its surface
And scatters abroad its inhabitants.
2 And it shall be:
As with the people, so with the ᵃpriest;
As with the servant, so with his
master;
As with the maid, so with her mistress;
ᵇAs with the buyer, so with the seller;
As with the lender, so with the borrower;
As with the creditor, so with the debtor.
3 The land shall be entirely emptied and
utterly plundered,
For the LORD has spoken this word.

4 The earth mourns *and* fades away,
The world languishes *and* fades away;
The ᶜhaughty people of the earth
languish.
5 ᵈThe earth is also defiled under its
inhabitants,
Because they have ᵉtransgressed the
laws,
Changed the ordinance,
Broken the ᶠeverlasting covenant.
6 Therefore ᵍthe curse has devoured the
earth,
And those who dwell in it are desolate.
Therefore the inhabitants of the earth
are ʰburned,
And few men *are* left.

7 ⁱThe new wine fails, the vine languishes,
All the merry-hearted sigh.
8 The mirth ʲof the tambourine ceases,
The noise of the jubilant ends,
The joy of the harp ceases.
9 They shall not drink wine with a song;
Strong drink is bitter to those who
drink it.
10 The city of confusion is broken down;
Every house is shut up, so that none
may go in.
11 *There is* a cry for wine in the streets,
All joy is darkened,
The mirth of the land is gone.
12 In the city desolation is left,
And the gate is stricken with destruction.

* **23:10** That is, the Nile

23:15 *seventy years.* Seventy years symbolizes a full measure of time, a lifetime.
23:18 *Her gain . . . set apart for the LORD.* This was not a violation of God's command (Deut. 23:18) which forbade bringing a harlot's pay (v. 17) to the temple. Tyre's destruction was part of the Lord's war against the unrighteous. The spoils would belong to Him as the Victor (Deut. 2:35; Josh. 6:17,19).
24:1—27:12 *Behold, the LORD.* The section describing the Lord's "burdens" against particular nations (chs. 13–23) is now placed in a larger framework that shows God's triumph over the entire earth for His elect. Chapter 24 focuses on God's overthrow of the corrupted earth; chapter 25 focuses on the responsive praise to His actions. Chapters 26 and 27 focus on God's efforts for His people.

24:4 *The earth mourns.* For a similar idea, see Romans 8:22.
24:5 *laws . . . ordinance . . . covenant.* The usual language concerning a breach of the covenant is applied more generally to the wicked nations. Perhaps these words speak of that innate sense of right and wrong—the conscience—that God has given to all mankind, but which everyone violates (Acts 24:16; Rom. 1:18–32).

23:9 ᶠIs. 14:26 ᵍDan. 4:37 **23:11** ʰZech. 9:2–4
23:12 ʲRev. 18:22 **23:13** ʲIs. 47:1 ᵏPs. 72:9
23:14 ˡEzek. 27:25–30 **23:17** ᵐRev. 17:2
23:18 ⁿZech. 14:20, 21 **24:2** ᵈHos. 4:9 ᵇEzek. 7:12, 13
24:4 ᶜIs. 25:11 **24:5** ᵈNum. 35:33 ᵉIs. 59:12 ᶠ1 Chr.
16:14–19 **24:6** ᵍMal. 4:6 ʰIs. 9:19 **24:7** ⁱJoel 1:10, 12
24:8 ʲEzek. 26:13

13 When it shall be thus in the midst of
the land among the people,
kIt shall be like the shaking of an olive
tree,
Like the gleaning of grapes when the
vintage is done.
14 They shall lift up their voice, they shall
sing;
For the majesty of the LORD
They shall cry aloud from the sea.
15 Therefore lglorify the LORD in the
dawning light,
mThe name of the LORD God of Israel in
the coastlands of the sea.
16 From the ends of the earth we have
heard songs:
"Glory to the righteous!"
But I said, "I am ruined, ruined!
Woe to me!
nThe treacherous dealers have dealt
treacherously,
Indeed, the treacherous dealers have
dealt very treacherously."
17 oFear and the pit and the snare
Are upon you, O inhabitant of the
earth.
18 And it shall be
That he who flees from the noise of
the fear
Shall fall into the pit,
And he who comes up from the midst
of the pit
Shall be caught in the snare;
For pthe windows from on high are
open,
And qthe foundations of the earth are
shaken.
19 rThe earth is violently broken,
The earth is split open,
The earth is shaken exceedingly.
20 The earth shall sreel to and fro like a
drunkard,
And shall totter like a hut;
Its transgression shall be heavy upon
it,
And it will fall, and not rise again.
21 It shall come to pass in that day
That the LORD will punish on high the
host of exalted ones,
And on the earth tthe kings of the
earth.

22 They will be gathered together,
As prisoners are gathered in the pit,
And will be shut up in the prison;
After many days they will be
punished.
23 Then the umoon will be disgraced
And the sun ashamed;
For the LORD of hosts will vreign
On wMount Zion and in Jerusalem
And before His elders, gloriously.

Praise to God

25 O LORD, You are my God.
aI will exalt You,
I will praise Your name,
bFor You have done wonderful things;
cYour counsels of old are faithfulness
and truth.
2 For You have made da city a ruin,
A fortified city a ruin,
A palace of foreigners to be a city no
more;
It will never be rebuilt.
3 Therefore the strong people will
eglorify You;
The city of the terrible nations will
fear You.
4 For You have been a strength to the
poor,
A strength to the needy in his
distress,
fA refuge from the storm,
A shade from the heat;
For the blast of the terrible ones is as a
storm against the wall.
5 You will reduce the noise of aliens,
As heat in a dry place;
As heat in the shadow of a cloud,
The song of the terrible ones will be
diminished.
6 And in gthis mountain
hThe LORD of hosts will make for iall
people
A feast of choice pieces,
A feast of wines on the lees,
Of fat things full of marrow,
Of well-refined wines on the lees.
7 And He will destroy on this mountain
The surface of the covering cast over
all people,
And jthe veil that is spread over all
nations.

24:14–16 lift up their voice. Isaiah cannot join in the chorus of praise, because he, like Daniel (Dan. 7:28; 8:27), was too overwhelmed by the tragedy that was to come. It is impossible to tell whether the people who praised the Lord were faithful followers who had been oppressed by the treacherous leaders, or whether those who praised were the unfaithful leaders who were beginning to remember the Lord. There comes a time when the Lord does not wait any more, but He carries out the promised punishment for sinful behavior. Those who have trusted in Him will always find their souls secure, but that does not mean that they will not see dreadful sights or perhaps even be martyred for their faith.

24:21 that day. "That day" is the day that the Lord will finally judge the whole world (Rev. 20:11–15).
25:5 terrible ones. The use of the term "terrible" three times in verses 3–5 emphasizes divine judgment on the nations represented.

24:13 k [Is. 17:5, 6; 27:12]   **24:15** l Is. 25:3   m Mal. 1:11   **24:16** n Jer. 3:20; 5:11   **24:17** o Jer. 48:43   **24:18** p Gen. 7:11   q Ps. 18:7; 46:2   **24:19** r Jer. 4:23   **24:20** s Is. 19:14; 24:1; 28:7   **24:21** t Ps. 76:12   **24:23** u Is. 13:10; 60:19   v Rev. 19:4, 6   w [Heb. 12:22]   **25:1** o Ex. 15:2   b Ps. 98:1   c Num. 23:19   **25:2** d Jer. 51:37   **25:3** e Is. 24:15   **25:4** f Is. 4:6   **25:6** g [Is. 2:2–4; 56:7]   h Prov. 9:2   i [Dan. 7:14]   **25:7** j [Eph. 4:18]

8 He will ᵏswallow up death forever,
And the Lord GOD will ˡwipe away
tears from all faces;
The rebuke of His people
He will take away from all the earth;
For the LORD has spoken.

9 And it will be said in that day:
"Behold, this *is* our God;
ᵐWe have waited for Him, and He will
save us.
This *is* the LORD;
We have waited for Him;
ⁿWe will be glad and rejoice in His
salvation."

10 For on this mountain the hand of the
LORD will rest,
And ᵒMoab shall be trampled down
under Him,
As straw is trampled down for the
refuse heap.

11 And He will spread out His hands in
their midst
As a swimmer reaches out to swim,
And He will bring down their ᵖpride
Together with the trickery of their
hands.

12 The ᵠfortress of the high fort of your
walls
He will bring down, lay low,
And bring to the ground, down to the
dust.

A Song of Salvation

26 In ᵃthat day this song will be sung in
the land of Judah:

"We have a strong city;
ᵇGod will appoint salvation *for* walls
and bulwarks.

2 ᶜOpen the gates,
That the righteous nation which keeps
the truth may enter in.

3 You will keep *him* in perfect ᵈpeace,
Whose mind *is* stayed *on You,*
Because he trusts in You.

4 Trust in the LORD forever,
ᵉFor in YAH, the LORD, *is* everlasting
strength.*

5 For He brings down those who dwell
on high,
ᶠThe lofty city;
He lays it low,

He lays it low to the ground,
He brings it down to the dust.

6 The foot shall tread it down—
The feet of the poor
And the steps of the needy."

7 The way of the just *is* uprightness;
ᵍO Most Upright,
You weigh the path of the just.

8 Yes, ʰin the way of Your judgments,
O LORD, we have ⁱwaited for You;
The desire of *our* soul *is* for Your name
And for the remembrance of You.

9 ʲWith my soul I have desired You in the
night,
Yes, by my spirit within me I will seek
You early;
For when Your judgments *are* in the
earth,
The inhabitants of the world will learn
righteousness.

10 ᵏLet grace be shown to the wicked,
Yet he will not learn righteousness;
In ˡthe land of uprightness he will deal
unjustly,
And will not behold the majesty of the
LORD.

11 LORD, *when* Your hand is lifted up,
ᵐthey will not see.
But they will see and be ashamed
For *their* envy of people;
Yes, the fire of Your enemies shall
devour them.

12 LORD, You will establish peace for us,
For You have also done all our works
in us.

13 O LORD our God, ⁿmasters besides You
Have had dominion over us;
But by You only we make mention of
Your name.

14 *They are* dead, they will not live;
They are deceased, they will not rise.
Therefore You have punished and
destroyed them,
And made all their memory to ᵒperish.

15 You have increased the nation, O LORD,
You have ᵖincreased the nation;
You are glorified;
You have expanded all the borders of
the land.

---

* **26:4** Or *Rock of Ages*

25:8 *wipe away tears.* When the first earth passes away and the tabernacle of God is among men, finally the whole creation will be as it should be, and God will tenderly wipe away the tears of His people (Rev. 7:17; 21:4).

26:3 *peace.* The result of a settled faith in God is "perfect peace." Faith in God is the only thing that brings inner peace to man. One must come to the point of recognizing his own utter sinfulness and his deep need of a redeemer before he can find peace. Only when one is at peace with God can he have peace with others. Only a mind settled in God can tolerate the changing circumstances of life.

26:8 *waited.* Waiting for—or on—the Lord is

a waiting with expectation. Perhaps one could describe it as the difference between waiting for the arrival of an airplane with a loved one arriving, and the waiting one does at a traffic light. (For a similar idea, see 40:31.)

25:8 ᵏ [Hos. 13:14] ˡ Rev. 7:17; 21:4   **25:9** ᵐ Gen. 49:18
ⁿ Ps. 20:5   **25:10** ᵒ Amos 2:1–3   **25:11** ᵖ Is. 24:4;
26:5   **25:12** ᵠ Is. 26:5   **26:1** ᵃ Is. 2:11; 12:1 ᵇ Is. 60:18
26:2 ᶜ Ps. 118:19, 20   **26:3** ᵈ Is. 57:19   **26:4** ᵉ Is. 12:2;
45:17   **26:5** ᶠ Is. 25:11, 12   **26:7** ᵍ Ps. 37:23   **26:8** ʰ Is.
64:5   ⁱ Is. 25:9; 33:2   **26:9** ʲ Ps. 63:6   **26:10** ᵏ [Rom.
2:4] ˡ Ps. 143:10   **26:11** ᵐ Is. 5:12   **26:13** ⁿ 2 Chr. 12:8
26:14 ᵒ Eccl. 9:5   **26:15** ᵖ Is. 9:3

16 LORD, [q]in trouble they have visited
You,
They poured out a prayer *when* Your
chastening *was* upon them.
17 As [r]a woman with child
Is in pain and cries out in her pangs,
When she draws near the time of her
delivery,
So have we been in Your sight,
O LORD.
18 We have been with child, we have
been in pain;
We have, as it were, brought forth
wind;
We have not accomplished any
deliverance in the earth,
Nor have [s]the inhabitants of the world
fallen.

19 [t]Your dead shall live;
Together with my dead body* they
shall arise.
[u]Awake and sing, you who dwell in
dust;
For your dew *is like* the dew of herbs,
And the earth shall cast out the dead.

Take Refuge from the Coming Judgment

20 Come, my people, [v]enter your
chambers,
And shut your doors behind you;
Hide yourself, as it were, [w]for a little
moment,
Until the indignation is past.
21 For behold, the LORD [x]comes out of
His place
To punish the inhabitants of the earth
for their iniquity;
The earth will also disclose her blood,
And will no more cover her slain.

27 In that day the LORD with His severe
sword, great and strong,
Will punish Leviathan the fleeing
serpent,
[a]Leviathan that twisted serpent;
And He will slay [b]the reptile that *is* in
the sea.

The Restoration of Israel

2 In that day [c]sing to her,
[d]"A vineyard of red wine!*
3 [e]I, the LORD, keep it,
I water it every moment;
Lest any hurt it,
I keep it night and day.
4 Fury *is* not in Me.
Who would set [f]briers *and* thorns
Against Me in battle?
I would go through them,
I would burn them together.
5 Or let him take hold [g]of My strength,
That he may [h]make peace with Me;
And he shall make peace with Me."

6 Those who come He shall cause [i]to
take root in Jacob;
Israel shall blossom and bud,
And fill the face of the world with
fruit.

7 [j]Has He struck Israel as He struck
those who struck him?
Or has He been slain according to the
slaughter of those who were slain
by Him?
8 [k]In measure, by sending it away,
You contended with it.
[l]He removes *it* by His rough wind
In the day of the east wind.
9 Therefore by this the iniquity of Jacob
will be covered;
And this *is* all the fruit of taking away
his sin:
When he makes all the stones of the
altar
Like chalkstones that are beaten to
dust,
Wooden images* and incense altars
shall not stand.

*26:19 Following Masoretic Text and Vulgate; Syriac and Targum read *their dead bodies;* Septuagint reads *those in the tombs.* *27:2 Following Masoretic Text (Kittel's *Biblia Hebraica*), Bomberg, and Vulgate; Masoretic Text (*Biblia Hebraica Stuttgartensia*), some Hebrew manuscripts, and Septuagint read *delight;* Targum reads *choice vineyard.* *27:9 Hebrew *Asherim,* Canaanite deities

26:18 *brought forth wind.* Even the faithful followers of the Lord cannot bring new life to the earth. Only God can regenerate the world and its inhabitants. The new life can come only through Jesus Christ, whose coming was still in the future at the time of Isaiah's writing.
26:21 *The earth will also disclose her blood.* In that day of judgment, there will be no unsolved murders, no injustice that is unrevealed.
27:1 *punish.* The punishment in this verse links it with 26:21; this verse is the climax of the preceding section. ***Leviathan.*** This creature was used to poetically describe various evil forces over which God has ultimate control and victory (Job 3:8; Ps. 74:14). Eventually Leviathan (Job 41:1) became a symbol for Satan, who is "the dragon, that serpent of old" (Rev. 20:2).
27:2 *vineyard.* The vineyard is Israel (5:7; 27:6). The language of the vineyard is used frequently in Scripture. The good vines are planted or cared for by God and His servants. They are supposed to bear good fruit and be worthy of the care of the Master. Sometimes the fruit is bad, sometimes the servants are unfaithful, but the vines always belong to God (Matt. 21:33–46; Mark 12:1–12; Luke 20:9–19).
27:3 *keep it . . . water it.* The "keeper" of the vineyard contrasts with the one who will lay waste, and watering it "every moment" contrasts with "no rain" (5:6).

26:16 [q] Hos. 5:15 **26:17** [r] [John 16:21] **26:18** [s] Ps. 17:14 **26:19** [t] [Ezek. 37:1–14] [u] [Dan. 12:2] **26:20** [v] Ex. 12:22, 23 [w] [Ps. 30:5] **26:21** [x] Mic. 1:3 **27:1** [a] Ps. 74:13, 14 [b] Is. 51:9 **27:2** [c] Is. 5:1 [d] Is. 5:7 **27:3** [e] Is. 31:5 **27:4** [f] 2 Sam. 23:6 **27:5** [g] Is. 25:4 [h] Job 22:21 **27:6** [i] Is. 37:31 **27:7** [j] Is. 10:12, 17; 30:30–33 **27:8** [k] Job 23:6 [l] [Ps. 78:38]

10 Yet the fortified city *will be* ^mdesolate,
   The habitation forsaken and left like a
      wilderness;
   There the calf will feed, and there it
      will lie down
   And consume its branches.
11 When its boughs are withered, they
      will be broken off;
   The women come *and* set them on fire.
   For ^nit *is* a people of no understanding;
   Therefore He who made them will ^onot
      have mercy on them,
   And ^pHe who formed them will show
      them no favor.

12 And it shall come to pass in that day
   That the LORD will thresh,
   From the channel of the River* to the
      Brook of Egypt;
   And you will be ^qgathered one by one,
   O you children of Israel.

13 ^rSo it shall be in that day:
   ^sThe great trumpet will be blown;
   They will come, who are about to
      perish in the land of Assyria,
   And they who are outcasts in the land
      of ^tEgypt,
   And shall ^uworship the LORD in the
      holy mount at Jerusalem.

Woe to Ephraim and Jerusalem

28 Woe to the crown of pride, to the
      drunkards of Ephraim,
   Whose glorious beauty *is* a fading
      flower
   Which *is* at the head of the verdant
      valleys,
   To those who are overcome with
      wine!
2 Behold, the Lord has a mighty and
      strong one,
   ^aLike a tempest of hail and a destroying
      storm,
   Like a flood of mighty waters
      overflowing,
   Who will bring *them* down to the
      earth with *His* hand.
3 The crown of pride, the drunkards of
      Ephraim,
   Will be trampled underfoot;

4 And the glorious beauty is a fading
      flower
   Which *is* at the head of the verdant
      valley,
   Like the first fruit before the summer,
   Which an observer sees;
   He eats it up while it is still in his hand.

5 In that day the LORD of hosts will be
   For a crown of glory and a diadem of
      beauty
   To the remnant of His people,
6 For a spirit of justice to him who sits in
      judgment,
   And for strength to those who turn
      back the battle at the gate.

7 But they also ^bhave erred through
      wine,
   And through intoxicating drink are
      out of the way;
   ^cThe priest and the prophet have erred
      through intoxicating drink,
   They are swallowed up by wine,
   They are out of the way through
      intoxicating drink;
   They err in vision, they stumble *in*
      judgment.
8 For all tables are full of vomit *and*
      filth;
   No place *is clean.*

9 "Whom^d will he teach knowledge?
   And whom will he make to understand
      the message?
   Those *just* weaned from milk?
   Those *just* drawn from the breasts?
10 ^eFor precept *must be* upon precept,
      precept upon precept,
   Line upon line, line upon line,
   Here a little, there a little."

11 For with ^fstammering lips and another
      tongue
   He will speak to this people,
12 To whom He said, "This *is* the ^grest
      with which
   You may cause the weary to rest,"
   And, "This *is* the refreshing";
   Yet they would not hear.

---

* **27:12** That is, the Euphrates

27:12 thresh . . . be gathered. Threshing and gathering describe how the grain is separated from the chaff. The grain is saved or "gathered," and the chaff is thrown away. Threshing can be accomplished by beating the grain heads with flails or driving a cart over the grain to separate the grain from the stalks and husks. The grain is then gathered in baskets and tossed in the air, where the wind blows away the chaff and bits of straw, and the ripe grain falls back down into the basket.
28:1 crown of pride. The "crown of pride" on Ephraim's drunkards is part of a word picture (v. 3) contrasting the debasing actions of a drunkard with the crown of flowers, which was customary to wear at feasts. The incongruity of this image parallels God's view of the debauchery of the Israelites in the beautiful land He had given them.

28:5 diadem of beauty. The crown of the Lord of Hosts, which is Himself, sits in true beauty on the remnant of His people. Unlike the fading beauty of the crown of flowers, the glorious crown will be a lasting beauty.
28:9 Those just weaned. A child was weaned between the ages of three and five, the time for elementary moral education, which is described in verse 10.

27:10 ^m Is. 5:6, 17; 32:14 **27:11** ^n Deut. 32:28 ^o Is. 9:17
^p Deut. 32:18 **27:12** ^q [Is. 11:11; 56:8] **27:13** ^r Is. 2:11
^s Rev. 11:15 ^t Is. 19:21, 22 ^u Zech. 14:16 **28:2** ^a Ezek.
13:11 **28:7** ^b Hos. 4:11 ^c Is. 56:10, 12 **28:9** ^d Jer. 6:10
28:10 ^e [2 Chr. 36:15] **28:11** ^f 1 Cor. 14:21 **28:12** ^g Is.
30:15

13 But the word of the LORD was to them,
"Precept upon precept, precept upon
precept,
Line upon line, line upon line,
Here a little, there a little,"
That they might go and fall backward,
and be broken
And snared and caught.

14 Therefore hear the word of the LORD,
you scornful men,
Who rule this people who *are* in
Jerusalem,

15 Because you have said, "We have
made a covenant with death,
And with Sheol we are in agreement.
When the overflowing scourge passes
through,
It will not come to us,
*h*For we have made lies our refuge,
And under falsehood we have hidden
ourselves."

A Cornerstone in Zion

16Therefore thus says the Lord GOD:

"Behold, I lay in Zion *i*a stone for a
foundation,
A tried stone, a precious cornerstone,
a sure foundation;
Whoever believes will not act hastily.

17 Also I will make justice the measuring
line,
And righteousness the plummet;
The hail will sweep away the refuge
of lies,
And the waters will overflow the
hiding place.

18 Your covenant with death will be
annulled,
And your agreement with Sheol will
not stand;
When the overflowing scourge passes
through,
Then you will be trampled down by it.

19 As often as it goes out it will take you;
For morning by morning it will pass
over,
And by day and by night;
It will be a terror just to understand
the report."

20 For the bed is too short to stretch out *on*,
And the covering so narrow that one
cannot wrap himself *in it*.

21 For the LORD will rise up as *at* Mount
*j*Perazim,
He will be angry as in the Valley of
*k*Gibeon—
That He may do His work, *l*His
awesome work,
And bring to pass His act, His unusual
act.

22 Now therefore, do not be mockers,
Lest your bonds be made strong;
For I have heard from the Lord GOD
of hosts,
*m*A destruction determined even upon
the whole earth.

Listen to the Teaching of God

23 Give ear and hear my voice,
Listen and hear my speech.

24 Does the plowman keep plowing all
day to sow?
Does he keep turning his soil and
breaking the clods?

25 When he has leveled its surface,
Does he not sow the black cummin
And scatter the cummin,
Plant the wheat in rows,
The barley in the appointed place,
And the spelt in its place?

26 For He instructs him in right judgment,
His God teaches him.

27 For the black cummin is not threshed
with a threshing sledge,
Nor is a cartwheel rolled over the
cummin;
But the black cummin is beaten out
with a stick,
And the cummin with a rod.

28 Bread *flour* must be ground;
Therefore he does not thresh it forever,
Break *it with* his cartwheel,
Or crush *it with* his horsemen.

29 This also comes from the LORD of hosts,
*n*Who is wonderful in counsel *and*
excellent in guidance.

Woe to Jerusalem

29 "Woe *a*to Ariel,* to Ariel, the city
*b*where David dwelt!
Add year to year;
Let feasts come around.

---

* **29:1** That is, Jerusalem

28:13 *fall backward, and be broken.* In keeping with their drunken habits, the people would not be able to hear the teaching of the Lord.

28:14 *scornful.* The scornful, or scoffers, are worse than fools. Beyond choosing what is bad, they despise what is good (Ps. 1:1).

28:16 *precious cornerstone.* The apostles identified the cornerstone as Jesus Christ (1 Pet. 2:4–6).

28:20 *bed . . . covering.* The word picture of the short bed and inadequate covering is an illustration of the inadequacy of any security that is not based on a relationship with the living God as He has outlined it in Scripture.

28:27 *cummin . . . threshing sledge.* Cummin cannot be threshed with a sledge. The cart and sledge are too large for such a fine seed (27:12).

28:29 *wonderful in counsel.* The wisdom that the farmer uses to tend his crops comes from God, the source of all good counsel.

29:1 *Ariel.* Ariel probably means "altar" (Ezek. 43:15–16). The destruction and bloodshed in Jeru-

28:15 *h* Is. 9:15   **28:16** *i* Matt. 21:42   **28:21** *j* 2 Sam. 5:20   *k* Josh. 10:10, 12   *l* [Lam. 3:33]   **28:22** *m* Is. 10:22   **28:29** *n* Ps. 92:5   **29:1** *a* Ezek. 24:6, 9   *b* 2 Sam. 5:9

2 Yet I will distress Ariel;
   There shall be heaviness and sorrow,
   And it shall be to Me as Ariel.
3 I will encamp against you all around,
   I will lay siege against you with a
      mound,
   And I will raise siegeworks against
      you.
4 You shall be brought down,
   You shall speak out of the ground;
   Your speech shall be low, out of the
      dust;
   Your voice shall be like a medium's,
      cout of the ground;
   And your speech shall whisper out of
      the dust.

5 "Moreover the multitude of your dfoes
      Shall be like fine dust,
   And the multitude of the terrible ones
      Like echaff that passes away;
   Yes, it shall be fin an instant,
      suddenly.
6 gYou will be punished by the LORD of
      hosts
   With thunder and hearthquake and
      great noise,
   With storm and tempest
   And the flame of devouring fire.
7 iThe multitude of all the nations who
      fight against Ariel,
   Even all who fight against her and her
      fortress,
   And distress her,
   Shall be jas a dream of a night vision.
8 kIt shall even be as when a hungry man
      dreams,
   And look—he eats;
   But he awakes, and his soul is still
      empty;
   Or as when a thirsty man dreams,
   And look—he drinks;
   But he awakes, and indeed he is faint,
   And his soul still craves:
   So the multitude of all the nations
      shall be,
   Who fight against Mount Zion."

The Blindness of Disobedience

9 Pause and wonder!
   Blind yourselves and be blind!
   lThey are drunk, mbut not with wine;
   They stagger, but not with intoxicating
      drink.

10 For nthe LORD has poured out on you
   The spirit of deep sleep,
   And has oclosed your eyes, namely, the
      prophets;
   And He has covered your heads,
      namely, pthe seers.

11 The whole vision has become to you
like the words of a book qthat is sealed,
which men deliver to one who is literate,
saying, "Read this, please."
   rAnd he says, "I cannot, for it is sealed."
12 Then the book is delivered to one who
is illiterate, saying, "Read this, please."
   And he says, "I am not literate."
13 Therefore the Lord said:

s"Inasmuch as these people draw near
      with their mouths
   And honor Me twith their lips,
   But have removed their hearts far
      from Me,
   And their fear toward Me is taught by
      the commandment of men,
14 uTherefore, behold, I will again do a
      marvelous work
   Among this people,
   A marvelous work and a wonder;
   vFor the wisdom of their wise men shall
      perish,
   And the understanding of their
      prudent men shall be hidden."

15 wWoe to those who seek deep to hide
      their counsel far from the LORD,
   And their works are in the dark;
   xThey say, "Who sees us?" and, "Who
      knows us?"
16 Surely you have things turned
      around!
   Shall the potter be esteemed as the
      clay;
   For shall the ything made say of him
      who made it,
   "He did not make me"?
   Or shall the thing formed say of him
      who formed it,
   "He has no understanding"?

Future Recovery of Wisdom

17 Is it not yet a very little while
   Till zLebanon shall be turned into a
      fruitful field,
   And the fruitful field be esteemed as
      a forest?

---

salem would make the city appear like an altar. The repetition of the term *Ariel* indicates the Lord's sorrow over the state to which His city had fallen. *where David dwelt.* David made Jerusalem his capital and planned the temple that Solomon later built in that city. These words show God's continuing love for His servant David.
29:7 *as a dream.* No city has suffered desolation and later been rebuilt like Jerusalem. One final time the fires of God's wrath will be allowed to burn on the City of Peace. God's eternal purpose will bring the city to its knees. Judgment is God's unwilling work. He never allows the fires of discipline to punish His

own for no reason. When His disciplines have accomplished His task, peace is sure to follow.
29:17 *Lebanon . . . fruitful field.* This is a statement of sharp changes. Lebanon was a land of forests. As valuable as a fertile field was, a forest was even more

29:4 c Is. 8:19   **29:5** d Is. 25:5   e Job 21:18   f Is. 30:13;
47:11   **29:6** g Is. 28:2; 30:30   h Rev. 16:18, 19   **29:7** i Mic.
4:11, 12   j Job 20:8   **29:8** k Ps. 73:20   **29:9** l Is. 28:7, 8
m Is. 51:21   **29:10** n Rom. 11:8   o Ps. 69:23   p Is. 44:18
29:11 q Is. 8:16   r Dan. 12:4, 9   **29:13** s Ezek. 33:31   t Col.
2:22   **29:14** u Is. 1:5   v Jer. 49:7   **29:15** w Is. 30:1   x Ps.
10:11; 94:7   **29:16** y Is. 45:9   **29:17** z Is. 32:15

18 *a*In that day the deaf shall hear the
    words of the book,
And the eyes of the blind shall see out
    of obscurity and out of darkness.
19 *b*The humble also shall increase *their*
    joy in the LORD,
And *c*the poor among men shall rejoice
    In the Holy One of Israel.
20 For the terrible one is brought to
    nothing,
    *d*The scornful one is consumed,
And all who *e*watch for iniquity are
    cut off—
21 Who make a man an offender by a
    word,
And *f*lay a snare for him who reproves
    in the gate,
And turn aside the just *g*by empty
    words.

22Therefore thus says the LORD, *h*who redeemed Abraham, concerning the house of
Jacob:

"Jacob shall not now be *i*ashamed,
    Nor shall his face now grow pale;
23 But when he sees his children,
    *j*The work of My hands, in his midst,
    They shall hallow My name,
And hallow the Holy One of Jacob,
    And fear the God of Israel.
24 These also *k*who erred in spirit will
    come to understanding,
And those who complained will learn
    doctrine."

Futile Confidence in Egypt

30 "Woe to the rebellious children,"
    says the LORD,
a"Who take counsel, but not of Me,
    And who devise plans, but not of My
    Spirit,
*b*That they may add sin to sin;
2 *c*Who walk to go down to Egypt,
    And *d*have not asked My advice,
    To strengthen themselves in the
      strength of Pharaoh,
    And to trust in the shadow of Egypt!
3 *e*Therefore the strength of Pharaoh
    Shall be your shame,
And trust in the shadow of Egypt
    Shall be *your* humiliation.

4 For his princes were at *f*Zoan,
    And his ambassadors came to Hanes.
5 *g*They were all ashamed of a people
    who could not benefit them,
    Or be help or benefit,
But a shame and also a reproach."

6*h*The burden against the beasts of the
South.

Through a land of trouble and anguish,
    From which *came* the lioness and lion,
    *i*The viper and fiery flying serpent,
They will carry their riches on the
      backs of young donkeys,
And their treasures on the humps of
      camels,
To a people *who* shall not profit;
7 *j*For the Egyptians shall help in vain
    and to no purpose.
Therefore I have called her
Rahab-Hem-Shebeth.*

A Rebellious People

8 Now go, *k*write it before them on a
    tablet,
    And note it on a scroll,
That it may be for time to come,
    Forever and ever:
9 That *l*this *is* a rebellious people,
    Lying children,
Children *who* will not hear the law of
    the LORD;
10 *m*Who say to the seers, "Do not see,"
    And to the prophets, "Do not prophesy
      to us right things;
    *n*Speak to us smooth things, prophesy
      deceits.
11 Get out of the way,
    Turn aside from the path,
    Cause the Holy One of Israel
To cease from before us."

12Therefore thus says the Holy One of
Israel:

"Because you *o*despise this word,
    And trust in oppression and
      perversity,
    And rely on them,

---

* **30:7** Literally *Rahab Sits Idle*

---

valuable in Israel and Judah, which did not have large
stands of trees suitable for lumber. It would indicate
some major economic and physical changes for Lebanon to become a field and for a fertile field to be as
valuable as a forest.
29:19 poor . . . rejoice. God always notices the
poor and commands His people to do likewise. The
poor and the humble are particularly vulnerable to
exploitation, and God in His justice does not forget
this when He is dealing with disobedient leaders.
29:21 by a word . . . lay a snare . . . empty words. The
central issue in this passage is justice. The evil ones
miscarry justice with "a word" or false testimony,
"snare" through legal technicalities, and win cases
with empty words or lies and clever arguments that
obscure true justice.

30:1 Woe. This is the fourth woe. The rebellious children are Hezekiah's advisors. To the sin of injustice
they add the sin of devising plans independently of
God.
30:4 Zoan . . . Hanes. Zoan, which was in the Nile
delta, was the capital of Egypt at this time (19:11–13).
Hanes was 50 miles south of Cairo.

29:18 *a* Is. 35:5   **29:19** *b* [Is. 11:4; 61:1]   *c* [James 2:5]
29:20 *d* Is. 28:14   *e* Mic. 2:1   **29:21** *f* Amos 5:10, 12 *g* Prov.
28:21   **29:22** *h* Josh. 24:3 *i* Is. 45:17   **29:23** *j* [Is. 45:11;
49:20–26]   **29:24** *k* Is. 28:7   **30:1** *a* Is. 29:15 *b* Deut. 29:19
30:2 *c* Is. 31:1 *d* Josh. 9:14   **30:3** *e* Is. 20:5   **30:4** *f* Is. 19:11
30:5 *g* Jer. 2:36   **30:6** *h* Is. 57:9 *Deut. 8:15   **30:7** *j* Jer.
37:7   **30:8** *k* Hab. 2:2   **30:9** *l* Is. 1:2, 4; 65:2   **30:10** *m* Jer.
11:21 *n* 1 Kin. 22:8, 13   **30:12** *o* Is. 5:24

13 Therefore this iniquity shall be to you
  pLike a breach ready to fall,
  A bulge in a high wall,
  Whose breaking qcomes suddenly, in
    an instant.
14 And rHe shall break it like the
    breaking of the potter's vessel,
  Which is broken in pieces;
  He shall not spare.
  So there shall not be found among its
    fragments
  A shard to take fire from the hearth,
  Or to take water from the cistern."

15For thus says the Lord GOD, the Holy
One of Israel:

s"In returning and rest you shall be
    saved;
  In quietness and confidence shall be
    your strength."
  tBut you would not,
16 And you said, "No, for we will flee on
    horses"—
  Therefore you shall flee!
  And, "We will ride on swift horses"—
  Therefore those who pursue you shall
    be swift!

17 uOne thousand shall flee at the threat of
    one,
  At the threat of five you shall flee,
  Till you are left as a pole on top of a
    mountain
  And as a banner on a hill.

God Will Be Gracious

18 Therefore the LORD will wait, that He
    may be vgracious to you;
  And therefore He will be exalted, that
    He may have mercy on you.
  For the LORD is a God of justice;
  wBlessed are all those who xwait for Him.

19 For the people yshall dwell in Zion at
    Jerusalem;
  You shall zweep no more.
  He will be very gracious to you at the
    sound of your cry;
  When He hears it, He will aanswer
    you.
20 And though the Lord gives you
  bThe bread of adversity and the water
    of affliction,
  Yet cyour teachers will not be moved
    into a corner anymore,
  But your eyes shall see your teachers.

21 Your ears shall hear a word behind
    you, saying,
  "This is the way, walk in it,"
  Whenever you dturn to the right hand
  Or whenever you turn to the left.
22 eYou will also defile the covering of
    your images of silver,
  And the ornament of your molded
    images of gold.
  You will throw them away as an
    unclean thing;
  fYou will say to them, "Get away!"

23 gThen He will give the rain for your
    seed
  With which you sow the ground,
  And bread of the increase of the
    earth;
  It will be fat and plentiful.
  In that day your cattle will feed
  In large pastures.
24 Likewise the oxen and the young
    donkeys that work the ground
  Will eat cured fodder,
  Which has been winnowed with the
    shovel and fan.
25 There will be hon every high mountain
  And on every high hill
  Rivers and streams of waters,
  In the day of the igreat slaughter,
  When the towers fall.
26 Moreover jthe light of the moon will be
    as the light of the sun,
  And the light of the sun will be
    sevenfold,
  As the light of seven days,
  In the day that the LORD binds up the
    bruise of His people
  And heals the stroke of their wound.

Judgment on Assyria

27 Behold, the name of the LORD comes
    from afar,
  Burning with His anger,
  And His burden is heavy;
  His lips are full of indignation,
  And His tongue like a devouring
    fire.
28 kHis breath is like an overflowing
    stream,
  lWhich reaches up to the neck,
  To sift the nations with the sieve of
    futility;
  And there shall be ma bridle in the
    jaws of the people,
  Causing them to err.

30:15 confidence. A quiet, patient trust in God provides more strength for a follower of God than any
alliance with any other person or system. When
danger threatens, it is difficult not to look for ways to
use one's own strength. It is also difficult to maintain
inward composure and not trust in external sources
of help. Even if we cannot imagine how we can be
helped, if we are trusting God, we can have confidence and therefore have peace that He will not forsake us in our hour of need. God may use our strength
or the help of others, but, when we turn to God first,
we can learn which resources, if any, are the ones He
wants us to use. When God is first, then our decisions
are wise.
30:23–24 give the rain. The promises that were part
of the original Mosaic covenant were in force again.

30:13 p Ps. 62:3, 4 q Is. 29:5   30:14 r Jer. 19:11
30:15 s Is. 7:4; 28:12 t Matt. 23:37   30:17 u Josh.
23:10   30:18 v Is. 33:2 w Jer. 17:7 x Is. 26:8   30:19 y Is.
65:9 z Is. 25:8 a Is. 65:24   30:20 b 1 Kin. 22:27 c Amos
8:11   30:21 d Josh. 1:7   30:22 e Is. 2:20; 31:7 f Hos. 14:8
30:23 g [Matt. 6:33]   30:25 h Is. 2:14, 15 i Is. 2:10–21; 34:2
30:26 j [Is. 60:19, 20]   30:28 k Is. 11:4 l Is. 8:8 m Is. 37:29

29 You shall have a song
As in the night *when* a holy festival is
kept,
And gladness of heart as when one
goes with a flute,
To come into ⁿthe mountain of the
LORD,
To the Mighty One of Israel.
30 ᵒThe LORD will cause His glorious
voice to be heard,
And show the descent of His arm,
With the indignation of *His* anger
And the flame of a devouring fire,
With scattering, tempest, ᵖand
hailstones.
31 For �q through the voice of the LORD
Assyria will be beaten down,
As He strikes with the ʳrod.
32 And *in* every place where the staff of
punishment passes,
Which the LORD lays on him,
It will be with tambourines and
harps;
And in battles of ˢbrandishing He will
fight with it.
33 ᵗFor Tophet *was* established of old,
Yes, for the king it is prepared.
He has made *it* deep and large;
Its pyre *is* fire with much wood;
The breath of the LORD, like a stream
of brimstone,
Kindles it.

The Folly of Not Trusting God

31 Woe to those ᵃwho go down to
Egypt for help,
And ᵇrely on horses,
Who trust in chariots because *they are*
many,
And in horsemen because they are
very strong,
But who do not look to the Holy One
of Israel,
ᶜNor seek the LORD!
2 Yet He also *is* wise and will bring
disaster,
And ᵈwill not call back His words,
But will arise against the house of
evildoers,

And against the help of those who
work iniquity.
3 Now the Egyptians *are* men, and not
God;
And their horses are flesh, and not
spirit.
When the LORD stretches out His
hand,
Both he who helps will fall,
And he who is helped will fall down;
They all will perish ᵉtogether.

God Will Deliver Jerusalem

⁴For thus the LORD has spoken to me:

ᶠ"As a lion roars,
And a young lion over his prey
(When a multitude of shepherds is
summoned against him,
He will not be afraid of their voice
Nor be disturbed by their noise),
So the LORD of hosts will come down
To fight for Mount Zion and for its hill.
5 ᵍLike birds flying about,
So will the LORD of hosts defend
Jerusalem.
Defending, He will also deliver *it*;
Passing over, He will preserve *it*."

⁶Return *to Him* against whom the children of Israel have ʰdeeply revolted. ⁷For
in that day every man shall ⁱthrow away
his idols of silver and his idols of gold—
ʲsin, which your own hands have made for
yourselves.

8 "Then Assyria shall ᵏfall by a sword
not of man,
And a sword not of mankind shall
ˡdevour him.
But he shall flee from the sword,
And his young men shall become
forced labor.
9 ᵐHe shall cross over to his stronghold
for fear,
And his princes shall be afraid of the
banner,"
Says the LORD,
Whose fire *is* in Zion
And whose furnace *is* in Jerusalem.

Blessing would extend from field to flock (Deut. 28:11–12).
30:30 descent of His arm. The strong arm of God had delivered the Israelites from Egypt. Now His arm would descend in judgment (Ex. 6:6).
30:33 Tophet. Tophet was a place where Judah made human sacrifices to the heathen god Molech. The prophet uses it as a picture of God's vengeance on the wicked. He is not picturing temporal punishment, but everlasting destruction. This punishment will be in a place that is "deep" or inescapable. Then Isaiah draws the picture of the punishment by fire in hell. Some claim that the fire is symbolic, but it should be remembered that the reality is always greater than the symbol. The bliss of the righteous cannot be fully comprehended, and neither can the terror that awaits the wicked.
31:1 Woe. The fifth woe reaffirms the fourth woe

(30:1–33). It, too, was addressed to those who replace faith in the Lord with reliance on Egypt.
31:2 house of evildoers . . . help. This "house" refers to Judah, and their "help" refers to Egypt.
31:7 that day. "That day" refers to the day when God will judge the rebellious (24:21; 26:1). God had judged nations from time to time over the ages (Canaan, Egypt, Babylon, Israel, etc.), but the final day of judgment when everything will be made new is still in the future (Rev. 20:11–15).

30:29 ⁿ [Is. 2:3]   **30:30** ᵒ Is. 29:6 ᵖ Is. 28:2   **30:31** q Is.
14:25; 37:36 ʳ Is. 10:5, 24   **30:32** ˢ Is. 11:15   **30:33** ᵗ Jer.
7:31   **31:1** ᵃ Is. 30:1, 2 ᵇ Ps. 20:7 ᶜ Dan. 9:13
31:2 ᵈ Num. 23:19   **31:3** ᵉ Is. 20:6   **31:4** ᶠ Hos. 11:10
31:5 ᵍ Deut. 32:11   **31:6** ʰ Hos. 9:9   **31:7** ⁱ Is. 2:20;
30:22 ʲ 1 Kin. 12:30   **31:8** ᵏ 2 Kin. 19:35, 36 ˡ Is. 37:36
31:9 ᵐ Is. 37:37

A Reign of Righteousness

32 Behold, ᵃa king will reign in righteousness,
And princes will rule with justice.
2 A man will be as a hiding place from the wind,
And ᵇa cover from the tempest,
As rivers of water in a dry place,
As the shadow of a great rock in a weary land.
3 ᶜThe eyes of those who see will not be dim,
And the ears of those who hear will listen.
4 Also the heart of the rash will ᵈunderstand knowledge,
And the tongue of the stammerers will be ready to speak plainly.
5 The foolish person will no longer be called generous,
Nor the miser said *to be* bountiful;
6 For the foolish person will speak foolishness,
And his heart will work ᵉiniquity:
To practice ungodliness,
To utter error against the LORD,
To keep the hungry unsatisfied,
And he will cause the drink of the thirsty to fail.
7 Also the schemes of the schemer *are* evil;
He devises wicked plans
To destroy the poor with ᶠlying words,
Even when the needy speaks justice.
8 But a generous man devises generous things,
And by generosity he shall stand.

Consequences of Complacency

9 Rise up, you women ᵍwho are at ease,
Hear my voice;
You complacent daughters,
Give ear to my speech.
10 In a year and *some* days
You will be troubled, you complacent women;
For the vintage will fail,
The gathering will not come.
11 Tremble, you *women* who are at ease;
Be troubled, you complacent ones;
Strip yourselves, make yourselves bare,
And gird *sackcloth* on *your* waists.

12 People shall mourn upon their breasts
For the pleasant fields, for the fruitful vine.
13 ʰOn the land of my people will come up thorns *and* briers,
Yes, on all the happy homes *in* ⁱthe joyous city;
14 ʲBecause the palaces will be forsaken,
The bustling city will be deserted.
The forts and towers will become lairs forever,
A joy of wild donkeys, a pasture of flocks—
15 Until ᵏthe Spirit is poured upon us from on high,
And ˡthe wilderness becomes a fruitful field,
And the fruitful field is counted as a forest.

The Peace of God's Reign

16 Then justice will dwell in the wilderness,
And righteousness remain in the fruitful field.
17 ᵐThe work of righteousness will be peace,
And the effect of righteousness,
quietness and assurance forever.
18 My people will dwell in a peaceful habitation,
In secure dwellings, and in quiet ⁿresting places,
19 ᵒThough hail comes down ᵖon the forest,
And the city is brought low in humiliation.

20 Blessed *are* you who sow beside all waters,
Who send out freely the feet of ᵠthe ox and the donkey.

A Prayer in Deep Distress

33 Woe to you ᵃwho plunder, though you *have* not *been* plundered;
And you who deal treacherously,
though they have not dealt treacherously with you!
ᵇWhen you cease plundering,
You will be ᶜplundered;
When you make an end of dealing treacherously,
They will deal treacherously with you.

32:1 Behold. The fifth woe concludes with a prophecy about leadership and its effects. *a king will reign in righteousness.* The prophecy concerning this king is fulfilled in the Lord Jesus Christ (7:14; 9:1–7; 11:1–5; 28:16; John 10:11). *princes.* The princes are Jesus' shepherds (1 Pet. 5:2–4).
32:9–11 complacent. The word "complacent" has connotations of "trust," as one who has taken refuge, or who is secure and without care. These women were complacent, but it was a false security. *sackcloth.* Mourning women removed their clothing and wore sackcloth around their waists (Gen. 37:34).

33:1 Woe. The sixth woe differs from the others in that it is addressed to Assyria, not to Judah. By focusing exclusively on Assyria's defeat and Judah's salvation, the prophecy magnifies Judah's exalted King.

32:1 ᵃ Ps. 45:1 **32:2** ᵇ Is. 4:6 **32:3** ᶜ Is. 29:18; 35:5 **32:4** ᵈ Is. 29:24 **32:6** ᵉ Prov. 24:7–9 **32:7** ᶠ Jer. 5:26–28 **32:9** ᵍ Amos 6:1 **32:13** ʰ Hos. 9:6 ⁱ Is. 22:2 **32:14** ʲ Is. 27:10 **32:15** ᵏ [Joel 2:28] ˡ Is. 29:17 **32:17** ᵐ James 3:18 **32:18** ⁿ [Zech. 2:5; 3:10] **32:19** ᵒ Is. 30:30 ᵖ Zech. 11:2 **32:20** ᵠ Is. 30:23, 24 **33:1** ᵃ Hab. 2:8 ᵇ Rev. 13:10 ᶜ Is. 10:12; 14:25; 31:8

2 O LORD, be gracious to us;
 dWe have waited for You.
 Be their* arm every morning,
 Our salvation also in the time of
  trouble.
3 At the noise of the tumult the people
  eshall flee;
 When You lift Yourself up, the nations
  shall be scattered;
4 And Your plunder shall be gathered
 Like the gathering of the caterpillar;
 As the running to and fro of locusts,
 He shall run upon them.

5 fThe LORD is exalted, for He dwells on
  high;
 He has filled Zion with justice and
  righteousness.
6 Wisdom and knowledge will be the
  stability of your times,
 And the strength of salvation;
 The fear of the LORD is His treasure.

7 Surely their valiant ones shall cry
  outside,
 gThe ambassadors of peace shall weep
  bitterly.
8 hThe highways lie waste,
 The traveling man ceases.
 iHe has broken the covenant,
 He has despised the cities,*
 He regards no man.
9 jThe earth mourns and languishes,
 Lebanon is shamed and shriveled;
 Sharon is like a wilderness,
 And Bashan and Carmel shake off
  their fruits.

Impending Judgment on Zion

10 "Nowk I will rise," says the LORD;
 "Now I will be exalted,
 Now I will lift Myself up.
11 lYou shall conceive chaff,
 You shall bring forth stubble;
 Your breath, as fire, shall devour you.
12 And the people shall be like the
  burnings of lime;
 mLike thorns cut up they shall be
  burned in the fire.
13 Hear, nyou who are afar off, what I
  have done;

And you who are near, acknowledge
 My might."

14 The sinners in Zion are afraid;
 Fearfulness has seized the hypocrites:
 "Who among us shall dwell with the
  devouring ofire?
 Who among us shall dwell with
  everlasting burnings?"
15 He who pwalks righteously and speaks
  uprightly,
 He who despises the gain of
  oppressions,
 Who gestures with his hands, refusing
  bribes,
 Who stops his ears from hearing of
  bloodshed,
 And qshuts his eyes from seeing evil:
16 He will dwell on high;
 His place of defense will be the
  fortress of rocks;
 Bread will be given him,
 His water will be sure.

The Land of the Majestic King

17 Your eyes will see the King in His
  rbeauty;
 They will see the land that is very far off.
18 Your heart will meditate on terror:
  s"Where is the scribe?
 Where is he who weighs?
 Where is he who counts the towers?"
19 tYou will not see a fierce people,
  uA people of obscure speech, beyond
   perception,
 Of a stammering tongue that you
  cannot understand.

20 vLook on Zion, the city of our
  appointed feasts;
 Your eyes will see wJerusalem, a quiet
  home,
 A tabernacle that will not be taken
  down;
  xNot one of yits stakes will ever be
   removed,
 Nor will any of its cords be broken.

---

* 33:2 Septuagint omits their; Syriac, Targum,
and Vulgate read our. * 33:8 Following Masoretic Text and Vulgate; Dead Sea Scrolls read
witnesses; Septuagint omits cities; Targum reads
They have been removed from their cities.

33:3 lift Yourself up. This passage refers to an exaltation of the heavenly King (vv. 5,10) as He rises to
demonstrate His glory and vindicate His justice.
33:4 plunder. The plunder of God's war with His enemies belongs to the Lord, the true Victor (23:18; 34:2).
33:9 Sharon . . . Bashan. Sharon was on the western
coastal plain, and Bashan was on the east side of the
Jordan.
33:15 walks righteously. For a similar description of
the person who can approach the Holy One, see Psalm
1:1–2; 15:2; Galatians 5:22–25; and Ephesians 5:1–2.
33:17 land that is very far off. The prophet's land
was continually threatened by the Assyrian army.
But, in prophetic vision, Isaiah saw a little picture of
the beauty of heaven. In the mind of the believer, the

trials of the present fade into insignificance if he only
contemplates that glorious time when he will dwell in
the presence of his King.
33:18 the scribe. The scribe who counted was the
one who took tribute (2 Kin. 18:14).
33:19 people of obscure speech. For a similar idea
concerning Israel's enemies, see Deuteronomy 28:49.

33:2 d Is. 25:9; 26:8   **33:3** e Is. 17:13   **33:5** f Ps.
97:9   **33:7** g 2 Kin. 18:18, 37   **33:8** h Judg. 5:6 i 2 Kin.
18:13–17   **33:9** j Is. 24:4   **33:10** k Ps. 12:5   **33:11** l [Ps.
7:14]   **33:12** m Is. 9:18   **33:13** n Is. 49:1   **33:14** o Heb.
12:29   **33:15** p Ps. 15:2; 24:3, 4 q Ps. 119:37   **33:17** r Ps.
27:4   **33:18** s 1 Cor. 1:20   **33:19** t 2 Kin. 19:32 u Jer. 5:15
33:20 v Ps. 48:12 w Ps. 46:5; 125:1 x Is. 37:33 y Is. 54:2

21 But there the majestic LORD *will be* for
   us
   A place of broad rivers *and* streams,
   In which no galley with oars will sail,
   Nor majestic ships pass by
22 (For the LORD *is* our ²Judge,
   The LORD *is* our ªLawgiver,
   ᵇThe LORD *is* our King;
   He will save us);
23 Your tackle is loosed,
   They could not strengthen their mast,
   They could not spread the sail.

   Then the prey of great plunder is
   divided;
   The lame take the prey.
24 And the inhabitant will not say, "I am
   sick";
   ᶜThe people who dwell in it *will be*
   forgiven *their* iniquity.

Judgment on the Nations

34 Come ªnear, you nations, to hear;
   And heed, you people!
   ᵇLet the earth hear, and all that is in it,
   The world and all things that come
   forth from it.
2 For the indignation of the LORD *is*
   against all nations,
   And *His* fury against all their armies;
   He has utterly destroyed them,
   He has given them over to the
   ᶜslaughter.
3 Also their slain shall be thrown out;
   ᵈTheir stench shall rise from their
   corpses,
   And the mountains shall be melted
   with their blood.
4 ᵉAll the host of heaven shall be
   dissolved,
   And the heavens shall be rolled up like
   a scroll;
   ᶠAll their host shall fall down
   As the leaf falls from the vine,
   And as ᵍ*fruit* falling from a fig tree.
5 "For ʰMy sword shall be bathed in
   heaven;
   Indeed it ⁱshall come down on Edom,
   And on the people of My curse, for
   judgment.
6 The ʲsword of the LORD is filled with
   blood,
   It is made overflowing with fatness,
   With the blood of lambs and goats,

With the fat of the kidneys of rams.
   For ᵏthe LORD has a sacrifice in
   Bozrah,
   And a great slaughter in the land of
   Edom.
7 The wild oxen shall come down with
   them,
   And the young bulls with the mighty
   bulls;
   Their land shall be soaked with blood,
   And their dust saturated with fatness."

8 For *it is* the day of the LORD's
   ˡvengeance,
   The year of recompense for the cause
   of Zion.
9 ᵐIts streams shall be turned into pitch,
   And its dust into brimstone;
   Its land shall become burning pitch.
10 It shall not be quenched night or day;
   ⁿIts smoke shall ascend forever.
   ᵒFrom generation to generation it shall
   lie waste;
   No one shall pass through it forever
   and ever.
11 ᵖBut the pelican and the porcupine
   shall possess it,
   Also the owl and the raven shall dwell
   in it.
   And ᑫHe shall stretch out over it
   The line of confusion and the stones of
   emptiness.
12 They shall call its nobles to the
   kingdom,
   But none *shall be* there, and all its
   princes shall be nothing.

13 And ʳthorns shall come up in its
   palaces,
   Nettles and brambles in its fortresses;
   ˢIt shall be a habitation of jackals,
   A courtyard for ostriches.
14 The wild beasts of the desert shall also
   meet with the jackals,
   And the wild goat shall bleat to its
   companion;
   Also the night creature shall rest
   there,
   And find for herself a place of rest.
15 There the arrow snake shall make her
   nest and lay *eggs*
   And hatch, and gather *them* under her
   shadow;
   There also shall the hawks be
   gathered,
   Every one with her mate.

33:22 The LORD is our Lawgiver. The Lawgiver is associated with other acts of mercy (Deut. 6:1–3; John 1:14–18); the giving of the law was God's way to point out the correct path for the Israelites to follow. His commitment to set our feet on the right path is one of His acts of mercy.

34:4 host of heaven. The host of heaven here refers to pagan deities (24:21; 2 Kin. 17:16). **heavens shall be rolled up like a scroll.** The old cosmos will give way to the new (51:6; Matt. 24:29; Rev. 6:13–14; 21:1).

34:8 vengeance. The Lord has promised that He will one day right the wrongs suffered by His followers,

but that vengeance is His and His alone (Deut. 32:35; Rom. 12:19).

34:9 brimstone . . . burning pitch. Brimstone and burning pitch may be allusions to Sodom and Gomorrah (30:33; Gen. 19:24; Ezek. 38:22).

33:22 ᶻ[Acts 10:42] ª James 4:12 ᵇ Ps. 89:18 **33:24** ᶜ Is. 40:2 **34:1** ª Ps. 49:1 ᵇ Deut. 32:1 **34:2** ᶜ Is. 13:5 **34:3** ᵈ Joel 2:20 **34:4** ᵉ Is. 13:13 ᶠ Is. 14:12 ᵍ Rev. 6:12–14 **34:5** ʰ Jer. 46:10 ⁱ Mal. 1:4 **34:6** ʲ Is. 66:16 ᵏ Zeph. 1:7 **34:8** ˡ Is. 63:4 **34:9** ᵐ Deut. 29:23 **34:10** ⁿ Rev. 14:11; 18:18; 19:3 ᵒ Mal. 1:3, 4 **34:11** ᵖ Zeph. 2:14 ᑫ Lam. 2:8 **34:13** ʳ Is. 32:13 ˢ Is. 13:21

16 "Search from *t*the book of the Lord,
and read:
Not one of these shall fail;
Not one shall lack her mate.
For My mouth has commanded it, and
His Spirit has gathered them.
17 He has cast the lot for them,
And His hand has divided it among
them with a measuring line.
They shall possess it forever;
From generation to generation they
shall dwell in it."

The Future Glory of Zion

35 The *a*wilderness and the wasteland
shall be glad for them,
And the *b*desert shall rejoice and
blossom as the rose;
2 *c*It shall blossom abundantly and
rejoice,
Even with joy and singing.
The glory of Lebanon shall be given
to it,
The excellence of Carmel and Sharon.
They shall see the *d*glory of the Lord,
The excellency of our God.

3 *e*Strengthen the weak hands,
And make firm the feeble knees.
4 Say to those *who are* fearful-hearted,
"Be strong, do not fear!
Behold, your God will come *with*
*f*vengeance,
With the recompense of God;
He will come and *g*save you."

5 Then the *h*eyes of the blind shall be
opened,
And *i*the ears of the deaf shall be
unstopped.
6 Then the *j*lame shall leap like a deer,
And the *k*tongue of the dumb sing.
For *l*waters shall burst forth in the
wilderness,
And streams in the desert.

7 The parched ground shall become a
pool,
And the thirsty land springs of water;
In *m*the habitation of jackals, where
each lay,
There shall be grass with reeds and
rushes.

8 A *n*highway shall be there, and a road,
And it shall be called the Highway of
Holiness.
*o*The unclean shall not pass over it,
But it *shall be* for others.
Whoever walks the road, although a
fool,
Shall not go astray.
9 *p*No lion shall be there,
Nor shall *any* ravenous beast go up on it;
It shall not be found there.
But the redeemed shall walk *there*,
10 And the *q*ransomed of the Lord shall
return,
And come to Zion with singing,
With everlasting joy on their heads.
They shall obtain joy and gladness,
And *r*sorrow and sighing shall flee away.

Sennacherib Boasts Against the Lord

36 Now *a*it came to pass in the fourteenth year of King Hezekiah *that*
Sennacherib king of Assyria came up
against all the fortified cities of Judah and
took them. 2 Then the king of Assyria sent
the Rabshakeh* with a great army from
Lachish to King Hezekiah at Jerusalem.
And he stood by the aqueduct from the
upper pool, on the highway to the Fuller's
Field. 3 And *b*Eliakim the son of Hilkiah,
who was over the household, *c*Shebna the
scribe, and Joah the son of Asaph, the recorder, came out to him.

---

* 36:2 A title, probably *Chief of Staff* or *Governor*

35:1–2 rejoice. Isaiah 35 stands in contrast to Isaiah 34. This chapter opens with the lilt of joy. The Arabah, or desert plain, shall blossom and break into bloom. Centuries before, Moses had warned of a day when the rain of this land would become "powder and dust" (Deut. 28:24). That day came because Israel was disobedient to God. But, at the second coming of Christ (Rev. 20:1–6), Israel will be restored spiritually, and with spiritual restoration comes physical bless-ing. When judgment is removed, great blessing fol-lows. Restoration follows repentance, and restoration is accompanied by joy.
35:3 Strengthen the weak hands. This phrase is cited in Hebrews 12:12 (Josh. 1:6–7,9,18). We can reassure ourselves with the knowledge that our Savior is coming. In that day, justice will be restored.
35:5–6 eyes…ears…lame…tongue. This proph-ecy of healings was fulfilled by Jesus (Matt. 12:22; Luke 4:18; 7:22), and it was this passage in Isaiah that Jesus referred to when He answered John the Baptist's disciples who asked if He was the Expected One. The reply was somewhat cryptic, but it was something that John would understand in prison, without requiring Jesus to reveal Himself before it was time (Matt. 11:27; Luke 7:22).
35:10 ransomed. Someone who is ransomed is someone who has had a price paid to set him free from captivity. This promise looked forward to the return of the political captives and, in a much fuller sense, to the salvation through Jesus Christ, who gave "His life a ransom for many" (Matt. 20:28; Mark 10:45; 1 Tim. 2:6).
36:1 fourteenth year. The 14th year of King Hezeki-ah's sole reign was 701 B.C. **all.** In his annals, Sennach-erib mentions 46 cities that he attacked.
36:2 the Rabshakeh. This was probably the title of one of Sennacherib's officials (2 Kin. 18:17).

34:16 *t* [Mal. 3:16]   35:1 *a* Is. 32:15; 55:12   *b* Is. 41:19; 51:3   35:2 *c* Is. 32:15   *d* Is. 40:5   35:3 *e* Heb. 12:12   35:4 *f* Is. 34:8   *g* Is. 33:22   35:5 *h* Is. 29:18   *i* [Matt. 11:5]   35:6 *j* Acts 8:7   *k* Is. 32:4   *l* [John 7:38]   35:7 *m* Is. 34:13   35:8 *n* Is. 19:23   *o* Joel 3:17   35:9 *p* Lev. 26:6   35:10 *q* Is. 51:11   *r* [Rev. 7:17; 21:4]   36:1 *a* 2 Chr. 32:1   36:3 *b* Is. 22:20   *c* Is. 22:15

4ᵈThen *the* Rabshakeh said to them, "Say now to Hezekiah, 'Thus says the great king, the king of Assyria: "What confidence is this in which you trust? ⁵I say you speak of having plans and power for war; but *they are* mere words. Now in whom do you trust, that you rebel against me? ⁶Look! You are trusting in the ᵉstaff of this broken reed, Egypt, on which if a man leans, it will go into his hand and pierce it. So *is* Pharaoh king of Egypt to all who ᶠtrust in him.

⁷"But if you say to me, 'We trust in the LORD our God,' *is it* not He whose high places and whose altars Hezekiah has taken away, and said to Judah and Jerusalem, 'You shall worship before this altar'?" ' ⁸Now therefore, I urge you, give a pledge to my master the king of Assyria, and I will give you two thousand horses—if you are able on your part to put riders on them! ⁹How then will you repel one captain of the least of my master's servants, and put your trust in Egypt for chariots and horsemen? ¹⁰Have I now come up without the LORD against this land to destroy it? The LORD said to me, 'Go up against this land, and destroy it.' "

¹¹Then Eliakim, Shebna, and Joah said to *the* Rabshakeh, "Please speak to your servants in Aramaic, for we understand *it;* and do not speak to us in Hebrew* in the hearing of the people who *are* on the wall."

¹²But *the* Rabshakeh said, "Has my master sent to your master and to you to speak these words, and not to the men who sit on the wall, who will eat and drink their own waste with you?"

¹³Then *the* Rabshakeh stood and called out with a loud voice in Hebrew, and said, "Hear the words of the great king, the king of Assyria! ¹⁴Thus says the king: 'Do not let Hezekiah deceive you, for he will not be able to deliver you; ¹⁵nor let Hezekiah make you trust in the LORD, saying, "The LORD will surely deliver us; this city will not be given into the hand of the king of Assyria." ' ¹⁶Do not listen to Hezekiah; for thus says the king of Assyria: 'Make *peace* with me *by a* present and come out to me; ᵍand every one of you eat from his own vine and every one from his own fig tree, and every one of you drink the waters of

his own cistern; ¹⁷until I come and take you away to a land like your own land, a land of grain and new wine, a land of bread and vineyards. ¹⁸*Beware* lest Hezekiah persuade you, saying, "The LORD will deliver us." Has any one of the ʰgods of the nations delivered its land from the hand of the king of Assyria? ¹⁹Where *are* the gods of Hamath and Arpad? Where *are* the gods of Sepharvaim? Indeed, have they delivered ⁱSamaria from my hand? ²⁰Who among all the gods of these lands have delivered their countries from my hand, that the LORD should deliver Jerusalem from my hand?' "

²¹But they held their peace and answered him not a word; for the king's commandment was, "Do not answer him." ²²Then Eliakim the son of Hilkiah, who *was* over the household, Shebna the scribe, and Joah the son of Asaph, the recorder, came to Hezekiah with *their* clothes torn, and told him the words of *the* Rabshakeh.

Isaiah Assures Deliverance

37 And ᵃso it was, when King Hezekiah heard *it,* that he tore his clothes, covered himself with sackcloth, and went into the house of the LORD. ²Then he sent Eliakim, who *was* over the household, Shebna the scribe, and the elders of the priests, covered with sackcloth, to Isaiah the prophet, the son of Amoz. ³And they said to him, "Thus says Hezekiah: 'This day *is* a day of ᵇtrouble and rebuke and blasphemy; for the children have come to birth, but *there is* no strength to bring them forth. ⁴It may be that the LORD your God will hear the words of *the* Rabshakeh, whom his master the king of Assyria has sent to ᶜreproach the living God, and will rebuke the words which the LORD your God has heard. Therefore lift up *your* prayer for the remnant that is left.' "

⁵So the servants of King Hezekiah came to Isaiah. ⁶And Isaiah said to them, "Thus you shall say to your master, 'Thus says the LORD: "Do not be afraid of the words which you have heard, with which the servants of the king of Assyria have blasphemed Me. ⁷Surely I will send a spirit upon him, and he shall hear a rumor and return to his

---

* **36:11** Literally *Judean*

36:7 taken away. Hezekiah had destroyed the idolatrous high places and altars that his father Ahaz had built (2 Kin. 18:1–5; 2 Chr. 31:1–3).

36:8 riders. Micah referred to Jerusalem's soldiers as merely "troops" (Mic. 5:1) compared to the enormous international army of Assyria.

36:10 The LORD said to me. Ancient Middle Eastern conquerors liked to claim that the gods of their defeated enemies had joined their side (2 Chr. 35:21). These words about the Lord were no more than a boast.

36:11 Aramaic. The Syrian language was Aramaic, which was the language of international diplomacy.

36:19 have they delivered Samaria. Like the

Assyrian king (10:11), the Rabshakeh assumed that different gods were worshiped in Samaria than in Jerusalem.

36:22 Shebna. Isaiah had earlier condemned Shebna for presumption (22:15–23). Apparently that was a warning which was heeded, for his attitude was of mourning, repentance, and humility at this time.

37:6 Do not be afraid. The Lord commonly reassured

36:4 ᵈ2 Kin. 18:19   **36:6** ᵉEzek. 29:6   ᶠPs. 146:3
36:16 ᵍZech. 3:10   **36:18** ʰIs. 37:12   **36:19** ⁱ2 Kin.
17:6   **37:1** ᵈ2 Kin. 19:1–37   **37:3** ᵇIs. 22:5; 26:16; 33:2
37:4 ᶜIs. 36:15, 18, 20

own land; and I will cause him to fall by the sword in his own land." ' "

Sennacherib's Threat and Hezekiah's Prayer

⁸Then *the* Rabshakeh returned, and found the king of Assyria warring against Libnah, for he heard that he had departed from Lachish. ⁹And the king heard concerning Tirhakah king of Ethiopia, "He has come out to make war with you." So when he heard *it*, he sent messengers to Hezekiah, saying, ¹⁰"Thus you shall speak to Hezekiah king of Judah, saying: 'Do not let your God in whom you trust deceive you, saying, "Jerusalem shall not be given into the hand of the king of Assyria." ¹¹Look! You have heard what the kings of Assyria have done to all lands by utterly destroying them; and shall you be delivered? ¹²Have the ᵈgods of the nations delivered those whom my fathers have destroyed, Gozan and Haran and Rezeph, and the people of Eden who *were* in Telassar? ¹³Where *is* the king of ᵉHamath, the king of Arpad, and the king of the city of Sepharvaim, Hena, and Ivah?' "

¹⁴And Hezekiah received the letter from the hand of the messengers, and read it; and Hezekiah went up to the house of the LORD, and spread it before the LORD. ¹⁵Then Hezekiah prayed to the LORD, saying: ¹⁶"O LORD of hosts, God of Israel, *the One* who dwells *between* the cherubim, You *are* God, You ᶠalone, of all the kingdoms of the earth. You have made heaven and earth. ¹⁷ᵍIncline Your ear, O LORD, and hear; open Your eyes, O LORD, and see; and ʰhear all the words of Sennacherib, which he has sent to reproach the living God. ¹⁸Truly, LORD, the kings of Assyria have laid waste all the nations and their ⁱlands, ¹⁹and have cast their gods into the fire; for they *were* ʲnot gods, but the work of men's hands—wood and stone. Therefore they destroyed them. ²⁰Now therefore, O LORD our God, ᵏsave us from his hand, that all the kingdoms of the earth may ˡknow that You *are* the LORD, You alone."

The Word of the LORD Concerning Sennacherib

²¹Then Isaiah the son of Amoz sent to Hezekiah, saying, "Thus says the LORD God of Israel, 'Because you have prayed to Me against Sennacherib king of Assyria, ²²this *is* the word which the LORD has spoken concerning him:

"The virgin, the daughter of Zion,
Has despised you, laughed you to
    scorn;
The daughter of Jerusalem
Has shaken *her* head behind your back!

²³ "Whom have you reproached and
    blasphemed?
Against whom have you raised *your*
    voice,
And lifted up your eyes on high?
Against the Holy One of Israel.
²⁴ By your servants you have reproached
    the Lord,
And said, 'By the multitude of my
    chariots
I have come up to the height of the
    mountains,
To the limits of Lebanon;
I will cut down its tall cedars
And its choice cypress trees;
I will enter its farthest height,
To its fruitful forest.
²⁵ I have dug and drunk water,
And with the soles of my feet I have
    dried up
All the brooks of defense.'
²⁶ "Did you not hear ᵐlong ago
How I made it,
From ancient times that I formed it?
Now I have brought it to pass,
That you should be
For crushing fortified cities *into* heaps
    of ruins.
²⁷ Therefore their inhabitants *had* little
    power;
They were dismayed and confounded;
They were *as* the grass of the field
And the green herb,
As the grass on the housetops
And *grain* blighted before it is
    grown.
²⁸ "But I know your dwelling place,
Your going out and your coming in,
And your rage against Me.
²⁹ Because your rage against Me and
    your tumult
Have come up to My ears,

His servants with these words (7:4; 35:4; Gen. 15:1; Josh. 1:9). We have no reason to fear if our trust is in the all-powerful God (Heb. 13:6).

37:10 *Thus you shall speak.* Blasphemous and malicious designs against God and His people should motivate us to rely completely on the Lord and earnestly seek His strength. The response of God's people to blasphemers must never be incited by personal feelings, but by the desire that "all the kingdoms of the earth may know that You are the LORD, You alone" (v. 20).

37:21 *Thus says the LORD God.* Hezekiah's plea for help against the Assyrian menace brought a word from the Lord. Hezekiah was assured that the Lord was in absolute charge, even to the extent that

the Assyrian king's activities were brought about through God's own plan (v. 26). Sennacherib's forces fell before the mighty power of the angel of the Lord (v. 36), as a witness to the truth of the Word of God that the king's heart is turned by the hand of the Lord (Prov. 21:1).

37:29 *My hook in your nose.* The Assyrians dragged prisoners away with a hook in the nose. The Lord's

37:12 ᵈ Is. 36:18, 19   **37:13** ᵉ Is. 49:23   **37:16** ᶠ Is. 43:10, 11   **37:17** ᵍ Dan. 9:18   ʰ Ps. 74:22   **37:18** ⁱ 2 Kin. 15:29; 16:9; 17:6, 24   **37:19** ʲ Is. 40:19, 20   **37:20** ᵏ Is. 33:22   ˡ Ps. 83:18   **37:26** ᵐ Is. 25:1; 40:21; 45:21

Therefore [n]I will put My hook in your nose
And My bridle in your lips,
And I will [o]turn you back
By the way which you came."'

30"This *shall be* a sign to you:

You shall eat this year such as grows of itself,
And the second year what springs from the same;
Also in the third year sow and reap,
Plant vineyards and eat the fruit of them.

31 And the remnant who have escaped of the house of Judah
Shall again take root downward,
And bear fruit upward.

32 For out of Jerusalem shall go a remnant,
And those who escape from Mount Zion.
The [p]zeal of the LORD of hosts will do this.

33"Therefore thus says the LORD concerning the king of Assyria:

'He shall not come into this city,
Nor shoot an arrow there,
Nor come before it with shield,
Nor build a siege mound against it.

34 By the way that he came,
By the same shall he return;
And he shall not come into this city,'
Says the LORD.

35 'For I will [q]defend this city, to save it
For My own sake and for My servant [r]David's sake.'"

Sennacherib's Defeat and Death

36Then the [s]angel* of the LORD went out, and killed in the camp of the Assyrians one hundred and eighty-five thousand; and when *people* arose early in the morning, there were the corpses—all dead. 37So Sennacherib king of Assyria departed and went away, returned *home*, and remained at Nineveh. 38Now it came to pass, as he was worshiping in the house of Nisroch his god, that his sons Adrammelech and Sharezer struck him down with the sword; and they escaped into the land of Ararat. Then [t]Esarhaddon his son reigned in his place.

Hezekiah's Life Extended

38 In [a]those days Hezekiah was sick and near death. And Isaiah the prophet, the son of Amoz, went to him and said to him, "Thus says the LORD: [b]'Set your house in order, for you shall die and not live.'"

2Then Hezekiah turned his face toward the wall, and prayed to the LORD, 3and said, [c]"Remember now, O LORD, I pray, how I have walked before You in truth and with a loyal heart, and have done *what is* good in Your [d]sight." And Hezekiah wept bitterly.

4And the word of the LORD came to Isaiah, saying, 5"Go and tell Hezekiah, 'Thus says the LORD, the God of David your father: "I have heard your prayer, I have seen your tears; surely I will add to your days fifteen years. 6I will deliver you and this city from the hand of the king of Assyria, and [e]I will defend this city."' 7And this *is* [f]the sign to you from the LORD, that the LORD will do this thing which He has spoken: 8Behold, I will bring the shadow on the sundial, which has gone down with the sun on the sundial of Ahaz, ten degrees backward." So the sun returned ten degrees on the dial by which it had gone down.

9This is the writing of Hezekiah king of Judah, when he had been sick and had recovered from his sickness:

10 I said,
"In the prime of my life
I shall go to the gates of Sheol;
I am deprived of the remainder of my years."

11 I said,
"I shall not see YAH,
The LORD* [g]in the land of the living;
I shall observe man no more among the inhabitants of the world.*

12 [h]My life span is gone,
Taken from me like a shepherd's tent;
I have cut off my life like a weaver.

---

* 37:36 Or *Angel*   * 38:11 Hebrew YAH, YAH • Following some Hebrew manuscripts; Masoretic Text and Vulgate read *rest;* Septuagint omits *among the inhabitants of the world;* Targum reads *land.*

---

judgment was coming, and soon the Assyrians would experience being pulled away where they did not want to go.
37:36 angel of the LORD . . . killed. This verse is the fulfillment of God's promise to take vengeance on those who trouble His people (34:8).
37:38 Esarhaddon. Esarhaddon began his reign in 681 B.C.
38:5 add to your days. Hezekiah had no male heir at the time of his illness. Manasseh, the successor to his throne, was 12 when Hezekiah died (2 Kin. 20:21 — 21:1).
38:9 writing of Hezekiah. Scriptures attest to King

Hezekiah's interest in devotional literature. Apparently, he instructed his scribes to compile some of the proverbs of Solomon (Prov. 25:1). He ordered the Levites to worship God with the psalms of David and Asaph (2 Chr. 29:30), and the song of praise (vv. 10–20) has some similarities with those psalms.

37:29 [n] Is. 30:28 [o] Ezek. 38:4; 39:2		37:32 [p] 2 Kin. 19:31
37:35 [q] Is. 31:5; 38:6 [r] 1 Kin. 11:13		37:36 [s] 2 Kin. 19:35
37:38 [t] Ezra 4:2	38:1 [a] 2 Chr. 32:24 [b] 2 Sam. 17:23	
38:3 [c] Neh. 13:14 [d] 2 Kin. 18:5, 6		38:6 [e] Is. 31:5; 37:35
38:7 [f] Is. 7:11	38:11 [g] Ps. 27:13; 116:9	38:12 [h] Job 7:6

He cuts me off from the loom;
From day until night You make an end of me.

13 I have considered until morning—
Like a lion,
So He breaks all my bones;
From day until night You make an end of me.

14 Like a crane *or* a swallow, so I chattered;
*i*I mourned like a dove;
My eyes fail *from looking* upward.
O LORD,* I am oppressed;
Undertake for me!

15 "What shall I say?
He has both spoken to me,*
And He Himself has done *it.*
I shall walk carefully all my years
*j*In the bitterness of my soul.

16 O Lord, by these *things men* live;
And in all these *things is* the life of my spirit;
So You will restore me and make me live.

17 Indeed *it was* for *my own* peace
That I had great bitterness;
But You have lovingly *delivered* my soul from the pit of corruption,
For You have cast all my sins behind Your back.

18 For *k*Sheol cannot thank You,
Death cannot praise You;
Those who go down to the pit cannot hope for Your truth.

19 The living, the living man, he shall praise You,
As I *do* this day;
*l*The father shall make known Your truth to the children.

20 "The LORD *was ready* to save me;
Therefore we will sing my songs with stringed instruments
All the days of our life, in the house of the LORD."

21Now *m*Isaiah had said, "Let them take a lump of figs, and apply *it* as a poultice on the boil, and he shall recover."

22And *n*Hezekiah had said, "What *is* the sign that I shall go up to the house of the LORD?"

The Babylonian Envoys

39 At *a*that time Merodach-Baladan* the son of Baladan, king of Babylon, sent letters and a present to Hezekiah, for he heard that he had been sick and had recovered. 2*b*And Hezekiah was pleased with them, and showed them the house of his treasures—the silver and gold, the spices and precious ointment, and all his armory—all that was found among his treasures. There was nothing in his house or in all his dominion that Hezekiah did not show them.

3Then Isaiah the prophet went to King Hezekiah, and said to him, "What did these men say, and from where did they come to you?"

So Hezekiah said, "They came to me from a *c*far country, from Babylon."

4And he said, "What have they seen in your house?"

So Hezekiah answered, "They have seen all that *is* in my house; there is nothing among my treasures that I have not shown them."

5Then Isaiah said to Hezekiah, "Hear the word of the LORD of hosts: 6'Behold, the days are coming *d*when all that *is* in your house, and what your fathers have accumulated until this day, shall be carried to Babylon; nothing shall be left,' says the LORD. 7'And they shall take away *some* of your *e*sons who will descend from you, whom you will beget; and they shall be eunuchs in the palace of the king of Babylon.'"

8So Hezekiah said to Isaiah, *f*"The word of the LORD which you have spoken *is* good!" For he said, "At least there will be peace and truth in my days."

God's People Are Comforted

40 "Comfort, yes, comfort My people!" Says your God.

---

* **38:14** Following Bomberg; Masoretic Text and Dead Sea Scrolls read *Lord.*   * **38:15** Following Masoretic Text and Vulgate; Dead Sea Scrolls and Targum read *And shall I say to Him;* Septuagint omits first half of this verse.   * **39:1** Spelled *Berodach-Baladan* in 2 Kings 20:12

38:22 *sign.* Depending on one's attitude, the request for a sign may express either unbelief (Matt. 12:39; John 6:30) or faith (v. 7). The healing of a boil would be the sign that the Lord would save Hezekiah (vv. 20–21).

39:1 *recovered.* The miracle of the sundial (38:8) would have held special interest for the astronomy-minded Babylonians (2 Chr. 32:31).

39:2 *showed them the house of his treasures.* Hezekiah was flattered to receive the attention of the Babylonian delegation and wanted to show how important he was.

40:1—55:13 *Comfort.* This section is addressed to the Babylonian exiles in a prophetic manner. This book of comfort, written about 150 years before the time of Cyrus, promised the exiles from Judah that they would return to Jerusalem (40:1–2). The restoration after the exile pointed to the coming of the Lord's kingdom. In Isaiah's prophecy, this first taste of salvation merges with predictions of the full salvation that Jesus Christ would bring.

38:14 *j* Is. 59:11   **38:15** *j* Job 7:11; 10:1   **38:18** *k* Ps. 6:5; 30:9; 88:11; 115:17   **38:19** *l* Deut. 4:9; 6:7   **38:21** *m* 2 Kin. 20:7   **38:22** *n* 2 Kin. 20:8   **39:1** *a* 2 Kin. 20:12–19   **39:2** *b* 2 Chr. 32:25, 31   **39:3** *c* Deut. 28:49   **39:6** *d* Jer. 20:5   **39:7** *e* Dan. 1:1–7   **39:8** *f* 1 Sam. 3:18

2 "Speak comfort to Jerusalem, and cry
  out to her,
  That her warfare is ended,
  That her iniquity is pardoned;
  *a*For she has received from the LORD's
  hand
  Double for all her sins."

3 *b*The voice of one crying in the
  wilderness:
  c"Prepare the way of the LORD;
  *d*Make straight in the desert*
  A highway for our God.

4 Every valley shall be exalted
  And every mountain and hill brought
  low;
  *e*The crooked places shall be made
  straight
  And the rough places smooth;

5 The *f*glory of the LORD shall be
  revealed,
  And all flesh shall see *it* together;
  For the mouth of the LORD has
  spoken."

6 The voice said, "Cry out!"
  And he* said, "What shall I cry?"

  g"All flesh *is* grass,
  And all its loveliness *is* like the flower
  of the field.

7 The grass withers, the flower
  fades,
  Because the breath of the LORD blows
  upon it;
  Surely the people *are* grass.

8 The grass withers, the flower fades,
  But *h*the word of our God stands
  forever."

9 O Zion,
  You who bring good tidings,
  Get up into the high mountain;
  O Jerusalem,
  You who bring good tidings,
  Lift up your voice with strength,
  Lift *it* up, be not afraid;
  Say to the cities of Judah, "Behold
  your God!"

10 Behold, the Lord GOD shall come with
  a strong *hand,*
  And *i*His arm shall rule for Him;
  Behold, *j*His reward *is* with Him,
  And His work before Him.

11 He will *k*feed His flock like a shepherd;
  He will gather the lambs with His arm,
  And carry *them* in His bosom,
  And gently lead those who are with
  young.

12 *l*Who has measured the waters* in the
  hollow of His hand,
  Measured heaven with a span

---

* **40:3** Following Masoretic Text, Targum,
and Vulgate; Septuagint omits *in the desert.*
* **40:6** Following Masoretic Text and Targum;
Dead Sea Scrolls, Septuagint, and Vulgate read *I.*
* **40:12** Following Masoretic Text, Septuagint, and
Vulgate; Dead Sea Scrolls read *waters of the sea;*
Targum reads *waters of the world.*

40:2–5 Preparing the Way—Biblical scholars think this passage was originally intended to encourage the Israelite exiles, who were looking forward to their return to Israel. The obstacles to getting back home included both a release from slavery and a journey of hundreds of miles on foot through hostile territory. There was also much to be apprehensive about when they arrived home. How were they ever going to be able to rebuild their communities when they were virtually penniless and without resources?

Scholars also see this passage as one of the key messianic prophecies. The image of verses 3–4 is that of the ancient Near Eastern practice of "rolling out the red carpet" for a visiting monarch. Mark makes use of these verses to describe the ministry of John the Baptist, as the prophet urges people to prepare for the coming of the Messiah.

Both applications point to the same concepts. God is saying, "Trust Me, I will make it right. I will make a way through the obstacles. No matter how large the obstacles, I will overcome them." We should see these as some of the strongest words of comfort in the Bible.

40:2 *Jerusalem.* In this case, Jerusalem represents the exiles. ***warfare.*** Warfare refers to Israel's hard service in Babylon.

40:3 *voice of one crying.* John referred to this passage to explain who he was (John 1:23) as the forerunner of Christ.

40:5 *glory . . . shall be revealed.* The glory of the Lord is revealed in the restoration of the captives, but in a fuller sense it is revealed in the coming of the Lord Jesus Christ (Luke 2:29–32; John 1:14).

40:9 *good tidings.* Good news from God to man can always be properly described as "gospel." Here, the glad tidings are that the God who once delivered His captive people from bondage in Egypt is again at hand to rescue and protect His beleaguered Israelites. The assurance that God is with us (7:14; John 1:14) to save is at the heart of the Christian gospel (1 Cor. 15:3–4), and it is always "good news," even when it is something we have heard before.

40:12–31 God's Sovereignty over the Nations—God controls the destinies of rulers and politicians and public figures, no matter how much power they think they have. When times are rough, we wonder if God is really in charge. We wonder why He lets us get moved around by so many economic and political forces beyond our control. We sometimes wonder if He really even cares about what is going on in the world or our lives. If He really is in charge, does He know what He is doing?

The testimony of Isaiah is a resounding Yes! Nations may rise and fall. Rulers may come and go. God remains both Starter and Finisher. The circumstances that surround us are temporary conditions in the scheme of eternity. As God sustains the stars in heaven and the whole universe, He sustains our lives. We may not be able to say that easily every day, but if we keep coming back to Him, He will not disappoint us.

40:12 *span.* A span is the width of an outstretched

40:2 *a* Is. 61:7   **40:3** *b* Matt. 3:3 *c* [Mal. 3:1; 4:5, 6] *d* Ps. 68:4   **40:4** *e* Is. 45:2   **40:5** *f* Is. 35:2   **40:6** *g* Job 14:2   **40:8** *h* [John 12:34]   **40:10** *i* Is. 59:16, 18 *j* Is. 62:11
40:11 *k* [John 10:11, 14–16]   **40:12** *l* Prov. 30:4

And calculated the dust of the earth in a measure?
Weighed the mountains in scales
And the hills in a balance?
13 [m]Who has directed the Spirit of the LORD,
Or *as* His counselor has taught Him?
14 With whom did He take counsel, and *who* instructed Him,
And [n]taught Him in the path of justice?
Who taught Him knowledge,
And showed Him the way of understanding?

15 Behold, the nations *are* as a drop in a bucket,
And are counted as the small dust on the scales;
Look, He lifts up the isles as a very little thing.
16 And Lebanon *is* not sufficient to burn,
Nor its beasts sufficient for a burnt offering.
17 All nations before Him *are* as [o]nothing,
And [p]they are counted by Him less than nothing and worthless.

18 To whom then will you [q]liken God?
Or what likeness will you compare to Him?
19 [r]The workman molds an image,
The goldsmith overspreads it with gold,
And the silversmith casts silver chains.
20 Whoever *is* too impoverished for *such* a contribution
Chooses a tree *that* will not rot;
He seeks for himself a skillful workman
[s]To prepare a carved image *that* will not totter.

21 [t]Have you not known?
Have you not heard?
Has it not been told you from the beginning?
Have you not understood from the foundations of the earth?
22 *It is* He who sits above the circle of the earth,
And its inhabitants *are* like grasshoppers,
Who [u]stretches out the heavens like a curtain,
And spreads them out like a [v]tent to dwell in.
23 He brings the [w]princes to nothing;
He makes the judges of the earth useless.

24 Scarcely shall they be planted,
Scarcely shall they be sown,
Scarcely shall their stock take root in the earth,
When He will also blow on them,
And they will wither,
And the whirlwind will take them away like stubble.

25 "To[x] whom then will you liken Me,
Or *to whom* shall I be equal?" says the Holy One.
26 Lift up your eyes on high,
And see who has created these *things*,
Who brings out their host by number;
[y]He calls them all by name,
By the greatness of His might
And the strength of *His* power;
Not one is missing.

27 [z]Why do you say, O Jacob,
And speak, O Israel:
"My way is hidden from the LORD,
And my just claim is passed over by my God"?
28 Have you not known?
Have you not heard?
The everlasting God, the LORD,
The Creator of the ends of the earth,
Neither faints nor is weary.
[a]His understanding is unsearchable.
29 He gives power to the weak,
And to *those who have* no might He increases strength.
30 Even the youths shall faint and be weary,
And the young men shall utterly fall,
31 But those who [b]wait on the LORD
[c]Shall renew *their* strength;
They shall mount up with wings like eagles,
They shall run and not be weary,
They shall walk and not faint.

---

hand. This verse dramatically imposes images of the grandeur of God.

40:15 ***nations are as a drop in a bucket.*** Wicked nations have no power to thwart the purposes of God (Ps. 2:1–6).

40:19–20 ***image.*** Many idols were made with wood, then overlaid with gold. The poor had to choose the best wood available and hope it was good enough. But of what value is the prayer of a poor man to a plain idol? What is the value of the rich to one covered with gold? To both questions, the answer is "none."

40:26 ***who has created these things.*** The Babylonian gods were identified with the heavenly bodies. These words would have been comforting and encouraging to the Israelites who had learned to say no to Babylon and yes to the Lord.

40:27 ***my just claim is passed over.*** The captives in their weariness may have complained that they were forgotten by God.

40:31 ***wait.*** To "wait" for the Lord entails confident expectation and active hope, never passive resignation.

40:13 [m] [1 Cor. 2:16] **40:14** [n] Job 36:22, 23 **40:17** [o] Dan. 4:35 [p] Ps. 62:9 **40:18** [q] Is. 46:5 **40:19** [r] Is. 41:7; 44:10 **40:20** [s] Is. 41:7; 46:7 **40:21** [t] Rom. 1:19 **40:22** [u] Jer. 10:12 [v] Ps. 19:4 **40:23** [w] Ps. 107:40 **40:25** [x] Is. 40:18 **40:26** [y] Ps. 147:4 **40:27** [z] Is. 54:7, 8 **40:28** [a] Rom. 11:33 **40:31** [b] Is. 30:15; 49:23 [c] Ps. 103:5

Israel Assured of God's Help

41 "Keep [a]silence before Me,
O coastlands,
And let the people renew *their*
strength!
Let them come near, then let them
speak;
Let us [b]come near together for
judgment.

2 "Who raised up one [c]from the east?
Who in righteousness called him to
His feet?
Who [d]gave the nations before him,
And made *him* rule over kings?
Who gave *them* as the dust *to* his
sword,
As driven stubble to his bow?
3 Who pursued them, *and* passed safely
By the way *that* he had not gone with
his feet?
4 [e]Who has performed and done *it*,
Calling the generations from the
beginning?
'I, the LORD, am [f]the first;
And with the last I *am* [g]He.'"

5 The coastlands saw *it* and feared,
The ends of the earth were afraid;
They drew near and came.
6 [h]Everyone helped his neighbor,
And said to his brother,
"Be of good courage!"
7 [i]So the craftsman encouraged the
[j]goldsmith;
He who smooths *with* the hammer
inspired him who strikes the
anvil,
Saying, "It *is* ready for the soldering";
Then he fastened it with pegs,
[k]*That* it might not totter.

8 "But you, Israel, *are* My servant,
Jacob whom I have [l]chosen,
The descendants of Abraham My
[m]friend.
9 *You* whom I have taken from the ends
of the earth,
And called from its farthest regions,
And said to you,
'You *are* My servant,
I have chosen you and have not cast
you away:
10 [n]Fear not, [o]for I *am* with you;
Be not dismayed, for I *am* your God.
I will strengthen you,
Yes, I will help you,
I will uphold you with My righteous
right hand.'

11 "Behold, all those who were incensed
against you
Shall be [p]ashamed and disgraced;
They shall be as nothing,
And those who strive with you shall
perish.
12 You shall seek them and not find
them—
Those who contended with you.
Those who war against you
Shall be as nothing,
As a nonexistent thing.
13 For I, the LORD your God, will hold
your right hand,
Saying to you, 'Fear not, I will help you.'

14 "Fear not, you [q]worm Jacob,
You men of Israel!
I will help you," says the LORD
And your Redeemer, the Holy One of
Israel.
15 "Behold, [r]I will make you into a new
threshing sledge with sharp
teeth;
You shall thresh the mountains and
beat *them* small,
And make the hills like chaff.
16 You shall [s]winnow them, the wind
shall carry them away,
And the whirlwind shall scatter them;
You shall rejoice in the LORD,
And[t] glory in the Holy One of Israel.

17 "The poor and needy seek water, but
there is none,
Their tongues fail for thirst.
I, the LORD, will hear them;
I, the God of Israel, will not [u]forsake
them.
18 I will open [v]rivers in desolate heights,
And fountains in the midst of the
valleys;
I will make the [w]wilderness a pool of
water,
And the dry land springs of water.
19 I will plant in the wilderness the cedar
and the acacia tree,
The myrtle and the oil tree;
I will set in the [x]desert the cypress tree
and the pine
And the box tree together,

41:2 *one from the east.* This refers to Cyrus, king of Persia (559–530 B.C.; see 46:11).

41:4 *first . . . last.* The Lord also refers to Himself as the first and last in Revelation 22:13, when He is speaking to the apostle John of the things that will happen at the end of the age. This description speaks of His sovereignty over all time.

41:14 *Redeemer.* For Israel, the redeemer was the family protector of distressed relatives, who could avenge murder (Num. 35:19) and redeem indentured slaves (Lev. 25:47–49). When the Lord is called the Redeemer, the title highlights His zeal to defend, protect, and purchase back His people (49:26).

41:16 *winnow them.* As threshed grain is tossed in the air or "winnowed" to separate the chaff, so the victorious people of God would be able to "blow away" their enemies.

41:1 [a] Zech. 2:13 [b] Is. 1:18 **41:2** [c] Is. 46:11 [d] Is. 45:1, 13 **41:4** [e] Is. 41:26 [f] Rev. 1:8, 17; 22:13 [g] Is. 43:10; 44:6 **41:6** [h] Is. 40:19 **41:7** [i] Is. 44:13 [j] Is. 40:19 [k] Is. 40:20 **41:8** [l] Deut. 7:6; 10:15 [m] James 2:23 **41:10** [n] Is. 41:13, 14; 43:5 [o] [Deut. 31:6] **41:11** [p] Zech. 12:3 **41:14** [q] Job 25:6 **41:15** [r] Mic. 4:13 **41:16** [s] Jer. 51:2 [t] Is. 45:25 **41:17** [u] Rom. 11:2 **41:18** [v] Is. 35:6, 7; 43:19; 44:3 [w] Ps. 107:35 **41:19** [x] Is. 35:1

20 ʸThat they may see and know,
And consider and understand together,
That the hand of the LORD has done
this,
And the Holy One of Israel has
created it.

The Futility of Idols

21 "Present your case," says the LORD.
"Bring forth your strong *reasons*," says
the ᶻKing of Jacob.
22 "Letᵃ them bring forth and show us
what will happen;
Let them show the ᵇformer things,
what they *were*,
That we may consider them,
And know the latter end of them;
Or declare to us things to come.
23 ᶜShow the things that are to come
hereafter,
That we may know that you *are* gods;
Yes, ᵈdo good or do evil,
That we may be dismayed and see *it*
together.
24 Indeed ᵉyou *are* nothing,
And your work *is* nothing;
He who chooses you *is* an abomination.

25 "I have raised up one from the north,
And he shall come;
From the rising of the sun ᶠhe shall call
on My name;
ᵍAnd he shall come against princes as
though mortar,
As the potter treads clay.
26 ʰWho has declared from the beginning,
that we may know?
And former times, that we may say,
'*He is* righteous'?
Surely *there is* no one who shows,
Surely *there is* no one who declares,
Surely *there is* no one who hears your
words.
27 ⁱThe first time ʲI said to Zion,
'Look, there they are!'
And I will give to Jerusalem one who
brings good tidings.
28 ᵏFor I looked, and *there was* no man;
I looked among them, but *there was*
no counselor,
Who, when I asked of them, could
answer a word.

29 ˡIndeed they *are* all worthless;*
Their works *are* nothing;
Their molded images *are* wind and
confusion.

The Servant of the LORD

42 "Behold! ᵃMy Servant whom I
uphold,
My Elect One *in whom* My soul
ᵇdelights!
ᶜI have put My Spirit upon Him;
He will bring forth justice to the
Gentiles.
2 He will not cry out, nor raise *His voice*,
Nor cause His voice to be heard in the
street.
3 A bruised reed He will not break,
And smoking flax He will not quench;
He will bring forth justice for truth.
4 He will not fail nor be discouraged,
Till He has established justice in the
earth;
ᵈAnd the coastlands shall wait for His
law."

5 Thus says God the LORD,
ᵉWho created the heavens and
stretched them out,
Who spread forth the earth and that
which comes from it,
ᶠWho gives breath to the people on it,
And spirit to those who walk on it:
6 "I,ᵍ the LORD, have called You in
righteousness,
And will hold Your hand;
I will keep You ʰand give You as a
covenant to the people,
As ⁱa light to the Gentiles,
7 ʲTo open blind eyes,
To ᵏbring out prisoners from the
prison,
Those who sit in ˡdarkness from the
prison house.
8 I *am* the LORD, that *is* My name;
And My ᵐglory I will not give to
another,
Nor My praise to carved images.

* **41:29** Following Masoretic Text and Vulgate;
Dead Sea Scrolls, Syriac, and Targum read *nothing*; Septuagint omits the first line.

41:21 *Present your case.* The Lord is addressing the idols in this passage. He is pointing out that only the Lord can tell the past or the future; He challenges the idols to prove themselves, but they cannot.
41:24 *abomination.* An abomination is something that causes revulsion. If the Lord regards idol worshipers as an abomination, we should too.
41:25 *from the north.* The conquest of Media by Cyrus (550 B.C.) made him master of the territories north of Babylon. Cyrus did not personally know God (45:4), but he nevertheless called on God's name when he released the exiles (2 Chr. 36:23; Ezra 1:1–4).
42:1 *My Servant.* The Lord formally presents His servant. This title is identified with Jesus Christ in the New Testament. This is the beginning of the first song of the Suffering Servant (vv. 1–13).

42:3 *bruised reed . . . smoking flax.* The Servant will restore that which is broken; He will not break or snuff out the needy.
42:6 *covenant.* The Servant will institute a new covenant binding Israel to the Lord (49:8). The prophets refer to this new covenant as a "covenant of peace" (54:10; Ezek. 34:25); an "everlasting covenant" (which

41:20ʸ Job 12:9   **41:21**ᶻ Is. 43:15   **41:22**ᵃ Is. 45:21 ᵇ Is. 43:9   **41:23**ᶜ [John 13:19] ᵈ Jer. 10:5   **41:24**ᵉ [1 Cor. 8:4]   **41:25**ᶠ Ezra 1:2 ᵍ Is. 41:2   **41:26**ʰ Is. 43:9   **41:27**ⁱ Is. 41:4 ʲ Is. 40:9   **41:28**ᵏ Is. 63:5   **41:29**ˡ Is. 41:24   **42:1**ᵃ [Phil. 2:7] ᵇ Matt. 3:17; 17:5 ᶜ [Is. 11:2]   **42:4**ᵈ [Gen. 49:10]   **42:5**ᵉ Zech. 12:1 ᶠ Acts 17:25   **42:6**ᵍ Is. 43:1 ʰ Is. 49:8 ⁱ Luke 2:32   **42:7**ʲ Is. 35:5 ᵏ Luke 4:18 ˡ Is. 9:2   **42:8**ᵐ Is. 48:11

9 Behold, the former things have come
 to pass,
 And new things I declare;
 Before they spring forth I tell you of
 them."

Praise to the LORD

10 ^{n}Sing to the LORD a new song,
 And His praise from the ends of the
 earth,
 ^{o}You who go down to the sea, and all
 that is in it,
 You coastlands and you inhabitants
 of them!
11 Let the wilderness and its cities lift up
 their voice,
 The villages *that* Kedar inhabits.
 Let the inhabitants of Sela sing,
 Let them shout from the top of the
 mountains.
12 Let them give glory to the LORD,
 And declare His praise in the
 coastlands.
13 The LORD shall go forth like a mighty
 man;
 He shall stir up *His* zeal like a man of
 war.
 He shall cry out, ^{p}yes, shout aloud;
 He shall prevail against His enemies.

Promise of the LORD's Help

14 "I have held My peace a long time,
 I have been still and restrained Myself.
 Now I will cry like a woman in labor,
 I will pant and gasp at once.
15 I will lay waste the mountains and
 hills,
 And dry up all their vegetation;
 I will make the rivers coastlands,
 And I will dry up the pools.
16 I will bring the blind by a way they did
 not know;
 I will lead them in paths they have not
 known.
 I will make darkness light before
 them,
 And crooked places straight.
 These things I will do for them,
 And not forsake them.
17 They shall be ^{q}turned back,
 They shall be greatly ashamed,

Who trust in carved images,
 Who say to the molded images,
 'You *are* our gods.'
18 "Hear, you deaf;
 And look, you blind, that you may see.
19 ^{r}Who *is* blind but My servant,
 Or deaf as My messenger *whom* I
 send?
 Who *is* blind as *he who is* perfect,
 And blind as the LORD's servant?
20 Seeing many things, ^{s}but you do not
 observe;
 Opening the ears, but he does not
 hear."

Israel's Obstinate Disobedience

21 The LORD is well pleased for His
 righteousness' sake;
 He will exalt the law and make *it*
 honorable.
22 But this *is* a people robbed and
 plundered;
 All of them are snared in holes,
 And they are hidden in prison houses;
 They are for prey, and no one delivers;
 For plunder, and no one says, "Restore!"
23 Who among you will give ear to this?
 Who will listen and hear for the time
 to come?
24 Who gave Jacob for plunder, and Israel
 to the robbers?
 Was it not the LORD,
 He against whom we have sinned?
 ^{t}For they would not walk in His ways,
 Nor were they obedient to His law.
25 Therefore He has poured on him the
 fury of His anger
 And the strength of battle;
 ^{u}It has set him on fire all around,
 ^{v}Yet he did not know;
 And it burned him,
 Yet he did not take *it* to ^{w}heart.

The Redeemer of Israel

43 But now, thus says the LORD, who
 created you, O Jacob,
 And He who formed you, O Israel:
 "Fear not, ^{a}for I have redeemed you;
 ^{b}I have called you by your name;
 You *are* Mine.

---

is also associated with the Davidic covenant, 55:3); a "new covenant" (Jer. 31:31–34); and most often simply as covenant. **people.** The "people" refers to the Gentiles.
42:17 molded images. Why is idolatry so terrible in God's sight? Several reasons may be given. It displays a total ignorance of the true nature and being of the Creator. He is invisible, eternal, all-knowing, and all-present Spirit, without limitations. Idolatry usually reduces the concept of God to an ugly metal or wooden object, which is almost always perceived as evil and bloodthirsty, selfish and capricious. Finally, idolatry provides absolutely no indication of those characteristics closest to God's heart—His love, mercy, grace, and holiness.

42:18–25 Hear, you deaf. This prophecy, justifying the exile as punishment, consists of two parts. First, the Lord addresses the fact that the people did not listen to Him.
42:24 sinned. The second part of the prophecy addresses the sin of the exiles, which was the reason for the punishment.
43:1 thus says the LORD. This statement emphasizes the authority of the words that will follow.

42:10 ^{n} Ps. 33:3; 40:3; 98:1 ^{o} Ps. 107:23 **42:13** ^{p} Is. 31:4
42:17 ^{q} Ps. 97:7 **42:19** ^{r} [John 9:39, 41] **42:20** ^{s} Rom.
2:21 **42:24** ^{t} Is. 65:2 **42:25** ^{u} 2 Kin. 25:9 ^{v} Hos. 7:9 ^{w} Is.
29:13 **43:1** ^{a} Is. 43:5; 44:6 ^{b} Is. 42:6; 45:4

2 cWhen you pass through the waters, dI
   will be with you;
And through the rivers, they shall not
   overflow you.
When you ewalk through the fire, you
   shall not be burned,
Nor shall the flame scorch you.
3 For I am the LORD your God,
The Holy One of Israel, your Savior;
fI gave Egypt for your ransom,
Ethiopia and Seba in your place.
4 Since you were precious in My sight,
You have been honored,
And I have gloved you;
Therefore I will give men for you,
And people for your life.
5 hFear not, for I am with you;
I will bring your descendants from the
   east,
And igather you from the west;
6 I will say to the jnorth, 'Give them up!'
And to the south, 'Do not keep them
   back!'
Bring My sons from afar,
And My daughters from the ends of
   the earth—
7 Everyone who is kcalled by My name,
Whom lI have created for My glory;
I have formed him, yes, I have made
   him."
8 mBring out the blind people who have
   eyes,
And the ndeaf who have ears.
9 Let all the nations be gathered
   together,
And let the people be assembled.
oWho among them can declare this,
And show us former things?
Let them bring out their witnesses,
   that they may be justified;
Or let them hear and say, "It is truth."
10 "Youp are My witnesses," says the
   LORD,
q"And My servant whom I have chosen,
That you may know and rbelieve Me,
And understand that I am He.
Before Me there was no God formed,
Nor shall there be after Me.
11 I, even I, sam the LORD,
And besides Me there is no savior.
12 I have declared and saved,
I have proclaimed,
And there was no tforeign god among
   you;
uTherefore you are My witnesses,"
Says the LORD, "that I am God.

13 vIndeed before the day was, I am He;
And there is no one who can deliver
   out of My hand;
I work, and who will wreverse it?"
14 Thus says the LORD, your Redeemer,
The Holy One of Israel:
"For your sake I will send to Babylon,
And bring them all down as
   fugitives—
The Chaldeans, who rejoice in their
   ships.
15 I am the LORD, your Holy One,
The Creator of Israel, your xKing."
16 Thus says the LORD, who ymakes a
   way in the sea
And a zpath through the mighty
   waters,
17 Who abrings forth the chariot and
   horse,
The army and the power
(They shall lie down together, they
   shall not rise;
They are extinguished, they are
   quenched like a wick):
18 "Dob not remember the former things,
Nor consider the things of old.
19 Behold, I will do a cnew thing,
Now it shall spring forth;
Shall you not know it?
dI will even make a road in the
   wilderness
And rivers in the desert.
20 The beast of the field will honor Me,
The jackals and the ostriches,
Because eI give waters in the
   wilderness
And rivers in the desert,
To give drink to My people, My
   chosen.
21 fThis people I have formed for
   Myself;
They shall declare My gpraise.

Pleading with Unfaithful Israel

22 "But you have not called upon Me,
   O Jacob;
And you hhave been weary of Me,
   O Israel.
23 iYou have not brought Me the sheep for
   your burnt offerings,
Nor have you honored Me with your
   sacrifices.
I have not caused you to serve with
   grain offerings,
Nor wearied you with incense.

43:14 Thus says the LORD. The same phrase (v. 1) is
used to emphasize the ultimate source of this prophecy, God Himself. Redeemer. The Lord is described as
Redeemer because He zealously defends, protects,
and purchases back His people (41:14).
43:22 But you. After the splendid and glorious declarations of His faithfulness, the Lord addresses the
unfaithfulness of His people.

43:2 c [Ps. 66:12; 91:3] d [Deut. 31:6] e Dan. 3:25
43:3 f [Prov. 11:8; 21:18] 43:4 g Is. 63:9 h Is.
41:10; 44:2 i Is. 54:7 43:6 j Is. 49:12 43:7 k James 2:7
l [2 Cor. 5:17] 43:8 m Ezek. 12:2 n Is. 29:18 43:9 o Is.
41:21, 22, 26 43:10 p Is. 44:8 q Is. 55:4 r Is. 41:4;
44:6 43:11 s Hos. 13:4 43:12 t Deut. 32:16 u Is.
44:8 43:13 v Ps. 90:2 w Job 9:12 43:15 x Is. 41:20,
21 43:16 y Ex. 14:16, 21, 22 z Josh. 3:13 43:17 a Ex.
14:4–9, 25 43:18 b Jer. 16:14 43:19 c [2 Cor. 5:17] d Ex.
17:6 43:20 e Is. 48:21 43:21 f Ps. 102:18 g Jer. 13:11
43:22 h Mal. 1:13; 3:14 43:23 i Amos 5:25

24 You have bought Me no sweet cane
    with money,
Nor have you satisfied Me with the fat
    of your sacrifices;
But you have burdened Me with your
    sins,
You have ʲwearied Me with your
    iniquities.

25 "I, *even* I, *am* He who ᵏblots out your
    transgressions ˡfor My own sake;
   ᵐAnd I will not remember your sins.

26 Put Me in remembrance;
Let us contend together;
State your *case,* that you may be
    acquitted.

27 Your first father sinned,
And your mediators have transgressed
    against Me.

28 Therefore I will profane the princes of
    the sanctuary;
   ⁿI will give Jacob to the curse,
And Israel to reproaches.

God's Blessing on Israel

44 "Yet hear now, O Jacob My servant,
    And Israel whom I have chosen.
2 Thus says the LORD who made you
And formed you from the womb, *who*
    will help you:
'Fear not, O Jacob My servant;
And you, Jeshurun, whom I have
    chosen.

3 For I will pour water on him who is
    thirsty,
And floods on the dry ground;
I will pour My Spirit on your
    descendants,
And My blessing on your offspring;

4 They will spring up among the grass
Like willows by the watercourses.'

5 One will say, 'I *am* the LORD's';
Another will call *himself* by the name
    of Jacob;
Another will write *with* his hand, 'The
    LORD's,'
And name *himself* by the name of
    Israel.

There Is No Other God

6 "Thus says the LORD, the King of Israel,
    And his Redeemer, the LORD of hosts:
ᵃ'I *am* the First and I *am* the Last;
Besides Me *there is* no God.

7 And ᵇwho can proclaim as I do?
Then let him declare it and set it in
    order for Me,
Since I appointed the ancient people.
And the things that are coming and
    shall come,
Let them show these to them.

8 Do not fear, nor be afraid;
ᶜHave I not told you from that time, and
    declared *it?*
ᵈYou *are* My witnesses.
Is there a God besides Me?
Indeed ᵉ*there is* no other Rock;
I know not *one.'* "

Idolatry Is Foolishness

9 ᶠThose who make an image, all of them
    are useless,
And their precious things shall not
    profit;
They *are* their own witnesses;
ᵍThey neither see nor know, that they
    may be ashamed.

10 Who would form a god or mold an
    image
ʰ*That* profits him nothing?

11 Surely all his companions would be
    ⁱashamed;
And the workmen, they *are* mere men.
Let them all be gathered together,
Let them stand up;
Yet they shall fear,
They shall be ashamed together.

12 ʲThe blacksmith with the tongs works
    one in the coals,
Fashions it with hammers,
And works it with the strength of his
    arms.
Even so, he is hungry, and his strength
    fails;
He drinks no water and is faint.

13 The craftsman stretches out *his* rule,
He marks one out with chalk;
He fashions it with a plane,
He marks it out with the compass,
And makes it like the figure of a man,
According to the beauty of a man, that
    it may remain in the house.

14 He cuts down cedars for himself,
And takes the cypress and the oak;
He secures *it* for himself among the
    trees of the forest.
He plants a pine, and the rain
    nourishes *it.*

43:25 *for My own sake.* The Lord chooses to save and forgive. This arises out of His own character (37:35; 42:21; 48:9,11).

44:2 *Jeshurun.* Jeshurun, meaning "upright one," is a poetic word for the nation of Israel (Deut. 32:15).

44:6 *King of Israel.* For background, read Psalm 99, which begins by declaring, "The LORD reigns."

44:8 *You are My witnesses.* The people of Israel had already witnessed great miracles on their behalf (43:10).

44:9–20 *Those who make an image.* This passage skillfully displays the utter absurdity of trusting in idols. Idolatry is a source of shame (v. 11), and it is

caused by a deceived heart (v. 20). This is a passage to remember and to come back to, for idolatry was a continual snare to the Israelites. We need to remember in our modern age that we are not immune to this sin; it is the Second Commandment, the reminder that nothing must come between us and our relationship to God.

43:24 ʲ Is. 1:14; 7:13   **43:25** ᵏ Jer. 50:20 ˡEzek. 36:22 ᵐ Is. 1:18   **43:28** ⁿ Dan. 9:11   **44:6** ᵃ Is. 41:4   **44:7** ᵇ Is. 41:4, 22, 26   **44:8** ᶜ Is. 41:22 ᵈ Is. 43:10, 12 ᵉ 1 Sam. 2:2   **44:9** ᶠ Is. 41:24 ᵍ Ps. 115:4   **44:10** ʰ Hab. 2:18   **44:11** ⁱ Ps. 97:7   **44:12** ʲ Jer. 10:3–5

15 Then it shall be for a man to burn,
For he will take some of it and warm
  himself;
Yes, he kindles *it* and bakes bread;
Indeed he makes a god and worships
  it;
He makes it a carved image, and falls
  down to it.

16 He burns half of it in the fire;
With this half he eats meat;
He roasts a roast, and is satisfied.
He even warms *himself* and says,
"Ah! I am warm,
I have seen the fire."

17 And the rest of it he makes into a
  god,
His carved image.
He falls down before it and worships
  it,
Prays to it and says,
"Deliver me, for you *are* my god!"

18 *k*They do not know nor understand;
For *l*He has shut their eyes, so that
  they cannot see,
And their hearts, so that they cannot
  *m*understand.

19 And no one *n*considers in his
  heart,
Nor *is there* knowledge nor
  understanding to say,
"I have burned half of it in the fire,
Yes, I have also baked bread on its
  coals;
I have roasted meat and eaten *it;*
And shall I make the rest of it an
  abomination?
Shall I fall down before a block of
  wood?"

20 He feeds on ashes;
*o*A deceived heart has turned him
  aside;
And he cannot deliver his soul,
Nor say, "*Is there* not a *p*lie in my right
  hand?"

Israel Is Not Forgotten

21 "Remember these, O Jacob,
And Israel, for you *are* My servant;
I have formed you, you *are* My
  servant;
O Israel, you will not be *q*forgotten by
  Me!

22 *r*I have blotted out, like a thick cloud,
  your transgressions,
And like a cloud, your sins.
Return to Me, for *s*I have redeemed
  you."

23 *t*Sing, O heavens, for the LORD has
  done *it!*
Shout, you lower parts of the earth;
Break forth into singing, you
  mountains,
O forest, and every tree in it!
For the LORD has redeemed
  Jacob,
And *u*glorified Himself in Israel.

Judah Will Be Restored

24 Thus says the LORD, *v*your
  Redeemer,
And *w*He who formed you from the
  womb:
"I *am* the LORD, who makes all
  things,
*x*Who stretches out the heavens all
  alone,
Who spreads abroad the earth by
  Myself;

25 Who *y*frustrates the signs *z*of the
  babblers,
And drives diviners mad;
Who turns wise men backward,
*a*And makes their knowledge
  foolishness;

26 *b*Who confirms the word of His
  servant,
And performs the counsel of His
  messengers;
Who says to Jerusalem, 'You shall be
  inhabited,'
To the cities of Judah, 'You shall be
  built,'
And I will raise up her waste
  places;

27 *c*Who says to the deep, 'Be dry!
And I will dry up your rivers';

28 Who says of *d*Cyrus, '*He is* My
  shepherd,
And he shall perform all My
  pleasure,
Saying to Jerusalem, *e*"You shall be
  built,"
And to the temple, "Your foundation
  shall be laid."'

44:22 blotted out. The idea of total forgiveness of sins is also found in 40:2 and 43:25.

44:23 glorified Himself. When He saves, the Lord demonstrates to the world His mercy and His power and His glory.

44:24 Thus says the LORD. Because the Lord says it, it will come to pass.

44:25 diviners. This term refers to people who attempt to foretell the future through occult practices. They are often mentioned along with other practitioners of the occult—all of whom were forbidden in Israel (Deut. 18:10–22). Diviners brought trouble on themselves, and on their nations as well (Deut. 18:10; 2 Kin. 17:17–18; Mic. 3:6–7).

44:28 Cyrus. Here, Isaiah mentions by name the king of Persia who would allow the Israelites to return to Jerusalem in 538 B.C. (Ezra 1:1–4). He was a chosen servant of God, even though he was not an Israelite. Isaiah's prophecy was made more than 150 years before it was fulfilled.

44:18 *k* Is. 45:20 *l* Is. 6:9, 10; 29:10 *m* Jer. 10:14 **44:19** *n* Is. 46:8 **44:20** *o* 2 Thess. 2:11 *p* Rom. 1:25 **44:21** *q* Is. 49:15 **44:22** *r* Is. 43:25 *s* 1 Cor. 6:20 **44:23** *t* Ps. 69:34 *u* Is. 49:3; 60:21 **44:24** *v* Is. 43:14 *w* Is. 43:1 *x* Job 9:8 **44:25** *y* Is. 47:13 *z* Jer. 50:36 *a* 1 Cor. 1:20, 27 **44:26** *b* Zech. 1:6 **44:27** *c* Jer. 50:38; 51:36 **44:28** *d* Ezra 1:1 *e* Ezra 6:7

Cyrus, God's Instrument

45 "Thus says the LORD to His anointed,
To [a]Cyrus, whose [b]right hand I have held—
[c]To subdue nations before him
And [d]loose the armor of kings,
To open before him the double doors,
So that the gates will not be shut:

2 'I will go before you
[e]And make the crooked places*
straight;
[f]I will break in pieces the gates of bronze
And cut the bars of iron.

3 I will give you the treasures of darkness
And hidden riches of secret places,
[g]That you may know that I, the LORD,
Who [h]call you by your name,
Am the God of Israel.

4 For [i]Jacob My servant's sake,
And Israel My elect,
I have even called you by your name;
I have named you, though you have not known Me.

5 I [j]*am* the LORD, and [k]*there is* no other;
There is no God besides Me.
[l]I will gird you, though you have not known Me,

6 [m]That they may [n]know from the rising of the sun to its setting
That *there is* none besides Me.
I *am* the LORD, and *there is* no other;

7 I form the light and create darkness,
I make peace and [o]create calamity;
I, the LORD, do all these *things*.'

8 "Rain[p] down, you heavens, from above,
And let the skies pour down righteousness;
Let the earth open, let them bring forth salvation,
And let righteousness spring up together.
I, the LORD, have created it.

9 "Woe to him who strives with [q]his Maker!
Let the potsherd *strive* with the potsherds of the earth!
[r]Shall the clay say to him who forms it,
'What are you making?'
Or shall your handiwork *say*, 'He has no hands'?

10 Woe to him who says to *his* father,
'What are you begetting?'
Or to the woman, 'What have you brought forth?'"

11 Thus says the LORD,
The Holy One of Israel, and his Maker:
[s]"Ask Me of things to come concerning [t]My sons;
And concerning [u]the work of My hands, you command Me.

12 [v]I have made the earth,
And [w]created man on it.
I—My hands—stretched out the heavens,
And [x]all their host I have commanded.

13 [y]I have raised him up in righteousness,
And I will direct all his ways;
He shall [z]build My city
And let My exiles go free,
[a]Not for price nor reward,"
Says the LORD of hosts.

The LORD, the Only Savior

14 Thus says the LORD:

[b]"The labor of Egypt and merchandise of Cush
And of the Sabeans, men of stature,
Shall come over to you, and they shall be yours;

---

* **45:2** Dead Sea Scrolls and Septuagint read *mountains*; Targum reads *I will trample down the walls*; Vulgate reads *I will humble the great ones of the earth*.

45:3 *treasures of darkness.* These treasures are an allusion to the fabled wealth of Sardis captured by Cyrus in 546 B.C. **Who call you by your name.** The Lord specifically named Cyrus and appointed his work before he became king, and even before he was born. Isaiah was ministering from approximately 740 to 701 B.C., which was at least 150 years before Cyrus became prominent. The Lord picked out Cyrus, but He picked out each of us, too, to do good works which He had planned beforehand for us to do (Eph. 2:10).
45:8 *have created it.* In the Middle East, pagan people commonly believed that the fertility of the earth and maintenance of the social order depended on the king's right relationship with a deity. Isaiah was proclaiming the Lord's clear statement that it is the Lord alone who made the earth and blesses it with rain and with righteousness.
45:9 *potsherds.* The ultimate act of insanity committed by the human soul is unfaithfulness. As the prophet Isaiah shows, how inconceivable and ridiculous it would be for a simple piece of pottery to lash out at the craftsman. And yet, that was what Israel had consistently done from the exodus of Egypt to

the destruction of the second temple by Titus in A.D. 70. Jonah was a classic example of unfaithfulness. In the Book of Jonah, all nature spontaneously obeyed its Creator. The ocean churned, the fish appeared, the gourd grew, the worm died, and the east wind blew at the command of God. The only object in that narrative that dared disobey was Jonah the prophet. What law of logic would allow a finite and sinful creature to brazenly speak out against the infinite and sovereign Creator of all things? (Compare Romans 9:20.)
45:13 *him.* That is, Cyrus.
45:14 *Shall come over to you, and they shall be yours.* The "you" and "yours" are both feminine singular, referring to the Daughter of Zion.

45:1 [d] Is. 44:28 [b] Is. 41:13 [c] Dan. 5:30 [d] Job 12:21
45:2 [e] Is. 40:4 [f] Ps. 107:16 **45:3** [g] Is. 41:23 [h] Ex. 33:12 **45:4** [i] Is. 44:1 **45:5** [j] Deut. 4:35; 32:39 [k] Is. 45:14, 18 [l] Ps. 18:32 **45:6** [m] Mal. 1:11 [n] [Is. 11:9; 52:10]
45:7 [o] Amos 3:6 **45:8** [p] Ps. 85:11 **45:9** [q] Is. 64:8 [r] Jer. 18:6 **45:11** [s] Is. 8:19 [t] Jer. 31:9 [u] Is. 29:23; 60:21; 64:8
45:12 [v] Is. 42:5 [w] Gen. 1:26 [x] Gen. 2:1 **45:13** [y] Is. 41:2 [z] 2 Chr. 36:22 [a] [Rom. 3:24] **45:14** [b] Zech. 8:22, 23

They shall walk behind you,
They shall come over cin chains;
And they shall bow down to you.
They will make supplication to you,
saying, d'Surely God *is* in you,
And *there is* no other;
e*There is* no other God.'"

15 Truly You *are* God, fwho hide
Yourself,
O God of Israel, the Savior!
16 They shall be gashamed
And also disgraced, all of them;
They shall go in confusion together,
Who are makers of idols.
17 hBut Israel shall be saved by the
LORD
With an ieverlasting salvation;
You shall not be ashamed or
jdisgraced
Forever and ever.

18 For thus says the LORD,
kWho created the heavens,
Who is God,
Who formed the earth and made it,
Who has established it,
Who did not create it in vain,
Who formed it to be linhabited:
m"I *am* the LORD, and *there is* no other.
19 I have not spoken in nsecret,
In a dark place of the earth;
I did not say to the seed of Jacob,
'Seek Me in vain';
oI, the LORD, speak righteousness,
I declare things that are right.

20 "Assemble yourselves and come;
Draw near together,
You *who have* escaped from the
nations.
pThey have no knowledge,
Who carry the wood of their carved
image,
And pray to a god *that* cannot save.
21 Tell and bring forth *your case*;
Yes, let them take counsel together.
qWho has declared this from ancient
time?

Who has told it from that time?
Have not I, the LORD?
rAnd *there is* no other God besides Me,
A just God and a Savior;
There is none besides Me.

22 "Look to Me, and be saved,
sAll you ends of the earth!
For I *am* God, and *there is* no other.
23 tI have sworn by Myself;
The word has gone out of My mouth *in*
righteousness,
And shall not return,
That to Me every uknee shall bow,
vEvery tongue shall take an oath.
24 He shall say,
'Surely in the LORD I have
wrighteousness and strength.
To Him *men* shall come,
And xall shall be ashamed
Who are incensed against Him.
25 yIn the LORD all the descendants of
Israel
Shall be justified, and zshall glory.'"

Dead Idols and the Living God

46 Bel abows down, Nebo stoops;
Their idols were on the beasts and
on the cattle.
Your carriages *were* heavily loaded,
bA burden to the weary *beast*.
2 They stoop, they bow down together;
They could not deliver the burden,
cBut have themselves gone into
captivity.

3 "Listen to Me, O house of Jacob,
And all the remnant of the house of
Israel,
dWho have been upheld *by Me* from
birth,
Who have been carried from the
womb:
4 Even to *your* old age, eI *am* He,
And *even* to gray hairs fI will carry
you!
I have made, and I will bear;
Even I will carry, and will deliver *you.*

45:19 in secret . . . dark. The diviners pronounced their mysterious and ambiguous oracles in secret and dark places. The Lord's prophets proclaimed the truth openly to all who would listen.
45:23 I have sworn by Myself. The Lord's promise to Abraham was sworn by Himself (Gen. 22:16; Heb. 6:13), and whatever God promises will come to pass, for He cannot lie. The certainty of the Word of the Lord is emphasized strongly in the Book of Isaiah (40:8). **to Me every knee shall bow.** This promise will be fulfilled in Jesus Christ (Rom. 14:11; 1 Cor. 15:24–25; Phil. 2:10–11).
45:24–25 justified. God breaks the stranglehold of nations to secure the release of His people from captivity. In the same way, God also breaks the stranglehold of sin to release His people from spiritual bondage. He does so by pouring forth righteousness through the atoning sacrifice of Jesus Christ on the cross. This is the centerpiece of God's salvation, which is worldwide in its scope. It is the only ground

for acceptance by God, the only foundation for fellowship with God, and the only platform of service to God. Those who embrace it find that they are released from sin's guilt and that they are also given strength to have victory over sin. No wonder this all evokes jubilant praise!
46:1 Bel . . . Nebo. Bel, meaning "Lord," was a title of Marduk, Babylon's chief deity. Nebo, Marduk's son, was the god of fate, writing, and wisdom.

45:14 cPs. 149:8 d1 Cor. 14:25 eIs. 45:5 45:15 fPs. 44:24 45:16 gIs. 44:11 45:17 hIs. 26:4 iIs. 51:6 jIs. 29:22 45:18 kIs. 42:5 lPs. 115:16 mIs. 45:5 45:19 nDeut. 30:11 oPs. 19:8 45:20 pIs. 44:9; 46:7 45:21 qIs. 41:22; 43:9 rIs. 44:8 45:22 sPs. 22:27; 65:5 45:23 t[Heb. 6:13] uRom. 14:11 vDeut. 6:13 45:24 w[1 Cor. 1:30] xIs. 41:11 45:25 yIs. 45:17 z1 Cor. 1:31 46:1 aJer. 50:2 bJer. 10:5 46:2 cJer. 48:7 46:3 dPs. 71:6 46:4 eMal. 3:6 fPs. 48:14

5 "To^g whom will you liken Me, and make
   Me equal
   And compare Me, that we should be
   alike?
6 ^hThey lavish gold out of the bag,
   And weigh silver on the scales;
   They hire a ⁱgoldsmith, and he makes
   it a god;
   They prostrate themselves, yes, they
   worship.
7 ^jThey bear it on the shoulder, they
   carry it
   And set it in its place, and it stands;
   From its place it shall not move.
   Though ^k*one* cries out to it, yet it
   cannot answer
   Nor save him out of his trouble.
8 "Remember this, and show yourselves
   men;
   ^lRecall to mind, O you transgressors.
9 ^mRemember the former things of old,
   For I *am* God, and ⁿ*there is* no other;
   I am God, and *there is* none like Me,
10 ^oDeclaring the end from the beginning,
   And from ancient times *things* that are
   not *yet* done,
   Saying, ^p'My counsel shall stand,
   And I will do all My pleasure,'
11 Calling a bird of prey ^qfrom the east,
   The man ^rwho executes My counsel,
   from a far country.
   Indeed ^sI have spoken *it;*
   I will also bring it to pass.
   I have purposed *it;*
   I will also do it.
12 "Listen to Me, you ^tstubborn-hearted,
   ^uWho *are* far from righteousness:
13 ^vI bring My righteousness near, it shall
   not be far off;
   My salvation ^wshall not linger.
   And I will place ^xsalvation in Zion,
   For Israel My glory.

The Humiliation of Babylon

47 "Come ^adown and ^bsit in the dust,
   O virgin daughter of ^cBabylon;
   Sit on the ground without a throne,
   O daughter of the Chaldeans!
   For you shall no more be called
   Tender and delicate.

2 ^dTake the millstones and grind meal.
   Remove your veil,
   Take off the skirt,
   Uncover the thigh,
   Pass through the rivers.
3 ^eYour nakedness shall be uncovered,
   Yes, your shame will be seen;
   ^fI will take vengeance,
   And I will not arbitrate with a man."
4 *As for* ^gour Redeemer, the LORD of
   hosts *is* His name,
   The Holy One of Israel.
5 "Sit in ^hsilence, and go into darkness,
   O daughter of the Chaldeans;
   ⁱFor you shall no longer be called
   The Lady of Kingdoms.
6 ^jI was angry with My people;
   ^kI have profaned My inheritance,
   And given them into your hand.
   You showed them no mercy;
   ^lOn the elderly you laid your yoke very
   heavily.
7 And you said, 'I shall be ^ma lady forever,'
   So that you did not ⁿtake these *things*
   to heart,
   ^oNor remember the latter end of them.
8 "Therefore hear this now, *you who are*
   given to pleasures,
   Who dwell securely,
   Who say in your heart, 'I *am,* and
   there is no one else besides me;
   I shall not sit *as* a widow,
   Nor shall I know the loss of children';
9 But these two *things* shall come to you
   ^pIn a moment, in one day:
   The loss of children, and widowhood.
   They shall come upon you in their
   fullness
   Because of the multitude of your
   sorceries,
   For the great abundance of your
   enchantments.
10 "For you have trusted in your wickedness;
   You have said, 'No one ^qsees me';
   Your wisdom and your knowledge
   have warped you;
   And you have said in your heart,
   'I *am,* and *there is* no one else besides
   me.'

46:11 *a bird of prey from the east.* The bird of prey refers to Cyrus (41:2) and to the speed and power of his conquests.
47:2 *grind meal.* Grinding meal was usually a job for female slaves (Ex. 11:5). ***Uncover the thigh.*** This phrase suggests doing menial labor with overtones of the shame of indecent exposure. A woman who was doing heavy labor may have needed more freedom of movement than was possible without shortening her skirts.
47:3 *nakedness.* Nakedness indicates disgrace, impropriety, lack of dignity, and vulnerability (Gen. 9:22–23).
47:6 *You showed them no mercy.* Babylon's cruel abuse of Israel when the Lord had given them into Babylon's hand would be avenged, as in the case of the Assyrians (10:1–19; 49:25). When God chooses

to punish, He is never pleased with a bystander who cheers over the downfall of another.
47:10 *trusted in your wickedness.* The selfish pride of the wicked is based in part on believing that there is not an all-knowing, all-seeing God in the universe.

46:5 ^g Is. 40:18, 25   **46:6** ^h Is. 40:19; 41:6   ⁱ Is. 44:12
46:7 ^j Jer. 10:5   ^k Is. 45:20   **46:8** ^l Is. 44:19   **46:9** ^m Deut.
32:7   ⁿ Is. 45:5, 21   **46:10** ^o Is. 45:21; 48:3   ^p Ps. 33:11
46:11 ^q Is. 41:2, 25   ^r Is. 44:28   ^s Num. 23:19   **46:12** ^t Ps.
76:5   ^u [Rom. 10:3]   **46:13** ^v [Rom. 1:17]   ^w Hab. 2:3
^x Is. 62:11   **47:1** ^a Jer. 48:18   ^b Is. 3:26   ^c Jer. 25:12;
50:1—51:64   **47:2** ^d Ex. 11:5   **47:3** ^e Is. 3:17; 20:4
^f [Rom. 12:19]   **47:4** ^g Jer. 50:34   **47:5** ^h 1 Sam. 2:9
ⁱ [Dan. 2:37]   **47:6** ^j 2 Sam. 24:14   ^k Is. 43:28   ^l Deut. 28:49,
50   **47:7** ^m Rev. 18:7   ⁿ Is. 42:25; 46:8   ^o Deut. 32:29
47:9 ^p 1 Thess. 5:3   **47:10** ^q Is. 29:15

11 Therefore evil shall come upon you;
   You shall not know from where it
      arises.
   And trouble shall fall upon you;
   You will not be able to put it off.
   And ʳdesolation shall come upon you
      ˢsuddenly,
   Which you shall not know.

12 "Stand now with your enchantments
   And the multitude of your sorceries,
   In which you have labored from your
      youth—
   Perhaps you will be able to profit,
   Perhaps you will prevail.
13 ᵗYou are wearied in the multitude of
      your counsels;
   Let now ᵘthe astrologers, the
      stargazers,
   And the monthly prognosticators
   Stand up and save you
   From what shall come upon you.
14 Behold, they shall be ᵛas stubble,
   The fire shall ʷburn them;
   They shall not deliver themselves
   From the power of the flame;
   It shall not be a coal to be warmed by,
   Nor a fire to sit before!
15 Thus shall they be to you
   With whom you have labored,
   ˣYour merchants from your youth;
   They shall wander each one to his
      quarter.
   No one shall save you.

Israel Refined for God's Glory

48 "Hear this, O house of Jacob,
   Who are called by the name of
      Israel,
   And have come forth from the
      wellsprings of Judah;
   Who swear by the name of the LORD,
   And make mention of the God of
      Israel,
   But ᵃnot in truth or in righteousness;
2 For they call themselves ᵇafter the holy
      city,
   And ᶜlean on the God of Israel;
   The LORD of hosts is His name:

3 "I have ᵈdeclared the former things
      from the beginning;
   They went forth from My mouth, and I
      caused them to hear it.
   Suddenly I did them, ᵉand they came
      to pass.

4 Because I knew that you were
      obstinate,
   And ᶠyour neck was an iron sinew,
   And your brow bronze,
5 Even from the beginning I have
      declared it to you;
   Before it came to pass I proclaimed it
      to you,
   Lest you should say, 'My idol has done
      them,
   And my carved image and my molded
      image
   Have commanded them.'

6 "You have heard;
   See all this.
   And will you not declare it?
   I have made you hear new things from
      this time,
   Even hidden things, and you did not
      know them.
7 They are created now and not from the
      beginning;
   And before this day you have not
      heard them,
   Lest you should say, 'Of course I knew
      them.'
8 Surely you did not hear,
   Surely you did not know;
   Surely from long ago your ear was not
      opened.
   For I knew that you would deal very
      treacherously,
   And were called ᵍa transgressor from
      the womb.

9 "For ʰMy name's sake ⁱI will defer My
      anger,
   And for My praise I will restrain it
      from you,
   So that I do not cut you off.
10 Behold, ʲI have refined you, but not as
      silver;
   I have tested you in the ᵏfurnace of
      affliction.
11 For My own sake, for My own sake,
      I will do it;
   For ˡhow should My name be
      profaned?
   And ᵐI will not give My glory to another.

God's Ancient Plan to Redeem Israel

12 "Listen to Me, O Jacob,
   And Israel, My called:
   I am He, ⁿI am the ᵒFirst,
   I am also the Last.

47:12 Stand now. The admonition to "stand" is face-tious. The sorcerers and astrologers have nothing real to offer a person or nation that is having trouble.
48:5 declared it to you. God told His people of events that would come to pass in the future so that they would know that it was He, and He alone, who controlled history.
48:6 new things . . . hidden things. God did not tell His people all that the future would unfold. He knew that, if they had possessed such knowledge, they would have misused that knowledge to the detriment of God's plan and themselves.

48:11 For My own sake. God's acts of mercy are His own initiative, springing from the depths of His mercy (37:35; 42:21; 43:25).

47:11 ʳ 1 Thess. 5:3 ˢ Is. 29:5   **47:13** ᵗ Is. 57:10 ᵘ Dan. 2:2, 10   **47:14** ᵛ Nah. 1:10 ʷ Jer. 51:58   **47:15** ˣ Rev. 18:11   **48:1** ᵃ Jer. 4:2; 5:2   **48:2** ᵇ Is. 52:1; 64:10 ᶜ Mic. 3:11   **48:3** ᵈ Is. 44:7, 8; 46:10 ᵉ Josh. 21:45   **48:4** ᶠ Deut. 31:27   **48:8** ᵍ Ps. 58:3   **48:9** ʰ Ezek. 20:9, 14, 22, 44 ⁱ Ps. 78:38   **48:10** ʲ Ps. 66:10 ᵏ Deut. 4:20   **48:11** ˡ Ezek. 20:9 ᵐ Is. 42:8   **48:12** ⁿ Deut. 32:39 ᵒ [Rev. 22:13]

13 Indeed [p]My hand has laid the foundation of the earth,
And My right hand has stretched out the heavens;
When [q]I call to them,
They stand up together.

14 "All of you, assemble yourselves, and hear!
Who among them has declared these *things?*
[r]The LORD loves him;
[s]He shall do His pleasure on Babylon,
And His arm *shall be against* the Chaldeans.
15 I, *even* I, have spoken;
Yes, [t]I have called him,
I have brought him, and his way will prosper.

16 "Come near to Me, hear this:
[u]I have not spoken in secret from the beginning;
From the time that it was, I *was* there.
And now [v]the Lord GOD and His Spirit
Have* sent Me."

17 Thus says [w]the LORD, your Redeemer,
The Holy One of Israel:
"I *am* the LORD your God,
Who teaches you to profit,
[x]Who leads you by the way you should go.
18 [y]Oh, that you had heeded My commandments!
[z]Then your peace would have been like a river,
And your righteousness like the waves of the sea.
19 [a]Your descendants also would have been like the sand,
And the offspring of your body like the grains of sand;
His name would not have been cut off
Nor destroyed from before Me."

20 [b]Go forth from Babylon!
Flee from the Chaldeans!
With a voice of singing,
Declare, proclaim this,
Utter it to the end of the earth;
Say, "The LORD has [c]redeemed
His servant Jacob!"
21 And they [d]did not thirst
When He led them through the deserts;
He [e]caused the waters to flow from the rock for them;
He also split the rock, and the waters gushed out.

22 "There[f] *is* no peace," says the LORD, "for the wicked."

The Servant, the Light to the Gentiles

49 "Listen, [a]O coastlands, to Me,
And take heed, you peoples from afar!
[b]The LORD has called Me from the womb;
From the matrix of My mother He has made mention of My name.
2 And He has made [c]My mouth like a sharp sword;
[d]In the shadow of His hand He has hidden Me,
And made Me [e]a polished shaft;
In His quiver He has hidden Me."

3 "And He said to me,
[f]'You *are* My servant, O Israel,
[g]In whom I will be glorified.'
4 [h]Then I said, 'I have labored in vain,
I have spent my strength for nothing and in vain;
Yet surely my just reward *is* with the LORD,
And my work with my God.'"

5 "And now the LORD says,
Who formed Me from the womb *to be* His Servant,
To bring Jacob back to Him,
So that Israel [i]is gathered to Him*
(For I shall be glorious in the eyes of the LORD,
And My God shall be My strength),

* **48:16** The Hebrew verb is singular. * **49:5** Qere, Dead Sea Scrolls, and Septuagint read *is gathered to Him;* Kethib reads *is not gathered.*

48:12 *Listen to Me.* This section (vv. 12–22) is directed to all Israel and encourages the unrighteous to participate in the Lord's redemption of the nation from Babylon.
48:16 *His Spirit.* One of the works of the Holy Spirit is to empower believers and their message. Isaiah recognized this task of the Spirit of God. The prophet had delivered unbelievable prophecies in a time when Assyria reigned supreme, speaking of a day when Babylon would replace the Assyrians. He even named the Persian King Cyrus, who would rescue Judah from Babylon. Knowing that these things were hard to believe, he urged the people to listen. He appealed to them on the basis that the Lord had sent him "and his Spirit." Isaiah's message was not simply the message of a man, but the Word of the Holy Spirit, the teacher and director of God's messengers.
48:20 *Declare.* By putting the command "declare" in the present tense, the future salvation is brought vividly into the present.
49:1–13 *Listen.* This second song of the Suffering Servant (42:1–13) consists of two parts: the Servant's soliloquy (vv. 1–6) and the Lord's oracles to Him (vv. 7–9). The song is followed by Isaiah's elaboration (vv. 9–12), and it concludes with a hymn of praise.
49:2 *mouth like a sharp sword.* The truth is "sharp." It cuts through lies and deception like a sharp sword (Eph. 6:17; Heb. 4:12; Rev. 1:16; 19:15).
49:5 *bring Jacob back.* The political mission of Cyrus to bring Jacob back from Babylon (44:28; 45:13) foreshadows the spiritually redemptive mission of the

48:13 [p] Ps. 102:25 [q] Is. 40:26 **48:14** [r] Is. 45:1 [s] Is. 44:28; 47:1–15 **48:15** [t] Is. 45:1, 2 **48:16** [u] Is. 45:19 [v] Zech. 2:8, 9, 11 **48:17** [w] Is. 43:14 [x] Ps. 32:8 **48:18** [y] Ps. 81:13 [z] Ps. 119:165 **48:19** [a] Gen. 22:17 **48:20** [b] Zech. 2:6, 7 [c] [Ex. 19:4–6] **48:21** [d] [Is. 41:17, 18] [e] Ex. 17:6 **48:22** [f] [Is. 57:21] **49:1** [a] Is. 41:1 [b] Jer. 1:5 **49:2** [c] Rev. 1:16; 2:12 [d] Is. 51:16 [e] Ps. 45:5 **49:3** [f] [Zech. 3:8] [g] Is. 44:23 **49:4** [h] [Ezek. 3:19] **49:5** [i] Matt. 23:37

6 Indeed He says,
'It is too small a thing that You should
be My Servant
To raise up the tribes of Jacob,
And to restore the preserved ones of
Israel;
I will also give You as a *j*light to the
Gentiles,
That You should be My salvation to the
ends of the earth.'"

7 Thus says the LORD,
The Redeemer of Israel, their Holy
One,
*k*To Him whom man despises,
To Him whom the nation abhors,
To the Servant of rulers:
l"Kings shall see and arise,
Princes also shall worship,
Because of the LORD who is faithful,
The Holy One of Israel;
And He has chosen You."

8 Thus says the LORD:

"In an *m*acceptable time I have heard
You,
And in the day of salvation I have
helped You;
I will preserve You *n*and give You
As a covenant to the people,
To restore the earth,
To cause them to inherit the desolate
heritages;
9 That You may say *o*to the prisoners,
'Go forth,'
To those who *are* in darkness, 'Show
yourselves.'

"They shall feed along the roads,
And their pastures *shall be* on all
desolate heights.
10 They shall neither *p*hunger nor thirst,
*q*Neither heat nor sun shall strike
them;
For He who has mercy on them *r*will
lead them,
Even by the springs of water He will
guide them.
11 *s*I will make each of My mountains a
road,
And My highways shall be
elevated.

12 Surely *t*these shall come from afar;
Look! Those from the north and the
west,
And these from the land of Sinim."

13 *u*Sing, O heavens!
Be joyful, O earth!
And break out in singing,
O mountains!
For the LORD has comforted His
people,
And will have mercy on His afflicted.

God Will Remember Zion

14 *v*But Zion said, "The LORD has forsaken
me,
And my Lord has forgotten me."

15 "Can*w* a woman forget her nursing child,
And not have compassion on the son
of her womb?
Surely they may forget,
*x*Yet I will not forget you.
16 See, *y*I have inscribed you on the
palms *of My hands;*
Your walls *are* continually before Me.
17 Your sons* shall make haste;
Your destroyers and those who laid
you waste
Shall go away from you.
18 *z*Lift up your eyes, look around and see;
All these gather together *and* come to
you.
As I live," says the LORD,
"You shall surely clothe yourselves with
them all *a*as an ornament,
And bind them *on you* as a bride *does.*

19 "For your waste and desolate places,
And the land of your destruction,
*b*Will even now be too small for the
inhabitants;
And those who swallowed you up will
be far away.
20 *c*The children you will have,
*d*After you have lost the others,
Will say again in your ears,
'The place *is* too small for me;
Give me a place where I may dwell.'

* **49:17** Dead Sea Scrolls, Septuagint, Targum, and
Vulgate read *builders.*

Servant to free His people from their captivity to sin
(42:7).
49:6 to the Gentiles. The "Gentiles" refers to those
who are not Israel.
49:9 Go forth. This is an allusion to Isaiah's command
for the exiles to leave Babylon (48:20).
49:14 has forsaken me. The complaint that the Lord
had forsaken Zion resembles that in 40:27–31. The
Lord disciplined the Israelites briefly because of their
sin (54:7; Lam. 5:20–22), but the things that Isaiah
was saying about captivity were still in the future. A
message such as this would be good to remember in
the days of captivity when it seemed that they were
waiting a long time for the Lord to rescue them.
49:15 Can a woman forget. In the strongest of
human ties, the tenderness of the mother for her

precious and dependent child, the Lord draws a parallel picture of Himself. Even if the mother could forget, the Lord will never forget. Human parents often
fail, but the Lord is the parent who never forgets how
much His child needs Him.
49:20 too small. The complaint that the place is too
small is in fact a cause for rejoicing (54:1–3; Zech.
2:4–5), because it means that the Lord would cause

49:6 *j* [Luke 2:32]   **49:7** *k* [Is. 53:3] *l* [Is. 52:15]
49:8 *m* 2 Cor. 6:2 *n* Is. 42:6   **49:9** *o* Is. 61:1   **49:10** *p* Rev.
7:16 *q* Ps. 121:6 *r* Ps. 23:2   **49:11** *s* Is. 40:4   **49:12** *t* Is.
43:5, 6   **49:13** *u* Is. 44:23   **49:14** *v* Is. 40:27
49:15 *w* Ps. 103:13 *x* Rom. 11:29   **49:16** *y* Song
8:6   **49:18** *z* Is. 60:4 *a* Prov. 17:6   **49:19** *b* Zech. 10:10
49:20 *c* Is. 60:4 *d* [Rom. 11:11]

21 Then you will say in your heart,
'Who has begotten these for me,
Since I have lost my children and am
desolate,
A captive, and wandering to and fro?
And who has brought these up?
There I was, left alone;
But these, where *were* they?'"

22 *e*Thus says the Lord GOD:

"Behold, I will lift My hand in an oath
to the nations,
And set up My standard for the
peoples;
They shall bring your sons in *their*
arms,
And your daughters shall be carried
on *their* shoulders;
23 *f*Kings shall be your foster fathers,
And their queens your nursing
mothers;
They shall bow down to you with *their*
faces to the earth,
And *g*lick up the dust of your feet.
Then you will know that I *am* the
LORD,
*h*For they shall not be ashamed who
wait for Me."
24 *i*Shall the prey be taken from the
mighty,
Or the captives of the righteous* be
delivered?

25 But thus says the LORD:

"Even the captives of the mighty shall
be taken away,
And the prey of the terrible be
delivered;
For I will contend with him who
contends with you,
And I will save your children.
26 I will *j*feed those who oppress you with
their own flesh,
And they shall be drunk with their
own *k*blood as with sweet wine.

All flesh *l*shall know
That I, the LORD, *am* your Savior,
And your Redeemer, the Mighty One
of Jacob."

The Servant, Israel's Hope

50 Thus says the LORD:

"Where *is* *a*the certificate of your
mother's divorce,
Whom I have put away?
Or which of My *b*creditors *is it* to
whom I have sold you?
For your iniquities *c*you have sold
yourselves,
And for your transgressions your
mother has been put away.
2 Why, when I came, *was there* no man?
Why, when I called, *was there* none to
answer?
Is My hand shortened at all that it
cannot redeem?
Or have I no power to deliver?
Indeed with My *d*rebuke I dry up the
sea,
I make the rivers a wilderness;
Their fish stink because *there is* no
water,
And die of thirst.
3 *e*I clothe the heavens with blackness,
*f*And I make sackcloth their covering."

4 "The*g* Lord GOD has given Me
The tongue of the learned,
That I should know how to speak
A word in season to *him who is* *h*weary.
He awakens Me morning by morning,
He awakens My ear
To hear as the learned.
5 The Lord GOD *i*has opened My ear;
And I was not *j*rebellious,
Nor did I turn away.

---

* **49:24** Following Masoretic Text and Targum;
Dead Sea Scrolls, Syriac, and Vulgate read *the
mighty*; Septuagint reads *unjustly.*

His people to grow. This prophecy points to the return of the exiles to Jerusalem, for under Ezra and Nehemiah the exiles built a relatively small city (Ezra 2; Neh. 7). Some view the ultimate fulfillment of this prophecy to be the gathering of the Lord's people at the coming of Jesus' kingdom.
49:22 lift My hand in an oath to the nations. The return of the Israelites from all the nations, not only from Babylon, shows that the future salvation of all Israel is in view (Rom. 11:26).
50:1 divorce. The Lord had put away Israel as a husband might put away a wife, but it was for only a short period of exile (54:5–7; 62:4) and not permanently. Permanent exile would have required a certificate of divorce (Deut. 24:1–4). If the Lord had issued one, He could not have taken Israel back (Jer. 3:1,8). No prophet suggested that God had completely broken His covenant; rather, they predicted God's faithfulness to a remnant who would return (Mic. 4:9–10). **creditors.** If the Lord had sold Israel to creditors (Ex. 21:7; 2 Kin. 4:1; Neh. 5:5), He would

not have any authority over its destiny. But the Israelites sold themselves because of their own iniquities (42:23–25). Therefore God as their Redeemer could buy them back (41:14; 52:3). **your mother.** The mother is Jerusalem—more specifically, the inhabitants of the preceding generation that had gone into exile.
50:2 I came. God came to Israel at the time of the exile through the prophets whom He sent. Later God came to this earth through His Servant and Son, Jesus (41:9).
50:4 tongue of the learned. The third Servant song consists of a reflection by the Servant (vv. 4–9) and the prophet's address to the believing and unbelieving Israel (vv. 10–11).

49:22 *e* Is. 60:4　**49:23** *f* Is. 52:15　*g* Ps. 72:9　*h* [Rom. 5:5]
49:24 *i* Luke 11:21, 22　**49:26** *j* Is. 9:20　*k* Rev. 14:20　*l* Ps.
9:16　**50:1** *a* Deut. 24:1　*b* Deut. 32:30; 2 Kin. 4:1　*c* Is. 52:3
50:2 *d* Nah. 1:4　**50:3** *e* Ex. 10:21　*f* Rev. 6:12　**50:4** *g* Ex.
4:11　*h* Matt. 11:28　**50:5** *i* Ps. 40:6　*j* Matt. 26:39

6 kI gave My back to those who struck
Me,
And lMy cheeks to those who plucked
out the beard;
I did not hide My face from shame and
mspitting.

7 "For the Lord GOD will help Me;
Therefore I will not be disgraced;
Therefore nI have set My face like a
flint,
And I know that I will not be
ashamed.

8 oHe is near who justifies Me;
Who will contend with Me?
Let us stand together.
Who is My adversary?
Let him come near Me.

9 Surely the Lord GOD will help Me;
Who is he who will condemn Me?
pIndeed they will all grow old like a
garment;
qThe moth will eat them up.

10 "Who among you fears the LORD?
Who obeys the voice of His Servant?
Who rwalks in darkness
And has no light?
sLet him trust in the name of the LORD
And rely upon his God.

11 Look, all you who kindle a fire,
Who encircle yourselves with
sparks:
Walk in the light of your fire and in
the sparks you have kindled—
tThis you shall have from My hand:
You shall lie down uin torment.

The LORD Comforts Zion

51 "Listen to Me, ayou who follow after
righteousness,
You who seek the LORD:
Look to the rock from which you were
hewn,
And to the hole of the pit from which
you were dug.

2 bLook to Abraham your father,
And to Sarah who bore you;
cFor I called him alone,
And dblessed him and increased him."

3 For the LORD will ecomfort Zion,
He will comfort all her waste places;
He will make her wilderness like
Eden,
And her desert flike the garden of the
LORD;
Joy and gladness will be found in it,
Thanksgiving and the voice of melody.

4 "Listen to Me, My people;
And give ear to Me, O My nation:
gFor law will proceed from Me,
And I will make My justice rest
hAs a light of the peoples.

5 iMy righteousness is near,
My salvation has gone forth,
jAnd My arms will judge the
peoples;
kThe coastlands will wait upon Me,
And lon My arm they will trust.

6 mLift up your eyes to the heavens,
And look on the earth beneath.
For nthe heavens will vanish away like
smoke,
oThe earth will grow old like a
garment,
And those who dwell in it will die in
like manner;
But My salvation will be pforever,
And My righteousness will not be
abolished.

7 "Listen to Me, you who know
righteousness,
You people qin whose heart is My law:
rDo not fear the reproach of men,
Nor be afraid of their insults.

8 For sthe moth will eat them up like a
garment,
And the worm will eat them like wool;
But My righteousness will be forever,
And My salvation from generation to
generation."

9 tAwake, awake, uput on strength,
O arm of the LORD!
Awake vas in the ancient days,
In the generations of old.
wAre You not the arm that cut xRahab
apart,
And wounded the yserpent?

50:6 shame and spitting. This prophecy was fulfilled in the suffering of Jesus Christ (Matt. 27:30).
50:7 face like a flint. Setting one's face like a flint indicates determination in the face of opposition (Ezek. 3:8–9; Luke 9:51).
50:8 justifies. God's Servant fully anticipates vindication before the bar of God's justice. He was told to obey God perfectly, and He did. He was sent to suffer sacrificially, and He did. No prosecutor has a case against Him. In a stupendous development, God discloses that the sinners who identify themselves with the Servant may expect the same, although they are not righteous. Sin does carry the death penalty, but identification with the Servant brings exchange and substitution, in which the Servant takes the sinners' place. This makes the justification of sinners both possible and just. Their sins are transferred to Him, and He dies in their place. His shed blood removes their guilt, and they will be declared not guilty. His perfection makes them righteous, and they will be declared righteous. Every accuser will be silenced. Every attempt to have them convicted will be thrown out of court. God is just when He justifies those who belong to the Servant Savior (Rom. 8:31–34).

50:6 k Matt. 27:26 l Matt. 26:67; 27:30 m Lam. 3:30
50:7 n Ezek. 3:8, 9 **50:8** o [Rom. 8:32–34] **50:9** p Job 13:28 q Is. 51:6, 8 **50:10** r Ps. 23:4 s 2 Chr. 20:20 **50:11** t [John 9:39] u Ps. 16:4 **51:1** a [Rom. 9:30–32] **51:2** b Heb. 11:11 c Gen. 12:1 d Gen. 24:35 **51:3** e Is. 40:1; 52:9 f Gen. 13:10 **51:4** g Is. 2:3 h Is. 42:6 **51:5** i Is. 46:13 j Ps. 67:4 k Is. 60:9 l [Rom. 1:16] **51:6** m Is. 40:26 n Matt. 24:35 o Is. 24:19, 20; 50:9 p Is. 45:17 **51:7** q Ps. 37:31 r [Matt. 5:11, 12; 10:28] **51:8** s Is. 50:9 **51:9** t Ps. 44:23 u Ps. 93:1 v Ps. 44:1 w Job 26:12 x Ps. 87:4 y Ps. 74:13

10 *Are* You not *the One* who [z]dried up the
sea,
The waters of the great deep;
That made the depths of the sea a road
For the redeemed to cross over?
11 So [a]the ransomed of the LORD shall
return,
And come to Zion with singing,
With everlasting joy on their heads.
They shall obtain joy and gladness;
Sorrow and sighing shall flee away.

12 "I, *even* I, *am* He [b]who comforts you.
Who *are* you that you should be afraid
[c]Of a man *who* will die,
And of the son of a man *who* will be
made [d]like grass?
13 And [e]you forget the LORD your Maker,
[f]Who stretched out the heavens
And laid the foundations of the earth;
You have feared continually every day
Because of the fury of the oppressor,
When *he has* prepared to destroy.
[g]And where *is* the fury of the oppressor?
14 The captive exile hastens, that he may
be loosed,
[h]That he should not die in the pit,
And that his bread should not fail.
15 But I *am* the LORD your God,
Who [i]divided the sea whose waves
roared—
The LORD of hosts *is* His name.
16 And [j]I have put My words in your
mouth;
[k]I have covered you with the shadow of
My hand,
[l]That I may plant the heavens,
Lay the foundations of the earth,
And say to Zion, 'You *are* My people.'"

God's Fury Removed

17 [m]Awake, awake!
Stand up, O Jerusalem,
You who [n]have drunk at the hand of
the LORD
The cup of His fury;
You have drunk the dregs of the cup of
trembling,
And drained *it* out.
18 *There is* no one to guide her
Among all the sons she has brought
forth;
Nor *is there any* who takes her by the
hand
Among all the sons she has
brought up.
19 [o]These two *things* have come to you;
Who will be sorry for you?—
Desolation and destruction, famine
and sword—
[p]By whom will I comfort you?
20 [q]Your sons have fainted,
They lie at the head of all the streets,
Like an antelope in a net;
They are full of the fury of the LORD,
The rebuke of your God.

21 Therefore please hear this, you
afflicted,
And drunk [r]but not with wine.
22 Thus says your Lord,
The LORD and your God,
Who [s]pleads the cause of His people:
"See, I have taken out of your hand
The cup of trembling,
The dregs of the cup of My fury;
You shall no longer drink it.
23 [t]But I will put it into the hand of those
who afflict you,
Who have said to you,*
'Lie down, that we may walk over you.'
And you have laid your body like the
ground,
And as the street, for those who walk
over."

God Redeems Jerusalem

52 Awake, awake!
Put on your strength, O Zion;
Put on your beautiful garments,
O Jerusalem, the holy city!
For the uncircumcised [a]and the
unclean
Shall no longer come to you.
2 [b]Shake yourself from the dust, arise;
Sit down, O Jerusalem!
[c]Loose yourself from the bonds of your
neck,
O captive daughter of Zion!

3 For thus says the LORD:

[d]"You have sold yourselves for nothing,
And you shall be redeemed [e]without
money."

4 For thus says the Lord GOD:

"My people went down at first
Into [f]Egypt to dwell there;
Then the Assyrian oppressed them
without cause.

*51:23 Literally *your soul*

50:11 *kindle a fire.* Those who kindle a fire instead of the Light from God are those who are self-reliant. When the Light comes into the world, some will choose darkness (John 3:17–18).

51:14 *exile . . . in the pit.* The exile refers to those who were captive in Babylon. The meaning also extends to all who experience the darkness of sin and alienation from God (48:20; 49:9).

51:19 *These two things.* The two things are the desolation of the land and the destruction of the people.

51:21 *drunk but not with wine.* The cause of drunkenness was not wine, but the "cup of trembling" (v. 22), the terror of God's judgment.

51:10 [z] Ex. 14:21 **51:11** [a] Is. 35:10 **51:12** [b] 2 Cor. 1:3 [c] Ps. 118:6 [d] Is. 40:6, 7 **51:13** [e] Is. 17:10 [f] Ps. 104:2 [g] Job 20:7 **51:14** [h] Zech. 9:11 **51:15** [i] Job 26:12 **51:16** [j] Deut. 18:18 [k] Is. 49:2 [l] Is. 65:17 **51:17** [m] Is. 52:1 [n] Job 21:20 **51:19** [o] Is. 47:9 [p] Amos 7:2 **51:20** [q] Lam. 2:11 **51:21** [r] Lam. 3:15 **51:22** [s] Jer. 50:34 **51:23** [t] Zech. 12:2 **52:1** [a] [Rev. 21:2–27] **52:2** [b] Is. 3:26 [c] Zech. 2:7 **52:3** [d] Ps. 44:12 [e] Is. 45:13 **52:4** [f] Gen. 46:6

5 Now therefore, what have I here," says the LORD,
"That My people are taken away for nothing?
Those who rule over them
Make them wail,"* says the LORD,
"And My name *is* [g]blasphemed continually every day.
6 Therefore My people shall know My name;
Therefore *they shall know* in that day
That I *am* He who speaks:
'Behold, *it is* I.'"

7 [h]How beautiful upon the mountains
Are the feet of him who brings good news,
Who proclaims peace,
Who brings glad tidings of good *things*,
Who proclaims salvation,
Who says to Zion,
[i]"Your God reigns!"
8 Your watchmen shall lift up *their* voices,
With their voices they shall sing together;
For they shall see eye to eye
When the LORD brings back Zion.
9 Break forth into joy, sing together,
You waste places of Jerusalem!
For the LORD has comforted His people,
He has redeemed Jerusalem.
10 [j]The LORD has made bare His holy arm
In the eyes of [k]all the nations;
And all the ends of the earth shall see
The salvation of our God.

11 [l]Depart! Depart! Go out from there,
Touch no unclean *thing*;
Go out from the midst of her,
[m]Be clean,
You who bear the vessels of the LORD.
12 For [n]you shall not go out with haste,
Nor go by flight;
[o]For the LORD will go before you,
[p]And the God of Israel *will be* your rear guard.

The Sin-Bearing Servant

13 Behold, [q]My Servant shall deal prudently;
[r]He shall be exalted and extolled and be very high.
14 Just as many were astonished at you,
So His [s]visage was marred more than any man,
And His form more than the sons of men;
15 [t]So shall He sprinkle* many nations.
Kings shall shut their mouths at Him;
For [u]what had not been told them they shall see,
And what they had not heard they shall consider.

53 Who [a]has believed our report?
And to whom has the arm of the LORD been revealed?
2 For He shall grow up before Him as a tender plant,
And as a root out of dry ground.
He has no form or comeliness;
And when we see Him,
There is no beauty that we should desire Him.
3 [b]He is despised and rejected by men,
A Man of sorrows and [c]acquainted with grief.

* 52:5 Dead Sea Scrolls read *Mock;* Septuagint reads *Marvel and wail;* Targum reads *Boast themselves;* Vulgate reads *Treat them unjustly.*
* 52:15 Or *startle*

52:6 *shall know My name.* The people are the redeemed exiles, as well as the people who believe in and follow the Servant (Messiah). Isaiah was speaking of a time beyond his own time, to people who were not yet born (1 Pet. 1:10–12). Jesus speaks strongly of this concept when He says, I "know My sheep, and am known by My own" (John 10:11–18).
52:12 *go before you . . . rear guard.* This is an allusion to the pillar of cloud and fire that protected Israel in its flight from Egypt (Ex. 13:21–22; 14:19–20).
52:13—53:12 *Behold.* The fourth of the Servant songs, which form the central unit of chapters 40–66, begins with the praise of the Father for the work of the Servant.
52:14 *visage was marred.* This speaks of the physical punishment that the Servant, Jesus Christ, endured when He was bearing the sins of the world on the cross. He was cruelly beaten, even before He was crucified (Matt. 27:27–31; Mark 15:16–20; John 19:1–3).
52:15 *shut their mouths.* The kings are silent in stunned respect.
53:1–12 The Suffering Servant—Along with Psalm 22, this Scripture is understood to be one of the key prophetic Old Testament passages pointing to the saving work of Christ. This passage presents the whole idea of the "Suffering Servant," which is one of the central concepts of Isaiah, and for many, Judaism. Christ's fulfillment of this passage in His passion is remarkable. The New Testament writers point often to Isaiah 53 and how Christ fulfilled this prophecy (Matt. 8:17; Luke 23:8–9; John 12:38; Rom. 10:16; 1 Pet. 2:25). It is also the Scripture that Philip explained to the Ethiopian eunuch in Acts 8:32–33.

In the Old Testament sacrificial system people offered animals to atone for sin (Lev. 16). The Bible presents Christ as the ultimate sacrifice that died once and for all for the sins of the world (Heb. 8–10). Our sins are forgiven and we become righteous through Christ's great work on the cross (2 Cor. 5:21).
53:2 *no form or comeliness.* There was nothing in the Promised Servant's appearance to mark His special calling.
53:3 *despised and rejected.* The Servant was not received joyfully by the people who needed Him so much (Mark 9:12). ***Man of sorrows.*** This phrase does

52:5 [g] Ezek. 36:20, 23 **52:7** [h] Rom. 10:15 [i] Ps. 93:1 **52:10** [j] Ps. 98:1–3 [k] Luke 3:6 **52:11** [l] Is. 48:20 [m] Lev. 22:2 **52:12** [n] Ex. 12:11, 33 [o] Mic. 2:13 [p] Ex. 14:19, 20 **52:13** [q] Is. 42:1 [r] Phil. 2:9 **52:14** [s] Ps. 22:6, 7 **52:15** [t] Ezek. 36:25 [u] Rom. 15:21 **53:1** [a] John 12:38 **53:3** [b] Ps. 22:6 [c] [Heb. 4:15]

And we hid, as it were, *our* faces from Him;
He was despised, and [d]we did not esteem Him.

4 Surely [e]He has borne our griefs
And carried our sorrows;
Yet we esteemed Him stricken,
Smitten by God, and afflicted.
5 But He *was* [f]wounded for our transgressions,
He was bruised for our iniquities;
The chastisement for our peace *was* upon Him,
And by His [g]stripes we are healed.
6 All we like sheep have gone astray;
We have turned, every one, to his own way;
And the LORD has laid on Him the iniquity of us all.

7 He was oppressed and He was afflicted,
Yet [h]He opened not His mouth;
[i]He was led as a lamb to the slaughter,
And as a sheep before its shearers is silent,
So He opened not His mouth.
8 He was [j]taken from prison and from judgment,
And who will declare His generation?
For [k]He was cut off from the land of the living;
For the transgressions of My people He was stricken.
9 [l]And they* made His grave with the wicked—
But with the rich at His death,
Because He had done no violence,
Nor *was any* [m]deceit in His mouth.

10 Yet it pleased the LORD to bruise Him;
He has put *Him* to grief.
When You make His soul [n]an offering for sin,
He shall see *His* seed, He shall prolong *His* days,
And the pleasure of the LORD shall prosper in His hand.

11 He shall see the labor of His soul,* *and* be satisfied.
By His knowledge [o]My righteous [p]Servant shall [q]justify many,
For He shall bear their iniquities.
12 [r]Therefore I will divide Him a portion with the great,
[s]And He shall divide the spoil with the strong,
Because He [t]poured out His soul unto death,
And He was [u]numbered with the transgressors,
And He bore the sin of many,
And [v]made intercession for the transgressors.

A Perpetual Covenant of Peace

54 "Sing, O [a]barren,
You *who* have not borne!
Break forth into singing, and cry aloud,
You *who* have not labored with child!
For more *are* the children of the desolate
Than the children of the married woman," says the LORD.

2 "Enlarge[b] the place of your tent,
And let them stretch out the curtains of your dwellings;
Do not spare;
Lengthen your cords,
And strengthen your stakes.
3 For you shall expand to the right and to the left,
And your descendants will [c]inherit the nations,
And make the desolate cities inhabited.

4 "Do[d] not fear, for you will not be ashamed;
Neither be disgraced, for you will not be put to shame;

---

* **53:9** Literally *he* or *He* * **53:11** Following Masoretic Text, Targum, and Vulgate; Dead Sea Scrolls and Septuagint read *From the labor of His soul He shall see light.*

---

not indicate that the Servant would be dour, but that He knew better than anyone the havoc that sin brings into human life, and, as the kindest of friends, He was sorry for the pain of His people.
53:4 *borne our griefs.* The Savior Jesus came to suffer and die for the sins of others (Matt. 8:17; Heb. 9:28; 1 Pet. 2.24). Griefs, sorrows, and affliction refer to the consequences of sin.
53:7 *He opened not His mouth.* Jesus did not open His mouth to defend Himself or to answer the false charges made against Him (Matt. 26:63; Mark 14:61; Luke 23:9; John 19:9).
53:10 *it pleased the LORD to bruise Him.* The Old Testament pointed to the doctrine of the atonement long before Jesus died for our sins (1 Cor. 15:3). In fact, the atonement was part of God's eternal plan (Eph. 1:4–7). The Father was pleased that His Son would die because it would cover up the sins of many and reconcile them to Himself. *offering for sin.* The offering for sin, or "trespass offering," was the sacrifice

of a ram to secure the Lord's atonement for sin (Lev. 5:6–7,15; 7:1; 14:12; 19:21). Here, the prophet Isaiah describes the Servant Jesus as a trespass offering. *His seed.* If the Spirit of God dwells in us (Rom. 8:9–11), and if we are led by the Spirit, then we are sons of God—His offspring (Rom. 8:14).
54:1 *have not labored.* The Israelites received a liberation (through the promised Cyrus for the Babylonian exiles, or through the Messiah, in the fullest sense) that they did not work for—it was God's idea.
54:4 *widowhood.* The widowhood was the time

53:3 [d][John 1:10, 11] **53:4** [e][Matt. 8:17] **53:5** [f][Rom. 4:25] [g][1 Pet. 2:24, 25] **53:7** [h]Matt. 26:63; 27:12–14 [i]Acts 8:32, 33 **53:8** [j]Luke 23:1–25 [k][Dan. 9:26] **53:9** [l]Matt. 27:57–60 [m]1 Pet. 2:22 **53:10** [n][2 Cor. 5:21] **53:11** [o][1 John 2:1] [p]Is. 42:1 [q][Rom. 5:15–19] **53:12** [r]Ps. 2:8 [s]Col. 2:15 [t]Is. 50:6 [u]Matt. 27:38 [v]Luke 23:34 **54:1** [a]Gal. 4:27 **54:2** [b]Is. 49:19, 20 **54:3** [c]Is. 14:2; 49:22, 23; 60:9 **54:4** [d]Is. 41:10

For you will forget the shame of your
youth,
And will not remember the reproach
of your widowhood anymore.
5 eFor your Maker is your husband,
The LORD of hosts is His name;
And your Redeemer is the Holy One
of Israel;
He is called fthe God of the whole
earth.
6 For the LORD ghas called you
Like a woman forsaken and grieved
in spirit,
Like a youthful wife when you were
refused,"
Says your God.
7 "Forh a mere moment I have forsaken
you,
But with great mercies iI will gather
you.
8 With a little wrath I hid My face from
you for a moment;
jBut with everlasting kindness I will
have mercy on you,"
Says the LORD, your Redeemer.

9 "For this is like the waters of kNoah to
Me;
For as I have sworn
That the waters of Noah would no
longer cover the earth,
So have I sworn
That I would not be angry with lyou,
nor rebuke you.
10 For mthe mountains shall depart
And the hills be removed,
nBut My kindness shall not depart from
you,
Nor shall My covenant of peace be
removed,"
Says the LORD, who has mercy on you.

11 "O you afflicted one,
Tossed with tempest, and not
comforted,
Behold, I will lay your stones with
ocolorful gems,
And lay your foundations with
sapphires.
12 I will make your pinnacles of rubies,
Your gates of crystal,
And all your walls of precious stones.
13 All your children shall be ptaught by
the LORD,

And qgreat shall be the peace of your
children.
14 In righteousness you shall be
established;
You shall be far from oppression, for
you shall not fear;
And from terror, for it shall not come
near you.
15 Indeed they shall surely assemble, but
not because of Me.
Whoever assembles against you shall
rfall for your sake.

16 "Behold, I have created the blacksmith
Who blows the coals in the fire,
Who brings forth an instrument for
his work;
And I have created the spoiler to
destroy.
17 No weapon formed against you shall
sprosper,
And every tongue which rises against
you in judgment
You shall condemn.
This is the heritage of the servants of
the LORD,
tAnd their righteousness is from Me,"
Says the LORD.

An Invitation to Abundant Life

55 "Ho! aEveryone who thirsts,
Come to the waters;
And you who have no money,
bCome, buy and eat.
Yes, come, buy wine and milk
Without money and without price.
2 Why do you spend money for what is
not bread,
And your wages for what does not
satisfy?
Listen carefully to Me, and eat what
is good,
And let your soul delight itself in
abundance.
3 Incline your ear, and ccome to Me.
Hear, and your soul shall live;
dAnd I will make an everlasting
covenant with you—
The esure mercies of David.
4 Indeed I have given him as fa witness
to the people,
gA leader and commander for the
people.

---

without the working presence of God in the lives of
the people of God, the time of exile. In the fullest
sense, every sinner is a "widow" without God, who
has the role of protector and provider.
54:11 foundations with sapphires. For a more
detailed description of the New Jerusalem, see Revelation 21:18–21. It will be a city of stunning beauty
and grand proportions.
54:17 the servants of the LORD. Throughout the rest
of Isaiah, the word "servants" refers to all saints, Jews
and Gentiles (56:6–8; 63:17; 65:8–9,13–15; 66:14), the
offspring of the Servant (Jesus).
55:4 witness. God's fulfillment of the promises to

the house of David, climaxing in the resurrection of
Christ, serves as a witness to the nations (43:10,12;
44:8). It shows that He has fulfilled His prophecies
and promises, and that He is who He says He is: the
King of the universe.

54:5 e Jer. 3:14 f Zech. 14:9 **54:6** g Is. 62:4 **54:7** h Is.
26:20; 60:10 i [Is. 43:5; 56:8] **54:8** j Jer. 31:3
54:9 k Gen. 8:21; 9:11 l Ezek. 39:29 **54:10** m Is. 51:6 n Ps.
89:33, 34 **54:11** o Rev. 21:18, 19 **54:13** p [John 6:45]
q Ps. 119:165 **54:15** r Is. 41:11–16 **54:17** s Is. 17:12–14;
29:8 t Is. 45:24, 25; 54:14 **55:1** a [John 4:14; 7:37]
b [Rev. 3:18] **55:3** c Matt. 11:28 d Jer. 32:40 e 2 Sam. 7:8
55:4 f [Rev. 1:5] g [Dan. 9:25]

5 [h]Surely you shall call a nation you do
   not know,
[i]And nations *who* do not know you
   shall run to you,
Because of the LORD your God,
And the Holy One of Israel;
[j]For He has glorified you."

6 [k]Seek the LORD while He may be [l]found,
   Call upon Him while He is near.
7 [m]Let the wicked forsake his way,
   And the unrighteous man [n]his
      thoughts;
   Let him return to the LORD,
   [o]And He will have mercy on him;
   And to our God,
   For He will abundantly pardon.

8 "For[p] My thoughts *are* not your
      thoughts,
   Nor *are* your ways My ways," says the
      LORD.
9 "For[q] *as* the heavens are higher than
      the earth,
   So are My ways higher than your
      ways,
   And My thoughts than your thoughts.

10 "For [r]as the rain comes down, and the
      snow from heaven,
   And do not return there,
   But water the earth,
   And make it bring forth and bud,
   That it may give seed to the sower
   And bread to the eater,
11 [s]So shall My word be that goes forth
      from My mouth;
   It shall not return to Me void,
   But it shall accomplish what I please,
   And it shall [t]prosper *in the thing* for
      which I sent it.

12 "For[u] you shall go out with joy,
   And be led out with peace;
   The mountains and the hills
   Shall [v]break forth into singing before
      you,
   And [w]all the trees of the field shall
      clap *their* hands.

13 [x]Instead of [y]the thorn shall come up the
      cypress tree,
   And instead of the brier shall come up
      the myrtle tree;
   And it shall be to the LORD [z]for a name,
   For an everlasting sign *that* shall not
      be cut off."

Salvation for the Gentiles

56 Thus says the LORD:

"Keep justice, and do righteousness,
   [a]For My salvation *is* about to come,
   And My righteousness to be revealed.
2 Blessed *is* the man *who* does this,
   And the son of man *who* lays hold on it;
   [b]Who keeps from defiling the Sabbath,
   And keeps his hand from doing any
      evil."

3 Do not let [c]the son of the foreigner
   Who has joined himself to the LORD
   Speak, saying,
   "The LORD has utterly separated me
      from His people";
   Nor let the [d]eunuch say,
   "Here I am, a dry tree."
4 For thus says the LORD:
   "To the eunuchs who keep My Sabbaths,
   And choose what pleases Me,
   And hold fast My covenant,
5 Even to them I will give in [e]My house
   And within My walls a place [f]and a
      name
   Better than that of sons and daughters;
   I will give them* an everlasting name
   That shall not be cut off.

6 "Also the sons of the foreigner
   Who join themselves to the LORD, to
      serve Him,
   And to love the name of the LORD, to
      be His servants—
   Everyone who keeps from defiling the
      Sabbath,
   And holds fast My covenant—

---

* **56:5** Literally *him*

55:6 *while He may be found.* Solomon warned his readers to remember their Creator in the days of their youth, when the evil days have not yet come (Eccl. 12:1). The writer to the Hebrews admonishes his readers, "Today, if you will hear His voice, do not harden your hearts" (Ps. 95:7–8; Heb. 4:7). Responding to the call of God is not something to be put off. Hardened hearts become a habit, or evil days may impair our ability to think clearly. If the Lord is calling, respond to Him. We do not know how long we have to live. No one knows whether "this night" his soul may be required (Luke 12:20).

55:9 *higher.* The gulf existing between human and divine nature is expressed here in graphic terms. God functions at the level of pure holiness, and He is motivated by complete love and service to others. The corruption of human nature by sin introduces carnal elements that are totally unknown to the nature of God, and by contrast are base both in character and execution. It is only when we are born again that we

can understand the things of the Spirit, the ways of God (John 3:9–21).

56:3 *foreigner.* In speaking of the foreigner who joined himself to the Lord, Isaiah was not speaking of the foreign wives that the returning exiles would have married (Ezra 9:1–4). Those foreign wives were considered a corrupting influence because they had not become followers of the living God. The foreigners that Isaiah was prophesying about would be converted to worship the true Lord (44:5).

56:5 *not be cut off.* This phrase is an idiom for preserving one's name through one's offspring. The phrase links this passage with 55:13.

55:5 [h] Eph. 2:11, 12 [i] Is. 60:5 [j] Is. 60:9   **55:6** [k] [Heb. 3:13]   [l] Ps. 32:6   **55:7** [m] Is. 1:16 [n] Zech. 8:17 [o] Jer. 3:12   **55:8** [p] 2 Sam. 7:19   **55:9** [q] Ps. 103:11   **55:10** [r] Deut. 32:2   **55:11** [s] Is. 45:23 [t] Is. 46:9–11   **55:12** [u] Is. 35:10 [v] Ps. 98:8   [w] 1 Chr. 16:33   **55:13** [x] Is. 41:19 [y] Mic. 7:4 [z] Jer. 13:11   **56:1** [a] Matt. 3:2; 4:17   **56:2** [b] Is. 58:13   **56:3** [c] [Eph. 2:12–19]   [d] Acts 8:27   **56:5** [e] 1 Tim. 3:15   [f] [1 John 3:1, 2]

7 Even them I will ^gbring to My holy
mountain,
And make them joyful in My ^hhouse
of prayer.
ⁱTheir burnt offerings and their
sacrifices
Will be ^jaccepted on My altar;
For ^kMy house shall be called a house
of prayer ^lfor all nations."
8 The Lord GOD, ^mwho gathers the
outcasts of Israel, says,
ⁿ"Yet I will gather to him
Others besides those who are gathered
to him."

Israel's Irresponsible Leaders

9 ^oAll you beasts of the field, come to
devour,
All you beasts in the forest.
10 His watchmen *are* ^pblind,
They are all ignorant;
^qThey *are* all dumb dogs,
They cannot bark;
Sleeping, lying down, loving to
slumber.
11 Yes, *they are* ^rgreedy dogs
Which ^snever have enough.
And they *are* shepherds
Who cannot understand;
They all look to their own way,
Every one for his own gain,
From his *own* territory.
12 "Come," *one says,* "I will bring
wine,
And we will fill ourselves with
intoxicating ^tdrink;
^uTomorrow will be ^vas today,
And much more abundant."

Israel's Futile Idolatry

57 The righteous perishes,
And no man takes *it* to heart;
^aMerciful men *are* taken away,
^bWhile no one considers
That the righteous is taken away from
evil.
2 He shall enter into peace;
They shall rest in ^ctheir beds,
Each one walking *in* his uprightness.
3 "But come here,
^dYou sons of the sorceress,
You offspring of the adulterer and the
harlot!

4 Whom do you ridicule?
Against whom do you make a wide
mouth
And stick out the tongue?
Are you not children of transgression,
Offspring of falsehood,
5 Inflaming yourselves with gods ^eunder
every green tree,
^fSlaying the children in the valleys,
Under the clefts of the rocks?
6 Among the smooth ^gstones of the
stream
Is your portion;
They, they, *are* your lot!
Even to them you have poured a drink
offering,
You have offered a grain offering.
Should I receive comfort in ^hthese?
7 "Onⁱ a lofty and high mountain
You have set ^jyour bed;
Even there you went up
To offer sacrifice.
8 Also behind the doors and their posts
You have set up your remembrance;
For you have uncovered yourself *to
those other* than Me,
And have gone up to them;
You have enlarged your bed
And made *a* covenant with them;
^kYou have loved their bed,
Where you saw *their* nudity.*
9 ^lYou went to the king with ointment,
And increased your perfumes;
You sent your ^mmessengers far off,
And *even* descended to Sheol.
10 You are wearied in the length of your
way;
ⁿYet you did not say, 'There is no hope.'
You have found the life of your hand;
Therefore you were not grieved.
11 "And ^oof whom have you been afraid,
or feared,
That you have lied
And not remembered Me,
Nor taken *it* to your heart?
Is it not because ^pI have held My peace
from of old
That you do not fear Me?
12 I will declare your righteousness
And your works,
For they will not profit you.

---

* 57:8 Literally *hand,* a euphemism

56:9 beasts. The unclean, ravenous beasts summoned to attack the ungodly community are hostile
nations (Jer. 12:8–9; Ezek. 34:5,8).
56:11 dogs. The dog was not highly regarded in biblical culture, and to the Jews they were unclean. In
Deuteronomy 23:18, a "dog" is discussed in the context of a prostitute.
57:5 Slaying the children. Killing the children was
associated with the worship of Molech and with
demon worship (30:33; 2 Kin. 23:10; Ps. 106:37–38;
Jer. 7:31).
57:12 your righteousness. This phrase is stated in
sarcasm or irony. The people had found a counterfeit
life in idolatry and immorality that would only lead
to death.

56:7 ^g [Is. 2:2, 3; 60:11] ^h Mark 11:17 ⁱ [Rom. 12:1] ^j Is.
60:7 ^k Matt. 21:13 ^l [Mal. 1:11] **56:8** ^m Is. 11:12; 27:12;
54:7 ⁿ [John 10:16] **56:9** ^o Jer. 12:9 **56:10** ^p Matt.
15:14 ^q Phil. 3:2 **56:11** ^r [Mic. 3:5, 11] ^s Ezek. 34:2–10
56:12 ^t Is. 28:7 ^u Luke 12:19 ^v 2 Pet. 3:4 **57:1** ^a Ps. 12:1
^b 1 Kin. 14:13 **57:2** ^c 2 Chr. 16:14 **57:3** ^d Matt. 16:4
57:5 ^e 2 Kin. 16:4 ^f Jer. 7:31 **57:6** ^g Jer. 3:9 ^h Jer. 5:9, 29;
9:9 **57:7** ⁱ Ezek. 16:16 ^j Ezek. 23:41 **57:8** ^k Ezek. 16:26
57:9 ^l Hos. 7:11 ^m Ezek. 23:16, 40 **57:10** ⁿ Jer. 2:25; 18:12
57:11 ^o Is. 51:12, 13 ^p Ps. 50:21

13 When you cry out,
Let your collection *of idols* deliver
you.
But the wind will carry them all away,
A breath will take *them.*
But he who puts his trust in Me shall
possess the land,
And shall inherit My holy mountain."

Healing for the Backslider

14 And one shall say,
a"Heap it up! Heap it up!
Prepare the way,
Take the stumbling block out of the
way of My people."

15 For thus says the High and Lofty One
Who inhabits eternity, *r*whose name
is Holy:
s"I dwell in the high and holy *place,*
*t*With him *who* has a contrite and
humble spirit,
*u*To revive the spirit of the humble,
And to revive the heart of the contrite
ones.

16 *v*For I will not contend forever,
Nor will I always be angry;
For the spirit would fail before Me,
And the souls *w*which I have made.

17 For the iniquity of *x*his covetousness
I was angry and struck him;
*y*I hid and was angry,
*z*And he went on backsliding in the way
of his heart.

18 I have seen his ways, and *a*will heal
him;
I will also lead him,
And restore comforts to him
And to *b*his mourners.

19 "I create *c*the fruit of the lips:
Peace, peace *d*to *him who is* far off and
to *him who is* near,"
Says the LORD,
"And I will heal him."

20 *e*But the wicked *are* like the troubled
sea,
When it cannot rest,
Whose waters cast up mire and dirt.

21 "There*f* *is* no peace,"
Says my God, "for the wicked."

Fasting that Pleases God

58 "Cry aloud, spare not;
Lift up your voice like a trumpet;
*a*Tell My people their transgression,
And the house of Jacob their sins.

2 Yet they seek Me daily,
And delight to know My ways,
As a nation that did righteousness,
And did not forsake the ordinance of
their God.
They ask of Me the ordinances of
justice;
They take delight in approaching God.

3 'Why*b* have we fasted,' *they say,* 'and
You have not seen?
Why have we *c*afflicted our souls, and
You take no notice?'
"In fact, in the day of your fast you find
pleasure,
And exploit all your laborers.

4 *d*Indeed you fast for strife and debate,
And to strike with the fist of wickedness.
You will not fast as *you do* this day,
To make your voice heard on high.

5 Is *e*it a fast that I have chosen,
*f*A day for a man to afflict his soul?
Is it to bow down his head like a
bulrush,
And *g*to spread out sackcloth and ashes?
Would you call this a fast,
And an acceptable day to the LORD?

6 "Is this not the fast that I have chosen:
To *h*loose the bonds of wickedness,
*i*To undo the heavy burdens,
*j*To let the oppressed go free,
And that you break every yoke?

7 *Is it* not *k*to share your bread with the
hungry,
And that you bring to your house the
poor who are cast out;
*l*When you see the naked, that you
cover him,
And not hide yourself from *m*your own
flesh?

8 *n*Then your light shall break forth like
the morning,
Your healing shall spring forth
speedily,

57:14 *Heap it up.* This verse is based on 40:1–4. The phrase "heap it up" resembles "every valley shall be exalted."
57:16 *will not contend forever.* God was addressing the human failure to keep His good laws, but humans will always fail. God knew this, so He created a way of salvation, a way to heal the problem of sin (v. 18). He knew that they needed to be radically rescued, for the law was powerless to save them (Rom. 2–8).
58:2 *delight to know My ways . . . delight in approaching God.* Unfortunately, one can really enjoy all the religious ritual without really wanting to know God. God can always tell the difference between the heart that is turned toward Him and the heart that is devoted to religious form.
58:6 *To loose . . . To undo . . . free.* Love is right at the

top of the list in relating to God and to other people (1 John 4:7–21). Once again, the Lord is defining true religion. It is always horizontal (directed toward other people) as well as vertical (directed toward God). If we love God, we will be just and merciful to other people (Mic. 6:8; James 1:26–27).

57:14 *q* Is. 40:3; 62:10 **57:15** *r* Job 6:10 *s* Zech. 2:13 *t* Ps. 34:18; 51:17 *u* Is. 61:1–3 **57:16** *v* [Mic. 7:18] *w* Num. 16:22 **57:17** *x* Jer. 6:13 *y* Is. 8:17; 45:15; 59:2 *z* Is. 9:13 **57:18** *a* Jer. 3:22 *b* Is. 61:2 **57:19** *c* Heb. 13:15 *d* Eph. 2:17 **57:20** *e* Job 15:20 **57:21** *f* Is. 48:22 **58:1** *a* Mic. 3:8 **58:3** *b* Mal. 3:13–18 *c* Lev. 16:29; 23:27 **58:4** *d* 1 Kin. 21:9 **58:5** *e* Zech. 7:5 *f* Lev. 16:29 *g* Esth. 4:3 **58:6** *h* Luke 4:18, 19 *i* Neh. 5:10–12 *j* Jer. 34:9 **58:7** *k* Ezek. 18:7 *l* Job 31:19–22 *m* Neh. 5:5 **58:8** *n* Job 11:17

And your righteousness shall go
before you;
*o*The glory of the LORD shall be your
rear guard.
9 Then you shall call, and the LORD will
answer;
You shall cry, and He will say, 'Here
I *am*.'

"If you take away the yoke from your
midst,
The pointing of the finger, and
*p*speaking wickedness,
10 *If* you extend your soul to the hungry
And satisfy the afflicted soul,
Then your light shall dawn in the
darkness,
And your darkness shall *be* as the
noonday.
11 The LORD will guide you continually,
And satisfy your soul in drought,
And strengthen your bones;
You shall be like a watered garden,
And like a spring of water, whose
waters do not fail.
12 Those from among you
*q*Shall build the old waste places;
You shall raise up the foundations of
many generations;
And you shall be called the Repairer
of the Breach,
The Restorer of Streets to Dwell In.

13 "If *r*you turn away your foot from the
Sabbath,
From doing your pleasure on My holy
day,
And call the Sabbath a delight,
The holy *day* of the LORD honorable,
And shall honor Him, not doing your
own ways,
Nor finding your own pleasure,
Nor speaking *your own* words,
14 *s*Then you shall delight yourself in the
LORD;
And I will cause you to *t*ride on the
high hills of the earth,
And feed you with the heritage of
Jacob your father.
*u*The mouth of the LORD has
spoken."

Separated from God

59 Behold, the LORD's hand is not
*a*shortened,
That it cannot save;
Nor His ear heavy,
That it cannot hear.
2 But your iniquities have separated you
from your God;
And your sins have hidden *His* face
from you,
So that He will *b*not hear.
3 For *c*your hands are defiled with
blood,
And your fingers with iniquity;
Your lips have spoken lies,
Your tongue has muttered
perversity.

4 No one calls for justice,
Nor does *any* plead for truth.
They trust in *d*empty words and speak
lies;
*e*They conceive evil and bring forth
iniquity.
5 They hatch vipers' eggs and weave the
spider's web;
He who eats of their eggs dies,
And *from* that which is crushed a
viper breaks out.

6 *f*Their webs will not become
garments,
Nor will they cover themselves with
their works;
Their works *are* works of iniquity,
And the act of violence *is* in their
hands.
7 *g*Their feet run to evil,
And they make haste to shed
*h*innocent blood;
*i*Their thoughts *are* thoughts of
iniquity;
Wasting and *j*destruction *are* in their
paths.
8 The way of *k*peace they have not
known,
And *there is* no justice in their ways;
*l*They have made themselves crooked
paths;
Whoever takes that way shall not
know peace.

59:2 The Effects of Sin—Sin, regardless of how serious, always has an effect—separation. Sin separates one from God. This separation from God is death. Adam was told that if he ate of the tree of the knowledge of good and evil he would die (Gen. 3:3). Adam ate of the tree anyway and immediately died spiritually—his soul was separated from God—and he then began to die physically. The entrance of sin into the world brought with it death (Rom. 5:12; 6:23). That man is a sinner is proven by the fact that he dies—where there is death, there is sin. Sin's penalty, death, can be remedied by life—union with God. This is achieved by belief in Jesus, who died to pay the penalty of man's sin (Rom. 5:21). For one who believes in Jesus, the penalty of sin is broken. He will die physically but physical death for him is only the doorway into the presence of God.

Sin has an effect upon the believer, for it mars his fellowship with God. Sin in the believer's life is a terrible thing and is not to be tolerated. While it is probable that the believer will sin, it is never necessary for him to do so (1 John 2:1).
59:5 vipers' eggs. The viper is a poisonous snake (Acts 28:3–6).
59:7–8 feet run to evil. This passage is cited in Romans 3:15–17 to document the universal aspect of sin.

58:8 *o* Ex. 14:19 **58:9** *p* Ps. 12:2 **58:12** *q* Is. 61:4
58:13 *r* Is. 56:2, 4, 6 **58:14** *s* Job 22:26 *t* Deut. 32:13;
33:29 *u* Is. 1:20; 40:5 **59:1** *a* Num. 11:23 **59:2** *b* Is. 1:15
59:3 *c* Ezek. 7:23 **59:4** *d* Jer. 7:4 *e* Job 15:35 **59:6** *f* Job
8:14 **59:7** *g* Rom. 3:15 *h* Prov. 6:17 *i* Is. 55:7 *j* Rom. 3:16,
17 **59:8** *k* Is. 57:20, 21 *l* Prov. 2:15

Sin Confessed

9 Therefore justice is far from us,
  Nor does righteousness overtake us;
  *m*We look for light, but there is
      darkness!
  For brightness, *but* we walk in
      blackness!

10 *n*We grope for the wall like the blind,
   And we grope as if *we had* no eyes;
   We stumble at noonday as at twilight;
   We are as dead *men* in desolate places.

11 We all growl like bears,
   And *o*moan sadly like doves;
   We look for justice, but *there is* none;
   For salvation, *but* it is far from us.

12 For our *p*transgressions are multiplied
      before You,
   And our sins testify against us;
   For our transgressions *are* with us,
   And *as for* our iniquities, we know
      them:

13 In transgressing and lying against the
      LORD,
   And departing from our God,
   Speaking oppression and revolt,
   Conceiving and uttering *q*from the
      heart words of falsehood.

14 Justice is turned back,
   And righteousness stands afar off;
   For truth is fallen in the street,
   And equity cannot enter.

15 So truth fails,
   And he *who* departs from evil makes
      himself a *r*prey.

The Redeemer of Zion

Then the LORD saw *it*, and it
   displeased Him
That *there was* no justice.

16 *s*He saw that *there was* no man,
   And *t*wondered that *there was* no
      intercessor;
   *u*Therefore His own arm brought
      salvation for Him;
   And His own righteousness, it
      sustained Him.

17 *v*For He put on righteousness as a
      breastplate,
   And a helmet of salvation on His head;
   He put on the garments of vengeance
      for clothing,
   And was clad with zeal as a cloak.

18 *w*According to *their* deeds, accordingly
      He will repay,
   Fury to His adversaries,
   Recompense to His enemies;
   The coastlands He will fully repay.

19 *x*So shall they fear
   The name of the LORD from the west,
   And His glory from the rising of the
      sun;
   When the enemy comes in *y*like a
      flood,
   The Spirit of the LORD will lift up a
      standard against him.

20 "The*z* Redeemer will come to Zion,
   And to those who turn from
      transgression in Jacob,"
   Says the LORD.

21"As*a* for Me," says the LORD, "this *is* My
covenant with them: My Spirit who *is* upon
you, and My words which I have put in your
mouth, shall not depart from your mouth,
nor from the mouth of your descendants,
nor from the mouth of your descendants'
descendants," says the LORD, "from this
time and forevermore."

59:9 Therefore. "Therefore" links Israel's repentance with the prophet's reprimand. With the pronoun "us," Isaiah identified himself with his people's sins (Ezek. 9:6–7; Dan. 9:5).
59:16 no man. God's salvation does not depend on humans (Ezek. 22:30).
59:17 righteousness as a breastplate. This idea of the righteous warrior is repeated in Ephesians 6:13–17. Right standing with God is our protection, as surely as the warrior depends on the heavy body shield over his heart to protect him from the arrows of the enemy.
59:20 The Redeemer will come. The Redeemer comes in the person of Jesus Christ.
59:21 My Spirit. God promised that His Spirit and His Word would never be lost to His people. The covenant that He made with them affirms that the Word is firm and unshakable. It may not be performed immediately, but the hearers can be assured of its truth. He also promised that He would always be present with His people through the Spirit. This is a promise that continues to be comforting to the people of God, and it must have brought particular comfort to the people who lived in the "silent" years between the preaching of Malachi and the coming of John the Baptist.
59:21 Inspiration of God's Word—The word *inspiration* occurs only once in the New Testament, in 2 Timothy 3:16. Paul says there "All Scripture is given

by inspiration of God," literally "God-breathed." God takes the initiative in communicating with us. Divine inspiration logically follows divine revelation. In revelation God speaks to man's ear, while by inspiration He guides the pen to ensure that the imparted message is correctly written down. God's intent is to give His people a right understanding of His revelation and a permanent record of His dealings with mankind. The authority of the Bible is from God Himself.

Bible authors understood that their writings were being guided by the Spirit of God, even as they wrote them. Peter said this was true of Old Testament authors (2 Pet. 1:20–21). He then stated his own letters were inspired by God (2 Pet. 3:1–2). Finally, he pointed out this was also true concerning Paul's writings (2 Pet. 3:15).

This means that the Bible is more than just the wise insights of men who desired to follow God. God worked in the thinking of the biblical writers so the message they wrote was also God's message. While the writings certainly display the individual

59:9 *m* Jer. 8:15　**59:10** *n* Job 5:14　**59:11** *o* Ezek. 7:16
59:12 *p* Is. 24:5; 58:1　**59:13** *q* Matt. 12:34　**59:15** *r* Is.
5:23; 10:2; 29:21; 32:7　**59:16** *s* Ezek. 22:30　*t* Mark
6:6　*u* Ps. 98:1　**59:17** *v* Eph. 6:14, 17　**59:18** *w* Is.
63:6　**59:19** *x* Mal. 1:11　*y* Rev. 12:15　**59:20** *z* Rom. 11:26
59:21 *a* [Heb. 8:10; 10:16]

The Gentiles Bless Zion

60 Arise, ^ashine;
For your light has come!
And ^bthe glory of the LORD is risen
upon you.
2 For behold, the darkness shall cover
the earth,
And deep darkness the people;
But the LORD will arise over you,
And His glory will be seen upon you.
3 The ^cGentiles shall come to your light,
And kings to the brightness of your
rising.

4 "Lift^d up your eyes all around, and see:
They all gather together, ^ethey come
to you;
Your sons shall come from afar,
And your daughters shall be nursed at
your side.
5 Then you shall see and become radiant,
And your heart shall swell with joy;
Because ^fthe abundance of the sea
shall be turned to you,
The wealth of the Gentiles shall come
to you.
6 The multitude of camels shall cover
your *land*,
The dromedaries of Midian and
^gEphah;
All those from ^hSheba shall come;
They shall bring ⁱgold and incense,
And they shall proclaim the praises of
the LORD.
7 All the flocks of ^jKedar shall be
gathered together to you,
The rams of Nebaioth shall minister
to you;
They shall ascend with ^kacceptance on
My altar,
And ^lI will glorify the house of My
glory.

8 "Who *are* these *who* fly like a cloud,
And like doves to their roosts?
9 ^mSurely the coastlands shall wait for Me;
And the ships of Tarshish *will come*
first,
ⁿTo bring your sons from afar,
^oTheir silver and their gold with them,
To the name of the LORD your God,
And to the Holy One of Israel,
^pBecause He has glorified you.

10 "The^q sons of foreigners shall build up
your walls,
^rAnd their kings shall minister to you;
For ^sin My wrath I struck you,
^tBut in My favor I have had mercy on
you.
11 Therefore your gates ^ushall be open
continually;
They shall not be shut day or night,
That *men* may bring to you the wealth
of the Gentiles,
And their kings in procession.
12 ^vFor the nation and kingdom which will
not serve you shall perish,
And *those* nations shall be utterly
ruined.

13 "The^w glory of Lebanon shall come to
you,
The cypress, the pine, and the box tree
together,
To beautify the place of My sanctuary;
And I will make ^xthe place of My feet
glorious.
14 Also the sons of those who afflicted
you
Shall come ^ybowing to you,
And all those who despised you shall
^zfall prostrate at the soles of your
feet;
And they shall call you The City of the
LORD,
^aZion of the Holy One of Israel.

15 "Whereas you have been forsaken and
hated,
So that no one went through *you*,
I will make you an eternal excellence,
A joy of many generations.
16 You shall drink the milk of the
Gentiles,
^bAnd milk the breast of kings;
You shall know that ^cI, the LORD, *am*
your Savior
And your Redeemer, the Mighty One
of Jacob.

17 "Instead of bronze I will bring gold,
Instead of iron I will bring silver,
Instead of wood, bronze,
And instead of stones, iron.
I will also make your officers peace,
And your magistrates righteousness.

---

characteristics of all of the different authors, there is
also an overall divine influence that unifies the Bible
as no other book.
60:1 Arise, shine. This command is directed to Zion
(v. 14), which is both the recipient of God's light and
the reflector of it. It is difficult to imagine the world
without the knowledge of Christ, yet each believer
who remembers his life before he was born again
can testify to the power of the light of the gospel. It
is a great joy to come from the darkness of sin and
doubt to the light of forgiveness and knowledge of
Jesus Christ. What a joyful command, to "shine" for
the Savior.
60:3 Gentiles. The Gentiles are the other nations.
60:9 ships of Tarshish. The reference to the ships of

Tarshish alludes to the wealth of King Solomon (2:16;
1 Kin. 10:22).
60:12 not serve you shall perish. The nation and
kingdom that does not serve Zion, where Christ now
reigns (Acts 2:29–36), shall perish (John 3:18; Heb. 2:3;
9:27; 10:27).

60:1 ^a Eph. 5:14 ^b Mal. 4:2 **60:3** ^c Is. 49:6, 23
60:4 ^d Is. 49:18 ^e Is. 49:20–22 **60:5** ^f [Rom. 11:25–27]
60:6 ^g Gen. 25:4 ^h Ps. 72:10 ⁱ Matt. 2:11 **60:7** ^j Gen.
25:13 ^k Is. 56:7 ^l Hag. 2:7, 9 **60:9** ^m Ps. 72:10 ⁿ [Gal. 4:26]
^o Jer. 3:17 ^p Is. 55:5 **60:10** ^q Zech. 6:15 ^r Rev. 21:24 ^s Is.
57:17 ^t Is. 54:7, 8 **60:11** ^u Rev. 21:25, 26 **60:12** ^v Zech.
14:17 **60:13** ^w Is. 35:2 ^x 1 Chr. 28:2 **60:14** ^y Is. 45:14
^z Rev. 3:9 ^a [Heb. 12:22] **60:16** ^b Is. 49:23 ^c Is. 43:3

18 Violence shall no longer be heard in
  your land,
Neither wasting nor destruction
  within your borders;
But you shall call ᵈyour walls
  Salvation,
And your gates Praise.

God the Glory of His People

19 "The ᵉsun shall no longer be your light
  by day,
Nor for brightness shall the moon give
  light to you;
But the LORD will be to you an
  everlasting light,
And ᶠyour God your glory.
20 ᵍYour sun shall no longer go down,
Nor shall your moon withdraw itself;
For the LORD will be your everlasting
  light,
And the days of your mourning shall
  be ended.
21 ʰAlso your people *shall* all *be*
  righteous;
ⁱThey shall inherit the land forever,
ʲThe branch of My planting,
ᵏThe work of My hands,
That I may be glorified.
22 ˡA little one shall become a thousand,
And a small one a strong nation.
I, the LORD, will hasten it in its time."

The Good News of Salvation

61 "The ᵃSpirit of the Lord GOD *is* upon
  Me,
Because the LORD ᵇhas anointed Me
To preach good tidings to the poor;
He has sent Me ᶜto heal the
  brokenhearted,
To proclaim ᵈliberty to the captives,
And the opening of the prison to *those
  who are* bound;
2 ᵉTo proclaim the acceptable year of the
  LORD,
And ᶠthe day of vengeance of our God;
ᵍTo comfort all who mourn,
3 To console those who mourn in Zion,
ʰTo give them beauty for ashes,
The oil of joy for mourning,

The garment of praise for the spirit of
  heaviness;
That they may be called trees of
  righteousness,
ⁱThe planting of the LORD, ʲthat He may
  be glorified."

4 And they shall ᵏrebuild the old ruins,
They shall raise up the former
  desolations,
And they shall repair the ruined
  cities,
The desolations of many generations.
5 ˡStrangers shall stand and feed your
  flocks,
And the sons of the foreigner
  Shall be your plowmen and your
  vinedressers.
6 ᵐBut you shall be named the priests of
  the LORD,
They shall call you the servants of our
  God.
ⁿYou shall eat the riches of the Gentiles,
And in their glory you shall boast.
7 ᵒInstead of your shame *you shall have*
  double *honor,*
And *instead of* confusion they shall
  rejoice in their portion.
Therefore in their land they shall
  possess double;
Everlasting joy shall be theirs.

8 "For ᵖI, the LORD, love justice;
ᑫI hate robbery for burnt offering;
I will direct their work in truth,
ʳAnd will make with them an
  everlasting covenant.
9 Their descendants shall be known
  among the Gentiles,
And their offspring among the people.
All who see them shall acknowledge
  them,
ˢThat they *are* the posterity *whom* the
  LORD has blessed."

10 ᵗI will greatly rejoice in the LORD,
My soul shall be joyful in my God;
For ᵘHe has clothed me with the
  garments of salvation,
He has covered me with the robe of
  righteousness,

60:18 Salvation . . . Praise. Judging from the figurative language in verses 15–22, especially verse 17, God's salvation and Israel's praise will be the city's defense (Zech. 2:4–5).
60:19–20 no longer. These verses form the basis for the description of the New Jerusalem in the new heaven and earth (Rev. 21:1,23; 22:5).
61:1 Me. The "Me" featured so prominently here is the same as the Servant in 42:1; 49:1; 50:4; 52:13. The Servant is the Messiah, the Lord Jesus Christ. This verse is the passage from Isaiah that Jesus read in the synagogue at the beginning of His ministry (Luke 4:16–21). When He finished reading it, He said, "Today this Scripture is fulfilled in your hearing."
61:2 day of vengeance. The day of God's vengeance is yet to come. This is the "day" that the Book of Revelation is talking about (Rev. 11:14–19).

61:10 Christ's Righteousness—One of the most awesome requirements made upon men and women by God is that they be righteous, that is, conform to His ethical and moral standards (Ps. 15:2; Mic. 6:8). Since God is holy He cannot allow sinners into His presence (Is. 6:3–5). We sinners cannot save ourselves or make ourselves righteous. Only God's intervention can save us and make us righteous. God sent Christ,

60:18 ᵈ Is. 26:1   **60:19** ᵉ Rev. 21:23; 22:5   ᶠ Zech. 2:5
60:20 ᵍ Amos 8:9   **60:21** ʰ Rev. 21:27   ⁱ Ps. 37:11   ʲ Is.
61:3   ᵏ [Eph. 2:10]   **60:22** ˡ Matt. 13:31, 32   **61:1** ᵃ Luke
4:18, 19   ᵇ Luke 7:22   ᶜ Ps. 147:3   ᵈ Is. 42:7   **61:2** ᵉ Lev. 25:9
ᶠ Is. 34:8   ᵍ Matt. 5:4   **61:3** ʰ Ps. 30:11   ⁱ Is. 60:21   ʲ [John
15:8]   **61:4** ᵏ Ezek. 36:33   **61:5** ˡ [Eph. 2:12]   **61:6** ᵐ Ex.
19:6   ⁿ Is. 60:5, 11   **61:7** ᵒ Zech. 9:12   **61:8** ᵖ Ps. 11:7
ᑫ Is. 1:11, 13   ʳ Is. 55:3   **61:9** ˢ Is. 65:23   **61:10** ᵗ Hab. 3:18
ᵘ Ps. 132:9, 16

ᵛAs a bridegroom decks *himself* with
ornaments,
And as a bride adorns *herself* with her
jewels.
11 For as the earth brings forth its bud,
As the garden causes the things that
are sown in it to spring forth,
So the Lord GOD will cause
ʷrighteousness and ˣpraise
to spring forth before all the
nations.

Assurance of Zion's Salvation

62 For Zion's sake I will not hold My
peace,
And for Jerusalem's sake I will not
rest,
Until her righteousness goes forth as
brightness,
And her salvation as a lamp *that* burns.
2 ᵃThe Gentiles shall see your
righteousness,
And all ᵇkings your glory.
ᶜYou shall be called by a new name,
Which the mouth of the LORD will
name.
3 You shall also be ᵈa crown of glory
In the hand of the LORD,
And a royal diadem
In the hand of your God.
4 ᵉYou shall no longer be termed
ᶠForsaken,
Nor shall your land any more be
termed ᵍDesolate;
But you shall be called Hephzibah,*
and your land Beulah;*
For the LORD delights in you,
And your land shall be married.
5 For *as* a young man marries a virgin,
So shall your sons marry you;
And *as* the bridegroom rejoices over
the bride,
ʰSo shall your God rejoice over you.
6 ⁱI have set watchmen on your walls,
O Jerusalem;
They shall never hold their peace day
or night.
You who make mention of the LORD,
do not keep silent,

7 And give Him no rest till He establishes
And till He makes Jerusalem ʲa praise
in the earth.
8 The LORD has sworn by His right hand
And by the arm of His strength:
"Surely I will no longer ᵏgive your grain
As food for your enemies;
And the sons of the foreigner shall not
drink your new wine,
For which you have labored.
9 But those who have gathered it shall
eat it,
And praise the LORD;
Those who have brought it together
shall drink it ⁱin My holy courts."
10 Go through,
Go through the gates!
ᵐPrepare the way for the people;
Build up,
Build up the highway!
Take out the stones,
ⁿLift up a banner for the peoples!
11 Indeed the LORD has proclaimed
To the end of the world:
ᵒ"Say to the daughter of Zion,
'Surely your salvation is coming;
Behold, His ᵖreward *is* with Him,
And His work before Him.'"
12 And they shall call them The Holy
People,
The Redeemed of the LORD;
And you shall be called Sought Out,
A City Not Forsaken.

The LORD in Judgment and Salvation

63 Who *is* this who comes from Edom,
With dyed garments from Bozrah,
This *One who is* glorious in His
apparel,
Traveling in the greatness of His
strength?—

"I who speak in righteousness, mighty
to save."

---

* **62:4** Literally *My Delight Is in Her* • Literally
Married

---

who never sinned, to die for our sins and thus satisfy His own wrath towards us and our sin. God, at the cross, treated Christ as though He had committed our sins even though He was righteous. On the other hand, when we believe in Christ, He treats us as though we were as righteous as Himself (2 Cor. 5:21). It is as if God deposits in our spiritual account the very worth of Christ, much as though He were a banker adding an inexhaustible deposit to our bank account.
62:2 *a new name.* A new name, like new clothing, signified a new status (Gen. 17:5,15; 32:28; Rev. 2:17).
62:4 *Hephzibah . . . Beulah.* The name "Hephzibah" means "my delight is in her"—in this case, it is the Lord's delight—and "Beulah" means "married." Both of these names are symbolic, pointing to a time when Israel's relationship with the Lord is restored.
62:6 *You who make mention of the LORD.* The

"watchmen," or prophets, were intercessors. They prayed that the Lord's promises would be fulfilled.
62:8 *The LORD has sworn.* When God made the promise to Abraham (Heb. 6:13), He swore by Himself; so here He again swears in His own name. There is no greater name than the name of the Lord, and He cannot lie—this is the surest promise man can receive.
63:1 *Edom.* Edom epitomized Israel's enemies (Ps. 137:7; Lam. 4:21–22; Ezek. 25:12; 35:1–5; Obad.

61:10 ᵛ Is. 49:18   **61:11** ʷ Ps. 72:3; 85:11   ˣ Is. 60:18; 62:7
62:2 ᵈ Is. 60:3 ᵇ Ps. 102:15, 16; 138:4, 5; 148:11, 13 ᶜ Is.
62:4, 12; 65:15   **62:3** ᵈ Zech. 9:16   **62:4** ᵉ Hos. 1:10 ᶠ Is.
49:14; 54:6, 7 ᵍ Is. 54:1   **62:5** ʰ Is. 65:19   **62:6** ⁱ Ezek.
3:17; 33:7   **62:7** ʲ Zeph. 3:19, 20   **62:8** ᵏ Deut. 28:31, 33
62:9 ⁱ Deut. 12:12; 14:23, 26   **62:10** ᵐ Is. 40:3; 57:14 ⁿ Is.
11:12   **62:11** ᵒ Zech. 9:9 ᵖ [Rev. 22:12]

2 Why [a]*is* Your apparel red,
And Your garments like one who treads in the winepress?
3 "I have [b]trodden the winepress alone,
And from the peoples no one *was* with Me.
For I have trodden them in My anger,
And trampled them in My fury;
Their blood is sprinkled upon My garments,
And I have stained all My robes.
4 For the [c]day of vengeance *is* in My heart,
And the year of My redeemed has come.
5 [d]I looked, but [e]*there was* no one to help,
And I wondered
That *there was* no one to uphold;
Therefore My own [f]arm brought salvation for Me;
And My own fury, it sustained Me.
6 I have trodden down the peoples in My anger,
Made them drunk in My fury,
And brought down their strength to the earth."

God's Mercy Remembered

7 I will mention the lovingkindnesses of the LORD
And the praises of the LORD,
According to all that the LORD has bestowed on us,
And the great goodness toward the house of Israel,
Which He has bestowed on them according to His mercies,
According to the multitude of His lovingkindnesses.
8 For He said, "Surely they *are* My people,
Children *who* will not lie."
So He became their Savior.
9 [g]In all their affliction He was afflicted,
[h]And the Angel of His Presence saved them;
[i]In His love and in His pity He redeemed them;
And [j]He bore them and carried them
All the days of old.
10 But they [k]rebelled and [l]grieved His Holy Spirit;
[m]So He turned Himself against them as an enemy,
And He fought against them.
11 Then he [n]remembered the days of old,
Moses *and* his people, *saying:*
"Where *is* He who [o]brought them up out of the sea
With the shepherd of His flock?
[p]Where *is* He who put His Holy Spirit within them,
12 Who led *them* by the right hand of Moses,
[q]With His glorious arm,
[r]Dividing the water before them
To make for Himself an everlasting name,
13 [s]Who led them through the deep,
As a horse in the wilderness,
That they might not stumble?"

14 As a beast goes down into the valley,
And the Spirit of the LORD causes him to rest,
So You lead Your people,
[t]To make Yourself a glorious name.

A Prayer of Penitence

15 [u]Look down from heaven,
And see [v]from Your habitation, holy and glorious.
Where *are* Your zeal and Your strength,
The yearning [w]of Your heart and Your mercies toward me?
Are they restrained?
16 [x]Doubtless You *are* our Father,
Though Abraham [y]was ignorant of us,
And Israel does not acknowledge us.
You, O LORD, *are* our Father;
Our Redeemer from Everlasting *is* Your name.
17 O LORD, why have You [z]made us stray from Your ways,
And hardened our heart from Your fear?
Return for Your servants' sake,
The tribes of Your inheritance.
18 [a]Your holy people have possessed *it* but a little while;
[b]Our adversaries have trodden down Your sanctuary.
19 We have become *like* those of old, over whom You never ruled,
Those who were never called by Your name.

64 Oh, that You would rend the heavens!
That You would come down!
That the mountains might shake at Your [a]presence—

13–14). It was famous for its winemaking (v. 3). ***Bozrah.*** Bozrah was the chief town of Edom.

63:3 ***I.*** The pronoun "I" refers to Christ in Revelation 19:5.

63:11 ***put His Holy Spirit within them.*** This refers to the presence of the Holy Spirit on Moses and his helpers in the desert (Num. 11:17,25).

63:12 ***glorious arm.*** This verse refers to God dividing the Red Sea (Ex. 15:6; 14:16,21; Ps. 78:13). Isaiah is reminding his hearers of the mighty acts that God did in the past, as well as the things that He has promised to do in the future. Such perspective is often helpful when one is bearing difficult times in the present.

63:2 [a][Rev. 19:13, 15] **63:3** [b]Rev. 14:19, 20; 19:15 **63:4** [c]Is. 34:8; 35:4; 61:2 **63:5** [d]Is. 41:28; 59:16 [e][John 16:32] [f]Ps. 98:1 **63:9** [g]Judg. 10:16 [h]Ex. 14:19 [i]Deut. 7:7 [j]Ex. 19:4 **63:10** [k]Ex. 15:24 [l]Ps. 78:40 [m]Ex. 23:21 **63:11** [n]Ps. 106:44, 45 [o]Ex. 14:30 [p]Num. 11:17, 25, 29 **63:12** [q]Ex. 15:6 [r]Ex. 14:21, 22 **63:13** [s]Ps. 106:9 **63:14** [t]2 Sam. 7:23 **63:15** [u]Deut. 26:15 [v]Ps. 33:14 [w]Jer. 31:20 **63:16** [x]Deut. 32:6 [y]Job 14:21 **63:17** [z]John 12:40 **63:18** [a]Deut. 7:6 [b]Ps. 74:3–7 **64:1** [a]Mic. 1:3, 4

2   As fire burns brushwood,
As fire causes water to boil—
To make Your name known to Your
    adversaries,
That the nations may tremble at Your
    presence!
3   When *b*You did awesome things *for
    which* we did not look,
You came down,
The mountains shook at Your presence.
4   For since the beginning of the world
cMen have not heard nor perceived by
    the ear,
Nor has the eye seen any God besides
    You,
Who acts for the one who waits for
    Him.
5   You meet him who rejoices and does
    righteousness,
Who remembers You in Your ways.
You are indeed angry, for we have
    sinned—
*d*In these ways we continue;
And we need to be saved.

6   But we are all like an unclean *thing,*
And all *e*our righteousnesses *are* like
    filthy rags;
We all *f*fade as a leaf,
And our iniquities, like the wind,
Have taken us away.
7   And *there is* no one who calls on Your
    name,
Who stirs himself up to take hold of
    You;
For You have hidden Your face from us,
And have consumed us because of our
    iniquities.

8   But now, O LORD,
You *are* our Father;
We *are* the clay, and You our *g*potter;
And all we *are* the work of Your hand.
9   Do not be furious, O LORD,
Nor remember iniquity forever;
Indeed, please look—we all *are* Your
    people!
10   Your holy cities are a wilderness,
Zion is a wilderness,
Jerusalem a desolation.
11   Our holy and beautiful temple,
Where our fathers praised You,
Is burned up with fire;
And all *h*our pleasant things are laid
    waste.
12   *i*Will You restrain Yourself because of
    these *things,* O LORD?
*j*Will You hold Your peace, and afflict
    us very severely?

The Righteousness of God's Judgment

65 "I was *a*sought by *those who* did not
    ask *for Me;*
I was found by *those who* did not
    seek Me.
I said, 'Here I am, here I am,'
To a nation *that b*was not called by My
    name.
2   *c*I have stretched out My hands all day
    long to a *d*rebellious people,
Who *e*walk in a way *that is* not good,
According to their own thoughts;
3   A people *f*who provoke Me to anger
    continually to My face;
*g*Who sacrifice in gardens,
And burn incense on altars of brick;
4   *h*Who sit among the graves,
And spend the night in the tombs;
*i*Who eat swine's flesh,
And the broth of abominable things is
    in their vessels;
5   *j*Who say, 'Keep to yourself,
Do not come near me,
For I am holier than you!'
These *are* smoke in My nostrils,
A fire that burns all the day.

6   "Behold, *k*it is* written before Me:
*l*I will not keep silence, *m*but will
    repay—
Even repay into their bosom—
7   Your iniquities and *n*the iniquities of
    your fathers together,"
Says the LORD,
o"Who have burned incense on the
    mountains
*p*And blasphemed Me on the hills;
Therefore I will measure their former
    work into their bosom."

8 Thus says the LORD:

"As the new wine is found in the cluster,
And *one* says, 'Do not destroy it,
For *q*a blessing *is* in it,'
So will I do for My servants' sake,
That I may not destroy them *r*all.
9   I will bring forth descendants from
    Jacob,
And from Judah an heir of My
    mountains;
My *s*elect shall inherit it,
And My servants shall dwell there.
10   *t*Sharon shall be a fold of flocks,
And *u*the Valley of Achor a place for
    herds to lie down,
For My people who have *v*sought Me.

64:4 *Nor has the eye seen.* Paul cites this verse with
some changes in 1 Corinthians 2:9.
64:10 *wilderness . . . desolation.* The prophetic picture of devastation of the land is probably referring to
the time of the Babylonian invasion.
65:1 *those who did not ask for Me.* Paul saw his ministry to the Gentiles as a fulfillment of this promise
(Rom. 10:20–21).
65:10 *Sharon . . . Valley of Achor.* Sharon, on the

64:3 *b* Ex. 34:10   **64:4** *c* Ps. 31:19   **64:5** *d* Mal.
3:6   **64:6** *e* [Phil. 3:9] *f* Ps. 90:5, 6   **64:8** *g* Is. 29:16;
45:9   **64:11** *h* Ezek. 24:21   **64:12** *i* Is. 42:14 *j* Ps.
83:1   **65:1** *a* Rom. 9:24; 10:20 *b* Is. 63:19   **65:2** *c* Rom.
10:21 *d* Is. 1:2, 23 *e* Is. 42:24   **65:3** *f* Deut. 32:21 *g* Is.
1:29   **65:4** *h* Deut. 18:11 *i* Is. 66:17   **65:5** *j* Matt. 9:11
65:6 *k* Deut. 32:34 *l* Ps. 50:3 *m* Ps. 79:12   **65:7** *n* Ex. 20:5
o Ezek. 18:6 *p* Ezek. 20:27, 28   **65:8** *q* Joel 2:14 *r* Is. 1:9
65:9 *s* Matt. 24:22   **65:10** *t* Is. 33:9 *u* Josh. 7:24 *v* Is. 55:6

11 "But you *are* those who forsake the
LORD,
Who forget [w]My holy mountain,
Who prepare [x]a table for Gad,*
And who furnish a drink offering for
Meni.*
12 Therefore I will number you for the
sword,
And you shall all bow down to the
slaughter;
[y]Because, when I called, you did not
answer;
When I spoke, you did not hear,
But did evil before My eyes,
And chose *that* in which I do not
delight."

13 Therefore thus says the Lord GOD:

"Behold, My servants shall eat,
But you shall be hungry;
Behold, My servants shall drink,
But you shall be thirsty;
Behold, My servants shall rejoice,
But you shall be ashamed;
14 Behold, My servants shall sing for joy
of heart,
But you shall cry for sorrow of heart,
And [z]wail for grief of spirit.
15 You shall leave your name [a]as a curse
to [b]My chosen;
For the Lord GOD will slay you,
And [c]call His servants by another
name;
16 [d]So that he who blesses himself in the
earth
Shall bless himself in the God of truth;
And [e]he who swears in the earth
Shall swear by the God of truth;
Because the former troubles are
forgotten,
And because they are hidden from My
eyes.

The Glorious New Creation

17 "For behold, I create [f]new heavens and
a new earth;
And the former shall not be
remembered or come to mind.
18 But be glad and rejoice forever in what
I create;
For behold, I create Jerusalem *as* a
rejoicing,
And her people a joy.
19 [g]I will rejoice in Jerusalem,
And joy in My people;
The [h]voice of weeping shall no longer
be heard in her,
Nor the voice of crying.

20 "No more shall an infant from there *live
but a few* days,
Nor an old man who has not fulfilled
his days;
For the child shall die one hundred
years old,
[i]But the sinner *being* one hundred
years old shall be accursed.
21 [j]They shall build houses and inhabit
them;
They shall plant vineyards and eat
their fruit.
22 They shall not build and another inhabit;
They shall not plant and [k]another eat;
For [l]as the days of a tree, *so shall be*
the days of My people,
And [m]My elect shall long enjoy the
work of their hands.
23 They shall not labor in vain,
[n]Nor bring forth children for trouble;
For [o]they *shall be* the descendants of
the blessed of the LORD,
And their offspring with them.

24 "It shall come to pass
That [p]before they call, I will answer;
And while they are still speaking, I
will [q]hear.
25 The [r]wolf and the lamb shall feed
together,
The lion shall eat straw like the ox,
[s]And dust *shall be* the serpent's food.
They shall not hurt nor destroy in all
My holy mountain,"
Says the LORD.

True Worship and False

66 Thus says the LORD:

[a]"Heaven *is* My throne,
And earth *is* My footstool.
Where *is* the house that you will build
Me?
And where *is* the place of My rest?

* **65:11** Literally *Troop* or *Fortune*, a pagan deity • Literally *Number* or *Destiny*, a pagan deity

coastal plain in the west, and the Valley of Achor, near Jericho in the east, represent the whole land.

65:17 *new heavens and a new earth.* As God fashioned the existing heavens and earth, so He will fashion a new cosmos that will be ready for His presence and for the enjoyment of His people (Rev. 21:4).

65:20 *child shall die one hundred years old.* In the coming kingdom the life spans will be much greater. People will not be affected by disease and aging in the same way as in our present age. This time probably refers to the millennial kingdom (Rev. 20:1–6).

65:25 *wolf . . . lamb.* This picture is also presented in 11:6–9. It is a picture of regenerated nature that will occur in the new heavens and new earth.

66:1 *Where is the house.* No place on earth can accommodate the transcendent God. Even the temple built by Solomon, which was filled with the glory of the Lord (1 Kin. 8:11), did not really contain the Lord. He called it a "a temple for My name" (1 Kin. 8:18).

65:11 [w]Is. 56:7 [x]Ezek. 23:41 **65:12** [y]Prov. 1:24 **65:14** [z]Matt. 8:12 **65:15** [a]Jer. 29:22 [b]Is. 65:9, 22 [c][Acts 11:26] **65:16** [d]Jer. 4:2 [e]Zeph. 1:5 **65:17** [f]Rev. 21:1 **65:19** [g]Is. 62:4, 5 [h]Rev. 7:17; 21:4 **65:20** [i]Eccl. 8:12, 13 **65:21** [j]Amos 9:14 **65:22** [k]Is. 62:8, 9 [l]Ps. 92:12 [m]Is. 65:9, 15 **65:23** [n]Hos. 9:12 [o]Is. 61:9 **65:24** [p]Is. 58:9 [q]Dan. 9:20–23 **65:25** [r]Is. 11:6–9 [s]Gen. 3:14 **66:1** [a]1 Kin. 8:27

2 For all those *things* My hand has made,
And all those *things* exist,"
Says the LORD.
b"But on this *one* will I look:
cOn *him who is* poor and of a contrite
spirit,
And who trembles at My word.

3 "Hed who kills a bull *is as if* he slays a
man;
He who sacrifices a lamb, *as if he*
ebreaks a dog's neck;
He who offers a grain offering, *as if he*
offers swine's blood;
He who burns incense, *as if* he blesses
an idol.
Just as they have chosen their own
ways,
And their soul delights in their
abominations,

4 So will I choose their delusions,
And bring their fears on them;
fBecause, when I called, no one
answered,
When I spoke they did not hear;
But they did evil before My eyes,
And chose *that* in which I do not
delight."

The LORD Vindicates Zion

5 Hear the word of the LORD,
You who tremble at His word:
"Your brethren who ghated you,
Who cast you out for My name's sake,
said,
h'Let the LORD be glorified,
That iwe may see your joy.'
But they shall be ashamed."

6 The sound of noise from the city!
A voice from the temple!
The voice of the LORD,
Who fully repays His enemies!

7 "Before she was in labor, she gave birth;
Before her pain came,
She delivered a male child.

8 Who has heard such a thing?
Who has seen such things?
Shall the earth be made to give birth
in one day?
Or shall a nation be born at once?
For as soon as Zion was in labor,
She gave birth to her children.

9 Shall I bring to the time of birth, and not
cause delivery?" says the LORD.
"Shall I who cause delivery shut up *the*
womb?" says your God.

10 "Rejoice with Jerusalem,
And be glad with her, all you who love
her;
Rejoice for joy with her, all you who
mourn for her;

11 That you may feed and be satisfied
With the consolation of her bosom,
That you may drink deeply and be
delighted
With the abundance of her glory."

12For thus says the LORD:

"Behold, jI will extend peace to her like
a river,
And the glory of the Gentiles like a
flowing stream.
Then you shall kfeed;
On *her* sides shall you be lcarried,
And be dandled on *her* knees.

13 As one whom his mother comforts,
So I will mcomfort you;
And you shall be comforted in
Jerusalem."

The Reign and Indignation of God

14 When you see *this*, your heart shall
rejoice,
And nyour bones shall flourish like
grass;
The hand of the LORD shall be known
to His servants,
And *His* indignation to His enemies.

15 oFor behold, the LORD will come with
fire
And with His chariots, like a
whirlwind,
To render His anger with fury,
And His rebuke with flames of fire.

16 For by fire and by pHis sword
The LORD will judge all flesh;
And the slain of the LORD shall be
qmany.

17 "Thoser who sanctify themselves and
purify themselves,
To go to the gardens
After an *idol* in the midst,
Eating swine's flesh and the
abomination and the mouse,
Shall be consumed together," says the
LORD.

18"For I *know* their works and their
sthoughts. It shall be that I will tgather all
nations and tongues; and they shall come
and see My glory. 19uI will set a sign among
them; and those among them who escape

66:3 *as if he slays a man.* This may refer to child sacrifice (57:5). ***as if he breaks a dog's neck ... offers
swine's blood.*** The dog and the pig were both
unclean animals; this may refer to a pagan practice.
**66:6 *sound of noise from the city ... voice from
the temple ... enemies.*** Isaiah heard the sound of
noise from the city and the temple, the Lord giving
His enemies what they deserved. This prophecy may
find its fulfillment at the Lord's second coming (66:17;
2 Thess. 1:7–10).

66:16 *fire ... sword.* The Divine Warrior comes
with fire and sword (Luke 21:24; Rev. 19:11–15).

66:2 b [Is. 57:15; 61:1] c Ps. 34:18; 51:17   **66:3** d [Is.
1:10–17; 58:1–7] e Deut. 23:18   **66:4** f Is. 65:12
66:5 g Is. 60:15 h Is. 5:19 i [Titus 2:13]   **66:12** j Is.
48:18; 60:5 k Is. 60:16 l Is. 49:22; 60:4   **66:13** m Is. 51:3
66:14 n Ezek. 37:1   **66:15** o Is. 9:5   **66:16** p Is. 27:1 q Is.
34:6   **66:17** r Is. 65:3–8   **66:18** s Is. 59:7 t Jer. 3:17
66:19 u Luke 2:34

I will send to the nations: *to* Tarshish and Pul* and Lud, who draw the bow, and Tubal and Javan, *to* the coastlands afar off who have not heard My fame nor seen My glory. ᵛAnd they shall declare My glory among the Gentiles. ²⁰Then they shall ʷbring all your brethren ˣfor an offering to the LORD out of all nations, on horses and in chariots and in litters, on mules and on camels, to My holy mountain Jerusalem," says the LORD, "as the children of Israel bring an offering in a clean vessel into the house of the LORD. ²¹And I will also take some of them for ʸpriests *and* Levites," says the LORD.

²² "For as ᶻthe new heavens and the new earth
Which I will make shall remain before Me," says the LORD,

"So shall your descendants and your
name remain.
²³ And ᵃit shall come to pass
That from one New Moon to
another,
And from one Sabbath to another,
ᵇAll flesh shall come to worship before
Me," says the LORD.

²⁴ "And they shall go forth and look
Upon the corpses of the men
Who have transgressed against Me.
For their ᶜworm does not die,
And their fire is not quenched.
They shall be an abhorrence to all
flesh."

---

* **66:19** Following Masoretic Text and Targum;
Septuagint reads *Put* (compare Jeremiah 46:9).

The word picture promises judgment and punishment.
66:23 All flesh shall come to worship before Me. In the end, every person will bow to the Lord, whether they were followers of God or not. This idea is repeated in more detail in Romans 14:11, 1 Corinthians 15:24–25, Philippians 2:10, and Revelation 15:4.
66:24 And their fire is not quenched. This verse is cited by Jesus in Mark 9:44, 46, and 48. The imagery is drawn from the Valley of Hinnom that was

Jerusalem's garbage dump, where unclean corpses decomposed and were burned. The final eternal punishment is the lake of fire (Rev. 20:1–15). Although the Book of Isaiah depicts God's coming salvation, it closes with a strong statement of the judgment of the wicked.

66:19 ᵛ Mal. 1:11   **66:20** ʷ Is. 49:22   ˣ [Rom. 15:16]
66:21 ʸ Ex. 19:6   **66:22** ᶻ Rev. 21:1   **66:23** ᵃ Zech. 14:16
ᵇ Zech. 14:17–21   **66:24** ᶜ Mark 9:44, 46, 48

THE BOOK OF
JEREMIAH

▶ **AUTHOR:** Jeremiah was the son of Hilkiah the priest and lived just over two miles north of Jerusalem. The book clearly states that Jeremiah is its author, and that he dictated all his prophecies to his secretary Baruch. A first copy of the work was destroyed by the king, after which Jeremiah produced a more complete edition (36:32). The only segment of this book not credited to Jeremiah is chapter 52. This supplement is almost identical to 2 Kings 24:18—25:30, and may have been added by Baruch. Daniel alludes to Jeremiah's prophecy of the seventy-year captivity (25:11–14; 29:10; Dan. 9:2), and Jeremiah's authorship is also confirmed by Ecclesiasticus, Josephus, and the Talmud.

▶ **TIME:** c. 627–580 B.C.   ▶ **KEY VERSES:** Jer. 7:23–24

▶ **THEME:** In the Book of Jeremiah we get an intimate picture of this prophet's life and thoughts. He was constantly rejected for speaking God's message, often lamenting to God. For this fact he is often called the weeping prophet. His ministry begins in 627 B.C., during the reign of King Josiah, who brought about reform after finding the Book of Deuteronomy in the temple. By that time Judah was a weak kingdom that was subject to the major political forces of the day, which were Egypt and Babylon. While Josiah's reform was certainly a step in the right direction, many of the people didn't follow through on the implications of what the law taught. Jeremiah demonstrated God's perspective on the political upheaval going on throughout Judah in his day.

---

1 The words of Jeremiah the son of Hilkiah, of the priests who *were* ᵃin Anathoth in the land of Benjamin, ²to whom the word of the LORD came in the days of ᵇJosiah the son of Amon, king of Judah, ᶜin the thirteenth year of his reign. ³It came also in the days of ᵈJehoiakim the son of Josiah, king of Judah, ᵉuntil the end of the eleventh year of Zedekiah the son of Josiah, king of Judah, ᶠuntil the carrying away of Jerusalem captive ᵍin the fifth month.

The Prophet Is Called
⁴Then the word of the LORD came to me, saying:

5 "Before I ʰformed you in the womb ⁱI knew you;

Before you were born I ʲsanctified you;
I ordained you a prophet to the nations."

⁶Then said I:

ᵏ"Ah, Lord GOD!
Behold, I cannot speak, for I *am* a youth."

⁷But the LORD said to me:

"Do not say, 'I *am* a youth,'
For you shall go to all to whom I send you,
And ˡwhatever I command you, you shall speak.

8 ᵐDo not be afraid of their faces,
For ⁿI *am* with you to deliver you,"
says the LORD.

1:1 *Jeremiah.* The name probably means either "the Lord exalts" or "the Lord establishes."
1:4 *Then the word of the LORD came to me, saying.* This was a standard way of introducing a divine oracle at the beginning of a prophetic book. Jeremiah did not speak out of his own imagination. He spoke as God revealed His word and will.
1:5 *Before I formed you in the womb I knew you.* Jeremiah was keenly aware that the call of God in his life had been determined by God from before his conception. As God's word became a reality in his life, the prophet understood that God knew him and had called him to proclaim a critical message at a crucial

point in the history of the nation. The word "knew" refers to an intimate knowledge that comes from relationship and personal commitment.
1:8 *I am with you to deliver you.* Twice in his call (v. 19), God reassured Jeremiah of His presence and protection. In moments of personal crisis, Jeremiah prays these words back to God (20:11).

1:1 ᵃ Josh. 21:18   **1:2** ᵇ 2 Kin. 21:24   ᶜ Jer. 25:3
1:3 ᵈ 2 Kin. 23:34   ᵉ Jer. 39:2   ᶠ Jer. 52:12   ᵍ 2 Kin. 25:8
1:5 ʰ Is. 49:1, 5   ⁱ Ex. 33:12   ʲ [Luke 1:15]   **1:6** ᵏ Ex. 4:10;
6:12, 30   **1:7** ˡ Num. 22:20, 38   **1:8** ᵐ Ezek. 2:6; 3:9   ⁿ Ex.
3:12

9Then the LORD put forth His hand and othouched my mouth, and the LORD said to me:

"Behold, I have pput My words in your mouth.
10 aSee, I have this day set you over the nations and over the kingdoms,
To rroot out and to pull down,
To destroy and to throw down,
To build and to plant."

11Moreover the word of the LORD came to me, saying, "Jeremiah, what do you see?" And I said, "I see a branch of an almond tree."

12Then the LORD said to me, "You have seen well, for I am ready to perform My word."

13And the word of the LORD came to me the second time, saying, "What do you see?"

And I said, "I see sa boiling pot, and it is facing away from the north."

14Then the LORD said to me:

"Out of the tnorth calamity shall break forth
On all the inhabitants of the land.
15 For behold, I am ucalling
All the families of the kingdoms of the north," says the LORD;
"They shall come and veach one set his throne
At the entrance of the gates of Jerusalem,
Against all its walls all around,
And against all the cities of Judah.
16 I will utter My judgments
Against them concerning all their wickedness,
Because wthey have forsaken Me,
Burned xincense to other gods,
And worshiped the works of their own yhands.

17 "Therefore zprepare yourself and arise,
And speak to them all that I command you.
aDo not be dismayed before their faces,
Lest I dismay you before them.

18 For behold, I have made you this day
bA fortified city and an iron pillar,
And bronze walls against the whole land—
Against the kings of Judah,
Against its princes,
Against its priests,
And against the people of the land.
19 They will fight against you,
But they shall not prevail against you.
For I am with you," says the LORD, "to deliver you."

God's Case Against Israel

2 Moreover the word of the LORD came to me, saying, 2"Go and cry in the hearing of Jerusalem, saying, 'Thus says the LORD:

"I remember you,
The kindness of your ayouth,
The love of your betrothal,
bWhen you went after Me in the wilderness,
In a land not sown.
3 cIsrael was holiness to the LORD,
dThe firstfruits of His increase.
eAll that devour him will offend;
Disaster will fcome upon them," says the LORD.'"

4Hear the word of the LORD, O house of Jacob and all the families of the house of Israel. 5Thus says the LORD:

g"What injustice have your fathers found in Me,
That they have gone far from Me,
hHave followed idols,
And have become idolaters?
6 Neither did they say, 'Where is the LORD,
Who ibrought us up out of the land of Egypt,
Who led us through jthe wilderness,
Through a land of deserts and pits,
Through a land of drought and the shadow of death,
Through a land that no one crossed
And where no one dwelt?'

1:9 I have put My words in your mouth. This verse gives us an understanding of the dual nature of Scripture. The message is the Lord's; its expression is accomplished through His servants the prophets (Heb. 1:1).

1:10 I have this day set you over the nations. The nations were instruments in God's purpose of revealing Himself. The Lord would use Babylon to punish Judah, and then He would use the Persians to punish Babylon.

1:11 I see a branch of an almond tree. God confirmed His call to Jeremiah with two visions. The first vision involved an almond tree, which blossoms when other trees are still dormant. The almond tree served as a harbinger of spring, as though it watched over the beginning of the season. In a similar fashion, God was watching over His word, ready to bring judgment on Israel.

1:13 I see a boiling pot, and it is facing away from

the north. This is the second vision God used to confirm Jeremiah's call. Judgment was coming from the north.

1:17 Therefore prepare yourself. This means tuck your robe into your belt so you can run, or "gird up your loins" (1 Sam. 2:4).

1:18 A fortified city. This military language indicates that God would fight for Jeremiah. His defense system could not be battered down or tunneled under by men and armies.

2:1–3 The love of your betrothal. Chapter 2 is

1:9 o Is. 6:7 P Is. 51:16   **1:10** q 1 Kin. 19:17 r [2 Cor. 10:4, 5]   **1:13** s Ezek. 11:3; 24:3   **1:14** t Jer. 6:1   **1:15** u Jer. 6:22; 25:9 v Jer. 39:3   **1:16** w Deut. 28:20 x Jer. 7:9 y Is. 37:19   **1:17** z Job 38:3 a Ezek. 2:6   **1:18** b Is. 50:7   **2:1** a Ezek. 16:8 b Deut. 2:7   **2:3** c [Ex. 19:5, 6] d Rev. 14:4 e Jer. 2:14 f Is. 41:11   **2:5** g Is. 5:4 h 2 Kin. 17:15   **2:6** i Is. 63:11 j Deut. 8:15; 32:10

7 I brought you into [k]a bountiful country,
To eat its fruit and its goodness.
But when you entered, you [l]defiled My land
And made My heritage an abomination.
8 The priests did not say, 'Where *is* the LORD?'
And those who handle the [m]law did not know Me;
The rulers also transgressed against Me;
[n]The prophets prophesied by Baal,
And walked after *things that* do not profit.
9 "Therefore [o]I will yet bring charges against you," says the LORD,
"And against your children's children I will bring charges.
10 For pass beyond the coasts of Cyprus* and see,
Send to Kedar* and consider diligently,
And see if there has been such *a* [p]*thing.*
11 [q]Has a nation changed *its* gods,
Which *are* [r]not gods?
[s]But My people have changed their Glory
For *what* does not profit.
12 Be astonished, O heavens, at this,
And be horribly afraid;
Be very desolate," says the LORD.
13 "For My people have committed two evils:
They have forsaken Me, the [t]fountain of living waters,
And hewn themselves cisterns—broken cisterns that can hold no water.
14 "*Is* Israel [u]a servant?
Is he a homeborn *slave*?
Why is he plundered?
15 [v]The young lions roared at him, *and* growled;
They made his land waste;
His cities are burned, without inhabitant.
16 Also the people of Noph* and [w]Tahpanhes
Have broken the crown of your head.
17 [x]Have you not brought this on yourself,
In that you have forsaken the LORD your God
When [y]He led you in the way?
18 And now why take [z]the road to Egypt,
To drink the waters of [a]Sihor?
Or why take the road to [b]Assyria,
To drink the waters of the River?*
19 Your own wickedness will [c]correct you,
And your backslidings will rebuke you.
Know therefore and see that *it is* an evil and bitter *thing*
That you have forsaken the LORD your God,
And the fear of Me *is* not in you,"
Says the Lord GOD of hosts.
20 "For of old I have [d]broken your yoke *and* burst your bonds;
And [e]you said, 'I will not transgress,'
When [f]on every high hill and under every green tree
You lay down, [g]playing the harlot.
21 Yet I had [h]planted you a noble vine, a seed of highest quality.
How then have you turned before Me
Into [i]the degenerate plant of an alien vine?
22 For though you wash yourself with lye, and use much soap,
Yet your iniquity is [j]marked before Me," says the Lord GOD.
23 "How[k] can you say, 'I am not polluted,
I have not gone after the Baals'?
See your way in the valley;
Know what you have done:
You are a swift dromedary breaking loose in her ways,
24 A wild donkey used to the wilderness,
That sniffs at the wind in her desire;
In her time of mating, who can turn her away?
All those who seek her will not weary themselves;
In her month they will find her.

* **2:10** Hebrew *Kittim,* western lands, especially Cyprus • In the northern Arabian desert, representative of the eastern cultures * **2:16** That is, Memphis in ancient Egypt * **2:18** That is, the Euphrates

presented in the form of a covenant lawsuit, an indictment brought by God against His people. Jeremiah challenged the people of Judah to remember God.

2:8 *priests . . . rulers . . . prophets.* Those who should have known God most intimately did not know Him at all. The rulers transgressed against God and His covenant. The prophets prophesied in the name of Baal rather than God.

2:13 *broken cisterns.* The people could have chosen a "fountain of living waters." Instead they chose broken cisterns that would have been useless for sustaining life.

2:15 *The young lions.* Assyria laid waste to Israel and Judah during several invasions between 734 and 701 B.C.

2:16 *the people of Noph and Tahpanhes.* Egypt forced Judah into a vassal relationship.

2:19 *backslidings.* Israel had turned in every direction for help except to the true source of safety and security.

2:23–25 *a swift dromedary.* The image is that of a

2:7 [k]Num. 13:27 [l]Num. 35:33 **2:8** [m]Rom. 2:20 [n]Jer. 23:13 **2:9** [o]Mic. 6:2 **2:10** [p]Jer. 18:13 **2:11** [q]Mic. 4:5 [r]Is. 37:19 [s]Rom. 1:23 **2:13** [t]Ps. 36:9 **2:14** [u][Ex. 4:22] **2:15** [v]Is. 1:7 **2:16** [w]Jer. 43:7–9 **2:17** [x]Jer. 4:18 [y]Deut. 32:10 **2:18** [z]Is. 30:1–3 [a]Josh. 13:3 [b]Hos. 5:13 **2:19** [c]Jer. 4:18 **2:20** [d]Lev. 26:13 [e]Judg. 10:16 [f]Deut. 12:2 [g]Ex. 34:15 **2:21** [h]Ex. 15:17 [i]Is. 5:4 **2:22** [j]Job 14:16, 17 **2:23** [k]Prov. 30:12

25 Withhold your foot from being unshod,
and your throat from thirst.
But you said, *l*"There is no hope.
No! For I have loved *m*aliens, and after
them I will go.'

26 "As the thief is ashamed when he is
found out,
So is the house of Israel ashamed;
They and their kings and their
princes, and their priests and
their *n*prophets,

27 Saying to a tree, 'You *are* my father,'
And to a *o*stone, 'You gave birth to me.'
For they have turned *their* back to Me,
and not *their* face.
But in the time of their *p*trouble
They will say, 'Arise and save us.'

28 But *q*where *are* your gods that you
have made for yourselves?
Let them arise,
If they *r*can save you in the time of
your trouble;
For *s*according to the number of your
cities
Are your gods, O Judah.

29 "Why will you plead with Me?
You all have transgressed against Me,"
says the LORD.

30 "In vain I have *t*chastened your children;
They *u*received no correction.
Your sword has *v*devoured your
prophets
Like a destroying lion.

31 "O generation, see the word of the
LORD!
Have I been a wilderness to Israel,
Or a land of darkness?
Why do My people say, 'We are lords;
*w*We will come no more to You'?

32 Can a virgin forget her ornaments,
Or a bride her attire?
Yet My people *x*have forgotten Me
days without number.

33 "Why do you beautify your way to seek
love?
Therefore you have also taught
The wicked women your ways.

34 Also on your skirts is found
*y*The blood of the lives of the poor
innocents.
I have not found it by secret search,
But plainly on all these things.

35 *z*Yet you say, 'Because I am innocent,
Surely His anger shall turn from me.'
Behold, *a*I will plead My case against
you,
*b*Because you say, 'I have not sinned.'

36 *c*Why do you gad about so much to
change your way?
Also *d*you shall be ashamed of Egypt
*e*as you were ashamed of Assyria.

37 Indeed you will go forth from him
With your hands on *f*your head;
For the LORD has rejected your trusted
allies,
And you will *g*not prosper by them.

Israel Is Shameless

3 "They say, 'If a man divorces his wife,
And she goes from him
And becomes another man's,
*a*May he return to her again?'
Would not that *b*land be greatly
polluted?
But you have *c*played the harlot with
many lovers;
*d*Yet return to Me," says the LORD.

2 "Lift up your eyes to *e*the desolate
heights and see:
Where have you not lain *with men*?
*f*By the road you have sat for them
Like an Arabian in the wilderness;
*g*And you have polluted the land
With your harlotries and your
wickedness.

3 Therefore the *h*showers have been
withheld,
And there has been no latter rain.
You have had a *i*harlot's forehead;
You refuse to be ashamed.

4 Will you not from this time cry to Me,
'My Father, You *are* *j*the guide of *k*my
youth?

5 *l*Will He remain angry forever?
Will He keep it to the end?'

---

camel who is in heat, vividly portraying Israel's lust
for foreign gods.
2:32 *Yet My people have forgotten Me.* In the
ancient world, those women who were not slaves
normally possessed a variety of rings, bracelets, and
ornaments made from gold, silver, or bronze. Many
of these were exquisite in appearance and were frequently inlaid with semiprecious stones. Ornaments
of this kind were commonly part of the wedding finery of a bride. The nation Israel, however, which was
God's bride, had behaved in a completely unnatural
fashion by presuming to forget the God to whom the
people were so intimately bound by the Sinai covenant. In forgetting their God for so long a time they
had actually rejected Him and His claims upon them,
a prospect which Jeremiah found almost impossible
to believe.
3:1 *If a man divorces his wife.* Deuteronomy 24:1–4

forbids a man to remarry his divorced wife if she
has remarried and been divorced in the meantime.
The implication is that the woman has been defiled
by the second marriage. After forsaking God, Israel
had taken many other lovers, that is, the nation worshiped many other gods. Yet the Lord in His mercy
still extended His loving hand to His unfaithful bride.
3:3 *showers . . . latter rain.* There were two types of

2:25 *l* Jer. 18:12 *m* Jer. 3:13 **2:26** *n* Is. 28:7 **2:27** *o* Jer.
3:9 *p* Is. 26:16 **2:28** *q* Judg. 10:14 *r* Is. 45:20 *s* Jer. 11:13
2:30 *t* Is. 9:13 *u* Jer. 5:3; 7:28 *v* Neh. 9:26 **2:31** *w* Deut.
32:15 **2:32** *x* Ps. 106:21 **2:34** *y* Ps. 106:38 **2:35** *z* Jer.
2:23, 29 *a* Jer. 2:9 *b* [Prov. 28:13] **2:36** *c* Hos. 5:13; 12:1
d Is. 30:3 *e* 2 Chr. 28:16 **2:37** *f* 2 Sam. 13:19 *g* Jer. 37:7–10
3:1 *a* Deut. 24:1–4 *b* Jer. 2:7 *c* Ezek. 16:26 *d* [Zech. 1:3]
3:2 *e* Deut. 12:2 *f* Prov. 23:28 *g* Jer. 2:7 **3:3** *h* Lev. 26:19
i Zeph. 3:5 **3:4** *j* Prov. 2:17 *k* Jer. 2:2 **3:5** *l* [Is. 57:16]

Behold, you have spoken and done evil
things,
As you were able."

A Call to Repentance

6The LORD said also to me in the days
of Josiah the king: "Have you seen what
[m]backsliding Israel has done? She has
[n]gone up on every high mountain and under every green tree, and there played the
harlot. 7[o]And I said, after she had done all
these *things*, 'Return to Me.' But she did not
return. And her treacherous [p]sister Judah
saw it. 8Then I saw that [q]for all the causes
for which backsliding Israel had committed adultery, I had [r]put her away and given
her a certificate of divorce; [s]yet her treacherous sister Judah did not fear, but went
and played the harlot also. 9So it came to
pass, through her casual harlotry, that she
[t]defiled the land and committed adultery
with [u]stones and trees. 10And yet for all
this her treacherous sister Judah has not
turned to Me [v]with her whole heart, but in
pretense," says the LORD.

11Then the LORD said to me, [w]"Backsliding Israel has shown herself more righteous than treacherous Judah. 12Go and
proclaim these words toward [x]the north,
and say:

'Return, backsliding Israel,' says the
LORD;
'I will not cause My anger to fall on
you.
For I *am* [y]merciful,' says the LORD;
'I will not remain angry forever.
13 [z]Only acknowledge your iniquity,
That you have transgressed against
the LORD your God,
And have [a]scattered your charms
To [b]alien deities [c]under every green
tree,
And you have not obeyed My voice,'
says the LORD.

14"Return, O backsliding children," says
the LORD; [d]"for I am married to you. I will
take you, [e]one from a city and two from a
family, and I will bring you to [f]Zion. 15And
I will give you [g]shepherds according to My
heart, who will [h]feed you with knowledge
and understanding.

16"Then it shall come to pass, when you
are multiplied and [i]increased in the land in
those days," says the LORD, "that they will
say no more, 'The ark of the covenant of
the LORD.' [j]It shall not come to mind, nor
shall they remember it, nor shall they visit
it, nor shall it be made anymore.

17"At that time Jerusalem shall be called
The Throne of the LORD, and all the nations
shall be gathered to it, [k]to the name of the
LORD, to Jerusalem. No more shall they
[l]follow the dictates of their evil hearts.

18"In those days [m]the house of Judah
shall walk with the house of Israel, and
they shall come together out of the land of
[n]the north to [o]the land that I have given as
an inheritance to your fathers.

19"But I said:

'How can I put you among the
children
And give you [p]a pleasant land,
A beautiful heritage of the hosts of
nations?'

"And I said:

'You shall call Me, [q]"My Father,"
And not turn away from Me.'
20 Surely, *as* a wife treacherously departs
from her husband,
So [r]have you dealt treacherously with
Me,
O house of Israel," says the LORD.

21 A voice was heard on [s]the desolate
heights,
Weeping *and* supplications of the
children of Israel.
For they have perverted their way;
They have forgotten the LORD their
God.

22 "Return, you backsliding
children,
And I will [t]heal your backslidings."

"Indeed we do come to You,
For You are the LORD our God.

---

rain that fell in Israel in the spring from March to early April. These were vital for the fields and crops.

3:6 *in the days of Josiah the king.* The reign of Josiah (640–609 B.C.) followed the idolatrous reigns of Manasseh (697–642 B.C.) and Amon (642–640 B.C.).

3:8 *backsliding Israel had committed adultery.* Because of Israel's adultery, the Lord presented her with a certificate of divorce based on Deuteronomy 24:1–4. As a consequence, in 722 B.C. Israel was taken captive by Assyria, and Samaria was destroyed. Judah looked on but did not learn from Israel's example.

3:15 *And I will give you shepherds.* Throughout the Bible God provides shepherds for His people to watch over them, guide them, care for them, and lead them. From Moses in the Old Testament to Jesus in the New, God provides faithful, devoted leaders after His own heart.

3:16 *when you are multiplied and increased.* God ordained that His shepherds would lead Israel through a time of blessing, increase in numbers, and material prosperity.

3:19 *give you a pleasant land.* The possession of the land was always dependent on the covenant faithfulness of Israel to their God. The Lord's desire has always been to bless His people.

3:6 [m] Jer. 7:24 [n] Jer. 2:20 **3:7** [o] 2 Kin. 17:13 [p] Ezek. 16:47, 48 **3:8** [q] Ezek. 23:9 [r] 2 Kin. 17:6 [s] Ezek. 23:11 **3:9** [t] Jer. 2:7 [u] Jer. 2:27 **3:10** [v] Jer. 12:2 **3:11** [w] Ezek. 16:51, 52 **3:12** [x] 2 Kin. 17:6 [y] Ps. 86:15 **3:13** [z] Deut. 30:1, 2 [a] Ezek. 16:15 [b] Jer. 2:25 [c] Deut. 12:2 **3:14** [d] Hos. 2:19, 20 [e] Jer. 31:6 [f] [Rom. 11:5] **3:15** [g] Eph. 4:11 [h] Acts 20:28 **3:16** [i] Is. 49:19 [j] Is. 65:17 **3:17** [k] Is. 60:9 [l] Deut. 29:19; Jer. 7:24 **3:18** [m] Is. 11:13 [n] Jer. 31:8 [o] Amos 9:15 **3:19** [p] Ps. 106:24 [q] Is. 63:16 **3:20** [r] Is. 48:8 **3:21** [s] Is. 15:2 **3:22** [t] Hos. 6:1; 14:4

23 ^uTruly, in vain *is salvation hoped for*
  from the hills,
  And from the multitude of mountains;
  ^vTruly, in the LORD our God
  Is the salvation of Israel.
24 ^wFor shame has devoured
  The labor of our fathers from our
  youth—
  Their flocks and their herds,
  Their sons and their daughters.
25 We lie down in our shame,
  And our reproach covers us.
  ^xFor we have sinned against the LORD
  our God,
  We and our fathers,
  From our youth even to this day,
  And ^yhave not obeyed the voice of the
  LORD our God."

4 "If you will return, O Israel," says the
  LORD,
  ^a"Return to Me;
  And if you will put away your
  abominations out of My sight,
  Then you shall not be moved.
2 ^bAnd you shall swear, 'The LORD lives,'
  ^cIn truth, in judgment, and in
  righteousness;
  ^dThe nations shall bless themselves in
  Him,
  And in Him they shall ^eglory."

3For thus says the LORD to the men of
Judah and Jerusalem:

^f"Break up your fallow ground,
  And ^gdo not sow among thorns.
4 ^hCircumcise yourselves to the LORD,
  And take away the foreskins of your
  hearts,
  You men of Judah and inhabitants of
  Jerusalem,
  Lest My fury come forth like fire,
  And burn so that no one can quench *it*,
  Because of the evil of your doings."

An Imminent Invasion

5Declare in Judah and proclaim in Jerusalem, and say:

ⁱ"Blow the trumpet in the land;
  Cry, 'Gather together,'
  And say, ^j'Assemble yourselves,
  And let us go into the fortified cities.'
6 Set up the standard toward Zion.
  Take refuge! Do not delay!
  For I will bring disaster from the
  ^knorth,
  And great destruction."

7 ^lThe lion has come up from his
  thicket,
  And ^mthe destroyer of nations is on
  his way.
  He has gone forth from his place
  ⁿTo make your land desolate.
  Your cities will be laid waste,
  Without inhabitant.
8 For this, ^oclothe yourself with
  sackcloth,
  Lament and wail.
  For the fierce anger of the LORD
  Has not turned back from us.

9 "And it shall come to pass in that day,"
  says the LORD,
  "*That* the heart of the king shall
  perish,
  And the heart of the princes;
  The priests shall be astonished,
  And the prophets shall wonder."

10 Then I said, "Ah, Lord GOD!
  ^pSurely You have greatly deceived this
  people and Jerusalem,
  ^qSaying, 'You shall have peace,'
  Whereas the sword reaches to the
  heart."

11 At that time it will be said
  To this people and to Jerusalem,
  ^r"A dry wind of the desolate heights
  blows in the wilderness
  Toward the daughter of My people—
  Not to fan or to cleanse—
12 A wind too strong for these will come
  for Me;
  Now ^sI will also speak judgment
  against them."

3:23 from the multitude of mountains. The mountains were centers of idol worship and thus were
strongholds of falsehood. True salvation or deliverance could be found only in the true God of Israel.
4:2 The LORD lives. This phrase was regularly used
in oaths. When spoken by those faithful to the covenant, it should have been a sign of truth, judgment,
and righteousness. Failure to be willing to owe God
their faithfulness and worship brought terrible consequences to Israel, the northern kingdom, and then
to Judah, and resulted in failure of the nations to
be converted as well. Because Israel would not give
glory to God, the rest of the world could not.
4:4 Circumcise yourselves to the LORD. Circumcision
was a sign of the covenant relationship between Israel and God (Gen. 17:10–14). The intent of God was
always that the outward symbol should be a sign of a
reality of total devotion to Him (Deut. 10:12–21).
4:5 Blow the trumpet in the land. Jeremiah

announced the judgment of Judah and Jerusalem
with the alarming sound of a trumpet, literally a shofar
made of a ram's horn. This was the instrument used to
sound the alarm when an enemy attacked a city.
4:7 from his thicket. Destruction would come as a
terrible surprise, like a lion hiding and then pouncing
on its prey. The desolation of the land and the deportation of the people would be the result.
4:8 clothe yourself with sackcloth. This material
was a rough-textured fabric that was worn as a sign
of mourning or distress (6:21).

3:23 ^uPs. 121:1, 2 ^vPs. 3:8   **3:24** ^wHos. 9:10
3:25 ^xEzra 9:6, 7 ^yJer. 22:21   **4:1** ^aJoel 2:12
4:2 ^bDeut. 10:20 ^cZech. 8:8 ^d[Gen. 22:18] ^e1 Cor. 1:31
4:3 ^fHos. 10:12 ^gMatt. 13:7   **4:4** ^hDeut. 10:16; 30:6
4:5 ⁱHos. 8:1 ^jJer. 8:14   **4:6** ^kJer. 1:13–15; 6:1, 22; 50:17
4:7 ^lDan. 7:4 ^mJer. 25:9 ⁿIs. 1:7; 6:11   **4:8** ^oIs. 22:12
4:10 ^pEzek. 14:9 ^qJer. 5:12; 14:13   **4:11** ^rHos. 13:15
4:12 ^sJer. 1:16

13 "Behold, he shall come up like clouds,
And ᵗhis chariots like a whirlwind.
ᵘHis horses are swifter than eagles.
Woe to us, for we are plundered!"

14 O Jerusalem, ᵛwash your heart from
wickedness,
That you may be saved.
How long shall your evil thoughts
lodge within you?

15 For a voice declares ᵂfrom Dan
And proclaims affliction from Mount
Ephraim:

16 "Make mention to the nations,
Yes, proclaim against Jerusalem,
That watchers come from a ˣfar
country
And raise their voice against the cities
of Judah.

17 ʸLike keepers of a field they are against
her all around,
Because she has been rebellious
against Me," says the LORD.

18 "Yourᶻ ways and your doings
Have procured these *things* for you.
This *is* your wickedness,
Because it is bitter,
Because it reaches to your heart."

Sorrow for the Doomed Nation

19 O my ᵃsoul, my soul!
I am pained in my very heart!
My heart makes a noise in me;
I cannot hold my peace,
Because you have heard, O my soul,
The sound of the trumpet,
The alarm of war.

20 ᵇDestruction upon destruction is cried,
For the whole land is plundered.
Suddenly ᶜmy tents are plundered,
And my curtains in a moment.

21 How long will I see the standard,
And hear the sound of the trumpet?

22 "For My people *are* foolish,
They have not known Me.
They *are* silly children,
And they have no understanding.

ᵈThey *are* wise to do evil,
But to do good they have no knowledge."

23 ᵉI beheld the earth, and indeed *it was*
ᶠwithout form, and void;
And the heavens, they *had* no light.

24 ᵍI beheld the mountains, and indeed
they trembled,
And all the hills moved back and
forth.

25 I beheld, and indeed *there was* no
man,
And ʰall the birds of the heavens had
fled.

26 I beheld, and indeed the fruitful land
was a ⁱwilderness,
And all its cities were broken down
At the presence of the LORD,
By His fierce anger.

27For thus says the LORD:

"The whole land shall be desolate;
ʲYet I will not make a full end.

28 For this ᵏshall the earth mourn,
And ˡthe heavens above be black,
Because I have spoken.
I have ᵐpurposed and ⁿwill not relent,
Nor will I turn back from it.

29 The whole city shall flee from the
noise of the horsemen and
bowmen.
They shall go into thickets and climb
up on the rocks.
Every city *shall be* forsaken,
And not a man shall dwell in it.

30 "And *when* you are plundered,
What will you do?
Though you clothe yourself with
crimson,
Though you adorn *yourself* with
ornaments of gold,
ᵒThough you enlarge your eyes with
paint,
In vain you will make yourself fair;
ᵖYour lovers will despise you;
They will seek your life.

4:13 Behold, he shall come up like clouds. Judah had become the foe of God, and He would use the nation's international foes to discipline the nation. The imagery of clouds and chariots like a whirlwind portrays the thoroughness and swiftness of God's judgment.

4:15 Dan . . . Mount Ephraim. Dan was the most northern tribe of Israel. Ephraim was the southernmost region of the northern kingdom of Israel. The message is that just as Israel had been subjugated, Judah was also in danger.

4:19 my soul, my soul. "Soul" here means *bowels* or *belly*, a reference to the internal organs. In ancient Middle Eastern thought, the internal organs were the seat of emotions and feelings. The phrase describes Jeremiah's anguish over the destruction of Jerusalem.

4:23 it was without form, and void. This Hebrew phrase is the same one used in Genesis 1:2 to describe the chaos before the ordering of the cosmos. **no light.** The prophets spoke of darkness as part of

God's judgment on the world. Here the lack of light describes the disastrous effects of sin on creation, particularly on the land of Judah.

4:24 they trembled. The symbols of stability and of strength would be shaken as by an earthquake. Birds would disappear as Hosea had proclaimed (Hos. 4:3). In Genesis 1, the creation of the birds of the heavens depicts the fulfillment of the creative process. In Jeremiah and Hosea, the removal of the birds symbolizes the reversal of creation.

4:28 the heavens above be black. The dark skies are associated with God's judgment.

4:13 ᵗ Is. 5:28 ᵘ Deut. 28:49 **4:14** ᵛ James 4:8
4:15 ᵂ Jer. 8:16; 50:17 **4:16** ˣ Is. 39:3 **4:17** ʸ 2 Kin.
25:1, 4 **4:18** ᶻ Is. 50:1 **4:19** ᵃ Is. 15:5; 16:11; 21:3;
22:4 **4:20** ᵇ Ezek. 7:26 ᶜ Jer. 10:20 **4:22** ᵈ Rom.
16:19 **4:23** ᵉ Is. 24:19 ᶠ Gen. 1:2 **4:24** ᵍ Ezek. 38:20
4:25 ʰ Zeph. 1:3 **4:26** ⁱ Jer. 9:10 **4:27** ʲ Jer. 5:10, 18;
30:11; 46:28 **4:28** ᵏ Hos. 4:3 ˡ Is. 5:30; 50:3 ᵐ [Dan. 4:35]
ⁿ [Num. 23:19] **4:30** ᵒ 2 Kin. 9:30 ᵖ Jer. 22:20, 22

31 "For I have heard a voice as of a woman in labor,
The anguish as of her who brings forth her first child,
The voice of the daughter of Zion bewailing herself;
She ^qspreads her hands, *saying*,
'Woe *is* me now, for my soul is weary
Because of murderers!'

The Justice of God's Judgment

5 "Run to and fro through the streets of Jerusalem;
See now and know;
And seek in her open places
^aIf you can find a man,
^bIf there is *anyone* who executes judgment,
Who seeks the truth,
^cAnd I will pardon her.
2 ^dThough they say, '*As* ^ethe LORD lives,'
Surely they ^fswear falsely."

3 O LORD, *are* not ^gYour eyes on the truth?
You have ^hstricken them,
But they have not grieved;
You have consumed them,
But ⁱthey have refused to receive correction.
They have made their faces harder than rock;
They have refused to return.

4 Therefore I said, "Surely these *are* poor.
They are foolish;
For ^jthey do not know the way of the LORD,
The judgment of their God.
5 I will go to the great men and speak to them,
For ^kthey have known the way of the LORD,
The judgment of their God."

But these have altogether ^lbroken the yoke
And burst the bonds.

6 Therefore ^ma lion from the forest shall slay them,
ⁿA wolf of the deserts shall destroy them;
^oA leopard will watch over their cities.
Everyone who goes out from there shall be torn in pieces,
Because their transgressions are many;
Their backslidings have increased.

7 "How shall I pardon you for this?
Your children have forsaken Me
And ^psworn by *those* ^q*that are* not gods.
^rWhen I had fed them to the full,
Then they committed adultery
And assembled themselves by troops in the harlots' houses.
8 ^sThey were *like* well-fed lusty stallions;
Every one neighed after his neighbor's wife.
9 Shall I not punish *them* for these things?" says the LORD.
"And shall I not ^tavenge Myself on such a nation as this?

10 "Go up on her walls and destroy,
But do not make a ^ucomplete end.
Take away her branches,
For they *are* not the LORD's.
11 For ^vthe house of Israel and the house of Judah
Have dealt very treacherously with Me," says the LORD.

12 ^wThey have lied about the LORD,
And said, ^x"*It is* not He.
^yNeither will evil come upon us,
Nor shall we see sword or famine.
13 And the prophets become wind,
For the word *is* not in them.
Thus shall it be done to them."

14 Therefore thus says the LORD God of hosts:

"Because you speak this word,
^zBehold, I will make My words in your mouth fire,
And this people wood,
And it shall devour them.

5:1 *anyone who executes judgment.* Similar to Abraham's plea that Sodom be saved on account of the few faithful people among its inhabitants (Gen. 18:16–33), so Jeremiah summoned the people to search the city of Jerusalem for one just and righteous person.

5:3 *they have refused to receive correction.* The Hebrew term translated *correction* means "chastisement" or "discipline." Sometimes it means "instruction." In the Prophets, it generally refers to God's attempt to teach His children faithfulness by means of discipline or punishment (7:28). But despite the words of Jeremiah and other prophets, Israel refused "correction" and continued down the path of self-destruction.

5:5 *broken the yoke.* Jeremiah paints a picture of Judah as oxen that are wandering aimlessly through the field, guided by their own desires. They are exposed to the elements and the wild animals of the forest and desert.

5:7 *they committed adultery.* The prophets generally refer to cultic prostitution as adultery. Such immoral behavior violated covenant law (Ex. 20:14) and set in motion the curses of the covenant.

5:9 *Shall I not punish them for these things?* The Hebrew word translated *punish* (9:9), literally meaning "to visit," can be used of the visitation of God in mercy (Ps. 65:9) or in wrath. Here it clearly refers to wrath.

5:13 *the prophets become wind.* False prophets like Hananiah (28:11) had foretold a time of peace

4:31 ^qLam. 1:17   5:1 ^aEzek. 22:30 ^bGen. 18:23–32 ^cGen. 18:26   5:2 ^dTitus 1:16 ^eJer. 4:2 ^fJer. 7:9 5:3 ^g[2 Chr. 16:9] ^hIs. 1:5; 9:13 ⁱZeph. 3:2   5:4 ^jJer. 8:7   5:5 ^kMic. 3:1 ^lPs. 2:3   5:6 ^mJer. 4:7 ⁿZeph. 3:3 ^oHos. 13:7   5:7 ^pZeph. 1:5 ^qDeut. 32:21 ^rDeut. 32:15   5:8 ^sEzek. 22:11   5:9 ^tJer. 9:9   5:10 ^uJer. 4:27 5:11 ^vJer. 3:6, 7, 20   5:12 ^w2 Chr. 36:16 ^xJer. 23:17 ^yJer. 14:13   5:14 ^zJer. 1:9; 23:29

15 Behold, I will bring a anation against
   you bfrom afar,
   O house of Israel," says the LORD.
"It is a mighty nation,
   It is an ancient nation,
   A nation whose language you do not
      know,
   Nor can you understand what they say.
16 Their quiver is like an open tomb;
   They are all mighty men.
17 And they shall eat up your charvest
      and your bread,
   Which your sons and daughters
      should eat.
   They shall eat up your flocks and your
      herds;
   They shall eat up your vines and your
      fig trees;
   They shall destroy your fortified cities,
   In which you trust, with the sword.

18"Nevertheless in those days," says the
LORD, "I dwill not make a complete end of
you. 19And it will be when you say, e'Why
does the LORD our God do all these things
to us?' then you shall answer them, 'Just
as you have fforsaken Me and served foreign gods in your land, so gyou shall serve
aliens in a land that is not yours.'

20 "Declare this in the house of Jacob
   And proclaim it in Judah, saying,
21 'Hear this now, O hfoolish people,
   Without understanding,
   Who have eyes and see not,
   And who have ears and hear not:
22 iDo you not fear Me?' says the LORD.
   'Will you not tremble at My
      presence,
   Who have placed the sand as the
      jbound of the sea,
   By a perpetual decree, that it cannot
      pass beyond it?
   And though its waves toss to and fro,
   Yet they cannot prevail;
   Though they roar, yet they cannot
      pass over it.
23 But this people has a defiant and
      rebellious heart;
   They have revolted and departed.
24 They do not say in their heart,
   "Let us now fear the LORD our God,

kWho gives rain, both the lformer and
   the latter, in its season.
mHe reserves for us the appointed
   weeks of the harvest."
25 nYour iniquities have turned these
      things away,
   And your sins have withheld good
      from you.

26 'For among My people are found
      wicked men;
   They olie in wait as one who sets snares;
   They set a trap;
   They catch men.
27 As a cage is full of birds,
   So their houses are full of deceit.
   Therefore they have become great and
      grown rich.
28 They have grown pfat, they are sleek;
   Yes, they surpass the deeds of the
      wicked;
   They do not plead qthe cause,
   The cause of the fatherless;
   rYet they prosper,
   And the right of the needy they do not
      defend.
29 sShall I not punish them for these
      things?' says the LORD.
   'Shall I not avenge Myself on such a
      nation as this?'

30 "An astonishing and thorrible thing
   Has been committed in the land:
31 The prophets prophesy ufalsely,
   And the priests rule by their own
      power;
   And My people vlove to have it so.
   But what will you do in the end?

Impending Destruction
from the North

6 "O you children of Benjamin,
   Gather yourselves to flee from the
      midst of Jerusalem!
   Blow the trumpet in Tekoa,
   And set up a signal-fire in aBeth
      Haccerem;
   bFor disaster appears out of the north,
   And great destruction.
2   I have likened the daughter of Zion
   To a lovely and delicate woman.

---

and deliverance from the domination and destructiveness of their enemies. But their word was like an
empty breeze. The very sword they denied would
seal their fate.
5:17 they shall eat up. The word devour is used four
times in this verse to paint an image of the enemy as
consuming field, flock, and fortifications.
5:20 house of Jacob. Even after the northern kingdom had been destroyed, the prophets still spoke of
Israel. There was not a complete destruction of the
northern tribes, as is commonly thought.
5:26–28 wicked men. Those responsible for the
welfare of the whole populace had abused their
positions by exploiting the lesser elements of Israelite society. The picture presented is one of birds, or
the poor, being ensnared by great men who were

building wealth at the expense of orphans and the
needy (Deut. 10:18).
5:31 prophets . . . priests. The deterioration of the
leadership of the land reached the very people who
were supposed to be the mainstays of righteousness
among the people. Both offices had succumbed to
the temptation of abusing their power, rejecting their
responsible roles as messengers and servants of God.

5:15 a Deut. 28:49 b Jer. 4:16 **5:17** c Lev. 26:16
5:18 d Jer. 30:11 **5:19** e Deut. 29:24–29 f Jer. 1:16; 2:13
g Deut. 28:48 **5:21** h Matt. 13:14 **5:22** i [Rev. 15:4]
j Job 26:10 **5:24** k Acts 14:17 l Joel 2:23 m [Gen. 8:22]
5:25 n Jer. 3:3 **5:26** o Hab. 1:15 **5:28** p Deut. 32:15
q Zech. 7:10 r Job 12:6 **5:29** s Mal. 3:5 **5:30** t Hos. 6:10
5:31 u Ezek. 13:6 v Mic. 2:11 **6:1** a Neh. 3:14 b Jer. 4:6

3 The ^cshepherds with their flocks shall
come to her.
They shall pitch *their* tents against her
all around.
Each one shall pasture in his own
place."

4 "Prepare^d war against her;
Arise, and let us go up ^eat noon.
Woe to us, for the day goes away,
For the shadows of the evening are
lengthening.

5 Arise, and let us go by night,
And let us destroy her palaces."

6For thus has the LORD of hosts said:

"Cut down trees,
And build a mound against Jerusalem.
This *is* the city to be punished.
She *is* full of oppression in her midst.

7 ^fAs a fountain wells up with water,
So she wells up with her wickedness.
^gViolence and plundering are heard in
her.
Before Me continually *are* grief and
wounds.

8 Be instructed, O Jerusalem,
Lest ^hMy soul depart from you;
Lest I make you desolate,
A land not inhabited."

9Thus says the LORD of hosts:

"They shall thoroughly glean as a vine
the remnant of Israel;
As a grape-gatherer, put your hand
back into the branches."

10 To whom shall I speak and give
warning,
That they may hear?
Indeed their ⁱear *is* uncircumcised,
And they cannot give heed.
Behold, ^jthe word of the LORD is a
reproach to them;
They have no delight in it.

11 Therefore I am full of the fury of the
LORD.
^kI am weary of holding *it* in.

"I will pour it out ^lon the children
outside,
And on the assembly of young men
together;
For even the husband shall be taken
with the wife,
The aged with *him who is* full of days.

12 And ^mtheir houses shall be turned over
to others,
Fields and wives together;
For I will stretch out My hand
Against the inhabitants of the land,"
says the LORD.

13 "Because from the least of them even to
the greatest of them,
Everyone *is* given to ⁿcovetousness;
And from the prophet even to the
^opriest,
Everyone deals falsely.

14 They have also ^phealed the hurt of My
people slightly,
^qSaying, 'Peace, peace!'
When *there is* no peace.

15 Were they ^rashamed when they had
committed abomination?
No! They were not at all ashamed;
Nor did they know how to blush.
Therefore they shall fall among those
who fall;
At the time I punish them,
They shall be cast down," says the
LORD.

16Thus says the LORD:

"Stand in the ways and see,
And ask for the ^sold paths, where the
good way *is*,
And walk in it;
Then you will find ^trest for your souls.
But they said, 'We will not walk *in it*.'

17 Also, I set ^uwatchmen over you,
saying,
^v'Listen to the sound of the trumpet!'
But they said, 'We will not listen.'

18 Therefore hear, you nations,
And know, O congregation, what *is*
among them.

6:4–5 *Prepare war against her.* Prepare can also be translated "make holy." It refers to ritual sanctification performed in preparation for battle. The words are overheard in the camps of the enemies who are about to come against Jerusalem. Sorcerers and diviners were called upon to perform sacrifices to determine the will of the gods and assure a successful outcome in battle.

6:6 *Cut down trees, and build a mound.* A siege mound was a ramp of wood, stone, and sand that sloped toward the wall of a city. Armored siege machines could go up the ramp and attack the city walls.

6:7 *Violence and plundering.* Jerusalem had once been a city that had peace, justice, and righteousness. Under the siege of the Babylonians in 588–586 B.C. conditions were unspeakable (see the Book of Lamentations).

6:11 *I am full of the fury of the LORD.* Jeremiah's own emotions reveal his identification with God's

feelings about Judah. The prophet was both angry and weary with the entire nation, both young and old.

6:13 *Everyone is given to covetousness.* The accusation of covetousness suggests monetary gain by means of deception and fraud. Even those called to guide the nation in its covenant relationship had defrauded God and man.

6:15 *Nor did they know how to blush.* The people had lost all sense of what was right before God.

6:16–17 *old paths.* This phrase probably refers to

6:3 ^c 2 Kin. 25:1–4   **6:4** ^d Joel 3:9   ^e Jer. 15:8   **6:7** ^f Is. 57:20   ^g Ps. 55:9   **6:8** ^h Hos. 9:12   **6:10** ⁱ [Acts 7:51]   ^j Jer. 8:9; 20:8   **6:11** ^k Jer. 20:9   ^l Jer. 9:21   **6:12** ^m Deut. 28:30   **6:13** ⁿ Is. 56:11; Jer. 8:10; 22:17   ^o Jer. 5:31; 23:11   **6:14** ^p Jer. 8:11–15   ^q Jer. 4:10; 23:17   **6:15** ^r Jer. 3:3; 8:12   **6:16** ^s Jer. 18:15   ^t Matt. 11:29   **6:17** ^u Hab. 2:1   ^v Deut. 4:1

19 ^wHear, O earth!
Behold, I will certainly bring
^xcalamity on this people—
^yThe fruit of their thoughts,
Because they have not heeded My words
Nor My law, but rejected it.
20 ^zFor what purpose to Me
Comes frankincense ^afrom Sheba,
And ^bsweet cane from a far country?
^cYour burnt offerings *are* not
acceptable,
Nor your sacrifices sweet to Me."

21 Therefore thus says the LORD:

"Behold, I will lay stumbling blocks
before this people,
And the fathers and the sons together
shall fall on them.
The neighbor and his friend shall
perish."

22 Thus says the LORD:

"Behold, a people comes from the
^dnorth country,
And a great nation will be raised from
the farthest parts of the earth.
23 They will lay hold on bow and spear;
They *are* cruel and have no mercy;
Their voice ^eroars like the sea;
And they ride on horses,
As men of war set in array against
you, O daughter of Zion."

24 We have heard the report of it;
Our hands grow feeble.
^fAnguish has taken hold of us,
Pain as of a woman in labor.
25 Do not go out into the field,
Nor walk by the way.
Because of the sword of the enemy,
Fear *is* on every side.
26 O daughter of my people,
^gDress in sackcloth

^hAnd roll about in ashes!
ⁱMake mourning *as for* an only son,
most bitter lamentation;
For the plunderer will suddenly come
upon us.

27 "I have set you *as* an assayer *and* ⁱa
fortress among My people,
That you may know and test their way.
28 ^kThey *are* all stubborn rebels, ^lwalking
as slanderers.
They are ^mbronze and iron,
They *are* all corrupters;
29 The bellows blow fiercely,
The lead is consumed by the fire;
The smelter refines in vain,
For the wicked are not drawn off.
30 *People* will call them ⁿrejected silver,
Because the LORD has rejected them."

Trusting in Lying Words

7 The word that came to Jeremiah from
the LORD, saying, 2^a"Stand in the gate
of the LORD's house, and proclaim there
this word, and say, 'Hear the word of the
LORD, all *you of* Judah who enter in at
these gates to worship the LORD!'" 3 Thus
says the LORD of hosts, the God of Israel:
^b"Amend your ways and your doings, and
I will cause you to dwell in this place. 4^cDo
not trust in these lying words, saying, 'The
temple of the LORD, the temple of the LORD,
the temple of the LORD *are* these.'

5 "For if you thoroughly amend your
ways and your doings, if you thoroughly
^dexecute judgment between a man and his
neighbor, 6 *if* you do not oppress the stranger, the fatherless, and the widow, and do
not shed innocent blood in this place, ^eor
walk after other gods to your hurt, 7 ^fthen
I will cause you to dwell in this place, in
^gthe land that I gave to your fathers forever
and ever.

---

the Sinai covenant and the Book of Deuteronomy,
as Jeremiah called the people back to former days of
steadfast devotion.
6:20 Your burnt offerings are not acceptable.
There is a common misconception that in the Old
Testament, prior to the cross, God was primarily
interested in outward and formal religious rites, such
as circumcision, Sabbath-day observance, and animal
sacrifices. Nothing could be more removed from the
truth. In both Testaments, God is basically concerned
with the attitudes of the heart (Deut. 10:6).
6:26 roll about in ashes. This action symbolically
expressed sorrow and despair.
6:27 I have set you as an assayer. Jeremiah would
act as the nation's assayer, the one who tests or evaluates quality or purity.
6:29–30 The smelter refines in vain. Jeremiah
assesses Judah as a refiner purifies silver, using lead
to remove impurities (9:7). The lead is consumed,
so the dross in the silver ore cannot be purged. This
results in the refiner discarding the ore because it is
so impure that the smelting process is not worth the
energy it takes. Similarly God rejects those whose
wickedness cannot be refined.

7:2 Stand in the gate. The parallel in 26:2 suggests
the proclamation was made in the outer court of the
temple, where Jeremiah would have been guaranteed a large audience.
7:4 Do not trust in these lying words. Trust conveys
the sense of security and confidence that the people
had in their holy place. They believed that since God
had chosen Jerusalem as His dwelling, had promised
that a Davidic king would remain on the throne forever, and had delivered the city from attack in the
days of Hezekiah and Isaiah, He would never allow
the city or the temple to be destroyed. *The temple
of the LORD.* The Israelites believed that the building guaranteed their security whether or not they
obeyed the provisions of the covenant. This false
hope was a lie (3:23; 7:9).

6:19 ^w Is. 1:2 ^x Jer. 19:3, 15 ^y Prov. 1:31 **6:20** ^z Mic. 6:6, 7
^a Is. 60:6 ^b Is. 43:24 ^c Jer. 7:21–23 **6:22** ^d Jer. 1:15; 10:22;
50:41–43 **6:23** ^e Is. 5:30 **6:24** ^f Jer. 4:31; 13:21; 49:24
6:26 ^g Jer. 4:8 ^h Mic. 1:10 ⁱ [Zech. 12:10] **6:27** ^j Jer.
1:18 **6:28** ^k Jer. 5:23 ^l Jer. 9:4 ^m Ezek. 22:18 **6:30** ⁿ Jer.
1:22 **7:2** ^a Jer. 17:19; 26:2 **7:3** ^b Jer. 4:1; 18:11; 26:13
7:4 ^c Mic. 3:11 **7:5** ^d Jer. 21:12; 22:3 **7:6** ^e Deut. 6:14, 15
7:7 ^f Deut. 4:40 ^g Jer. 3:18

8"Behold, you trust in [h]lying words that cannot profit. 9[i]Will you steal, murder, commit adultery, swear falsely, burn incense to Baal, and [j]walk after other gods whom you do not know, 10[k]and *then* come and stand before Me in this house [l]which is called by My name, and say, 'We are delivered to do all these abominations'? 11Has [m]this house, which is called by My name, become a [n]den of thieves in your eyes? Behold, I, even I, have seen *it*," says the LORD.

12"But go now to [o]My place which *was* in Shiloh, [p]where I set My name at the first, and see [q]what I did to it because of the wickedness of My people Israel. 13And now, because you have done all these works," says the LORD, "and I spoke to you, [r]rising up early and speaking, but you did not hear, and I [s]called you, but you did not answer, 14therefore I will do to the house which is called by My name, in which you trust, and to this place which I gave to you and your fathers, as I have done to [t]Shiloh. 15And I will cast you out of My sight, [u]as I have cast out all your brethren—[v]the whole posterity of Ephraim.

16"Therefore [w]do not pray for this people, nor lift up a cry or prayer for them, nor make intercession to Me; [x]for I will not hear you. 17Do you not see what they do in the cities of Judah and in the streets of Jerusalem? 18[y]The children gather wood, the fathers kindle the fire, and the women knead dough, to make cakes for the queen of heaven; and *they* [z]pour out drink offerings to other gods, that they may provoke Me to anger. 19[a]Do they provoke Me to anger?"

says the LORD. "*Do they* not *provoke* themselves, to the shame of their own faces?"

20Therefore thus says the Lord GOD: "Behold, My anger and My fury will be poured out on this place—on man and on beast, on the trees of the field and on the fruit of the ground. And it will burn and not be quenched."

21Thus says the LORD of hosts, the God of Israel: [b]"Add your burnt offerings to your sacrifices and eat meat. 22[c]For I did not speak to your fathers, or command them in the day that I brought them out of the land of Egypt, concerning burnt offerings or sacrifices. 23But this is what I commanded them, saying, [d]'Obey My voice, and [e]I will be your God, and you shall be My people. And walk in all the ways that I have commanded you, that it may be well with you.' 24[f]Yet they did not obey or incline their ear, but [g]followed the counsels *and* the dictates of their evil hearts, and [h]went backward and not forward. 25Since the day that your fathers came out of the land of Egypt until this day, I have even [i]sent to you all My servants the prophets, daily rising up early and sending *them*. 26[j]Yet they did not obey Me or incline their ear, but [k]stiffened their neck. [l]They did worse than their fathers.

27"Therefore [m]you shall speak all these words to them, but they will not obey you. You shall also call to them, but they will not answer you.

Judgment on Obscene Religion

28"So you shall say to them, 'This *is* a nation that does not obey the voice of the

---

7:10 stand before Me. This means "to place (oneself) in submissive service to someone." Entering the temple of God in such a manner, while worshiping other gods, was incomprehensible. Furthermore, for the people to think that they were secure enough to perform perverted abominations was the ultimate hypocrisy.

7:11 den of thieves. Like thieves hiding in a cave for safety, Judah attempted to hide behind the sanctuary of the temple for protection from the divine hand of judgment. But the Lord had seen the hypocrisy of Israel's ways. Jesus quoted this verse when He cleansed the second temple (Matt. 21:13).

7:16 do not pray for this people. God's instruction to Jeremiah indicates the extreme depravity of Jerusalem's inhabitants (11:14; 14:11). No manner of intercession was to be made on behalf of Judah. God would not hear Jeremiah's appeals.

7:18 the queen of heaven. This is a reference to the goddess Ishtar, who was worshiped in open-air cultic centers throughout the eastern Mediterranean region and Mesopotamia. Worship of Ishtar involved the preparation of special cakes that bore the goddess's image, as well as drink offerings (44:19). The family cooperation in the idolatrous worship of Ishtar stood in direct opposition to the covenant demands that a father instruct his children in the ways of the Lord (Deut. 6:4–9).

7:21 Add your burnt offerings to your sacrifices. Because the people had missed the true meaning of

the Lord's worship, they could multiply their offerings as much as they liked and it would do them no good. The Lord cared for none of their sacrifices. To Him they were simply meat.

7:23 that it may be well with you. God required that His people obey His voice. Obedience would bring blessing. When the prophets lashed out against sacrifice, it was not against the sacrificial system as God had established it, but against the corruption of that system as the people practiced it. The same thing is found in the New Testament passages that seemingly speak against the law. Both the New Testament writers and the Hebrew prophets denounce the abuses of divine systems in human hands.

7:26 or incline their ear, but stiffened their neck. These phrases suggest a cold rebuff to the will and work of God. Jeremiah, like Isaiah before him (Is. 6:9–10), was told that the people would not respond to his message.

7:8 [h] Jer. 5:31; 14:13, 14 **7:9** [i] 1 Kin. 18:21 [j] Ex. 20:3 **7:10** [k] Ezek. 23:39 [l] Jer. 7:11, 14; 32:34; 34:15 **7:11** [m] Is. 56:7 [n] Matt. 21:13 **7:12** [o] Josh. 18:1 [p] Deut. 12:11 [q] 1 Sam. 4:10 **7:13** [r] 2 Chr. 36:15 [s] Prov. 1:24 **7:14** [t] 1 Sam. 4:10, 11 **7:15** [u] 2 Kin. 17:23 [v] Ps. 78:67 **7:16** [w] Ex. 32:10; Jer. 11:14 [x] Jer. 15:1 **7:18** [y] Jer. 44:17 [z] Jer. 19:13 **7:19** [a] Deut. 32:16, 21 **7:21** [b] Jer. 6:20 **7:22** [c] [Hos. 6:6] **7:23** [d] Deut. 6:3 [e] [Ex. 19:5, 6] **7:24** [f] Ps. 81:11 [g] Deut. 29:19 [h] Jer. 32:33 **7:25** [i] 2 Chr. 36:15 **7:26** [j] Jer. 11:8 [k] Neh. 9:17 [l] Jer. 16:12 **7:27** [m] Ezek. 2:7

LORD their God *n*nor receive correction. *o*Truth has perished and has been cut off from their mouth. **29***p*Cut off your hair and cast *it* away, and take up a lamentation on the desolate heights; for the LORD has rejected and forsaken the generation of His wrath.' **30**For the children of Judah have done evil in My sight," says the LORD. *q*"They have set their abominations in the house which is called by My name, to pollute it. **31**And they have built the *r*high places of Tophet, which *is* in the Valley of the Son of Hinnom, to *s*burn their sons and their daughters in the fire, *t*which I did not command, nor did it come into My heart.

32"Therefore behold, *u*the days are coming," says the LORD, "when it will no more be called Tophet, or the Valley of the Son of Hinnom, but the Valley of Slaughter; *v*for they will bury in Tophet until there is no room. **33**The *w*corpses of this people will be food for the birds of the heaven and for the beasts of the earth. And no one will frighten *them away.* **34**Then I will cause to *x*cease from the cities of Judah and from the streets of Jerusalem the voice of mirth and the voice of gladness, the voice of the bridegroom and the voice of the bride. For *y*the land shall be desolate.

8 "At that time," says the LORD, "they shall bring out the bones of the kings of Judah, and the bones of its princes, and the bones of the priests, and the bones of the prophets, and the bones of the inhabitants of Jerusalem, out of their graves. **2**They shall spread them before the sun and the moon and all the host of heaven, which they have loved and which they have served and after which they have walked, which they have sought and *a*which they have worshiped. They shall not be gathered *b*nor buried; they shall be like refuse on the face of the earth. **3**Then *c*death shall be chosen rather than life by all the residue of those who remain of this evil family, who remain in all the places where I have driven them," says the LORD of hosts.

The Peril of False Teaching

4"Moreover you shall say to them, 'Thus says the LORD:

"Will they fall and not rise?
   Will one turn away and not return?
5 Why has this people *d*slidden back,
   Jerusalem, in a perpetual
      backsliding?
  *e*They hold fast to deceit,
  *f*They refuse to return.
6 *g*I listened and heard,
  But they do not speak aright.
  *h*No man repented of his wickedness,
   Saying, 'What have I done?'
  Everyone turned to his own course,
   As the horse rushes into the battle.
7 "Even *i*the stork in the heavens
   Knows her appointed times;
  And the turtledove, the swift, and the
     swallow
  Observe the time of their coming.
  But *j*My people do not know the
    judgment of the LORD.
8 "How can you say, 'We *are* wise,
  *k*And the law of the LORD *is* with us'?
  Look, the false pen of the scribe
    certainly works falsehood.
9 *l*The wise men are ashamed,
   They are dismayed and taken.
  Behold, they have rejected the word of
    the LORD;
  So *m*what wisdom do they have?
10 Therefore *n*I will give their wives to
    others,
  And their fields to those who will
    inherit *them;*
  Because from the least even to the
    greatest
  Everyone is given to *o*covetousness;
  From the prophet even to the priest
   Everyone deals falsely.
11 For they have *p*healed the hurt of the
    daughter of My people slightly,
  Saying, *q*'Peace, peace!'
  When *there is* no peace.
12 Were they *r*ashamed when they had
    committed abomination?
  No! They were not at all ashamed,
  Nor did they know how to blush.
  Therefore they shall fall among those
    who fall;
  In the time of their punishment
  They shall be cast down," says the
    LORD.

7:29 *Cut off your hair.* This practice was a way of expressing mourning and grief. The act may also have symbolized that Judah had rejected the covenant relationship just as if they had broken a Nazirite vow, a sign of personal devotion that required the hair not to be cut (Num. 6:1–21).

7:33 *corpses of this people.* Unburied corpses left to the elements and animals were regarded as a horrible desecration in the ancient Middle East.

8:1–3 *the sun and the moon and all the host of heaven.* The gods and goddesses to whom Jerusalem looked for deliverance would stand over the people's desecrated corpses, which are pictured here as dung. Those who survived the siege and attack as exiles and slaves would prefer death over life.

8:7 *appointed times.* Whereas the birds follow their instincts to migrate, the people of Israel refused to follow God's promptings to obey His covenant. Note that God still refers to the people of Judah as "my people" even though they continued to rebel against Him.

7:28 *n* Jer. 5:3 *o* Jer. 9:3 **7:29** *p* Mic. 1:16 **7:30** *q* Dan. 9:27; 11:31 **7:31** *r* 2 Kin. 23:10 *s* Ps. 106:38 *t* Deut. 17:3 **7:32** *u* Jer. 19:6 *v* 2 Kin. 23:10 **7:33** *w* Jer. 9:22; 19:11 **7:34** *x* Is. 24:7, 8 *y* Lev. 26:33 **8:2** *a* 2 Kin. 23:5 *b* Jer. 22:19 **8:3** *c* Rev. 9:6 **8:5** *d* Jer. 7:24 *e* Jer. 9:6 *f* Jer. 5:3 **8:6** *g* Ps. 14:2 *h* Mic. 7:2 **8:7** *i* Song 2:12 *j* Jer. 5:4; 9:3 **8:8** *k* Rom. 2:17 **8:9** *l* Jer. 6:15 *m* Jer. 4:22 **8:10** *n* Deut. 28:30 *o* Is. 56:11; 57:17 **8:11** *p* Jer. 6:14 *q* Ezek. 13:10 **8:12** *r* Jer. 3:3; 6:15

13 "I will surely consume them," says the LORD.

"No grapes *shall be* ᵍon the vine,
Nor figs on the ᵗfig tree,
And the leaf shall fade;
And *the things* I have given them shall
ᵘpass away from them." ' "

14 "Why do we sit still?
ᵛAssemble yourselves,
And let us enter the fortified cities,
And let us be silent there.
For the LORD our God has put us to
silence
And given us ʷwater of gall to drink,
Because we have sinned against the
LORD.

15 "*We* ˣlooked for peace, but no good
came;
And for a time of health, and there
was trouble!

16 The snorting of His horses was heard
from ʸDan.
The whole land trembled at the sound
of the neighing of His ᶻstrong
ones;
For they have come and devoured the
land and all that is in it,
The city and those who dwell in it."

17 "For behold, I will send serpents among
you,
Vipers which cannot be ᵃcharmed,
And they shall bite you," says the LORD.

The Prophet Mourns for the People

18 I would comfort myself in sorrow;
My heart *is* faint in me.

19 Listen! The voice,
The cry of the daughter of my people
From ᵇa far country:
"*Is* not the LORD in Zion?
Is not her King in her?"

"Why have they provoked Me to anger
With their carved images—
With foreign idols?"

20 "The harvest is past,
The summer is ended,
And we are not saved!"

21 ᶜFor the hurt of the daughter of my
people I am hurt.
I am ᵈmourning;
Astonishment has taken hold of me.

22 *Is there* no ᵉbalm in Gilead,
Is there no physician there?
Why then is there no recovery
For the health of the daughter of my
people?

9 Oh, ᵃthat my head were waters,
And my eyes a fountain of tears,
That I might weep day and night
For the slain of the daughter of my
people!

2 Oh, that I had in the wilderness
A lodging place for travelers;
That I might leave my people,
And go from them!
For ᵇthey *are* all adulterers,
An assembly of treacherous men.

3 "And *like* their bow ᶜthey have bent
their tongues *for* lies.
They are not valiant for the truth on
the earth.
For they proceed from ᵈevil to evil,
And they ᵉdo not know Me," says the
LORD.

4 "Everyoneᶠ take heed to his neighbor,
And do not trust any brother;
For every brother will utterly
supplant,
And every neighbor will ᵍwalk with
slanderers.

5 Everyone will ʰdeceive his neighbor,
And will not speak the truth;
They have taught their tongue to
speak lies;
They weary themselves to commit
iniquity.

6 Your dwelling place *is* in the midst of
deceit;
Through deceit they refuse to know
Me," says the LORD.

7 Therefore thus says the LORD of hosts:

"Behold, ⁱI will refine them and try
them;
ʲFor how shall I deal with the daughter
of My people?

8:17 *I will send serpents among you.* Judgment by means of poisonous snakes is described in Numbers 21:6.

8:20 *harvest is past.* This proverb reflects the sense of helplessness in the early fall. The harvest was meager and the oppression persisted. Even Jeremiah was deeply hurt—this translates a Hebrew word derived from the verb meaning "to break," "to shatter"; in other words, the prophet's spirit was broken over the fate of his people.

8:22 *Is there no balm in Gilead.* The region of Gilead was known for its balsam ointment (Gen. 37:25). There is no healing, physical or spiritual, for a people intent on rebelling against God.

9:1 *my eyes a fountain of tears.* Jeremiah, who is known as the "weeping prophet," identified personally with the suffering of his people. Here he

expresses his desire for a reserve of tears that would flow without stopping.

9:3 *like their bow they have bent their tongues.* Once falseness takes hold in a community or nation, it seems to pervade every area of life. Such a condition is what Jeremiah describes here. There was falsity in every relation. There was a lack of fidelity and trust.

9:4 *Everyone take heed to his neighbor.* The personal affairs of the people were characterized by

8:13 ˢ Joel 1:17 ᵗ Matt. 21:19 ᵘ Deut. 28:39, 40 8:14 ᵛ Jer. 4:5 ʷ Jer. 9:15 8:15 ˣ Jer. 14:19 8:16 ʸ Jer. 4:15 ᶻ Jer. 47:3 8:17 ᵃ Ps. 58:4, 5 8:19 ᵇ Is. 39:3 8:21 ᶜ Jer. 9:1 ᵈ Joel 2:6 8:22 ᵉ Jer. 46:11 9:1 ᵃ Is. 22:4 9:2 ᵇ Jer. 5:7, 8; 23:10 9:3 ᶜ Ps. 64:3 ᵈ Jer. 4:22; 13:23 ᵉ 1 Sam. 2:12 9:4 ᶠ Mic. 7:5, 6 ᵍ Jer. 6:28 9:5 ʰ Is. 59:4 9:7 ⁱ Is. 1:25 ʲ Hos. 11:8

8 Their tongue *is* an arrow shot out;
    It speaks *k*deceit;
    One speaks *l*peaceably to his neighbor
        with his mouth,
    But in his heart he lies in wait.
9 *m*Shall I not punish them for these
        things?" says the LORD.
    "Shall I not avenge Myself on such a
        nation as this?"

10 I will take up a weeping and wailing
        for the mountains,
    And *n*for the dwelling places of the
        wilderness a lamentation,
    Because they are burned up,
    So that no one can pass through;
    Nor can *men* hear the voice of the
        cattle.
    *o*Both the birds of the heavens and the
        beasts have fled;
    They are gone.

11 "I will make Jerusalem *p*a heap of
        ruins, *q*a den of jackals.
    I will make the cities of Judah
        desolate, without an inhabitant."

12*r*Who *is* the wise man who may understand this? And *who is he* to whom the
mouth of the LORD has spoken, that he may
declare it? Why does the land perish *and*
burn up like a wilderness, so that no one
can pass through?

13And the LORD said, "Because they have
forsaken My law which I set before them,
and have *s*not obeyed My voice, nor walked
according to it, 14but they have *t*walked according to the dictates of their own hearts
and after the Baals, *u*which their fathers
taught them," 15therefore thus says the
LORD of hosts, the God of Israel: "Behold,
I will *v*feed them, this people, *w*with wormwood, and give them water of gall to drink.
16I will *x*scatter them also among the Gentiles, whom neither they nor their fathers
have known. *y*And I will send a sword after
them until I have consumed them."

The People Mourn in Judgment

17Thus says the LORD of hosts:

"Consider and call for *z*the mourning
    women,

That they may come;
    And send for skillful *wailing* women,
    That they may come.
18 Let them make haste
    And take up a wailing for us,
    That *a*our eyes may run with tears,
    And our eyelids gush with water.
19 For a voice of wailing is heard from
        Zion:
    'How we are plundered!
    We are greatly ashamed,
    Because we have forsaken the land,
    Because we have been cast out of *b*our
        dwellings.'"

20 Yet hear the word of the LORD,
        O women,
    And let your ear receive the word of
        His mouth;
    Teach your daughters wailing,
    And everyone her neighbor a
        lamentation.
21 For death has come through our
        windows,
    Has entered our palaces,
    To kill off *c*the children—*no longer to
        be* outside!
    And the young men—*no longer* on the
        streets!

22Speak, "Thus says the LORD:

'Even the carcasses of men shall fall
    *d*as refuse on the open field,
    Like cuttings after the harvester,
    And no one shall gather *them*.'"

23Thus says the LORD:

e"Let not the wise *man* glory in his
        wisdom,
    Let not the mighty *man* glory in his
        *f*might,
    Nor let the rich *man* glory in his
        riches;
24 But *g*let him who glories glory in this,
    That he understands and knows Me,
    That I *am* the LORD, exercising
        lovingkindness, judgment, and
        righteousness in the earth.
    *h*For in these I delight," says the
        LORD.

---

deceit, slander, and mistrust. Ethical standards had
collapsed.

9:8 *Their tongue is an arrow shot out.* Jeremiah
returns to the imagery of bow and arrow to depict
Judah's deceit (v. 3). The picture is of a person speaking peaceably to his neighbor while lying in wait to
ambush him.

9:13 *have not obeyed.* The word "obey," which
comes from the Hebrew word meaning "to hear,"
implies an active response to the hearing of God's
word. Instead of walking according to God's law, the
people walked according to the dictates or stubbornness of their own hearts.

9:18 *Let them make haste.* There is urgency in summoning the skilled mourners to lead the people in
tearful lament over the imminent destruction of
Judah.

9:21 *death has come.* The Canaanite god of death,
Mot, was believed to enter a household through an
open window to bring adversity, destruction, and
death.

**9:24 *lovingkindness, judgment, and righteous-
ness in the earth.*** True knowledge of God resulting from an intimate relationship with Him will be

9:8 *k* Ps. 12:2 *l* Ps. 55:21 **9:9** *m* Jer. 5:9, 29 **9:10** *n* Hos.
4:3 *o* Jer. 4:25 **9:11** *p* Is. 25:2 *q* Is. 13:22; 34:13
9:12 *r* Hos. 14:9 **9:13** *s* Jer. 3:25; 7:24 **9:14** *t* Jer. 7:24;
11:8 *u* Gal. 1:14 **9:15** *v* Ps. 80:5 *w* Lam. 3:15 **9:16** *x* Lev.
26:33 *y* Ezek. 5:2 **9:17** *z* 2 Chr. 35:25 **9:18** *a* Jer.
9:1; 14:17 **9:19** *b* Lev. 18:28 **9:21** *c* Jer. 6:11; 18:21
9:22 *d* Jer. 8:1, 2 **9:23** *e* [Eccl. 9:11] *f* Ps. 33:16–18
9:24 *g* 1 Cor. 1:31 *h* Mic. 7:18

25"Behold, the days are coming," says the LORD, "that *i*I will punish all *who are* circumcised with the uncircumcised— 26Egypt, Judah, Edom, the people of Ammon, Moab, and all *who are* in the *j*farthest corners, who dwell in the wilderness. For all *these* nations *are* uncircumcised, and all the house of Israel *are* *k*uncircumcised in the heart."

Idols and the True God

10 Hear the word which the LORD speaks to you, O house of Israel.
2Thus says the LORD:

a"Do not learn the way of the Gentiles;
  Do not be dismayed at the signs of
     heaven,
  For the Gentiles are dismayed at them.
3 For the customs of the peoples *are*
     futile;
  For *b*one cuts a tree from the forest,
  The work of the hands of the
     workman, with the ax.
4 They decorate it with silver and gold;
  They *c*fasten it with nails and hammers
  So that it will not topple.
5 They *are* upright, like a palm tree,
  And *d*they cannot speak;
  They must be *e*carried,
  Because they cannot go by
     themselves.
  Do not be afraid of them,
  For *f*they cannot do evil,
  Nor can they do any good."

6 Inasmuch as *there is* none *g*like You,
     O LORD
  (You *are* great, and Your name *is* great
     in might),
7 *h*Who would not fear You, O King of the
     nations?
  For this is Your rightful due.
  For *i*among all the wise *men* of the
     nations,
  And in all their kingdoms,
  There is none like You.

8 But they are altogether *j*dull-hearted
     and foolish;
  A wooden idol *is* a worthless doctrine.
9 Silver is beaten into plates;
  It is brought from Tarshish,
  And *k*gold from Uphaz,
  The work of the craftsman
  And of the hands of the metalsmith;
  Blue and purple *are* their clothing;
  They *are* all *l*the work of skillful *men*.
10 But the LORD *is* the true God;
  He *is* *m*the living God and the
     *n*everlasting King.
  At His wrath the earth will tremble,
  And the nations will not be able to
     endure His indignation.

11Thus you shall say to them: *o*"The gods that have not made the heavens and the earth *p*shall perish from the earth and from under these heavens."

12 He *q*has made the earth by His power,
  He has *r*established the world by His
     wisdom,
  And *s*has stretched out the heavens at
     His discretion.
13 *t*When He utters His voice,
  There is a multitude of waters in the
     heavens;
  u"And He causes the vapors to ascend
     from the ends of the earth.
  He makes lightning for the rain,
  He brings the wind out of His
     treasuries."*

14 *v*Everyone is *w*dull-hearted, without
     knowledge;
  *x*Every metalsmith is put to shame by
     an image;
  *y*For his molded image *is* falsehood,
  And *there is* no breath in them.
15 They *are* futile, a work of errors;
  In the time of their punishment they
     shall perish.

* **10:13** Psalm 135:7

---

demonstrated in a person's character. God demands these attributes of His followers.
10:2 *the way of the Gentiles.* The Gentiles worshiped natural phenomena by means of handmade icons and symbolic imagery. ***the signs of heaven.*** These were astral deities (8:1–3) worshiped in the days of Manasseh and reinstituted following the death of Josiah and the collapse of his reforms.
10:6–7 *there is none like You, O LORD.* This phrase expresses one of the great teachings of the prophets—the incomparability of God. God is not simply better than other gods; He alone is the living God.
10:9 *the work of skillful men.* No matter how skilled the idol makers were, the fabricated icons were lifeless, deteriorating, false gods who were no more powerful or wise than their makers.
10:10 *the LORD is the true God.* Jeremiah speaks of Israel's God not only as living, but also as being the true God and the nation's everlasting King. He thus governs His covenant people by principles of truth, and with a power that far surpasses the might of

earthly kings. Whereas pagan gods cannot alter the course of nature in the slightest degree, even though their worshipers believed very much to the contrary, the God of Sinai is the Creator of nature. He can punish the wicked by storm, flood, earthquake, or pestilence, and strike terror into the hearts of all those who oppose Him.
10:12 *He has made the earth.* Jeremiah emphasizes the creative power of God, drawing on the imagery of Job 38 and Psalm 8. Jeremiah was reminding the people of Judah that their God not only created the universe but also governs its ongoing life.

9:25 *i* [Rom. 2:28, 29]   **9:26** *j* Jer. 25:23 *k* [Rom. 2:28]   **10:2** *a* [Lev. 18:3; 20:23]   **10:3** *b* Is. 40:19; 45:20   **10:4** *c* Is. 41:7   **10:5** *d* Ps. 115:5 *e* Ps. 115:7 *f* Is. 41:23, 24   **10:6** *g* Ex. 15:11   **10:7** *h* Rev. 15:4 *i* Ps. 89:6   **10:8** *j* Hab. 2:18   **10:9** *k* Dan. 10:5 *l* Ps. 115:4   **10:10** *m* 1 Tim. 6:17 *n* Ps. 10:16   **10:11** *o* Ps. 96:5 *p* Zeph. 2:11   **10:12** *q* Jer. 51:15 *r* Ps. 93:1 *s* Job 9:8   **10:13** *t* Job 38:34 *u* Ps. 135:7   **10:14** *v* Jer. 51:17 *w* Prov. 30:2 *x* Is. 42:17; 44:11 *y* Hab. 2:18

16 [z]The Portion of Jacob *is* not like them,
For He *is* the Maker of all *things*,
And [a]Israel *is* the tribe of His inheritance;
[b]The LORD of hosts *is* His name.

The Coming Captivity of Judah

17 [c]Gather up your wares from the land,
O inhabitant of the fortress!

18For thus says the LORD:

"Behold, I will [d]throw out at this time
The inhabitants of the land,
And will distress them,
[e]That they may find *it so*."

19 [f]Woe is me for my hurt!
My wound is severe.
But I say, [g]"Truly this *is* an infirmity,
And [h]I must bear it."
20 [i]My tent is plundered,
And all my cords are broken;
My children have gone from me,
And they *are* [j]no more.
There is no one to pitch my tent anymore,
Or set up my curtains.

21 For the shepherds have become dull-hearted,
And have not sought the LORD;
Therefore they shall not prosper,
And all their flocks shall be [k]scattered.
22 Behold, the noise of the report has come,
And a great commotion out of the [l]north country,
To make the cities of Judah desolate, a [m]den of jackals.

23 O LORD, I know the [n]way of man *is* not in himself;
It is not in man who walks to direct his own steps.
24 O LORD, [o]correct me, but with justice;
Not in Your anger, lest You bring me to nothing.
25 [p]Pour out Your fury on the Gentiles,
[q]who do not know You,
And on the families who do not call on Your name;
For they have eaten up Jacob,
[r]Devoured him and consumed him,
And made his dwelling place desolate.

The Broken Covenant

11 The word that came to Jeremiah from
the LORD, saying, 2"Hear the words
of this covenant, and speak to the men of
Judah and to the inhabitants of Jerusalem;
3and say to them, 'Thus says the LORD
God of Israel: [a]"Cursed *is* the man who
does not obey the words of this covenant
4which I commanded your fathers in the
day I brought them out of the land of Egypt,
[b]from the iron furnace, saying, [c]'Obey My
voice, and do according to all that I command you; so shall you be My people, and I
will be your God,' 5that I may establish the
[d]oath which I have sworn to your fathers,
to give them [e]'a land flowing with milk and
honey,'* as *it is* this day."'"

And I answered and said, "So be it, LORD."

6Then the LORD said to me, "Proclaim all
these words in the cities of Judah and in
the streets of Jerusalem, saying: 'Hear the
words of this covenant [f]and do them. 7For I
earnestly exhorted your fathers in the day
I brought them up out of the land of Egypt,
until this day, [g]rising early and exhorting,
saying, "Obey My voice." 8[h]Yet they did not
obey or incline their ear, but [i]everyone followed the dictates of his evil heart; therefore I will bring upon them all the words of
this covenant, which I commanded *them* to
do, but *which* they have not done.'"

9And the LORD said to me, [j]"A conspiracy has been found among the men of Judah
and among the inhabitants of Jerusalem.
10They have turned back to [k]the iniquities
of their forefathers who refused to hear My
words, and they have gone after other gods
to serve them; the house of Israel and the
house of Judah have broken My covenant
which I made with their fathers."

11Therefore thus says the LORD: "Behold,

* **11:5** Exodus 3:8

10:17 ***Gather up your wares from the land.*** The Assyrian stone reliefs of Shalmaneser III depict captives transporting household goods on their heads as they go into exile in the eastern reaches of the empire. Soon this would be the fate of the people of Judah.
10:19 ***Woe is me.*** Jeremiah personally identified with Judah and the destruction of Jerusalem. The injuries inflicted upon Judah were severe.
11:2 ***Hear the words of this covenant.*** Jeremiah's message from the Lord here is strongly associated with the Book of Deuteronomy. The term "words" is the Hebrew name of the Book of Deuteronomy; it is also used to refer to the terms of the covenant. A covenant is a legal treaty or relationship between individuals, between nations, or—in the case of Israel—between a nation and its God. The covenant specified rights, obligations, and responsibilities of the parties entering into the agreement.
11:4 ***iron furnace.*** This terminology comes directly from Deuteronomy 4:20, which is set in a context of a warning against worshiping idols.
11:5 ***that I may establish the oath.*** The blessing of land, as promised to Abraham, was dependent upon the covenant loyalty of the people.
11:11 ***bring calamity on them.*** Because the heart of the nation was evil, God would bring disaster upon

10:16 [z]Lam. 3:24 [a]Deut. 32:9 [b]Is. 47:4 **10:17** [c]Jer. 6:1 **10:18** [d]1 Sam. 25:29 [e]Ezek. 6:10 **10:19** [f]Jer. 8:21 [g]Ps. 77:10 [h]Mic. 7:9 **10:20** [i]Jer. 4:20 [j]Jer. 31:15 **10:21** [k]Jer. 23:2 **10:22** [l]Jer. 5:15 [m]Jer. 9:11 **10:23** [n]Prov. 16:1; 20:24 **10:24** [o]Jer. 30:11 **10:25** [p]Ps. 79:6, 7 [q]Job 18:21 [r]Jer. 8:16 **11:3** [a]Deut. 27:26 **11:4** [b]Deut. 4:20 [c]Lev. 26:3 **11:5** [d]Ps. 105:9 [e]Ex. 3:8 **11:6** [f][Rom. 2:13] **11:7** [g]Jer. 35:15 **11:8** [h]Jer. 7:26 [i]Jer. 13:10 **11:9** [j]Ezek. 22:25 **11:10** [k]Ezek. 20:18

I will surely bring calamity on them which they will not be able to escape; and [though they cry out to Me, I will not listen to them. [12]Then the cities of Judah and the inhabitants of Jerusalem will go and [m]cry out to the gods to whom they offer incense, but they will not save them at all in the time of their trouble. [13]For *according to* the number of your [n]cities were your gods, O Judah; and *according to* the number of the streets of Jerusalem you have set up altars to *that* shameful thing, altars to burn incense to Baal.

[14]"So [o]do not pray for this people, or lift up a cry or prayer for them; for I will not hear *them* in the time that they cry out to Me because of their trouble.

[15] "What[p] has My beloved to do in My house,
Having [q]done lewd deeds with many?
And [r]the holy flesh has passed from you.
When you do evil, then you [s]rejoice.
[16] The LORD called your name,
[t]Green Olive Tree, Lovely *and* of Good Fruit.
With the noise of a great tumult He has kindled fire on it,
And its branches are broken.

[17]"For the LORD of hosts, [u]who planted you, has pronounced doom against you for the evil of the house of Israel and of the house of Judah, which they have done against themselves to provoke Me to anger in offering incense to Baal."

Jeremiah's Life Threatened

[18]Now the LORD gave me knowledge *of it*, and I know *it*; for You showed me their doings. [19]But I *was* like a docile lamb brought to the slaughter; and I did not know that they had devised schemes against me, *saying*, "Let us destroy the tree with its fruit, [v]and let us cut him off from [w]the land of the living, that his name may be remembered no more."

[20] But, O LORD of hosts,
You who judge righteously,
[x]Testing the mind and the heart,
Let me see Your [y]vengeance on them,
For to You I have revealed my cause.

[21]"Therefore thus says the LORD concerning the men of [z]Anathoth who seek your life, saying, [a]"Do not prophesy in the name of the LORD, lest you die by our hand'—[22]therefore thus says the LORD of hosts: 'Behold, I will punish them. The young men shall die by the sword, their sons and their daughters shall [b]die by famine; [23]and there shall be no remnant of them, for I will bring catastrophe on the men of Anathoth, *even* [c]the year of their punishment.'"

Jeremiah's Question

12 Righteous *are* You, O LORD, when I plead with You;
Yet let me talk with You about *Your* judgments.
[b]Why does the way of the wicked prosper?
Why are those happy who deal so treacherously?
[2] You have planted them, yes, they have taken root;
They grow, yes, they bear fruit.
[c]You *are* near in their mouth But far from their mind.

[3] But You, O LORD, [d]know me;
You have seen me,
And You have [e]tested my heart toward You.
Pull them out like sheep for the slaughter,
And prepare them for [f]the day of slaughter.
[4] How long will [g]the land mourn,
And the herbs of every field wither?
[h]The beasts and birds are consumed,
[i]For the wickedness of those who dwell there,
Because they said, "He will not see our final end."

---

the people. God's justice is inescapable when sin is intrinsic to one's character. Even if the people were to cry out in distress, God would not listen.

11:17 planted. This term recalls the theme of Jeremiah 2:21, the idea that God had established Israel as His choicest vine. However, here the context is the impending doom that would result from the evil done by the Lord's people.

11:20 Let me see Your vengeance on them. Jeremiah appealed for vindication to God as the one true righteous judge. "Heart" refers to the seat of intellect and will. "Vengeance" describes God's fury and anger against sin that demands punishment.

11:21–23 the men of Anathoth. These men insisted that Jeremiah not prophesy in the name of the Lord. If Jeremiah had yielded to their demand, he would have repudiated his calling, his person, and his God. The threat of death to Jeremiah was answered by punishment of the young men as well as their children. The

prediction of death by famine was fulfilled when the city was besieged by the Babylonians in the days of Zedekiah.

12:4 How long will the land mourn. Jeremiah's question related to God's delay of judgment on the people of the land. "Land mourn . . . herbs of every field wither . . . beasts and birds are consumed" are phrases that are recurring themes in Jeremiah and other prophetic texts (4:28; 40:7; Zeph. 1:3). In spite of past chastisement, the people believed that God would not bring their country to an end.

11:11 [l] Prov. 1:28   **11:12** [m] Deut. 32:37   **11:13** [n] Jer. 2:28   **11:14** [o] Ex. 32:10   **11:15** [p] Ps. 50:16   [q] Ezek. 16:25   [r] [Titus 1:15]   [s] Prov. 2:14   **11:16** [t] Ps. 52:8   **11:17** [u] Is. 5:2   **11:19** [v] Ps. 83:4   [w] Ps. 27:13   **11:20** [x] Ps. 7:9   [y] Jer. 15:15   **11:21** [z] Jer. 1:1; 12:5, 6   [a] Mic. 2:6   **11:22** [b] Jer. 9:21   **11:23** [c] Jer. 23:12   **12:1** [a] Ps. 51:4   [b] Mal. 3:15   **12:2** [c] Matt. 15:8   **12:3** [d] Ps. 17:3   [e] Jer. 11:20   [f] James 5:5   **12:4** [g] Hos. 4:3   [h] Jer. 9:10   [i] Ps. 107:34

The LORD Answers Jeremiah

5 "If you have run with the footmen, and
they have wearied you,
Then how can you contend with
horses?
And *if* in the land of peace,
In which you trusted, *they wearied
you,*
Then how will you do in *j*the
floodplain* of the Jordan?
6 For even *k*your brothers, the house of
your father,
Even they have dealt treacherously
with you;
Yes, they have called a multitude after
you.
*l*Do not believe them,
Even though they speak smooth words
to you.

7 "I have forsaken My house, I have left
My heritage;
I have given the dearly beloved of My
soul into the hand of her enemies.
8 My heritage is to Me like a lion in the
forest;
It cries out against Me;
Therefore I have *m*hated it.
9 My heritage *is* to Me *like* a speckled
vulture;
The vultures all around *are* against
her.
Come, assemble all the beasts of the
field,
*n*Bring them to devour!

10 "Many *o*rulers* have destroyed *p*My
vineyard,
They have *q*trodden My portion
underfoot;
They have made My pleasant portion a
desolate wilderness.
11 They have made it *r*desolate;
Desolate, it mourns to Me;

The whole land is made desolate,
Because *s*no one takes *it* to heart.
12 The plunderers have come
On all the desolate heights in the
wilderness,
For the sword of the LORD shall devour
From *one* end of the land to the *other*
end of the land;
No flesh shall have peace.
13 *t*They have sown wheat but reaped
thorns;
They have put themselves to pain *but*
do not profit.
But be ashamed of your harvest
Because of the fierce anger of the
LORD."

14Thus says the LORD: "Against all My
evil neighbors who *u*touch the inheritance
which I have caused My people Israel to
inherit—behold, I will *v*pluck them out of
their land and pluck out the house of Judah from among them. 15*w*Then it shall be,
after I have plucked them out, that I will
return and have compassion on them *x*and
bring them back, everyone to his heritage
and everyone to his land. 16And it shall
be, if they will learn carefully the ways of
My people, *y*to swear by My name, 'As the
LORD lives,' as they taught My people to
swear by Baal, then they shall be *z*established in the midst of My people. 17But if
they do not *a*obey, I will utterly pluck up
and destroy that nation," says the LORD.

Symbol of the Linen Sash

13 Thus the LORD said to me: "Go and
get yourself a linen sash, and put it
around your waist, but do not put it in water." 2So I got a sash according to the word
of the LORD, and put *it* around my waist.

---

* **12:5** Or *thicket*   * **12:10** Literally *shepherds* or
pastors

12:5–6 *If you have run with the footmen.* God's
response to Jeremiah's question (v. 4) comes in the
form of two metaphorical questions. The first metaphor of foot racing was designed to teach Jeremiah
that the obstacles he faced in his hometown were
meager compared to those he would encounter
before the kings of Judah and Babylon (the horses).
land of peace. This second metaphor was designed
to remind the prophet of the impending turmoil he
would have to endure in proclaiming the message
of judgment to an unrepentant leadership. The relatively peaceful setting of Anathoth, with its minor
opposition from treacherous family members, served
to prepare Jeremiah to struggle against greater
antagonists.
12:10–11 *Many rulers.* This phrase refers to the
foreign kings who had come as agents of God to
judge Judah. The repetition of the word "desolate"
describes the complete devastation of Judah (Is.
6:11). Because of sin, the land that once saw God's
bounteous blessing would experience His devastating judgment.
12:15 *after I have plucked them out.* This verse

offers a glimmer of hope in the middle of a prophecy of judgment. In the midst of His judgment, God
would remember His covenant with Abraham. Eventually He would return and have compassion on His
people.
12:16 *swear by My name.* Only the everlasting love
of God provides an answer to what God will do in a
life that turns from an oath to a false god to an oath
to serve the Lord. What unfathomable blessing can
be ours from a God like this when we pledge our allegiance to Him. He asks our allegiance, and He asks us
to truly learn the ways that He has established for His
people.
13:1–5 *linen sash.* This was an article of clothing that
was like a short skirt or kilt worn by men. Jeremiah
was not supposed to wash it.

12:5 *j* Josh. 3:15   **12:6** *k* Jer. 9:4, 5   *l* Prov. 26:25
12:8 *m* Hos. 9:15   **12:9** *n* Lev. 26:22   **12:10** *o* Jer. 6:3;
23:1   *p* Is. 5:1–7   *q* Is. 63:18   **12:11** *r* Jer. 10:22; 22:6   *s* Is.
42:25   **12:13** *t* Hag. 1:6   **12:14** *u* Zech. 2:8   *v* Deut.
30:3   **12:15** *w* Ezek. 28:25   *x* Amos 9:14   **12:16** *y* [Jer. 4:2]
z [1 Pet. 2:5]   **12:17** *a* Is. 60:12

³And the word of the LORD came to me the second time, saying, ⁴"Take the sash that you acquired, which *is* around your waist, and arise, go to the Euphrates,* and hide it there in a hole in the rock." ⁵So I went and hid it by the Euphrates, as the LORD commanded me.

⁶Now it came to pass after many days that the LORD said to me, "Arise, go to the Euphrates, and take from there the sash which I commanded you to hide there." ⁷Then I went to the Euphrates and dug, and I took the sash from the place where I had hidden it; and there was the sash, ruined. It was profitable for nothing.

⁸Then the word of the LORD came to me, saying, ⁹"Thus says the LORD: 'In this manner ᵃI will ruin the pride of Judah and the great ᵇpride of Jerusalem. ¹⁰This evil people, who ᶜrefuse to hear My words, who ᵈfollow the dictates of their hearts, and walk after other gods to serve them and worship them, shall be just like this sash which is profitable for nothing. ¹¹For as the sash clings to the waist of a man, so I have caused the whole house of Israel and the whole house of Judah to cling to Me,' says the LORD, 'that ᵉthey may become My people, ᶠfor renown, for praise, and for ᵍglory; but they would ʰnot hear.'

Symbol of the Wine Bottles

¹²"Therefore you shall speak to them this word: 'Thus says the LORD God of Israel: "Every bottle shall be filled with wine." '

"And they will say to you, 'Do we not certainly know that every bottle will be filled with wine?'

¹³"Then you shall say to them, 'Thus says the LORD: "Behold, I will fill all the inhabitants of this land—even the kings who sit on David's throne, the priests, the prophets, and all the inhabitants of Jerusalem—ⁱwith drunkenness! ¹⁴And ʲI will dash them one against another, even the fathers and the sons together," says the LORD. "I will not pity nor spare nor have mercy, but will destroy them." ' "

Pride Precedes Captivity

¹⁵ Hear and give ear:
  Do not be proud,
  For the LORD has spoken.

¹⁶ ᵏGive glory to the LORD your God
  Before He causes ˡdarkness,
  And before your feet stumble
  On the dark mountains,
  And while you are ᵐlooking for light,
  He turns it into ⁿthe shadow of death
  And makes *it* dense darkness.

¹⁷ But if you will not hear it,
  My soul will ᵒweep in secret for *your* pride;
  My eyes will weep bitterly
  And run down with tears,
  Because the LORD's flock has been taken captive.

¹⁸ Say to ᵖthe king and to the queen mother,
  "Humble yourselves;
  Sit down,
  For your rule shall collapse, the crown of your glory."

¹⁹ The cities of the South shall be shut up,
  And no one shall open *them;*
  Judah shall be carried away captive, all of it;
  It shall be wholly carried away captive.

²⁰ Lift up your eyes and see
  Those who come from the �q north.
  Where *is* the flock *that* was given to you,
  Your beautiful sheep?

²¹ What will you say when He punishes you?
  For you have taught them
  To be chieftains, to be head over you.
  Will not ʳpangs seize you,
  Like a woman in labor?

²² And if you say in your heart,
  ˢ"Why have these things come upon me?"
  For the greatness of your iniquity
  ᵗYour skirts have been uncovered,
  Your heels made bare.

²³ Can the Ethiopian change his skin or the leopard its spots?
  Then may you also do good who are accustomed to do evil.

---

* 13:4 Hebrew *Perath*

13:6–7 *profitable for nothing.* Because Jeremiah's sash was dirty and then was exposed to the elements, it was ruined and useless.

13:8–11 *refuse to hear My words . . . follow the dictates of their hearts . . . walk after other gods.* As Jeremiah's sash was ruined, so Judah's pride would be reduced to ruin. Pride describes the self-exalting conduct that characterized Israel in its love for idols. This pride is explained in a triplet of verbal phrases.

13:14 *I will dash them one against another.* The wine jars of God's wrath would be smashed and broken together, a picture of a devastated nation.

13:16 *Give glory to the LORD your God.* This means exalt and worship Him. The verse warns of the consequences of failing to glorify God. Four Hebrew synonyms for darkness are found in this verse, deepening the impression of divine displeasure meted out against God's people.

13:20 *Those who come from the north.* This phrase refers to Babylon.

13:23 *Can the Ethiopian change his skin.* The negative rhetorical question confirmed Judah's inability

---

13:9 ᵃ Lev. 26:19 ᵇ Zeph. 3:11 **13:10** ᶜ Jer. 16:12 ᵈ Jer. 7:24; 16:12 **13:11** ᵉ [Ex. 19:5, 6] ᶠ Jer. 33:9 ᵍ Is. 43:21 ʰ Jer. 7:13, 24, 26 **13:13** ⁱ Is. 51:17; 63:6 **13:14** ʲ Jer. 19:9–11 **13:16** ᵏ Josh. 7:19 ˡ Amos 8:9 ᵐ Is. 59:9 ⁿ Ps. 44:19 **13:17** ᵒ Jer. 9:1; 14:17 **13:18** ᵖ Jer. 22:26 **13:20** �q Jer. 10:22; 46:20 **13:21** ʳ Jer. 6:24 **13:22** ˢ Jer. 16:10 ᵗ Is. 47:2

24 "Therefore I will *u*scatter them *v*like
     stubble
   That passes away by the wind of the
     wilderness.
25 *w*This is your lot,
   The portion of your measures from
     Me," says the LORD,
   "Because you have forgotten Me
   And trusted in *x*falsehood.
26 Therefore *y*I will uncover your skirts
     over your face,
   That your shame may appear.
27 I have seen your adulteries
   And your *lustful* *z*neighings,
   The lewdness of your harlotry,
   Your abominations *a*on the hills in the
     fields.
   Woe to you, O Jerusalem!
   Will you still not be made clean?"

Sword, Famine, and Pestilence

14 The word of the LORD that came to
     Jeremiah concerning the droughts.

2 "Judah mourns,
   And *a*her gates languish;
   They *b*mourn for the land,
   And *c*the cry of Jerusalem has
     gone up.
3 Their nobles have sent their lads for
     water;
   They went to the cisterns *and* found
     no water.
   They returned with their vessels
     empty;
   They were *d*ashamed and confounded
   *e*And covered their heads.
4 Because the ground is parched,
   For there was *f*no rain in the land,
   The plowmen were ashamed;
   They covered their heads.
5 Yes, the deer also gave birth in the
     field,
   But left because there was no grass.
6 And *g*the wild donkeys stood in the
     desolate heights;
   They sniffed at the wind like jackals;
   Their eyes failed because *there was*
     no grass."

7 O LORD, though our iniquities testify
     against us,
   Do it *h*for Your name's sake;
   For our backslidings are many,
   We have sinned against You.
8 *i*O the Hope of Israel, his Savior in time
     of trouble,
   Why should You be like a stranger in
     the land,
   And like a traveler *who* turns aside to
     tarry for a night?
9 Why should You be like a man
     astonished,
   Like a mighty one *j*who cannot save?
   Yet You, O LORD, *k*are in our midst,
   And we are called by Your name;
   Do not leave us!

10 Thus says the LORD to this people:

l"Thus they have loved to wander;
   They have not restrained their feet.
   Therefore the LORD does not accept
     them;
*m*He will remember their iniquity now,
   And punish their sins."

11 Then the LORD said to me, *n*"Do
not pray for this people, for *their* good.
12 *o*When they fast, I will not hear their cry;
and *p*when they offer burnt offering and
grain offering, I will not accept them. But
*q*I will consume them by the sword, by the
famine, and by the pestilence."

13 *r*Then I said, "Ah, Lord GOD! Behold,
the prophets say to them, 'You shall not see
the sword, nor shall you have famine, but I
will give you assured *s*peace in this place.'"

14 And the LORD said to me, *t*"The prophets prophesy lies in My name. *u*I have not
sent them, commanded them, nor spoken
to them; they prophesy to you a false vision, divination, a worthless thing, and the
*v*deceit of their heart. 15 Therefore thus says
the LORD concerning the prophets who
prophesy in My name, whom I did not send,
*w*and who say, 'Sword and famine shall
not be in this land'—'By sword and famine
those prophets shall be consumed! 16 And
the people to whom they prophesy shall be

---

to change its own ways. The nation had reinforced
its habit of doing evil (4:22) for so long that it did not
know how to do good.

13:26–27 *your skirts over your face.* This phrase
meant public exposure (v. 22). Since Judah had lust-
fully sought adulterous relationships with foreign
gods and goddesses, God would expose and bring to
shame its actions.

14:2 *mourn.* This is a general word for grief over the
dead. It describes the dark gloom of weeping and
wailing.

14:8 *Hope . . . Savior.* Jeremiah pleaded with God
on the basis of God's name and character. Instead
of having an intimate relationship with Judah, God
had become like a stranger or a traveler in the land,
because the people worshiped other gods.

14:10 *Thus they have loved to wander.* "Loved"
describes voluntary desire. "Wander" describes a

repetitive back and forth movement—in this case, of
seeking every possible occasion for sin. Because no
one displayed any restraint from sin, God could not
violate His holy character and accept the people of
Judah.

14:13 *I will give you assured peace.* Jeremiah complained to the Lord about false prophets who were
proclaiming a message of peace instead of war and
pestilence. These pretentious prophets presumed

13:24 *u* Jer. 9:16 *v* Hos. 13:3   **13:25** *w* Job 20:29 *x* Jer.
10:14   **13:26** *y* Lam. 1:8   **13:27** *z* Jer. 5:7, 8 *a* Is.
65:7; Ezek. 6:13   **14:2** *a* Is. 3:26 *b* Jer. 8:21 *c* 1 Sam.
5:12   **14:3** *d* Ps. 40:14 *e* 2 Sam. 15:30   **14:4** *f* Jer.
3:3   **14:6** *g* Jer. 2:24   **14:7** *h* Ps. 25:11   **14:8** *i* Jer. 17:13
14:9 *j* Is. 59:1 *k* Ex. 29:45   **14:10** *l* Jer. 2:23–25 *m* Hos. 8:13
14:11 *n* Ex. 32:10   **14:12** *o* Ezek. 8:18 *p* Jer. 6:20 *q* Jer. 9:16
14:13 *r* Jer. 4:10 *s* Jer. 8:11; 23:17   **14:14** *t* Jer. 27:10 *u* Jer.
29:8, 9 *v* Jer. 23:16   **14:15** *w* Ezek. 14:10

cast out in the streets of Jerusalem because of the famine and the sword; ˣthey will have no one to bury them—them nor their wives, their sons nor their daughters—for I will pour their wickedness on them.'

17"Therefore you shall say this word to them:

ʸ"Let my eyes flow with tears night and
day,
And let them not cease;
ᶻFor the virgin daughter of my people
Has been broken with a mighty stroke,
with a very severe blow.
18 If I go out to ᵃthe field,
Then behold, those slain with the
sword!
And if I enter the city,
Then behold, those sick from
famine!
Yes, both prophet and ᵇpriest go about
in a land they do not know.' "

The People Plead for Mercy

19 ᶜHave You utterly rejected Judah?
Has Your soul loathed Zion?
Why have You stricken us so that
ᵈthere is no healing for us?
ᵉWe looked for peace, but there was no
good;
And for the time of healing, and there
was trouble.
20 We acknowledge, O LORD, our
wickedness
And the iniquity of our ᶠfathers,
For ᵍwe have sinned against You.
21 Do not abhor us, for Your name's
sake;
Do not disgrace the throne of Your
glory.
ʰRemember, do not break Your
covenant with us.
22 ⁱAre there any among ʲthe idols of the
nations that can cause ᵏrain?
Or can the heavens give
showers?
ˡAre You not He, O LORD our God?
Therefore we will wait for You,
Since You have made all these.

The LORD Will Not Relent

15 Then the LORD said to me, ᵃ"Even if ᵇMoses and ᶜSamuel stood before Me, My mind would not be favorable toward this people. Cast them out of My sight, and let them go forth. 2And it shall be, if they say to you, 'Where should we go?' then you shall tell them, 'Thus says the LORD:

ᵈ"Such as are for death, to death;
And such as are for the sword, to the
sword;
And such as are for the famine, to the
famine;
And such as are for the ᵉcaptivity, to
the captivity." '

3"And I will ᶠappoint over them four forms of destruction," says the LORD: "the sword to slay, the dogs to drag, ᵍthe birds of the heavens and the beasts of the earth to devour and destroy. 4I will hand them over to ʰtrouble, to all kingdoms of the earth, because of ⁱManasseh the son of Hezekiah, king of Judah, for what he did in Jerusalem.

5 "For who will have pity on you,
O Jerusalem?
Or who will bemoan you?
Or who will turn aside to ask how you
are doing?
6 ʲYou have forsaken Me," says the LORD,
"You have ᵏgone backward.
Therefore I will stretch out My hand
against you and destroy you;
ˡI am weary of relenting!
7 And I will winnow them with a
winnowing fan in the gates of the
land;
I will ᵐbereave them of children;
I will destroy My people,
Since they ⁿdo not return from their
ways.
8 Their widows will be increased to Me
more than the sand of the seas;
I will bring against them,
Against the mother of the young men,
A plunderer at noonday;
I will cause anguish and terror to fall
on them ᵒsuddenly.

---

upon God's mercy and promise of deliverance as demonstrated in the days of Hezekiah and Isaiah, when Jerusalem was miraculously rescued from the siege of Sennacherib's army.

14:21–22 for Your name's sake. The people's plea for God's mercy was based on His character. Entreaties based on divine character and attributes are common in the Psalms. At stake was God's reputation and the blessing that would come to the people, but here the obligations of the people to the Lord are disregarded.

15:2 death . . . sword . . . famine . . . captivity. These all would be the outcome of God's judgment. He would use foreign armies as instruments of judgment (14:11–12).

15:3–4 I will appoint over them four forms. The judgment of Judah is described. The imagery of dogs, birds, and beasts devouring human flesh vividly

illustrates not only death, but desecration. The basis for this desecration is the defilement of Jerusalem that took place during the reign of Manasseh, when idolatry reigned in the temple courts and children were sacrificed to Molech (7:31).

15:7–8 winnow them with a winnowing fan. Like wheat chaff that is scattered by the winnowing fork and the wind, the people of Judah would be

14:16 ˣPs. 79:2, 3   14:17 ʸJer. 9:1; 13:17 ᶻJer. 8:21
14:18 ᵈEzek. 7:15 ᵇJer. 23:11   14:19 ᶜLam. 5:22 ᵈJer.
15:18 ᵉJer. 8:15   14:20 ᶠJer. 3:25 ᵍDan. 9:8   14:21 ʰPs.
106:45   14:22 ⁱZech. 10:1 ʲDeut. 32:21 ᵏJer. 5:24 ˡPs.
135:7   15:1 ᵈEzek. 14:14 ᵇEx. 32:11–14 ᶜ1 Sam. 7:9
15:2 ᵈZech. 11:9 ᵉJer. 9:16; 16:13   15:3 ᶠEzek. 14:21
ᵍJer. 7:33   15:4 ʰDeut. 28:25 ⁱ2 Kin. 24:3, 4   15:6 ʲJer.
2:13 ᵏJer. 7:24 ˡJer. 20:16   15:7 ᵐJer. 18:21 ⁿJer. 9:13
15:8 ᵒIs. 29:5

9 "She[p] languishes who has borne seven;
　She has breathed her last;
　[q]Her sun has gone down
　While *it was* yet day;
　She has been ashamed and confounded.
　And the remnant of them I will deliver
　　to the sword
　Before their enemies," says the LORD.

Jeremiah's Dejection

10 [r]Woe is me, my mother,
　That you have borne me,
　A man of strife and a man of
　　contention to the whole earth!
　I have neither lent for interest,
　Nor have men lent to me for interest.
　Every one of them curses me.

11 The LORD said:

"Surely it will be well with your
　remnant;
Surely I will cause [s]the enemy to
　intercede with you
In the time of adversity and in the time
　of affliction.

12 Can anyone break iron,
　The northern iron and the bronze?
13 Your wealth and your treasures
　I will give as [t]plunder without price,
　Because of all your sins,
　Throughout your territories.
14 And I will make you cross over with*
　　your enemies
　[u]Into a land *which* you do not know;
　For a [v]fire is kindled in My anger,
　Which shall burn upon you."

15 O LORD, [w]You know;
　Remember me and visit me,
　And [x]take vengeance for me on my
　　persecutors.
　In Your enduring patience, do not take
　　me away.
　Know that [y]for Your sake I have
　　suffered rebuke.
16 Your words were found, and I [z]ate
　them,
　And [a]Your word was to me the joy and
　　rejoicing of my heart;
　For I am called by Your name,
　O LORD God of hosts.

17 [b]I did not sit in the assembly of the
　　mockers,
　Nor did I rejoice;
　I sat alone because of Your hand,
　For You have filled me with indignation.
18 Why is my [c]pain perpetual
　And my wound incurable,
　Which refuses to be healed?
　Will You surely be to me [d]like an
　　unreliable stream,
　As waters *that* fail?

The LORD Reassures Jeremiah

19 Therefore thus says the LORD:

[e]"If you return,
　Then I will bring you back;
　You shall [f]stand before Me;
　If you [g]take out the precious from the
　　vile,
　You shall be as My mouth.
　Let them return to you,
　But you must not return to them.
20 And I will make you to this people a
　　fortified bronze [h]wall;
　And they will fight against you,
　But [i]they shall not prevail against you;
　For I *am* with you to save you
　And deliver you," says the LORD.
21 "I will deliver you from the hand of the
　　wicked,
　And I will redeem you from the grip of
　　the terrible."

Jeremiah's Lifestyle and Message

16 The word of the LORD also came to
me, saying, 2"You shall not take a
wife, nor shall you have sons or daughters
in this place." 3For thus says the LORD concerning the sons and daughters who are
born in this place, and concerning their
mothers who bore them and their fathers
who begot them in this land: 4"They shall
die [a]gruesome deaths; they shall not be
[b]lamented nor shall they be [c]buried, *but*
they shall be [d]like refuse on the face of
the earth. They shall be consumed by the
sword and by famine, and their [e]corpses

---

* **15:14** Following Masoretic Text and Vulgate;
Septuagint, Syriac, and Targum read *cause you to
serve* (compare 17:4).

---

dispersed. The population would be decimated. The
further ravaging of the land is revealed in the numerous widows who would be left in the wake of the
death of the men of Judah.
15:9 who has borne seven. The blessing of seven
sons was the ultimate hope for ancient mothers and
fathers. But the utmost horror was to lose all seven in
death, resulting in the loss of an heir.
15:10 Every one of them curses me. To curse someone in ancient Israel was to invoke condemnation on
that person with a prescribed formula.
15:16 Your words were found, and I ate them. Eating the words of the Lord means to internalize them
and allow their meaning to become a reality in one's
life.
15:17 I did not sit in the assembly of the mockers.

Jeremiah's isolation was the result of his obedience to
the word and calling of God.
15:18 As waters that fail. This simile is a vivid picture
of the arid regions in the Middle East, where water is
at a premium.
16:1–2 You shall not take a wife. In the case of Jeremiah, the prohibition against marriage was both

---

15:9[p] 1 Sam. 2:5 [q] Amos 8:9　**15:10** [r] Job 3:1
15:11 [s] Jer. 40:4, 5　**15:13** [t] Ps. 44:12　**15:14** [u] Jer. 16:13
[v] Deut. 32:22　**15:15** [w] Jer. 12:3 [x] Jer. 20:12 [y] Ps. 69:7–9
15:16 [z] Ezek. 3:1, 3 [a] [Job 23:12]　**15:17** [b] Ps. 26:4, 5
15:18 [c] Jer. 10:19; 30:15 [d] Job 6:15　**15:19** [e] Zech. 3:7
[f] Jer. 15:1 [g] Ezek. 22:26; 44:23　**15:20** [h] Ezek. 3:9 [i] Jer.
1:8, 19; 20:11; 37:21; 38:13; 39:11, 12　**16:4** [a] Jer. 15:2 [b] Jer.
22:18; 25:33 [c] Jer. 14:16; 19:11 [d] Ps. 83:10 [e] Ps. 79:2

shall be meat for the birds of heaven and for the beasts of the earth."

5For thus says the LORD: f"Do not enter the house of mourning, nor go to lament or bemoan them; for I have taken away My peace from this people," says the LORD, "lovingkindness and mercies. 6Both the great and the small shall die in this land. They shall not be buried; gneither shall men lament for them, hcut themselves, nor imake themselves bald for them. 7Nor shall men break bread in mourning for them, to comfort them for the dead; nor shall men give them the cup of consolation to jdrink for their father or their mother. 8Also you shall not go into the house of feasting to sit with them, to eat and drink."

9For thus says the LORD of hosts, the God of Israel: "Behold, kI will cause to cease from this place, before your eyes and in your days, the voice of mirth and the voice of gladness, the voice of the bridegroom and the voice of the bride.

10"And it shall be, when you show this people all these words, and they say to you, l"Why has the LORD pronounced all this great disaster against us? Or what is our iniquity? Or what is our sin that we have committed against the LORD our God?' 11then you shall say to them, m'Because your fathers have forsaken Me,' says the LORD; 'they have walked after other gods and have served them and worshiped them, and have forsaken Me and not kept My law. 12And you have done nworse than your fathers, for behold, oeach one follows the dictates of his own evil heart, so that no one listens to Me. 13pTherefore I will cast you out of this land qinto a land that you do not know, neither you nor your fathers; and there you shall serve other gods day and night, where I will not show you favor.'

God Will Restore Israel

14"Therefore behold, the rdays are coming," says the LORD, "that it shall no more be said, 'The LORD lives who brought up the children of Israel from the land of Egypt,' 15but, 'The LORD lives who brought

up the children of Israel from the land of the snorth and from all the lands where He had driven them.' For tI will bring them back into their land which I gave to their fathers.

16"Behold, I will send for many ufishermen," says the LORD, "and they shall fish them; and afterward I will send for many hunters, and they shall hunt them from every mountain and every hill, and out of the holes of the rocks. 17For My veyes are on all their ways; they are not hidden from My face, nor is their iniquity hidden from My eyes. 18And first I will repay wdouble for their iniquity and their sin, because xthey have defiled My land; they have filled My inheritance with the carcasses of their detestable and abominable idols."

19 O LORD, ymy strength and my
          fortress,
       zMy refuge in the day of affliction,
       The Gentiles shall come to You
       From the ends of the earth and say,
     "Surely our fathers have inherited
          lies,
       Worthlessness and aunprofitable
          things."
20 Will a man make gods for himself,
       bWhich are not gods?
21 "Therefore behold, I will this once
          cause them to know,
       I will cause them to know
       My hand and My might;
       And they shall know that cMy name is
       the LORD.

Judah's Sin and Punishment

17 "The sin of Judah is awritten with a
       bpen of iron;
    With the point of a diamond it is
       cengraved
    On the tablet of their heart,
    And on the horns of your altars,
2   While their children remember
       Their altars and their dwooden
          images*
    By the green trees on the high hills.

---

* 17:2 Hebrew Asherim, Canaanite deities

---

a sign to the nation and a blight against his name among the people. Celibacy was abnormal; large families were indicative of God's blessing upon a household. Jeremiah faced life with God as his sole comfort and support.

16:10 Why has the LORD pronounced. The trio of questions posed by the people indicates their lack of understanding of God's word. The people of Judah had missed the purpose for which they were chosen, to manifest to the world the nature and character of God by living as the people of God.

16:16 many fishermen . . . many hunters. These words refer to the Babylonian armies that would scour the land for Judah's rebels. Hunting and fishing imagery as a metaphor for deportation is also found in Ezekiel 12:3 and Amos 4:2.

16:19–20 strength . . . fortress . . . refuge. Jeremiah knew that his only place of safety was in God. The scope of Jeremiah's hope is universal. The Gentiles, among whom the people of Judah would be exiled, would come to the God of Israel in fulfillment of the promise of Genesis 12:1–3.

16:5 f Ezek. 24:17, 22, 23   **16:6** g Jer. 22:18   h Deut. 14:1   i Is. 22:12   **16:7** j Prov. 31:6   **16:9** k Rev. 18:23   **16:10** l Deut. 29:24   **16:11** m Jer. 22:9   **16:12** n Jer. 7:26   o Jer. 3:17; 18:12   **16:13** p Deut. 4:26; 28:36, 63   q Jer. 15:14   **16:14** r Jer. 23:7, 8   **16:15** s Jer. 3:18   t Jer. 24:6; 30:3; 32:37   **16:16** u Amos 4:2   **16:17** v Heb. 4:13   **16:18** w Jer. 17:18   x [Ezek. 43:7]   **16:19** y Ps. 18:1, 2   z Jer. 17:17   a Is. 44:10   **16:20** b Gal. 4:8   **16:21** c Amos 5:8   **17:1** a Jer. 2:22   b Job 19:24   c 2 Cor. 3:3   **17:2** d Judg. 3:7

3 O My mountain in the field,
I will give as plunder your wealth, all
your treasures,
And your high places of sin within all
your borders.
4 And you, even yourself,
Shall let go of your heritage which I
gave you;
And I will cause you to serve your
enemies
In *e*the land which you do not know;
For *f*you have kindled a fire in My
anger *which* shall burn forever."

5 Thus says the LORD:

g"Cursed *is* the man who trusts in man
And makes *h*flesh his strength,
Whose heart departs from the LORD.
6 For he shall be *i*like a shrub in the
desert,
And *j*shall not see when good comes,
But shall inhabit the parched places in
the wilderness,
*k*In a salt land *which is* not inhabited.

7 "Blessed*l is* the man who trusts in the
LORD,
And whose hope is the LORD.
8 For he shall be *m*like a tree planted by
the waters,
Which spreads out its roots by the
river,
And will not fear* when heat comes;
But its leaf will be green,
And will not be anxious in the year of
drought,
Nor will cease from yielding fruit.

9 "The *n*heart *is* deceitful above all
things,
And desperately wicked;
Who can know it?
10 I, the LORD, *o*search the heart,
I test the mind,
*p*Even to give every man according to
his ways,
According to the fruit of his doings.

11 "*As* a partridge that broods but does
not hatch,
So is he who gets riches, but not by
right;
It *q*will leave him in the midst of his
days,
And at his end he will be *r*a fool."

12 A glorious high throne from the
beginning
Is the place of our sanctuary.
13 O LORD, *s*the hope of Israel,
*t*All who forsake You shall be
ashamed.

"Those who depart from Me
Shall be *u*written in the earth,
Because they have forsaken the
LORD,
The *v*fountain of living waters."

Jeremiah Prays for Deliverance

14 Heal me, O LORD, and I shall be
healed;
Save me, and I shall be saved,
For *w*You *are* my praise.
15 Indeed they say to me,
x"Where *is* the word of the LORD?
Let it come now!"
16 As for me, *y*I have not hurried away
from *being* a shepherd *who*
follows You,
Nor have I desired the woeful day;
You know what came out of my lips;
It was right there before You.
17 Do not be a terror to me;
*z*You *are* my hope in the day of doom.
18 *a*Let them be ashamed who persecute
me,
But *b*do not let me be put to shame;
Let them be dismayed,
But do not let me be dismayed.
Bring on them the day of doom,
And *c*destroy them with double
destruction!

---

* 17:8 Qere and Targum read *see*.

17:3 your high places of sin. Jerusalem and the other cities of Judah were demolished and plundered by the Babylonians. The remaining treasures of the temple of God were carried by Nebuchadnezzar's army to Babylon. Even the idolatrous cultic centers were destroyed (15:13–14).
17:4 let go of your heritage. This phrase, when used in the context of land, usually refers to letting the land lie fallow during the sabbatical year (Ex. 23:10–11). Judah's captivity would provide rest for the land from the idolatrous activities of its people.
17:5 Cursed is the man. One cannot trust in both God and humankind.
17:7 Blessed is the man who trusts in the LORD. The basic element in a life of faith is stability. Man depending upon his own strength is unstable. But faith in God brings stability.
17:11 As a partridge that broods but does not hatch. The teaching of Jeremiah 17:1–10 is supported by a proverb based on the common belief that the partridge hatched eggs other than its own.

When the young birds recognized that the partridge was not their mother, they would leave her. Similarly, a man who unjustly gains wealth will be abandoned by the wealth and then be known as a fool.
17:12–13 A glorious high throne. This phrase refers to the temple in Jerusalem and the ark of the covenant, the symbol of God's presence and sovereignty over the nations.
17:17 Do not be a terror to me. This refers to physical, emotional, or mental horror.
17:18 Let them be ashamed. Jeremiah called for his persecutors to be ashamed and dismayed, to be

---

17:4 *e* Jer. 16:13 *f* Jer. 15:14 **17:5** *g* Is. 30:1, 2; 31:1
h Is. 31:3 **17:6** *i* Jer. 48:6 *j* Job 20:17 *k* Deut. 29:23
17:7 *l* [Is. 30:18] **17:8** *m* [Ps. 1:3] **17:9** *n* [Eccl. 9:3]
17:10 *o* Rev. 2:23 *p* Rom. 2:6 **17:11** *q* Ps. 55:23 *r* Luke
12:20 **17:13** *s* Jer. 14:8 *t* [Is. 1:28] *u* Luke 10:20 *v* Jer.
2:13 **17:14** *w* Deut. 10:21 **17:15** *x* Is. 5:19 **17:16** *y* Jer.
1:4–12 **17:17** *z* Jer. 16:19 **17:18** *a* Ps. 35:4; 70:2 *b* Ps.
25:2 *c* Jer. 11:20

Hallow the Sabbath Day

19 Thus the LORD said to me: "Go and stand in the gate of the children of the people, by which the kings of Judah come in and by which they go out, and in all the gates of Jerusalem; 20 and say to them, d'Hear the word of the LORD, you kings of Judah, and all Judah, and all the inhabitants of Jerusalem, who enter by these gates. 21 Thus says the LORD: e'Take heed to yourselves, and bear no burden on the Sabbath day, nor bring it in by the gates of Jerusalem; 22 nor carry a burden out of your houses on the Sabbath day, nor do any work, but hallow the Sabbath day, as I fcommanded your fathers. 23g But they did not obey nor incline their ear, but made their neck stiff, that they might not hear nor receive instruction.

24 "And it shall be, hif you heed Me carefully," says the LORD, "to bring no burden through the gates of this city on the iSabbath day, but hallow the Sabbath day, to do no work in it, 25j then shall enter the gates of this city kings and princes sitting on the throne of David, riding in chariots and on horses, they and their princes, accompanied by the men of Judah and the inhabitants of Jerusalem; and this city shall remain forever. 26 And they shall come from the cities of Judah and from kthe places around Jerusalem, from the land of Benjamin and from lthe lowland, from the mountains and from mthe South, bringing burnt offerings and sacrifices, grain offerings and incense, bringing nsacrifices of praise to the house of the LORD.

27 "But if you will not heed Me to hallow the Sabbath day, such as not carrying a burden when entering the gates of Jerusalem on the Sabbath day, then oI will kindle a fire in its gates, pand it shall devour the palaces of Jerusalem, and it shall not be qquenched." ' "

The Potter and the Clay

18 The word which came to Jeremiah from the LORD, saying: 2 "Arise and go down to the potter's house, and there I will cause you to hear My words." 3 Then I went down to the potter's house, and there he was, making something at the wheel. 4 And the vessel that he made of clay was marred in the hand of the potter; so he made it again into another vessel, as it seemed good to the potter to make.

5 Then the word of the LORD came to me, saying: 6 "O house of Israel, acan I not do with you as this potter?" says the LORD. "Look, bas the clay is in the potter's hand, so are you in My hand, O house of Israel! 7 The instant I speak concerning a nation and concerning a kingdom, to cpluck up, to pull down, and to destroy it, 8dif that nation against whom I have spoken turns from its evil, eI will relent of the disaster that I thought to bring upon it. 9 And the instant I speak concerning a nation and concerning a kingdom, to build and to plant it, 10 if it does evil in My sight so that it does not obey My voice, then I will relent concerning the good with which I said I would benefit it.

11 "Now therefore, speak to the men of Judah and to the inhabitants of Jerusalem, saying, 'Thus says the LORD: "Behold, I am fashioning a disaster and devising a plan against you. fReturn now every one from his evil way, and make your ways and your doings ggood." ' "

God's Warning Rejected

12 And they said, h"That is hopeless! So we will walk according to our own plans, and we will every one obey the idictates of his evil heart."

13 Therefore thus says the LORD:

> j"Ask now among the Gentiles,
> Who has heard such things?
> The virgin of Israel has done ka very
> horrible thing.
> 14 Will a man leave the snow water of
> Lebanon,
> Which comes from the rock of the
> field?
> Will the cold flowing waters be
> forsaken for strange
> waters?

---

dishonored and demoralized. The prophet also called upon the Lord to confirm the message of judgment in the day of doom and double destruction.

17:21–22 Take heed to yourselves. This same phrasing is used in Deuteronomy 4:15 in a warning against idolatry. The sanctity of the Sabbath was a most serious matter. The Sabbath stood as a sign of creation and the covenant relationship between God and Israel.

18:4–6 was marred in the hand of the potter. The potter's vessel was marred and thus unsuitable for its intended purpose. The potter's remolding of the clay into an acceptable and unblemished work symbolized God's action in reforming Israel. The people had become marred and defiled and had to be reformed into a vessel fit to be identified with the Lord.

18:13–14 Who has heard such things. Negative rhetorical questions show the absurdity of Israel's rebellion. **snow water of Lebanon.** This describes the Mount Hermon watershed that erupts in numerous springs, providing most of the water for the Jordan River. God's blessing was often demonstrated in the provision of water from rocks in arid regions (Ex. 17:6).

17:20 d Jer. 19:3, 4 **17:21** e Neh. 13:19 **17:22** f Ex. 20:8; 31:13 **17:23** g Jer. 7:24, 26 **17:24** h Jer. 11:4; 26:3 i Ex. 16:23–30; 20:8–10 **17:25** j Jer. 22:4 **17:26** k Jer. 33:13 l Zech. 7:7 m Judg. 1:9 n Ps. 107:22; 116:17 **17:27** o Lam. 4:11 p 2 Kin. 25:9 q Jer. 7:20 **18:6** a Rom. 9:20, 21 b Is. 64:8 **18:7** c Jer. 1:10 **18:8** d [Ezek. 18:21; 33:11] e Jer. 26:3 **18:11** f 2 Kin. 17:13 g Jer. 7:3–7 **18:12** h Jer. 2:25 i Jer. 3:17; 23:17 **18:13** j Jer. 2:10, 11 k Jer. 5:30

15 "Because My people have forgotten
[l]Me,
They have burned incense to
worthless idols.
And they have caused themselves to
stumble in their ways,
From the [m]ancient paths,
To walk in pathways and not on a
highway,
16 To make their land [n]desolate *and* a
perpetual [o]hissing;
Everyone who passes by it will be
astonished
And shake his head.
17 [p]I will scatter them [q]as with an east
wind before the enemy;
[r]I will show them* the back and not the
face
In the day of their calamity."

Jeremiah Persecuted

18Then they said, [s]"Come and let us devise plans against Jeremiah; [t]for the law
shall not perish from the priest, nor counsel from the wise, nor the word from the
prophet. Come and let us attack him with
the tongue, and let us not give heed to any
of his words."

19 Give heed to me, O LORD,
And listen to the voice of those who
contend with me!
20 [u]Shall evil be repaid for good?
For they have [v]dug a pit for my life.
Remember that I [w]stood before You
To speak good for them,
To turn away Your wrath from them.
21 Therefore [x]deliver up their children to
the famine,
And pour out their *blood*
By the force of the sword;
Let their wives *become* widows
And [y]bereaved of their children.
Let their men be put to death,
Their young men *be* slain
By the sword in battle.
22 Let a cry be heard from their houses,
When You bring a troop suddenly
upon them;
For they have dug a pit to take me,
And hidden snares for my feet.
23 Yet, LORD, You know all their counsel
Which is against me, to slay *me*.
[z]Provide no atonement for their
iniquity,
Nor blot out their sin from Your
sight;
But let them be overthrown before
You.
Deal *thus* with them
In the time of Your [a]anger.

The Sign of the Broken Flask

19 Thus says the LORD: "Go and get a
potter's earthen flask, and *take* some
of the elders of the people and some of the
elders of the priests. 2And go out to [a]the
Valley of the Son of Hinnom, which *is* by
the entry of the Potsherd Gate; and proclaim there the words that I will tell you,
3[b]and say, 'Hear the word of the LORD, O
kings of Judah and inhabitants of Jerusalem. Thus says the LORD of hosts, the God
of Israel: "Behold, I will bring such a catastrophe on this place, that whoever hears
of it, his ears will [c]tingle.
4"Because they [d]have forsaken Me and
made this an alien place, because they
have burned incense in it to other gods
whom neither they, their fathers, nor the
kings of Judah have known, and have
filled this place with [e]the blood of the innocents 5[f](they have also built the high
places of Baal, to burn their sons with fire
for burnt offerings to Baal, [g]which I did
not command or speak, nor did it come
into My mind), 6therefore behold, the
days are coming," says the LORD, "that
this place shall no more be called Tophet
or [h]the Valley of the Son of Hinnom, but
the Valley of Slaughter. 7And I will make
void the counsel of Judah and Jerusalem
in this place, [i]and I will cause them to fall
by the sword before their enemies and by
the hands of those who seek their lives;
their [j]corpses I will give as meat for the
birds of the heaven and for the beasts of
the earth. 8I will make this city [k]desolate
and a hissing; everyone who passes by

* **18:17** Following Septuagint, Syriac, Targum, and Vulgate; Masoretic Text reads *look them in*.

18:15 *burned incense to worthless idols.* Foreign deities such as Baal and Asherah were represented by empty and ineffective cultic figurines.
18:17 *as with an east wind.* This line refers to the scorching late-spring sirocco wind from the northern Arabian desert.
18:19–20 *they have dug a pit for my life.* Jeremiah reminded the Lord how he had interceded for the people and had asked God to turn away His wrath and judgment. But instead of showing their appreciation for Jeremiah's intervention, the people prepared his grave.
19:3 *Hear the word of the LORD.* This key word of the Deuteronomic code (Deut. 6:4) calls for a decision regarding the content of the message. ***his ears will tingle.*** This expression is used to refer to a harsh, ringing judgment announcement (1 Sam. 3:11).
19:4–5 *the blood of the innocents.* This phrase refers to the murderous act of child sacrifice (7:31). Human sacrifice was known among the Phoenicians, Moabites, and Canaanites. This abominable practice, performed in the name of religious worship, was explicitly forbidden in the covenant (Deut. 12:31).

18:15 [l] Jer. 2:13, 32 [m] Jer. 6:16 **18:16** [n] Jer. 19:8 [o] 1 Kin. 9:8 **18:17** [p] Jer. 13:24 [q] Ps. 48:7 [r] Jer. 2:27 **18:18** [s] Jer. 11:19 [t] Lev. 10:11 **18:20** [u] Ps. 109:4 [v] Jer. 5:26 [w] Jer. 14:7—15:1 **18:21** [x] Ps. 109:9–20 [y] Jer. 15:7, 8 **18:23** [z] Ps. 35:14; 109:14 [a] Jer. 7:20 **19:2** [a] Josh. 15:8 **19:3** [b] Jer. 17:20 [c] 1 Sam. 3:11 **19:4** [d] Is. 65:11 [e] 2 Kin. 21:12 **19:5** [f] Jer. 7:31; 32:35 [g] Lev. 18:21 **19:6** [h] Josh. 15:8 **19:7** [i] Lev. 26:17 [j] Ps. 79:2 **19:8** [k] Jer. 18:16; 49:13; 50:13

it will be astonished and hiss because of all its plagues. 9And I will cause them to eat the *flesh of their sons and the flesh of their daughters, and everyone shall eat the flesh of his friend in the siege and in the desperation with which their enemies and those who seek their lives shall drive them to despair." '

10m"Then you shall break the flask in the sight of the men who go with you, 11and say to them, 'Thus says the LORD of hosts: n"Even so I will break this people and this city, as *one* breaks a potter's vessel, which cannot be made whole again; and they shall °bury *them* in Tophet till *there is* no place to bury. 12Thus I will do to this place," says the LORD, "and to its inhabitants, and make this city like Tophet. 13And the houses of Jerusalem and the houses of the kings of Judah shall be defiled plike the place of Tophet, because of all the houses on whose qroofs they have burned incense to all the host of heaven, and rpoured out drink offerings to other gods." ' "

14Then Jeremiah came from Tophet, where the LORD had sent him to prophesy; and he stood in sthe court of the Lord's house and said to all the people, 15"Thus says the LORD of hosts, the God of Israel: 'Behold, I will bring on this city and on all her towns all the doom that I have pronounced against it, because tthey have stiffened their necks that they might not hear My words.'"

The Word of God to Pashhur

20 Now aPashhur the son of bImmer, the priest who *was* also chief governor in the house of the LORD, heard that Jeremiah prophesied these things. 2Then Pashhur struck Jeremiah the prophet, and put him in the stocks that *were* in the high cgate of Benjamin, which *was* by the house of the LORD.

3And it happened on the next day that Pashhur brought Jeremiah out of the stocks. Then Jeremiah said to him, "The LORD has not called your name Pashhur, but Magor-Missabib.* 4For thus says the LORD: 'Behold, I will make you a terror to yourself and to all your friends; and they shall fall by the sword of their enemies, and your eyes shall see *it*. I will dgive all Judah into the hand of the king of Babylon, and he shall carry them captive to Babylon and slay them with the sword. 5Moreover I ewill deliver all the wealth of this city, all its produce, and all its precious things; all the treasures of the kings of Judah I will give into the hand of their enemies, who will plunder them, seize them, and fcarry them to Babylon. 6And you, Pashhur, and all who dwell in your house, shall go into captivity. You shall go to Babylon, and there you shall die, and be buried there, you and all your friends, to whom you have gprophesied lies.'"

Jeremiah's Unpopular Ministry

7 O LORD, You induced me, and I was persuaded;
    hYou are stronger than I, and have prevailed.
    iI am in derision daily;
    Everyone mocks me.
8 For when I spoke, I cried out;
    jI shouted, "Violence and plunder!"
    Because the word of the LORD was made to me
    A reproach and a derision daily.
9 Then I said, "I will not make mention of Him,
    Nor speak anymore in His name."
    But *His word* was in my heart like a kburning fire
    Shut up in my bones;
    I was weary of holding *it* back,
    And lI could not.

* **20:3** Literally *Fear on Every Side*

19:9 *I will cause them to eat the flesh of their sons.* The gruesome practice of cannibalism appears, recalling the words of Deuteronomy 28:53. After years of siege resulting in severe famine, the people would resort to eating human flesh in order to survive. This prophecy was literally fulfilled in 586 B.C. when Nebuchadnezzar invaded Judah, and again in A.D. 70 when Titus destroyed Jerusalem.

20:1 *Pashhur . . . chief governor.* A person in this position had to be a priest. He had oversight of the temple, the temple guards, entry into the courts, and so on. Jeremiah's proclamations against the city and the temple were of grave concern to Pashhur because of the threat to the continuation of the cult in which he was involved.

20:2 *high gate of Benjamin.* This portal provided access into the temple courtyards from the north, the direction of Benjamin's territory.

20:3–4 *Magor-Missabib.* This means "terror on every side." As Pashhur had been a terror to Jeremiah, so he would become a terror to himself, his family, and his associates.

20:6 *Pashhur, and all who dwell in your house.* Pashhur's whole family and his close associates, who had opposed Jeremiah, would be deported to Babylon because Pashhur had prophesied lies. Pashhur apparently had announced that Jerusalem would not suffer destruction.

20:7 *You induced me, and I was persuaded.* A play on words is intended by using two forms of the same word, which means "to entice." Jeremiah claimed that the Lord had seduced him and that he had succumbed to the temptation.

20:8 *A reproach and a derision.* Jeremiah had faithfully proclaimed the Lord's word of judgment and

19:9 *l* Lev. 26:29   **19:10** *m* Jer. 51:63, 64   **19:11** *n* Is. 30:14 *o* Jer. 7:32   **19:13** *p* 2 Kin. 23:10 *q* Zeph. 1:5 *r* Jer. 7:18   **19:14** *s* 2 Chr. 20:5   **19:15** *t* Neh. 9:17, 29   **20:1** *a* Ezra 2:37, 38 *b* 1 Chr. 24:14   **20:2** *c* Jer. 37:13   **20:4** *d* Jer. 21:4–10   **20:5** *e* 2 Kin. 20:17 *f* Is. 39:6   **20:6** *g* Jer. 14:13–15   **20:7** *h* Jer. 1:6, 7 *i* Lam. 3:14   **20:8** *j* Jer. 6:7   **20:9** *k* Ps. 39:3 *l* Job 32:18

10 [m]For I heard many mocking:
"Fear on every side!"
"Report," *they say,* "and we will report it!"
[n]All my acquaintances watched for my stumbling, *saying,*
"Perhaps he can be induced;
Then we will prevail against him,
And we will take our revenge on him."

11 But the LORD *is* [o]with me as a mighty, awesome One.
Therefore my persecutors will stumble, and will not [p]prevail.
They will be greatly ashamed, for they will not prosper.
Their [q]everlasting confusion will never be forgotten.
12 But, O LORD of hosts,
You who [r]test the righteous,
And see the mind and heart,
[s]Let me see Your vengeance on them;
For I have pleaded my cause before You.

13 Sing to the LORD! Praise the LORD!
For [t]He has delivered the life of the poor
From the hand of evildoers.

14 [u]Cursed *be* the day in which I was born!
Let the day not be blessed in which my mother bore me!
15 Let the man *be* cursed
Who brought news to my father, saying,
"A male child has been born to you!"
Making him very glad.
16 And let that man be like the cities
Which the LORD [v]overthrew, and did not relent;
Let him [w]hear the cry in the morning
And the shouting at noon,
17 [x]Because he did not kill me from the womb,
That my mother might have been my grave,
And her womb always enlarged *with me.*
18 [y]Why did I come forth from the womb
to [z]see labor and sorrow,
That my days should be consumed with shame?

Jerusalem's Doom Is Sealed

21 The word which came to Jeremiah
from the LORD when [a]King Zedekiah
sent to him [b]Pashhur the son of Melchiah,
and [c]Zephaniah the son of Maaseiah, the
priest, saying, 2 [d]"Please inquire of the
LORD for us, for Nebuchadnezzar* king of
Babylon makes war against us. Perhaps
the LORD will deal with us according to all
His wonderful works, that *the king* may go
away from us."
3 Then Jeremiah said to them, "Thus you
shall say to Zedekiah, 4 'Thus says the LORD
God of Israel: "Behold, I will turn back the
weapons of war that *are* in your hands,
with which you fight against the king of
Babylon and the Chaldeans* who besiege
you outside the walls; and [e]I will assemble
them in the midst of this city. 5 I [f]Myself will
fight against you with an [g]outstretched
hand and with a strong arm, even in anger and fury and great wrath. 6 I will strike
the inhabitants of this city, both man and
beast; they shall die of a great pestilence.
7 And afterward," says the LORD, [h]"I will deliver Zedekiah king of Judah, his servants
and the people, and such as are left in this
city from the pestilence and the sword and
the famine, into the hand of Nebuchadnezzar king of Babylon, into the hand of their
enemies, and into the hand of those who
seek their life; and he shall strike them
with the edge of the sword. [i]He shall not
spare them, or have pity or mercy."'
8 "Now you shall say to this people, 'Thus
says the LORD: "Behold, [j]I set before you the
way of life and the way of death. 9 He who
[k]remains in this city shall die by the sword,
by famine, and by pestilence; but he who
goes out and defects to the Chaldeans who
besiege you, he shall [l]live, and his life shall

* **21:2** Hebrew *Nebuchadrezzar,* and so elsewhere
* **21:4** Or *Babylonians*

destruction, but the prophecy had not been fulfilled, thus opening the prophet up to criticism.

20:11 ***the LORD is with me.*** In order for a prophet to endure the pain and suffering that goes with the job, he needs to be aware of God's presence, power, and approval.

20:12 ***who test the righteous.*** God tests (6:27; 17:10) and judges the righteous, those who walk uprightly in His ways and truth.

20:14–15 ***Cursed be the day.*** In ancient Israel, to curse God or one's parents was an offense punishable by death. Jeremiah avoided committing a capital offense by cursing his conception and birth, and hence his call from God.

21:2 ***inquire of the LORD.*** This phrase means to seek His will.

21:5 ***with an outstretched hand.*** Because the people of Judah had become God's enemies, God would fight against them. The divine instruments by which Israel had gained freedom from Egypt (Ex. 15:6; Deut. 6:21) and deliverance from their enemies would be used against them.

21:8–9 ***the way of life and the way of death.*** Death would come to those who attempted to survive the siege of Jerusalem; life was possible through surrender to the Chaldeans (Babylonians).

20:10 [m] Ps. 31:13 [n] Ps. 41:9; 55:13, 14 **20:11** [o] Jer. 1:18, 19 [p] Jer. 15:20; 17:18 [q] Jer. 23:40 **20:12** [r] [Jer. 11:20; 17:10] [s] Ps. 54:7; 59:10 **20:13** [t] Ps. 35:9, 10; 109:30, 31 **20:14** [u] Job 3:3 **20:16** [v] Gen. 19:25 [w] Jer. 18:22 **20:17** [x] Job 3:10, 11 **20:18** [y] Job 3:20 [z] Lam. 3:1 **21:1** [a] 2 Kin. 24:17, 18 [b] Jer. 38:1 [c] 2 Kin. 25:18 **21:2** [d] Jer. 37:3, 7 **21:4** [e] Is. 13:4 **21:5** [f] Is. 63:10 [g] Ex. 6:6 **21:7** [h] Jer. 37:17; 39:5; 52:9 [i] 2 Chr. 36:17 **21:8** [j] Deut. 30:15, 19 **21:9** [k] Jer. 38:2 [l] Jer. 39:18

be as a prize to him. 10 For I have [m]set My
face against this city for adversity and not
for good," says the LORD. [n]"It shall be given
into the hand of the king of Babylon, and he
shall [o]burn it with fire."'

Message to the House of David

11 "And concerning the house of the king
of Judah, *say*, 'Hear the word of the LORD,
12 O house of David! Thus says the LORD:

[p]"Execute judgment [q]in the morning;
And deliver *him who is* plundered
Out of the hand of the oppressor,
Lest My fury go forth like fire
And burn so that no one can quench *it*,
Because of the evil of your doings.

13 "Behold, [r]I *am* against you,
O inhabitant of the valley,
And rock of the plain," says the LORD,
"Who say, [s]'Who shall come down
against us?
Or who shall enter our dwellings?'
14 But I will punish you according to the
[t]fruit of your doings," says the
LORD;
"I will kindle a fire in its forest,
And [u]it shall devour all things around
it."'"

22 Thus says the LORD: "Go down to
the house of the king of Judah, and
there speak this word, 2 and say, [a]'Hear
the word of the LORD, O king of Judah,
you who sit on the throne of David, you
and your servants and your people who
enter these gates! 3 Thus says the LORD:
[b]"Execute judgment and righteousness,
and deliver the plundered out of the hand
of the oppressor. Do no wrong and do no
violence to the stranger, the [c]fatherless,
or the widow, nor shed innocent blood in
this place. 4 For if you indeed do this thing,
[d]then shall enter the gates of this house,
riding on horses and in chariots, accompanied by servants and people, kings who sit
on the throne of David. 5 But if you will not
hear these words, [e]I swear by Myself," says
the LORD, "that this house shall become a
desolation."'"

6 For thus says the LORD to the house of
the king of Judah:

"You *are* [f]Gilead to Me,
The head of Lebanon;
Yet I surely will make you a
wilderness,
Cities *which* are not inhabited.
7 I will prepare destroyers against you,
Everyone with his weapons;
They shall cut down [g]your choice
cedars
[h]And cast *them* into the fire.

8 And many nations will pass by this city;
and everyone will say to his neighbor,
[i]'Why has the LORD done so to this great
city?' 9 Then they will answer, [j]'Because
they have forsaken the covenant of the
LORD their God, and worshiped other gods
and served them.'"

10 Weep not for [k]the dead, nor bemoan
him;
Weep bitterly for him [l]who goes
away,
For he shall return no more,
Nor see his native country.

Message to the Sons of Josiah

11 For thus says the LORD concerning
[m]Shallum* the son of Josiah, king of Judah,
who reigned instead of Josiah his father,
[n]who went from this place: "He shall not
return here anymore, 12 but he shall die in
the place where they have led him captive,
and shall see this land no more.

---

* **22:11** Also called *Jehoahaz*

21:10 *For I have set My face.* This phrase describes the fixed intention of God, which in this context was against Jerusalem. The result would be adversity rather than good.

21:13 *come down against us.* Attacking armies generally approached Jerusalem from the north along an elevated ridge.

22:1 *Go . . . king of Judah . . . speak this word.* This is the first of three messages directed at specific kings of Judah. Shallum, the fourth son of Josiah, was placed on the throne by the people of Judah, but he was dethroned after three months by Pharaoh Necho. Shallum was imprisoned and taken captive to Egypt (2 Chr. 36:1–4). Eliakim (Jehoiakim), Shallum's brother, was placed on the throne as an Egyptian vassal. Necho maintained control of Palestine until Nebuchadnezzar defeated Egypt at the Battle of Carchemish in 605 B.C. Shallum died without returning from Egypt, in fulfillment of Jeremiah's prophecy.

22:2 *who sit on the throne of David.* Jeremiah's prophecy was addressed to three groups: the kings who are of David's lineage, the kings' servants, and "your people who enter these gates." The last phrase may refer to the citizens in general or to personnel who regularly entered the palace gates.

22:3 *Execute judgment and righteousness.* For all practical purposes these two terms are synonymous. One could not have one without the other.

22:6–7 *Gilead . . . Lebanon.* The territories were sources for timber for the royal palaces. These luxurious residences would be reduced to deserted wilderness and set ablaze if the kings disobeyed the covenant.

22:9 *worshiped other gods.* The pagan nations would recognize that the destruction of Jerusalem was the result of Judah's violation of its covenant with God. The people of Judah had exchanged their God for alien deities, whom they worshiped and served.

21:10 [m] Amos 9:4 [n] Jer. 38:3 [o] Jer. 34:2, 22; 37:10 **21:12** [p] Zech. 7:9 [q] Ps. 101:8 **21:13** [r] [Ezek. 13:8] [s] Jer. 49:4 **21:14** [t] Is. 3:10, 11 [u] 2 Chr. 36:19 **22:2** [a] Jer. 17:20 **22:3** [b] Jer. 21:12 [c] Jer. 7:6 **22:4** [d] Jer. 17:25 **22:5** [e] Heb. 6:13, 17 **22:6** [f] Song 4:1 **22:7** [g] Is. 37:24 [h] Jer. 21:14 **22:8** [i] Deut. 29:24–26 **22:9** [j] 2 Chr. 34:25 **22:10** [k] 2 Kin. 22:20 [l] Jer. 14:17; 22:11 **22:11** [m] 1 Chr. 3:15 [n] 2 Kin. 23:34

13 "Woe[o] to him who builds his house by
    unrighteousness
And his chambers by injustice,
[p]Who uses his neighbor's service
    without wages
And gives him nothing for his work,
14 Who says, 'I will build myself a wide
    house with spacious chambers,
And cut out windows for it,
Paneling *it* with cedar
And painting *it* with vermilion.'

15 "Shall you reign because you enclose
    yourself in cedar?
Did not your father eat and drink,
And do justice and righteousness?
Then [q]*it was* well with him.
16 He judged the cause of the poor and
    needy;
Then *it was* well.
Was not this knowing Me?" says the
    LORD.
17 "Yet[r] your eyes and your heart *are* for
    nothing but your covetousness,
For shedding innocent blood,
And practicing oppression and
    violence."

18Therefore thus says the LORD concerning Jehoiakim the son of Josiah, king
of Judah:

[s]"They shall not lament for him,
    Saying, [t]'Alas, my brother!' or 'Alas,
    my sister!'
They shall not lament for him,
    Saying, 'Alas, master!' or 'Alas, his
    glory!'
19 [u]He shall be buried with the burial of a
    donkey,
Dragged and cast out beyond the gates
    of Jerusalem.

20 "Go up to Lebanon, and cry out,
And lift up your voice in Bashan;
Cry from Abarim,
For all your lovers are destroyed.
21 I spoke to you in your prosperity,
But you said, 'I will not hear.'
[v]This *has been* your manner from your
    youth,
That you did not obey My voice.
22 The wind shall eat up all [w]your rulers,
And your lovers shall go into captivity;

Surely then you will be ashamed and
    humiliated
For all your wickedness.
23 O inhabitant of Lebanon,
Making your nest in the cedars,
How gracious will you be when pangs
    come upon you,
Like [x]the pain of a woman in labor?

Message to Coniah

24"As I live," says the LORD, [y]"though Coniah* the son of Jehoiakim, king of Judah,
[z]were the signet on My right hand, yet I
would pluck you off; 25[a]and I will give you
into the hand of those who seek your life,
and into the hand *of those* whose face you
fear—the hand of Nebuchadnezzar king
of Babylon and the hand of the Chaldeans.
26[b]So I will cast you out, and your mother
who bore you, into another country where
you were not born; and there you shall die.
27But to the land to which they desire to return, there they shall not return.

28 "Is this man Coniah a despised, broken
    idol—
[c]A vessel in which *is* no pleasure?
Why are they cast out, he and his
    descendants,
And cast into a land which they do not
    know?
29 [d]O earth, earth, earth,
Hear the word of the LORD!
30 Thus says the LORD:
'Write this man down as [e]childless,
A man *who* shall not prosper in his
    days;
For [f]none of his descendants shall
    prosper,
Sitting on the throne of David,
And ruling anymore in Judah.'"

The Branch of Righteousness

23 "Woe [a]to the shepherds who destroy
and scatter the sheep of My pasture!"
says the LORD. 2Therefore thus says the
LORD God of Israel against the shepherds
who feed My people: "You have scattered
My flock, driven them away, and not attended to them. [b]Behold, I will attend to

---

* 22:24 Also called *Jeconiah* and *Jehoiachin*

22:13 *uses his neighbor's service without wages.*
The king was supposed to be the guardian of his people, but Jehoiakim enslaved his fellow Israelites to
build his self-aggrandizing palaces.
**22:18–19 *He shall be buried with the burial of
a donkey.*** A king of such despicable character as
Jehoiakim deserved no lament. Instead of proper
funeral rites due a king, Jehoiakim would receive an
ignoble burial, like an animal, alone and unlamented.
22:22–23 *The wind shall eat up all your rulers.*
The winds of adversity and invasion would carry off
Judah's leaders and allies alike. The nation would be
ashamed that it had entered into such futile associations.
22:24–27 *Coniah.* This was another name for

Jehoiachin. He succeeded his father in 598 B.C.
under the threat of siege from Babylon as a result of
Jehoiakim's rebellion. Jehoiachin reigned for three
months until he and his family were exiled to Babylon by Nebuchadnezzar (2 Kin. 24:6–16). Eventually
Jehoiachin was released from prison after the death
of Nebuchadnezzar.

22:13 [o] 2 Kin. 23:35 [p] James 5:4   **22:15** [q] Ps. 128:2
22:17 [r] Ezek. 19:6   **22:18** [s] Jer. 16:4, 6 [t] 1 Kin. 13:30
22:19 [u] Jer. 36:30   **22:21** [v] Jer. 3:24, 25; 32:30
22:22 [w] Jer. 23:1   **22:23** [x] Jer. 6:24   **22:24** [y] 2 Kin. 24:6, 8
[z] Hag. 2:23   **22:25** [a] Jer. 34:20   **22:26** [b] 2 Kin. 24:15
22:28 [c] Hos. 8:8   **22:29** [d] Deut. 32:1   **22:30** [e] Matt. 1:12
[f] Jer. 36:30   **23:1** [a] Jer. 10:21   **23:2** [b] Ex. 32:34

you for the evil of your doings," says the
LORD. 3"But [c]I will gather the remnant of
My flock out of all countries where I have
driven them, and bring them back to their
folds; and they shall be fruitful and increase. 4I will set up [d]shepherds over them
who will feed them; and they shall fear no
more, nor be dismayed, nor shall they be
lacking," says the LORD.

5 "Behold, [e]*the* days are coming," says
the LORD,
"That I will raise to David a Branch of
righteousness;
A King shall reign and prosper,
[f]And execute judgment and
righteousness in the earth.
6 [g]In His days Judah will be saved,
And Israel [h]will dwell safely;
Now [i]this *is* His name by which He
will be called:

THE LORD OUR RIGHTEOUSNESS.*

7"Therefore, behold, [j]*the* days are coming," says the LORD, "that they shall no
longer say, 'As the LORD lives who brought
up the children of Israel from the land
of Egypt,' 8but, 'As the LORD lives who
brought up and led the descendants of the
house of Israel from the north country [k]and
from all the countries where I had driven
them.' And they shall dwell in their own
[l]land."

False Prophets and Empty Oracles

9 My heart within me is broken
Because of the prophets;
[m]All my bones shake.
I am like a drunken man,
And like a man whom wine has
overcome,
Because of the LORD,
And because of His holy words.
10 For [n]the land is full of adulterers;
For [o]because of a curse the land mourns.
[p]The pleasant places of the wilderness
are dried up.
Their course of life is evil,
And their might *is* not right.

11 "For [q]both prophet and priest are
profane;
Yes, [r]in My house I have found their
wickedness," says the LORD.
12 "Therefore[s] their way shall be to them
Like slippery *ways;*
In the darkness they shall be driven on
And fall in them;
For I [t]will bring disaster on them,
The year of their punishment," says
the LORD.
13 "And I have seen folly in the prophets of
Samaria:
[u]They prophesied by Baal
And [v]caused My people Israel to err.
14 Also I have seen a horrible thing in the
prophets of Jerusalem:
[w]They commit adultery and walk in
lies;
They also [x]strengthen the hands of
evildoers,
So that no one turns back from his
wickedness.
All of them are like [y]Sodom to Me,
And her inhabitants like Gomorrah.

15"Therefore thus says the LORD of hosts
concerning the prophets:

'Behold, I will feed them with
[z]wormwood,
And make them drink the water of
gall;
For from the prophets of Jerusalem
Profaneness has gone out into all the
land.'"

16Thus says the LORD of hosts:

"Do not listen to the words of the
prophets who prophesy to you.
They make you worthless;
[a]They speak a vision of their own
heart,
Not from the mouth of the LORD.

* **23:6** Hebrew *YHWH Tsidkenu*

23:3 *I will gather the remnant.* The kings of Israel had caused the dispersion of the nation; but the Lord would mercifully bring about the restoration of the remnant. This concept was a popular one with many of the prophets (Is. 1:9; 10:20–23). The blessing of restoration and prosperity as a consequence of repentance is outlined in Deuteronomy 30:1–10.

23:5 *a Branch of righteousness.* Beginning with Isaiah 4:2 this term is used of the promised Messiah (33:15; Zech. 3:8). This great king will reign with justice and righteousness. This ideal was founded on God's promise to David (2 Sam. 7:16).

23:7–8 *the days are coming.* The future restoration of Israel would exceed anything in the past; it would surpass even the first exodus, the deliverance from Egypt.

23:9–10 *My heart within me is broken.* Jeremiah's dismay over the false prophets weakened him mentally and physically, so much so that he felt drunken from the inner turmoil.

23:15 *I will feed them with wormwood.* This word refers to bitterness and death by poison. According to Deuteronomy 18:20, the consequence of false prophecy was death.

23:16 *a vision of their own heart.* Visions were commonly understood to be a means of receiving a message from God (or the gods). The term *vision* used here and in Jeremiah 14:14 is also found in Daniel 1:17 and 8:1; plus it is used in other prophetic books to describe a divine revelation (Is. 1:1; Mic. 3:6).

23:3 [c] Jer. 32:37 **23:4** [d] Jer. 3:15 **23:5** [e] Jer. 33:14; Matt. 1:1, 6; Luke 3:31; [John 1:45; 7:42]; Rev. 22:16 [f] Ps. 72:2 **23:6** [g] Zech. 14:11 [h] Jer. 32:37 [i] [Rom. 3:22; 1 Cor. 1:30] **23:7** [j] Jer. 16:14 **23:8** [k] Is. 43:5, 6 [l] Gen. 12:7 **23:9** [m] Hab. 3:16 **23:10** [n] Jer. 9:2 [o] Hos. 4:2 [p] Jer. 9:10 **23:11** [q] Zeph. 3:4 [r] Jer. 7:30; 32:34 **23:12** [s] [Prov. 4:19] [t] Jer. 11:23 **23:13** [u] Jer. 2:8 [v] Is. 9:16 **23:14** [w] Jer. 29:23 [x] Ezek. 13:22, 23 [y] Is. 1:9, 10 **23:15** [z] Jer. 9:15 **23:16** [a] Jer. 14:14

17 They continually say to those who
　despise Me,
'The LORD has said, b"You shall have
　peace"';
And to everyone who cwalks
　according to the dictates of his
　own heart, they say,
d'No evil shall come upon you.'"

18 For ewho has stood in the counsel of
　the LORD,
And has perceived and heard His
　word?
Who has marked His word and heard
　it?

19 Behold, a fwhirlwind of the LORD has
　gone forth in fury—
A violent whirlwind!
It will fall violently on the head of the
　wicked.

20 The ganger of the LORD will not turn
　back
Until He has executed and performed
　the thoughts of His heart.
hIn the latter days you will understand
　it perfectly.

21 "Ii have not sent these prophets, yet
　they ran.
I have not spoken to them, yet they
　prophesied.

22 But if they had stood in My counsel,
And had caused My people to hear My
　words,
Then they would have jturned them
　from their evil way
And from the evil of their doings.

23 "Am I a God near at hand," says the
　LORD,
"And not a God afar off?

24 Can anyone khide himself in secret
　places,
So I shall not see him?" says the LORD;
l"Do I not fill heaven and earth?" says
　the LORD.

25"I have heard what the prophets have
said who prophesy lies in My name, saying, 'I have dreamed, I have dreamed!'
26How long will this be in the heart of the
prophets who prophesy lies? Indeed they
are prophets of the deceit of their own
heart, 27who try to make My people forget

My name by their dreams which everyone
tells his neighbor, mas their fathers forgot
My name for Baal.

28 "The prophet who has a dream, let him
　tell a dream;
And he who has My word, let him
　speak My word faithfully.
What is the chaff to the wheat?" says
　the LORD.

29 "Is not My word like a nfire?" says the
　LORD,
"And like a hammer that breaks the
　rock in pieces?

30"Therefore behold, oI am against the
prophets," says the LORD, "who steal My
words every one from his neighbor. 31Be-
hold, I am pagainst the prophets," says the
LORD, "who use their tongues and say, 'He
says.' 32Behold, I am against those who
prophesy false dreams," says the LORD,
"and tell them, and cause My people to err
by their qlies and by rtheir recklessness.
Yet I did not send them or command them;
therefore they shall not sprofit this people
at all," says the LORD.

33"So when these people or the prophet
or the priest ask you, saying, 'What is tthe
oracle of the LORD?' you shall then say to
them, 'What oracle?'* I will even forsake
you," says the LORD. 34"And as for the
prophet and the priest and the people who
say, 'The oracle of the LORD!' I will even
punish that man and his house. 35Thus
every one of you shall say to his neighbor, and every one to his brother, 'What
has the LORD answered?' and, 'What has
the LORD spoken?' 36And the oracle of the
LORD you shall mention no more. For every
man's word will be his oracle, for you have
uperverted the words of the living God, the
LORD of hosts, our God. 37Thus you shall
say to the prophet, 'What has the LORD
answered you?' and, 'What has the LORD
spoken?' 38But since you say, 'The oracle
of the LORD!' therefore thus says the LORD:
'Because you say this word, "The oracle of
the LORD!" and I have sent to you, saying,
"Do not say, 'The oracle of the LORD!'"'"

* 23:33 Septuagint, Targum, and Vulgate read 'You
are the burden.'

23:19 a whirlwind of the LORD. This is a symbol of
God's judgment (Is. 29:6).
23:21–22 I have not sent these prophets. A true
prophet must be sent by God with a word from God.
A true prophet of God calls people to repentance of
sin or evil and to renewed faith.
23:26 the deceit of their own heart. The character
of the false prophets was based on lies and deceit.
Their deception was apparent because their goal was
to draw the people into idolatry with their fanciful
dreams, leading people to forget God and follow Baal
(2:8).
23:28–29 What is the chaff to the wheat. This
poetic interlude compares dream and word. A dream

is fleeting, like chaff in the wind. God's word has the
force of fire and a hammer.
23:38–40 The oracle of the LORD. False prophets
could not speak an oracle. The disgrace that resulted
from the false prophets would last for an extended
period of time: Its memory would endure forever
(20:11).

23:17 b Ezek. 13:10 c Deut. 29:19; Jer. 3:17 d Mic. 3:11
23:18 e [1 Cor. 2:16] 23:19 f Amos 1:14 23:20 g Jer.
30:24 h Gen. 49:1 23:21 i Jer. 14:14; 23:32; 27:15
23:22 j Jer. 25:5 23:24 k [Ps. 139:7] l [1 Kin. 8:27]
23:27 m Judg. 3:7 23:29 n Jer. 5:14 23:30 o Deut.
18:20 23:31 p Ezek. 13:9 23:32 q Lam. 2:14; 3:37
r Zeph. 3:4 s Jer. 7:8 23:33 t Mal. 1:1 23:36 u Deut. 4:2

³⁹therefore behold, I, even I, ᵛwill utterly forget you and forsake you, and the city that I gave you and your fathers, and *will* cast you out of My presence. ⁴⁰And I will bring ʷan everlasting reproach upon you, and a perpetual ˣshame, which shall not be forgotten.'"

The Sign of Two Baskets of Figs

24 The ᵃLORD showed me, and there were two baskets of figs set before the temple of the LORD, after Nebuchadnezzar ᵇking of Babylon had carried away captive ᶜJeconiah the son of Jehoiakim, king of Judah, and the princes of Judah with the craftsmen and smiths, from Jerusalem, and had brought them to Babylon. ²One basket *had* very good figs, like the figs *that are* first ripe; and the other basket *had* very bad figs which could not be eaten, they were so ᵈbad. ³Then the LORD said to me, "What do you see, Jeremiah?"

And I said, "Figs, the good figs, very good; and the bad, very bad, which cannot be eaten, they are so bad."

⁴Again the word of the LORD came to me, saying, ⁵"Thus says the LORD, the God of Israel: 'Like these good figs, so will I acknowledge those who are carried away captive from Judah, whom I have sent out of this place for *their own* good, into the land of the Chaldeans. ⁶For I will set My eyes on them for good, and ᵉI will bring them back to this land; ᶠI will build them and not pull *them* down, and I will plant them and not pluck *them* up. ⁷Then I will give them ᵍa heart to know Me, that I *am* the LORD; and they shall be ʰMy people, and I will be their God, for they shall return to Me ⁱwith their whole heart.

⁸'And as the bad ʲfigs which cannot be eaten, they are so bad'—surely thus says the LORD—'so will I give up Zedekiah the king of Judah, his princes, the ᵏresidue of Jerusalem who remain in this land, and ˡthose who dwell in the land of Egypt. ⁹I will deliver them to ᵐtrouble into all the kingdoms of the earth, for *their* harm, ⁿto be a reproach and a byword, a taunt and a curse, in all places where I shall drive them. ¹⁰And I will send the sword, the famine, and the pestilence among them, till they are consumed from the land that I gave to them and their fathers.'"

Seventy Years of Desolation

25 The word that came to Jeremiah concerning all the people of Judah, ᵃin the fourth year of ᵇJehoiakim the son of Josiah, king of Judah (which *was* the first year of Nebuchadnezzar king of Babylon), ²which Jeremiah the prophet spoke to all the people of Judah and to all the inhabitants of Jerusalem, saying: ³ᶜ"From the thirteenth year of Josiah the son of Amon, king of Judah, even to this day, this *is* the twenty-third year in which the word of the LORD has come to me; and I have spoken to you, rising early and speaking, ᵈbut you have not listened. ⁴And the LORD has sent to you all His servants the prophets, ᵉrising early and sending *them*, but you have not listened nor inclined your ear to hear. ⁵They said, ᶠ'Repent now everyone of his evil way and his evil doings, and dwell in the land that the LORD has given to you and your fathers forever and ever. ⁶Do not go after other gods to serve them and worship them, and do not provoke Me to anger with the works of your hands; and I will not harm you.' ⁷Yet you have not listened to Me," says the LORD, "that you might ᵍprovoke Me to anger with the works of your hands to your own hurt.

⁸"Therefore thus says the LORD of hosts: 'Because you have not heard My words, ⁹behold, I will send and take ʰall the families of the north,' says the LORD, 'and Nebuchadnezzar the king of Babylon, ⁱMy servant, and will bring them against this land, against its inhabitants, and against these nations all around, and will utterly destroy them, and ʲmake them an astonishment, a hissing, and perpetual desolations. ¹⁰Moreover I will take from them the ᵏvoice of mirth and the voice of gladness, the voice of the bridegroom and the voice of the bride, ˡthe sound of the millstones and the light of the lamp. ¹¹And this whole land shall be a desolation *and* an astonishment, and these nations shall serve the king of Babylon seventy ᵐyears.

¹²'Then it will come to pass, ⁿwhen seventy years are completed, *that* I will punish the king of Babylon and that nation, the land of the Chaldeans, for their iniquity,' says the LORD; ᵒ'and I will make it a perpetual desolation. ¹³So I will bring on that land

24:4–7 *Like these good figs.* These are identified with the deported exiles, including Jeconiah's royal household, whom God set apart. God would bring back the captives, establish them in the land, and multiply their crops.

25:3 *I have spoken to you, rising early and speaking.* This phrase describes Jeremiah's diligence and persistence.

25:9 *Nebuchadnezzar . . . My servant.* This expression does not imply that the Babylonian monarch worshiped Israel's God, but simply that he was used by God to fulfill His purposes (as in the case of Cyrus, who is called the Lord's "anointed" in Is. 45:1).

23:39 ᵛHos. 4:6 23:40 ʷJer. 20:11 ˣMic. 3:5–7 24:1 ᵃAmos 7:1, 4; 8:1 ᵇ2 Kin. 24:12–16 ᶜJer. 22:24–28; 29:2 24:2 ᵈJer. 29:17 24:6 ᵉJer. 12:15; 29:10 ᶠJer. 32:41; 33:7; 42:10 24:7 ᵍ[Deut. 30:6] ʰJer. 30:22; 31:33; 32:38 ⁱJer. 29:13 24:8 ʲJer. 29:17 ᵏJer. 39:9 ˡJer. 44:1, 26–30 24:9 ᵐDeut. 28:25, 37 ⁿPs. 44:13, 14 25:1 ᵃJer. 36:1 ᵇ2 Kin. 24:1, 2 25:3 ᶜJer. 1:2 ᵈJer. 7:13; 11:7, 8, 10 25:4 ᵉJer. 7:13, 25 25:5 ᶠJer. 18:11 25:7 ᵍDeut. 32:21 25:9 ʰJer. 1:15 ⁱIs. 45:1 ʲJer. 18:16 25:10 ᵏRev. 18:23 ˡEccl. 12:4 25:11 ᵐJer. 29:10 25:12 ⁿEzra 1:1 ᵒIs. 13:20

all My words which I have pronounced against it, all that is written in this book, which Jeremiah has prophesied concerning all the nations. [14]p(For many nations qand great kings shall rbe served by them also; sand I will repay them according to their deeds and according to the works of their own hands.)' "

Judgment on the Nations

[15]For thus says the LORD God of Israel to me: "Take this twine cup of fury from My hand, and cause all the nations, to whom I send you, to drink it. [16]And uthey will drink and stagger and go mad because of the sword that I will send among them."

[17]Then I took the cup from the LORD's hand, and made all the nations drink, to whom the LORD had sent me: [18]Jerusalem and the cities of Judah, its kings and its princes, to make them va desolation, an astonishment, a hissing, and wa curse, as it is this day; [19]Pharaoh king of Egypt, his servants, his princes, and all his people; [20]all the mixed multitude, all the kings of xthe land of Uz, all the kings of the land of the yPhilistines (namely, Ashkelon, Gaza, Ekron, and zthe remnant of Ashdod); [21]aEdom, Moab, and the people of Ammon; [22]all the kings of bTyre, all the kings of Sidon, and the kings of the coastlands which are across the csea; [23]dDedan, Tema, Buz, and all who are in the farthest corners; [24]all the kings of Arabia and all the kings of the emixed multitude who dwell in the desert; [25]all the kings of Zimri, all the kings of fElam, and all the kings of the gMedes; [26]hall the kings of the north, far and near, one with another; and all the kingdoms of the world which are on the face of the earth. Also the king of She-shach* shall drink after them.

[27]"Therefore you shall say to them, 'Thus says the LORD of hosts, the God of Israel: i"Drink, jbe drunk, and vomit! Fall and rise no more, because of the sword which I will send among you." ' [28]And it shall be, if they refuse to take the cup from your hand to drink, then you shall say to them, 'Thus

says the LORD of hosts: "You shall certainly drink! [29]For behold, kI begin to bring calamity on the city lwhich is called by My name, and should you be utterly unpunished? You shall not be unpunished, for mI will call for a sword on all the inhabitants of the earth," says the LORD of hosts.'

[30]"Therefore prophesy against them all these words, and say to them:

'The LORD will nroar from on high,
And utter His voice from oHis holy
    habitation;
He will roar mightily against pHis fold.
He will give qa shout, as those who
    tread the grapes,
Against all the inhabitants of the
    earth.
[31] A noise will come to the ends of the
    earth—
For the LORD has ra controversy with
    the nations;
sHe will plead His case with all flesh.
He will give those who are wicked to
    the sword,' says the LORD."

[32]Thus says the LORD of hosts:

"Behold, disaster shall go forth
From nation to nation,
And ta great whirlwind shall be
    raised up
From the farthest parts of the earth.

[33]uAnd at that day the slain of the LORD shall be from one end of the earth even to the other end of the earth. They shall not be vlamented, wor gathered, or buried; they shall become refuse on the ground.

[34] "Wail,x shepherds, and cry!
Roll about in the ashes,
You leaders of the flock!
For the days of your slaughter and
    your dispersions are fulfilled;
You shall fall like a precious vessel.
[35] And the shepherds will have no way to
    flee,
Nor the leaders of the flock to escape.

---

* 25:26 A code word for Babylon (compare 51:41)

25:16 drink and stagger and go mad. This triad sequence depicts the judgment process by which the sword of the Lord subdues those opposed to Him. The state of drunkenness was condemned in the Old Testament: to drink the cup and stagger was to display one's guilt (Num. 5:19–28).

25:18 to make them a desolation, an astonishment. The list of nations that would be made to drink from the cup of the Lord's judgment begins with Judah and Jerusalem, which would be made a source of derision (19:8).

25:27–28 Drink, be drunk, and vomit. These terms for progressive inebriation emphasize the extent of judgment that would flow from God's cup of wrath. Those who refused the cup would be forced to drink.

25:30 The LORD will roar from on high. Generally this phrase refers to God's abode on Mount Zion (Joel 3:16; Amos 1:2).

25:31 A noise will come. This noise refers to a thunderous judgment resulting from God's "covenant lawsuit" against the nations. Though they had not received the law like Judah and Israel, the Gentiles would be judged because they were "wicked." The word "wicked" refers to the guilt associated with the

25:14 p Jer. 50:9; 51:27, 28 q Jer. 51:27 r Jer. 27:7 s Jer. 50:29; 51:6, 24 **25:15** t Rev. 14:10 **25:16** u Nah. 3:11 **25:18** v Jer. 25:9, 11 w Jer. 24:9 **25:20** x Job 1:1 y Jer. 47:1–7 z Is. 20:1 **25:21** a Jer. 49:7 **25:22** b Jer. 47:4 c Jer. 49:23 **25:23** d Jer. 49:7, 8 **25:24** e Ezek. 30:5 **25:25** f Jer. 49:34 g Jer. 51:11, 28 **25:26** h Jer. 50:9 **25:27** i Hab. 2:16 j Is. 63:6 **25:29** k Ezek. 9:6 l Dan. 9:18 m Ezek. 38:21 **25:30** n Amos 1:2 o Ps. 11:4 p 1 Kin. 9:3 q Is. 16:9 **25:31** r Mic. 6:2 s Is. 66:16 **25:32** t Jer. 23:19; 30:23 **25:33** u Is. 34:2; 3; 66:16 v Jer. 16:4, 6 w Ps. 79:3 **25:34** x Jer. 4:8; 6:26

36 A voice of the cry of the
shepherds,
And a wailing of the leaders to the
flock *will be heard.*
For the LORD has plundered their
pasture,
37 And the peaceful dwellings are cut
down
Because of the fierce anger of the
LORD.
38 He has left His lair like the lion;
For their land is desolate
Because of the fierceness of the
Oppressor,
And because of His fierce anger."

Jeremiah Saved from Death

26 In the beginning of the reign of Jehoiakim the son of Josiah, king of
Judah, this word came from the LORD, saying, 2"Thus says the LORD: 'Stand in [a]the
court of the LORD's house, and speak to all
the cities of Judah, which come to worship
in the LORD's house, [b]all the words that I
command you to speak to them. [c]Do not
diminish a word. 3[d]Perhaps everyone will
listen and turn from his evil way, that I may
[e]relent concerning the calamity which I
purpose to bring on them because of the
evil of their doings.' 4And you shall say to
them, 'Thus says the LORD: [f]"If you will
not listen to Me, to walk in My law which
I have set before you, 5to heed the words
of My servants the prophets [g]whom I sent
to you, both rising up early and sending
them (but you have not heeded), 6then I
will make this house like [h]Shiloh, and will
make this city [i]a curse to all the nations of
the earth."'"
7So the priests and the prophets and all
the people heard Jeremiah speaking these
words in the house of the LORD. 8Now it
happened, when Jeremiah had made an
end of speaking all that the LORD had
commanded *him* to speak to all the people,
that the priests and the prophets and all the
people seized him, saying, "You will surely
die! 9Why have you prophesied in the name
of the LORD, saying, 'This house shall be
like Shiloh, and this city shall be [j]desolate,
without an inhabitant'?" And all the people were gathered against Jeremiah in the
house of the LORD.
10When the princes of Judah heard these
things, they came up from the king's house
to the house of the LORD and sat down in
the entry of the New Gate of the LORD's
house. 11And the priests and the prophets
spoke to the princes and all the people, saying, "This man deserves to [k]die! For he has
prophesied against this city, as you have
heard with your ears."
12Then Jeremiah spoke to all the princes and all the people, saying: "The LORD
sent me to prophesy against this house and
against this city with all the words that you
have heard. 13Now therefore, [l]amend your
ways and your doings, and obey the voice
of the LORD your God; then the LORD will
relent concerning the doom that He has
pronounced against you. 14As for me, here
[m]I am, in your hand; do with me as seems
good and proper to you. 15But know for certain that if you put me to death, you will
surely bring innocent blood on yourselves,
on this city, and on its inhabitants; for truly
the LORD has sent me to you to speak all
these words in your hearing."
16So the princes and all the people said
to the priests and the prophets, "This man
does not deserve to die. For he has spoken
to us in the name of the LORD our God."
17[n]Then certain of the elders of the land
rose up and spoke to all the assembly of
the people, saying: 18[o]"Micah of Moresheth
prophesied in the days of Hezekiah king of
Judah, and spoke to all the people of Judah,
saying, 'Thus says the LORD of hosts:

[p]"Zion shall be plowed *like* a field,
Jerusalem shall become [q]heaps of
ruins,
And the mountain of the temple*
Like the bare hills of the forest."'*

*26:18 Literally *house* • Compare Micah 3:12

breach of ethical standards, including violating the poor and needy and abusing the oppressed.

25:37 ***Because of the fierce anger of the LORD.*** Human anger is an emotion. God's anger is an aspect of the righteous administration of His laws—natural, moral, and spiritual.

26:2 ***Do not diminish a word.*** Jeremiah was told to speak unsparingly with unwavering boldness.

26:3 ***Perhaps everyone will listen.*** The introduction to the judgment oracle is expressed in conditional terms. If the people repented of evil, the Lord would relent from the calamity He was threatening to bring on them.

26:6 ***then I will make this house like Shiloh.*** This city was not far from Jerusalem. The people could see the effects of its destruction by the Philistines in 1050 B.C., a destruction that overtook it even though it was the first resting place of the ark of the covenant. Jeremiah uses Shiloh as an illustration of the coming judgment of Jerusalem even though the temple of God had been built there.

26:13 ***obey the voice of the LORD your God.*** Jeremiah gives the Lord's assurance that if we, like Judah, turn to obey Him, our future will be changed from punishment to blessing.

26:15 ***if you put me to death.*** Jeremiah defended himself and pointed to the potential sin of shedding innocent blood. He had already accused the leaders of Jerusalem of child sacrifices in the Hinnom valley (2:34; 19:4).

26:18 ***Micah of Moresheth.*** In the reign of Hezekiah, Micah had announced the impending destruction of

26:2 [a] Jer. 19:14 [b] Matt. 28:20 [c] Acts 20:27 **26:3** [d] Jer. 36:3–7 [e] Jer. 18:8 **26:4** [f] Lev. 26:14, 15 **26:5** [g] Jer. 25:4; 29:19 **26:6** [h] 1 Sam. 4:10, 11 [i] Is. 65:15 **26:9** [j] Jer. 9:11 **26:11** [k] Jer. 38:4 **26:13** [l] Jer. 7:3 **26:14** [m] Jer. 38:5 **26:17** [n] Acts 5:34 **26:18** [o] Mic. 1:1 [p] Mic. 3:12 [q] Jer. 9:11

[19]Did Hezekiah king of Judah and all Judah ever put him to death? [r]Did he not fear the LORD and [s]seek the LORD's favor? And the LORD [t]relented concerning the doom which He had pronounced against them. [u]But we are doing great evil against ourselves."

[20]Now there was also a man who prophesied in the name of the LORD, Urijah the son of Shemaiah of Kirjath Jearim, who prophesied against this city and against this land according to all the words of Jeremiah. [21]And when Jehoiakim the king, with all his mighty men and all the princes, heard his words, the king sought to put him to death; but when Urijah heard it, he was afraid and fled, and went to Egypt. [22]Then Jehoiakim the king sent men to Egypt: Elnathan the son of Achbor, and other men who went with him to Egypt. [23]And they brought Urijah from Egypt and brought him to Jehoiakim the king, who killed him with the sword and cast his dead body into the graves of the common people.

[24]Nevertheless [v]the hand of Ahikam the son of Shaphan was with Jeremiah, so that they should not give him into the hand of the people to put him to death.

Symbol of the Bonds and Yokes

27 In the beginning of the reign of Jehoiakim* the son of Josiah, [a]king of Judah, this word came to Jeremiah from the LORD, saying,* [2]"Thus says the LORD to me: 'Make for yourselves bonds and yokes, [b]and put them on your neck, [3]and send them to the king of Edom, the king of Moab, the king of the Ammonites, the king of Tyre, and the king of Sidon, by the hand of the messengers who come to Jerusalem to Zedekiah king of Judah. [4]And command them to say to their masters, "Thus says the LORD of hosts, the God of Israel—thus you shall say to your masters: [5c]'I have made the earth, the man and the beast that are on the ground, by My great power and by My outstretched arm, and [d]have given it to whom it seemed proper to Me. [6e]And now I have given all these lands into the hand of Nebuchadnezzar the king of Babylon, [f]My servant; and [g]the beasts of the field I

have also given him to serve him. [7h]So all nations shall serve him and his son and his son's son, [i]until the time of his land comes; [j]and then many nations and great kings shall make him serve them. [8]And it shall be, that the nation and kingdom which will not serve Nebuchadnezzar the king of Babylon, and which will not put its neck under the yoke of the king of Babylon, that nation I will punish,' says the LORD, 'with the sword, the famine, and the pestilence, until I have consumed them by his hand. [9]Therefore do not listen to your prophets, your diviners, your dreamers, your soothsayers, or your sorcerers, who speak to you, saying, "You shall not serve the king of Babylon." [10]For they prophesy a [k]lie to you, to remove you far from your land; and I will drive you out, and you will perish. [11]But the nations that bring their necks under the yoke of the king of Babylon and serve him, I will let them remain in their own land,' says the LORD, 'and they shall till it and dwell in it.'"'"

[12]I also spoke to [l]Zedekiah king of Judah according to all these words, saying, "Bring your necks under the yoke of the king of Babylon, and serve him and his people, and live! [13m]Why will you die, you and your people, by the sword, by the famine, and by the pestilence, as the LORD has spoken against the nation that will not serve the king of Babylon? [14]Therefore [n]do not listen to the words of the prophets who speak to you, saying, 'You shall not serve the king of Babylon,' for they prophesy [o]a lie to you; [15]for I have [p]not sent them," says the LORD, "yet they prophesy a lie in My name, that I may drive you out, and that you may perish, you and the prophets who prophesy to you."

[16]Also I spoke to the priests and to all this people, saying, "Thus says the LORD: 'Do not listen to the words of your prophets who prophesy to you, saying, "Behold, [q]the vessels of the LORD's house will now shortly be brought back from Babylon";

---

* **27:1** Following Masoretic Text, Targum, and Vulgate; some Hebrew manuscripts, Arabic, and Syriac read *Zedekiah* (compare 27:3, 12; 28:1). • Septuagint omits verse 1.

Jerusalem by the Assyrians (Mic. 3:12). Yet because of the repentance of Hezekiah and the inhabitants, the city was spared from the onslaught of the Assyrian army under Sennacherib (701 B.C.).

26:24 Ahikam the son of Shaphan. This man, along with his father, served as a scribe under Josiah when the Book of the Law was found in the temple (2 Kin. 22:8–14). Ahikam's brother Gemariah also opposed Jehoiakim's burning of Jeremiah's scroll (36:25). This faithful family was supportive of Jeremiah and was instrumental in saving his life.

27:2–3 bonds and yokes. These are wooden bars or beams that attach to a pair of oxen with leather bands. The symbolic act of wearing the yoke would communicate bondage, restraint, and enslavement.

27:7 all nations shall serve him and his son and his

son's son. Following the death of Nebuchadnezzar in 562 B.C., his heirs and successors retained control of Babylon for only 24 years. Babylon fell without a battle to Cyrus and the Persian armies in 539 B.C., and later to Alexander the Great of Greece.

27:9–10 do not listen. The way kings summoned various prophet-diviners to give them direction is

26:19 [r] 2 Chr. 32:26 [s] 2 Kin. 20:1–19 [t] Ex. 32:14 [u] [Acts 5:39] **26:24** [v] 2 Kin. 22:12–14 **27:1** [a] Jer. 27:3, 12, 20; 28:1 **27:2** [b] Jer. 28:10, 12 **27:5** [c] Is. 45:12 [d] Dan. 4:17, 25, 32 **27:6** [e] Jer. 28:14 [f] Jer. 25:9; 43:10 [g] Dan. 2:38 **27:7** [h] 2 Chr. 36:20 [i] [Dan. 5:26] [j] Jer. 25:14 **27:10** [k] Jer. 23:16, 32; 28:15 **27:12** [l] Jer. 28:1; 38:17 **27:13** [m] [Ezek. 18:31] **27:14** [n] Jer. 23:16 [o] Jer. 14:14; 23:21; 29:8, 9 **27:15** [p] Jer. 23:21; 29:9 **27:16** [q] Dan. 1:2

for they prophesy a lie to you. ¹⁷Do not listen to them; serve the king of Babylon, and live! Why should this city be laid waste? ¹⁸But if they *are* prophets, and if the word of the LORD is with them, let them now make intercession to the LORD of hosts, that the vessels which are left in the house of the LORD, *in* the house of the king of Judah, and at Jerusalem, do not go to Babylon.'

¹⁹"For thus says the LORD of hosts ^rconcerning the pillars, concerning the Sea, concerning the carts, and concerning the remainder of the vessels that remain in this city, ²⁰which Nebuchadnezzar king of Babylon did not take, when he carried away ^scaptive Jeconiah the son of Jehoiakim, king of Judah, from Jerusalem to Babylon, and all the nobles of Judah and Jerusalem— ²¹yes, thus says the LORD of hosts, the God of Israel, concerning the ^tvessels that remain in the house of the LORD, and in the house of the king of Judah and of Jerusalem: ²²'They shall be ^ucarried to Babylon, and there they shall be until the day that I ^vvisit them,' says the LORD. 'Then ^wI will bring them up and restore them to this place.'"

Hananiah's Falsehood and Doom

28 And ^ait happened in the same year, at the beginning of the reign of Zedekiah king of Judah, in the ^bfourth year *and* in the fifth month, *that* Hananiah the son of ^cAzur the prophet, who *was* from Gibeon, spoke to me in the house of the LORD in the presence of the priests and of all the people, saying, ²"Thus speaks the LORD of hosts, the God of Israel, saying: 'I have broken ^dthe yoke of the king of Babylon. ^{3e}Within two full years I will bring back to this place all the vessels of the LORD's house, that Nebuchadnezzar king of Babylon ^ftook away from this place and carried to Babylon. ⁴And I will bring back to this place Jeconiah the son of Jehoiakim,

king of Judah, with all the captives of Judah who went to Babylon,' says the LORD, 'for I will break the yoke of the king of Babylon.'"

⁵Then the prophet Jeremiah spoke to the prophet Hananiah in the presence of the priests and in the presence of all the people who stood in the house of the LORD, ⁶and the prophet Jeremiah said, ^g"Amen! The LORD do so; the LORD perform your words which you have prophesied, to bring back the vessels of the LORD's house and all who were carried away captive, from Babylon to this place. ⁷Nevertheless hear now this word that I speak in your hearing and in the hearing of all the people: ⁸The prophets who have been before me and before you of old prophesied against many countries and great kingdoms—of war and disaster and pestilence. ⁹As for ^hthe prophet who prophesies of ⁱpeace, when the word of the prophet comes to pass, the prophet will be known *as* one whom the LORD has truly sent."

¹⁰Then Hananiah the prophet took the ^jyoke off the prophet Jeremiah's neck and broke it. ¹¹And Hananiah spoke in the presence of all the people, saying, "Thus says the LORD: 'Even so I will break the yoke of Nebuchadnezzar king of Babylon ^kfrom the neck of all nations within the space of two full years.'" And the prophet Jeremiah went his way.

¹²Now the word of the LORD came to Jeremiah, after Hananiah the prophet had broken the yoke from the neck of the prophet Jeremiah, saying, ¹³"Go and tell Hananiah, saying, 'Thus says the LORD: "You have broken the yokes of wood, but you have made in their place yokes of iron." ¹⁴For thus says the LORD of hosts, the God of Israel: ^l"I have put a yoke of iron on the neck of all these nations, that they may serve Nebuchadnezzar king of Babylon; and they shall serve him. ^mI have given him the beasts of the field also."'"

---

well known from the Book of Daniel (Dan. 2:2; 5:7). Besides prophets, there were diviners, like Balaam (Num. 22–24), who were prohibited from practicing their craft in Israel (Deut. 18:9–14). The collective effort of these diviners to determine the fate of their nations failed. Like the false prophets of Judah, they heralded a message of rebellion and resistance against Babylon. Only Jeremiah stood for the truth. The Lord would punish Judah through Nebuchadnezzar.

27:21–22 *concerning the vessels.* Jeremiah's message from the Lord is presented in detail. The remaining vessels in the temple, as well as in the king's palace, would be carried to Babylon until the Lord restored His people. In the midst of a prophetic message against the false prophets, Jeremiah spoke a message of hope and restoration. Destruction was imminent, but God does not forget His people. He would restore the righteous remnant.

28:1–4 *Hananiah the son of Azur.* This prophet believed that God's message for Judah was one of

imminent deliverance—within two years—from servitude to the king of Babylon. Hananiah also prophesied the return of the holy vessels taken by Nebuchadnezzar from the temple. Furthermore, Hananiah espoused the popular belief that the kingship of Zedekiah was illegitimate and that God would restore Jeconiah (Jehoiachin) to the throne in Jerusalem.

28:7–9 *war and disaster and pestilence.* Hananiah's message of peace and prosperity ran contrary to the long tradition of the genuine Hebrew prophets. Amos, Hosea, Micah, Joel, and Nahum spoke words of judgment and destruction against the great kingdoms like Assyria and Egypt.

27:19 ^r 2 Kin. 25:13–17   **27:20** ^s Jer. 24:1   **27:21** ^t Jer. 20:5   **27:22** ^u 2 Kin. 25:13   ^v 2 Chr. 36:21; Jer. 29:10; 32:5   ^w Ezra 1:7; 7:19   **28:1** ^a Jer. 27:1   ^b Jer. 51:59   ^c Ezek. 11:1   **28:2** ^d Jer. 27:12   **28:3** ^e Jer. 27:16   ^f Dan. 1:2   **28:6** ^g 1 Kin. 1:36   **28:9** ^h Deut. 18:22   ⁱ Jer. 23:17   **28:10** ^j Jer. 27:2   **28:11** ^k Jer. 27:7   **28:14** ^l Deut. 28:48   ^m Jer. 27:6

15 Then the prophet Jeremiah said to
Hananiah the prophet, "Hear now, Hananiah, the LORD has not sent you, but [n]you
make this people trust in a [o]lie. 16 Therefore
thus says the LORD: 'Behold, I will cast you
from the face of the earth. This year you
shall [p]die, because you have taught [q]rebel-
lion against the LORD.' "
17 So Hananiah the prophet died the
same year in the seventh month.

Jeremiah's Letter to the Captives

29 Now these *are* the words of the letter
that Jeremiah the prophet sent from
Jerusalem to the remainder of the elders
who were [a]carried away captive—to the
priests, the prophets, and all the people
whom Nebuchadnezzar had carried away
captive from Jerusalem to Babylon. 2 (This
happened after [b]Jeconiah the king, the
[c]queen mother, the eunuchs, the princes of
Judah and Jerusalem, the craftsmen, and
the smiths had departed from Jerusalem.)
3 *The letter was sent* by the hand of Elasah
the son of [d]Shaphan, and Gemariah the son
of Hilkiah, whom Zedekiah king of Judah
sent to Babylon, to Nebuchadnezzar king
of Babylon, saying,

4 Thus says the LORD of hosts, the God
of Israel, to all who were carried away
captive, whom I have caused to be carried away from Jerusalem to Babylon:

5 Build houses and dwell *in them;* plant
gardens and eat their fruit. 6 Take
wives and beget sons and daughters;
and take wives for your sons and give
your daughters to husbands, so that
they may bear sons and daughters—
that you may be increased there, and
not diminished. 7 And seek the peace
of the city where I have caused you to
be carried away captive, [e]and pray to
the LORD for it; for in its peace you will
have peace. 8 For thus says the LORD of
hosts, the God of Israel: Do not let your
prophets and your diviners who are
in your midst [f]deceive you, nor listen
to your dreams which you cause to be
dreamed. 9 For they prophesy [g]falsely to
you in My name; I have not sent them,
says the LORD.

10 For thus says the LORD: After [h]seventy
years are completed at Babylon, I will
visit you and perform My good word
toward you, and cause you to [i]return
to this place. 11 For I know the thoughts
that I think toward you, says the LORD,
thoughts of peace and not of evil, to
give you a future and a hope. 12 Then
you will [j]call upon Me and go and pray
to Me, and I will [k]listen to you. 13 And
[l]you will seek Me and find *Me,* when
you search for Me [m]with all your heart.
14 [n]I will be found by you, says the LORD,
and I will bring you back from your
captivity; [o]I will gather you from all the
nations and from all the places where
I have driven you, says the LORD, and I
will bring you to the place from which I
cause you to be carried away captive.

28:15–16 *you make this people trust in a lie.* Hananiah had not been sent by God, but he had led the people astray with a lie. As a result, Hananiah would die that very year.

29:2 *after.* This parenthetical passage provides background from 2 Kings 24:12–16 concerning the deportation of Jeconiah (Jehoiachin) to Babylon in 597 B.C. This method of eliminating leaders and leaving the peasant population to pay taxes to the kingdom was learned from the Assyrians and was designed to reduce the likelihood of rebellion.

29:4 *to all who were carried away captive.* Jeremiah reminded the exiled community that ultimately it was God, not Nebuchadnezzar, who had caused them to be taken to Babylon.

29:10 *After seventy years are completed.* The concept of seventy years of Babylonian captivity is reiterated from Jeremiah 25:12. The number 70 symbolizes completion and fulfillment of God's sovereign plans for creation and human history. The completion of the years of the kingdom of Babylon would also be the completion of Judah's exile.

29:11 A Future and a Hope—This text comes from a letter from Jeremiah to the exiles from Judah who were living in Babylon (vv. 4–9). The exiles must have had a lot of questions about their situation before they heard from Jeremiah. Had God abandoned them forever? How could they serve God properly while under the domination of the nation of Babylon? When would the exile end? Would they ever see Jerusalem again? What was the plan?

The answer that Jeremiah wrote to them probably wasn't satisfactory for all. They still would have had questions. Many would have wanted more specific answers. They would have wanted to know how long they would be in Babylon. They would have asked if they could do anything to hasten their return. These are not unlike the questions we ask God on a daily basis.

Perhaps the best way to describe the content of Jeremiah's letter is to say that he is pointing to the fact that all the specifics are wrapped up in their relationship with God. The promises are ultimate promises. If we seek Him, we will find Him. God Himself is our hope. Shouldn't knowing this give us all the direction we need? Isn't this what our faith is all about? On the basis of knowing what God has done and what He has promised to do, we will move ahead in trust. We may not see the path clearly, but we know He does lead and He is leading us.

29:14 *I will be found by you.* Those who seek God with a whole heart will find Him and experience His renewal. ***I will bring you back.*** God was the captor, and He would restore His people from captivity.

28:15 [n] Ezek. 13:22 [o] Jer. 27:10; 29:9 **28:16** [p] Jer. 20:6 [q] Deut. 13:5 **29:1** [a] Jer. 27:20 **29:2** [b] 2 Kin. 24:12–16 [c] Jer. 13:18 **29:3** [d] 2 Chr. 34:8 **29:7** [e] 1 Tim. 2:2 **29:8** [f] Eph. 5:6 **29:9** [g] Jer. 28:15; 37:19 **29:10** [h] Dan. 9:2 [i] [Jer. 24:6, 7] **29:12** [j] Ps. 50:15 [k] Ps. 145:19 **29:13** [l] Deut. 30:1–3 [m] Jer. 24:7 **29:14** [n] [Is. 55:6, 7] [o] Jer. 23:8; 32:37

15 Because you have said, "The LORD has raised up prophets for us in Babylon"— **16**^ptherefore thus says the LORD concerning the king who sits on the throne of David, concerning all the people who dwell in this city, and concerning your brethren who have not gone out with you into captivity— **17**thus says the LORD of hosts: Behold, I will send on them the sword, the famine, and the pestilence, and will make them like ^qrotten figs that cannot be eaten, they are so bad. **18**And I will pursue them with the sword, with famine, and with pestilence; and I ^rwill deliver them to trouble among all the kingdoms of the earth—to be ^sa curse, an astonishment, a hissing, and a reproach among all the nations where I have driven them, **19**because they have not heeded My words, says the LORD, which ^tI sent to them by My servants the prophets, rising up early and sending *them*; neither would you heed, says the LORD. **20**Therefore hear the word of the LORD, all you of the captivity, whom I have sent from Jerusalem to Babylon.

21 Thus says the LORD of hosts, the God of Israel, concerning Ahab the son of Kolaiah, and Zedekiah the son of Maaseiah, who prophesy a ^ulie to you in My name: Behold, I will deliver them into the hand of Nebuchadnezzar king of Babylon, and he shall slay them before your eyes. **22**^vAnd because of them a curse shall be taken up by all the captivity of Judah who *are* in Babylon, saying, "The LORD make you like Zedekiah and Ahab, ^wwhom the king of Babylon roasted in the fire"; **23**because ^xthey have done disgraceful things in Israel, have committed adultery with their neighbors' wives, and have spoken lying words in My name, which I have not commanded them. Indeed I ^yknow, and *am* a witness, says the LORD.

24 You shall also speak to Shemaiah the Nehelamite, saying, **25**Thus speaks the LORD of hosts, the God of Israel, saying: You have sent letters in your name to all the people who *are* at Jerusalem, ^zto Zephaniah the son of Maaseiah the priest, and to all the priests, saying, **26**"The LORD has made you priest instead of Jehoiada the priest, so that there should be ^aofficers *in* the house of the LORD over every man *who* is ^bdemented and considers himself a prophet, that you should ^cput him in prison and in the stocks. **27**Now therefore, why have you not rebuked Jeremiah of Anathoth who makes himself a prophet to you? **28**For he has sent to us *in* Babylon, saying, 'This *captivity is* long; build houses and dwell *in them*, and plant gardens and eat their fruit.' "

29Now Zephaniah the priest read this letter in the hearing of Jeremiah the prophet. **30**Then the word of the LORD came to Jeremiah, saying: **31**Send to all those in captivity, saying, Thus says the LORD concerning Shemaiah the Nehelamite: Because Shemaiah has prophesied to you, ^dand I have not sent him, and he has caused you to trust in a ^elie— **32**therefore thus says the LORD: Behold, I will punish Shemaiah the Nehelamite and his family: he shall not have anyone to dwell among this people, nor shall he see the good that I will do for My people, says the LORD, ^fbecause he has taught rebellion against the LORD.

Restoration of Israel and Judah

30 The word that came to Jeremiah from the LORD, saying, **2**"Thus speaks the LORD God of Israel, saying: 'Write in a book for yourself all the words that I have spoken to you. **3**For behold, the days are coming,' says the LORD, 'that ^aI will bring back from captivity My people Israel and Judah,' says the LORD. ^bAnd I will cause them to return to the land that I gave to their fathers, and they shall possess it.' "

4Now these *are* the words that the LORD spoke concerning Israel and Judah.

5"For thus says the LORD:

'We have heard a voice of trembling,
Of fear, and not of peace.
6 Ask now, and see,
 Whether a man is ever in labor with
  child?
So why do I see every man *with* his
  hands on his loins
 ^cLike a woman in labor,
 And all faces turned pale?

29:21 *Ahab the son of Kolaiah, and Zedekiah the son of Maaseiah.* These two were the prophets spoken of in Jeremiah 29:15. They were accused by Jeremiah of a deplorable crime; prophesying the imminent collapse of Babylon and the restoration of the captives to Jerusalem. Such false prophecy urging rebellion against God was a capital offense (Deut. 14:5–10). The prophetic punishment of Ahab and Zedekiah was death by command of Nebuchadnezzar.
30:2 *Write . . . all the words.* The oracles of Jeremiah were recorded by the scribe Baruch (ch. 36). "Book" refers to any type of writing medium, from a clay tablet to a parchment scroll. Jeremiah's oracles were recorded on a scroll (36:2).
30:6 *hands on his loins.* This phrase symbolizes the agony of God's people who had become like

29:16 ^p Jer. 38:2, 3, 17–23   **29:17** ^q Jer. 24:3, 8–10
29:18 ^r Deut. 28:25   ^s Jer. 26:6; 42:18   **29:19** ^t Jer. 25:4;
26:5; 35:15   **29:21** ^u Lam. 2:14   **29:22** ^v Is. 65:15   ^w Dan.
3:6, 21   **29:23** ^x Jer. 23:14   ^y [Prov. 5:21]   **29:25** ^z Jer. 21:1
29:26 ^a Jer. 20:1   ^b John 10:20   ^c Jer. 20:1, 2   **29:31** ^d Jer.
28:15   ^e Ezek. 13:8–16, 22, 23   **29:32** ^f Jer. 28:16
30:3 ^a Ezek. 39:25   ^b Jer. 16:15   **30:6** ^c Jer. 4:31; 6:24

7 ^dAlas! For that day *is* great,
 ^eSo that none is like it;
 And it *is* the time of Jacob's trouble,
 But he shall be saved out of it.

8 'For it shall come to pass in that day,'
 Says the LORD of hosts,
 'That I will break his yoke from your
   neck,
 And will burst your bonds;
 Foreigners shall no more enslave
   them.

9 But they shall serve the LORD their
   God,
 And ^fDavid their king,
 Whom I will ^graise up for them.

10 'Therefore ^hdo not fear, O My servant
   Jacob,' says the LORD,
 'Nor be dismayed, O Israel;
 For behold, I will save you from afar,
 And your seed ⁱfrom the land of their
   captivity.
 Jacob shall return, have rest and be
   quiet,
 And no one shall make *him* afraid.

11 For I *am* with ^jyou,' says the LORD, 'to
   save you;
 ^kThough I make a full end of all nations
   where I have scattered you,
 ^lYet I will not make a complete end of
   you.
 But I will correct you ^min justice,
 And will not let you go altogether
   unpunished.'

12 "For thus says the LORD:

 ⁿ"Your affliction *is* incurable,
 Your wound *is* severe.

13 *There is* no one to plead your cause,
 That you may be bound up;
 ^oYou have no healing medicines.

14 ^pAll your lovers have forgotten you;
 They do not seek you;
 For I have wounded you with the
   wound ^qof an enemy,
 With the chastisement ^rof a cruel one,
 For the multitude of your iniquities,
 ^sBecause your sins have increased.

15 Why ^tdo you cry about your
   affliction?
 Your sorrow *is* incurable.
 Because of the multitude of your
   iniquities,
 Because your sins have increased,
 I have done these things to you.

16 'Therefore all those who devour you
   ^ushall be devoured;
 And all your adversaries, every one of
   them, shall go into ^vcaptivity;
 Those who plunder you shall become
   ^wplunder,
 And all who prey upon you I will make
   a ^xprey.

17 ^yFor I will restore health to you
 And heal you of your wounds,' says
   the LORD,
 'Because they called you an outcast
   saying:
 "This *is* Zion;
 No one seeks her."'

18 "Thus says the LORD:

 'Behold, I will bring back the captivity
   of Jacob's tents,
 And ^zhave mercy on his dwelling
   places;
 The city shall be built upon its own
   mound,
 And the palace shall remain according
   to its own plan.

19 Then ^aout of them shall proceed
   thanksgiving
 And the voice of those who make
   merry;
 ^bI will multiply them, and they shall not
   diminish;
 I will also glorify them, and they shall
   not be small.

20 Their children also shall be ^cas before,
 And their congregation shall be
   established before Me;
 And I will punish all who oppress
   them.

21 Their nobles shall be from among
   them,

---

defenseless pregnant women in the midst of delivery before their enemies (4:31; 6:24).
30:8 *it shall come to pass in that day.* The day of the Lord was an ordained time of horror and distress for Israel and Judah, out of which the Lord would save them. Jeremiah expressed the hope of release from the bondage of the yoke of Babylon according to the Lord's timing (25:12) and not that of men (28:11).
30:12 *Your affliction is incurable.* God's hand of judgment had brought serious harm to the nation, a mortal wound unless God intervened.
30:13 *That you may be bound up.* This refers to the growth of new skin over an open wound.
30:14 *All your lovers have forgotten you.* Israel's lovers were the surrounding nations like Assyria, Egypt, Phoenicia, Ammon, and Edom, with whom it had made political and religious alliances. These nations had quickly forgotten Judah; they shrank back or were defeated by Nebuchadnezzar.

30:17 *For I will restore health to you.* Restoration and healing of Israel came in two forms: retribution against its enemies and healing of its wounds.
30:18 *Jacob's tents . . . dwelling places . . . city . . . palace.* These phrases emphasize God's work in rebuilding the homes and cities of His returning exiles, from the peasant population to the administration.
30:21 *Their nobles shall be from among them.* Israel's leaders would no longer be appointed by

30:7 ^d Amos 5:18 ^e Dan. 9:12; 12:1 **30:9** ^f Hos. 3:5 ^g [Luke 1:69] **30:10** ^h Is. 41:13; 43:5; 44:2 ⁱ Jer. 3:18 **30:11** ^j [Is. 43:2–5] ^k Amos 9:8 ^l Jer. 4:27; 46:27, 28 ^m Ps. 6:1 **30:12** ⁿ Jer. 15:18 **30:13** ^o Jer. 8:22 **30:14** ^p Lam. 1:2 ^q Job 13:24; 16:9; 19:11 ^r Job 30:21 ^s Jer. 5:6 **30:15** ^t Jer. 15:18 **30:16** ^u Jer. 10:25 ^v Is. 14:2 ^w Ezek. 39:10 ^x Jer. 2:3 **30:17** ^y Jer. 33:6 **30:18** ^z Ps. 102:13 **30:19** ^a Is. 51:11 ^b Zech. 10:8 **30:20** ^c Is. 1:26

[d]And their governor shall come from
their midst;
Then I will [e]cause him to draw near,
And he shall approach Me;
For who *is* this who pledged his heart
to approach Me?' says the LORD.
22 'You shall be [f]My people,
And I will be your God.'"

23 Behold, the [g]whirlwind of the LORD
Goes forth with fury,
A continuing whirlwind;
It will fall violently on the head of the
wicked.
24 The fierce anger of the LORD will not
return until He has done it,
And until He has performed the
intents of His heart.

[h]In the latter days you will consider it.

The Remnant of Israel Saved

31 "At [a]the same time," says the LORD,
[b]"I will be the God of all the families
of Israel, and they shall be My people."
2 Thus says the LORD:

"The people who survived the sword
Found grace in the wilderness—
Israel, when [c]I went to give him rest."

3 The LORD has appeared of old to me,
saying:
"Yes, [d]I have loved you with [e]an
everlasting love;
Therefore with lovingkindness I have
[f]drawn you.
4 Again [g]I will build you, and you shall
be rebuilt,
O virgin of Israel!
You shall again be adorned with your
[h]tambourines,
And shall go forth in the dances of
those who rejoice.
5 [i]You shall yet plant vines on the
mountains of Samaria;
The planters shall plant and eat *them*
as ordinary food.

6 For there shall be a day
When the watchmen will cry on
Mount Ephraim,
[i]'Arise, and let us go up *to* Zion,
To the LORD our God.'"

7 For thus says the LORD:

[k]"Sing with gladness for Jacob,
And shout among the chief of the
nations;
Proclaim, give praise, and say,
'O LORD, save Your people,
The remnant of Israel!'
8 Behold, I will bring them [l]from the
north country,
And [m]gather them from the ends of
the earth,
Among them the blind and the lame,
The woman with child
And the one who labors with child,
together;
A great throng shall return there.
9 [n]They shall come with weeping,
And with supplications I will lead
them.
I will cause them to walk [o]by the rivers
of waters,
In a straight way in which they shall
not stumble;
For I am a Father to Israel,
And Ephraim *is* My [p]firstborn.

10 "Hear the word of the LORD, O nations,
And declare *it* in the isles afar off, and
say,
'He who scattered Israel [q]will gather
him,
And keep him as a shepherd *does* his
flock.'
11 For [r]the LORD has redeemed Jacob,
And ransomed him [s]from the hand of
one stronger than he.
12 Therefore they shall come and sing in
[t]the height of Zion,
Streaming to [u]the goodness of the
LORD—
For wheat and new wine and oil,

---

foreign kings, and foreign rulers would not preside
over Israel's lands.
31:3 everlasting love . . . lovingkindness. These
strong words are in parallel and point toward a love
characterized by loyalty, a king of covenant love. Out
of His faithfulness to the covenants God established
with Abraham and Moses, and out of His great love,
God established the nation Israel for His glory and
for hers. The Lord would also deliver His people from
captivity and reestablish them by His love.
31:4 O virgin of Israel. Earlier in Jeremiah, this
expression was used sadly in depicting the departure of Israel from faith in God (2:32; 14:17). Here the
image is reversed. Israel is rebuilt in the manner of her
former betrothal (2:2), having become again a virgin
bride to God. **go forth in the dances of those who
rejoice.** A joyful celebration of marriage and festival
throughout villages is in view here (v. 13).
31:6 watchmen. This time the watchman's purpose

is not to warn the people about oncoming armies but
to call them to come with joy to the holy city.
31:9 I am a Father to Israel. This text is one of the
few cases in the Old Testament where the fatherhood
of God is portrayed directly (Deut. 32:6; Is. 63:16). Israel was familiar with the idea of God as Father, but
it was not until the teaching of Jesus that the phrase
took on the importance that we understand it to have
in our lives today.
31:12 the goodness of the LORD. The blessings of the

30:21 [d] Gen. 49:10 [e] Num. 16:5   **30:22** [f] Ezek.
36:28   **30:23** [g] Jer. 23:19, 20; 25:32   **30:24** [h] Gen.
49:1   **31:1** [a] Jer. 30:24 [b] Jer. 30:22   **31:2** [c] Num. 10:33
31:3 [d] Mal. 1:2 [e] Rom. 11:28 [f] Hos. 11:4   **31:4** [g] Jer.
33:7 [h] Judg. 11:34   **31:5** [i] Amos 9:14   **31:6** [j] [Mic. 4:2]
31:7 [k] Is. 12:5, 6   **31:8** [l] Jer. 3:12, 18; 23:8 [m] Ezek. 20:34,
41; 34:13   **31:9** [n] [Jer. 50:4] [o] Is. 35:8; 43:19; 49:10, 11
[p] Ex. 4:22   **31:10** [q] Is. 40:11   **31:11** [r] Is. 44:23; 48:20 [s] Is.
49:24   **31:12** [t] Ezek. 17:23 [u] Hos. 3:5

For the young of the flock and the
herd;
Their souls shall be like a [v]well-
watered garden,
[w]And they shall sorrow no more at all.

13 "Then shall the virgin rejoice in the
dance,
And the young men and the old,
together;
For I will turn their mourning to joy,
Will comfort them,
And make them rejoice rather than
sorrow.
14 I will satiate the soul of the priests
with abundance,
And My people shall be satisfied with
My goodness, says the LORD."

Mercy on Ephraim

15 Thus says the LORD:

[x]"A voice was heard in [y]Ramah,
Lamentation *and* bitter [z]weeping,
Rachel weeping for her children,
Refusing to be comforted for her
children,
Because [a]they *are* no more."

16 Thus says the LORD:

"Refrain your voice from [b]weeping,
And your eyes from tears;
For your work shall be rewarded, says
the LORD,
And they shall come back from the
land of the enemy.
17 There is [c]hope in your future, says the
LORD,
That *your* children shall come back to
their own border.

18 "I have surely heard Ephraim
bemoaning himself:
'You have [d]chastised me, and I was
chastised,
Like an untrained bull;
[e]Restore me, and I will return,
For You *are* the LORD my God.
19 Surely, [f]after my turning, I
repented;
And after I was instructed, I struck
myself on the thigh;
I was [g]ashamed, yes, even
humiliated,
Because I bore the reproach of my
youth.'
20 *Is* Ephraim My dear son?
Is he a pleasant child?
For though I spoke against him,
I earnestly remember him still;
[h]Therefore My heart yearns for him;
[i]I will surely have mercy on him, says
the LORD.

21 "Set up signposts,
Make landmarks;
[j]Set your heart toward the highway,
The way in *which* you went.
Turn back, O virgin of Israel,
Turn back to these your cities.
22 How long will you [k]gad about,
O you [l]backsliding daughter?
For the LORD has created a new thing
in the earth—
A woman shall encompass a man."

Future Prosperity of Judah

23 Thus says the LORD of hosts, the God
of Israel: "They shall again use this speech
in the land of Judah and in its cities, when
I bring back their captivity: [m]'The LORD
bless you, O home of justice, *and* [n]moun-
tain of holiness!' 24 And there shall dwell in
Judah itself, and [o]in all its cities together,
farmers and those going out with flocks.
25 For I have satiated the weary soul, and
I have replenished every sorrowful soul."
26 After this I awoke and looked around,
and my sleep was [p]sweet to me.
27 "Behold, the days are coming, says the
LORD, that [q]I will sow the house of Israel
and the house of Judah with the seed of
man and the seed of beast. 28 And it shall
come to pass, *that* as I have [r]watched over
them [s]to pluck up, to break down, to throw
down, to destroy, and to afflict, so I will
watch over them [t]to build and to plant, says
the LORD. 29 [u]In those days they shall say
no more:

'The fathers have eaten sour grapes,
And the children's teeth are set on
edge.'

30 [v]But every one shall die for his own iniquity; every man who eats the sour grapes,
his teeth shall be set on edge.

---

goodness of the Lord are bountiful crops, flocks, and vineyards (Ps. 65).

31:14 *I will satiate the soul of the priests with abundance.* The theme of joy is summarized in God's intention to fill the priests and the people with abundance. Jeremiah gave the people hope and comfort in facing the poverty and oppression of exile and captivity.

31:19 *I struck myself on the thigh.* This indicates an outward demonstration of remorse over sin and change of life (Ezek. 21:12).

31:21 *signposts . . . landmarks.* These would point out the way to the people's homeland. More importantly, Israel was instructed to set its heart toward the way that is the path of faith in its God.

31:27 *I will sow the house of Israel.* God would plant and multiply the seed of man and animal in the land of Judah.

31:28 *to build and to plant.* These are the same terms used in Jeremiah's call (1:10).

31:12 [v] Is. 58:11 [w] Is. 35:10; 65:19 **31:15** [x] Matt. 2:17, 18 [y] Josh. 18:25 [z] Gen. 37:35 [a] Jer. 10:20 **31:16** [b] [Is. 25:8; 30:19] **31:17** [c] Jer. 29:11 **31:18** [d] Ps. 94:12 [e] Lam. 5:21 **31:19** [f] Deut. 30:2 [g] Ezek. 36:31 **31:20** [h] Is. 63:15 [i] [Hos. 14:4] **31:21** [j] Jer. 50:5 **31:22** [k] Jer. 2:18, 23, 36 [l] Jer. 3:6, 8, 11, 12, 14, 22 **31:23** [m] Is. 1:26 [n] [Zech. 8:3] **31:24** [o] Jer. 33:12 **31:26** [p] Prov. 3:24 **31:27** [q] Ezek. 36:9–11 **31:28** [r] Jer. 44:27 [s] Jer. 1:10; 18:7 [t] Jer. 24:6 **31:29** [u] Ezek. 18:2, 3 **31:30** [v] [Gal. 6:5, 7]

A New Covenant

³¹"Behold, the ʷdays are coming, says the LORD, when I will make a new covenant with the house of Israel and with the house of Judah— ³²not according to the covenant that I made with their fathers in the day *that* ˣI took them by the hand to lead them out of the land of Egypt, My covenant which they broke, though I was a husband to them,* says the LORD. ³³ʸBut this *is* the covenant that I will make with the house of Israel after those days, says the LORD: ᶻI will put My law in their minds, and write it on their hearts; ᵃand I will be their God, and they shall be My people. ³⁴No more shall every man teach his neighbor, and every man his brother, saying, 'Know the LORD,' for ᵇthey all shall know Me, from the least of them to the greatest of them, says the LORD. For ᶜI will forgive their iniquity, and their sin I will remember no more."

35 Thus says the LORD,
     ᵈWho gives the sun for a light by
          day,
     The ordinances of the moon and the
          stars for a light by night,
     Who disturbs ᵉthe sea,
     And its waves roar
     ᶠ(The LORD of hosts *is* His name):

36 "If ᵍthose ordinances depart
     From before Me, says the LORD,

     Then the seed of Israel shall also
          cease
     From being a nation before Me
          forever."

³⁷Thus says the LORD:

     ʰ"If heaven above can be measured,
     And the foundations of the earth
          searched out beneath,
     I will also ᶦcast off all the seed of
          Israel
     For all that they have done, says the
          LORD.

³⁸"Behold, the days are coming, says the LORD, that the city shall be built for the LORD ʲfrom the Tower of Hananel to the Corner Gate. ³⁹ᵏThe surveyor's line shall again extend straight forward over the hill Gareb; then it shall turn toward Goath. ⁴⁰And the whole valley of the dead bodies and of the ashes, and all the fields as far as the Brook Kidron, ˡto the corner of the Horse Gate toward the east, ᵐ*shall be* holy to the LORD. It shall not be plucked up or thrown down anymore forever."

Jeremiah Buys a Field

32 The word that came to Jeremiah from the LORD ᵃin the tenth year of

---

* **31:32** Following Masoretic Text, Targum, and Vulgate; Septuagint and Syriac read *and I turned away from them.*

31:31–34 The New Covenant—The new covenant is called "new" in contrast to the covenant with Moses which is called "old" (Jer. 31:32; Heb. 8:6–13) because it actually accomplishes what the Mosaic covenant could only point to, that is, the child of God living in a manner that is consistent with the character of God. Four provisions are made in this covenant: (1) *Regeneration*—God will put His law in their inward parts and write it in their hearts (31:33), (2) *A national restoration*—Yahweh will be their God and the nation will be His people (31:33), (3) *Personal ministry of the Holy Spirit*—they will all be taught individually by God (31:34), and (4) *Full justification*—their sins will be forgiven and completely removed (31:34). The new covenant is made sure by the blood that Jesus shed on Calvary's cross. The blood that guarantees to Israel its new covenant also provides for the forgiveness of sins for the believers who comprise the church. Jesus' payment for sin is more than adequate to pay for the sins of all who will believe in Him.

31:32 the covenant that I made with their fathers. The old covenant demanded adherence to stipulations (Ex. 19:1—23:33) which the people were unable to keep. Above all other commandments, the people were commanded to love and serve God and abandon all others (Deut. 6:4–5). This they did not do. From the wilderness period (Ex. 32:1–10; Num. 25:1–9) until the days of Manasseh, the history of Israel was permeated with idolatrous activity, only occasionally broken by periods of true faithfulness to God. The people seemed incapable of acting in sustained obedience to the covenant. **husband.** As Hosea was to Gomer, the Lord had been a faithful and devoted husband to Israel.

31:33 the covenant that I will make. The new covenant would be initiated by God Himself, assuring its effectiveness. **after those days.** This expression looks forward to the time of fulfillment of the new covenant, which found fruition in the life, death, and resurrection of Jesus Christ.

31:34 No more shall every man teach. No longer would intermediaries like priests or prophets be needed to show the people how to know the Lord. Knowledge of God is a major theme of Jeremiah (2:8; 4:22; 5:4; 8:7). This knowledge is an intimate relationship with God evidenced by faith, obedience, and devotion.

31:36–37 If those ordinances depart. The foundation of the new covenant is as sure as the God who maintains creation. At the peak of Judah's apostasy, shortly before the destruction of the nation by Babylon in divine judgment, the Lord emphatically reaffirmed His covenant relationship with the Jewish people in such strong terms that the promise was unbreakable, even by Him. When we observe the sun, moon, or stars in the sky, we should remember God's promise to the Jewish people, even as God does.

31:31 ʷ Heb. 8:8–12; 10:16, 17   **31:32** ˣ Deut. 1:31   **31:33** ʸ Jer. 32:40 ᶻ Ps. 40:8 ᵃ Jer. 24:7; 30:22; 32:38   **31:34** ᵇ [John 6:45] ᶜ [Rom. 11:27]   **31:35** ᵈ Gen. 1:14–18 ᵉ Is. 51:15 ᶠ Jer. 10:16   **31:36** ᵍ Ps. 148:6   **31:37** ʰ Jer. 33:22 ᶦ [Rom. 11:2–5, 26, 27]   **31:38** ʲ Zech. 14:10   **31:39** ᵏ Zech. 2:1, 2   **31:40** ˡ Neh. 3:28 ᵐ [Joel 3:17]   **32:1** ᵃ Jer. 39:1, 2

Zedekiah king of Judah, which was the eighteenth year of Nebuchadnezzar. ²For then the king of Babylon's army besieged Jerusalem, and Jeremiah the prophet was shut up ^bin the court of the prison, which *was in* the king of Judah's house. ³For Zedekiah king of Judah had shut him up, saying, "Why do you ^cprophesy and say, 'Thus says the LORD: ^d"Behold, I will give this city into the hand of the king of Babylon, and he shall take it; ⁴and Zedekiah king of Judah ^eshall not escape from the hand of the Chaldeans, but shall surely be delivered into the hand of the king of Babylon, and shall speak with him face to face,* and see him ^feye to eye; ⁵then he shall ^glead Zedekiah to Babylon, and there he shall be ^huntil I visit him," says the LORD; ⁱ"though you fight with the Chaldeans, you shall not succeed"'?"

⁶And Jeremiah said, "The word of the LORD came to me, saying, ⁷'Behold, Hanamel the son of Shallum your uncle will come to you, saying, "Buy my field which *is* in Anathoth, for the ^jright of redemption *is* yours to buy *it*."' ⁸Then Hanamel my uncle's son came to me in the court of the prison according to the word of the LORD, and said to me, 'Please buy my field that *is* in Anathoth, which *is* in the country of Benjamin; for the right of inheritance *is* yours, and the redemption *yours*; buy *it* for yourself.' Then I knew that this was the word of the LORD. ⁹So I bought the field from Hanamel, the son of my uncle who *was* in Anathoth, and ^kweighed *out to* him the money—seventeen shekels of silver. ¹⁰And I signed the deed and sealed *it*, took witnesses, and weighed the money on the scales. ¹¹So I took the purchase deed, *both* that which was sealed *according* to the law and custom, and that which was open; ¹²and I gave the purchase deed to ^lBaruch the son of Neriah, son of Mahseiah, in the presence of Hanamel my uncle's *son*, and in the presence of the ^mwitnesses who signed the purchase deed, before all the Jews who sat in the court of the prison.

¹³"Then I charged ⁿBaruch before them, saying, ¹⁴'Thus says the LORD of hosts, the God of Israel: "Take these deeds, both this purchase deed which is sealed and this deed which is open, and put them in an earthen vessel, that they may last many days." ¹⁵For thus says the LORD of hosts, the God of Israel: "Houses and fields and vineyards shall be ^opossessed again in this land."'

Jeremiah Prays for Understanding

¹⁶"Now when I had delivered the purchase deed to Baruch the son of Neriah, I prayed to the LORD, saying: ¹⁷'Ah, Lord GOD! Behold, ^pYou have made the heavens and the earth by Your great power and outstretched arm. ^qThere is nothing too hard for You. ¹⁸*You* show ^rlovingkindness to thousands, and repay the iniquity of the fathers into the bosom of their children after them—the Great, ^sthe Mighty God, whose name *is* ^tthe LORD of hosts. ¹⁹*You are* ^ugreat in counsel and mighty in work, for Your ^veyes *are* open to all the ways of the sons of men, ^wto give everyone according to his ways and according to the fruit of his doings. ²⁰You have set signs and wonders in the land of Egypt, to this day, and in Israel and among *other* men; and You have made Yourself ^xa name, as it is this day. ²¹You ^yhave brought Your people Israel out of the land of Egypt with signs and wonders, with a strong hand and an outstretched arm, and with great terror; ²²You have given them this land, of which You swore to their fathers to give them—^z"a land flowing with milk and honey."* ²³And they came in and took possession of it, but ^athey have not obeyed Your voice or walked in Your law. They have done nothing of all that You commanded them to do; therefore You have caused all this calamity to come upon them.

²⁴'Look, the siege mounds! They have come to the city to take it; and the city has been given into the hand of the Chaldeans who fight against it, because of ^bthe sword and famine and pestilence. What You have spoken has happened; there You see it! ²⁵And You have said to me, O Lord GOD, "Buy the field for money, and take witnesses"!—yet the city has been given into the hand of the Chaldeans.'"

---

* **32:4** Literally *mouth to mouth*   * **32:22** Exodus 3:8

32:6–8 which is in Anathoth. The Lord instructed Jeremiah to purchase a field in his hometown three miles north of Jerusalem.

32:13–15 earthen vessel. Examples of storage jars that served as safety-deposit vessels have been excavated in Judah. The Dead Sea Scrolls were also stored in ceramic vessels, aiding their preservation for almost two thousand years. The illustrated message of the purchase was assurance and confirmation that restoration of the land was certain.

32:20–21 signs and wonders in the land of Egypt. The great historical demonstration of God's loyal love was the exodus of Israel from Egypt. The miracles that accompanied the exodus made God known among the nations such as Moab (Num. 22–24).

32:2 ^b Jer. 33:1; 37:21; 39:14   **32:3** ^c Jer. 26:8, 9 ^d Jer. 21:3–7; 34:2   **32:4** ^e Jer. 34:3; 38:18, 23; 39:5; 52:9 ^f Jer. 39:5   **32:5** ^g Ezek. 12:12, 13 ^h Jer. 27:22 ⁱ Jer. 21:4; 33:5   **32:7** ^j Ruth 4:4   **32:9** ^k Zech. 11:12   **32:12** ^l Jer. 36:4 ^m Is. 8:2   **32:13** ⁿ Jer. 36:4   **32:15** ^o [Jer. 31:5, 12, 14]   **32:17** ^p 2 Kin. 19:15 ^q Luke 18:27   **32:18** ^r Deut. 5:9, 10 ^s [Is. 9:6] ^t Jer. 10:16   **32:19** ^u Is. 28:29 ^v Prov. 5:21 ^w Jer. 17:10   **32:20** ^x Is. 63:12   **32:21** ^y Ex. 6:6   **32:22** ^z Ex. 3:8, 17   **32:23** ^a [Neh. 9:26]   **32:24** ^b Jer. 14:12

God's Assurance of the People's Return

26Then the word of the LORD came to Jeremiah, saying, 27"Behold, I *am* the LORD, the cGod of all flesh. Is there anything too hard for Me? 28Therefore thus says the LORD: 'Behold, I will give this city into the hand of the Chaldeans, into the hand of Nebuchadnezzar king of Babylon, and he shall take it. 29And the Chaldeans who fight against this city shall come and dset fire to this city and burn it, with the houses eon whose roofs they have offered incense to Baal and poured out drink offerings to other gods, to provoke Me to anger; 30because the children of Israel and the children of Judah fhave done only evil before Me from their youth. For the children of Israel have provoked Me only to anger with the work of their hands,' says the LORD. 31'For this city has been to Me *a provocation of* My anger and My fury from the day that they built it, even to this day; gso I will remove it from before My face 32because of all the evil of the children of Israel and the children of Judah, which they have done to provoke Me to anger—hthey, their kings, their princes, their priests, itheir prophets, the men of Judah, and the inhabitants of Jerusalem. 33And they have turned to Me the jback, and not the face; though I taught them, krising up early and teaching *them,* yet they have not listened to receive instruction. 34But they lset their abominations in the house which is called by My name, to defile it. 35And they built the high places of Baal which *are* in the Valley of the Son of Hinnom, to mcause their sons and their daughters to pass through *the fire* to nMolech, owhich I did not command them, nor did it come into My mind that they should do this abomination, to cause Judah to sin."

36"Now therefore, thus says the LORD, the God of Israel, concerning this city of which you say, 'It shall be delivered into the hand of the king of Babylon by the sword, by the famine, and by the pestilence: 37Behold, I will pgather them out of all countries where I have driven them in My anger, in My fury, and in great wrath; I will bring them back to this place, and I will cause them qto dwell safely. 38They shall be rMy people, and I will be their God; 39then I will sgive them one heart and one way, that they may fear Me forever, for the good of them and their children after them. 40And tI will make an everlasting covenant with them, that I will not turn away from doing them good; but uI will put My fear in their hearts so that they will not depart from Me. 41Yes, vI will rejoice over them to do them good, and wI will assuredly plant them in this land, with all My heart and with all My soul."

42"For thus says the LORD: x'Just as I have brought all this great calamity on this people, so I will bring on them all the good that I have promised them. 43And fields will be bought in this land yof which you say, *"It is* desolate, without man or beast; it has been given into the hand of the Chaldeans." 44Men will buy fields for money, sign deeds and seal *them,* and take witnesses, in zthe land of Benjamin, in the places around Jerusalem, in the cities of Judah, in the cities of the mountains, in the cities of the lowland, and in the cities of the South; for aI will cause their captives to return,' says the LORD."

Excellence of the Restored Nation

33 Moreover the word of the LORD came to Jeremiah a second time, while he was still ashut up in the court of the prison, saying, 2"Thus says the LORD bwho made it, the LORD who formed it to establish it c(the LORD *is* His name): 3d'Call to Me, and I will answer you, and show you great and mighty things, which you do not know.'

4"For thus says the LORD, the God of Israel, concerning the houses of this city and the houses of the kings of Judah, which have been pulled down *to fortify** against ethe siege mounds and the sword: 5'They come to fight with the Chaldeans, but *only* to ffill their places* with the dead bodies of men whom I will slay in My anger and My fury, all for whose wickedness I have

---

* **33:4** Compare Isaiah 22:10   * **33:5** Compare 2 Kings 23:14

32:27 the God of all flesh. God was Lord over Israel and Judah, and Lord over the nations (27:11), including mighty Babylon (25:15–26).

32:39 one heart and one way. Because the Lord had written on the heart of the people a new covenant (31:33), no longer would they worship other deities and turn to foreign nations for help. The word "way" is often used in Jeremiah to denote the character of a person's life, whether evil (4:18) or good (7:23).

32:40 everlasting covenant. This expression is also found in Isaiah 55:3; Ezekiel 16:60; 37:26. In Ezekiel it is equated with a covenant of peace that God will establish with His people. This covenant will be everlasting, unlike the Sinai covenant which had been broken and ignored for so long.

33:1 while he was still shut up. A chronological tie is made to 32:2 (588 B.C.). Jeremiah had been placed under palace court guard because of what his enemies regarded as seditious speeches, announcing

---

32:27 c [Num. 16:22]   **32:29** d 2 Chr. 36:19   e Jer. 19:13
32:30 f Jer. 2:7; 3:25; 7:22–26   **32:31** g 2 Kin. 23:27; 24:3
32:32 h Dan. 9:8   i Jer. 23:14   **32:33** j Jer. 2:27; 7:24   k Jer.
7:13   **32:34** l Jer. 7:10–12, 30; 23:11   **32:35** m Jer. 7:31;
19:5   n Lev. 18:21   o Jer. 7:31   **32:37** p Deut. 30:3   q Jer.
33:16   **32:38** r [Jer. 24:7; 30:22; 31:33]   **32:39** s [Ezek.
11:19]   **32:40** t Is. 55:3   u [Jer. 31:33]   **32:41** v Deut.
30:9   w Amos 9:15   **32:42** x Jer. 31:28   **32:43** y Jer. 33:10
32:44 z Jer. 17:26   a Jer. 33:7, 11   **33:1** a Jer. 32:2, 3
33:2 b Is. 37:26   c Ex. 15:3   **33:3** d Jer. 29:12   **33:4** e Is.
22:10   **33:5** f 2 Kin. 23:14

hidden My face from this city. ⁶Behold, ᵍI will bring it health and healing; I will heal them and reveal to them the abundance of peace and truth. ⁷And ʰI will cause the captives of Judah and the captives of Israel to return, and will rebuild those places ⁱas at the first. ⁸I will ʲcleanse them from all their iniquity by which they have sinned against Me, and I will pardon all their iniquities by which they have sinned and by which they have transgressed against Me. ⁹ᵏThen it shall be to Me a name of joy, a praise, and an honor before all nations of the earth, who shall hear all the good that I do to them; they shall ˡfear and tremble for all the goodness and all the prosperity that I provide for it.'

¹⁰"Thus says the LORD: 'Again there shall be heard in this place—ᵐof which you say, "It *is* desolate, without man and without beast"—in the cities of Judah, in the streets of Jerusalem that are desolate, without man and without inhabitant and without beast, ¹¹the ⁿvoice of joy and the voice of gladness, the voice of the bridegroom and the voice of the bride, the voice of those who will say:

ᵒ"Praise the LORD of hosts,
 For the LORD *is* good,
 For His mercy *endures* forever"—

and of those *who will* bring ᵖthe sacrifice of praise into the house of the LORD. For I will cause the captives of the land to return as at the first,' says the LORD.

¹²"Thus says the LORD of hosts: ᵠ'In this place which is desolate, without man and without beast, and in all its cities, there shall again be a dwelling place of shepherds causing *their* flocks to lie down. ¹³ʳIn the cities of the mountains, in the cities of the lowland, in the cities of the South, in the land of Benjamin, in the places around Jerusalem, and in the cities of Judah, the flocks shall again ˢpass under the hands of him who counts *them*,' says the LORD.

¹⁴ᵗ'Behold, the days are coming,' says the LORD, 'that ᵘI will perform that good thing which I have promised to the house of Israel and to the house of Judah:

¹⁵ 'In those days and at that time
 I will cause to grow up to David

A ᵛBranch of righteousness;
 He shall execute judgment and
  righteousness in the earth.
¹⁶ In those days Judah will be saved,
 And Jerusalem will dwell safely.
 And this *is the name* by which she will
  be called:

THE LORD OUR RIGHTEOUSNESS.'*

¹⁷"For thus says the LORD: 'David shall never ʷlack a man to sit on the throne of the house of Israel; ¹⁸nor shall the ˣpriests, the Levites, lack a man to ʸoffer burnt offerings before Me, to kindle grain offerings, and to sacrifice continually.'"

The Permanence of God's Covenant

¹⁹And the word of the LORD came to Jeremiah, saying, ²⁰"Thus says the LORD: 'If you can break My covenant with the day and My covenant with the night, so that there will not be day and night in their season, ²¹then ᶻMy covenant may also be broken with David My servant, so that he shall not have a son to reign on his throne, and with the Levites, the priests, My ministers. ²²As ᵃthe host of heaven cannot be numbered, nor the sand of the sea measured, so will I ᵇmultiply the descendants of David My servant and the ᶜLevites who minister to Me.'"

²³Moreover the word of the LORD came to Jeremiah, saying, ²⁴"Have you not considered what these people have spoken, saying, 'The two families which the LORD has chosen, He has also cast them off'? Thus they have ᵈdespised My people, as if they should no more be a nation before them.

²⁵"Thus says the LORD: 'If ᵉMy covenant *is* not with day and night, *and if* I have not ᶠappointed the ordinances of heaven and earth, ²⁶ᵍthen I will ʰcast away the descendants of Jacob and David My servant, *so* that I will not take *any* of his descendants *to be* rulers over the descendants of Abraham, Isaac, and Jacob. For I will cause their captives to return, and will have mercy on them.'"

---

* 33:16 Compare 23:5, 6

---

the fall of Jerusalem and giving advice to Zedekiah to surrender to Nebuchadnezzar.
33:8 cleanse . . . pardon. Forgiveness is described with these two terms. The word "cleanse" describes ritual purification of what is physically or spiritually unclean or defiled, like Israel and Judah (2:23; 7:30). "Pardon" means "to forgive," and in the Old Testament is used only with God as the subject as He forgives man. This fact helps us understand the reaction of the scribes when they heard Jesus forgiving sins (Mark 2:7).
33:13 flocks shall again pass under. The term "flocks" is used to depict the Israelites as they returned from captivity into the fold of the holy city of Jerusalem.
33:16 will dwell safely. Following the devastation

of the Babylonian onslaught, Jerusalem would exist under divine protection.
33:17 David shall never lack. The Davidic covenant of divine succession is reiterated (2 Sam. 7:12–16). The Levitical priesthood would likewise be heirs to a

---

33:6 ᵍ Jer. 30:17   33:7 ʰ Jer. 30:3; 32:44   ⁱ Is. 1:26
33:8 ʲ Zech. 13:1   33:9 ᵏ Is. 62:7   ˡ Is. 60:5   33:10 ᵐ Jer.
32:43   33:11 ⁿ Rev. 18:23   ᵒ Is. 12:4   ᵖ Lev. 7:12
33:12 ᵠ Is. 65:10   33:13 ʳ Jer. 17:26; 32:44   ˢ Lev. 27:32
33:14 ᵗ Jer. 23:5; 31:27, 31   ᵘ Jer. 29:10; 32:42   33:15 ᵛ Jer.
23:5   33:17 ʷ 2 Sam. 7:16   ˣ Ezek. 44:15   ʸ [1 Pet.
2:5, 9]   33:21 ᶻ 2 Sam. 23:5; Ps. 89:34   33:22 ᵃ Gen.
15:5; 22:17   ᵇ Jer. 30:19   ᶜ Is. 66:21   33:24 ᵈ Esth. 3:6–8
33:25 ᵉ Gen. 8:22   ᶠ Ps. 74:16; 104:19   33:26 ᵍ Jer. 31:37
ʰ Rom. 11:1, 2

Zedekiah Warned by God

34 The word which came to Jeremiah from the LORD, *a*when Nebuchadnezzar king of Babylon and all his army, *b*all the kingdoms of the earth under his dominion, and all the people, fought against Jerusalem and all its cities, saying, 2"Thus says the LORD, the God of Israel: 'Go and *c*speak to Zedekiah king of Judah and tell him, "Thus says the LORD: 'Behold, *d*I will give this city into the hand of the king of Babylon, and he shall burn it with fire. 3And *e*you shall not escape from his hand, but shall surely be taken and delivered into his hand; your eyes shall see the eyes of the king of Babylon, he shall speak with you *f*face to face,* and you shall go to Babylon.' " ' 4Yet hear the word of the LORD, O Zedekiah king of Judah! Thus says the LORD concerning you: 'You shall not die by the sword. 5You shall die in peace; as in *g*the ceremonies of your fathers, the former kings who were before you, *h*so they shall burn *incense* for you and *i*lament for you, *saying*, "Alas, lord!" For I have pronounced the word, says the LORD.' "

6Then Jeremiah the prophet spoke all these words to Zedekiah king of Judah in Jerusalem, 7when the king of Babylon's army fought against Jerusalem and all the cities of Judah that were left, against Lachish and Azekah; for *only j*these fortified cities remained of the cities of Judah.

Treacherous Treatment of Slaves

8*This is* the word that came to Jeremiah from the LORD, after King Zedekiah had made a covenant with all the people who *were* at Jerusalem to proclaim *k*liberty to them: 9*l*that every man should set free his male and female slave—a Hebrew man or woman—*m*that no one should keep a Jewish brother in bondage. 10Now when all the princes and all the people, who had entered into the covenant, heard that everyone should set free his male and female slaves, that no one should keep them in bondage anymore, they obeyed and let *them* go. 11But afterward they changed their minds and made the male and female slaves return, whom they had set free, and brought them into subjection as male and female slaves.

12Therefore the word of the LORD came to Jeremiah from the LORD, saying, 13"Thus says the LORD, the God of Israel: 'I made a *n*covenant with your fathers in the day that I brought them out of the land of Egypt, out of the house of bondage, saying, 14"At the end of *o*seven years let every man set free his Hebrew brother, who has been sold to him; and when he has served you six years, you shall let him go free from you." But your fathers did not obey Me nor incline their ear. 15Then you recently turned and did what was right in My sight—every man proclaiming liberty to his neighbor; and you *p*made a covenant before Me *q*in the house which is called by My name. 16Then you turned around and *r*profaned My name, and every one of you brought back his male and female slaves, whom you had set at liberty, at their pleasure, and brought them back into subjection, to be your male and female slaves.'

17"Therefore thus says the LORD: 'You have not obeyed Me in proclaiming liberty, every one to his brother and every one to his neighbor. *s*Behold, I proclaim liberty to you,' says the LORD—*t*'to the sword, to pestilence, and to famine! And I will deliver you to *u*trouble among all the kingdoms of the earth. 18And I will give the men who have transgressed My covenant, who have

---

* **34:3** Literally *mouth to mouth*

---

divine succession in overseeing the sacrificial system in the Jerusalem temple. Jesus, as Priest and King, fulfills both offices in the new covenant.

34:3 *you shall not escape from his hand.* Though Zedekiah attempted to flee to Jericho, Nebuchadnezzar's forces captured and brought him to Riblah for a face-to-face meeting with Nebuchadnezzar (32:3–4).

34:5 *You shall die in peace.* Jeremiah proclaimed the destruction of Jerusalem and the death of its inhabitants by sword, pestilence, and famine. The particular implications for Zedekiah are outlined here. He would not be executed by the sword. According to 2 Kings 25:6–7, his sons were killed before his eyes and then his eyes were put out before being taken to Babylon.

34:8 *Zedekiah had made a covenant with all the people.* A legal agreement was made between Zedekiah and the people of Jerusalem during the Babylonian siege to release from bondage all Hebrew slaves.

34:12–14 *Thus says the LORD.* Jeremiah, a faithful steward of the word of God, began his attack against Judah's leaders by recounting the teaching of the law on the matter of emancipating slaves (Ex. 21:2–6;

Deut. 15:12–15). He reminded the people that their forefathers were slaves in Egypt, and that God had freed them from slavery and oppression.

34:16 *turned around and profaned My name.* When the princes of Judah emancipated their Hebrew slaves, it demonstrated their covenant faithfulness and devotion to God (v. 10). But when the righteous decision was reversed (v. 11), the name of God was profaned. The name of God sums up and represents His attributes, character, and work. That name had been defiled by the breach of covenant in the same way that the people had defiled the land with their idolatry (16:18).

34:18–19 *they cut the calf in two.* The covenant ceremony is outlined. The main ritual of the two-party covenant began with cutting the sacrificial animal

34:1 *a* 2 Kin. 25:1 *b* Jer. 1:15; 25:9   **34:2** *c* 2 Chr. 36:11, 12 *d* Jer. 21:10; 32:3, 28   **34:3** *e* 2 Kin. 25:4, 5 *f* Jer. 32:4; 39:5, 6   **34:5** *g* 2 Chr. 16:14; 21:19 *h* Dan. 2:46 *i* Jer. 22:18   **34:7** *j* 2 Kin. 18:13; 19:8   **34:8** *k* Ex. 21:2   **34:9** *l* Neh. 5:11 *m* Lev. 25:39–46   **34:13** *n* Ex. 24:3, 7, 8   **34:14** *o* Deut. 15:12   **34:15** *p* Neh. 10:29 *q* Jer. 7:10   **34:16** *r* Ex. 20:7   **34:17** *s* [Matt. 7:2] *t* Jer. 32:24, 36 *u* Deut. 28:25, 64

not performed the words of the covenant which they made before Me, when ᵛthey cut the calf in two and passed between the parts of it— ¹⁹the princes of Judah, the princes of Jerusalem, the eunuchs, the priests, and all the people of the land who passed between the parts of the calf— ²⁰I will ʷgive them into the hand of their enemies and into the hand of those who seek their life. Their ˣdead bodies shall be for meat for the birds of the heaven and the beasts of the earth. ²¹And I will give Zedekiah king of Judah and his princes into the hand of their enemies, into the hand of those who seek their life, and into the hand of the king of Babylon's army ʸwhich has gone back from you. ²²ᶻBehold, I will command,' says the LORD, 'and cause them to return to this city. They will fight against it ᵃand take it and burn it with fire; and ᵇI will make the cities of Judah a desolation without inhabitant.'"

The Obedient Rechabites

35 The word which came to Jeremiah from the LORD in the days of Jehoiakim the son of Josiah, king of Judah, saying, ²"Go to the house of the ᵃRechabites, speak to them, and bring them into the house of the LORD, into one of ᵇthe chambers, and give them wine to drink."

³Then I took Jaazaniah the son of Jeremiah, the son of Habazziniah, his brothers and all his sons, and the whole house of the Rechabites, ⁴and I brought them into the house of the LORD, into the chamber of the sons of Hanan the son of Igdaliah, a man of God, which was by the chamber of the princes, above the chamber of Maaseiah the son of Shallum, ᶜthe keeper of the door. ⁵Then I set before the sons of the house of the Rechabites bowls full of wine, and cups; and I said to them, "Drink wine."

⁶But they said, "We will drink no wine, for ᵈJonadab the son of Rechab, our father, commanded us, saying, 'You shall drink ᵉno wine, you nor your sons, forever. ⁷You shall not build a house, sow seed, plant a vineyard, nor have any of these; but all your days you shall dwell in tents, ᶠthat you may live many days in the land where you are sojourners.' ⁸Thus we have ᵍobeyed the voice of Jonadab the son of Rechab, our father, in all that he charged us, to drink no wine all our days, we, our wives, our sons, or our daughters, ⁹nor to build ourselves houses to dwell in; nor do we have vineyard, field, or seed. ¹⁰But we have dwelt in tents, and have obeyed and done according to all that Jonadab our father commanded us. ¹¹But it came to pass, when Nebuchadnezzar king of Babylon came up into the land, that we said, 'Come, let us ʰgo to Jerusalem for fear of the army of the Chaldeans and for fear of the army of the Syrians.' So we dwell at Jerusalem."

¹²Then came the word of the LORD to Jeremiah, saying, ¹³"Thus says the LORD of hosts, the God of Israel: 'Go and tell the men of Judah and the inhabitants of Jerusalem, "Will you not ⁱreceive instruction to obey My words?" says the LORD. ¹⁴The words of Jonadab the son of Rechab, which he commanded his sons, not to drink wine, are performed; for to this day they drink none, and obey their father's commandment. ʲBut although I have spoken to you, ᵏrising early and speaking, you did not obey Me. ¹⁵I have also sent to you all My ˡservants the prophets, rising up early and sending them, saying, ᵐ"Turn now everyone from his evil way, amend your doings, and do not go after other gods to serve them; then you will ⁿdwell in the land which I have given you and your fathers.' But you have not inclined your ear, nor obeyed Me. ¹⁶Surely the sons of Jonadab the son of Rechab have performed the commandment of their ᵒfather, which he commanded them, but this people has not obeyed Me."'

¹⁷"Therefore thus says the LORD God of hosts, the God of Israel: 'Behold, I will bring on Judah and on all the inhabitants of Jerusalem all the doom that I have pronounced against them; ᵖbecause I have spoken to them but they have not heard, and I have called to them but they have not answered.'"

¹⁸And Jeremiah said to the house of the Rechabites, "Thus says the LORD of hosts, the God of Israel: 'Because you have obeyed the commandment of Jonadab your father, and kept all his precepts and done according to all that he commanded you, ¹⁹therefore thus says the LORD of hosts, the

---

in half, after which the two participants would walk together between the parts (Gen. 15). The divided animal portrayed the potential fate of one who broke the covenant stipulations.

35:2 the house of the Rechabites. This clan was a tightly knit group of descendants of the Kenites (Judg. 1:16; 1 Chr. 2:55). They lived as nomads, rejecting all forms of urban and agrarian life. They refused to drink wine or strong drink and would not cultivate vineyards. They also would not plant any other crops. They were invited by Jeremiah into one of the chambers surrounding the courtyard of the temple of God for a symbolic demonstration.

35:13–16 obey their father's commandment. The Rechabites held to the teaching of their forefather, while the Israelites continually rebelled against the teaching of God.

34:18 ᵛGen. 15:10, 17 **34:20** ʷJer. 22:25 ˣJer. 7:33; 16:4; 19:7 **34:21** ʸJer. 37:5–11; 39:4–7 **34:22** ᶻJer. 37:8, 10 ᵃJer. 38:3; 39:1, 2, 8; 52:7, 13 ᵇJer. 9:11; 44:2, 6 **35:2** ᵃ1 Chr. 2:55 ᵇ1 Kin. 6:5, 8 **35:4** ᶜ1 Chr. 9:18, 19 **35:6** ᵈ2 Kin. 10:15, 23 ᵉLuke 1:15 **35:7** ᶠEx. 20:12 **35:8** ᵍ[Col. 3:20] **35:11** ʰJer. 4:5–7; 8:14 **35:13** ⁱJer. 6:10; 17:23; 32:33 **35:14** ʲ2 Chr. 36:15 ᵏJer. 7:13; 25:3 **35:15** ˡJer. 26:4, 5; 29:19 ᵐJer. 18:11; 25:5, 6 ⁿJer. 7:7; 25:5, 6 **35:16** ᵒ[Heb. 12:9] **35:17** ᵖProv. 1:24

God of Israel: "Jonadab the son of Rechab shall not lack a man to ᵃstand before Me forever."'"

The Scroll Read in the Temple

36 Now it came to pass in the ᵃfourth year of Jehoiakim the son of Josiah, king of Judah, *that* this word came to Jeremiah from the LORD, saying: ²"Take a ᵇscroll of a book and ᶜwrite on it all the words that I have spoken to you against Israel, against Judah, and against ᵈall the nations, from the day I spoke to you, from the days of ᵉJosiah even to this day. ³It ᶠmay be that the house of Judah will hear all the adversities which I purpose to bring upon them, that everyone may ᵍturn from his evil way, that I may forgive their iniquity and their sin."

⁴Then Jeremiah ʰcalled Baruch the son of Neriah; and ⁱBaruch wrote on a scroll of a book, at the instruction of Jeremiah,* all the words of the LORD which He had spoken to him. ⁵And Jeremiah commanded Baruch, saying, "I *am* confined, I cannot go into the house of the LORD. ⁶You go, therefore, and read from the scroll which you have written at my instruction,* the words of the LORD, in the hearing of the people in the LORD's house on ʲthe day of fasting. And you shall also read them in the hearing of all Judah who come from their cities. ⁷It may be that they will present their supplication before the LORD, and everyone will turn from his evil way. For great *is* the anger and the fury that the LORD has pronounced against this people." ⁸And Baruch the son of Neriah did according to all that Jeremiah the prophet commanded him, reading from the book the words of the LORD in the LORD's house.

⁹Now it came to pass in the fifth year of Jehoiakim the son of Josiah, king of Judah, in the ninth month, *that* they proclaimed a fast before the LORD to all the people in Jerusalem, and to all the people who came from the cities of Judah to Jerusalem. ¹⁰Then Baruch read from the book the words of Jeremiah in the house of the LORD, in the chamber of Gemariah the son of Shaphan the scribe, in the upper court at the ᵏentry of the New Gate of the LORD's house, in the hearing of all the people.

The Scroll Read in the Palace

¹¹When Michaiah the son of Gemariah, the son of Shaphan, heard all the words of the LORD from the book, ¹²he then went down to the king's house, into the scribe's chamber; and there all the princes were sitting—ˡElishama the scribe, Delaiah the son of Shemaiah, ᵐElnathan the son of Achbor, Gemariah the son of Shaphan, Zedekiah the son of Hananiah, and all the princes. ¹³Then Michaiah declared to them all the words that he had heard when Baruch read the book in the hearing of the people. ¹⁴Therefore all the princes sent Jehudi the son of Nethaniah, the son of Shelemiah, the son of Cushi, to Baruch, saying, "Take in your hand the scroll from which you have read in the hearing of the people, and come." So Baruch the son of Neriah took the scroll in his hand and came to them. ¹⁵And they said to him, "Sit down now, and read it in our hearing." So Baruch read *it* in their hearing.

¹⁶Now it happened, when they had heard all the words, that they looked in fear from one to another, and said to Baruch, "We will surely tell the king of all these words." ¹⁷And they asked Baruch, saying, "Tell us now, how did you write all these words—at his instruction?"*

¹⁸So Baruch answered them, "He proclaimed with his mouth all these words to me, and I wrote *them* with ink in the book." ¹⁹Then the princes said to Baruch, "Go and hide, you and Jeremiah; and let no one know where you are."

The King Destroys Jeremiah's Scroll

²⁰And they went to the king, into the court; but they stored the scroll in the chamber of Elishama the scribe, and told all the words in the hearing of the king. ²¹So the king sent Jehudi to bring the scroll, and he took it from Elishama the scribe's chamber. And Jehudi read it in the hearing of the king and in the hearing of all the princes who stood beside the king. ²²Now the king was sitting in ⁿthe

* **36:4** Literally *from Jeremiah's mouth* * **36:6** Literally *from my mouth* * **36:17** Literally *with his mouth*

36:2 *Take a scroll of a book and write on it.* The usual material for a scroll was parchment (a kind of leather), though Egyptian papyrus was also available. The contents of the scroll were the oracles dating from the days of Josiah, at the advent of Jeremiah's ministry (626 B.C.).

36:6 *read from the scroll.* This scroll was to be read on a day of fasting, a time set aside by official declaration of the king or priests (v. 9) in a period of national crisis.

36:8 *Baruch . . . did according to all that Jeremiah the prophet commanded him.* As a faithful disciple, Baruch read from the book of God's words in the temple of the Lord. This act closely parallels the reading

of the Book of the Law in the temple after it was discovered there under Josiah.

36:20–24 *cut it with the scribe's knife.* Jehoiakim showed no signs of fear or lamentation, unlike Josiah when the Book of the Law was read in his hearing (2 Kin. 22:11–13). Instead he cuts the scroll up and throws it into a fire.

35:19 ᵍ Jer. 15:19 **36:1** ᵃ Jer. 25:1, 3; 45:1 **36:2** ᵇ Zech. 5:1 ᶜ Jer. 30:2 ᵈ Jer. 25:15 ᵉ Jer. 25:3 **36:3** ᶠ Jer. 26:3 ᵍ Jon. 3:8 **36:4** ʰ Jer. 32:12 ⁱ Jer. 45:1 **36:6** ʲ Acts 27:9 **36:10** ᵏ Jer. 26:10 **36:12** ˡ Jer. 41:1 ᵐ Jer. 26:22 **36:22** ⁿ Amos 3:15

winter house in the ninth month, with *a fire* burning on the hearth before him. ²³And it happened, when Jehudi had read three or four columns, *that the king* cut it with the scribe's knife and cast *it* into the fire that *was* on the hearth, until all the scroll was consumed in the fire that *was* on the hearth. ²⁴Yet they were ^onot afraid, nor did they ^ptear their garments, the king nor any of his servants who heard all these words. ²⁵Nevertheless Elnathan, Delaiah, and Gemariah implored the king not to burn the scroll; but he would not listen to them. ²⁶And the king commanded Jerahmeel the king's* son, Seraiah the son of Azriel, and Shelemiah the son of Abdeel, to seize Baruch the scribe and Jeremiah the prophet, but the LORD hid them.

Jeremiah Rewrites the Scroll

²⁷Now after the king had burned the scroll with the words which Baruch had written at the instruction of Jeremiah,* the word of the LORD came to Jeremiah, saying: ²⁸"Take yet another scroll, and write on it all the former words that were in the first scroll which Jehoiakim the king of Judah has burned. ²⁹And you shall say to Jehoiakim king of Judah, 'Thus says the LORD: "You have burned this scroll, saying, ^q'Why have you written in it that the king of Babylon will certainly come and destroy this land, and cause man and beast to ^rcease from here?'"' ³⁰Therefore thus says the LORD concerning Jehoiakim king of Judah: ^s"He shall have no one to sit on the throne of David, and his dead body shall be ^tcast out to the heat of the day and the frost of the night. ³¹I will punish him, his family, and his servants for their iniquity; and I will bring on them, on the inhabitants of Jerusalem, and on the men of Judah all the doom that I have pronounced against them; but they did not heed."'"

³²Then Jeremiah took another scroll and gave it to Baruch the scribe, the son of Neriah, who wrote on it at the instruction of Jeremiah* all the words of the book which Jehoiakim king of Judah had burned in the fire. And besides, there were added to them many similar words.

Zedekiah's Vain Hope

37 Now King ^aZedekiah the son of Josiah reigned instead of Coniah the son of Jehoiakim, whom Nebuchadnezzar king of Babylon made king in the land of Judah. ^{2b}But neither he nor his servants nor the people of the land gave heed to the words of the LORD which He spoke by the prophet Jeremiah.

³And Zedekiah the king sent Jehucal the son of Shelemiah, and ^cZephaniah the son of Maaseiah, the priest, to the prophet Jeremiah, saying, ^d"Pray now to the LORD our God for us." ⁴Now Jeremiah was coming and going among the people, for they had not yet put him in prison. ⁵Then ^ePharaoh's army came up from Egypt; and when the Chaldeans who were besieging Jerusalem heard news of them, they departed from Jerusalem.

⁶Then the word of the LORD came to the prophet Jeremiah, saying, ⁷"Thus says the LORD, the God of Israel, 'Thus you shall say to the king of Judah, ^fwho sent you to Me to inquire of Me: "Behold, Pharaoh's army which has come up to help you will return to Egypt, to their own land. ^{8g}And the Chaldeans shall come back and fight against this city, and take it and burn it with fire."' ⁹Thus says the LORD: 'Do not deceive yourselves, saying, "The Chaldeans will surely depart from us," for they will not depart. ^{10h}For though you had defeated the whole army of the Chaldeans who fight against you, and there remained *only* wounded men among them, they would rise up, every man in his tent, and burn the city with fire.'"

---

* **36:26** Hebrew *Hammelech*   * **36:27** Literally *from Jeremiah's mouth*   * **36:32** Literally *from Jeremiah's mouth*

36:29–31 to Jehoiakim king of Judah. Indictment and judgment against Jehoiakim is pronounced. The indictment was declared because he destroyed the scroll of the Word of the Lord. First, the Davidic lineage would not continue through him. His son would rule for only three months before Nebuchadnezzar deported Jehoiachin to Babylon, where he died. Second, the king's body would be treated disgracefully after his death. As the king had cast the scroll into the fire, so his body would be cast from the royal palace. Third, the royal household would experience the destructive judgment that had been proclaimed in the words of the original scroll.

37:2 neither he nor his servants nor the people of the land gave heed. It is eminently possible and easy to reject God's message. As Zedekiah and all the people did, so can we deliberately refuse to heed the Lord, even when events have shown the truth of His message.

37:5 Pharaoh's army came up from Egypt. In late spring or early summer 588 B.C., Pharaoh Hophra led the Egyptian army into southern Palestine. The Babylonian forces withdrew their siege of Jerusalem to confront the Egyptians. Zedekiah hoped the Babylonians would be defeated, but his hopes proved to be in vain.

37:9 Do not deceive yourselves. To think that the brief respite caused by the Egyptian appearance in the southern coastal plain was proof of imminent deliverance, as the false prophets declared, was an exercise in self-deception and futile imagination.

36:24 ^o[Ps. 36:1] ^pIs. 36:22; 37:1   **36:29** ^qJer. 32:3
^rJer. 25:9–11; 26:9   **36:30** ^sJer. 22:30 ^tJer. 22:19
37:1 ^a2 Kin. 24:17   **37:2** ^b2 Chr. 36:12–16   **37:3** ^cJer. 21:1, 2; 29:25; 52:24   ^dJer. 42:2   **37:5** ^eEzek. 17:15
37:7 ^fJer. 21:2   **37:8** ^gJer. 34:22   **37:10** ^hJer. 21:4, 5

Jeremiah Imprisoned

¹¹And it happened, when the army of the Chaldeans left *the siege* of Jerusalem for fear of Pharaoh's army, ¹²that Jeremiah went out of Jerusalem to go into the land of Benjamin to claim his property there among the people. ¹³And when he was in the Gate of Benjamin, a captain of the guard *was* there whose name *was* Irijah the son of Shelemiah, the son of Hananiah; and he seized Jeremiah the prophet, saying, "You are defecting to the Chaldeans!"

¹⁴Then Jeremiah said, "False! I am not defecting to the Chaldeans." But he did not listen to him.

So Irijah seized Jeremiah and brought him to the princes. ¹⁵Therefore the princes were angry with Jeremiah, and they struck him ⁱand put him in prison in the ʲhouse of Jonathan the scribe. For they had made that the prison.

¹⁶When Jeremiah entered ᵏthe dungeon and the cells, and Jeremiah had remained there many days, ¹⁷then Zedekiah the king sent and took him *out*. The king asked him secretly in his house, and said, "Is there *any* word from the LORD?"

And Jeremiah said, "There is." Then he said, "You shall be ˡdelivered into the hand of the king of Babylon!"

¹⁸Moreover Jeremiah said to King Zedekiah, "What offense have I committed against you, against your servants, or against this people, that you have put me in prison? ¹⁹Where now *are* your prophets who prophesied to you, saying, 'The king of Babylon will not come against you or against this land'? ²⁰Therefore please hear now, O my lord the king. Please, let my petition be accepted before you, and do not make me return to the house of Jonathan the scribe, lest I die there."

²¹Then Zedekiah the king commanded that they should commit Jeremiah ᵐto the court of the prison, and that they should give him daily a piece of bread from the bakers' street, ⁿuntil all the bread in the city was gone. Thus Jeremiah remained in the court of the prison.

Jeremiah in the Dungeon

38 Now Shephatiah the son of Mattan, Gedaliah the son of Pashhur, ᵃJucal* the son of Shelemiah, and ᵇPashhur the son of Malchiah ᶜheard the words that Jeremiah had spoken to all the people, saying, ²"Thus says the LORD: ᵈ'He who remains in this city shall die by the sword, by famine, and by pestilence; but he who goes over to the Chaldeans shall live; his life shall be as a prize to him, and he shall live.'* ³Thus says the LORD: ᵉ'This city shall surely be ᶠgiven into the hand of the king of Babylon's army, which shall take it.'"

⁴Therefore the princes said to the king, "Please, ᵍlet this man be put to death, for thus he weakens the hands of the men of war who remain in this city, and the hands of all the people, by speaking such words to them. For this man does not seek the welfare of this people, but their harm."

⁵Then Zedekiah the king said, "Look, he *is* in your hand. For the king can *do* nothing against you." ⁶ʰSo they took Jeremiah and cast him into the dungeon of Malchiah the king's* son, which *was* in the court of the prison, and they let Jeremiah down with ropes. And in the dungeon *there was* no water, but mire. So Jeremiah sank in the mire.

⁷ⁱNow Ebed-Melech the Ethiopian, one of the eunuchs, who was in the king's house, heard that they had put Jeremiah in the dungeon. When the king was sitting at the Gate of Benjamin, ⁸Ebed-Melech went out of the king's house and spoke to the king, saying, ⁹"My lord the king, these men have done evil in all that they have done to Jeremiah the prophet, whom they have cast into the dungeon, and he is likely to die from hunger in the place where he is. For *there is* ʲno more bread in the city." ¹⁰Then the king commanded Ebed-Melech the Ethiopian, saying, "Take from here thirty men with you, and lift Jeremiah the prophet out of the dungeon before he dies." ¹¹So Ebed-Melech took the men with

---

* **38:1** Same as *Jehucal* (compare 37:3)
* **38:2** Compare 21:9   * **38:6** Hebrew *Hammelech*

37:14–16 *I am not defecting to the Chaldeans.* Jeremiah denied the accusation of defection, but to no avail. Irijah arrested the prophet and arraigned him before the court of princes. Prison space was lacking in Jerusalem due to the crowded conditions of the siege, so a prison had to be devised.

37:17–19 *then Zedekiah the king sent and took him out.* Fearing possible exposure and opposition from his courtiers, Zedekiah secretly summoned Jeremiah and asked of him a word from the Lord. He seems to have earnestly desired a word from God but could not come to grips with the reality and respond appropriately. Jeremiah appealed to Zedekiah's sense of justice and decency and asked to be released from prison. Zedekiah consented.

38:2–3 *He who remains in this city.* Verse 2 is almost an exact duplicate of 21:9. Jeremiah said the choice

was between life under the Babylonians and death among the ruins of Jerusalem. Such a statement was treasonous, as was the statement that Jerusalem must fall.

38:7 *Ebed-Melech.* This man took special care to obtain rags for Jeremiah to cushion his armpits, preventing the ropes from cutting his skin. A foreigner, a once despised Cushite (from Egypt), cared more for the prophet of God than did the king and the princes of Jeremiah's own people.

37:15 ⁱ Jer. 20:2 ʲ Jer. 38:26   **37:16** ᵏ Jer. 38:6
37:17 ˡ Jer. 21:7   **37:21** ᵐ Jer. 32:2; 38:13, 28   ⁿ Jer. 38:9;
52:6   **38:1** ᵃ Jer. 37:3 ᵇ Jer. 21:1 ᶜ Jer. 21:8   **38:2** ᵈ Jer.
21:9   **38:3** ᵉ Jer. 21:10; 32:3 ᶠ Jer. 34:2   **38:4** ᵍ Jer. 26:11
38:6 ʰ Jer. 37:21   **38:7** ⁱ Jer. 39:16   **38:9** ʲ Jer. 37:21

him and went into the house of the king under the treasury, and took from there old clothes and old rags, and let them down by ropes into the dungeon to Jeremiah. [12]Then Ebed-Melech the Ethiopian said to Jeremiah, "Please put these old clothes and rags under your armpits, under the ropes." And Jeremiah did so. [13]So they pulled Jeremiah up with ropes and lifted him out of the dungeon. And Jeremiah remained [k]in the court of the prison.

Zedekiah's Fears and Jeremiah's Advice

[14]Then Zedekiah the king sent and had Jeremiah the prophet brought to him at the third entrance of the house of the LORD. And the king said to Jeremiah, "I will [l]ask you something. Hide nothing from me." [15]Jeremiah said to Zedekiah, "If I declare it to you, will you not surely put me to death? And if I give you advice, you will not listen to me." [16]So Zedekiah the king swore secretly to Jeremiah, saying, "As the LORD lives, [m]who made our very souls, I will not put you to death, nor will I give you into the hand of these men who seek your life." [17]Then Jeremiah said to Zedekiah, "Thus says the LORD, the God of hosts, the God of Israel: 'If you surely [n]surrender [o]to the king of Babylon's princes, then your soul shall live; this city shall not be burned with fire, and you and your house shall live. [18]But if you do not surrender to the king of Babylon's princes, then this city shall be given into the hand of the Chaldeans; they shall burn it with fire, and [p]you shall not escape from their hand.'" [19]And Zedekiah the king said to Jeremiah, "I am afraid of the Jews who have [q]defected to the Chaldeans, lest they deliver me into their hand, and they [r]abuse me." [20]But Jeremiah said, "They shall not deliver you. Please, obey the voice of the LORD which I speak to you. So it shall be [s]well with you, and your soul shall live. [21]But if you refuse to surrender, this is the word that the LORD has shown me: [22]'Now behold, all the [t]women who are left in the king of Judah's house shall be surrendered to the king of Babylon's princes, and those women shall say:

"'Your close friends have set upon you
And prevailed against you;
Your feet have sunk in the mire,
And they have turned away again.'"

[23]'So they shall surrender all your wives and [u]children to the Chaldeans. [v]You shall not escape from their hand, but shall be taken by the hand of the king of Babylon. And you shall cause this city to be burned with fire.'"

[24]Then Zedekiah said to Jeremiah, "Let no one know of these words, and you shall not die. [25]But if the princes hear that I have talked with you, and they come to you and say to you, 'Declare to us now what you have said to the king, and also what the king said to you; do not hide it from us, and we will not put you to death,' [26]then you shall say to them, [w]'I presented my request before the king, that he would not make me return [x]to Jonathan's house to die there.'" [27]Then all the princes came to Jeremiah and asked him. And he told them according to all these words that the king had commanded. So they stopped speaking with him, for the conversation had not been heard. [28]Now [y]Jeremiah remained in the court of the prison until the day that Jerusalem was taken. And he was there when Jerusalem was taken.

The Fall of Jerusalem

39 In the [a]ninth year of Zedekiah king of Judah, in the tenth month, Nebuchadnezzar king of Babylon and all his army came against Jerusalem, and besieged it. [2]In the [b]eleventh year of Zedekiah, in the fourth month, on the ninth day of the month, the city was penetrated. [3c]Then all the princes of the king of Babylon came in and sat in the Middle Gate: Nergal-Sharezer, Samgar-Nebo, Sarsechim, Rabsaris,* Nergal-Sarezer, Rabmag,* with the rest of the princes of the king of Babylon.

---

* **39:3** A title, probably *Chief Officer;* also verse 13 • A title, probably *Troop Commander;* also verse 13

38:17 Then Jeremiah said to Zedekiah. Jeremiah repeated to the king the message recorded in Jeremiah 38:2–3. Surrender would spare the life of the king, and the city's failure to surrender would bring death and destruction.
38:20–23 So it shall be well with you. Jeremiah tried to settle Zedekiah's fears and to resolve his moral and ethical dilemma by reassuring him that surrender would result in his personal safety. But if the king refused to surrender to Nebuchadnezzar, the word of judgment would fall. Women and children would be handed over to Nebuchadnezzar and Jerusalem would be destroyed.
39:1 king of Babylon and all his army came against Jerusalem, and besieged it. The Babylonian siege

began in December 589 B.C. and ended about 30 months later when the walls of Jerusalem were breached.
39:3–7 all the princes of the king of Babylon. When Zedekiah saw the Babylonian officers enter the gate on the north side of Jerusalem, he and his men left at night through another gate on the south side of the

38:13 [k] Jer. 37:21 **38:14** [l] Jer. 21:1, 2; 37:17 **38:16** [m] Is. 57:16 **38:17** [n] 2 Kin. 24:12 [o] Jer. 39:3 **38:18** [p] Jer. 32:4; 34:3 **38:19** [q] Jer. 39:9 [r] 1 Sam. 31:4 **38:20** [s] Jer. 40:9 **38:22** [t] Jer. 8:10 **38:23** [u] Jer. 39:6; 41:10 [v] Jer. 39:5 **38:26** [w] Jer. 37:20 [x] Jer. 37:15 **38:28** [y] Jer. 37:21; 39:14 **39:1** [a] 2 Kin. 25:1–12 **39:2** [b] Jer. 1:3 **39:3** [c] Jer. 1:15; 38:17

4*d*So it was, when Zedekiah the king of Judah and all the men of war saw them, that they fled and went out of the city by night, by way of the king's garden, by the gate between the two walls. And he went out by way of the plain.* 5But the Chaldean army pursued them and *e*overtook Zedekiah in the plains of Jericho. And when they had captured him, they brought him up to Nebuchadnezzar king of Babylon, to *f*Riblah in the land of Hamath, where he pronounced judgment on him. 6Then the king of Babylon killed the sons of Zedekiah before his *g*eyes in Riblah; the king of Babylon also killed all the *h*nobles of Judah. 7Moreover *i*he put out Zedekiah's eyes, and bound him with bronze fetters to carry him off to Babylon. 8*j*And the Chaldeans burned the king's house and the houses of the people with *k*fire, and broke down the *l*walls of Jerusalem. 9*m*Then Nebuzaradan the captain of the guard carried away captive to Babylon the remnant of the people who remained in the city and those who *n*defected to him, with the rest of the people who remained. 10But Nebuzaradan the captain of the guard left in the land of Judah the *o*poor people, who had nothing, and gave them vineyards and fields at the same time.

Jeremiah Goes Free

11Now Nebuchadnezzar king of Babylon gave charge concerning Jeremiah to Nebuzaradan the captain of the guard, saying, 12"Take him and look after him, and do him no *p*harm; but do to him just as he says to you." 13So Nebuzaradan the captain of the guard sent Nebushasban, Rabsaris, Nergal-Sharezer, Rabmag, and all the king of Babylon's chief officers; 14then they sent *someone* *q*to take Jeremiah from the court of the prison, and committed him *r*to Gedaliah the son of *s*Ahikam, the son of Shaphan, that he should take him home. So he dwelt among the people.

15Meanwhile the word of the LORD had come to Jeremiah while he was shut up in the court of the prison, saying, 16"Go and speak to *t*Ebed-Melech the Ethiopian, saying, 'Thus says the LORD of hosts, the God of Israel: "Behold, *u*I will bring My words upon

this city for adversity and not for good, and they shall be *performed* in that day before you. 17But I will deliver you in that day," says the LORD, "and you shall not be given into the hand of the men of whom you *are* afraid. 18For I will surely deliver you, and you shall not fall by the sword; but *v*your life shall be as a prize to you, *w*because you have put your trust in Me," says the LORD.'"

Jeremiah with Gedaliah the Governor

40 The word that came to Jeremiah from the LORD *a*after Nebuzaradan the captain of the guard had let him go from Ramah, when he had taken him bound in chains among all who were carried away captive from Jerusalem and Judah, who were carried away captive to Babylon.

2And the captain of the guard took Jeremiah and *b*said to him: "The LORD your God has pronounced this doom on this place. 3Now the LORD has brought *it*, and has done just as He said. *c*Because you *people* have sinned against the LORD, and not obeyed His voice, therefore this thing has come upon you. 4And now look, I free you this day from the chains that *were* on your hand. *d*If it seems good to you to come with me to Babylon, come, and I will look after you. But if it seems wrong for you to come with me to Babylon, remain here. See, *e*all the land *is* before you; wherever it seems good and convenient for you to go, go there."

5Now while Jeremiah had not yet gone back, *Nebuzaradan said*, "Go back to *f*Gedaliah the son of Ahikam, the son of Shaphan, *g*whom the king of Babylon has made governor over the cities of Judah, and dwell with him among the people. Or go wherever it seems convenient for you to go." So the captain of the guard gave him rations and a gift and let him go. 6*h*Then Jeremiah went to Gedaliah the son of Ahikam, to *i*Mizpah, and dwelt with him among the people who were left in the land.

---

* **39:4** Or *the Arabah,* that is, the Jordan Valley

---

city. They were captured near Jericho and taken to Riblah to meet Nebuchadnezzar.

39:8–10 And the Chaldeans burned. In addition to the royal palace and homes of the inhabitants, Jeremiah 52:13 includes the "house of the LORD" among the buildings burned in Jerusalem. *poor people.* Typically the Babylonians deported the upper classes, such as court officials, merchants, artisans, and craftsmen, and left behind peasants to work the fields.

39:18 your life shall be as a prize . . . your trust in Me. Ebed-Melech experienced the power and grace of God in the deliverance of his life simply because he exercised faith.

40:2–3 The LORD has brought it, and has done just as He said. Prophets whose words were deemed verified were generally treated well by peoples of the ancient Middle East.

40:4–5 I free you this day from the chains. Jeremiah was released from bondage and given three options: (1) to go with Nebuzaradan to Babylon and enjoy special treatment and protection there; (2) to remain in the care of Gedaliah, the district governor at Mizpah; or (3) to live in the land as he chose.

39:4 *d* Jer. 52:7 **39:5** *e* Jer. 21:7; 32:4; 38:18, 23 *f* 2 Kin. 23:33 **39:6** *g* Deut. 28:34 *h* Jer. 34:19–21 **39:7** *i* Ezek. 12:13 **39:8** *j* 2 Kin. 25:9 *k* Jer. 21:10 *l* Neh. 1:3 **39:9** *m* 2 Kin. 25:8, 11, 12, 20 *n* Jer. 38:19 **39:10** *o* Jer. 40:7 **39:12** *p* Jer. 1:18, 19; 15:20, 21 **39:14** *q* Jer. 38:28 *r* Jer. 40:5 *s* Jer. 26:24 **39:16** *t* Jer. 38:7, 12 *u* [Dan. 9:12] **39:18** *v* Jer. 21:9; 45:5 *w* Ps. 37:40 **40:1** *a* Jer. 39:9, 11 **40:2** *b* Jer. 50:7 **40:3** *c* Dan. 9:11 **40:4** *d* Jer. 39:12 *e* Gen. 20:15 **40:5** *f* Jer. 39:14 *g* Jer. 41:10 **40:6** *h* Jer. 39:14 *i* Judg. 20:1

7[j]And when all the captains of the armies who *were* in the fields, they and their men, heard that the king of Babylon had made Gedaliah the son of Ahikam governor in the land, and had committed to him men, women, children, and [k]the poorest of the land who had not been carried away captive to Babylon, 8then they came to Gedaliah at Mizpah—[l]Ishmael the son of Nethaniah, [m]Johanan and Jonathan the sons of Kareah, Seraiah the son of Tanhumeth, the sons of Ephai the Netophathite, and [n]Jezaniah* the son of a [o]Maachathite, they and their men. 9And Gedaliah the son of Ahikam, the son of Shaphan, took an oath before them and their men, saying, "Do not be afraid to serve the Chaldeans. Dwell in the land and serve the king of Babylon, and it shall be [p]well with you. 10As for me, I will indeed dwell at Mizpah and serve the Chaldeans who come to us. But you, gather wine and summer fruit and oil, put *them* in your vessels, and dwell in your cities that you have taken." 11Likewise, when all the Jews who *were* in Moab, among the Ammonites, in Edom, and who *were* in all the countries, heard that the king of Babylon had left a remnant of Judah, and that he had set over them Gedaliah the son of Ahikam, the son of Shaphan, 12then all the Jews [q]returned out of all places where they had been driven, and came to the land of Judah, to Gedaliah at Mizpah, and gathered wine and summer fruit in abundance.

13Moreover Johanan the son of Kareah and all the captains of the forces that *were* in the fields came to Gedaliah at Mizpah, 14and said to him, "Do you certainly know that [r]Baalis the king of the Ammonites has sent Ishmael the son of Nethaniah to murder you?" But Gedaliah the son of Ahikam did not believe them.

15Then Johanan the son of Kareah spoke secretly to Gedaliah in Mizpah, saying, "Let me go, please, and I will kill Ishmael the son of Nethaniah, and no one will know *it*. Why should he murder you, so that all the Jews who are gathered to you would be scattered, and the [s]remnant in Judah perish?"

16But Gedaliah the son of Ahikam said to Johanan the son of Kareah, "You shall not do this thing, for you speak falsely concerning Ishmael."

Insurrection Against Gedaliah

41 Now it came to pass in the seventh month [a]that Ishmael the son of Nethaniah, the son of Elishama, of the royal family and of the officers of the king, came with ten men to Gedaliah the son of Ahikam, at [b]Mizpah. And there they ate bread together in Mizpah. 2Then Ishmael the son of Nethaniah, and the ten men who were with him, arose and [c]struck Gedaliah the son of Ahikam, the son of Shaphan, with the sword, and killed him whom the king of Babylon had made [e]governor over the land. 3Ishmael also struck down all the Jews who were with him, *that is*, with Gedaliah at Mizpah, and the Chaldeans who were found there, the men of war.

4And it happened, on the second day after he had killed Gedaliah, when as yet no one knew *it*, 5that certain men came from Shechem, from Shiloh, and from Samaria, eighty men [f]with their beards shaved and their clothes torn, having cut themselves, with offerings and incense in their hand, to bring *them* to [g]the house of the LORD. 6Now Ishmael the son of Nethaniah went out from Mizpah to meet them, weeping as he went along; and it happened as he met them that he said to them, "Come to Gedaliah the son of Ahikam!" 7So it was, when they came into the midst of the city, that Ishmael the son of Nethaniah [h]killed them *and cast them* into the midst of a pit, he and the men who were with him. 8But ten men were found among them who said to Ishmael, "Do not kill us, for we have treasures of wheat, barley, oil, and honey in the field." So he desisted and did not kill them among their brethren. 9Now the pit into which Ishmael had cast all the dead bodies of the men whom he had slain, because of Gedaliah, *was* [i]the same one Asa the king had made for fear of Baasha king of Israel. Ishmael the son of Nethaniah filled it with *the* slain. 10Then Ishmael carried away captive all the [j]rest of the people who *were* in Mizpah, [k]the king's daughters and all the people who remained in Mizpah, [l]whom Nebuzaradan the captain of the guard had committed to Gedaliah the son of Ahikam. And Ishmael the son of Nethaniah carried them away captive and departed to go over to [m]the Ammonites.

* **40:8** Spelled *Jaazaniah* in 2 Kings 25:23

40:7–10 the captains of the armies. This phrase refers to the surviving Jewish commanders of the armies in the towns throughout Judah who had fled into the rugged hill country. Among the list of escaped leaders was Ishmael, a member of the royal family and a court officer (41:1).
40:11–12 the Jews. Those who had escaped the Babylonian onslaught into neighboring states returned home and began working the fields, vineyards, and orchards.
40:13–16 Johanan. This man led a group of leaders to Gedaliah to warn him of a plot by Ishmael.

He even asked for permission to kill the plotter, Ishmael. Unfortunately, Gedaliah was far too trusting of Ishmael and didn't take the warning seriously enough.

40:7 [j]2 Kin. 25:23, 24 [k]Jer. 39:10 **40:8** [l]Jer. 41:1–10 [m]Jer. 41:11; 43:2 [n]Jer. 42:1 [o]Deut. 3:14 **40:9** [p]Jer. 27:11; 38:17–20 **40:12** [q]Jer. 43:5 **40:14** [r]Jer. 41:10 **40:15** [s]Jer. 42:2 **41:1** [a]2 Kin. 25:25 [b]Jer. 40:6, 10 **41:2** [c]2 Kin. 25:25 [d]Jer. 26:24 [e]Jer. 40:5 **41:5** [f]Deut. 14:1 [g]1 Sam. 1:7 **41:7** [h]Ps. 55:23 **41:9** [i]1 Kin. 15:22 **41:10** [j]Jer. 40:11, 12 [k]Jer. 43:6 [l]Jer. 40:7 [m]Jer. 40:14

[11]But when [n]Johanan the son of Kareah and all the captains of the forces that *were* with him heard of all the evil that Ishmael the son of Nethaniah had done, [12]they took all the men and went to fight with Ishmael the son of Nethaniah; and they found him by [o]the great pool that *is* in Gibeon. [13]So it was, when all the people who *were* with Ishmael saw Johanan the son of Kareah, and all the captains of the forces who *were* with him, that they were glad. [14]Then all the people whom Ishmael had carried away captive from Mizpah turned around and came back, and went to Johanan the son of Kareah. [15]But Ishmael the son of Nethaniah escaped from Johanan with eight men and went to the Ammonites.

[16]Then Johanan the son of Kareah, and all the captains of the forces that were with him, took from Mizpah all the [p]rest of the people whom he had recovered from Ishmael the son of Nethaniah after he had murdered Gedaliah the son of Ahikam—the mighty men of war and the women and the children and the eunuchs, whom he had brought back from Gibeon. [17]And they departed and dwelt in the habitation of [q]Chimham, which is near Bethlehem, as they went on their way to [r]Egypt, [18]because of the Chaldeans; for they were afraid of them, because Ishmael the son of Nethaniah had murdered Gedaliah the son of Ahikam, [s]whom the king of Babylon had made governor in the land.

The Flight to Egypt Forbidden

42 Now all the captains of the forces, [a]Johanan the son of Kareah, Jezaniah the son of Hoshaiah, and all the people, from the least to the greatest, came near [2]and said to Jeremiah the prophet, [b]"Please, let our petition be acceptable to you, and [c]pray for us to the LORD your God, for all this remnant (since we are left *but* [d]a few of many, as you can see), [3]that the LORD your God may show us [e]the way in which we should walk and the thing we should do."

[4]Then Jeremiah the prophet said to them, "I have heard. Indeed, I will pray to the LORD your God according to your words, and it shall be, *that* [f]whatever the LORD answers you, I will declare *it* to you. I will [g]keep nothing back from you."

[5]So they said to Jeremiah, [h]"Let the LORD be a true and faithful witness between us, if we do not do according to everything which the LORD your God sends us by you. [6]Whether *it is* pleasing or displeasing, we will [i]obey the voice of the LORD our God to whom we send you, [j]that it may be well with us when we obey the voice of the LORD our God."

[7]And it happened after ten days that the word of the LORD came to Jeremiah. [8]Then he called Johanan the son of Kareah, all the captains of the forces which *were* with him, and all the people from the least even to the greatest, [9]and said to them, "Thus says the LORD, the God of Israel, to whom you sent me to present your petition before Him: [10]'If you will still remain in this land, then [k]I will build you and not pull *you* down, and I will plant you and not pluck *you* up. For I [l]relent concerning the disaster that I have brought upon you. [11]Do not be afraid of the king of Babylon, of whom you are afraid; do not be afraid of him,' says the LORD, [m]'for I *am* with you, to save you and deliver you from his hand. [12]And [n]I will show you mercy, that he may have mercy on you and cause you to return to your own land.'

[13]"But if [o]you say, 'We will not dwell in this land,' disobeying the voice of the LORD your God, [14]saying, 'No, but we will go to the land of [p]Egypt where we shall see no war, nor hear the sound of the trumpet, nor be hungry for bread, and there we will dwell'— [15]Then hear now the word of the LORD, O remnant of Judah! Thus says the LORD of hosts, the God of Israel: 'If you [q]wholly set [r]your faces to enter Egypt, and go to dwell there, [16]then it shall be *that* the [s]sword which you feared shall overtake you there in the land of Egypt; the famine of which you were afraid shall follow close after you there *in* Egypt; and there you shall die. [17]So shall it be with all the men who set their faces to go to Egypt to dwell there. They shall die by the sword, by famine, and by pestilence. And [t]none of them shall remain or escape from the disaster that I will bring upon them.'

41:11–12 they took all the men. After Ishmael assassinated Gedaliah, Johanan gathered forces to fight Ishmael's army at Gibeon. Then he started for Egypt and safety.

42:1–3 said to Jeremiah. The people asked Jeremiah to intercede with the Lord on their behalf.

42:4–6 I will pray. Jeremiah cautiously agreed to pray to God. He asked the people to agree to abide by the answer he received. The people responded with an oath of obedience, calling upon the Lord as witness.

42:15 set your faces. This expression indicates the fixed intentions of the people. The announcement of judgment against the disobedient evacuees echoes

Jeremiah's earlier pronouncements against Judah. The very thing they were trying to escape from would meet them in Egypt.

41:11 [n] Jer. 40:7, 8, 13–16   **41:12** [o] 2 Sam. 2:13
41:16 [p] Jer. 40:11, 12; 43:4–7   **41:17** [q] 2 Sam. 19:37, 38
[r] Jer. 43:7   **41:18** [s] Jer. 40:5   **42:1** [a] Jer. 40:8, 13; 41:11
42:2 [b] Jer. 15:11   [c] Is. 37:4   [d] Lev. 26:22   **42:3** [e] Ezra
8:21   **42:4** [f] 1 Kin. 22:14   [g] 1 Sam. 3:17, 18   **42:5** [h] Gen.
31:50   **42:6** [i] Ex. 24:7   [j] Jer. 7:23   **42:10** [k] Jer. 24:6; 31:28;
33:7   [l] [Jer. 18:8]   **42:11** [m] Rom. 8:31   **42:12** [n] Ps. 106:46
42:13 [o] Jer. 44:16   **42:14** [p] Jer. 41:17; 43:7   **42:15** [q] Deut.
17:16   [r] Luke 9:51   **42:16** [s] Ezek. 11:8   **42:17** [t] Jer.
44:14, 28

18"For thus says the LORD of hosts, the God of Israel: 'As My anger and My fury have been uupoured out on the inhabitants of Jerusalem, so will My fury be poured out on you when you enter Egypt. And vyou shall be an oath, an astonishment, a curse, and a reproach; and you shall see this place no more.'

19"The LORD has said concerning you, O remnant of Judah, w'Do not go to Egypt!' Know certainly that I have admonished you this day. 20For you were hypocrites in your hearts when you sent me to the LORD your God, saying, 'Pray for us to the LORD our God, and according to all that the LORD your God says, so declare to us and we will do it.' 21And I have this day declared it to you, but you have xnot obeyed the voice of the LORD your God, or anything which He has sent you by me. 22Now therefore, know certainly that you yshall die by the sword, by famine, and by pestilence in the place where you desire to go to dwell."

Jeremiah Taken to Egypt

43 Now it happened, when Jeremiah had stopped speaking to all the people all the awords of the LORD their God, for which the LORD their God had sent him to them, all these words, 2bthat Azariah the son of Hoshaiah, Johanan the son of Kareah, and all the proud men spoke, saying to Jeremiah, "You speak falsely! The LORD our God has not sent you to say, 'Do not go to Egypt to dwell there.' 3But cBaruch the son of Neriah has set you against us, to deliver us into the hand of the Chaldeans, that they may put us to death or carry us away captive to Babylon." 4So Johanan the son of Kareah, all the captains of the forces, and all the people would dnot obey the voice of the LORD, to remain in the land of Judah. 5But Johanan the son of Kareah and all the captains of the forces took eall the remnant of Judah who had returned to dwell in the land of Judah, from all nations where they had been driven— 6men, women, children, fthe king's daughters, gand every person whom Nebuzaradan the captain of the guard had left with Gedaliah the son of Ahikam, the son of Shaphan, and Jeremiah the prophet and Baruch the son of Neriah. 7hSo they went to the land of Egypt, for they did not obey the voice of the LORD. And they went as far as iTahpanhes.

8Then the jword of the LORD came to Jeremiah in Tahpanhes, saying, 9"Take large stones in your hand, and hide them in the sight of the men of Judah, in the clay in the brick courtyard which is at the entrance to Pharaoh's house in Tahpanhes; 10and say to them, 'Thus says the LORD of hosts, the God of Israel: "Behold, I will send and bring Nebuchadnezzar the king of Babylon, kMy servant, and will set his throne above these stones that I have hidden. And he will spread his royal pavilion over them. 11lWhen he comes, he shall strike the land of Egypt and deliver to death mthose appointed for death, and to captivity those appointed for captivity, and to the sword those appointed for the sword. 12I* will kindle a fire in the houses of nthe gods of Egypt, and he shall burn them and carry them away captive. And he shall array himself with the land of Egypt, as a shepherd puts on his garment, and he shall go out from there in peace. 13He shall also break the sacred pillars of Beth Shemesh* that are in the land of Egypt; and the houses of the gods of the Egyptians he shall burn with fire." ' "

Israelites Will Be Punished in Egypt

44 The word that came to Jeremiah concerning all the Jews who dwell in the land of Egypt, who dwell at aMigdol, at bTahpanhes, at cNoph,* and in the country of dPathros, saying, 2"Thus says the LORD of hosts, the God of Israel: 'You have seen all the calamity that I have brought on Jerusalem and on all the cities of Judah; and behold, this day they are ea desolation, and no one dwells in them, 3because of their wickedness which they have committed to provoke Me to anger, in that they went fto burn incense and to gserve other gods whom they did not know, they nor you nor your fathers. 4However hI have sent to you all My servants the prophets, rising early and sending them, saying, "Oh, do not do this abominable thing that I hate!" 5But they did not listen or incline their ear to turn from their wickedness, to burn no incense to other gods. 6So My fury and My anger were poured out and kindled in the cities of Judah and in the streets of Jerusalem; and they are wasted and desolate, as it is this day.'

---

* **43:12** Following Masoretic Text and Targum; Septuagint, Syriac, and Vulgate read *He.*
* **43:13** Literally *House of the Sun,* ancient On; later called Heliopolis   * **44:1** That is, ancient Memphis

---

43:4–7 *all the people would not obey.* Johanan led the migration to Egypt, against the direction of the Lord through Jeremiah.

43:10 *these stones.* These symbolized the strong foundation of Nebuchadnezzar's empire, the point from which he would spread his canopy.

42:18 u Jer. 7:20 v Is. 65:15   **42:19** w Deut. 17:16
42:21 x Is. 30:1–7   **42:22** y Ezek. 6:11   **43:1** a Jer. 42:9–
18   **43:2** b Jer. 42:1   **43:3** c Jer. 36:4; 45:1   **43:4** d 2 Kin.
25:26   **43:5** e Jer. 40:11, 12   **43:6** f Jer. 41:10 g Jer.
39:10; 40:7   **43:7** h Jer. 42:19 i Jer. 2:16; 44:1   **43:8** i Jer.
44:1–30   **43:10** k Jer. 25:9; 27:6   **43:11** l Jer. 25:15–19;
44:13; 46:1, 2, 13–26 m Jer. 15:2   **43:12** n Jer. 46:25
44:1 a Jer. 46:14 b Jer. 43:7 c Is. 19:13 d Ezek. 29:14; 30:14
44:2 e Jer. 4:7; 9:11; 34:22   **44:3** f Jer. 19:4 g Deut. 13:6;
32:17   **44:4** h Jer. 7:25; 25:4; 26:5; 29:19

⁷"Now therefore, thus says the LORD, the God of hosts, the God of Israel: 'Why do you commit *this* great evil ⁱagainst yourselves, to cut off from you man and woman, child and infant, out of Judah, leaving none to remain, ⁸in that you ʲprovoke Me to wrath with the works of your hands, burning incense to other gods in the land of Egypt where you have gone to dwell, that you may cut yourselves off and be ᵏa curse and a reproach among all the nations of the earth? ⁹Have you forgotten the wickedness of your fathers, the wickedness of the kings of Judah, the wickedness of their wives, your own wickedness, and the wickedness of your wives, which they committed in the land of Judah and in the streets of Jerusalem? ¹⁰They have not been ˡhumbled, to this day, nor have they ᵐfeared; they have not walked in My law or in My statutes that I set before you and your fathers.'

¹¹"Therefore thus says the LORD of hosts, the God of Israel: 'Behold, ⁿI will set My face against you for catastrophe and for cutting off all Judah. ¹²And I will take the remnant of Judah who have set their faces to go into the land of Egypt to dwell there, and ᵒthey shall all be consumed *and* fall in the land of Egypt. They shall be consumed by the sword *and* by famine. They shall die, from the least to the greatest, by the sword and by famine; and ᵖthey shall be an oath, an astonishment, a curse and a reproach! ¹³ᑫFor I will punish those who dwell in the land of Egypt, as I have punished Jerusalem, by the sword, by famine, and by pestilence, ¹⁴so that none of the remnant of Judah who have gone into the land of Egypt to dwell there shall escape or survive, lest they return to the land of Judah, to which they ʳdesire to return and dwell. For ˢnone shall return except those who escape.'"

¹⁵Then all the men who knew that their wives had burned incense to other gods, with all the women who stood by, a great multitude, and all the people who dwelt in the land of Egypt, in Pathros, answered Jeremiah, saying: ¹⁶"*As for* the word that you have spoken to us in the name of the LORD, ᵗwe will not listen to you! ¹⁷But we will certainly do ᵘwhatever has gone out of our own mouth, to burn incense to the ᵛqueen of heaven and pour out drink offerings to her, as we have done, we and our fathers, our kings and our princes, in the cities of Judah and in the streets of Jerusalem. For *then* we had plenty of food, were well-off, and saw no trouble. ¹⁸But since we stopped burning incense to the queen of heaven and pouring out drink offerings to her, we have lacked everything and have been consumed by the sword and by famine."

¹⁹*The women also said,* ʷ"And when we burned incense to the queen of heaven and poured out drink offerings to her, did we make cakes for her, to worship her, and pour out drink offerings to her without our husbands' *permission?*"

²⁰Then Jeremiah spoke to all the people—the men, the women, and all the people who had given him *that* answer—saying: ²¹"The incense that you burned in the cities of Judah and in the streets of Jerusalem, you and your fathers, your kings and your princes, and the people of the land, did not the LORD remember them, and did it *not* come into His mind? ²²So the LORD could no longer bear *it*, because of the evil of your doings *and* because of the abominations which you committed. Therefore your land is a desolation, an astonishment, a curse, and without an inhabitant, ˣas *it* is this day. ²³Because you have burned incense and because you have sinned against the LORD, and have not obeyed the voice of the LORD or walked in His law, in His statutes or in His testimonies, ʸtherefore this calamity has happened to you, as *at* this day."

²⁴Moreover Jeremiah said to all the people and to all the women, "Hear the word of the LORD, all Judah who *are* in the land of Egypt! ²⁵Thus says the LORD of hosts, the God of Israel, saying: 'You and your wives have spoken with your mouths and fulfilled with your hands, saying, "We will surely keep our vows that we have made, to burn incense to the queen of heaven and pour out drink offerings to her." You will surely keep your vows and perform your vows!' ²⁶Therefore hear the word of the LORD, all Judah who dwell in the land of Egypt: 'Behold, ᶻI have sworn by My ᵃgreat name,' says the LORD, 'that ᵇMy name shall

---

44:8 provoke. This term indicates willful, stubborn rebellion against God, which roused His anger.

44:10 They have not been humbled. The present generation of Jews had learned nothing from the past failures of the nation. The people were not broken in heart, only more stubborn.

44:13 I will punish those who dwell in the land of Egypt. The Jews in Egypt would suffer the same judgment as those in Jerusalem. Only a small remnant would survive to tell their story.

44:18 queen of heaven. The people reasoned that when they stopped worshiping the queen of heaven in the days of Josiah's reform, their king was killed and their land was overrun and destroyed.

44:24 and to all the women. The focus here is on the

stubbornness of the women who persisted in their idolatry. Nothing could make them abandon their vows to worship Ishtar.

44:26–27 by My great name. The name of God reveals His quality and character in dealing with humankind.

44:7 ⁱNum. 16:38   **44:8** ʲJer. 25:6, 7; 44:3   ᵏJer. 42:18
44:10 ˡJer. 6:15; 8:12   ᵐ[Prov. 28:14]   **44:11** ⁿAmos
9:4   **44:12** ᵒJer. 42:15–17, 22   ᵖIs. 65:15   **44:13** ᑫJer.
43:11   **44:14** ʳJer. 22:26, 27   ˢJer. 44:28   **44:16** ᵗJer.
6:16   **44:17** ᵘNum. 30:12   ᵛJer. 7:18   **44:19** ʷJer.
7:18   **44:22** ˣJer. 25:11, 18, 38   **44:23** ʸDan. 9:11, 12
44:26 ᶻHeb. 6:13   ᵃJer. 10:6   ᵇEzek. 20:39

no more be named in the mouth of any man of Judah in all the land of Egypt, saying, "The Lord GOD lives." 27Behold, I will watch over them for adversity and not for good. And all the men of Judah who *are* in the land of Egypt cshall be consumed by the sword and by famine, until there is an end to them. 28Yet da small number who escape the sword shall return from the land of Egypt to the land of Judah; and all the remnant of Judah, who have gone to the land of Egypt to dwell there, shall know whose words will stand, Mine or theirs. 29And this *shall be* a sign to you,' says the LORD, 'that I will punish you in this place, that you may know that My words will surely estand against you for adversity.'

30"Thus says the LORD: 'Behold, fI will give Pharaoh Hophra king of Egypt into the hand of his enemies and into the hand of those who seek his life, as I gave gZedekiah king of Judah into the hand of Nebuchadnezzar king of Babylon, his enemy who sought his life.'"

Assurance to Baruch

45 The aword that Jeremiah the prophet spoke to bBaruch the son of Neriah, when he had written these words in a book at the instruction of Jeremiah,* in the cfourth year of Jehoiakim the son of Josiah, king of Judah, saying, 2"Thus says the LORD, the God of Israel, to you, O Baruch: 3'You said, "Woe is me now! For the LORD has added grief to my sorrow. I dfainted in my sighing, and I find no rest."'

4"Thus you shall say to him, 'Thus says the LORD: "Behold, ewhat I have built I will break down, and what I have planted I will pluck up, that is, this whole land. 5And do you seek great things for yourself? Do not seek *them;* for behold, fI will bring adversity on all flesh," says the LORD. "But I will give your glife to you as a prize in all places, wherever you go."'"

Judgment on Egypt

46 The word of the LORD which came to Jeremiah the prophet against athe nations. 2Against bEgypt.

cConcerning the army of Pharaoh Necho, king of Egypt, which was by the River Euphrates in Carchemish, and which Nebuchadnezzar king of Babylon ddefeated in the efourth year of Jehoiakim the son of Josiah, king of Judah:

3 "Order the buckler and shield,
  And draw near to battle!
4 Harness the horses,
  And mount up, you horsemen!
  Stand forth with *your* helmets,
  Polish the spears,
  fPut on the armor!
5 Why have I seen them dismayed *and* turned back?
  Their mighty ones are beaten down;
  They have speedily fled,
  And did not look back,
  For gfear *was* all around," says the LORD.
6 "Do not let the swift flee away,
  Nor the mighty man escape;
  They will hstumble and fall
  Toward the north, by the River Euphrates.

7 "Who *is* this coming up ilike a flood,
  Whose waters move like the rivers?
8 Egypt rises up like a flood,
  And *its* waters move like the rivers;
  And he says, 'I will go up *and* cover the earth,
  I will destroy the city and its inhabitants.'
9 Come up, O horses, and rage, O chariots!
  And let the mighty men come forth:
  The Ethiopians and the Libyans who handle the shield,
  And the Lydians jwho handle *and* bend the bow.
10 For this is kthe day of the Lord GOD of hosts,
  A day of vengeance,
  That He may avenge Himself on His adversaries.
  lThe sword shall devour;
  It shall be satiated and made drunk with their blood;
  For the Lord GOD of hosts mhas a sacrifice

---

* 45:1 Literally *from Jeremiah's mouth*

44:28 all the remnant of Judah. A small remnant would survive and see the fulfillment of God's word as revealed through Jeremiah. Their own hopes of prosperity in Egypt would vanish, and the sign of God's work against them would be the fall of Pharaoh Hophra of Egypt. In 570 B.C., Hophra was overthrown in a military coup by his own general, Amasis. Three years later he was executed in fulfillment of Jeremiah's prophecy.

45:2–3 to you, O Baruch. Jeremiah addressed Baruch in light of the scribe's sorrow. Baruch lamented his plight in the same manner that Jeremiah had done (15:10). He also suffered mental anguish and personal rejection from his people due to his association with Jeremiah (36:15–19).

46:1 against the nations. This verse introduces a collection of oracles. The text moves generally from the west—Egypt—to the east—Elam and Babylon.

Scattered throughout the oracles are brief messages of the restoration of Israel and Judah. The main message of these oracles is the sovereignty of God over all the nations of the earth.

46:10–12 day of the Lord. This time the day is a day of vengeance in which Egypt is punished for the death of Josiah. The imagery of a devouring sword is also found in Jeremiah 2:30. Egypt's demise is

44:27 c Ezek. 7:6   **44:28** d Is. 10:19; 27:12, 13
44:29 e [Ps. 33:11]   **44:30** f Ezek. 29:3; 30:21   g Jer.
39:5   **45:1** a Jer. 36:1, 4, 32   b Jer. 32:12, 16; 43:3   c Jer.
25:1; 36:1; 46:2   **45:3** d Ps. 6:6; 69:3   **45:4** e Is. 5:5
45:5 f Jer. 25:17–26   g Jer. 21:9; 38:2; 39:18   **46:1** a Jer.
25:15   **46:2** b Jer. 25:17–19   c 2 Kin. 23:33–35   d 2 Chr.
35:20   e Jer. 45:1   **46:4** f Jer. 51:11, 12   **46:5** g Jer. 49:29
46:6 h Dan. 11:19   **46:7** i Jer. 47:2   **46:9** j Is. 66:19
46:10 k Joel 1:15   l Deut. 32:42   m Is. 34:6

In the north country by the River
Euphrates.

11 "Go[n] up to Gilead and take balm,
[o]O virgin, the daughter of Egypt;
In vain you will use many medicines;
[p]You shall not be cured.
12 The nations have heard of your
[q]shame,
And your cry has filled the land;
For the mighty man has stumbled
against the mighty;
They both have fallen together."

Babylonia Will Strike Egypt

13The word that the LORD spoke to Jeremiah the prophet, how Nebuchadnezzar king of Babylon would come and [r]strike the land of Egypt.

14 "Declare in Egypt, and proclaim in
[s]Migdol;
Proclaim in Noph* and in [t]Tahpanhes;
Say, 'Stand fast and prepare
yourselves,
For the sword devours all around you.'
15 Why are your valiant men swept
away?
They did not stand
Because the LORD drove them away.
16 He made many fall;
Yes, [u]one fell upon another.
And they said, 'Arise!
[v]Let us go back to our own people
And to the land of our nativity
From the oppressing sword.'
17 They cried there,
'Pharaoh, king of Egypt, is but a noise.
He has passed by the appointed time!'

18 "As I live," says the King,
[w]Whose name is the LORD of hosts,
"Surely as Tabor is among the
mountains
And as Carmel by the sea, so he shall
come.
19 O [x]you daughter dwelling in Egypt,
Prepare yourself [y]to go into captivity!
For Noph* shall be waste and desolate,
without inhabitant.

20 "Egypt is a very pretty [z]heifer,
But destruction comes, it comes [a]from
the north.
21 Also her mercenaries are in her midst
like fat bulls;
For they also are turned back,

They have fled away together.
They did not stand,
For [b]the day of their calamity had
come upon them,
The time of their punishment.
22 [c]Her noise shall go like a serpent,
For they shall march with an army
And come against her with axes,
Like those who chop wood.

23 "They shall [d]cut down her forest," says
the LORD,
"Though it cannot be searched,
Because they are innumerable,
And more numerous than
[e]grasshoppers.
24 The daughter of Egypt shall be
ashamed;
She shall be delivered into the hand
Of [f]the people of the north."

25The LORD of hosts, the God of Israel, says: "Behold, I will bring punishment on Amon* of [g]No,* and Pharaoh and Egypt, [h]with their gods and their kings—Pharaoh and those who [i]trust in him. 26[j]And I will deliver them into the hand of those who seek their lives, into the hand of Nebuchadnezzar king of Babylon and the hand of his servants. [k]Afterward it shall be inhabited as in the days of old," says the LORD.

God Will Preserve Israel

27 "But[l] do not fear, O My servant Jacob,
And do not be dismayed, O Israel!
For behold, I will [m]save you from afar,
And your offspring from the land of
their captivity;
Jacob shall return, have rest and be
at ease;
No one shall make him afraid.
28 Do not fear, O Jacob My servant," says
the LORD,
"For I am with you;
For I will make a complete end of all
the nations
To which I have driven you,
But I will not make [n]a complete end
of you.
I will rightly [o]correct you,
For I will not leave you wholly
unpunished."

---

* **46:14** That is, ancient Memphis * **46:19** That is, ancient Memphis * **46:25** A sun god • That is, ancient Thebes

---

pictured as a sacrificial feast. As there was no healing balm for sinful Judah, so now Egypt was mortally wounded, stumbling to its death.

46:15–17 Why are your valiant men swept away? The fall of the gods before God in judgment is a prominent theme in the oracles against the nations (v. 25).

46:18 King . . . LORD of hosts. The term "hosts" can also be translated "armies." God is the true and sovereign King over all the armies of heaven and earth.

46:25–26 with their gods and their kings. The gods

and goddesses of Egypt were punished in the defeat of the people who worshiped them.

46:11 [n] Jer. 8:22 [o] Is. 47:1 [p] Ezek. 30:21 **46:12** [q] Jer. 2:36 **46:13** [r] Is. 19:1 **46:14** [s] Jer. 44:1 [t] Ezek. 30:18 **46:16** [u] Lev. 26:36, 37 [v] Jer. 51:9 **46:18** [w] Jer. 48:15 **46:19** [x] Jer. 48:18 [y] Is. 20:4 **46:20** [z] Hos. 10:11 [a] Jer. 1:14 **46:21** [b] [Ps. 37:13] **46:22** [c] [Is. 29:4] **46:23** [d] Is. 10:34 [e] Judg. 6:5; 7:12 **46:24** [f] Jer. 1:15 **46:25** [g] Ezek. 30:14–16 [h] Jer. 43:12, 13 [i] Is. 30:1–5; 31:1–3 **46:26** [j] Ezek. 32:11 [k] Ezek. 29:8–14 **46:27** [l] Is. 41:13, 14; 43:5; 44:2 [m] Is. 11:11 **46:28** [n] Amos 9:8, 9 [o] Jer. 30:11

Judgment on Philistia

47 The word of the LORD that came to Jeremiah the prophet ªagainst the Philistines, ᵇbefore Pharaoh attacked Gaza.

2 Thus says the LORD:

"Behold, ᶜwaters rise ᵈout of the north,
And shall be an overflowing flood;
They shall overflow the land and all
   that is in it,
The city and those who dwell within;
Then the men shall cry,
And all the inhabitants of the land
   shall wail.
3 At the ᵉnoise of the stamping hooves of
   his strong horses,
At the rushing of his chariots,
At the rumbling of his wheels,
The fathers will not look back for *their*
   children,
Lacking courage,
4 Because of the day that comes to
   plunder all the ᶠPhilistines,
To cut off from ᵍTyre and Sidon every
   helper who remains;
For the LORD shall plunder the
   Philistines,
ʰThe remnant of the country of
   ⁱCaphtor.
5 ʲBaldness has come upon Gaza,
   ᵏAshkelon is cut off
With the remnant of their valley.
How long will you cut yourself?

6 "O you ˡsword of the LORD,
How long until you are quiet?
Put yourself up into your scabbard,
Rest and be still!
7 How can it be quiet,
Seeing the LORD has ᵐgiven it a
   charge
Against Ashkelon and against the
   seashore?
There He has ⁿappointed it."

Judgment on Moab

48 Against ªMoab.
Thus says the LORD of hosts, the God of Israel:

"Woe to ᵇNebo!
For it is plundered,
ᶜKirjathaim is shamed *and* taken;
The high stronghold* is shamed and
   dismayed—
2 ᵈNo more praise of Moab.
In ᵉHeshbon they have devised evil
   against her:

'Come, and let us cut her off as a
   nation.'
You also shall be cut down,
   O ᶠMadmen!*
The sword shall pursue you;
3 A voice of crying *shall be* from
   ᵍHoronaim:
'Plundering and great destruction!'
4 "Moab is destroyed;
Her little ones have caused a cry to be
   heard;*
5 ʰFor in the Ascent of Luhith they
   ascend with continual weeping;
For in the descent of Horonaim the
   enemies have heard a cry of
   destruction.

6 "Flee, save your lives!
And be like the ⁱjuniper* in the
   wilderness.
7 For because you have trusted in your
   works and your ʲtreasures,
You also shall be taken.
And ᵏChemosh shall go forth into
   captivity,
His ˡpriests and his princes together.
8 And ᵐthe plunderer shall come against
   every city;
No one shall escape.
The valley also shall perish,
And the plain shall be destroyed,
As the LORD has spoken.

9 "Giveⁿ wings to Moab,
That she may flee and get away;
For her cities shall be desolate,
Without any to dwell in them.
10 ᵒCursed *is* he who does the work of the
   LORD deceitfully,
And cursed *is* he who keeps back his
   sword from blood.

11 "Moab has been at ease from his*
   youth;
He ᵖhas settled on his dregs,
And has not been emptied from vessel
   to vessel,
Nor has he gone into captivity.
Therefore his taste remained in him,
And his scent has not changed.

12 "Therefore behold, the days are
   coming," says the LORD,

---

* **48:1** Hebrew *Misgab*   * **48:2** A city of Moab
* **48:4** Following Masoretic Text, Targum, and Vulgate; Septuagint reads *Proclaim it in Zoar.*
* **48:6** Or *Aroer,* a city of Moab   * **48:11** The Hebrew uses masculine and feminine pronouns interchangeably in this chapter.

47:6–7 sword of the LORD. This image is used often to portray divine judgment (12:2; 46:10,14,16).
48:6–8 the juniper. This tree ekes out its stunted growth in the wilderness, hiding in crevasses of rock. **captivity.** Taking a deity captive was a well-known Middle Eastern custom. The national statue of the patron deity was seized, and it was believed that the captured god could no longer protect its people.

47:1 ª Zeph. 2:4, 5 ᵇ Amos 1:6   **47:2** ᶜ Is. 8:7, 8 ᵈ Jer. 1:14   **47:3** ᵉ Jer. 8:16   **47:4** ᶠ Is. 14:29–31 ᵍ Jer. 25:22 ʰ Ezek. 25:16 ⁱ Gen. 10:14   **47:5** ʲ Mic. 1:16 ᵏ Jer. 25:20   **47:6** ˡ Ezek. 21:3–5   **47:7** ᵐ Ezek. 14:17 ⁿ Mic. 6:9   **48:1** ª Is. 15:1—16:14; 25:10 ᵇ Is. 15:2 ᶜ Num. 32:37   **48:2** ᵈ Is. 16:14 ᵉ Jer. 49:3 ᶠ Is. 10:31   **48:3** ᵍ Is. 15:5   **48:5** ʰ Is. 15:5   **48:6** ⁱ Jer. 17:6   **48:7** ʲ Jer. 9:23 ᵏ Jer. 48:13 ˡ Jer. 49:3   **48:8** ᵐ Jer. 6:26   **48:9** ⁿ Ps. 55:6   **48:10** ᵒ 1 Sam. 15:3, 9   **48:11** ᵖ Zeph. 1:12

"That I shall send him wine-workers
Who will tip him over
And empty his vessels
And break the bottles.
13 Moab shall be ashamed of [q]Chemosh,
As the house of Israel [r]was ashamed of
[s]Bethel, their confidence.

14 "How can you say, [t]'We *are* mighty
And strong men for the war'?
15 Moab is plundered and gone up *from*
her cities;
Her chosen young men have [u]gone
down to the slaughter," says [v]the
King,
Whose name *is* the LORD of hosts.

16 "The calamity of Moab *is* near at hand,
And his affliction comes quickly.
17 Bemoan him, all you who are around
him;
And all you who know his name,
Say, [w]'How the strong staff is broken,
The beautiful rod!'

18 "O [x]daughter inhabiting [y]Dibon,
Come down from *your* glory,
And sit in thirst;
For the plunderer of Moab has come
against you,
He has destroyed your strongholds.
19 O inhabitant of [z]Aroer,
[a]Stand by the way and watch;
Ask him who flees
And her who escapes;
Say, 'What has happened?'
20 Moab is shamed, for he is broken down.
[b]Wail and cry!
Tell it in [c]Arnon, that Moab is plundered.

21 "And judgment has come on the plain
country:
On Holon and Jahzah and Mephaath,
22 On Dibon and Nebo and Beth
Diblathaim,
23 On Kirjathaim and Beth Gamul and
Beth Meon,
24 On [d]Kerioth and Bozrah,
On all the cities of the land of Moab,
Far or near.
25 [e]The horn of Moab is cut off,
And his [f]arm is broken," says the LORD.

26 "Make[g] him drunk,
Because he exalted *himself* against the
LORD.
Moab shall wallow in his vomit,
And he shall also be in derision.
27 For [h]was not Israel a derision to you?
[i]Was he found among thieves?
For whenever you speak of him,
You shake *your head in* [j]*scorn.*
28 You who dwell in Moab,
Leave the cities and [k]dwell in the rock,
And be like [l]the dove *which* makes
her nest
In the sides of the cave's mouth.

29 "We have heard the [m]pride of Moab
(He *is* exceedingly proud),
Of his loftiness and arrogance and
[n]pride,
And of the haughtiness of his heart."

30 "I know his wrath," says the LORD,
"But it *is* not right;
[o]His lies have made nothing right.
31 Therefore [p]I will wail for Moab,
And I will cry out for all Moab;
I* will mourn for the men of Kir Heres.
32 [q]O vine of Sibmah! I will weep for you
with the weeping of [r]Jazer.
Your plants have gone over the sea,
They reach to the sea of Jazer.
The plunderer has fallen on your
summer fruit and your vintage.
33 [s]Joy and gladness are taken
From the plentiful field
And from the land of Moab;
I have caused wine to fail from the
winepresses;
No one will tread with joyous
shouting—
Not joyous shouting!

34 "From[t] the cry of Heshbon to [u]Elealeh
and to Jahaz
They have uttered their voice,
[v]From Zoar to Horonaim,
Like a three-year-old heifer;*
For the waters of Nimrim also shall be
desolate.

35 "Moreover," says the LORD,
"I will cause to cease in Moab
[w]The one who offers *sacrifices* in the
high places
And burns incense to his gods.

* **48:31** Following Dead Sea Scrolls, Septuagint, and Vulgate; Masoretic Text reads *He.* * **48:34** Or *The Third Eglath,* an unknown city (compare Isaiah 15:5)

48:17 ***Bemoan him, all you who are around him.*** A note of sarcasm is communicated. The nations around Moab, like Judah, who was attacked by Moab's mercenaries, were called upon to lament Moab's destruction.

48:18 ***Come down from your glory.*** The haughty Moab was shamed by the destruction of its fortresses.

48:26–29 ***Make him drunk.*** Judgment is portrayed in the form of drunkenness to the point of vomiting, the result of Moab's mockery of Israel (25:15–29).

48:33 ***Joy and gladness are taken.*** The joy once heard echoing from the vineyards and winepresses had vanished before the horrifying sound of horses' hoofbeats and clashing weapons.

48:13 [q] 1 Kin. 11:7 [r] Hos. 10:6 [s] 1 Kin. 12:29; 13:32–34 **48:14** [t] Is. 16:6 **48:15** [u] Jer. 50:27 [v] Jer. 46:18; 51:57 **48:17** [w] Is. 9:4; 14:4, 5 **48:18** [x] Is. 47:1 [y] Is. 15:2 **48:19** [z] Deut. 2:36 [a] 1 Sam. 4:13, 14, 16 **48:20** [b] Is. 16:7 [c] Num. 21:13 **48:24** [d] Amos 2:2 **48:25** [e] Ps. 75:10 [f] Ezek. 30:21 **48:26** [g] Jer. 25:15 **48:27** [h] Zeph. 2:8 [i] Jer. 2:26 [j] Lam. 2:15 **48:28** [k] Ps. 55:6, 7 [l] Song 2:14 **48:29** [m] Is. 16:6 [n] Jer. 49:16 **48:30** [o] Jer. 50:36 **48:31** [p] Is. 15:5; 16:7, 11 **48:32** [q] Is. 16:8, 9 [r] Num. 21:32 **48:33** [s] Joel 1:12 **48:34** [t] Is. 15:4–6 [u] Num. 32:3, 37 [v] Is. 15:5, 6 **48:35** [w] Is. 15:2; 16:12

36 Therefore ˣMy heart shall wail like
flutes for Moab,
And like flutes My heart shall wail
For the men of Kir Heres.
Therefore ʸthe riches they have
acquired have perished.

37 "For ᶻevery head *shall be* bald, and
every beard clipped;
On all the hands *shall be* cuts, and ᵃon
the loins sackcloth—
38 A general lamentation
On all the ᵇhousetops of Moab,
And in its streets;
For I have ᶜbroken Moab like a vessel
in which *is* no pleasure," says the
LORD.
39 "They shall wail:
'How she is broken down!
How Moab has turned her back with
shame!'
So Moab shall be a derision
And a dismay to all those about her."

40For thus says the LORD:

"Behold, ᵈone shall fly like an eagle,
And ᵉspread his wings over Moab.
41 Kerioth is taken,
And the strongholds are surprised;
ᶠThe mighty men's hearts in Moab on
that day shall be
Like the heart of a woman in birth
pangs.
42 And Moab shall be destroyed ᵍas a
people,
Because he exalted *himself* against the
LORD.
43 ʰFear and the pit and the snare *shall be*
upon you,
O inhabitant of Moab," says the LORD.
44 "He who flees from the fear shall fall
into the pit,
And he who gets out of the pit shall be
caught in the ⁱsnare.
For upon Moab, upon it ʲI will bring
The year of their punishment," says
the LORD.

45 "Those who fled stood under the
shadow of Heshbon
Because of exhaustion.
But ᵏa fire shall come out of Heshbon,
A flame from the midst of ˡSihon,
And ᵐshall devour the brow of Moab,
The crown of the head of the sons of
tumult.

46 ⁿWoe to you, O Moab!
The people of Chemosh perish;
For your sons have been taken captive,
And your daughters captive.

47 "Yet I will bring back the captives of
Moab
ᵒIn the latter days," says the LORD.

Thus far *is* the judgment of Moab.

Judgment on Ammon

49 Against the ᵃAmmonites.
Thus says the LORD:

"Has Israel no sons?
Has he no heir?
Why *then* does Milcom* inherit ᵇGad,
And his people dwell in its cities?
2 ᶜTherefore behold, the days are
coming," says the LORD,
"That I will cause to be heard an alarm
of war
In ᵈRabbah of the Ammonites;
It shall be a desolate mound,
And her villages shall be burned with
fire.
Then Israel shall take possession of
his inheritance," says the LORD.

3 "Wail, O ᵉHeshbon, for Ai is plundered!
Cry, you daughters of Rabbah,
ᶠGird yourselves with sackcloth!
Lament and run to and fro by the
walls;
For Milcom shall go into captivity
With his ᵍpriests and his princes
together.
4 Why ʰdo you boast in the valleys,
Your flowing valley, O ⁱbacksliding
daughter?
Who trusted in her ʲtreasures, ᵏ*saying,*
'Who will come against me?'
5 Behold, I will bring fear upon you,"
Says the Lord GOD of hosts,
"From all those who are around you;
You shall be driven out, everyone
headlong,
And no one will gather those who
wander off.
6 But ˡafterward I will bring back
The captives of the people of Ammon,"
says the LORD.

* 49:1 Hebrew *Malcam,* literally *their king,* a god
of the Ammonites; also called *Molech* (compare
verse 3)

48:40–44 one shall fly like an eagle. The imagery
is that of Babylon spreading its ravaging armies over
Moab like an eagle spreading its wings. **he exalted
himself.** Moab's chief sin was pride, considering itself
greater than the God of Israel. Its pride would be
turned to fear and terror, and then the nation would
be taken captive.
49:1–2 Milcom. This was the patron deity of the Ammonites and is pictured here as taking possession of
the land formerly belonging to the Gadites, a process
that began in the days of the judges.

48:36 ˣ Is. 15:5; 16:11 ʸ Is. 15:7 **48:37** ᶻ Is. 15:2, 3 ᵃ Gen.
37:34 **48:38** ᵇ Is. 15:3 ᶜ Jer. 22:28 **48:40** ᵈ Deut.
28:49 ᵉ Is. 8:8 **48:41** ᶠ Is. 13:8; 21:3 **48:42** ᵍ Ps. 83:4
48:43 ʰ Is. 24:17, 18 **48:44** ⁱ Is. 24:18 ʲ Jer. 11:23
48:45 ᵏ Num. 21:28, 29 ˡ Ps. 135:11 ᵐ Num. 24:17
48:46 ⁿ Num. 21:29 **48:47** ᵒ Jer. 49:6, 39 **49:1** ᵃ Ezek.
21:28–32; 25:1–7 ᵇ Amos 1:13–15 **49:2** ᶜ Amos
1:13–15 ᵈ Ezek. 25:5 **49:3** ᵉ Jer. 48:2 ᶠ Is. 32:11 ᵍ Jer.
48:7 **49:4** ʰ Jer. 9:23 ⁱ Jer. 3:14 ʲ Jer. 48:7 ᵏ Jer. 21:13
49:6 ˡ Jer. 48:47

Judgment on Edom

7mAgainst Edom.
Thus says the LORD of hosts:

n"Is wisdom no more in Teman?
oHas counsel perished from the prudent?
Has their wisdom pvanished?
8 Flee, turn back, dwell in the depths,
O inhabitants of qDedan!
For I will bring the calamity of Esau
upon him,
The time that I will punish him.
9 rIf grape-gatherers came to you,
Would they not leave some gleaning
grapes?
If thieves by night,
Would they not destroy until they have
enough?
10 sBut I have made Esau bare;
I have uncovered his secret places,*
And he shall not be able to hide himself.
His descendants are plundered,
His brethren and his neighbors,
And the is no more.
11 Leave your fatherless children,
I will preserve them alive;
And let your widows trust in Me."

12For thus says the LORD: "Behold, uthose
whose judgment was not to drink of the cup
have assuredly drunk. And are you the one
who will altogether go unpunished? You
shall not go unpunished, but you shall surely drink of it. 13For vI have sworn by Myself,"
says the LORD, "that wBozrah shall become a
desolation, a reproach, a waste, and a curse.
And all its cities shall be perpetual wastes."

14 xI have heard a message from the LORD,
And an ambassador has been sent to
the nations:
"Gather together, come against her,
And rise up to battle!

15 "For indeed, I will make you small
among nations,
Despised among men.
16 Your fierceness has deceived you,
The ypride of your heart,
O you who dwell in the clefts of the rock,
Who hold the height of the hill!
zThough you make your anest as high
as the eagle,
bI will bring you down from there," says
the LORD.*

17 "Edom also shall be an astonishment;
cEveryone who goes by it will be
astonished

And will hiss at all its
plagues.
18 dAs in the overthrow of Sodom and
Gomorrah
And their neighbors," says the LORD,
"No one shall remain there,
Nor shall a son of man dwell in it.

19 "Behold,e he shall come up like a lion
from fthe floodplain* of the Jordan
Against the dwelling place of the
strong;
But I will suddenly make him run
away from her.
And who is a chosen man that I may
appoint over her?
For gwho is like Me?
Who will arraign Me?
And hwho is that shepherd
Who will withstand Me?"

20 iTherefore hear the counsel of the LORD
that He has taken against Edom,
And His purposes that He has
proposed against the inhabitants
of Teman:
Surely the least of the flock shall draw
them out;
Surely He shall make their dwelling
places desolate with them.
21 jThe earth shakes at the noise of their
fall;
At the cry its noise is heard at the Red
Sea.
22 Behold, kHe shall come up and fly like
the eagle,
And spread His wings over Bozrah;
The heart of the mighty men of Edom
in that day shall be
Like the heart of a woman in birth
pangs.

Judgment on Damascus

23lAgainst Damascus.

m"Hamath and Arpad are shamed,
For they have heard bad news.
They are fainthearted;
nThere is trouble on the sea;
It cannot be quiet.
24 Damascus has grown feeble,
She turns to flee,
And fear has seized her.
oAnguish and sorrows have taken her
like a woman in labor.

---

* 49:10 Compare Obadiah 5, 6   * 49:16 Compare
Obadiah 3, 4   * 49:19 Or thicket

49:9–11 grape-gatherers. This imagery is derived
from 6:9, but there was no real remnant left in Edom.
The nation had been totally ravaged and stripped
bare, with only women and children left alive to work
the land.
49:17–19 astonishment. Like Israel, Judah, Egypt,
Moab, and Ammon, Edom would be destroyed and
would become an object of derision. Like the lion that
emerges from the thickets along the lower Jordan
and seizes its prey, God would attack the Edomites
through His appointed instrument.

49:7 m Ezek. 25:12–14; 35:1–15   n Gen. 36:11   o Is. 19:11
p Jer. 8:9   **49:8** q Jer. 25:23   **49:9** r Obad. 5, 6
49:10 s Mal. 1:3   t Is. 17:14   **49:12** u Jer. 25:29
49:13 v Amos 6:8   w Is. 34:6; 63:1   **49:14** x Obad. 1–4
49:16 y Jer. 48:29   z Obad. 3, 4   a Job 39:27   b Amos 9:2
49:17 c Jer. 18:16; 49:13; 50:13   **49:18** d Deut. 29:23
49:19 e Jer. 50:44   f Jer. 12:5   g Ex. 15:11   h Job 41:10
49:20 i Jer. 50:45   **49:21** j Jer. 50:46   **49:22** k Jer.
48:40, 41   **49:23** l Amos 1:3, 5   m Jer. 39:5   n [Is. 57:20]
49:24 o Is. 13:8

25 Why is ᵖthe city of praise not deserted,
the city of My joy?
26 ᵃTherefore her young men shall fall in
her streets,
And all the men of war shall be cut
off in that day," says the LORD of
hosts.
27 "Iʳ will kindle a fire in the wall of
Damascus,
And it shall consume the palaces of
Ben-Hadad."*

Judgment on Kedar and Hazor

28ˢAgainst Kedar and against the kingdoms of Hazor, which Nebuchadnezzar
king of Babylon shall strike.

Thus says the LORD:

"Arise, go up to Kedar,
And devastate ᵗthe men of the East!
29 Their ᵘtents and their flocks they shall
take away.
They shall take for themselves their
curtains,
All their vessels and their camels;
And they shall cry out to them,
ᵛ'Fear is on every side!'
30 "Flee, get far away! Dwell in the
depths,
O inhabitants of Hazor!" says the
LORD.
"For Nebuchadnezzar king of Babylon
has taken counsel against
you,
And has conceived a plan against
you.
31 "Arise, go up to ʷthe wealthy nation
that dwells securely," says the
LORD,
"Which has neither gates nor bars,
ˣDwelling alone.
32 Their camels shall be for booty,
And the multitude of their cattle for
plunder.
I will ʸscatter to all winds those in the
farthest corners,
And I will bring their calamity from
all its sides," says the LORD.
33 "Hazor ᶻshall be a dwelling for jackals,
a desolation forever;
No one shall reside there,
Nor son of man dwell in it."

Judgment on Elam

34The word of the LORD that came to
Jeremiah the prophet against ᵃElam, in the
ᵇbeginning of the reign of Zedekiah king
of Judah, saying, 35"Thus says the LORD of
hosts:

'Behold, I will break ᶜthe bow of Elam,
The foremost of their might.
36 Against Elam I will bring the four
winds
From the four quarters of heaven,
And scatter them toward all those
winds;
There shall be no nations where the
outcasts of Elam will not go.
37 For I will cause Elam to be dismayed
before their enemies
And before those who seek their life.
ᵈI will bring disaster upon them,
My fierce anger,' says the LORD;
'And I will send the sword after them
Until I have consumed them.
38 I will ᵉset My throne in Elam,
And will destroy from there the king
and the princes,' says the LORD.
39 'But it shall come to pass ᶠin the latter
days:
I will bring back the captives of Elam,'
says the LORD."

Judgment on Babylon and Babylonia

50 The word that the LORD spoke
ᵃagainst Babylon and against the
land of the Chaldeans by Jeremiah the
prophet.

2 "Declare among the nations,
Proclaim, and set up a standard;
Proclaim—do not conceal it—
Say, 'Babylon is ᵇtaken, ᶜBel is shamed.
Merodach* is broken in pieces;
ᵈHer idols are humiliated,
Her images are broken in pieces.'
3 ᵉFor out of the north ᶠa nation comes up
against her,
Which shall make her land desolate,
And no one shall dwell therein.
They shall move, they shall depart,
Both man and beast.

---

* 49:27 Compare Amos 1:4   * 50:2 A Babylonian
god; sometimes spelled *Marduk*

49:30–33 Hazor shall be a dwelling for jackals.
Nebuchadnezzar's destructive army would attack
the tent villages of Kedar and Hazor. The oases would
be left to the jackals for habitation (9:11; 10:22). The
Bedouin peoples would be scattered afar, as if by the
hot desert winds.
49:34–36 break the bow. The Elamites were famous
for their skilled archers (Is. 22:6), who became an
important part of the Persian army under Cyrus. **four
winds.** This expression indicates the military might
that the Lord musters against His enemies (Ezek.
37:9).
50:2–3 Bel is shamed. Bel was a title like Baal,

meaning "Lord," another name for Babylon's patron
deity, Marduk. The oracle begins with a defamation
of the gods of Babylon. The term translated "images"
means animal droppings. The Hebrew prophets are
openly contemptuous of idols and speak of them with
ridicule.

49:25 ᵖ Jer. 33:9   49:26 ᵃ Jer. 50:30   49:27 ʳ Amos 1:4
49:28 ˢ Ezek. 27:21 ᵗ Judg. 6:3   49:29 ᵘ Ps. 120:5 ᵛ Jer.
46:5   49:31 ʷ Ezek. 38:11 ˣ Num. 23:9   49:32 ʸ Ezek.
5:10   49:33 ᶻ Mal. 1:3   49:34 ᵃ Jer. 25:25 ᵇ 2 Kin. 24:17,
18   49:35 ᶜ Is. 22:6   49:37 ᵈ Jer. 9:16   49:38 ᵉ Jer. 43:10
49:39 ᶠ Jer. 48:47   50:1 ᵃ Is. 13:1; 47:1   50:2 ᵇ Is. 21:9 ᶜ Is.
46:1 ᵈ Jer. 43:12, 13   50:3 ᵉ Jer. 51:48 ᶠ Is. 13:17, 18, 20

4 "In those days and in that time," says
the LORD,
"The children of Israel shall come,
gThey and the children of Judah
together;
hWith continual weeping they shall
come,
iAnd seek the LORD their God.
5 They shall ask the way to Zion,
With their faces toward it, *saying,*
'Come and let us join ourselves to the
LORD
In ja perpetual covenant
That will not be forgotten.'

6 "My people have been klost sheep.
Their shepherds have led them lastray;
They have turned them away *on* mthe
mountains.
They have gone from mountain to hill;
They have forgotten their resting place.
7 All who found them have ndevoured
them;
And otheir adversaries said, p'We have
not offended,
Because they have sinned against the
LORD, qthe habitation of justice,
The LORD, rthe hope of their fathers.'

8 "Moves from the midst of Babylon,
Go out of the land of the Chaldeans;
And be like the rams before the
flocks.
9 tFor behold, I will raise and cause to
come up against Babylon
An assembly of great nations from the
north country,
And they shall array themselves
against her;
From there she shall be captured.
Their arrows *shall be* like *those* of an
expert warrior;*
uNone shall return in vain.
10 And Chaldea shall become plunder;
vAll who plunder her shall be satisfied,"
says the LORD.

11 "Becausew you were glad, because you
rejoiced,
You destroyers of My heritage,
Because you have grown fat xlike a
heifer threshing grain,
And you bellow like bulls,
12 Your mother shall be deeply
ashamed;
She who bore you shall be ashamed.
Behold, the least of the nations *shall be*
a ywilderness,
A dry land and a desert.

13 Because of the wrath of the LORD
She shall not be inhabited,
zBut she shall be wholly desolate.
aEveryone who goes by Babylon shall
be horrified
And hiss at all her plagues.

14 "Putb yourselves in array against
Babylon all around,
All you who bend the bow;
Shoot at her, spare no arrows,
For she has sinned against the LORD.
15 Shout against her all around;
She has cgiven her hand,
Her foundations have fallen,
dHer walls are thrown down;
For eit *is* the vengeance of the LORD.
Take vengeance on her.
As she has done, so do to her.
16 Cut off the sower from Babylon,
And him who handles the sickle at
harvest time.
For fear of the oppressing sword
fEveryone shall turn to his own people,
And everyone shall flee to his own
land.

17 "Israel *is* like gscattered sheep;
hThe lions have driven *him* away.
First ithe king of Assyria devoured
him;
Now at last this jNebuchadnezzar king
of Babylon has broken his bones."

18Therefore thus says the LORD of hosts,
the God of Israel:

"Behold, I will punish the king of
Babylon and his land,
As I have punished the king of
kAssyria.
19 lBut I will bring back Israel to his
home,
And he shall feed on Carmel and
Bashan;
His soul shall be satisfied on Mount
Ephraim and Gilead.
20 In those days and in that time," says
the LORD,
m"The iniquity of Israel shall be sought,
but *there shall be* none;
And the sins of Judah, but they shall
not be found;
For I will pardon those nwhom I
preserve.

* 50:9 Following some Hebrew manuscripts, Septuagint, and Syriac; Masoretic Text, Targum, and
Vulgate read *a warrior who makes childless.*

50:11–13 *You destroyers of My heritage.* Babylon's
plunder would be its punishment for gloating over
Judah's demise and the abuse of God's heritage. Babylon would "be a wilderness." Defamation, drought,
dehabitation, desolation, and derision were Babylon's destiny (18:16; 19:8; 49:17).

50:4 gHos. 1:11 hEzra 3:12, 13 iHos. 3:5 **50:5** jJer. 31:31 **50:6** kIs. 53:6 lJer. 23:1 m[Jer. 2:20; 3:6, 23] **50:7** nPs. 79:7 oZech. 11:5 pJer. 2:3 q[Ps. 90:1; 91:1] rPs. 22:4 **50:8** sIs. 48:20 **50:9** tJer. 15:14; 51:27 u2 Sam. 1:22 **50:10** v[Rev. 17:16] **50:11** wIs. 47:6 xHos. 10:11 **50:12** yJer. 51:43 **50:13** zJer. 25:12 aJer. 49:17 **50:14** bJer. 51:2 **50:15** cLam. 5:6 dJer. 51:58 eJer. 51:6, 11 **50:16** fIs. 13:14 **50:17** g2 Kin. 24:10, 14 hJer. 2:15 i2 Kin. 15:29; 17:6; 18:9–13 j2 Kin. 24:10–14; 25:1–7 **50:18** kEzek. 31:3, 11, 12 **50:19** lIs. 65:10 **50:20** m[Jer. 31:34] nIs. 1:9

21 "Go up against the land of Merathaim, against it,
And against the inhabitants of [o]Pekod.
Waste and utterly destroy them," says the LORD,
"And do [p]according to all that I have commanded you.
22 [q]A sound of battle *is* in the land,
And of great destruction.
23 How [r]the hammer of the whole earth has been cut apart and broken!
How Babylon has become a desolation among the nations!
24 I have laid a snare for you;
You have indeed been [s]trapped, O Babylon,
And you were not aware;
You have been found and also caught,
Because you have [t]contended against the LORD.
25 The LORD has opened His armory,
And has brought out [u]the weapons of His indignation;
For this *is* the work of the Lord GOD of hosts
In the land of the Chaldeans.
26 Come against her from the farthest border;
Open her storehouses;
Cast her up as heaps of ruins,
And destroy her utterly;
Let nothing of her be left.
27 Slay all her [v]bulls,
Let them go down to the slaughter.
Woe to them!
For their day has come, the time of [w]their punishment.
28 The voice of those who flee and escape from the land of Babylon
[x]Declares in Zion the vengeance of the LORD our God,
The vengeance of His temple.

29 "Call together the archers against Babylon.
All you who bend the bow, encamp against it all around;
Let none of them escape.*
[y]Repay her according to her work;
According to all she has done, do to her;
[z]For she has been proud against the LORD,
Against the Holy One of Israel.
30 [a]Therefore her young men shall fall in the streets,
And all her men of war shall be cut off in that day," says the LORD.

31 "Behold, I *am* against you,
O most haughty one!" says the Lord GOD of hosts;
"For your day has come,
The time *that* I will punish you.*
32 The most [b]proud shall stumble and fall,
And no one will raise him up;
[c]I will kindle a fire in his cities,
And it will devour all around him."

33 Thus says the LORD of hosts:

"The children of Israel *were* oppressed,
Along with the children of Judah;
All who took them captive have held them fast;
They have refused to let them go.
34 [d]Their Redeemer *is* strong;
[e]The LORD of hosts *is* His name.
He will thoroughly plead their [f]case,
That He may give rest to the land,
And disquiet the inhabitants of Babylon.

35 "A sword *is* against the Chaldeans," says the LORD,
"Against the inhabitants of Babylon,
And [g]against her princes and [h]her wise men.
36 A sword *is* [i]against the soothsayers, and they will be fools.
A sword *is* against her mighty men, and they will be dismayed.
37 A sword *is* against their horses,
Against their chariots,
And against all [j]the mixed peoples who *are* in her midst;
And [k]they will become like women.
A sword *is* against her treasures, and they will be robbed.
38 [l]A drought* *is* against her waters, and they will be dried up.
For it *is* the land of carved images,
And they are insane with *their* idols.

39 "Therefore[m] the wild desert beasts shall dwell *there* with the jackals,
And the ostriches shall dwell in it.
[n]It shall be inhabited no more forever,
Nor shall it be dwelt in from generation to generation.

* **50:29** Qere, some Hebrew manuscripts, Septuagint, and Targum add *to her.* * **50:31** Following Masoretic Text and Targum; Septuagint and Vulgate read *The time of your punishment.* * **50:38** Following Masoretic Text, Targum, and Vulgate; Syriac reads *sword;* Septuagint omits *A drought is.*

50:21–28 ***utterly destroy them.*** The tables would be turned on Babylon. The Lord God had launched His vengeful weapons upon the city through His anointed servant Cyrus (2 Chr. 36:22–23; Is 45:1).

50:34 ***Their Redeemer is strong.*** One who secured the freedom of a kinsman, protecting family rights, was called a kinsmen redeemer. Here God, the Redeemer of Israel (Is. 47:4), offers to obtain the legal freedom of His people from captivity.

50:21 [o] Ezek. 23:23 [p] 2 Sam. 16:11 **50:22** [q] Jer. 51:54 **50:23** [r] Jer. 51:20–24 **50:24** [s] Dan. 5:30 [t] [Is. 45:9] **50:25** [u] Is. 13:5 **50:27** [v] Is. 34:7 [w] Jer. 48:44 **50:28** [x] Jer. 51:10 **50:29** [y] Jer. 51:56 [z] [Is. 47:10] **50:30** [a] Jer. 49:26; 51:4 **50:32** [b] Mal. 4:1 [c] Jer. 21:14 **50:34** [d] Rev. 18:8 [e] Is. 47:4 [f] Jer. 51:36; Mic. 7:9 **50:35** [g] Dan. 5:30 [h] Is. 47:13 **50:36** [i] Is. 44:25 **50:37** [j] Jer. 25:20 [k] Jer. 51:30 **50:38** [l] Rev. 16:12 **50:39** [m] Rev. 18:2 [n] Is. 13:20

40 oAs God overthrew Sodom and
    Gomorrah
    And their neighbors," says the LORD,
    "So no one shall reside there,
    Nor son of man pdwell in it.

41 "Behold,q a people shall come from the
    north,
    And a great nation and many kings
    Shall be raised up from the ends of the
    earth.

42 rThey shall hold the bow and the lance;
    sThey are cruel and shall not show
    mercy.
    tTheir voice shall roar like the sea;
    They shall ride on horses,
    Set in array, like a man for the battle,
    Against you, O daughter of Babylon.

43 "The king of Babylon has uheard the
    report about them,
    And his hands grow feeble;
    Anguish has taken hold of him,
    Pangs as of a woman in vchildbirth.

44 "Behold,w he shall come up like a
    lion from the floodplain* of the
    Jordan
    Against the dwelling place of the
    strong;
    But I will make them suddenly run
    away from her.
    And who is a chosen man that I may
    appoint over her?
    For who is like Me?
    Who will arraign Me?
    And xwho is that shepherd
    Who will withstand Me?"

45 Therefore hear ythe counsel of the
    LORD that He has taken against
    Babylon,
    And His zpurposes that He has
    proposed against the land of the
    Chaldeans:
    aSurely the least of the flock shall draw
    them out;
    Surely He will make their dwelling
    place desolate with them.

46 bAt the noise of the taking of Babylon
    The earth trembles,
    And the cry is heard among the
    nations.

The Utter Destruction of Babylon

51 Thus says the LORD:

    "Behold, I will raise up against
    aBabylon,

    Against those who dwell in Leb
        Kamai,*
    bA destroying wind.

2   And I will send cwinnowers to
        Babylon,
    Who shall winnow her and empty her
        land.
    dFor in the day of doom
    They shall be against her all
        around.

3   Against her elet the archer bend his
        bow,
    And lift himself up against her in his
        armor.
    Do not spare her young men;
    fUtterly destroy all her army.

4   Thus the slain shall fall in the land of
        the Chaldeans,
    gAnd those thrust through in her
        streets.

5   For Israel is hnot forsaken, nor
        Judah,
    By his God, the LORD of hosts,
    Though their land was filled with sin
        against the Holy One of Israel."

6   iFlee from the midst of Babylon,
    And every one save his life!
    Do not be cut off in her iniquity,
    For jthis is the time of the LORD's
        vengeance;
    kHe shall recompense her.

7   lBabylon was a golden cup in the
        LORD's hand,
    That made all the earth drunk.
    mThe nations drank her wine;
    Therefore the nations nare
        deranged.

8   Babylon has suddenly ofallen and been
        destroyed.
    pWail for her!
    qTake balm for her pain;
    Perhaps she may be healed.

9   We would have healed Babylon,
    But she is not healed.
    Forsake her, and rlet us go everyone to
        his own country;
    sFor her judgment reaches to heaven
        and is lifted up to the skies.

10 The LORD has trevealed our
        righteousness.
    Come and let us udeclare in Zion the
        work of the LORD our God.

---

*50:44 Or thicket   *51:1 A code word for Chal-
dea (Babylonia); may be translated The Midst of
Those Who Rise Up Against Me

51:6–10 Babylon was a golden cup. The imagery
of Babylon's cup of fury from 25:15–19 is reversed.
Here Babylon's cup is broken by the Lord. **Take balm.**
As in the case of Judah (8:22), decadent Babylon
was beyond healing and had to be abandoned. The
destruction of Babylon was the vindication of the justice of God. Jeremiah's prediction (25:12–14) would
be realized: Israel would be made righteous through
God's work.

50:40 oIs. 13:19 pIs. 13:20   **50:41** qJer. 6:22; 25:14; 51:27
50:42 rJer. 6:23 sIs. 13:18 tIs. 5:30   **50:43** uJer. 51:31
vJer. 6:24   **50:44** wJer. 49:19–21 xJob 41:10   **50:45** yJer.
51:10, 11 zJer. 51:29 aJer. 49:19, 20   **50:46** bRev. 18:9
51:1 aIs. 47:1 bJer. 4:11   **51:2** cJer. 15:7 dJer. 50:14
51:3 eJer. 50:14, 29 fJer. 50:21   **51:4** gJer. 49:26; 50:30,
37   **51:5** hJer. 33:24–26; 46:28]   **51:6** iRev. 18:4 jJer.
50:15 kJer. 25:14   **51:7** lRev. 17:4 mRev. 14:8 nJer. 25:16
51:8 oIs. 21:9 pRev. 18:9, 11, 19 qJer. 46:11   **51:9** rIs. 13:14
sRev. 18:5   **51:10** tPs. 37:6 uJer. 50:28

11 vMake the arrows bright!
Gather the shields!
wThe LORD has raised up the spirit of
the kings of the Medes.
xFor His plan *is* against Babylon to
destroy it,
Because it *is* ythe vengeance of the
LORD,
The vengeance for His temple.
12 zSet up the standard on the walls of
Babylon;
Make the guard strong,
Set up the watchmen,
Prepare the ambushes.
For the LORD has both devised and
done
What He spoke against the inhabitants
of Babylon.
13 aO you who dwell by many waters,
Abundant in treasures,
Your end has come,
The measure of your covetousness.
14 bThe LORD of hosts has sworn by
Himself:
"Surely I will fill you with men, cas with
locusts,
And they shall lift dup a shout against
you."
15 eHe has made the earth by His power;
He has established the world by His
wisdom,
And fstretched out the heaven by His
understanding.
16 When He utters *His* voice—
There is a multitude of waters in the
heavens;
g"He causes the vapors to ascend from
the ends of the earth;
He makes lightnings for the rain;
He brings the wind out of His
treasuries."*
17 hEveryone is dull-hearted, without
knowledge;
Every metalsmith is put to shame by
the carved image;
iFor his molded image *is* falsehood,
And *there is* no breath in them.
18 They *are* futile, a work of errors;
In the time of their punishment they
shall perish.
19 The Portion of Jacob *is* not like them,
For He *is* the Maker of all things;
And Israel *is* the tribe of His
inheritance.
The LORD of hosts *is* His name.
20 "Youj *are* My battle-ax *and* weapons of
war:

For with you I will break the nation in
pieces;
With you I will destroy kingdoms;
21 With you I will break in pieces the
horse and its rider;
With you I will break in pieces the
chariot and its rider;
22 With you also I will break in pieces
man and woman;
With you I will break in pieces kold
and young;
With you I will break in pieces the
young man and the maiden;
23 With you also I will break in pieces the
shepherd and his flock;
With you I will break in pieces the
farmer and his yoke of oxen;
And with you I will break in pieces
governors and rulers.

24 "Andl I will repay Babylon
And all the inhabitants of Chaldea
For all the evil they have done
In Zion in your sight," says the LORD.
25 "Behold, I *am* against you,
mO destroying mountain,
Who destroys all the earth," says the
LORD.
"And I will stretch out My hand against
you,
Roll you down from the rocks,
nAnd make you a burnt mountain.
26 They shall not take from you a stone
for a corner
Nor a stone for a foundation,
oBut you shall be desolate forever," says
the LORD.
27 pSet up a banner in the land,
Blow the trumpet among the nations!
qPrepare the nations against her,
Call rthe kingdoms together against
her:
Ararat, Minni, and Ashkenaz.
Appoint a general against her;
Cause the horses to come up like the
bristling locusts.
28 Prepare against her the nations,
With the kings of the Medes,
Its governors and all its rulers,
All the land of his dominion.
29 And the land will tremble and
sorrow;
For every spurpose of the LORD shall
be performed against Babylon,
tTo make the land of Babylon a
desolation without inhabitant.

* 51:16 Psalm 135:7

51:20–26 *You are My battle-ax.* Babylon had been
God's implement for judgment against the nations,
and Judah in particular.
**51:29–32 *The mighty men of Babylon have ceased
fighting.*** The Nabonidus Chronicle, an ancient text
describing the fall of Babylon, reports that "Cyrus
entered Babylon without a battle." By the time Cyrus
reached Babylon, he had conquered all of Babylonia

51:11 v Jer. 46:4, 9 w Is. 13:17 x Jer. 50:45 y Jer. 50:28
51:12 z Nah. 2:1; 3:14 **51:13** a Rev. 17:1, 15 **51:14** b Jer.
49:13 c Nah. 3:15 d Jer. 50:15 **51:15** e Gen. 1:1, 6 f Job
9:8 **51:16** g Ps. 135:7 **51:17** h Jer. 10:14 i Jer. 50:2
51:20 j Is. 10:5, 15 **51:22** k 2 Chr. 36:17 **51:24** l Jer.
50:15, 29 **51:25** m Zech. 4:7 n Rev. 8:8 **51:26** o Jer.
50:26, 40 **51:27** p Is. 13:2 q Jer. 25:14 r Jer. 50:41, 42
51:29 s Jer. 50:45 t Jer. 50:13; 51:26, 43

30 The mighty men of Babylon have
    ceased fighting,
They have remained in their strongholds;
    Their might has failed,
uThey became *like* women;
They have burned her dwelling places,
vThe bars of her *gate* are broken.
31 wOne runner will run to meet another,
    And one messenger to meet another,
To show the king of Babylon that his
    city is taken on *all* sides;
32 xThe passages are blocked,
The reeds they have burned with fire,
And the men of war are terrified.

33For thus says the LORD of hosts, the
God of Israel:

"The daughter of Babylon *is* ylike a
    threshing floor
When zit *is* time to thresh her;
    Yet a little while
aAnd the time of her harvest will come."

34 "Nebuchadnezzar the king of Babylon
    Has bdevoured me, he has crushed me;
He has made me an cempty vessel,
He has swallowed me up like a monster;
He has filled his stomach with my
    delicacies,
He has spit me out.
35 Let the violence *done* to me and my
    flesh *be* upon Babylon,"
The inhabitant of Zion will say;
"And my blood be upon the inhabitants
    of Chaldea!"
Jerusalem will say.

36Therefore thus says the LORD:

"Behold, dI will plead your case and
    take vengeance for you.
eI will dry up her sea and make her
    springs dry.
37 fBabylon shall become a heap,
    A dwelling place for jackals,
gAn astonishment and a hissing,
    Without an inhabitant.
38 They shall roar together like lions,
They shall growl like lions' whelps.
39 In their excitement I will prepare their
    feasts;
hI will make them drunk,
    That they may rejoice,
And sleep a perpetual sleep
    And not awake," says the LORD.
40 "I will bring them down

Like lambs to the slaughter,
Like rams with male goats.
41 "Oh, how iSheshach* is taken!
Oh, how jthe praise of the whole earth
    is seized!
How Babylon has become desolate
    among the nations!
42 kThe sea has come up over Babylon;
She is covered with the multitude of
    its waves.
43 lHer cities are a desolation,
    A dry land and a wilderness,
A land where mno one dwells,
Through which no son of man passes.
44 I will punish nBel in Babylon,
    And I will bring out of his mouth what
        he has swallowed;
And the nations shall not stream to
    him anymore.
Yes, othe wall of Babylon shall fall.

45 "Myp people, go out of the midst of her!
And let everyone deliver himself from
    the fierce anger of the LORD.
46 And lest your heart faint,
    And you fear qfor the rumor that *will*
        be heard in the land
(A rumor will come *one* year,
And after that, in *another* year
A rumor *will* come,
And violence in the land,
Ruler against ruler),
47 Therefore behold, the days are coming
    That I will bring judgment on the
        carved images of Babylon;
Her whole land shall be ashamed,
And all her slain shall fall in her
    midst.
48 Then rthe heavens and the earth and
    all that *is* in them
Shall sing joyously over Babylon;
sFor the plunderers shall come to her
    from the north," says the LORD.

49 As Babylon *has caused* the slain of
    Israel to fall,
So at Babylon the slain of all the earth
    shall fall.
50 tYou who have escaped the sword,
    Get away! Do not stand still!
uRemember the LORD afar off,
    And let Jerusalem come to your mind.

* **51:41** A code word for Babylon (compare Jeremiah 25:26)

---

except for the capital city, cutting off roads and supply routes.
51:47–48 the days are coming. This expression
usually introduces a message of divine intervention
into history. *judgment on the carved images of Babylon.* The city was known for its thousands of images
of its numerous gods and goddesses. As the king
claimed to conquer nations in the name of his patron
deity, so the gods of the defeated would be punished along with their worshipers. The devastation of
decadent Babylon would be no cause for mourning

among the nations. Instead, the nations would sing
joyfully of Babylon's fall.

51:30 u Is. 19:16 j Lam. 2:9 **51:31** w Jer. 50:24
51:32 x Jer. 50:38 **51:33** y Is. 21:10 z Hab. 3:12 a Rev.
14:15 **51:34** b Jer. 50:17 c Is. 24:1–3 **51:36** d Jer. 50:34
e Jer. 50:38 **51:37** f Is. 13:22 g Jer. 25:9, 11 **51:39** h Jer.
51:57 **51:41** i Jer. 25:26 j Is. 13:19 **51:42** k Is. 8:7, 8
51:43 l Jer. 50:39, 40 m Is. 13:20 **51:44** n Jer. 50:2
o Jer. 50:15 **51:45** p [Rev. 18:4] **51:46** q 2 Kin. 19:7
51:48 r Is. 44:23; 48:20; 49:13 s Jer. 50:3, 41 **51:50** t Jer.
44:28 u [Deut. 4:29–31]

⁵¹ ᵛWe are ashamed because we have
heard reproach.
Shame has covered our faces,
For strangers ʷhave come into the
sanctuaries of the LORD's house.

⁵² "Therefore behold, the days are
coming," says the LORD,
"That I will bring judgment on her
carved images,
And throughout all her land the
wounded shall groan.

⁵³ ˣThough Babylon were to mount up to
heaven,
And though she were to fortify the
height of her strength,
Yet from Me plunderers would come to
her," says the LORD.

⁵⁴ ʸThe sound of a cry comes from
Babylon,
And great destruction from the land of
the Chaldeans,
⁵⁵ Because the LORD is plundering
Babylon
And silencing her loud voice,
Though her waves roar like great
waters,
And the noise of their voice is uttered,
⁵⁶ Because the plunderer comes against
her, against Babylon,
And her mighty men are taken.
Every one of their bows is broken;
ᶻFor the LORD is the God of
recompense,
He will surely repay.

⁵⁷ "And I will make drunk
Her princes and ᵃwise men,
Her governors, her deputies, and her
mighty men.
And they shall sleep a perpetual
sleep
And not awake," says ᵇthe King,
Whose name is the LORD of hosts.

⁵⁸Thus says the LORD of hosts:

"The broad walls of Babylon shall be
utterly ᶜbroken,
And her high gates shall be burned
with fire;
ᵈThe people will labor in vain,
And the nations, because of the fire;
And they shall be weary."

Jeremiah's Command to Seraiah

⁵⁹The word which Jeremiah the prophet
commanded Seraiah the son of ᵉNeriah, the
son of Mahseiah, when he went with Zedekiah the king of Judah to Babylon in the
fourth year of his reign. And Seraiah was
the quartermaster. ⁶⁰So Jeremiah ᶠwrote in
a book all the evil that would come upon
Babylon, all these words that are written
against Babylon. ⁶¹And Jeremiah said to
Seraiah, "When you arrive in Babylon
and see it, and read all these words, ⁶²then
you shall say, 'O LORD, You have spoken
against this place to cut it off, so that ᵍnone
shall remain in it, neither man nor beast,
but it shall be desolate forever.' ⁶³Now it
shall be, when you have finished reading
this book, ʰthat you shall tie a stone to it
and throw it out into the Euphrates. ⁶⁴Then
you shall say, 'Thus Babylon shall sink and
not rise from the catastrophe that I will
bring upon her. And they shall be weary.' "

Thus far are the words of Jeremiah.

The Fall of Jerusalem Reviewed

52 Zedekiah was ᵃtwenty-one years
old when he became king, and he
reigned eleven years in Jerusalem. His
mother's name was Hamutal the daughter
of Jeremiah of ᵇLibnah. ²He also did evil in
the sight of the LORD, according to all that
Jehoiakim had done. ³For because of the
anger of the LORD this happened in Jerusalem and Judah, till He finally cast them
out from His presence. Then Zedekiah ᶜre-
belled against the king of Babylon.

⁴Now it came to pass in the ᵈninth year
of his reign, in the tenth month, on the
tenth day of the month, that Nebuchadnezzar king of Babylon and all his army came
against Jerusalem and encamped against
it; and they built a siege wall against it all
around. ⁵So the city was besieged until
the eleventh year of King Zedekiah. ⁶By
the fourth month, on the ninth day of the
month, the famine had become so severe
in the city that there was no food for the
people of the land. ⁷Then the city wall was
broken through, and all the men of war
fled and went out of the city at night by way
of the gate between the two walls, which
was by the king's garden, even though the
Chaldeans were near the city all around.
And they went by way of the plain.*

⁸But the army of the Chaldeans pursued
the king, and they overtook Zedekiah in
the plains of Jericho. All his army was
scattered from him. ⁹ᵉSo they took the king
and brought him up to the king of Babylon
at Riblah in the land of Hamath, and he
pronounced judgment on him. ¹⁰ᶠThen the
king of Babylon killed the sons of Zedekiah before his eyes. And he killed all the
princes of Judah in Riblah. ¹¹He also ᵍput
out the eyes of Zedekiah; and the king of
Babylon bound him in bronze fetters, took
him to Babylon, and put him in prison till
the day of his death.

---

* **52:7** Or the Arabah, that is, the Jordan Valley

51:51 ᵛPs. 44:15; 79:4 ʷLam. 1:10 **51:53** ˣAmos 9:2
51:54 ʸJer. 50:22 **51:56** ᶻJer. 50:29 **51:57** ᵃJer.
50:35 ᵇJer. 46:18; 48:15 **51:58** ᶜJer. 50:15
ᵈHab. 2:13 **51:59** ᵉJer. 32:12 **51:60** ᶠJer. 36:2

51:62 ᵍJer. 50:3, 39 **51:63** ʰRev. 18:21 **52:1** ᵃ2 Kin.
24:18 ᵇJosh. 10:29 **52:3** ᶜ2 Chr. 36:13 **52:4** ᵈJer.
39:1 **52:9** ᵉJer. 32:4; 39:5 **52:10** ᶠEzek. 12:13
52:11 ᵍEzek. 12:13

The Temple and City Plundered and Burned

¹²ʰNow in the fifth month, on the tenth day of the month (ⁱwhich was the nineteenth year of King Nebuchadnezzar king of Babylon), ʲNebuzaradan, the captain of the guard, who served the king of Babylon, came to Jerusalem. ¹³He burned the house of the LORD and the king's house; all the houses of Jerusalem, that is, all the houses of the great, he burned with fire. ¹⁴And all the army of the Chaldeans who were with the captain of the guard broke down all the walls of Jerusalem all around. ¹⁵ᵏThen Nebuzaradan the captain of the guard carried away captive some of the poor people, the rest of the people who remained in the city, the defectors who had deserted to the king of Babylon, and the rest of the craftsmen. ¹⁶But Nebuzaradan the captain of the guard left some of the poor of the land as vinedressers and farmers.

¹⁷ˡThe ᵐbronze pillars that were in the house of the LORD, and the carts and the bronze Sea that were in the house of the LORD, the Chaldeans broke in pieces, and carried all their bronze to Babylon. ¹⁸They also took away ⁿthe pots, the shovels, the trimmers, the bowls, the spoons, and all the bronze utensils with which the priests ministered. ¹⁹The basins, the firepans, the bowls, the pots, the lampstands, the spoons, and the cups, whatever was solid gold and whatever was solid silver, the captain of the guard took away. ²⁰The two pillars, one Sea, the twelve bronze bulls which were under it, and the carts, which King Solomon had made for the house of the LORD—ᵒthe bronze of all these articles was beyond measure. ²¹Now concerning the ᵖpillars: the height of one pillar was eighteen cubits, a measuring line of twelve cubits could measure its circumference, and its thickness was four fingers; it was hollow. ²²A capital of bronze was on it; and the height of one capital was five cubits, with a network and pomegranates all around the capital, all of bronze. The second pillar, with pomegranates was the same. ²³There were ninety-six pomegranates on the sides; ᵠall the pomegranates, all around on the network, were one hundred.

The People Taken Captive to Babylonia

²⁴ʳThe captain of the guard took Seraiah the chief priest, ˢZephaniah the second priest, and the three doorkeepers. ²⁵He also took out of the city an officer who had charge of the men of war, seven men of the king's close associates who were found in the city, the principal scribe of the army who mustered the people of the land, and sixty men of the people of the land who were found in the midst of the city. ²⁶And Nebuzaradan the captain of the guard took these and brought them to the king of Babylon at Riblah. ²⁷Then the king of Babylon struck them and put them to death at Riblah in the land of Hamath. Thus Judah was carried away captive from its own land.

²⁸ᵗThese are the people whom Nebuchadnezzar carried away captive: ᵘin the seventh year, ᵛthree thousand and twenty-three Jews; ²⁹ʷin the eighteenth year of Nebuchadnezzar he carried away captive from Jerusalem eight hundred and thirty-two persons; ³⁰in the twenty-third year of Nebuchadnezzar, Nebuzaradan the captain of the guard carried away captive of the Jews seven hundred and forty-five persons. All the persons were four thousand six hundred.

Jehoiachin Released from Prison

³¹ˣNow it came to pass in the thirty-seventh year of the captivity of Jehoiachin king of Judah, in the twelfth month, on the twenty-fifth day of the month, that Evil-Merodach* king of Babylon, in the first year of his reign, ʸlifted up the head of Jehoiachin king of Judah and brought him out of prison. ³²And he spoke kindly to him and gave him a more prominent seat than those of the kings who were with him in Babylon. ³³So Jehoiachin changed from his prison garments, ᶻand he ate bread regularly before the king all the days of his life. ³⁴And as for his provisions, there was a regular ration given him by the king of Babylon, a portion for each day until the day of his death, all the days of his life.

---

* 52:31 Or Awil-Marduk

52:13–16 burned the house of the LORD. The entire city of Jerusalem was burned, from the temple to the royal palace to the houses. The city walls were demolished. Leading citizens and some of the poor were deported under Nebuzaradan's command, leaving only a remnant of peasant farmers to work the fields, vineyards, and orchards.

52:31–34 Evil-Merodach. Nebuchadnezzar's son became king next but reigned for only two years. Jehoiachin was released from prison during his reign and pardoned. He was provided with food and given a seat of honor in Babylon. This restoration was symbolic of the future restoration of Israel and Judah to their homeland.

52:12 ʰ 2 Kin. 25:8–21 ⁱ Jer. 52:29 ʲ Jer. 39:9   **52:15** ᵏ Jer. 39:9   **52:17** ˡ Jer. 27:19 ᵐ 1 Kin. 7:15, 23, 27, 50   **52:18** ⁿ Ex. 27:3   **52:20** ᵒ 1 Kin. 7:47   **52:21** ᵖ 2 Kin. 25:17   **52:23** ᵠ 1 Kin. 7:20   **52:24** ʳ 2 Kin. 25:18 ˢ Jer. 21:1; 29:25   **52:28** ᵗ 2 Kin. 24:2 ᵘ 2 Kin. 24:12 ᵛ 2 Kin. 24:14   **52:29** ʷ Jer. 39:9   **52:31** ˣ 2 Kin. 25:27–30 ʸ Gen. 40:13, 20   **52:33** ᶻ 2 Sam. 9:7, 13

THE BOOK OF
LAMENTATIONS

▶ **AUTHOR:** The universal consensus of early Jewish and Christian tradition attributes this book to Jeremiah. Even though the author is unnamed in the book, the superscription to Lamentations in the Septuagint states: "And it came to pass, after Israel had been carried away captive and Jerusalem had become desolate, that Jeremiah sat weeping, and lamented with this lamentation over Jerusalem saying. . . ." The Talmud, as well as many other ancient sources, also supports this position.

▶ **TIME:** c. 586 B.C.   ▶ **KEY VERSES:** Lam. 3:22–23

▶ **THEME:** A lament is a vehicle for working through sorrow. While grief is expressed in words, its resolution is in God and the hope He gives for the future. In a way, the lamentation process is one of coming to grips with all that God wants us to see about our present circumstances. For the people of Judah to lose a country meant not only the loss of the homeland, but the loss of God's presence and power to sustain the people in that land. It is hard for people who have never experienced such loss to understand the depth of grief expressed in this book.

Jerusalem in Affliction

1 How lonely sits the city
  That was full of people!
 ªHow like a widow is she,
  Who *was* great among the nations!
  The ᵇprincess among the provinces
  Has become a slave!

2 She ᶜweeps bitterly in the ᵈnight,
  Her tears *are* on her cheeks;
  Among all her lovers
  She has none to comfort *her.*
  All her friends have dealt
      treacherously with her;
  They have become her enemies.

3 ᵉJudah has gone into captivity,
  Under affliction and hard servitude;
  ᶠShe dwells among the nations,
  She finds no ᵍrest;
  All her persecutors overtake her in
      dire straits.

4 The roads to Zion mourn
  Because no one comes to the set feasts.
  All her gates are ʰdesolate;

Her priests sigh,
Her virgins are afflicted,
And she *is* in bitterness.

5 Her adversaries ⁱhave become the
    master,
  Her enemies prosper;
  For the LORD has afflicted her
  ʲBecause of the multitude of her
      transgressions.
  Her ᵏchildren have gone into captivity
      before the enemy.

6 And from the daughter of Zion
  All her splendor has departed.
  Her princes have become like deer
  That find no pasture,
  That flee without strength
  Before the pursuer.

7 In the days of her affliction and
    roaming,
  Jerusalem ˡremembers all her pleasant
    things
  That she had in the days of old.
  When her people fell into the hand of
    the enemy,

1:1 How. This exclamatory word is used frequently in laments and funeral songs. It expresses astonishment, sorrow, and dismay (2:1; 4:1).
1:2 Among all her lovers. Verse 19 describes Judah's sin of turning away from God and toward the gods of Canaan (Jer. 3:1–6). Also, the sins of Judah often involved the sexual forms of pagan worship that characterized the Canaanite people.
1:4 The roads to Zion mourn. When the temple was built, Zion was used to describe the hill on which the temple was located. Later, the name came to stand for the whole city. The roads "mourned" because

there would no longer be throngs of pilgrims traveling to Jerusalem to worship at the temple.
1:5 Her children have gone into captivity. God had warned Israel in Leviticus 26:41 that captivity in a foreign land would be the result of continued sinning.
1:7 In the days of her affliction and roaming. The emphasis is on Jerusalem's utter helplessness as her enemies ridiculed her miseries (v. 21).

1:1 ª Is. 47:7–9 ᵇ Ezra 4:20   **1:2** ᶜ Jer. 13:17 ᵈ Job 7:3
1:3 ᵉ Jer. 52:27 ᶠ Lam. 2:9 ᵍ Deut. 28:65   **1:4** ʰ Is. 27:10
1:5 ⁱ Deut. 28:43 ʲ Dan. 9:7, 16 ᵏ Jer. 52:28   **1:7** ˡ Ps. 137:1

With no one to help her,
The adversaries saw her
And mocked at her downfall.*

8 *m*Jerusalem has sinned gravely,
Therefore she has become vile.*
All who honored her despise her
Because *n*they have seen her
nakedness;
Yes, she sighs and turns away.

9 Her uncleanness *is* in her skirts;
She *o*did not consider her destiny;
Therefore her collapse was awesome;
She had no comforter.
"O LORD, behold my affliction,
For *the* enemy is exalted!"

10 The adversary has spread his hand
Over all her pleasant things;
For she has seen *p*the nations enter her
sanctuary,
Those whom You commanded
*q*Not to enter Your assembly.

11 All her people sigh,
*r*They seek bread;
They have given their valuables for
food to restore life.
"See, O LORD, and consider,
For I am scorned."

12 "*Is it* nothing to you, all you who pass
by?
Behold and see
*s*If there is any sorrow like my sorrow,
Which has been brought on me,
Which the LORD has inflicted
In the day of His fierce anger.

13 "From above He has sent fire into my
bones,
And it overpowered them;
He has *t*spread a net for my feet
And turned me back;
He has made me desolate
And faint all the day.

14 "The*u* yoke of my transgressions was
bound;*
They were woven together by His
hands,
And thrust upon my neck.
He made my strength fail;

The Lord delivered me into the hands
of *those whom* I am not able to
withstand.

15 "The Lord has trampled underfoot all
my mighty *men* in my midst;
He has called an assembly against me
To crush my young men;
*v*The Lord trampled *as* in a winepress
The virgin daughter of Judah.

16 "For these *things* I weep;
My eye, *w*my eye overflows with water;
Because the comforter, who should
restore my life,
Is far from me.
My children are desolate
Because the enemy prevailed."

17 *x*Zion spreads out her hands,
But no one comforts her;
The LORD has commanded concerning
Jacob
That those *y*around him *become* his
adversaries;
Jerusalem has become an unclean
thing among them.

18 "The LORD is *z*righteous,
For I *a*rebelled against His
commandment.
Hear now, all peoples,
And behold my sorrow;
My virgins and my young men
Have gone into captivity.

19 "I called for my lovers,
But they deceived me;
My priests and my elders
Breathed their last in the city,
While they sought food
To restore their life.

20 "See, O LORD, that I *am* in distress;
My *b*soul is troubled;
My heart is overturned within me,
For I have been very rebellious.
*c*Outside the sword bereaves,
At home *it is* like death.

21 "They have heard that I sigh,
But no one comforts me.

---

* 1:7 Vulgate reads *her Sabbaths.*   * 1:8 Septuagint and Vulgate read *moved* or *removed.*
* 1:14 Following Masoretic Text and Targum; Septuagint, Syriac, and Vulgate read *watched over.*

1:10 *the nations enter her sanctuary.* Since God's people had not preserved the sanctuary of their hearts from pollution, they had no reason to be amazed when their enemies desecrated the earthly sanctuary. As a rule, Gentiles were forbidden to enter the congregation of the Lord.

1:13 *He has sent fire into my bones.* Jerusalem's suffering is portrayed, using several metaphors: (1) fire from heaven, (2) a hunter's net spread to trap animals, (3) an animal yoke fastened about the head of a person, and (4) the crushing of grapes in a winepress. The purpose of Jerusalem's suffering was to bring about a turning or repentance.

1:15 *The virgin daughter of Judah.* Jerusalem (Judah) was supposed to be the chaste bride of God. Instead, she had become a polluted harlot because

her people worshiped gods other than the God with whom they covenanted.

1:16 *comforter.* The real comforter of Judah is God. But because of Judah's sin, God would not come to their assistance.

1:21 *All my enemies.* Those who previously had been friends of Judah (v. 2) became Judah's enemies. ***Bring on the day.*** Several times the "day" of God's wrath is mentioned in the Book of Lamentations (2:1,21–22).

1:8 *m* [1 Kin. 8:46] *n* Ezek. 16:37   **1:9** *o* Is. 47:7
1:10 *p* Jer. 51:51   *q* Deut. 23:3   **1:11** *r* Jer. 38:9; 52:6
1:12 *s* Dan. 9:12   **1:13** *t* Ezek. 12:13; 17:20   **1:14** *u* Deut.
28:48   **1:15** *v* [Rev. 14:19]   **1:16** *w* Eccl. 4:1   **1:17** *x* Jer.
4:31   *y* 2 Kin. 24:2–4   **1:18** *z* Dan. 9:7, 14   *a* 1 Sam. 12:14, 15
1:20 *b* Is. 16:11   *c* Ezek. 7:15

All my enemies have heard of my
trouble;
They are ^dglad that You have done *it*.
Bring on ^ethe day You have
announced,
That they may become like me.

22 "Let^f all their wickedness come before
You,
And do to them as You have done to
me
For all my transgressions;
For my sighs *are* many,
And my heart *is* faint."

God's Anger with Jerusalem

2 How the Lord has covered the
daughter of Zion
With a ^acloud in His anger!
^bHe cast down from heaven to the
earth
^cThe beauty of Israel,
And did not remember ^dHis footstool
In the day of His anger.

2 The Lord has swallowed up and has
^enot pitied
All the dwelling places of Jacob.
He has thrown down in His wrath
The strongholds of the daughter of
Judah;
He has brought *them* down to the
ground;
^fHe has profaned the kingdom and its
princes.

3 He has cut off in fierce anger
Every horn of Israel;
^gHe has drawn back His right hand
From before the enemy.
^hHe has blazed against Jacob like a
flaming fire
Devouring all around.

4 ⁱStanding like an enemy, He has bent
His bow;
With His right hand, like an
adversary,
He has slain ^jall *who were* pleasing to
His eye;
On the tent of the daughter of Zion,
He has poured out His fury like fire.

5 ^kThe Lord was like an enemy.
He has swallowed up Israel,
He has swallowed up all her palaces;
^lHe has destroyed her strongholds,
And has increased mourning and
lamentation
In the daughter of Judah.

6 He has done violence ^mto His
tabernacle,
ⁿAs if it were a garden;
He has destroyed His place of
assembly;
The LORD has caused
The appointed feasts and Sabbaths to
be forgotten in Zion.
In His burning indignation He has
^ospurned the king and the priest.

7 The Lord has spurned His altar,
He has ^pabandoned His sanctuary;
He has given up the walls of her
palaces
Into the hand of the enemy.
^qThey have made a noise in the house
of the LORD
As on the day of a set feast.

8 The LORD has purposed to destroy
The ^rwall of the daughter of Zion.
^sHe has stretched out a line;
He has not withdrawn His hand from
destroying;
Therefore He has caused the rampart
and wall to lament;
They languished together.

9 Her gates have sunk into the ground;
He has destroyed and ^tbroken her
bars.
^uHer king and her princes *are* among
the nations;
^vThe Law *is* no *more*,
And her ^wprophets find no vision from
the LORD.

10 The elders of the daughter of Zion
^xSit on the ground *and* keep silence;
They ^ythrow dust on their heads
And ^zgird themselves with
sackcloth.
The virgins of Jerusalem
Bow their heads to the ground.

The term is used to refer not only to the time of Jerusalem's fall in the past, but also to a future day when God would rectify all of the wrongs that the nations had committed against Israel and God.
2:1 His anger. This word is a firm expression of God's displeasure with wickedness and sin. Yet God's anger never shuts us off from His compassion (Ps. 77:9).
2:3 drawn back His right hand. Usually the right hand of God is understood as the instrument of help for God's people stretched out against their enemies (Ex. 15:6; Ps. 20:6). Here God's hand is withdrawn from the enemies, leaving the people of God at their mercy.
2:9 the Law is no more. These words do not suggest the end of the law, but rather the ceasing of the work of the law in the lives of the people for their blessing (Deut. 6:1–3).

2:10 They throw dust on their heads. This custom was a common sign of mourning in Israel and in other countries of the ancient world. *virgins of Jerusalem.* Their sadness was increased by the knowledge that this was not a time for marriage and family. Even though their lives had been spared, they had lost their futures.

1:21 ^dPs. 35:15 ^e[Jer. 46] **1:22** ^fPs. 109:15; 137:7, 8 **2:1** ^a[Lam. 3:44] ^bMatt. 11:23 ^c2 Sam. 1:19 ^dPs. 99:5 **2:2** ^eLam. 3:43 ^fPs. 89:39, 40 **2:3** ^gPs. 74:11 ^hPs. 89:46 **2:4** ⁱIs. 63:10 ^jEzek. 24:25 **2:5** ^kJer. 30:14 ^lJer. 52:13 **2:6** ^mPs. 80:12; 89:40 ⁿIs. 1:8 ^oIs. 43:28 **2:7** ^pEzek. 24:21 ^qPs. 74:3–8 **2:8** ^rJer. 52:14 ^s[Is. 34:11] **2:9** ^tJer. 51:30 ^uDeut. 28:36 ^v2 Chr. 15:3 ^wPs. 74:9 **2:10** ^xIs. 3:26 ^yJob 2:12 ^zIs. 15:3

11 aMy eyes fail with tears,
My heart is troubled;
bMy bile is poured on the ground
Because of the destruction of the
daughter of my people,
Because cthe children and the infants
Faint in the streets of the city.

12 They say to their mothers,
"Where is grain and wine?"
As they swoon like the wounded
In the streets of the city,
As their life is poured out
In their mothers' bosom.

13 How shall I dconsole you?
To what shall I liken you,
O daughter of Jerusalem?
What shall I compare with you, that I
may comfort you,
O virgin daughter of Zion?
For your ruin is spread wide as the
sea;
Who can heal you?

14 Your eprophets have seen for you
False and deceptive visions;
They have not funcovered your iniquity,
To bring back your captives,
But have envisioned for you false
gprophecies and delusions.

15 All who pass by hclap their hands at
you;
They hiss iand shake their heads
At the daughter of Jerusalem:
"Is this the city that is called
j'The perfection of beauty,
The joy of the whole earth'?"

16 kAll your enemies have opened their
mouth against you;
They hiss and gnash their teeth.
They say, l"We have swallowed her up!
Surely this is the mday we have waited
for;
We have found it, nwe have seen it!"

17 The LORD has done what He opurposed;
He has fulfilled His word
Which He commanded in days of old.
He has thrown down and has not
pitied,
And He has caused an enemy to
prejoice over you;
He has exalted the horn of your
adversaries.

18 Their heart cried out to the Lord,
"O wall of the daughter of Zion,
qLet tears run down like a river day and
night;
Give yourself no relief;
Give your eyes no rest.

19 "Arise, rcry out in the night,
At the beginning of the watches;
sPour out your heart like water before
the face of the Lord.
Lift your hands toward Him
For the life of your young children,
Who faint from hunger tat the head of
every street."

20 "See, O LORD, and consider!
To whom have You done this?
uShould the women eat their offspring,
The children they have cuddled?*
Should the priest and prophet be slain
In the sanctuary of the Lord?

21 "Youngv and old lie
On the ground in the streets;
My virgins and my young men
Have fallen by the wsword;
You have slain them in the day of Your
anger,
You have slaughtered and not pitied.

22 "You have invited as to a feast day
xThe terrors that surround me.
In the day of the LORD's anger
There was no refugee or survivor.
yThose whom I have borne and
brought up
My enemies have zdestroyed."

The Prophet's Anguish and Hope

3 I am the man who has seen affliction
by the rod of His wrath.
2 He has led me and made me walk
In darkness and not in light.
3 Surely He has turned His hand
against me
Time and time again throughout the
day.

4 He has aged amy flesh and my skin,
And bbroken my bones.
5 He has besieged me
And surrounded me with bitterness
and woe.

---

* **2:20** Vulgate reads a span long.

2:15 shake their heads. This was a common expression of derision (Ps. 22:7; 109:25; Jer. 19:8). Losing face in the ancient Middle East was a terrible evil.
2:18 O wall. The wall of the people's hearts was more impenetrable than the wall of the city of Jerusalem (2:7–8).
2:19 Arise. The call is for people to awaken and scream for mercy from the Lord. **Lift your hands.** This refers to a posture of prayer (1:17; Ps. 134:2).
2:20 Should the women eat their offspring. So desperate were the scenes of starvation in Jerusalem that women actually fought over whose deceased child would be eaten next.

3:4 He has aged my flesh and my skin. This imagery suggests the ebbing and wasting away of Jeremiah's life and that of the nation.

2:11 a Lam. 3:48 b Job 16:13 c Lam. 4:4 **2:13** d Lam. 1:12
2:14 e Jer. 2:8; 23:25–29; 29:8, 9; 37:19 f Is. 58:1 g Jer.
23:33–36 **2:15** h Ezek. 25:6 i Ps. 44:14 j [Ps. 48:2; 50:2]
2:16 k Job 16:9, 10 l Ps. 56:2; 124:3 m Lam. 1:21 n Ps. 35:21
2:17 o Lev. 26:16 p Ps. 38:16 **2:18** q Jer. 14:17 **2:19** r Ps.
119:147 s Ps. 42:4; 62:8 t Is. 51:20 **2:20** u Lev. 26:29
2:21 v 2 Chr. 36:17 w Jer. 18:21 **2:22** x Ps. 31:13 y Hos.
9:12 z Jer. 16:2–4; 44:7 **3:4** a Job 16:8 b Ps. 51:8

6 cHe has set me in dark places
Like the dead of long ago.
7 dHe has hedged me in so that I cannot
get out;
He has made my chain heavy.
8 Even ewhen I cry and shout,
He shuts out my prayer.
9 He has blocked my ways with hewn
stone;
He has made my paths crooked.
10 fHe *has been* to me a bear lying in wait,
Like a lion in ambush.
11 He has turned aside my ways and
gtorn me in pieces;
He has made me desolate.
12 He has bent His bow
And hset me up as a target for the
arrow.
13 He has caused ithe arrows of His
quiver
To pierce my loins.*
14 I have become the jridicule of all my
people—
kTheir taunting song all the day.
15 lHe has filled me with bitterness,
He has made me drink wormwood.
16 He has also broken my teeth mwith
gravel,
And covered me with ashes.
17 You have moved my soul far from
peace;
I have forgotten prosperity.
18 nAnd I said, "My strength and my hope
Have perished from the LORD."

19 Remember my affliction and roaming,
oThe wormwood and the gall.
20 My soul still remembers
And sinks within me.
21 This I recall to my mind,
Therefore I have phope.

22 qThrough the LORD's mercies we are
not consumed,
Because His compassions rfail not.
23 *They are* new severy morning;
Great *is* Your faithfulness.

24 "The LORD *is* my tportion," says my
soul,
"Therefore I uhope in Him!"
25 The LORD *is* good to those who vwait
for Him,
To the soul *who* seeks Him.
26 *It is* good that *one* should whope xand
wait quietly
For the salvation of the LORD.
27 yIt *is* good for a man to bear
The yoke in his youth.
28 zLet him sit alone and keep silent,
Because *God* has laid *it* on him;
29 aLet him put his mouth in the dust—
There may yet be hope.
30 bLet him give *his* cheek to the one who
strikes him,
And be full of reproach.

31 cFor the Lord will not cast off forever.
32 Though He causes grief,
Yet He will show compassion
According to the multitude of His
mercies.
33 For dHe does not afflict willingly,
Nor grieve the children of men.

34 To crush under one's feet
All the prisoners of the earth,
35 To turn aside the justice *due* a man
Before the face of the Most High,
36 Or subvert a man in his cause—
eThe Lord does not approve.

37 Who *is* he fwho speaks and it comes to
pass,
When the Lord has not commanded *it*?
38 *Is it* not from the mouth of the Most
High
That gwoe and well-being proceed?
39 hWhy should a living man complain,
iA man for the punishment of his
sins?

40 Let us search out and examine our
ways,
And turn back to the LORD;

---

* **3:13** Literally *kidneys*

3:9 He has blocked my ways with hewn stone. A common practice of the Assyrians was to wall up prisoners in extremely confined places and leave them to die.
3:15 drink wormwood. This was a bitter herb used to flavor some drinks.
3:16 He has also broken my teeth with gravel. The people had sensed that they were so associated with dust and sackcloth—symbols of mourning—that it was as though they fed on dirt. The dust became gravel which broke the people's teeth.
3:22 Because His compassions fail not. This verse seems to contradict all that had been written up to this point (2:1–5). Yet the very fact that there was a prophet left to write these words and a remnant left to read them showed that not every person in Jerusalem had been consumed.
3:23 Great is Your faithfulness. Here is the heart of the Book of Lamentations. The comforting, compassionate character of God dominates the wreckage of every other institution and office. God remains "full of grace and truth" in every situation (Ex. 34:6; John 1:14).
3:29 put his mouth in the dust. This expression is a figure of speech for conquest. The phrase pictures a captive lying face down with the conqueror's foot on his back.

3:6 c [Ps. 88:5, 6; 143:3] **3:7** d Hos. 2:6 **3:8** e Job 30:20 **3:10** f Is. 38:13 **3:11** g Hos. 6:1 **3:12** h Job 7:20; 16:12 **3:13** i Job 6:4 **3:14** j Jer. 20:7 k Job 30:9 **3:15** l Jer. 9:15 **3:16** m [Prov. 20:17] **3:18** n Ps. 31:22 **3:19** o Jer. 9:15 **3:21** p Ps. 130:7 **3:22** q [Mal. 3:6] r Ps. 78:38 **3:23** s Is. 33:2 **3:24** t Ps. 16:5; 73:26; 119:57 u Mic. 7:7 **3:25** v Is. 30:18 **3:26** w [Rom. 4:16–18] x Ps. 37:7 **3:27** y Ps. 94:12 **3:28** z Jer. 15:17 **3:29** a Job 42:6 **3:30** b Is. 50:6 **3:31** c Ps. 77:7; 94:14 **3:33** d [Ezek. 33:11] **3:36** e [Hab. 1:13] **3:37** f [Ps. 33:9–11] **3:38** g Job 2:10 **3:39** h Prov. 19:3 i Mic. 7:9

41 [j]Let us lift our hearts and hands
To God in heaven.
42 [k]We have transgressed and rebelled;
You have not pardoned.

43 You have covered *Yourself* with anger
And pursued us;
You have slain *and* not pitied.
44 You have covered Yourself with a cloud,
That prayer should not pass through.
45 You have made us an [l]offscouring and refuse
In the midst of the peoples.

46 [m]All our enemies
Have opened their mouths against us.
47 [n]Fear and a snare have come upon us,
[o]Desolation and destruction.
48 [p]My eyes overflow with rivers of water
For the destruction of the daughter of my people.

49 [q]My eyes flow and do not cease,
Without interruption,
50 Till the LORD from heaven
[r]Looks down and sees.
51 My eyes bring suffering to my soul
Because of all the daughters of my city.

52 My enemies [s]without cause
Hunted me down like a bird.
53 They silenced* my life [t]in the pit
And [u]threw stones at me.
54 [v]The waters flowed over my head;
[w]I said, "I am cut off!"

55 [x]I called on Your name, O LORD,
From the lowest [y]pit.
56 [z]You have heard my voice:
"Do not hide Your ear
From my sighing, from my cry for help."
57 You [a]drew near on the day I called on You,
And said, [b]"Do not fear!"

58 O Lord, You have [c]pleaded the case for my soul;
[d]You have redeemed my life.
59 O LORD, You have seen *how* I am wronged;
[e]Judge my case.
60 You have seen all their vengeance,
All their [f]schemes against me.

61 You have heard their reproach, O LORD,
All their schemes against me,
62 The lips of my enemies
And their whispering against me all the day.
63 Look at their [g]sitting down and their rising up;
I *am* their taunting song.

64 [h]Repay them, O LORD,
According to the work of their hands.
65 Give them a veiled* heart;
Your curse *be* upon them!
66 In Your anger,
Pursue and destroy them
[i]From under the heavens of the [j]LORD.

The Degradation of Zion

4 How the gold has become dim!
How changed the fine gold!
The stones of the sanctuary are scattered
At the head of every street.

2 The precious sons of Zion,
Valuable as fine gold,
How they are regarded [a]as clay pots,
The work of the hands of the potter!

3 Even the jackals present their breasts
To nurse their young;
But the daughter of my people *is* cruel,
[b]Like ostriches in the wilderness.

4 The tongue of the infant clings
To the roof of its mouth for thirst;
[c]The young children ask for bread,
But no one breaks *it* for them.

5 Those who ate delicacies
Are desolate in the streets;
Those who were brought up in scarlet
[d]Embrace ash heaps.

6 The punishment of the iniquity of the daughter of my people
Is greater than the punishment of the [e]sin of Sodom,
Which was [f]overthrown in a moment,
With no hand to help her!

* **3:53** Septuagint reads *put to death.*
* **3:65** A Jewish tradition reads *sorrow of.*

3:44 *with a cloud.* So long as sin festered, God's wrath was a cloud or veil through which no prayer could penetrate—including the prayers of the people and the prayers of Jeremiah.
3:52–54 *silenced my life in the pit.* Jeremiah speaks not only of his own experience of being cast into a pit (Jer. 38:4–6), but also of his pain and grief over the wretched condition of his fellow countrymen. The pit is a metaphor for the grave or extreme danger (Ps. 28:1; 40:2).
3:64–66 *Repay them.* The request for divine vindication is an expression of a longing for God's righteousness and the success of His kingdom and His truth.
4:1–2 *stones of the sanctuary are scattered.* The Babylonian army looted the temple and overturned all its huge stones.
4:4 *The tongue of the infant.* The theme of thirsting and starving children is revisited (2:11–13).

3:41 [j] Ps. 86:4 **3:42** [k] Dan. 9:5 **3:45** [l] 1 Cor. 4:13 **3:46** [m] Lam. 2:16 **3:47** [n] Is. 24:17, 18 [o] Is. 51:19 **3:48** [p] Jer. 4:19; 14:17 **3:49** [q] Jer. 14:17 **3:50** [r] Is. 63:15 **3:52** [s] Ps. 35:7, 19 **3:53** [t] Jer. 37:16 [u] Dan. 6:17 **3:54** [v] Ps. 69:2 [w] Is. 38:10 **3:55** [x] Ps. 130:1 [y] Jer. 38:6–13 **3:56** [z] Ps. 3:4 **3:57** [a] James 4:8 [b] Is. 41:10, 14 **3:58** [c] Jer. 51:36 [d] Ps. 71:23 **3:59** [e] Ps. 9:4 **3:60** [f] Jer. 11:19 **3:63** [g] Ps. 139:2 **3:64** [h] Ps. 28:4 **3:66** [i] Deut. 25:19 [j] Ps. 8:3 **4:2** [a] Is. 30:14 **4:3** [b] Job 39:14–17 **4:4** [c] Ps. 22:15 **4:5** [d] Job 24:8 **4:6** [e] Ezek. 16:48 [f] Gen. 19:25

7 Her Nazirites* were brighter than
   snow
And whiter than milk;
They were more ruddy in body than
   rubies,
Like sapphire in their appearance.

8 *Now* their appearance is blacker than
   soot;
They go unrecognized in the streets;
ᵍTheir skin clings to their bones,
It has become as dry as wood.

9 *Those* slain by the sword are better off
Than *those* who die of hunger;
For these ʰpine away,
Stricken *for lack* of the fruits of the
   ⁱfield.

10 The hands of the ʲcompassionate
   women
Have cooked their ᵏown children;
They became ˡfood for them
In the destruction of the daughter of
   my people.

11 The LORD has fulfilled His fury,
ᵐHe has poured out His fierce anger.
ⁿHe kindled a fire in Zion,
And it has devoured its foundations.

12 The kings of the earth,
And all inhabitants of the world,
Would not have believed
That the adversary and the enemy
Could ᵒenter the gates of Jerusalem—

13 ᵖBecause of the sins of her prophets
And the iniquities of her priests,
ᑫWho shed in her midst
The blood of the just.

14 They wandered blind in the streets;
ʳThey have defiled themselves with
   blood,
ˢSo that no one would touch their
   garments.

15 They cried out to them,
"Go away, ᵗunclean!
Go away, go away,
Do not touch us!"
When they fled and wandered,
Those among the nations said,
"They shall no longer dwell *here*."

16 The face* of the LORD scattered
   them;
He no longer regards them.

ᵘ*The people* do not respect the
   priests
Nor show favor to the elders.

17 Still ᵛour eyes failed us,
Watching vainly for our help;
In our watching we watched
For a nation *that* could not save *us*.

18 ʷThey tracked our steps
So that we could not walk in our
   streets.
ˣOur end was near;
Our days were over,
For our end had come.

19 Our pursuers were ʸswifter
Than the eagles of the heavens.
They pursued us on the mountains
And lay in wait for us in the
   wilderness.

20 The ᶻbreath of our nostrils, the
   anointed of the LORD,
ᵃWas caught in their pits,
Of whom we said, "Under his shadow
We shall live among the nations."

21 Rejoice and be glad, O daughter of
   ᵇEdom,
You who dwell in the land of Uz!
ᶜThe cup shall also pass over to you
And you shall become drunk and
   make yourself naked.

22 ᵈ*The punishment of* your iniquity is
   accomplished,
O daughter of Zion;
He will no longer send you into
   captivity.
ᵉHe will punish your iniquity,
O daughter of Edom;
He will uncover your sins!

Prayer for Restoration

5 Remember, ᵃO LORD, what has come
upon us;
Look, and behold ᵇour reproach!

2 ᶜOur inheritance has been turned over
   to aliens,
And our houses to foreigners.

3 We have become orphans and waifs,
Our mothers *are* like ᵈwidows.

4 We pay for the water we drink,
And our wood comes at a price.

---

* 4:7 Or *nobles*   * 4:16 Targum reads *anger*.

4:10 cooked their own children. This verse describes the horrible effects of the long siege that were alluded to in 2:20. This unimaginable horror could only have occurred in the most inhumane conditions of human suffering.

5:2–3 Our inheritance. The Promised Land had been a gift from the Lord to Abraham. This inheritance was a kind of "down payment" on the future reign of God that would include the restoration of His people to that land. God demonstrated that He owned all nations and that Israel was to be His instrument for blessing all the nations on the earth. Yet in

their present condition, the people of Israel seemed to be the most helpless of all peoples.

4:8 ᵍPs. 102:5   4:9 ʰLev. 26:39   ⁱJer. 16:4   4:10 ʲLam. 2:20   ᵏIs. 49:15   ˡDeut. 28:57   4:11 ᵐJer. 7:20   ⁿDeut. 32:22   4:12 ᵒJer. 21:13   4:13 ᵖJer. 5:31   ᑫMatt. 23:31   4:14 ʳJer. 2:34   ˢNum. 19:16   4:15 ᵗLev. 13:45, 46   4:16 ᵘLam. 5:12   4:17 ᵛ2 Kin. 24:7   4:18 ʷ2 Kin. 25:4   ˣEzek. 7:2, 3, 6   4:19 ʸDeut. 28:49   4:20 ᶻGen. 2:7   ᵃJer. 52:9   4:21 ᵇPs. 83:3–6   ᶜJer. 25:15   4:22 ᵈ[Is. 40:2]   ᵉPs. 137:7   5:1 ᵃPs. 89:50   ᵇLam. 2:15   5:2 ᶜPs. 79:1   5:3 ᵈJer. 15:8; 18:21

5 *eThey* pursue at our heels;*
We labor *and* have no rest.
6 fWe have given our hand gto the
Egyptians
And the hAssyrians, to be satisfied
with bread.
7 iOur fathers sinned *and are* no more,
But we bear their iniquities.
8 Servants rule over us;
There is none to deliver *us* from their
hand.
9 We get our bread *at the risk* of our
lives,
Because of the sword in the
wilderness.
10 Our skin is hot as an oven,
Because of the fever of famine.
11 They jravished the women in Zion,
The maidens in the cities of Judah.
12 Princes were hung up by their hands,
And elders were not respected.
13 Young men kground at the millstones;
Boys staggered under *loads of* wood.
14 The elders have ceased *gathering* at
the gate,
And the young men from their
lmusic.
15 The joy of our heart has ceased;
Our dance has turned into
mmourning.
16 nThe crown has fallen *from* our head.
Woe to us, for we have sinned!
17 Because of this our heart is faint;
oBecause of these *things* our eyes grow
dim;
18 Because of Mount Zion which is
pdesolate,
With foxes walking about on it.
19 You, O LORD, qremain forever;
rYour throne from generation to
generation.
20 sWhy do You forget us forever,
And forsake us for so long a time?
21 tTurn us back to You, O LORD, and we
will be restored;
Renew our days as of old,
22 Unless You have utterly rejected us,
And are very angry with us!

---

* 5:5 Literally *necks*

5:10 *Our skin is hot as an oven.* Disease would have been rampant during the siege.
5:16 *The crown has fallen from our head.* This phrase expresses the loss of Judah's position of honor.
5:17 *our heart is faint . . . our eyes grow dim.* The normal zest for life was gone. Death would be better than a horrible existence during the siege of Jerusalem.
5:18 *foxes walking about on it.* The idea of wild animals roaming the holy city where the people of God once came in glad worship was the final indignity.

5:19 *You, O LORD, remain forever.* God's eternal rule and reign are a hope and support during the bleakest moments of suffering and despair (Ps. 80:1; 103:19).

5:5 e Jer. 28:14   5:6 f Gen. 24:2 g Hos. 9:3; 12:1 h Hos. 5:13   5:7 i Jer. 31:29   5:11 j Zech. 14:2   5:13 k Judg. 16:21   5:14 l Jer. 7:34   5:15 m Amos 8:10   5:16 n Ps. 89:39   5:17 o Ps. 6:7   5:18 p Is. 27:10   5:19 q Ps. 9:7 r Ps. 45:6   5:20 s Ps. 13:1; 44:24   5:21 t Jer. 31:18

THE BOOK OF
EZEKIEL

▶ **AUTHOR:** There is strong evidence in favor of Ezekiel's authorship of this book. The first person singular is used throughout the book, indicating that it is the work of one person. This person is actually identified in 1:3 and 24:24 as Ezekiel. The unity and integrity of Ezekiel's prophetic record are supported and the style, language, and thematic development are consistent throughout the book. Like Jeremiah, Ezekiel was a priest who was called to be a prophet of the Lord. Ezekiel was privileged to receive a number of visions of the power and plan of God, and he was careful and artistic in his written presentation.

▶ **TIME:** c. 592–570 B.C.   ▶ **KEY VERSES:** Ezek. 36:33–35

▶ **THEME:** Ezekiel was an exilic prophet, meaning he prophesied to the exiles in Babylon. He was one of the 10,000 taken there by Nebuchadnezzar in 597 B.C. (2 Kin. 24:14). The book contains a series of prophetic messages, which represents a lifetime of ministry to the exiles in Babylon. Ezekiel sees himself as a watchman or lookout, compelled to warn people of coming danger and of the need for personal responsibility to an awesome, all-seeing, all-knowing God. The last half of the book is more concerned with encouraging the people to hope for God's promise of restoration back to the land of Israel. The restoration of the temple is a key element of chapters 40–48.

Ezekiel's Vision of God

1 Now it came to pass in the thirtieth year, in the fourth *month*, on the fifth *day* of the month, as I *was* among the captives by ᵃthe River Chebar, *that* ᵇthe heavens were opened and I saw ᶜvisions* of God. ²On the fifth *day* of the month, which *was* in the fifth year of King Jehoiachin's captivity, ³the word of the LORD came expressly to Ezekiel the priest, the son of Buzi, in the land of the Chaldeans* by the River Chebar; and ᵈthe hand of the LORD was upon him there.

⁴Then I looked, and behold, ᵉa whirlwind was coming ᶠout of the north, a great cloud with raging fire engulfing itself; and brightness *was* all around it and radiating

out of its midst like the color of amber, out of the midst of the fire. ⁵ᵍAlso from within it *came* the likeness of four living creatures. And ʰthis *was* their appearance: they had ⁱthe likeness of a man. ⁶Each one had four faces, and each one had four wings. ⁷Their legs *were* straight, and the soles of their feet *were* like the soles of calves' feet. They sparkled ʲlike the color of burnished bronze. ⁸ᵏThe hands of a man *were* under their wings on their four sides; and each of the four had faces and wings. ⁹Their wings

---

* **1:1** Following Masoretic Text, Septuagint, and Vulgate; Syriac and Targum read *a vision.*
* **1:3** Or *Babylonians,* and so elsewhere in this book

1:1 in the thirtieth year. This most likely refers to Ezekiel's age. He was preparing to become a priest when the Babylonians attacked Judah in 597 B.C. **I saw visions of God.** As with all the true prophets of ancient Israel, the visitation of God was at His initiative, calling certain people to special responsibilities. The word "vision" is derived from the common Hebrew verb meaning "to see," rather than from the specific verb used for prophetic vision as in Isaiah 1.
1:3 the word of the LORD. Ezekiel uses this introductory phrase 50 times in this book. It always introduces a divine message and sometimes a new section.
Ezekiel. The name comes from the verb meaning "to seize, to hold fast," coupled with the term meaning "God." Thus Ezekiel's name indicates that he was a man whom God had seized.

1:4 whirlwind . . . great cloud . . . fire engulfing itself. Compare the descriptions of divine appearance in Exodus 19:16–20; Psalm 18:7–15; and Micah 1:2–4.
1:5 four living creatures. These creatures are related to the cherubim—celestial beings associated with God's holiness and glory, and sometimes poetically with storm winds upon which God travels (Ps. 18:10). There are two basic approaches to understanding them: as a highly symbolic representation of deity, or as highly symbolic representations of angelic

1:1 ᵃ Ezek. 3:15, 23; 10:15 ᵇ Rev. 4:1; 19:11 ᶜ Ezek. 8:3
1:3 ᵈ Ezek. 3:14, 22   **1:4** ᵉ Jer. 23:19; 25:32 ᶠ Jer. 1:14
1:5 ᵍ Rev. 4:6–8 ʰ Ezek. 10:8 ⁱ Ezek. 10:14   **1:7** ʲ Dan. 10:6
1:8 ᵏ Ezek. 10:8, 21

touched one another. *The creatures* did not turn when they went, but each one went straight *f*forward.

¹⁰As for *m*the likeness of their faces, each *n*had the face of a man; each of the four had *o*the face of a lion on the right side, *p*each of the four had the face of an ox on the left side, *q*and each of the four had the face of an eagle. ¹¹Thus *were* their faces. Their wings stretched upward; two *wings* of each one touched one another, and *r*two covered their bodies. ¹²And *s*each one went straight forward; they went wherever the spirit wanted to go, and they did not turn when they went.

¹³As for the likeness of the living creatures, their appearance *was* like burning coals of fire, *t*like the appearance of torches going back and forth among the living creatures. The fire was bright, and out of the fire went lightning. ¹⁴And the living creatures ran back and forth, *u*in appearance like a flash of lightning.

¹⁵Now as I looked at the living creatures, behold, *v*a wheel *was* on the earth beside each living creature with its four faces. ¹⁶*w*The appearance of the wheels and their workings *was* *x*like the color of beryl, and all four had the same likeness. The appearance of their workings *was,* as it were, a wheel in the middle of a wheel. ¹⁷When they moved, they went toward any one of four directions; they did not turn aside when they went. ¹⁸As for their rims, they were so high they were awesome; and their rims *were* *y*full of eyes, all around the four of them. ¹⁹*z*When the living creatures went, the wheels went beside them; and when the living creatures were lifted up from the earth, the wheels were lifted up. ²⁰Wherever the spirit wanted to go, they went, *because* there the spirit went; and the wheels were lifted together with them, *a*for the spirit of the living creatures* *was* in the wheels. ²¹When those went, *these* went; when those stood, *these* stood; and

when those were lifted up from the earth, the wheels were lifted up together with them, for the spirit of the living creatures* *was* in the wheels.

²²*b*The likeness of the firmament above the heads of the living creatures* *was* like the color of an awesome *c*crystal, stretched out *d*over their heads. ²³And under the firmament their wings *spread out* straight, one toward another. Each one had two which covered one side, and each one had two which covered the other side of the body. ²⁴*e*When they went, I heard the noise of their wings, *f*like the noise of many waters, like *g*the voice of the Almighty, a tumult like the noise of an army; and when they stood still, they let down their wings. ²⁵A voice came from above the firmament that *was* over their heads; whenever they stood, they let down their wings.

²⁶*h*And above the firmament over their heads *was* the likeness of a throne, *i*in appearance like a sapphire stone; on the likeness of the throne *was* a likeness with the appearance of a man high above *j*it. ²⁷Also from the appearance of His waist and upward *k*I saw, as it were, the color of amber with the appearance of fire all around within it; and from the appearance of His waist and downward I saw, as it were, the appearance of fire with brightness all around. ²⁸*l*Like the appearance of a rainbow in a cloud on a rainy day, so *was* the appearance of the brightness all around it. *m*This *was* the appearance of the likeness of the glory of the LORD.

Ezekiel Sent to Rebellious Israel

So when I saw *it,* *n*I fell on my face, and I heard a voice of One speaking.

---

* **1:20** Literally *living creature*; Septuagint and Vulgate read *spirit of life*; Targum reads *creatures.*
* **1:21** Literally *living creature*; Septuagint and Vulgate read *spirit of life*; Targum reads *creatures.*
* **1:22** Following Septuagint, Targum, and Vulgate; Masoretic Text reads *living creature.*

---

beings who serve in God's presence. Probably they are angels, since God Himself is not revealed until the end of the section (v. 26).

1:10 man . . . lion . . . ox . . . eagle. Composite fantastic figures in these classic combinations have been found in Mesopotamian and Egyptian iconography. The idealized strengths of each figure were thus presumed to reside in these living beings.

1:18 rims . . . full of eyes. The wheels had an exquisite beauty and an animate intelligence.

1:19–21 spirit . . . in the wheels. The prophet stresses the association of the wheels with the living beings, as well as the beings' ability to travel where they wished. It appears that the wheels represented the flexibility and mobility of the living beings. This is a pictorial representation of God's omnipresence.

1:24 Almighty. This is the divine name *Shaddai,* most likely based on a word meaning "mountain," to suggest God's omnipotence and majesty (10:5).

1:26 throne. While Isaiah describes the elevation

of the Lord's throne (Is. 6:1), Ezekiel focuses on its beauty.

1:27–28 glory of the LORD. The "glory" indicates the wonder, majesty, and worthiness of the living God. Amid the wheels, the beings, the colors, and the dazzling light was a figure who appeared like a man (v. 26). Compare the vision of Daniel who saw One "like the Son of Man" (Dan. 7:13). **I fell on my face.** The prophet's response was to fall down in worship and submission. All believers should recognize God's great glory and fall down in humble submission before Him (Phil. 2:10–11).

1:9 *f* Ezek. 1:12; 10:20–22   **1:10** *m* Rev. 4:7   *n* Num. 2:10   *o* Num. 2:3   *p* Num. 2:18   *q* Num. 2:25   **1:11** *r* Is. 6:2   **1:12** *s* Ezek. 10:11, 22   **1:13** *t* Rev. 4:5   **1:14** *u* [Matt. 24:27]   **1:15** *v* Ezek. 10:9   **1:16** *w* Ezek. 10:9, 10   *x* Dan. 10:6   **1:18** *y* Ezek. 10:12   **1:19** *z* Ezek. 10:16, 17   **1:20** *a* Ezek. 10:17   **1:22** *b* Ezek. 10:1   *c* Rev. 4:6   *d* Ezek. 10:1   **1:24** *e* Ezek. 3:13; 10:5   *f* Rev. 1:15   *g* Job 37:4, 5   **1:26** *h* Ezek. 10:1   *i* Ex. 24:10, 16   *j* Ezek. 8:2   **1:27** *k* Ezek. 8:2   **1:28** *l* Rev. 4:3; 10:1   *m* Ezek. 3:23; 8:4   *n* Dan. 8:17

2 And He said to me, "Son of man, *a*stand on your feet, and I will speak to you." [2]Then *b*the Spirit entered me when He spoke to me, and set me on my feet; and I heard Him who spoke to me. [3]And He said to me: "Son of man, I am sending you to the children of Israel, to a rebellious nation that has *c*rebelled against Me; *d*they and their fathers have transgressed against Me to this very day. [4e]For *they are* impudent and stubborn children. I am sending you to them, and you shall say to them, 'Thus says the Lord GOD.' [5f]As for them, whether they hear or whether they refuse—for they *are* a *g*rebellious house—yet they *h*will know that a prophet has been among them.

[6]"And you, son of man, *i*do not be afraid of them nor be afraid of their words, though *j*briers and thorns *are* with you and you dwell among scorpions; *k*do not be afraid of their words or dismayed by their looks, *l*though they *are* a rebellious house. [7m]You shall speak My words to them, whether they hear or whether they refuse, for they *are* rebellious. [8]But you, son of man, hear what I say to you. Do not be rebellious like that rebellious house; open your mouth and *n*eat what I give you."

[9]Now when I looked, there was *o*a hand stretched out to me; and behold, *p*a scroll of a book *was* in it. [10]Then He spread it before me; and *there was* writing on the inside and on the outside, and written on it *were* lamentations and mourning and woe.

3 Moreover He said to me, "Son of man, eat what you find; *a*eat this scroll, and go, speak to the house of Israel." [2]So I opened my mouth, and He caused me to eat that scroll.

[3]And He said to me, "Son of man, feed your belly, and fill your stomach with this scroll that I give you." So I *b*ate, and it was in my mouth *c*like honey in sweetness.

[4]Then He said to me: "Son of man, go to the house of Israel and speak with My words to them. [5]For you *are* not sent to a people of unfamiliar speech and of hard language, *but* to the house of Israel, [6]not to many people of unfamiliar speech and of hard language, whose words you cannot understand. Surely, *d*had I sent you to them, they would have listened to you. [7]But the house of Israel will not listen to you, *e*because they will not listen to Me; *f*for all the house of Israel *are* impudent and hard-hearted. [8]Behold, I have made your face strong against their faces, and your forehead strong against their foreheads. [9g]Like adamant stone, harder than flint, I have made your forehead; *h*do not be afraid of them, nor be dismayed at their looks, though they *are* a rebellious house."

[10]Moreover He said to me: "Son of man, receive into your heart all My words that I speak to you, and hear with your ears. [11]And go, get to the captives, to the children of your people, and speak to them and tell them, *i*'Thus says the Lord GOD,' whether they hear, or whether they refuse."

[12]Then *j*the Spirit lifted me up, and I heard behind me a great thunderous voice: "Blessed *is* the *k*glory of the LORD from His place!" [13]*I* also *heard* the *l*noise of the wings of the living creatures that touched one another, and the noise of the wheels beside them, and a great thunderous noise. [14]So the Spirit lifted me up and took me away, and I went in bitterness, in the heat of my spirit; but *m*the hand of the LORD was strong upon me. [15]Then I came to the

---

2:1 *Son of man.* Ezekiel uses this phrase more than 90 times to refer to himself. It emphasizes his humanity in his God-given role as a spokesman for God. The meaning of the phrase is "human one." In the Old Testament, only Daniel 7:13 and 8:17 also employ this phrase. In the New Testament, "Son of Man" is used frequently by Jesus for Himself. With this phrase Jesus was calling Himself "the Human One"—the long-awaited Messiah who came as God in the flesh (Luke 21:27; John 1:14; 2 John 7).

2:2 *the Spirit entered me.* This reference to the indwelling of the Holy Spirit in God's prophet is of great importance. The visions and messages of Ezekiel were revelations from the living God.

2:5 *they are a rebellious house.* God told Ezekiel to take His Word to the sons of Israel. These people were to hear what the Lord Himself was to say to them. Listening or not listening, belief or unbelief, would not change what was spoken. Our belief or unbelief has no effect on what God tells us or what the Bible says. His word remains true. By its very nature, it is worthy of belief.

2:6 *briers . . . thorns . . . scorpions.* These images vividly portray the nature of the rebellious opponents of Ezekiel's warnings. God told Ezekiel not to allow fear to hinder his message, whether or not the message was wanted (v. 7).

2:10 *lamentations and mourning and woe.* The unusual feature of writing on both sides of a scroll indicates the magnitude of the nation's transgressions and its need for words of grief (Zech. 5:3; Rev. 5:1). Although Ezekiel would later bring words of comfort and consolation (chs. 33–48), his first prophecies from God contained only sorrow and sadness.

3:1–3 *eat this scroll.* The symbolic act of eating the scroll demonstrated that Ezekiel internalized the message in preparation for speaking to the people.

3:8–9 *I have made your face strong against their faces.* There may have been an intentional pun on Ezekiel's name, which means "strongly seized by God" (1:3) or "God strengthens." Double meanings in biblical names are common.

3:14 *I went in bitterness, in the heat of my spirit.* Ezekiel's human perspective caused him to focus on

---

2:1 *a* Dan. 10:11 **2:2** *b* Ezek. 3:24 **2:3** *c* Ezek. 5:6; 20:8, 13, 18 *d* Jer. 3:25 **2:4** *e* Ezek. 3:7 **2:5** *f* Ezek. 3:11, 26, 27 *g* Ezek. 3:26 *h* Ezek. 33:33 **2:6** *i* Jer. 1:8, 17 *j* Mic. 7:4 *k* [1 Pet. 3:14] *l* Ezek. 3:9, 26, 27 **2:7** *m* Jer. 1:7, 17 **2:8** *n* Rev. 10:9 **2:9** *o* [Ezek. 8:3] *p* Ezek. 3:1 **3:1** *a* Ezek. 2:8, 9 **3:3** *b* Rev. 10:9 *c* Ps. 19:10; 119:103 **3:6** *d* Matt. 11:21 **3:7** *e* John 15:20, 21 *f* Ezek. 2:4 **3:9** *g* Mic. 3:8 *h* Jer. 1:8, 17 **3:11** *i* Ezek. 2:5, 7 **3:12** *j* Acts 8:39 *k* Ezek. 1:28; 8:4 **3:13** *l* Ezek. 1:24; 10:5 **3:14** *m* 2 Kin. 3:15

captives at Tel Abib, who dwelt by the River Chebar; and [n]I sat where they sat, and remained there astonished among them seven days.

Ezekiel Is a Watchman

16 Now it [o]came to pass at the end of seven days that the word of the LORD came to me, saying, 17 [p]"Son of man, I have made you [q]a watchman for the house of Israel; therefore hear a word from My mouth, and give them [r]warning from Me: 18 When I say to the wicked, 'You shall surely die,' and you give him no warning, nor speak to warn the wicked from his wicked way, to save his life, that same wicked *man* [s]shall die in his iniquity; but his blood I will require at your hand. 19 Yet, if you warn the wicked, and he does not turn from his wickedness, nor from his wicked way, he shall die in his iniquity; [t]but you have delivered your soul.

20 "Again, when a [u]righteous *man* turns from his righteousness and commits iniquity, and I lay a stumbling block before him, he shall die; because you did not give him warning, he shall die in his sin, and his righteousness which he has done shall not be remembered; but his blood I will require at your hand. 21 Nevertheless if you warn the righteous *man* that the righteous should not sin, and he does not sin, he shall surely live because he took warning; also you will have delivered your soul."

22 [v]Then the hand of the LORD was upon me there, and He said to me, "Arise, go out [w]into the plain, and there I shall talk with you."

23 So I arose and went out into the plain, and behold, [x]the glory of the LORD stood there, like the glory which I [y]saw by the River Chebar; [z]and I fell on my face. 24 Then [a]the Spirit entered me and set me on my feet, and spoke with me and said to me: "Go, shut yourself inside your house. 25 And you, O son of man, surely [b]they will put ropes on you and bind you with them, so that you cannot go out among them. 26 [c]I will make your tongue cling to the roof of your mouth, so that you shall be mute and [d]not be one to rebuke them, [e]for they *are* a rebellious house. 27 [f]But when I speak with you, I will open your mouth, and you shall say to them, [g]'Thus says the Lord GOD.' He who hears, let him hear; and he who refuses, let him refuse; for they *are* a rebellious house.

The Siege of Jerusalem Portrayed

4 "You also, son of man, take a clay tablet and lay it before you, and portray on it a city, Jerusalem. 2 [a]Lay siege against it, build a [b]siege wall against it, and heap up a mound against it; set camps against it also, and place battering rams against it all around. 3 Moreover take for yourself an iron plate, and set it *as* an iron wall between you and the city. Set your face against it, and it shall be [c]besieged, and you shall lay siege against it. [d]This *will be* a sign to the house of Israel.

4 "Lie also on your left side, and lay the iniquity of the house of Israel upon it. *According* to the number of the days that you lie on it, you shall bear their iniquity. 5 For I have laid on you the years of their iniquity, according to the number of the days, three hundred and ninety days; [e]so you shall bear the iniquity of the house

---

the distasteful calling of delivering a message that would not be well received. The prophet was angry and appalled. But God was present to help him deal with these feelings and then move him on to live and work among the captives.

3:17 ***a watchman.*** He stood on the city wall guarding against any external or internal threat. He would sound an alarm upon sighting impending danger (2 Sam. 18:24). God made Ezekiel a spiritual watchman over His people.

3:20 ***when a righteous man turns from his righteousness and commits iniquity.*** The prophet's responsibility was to warn, if he saw apostasy taking place. If he did not, he became culpable too. Even for the most devoted and the most saintly, righteousness can become something to spurn and iniquity can become something to embrace. God says that repudiation of righteousness leads to death.

3:26 ***not be one to rebuke them.*** This phrase qualified what was meant by Ezekiel's being mute. The idea may be better stated as "not be a legal mediator." During his "mute" period, Ezekiel would not be allowed to speak as a mediator on behalf of the people before God, their Judge.

3:27 ***He who hears, let him hear.*** Jesus used this warning often in His teaching (Mark 4:23). The phrasing emphasizes individual responsibility and readiness to accept the divine message.

4:1 ***take a clay tablet.*** The tablet would have been soft enough to inscribe with a stylus.

4:2 ***Lay siege.*** The city of Jerusalem would come under siege, meaning that the Babylonians would surround the city and cut off its outside supplies. The purpose was to starve its inhabitants into submission. By his symbolic drawing, Ezekiel may have been commanded to do what other "prophets" of the nations might do. That is, the hired "prophets" of pagan nations might use such a drawing as a device for invoking the gods to bring about the event graphically described. In Ezekiel's case, the drawing was the opposite of what the people wanted. As they sat in captivity, the worst news would have been that the holy city had been destroyed.

4:3 ***an iron plate.*** This was a plate that Ezekiel possessed as a priest; it was for baking grain for the grain offerings (Lev. 2:5; 6:21). Here its purpose was to represent a wall between Ezekiel and the city.

3:15 [n]Job 2:13 **3:16** [o]Jer. 42:7 **3:17** [p]Ezek. 33:7–9 [q]Jer. 6:17 [r][Lev. 19:17] **3:18** [s][John 8:21, 24] **3:19** [t]Acts 18:6; 20:26 **3:20** [u]Ezek. 18:24; 33:18 **3:22** [v]Ezek. 1:3 [w]Ezek. 8:4 **3:23** [x]Ezek. 1:28 [y]Ezek. 1:1 [z]Ezek. 1:28 **3:24** [a]Ezek. 2:2 **3:25** [b]Ezek. 4:8 **3:26** [c]Luke 1:20, 22 [d]Hos. 4:17 [e]Ezek. 2:5–7 **3:27** [f]Ezek. 24:27; 33:22 [g]Ezek. 3:11 **4:2** [a]Jer. 6:6 [b]2 Kin. 25:1 **4:3** [c]Jer. 39:1, 2 [d]Ezek. 12:6, 11; 24:24, 27 **4:5** [e]Num. 14:34

of Israel. **6**And when you have completed them, lie again on your right side; then you shall bear the iniquity of the house of Judah forty days. I have laid on you a day for each year.

7"Therefore you shall set your face toward the siege of Jerusalem; your arm *shall be* uncovered, and you shall prophesy against it. **8**/And surely I will restrain you so that you cannot turn from one side to another till you have ended the days of your siege.

9"Also take for yourself wheat, barley, beans, lentils, millet, and spelt; put them into one vessel, and make bread of them for yourself. *During* the number of days that you lie on your side, three hundred and ninety days, you shall eat it. **10**And your food which you eat *shall be* by weight, twenty shekels a day; from time to time you shall eat it. **11**You shall also drink water by measure, one-sixth of a hin; from time to time you shall drink. **12**And you shall eat it *as* barley cakes; and bake it using fuel of human waste in their sight."

13Then the LORD said, "So *g*shall the children of Israel eat their defiled bread among the Gentiles, where I will drive them."

14So I said, *h*"Ah, Lord GOD! Indeed I have never defiled myself from my youth till now; I have never eaten *i*what died of itself or was torn by beasts, nor has *j*abominable flesh ever come into my mouth."

15Then He said to me, "See, I am giving you cow dung instead of human waste, and you shall prepare your bread over it."

16Moreover He said to me, "Son of man, surely I will cut off the *k*supply of bread in Jerusalem; they shall *l*eat bread by weight and with anxiety, and shall *m*drink water by measure and with dread, **17**that they may lack bread and water, and be dismayed with one another, and *n*waste away because of their iniquity.

A Sword Against Jerusalem

5 "And you, son of man, take a sharp sword, take it as a barber's razor, *a*and pass *it* over your head and your beard; then take scales to weigh and divide the *hair.* **2b**You shall burn with fire one-third in the midst of *c*the city, when *d*the days of the siege are finished; then you shall take one-third and strike around *it* with the sword, and one-third you shall scatter in the wind: I will draw out a sword after *e*them. **3f**You shall also take a small number of them and bind them in the edge of your *garment.* **4**Then take some of them again and *g*throw them into the midst of the fire, and burn them in the fire. From there a fire will go out into all the house of Israel.

5"Thus says the Lord GOD: 'This *is* Jerusalem; I have set her in the midst of the nations and the countries all around her. **6**She has rebelled against My judgments by doing wickedness more than the nations, and against My statutes more than the countries that *are* all around her; for they have refused My judgments, and they have not walked in My statutes.' **7**Therefore thus says the Lord GOD: 'Because you have multiplied *disobedience* more than the nations that *are* all around you, have not walked in My statutes *h*nor kept My judgments, nor even done* according to the judgments of the nations that *are* all around you'— **8**therefore thus says the Lord GOD: 'Indeed I, even I, *am* against you and will execute judgments in your midst in the sight of the nations. **9i**And I will do among you what I have never done, and the like of which I will never do again, because of all your abominations. **10**Therefore fathers *j*shall eat *their* sons in your midst, and sons shall

* **5:7** Following Masoretic Text, Septuagint, Targum, and Vulgate; many Hebrew manuscripts and Syriac read *but have done* (compare 11:12).

4:7 *set your face toward the siege.* As horrible as it was, the siege ultimately showed God's faithfulness to His covenant established in the days of Moses—that idolatry and disobedience would bring curses, which would include being conquered, captured and removed from the land (Deut. 28:15–68).
4:8 *restrain you.* Ezekiel was bound while lying on either side for the entire 430 days, but the activities described in Ezekiel 4:9–17 show that lying down and being tied up occurred only during parts of each day.
4:17 *waste away because of their iniquity.* The people had broken their covenant with God, and He had no choice but to bring upon them the promised consequences of their disobedience (Lev. 26:14–29).
5:1 *a barber's razor, and pass it over your head and your beard.* Shaving the head was an act showing shame or disgrace in Hebrew culture (7:18). It also represented a type of pagan mourning forbidden by the law (27:31). Shaving the head was a mark of defilement, making a priest like Ezekiel ritually unclean, and so unable to perform his duties in the temple (Lev. 21:5). This message was telling the people that they were about to be humiliated and defiled.

5:2 *one-third.* Each citizen of Jerusalem would suffer one of the three fates depicted by each of the three mounds of hair: (1) some would be burned along with the city or would die from plague, famine, or other siege conditions (5:12; 2 Kin. 25:9); (2) some would be murdered by the sword during the attack (5:12; 2 Kin. 25:18–21); and (3) some would be scattered in the wind—referring to the exile (5:12; 2 Kin. 25:11–17).
5:9–17 *what I have never done.* The elements in God's judgment on the people for their sins can be enumerated in this way: (1) a judgment that will be worse in extent than ever before; (2) a terrible famine that will lead to cannibalism; (3) pestilence, meaning plagues and diseases associated with famine; (4) violent death by sword or wild beasts; and (5) the scattering and killing of a remnant. These

4:8 *f* Ezek. 3:25 **4:13** *g* Hos. 9:3 **4:14** *h* Acts 10:14
i Lev. 17:15; 22:8 *j* Deut. 14:3 **4:16** *k* Is. 3:1 *l* Ezek. 4:10,
11; 12:19 *m* Ezek. 4:11 **4:17** *n* Lev. 26:39 **5:1** *a* Is. 7:20
5:2 *b* Ezek. 5:12 *c* Ezek. 4:1 *d* Ezek. 4:8; 9 *e* Lev. 26:25
5:3 *f* Jer. 40:6; 52:16 **5:4** *g* Jer. 41:1, 2; 44:14 **5:7** *h* Jer.
2:10, 11 **5:9** *i* [Amos 3:2] **5:10** *j* Jer. 19:9

eat their fathers; and I will execute judgments among you, and all of you who remain I will *k*scatter to all the winds.

11'Therefore, *as* I live,' says the Lord GOD, 'surely, because you have *l*defiled My sanctuary with all your *m*detestable things and with all your abominations, therefore I will also diminish *you;* *n*My eye will not spare, nor will I have any pity. 12*o*One-third of you shall die of the pestilence, and be consumed with famine in your midst; and one-third shall fall by the sword all around you; and *p*I will scatter another third to all the winds, and I will draw out a sword after *q*them.

13'Thus shall My anger *r*be spent, and I will *s*cause My fury to rest upon them, *t*and I will be avenged; *u*and they shall know that I, the LORD, have spoken *it* in My zeal, when I have spent My fury upon them. 14Moreover *v*I will make you a waste and a reproach among the nations that *are* all around you, in the sight of all who pass by.

15'So it* shall be a *w*reproach, a taunt, a *x*lesson, and an astonishment to the nations that *are* all around you, when I execute judgments among you in anger and in fury and in *y*furious rebukes. I, the LORD, have spoken. 16When I *z*send against them the terrible arrows of famine which shall be for destruction, which I will send to destroy you, I will increase the famine upon you and cut off your *a*supply of bread. 17So I will send against you famine and *b*wild beasts, and they will bereave you. *c*Pestilence and blood shall pass through you, and I will bring the sword against you. I, the LORD, have spoken.' "

Judgment on Idolatrous Israel

6 Now the word of the LORD came to me, saying: 2"Son of man, *a*set your face toward the *b*mountains of Israel, and prophesy against them, 3and say, 'O mountains of Israel, hear the word of the Lord GOD! Thus says the Lord GOD to the mountains, to the hills, to the ravines, and to the valleys:

"Indeed I, *even* I, will bring a sword against you, and *c*I will destroy your high places. 4Then your altars shall be desolate, your incense altars shall be broken, and *d*I will cast down your slain *men* before your idols. 5And I will lay the corpses of the children of Israel before their idols, and I will scatter your bones all around your altars. 6In all your dwelling places the cities shall be laid waste, and the high places shall be desolate, so that your altars may be laid waste and made desolate, your idols may be broken and made to cease, your incense altars may be cut down, and your works may be abolished. 7The slain shall fall in your midst, and *e*you shall know that I *am* the LORD.

8'"Yet I will leave a remnant, so that you may have *some* who escape the sword among the nations, when you are *g*scattered through the countries. 9Then those of you who escape will *h*remember Me among the nations where they are carried captive, because *i*I was crushed by their adulterous heart which has departed from Me, and *j*by their eyes which play the harlot after their idols; *k*they will loathe themselves for the evils which they committed in all their abominations. 10And they shall know that I *am* the LORD; I have not said in vain that I would bring this calamity upon them."

11'Thus says the Lord GOD: "*l*Pound your fists and stamp your feet, and say, 'Alas, for all the evil abominations of the house of Israel! *m*For they shall fall by the sword, by famine, and by pestilence. 12He who is far off shall die by the pestilence, he who is near shall fall by the sword, and he who remains and is besieged shall die by the famine. *n*Thus will I spend My fury upon them. 13Then you shall know that I *am* the LORD, when their slain are among their idols all around their altars, *o*on every high hill, *p*on all the mountaintops, *q*under every green tree, and under every thick oak, wherever they offered sweet incense to all their idols.

---

* **5:15** Septuagint, Syriac, Targum, and Vulgate read *you.*

5:10 *k* Zech. 2:6; 7:14   **5:11** *l* [Jer. 7:9–11]   *m* Ezek. 11:21   *n* Ezek. 7:4, 9; 8:18; 9:10   **5:12** *o* Ezek. 6:12   *p* Jer. 9:16   *q* Jer. 43:10, 11; 44:27   **5:13** *r* Lam. 4:11   *s* Ezek. 21:17   *t* Is. 1:24   *u* Ezek. 36:6; 38:19   **5:14** *v* Ezek. 26:31   **5:15** *w* Jer. 24:9   *x* [Is. 26:9]   *y* Ezek. 5:8; 25:17   **5:16** *z* Deut. 32:23   *a* Lev. 26:26   **5:17** *b* Lev. 26:22   *c* Ezek. 38:22   **6:2** *a* Ezek. 20:46; 21:2; 25:2   *b* Ezek. 36:1   **6:3** *c* Lev. 26:30   **6:4** *d* Lev. 26:30   **6:7** *e* Ezek. 7:4, 9   **6:8** *f* Jer. 44:28   *g* Ezek. 5:12   **6:9** *h* [Deut. 4:29]   *i* Ps. 78:40   *j* Ezek. 20:7, 24   *k* Ezek. 20:43; 36:31   **6:11** *l* Ezek. 21:14   *m* Ezek. 5:12   **6:12** *n* Ezek. 5:13   **6:13** *o* Jer. 2:20; 3:6   *p* Hos. 4:13   *q* Is. 57:5

---

punishments would come as the result of the people's idolatry.

6:2–3 high places. These were originally elevated locations for worship of the god Baal and other deities of the Canaanite pantheon. The term "high place" could be used of any location, whether hilltop or valley. Before entering the Promised Land, the Hebrews had been commanded to abolish all the high places where idols were worshiped (Num. 33:52).

6:4–6 cast down your slain men . . . lay the corpses . . . scatter your bones. These phrases refer to God's judgment. Dead people lying unburied and bones scattered around signify the ultimate defilement of the land. God would bring this upon them because they had defiled and desecrated themselves by worshiping in the pagan high places.

6:13 Then you shall know that I am the LORD. As in verses 7 and 10, the Lord states the purpose of the coming destruction of His city and many of its people. The use of God's personal name further emphasizes

the intent to bring His people back to a personal, intimate relationship with Himself.

6:13 God's Desire for Exclusiveness—God's point throughout the Book of Ezekiel is the same; His relationship with us is exclusive. He doesn't share that primary God-man relationship with anybody else or anything. As a model for exclusiveness, Ezekiel uses the marriage relationship. Exclusiveness is the

14So I will [r]stretch out My hand against them and make the land desolate, yes, more desolate than the wilderness toward [s]Diblah, in all their dwelling places. Then they shall know that I *am* the LORD.' " ' "

Judgment on Israel Is Near

7 Moreover the word of the LORD came to me, saying, 2"And you, son of man, thus says the Lord GOD to the land of Israel:

[a]'An end! The end has come upon the
four corners of the land.
3 Now the end *has come* upon you,
And I will send My anger against you;
I will judge you [b]according to your ways,
And I will repay you for all your
abominations.
4 [c]My eye will not spare you,
Nor will I have pity;
But I will repay your ways,
And your abominations will be in your
midst;
[d]Then you shall know that I *am* the
LORD!'

5"Thus says the Lord GOD:

'A disaster, a singular [e]disaster;
Behold, it has come!
6 An end has come,
The end has come;
It has dawned for you;
Behold, it has come!
7 [f]Doom has come to you, you who dwell
in the land;
[g]The time has come,
A day of trouble *is* near,
And not of rejoicing in the mountains.
8 Now upon you I will soon [h]pour out
My fury,
And spend My anger upon you;
I will judge you according to your ways,
And I will repay you for all your
abominations.
9 'My eye will not spare,
Nor will I have pity;
I will repay you according to your ways,
And your abominations will be in your
midst.
Then you shall know that I *am* the
LORD who strikes.

10 'Behold, the day!
Behold, it has come!
[i]Doom has gone out;
The rod has blossomed,
Pride has budded.
11 [j]Violence has risen up into a rod of
wickedness;
None of them *shall remain,*
None of their multitude,
None of them;
[k]Nor *shall there be* wailing for them.
12 The time has come,
The day draws near.
'Let not the buyer [l]rejoice,
Nor the seller [m]mourn,
For wrath *is* on their whole
multitude.
13 For the seller shall not return to what
has been sold,
Though he may still be alive;
For the vision concerns the whole
multitude,
And it shall not turn back;
No one will strengthen himself
Who lives in iniquity.
14 'They have blown the trumpet and
made everyone ready,
But no one goes to battle;
For My wrath *is* on all their multitude.
15 [n]The sword *is* outside,
And the pestilence and famine within.
Whoever *is* in the field
Will die by the sword;
And whoever *is* in the city,
Famine and pestilence will devour
him.

16 'Those who [o]survive will escape and be
on the mountains
Like doves of the valleys,
All of them mourning,
Each for his iniquity.
17 Every [p]hand will be feeble,
And every knee will be *as* weak *as*
water.
18 They will also [q]be girded with
sackcloth;
Horror will cover them;
Shame *will be* on every face,
Baldness on all their heads.

---

boundary that provides the shape to that relationship. It is the same with our relationship with God. When we violate God's desire for exclusiveness, we ruin our relationship with Him. God designed us for Himself alone. If we have anything less than an exclusive relationship with Him, we become less than what we were created to be.

7:2–3 *the end.* Three uses of this key word stressed that the fulfillment of the prophecy was at hand.

7:10 *the rod has blossomed.* The flowering of the rod indicates that the time to bring judgment was ripe. These words describe one whose time had come, a person marked by arrogance. In this case, it pictures the chosen instrument of God (Num. 17:5) with whom He would discipline Jerusalem and Judah—namely Nebuchadnezzar, king of Babylon and the characteristic representative of the arrogant and evil Babylonians.

7:12 *Let not the buyer rejoice.* The fact of coming judgment was so certain, and its effects would be so lasting and devastating, that transactions of buying and selling would be concluded improperly or not at all.

7:16–19 *Those who survive will escape.* Those left alive would hide in the hills and be characterized by

6:14 [r]Is. 5:25 [s]Num. 33:46 **7:2** [a]Amos 8:2, 10 **7:3** [b][Rom. 2:6] **7:4** [c]Ezek. 5:11 [d]Ezek. 12:20 **7:5** [e]2 Kin. 21:12, 13 **7:7** [f]Ezek. 7:10 [g]Zeph. 1:14, 15 **7:8** [h]Ezek. 20:8, 21 **7:10** [i]Ezek. 7:7 **7:11** [j]Jer. 6:7 [k]Jer. 16:5, 6 **7:12** [l]Prov. 20:14 [m]Is. 24:2 **7:15** [n]Jer. 14:18 **7:16** [o]Ezek. 6:8; 14:22 **7:17** [p]Is. 13:7 **7:18** [q]Amos 8:10

¹⁹ 'They will throw their silver into the streets,
And their gold will be like refuse;
Their ^rsilver and their gold will not be able to deliver them
In the day of the wrath of the LORD;
They will not satisfy their souls,
Nor fill their stomachs,
Because it became their stumbling block of iniquity.

²⁰ 'As for the beauty of his ornaments,
He set it in majesty;
^sBut they made from it
The images of their abominations—
Their detestable things;
Therefore I have made it
Like refuse to them.

²¹ I will give it as ^tplunder
Into the hands of strangers,
And to the wicked of the earth as spoil;
And they shall defile it.

²² I will turn My face from them,
And they will defile My secret place;
For robbers shall enter it and defile it.

²³ 'Make a chain,
For ^uthe land is filled with crimes of blood,
And the city is full of violence.

²⁴ Therefore I will bring the ^vworst of the Gentiles,
And they will possess their houses;
I will cause the pomp of the strong to cease,
And their holy places shall be ^wdefiled.

²⁵ Destruction comes;
They will seek peace, but *there shall be* none.

²⁶ ^xDisaster will come upon disaster,
And rumor will be upon rumor.
^yThen they will seek a vision from a prophet;
But the law will perish from the priest,
And counsel from the elders.

²⁷ 'The king will mourn,
The prince will be clothed with desolation,
And the hands of the common people will tremble.
I will do to them according to their way,
And according to what they deserve I will judge them;
Then they shall know that I *am* the LORD!' "

Abominations in the Temple

8 And it came to pass in the sixth year, in the sixth *month*, on the fifth *day* of the month, as I sat in my house with ^athe elders of Judah sitting before me, that ^bthe hand of the Lord GOD fell upon me there. ²^cThen I looked, and there was a likeness, like the appearance of fire—from the appearance of His waist and downward, fire; and from His waist and upward, like the appearance of brightness, ^dlike the color of amber. ³He ^estretched out the form of a hand, and took me by a lock of my hair; and ^fthe Spirit lifted me up between earth and heaven, and ^gbrought me in visions of God to Jerusalem, to the door of the north gate of the inner *court*, ^hwhere the seat of the image of jealousy *was*, which ⁱprovokes to jealousy. ⁴And behold, the ^jglory of the God of Israel *was* there, like the vision that I ^ksaw in the plain.

⁵Then He said to me, "Son of man, lift your eyes now toward the north." So I lifted my eyes toward the north, and there, north of the altar gate, was this image of jealousy in the entrance.

⁶Furthermore He said to me, "Son of man, do you see what they are doing, the great ^labominations that the house of Israel commits here, to make Me go far away from My sanctuary? Now turn again, you will see greater abominations." ⁷So He brought me to the door of the court; and when I looked, there was a hole in the wall. ⁸Then He said to me, "Son of man, dig into the wall"; and when I dug into the wall, there was a door.

⁹And He said to me, "Go in, and see the wicked abominations which they are doing there." ¹⁰So I went in and saw, and there—every ^msort of ⁿcreeping thing, abominable beasts, and all the idols of the house of Israel, portrayed all around on the walls. ¹¹And there stood before them ^oseventy men of the elders of the house of Israel, and in their midst stood Jaazaniah the son of Shaphan. Each man had a censer in his hand, and a thick cloud of incense went up. ¹²Then He said to me, "Son of man, have you seen what the elders of the house of Israel do in the dark, every man in the room of his idols? For they say, ^p'The LORD does not see us, the LORD has forsaken the land.' "

---

four things: (1) mourning; displaying their humiliation over sin by wearing sackcloth and shaving their heads (Is. 15:2); (2) weakness; (3) horror; and (4) disgust and disillusionment over wealth.

7:20 the beauty of his ornaments. The people had sinned horribly when they crafted idols out of the temple treasures and then worshiped what their hands had made (Rom. 1:25).

8:5–6 to make Me go far away from My sanctuary. The people thought that just because the temple stood among them, whatever wrong they might do could not bring ultimate disaster. They thought the temple guaranteed their security. They did not realize

that their evil had caused God to leave His temple, which would then no longer be their protection.

8:11 seventy men. These men were the nation's leaders (Num. 11:16–25).

7:19 ^r Zeph. 1:18   **7:20** ^s Jer. 7:30   **7:21** ^t 2 Kin. 24:13   **7:23** ^u 2 Kin. 21:16   **7:24** ^v Ezek. 21:31; 28:7   ^w Ezek. 24:21   **7:26** ^x Jer. 4:20   ^y Ps. 74:9   **8:1** ^a Ezek. 14:1; 20:1; 33:31   ^b Ezek. 1:3; 3:22   **8:2** ^c Ezek. 1:26, 27   ^d Ezek. 1:4, 27   **8:3** ^e Dan. 5:5   ^f Ezek. 3:14   ^g Ezek. 11:1, 24; 40:2   ^h Ezek. 5:11   ⁱ Deut. 32:16, 21   **8:4** ^j Ezek. 3:12; 9:3   ^k Ezek. 1:28; 3:22, 23   **8:6** ^l 2 Kin. 23:4, 5   **8:10** ^m Ex. 20:4   ⁿ Rom. 1:23   **8:11** ^o Num. 11:16, 25   **8:12** ^p Ezek. 9:9

13And He said to me, "Turn again, *and* you will see greater abominations that they are doing." 14So He brought me to the door of the north gate of the LORD's house; and to my dismay, women were sitting there weeping for Tammuz.

15Then He said to me, "Have you seen *this*, O son of man? Turn again, you will see greater abominations than these." 16So He brought me into the inner court of the LORD's house; and there, at the door of the temple of the LORD, qbetween the porch and the altar, rwere about twenty-five men swith their backs toward the temple of the LORD and their faces toward the east, and they were worshiping tthe sun toward the east.

17And He said to me, "Have you seen *this*, O son of man? Is it a trivial thing to the house of Judah to commit the abominations which they commit here? For they have ufilled the land with violence; then they have returned to provoke Me to anger. Indeed they put the branch to their nose. 18vTherefore I also will act in fury. My weye will not spare nor will I have pity; and though they xcry in My ears with a loud voice, I will not hear them."

The Wicked Are Slain

9 Then He called out in my hearing with a loud voice, saying, "Let those who have charge over the city draw near, each *with* a deadly weapon in his hand." 2And suddenly six men came from the direction of the upper gate, which faces north, each with his battle-ax in his hand. aOne man among them *was* clothed with linen and had a writer's inkhorn at his side. They went in and stood beside the bronze altar.

3Now bthe glory of the God of Israel had gone up from the cherub, where it had been, to the threshold of the temple.* And He called to the man clothed with linen, who *had* the writer's inkhorn at his side; 4and the LORD said to him, "Go through the midst of the city, through the midst of Jerusalem, and put ca mark on the foreheads of the men dwho sigh and cry over all the abominations that are done within it."

5To the others He said in my hearing, "Go after him through the city and ekill; fdo not let your eye spare, nor have any pity. 6gUtterly slay old *and* young men, maidens and little children and women; but hdo not come near anyone on whom *is* the mark; and ibegin at My sanctuary." jSo they began with the elders who *were* before the temple. 7Then He said to them, "Defile the temple, and fill the courts with the slain. Go out!" And they went out and killed in the city.

8So it was, that while they were killing them, I was left *alone*; and I kfell on my face and cried out, and said, l"Ah, Lord God! Will You destroy all the remnant of Israel in pouring out Your fury on Jerusalem?"

9Then He said to me, "The iniquity of the house of Israel and Judah *is* exceedingly great, and mthe land is full of bloodshed, and the city full of perversity; for they say, n'The LORD has forsaken the land, and othe LORD does not see!' 10And as for Me also, My peye will neither spare, nor will I have pity, *but* qI will recompense their deeds on their own head."

11Just then, the man clothed with linen, who *had* the inkhorn at his side, reported back and said, "I have done as You commanded me."

The Glory Departs from the Temple

10 And I looked, and there in the afirmament that was above the head of the cherubim, there appeared something like a sapphire stone, having the appearance of the likeness of a throne. 2bThen He spoke to the man clothed with linen, and said, "Go in among the wheels, under the cherub, fill your hands with ccoals of fire from among the cherubim, and dscatter *them* over the city." And he went in as I watched.

3Now the cherubim were standing on the south side of the temple* when the man went in, and the ecloud filled the inner

---

* 9:3 Literally *house*   * 10:3 Literally *house*, also in verses 4 and 18

8:13–14 *Tammuz.* This was a fertility god. The women were crying out to the idol because they had no children or because the crops were failing. In the sixth month, August-September, Tammuz was thought to "die" with the scorched land. Worshipers would wail over his death and cry for his resurgence.

8:17–18 *they put the branch to their nose.* This action is not mentioned elsewhere. In the context it appears to be (1) a ritualistic gesture used in idol worship, or (2) an action indicative of the extensive violence which was occurring in Judah as a result of idolatry.

9:5–6 *Go after him through the city.* The universality of this judgment is shocking to us; but this is in line with divine judgments from the time of the flood in Genesis to the final judgment described in Revelation.

9:6–7 *My sanctuary.* The corrupt spiritual leaders had been practicing idolatry and immorality in the

temple itself (8:3–16). Judgment would begin with them because they had led the nation astray.

9:9 *iniquity . . . bloodshed . . . perversity.* These three reasons are given as the offenses that deserve this terrible outpouring of God's wrath. The people and especially rich rulers willfully chose to believe that God did not see or care what injustices went on.

10:3–5 *the cloud filled the inner court.* The cloud

8:16 qJoel 2:17 rEzek. 11:1 sJer. 2:27; 32:33 tDeut. 4:19   8:17 uEzek. 9:9   8:18 vEzek. 5:13; 16:42; 24:13 wEzek. 5:11; 7:4, 9; 9:5, 10 xMic. 3:4   9:2 aLev. 16:4   9:3 bEzek. 3:23; 8:4; 10:4, 18; 11:22, 23   9:4 cRev. 7:2, 3; 9:4; 14:1 dEzek. 13:17   9:5 eEzek. 7:9 fEzek. 5:11   9:6 g2 Chr. 36:17 hRev. 9:4 iJer. 25:29 jEzek. 8:11, 12, 16   9:8 kJosh. 7:6 lEzek. 11:13   9:9 m2 Kin. 21:16 nEzek. 8:12 oIs. 29:15   9:10 pEzek. 5:11; 7:4; 8:18 qEzek. 11:21   10:1 aEzek. 1:22, 26   10:2 bDan. 10:5 cEzek. 1:13 dRev. 8:5   10:3 e1 Kin. 8:10, 11

court. 4fThen the glory of the LORD went up from the cherub, *and paused* over the threshold of the temple; and *g*the house was filled with the cloud, and the court was full of the brightness of the LORD's *h*glory. 5And the *i*sound of the wings of the cherubim was heard *even* in the outer court, like *j*the voice of Almighty God when He speaks.

6Then it happened, when He commanded the man clothed in linen, saying, "Take fire from among the wheels, from among the cherubim," that he went in and stood beside the wheels. 7And the cherub stretched out his hand from among the cherubim to the fire that *was* among the cherubim, and took *some of it* and put *it* into the hands of the *man* clothed with linen, who took *it* and went out. 8kThe cherubim appeared to have the form of a man's hand under their wings.

9lAnd when I looked, there were four wheels by the cherubim, one wheel by one cherub and another wheel by each other cherub; the wheels appeared *to have* the color of a *m*beryl stone. 10As *for* their appearance, all four looked alike—as it were, a wheel in the middle of a wheel. 11nWhen they went, they went toward *any of* their four directions; they did not turn aside when they went, but followed in the direction the head was facing. They did not turn aside when they went. 12And their whole body, with their back, their hands, their wings, and the wheels that the four had, *were* ofull of eyes all around. 13As for the wheels, they were called in my hearing, "Wheel."

14pEach one had four faces: the first face *was* the face of a cherub, the second face the face of a man, the third the face of a lion, and the fourth the face of an eagle. 15And the cherubim were lifted up. This *was* qthe living creature I saw by the River Chebar. 16rWhen the cherubim went, the wheels went beside them; and when the cherubim lifted their wings to mount up from the earth, the same wheels also did not turn from beside them. 17sWhen *the cherubim*** stood still, *the wheels* stood still, and when *one*** was lifted up, *the*

other* lifted itself up, for the spirit of the living creature *was* in them. 18Then *t*the glory of the LORD *u*departed from the threshold of the temple and stood over the cherubim. 19And *v*the cherubim lifted their wings and mounted up from the earth in my sight. When they went out, the wheels *were* beside them; and they stood at the door of the *w*east gate of the LORD's house, and the glory of the God of Israel *was* above them.

20xThis *is* the living creature I saw under the God of Israel *y*by the River Chebar, and I knew they *were* cherubim. 21zEach one had four faces and each one four wings, and the likeness of the hands of a man *was* under their wings. 22And *a*the likeness of their faces *was* the same *as* the faces which I had seen by the River Chebar, their appearance and their persons. *b*They each went straight forward.

Judgment on Wicked Counselors

11 Then *a*the Spirit lifted me up and brought me to *b*the East Gate of the LORD's house, which faces eastward; and there *c*at the door of the gate were twenty-five men, among whom I saw Jaazaniah the son of Azzur, and Pelatiah the son of Benaiah, princes of the people. 2And He said to me: "Son of man, these *are* the men who devise iniquity and give wicked counsel in this city, 3who say, '*The time is* not *d*near to build houses; *e*this *city is* the caldron, and we *are* the meat.' 4Therefore prophesy against them, prophesy, O son of man!"

5Then *f*the Spirit of the LORD fell upon me, and said to me, "Speak! 'Thus says the LORD: "Thus you have said, O house of Israel; for *g*I know the things that come into your mind. 6hYou have multiplied your slain in this city, and you have filled its streets with the slain." 7Therefore thus says the Lord GOD: *i*"Your slain whom you have laid in its midst, they *are* the meat, and this *city is* the caldron; *j*but I shall bring you out of the midst of it. 8You have

---

* **10:17** Literally *they* • Literally *they* • Literally *they*

---

represented God's glory (as in 1:4), which was seen moving from the inner court to the threshold of the temple. From there it filled the temple.

10:9–17 *the first face was the face of a cherub.* Whereas one of the four faces in 1:10 is an ox, here it is a cherub. These are ancient sculptures with animal bodies and wings but human faces. The difference of the faces between 1:10 and 10:14 should not be called an error; it is possible that the images that Ezekiel saw were changing from time to time.

10:20–22 *and I knew they were cherubim.* They sometimes serve as guardians (Gen. 3:24). They are associated with God's throne and presence (the mercy seat on the ark, Ex. 25:18–22; 1 Chr. 13:6). They are also associated with God's chariot-like throne (v. 1; 1:20–26; Ps. 18:10).

11:3 *build houses.* These officials were proclaiming

that the inhabitants of Jerusalem were as secure behind the city's walls as meat was safe in its cooking pot. There was no impending doom, they said; therefore, new construction projects were encouraged.

10:4 *f* Ezek. 1:28 *g* Ezek. 43:5 *h* Ezek. 11:22, 23 **10:5** *i* Ezek. 1:24 *j* [Ps. 29:3] **10:8** *k* Ezek. 1:8; 10:21 **10:9** *l* Ezek. 1:15 *m* Ezek. 1:16 **10:11** *n* Ezek. 1:17 **10:12** *o* Rev. 4:6, 8 **10:14** *p* Ezek. 1:6, 10, 11 **10:15** *q* Ezek. 1:3, 5 **10:16** *r* Ezek. 1:19 **10:17** *s* Ezek. 1:12, 20, 21 **10:18** *t* Ezek. 10:4 *u* Hos. 9:12 **10:19** *v* Ezek. 11:22 *w* Ezek. 11:1 **10:20** *x* Ezek. 1:22 *y* Ezek. 1:1 **10:21** *z* Ezek. 1:6, 8; 10:14; 41:18, 19 **10:22** *a* Ezek. 1:10 *b* Ezek. 1:9, 12 **11:1** *a* Ezek. 3:12, 14 *b* Ezek. 10:19 *c* Ezek. 8:16 **11:3** *d* 2 Pet. 3:4 *e* Jer. 1:13 **11:5** *f* Ezek. 2:2; 3:24 *g* [Jer. 16:17; 17:10] **11:6** *h* Ezek. 7:23; 22:2–6, 9, 12, 27 **11:7** *i* Mic. 3:2, 3 *j* Ezek. 11:9

kfeared the sword; and I will bring a sword upon you," says the Lord GOD. 9"And I will bring you out of its midst, and deliver you into the hands of strangers, and lexecute judgments on you. 10mYou shall fall by the sword. I will judge you at nthe border of Israel. oThen you shall know that I am the LORD. 11pThis city shall not be your caldron, nor shall you be the meat in its midst. I will judge you at the border of Israel. 12And you shall know that I am the LORD; for you have not walked in My statutes nor executed My judgments, but qhave done according to the customs of the Gentiles which are all around you." ' "

13Now it happened, while I was prophesying, that rPelatiah the son of Benaiah died. Then sI fell on my face and cried with a loud voice, and said, "Ah, Lord GOD! Will You make a complete end of the remnant of Israel?"

God Will Restore Israel

14Again the word of the LORD came to me, saying, 15"Son of man, your brethren, your relatives, your countrymen, and all the house of Israel in its entirety, are those about whom the inhabitants of Jerusalem have said, 'Get far away from the LORD; this land has been given to us as a possession.' 16Therefore say, 'Thus says the Lord GOD: "Although I have cast them far off among the Gentiles, and although I have scattered them among the countries, tyet I shall be a little sanctuary for them in the countries where they have gone." ' 17Therefore say, 'Thus says the Lord GOD: u"I will gather you from the peoples, assemble you from the countries where you have been scattered, and I will give you the land of Israel." ' 18And they will go there, and they will take away all its vdetestable things and

all its abominations from there. 19Then wI will give them one heart, and I will put xa new spirit within them,* and take ythe stony heart out of their flesh, and give them a heart of flesh, 20zthat they may walk in My statutes and keep My judgments and do them; qand they shall be My people, and I will be their God. 21But as for those whose hearts follow the desire for their detestable things and their abominations, bI will recompense their deeds on their own heads," says the Lord GOD.

22So the cherubim clifted up their wings, with the wheels beside them, and the glory of the God of Israel was high above them. 23And dthe glory of the LORD went up from the midst of the city and stood eon the mountain, fwhich is on the east side of the city.

24Then gthe Spirit took me up and brought me in a vision by the Spirit of God into Chaldea,* to those in captivity. And the vision that I had seen went up from me. 25So I spoke to those in captivity of all the things the LORD had shown me.

Judah's Captivity Portrayed

12 Now the word of the LORD came to me, saying: 2"Son of man, you dwell in the midst of aa rebellious house, which bhas eyes to see but does not see, and ears to hear but does not hear; cfor they are a rebellious house.

3"Therefore, son of man, prepare your belongings for captivity, and go into captivity by day in their sight. You shall go from your place into captivity to another place in their sight. It may be that they will consider, though they are a rebellious

* 11:19 Literally you   * 11:24 Or Babylon, and so elsewhere in this book

---

11:13 Ah, Lord GOD. Ezekiel's reaction showed that Pelatiah, one of the corrupt city leaders (v. 1), was struck dead by God as undeniable proof that the prophet's message would come true. Ezekiel himself was awestruck and asked if this meant that God would not after all preserve a remnant.
11:15 your countrymen. The people in Jerusalem (representative of Judah) regarded the exiles as sinners because they had been deported to Babylon.
11:16 I shall be a little sanctuary. God explained to Ezekiel that the Hebrews taken captive and spread among foreign lands were actually the remnant whom God was protecting. God Himself would continue as their sanctuary—a word in Hebrew that literally means a "holy place."
11:18-20 they will take away all the detestable things. When the remnant returned to the land, they would abolish idolatry. At that time God would establish a new covenant with them (Jer. 31:31–34). Then God would pour out His Spirit (36:26–27; Joel 2:28–29) so that His people would become united in purpose and empowered to maintain their righteousness. They would finally and truly become His people (Ex. 6:6–8).

11:23 the glory of the LORD went up. The Hebrew term for "glory" literally means "weight" or "significance" and refers to the wonder and majesty of the living God.
11:24-25 Then the Spirit took me up. Ezekiel's visions are not merely dreams; they were inspired by God Himself and thus were prophetic. **Chaldea.** This is an alternative term for Babylon.
12:3-7 prepare your belongings for captivity. Ezekiel's next visual demonstration warned the captives already in Babylon that they should not expect a quick return to Jerusalem. He had already shown that the city would soon fall (chs. 4–5) and those not killed would be led into exile. These exiles should have understood Ezekiel's meaning.

11:8 k Jer. 42:16   **11:9** l Ezek. 5:8   **11:10** m Jer. 39:6; 52:10   n 2 Kin. 14:25   o Ps. 9:16   **11:11** p Ezek. 11:3, 7   **11:12** q Deut. 12:30, 31   **11:13** r Acts 5:5   s Ezek. 9:8   **11:16** l Is. 8:14   **11:17** u Jer. 3:12, 18; 24:5   **11:18** v Ezek. 37:23   **11:19** w Jer. 32:39   x Ezek. 18:31   y Zech. 7:12   **11:20** z Ps. 105:45   a Jer. 24:7   **11:21** b Ezek. 9:10   **11:22** c Ezek. 1:19   **11:23** d Ezek. 8:4; 9:3   e Zech. 14:4   f Ezek. 43:2   **11:24** g Ezek. 8:3   **12:2** a Ezek. 2:3, 6–8   b Jer. 5:21   c Ezek. 2:5

house. [4]By day you shall bring out your belongings in their sight, as though going into captivity; and at evening you shall go in their sight, like those who go into captivity. [5]Dig through the wall in their sight, and carry your belongings out through it. [6]In their sight you shall bear them on your shoulders and carry them out at twilight; you shall cover your face, so that you cannot see the ground, [d]for I have made you a sign to the house of Israel."

[7]So I did as I was commanded. I brought out my belongings by day, as though going into captivity, and at evening I dug through the wall with my hand. I brought them out at twilight, and I bore them on my shoulder in their sight.

[8]And in the morning the word of the LORD came to me, saying, [9]"Son of man, has not the house of Israel, [e]the rebellious house, said to you, [f]'What are you doing?' [10]Say to them, 'Thus says the Lord GOD: "This [g]burden concerns the prince in Jerusalem and all the house of Israel who are among them."' [11]Say, [h]'I am a sign to you. As I have done, so shall it be done to them; [i]they shall be carried away into captivity.' [12]And [j]the prince who is among them shall bear his belongings on his shoulder at twilight and go out. They shall dig through the wall to carry them out through it. He shall cover his face, so that he cannot see the ground with his eyes. [13]I will also spread My [k]net over him, and he shall be caught in My snare. [l]I will bring him to Babylon, to the land of the Chaldeans; yet he shall not see it, though he shall die there. [14m]I will scatter to every wind all who are around him to help him, and all his troops; and [n]I will draw out the sword after them.

[15o]"Then they shall know that I am the LORD, when I scatter them among the nations and disperse them throughout the countries. [16p]But I will spare a few of their men from the sword, from famine, and from pestilence, that they may declare all their abominations among the Gentiles wherever they go. Then they shall know that I am the LORD."

Judgment Not Postponed

[17]Moreover the word of the LORD came to me, saying, [18]"Son of man, [q]eat your bread with quaking, and drink your water with trembling and anxiety. [19]And say to the people of the land, 'Thus says the Lord GOD to the inhabitants of Jerusalem and to the land of Israel: "They shall eat their bread with anxiety, and drink their water with dread, so [t]that her land may [r]be emptied of all who are in it, [s]because of the violence of all those who dwell in it. [20]Then the cities that are inhabited shall be laid waste, and the land shall become desolate; and you shall know that I am the LORD."

[21]And the word of the LORD came to me, saying, [22]"Son of man, what is this proverb that you people have about the land of Israel, which says, [t]'The days are prolonged, and every vision fails'? [23]Tell them therefore, 'Thus says the Lord GOD: "I will lay this proverb to rest, and they shall no more use it as a proverb in Israel."' But say to them, [u]"The days are at hand, and the fulfillment of every vision. [24]For [v]no more shall there be any [w]false vision or flattering divination within the house of Israel. [25]For I am the LORD. I speak, and [x]the word which I speak will come to pass; it will no more be postponed; for in your days, O rebellious house, I will say the word and [y]perform it," says the Lord GOD.'"

[26]Again the word of the LORD came to me, saying, [27z]"Son of man, look, the house of Israel is saying, 'The vision that he sees is [a]for many days from now, and he prophesies of times far off.' [28b]Therefore say to them, 'Thus says the Lord GOD: "None of My words will be postponed any more, but the word which I speak [c]will be done," says the Lord GOD.'"

12:11–14 they shall be carried away into captivity. Speaking in 592 B.C., Ezekiel predicted the deportation of Jerusalem's population to Babylon six years later and prophesied exactly what would happen to their leader Zedekiah. The king would attempt to escape by night, secretly and in disguise; but he would be caught and blinded by the Babylonians, then carried off to Babylon where he would later die.
12:15–16 Then they shall know that I am the LORD. The defeat of God's people would not indicate the Lord's lack of strength, but the serious consequences of sin against Him. Yet He would demonstrate that His purpose had always been to restore His people to Himself (Heb. 12:1–11). Through the difficult experience, His people would learn that their God was both holy and loving. Sin offended Him, but He still would reach out to restore the sinner.
12:22 The days are prolonged, and every vision fails. This proverb among the exiles indicates how hardened they were to Ezekiel's prophecies.

Although already captive, the people were cynical and apathetic, mistakenly thinking that a delay in judgment meant no judgment, at least in their lifetime (vv. 25,27–28; 2 Pet. 3:3–4).
12:23–25 The days are at hand, and the fulfillment of every vision. This proverb would replace the old one (v. 22), and false prophets opposing Ezekiel would cease to speak. The exiles would live to see the judgment on Jerusalem fulfilled.

12:6 [d]Ezek. 4:3; 24:24   **12:9** [e]Ezek. 2:5   [f]Ezek. 17:12; 24:19   **12:10** [g]Mal. 1:1   **12:11** [h]Ezek. 12:6   [i]2 Kin. 25:4, 5, 7   **12:12** [j]Jer. 39:4; 52:7   **12:13** [k]Jer. 52:9   [l]Jer. 52:11   **12:14** [m]Ezek. 5:10   [n]Ezek. 5:2, 12   **12:15** [o]Ezek. 6:7, 14; 12:16, 20   **12:16** [p]Ezek. 6:8–10   **12:18** [q]Ezek. 4:16   **12:19** [r]Zech. 7:14   [s]Ps. 107:34   **12:22** [t]Ezek. 11:3; 12:27   **12:23** [u]Zeph. 1:14   **12:24** [v]Ezek. 13:6   [w]Lam. 2:14   **12:25** [x]Luke 21:33   [y][Is. 14:24]   **12:27** [z]Ezek. 12:22   [a]Dan. 10:14   **12:28** [b]Ezek. 12:23, 25   [c]Jer. 4:7

Woe to Foolish Prophets

13 And the word of the LORD came to me, saying, 2"Son of man, prophesy ^aagainst the prophets of Israel who prophesy, and say to ^bthose who prophesy out of their own ^cheart, 'Hear the word of the LORD!'"

3Thus says the Lord GOD: "Woe to the foolish prophets, who follow their own spirit and have seen nothing! 4O Israel, your prophets are ^dlike foxes in the deserts. 5You ^ehave not gone up into the gaps to build a wall for the house of Israel to stand in battle on the day of the LORD. 6^fThey have envisioned futility and false divination, saying, 'Thus says the LORD!' But the LORD has ^gnot sent them; yet they hope that the word may be confirmed. 7Have you not seen a futile vision, and have you not spoken false divination? You say, 'The LORD says,' but I have not spoken.

8Therefore thus says the Lord GOD: "Because you have spoken nonsense and envisioned lies, therefore I *am* indeed against you," says the Lord GOD. 9"My hand will be ^hagainst the prophets who envision futility and who ⁱdivine lies; they shall not be in the assembly of My people, ^jnor be written in the record of the house of Israel, ^knor shall they enter into the land of Israel. ^lThen you shall know that I *am* the Lord GOD.

10"Because, indeed, because they have seduced My people, saying, ^m'Peace!' when *there is* no peace—and one builds a wall, and they ⁿplaster it with untempered *mortar*— 11say to those who plaster *it* with untempered *mortar*, that it will fall. ^oThere will be flooding rain, and you, O great hailstones, shall fall; and a stormy wind shall tear *it* down. 12Surely, when the wall has fallen, will it not be said to you, 'Where *is* the mortar with which you plastered *it?*'"

13Therefore thus says the Lord GOD: "I will cause a stormy wind to break forth in My fury; and there shall be a flooding rain in My anger, and great hailstones in fury to consume *it*. 14So I will break down the wall you have plastered with untempered *mortar*, and bring it down to the ground, so that its foundation will be uncovered; it will fall, and you shall be consumed in the midst of it. ^pThen you shall know that I *am* the LORD.

15"Thus will I accomplish My wrath on the wall and on those who have plastered it with untempered *mortar*; and I will say to you, 'The wall *is* no more, nor those who plastered it, 16*that is*, the prophets of Israel who prophesy concerning Jerusalem, and who ^qsee visions of peace for her when *there is* no peace,'" says the Lord GOD.

17"Likewise, son of man, ^rset your face against the daughters of your people, ^swho prophesy out of their own heart; prophesy against them, 18and say, 'Thus says the Lord GOD: "Woe to the *women* who sew *magic* charms on their sleeves* and make veils for the heads of people of every height to hunt souls! Will you ^thunt the souls of My people, and keep yourselves alive? 19And will you profane Me among My people ^ufor handfuls of barley and for pieces of bread, killing people who should not die, and keeping people alive who should not live, by your lying to My people who listen to lies?"

20'Therefore thus says the Lord GOD: "Behold, I *am* against your *magic* charms by which you hunt souls like birds. I will tear them from your arms, and let the souls go, the souls you hunt like birds. 21I will also tear off your veils and deliver My people out of your hand, and they shall no longer be as prey in your hand. ^vThen you shall know that I *am* the LORD.

---

* **13:18** Literally *over all the joints of My hands;* Vulgate reads *under every elbow;* Septuagint and Targum read *on all elbows of the hands.*

13:2–4 foxes in the deserts. The word translated "deserts" conveys the idea of open, desolate places. In the immediate context (v. 5), the foxes are pictured roaming amid the rubble of ruined city walls. The prophets were fools because they confused their own thoughts with God's. They were like foxes among the ruins because they scavenged for themselves while causing, ignoring, and profiting from the human wreckage surrounding them.

13:5 the day of the LORD. This phrase refers to times when God triumphs (7:19; 30:3). It is particularly used by the prophets to describe those periods in which God is unusually active in the affairs of His people, either for deliverance or for judgment (Joel 2:1; Zeph. 1:7). In that day, God will actively bring about His purposes for the world; He will rescue the righteous and judge evildoers.

13:10–16 you shall be consumed in the midst of it. The false prophets would experience God's wrath—just as the walls of Jerusalem which were being constructed at that time would be destroyed. Jerusalem would be conquered and captured for the sins of its inhabitants. The preaching of a false peace had prompted people to build for a "certain" future, but only the opposite was certain. The false prophets had deceived the people with false hopes of comfort and prosperity (v. 10). Their deception placed them not only at odds with God's truth, but also with God Himself. Their destruction was certain.

13:17–19 set your face against the daughters of your people. The Hebrew women who were false prophetesses were confusing their own ideas with God's and casting magic death spells through sorcery or witchcraft (Lev. 19:26).

13:2 ^a Ezek. 22:25–28 ^b Ezek. 13:17 ^c Jer. 14:14; 23:16, 26 **13:4** ^d Song 2:15 **13:5** ^e Ps. 106:23 **13:6** ^f Ezek. 22:28 ^g Jer. 27:8–15 **13:9** ^h Jer. 23:30 ⁱ Jer. 20:3–6 ^j Ezra 2:59, 62 ^k Jer. 20:3–6 ^l Ezek. 11:10, 12 **13:10** ^m Jer. 6:14; 8:11 ⁿ Ezek. 22:28 **13:11** ^o Ezek. 38:22 **13:14** ^p Ezek. 13:9, 21, 23; 14:8 **13:16** ^q Jer. 6:14; 8:11; 28:9 **13:17** ^r Ezek. 20:46; 21:2 ^s Ezek. 13:2 **13:18** ^t [2 Pet. 2:14] **13:19** ^u Mic. 3:5 **13:21** ^v Ezek. 13:9

22"Because with ʷlies you have made the heart of the righteous sad, whom I have not made sad; and you have ˣstrengthened the hands of the wicked, so that he does not turn from his wicked way to save his life. 23Therefore ʸyou shall no longer envision futility nor practice divination; for I will deliver My people out of your hand, and you shall know that I *am* the LORD."'"

Idolatry Will Be Punished

14 Now ᵃsome of the elders of Israel came to me and sat before me. 2And the word of the LORD came to me, saying, 3"Son of man, these men have set up their idols in their hearts, and put before their ᵇthat which causes them to stumble into iniquity. ᶜShould I let Myself be inquired of at all by them?

4"Therefore speak to them, and say to them, 'Thus says the Lord GOD: "Everyone of the house of Israel who sets up his idols in his heart, and puts before him what causes him to stumble into iniquity, and then comes to the prophet, I the LORD will answer him who comes, according to the multitude of his idols, 5that I may seize the house of Israel by their heart, because they are all estranged from Me by their idols."'

6"Therefore say to the house of Israel, 'Thus says the Lord GOD: "Repent, turn away from your idols, and ᵈturn your faces away from all your abominations. 7For anyone of the house of Israel, or of the strangers who dwell in Israel, who separates himself from Me and sets up his idols in his heart and puts before him what causes him to stumble into iniquity, then comes to a prophet to inquire of him concerning Me, I the LORD will answer him by Myself. 8ᵉI will set My face against that man and make him a ᶠsign and a proverb, and I will cut him off from the midst of My people. ᵍThen you shall know that I *am* the LORD.

9"And if the prophet is induced to speak anything, I the LORD ʰhave induced that prophet, and I will stretch out My hand against him and destroy him from among My people Israel. 10And they shall bear their iniquity; the punishment of the prophet shall be the same as the punishment of the one who inquired, 11that the house of Israel may ⁱno longer stray from Me, nor be profaned anymore with all their transgressions, ʲbut that they may be My people and I may be their God," says the Lord GOD.'"

Judgment on Persistent Unfaithfulness

12The word of the LORD came again to me, saying: 13"Son of man, when a land sins against Me by persistent unfaithfulness, I will stretch out My hand against it; I will cut off its ᵏsupply of bread, send famine on it, and cut off man and beast from it. 14ˡEven *if* these three men, Noah, Daniel, and Job, were in it, they would deliver *only* themselves ᵐby their righteousness," says the Lord GOD.

15"If I cause ⁿwild beasts to pass through the land, and they empty it, and make it so desolate that no man may pass through because of the beasts, 16*even* ᵒ*though* these three men *were* in it, *as* I live," says the Lord GOD, "they would deliver neither sons nor daughters; only they would be delivered, and the land would be ᵖdesolate.

17"Or *if* ᑫI bring a sword on that land, and say, 'Sword, go through the land,' and I ʳcut off man and beast from it, 18*even* ˢ*though* these three men *were* in it, *as* I live," says the Lord GOD, "they would deliver neither sons nor daughters, but only they themselves would be delivered.

19"Or *if* I send ᵗa pestilence into that land and ᵘpour out My fury on it in blood, and cut off from it man and beast, 20even ᵛ*though* Noah, Daniel, and Job *were* in it, *as* I live," says the Lord GOD, "they would deliver neither son nor daughter; they would deliver *only* themselves by their righteousness."

21For thus says the Lord GOD: "How much more it shall be when ʷI send My four severe judgments on Jerusalem—the sword and famine and wild beasts and pestilence—to cut off man and beast from it? 22ˣYet behold, there shall be left in it a remnant who will be ʸbrought out, *both* sons and daughters; surely they will come out to you, and ᶻyou will see their ways and

---

14:1-3 *some of the elders of Israel.* God revealed to Ezekiel that this group consisted of double-minded men (1 Kin. 18:21; Matt. 6:24; James 1:5–8). Outwardly, they came to seek a word from God through His true prophet Ezekiel, but in their hearts they harbored loyalties to other gods.

14:5 *seize the house of Israel by their heart.* These words announce God's restorative purpose (Prov. 3:12; Rev. 3:19) in allowing sin to run its course.

14:8 *I will cut him off from the midst of My people.* The unrepentant idolater would be separated not only from God, but also from God's people (13:9). This experience would be a strong visual warning and an international example—proverb—of God's absolute honoring of His promise to punish disobedience with cursing (Lev. 20:1–7).

14:9–11 *they shall bear their iniquity.* The relationship between God's sovereignty and human responsibility is implicit in these verses. God allows false preaching for His own inscrutable purposes,

13:22 ʷ Jer. 28:15 ˣ Jer. 23:14   **13:23** ʸ Mic. 3:5, 6   **14:1** ᵃ Ezek. 8:1; 20:1; 33:31   **14:3** ᵇ Ezek. 7:19 ᶜ Ezek. 20:3, 31   **14:6** ᵈ Is. 2:20; 30:22; 55:6, 7   **14:8** ᵉ Jer. 44:11 ᶠ Num. 26:10 ᵍ Ezek. 6:7; 13:14   **14:9** ʰ 2 Thess. 2:11   **14:11** ⁱ 2 Pet. 2:15 ʲ Ezek. 11:20; 37:27   **14:13** ᵏ Is. 3:1   **14:14** ˡ Jer. 15:1 ᵐ [Prov. 11:4]   **14:15** ⁿ Lev. 26:22   **14:16** ᵒ Ezek. 14:14, 18, 20 ᵖ Ezek. 15:8; 33:28, 29   **14:17** ᑫ Lev. 26:25 ʳ Zeph. 1:3   **14:18** ˢ Ezek. 14:14   **14:19** ᵗ 2 Sam. 24:15 ᵘ Ezek. 7:8   **14:20** ᵛ Ezek. 14:14   **14:21** ʷ Ezek. 5:17; 33:27   **14:22** ˣ Ezek. 12:16; 36:20 ʸ Ezek. 6:8 ᶻ Ezek. 20:43

their doings. Then you will be comforted concerning the disaster that I have brought upon Jerusalem, all that I have brought upon it. 23And they will comfort you, when you see their ways and their doings; and you shall know that I have done nothing *a*without cause that I have done in it," says the Lord GOD.

The Outcast Vine

15 Then the word of the LORD came to me, saying: 2"Son of man, how is the wood of the vine *better* than any other wood, the vine branch which is among the trees of the forest? 3Is wood taken from it to make any object? Or can *men* make a peg from it to hang any vessel on? 4Instead, *a*it is thrown into the fire for fuel; the fire devours both ends of it, and its middle is burned. Is it useful for *any* work? 5Indeed, when it was whole, no object could be made from it. How much less will it be useful for *any* work when the fire has devoured it, and it is burned?

6"Therefore thus says the Lord GOD: 'Like the wood of the vine among the trees of the forest, which I have given to the fire for fuel, so I will give up the inhabitants of Jerusalem; 7and *b*I will set My face against them. *c*They will go out from *one* fire, but *another* fire shall devour them. *d*Then you shall know that I *am* the LORD, when I set My face against them. 8Thus I will make the land desolate, because they have persisted in unfaithfulness,' says the Lord GOD."

God's Love for Jerusalem

16 Again the word of the LORD came to me, saying, 2"Son of man, *a*cause Jerusalem to know her abominations, 3and say, 'Thus says the Lord GOD to Jerusalem: "Your birth *b*and your nativity *are* from the land of Canaan; *c*your father *was* an Amorite and your mother a Hittite. 4As for your nativity, *d*on the day you were born your navel cord was not cut, nor were you washed in water to cleanse you; you were not rubbed with salt nor wrapped in swaddling cloths. 5No eye pitied you, to do any of these things for you, to have compassion on you; but you were thrown out into the open field, when you yourself were loathed on the day you were born.

6"And when I passed by you and saw you struggling in your own blood, I said to you in your blood, 'Live!' Yes, I said to you in your blood, 'Live!' 7*e*I made you thrive like a plant in the field; and you grew, matured, and became very beautiful. *Your* breasts were formed, your hair grew, but you *were* naked and bare.

8"When I passed by you again and looked upon you, indeed your time *was* the time of love; *f*so I spread My wing over you and covered your nakedness. Yes, I *g*swore an oath to you and entered into a *h*covenant with you, and *i*you became Mine," says the Lord GOD.

9"Then I washed you in water; yes, I thoroughly washed off your blood, and I anointed you with oil. 10I clothed you in embroidered cloth and gave you sandals of badger skin; I clothed you with fine linen and covered you with silk. 11I adorned you with ornaments, *j*put bracelets on your wrists, *k*and a chain on your neck. 12And I put a jewel in your nose, earrings in your ears, and a beautiful crown on your head. 13Thus you were adorned with gold and silver, and your clothing *was* of fine linen,

---

but the preacher is held accountable for the content of the message. These were Israelite false prophets who deliberately ignored the truth and mixed it with falsehood.

15:6 the vine among the trees of the forest. Unlike an olive tree whose wood is also useful, the vine has only one use, to bear grapes.

15:6–8 another fire shall devour them. God had designed the people of Israel for a particular purpose, to bring glory to His name by living faithfully to His covenant and by bringing the nations to the knowledge of the Lord. Instead, Israel had become like the pagan nations around them.

16:2 cause Jerusalem to know her abominations. What follows is an animated development of the dreary story, designed to teach errant Jerusalem the real nature of her character in the eyes of God. The word "abominations" describes that which makes one physically ill.

16:3 your father was an Amorite and your mother a Hittite. These shocking words refer to the cultural and moral origins of Jerusalem. Ancient Canaan was inhabited by Semitic and non-Semitic peoples. The Amorites and Hittites are associated in Scripture with the southern hill country, where Jerusalem is (Num. 13:29). The point is that non-Israelites founded this city. Jebusites controlled it when the Israelites

entered the land under Joshua (Josh. 15:8). Israel did not obtain full control of the city until David conquered it (2 Sam. 5:6–7). In other words, Israel was not as pure as it thought it was.

16:4 you were not rubbed with salt. God reminds Jerusalem that He had rescued them from being like an abandoned newborn child—unwashed, unsanitary, and exposed to the elements to die. God alone has given her glory.

16:6 Live. Ezekiel warned the Jews remaining in Jerusalem to repent, reminding them that not merely their existence, but their living relation to God, was dependent upon His free grace. God alone is the Author of eternal life, just as He is Creator of all life (John 5:24).

16:7–9 Your breasts were formed. The city is compared to a young woman, mature and lovely. Yet it was naked and bare until God covered it with a relationship of covenantal love. This began when David moved the ark of the covenant there and

14:23 *a* Jer. 22:8, 9   15:4 *a* [John 15:6]   15:7 *b* Ezek. 14:8 *c* Is. 24:18 *d* Ezek. 7:4   16:2 *a* Ezek. 20:4; 22:2   16:3 *b* Ezek. 21:30 *c* Ezek. 16:45   16:4 *d* Hos. 2:3   16:7 *e* Ex. 1:7   16:8 *f* Ruth 3:9 *g* Gen. 22:16–18 *h* Ex. 24:6–8 *i* [Ex. 19:5]   16:11 *j* Gen. 24:22, 47 *k* Prov. 1:9

silk, and embroidered cloth. [l]You ate *pas-*
try of fine flour, honey, and oil. You were
exceedingly [m]beautiful, and succeeded to
royalty. 14 [n]Your fame went out among the
nations because of your beauty, for it *was*
perfect through My splendor which I had
bestowed on you," says the Lord GOD.

Jerusalem's Harlotry

15 [o]"But you trusted in your own beauty,
[p]played the harlot because of your fame,
and poured out your harlotry on everyone passing by who *would have* it. 16 [q]You
took some of your garments and adorned
multicolored high places for yourself, and
played the harlot on them. *Such* things
should not happen, nor be. 17 You have also
taken your beautiful jewelry from My gold
and My silver, which I had given you, and
made for yourself male images and played
the harlot with them. 18 You took your embroidered garments and covered them, and
you set My oil and My incense before them.
19 Also [r]My food which I gave you—the
pastry of fine flour, oil, and honey *which*
I fed you—you set it before them as sweet
incense; and so it was," says the Lord GOD.
20 [s]"Moreover you took your sons and
your daughters, whom you bore to Me,
and these you sacrificed to them to be devoured. *Were* your *acts* of harlotry a small
matter, 21 that you have slain My children
and offered them up to them by causing
them to pass through *the* [t]*fire?* 22 And in
all your abominations and acts of harlotry you did not remember the days of your
[u]youth, [v]when you were naked and bare,
struggling in your blood.
23 "Then it was so, after all your
wickedness—'Woe, woe to you!' says the
Lord GOD—24 *that* [w]you also built for yourself a shrine, and [x]made a high place for
yourself in every street. 25 You built your
high places [y]at the head of every road, and
made your beauty to be abhorred. You offered yourself to everyone who passed by,
and multiplied your acts of harlotry. 26 You
also committed harlotry with [z]the Egyptians, your very fleshly neighbors, and increased your acts of harlotry to [a]provoke
Me to anger.
27 "Behold, therefore, I stretched out My
hand against you, diminished your allotment, and gave you up to the will of those
who hate you, [b]the daughters of the Philistines, who were ashamed of your lewd
behavior. 28 You also played the harlot with
the [c]Assyrians, because you were insatia-
ble; indeed you played the harlot with them
and still were not satisfied. 29 Moreover you
multiplied your acts of harlotry as far as
the land of the trader, [d]Chaldea; and even
then you were not satisfied.
30 "How degenerate is your heart!" says
the Lord GOD, "seeing you do all these
things, the deeds of a brazen harlot.

Jerusalem's Adultery

31 [e]"You erected your shrine at the head
of every road, and built your high place in
every street. Yet you were not like a harlot,
because you scorned [f]payment. 32 *You are*
an adulterous wife, *who* takes strangers instead of her husband. 33 Men make payment
to all harlots, but [g]you made your payments
to all your lovers, and hired them to come
to you from all around for your harlotry.
34 You are the opposite of *other* women in
your harlotry, because no one solicited you
to be a harlot. In that you gave payment but
no payment was given you, therefore you
are the opposite."

Jerusalem's Lovers Will Abuse Her

35 'Now then, O harlot, hear the word of
the LORD! 36 Thus says the Lord GOD: "Because your filthiness was poured out and
your nakedness uncovered in your harlotry with your lovers, and with all your
abominable idols, and because of [h]the
blood of your children which you gave to
them, 37 surely, therefore, [i]I will gather all
your lovers with whom you took pleasure,
all those you loved, *and* all those you hated;
I will gather them from all around against
you and will uncover your nakedness to
them, that they may see all your nakedness. 38 And I will judge you as [j]women who
break wedlock or [k]shed blood are judged; I
will bring blood upon you in fury and jealousy. 39 I will also give you into their hand,
and they shall throw down your shrines
and break down [l]your high places. [m]They

God established the covenant with David (2 Sam. 6:1—7:17).

16:15 ***you trusted in your own beauty.*** These words indict God's people for forgetting that their fame and fortune were God's gifts and not their own doing (v. 14). They relied on themselves and their gifts instead of on God. They came to believe that their material wealth and health as a nation absolutely demonstrated God's approval of their spiritual life, even though they were becoming spiritually corrupt.

16:27–29 ***played the harlot.*** Jerusalem's kings had sought political alliances with Assyria (2 Kin. 15:17–20) and Babylon (2 Kin. 20:12–19) instead of relying on their God for security. Probably a part of the treaty-making ceremonies was to worship the other nation's god. For Israel to do this would be a violation of the First Commandment.

16:36 ***your filthiness was poured out.*** Jerusalem was filthy spiritually because the city had soiled itself

16:13 [l]Deut. 32:13, 14 [m]Ps. 48:2 **16:14** [n]Lam. 2:15 **16:15** [o]Mic. 3:11 [p]Is. 1:21; 57:8 **16:16** [q]Ezek. 7:20 **16:19** [r]Hos. 2:8 **16:20** [s]Jer. 7:31 **16:21** [t]Jer. 19:5 **16:22** [u]Jer. 2:2 [v]Ezek. 16:4–6 **16:24** [w]Jer. 11:13 [x]Jer. 2:20; 3:2 **16:25** [y]Prov. 9:14 **16:26** [z]Ezek. 16:26; 20:7, 8 [a]Deut. 31:20 **16:27** [b]Ezek. 16:57 **16:28** [c]Jer. 2:18, 36 **16:29** [d]Ezek. 23:14–17 **16:31** [e]Ezek. 16:24, 39 [f]Is. 52:3 **16:33** [g]Hos. 8:9, 10 **16:36** [h]Jer. 2:34 **16:37** [i]Lam. 1:8 **16:38** [j]Lev. 20:10 [k]Gen. 9:6 **16:39** [l]Ezek. 16:24, 31 [m]Hos. 2:3

shall also strip you of your clothes, take your beautiful jewelry, and leave you naked and bare.

⁴⁰ⁿ"They shall also bring up an assembly against you, ᵒand they shall stone you with stones and thrust you through with their swords. ⁴¹They shall ᵖburn your houses with fire, and ᑫexecute judgments on you in the sight of many women; and I will make you ʳcease playing the harlot, and you shall no longer hire lovers. ⁴²So ˢI will lay to rest My fury toward you, and My jealousy shall depart from you. I will be quiet, and be angry no more. ⁴³Because ᵗyou did not remember the days of your youth, but agitated Me* with all these *things*, surely ᵘI will also recompense your deeds on *your own* head," says the Lord GOD. "And you shall not commit lewdness in addition to all your abominations.

More Wicked than Samaria and Sodom

⁴⁴"Indeed everyone who quotes proverbs will use *this* proverb against you: 'Like mother, like daughter!' ⁴⁵You *are* your mother's daughter, loathing husband and children; and you *are* the ᵛsister of your sisters, who loathed their husbands and children; ʷyour mother *was* a Hittite and your father an Amorite.

⁴⁶"Your elder sister *is* Samaria, who dwells with her daughters to the north of you; and ˣyour younger sister, who dwells to the south of you, *is* Sodom and her daughters. ⁴⁷You did not walk in their ways nor act according to their abominations; but, as if that were too little, ʸyou became more corrupt than they in all your ways. ⁴⁸"As I live," says the Lord GOD, "neither ᶻyour sister Sodom nor her daughters have done as you and your daughters have done. ⁴⁹Look, this was the iniquity of your sister Sodom: She and her daughter had pride, ᵃfullness of food, and abundance of idleness; neither did she strengthen the hand of the poor and needy. ⁵⁰And they were haughty and ᵇcommitted abomination before Me; therefore ᶜI took them away as I saw *fit*.*

⁵¹"Samaria did not commit ᵈhalf of your sins; but you have multiplied your abominations more than they, and ᵉhave justified your sisters by all the abominations which you have done. ⁵²You who judged your sisters, bear your own shame also, because the sins which you committed were more abominable than theirs; they are more righteous than you. Yes, be disgraced also, and bear your own shame, because you justified your sisters.

⁵³ᶠ"When I bring back their captives, the captives of Sodom and her daughters, and the captives of Samaria and her daughters, then *I will also bring back* ᵍthe captives of your captivity among them, ⁵⁴that you may bear your own shame and be disgraced by all that you did when ʰyou comforted them. ⁵⁵When your sisters, Sodom and her daughters, return to their former state, and Samaria and her daughters return to their former state, then you and your daughters will return to your former state. ⁵⁶For your sister Sodom was not a byword in your mouth in the days of your pride, ⁵⁷before your wickedness was uncovered. It was like the time of the ⁱreproach of the daughters of Syria* and all *those* around her, and of ʲthe daughters of the Philistines, who despise you everywhere. ⁵⁸ᵏYou have paid for your lewdness and your abominations," says the LORD. ⁵⁹For thus says the Lord GOD: "I will deal with you as you have done, who ˡdespised ᵐthe oath by breaking the covenant.

An Everlasting Covenant

⁶⁰"Nevertheless I will ⁿremember My covenant with you in the days of your youth, and I will establish ᵒan everlasting covenant with you. ⁶¹Then ᵖyou will remember your ways and be ashamed, when you receive your older and your

---

* **16:43** Following Septuagint, Syriac, Targum, and Vulgate; Masoretic Text reads *were agitated with Me*. * **16:50** Vulgate reads *you saw*; Septuagint reads *he saw*; Targum reads *as was revealed to Me*. * **16:57** Following Masoretic Text, Septuagint, Targum, and Vulgate; many Hebrew manuscripts and Syriac read *Edom*.

---

by worshiping foreign idols and practicing infanticide (vv. 20–21; Deut. 12:29–32).

16:41 *I will make you cease playing the harlot.* During the captivity, Israel would abandon idolatry and polytheism, as Ezekiel predicted. God's anger over the people's sin would be satisfied.

16:44–47 *Samaria ... Sodom.* Along with Jerusalem, these three are presented as sisters in the religiously and morally corrupt cultures in Canaan. Ezekiel even makes the point that Jerusalem had become more corrupt than the other two.

16:53–59 *who despised the oath by breaking the covenant.* The punishment of the exile and captivity was appropriate. The clear promise of the covenant was that blessings and curses were dependent upon Israel's obedience or disobedience (Ex. 24; Lev. 26; Deut. 28–29).

16:60–63 *Nevertheless I will remember.* Despite Jerusalem's disobedience to the Mosaic covenant and the resulting punishment, the covenant with Abraham—*My covenant*—would still be honored. Fulfillment of the covenant with Abraham did not depend on the people's faithfulness; God had made

16:40 ⁿ Ezek. 23:45–47 ᵒ John 8:5, 7 **16:41** ᵖ Deut. 13:16 ᑫ Ezek. 5:8; 23:10, 48 ʳ Ezek. 23:27 **16:42** ˢ Ezek. 5:13; 21:17 **16:43** ᵗ Ps. 78:42 ᵘ Ezek. 9:10; 11:21; 22:31 **16:45** ᵛ Ezek. 23:2–4 ʷ Ezek. 16:3 **16:46** ˣ Is. 1:10 **16:47** ʸ Ezek. 5:6, 7 **16:48** ᶻ Matt. 10:15; 11:24 **16:49** ᵃ Gen. 13:10 **16:50** ᵇ Gen. 13:13; 18:20; 19:5 ᶜ Gen. 19:24 **16:51** ᵈ Ezek. 23:11 ᵉ Jer. 3:8–11 **16:53** ᶠ Is. 1:9 ᵍ Jer. 20:16 **16:54** ʰ Ezek. 14:22 **16:57** ⁱ 2 Kin. 16:5 ʲ Ezek. 16:27 **16:58** ᵏ Ezek. 23:49 **16:59** ˡ Ezek. 17:13 ᵐ Deut. 29:12 **16:60** ⁿ Ps. 106:45 ᵒ Is. 55:3 **16:61** ᵖ Ezek. 20:43; 36:31

younger sisters; for I will give them to you for ^qdaughters, ^rbut not because of My covenant with you. ^{62s}And I will establish My covenant with you. Then you shall know that I *am* the LORD, ⁶³that you may ^tremember and be ashamed, ^uand never open your mouth anymore because of your shame, when I provide you an atonement for all you have done," says the Lord GOD.' "

The Eagles and the Vine

17 And the word of the LORD came to me, saying, ²"Son of man, pose a riddle, and speak a ^aparable to the house of Israel, ³and say, 'Thus says the Lord GOD:

> ^b"A great eagle with large wings and
> long pinions,
> Full of feathers of various colors,
> Came to Lebanon
> And ^ctook from the cedar the highest
> branch.
> ⁴ He cropped off its topmost young twig
> And carried it to a land of trade;
> He set it in a city of merchants.
> ⁵ Then he took some of the seed of the
> land
> And planted it in ^da fertile field;
> He placed *it* by abundant waters
> *And* set it ^elike a willow tree.
> ⁶ And it grew and became a spreading
> vine ^fof low stature;
> Its branches turned toward him,
> But its roots were under it.
> So it became a vine,
> Brought forth branches,
> And put forth shoots.
>
> ⁷ "But there was another* great eagle
> with large wings and many
> feathers;
> And behold, ^gthis vine bent its roots
> toward him,
> And stretched its branches toward
> him,

> From the garden terrace where it had
> been planted,
> That he might water it.
> ⁸ It was planted in good soil by many
> waters,
> To bring forth branches, bear fruit,
> *And* become a majestic vine." '

⁹"Say, 'Thus says the Lord GOD:

> "Will it thrive?
> ^hWill he not pull up its roots,
> Cut off its fruit,
> And leave it to wither?
> All of its spring leaves will wither,
> And no great power or many people
> Will be needed to pluck it up by its
> roots.
> ¹⁰ Behold, *it is* planted,
> Will it thrive?
> ⁱWill it not utterly wither when the east
> wind touches it?
> It will wither in the garden terrace
> where it grew." ' "

¹¹Moreover the word of the LORD came to me, saying, ¹²"Say now to ^jthe rebellious house: 'Do you not know what these *things mean?*' Tell *them,* 'Indeed ^kthe king of Babylon went to Jerusalem and took its king and princes, and led them with him to Babylon. ^{13l}And he took the king's offspring, made a covenant with him, ^mand put him under oath. He also took away the mighty of the land, ¹⁴that the kingdom might be ⁿbrought low and not lift itself up, *but* that by keeping his covenant it might stand. ¹⁵But ^ohe rebelled against him by sending his ambassadors to Egypt, ^pthat they might give him horses and many people. ^qWill he prosper? Will he who does such *things* escape? Can he break a covenant and still be delivered?

---

* **17:7** Following Septuagint, Syriac, and Vulgate; Masoretic Text and Targum read *one.*

---

the promise and He would keep it (Gen. 15; 17:7–8; Lev. 26:40–45; Ps. 145:13). The everlasting covenant had been made with Abraham before the Hebrew nation even existed. This covenant would be remembered and reestablished with the exiled Judeans. At that time, God's people would be ashamed by the contrast between their faithlessness and God's faithfulness and the fact that they were being exalted over those who were less sinful—Sodom and Samaria. The people of these other sinful nations would also inherit land, but only by God's grace, because no such covenant was made with them.

17:2–10 *pose a riddle, and speak a parable.* Both of these words can be used to refer to an allegory. The "parable" primarily refers to a comparison between two things. A "riddle" was sometimes used as a political contest of mental competition between kings, in which the loser would submit to the winner and be killed. The details of the allegory: *great eagle* is the king of Babylon (v. 12); *Lebanon* symbolizes Canaan, of which Jerusalem (v. 12) is the major city; *the highest branch of the cedar* is the king of Jerusalem and

Judah (v. 12); *the young twigs* refers to the nobility of Judah; the *city of merchants* is Babylon; *the seed* is a member of the royal family (v. 13); the *fertile field* is the land where this royal offspring would rule (vv. 13–14); *another great eagle* is the king of Egypt (v. 15); and the *vine* is the remnant and ruler left in Judah. This remnant failed to prosper because they made a treaty with the Egyptian Pharaoh. As a result, even the remnant was slain and scattered by Babylon's army (vv. 15–21).

17:11–21 *Say now to the rebellious house.* Since Ezekiel had preached earlier about Jerusalem's past abominations (ch. 16), the people were likely

16:61 ^q [Gal. 4:26] ^r Jer. 31:31   **16:62** ^s Hos. 2:19, 20
16:63 ^t Ezek. 36:31, 32 ^u [Rom. 3:19]   **17:2** ^a Ezek. 20:49;
24:3   **17:3** ^b Ezek. 17:12 ^c 2 Kin. 24:12   **17:5** ^d Deut.
8:7–9 ^e Is. 44:4   **17:6** ^f Ezek. 17:14   **17:7** ^g Ezek. 17:15
17:9 ^h 2 Kin. 25:7   **17:10** ⁱ Hos. 13:15   **17:12** ^j Ezek.
2:3–5; 12:9 ^k 2 Kin. 24:11–16   **17:13** ^l 2 Kin. 24:17 ^m 2 Chr.
36:13   **17:14** ⁿ Ezek. 29:14   **17:15** ^o 2 Kin. 24:20 ^p Deut.
17:16 ^q Ezek. 17:9

16'As I live,' says the Lord GOD, 'surely *r*in the place *where* the king *dwells* who made him king, whose oath he despised and whose covenant he broke—with him in the midst of Babylon he shall die. 17*s*Nor will Pharaoh with *his* mighty army and great company do anything in the war, *t*when they heap up a siege mound and build a wall to cut off many persons. 18Since he despised the oath by breaking the covenant, and in fact *u*gave his hand and still did all these *things,* he shall not escape.'"

19Therefore thus says the Lord GOD: "*As* I live, surely My oath which he despised, and My covenant which he broke, I will recompense on his own head. 20I will *v*spread My net over him, and he shall be taken in My snare. I will bring him to Babylon and *w*try him there for the treason which he committed against Me. 21*x*All his fugitives* with all his troops shall fall by the sword, and those who remain shall be *y*scattered to every wind; and you shall know that I, the LORD, have spoken."

Israel Exalted at Last

22Thus says the Lord GOD: "I will take also *one* of the highest *z*branches of the high cedar and set *it* out. I will crop off from the topmost of its young twigs *a*a tender one, and will *b*plant *it* on a high and prominent mountain. 23*c*On the mountain height of Israel I will plant it; and it will bring forth boughs, and bear fruit, and be a majestic cedar. *d*Under it will dwell birds of every sort; in the shadow of its branches they will dwell. 24And all the trees of the field shall know that I, the LORD, *e*have brought down the high tree and exalted the low tree, dried up the green tree and made the dry tree flourish; *f*I, the LORD, have spoken and have done *it.*"

A False Proverb Refuted

18 The word of the LORD came to me again, saying, 2"What do you mean when you use this proverb concerning the land of Israel, saying:

'The *a*fathers have eaten sour grapes, And the children's teeth are set on edge'?

3"*As* I live," says the Lord GOD, "you shall no longer use this proverb in Israel. 4 "Behold, all souls are *b*Mine; The soul of the father As well as the soul of the son is Mine; *c*The soul who sins shall die. 5 But if a man is just And does what is lawful and right; 6 *d*If he has not eaten on the mountains, Nor lifted up his eyes to the idols of the house of Israel, Nor *e*defiled his neighbor's wife, Nor approached *f*a woman during her impurity; 7 If he has not *g*oppressed anyone, *But* has restored to the debtor his *h*pledge; Has robbed no one by violence, *But* has *i*given his bread to the hungry And covered the naked with *j*clothing; 8 If he has not exacted *k*usury Nor taken any increase, *But* has withdrawn his hand from iniquity And *l*executed true judgment between man and man; 9 *If* he has walked in My statutes And kept My judgments faithfully— He *is* just; He shall surely *m*live!" Says the Lord GOD.

* **17:21** Following Masoretic Text and Vulgate; many Hebrew manuscripts and Syriac read *choice men*; Targum reads *mighty men*; Septuagint omits *All his fugitives.*

---

charging God with unfairness in punishing the present population. Ezekiel points out that present and past sins make God's actions just and fair. In this section, the Lord explains His grounds for using Babylon to judge Judah.

17:22 I will take also. The Hebrew is emphatic: "I Myself will take." In contrast to human kings, God declared that He personally would pick out, plant, and make prominent "a tender one," that is a twig or a sprig. Cedar branches are symbolic of rulers on the Davidic throne (17:3–4,12–13) and elsewhere of a line of David's descendants prophesied to produce the Messiah (2 Sam. 7:16; Is. 11:1–5; Jer. 22:24–30; Zech. 6:9–13; Matt. 1:1–17).

17:23–24 made the dry tree flourish. What was accomplished in the restoration under Zerubbabel was a fulfillment of this promise. But as is often the case, in biblical prophecy, the greater fulfillment is still to come in the reign of the Savior King.

18:2–3 set on edge. The Hebrew word that is rendered here is literally "made dull" but can refer to a sour sensation. The main idea of the proverb is that children are affected by their parents' behavioral

choices just as eating sour grapes produces a bitter taste. However, the people were interpreting and applying this proverb incorrectly; therefore, God said they should not use it any longer.

18:4 The soul who sins shall die. In this verse, the physical, earthly consequences of sinful behavior are being addressed (3:16–21; 33:12–20; Deut. 30:15–20).

18:6 approached a woman during her impurity. In ancient Israel, intimacy during the woman's menstrual period was prohibited. The Old Testament does not explain the reason for this, but it may be tied to the special role of blood for the atoning of sin (Lev. 15:19–33).

17:16 *r* Ezek. 12:13   **17:17** *s* Jer. 37:7   *t* Jer. 52:4   **17:18** *u* 1 Chr. 29:24   **17:20** *v* Ezek. 12:13   *w* Ezek. 20:36   **17:21** *x* Ezek. 12:14   *y* Ezek. 12:15; 22:15   **17:22** *z* [Zech. 3:8]   *a* Is. 53:2   *b* [Ps. 2:6]   **17:23** *c* [Is. 2:2, 3]   *d* Dan. 4:12   **17:24** *e* Amos 9:11   *f* Ezek. 22:14   **18:2** *a* Lam. 5:7   **18:4** *b* Num. 16:22; 27:16   *c* [Rom. 6:23]   **18:6** *d* Ezek. 22:9   *e* Lev. 18:20; 20:10   *f* Lev. 18:19; 20:18   **18:7** *g* Ex. 22:21   *h* Deut. 24:12   *i* Deut. 15:7, 11   *j* Is. 58:7   **18:8** *k* Ex. 22:25   *l* Zech. 8:16   **18:9** *m* Amos 5:4

10 "If he begets a son *who is* a robber
Or [n]a shedder of blood,
Who does any of these *things*
11 And does none of those *duties,*
But has eaten on the mountains
Or defiled his neighbor's wife;
12 If he has oppressed the poor and needy,
Robbed by violence,
Not restored the pledge,
Lifted his eyes to the idols,
Or [o]committed abomination;
13 If he has exacted usury
Or taken increase—
Shall he then live?
He shall not live!
If he has done any of these abominations,
He shall surely die;
[p]His blood shall be upon him.

14 "*If,* however, he begets a son
Who sees all the sins which his father
has done,
And considers but does not do likewise;
15 [q]*Who* has not eaten on the mountains,
Nor lifted his eyes to the idols of the
house of Israel,
Nor defiled his neighbor's wife;
16 Has not oppressed anyone,
Nor withheld a pledge,
Nor robbed by violence,
But has given his bread to the hungry
And covered the naked with clothing;
17 *Who* has withdrawn his hand from the
poor*,
And not received usury or increase,
But has executed My judgments
And walked in My statutes—
He shall not die for the iniquity of his
father;
He shall surely live!

18 "*As for* his father,
Because he cruelly oppressed,
Robbed his brother by violence,
And did what *is* not good among his
people,
Behold, [r]he shall die for his iniquity.

Turn and Live

19 "Yet you say, 'Why [s]should the son
not bear the guilt of the father?' Because
the son has done what is lawful and right,
and has kept all My statutes and observed
them, he shall surely live. 20[t]The soul who
sins shall die. [u]The son shall not bear the
guilt of the father, nor the father bear the
guilt of the son. [v]The righteousness of the
righteous shall be upon himself, [w]and the
wickedness of the wicked shall be upon
himself.

21 "But [x]if a wicked man turns from all
his sins which he has committed, keeps all
My statutes, and does what is lawful and
right, he shall surely live; he shall not die.
22[y]None of the transgressions which he has
committed shall be remembered against
him; because of the righteousness which
he has done, he shall [z]live. 23[a]Do I have any
pleasure at all that the wicked should die?"
says the Lord GOD, "*and* not that he should
turn from his ways and live?

24 "But [b]when a righteous man turns
away from his righteousness and commits iniquity, and does according to all the
abominations that the wicked *man* does,
shall he live? [c]All the righteousness which
he has done shall not be remembered; because of the unfaithfulness of which he is
guilty and the sin which he has committed,
because of them he shall die.

25 "Yet you say, [d]'The way of the Lord is
not fair.' Hear now, O house of Israel, is it
not My way which is fair, and your ways
which are not fair? 26[e]When a righteous
man turns away from his righteousness,
commits iniquity, and dies in it, it is because of the iniquity which he has done
that he dies. 27Again, [f]when a wicked *man*
turns away from the wickedness which he
committed, and does what is lawful and
right, he preserves himself alive. 28Because
he [g]considers and turns away from all the
transgressions which he committed, he
shall surely live; he shall not die. 29[h]Yet the
house of Israel says, 'The way of the Lord
is not fair.' O house of Israel, is it not My
ways which are fair, and your ways which
are not fair?

30[i]"Therefore I will judge you, O house
of Israel, every one according to his ways,"
says the Lord GOD. [j]"Repent, and turn from
all your transgressions, so that iniquity
will not be your ruin. 31[k]Cast away from
you all the transgressions which you have
committed, and get yourselves a [l]new heart
and a new spirit. For why should you die, O
house of Israel? 32For [m]I have no pleasure
in the death of one who dies," says the Lord
GOD. "Therefore turn and [n]live!"

---

* **18:17** Following Masoretic Text, Targum, and
Vulgate; Septuagint reads *iniquity* (compare
verse 8).

**18:19–32 Why should the son not bear the guilt
of the father?** In this passage, Ezekiel further clarifies his teaching on individual responsibility for sin
by answering certain questions that reflect what his
audience might be thinking in response to his previous message. God's response to their questions
through Ezekiel is, in part, also composed of questions.

18:10 [n] Num. 35:31 **18:12** [o] Ezek. 8:6, 17 **18:13** [p] Lev.
20:9, 11–13, 16, 27 **18:15** [q] Ezek. 18:6 **18:18** [r] Ezek.
3:18 **18:19** [s] Ex. 20:5 **18:20** [t] Ezek. 18:4 [u] Deut. 24:16
[v] Is. 3:10, 11 [w] Rom. 2:6–9 **18:21** [x] Ezek. 18:27; 33:12, 19
18:22 [y] Ezek. 18:24; 33:16 [z] Ps. 18:20–24] **18:23** [a] [Ezek.
18:32; 33:11] **18:24** [b] Ezek. 3:20; 18:26; 33:18 [c] [2 Pet.
2:20] **18:25** [d] Ezek. 18:29; 33:17, 20 **18:26** [e] Ezek.
18:24 **18:27** [f] Ezek. 18:21 **18:28** [g] Ezek. 18:14
18:29 [h] Ezek. 18:25 **18:30** [i] Ezek. 7:3; 33:20 [j] Matt. 3:2
18:31 [k] Eph. 4:22, 23 [l] Jer. 32:39 **18:32** [m] Lam. 3:33
[n] [Prov. 4:2, 5, 6]

Israel Degraded

19 "Moreover ᵃtake up a lamentation for the princes of Israel, ²and say:

'What *is* your mother? A lioness:
She lay down among the lions;
Among the young lions she nourished her cubs.
³ She brought up one of her cubs,
And ᵇhe became a young lion;
He learned to catch prey,
And he devoured men.
⁴ The nations also heard of him;
He was trapped in their pit,
And they brought him with chains to the land of ᶜEgypt.

⁵ 'When she saw that she waited, *that* her hope was lost,
She took ᵈanother of her cubs *and* made him a young lion.
⁶ ᵉHe roved among the lions,
And ᶠbecame a young lion;
He learned to catch prey;
He devoured men.
⁷ He knew their desolate places,*
And laid waste their cities;
The land with its fullness was desolated
By the noise of his roaring.
⁸ ᵍThen the nations set against him from the provinces on every side,
And spread their net over him;
ʰHe was trapped in their pit.
⁹ ⁱThey put him in a cage with chains,
And brought him to the king of Babylon;
They brought him in nets,
That his voice should no longer be heard on ʲthe mountains of Israel.

¹⁰ 'Your mother *was* ᵏlike a vine in your bloodline,*
Planted by the waters,
ˡFruitful and full of branches
Because of many waters.
¹¹ She had strong branches for scepters of rulers.
ᵐShe towered in stature above the thick branches,
And was seen in her height amid the dense foliage.

¹² But she was ⁿplucked up in fury,
She was cast down to the ground,
And the ᵒeast wind dried her fruit.
Her strong branches were broken and withered;
The fire consumed them.
¹³ And now she *is* planted in the wilderness,
In a dry and thirsty land.
¹⁴ ᵖFire has come out from a rod of her branches
And devoured her fruit,
So that she has no strong branch—
a scepter for ruling.' "

ᵠThis *is* a lamentation, and has become a lamentation.

The Rebellions of Israel

20 It came to pass in the seventh year, in the fifth *month*, on the tenth *day* of the month, *that* ᵃcertain of the elders of Israel came to inquire of the LORD, and sat before me. ²Then the word of the LORD came to me, saying, ³"Son of man, speak to the elders of Israel, and say to them, 'Thus says the Lord GOD: "Have you come to inquire of Me? *As* I live," says the Lord GOD, ᵇ"I will not be inquired of by you." ' ⁴Will you judge them, son of man, will you judge *them*? Then ᶜmake known to them the abominations of their fathers.

⁵"Say to them, 'Thus says the Lord GOD: "On the day when ᵈI chose Israel and raised My hand in an oath to the descendants of the house of Jacob, and made Myself ᵉknown to them in the land of Egypt, I raised My hand in an oath to them, saying, ᶠ'I *am* the LORD your God.' ⁶On that day I raised My hand in an oath to them, ᵍto bring them out of the land of Egypt into a land that I had searched out for them, ʰ'flowing with milk and honey,'* ⁱthe glory

---

* **19:7** Septuagint reads *He stood in insolence;* Targum reads *He destroyed its palaces;* Vulgate reads *He learned to make widows.* * **19:10** Literally *blood,* following Masoretic Text, Syriac, and Vulgate; Septuagint reads *like a flower on a pomegranate tree;* Targum reads *in your likeness.* * **20:6** Exodus 3:8

19:2–10 lioness . . . vine in your bloodline. Most likely both of these terms represented the nation of Israel since each was a "mother" of kings—the "cubs" and the "branches." The vine and lion images are common symbols for Hebrew royalty and nationality (15:1–6; 17:1–10; Gen. 49:9).

19:13 In a dry and thirsty land. To anyone who loved the covenantal promises focused on God's worship in Jerusalem, any alternative to Jerusalem was akin to living in the desert.

20:2–4 I will not be inquired of by you. God explains to Ezekiel that the elders of Israel had forfeited any right to inquire of Him due to the abominations of their fathers. All the people are responsible for their own sins, and this does not mean that these Hebrews were paying for sins their ancestors had committed. Instead, the present generation of Hebrews in exile

had clearly shown their failure to learn practical lessons from history, and thus had condemned themselves to repeat many mistakes. These leaders came to God with questions, but the questions were foolish and demonstrated the people's sinfulness. God gives a remedial review of their past.

19:1 ᵃEzek. 26:17; 27:2 **19:3** ᵇ2 Kin. 23:31, 32 **19:4** ᶜ2 Kin. 23:33, 34 **19:5** ᵈ2 Kin. 23:34 **19:6** ᵉ2 Kin. 24:8, 9 ᶠEzek. 19:3 **19:8** ᵍ2 Kin. 24:2, 11 ʰEzek. 19:4 **19:9** ⁱ2 Chr. 36:6 ʲEzek. 6:2 **19:10** ᵏEzek. 17:6 ˡDeut. 8:7–9 **19:11** ᵐDan. 4:11 **19:12** ⁿJer. 31:27, 28 ᵒHos. 13:5 **19:14** ᵖJudg. 9:15 ᵠLam. 2:5 **20:1** ᵃEzek. 8:1, 11, 12; 14:1 **20:3** ᵇEzek. 7:26; 14:3 **20:4** ᶜEzek. 16:2; 22:2 **20:5** ᵈEx. 6:6–8 ᵉDeut. 4:34 ᶠEx. 20:2 **20:6** ᵍJer. 32:22 ʰEx. 3:8 ⁱJer. 11:5; 32:22

of all lands. **7**Then I said to them, 'Each of you, *j*throw away *k*the abominations which are before his eyes, and do not defile yourselves with *l*the idols of Egypt. I *am* the LORD your God.' **8**But they rebelled against Me and would not obey Me. They did not all cast away the abominations which were before their eyes, nor did they forsake the idols of Egypt. Then I said, 'I will *m*pour out My fury on them and fulfill My anger against them in the midst of the land of Egypt.' **9**nBut I acted for My name's sake, that it should not be profaned before the Gentiles among whom they *were,* in whose sight I had made Myself *o*known to them, to bring them out of the land of Egypt.

10"Therefore I *p*made them go out of the land of Egypt and brought them into the wilderness. **11**qAnd I gave them My statutes and showed them My judgments, *r*'which, *if* a man does, he shall live by them.'* **12**Moreover I also gave them My *s*Sabbaths, to be a sign between them and Me, that they might know that I *am* the LORD who sanctifies them. **13**Yet the house of Israel *t*rebelled against Me in the wilderness; they did not walk in My statutes; they *u*despised My judgments, *v*'which, *if* a man does, he shall live by them';* and they greatly *w*defiled My Sabbaths. Then I said I would pour out My fury on them in the *x*wilderness, to consume them. **14**yBut I acted for My name's sake, that it should not be profaned before the Gentiles, in whose sight I had brought them out. **15**So *z*I also raised My hand in an oath to them in the wilderness, that I would not bring them into the land which I had given *them,* *a*'flowing with milk and honey,'* *b*the glory of all lands, **16**cbecause they despised My judgments and did not walk in My statutes; but profaned My Sabbaths; for *d*their heart went after their idols. **17**eNevertheless My eye spared them from destruction. I did not make an end of them in the wilderness.

18"But I said to their children in the wilderness, 'Do not walk in the statutes of your fathers, nor observe their judgments, nor defile yourselves with their idols. **19**I *am* the LORD your God: *f*Walk in My statutes, keep My judgments, and do them;

20ghallow My Sabbaths, and they will be a sign between Me and you, that you may know that I *am* the LORD your God.'

21"Notwithstanding, *h*the children rebelled against Me; they did not walk in My statutes, and were not careful to observe My judgments, *i*'which, *if* a man does, he shall live by them';* but they profaned My Sabbaths. Then I said I would pour out My fury on them and fulfill My anger against them in the wilderness. **22**Nevertheless I withdrew My hand and acted for My name's sake, that it should not be profaned in the sight of the Gentiles, in whose sight I had brought them out. **23**Also I raised My hand in an oath to those in the wilderness, that *j*I would scatter them among the Gentiles and disperse them throughout the countries, **24**kbecause they had not executed My judgments, but had despised My statutes, profaned My Sabbaths, and *l*their eyes were fixed on their fathers' idols.

25"Therefore *m*I also gave them up to statutes *that were* not good, and judgments by which they could not live; **26**and I pronounced them unclean because of their ritual gifts, in that they caused all their firstborn to pass *n*through *the fire,* that I might make them desolate and that they *o*might know that I am the LORD." '

27"Therefore, son of man, speak to the house of Israel, and say to them, 'Thus says the Lord GOD: "In this too your fathers have *p*blasphemed Me, by being unfaithful to Me. **28**When I brought them into the land *concerning* which I had raised My hand in an oath to give them, and *q*they saw all the high hills and all the thick trees, there they offered their sacrifices and provoked Me with their offerings. There they also sent up their *r*sweet aroma and poured out their drink offerings. **29**Then I said to them, 'What *is* this high place to which you go?' So its name is called Bamah* to this day." ' **30**Therefore say to the house of Israel, 'Thus says the Lord GOD: "Are you defiling yourselves in the manner of your

---

* **20:11** Leviticus 18:5 * **20:13** Leviticus 18:5
* **20:15** Exodus 3:8 * **20:21** Leviticus 18:5
* **20:29** Literally *High Place*

20:11 *if a man does, he shall live by them.* Following their exodus from slavery in Egypt, God began to sanctify the Israelites by revealing to them a code of law and entering a covenant relationship with them on a Creator-creature basis. This does not teach that eternal salvation can be earned by good works, but that the quality of the believer's physical and spiritual life on earth are related to his or her obedience to the living God.

20:12 *gave them My Sabbaths.* This is an important verse for understanding the Sabbath (Ex. 20:8–11; Deut. 5:12–15). Sabbath means "rest." That is, the Sabbath was a day to cease all ordinary work or labor, as clearly emphasized in Exodus 20:8–11. The Sabbath was to serve as a sign of God's covenantal relationship with His people, Israel.

20:20 *hallow My Sabbaths.* This word means "to treat as holy," "to observe as distinct," and "to consecrate." God commands that His Sabbaths be continually maintained by His people as sacred—distinct and separate from ordinary days.

20:7 *j* Ezek. 18:31 *k* 2 Chr. 15:8 *l* Lev. 18:3 **20:8** *m* Ezek. 7:8 **20:9** *n* Num. 14:13 *o* Josh. 2:10; 9:9, 10 **20:10** *p* Ex. 13:18 **20:11** *q* Neh. 9:13 *r* Lev. 18:5 **20:12** *s* Deut. 5:12 **20:13** *t* Num. 14:22 *u* Prov. 1:25 *v* Lev. 18:5 *w* Ex. 16:27 *x* Num. 14:29 **20:14** *y* Ezek. 20:9, 20 **20:15** *z* Num. 14:28 *a* Ex. 3:8 *b* Ezek. 20:6 **20:16** *c* Ezek. 20:13, 24 *d* Amos 5:25 **20:17** *e* [Ps. 78:38] **20:19** *f* Deut. 5:32 **20:20** *g* Jer. 17:22 **20:21** *h* Num. 25:1 *i* Lev. 18:5 **20:23** *j* Lev. 26:33 **20:24** *k* Ezek. 20:13, 16 *l* Ezek. 6:9 **20:25** *m* Rom. 1:24 **20:26** *n* Jer. 32:35 *o* Ezek. 6:7; 20:12, 20 **20:27** *p* Rom. 2:24 **20:28** *q* Ezek. 6:13 *r* Ezek. 16:19

ˢfathers, and committing harlotry according to their ᵗabominations? ³¹For when you offer ᵘyour gifts and make your sons pass through the fire, you defile yourselves with all your idols, even to this day. So shall I be inquired of by you, O house of Israel? As I live," says the Lord GOD, "I will ᵛnot be inquired of by you. ³²ʷWhat you have in your mind shall never be, when you say, 'We will be like the Gentiles, like the families in other countries, serving wood and stone.'

God Will Restore Israel

³³"As I live," says the Lord GOD, "surely with a mighty hand, ˣwith an outstretched arm, and with fury poured out, I will rule over you. ³⁴I will bring you out from the peoples and gather you out of the countries where you are scattered, with a mighty hand, with an outstretched arm, and with fury poured out. ³⁵And I will bring you into the wilderness of the peoples, and there ʸI will plead My case with you face to face. ³⁶ᶻJust as I pleaded My case with your fathers in the wilderness of the land of Egypt, so I will plead My case with you," says the Lord GOD.

³⁷"I will make you ᵃpass under the rod, and I will bring you into the bond of the ᵇcovenant; ³⁸ᶜI will purge the rebels from among you, and those who transgress against Me; I will bring them out of the country where they dwell, but ᵈthey shall not enter the land of Israel. Then you will know that I am the LORD.

³⁹"As for you, O house of Israel," thus says the Lord GOD: ᵉ"Go, serve every one of you his idols—and hereafter—if you will not obey Me; ᶠbut profane My holy name no more with your gifts and your idols. ⁴⁰For ᵍon My holy mountain, on the mountain height of Israel," says the Lord GOD, "there ʰall the house of Israel, all of them in the land, shall serve Me; there ⁱI will accept them, and there I will require your offerings

and the firstfruits of your sacrifices, together with all your holy things. ⁴¹I will accept you as a ʲsweet aroma when I bring you out from the peoples and gather you out of the countries where you have been scattered; and I will be hallowed in you before the Gentiles. ⁴²ᵏThen you shall know that I am the LORD, ˡwhen I bring you into the land of Israel, into the country for which I raised My hand in an oath to give to your fathers. ⁴³And ᵐthere you shall remember your ways and all your doings with which you were defiled; and ⁿyou shall loathe yourselves in your own sight because of all the evils that you have committed. ⁴⁴ᵒThen you shall know that I am the LORD, when I have dealt with you ᵖfor My name's sake, not according to your wicked ways nor according to your corrupt doings, O house of Israel," says the Lord GOD.'"

Fire in the Forest

⁴⁵Furthermore the word of the LORD came to me, saying, ⁴⁶ᑫ"Son of man, set your face toward the south; preach against the south and prophesy against the forest land, the South,* ⁴⁷and say to the forest of the South, 'Hear the word of the LORD! Thus says the Lord GOD: "Behold, ʳI will kindle a fire in you, and it shall devour ˢevery green tree and every dry tree in you; the blazing flame shall not be quenched, and all faces ᵗfrom the south to the north shall be scorched by it. ⁴⁸All flesh shall see that I, the LORD, have kindled it; it shall not be quenched."'"

⁴⁹Then I said, "Ah, Lord GOD! They say of me, 'Does he not speak ᵘparables?'"

Babylon, the Sword of God

21 And the word of the LORD came to me, saying, ²ᵃ"Son of man, set your face toward Jerusalem, ᵇpreach against the

* **20:46** Hebrew *Negev*

20:32 We will be like the Gentiles. Chosen to be a nation separate from sin and secular ways—a special instrument to reveal God's glory—Israel's consistent tendency was to identify with the neighboring ungodly nations and to take on their idolatrous ways (Ex. 19:5).

20:33–36 I will bring you out from the peoples. The judgment of captivity in Babylon had begun in the deportations of 605 and 597 B.C. and would be continued with Jerusalem's fall in 586 B.C. However, God also promised to restore Judah and to judge her enemies with fury (Deut. 4:34). This refers to the Persian conquest of Babylon in 539 B.C. and to the three returns of the Jews to their land and the rebuilding of their homeland (538–330 B.C.), yet Israel would again be taken captive and made to wander throughout the nations during the Roman occupation.

20:37 I will make you pass under the rod. This is the way a shepherd counts and controls his sheep (Lev. 27:32; Jer. 33:13).

20:39 Go, serve every one of you his idols. This is an

ironic command; the rest of the verse indicates that God was giving the stubborn people over to what they had decided. God grants each one a destiny consistent with his or her decisions.

20:44 you shall know that I am the LORD. The promise of this verse is that the Lord will gather the nation of Israel from places where they have been dispersed and that they will repent because of the evil things they have done.

20:46–47 the forest of the South. This refers to the

20:30 ˢ Judg. 2:19 ᵗ Jer. 7:26; 16:12 **20:31** ᵘ Ezek. 16:20; 20:26 ᵛ Ezek. 20:3 **20:32** ʷ Ezek. 11:5 **20:33** ˣ Jer. 21:5 **20:35** ʸ Jer. 2:9, 35; Ezek. 17:20 **20:36** ᶻ Num. 14:21–23, 28 **20:37** ᵃ Lev. 27:32 ᵇ Ps. 89:30–34 **20:38** ᶜ Ezek. 34:17 ᵈ Jer. 44:14 **20:39** ᵉ Amos 4:4 ᶠ Is. 1:13–15 **20:40** ᵍ Is. 2:2, 3 ʰ Ezek. 37:22 ⁱ Zech. 8:20–22 **20:41** ʲ Phil. 4:18 **20:42** ᵏ Ezek. 36:23; 38:23 ˡ Ezek. 11:17; 34:13; 36:24 **20:43** ᵐ Ezek. 16:61 ⁿ Lev. 26:39 **20:44** ᵒ Ezek. 24:24 ᵖ Ezek. 36:22 **20:46** ᑫ Ezek. 21:2 **20:47** ʳ Jer. 21:14 ˢ Luke 23:31 ᵗ Ezek. 21:4 **20:49** ᵘ Ezek. 12:9; 17:2 **21:2** ᵃ Ezek. 20:46 ᵇ Amos 7:16

holy places, and prophesy against the land
of Israel; 3and say to the land of Israel, 'Thus
says the LORD: "Behold, I *am* [c]against you,
and I will draw My sword out of its sheath
and cut off both [d]righteous and wicked
from you. 4Because I will cut off both righteous and wicked from you, therefore My
sword shall go out of its sheath against all
flesh [e]from south *to* north, 5that all flesh
may know that I, the LORD, have drawn My
sword out of its sheath; it [f]shall not return
anymore."' 6[g]Sigh therefore, son of man,
with a breaking heart, and sigh with bitterness before their eyes. 7And it shall be
when they say to you, 'Why are you sighing?' that you shall answer, 'Because of the
news; when it comes, every heart will melt,
[h]all hands will be feeble, every spirit will
faint, and all knees will be weak *as* water.
Behold, it is coming and shall be brought to
pass,' says the Lord GOD."
8Again the word of the LORD came to
me, saying, 9"Son of man, prophesy and
say, 'Thus says the LORD!' Say:

[i]'A sword, a sword is sharpened
And also polished!
10 Sharpened to make a dreadful
slaughter,
Polished to flash like lightning!
Should we then make mirth?
It despises the scepter of My son,
As it does all wood.
11 And He has given it to be polished,
That it may be handled;
This sword is sharpened, and it is
polished
To be given into the hand of [j]the slayer.'

12 "Cry and wail, son of man;
For it will be against My people,
Against all the princes of Israel.
Terrors including the sword will be
against My people;
Therefore [k]strike *your* thigh.

13 "Because *it is* [l]a testing,
And what if *the sword* despises even
the scepter?
[m]*The scepter* shall be no *more,*"

says the Lord GOD.

14 "You therefore, son of man, prophesy,
And [n]strike *your* hands together.
The third time let the sword do double
damage.
It *is* the sword *that* slays,
The sword that slays the great *men,*
That enters their [o]private chambers.
15 I have set the point of the sword
against all their gates,
That the heart may melt and many
may stumble.
Ah! [p]*It is* made bright;
It is grasped for slaughter:

16 "Swords[q] at the ready!
Thrust right!
Set your blade!
Thrust left—
Wherever your edge is ordered!

17 "I also will [r]beat My fists together,
And [s]I will cause My fury to rest;
I, the LORD, have spoken."

18The word of the LORD came to me
again, saying: 19"And son of man, appoint
for yourself two ways for the sword of the
king of Babylon to go; both of them shall go
from the same land. Make a sign; put *it* at
the head of the road to the city. 20Appoint
a road for the sword to go to [t]Rabbah of
the Ammonites, and to Judah, into fortified Jerusalem. 21For the king of Babylon
stands at the parting of the road, at the
fork of the two roads, to use divination: he
shakes the arrows, he consults the images,
he looks at the liver. 22In his right hand is
the divination for Jerusalem: to set up battering rams, to call for a slaughter, to [u]lift
the voice with shouting, [v]to set battering
rams against the gates, to heap up a *siege*
mound, and to build a wall. 23And it will be
to them like a false divination in the eyes
of those who [w]have sworn oaths with them;
but he will bring their iniquity to remembrance, that they may be taken.
24"Therefore thus says the Lord GOD:
'Because you have made your iniquity to
be remembered, in that your transgressions are uncovered, so that in all your doings your sins appear—because you have
come to remembrance, you shall be taken
in hand.

---

land of Judah—the southern kingdom—which had more trees then than now.

21:6 ***a breaking heart.*** This phrase translates words that literally mean "breaking loins," suggesting great emotional upheaval.

21:12 ***Cry and wail . . . strike your thigh.*** Ezekiel was told to add verbal groans and a physical gesture to his musical message. In that culture, these actions displayed great grief and sorrow (Jer. 31:19).

21:14–17 ***The third time . . . double damage.*** This was a numeric device (Prov. 6:16) used here to emphasize the extent and effectiveness of the sword's employment against Judah.

21:19–20 ***Make a sign.*** Ezekiel was to place a signpost at a fork in the road leading to the capital cities of Ammon and Judah.

21:21 ***shakes the arrows.*** There was a method of casting lots using arrows inscribed with names. They were shaken about in the quiver and then dropped to the ground like throwing dice. ***looks at the liver.*** Sheep livers from sacrificed animals were studied. The shades and shapes of various sections of the organ were the basis for a positive or negative prediction.

21:3 [c]Ezek. 5:8 [d]Job 9:22 **21:4** [e]Ezek. 20:47 **21:5** [f][Is. 45:23; 55:11] **21:6** [g]Is. 22:4 **21:7** [h]Ezek. 7:17 **21:9** [i]Deut. 32:41 **21:11** [j]Ezek. 21:19 **21:12** [k]Jer. 31:19 **21:13** [l]Job 9:23 [m]Ezek. 21:27 **21:14** [n]Num. 24:10 [o]1 Kin. 20:30 **21:15** [p]Ezek. 21:10, 28 **21:16** [q]Ezek. 14:17 **21:17** [r]Ezek. 22:13 [s]Ezek. 5:13; 16:42; 24:13 **21:20** [t]Jer. 49:2 **21:22** [u]Jer. 51:14 [v]Ezek. 4:2 **21:23** [w]Ezek. 17:16, 18

25'Now to you, O *profane, wicked prince of Israel, ʸwhose day has come, whose iniquity *shall* end, 26thus says the Lord GOD:

"Remove the turban, and take off the crown;
Nothing *shall remain* the same.
ᶻExalt the humble, and humble the exalted.
27 Overthrown, overthrown,
I will make it overthrown!
ᵃIt shall be no *longer*,
Until He comes whose right it is,
And I will give it *to* ᵇHim."'

A Sword Against the Ammonites

28"And you, son of man, prophesy and say, 'Thus says the Lord GOD ᶜconcerning the Ammonites and concerning their reproach,' and say:

'A sword, a sword *is* drawn,
Polished for slaughter,
For consuming, for flashing—
29 While they ᵈsee false visions for you,
While they divine a lie to you,
To bring you on the necks of the wicked, the slain
ᵉWhose day has come,
Whose iniquity *shall* end.

30 'Return ᶠit to its sheath.
ᵍI will judge you
In the place where you were created,
ʰIn the land of your nativity.
31 I will ⁱpour out My indignation on you;
I will ʲblow against you with the fire of My wrath,
And deliver you into the hands of brutal men *who are* skillful to ᵏdestroy.
32 You shall be fuel for the fire;
Your blood shall be in the midst of the land.
ˡYou shall not be remembered,
For I the LORD have spoken.'"

Sins of Jerusalem

22 Moreover the word of the LORD came to me, saying, 2"Now, son of man,

ᵃwill you judge, will you judge ᵇthe bloody city? Yes, show her all her abominations! ³Then say, 'Thus says the Lord GOD: "The city sheds ᶜblood in her own midst, that her time may come; and she makes idols within herself to defile herself. ⁴You have become guilty by the blood which you have ᵈshed, and have defiled yourself with the idols which you have made. You have caused your days to draw near, and have come to the *end of* your years; ᵉtherefore I have made you a reproach to the nations, and a mockery to all countries. ⁵*Those* near and *those* far from you will mock you as infamous and full of tumult.

⁶"Look, ᶠthe princes of Israel: each one has used his power to shed blood in you. ⁷In you they have ᵍmade light of father and mother; in your midst they have ʰoppressed the stranger; in you they have mistreated the fatherless and the widow. ⁸You have despised My holy things and ⁱprofaned My Sabbaths. ⁹In you are ʲmen who slander to cause bloodshed; ᵏin you are those who eat on the mountains; in your midst they commit lewdness. ¹⁰In you men ˡuncover their fathers' nakedness; in you they violate women who are ᵐset apart during their impurity. ¹¹One commits abomination ⁿwith his neighbor's wife; ᵒanother lewdly defiles his daughter-in-law; and another in you violates his sister, his father's ᵖdaughter. ¹²In you ᑫthey take bribes to shed blood; ʳyou take usury and increase; you have made profit from your neighbors by extortion, and ˢhave forgotten Me," says the Lord GOD.

¹³"Behold, therefore, I ᵗbeat My fists at the dishonest profit which you have made, and at the bloodshed which has been in your midst. ¹⁴ᵘCan your heart endure, or can your hands remain strong, in the days when I shall deal with you? ᵛI, the LORD, have spoken, and will do *it*. ¹⁵ʷI will scatter you among the nations, disperse you throughout the countries, and ˣremove your filthiness completely from you. ¹⁶You shall defile yourself in the sight of the nations; then ʸyou shall know that I *am* the LORD."'"

21:26–27 turban . . . crown. These stand for the priesthood and kingship. Both would be removed from Judah.
21:28 concerning the Ammonites. The Ammonites joined other nations east of the Jordan in raiding Judean territory, in return for protection from Nebuchadnezzar. Later, during the reign of Zedekiah, Ammon, Moab, Edom, and others conspired against Babylon, but with false hopes of help from Egypt (Jer. 27:3–11).
22:1–5 You have caused your days to draw near. The city was ripe for judgment. When such hypocrisy is exposed and punishment is executed before the world, God's people become lasting objects of ridicule.
22:6–12 the princes of Israel. Jerusalem's princes had shed the blood of innocent people (7:27; 11:1; 12:10; 19:1; 21:13). These evil leaders had been (1) taking advantage of parents and the weak; (2) rejecting

God and His covenant, leading to ungodliness and inhumanity; (3) murdering the innocent by slandering them; (4) preferring idolatrous religion and its immoral rituals; (5) engaging in sexual immorality with neighbors, family, and relatives; and (6) loving money and using it to get ahead of fellow citizens.

21:25 ˣ Jer. 52:2 ʸEzek. 21:29 **21:26** ᶻLuke 1:52 **21:27** ᵃ[Luke 1:32, 33] ᵇ[Jer. 23:5, 6] **21:28** ᶜEzek. 25:1-7 **21:29** ᵈEzek. 12:24; 13:6-9; 22:28 ᵉJob 18:20 **21:30** ᶠJer. 47:6, 7 ᵍGen. 15:14 ʰEzek. 16:3 **21:31** ⁱEzek. 7:8 ʲEzek. 22:20, 21 ᵏHab. 1:6-10 **21:32** ˡEzek. 25:10 **22:2** ᵃEzek. 20:4 ᵇNah. 3:1 **22:3** ᶜEzek. 24:6, 7 **22:4** ᵈ2 Kin. 21:16 ᵉDeut. 28:37 **22:6** ᶠIs. 1:23 **22:7** ᵍLev. 20:9 ʰEx. 22:22 **22:8** ⁱLev. 19:30 **22:9** ʲLev. 19:16 ᵏEzek. 18:6, 11 **22:10** ˡLev. 18:7, 8 ᵐLev. 18:19; 20:18 **22:11** ⁿEzek. 18:11 ᵒLev. 18:15 ᵖLev. 18:9 **22:12** ᑫEx. 23:8 ʳEx. 22:25 ˢEzek. 23:35 **22:13** ᵗEzek. 21:17 **22:14** ᵘEzek. 21:7 ᵛEzek. 17:24 **22:15** ʷDeut. 4:27 ˣEzek. 23:27, 48 **22:16** ʸPs. 9:16

Israel in the Furnace

17The word of the LORD came to me, saying, 18"Son of man, zthe house of Israel has become dross to Me; they *are* all bronze, tin, iron, and lead, in the midst of a afurnace; they have become dross from silver. 19Therefore thus says the Lord GOD: 'Because you have all become dross, therefore behold, I will gather you into the midst of Jerusalem. 20As *men* gather silver, bronze, iron, lead, and tin into the midst of a furnace, to blow fire on it, to bmelt *it*; so I will gather *you* in My anger and in My fury, and I will leave *you there* and melt you. 21Yes, I will gather you and blow on you with the fire of My wrath, and you shall be melted in its midst. 22As silver is melted in the midst of a furnace, so shall you be melted in its midst; then you shall know that I, the LORD, have cpoured out My fury on you.'"

Israel's Wicked Leaders

23And the word of the LORD came to me, saying, 24"Son of man, say to her: 'You *are* a land that is dnot cleansed' or rained on in the day of indignation.' 25eThe conspiracy of her prophets* in her midst is like a roaring lion tearing the prey; they fhave devoured people; gthey have taken treasure and precious things; they have made many widows in her midst. 26hHer priests have violated My law and iprofaned My holy things; they have not jdistinguished between the holy and unholy, nor have they made known *the difference* between the unclean and the clean; and they have hidden their eyes from My Sabbaths, so that I am profaned among them. 27Her kprinces in her midst *are* like wolves tearing the prey, to shed blood, to destroy people, and to get dishonest gain. 28lHer prophets plastered them with untempered *mortar,* mseeing false visions, and divining nlies for them, saying, 'Thus says the Lord GOD,' when the LORD had not spoken. 29The people of the land have used oppressions, committed robbery, and mistreated the poor and needy; and they wrongfully ooppress the stranger. 30pSo I sought for a man among them who would qmake a wall, and rstand in the gap before Me on behalf of the land, that I should not destroy it; but I found no one. 31Therefore I have spoured

out My indignation on them; I have consumed them with the fire of My wrath; and I have recompensed ttheir deeds on their own heads," says the Lord GOD.

Two Harlot Sisters

23 The word of the LORD came again to me, saying:

2 "Son of man, there were atwo women,
   The daughters of one mother.
3 bThey committed harlotry in Egypt,
   They committed harlotry in ctheir
      youth;
   Their breasts were there embraced,
   Their virgin bosom was there pressed.
4 Their names: Oholah* the elder and
      Oholibah* dher sister;
   eThey were Mine,
   And they bore sons and daughters.
   As for their names,
   Samaria *is* Oholah, and Jerusalem *is*
      Oholibah.

The Older Sister, Samaria

5 "Oholah played the harlot even though
      she was Mine;
   And she lusted for her lovers, the
      neighboring fAssyrians,
6 *Who were* clothed in purple,
   Captains and rulers,
   All of them desirable young men,
   Horsemen riding on horses.
7 Thus she committed her harlotry with
      them,
   All of them choice men of Assyria;
   And with all for whom she lusted,
   With all their idols, she defiled herself.
8 She has never given up her harlotry
      brought gfrom Egypt,
   For in her youth they had lain with her,
   Pressed her virgin bosom,
   And poured out their immorality upon
      her.
9 "Therefore I have delivered her
   Into the hand of her lovers,
   Into the hand of the hAssyrians,
   For whom she lusted.

---

* 22:24 Following Masoretic Text, Syriac, and Vulgate; Septuagint reads *showered upon.*
* 22:25 Following Masoretic Text and Vulgate; Septuagint reads *princes;* Targum reads *scribes.*
* 23:4 Literally *Her Own Tabernacle* • Literally *My Tabernacle Is in Her*

22:26 Her priests. Those who were supposed to be leaders were not examples of separation from worldly ways (Ex. 19:6). Some at least were motivated by monetary gain (Mic. 3:11).
22:28 plastered them with untempered mortar. The false prophets were involved in "whitewashing" the sins of the nation's leaders.
22:30 sought for a man among them. God could not find a spiritual leader to guide the people in godliness.
23:4 Oholah. In Hebrew, Oholah means "her own tabernacle" and **Oholibah** means "My tabernacle is in her." These seem to refer to God's sanctuaries in

each land or, in a distinct usage, to the tent shrines for Canaanite idols as opposed to God's true temple.
23:9-10 They uncovered her nakedness. This means to be stripped bare and so put to great shame.

22:18 z Is. 1:22 a Prov. 17:3 **22:20** b Is. 1:25 **22:22** c Ezek. 20:8, 33 **22:24** d Ezek. 24:13 **22:25** e Hos. 6:9 f Matt. 23:14 g Mic. 3:11 **22:26** h Mal. 2:8 i 1 Sam. 2:29 j Lev. 10:10 **22:27** k Is. 1:23 **22:28** l Ezek. 13:10 m Ezek. 13:6, 7 n Jer. 23:25-32 **22:29** o Ex. 23:9 **22:30** p Jer. 5:1 q Ezek. 13:5 r Ps. 106:23 **22:31** s Ezek. 22:22 t Ezek. 9:10 **23:2** a Ezek. 16:44-46 **23:3** b Lev. 17:7 c Ezek. 16:22 **23:4** d Jer. 3:6, 7 e Ezek. 16:8, 20 **23:5** f Hos. 5:13; 8:9, 10 **23:8** g Ezek. 23:3, 19 **23:9** h 2 Kin. 17:3

10 They uncovered her nakedness,
  Took away her sons and daughters,
  And slew her with the sword;
  She became a byword among women,
  For they had executed judgment on her.

The Younger Sister, Jerusalem

11"Now *i*although her sister Oholibah saw *this*, *j*she became more corrupt in her lust than she, and in her harlotry more corrupt than her sister's harlotry.

12 "She lusted for the neighboring
     *k*Assyrians,
  *l*Captains and rulers,
  Clothed most gorgeously,
  Horsemen riding on horses,
  All of them desirable young men.
13 Then I saw that she was defiled;
  Both *took* the same way.
14 But she increased her harlotry;
  She looked at men portrayed on the
     wall,
  Images of *m*Chaldeans portrayed in
     vermilion,
15 Girded with belts around their waists,
  Flowing turbans on their heads,
  All of them looking like captains,
  In the manner of the Babylonians of
     Chaldea,
  The land of their nativity.
16 *n*As soon as her eyes saw them,
  She lusted for them
  And sent *o*messengers to them in
     Chaldea.
17 "Then the Babylonians came to her,
     into the bed of love,
  And they defiled her with their
     immorality;
  So she was defiled by them, *p*and
     alienated herself from them.
18 She revealed her harlotry and
     uncovered her nakedness.
  Then *q*I *r*alienated Myself from her,
  As I had alienated Myself from her
     sister.

19 "Yet she multiplied her harlotry
  In calling to remembrance the days of
     her youth,
  *s*When she had played the harlot in the
     land of Egypt.
20 For she lusted for her paramours,
  Whose flesh *is like* the flesh of
     donkeys,

And whose issue *is like* the issue of
     horses.
21 Thus you called to remembrance the
     lewdness of your youth,
  When the *t*Egyptians pressed your
     bosom
  Because of your youthful breasts.

Judgment on Jerusalem

22"Therefore, Oholibah, thus says the Lord GOD:

  u'Behold, I will stir up your lovers
     against you,
  From whom you have alienated
     yourself,
  And I will bring them against you
     from every side:
23 The Babylonians,
  All the Chaldeans,
  *v*Pekod, Shoa, Koa,
  *w*All the Assyrians with them,
  All of them desirable young men,
  Governors and rulers,
  Captains and men of renown,
  All of them riding on horses.
24 And they shall come against you
  With chariots, wagons, and
     war-horses,
  With a horde of people.
  They shall array against you
  Buckler, shield, and helmet all around.

  'I will delegate judgment to them,
  And they shall judge you according to
     their judgments.
25 I will set My *x*jealousy against you,
  And they shall deal furiously with you;
  They shall remove your nose and your
     ears,
  And your remnant shall fall by the
     sword;
  They shall take your sons and your
     daughters,
  And your remnant shall be devoured
     by fire.
26 *y*They shall also strip you of your
     clothes
  And take away your beautiful jewelry.
27 'Thus *z*I will make you cease your
     lewdness and your *a*harlotry
  Brought from the land of Egypt,
  So that you will not lift your eyes to
     them,
  Nor remember Egypt anymore.'

Ezekiel is reminding his audience of how God already had judged Samaria through Assyrian conquest and captivity in 722 B.C. (2 Kin. 17:5–41).
23:14 She looked at men portrayed on the wall. These lines tell how Judean envoys to Babylon became enamored of Babylonian rulers and their power through pictures (Jer. 22:14) on their palace and temple walls.
23:17–18 she was defiled by them. This is an allusion to Judah's turning in disappointment and disgust from relying on Babylon to relying on Egypt (2 Kin. 23:28—24:1). God's alienation from Jerusalem

is an allusion to the city's coming defeat by Nebuchadnezzar.
23:24 Buckler. This was a large rectangular shield.

23:11 *i* Jer. 3:8 *j* Jer. 3:8–11 **23:12** *k* 2 Kin. 16:7, 8 *l* Ezek. 23:6, 23 **23:14** *m* Ezek. 8:10; 16:29 **23:16** *n* 2 Kin. 24:1 *o* Is. 57:9 **23:17** *p* Ezek. 23:22, 28 **23:18** *q* Jer. 6:8 *r* Jer. 12:8 **23:19** *s* Ezek. 23:2 **23:21** *t* Ezek. 16:26 **23:22** *u* Ezek. 16:37–41; 23:28 **23:23** *v* Jer. 50:21 *w* Ezek. 23:12 **23:25** *x* Ex. 34:14 **23:26** *y* Is. 3:18–23 **23:27** *z* Ezek. 16:41; 22:15 *a* Ezek. 23:3, 19

28"For thus says the Lord GOD: 'Surely I will deliver you into the hand of *b*those you hate, into the hand of *those* *c*from whom you alienated yourself. 29*d*They will deal hatefully with you, take away all you have worked for, and *e*leave you naked and bare. The nakedness of your harlotry shall be uncovered, both your lewdness and your harlotry. 30I will do these *things* to you because you have *f*gone as a harlot after the Gentiles, because you have become defiled by their idols. 31You have walked in the way of your sister; therefore I will put her *g*cup in your hand.'

32"Thus says the Lord GOD:

'You shall drink of your sister's cup,
　The deep and wide one;
*h*You shall be laughed to scorn
　And held in derision;
　It contains much.
33　You will be filled with drunkenness
　　　and sorrow,
　The cup of horror and desolation,
　The cup of your sister Samaria.
34　You shall *i*drink and drain it,
　You shall break its shards,
　And tear at your own breasts;
　For I have spoken,'
Says the Lord GOD.

35"Therefore thus says the Lord GOD:

'Because you *j*have forgotten Me and
　*k*cast Me behind your back,
Therefore you shall bear the *penalty*
Of your lewdness and your harlotry.'"

Both Sisters Judged

36The LORD also said to me: "Son of man, will you *l*judge Oholah and Oholibah? Then *m*declare to them their abominations. 37For they have committed adultery, and *n*blood *is* on their hands. They have committed adultery with their idols, and even *sacrificed* their sons *o*whom they bore to Me, passing them through *the fire*, to devour *them*. 38Moreover they have done this to Me: They have *p*defiled My sanctuary on the same day and *q*profaned My Sabbaths. 39For after they had slain their children for their idols, on the same day they came into My sanctuary to profane it; and indeed *r*thus they have done in the midst of My house.

40"Furthermore you sent for men to come from afar, *s*to whom a messenger *was* sent;

and there they came. And you *t*washed yourself for them, *u*painted your eyes, and adorned yourself with ornaments. 41You sat on a stately *v*couch, with a table prepared before it, *w*on which you had set My incense and My oil. 42The sound of a carefree multitude *was* with her, and Sabeans *were* brought from the wilderness with men of the common sort, who put bracelets on their wrists and beautiful crowns on their heads. 43Then I said concerning *her who had grown* old in adulteries, 'Will they commit harlotry with her now, and she *with them?*' 44Yet they went in to her, as men go in to a woman who plays the harlot; thus they went in to Oholah and Oholibah, the lewd women. 45But righteous men will *x*judge them after the manner of adulteresses, and after the manner of women who shed blood, because they *are* adulteresses, and *y*blood *is* on their hands.

46"For thus says the Lord GOD: *z*'Bring up an assembly against them, give them up to trouble and plunder. 47*a*The assembly shall stone them with stones and execute them with their swords; *b*they shall slay their sons and their daughters, and burn their houses with fire. 48Thus *c*I will cause lewdness to cease from the land, *d*that all women may be taught not to practice your lewdness. 49They shall repay you for your lewdness, and you shall *e*pay for your idolatrous sins. *f*Then you shall know that I *am* the Lord GOD.'"

Symbol of the Cooking Pot

24 Again, in the ninth year, in the tenth month, on the tenth *day* of the month, the word of the LORD came to me, saying, 2"Son of man, write down the name of the day, this very day—the king of Babylon started his siege against Jerusalem *a*this very day. 3*b*And utter a parable to the rebellious house, and say to them, 'Thus says the Lord GOD:

c"Put on a pot, set *it* on,
　And also pour water into it.
4　Gather pieces *of meat* in it,
　Every good piece,
　The thigh and the shoulder.
　Fill *it* with choice cuts;
5　Take the choice of the flock.
　Also pile *fuel* bones under it,
　Make it boil well,
　And let the cuts simmer in it."

23:32–34 You shall drink of your sister's cup. The cup is often symbolic of God's judgment (Ps. 75:7–8; Jer. 25:15–29). The phrase portrays how completely Judah would drink the cup of wrath, breaking what was already broken. **tear at your own breasts.** This image gives a picture of the resultant agony and anguish.

24:1–2 write down the name of the day. This would be a bitter reminder of God's trustworthiness to do what He promised through the prophets.

24:5 flock. The flock was symbolic of God's chosen

23:28 *b* Ezek. 16:37–41　*c* Ezek. 23:17　**23:29** *d* Deut. 28:48　*e* Ezek. 16:39　**23:30** *f* Ezek. 6:9　**23:31** *g* Jer. 7:14, 15; 25:15　**23:32** *h* Ezek. 22:4, 5　**23:34** *i* Is. 51:17　**23:35** *j* Jer. 3:21　*k* 1 Kin. 14:9　**23:36** *l* Ezek. 20:4; 22:2　*m* Is. 58:1　**23:37** *n* Ezek. 16:38　*o* Ezek. 16:20, 21, 36, 45; 20:26, 31　**23:38** *p* 2 Kin. 21:4, 7　*q* Ezek. 22:8　**23:39** *r* 2 Kin. 21:2–8　**23:40** *s* Is. 57:9　*t* Ruth 3:3　*u* Jer. 4:30　**23:41** *v* Is. 57:7　*w* Prov. 7:17　**23:45** *x* Ezek. 16:38　*y* Ezek. 23:37　**23:46** *z* Ezek. 16:40　**23:47** *a* Ezek. 16:40　*b* Ezek. 24:21　**23:48** *c* Ezek. 22:15　*d* Deut. 13:11　**23:49** *e* Ezek. 23:35　*f* Ezek. 20:38, 42, 44; 25:5　**24:2** *a* 2 Kin. 25:1　**24:3** *b* Ezek. 17:12　*c* Jer. 1:13

6'Therefore thus says the Lord GOD:

"Woe to dthe bloody city,
To the pot whose scum is in it,
And whose scum is not gone from it!
Bring it out piece by piece,
On which no elot has fallen.
7 For her blood is in her midst;
She set it on top of a rock;
fShe did not pour it on the ground,
To cover it with dust.
8 That it may raise up fury and take
vengeance,
gI have set her blood on top of a rock,
That it may not be covered."

9'Therefore thus says the Lord GOD:

h"Woe to the bloody city!
I too will make the pyre great.
10 Heap on the wood,
Kindle the fire;
Cook the meat well,
Mix in the spices,
And let the cuts be burned up.

11 "Then set the pot empty on the coals,
That it may become hot and its bronze
may burn,
That iits filthiness may be melted in it,
That its scum may be consumed.
12 She has grown weary with lies,
And her great scum has not gone from
her.
Let her scum be in the fire!
13 In your jfilthiness is lewdness.
Because I have cleansed you, and you
were not cleansed,
You will know not be cleansed of your
filthiness anymore,
lTill I have caused My fury to rest upon
you.
14 mI, the LORD, have spoken it;
nIt shall come to pass, and I will do it;
I will not hold back,
oNor will I spare,
Nor will I relent;
According to your ways
And according to your deeds
They* will judge you,"
Says the Lord GOD.'"

The Prophet's Wife Dies

15Also the word of the LORD came to me, saying, 16"Son of man, behold, I take away from you the desire of your eyes with one stroke; yet you shall pneither mourn nor weep, nor shall your tears run down. 17Sigh in silence, qmake no mourning for the dead; rbind your turban on your head, and sput your sandals on your feet; tdo not cover your lips, and do not eat man's bread of sorrow."

18So I spoke to the people in the morning, and at evening my wife died; and the next morning I did as I was commanded.

19And the people said to me, u"Will you not tell us what these things signify to us, that you behave so?"

20Then I answered them, "The word of the LORD came to me, saying, 21'Speak to the house of Israel, "Thus says the Lord GOD: 'Behold, vI will profane My sanctuary, your arrogant boast, the desire of your eyes, the delight of your soul; wand your sons and daughters whom you left behind shall fall by the sword. 22And you shall do as I have done; xyou shall not cover your lips nor eat man's bread of sorrow. 23Your turbans shall be on your heads and your sandals on your feet; yyou shall neither mourn nor weep, but zyou shall pine away in your iniquities and mourn with one another. 24Thus aEzekiel is a sign to you; according to all that he has done you shall do; band when this comes, cyou shall know that I am the Lord GOD.'"

25'And you, son of man—will it not be in the day when I take from them dtheir stronghold, their joy and their glory, the desire of their eyes, and that on which they set their minds, their sons and their daughters: 26that on that day eone who escapes will come to you to let you hear it with your ears? 27fOn that day your mouth will be opened to him who has escaped; you shall speak and no longer be mute. Thus you will be a sign to them, and they shall know that I am the LORD.'"

* 24:14 Septuagint, Syriac, Targum, and Vulgate read I.

---

people (ch. 34). **bones.** Bones were sometimes used as fuel for fire.
24:6 no lot has fallen. God does not play favorites; His judgment would fall equally on all inhabitants of the city, for they all had sinned.
24:16 you shall neither mourn nor weep. This command of God may be one of the hardest ever given to one of His servants. The picture of Ezekiel's wife dying and Ezekiel not being allowed to grieve illustrated God's pain over the death of His wife—Jerusalem—and His inability to mourn because the nation deserved the punishment. Ezekiel was called by God to be a sign to the exiles by demonstrating what they should do in response to the "death" of their desire and delight—their nation and its capital city. What Ezekiel was commanded to accept and do illustrated the degree of personal sacrifice and separation from ordinary life that the prophetic ministry often required. A long

period of mourning was normal in the ancient Middle East.
24:21 the delight of your soul. The entire phrase means something like the "object of your affections." The Judeans had the wrong kind of pride about the temple. Instead of the temple being a place of worship and the house of God, the Judeans took pride in the building as a sign of their importance.
24:22–24 sign. When Jerusalem fell, God would

24:6 d Ezek. 22:2, 3, 27 e Nah. 3:10 **24:7** f Lev. 17:13
24:8 g [Matt. 7:2] **24:9** h Hab. 2:12 **24:11** i Ezek.
22:15 **24:13** j Ezek. 23:36–48 k Jer. 6:28–30 l Ezek.
5:13; 8:18; 16:42 **24:14** m [1 Sam. 15:29] n Is. 55:11
o Ezek. 5:11 **24:16** p Jer. 16:5 **24:17** q Jer. 16:5 r Lev.
10:6; 21:10 s 2 Sam. 15:30 t Mic. 3:7 **24:19** u Ezek. 12:9;
37:18 **24:21** v Jer. 7:14 w Ezek. 23:25, 47 **24:22** x Jer.
16:6, 7 **24:23** y Job 27:15 z Lev. 26:39 **24:24** a Is.
20:3 b Jer. 17:15 c Ezek. 6:7; 25:5 **24:25** d Ezek. 24:21
24:26 e Ezek. 33:21 **24:27** f Ezek. 3:26; 33:22

Proclamation Against Ammon

25 The word of the LORD came to me, saying, [2]"Son of man, [a]set your face [b]against the Ammonites, and prophesy against them. [3]Say to the Ammonites, 'Hear the word of the Lord GOD! Thus says the Lord GOD: [c]"Because you said, 'Aha!' against My sanctuary when it was profaned, and against the land of Israel when it was desolate, and against the house of Judah when they went into captivity, [4]indeed, therefore, I will deliver you as a possession to the men of the East, and they shall set their encampments among you and make their dwellings among you; they shall eat your fruit, and they shall drink your milk. [5]And I will make [d]Rabbah [e]a stable for camels and Ammon a resting place for flocks. [f]Then you shall know that I am the LORD."

[6]'For thus says the Lord GOD: "Because you [g]clapped your hands, stamped your feet, and [h]rejoiced in heart with all your disdain for the land of Israel, [7]indeed, therefore, I will [i]stretch out My hand against you, and give you as plunder to the nations; I will cut you off from the peoples, and I will cause you to perish from the countries; I will destroy you, and you shall know that I am the LORD."

Proclamation Against Moab

[8]'Thus says the Lord GOD: "Because [j]Moab and [k]Seir say, 'Look! The house of Judah is like all the nations,' [9]therefore, behold, I will clear the territory of Moab of cities, of the cities on its frontier, the glory of the country, Beth Jeshimoth, Baal Meon, and [l]Kirjathaim. [10m]To the men of the East I will give it as a possession, together with the Ammonites, that the Ammonites [n]may not be remembered among the nations. [11]And I will execute judgments upon Moab, and they shall know that I am the LORD."

Proclamation Against Edom

[12]'Thus says the Lord GOD: [o]"Because of what Edom did against the house of Judah by taking vengeance, and has greatly offended by avenging itself on them," [13]therefore thus says the Lord GOD: "I will also stretch out My hand against Edom, cut off man and beast from it, and make it desolate from Teman; Dedan shall fall by the sword. [14p]I will lay My vengeance on Edom by the hand of My people Israel, that they may do in Edom according to My anger and according to My fury; and they shall know My vengeance," says the Lord GOD.

Proclamation Against Philistia

[15]'Thus says the Lord GOD: [q]"Because [r]the Philistines dealt vengefully and took vengeance with a spiteful heart, to destroy because of the old hatred," [16]therefore thus says the Lord GOD: [s]"I will stretch out My hand against the Philistines, and I will cut off the [t]Cherethites [u]and destroy the remnant of the seacoast. [17]I will [v]execute great vengeance on them with furious rebukes; [w]and they shall know that I am the LORD, when I lay My vengeance upon them." '"

Proclamation Against Tyre

26 And it came to pass in the eleventh year, on the first day of the month, that the word of the LORD came to me, saying, [2]"Son of man, [a]because Tyre has said against Jerusalem, [b]'Aha! She is broken who was the gateway of the peoples; now she is turned over to me; I shall be filled; she is laid waste.'

[3]"Therefore thus says the Lord GOD: 'Behold, I am against you, O Tyre, and will cause many nations to come up against you, as the sea causes its waves to come up. [4]And they shall destroy the walls of Tyre and break down her towers; I will also scrape her dust from her, and [c]make her like the top of a rock. [5]It shall be a place for spreading nets [d]in the midst of the sea, for I have spoken,' says the Lord GOD; 'it shall become plunder for the nations. [6]Also her daughter villages which are in the fields shall be slain by the sword. [e]Then they shall know that I am the LORD.'

---

prove Himself as trustworthy and righteous, and Ezekiel as His true prophet (v. 27). **you shall know that I am the Lord GOD.** The trials that the Israelites were going through would prompt them to depend on the Lord and know that He is holy.

25:2 set your face against the Ammonites. This country corresponds roughly to the present-day country of Jordan with its capital Amman.

25:4 men of the East. This is another title for the Babylonians (21:31). Ancient historical records mention Ammon's subjugation by Nebuchadnezzar five years after the fall of Jerusalem. Arab invaders came to dominate the territory, and Persian control began about 530 B.C.

25:8–12 Moab and Seir. Moab was south of Ammon and east of the Dead Sea. Seir (Edom) was located south of Moab. They were the descendants of Esau.

25:15 Philistines. The Philistines were along the Mediterranean coast in southwest Palestine.

25:16 Cherethites. This term was used here as a substitute term for some or all of the Philistines who had migrated from Crete. Their remote ancestors were Aegeans.

26:2 Tyre. Tyre was a major seaport and the leading

25:2 [a] Ezek. 35:2 [b] Jer. 49:1 **25:3** [c] Ezek. 26:2 **25:5** [d] Ezek. 21:20 [e] Is. 17:2 [f] Ezek. 24:24 **25:6** [g] Job 27:23 [h] Ezek. 36:5 **25:7** [i] Ezek. 35:3 **25:8** [j] Amos 2:1, 2 [k] Ezek. 35:2, 5 **25:9** [l] Jer. 48:23 **25:10** [m] Ezek. 25:4 [n] Ezek. 21:32 **25:12** [o] Obad. 10–14 **25:14** [p] Is. 11:14 **25:15** [q] Jer. 25:20 [r] 2 Chr. 28:18 **25:16** [s] Zeph. 2:4 [t] 1 Sam. 30:14 [u] Jer. 47:4 **25:17** [v] Ezek. 5:15 [w] Ps. 9:16 **26:2** [a] Jer. 25:22 [b] Ezek. 25:3 **26:4** [c] Ezek. 26:14 **26:5** [d] Ezek. 27:32 **26:6** [e] Ezek. 25:5

7"For thus says the Lord God: 'Behold, I will bring against Tyre from the north *f*Nebuchadnezzar* king of Babylon, *g*king of kings, with horses, with chariots, and with horsemen, and an army with many people. 8He will slay with the sword your daughter *villages* in the fields; he will *h*heap up a siege mound against you, build a wall against you, and raise a defense against you. 9He will direct his battering rams against your walls, and with his axes he will break down your towers. 10Because of the abundance of his horses, their dust will cover you; your walls will shake at the noise of the horsemen, the wagons, and the chariots, when he enters your gates, as men enter a city that has been breached. 11With the hooves of his *i*horses he will trample all your streets; he will slay your people by the sword, and your strong pillars will fall to the ground. 12They will plunder your riches and pillage your merchandise; they will break down your walls and destroy your pleasant houses; they will lay your stones, your timber, and your soil in the *j*midst of the water. 13*k*I will put an end to the sound of *l*your songs, and the sound of your harps shall be heard no more. 14*m*I will make you like the top of a rock; you shall be *a place for* spreading nets, and you shall never be rebuilt, for I the Lord have spoken,' says the Lord God.

15"Thus says the Lord God to Tyre: 'Will the coastlands not *n*shake at the sound of your fall, when the wounded cry, when slaughter is made in the midst of you? 16Then all the *o*princes of the sea will *p*come down from their thrones, lay aside their robes, and take off their embroidered garments; they will clothe themselves with trembling; *q*they will sit on the ground, *r*tremble *every* moment, and *s*be astonished at you. 17And they will take up a *t*lamentation for you, and say to you:

"How you have perished,
O one inhabited by seafaring men,
O renowned city,
Who was *u*strong at sea,
She and her inhabitants,
Who caused their terror *to be* on all
    her inhabitants!
18   Now *v*the coastlands tremble on the
        day of your fall;
    Yes, the coastlands by the sea are
        troubled at your departure."'

19"For thus says the Lord God: 'When I make you a desolate city, like cities that are not inhabited, when I bring the deep upon you, and great waters cover you, 20then I will bring you down *w*with those who descend into the Pit, to the people of old, and I will make you dwell in the lowest part of the earth, in places desolate from antiquity, with those who go down to the Pit, so that you may never be inhabited; and I shall establish glory *x*in the land of the living. 21*y*I will make you a terror, and you *shall be* no more; *z*though you are sought for, you will never be found again,' says the Lord God."

Lamentation for Tyre

27 The word of the Lord came again to me, saying, 2"Now, son of man, *a*take up a lamentation for Tyre, 3and say to Tyre, *b*'You who are situated at the entrance of the sea, *c*merchant of the peoples on many coastlands, thus says the Lord God:

"O Tyre, you have said,
d'I *am* perfect in beauty.'
4   Your borders *are* in the midst of the
        seas.
    Your builders have perfected your
        beauty.
5   They made all *your* planks of fir trees
        from *e*Senir;
    They took a cedar from Lebanon to
        make you a mast.
6   Of *f*oaks from Bashan they made your
        oars;
    The company of Ashurites have inlaid
        your planks
    With ivory from *g*the coasts of
        Cyprus.*

---

* 26:7 Hebrew *Nebuchadrezzar*, and so elsewhere in this book   * 27:6 Hebrew *Kittim*, western lands, especially Cyprus

---

city in Phoenicia (present-day Lebanon). **has said.** The past tense could refer to an event that had not yet taken place, using a Hebrew idiom which describes a future event so certain that it can be expressed as having already been accomplished (Is. 9:6; 52:13—53:12).
26:7–14 I will make you like the top of a rock. This prophecy of Tyre's fate had two steps. First the Babylonian army under Nebuchadnezzar laid siege to it, and Persia defeated it in about 525 B.C. Then in 322 B.C. Alexander the Great defeated it again when his army built a causeway a half mile long between the shore and the city on its island. He tore down defensive walls to build the causeway.
27:1–25 take up a lamentation for Tyre. Prosperity often leads to pride, which results in the abandonment of God (Deut. 18:11–14). Jerusalem and Tyre

both claimed to be unique, the former because of her exclusive claim to true religion and the latter because of the exclusive emphasis on material gain. Yet the wealth of Tyre vanished quickly.
27:6 Bashan. This was the broad and fertile plateau east of the Sea of Galilee and the upper Jordan.

26:7 *f* Jer. 27:3–6 *g* Dan. 2:37, 47   **26:8** *h* Ezek. 21:22   **26:11** *i* Hab. 1:8   **26:12** *j* Ezek. 27:27, 32
26:13 *k* Is. 14:11; 24:8 *l* Rev. 18:22   **26:14** *m* Ezek. 26:4, 5
26:15 *n* Jer. 49:21   **26:16** *o* Is. 23:8 *p* Jon. 3:6 *q* Job 2:13 *r* Ezek. 32:10 *s* Ezek. 27:35   **26:17** *t* Ezek. 27:2–36
u Is. 23:4   **26:18** *v* Ezek. 26:15   **26:20** *w* Ezek. 32:18
x Ezek. 32:23   **26:21** *y* Ezek. 27:36; 28:19 *z* Ps. 37:10, 36   **27:2** *a* Ezek. 26:17   **27:3** *b* Ezek. 26:17; 28:2 *c* Is. 23:3   *d* Ezek. 28:12   **27:5** *e* Deut. 3:9   **27:6** *f* Is. 2:12, 13
g Jer. 2:10

7 Fine embroidered linen from Egypt was
   what you spread for your sail;
   Blue and purple from the coasts of
   Elishah was what covered you.

8 "Inhabitants of Sidon and Arvad were
   your oarsmen;
   Your wise men, O Tyre, were in you;
   They became your pilots.

9 Elders of ʰGebal and its wise men
   Were in you to caulk your seams;
   All the ships of the sea
   And their oarsmen were in you
   To market your merchandise.

10 "Those from Persia, Lydia,* and Libya*
   Were in your army as men of war;
   They hung shield and helmet in you;
   They gave splendor to you.

11 Men of Arvad with your army *were* on
   your walls *all* around,
   And the men of Gammad were in your
   towers;
   They hung their shields on your walls
   all around;
   They made ʲyour beauty perfect.

12ʲ"Tarshish *was* your merchant because
of your many luxury goods. They gave you
silver, iron, tin, and lead for your goods.
13ᵏJavan, Tubal, and Meshech *were* your
traders. They bartered ˡhuman lives and
vessels of bronze for your merchandise.
14Those from the house of ᵐTogarmah
traded for your wares with horses, steeds,
and mules. 15The men of ⁿDedan *were* your
traders; many isles *were* the market of your
hand. They brought you ivory tusks and
ebony as payment. 16Syria *was* your merchant because of the abundance of goods
you made. They gave you for your wares
emeralds, purple, embroidery, fine linen,
corals, and rubies. 17Judah and the land
of Israel *were* your traders. They traded
for your merchandise wheat of ᵒMinnith,
millet, honey, oil, and ᵖbalm. 18Damascus
was your merchant because of the abundance of goods you made, because of your
many luxury items, with the wine of Hel-
bon and with white wool. 19Dan and Javan
paid for your wares, traversing back and

forth. Wrought iron, cassia, and cane were
among your merchandise. 20ᑫDedan *was*
your merchant in saddlecloths for riding.
21Arabia and all the princes of ʳKedar *were*
your regular merchants. They traded with
you in lambs, rams, and goats. 22The merchants of ˢSheba and Raamah *were* your
merchants. They traded for your wares
the choicest spices, all kinds of precious
stones, and gold. 23ᵗHaran, Canneh, Eden,
the merchants of ᵘSheba, Assyria, *and*
Chilmad *were* your merchants. 24These
were your merchants in choice items—in
purple clothes, in embroidered garments,
in chests of multicolored apparel, in sturdy
woven cords, which were in your marketplace.

25 "The ᵛships of Tarshish were carriers of
   your merchandise.
   You were filled and very glorious ʷin
   the midst of the seas.

26 Your oarsmen brought you into many
   waters,
   But ˣthe east wind broke you in the
   midst of the seas.

27 "Your ʸriches, wares, and merchandise,
   Your mariners and pilots,
   Your caulkers and merchandisers,
   All your men of war who *are* in you,
   And the entire company which *is* in
   your midst,
   Will fall into the midst of the seas on
   the day of your ruin.

28 The ᶻcommon-land will shake at the
   sound of the cry of your pilots.

29 "All ᵃwho handle the oar,
   The mariners,
   All the pilots of the sea
   Will come down from their ships *and*
   stand on the shore.

30 They will make their voice heard
   because of you;
   They will cry bitterly and ᵇcast dust on
   their heads;
   They ᶜwill roll about in ashes;

---

* 27:10 Hebrew *Lud* • Hebrew *Put*

27:8 **Sidon.** Sidon was a Phoenician seaport about 30 miles north of Tyre. The two cities were rivals but Tyre tended to dominate.

27:10–11 **Lydia, and Libya.** Or *Lud*, in western Asia Minor, and Put, in northern Africa.

27:13 **Javan, Tubal, and Meshech.** Javan is Greece. Tubal and Meshech are thought to have been in east-ern Asia Minor or modern Turkey.

27:14 **Togarmah.** This phrase may refer to the people of Armenia in eastern Asia Minor (38:6).

27:15 **Dedan.** This may have been "Redan" or Rhodes, which was a major trading center in the southern Aegean Sea.

27:17 **balm.** Balm was an aromatic resin or other gummy substance that may have had medicinal value (Jer. 8:22).

27:19 **cassia.** Cassia was either a type of cinnamon

tree or a plant from which perfume and incense were made. **cane.** This refers to an oil-producing reed found in swamps.

27:21 **Kedar.** Kedar was a nomadic tribe in Arabia.

27:22 **Sheba and Raamah.** These places were located near Arabia (Gen. 10:6–7).

27:23 **Canneh, Eden . . . Chilmad.** These three places were probably in Mesopotamia, most likely south of Haran.

27:9 ʰ 1 Kin. 5:18   27:11 ⁱ Ezek. 27:3   27:12 ʲ Gen.
10:4   27:13 ᵏ Gen. 10:2 ˡ Rev. 18:13   27:14 ᵐ Gen.
10:3   27:15 ⁿ Gen. 10:7   27:17 ᵒ Judg. 11:33 ᵖ Jer.
8:22   27:21 ᑫ Gen. 25:3   27:21 ʳ Is. 60:7   27:22 ˢ Gen.
10:7   27:23 ᵗ 2 Kin. 19:12 ᵘ Gen. 25:3   27:25 ᵛ Is. 2:16
ʷ Ezek. 27:4   27:26 ˣ Ps. 48:7   27:27 ʸ [Prov. 11:4]
27:28 ᶻ Ezek. 26:15   27:29 ᵃ Rev. 18:17   27:30 ᵇ Rev.
18:19 ᶜ Jer. 6:26

31 They will ^dshave themselves
   completely bald because of you,
   Gird themselves with sackcloth,
   And weep for you
   With bitterness of heart *and* bitter
   wailing.
32 In their wailing for you
   They will ^etake up a lamentation,
   And lament for you:
   ^f'What *city is* like Tyre,
   Destroyed in the midst of the sea?
33 'When^g your wares went out by sea,
   You satisfied many people;
   You enriched the kings of the earth
   With your many luxury goods and
   your merchandise.
34 But ^hyou are broken by the seas in the
   depths of the waters;
   ⁱYour merchandise and the entire
   company will fall in your midst.
35 ^jAll the inhabitants of the isles will be
   astonished at you;
   Their kings will be greatly afraid,
   And *their* countenance will be troubled.
36 The merchants among the peoples
   ^kwill hiss at you;
   ^lYou will become a horror, and *be* no
   ^mmore forever.' ' ' "

Proclamation Against the King of Tyre

28 The word of the LORD came to me
again, saying, ²"Son of man, say to
the prince of Tyre, 'Thus says the Lord
GOD:

"Because your heart *is* ^alifted up,
   And ^byou say, 'I *am* a god,
   I sit *in* the seat of gods,
   ^cIn the midst of the seas,'
   ^dYet you *are* a man, and not a god,
   Though you set your heart as the heart
   of a god
3 (Behold, ^eyou *are* wiser than Daniel!
   There is no secret that can be hidden
   from you!
4 With your wisdom and your
   understanding
   You have gained ^friches for yourself,
   And gathered gold and silver into your
   treasuries;
5 ^gBy your great wisdom in trade you
   have increased your riches,

And your heart is lifted up because of
   your riches),"

6 'Therefore thus says the Lord GOD:

"Because you have set your heart as the
   heart of a god,
7 Behold, therefore, I will bring
   ^hstrangers against you,
   ⁱThe most terrible of the nations;
   And they shall draw their swords
   against the beauty of your
   wisdom,
   And defile your splendor.
8 They shall throw you down into the ^jPit,
   And you shall die the death of the slain
   In the midst of the seas.
9 "Will you still ^ksay before him who
   slays you,
   'I *am* a god'?
   But you *shall be* a man, and not a god,
   In the hand of him who slays you.
10 You shall die the death of ^lthe
   uncircumcised
   By the hand of aliens;
   For I have spoken," says the Lord GOD.' "

Lamentation for the King of Tyre

¹¹Moreover the word of the LORD came
to me, saying, ¹²"Son of man, ^mtake up a
lamentation for the king of Tyre, and say
to him, 'Thus says the Lord GOD:

ⁿ"You *were* the seal of perfection,
   Full of wisdom and perfect in beauty.
13 You were in ^oEden, the garden of God;
   Every precious stone *was* your
   covering:
   The sardius, topaz, and diamond,
   Beryl, onyx, and jasper,
   Sapphire, turquoise, and emerald with
   gold.
   The workmanship of ^pyour timbrels
   and pipes
   Was prepared for you on the day you
   were created.
14 "You *were* the anointed ^qcherub who
   covers;
   I established you;
   You were on ^rthe holy mountain of
   God;
   You walked back and forth in the
   midst of fiery stones.

28:2 *Because your heart is lifted up.* Ezekiel
rebuked the king of Tyre for imagining that by his
wisdom he had acquired his riches of silver and gold.
He had filled the city with violence because of the
abundance and unrighteousness of his trade. God
would therefore bring a ruthless nation against him.
28:10 *the death of the uncircumcised.* This term
denotes a disgraceful death (31:18).
28:12 *king of Tyre.* The lamentation is for the king of
Tyre because he is exhibiting the character and attitudes of Satan. *seal of perfection.* This is more literally
"the one sealing a plan." In effect, the king affixed the
official seal of his signet ring to the plans that made Tyre
one of the leading centers of commerce in that day.

28:14 *cherub.* Satan was a created being (v. 13).
He does not have the characteristics of God. He
belonged to the order of angels called cherubim. *the*

27:31 ^dEzek. 29:18 **27:32** ^eEzek. 26:17 ^fRev. 18:18
27:33 ^gRev. 18:19 **27:34** ^hEzek. 26:19 ⁱEzek. 27:27
27:35 ^jEzek. 26:15, 16 **27:36** ^kJer. 18:16 ^lEzek. 26:2
^mPs. 37:10, 36 **28:2** ^aJer. 49:16 ^bEzek. 28:9 ^cEzek.
27:3, 4 ^dIs. 31:3 **28:3** ^eDan. 1:20; 2:20–23, 28; 5:11,
12 **28:4** ^fZech. 9:1–3 **28:5** ^gPs. 62:10 **28:7** ^hEzek.
26:7 ⁱEzek. 7:24; 21:31; 30:11 **28:8** ^jIs. 14:15
28:9 ^kEzek. 28:2 **28:10** ^lEzek. 31:18; 32:19, 21, 25, 27
28:12 ^mEzek. 27:2 ⁿEzek. 27:3; 28:3 **28:13** ^oEzek. 31:8,
9; 36:35 ^pEzek. 26:13 **28:14** ^qEx. 25:20 ^rEzek. 20:40

¹⁵ You *were* perfect in your ways from
　　the day you were created,
　　Till ˢiniquity was found in you.
¹⁶ "By the abundance of your trading
　　You became filled with violence within,
　　And you sinned;
　　Therefore I cast you as a profane thing
　　Out of the mountain of God;
　　And I destroyed you, ᵗO covering
　　　cherub,
　　From the midst of the fiery stones.
¹⁷ "Your ᵘheart was lifted up because of
　　your beauty;
　　You corrupted your wisdom for the
　　sake of your splendor;
　　I cast you to the ground,
　　I laid you before kings,
　　That they might gaze at you.
¹⁸ "You defiled your sanctuaries
　　By the multitude of your iniquities,
　　By the iniquity of your trading;
　　Therefore I brought fire from your
　　　midst;
　　It devoured you,
　　And I turned you to ashes upon the
　　　earth
　　In the sight of all who saw you.
¹⁹ All who knew you among the peoples
　　are astonished at you;
　　ᵛYou have become a horror,
　　And *shall be* no ᵂmore forever."'"

Proclamation Against Sidon

²⁰Then the word of the LORD came to
me, saying, ²¹"Son of man, ˣset your face
ʸtoward Sidon, and prophesy against her,
²²and say, 'Thus says the Lord GOD:

ᶻ"Behold, I *am* against you, O Sidon;
　　I will be glorified in your midst;
　　And ᵃthey shall know that I *am* the
　　　LORD,
　　When I execute judgments in her and
　　　am ᵇhallowed in her.
²³ ᶜFor I will send pestilence upon her,
　　And blood in her streets;
　　The wounded shall be judged in her
　　　midst

By the sword against her on every side;
　　Then they shall know that I *am* the
　　　LORD.

²⁴"And there shall no longer be a pricking brier or ᵈa painful thorn for the house
of Israel from among all *who are* around
them, who ᵉdespise them. Then they shall
know that I *am* the Lord GOD."

Israel's Future Blessing

²⁵'Thus says the Lord GOD: "When I
have ᶠgathered the house of Israel from the
peoples among whom they are scattered,
and am ᵍhallowed in them in the sight of
the Gentiles, then they will dwell in their
own land which I gave to My servant Jacob.
²⁶And they will ʰdwell safely there, ⁱbuild
houses, and ʲplant vineyards; yes, they will
dwell securely, when I execute judgments
on all those around them who despise
them. Then they shall know that I *am* the
LORD their God."'"

Proclamation Against Egypt

29 In the tenth year, in the tenth *month*,
on the twelfth *day* of the month, the
word of the LORD came to me, saying,
²"Son of man, ᵃset your face against Pharaoh king of Egypt, and prophesy against
him, and ᵇagainst all Egypt. ³Speak, and
say, 'Thus says the Lord GOD:

ᶜ"Behold, I *am* against you,
　　O Pharaoh king of Egypt,
　　O great ᵈmonster who lies in the midst
　　　of his rivers,
　　ᵉWho has said, 'My River* *is* my
　　　own;
　　I have made *it* for myself.'
⁴ But ᶠI will put hooks in your jaws,
　　And cause the fish of your rivers to
　　　stick to your scales;
　　I will bring you up out of the midst of
　　　your rivers,
　　And all the fish in your rivers will
　　　stick to your scales.

---

* **29:3** That is, the Nile

---

holy mountain of God. The focus here seems to be
on the king of Tyre's attempt to enter into the council
of the gods. So instead of the verse referring to the
king's presence in Jerusalem, it could refer more logically to a Phoenician ritual, the celebration of their
patron god Melqart's fiery resurrection. This king
wanted to imitate Melqart.
28:15 perfect. Satan was not created evil. **iniquity.**
The Bible does not say where this iniquity came from,
but his sin was pride (1 Tim. 3:6).
28:16–19 the abundance of your trading. The
expression is most easily and appropriately applied
to the human king who was the driving force behind
the development of Tyre's commercial empire.
28:17 because of your beauty. This was part of the
sin of pride, which made Satan want to be like the
Most High (Is. 14:13–14). **cast you to the ground.**
Jesus said that He saw Satan fall (Luke 10:18).
28:24 a pricking brier or a painful thorn. These

words refer to the nations around Israel who had
been enemies and evil influences. When the judgments were executed fully, these nations would no
longer be able to harass and oppress Israel.
29:3 great monster. The Pharaoh is pictured here
as a crocodile. Pharaoh's arrogant pride is described
by his words about the Nile River, "I have made it for
myself."
29:4–5 I will put hooks in your jaws. Whereas verse
3 explains why Pharaoh would be punished, these

28:15 ˢ [Is. 14:12]　**28:16** ᵗ Ezek. 28:14　**28:17** ᵘ Ezek.
28:2, 5　**28:19** ᵛ Ezek. 26:21　ᵂ Ezek. 27:36
28:21 ˣ Ezek. 6:2; 25:2; 29:2　ʸ Is. 23:2, 4, 12　**28:22** ᶻ Ex.
14:4, 17　ᵃ Ps. 9:16　ᵇ Ezek. 28:25　**28:23** ᶜ Ezek. 38:22
28:24 ᵈ Josh. 23:13　ᵉ Ezek. 16:57; 25:6, 7　**28:25** ᶠ Is.
11:12, 13　ᵍ Ezek. 28:22　**28:26** ʰ Jer. 23:6　ⁱ Amos 9:13,
14　ʲ Jer. 31:5　**29:2** ᵃ Ezek. 28:21　ᵇ Is. 19:1　**29:3** ᶜ Jer.
44:30　ᵈ Ps. 74:13, 14　ᵉ Ezek. 28:2　**29:4** ᶠ Ezek. 38:4

5 I will leave you in the wilderness,
You and all the fish of your rivers;
You shall fall on the open [g]field;
[h]You shall not be picked up or
gathered.*
[i]I have given you as food
To the beasts of the field
And to the birds of the heavens.

6 "Then all the inhabitants of Egypt
Shall know that I *am* the LORD,
Because they have been a [j]staff of reed
to the house of Israel.
7 [k]When they took hold of you with the
hand,
You broke and tore all their shoulders;*
When they leaned on you,
You broke and made all their backs
quiver."

8'Therefore thus says the Lord GOD:
"Surely I will bring [l]a sword upon you and
cut off from you man and beast. 9And the
land of Egypt shall become [m]desolate and
waste; then they will know that I *am* the
LORD, because he said, 'The River *is* mine,
and I have made *it*.' 10Indeed, therefore, I
am against you and against your rivers,
[n]and I will make the land of Egypt utterly
waste and desolate, [o]from Migdol* *to* Syene, as far as the border of Ethiopia. 11[p]Nei-
ther foot of man shall pass through it nor
foot of beast pass through it, and it shall be
uninhabited forty years. 12[q]I will make the
land of Egypt desolate in the midst of the
countries *that are* desolate; and among
the cities *that are* laid waste, her cities shall
be desolate forty years; and I will [r]scatter
the Egyptians among the nations and disperse them throughout the countries."
13'Yet, thus says the Lord GOD: "At the
[s]end of forty years I will gather the Egyptians from the peoples among whom they
were scattered. 14I will bring back the captives of Egypt and cause them to return to
the land of Pathros, to the land of their origin, and there they shall be a [t]lowly kingdom. 15It shall be the lowliest of kingdoms;
it shall never again exalt itself above the
nations, for I will diminish them so that
they will not rule over the nations anymore.
16No longer shall it be [u]the confidence of
the house of Israel, but will remind them of
their iniquity when they turned to follow
them. Then they shall know that I *am* the
Lord GOD." ' "

Babylonia Will Plunder Egypt

17And it came to pass in the twenty-
seventh year, in the first *month*, on the
first *day* of the month, *that* the word of the
LORD came to me, saying, 18"Son of man,
[v]Nebuchadnezzar king of Babylon caused
his army to labor strenuously against Tyre;
every head *was* made [w]bald, and every
shoulder rubbed raw; yet neither he nor his
army received wages from Tyre, for the labor which they expended on it. 19Therefore
thus says the Lord GOD: 'Surely I will give
the land of Egypt to [x]Nebuchadnezzar king
of Babylon; he shall take away her wealth,
carry off her spoil, and remove her pillage;
and that will be the wages for his army. 20I
have given him the land of Egypt *for* his
labor, because they [y]worked for Me,' says
the Lord GOD.
21'In that day [z]I will cause the horn of the
house of Israel to spring forth, and I will
[a]open your mouth to speak in their midst.
Then they shall know that I *am* the LORD.' "

Egypt and Her Allies Will Fall

30 The word of the LORD came to me
again, saying, 2"Son of man, prophesy and say, 'Thus says the Lord GOD:

[a]"Wail, 'Woe to the day!'
3 For [b]the day *is* near,
Even the day of the LORD *is* near;
It will be a day of clouds, the time of
the Gentiles.
4 The sword shall come upon Egypt,
And great anguish shall be in
Ethiopia,
When the slain fall in Egypt,
And they [c]take away her wealth,
And [d]her foundations are broken down.

* 29:5 Following Masoretic Text, Septuagint, and Vulgate; some Hebrew manuscripts and Targum read *buried*. * 29:7 Following Masoretic Text and Vulgate; Septuagint and Syriac read *hand*. * 29:10 Or *tower*

verses explain how the punishment would be accomplished. The imagery pictures a crocodile being caught, carried out of the water onto land, and left as carrion.

29:8 ***sword.*** Here is another reference to the Babylonian army under Nebuchadnezzar, the predicted human instrument of God's coming wrath (21:1–7, 9–11,19–20).

29:10 ***Migdol to Syene, as far as the border of Ethiopia.*** This phrase refers to places most likely near the northern and southern boundaries of ancient Egypt, indicating the totality of the land (Judg. 20:1). The desolation would extend to the land south of Egypt—ancient Nubia, which is modern Sudan.

29:14–15 ***land of Pathros.*** This was southern Egypt. It would thereafter never again dominate other nations.

29:18 ***every head was made bald.*** The siege of Tyre was protracted, lasting about 13 years.

29:21 ***In that day.*** This refers to the day when Egypt would fall to Babylon, and a prophecy about the Messiah should not be read into this text.

29:5 [g] Ezek. 32:4–6 [h] Jer. 8:2; 16:4; 25:33 [i] Jer. 7:33; 34:20 **29:6** [j] Is. 36:6 **29:7** [k] Ezek. 17:17 **29:8** [l] Ezek. 14:17; 32:11–13 **29:9** [m] Ezek. 30:7, 8 **29:10** [n] Ezek. 30:12 [o] Ezek. 30:6 **29:11** [p] Ezek. 32:13 **29:12** [q] Ezek. 30:7, 26 [r] Ezek. 30:23, 26 **29:13** [s] Jer. 46:26 **29:14** [t] Ezek. 17:6, 14 **29:16** [u] Is. 30:2, 3; 36:4, 6 **29:18** [v] Jer. 25:9; 27:6 [w] Ezek. 27:31 **29:19** [x] Jer. 43:10–13 **29:20** [y] Jer. 25:9 **29:21** [z] Ps. 92:10; 132:17 [a] Ezek. 24:27 **30:2** [a] Is. 13:6; 15:2 **30:3** [b] Joel 2:1 **30:4** [c] Ezek. 29:19 [d] Jer. 50:15

5"Ethiopia, Libya,* Lydia,* *e*all the mingled people, Chub, and the men of the lands who are allied, shall fall with them by the sword."

6'Thus says the LORD:

"Those who uphold Egypt shall fall,
And the pride of her power shall come down.
*f*From Migdol *to* Syene
Those within her shall fall by the sword,"
Says the Lord GOD.

7 "They*g* shall be desolate in the midst of the desolate countries,
And her cities shall be in the midst of the cities *that are* laid waste.

8 Then they will know that I *am* the LORD,
When I have set a fire in Egypt
And all her *h*elpers are destroyed.

9 On that day *h*messengers shall go forth from Me in ships
To make the careless Ethiopians afraid,
And great anguish shall come upon them,
As on the day of Egypt;
For indeed it is coming!"

10'Thus says the Lord GOD:

i"I will also make a multitude of Egypt to cease
By the hand of Nebuchadnezzar king of Babylon.

11 He and his people with him, *j*the most terrible of the nations,
Shall be brought to destroy the land;
They shall draw their swords against Egypt,
And fill the land with the slain.

12 *k*I will make the rivers dry,
And *l*sell the land into the hand of the wicked;
I will make the land waste, and all that is in it,
By the hand of aliens.
I, the LORD, have spoken."

13'Thus says the Lord GOD:

"I will also *m*destroy the idols,
And cause the images to cease from Noph;*
*n*There shall no longer be princes from the land of Egypt;
*o*I will put fear in the land of Egypt.

14 I will make *p*Pathros desolate,
Set fire to *q*Zoan,
*r*And execute judgments in No.*

15 I will pour My fury on Sin,* the strength of Egypt;
*s*I will cut off the multitude of No,

16 And *t*set a fire in Egypt;
Sin shall have great pain,
No shall be split open,
And Noph *shall be in* distress daily.

17 The young men of Aven* and Pi Beseth shall fall by the sword,
And these *cities* shall go into captivity.

18 *u*At Tehaphnehes* the day shall also be darkened,*
When I break the yokes of Egypt there.
And her arrogant strength shall cease in her;
As for her, a cloud shall cover her,
And her daughters shall go into captivity.

19 Thus I will *v*execute judgments on Egypt,
Then they shall know that I *am* the LORD."'"

Proclamation Against Pharaoh

20And it came to pass in the eleventh year, in the first *month,* on the seventh *day* of the month, *that* the word of the LORD came to me, saying, 21"Son of man, I have *w*broken the arm of Pharaoh king of Egypt; and see, *x*it has not been bandaged for healing, nor a splint put on to bind it, to make it strong enough to hold a sword. 22Therefore thus says the Lord GOD: 'Surely I *am* *y*against Pharaoh king of Egypt, and will *z*break his arms, both the strong one and the one that was broken; and I will make the sword fall out of his hand. 23a I will scatter the Egyptians among the nations, and disperse them throughout the countries. 24I will strengthen the arms of the king of Babylon and put My sword in his hand; but I will break Pharaoh's arms, and he will groan before him with the groanings

---

* **30:5** Hebrew *Put* • Hebrew *Lud* * **30:13** That is, ancient Memphis * **30:14** That is, ancient Thebes * **30:15** That is, ancient Pelusium * **30:17** That is, ancient On (Heliopolis) * **30:18** Spelled *Tahpanhes* in Jeremiah 43:7 and elsewhere • Following many Hebrew manuscripts, Bomberg, Septuagint, Syriac, Targum, and Vulgate; Masoretic Text reads *refrained.*

30:5 Ethiopia. This is the Hebrew Cush, and refers to the area south of Egypt toward modern Ethiopia.
30:9 day of Egypt. This was the day that Egypt and her allies would be conquered. It was part of a larger period of God's judgment on the nations outside Israel by means of Babylon; in fact, Ezekiel describes the Babylonians as "messengers" sent from God Himself.
30:13–19 Noph. Ancient Noph, or Memphis, was a significant city in Egypt. It was capital of the Old Kingdom in the third century B.C.
30:21 I have broken the arm of Pharaoh. The prophecy refers to Pharaoh Hophra's unsuccessful attempt to relieve the siege of Jerusalem just a few months earlier (29:2,6–7). God used Nebuchadnezzar to defeat the Egyptian army.

30:5 *e* Jer. 25:20, 24 **30:6** *f* Ezek. 29:10 **30:7** *g* Ezek. 29:12 **30:9** *h* Is. 18:1, 2 **30:10** *i* Ezek. 29:19 **30:11** *j* Ezek. 28:7; 31:12 **30:12** *k* Is. 19:5, 6 *l* Is. 19:4 **30:13** *m* Is. 19:1 *n* Zech. 10:11 *o* Is. 19:16 **30:14** *p* Ezek. 29:14 *q* Ps. 78:12, 43 *r* Nah. 3:8–10 **30:15** *s* Jer. 46:25 **30:16** *t* Ezek. 30:8 **30:18** *u* Jer. 2:16 **30:19** *v* [Ps. 9:16] **30:21** *w* Jer. 48:25 *x* Jer. 46:11 **30:22** *y* Jer. 46:25 *z* Ps. 37:17 **30:23** *a* Ezek. 29:12; 30:17, 18, 26

of a mortally wounded *man*. [25]Thus I will strengthen the arms of the king of Babylon, but the arms of Pharaoh shall fall down; [b]they shall know that I *am* the LORD, when I put My sword into the hand of the king of Babylon and he stretches it out against the land of Egypt. [26c]I will scatter the Egyptians among the nations and disperse them throughout the countries. Then they shall know that I *am* the LORD.'"

Egypt Cut Down Like a Great Tree

31 Now it came to pass in the [a]eleventh year, in the third *month*, on the first *day* of the month, *that* the word of the LORD came to me, saying, [2]"Son of man, say to Pharaoh king of Egypt and to his multitude:

[b]'Whom are you like in your greatness?
[3] [c]Indeed Assyria *was* a cedar in Lebanon,
    With fine branches that shaded the forest,
    And of high stature;
    And its top was among the thick boughs.
[4] [d]The waters made it grow;
    Underground waters gave it height,
    With their rivers running around the place where it was planted,
    And sent out rivulets to all the trees of the field.
[5] 'Therefore [e]its height was exalted above all the trees of the field;
    Its boughs were multiplied,
    And its branches became long because of the abundance of water,
    As it sent them out.
[6] All the [f]birds of the heavens made their nests in its boughs;
    Under its branches all the beasts of the field brought forth their young;
    And in its shadow all great nations made their home.
[7] 'Thus it was beautiful in greatness and in the length of its branches,
    Because its roots reached to abundant waters.
[8] The cedars in the [g]garden of God could not hide it;
    The fir trees were not like its boughs,
    And the chestnut* trees were not like its branches;
    No tree in the garden of God was like it in beauty.

[9] I made it beautiful with a multitude of branches,
    So that all the trees of Eden envied it,
    That *were* in the garden of God.'

[10]"Therefore thus says the Lord GOD: 'Because you have increased in height, and it set its top among the thick boughs, and [h]its heart was lifted up in its height, [11]therefore I will deliver it into the hand of the [i]mighty one of the nations, and he shall surely deal with it; I have driven it out for its wickedness. [12]And aliens, [j]the most terrible of the nations, have cut it down and left it; its branches have fallen [k]on the mountains and in all the valleys; its boughs lie [l]broken by all the rivers of the land; and all the peoples of the earth have gone from under its shadow and left it.

[13] 'On [m]its ruin will remain all the birds of the heavens,
    And all the beasts of the field will come to its branches—

[14]'So that no trees by the waters may ever again exalt themselves for their height, nor set their tops among the thick boughs, that no tree which drinks water may ever be high enough to reach up to them.

    'For [n]they have all been delivered to death,
    [o]To the depths of the earth,
    Among the children of men who go down to the Pit.'

[15]"Thus says the Lord GOD: 'In the day when it [p]went down to hell, I caused mourning. I covered the deep because of it. I restrained its rivers, and the great waters were held back. I caused Lebanon to mourn for it, and all the trees of the field wilted because of it. [16]I made the nations [q]shake at the sound of its fall, when I [r]cast it down to hell together with those who descend into the Pit; and [s]all the trees of Eden, the choice and best of Lebanon, all that drink water, [t]were comforted in the depths of the earth. [17]They also went down to hell with it, with those slain by the sword; and *those who were* its *strong* arm [u]dwelt in its shadows among the nations.

[18v]'To which of the trees in Eden will you then be likened in glory and greatness? Yet you shall be brought down with the trees of Eden to the depths of the earth; [w]you shall

---

* **31:8** Hebrew *armon*

31:4 *The waters made it grow.* These waters were the Tigris and Euphrates rivers. They were important for agricultural fertility and fostered the development of great cities along trade routes.
31:10–14 *the hand of the mighty one of the nations.* The meaning is that Assyria had been cut down by Babylon. The picturesque conclusion to this second message of chapter 31 indicates that all the other nations that observe Assyria's ruin would share its destiny of death.
31:18 *Pharaoh and all his multitude.* If Assyria, the

30:25 [b] Ps. 9:16 **30:26** [c] Ezek. 29:12 **31:1** [a] Ezek. 30:20; 32:1 **31:2** [b] Ezek. 31:18 **31:3** [c] Dan. 4:10, 20–23 **31:4** [d] Jer. 51:36 **31:5** [e] Dan. 4:11 **31:6** [f] Dan. 4:12, 21 **31:8** [g] Gen. 2:8, 9; 13:10 **31:10** [h] Dan. 5:20 **31:11** [i] Ezek. 30:10 **31:12** [j] Ezek. 28:7; 30:11; 32:12 [k] Ezek. 32:5; 35:8 [l] Ezek. 30:24, 25 **31:13** [m] Is. 18:6 **31:14** [n] Ps. 82:7 [o] Ezek. 32:18 **31:15** [p] Ezek. 32:22, 23 **31:16** [q] Ezek. 26:15 [r] Is. 14:15 [s] Is. 14:8 [t] Ezek. 32:31 **31:17** [u] Lam. 4:20 **31:18** [v] Ezek. 32:19 [w] Ezek. 28:10; 32:19, 21

lie in the midst of the uncircumcised, with *those* slain by the sword. This *is* Pharaoh and all his multitude,' says the Lord GOD."

Lamentation for Pharaoh and Egypt

32 And it came to pass in the twelfth year, in the [a]twelfth *month*, on the first *day* of the month, *that* the word of the LORD came to me, saying, 2"Son of man, [b]take up a lamentation for Pharaoh king of Egypt, and say to him:

[c]'You are like a young lion among the nations,
And [d]you *are* like a monster in the seas,
[e]Bursting forth in your rivers,
Troubling the waters with your feet,
And [f]fouling their rivers.

3'Thus says the Lord GOD:

"I will therefore [g]spread My net over you with a company of many people,
And they will draw you up in My net.
4   Then [h]I will leave you on the land;
I will cast you out on the open fields,
[i]And cause to settle on you all the birds of the heavens.
And with you I will fill the beasts of the whole earth.
5   I will lay your flesh [j]on the mountains,
And fill the valleys with your carcass.
6   "I will also water the land with the flow of your blood,
Even to the mountains;
And the riverbeds will be full of you.
7   When *I* put out your light,
[k]I will cover the heavens, and make its stars dark;
I will cover the sun with a cloud,
And the moon shall not give her light.
8   All the bright lights of the heavens I will make dark over you,
And bring darkness upon your land,"
Says the Lord GOD.

9'I will also trouble the hearts of many peoples, when I bring your destruction among the nations, into the countries which you have not known. 10Yes, I will make many peoples astonished at you, and their kings shall be horribly afraid of you when I brandish My sword before them; and [l]they shall tremble *every* moment, every man for his own life, in the day of your fall.

11[m]'For thus says the Lord GOD: "The sword of the king of Babylon shall come upon you. 12By the swords of the mighty

warriors, all of them [n]the most terrible of the nations, I will cause your multitude to fall.

[o]"They shall plunder the pomp of Egypt,
And all its multitude shall be destroyed.
13   Also I will destroy all its animals
From beside its great waters;
[p]The foot of man shall muddy them no more,
Nor shall the hooves of animals muddy them.
14   Then I will make their waters clear,
And make their rivers run like oil,"
Says the Lord GOD.

15   "When I make the land of Egypt desolate,
And the country is destitute of all that once filled it,
When I strike all who dwell in it,
[q]Then they shall know that I *am* the LORD.

16   "This *is* the [r]lamentation
With which they shall lament her;
The daughters of the nations shall lament her;
They shall lament for her, for Egypt,
And for all her multitude,"
Says the Lord GOD.'"

Egypt and Others Consigned to the Pit

17It came to pass also in the twelfth year, on the fifteenth *day* of the month, [s]*that* the word of the LORD came to me, saying:

18   "Son of man, wail over the multitude of Egypt,
And [t]cast them down to the depths of the earth,
Her and the daughters of the famous nations,
With those who go down to the Pit:
19   'Whom [u]do you surpass in beauty?
[v]Go down, be placed with the uncircumcised.'
20   "They shall fall in the midst of *those* slain by the sword;
She is delivered to the sword,
[w]Drawing her and all her multitudes.
21   [x]The strong among the mighty
Shall speak to him out of the midst of hell
With those who help him:
'They have [y]gone down,
They lie with the uncircumcised, slain by the sword.'

---

greatest nation, had fallen to the Babylonians, surely a nation less great (Egypt) would also fall.
32:2 *lion . . . monster.* These words depict Egypt as proud and powerful.
32:14 *rivers run like oil.* This phrase is not used anywhere else. It pictures the time following massive killing when the Nile and its tributaries would experience a "deadly" calm.

32:1 [a] Ezek. 31:1; 33:21   **32:2** [b] Ezek. 27:2 [c] Ezek. 19:2–6
[d] Ezek. 29:3 [e] Jer. 46:7, 8 [f] Ezek. 34:18   **32:3** [g] Ezek.
12:13; 17:20   **32:4** [h] Ezek. 29:5 [i] Is. 18:6; Ezek. 31:13
32:5 [j] Ezek. 31:12   **32:7** [k] Rev. 6:12, 13; 8:12
32:10 [l] Ezek. 26:16   **32:11** [m] Jer. 46:26   **32:12** [n] Ezek.
28:7; 30:11; 31:12 [o] Ezek. 29:19   **32:13** [p] Ezek. 29:11
32:15 [q] Ps. 9:16   **32:16** [r] Ezek. 26:17   **32:17** [s] Ezek. 32:1;
33:21   **32:18** [t] Ezek. 26:20; 31:14   **32:19** [u] Ezek. 31:2, 18
[v] Ezek. 28:10   **32:20** [w] Ps. 28:3   **32:21** [x] Is. 1:31; 14:9, 10
[y] Ezek. 32:19, 25

22 "Assyria[z] *is* there, and all her company,
With their graves all around her,
All of them slain, fallen by the sword.
23 [a]Her graves are set in the recesses of
the Pit,
And her company is all around her
grave,
All of them slain, fallen by the sword,
Who [b]caused terror in the land of the
living.

24 "There *is* [c]Elam and all her multitude,
All around her grave,
All of them slain, fallen by the sword,
Who have [d]gone down uncircumcised
to the lower parts of the earth,
[e]Who caused their terror in the land of
the living;
Now they bear their shame with those
who go down to the Pit.

25 They have set her [f]bed in the midst of
the slain,
With all her multitude,
With her graves all around it,
All of them uncircumcised, slain by
the sword;
Though their terror was caused
In the land of the living,
Yet they bear their shame
With those who go down to the Pit;
It was put in the midst of the slain.

26 "There *are* [g]Meshech and Tubal and all
their multitudes,
With all their graves around it,
All of them [h]uncircumcised, slain by
the sword,
Though they caused their terror in the
land of the living.

27 [i]They do not lie with the mighty
Who are fallen of the uncircumcised,
Who have gone down to hell with their
weapons of war;
They have laid their swords under
their heads,
But their iniquities will be on their
bones,
Because of the terror of the mighty in
the land of the living.

28 Yes, you shall be broken in the midst
of the uncircumcised,
And lie with *those* slain by the sword.

29 "There *is* [j]Edom,
Her kings and all her princes,
Who despite their might

Are laid beside *those* slain by the
sword;
They shall lie with the uncircumcised,
And with those who go down to the Pit.
30 [k]There *are* the princes of the north,
All of them, and all the [l]Sidonians,
Who have gone down with the slain
In shame at the terror which they
caused by their might;
They lie uncircumcised with *those*
slain by the sword,
And bear their shame with those who
go down to the Pit.

31 "Pharaoh will see them
And be [m]comforted over all his
multitude,
Pharaoh and all his army,
Slain by the sword,"
Says the Lord GOD.

32 "For I have caused My terror in the land
of the living;
And he shall be placed in the midst of
the uncircumcised
With *those* slain by the sword,
Pharaoh and all his multitude,"
Says the Lord GOD.

The Watchman and His Message

33 Again the word of the LORD came
to me, saying, 2"Son of man, speak
to [a]the children of your people, and say
to them: [b]'When I bring the sword upon
a land, and the people of the land take a
man from their territory and make him
their [c]watchman, 3when he sees the sword
coming upon the land, if he blows the trumpet and warns the people, 4then whoever
hears the sound of the trumpet and does
[d]not take warning, if the sword comes
and takes him away, [e]his blood shall be
on his *own* head. 5He heard the sound of
the trumpet, but did not take warning; his
blood shall be upon himself. But he who
takes warning will save his life. 6But if
the watchman sees the sword coming and
does not blow the trumpet, and the people
are not warned, and the sword comes and
takes *any* person from among them, [f]he is
taken away in his iniquity; but his blood I
will require at the watchman's hand.'

7[g]"So you, son of man: I have made you a
watchman for the house of Israel; therefore
you shall hear a word from My mouth and

32:24 *There is Elam.* Elam was east and southeast of
Assyria in what is now Iran. The people of Elam were
descended from one of the sons of Shem (Gen. 10:22;
1 Chr. 1:17).

32:30 *princes of the north.* This is a reference to
lands that are north of Israel like Tyre and Sidon.

32:31 *Pharaoh will see.* Now the message (vv.
17–32) comes full circle. The point is that Egypt and
Pharaoh will die like the other nations at the hand of
the living God who judges every nation with justice.

33:2 *the children of your people.* This phrase refers

to fellow Israelites in exile with Ezekiel, now including
the people of Judah deported to Babylon after Nebuchadnezzar's third invasion.

32:22 [z] Ezek. 31:3, 16 **32:23** [a] Is. 14:15 [b] Ezek. 32:24–27,
32 **32:24** [c] Jer. 25:25; 49:34–39 [d] Ezek. 32:21 [e] Ezek.
32:23 **32:25** [f] Ps. 139:8 **32:26** [g] Gen. 10:2 [h] Ezek.
32:19 **32:27** [i] Is. 14:18, 19 **32:29** [j] Ezek. 25:12–14
32:30 [k] Jer. 1:15; 25:26 [l] Ezek. 28:21–23 **32:31** [m] Ezek.
14:21; 31:16 **33:2** [a] Ezek. 3:11 [b] Ezek. 14:17 [c] 2 Sam.
18:24, 25 **33:4** [d] Zech. 1:4 [e] [Acts 18:6] **33:6** [f] Ezek.
33:8 **33:7** [g] Is. 62:6

warn them for Me. 8When I say to the wicked, 'O wicked *man*, you shall surely die!' and you do not speak to warn the wicked from his way, that wicked *man* shall die in his iniquity; but his blood I will require at your hand. 9Nevertheless if you warn the wicked to turn from his way, and he does not turn from his way, he shall die in his iniquity; but you have delivered your soul.

10"Therefore you, O son of man, say to the house of Israel: 'Thus you say, "If our transgressions and our sins *lie* upon us, and we *h*pine away in them, *i*how can we then live?"' 11Say to them: '*As* I live,' says the Lord GOD, *j*'I have no pleasure in the death of the wicked, but that the wicked *k*turn from his way and live. Turn, turn from your evil ways! For *l*why should you die, O house of Israel?'

The Fairness of God's Judgment

12"Therefore you, O son of man, say to the children of your people: 'The *m*righteousness of the righteous man shall not deliver him in the day of his transgression; as for the wickedness of the wicked, *n*he shall not fall because of it in the day that he turns from his wickedness; nor shall the righteous be able to live because of *his righteousness* in the day that he sins.' 13When I say to the righteous *that* he shall surely live, *o*but he trusts in his own righteousness and commits iniquity, none of his righteous works shall be remembered; but because of the iniquity that he has committed, he shall die. 14Again, *p*when I say to the wicked, 'You shall surely die,' if he turns from his sin and does what is lawful and right, 15if the wicked *q*restores the pledge, *r*gives back what he has stolen, and walks in *s*the statutes of life without committing iniquity, he shall surely live; he shall not die. 16*t*None of his sins which he has committed shall be remembered against him; he has done what is lawful and right; he shall surely live.

17*u*"Yet the children of your people say, 'The way of the Lord is not fair.' But it is their way which is not fair! 18*v*When the righteous turns from his righteousness and commits iniquity, he shall die because of it. 19But when the wicked turns from his wickedness and does what is lawful and right, he shall live because of it. 20Yet you say, *w*'The way of the Lord is not fair.' O house of Israel, I will judge every one of you according to his own ways."

The Fall of Jerusalem

21And it came to pass in the twelfth year *x*of our captivity, in the tenth *month*, on the fifth *day* of the month, *y*that one who had escaped from Jerusalem came to me and said, *z*"The city has been captured!" 22Now *a*the hand of the LORD had been upon me the evening before the man came who had escaped. And He had *b*opened my mouth; so when he came to me in the morning, my mouth was opened, and I was no longer mute.

The Cause of Judah's Ruin

23Then the word of the LORD came to me, saying: 24"Son of man, *c*they who inhabit those *d*ruins in the land of Israel are saying, *e*'Abraham was only one, and he inherited the land. *f*But we *are* many; the land has been given to us as a *g*possession.' 25"Therefore say to them, 'Thus says the Lord GOD: *h*"You eat *meat* with blood, you *i*lift up your eyes toward your idols, and *j*shed blood. Should you then possess the *k*land? 26You rely on your sword, you commit abominations, and you *l*defile one another's wives. Should you then possess the land?" '

27"Say thus to them, 'Thus says the Lord GOD: "As I live, surely *m*those who *are* in the ruins shall fall by the sword, and the one who *is* in the open field *n*I will give to the beasts to be devoured, and those who *are* in the strongholds and *o*caves shall die of the pestilence. 28*p*For I will make the land most desolate, her *q*arrogant strength shall cease, and *r*the mountains of Israel shall be so desolate that no one will pass through. 29Then they shall know that I *am* the LORD, when I have made the land most desolate because of all their abominations which they have committed." '

33:12–20 *I will judge every one of you according to his own ways.* God presents His rationale in these verses for deciding who would be rewarded with life and who would suffer death; He would save those who repent and turn to Him, but would condemn those who trust in themselves and do evil. After presenting His rationale, God declares that His judgment is just and fair—certainly more just than the practices of the Israelites.

33:25–26 *Should you then possess the land.* Ezekiel confronted his people with specific examples of their past and present refusal to obey God's revealed will for their lives (18:6,10; 22:11; Ex. 20:4–5,13; Lev. 7:26–27; 17:10–14; Deut. 12:16,23). Was it not then reasonable that God would punish the present generation by removing them from the land, at least

temporarily? The writer of Hebrews, after using the example of Israel's failure to enter the land, admonished the church in a similar way (Heb. 4:1).

33:10 *h* Ezek. 24:23 *i* Is. 49:14 **33:11** *j* [2 Sam. 14:14] *k* [Acts 3:19] *l* Ezek. 18:30, 31 **33:12** *m* Ezek. 3:20; 18:24, 26 *n* [2 Chr. 7:14] **33:13** *o* Ezek. 3:20; 18:24 **33:14** *p* Ezek. 3:18, 19; 18:27 **33:15** *q* Ezek. 18:7 *r* Lev. 6:2, 4, 5 *s* Ezek. 20:11, 13, 21 **33:16** *t* [Is. 1:18; 43:25] **33:17** *u* Ezek. 18:25, 29 **33:18** *v* Ezek. 18:26 **33:20** *w* Ezek. 18:25, 29 **33:21** *x* Ezek. 1:2 *y* Ezek. 24:26 *z* 2 Kin. 25:4 **33:22** *a* Ezek. 1:3; 8:1; 37:1 *b* Ezek. 24:27 **33:24** *c* Ezek. 34:2 *d* Ezek. 36:4 *e* Is. 51:2 *f* [Matt. 3:9] *g* Ezek. 11:15 **33:25** *h* Lev. 3:17; 7:26; 17:10–14; 19:26 *i* Ezek. 18:6 *j* Ezek. 22:6, 9 *k* Deut. 29:28 **33:26** *l* Ezek. 18:6; 22:11 **33:27** *m* Ezek. 33:24 *n* Ezek. 39:4 *o* 1 Sam. 13:6 **33:28** *p* Jer. 44:2, 6, 22 *q* Ezek. 7:24; 24:21 *r* Ezek. 6:2, 3, 6

Hearing and Not Doing

30“As for you, son of man, the children of
your people are talking about you beside
the walls and in the doors of the houses;
and they [s]speak to one another, everyone
saying to his brother, ‘Please come and
hear what the word is that comes from the
LORD.’ 31So [t]they come to you as people do,
they [u]sit before you *as* My people, and they
[v]hear your words, but they do not do them;
[w]for with their mouth they show much love,
but [x]their hearts pursue their *own* gain.
32Indeed you *are* to them as a very lovely
song of one who has a pleasant voice and
can play well on an instrument; for they
hear your words, but they do [y]not do them.
33[z]And when this comes to pass—surely
it will come—then [a]they will know that a
prophet has been among them.”

Irresponsible Shepherds

34 And the word of the LORD came to
me, saying, 2“Son of man, prophesy
against the shepherds of Israel, prophesy
and say to them, ‘Thus says the Lord GOD
to the shepherds: [a]“Woe to the shepherds of
Israel who feed themselves! Should not the
shepherds feed the flocks? 3[b]You eat the
fat and clothe yourselves with the wool;
you [c]slaughter the fatlings, *but* you do not
feed the flock. 4[d]The weak you have not
strengthened, nor have you healed those
who were sick, nor bound up the broken,
nor brought back what was driven away,
nor [e]sought what was lost; but with [f]force
and cruelty you have ruled them. 5[g]So
they were [h]scattered because *there was*
no shepherd; [i]and they became food for
all the beasts of the field when they were
scattered. 6My sheep [j]wandered through
all the mountains, and on every high hill;
yes, My flock was scattered over the whole
face of the earth, and no one was seeking
or searching *for them.*”
7‘Therefore, you shepherds, hear the
word of the LORD: 8“*As* I live,” says the
Lord GOD, “surely because My flock became a prey, and My flock [k]became food
for every beast of the field, because *there
was* no shepherd, nor did My shepherds
search for My flock, [l]but the shepherds fed
themselves and did not feed My flock”—
9therefore, O shepherds, hear the word of
the LORD! 10Thus says the Lord GOD: “Behold, I *am* [m]against the shepherds, and [n]I
will require My flock at their hand; I will
cause them to cease feeding the sheep,
and the shepherds shall [o]feed themselves
no more; for I will [p]deliver My flock from
their mouths, that they may no longer be
food for them.”

God, the True Shepherd

11‘For thus says the Lord GOD: “Indeed I
Myself will search for My sheep and seek
them out. 12As a [q]shepherd seeks out his
flock on the day he is among his scattered
sheep, so will I seek out My sheep and deliver them from all the places where they
were scattered on [r]a cloudy and dark day.
13And [s]I will bring them out from the peoples and gather them from the countries,
and will bring them to their own land; I will
feed them on the mountains of Israel, in
the valleys and in all the inhabited places
of the country. 14[t]I will feed them in good
pasture, and their fold shall be on the high
mountains of Israel. [u]There they shall lie
down in a good fold and feed in rich pasture on the mountains of Israel. 15I will feed
My flock, and I will make them lie down,”
says the Lord GOD. 16[v]“I will seek what was
lost and bring back what was driven away,
bind up the broken and strengthen what
was sick; but I will destroy [w]the fat and the
strong, and feed them [x]in judgment.”
17‘And *as for* you, O My flock, thus says
the Lord GOD: [y]“Behold, I shall judge between sheep and sheep, between rams and
goats. 18*Is it* too little for you to have eaten
up the good pasture, that you must tread
down with your feet the residue of your
pasture—and to have drunk of the clear
waters, that you must foul the residue with
your feet? 19And *as for* My flock, they eat
what you have trampled with your feet, and
they drink what you have fouled with your
feet.”
20‘Therefore thus says the Lord GOD to
them: [z]“Behold, I Myself will judge between

33:30–33 *they hear your words, but they do not do them.* This section contrasts the actions and attitudes of the exiles with the life of God's prophet Ezekiel. The exiles had claimed to go to the prophet to receive God's revelation, but their behavior was inconsistent with their stated beliefs. Their true desire was for entertainment, not for divine enlightenment. If the fall of Jerusalem failed to awaken them spiritually, nothing would. Yet it certainly would open their eyes to the divine truth of Ezekiel's preaching. In these verses then, God also comforted and consoled Ezekiel.

34:7–10 *did not feed My flock.* The crimes of Israel's leaders come under review before their punishment is pronounced.

34:11–16 *a cloudy and dark day.* This was the day Jerusalem fell (30:1–5). It may also speak of the future day of deliverance when God will seek out His sheep. Israel, though guilty and misguided, would eventually be rescued by the divine Good Shepherd and restored to the Promised Land (chs. 33–39).

33:30 [s] Is. 29:13 **33:31** [t] Ezek. 14:1 [u] Ezek. 8:1 [v] Is. 58:2 [w] Ps. 78:36, 37 [x] [Matt. 13:22] **33:32** [y] [Matt. 7:21–28] **33:33** [z] 1 Sam. 3:20 [a] Ezek. 2:5 **34:2** [a] Zech. 11:17 **34:3** [b] Zech. 11:16 [c] Ezek. 33:25, 26 **34:4** [d] Zech. 11:16 [e] Luke 15:4 [f] [1 Pet. 5:3] **34:5** [g] Ezek. 33:21 [h] Matt. 9:36 [i] Is. 56:9 **34:6** [j] 1 Pet. 2:25 **34:8** [k] Ezek. 34:5, 6 [l] Ezek. 34:2, 10 **34:10** [m] Jer. 21:13; 52:24–27 [n] Heb. 13:17 [o] Ezek. 34:2, 8 [p] Ezek. 13:23 **34:12** [q] Jer. 31:10 [r] Ezek. 30:3 **34:13** [s] Jer. 23:3 **34:14** [t] [John 10:9] [u] Jer. 33:12 **34:16** [v] Mic. 4:6 [w] Is. 10:16 [x] Jer. 10:24 **34:17** [y] [Matt. 25:32] **34:20** [z] Ezek. 34:17

the fat and the lean sheep. 21Because you have pushed with side and shoulder, butted all the weak ones with your horns, and scattered them abroad, 22therefore I will save My flock, and they shall no longer be a prey; and I will judge between sheep and sheep. 23I will establish one ashepherd over them, and he shall feed them—bMy servant David. He shall feed them and be their shepherd. 24And cI, the LORD, will be their God, and My servant David da prince among them; I, the LORD, have spoken.

25e"I will make a covenant of peace with them, and fcause wild beasts to cease from the land; and they gwill dwell safely in the wilderness and sleep in the woods. 26I will make them and the places all around hMy hill ia blessing; and I will jcause showers to come down in their season; there shall be kshowers of blessing. 27Then lthe trees of the field shall yield their fruit, and the earth shall yield her increase. They shall be safe in their land; and they shall know that I am the LORD, when I have mbroken the bands of their yoke and delivered them from the hand of those who nenslaved them. 28And they shall no longer be a prey for the nations, nor shall beasts of the land devour them; but othey shall dwell safely, and no one shall make them afraid. 29I will raise up for them a pgarden of renown, and they shall qno longer be consumed with hunger in the land, rnor bear the shame of the Gentiles anymore. 30Thus they shall know that sI, the LORD their God, am with them, and they, the house of Israel, are tMy people," says the Lord GOD.' 31"You are My uflock, the flock of My pasture; you are men, and I am your God," says the Lord GOD.

Judgment on Mount Seir

35 Moreover the word of the LORD came to me, saying, 2"Son of man, set your face against aMount Seir and bprophesy against it, 3and say to it, 'Thus says the Lord GOD:

"Behold, O Mount Seir, I am against you;
cI will stretch out My hand against you,
    And make you most desolate;
4   I shall lay your cities waste,
    And you shall be desolate.
    Then you shall know that I am the
    LORD.

5d"Because you have had an ancient hatred, and have shed the blood of the children of Israel by the power of the sword at the time of their calamity, ewhen their iniquity came to an end, 6therefore, as I live," says the Lord GOD, "I will prepare you for fblood, and blood shall pursue you; gsince you have not hated blood, therefore blood shall pursue you. 7Thus I will make Mount Seir most desolate, and cut off from it the hone who leaves and the one who returns. 8And I will fill its mountains with the slain; on your hills and in your valleys and in all your ravines those who are slain by the sword shall fall. 9iI will make you perpetually desolate, and your cities shall be uninhabited; jthen you shall know that I am the LORD.

10"Because you have said, 'These two nations and these two countries shall be mine, and we will kpossess them,' although lthe LORD was there, 11therefore, as I live," says the Lord GOD, "I will do maccording to your anger and according to the envy which you showed in your hatred against them; and I will make Myself known among them when I judge you. 12nThen you shall know that I am the LORD. I have oheard all your pblasphemies which you have spoken against the mountains of Israel, saying, 'They are desolate; they are given to us to consume.' 13Thus qwith your mouth you have boasted against Me and multiplied your rwords against Me; I have heard them."

14'Thus says the Lord GOD: s"The whole earth will rejoice when I make you desolate. 15tAs you rejoiced because the inheritance of the house of Israel was desolate, uso I will do to you; you shall be desolate, O Mount Seir, as well as all of Edom—all of it! Then they shall know that I am the LORD."'

34:23–24 I will establish . . . he shall feed. The change from the pronoun I to he in this verse indicates that God would continue operating as the Chief Shepherd through this chosen future ruler from the Davidic line. He is the Messiah—God's only Son and His servant.

34:25–31 covenant of peace. These exiles were encouraged through these promises (37:26–28; 38:11–13; 39:25–29; Is. 54:10): (1) security from foreign aggressor nations; (2) showers of blessing, meaning productivity and prosperity; and (3) the certainty that the Lord is Israel's God and desires reunion with His people and a lasting relationship built on a new covenant (Jer. 31:31–34; Heb. 8:6).

35:6–9 perpetually desolate. Having stated why Edom deserved judgment, Ezekiel explained how the

nation would be punished. The punishment would include widespread death and unrelieved destruction (Is. 34.6–8; 63:1–6; Jer. 49:7–13).

34:23 a [Is. 40:11] b Jer. 30:9 **34:24** c Ex. 29:45 d Ezek. 37:24, 25 **34:25** e Ezek. 37:26 f Is. 11:6–9 g Jer. 23:6 **34:26** h Is. 56:7 i Zech. 8:13 j Lev. 26:4 k Ps. 68:9 **34:27** l Is. 4:2 m Jer. 2:20 n Jer. 25:14 **34:28** o Jer. 30:10 **34:29** p [Is. 11:1] q Ezek. 36:29 r Ezek. 36:3, 6, 15 **34:30** s Ezek. 34:24 t Ezek. 14:11; 36:28 **34:31** u Ps. 100:3 **35:2** a Ezek. 25:12–14 b Amos 1:11 **35:3** c Ezek. 6:14 **35:5** d Ezek. 25:12 e Ps. 137:7 **35:6** f Is. 63:1–6 g Ps. 109:17 **35:7** h Judg. 5:6 **35:9** i Jer. 49:13 j Ezek. 36:11 **35:10** k Ps. 83:4–12 l [Ps. 48:1–3; 132:13, 14] **35:11** m [James 2:13] **35:12** n Ps. 9:16 o Zeph. 2:8 p Is. 52:5 **35:13** q [1 Sam. 2:3] r Ezek. 36:3 **35:14** s Is. 65:13, 14 **35:15** t Obad. 12, 15 u Lam. 4:21

Blessing on Israel

36 "And you, son of man, prophesy to the *a*mountains of Israel, and say, 'O mountains of Israel, hear the word of the LORD! ²Thus says the Lord GOD: "Because *b*the enemy has said of you, 'Aha! *c*The ancient heights *d*have become our possession,'"' ³therefore prophesy, and say, 'Thus says the Lord GOD: "Because they made *you* desolate and swallowed you up on every side, so that you became the possession of the rest of the nations, *e*and you are taken up by the lips of *f*talkers and slandered by the people"—⁴therefore, O mountains of Israel, hear the word of the Lord GOD! Thus says the Lord GOD to the mountains, the hills, the rivers, the valleys, the desolate wastes, and the cities that have been forsaken, which *g*became plunder and *h*mockery to the rest of the nations all around—⁵therefore thus says the Lord GOD: *i*"Surely I have spoken in My burning jealousy against the rest of the nations and against all Edom, *j*who gave My land to themselves as a possession, with wholehearted joy *and* spiteful minds, in order to plunder its open country."'

⁶"Therefore prophesy concerning the land of Israel, and say to the mountains, the hills, the rivers, and the valleys, 'Thus says the Lord GOD: "Behold, I have spoken in My jealousy and My fury, because you have *k*borne the shame of the nations." ⁷Therefore thus says the Lord GOD: "I have *l*raised My hand in an oath that surely the nations that *are* around you shall *m*bear their own shame. ⁸But you, O mountains of Israel, you shall shoot forth your branches and yield your fruit to My people Israel, for they are about to come. ⁹For indeed I *am* for you, and I will turn to you, and you shall be tilled and sown. ¹⁰I will multiply men upon you, all the house of Israel, all of it; and the cities shall be inhabited and *n*the ruins rebuilt. ¹¹o I will multiply upon you man and beast; and they shall increase and bear young; I will make you inhabited as in former times, and do *p*better *for you* than at your beginnings. *q*Then you shall know that I *am* the LORD. ¹²Yes, I will cause men

to walk on you, My people Israel; *r*they shall take possession of you, and you shall be their inheritance; no more shall you *s*bereave them *of children."*

¹³'Thus says the Lord GOD: "Because they say to you, *t*'You devour men and bereave your nation *of children,'* ¹⁴therefore you shall devour men no more, nor bereave your nation anymore," says the Lord GOD. ¹⁵u"Nor will I let you hear the taunts of the nations anymore, nor bear the reproach of the peoples anymore, nor shall you cause your nation to stumble anymore," says the Lord GOD.'"

The Renewal of Israel

¹⁶Moreover the word of the LORD came to me, saying: ¹⁷"Son of man, when the house of Israel dwelt in their own land, *v*they defiled it by their own ways and deeds; to Me their way was like *w*the uncleanness of a woman in her customary impurity. ¹⁸Therefore I poured out My fury on them *x*for the blood they had shed on the land, and for their idols *with which* they had defiled it. ¹⁹So I *y*scattered them among the nations, and they were dispersed throughout the countries; I judged them *z*according to their ways and their deeds. ²⁰When they came to the nations, wherever they went, they *a*profaned My holy name—when they said of them, 'These *are* the people of the LORD, *and* yet they have gone out of His land.' ²¹But I had concern *b*for My holy name, which the house of Israel had profaned among the nations wherever they went.

²²"Therefore say to the house of Israel, 'Thus says the Lord GOD: "I do not do *this* for your sake, O house of Israel, *c*but for My holy name's sake, which you have profaned among the nations wherever you went. ²³And I will sanctify My great name, which has been profaned among the nations, which you have profaned in their midst; and the nations shall know that I *am* the LORD," says the Lord GOD, "when I am *d*hallowed in you before their eyes. ²⁴For *e*I will take you from among the nations, gather you out of all countries, and

---

36:1–7 The ancient heights. This was a term for Israel because the hill country was central to the country's geography. God is glorified and the exiles comforted by the following: (1) exposing the crimes of the enemies of His nation; (2) exonerating His land from false charges; and (3) executing judgment and justice against the foreign nations.

36:12 My people Israel. Despite all their sinfulness, which the book has taken enormous pains to detail and describe, the nation was still referred to as the people of God. They would finally and forever take possession of their land, symbolized by the mountains and the central hills of Palestine, which are personified as "you" in this verse.

36:19 according to their ways and their deeds. Israel had been hypocritical and unholy; they had not separated themselves or made themselves distinct from the pagan world around them (v. 18). God had

given His people the Promised Land as a place where they could show the world the difference it makes to follow the true God (Deut. 7:1–11). They failed to follow God, so He forced them out of the land. Through either their obedience or their disobedience, God would demonstrate to the watching world His personality, power, and plans.

36:1 *a* Ezek. 6:2, 3 **36:2** *b* Ezek. 25:3; 26:2 *c* Deut. 32:13 *d* Ezek. 35:10 **36:3** *e* Deut. 28:37 *f* Ezek. 35:13 **36:4** *g* Ezek. 34:8, 28 *h* Ps. 79:4 **36:5** *i* Deut. 4:24 *j* Ezek. 35:10, 12 **36:6** *k* Ps. 74:10; 123:3, 4 **36:7** *l* Ezek. 20:5 *m* Jer. 25:9, 15, 29 **36:10** *n* Amos 9:14 **36:11** *o* Jer. 31:27; 33:12 *p* Is. 51:3 *q* Ezek. 35:9; 37:6, 13 **36:12** *r* Obad. 17 *s* Jer. 15:7 **36:13** *t* Num. 13:32 **36:15** *u* Ezek. 34:29 **36:17** *v* Jer. 2:7 *w* Lev. 15:19 **36:18** *x* Ezek. 16:36, 38; 23:37 **36:19** *y* Deut. 28:64 *z* [Rom. 2:6] **36:20** *a* Rom. 2:24 **36:21** *b* Ezek. 20:9, 14 **36:22** *c* Ps. 106:8 **36:23** *d* Ezek. 20:41; 28:22 **36:24** *e* Ezek. 34:13; 37:21

bring you into your own land. 25fThen I will sprinkle clean water on you, and you shall be clean; I will cleanse you gfrom all your filthiness and from all your idols. 26I will give you a hnew heart and put a new spirit within you; I will take the heart of stone out of your flesh and give you a heart of flesh. 27I will put My iSpirit within you and cause you to walk in My statutes, and you will keep My judgments and do *them*. 28jThen you shall dwell in the land that I gave to your fathers; kyou shall be My people, and I will be your God. 29I will ldeliver you from all your uncleannesses. mI will call for the grain and multiply it, and nbring no famine upon you. 30oAnd I will multiply the fruit of your trees and the increase of your fields, so that you need never again bear the reproach of famine among the nations. 31Then pyou will remember your evil ways and your deeds that *were* not good; and you qwill loathe yourselves in your own sight, for your iniquities and your abominations. 32rNot for your sake do I do *this*," says the Lord GOD, "let it be known to you. Be ashamed and confounded for your own ways, O house of Israel!"

33'Thus says the Lord GOD: "On the day that I cleanse you from all your iniquities, I will also enable *you* to dwell in the cities, sand the ruins shall be rebuilt. 34The desolate land shall be tilled instead of lying desolate in the sight of all who pass by. 35So they will say, 'This land that was desolate has become like the garden of tEden; and the wasted, desolate, and ruined cities *are now* fortified *and* inhabited.' 36Then the nations which are left all around you shall know that I, the LORD, have rebuilt the ruined places *and* planted what was desolate. uI, the LORD, have spoken *it*, and I will do *it*."

37'Thus says the Lord GOD: v"I will also let the house of Israel inquire of Me to do this for them: I will wincrease their men like a flock. 38Like a flock *offered as* holy *sacrifices*, like the flock at Jerusalem on its feast days, so shall the ruined cities be filled with flocks of men. Then they shall know that I *am* the LORD." '"

The Dry Bones Live

37 The ahand of the LORD came upon me and brought me out bin the Spirit of the LORD, and set me down in the midst of the valley; and it *was* full of bones. 2Then He caused me to pass by them all around, and behold, *there were* very many in the open valley; and indeed *they were* very dry. 3And He said to me, "Son of man, can these bones live?"

So I answered, "O Lord GOD, cYou know."

4Again He said to me, "Prophesy to these bones, and say to them, 'O dry bones, hear the word of the LORD! 5Thus says the Lord GOD to these bones: "Surely I will dcause breath to enter into you, and you shall live. 6I will put sinews on you and bring flesh upon you, cover you with skin and put breath in you; and you shall live. eThen you shall know that I *am* the LORD." '"

7So I prophesied as I was commanded; and as I prophesied, there was a noise, and suddenly a rattling; and the bones came together, bone to bone. 8Indeed, as I looked, the sinews and the flesh came upon them, and the skin covered them over; but *there was* no breath in them.

9Also He said to me, "Prophesy to the breath, prophesy, son of man, and say to the breath, 'Thus says the Lord GOD: f"Come from the four winds, O breath, and breathe on these slain, that they may live." '" 10So I prophesied as He commanded me, gand breath came into them, and they lived, and stood upon their feet, an exceedingly great army.

36:25 *sprinkle clean water on you.* This symbolized cleansing from sin.

36:27 *I will put My Spirit within you.* The regenerating and empowering work of the Holy Spirit on individuals would not only restore the people physically to the land, but would restore them spiritually, by giving them a new heart and new spirit to help them follow Him and do His will (11:19–20; 18:31; 37:14; Jer. 31:31–34; Joel 2:28–29; Rom. 7:7—8:11).

36:28-30 *you shall be My people.* The purpose of the Mosaic covenant would finally be realized (Deut. 26:16–19; 29:13; 30:8). The Israelites would become a people dedicated to God's ways.

36:31-32 *Not for your sake do I do this.* The restoration from the exile would recover God's glorious reputation among the nations and erase the guilt of the Israelites' sin. This is all a product of God's favor on the Israelites—even though they had done nothing to merit such mercy.

37:4 *Prophesy to these bones.* Ezekiel's prophecies had often been directed to people as deaf as these old, dry bones.

37:5 *breath.* This word is translated as wind or spirit in other places. The breath sent by God into the lifeless bodies symbolizes the Holy Spirit who brings renewal, regeneration, and rebirth (John 3:5–8; 6:44; 7:37–39; Rom. 8:9–11).

37:6 *you shall live.* This passage is not about resurrection from physical death, but rebirth from spiritual death brought about by divine power. Psalm 87 is another text that speaks of spiritual rebirth. The point of Jesus' words to Nicodemus in John 3 was that he should have known and understood the concept of a second birth.

37:10 *an exceedingly great army.* The dead bones

36:25 fHeb. 9:13, 19; 10:22 gJer. 33:8 **36:26** hEzek. 11:19 **36:27** iEzek. 11:19; 37:14 **36:28** jEzek. 28:25; 37:25 kJer. 30:22 **36:29** l[Rom. 11:26] mPs. 105:16 nEzek. 34:27, 29 **36:30** oEzek. 34:27 **36:31** pEzek. 16:61, 63 qEzek. 6:9; 20:43 **36:32** rDeut. 9:5 **36:33** sEzek. 36:10 **36:35** tJoel 2:3 **36:36** uEzek. 17:24; 22:14; 37:14 **36:37** vEzek. 14:3; 20:3, 31 wEzek. 36:10 **37:1** aEzek. 1:3 bEzek. 3:14; 8:3; 11:24 **37:3** c[1 Sam. 2:6] **37:5** dPs. 104:29, 30 **37:6** eJoel 2:27; 3:17 **37:9** f[Ps. 104:30] **37:10** gRev. 11:11

11 Then He said to me, "Son of man, these
bones are the [h]whole house of Israel. They
indeed say, [i]'Our bones are dry, our hope is
lost, and we ourselves are cut off!' 12 Therefore prophesy and say to them, 'Thus says
the Lord GOD: "Behold, [j]O My people, I will
open your graves and cause you to come up
from your graves, and [k]bring you into the
land of Israel. 13 Then you shall know that
I *am* the LORD, when I have opened your
graves, O My people, and brought you up
from your graves. 14 I [l]will put My Spirit in
you, and you shall live, and I will place you
in your own land. Then you shall know that
I, the LORD, have spoken *it* and performed
it," says the LORD.' "

One Kingdom, One King

15 Again the word of the LORD came
to me, saying, 16 "As for you, son of man,
[m]take a stick for yourself and write on it:
'For Judah and for [n]the children of Israel,
his companions.' Then take another stick
and write on it, 'For Joseph, the stick of
Ephraim, and *for* all the house of Israel, his
companions.' 17 Then [o]join them one to another for yourself into one stick, and they
will become one in your hand.

18 "And when the children of your people
speak to you, saying, [p]'Will you not show
us what you *mean* by these?'— 19 [q]say to
them, 'Thus says the Lord GOD: "Surely I
will take [r]the stick of Joseph, which *is* in
the hand of Ephraim, and the tribes of Israel, his companions; and I will join them
with it, with the stick of Judah, and make
them one stick, and they will be one in
My hand." ' 20 And the sticks on which you
write will be in your hand [s]before their
eyes.

21 "Then say to them, 'Thus says the Lord
GOD: "Surely [t]I will take the children of
Israel from among the nations, wherever
they have gone, and will gather them from
every side and bring them into their own
land; 22 and [u]I will make them one nation
in the land, on the mountains of Israel; and
[v]one king shall be king over them all; they
shall no longer be two nations, nor shall
they ever be divided into two kingdoms
again. 23 [w]They shall not defile themselves
anymore with their idols, nor with their
detestable things, nor with any of their
transgressions; but [x]I will deliver them
from all their dwelling places in which
they have sinned, and will cleanse them.
Then they shall be My people, and I will
be their God.

24 [y]"David My servant *shall be* king over
them, and [z]they shall all have one shepherd;
[a]they shall also walk in My judgments and
observe My statutes, and do them. 25 [b]Then
they shall dwell in the land that I have
given to Jacob My servant, where your
fathers dwelt; and they shall dwell there,
they, their children, and their children's
children, [c]forever; and [d]My servant David
shall be their prince forever. 26 Moreover I
will make [e]a covenant of peace with them,
and it shall be an everlasting covenant with
them; I will establish them and [f]multiply
them, and I will set My [g]sanctuary in their
midst forevermore. 27 [h]My tabernacle also
shall be with them; indeed I will be [i]their
God, and they shall be My people. 28 [j]The
nations also will know that I, the LORD,
[k]sanctify Israel, when My sanctuary is in
their midst forevermore." ' "

Gog and Allies Attack Israel

38 Now the word of the LORD came to
me, saying, 2 [a]"Son of man, [b]set your
face against [c]Gog, of the land of [d]Magog,
the prince of Rosh,* [e]Meshech, and Tubal,
and prophesy against him, 3 and say, 'Thus
says the Lord GOD: "Behold, I *am* against
you, O Gog, the prince of Rosh, Meshech,

* **38:2** Targum, Vulgate, and Aquila read *chief prince of* (also verse 3).

---

in the valley (vv. 1–2) must have looked like the aftermath of a horrible military defeat in which there were no survivors even to bury the dead.

37:11–14 ***these bones.*** The bones symbolize the whole house of Israel. This identification picks up on imagery already used: (1) those identified as dry or spiritually dead; (2) those identified as despondent and dejected, with no apparent hope of being "resurrected" as the people of the living God; and (3) those described as disassembled and dispersed before being rejoined and rebuilt. The major thrust of this passage is the coming spiritual rebirth of God's chosen people through the agency of His Spirit.

37:24–25 ***David my servant.*** This title refers to the Messiah and King who would come from David's line to save Israel (2 Sam. 7:8–16).

37:26–28 ***My sanctuary in their midst.*** The sanctuary or holy place of the living God is His dwelling place among His people (Zeph. 3:15–18). ***My tabernacle.*** This is a synonym for sanctuary. Both can be used of God's dwelling in the midst of His people in the wilderness. Here they point to the future dwelling of the living God in the midst of His people forevermore.

38:2 ***Son of man.*** This is a title for Ezekiel emphasizing his humanity, even though his message was from God. The proper names in this prophecy do not have to be specifically identified for an understanding of the main message.

38:3 ***Gog.*** This leader or king only appears in Scripture here and in Revelation 20:8. Several ideas about

37:11 [h] Ezek. 36:10 [i] Ps. 141:7 **37:12** [j] Is. 26:19; 66:14 [k] Ezek. 36:24 **37:14** [l] Ezek. 36:27 **37:16** [m] Num. 17:2, 3 [n] 2 Chr. 11:12, 13, 16; 15:9; 30:11, 18 **37:17** [o] Hos. 1:11 **37:18** [p] Ezek. 12:9; 24:19 **37:19** [q] Zech. 10:6 [r] Ezek. 37:16, 17 **37:20** [s] Ezek. 12:3 **37:21** [t] Ezek. 36:24 **37:22** [u] Jer. 3:18 [v] Ezek. 34:23 **37:23** [w] Ezek. 36:25 [x] Ezek. 36:28, 29 **37:24** [y] Is. 40:11; [Luke 1:32]; 1 Pet. 2:25 [z] [John 10:16] [a] Ezek. 36:27 **37:25** [b] Ezek. 36:28; Rev. 21:3; 22:3 [c] Is. 60:21 [d] John 12:34 **37:26** [e] Is. 55:3 [f] Ezek. 36:10 [g] [2 Cor. 6:16] **37:27** [h] [John 1:14] [i] Ezek. 11:20 **37:28** [j] Ezek. 36:23 [k] Ezek. 20:12 **38:2** [a] Ezek. 39:1 [b] Ezek. 35:2, 3 [c] Rev. 20:8 [d] Gen. 10:2 [e] Ezek. 32:26

and Tubal. 4fI will turn you around, put hooks into your jaws, and glead you out, with all your army, horses, and horsemen, hall splendidly clothed, a great company with bucklers and shields, all of them handling swords. 5Persia, Ethiopia,* and Libya* are with them, all of them with shield and helmet; 6iGomer and all its troops; the house of jTogarmah from the far north and all its troops—many people are with you.

7k"Prepare yourself and be ready, you and all your companies that are gathered about you; and be a guard for them. 8lAfter many days myou will be visited. In the latter years you will come into the land of those brought back from the sword nand gathered from many people on othe mountains of Israel, which had long been desolate; they were brought out of the nations, and now all of them pdwell safely. 9You will ascend, coming qlike a storm, covering the rland like a cloud, you and all your troops and many peoples with you."

10'Thus says the Lord GOD: "On that day it shall come to pass that thoughts will arise in your mind, and you will make an evil plan: 11You will say, 'I will go up against a land of sunwalled villages; I will tgo to a peaceful people, uwho dwell safely, all of them dwelling without walls, and having neither bars nor gates'— 12to take plunder and to take booty, to stretch out your hand against the waste places that are again inhabited, vand against a people gathered from the nations, who have acquired livestock and goods, who dwell in the midst of the land. 13wSheba, xDedan, the merchants yof Tarshish, and all ztheir young lions will say to you, 'Have you come to take plunder? Have you gathered your army to take booty, to carry away silver and gold, to take away livestock and goods, to take great plunder?'"'

14"Therefore, son of man, prophesy and say to Gog, 'Thus says the Lord GOD: a"On that day when My people Israel bdwell safely, will you not know it? 15cThen you will come from your place out of the far north, you and many peoples with you, all of them riding on horses, a great company and a

mighty army. 16You will come up against My people Israel like a cloud, to cover the land. It will be in the latter days that I will bring you against My land, so that the nations may dknow Me, when I am ehallowed in you, O Gog, before their eyes." 17Thus says the Lord GOD: "Are you he of whom I have spoken in former days by My servants the prophets of Israel, who prophesied for years in those days that I would bring you against them?

Judgment on Gog

18"And it will come to pass at the same time, when Gog comes against the land of Israel," says the Lord GOD, "that My fury will show in My face. 19For fin My jealousy gand in the fire of My wrath I have spoken: h'Surely in that day there shall be a great earthquake in the land of Israel, 20so that ithe fish of the sea, the birds of the heavens, the beasts of the field, all creeping things that creep on the earth, and all men who are on the face of the earth shall shake at My presence. jThe mountains shall be thrown down, the steep places shall fall, and every wall shall fall to the ground.' 21I will kcall for la sword against Gog throughout all My mountains," says the Lord GOD. m"Every man's sword will be against his brother. 22And I will nbring him to judgment with opestilence and bloodshed; pI will rain down on him, on his troops, and on the many peoples who are with him, flooding rain, qgreat hailstones, fire, and brimstone. 23Thus I will magnify Myself and rsanctify Myself, sand I will be known in the eyes of many nations. Then they shall know that I am the LORD."'

Gog's Armies Destroyed

39 "And ayou, son of man, prophesy against Gog, and say, 'Thus says the Lord GOD: "Behold, I am against you, O Gog, the prince of Rosh,* Meshech, and Tubal; 2and I will bturn you around and lead you on, cbringing you up from

---

* **38:5** Hebrew Cush • Hebrew Put • **39:1** Targum, Vulgate and Aquila read chief prince of.

---

his identity have been suggested but none are completely convincing.

38:8 After many days . . . In the latter years. The first phrase usually denotes an indefinite time period, sometimes extending into the distant future or the end times (Dan. 8:26). The second phrase frequently points to messianic times or to the times when Israel is regathered. From Ezekiel's viewpoint, he was predicting a time in the very distant future—the end times. Unless the passage refers to spiritual warfare, the invasion of Israel and the subsequent time of confident and carefree peace are still future events. **dwell safely.** This phrase indicates that the Israel of this passage is secure; the nation is not safe from attack, but it is safe from defeat.

38:18–23 My fury will show in My face. These verses

speak of God defending His nation against Gog and his army with supernatural and earthshaking methods. Unusually strong language concerning the wrath of God is found in these verses.

38:4 f2 Kin. 19:28 gIs. 43:17 hEzek. 23:12 **38:6** iGen. 10:2 jEzek. 27:14 **38:7** kIs. 8:9, 10 **38:8** lIs. 24:22 mIs. 29:6 nEzek. 34:13 oEzek. 36:1, 4 pEzek. 34:25; 39:26 **38:9** qIs. 28:2 rJer. 4:13 **38:11** sZech. 2:4 tJer. 49:31 uEzek. 38:8 **38:12** vEzek. 38:8 **38:13** wEzek. 27:22 xEzek. 27:15, 20 yEzek. 27:12 zEzek. 19:3, 5 **38:14** aIs. 4:1 bEzek. 38:8, 11 **38:15** cEzek. 38:2 **38:16** dEzek. 35:11 eEzek. 28:22 **38:19** fEzek. 36:5, 6 gPs. 89:46 hRev. 16:18 **38:20** iHos. 4:3 jJer. 4:24 **38:21** kPs. 105:16 lEzek. 14:17 m1 Sam. 14:20 **38:22** nIs. 66:16 oEzek. 5:17 pPs. 11:6 qRev. 16:21 **38:23** rEzek. 36:23 sEzek. 37:28; 38:16 **39:1** aEzek. 38:2, 3 **39:2** bEzek. 38:8 cEzek. 38:15

the far north, and bring you against the mountains of Israel. [3]Then I will knock the bow out of your left hand, and cause the arrows to fall out of your right hand. [4d]You shall fall upon the mountains of Israel, you and all your troops and the peoples who *are* with you; [e]I will give you to birds of prey of every sort and *to* the beasts of the field to be devoured. [5]You shall fall on the open field; for I have spoken," says the Lord GOD. [6f]"And I will send fire on Magog and on those who live in security in [g]the coastlands. Then they shall know that I *am* the LORD. [7h]So I will make My holy name known in the midst of My people Israel, and I will not let them [i]profane My holy name anymore. [j]Then the nations shall know that I *am* the LORD, the Holy One in Israel. [8k]Surely it is coming, and it shall be done," says the Lord GOD. "This *is* the day [l]of which I have spoken.

[9]"Then those who dwell in the cities of Israel will go out and set on fire and burn the weapons, both the shields and bucklers, the bows and arrows, the javelins and spears; and they will make fires with them for seven years. [10]They will not take wood from the field nor cut down *any* from the forests, because they will make fires with the weapons; [m]and they will plunder those who plundered them, and pillage those who pillaged them," says the Lord GOD.

The Burial of Gog

[11]"It will come to pass in that day *that* I will give Gog a burial place there in Israel, the valley of those who pass by east of the sea; and it will obstruct travelers, because there they will bury Gog and all his multitude. Therefore they will call *it* the Valley of Hamon Gog.* [12]For seven months the house of Israel will be burying them, [n]in order to cleanse the land. [13]Indeed all the people of the land will be burying, and they will gain [o]renown for it on the day that [p]I am glorified," says the Lord GOD. [14]"They will set apart men regularly employed, with the help of a search party,* to pass through the land and bury those bodies remaining on the ground, in order [q]to

cleanse it. At the end of seven months they will make a search. [15]The search party will pass through the land; and *when anyone* sees a man's bone, he shall set up a marker by it, till the buriers have buried it in the Valley of Hamon Gog. [16]*The* name of *the* city *will* also *be* Hamonah. Thus they shall [r]cleanse the land."'

A Triumphant Festival

[17]"And as for you, son of man, thus says the Lord GOD, [s]'Speak to every sort of bird and to every beast of the field:

[t]"Assemble yourselves and come;
  Gather together from all sides to My
    [u]sacrificial meal
  Which I am sacrificing for you,
  A great sacrificial meal [v]on the
    mountains of Israel,
  That you may eat flesh and drink blood.
[18] [w]You shall eat the flesh of the mighty,
  Drink the blood of the princes of the
    earth,
  Of rams and lambs,
  Of goats and bulls,
  All of them [x]fatlings of Bashan.
[19] You shall eat fat till you are full,
  And drink blood till you are drunk,
  At My sacrificial meal
  Which I am sacrificing for you.
[20] [y]You shall be filled at My table
  With horses and riders,
  [z]With mighty men
  And with all the men of war," says the
    Lord GOD.

Israel Restored to the Land

[21a]"I will set My glory among the nations; all the nations shall see My judgment which I have executed, and [b]My hand which I have laid on them. [22c]So the house of Israel shall know that I *am* the LORD their God from that day forward. [23d]The Gentiles shall know that the house of Israel went into captivity for their iniquity; because they were unfaithful to Me, therefore [e]I hid My face from them. I [f]gave

---

* 39:11 Literally *The Multitude of Gog*
* 39:14 Literally *those who pass through*

39:6 *I will send fire.* Often fire from the Lord has the form of lightning bolts (1 Kin. 18:38).
39:12 *cleanse the land.* The law of Moses prescribed the sacrifice of a heifer to cleanse the land if a murdered person was found in a region (Deut. 21:1–9).
39:17–20 *Speak to every sort of bird.* A poem or song is addressed to the scavenging birds and beasts who come to the multitude of dead bodies (vv. 14–16). Whether figurative or not, the passage powerfully pictures God's sovereign control over the complete conquest of Israel's future and most ferocious enemies (Rev. 19:11–21). The meal would be a divinely prepared sacrifice served at God's table.
39:21–22 *My glory among the nations.* The universal knowledge of the living God of Israel will be based finally on the outcome of the battle described in

chapters 38 and 39. Ezekiel followed the great theme of biblical theology begun in Genesis 12:3 that the ultimate purpose of God in His choice of Abraham and Sarah was to make His blessings known to all the families of the earth. God will demonstrate His glory both among the nations and among His chosen people Israel.

39:4 [d]Ezek. 38:4, 21 [e]Ezek. 33:27   **39:6** [f]Amos 1:4, 7, 10 [g]Ps. 72:10   **39:7** [h]Ezek. 39:25 [i]Lev. 18:21 [j]Ezek. 38:16   **39:8** [k]Rev. 16:17; 21:6 [l]Ezek. 38:17   **39:10** [m]Is. 14:2; 33:1   **39:12** [n]Deut. 21:23   **39:13** [o]Zeph. 3:19, 20 [p]Ezek. 28:22   **39:14** [q]Ezek. 39:12   **39:16** [r]Ezek. 39:12   **39:17** [s]Rev. 19:17, 18 [t]Is. 18:6 [u]Zeph. 1:7 [v]Ezek. 39:4   **39:18** [w]Rev. 19:18 [x]Deut. 32:14   **39:20** [y]Ps. 76:5, 6 [z]Rev. 19:18   **39:21** [a]Ezek. 36:23; 38:23 [b]Ex. 7:4   **39:22** [c]Ex. 39:7, 28   **39:23** [d]Ezek. 36:18–20, 23 [e]Is. 1:15; 59:2 [f]Lev. 26:25

them into the hand of their enemies, and
they all fell by the sword. 24 [g]According to
their uncleanness and according to their
transgressions I have dealt with them, and
hidden My face from them."'
25 "Therefore thus says the Lord GOD:
[h]'Now I will bring back the captives of
Jacob, and have mercy on the [i]whole
house of Israel; and I will be jealous for
My holy name— 26 [j]after they have borne
their shame, and all their unfaithfulness
in which they were unfaithful to Me, when
they [k]dwelt safely in their *own* land and
no one made *them* afraid. 27 [l]When I have
brought them back from the peoples and
gathered them out of their enemies' lands,
and I [m]am hallowed in them in the sight of
many nations, 28 [n]then they shall know that
I *am* the LORD their God, who sent them
into captivity among the nations, but also
brought them back to their land, and left
none of them captive any longer. 29 [o]And I
will not hide My face from them anymore;
for I shall have [p]poured out My Spirit on
the house of Israel,' says the Lord GOD."

A New City, a New Temple

40 In the twenty-fifth year of our captivity, at the beginning of the year,
on the tenth *day* of the month, in the fourteenth year after [a]the city was captured, on
the very same day [b]the hand of the LORD
was upon me; and He took me there. 2 [c]In
the visions of God He took me into the land
of Israel and [d]set me on a very high mountain; on it toward the south *was* something
like the structure of a city. 3 He took me
there, and behold, *there was* a man whose
appearance *was* [e]like the appearance of
bronze. [f]He had a line of flax [g]and a measuring rod in his hand, and he stood in the
gateway.
4 And the man said to me, [h]"Son of man,
look with your eyes and hear with your
ears, and fix your mind on everything I
show you; for you *were* brought here so
that I might show *them* to you. [i]Declare
to the house of Israel everything you see."
5 Now there was [j]a wall all around the outside of the temple.* In the man's hand was a
measuring rod six cubits *long, each being a*
cubit and a handbreadth; and he measured
the width of the wall structure, one rod;
and the height, one rod.

The Eastern Gateway of the Temple

6 Then he went to the gateway which
faced [k]east; and he went up its stairs and
measured the threshold of the gateway,
which was one rod wide, and the other
threshold *was* one rod wide. 7 Each gate
chamber *was* one rod long and one rod
wide; between the gate chambers *was a*
space of five cubits; and the threshold of
the gateway by the vestibule of the inside
gate *was* one rod. 8 He also measured the
vestibule of the inside gate, one rod. 9 Then
he measured the vestibule of the gateway,
eight cubits; and the gateposts, two cubits.
The vestibule of the gate *was* on the inside.
10 In the eastern gateway *were* three gate
chambers on one side and three on the other; the three *were* all the same size; also the
gateposts were of the same size on this side
and that side.
11 He measured the width of the entrance
to the gateway, ten cubits; *and* the length
of the gate, thirteen cubits. 12 *There was* a
space in front of the gate chambers, one cubit *on this side* and one cubit on that side;
the gate chambers *were* six cubits on this
side and six cubits on that side. 13 Then he
measured the gateway from the roof of *one*
gate chamber to the roof of the other; the
width *was* twenty-five cubits, as door faces door. 14 He measured the gateposts, sixty
cubits high, and the court all around the
gateway *extended* to the gatepost. 15 *From*
the front of the entrance gate to the front
of the vestibule of the inner gate *was* fifty cubits. 16 *There were* [l]beveled window
frames in the gate chambers and in their
intervening archways on the inside of the
gateway all around, and likewise in the
vestibules. *There were* windows all around
on the inside. And on each gatepost *were*
[m]palm trees.

---

*40:5 Literally *house*, and so elsewhere in this book

40:1 *In the twenty-fifth year of our captivity.* The actual date would have been about 573 B.C. This final vision of the temple in the book is one of God returning to dwell in the midst of His people who are now restored in their homeland. These are difficult chapters to interpret because of how easy it is to get bogged down in the architectural details. The writing is apocalyptic in style and expresses in symbolic manner how God would restore Israel in the future.

40:3–5 *a line of flax and a measuring rod in his hand.* This man with a measuring rod is a kind of angelic architect who serves as both a guide and an interpreter for Ezekiel. ***Declare to the house of Israel everything you see.*** The details of the temple would have been of great importance and enormous interest to the exiles because the temple was the focal point of all of their worship.

40:7 *cubits . . . rod.* A cubit was about 18 inches long. A measuring rod was six cubits or nine feet in length.

40:16 *palm trees.* These were common decorations that were also found in Solomon's temple (1 Kin. 6:29–35).

39:24 [g] Ezek. 36:19 **39:25** [h] Ezek. 34:13; 36:24 [i] Hos. 1:11 **39:26** [j] Dan. 9:16 [k] Lev. 26:5, 6 **39:27** [l] Ezek. 28:25, 26 [m] Ezek. 36:23, 24; 38:16 **39:28** [n] Ezek. 34:30 **39:29** [o] Is. 54:8, 9 [p] [Joel 2:28] **40:1** [a] Ezek. 33:21 [b] Ezek. 1:3; 3:14, 22; 37:1 **40:2** [c] Ezek. 1:1; 3:14; 8:3; 37:1 [d] Rev. 21:10 **40:3** [e] Dan. 10:6 [f] Ezek. 47:3 [g] Rev. 11:1; 21:15 **40:4** [h] Ezek. 44:5 [i] Ezek. 43:10 **40:5** [j] Ezek. 42:20 **40:6** [k] Ezek. 43:1 **40:16** [l] 1 Kin. 6:4 [m] 1 Kin. 6:29, 32, 35

The Outer Court

[17]Then he brought me into [n]the outer court; and *there were* [o]chambers and a pavement made all around the court; [p]thirty chambers faced the pavement. [18]The pavement was by the side of the gateways, corresponding to the length of the gateways; *this was* the lower pavement. [19]Then he measured the width from the front of the lower gateway to the front of the inner court exterior, one hundred cubits toward the east and the north.

The Northern Gateway

[20]On the outer court was also a gateway facing north, and he measured its length and its width. [21]Its gate chambers, three on this side and three on that side, its gateposts and its archways, had the same measurements as the first gate; its length *was* fifty cubits and its width twenty-five cubits. [22]Its windows and those of its archways, and also its palm trees, *had* the same measurements as the gateway facing east; it was ascended by seven steps, and its archway *was* in front of it. [23]A gate of the inner court was opposite the northern gateway, just as the eastern *gateway*; and he measured from gateway to gateway, one hundred cubits.

The Southern Gateway

[24]After that he brought me toward the south, and there a gateway was facing south; and he measured its gateposts and archways according to these same measurements. [25]*There were* windows in it and in its archways all around like those windows; its length *was* fifty cubits and its width twenty-five cubits. [26]Seven steps led up to it, and its archway *was* in front of them; and it had palm trees on its gateposts, one on this side and one on that side. [27]*There was* also a gateway on the inner court, facing south; and he measured from gateway to gateway toward the south, one hundred cubits.

Gateways of the Inner Court

[28]Then he brought me to the inner court through the southern gateway; he measured the southern gateway according to these same measurements. [29]Also its gate chambers, its gateposts, and its archways *were* according to these same measurements; *there were* windows in it and in its archways all around; *it was* fifty cubits long and twenty-five cubits wide. [30]*There* were archways all around, [q]twenty-five cubits long and five cubits wide. [31]Its archways faced the outer court, palm trees *were* on its gateposts, and going up to it *were* eight steps.

[32]And he brought me into the inner court facing east; he measured the gateway according to these same measurements. [33]Also its gate chambers, its gateposts, and its archways *were* according to these same measurements; and *there were* windows in it and in its archways all around; *it was* fifty cubits long and twenty-five cubits wide. [34]Its archways faced the outer court, and palm trees *were* on its gateposts on this side and on that side; and going up to it *were* eight steps.

[35]Then he brought me to the north gateway and measured *it* according to these same measurements— [36]also its gate chambers, its gateposts, and its archways. It had windows all around; its length *was* fifty cubits and its width twenty-five cubits. [37]Its gateposts faced the outer court, palm trees *were* on its gateposts on this side and on that side, and going up to it *were* eight steps.

Where Sacrifices Were Prepared

[38]*There was* a chamber and its entrance by the gateposts of the gateway, where they [r]washed the burnt offering. [39]In the vestibule of the gateway *were* two tables on this side and two tables on that side, on which to slay the burnt offering, [s]the sin offering, and [t]the trespass offering. [40]At the outer side of the *vestibule*, as one goes up to the entrance of the northern gateway, *were* two tables; and on the other side of the vestibule of the gateway *were* two tables. [41]Four tables *were* on this side and four tables on that side, by the side of the gateway, eight tables on which they slaughtered *the sacrifices*. [42]*There were* also four tables of hewn stone for the burnt offering, one cubit and a half long, one cubit and a half wide, and one cubit high; on these they laid the instruments with which they slaughtered the burnt offering and the sacrifice. [43]Inside *were* hooks, a handbreadth wide, fastened all around; and the flesh of the sacrifices *was* on the tables.

Chambers for Singers and Priests

[44]Outside the inner gate *were* the chambers for [u]the singers in the inner court,

---

40:22 *ascended by seven steps.* This would indicate that the temple area is a huge raised area, built up above the level of the surrounding land.
40:38–43 *Four tables were on this side . . . on which they slaughtered the sacrifices.* Ezekiel observes a room where the animals are slaughtered and washed for sacrificial offerings. These sacrifices point to the ultimate sacrifice; the sacrifice of God's only Son on the cross once for all (Heb. 7:20–28; 9:25–30).

40:44–47 *chamber . . . for the priests.* The guide explains that the chamber on the north side is for the priests who run the day-to-day operations of the

one facing south at the side of the northern gateway, and the other facing north at the side of the southern* gateway. ⁴⁵Then he said to me, "This chamber which faces south *is* for ᵛthe priests who have charge of the temple. ⁴⁶The chamber which faces north *is* for the priests ʷwho have charge of the altar; these *are* the sons of ˣZadok, from the sons of Levi, who come near the LORD to minister to Him."

Dimensions of the Inner Court and Vestibule

⁴⁷And he measured the court, one hundred cubits long and one hundred cubits wide, foursquare. The altar *was* in front of the temple. ⁴⁸Then he brought me to the ʸvestibule of the temple and measured the doorposts of the vestibule, five cubits on this side and five cubits on that side; and the width of the gateway was three cubits on this side and three cubits on that side. ⁴⁹ᶻThe length of the vestibule *was* twenty cubits, and the width eleven cubits; and by the steps which led up to it *there were* ᵃpillars by the doorposts, one on this side and another on that side.

Dimensions of the Sanctuary

41 Then he ᵃbrought me into the sanctuary* and measured the doorposts, six cubits wide on one side and six cubits wide on the other side—the width of the tabernacle. ²The width of the entryway *was* ten cubits, and the side walls of the entrance *were* five cubits on this side and five cubits on the other side; and he measured its length, forty cubits, and its width, twenty cubits.

³Also he went inside and measured the doorposts, two cubits; and the entrance, six cubits *high*; and the width of the entrance, seven cubits. ⁴ᵇHe measured the length, twenty cubits; and the width, twenty cubits, beyond the sanctuary; and he said to me, "This *is* the Most Holy *Place*."

The Side Chambers on the Wall

⁵Next, he measured the wall of the temple, six cubits. The width of each side chamber *was* four cubits all around the temple on every side. ⁶ᶜThe side chambers *were* in three stories, one above the other, thirty chambers in each story; they rested on ledges which *were* for the side chambers all around, that they might be supported,

but ᵈnot fastened to the wall of the temple. ⁷As one went up from story to story, the side chambers ᵉbecame wider all around, because their supporting ledges in the wall of the temple ascended like steps; therefore the width of the structure increased as one went up *from* the lowest *story* to the highest by way of the middle one. ⁸I also saw an elevation all around the temple; it was the foundation of the side chambers, ᶠa full rod, *that is,* six cubits *high*. ⁹The thickness of the outer wall of the side chambers *was* five cubits, and so also the remaining terrace by the place of the side chambers of the temple. ¹⁰And between *it and* the *wall* chambers was a width of twenty cubits all around the temple on every side. ¹¹The doors of the side chambers opened on the terrace, one door toward the north and another toward the south; and the width of the terrace *was* five cubits all around.

The Building at the Western End

¹²The building that faced the separating courtyard at its western end *was* seventy cubits wide; the wall of the building *was* five cubits thick all around, and its length ninety cubits.

Dimensions and Design of the Temple Area

¹³So he measured the temple, one ᵍhundred cubits long; and the separating courtyard with the building and its walls *was* one hundred cubits long; ¹⁴also the width of the eastern face of the temple, including the separating courtyard, *was* one hundred cubits. ¹⁵He measured the length of the building behind it, facing the separating courtyard, with its ʰgalleries on the one side and on the other side, one hundred cubits, as well as the inner temple and the porches of the court, ¹⁶ⁱthe doorposts and ⁱthe beveled window frames. And the galleries all around their three stories opposite the threshold were paneled with ʲwood from the ground to the windows—the windows were covered— ¹⁷from the space above the door, even to the inner room,*

---

* **40:44** Following Septuagint; Masoretic Text and Vulgate read *eastern.* * **41:1** Hebrew *heykal,* here the main room of the temple, sometimes called the *holy place* (compare Exodus 26:33) * **41:17** Literally *house,* here the Most Holy Place

---

temple. The chamber on the south side is for the priests who perform the sacrifices.

41:1–4 *Then he brought me into the sanctuary.* The basic temple has three areas: the outer area, the holy place or "nave," and the inner area or the "Most Holy Place." The innermost room is the focal point of the whole structure. Only the high priest could enter it and then only once a year on the Day of Atonement.
41:13–15 *So he measured the temple.* Ezekiel would have found pleasure in the symmetrical precision of the temple. It would have meant that it all fit

together perfectly. There was nothing that was out of place. This may represent the order and harmony in God's future kingdom.

40:45 ᵛ Lev. 8:35 **40:46** ʷ Num. 18:5 ˣ 1 Kin. 2:35 **40:48** ʸ 1 Kin. 6:3 **40:49** ᶻ 1 Kin. 6:3 ᵃ 1 Kin. 7:15–22 **41:1** ᵃ Ezek. 40:2, 3, 17 **41:4** ᵇ 1 Kin. 6:20 **41:6** ᶜ 1 Kin. 6:5–10 ᵈ 1 Kin. 6:6, 10 **41:7** ᵉ 1 Kin. 6:8 **41:8** ᶠ Ezek. 40:5 **41:13** ᵍ Ezek. 40:47 **41:15** ʰ Ezek. 42:3, 5 **41:16** ⁱ Ezek. 40:16, 25 ʲ 1 Kin. 6:15

as well as outside, and on every wall all around, inside and outside, by measure.

18And *it was* made [k]with cherubim and [l]palm trees, a palm tree between cherub and cherub. *Each* cherub had two faces, 19[m]so that the face of a man *was* toward a palm tree on one side, and the face of a young lion toward a palm tree on the other side; thus *it was* made throughout the temple all around. 20From the floor to the space above the door, and on the wall of the sanctuary, cherubim and palm trees *were* carved.

21The [n]doorposts of the temple *were* square, *as was* the front of the sanctuary; their appearance was similar. 22[o]The altar *was* of wood, three cubits high, and its length two cubits. Its corners, its length, and its sides *were* of wood; and he said to me, "This *is* [p]the table that *is* [q]before the LORD."

23[r]The temple and the sanctuary had two doors. 24The doors had two [s]panels *apiece,* two folding panels: two *panels* for one door and two panels for the other *door.* 25Cherubim and palm trees *were* carved on the doors of the temple just as they *were* carved on the walls. A wooden canopy *was* on the front of the vestibule outside. 26*There were* [t]beveled window *frames* and palm trees on one side and on the other, on the sides of the vestibule—also on the side chambers of the temple and on the canopies.

The Chambers for the Priests

42 Then he [a]brought me out into the outer court, by the way toward the [b]north; and he brought me into [c]the chamber which *was* opposite the separating courtyard, and which *was* opposite the building toward the north. 2Facing the length, *which was* one hundred cubits (the width was fifty cubits), was the north door. 3Opposite the inner court of twenty *cubits,* and opposite the [d]pavement of the outer court, *was* [e]gallery against gallery in three *stories.* 4In front of the chambers, toward the inside, *was* a walk ten cubits wide, at a distance of one cubit; and their doors faced north. 5Now the upper chambers *were* shorter, because the galleries

took away *space* from them more than from the lower and middle stories of the building. 6For they *were* in three *stories* and did not have pillars like the pillars of the courts; therefore *the upper level* was shortened more than the lower and middle levels from the ground up. 7And a wall which *was* outside ran parallel to the chambers, at the front of the chambers, toward the outer court; its length *was* fifty cubits. 8The length of the chambers toward the outer court *was* fifty cubits, whereas that facing the temple *was* one [f]hundred cubits. 9At the lower chambers *was* the entrance on the east side, as one goes into them from the outer court.

10Also *there were* chambers in the thickness of the wall of the court toward the east, opposite the separating courtyard and opposite the building. 11[g]*There was* a walk in front of them also, and their appearance *was* like the chambers which *were* toward the north; they *were* as long and as wide as the others, and all their exits and entrances *were* according to plan. 12And corresponding to the doors of the chambers that *were* facing south, as one enters them, *there was* a door in front of the walk, the way directly in front of the wall toward the east.

13Then he said to me, "The north chambers *and* the south chambers, which *are* opposite the separating courtyard, *are* the holy chambers where the priests who approach the LORD [h]shall eat the most holy offerings. There they shall lay the most holy offerings—[i]the grain offering, the sin offering, and the trespass offering—for the place *is* holy. 14[i]When the priests enter them, they shall not go out of the holy *chamber* into the outer court; but there they shall leave their garments in which they minister, for they *are* holy. They shall put on other garments; then they may approach *that* which *is* for the people."

Outer Dimensions of the Temple

15Now when he had finished measuring the inner temple, he brought me out through the gateway that faces toward the [k]east, and measured it all around. 16He measured the east side with the

---

41:22 *This is the table that is before the LORD.* This is a reference to the table that held the showbread or bread of the Presence (Ex. 25:23–30), a reminder that man lives his whole life constantly in the divine presence. When God is not present to bless His people, their worship is unacceptable, because such worship will inevitably be merely formal and devoid of blessing. When God is present with His people in worship, they are then enabled to worship.

42:1–14 *Then he brought me out into the outer court.* At this point the text has given us many details of the physical descriptions of the temple. No references have been made to God's spiritual presence. Ezekiel has set the scene for the return of the Lord to His temple and city.

42:13–14 *holy chambers where the priests who*

approach the LORD shall eat. This chapter focuses on the buildings designed for the use of the priests. They were used for storage, changing, and eating.

42:15–20 *he brought me out.* After seeing the inside of the temple area, the guide takes Ezekiel to see the surrounding grounds.

41:18 [k] 1 Kin. 6:29 [l] Ezek. 40:16 41:19 [m] Ezek. 1:10; 10:14 41:21 [n] 1 Kin. 6:33 41:22 [o] Ex. 30:1–3 [p] Ex. 25:23, 30 [q] Ex. 30:8 41:23 [r] 1 Kin. 6:31–35 41:24 [s] 1 Kin. 6:34 41:26 [t] Ezek. 40:16 42:1 [a] Ezek. 41:1 [b] Ezek. 40:20 [c] Ezek. 41:12, 15 42:3 [d] Ezek. 40:17 [e] Ezek. 41:15, 16; 42:5 42:8 [f] Ezek. 41:13, 14 42:11 [g] Ezek. 42:4 42:13 [h] Lev. 6:16, 26; 24:9 [i] Lev. 2:3, 10; 6:14, 17, 25 42:14 [i] Ezek. 44:19 42:15 [k] Ezek. 40:6; 43:1

measuring rod,* five hundred rods by the measuring rod all around. [17]He measured the north side, five hundred rods by the measuring rod all around. [18]He measured the south side, five hundred rods by the measuring rod. [19]He came around to the west side and measured five hundred rods by the measuring rod. [20]He measured it on the four sides; [l]it had a wall all around, [m]five hundred cubits long and five hundred wide, to separate the holy areas from the common.

The Temple, the LORD's Dwelling Place

43 Afterward he brought me to the gate, the gate [a]that faces toward the east. [2b]And behold, the glory of the God of Israel came from the way of the east. [c]His voice was like the sound of many waters; [d]and the earth shone with His glory. [3]It was [e]like the appearance of the vision which I saw—like the vision which I saw when I* came [f]to destroy the city. The visions were like the vision which I saw [g]by the River Chebar; and I fell on my face. [4h]And the glory of the LORD came into the temple by way of the gate which faces toward the east. [5i]The Spirit lifted me up and brought me into the inner court; and behold, [j]the glory of the LORD filled the temple.

[6]Then I heard Him speaking to me from the temple, while [k]a man stood beside me. [7]And He said to me, "Son of man, this is [l]the place of My throne and [m]the place of the soles of My feet, [n]where I will dwell in the midst of the children of Israel forever. [o]No more shall the house of Israel defile My holy name, they nor their kings, by their harlotry or with [p]the carcasses of their kings on their high places. [8q]When they set their threshold by My threshold, and their doorpost by My doorpost, with a wall between them and Me, they defiled My holy name by the abominations which they committed; therefore I have consumed them in My anger. [9]Now let them put their harlotry and the carcasses of their kings far away from Me, and I will dwell in their midst forever.

[10]"Son of man, [r]describe the temple to the house of Israel, that they may be ashamed of their iniquities; and let them measure the pattern. [11]And if they are ashamed of all that they have done, make known to them the design of the temple and its arrangement, its exits and its entrances, its entire design and all its [s]ordinances, all its forms and all its laws. Write it down in their sight, so that they may keep its whole design and all its ordinances, and [t]perform them. [12]This is the law of the temple: The whole area surrounding [u]the mountaintop is most holy. Behold, this is the law of the temple.

Dimensions of the Altar

[13]"These are the measurements of the [v]altar in cubits [w](the cubit is one cubit and a handbreadth): the base one cubit high and one cubit wide, with a rim all around its edge of one span. This is the height of the altar: [14]from the base on the ground to the lower ledge, two cubits; the width of the ledge, one cubit; from the smaller ledge to the larger ledge, four cubits; and the width of the ledge, one cubit. [15]The altar hearth is four cubits high, with four [x]horns extending upward from the hearth. [16]The altar hearth is twelve cubits long, twelve wide, [y]square at its four corners; [17]the ledge, fourteen cubits long and fourteen wide on its four sides, with a rim of half a cubit around it; its base, one cubit all around; and [z]its steps face toward the east."

Consecrating the Altar

[18]And He said to me, "Son of man, thus says the Lord GOD: 'These are the ordinances for the altar on the day when it is made, for sacrificing [a]burnt offerings on it, and for [b]sprinkling blood on it. [19]You shall give [c]a young bull for a sin offering to [d]the priests, the Levites, who are of the seed of [e]Zadok, who approach Me to minister to Me,' says the Lord GOD. [20]'You shall take some of its blood and put it on the four horns of the altar, on the four corners of the ledge, and on the rim around it; thus you shall cleanse it and make atonement for it. [21]Then you shall also take the bull of the sin offering, and [f]burn it in the appointed place of the temple, [g]outside the

---

* **42:16** Compare 40:5   * **43:3** Some Hebrew manuscripts and Vulgate read He.

43:2 the glory of the God of Israel came. Nineteen years before, Ezekiel had a vision of the Lord leaving His temple (10:18–22; 11:22–24). Now he gets a chance to see His return. Ezekiel's response is one of being overwhelmed with awe.
43:3 the River Chebar. This was where the Jewish exiles were located in Babylonia.
43:7–12 I will dwell in the midst of the children of Israel forever. When God left Jerusalem, it rapidly moved towards destruction. Here, when God returned, everything was rebuilt as a permanent dwelling. The Lord stipulated that Israel was not to defile God's holiness as it had done in the past.
43:20–23 cleanse . . . sin offering. These suggest

purification and cleansing from sin. Because of the sinlessness—without blemish—of the sacrifice, the

42:20 [l] Ezek. 40:5   [m] Ezek. 45:2   **43:1** [a] Ezek. 10:19; 46:1   **43:2** [b] Ezek. 11:23   [c] Rev. 1:15; 14:2   [d] Rev. 18:1   **43:3** [e] Ezek. 1:4–28   [f] Jer. 1:10   [g] Ezek. 1:28; 3:23   **43:4** [h] Ezek. 10:19; 11:23   **43:5** [i] Ezek. 3:12, 14; 8:3   [j] 1 Kin. 8:10, 11   **43:6** [k] Ezek. 1:26; 40:3   **43:7** [l] Ps. 99:1   [m] 1 Chr. 28:2   [n] Joel 3:17   [o] Ezek. 39:7   [p] Lev. 26:30   **43:8** [q] Ezek. 8:3; 23:39; 44:7   **43:10** [r] Ezek. 40:4   **43:11** [s] Ezek. 44:5   [t] Ezek. 11:20   **43:12** [u] Ezek. 40:2   **43:13** [v] Ex. 27:1–8   [w] Ezek. 41:8   **43:15** [x] Ex. 27:2   **43:16** [y] Ex. 27:1   **43:17** [z] Ex. 20:26   **43:18** [a] Ex. 40:29   [b] Lev. 1:5, 11   **43:19** [c] Lev. 8:14   [d] Ezek. 44:15, 16   [e] Ezek. 40:46   **43:21** [f] Ex. 29:14   [g] Heb. 13:11

sanctuary. [22]On the second day you shall offer a kid of the goats without blemish for a sin offering; and they shall cleanse the altar, as they cleansed it with the bull. [23]When you have finished cleansing it, you shall offer a young bull without blemish, and a ram from the flock without blemish. [24]When you offer them before the LORD, [h]the priests shall throw salt on them, and they will offer them up as a burnt offering to the LORD. [25]Every day for [i]seven days you shall prepare a goat for a sin offering; they shall also prepare a young bull and a ram from the flock, both without blemish. [26]Seven days they shall make atonement for the altar and purify it, and so consecrate it. [27j]When these days are over it shall be, on the eighth day and thereafter, that the priests shall offer your burnt offerings and your peace offerings on the altar; and I will [k]accept you,' says the Lord GOD."

The East Gate and the Prince

44 Then He brought me back to the outer gate of the sanctuary [a]which faces toward the east, but it was shut. [2]And the LORD said to me, "This gate shall be shut; it shall not be opened, and no man shall enter by it, [b]because the LORD God of Israel has entered by it; therefore it shall be shut. [3]As for the [c]prince, because he is the prince, he may sit in it to [d]eat bread before the LORD; he shall enter by way of the vestibule of the gateway, and go out the same way."

Those Admitted to the Temple

[4]Also He brought me by way of the north gate to the front of the temple; so I looked, and [e]behold, the glory of the LORD filled the house of the LORD; [f]and I fell on my face. [5]And the LORD said to me, [g]"Son of man, mark well, see with your eyes and hear with your ears, all that I say to you concerning all the [h]ordinances of the house of the LORD and all its laws. Mark well who may enter the house and all who go out from the sanctuary.

[6]"Now say to the [i]rebellious, to the house of Israel, 'Thus says the Lord GOD: "O house of Israel, [j]let Us have no more of all your abominations. [7k]When you brought in [l]foreigners, [m]uncircumcised in heart and uncircumcised in flesh, to be in My sanctuary to defile it—My house—and when you offered [n]My food, [o]the fat and the blood, then they broke My covenant because of all your abominations. [8]And you have not [p]kept charge of My holy things, but you have set others to keep charge of My sanctuary for you." [9]Thus says the Lord GOD: [q]"No foreigner, uncircumcised in heart or uncircumcised in flesh, shall enter My sanctuary, including any foreigner who is among the children of Israel.

Laws Governing Priests

[10r]"And the Levites who went far from Me, when Israel went astray, who strayed away from Me after their idols, they shall bear their iniquity. [11]Yet they shall be ministers in My sanctuary, [s]as gatekeepers of the house and ministers of the house; [t]they shall slay the burnt offering and the sacrifice for the people, and [u]they shall stand before them to minister to them. [12]Because they ministered to them before their idols and [v]caused the house of Israel to fall into iniquity, therefore I have [w]raised My hand in an oath against them," says the Lord GOD, "that they shall bear their iniquity. [13x]And they shall not come near Me to minister to Me as priest, nor come near any of My holy things, nor into the Most Holy Place; but they shall [y]bear their shame and their abominations which they have committed. [14]Nevertheless I will make them [z]keep charge of the temple, for all its work, and for all that has to be done in it.

[15a]"But the priests, the Levites, [b]the sons of Zadok, who kept charge of My sanctuary [c]when the children of Israel went astray from Me, they shall come near Me to minister to Me; and they [d]shall stand before Me to offer to Me the [e]fat and the blood," says the Lord GOD. [16]"They shall [f]enter My sanctuary, and they shall come near [g]My table to minister to Me, and they shall keep My charge. [17]And it shall be, whenever they enter the gates of the inner court, that [h]they shall put on linen garments; no wool shall

---

people for whom the sacrifice is made are declared acceptable before God (v. 27; Ex. 29:14; Lev. 3; 4:12).

44:1–3 This gate shall be shut. Today this is known as the "Golden Gate" and dates from several centuries after Christ. It is walled shut today in accordance with an Islamic tradition.

44:4–9 I looked . . . I fell on my face. Ezekiel experiences another awe-inspiring vision of God's glory leading him to bow in worship (1:28—2:1). God demands that His renewed people follow His regulations exactly. He emphasizes the necessity of holiness and righteousness, especially in light of Israel's past.

44:11–14 Yet they shall be ministers in My sanctuary. God explains to Ezekiel why the Levites would be limited to certain types of temple ministry. The Levites (with the exception of the sons of Zadok; v. 15) could not be priests but could be ministers (servants

or attendants). They could not serve in the inner court or temple, where the holy things are located; but they could oversee the general operation of the temple complex.

43:24 [h] Lev. 2:13   **43:25** [i] Ex. 29:35   **43:27** [j] Lev. 9:1–4
[k] Ezek. 20:40, 41   **44:1** [a] Ezek. 43:1   **44:2** [b] Ezek. 43:2–4
44:3 [c] Gen. 31:54   [d] Ezek. 46:2, 8   **44:4** [e] Ezek. 3:23; 43:5
[f] Ezek. 1:28; 43:3   **44:5** [g] Ezek. 40:4   [h] Ezek. 43:10, 11
44:6 [i] Ezek. 2:5   [j] 1 Pet. 4:3   **44:7** [k] Acts 21:28   [l] Lev. 22:25
[m] Lev. 26:41   [n] Lev. 21:17   [o] Lev. 3:16   **44:8** [p] Lev. 22:2
44:9 [q] Ezek. 44:7   **44:10** [r] 2 Kin. 23:8   **44:11** [s] 1 Chr.
26:1–19   [t] 2 Chr. 29:34; 30:17   [u] Num. 16:9   **44:12** [v] Is.
9:16   [w] Ps. 106:26   **44:13** [x] 2 Kin. 23:9   [y] Ezek. 32:30
44:14 [z] Num. 18:4   **44:15** [a] Ezek. 40:46   [b] [1 Sam. 2:35]
[c] Ezek. 44:10   [d] Deut. 10:8   [e] Ezek. 44:7   **44:16** [f] Num.
18:5, 7, 8   [g] Ezek. 41:22   **44:17** [h] Ex. 28:39–43; 39:27–29

come upon them while they minister within the gates of the inner court or within the house. [18i]They shall have linen turbans on their heads and linen trousers on their bodies; they shall not clothe themselves with *anything that causes* sweat. [19]When they go out to the outer court, to the outer court to the people, [j]they shall take off their garments in which they have ministered, leave them in the holy chambers, and put on other garments; and in their holy garments they shall [k]not sanctify the people.

[20l]"They shall neither shave their heads nor let their hair grow [m]long, but they shall keep their hair well trimmed. [21n]No priest shall drink wine when he enters the inner court. [22]They shall not take as wife a [o]widow or a divorced woman, but take virgins of the descendants of the house of Israel, or widows of priests.

[23]"And [p]they shall teach My people the difference between the holy and the unholy, and cause them to [q]discern between the unclean and the clean. [24r]In controversy they shall stand as judges, *and* judge it according to My judgments. They shall keep My laws and My statutes in all My appointed meetings, [s]and they shall hallow My Sabbaths.

[25]"They shall not defile *themselves* by coming near a dead person. Only for father or mother, for son or daughter, for brother or unmarried sister may they defile themselves. [26t]After he is cleansed, they shall count seven days for him. [27]And on the day that he goes to the sanctuary to minister in the sanctuary, [u]he must offer his sin offering [v]in the inner court," says the Lord GOD.

[28]"It shall be, in regard to their inheritance, *that* I [w]am their inheritance. You shall give them no [x]possession in Israel, for I *am* their possession. [29y]They shall eat the grain offering, the sin offering, and the trespass offering; [z]every dedicated thing in Israel shall be theirs. [30]The [a]best of all firstfruits of any kind, and every sacrifice of any kind from all your sacrifices, shall

be the priest's; also you [b]shall give to the priest the first of your ground meal, [c]to cause a blessing to rest on your house. [31]The priests shall not eat anything, bird or beast, that [d]died naturally or was torn *by wild beasts.*

The Holy District

45 "Moreover, when you [a]divide the land by lot into inheritance, you shall [b]set apart a district for the LORD, a holy section of the land; its length *shall be* twenty-five thousand *cubits*, and the width ten thousand. It *shall be* holy throughout its territory all around. [2]Of this there shall be a square plot for the sanctuary, [c]five hundred by five hundred *rods*, with fifty cubits around it for an open space. [3]So this is the district you shall measure: twenty-five thousand *cubits* long and ten thousand wide; [d]in it shall be the sanctuary, the Most Holy *Place.* [4]It shall be [e]a holy *section* of the land, belonging to the priests, the ministers of the sanctuary, who come near to minister to the LORD; it shall be a place for their houses and a holy place for the sanctuary. [5f]*An area* twenty-five thousand *cubits* long and ten thousand wide shall belong to the Levites, the ministers of the temple; they shall have [g]twenty chambers as a possession.*

Properties of the City and the Prince

[6h]"You shall appoint as the property of the city *an area* five thousand *cubits* wide and twenty-five thousand long, adjacent to the district of the holy *section*; it shall belong to the whole house of Israel.

[7i]"The prince shall have *a section* on one side and the other of the holy district and the city's property; and bordering on the holy district and the city's property,

---

* **45:5** Following Masoretic Text, Targum, and Vulgate; Septuagint reads *a possession, cities of dwelling.*

44:23 they shall teach My people the difference between the holy and the unholy. These verses speak of holiness in conduct. These regulations continued practices already prescribed in the law of Moses (Lev. 10:6,9; 21:1–7,10,14). Their aim was to help the priests avoid conformity to the immoral and idolatrous religious rituals and conduct among the pagan nations. The priests, then and in the future, have the responsibility of modeling and maintaining the highest standards of morality, self-control, self-denial, discipline, and obedience to God's will.

44:28 I am their possession. God was to be the priests' inheritance in all respects; they were not to inherit land or cities.

45:1–5 a holy section of the land. A distinct or holy section was to be allocated for God. This area would be divided into two equal sections. One would be the portion for the Zadokites. In the center of this part of the holy district is the holy square-mile environs for the temple. The other half of the holy district would

be the portion given to the Levites. All this is holy; God owns it.

45:6 the city. Most likely the city is Jerusalem.

45:7–8 The prince . . . My princes. Their identity is unknown (44:3), but the allotted area is on both sides of the holy district. The prince and God's princes of the messianic period—in contrast to previous leaders of Israel (11:1–13; 14:1–11,20–22; 34:1–10)—will

44:18 [i]Ex. 28:40; 39:28   **44:19** [j]Ezek. 42:14   [k]Lev. 6:27   **44:20** [l]Lev. 21:5   [m]Num. 6:5   **44:21** [n]Lev. 10:9   **44:22** [o]Lev. 21:7, 13, 14   **44:23** [p]Mal. 2:6–8   [q]Lev. 20:25   **44:24** [r]Deut. 17:8, 9   [s]Ezek. 22:26   **44:26** [t]Num. 6:10; 19:11, 13–19   **44:27** [u]Lev. 5:3, 6   [v]Ezek. 44:17   **44:28** [w]Num. 18:20   [x]Ezek. 45:4   **44:29** [y]Lev. 7:6   [z]Lev. 27:21, 28   **44:30** [a]Num. 3:13; 18:12   [b]Neh. 10:37   [c][Mal. 3:10]   **44:31** [d]Lev. 22:8   **45:1** [a]Ezek. 47:22   [b]Ezek. 48:8, 9   **45:2** [c]Ezek. 42:20   **45:3** [d]Ezek. 48:10   **45:4** [e]Ezek. 48:10, 11   **45:5** [f]Ezek. 48:13   [g]Ezek. 40:17   **45:6** [h]Ezek. 48:15   **45:7** [i]Ezek. 48:21

extending westward on the west side and eastward on the east side, the length *shall be* side by side with one of the *tribal* portions, from the west border to the east border. [8]The land shall be his possession in Israel; and [i]My princes shall no more oppress My people, but they shall give *the rest of* the land to the house of Israel, according to their tribes."

Laws Governing the Prince

[9]'Thus says the Lord GOD: [k]"Enough, O princes of Israel! [l]Remove violence and plundering, execute justice and righteousness, and stop dispossessing My people," says the Lord GOD. [10]"You shall have [m]honest scales, an honest ephah, and an honest bath. [11]The ephah and the bath shall be of the same measure, so that the bath contains one-tenth of a homer, and the ephah one-tenth of a homer; their measure shall be according to the homer. [12]The [n]shekel *shall be* twenty gerahs; twenty shekels, twenty-five shekels, *and* fifteen shekels shall be your mina.

[13]"This *is* the offering which you shall offer: you shall give one-sixth of an ephah from a homer of wheat, and one-sixth of an ephah from a homer of barley. [14]The ordinance concerning oil, the bath of oil, *is* one-tenth of a bath from a kor. *A kor is* a homer or ten baths, for ten baths *are* a homer. [15]And one lamb shall be given from a flock of two hundred, from the rich pastures of Israel. These shall be for grain offerings, burnt offerings, and peace offerings, [o]to make atonement for them," says the Lord GOD. [16]"All the people of the land shall give this offering for the prince in Israel. [17]Then it shall be the [p]prince's part *to give* burnt offerings, grain offerings, and drink offerings, at the feasts, the New Moons, the Sabbaths, and at all the appointed seasons of the house of Israel. He shall prepare the sin offering, the grain offering, the burnt offering, and the peace offerings to make atonement for the house of Israel."

Keeping the Feasts

[18]'Thus says the Lord GOD: "In the first *month*, on the first *day* of the month, you shall take a young bull without blemish and [q]cleanse the sanctuary. [19][r]The priest shall take some of the blood of the sin offering and put *it* on the doorposts of the temple, on the four corners of the ledge of the altar, and on the gateposts of the gate of the inner court. [20]And so you shall do on the seventh *day* of the month [s]for everyone who has sinned unintentionally or in ignorance. Thus you shall make atonement for the temple.

[21][t]"In the first *month*, on the fourteenth day of the month, you shall observe the Passover, a feast of seven days; unleavened bread shall be eaten. [22]And on that day the prince shall prepare for himself and for all the people of the land [u]a bull *for* a sin offering. [23]On the [v]seven days of the feast he shall prepare a burnt offering to the LORD, seven bulls and seven rams without blemish, daily for seven days, [w]and a kid of the goats daily *for* a sin offering. [24][x]And he shall prepare a grain offering of one ephah for each bull and one ephah for each ram, together with a hin of oil for each ephah.

[25]"In the seventh *month*, on the fifteenth day of the month, at the [y]feast, he shall do likewise for seven days, according to the sin offering, the burnt offering, the grain offering, and the oil."

The Manner of Worship

46 'Thus says the Lord GOD: "The gateway of the inner court that faces toward the east shall be shut the six [a]working days; but on the Sabbath it shall be opened, and on the day of the New Moon it shall be opened. [2][b]The prince shall enter by way of the vestibule of the gateway from the outside, and stand by the gatepost. The priests shall prepare his burnt offering and his peace offerings. He shall worship at the threshold of the gate. Then he shall go out, but the gate shall not be shut until evening. [3]Likewise the people of the land shall

---

not be greedy for riches and real estate but will give the land that remains to the people.
45:10–11 You shall have honest scales. The merchants were exhorted to use accurate measures. They must not cheat anymore when weighing produce (Lev. 19:35; Amos 8:5; Mic. 6:10–12). God called for an end to dishonesty and deceit; a time is coming when all such scheming will end (37:15–28).
45:18 In the first month, on the first day of the month. This is an annual day of purifying the temple sanctuary. In the light of Jesus' death on the cross, the actions of the prince symbolize and emphasize that God has made atonement for all through the sacrifice of the Messiah. The prince represents the people in these actions of worship.
45:21 you shall observe the Passover, a feast of seven days. In this passage the Feasts of Passover and Tabernacles are observed (Ex. 12:1–14; Lev.

23:5–8,33–43; Num. 28:16–25). The dates are in relation to the Levitical calendar, the Jewish religious year. The procedures as well are very similar to those of the Mosaic system. These feasts commemorate God's faithfulness to His promises.
46:1–8 The prince shall enter. What the rituals signified under the law was fulfilled by the Messiah. At the time of this prince, certain promises were being fulfilled and the covenants consummated in the messianic age (40:6–16,28–37; 43:18–27; Ex. 20:8–11).

45:8 [j]Ezek. 22:27   **45:9** [k]Ezek. 44:6   [l]Jer. 22:3
45:10 [m]Lev. 19:36   **45:12** [n]Ex. 30:13   **45:15** [o]Lev. 1:4;
6:30   **45:17** [p]Ezek. 46:4–12   **45:18** [q]Lev. 16:16, 33
45:19 [r]Ezek. 43:20   **45:20** [s]Lev. 4:27   **45:21** [t]Ex. 12:18
45:22 [u]Lev. 4:14   **45:23** [v]Lev. 23:8   [w]Num. 28:15, 22,
30; 29:5, 11, 16, 19   **45:24** [x]Ezek. 46:5, 7   **45:25** [y]Num.
29:12   **46:1** [a]Ex. 20:9   **46:2** [b]Ezek. 44:3

worship at the entrance to this gateway
before the LORD on the Sabbaths and the
New Moons. 4 The burnt offering that [c]the
prince offers to the LORD on the [d]Sabbath
day *shall be* six lambs without blemish,
and a ram without blemish; 5 [e]and the grain
offering *shall be one* ephah for a ram, and
the grain offering for the lambs, as much as
he wants to give, as well as a hin of oil with
every ephah. 6 On the day of the New Moon
it shall be a young bull without blemish,
six lambs, and a ram; they shall be without
blemish. 7 He shall prepare a grain offering
of an ephah for a bull, an ephah for a ram,
as much as he wants to give for the lambs,
and a hin of oil with every ephah. 8 [f]When
the prince enters, he shall go in by way of
the vestibule of the gateway, and go out the
same way.

9 "But when the people of the land [g]come
before the LORD on the appointed feast
days, whoever enters by way of the north
[h]gate to worship shall go out by way of the
south gate; and whoever enters by way of
the south gate shall go out by way of the
north gate. He shall not return by way of
the gate through which he came, but shall
go out through the opposite gate. 10 The
prince shall then be in their midst. When
they go in, he shall go in; and when they
go out, he shall go out. 11 At the festivals
and the appointed feast days [i]the grain
offering shall be an ephah for a bull, an
ephah for a ram, as much as he wants to
give for the lambs, and a hin of oil with
every ephah.

12 "Now when the prince makes a voluntary burnt offering or voluntary peace
offering to the LORD, the gate that faces toward the east [j]shall then be opened for him;
and he shall prepare his burnt offering and
his peace offerings as he did on the Sabbath day. Then he shall go out, and after he
goes out the gate shall be shut.

13 [k]"You shall daily make a burnt offering to the LORD *of* a lamb of the first year
without blemish; you shall prepare it every
morning. 14 And you shall prepare a grain
offering with it every morning, a sixth
of an ephah, and a third of a hin of oil to
moisten the fine flour. This grain offering
is a perpetual ordinance, to be made regularly to the LORD. 15 Thus they shall prepare
the lamb, the grain offering, and the oil, *as*
a [l]regular burnt offering every morning."

The Prince and Inheritance Laws

16 'Thus says the Lord GOD: "If the prince
gives a gift *of some* of his inheritance to
any of his sons, it shall belong to his sons;
it is their possession by inheritance. 17 But if
he gives a gift of some of his inheritance to
one of his servants, it shall be his until [m]the
year of liberty, after which it shall return to
the prince. But his inheritance shall belong
to his sons; it shall become theirs. 18 Moreover [n]the prince shall not take any of the
people's inheritance by evicting them from
their property; he shall provide an inheritance for his sons from his own property,
so that none of My people may be scattered
from his property." ' "

How the Offerings Were Prepared

19 Now he brought me through the entrance, which *was* at the side of the gate,
into the holy [o]chambers of the priests
which face toward the north; and there a
place *was* situated at their extreme western
end. 20 And he said to me, "This *is* the place
where the priests shall [p]boil the trespass
offering and the sin offering, *and* where
they shall [q]bake the grain offering, so that
they do not bring *them* out into the outer
court [r]to sanctify the people."

21 Then he brought me out into the outer
court and caused me to pass by the four
corners of the court; and in fact, in every
corner of the court *there was another*
court. 22 In the four corners of the court
were enclosed courts, forty *cubits* long and
thirty wide; all four corners *were* the same
size. 23 *There was* a row *of building stones*
all around in them, all around the four of
them; and cooking hearths were made under the rows of stones all around. 24 And he
said to me, "These *are* the kitchens where
the ministers of the temple shall [s]boil the
sacrifices of the people."

The Healing Waters and Trees

47 Then he brought me back to the door
of the temple; and there was [a]water,
flowing from under the threshold of the
temple toward the east, for the front of the
temple faced east; the water was flowing
from under the right side of the temple,
south of the altar. 2 He brought me out by
way of the north gate, and led me around
on the outside to the outer gateway that

46:9 ***He shall not return by the way of the gate through which he came.*** The prescribed protocol was probably to ensure an orderly procession and service. Such regulations would be needed on the special feast days due to the participation of large numbers of people.

46:14 ***a perpetual ordinance.*** This is a change from the provisions in the law (Num. 28:5). God's people cannot be reminded too often of God's provisions for them; nor can they thank Him too much or too frequently.

46:24 ***These are the kitchens.*** These were kitchen areas for the people to boil their sacrifices. The temple was a place for sacrificing, cooking, and eating. To combine the two elements is healthy for spiritual fellowship.

46:4 [c] Ezek. 45:17 [d] Num. 28:9, 10 **46:5** [e] Ezek. 45:24; 46:7, 11 **46:8** [f] Ezek. 44:3; 46:2 **46:9** [g] Ex. 23:14–17; 34:23 [h] Ezek. 48:31, 33 **46:11** [i] Ezek. 46:5, 7 **46:12** [j] Ezek. 44:3; 46:1, 2, 8 **46:13** [k] Num. 28:3–5 **46:15** [l] Ex. 29:42 **46:17** [m] Lev. 25:10 **46:18** [n] Ezek. 45:8 **46:19** [o] Ezek. 42:13 **46:20** [p] 2 Chr. 35:13 [q] Lev. 2:4, 5, 7 [r] Ezek. 44:19 **46:24** [s] Ezek. 46:20 **47:1** [a] Joel 3:18

faces *b*east; and there was water, running out on the right side.

³And when *c*the man went out to the east with the line in his hand, he measured one thousand cubits, and he brought me through the waters; the water *came up to my* ankles. ⁴Again he measured one thousand and brought me through the waters; the water *came up to my* knees. Again he measured one thousand and brought me through; the water *came up to my* waist. ⁵Again he measured one thousand, *and it was* a river that I could not cross; for the water was too deep, water in which one must swim, a river that could not be crossed. ⁶He said to me, "Son of man, have you seen *this*?" Then he brought me and returned me to the bank of the river.

⁷When I returned, there, along the bank of the river, *were* very many *d*trees on one side and the other. ⁸Then he said to me: "This water flows toward the eastern region, goes down into the valley, and enters the sea. *When it* reaches the sea, *its* waters are healed. ⁹And it shall be *that* every living thing that moves, wherever the rivers go, will live. There will be a very great multitude of fish, because these waters go there; for they will be healed, and everything will live wherever the river goes. ¹⁰It shall be *that* fishermen will stand by it from En Gedi to En Eglaim; they will be *places* for spreading their nets. Their fish will be of the same kinds as the fish *e*of the Great Sea, exceedingly many. ¹¹But its swamps and marshes will not be healed; they will be given over to salt. ¹²*f*Along the bank of the river, on this side and that, will grow all *kinds of* trees used for food; *g*their leaves will not wither, and their fruit will not fail. They will bear fruit every month, because their water flows from the sanctuary. Their fruit will be for food, and their leaves for *h*medicine."

Borders of the Land

¹³Thus says the Lord GOD: "These *are* the *i*borders by which you shall divide the land as an inheritance among the twelve tribes of Israel. *j*Joseph *shall have two* portions. ¹⁴You shall inherit it equally with one another; for I *k*raised My hand in an oath to give it to your fathers, and this land shall *l*fall to you as your inheritance.

¹⁵"This *shall be* the border of the land on the north: from the Great Sea, by *m*the road to Hethlon, as one goes to *n*Zedad, ¹⁶*o*Hamath, *p*Berothah, Sibraim (which *is* between the border of Damascus and the border of Hamath), to Hazar Hatticon (which *is* on the border of Hauran). ¹⁷Thus the boundary shall be from the Sea to *q*Hazar Enan, the border of Damascus; and as for the north, northward, it is the border of Hamath. *This is* the north side.

¹⁸"On the east side you shall mark out the border from between Hauran and Damascus, and between Gilead and the land of Israel, along the Jordan, and along the eastern side of the sea. *This is* the east side.

¹⁹"The south side, toward the South,* *shall be* from Tamar to *r*the waters of Meribah by Kadesh, along the brook to the Great Sea. *This is* the south side, toward the South.

²⁰"The west side *shall be* the Great Sea, from the *southern* boundary until one comes to a point opposite Hamath. This *is* the west side.

²¹"Thus you shall *s*divide this land among yourselves according to the tribes of Israel. ²²It shall be that you will divide it by *t*lot as an inheritance for yourselves, *u*and for the strangers who dwell among you and who bear children among you. *v*They shall be to you as native-born among the children of Israel; they shall have an inheritance with you among the tribes of Israel. ²³And it shall be *that* in whatever tribe the stranger dwells, there you shall give *him* his inheritance," says the Lord GOD.

Division of the Land

48 "Now these *are* the names of the tribes: *a*From the northern border along the road to Hethlon at the entrance of Hamath, to Hazar Enan, the border of Damascus northward, in the direction of Hamath, there shall *be* one *section for* *b*Dan from its east to its west side; ²by the border of Dan, from the east side to the west, one *section for* *c*Asher; ³by the border of Asher, from the east side to the west, one *section for* *d*Naphtali; ⁴by the border

* **47:19** Hebrew *Negev*

47:7–12 their water flows from the sanctuary. The living water that God will provide has immeasurable power to renew, restore, and resurrect life. The water is a river of healing and the source of abundant life for everything and everyone.

47:14 You shall inherit it equally. Equality of inheritance is stressed. The unilateral and unconditional nature of the Abrahamic covenant is suggested; this inheritance is a free gift of God's grace which God's people did and could do nothing to deserve.

47:21–23 and for the strangers. Non-Israelites who married and settled within the Jewish communities were to be accepted as native Israelites, qualified to

share in the territorial inheritance of whatever tribe they joined (Lev. 19:34).

48:1 Now these are the names. The land would be

47:2 *b* Ezek. 44:1, 2   **47:3** *c* Ezek. 40:3   **47:7** *d* [Rev. 22:2]   **47:10** *e* Num. 34:3   **47:12** *f* Ezek. 47:7 *g* [Jer. 17:8] *h* [Rev. 22:2]   **47:13** *i* Num. 34:1–29 *j* Gen. 48:5   **47:14** *k* Ezek. 20:5, 6, 28, 42 *l* Ezek. 48:29   **47:15** *m* Ezek. 48:1 *n* Num. 34:7, 8   **47:16** *o* Num. 34:8 *p* 2 Sam. 8:8   **47:17** *q* Num. 34:9   **47:19** *r* Ps. 81:7   **47:21** *s* Ezek. 45:1   **47:22** *t* Num. 26:55, 56 *u* [Eph. 3:6] *v* [Col. 3:11]   **48:1** *a* Ezek. 47:15 *b* Josh. 19:40–48   **48:2** *c* Josh. 19:24–31   **48:3** *d* Josh. 19:32–39

of Naphtali, from the east side to the west, one *section for* eManasseh; 5by the border of Manasseh, from the east side to the west, one *section for* fEphraim; 6by the border of Ephraim, from the east side to the west, one *section for* gReuben; 7by the border of Reuben, from the east side to the west, one *section for* hJudah; 8by the border of Judah, from the east side to the west, shall be ithe district which you shall set apart, twenty-five thousand *cubits* in width, and *in* length the same as one of the *other* portions, from the east side to the west, with the jsanctuary in the center.

9"The district that you shall set apart for the LORD *shall be* twenty-five thousand *cubits* in length and ten thousand in width. 10To these—to the priests—the holy district shall belong: on the north twenty-five thousand *cubits in length*, on the west ten thousand in width, on the east ten thousand in width, and on the south twenty-five thousand in length. The sanctuary of the LORD shall be in the center. 11k*It shall be* for the priests of the sons of Zadok, who are sanctified, who have kept My charge, who did not go astray when the children of Israel went astray, las the Levites went astray. 12And *this* district of land that is set apart shall be to them a thing most mholy by the border of the Levites.

13"Opposite the border of the priests, the nLevites *shall have an area* twenty-five thousand *cubits* in length and ten thousand in width; its entire length *shall be* twenty-five thousand and its width ten thousand. 14oAnd they shall not sell or exchange any of it; they may not alienate this best *part* of the land, for *it is* holy to the LORD.

15p"The five thousand *cubits* in width that remain, along the edge of the twenty-five thousand, shall be qfor general use by the city, for dwellings and common-land; and the city shall be in the center. 16These *shall be* its measurements: the north side four thousand five hundred *cubits*, the south side four thousand five hundred, the east side four thousand five hundred, and the west side four thousand five hundred. 17The common-land of the city shall be: to the north two hundred and fifty *cubits*, to the south two hundred and fifty, to the east two hundred and fifty, and to the west two hundred and fifty. 18The rest of the length, alongside the district of the holy *section*,

shall be ten thousand *cubits* to the east and ten thousand to the west. It shall be adjacent to the district of the holy *section*, and its produce shall be food for the workers of the city. 19rThe workers of the city, from all the tribes of Israel, shall cultivate it. 20The entire district *shall be* twenty-five thousand *cubits* by twenty-five thousand *cubits*, foursquare. You shall set apart the holy district with the property of the city.

21s"The rest *shall belong* to the prince, on one side and on the other of the holy district and of the city's property, next to the twenty-five thousand *cubits* of the *holy* district as far as the eastern border, and westward next to the twenty-five thousand as far as the western border, adjacent to the *tribal* portions; *it shall belong* to the prince. It shall be the holy district, tand the sanctuary of the temple *shall be* in the center. 22Moreover, apart from the possession of the Levites and the possession of the city *which are* in the midst of what *belongs* to the prince, *the area* between the border of Judah and the border of uBenjamin shall belong to the prince.

23"As for the rest of the tribes, from the east side to the west, Benjamin *shall have* one *section*; 24by the border of Benjamin, from the east side to the west, vSimeon *shall have* one *section*; 25by the border of Simeon, from the east side to the west, wIssachar *shall have* one *section*; 26by the border of Issachar, from the east side to the west, xZebulun *shall have* one *section*; 27by the border of Zebulun, from the east side to the west, yGad *shall have* one *section*; 28by the border of Gad, on the south side, toward the South,* the border shall be from Tamar *to* zthe waters of Meribah *by* Kadesh, along the brook to the aGreat Sea. 29bThis *is* the land which you shall divide by lot as an inheritance among the tribes of Israel, and these *are* their portions," says the Lord GOD.

The Gates of the City and Its Name

30"These *are* the exits of the city. On the north side, measuring four thousand five hundred *cubits* 31c(the gates of the city *shall be* named after the tribes of Israel), the three gates northward: one gate for Reuben, one gate for Judah, and one gate

---

*48:28 Hebrew *Negev*

---

divided into thirteen parts. The division makes it clear that all who believe have a place.
48:28 Great Sea. This would have been the Mediterranean Sea.
48:31 named after the tribes of Israel. The gates are named after the original twelve tribes (Rev. 21:12–13). The gate for Joseph represents the two tribes of Manasseh and Ephraim.

48:4 eJosh. 13:29–31; 17:1–11, 17, 18   48:5 fJosh.

16:5–10; 17:8–10, 14–18   48:6 gJosh. 13:15–23
48:7 hJosh. 15:1–63; 19:9   48:8 iEzek. 45:1–6 j[Is. 12:6; 33:20–22]   48:11 kEzek. 40:46; 44:15 lEzek. 44:10, 12
48:12 mEzek. 45:4   48:13 nEzek. 45:5   48:14 oLev. 27:10, 28, 33   48:15 pEzek. 45:6 qEzek. 42:20
48:19 rEzek. 45:6   48:21 sEzek. 34:24; 45:7; 48:22
tEzek. 48:8, 10   48:22 uJosh. 18:21–28   48:24 vJosh. 19:1–9   48:25 wJosh. 19:17–23   48:26 xJosh. 19:10–16
48:27 yJosh. 13:24–28   48:28 zEzek. 47:19 aEzek. 47:10, 15, 19, 20   48:29 bEzek. 47:14, 21, 22   48:31 c[Rev. 21:10–14]

for Levi; ³²on the east side, four thousand five hundred *cubits*, three gates: one gate for Joseph, one gate for Benjamin, and one gate for Dan; ³³on the south side, measuring four thousand five hundred *cubits*, three gates: one gate for Simeon, one gate for Issachar, and one gate for Zebulun; ³⁴on the west side, four thousand five hundred *cubits* with their three gates: one gate for Gad, one gate for Asher, and one gate for Naphtali. ³⁵All the way around *shall be* eighteen thousand *cubits;* ^dand the name of the city from *that* day *shall be:* ^eTHE LORD *IS* THERE."*

---

* **48:35** Hebrew *YHWH Shammah*

48:35 *THE LORD IS THERE.* This return of the Lord and the regathering of His people are predicted by Ezekiel in 11:17; 20:33–44; 37:15–28; and 39:21–29. The Lord was forced to depart from the city and the temple because of the wickedness of the Israelites (8:6; 10:18). But here, Ezekiel foresees the return of God in all His glory to His people, His temple, and His land. This was a powerful message in its context. Ezekiel and his immediate audience were far away from their homeland. This vision of the coming restoration would have inspired much hope in the faithful.

48:35 ^d Jer. 23:6; 33:16 ^e Joel 3:21

THE BOOK OF

DANIEL

▶ **AUTHOR:** Daniel's life and ministry bridge the entire seventy-year period of Babylonian captivity. This claims Daniel as author, and it uses the first person from 7:2 onward. The Jewish Talmud supports this claim, and Christ attributed a quote from 9:27 to "Daniel the prophet" (Matt. 24:15). Daniel's wisdom and divinely given interpretive abilities brought him into a position of prominence, especially in the courts of Nebuchadnezzar and Darius.

▶ **TIME:** c. 605–536 B.C.   ▶ **KEY VERSES:** Dan. 2:20–22

▶ **THEME:** Daniel is one of very few heroes in the Bible whose record is flawless. He is an example of how to live and work as a believer in a hostile environment; a man of action while at the same time fully aware of his dependence on God. The important prophecies in Daniel have inspired many interpretations over the years. Many have attempted to identify the various elements of the prophecies and apply them to contemporary figures.

Daniel and His Friends Obey God

1 In the third year of the reign of ᵃJehoiakim king of Judah, Nebuchadnezzar king of Babylon came to Jerusalem and besieged it. ²And the Lord gave Jehoiakim king of Judah into his hand, with ᵇsome of the articles of the house of God, which he carried ᶜinto the land of Shinar to the house of his god; ᵈand he brought the articles into the treasure house of his god.

³Then the king instructed Ashpenaz, the master of his eunuchs, to bring ᵉsome of the children of Israel and some of the king's descendants and some of the nobles, ⁴young men ᶠin whom *there was* no blemish, but good-looking, gifted in all wisdom, possessing knowledge and quick to understand, who *had* ability to serve in the king's palace, and ᵍwhom they might teach the language and literature of the Chaldeans. ⁵And the king appointed for them a daily provision of the king's delicacies and of the wine which he drank, and three years of training for them, so that at the end of *that time* they might ʰserve before the king. ⁶Now from among those of the sons of Judah were Daniel, Hananiah, Mishael, and Azariah. ⁷ⁱTo them the chief of the eunuchs gave names: ʲhe gave Daniel *the name* Belteshazzar; to Hananiah, Shadrach; to Mishael, Meshach; and to Azariah, Abed-Nego.

1:1 Jehoiakim king of Judah. Jehoiakim was an evil king who sided first with the Egyptians and then with the Babylonians, until he finally decided to rebel. His independence was short-lived, however, and he remained under Babylonian domination until his death (2 Kin. 23:34—24:6).

1:2 the treasure house of his god. These articles taken from the temple appear later, on the night of Belshazzar's feast (ch. 5). Eventually they were returned to Zerubbabel, who brought them back to Israel (Ezra 1:7).

1:3 master of his eunuchs. A term which became synonymous with "official." In ancient Middle Eastern monarchies, royal harems were typically superintended by men who had been emasculated and were considered reliable to serve in that capacity. A eunuch was often regarded as a privileged official. Some have speculated that Daniel and his friends were eunuchs, but there is no specific statement in the book to this effect.

1:4 language and literature. The language of most of Mesopotamia was Akkadian, which was written in cuneiform script. Over the centuries the Babylonians and Assyrians produced a massive body of literature of all types. Though Aramaic had begun to replace Akkadian by the time of Nebuchadnezzar, scholars continued to study and write literature in their classical tongue. **Chaldeans.** This name was commonly applied to Babylonians in general, and also to the guild of astrologers, diviners, and other practitioners of wisdom to which Daniel was being introduced (1:17; 2:2; 3:8).

1:7 names. Daniel means "God is my judge"; Belteshazzar means "lady protect the king," referring to the goddess Sarpanitu, wife of the god Marduk. Hananiah means "the Lord is gracious"; Shadrach means "I am fearful of the God." Mishael means "who is what God is?" Meshach means "I am of little

---

1:1 ᵈ 2 Kin. 24:1, 2   **1:2** ᵇ Jer. 27:19, 20   ᶜ Zech. 5:11   ᵈ 2 Chr. 36:7   **1:3** ᵉ Is. 39:7   **1:4** ᶠ Lev. 24:19, 20   ᵍ Acts 7:22   **1:5** ʰ Dan. 1:19   **1:7** ⁱ 2 Kin. 24:17   ʲ Dan. 2:26; 4:8; 5:12

⁸But Daniel purposed in his heart that he would not defile himself ᵏwith the portion of the king's delicacies, nor with the wine which he drank; therefore he requested of the chief of the eunuchs that he might not defile himself. ⁹Now ˡGod had brought Daniel into the favor and goodwill of the chief of the eunuchs. ¹⁰And the chief of the eunuchs said to Daniel, "I fear my lord the king, who has appointed your food and drink. For why should he see your faces looking worse than the young men who *are* your age? Then you would endanger my head before the king."

¹¹So Daniel said to the steward* whom the chief of the eunuchs had set over Daniel, Hananiah, Mishael, and Azariah, ¹²"Please test your servants for ten days, and let them give us vegetables to eat and water to drink. ¹³Then let our appearance be examined before you, and the appearance of the young men who eat the portion of the king's delicacies; and as you see fit, *so* deal with your servants." ¹⁴So he consented with them in this matter, and tested them ten days.

¹⁵And at the end of ten days their features appeared better and fatter in flesh than all the young men who ate the portion of the king's delicacies. ¹⁶Thus the steward took away their portion of delicacies and the wine that they were to drink, and gave them vegetables.

¹⁷As for these four young men, ᵐGod gave them ⁿknowledge and skill in all literature and wisdom; and Daniel had ᵒunderstanding in all visions and dreams.

¹⁸Now at the end of the days, when the king had said that they should be brought in, the chief of the eunuchs brought them in before Nebuchadnezzar. ¹⁹Then the king interviewed* them, and among them all none was found like Daniel, Hananiah, Mishael, and Azariah; therefore ᵖthey served before the king. ²⁰ᵠAnd in all matters of wisdom *and* understanding about which the king examined them, he found them ten times better than all the magicians *and* astrologers who *were* in all his realm. ²¹ʳThus Daniel continued until the first year of King Cyrus.

Nebuchadnezzar's Dream

2 Now in the second year of Nebuchadnezzar's reign, Nebuchadnezzar had

dreams; ᵃand his spirit was *so* troubled that ᵇhis sleep left him. ²ᶜThen the king gave the command to call the magicians, the astrologers, the sorcerers, and the Chaldeans to tell the king his dreams. So they came and stood before the king. ³And the king said to them, "I have had a dream, and my spirit is anxious to know the dream."

⁴Then the Chaldeans spoke to the king in Aramaic,* ᵈ"O king, live forever! Tell your servants the dream, and we will give the interpretation."

⁵The king answered and said to the Chaldeans, "My decision is firm: if you do not make known the dream to me, and its interpretation, you shall be ᵉcut in pieces, and your houses shall be made an ash heap. ⁶ᶠHowever, if you tell the dream and its interpretation, you shall receive from me gifts, rewards, and great honor. Therefore tell me the dream and its interpretation."

⁷They answered again and said, "Let the king tell his servants the dream, and we will give its interpretation."

⁸The king answered and said, "I know for certain that you would gain time, because you see that my decision is firm: ⁹if you do not make known the dream to me, *there is only* one decree for you! For you have agreed to speak lying and corrupt words before me till the time has changed. Therefore tell me the dream, and I shall know that you can give me its interpretation."

¹⁰The Chaldeans answered the king, and said, "There is not a man on earth who can tell the king's matter; therefore no king, lord, or ruler has *ever* asked such things of any magician, astrologer, or Chaldean. ¹¹*It is* a difficult thing that the king requests, and there is no other who can tell it to the king ᵍexcept the gods, whose dwelling is not with flesh."

¹²For this reason the king was angry and very furious, and gave the command to destroy all the wise *men* of Babylon. ¹³So the decree went out, and they began killing the wise *men;* and they sought ʰDaniel and his companions, to kill *them.*

---

* **1:11** Hebrew *Melzar,* also in verse 16   * **1:19** Literally *talked with them*   * **2:4** The original language of Daniel 2:4b through 7:28 is Aramaic.

---

account." Azariah means "the Lord has helped me"; Abed-Nego means "servant of [the god] Nebo."
1:8 defile himself. The issue here was not the richness of the food or the alcohol. The king's table no doubt included unclean meats and food which had not been prepared according to the law. In addition, both meat and wines may well have already been offered to idols.
2:2 magicians. The word translated "magicians" refers to those who use a pen—most likely, those learned in the sacred writings of the Babylonians.
2:4 in Aramaic. Daniel 2:4b—7:28 is written in Aramaic, the common language of the day.

2:8 gain time. Nebuchadnezzar obviously did not have any faith in the integrity of his wise men or in the reality of their wisdom. He wanted to know for sure that the interpretation of his dream was a supernatural revelation, not just a clever story to please a king.

1:8 ᵏ Hos. 9:3   **1:9** ˡ Gen. 39:21   **1:17** ᵐ [James 1:5–7] ⁿ Acts 7:22 ᵒ 2 Chr. 26:5   **1:19** ᵖ Gen. 41:46
1:20 ᵠ 1 Kin. 10:1   **1:21** ʳ Dan. 6:28; 10:1   **2:1** ᵃ Gen. 40:5–8; 41:1, 8 ᵇ Esth. 6:1   **2:2** ᶜ Ex. 7:11   **2:4** ᵈ Dan. 3:9; 5:10; 6:6, 21   **2:5** ᵉ Ezra 6:11   **2:6** ᶠ Dan. 5:16
2:11 ᵍ Dan. 5:11   **2:13** ʰ Dan. 1:19, 20

God Reveals Nebuchadnezzar's Dream

14 Then with counsel and wisdom Daniel
answered Arioch, the captain of the king's
guard, who had gone out to kill the wise
men of Babylon; 15 he answered and said
to Arioch the king's captain, "Why is the
decree from the king so urgent?" Then Arioch made the decision known to Daniel.
16 So Daniel went in and asked the king
to give him time, that he might tell the king
the interpretation. 17 Then Daniel went to
his house, and made the decision known to
Hananiah, Mishael, and Azariah, his companions, 18 [i]that they might seek mercies
from the God of heaven concerning this
secret, so that Daniel and his companions
might not perish with the rest of the wise
men of Babylon. 19 Then the secret was revealed to Daniel [j]in a night vision. So Daniel blessed the God of heaven.
20 Daniel answered and said:

[k]"Blessed be the name of God forever
and ever,
[l]For wisdom and might are His.
21 And He changes [m]the times and the
seasons;
[n]He removes kings and raises up kings;
[o]He gives wisdom to the wise
And knowledge to those who have
understanding.
22 [p]He reveals deep and secret things;
[q]He knows what *is* in the darkness,
And [r]light dwells with Him.

23 "I thank You and praise You,
O God of my fathers;
You have given me wisdom and might,
And have now made known to me
what we [s]asked of You,
For You have made known to us the
king's demand."

Daniel Explains the Dream

24 Therefore Daniel went to Arioch,
whom the king had appointed to destroy
the wise *men* of Babylon. He went and said
thus to him: "Do not destroy the wise *men*
of Babylon; take me before the king, and I
will tell the king the interpretation."
25 Then Arioch quickly brought Daniel
before the king, and said thus to him, "I
have found a man of the captives* of Judah, who will make known to the king the
interpretation."
26 The king answered and said to Daniel, whose name *was* Belteshazzar, "Are
you able to make known to me the dream
which I have seen, and its interpretation?"
27 Daniel answered in the presence of the
king, and said, "The secret which the king
has demanded, the wise *men,* the astrologers, the magicians, and the soothsayers
cannot declare to the king. 28 [t]But there is
a God in heaven who reveals secrets, and
He has made known to King Nebuchadnezzar [u]what will be in the latter days. Your
dream, and the visions of your head upon
your bed, were these: 29 As for you, O king,
thoughts came *to* your *mind while* on your
bed, *about* what would come to pass after
this; [v]and He who reveals secrets has made
known to you what will be. 30 [w]But as for
me, this secret has not been revealed to me
because I have more wisdom than anyone
living, but for *our* sakes who make known
the interpretation to the king, [x]and that you
may know the thoughts of your heart.
31 "You, O king, were watching; and
behold, a great image! This great image,
whose splendor *was* excellent, stood before
you; and its form *was* awesome. 32 [y]This
image's head *was* of fine gold, its chest
and arms of silver, its belly and thighs*
of bronze, 33 its legs of iron, its feet partly
of iron and partly of clay.* 34 You watched
while a stone was cut out [z]without hands,
which struck the image on its feet of iron
and clay, and broke them in pieces. 35 [a]Then
the iron, the clay, the bronze, the silver, and
the gold were crushed together, and became [b]like chaff from the summer threshing floors; the wind carried them away
so that [c]no trace of them was found. And
the stone that struck the image [d]became a
great mountain [e]and filled the whole earth.
36 "This *is* the dream. Now we will tell the
interpretation of it before the king. 37 [f]You,
O king, *are* a king of kings. [g]For the God

* **2:25** Literally *of the sons of the captivity*
* **2:32** Or *sides* * **2:33** Or *baked clay,* and so in verses 34, 35, and 42

2:11 ***except the gods.*** The wise men were forced to acknowledge their own limitations. As far as they knew, they were doomed because the gods who had the answers did not speak with men.

2:18 ***that they might seek mercies from the God of heaven.*** Daniel and his friends knew the same thing that the other wise men did: only God could possibly reveal the king's dream. But, unlike the other wise men, they knew that their God would answer when they called on Him.

2:28 ***the latter days.*** This is an expression used frequently for the end times when God will intervene in human history to establish His eternal kingdom (Is. 2:2; Hos. 3:5; Mic. 4:1–3).

2:31 ***a great image.*** The image that Nebuchadnezzar saw represented four kingdoms that would rule over all the earth.

2:37 ***the God of heaven has given you a kingdom.*** The rulers of the nations of the world may not recognize God's authority, but that does not alter the fact that they have their positions only through His permission.

2:18 [i] [Matt. 18:19] **2:19** [j] Job 33:15 **2:20** [k] Ps. 113:2 [l] [Jer. 32:19] **2:21** [m] Esth. 1:13 [n] [Ps. 75:6, 7] [o] [James 1:5] **2:22** [p] Ps. 25:14 [q] [Heb. 4:13] [r] Dan. 5:11, 14 **2:23** [s] Dan. 2:18, 29, 30 **2:28** [t] Gen. 40:8 [u] Gen. 49:1 **2:29** [v] [Dan. 2:22, 28] **2:30** [w] Acts 3:12 [x] Dan. 2:47 **2:32** [y] Dan. 2:38, 45 **2:34** [z] [Zech. 4:6] **2:35** [a] [Rev. 16:14] [b] Hos. 13:3 [c] Ps. 37:10, 36 [d] [Is. 2:2, 3] [e] Ps. 80:9 **2:37** [f] Jer. 27:6, 7 [g] Ezra 1:2

of heaven has given you a kingdom, power, strength, and glory; [38h]and wherever the children of men dwell, or the beasts of the field and the birds of the heaven, He has given *them* into your hand, and has made you ruler over them all—[i]you *are* this head of gold. [39]But after you shall arise [j]another kingdom [k]inferior to yours; then another, a third kingdom of bronze, which shall rule over all the earth. [40]And [l]the fourth kingdom shall be as strong as iron, inasmuch as iron breaks in pieces and shatters everything; and like iron that crushes, *that kingdom* will break in pieces and crush all the others. [41]Whereas you saw the feet and toes, partly of potter's clay and partly of iron, the kingdom shall be divided; yet the strength of the iron shall be in it, just as you saw the iron mixed with ceramic clay. [42]And *as* the toes of the feet *were* partly of iron and partly of clay, [m]so the kingdom shall be partly strong and partly fragile. [43]As you saw iron mixed with ceramic clay, they will mingle with the seed of men; but they will not adhere to one another, just as iron does not mix with clay. [44]And in the days of these kings [n]the God of heaven will set up a kingdom [o]which shall never be destroyed; and the kingdom shall not be left to other people; [p]it shall break in pieces and consume all these kingdoms, and it shall stand forever. [45q]Inasmuch as you saw that the stone was cut out of the mountain without hands, and that it broke in pieces the iron, the bronze, the clay, the silver, and the gold—the great God has made known to the king what will come to pass after this. The dream is certain, and its interpretation is sure."

Daniel and His Friends Promoted

[46r]Then King Nebuchadnezzar fell on his face, prostrate before Daniel, and commanded that they should present an offering [s]and incense to him. [47]The king answered Daniel, and said, "Truly [t]your God *is* the God of [u]gods, the Lord of kings, and a revealer of secrets, since you could reveal this secret." [48v]Then the king promoted Daniel [w]and gave him many great gifts; and he made him ruler over the whole province of Babylon, and [x]chief administrator over all the wise *men* of Babylon. [49]Also Daniel petitioned the king, [y]and he set Shadrach, Meshach, and Abed-Nego over the affairs of the province of Babylon; but Daniel [z]sat in the gate* of the king.

The Image of Gold

3 Nebuchadnezzar the king made an image of gold, whose height *was* sixty cubits *and* its width six cubits. He set it up in the plain of Dura, in the province of Babylon. [2]And King Nebuchadnezzar sent word to gather together the satraps, the administrators, the governors, the counselors, the treasurers, the judges, the magistrates, and all the officials of the provinces, to come to the dedication of the image which King Nebuchadnezzar had set up. [3]So the satraps, the administrators, the governors, the counselors, the treasurers, the judges, the magistrates, and all the officials of the provinces gathered together for the dedication of the image that King Nebuchadnezzar had set up; and they stood before the image that Nebuchadnezzar had set up. [4]Then a herald cried aloud:

---

* **2:49** That is, the king's court

2:38 head of gold. The first worldwide empire, the head of gold, was Babylon.

2:39 another kingdom inferior to yours. The second empire, the chest and arms of silver, was Medo-Persia. Just as silver is inferior to gold, Medo-Persia was inferior to Babylon, not in size but in its effectiveness in governing its people. **third kingdom of bronze.** The third kingdom would be the Greek Empire.

2:40 fourth kingdom . . . strong as iron. The fourth kingdom, the legs of iron, is the only one not specifically identified within the Book of Daniel. Rome is the most likely choice, for it succeeded Greece, and was certainly a very strong empire.

2:41–45 the kingdom shall be divided. Some believe that this is a reference to the Roman Empire's decline, when the kingdom was divided and the fabric of the empire was weakening in the early centuries after Christ. In this case the "kingdom which shall never be destroyed" (obviously the kingdom of God) is a spiritual kingdom introduced by Christ at His first coming, and the mountain that grew from the rock would be a reference to the spread of Christianity, which eventually was named the state religion of the Roman Empire.

Others believe that verses 41–45 point to future events that have not yet been fulfilled. When this vision is compared with the four beasts of chapter 7,

it seems clear that the fourth kingdom is yet to come. It is theorized that the kingdom of iron does actually refer to the Roman Empire, which will be revived in some form in the last days, perhaps as a ten-nation confederacy (the ten toes, or the ten horns of the beast of chapter 7). In this case, the "kingdom which shall never be destroyed" is a literal kingdom to be established by Jesus Christ at the second coming, at which time He will destroy the kingdoms of the world (Rev. 19:15).

3:1 cubits. A cubit in Israel was approximately 18 inches; in Babylon it was about 20 inches. Nebuchadnezzar's image was 90 to 100 feet tall. The odd proportions of this figure (a normal human height-to-width ratio is about 4:1 rather than 10:1) may indicate that the height includes a base or pedestal.

3:2 satraps. Satraps were the chief officials of the provinces of the empire.

2:38 [h] Dan. 4:21, 22 [i] Dan. 2:32 **2:39** [j] Dan. 5:28, 31 [k] Dan. 2:32 **2:40** [l] Dan. 7:7, 23 **2:42** [m] Dan. 7:24 **2:44** [n] Dan. 2:28, 37 [o] [Luke 1:32, 33] [p] Is. 60:12 **2:45** [q] Dan. 2:35 **2:46** [r] Acts 10:25; 14:13 [s] Ezra 6:10 **2:47** [t] Dan. 3:28, 29; 4:34–37 [u] [Deut. 10:17] **2:48** [v] [Prov. 14:35; 21:1] [w] Dan. 2:6 [x] Dan. 4:9; 5:11 **2:49** [y] Dan. 1:7; 3:12 [z] Esth. 2:19, 21; 3:2

"To you it is commanded, *a*O peoples, nations, and languages, *5that* at the time you hear the sound of the horn, flute, harp, lyre, *and* psaltery, in symphony with all kinds of music, you shall fall down and worship the gold image that King Nebuchadnezzar has set up; *6*and whoever does not fall down and worship shall *b*be cast immediately into the midst of a burning fiery furnace."

*7*So at that time, when all the people heard the sound of the horn, flute, harp, *and* lyre, in symphony with all kinds of music, all the people, nations, and languages fell down *and* worshiped the gold image which King Nebuchadnezzar had set up.

Daniel's Friends Disobey the King

*8*Therefore at that time certain Chaldeans *c*came forward and accused the Jews. *9*They spoke and said to King Nebuchadnezzar, *d*"O king, live forever! *10*You, O king, have made a decree that everyone who hears the sound of the horn, flute, harp, lyre, *and* psaltery, in symphony with all kinds of music, shall fall down and worship the gold image; *11*and whoever does not fall down and worship shall be cast into the midst of a burning fiery furnace. *12e*There are certain Jews whom you have set over the affairs of the province of Babylon: Shadrach, Meshach, and Abed-Nego; these men, O king, have *f*not paid due regard to you. They do not serve your gods or worship the gold image which you have set up."

*13*Then Nebuchadnezzar, in *g*rage and fury, gave the command to bring Shadrach, Meshach, and Abed-Nego. So they brought these men before the king. *14*Nebuchadnezzar spoke, saying to them, *"Is it* true, Shadrach, Meshach, and Abed-Nego, *that* you do not serve my gods or worship the gold image which I have set up? *15*Now if you are ready at the time you hear the sound of the horn, flute, harp, lyre, *and* psaltery, in symphony with all kinds of music, and you fall down and worship the image which I have made, *h*good! But if you do not worship, you shall be cast immediately into the midst of a burning fiery furnace. *i*And who *is* the god who will deliver you from my hands?"

*16*Shadrach, Meshach, and Abed-Nego answered and said to the king, "O Nebuchadnezzar, *j*we have no need to answer you in this matter. *17*If *that is the case,* our *k*God whom we serve is able to *l*deliver us

from the burning fiery furnace, and He will deliver *us* from your hand, O king. *18*But if not, let it be known to you, O king, that we do not serve your gods, nor will we *m*worship the gold image which you have set up."

Saved in Fiery Trial

*19*Then Nebuchadnezzar was full of fury, and the expression on his face changed toward Shadrach, Meshach, and Abed-Nego. He spoke and commanded that they heat the furnace seven times more than it was usually heated. *20*And he commanded certain mighty men of valor who *were* in his army to bind Shadrach, Meshach, and Abed-Nego, *and* cast *them* into the burning fiery furnace. *21*Then these men were bound in their coats, their trousers, their turbans, and their *other* garments, and were cast into the midst of the burning fiery furnace. *22*Therefore, because the king's command was urgent, and the furnace exceedingly hot, the flame of the fire killed those men who took up Shadrach, Meshach, and Abed-Nego. *23*And these three men, Shadrach, Meshach, and Abed-Nego, fell down bound into the midst of the burning fiery furnace.

*24*Then King Nebuchadnezzar was astonished; and he rose in haste *and* spoke, saying to his counselors, "Did we not cast three men bound into the midst of the fire?"

They answered and said to the king, "True, O king."

25"Look!" he answered, "I see four men loose, *n*walking in the midst of the fire; and they are not hurt, and the form of the fourth is like *o*the Son of God."*

Nebuchadnezzar Praises God

*26*Then Nebuchadnezzar went near the mouth of the burning fiery furnace *and* spoke, saying, "Shadrach, Meshach, and Abed-Nego, servants of the *p*Most High God, come out, and come *here.*" Then Shadrach, Meshach, and Abed-Nego came from the midst of the fire. *27*And the satraps, administrators, governors, and the king's counselors gathered together, and they saw these men *q*on whose bodies the fire had no power; the hair of their head was not singed nor were their garments affected, and the smell of fire was not on them.

* 3:25 Or *a son of the gods*

3:18 But if not. The faithful men knew that God could deliver them (v. 17), yet they were also aware that God could have chosen not to do so. Faith in God may not translate into victory in every circumstance (Heb. 11:32–39). To these men the outcome was irrelevant, for what was at stake was not God's ability or their own lives, but their faith and obedience to serve Him regardless of the cost.

3:25 I see four men loose. The fourth man walking with the three friends in the furnace may have been

an angel. Many believe that this was an appearance of the preincarnate Christ.

3:4 *a* Dan. 4:1; 6:25   3:6 *b* Jer. 29:22   3:8 *c* Dan. 6:12, 13   3:9 *d* Dan. 2:4; 5:10; 6:6, 21   3:12 *e* Dan. 2:49   *f* Dan. 1:8; 6:12, 13   3:13 *g* Dan. 2:12; 3:19   3:15 *h* Luke 13:9   *i* Ex. 5:2   3:16 *j* [Matt. 10:19]   3:17 *k* [Is. 26:3, 4]   *l* 1 Sam. 17:37   3:18 *m* Job 13:15   3:25 *n* Is. 43:2   *o* [Ps. 34:7]   3:26 *p* [Dan. 4:2, 3, 17, 34, 35]   3:27 *q* Heb. 11:34

28Nebuchadnezzar spoke, saying, "Blessed be the God of Shadrach, Meshach, and Abed-Nego, who sent His rAngel* and delivered His servants who trusted in Him, and they have frustrated the king's word, and yielded their bodies, that they should not serve nor worship any god except their own God! 29sTherefore I make a decree that any people, nation, or language which speaks anything amiss against the tGod of Shadrach, Meshach, and Abed-Nego shall be ucut in pieces, and their houses shall be made an ash heap; vbecause there is no other God who can deliver like this."

30Then the king promoted Shadrach, Meshach, and Abed-Nego in the province of Babylon.

Nebuchadnezzar's Second Dream

4 Nebuchadnezzar the king,

aTo all peoples, nations, and languages that dwell in all the earth:

Peace be multiplied to you.

2 I thought it good to declare the signs and wonders bthat the Most High God has worked for me.

3 cHow great are His signs,
And how mighty His wonders!
His kingdom is dan everlasting kingdom,
And His dominion is from generation
to generation.

4 I, Nebuchadnezzar, was at rest in my house, and flourishing in my palace. 5I saw a dream which made me afraid, eand the thoughts on my bed and the visions of my head ftroubled me. 6Therefore I issued a decree to bring in all the wise men of Babylon before me, that they might make known to me the interpretation of the dream. 7gThen the magicians, the astrologers, the Chaldeans, and the soothsayers came in, and I told them the dream; but they did not make known to me its interpretation. 8But at last Daniel came before me h(his name is Belteshazzar, according

to the name of my god; iin him is the Spirit of the Holy God), and I told the dream before him, saying: 9"Belteshazzar, jchief of the magicians, because I know that the Spirit of the Holy God is in you, and no secret troubles you, explain to me the visions of my dream that I have seen, and its interpretation.

10 "These were the visions of my head while on my bed:

I was looking, and behold,
kA tree in the midst of the earth,
And its height was great.
11 The tree grew and became strong;
Its height reached to the heavens,
And it could be seen to the ends of all
the earth.
12 Its leaves were lovely,
Its fruit abundant,
And in it was food for all.
lThe beasts of the field found shade
under it,
The birds of the heavens dwelt in its
branches,
And all flesh was fed from it.

13 "I saw in the visions of my head while on my bed, and there was ma watcher, na holy one, coming down from heaven. 14He cried aloud and said thus:

o'Chop down the tree and cut off its
branches,
Strip off its leaves and scatter its fruit.
pLet the beasts get out from under it,
And the birds from its branches.
15 Nevertheless leave the stump and
roots in the earth,
Bound with a band of iron and bronze,
In the tender grass of the field.
Let it be wet with the dew of heaven,
And let him graze with the beasts
On the grass of the earth.
16 Let his heart be changed from that of
a man,
Let him be given the heart of a beast,
And let seven qtimes* pass over him.

* 3:28 Or angel   * 4:16 Possibly seven years, and so in verses 23, 25, and 32

3:28 Blessed be the God of Shadrach, Meshach, and Abed-Nego. Pagan cultures did not deny the existence of other gods, even those of other peoples. Nebuchadnezzar was impressed with the God of Israel, but that did not mean that he recognized that God is the only true god.

4:1 Nebuchadnezzar the king. These verses are a royal proclamation by Nebuchadnezzar concerning the God of Israel, in which the king celebrated what God had done for him and extolled His power and dominion.

4:8 my god. This refers to Marduk. Nebuchadnezzar was still a pagan, but he also recognized that Daniel had the spirit of his god, and that Daniel's God was different from other gods.

4:9 chief of the magicians. Daniel's position as head magician did not mean that he practiced sorcery or witchcraft, a thing clearly forbidden by the law (Deut.

18:10–11). In the pluralistic Babylonian society, Daniel's relationship with the God of Israel would automatically have been categorized as another form of magic, or astrology, or divination, the "wisdom" of the day. He received the honor and position of one who has favor with the gods.

4:16 seven times. These times could refer to years, months, weeks, days, or hours. Most take them as years, as elsewhere in the book (7:25).

3:28 r [Ps. 34:7, 8]   **3:29** s Dan. 6:26   t Dan. 2:46, 47;
4:34–37   u Dan. 2:5   v Dan. 6:27   **4:1** a Dan. 3:4; 6:25
4:2 b Dan. 3:26   **4:3** c 2 Sam. 7:16   d [Dan. 2:44; 4:34; 6:26]
4:5 e Dan. 2:28, 29   f Dan. 2:1   **4:7** g Dan. 2:2   **4:8** h Dan.
1:7   i Dan. 2:11; 4:18; 5:11, 14   **4:9** j Dan. 2:48; 5:11
4:10 k Ezek. 31:3   **4:12** l Lam. 4:20   **4:13** m [Dan. 4:17,
23]   n Deut. 33:2   **4:14** o Ezek. 31:10–14   p Ezek. 31:12, 13
4:16 q Dan. 11:13; 12:7

17 'This decision *is* by the decree of the watchers,
And the sentence by the word of the holy ones,
In order ^rthat the living may know
^sThat the Most High rules in the kingdom of men,
^tGives it to whomever He will,
And sets over it the ^ulowest of men.'

18 "This dream I, King Nebuchadnezzar, have seen. Now you, Belteshazzar, declare its interpretation, ^vsince all the wise *men* of my kingdom are not able to make known to me the interpretation; but you *are* able, ^wfor the Spirit of the Holy God *is* in you."

Daniel Explains the Second Dream

19 Then Daniel, ^xwhose name *was* Belteshazzar, was astonished for a time, and his thoughts ^ytroubled him. *So* the king spoke, and said, "Belteshazzar, do not let the dream or its interpretation trouble you."

Belteshazzar answered and said, "My lord, *may* ^zthe dream concern those who hate you, and its interpretation concern your enemies!

20 ^a"The tree that you saw, which grew and became strong, whose height reached to the heavens and which *could be* seen by all the earth, 21whose leaves *were* lovely and its fruit abundant, in which *was* food for all, under which the beasts of the field dwelt, and in whose branches the birds of the heaven had their home— 22^bit *is* you, O king, who have grown and become strong; for your greatness has grown and reaches to the heavens, ^cand your dominion to the end of the earth.

23 ^d"And inasmuch as the king saw a watcher, a holy one, coming down from heaven and saying, 'Chop down the tree and destroy it, but leave its stump and roots in the earth, *bound* with a band of iron and bronze in the tender grass of the field; let it be wet with the dew of heaven, ^eand let him graze with the beasts of the field, till seven times pass over him'; 24this is the interpretation, O king, and this is the decree of the Most High, which has come upon

my lord the king: 25They shall ^fdrive you from men, your dwelling shall be with the beasts of the field, and they shall make you ^geat grass like oxen. They shall wet you with the dew of heaven, and seven times shall pass over you, ^htill you know that the Most High rules in the kingdom of men, and ⁱgives it to whomever He chooses.

26 "And inasmuch as they gave the command to leave the stump *and* roots of the tree, your kingdom shall be assured to you, after you come to know that ^jHeaven rules. 27Therefore, O king, let my advice be acceptable to you; ^kbreak off your sins by *being* righteous, and your iniquities by showing mercy to *the* poor. ^lPerhaps there may be ^ma lengthening of your prosperity."

Nebuchadnezzar's Humiliation

28 All *this* came upon King Nebuchadnezzar. 29At the end of the twelve months he was walking about the royal palace of Babylon. 30The king ⁿspoke, saying, "Is not this great Babylon, that I have built for a royal dwelling by my mighty power and for the honor of my majesty?"

31 ^oWhile the word *was* still in the king's mouth, ^pa voice fell from heaven: "King Nebuchadnezzar, to you it is spoken: the kingdom has departed from you! 32And ^qthey shall drive you from men, and your dwelling *shall be* with the beasts of the field. They shall make you eat grass like oxen; and seven times shall pass over you, until you know that the Most High rules in the kingdom of men, and gives it to whomever He chooses."

33 That very hour the word was fulfilled concerning Nebuchadnezzar; he was driven from men and ate grass like oxen; his body was wet with the dew of heaven till his hair had grown like eagles' *feathers* and his nails like birds' *claws*.

Nebuchadnezzar Praises God

34 And ^rat the end of the time* I, Nebuchadnezzar, lifted my eyes to heaven, and my understanding returned to

---

* 4:34 Literally *days*

4:20 tree. In the Old Testament, a tree is a common symbol for a ruler (Judg. 9:7–15; Ezek. 31:2–14; Zech. 11:1–2).
4:23 a watcher. The term "watcher" means "waking one," one who is constantly alert. The parallel "holy one" suggests that the watcher is either the Lord Himself or one of His angels (3:28; 6:22; 8:16; 10:13).
4:32 until you know that the Most High rules. Nebuchadnezzar would become insane, yet in his animal-like state he would learn more of God than he ever had before. The chastisement of God is always for a holy and helpful purpose, if we will accept it.

4:17 ^r Ps. 9:16; 83:18 ^s Dan. 2:21; 4:25, 32; 5:21 ^t Jer. 27:5–7 ^u 1 Sam. 2:8 **4:18** ^v Gen. 41:8, 15 ^w Dan. 4:8, 9; 5:11, 14 **4:19** ^x Dan. 4:8 ^y Dan. 7:15, 28; 8:27 ^z 2 Sam. 18:32 **4:20** ^a Dan. 4:10–12 **4:22** ^b Dan. 2:37, 38 ^c Jer. 27:6–8 **4:23** ^d Dan. 4:13–15 ^e Dan. 5:21 **4:25** ^f Dan. 4:32; 5:21 ^g Ps. 106:20 ^h Dan. 4:2, 17, 32 ⁱ Jer. 27:5 **4:26** ^j Matt. 21:25 **4:27** ^k [1 Pet. 4:8] ^l [Ps. 41:1–3] ^m 1 Kin. 21:29 **4:30** ⁿ Prov. 16:18 **4:31** ^o Luke 12:20 ^p Dan. 4:24 **4:32** ^q [Dan. 4:25] **4:34** ^r Dan. 4:26

me; and I blessed the Most High and praised and honored Him ^swho lives forever:

For His dominion *is* ^tan everlasting dominion,
And His kingdom *is* from generation to generation.
35 ^uAll the inhabitants of the earth *are* reputed as nothing;
^vHe does according to His will in the army of heaven
And *among* the inhabitants of the earth.
^wNo one can restrain His hand
Or say to Him, ^x"What have You done?"

36 At the same time my reason returned to me, ^yand for the glory of my kingdom, my honor and splendor returned to me. My counselors and nobles resorted to me, I was ^zrestored to my kingdom, and excellent majesty was ^aadded to me. 37Now I, Nebuchadnezzar, ^bpraise and extol and honor the King of heaven, ^call of whose works *are* truth, and His ways justice. ^dAnd those who walk in pride He is able to put down.

Belshazzar's Feast

5 Belshazzar the king ^amade a great feast for a thousand of his lords, and drank wine in the presence of the thousand. 2While he tasted the wine, Belshazzar gave the command to bring the gold and silver vessels ^bwhich his father Nebuchadnezzar had taken from the temple which *had been* in Jerusalem, that the king and his lords, his wives, and his concubines might drink from them. 3Then they brought the gold ^cvessels that had been taken from the temple of the house of God which *had been* in Jerusalem; and the king and his lords, his wives, and his concubines drank from them. 4They drank wine, ^dand praised the gods of gold and silver, bronze and iron, wood and stone.

5^eIn the same hour the fingers of a man's hand appeared and wrote opposite the lampstand on the plaster of the wall of the king's palace; and the king saw the part of the hand that wrote. 6Then the king's countenance changed, and his thoughts troubled him, so that the joints of his hips were loosened and his ^fknees knocked against each other. 7^gThe king cried aloud to bring in ^hthe astrologers, the Chaldeans, and the soothsayers. The king spoke, saying to the wise *men* of Babylon, "Whoever reads this writing, and tells me its interpretation, shall be clothed with purple and *have* a chain of gold around his neck; ⁱand he shall be the third ruler in the kingdom." 8Now all the king's wise *men* came, ^jbut they could not read the writing, or make known to the king its interpretation. 9Then King Belshazzar was greatly ^ktroubled, his countenance was changed, and his lords were astonished.

10The queen, because of the words of the king and his lords, came to the banquet hall. The queen spoke, saying, "O king, live forever! Do not let your thoughts trouble you, nor let your countenance change. 11There is a man in your kingdom in whom *is* the Spirit of the Holy God. And in the days of your father, light and understanding and wisdom, like the wisdom of the gods, were found in him; and King Nebuchadnezzar your father— your father the king—made him chief of the magicians, astrologers, Chaldeans, *and* soothsayers. 12Inasmuch as an excellent spirit, knowledge, understanding, interpreting dreams, solving riddles, and explaining enigmas* were found in this Daniel, ^mwhom the king named Belteshazzar, now let Daniel be called, and he will give the interpretation."

The Writing on the Wall Explained

13Then Daniel was brought in before the king. The king spoke, and said to Daniel, "*Are* you that Daniel who is one of the captives* from Judah, whom my father the king brought from Judah? 14I have heard of you, that ⁿthe Spirit of God *is* in you, and *that* light and understanding and excellent

---

* **5:12** Literally *untying knots*, and so in verse 16
* **5:13** Literally *of the sons of the captivity*

5:1 *Belshazzar the king.* Belshazzar is called the king and the son of Nebuchadnezzar. Other ancient records, however, seem to dispute both facts. These records indicate that Belshazzar was the son of Nabonidus, the last king of Babylon. It is possible that Belshazzar was the grandson of Nebuchadnezzar. In ancient writings, the term *father* is often used to indicate ancestry rather than immediate family (2 Kin. 14:3). Belshazzar may have served as vice-regent while his father was still living (Nabonidus seems to have spent a number of the years of his reign in Arabia). Thus, he would have been acting as king, even if he was not officially king. Note that Darius the Mede was also called king, even though he served Cyrus (5:31; 6:6).
5:7 *third ruler.* Assuming that Belshazzar was acting

as regent for his father Nabonidus, the "third ruler" would have been next in line for the throne.
5:11 *the Spirit of the Holy God.* This is the same expression used by Nebuchadnezzar (4:8–9,18).
5:13 *that Daniel who is one of the captives.* Daniel was an old man by this time, possibly 80 years old or older.

4:34 ^s[Rev. 4:10] ^t[Luke 1:33]   **4:35** ^uIs. 40:15, 17 ^vPs. 115:3; 135:6 ^wJob 34:29 ^xRom. 9:20   **4:36** ^yDan. 4:26 ^z2 Chr. 20:20 ^a[Prov. 22:4]   **4:37** ^bDan. 2:46, 47; 3:28, 29 ^c[Ps. 33:4] ^dEx. 18:11   **5:1** ^a Esth. 1:3   **5:2** ^bDan. 1:2   **5:3** ^c2 Chr. 36:10   **5:4** ^dRev. 9:20   **5:5** ^eDan. 4:31   **5:6** ^fEzek. 7:17; 21:7   **5:7** ^gDan. 4:6, 7; 5:11, 15 ^hIs. 47:13 ⁱDan. 6:2, 3   **5:8** ^jDan. 2:27; 4:7; 5:15   **5:9** ^kDan. 2:1; 5:6   **5:11** ^lDan. 2:48; 4:8, 9, 18   **5:12** ^mDan. 1:7; 4:8   **5:14** ⁿDan. 4:8, 9, 18; 5:11, 12

wisdom are found in you. ¹⁵Now ᵒthe wise *men*, the astrologers, have been brought in before me, that they should read this writing and make known to me its interpretation, but they could not give the interpretation of the thing. ¹⁶And I have heard of you, that you can give interpretations and explain enigmas. ᵖNow if you can read the writing and make known to me its interpretation, you shall be clothed with purple and *have* a chain of gold around your neck, and shall be the third ruler in the kingdom."

¹⁷Then Daniel answered, and said before the king, "Let your gifts be for yourself, and give your rewards to another; yet I will read the writing to the king, and make known to him the interpretation. ¹⁸O king, �q the Most High God gave Nebuchadnezzar your father a kingdom and majesty, glory and honor. ¹⁹And because of the majesty that He gave him, ʳall peoples, nations, and languages trembled and feared before him. Whomever he wished, he ˢexecuted; whomever he wished, he kept alive; whomever he wished, he set up; and whomever he wished, he put down. ²⁰ᵗBut when his heart was lifted up, and his spirit was hardened in pride, he was deposed from his kingly throne, and they took his glory from him. ²¹Then he was ᵘdriven from the sons of men, his heart was made like the beasts, and his dwelling *was* with the wild donkeys. They fed him with grass like oxen, and his body was wet with the dew of heaven, ᵛtill he knew that the Most High God rules in the kingdom of men, and appoints over it whomever He chooses.

²²"But you his son, Belshazzar, ʷhave not humbled your heart, although you knew all this. ²³ˣAnd you have lifted yourself up against the Lord of heaven. They have brought the ʸvessels of His house before you, and you and your lords, your wives and your concubines, have drunk wine from them. And you have praised the gods of silver and gold, bronze and iron, wood and stone, ᶻwhich do not see or hear or know; and the God who *holds*

your breath in His hand ᵃand owns all your ways, you have not glorified. ²⁴Then the fingers* of the hand were sent from Him, and this writing was written. ²⁵"And this is the inscription that was written:

MENE,* MENE, TEKEL,*
UPHARSIN.*

²⁶This *is* the interpretation of *each* word. MENE: God has numbered your kingdom, and finished it; ²⁷TEKEL: ᵇYou have been weighed in the balances, and found wanting; ²⁸PERES: Your kingdom has been divided, and given to the ᶜMedes and ᵈPersians."* ²⁹Then Belshazzar gave the command, and they clothed Daniel with purple and *put* a chain of gold around his neck, and made a proclamation concerning him ᵉthat he should be the third ruler in the kingdom.

Belshazzar's Fall

³⁰ᶠThat very night Belshazzar, king of the Chaldeans, was slain. ³¹ᵍAnd Darius the Mede received the kingdom, *being* about sixty-two years old.

The Plot Against Daniel

6 It pleased Darius to set over the kingdom one hundred and twenty satraps, to be over the whole kingdom; ²and over these, three governors, of whom Daniel *was* one, that the satraps might give account to them, so that the king would suffer no loss. ³Then this Daniel distinguished himself above the governors and satraps, ᵃbecause an excellent spirit *was* in him; and the king gave thought to setting him over the whole realm. ⁴ᵇSo the governors and satraps sought to find *some* charge against Daniel concerning the kingdom; but they could find no charge or fault, because he *was* faithful; nor was there any error or

---

* **5:24** Literally *palm* * **5:25** Literally *a mina* (50 shekels) from the verb "to number" • Literally *a shekel* from the verb "to weigh" • Literally *and half-shekels* from the verb "to divide" * **5:28** Aramaic *Paras*, consonant with *Peres*

5:25–28 MENE, MENE, TEKEL, UPHARSIN. MENE means "numbered." The repetition is for emphasis. God had numbered the days of Belshazzar's kingdom, and the time was up. TEKEL means "weighed." God had weighed Belshazzar's character, and he did not measure up. UPHARSIN (the plural of PERES) means "divided." That very night Babylon would be divided and defeated by the Medes and the Persians.

5:30 That very night. That very evening (October 12, 539 B.C.), Babylon fell to the Persian army commanded by Gubaru.

5:31 Darius the Mede. Darius the Mede is mentioned by name only in the Book of Daniel. He cannot be the famous Darius I Hystaspes because Darius I was not a Mede, and he lived too late (522–486 B.C.) to be a contemporary of Daniel. It is believed that "Darius the Mede" was Gubaru, a governor appointed by Cyrus.

Ancient literary sources indicate that this official took over immediately in Babylon until Cyrus appointed his own son Cambyses as co-ruler around 538 B.C. Why Gubaru might have been called Darius is uncertain, though ancient rulers often took other names for themselves.

6:3 an excellent spirit. This probably refers to Daniel's surpassing ability to do his job well and perhaps also indicates a commendable attitude.

5:15 ᵒ Dan. 5:7, 8 **5:16** ᵖ Dan. 5:7, 29 **5:18** �q Dan. 2:37, 38; 4:17, 22, 25 **5:19** ʳ Jer. 27:7 ˢ Dan. 2:12, 13; 3:6 **5:20** ᵗ Dan. 4:30, 37 **5:21** ᵘ Dan. 4:32, 33 ᵛ Ezek. 17:24 **5:22** ʷ 2 Chr. 33:23; 36:12 **5:23** ˣ Dan. 5:3, 4 ʸ Ex. 40:9 ᶻ Ps. 115:5, 6 ᵃ [Jer. 10:23] **5:27** ᵇ Ps. 62:9 **5:28** ᶜ Dan. 5:31; 9:1 ᵈ Dan. 6:28 **5:29** ᵉ Dan. 5:7, 16 **5:30** ᶠ Jer. 51:31, 39, 57 **5:31** ᵍ Dan. 2:39; 9:1 **6:3** ᵃ Dan. 5:12 **6:4** ᵇ Eccl. 4:4

fault found in him. 5Then these men said, "We shall not find any charge against this Daniel unless we find *it* against him concerning the law of his God."

6So these governors and satraps thronged before the king, and said thus to him: c"King Darius, live forever! 7All the governors of the kingdom, the administrators and satraps, the counselors and advisors, have dconsulted together to establish a royal statute and to make a firm decree, that whoever petitions any god or man for thirty days, except you, O king, shall be cast into the den of lions. 8Now, O king, establish the decree and sign the writing, so that it cannot be changed, according to the elaw of the Medes and Persians, which does not alter." 9Therefore King Darius signed the written decree.

Daniel in the Lions' Den

10Now when Daniel knew that the writing was signed, he went home. And in his upper room, with his windows open ftoward Jerusalem, he knelt down on his knees gthree times that day, and prayed and gave thanks before his God, as was his custom since early days.

11Then these men assembled and found Daniel praying and making supplication before his God. 12hAnd they went before the king, and spoke concerning the king's decree: "Have you not signed a decree that every man who petitions any god or man within thirty days, except you, O king, shall be cast into the den of lions?"

The king answered and said, "The thing *is* true, iaccording to the law of the Medes and Persians, which does not alter."

13So they answered and said before the king, "That Daniel, jwho is one of the captives* from Judah, kdoes not show due regard for you, O king, or for the decree that you have signed, but makes his petition three times a day."

14And the king, when he heard *these* words, lwas greatly displeased with himself, and set *his* heart on Daniel to deliver him; and he labored till the going down of the sun to deliver him. 15Then these men approached the king, and said to the king,

"Know, O king, that *it is* mthe law of the Medes and Persians that no decree or statute which the king establishes may be changed."

16So the king gave the command, and they brought Daniel and cast *him* into the den of lions. *But* the king spoke, saying to Daniel, "Your God, whom you serve continually, He will deliver you." 17nThen a stone was brought and laid on the mouth of the den, oand the king sealed it with his own signet ring and with the signets of his lords, that the purpose concerning Daniel might not be changed.

Daniel Saved from the Lions

18Now the king went to his palace and spent the night fasting; and no musicians* were brought before him. pAlso his sleep went from him. 19Then the qking arose very early in the morning and went in haste to the den of lions. 20And when he came to the den, he cried out with a lamenting voice to Daniel. The king spoke, saying to Daniel, "Daniel, servant of the living God, rhas your God, whom you serve continually, been able to deliver you from the lions?"

21Then Daniel said to the king, s"O king, live forever! 22tMy God sent His angel and ushut the lions' mouths, so that they have not hurt me, because I was found innocent before Him; and also, O king, I have done no wrong before you."

23Now the king was exceedingly glad for him, and commanded that they should take Daniel up out of the den. So Daniel was taken up out of the den, and no injury whatever was found on him, vbecause he believed in his God.

Darius Honors God

24And the king gave the command, wand they brought those men who had accused Daniel, and they cast *them* into the den of lions—them, xtheir children, and their wives; and the lions overpowered them, and broke all their bones in pieces before they ever came to the bottom of the den.

* 6:13 Literally *of the sons of the captivity*
* 6:18 Exact meaning unknown

6:5 *the law of his God.* Daniel had such integrity that, even after a life spent in government circles, his enemies could find nothing against him. His devotion to God was so well known that these men were confident that Daniel would obey His law even if it would cost him his life.

6:13 *who is one of the captives from Judah.* Daniel's accusers did not describe him as governor (v. 2), but as a captive from another land, in order to implicate him as a treasonous and dangerous person.

6:14 *was greatly displeased.* It is clear that Darius had not factored Daniel into the situation in the beginning. He never had the intention of harming him.

6:23 *he believed in his God.* Daniel's faithfulness got him into trouble; faith got him out of it (Heb. 11:33).

6:24 *their children, and their wives.* The entire families of the wicked conspirators were destroyed because the Persians, like the Hebrews and other peoples, considered guilt a collective responsibility (Num. 16:1–35; Josh. 7).

6:6 c Neh. 2:3   **6:7** d Ps. 59:3; 62:4; 64:2–6   **6:8** e Esth. 1:19, 8:8   **6:10** f Jon. 2:4   g Ps. 55:17   **6:12** h Dan. 3:8–12   i Dan. 6:8, 15   **6:13** j Dan. 1:6; 5:13   k Dan. 3:12   **6:14** l Mark 6:26   **6:15** m Dan. 6:8, 12   **6:17** n Lam. 3:53   o Matt. 27:66   **6:18** p Dan. 2:1   **6:19** q Dan. 3:24   **6:20** r Dan. 3:17   **6:21** s Dan. 2:4; 6:6   **6:22** t Dan. 3:28   u Heb. 11:33   **6:23** v Heb. 11:33   **6:24** w Deut. 19:18, 19   x Deut. 24:16

25yThen King Darius wrote:

To all peoples, nations, and languages
that dwell in all the earth:

Peace be multiplied to you.

26zI make a decree that in every dominion
of my kingdom men must atremble and
fear before the God of Daniel.

bFor He is the living God,
And steadfast forever;
His kingdom is the one which shall
not be cdestroyed,
And His dominion shall endure to the
end.
27 He delivers and rescues,
dAnd He works signs and wonders
In heaven and on earth,
Who has delivered Daniel from the
power of the lions.

28So this Daniel prospered in the reign
of Darius eand in the reign of fCyrus the
Persian.

Vision of the Four Beasts

7 In the first year of Belshazzar king of
Babylon, aDaniel had a dream and bvi-
sions of his head while on his bed. Then
he wrote down the dream, telling the main
facts.*

2Daniel spoke, saying, "I saw in my vision by night, and behold, the four winds
of heaven were stirring up the Great Sea.
3And four great beasts ccame up from the
sea, each different from the other. 4The first
was alike a lion, and had eagle's wings. I
watched till its wings were plucked off; and
it was lifted up from the earth and made to
stand on two feet like a man, and a eman's
heart was given to it.

5f"And suddenly another beast, a second,
like a bear. It was raised up on one side,
and had three ribs in its mouth between
its teeth. And they said thus to it: 'Arise,
devour much flesh!'

6"After this I looked, and there was

another, like a leopard, which had on its
back four wings of a bird. The beast also had
gfour heads, and dominion was given to it.
7"After this I saw in the night visions, and
behold, ha fourth beast, dreadful and terrible, exceedingly strong. It had huge iron
teeth; it was devouring, breaking in pieces,
and trampling the residue with its feet. It
was different from all the beasts that were
before it, iand it had ten horns. 8I was considering the horns, and jthere was another
horn, a little one, coming up among them,
before whom three of the first horns were
plucked out by the roots. And there, in this
horn, were eyes like the eyes kof a man, land
a mouth speaking pompous words.

Vision of the Ancient of Days

9 "Im watched till thrones were put in
place,
And nthe Ancient of Days was seated;
oHis garment was white as snow,
And the hair of His head was like pure
wool.
His throne was a fiery flame,
pIts wheels a burning fire;
10 qA fiery stream issued
And came forth from before Him.
rA thousand thousands ministered to
Him;
Ten thousand times ten thousand
stood before Him.
sThe court* was seated,
And the books were opened.

11"I watched then because of the sound
of the pompous words which the horn was
speaking; tI watched till the beast was
slain, and its body destroyed and given
to the burning flame. 12As for the rest of
the beasts, they had their dominion taken
away, yet their lives were prolonged for a
season and a time.

---

* 7:1 Literally the head (or chief) of the words
* 7:10 Or judgment

6:28 and in the reign of Cyrus. Gubaru, or Darius,
served Cyrus for about one year, after which Cyrus
appointed his son Cambyses as regent over Babylon.
7:1 the first year of Belshazzar. Chapter 5 records
Belshazzar's death, indicating that the Book of Daniel
is not arranged chronologically.
7:3 four great beasts. These four beasts represent
kings or kingdoms, like the four metals of the statue
in chapter 2.
7:4 like a lion, and had eagle's wings. There has
been almost universal agreement from the early centuries until today that this beast represents Babylon.
It is also agreed that the visions of chapters 2 and 7
speak of the same four kingdoms.
7:5 like a bear. The bear seems to represent Babylon's successor, the Medo-Persian Empire (2:38–39).
The three ribs may represent the three kingdoms that
Medo-Persia devoured—Babylon, Libya, and Egypt.
7:6 like a leopard. The leopard is believed to represent Greece. The Greeks, under the leadership of Alexander the Great, rapidly conquered the known world.

four heads. After Alexander's death, his empire was
divided into four different parts (8:8–22)—Macedonia, Egypt, Syria, and Thracia.
7:7 fourth beast. The last of the beasts may represent Rome (2:40).
7:9 Ancient of Days. "Ancient of Days" is a reference
to God the Father as certified by the submission of the
"One like the Son of Man" (vv. 13–14) and His role in
judgment (v. 22).
7:10 And the books were opened. The books record
the names and deeds of those who will be judged
(Rev. 20:12).

6:25 yDan. 4:1 **6:26** zDan. 3:29 aPs. 99:1 bDan.
4:34; 6:20 cDan. 2:44; 4:3; 7:14, 27 **6:27** dDan. 4:2, 3
6:28 eDan. 1:21 fEzra 1:1, 2 **7:1** a[Amos 3:7] b[Dan.
2:28] **7:3** cRev. 13:1; 17:8 **7:4** dDeut. 28:49 eDan.
4:16, 34 **7:5** fDan. 2:39 **7:6** gDan. 8:8, 22 **7:7** hDan.
2:40 iRev. 12:3; 13:1 **7:8** jDan. 8:9 kRev. 9:7 lRev.
13:5; 6 **7:9** mRev. 20:4] nPs. 90:2 oRev. 1:14 pEzek.
1:15 **7:10** qIs. 30:33; 66:15 rRev. 5:11 s[Rev. 20:11–15]
7:11 t[Rev. 19:20; 20:10]

13 "I was watching in the night visions,
And behold, [u]*One* like the Son of Man,
Coming with the clouds of heaven!
He came to the Ancient of Days,
And they brought Him near before Him.
14 [v]Then to Him was given dominion and
glory and a kingdom,
That all [w]peoples, nations, and
languages should serve Him.
His dominion *is* [x]an everlasting
dominion,
Which shall not pass away,
And His kingdom *the one*
Which shall not be destroyed.

Daniel's Visions Interpreted

15"I, Daniel, was grieved in my spirit
within *my* body, and the visions of my head
troubled me. 16I came near to one of those
who stood by, and asked him the truth of
all this. So he told me and made known
to me the interpretation of these things:
17'Those great beasts, which are four, *are*
four kings* which arise out of the earth.
18But [y]the saints of the Most High shall receive the kingdom, and possess the kingdom forever, even forever and ever.'
19"Then I wished to know the truth about
the fourth beast, which was different from
all the others, exceedingly dreadful, *with*
its teeth of iron and its nails of bronze,
which devoured, broke in pieces, and trampled the residue with its feet; 20and the ten
horns that *were* on its head, and the other
horn which came up, before which three
fell, namely, that horn which had eyes and
a mouth which spoke pompous words,
whose appearance *was* greater than his
fellows.
21"I was watching; [z]and the same horn
was making war against the saints, and
prevailing against them, 22until the Ancient of Days came, [a]and a judgment was
made *in favor* of the saints of the Most
High, and the time came for the saints to
possess the kingdom.

23"Thus he said:

'The fourth beast shall be
[b]A fourth kingdom on earth,
Which shall be different from all *other*
kingdoms,
And shall devour the whole earth,
Trample it and break it in pieces.
24 [c]The ten horns *are* ten kings
Who shall arise from this
kingdom.
And another shall rise after them;
He shall be different from the first
ones,
And shall subdue three kings.
25 [d]He shall speak *pompous* words
against the Most High,
Shall [e]persecute* the saints of the
Most High,
And shall [f]intend to change times and
law.
Then [g]*the saints* shall be given into
his hand
[h]For a time and times and half a
time.
26 'But[i] the court shall be seated,
And they shall [j]take away his
dominion,
To consume and destroy *it* forever.
27 Then the [k]kingdom and dominion,
And the greatness of the kingdoms
under the whole heaven,
Shall be given to the people, the saints
of the Most High.
[l]His kingdom *is* an everlasting
kingdom,
[m]And all dominions shall serve and
obey Him.'

28"This *is* the end of the account.* As for
me, Daniel, [n]my thoughts greatly troubled
me, and my countenance changed; but I
[o]kept the matter in my heart."

---

* **7:17** Representing their kingdoms (compare
verse 23) * **7:25** Literally *wear out* * **7:28** Literally *the word*

7:13 with the clouds of heaven. John uses the same
expression to speak of Jesus coming in judgment
(Rev. 1:7). **One like the Son of Man.** The term "son of
man" is an expression meaning "human," but clearly
this "One like the Son of Man" was no ordinary human.
Jewish and Christian expositors have both identified
this individual as the Messiah. Jesus Himself used this
name to emphasize His humanity (Matt. 9:6; 10:23).
7:14 to Him was given dominion. Jesus will reign
over all things (1 Cor. 15:27–28; Eph. 1:20–23; Phil.
2:9–11; Rev. 17:14; 19:10).
7:21 the same horn was making war. The little
horn's militaristic character is seen also in 11:38–39
and particularly in Revelation 13:1–10. There, in
the guise of a beast, this blasphemous enemy of
the saints prevails for 42 months. The connection
between Daniel's little horn and John's beast from
the sea is unmistakable.
7:24 The ten horns. Some perceive the fourth beast
as representing Rome, and the ten horns as the fragments of the Roman Empire. Others see the fourth

beast as a revived Roman Empire and the ten horns as
kings of a future realm.
7:25 a time and times and half a time. If the expression "time" is taken to mean a year, and "times" as
two years, the three and a half years would exactly
equal the 42 months mentioned in the Book of Revelation (Rev. 13:1–10), half of the 70th "week" of years
of 9:27. Some also believe that the expression does
not indicate a specific number of years but instead a
period of time that God in His mercy would shorten.

7:13 [u] [Matt. 24:30; 26:64; Mark 13:26; 14:62; Luke
21:27; Rev. 1:7, 12; 14:14]   **7:14** [v] [Matt. 28:18; John
3:35, 36; 1 Cor. 15:27; Eph. 1:22; Phil. 2:9–11; Rev. 1:6;
11:15] [w] Dan. 3:4 [x] Mic. 4:7 [Luke 1:33]; John 12:34; Heb.
12:28   **7:18** [y] Is. 60:12–14   **7:21** [z] Rev. 11:7; 13:7; 17:14
7:22 [a] [Rev. 1:6]   **7:23** [b] Dan. 2:40   **7:24** [c] Rev. 13:1;
17:12   **7:25** [d] Rev. 13:1–6 [e] Rev. 17:6 [f] Dan. 2:21 [g] Rev.
13:7; 18:24 [h] Rev. 12:14   **7:26** [i] [Dan. 2:35; 7:10, 22] [j] Rev.
19:20   **7:27** [k] Dan. 7:14, 18, 22 [l] [Luke 1:32, 33] [m] Is. 60:12
7:28 [n] Dan. 8:27 [o] Luke 2:19, 51

Vision of a Ram and a Goat

8 In the third year of the reign of King Belshazzar a vision appeared *to* me—to me, Daniel—after the one that appeared to me *a*the first time. **2**I saw in the vision, and it so happened while I was looking, that I *was* in *b*Shushan, the citadel, which *is* in the province of Elam; and I saw in the vision that I was by the River Ulai. **3**Then I lifted my eyes and saw, and there, standing beside the river, was a ram which had two horns, and the two horns *were* high; but one *was* *c*higher than the other, and the higher *one* came up last. **4**I saw the ram pushing westward, northward, and southward, so that no animal could withstand him; nor *was there any* that could deliver from his hand, *d*but he did according to his will and became great.

5And as I was considering, suddenly a male goat came from the west, across the surface of the whole earth, without touching the ground; and the goat *had* a notable *e*horn between his eyes. **6**Then he came to the ram that had two horns, which I had seen standing beside the river, and ran at him with furious power. **7**And I saw him confronting the ram; he was moved with rage against him, attacked the ram, and broke his two horns. There was no power in the ram to withstand him, but he cast him down to the ground and trampled them; and there was no one that could deliver the ram from his hand.

8Therefore the male goat grew very great; but when he became strong, the large horn was broken, and in place of it *f*four notable ones came up toward the four winds of heaven. **9**gAnd out of one of them came a little horn which grew exceedingly great toward the south, *h*toward the east, and toward the *i*Glorious *Land*. **10***j*And it grew up to *k*the host of heaven; and *l*it cast down *some* of the host and *some* of the stars to the ground, and trampled them. **11***m*He even exalted *himself* as high as *n*the Prince of the host; *o*and by him *p*the daily *sacrifices* were taken away, and the place

of His sanctuary was cast down. **12**Because of transgression, *q*an army was given over *to the horn* to oppose the daily *sacrifices;* and he cast *r*truth down to the ground. He *s*did *all this* and prospered.

13Then I heard *t*a holy one speaking; and *another* holy one said to that certain *one* who was speaking, "How long *will* the vision *be, concerning* the daily *sacrifices* and the transgression of desolation, the giving of both the sanctuary and the host to be trampled underfoot?"

14And he said to me, "For two thousand three hundred days;* then the sanctuary shall be cleansed."

Gabriel Interprets the Vision

15Then it happened, when I, Daniel, had seen the vision and *u*was seeking the meaning, that suddenly *u*there stood before me *v*one having the appearance of a man. **16**And I heard a man's voice *w*between *the* banks of the Ulai, who called, and said, *x*"Gabriel, make this *man* understand the vision." **17**So he came near where I stood, and when he came I was afraid and *y*fell on my face; but he said to me, "Understand, son of man, that the vision *refers* to the time of the end."

18*z*Now, as he was speaking with me, I was in a deep sleep with my face to the ground; *a*but he touched me, and stood me upright. **19**And he said, "Look, I am making known to you what shall happen in the latter time of the indignation; *b*for at the appointed time the end *shall be*. **20**The ram which you saw, having the two horns—*they are* the kings of Media and Persia. **21**And the male goat *is* the kingdom* of Greece. The large horn that *is* between its eyes *c*is the first king. **22***d*As for the broken *horn* and the four that stood up in its place, four kingdoms shall arise out of that nation, but not with its power.

* **8:14** Literally *evening-mornings*   * **8:21** Literally *king*, representing his kingdom (compare 7:17, 23)

8:1 *In the third year.* After writing in Aramaic from 2:4—7:28, Daniel returns to writing in Hebrew.

8:3 *a ram which had two horns.* The ram represents Medo-Persia (v. 20). The two horns symbolize the peoples of Media and Persia.

8:5 *a male goat.* The goat represents Greece (v. 21). The notable horn symbolizes Alexander the Great (v. 21) who launched his attack against Persia in 334 B.C. Within two years, he had essentially subdued the Persian Empire. His conquest was so rapid that it seemed as if he never touched the ground.

8:8 *the large horn was broken.* Alexander the Great died at the height of his career, before he was 33 years old. After his death, his empire was divided among his four generals (11:4).

8:9 *a little horn.* This horn is Antiochus Epiphanes, who ruled part of the Greek Empire from 175 to 164 B.C.

8:11 *Prince of the host.* This is clearly God Himself. The "host" refers to God's people (12:3; Gen. 15:5).

Antiochus is remembered in infamy by the Jews because he desecrated the temple by setting up a statue of Zeus and sacrificing a pig on the holy altar.

8:14 *two thousand three hundred days.* This was the amount of time between Antiochus' pollution of the temple and the Maccabees' cleansing of it.

8:16 *Gabriel.* This is the first mention of the angel Gabriel. This angel is mentioned by name three other times (9:21; Luke 1:19,26).

8:1 *a* Dan. 7:1   **8:2** *b* Esth. 1:2, 2:8   **8:3** *c* Dan. 7:5   **8:4** *d* Dan. 5:19   **8:5** *e* Dan. 8:8, 21; 11:3   **8:8** *f* Dan. 7:6; 8:22; 11:4   **8:9** *g* Dan. 11:21   *h* Dan. 11:25   *i* Ps. 48:2   **8:10** *j* Dan. 11:28   *k* Is. 14:13   *l* Rev. 12:4   **8:11** *m* Dan. 8:25; 11:36, 37   *n* Josh. 5:14   *o* Dan. 11:31; 12:11   *p* Ex. 29:38   **8:12** *q* Dan. 11:31   *r* Is. 59:14   *s* Dan. 8:4; 11:36   **8:13** *t* Dan. 4:13, 23   **8:15** *u* 1 Pet. 1:10   *v* Ezek. 1:26   **8:16** *w* Dan. 12:6, 7   *x* Luke 1:19, 26   *y* Rev. 1:17   **8:18** *z* Luke 9:32   *a* Ezek. 2:2   **8:19** *b* Hab. 2:3   **8:21** *c* Dan. 11:3   **8:22** *d* Dan. 11:4

23 "And in the latter time of their kingdom,
    When the transgressors have reached
        their fullness,
    A king shall arise,
    eHaving fierce features,
    Who understands sinister schemes.
24 His power shall be mighty, fbut not by
        his own power;
    He shall destroy fearfully,
    gAnd shall prosper and thrive;
    hHe shall destroy the mighty, and *also*
        the holy people.

25 "Throughi his cunning
    He shall cause deceit to prosper under
        his rule;*
    iAnd he shall exalt *himself* in his heart.
    He shall destroy many in *their*
        prosperity.
    kHe shall even rise against the Prince
        of princes;
    But he shall be lbroken without *human*
        means.*

26 "And the vision of the evenings and
        mornings
    Which was told is true;
    mTherefore seal up the vision,
    For *it refers* to many days *in the future.*"

27nAnd I, Daniel, fainted and was sick
for days; afterward I arose and went about
the king's business. I was astonished by the
vision, but no one understood it.

Daniel's Prayer for the People

9 In the first year aof Darius the son of
Ahasuerus, of the lineage of the Medes,
who was made king over the realm of the
Chaldeans—2in the first year of his reign I,
Daniel, understood by the books the num-
ber of the years *specified* by the word of the
LORD through bJeremiah the prophet, that

He would accomplish seventy years in the
desolations of Jerusalem.

3cThen I set my face toward the Lord
God to make request by prayer and supplications, with fasting, sackcloth, and ashes. 4And I prayed to the LORD my God, and
made confession, and said, "O dLord, great
and awesome God, who keeps His covenant
and mercy with those who love Him, and
with those who keep His commandments,
5ewe have sinned and committed iniquity,
we have done wickedly and rebelled, even
by departing from Your precepts and Your
judgments. 6fNeither have we heeded Your
servants the prophets, who spoke in Your
name to our kings and our princes, to our
fathers and all the people of the land. 7O
Lord, grighteousness *belongs* to You, but to
us shame of face, as *it is* this day—to the
men of Judah, to the inhabitants of Jerusalem and all Israel, those near and those far
off in all the countries to which You have
driven them, because of the unfaithfulness
which they have committed against You.

8"O Lord, to us *belongs* shame of face,
to our kings, our princes, and our fathers,
because we have sinned against You. 9hTo
the Lord our God *belong* mercy and forgiveness, though we have rebelled against
Him. 10We have not obeyed the voice of
the LORD our God, to walk in His laws,
which He set before us by His servants the
prophets. 11Yes, iall Israel has transgressed
Your law, and has departed so as not to
obey Your voice; therefore the curse and
the oath written in the jLaw of Moses the
servant of God have been poured out on
us, because we have sinned against Him.
12And He has kconfirmed His words, which
He spoke against us and against our judges
who judged us, by bringing upon us a great
disaster; lfor under the whole heaven such

---

* **8:25** Literally *hand* • Literally *hand*

8:24 not by his own power. Like the antichrist
(2 Thess. 2:9), Antiochus would be energized by
Satan.
8:25 broken without human means. According to
the book of 2 Maccabees, Antiochus died of a painful
disease.
9:2 by the books. The "books" were the Scriptures,
specifically the Book of Jeremiah, which states that
the captivity would last 70 years (Jer. 25:11–12;
29:10–14). By this time, Daniel himself had been in
captivity for about 67 years, and he knew that the
punishment was nearly over.
9:3–4 Prayer and Fasting—There are many examples in Scripture of people who pray to learn the will
of God. There are also some examples of people who
do not pray and find themselves in trouble (Josh. 9).
Most Christians quickly learn that one of the most
important ways we learn the will of God for our lives
is through prayer. "If any of you lacks wisdom, let
him ask of God, who gives to all liberally and without
reproach, and it will be given to him" (James 1:5). See
also Psalm 143:8–10 and James 4:2.
    Other verses in the Bible link prayer with fasting.
To fast is to abstain for a period of time from some

important and necessary activity in our lives. The
purpose of fasting is to be able to spend that time in
prayer before God. Different kinds of fasting are possible. One may for a time refrain from sleep (2 Cor. 6:5;
11:27), marital sex (1 Cor. 7:1–5), or food (Matt. 4:1–2).
There are also many examples of fasting in the Word:
Moses in Deuteronomy 9:9, Elijah in 1 Kings 19:8, Daniel in Daniel 9:3, Ezra in Ezra 10:6, and Nehemiah in
Nehemiah 1:4.
9:11 the curse and the oath. Covenant documents
typically contained statements concerning the pen-
alties for covenant violation (Lev. 26:3–45; Deut.
27–28). The most feared and devastating curse of all
had come to pass when the people were deported
from the land.

8:23 e Deut. 28:50   **8:24** f Rev. 17:13 g Dan. 11:36
h Dan. 7:25   **8:25** i Dan. 11:21 j Dan. 8:11–13; 11:36;
12:7 k Rev. 19:19, 20 l Job 34:20   **8:26** m Ezek. 12:27
8:27 n Dan. 7:28; 8:17   **9:1** a Dan. 1:21   **9:2** b 2 Chr.
36:21   **9:3** c Neh. 1:4   **9:4** d Ex. 20:6   **9:5** e 1 Kin. 8:47,
48   **9:6** f 2 Chr. 36:15   **9:7** g Neh. 9:33
9:9 h [Ps. 130:4, 7]   **9:11** i Is. 1:3–6 j Lev. 26:14
9:12 k Zech. 1:6 l Lam. 1:12; 2:13

has never been done as what has been done to Jerusalem.

¹³ᵐ"As *it is* written in the Law of Moses, all this disaster has come upon us; ⁿyet we have not made our prayer before the LORD our God, that we might turn from our iniquities and understand Your truth. ¹⁴Therefore the LORD has ᵒkept the disaster in mind, and brought it upon us; for ᵖthe LORD our God *is* righteous in all the works which He does, though we have not obeyed His voice. ¹⁵And now, O Lord our God, qwho brought Your people out of the land of Egypt with a mighty hand, and made Yourself ʳa name, as *it is* this day— we have sinned, we have done wickedly!

¹⁶"O Lord, ˢaccording to all Your righteousness, I pray, let Your anger and Your fury be turned away from Your city Jerusalem, ᵗYour holy mountain; because for our sins, ᵘand for the iniquities of our fathers, ᵛJerusalem and Your people ʷ*are* a reproach to all *those* around us. ¹⁷Now therefore, our God, hear the prayer of Your servant, and his supplications, ˣand ʸfor the Lord's sake cause Your face to shine on Your sanctuary, ᶻwhich is desolate. ¹⁸ᵃO my God, incline Your ear and hear; open Your eyes ᵇand see our desolations, and the city ᶜwhich is called by Your name; for we do not present our supplications before You because of our righteous deeds, but because of Your great mercies. ¹⁹O Lord, hear! O Lord, forgive! O Lord, listen and act! Do not delay for Your own sake, my God, for Your city and Your people are called by Your name."

The Seventy-Weeks Prophecy

²⁰Now while I *was* speaking, praying, and confessing my sin and the sin of my people Israel, and presenting my supplication before the LORD my God for the holy mountain of my God, ²¹yes, while I *was* speaking in prayer, the man ᵈGabriel, whom I had seen in the vision at the beginning, being caused to fly swiftly, reached me about the time of the evening offering. ²²And he informed *me*, and talked with me,

and said, "O Daniel, I have now come forth to give you skill to understand. ²³At the beginning of your supplications the command went out, and I have come to tell *you*, for you *are* greatly ᵉbeloved; therefore ᶠconsider the matter, and understand the vision:

²⁴ "Seventy weeks* are determined
   For your people and for your holy city,
   To finish the transgression,
   To make an end of* sins,
   ᵍTo make reconciliation for iniquity,
   ʰTo bring in everlasting righteousness,
   To seal up vision and prophecy,
   ⁱAnd to anoint the Most Holy.

²⁵ "Know therefore and understand,
   That from the going forth of the
      command
   To restore and build Jerusalem
   Until ʲMessiah ᵏthe Prince,
   There shall be seven weeks and sixty-
      two weeks;
   The street* shall be built again, and
      the wall,*
   Even in troublesome times.

²⁶ "And after the sixty-two weeks
   ˡMessiah shall be cut off, ᵐbut not for
      Himself;
   And ⁿthe people of the prince who is
      to come
   ᵒShall destroy the city and the sanctuary.
   The end of it *shall be* with a flood,
   And till the end of the war desolations
      are determined.
²⁷ Then he shall confirm ᵖa covenant
      with qmany for one week;
   But in the middle of the week
   He shall bring an end to sacrifice and
      offering.
   And on the wing of abominations shall
      be one who makes desolate,
   ʳEven until the consummation, which is
      determined,
   Is poured out on the desolate."

---

* 9:24 Literally *sevens*, and so throughout the chapter • Following Qere, Septuagint, Syriac, and Vulgate; Kethib and Theodotion read *To seal up.*
* 9:25 Or *open square* • Or *moat*

9:21 *the time of the evening offering.* The temple was in ruins, and regular daily sacrifices were impossible. Nevertheless, Daniel observed the ritual of worship by praying at the hour of the evening sacrifice. Daniel's prayer was his evening offering.
9:24 *Seventy weeks.* The word "weeks" can also be translated "sevens." Many scholars agree that the "sevens" are periods of seven years.
9:25 *the going forth of the command to restore and build Jerusalem.* This may refer to the decree of Cyrus in Ezra 1, the decree of Darius in Ezra 6, the decree of Artaxerxes in Ezra 7, or the decree of Artaxerxes in Nehemiah 2.
9:26 *sixty-two weeks.* When the 7 weeks and 62 weeks (v. 25) are added together, they equal 483 years. If these years are added to the date of the decree of Artaxerxes in Nehemiah 2 (445 B.C.), with an adjustment to allow for a 360-day year, the end of

the 69 weeks coincides with the date of the triumphal entry into Jerusalem just before the crucifixion. ***the prince who is to come.*** This seems to be a reference to the antichrist.
9:27 *in the middle of the week.* That is, 3-1/2 years later. These 3-1/2 years of the rule of the antichrist

---

9:13 ᵐDeut. 28:15–68 ⁿIs. 9:13   **9:14** ᵒ Jer. 31:28;
44:27 ᵖNeh. 9:33   **9:15** qNeh. 1:10 ʳNeh. 9:10
9:16 ˢ1 Sam. 12:7 ᵗZech. 8:3 ᵘEx. 20:5 ᵛLam. 2:16 ʷPs.
79:4   **9:17** ˣNum. 6:24–26 ʸLam. 5:18 ᶻ[John 16:24]
9:18 ᵃIs. 37:17 ᵇEx. 3:7 ᶜJer. 25:29   **9:21** ᵈDan. 8:16
9:23 ᵉDan. 10:11, 19 ᶠMatt. 24:15   **9:24** ᵍ[Is. 53:10]
ʰRev. 14:6 ⁱPs. 45:7   **9:25** ʲJohn 1:41; 4:25 ᵏIs. 55:4
9:26 ˡ[Is. 53:8]; Matt. 27:50; Mark 9:12; 15:37; [Luke 23:46;
24:26]; John 19:30; Acts 8:32 ᵐ[1 Pet. 2:21] ⁿMatt. 22:7
ᵒMatt. 24:2; Mark 13:2; Luke 19:43, 44   **9:27** ᵖIs. 42:6
q[Matt. 26:28] ʳDan. 11:36

Vision of the Glorious Man

10 In the third year of Cyrus king of Persia a message was revealed to Daniel, whose *a*name was called Belteshazzar. The message *was* true, but the appointed time *was* long;* and he understood the message, and had understanding of the vision. ²In those days I, Daniel, was mourning three full weeks. ³I ate no pleasant food, no meat or wine came into my mouth, nor did I anoint myself at all, till three whole weeks were fulfilled.

⁴Now on the twenty-fourth day of the first month, as I was by the side of the great river, that *is*, the Tigris,* ⁵I lifted my eyes and looked, and behold, a certain man clothed in *b*linen, whose waist *was* *c*girded with gold of Uphaz! ⁶His body *was* like beryl, his face like the appearance of lightning, his eyes like torches of fire, his arms and feet like burnished bronze in color, *d*and the sound of his words like the voice of a multitude.

⁷And I, Daniel, alone saw the vision, for the men who were with me did not see the vision; but a great terror fell upon them, so that they fled to hide themselves. ⁸Therefore I was left alone when I saw this great vision, and no strength remained in me; for my vigor was turned to frailty in me, and I retained no strength. ⁹Yet I heard the sound of his words; and while I heard the sound of his words I was in a deep sleep on my face, with my face to the ground.

Prophecies Concerning Persia and Greece

¹⁰*e*Suddenly, a hand touched me, which made me tremble on my knees and *on* the palms of my hands. ¹¹And he said to me, "O Daniel, *f*man greatly beloved, understand the words that I speak to you, and stand upright, for I have now been sent to you."

While he was speaking this word to me, I stood trembling.

¹²Then he said to me, *g*"Do not fear, Daniel, for from the first day that you set your heart to understand, and to humble yourself before your God, *h*your words were heard; and I have come because of your words. ¹³*i*But the prince of the kingdom of Persia withstood me twenty-one days; and behold, *j*Michael, one of the chief princes, came to help me, for I had been left alone there with the kings of Persia. ¹⁴Now I have come to make you understand what will happen to your people *k*in the latter days, *l*for the vision *refers* to *many* days yet *to come*."

¹⁵When he had spoken such words to me, *m*I turned my face toward the ground and became speechless. ¹⁶And suddenly, *n*one having the likeness of the sons* of men *o*touched my lips; then I opened my mouth and spoke, saying to him who stood before me, "My lord, because of the vision *p*my sorrows have overwhelmed me, and I have retained no strength. ¹⁷For how can this servant of my lord talk with you, my lord? As for me, no strength remains in me now, nor is any breath left in me."

¹⁸Then again, the one having the likeness of a man touched me and strengthened me. ¹⁹*q*And he said, "O man greatly beloved, *r*fear not! Peace *be* to you; be strong, yes, be strong!"

So when he spoke to me I was strengthened, and said, "Let my lord speak, for you have strengthened me."

²⁰Then he said, "Do you know why I have come to you? And now I must return to fight *s*with the prince of Persia; and when I have gone forth, indeed the prince of Greece will come. ²¹But I will tell you

* **10:1** Or *and of great conflict* * **10:4** Hebrew *Hiddekel* * **10:16** Theodotion and Vulgate read *the son*; Septuagint reads *a hand*.

---

seem to correspond with the "time and times and half a time" when the fourth beast rules (7:25) and with the 42-month rule of the beast from the sea (Rev. 13:1–10). **one who makes desolate.** Antiochus committed an abomination by setting up an altar to the god Zeus in the holy place in the temple in Jerusalem (11:31). The antichrist will also commit an abomination of desolation against the living God. Jesus' reference to "the abomination of desolation, spoken of by Daniel the prophet" (Matt. 24:15) occurred long after the desolation caused by Antiochus and indicates that this verse is describing the abomination of the antichrist and not that of Antiochus.

10:2 three full weeks. This period of time refers to Daniel's observance of the Passover and the Feast of Unleavened Bread, which took place during the first month of the year (Ex. 12:1–20).

10:6 his face like the appearance of lightning. The description of this man is very much like Ezekiel's description of the glory of God (Ezek. 1:4–28) and John's description of the risen Christ (Rev. 1:9–20).

10:13 the prince of the kingdom of Persia. This prince cannot be a human ruler because the conflict

referred to here is in the spiritual, heavenly realm, as the allusion to the angel Michael (also referred to as a prince) makes clear. This prince, therefore, must be understood as a satanic figure who was to supervise the affairs of Persia, inspiring its religious, social, and political structures to evil. The apostle Paul refers to "spiritual hosts of wickedness in the heavenly places" (Eph. 6:12). The prince of Persia apparently sought to detain the angel so that Daniel would be prevented from hearing more of God's revelation (vv. 12–14). **Michael.** Michael seems to be one of the most powerful angels. He is mentioned three times in the Old Testament, all in the Book of Daniel (v. 21; 12:1), and twice in the New Testament (Jude 9; Rev. 12:7).

10:20 with the prince of Persia. Persia was under

10:1 *a* Dan. 1:7   **10:5** *b* Ezek. 9:2; 10:2   *c* Rev. 1:13; 15:6   **10:6** *d* [Rev. 1:15]   **10:10** *e* Dan. 9:21   **10:11** *f* Dan. 9:23   **10:12** *g* Rev. 1:17   *h* Acts 10:4   **10:13** *i* Dan. 10:20   *j* Dan. 10:21; 12:1   **10:14** *k* Dan. 2:28   *l* Dan. 8:26; 10:1   **10:15** *m* Dan. 8:18; 10:9   **10:16** *n* Dan. 8:15   *o* Jer. 1:9   *p* Dan. 10:8, 9   **10:19** *q* Dan. 10:11   *r* Judg. 6:23   **10:20** *s* Dan. 10:13

what is noted in the Scripture of Truth. (No one upholds me against these, [t]except Michael your prince.

11 "Also [a]in the first year of [b]Darius the Mede, I, *even* I, stood up to confirm and strengthen him.) [2]And now I will tell you the truth: Behold, three more kings will arise in Persia, and the fourth shall be far richer than *them* all; by his strength, through his riches, he shall stir up all against the realm of Greece. [3]Then [c]a mighty king shall arise, who shall rule with great dominion, and [d]do according to his will. [4]And when he has arisen, [e]his kingdom shall be broken up and divided toward the four winds of heaven, but not among his posterity [f]nor according to his dominion with which he ruled; for his kingdom shall be uprooted, even for others besides these.

Warring Kings of North and South

[5]"Also the king of the South shall become strong, as well as *one* of his princes; and he shall gain power over him and have dominion. His dominion *shall be* a great dominion. [6]And at the end of *some* years they shall join forces, for the daughter of the king of the South shall go to the king of the North to make an agreement; but she shall not retain the power of her authority,* and neither he nor his authority* shall stand; but she shall be given up, with those who brought her, and with him who begot her, and with him who strengthened her in *those* times. [7]But from a branch of her roots *one* shall arise in his place, who shall come with an army, enter the fortress of the king of the North, and deal with them and prevail. [8]And he shall also carry their gods captive to Egypt, with their princes* *and* their precious articles of silver and gold; and he shall continue *more* years than the king of the North.

[9]"Also *the king of the North* shall come to the kingdom of the king of the South, but shall return to his own land. [10]However his sons shall stir up strife, and assemble a multitude of great forces; and *one* shall certainly come [g]and overwhelm and pass through; then he shall return [h]to his fortress and stir up strife.

[11]"And the king of the South shall be [i]moved with rage, and go out and fight with him, with the king of the North, who shall muster a great multitude; but the [j]multitude shall be given into the hand of his *enemy*. [12]When he has taken away the multitude, his heart will be lifted up; and he will cast down tens of thousands, but he will not prevail. [13]For the king of the North will return and muster a multitude greater than the former, and shall certainly come at the end of some years with a great army and much equipment.

[14]"Now in those times many shall rise up against the king of the South. Also, violent men* of your people shall exalt themselves in fulfillment of the vision, but they shall [k]fall. [15]So the king of the North shall come and [l]build a siege mound, and take a fortified city; and the forces* of the South shall not withstand *him*. Even his choice troops *shall have* no strength to resist. [16]But he who comes against him [m]shall do according to his own will, and [n]no one shall stand against him. He shall stand in the Glorious Land with destruction in his power.*

[17]"He shall also [o]set his face to enter with the strength of his whole kingdom, and upright ones* with him; thus shall he do. And he shall give him the daughter of women to destroy it; but she shall not stand *with him*,

---

* **11:6** Literally *arm* • Literally *arm* * **11:8** Or *molded images* * **11:14** Or *robbers*, literally *sons of breakage* * **11:15** Literally *arms* * **11:16** Literally *hand* * **11:17** Or *bring equitable terms*

---

the ultimate dominion of an evil spirit from Satan (vv. 13–14), and so also was Greece. The succession of world powers follows the pattern of Daniel's second vision (8:20–22).

11:1 the first year of Darius. This is the same year as that of the revelation of the 70 weeks, 539 B.C.

11:2 three more kings. Darius (under Cyrus) was followed by Cambyses (530–522 B.C.), Gaumata (522 B.C.), Darius I (522–486 B.C.), and Xerxes (486–465 B.C.)—who was the richest king of all, due to the extent of the empire's conquests and the severe taxation.

11:4 but not among his posterity. The "mighty king" of verse 3 fits with Alexander the Great, the first ruler of the Greek Empire. When Alexander died, his four generals carved up the Macedonian Empire. Antigonus ruled from southern Syria to central Asia; Cassander ruled over Macedonia; Ptolemy ruled in Egypt and southern Syria, including Palestine; Lysimachus ruled over Thrace.

11:5 the king of the South. Alexander's general Ptolemy I Soter was the first king of the southern kingdom—that is, Egypt.

11:6–15 at the end of some years. The events described in these verses fit with the actual history

of the divided Greek Empire. **the daughter of the king.** This refers to Berenice, the daughter of Ptolemy Philadelphus (285–246 B.C.) of Egypt. **the king of the North.** This is Antiochus II Theos (261–246 B.C.) of Syria. **a branch of her roots.** This is Berenice's brother, Ptolemy III Eurgetes (246–221 B.C.), who conquered Seleucus Callinicus (246–226 B.C.) of Syria (the king of the North). Seleucus did attempt a return attack on Egypt, but returned to Syria without accomplishing his goal. The kings of Egypt and Syria (the south and the north) continued to war against each other in the manner described in the prophecy. **take a fortified city.** Antiochus of Syria defeated the fortified city of Sidon in 198 B.C.

11:17 the daughter of women. Antiochus III's daughter Cleopatra was given in marriage to Ptolemy V Epiphanes of Egypt in order to destroy or undermine

---

10:21 [t][Rev. 12:7] **11:1** [a]Dan. 9:1 [b]Dan. 5:31 **11:3** [c]Dan. 7:6; 8:5 [d]Dan. 8:4; 11:16, 36 **11:4** [e]Zech. 2:6 [f]Dan. 8:22 **11:10** [g]Is. 8:8 [h]Dan. 11:7 **11:11** [i]Prov. 16:14 [j][Ps. 33:10, 16] **11:14** [k]Job 9:13 **11:15** [l]Ezek. 4:2; 17:17 **11:16** [m]Dan. 8:4, 7 [n]Josh. 1:5 **11:17** [o]2 Chr. 20:3

*or be for him. **18**After this he shall turn his face to the coastlands, and shall take many. But a ruler shall bring the reproach against them to an end; and with the reproach removed, he shall turn back on him. **19**Then he shall turn his face toward the fortress of his own land; but he shall *q*stumble and fall, *r*and not be found.

20"There shall arise in his place one who imposes taxes *on* the glorious kingdom; but within a few days he shall be destroyed, but not in anger or in battle. **21**And in his place *s*shall arise a vile person, to whom they will not give the honor of royalty; but he shall come in peaceably, and seize the kingdom by intrigue. **22**With the force* of a *t*flood they shall be swept away from before him and be broken, *u*and also the prince of the covenant. **23**And after the league *is made* with him *v*he shall act deceitfully, for he shall come up and become strong with a small *number of* people. **24**He shall enter peaceably, even into the richest places of the province; and he shall do *what* his fathers have not done, nor his forefathers: he shall disperse among them the plunder, spoil, and riches; and he shall devise his plans against the strongholds, but *only* for a time.

25"He shall stir up his power and his courage against the king of the South with a great army. And the king of the South shall be stirred up to battle with a very great and mighty army; but he shall not stand, for they shall devise plans against him. **26**Yes, those who eat of the portion of his delicacies shall destroy him; his army shall be swept away, and many shall fall down slain. **27**Both these kings' hearts *shall be* bent on evil, and they shall speak lies at the same table; but it shall not prosper, for the end *will* still *be* at the *w*appointed time. **28**While returning to his land with great riches, his heart shall be *moved* against the holy covenant; so he shall do *damage* and return to his own land.

The Northern King's Blasphemies

29"At the appointed time he shall return and go toward the south; but it shall not be like the former or the latter. **30**xFor ships from Cyprus* shall come against him; therefore he shall be grieved, and return in rage against the holy covenant, and do *damage.*

"So he shall return and show regard for those who forsake the holy covenant. **31**And forces* shall be mustered by him, *y*and they shall defile the sanctuary fortress; then they shall take away the daily *sacrifices,* and place *there* the abomination of desolation. **32**Those who do wickedly against the covenant he shall corrupt with flattery; but the people who know their God shall be strong, and carry out *great exploits.* **33**And those of the people who understand shall instruct many; yet *for many* days they shall fall by sword and flame, by captivity and plundering. **34**Now when they fall, they shall be aided with a little help; but many shall join with them by intrigue. **35**And *some* of those of understanding shall fall, *z*to refine them, purify *them,* and make *them* white, *until* the time of the end; because *it is* still for the appointed time.

---

* **11:22** Literally *arms*   * **11:30** Hebrew *Kittim,* western lands, especially Cyprus   * **11:31** Literally *arms*

Egypt, but Cleopatra sided with her husband over her father.

11:18–19 the coastlands . . . his own land. Antiochus III undertook a vigorous campaign into Asia Minor and the Aegean region. The Roman Lucius Cornelius Scipio defeated Antiochus. Having lost all that he had gained, Antiochus returned to his own land, where he was defeated and killed while trying to plunder a temple.

11:21 a vile person. Antiochus IV Epiphanes seized the throne through treachery and later defiled the temple in Jerusalem (v. 31; 9:27).

11:29 he shall return and go toward the south. After learning that Ptolemy VI and Ptolemy VII had formed a union against him, Antiochus returned to Egypt in 168 B.C., but he was driven out by the Romans.

11:31 abomination of desolation. Antiochus defiled the sanctuary by sacrificing a pig on the altar. He put a stop to the daily sacrifices, and he set up an image of Zeus in the holy place. Jesus said that a similar thing would happen just prior to His return (Matt. 24:15).

11:32 the people who know their God. The books of Maccabees record the story of Mattathias, the father of five sons, who refused to offer profane sacrifices and killed the king's agents. He and his sons then fled to the mountains and began the famous Maccabean revolt.

11:32 Know God Through His Word—The highest knowledge to which men and women can attain is personal knowledge of God (Jer. 9:24). One of the most valuable teachings of Scripture is that we can actually know God through His Word. To know God personally is to be saved and have eternal life (Job 17:3). We gain this knowledge primarily through interaction with His Word in four ways: First, we listen to and receive God's Word as the Holy Spirit interprets it and applies it to our hearts. Second, Scripture reveals God's nature and character. We know God through understanding of the works He has done, which are explained in Scripture. Third, our knowledge of God moves from intellectual to personal when we accept the invitation He has given us and do what He commands. Fourth, our personal knowledge of God grows as we rejoice in the love He shows us in Scripture and express joy in response to what He has done for us and given us. The Word leads to knowledge of all that is true about God. This knowledge of God then produces fellowship with Him.

11:35 it is still for the appointed time. Clearly, the trouble and wickedness of Antiochus' reign was not the end. That is yet to come.

11:17 *p* Dan. 9:26   **11:19** *q* Jer. 46:6   *r* Ps. 37:36
11:21 *s* Dan. 7:8   **11:22** *t* Dan. 9:26   *u* Dan. 8:10, 11
11:23 *v* Dan. 8:25   **11:27** *w* Hab. 2:3   **11:30** *x* Jer. 2:10
11:31 *y* Dan. 8:11–13; 12:11   **11:35** *z* Dan. 12:10

36"Then the king shall do according to his own will: he shall ^aexalt and magnify himself above every god, shall speak blasphemies against the God of gods, and shall prosper till the wrath has been accomplished; for what has been determined shall be done. 37He shall regard neither the God* of his fathers nor the desire of women, ^bnor regard any god; for he shall exalt himself above *them* all. 38But in their place he shall honor a god of fortresses; and a god which his fathers did not know he shall honor with gold and silver, with precious stones and pleasant things. 39Thus he shall act against the strongest fortresses with a foreign god, which he shall acknowledge, *and* advance *its* glory; and he shall cause them to rule over many, and divide the land for gain.

The Northern King's Conquests

40"At the ^ctime of the end the king of the South shall attack him; and the king of the North shall come against him ^dlike a whirlwind, with chariots, ^ehorsemen, and with many ships; and he shall enter the countries, overwhelm *them*, and pass through. 41He shall also enter the Glorious Land, and many *countries* shall be overthrown; but these shall escape from his hand: ^fEdom, Moab, and the prominent people of Ammon. 42He shall stretch out his hand against the countries, and the land of ^gEgypt shall not escape. 43He shall have power over the treasures of gold and silver, and over all the precious things of Egypt; also the Libyans and Ethiopians *shall follow* ^hat his heels. 44But news from the east and the north shall trouble him; therefore he shall go out with great fury to destroy and annihilate many. 45And he shall plant the tents of his palace between the seas and ⁱthe glorious holy mountain; ^jyet he shall come to his end, and no one will help him.

Prophecy of the End Time

12 "At that time Michael shall stand up,
The great prince who stands *watch*
over the sons of your people;
^aAnd there shall be a time of
trouble,
Such as never was since there was a
nation,
Even to that time.
And at that time your people ^bshall be
delivered,
Every one who is found ^cwritten in the
book.
2 And many of those who sleep in the
dust of the earth shall awake,
^dSome to everlasting life,
Some to shame ^e*and* everlasting
contempt.
3 Those who are wise shall ^fshine
Like the brightness of the
firmament,
^gAnd those who turn many to
righteousness
^hLike the stars forever and ever.

4"But you, Daniel, ⁱshut up the words, and seal the book until the time of the end; many shall ^jrun to and fro, and knowledge shall increase."

5Then I, Daniel, looked; and there stood two others, one on this riverbank and the other on that ^kriverbank. 6And *one* said to the man clothed in ^llinen, who *was* above the waters of the river, ^m"How long shall the fulfillment of these wonders *be?*"

7Then I heard the man clothed in linen, who *was* above the waters of the river, when he ⁿheld up his right hand and his left hand to heaven, and swore by Him ^owho lives forever, ^pthat *it shall be* for a time, times, and half *a time;* ^qand when the power of ^rthe holy people has been completely shattered, all these *things* shall be finished.

* 11:37 Or gods

11:36 *Then the king.* Many ancient and modern interpreters have concluded that at this point a new person, the antichrist, is introduced. This king is distinguished from the king of the North (v. 40); therefore, he cannot be Antiochus Epiphanes. It appears that there is a gap of many years between verses 35 and 36, and this refers back to "the time of the end" which will come at the "appointed time" (v. 35).
11:38 *a god which his fathers did not know.* This is probably a reference to self-worship (v. 37; 2 Thess. 2:4).
11:40 *time of the end.* This is the period just before the return of Christ (Matt. 24:14).
11:45 *no one will help him.* The end of the king is sealed at Christ's second coming (Rev. 19:11–21).
12:1 *written in the book.* The Book of Life is God's record of those who are justified by faith (Ex. 32:32; Ps. 69:28; Luke 10:20; Rev. 20:12).
12:2 *many . . . who sleep . . . shall awake.* This passage appears to refer to a general resurrection, while other passages suggest that there is more than one (John 5:25). It is not unusual for prophecy in the Old

Testament to present events separated by a considerable span of time as if they occurred in immediate relationship to each other (see, for example, Is. 61:1–2).
12:6 *How long.* This question refers to the duration of the trials, not the dates of the events.
12:7 *a time, times, and half a time.* If a "time" is a year, this adds up to 3-1/2 years (7:25), which may refer to the period immediately preceding the second coming of Christ (7:27). Some believe that this expression is not meant to indicate anything more specific than a length of time.

11:36 ^aDan. 7:8, 25   11:37 ^bIs. 14:13   11:40 ^cDan. 11:27, 35; 12:4, 9 ^dIs. 21:1 ^eRev. 9:16   11:41 ^fIs. 11:14   11:42 ^gJoel 3:19   11:43 ^hEx. 11:8   11:45 ⁱPs. 48:2 ^jRev. 19:20   12:1 ^aJer. 30:7 ^bRom. 11:26 ^cEx. 32:32 12:2 ^d[John 5:28, 29] ^e[Is. 66:24]   12:3 ^fMatt. 13:43 ^g[James 5:19, 20] ^h1 Cor. 15:41   12:4 ⁱRev. 22:10 ^jAmos 8:12   12:5 ^kDan. 10:4   12:6 ^lEzek. 9:2 ^mDan. 8:13; 12:8   12:7 ⁿDeut. 32:40 ^oDan. 4:34 ^pDan. 7:25 ^qLuke 21:24 ^rDan. 8:24

⁸Although I heard, I did not understand. Then I said, "My lord, what *shall be* the end of these *things*?"

⁹And he said, "Go *your way*, Daniel, for the words *are* closed up and sealed till the time of the end. ¹⁰ˢMany shall be purified, made white, and refined, ᵗbut the wicked shall do wickedly; and none of the wicked shall understand, but ᵘthe wise shall understand.

¹¹"And from the time *that* the daily *sacrifice* is taken away, and the abomination of desolation is set up, *there shall be* one thousand two hundred and ninety days. ¹²Blessed *is* he who waits, and comes to the one thousand three hundred and thirty-five days.

¹³"But you, go *your way* till the end; ᵛfor you shall rest, ʷand will arise to your inheritance at the end of the days."

12:11 one thousand two hundred and ninety days. Various interpretations have been suggested. One significant interpretation is that these days refer to the time following a point halfway through a seven-year period of tribulation prior to the coming of Christ (9:27).

12:12 the one thousand three hundred and thirty-five days. The extra 45 days may be the amount of

time that the last battles will take before the victory is completely established.

12:13 you shall rest, and will arise to your inheritance. Daniel died before these things came to pass, but at the end he will be among those resurrected (v. 2).

12:10 ˢ Zech. 13:9 ᵗ Is. 32:6, 7 ᵘ John 7:17; 8:47
12:13 ᵛ Rev. 14:13 ʷ Ps. 1:5

THE BOOK OF
HOSEA

▶ **AUTHOR:** Few critics argue with the claim in 1:1 that Hosea is the author of this book. The author's place of birth is not given but his familiarity and obvious concern with the northern kingdom point to his living in Israel, rather than Judah. Hosea had a real compassion for his people. His personal suffering because of his wife, Gomer, gave him some understanding of God's grief over the people's sin, and this grief becomes the source of the unique tenderness and hope that characterizes Hosea's book.

▶ **TIME:** c. 755–710 B.C.   ▶ **KEY VERSE:** Hos. 4:1

▶ **THEME:** Hosea was a contemporary of Isaiah, prophesying near the end of Israel's existence. It is clear from reading the text that Assyria was about to take over. In the second verse of Hosea, God tells Hosea to marry a prostitute named Gomer to provide a living illustration of God's faithfulness and Israel's unfaithfulness. By this, Hosea demonstrates that God loves us, as He did Israel, knowingly and in spite of all our propensities to reject His love for us.

---

1 The word of the LORD that came to Hosea the son of Beeri, in the days of *a*Uzziah, *b*Jotham, *c*Ahaz, *and* *d*Hezekiah, kings of Judah, and in the days of *e*Jeroboam the son of Joash, king of Israel.

The Family of Hosea
2When the LORD began to speak by Hosea, the LORD said to Hosea:

f"Go, take yourself a wife of harlotry
And children of harlotry,
  For *g*the land has committed great harlotry
  By departing from the LORD."

3So he went and took Gomer the daughter of Diblaim, and she conceived and bore him a son. **4**Then the LORD said to him:

"Call his name Jezreel,
  For in a little *while*
  *h*I will avenge the bloodshed of Jezreel on the house of Jehu,
  *i*And bring an end to the kingdom of the house of Israel.

5 *j*It shall come to pass in that day
That I will break the bow of Israel in the Valley of Jezreel."

6And she conceived again and bore a daughter. Then *God* said to him:

"Call her name Lo-Ruhamah,*
  *k*For I will no longer have mercy on the house of Israel,
  But I will utterly take them away.*
7 *l*Yet I will have mercy on the house of Judah,
  Will save them by the LORD their God,
  And *m*will not save them by bow,
  Nor by sword or battle,
  By horses or horsemen."

8Now when she had weaned Lo-Ruhamah, she conceived and bore a son. **9**Then *God* said:

---

* **1:6** Literally *No-Mercy* • Or *That I may forgive them at all*

1:2–3 *wife of harlotry.* Gomer may have been a common prostitute at the time Hosea married her, or perhaps she had participated in a ritual sexual act as part of a Baal cult. However, it is more likely that the descriptive phrase anticipates what Gomer would become following her marriage to Hosea. *children of harlotry.* If Gomer was a prostitute when she married Hosea, this could refer to children that Gomer already had and that Hosea adopted at the time of marriage. A more likely possibility is that the title anticipates children born to a mother whose reputation and escapades would make their lineage suspect. Gomer's marital infidelity is a picture of Israel's idolatry and unfaithfulness to its covenant with God.

1:5 *break the bow.* This phrase means to destroy an opponent's military strength (1 Sam. 2:4; Ps. 46:9; Jer. 49:35).

1:6 *Lo-Ruhamah.* This means "no mercy" or "not loved," foreshadowing the Lord's rejection of Israel.

1:9 *Lo-Ammi.* This means "not my people,"

1:1 *a* Amos 1:1   *b* 2 Chr. 27   *c* 2 Chr. 28   *d* 2 Chr. 29:1—32:33   *e* 2 Kin. 13:13; 14:23–29   **1:2** *f* Hos. 3:1 *g* Jer. 2:13   **1:4** *h* 2 Kin. 10:11 *i* 2 Kin. 15:8–10; 17:6, 23; 18:11   **1:5** *j* 2 Kin. 15:29   **1:6** *k* 2 Kin. 17:6   **1:7** *l* 2 Kin. 19:29–35 *m* [Zech. 4:6]

"Call his name Lo-Ammi,*
For you *are* not My people,
And I will not be your *God.*

The Restoration of Israel

10 "Yet *n*the number of the children of Israel
Shall be as the sand of the sea,
Which cannot be measured or
numbered.
*o*And it shall come to pass
In the place where it was said to them,
'You *are* not My *p*people,'*
There it shall be said to them,
'You *are* *q*sons of the living God.'
11 *r*Then the children of Judah and the
children of Israel
Shall be gathered together,
And appoint for themselves one head;
And they shall come up out of the
land,
For great *will be* the day of Jezreel!

2 Say to your brethren, 'My people,'*
And to your sisters, 'Mercy* *is shown.'*

God's Unfaithful People

2 "Bring charges against your mother,
bring charges;
For *a*she *is* not My wife, nor *am* I her
Husband!
Let her put away her *b*harlotries from
her sight,
And her adulteries from between her
breasts;
3 Lest *c*I strip her naked
And expose her, as in the day she was
*d*born,
And make her like a wilderness,
And set her like a dry land,
And slay her with *e*thirst.
4 "I will not have mercy on her children,
For they *are* the *f*children of harlotry.
5 For their mother has played the
harlot;
She who conceived them has behaved
shamefully.
For she said, 'I will go after my lovers,
*g*Who give *me* my bread and my water,
My wool and my linen,
My oil and my drink.'
6 "Therefore, behold,
*h*I will hedge up your way with thorns,

And wall her in,
So that she cannot find her paths.
7 She will chase her lovers,
But not overtake them;
Yes, she will seek them, but not find
them.
Then she will say,
i'I will go and return to my *j*first
husband,
For then *it was* better for me than now.'
8 For she did not *k*know
That I gave her grain, new wine, and
oil,
And multiplied her silver and gold—
Which they prepared for Baal.

9 "Therefore I will return and take
away
My grain in its time
And My new wine in its season,
And will take back My wool and My
linen,
Given to cover her nakedness.
10 Now *l*I will uncover her lewdness in
the sight of her lovers,
And no one shall deliver her from My
hand.
11 *m*I will also cause all her mirth to
cease,
Her feast days,
Her New Moons,
Her Sabbaths—
All her appointed feasts.

12 "And I will destroy her vines and her
fig trees,
Of which she has said,
'These *are* my wages that my lovers
have given me.'
So I will make them a forest,
And the beasts of the field shall eat
them.
13 I will punish her
For the days of the Baals to which she
burned incense.
She decked herself with her earrings
and jewelry,
And went after her lovers;
But Me she forgot," says the LORD.

---

* **1:9** Literally *Not-My-People* • * **1:10** Hebrew
lo-ammi (compare verse 9) • * **2:1** Hebrew *Ammi*
(compare 1:9, 10) • Hebrew *Ruhamah* (compare
1:6)

---

threatening the termination of the Lord's covenant
relationship with His people (Lev. 26:12).
1:10 Shall be as the sand of the sea. The Lord would
not reject His people forever. God would fulfill His
promise to Abraham (Gen. 22:17; 32:12).
2:2 she is not My wife. This may be a formal
announcement of divorce or a realistic confession
that the relationship between God and Israel had lost
its vitality.
2:3 And make her like a wilderness. This simile pictures the loss of fertility, an appropriate punishment
for a nation that had sought fertility by worshiping
another god.
2:6–7 She will chase her lovers. This word draws

attention to the strong passion the people of Israel
felt for Baal. These verses anticipate the exile, when
Israel would be separated from the idols of Baal.
2:12 beasts of the field. The Lord would break down
the nation's defenses and turn them into overgrown
thickets inhabited by wild animals.

1:10 *n* Gen. 22:17; 32:12 *o* 1 Pet. 2:10 *p* Rom. 9:26 *q* [John
1:12] **1:11** *r* Is. 11:11–13 **2:2** *a* Is. 50:1 *b* Ezek. 16:25
2:3 *c* Jer. 13:22, 26 *d* Ezek. 16:4–7, 22 *e* Amos 8:11–13
2:4 *f* John 8:41 **2:5** *g* Hos. 2:8, 12 **2:6** *h* Lam. 3:7, 9
2:7 *i* Luke 15:17, 18 *j* Ezek. 16:8; 23:4 **2:8** *k* Is. 1:3
2:10 *l* Ezek. 16:37 **2:11** *m* Amos 5:21; 8:10

God's Mercy on His People

14 "Therefore, behold, I will allure her,
Will bring her into the wilderness,
And speak comfort to her.
15 I will give her her vineyards from there,
And [n]the Valley of Achor as a door of hope;
She shall sing there,
As in [o]the days of her youth,
[p]As in the day when she came up from the land of Egypt.

16 "And it shall be, in that day,"
Says the LORD,
"*That* you will call Me 'My Husband,'*
And no longer call Me 'My Master,'*
17 For [q]I will take from her mouth the names of the Baals,
And they shall be remembered by their name no more.
18 In that day I will make a [r]covenant for them
With the beasts of the field,
With the birds of the air,
And *with* the creeping things of the ground.
Bow and sword of battle [s]I will shatter from the earth,
To make them [t]lie down safely.

19 "I will betroth you to Me forever;
Yes, I will betroth you to Me
In righteousness and justice,
In lovingkindness and mercy;
20 I will betroth you to Me in faithfulness,
And [u]you shall know the LORD.

21 "It shall come to pass in that day
That [v]I will answer," says the LORD;
"I will answer the heavens,
And they shall answer the earth.
22 The earth shall answer
With grain,
With new wine,
And with oil;
They shall answer Jezreel.*
23 Then [w]I will sow her for Myself in the earth,
[x]And I will have mercy on *her who had* not obtained mercy;*
Then [y]I will say to *those who were* not My people,*
'You *are* My people!'
And they shall say, '*You are* my God!'"

Israel Will Return to God

3 Then the LORD said to me, "Go again, love a woman *who is* loved by a [a]lover* and is committing adultery, just like the love of the LORD for the children of Israel, who look to other gods and love *the* raisin cakes *of the pagans*."

2So I bought her for myself for fifteen *shekels* of silver, and one and one-half homers of barley. 3And I said to her, "You shall [b]stay with me many days; you shall not play the harlot, nor shall you have a man—so, too, *will* I *be* toward you."

4For the children of Israel shall abide many days [c]without king or prince, without sacrifice or *sacred* pillar, without [d]ephod or [e]teraphim. 5Afterward the children of Israel shall return and [f]seek the LORD their God and [g]David their king. They shall fear the LORD and His goodness in the [h]latter days.

*2:16 Hebrew *Ishi* • Hebrew *Baali* *2:22 Literally *God Will Sow* *2:23 Hebrew *lo-ruhamah* • Hebrew *lo-ammi* *3:1 Literally *friend* or *husband*

2:14 *I will allure her.* Having separated Israel from her lovers, the Lord would seek to win her back by making romantic overtures and wooing her with tender words of love.
2:15 *Valley of Achor.* This meant "valley of trouble." It was a reminder of the sin of Achan and God's discipline of the nation of Israel for his sin (Josh. 7:24–26).
2:19–20 *betroth.* Betrothal was a binding commitment, the last step before the wedding and consummation of the marriage.
3:1–2 *I bought her.* Gomer had become the property of another man. Hosea's purchase of Gomer symbolized God's great devotion, which moves Him to seek reconciliation even if it means subjecting Himself to humiliation (Phil. 2:8). One of the great truths presented in the Old Testament is God's undying love for Israel. From among all the ancient nations on earth, He had chosen Israel.
3:1 The Extent of God's Love—People who think of the God of the Old Testament as a God of judgment and the God of the New Testament as a God of love should spend some time studying Hosea. In the book God instructs Hosea to marry a woman named Gomer who is consistently unfaithful. The Book of Hosea is a living parable about how far God will go to love Israel. While there is definitely judgment in Hosea, the consistent ongoing message is God will go to any extreme to demonstrate His love.

He is even willing to play the betrayed spouse in order to save us. He is willing to be an object of scorn and disrespect if that is what it takes to win us back to Him. God's own given law allows for the execution of both parties in an adulterous affair (Lev. 20:10). God cares deeply about this sin. He cares more deeply about His people.

It is important to understand how much He takes the initiative. He does not wait passively for us to come to Him. He is faithful about the task of going after us. Even though there is every reason to reject and ignore us, God is right there working to win us in spite of the fact that we reject Him at every turn.
3:4 *sacred pillar.* These were stone pillars used by the Canaanites in their worship of Baal and other gods (2 Kin. 3:2; 10:26–27; 17:10). ***ephod.*** This was a priestly garment.

2:15 [n] Josh. 7:26 [o] Ezek. 16:8–14 [p] Ex. 15:1 **2:17** [q] Ex. 23:13 **2:18** [r] Job 5:23 [s] Is. 2:4 [t] Lev. 26:5 **2:20** [u] [Jer. 31:33, 34] **2:21** [v] Zech. 8:12 **2:23** [w] Jer. 31:27 [x] Hos. 1:6 [y] Hos. 1:10 **3:1** [a] Jer. 3:20 **3:3** [b] Deut. 21:13 **3:4** [c] Hos. 10:3 [d] Ex. 28:4–12 [e] Judg. 17:5; 18:14, 17 **3:5** [f] Jer. 50:4 [g] Jer. 30:9 [h] [Is. 2:2, 3]

God's Charge Against Israel

4 Hear the word of the LORD,
You children of Israel,
For the LORD *brings* a [a]charge against
the inhabitants of the land:

"There is no truth or mercy
Or [b]knowledge of God in the land.
2 *By* swearing and lying,
Killing and stealing and committing
adultery,
They break all restraint,
With bloodshed upon bloodshed.
3 Therefore [c]the land will mourn;
And [d]everyone who dwells there will
waste away
With the beasts of the field
And the birds of the air;
Even the fish of the sea will be taken
away.

4 "Now let no man contend, or rebuke
another;
For your people *are* like those [e]who
contend with the priest.
5 Therefore you shall stumble [f]in the
day;
The prophet also shall stumble with
you in the night;
And I will destroy your mother.
6 [g]My people are destroyed for lack of
knowledge.
Because you have rejected knowledge,
I also will reject you from being priest
for Me;
[h]Because you have forgotten the law of
your God,
I also will forget your children.

7 "The more they increased,
The more they sinned against Me;
[i]I will change* their glory* into shame.
8 They eat up the sin of My people;
They set their heart on their iniquity.
9 And it shall be: [j]like people, like priest.
So I will punish them for their ways,
And reward them for their deeds.
10 For [k]they shall eat, but not have enough;
They shall commit harlotry, but not
increase;

Because they have ceased obeying the
LORD.

The Idolatry of Israel

11 "Harlotry, wine, and new wine [l]enslave
the heart.
12 My people ask counsel from their
[m]wooden *idols*,
And their staff informs them.
For [n]the spirit of harlotry has caused
them to stray,
And they have played the harlot
against their God.
13 [o]They offer sacrifices on the
mountaintops,
And burn incense on the hills,
Under oaks, poplars, and terebinths,
Because their shade *is* good.
[p]Therefore your daughters commit
harlotry,
And your brides commit adultery.

14 "I will not punish your daughters when
they commit harlotry,
Nor your brides when they commit
adultery;
For *the men* themselves go apart with
harlots,
And offer sacrifices with a [q]ritual
harlot.*
Therefore people *who* do not
understand will be trampled.

15 "Though you, Israel, play the harlot,
Let not Judah offend.
[r]Do not come up to Gilgal,
Nor go up to [s]Beth Aven,
[t]Nor swear an oath, *saying*, 'As the
LORD lives'—

16 "For Israel [u]is stubborn
Like a stubborn calf;
Now the LORD will let them forage
Like a lamb in open country.

---

* 4:7 Following Masoretic Text, Septuagint, and
Vulgate; scribal tradition, Syriac, and Targum
read *They will change.* • Following Masoretic
Text, Septuagint, Syriac, Targum, and Vulgate;
scribal tradition reads *My glory.* * 4:14 Compare
Deuteronomy 23:18

4:1 charge. The Hebrew word refers to a formal complaint charging Israel with breaking the covenant. **mercy.** This means loyalty or devotion. **knowledge.** This does not refer to intellectual awareness, but to recognition of God's authority as Israel's covenant Lord.
4:2 swearing and lying, killing and stealing and committing adultery. Five of the Ten Commandments are mentioned here.
4:5–6 lack of knowledge. The priests had failed to teach God's law to the people (Mal. 2:7). As a result, the priests would be the special object of God's judgment. He would terminate the priestly line.
4:7–8 They eat up the sin of My people. The priests greedily accepted the meat from the people's hypocritical and empty sacrifices (6:6; 8:11–13).
4:10 harlotry. This refers to religious prostitution associated with Baal worship, not to immorality in general. The Israelites worshiped Baal in order to

have good crops and many children, but they still would not have enough to eat, nor would they multiply in number.
4:12 their staff. This refers to wooden idols that Baal worshipers consulted for guidance.
4:15 Gilgal. This was an important religious center in the north, known in Hosea's time for its hypocritical religious practices (9:15; 12:11; Amos 4:4). **Beth Aven.** This means "house of iniquity," and is a sarcastic reference to the important religious center Bethel, which means "house of God" (Amos 5:5).

4:1 [a]Is. 1:18 [b]Jer. 4:22 **4:3** [c]Amos 5:16; 8:8 [d]Zeph. 1:3
4:4 [e]Deut. 17:12 **4:5** [f]Jer. 15:8 **4:6** [g]Is. 5:13 [h]Ezek.
22:26 **4:7** [i]1 Sam. 2:30 **4:9** [j]Is. 24:2 **4:10** [k]Lev.
26:26 **4:11** [l]Is. 5:12; 28:7 **4:12** [m]Jer. 2:27 [n]Is. 44:19,
20 **4:13** [o]Is. 1:29; 57:5, 7 [p]Amos 7:17 **4:14** [q]Deut.
23:18 **4:15** [r]Hos. 9:15; 12:11 [s]1 Kin. 12:29 [t]Amos 8:14
4:16 [u]Jer. 3:6; 7:24; 8:5

17 "Ephraim *is* joined to idols,
   vLet him alone.
18 Their drink is rebellion,
   They commit harlotry continually.
   wHer rulers dearly* love dishonor.
19 xThe wind has wrapped her up in its
      wings,
   And ythey shall be ashamed because
      of their sacrifices.

Impending Judgment on Israel and Judah

5 "Hear this, O priests!
   Take heed, O house of Israel!
   Give ear, O house of the king!
   For yours *is* the judgment,
   Because ayou have been a snare to
      Mizpah
   And a net spread on Tabor.
2 The revolters are bdeeply involved in
      slaughter,
   Though I rebuke them all.
3 cI know Ephraim,
   And Israel is not hidden from Me;
   For now, O Ephraim, dyou commit
      harlotry;
   Israel is defiled.
4 "They do not direct their deeds
   Toward turning to their God,
   For ethe spirit of harlotry is in their
      midst,
   And they do not know the LORD.
5 The fpride of Israel testifies to his face;
   Therefore Israel and Ephraim stumble
      in their iniquity;
   Judah also stumbles with them.
6 "With their flocks and herds
   gThey shall go to seek the LORD,
   But they will not find *Him*;
   He has withdrawn Himself from them.
7 They have hdealt treacherously with
      the LORD,
   For they have begotten pagan children.
   Now a New Moon shall devour them
      and their heritage.
8 "Blowi the ram's horn in Gibeah,
   The trumpet in Ramah!

iCry aloud *at* kBeth Aven,
   '*Look* behind you, O Benjamin!'
9 Ephraim shall be desolate in the day of
      rebuke;
   Among the tribes of Israel I make
      known what is sure.
10 "The princes of Judah are like those
      who lremove a landmark;
   I will pour out My wrath on them like
      water.
11 Ephraim is moppressed *and* broken in
      judgment,
   Because he willingly walked by
      n*human* precept.
12 Therefore I *will be* to Ephraim like a
      moth,
   And to the house of Judah olike
      rottenness.
13 "When Ephraim saw his sickness,
   And Judah *saw* his pwound,
   Then Ephraim went qto Assyria
   And sent to King Jareb;
   Yet he cannot cure you,
   Nor heal you of your wound.
14 For rI *will be* like a lion to Ephraim,
   And like a young lion to the house of
      Judah.
   sI, *even* I, will tear *them* and go away;
   I will take *them* away, and no one
      shall rescue.
15 I will return again to My place
   Till they acknowledge their offense.
   Then they will seek My face;
   In their affliction they will earnestly
      seek Me."

A Call to Repentance

6 Come,a and let us return to the LORD;
   For bHe has torn, but cHe will heal us;
   He has stricken, but He will bind
      us up.
2 dAfter two days He will revive us;
   On the third day He will raise us up,
   That we may live in His sight.

---

* 4:18 Hebrew is difficult; a Jewish tradition reads
Her rulers shamefully love, 'Give!'

4:17–19 Ephraim. This tribe was one of the largest tribes of Israel. It is used here to represent the entire northern kingdom.

5:1 spirit of harlotry. The people had an uncontrollable desire to worship other gods.

5:8–9 Blow the ram's horn. This act signaled an emergency and mustered the fighting men to defend the land. The towns mentioned were north of Jerusalem, within or near the borders of Benjamin. The implication is that the enemy army had already swept through the north and was ready to invade Judah.

5:10 remove a landmark. Stones were used to mark the boundaries of property. A thief could steal a part of someone's land by moving one. The law warned that altering a boundary in this way would bring a special judgment from God (Deut. 19:14; 27:17; Prov. 22:28).

5:12 I will be to Ephraim like a moth. As a moth

slowly destroys clothing, so the Lord would destroy Israel (Job 13:28; Is. 50:9; 51:8). **rottenness.** Elsewhere this word refers to bone or to decay (Prov. 12:4; 14:30; Hab. 3:16).

5:14–15 like a young lion. God would scatter His people as judgment for their treachery. But the purpose of the Lord's discipline was to drive the people to earnestly seek Him.

4:17 v Matt. 15:14 4:18 w Mic. 3:11 4:19 x Jer. 51:1
y Is. 1:29 5:1 a Hos. 6:9 5:2 b Is. 29:15 5:3 c Amos
3:2; 5:12 d Hos. 4:17 5:4 e Hos. 4:12 5:5 f Hos. 7:10
5:6 g Prov. 1:28 5:7 h Jer. 3:20 5:8 i Joel 2:1 j Is. 10:30
k Josh. 7:2 5:10 l Deut. 19:14; 27:17 5:11 m Deut.
28:33 n Mic. 6:16 5:12 o Prov. 12:4 5:13 p Jer. 30:12–15
q 2 Kin. 15:19 5:14 r Lam. 3:10 s Ps. 50:22 6:1 a Is. 1:18
b Deut. 32:39 c Jer. 30:17 6:2 d Luke 24:26; Acts 10:40;
[1 Cor. 15:4]

3 eLet us know,
  Let us pursue the knowledge of the
    LORD.
  His going forth is established fas the
    morning;
  gHe will come to us hlike the rain,
  Like the latter and former rain to the
    earth.

Impenitence of Israel and Judah

4 "O Ephraim, what shall I do to you?
  O Judah, what shall I do to you?
  For your faithfulness is like a morning
    cloud,
  And like the early dew it goes away.
5 Therefore I have hewn them by the
    prophets,
  I have slain them by ithe words of My
    mouth;
  And your judgments are like light that
    goes forth.
6 For I desire jmercy and knot sacrifice,
  And the lknowledge of God more than
    burnt offerings.
7 "But like men* they transgressed the
    covenant;
  There they dealt treacherously with Me.
8 mGilead is a city of evildoers
  And defiled with blood.
9 As bands of robbers lie in wait for a
    man,
  So the company of npriests omurder on
    the way to Shechem;
  Surely they commit plewdness.
10 I have seen a horrible thing in the
    house of Israel:
  There is the harlotry of Ephraim;
  Israel is defiled.
11 Also, O Judah, a harvest is appointed
    for you,
  When I return the captives of My
    people.

7 "When I would have healed Israel,
  Then the iniquity of Ephraim was
    uncovered,
  And the wickedness of Samaria.

For athey have committed fraud;
  A thief comes in;
  A band of robbers takes spoil outside.
2 They do not consider in their hearts
  That bI remember all their wickedness;
  Now their own deeds have surrounded
    them;
  They are before My face.
3 They make a cking glad with their
    wickedness,
  And princes dwith their lies.
4 "Theye are all adulterers.
  Like an oven heated by a baker—
  He ceases stirring the fire after
    kneading the dough,
  Until it is leavened.
5 In the day of our king
  Princes have made him sick, inflamed
    with fwine;
  He stretched out his hand with
    scoffers.
6 They prepare their heart like an oven,
  While they lie in wait;
  Their baker* sleeps all night;
  In the morning it burns like a flaming
    fire.
7 They are all hot, like an oven,
  And have devoured their judges;
  All their kings have fallen.
  gNone among them calls upon Me.
8 "Ephraim hhas mixed himself among
    the peoples;
  Ephraim is a cake unturned.
9 iAliens have devoured his strength,
  But he does not know it;
  Yes, gray hairs are here and there on
    him,
  Yet he does not know it.
10 And the jpride of Israel testifies to his
    face,
  But kthey do not return to the LORD
    their God,
  Nor seek Him for all this.

* 6:7 Or like Adam * 7:6 Following Masoretic
Text and Vulgate; Syriac and Targum read Their
anger; Septuagint reads Ephraim.

6:3 **like the latter and former rain.** Two periods of
rain are alluded to here. The former rains came in
the autumn and softened the ground for plowing
and sowing. The latter rains came in the spring and
caused the plants to grow.
6:5 **judgments are like light that goes forth.** This
comparison suggests that God's judgment, like
bright sunlight, was obvious to all; or that, like a bolt
of lightning or a blinding flash of light, it came swiftly.
6:11 **a harvest is appointed for you.** The comparison of God's judgment to a harvest indicates that the
judgment was inevitable and implies that it would be
thorough in its destruction.
7:4–7 **Like an oven.** The background for these verses
is the political turmoil of the northern kingdom.
During a 20-year period (752–732 B.C.), four Israelite
kings were assassinated (2 Kin. 15). The dangerous,
uncontrollable perpetuators of these crimes are
described here. These conspirators were like a large

baker's oven that has been heating up for several
hours while the bread dough rises. By morning the
fire in the oven can be destructive.
7:8 **Ephraim has mixed himself among the peoples.** Instead of depending on the Lord for political
stability, Israel formed alliances with surrounding
nations. The destructive outcome of this policy is
compared to a cake that has been placed over a fire
and left unturned.
7:9–10 **gray hairs.** Israel did not recognize that its
power was declining and its freedom was slipping

6:3 eIs. 54:13 f2 Sam. 23:4 gPs. 72:6 hJob 29:23
6:5 i[Jer. 23:29] 6:6 jMatt. 9:13; 12:7 k[Mic. 6:6–8]
l[John 17:3] 6:8 mHos. 12:11 6:9 nHos. 5:1 oJer.
7:9, 10 pEzek. 22:9; 23:27 7:1 aHos. 5:1 7:2 bJer.
14:10; 17:1 7:3 cHos. 11:4 d[Rom. 1:32] 7:4 eJer. 9:2;
23:10 7:5 fIs. 28:1, 7 7:7 gIs. 64:7 7:8 hPs. 106:35
7:9 iHos. 8:7 7:10 jHos. 5:5 kIs. 9:13

Futile Reliance on the Nations

11 "Ephraim[l] also is like a silly dove,
without sense—
[m]They call to Egypt,
They go to [n]Assyria.
12 Wherever they go, I will [o]spread My
net on them;
I will bring them down like birds of
the air;
I will chastise them
[p]According to what their congregation
has heard.

13 "Woe to them, for they have fled from
Me!
Destruction to them,
Because they have transgressed
against Me!
Though [q]I redeemed them,
Yet they have spoken lies against Me.
14 [r]They did not cry out to Me with their
heart
When they wailed upon their beds.

"They assemble together for* grain and
new [s]wine,
They rebel against Me;*
15 Though I disciplined and strengthened
their arms,
Yet they devise evil against Me;
16 They return, but not to the Most High;*
[t]They are like a treacherous bow.
Their princes shall fall by the sword
For the [u]cursings of their tongue.
This shall be their derision [v]in the land
of Egypt.

The Apostasy of Israel

8 "Set the trumpet* to your mouth!
He shall come [a]like an eagle against
the house of the LORD,
Because they have transgressed My
covenant
And rebelled against My law.

2 [b]Israel will cry to Me,
'My God, [c]we know You!'
3 Israel has rejected the good;
The enemy will pursue him.

4 "They[d] set up kings, but not by Me;
They made princes, but I did not
acknowledge them.
From their silver and gold
They made idols for themselves—
That they might be cut off.
5 Your calf is rejected, O Samaria!
My anger is aroused against them—
[e]How long until they attain to innocence?
6 For from Israel is even this:
A [f]workman made it, and it is not God;
But the calf of Samaria shall be
broken to pieces.

7 "They[g] sow the wind,
And reap the whirlwind.
The stalk has no bud;
It shall never produce meal.
If it should produce,
[h]Aliens would swallow it up.
8 [i]Israel is swallowed up;
Now they are among the Gentiles
[j]Like a vessel in which is no pleasure.
9 For they have gone up to Assyria,
Like [k]a wild donkey alone by itself;
Ephraim [l]has hired lovers.
10 Yes, though they have hired among
the nations,
Now [m]I will gather them;
And they shall sorrow a little,*
Because of the burden* of [n]the king of
princes.

---

* 7:14 Following Masoretic Text and Targum; Vulgate reads thought upon; Septuagint reads slashed themselves for (compare 1 Kings 18:28). • Following Masoretic Text, Syriac, and Targum; Septuagint omits They rebel against Me; Vulgate reads They departed from Me. * 7:16 Or upward * 8:1 Hebrew shophar, ram's horn * 8:10 Or begin to diminish • Or oracle

---

away, like an aging man who is gradually overtaken by the signs of old age.
7:11–12 Egypt ... Assyria. Israel was caught between these two superpowers. It tried to maintain its independence by playing one power against the other, but this vacillating policy didn't work. Israel was like a silly dove, flitting about from place to place.
7:13 Woe to them. When prophets spoke this way, they were saying a funeral dirge for those under the sentence of God's judgment.
7:14 grain and new wine. God sent a drought on Israel, but instead of the people turning to Him in repentance, the idolatrous Israelites demonstrated their devotion to Baal. According to Canaanite religious beliefs, prolonged drought was a signal that the storm god Baal had been temporarily defeated by the god of death and was imprisoned by the underworld. Baal's worshipers would mourn his death in hopes that their tears might facilitate his resurrection and the restoration of crops.
8:1–3 like an eagle. As a bird of prey would do, Assyria would invade Israel and take its people into captivity. **we know You.** Though Israel claimed to

acknowledge the Lord's authority, it had violated His covenant and rejected the qualities the Lord regarded as good, such as justice, loyalty, and humility (Amos 5:14–15; Mic. 6:8).
8:4 They set up kings. This phrase alludes to the political turmoil surrounding the throne of the northern kingdom during the eighth century B.C., when four kings were assassinated during a 20-year period (7:4–7).
8:6 A workman made it. Hosea reasoned that anything that is made with human hands cannot possibly qualify as a god.
8:9–10 a wild donkey. This comparison draws attention to Israel's free-spirited attitude and desire to live unrestrained by God's standards.

7:11 [l]Hos. 11:11 [m]Is. 30:3 [n]Hos. 5:13; 8:9 **7:12** [o]Ezek. 12:13 [p]Lev. 26:14 **7:13** [q]Mic. 6:4 **7:14** [r]Job 35:9, 10 [s]Amos 2:8 **7:16** [t]Ps. 78:57 [u]Ps. 73:9 [v]Hos. 8:13; 9:3 **8:1** [a]Deut. 28:49 **8:2** [b]Ps. 78:34 [c]Titus 1:16 **8:4** [d]2 Kin. 15:23, 25 **8:5** [e]Jer. 13:27 **8:6** [f]Is. 40:19 **8:7** [g]Prov. 22:8 [h]Hos. 7:9 **8:8** [i]2 Kin. 17:6 [j]Jer. 22:28; 25:34 **8:9** [k]Jer. 2:24 [l]Ezek. 16:33, 34 **8:10** [m]Ezek. 16:37; 22:20 [n]Is. 10:8

11 "Because Ephraim has made many
altars for sin,
They have become for him altars for
sinning.
12 I have written for him [o]the great
things of My law,
But they were considered a strange
thing.
13 *For* the sacrifices of My offerings
[p]they sacrifice flesh and eat *it,*
[q]*But* the LORD does not accept them.
[r]Now He will remember their iniquity
and punish their sins.
They shall return to Egypt.

14 "For[s] Israel has forgotten [t]his Maker,
And has built temples;*
Judah also has multiplied [u]fortified
cities;
But [v]I will send fire upon his cities,
And it shall devour his palaces."

Judgment of Israel's Sin

9 Do[a] not rejoice, O Israel, with joy like
other peoples,
For you have played the harlot against
your God.
You have made love *for* [b]hire on every
threshing floor.
2 The threshing floor and the winepress
Shall not feed them,
And the new wine shall fail in her.

3 They shall not dwell in [c]the LORD's
land,
[d]But Ephraim shall return to Egypt,
And [e]shall eat unclean *things* in
Assyria.
4 They shall not offer wine *offerings* to
the LORD,
Nor [f]shall their [g]sacrifices be pleasing
to Him.
It shall be like bread of mourners to
them;
All who eat it shall be defiled.
For their bread *shall be* for their *own*
life;
It shall not come into the house of the
LORD.
5 What will you do in the appointed day,
And in the day of the feast of the
LORD?
6 For indeed they are gone because of
destruction.
Egypt shall gather them up;
Memphis shall bury them.
[h]Nettles shall possess their valuables
of silver;
Thorns *shall be* in their tents.

7 The [i]days of punishment have come;
The days of recompense have come.
Israel knows!
The prophet *is* a [j]fool,
[k]The spiritual man *is* insane,
Because of the greatness of your
iniquity and great enmity.
8 The [l]watchman of Ephraim *is* with my
God;
But the prophet *is* a fowler's* snare in
all his ways—
Enmity in the house of his God.
9 [m]They are deeply corrupted,
As in the days of [n]Gibeah.
He will remember their iniquity;
He will punish their sins.

10 "I found Israel
Like grapes in the [o]wilderness;
I saw your fathers
As the [p]firstfruits on the fig tree in its
first season.
But they went to [q]Baal Peor,
And separated themselves *to that*
shame;
[r]They became an abomination like the
thing they loved.
11 *As for* Ephraim, their glory shall fly
away like a bird—
No birth, no pregnancy, and no
conception!
12 Though they bring up their children,
Yet I will bereave them to the last man.
Yes, [s]woe to them when I depart from
them!

* **8:14** Or *palaces* * **9:8** That is, one who catches birds in a trap or snare

8:14 ***temples . . . multiplied fortified cities.*** True security comes from the Creator, but God's people trusted instead in their own efforts, symbolized by their important buildings.

9:1–2 ***threshing floor.*** Because of their association with the harvest, threshing floors were the site of agricultural festivals in which Israel offered up sacrifices to Baal. The Lord would take away the joy of the harvest by destroying the crops and leaving the threshing floors and wine vats empty.

9:3 ***the LORD's land.*** Israel had forgotten that their land belonged to the Lord. He alone decided who would or would not live in it (Lev. 25:23).

9:7 ***the spiritual man is insane.*** The word translated "insane" is used in 1 Samuel 21:15 of David when he pretended to be insane before the Philistine king.

9:8 ***watchman.*** He would look for approaching armies and then warn the people so that they could secure the city and prepare for battle (Ezek. 33:6). The prophets were like watchmen because they were sent by God to warn the people of judgment and urge them to repent (Ezek. 3:17).

9:9 ***As in the days of Gibeah.*** The reference here is to the rape and murder of a young woman by men of Gibeah, an event that started a civil war (Judg. 19). Those who witnessed this violent deed remarked that it was the worst crime committed in Israel's history until that time. However, the sins of Hosea's generation rivaled the infamous Gibeah.

8:12 [o] [Deut. 4:6–8] **8:13** [p] Zech. 7:6 [q] Jer. 14:10 [r] Amos 8:7 **8:14** [s] Deut. 32:18 [t] Is. 29:23 [u] Num. 32:17 [v] Jer. 17:27 **9:1** [a] Is. 22:12, 13 [b] Jer. 44:17 **9:3** [c] [Lev. 25:23] [d] Hos. 7:16; 8:13 [e] Ezek. 4:13 **9:4** [f] Jer. 6:20 [g] Hos. 8:13 **9:6** [h] Is. 5:6; 7:23 **9:7** [i] Is. 10:3 [j] Lam. 2:14 [k] Mic. 2:11 **9:8** [l] Ezek. 3:17; 33:7 **9:9** [m] Hos. 10:9 [n] Judg. 19:22 **9:10** [o] Jer. 2:2 [p] Is. 28:4 [q] Num. 25:3 [r] Ps. 81:12 **9:12** [s] Deut. 31:17

13 Just *t*as I saw Ephraim like Tyre,
    planted in a pleasant place,
So Ephraim will bring out his children
    to the murderer."

14 Give them, O LORD—
    What will You give?
Give them *u*a miscarrying womb
    And dry breasts!

15 "All their wickedness *is* in *v*Gilgal,
    For there I hated them.
Because of the evil of their deeds
    I will drive them from My house;
I will love them no more.
    *w*All their princes *are* rebellious.
16 Ephraim is *x*stricken,
    Their root is dried up;
They shall bear no fruit.
    Yes, were they to bear children,
I would kill the darlings of their womb."

17 My God will *y*cast them away,
    Because they did not obey Him;
And they shall be *z*wanderers among
    the nations.

Israel's Sin and Captivity

10 Israel *a*empties *his* vine;
    He brings forth fruit for himself.
According to the multitude of his fruit
    *b*He has increased the altars;
According to the bounty of his land
    They have embellished *his sacred*
        pillars.
2 Their heart is *c*divided;
    Now they are held guilty.
He will break down their altars;
    He will ruin their *sacred* pillars.
3 For now they say,
    "We have no king,
Because we did not fear the LORD.
    And as for a king, what would he do
        for us?"
4 They have spoken words,
    Swearing falsely in making a covenant.
Thus judgment springs up *d*like
    hemlock in the furrows of the
        field.
5 The inhabitants of Samaria fear
    Because of the *e*calf* of Beth Aven.

For its people mourn for it,
    And its priests shriek for it—
Because its *f*glory has departed
    from it.
6 *The idol* also shall be carried to
        Assyria
    As a present for King *g*Jareb.
Ephraim shall receive shame,
    And Israel shall be ashamed of his
        own counsel.

7 *As for* Samaria, her king is cut off
    Like a twig on the water.
8 Also the *h*high places of Aven, *i*the sin
        of Israel,
    Shall be destroyed.
The thorn and thistle shall grow on
        their altars;
    *j*They shall say to the mountains,
        "Cover us!"
And to the hills, "Fall on us!"

9 "O Israel, you have sinned from the
        days of *k*Gibeah;
    There they stood.
The *l*battle in Gibeah against the
        children of iniquity*
    Did not overtake them.
10 When *it is* My desire, I will chasten
        them.
    *m*Peoples shall be gathered against
        them
When I bind them for their two
        transgressions.*
11 Ephraim *is* *n*a trained heifer
    That loves to thresh *grain;*
But I harnessed her fair neck,
    I will make Ephraim pull *a plow.*
Judah shall plow;
    Jacob shall break his clods."

12 Sow for yourselves righteousness;
    Reap in mercy;
*o*Break up your fallow ground,
    For *it is* time to seek the LORD,
Till He *p*comes and rains
    righteousness on you.

---

* **10:5** Literally *calves*   * **10:9** So read many
Hebrew manuscripts, Septuagint, and Vulgate;
Masoretic Text reads *unruliness.*   * **10:10** Or *in
their two habitations*

9:14 *miscarrying womb.* Some women of Israel
would be barren (v. 11); others would bear children,
only to lose them to the invader's sword (vv. 12–13).
Still others would conceive but miscarry.
10:1 *Israel empties his vine.* This refers to God's
blessings upon the nation, which contrast with the
nation's ingratitude and idolatry.
**10:4 *judgment springs up like hemlock in the fur-
rows of the field.*** In much the same way judgment
would replace God's blessings.
10:11 *loves to thresh grain.* Israel preferred to be
unrestrained, like an unmuzzled heifer at the threshing floor that can simply lean down and eat grain.
I will make Ephraim pull a plow. Israel's rebellious
spirit necessitated harsh treatment, compared here
to a farmer binding his calf to the yoke and forcing

it to do hard labor. Threshing in this context refers to
Israel's service to the Lord; plowing refers to the discipline that Israel had to acquire through judgment
and exile.
10:12 *Break up your fallow ground.* Plowing and
planting are necessary preliminary steps for growing
a crop, which eventually sprouts when the rain falls

9:13 *t* Ezek. 26–28   **9:14** *u* Luke 23:29   **9:15** *v* Hos.
4:15; 12:11   *w* Is. 1:23   **9:16** *x* Hos. 5:11   **9:17** *y* [Zech.
10:6]   *z* Lev. 26:33   **10:1** *a* Nah. 2:2   *b* Jer. 2:28
10:2 *c* 1 Kin. 18:21   **10:4** *d* Amos 5:7   **10:5** *e* Hos. 8:5,
6; 13:2   *f* Hos. 9:11   **10:6** *g* Hos. 5:13   **10:8** *h* Hos. 4:15
i 1 Kin. 13:34   *j* Luke 23:30   **10:9** *k* Hos. 9:9   *l* Judg. 20
10:10 *m* Jer. 16:16   **10:11** *n* [Mic. 4:13]   **10:12** *o* Jer. 4:3
p Hos. 6:3

13 aYou have plowed wickedness;
  You have reaped iniquity.
  You have eaten the fruit of lies,
  Because you trusted in your own way,
  In the multitude of your mighty men.
14 Therefore tumult shall arise among
      your people,
  And all your fortresses shall be
      plundered
  As Shalman plundered Beth Arbel in
      the day of battle—
  A mother dashed in pieces upon her
      children.
15 Thus it shall be done to you, O Bethel,
  Because of your great wickedness.
  At dawn the king of Israel
  Shall be cut off utterly.

God's Continuing Love for Israel

11 "When Israel was a child, I loved
      him,
  And out of Egypt aI called My bson.
2 As they called them,*
  So they cwent from them;*
  They sacrificed to the Baals,
  And burned incense to carved images.

3 "Id taught Ephraim to walk,
  Taking them by their arms;*
  But they did not know that eI healed
      them.
4 I drew them with gentle cords,*
  With bands of love,
  And fI was to them as those who take
      the yoke from their neck.*
  gI stooped and fed them.

5 "He shall not return to the land of
      Egypt;
  But the Assyrian shall be his king,
  Because they refused to repent.
6 And the sword shall slash in his cities,
  Devour his districts,
  And consume them,
  Because of their own counsels.
7 My people are bent on hbacksliding
      from Me.
  Though they call to the Most High,*
  None at all exalt Him.

8 "Howi can I give you up, Ephraim?
  How can I hand you over, Israel?

How can I make you like iAdmah?
  How can I set you like Zeboiim?
  My heart churns within Me;
  My sympathy is stirred.
9 I will not execute the fierceness of My
      anger;
  I will not again destroy Ephraim.
  kFor I am God, and not man,
  The Holy One in your midst;
  And I will not come with terror.*

10 "They shall walk after the LORD.
  lHe will roar like a lion.
  When He roars,
  Then His sons shall come trembling
      from the west;
11 They shall come trembling like a bird
      from Egypt,
  mLike a dove from the land of Assyria.
  nAnd I will let them dwell in their houses,"
  Says the LORD.

God's Charge Against Ephraim

12 "Ephraim has encircled Me with lies,
  And the house of Israel with deceit;
  But Judah still walks with God,
  Even with the Holy One* who is
      faithful.

12 "Ephraim afeeds on the wind,
      And pursues the east wind;
  He daily increases lies and desolation.
  bAlso they make a covenant with the
      Assyrians,
  And coil is carried to Egypt.

2 "Thed LORD also brings a charge
      against Judah,
  And will punish Jacob according to
      his ways;
  According to his deeds He will
      recompense him.

---

* **11:2** Following Masoretic Text and Vulgate;
Septuagint reads Just as I called them; Targum
interprets as I sent prophets to a thousand of
them. • Following Masoretic Text, Targum,
and Vulgate; Septuagint reads from My face.
* **11:3** Some Hebrew manuscripts, Septuagint, Syriac, and Vulgate read My arms. * **11:4** Literally
cords of a man • Literally jaws * **11:7** Or upward
* **11:9** Or I will not enter a city * **11:12** Or holy
ones

---

in season. In the same way, repentance would set the
stage for restored blessing, which God would eventually rain down on His people.
11:3 I taught Ephraim to walk. Like a father teaching
his child to walk, the Lord patiently gave the people
of Israel direction and cared for them tenderly when
they experienced pain or injury.
11:4 cords . . . bands. The Lord had placed restraints
on Israel, but His regulations, rather than being overly
strict or harsh, reflected His concern for the people's
well-being. God did not drive them mercilessly but
provided for their needs, like a farmer who periodi-
cally removes the yoke from an animal's neck so that
it can eat.
11:6 consume. This is the same Hebrew word
translated "fed" in verse 4. The people of Israel had

rejected the gentle Master who fed them and provided for their needs. As a result, they would be
devoured by the swords of the invading Assyrians.
11:9 For I am God, and not man. When human
beings get angry, they are often incapable of temper-
ing their anger with compassion, but God's emotions
operate in perfect balance.
12:1 oil is carried to Egypt. Oil may have been used

10:13 q [Prov. 22:8] **11:1** a Matt. 2:15 b Ex. 4:22, 23
11:2 c 2 Kin. 17:13–15 **11:3** d Deut. 1:31; 32:10, 11 e Ex.
15:26 **11:4** f Lev. 26:13 g Ps. 78:25 **11:7** h Jer. 3:6, 7;
8:5 **11:8** i Jer. 9:7 j Gen. 14:8; 19:24, 25 **11:9** k Num.
23:19 **11:10** l [Joel 3:16] **11:11** m Is. 11:11; 60:8 n Ezek.
28:25, 26; 34:27, 28 **12:1** a Job 15:2, 3 b 2 Kin. 17:4 c Is.
30:6 **12:2** d Mic. 6:2

3 He took his brother eby the heel in the
womb,
And in his strength he fstruggled with
God.*
4 Yes, he struggled with the Angel and
prevailed;
He wept, and sought favor from Him.
He found Him in gBethel,
And there He spoke to us—
5 That is, the LORD God of hosts.
The LORD is His hmemorable
name.
6 iSo you, by the help of your God,
return;
Observe mercy and justice,
And wait on your God continually.

7 "A cunning Canaanite!
jDeceitful scales are in his hand;
He loves to oppress.
8 And Ephraim said,
k'Surely I have become rich,
I have found wealth for myself;
In all my labors
They shall find in me no iniquity that
is sin.'

9 "But I am the LORD your God,
Ever since the land of Egypt;
lI will again make you dwell in tents,
As in the days of the appointed feast.
10 mI have also spoken by the prophets,
And have multiplied visions;
I have given symbols through the
witness of the prophets."

11 Though nGilead has idols—
Surely they are vanity—
Though they sacrifice bulls in
oGilgal,
Indeed their altars shall be heaps in
the furrows of the field.

12 Jacob pfled to the country of Syria;
qIsrael served for a spouse,
And for a wife he tended sheep.
13 rBy a prophet the LORD brought Israel
out of Egypt,
And by a prophet he was preserved.
14 Ephraim sprovoked Him to anger most
bitterly;
Therefore his Lord will leave the guilt
of his bloodshed upon him,
tAnd return his reproach upon him.

Relentless Judgment on Israel

13 When Ephraim spoke, trembling,
He exalted himself in Israel;
But when he offended through Baal
worship, he died.
2 Now they sin more and more,
And have made for themselves molded
images,
Idols of their silver, according to their
skill;
All of it is the work of craftsmen.
They say of them,
"Let the men who sacrifice* kiss the
calves!"
3 Therefore they shall be like the
morning cloud
And like the early dew that passes away,
aLike chaff blown off from a threshing
floor
And like smoke from a chimney.

4 "Yet bI am the LORD your God
Ever since the land of Egypt,
And you shall know no God but Me;
For cthere is no savior besides Me.
5 dI knew you in the wilderness,
eIn the land of great drought.
6 fWhen they had pasture, they were
filled;
They were filled and their heart was
exalted;
Therefore they forgot Me.

7 "So gI will be to them like a lion;
Like ha leopard by the road I will lurk;
8 I will meet them ilike a bear deprived
of her cubs;
I will tear open their rib cage,
And there I will devour them like a lion.
The wild beast shall tear them.

9 "O Israel, you are destroyed,*
But your help* is from Me.
10 I will be your King;*
jWhere is any other,
That he may save you in all your cities?
And your judges to whom kyou said,
'Give me a king and princes'?

* 12:3 Compare Genesis 32:28 * 13:2 Or those
who offer human sacrifice * 13:9 Literally it
or he destroyed you • Literally in your help
* 13:10 Septuagint, Syriac, Targum, and Vulgate
read Where is your king?

---

in a ritual ratifying a treaty or given as a sign of loyalty.
12:7 Deceitful scales are in his hand. In violation of
the Old Testament law (Lev. 19:36), dishonest merchants sometimes rigged their scales so that they
could give buyers less than what they thought they
were purchasing (Prov. 11:1; 16:11).
12:9 I will again make you dwell in tents. During the
Feast of the Tabernacles people lived in tents to commemorate the wilderness wandering (Lev. 23:33–43).
13:2 kiss the calves. This is a reference to the idolatrous practice of kissing images as a sign of homage
(1 Kin. 19:18).
13:6–9 I will be to them like a lion. God provided
for Israel's needs and richly blessed the people, like

a shepherd leading his flock to lush pasturelands.
In return, Israel forgot the Lord. The Lord's relationship with Israel would change drastically from caring Shepherd to ravaging Predator. Ironically and

12:3 e Gen. 25:26 f Gen. 32:24–28 **12:4** g [Gen.
28:12–19; 35:9–15] **12:5** h Ex. 3:15 **12:6** i Mic.
6:8 **12:7** j Amos 8:5 **12:8** k Rev. 3:17 **12:9** l Lev.
23:42 **12:10** m 2 Kin. 17:13 **12:11** n Hos. 6:8 o Hos.
9:15 **12:12** p Gen. 28:5 q Gen. 29:20, 28 **12:13** r Ex.
12:50, 51; 13:3 **12:14** s Ezek. 18:10–13 t Dan. 11:18
13:3 a Dan. 2:35 **13:4** b Is. 43:11 c Is. 43:11; 45:21, 22
13:5 d Deut. 2:7; 32:10 e Deut. 8:15 **13:6** f Deut. 8:12, 14;
32:13–15 **13:7** g Lam. 3:10 h Jer. 5:6 **13:8** i 2 Sam. 17:8
13:10 j Deut. 32:38 k 1 Sam. 8:5, 6

11 lI gave you a king in My anger,
And took *him* away in My wrath.
12 "The^m iniquity of Ephraim *is* bound up;
His sin *is* stored up.
13 ⁿThe sorrows of a woman in childbirth
shall come upon him.
He *is* an unwise son,
For he should not stay long where
children are born.
14 "I will ransom them from the power of
the grave;*
I will redeem them from death.
^oO Death, I will be your plagues!*
O Grave,* I will be your destruction!*
^pPity is hidden from My eyes."
15 Though he is fruitful among *his*
brethren,
^qAn east wind shall come;
The wind of the Lᴏʀᴅ shall come up
from the wilderness.
Then his spring shall become dry,
And his fountain shall be dried up.
He shall plunder the treasury of every
desirable prize.
16 Samaria is held guilty,*
For she has ^rrebelled against her God.
They shall fall by the sword,
Their infants shall be dashed in pieces,
And their women with child ^sripped
open.

Israel Restored at Last

14 O Israel, ^areturn to the Lᴏʀᴅ your
God,
For you have stumbled because of your
iniquity;
2 Take words with you,
And return to the Lᴏʀᴅ.
Say to Him,
"Take away all iniquity;
Receive *us* graciously,

For we will offer the ^bsacrifices* of
our lips.
3 Assyria shall ^cnot save us,
^dWe will not ride on horses,
Nor will we say anymore to the work
of our hands, 'You *are* our gods.'
^eFor in You the fatherless finds mercy."
4 "I will heal their ^fbacksliding,
I will ^glove them freely,
For My anger has turned away from
him.
5 I will be like the ^hdew to Israel;
He shall grow like the lily,
And lengthen his roots like Lebanon.
6 His branches shall spread;
ⁱHis beauty shall be like an olive tree,
And ^jhis fragrance like Lebanon.
7 ^kThose who dwell under his shadow
shall return;
They shall be revived *like* grain,
And grow like a vine.
Their scent* *shall be* like the wine of
Lebanon.
8 "Ephraim *shall say*, 'What have I to do
anymore with idols?'
I have heard and observed him.
I *am* like a green cypress tree;
^lYour fruit is found in Me."
9 Who *is* wise?
Let him understand these things.
Who is prudent?
Let him know them.
For ^mthe ways of the Lᴏʀᴅ *are* right;
The righteous walk in them,
But transgressors stumble in them.

---

* **13:14** Or *Sheol* • Septuagint reads *where is
your punishment?* • Or *Sheol* • Septuagint
reads *where is your sting?* * **13:16** Septuagint
reads *shall be disfigured* * **14:2** Literally *bull
calves*; Septuagint reads *fruit.* * **14:7** Literally
remembrance

---

tragically, Israel's rebellion had turned its Helper into
a Destroyer.
13:12 bound up ... stored up. God had kept a careful
record of Israel's sins, to be revealed as evidence of
guilt in the day of judgment.
13:13 *The sorrows of a woman in childbirth.* This
metaphor illustrates Israel's spiritual insensitivity.
When the crucial time of judgment arrived, Israel
would respond unwisely, resulting in death. The
nation's failure to repent is compared to a baby that is
not positioned properly during labor and jeopardizes
the life of both mother and child.
14:1–3 *Take away all iniquity.* The final section of
Hosea's prophecy begins with a call to repentance
that includes a model prayer. The people of Israel
were to pray for God's gracious forgiveness and
renew their allegiance to Him by renouncing foreign
alliances, their own military strength, and artificial
gods.
14:4 *I will heal their backsliding.* The grief-stricken

Hosea does not tell us whether a reconciliation took
place between him and his adulterous wife Gomer.
But there is no question concerning the outcome
between God and faithless Israel. Several beautiful
figures of speech are employed by Hosea to describe
the results and effects of God's love for Israel.
14:9 *For the ways of the Lᴏʀᴅ are right.* God's
demands and principles are completely true. The
wise person will choose to obey them, but the foolish
person will ignore them and consequently stumble
into judgment.

13:11 ^l 1 Sam. 8:7; 10:17–24   **13:12** ^m Deut. 32:34,
35   **13:13** ⁿ Is. 13:8   **13:14** ^o [1 Cor. 15:54, 55] ^p Jer. 15:6
13:15 ^q Jer. 4:11, 12   **13:16** ^r 2 Kin. 18:12 ^s 2 Kin. 15:16
14:1 ^a [Joel 2:13]   **14:2** ^b [Heb. 13:15]   **14:3** ^c Hos.
7:11; 10:13; 12:1 ^d [Ps. 33:17] ^e Ps. 10:14; 68:5   **14:4** ^f Jer.
14:7 ^g [Eph. 1:6]   **14:5** ^h Prov. 19:12   **14:6** ⁱ Ps. 52:8;
128:3 ^j Gen. 27:27   **14:7** ^k Dan. 4:12   **14:8** ^l [John 15:4]
14:9 ^m [Prov. 10:29]

THE BOOK OF JOEL

▶ **AUTHOR:** Although there are several other Joels in the Bible, the prophet Joel is known only from this book. It has been suggested that he lived not far from Jerusalem and some think that Joel was possibly a priest as well as a prophet on account of references to the priesthood throughout the book (1:13–14; 2:17).

▶ **TIME:** c. 835 B.C. ▶ **KEY VERSE:** Joel 2:11

▶ **THEME:** For the true agrarian society, crops are life itself. It is hard to imagine how devastating the natural disasters described in Joel are, and he uses these painful events as a megaphone to get the attention of the people. There is urgency in this call, because the day of the Lord is coming. This day will be a day of judgment or a day of blessing depending on where one stands with God.

1 The word of the LORD that came to [a]Joel
the son of Pethuel.

The Land Laid Waste

2 Hear this, you elders,
And give ear, all you inhabitants of the land!
[b]Has *anything like* this happened in your days,
Or even in the days of your fathers?
3 [c]Tell your children about it,
Let your children *tell* their children,
And their children another generation.

4 [d]What the chewing locust* left, the [e]swarming locust has eaten;
What the swarming locust left, the crawling locust has eaten;
And what the crawling locust left, the consuming locust has eaten.

5 Awake, you [f]drunkards, and weep;
And wail, all you drinkers of wine,
Because of the new wine,
[g]For it has been cut off from your mouth.
6 For [h]a nation has come up against My land,
Strong, and without number;
[i]His teeth *are* the teeth of a lion,
And he has the fangs of a fierce lion.
7 He has [j]laid waste My vine,
And ruined My fig tree;
He has stripped it bare and thrown *it* away;
Its branches are made white.

8 [k]Lament like a virgin girded with sackcloth
For [l]the husband of her youth.
9 [m]The grain offering and the drink offering
Have been cut off from the house of the LORD;
The priests [n]mourn, who minister to the LORD.
10 The field is wasted,
[o]The land mourns;
For the grain is ruined,
[p]The new wine is dried up,
The oil fails.

11 [q]Be ashamed, you farmers,
Wail, you vinedressers,
For the wheat and the barley;
Because the harvest of the field has perished.

* **1:4** Exact identity of these locusts is unknown.

1:2 ***happened in your days.*** The calamity of recent days was unprecedented in the memory of the people.
1:4 ***locust.*** Many interpreters have viewed these locusts as foreign armies that attacked Judah in successive waves—Assyria, Babylon, Greece, and Rome. Yet literal locust plagues were one of the judgments promised if the people disobeyed God and broke their covenant with Him (Deut. 28:38–42). Further, Joel's description of the damage done by the locusts compares with eyewitness reports. The impression given is one of overwhelming devastation.
1:9 ***The grain offering and the drink offering.*** This phrase refers to the wine offerings that accompanied the priests' morning and evening sacrifices (Ex. 29:38–41). The devastation of the locust meant that no sacrifice could be offered.
1:10 ***The land mourns.*** The land is personified as mourning because the three principal crops it produced—grain, grapes, and olives—had been destroyed (Deut. 7:13; Ps. 104:15).

1:1 [a] Acts 2:16 **1:2** [b] Joel 2:2 **1:3** [c] Ps. 78:4 **1:4** [d] Deut. 28:38 [e] Is. 33:4 **1:5** [f] Is. 5:11; 28:1 [g] Is. 32:10 **1:6** [h] Joel 2:2, 11, 25 [i] Rev. 9:8 **1:7** [j] Is. 5:6 **1:8** [k] Is. 22:12 [l] Jer. 3:4 **1:9** [m] Joel 1:13; 2:14 [n] Joel 2:17 **1:10** [o] Jer. 12:11 [p] Is. 24:7 **1:11** [q] Jer. 14:3, 4

12 ʳThe vine has dried up,
  And the fig tree has withered;
  The pomegranate tree,
  The palm tree also,
  And the apple tree—
  All the trees of the field are withered;
  Surely ˢjoy has withered away from
    the sons of men.

Mourning for the Land

13 ᵗGird yourselves and lament, you
    priests;
  Wail, you who minister before the altar;
  Come, lie all night in sackcloth,
  You who minister to my God;
  For the grain offering and the drink
    offering
  Are withheld from the house of your
    God.
14 ᵘConsecrate a fast,
  Call ᵛa sacred assembly;
  Gather the elders
  And ʷall the inhabitants of the land
  Into the house of the LORD your God,
  And cry out to the LORD.

15 ˣAlas for the day!
  For ʸthe day of the LORD is at hand;
  It shall come as destruction from the
    Almighty.

16 Is not the food ᶻcut off before our
    eyes,
  ᵃJoy and gladness from the house of
    our God?
17 The seed shrivels under the clods,
  Storehouses are in shambles;
  Barns are broken down,
  For the grain has withered.
18 How ᵇthe animals groan!
  The herds of cattle are restless,
  Because they have no pasture;
  Even the flocks of sheep suffer
    punishment.*
19 O LORD, ᶜto You I cry out;
  For ᵈfire has devoured the open
    pastures,
  And a flame has burned all the trees of
    the field.
20 The beasts of the field also ᵉcry out to
    You,
  For ᶠthe water brooks are dried up,
  And fire has devoured the open
    pastures.

The Day of the LORD

2 Blow ᵃthe trumpet in Zion,
  And ᵇsound an alarm in My holy
    mountain!
  Let all the inhabitants of the land
    tremble;
  For ᶜthe day of the LORD is coming,
  For it is at hand:
2 ᵈA day of darkness and gloominess,
  A day of clouds and thick darkness,
  Like the morning *clouds* spread over
    the mountains.
  ᵉA people *come*, great and strong,
  ᶠThe like of whom has never been;
  Nor will there ever be any *such* after
    them,
  Even for many successive generations.

3 A fire devours before them,
  And behind them a flame burns;
  The land *is* like ᵍthe Garden of Eden
    before them,
  ʰAnd behind them a desolate wilderness;
  Surely nothing shall escape them.
4 ⁱTheir appearance is like the
    appearance of horses;
  And like swift steeds, so they run.
5 ʲWith a noise like chariots
  Over mountaintops they leap,
  Like the noise of a flaming fire that
    devours the stubble,
  Like a strong people set in battle array.
6 Before them the people writhe in pain;
  ᵏAll faces are drained of color.*
7 They run like mighty men,
  They climb the wall like men of war;
  Every one marches in formation,
  And they do not break ˡranks.
8 They do not push one another;
  Every one marches in his own column.*
  Though they lunge between the
    weapons,
  They are not cut down.*
9 They run to and fro in the city,
  They run on the wall;
  They climb into the houses,
  They ᵐenter at the windows ⁿlike a
    thief.

* 1:18 Septuagint and Vulgate read *are made desolate.*   * 2:6 Septuagint, Targum, and Vulgate read *gather blackness.*   * 2:8 Literally *his own highway* • That is, they are not halted by losses

1:15 the day of the LORD. This phrase refers to a time of judgment and deliverance. Joel views the locust plague as a contemporary day of judgment that was serving as a token or forewarning of an even greater, future "day of the LORD."

1:17 The seed shrivels. This indicated further devastation in the land and an inability to replant the following year.

2:1 at hand. The Bible presents the day of the Lord as an imminent reality. It is not something that we are gradually moving toward; rather, it is ever ready to burst in on us. At any moment, the day that is "at hand" may become present.

2:2 darkness and of gloominess. This phrase is used as a figure for misery, distress, and judgment (Is. 8:22; 60:2; Jer. 13:16).

2:4 the appearance of horses. Joel compared the speed and strength of the invaders to galloping horses.

1:12 ʳJoel 1:10 ˢJer. 48:33   **1:13** ᵗJer. 4:8   **1:14** ᵘJoel 2:15, 16 ᵛLev. 23:36 ʷ2 Chr. 20:13   **1:15** ˣ[Jer. 30:7] ʸIs. 13:6   **1:16** ᶻIs. 3:1 ᵃDeut. 12:7   **1:18** ᵇHos. 4:3   **1:19** ᶜ[Ps. 50:15] ᵈJer. 9:10   **1:20** ᵉPs. 104:21; 147:9 ᶠ1 Kin. 17:7; 18:5   **2:1** ᵃJer. 4:5 ᵇNum. 10:5 ᶜ[Obad. 15] **2:2** ᵈAmos 5:18 ᵉJoel 2:11, 25 ᶠDan. 9:12; 12:1   **2:3** ᵍIs. 51:3 ʰZech. 7:14   **2:4** ⁱRev. 9:7   **2:5** ʲRev. 9:9   **2:6** ᵏNah. 2:10   **2:7** ˡProv. 30:27   **2:9** ᵐJer. 9:21 ⁿJohn 10:1

10 *o*The earth quakes before them,
　The heavens tremble;
　*p*The sun and moon grow dark,
　And the stars diminish their brightness.
11 *q*The LORD gives voice before His army,
　For His camp is very great;
　*r*For strong *is the One* who executes
　　His word.
　For the *s*day of the LORD *is* great and
　　very terrible;
　*t*Who can endure it?

A Call to Repentance

12 "Now, therefore," says the LORD,
　u"Turn to Me with all your heart,
　With fasting, with weeping, and with
　　mourning."
13 So *v*rend your heart, and not *w*your
　　garments;
　Return to the LORD your God,
　For He *is* *x*gracious and merciful,
　Slow to anger, and of great kindness;
　And He relents from doing harm.
14 *y*Who knows *if* He will turn and relent,
　And leave *z*a blessing behind Him—
　*a*A grain offering and a drink offering
　For the LORD your God?

15 *b*Blow the trumpet in Zion,
　*c*Consecrate a fast,
　Call a sacred assembly;
16 Gather the people,
　*d*Sanctify the congregation,
　Assemble the elders,
　Gather the children and nursing babes;
　*e*Let the bridegroom go out from his
　　chamber,
　And the bride from her dressing room.
17 Let the priests, who minister to the
　　LORD,
　Weep *f*between the porch and the altar;
　Let them say, *g*"Spare Your people,
　O LORD,
　And do not give Your heritage to
　　reproach,
　That the nations should rule over them.

*h*Why should they say among the
　　peoples,
　'Where *is* their God?'"

The Land Refreshed

18 Then the LORD will *i*be zealous for His
　　land,
　And pity His people.
19 The LORD will answer and say to His
　　people,
　"Behold, I will send you *j*grain and new
　　wine and oil,
　And you will be satisfied by them;
　I will no longer make you a reproach
　　among the nations.

20 "But *k*I will remove far from you *l*the
　　northern *army*,
　And will drive him away into a barren
　　and desolate land,
　With his face toward the eastern sea
　And his back *m*toward the western sea;
　His stench will come up,
　And his foul odor will rise,
　Because he has done monstrous
　　things."

21 Fear not, O land;
　Be glad and rejoice,
　For the LORD has done marvelous
　　things!
22 Do not be afraid, you beasts of the field;
　For *n*the open pastures are springing up,
　And the tree bears its fruit;
　The fig tree and the vine yield their
　　strength.
23 Be glad then, you children of Zion,
　And *o*rejoice in the LORD your God;
　For He has given you the former rain
　　faithfully,*
　And He *p*will cause the rain to come
　　down for you—
　The former rain,
　And the latter rain in the first *month*.

***

* **2:23** Or *the teacher of righteousness*

***

2:11 *Who can endure it.* Nothing will be able to withstand the wrath of God (Matt. 24:21–22).
2:13 *rend your heart.* God is not satisfied with outward acts of repentance. Tearing one's garments was a customary way of expressing grief or remorse (Josh. 7:6; 1 Sam. 4:12). However, like all outward acts, the tearing of a garment could be done without true sorrow or repentance. God required more than mere external words or actions; He wanted a change of heart and sorrow over sin.
2:14 *Who knows.* These words suggest that even at the last moment, the Lord would withhold His wrath and display His grace if the people would truly repent. As a result, agriculture would be restored and productivity would return. There would be food and drink for the people and for offerings to the Lord.
2:16 *bridegroom . . . bride.* According to Jewish tradition codified in the Mishnah, a couple could be excused from reciting daily prayers on their wedding day. But Joel excused no one from prayer at this time of spiritual emergency.
2:17 *Why should they say among the peoples.*

This rhetorical question was designed to move God to intervene. Failure to come to Judah's aid might encourage the nations to make a mockery of Judah's God.
2:18–19 *zealous for His land.* The deep love of God for the land of Israel is coupled with His abiding love for the people. On every occasion in which God brought judgment on the land, there was the hope that one day His zeal for the land would lead to a renewal of blessing. Genuine repentance is the prerequisite for God's blessing. In response to repentance, God would bring restoration and blessing.
2:22 *the open pastures are springing up . . . the tree*

***

2:10 *o* Ps. 18:7 *p* Is. 13:10; 34:4　**2:11** *q* Jer. 25:30 *r* Rev. 18:8 *s* Amos 5:18 *t* [Mal. 3:2]　**2:12** *u* Jer. 4:1　**2:13** *v* [Ps. 34:18; 51:17] *w* Gen. 37:34 *x* [Ex. 34:6]　**2:14** *y* Jer. 26:3 *z* Hag. 2:19 *a* Joel 1:9, 13　**2:15** *b* Num. 10:3 *c* Joel 1:14　**2:16** *d* Ex. 19:10 *e* Ps. 19:5　**2:17** *f* Matt. 23:35 *g* Ex. 32:11, 12 *h* Ps. 42:10　**2:18** *i* [Is. 60:10; 63:9, 15]　**2:19** *j* [Mal. 3:10]　**2:20** *k* Ex. 10:19 *l* Jer. 1:14, 15 *m* Deut. 11:24　**2:22** *n* Joel 1:19　**2:23** *o* Is. 41:16 *p* Lev. 26:4

24 The threshing floors shall be full of
wheat,
And the vats shall overflow with new
wine and oil.
25 "So I will restore to you the years ᵍthat
the swarming locust has eaten,
The crawling locust,
The consuming locust,
And the chewing locust,*
My great army which I sent among you.
26 You shall ʳeat in plenty and be satisfied,
And praise the name of the LORD your
God,
Who has dealt wondrously with you;
And My people shall never be put to
ˢshame.
27 Then you shall know that I *am* ᵗin the
midst of Israel:
ᵘI *am* the LORD your God
And there is no other.
My people shall never be put to shame.

God's Spirit Poured Out

28 "Andᵛ it shall come to pass afterward
That ʷI will pour out My Spirit on all
flesh;
ˣYour sons and your ʸdaughters shall
prophesy,
Your old men shall dream dreams,
Your young men shall see visions.
29 And also on *My* ᶻmenservants and on
My maidservants
I will pour out My Spirit in those days.

30 "And ᵃI will show wonders in the
heavens and in the earth:
Blood and fire and pillars of smoke.
31 ᵇThe sun shall be turned into darkness,
And the moon into blood,
ᶜBefore the coming of the great and
awesome day of the LORD.
32 And it shall come to pass
That ᵈwhoever calls on the name of
the LORD
Shall be saved.
For ᵉin Mount Zion and in Jerusalem
there shall be deliverance,
As the LORD has said,
Among ᶠthe remnant whom the LORD
calls.

God Judges the Nations

3 "For behold, ᵃin those days and at that
time,
When I bring back the captives of
Judah and Jerusalem,
2 ᵇI will also gather all nations,
And bring them down to the Valley of
Jehoshaphat;
And I ᶜwill enter into judgment with
them there
On account of My people, My heritage
Israel,
Whom they have scattered among the
nations;
They have also divided up My land.
3 They have ᵈcast lots for My people,
Have given a boy *as payment* for a
harlot,
And sold a girl for wine, that they may
drink.

4 "Indeed, what have you to do with Me,
ᵉO Tyre and Sidon, and all the coasts of
Philistia?
Will you retaliate against Me?
But if you retaliate against Me,
Swiftly and speedily I will return your
retaliation upon your own head;
5 Because you have taken My silver and
My gold,
And have carried into your temples
My prized possessions.
6 Also the people of Judah and the
people of Jerusalem
You have sold to the Greeks,
That you may remove them far from
their borders.

7 "Behold, ᶠI will raise them
Out of the place to which you have sold
them,
And will return your retaliation upon
your own head.
8 I will sell your sons and your
daughters
Into the hand of the people of Judah,
And they will sell them to the ᵍSabeans,*
To a people ʰfar off;
For the LORD has spoken."

---

* **2:25** Compare 1:4 * **3:8** Literally *Shebaites*
(compare Isaiah 60:6 and Ezekiel 27:22)

---

bears its fruit. The renewal of agriculture would be a
sign that God had renewed prosperity and peace to
His land.
2:28–32 I will pour out My Spirit on all flesh.
Peter quotes this passage on the Day of Pentecost
(Acts 2:17–21) to explain the miracle of speaking in
tongues. There are three main viewpoints regarding
how Peter uses Joel's prophecy: (1) Some interpreters
see a complete fulfillment of Joel's prophecy in the
experience of the first believers on the Day of Pentecost. The outpouring of the Spirit ushered in the kingdom age; (2) some interpreters believe that Peter was
simply using Joel's prophecy as an illustration of what
was happening. In effect, Peter was saying, "This is
that same Holy Spirit which was spoken of by Joel";
(3) some others suggest that Joel's prophecy was
partially fulfilled on the Day of Pentecost. The gift of

the Holy Spirit was given, but the signs mentioned in
verses 30–32 will be fulfilled later in connection with
the return of Christ in great glory.
3:2 Valley of Jehoshaphat. The name Jehoshaphat
means "the Lord judges." The location of this valley
is not known. Perhaps this was merely a symbolic
name for the location of the great battle in the end
times.

2:25 ᵍ Joel 1:4–7; 2:2–11 **2:26** ʳ Lev. 26:5 ˢ Is. 45:17
2:27 ᵗ Lev. 26:11, 12 ᵘ [Is. 45:5, 6] **2:28** ᵛ Ezek. 39:29
ʷ Zech. 12:10 ˣ Is. 54:13 ʸ Acts 21:9 **2:29** ᶻ [Gal. 3:28]
2:30 ᵃ Matt. 24:29 **2:31** ᵇ Is. 13:9, 10; 34:4
ᶜ [Mal. 4:1, 5, 6] **2:32** ᵈ Rom. 10:13 ᵉ Is. 46:13 ᶠ [Mic. 4:7]
3:1 ᵃ Jer. 30:3 **3:2** ᵇ Zech. 14:2 ᶜ Is. 66:16 **3:3** ᵈ Nah.
3:10 **3:4** ᵉ Amos 1:6–8 **3:7** ᶠ Jer. 23:8 **3:8** ᵍ Ezek.
23:42 ʰ Jer. 6:20

9 *Proclaim this among the nations:
"Prepare for war!
Wake up the mighty men,
Let all the men of war draw near,
Let them come up.
10 *Beat your plowshares into swords
And your pruning hooks into spears;
*Let the weak say, 'I *am* strong.'"
11 Assemble and come, all you nations,
And gather together all around.
Cause *Your mighty ones to go down
there, O LORD.

12 "Let the nations be wakened, and come
up to the Valley of Jehoshaphat;
For there I will sit to *judge all the
surrounding nations.
13 *Put in the sickle, for *the harvest is
ripe.
Come, go down;
For the *winepress is full,
The vats overflow—
For their wickedness *is* great."

14 Multitudes, multitudes in the valley of
decision!
For *the day of the LORD *is* near in the
valley of decision.
15 The sun and moon will grow dark,
And the stars will diminish their
brightness.
16 The LORD also will roar from Zion,
And utter His voice from Jerusalem;
The heavens and earth will shake;
*But the LORD will be a shelter for His
people,

And the strength of the children of
Israel.

17 "So you shall know that I *am* the LORD
your God,
Dwelling in Zion My *holy
mountain.
Then Jerusalem shall be holy,
And no aliens shall ever pass through
her again."

God Blesses His People

18 And it will come to pass in that
day
That the mountains shall drip with
new wine,
The hills shall flow with milk,
And all the brooks of Judah shall be
flooded with water;
A *fountain shall flow from the house
of the LORD
And water the Valley of Acacias.

19 "Egypt shall be a desolation,
And Edom a desolate wilderness,
Because of violence *against* the people
of Judah,
For they have shed innocent blood in
their land.
20 But Judah shall abide forever,
And Jerusalem from generation to
generation.
21 For I will *acquit them of the guilt
of bloodshed, whom I had not
acquitted;
For the LORD dwells in Zion."

3:11 nations ... mighty ones. Joel saw two different armies assembling for battle (Mark 8:38; Rev. 19:14).
3:14 the valley of decision. This may be a symbolic name for the Valley of Jehoshaphat (3:2), or it may refer to the option before the people to continue toward certain judgment or to turn to God in repentance (vv. 12–13).
3:18 in that day. These words indicate the prophetic future. Joel uses poetic imagery to describe the

productivity of the land in the messianic age. The Valley of Acacias was the location of the last encampment before the Israelites entered Canaan (Num. 25:1; Josh. 3:1).

3:9 *Ezek. 38:7 **3:10** *[Is. 2:4] *Zech. 12:8 **3:11** *Is. 13:3 **3:12** *Is. 2:4 **3:13** *Rev. 14:15 *Jer. 51:33 *[Is. 63:3] **3:14** *Joel 2:1 **3:16** *[Is. 51:5, 6] **3:17** *Zech. 8:3 **3:18** *Ezek. 47:1 **3:21** *Is. 4:4

THE BOOK OF
AMOS

▶ **AUTHOR:** The only Old Testament appearance of the name Amos is in this book. Amos's objective appraisal of Israel's spiritual condition was not well received, not least because he was just a farmer from Judah. The author said of his background, "I was no prophet, nor was I a son of a prophet, but I was a sheepbreeder and a tender of sycamore fruit" (7:14). He delivered his message in Bethel because it was the residence of the king of Israel and a center of idolatry.

▶ **TIME:** c. 760–753 B.C.   ▶ **KEY VERSES:** Amos 3:1–2

▶ **THEME:** Amos was a contemporary of Isaiah and Hosea. The unusual aspect of his ministry is that he was a farmer and herdsman from Judah prophesying to the northern kingdom of Israel. The issues he addresses are the usual prophetic concerns, but with a heavy emphasis on social justice. When injustice is rampant, expect God's judgment. No one is immune. In fact, the more God has given, the more God expects in response.

---

1 The words of Amos, who was among the *a*sheepbreeders* of *b*Tekoa, which he saw concerning Israel in the days of *c*Uzziah king of Judah, and in the days of *d*Jeroboam the son of Joash, king of Israel, two years before the *e*earthquake.
²And he said:

"The LORD *f*roars from Zion,
And utters His voice from Jerusalem;
The pastures of the shepherds mourn,
And the top of *g*Carmel withers."

Judgment on the Nations
³Thus says the LORD:

"For three transgressions of
   *h*Damascus, and for four,
I will not turn away its *punishment*,
Because they have *i*threshed Gilead
   with implements of iron.

⁴ *i*But I will send a fire into the house of
      Hazael,
Which shall devour the palaces of
   *k*Ben-Hadad.
⁵ I will also break the *gate l*bar of
      Damascus,
And cut off the inhabitant from the
      Valley of Aven,
And the one who holds the scepter
      from Beth Eden.
The people of Syria shall go captive
      to Kir,"
Says the LORD.

⁶Thus says the LORD:

"For three transgressions of *m*Gaza,
      and for four,

---

* **1:1** Compare 2 Kings 3:4

1:1—2:16 The words of Amos. The Lord sent Amos, a Judean, to Bethel to prophesy of coming judgment on Israel. But in Bethel, Amos faced a hostile audience. Israel's first king, Jeroboam I, had made the town a center of pagan worship. Because the temple in Jerusalem was in Judah and not in the nation of Israel, Jeroboam had encouraged the Israelites to worship at Bethel instead of Jerusalem. Thus the Israelites who gathered at Bethel would regard Amos, a Judean, with suspicion. Yet Amos bravely condemned there the sins of Israel's neighbors. He also points to the iniquity of Israel and Judah. They both had rejected the God who had covenanted with them.
1:1 Tekoa. This town was about ten miles south of Jerusalem, in a region well suited for raising sheep and goats.
1:3 For three . . . and for four. This stylistic device indicated the exhaustion of God's patience—the Syrians had continued to sin, again and again. This

device is repeated as Amos speaks God's words against nation after sinful nation. **Gilead.** This was the region on the east side of the Jordan from the Yarmuk River to the Dead Sea.
1:4 I will send a fire . . . devour the palaces. Fire in an ancient city was a real threat. Cities were crowded with houses close together on very narrow streets; there was too little water to effectively fight them.
1:5 the gate bar. This was a large timber that barred the city gate from the inside. If it was broken, the city would lose its security and could be captured easily.
1:6 Gaza. This was one of the five principal cities of the Philistines.

1:1 *a* 2 Kin. 3:4; Amos 7:14 *b* 2 Sam. 14:2 *c* 2 Chr. 26:1–23
d Amos 7:10 *e* Zech. 14:5   **1:2** *f* Joel 3:16 *g* 1 Sam. 25:2
1:3 *h* Is. 8:4; 17:1–3 *i* 2 Kin. 10:32, 33   **1:4** *j* Jer. 49:27;
51:30 *k* 2 Kin. 6:24   **1:5** *l* Jer. 51:30   **1:6** *m* Jer. 47:1, 5

I will not turn away its *punishment*,
Because they took captive the whole
captivity
To deliver *them* up to Edom.
7 [n]But I will send a fire upon the wall of
Gaza,
Which shall devour its palaces.
8 I will cut off the inhabitant [o]from
Ashdod,
And the one who holds the scepter
from Ashkelon;
I will [p]turn My hand against
Ekron,
And [q]the remnant of the Philistines
shall perish,"
Says the Lord GOD.

9 Thus says the LORD:

"For three transgressions of [r]Tyre, and
for four,
I will not turn away its
punishment,
Because they delivered up the whole
captivity to Edom,
And did not remember the covenant of
brotherhood.
10 But I will send a fire upon the wall of
Tyre,
Which shall devour its palaces."

11 Thus says the LORD:

"For three transgressions of [s]Edom,
and for four,
I will not turn away its *punishment*,
Because he pursued his [t]brother with
the sword,
And cast off all pity;
His anger tore perpetually,
And he kept his wrath forever.
12 But [u]I will send a fire upon Teman,
Which shall devour the palaces of
Bozrah."

13 Thus says the LORD:

"For three transgressions of [v]the people
of Ammon, and for four,
I will not turn away its *punishment*,
Because they ripped open the women
with child in Gilead,
That they might enlarge their
territory.

14 But I will kindle a fire in the wall of
[w]Rabbah,
And it shall devour its palaces,
[x]Amid shouting in the day of battle,
And a tempest in the day of the
whirlwind.
15 [y]Their king shall go into captivity,
He and his princes together,"
Says the LORD.

2 Thus says the LORD:

[a]"For three transgressions of Moab, and
for four,
I will not turn away its *punishment*,
Because he [b]burned the bones of the
king of Edom to lime.
2 But I will send a fire upon Moab,
And it shall devour the palaces of
[c]Kerioth;
Moab shall die with tumult,
With shouting *and* trumpet sound.
3 And I will cut off [d]the judge from its
midst,
And slay all its princes with him,"
Says the LORD.

Judgment on Judah
4 Thus says the LORD:

"For three transgressions of [e]Judah,
and for four,
I will not turn away its *punishment*,
[f]Because they have despised the law of
the LORD,
And have not kept His
commandments.
[g]Their lies lead them astray,
Lies [h]which their fathers followed.
5 [i]But I will send a fire upon Judah,
And it shall devour the palaces of
Jerusalem."

Judgment on Israel
6 Thus says the LORD:

"For three transgressions of [j]Israel, and
for four,
I will not turn away its *punishment*,
Because [k]they sell the righteous for
silver,
And the [l]poor for a pair of sandals.

1:11 *Edom.* This nation was located southeast of the Dead Sea. It controlled important caravan trade routes, and thus was deeply involved in commerce. Its citizens were descendants of Esau.

1:13 *Ammon.* The nation of Ammon was located east of Gilead on the edge of the desert. Its people were descended from one of the sons of Lot (Gen. 19:36–38).

2:1 *burned the bones.* This act was believed to desecrate the remains of a deceased person, a heinous act in ancient times and a great dishonor to the person's memory.

2:6 *sell the righteous for silver.* In His law, God had instructed the Israelites to work off their debts through indentured service—administered humanely and for a strictly limited time (Lev. 25:39–43; Deut. 15:12). By Amos's day, those in power in Israel were taking advantage of the courts to sell debtors as slaves, termed "the righteous" here because they were the innocent victims of the corruption of the courts. ***for a pair of sandals.*** This means for little or nothing.

1:7 [n] Jer. 47:1 1:8 [o] Zeph. 2:4 [p] Ps. 81:14 [q] Ezek. 25:16
1:9 [r] Is. 23:1–18 1:11 [s] Is. 21:11 [t] Obad. 10–12
1:12 [u] Obad. 9, 10 1:13 [v] Ezek. 25:2 1:14 [w] Deut.
3:11 [x] Amos 2:2 1:15 [y] Jer. 49:3 2:1 [a] Zeph. 2:8–11
[b] 2 Kin. 3:26, 27 2:2 [c] Jer. 48:24, 41 2:3 [d] Num. 24:17
2:4 [e] Hos. 12:2 [f] Lev. 26:14 [g] Jer. 16:19 [h] Ezek. 20:13, 16,
18 2:5 [i] Hos. 8:14 2:6 [j] 2 Kin. 17:7–18; 18:12 [k] Is. 29:21
[l] Amos 4:1; 5:11; 8:6

7 They pant after* the dust of the earth
which is on the head of the poor,
And [m]pervert the way of the humble.
[n]A man and his father go in to the *same* girl,
[o]To defile My holy name.
8 They lie down [p]by every altar on clothes [q]taken in pledge,
And drink the wine of the condemned *in* the house of their god.

9 "Yet *it was* I *who* destroyed the [r]Amorite before them,
Whose height *was* like the [s]height of the cedars,
And he *was as* strong as the oaks;
Yet I [t]destroyed his fruit above
And his roots beneath.
10 Also *it was* [u]I *who* brought you up from the land of Egypt,
And [v]led you forty years through the wilderness,
To possess the land of the Amorite.
11 I raised up some of your sons as [w]prophets,
And some of your young men as [x]Nazirites.
Is it not so, O you children of Israel?"
Says the LORD.
12 "But you gave the Nazirites wine to drink,
And commanded the prophets [y]saying,
'Do not prophesy!'

13 "Behold,[z] I am weighed down by you,
As a cart full of sheaves is weighed down.
14 [a]Therefore flight shall perish from the swift,
The strong shall not strengthen his power,
[b]Nor shall the mighty deliver himself;
15 He shall not stand who handles the bow,
The swift of foot shall not escape,
Nor shall he who rides a horse deliver himself.
16 The most courageous men of might
Shall flee naked in that day,"
Says the LORD.

Authority of the Prophet's Message

3 Hear this word that the LORD has spoken against you, O children of Israel, against the whole family which I brought up from the land of Egypt, saying:

2 "You[a] only have I known of all the families of the earth;
[b]Therefore I will punish you for all your iniquities."

3 Can two walk together, unless they are agreed?
4 Will a lion roar in the forest, when he has no prey?
Will a young lion cry out of his den, if he has caught nothing?
5 Will a bird fall into a snare on the earth, where there is no trap for it?
Will a snare spring up from the earth, if it has caught nothing at all?
6 If a trumpet is blown in a city, will not the people be afraid?
[c]If there is calamity in a city, will not the LORD have done *it*?

7 Surely the Lord GOD does nothing,
Unless [d]He reveals His secret to His servants the prophets.

* 2:7 Or *trample on*

2:7 *humble.* Those without power or influence should have been able to depend on the justice due them. Instead, justice was denied them. As a result, their lives were turned to poverty, oppression, and insecurity.
2:8 *clothes taken in pledge.* Clothing taken as security for a loan was supposed to be returned in the evening so that it could be used as bedding for the poor (Ex. 22:26–27). The powerful in Israel were spreading the clothes out as beds for themselves beside the altars, in a show of empty, merciless piety.
2:9 *it was I who destroyed.* This emphatic statement underscores the fact that God had been Israel's champion, and the nation's success had not been its own doing. ***the Amorite.*** This refers to the previous inhabitants of the land of Canaan.
2:13 *I am weighed down by you.* This is a powerful metaphor of the burden of Israel's sin on the Lord. This is the same God Isaiah describes as measuring the waters of the earth in the hollow of His hand, measuring the heavens with the span of His hand, and weighing the mountains in His balance (Is. 40:12).
3:1 *the whole family which I brought up.* This phrase emphasizes the personal, intimate relationship that God had with Israel.
3:2 *You only have I known.* God's relationship with Israel was not only intimate, it was exclusive. God had been faithful to Israel, yet Israel had not been faithful to God. For this reason, the nation would be judged.
3:2 Selection of Israel—The selection of Israel as a special nation to God was part of God's plan (Rom. 11:2). Historically, the selection of Israel began with the Lord's promise to Abraham, "I will make you a great nation" (Gen. 12:2). The name Israel actually comes from the new name which God gave to Abraham's grandson Jacob when they fought at the ford of Jabbok (Gen. 32:28). This fact explains why his descendants are often called the children of Israel.

The motivation for the Lord's choice of Israel as His select nation did not lie in any special attraction the nation possessed. Its people were, in fact, the least in number among all the nations (Deut. 7:6–8). Rather, the Lord chose them because of His love for them and because of His covenant with Abraham. This fact does not mean that God did not love other nations, because it was through Israel that He blessed all nations in Christ.
3:3–6 *Can two walk together.* This series of rhetorical questions illustrates the seriousness, certainty, and righteousness of God's impending action against

2:7 [m] Amos 5:12 [n] Ezek. 22:11 [o] Lev. 20:3 **2:8** [p] 1 Cor. 8:10 [q] Ex. 22:26 **2:9** [r] Num. 21:25 [s] Ezek. 31:3 [t] [Mal. 4:1] **2:10** [u] Ex. 12:51 [v] Deut. 2:7 **2:11** [w] Num. 12:6 [x] Num. 6:2, 3 **2:12** [y] Is. 30:10 **2:13** [z] Is. 1:14 **2:14** [a] Jer. 46:6 [b] Ps. 33:16 **3:2** [a] [Deut. 7:6] [b] [Rom. 2:9] **3:6** [c] Is. 45:7 **3:7** [d] [John 15:15]

8 A lion has roared!
  Who will not fear?
  The Lord GOD has spoken!
  eWho can but prophesy?

Punishment of Israel's Sins

9 "Proclaim in the palaces at Ashdod,*
  And in the palaces in the land of
    Egypt, and say:
  'Assemble on the mountains of
    Samaria;
  See great tumults in her midst,
  And the oppressed within her.
10 For they fdo not know to do right,'
  Says the LORD,
  'Who store up violence and robbery in
    their palaces.'"

11 Therefore thus says the Lord GOD:

  "An adversary shall be all around the
    land;
  He shall sap your strength from you,
  And your palaces shall be
    plundered."

12 Thus says the LORD:

  "As a shepherd takes from the mouth
    of a lion
  Two legs or a piece of an ear,
  So shall the children of Israel be taken
    out
  Who dwell in Samaria—
  In the corner of a bed and on the edge*
    of a couch!
13 Hear and testify against the house of
    Jacob,"
  Says the Lord GOD, the God of hosts,
14 "That in the day I punish Israel for their
    transgressions,
  I will also visit destruction on the
    altars of gBethel;
  And the horns of the altar shall be
    cut off
  And fall to the ground.

15 I will destroy hthe winter house along
    with the summer house;
  The ihouses of ivory shall perish,
  And the great houses shall have an
    end,"
  Says the LORD.

4 Hear this word, you acows of Bashan,
  who are on the mountain of
    Samaria,
  Who oppress the bpoor,
  Who crush the needy,
  Who say to your husbands,* "Bring
    wine, let us cdrink!"
2 dThe Lord GOD has sworn by His
    holiness:
  "Behold, the days shall come upon you
  When He will take you away ewith
    fishhooks,
  And your posterity with fishhooks.
3 fYou will go out through broken walls,
  Each one straight ahead of her,
  And you will be cast into Harmon,"
  Says the LORD.

4 "Comeg to Bethel and transgress,
  At hGilgal multiply transgression;
  iBring your sacrifices every morning,
  jYour tithes every three days.*
5 kOffer a sacrifice of thanksgiving with
    leaven,
  Proclaim and announce lthe freewill
    offerings;
  For this you love,
  You children of Israel!"
  Says the Lord GOD.

Israel Did Not Accept Correction

6 "Also I gave you cleanness of teeth in
    all your cities,

---

* 3:9 Following Masoretic Text; Septuagint
reads Assyria. * 3:12 The Hebrew is uncertain. * 4:1 Literally their lords or their masters
* 4:4 Or years (compare Deuteronomy 14:28)

Israel. Each question is framed so as to require a resounding "no" as its answer.
3:11 An adversary shall be all around the land. This verse pictures a formal sentencing of Israel in the presence of the witnesses whom God had called (v. 9). Sapping Israel's strength was exactly what Assyria did in the years following Amos's prophecies, finally putting an end to the nation in 722 B.C.
3:12 As a shepherd takes from the mouth of a lion. The hired shepherd was responsible to the owner for the safety of the sheep. He had to make good any loss, unless he could prove it was unavoidable. A lion taking a sheep was an unavoidable loss, but the shepherd had to prove that the lion had taken it. A couple of small bones or a piece of an ear was sufficient; the owner would recognize the lion's work. As complete as the destruction of a sheep by a lion would be the destruction of Israel that God would bring.
3:15 the great houses shall have an end. The four houses mentioned here were all symbols of oppression. Many small inheritances had been stolen to form the large estates of the wealthy and powerful, where they built their opulent houses.

4:1 cows of Bashan. This phrase refers to the well-fed women of Samaria. Bashan, the region east and northeast of the Sea of Galilee, was a prime grassland area renowned for its cattle.
4:3 broken walls. These were a symbol of the thoroughness of the destruction of the city and the homes that the people held so dear. In an undamaged city, the usual way in and out was the one main gate. But Samaria would be so ruined that the deportees would be driven straight through the breaches in the walls of their houses and their city.
4:6–11 you have not returned to Me. This passage describes a series of five calamities that God had already sent upon the Israelites in an effort to drive them to repentance. A striking feature of this narrative is God's emphatic claim that the Israelites had brought these disasters on themselves. They had

---

3:8 e Acts 4:20 **3:10** f Jer. 4:22 **3:14** g Amos 4:4
3:15 h Jer. 36:22 i Judg. 3:20 j 1 Kin. 22:39 **4:1** a Ps. 22:12
b Amos 2:6 c Prov. 23:20 **4:2** d Ps. 89:35 e Jer. 16:16
4:3 f Ezek. 12:5 **4:4** g Ezek. 20:39 h Hos. 4:15 i Num. 28:3
j Deut. 14:28 **4:5** k Lev. 7:13 l Lev. 22:18

And lack of bread in all your places;
[m]Yet you have not returned to Me,"
Says the LORD.

7 "I also withheld rain from you,
When *there were* still three months to the harvest.
I made it rain on one city,
I withheld rain from another city.
One part was rained upon,
And where it did not rain the part withered.
8 So two *or* three cities wandered to another city to drink water,
But they were not satisfied;
Yet you have not returned to Me,"
Says the LORD.

9 "I[n] blasted you with blight and mildew.
When your gardens increased,
Your vineyards,
Your fig trees,
And your olive trees,
[o]The locust devoured *them;*
Yet you have not returned to Me,"
Says the LORD.

10 "I sent among you a plague [p]after the manner of Egypt;
Your young men I killed with a sword,
Along with your captive horses;
I made the stench of your camps come up into your nostrils;
Yet you have not returned to Me,"
Says the LORD.

11 "I overthrew *some* of you,
As God overthrew [q]Sodom and Gomorrah,
And you were like a firebrand plucked from the burning;
Yet you have not returned to Me,"
Says the LORD.

12 "Therefore thus will I do to you, O Israel;
Because I will do this to you,
[r]Prepare to meet your God, O Israel!"

13 For behold,
He who forms mountains,
And creates the wind,
[s]Who declares to man what his* thought *is,*
And makes the morning darkness,
[t]Who treads the high places of the earth—
[u]The LORD God of hosts *is* His name.

A Lament for Israel

5 Hear this word which I [a]take up against you, a lamentation, O house of Israel:

2 The virgin of Israel has fallen;
She will rise no more.
She lies forsaken on her land;
There is no one to raise her up.

3For thus says the Lord GOD:

"The city that goes out by a thousand
Shall have a hundred left,
And that which goes out by a hundred
Shall have ten left to the house of Israel."

A Call to Repentance

4For thus says the LORD to the house of Israel:

[b]"Seek Me [c]and live;
5 But do not seek [d]Bethel,
Nor enter Gilgal,
Nor pass over to [e]Beersheba;
For Gilgal shall surely go into captivity,
And [f]Bethel shall come to nothing.
6 [g]Seek the LORD and live,
Lest He break out like fire *in* the house of Joseph,
And devour *it,*
With no one to quench *it* in Bethel—
7 You who [h]turn justice to wormwood,
And lay righteousness to rest in the earth!"

8 He made the [i]Pleiades and Orion;
He turns the shadow of death into morning
[j]And makes the day dark as night;
He [k]calls for the waters of the sea
And pours them out on the face of the earth;
[l]The LORD *is* His name.

---

* **4:13** Or *His*

---

repeatedly failed to understand the implications of the disasters.
4:10 *after the manner of Egypt.* This fourth calamity suggests that God was reminding Israel of the ten plagues that preceded their exodus from Egypt; these included epidemic diseases and other disasters.
4:11 *like a firebrand plucked from the burning.* This refers to a stick snatched from a fire with one end already ablaze. Here it was a vivid metaphor for God's last-minute rescue of most of Israel from the fate He brought upon some of its cities and territories.
4:12 *Prepare to meet your God.* Because Israel had not returned to God through these five calamities, it would have to meet God Himself. To be confronted—inescapably—by the God it had scorned and rejected would be a fate more terrible than Israel could imagine.
5:2 *The virgin of Israel.* This term depicts the nation as a young maiden, cut off from her life before it had really begun. ***on her land.*** This is a reminder that the land had been God's gift to Israel. By their faithlessness, the people had turned God's gift into the place of their death and burial.
5:6 *in the house of Joseph.* This phrase refers to the whole nation.
5:8 *the Pleiades.* This refers to a cluster of stars within the constellation Taurus, one of the twelve signs of the Zodiac. One of Israel's idolatries was astral worship. Far from being deities, Amos asserted,

4:6 [m] Jer. 5:3 **4:9** [n] Hag. 2:17 [o] Joel 1:4, 7 **4:10** [p] Ps. 78:50 **4:11** [q] Is. 13:19 **4:12** [r] Jer. 5:22 **4:13** [s] Ps. 139:2 [t] Mic. 1:3 [u] Is. 47:4 **5:1** [a] Jer. 7:29; 9:10, 17 **5:4** [b] [Jer. 29:13] [c] [Is. 55:3] **5:5** [d] Amos 4:4 [e] Amos 8:14 [f] Hos. 4:15 **5:6** [g] [Is. 55:3, 6, 7] **5:7** [h] Amos 6:12 **5:8** [i] Job 9:9; 38:31 [j] Ps. 104:20 [k] Job 38:34 [l] [Amos 4:13]

9 He rains ruin upon the strong,
So that fury comes upon the fortress.

10 mThey hate the one who rebukes in the gate,
And they nabhor the one who speaks uprightly.

11 oTherefore, because you tread down the poor
And take grain taxes from him,
Though pyou have built houses of hewn stone,
Yet you shall not dwell in them;
You have planted pleasant vineyards,
But you shall not drink wine from them.

12 For I qknow your manifold transgressions
And your mighty sins:
rAfflicting the just and taking bribes;
sDiverting the poor from justice at the gate.

13 Therefore tthe prudent keep silent at that time,
For it is an evil time.

14 Seek good and not evil,
That you may live;
So the LORD God of hosts will be with you,
uAs you have spoken.

15 vHate evil, love good;
Establish justice in the gate.
wIt may be that the LORD God of hosts
Will be gracious to the remnant of Joseph.

The Day of the LORD

16Therefore the LORD God of hosts, the Lord, says this:

"There shall be wailing in all streets,
And they shall say in all the highways,
'Alas! Alas!'
They shall call the farmer to mourning,
xAnd skillful lamenters to wailing.

17 In all vineyards there shall be wailing,
For yI will pass through you,"
Says the LORD.

18 zWoe to you who desire the day of the LORD!
For what good is athe day of the LORD to you?
It will be darkness, and not light.

19 It will be bas though a man fled from a lion,
And a bear met him!
Or as though he went into the house,
Leaned his hand on the wall,
And a serpent bit him!

20 Is not the day of the LORD darkness, and not light?
Is it not very dark, with no brightness in it?

21 "Ic hate, I despise your feast days,
And dI do not savor your sacred assemblies.

22 eThough you offer Me burnt offerings and your grain offerings,
I will not accept them,
Nor will I regard your fattened peace offerings.

---

the constellations also were God's creations. **Orion.** This is a reference to a prominent constellation in the southern sky in the shape of a hunter.

5:10 the gate. This was the location of the town court, where justice was to be upheld in all legal proceedings whether civil or criminal.

5:11–15 God's Justice—The Israelites in Amos's day had lost sight of God's commands to treat the poor compassionately. There is no record that Israel ever practiced the year of Jubilee (Lev. 25:11) that is part of Old Testament law, for instance.

As many of the prophets did, Amos called on the Israelites to practice justice and see to it that the poor were not abused. He made it clear that the rich in his day were taking advantage of the poor. The justice system was ineffective because of rampant bribery. The prophets repeatedly made the point that the sacrifices were not enough. The sacrificial process needed to be connected with a response in behavior. God's justice demanded more than the sacrifices. It demanded obedience.

Amos teaches us to be observant about where this injustice is being practiced. He teaches us to look for movements, forces, or programs that can work against the accumulation of power and unjustly gained wealth.

One of the first things the Jerusalem church did when it formed was to put in place a system of some kind to care for the widows and orphans (Acts 6:1–4). Belief in God included an understanding of His desire for justice and the believer's need to act on it.

5:11 grain taxes. To take grain taxes from the poor

was to put them at risk of starvation if the harvest had not been bountiful. Yet the rich and powerful had sufficient resources to build luxurious houses for themselves. God promised that the rich would not enjoy their luxury stolen from the lifeblood of the poor and powerless.

5:12 your mighty sins. Israel's leaders did not sin incidentally or furtively; they sinned brazenly and habitually, as though God had never revealed Himself and His standards of justice and mercy.

5:18 the day of the LORD. The popular theology of Amos's time apparently looked forward to this day as the time of Israel's restoration to military, political, and economic greatness, perhaps to the greatness of the reigns of David and Solomon. Amos declared such hopes futile, even pitiable. What the people looked forward to as a day of light and triumph would rise upon them instead as a day of darkness and ruin.

5:19 bear . . . serpent. These images evoke the terror that follows when a person escapes a terrible danger and is exhausted and relieved, only to find a worse danger so close at hand that it is inescapable.

5:21–23 feast days . . . sacred assemblies. By stating He would no longer accept Israel's sacrifices or

5:10 m Is. 29:21; 66:5 n 1 Kin. 22:8 **5:11** o Amos 2:6
p Mic. 6:15 **5:12** q Hos. 5:3 r Amos 2:6 s Is. 29:21
5:13 t Amos 6:10 **5:14** u Mic. 3:11 **5:15** v Rom. 12:9
w Joel 2:14 **5:16** x Jer. 9:17 **5:17** y Ex. 12:12 **5:18** z Is.
5:19 a Joel 2:2 **5:19** b Jer. 48:44 **5:21** c Is. 1:11–16
d Lev. 26:31 **5:22** e Mic. 6:6, 7

23 Take away from Me the noise of your songs,
For I will not hear the melody of your stringed instruments.
24 [f]But let justice run down like water,
And righteousness like a mighty stream.

25 "Did[g] you offer Me sacrifices and offerings
In the wilderness forty years, O house of Israel?
26 You also carried Sikkuth* [h]your king*
And Chiun,* your idols,
The star of your gods,
Which you made for yourselves.
27 Therefore I will send you into captivity [i]beyond Damascus,"
Says the LORD, [j]whose name *is* the God of hosts.

Warnings to Zion and Samaria

6 Woe [a]to you *who are* at [b]ease in Zion,
And [c]trust in Mount Samaria,
Notable persons in the [d]chief nation,
To whom the house of Israel comes!
2 [e]Go over to [f]Calneh and see;
And from there go to [g]Hamath the great;
Then go down to Gath of the Philistines.
[h]*Are you* better than these kingdoms?
Or is their territory greater than your territory?

3 *Woe to* you who [i]put far off the day of [j]doom,
[k]Who cause [l]the seat of violence to come near;
4 Who lie on beds of ivory,
Stretch out on your couches,
Eat lambs from the flock
And calves from the midst of the stall;
5 [m]Who sing idly to the sound of stringed instruments,
And invent for yourselves [n]musical instruments [o]like David;
6 Who [p]drink wine from bowls,
And anoint yourselves with the best ointments,
[q]But are not grieved for the affliction of Joseph.

7 Therefore they shall now go [r]captive as the first of the captives,
And those who recline at banquets shall be removed.

8 [s]The Lord GOD has sworn by Himself,
The LORD God of hosts says:
"I abhor [t]the pride of Jacob,
And hate his palaces;
Therefore I will deliver up *the* city
And all that is in it."

9 Then it shall come to pass, that if ten
men remain in one house, they shall die.
10 And when a relative *of the dead,* with one
who will burn *the bodies,* picks up the bodies* to take them out of the house, he will
say to one inside the house, "*Are there* any
more with you?"
Then someone will say, "None."
And he will say, [u]"Hold your tongue!
[v]For we dare not mention the name of the
LORD."

11 For behold, [w]the LORD gives a command:
[x]He will break the great house into bits,
And the little house into pieces.

12 Do horses run on rocks?
Does *one* plow *there* with oxen?
Yet [y]you have turned justice into gall,
And the fruit of righteousness into wormwood,
13 You who rejoice over Lo Debar,*
Who say, "Have we not taken Karnaim* for ourselves
By our own strength?"

14 "But, behold, [z]I will raise up a nation against you,
O house of Israel,"
Says the LORD God of hosts;
"And they will afflict you from the [a]entrance of Hamath
To the Valley of the Arabah."

Vision of the Locusts

7 Thus the Lord GOD showed me: Behold,
He formed locust swarms at the beginning of the late crop; indeed *it was* the late

*5:26 A pagan deity • Septuagint and Vulgate read *tabernacle of Moloch.* • *A pagan deity* *6:10 Literally *bones* *6:13 Literally *Nothing* • Literally *Horns,* symbol of strength

listen to them, God was rejecting Israel's worship as hypocritical, dishonest, and meaningless.

5:25 *Did you offer Me.* This verse is a rhetorical question with "yes" as the expected answer.

6:3 *you who put far off the day of doom.* This refers to those who insisted that Israel was too strong for destruction to fall upon the nation any time soon.

6:4–6 *lambs . . . calves.* This passage describes the extravagant living indulged in by the rich and paid for with the wealth stolen from the poor. Meat was a luxury for most families of the ancient Middle East, consumed only on special occasions. Meat on a daily basis was the privilege only of the rich and powerful. The upper classes of Israel were so engrossed in their own privileges and luxuries that they cared nothing for the affliction of their fellow Israelites, though it was their transgressions that had caused it.

7:1 *the king's mowings.* These words imply that

5:24 [f]Mic. 6:8 **5:25** [g]Deut. 32:17 **5:26** [h]1 Kin. 11:33 **5:27** [i]2 Kin. 17:6 [j]Amos 4:13 **6:1** [a]Luke 6:24 [b]Zeph. 1:12 [c]Is. 31:1 [d]Ex. 19:5 **6:2** [e]Jer. 2:10 [f]Is. 10:9 [g]2 Kin. 18:34 [h]Nah. 3:8 **6:3** [i]Is. 56:12 [j]Amos 5:18 [k]Amos 5:12 [l]Ps. 94:20 **6:5** [m]Is. 5:12; Amos 5:23 [n]1 Chr. 15:16; 16:42 [o]1 Chr. 23:5 **6:6** [p]Amos 2:8; 4:1 [q]Gen. 37:25 **6:7** [r]Amos 5:27 **6:8** [s]Jer. 51:14 [t]Amos 8:7 **6:10** [u]Amos 5:13 [v]Amos 8:3 **6:11** [w]Is. 55:11 [x]Amos 3:15 **6:12** [y]Hos. 10:4 **6:14** [z]Jer. 5:15 [a]1 Kin. 8:65

crop after the king's mowings. 2And so it
was, when they had finished eating the
grass of the land, that I said:

"O Lord GOD, forgive, I pray!
[a]Oh, that Jacob may stand,
For he *is* small!"
3 *So* [b]the LORD relented concerning
this.
"It shall not be," said the LORD.

Vision of the Fire

4Thus the Lord GOD showed me: Behold, the Lord GOD called for conflict by
fire, and it consumed the great deep and
devoured the territory. 5Then I said:

"O Lord GOD, cease, I pray!
[c]Oh, that Jacob may stand,
For he *is* small!"
6 *So* the LORD relented concerning this.
"This also shall not be," said the Lord
GOD.

Vision of the Plumb Line

7Thus He showed me: Behold, the Lord
stood on a wall *made* with a plumb line,
with a plumb line in His hand. 8And the
LORD said to me, "Amos, what do you see?"
And I said, "A plumb line."
Then the Lord said:

"Behold, [d]I am setting a plumb line
In the midst of My people Israel;
[e]I will not pass by them anymore.
9 [f]The high places of Isaac shall be
desolate,
And the sanctuaries of Israel shall be
laid waste.
[g]I will rise with the sword against the
house of Jeroboam."

Amaziah's Complaint

10Then Amaziah the [h]priest of [i]Bethel
sent to [j]Jeroboam king of Israel, saying,
"Amos has conspired against you in the
midst of the house of Israel. The land is not
able to bear all his words. 11For thus Amos
has said:

'Jeroboam shall die by the sword,
And Israel shall surely be led away
[k]captive
From their own land.'"

12Then Amaziah said to Amos:

"Go, you seer!
Flee to the land of Judah.
There eat bread,
And there prophesy.
13 But [l]never again prophesy at Bethel,
[m]For it *is* the king's sanctuary,
And it *is* the royal residence."

14Then Amos answered, and said to
Amaziah:

"I *was* no prophet,
Nor *was* I [n]a son of a prophet,
But I *was* a [o]sheepbreeder*
And a tender of sycamore fruit.
15 Then the LORD took me as I followed
the flock,
And the LORD said to me,
'Go, [p]prophesy to My people Israel.'
16 Now therefore, hear the word of the
LORD:
You say, 'Do not prophesy against
Israel,
And [q]do not spout against the house
of Isaac.'

* **7:14** Compare 2 Kings 3:4

---

the king took the first harvest of hay as a tax. Thus a swarm of locusts devouring the late crop would leave the people with nothing for themselves, inflicting a crippling economic blow.

7:2–3 *that Jacob may stand.* If God carried out the threatened punishment, Jacob (the nation of Israel) might be destroyed. One function of the prophet was to serve as intercessor for the people before God. Amos prayed that the vision decreed in heaven might be halted before it was accomplished on earth. The basis of Amos's petition lay in the true assessment of Israel's position. They were not large and strong, as they thought; rather they were small and weak. In response to Amos's intercession, and out of His own love for Israel, God stayed His decree.

7:7–9 *a plumb line.* This apparatus is a string with a weight tied to one end, used to establish a vertical line so that a wall can be built straight. ***what do you see.*** Unlike the first two visions of natural disasters, the visions of the plumb line and the basket of summer fruit were not self-explanatory. God asked Amos what he saw, then explained the visions' meaning. Also unlike the first two visions, God did not give Amos opportunity to intercede, nor did He relent. These judgments would be executed. ***the house of Jeroboam.*** This is a metaphor for the nation.

7:10–11 *Amaziah.* Amaziah was the priest in charge of the temple at Bethel, who informed the king about the prophet who was making threats against the king's house. Amaziah was reacting to Amos's third vision which ended with God's promise to bring the sword against the house of Jeroboam. Amaziah regarded Amos's words as a political threat, and reported them not as a prophecy from God, but as Amos's call to revolt.

7:14–17 *Nor was I a son of a prophet.* Amos's answer to Amaziah came in two parts. First, he denied being a prophet by profession. He did not come from a family of prophets, nor had he been trained in prophecy. Amos made it clear that he had neither desired nor sought his prophetic task. ***Your wife shall be a harlot.*** The only way the spouse of an important official like Amaziah would be reduced to prostitution would be if all her family and all her resources were taken away and she were left to fend entirely for herself.

7:2 [a] Is. 51:19 **7:3** [b] Jon. 3:10 **7:5** [c] Amos 7:2, 3 **7:8** [d] 2 Kin. 21:13 [e] Mic. 7:18 **7:9** [f] Gen. 46:1 [g] 2 Kin. 15:8–10 **7:10** [h] 1 Kin. 12:31, 32; 13:33 [i] Amos 4:4 [j] 2 Kin. 14:23 **7:11** [k] Amos 5:27; 6:7 **7:13** [l] Amos 2:12 [m] 1 Kin. 12:29, 32 **7:14** [n] 1 Kin. 20:35 [o] Zech. 13:5 **7:15** [p] Amos 3:8 **7:16** [q] Ezek. 21:2

17"Therefore[r] thus says the LORD:

s'Your wife shall be a harlot in the city;
Your sons and daughters shall fall by
the sword;
Your land shall be divided by *survey* line;
You shall die in a [t]defiled land;
And Israel shall surely be led away
captive
From his own land.'"

Vision of the Summer Fruit

8 Thus the Lord GOD showed me: Behold,
a basket of summer fruit. 2And He said,
"Amos, what do you see?"
So I said, "A basket of summer fruit."
Then the LORD said to me:

a"The end has come upon My people
Israel;
bI will not pass by them anymore.
3 And cthe songs of the temple
Shall be wailing in that day,"
Says the Lord GOD—
"Many dead bodies everywhere,
dThey shall be thrown out in silence."

4 Hear this, you who swallow up* the
needy,
And make the poor of the land fail,

5Saying:

"When will the New Moon be past,
That we may sell grain?
And ethe Sabbath,
That we may trade wheat?
fMaking the ephah small and the
shekel large,
Falsifying the scales by gdeceit,
6 That we may buy the poor for hsilver,
And the needy for a pair of sandals—
Even sell the bad wheat?"

7 The LORD has sworn by ithe pride of
Jacob:
"Surely jI will never forget any of their
works.
8 kShall the land not tremble for this,
And everyone mourn who dwells in it?
All of it shall swell like the River,*
Heave and subside
lLike the River of Egypt.

9 "And it shall come to pass in that day,"
says the Lord GOD,

m"That I will make the sun go down at
noon,
And I will darken the earth in broad
daylight;
10 I will turn your feasts into nmourning,
oAnd all your songs into lamentation;
pI will bring sackcloth on every waist,
And baldness on every head;
I will make it like mourning for an
only *son*,
And its end like a bitter day.

11 "Behold, the days are coming," says the
Lord GOD,
"That I will send a famine on the land,
Not a famine of bread,
Nor a thirst for water,
But qof hearing the words of the LORD.
12 They shall wander from sea to sea,
And from north to east;
They shall run to and fro, seeking the
word of the LORD,
But shall rnot find *it*.
13 "In that day the fair virgins
And strong young men
Shall faint from thirst.
14 Those who sswear by tthe sin* of
Samaria,
Who say,
'As your god lives, O Dan!'
And, 'As the way of uBeersheba lives!'
They shall fall and never rise again."

The Destruction of Israel

9 I saw the Lord standing by the altar, and
He said:

"Strike the doorposts, that the
thresholds may shake,
And abreak them on the heads of them
all.
I will slay the last of them with the
sword.
bHe who flees from them shall not get
away,
And he who escapes from them shall
not be delivered.

---

* **8:4** Or *trample on* (compare 2:7)   * **8:8** That is,
the Nile; some Hebrew manuscripts, Septuagint,
Syriac, Targum, and Vulgate read *River*; Masoretic
Text reads *the light*.   * **8:14** Or *Ashima*, a Syrian
goddess

8:1–3 *a basket of summer fruit.* The fruits that came
at the end of the harvest in late summer included
grapes, pomegranates, and figs. ***The end has come.***
Amos could not have discerned the meaning of this
vision until God's pronouncement. Israel's wickedness was about to result in a harvest of judgment.
8:5 *Making the ephah small.* This was a way of
cheating the customer of value received for price
paid. ***shekel.*** This was a unit of money so making it
"great" was also a way of cheating.
8:12–13 *sea to sea.* This meant from the Dead Sea to
the Mediterranean. ***fair virgins . . . young men.*** This
refers to those who are most vigorous to survive.
8:14 *Dan . . . Beersheba.* This was a phrase that indicated the limits of the Israelite territory. In Amos's

day, Beersheba was in the kingdom of Judah. Israel
could swear oaths by the Lord, claiming they loy-
ally worshiped Him from the extreme north to the
extreme south of His land, but that would not relieve
the famine of God's word.

7:17 r Jer. 28:12; 29:21, 32   s Zech. 14:2   t Hos. 9:3
8:2 a Ezek. 7:2   b Amos 7:8   **8:3** c Amos 5:23   d Amos
6:9, 10   **8:5** e Neh. 13:15   f Mic. 6:10, 11   g Lev. 19:35,
36   **8:6** h Amos 2:6   **8:7** i Amos 6:8   j Hos. 7:2; 8:13
8:8 k Hos. 4:3   l Amos 9:5   **8:9** m Job 5:14   **8:10** n Ezek.
7:18   o Ezek. 27:31   p [Zech. 12:10]   **8:11** q Ezek. 7:26
8:12 r Hos. 5:6   **8:14** s Hos. 4:15   t Deut. 9:21   u Amos 5:5
9:1 a Hab. 3:13   b Amos 2:14

2 "Though[c] they dig into hell,*
From there My hand shall take
them;
[d]Though they climb up to heaven,
From there I will bring them down;
3 And though they [e]hide themselves on
top of Carmel,
From there I will search and take
them;
Though they hide from My sight at the
bottom of the sea,
From there I will command the
serpent, and it shall bite them;
4 Though they go into captivity before
their enemies,
From there [f]I will command the sword,
And it shall slay them.
[g]I will set My eyes on them for harm
and not for good."

5 The Lord GOD of hosts,
He who touches the earth and it
[h]melts,
[i]And all who dwell there mourn;
All of it shall swell like the River,*
And subside like the River of Egypt.
6 He who builds His [j]layers in the sky,
And has founded His strata in the
earth;
Who [k]calls for the waters of the sea,
And pours them out on the face of the
earth—
[l]The LORD is His name.

7 "Are you not like the people of Ethiopia
to Me,
O children of Israel?" says the LORD.
"Did I not bring up Israel from the land
of Egypt,
The [m]Philistines from [n]Caphtor,
And the [o]Syrians from [o]Kir?

8 "Behold, [p]the eyes of the Lord GOD are
on the sinful kingdom,
And I [q]will destroy it from the face of
the earth;
Yet I will not utterly destroy the house
of Jacob,"
Says the LORD.

9 "For surely I will command,
And will sift the house of Israel among
all nations,
As grain is sifted in a sieve;
[r]Yet not the smallest grain shall fall to
the ground.
10 All the sinners of My people shall die
by the sword,
[s]Who say, 'The calamity shall not
overtake nor confront us.'

Israel Will Be Restored

11 "On[t] that day I will raise up
The tabernacle* of David, which has
fallen down,
And repair its damages;
I will raise up its ruins,
And rebuild it as in the days of old;
12 [u]That they may possess the remnant of
[v]Edom,*
And all the Gentiles who are called by
My name,"
Says the LORD who does this thing.

13 "Behold, [w]the days are coming," says
the LORD,
"When the plowman shall overtake the
reaper,
And the treader of grapes him who
sows seed;
[x]The mountains shall drip with sweet
wine,
And all the hills shall flow with it.
14 [y]I will bring back the captives of My
people Israel;
[z]They shall build the waste cities and
inhabit them;
They shall plant vineyards and drink
wine from them;
They shall also make gardens and eat
fruit from them.
15 I will plant them in their land,
[a]And no longer shall they be pulled up
From the land I have given them,"
Says the LORD your God.

---

* 9:2 Or Sheol   * 9:5 That is, the Nile   * 9:11 Literally booth, figure of a deposed dynasty
* 9:12 Septuagint reads mankind.

9:2 hell . . . heaven. In this imagery, Israel's fugitives from God's judgment could escape neither up nor down; God would find them no matter where in the universe they fled.

9:3 top of Carmel. This peak represented the highest point on earth. Whether as high as that, or as low as the bottom of the sea, the earth would provide no escape.

9:8 the sinful kingdom. This is Israel. *I will not utterly destroy.* This was a glimmer of hope in a long passage of judgment and doom. God's judgment would be thorough, but a remnant would survive.

9:9 As grain is sifted in a sieve. Sifting grain was the final operation in cleaning it before gathering it into storage. In winnowing, all the chaff was blown away; only pebbles and small clumps of mud remained with the grain. The sieve was constructed with holes that were sized so debris were retained in the sieve.

9:13 the plowman shall overtake the reaper. For this to happen it would mean such an abundant harvest that it would last all summer and would not be gathered until the plowing had started again. Grapes were harvested from mid-summer to early fall. The grain crop was sown after the plowing in late fall.

9:15 plant them in their land. God does not abandon His promises or His covenant, nor does He leave His people without hope. God's punishment is certain, but His restoration is just as certain. The word of hope for God's people of old is valid also for God's people of today.

9:2 [c]Ps. 139:8 [d]Jer. 51:53   9:3 [e]Jer. 23:24   9:4 [f]Lev. 26:33 [g]Jer. 21:10; 39:16; 44:11   9:5 [h]Mic. 1:4 [i]Amos 8:8   9:6 [j]Ps. 104:3, 13 [k]Amos 5:8 [l]Amos 4:13; 5:27   9:7 [m]Jer. 47:4 [n]Deut. 2:23 [o]Amos 1:5   9:8 [p]Amos 9:4 [q]Jer. 5:10; 30:11   9:9 [r][Is. 65:8–16]   9:10 [s]Amos 6:3   9:11 [t]Acts 15:16–18   9:12 [u]Obad. 19 [v]Num. 24:18   9:13 [w]Lev. 26:5 [x]Joel 3:18   9:14 [y]Jer. 30:3, 18 [z]Is. 61:4   9:15 [a]Ezek. 34:28; 37:25

THE BOOK OF
OBADIAH

▶ **AUTHOR:** Obadiah was an obscure prophet who probably lived in the southern kingdom of Judah. It is assumed, however, that he was not a priest, since his father is not mentioned and nothing is given of his background. There are 13 Obadiahs in the Old Testament. Four of the better prospects for this Obadiah are: (1) the officer in Ahab's palace that hid God's prophets in a cave (1 Kin. 18:3); (2) one of the officials sent out by Jehoshaphat to teach the law in the cities of Judah (2 Chr. 17:7); (3) one of the overseers who took part in repairing the temple under Josiah (2 Chr. 34:12); or (4) a priest in the time of Nehemiah (Neh. 10:5).

▶ **TIME:** c. 840 B.C.   ▶ **KEY VERSE:** Obad. 10

▶ **THEME:** Obadiah is a prophecy against Edom, the nation that descended from Esau. Edom included the area south and east of the Dead Sea. Throughout most of Old Testament history, if Edom is mentioned, it is in the context of some kind of skirmish. This friction started when the king of Edom refused to let the Israelites cross his territory as they journeyed towards the Promised Land in Numbers 20:14–21. When Israel and Judah were taken into exile, Edom stood by and watched. The purpose of Obadiah seems clear. He is out to encourage the Israelites in the context of captivity. God will rescue His people.

The Coming Judgment on Edom

The vision of Obadiah.

Thus says the Lord GOD ᵃconcerning Edom
ᵇ(We have heard a report from the LORD,
And a messenger has been sent among the nations, *saying,*
"Arise, and let us rise up against her for battle"):

2 "Behold, I will make you small among the nations;
You shall be greatly despised.
3 The ᶜpride of your heart has deceived you,
You who dwell in the clefts of the rock,
Whose habitation is high;
ᵈ*You* who say in your heart, 'Who will bring me down to the ground?'
4 ᵉThough you ascend *as* high as the eagle,
And though you ᶠset your nest among the stars,

From there I will bring you down,"
says the LORD.

5 "If ᵍthieves had come to you,
If robbers by night—
Oh, how you will be cut off!—
Would they not have stolen till they had enough?
If grape-gatherers had come to you,
ʰWould they not have left *some* gleanings?
6 "Oh, how Esau shall be searched out!
How his hidden treasures shall be sought after!
7 All the men in your confederacy
Shall force you to the border;
ⁱThe men at peace with you
Shall deceive you *and* prevail against you.
Those who eat your bread shall lay a trap* for you.
ʲNo one is aware of it.

* **1:7** Or *wound,* or *plot*

---

2 *I will make you small.* God would bring about a reversal of Edom's inflated self-importance.
3 *Whose habitation is high.* Some of the mountain peaks of Edom reached over 6,000 feet. Jerusalem is about 2,300 feet above sea level. *Who will bring me down to the ground?* Edom's presumed physical safety led the Edomites to become haughty; this would be their downfall.
4 *ascend as high as the eagle.* Edom's physical

location became a metaphor of the proud and haughty spirit that the nation had displayed at the time of Judah's distress. Trusting in its high places and mountainous strongholds, Edom reckoned that no one could bring it to account for its actions.

1 ᵃ Is. 21:11 ᵇ Jer. 49:14–16   **3** ᶜ Jer. 49:16 ᵈ Rev. 18:7
4 ᵉ Job 20:6 ᶠ Hab. 2:9   **5** ᵍ Jer. 49:9 ʰ Deut. 24:21
7 ⁱ Jer. 38:22 ʲ Is. 19:11

8 "Will[k] I not in that day," says the LORD,
"Even destroy the wise *men* from
Edom,
And understanding from the
mountains of Esau?
9 Then your [l]mighty men, O [m]Teman,
shall be dismayed,
To the end that everyone from the
mountains of Esau
May be cut off by slaughter.

Edom Mistreated His Brother

10 "For [n]violence against your brother
Jacob,
Shame shall cover you,
And [o]you shall be cut off forever.
11 In the day that you [p]stood on the other
side—
In the day that strangers carried
captive his forces,
When foreigners entered his gates
And [q]cast lots for Jerusalem—
Even you *were* as one of them.

12 "But you should not have [r]gazed on the
day of your brother
In the day of his captivity;*
Nor should you have [s]rejoiced over the
children of Judah
In the day of their destruction;
Nor should you have spoken proudly
In the day of distress.
13 You should not have entered the gate
of My people
In the day of their calamity.
Indeed, you should not have gazed on
their affliction
In the day of their calamity,
Nor laid *hands* on their substance
In the day of their calamity.
14 You should not have stood at the
crossroads
To cut off those among them who
escaped;
Nor should you have delivered up
those among them who remained
In the day of distress.

15 "For[t] the day of the LORD upon all the
nations *is* near;
[u]As you have done, it shall be done to
you;
Your reprisal shall return upon your
own head.
16 [v]For as you drank on My holy
mountain,
So shall all the nations drink
continually;
Yes, they shall drink, and swallow,
And they shall be as though they had
never been.

Israel's Final Triumph

17 "But on Mount Zion there [w]shall be
deliverance,
And there shall be holiness;
The house of Jacob shall possess their
possessions.
18 The house of Jacob shall be a fire,
And the house of Joseph [x]a flame;
But the house of Esau *shall be* stubble;
They shall kindle them and devour
them,
And no survivor shall *remain* of the
house of Esau,"
For the LORD has spoken.

19 The South* [y]shall possess the
mountains of Esau,
[z]And the Lowland shall possess
Philistia.
They shall possess the fields of
Ephraim
And the fields of Samaria.
Benjamin *shall possess* Gilead.
20 And the captives of this host of the
children of Israel
Shall possess the land of the
Canaanites
As [a]far as Zarephath.
The captives of Jerusalem who are in
Sepharad

---

* **1:12** Literally *on the day he became a foreigner*
* **1:19** Hebrew *Negev*

---

8 destroy the wise men from Edom. The nation had
a reputation for having many wise men among its
citizens (Jer. 49:7).
9 O Teman. This name comes from a son of Eliphaz,
who was the firstborn son of Esau (Gen. 36:9–11).
11 In the day. This refers to the time of Judah's distress. **strangers ... foreigners.** These words are used
to describe Judah's principal enemies, contrasted
with the words of verse 10, "your brother." It was one
thing for the Babylonians to attack Judah; for a nation
like Edom to join the Babylonians against their own
brothers was unthinkable.
13 the day of their calamity. This phrase is repeated
three times in this verse. It refers to the day of God's
judgment upon Judah, carried out by the hand of
Nebuchadnezzar.
15 the day of the LORD. This is a technical term used
by the prophets to indicate the day of God's judgment (Amos 5:18–20). Here the term likely refers
to the time when God would judge all the nations,

including Edom, that had participated in Judah's
destruction.
18 house of Jacob ... house of Joseph. Together
these signify a unified Israel. God intends to rejoin the
kingdoms of Israel and Judah as one people again.
20 Zarephath. This was a Phoenician city 14 miles
north of Tyre (1 Kin. 17:8–24). **Sepharad.** This was
a city to which some Judeans were exiled. The restoration of Judah from exile, which these verses
predict, was a sign to Judah and all nations that the
God of Israel was not just a local god. He had not
been defeated by the Babylonian god Marduk. The
fact that He could allow His people to be carried into
captivity in a foreign land and then bring them back

---

8 [k] [Job 5:12–14]　**9** [l] Ps. 76:5　[m] Jer. 49:7　**10** [n] Gen.
27:41　[o] Ezek. 35:9　**11** [p] Ps. 83:5–8　[q] Nah. 3:10　**12** [r] Mic.
4:11; 7:10　[s] [Prov. 17:5]　**15** [t] Ezek. 30:3　[u] Hab. 2:8
16 [v] Joel 3:17　**17** [w] Amos 9:8　**18** [x] Zech. 12:6　**19** [y] Is.
11:14　[z] Zeph. 2:7　**20** [a] 1 Kin. 17:9

*b*Shall possess the cities of the
South.*
21 Then *c*saviors* shall come to Mount
Zion

To judge the mountains of Esau,
And the *d*kingdom shall be the LORD's.

---

* **1:20** Hebrew *Negev*   * **1:21** Or *deliverers*

---

to their own land was proof of His power and sovereignty over all the earth.

21 saviors. The Judeans who had been taken into captivity would come back as deliverers, and they would reign over the people of Edom. **the kingdom shall be the LORD's.** These were Obadiah's last words against all human arrogance, pride, and rebellion. Edom had thought itself indestructible; but the Lord humbled that nation and restored the fallen Judah.

Many people are tempted to consider themselves beyond the reach of God. But God will bring them low, just as He will lift those who humble themselves before Him. And one great day, He will establish His just rule over all.

---

20 *b* Jer. 32:44   **21** *c* [James 5:20]   *d* [Rev. 11:15]

THE BOOK OF
JONAH

▶ **AUTHOR:** Jonah was "the son of Amittai" and nothing more would be known about him were it not for a reference in 2 Kings 14:25 calling him a prophet in the reign of Jeroboam II of Israel. Jonah was a Galilean, contrary to the Pharisees' claim that "no prophet has arisen out of Galilee" (John 7:52). One Jewish tradition says that Jonah was the son of the widow of Zarephath whom Elijah raised from the dead (1 Kin. 17:8–24).

▶ **TIME:** c. 760 B.C.   ▶ **KEY VERSES:** Jon. 2:8–9

▶ **THEME:** The Book of Jonah directs us towards God's greatness and mercy. He will go to any lengths in order to assure that His message is heard. He makes it possible for people to repent and be redeemed no matter how decadent and far away from God they are. Jonah himself is a prime example of the power of storytelling, as he gives us an amazingly visual and memorable image of God's far-reaching grace and His involvement in individual lives to accomplish His purposes.

Jonah's Disobedience

1 Now the word of the LORD came to ᵃJonah the son of Amittai, saying, ²"Arise, go to ᵇNineveh, that ᶜgreat city, and cry out against it; for ᵈtheir wickedness has come up before Me." ³But Jonah arose to flee to Tarshish from the presence of the LORD. He went down to ᵉJoppa, and found a ship going to Tarshish; so he paid the fare, and went down into it, to go with them to ᶠTarshish ᵍfrom the presence of the LORD.

The Storm at Sea

⁴But ʰthe LORD sent out a great wind on the sea, and there was a mighty tempest on the sea, so that the ship was about to be broken up. ⁵Then the mariners were afraid; and every man cried out to his god, and threw the cargo that *was* in the ship into the sea, to lighten the load.* But Jonah had gone down ⁱinto the lowest parts of the ship, had lain down, and was fast asleep.

⁶So the captain came to him, and said to him, "What do you mean, sleeper? Arise, ʲcall on your God; ᵏperhaps your God will consider us, so that we may not perish."

⁷And they said to one another, "Come, let us ˡcast lots, that we may know for whose cause this trouble *has come* upon us." So they cast lots, and the lot fell on Jonah. ⁸Then they said to him, ᵐ"Please tell us! For whose cause *is* this trouble upon us? What is your occupation? And where do you come from? What is your country? And of what people are you?"

⁹So he said to them, "I *am* a Hebrew; and I fear the LORD, the God of heaven, ⁿwho made the sea and the dry *land*."

Jonah Thrown into the Sea

¹⁰Then the men were exceedingly afraid, and said to him, "Why have you done this?" For the men knew that he fled

---

* 1:5 Literally *from upon them*

1:1 *the word of the LORD.* This phrase affirms the divine source of the message to Jonah (Jer. 1:4; Hos. 1:1; Joel 1:1; Mic. 1:1). The name "Jonah" means "dove."
1:2 *Nineveh.* Nineveh is located on the Tigris River, the capital of ancient Assyria (2 Kin. 19:36) for about a century. It was over 500 miles from Jonah's home near Nazareth.
1:3 *a ship going to Tarshish.* The location of this port city is uncertain, but it could be Tartessus on the southeast coast of Spain. The city represents the most distant place known to the Israelites. Joppa was about 50 miles southwest of Jonah's hometown in the opposite direction from Nineveh.
1:4–5 *the LORD sent out a great wind.* Throughout the Book of Jonah, the Lord shows Himself sovereign over every aspect of creation. In this case, the storm

at sea was so ferocious that even the experienced mariners were afraid.
1:9 *I am a Hebrew.* With these words, Jonah identified himself with the people of the Lord's covenant (Gen. 14:13). *I fear the LORD.* Fear here indicates an ongoing activity of awe before the Lord, of piety in His presence, of obedience to His word, and of saving faith (Gen. 22:12; Ex. 20:20; Prov. 1:7). Yet Jonah's actions contradicted his words.
1:10 *exceedingly afraid.* This is the same term for

1:1 ᵃ 2 Kin. 14:25   **1:2** ᵇ Is. 37:37 ᶜ Gen. 10:11, 12 ᵈ Gen. 18:20   **1:3** ᵉ Josh. 19:46 ᶠ Is. 23:1 ᵍ Gen. 4:16   **1:4** ʰ Ps. 107:25   **1:5** ⁱ 1 Sam. 24:3   **1:6** ʲ Ps. 107:28 ᵏ Joel 2:14   **1:7** ˡ Josh. 7:14   **1:8** ᵐ Josh. 7:19   **1:9** ⁿ [Neh. 9:6]

from the presence of the LORD, because
he had told them. 11Then they said to him,
"What shall we do to you that the sea may
be calm for us?"—for the sea was growing
more tempestuous.

12And he said to them, [o]"Pick me up and
throw me into the sea; then the sea will
become calm for you. For I know that this
great tempest *is* because of me."

13Nevertheless the men rowed hard to
return to land, [p]but they could not, for the
sea continued to grow more tempestuous
against them. 14Therefore they cried out
to the LORD and said, "We pray, O LORD,
please do not let us perish for this man's
life, and [q]do not charge us with innocent
blood; for You, O LORD, [r]have done as it
pleased You." 15So they picked up Jonah
and threw him into the sea, [s]and the sea
ceased from its raging. 16Then the men
[t]feared the LORD exceedingly, and offered
a sacrifice to the LORD and took vows.

Jonah's Prayer and Deliverance

17Now the LORD had prepared a great
fish to swallow Jonah. And [u]Jonah was in
the belly of the fish three days and three
nights.

2 Then Jonah prayed to the LORD his God
from the fish's belly. 2And he said:

"I [a]cried out to the LORD because of my
affliction,
[b]And He answered me.

"Out of the belly of Sheol I cried,
And You heard my voice.
3 [c]For You cast me into the deep,
Into the heart of the seas,
And the floods surrounded me;
[d]All Your billows and Your waves
passed over me.
4 [e]Then I said, 'I have been cast out of
Your sight;
Yet I will look again [f]toward Your holy
temple.'
5 The [g]waters surrounded me, *even* to
my soul;
The deep closed around me;
Weeds were wrapped around my head.
6 I went down to the moorings of the
mountains;
The earth with its bars *closed* behind
me forever;
Yet You have brought up my [h]life from
the pit,
O LORD, my God.

7 "When my soul fainted within me,
I remembered the LORD;
[i]And my prayer went *up* to You,
Into Your holy temple.

8 "Those who regard [j]worthless idols
Forsake their own Mercy.
9 But I will [k]sacrifice to You
With the voice of thanksgiving;
I will pay what I have [l]vowed.
[m]Salvation *is* of the [n]LORD."

10So the LORD spoke to the fish, and it
vomited Jonah onto dry *land*.

Jonah Preaches at Nineveh

3 Now the word of the LORD came to Jonah the second time, saying, 2"Arise, go
to Nineveh, that great city, and preach to
it the message that I tell you." 3So Jonah
arose and went to Nineveh, according to
the word of the LORD. Now Nineveh was

"fear" that Jonah used in his statement of piety (v. 9). But here the word means to be in terror; it refers to overwhelming dread (v. 16). God, the Creator of the universe, was after Jonah. And because God was after Jonah, He was after the sailors as well. They had every right to be afraid (Gen. 12:18; Judg. 15:11).

1:14 ***they cried out to the LORD.*** Ironically, the pagan sailors prayed to the Lord on behalf of the Lord's rebellious prophet. Jonah needed God's grace as much as Nineveh did. ***as it pleased You.*** The narrator skillfully uses the sailors' words to express one of the book's themes: the Lord is free to act as He wills.

1:17 ***the LORD had prepared a great fish.*** God sent the fish—not a whale, as is commonly thought—to rescue Jonah from drowning, not to punish him (ch. 2). Three days and three nights may refer to one full day and portions of two more (Gen. 30:36; Ex. 3:18; 1 Sam. 30:12). Jesus Christ said that His death and resurrection were foreshadowed by Jonah's experience (Matt. 12:39–40; 16:4; Luke 11:29).

2:2 ***I cried . . . I cried.*** These terms come from two different verbs. The first is a more general term meaning "to call aloud," with a wide range of usage in the Bible. The second is a term that means a "cry for help," particularly as a scream to God (Ps. 5:2; 18:6; 22:24; 88:13; 119:146).

2:4 ***I will look again toward Your holy temple.*** The man who had run from God's presence was alone, yet he clung to the hope that God would not abandon him. The temple, the sanctuary in Jerusalem (Deut. 12:5–7; Ps. 48; 79:1; Heb. 9:24), was the symbol of God's presence.

2:6 ***the moorings of the mountains.*** Jonah pictures himself so deep in the sea that it is as if he had found the deepest place possible. ***pit.*** This term, along with hell (v. 2), is used to describe the realm of the dead (Job 33:24; Ps. 30:9; 49:9).

2:9 ***I will sacrifice to You . . . voice of thanksgiving.*** This vow is common in the Psalms (Ps. 13:6; 142:7). ***I will pay what I have vowed.*** Jonah declares that he will keep his promise, a pledge both to sacrifice and to acknowledge God's help (Job 22:27; Ps. 50:14; 66:13; Rom. 6:13; 1 Pet. 2:5).

2:10 ***the LORD spoke to the fish.*** The focus in the story of Jonah is on the Lord's sovereign control over creation to bring about His purpose.

3:1–2 ***the word of the LORD came to Jonah the second time.*** Jonah's new commission was essentially the same as the one he had received in 1:1.

1:12 [o] John 11:50 **1:13** [p] [Prov. 21:30] **1:14** [q] Deut. 21:8 [r] Ps. 115:3 **1:15** [s] [Ps. 89:9; 107:29] **1:16** [t] Acts 5:11 **1:17** [u] [Matt. 12:40] **2:2** [a] Ps. 120:1 [b] Ps. 65:2 **2:3** [c] Ps. 88:6 [d] Ps. 42:7 **2:4** [e] Ps. 31:22 [f] 1 Kin. 8:38 **2:5** [g] Lam. 3:54 **2:6** [h] [Ps. 16:10] **2:7** [i] Ps. 18:6 **2:8** [j] Jer. 10:8 **2:9** [k] Hos. 14:2 [l] [Eccl. 5:4, 5] [m] Ps. 3:8 [n] [Jer. 3:23]

an exceedingly great city, a three-day journey* in extent. 4And Jonah began to enter the city on the first day's walk. Then ᵃhe cried out and said, "Yet forty days, and Nineveh shall be overthrown!"

The People of Nineveh Believe

5So the ᵇpeople of Nineveh believed God, proclaimed a fast, and put on sackcloth, from the greatest to the least of them. 6Then word came to the king of Nineveh; and he arose from his throne and laid aside his robe, covered himself with sackcloth ᶜand sat in ashes. 7ᵈAnd he caused it to be proclaimed and published throughout Nineveh by the decree of the king and his nobles, saying,

Let neither man nor beast, herd nor flock, taste anything; do not let them eat, or drink water. 8But let man and beast be covered with sackcloth, and cry mightily to God; yes, ᵉlet every one turn from his evil way and from ᶠthe violence that is in his hands. 9ᵍWho can tell if God will turn and relent, and turn away from His fierce anger, so that we may not perish?

10ʰThen God saw their works, that they turned from their evil way; and God relented from the disaster that He had said He would bring upon them, and He did not do it.

Jonah's Anger and God's Kindness

4 But it displeased Jonah exceedingly, and he became angry. 2So he prayed to the LORD, and said, "Ah, LORD, was not this what I said when I was still in my country? Therefore I ᵃfled previously to Tarshish; for

I know that You are a ᵇgracious and merciful God, slow to anger and abundant in lovingkindness, One who relents from doing harm. 3ᶜTherefore now, O LORD, please take my life from me, for ᵈit is better for me to die than to live!"

4Then the LORD said, "Is it right for you to be angry?"

5So Jonah went out of the city and sat on the east side of the city. There he made himself a shelter and sat under it in the shade, till he might see what would become of the city. 6And the LORD God prepared a plant* and made it come up over Jonah, that it might be shade for his head to deliver him from his misery. So Jonah was very grateful for the plant. 7But as morning dawned the next day God prepared a worm, and it so damaged the plant that it withered. 8And it happened, when the sun arose, that God prepared a vehement east wind; and the sun beat on Jonah's head, so that he grew faint. Then he wished death for himself, and said, ᵉ"It is better for me to die than to live."

9Then God said to Jonah, "Is it right for you to be angry about the plant?"

And he said, "It is right for me to be angry, even to death!"

10But the LORD said, "You have had pity on the plant for which you have not labored, nor made it grow, which came up in a night and perished in a night. 11And should I not pity Nineveh, ᶠthat great city, in which are more than one hundred and twenty thousand persons ᵍwho cannot discern between their right hand and their left—and much livestock?"

* 3:3 Exact meaning unknown   * 4:6 Hebrew kikayon, exact identity unknown

---

3:5 the people of Nineveh believed God. The term used for God here is the general term for deity. In contrast, the sailors in chapter 1 proclaimed faith in the Lord, using the personal, covenant name for God (1:16). The fact that the writer does not use the personal name for God here may suggest that the Ninevites had a short-lived or imperfect understanding of God's message. History bears this out. We have no historical record of a lasting period of belief in Nineveh. Eventually the city was destroyed in 612 B.C.
3:10 God relented. The Ninevites' repentance moved the Lord to extend grace and mercy to them.
4:1 displeased. Jonah's irritation belied the good news that the city would be spared God's judgment, but he was unable to appreciate the parallel. **Jonah . . . became angry.** In contrast to God, Jonah had no compassion on the people of Nineveh.
4:5 till he might see what would become of the city. In his continuing stubbornness and lack of compassion, Jonah held out hope that God would judge Nineveh. This was God's chief complaint against him (Ps. 58).

4:7 God prepared a worm. The Book of Jonah depicts the Lord as both sovereign and free to act in creation. God placed the worm in the plant to serve as His agent in Jonah's life.
4:9 right for me to be angry. Jonah's anger (v. 1) did not arise from a desire for justice, but from his own selfishness. He continued to justify his rebellious attitude. And again, God was merciful.
4:11 pity. The same word used to describe Jonah's feeling toward the plant in verse 10 is used for God's feeling toward the people of Nineveh. People are of more value than animals and animals of more value than plants, but the Lord has a concern that extends to all of His creation. The Lord's compassion comes from His character (v. 2; Joel 2:13–14).

3:4 ᵃ [Deut. 18:22]   3:5 ᵇ [Matt. 12:41]   3:6 ᶜ Job 2:8   3:7 ᵈ 2 Chr. 20:3   3:8 ᵉ Is. 58:6   ᶠ Is. 59:6   3:9 ᵍ Joel 2:14   3:10 ʰ Jer. 18:8   4:2 ᵃ Jon. 1:3   ᵇ Joel 2:13   4:3 ᶜ 1 Kin. 19:4   ᵈ Jon. 4:8   4:8 ᵉ Jon. 4:3   4:11 ᶠ Jon. 1:2; 3:2, 3   ᵍ Deut. 1:39

THE BOOK OF
MICAH

▶ **AUTHOR:** Micah was from Moresheth Gath (1:14) which was located about 25 miles southwest of Jerusalem, near Gath. Although Micah was not as politically aware as Isaiah or Daniel, he showed a profound concern for the suffering of the people and had a clear sense of his prophetic calling. A contemporary of Isaiah and Hosea, Micah may have been a farmer-turned-prophet like Amos.

▶ **TIME:** c. 735–710 B.C.   ▶ **KEY VERSE:** Mic. 6:8

▶ **THEME:** Micah was from a town in southwestern Judah. His message was directed at both capital cities, Samaria and Jerusalem. He was probably around when the Assyrians destroyed Samaria in 722 B.C., and may have even lived through the siege of Jerusalem by Assyria. Micah's message comes out of unique visions from God. In effect he saw things that others couldn't, such as the prophecy of Bethlehem as the birthplace of Christ.

1 The word of the LORD that came to ᵃMicah of Moresheth in the days of ᵇJotham, Ahaz, *and* Hezekiah, kings of Judah, which he saw concerning Samaria and Jerusalem.

The Coming Judgment on Israel
2 Hear, all you peoples!
   Listen, O earth, and all that is in it!
   Let the Lord GOD be a witness against
      you,
   The Lord from ᶜHis holy temple.
3 For behold, the LORD is coming out of
      His place;
   He will come down
   And tread on the high places of the
      earth.
4 ᵈThe mountains will melt under Him,
   And the valleys will split
   Like wax before the fire,
   Like waters poured down a steep
      place.
5 All this is for the transgression of
      Jacob

And for the sins of the house of
      Israel.
   What *is* the transgression of
      Jacob?
   Is it not Samaria?
   And what *are* the ᵉhigh places of
      Judah?
   Are they not Jerusalem?

6 "Therefore I will make Samaria ᶠa heap
      of ruins in the field,
   Places for planting a vineyard;
   I will pour down her stones into the
      valley,
   And I will ᵍuncover her
      foundations.
7 All her carved images shall be beaten
      to pieces,
   And all her ʰpay as a harlot shall be
      burned with the fire;
   All her idols I will lay desolate,
   For she gathered *it* from the pay of a
      harlot,
   And they shall return to the ⁱpay of a
      harlot."

1:1 Micah. The name means "who is like the Lord?" The question presents a major biblical theme, the idea that God is incomparable (7:18; Deut. 4:32–40; Ps. 113:4–6). Micah's ministry centered on the Assyrian threat to Samaria, the capital of Israel, that was destroyed in 722 B.C. and Jerusalem, the capital of Judah.
1:3 the LORD is coming. This is the language of epiphany, the dramatic coming of God to earth, here in a solemn procession of judgment. In other texts the language of epiphany is used to describe God's dramatic acts of deliverance (Ps. 18:7–19).
1:5 Jacob. The name is used to refer to the northern kingdom of Israel, whose transgression was centered

in its capital Samaria. **high places.** Jerusalem, which was once "beautiful in elevation" (Ps. 48:2), was nothing more than another platform of pagan worship, like the "high places" of the Canaanites.
1:7 she gathered it from the pay of a harlot. Idolatry is often described in the Hebrew Bible as spiritual adultery (Jer. 3:1; Hos. 4:15). Israel is pictured here as a wife who is unfaithful to her husband. This is not just a metaphor, however; the worship system of Canaan was sexual in nature.

1:1 ᵃ Jer. 26:18 ᵇ Is. 1:1   **1:2** ᶜ [Ps. 11:4]   **1:4** ᵈ Amos 9:5
1:5 ᵉ Deut. 32:13; 33:29   **1:6** ᶠ 2 Kin. 19:25 ᵍ Ezek. 13:14
1:7 ʰ Hos. 2:5 ⁱ Deut. 23:18

Mourning for Israel and Judah

8 Therefore I will wail and howl,
I will go stripped and naked;
[j]I will make a wailing like the jackals
And a mourning like the ostriches,
9 For her wounds *are* incurable.
For [k]it has come to Judah;
It has come to the gate of My people—
To Jerusalem.

10 [l]Tell *it* not in Gath,
Weep not at all;
In Beth Aphrah*
Roll yourself in the dust.
11 Pass by in naked shame, you inhabitant of Shaphir;
The inhabitant of Zaanan* does not go out.
Beth Ezel mourns;
Its place to stand is taken away from you.

12 For the inhabitant of Maroth pined* for good,
But [m]disaster came down from the LORD
To the gate of Jerusalem.
13 O inhabitant of [n]Lachish,
Harness the chariot to the swift steeds
(She *was* the beginning of sin to the daughter of Zion),
For the transgressions of Israel were [o]found in you.

14 Therefore you shall [p]give presents to Moresheth Gath;*
The houses of [q]Achzib* *shall be* a lie to the kings of Israel.
15 I will yet bring an heir to you,
O inhabitant of [r]Mareshah;*
The glory of Israel shall come to [s]Adullam.
16 Make yourself [t]bald and cut off your hair,
Because of your [u]precious children;
Enlarge your baldness like an eagle,
For they shall go from you into [v]captivity.

Woe to Evildoers

2 Woe to those who devise iniquity,
And work out evil on their beds!
At [a]morning light they practice it,
Because it is in the power of their hand.
2 They [b]covet fields and take *them* by violence,
Also houses, and seize *them*.
So they oppress a man and his house,
A man and his inheritance.

3 Therefore thus says the LORD:

"Behold, against this [c]family I am devising [d]disaster,
From which you cannot remove your necks;
Nor shall you walk haughtily,
For this *is* an evil time.
4 In that day *one* shall take up a proverb against you,
And [e]lament with a bitter lamentation, saying:
'We are utterly destroyed!
He has changed the heritage of my people;
How He has removed *it* from me!
To a turncoat He has divided our fields.'"

5 Therefore you will have no one to determine boundaries* by lot
In the assembly of the LORD.

* **1:10** Literally *House of Dust* * **1:11** Literally *Going Out* * **1:12** Literally *was sick* * **1:14** Literally *Possession of Gath* • Literally *Lie* * **1:15** Literally *Inheritance* * **2:5** Literally *one casting a surveyor's line*

1:8 *stripped and naked.* Micah's words describe mourning rites in which outer garments were laid aside in deep humility. The mourning person thought no longer about himself but only about the calamity that had overcome his senses.
1:10 *in Gath.* The reference here is to the lament of David in his mourning over the death of Saul and Jonathan (2 Sam. 1:20). Just as it was unseemly then to have the bad news of God's people profaned in a foreign city, so it would be in the present circumstance.
1:12 *Maroth.* This name means "bitterness." The name Jerusalem suggests "peace." Thus, the inhabitants of the "town of bitterness" would be sickened with dread, and the inhabitants of the "town of peace" would experience God's judgments.
1:16 *cut off your hair.* This would have been the ultimate sign of mourning in a culture in which a man's hair was highly valued.
2:1–2 *devise iniquity . . . covet.* The ethical teaching of the prophets regularly included oracles of judgment against greed, theft, and oppression, actions of the powerful in attacking the weak. To covet is not just to have a passing thought; it is a determination to seize what is not one's own.
2:4 *To a turncoat He has divided our fields.* God would take the property rights from those who had seized them illegally and give them to people who were even more reprobate than they were.
2:5–6 *no one to determine boundaries.* Land-grabbers would no longer have a legitimate claim among God's people. God would dispossess them even as they had dispossessed others. ***Do not prattle.*** These words may have been a strong warning to Micah not to be like the lying prophets who counseled that all was well in the land.

1:8 [j] Ps. 102:6 **1:9** [k] 2 Kin. 18:13 **1:10** [l] 2 Sam. 1:20 **1:12** [m] Is. 59:9–11 **1:13** [n] Is. 36:2 [o] Ezek. 23:11 **1:14** [p] 2 Sam. 8:2 [q] Josh. 15:44 **1:15** [r] Josh. 15:44 [s] 2 Chr. 11:7 **1:16** [t] Job 1:20 [u] Lam. 4:5 [v] Amos 7:11, 17 **2:1** [a] Hos. 7:6, 7 **2:2** [b] Is. 5:8 **2:3** [c] Jer. 8:3 [d] Amos 5:13 **2:4** [e] 2 Sam. 1:17

Lying Prophets

6 "Do not prattle," *you say to those* who prophesy.
So they shall not prophesy to you;*
They shall not return insult for insult.*
7 *You who are* named the house of Jacob:
"Is the Spirit of the LORD restricted?
Are these His doings?
Do not My words do good
To him who walks uprightly?

8 "Lately My people have risen up as an enemy—
You pull off the robe with the garment
From those who trust *you,* as they pass by,
Like men returned from war.
9 The women of My people you cast out
From their pleasant houses;
From their children
You have taken away My glory forever.

10 "Arise and depart,
For this *is* not *your* ʃrest;
Because it is ᵍdefiled, it shall destroy,
Yes, with utter destruction.
11 If a man should walk in a false spirit
And speak a lie, *saying,*
'I will prophesy to you of wine and drink,'
Even he would be the ʰprattler of this people.

Israel Restored

12 "Iⁱ will surely assemble all of you,
O Jacob,
I will surely gather the remnant of Israel;
I will put them together ʲlike sheep of the fold,*
Like a flock in the midst of their pasture;
ᵏThey shall make a loud noise because of *so many* people.
13 The one who breaks open will come up before them;
They will break out,
Pass through the gate,
And go out by it;
ˡTheir king will pass before them,
ᵐWith the LORD at their head."

Wicked Rulers and Prophets

3 And I said:

"Hear now, O heads of Jacob,
And you ᵃrulers of the house of Israel:
ᵇIs it not for you to know justice?
2 You who hate good and love evil;
Who strip the skin from My people,*
And the flesh from their bones;
3 Who also ᶜeat the flesh of My people,
Flay their skin from them,
Break their bones,
And chop *them* in pieces
Like *meat* for the pot,
ᵈLike flesh in the caldron."

4 Then ᵉthey will cry to the LORD,
But He will not hear them;
He will even hide His face from them at that time,
Because they have been evil in their deeds.

5 Thus says the LORD ʃconcerning the prophets
Who make my people stray;
Who chant "Peace"
While they ᵍchew with their teeth,
But who prepare war against him
ʰWho puts nothing into their mouths:
6 "Therefore ⁱ you shall have night without vision,
And you shall have darkness without divination;
The sun shall go down on the prophets,
And the day shall be dark for ʲthem.
7 So the seers shall be ashamed,
And the diviners abashed;
Indeed they shall all cover their lips;
ᵏFor *there is* no answer from God."

8 But truly I am full of power by the Spirit of the LORD,
And of justice and might,
ˡTo declare to Jacob his transgression
And to Israel his sin.

---

* 2:6 Literally *to these* • Vulgate reads *He shall not take shame.* * 2:12 Hebrew *Bozrah*
* 3:2 Literally *them*

2:12–13 *assemble . . . gather . . . put them together.* The verbs are emphatic, demonstrating the certainty of God's determination to bring to pass His good pleasure on His people (Deut. 30:1–6). **They will break out.** This phrase speaks of regathering Israel from wherever the people may have been scattered.
3:1 *Is it not for you to know justice?* The idea here is that one might not expect justice from pagan leaders in a faraway place. But the rulers of the people of God were expected to emphasize justice. Justice is one of the key concepts of the law (Deut. 10:18; 32:4; 33:21). Perverting justice was strongly prohibited by God (Deut. 16:19; 24:17), yet this was precisely what the leaders of Judah were doing. They had used their authority to destroy justice rather than to establish it among the people.

3:5–7 *concerning the prophets.* This oracle was against false prophets who proclaimed peace, causing the people to be unprepared for trouble. These prophets would have neither true prophetic insight, nor help from the forbidden arts of divination. Finally, they would have nothing to say, for there would be no answer from God.

2:10 ʃDeut. 12:9 ᵍLev. 18:25   2:11 ʰIs. 30:10   2:12 ⁱ[Mic. 4:6, 7] ʲJer. 31:10 ᵏEzek. 33:22; 36:37   2:13 ˡ[Hos. 3:5] ᵐIs. 52:12   3:1 ᵃEzek. 22:27 ᵇJer. 5:4, 5   3:3 ᶜPs. 14:4; 27:2 ᵈEzek. 11:3, 6, 7   3:4 ᵉJer. 11:11   3:5 ʃEzek. 13:10, 19 ᵍMatt. 7:15 ʰEzek. 13:18   3:6 ⁱIs. 8:20–22; 29:10–12 ʲIs. 29:10   3:7 ᵏAmos 8:11   3:8 ˡIs. 58:1

9 Now hear this,
   You heads of the house of Jacob
   And rulers of the house of Israel,
   Who abhor justice
   And pervert all equity,
10 *m*Who build up Zion with *n*bloodshed
   And Jerusalem with iniquity:
11 *o*Her heads judge for a bribe,
   *p*Her priests teach for pay,
   And her prophets divine for money.
   *q*Yet they lean on the LORD, and say,
   "Is not the LORD among us?
   No harm can come upon us."
12 Therefore because of you
   Zion shall be *r*plowed *like* a field,
   *s*Jerusalem shall become heaps of
      ruins,
   And *t*the mountain of the temple*
   Like the bare hills of the forest.

The LORD's Reign in Zion

4 Now *a*it shall come to pass in the latter
   days
   That the mountain of the LORD's
      house
   Shall be established on the top of the
      mountains,
   And shall be exalted above the hills;
   And peoples shall flow to it.
2 Many nations shall come and say,
   "Come, and let us go up to the mountain
      of the LORD,
   To the house of the God of Jacob;
   He will teach us His ways,
   And we shall walk in His paths."
   For out of Zion the law shall go forth,
   And the word of the LORD from
      Jerusalem.
3 He shall judge between many peoples,
   And rebuke strong nations afar off;
   They shall beat their swords into
      *b*plowshares,
   And their spears into pruning hooks;
   Nation shall not lift up sword against
      nation,
   *c*Neither shall they learn war
      anymore.*

4 *d*But everyone shall sit under his vine
   and under his fig tree,
   And no one shall make *them* afraid;
   For the mouth of the LORD of hosts has
      spoken.
5 For all people walk each in the name
      of his god,
   But *e*we will walk in the name of the
   LORD our God
   Forever and ever.

Zion's Future Triumph

6 "In that day," says the LORD,
   f"I will assemble the lame,
   *g*I will gather the outcast
   And those whom I have afflicted;
7 I will make the lame *h*a remnant,
   And the outcast a strong nation;
   So the LORD *i*will reign over them in
      Mount Zion
   From now on, even forever.
8 And you, O tower of the flock,
   The stronghold of the daughter of
      Zion,
   To you shall it come,
   Even the former dominion shall
      come,
   The kingdom of the daughter of
      Jerusalem."

9 Now why do you cry aloud?
   *i*Is there no king in your midst?
   Has your counselor perished?
   For *k*pangs have seized you like a
      woman in labor.
10 Be in pain, and labor to bring forth,
   O daughter of Zion,
   Like a woman in birth pangs.
   For now you shall go forth from the
      city,
   You shall dwell in the field,
   And to *l*Babylon you shall go.
   There you shall be delivered;
   There the *m*LORD will *n*redeem you
   From the hand of your enemies.

---

* **3:12** Literally *house*   * **4:3** Compare Isaiah 2:2–4

3:11 *bribe . . . pay . . . money.* The wicked leaders and prophets of Israel worked only when they could gain something from it. Needless to say, if justice had to be paid for, it would not be justice. *Is not the LORD among us?* Many people of Jerusalem believed that they would not be affected by God's judgment because God Himself dwelled in the holy temple in Jerusalem. They reasoned that, despite their evils, as long as God was in His temple they were safe—even from divine judgment. What people refused to believe was that God might leave His temple because of the sinfulness of the people (Ezek. 10).
4:1 *in the latter days.* This is an indication of a prophecy of end times.
4:2 *we shall walk in His paths.* Unlike the people of Micah's generation who were strangers to justice (3:1), the peoples of the coming kingdom will be obedient to God.
4:3 *swords . . . spears.* All weapons of destruction will be recycled into tools of production. There will

finally be an end to conflict. War will not even be a subject for study any more.
4:4 *vine . . . fig tree.* Both are symbols of peace and prosperity (Zech. 3:10).
4:7 *remnant.* The majority of people in Israel did not live their lives in faith and dedication to the Lord. However, true faith never really died out in Israel, even in the worst of times.
4:9–10 *like a woman in labor.* The troubles of the present moment would lead finally to the birth of a deliverer. *to Babylon you shall go.* This refers to the exile.

3:10 *m* Jer. 22:13, 17 *n* Hab. 2:12   **3:11** *o* Is. 1:23 *p* Jer. 6:13 *q* Is. 48:2   **3:12** *r* Jer. 26:18 *s* Ps. 79:1 *t* Mic. 4:1, 2   **4:1** *a* Is. 2:2–4 *b* Is. 2:4 *c* Ps. 72:7   **4:4** *d* Zech. 3:10   **4:5** *e* Zech. 10:12   **4:6** *f* Ezek. 34:16 *g* Ps. 147:2   **4:7** *h* Mic. 2:12 *i* [Is. 9:6; 24:23]   **4:9** *j* Jer. 8:19 *k* Is. 13:8   **4:10** *l* Amos 5:27 *m* [Is. 45:13] *n* Ps. 18:17

11 ᵒNow also many nations have gathered
against you,
Who say, "Let her be defiled,
And let our eye ᵖlook upon Zion."
12 But they do not know ᑫthe thoughts of
the LORD,
Nor do they understand His counsel;
For He will gather them ʳlike sheaves
to the threshing floor.
13 "Ariseˢ and ᵗthresh, O daughter of Zion;
For I will make your horn iron,
And I will make your hooves bronze;
You shall ᵘbeat in pieces many
peoples;
ᵛI will consecrate their gain to the LORD,
And their substance to ʷthe Lord of
the whole earth."

5 Now gather yourself in troops,
O daughter of troops;
He has laid siege against us;
They will ᵃstrike the judge of Israel
with a rod on the cheek.

The Coming Messiah

2 "But you, ᵇBethlehem ᶜEphrathah,
Though you are little ᵈamong the
ᵉthousands of Judah,
Yet out of you shall come forth to Me
The One to be ᶠRuler in Israel,
ᵍWhose goings forth *are* from of old,
From everlasting."

3 Therefore He shall give them up,
Until the time *that* ʰshe who is in labor
has given birth;
Then ⁱthe remnant of His brethren
Shall return to the children of Israel.
4 And He shall stand and ʲfeed *His flock*
In the strength of the LORD,
In the majesty of the name of the LORD
His God;
And they shall abide,
For now He ᵏshall be great
To the ends of the earth;
5 And this *One* ˡshall be peace.

Judgment on Israel's Enemies

When the Assyrian comes into our
land,
And when he treads in our palaces,

Then we will raise against him
Seven shepherds and eight princely
men.
6 They shall waste with the sword the
land of Assyria,
And the land of ᵐNimrod at its
entrances;
Thus He shall ⁿdeliver *us* from the
Assyrian,
When he comes into our land
And when he treads within our borders.

7 Then ᵒthe remnant of Jacob
Shall be in the midst of many peoples,
ᵖLike dew from the LORD,
Like showers on the grass,
That tarry for no man
Nor wait for the sons of men.
8 And the remnant of Jacob
Shall be among the Gentiles,
In the midst of many peoples,
Like a ᑫlion among the beasts of the
forest,
Like a young lion among flocks of
sheep,
Who, if he passes through,
Both treads down and tears in pieces,
And none can deliver.
9 Your hand shall be lifted against your
adversaries,
And all your enemies shall be cut off.

10 "And it shall be in that day," says the
LORD,
"That I will ʳcut off your ˢhorses from
your midst
And destroy your ᵗchariots.
11 I will cut off the cities of your land
And throw down all your
strongholds.
12 I will cut off sorceries from your hand,
And you shall have no ᵘsoothsayers.
13 ᵛYour carved images I will also cut off,
And your *sacred* pillars from your
midst;
You shall ʷno more worship the work
of your hands;
14 I will pluck your wooden images* from
your midst;
Thus I will destroy your cities.

---

* 5:14 Hebrew *Asherim,* Canaanite deities

4:13 Arise and thresh. The nations would be gathered by the Lord like sheaves on the threshing floor (v. 12). This is a way of speaking of the final victory over all of Israel's foes.

5:2 Bethlehem. This name means "house of bread." **Ephrathah.** This locates the village in a known region in Judah (Gen. 35:16). This prophecy figures significantly in the New Testament story of the visit of the wise men to the Christ child (Matt. 2:1–12). **goings forth.** The birth of this Savior King would be unlike the birth of any other, because He was preexistent. He is "from everlasting."

5:3 she who is in labor. This probably refers to Zion (4:10). The metaphor refers to the deliverance in the end time of those who will be able to delight in the coming of God's kingdom (4:9—5:1).

5:7 dew . . . showers. Jewish people are blessings from God on their neighbors.

5:10 I will cut off. It was God's intention to destroy the evils in Israel's society. Horses and chariots represent the pride of Israel's military power. Israel's

---

4:11 ᵒLam. 2:16 ᵖObad. 12 4:12 ᑫIs. 55:8, 9] ʳIs. 21:10 4:13 ˢJer. 51:33 ᵗIs. 41:15 ᵘDan. 2:44 ᵛIs. 18:7 ʷZech. 4:14 5:1 ᵃLam. 3:30; Matt. 27:30; Mark 15:19 5:2 ᵇJohn 7:42 ᶜGen. 35:19; 48:7; 1 Sam. 23:23 ᵉEx. 18:25 ᶠ[Is. 9:6] ᵍPs. 90:2; [John 1:1] 5:3 ʰMic. 4:10 ⁱMic. 4:7; 7:18 5:4 ʲ[Is. 40:11; 49:9] ᵏPs. 72:8 5:5 ˡ[Is. 9:6] 5:6 ᵐGen. 10:8–11 ⁿIs. 14:25 5:7 ᵒMic. 5:3 ᵖDeut. 32:2 5:8 ᑫNum. 24:9 5:10 ʳZech. 9:10 ˢDeut. 17:16 ᵗIs. 2:7; 22:18 5:12 ᵘIs. 2:6 5:13 ᵛZech. 13:2 ʷIs. 2:8

15 And I will [x]execute vengeance in anger and fury
On the nations that have not heard."*

God Pleads with Israel

6 Hear now what the LORD says:

"Arise, plead your case before the mountains,
And let the hills hear your voice.
2 [a]Hear, O you mountains, [b]the LORD's complaint,
And you strong foundations of the earth;
For [c]the LORD has a complaint against His people,
And He will contend with Israel.

3 "O My people, what [d]have I done to you?
And how have I [e]wearied you?
Testify against Me.
4 [f]For I brought you up from the land of Egypt,
I redeemed you from the house of bondage;
And I sent before you Moses, Aaron, and Miriam.
5 O My people, remember now
What [g]Balak king of Moab counseled,
And what Balaam the son of Beor answered him,
From Acacia Grove* to Gilgal,
That you may know [h]the righteousness of the LORD."

6 With what shall I come before the LORD,
And bow myself before the High God?
Shall I come before Him with burnt offerings,
With calves a year old?
7 [i]Will the LORD be pleased with thousands of rams,
Ten thousand [j]rivers of oil?
[k]Shall I give my firstborn *for* my transgression,
The fruit of my body *for* the sin of my soul?

8 He has [l]shown you, O man, what *is* good;
And what does the LORD require of you
But [m]to do justly,
To love mercy,
And to walk humbly with your God?

Punishment of Israel's Injustice

9 The LORD's voice cries to the city—
Wisdom shall see Your name:

"Hear the rod!
Who has appointed it?
10 Are there yet the treasures of wickedness
In the house of the wicked,
And the short measure *that is* an abomination?
11 Shall I count pure *those* with [n]the wicked scales,
And with the bag of deceitful weights?
12 For her rich men are full of [o]violence,
Her inhabitants have spoken lies,
And [p]their tongue is deceitful in their mouth.

13 "Therefore I will also [q]make *you* sick by striking you,
By making *you* desolate because of your sins.
14 [r]You shall eat, but not be satisfied;
Hunger* *shall be* in your midst.
You may carry *some* away,* but shall not save *them;*
And what you do rescue I will give over to the sword.

15 "You shall [s]sow, but not reap;
You shall tread the olives, but not anoint yourselves with oil;
And *make* sweet wine, but not drink wine.
16 For the statutes of [t]Omri are [u]kept;
All the works of Ahab's house *are done;*
And you walk in their counsels,
That I may make you a desolation,
And your inhabitants a hissing.
Therefore you shall bear the [v]reproach of My people."*

Sorrow for Israel's Sins

7 Woe is me!
For I am like those who gather summer fruits,

*5:15 Or *obeyed* *6:5 Hebrew *Shittim* (compare Numbers 25:1; Joshua 2:1; 3:1) *6:14 Or *Emptiness* or *Humiliation* • Targum and Vulgate read *You shall take hold.* *6:16 Following Masoretic Text, Targum, and Vulgate; Septuagint reads *of nations.*

---

tendency was to rely on its own military power rather than on the Lord.

6:1–2 ***mountains . . . hills.*** These were among the witnesses to the covenant that God made with His people (Deut. 4:26; 32:1; Is. 1:2).

6:7 ***Will the LORD be pleased.*** The idea of bringing pleasure to God through sacrifice is found elsewhere in the Bible. God is pleased with those who do as He commands (Gen. 4:1–8).

6:8 ***what does the LORD require of you.*** This verse speaks of the underlying attitudes that must accompany all true worship. The idea here is that God seeks certain characteristics of true worship from His people. ***do justly . . . love mercy . . . walk humbly.*** These three phrases summarize biblical piety in true worship. The majority of the people of Israel had violated each of these standards repeatedly. ***with your God.*** It is the Lord who ultimately gives a person strength, courage, and ability to exercise the virtues of godly living.

7:1–2 ***Woe is me.*** Micah was moved by the oracles of judgment that God delivered through him (1:8).

5:15 [x] [2 Thess. 1:8] **6:2** [a] Ps. 50:1, 4 [b] Hos. 12:2 [c] [Is. 1:18] **6:3** [d] Jer. 2:5, 31 [e] Is. 43:22, 23 **6:4** [f] [Deut. 4:20] **6:5** [g] Num. 22:5, 6 [h] Judg. 5:11 **6:7** [i] Is. 1:11 [j] Job 29:6 [k] 2 Kin. 16:3 **6:8** [l] [Deut. 10:12] [m] Gen. 18:19 **6:11** [n] Hos. 12:7 **6:12** [o] Mic. 2:1, 2 [p] Jer. 9:2–6, 8 **6:13** [q] Lev. 26:16 **6:14** [r] Lev. 26:26 **6:15** [s] Amos 5:11 **6:16** [t] 1 Kin. 16:25, 26 [u] Hos. 5:11 [v] Is. 25:8

Like those who [a]glean vintage
grapes;
There is no cluster to eat
Of the first-ripe fruit *which* [b]my soul
desires.
2 The [c]faithful *man* has perished from
the earth,
And *there is* no one upright among
men.
They all lie in wait for blood;
[d]Every man hunts his brother with a
net.

3 That they may successfully do evil
with both hands—
The prince asks *for gifts,*
The judge *seeks* a [e]bribe,
And the great *man* utters his evil
desire;
So they scheme together.
4 The best of them *is* [f]like a brier;
The most upright *is sharper* than a
thorn hedge;
The day of your watchman and your
punishment comes;
Now shall be their perplexity.

5 [g]Do not trust in a friend;
Do not put your confidence in a
companion;
Guard the doors of your mouth
From her who lies in your [h]bosom.
6 For [i]son dishonors father,
Daughter rises against her mother,
Daughter-in-law against her mother-
in-law;
A man's enemies *are* the men of his
own household.
7 Therefore I will look to the LORD;
I will [j]wait for the God of my
salvation;
My God will hear me.

Israel's Confession and Comfort

8 [k]Do not rejoice over me, my enemy;
[l]When I fall, I will arise;
When I sit in darkness,
The LORD *will be* a light to me.
9 [m]I will bear the indignation of the LORD,
Because I have sinned against Him,
Until He pleads my [n]case
And executes justice for me.
He will bring me forth to the light;
I will see His righteousness.
10 Then *she who is* my enemy will see,
And [o]shame will cover her who said
to me,
[p]"Where is the LORD your God?"
My eyes will see her;
Now she will be trampled down
Like mud in the streets.

11 *In* the day when your [q]walls are to be
built,
In that day the decree shall go far and
wide.*
12 *In* that day [r]they* shall come to you
From Assyria and the fortified cities,*
From the fortress* to the River,*
From sea to sea,
And mountain *to* mountain.
13 Yet the land shall be desolate
Because of those who dwell in it,
And [s]for the fruit of their deeds.

God Will Forgive Israel

14 Shepherd Your people with Your staff,
The flock of Your heritage,
Who dwell solitarily *in* a [t]woodland,
In the midst of Carmel;
Let them feed *in* Bashan and Gilead,
As in days of old.

15 "As[u] in the days when you came out of
the land of Egypt,
I will show them* [v]wonders."

16 The nations [w]shall see and be
ashamed of all their might;
[x]They shall put *their* hand over *their*
mouth;
Their ears shall be deaf.
17 They shall lick the [y]dust like a serpent;
[z]They shall crawl from their holes like
snakes of the earth.
[a]They shall be afraid of the LORD our
God,
And shall fear because of You.

* **7:11** Or *the boundary shall be extended* * **7:12** Literally *he,* collective of the captives • Hebrew *arey mazor,* possibly *cities of Egypt* • Hebrew *mazor,* possibly *Egypt* • That is, the Euphrates * **7:15** Literally *him,* collective for the captives

There is not a cluster. For Micah, the harvest was over. There was nothing around him but undesirable fruit. ***The faithful man has perished.*** The norms of society had broken down; everyone was out to destroy someone else.

7:3–4 ***with both hands.*** The people were pursuing evil with gusto. The leaders of the state were leading the way in evil (3:11). ***The day of your watchman.*** This refers to the time when people needed to be alert for the approach of an enemy army. In this context, judgment was imminent.

7:7 ***I will look to the LORD.*** While there would need to be a watchman for the coming of an enemy army, Micah was going to look for the advent of the Lord.

7:8–9 ***I have sinned.*** This is the confession of the people in saving faith.

7:11–12 ***In the day.*** These words call attention to a future day, the time of the end.

7:16–17 ***nations shall see and be ashamed.*** The response of the wicked nations to the renewed mercies of God on His people would be terror. The nations would be humiliated because they had taunted Israel in the day of its trouble (vv. 8–10).

7:1 [a]Is. 17:6 [b]Is. 28:4 **7:2** [c]Is. 57:1 [d]Hab. 1:15 **7:3** [e]Mic. 3:11 **7:4** [f]Ezek. 2:6 **7:5** [g]Jer. 9:4 [h]Deut. 28:56 **7:6** [i]Matt. 10:36 **7:7** [j]Is. 25:9 **7:8** [k]Prov. 24:17 [l][Prov. 24:16] **7:9** [m]Lam. 3:39, 40 [n]Jer. 50:34 **7:10** [o]Ps. 35:26 [p]Ps. 42:3 **7:11** [q][Amos 9:11] **7:12** [r][Is. 11:16; 19:23–25] **7:13** [s]Jer. 21:14 **7:14** [t]Is. 37:24 **7:15** [u]Ps. 68:22; 78:12 [v]Ex. 34:10 **7:16** [w]Is. 26:11 [x]Job 21:5 **7:17** [y][Is. 49:23] [z]Ps. 18:45 [a]Jer. 33:9

18 ᵇWho *is* a God like You,
  ᶜPardoning iniquity
  And passing over the transgression of
    ᵈthe remnant of His heritage?

  ᵉHe does not retain His anger forever,
  Because He delights *in* ᶠmercy.
19 He will again have compassion on us,
  And will subdue our iniquities.

You will cast all our* sins
  Into the depths of the sea.
20 ᵍYou will give truth to Jacob
  And mercy to Abraham,
  ʰWhich You have sworn to our fathers
  From days of old.

* **7:19** Literally *their*

7:18–20 God's Mercy—There is a significant passage on mercy or love like this in every book in the Old Testament. God wants His people to succeed and be prosperous. He wants the best for them. He is always eager to restore them. He protects, directs, sustains, and covenants with them. His steadfast love is characterized by faithfulness in spite of constant wandering in unfaithfulness.

In the New Testament, it is also easy to find passages in every book where someone is being judged. Usually it's the religious people who have set themselves up in God's place or those who have turned away from God when they should know better who are condemned.

The Old Testament predicts, leads toward, and sets the scene for the ultimate judgment of the New Testament. The entire Bible consistently points to the kind of creatures we are because of the fall and sin. Only God has the ultimate solution in Christ. God subjects Himself to that ultimate judgment for us so that all of His love for us may be realized. It's a mystery that we can solve only in our hearts by accepting and believing its implications.

Every day our prayer needs to be, "Lord, my sins are ever with me. I deserve Your judgment. Thank You for the great mercy I've received through Jesus' death for me. That He died in my place must always be the primary reality in my life."

7:18 *Who is a God like You.* These words speak of the incomparability of God. There is nothing in all of creation to compare with God (Is. 40:25).

7:20 *which You have sworn.* This last verse is reminiscent of God's promise to Abraham in Genesis 12; 15; 22 and His promises to Jacob in Genesis 32. The Lord had sworn to fulfill His promises to the patriarchs. He would not—could not—leave His promise unfulfilled (Ps. 89:33).

7:18 ᵇEx. 15:11 ᶜEx. 34:6, 7, 9 ᵈMic. 4:7 ᵉPs. 103:8, 9, 13 ᶠ[Ezek. 33:11] **7:20** ᵍLuke 1:72, 73 ʰPs. 105:9

THE BOOK OF
NAHUM

▶ **AUTHOR:** The only mention of Nahum in the Old Testament is found in 1:1 where he is called an Elkoshite. Scholars have been unable to determine the exact location of Elkosh and numerous theories exist, but due to his interest in the triumph of Judah (1:15; 2:2), some believe Nahum to be a prophet of the southern kingdom.

▶ **TIME:** c. 660 B.C.   ▶ **KEY VERSES:** Nah. 1:7–8

▶ **THEME:** Nahum is unique in that it is a prophecy addressed completely to a nation other than Israel: Assyria and its capital Nineveh. While Nineveh may be powerful, her day of destruction is coming. Nineveh is not invincible. The message is that God's standards apply to all nations, not just Israel and Judah. They need to be prepared to live by those standards or face judgment.

---

1 The burden* ᵃagainst Nineveh. The book of the vision of Nahum the Elkoshite.

God's Wrath on His Enemies

2 God *is* ᵇjealous, and the LORD avenges;
   The LORD avenges and *is* furious.
   The LORD will take vengeance on His adversaries,
   And He reserves *wrath* for His enemies;
3 The LORD *is* ᶜslow to anger and ᵈgreat in power,
   And will not at all acquit *the wicked*.

   ᵉThe LORD has His way
   In the whirlwind and in the storm,
   And the clouds *are* the dust of His feet.
4 ᶠHe rebukes the sea and makes it dry,
   And dries up all the rivers.
   ᵍBashan and Carmel wither,
   And the flower of Lebanon wilts.
5 The mountains quake before Him,
   The hills melt,
   And the earth heaves* at His presence,
   Yes, the world and all who dwell in it.

6 Who can stand before His indignation?
   And ʰwho can endure the fierceness of His anger?
   His fury is poured out like fire,

And the rocks are thrown down by Him.

7 ⁱThe LORD *is* good,
   A stronghold in the day of trouble;
   And ʲHe knows those who trust in Him.
8 But with an overflowing flood
   He will make an utter end of its place,
   And darkness will pursue His enemies.

9 ᵏWhat do you conspire against the LORD?
   ˡHe will make an utter end *of it*.
   Affliction will not rise up a second time.
10 For while tangled ᵐlike thorns,
   ⁿAnd while drunken *like* drunkards,
   ᵒThey shall be devoured like stubble fully dried.
11 From you comes forth *one*
   Who plots evil against the LORD,
   A wicked counselor.

12 Thus says the LORD:

"Though *they are* safe, and likewise many,
   Yet in this manner they will be ᵖcut down

---

* 1:1 Or *oracle*   * 1:5 Targum reads *burns*.

1:2 *jealous, and the LORD avenges.* The repetition of words and the use of parallel terms are typical devices in Hebrew poetry for intensifying and sharpening the poet's message.

1:3 *whirlwind . . . storm . . . clouds.* The peoples of the ancient Middle East worshiped nature gods, particularly deities associated with storms, clouds, and rainfall. In Canaan, this fixation on storms was centered in the worship of Baal and his consorts Anat and Asherah. The Scriptures testify that there are no gods but the Lord; it is He who rules and is above all creation.

1:8 *flood . . . end . . . darkness.* The judgment of the

Lord will be inescapable. The word "flood" is both a poetic term for overwhelming devastation and a specific reference to the actual manner of Nineveh's fall. It is believed that the invaders of Nineveh entered the city through its flooded waterways (2:6).

1:11 *A wicked counselor.* "Wicked" is one of the harshest terms in biblical language, nearly a curse

---

1:1 ᵃ Zeph. 2:13   1:2 ᵇ Ex. 20:5   1:3 ᶜ Ex. 34:6, 7   ᵈ [Job 9:4]   ᵉ Ps. 18:17   1:4 ᶠ Matt. 8:26   ᵍ Is. 33:9   1:6 ʰ [Mal. 3:2]   1:7 ⁱ [Jer. 33:11]   ʲ 2 Tim. 2:19   1:9 ᵏ Ps. 2:1   ˡ 1 Sam. 3:12   1:10 ᵐ 2 Sam. 23:6   ⁿ Nah. 3:11   ᵒ Mal. 4:1   1:12 ᵖ [Is. 10:16–19, 33, 34]

When he passes through.
Though I have afflicted you,
I will afflict you no more;

13 For now I will break off his yoke from
you,
And burst your bonds apart."

14 The LORD has given a command
concerning you:
"Your name shall be perpetuated no
longer.
Out of the house of your gods
I will cut off the carved image and the
molded image.
I will dig your *a*grave,
For you are *r*vile."

15 Behold, on the mountains
The *s*feet of him who brings good
tidings,
Who proclaims peace!
O Judah, keep your appointed feasts,
Perform your vows.
For the wicked one shall no more pass
through you;
He is *t*utterly cut off.

The Destruction of Nineveh

2 He who scatters* has come up before
your face.
Man the fort!
Watch the road!
Strengthen *your* flanks!
Fortify *your* power mightily.

2 For the LORD will restore the
excellence of Jacob
Like the excellence of Israel,
For the emptiers have emptied them
out
And ruined their vine branches.

3 The shields of his mighty men *are*
made red,
The valiant men *are* in scarlet.
The chariots *come* with flaming
torches

In the day of his preparation,
And the spears are brandished.*

4 The chariots rage in the streets,
They jostle one another in the broad
roads;
They seem like torches,
They run like lightning.

5 He remembers his nobles;
They stumble in their walk;
They make haste to her walls,
And the defense is prepared.

6 The gates of the rivers are opened,
And the palace is dissolved.

7 It is decreed:*
She shall be led away captive,
She shall be brought up;
And her maidservants shall lead *her*
as with the voice of doves,
Beating their breasts.

8 Though Nineveh of old *was* like a pool
of water,
Now they flee away.
"Halt! Halt!" *they cry;*
But no one turns back.

9 Take spoil of silver!
Take spoil of *a*gold!
There is no end of treasure,
Or wealth of every desirable prize.

10 She is empty, desolate, and waste!
The heart melts, and the knees shake;
Much pain *is* in every side,
And all their faces are drained of color.*

11 Where *is* the dwelling of the *b*lions,
And the feeding place of the young
lions,
Where the lion walked, the lioness *and*
lion's cub,
And no one made *them* afraid?

---

* **2:1** Vulgate reads *He who destroys.*   * **2:3** Literally *the cypresses are shaken;* Septuagint and
Syriac read *the horses rush about;* Vulgate reads
the drivers are stupefied.   * **2:7** Hebrew *Huzzab*
* **2:10** Compare Joel 2:6

---

word. The term speaks of someone who is utterly
worthless.
1:14 *you are vile.* The only thing to be done with
Nineveh was to dig a grave and bury it. The prophecy came true literally—the city was destroyed so
completely that its very existence was questioned
until its discovery by archaeologists in the nineteenth
century (3:13–15).
2:1 *Man the fort.* These were sarcastic words to the
people of Nineveh and its leaders, as if they would be
able to protect themselves against the wrath of the
Lord.
2:3 *red . . . scarlet . . . flaming torches.* These images
speak of blood, violence, and warfare. Isaiah refers
to the custom of the Assyrians of rolling their outer
garments in blood before a battle (Is. 9:5) to strike terror in the hearts of their opponents. Here the tables
would be turned. While others would have shields,
chariots, and spears, the people of Nineveh would be
bathed in blood—their own blood.
2:4 *The chariots rage.* The Assyrians used chariots
as formidable war machines. The proficiency of the

chariot drivers underlies the imagery of this verse.
But, as in the case of the shields and spears of verse 3,
the chariots of Nineveh would not prevail, no matter
how fast they drove.
2:6 *gates of the rivers.* The destruction of Nineveh
is believed to have taken place when the besiegers
entered the city through its flooded waterways. The
attack came at flood time, when rivers undermined
the walls and defenses of the city. Archaeologists
have found evidence of flood debris that may be
associated with the destruction of the city. Thus, the
words of Nahum were fulfilled exactly.
2:11–12 *dwelling of the lions.* Nineveh was the city
of lions (v. 13). Yet, despite all the horrors that the lion
of Nineveh had brought to other nations, it would no
longer need to be feared by anyone. Although the
Babylonians conquered the city, they were only God's
instruments. Nineveh's greatest foe was God Himself.

1:14 *a* Ezek. 32:22, 23   *r* Nah. 3:6   **1:15** *s* Rom. 10:15   *t* Is.
29:7, 8   **2:9** *a* Zeph. 1:18   **2:11** *b* Job 4:10, 11

12 The lion tore in pieces enough for his
   cubs,
      Killed for his lionesses,
   cFilled his caves with prey,
      And his dens with flesh.

13"Behold, dI *am* against you," says the
LORD of hosts, "I will burn your* chariots
in smoke, and the sword shall devour your
young lions; I will cut off your prey from
the earth, and the voice of your emessen-
gers shall be heard no more."

The Woe of Nineveh

3 Woe to the abloody city!
   It *is* all full of lies *and* robbery.
      Its victim never departs.
2   The noise of a whip
      And the noise of rattling wheels,
   Of galloping horses,
      Of clattering chariots!
3   Horsemen charge with bright sword
         and glittering spear.
   There is a multitude of slain,
      A great number of bodies,
   Countless corpses—
      They stumble over the corpses—
4   Because of the multitude of harlotries
         of the seductive harlot,
   bThe mistress of sorceries,
      Who sells nations through her
         harlotries,
   And families through her
      sorceries.

5   "Behold, I *am* cagainst you," says the
         LORD of hosts;
   d"I will lift your skirts over your face,
      I will show the nations your
         nakedness,
   And the kingdoms your shame.
6   I will cast abominable filth upon you,
      Make you evile,
   And make you fa spectacle.
7   It shall come to pass *that* all who look
         upon you
   gWill flee from you, and say,
   h'Nineveh is laid waste!
      iWho will bemoan her?'
   Where shall I seek comforters for
      you?"

8   iAre you better than kNo Amon*
      That was situated by the River,*
   That had the waters around her,
      Whose rampart *was* the sea,
   Whose wall *was* the sea?
9   Ethiopia and Egypt *were* her
         strength,
      And *it was* boundless;
   lPut and Lubim were your* helpers.
10   Yet she *was* carried away,
      She went into captivity;
   mHer young children also were dashed
      to pieces
   nAt the head of every street;
      They ocast lots for her honorable men,
   And all her great men were bound in
      chains.
11   You also will be pdrunk;
      You will be hidden;
   You also will seek refuge from the
      enemy.

12   All your strongholds *are* qfig trees
      with ripened figs:
   If they are shaken,
      They fall into the mouth of the eater.
13   Surely, ryour people in your midst *are*
      women!
   The gates of your land are wide open
      for your enemies;
   Fire shall devour the sbars of your
      gates.

14   Draw your water for the siege!
   tFortify your strongholds!
      Go into the clay and tread the mortar!
   Make strong the brick kiln!
15   There the fire will devour you,
      The sword will cut you off;
   It will eat you up like a ulocust.

   Make yourself many—like the locust!
      Make yourself many—like the
         swarming locusts!
16   You have multiplied your vmerchants
      more than the stars of heaven.
   The locust plunders and flies away.

* **2:13** Literally *her*   * **3:8** That is, ancient Thebes;
Targum and Vulgate read *populous Alexandria.*
• Literally *rivers,* that is, the Nile and the sur-
rounding canals   * **3:9** Septuagint reads *her.*

3:4 harlotries. Any worship of gods other than the
God of Scriptures is an act of spiritual prostitution.
Nineveh was so adept at pagan practices that the city
earned the descriptive title, "the mistress of witch-
crafts."
3:6–7 I will cast abominable filth upon you. The
Lord described the fate of Nineveh as comparable
to a person on whom unspeakable filth was thrown.
When Nineveh lay in ruins, no one would grieve for
her. The nations would be glad that the city was gone.
3:8 No Amon. This is the Hebrew name for Thebes,
derived from the Egyptian name meaning "city of
the god Amon." The argument here was to suggest
that, before its destruction, no one would have even
dreamed of the fall of Thebes. But the destruction
had happened—not long before the writing of the
Book of Nahum. The city of Thebes was rebuilt only to

be destroyed later during the Roman period (29 B.C.).
Nineveh, however, would never be rebuilt.
3:11 drunk . . . hidden . . . seek refuge. Nineveh
would be like a helpless drunk hoping for strength
but finding nowhere to turn for it.
3:16–17 When the sun rises. The people of Nineveh
would be like nocturnal insects that disappear at daylight.

2:12 c Jer. 51:34   **2:13** d Nah. 3:5   e 2 Kin. 18:17–25;
19:9–13, 23   **3:1** a Hab. 2:12   **3:4** b Is. 47:9–12
3:5 c Nah. 2:13   d Is. 47:2, 3   **3:6** e Nah. 1:14   f Heb. 10:33
3:7 g Rev. 18:10   h Jon. 3:3; 4:11   i Jer. 15:5   **3:8** j Amos 6:2
k Jer. 46:25   **3:9** l Ezek. 27:10   **3:10** m Hos. 13:16   n Lam.
2:19   o Joel 3:3   **3:11** p Nah. 1:10   **3:12** q Rev. 6:12, 13
3:13 r Is. 19:16   s Jer. 51:30   **3:14** t Nah. 2:1   **3:15** u Joel
1:4   **3:16** v Rev. 18:3, 11–19

17 wYour commanders *are* like *swarming*
    locusts,
And your generals like great
    grasshoppers,
Which camp in the hedges on a cold
    day;
When the sun rises they flee away,
And the place where they *are* is not
    known.

18 xYour shepherds slumber, O yking of
    Assyria;

Your nobles rest *in the dust.*
Your people are zscattered on the
    mountains,
And no one gathers them.
19 Your injury *has* no healing,
    aYour wound is severe.
    bAll who hear news of you
Will clap *their* hands over you,
For upon whom has not your
    wickedness passed
    continually?

3:19 *All who hear.* Every nation and people that had
suffered under the abusive power of Nineveh would
shout and clap upon hearing of the city's destruction.
There would be no mourning for Nineveh.

3:17 w Rev. 9:7   **3:18** x Ps. 76:5, 6 y Jer. 50:18 z 1 Kin. 22:17   **3:19** a Mic. 1:9 b Lam. 2:15

THE BOOK OF
HABAKKUK

▶ **AUTHOR:** In both the introduction to the book (1:1) and the closing psalm (3:1) the author identifies himself as Habakkuk the prophet. It is believed that he might have been a priest as he mentions in the closing psalm, "To the Chief Musician. With my stringed instruments" (3:19). Also, in the apocryphal book of Bel and the Dragon, Daniel is rescued a second time by the prophet Habakkuk.

▶ **TIME:** c. 607 B.C.   ▶ **KEY VERSE:** Hab. 2:4

▶ **THEME:** This whole book of Habakkuk is really devoted to the question of "Lord, if You are all powerful, why is evil allowed to exist?" The events that seem to be precipitating this question are the victories of Babylon. God was using Babylon, a nation without God, to punish Israel, God's own people. The answers God gives us to this question in Habakkuk solidly point us in one direction, but ultimately the answers are in faith in Him alone.

---

1 The burden* which the prophet Habakkuk saw.

The Prophet's Question

2 O LORD, how long shall I cry,
   ᵃAnd You will not hear?
   Even cry out to You, ᵇ"Violence!"
   And You will ᶜnot save.
3 Why do You show me iniquity,
   And cause *me* to see trouble?
   For plundering and violence *are* before me;
   There is strife, and contention arises.
4 Therefore the law is powerless,
   And justice never goes forth.
   For the ᵈwicked surround the righteous;
   Therefore perverse judgment proceeds.

The LORD's Reply

5 "Lookᵉ among the nations and watch—
   Be utterly astounded!
   For *I will* work a work in your days
   Which you would not believe, though
   it were told *you.*
6 For indeed I am ᶠraising up the Chaldeans,
   A bitter and hasty ᵍnation

Which marches through the breadth of the earth,
To possess dwelling places *that are* not theirs.
7 They are terrible and dreadful;
   Their judgment and their dignity proceed from themselves.
8 Their horses also are ʰswifter than leopards,
   And more fierce than evening wolves.
   Their chargers charge ahead;
   Their cavalry comes from afar;
   They fly as the ⁱeagle *that* hastens to eat.
9 "They all come for violence;
   Their faces are set *like* the east wind.
   They gather captives like sand.
10 They scoff at kings,
   And princes are scorned by them.
   They deride every stronghold,
   For they heap up earthen *mounds* and seize it.
11 Then *his* mind* changes, and he transgresses;
   He commits offense,
   ʲAscribing this power to his god."

---

* 1:1 Or *oracle*   * 1:11 Literally *spirit* or *wind*

1:2 O LORD, how long. This question is phrased as a formal complaint (Ps. 13:1–2).
1:4 the law is powerless. The revelation of God given at Mount Sinai had little impact on the hearts of people whose lives were focused on material success. These people had little interest in living by God's definition of what is fair and humane. **wicked.** God's chosen people committed and tolerated heinous acts through the corruption of the courts.
1:5 Look among the nations. The international scene during Habakkuk's lifetime was full of turmoil, with Assyria on the decline and Babylonia on the rise.

1:6 I am raising up. God controls the nations for His own purposes (Dan. 2:21), sometimes indirectly and at other times directly.
1:7 terrible and dreadful. Far from being humane, the Babylonians prided themselves on their arrogant use of raw power.
1:9 They gather captives like sand. The Babylonians

1:2 ᵃLam. 3:8 ᵇMic. 2:1, 2; 3:1–3 ᶜ[Job 21:5–16]
1:4 ᵈJer. 12:1 1:5 ᵉIs. 29:14 1:6 ᶠ2 Kin. 24:2 ᵍEzek.
7:24; 21:31 1:8 ʰJer. 4:13 ⁱHos. 8:1 1:11 ʲDan. 5:4

The Prophet's Second Question

12 Are You not [k]from everlasting,
O LORD my God, my Holy One?
We shall not die.
O LORD, [l]You have appointed them for
judgment;
O Rock, You have marked them for
[m]correction.

13 *You are* of purer eyes than to behold
evil,
And cannot look on wickedness.
Why do You look on those who deal
treacherously,
And hold Your tongue when the
wicked devours
A *person* more righteous than he?

14 *Why* do You make men like fish of the
sea,
Like creeping things *that have* no
ruler over them?

15 They take up all of them with a hook,
They catch them in their net,
And gather them in their dragnet.
Therefore they rejoice and are glad.

16 Therefore [n]they sacrifice to their net,
And burn incense to their dragnet;
Because by them their share *is*
sumptuous
And their food plentiful.

17 Shall they therefore empty their net,
And continue to slay nations without
pity?

2 I will [a]stand my watch
And set myself on the rampart,
And watch to see what He will say to me,
And what I will answer when I am
corrected.

The Just Live by Faith

2 Then the LORD answered me and said:

[b]"Write the vision
And make *it* plain on tablets,
That he may run who reads it.

3 For [c]the vision *is* yet for an appointed
time;
But at the end it will speak, and it will
[d]not lie.
Though it tarries, [e]wait for it;
Because it will [f]surely come,
It will not tarry.

4 "Behold the proud,
His soul is not upright in him;
But the [g]just shall live by his faith.

Woe to the Wicked

5 "Indeed, because he transgresses by
wine,
He is a proud man,
And he does not stay at home.
Because he [h]enlarges his desire as hell,*
And he *is* like death, and cannot be
satisfied,
He gathers to himself all nations
And heaps up for himself all peoples.

6 "Will not all these [i]take up a proverb
against him,
And a taunting riddle against him,
and say,
'Woe to him who increases
What is not his—how long?
And to him who loads himself with
many pledges'?*

7 Will not your creditors* rise up
suddenly?
Will they not awaken who oppress you?
And you will become their booty.

8 [j]Because you have plundered many
nations,
All the remnant of the people shall
plunder you,
Because of men's blood
And the violence of the land *and* the
city,
And of all who dwell in it.

---

* **2:5** Or *Sheol*   * **2:6** Syriac and Vulgate read
thick clay.   * **2:7** Literally *those who bite you*

---

resettled numerous conquered peoples with little
regard for them as individuals.
1:12 *Are You not from everlasting.* Habakkuk's
point seems to be that God's holiness should have
prohibited Him from using a dirty instrument such as
Babylon to accomplish His purposes in judging and
reproving His own people.
1:16 *they sacrifice to their net.* This phrase speaks of
the contemptuous pride of the Babylonians in their
devices of destruction.
2:1 *I will stand . . . on the rampart.* Habakkuk stationed himself as a watchman to look at the nations,
as God had commanded him. ***what He will say to
me.*** Habakkuk's faith is seen in his anticipation of
a response from God. ***when I am corrected.*** This
phrase indicates the prophet's submission to God.
2:3 *an appointed time.* This speaks of a determined time in God's eyes. ***Though it tarries, wait
for it.*** God knows His plan and the outworking of all
things in accordance with His purposes. The godly
are responsible to study and proclaim His revelation
while awaiting its fulfillment. ***it will surely come.*** The

fulfillment of the vision would not take any longer
than God had planned.
2:4 *the just shall live by his faith.* True righteousness
before God is linked to genuine faith in God. A proud
person relies on self, power, position, and accomplishment; a righteous person relies on the Lord.
2:5 *all nations . . . all peoples.* These peoples of the
earth should have been gathered together before the
Lord in holy worship (Ps. 117:1); instead, they became
morsels for the rapacious appetite of Babylon.
2:6 *Woe to him.* A woe is an oracle of judgment consisting of two parts: a declaration of the wrong and
a notice of impending judgment. The judgment usually applies the principle of the law of retribution.
2:7 *creditors.* This Hebrew term has the idea of "those
who bite," suggesting sudden attacks (Mic. 3:5).

1:12 [k] Ps. 90:2; 93:2 [l] Is. 10:5–7 [m] Jer. 25:9 **1:16** [n] Deut.
8:17 **2:1** [a] Is. 21:8, 11 **2:2** [b] Is. 8:1 **2:3** [c] Dan. 8:17,
19; 10:14 [d] Ezek. 12:24, 25 [e] [Heb. 10:37, 38] [f] [2 Pet. 3:9]
2:4 [g] [John 3:36]; Rom. 1:17 **2:5** [h] Is. 5:11–15 **2:6** [i] Mic.
2:4 **2:8** [j] Is. 33:1

9 "Woe to him who covets evil gain for
his house,
That he may *k*set his nest on high,
That he may be delivered from the
power of disaster!
10 You give shameful counsel to your
house,
Cutting off many peoples,
And sin *against* your soul.
11 For the stone will cry out from the wall,
And the beam from the timbers will
answer it.
12 "Woe to him who builds a town with
bloodshed,
Who establishes a city by iniquity!
13 Behold, *is it* not of the LORD of hosts
That the peoples labor to feed the fire,*
And nations weary themselves in vain?
14 For the earth will be filled
With the knowledge of the glory of the
LORD,
As the waters cover the sea.
15 "Woe to him who gives drink to his
neighbor,
Pressing* *him to* your *l*bottle,
Even to make *him* drunk,
That you may look on his nakedness!
16 You are filled with shame instead of
glory.
You also—drink!
And be exposed as uncircumcised!*
The cup of the LORD's right hand *will
be* turned against you,
And utter shame will be on your glory.
17 For the violence *done to* Lebanon will
cover you,
And the plunder of beasts *which* made
them afraid,
Because of men's blood
And the violence of the land *and* the
city,
And of all who dwell in it.
18 "What profit is the image, that its
maker should carve it,
The molded image, a teacher of lies,
That the maker of its mold should trust
in it,
To make mute idols?

19 Woe to him who says to wood,
'Awake!'
To silent stone, 'Arise! It shall teach!'
Behold, it is overlaid with gold and
silver,
Yet in it there is no breath at all.
20 "But*m* the LORD is in His holy temple.
Let all the earth keep silence before
Him."

The Prophet's Prayer

3 A prayer of Habakkuk the prophet, on
Shigionoth.*

2 O LORD, I have heard Your speech *and*
was afraid;
O LORD, revive Your work in the midst
of the years!
In the midst of the years make *it*
known;
In wrath remember mercy.

3 God came from Teman,
The Holy One from Mount Paran.
Selah

His glory covered the heavens,
And the earth was full of His
praise.
4 *His* brightness was like the light;
He had rays *flashing* from His hand,
And there His power *was* hidden.
5 Before Him went pestilence,
And fever followed at His feet.
6 He stood and measured the earth;
He looked and startled the nations.
*a*And the everlasting mountains were
scattered,
The perpetual hills bowed.
His ways *are* everlasting.
7 I saw the tents of Cushan in
affliction;
The curtains of the land of Midian
trembled.

---

* **2:13** Literally *for what satisfies fire,* that is,
for what is of no lasting value   * **2:15** Literally
Attaching or *Joining*   * **2:16** Dead Sea Scrolls
and Septuagint read *And reel!*; Syriac and Vulgate
read *And fall fast asleep!*   * **3:1** Exact meaning
unknown

2:11 *the stone will cry out . . . the beam from the
timbers will answer it.* The whole structure of Israel's
society called out for justice; every part reverberated
with the need for righting wrongs.
2:14 *the glory of the LORD.* This speaks to the full
manifestation of His person, significance, presence,
and wonder. The true knowledge of God in the time of
His kingdom on earth will be like the waters—all-em-
bracing, inescapable, and fully enveloping.
2:16 *The cup of the LORD's right hand.* This represents the wrath of God (Is. 51:17,22; Rev. 14:10;
16:19).
2:18 *teacher of lies.* Idolatry begins with deception,
encourages deception, and calls for a commitment to
deception (Is. 44:20).
2:20 *keep silence before Him.* The call to silence
is not an invitation to worship, but a command to

reflect on the terrible state of all who fall into the
hands of the angry God (Zeph. 1:7).
3:2 *I have heard.* Habakkuk knew the stories of God's
mighty acts as celebrated in song and in the feasts
and festivals of Israel. These mighty acts included the
exodus from Egypt, the miracles by the Red Sea, and
the conquest of the land. *revive . . . make it known.*
Habakkuk prayed for God's renewed involvement in
Israel. *in the midst of the years.* This was a way of
calling for a quick response.
3:4 *His power was hidden.* God reveals evidence of
His power, but its totality and greatness remain hidden.

2:9 *k* Obad. 4	**2:15** *l* Hos. 7:5	**2:20** *m* Zeph. 1:7
3:6 *a* Nah. 1:5		

8 O LORD, were *You* displeased with the
    rivers,
Was Your anger against the rivers,
Was Your wrath against the sea,
That You rode on Your horses,
Your chariots of salvation?
9 Your bow was made quite ready;
Oaths were sworn over *Your* arrows.*
                     Selah

You divided the earth with rivers.
10 The mountains saw You *and*
    trembled;
The overflowing of the water
    passed by.
The deep uttered its voice,
And ᵇlifted its hands on high.
11 The ᶜsun and moon stood still in their
    habitation;
At the light of Your arrows they went,
At the shining of Your glittering
    spear.

12 You marched through the land in
    indignation;
You trampled the nations in anger.
13 You went forth for the salvation of
    Your people,
For salvation with Your Anointed.
You struck the head from the house of
    the wicked,
By laying bare from foundation to
    neck.   *Selah*

14 You thrust through with his own
    arrows
The head of his villages.

They came out like a whirlwind to
    scatter me;
Their rejoicing was like feasting on
    the poor in secret.
15 ᵈYou walked through the sea with Your
    horses,
Through the heap of great waters.

16 When I heard, ᵉmy body trembled;
My lips quivered at *the* voice;
Rottenness entered my bones;
And I trembled in myself,
That I might rest in the day of trouble.
When he comes up to the people,
He will invade them with his troops.

A Hymn of Faith

17 Though the fig tree may not blossom,
Nor fruit be on the vines;
Though the labor of the olive may fail,
And the fields yield no food;
Though the flock may be cut off from
    the fold,
And there be no herd in the stalls—
18 Yet I will ᶠrejoice in the LORD,
I will joy in the God of my salvation.

19 The LORD God* is my strength;
He will make my feet like ᵍdeer's *feet*,
And He will make me ʰwalk on my
    high hills.

To the Chief Musician. With my stringed
instruments.

---

* **3:9** Literally *rods* or *tribes* (compare verse 14)
* **3:19** Hebrew *YHWH Adonai*

3:8 *rivers . . . sea.* The Lord had divided the Red Sea and the Jordan River for His people to cross (Ex. 14:26—15:5; Josh. 3:14–17). *chariots of salvation.* The appearance of the Lord was for the purpose of bringing deliverance to His people.
3:16 *I might rest in the day of trouble.* The prophet encouraged the godly not to be anxious in adversity.
3:17 God and Politics—Living in this physical, time-bound reality we see only a small portion of what God created. It is the bigger part of creation we need to be aware of and try to understand. We ultimately live beyond what we see and feel now. Life, as currently defined, is only that proverbial shadow of what it shall be. Our struggle is to have the vision to see beyond.
    The same can be said for the political realities Habakkuk complains about. A season of failing crops isn't that much different than living a few years under the rule of an incompetent or cruel despot. It is tough

and life can be severely affected, but the ultimate realities of how the world functions and how God relates to it remain unchanged.
    God is a just God and will bring about justice. A period of injustice does not imply God has lost sight of what is going on or that He is losing His grip on the events of the world. He has different immediate purposes or works in a completely different timeframe.
    Despots usually don't last more than a generation. We had many in recent times and most are gone, along with their whole empires.
3:19 *my strength.* God will strengthen those who trust in Him (Ps. 18:32,39). He will give those who live by faith the same confidence that a sure-footed deer has in climbing mountains.

3:10 ᵇ Ex. 14:22   **3:11** ᶜ Josh. 10:12–14   **3:15** ᵈ Ps. 77:19
3:16 ᵉ Ps. 119:120   **3:18** ᶠ Is. 41:16; 61:10   **3:19** ᵍ 2 Sam.
22:34 ʰ Deut. 32:13; 33:29

THE BOOK OF
ZEPHANIAH

▶ **AUTHOR:** In the beginning of the book, Zephaniah traces his lineage back four generations to the godly King Hezekiah. This would make him the only prophet of royal descent. His use of the phrase "this place" in reference to Jerusalem indicates that he was probably an inhabitant of Judah's royal city.

▶ **TIME:** c. 630 B.C.   ▶ **KEY VERSES:** Zeph. 1:14–15

▶ **THEME:** Contemporary with Jeremiah, Zephaniah was written during the reign of Josiah, one of the good kings of Judah. The book follows a fairly familiar pattern for the prophets. Judgment is pronounced on Judah as well as several surrounding nations. After the judgment of the first two chapters, the third declares a restoration process that sounds strongly encouraging.

1 The word of the LORD which came to Zephaniah the son of Cushi, the son of Gedaliah, the son of Amariah, the son of Hezekiah, in the days of ªJosiah the son of Amon, king of Judah.

The Great Day of the LORD

2 "I will utterly consume everything
From the face of the land,"
Says the LORD;
3 "I b will consume man and beast;
I will consume the birds of the heavens,
The fish of the sea,
And the stumbling blocks* along with
the wicked.
I will cut off man from the face of the
land,"
Says the LORD.

4 "I will stretch out My hand against
Judah,
And against all the inhabitants of
Jerusalem.
I will cut off every trace of Baal from
this place,
The names of the cidolatrous priests*
with the *pagan* priests—

5 Those dwho worship the host of
heaven on the housetops;
Those who worship and swear *oaths*
by the LORD,
But who *also* swear eby Milcom;*
6 fThose who have turned back from
following the LORD,
And ghave not sought the LORD, nor
inquired of Him."

7 hBe silent in the presence of the Lord
GOD;
iFor the day of the LORD *is* at hand,
For jthe LORD has prepared a
sacrifice;
He has invited* His guests.

8 "And it shall be,
In the day of the LORD's sacrifice,
That I will punish kthe princes and the
king's children,
And all such as are clothed with
foreign apparel.

---

* **1:3** Figurative of idols   * **1:4** Hebrew *chemarim*
* **1:5** Or *Malcam,* an Ammonite god, also called
Molech (compare Leviticus 18:21)   * **1:7** Literally
set apart, consecrated

1:1 *Zephaniah* means "hidden in the Lord," a name that relates to the principal message the prophet presented (2:3). The names of the prophets were often significantly associated with the message that God gave them to present to the people.
1:2–3 *I will utterly consume everything.* The message of Zephaniah begins with a pronouncement of universal judgment (Gen. 6–8). These words not only introduce the particular judgment that would be pronounced upon Judah (v. 4), but they also speak of the final judgment that will usher in the kingdom of God on earth (Rev. 20:11–15).
1:4–6 *I will cut off every trace of Baal.* Baal worship and its evils had led to the destruction of Israel and its capital Samaria in 722 B.C. Likewise Baal worship

and its associations would lead to the destruction of Judah and its capital Jerusalem in 586 B.C.
1:7 *Be silent.* This prophetic call for silence is for solemn preparation for the horror of divine wrath (Hab. 2:20; Zech. 2:13). *sacrifice.* The people of God were expected to prepare sacrifices for the Lord as acts of contrition and celebration. But rebels, scofflaws, idolaters, and apostates would themselves become God's sacrifice.
1:8–9 *foreign apparel.* This suggests two things:

1:1 d 2 Kin. 22:1, 2   **1:3** b Hos. 4:3   **1:4** c Hos. 10:5
1:5 d 2 Kin. 23:12 e Josh. 23:7   **1:6** f Is. 1:4 g Hos. 7:7
1:7 h Zech. 2:13 i Is. 13:6 j Jer. 46:10   **1:8** k Jer. 39:6

9 In the same day I will punish
　All those who *l*leap over the threshold,*
　Who fill their masters' houses with
　　　violence and deceit.

10 "And there shall be on that day," says
　　　the LORD,
　"The sound of a mournful cry from
　　　*m*the Fish Gate,
　A wailing from the Second Quarter,
　And a loud crashing from the hills.
11 *n*Wail, you inhabitants of Maktesh!*
　For all the merchant people are cut down;
　All those who handle money are cut off.

12 "And it shall come to pass at that time
　That I will search Jerusalem with
　　　lamps,
　And punish the men
　Who are *o*settled in complacency,*
　*p*Who say in their heart,
　'The LORD will not do good,
　Nor will He do evil.'
13 Therefore their goods shall become booty,
　And their houses a desolation;
　They shall build houses, but not
　　　inhabit *them*;
　They shall plant vineyards, but *q*not
　　　drink their wine."

14 *r*The great day of the LORD *is* near;
　It is near and hastens quickly.
　The noise of the day of the LORD is bitter;
　There the mighty men shall cry out.
15 *s*That day *is* a day of wrath,
　A day of trouble and distress,
　A day of devastation and desolation,
　A day of darkness and gloominess,
　A day of clouds and thick darkness,
16 A day of *t*trumpet and alarm
　Against the fortified cities
　And against the high towers.

17 "I will bring distress upon men,
　And they shall *u*walk like blind men,
　Because they have sinned against the
　　　LORD;
　Their blood shall be poured out like
　　　dust,
　And their flesh like refuse."

18 *v*Neither their silver nor their gold

Shall be able to deliver them
In the day of the LORD's wrath;
But the whole land shall be devoured
By the fire of His jealousy,
For He will make speedy riddance
Of all those who dwell in the land.

A Call to Repentance

2 Gather*a* yourselves together, yes,
　　　gather together,
　O undesirable* nation,
2 Before the decree is issued,
　Or the day passes like chaff,
　Before the LORD's fierce anger comes
　　　upon you,
　Before the day of the LORD's anger
　　　comes upon you!
3 *b*Seek the LORD, *c*all you meek of the
　　　earth,
　Who have upheld His justice.
　Seek righteousness, seek humility.
　*d*It may be that you will be hidden
　In the day of the LORD's anger.

Judgment on Nations

4 For *e*Gaza shall be forsaken,
　And Ashkelon desolate;
　They shall drive out Ashdod *f*at
　　　noonday,
　And Ekron shall be uprooted.
5 Woe to the inhabitants of *g*the seacoast,
　The nation of the Cherethites!
　The word of the LORD *is* against you,
　O *h*Canaan, land of the Philistines:
　"I will destroy you;
　So there shall be no inhabitant."

6 The seacoast shall be pastures,
　With shelters* for shepherds *i*and folds
　　　for flocks.
7 The coast shall be for *j*the remnant of
　　　the house of Judah;
　They shall feed *their* flocks there;

---

* **1:9** Compare 1 Samuel 5:5　* **1:11** Literally *Mortar*, a market district of Jerusalem　* **1:12** Literally *on their lees*, that is, settled like the dregs of wine　* **2:1** Or *shameless*　* **2:6** Literally *excavations*, either underground huts or cisterns

---

(1) acts of greed and extortion against the populace, amassing funds for exotic clothing; and (2) participation in foreign religious rites associated with exotic clothing. ***leap over the threshold.*** This may refer to a pagan practice like the one mentioned in 1 Samuel 5:5. The priests of Dagon would not step on the doorway of the temple to Dagon because the hands and the head of Dagon had fallen there.
1:12–13 *The LORD will not do good, nor will He do evil.* The complacency of the wicked people led them to believe that God is similarly complacent. Foolishly these people believed that the Lord would be inactive, neither blessing nor cursing, neither benefiting nor punishing His people.
1:17–18 *like blind men.* God's judgment would be so sudden and so overwhelming that the survivors would be in a state of shock, stumbling around in the dark.

2:1–3 *you will be hidden.* Zephaniah used a play on words with the meaning of his own name, "hidden in the Lord." Even in the midst of the most calamitous of judgment scenes, the mercy and grace of the Lord is still available to a repentant people.
2:4–5 *Gaza . . . Ashkelon . . . Ashdod . . . Ekron.* The focus of the book moves from the description of divine judgment on Judah and Jerusalem to a description of divine judgment on the surrounding nations. The judgment begins with the nation to the west, Philistia and its major cities.

1:9 *l* 1 Sam. 5:5　**1:10** *m* 2 Chr. 33:14　**1:11** *n* James 5:1　**1:12** *o* Jer. 48:11　*p* Ps. 94:7　**1:13** *q* Deut. 28:39　**1:14** *r* Joel 2:1, 11　**1:15** *s* Is. 22:5　**1:16** *t* Jer. 4:19　**1:17** *u* Deut. 28:29　**1:18** *v* Ezek. 7:19　**2:1** *a* Joel 1:14; 2:16　**2:3** *b* Amos 5:6　*c* Ps. 76:9　*d* Amos 5:14, 15　**2:4** *e* Zech. 9:5　*f* Jer. 6:4　**2:5** *g* Ezek. 25:15–17　*h* Josh. 13:3　**2:6** *i* Is. 17:2　**2:7** *j* [Mic. 5:7, 8]

In the houses of Ashkelon they shall
lie down at evening.
For the LORD their God will [k]intervene
for them,
And [l]return their captives.

8 "I[m] have heard the reproach of Moab,
And [n]the insults of the people of Ammon,
With which they have reproached My
people,
And [o]made arrogant threats against
their borders.

9 Therefore, as I live,"
Says the LORD of hosts, the God of Israel,
"Surely [p]Moab shall be like Sodom,
And [q]the people of Ammon like
Gomorrah—
[r]Overrun with weeds and saltpits,
And a perpetual desolation.
The residue of My people shall plunder
them,
And the remnant of My people shall
possess them."

10 This they shall have [s]for their pride,
Because they have reproached and
made arrogant threats
Against the people of the LORD of hosts.

11 The LORD will be awesome to them,
For He will reduce to nothing all the
gods of the earth;
[t]People shall worship Him,
Each one from his place,
Indeed all [u]the shores of the nations.

12 "You[v] Ethiopians also,
You shall be slain by [w]My sword."

13 And He will stretch out His hand
against the north,
[x]Destroy Assyria,
And make Nineveh a desolation,
As dry as the wilderness.

14 The herds shall lie down in her midst,
[y]Every beast of the nation.
Both the [z]pelican and the bittern
Shall lodge on the capitals of her pillars;
Their voice shall sing in the windows;
Desolation shall be at the threshold;
For He will lay bare the [a]cedar work.

15 This is the rejoicing city
[b]That dwelt securely,
[c]That said in her heart,

"I am it, and there is none besides me."
How has she become a desolation,
A place for beasts to lie down!
Everyone who passes by her
[d]Shall hiss and [e]shake his fist.

The Wickedness of Jerusalem

3 Woe to her who is rebellious and
polluted,
To the oppressing city!

2 She has not obeyed His voice,
She has not received correction;
She has not trusted in the LORD,
She has not drawn near to her God.

3 [a]Her princes in her midst are roaring lions;
Her judges are [b]evening wolves
That leave not a bone till morning.

4 Her [c]prophets are insolent,
treacherous people;
Her priests have polluted the sanctuary,
They have done [d]violence to the law.

5 The LORD is righteous in her midst,
He will do no unrighteousness.
Every morning He brings His justice
to light;
He never fails,
But [e]the unjust knows no shame.

6 "I have cut off nations,
Their fortresses are devastated;
I have made their streets desolate,
With none passing by.
Their cities are destroyed;
There is no one, no inhabitant.

7 [f]I said, 'Surely you will fear Me,
You will receive instruction'—
So that her dwelling would not be cut
off,
Despite everything for which I
punished her.
But they rose early and [g]corrupted all
their deeds.

A Faithful Remnant

8 "Therefore [h]wait for Me," says the LORD,
"Until the day I rise up for plunder;*

* 3:8 Septuagint and Syriac read for witness;
Targum reads for the day of My revelation for
judgment; Vulgate reads for the day of My resurrection that is to come.

2:11 *The LORD will be awesome to them.* There may
be a double meaning in these words. For the righteous people of Judah and Jerusalem, there would be
a response of awe and wonder before God, who had
responded to the prayer of His servant. But for the
wicked there would be quite another response, one
of terror and dread. *all the shores of the nations.*
Not only would there be a righteous remnant in
Judah, there would also be people coming to God
from the nations of the earth.
2:13–15 *Their voice shall sing in the windows.* The
presence of birds in the ruins of Nineveh attests to
the severity of the destruction announced on these
people. *the rejoicing city.* The rejoicing here is ironic,
seen as an act of the city's complacency. Soon the
judgment of God would descend suddenly, and the
region would be useful only for herding animals.

3:3–4 *princes...judges...prophets...priests.* God
had designated these people to work for righteousness, but they were more wicked than the "regular"
citizens of Jerusalem. These leaders were destroying
and defrauding the weak, the needy, and the helpless.
3:8 *All My fierce anger.* God's response to the wickedness of Jerusalem was to declare His judgment.

2:7 [k] Luke 1:68 [l] Jer. 29:14   2:8 [m] Jer. 48:27 [n] Ezek.
25:3 [o] Jer. 49:1   2:9 [p] Is. 15:1–9 [q] Amos 1:13 [r] Deut.
29:23   2:10 [s] Is. 16:6   2:11 [t] Mal. 1:11 [u] Gen. 10:5
2:12 [v] Is. 18:1–7 [w] Ps. 17:13   2:13 [x] Is. 10:5–27; 14:24–27
2:14 [y] Is. 13:21 [z] Is. 14:23; 34:11 [a] Jer. 22:14   2:15 [b] Is.
47:8 [c] Rev. 18:7 [d] Lam. 2:15 [e] Nah. 3:19   3:3 [a] Ezek. 22:27
[b] Hab. 1:8   3:4 [c] Hos. 9:7 [d] Ezek. 22:26   3:5 [e] Jer. 3:3
3:7 [f] Jer. 8:6 [g] Gen. 6:12   3:8 [h] Hab. 2:3

My determination *is* to [i]gather the nations
To My assembly of kingdoms,
To pour on them My indignation,
All My fierce anger;
All the earth [j]shall be devoured
With the fire of My jealousy.

9 "For then I will restore to the peoples [k]a pure language,
That they all may call on the name of the LORD,
To serve Him with one accord.
10 [l]From beyond the rivers of Ethiopia
My worshipers,
The daughter of My dispersed ones,
Shall bring My offering.
11 In that day you shall not be shamed for any of your deeds
In which you transgress against Me;
For then I will take away from your midst
Those who [m]rejoice in your pride,
And you shall no longer be haughty
In My holy mountain.
12 I will leave in your midst
[n]A meek and humble people,
And they shall trust in the name of the LORD.
13 [o]The remnant of Israel [p]shall do no unrighteousness
[q]And speak no lies,
Nor shall a deceitful tongue be found in their mouth;
For [r]they shall feed *their* flocks and lie down,
And no one shall make *them* afraid."

Joy in God's Faithfulness

14 [s]Sing, O daughter of Zion!
Shout, O Israel!
Be glad and rejoice with all *your* heart,
O daughter of Jerusalem!
15 The LORD has taken away your judgments,
He has cast out your enemy.
[t]The King of Israel, the LORD, [u]*is* in your midst;
You shall see* disaster no more.

16 In that day [v]it shall be said to Jerusalem:
"Do not fear;
Zion, [w]let not your hands be weak.
17 The LORD your God [x]in your midst,
The Mighty One, will save;
[y]He will rejoice over you with gladness,
He will quiet *you* with His love,
He will rejoice over you with singing."

18 "I will gather those who [z]sorrow over the appointed assembly,
Who are among you,
To whom its reproach *is* a burden.
19 Behold, at that time
I will deal with all who afflict you;
I will save the [a]lame,
And gather those who were driven out;
I will appoint them for praise and fame
In every land where they were put to shame.
20 At that time [b]I will bring you back,
Even at the time I gather you;
For I will give you fame and praise
Among all the peoples of the earth,
When I return your captives before your eyes,"
Says the LORD.

* **3:15** Some Hebrew manuscripts, Septuagint, and Bomberg read *see;* Masoretic Text and Vulgate read *fear.*

He would use other nations to punish the city for its rebellion.

3:8 God's Purpose in Judgment—What we don't properly understand is that judgment should lead us to a restoration or improvement in a relationship. We live with the tension of knowing God's judgment hangs over us while at the same time knowing that forgiveness is readily available to us too. Such is the message of Zephaniah.

Judgment implies a necessary purification process. You can't get the impurities out without first identifying their presence. We want to think of ourselves as pure without going through any process of purification. We want grace without judgment, but it doesn't work that way. Judgment reflects the true state of our being, namely that we are sinful and in need of grace. Often the only way to understand our reality is to go through a judgment process.

Once the judgment is accepted and the proper response is made, we fully experience God's grace. He deals with our enemies (3:15). He quiets us with His love (3:17). He removes our burdens (3:18). God stands ready to gather us back to Himself (3:19). He restores our fortunes (3:20).

The commonly held thought that the writings of the Old Testament prophets are all gloom and doom is actually myth and misnomer. There's always hope and renewal in the prophetic message. There are always opportunities for repentance, forgiveness, and restoration. God's judgment is in fact good for us because the sin in our lives needs to be brought to light in order for us to be restored to full fellowship with God.

3:9–13 ***a pure language.*** One day human language will become a unifying element in the true worship of God. ***My worshipers.*** God's people would come from all nations to worship Him.

3:20 ***I will give you fame and praise.*** Ordinarily Scripture speaks of the praise that should be brought to God. Here we find the praise that God will bring to His people. ***Says the LORD.*** This is a solemn vow of God to do what He has promised. Zephaniah begins and ends with the strong assertion that the Lord is speaking. The implication is clear: "Listen and live!"

3:8 [i] Joel 3:2 [j] Zeph. 1:18 **3:9** [k] Is. 19:18; 57:19
3:10 [l] Ps. 68:31 **3:11** [m] Is. 2:12; 5:15 **3:12** [n] Is. 14:32
3:13 [o] [Mic. 4:7] [p] Is. 60:21 [q] Rev. 14:5 [r] Ezek. 34:13–15, 28
3:14 [s] Is. 12:6 **3:15** [t] [John 1:49] [u] Ezek. 48:35 **3:16** [v] Is. 35:3, 4 [w] Heb. 12:12 **3:17** [x] Zeph. 3:5, 15 [y] Is. 62:5; 65:19
3:18 [z] Lam. 2:6 **3:19** [a] [Mic. 4:6, 7] **3:20** [b] Is. 11:12

THE BOOK OF
HAGGAI

▶ **AUTHOR:** The authorship of the book is virtually uncontested as Haggai's name is mentioned nine times. Haggai is known only from this book and two other references to him in Ezra 5:1 and 6:14. Haggai returned from Babylon with the remnant and may well have been one of the few people who could remember the former temple before its destruction. Haggai was therefore very instrumental in the rebuilding of the temple.

▶ **TIME:** c. 520 B.C.   ▶ **KEY VERSES:** Hag. 1:7–8

▶ **THEME:** Haggai is the first of the postexilic prophets, addressing the immediate problem of the rebuilding of the temple. The people had returned about 20 years earlier, but apathy and opposition were keeping the work from being completed. Haggai's concern is that neglect of the temple is a symptom of a bigger problem. God has dropped out of the Israelites' sight as a priority. The people are more concerned with building their materialistic lifestyles than they are with their relationship with God.

The Command to Build God's House

1 In *a*the second year of King Darius, in the sixth month, on the first day of the month, the word of the LORD came by *b*Haggai the prophet to *c*Zerubbabel the son of Shealtiel, governor of Judah, and to *d*Joshua the son of *e*Jehozadak, the high priest, saying, 2"Thus speaks the LORD of hosts, saying: 'This people says, "The time has not come, the time that the LORD's house should be built." ' "

3Then the word of the LORD *f*came by Haggai the prophet, saying, 4"*Is it g*time for you yourselves to dwell in your paneled houses, and this temple* *to lie* in ruins?" 5Now therefore, thus says the LORD of hosts: *h*"Consider your ways!

6   "You have *i*sown much, and bring in little;
You eat, but do not have enough;
You drink, but you are not filled with drink;
You clothe yourselves, but no one is warm;
And *j*he who earns wages,

Earns wages *to put* into a bag with holes."

7Thus says the LORD of hosts: "Consider your ways! 8Go up to the *k*mountains and bring wood and build the temple, that I may take pleasure in it and be glorified," says the LORD. 9*l*"You looked for much, but indeed *it came to* little; and when you brought it home, *m*I blew it away. Why?" says the LORD of hosts. "Because of My house that *is in* ruins, while every one of you runs to his own house. 10Therefore *n*the heavens above you withhold the dew, and the earth withholds its fruit. 11For I *o*called for a drought on the land and the mountains, on the grain and the new wine and the oil, on whatever the ground brings forth, on men and livestock, and on *p*all the labor of *your* hands."

The People's Obedience

12*q*Then Zerubbabel the son of Shealtiel, and Joshua the son of Jehozadak, the high

---

* **1:4** Literally *house*, and so in verse 8

1:2 *The time has not come.* The people had decided that rebuilding the Lord's dwelling among His people was not important.
1:4 *your paneled houses.* Those who wanted to make their houses elaborate installed wood panels. The people of Haggai's time were making their homes elegant, rivaling royal residences and the holy temple itself. But they still did not feel that the time was right to begin working on the renewed temple. While this verse is not a blanket condemnation of elegant living among God's people, it certainly calls for a re-evaluation of priorities.

1:8 *that I may take pleasure in it.* God's joy in the temple is related to His pleasure in the people who would worship Him there. ***be glorified.*** Clearly God does not need to receive more glory (Ps. 24:7–10); however, He gladly receives the adoration of His people.

1:1 *a* Ezra 4:24 *b* Ezra 5:1; 6:14 *c* Ezra 2:2 *d* Ezra 5:2, 3 *e* 1 Chr. 6:15 **1:3** *f* Ezra 5:1 **1:4** *g* 2 Sam. 7:2 **1:5** *h* Lam. 3:40 **1:6** *i* Deut. 28:38–40 *j* Zech. 8:10 **1:8** *k* Ezra 3:7 **1:9** *l* Hag. 2:16 *m* Hag. 2:17 **1:10** *n* Deut. 28:23 **1:11** *o* 1 Kin. 17:1 *p* Hag. 2:17 **1:12** *q* Ezra 5:2

priest, with all the remnant of the people, obeyed the voice of the LORD their God, and the words of Haggai the prophet, as the LORD their God had sent him; and the people feared the presence of the LORD. 13 Then Haggai, the LORD's messenger, spoke the LORD's message to the people, saying, r"I *am* with you, says the LORD." 14 So sthe LORD stirred up the spirit of Zerubbabel the son of Shealtiel, tgovernor of Judah, and the spirit of Joshua the son of Jehozadak, the high priest, and the spirit of all the remnant of the people; uand they came and worked on the house of the LORD of hosts, their God, 15 on the twenty-fourth day of the sixth month, in the second year of King Darius.

The Coming Glory of God's House

2 In the seventh *month*, on the twenty-first of the month, the word of the LORD came by Haggai the prophet, saying: 2 "Speak now to Zerubbabel the son of Shealtiel, governor of Judah, and to Joshua the son of Jehozadak, the high priest, and to the remnant of the people, saying: 3 a 'Who is left among you who saw this temple* in its former glory? And how do you see it now? In comparison with it, bis *this* not in your eyes as nothing? 4 Yet now cbe strong, Zerubbabel,' says the LORD; 'and be strong, Joshua, son of Jehozadak, the high priest; and be strong, all you people of the land,' says the LORD, 'and work; for I *am* with you,' says the LORD of hosts. 5 d 'According *to* the word that I covenanted with you when you came out of Egypt, so eMy Spirit remains among you; do not fear!'

6 "For thus says the LORD of hosts: f 'Once more (it *is* a little while) gI will shake heaven and earth, the sea and dry land; 7 and I will shake all nations, and they shall come to hthe Desire of All Nations,* and I will fill this temple with iglory,' says the LORD of hosts. 8 'The silver *is* Mine, and the gold *is*

Mine,' says the LORD of hosts. 9 i 'The glory of this latter temple shall be greater than the former,' says the LORD of hosts. 'And in this place I will give kpeace,' says the LORD of hosts."

The People Are Defiled

10 On the twenty-fourth *day* of the ninth *month*, in the second year of Darius, the word of the LORD came by Haggai the prophet, saying, 11 "Thus says the LORD of hosts: 'Now, lask the priests concerning the law, saying, 12 "If one carries holy meat in the fold of his garment, and with the edge he touches bread or stew, wine or oil, or any food, will it become holy?" ' "

Then the priests answered and said, "No."

13 And Haggai said, "If one who is m unclean because of a dead body touches any of these, will it be unclean?"

So the priests answered and said, "It shall be unclean."

14 Then Haggai answered and said, n" 'So is this people, and so is this nation before Me,' says the LORD, 'and so is every work of their hands; and what they offer there is unclean.

Promised Blessing

15 'And now, carefully oconsider from this day forward: from before stone was laid upon stone in the temple of the LORD— 16 since those *days*, pwhen *one* came to a heap of twenty ephahs, there were *but* ten; when *one* came to the wine vat to draw out fifty baths from the press, there were *but* twenty. 17 qI struck you with blight and mildew and hail rin all the labors of your hands; syet you did not *turn* to Me,' says the LORD. 18 'Consider now from this day forward, from the twenty-fourth day

---

* **2:3** Literally *house*, and so in verses 7 and 9
* **2:7** Or *the desire of all nations*

1:13 *I am with you.* God's promise to Moses was, "I will certainly be with you" (Ex. 3:12). God's promise to the people of Judah was that the name of the Coming One would be Immanuel, meaning "God is with us" (Is. 7:14). Here God repeated the same message of comfort and encouragement.

2:3 *this temple in its former glory.* The temple of Solomon was one of the wonders of the ancient world (1 Kin. 6). The older temple would have loomed large and magnificent, far outstripping the present structure. So even though the building was completed, there may have been the sense among some of the people that it was "as nothing."

2:6 *I will shake heaven.* This is another way of speaking of the day of the Lord. The purpose of the day of the Lord is to prepare the earth for the glorious reign of Jesus Christ on earth (Matt. 24:29; Rev. 6:12–17).

2:9 *I will give peace.* Peace includes good health, well-being, and an abundant life. The term speaks of everything being as it ought to be.

2:12 *will it become holy.* Since the role of the priest

was to interpret God's law, it was reasonable that questions on holiness should be addressed to them. Haggai asked whether holiness could be transferred by contact. The answer was no.

2:13–14 *It shall be unclean.* The priests were asked if a religiously unclean person, someone who had touched a corpse, could contaminate someone else by touch. The answer was yes (Num. 19:11–13). The people had worked hard to rebuild the temple, only to be told that their worship would be unacceptable in the new temple. The existence of the temple itself guaranteed nothing. The hearts of the people had to be in harmony with the sacrifices being made.

1:13 r [Matt. 28:20]   **1:14** s Ezra 1:1 t Hag. 2:21 u Ezra 5:2, 8   **2:3** d Ezra 3:12, 13 b Zech. 4:10   **2:4** c Zech. 8:9   **2:5** d Ex. 29:45, 46 e [Neh. 9:20]   **2:6** f Heb. 12:26 g [Joel 3:16]   **2:7** h Gen. 49:10 i Is. 60:7   **2:9** j [John 1:14] k Ps. 85:8, 9   **2:11** l Mal. 2:7   **2:13** m Num. 19:11, 22   **2:14** n [Titus 1:15]   **2:15** o Hag. 1:5, 7; 2:18   **2:16** p Zech. 8:10   **2:17** q Deut. 28:22 r Hag. 1:11 s Amos 4:6–11

of the ninth month, from ^tthe day that the foundation of the LORD's temple was laid—consider it: ^{19u}Is the seed still in the barn? As yet the vine, the fig tree, the pomegranate, and the olive tree have not yielded *fruit. But* from this day I will ^vbless *you.*'"

Zerubbabel Chosen as a Signet

²⁰And again the word of the LORD came to Haggai on the twenty-fourth day of the month, saying, ²¹"Speak to Zerubbabel, ^wgovernor of Judah, saying:

^x'I will shake heaven and earth.
²² ^yI will overthrow the throne of kingdoms;

I will destroy the strength of the
 Gentile kingdoms.
^zI will overthrow the chariots
 And those who ride in them;
 The horses and their riders shall come
 down,
Every one by the sword of his
 brother.

²³'In that day,' says the LORD of hosts, 'I will take you, Zerubbabel My servant, the son of Shealtiel,' says the LORD, ^a'and will make you like a signet *ring;* for ^bI have chosen you,' says the LORD of hosts."

2:23 signet ring. This was an item of great value in the ancient world. The owner used it much like we use our personal signature on checks or other important documents. God used this imagery to indicate that Zerubbabel was in His hand, that he was highly valued, and that he represented God's authority in his leadership of the people. Even though the people had been told they were still unclean in God's eyes

(2:10–14), their leader Zerubbabel was encouraged to guide them through those spiritually trying times.

2:18 ^t Zech. 8:9   **2:19** ^u Zech. 8:12 ^v [Mal. 3:10]
2:21 ^w Zech. 4:6–10 ^x Hag. 2:6, 7   **2:22** ^y [Dan. 2:44]
^z Mic. 5:10   **2:23** ^a Song 8:6 ^b Is. 42:1; 43:10

THE BOOK OF
ZECHARIAH

▶ **AUTHOR:** The universal testimony of the Jewish and Christian tradition affirms Zechariah as the author of the entire book. Like Jeremiah and Ezekiel, he was of priestly lineage and was a young man when he was called to prophesy. According to Jewish tradition, Zechariah was a member of the Great Synagogue that collected and preserved the canon of revealed Scripture. He was born in Babylon and brought to Palestine by his grandfather when the Jewish exiles returned under Zerubbabel and Joshua the high priest.

▶ **TIME:** 520–470 B.C.   ▶ **KEY VERSE:** Zech. 9:9

▶ **THEME:** Zechariah's writings were designed to encourage the Israelites and inspire energy, identity, and vision during the rebuilding of the temple. Like Isaiah, Daniel, and Ezekiel, his prophecies are characterized by visions of God and the future. In this context, many would describe the book to be apocalyptic with similarities to Revelation. Probably more than any of the other books, Zechariah makes concrete predictions about Christ, which are fulfilled in the New Testament. He also makes some startling predictions about Israel in the end times that have already seen fulfillment.

A Call to Repentance

1 In the eighth month ᵃof the second year of Darius, the word of the LORD came ᵇto Zechariah the son of Berechiah, the son of ᶜIddo the prophet, saying, ²"The LORD has been very angry with your fathers. ³Therefore say to them, 'Thus says the LORD of hosts: "Return ᵈto Me," says the LORD of hosts, "and I will return to you," says the LORD of hosts. ⁴"Do not be like your fathers, ᵉto whom the former prophets preached, saying, 'Thus says the LORD of hosts: ᶠ"Turn now from your evil ways and your evil deeds."' But they did not hear nor heed Me," says the LORD.

5 "Your fathers, where *are* they?
   And the prophets, do they live forever?
6 Yet surely ᵍMy words and My statutes,
   Which I commanded My servants the
      prophets,
   Did they not overtake your fathers?

"So they returned and said:

ʰ'Just as the LORD of hosts determined
   to do to us,
   According to our ways and according
      to our deeds,
   So He has dealt with us.'"'"

Vision of the Horses

⁷On the twenty-fourth day of the eleventh month, which is the month Shebat, in the second year of Darius, the word of the LORD came to Zechariah the son of Berechiah, the son of Iddo the prophet, saying, ⁸I saw by night, and behold, ⁱa man riding on a red horse, and it stood among the myrtle trees in the hollow; and behind him *were* ʲhorses: red, sorrel, and white. ⁹Then I said, ᵏ"My lord, what *are* these?" So the angel who talked with me said to me, "I will show you what they *are*."

¹⁰And the man who stood among the

1:1 Zechariah. The name means "Yahweh remembers," emphasizing God's faithfulness to His covenant promises and to His people.
1:3 Return to Me. These words remind us of the depth of God's unconditional love. **says the LORD of hosts.** The personal name translated "LORD" speaks of God's gracious nature as He relates to His people (Ex. 3:14–16); the hosts are the angelic armies that await His every command.
1:5–6 fathers . . . prophets. The previous generation had been overtaken by God's judgment (Deut. 28:15–68).
1:7—6:15 the word of the LORD. This section

contains a sequence of eight night visions concerning Israel's future, followed by the symbolic crowning of the high priest Joshua. Here Zechariah pursues the same end as Haggai, rebuilding the temple as the center of worship and world rule, and as a place of pilgrimage for the nations (8:20–23).
1:8 myrtle. This was an evergreen tree that was once very common in the vicinity of Jerusalem (Neh. 8:15).

1:1 ᵃ Zech. 7:1 ᵇ Matt. 23:35 ᶜ Neh. 12:4, 16   **1:3** ᵈ [Mal. 3:7–10]   **1:4** ᵉ 2 Chr. 36:15, 16 ᶠ Is. 31:6   **1:6** ᵍ [Is. 55:11] ʰ Lam. 1:18; 2:17   **1:8** ⁱ [Rev. 6:4] ʲ [Zech. 6:2–7]   **1:9** ᵏ Zech. 4:4, 5, 13; 6:4

myrtle trees answered and said, *l*"These *are the ones* whom the LORD has sent to walk to and fro throughout the earth."

11*m*So they answered the Angel of the LORD, who stood among the myrtle trees, and said, "We have walked to and fro throughout the earth, and behold, all the earth is resting quietly."

The LORD Will Comfort Zion

12Then the Angel of the LORD answered and said, "O LORD of hosts, *n*how long will You not have mercy on Jerusalem and on the cities of Judah, against which You were angry *o*these seventy years?"

13And the LORD answered the angel who talked to me, *with* *p*good *and* comforting words. **14**So the angel who spoke with me said to me, "Proclaim, saying, 'Thus says the LORD of hosts:

"I am *q*zealous for Jerusalem
And for Zion with great zeal.
15 I am exceedingly angry with the nations at ease;
For *r*I was a little angry,
And they helped—*but* with evil *intent*."

16'Therefore thus says the LORD:

s"I am returning to Jerusalem with mercy;
My *t*house *u*shall be built in it," says the LORD of hosts,
"And *v*a *surveyor's* line shall be stretched out over Jerusalem."'

17"Again proclaim, saying, 'Thus says the LORD of hosts:

"My cities shall again spread out through prosperity;
*w*The LORD will again comfort Zion,
And *x*will again choose Jerusalem."'"

Vision of the Horns

18Then I raised my eyes and looked, and there *were* four *y*horns. **19**And I said to the angel who talked with me, "What *are* these?"

So he answered me, *z*"These *are* the horns that have scattered Judah, Israel, and Jerusalem."

20Then the LORD showed me four craftsmen. **21**And I said, "What are these coming to do?"

So he said, "These *are* the *a*horns that scattered Judah, so that no one could lift up his head; but the craftsmen* are coming to terrify them, to cast out the horns of the nations that *b*lifted up *their* horn against the land of Judah to scatter it."

Vision of the Measuring Line

2 Then I raised my eyes and looked, and behold, *a*a man with a measuring line in his hand. **2**So I said, "Where are you going?"

And he said to me, *b*"To measure Jerusalem, to see what *is* its width and what *is* its length."

3And there *was* the angel who talked with me, going out; and another angel was coming out to meet him, **4**who said to him, "Run, speak to this young man, saying: *c*'Jerusalem shall be inhabited *as* towns without walls, because of the multitude of men and livestock in it. **5**For I,' says the LORD, 'will be *d*a wall of fire all around her, *e*and I will be the glory in her midst.'"

Future Joy of Zion and Many Nations

6"Up, up! Flee *f*from the land of the north," says the LORD; "for I have *g*spread you abroad like the four winds of heaven," says the LORD. **7**"Up, Zion! *h*Escape, you who dwell with the daughter of Babylon."

8For thus says the LORD of hosts: "He sent Me after glory, to the nations which plunder you; for he who *i*touches you touches the apple of His eye. **9**For surely I will *j*shake My hand against them, and they shall become spoil for their servants. Then *k*you will know that the LORD of hosts has sent Me.

---

* **1:21** Literally *these*

1:12–13 *Angel of the LORD.* This may be a conversation between the preincarnate Jesus and the first Person of the Trinity, God the Father (Ps. 110:1–3). It is certainly an allusion to Jesus' role as Intercessor.

1:15 *I am exceedingly angry.* Here the anger of God was against the nations that He had used to punish His unrepentant people.

1:16 *line shall be stretched.* A measuring line was used to make measurements in preparation for new construction. The stretching of the line was a promise that the work would begin and that the completion of the task would follow.

1:18 *four horns.* Animal horns were often used by poets and prophets as symbols of powerful nations and their kings (Dan. 7:7–8,24). The horns that persecuted Israel and Judah included Assyria, Babylon, Medo-Persia, and later Greece.

2:4–5 *inhabited as towns without walls.* Jerusalem will have no need for defensive fortifications because

God's presence will guarantee its safety and security. These words refer ultimately to the future Jerusalem under the rule of its glorious king (Zeph. 3:15–19).

2:8–9 *the apple of His eye.* This refers to the pupil, an endearing expression suggesting how enormously important the Hebrew people are to God because of His covenant with them. Just as we protect our eyes from even the smallest particles of dust, so God protects and cares for His people.

1:10 *l* [Heb. 1:14]   **1:11** *m* [Ps. 103:20, 21]   **1:12** *n* Ps. 74:10 *o* Jer. 25:11, 12; 29:10   **1:13** *p* Jer. 29:10   **1:14** *q* Zech. 8:2   **1:15** *r* Is. 47:6   **1:16** *s* [Zech. 2:10; 8:3] *t* Ezra 6:14, 15 *u* Is. 44:28 *v* Zech. 2:1–3   **1:17** *w* [Is. 40:1, 2; 51:3] *x* Zech. 2:12   **1:18** *y* [Lam. 2:17]   **1:19** *z* Ezra 4:1, 4, 7   **1:21** *a* [Ps. 75:10] *b* Ps. 75:4, 5   **2:1** *a* Jer. 31:39   **2:2** *b* Rev. 11:1   **2:4** *c* Jer. 31:27   **2:5** *d* [Is. 26:1] *e* [Is. 60:19]   **2:6** *f* Is. 48:20 *g* Deut. 28:64   **2:7** *h* Is. 48:20   **2:8** *i* Deut. 32:10   **2:9** *j* Is. 19:16 *k* Zech. 4:9

10 l"Sing and rejoice, O daughter of Zion!
For behold, I am coming and I mwill dwell
in your midst," says the LORD. 11n"Many
nations shall be joined to the LORD oin
that day, and they shall become pMy people. And I will dwell in your midst. Then
qyou will know that the LORD of hosts has
sent Me to you. 12And the LORD will rtake
possession of Judah as His inheritance in
the Holy Land, and will again choose Jerusalem. 13sBe silent, all flesh, before the
LORD, for He is aroused tfrom His holy
habitation!"

Vision of the High Priest

3 Then he showed me aJoshua the high
priest standing before the Angel of the
LORD, and bSatan standing at his right
hand to oppose him. 2And the LORD said to
Satan, c"The LORD rebuke you, Satan! The
LORD who dhas chosen Jerusalem rebuke
you! eIs this not a brand plucked from the
fire?"

3Now Joshua was clothed with ffilthy
garments, and was standing before the
Angel.

4Then He answered and spoke to those
who stood before Him, saying, "Take away
the filthy garments from him." And to him
He said, "See, I have removed your iniquity
from you, gand I will clothe you with rich
robes."

5And I said, "Let them put a clean htur-
ban on his head."

So they put a clean turban on his head,
and they put the clothes on him. And the
Angel of the LORD stood by.

The Coming Branch

6Then the Angel of the LORD admonished Joshua, saying, 7"Thus says the LORD
of hosts:

'If you will walk in My ways,
    And if you will ikeep My command,
    Then you shall also judge My
        house,

And likewise have charge of My
        courts;
    I will give you places to walk
    Among these who kstand here.

8 'Hear, O Joshua, the high priest,
    You and your companions who sit
        before you,
    For they are la wondrous sign;
    For behold, I am bringing forth mMy
        Servant the nBRANCH.
9   For behold, the stone
    That I have laid before Joshua:
    oUpon the stone are pseven eyes.
    Behold, I will engrave its inscription,'
    Says the LORD of hosts,
    'And qI will remove the iniquity of that
        land in one day.
10 rIn that day,' says the LORD of hosts,
    'Everyone will invite his neighbor
    sUnder his vine and under his fig tree.'"

Vision of the Lampstand and Olive Trees

4 Now athe angel who talked with me
came back and wakened me, bas a man
who is wakened out of his sleep. 2And he
said to me, "What do you see?"

So I said, "I am looking, and there is ca
lampstand of solid gold with a bowl on top
of it, dand on the stand seven lamps with
seven pipes to the seven lamps. 3eTwo olive
trees are by it, one at the right of the bowl
and the other at its left." 4So I answered
and spoke to the angel who talked with me,
saying, "What are these, my lord?"

5Then the angel who talked with me answered and said to me, "Do you not know
what these are?"

And I said, "No, my lord."

6So he answered and said to me:

"This is the word of the LORD to
        fZerubbabel:
    g"Not by might nor by power, but by My
        Spirit,'
    Says the LORD of hosts.

2:12 the Holy Land. Surprisingly, this phrase occurs in the Old Testament only here. The land is "holy" because of the presence of God among His believing people.

3:1 Satan. The Hebrew is literally "the Satan," meaning "the Accuser." The picture is not unlike that of Job 1, where Satan stands before the Lord making accusations against people who follow God.

3:3 with filthy garments. The high priest represented the people before God (Ex. 28:29) and under no circumstances was he to become defiled or unclean (Ex. 28:2; Lev. 21:10–15). Joshua's garments were literally "befouled with excrement."

3:8 the BRANCH. Isaiah used this word and a similar one to describe the Messiah who will grow out of the root of the family of Jesse as a tender sprout shoots up from the ground (6:12; Is. 4:2; 11:1; 53:2). Joshua and his companions were "men wondered at" because the reinstitution of the priesthood made

public God's continuing intention to fulfill His promises to His people.

4:2–3 a lampstand of solid gold. This would remind people of the lampstand in the tabernacle and the temple.

4:6 but by My Spirit. The rebuilding of the temple, which had at last begun in earnest (Ezra 5:1–2; Hag. 1:14), would be accomplished not by human strength or resources, but by the power of God's Spirit.

2:10 l Is. 12:6 m [Lev. 26:12]   **2:11** n [Is. 2:2, 3] o Zech.
3:10 p Ex. 12:49 q Ezek. 33:33   **2:12** r [Deut. 32:9]
2:13 s Hab. 2:20 t Ps. 68:5   **3:1** d Hag. 1:1 b Ps. 109:6
3:2 c [Jude 9] d [Rom. 8:33] e Amos 4:11   **3:3** f Is. 64:6
3:4 g Is. 61:10   **3:5** h Ex. 29:6   **3:7** i Lev. 8:35 j Deut.
17:9, 12 k Zech. 3:4   **3:8** l Ps. 71:7 m Is. 42:1 n Is. 11:1;
53:2; Jer. 23:5   **3:9** o [Zech. 4:10] p Ps. 118:22 q Jer. 31:34;
50:20   **3:10** r Zech. 2:11 s Is. 36:16   **4:1** a Zech. 1:9; 2:3
b Dan. 8:18   **4:2** c Rev. 1:12 d [Rev. 4:5]   **4:3** e Rev. 11:3, 4
4:6 f Hag. 1:1 g Hos. 1:7

7 'Who *are* you, [h]O great mountain?
Before Zerubbabel *you shall become*
a plain!
And he shall bring forth [i]the capstone
[j]With shouts of "Grace, grace to it!"'"

8Moreover the word of the LORD came
to me, saying:

9 "The hands of Zerubbabel
[k]Have laid the foundation of this
temple;*
His hands [l]shall also finish *it.*
Then [m]you will know
That the [n]LORD of hosts has sent Me
to you.
10 For who has despised the day of [o]small
things?
For these seven rejoice to see
The plumb line in the hand of
Zerubbabel.
[p]They are the eyes of the LORD,
Which scan to and fro throughout the
whole earth."

11Then I answered and said to him,
"What *are* these [q]two olive trees—at the
right of the lampstand and at its left?"
12And I further answered and said to him,
"What *are these* two olive branches that
drip into the receptacles* of the two gold
pipes from which the golden *oil* drains?"
13Then he answered me and said, "Do
you not know what these *are?*"
And I said, "No, my lord."
14So he said, [r]"These *are* the two anointed ones, [s]who stand beside the Lord of the
whole earth."

Vision of the Flying Scroll

5 Then I turned and raised my eyes, and
saw there a flying [a]scroll.
2And he said to me, "What do you see?"
So I answered, "I see a flying scroll. Its
length *is* twenty cubits and its width ten
cubits."
3Then he said to me, "This *is* the [b]curse
that goes out over the face of the whole
earth: 'Every thief shall be expelled,' according *to* this side of *the scroll;* and, 'Every perjurer shall be expelled,' according
to that side of it.'

4 "I will send out *the curse*," says the
LORD of hosts;
"It shall enter the house of the [c]thief
And the house of [d]the one who swears
falsely by My name.
It shall remain in the midst of his
house
And consume [e]it, with its timber and
stones."

Vision of the Woman in a Basket

5Then the angel who talked with me
came out and said to me, "Lift your eyes
now, and see what this *is* that goes forth."
6So I asked, "What *is* it?" And he said, "It
is a basket* that is going forth."
He also said, "This *is* their resemblance
throughout the earth: 7Here *is* a lead disc
lifted up, and this *is* a woman sitting inside
the basket"; 8then he said, "This *is* Wickedness!" And he thrust her down into the
basket, and threw the lead cover* over its
mouth. 9Then I raised my eyes and looked,
and there *were* two women, coming with
the wind in their wings; for they had wings
like the wings of a [f]stork, and they lifted up
the basket between earth and heaven.
10So I said to the [g]angel who talked with
me, "Where are they carrying the basket?"
11And he said to me, "To [h]build a house
for it in [i]the land of Shinar;* when it is
ready, *the basket* will be set there on its
base."

Vision of the Four Chariots

6 Then I turned and raised my eyes and
looked, and behold, four chariots *were*
coming from between two mountains, and
the mountains *were* mountains of bronze.
2With the first chariot *were* [a]red horses,
with the second chariot [b]black horses,
3with the third chariot white horses, and
with the fourth chariot dappled horses—
strong *steeds.* 4Then I answered [c]and said
to the angel who talked with me, "What *are*
these, my lord?"

---

* **4:9** Literally *house*   * **4:12** Literally *into the
hands of*   * **5:6** Hebrew *ephah,* a measuring
container, and so elsewhere   * **5:8** Literally *stone*
* **5:11** That is, Babylon

4:7 *O great mountain.* This was a figurative reference to the great obstacles the people faced in
rebuilding the temple (Ezra 5:3–17). The setting of
the "capstone" would mark the completion of the
project. ***Grace, grace to it.*** This may be understood
as a prayer for God's favor, or as a cry of admiration
over the grace and beauty of the newly built temple.
4:11–14 *two olive trees . . . two anointed ones.*
These are identified as representatives of the religious and political offices in Israel, or of priest and
king. Many identify the two branches with the high
priest Joshua and the governor Zerubbabel.
5:4 *And consume it.* God's great love does not preclude the exercise of His judgment on those who
violate His will. The judgment upon the disobedient
would be certain and severe.

5:7–8 *This is Wickedness.* The woman sitting inside
the basket is a personification of sin.
6:1 *chariots.* In ancient times two-wheeled and
four-wheeled horse-drawn carts served as vehicles
for transportation and for warfare. The war chariots
usually had a crew of two or three men including a
driver, an archer, and a defender who used a shield to
protect the others.

4:7 [h] Jer. 51:25   [i] Ps. 118:22   [j] Ezra 3:10, 11, 13   **4:9** [k] Ezra
3:8–10; 5:16   [l] Ezra 6:14, 15   [m] Zech. 2:9, 11; 6:15   [n] [Is.
43:16]   **4:10** [o] Hag. 2:3   [p] 2 Chr. 16:9   **4:11** [q] Zech.
4:3   **4:14** [r] Rev. 11:4   [s] Zech. 3:1–7   **5:1** [a] Ezek. 2:9
5:3 [b] Mal. 4:6   **5:4** [c] Ex. 20:15   [d] Lev. 19:12   [e] Lev. 14:34, 35
5:9 [f] Lev. 11:13, 19   **5:10** [g] Zech. 5:5   **5:11** [h] Jer. 29:5, 28
[i] Gen. 10:10   **6:2** [a] Zech. 1:8   [b] Rev. 6:5   **6:4** [c] Zech. 5:10

⁵And the angel answered and said to me, ᵈ"These *are* four spirits of heaven, who go out from *their* ᵉstation before the Lord of all the earth. ⁶The one with the black horses is going to ᶠthe north country, the white are going after them, and the dappled are going toward the south country." ⁷Then the strong *steeds* went out, eager to go, that they might ᵍwalk to and fro throughout the earth. And He said, "Go, walk to and fro throughout the earth." So they walked to and fro throughout the earth. ⁸And He called to me, and spoke to me, saying, "See, those who go toward the north country have given rest to My ʰSpirit in the north country."

The Command to Crown Joshua

⁹Then the word of the LORD came to me, saying: ¹⁰"Receive *the gift* from the captives—from Heldai, Tobijah, and Jedaiah, who have come from Babylon—and go the same day and enter the house of Josiah the son of Zephaniah. ¹¹Take the silver and gold, make ⁱan elaborate crown, and set *it* on the head of ʲJoshua the son of Jehozadak, the high priest. ¹²Then speak to him, saying, 'Thus says the LORD of hosts, saying:

"Behold, ᵏthe Man whose name *is* the ˡBRANCH!
From His place He shall branch out,
ᵐAnd He shall build the temple of the LORD;
¹³ Yes, He shall build the temple of the LORD.
He ⁿshall bear the glory,
And shall sit and rule on His throne;
So ᵒHe shall be a priest on His throne,
And the counsel of peace shall be between them both."'

¹⁴"Now the elaborate crown shall be ᵖfor a memorial in the temple of the LORD for Helem,* Tobijah, Jedaiah, and Hen the son of Zephaniah. ¹⁵Even ᑫthose from afar shall come and build the temple of the LORD. Then you shall know that the LORD of hosts has sent Me to you. And *this* shall come to pass if you diligently obey the voice of the LORD your God."

Obedience Better than Fasting

7 Now in the fourth year of King Darius it came to pass *that* the word of the LORD came to Zechariah, on the fourth *day* of the ninth month, Chislev, ²when *the people** sent Sherezer,* with Regem-Melech and his men, *to* the house of God,* to pray before the LORD, ³*and* to ᵃask the priests who *were* in the house of the LORD of hosts, and the prophets, saying, "Should I weep in ᵇthe fifth month and fast as I have done for so many years?"

⁴Then the word of the LORD of hosts came to me, saying, ⁵"Say to all the people of the land, and to the priests: 'When you ᶜfasted and mourned in the fifth ᵈand seventh *months* ᵉduring those seventy years, did you really fast ᶠfor Me—for Me? ⁶ᵍWhen you eat and when you drink, do you not eat and drink *for yourselves*? ⁷*Should you* not *have obeyed* the words which the LORD proclaimed through the ʰformer prophets when Jerusalem and the cities around it were inhabited and prosperous, and ⁱthe South* and the Lowland were inhabited?'"

Disobedience Resulted in Captivity

⁸Then the word of the LORD came to Zechariah, saying, ⁹"Thus says the LORD of hosts:

ʲ'Execute true justice,
Show mercy and compassion
Everyone to his brother.
¹⁰ ᵏDo not oppress the widow or the fatherless,
The alien or the poor.
ˡLet none of you plan evil in his heart
Against his brother.'

---

* 6:14 Following Masoretic Text, Targum, and Vulgate; Syriac reads *for Heldai* (compare verse 10); Septuagint reads *for the patient ones.*
* 7:2 Literally *they* (compare verse 5) • Or *Sar-Ezer* • Hebrew *Bethel* * 7:7 Hebrew *Negev*

6:5 *four spirits of heaven.* These spirits were probably angels.
6:11 *make an elaborate crown.* This crown was to be placed on the head of Joshua the high priest.
6:12 *He shall build the temple of the LORD.* Since the restoration temple (the second temple) was already being built and would be completed by Zerubbabel (4:9), the temple referred to here may be the future temple of the messianic kingdom (Is. 2:2–4; Ezek. 40–42; Mic. 4:1–5; Hag. 2:7–9). The Messiah Himself will build it. The temple of Zerubbabel was a prophetic symbol of the temple that is still to come.
6:13 *sit and rule . . . be a priest.* In the Messiah the two offices of king and priest will be united (John 1:49; Heb. 3:1).
7:3 *the house of the LORD of hosts.* This refers to the temple in Jerusalem.
7:5–6 *did you really fast for Me.* The rhetorical question was designed to confront the people and priests with the selfish motives of their self-righteous fasting. Biblical fasting is meant to be time taken from the normal routines of preparing and eating food to express humility and dependence on God during a time of prayer. There was only one required fast in the law of Moses, the fast on the Day of Atonement (Lev. 23:27).
7:9–10 *Execute true justice.* Judicial decisions must

6:5 ᵈ [Heb. 1:7, 14] ᵉ Dan. 7:10 **6:6** ᶠ Jer. 1:14
6:7 ᵍ Zech. 1:10 **6:8** ʰ Eccl. 10:4 **6:11** ⁱ Ex. 29:6 ʲ Hag. 1:1 **6:12** ᵏ John 1:45 ˡ Zech. 3:8 ᵐ [Matt. 16:18; Eph. 2:20; Heb. 3:3] **6:13** ⁿ Is. 22:24 ᵒ Ps. 110:4; [Heb. 3:1] **6:14** ᵖ Ex. 12:14 **6:15** ᑫ Is. 57:19 **7:3** ᵃ Mal. 2:7 ᵇ Zech. 8:19 **7:5** ᶜ [Is. 58:1–9] ᵈ Jer. 41:1 ᵉ Zech. 1:12 ᶠ [Rom. 14:6] **7:6** ᵍ 1 Chr. 29:22 **7:7** ʰ Zech. 1:4 ⁱ Jer. 17:26 **7:9** ʲ Jer. 7:28 **7:10** ᵏ Ex. 22:22 ˡ Mic. 2:1

11"But they refused to heed, *m*shrugged their shoulders, and *n*stopped their ears so that they could not hear. 12Yes, they made their *o*hearts like flint, *p*refusing to hear the law and the words which the LORD of hosts had sent by His Spirit through the former prophets. *q*Thus great wrath came from the LORD of hosts. 13Therefore it happened, *that* just as He proclaimed and they would not hear, so *r*they called out and I would not listen," says the LORD of hosts. 14"But *s*I scattered them with a whirlwind among all the nations which they had not known. Thus the land became desolate after them, so that no one passed through or returned; for they made the pleasant land desolate."

Jerusalem, Holy City of the Future

8 Again the word of the LORD of hosts came, saying, 2"Thus says the LORD of hosts:

a'I am zealous for Zion with great zeal;
With great fervor I am zealous for her.'

3"Thus says the LORD:

b'I will return to Zion,
And *c*dwell in the midst of Jerusalem.
Jerusalem *d*shall be called the City of Truth,
*e*The Mountain of the LORD of hosts,
*f*The Holy Mountain.'

4"Thus says the LORD of hosts:

g"Old men and old women shall again sit
In the streets of Jerusalem,
Each one with his staff in his hand
Because of great age.
5 The streets of the city
Shall be *h*full of boys and girls
Playing in its streets.'

6"Thus says the LORD of hosts:

'If it is marvelous in the eyes of the remnant of this people in these days,
*i*Will it also be marvelous in My eyes?'
Says the LORD of hosts.

7"Thus says the LORD of hosts:

'Behold, *j*I will save My people from the land of the east
And from the land of the west;
8 I will *k*bring them *back*,
And they shall dwell in the midst of Jerusalem.
*l*They shall be My people
And I will be their God,
*m*In truth and righteousness.'

9"Thus says the LORD of hosts:

n'Let your hands be strong,
You who have been hearing in these days
These words by the mouth of *o*the prophets,
Who *spoke* in *p*the day the foundation was laid
For the house of the LORD of hosts,
That the temple might be built.
10 For before these days
There were no *q*wages for man nor any hire for beast;
There was no peace from the enemy for whoever went out or came in;
For I set all men, everyone, against his neighbor.

11*r*But now I *will* not *treat* the remnant of this people as in the former days,' says the LORD of hosts.

12 'For*s* the seed *shall be* prosperous,
The vine shall give its fruit,
*t*The ground shall give her increase,
And *u*the heavens shall give their dew—
I will cause the remnant of this people
To possess all these.
13 And it shall come to pass
That just as you were *v*a curse among the nations,
O house of Judah and house of Israel,
So I will save you, and *w*you shall be a blessing.
Do not fear,
Let your hands be strong.'

---

be made without partiality or bias. **Show mercy and compassion.** Loving commitment and concern should guide our relationships with others. **Do not oppress.** No advantage is to be taken of the helpless and less fortunate. **none of you plan evil in his heart.** Evil scheming against others is prohibited. Sacrifices and worship are of little interest to God if they are not accompanied by practical piety. Zechariah's four admonitions highlight the practical social concerns that many of the prophets emphasized (Is. 1:11–17; Hos. 6:6; Mic. 6:6–8).

8:1–3 City of Truth. This label will be valid only when the Messiah brings His righteous reign to that city. Then the land will be holy (2:12).

8:7–8 land of the east . . . land of the west. These terms together represent all parts of the earth. **My people . . . their God.** This expression occurs in the descriptions of God's covenant relationship with His people (Ex. 19:5; 29:45; Lev. 26:12; Hos. 2:23). With

these words, Zechariah anticipates a renewal of God's covenant with His people (Jer. 31:34).

8:10 no wages . . . no peace. Zechariah recounts the desperate situation in Judea before the work on the temple resumed in 520 B.C. (Hag. 1:1,6,10–11; 2:16–17).

8:11–13 Let your hands be strong. In view of God's gracious purposes and future plans for His people, they were called to be diligent in their present efforts to serve Him with sincere hearts (1 Cor. 15:58).

7:11 *m* Neh. 9:29 *n* Jer. 17:23   **7:12** *o* Ezek. 11:19 *p* Neh. 9:29, 30 *q* Dan. 9:11, 12   **7:13** *r* Prov. 1:24–28 **7:14** *s* Deut. 4:27; 28:64   **8:2** *a* Zech. 1:14   **8:3** *b* Zech. 1:16 *c* Zech. 2:10, 11 *d* Is. 1:21 *e* [Is. 2:2, 3] *f* Jer. 31:23 **8:4** *g* Is. 65:20   **8:5** *h* Jer. 30:19, 20   **8:6** *i* [Luke 1:37] **8:7** *j* Is. 11:11   **8:8** *k* Zeph. 3:20 *l* [Jer. 30:22; 31:1, 33] *m* Jer. 4:2   **8:9** *n* Hag. 2:4 *o* Ezra 5:1, 2; 6:14 *p* Hag. 2:18 **8:10** *q* Hag. 1:6, 9   **8:11** *r* Hag. 2:15–19   **8:12** *s* Joel 2:22 *t* Ps. 67:6 *u* Hag. 1:10   **8:13** *v* Jer. 42:18 *w* Gen. 12:2

14"For thus says the LORD of hosts:

x'Just as I determined to punish you
   When your fathers provoked Me to
     wrath,'
   Says the LORD of hosts,
y'And I would not relent,
15 So again in these days
   I am determined to do good
   To Jerusalem and to the house of
     Judah.
   Do not fear.
16 These *are* the things you shall ᶻdo:
  ᵃSpeak each man the truth to his
     neighbor;
   Give judgment in your gates for truth,
     justice, and peace;
17 ᵇLet none of you think evil in your*
     heart against your neighbor;
   And do not love a false oath.
   For all these *are things* that I hate,'
   Says the LORD."

18Then the word of the LORD of hosts
came to me, saying, 19"Thus says the LORD
of hosts:

c'The fast of the fourth *month,*
ᵈThe fast of the fifth,
ᵉThe fast of the seventh,
ᶠAnd the fast of the tenth,
   Shall be ᵍjoy and gladness and
     cheerful feasts
   For the house of Judah.
ʰTherefore love truth and peace.'

20"Thus says the LORD of hosts:

'Peoples shall yet come,
   Inhabitants of many cities;
21 The inhabitants of one *city* shall go to
     another, saying,
ⁱ"Let us continue to go and pray before
     the LORD,
   And seek the LORD of hosts.
   I myself will go also."
22 Yes, ʲmany peoples and strong nations
   Shall come to seek the LORD of hosts
     in Jerusalem,
   And to pray before the LORD.'

23"Thus says the LORD of hosts: 'In those
days ten men ᵏfrom every language of the
nations shall ˡgrasp the sleeve of a Jewish
man, saying, "Let us go with you, for we
have heard ᵐthat God *is* with you."'"

Israel Defended Against Enemies

9 The burden* of the word of the LORD
   Against the land of Hadrach,
   And ᵃDamascus its resting place
   (For ᵇthe eyes of men
   And all the tribes of Israel
   Are on the LORD);
2 Also *against* ᶜHamath, *which* borders
     on it,
   And *against* ᵈTyre and ᵉSidon, though
     they are very ᶠwise.

3 For Tyre built herself a tower,
   Heaped up silver like the dust,
   And gold like the mire of the streets.
4 Behold, ᵍthe Lord will cast her out;
   He will destroy ʰher power in the sea,
   And she will be devoured by fire.

5 Ashkelon shall see *it* and fear;
   Gaza also shall be very sorrowful;
   And ⁱEkron, for He dried up her
     expectation.
   The king shall perish from Gaza,
   And Ashkelon shall not be inhabited.
6 "A mixed race shall settle ʲin Ashdod,
   And I will cut off the pride of the
     ᵏPhilistines.
7 I will take away the blood from his
     mouth,
   And the abominations from between
     his teeth.
   But he who remains, even he *shall be*
     for our God,
   And shall be like a leader in Judah,
   And Ekron like a Jebusite.
8 ˡI will camp around My house
   Because of the army,
   Because of him who passes by and
     him who returns.
   No more shall an oppressor pass
     through them,
   For now I have seen with My eyes.

The Coming King

9 "Rejoice ᵐgreatly, O daughter of Zion!
   Shout, O daughter of Jerusalem!
   Behold, ⁿyour King is coming to you;
   He *is* just and having salvation,
   Lowly and riding on a donkey,
   A colt, the foal of a donkey.

---

* 8:17 Literally *his*   * 9:1 Or *oracle*

8:16–17 truth, justice, and peace. Zechariah set
forth the ethical obligations of a life of faith. He
upheld these important values and condemned evil
plans and false oaths.
8:20–23 Peoples shall yet come. Here Zechariah
announces a great turning of the nations to God.
During the messianic era, a multitude of people from
many cities will go to Jerusalem to "seek the LORD."
These Gentiles will be included among the people of
God by faith (Eph. 2:13–19).
9:1 burden. This word suggests that a weighty judgment must be declared.
**9:7 blood from his mouth . . . abominations from
between his teeth.** These phrases refer to the

cessation of unlawful and idolatrous practices (Lev.
17:14; Is. 65:4; 66:17).
9:9 Lowly and riding on a donkey. This prophecy

8:14 ˣ Jer. 31:28 ʸ [2 Chr. 36:16]   **8:16** ᶻ Zech. 7:9, 10
ᵃ [Eph. 4:25]   **8:17** ᵇ Prov. 3:29   **8:19** ᶜ Jer. 52:6 ᵈ Jer.
52:12 ᵉ 2 Kin. 25:25 ᶠ Jer. 52:4 ᵍ Esth. 8:17 ʰ Zech. 8:16
8:21 ⁱ [Is. 2:2, 3]   **8:22** ʲ Is. 60:3; 66:23   **8:23** ᵏ Is. 3:6
ˡ [Is. 45:14] ᵐ 1 Cor. 14:25   **9:1** ᵃ Is. 17:1 ᵇ Amos 1:3–5
9:2 ᶜ Jer. 49:23 ᵈ Is. 23 ᵉ 1 Kin. 17:9 ᶠ Ezek. 28:3   **9:4** ᵍ Is.
23:1 ʰ Ezek. 26:17   **9:5** ⁱ Zeph. 2:4, 5   **9:6** ʲ Amos 1:8
ᵏ Ezek. 25:15–17   **9:8** ˡ [Ps. 34:7]   **9:9** ᵐ Zech. 2:10
ⁿ [Jer. 23:5, 6]; Matt. 21:5; Mark 11:7, 9; Luke 19:35–38;
John 12:15

10 I [o]will cut off the chariot from
Ephraim
And the horse from Jerusalem;
The [p]battle bow shall be cut off.
He shall speak peace to the nations;
His dominion *shall be* [q]'from sea to sea,
And from the River to the ends of the
earth.'*

God Will Save His People

11 "As for you also,
Because of the blood of your covenant,
I will set your [r]prisoners free from the
waterless pit.
12 Return to the stronghold,
[s]You prisoners of hope.
Even today I declare
That I will restore [t]double to you.
13 For I have bent Judah, My *bow,*
Fitted the bow with Ephraim,
And raised up your sons, O Zion,
Against your sons, O Greece,
And made you like the sword of a
mighty man."

14 Then the LORD will be seen over them,
And [u]His arrow will go forth like
lightning.
The Lord GOD will blow the trumpet,
And go [v]with whirlwinds from the
south.
15 The LORD of hosts will [w]defend them;
They shall devour and subdue with
slingstones.
They shall drink *and* roar as if with
wine;
They shall be filled *with blood* like
basins,
Like the corners of the altar.
16 The LORD their God will [x]save them in
that day,
As the flock of His people.
For [y]they *shall be like* the jewels of a
crown,
[z]Lifted like a banner over His land—
17 For [a]how great is its* goodness
And how great its* [b]beauty!
[c]Grain shall make the young men
thrive,
And new wine the young women.

Restoration of Judah and Israel

10 Ask [a]the LORD for [b]rain
In [c]the time of the latter rain.*
The LORD will make flashing clouds;
He will give them showers of rain,
Grass in the field for everyone.

2 For the [d]idols* speak delusion;
The diviners envision [e]lies,
And tell false dreams;
They [f]comfort in vain.
Therefore *the people* wend their way
like [g]sheep;
They are in trouble [h]because *there is*
no shepherd.

3 "My anger is kindled against the
[i]shepherds,
[j]And I will punish the goatherds.
For the LORD of hosts [k]will visit His
flock,
The house of Judah,
And [l]will make them as His royal
horse in the battle.
4 From him comes [m]the cornerstone,
From him [n]the tent peg,
From him the battle bow,
From him every ruler* together.
5 They shall be like mighty men,
Who [o]tread down *their enemies*
In the mire of the streets in the battle.
They shall fight because the LORD is
with them,
And the riders on horses shall be put
to shame.

6 "I will strengthen the house of Judah,
And I will save the house of Joseph.
[p]I will bring them back,
Because I [q]have mercy on them.
They shall be as though I had not cast
them aside;
For I *am* the LORD their God,
And I [r]will hear them.
7 *Those of* Ephraim shall be like a
mighty man,
And their [s]heart shall rejoice as if with
wine.

***9:10** Psalm 72:8 ***9:17** Or *His* • Or *His* ***10:1** That is, spring rain ***10:2** Hebrew *teraphim* ***10:4** Or *despot*

---

was fulfilled on the day of the triumphal entry, when Jesus rode into Jerusalem on the colt of a donkey (Matt. 21:2–7). The donkey was the mount of princes (Judg. 5:10; 10:4) and kings (2 Sam. 16:1–2).

9:14 *whirlwinds from the south.* This description, patterned after God's appearance at Sinai (Ex. 19), reveals God's sovereignty and power to protect His own.

9:15 *They shall drink.* The people will be filled with drink like sacrificial basins were filled with blood, and they will be filled with meat like the corners of a sacrificial altar (Ps. 110:6).

10:2 *no shepherd.* The metaphor of *shepherd* was often used in the ancient Middle East to represent a king or ruler (Ezek. 34:6–8,23–24). Here the emphasis was on the lack of spiritual leadership.

10:3 *The house of Judah.* God will strengthen Judah so that she can overthrow the oppressors.

10:4–5 *tent peg.* A peg firmly in place suggests permanence and endurance (Is. 22:23). ***battle bow.*** This image pictures the strength necessary for military conquest (2 Kin. 13:17).

10:7 *as if with wine.* What was promised to Judah in verse 5 is here promised to Ephraim. Wine is used here as a symbol of abundant joy (Ps. 104:15; Amos 9:13; John 2:1–11).

9:10 [o] Hos. 1:7 [p] Hos. 2:18 [q] Ps. 72:8 **9:11** [r] Is. 42:7 **9:12** [s] Is. 49:9 [t] Is. 61:7 **9:14** [u] Ps. 18:14 [v] Is. 21:1 **9:15** [w] Zech. 12:8 **9:16** [x] Jer. 31:10, 11 [y] Is. 62:3 [z] Is. 11:12 **9:17** [a] [Ps. 31:19] [b] [Ps. 45:1–16] [c] Joel 3:18 **10:1** [a] [Jer. 14:22] [b] [Deut. 11:13, 14] [c] [Joel 2:23] **10:2** [d] Jer. 10:8 [e] Jer. 27:9 [f] Job 13:4 [g] Jer. 50:6, 17 [h] Ezek. 34:5–8 **10:3** [i] Jer. 25:34–36 [j] Ezek. 34:17 [k] Luke 1:68 [l] Song 1:9 **10:4** [m] Is. 28:16 [n] Is. 22:23 **10:5** [o] Ps. 18:42 **10:6** [p] Jer. 3:18 [q] Hos. 1:7 [r] Zech. 13:9 **10:7** [s] Ps. 104:15

Yes, their children shall see *it* and be
glad;
Their heart shall rejoice in the LORD.
8 I will ^twhistle for them and gather
them,
For I will redeem them;
^uAnd they shall increase as they once
increased.

9 "I^v will sow them among the peoples,
And they shall ^wremember Me in far
countries;
They shall live, together with their
children,
And they shall return.
10 ^xI will also bring them back from the
land of Egypt,
And gather them from Assyria.
I will bring them into the land of
Gilead and Lebanon,
^yUntil no *more room* is found for them.
11 ^zHe shall pass through the sea with
affliction,
And strike the waves of the sea:
All the depths of the River* shall
dry up.
Then ^athe pride of Assyria shall be
brought down,
And ^bthe scepter of Egypt shall depart.

12 "So I will strengthen them in the LORD,
And ^cthey shall walk up and down in
His name,"
Says the LORD.

Desolation of Israel

11 Open ^ayour doors, O Lebanon,
That fire may devour your cedars.
2 Wail, O cypress, for the ^bcedar has
fallen,
Because the mighty *trees* are ruined.
Wail, O oaks of Bashan,
^cFor the thick forest has come down.
3 *There is* the sound of wailing
^dshepherds!
For their glory is in ruins.
There is the sound of roaring lions!
For the pride* of the Jordan is in
ruins.

Prophecy of the Shepherds

4 Thus says the LORD my God, "Feed the
flock for slaughter, ⁵whose owners slaughter them and ^efeel no guilt; those who sell
them ^fsay, 'Blessed be the LORD, for I am
rich'; and their shepherds do ^gnot pity them.
6For I will no longer pity the inhabitants of
the land," says the LORD. "But indeed I will
give everyone into his neighbor's hand and
into the hand of his king. They shall attack
the land, and I will not deliver *them* from
their hand."

7So I fed the flock for slaughter, in particular ^hthe poor of the flock.* I took for
myself two staffs: the one I called Beauty,*
and the other I called Bonds;* and I fed the
flock. 8I dismissed the three shepherds ⁱin
one month. My soul loathed them, and their
soul also abhorred me. 9Then I said, "I will
not feed you. ^jLet what is dying die, and
what is perishing perish. Let those that are
left eat each other's flesh." 10And I took my
staff, Beauty, and cut it in two, that I might
break the covenant which I had made with
all the peoples. 11So it was broken on that
day. Thus ^kthe poor* of the flock, who were
watching me, knew that it *was* the word of
the LORD. 12Then I said to them, "If it is
agreeable to you, give *me* my wages; and if
not, refrain." So they ^lweighed out for my
wages thirty *pieces* of silver.

13And the LORD said to me, "Throw it to
the ^mpotter"—that princely price they set
on me. So I took the thirty *pieces* of silver
and threw them into the house of the LORD
for the potter. 14Then I cut in two my other
staff, Bonds, that I might break the brotherhood between Judah and Israel.

15And the LORD said to me, ⁿ"Next, take
for yourself the implements of a foolish

---

* **10:11** That is, the Nile * **11:3** Or *floodplain,
thicket* * **11:7** Following Masoretic Text, Targum,
and Vulgate; Septuagint reads *for the Canaanites.* • Or *Grace,* and so in verse 10 • Or *Unity,*
and so in verse 14 * **11:11** Following Masoretic
Text, Targum, and Vulgate; Septuagint reads *the
Canaanites.*

10:9 they shall remember Me. This phrase anticipates their turning to the Lord in repentance. **shall
live.** This implies more than mere survival. God promises spiritual life and blessing to the repentant.
10:12 I will strengthen them. The regathering will
be accomplished by God's power as He gives strength
to His people. **they shall walk up and down in His
name.** In the last days, Israel will return to the land
as a believing nation (v. 8; 12:10—13:1; Rom. 11:26).
11:7 Beauty . . . Bonds. These were the names of
Zechariah's two staffs. The images suggest that he
wanted the flock to enjoy God's favor and to experience national unity. According to Canaanite legend,
the god Baal was given the two clubs named Driver
and Chaser to battle the dark deities of the sea. It is
appropriate that God's messenger Zechariah is given
shepherd's staffs to guide the people, instead of
clubs for fighting.
11:8 three shepherds. Some have suggested that

the three shepherds represent classes of rulers in Israel: kings, priests, and prophets. Others suggest that
they refer to the last three kings of Judah or to certain
high priests of the Maccabean era.
11:12 thirty pieces of silver. Zechariah, taking the
role of the messianic shepherd, requested his wages
for service rendered. This amount was the price of a
slave. It was also the price paid to Judas for betraying
Jesus (Matt. 27:6–10).
11:15–16 take for yourself the implements of a

10:8 ^tIs. 5:26 ^uEzek. 36:37 **10:9** ^vHos. 2:23 ^wDeut.
30:1 **10:10** ^xIs. 11:11 ^yIs. 49:19, 20 **10:11** ^zIs. 11:15
^aZeph. 2:13 ^bEzek. 30:13 **10:12** ^cMic. 4:5 **11:1** ^aZech.
10:10 **11:5** ^bEzek. 31:3 ^cIs. 32:19 **11:3** ^dJer.
25:34–36 **11:5** ^e[Jer. 2:3]; 50:7 ^fHos. 12:8 ^gEzek.
34:2, 3 **11:7** ^hZeph. 3:12 **11:8** ⁱHos. 5:7 **11:9** ^jJer.
15:2 **11:11** ^kZeph. 3:12 **11:12** ^lEx. 21:32; Matt. 26:15;
27:9, 10 **11:13** ^mMatt. 27:3–10 **11:15** ⁿIs. 56:11

shepherd. ¹⁶For indeed I will raise up a shepherd in the land *who* will not care for those who are cut off, nor seek the young, nor heal those that are broken, nor feed those that still stand. But he will eat the flesh of the fat and tear their hooves in ⁰pieces.

¹⁷ "Woeᵖ to the worthless shepherd,
Who leaves the flock!
A sword *shall be* against his arm
And against his right eye;
His arm shall completely wither,
And his right eye shall be totally
    blinded."

The Coming Deliverance of Judah

12 The burden* of the word of the LORD against Israel. Thus says the LORD, ᵃwho stretches out the heavens, lays the foundation of the earth, and ᵇforms the spirit of man within him: ²"Behold, I will make Jerusalem ᶜa cup of drunkenness to all the surrounding peoples, when they lay siege against Judah and Jerusalem. ³ᵈAnd it shall happen in that day that I will make Jerusalem ᵉa very heavy stone for all peoples; all who would heave it away will surely be cut in pieces, though all nations of the earth are gathered against it. ⁴In that day," says the LORD, ᶠ"I will strike every horse with confusion, and its rider with madness; I will open My eyes on the house of Judah, and will strike every horse of the peoples with blindness. ⁵And the governors of Judah shall say in their heart, 'The inhabitants of Jerusalem *are* my strength in the LORD of hosts, their God.' ⁶In that day I will make the governors of Judah ᵍlike a firepan in the woodpile, and like a fiery torch in the sheaves; they shall devour all the surrounding peoples on the right hand and on the left, but Jerusalem shall be inhabited again in her own place—Jerusalem.

⁷"The LORD will save the tents of Judah first, so that the glory of the house of David and the glory of the inhabitants of Jerusalem shall not become greater than that of Judah. ⁸In that day the LORD will defend the inhabitants of Jerusalem; the one who is feeble among them in that day shall be like David, and the house of David *shall be* like God, like the Angel of the LORD before them. ⁹It shall be in that day *that* I will seek to ʰdestroy all the nations that come against Jerusalem.

Mourning for the Pierced One

¹⁰ⁱ"And I will pour on the house of David and on the inhabitants of Jerusalem the Spirit of grace and supplication; then they will ʲlook on Me whom they pierced. Yes, they will mourn for Him ᵏas one mourns for *his* only *son*, and grieve for Him as one grieves for a firstborn. ¹¹In that day there shall be a great ˡmourning in Jerusalem, ᵐlike the mourning at Hadad Rimmon in the plain of Megiddo.* ¹²ⁿAnd the land shall mourn, every family by itself: the family of the house of David by itself, and their wives by themselves; the family of the house of ⁰Nathan by itself, and their wives by themselves; ¹³the family of the house of Levi by itself, and their wives by themselves; the family of Shimei by itself, and their wives by themselves; ¹⁴all the families that remain, every family by itself, and their wives by themselves.

Idolatry Cut Off

13 "In that ᵃday ᵇa fountain shall be opened for the house of David and for the inhabitants of Jerusalem, for sin and for ᶜuncleanness.

²"It shall be in that day," says the LORD of hosts, "*that* I will ᵈcut off the names of the idols from the land, and they shall no longer be remembered. I will also cause ᵉthe prophets and the unclean spirit to

---

* **12:1** Or *oracle*   * **12:11** Hebrew *Megiddon*

═══════════════

foolish shepherd. This phrase means to behave like one. **eat the flesh of the fat and tear their hooves in pieces.** These phrases express the savagery of a foolish shepherd.
11:17 worthless shepherd. He will be judged. His "arm," which should have been used to protect the sheep, will wither. His "right eye," which should have watched over the sheep, will be blinded.
12:1 The burden. As in 9:1, the burden is a weighty judgment that the prophet must discharge. **heavens ... the earth ... the spirit of man.** Three phrases are used here in describing the greatness of God as Creator.
12:3 heavy stone. Jerusalem is compared to a heavy stone that brings injury to anyone who tries to remove it from its place.
12:6 Judah. Here, Judah is likened to (1) "a firepan" used to carry hot coals for the purpose of starting a fire, and (2) "a fiery torch" that could easily ignite a field of cut grain.
12:10 Spirit of grace. These words refer to the gracious working of the Holy Spirit that leads to

conviction and repentance (John 16:8–11). **supplication.** The Spirit will stimulate an attitude of repentance and prayer for God's mercy. There are many significant ministries of the Holy Spirit in the period of the Hebrew kingdom.
12:12–14 the house of David ... the house of Levi ... their wives by themselves. These words are quoted in the Talmud as an argument for separating men and women in worship. But the verse seems to indicate that each mourner will face his or her sorrow alone, without the comfort of companionship.
13:2 cut off the names of the idols. In ancient times, a person's name reflected his or her reputation.

11:16 ⁰Ezek. 34:1–10   **11:17** ᵖJer. 23:1   **12:1** ᵃIs. 42:5; 44:24 ᵇ[Is. 57:16]   **12:2** ᶜIs. 51:17   **12:3** ᵈZech. 12:4, 6, 8; 13:1 ᵉMatt. 21:44   **12:4** ᶠEzek. 38:4   **12:6** ᵍObad. 18   **12:9** ʰHag. 2:22   **12:10** ⁱ[Joel 2:28, 29] ʲJohn 19:34, 37; 20:27; [Rev. 1:7] ᵏJer. 6:26   **12:11** ˡ[Rev. 1:7] ᵐ2 Kin. 23:29   **12:12** ⁿ[Matt. 24:30] ⁰Luke 3:31   **13:1** ᵃ[Rev. 21:6, 7] ᵇ[Heb. 9:14] ᶜEzek. 36:25   **13:2** ᵈEx. 23:13 ᵉJer. 23:14, 15

depart from the land. 3It shall come to pass
that if anyone still prophesies, then his father and mother who begot him will say to
him, 'You shall [f]not live, because you have
spoken lies in the name of the LORD.' And
his father and mother who begot him [g]shall
thrust him through when he prophesies.
4"And it shall be in that day *that* [h]every
prophet will be ashamed of his vision when
he prophesies; they will not wear [i]a robe of
coarse hair to deceive. 5[j]But he will say, 'I
am no prophet, I *am* a farmer; for a man
taught me to keep cattle from my youth.'
6And *one* will say to him, 'What are these
wounds between your arms?'* Then he will
answer, '*Those* with which I was wounded
in the house of my friends.'

The Shepherd Savior

7 "Awake, O sword, against [k]My Shepherd,
Against the Man [l]who is My Companion,"
Says the LORD of hosts.
[m]"Strike the Shepherd,
And the sheep will be scattered;
Then I will turn My hand against [n]the little ones.
8 And it shall come to pass in all the land,"
Says the LORD,
"*That* [o]two-thirds in it shall be cut off *and* die,
[p]But *one*-third shall be left in it:
9 I will bring the *one*-third [q]through the fire,
Will [r]refine them as silver is refined,
And test them as gold is tested.
[s]They will call on My name,
And I will answer them.
[t]I will say, 'This *is* My people';
And each one will say, 'The LORD *is* my God.'"

The Day of the LORD

14 Behold, [a]the day of the LORD is coming,
And your spoil will be divided in your midst.
2 For [b]I will gather all the nations to battle against Jerusalem;
The city shall be taken,
The houses rifled,
And the women ravished.
Half of the city shall go into captivity,
But the remnant of the people shall not be cut off from the city.

3 Then the LORD will go forth
And fight against those nations,
As He fights in the day of battle.
4 And in that day His feet will stand [c]on the Mount of Olives,
Which faces Jerusalem on the east.
And the Mount of Olives shall be split in two,
From east to west,
[d]*Making* a very large valley;
Half of the mountain shall move toward the north
And half of it toward the south.

5 Then you shall flee *through* My mountain valley,
For the mountain valley shall reach to Azal.
Yes, you shall flee
As you fled from the [e]earthquake
In the days of Uzziah king of Judah.

[f]Thus the LORD my God will come,
And [g]all the saints with You.*

6 It shall come to pass in that day
That there will be no light;
The lights will diminish.
7 It shall be one day
[h]Which is known to the LORD—
Neither day nor night.
But at [i]evening time it shall happen
That it will be light.

* **13:6** Or *hands* * **14:5** Or *you;* Septuagint, Targum, and Vulgate read *Him.*

Zechariah anticipated the complete removal of the reputation and acknowledgment of false gods.
13:4 ***a robe of coarse hair.*** This was the traditional clothing of a prophet. False prophets will deny that they are prophets for fear of punishment, and will refuse to wear one (2 Kin. 1:8; Matt. 3:4).
13:6 ***wounds between your arms.*** This is probably a reference to the profession of an ecstatic prophet who slashed himself on the back or breast. Self-inflicted wounds were thought to gain the attention and blessing of the gods (1 Kin. 18:28). Under questioning, the man declares that the wounds were received from friends so that he will not be found out as a false prophet and be put to death (v. 3).
13:7 ***O sword.*** The sword, an instrument of death, is likened to a warrior being roused for action. The Lord commands the sword to strike the Messiah. ***My Shepherd.*** This clearly indicates that the death of Jesus was not accident, but was divinely determined.
13:9 ***refine them.*** The smelting pot uses intense heat to separate the dross from pure metal. ***test them.*** Once refined, precious metal must be analyzed to determine its value.
14:4 ***Mount of Olives.*** This is located east of Jerusalem and the Kidron valley; it is a north-south hill about 2,700 feet in elevation. The Messiah will return to the Mount of Olives, the very mountain from which He will have ascended after His time on earth (Acts 1:10–11). On the day of Messiah's return, the mount will be split by a deep east-west valley.

13:3 [f]Deut. 18:20 [g]Deut. 13:6–11 **13:4** [h][Mic. 3:6, 7] [i]2 Kin. 1:8 **13:5** [j]Amos 7:14 **13:7** [k]Is. 40:11 [l][John 10:30] [m]Matt. 26:31, 56, 67; Mark 14:27; 1 Pet. 5:4; Rev. 7:16, 17 [n]Luke 12:32 **13:8** [o]Ezek. 5:2, 4, 12 [p][Rom. 11:5] **13:9** [q]Is. 48:10 [r]1 Pet. 1:6, 7 [s]Ps. 50:15 [t]Hos. 2:23 **14:1** [a][Is. 13:6, 9] **14:2** [b]Zech. 12:2, 3 **14:4** [c]Ezek. 11:23 [d]Joel 3:12 **14:5** [e]Amos 1:1 [f]Matt. 24:30, 31; 25:31 [g]Joel 3:11 **14:7** [h]Matt. 24:36 [i]Is. 30:26

8 And in that day it shall be
  That living *j*waters shall flow from
    Jerusalem,
  Half of them toward the eastern sea
  And half of them toward the western
    sea;
  In both summer and winter it shall
    occur.
9 And the LORD shall be *k*King over all
    the earth.
  In that day it shall be—
  l"The LORD *is* one,"*
  And His name one.

10All the land shall be turned into a plain from Geba to Rimmon south of Jerusalem. *Jerusalem** shall be raised up and *m*inhabited in her place from Benjamin's Gate to the place of the First Gate and the Corner Gate, *n*and *from* the Tower of Hananel to the king's winepresses.

11 *The people* shall dwell in it;
  And *o*no longer shall there be utter
    destruction,
  *p*But Jerusalem shall be safely
    inhabited.

12And this shall be the plague with which the LORD will strike all the people who fought against Jerusalem:

  Their flesh shall dissolve while they
    stand on their feet,
  Their eyes shall dissolve in their
    sockets,
  And their tongues shall dissolve in
    their mouths.
13 It shall come to pass in that day
  That *q*a great panic from the LORD will
    be among them.
  Everyone will seize the hand of his
    neighbor,
  And raise *r*his hand against his
    neighbor's hand;
14 Judah also will fight at
    Jerusalem.

*s*And the wealth of all the surrounding
    nations
  Shall be gathered together:
  Gold, silver, and apparel in great
    abundance.
15 *t*Such also shall be the plague
  On the horse *and* the mule,
  On the camel and the donkey,
  And on all the cattle that will be in
    those camps.
  So *shall* this plague *be*.

The Nations Worship the King

16And it shall come to pass *that* everyone who is left of all the nations which came against Jerusalem shall *u*go up from year to year to *v*worship the King, the LORD of hosts, and to keep *w*the Feast of Tabernacles. 17*x*And it shall be *that* whichever of the families of the earth do not come up to Jerusalem to worship the King, the LORD of hosts, on them there will be no rain. 18If the family of *y*Egypt will not come up and enter in, *z*they *shall have* no rain; they shall receive the plague with which the LORD strikes the nations who do not come up to keep the Feast of Tabernacles. 19This shall be the punishment of Egypt and the punishment of all the nations that do not come up to keep the Feast of Tabernacles.

20In that day *a*"HOLINESS TO THE LORD" shall be *engraved* on the bells of the horses. The *b*pots in the LORD's house shall be like the bowls before the altar. 21Yes, every pot in Jerusalem and Judah shall be holiness to the LORD of hosts.* Everyone who sacrifices shall come and take them and cook in them. In that day there shall no longer be a *c*Canaanite *d*in the house of the LORD of hosts.

---

* **14:9** Compare Deuteronomy 6:4 * **14:10** Literally *She* * **14:21** Or *on every pot ... shall be (engraved)* "HOLINESS TO THE LORD OF HOSTS"

14:8 *living waters.* This term describes running water from a spring or river, in contrast to the stale and stagnant water of a cistern (Jer. 2:13). The water will flow from Jerusalem toward the eastern sea (the Dead Sea) and the western sea (the Mediterranean). In contrast with the seasonal streams that flow only during the rainy season, these streams will irrigate the land in both summer and winter.
14:11 *shall be safely inhabited.* This is a contrast to the time of Nehemiah when the population of Jerusalem was sparse (Neh. 7:4; 11:1). In the Lord's coming kingdom, the city will be inhabited and its citizens secure.
14:18–19 *Egypt.* In this passage, Egypt is used as an example of the nations that are unwilling to come to Jerusalem to worship King Messiah and celebrate the feast. It will be subject to divine judgment because it was a traditional enemy of Israel.
14:20–21 *HOLINESS TO THE LORD.* These words will be inscribed on the gold headband worn by the high priest (Ex. 28:36). Holiness will so permeate Messiah's kingdom that even the lowly cooking pots will be holy. The name "Canaanite" here refers to the merchants who frequented Jerusalem and the temple courts with their wares (Neh. 13:19–22; Matt. 21:12; John 2:14). None will profiteer in the worship of God in the coming age. God's search for true worshipers will be realized in the company of devoted, holy people.

14:8 *j* Ezek. 47:1–12 **14:9** *k* [Rev. 11:15] *l* Deut. 6:4 **14:10** *m* Zech. 12:6 *n* Jer. 31:38 **14:11** *o* Jer. 31:40 *p* Jer. 23:6 **14:13** *q* 1 Sam. 14:15, 20 *r* Judg. 7:22 **14:14** *s* Ezek. 39:10, 17 **14:15** *t* Zech. 14:12 **14:16** *u* [Is. 2:2, 3; 60:6–9; 66:18–21] *v* Is. 27:13 *w* Lev. 23:34–44 **14:17** *x* Is. 60:12 **14:18** *y* Is. 19:21 *z* Deut. 11:10 **14:20** *a* Is. 23:18 *b* Ezek. 46:20 **14:21** *c* Is. 35:8 *d* [Eph. 2:19–22]

THE BOOK OF
MALACHI

▶ **AUTHOR:** The only Old Testament mention of Malachi is in 1:1. Nothing else is known of Malachi, not even his father's name. But tradition holds that he too, like Zechariah, was a member of the Great Synagogue. He is generally accepted as the author of this book. It is likely that Malachi proclaimed his message when Nehemiah was absent from Judah between 432 B.C. and 425 B.C., almost a century after Haggai and Zechariah began to prophesy. Thus, because of its place in history and the Old Testament, Malachi is a transitional book. Its primary themes are consistent with the rest of the Old Testament, but it also serves as a precursor to the New Testament.

▶ **TIME:** c. 432–425 B.C.   ▶ **KEY VERSE:** Mal. 2:17

▶ **THEME:** In Malachi, the days of political upheaval are past, and the country is living in an uneventful waiting period. The people are waiting for Messiah to bring the glorious restoration of their nation to the renewed prominence of the Davidic and Solomonic period. There is a sense the people are losing touch with God during this rather uneventful time. The old problem with idol worship is gone, but other problems have taken its place. Malachi's role is to call the people back to a genuine, enduring faith in God. His dominant admonition is for a personal relationship with the living God, who seeks men to walk with Him (2:6).

---

1 The burden* of the word of the LORD to Israel by Malachi.

Israel Beloved of God

2 "I[a] have loved you," says the LORD.
"Yet you say, 'In what way have You loved us?'
Was not Esau Jacob's brother?"
Says the LORD.
"Yet [b]Jacob I have loved;
3 But Esau I have hated,
And [c]laid waste his mountains and his heritage
For the jackals of the wilderness."

4 Even though Edom has said,
"We have been impoverished,
But we will return and build the desolate places,"

Thus says the LORD of hosts:

"They may build, but I will [d]throw down;

They shall be called the Territory of Wickedness,
And the people against whom the LORD will have indignation forever.
5 Your eyes shall see,
And you shall say,
[e]'The LORD is magnified beyond the border of Israel.'

Polluted Offerings

6 "A son [f]honors *his* father,
And a servant *his* master.
[g]If then I am the Father,
Where *is* My honor?
And if I *am* a Master,
Where *is* My reverence?
Says the LORD of hosts
To you priests who despise My name.
[h]Yet you say, 'In what way have we despised Your name?'

---

* **1:1** Or *oracle*

1:1 to Israel. In the postexilic period, the use of the word Israel for the people of Judah expresses the hope that the Lord was in the process of reasserting the fullness of His original promises to His people. The name "Malachi" means "My messenger."
1:3 *Esau I have hated.* The contrast between the words *love* and *hate* here and in verse 2 seems too strong. But on many occasions in the Old Testament, the verb *hate* has the basic meaning "not to choose." God's love for Jacob was expressed in His electing grace in extending His covenant to Jacob and to his descendants (Gen. 25:21–26; Is. 44:1–5). In His

sovereign purpose, God set His love on the one and not the other. The term *hate* may carry the idea of indifference as well.
1:6 *A son honors his father.* Here the Lord uses truisms: A father and a master can expect honor from those beneath them, but God was not receiving the honor due Him. ***If then I am the Father.*** The image

---

1:2 [a] Deut. 4:37; 7:8; 23:5   [b] Rom. 9:13   **1:3** [c] Jer. 49:18
1:4 [d] Jer. 49:16–18   **1:5** [e] Ps. 35:27   **1:6** [f] [Ex. 20:12]
[g] Luke 6:46 [h] Mal. 2:14

7 "You offer ⁱdefiled food on My altar,
But say,
'In what way have we defiled You?'
By saying,
ʲ'The table of the LORD is contemptible.'
8 And ᵏwhen you offer the blind as a
sacrifice,
Is it not evil?
And when you offer the lame and sick,
Is it not evil?
Offer it then to your governor!
Would he be pleased with you?
Would he ˡaccept you favorably?"
Says the LORD of hosts.

9 "But now entreat God's favor,
That He may be gracious to us.
ᵐ*While* this is being *done* by your hands,
Will He accept you favorably?"
Says the LORD of hosts.
10 "Who *is there* even among you who
would shut the doors,
ⁿSo that you would not kindle fire *on*
My altar in vain?
I have no pleasure in you,"
Says the LORD of hosts,
ᵒ"Nor will I accept an offering from your
hands.
11 For ᵖfrom the rising of the sun, even to
its going down,
My name *shall be* great ᑫamong the
Gentiles;
ʳIn every place ˢincense *shall be* offered
to My name,
And a pure offering;
ᵗFor My name shall be great among the
nations,"
Says the LORD of hosts.
12 "But you profane it,
In that you say,
ᵘ'The table of the LORD* is defiled;
And its fruit, its food, *is* contemptible.'
13 You also say,
'Oh, what a ᵛweariness!'
And you sneer at it,"
Says the LORD of hosts.
"And you bring the stolen, the lame,
and the sick;

Thus you bring an offering!
ʷShould I accept this from your hand?"
Says the LORD.
14 "But cursed *be* ˣthe deceiver
Who has in his flock a male,
And takes a vow,
But sacrifices to the Lord ʸwhat is
blemished—
For ᶻI *am* a great King,"
Says the LORD of hosts,
"And My name *is to be* feared among
the nations.

Corrupt Priests

2 "And now, O ᵃpriests, this
commandment is for you.
2 ᵇIf you will not hear,
And if you will not take *it* to heart,
To give glory to My name,"
Says the LORD of hosts,
"I will send a curse upon you,
And I will curse your blessings.
Yes, I have cursed them ᶜalready,
Because you do not take *it* to heart.

3 "Behold, I will rebuke your descendants
And spread ᵈrefuse on your faces,
The refuse of your solemn feasts;
And *one* will ᵉtake you away with it.
4 Then you shall know that I have sent
this commandment to you,
That My covenant with Levi may
continue,"
Says the LORD of hosts.
5 "My ᶠcovenant was with him, *one* of life
and peace,
And I gave them to him ᵍ*that he might
fear Me*;
So he feared Me
And was reverent before My name.
6 ʰThe law of truth* was in his mouth,
And injustice was not found on his lips.
He walked with Me in peace and
equity,
And ⁱturned many away from iniquity.

---

* **1:12** Following Bomberg; Masoretic Text reads
Lord. * **2:6** Or *true instruction*

---

of God as Father is common in the New Testament,
but less frequent in the Old Testament (Is. 63:16; 64:8).
1:8 *the blind . . . lame and sick.* The demands of the
holy worship of God had been made clear in the law.
Only the very best should be presented as an offering to the Lord (Lev. 1:3); no one was to come with an
offering that was blemished or unclean (Lev. 7:19–21).
1:11 *great among the Gentiles.* God would one day
receive praise from all the nations. Even the despised
Gentiles would offer praise, while God's own people
were profaning His holy name (Ps. 87; 117).
1:14 *I am a great King.* The reputation of the Lord
among His people was to have been the means
whereby all the nations would be drawn to worship
Him as well.
2:2 *I will send a curse.* At the passage of the people
into the Promised Land, the Levites spread before the
people the blessings of obedience and the curses on
disobedience (Deut. 27; 28). But the priests were not

obeying the law that they were supposed to uphold.
They would therefore receive the curses.
2:3 *refuse.* This was the refuse in the sacrificed animal that should have been removed when the animal
was prepared for sacrifice to the Lord.
2:6 *The law of truth.* The priests of the Old Testament period had a twofold responsibility: they were
to represent the people in holy worship before the
living God, and they were to teach and apply God's
law to the people. ***in peace and equity.*** This refers to
complete moral virtue in all things before the Lord.

1:7 ⁱDeut. 15:21 ʲEzek. 41:22 **1:8** ᵏLev. 22:22 ˡ[Job
42:8] **1:9** ᵐHos. 13:9 **1:10** ⁿ1 Cor. 9:13 ᵒIs. 1:11
1:11 ᵖIs. 59:19 ᑫIs. 60:3, 5 ʳ1 Tim. 2:8 ˢRev. 8:3 ᵗIs.
66:18, 19 **1:12** ᵘMal. 1:7 **1:13** ᵛIs. 43:22 ʷLev. 22:20
1:14 ˣMal. 1:8 ʸLev. 22:18–20 ᶻPs. 47:2 **2:1** ᵃMal. 1:6
2:2 ᵇ[Deut. 28:15] ᶜMal. 3:9 **2:3** ᵈEx. 29:14 ᵉ1 Kin.
14:10 **2:5** ᶠNum. 25:12 ᵍDeut. 33:9 **2:6** ʰDeut. 33:10
ⁱJer. 23:22

7 "For[j] the lips of a priest should keep
   knowledge,
  And *people* should seek the law from
   his mouth;
  [k]For he is the messenger of the Lord
   of hosts.
8 But you have departed from the way;
  You [l]have caused many to stumble at
   the law.
  [m]You have corrupted the covenant of
   Levi,"
  Says the Lord of hosts.
9 "Therefore [n]I also have made you
   contemptible and base
  Before all the people,
  Because you have not kept My ways
  But have shown [o]partiality in the law."

Treachery of Infidelity

10 [p]Have we not all one Father?
  [q]Has not one God created us?
  Why do we deal treacherously with
   one another
  By profaning the covenant of the fathers?
11 Judah has dealt treacherously,
  And an abomination has been committed
   in Israel and in Jerusalem,
  For Judah has [r]profaned
  The Lord's holy *institution* which He
   loves:

He has married the daughter of a
   foreign god.
12 May the Lord cut off from the tents of
   Jacob
  The man who does this, being awake
   and aware,*
  Yet [s]who brings an offering to the
   Lord of hosts!

13 And this is the second thing you do:
  You cover the altar of the Lord with
   tears,
  With weeping and crying;
  So He does not regard the offering
   anymore,
  Nor receive *it* with goodwill from your
   hands.
14 Yet you say, "For what reason?"
  Because the Lord has been witness
  Between you and [t]the wife of your
   youth,
  With whom you have dealt
   treacherously;
  [u]Yet she is your companion
  And your wife by covenant.
15 But [v]did He not make *them* one,
  Having a remnant of the Spirit?
  And why one?

---

* **2:12** Talmud and Vulgate read *teacher and student.*

2:7 *messenger.* In the Old Testaments, prophets were commonly called messengers. But apparently this is the only time in the Old Testament that priests are specifically called the messengers of the Lord (3:1).

2:10 God the Father of All—The Fatherhood of God applies in a general sense to everyone since all men and women are created by God in His image. God is the Father of the human race. Several Scriptures speak of God as "the Father of spirits" (Heb. 12:9; Num. 16:22; Eccl. 12:7). Paul even agrees with a heathen poet that all men are God's offspring (Acts 17:28). James 3:9 says that men have been made in God's image.

God is also the Father of all as sustainer of life. Every person is an object of His fatherly care (Matt. 18:10) and a candidate for His Kingdom (Luke 18:16). Furthermore, God is not willing that any should perish (Matt. 18:14; 1 Tim. 2:4). Even when men and women reject God He still provides for them as He does believers with rain, fruitful seasons, food, and gladness (Matt. 5:45; Acts 14:17).

2:11 the Lord's holy institution which He loves. The text presents the ideas of affection and revulsion which we usually think of in the verbs *to love* and *to hate*. Marriage is something God loves; divorce is something He hates (v. 16). The Lord's people had polluted something in which God takes great pleasure.

2:13 the second thing you do. The prophets at times spoke of the compounding sins of the people (Jer. 2:13). Here, tears seem to be judged as hypocritical acts of insincere repentance (Is. 1:10–15).

2:14 what reason. The feigned surprise of the people fooled no one, certainly not the Lord. *witness.* There are some whose witness may be challenged, but the Lord is not among them (3:5). **wife of your youth.** These men had not only married pagan wives, but they had divorced their first wives to make room for their new ones.

2:15–16 God and Marriage—While couples make the marriage covenant with each other, God is a party in the relationship too. He owns us and makes us one, all at the same time. Going back to Genesis 2:24, He designed man and woman for each other; to be in relationship with each other, out of His wisdom for what was best for them. This design was the culminating action in the creation process. Out of it was to be the future of this race, this species that God created to rule with Him. Marriage is not just an institution for couples, but for society and God. In marriage we fulfill God's plan for the universe. God not only made the couple one, in a way He made Himself one with the couple too. It grieves Him when we cannot or will not follow through with our part of this covenant.

The best way to carry on the faith is through children of functioning covenant marriages. This only confirms what all the statistics are increasingly telling us. When divorce rates started soaring in the mid-twentieth century, many thought children were resilient and handling the dissolution of their families well. Current studies, years later, indicate children of these divorces have significantly greater problems coping with life when compared with children from intact families. While there is enormous complexity involved in a marriage relationship, nothing about it is more important in making it work than the commitment to maintain it.

2:15 a remnant of the Spirit. This somewhat difficult phrase most likely indicates the work of God's Holy Spirit in the life of the married couple. God has joined

2:7 [j] Deut. 17:8–11 [k] [Gal. 4:14] **2:8** [l] Jer. 18:15 [m] Neh. 13:29 **2:9** [n] 1 Sam. 2:30 [o] Deut. 1:17 **2:10** [p] 1 Cor. 8:6 [q] Job 31:15 **2:11** [r] Ezra 9:1, 2 **2:12** [s] Neh. 13:29 **2:14** [t] Mal. 3:5 [u] Prov. 2:17 **2:15** [v] Matt. 19:4, 5

He seeks [w]godly offspring.
Therefore take heed to your spirit,
And let none deal treacherously with
the wife of his youth.

16 "For [x]the LORD God of Israel says
That He hates divorce,
For it covers one's garment with violence,"
Says the LORD of hosts.
"Therefore take heed to your spirit,
That you do not deal treacherously."

17 [y]You have wearied the LORD with your
words;
Yet you say,
"In what way have we wearied *Him?*"
In that you say,
[z]"Everyone who does evil
Is good in the sight of the LORD,
And He delights in them,"
Or, "Where *is* the God of justice?"

The Coming Messenger

3 "Behold, [a]I send My messenger,
And he will [b]prepare the way
before Me.
And the Lord, whom you seek,
Will suddenly come to His temple,
[c]Even the Messenger of the covenant,
In whom you delight.
Behold, [d]He is coming,"
Says the LORD of hosts.

2 "But who can endure [e]the day of His
coming?
And [f]who can stand when He appears?
For [g]He *is* like a refiner's fire
And like launderers' soap.
3 [h]He will sit as a refiner and a purifier of
silver;
He will purify the sons of Levi,
And purge them as gold and silver,
That they may [i]offer to the LORD
An offering in righteousness.

4 "Then [j]the offering of Judah and
Jerusalem
Will be pleasant to the LORD,
As in the days of old,
As in former years.
5 And I will come near you for judgment;
I will be a swift witness
Against sorcerers,
Against adulterers,
[k]Against perjurers,
Against those who [l]exploit wage earners
and [m]widows and orphans,
And against those who turn away an
alien—
Because they do not fear Me,"
Says the LORD of hosts.

6 "For I *am* the LORD, [n]I do not change;
[o]Therefore you are not consumed,
O sons of Jacob.
7 Yet from the days of [p]your fathers
You have gone away from My ordinances
And have not kept *them.*
[q]Return to Me, and I will return to you,"
Says the LORD of hosts.
[r]"But you said,
'In what way shall we return?'

Do Not Rob God

8 "Will a man rob God?
Yet you have robbed Me!
But you say,
'In what way have we robbed You?'
[s]In tithes and offerings.
9 You are cursed with a curse,
For you have robbed Me,
Even this whole nation.
10 [t]Bring all the tithes into the
[u]storehouse,
That there may be food in My house,
And try Me now in this,"
Says the LORD of hosts,
"If I will not open for you the [v]windows
of heaven
And [w]pour out for you *such* blessing
That *there will* not *be room* enough *to
receive it.*

11 "And I will rebuke [x]the devourer for
your sakes,

---

them, and by His Spirit He has worked on their behalf to strengthen them.

2:16 ***treacherously.*** To the Lord, attitudes of indifference to marriage vows and duties are the actions of a traitor.

2:17 ***You have wearied the LORD.*** God is wearied by people who do not submit to Him but who argue their points against His revelation. When justice comes, they will be sorry they asked (3:5).

3:1 ***Messenger of the covenant.*** This is a messianic title, referring to the One who will initiate the new covenant (Jer. 31:33–34; Matt. 26:28; Heb. 12:24). ***He is coming.*** As in Psalm 96:13, this dramatic wording indicates something that was just about to occur. However, it would be 400 years before these words would be fulfilled.

3:2 ***like a refiner's fire and like launderer's soap.*** These two images are vivid illustrations of the purifying process. The Savior King Himself will sift all people to prepare for His reign.

3:3 ***purify the sons of Levi.*** Since the priests had come under such strong censure in this book (1:6—2:9), and since the prophet himself was likely a priest, these words would have had a special significance for him.

3:6 ***For I am the LORD, I do not change.*** We might expect these opening words to ensure the nation's doom. Instead, they give assurance of God's continuing mercy.

3:8 ***tithes.*** These were gifts to the Lord that the law required. There were three: two that were annual and one that came every three years. The tithe supported the priests and Levites, and also widows, orphans, and foreigners (Deut. 14:28–29).

2:15 [w] [1 Cor. 7:14] **2:16** [x] [Matt. 5:31; 19:6–8] **2:17** [y] Is. 43:22, 24 [z] Is. 5:20 **3:1** [a] Matt. 11:10; Mark 1:2; Luke 1:76; 7:27; John 1:23; 2:14, 15 [b] [Is. 40:3] [c] Is. 63:9 [d] Hag. 2:7 **3:2** [e] [Mal. 4:1] [f] Rev. 6:17 [g] [Matt. 3:10–12] **3:3** [h] Is. 1:25 [i] [1 Pet. 2:5] **3:4** [j] Mal. 1:11 **3:5** [k] Zech. 5:4 [l] James 5:4 [m] Ex. 22:22 **3:6** [n] [Rom. 11:29] [o] [Lam. 3:22] **3:7** [p] Acts 7:51 [q] Zech. 1:3 [r] Mal. 1:6 **3:8** [s] Neh. 13:10–12 **3:10** [t] Prov. 3:9, 10 [u] 1 Chr. 26:20 [v] Gen. 7:11 [w] 2 Chr. 31:10 **3:11** [x] Amos 4:9

So that he will not destroy the fruit of
    your ground,
Nor shall the vine fail to bear fruit for
    you in the field,"
Says the LORD of hosts;
12 "And all nations will call you blessed,
For you will be *y*a delightful land,"
Says the LORD of hosts.

The People Complain Harshly

13 "Your*z* words have been harsh against Me,"
Says the LORD,
"Yet you say,
'What have we spoken against You?'
14 *a*You have said,
'It is useless to serve God;
What profit *is it* that we have kept His
    ordinance,
And that we have walked as mourners
Before the LORD of hosts?
15 So now *b*we call the proud blessed,
For those who do wickedness are
    raised up;
They even *c*tempt God and go free.'"

A Book of Remembrance

16 Then those *d*who feared the LORD
    *e*spoke to one another,
And the LORD listened and heard *them;*
So *f*a book of remembrance was
    written before Him
For those who fear the LORD
And who meditate on His name.

17 "They*g* shall be Mine," says the LORD of
    hosts,
"On the day that I make them My *h*jewels.*
And *i*I will spare them
As a man spares his own son who
    serves him."
18 *j*Then you shall again discern
Between the righteous and the wicked,

Between one who serves God
And one who does not serve Him.

The Great Day of God

4 "For behold, *a*the day is coming,
Burning like an oven,
And all *b*the proud, yes, all who do
    wickedly will be *c*stubble.
And the day which is coming shall
    burn them up,"
Says the LORD of hosts,
"That will *d*leave them neither root nor
    branch.
2 But to you who *e*fear My name
The *f*Sun of Righteousness shall arise
With healing in His wings;
And you shall go out
And grow fat like stall-fed calves.
3 *g*You shall trample the wicked,
For they shall be ashes under the soles
    of your feet
On the day that I do *this*,"
Says the LORD of hosts.

4 "Remember the *h*Law of Moses, My
    servant,
Which I commanded him in Horeb for
    all Israel,
*With i*the statutes and judgments.
5 Behold, I will send you *j*Elijah the
    prophet
*k*Before the coming of the great and
    dreadful day of the LORD.
6 And *l*he will turn
The hearts of the fathers to the
    children,
And the hearts of the children to their
    fathers,
Lest I come and *m*strike the earth with
    *n*a curse."

---

* 3:17 Literally *special treasure*

3:12 *all nations.* One of the ways in which other countries would be drawn to the worship of the Lord was by seeing how the people of Israel fared with the Lord as their God. ***a delightful land.*** The adjective indicates enjoyment, life that is genuinely pleasurable (1:10).

3:14 *What profit.* The people secretly entertained doubts about the value of following the Lord. In fact, they had not really "kept His ordinance." The proper attitude is encouraged in Malachi 4:4.

3:16 *a book of remembrance.* God never forgets His promises. God teaches us to remember and value the good that people do (Phil. 4:8); He does the same as He commands us.

3:17 *They shall be Mine.* These words are exciting because we can sense in them the pride God has in His children.

3:18 *one who serves God.* Serving God means putting Him first, obeying His commands, and finding one's chief joy in life the advancement of the glory of His name.

4:2 *With healing in His wings.* The prophet compares the Savior to a bird whose comforting wings bring healing to the chicks that gather underneath (Ps. 91:1–4).

4:5 *Elijah the prophet.* There are three ways in which

this prophecy might be fulfilled: (1) John the Baptist, whom Malachi had already prophesied (3:1), was the first to fill the promise of the Elijah figure. John, like Elijah, was a minister of the Lord calling the people to repent and prepare for the coming of the Messiah (Matt. 11:14). (2) Elijah appeared in person along with Moses at the transfiguration (Matt. 17:1–8). (3) An Elijah-like figure will appear at the end times; he will call fire down from heaven just as Elijah did (1 Kin. 18:36; Rev. 11:1–7).

4:6 *fathers to the children . . . children to their fathers.* Malachi ends with a promise and a warning. As in every act of God announcing judgment, there is also an offer of His mercy (Jon. 4:2). ***a curse.*** The term is one of the harshest in Scripture. The Hebrew word suggests complete annihilation. This is the term translated "accursed" in the account of the destruction of Jericho (Josh. 6).

3:12 *y* Dan. 8:9   3:13 *z* Mal. 2:17   3:14 *a* Job 21:14
3:15 *b* Ps. 73:12   *c* Ps. 95:9   3:16 *d* Ps. 66:16 *e* Heb.
3:13 *f* Ps. 56:8   3:17 *g* Ex. 19:5 *h* Is. 62:3 *i* Ps. 103:13
3:18 *j* [Ps. 58:11] 4:1 *a* [2 Pet. 3:7] *b* Mal. 3:18 *c* Obad.
18 *d* Amos 2:9 4:2 *e* Mal. 3:16 *f* Luke 1:78 4:3 *g* Mic.
7:10 4:4 *h* Ex. 20:3 *i* Deut. 4:10 4:5 *j* [Matt. 11:14;
17:10–13; Mark 9:11–13; Luke 1:17]; John 1:21 *k* Joel 2:31
4:6 *l* Zech. 1:17 *m* Zech. 14:12 *n* Zech. 5:3

THE
NEW TESTAMENT

The Words of Christ in Red

THE GOSPEL ACCORDING TO
MATTHEW

▶ **AUTHOR:** The early church uniformly attributed this Gospel to Matthew, and no tradition to the contrary ever emerged. This book was known early and accepted quickly. Matthew occupied the unpopular post of tax collector in Capernaum for the Roman government, and as a result he was no doubt disliked by his Jewish countrymen. He was chosen as one of the twelve apostles, and the last appearance of his name in the Bible is in Acts 1:13. Matthew's life from that point on is veiled in tradition.

▶ **TIME:** C. 4 B.C.–A.D. 33   ▶ **KEY VERSES:** Matt. 16:16–19

▶ **THEME:** Matthew is typically described as the story of Jesus written by a Jew for Jewish people. In this context it contains the most references to Jewish culture and the Old Testament of the Gospels. The author's main purpose seems to be proving to his Jewish readers that Jesus is their Messiah. Matthew is also the fullest systematic account of Christ's teachings. These five "blocks" of teaching are one of the key differences with the other Gospels: Chapters 5–7, The Sermon on the Mount; chapter 10, The Mission Charge; chapter 13, The Parables of the Kingdom; chapter 18, The Church; chapters 23–25, Judgment and the End of the Age.

The Genealogy of Jesus Christ

1 The book of the ^{a}genealogy of Jesus Christ, ^{b}the Son of David, ^{c}the Son of Abraham:

^{2d}Abraham begot Isaac, ^{e}Isaac begot Jacob, and Jacob begot ^{f}Judah and his brothers. ^{3g}Judah begot Perez and Zerah by Tamar, ^{h}Perez begot Hezron, and Hezron begot Ram. ^{4}Ram begot Amminadab, Amminadab begot Nahshon, and Nahshon begot Salmon. ^{5}Salmon begot ^{i}Boaz by Rahab, Boaz begot Obed by Ruth, Obed begot Jesse, ^{6}and ^{j}Jesse begot David the king.

^{k}David the king begot Solomon by her *who had been the wife** of Uriah. ^{7l}Solomon begot Rehoboam, Rehoboam begot ^{m}Abijah, and Abijah begot Asa.* ^{8}Asa begot ^{n}Jehoshaphat, Jehoshaphat begot Joram, and Joram begot ^{o}Uzziah. ^{9}Uzziah begot Jotham, Jotham begot ^{p}Ahaz, and

Ahaz begot Hezekiah. ^{10a}Hezekiah begot Manasseh, Manasseh begot Amon,* and Amon begot ^{r}Josiah. ^{11s}Josiah begot Jeconiah and his brothers about the time they were ^{t}carried away to Babylon.

^{12}And after they were brought to Babylon, ^{u}Jeconiah begot Shealtiel, and Shealtiel begot ^{v}Zerubbabel. ^{13}Zerubbabel begot Abiud, Abiud begot Eliakim, and Eliakim begot Azor. ^{14}Azor begot Zadok, Zadok begot Achim, and Achim begot Eliud. ^{15}Eliud begot Eleazar, Eleazar begot Matthan, and Matthan begot Jacob. ^{16}And Jacob begot Joseph the husband of ^{w}Mary, of whom was born Jesus who is called Christ.

---

* **1:6** Words in italic type have been added for clarity. They are not found in the original Greek.
* **1:7** NU-Text reads *Asaph*.   * **1:10** NU-Text reads *Amos*.

1:1 genealogy. Jesus' genealogy is crucial to His claim to be the Messiah, as it traces the lineage of Joseph, His recognized father, back to Abraham through David. It shows that from a legal standpoint, Jesus is qualified to rule from the throne of David.
1:3 Tamar. The mention of women in a Jewish genealogy is unusual. But in addition to Mary, four women are listed in this catalogue of names: Tamar , who was involved in a scandal with Judah (Gen. 38); Rahab, the Canaanite harlot of Jericho (Josh. 2:1–21); Ruth, who was not an Israelite, but a Moabite (Ruth 1:4); and Bathsheba, the wife of Uriah, who committed adultery with David (2 Sam. 11:1–5). At the beginning of his Gospel, Matthew shows how God's grace forgives the darkest of sins and reaches beyond the nation of

Israel to the world. He also points out that God can lift the lowest and place them in royal lineage.
1:16 the husband of Mary. Matthew was careful not to identify Jesus as the physical son of Joseph. The Greek pronoun translated "of whom" is feminine and refers to Mary. **called Christ.** The words "Messiah"

1:1 ^{a} Luke 3:23 ^{b} John 7:42 ^{c} Gen. 12:3; 22:18   **1:2** ^{d} Gen. 21:2, 12 ^{e} Gen. 25:26; 28:14 ^{f} Gen. 29:35   **1:3** ^{g} Gen. 38:27; 49:10 ^{h} Ruth 4:18–22   **1:5** ^{i} Ruth 2:1; 4:1–13   **1:6** ^{j} 1 Sam. 16:1 ^{k} 2 Sam. 7:12; 12:24   **1:7** ^{l} 1 Chr. 3:10 ^{m} 2 Chr. 11:20   **1:8** ^{n} 1 Chr. 3:10 ^{o} 2 Kin. 15:13   **1:9** ^{p} 2 Kin. 15:38   **1:10** ^{q} 2 Kin. 20:21 ^{r} 1 Kin. 13:2   **1:11** ^{s} 1 Chr. 3:15, 16 ^{t} 2 Kin. 24:14–16   **1:12** ^{u} 1 Chr. 3:17 ^{v} Ezra 3:2   **1:16** ^{w} Matt. 13:55

¹⁷So all the generations from Abraham to David *are* fourteen generations, from David until the captivity in Babylon *are* fourteen generations, and from the captivity in Babylon until the Christ *are* fourteen generations.

Christ Born of Mary

¹⁸Now the ^xbirth of Jesus Christ was as follows: After His mother Mary was betrothed to Joseph, before they came together, she was found with child ^yof the Holy Spirit. ¹⁹Then Joseph her husband, being a just *man*, and not wanting ^zto make her a public example, was minded to put her away secretly. ²⁰But while he thought about these things, behold, an angel of the Lord appeared to him in a dream, saying, "Joseph, son of David, do not be afraid to take to you Mary your wife, ^afor that which is conceived in her is of the Holy Spirit. ^{21b}And she will bring forth a Son, and you shall call His name JESUS, ^cfor He will save His people from their sins." ²²So all this was done that it might be fulfilled which was spoken by the Lord through the prophet, saying: ^{23d}*"Behold, the virgin shall be with child, and bear a Son, and they shall call His name Immanuel,"** which is translated, "God with us."

²⁴Then Joseph, being aroused from sleep, did as the angel of the Lord commanded him and took to him his wife, ²⁵and did not know her till she had brought forth ^eher firstborn Son.* And he called His name JESUS.

Wise Men from the East

2 Now after ^aJesus was born in Bethlehem of Judea in the days of Herod the king, behold, wise men ^bfrom the East came to Jerusalem, ²saying, ^c"Where is He who has been born King of the Jews? For we have seen ^dHis star in the East and have come to worship Him."

³When Herod the king heard *this*, he was troubled, and all Jerusalem with him. ⁴And when he had gathered all ^ethe chief priests and ^fscribes of the people together, ^ghe inquired of them where the Christ was to be born.

⁵So they said to him, "In Bethlehem of Judea, for thus it is written by the prophet:

⁶ 'But^h you, Bethlehem, in the land of
         Judah,
     Are not the least among the rulers of
         Judah;
     For out of you shall come a Ruler
   ⁱ Who will shepherd My people Israel.'"*

⁷Then Herod, when he had secretly called the wise men, determined from them what time the ^jstar appeared. ⁸And he sent them to Bethlehem and said, "Go and search carefully for the young Child, and when you have found *Him*, bring back word to me, that I may come and worship Him also."

⁹When they heard the king, they departed; and behold, the star which they had seen in the East went before them, till it came and stood over where the young Child was. ¹⁰When they saw the star, they rejoiced with exceedingly great joy. ¹¹And when they had come into the house, they saw the young Child with Mary His mother, and fell down and worshiped Him. And when they had opened their treasures, ^kthey presented gifts to Him: gold, frankincense, and myrrh.

---

* **1:23** Isaiah 7:14. Words in oblique type in the New Testament are quoted from the Old Testament. * **1:25** NU-Text reads *a Son*. * **2:6** Micah 5:2

(from the Hebrew) and "Christ" (from the Greek) both mean "Anointed One."

1:17 Abraham . . . until the Christ. The genealogy is broken down into three groups of names with 14 generations in each list. A basic covenant is set forth in each period: the Abrahamic covenant, the Davidic covenant, and the new covenant.

1:18 betrothed. In Jewish culture, this covenant was made about a year before the marriage. Engagement was understood to be as binding as a marriage covenant, therefore a legal divorce was required to withdraw from the agreement.

1:23 Behold . . . Immanuel. The angel's message to Joseph indicated that Mary would fulfill the prophecy of Isaiah (Is. 7:14). "Jesus," the Greek form of "Joshua," means "salvation."

1:25 did not know her till. The clear implication is that Mary was a virgin only until the birth of Jesus. The brothers and sisters of Jesus (13:55–56) were probably younger siblings born to Joseph and Mary after Jesus' birth. Joseph could not have had children by a previous marriage, as some suppose, for then Jesus would not have been heir to the Davidic throne as the oldest son of Joseph.

2:1 wise men from the East. These "wise men" would have been of the same class as the "wise men" of Babylon over whom Daniel was made ruler (Dan. 2:48). **to Jerusalem.** Contrary to popular belief, the events of chapter two probably took place some months after Jesus' birth. Herod murdered all the male children age two and under, going by the time the wise men said the star had appeared (and probably leaving a significant margin for error). In addition, it would have been strange for Mary and Joseph to offer the sacrifice of the poor (see Lev. 12:8; Luke 2:24) if the wise men had just given them rich gifts.

2:7 Then Herod. This is Herod the Great, who reigned over Palestine for over thirty years. A crafty ruler and lavish builder, Herod had a reign marked by cruelty and bloodshed.

1:18 ^xLuke 1:27 ^yLuke 1:35   **1:19** ^zDeut. 24:1
1:20 ^aLuke 1:35   **1:21** ^bLuke 1:31; 2:21 ^cJohn 1:29
1:23 ^dIs. 7:14   **1:25** ^eLuke 2:7, 21   **2:1** ^aMic. 5:2;
Luke 2:4 ^bGen. 25:6   **2:2** ^cLuke 2:11 ^d[Num. 24:17]
2:4 ^e2 Chr. 36:14 ^f2 Chr. 34:13 ^gMal. 2:7   **2:6** ^hMic. 5:2
ⁱ[Rev. 2:27]   **2:7** ^jNum. 24:17   **2:11** ^kIs. 60:6

[12]Then, being divinely warned [l]in a dream that they should not return to Herod, they departed for their own country another way.

The Flight into Egypt

[13]Now when they had departed, behold, an angel of the Lord appeared to Joseph in a dream, saying, "Arise, take the young Child and His mother, flee to Egypt, and stay there until I bring you word; for Herod will seek the young Child to destroy Him."

[14]When he arose, he took the young Child and His mother by night and departed for Egypt, [15]and was there until the death of Herod, that it might be fulfilled which was spoken by the Lord through the prophet, saying, [m]"Out of Egypt I called My Son."*

Massacre of the Innocents

[16]Then Herod, when he saw that he was deceived by the wise men, was exceedingly angry; and he sent forth and put to death all the male children who were in Bethlehem and in all its districts, from two years old and under, according to the time which he had determined from the wise men. [17]Then was fulfilled what was spoken by Jeremiah the prophet, saying:

[18] "A [n]voice was heard in Ramah,
    Lamentation, weeping, and great
        mourning,
    Rachel weeping for her children,
    Refusing to be comforted,
    Because they are no more."*

The Home in Nazareth

[19]Now when Herod was dead, behold, an angel of the Lord appeared in a dream to Joseph in Egypt, [20]osaying, "Arise, take the young Child and His mother, and go to the land of Israel, for those who [p]sought the young Child's life are dead." [21]Then he arose, took the young Child and His mother, and came into the land of Israel.

[22]But when he heard that Archelaus was reigning over Judea instead of his father Herod, he was afraid to go there. And being warned by God in a [q]dream, he turned aside [r]into the region of Galilee. [23]And he came and dwelt in a city called [s]Nazareth, that it might be fulfilled [t]which was spoken by the prophets, "He shall be called a Nazarene."

John the Baptist Prepares the Way

3 In those days [a]John the Baptist came preaching [b]in the wilderness of Judea, [2]and saying, "Repent, for [c]the kingdom of heaven is at hand!" [3]For this is he who was spoken of by the prophet Isaiah, saying:

[d]"The voice of one crying in the
        wilderness:
    [e]'Prepare the way of the LORD;
    Make His paths straight.'"*

[4]Now [f]John himself was clothed in camel's hair, with a leather belt around his waist; and his food was [g]locusts and [h]wild honey. [5][i]Then Jerusalem, all Judea, and all the region around the Jordan went out to him [6][j]and were baptized by him in the Jordan, confessing their sins.

[7]But when he saw many of the Pharisees and Sadducees coming to his baptism, he said to them, [k]"Brood of vipers! Who warned you to flee from [l]the wrath to come? [8]Therefore bear fruits worthy of repentance, [9]and do not think to say to yourselves, [m]'We have Abraham as our father.' For I say to you that God is able to raise

---

* **2:15** Hosea 11:1   * **2:18** Jeremiah 31:15
* **3:3** Isaiah 40:3

2:15 might be fulfilled. The prophecy quoted here, from Hosea 11:1, refers to the nation of Israel as God's son coming out of Egypt in the Exodus. Jesus is the genuine Son of God, and, as Israel's Messiah, is the true Israel (John 15:1); therefore He gives fuller meaning to the prophecy of Hosea.

2:18 Rachel weeping for her children. This prophecy comes from Jeremiah 31:15, in which Rachel, entombed near Bethlehem some 13 centuries before the Babylonian captivity, is seen weeping for her children as they are led away in 586 B.C. In the slaughter of the male infants at the time of Christ's birth, Rachel is again seen weeping for the violent loss of her sons.

2:23 Nazareth. Those who lived in Nazareth were looked down upon (John 1:46). Perhaps God chose this place for His Son to emphasize His humanness.

3:2 Repent. The Greek verb translated "repent" indicates a change of attitude. The basic idea is a recognition of sin and a reversal of thinking which changes one's life.

3:3 Prepare the way of the LORD. As roads were smoothed and straightened for the arrival of a king, so John was preparing a spiritual path for the Messiah. The quotation is from Isaiah 40:3.

3:7 Pharisees and Sadducees. The Pharisees and Sadducees were two prominent groups in Judaism at the time of Christ. The groups differed considerably in their beliefs. The Pharisees based their beliefs not only on the law of Moses, but also on a large body of oral tradition. They were devout and zealous, concerned with outward righteousness. The Sadducees were associated with a priestly caste, and in doctrine they held primarily to the first five books of Moses. They did not believe in the resurrection of the dead, and did not adhere to all the detailed laws of the Pharisees. Formerly enemies, the two groups seemed to unite against a common enemy: the long awaited Messiah.

2:12 [l]Matt. 1:20   **2:15** [m]Hos. 11:1   **2:18** [n]Jer. 31:15   **2:20** [o]Luke 2:39   [p]Matt. 2:16   **2:22** [q]Matt. 2:12, 13, 19   [r]Luke 2:39   **2:23** [s]John 1:45, 46   [t]Judg. 13:5   **3:1** [a]Mark 1:3–8   [b]Josh. 14:10   **3:2** [c]Dan. 2:44   **3:3** [d]Is. 40:3   [e]Luke 1:76   **3:4** [f]Mark 1:6   [g]Lev. 11:22   [h]1 Sam. 14:25, 26   **3:5** [i]Mark 1:5   **3:6** [j]Acts 19:4, 18   **3:7** [k]Matt. 12:34   [l][1 Thess. 1:10]   **3:9** [m]John 8:33

up children to Abraham from these stones. [10]And even now the ax is laid to the root of the trees. [n]Therefore every tree which does not bear good fruit is cut down and thrown into the fire. [11]oI indeed baptize you with water unto repentance, but He who is coming after me is mightier than I, whose sandals I am not worthy to carry. [p]He will baptize you with the Holy Spirit and fire.* [12]qHis winnowing fan *is* in His hand, and He will thoroughly clean out His threshing floor, and gather His wheat into the barn; but He will [r]burn up the chaff with unquenchable fire."

John Baptizes Jesus

[13]sThen Jesus came [t]from Galilee to John at the Jordan to be baptized by him. [14]And John *tried to* prevent Him, saying, "I need to be baptized by You, and are You coming to me?"

[15]But Jesus answered and said to him, "Permit *it to be so* now, for thus it is fitting for us to fulfill all righteousness." Then he allowed Him.

[16]uWhen He had been baptized, Jesus came up immediately from the water; and behold, the heavens were opened to Him, and He* saw [v]the Spirit of God descending like a dove and alighting upon Him. [17]wAnd suddenly a voice *came* from heaven, saying, [x]"This is My beloved Son, in whom I am well pleased."

Satan Tempts Jesus

4 Then [a]Jesus was led up by [b]the Spirit into the wilderness to be tempted by the devil. [2]And when He had fasted forty days and forty nights, afterward He was hungry. [3]Now when the tempter came to Him, he said, "If You are the Son of God, command that these stones become bread."

[4]But He answered and said, "It is written, [c]'Man shall not live by bread alone, but by every word that proceeds from the mouth of God.' "*

[5]Then the devil took Him up [d]into the holy city, set Him on the pinnacle of the temple, [6]and said to Him, "If You are the Son of God, throw Yourself down. For it is written:

[e]'He shall give His angels charge over you,'

and,

[f]'In their hands they shall bear you up, Lest you dash your foot against a stone.' "*

[7]Jesus said to him, "It is written again, [g]'You shall not tempt the LORD your God.' "*

[8]Again, the devil took Him up on an exceedingly high mountain, and [h]showed Him all the kingdoms of the world and their glory. [9]And he said to Him, "All these things I will give You if You will fall down and worship me."

[10]Then Jesus said to him, "Away with you,* Satan! For it is written, [i]'You shall worship the LORD your God, and Him only you shall serve.' "*

[11]Then the devil [j]left Him, and behold, [k]angels came and ministered to Him.

---

* **3:11** M-Text omits *and fire.* * **3:16** Or *he*
* **4:4** Deuteronomy 8:3 * **4:6** Psalm 91:11, 12
* **4:7** Deuteronomy 6:16 * **4:10** M-Text reads *Get behind Me.* • Deuteronomy 6:13

3:11 baptize. Sometimes fire has connotations of judgment in Scripture, but here the fire of God's Spirit represents the transforming power of His grace and love. The baptism of all Jesus' disciples with water is an outward sign of the inward work of the Holy Spirit. It is the symbol of obedience to the command to believe in Christ's saving work of grace on the cross.
3:15 to fulfill all righteousness. This phrase does not suggest that Jesus came for baptism because He had sinned; the Lord Jesus was without sin (2 Cor. 5:21; Heb. 4:15). His baptism probably served several purposes. By being baptized, He confirmed the ministry of John and fulfilled the Father's will.
3:17 God, the Father of Christ—Most Christians eventually wonder how God may be called the Father of Christ, and Christ the Son of God. First, one must recognize that God is spirit (John 4:24), and Christ was the Son of God before He assumed a human body in Bethlehem (John 3:16; Gal. 4:4). Passages which use terms implying physical origin must be taken in a figurative sense (Heb. 1:5). Second, the title expresses a sonship relationship, unique from that of His disciples (John 20:17). He was begotten of God unlike anyone else (John 1:14; 3:16). The Nicene council in the fourth century used the phrase "very God of very God; begotten, not made, being of one substance with the Father" to describe this unique relationship. Third, the title describes equality with God. When Jesus claimed to be "one" with the Father, He was speaking of a unity of "substance" with the Father and thus equality in all the attributes of deity (John 10:30). The Jews understood this claim, because they took up stones to stone Him, protesting that "You . . . make Yourself God" (John 10:33). Fourth, the title emphasizes Christ's role as the revealer of God. He alone possesses the knowledge of the Father (John 14:6–9; 1 John 1:2), and He is the sole mediator of that knowledge (1 Tim. 2:5). Therefore, no one can know the Father except through the Son (John 14:6).
4:1–4 It is written. Satan did not lead Jesus into the place of temptation, the Holy Spirit did. Perhaps part of the reason for this was to show us how to deal with temptation. Jesus quoted the Word of God, showing the power of Scripture in battling with the evil one.
4:10 Satan. Satan is not dispatched easily by anyone who merely says, "Go." The only way we can be victorious in temptation is through the blood and authority of Jesus Christ.

3:10 [n] Matt. 7:19   **3:11** [o] Luke 3:16 [p] [Acts 2:3, 4]
3:12 [q] Mal. 3:3 [r] Matt. 13:30   **3:13** [s] Mark 1:9–11
[t] Matt. 2:22   **3:16** [u] Mark 1:10 [v] [Is. 11:2]; John 1:32
3:17 [w] John 12:28 [x] Ps. 2:7   **4:1** [a] Mark 1:12 [b] Ezek. 3:14
4:4 [c] Deut. 8:3   **4:5** [d] Neh. 11:1, 18   **4:6** [e] Ps. 91:11
[f] Ps. 91:12   **4:7** [g] Deut. 6:16   **4:8** [h] [1 John 2:15–17]
4:10 [i] Deut. 6:13; 10:20   **4:11** [j] [James 4:7] [k] [Heb. 1:14]

Jesus Begins His Galilean Ministry

12*l*Now when Jesus heard that John had been put in prison, He departed to Galilee. 13And leaving Nazareth, He came and dwelt in Capernaum, which is by the sea, in the regions of Zebulun and Naphtali, 14that it might be fulfilled which was spoken by Isaiah the prophet, saying:

15 "The*m* land of Zebulun and the land of
Naphtali,
By the way of the sea, beyond the
Jordan,
Galilee of the Gentiles:
16 *n*The people who sat in darkness have
seen a great light,
And upon those who sat in the region
and shadow of death
Light has dawned."*

17*o*From that time Jesus began to preach and to say, *p*"Repent, for the kingdom of heaven is at hand."

Four Fishermen Called as Disciples

18*q*And Jesus, walking by the Sea of Galilee, saw two brothers, Simon *r*called Peter, and Andrew his brother, casting a net into the sea; for they were fishermen. 19Then He said to them, "Follow Me, and *s*I will make you fishers of men." 20*t*They immediately left *their* nets and followed Him.

21*u*Going on from there, He saw two other brothers, James *the son* of Zebedee, and John his brother, in the boat with Zebedee their father, mending their nets. He called them, 22and immediately they left the boat and their father, and followed Him.

Jesus Heals a Great Multitude

23And Jesus went about all Galilee, *v*teaching in their synagogues, preaching *w*the gospel of the kingdom, *x*and healing all kinds of sickness and all kinds of disease among the people. 24Then His fame went throughout all Syria; and they *y*brought to Him all sick people who were afflicted with various diseases and torments, and

those who were demon-possessed, epileptics, and paralytics; and He healed them. 25*z*Great multitudes followed Him—from Galilee, and *from* Decapolis, Jerusalem, Judea, and beyond the Jordan.

The Beatitudes

5 And seeing the multitudes, *a*He went up on a mountain, and when He was seated His disciples came to Him. 2Then He opened His mouth and *b*taught them, saying:

3 "Blessed*c* *are* the poor in spirit,
For theirs is the kingdom of heaven.
4 *d*Blessed *are* those who mourn,
For they shall be comforted.
5 *e*Blessed *are* the meek,
For *f*they shall inherit the earth.
6 Blessed *are* those who *g*hunger and
thirst for righteousness,
*h*For they shall be filled.
7 Blessed *are* the merciful,
*i*For they shall obtain mercy.
8 *j*Blessed *are* the pure in heart,
For *k*they shall see God.
9 Blessed *are* the peacemakers,
For they shall be called sons of God.
10 *l*Blessed *are* those who are persecuted
for righteousness' sake,
For theirs is the kingdom of heaven.

11*m*"Blessed are you when they revile and persecute you, and say all kinds of *n*evil against you falsely for My sake. 12*o*Rejoice and be exceedingly glad, for great *is* your reward in heaven, for *p*so they persecuted the prophets who were before you.

Believers Are Salt and Light

13"You are the salt of the earth; *q*but if the salt loses its flavor, how shall it be seasoned? It is then good for nothing but to be thrown out and trampled underfoot by men.

14*r*"You are the light of the world. A city

---

* 4:16 Isaiah 9:1, 2

4:15–16 *great light.* The passage quoted here (Is. 9:1–2) foretells the reign of the Messiah in the coming kingdom.

4:18–20 *I will make you fishers of men.* This allusion to Jeremiah 16:16 was used to call Peter and Andrew to a life of ministry.

4:23 *teaching . . . preaching . . . healing.* These words summarize Jesus' early ministry.

5:2 *He . . . taught them.* The Sermon on the Mount wasn't given as the way of salvation for the lost, but as the way of life for the children of the kingdom. It was instruction for those who had responded to Jesus' invitation to repent.

5:3–12 The Beatitudes—In the Sermon on the Mount, Christ succinctly describes the basic character traits of those who will inherit the kingdom. The word *kingdom* usually implies someone who is on top, who rules and has authority over others. They are the privileged. In God's kingdom the people are not

privileged because they are on top but because, by being on the bottom, they are in a better position to receive God's grace and favor. These characteristics are the reverse of what man generally values in the world. "Blessed" can also be translated as "Happy." The signs of being blessed aren't power or material wealth. The sign of being blessed is receiving the benefits of God's grace.

4:12 *l* John 4:43   **4:15** *m* Is. 9:1, 2   **4:16** *n* Luke 2:32
4:17 *o* Matt. 1:14, 15 *p* Matt. 3:2; 10:7   **4:18** *q* Mark
1:16–20 *r* John 1:40–42   **4:19** *s* Luke 5:10   **4:20** *t* Mark
10:28   **4:21** *u* Mark 1:19   **4:23** *v* Matt. 9:35 *w* [Matt.
24:14] *x* Mark 1:34   **4:24** *y* Luke 4:40   **4:25** *z* Mark
3:7, 8   **5:1** *a* Mark 3:13   **5:2** *b* [Matt. 7:29]   **5:3** *c* Luke
6:20–23   **5:4** *d* Rev. 21:4   **5:5** *e* Ps. 37:11 *f* [Rom. 4:13]
5:6 *g* Luke 1:53 *h* [Is. 55:1; 65:13]   **5:7** *i* Ps. 41:1   **5:8** *j* Ps.
15:2; 24:4 *k* 1 Cor. 13:12   **5:10** *l* 1 Pet. 3:14   **5:11** *m* Luke
6:22   *n* 1 Pet. 4:14   **5:12** *o* 1 Pet. 4:13, 14 *p* Acts 7:52
5:13 *q* Luke 14:34   **5:14** *r* [John 8:12]

that is set on a hill cannot be hidden. 15Nor do they 5light a lamp and put it under a basket, but on a lampstand, and it gives light to all *who are* in the house. 16Let your light so shine before men, *t*that they may see your good works and *u*glorify your Father in heaven.

Christ Fulfills the Law

17*v*"Do not think that I came to destroy the Law or the Prophets. I did not come to destroy but to fulfill. 18For assuredly, I say to you, *w*till heaven and earth pass away, one jot or one tittle will by no means pass from the law till all is fulfilled. 19*x*Whoever therefore breaks one of the least of these commandments, and teaches men so, shall be called least in the kingdom of heaven; but whoever does and teaches *them*, he shall be called great in the kingdom of heaven. 20For I say to you, that unless your righteousness exceeds *y*the righteousness of the scribes and Pharisees, you will by no means enter the kingdom of heaven.

Murder Begins in the Heart

21"You have heard that it was said to those of old, *z*'You shall not murder,*** and whoever murders will be in danger of the judgment.' 22But I say to you that *a*whoever is angry with his brother without a cause* shall be in danger of the judgment. And whoever says to his brother, *b*'Raca!' shall be in danger of the council. But whoever says, 'You fool!' shall be in danger of hell fire. 23Therefore *c*if you bring your gift to the altar, and there remember that your brother has something against you, 24*d*leave your gift there before the altar, and go your way. First be reconciled to your brother, and then come and offer your gift. 25*e*Agree with your adversary quickly, *f*while you are on the way with him, lest your adversary deliver you to the judge, the judge hand you over to the officer, and you be thrown into prison. 26Assuredly, I say to you, you will by no means get out of there till you have paid the last penny.

Adultery in the Heart

27"You have heard that it was said to those of old,* *g*'You shall not commit adultery.'* 28But I say to you that whoever *h*looks at a woman to lust for her has already committed adultery with her in his heart. 29*i*If your right eye causes you to sin, *j*pluck it out and cast *it* from you; for it is more profitable for you that one of your members perish, than for your whole body to be cast into hell. 30And if your right hand causes you to sin, cut it off and cast *it* from you; for it is more profitable for you that one of your members perish, than for your whole body to be cast into hell.

Marriage Is Sacred and Binding

31"Furthermore it has been said, *k*'Whoever divorces his wife, let him give her a certificate of divorce.' 32But I say to you that *l*whoever divorces his wife for any reason except sexual immorality* causes her to commit adultery; and whoever marries a woman who is divorced commits adultery.

Jesus Forbids Oaths

33"Again you have heard that *m*it was said to those of old, *n*'You shall not swear falsely, but *o*shall perform your oaths to the Lord.' 34But I say to you, *p*do not swear at all: neither by heaven, for it is *q*God's throne; 35nor by the earth, for it is His footstool; nor by Jerusalem, for it is the city of *r*the great King. 36Nor shall you swear by your head, because you cannot make one hair white or black. 37*s*But let your 'Yes' be 'Yes,' and your 'No,' 'No.' For whatever is more than these is from the evil one.

Go the Second Mile

38"You have heard that it was said, *t*'An eye for an eye and a tooth for a tooth.'*

---

* **5:21** Exodus 20:13; Deuteronomy 5:17
* **5:22** NU-Text omits *without a cause*. * **5:27** NU-Text and M-Text omit *to those of old.* • Exodus 20:14; Deuteronomy 5:18 * **5:32** Or *fornication* * **5:38** Exodus 21:24; Leviticus 24:20; Deuteronomy 19:21

5:16 *Let your light so shine.* The believer does not have inherent light; rather, we have reflective light. As Christ followers, we must make sure that we do not allow anything to come between us and our Source of light.

5:27 *adultery.* Control of the heart and body begins with control of the eyes. Deeds of shame result from fantasies of shame. Jesus gives the sobering advice "if your right eye causes you to sin, pluck it out and cast it from you" (v. 29). It should be clear here that Jesus is not advocating mutilating our bodies, but He is using a strong figure of speech to emphasize removing any temptation for evil, whatever the cost.

5:32 *sexual immorality.* This is a general term that includes premarital sex, extramarital infidelity, homosexuality, and bestiality.

5:38 *An eye for an eye.* This important Old Testament

law (Ex. 21:24–25; Lev. 24:20; Deut. 19:21), known as the *lex talionis* (law of retaliation), covered what type of punishment should be meted out to transgressors. It limited the retribution the offender would have to bear, preventing the "head for eye, jaw for tooth" vengeance typical of humans.

5:15 5 Luke 8:16 **5:16** *t* 1 Pet. 2:12 *u* [John 15:8] **5:17** *v* Rom. 10:4 **5:18** *w* Luke 16:17 **5:19** *x* [James 2:10] **5:20** *y* [Rom. 10:3] **5:21** *z* Ex. 20:13; Deut. 5:17 **5:22** *a* [1 John 3:15] *b* [James 2:20; 3:6] **5:23** *c* Matt. 8:4 **5:24** *d* [Job 42:8] **5:25** *e* Luke 12:58, 59 *f* [Is. 55:6] **5:27** *g* Ex. 20:14; Deut. 5:18 **5:28** *h* Prov. 6:25 **5:29** *i* Mark 9:43 *j* [Col. 3:5] **5:31** *k* Deut. 24:1 **5:32** *l* [Luke 16:18] **5:33** *m* Matt. 23:16 *n* Lev. 19:12 *o* Deut. 23:23 **5:34** *p* James 5:12 *q* Is. 66:1 **5:35** *r* Ps. 48:2 **5:37** *s* [Col. 4:6] **5:38** *t* Ex. 21:24; Lev. 24:20; Deut. 19:21

39uBut I tell you not to resist an evil person. vBut whoever slaps you on your right cheek, turn the other to him also. 40If anyone wants to sue you and take away your tunic, let him have your cloak also. 41And whoever wcompels you to go one mile, go with him two. 42Give to him who asks you, and xfrom him who wants to borrow from you do not turn away.

Love Your Enemies

43"You have heard that it was said, y'You shall love your neighbor* zand hate your enemy.' 44But I say to you, alove your enemies, bless those who curse you, bdo good to those who hate you, and pray cfor those who spitefully use you and persecute you,* 45that you may be sons of your Father in heaven; for dHe makes His sun rise on the evil and on the good, and sends rain on the just and on the unjust. 46eFor if you love those who love you, what reward have you? Do not even the tax collectors do the same? 47And if you greet your brethren* only, what do you do more than others? Do not even the tax collectors* do so? 48fTherefore you shall be perfect, just gas your Father in heaven is perfect.

Do Good to Please God

6 "Take heed that you do not do your charitable deeds before men, to be seen by them. Otherwise you have no reward from your Father in heaven. 2Therefore, awhen you do a charitable deed, do not sound a trumpet before you as the hypocrites do in the synagogues and in the streets, that they may have glory from men. Assuredly, I say to you, they have their reward. 3But when you do a charitable deed, do not let your left hand know what your right hand is doing, 4that your charitable deed may be in secret; and your Father who sees in secret bwill Himself reward you openly.*

The Model Prayer

5"And when you pray, you shall not be like the hypocrites. For they love to pray standing in the synagogues and on the corners of the streets, that they may be seen by men. Assuredly, I say to you, they have their reward. 6But you, when you pray, cgo into your room, and when you have shut your door, pray to your Father who is in the secret place; and your Father who sees in secret will reward you openly.* 7And when you pray, ddo not use vain repetitions as the heathen do. eFor they think that they will be heard for their many words.

8"Therefore do not be like them. For your Father fknows the things you have need of before you ask Him. 9In this gmanner, therefore, pray:

hOur Father in heaven,
Hallowed be Your iname.
10 Your kingdom come.
jYour will be done
On earth kas it is in heaven.
11 Give us this day our ldaily
bread.
12 And mforgive us our debts,
As we forgive our debtors.
13 nAnd do not lead us into
temptation,
But odeliver us from the evil one.
For Yours is the kingdom and the
power and the glory forever.
Amen.*

14p"For if you forgive men their trespasses, your heavenly Father will also forgive you. 15But qif you do not forgive men their trespasses, neither will your Father forgive your trespasses.

Fasting to Be Seen Only by God

16"Moreover, rwhen you fast, do not be like the hypocrites, with a sad countenance. For they disfigure their faces that they may appear to men to be fasting. Assuredly, I say to you, they have their reward. 17But you, when you fast, sanoint your head and wash your face, 18so that you do not appear to men to be fasting, but to your Father who is in the secret place; and your Father who sees in secret will reward you openly.*

---

* **5:43** Compare Leviticus 19:18   * **5:44** NU-Text omits three clauses from this verse, leaving, "But I say to you, love your enemies and pray for those who persecute you."   * **5:47** M-Text reads friends. • NU-Text reads Gentiles.   * **6:4** NU-Text omits openly.   * **6:6** NU-Text omits openly. * **6:13** NU-Text omits For Yours through Amen. * **6:18** NU-Text and M-Text omit openly.

5:41 compels. The Roman government could press anyone to carry a load as far as one mile.
5:45 sons of your Father. In other words, "that you be like your heavenly Father who displays His love without discrimination."
5:48 be perfect. God does not lower the standard to accommodate our sinfulness. He gives us the power to keep this righteousness standard.
6:2 they have their reward. The only reward the hypocrites will ever receive is to be honored by man.
6:9 In this manner. This does not mean to pray only these words, but to pray in this way, remembering the general topics of worship, request for both

physical and spiritual needs, confession, and repentance of sins.

5:39 u Luke 6:29   v Is. 50:6   **5:41** w Matt. 27:32
5:42 x Luke 6:30–34   **5:43** y Lev. 19:18   z Deut. 23:3–6
5:44 a Luke 6:27   b [Rom. 12:20]   c Acts 7:60   **5:45** d Job
25:3   **5:46** e Luke 6:32   **5:48** f [Col. 1:28; 4:12]   g Eph.
5:1   **6:2** a Rom. 12:8   **6:4** b Luke 14:12–14   **6:6** c 2 Kin.
4:33   **6:7** d Eccl. 5:2   e 1 Kin. 18:26   **6:8** f [Rom.
8:26, 27]   **6:9** g Luke 11:2–4   h [Matt. 5:16]   i Mal.
1:11   **6:10** j Matt. 26:42   k Ps. 103:20   **6:11** l Prov. 30:8
6:12 m [Matt. 18:21, 22]   **6:13** n [2 Pet. 2:9]   o John 17:15
6:14 p Mark 11:25   **6:15** q Matt. 18:35   **6:16** r Is. 58:3–7
6:17 s Ruth 3:3

Lay Up Treasures in Heaven

19t"Do not lay up for yourselves treasures on earth, where moth and rust destroy and where thieves break in and steal; 20u but lay up for yourselves treasures in heaven, where neither moth nor rust destroys and where thieves do not break in and steal. 21For where your treasure is, there your heart will be also.

The Lamp of the Body

22v"The lamp of the body is the eye. If therefore your eye is good, your whole body will be full of light. 23But if your eye is bad, your whole body will be full of darkness. If therefore the light that is in you is darkness, how great is that darkness!

You Cannot Serve God and Riches

24w"No one can serve two masters; for either he will hate the one and love the other, or else he will be loyal to the one and despise the other. xYou cannot serve God and mammon.

Do Not Worry

25"Therefore I say to you, ydo not worry about your life, what you will eat or what you will drink; nor about your body, what you will put on. Is not life more than food and the body more than clothing? 26zLook at the birds of the air, for they neither sow nor reap nor gather into barns; yet your heavenly Father feeds them. Are you not of more value than they? 27Which of you by worrying can add one cubit to his stature? 28"So why do you worry about clothing? Consider the lilies of the field, how they grow: they neither toil nor spin; 29and yet I say to you that even Solomon in all his glory was not arrayed like one of these. 30Now if God so clothes the grass of the field, which today is, and tomorrow is thrown into the oven, will He not much more clothe you, O you of little faith? 31"Therefore do not worry, saying, 'What shall we eat?' or 'What shall we drink?' or 'What shall we wear?' 32For after all these things the Gentiles seek. For your heavenly Father knows that you need all

these things. 33But aseek first the kingdom of God and His righteousness, and all these things shall be added to you. 34Therefore do not worry about tomorrow, for tomorrow will worry about its own things. Sufficient for the day is its own trouble.

Do Not Judge

7 "Judge anot, that you be not judged. 2For with what judgment you judge, you will be judged; band with the measure you use, it will be measured back to you. 3cAnd why do you look at the speck in your brother's eye, but do not consider the plank in your own eye? 4Or how can you say to your brother, 'Let me remove the speck from your eye'; and look, a plank is in your own eye? 5Hypocrite! First remove the plank from your own eye, and then you will see clearly to remove the speck from your brother's eye.

6d"Do not give what is holy to the dogs; nor cast your pearls before swine, lest they trample them under their feet, and turn and tear you in pieces.

Keep Asking, Seeking, Knocking

7e"Ask, and it will be given to you; seek, and you will find; knock, and it will be opened to you. 8For feveryone who asks receives, and he who seeks finds, and to him who knocks it will be opened. 9gOr what man is there among you who, if his son asks for bread, will give him a stone? 10Or if he asks for a fish, will he give him a serpent? 11If you then, hbeing evil, know how to give good gifts to your children, how much more will your Father who is in heaven give good things to those who ask Him! 12Therefore, iwhatever you want men to do to you, do also to them, for jthis is the Law and the Prophets.

The Narrow Way

13k"Enter by the narrow gate; for wide is the gate and broad is the way that leads to destruction, and there are many who go in by it. 14Because* narrow is the gate and

* 7:14 NU-Text and M-Text read How … !

6:19 Do not lay up . . . on earth. In other words, don't give priority to things that only last on earth, but instead put priority and energy into serving God.
6:24 Covetousness—God requires total allegiance and continuous subjection of our wills to Him. He asks for full commitment of our hearts and love for His service. We cannot serve God like that while under the influence of the god of money, urging us to make present, tangible, and worldly things the object of our thoughts and affections.
6:27 add one cubit. Some translations say, "add a single hour to his life." It seems that Jesus would bring a smile here; the mental picture either of growing taller, or of stretching time by worrying, helps us to see the futility of it.
7:1–2 Judge not. The point of this verse is that a

Christian must not judge or criticize in a way that they themselves would not want to be judged or criticized. Every judgment that a person makes becomes a basis for his or her own judgment (James 3:1–2).
7:6 dogs . . . swine. These insulting terms refer to people who are enemies of the gospel, as opposed to those who are merely unbelievers.

6:19 t Prov. 23:4   6:20 u Matt. 19:21   6:22 v Luke 11:34, 35   6:24 w Luke 16:9, 11, 13   x [Gal. 1:10]
6:25 y Luke 12:22   6:26 z Luke 12:24   6:33 a [1 Tim. 4:8]   7:1 a Rom. 14:3   7:2 b Luke 6:38   7:3 c Luke 6:41
7:6 d Prov. 9:7, 8   7:7 e [Mark 11:24]   7:8 f Prov. 8:17
7:9 g Luke 11:11   7:11 h Gen. 6:5; 8:21   7:12 i Luke 6:31
j Gal. 5:14   7:13 k Luke 13:24

difficult *is* the way which leads to life, and there are few who find it.

You Will Know Them by Their Fruits

15 [i]"Beware of false prophets, [m]who come to you in sheep's clothing, but inwardly they are ravenous wolves. 16 [n]You will know them by their fruits. [o]Do men gather grapes from thornbushes or figs from thistles? 17 Even so, [p]every good tree bears good fruit, but a bad tree bears bad fruit. 18 A good tree cannot bear bad fruit, nor *can* a bad tree bear good fruit. 19 [q]Every tree that does not bear good fruit is cut down and thrown into the fire. 20 Therefore by their fruits you will know them.

I Never Knew You

21 "Not everyone who says to Me, [r]'Lord, Lord,' shall enter the kingdom of heaven, but he who [s]does the will of My Father in heaven. 22 Many will say to Me in that day, 'Lord, Lord, have we [t]not prophesied in Your name, cast out demons in Your name, and done many wonders in Your name?' 23 And [u]then I will declare to them, 'I never knew you; [v]depart from Me, you who practice lawlessness!'

Build on the Rock

24 "Therefore [w]whoever hears these sayings of Mine, and does them, I will liken him to a wise man who built his house on the rock: 25 and the rain descended, the floods came, and the winds blew and beat on that house; and it did not fall, for it was founded on the rock.

26 "But everyone who hears these sayings of Mine, and does not do them, will be like a foolish man who built his house on the sand: 27 and the rain descended, the floods came, and the winds blew and beat on that house; and it fell. And great was its fall."

28 And so it was, when Jesus had ended these sayings, that [x]the people were astonished at His teaching, 29 [y]for He taught them as one having authority, and not as the scribes.

Jesus Cleanses a Leper

8 When He had come down from the mountain, great multitudes followed

Him. 2 [a]And behold, a leper came and [b]worshiped Him, saying, "Lord, if You are willing, You can make me clean."

3 Then Jesus put out *His* hand and touched him, saying, "I am willing; be cleansed." Immediately his leprosy [c]was cleansed.

4 And Jesus said to him, [d]"See that you tell no one; but go your way, show yourself to the priest, and offer the gift that [e]Moses [f]commanded, as a testimony to them."

Jesus Heals a Centurion's Servant

5 [g]Now when Jesus had entered Capernaum, a [h]centurion came to Him, pleading with Him, 6 saying, "Lord, my servant is lying at home paralyzed, dreadfully tormented."

7 And Jesus said to him, "I will come and heal him."

8 The centurion answered and said, "Lord, [i]I am not worthy that You should come under my roof. But only [j]speak a word, and my servant will be healed. 9 For I also am a man under authority, having soldiers under me. And I say to this *one,* 'Go,' and he goes; and to another, 'Come,' and he comes; and to my servant, 'Do this,' and he does *it.*"

10 When Jesus heard *it,* He marveled, and said to those who followed, "Assuredly, I say to you, I have not found such great faith, not even in Israel! 11 And I say to you that [k]many will come from east and west, and sit down with Abraham, Isaac, and Jacob in the kingdom of heaven. 12 But [l]the sons of the kingdom [m]will be cast out into outer darkness. There will be weeping and gnashing of teeth." 13 Then Jesus said to the centurion, "Go your way; and as you have believed, *so* let it be done for you." And his servant was healed that same hour.

Peter's Mother-in-Law Healed

14 [n]Now when Jesus had come into Peter's house, He saw [o]his wife's mother lying sick with a fever. 15 So He touched her hand, and the fever left her. And she arose and served them.*

---

* **8:15** NU-Text and M-Text read *Him.*

7:15 *Beware of false prophets.* Deuteronomy 13.1–11 and 18:20–22 provide information on discerning and responding to false prophets. The way to tell a false teacher from teachers of the truth is by their fruits. Fruit does not only refer to deeds, but also to doctrine (16:12; 1 John 4:1–3).

8:4 *show yourself to the priest.* This was no small undertaking. The sacrifice required was long and involved (Lev. 14:4–32). In obeying the law of Moses, the leper would be a powerful testimony to the religious authorities in Jerusalem that the Messiah had arrived.

8:10 *I have not found . . . not even in Israel.* Jesus makes it clear that just being a physical descendant of

Abraham does not guarantee entrance into His kingdom. The true children of Abraham are those who share his faith in God (Gal. 5:6–9).

7:15 [i] Jer. 23:16 [m] Mic. 3:5 **7:16** [n] Matt. 7:20; 12:33 [o] Luke 6:43 **7:17** [p] Matt. 12:33 **7:19** [q] [John 15:2, 6] **7:21** [r] Luke 6:46 [s] Rom. 2:13 **7:22** [t] Num. 24:4 **7:23** [u] [2 Tim. 2:19] [v] Ps. 5:5; 6:8 **7:24** [w] Luke 6:47–49 **7:28** [x] Matt. 13:54 **7:29** [y] [John 7:46] **8:2** [a] Mark 1:40–45 [b] John 9:38 **8:3** [c] Luke 4:27 **8:4** [d] Mark 5:43 [e] Luke 5:14 [f] Deut. 24:8 **8:5** [g] Luke 7:1–3 [h] Matt. 27:54 **8:8** [i] Luke 15:19, 21 [j] Ps. 107:20 **8:11** [k] Is. 2:2, 3; Mal. 1:11 **8:12** [l] [Matt. 21:43] [m] Luke 13:28 **8:14** [n] Mark 1:29–31 [o] 1 Cor. 9:5

Many Healed in the Evening

16pWhen evening had come, they brought to Him many who were demon-possessed. And He cast out the spirits with a word, and healed all who were sick, 17that it might be fulfilled which was spoken by Isaiah the prophet, saying:

q"*He Himself took our infirmities
And bore our sicknesses.*"*

The Cost of Discipleship

18And when Jesus saw great multitudes about Him, He gave a command to depart to the other side. 19rThen a certain scribe came and said to Him, "Teacher, I will follow You wherever You go."

20And Jesus said to him, "Foxes have holes and birds of the air *have* nests, but the Son of Man has nowhere to lay *His* head."

21sThen another of His disciples said to Him, "Lord, tlet me first go and bury my father."

22But Jesus said to him, "Follow Me, and let the dead bury their own dead."

Wind and Wave Obey Jesus

23Now when He got into a boat, His disciples followed Him. 24uAnd suddenly a great tempest arose on the sea, so that the boat was covered with the waves. But He was asleep. 25Then His disciples came to *Him* and awoke Him, saying, "Lord, save us! We are perishing!"

26But He said to them, "Why are you fearful, O you of little faith?" Then vHe arose and rebuked the winds and the sea, and there was a great calm. 27So the men marveled, saying, "Who can this be, that even the winds and the sea obey Him?"

Two Demon-Possessed Men Healed

28wWhen He had come to the other side, to the country of the Gergesenes,* there met Him two demon-possessed *men,* coming out of the tombs, exceedingly fierce, so that no one could pass that way. 29And suddenly they cried out, saying, "What have we to do with You, Jesus, You Son of God? Have You come here to torment us before the time?"

30Now a good way off from them there

was a herd of many swine feeding. 31So the demons begged Him, saying, "If You cast us out, permit us to go away* into the herd of swine."

32And He said to them, "Go." So when they had come out, they went into the herd of swine. And suddenly the whole herd of swine ran violently down the steep place into the sea, and perished in the water.

33Then those who kept *them* fled; and they went away into the city and told everything, including what *had happened* to the demon-possessed *men.* 34And behold, the whole city came out to meet Jesus. And when they saw Him, xthey begged *Him* to depart from their region.

Jesus Forgives and Heals a Paralytic

9 So He got into a boat, crossed over, aand came to His own city. 2bThen behold, they brought to Him a paralytic lying on a bed. cWhen Jesus saw their faith, He said to the paralytic, "Son, be of good cheer; your sins are forgiven you."

3And at once some of the scribes said within themselves, "This Man blasphemes!"

4But Jesus, dknowing their thoughts, said, "Why do you think evil in your hearts? 5For which is easier, to say, 'Your sins are forgiven you,' or to say, 'Arise and walk'? 6But that you may know that the Son of Man has power on earth to forgive sins"—then He said to the paralytic, "Arise, take up your bed, and go to your house." 7And he arose and departed to his house.

8Now when the multitudes saw *it,* they emarveled* and glorified God, who had given such power to men.

Matthew the Tax Collector

9fAs Jesus passed on from there, He saw a man named Matthew sitting at the tax office. And He said to him, "Follow Me." So he arose and followed Him.

10gNow it happened, as Jesus sat at the table in the house, *that* behold, many tax collectors and sinners came and sat down with Him and His disciples. 11And when

* 8:17 Isaiah 53:4   * 8:28 NU-Text reads *Gadarenes.*   * 8:31 NU-Text reads *send us.*
* 9:8 NU-Text reads *were afraid.*

8:17 took our infirmities and bore our sicknesses. This verse quotes Isaiah 53:4. Jesus healed because He had compassion on the people.

8:28–29 demon-possessed. We learn several things about demons in this passage. They recognize the deity of Christ, they are limited in their knowledge, they know they will ultimately be judged by Christ (25:41; James 2:19; 2 Pet. 2:4; Jude 6; Rev. 12:7–17), and they cannot act without the permission of higher authority.

9:2 their faith. This refers to the faith of the paralytic as well as that of the men who were carrying him.

9:10 tax collectors. Publicans or tax collectors were often despised not only because they were seen as traitors, working for the hated Roman government, but also because they generally collected more than necessary and pocketed the difference.

8:16 P Luke 4:40, 41   8:17 q Is. 53:4   8:19 r Luke 9:57, 58   8:21 s Luke 9:59, 60   t 1 Kin. 19:20   8:24 u Mark 4:37   8:26 v Ps. 65:7; 89:9; 107:29   8:28 w Mark 5:1–4   8:34 x Luke 5:8; Acts 16:39   9:1 a Matt. 4:13; 11:23   9:2 b Luke 5:18–26   c Matt. 8:10   9:4 d Matt. 12:25   9:8 e John 7:15   9:9 f Luke 5:27   9:10 g Mark 2:15

the Pharisees saw *it*, they said to His disciples, "Why does your Teacher eat with *h*tax collectors and *i*sinners?"

¹²When Jesus heard *that*, He said to them, "Those who are well have no need of a physician, but those who are sick. ¹³But go and learn what *this* means: *j*'I desire mercy and not sacrifice.'** For I did not come to call the righteous, *k*but sinners, to repentance."**

Jesus Is Questioned About Fasting

¹⁴Then the disciples of John came to Him, saying, *l*"Why do we and the Pharisees fast often,* but Your disciples do not fast?"

¹⁵And Jesus said to them, "Can *m*the friends of the bridegroom mourn as long as the bridegroom is with them? But the days will come when the bridegroom will be taken away from them, and *n*then they will fast. ¹⁶No one puts a piece of unshrunk cloth on an old garment; for the patch pulls away from the garment, and the tear is made worse. ¹⁷Nor do they put new wine into old wineskins, or else the wineskins break, the wine is spilled, and the wineskins are ruined. But they put new wine into new wineskins, and both are preserved."

A Girl Restored to Life and a Woman Healed

¹⁸*o*While He spoke these things to them, behold, a ruler came and worshiped Him, saying, "My daughter has just died, but come and lay Your hand on her and she will live." ¹⁹So Jesus arose and followed him, and so *did* His *p*disciples.

²⁰*q*And suddenly, a woman who had a flow of blood for twelve years came from behind and *r*touched the hem of His garment. ²¹For she said to herself, "If only I may touch His garment, I shall be made well." ²²But Jesus turned around, and when He saw her He said, "Be of good cheer, daughter; *s*your faith has made you well." And the woman was made well from that hour.

²³*t*When Jesus came into the ruler's house, and saw *u*the flute players and the noisy crowd wailing, ²⁴He said to them, *v*"Make room, for the girl is not dead, but sleeping." And they ridiculed Him. ²⁵But when the crowd was put outside, He went in and *w*took her by the hand, and the girl arose. ²⁶And the *x*report of this went out into all that land.

Two Blind Men Healed

²⁷When Jesus departed from there, *y*two blind men followed Him, crying out and saying, *z*"Son of David, have mercy on us!"

²⁸And when He had come into the house, the blind men came to Him. And Jesus said to them, "Do you believe that I am able to do this?"

They said to Him, "Yes, Lord."

²⁹Then He touched their eyes, saying, "According to your faith let it be to you." ³⁰And their eyes were opened. And Jesus sternly warned them, saying, *a*"See *that* no one knows *it*." ³¹*b*But when they had departed, they spread the news about Him in all that country.

A Mute Man Speaks

³²*c*As they went out, behold, they brought to Him a man, mute and demon-possessed. ³³And when the demon was cast out, the mute spoke. And the multitudes marveled, saying, "It was never seen like this in Israel!"

³⁴But the Pharisees said, *d*"He casts out demons by the ruler of the demons."

The Compassion of Jesus

³⁵Then Jesus went about all the cities and villages, *e*teaching in their synagogues, preaching the gospel of the kingdom, and healing every sickness and every disease among the people.* ³⁶*f*But when He saw the multitudes, He was moved with compassion for them, because they were weary* and scattered, *g*like sheep having no shepherd. ³⁷Then He said to His disciples, *h*"The harvest truly *is* plentiful, but the laborers *are* few. ³⁸*i*Therefore pray the Lord of the harvest to send out laborers into His harvest."

---

* **9:13** Hosea 6:6 • NU-Text omits *to repentance.* * **9:14** NU-Text brackets *often* as disputed. * **9:35** NU-Text omits *among the people.* * **9:36** NU-Text and M-Text read *harassed.*

9:12–13 *Those who are well.* Jesus refers ironically to the Pharisees as "the righteous." They were not righteous; that was only how they perceived themselves because of their pious and scrupulous law keeping (Phil. 3:6). But God is more interested in a person's loyal love than the observance of external rituals.

9:30 *See that no one knows it.* Jesus may have wanted to discourage the masses from coming to Him for physical healing alone, because His primary purpose was spiritual healing.

9:37 *harvest.* The harvest will mark the beginning of

the kingdom age. For the lost it will mean doom, but for the saved it will mean blessing.

9:11 *h* Matt. 11:19 *i* [Gal. 2:15] **9:13** *j* Hos. 6:6 *k* 1 Tim. 1:15 **9:14** *l* Luke 5:33–35; 18:12 **9:15** *m* John 3:29 *n* Acts 13:2, 3; 14:23 **9:18** *o* Luke 8:41–56 **9:19** *p* Matt. 10:2–4 **9:20** *q* Luke 8:43 *r* Matt. 14:36; 23:5 **9:22** *s* Luke 7:50; 8:48; 17:19; 18:42 **9:23** *t* Mark 5:38 *u* 2 Chr. 35:25 **9:24** *v* Acts 20:10 *w* Mark 1:31 **9:26** *x* Matt. 4:24 **9:27** *y* Matt. 20:29–34 *z* Luke 18:38, 39 **9:30** *a* Matt. 8:4 **9:31** *b* Mark 7:36 **9:32** *c* Matt. 12:22, 24 **9:34** *d* Luke 11:15 **9:35** *e* Matt. 4:23 **9:36** *f* Mark 6:34 *g* Num. 27:17 **9:37** *h* Luke 10:2 **9:38** *i* 2 Thess. 3:1

The Twelve Apostles

10 And [a]when He had called His twelve disciples to *Him*, He gave them power *over* unclean spirits, to cast them out, and to heal all kinds of sickness and all kinds of disease. 2Now the names of the twelve apostles are these: first, Simon, [b]who is called Peter, and Andrew his brother; James the *son* of Zebedee, and John his brother; 3Philip and Bartholomew; Thomas and Matthew the tax collector; James the *son* of Alphaeus, and Lebbaeus, whose surname was* Thaddaeus; 4[c]Simon the Cananite,* and Judas [d]Iscariot, who also betrayed Him.

Sending Out the Twelve

5These twelve Jesus sent out and commanded them, saying: [e]"Do not go into the way of the Gentiles, and do not enter a city of [f]the Samaritans. 6[g]But go rather to the [h]lost sheep of the house of Israel. 7[i]And as you go, preach, saying, [j]'The kingdom of heaven is at hand.' 8Heal the sick, cleanse the lepers, raise the dead,* cast out demons. [k]Freely you have received, freely give. 9[l]Provide neither gold nor silver nor [m]copper in your money belts, 10nor bag for *your* journey, nor two tunics, nor sandals, nor staffs; [n]for a worker is worthy of his food.

11[o]"Now whatever city or town you enter, inquire who in it is worthy, and stay there till you go out. 12And when you go into a household, greet it. 13[p]If the household is worthy, let your peace come upon it. [q]But if it is not worthy, let your peace return to you. 14[r]And whoever will not receive you nor hear your words, when you depart from that house or city, [s]shake off the dust from your feet. 15Assuredly, I say to you, [t]it will be more tolerable for the land of Sodom and Gomorrah in the day of judgment than for that city!

Persecutions Are Coming

16[u]"Behold, I send you out as sheep in the midst of wolves. [v]Therefore be wise as serpents and [w]harmless as doves. 17But beware of men, for [x]they will deliver you up to councils and [y]scourge you in their synagogues. 18[z]You will be brought before governors and kings for My sake, as a testimony to them and to the Gentiles. 19[a]But when they deliver you up, do not worry about how or what you should speak. For [b]it will be given to you in that hour what you should speak; 20[c]for it is not you who speak, but the Spirit of your Father who speaks in you.

21[d]"Now brother will deliver up brother to death, and a father *his* child; and children will rise up against parents and cause them to be put to death. 22And [e]you will be hated by all for My name's sake. [f]But he who endures to the end will be saved. 23[g]When they persecute you in this city, flee to another. For assuredly, I say to you, you will not have [h]gone through the cities of Israel [i]before the Son of Man comes.

24[j]"A disciple is not above *his* teacher, nor a servant above his master. 25It is enough for a disciple that he be like his teacher, and a servant like his master. If [k]they have called the master of the house Beelzebub,* how much more *will they call* those of his household! 26Therefore do not fear them. [l]For there is nothing covered that will not be revealed, and hidden that will not be known.

Jesus Teaches the Fear of God

27"Whatever I tell you in the dark, [m]speak in the light; and what you hear in the ear, preach on the housetops. 28[n]And do not fear those who kill the body but cannot kill the soul. But rather [o]fear Him who is able to destroy both soul and body in hell. 29Are not two [p]sparrows sold for a copper coin? And not one of them falls to the ground apart from your Father's will. 30[q]But the very hairs of your head are all numbered. 31Do not fear therefore; you are of more value than many sparrows.

* 10:3 NU-Text omits *Lebbaeus, whose surname was.* * 10:4 NU-Text reads *Cananaean.* * 10:8 NU-Text reads *raise the dead, cleanse the lepers;* M-Text omits *raise the dead.* * 10:25 NU-Text and M-Text read *Beelzebul.*

10:2 *the twelve.* The twelve are called disciples in verse 1; here they are called apostles. The word "apostle" emphasizes delegated authority (1 Thess. 2:6).

10:15 *more tolerable for the land of Sodom and Gomorrah.* This verse, together with 11:22–24, implies that there will be different degrees of judgment and torment for those who reject Christ.

10:18 *for My sake.* God would use Jewish rejection and persecution of the messengers to bring the gospel message to the Gentiles.

10:25 Persecution—Believers must know that what the world has called our Lord, it will call us. The world has hated Jesus without cause, and they will hate those who bear His name in the same way.

10:1 [a] Luke 6:13 **10:2** [b] John 1:42 **10:4** [c] Acts 1:13 [d] John 13:2, 26 **10:5** [e] Matt. 4:15 [f] John 4:9 **10:6** [g] Matt. 15:24 [h] Jer. 50:6 **10:7** [i] Luke 9:2 [j] Matt. 3:2 **10:8** [k] [Acts 8:18] **10:9** [l] 1 Sam. 9:7 [m] Mark 6:8 **10:10** [n] 1 Tim. 5:18 **10:11** [o] Luke 10:8 **10:13** [p] Luke 10:5 [q] Ps. 35:13 **10:14** [r] Mark 6:11 [s] Acts 13:51 **10:15** [t] Matt. 11:22, 24 **10:16** [u] Luke 10:3 [v] Eph. 5:15 [w] [Phil. 2:14–16] **10:17** [x] Mark 13:9 [y] Acts 5:40; 22:19; 26:11 **10:18** [z] 2 Tim. 4:16 **10:19** [a] Luke 12:11, 12; 21:14, 15 [b] Ex. 4:12 **10:20** [c] 2 Sam. 23:2 **10:21** [d] Mic. 7:6 **10:22** [e] Luke 21:17 [f] Mark 13:13 **10:23** [g] Acts 8:1 [h] [Mark 13:10] [i] Matt. 16:28 **10:24** [j] John 15:20 **10:25** [k] John 8:48, 52 **10:26** [l] Mark 4:22 **10:27** [m] Acts 5:20 **10:28** [n] Luke 12:4 [o] Luke 12:5 **10:29** [p] Luke 12:6, 7 **10:30** [q] Luke 21:18

Confess Christ Before Men

32*r*"Therefore whoever confesses Me before men, *s*him I will also confess before My Father who is in heaven. **33***t*But whoever denies Me before men, him I will also deny before My Father who is in heaven.

Christ Brings Division

34*u*"Do not think that I came to bring peace on earth. I did not come to bring peace but a sword. **35**For I have come to *v*'set a man against his father, a daughter against her mother, and a daughter-in-law against her mother-in-law'; **36**and *w*'a man's enemies will be those of his own household.'* **37***x*He who loves father or mother more than Me is not worthy of Me. And he who loves son or daughter more than Me is not worthy of Me. **38***y*And he who does not take his cross and follow after Me is not worthy of Me. **39***z*He who finds his life will lose it, and he who loses his life for My sake will find it.

A Cup of Cold Water

40*a*"He who receives you receives Me, and he who receives Me receives Him who sent Me. **41***b*He who receives a prophet in the name of a prophet shall receive a prophet's reward. And he who receives a righteous man in the name of a righteous man shall receive a righteous man's reward. **42***c*And whoever gives one of these little ones only a cup of cold *water* in the name of a disciple, assuredly, I say to you, he shall by no means lose his reward."

John the Baptist Sends Messengers to Jesus

11 Now it came to pass, when Jesus finished commanding His twelve disciples, that He departed from there to *a*teach and to preach in their cities.

2*b*And when John had heard *c*in prison about the works of Christ, he sent two of* his disciples **3**and said to Him, "Are You *d*the Coming One, or do we look for another?"

4Jesus answered and said to them, "Go and tell John the things which you hear

and see: **5***e*The blind see and *the* lame walk; *the* lepers are cleansed and *the* deaf hear; *the* dead are raised up and *f the* poor have the gospel preached to them. **6**And blessed is he who is not *g*offended because of Me."

7*h*As they departed, Jesus began to say to the multitudes concerning John: "What did you go out into the wilderness to see? *i*A reed shaken by the wind? **8**But what did you go out to see? A man clothed in soft garments? Indeed, those who wear soft *clothing* are in kings' houses. **9**But what did you go out to see? A prophet? Yes, I say to you, *j*and more than a prophet. **10**For this is he of whom it is written:

k'Behold, I send My messenger before Your face,
Who will prepare Your way before You.'*

11"Assuredly, I say to you, among those born of women there has not risen one greater than John the Baptist; but he who is least in the kingdom of heaven is greater than he. **12***l*And from the days of John the Baptist until now the kingdom of heaven suffers violence, and the violent take it by force. **13***m*For all the prophets and the law prophesied until John. **14**And if you are willing to receive *it,* he is *n*Elijah who is to come. **15***o*He who has ears to hear, let him hear!

16*p*"But to what shall I liken this generation? It is like children sitting in the marketplaces and calling to their companions, **17**and saying:

'We played the flute for you,
And you did not dance;
We mourned to you,
And you did not lament.'

18For John came neither eating nor drinking, and they say, 'He has a demon.' **19**The Son of Man came eating and drinking, and they say, 'Look, a glutton and a winebibber, *q*a friend of tax collectors and sinners!' *r*But wisdom is justified by her children."*

* **10:36** Micah 7:6   * **11:2** NU-Text reads *by* for *two of.*   * **11:10** Malachi 3:1   * **11:19** NU-Text reads *works.*

10:32 *whoever confesses.* Every act of our lives will be evaluated at the judgment seat of Christ (2 Cor. 5:10). To refuse to speak up for Christ because of intimidation or persecution will result in the believer's loss of reward and consequent loss of glory in the kingdom (Rom. 8:17; 2 Tim. 2:12).

10:38 *does not take his cross.* "Taking up a cross" stands for commitment to the extent of being willing to die for something.

11:3 *do we look.* John probably expected the Messiah to immediately judge Israel and establish His kingdom (3:2–12). Jesus' failure to do what John anticipated may have planted seeds of doubt in John's mind about whether Jesus was the Messiah. But doubt that inquires and does not weaken faith is not evil. John went to the right person for answers,

and Jesus reassured him by pointing out the fulfillment of prophecy.

11:12 *violent take it by force.* This probably means that violent people forcibly oppose the kingdom with their hostility (23:13).

10:32 *r* Luke 12:8 *s* [Rev. 3:5]   **10:33** *t* 2 Tim. 2:12   **10:34** *u* [Luke 12:49]   **10:35** *v* Mic. 7:6   **10:36** *w* John 13:18   **10:37** *x* Luke 14:26   **10:38** *y* [Mark 8:34]   **10:39** *z* John 12:25   **10:40** *a* Luke 9:48   **10:41** *b* 1 Kin. 17:10   **10:42** *c* Mark 9:41   **11:1** *a* Luke 23:5   **11:2** *b* Luke 7:18–35 *c* Matt. 4:12; 14:3   **11:3** *d* John 6:14   **11:5** *e* Is. 29:18; 35:4–6 *f* Ps. 22:26; Is. 61:1   **11:6** *g* [Rom. 9:32]   **11:7** *h* Luke 7:24 *i* [Eph. 4:14]   **11:9** *j* Luke 1:76; 20:6   **11:10** *k* Mal. 3:1   **11:12** *l* Luke 16:16   **11:13** *m* Mal. 4:4–6   **11:14** *n* Luke 1:17   **11:15** *o* Luke 8:8   **11:16** *p* Luke 7:31   **11:19** *q* Matt. 9:10 *r* Luke 7:35

Woe to the Impenitent Cities

20sThen He began to rebuke the cities in which most of His mighty works had been done, because they did not repent: 21"Woe to you, Chorazin! Woe to you, Bethsaida! For if the mighty works which were done in you had been done in Tyre and Sidon, they would have repented long ago tin sackcloth and ashes. 22But I say to you, uit will be more tolerable for Tyre and Sidon in the day of judgment than for you. 23And you, Capernaum, vwho are exalted to heaven, will be* brought down to Hades; for if the mighty works which were done in you had been done in Sodom, it would have remained until this day. 24But I say to you wthat it shall be more tolerable for the land of Sodom in the day of judgment than for you."

Jesus Gives True Rest

25xAt that time Jesus answered and said, "I thank You, Father, Lord of heaven and earth, that yYou have hidden these things from the wise and prudent zand have revealed them to babes. 26Even so, Father, for so it seemed good in Your sight. 27aAll things have been delivered to Me by My Father, and no one knows the Son except the Father. bNor does anyone know the Father except the Son, and the one to whom the Son wills to reveal Him. 28Come to cMe, all you who labor and are heavy laden, and I will give you rest. 29Take My yoke upon you dand learn from Me, for I am gentle and elowly in heart, fand you will find rest for your souls. 30gFor My yoke is easy and My burden is light."

Jesus Is Lord of the Sabbath

12 At that time aJesus went through the grainfields on the Sabbath. And His disciples were hungry, and began to bpluck heads of grain and to eat. 2And when the Pharisees saw it, they said to Him, "Look, Your disciples are doing what is not lawful to do on the Sabbath!"

3But He said to them, "Have you not read cwhat David did when he was hungry, he and those who were with him: 4how he entered the house of God and ate dthe showbread which was not lawful for him to eat, nor for those who were with him, ebut only for the priests? 5Or have you not read in the flaw that on the Sabbath the priests in the temple profane the Sabbath, and are blameless? 6Yet I say to you that in this place there is gOne greater than the temple. 7But if you had known what this means, h'I desire mercy and not sacrifice,'* you would not have condemned the guiltless. 8For the Son of Man is Lord even* of the Sabbath."

Healing on the Sabbath

9iNow when He had departed from there, He went into their synagogue. 10And behold, there was a man who had a withered hand. And they asked Him, saying, j"Is it lawful to heal on the Sabbath?"—that they might accuse Him.

11Then He said to them, "What man is there among you who has one sheep, and if it falls into a pit on the Sabbath, will not lay hold of it and lift it out? 12Of how much more value then is a man than a sheep? Therefore it is lawful to do good on the Sabbath." 13Then He said to the man, "Stretch out your hand." And he stretched it out, and it was restored as whole as the other. 14Then kthe Pharisees went out and plotted against Him, how they might destroy Him.

Behold, My Servant

15But when Jesus knew it, lHe withdrew from there. mAnd great multitudes* followed Him, and He healed them all. 16Yet He nwarned them not to make Him known, 17that it might be fulfilled which was spoken by Isaiah the prophet, saying:

18 "Behold! oMy Servant whom I have chosen,
My Beloved pin whom My soul is well pleased!
I will put My Spirit upon Him,
And He will declare justice to the Gentiles.

---

* 11:23 NU-Text reads will you be exalted to heaven? No, you will be. * 12:7 Hosea 6:6 * 12:8 NU-Text and M-Text omit even.
* 12:15 NU-Text brackets multitudes as disputed.

11:21 Woe. Jesus pronounced a direct judgment on Israel. They would be judged for seeing the Messiah and then rejecting Him.
11:23 Capernaum. Capernaum, which is on the north shore of the Sea of Galilee, was called "His own city" (9:1).
12:2 is not lawful. To desecrate the Sabbath was flagrant disobedience to the law of Moses (Num. 15:30–36). The Pharisees were trying to make Jesus into a lawbreaker and accuse Him of wrongdoing.
12:14 how they might destroy Him. Because of Jesus' view of the Sabbath, the Pharisees concluded that He was trying to overthrow the entire Mosaic system, and therefore had to be destroyed. Their antagonism toward Jesus was growing.
12:17–21 spoken by Isaiah the prophet. This quotation of Isaiah 42:1–4 shows that the Messiah's gentleness was just as had been prophesied, and also that the Gentiles would be included in His blessing.

11:20 s Luke 10:13–15, 18   **11:21** t Jon. 3:6–8
11:22 u Matt. 10:15; 11:24   **11:23** v Is. 14:13
11:24 w Matt. 10:15   **11:25** x Luke 10:21, 22   y Ps. 8:2
z Matt. 16:17   **11:27** a Matt. 28:18   b John 1:18; 6:46;
10:15   **11:28** c [John 6:35–37]   **11:29** d [Phil. 2:5]
e Zech. 9:9   f Jer. 6:16   **11:30** g [1 John 5:3]   **12:1** a Luke
6:1–5   b Deut. 23:25   **12:3** c 1 Sam. 21:6   **12:4** d Lev.
24:5   e Ex. 29:32   **12:5** f Num. 28:9   **12:6** g [Is. 66:1, 2]
12:7 h [Hos. 6:6]   **12:9** i Mark 3:1–6   **12:10** j John
9:16   **12:14** k Mark 3:6   **12:15** l Mark 3:7   m Matt. 19:2
12:16 n Matt. 8:4; 9:30; 17:9   **12:18** o Is. 42:1–4; 49:3
p Matt. 3:17; 17:5

19 *He will not quarrel nor cry out,*
Nor will anyone hear His voice in the streets.
20 *A bruised reed He will not break,*
And smoking flax He will not quench,
Till He sends forth justice to victory;
21 *And in His name Gentiles will trust."**

A House Divided Cannot Stand

22[q]Then one was brought to Him who was demon-possessed, blind and mute; and He healed him, so that the blind and* mute man both spoke and saw. 23And all the multitudes were amazed and said, "Could this be the [r]Son of David?"

24[s]Now when the Pharisees heard *it* they said, "This *fellow* does not cast out demons except by Beelzebub,* the ruler of the demons."

25But Jesus [t]knew their thoughts, and said to them: "Every kingdom divided against itself is brought to desolation, and every city or house divided against itself will not stand. 26If Satan casts out Satan, he is divided against himself. How then will his kingdom stand? 27And if I cast out demons by Beelzebub, by whom do your sons cast *them* out? Therefore they shall be your judges. 28But if I cast out demons by the Spirit of God, [u]surely the kingdom of God has come upon you. 29[v]Or how can one enter a strong man's house and plunder his goods, unless he first binds the strong man? And then he will plunder his house. 30He who is not with Me is against Me, and he who does not gather with Me scatters abroad.

The Unpardonable Sin

31"Therefore I say to you, [w]every sin and blasphemy will be forgiven men, [x]but the blasphemy *against* the Spirit will not be forgiven men. 32Anyone who [y]speaks a word against the Son of Man, [z]it will be forgiven him; but whoever speaks against the Holy Spirit, it will not be forgiven him, either in this age or in the *age* to come.

A Tree Known by Its Fruit

33"Either make the tree good and [a]its fruit good, or else make the tree bad and its fruit bad; for a tree is known by *its* fruit. 34[b]Brood of vipers! How can you, being evil, speak good things? [c]For out of the abundance of the heart the mouth speaks. 35A good man out of the good treasure of his heart* brings forth good things, and an evil man out of the evil treasure brings forth evil things. 36But I say to you that for every idle word men may speak, they will give account of it in the day of judgment. 37For by your words you will be justified, and by your words you will be condemned."

The Scribes and Pharisees Ask for a Sign

38[d]Then some of the scribes and Pharisees answered, saying, "Teacher, we want to see a sign from You."

39But He answered and said to them, "An evil and [e]adulterous generation seeks after a sign, and no sign will be given to it except the sign of the prophet Jonah. 40[f]For as Jonah was three days and three nights in the belly of the great fish, so will the Son of Man be three days and three nights in the heart of the earth. 41[g]The men of Nineveh will rise up in the judgment with this generation and [h]condemn it, [i]because they repented at the preaching of Jonah; and indeed a greater than Jonah *is* here. 42[j]The queen of the South will rise up in the judgment with this generation and condemn it, for she came from the ends of the earth to hear the wisdom of Solomon; and indeed a greater than Solomon *is* here.

An Unclean Spirit Returns

43[k]"When an unclean spirit goes out of a man, [l]he goes through dry places, seeking rest, and finds none. 44Then he says,

* **12:21** Isaiah 42:1–4 * **12:22** NU-Text omits *blind and.* * **12:24** NU-Text and M-Text read *Beelzebul.* * **12:35** NU-Text and M-Text omit *of his heart.*

12:31–32 *blasphemy.* The sin that shall not be forgiven is the stubborn refusal to heed the Holy Spirit's conviction and accept the salvation that Christ offers. Particularly in reference to the leaders of Israel, Jesus had offered them all the proof that could be expected, such as the ministry of John, the testimony of the Father, the prophecies of the Old Testament, His own testimony, and the substantiation of the Holy Spirit. Because the leaders rejected all proofs regarding Jesus as Messiah, nothing else would be given.

12:39 *the sign of the prophet Jonah.* The demand for signs was evidence of unbelief. The "sign of the prophet Jonah" is explained in verse 40 as the resurrection.

12:41–42 *The men of Nineveh . . . The queen of the South.* These terms represent Gentiles who come to faith because of the words of God's prophets and kings, lesser messengers than God's only Son.

12:43 *an unclean spirit.* This analogy seems to be describing the moral reformation that took place in Israel as a result of the ministries of John the Baptist and Jesus. The reformation, however, was not genuine, and therefore Israel's unbelief and hardness of heart was worse than before. In the same way, a person who decides to try religion without being born again, and then decides "it's not for me," is worse off than if they had never tried, because their hearts are hardened to God's voice.

12:22 [q] Luke 11:14, 15 **12:23** [r] Matt. 9:27; 21:9 **12:24** [s] Matt. 9:34 **12:25** [t] Matt. 9:4 **12:28** [u] [Dan. 2:44; 7:14] **12:29** [v] Is. 49:24 **12:31** [w] Mark 3:28–30 [x] Acts 7:51 **12:32** [y] John 7:12, 52 [z] 1 Tim. 1:13 **12:33** [a] Matt. 7:16–18 **12:34** [b] Matt. 3:7; 23:33 [c] Luke 6:45 **12:38** [d] Mark 8:11 **12:39** [e] Matt. 16:4 **12:40** [f] Jon. 1:17 **12:41** [g] Luke 11:32 [h] Jer. 3:11 [i] Jon. 3:5 **12:42** [j] 1 Kin. 10:1–13 **12:43** [k] Luke 11:24–26 [l] [1 Pet. 5:8]

'I will return to my house from which I came.' And when he comes, he finds *it* empty, swept, and put in order. 45Then he goes and takes with him seven other spirits more wicked than himself, and they enter and dwell there; *m*and the last *state* of that man is worse than the first. So shall it also be with this wicked generation."

Jesus' Mother and Brothers Send for Him

46While He was still talking to the multitudes, *n*behold, His mother and *o*brothers stood outside, seeking to speak with Him. 47Then one said to Him, "Look, *p*Your mother and Your brothers are standing outside, seeking to speak with You." 48But He answered and said to the one who told Him, "Who is My mother and who are My brothers?" 49And He stretched out His hand toward His disciples and said, "Here are My mother and My *q*brothers! 50For *r*whoever does the will of My Father in heaven is My brother and sister and mother."

The Parable of the Sower

13 On the same day Jesus went out of the house *a*and sat by the sea. 2*b*And great multitudes were gathered together to Him, so that *c*He got into a boat and sat; and the whole multitude stood on the shore.

3Then He spoke many things to them in parables, saying: *d*"Behold, a sower went out to sow. 4And as he sowed, some *seed* fell by the wayside; and the birds came and devoured them. 5Some fell on stony places, where they did not have much earth; and they immediately sprang up because they had no depth of earth. 6But when the sun was up they were scorched, and because they had no root they withered away. 7And some fell among thorns, and the thorns sprang up and choked them. 8But others fell on good ground and yielded a crop: some *e*a hundredfold, some sixty, some thirty. 9*f*He who has ears to hear, let him hear!"

The Purpose of Parables

10And the disciples came and said to Him, "Why do You speak to them in parables?"

11He answered and said to them, "Because *g*it has been given to you to know the mysteries of the kingdom of heaven, but to them it has not been given. 12*h*For whoever has, to him more will be given, and he will have abundance; but whoever does not have, even what he has will be taken away from him. 13Therefore I speak to them in parables, because seeing they do not see, and hearing they do not hear, nor do they understand. 14And in them the prophecy of Isaiah is fulfilled, which says:

i'Hearing you will hear and shall not understand,
And seeing you will see and not *i*perceive;
15 For the hearts of this people have grown dull,
Their ears *k*are hard of hearing,
And their eyes they have *l*closed,
Lest they should see with their eyes and hear with their ears,
Lest they should understand with their hearts and turn,
So that I should* *m*heal them.'*

16But *n*blessed *are* your eyes for they see, and your ears for they hear; 17for assuredly, I say to you *o*that many prophets and righteous *men* desired to see what you see, and did not see *it*, and to hear what you hear, and did not hear *it*.

The Parable of the Sower Explained

18*p*"Therefore hear the parable of the sower: 19When anyone hears the word *q*of the kingdom, and does not understand *it*, then the wicked *one* comes and snatches away what was sown in his heart. This is he who received seed by the wayside. 20But he who received the seed on stony places, this is he who hears the word and immediately *r*receives it with joy; 21yet he has no root in himself, but endures only for a while. For when *s*tribulation or persecution arises because of the word, immediately *t*he stumbles. 22Now *u*he who received seed *v*among the thorns is he who hears the word, and the cares of this world and the deceitfulness of riches choke the word,

---

* **13:15** NU-Text and M-Text read *would.* • Isaiah 6:9, 10

13:11 *it has been given to you.* The purpose of this parable was to both reveal and conceal the truth. This hiding of the truth was a judgment for unbelief, as happened during Isaiah's ministry (Is. 6:9–10).
13:14–15 Spiritual Death—Genesis 3 teaches us that, through sin, man died spiritually. Here, Christ quotes from Isaiah 6 to detail the meaning of spiritual death: Our ability to perceive spiritual reality is absent. Key spiritual senses don't work as they were originally designed to work. We can't see the implications of spiritual events. We can't understand the meaning of spiritual words. It is as if our senses are dead. In order to have our spiritual senses restored, we need someone to heal us. Only Christ can provide the necessary healing to open our spiritual eyes and ears.

12:45 *m* [2 Pet. 2:20–22]   **12:46** *n* Luke 8:19–21   *o* John 2:12; 7:3, 5   **12:47** *p* Matt. 13:55, 56   **12:49** *q* John 20:17   **12:50** *r* John 15:14   **13:1** *a* Mark 4:1–12   **13:2** *b* Luke 8:4   *c* Luke 5:3   **13:3** *d* Luke 8:5   **13:8** *e* Gen. 26:12   **13:9** *f* Matt. 11:15   **13:11** *g* Mark 4:10, 11   **13:12** *h* Matt. 13:29   **13:14** *i* Is. 6:9, 10; Ezek. 12:2   *j* [John 3:36]   **13:15** *k* Heb. 5:11   *l* Luke 19:42   *m* Acts 28:26, 27   **13:16** *n* Luke 10:23, 24   **13:17** *o* Heb. 11:13   **13:18** *p* Mark 4:13–20   **13:19** *q* Matt. 4:23   **13:20** *r* Is. 58:2   **13:21** *s* [Acts 14:22]   *t* Matt. 11:6   **13:22** *u* 1 Tim. 6:9   *v* Jer. 4:3

and he becomes unfruitful. ²³But he who received seed on the good ground is he who hears the word and understands *it*, who indeed bears ʷfruit and produces: some a hundredfold, some sixty, some thirty."

The Parable of the Wheat and the Tares

²⁴Another parable He put forth to them, saying: "The kingdom of heaven is like a man who sowed good seed in his field; ²⁵but while men slept, his enemy came and sowed tares among the wheat and went his way. ²⁶But when the grain had sprouted and produced a crop, then the tares also appeared. ²⁷So the servants of the owner came and said to him, 'Sir, did you not sow good seed in your field? How then does it have tares?' ²⁸He said to them, 'An enemy has done this.' The servants said to him, 'Do you want us then to go and gather them up?' ²⁹But he said, 'No, lest while you gather up the tares you also uproot the wheat with them. ³⁰Let both grow together until the harvest, and at the time of harvest I will say to the reapers, "First gather together the tares and bind them in bundles to burn them, but ˣgather the wheat into my barn." ' "

The Parable of the Mustard Seed

³¹Another parable He put forth to them, saying: ʸ"The kingdom of heaven is like a mustard seed, which a man took and sowed in his field, ³²which indeed is the least of all the seeds; but when it is grown it is greater than the herbs and becomes a ᶻtree, so that the birds of the air come and nest in its branches."

The Parable of the Leaven

³³ᵃAnother parable He spoke to them: "The kingdom of heaven is like leaven, which a woman took and hid in three measures* of meal till ᵇit was all leavened."

Prophecy and the Parables

³⁴ᶜAll these things Jesus spoke to the multitude in parables; and without a parable He did not speak to them, ³⁵that it might be fulfilled which was spoken by the prophet, saying:

> ᵈ"I will open My mouth in
> parables;
> ᵉI will utter things kept secret from the
> foundation of the world."*

The Parable of the Tares Explained

³⁶Then Jesus sent the multitude away and went into the house. And His disciples came to Him, saying, "Explain to us the parable of the tares of the field."

³⁷He answered and said to them: "He who sows the good seed is the Son of Man. ³⁸ᶠThe field is the world, the good seeds are the sons of the kingdom, but the tares are ᵍthe sons of the wicked *one*. ³⁹The enemy who sowed them is the devil, ʰthe harvest is the end of the age, and the reapers are the angels. ⁴⁰Therefore as the tares are gathered and burned in the fire, so it will be at the end of this age. ⁴¹The Son of Man will send out His angels, ⁱand they will gather out of His kingdom all things that offend, and those who practice lawlessness, ⁴²ʲand will cast them into the furnace of fire. ᵏThere will be wailing and gnashing of teeth. ⁴³ˡThen the righteous will shine forth as the sun in the kingdom of their Father. ᵐHe who has ears to hear, let him hear!

The Parable of the Hidden Treasure

⁴⁴"Again, the kingdom of heaven is like treasure hidden in a field, which a man found and hid; and for joy over it he goes and ⁿsells all that he has and ᵒbuys that field.

---

* **13:33** Greek *sata*, approximately two pecks in all
* **13:35** Psalm 78:2

13:25 *his enemy came and sowed tares.* Tares are weeds which closely resemble wheat, but which do not produce good food. They are indistinguishable from the real wheat until the fruit appears. Just like the tares among the wheat, genuine believers and counterfeits will be allowed to remain together.
13:31 *like a mustard seed.* The parable of the mustard seed shows that the number of people who will inherit the kingdom will be very small at first, but it will grow to be completely out of proportion to its initial size.
13:33 *like leaven.* Although leaven is sometimes used in Scripture to symbolize evil, here the kingdom of heaven is being compared to the dynamic character of yeast. When yeast is mixed with the dough, it expands from within, causing the dough to grow. Rather than being powered by outward armies or organizations, the kingdom of God will grow by the internal power of the Holy Spirit.
13:42 *Hell*—This verse describes the separation that comes between the righteous and the wicked at the end of the age. The place of their eternal dwelling is described as a "furnace of fire," perhaps because fire is one of man's most vivid concepts of suffering. Some think that there is no real, actual hell of fire, and that instead the wicked simply cease to exist, but this is difficult to support. The Scriptures consistently speak of hell as a real place of torment and anguish for all who do not receive the salvation that Jesus offers.
13:44 *like treasure.* The main point here is the immense value of the kingdom, which far outweighs any sacrifice or inconvenience one might encounter on earth.

13:23 ʷ Col. 1:6   **13:30** ˣ Matt. 3:12   **13:31** ʸ Luke 13:18, 19   **13:32** ᶻ Ezek. 17:22–24; 31:3–9   **13:33** ᵃ Luke 13:20, 21   ᵇ [1 Cor. 5:6]   **13:34** ᶜ Ps. 78:2; Mark 4:33, 34   **13:35** ᵈ Ps. 78:2   ᵉ Eph. 3:9   **13:38** ᶠ Rom. 10:18   ᵍ John 8:44   **13:39** ʰ Rev. 14:15   **13:41** ⁱ Matt. 18:7   **13:42** ʲ Rev. 19:20; 20:10   ᵏ Matt. 8:12; 13:50   **13:43** ˡ [Dan. 12:3]   ᵐ Matt. 13:9   **13:44** ⁿ Phil. 3:7, 8   ᵒ [Is. 55:1]

The Parable of the Pearl of Great Price

45"Again, the kingdom of heaven is like a merchant seeking beautiful pearls, 46who, when he had found [p]one pearl of great price, went and sold all that he had and bought it.

The Parable of the Dragnet

47"Again, the kingdom of heaven is like a dragnet that was cast into the sea and [q]gathered some of every kind, 48which, when it was full, they drew to shore; and they sat down and gathered the good into vessels, but threw the bad away. 49So it will be at the end of the age. The angels will come forth, [r]separate the wicked from among the just, 50and cast them into the furnace of fire. There will be wailing and gnashing of teeth."

51Jesus said to them,* "Have you understood all these things?"

They said to Him, "Yes, Lord."*

52Then He said to them, "Therefore every scribe instructed concerning* the kingdom of heaven is like a householder who brings out of his treasure [s]*things* new and old."

Jesus Rejected at Nazareth

53Now it came to pass, when Jesus had finished these parables, that He departed from there. 54[t]When He had come to His own country, He taught them in their synagogue, so that they were astonished and said, "Where did this *Man* get this wisdom and *these* mighty works? 55[u]Is this not the carpenter's son? Is not His mother called Mary? And [v]His brothers [w]James, Joses,* Simon, and Judas? 56And His sisters, are they not all with us? Where then did this *Man* get all these things?" 57So they [x]were offended at Him.

But Jesus said to them, [y]"A prophet is not without honor except in his own country and in his own house." 58Now [z]He did not do many mighty works there because of their unbelief.

John the Baptist Beheaded

14 At that time [a]Herod the tetrarch heard the report about Jesus 2and said to his servants, "This is John the Baptist; he is risen from the dead, and therefore these powers are at work in him." 3[b]For Herod had laid hold of John and bound him, and put *him* in prison for the sake of Herodias, his brother Philip's wife. 4Because John had said to him, [c]"It is not lawful for you to have her." 5And although he wanted to put him to death, he feared the multitude, [d]because they counted him as a prophet.

6But when Herod's birthday was celebrated, the daughter of Herodias danced before them and pleased Herod. 7Therefore he promised with an oath to give her whatever she might ask.

8So she, having been prompted by her mother, said, "Give me John the Baptist's head here on a platter."

9And the king was sorry; nevertheless, because of the oaths and because of those who sat with him, he commanded *it* to be given to *her.* 10So he sent and had John beheaded in prison. 11And his head was brought on a platter and given to the girl, and she brought *it* to her mother. 12Then his disciples came and took away the body and buried it, and went and told Jesus.

Feeding the Five Thousand

13[e]When Jesus heard *it,* He departed from there by boat to a deserted place by Himself. But when the multitudes heard it, they followed Him on foot from the cities. 14And when Jesus went out He saw a great multitude; and He [f]was moved with compassion for them, and healed their sick. 15[g]When it was evening, His disciples came to Him, saying, "This is a deserted place, and the hour is already late. Send the multitudes away, that they may go into the villages and buy themselves food."

16But Jesus said to them, "They do not need to go away. You give them something to eat."

17And they said to Him, "We have here only five loaves and two fish."

18He said, "Bring them here to Me." 19Then He commanded the multitudes to sit down on the grass. And He took the five loaves and the two fish, and looking up to heaven, [h]He blessed and broke and gave the loaves to the disciples; and the disciples gave to the multitudes. 20So they all ate and were filled, and they took up twelve baskets full of the fragments that remained. 21Now those who had eaten were

* **13:51** NU-Text omits *Jesus said to them.* • NU-Text omits *Lord.* * **13:52** Or *for* * **13:55** NU-Text reads *Joseph.*

13:47 of every kind. The responsibility of the disciples would be to catch as many "fish" of every kind as possible. The work of judging or sorting out the false catch, however, is a job that disciples are neither called nor equipped to do. That work is assigned to angels at Christ's return.

14:3 for the sake of Herodias. Herod had gone to Rome, where he met Herodias, the wife of his half brother Philip. After seducing Herodias, Herod divorced his own wife and married his sister-in-law. John had rebuked the king for his moral transgressions.

13:46 [p] Prov. 2:4; 3:14, 15; 8:10, 19 **13:47** [q] Matt. 22:9, 10 **13:49** [r] Matt. 25:32 **13:52** [s] Song 7:13 **13:54** [t] Luke 4:16 **13:55** [u] John 6:42 [v] Matt. 12:46 [w] Mark 15:40 **13:57** [x] Matt. 11:6 [y] Luke 4:24 **13:58** [z] Mark 6:5, 6 **14:1** [a] Mark 6:14–29 **14:3** [b] Luke 3:19, 20 **14:4** [c] Lev. 18:16; 20:21 **14:5** [d] Luke 20:6 **14:13** [e] John 6:1, 2 **14:14** [f] Mark 6:34 **14:15** [g] Luke 9:12 **14:19** [h] Matt. 15:36; 26:26

about five thousand men, besides women and children.

Jesus Walks on the Sea

22Immediately Jesus made His disciples get into the boat and go before Him to the other side, while He sent the multitudes away. 23*i*And when He had sent the multitudes away, He went up on the mountain by Himself to pray. *j*Now when evening came, He was alone there. 24But the boat was now in the middle of the sea,* tossed by the waves, for the wind was contrary.

25Now in the fourth watch of the night Jesus went to them, walking on the sea. 26And when the disciples saw Him *k*walking on the sea, they were troubled, saying, "It is a ghost!" And they cried out for fear.

27But immediately Jesus spoke to them, saying, "Be of good *l*cheer! It is I; do not be afraid."

28And Peter answered Him and said, "Lord, if it is You, command me to come to You on the water."

29So He said, "Come." And when Peter had come down out of the boat, he walked on the water to go to Jesus. 30But when he saw that the wind *was* boisterous,* he was afraid; and beginning to sink he cried out, saying, "Lord, save me!"

31And immediately Jesus stretched out *His* hand and caught him, and said to him, "O you of *m*little faith, why did you doubt?" 32And when they got into the boat, the wind ceased.

33Then those who were in the boat came and* worshiped Him, saying, "Truly *n*You are the Son of God."

Many Touch Him and Are Made Well

34*o*When they had crossed over, they came to the land of* Gennesaret. 35And when the men of that place recognized Him, they sent out into all that surrounding region, brought to Him all who were sick, 36and begged Him that they might only *p*touch the hem of His garment. And *q*as many as touched *it* were made perfectly well.

Defilement Comes from Within

15 Then *a*the scribes and Pharisees who were from Jerusalem came to Jesus, saying, 2*b*"Why do Your disciples transgress the tradition of the elders? For they do not wash their hands when they eat bread."

3He answered and said to them, "Why do you also transgress the commandment of God because of your tradition? 4For God commanded, saying, *c*'Honor your father and your mother';* and, *d*'He who curses father or mother, let him be put to death.'* 5But you say, 'Whoever says to his father or mother, *e*"Whatever profit you might have received from me *is* a gift *to* God"— 6then he need not honor his father or mother.'* Thus you have made the commandment* of God of no effect by your tradition. 7*f*Hypocrites! Well did Isaiah prophesy about you, saying:

8 'These*g* people draw near to Me with
     their mouth,
And* honor Me with their lips,
But their heart is far from Me.
9 And in vain they worship Me,
  *h*Teaching as doctrines the
    commandments of men.' "*

10*i*When He had called the multitude to *Himself,* He said to them, "Hear and understand: 11*j*Not what goes into the mouth defiles a man; but what comes out of the mouth, this defiles a man."

12Then His disciples came and said to Him, "Do You know that the Pharisees were offended when they heard this saying?"

13But He answered and said, *k*"Every plant which My heavenly Father has not planted will be uprooted. 14Let them alone. *l*They are blind leaders of the blind. And if the blind leads the blind, both will fall into a ditch."

---

* **14:24** NU-Text reads *many furlongs away from the land.*   * **14:30** NU-Text brackets *that* and *boisterous* as disputed.   * **14:33** NU-Text omits *came and.*   * **14:34** NU-Text reads *came to land at.*   * **15:4** Exodus 20:12; Deuteronomy 5:16 • Exodus 21:17   * **15:6** NU-Text omits *or mother.* • NU-Text reads *word.*   * **15:8** NU-Text omits *draw near to Me with their mouth, And.*   * **15:9** Isaiah 29:13

14:25 *the fourth watch.* This would be between 3:00 and 6:00 A.M.

15:2 *the tradition of the elders.* This was not the law of Moses, but oral tradition, based on interpretations of the law.

15:3 *tradition.* The scribes and Pharisees were placing their own views above the revelation of God, and yet claimed to be following Him.

15:7 *Hypocrites.* The Pharisees had laid down many rigid and inflexible laws concerning diet, Sabbath day activities, ceremonial washings, and many other traditions. Not only did this reduce spiritual service to a harsh system of dos and don'ts, it also caused everyone, Pharisees included, to look for loopholes of escape from the burden of so many laws and rules. The ultimate outcome was religious hypocrisy. Christ came both to fulfill the law (5:17–18) and also to free us from its penalty (Gal. 3:13).

14:23 *i* Mark 6:46   *j* John 6:16   **14:26** *k* Job 9:8   **14:27** *l* Acts 23:11; 27:22, 25, 36   **14:31** *m* Matt. 6:30; 8:26   **14:33** *n* Ps. 2:7   **14:34** *o* Mark 6:53   **14:36** *p* [Mark 5:24–34]   *q* [Luke 6:19]   **15:1** *a* Mark 7:1   **15:2** *b* Mark 7:5   **15:4** *c* [Deut. 5:16]   *d* Ex. 21:17   **15:5** *e* Mark 7:11, 12   **15:7** *f* Mark 7:6   **15:8** *g* Ps. 78:36; Is. 29:13   **15:9** *h* [Col. 2:18–22]   **15:10** *i* Mark 7:14   **15:11** *j* [Acts 10:15]   **15:13** *k* [John 15:2]   **15:14** *l* Luke 6:39

15*m*Then Peter answered and said to Him, "Explain this parable to us."

16So Jesus said, *n*"Are you also still without understanding? 17Do you not yet understand that *o*whatever enters the mouth goes into the stomach and is eliminated? 18But *p*those things which proceed out of the mouth come from the heart, and they defile a man. 19*q*For out of the heart proceed evil thoughts, murders, adulteries, fornications, thefts, false witness, blasphemies. 20These are *the things* which defile a man, but to eat with unwashed hands does not defile a man."

A Gentile Shows Her Faith

21*r*Then Jesus went out from there and departed to the region of Tyre and Sidon. 22And behold, a woman of Canaan came from that region and cried out to Him, saying, "Have mercy on me, O Lord, *s*Son of David! My daughter is severely demon-possessed."

23But He answered her not a word.

And His disciples came and urged Him, saying, "Send her away, for she cries out after us."

24But He answered and said, *t*"I was not sent except to the lost sheep of the house of Israel."

25Then she came and worshiped Him, saying, "Lord, help me!"

26But He answered and said, "It is not good to take the children's bread and throw *it* to the little *u*dogs."

27And she said, "Yes, Lord, yet even the little dogs eat the crumbs which fall from their masters' table."

28Then Jesus answered and said to her, "O woman, *v*great *is* your faith! Let it be to you as you desire." And her daughter was healed from that very hour.

Jesus Heals Great Multitudes

29*w*Jesus departed from there, *x*skirted the Sea of Galilee, and went up on the mountain and sat down there. 30*y*Then great multitudes came to Him, having with them *the* lame, blind, mute, maimed, and many others; and they laid them down at Jesus' *z*feet, and He healed them. 31So the multitude marveled when they saw *the* mute speaking, *the* maimed made whole, *the* lame walking, and *the* blind seeing; and they *a*glorified the God of Israel.

Feeding the Four Thousand

32*b*Now Jesus called His disciples to *Himself* and said, "I have compassion on the multitude, because they have now continued with Me three days and have nothing to eat. And I do not want to send them away hungry, lest they faint on the way."

33*c*Then His disciples said to Him, "Where could we get enough bread in the wilderness to fill such a great multitude?"

34Jesus said to them, "How many loaves do you have?"

And they said, "Seven, and a few little fish."

35So He commanded the multitude to sit down on the ground. 36And *d*He took the seven loaves and the fish and *e*gave thanks, broke *them* and gave *them* to His disciples; and the disciples *gave* to the multitude. 37So they all ate and were filled, and they took up seven large baskets full of the fragments that were left. 38Now those who ate were four thousand men, besides women and children. 39*f*And He sent away the multitude, got into the boat, and came to the region of Magdala.*

The Pharisees and Sadducees Seek a Sign

16 Then the *a*Pharisees and Sadducees came, and testing Him asked that He would show them a sign from heaven. 2He answered and said to them, "When it is evening you say, '*It will be* fair weather, for the sky is red'; 3and in the morning, '*It will be* foul weather today, for the sky is red and threatening.' Hypocrites!* You know how to discern the face of the sky, but you cannot *discern* the signs of the times. 4*b*A wicked and adulterous generation seeks after a sign, and no sign shall be given to it except the sign of the prophet* Jonah." And He left them and departed.

* **15:39** NU-Text reads *Magadan.* * **16:3** NU-Text omits *Hypocrites.* * **16:4** NU-Text omits *the prophet.*

15:18 *come from the heart.* As we think in our hearts, or inner beings, so we are. The raw material of our actions is what we take into our minds and allow to settle in our hearts. David put it this way: "Your word I have hidden in my heart, that I might not sin against You" (Ps. 119:11). The other side is seen in Psalm 101:3 "I will set nothing wicked before my eyes." Paul says the believer must bring "every thought into captivity to the obedience of Christ" (2 Cor. 10:5).

15:22 *Have mercy on me, O Lord, Son of David.* The woman was a Gentile who would have had no natural claim on the Jewish Messiah.

15:31 *glorified the God of Israel.* The Gentiles believed and glorified Israel's God, while many in Israel remained blind to their Messiah.

15:15 *m* Mark 7:17　**15:16** *n* Matt. 16:9　**15:17** *o* [1 Cor. 6:13]　**15:18** *p* [James 3:6]　**15:19** *q* Prov. 6:14　**15:21** *r* Mark 7:24–30　**15:22** *s* Matt. 1:1; 22:41, 42　**15:24** *t* Matt. 10:5, 6　**15:26** *u* Matt. 7:6　**15:28** *v* Luke 7:9　**15:29** *w* Mark 7:31–37　*x* Matt. 4:18　**15:30** *y* Is. 35:5, 6　*z* Luke 7:38; 8:41; 10:39　**15:31** *a* Luke 5:25, 26; 19:37, 38　**15:32** *b* Mark 8:1–10　**15:33** *c* 2 Kin. 4:43　**15:36** *d* Matt. 14:19; 26:27　*e* Luke 22:19　**15:39** *f* Mark 8:10　**16:1** *a* Mark 8:11　**16:4** *b* Matt. 12:39

The Leaven of the Pharisees and Sadducees

5Now cwhen His disciples had come to the other side, they had forgotten to take bread. 6Then Jesus said to them, d"Take heed and beware of the leaven of the Pharisees and the Sadducees."

7And they reasoned among themselves, saying, "It is because we have taken no bread."

8But Jesus, being aware of it, said to them, "O you of little faith, why do you reason among yourselves because you have brought no bread?* 9eDo you not yet understand, or remember the five loaves of the five thousand and how many baskets you took up? 10fNor the seven loaves of the four thousand and how many large baskets you took up? 11How is it you do not understand that I did not speak to you concerning bread?—but to beware of the leaven of the Pharisees and Sadducees."

12Then they understood that He did not tell them to beware of the leaven of bread, but of the doctrine of the Pharisees and Sadducees.

Peter Confesses Jesus as the Christ

13When Jesus came into the region of Caesarea Philippi, He asked His disciples, saying, g"Who do men say that I, the Son of Man, am?"

14So they said, h"Some say John the Baptist, some Elijah, and others Jeremiah or ione of the prophets."

15He said to them, "But who do jyou say that I am?"

16Simon Peter answered and said, k"You are the Christ, the Son of the living God."

17Jesus answered and said to him, "Blessed are you, Simon Bar-Jonah, lfor flesh and blood has not revealed this to you, but mMy Father who is in heaven. 18And I also say to you that nyou are Peter, and oon this rock I will build My church, and pthe gates of Hades shall not prevail

against it. 19qAnd I will give you the keys of the kingdom of heaven, and whatever you bind on earth will be bound in heaven, and whatever you loose on earth will be loosed* in heaven."

20rThen He commanded His disciples that they should tell no one that He was Jesus the Christ.

Jesus Predicts His Death and Resurrection

21From that time Jesus began sto show to His disciples that He must go to Jerusalem, and suffer many things from the elders and chief priests and scribes, and be killed, and be raised the third day.

22Then Peter took Him aside and began to rebuke Him, saying, "Far be it from You, Lord; this shall not happen to You!"

23But He turned and said to Peter, "Get behind Me, tSatan! uYou are an offense to Me, for you are not mindful of the things of God, but the things of men."

Take Up the Cross and Follow Him

24vThen Jesus said to His disciples, "If anyone desires to come after Me, let him deny himself, and take up his cross, and wfollow Me. 25For xwhoever desires to save his life will lose it, but whoever loses his life for My sake will find it. 26For what yprofit is it to a man if he gains the whole world, and loses his own soul? Or zwhat will a man give in exchange for his soul? 27For athe Son of Man will come in the glory of His Father bwith His angels, cand then He will reward each according to his works. 28Assuredly, I say to you, dthere are some standing here who shall not taste death till they see the Son of Man coming in His kingdom."

---

* 16:8 NU-Text reads you have no bread.
* 16:19 Or will have been bound ... will have been loosed

16:11–12 leaven. In Scripture, leaven is often used as a symbol of evil. The doctrine of the Pharisees and Sadducees was hypocrisy and legalism, political opportunism, and spiritual hardness.

16:16 Church—Peter's confession "You are the Christ, the Son of the living God" is the foundation on which the church is built. Never mind how small the apostolic band may be, the church is indestructible, and with unsurpassed power overcomes Satan and cannot be overcome. The power comes from God, the Creator of the universe, Owner and Master of the church. All the church has is derived from and dependent on the Almighty Son of God.

16:18 The Origin of the Church—The church was a mystery (not clearly revealed) in the Old Testament. Christ prophesied in these words spoken to Peter, "on this rock I will build My church." There is a play here on the word rock, which also happens to be Peter's name. Jesus said, "you are Peter" (masculine, petros) and "on this rock" (feminine, petra) "I will build My

church." The Holy Spirit came upon the church on the Day of Pentecost in response to Peter's sermon when "three thousand souls were added to them" (Acts 2:41). This group, along with the original disciples, became "the church."

16:28 not taste death. In the transfiguration, Peter, James, and John saw a preview of the kingdom. Jesus was explaining that very soon those three disciples would see Him glorified as He will be in the kingdom.

16:5 c Mark 8:14   16:6 d Luke 12:1   16:9 e Matt. 14:15–21   16:10 f Matt. 15:32–38   16:13 g Luke 9:18   16:14 h Matt. 14:2 i Matt. 21:11   16:15 j John 6:67   16:16 k Acts 8:37; 9:20   16:17 l [Eph. 2:8] m Gal. 1:16   16:18 n John 1:42 o [Eph. 2:20] p Is. 38:10   16:19 q Matt. 18:18   16:20 r Luke 9:21   16:21 s Luke 9:22; 18:31; 24:46   16:23 t Matt. 4:10 u [Rom. 8:7]   16:24 v [2 Tim. 3:12] w [1 Pet. 2:21]   16:25 x John 12:25   16:26 y Luke 12:20, 21 z Ps. 49:7, 8   16:27 a Mark 8:38 b [Dan. 7:10] c Rom. 2:6   16:28 d Luke 9:27

Jesus Transfigured on the Mount

17 Now *a*after six days Jesus took Peter, James, and John his brother, led them up on a high mountain by themselves; 2and He was transfigured before them. His face shone like the sun, and His clothes became as white as the light. 3And behold, Moses and Elijah appeared to them, talking with Him. 4Then Peter answered and said to Jesus, "Lord, it is good for us to be here; if You wish, let us* make here three tabernacles: one for You, one for Moses, and one for Elijah."

5bWhile he was still speaking, behold, a bright cloud overshadowed them; and suddenly a voice came out of the cloud, saying, c"This is My beloved Son, din whom I am well pleased. eHear Him!" 6fAnd when the disciples heard it, they fell on their faces and were greatly afraid. 7But Jesus came and gtouched them and said, "Arise, and do not be afraid." 8When they had lifted up their eyes, they saw no one but Jesus only.

9Now as they came down from the mountain, Jesus commanded them, saying, "Tell the vision to no one until the Son of Man is risen from the dead."

10And His disciples asked Him, saying, h"Why then do the scribes say that Elijah must come first?"

11Jesus answered and said to them, "Indeed, Elijah is coming first* and will irestore all things. 12jBut I say to you that Elijah has come already, and they kdid not know him but did to him whatever they wished. Likewise lthe Son of Man is also about to suffer at their hands." 13mThen the disciples understood that He spoke to them of John the Baptist.

A Boy Is Healed

14nAnd when they had come to the multitude, a man came to Him, kneeling down to Him and saying, 15"Lord, have mercy on my son, for he is an epileptic* and suffers severely; for he often falls into the fire and often into the water. 16So I brought him to Your disciples, but they could not cure him."

17Then Jesus answered and said, "O faithless and operverse generation, how long shall I be with you? How long shall I bear with you? Bring him here to Me." 18And Jesus prebuked the demon, and it came out of him; and the child was cured from that very hour.

19Then the disciples came to Jesus privately and said, "Why could we not cast it out?"

20So Jesus said to them, "Because of your unbelief;* for assuredly, I say to you, qif you have faith as a mustard seed, you will say to this mountain, 'Move from here to there,' and it will move; and nothing will be impossible for you. 21However, this kind does not go out except by prayer and fasting."*

Jesus Again Predicts His Death and Resurrection

22rNow while they were staying* in Galilee, Jesus said to them, "The Son of Man is about to be betrayed into the hands of men, 23and they will kill Him, and the third day He will be raised up." And they were exceedingly ssorrowful.

Peter and His Master Pay Their Taxes

24tWhen they had come to Capernaum,* those who received the temple tax came to Peter and said, "Does your Teacher not pay the temple tax?"

25He said, "Yes."

And when he had come into the house, Jesus anticipated him, saying, "What do you think, Simon? From whom do the kings of the earth take customs or taxes, from their sons or from ustrangers?"

26Peter said to Him, "From strangers."

Jesus said to him, "Then the sons are free. 27Nevertheless, lest we offend them, go to the sea, cast in a hook, and take the fish that comes up first. And when you have opened its mouth, you will find a piece of money;* take that and give it to them for Me and you."

---

* 17:4 NU-Text reads *I will.* * 17:11 NU-Text omits *first.* * 17:15 Literally *moonstruck* * 17:20 NU-Text reads *little faith.* * 17:21 NU-Text omits this verse. * 17:22 NU-Text reads *gathering together.* * 17:24 NU-Text reads *Capharnaum* (here and elsewhere). * 17:27 Greek *stater*, the exact amount to pay the temple tax (didrachma) for two

---

17:3 Moses and Elijah. This amazing experience was not only to show the disciples that Jesus was God's Son, but also to show them that He supersedes the law and the prophets and that they were subordinate to Him. It also explained that what Jesus was doing was no mystery to the Old Testament. The Old Testament people had been long looking forward to the Messiah and His kingdom.

17:11–13 Elijah. Jesus indicates that the prophecies concerning Elijah had their fulfillment in John the Baptist, yet because the restoration is not complete, many conclude that the role of Elijah will be taken up by one of the two witnesses of Revelation 11:3–6.

17:24 temple tax. This was a tax given annually by every adult Jewish male over 20 years of age for maintaining the temple. It was based on Exodus 30:13, and amounted to two days' wages for a common laborer.

17:25 strangers. Most likely this means the king taxed the common people and not the imperial family.

17:1 *a* Mark 9:2–8   **17:5** *b* 2 Pet. 1:17 *c* Mark 1:11
d Matt. 3:17; 12:18 *e* [Deut. 18:15, 19]   **17:6** *f* 2 Pet.
1:18   **17:7** *g* Dan. 8:18   **17:10** *h* Mal. 4:5   **17:11** *i* [Mal.
4:6]   **17:12** *j* Mark 9:12, 13 *k* Matt. 14:3, 10 *l* Matt.
16:21   **17:13** *m* Matt. 11:14   **17:14** *n* Mark 9:14–28
17:17 *o* Phil. 2:15   **17:18** *p* Luke 4:41   **17:20** *q* Luke
17:6   **17:22** *r* Mark 8:31   **17:23** *s* John 16:6; 19:30
17:24 *t* Mark 9:33   **17:25** *u* [Is. 60:10–17]

Who Is the Greatest?

18 At *a*that time the disciples came to Jesus, saying, "Who then is greatest in the kingdom of heaven?"

2Then Jesus called a little *b*child to Him, set him in the midst of them, 3and said, "Assuredly, I say to you, *c*unless you are converted and become as little children, you will by no means enter the kingdom of heaven. 4*d*Therefore whoever humbles himself as this little child is the greatest in the kingdom of heaven. 5*e*Whoever receives one little child like this in My name receives Me.

Jesus Warns of Offenses

6*f*"Whoever causes one of these little ones who believe in Me to sin, it would be better for him if a millstone were hung around his neck, and he were drowned in the depth of the sea. 7Woe to the world because of offenses! For *g*offenses must come, but *h*woe to that man by whom the offense comes!

8*i*"If your hand or foot causes you to sin, cut it off and cast *it* from you. It is better for you to enter into life lame or maimed, rather than having two hands or two feet, to be cast into the everlasting fire. 9And if your eye causes you to sin, pluck it out and cast *it* from you. It is better for you to enter into life with one eye, rather than having two eyes, to be cast into hell fire.

The Parable of the Lost Sheep

10"Take heed that you do not despise one of these little ones, for I say to you that in heaven *j*their angels always *k*see the face of My Father who is in heaven. 11*l*For the Son of Man has come to save that which was lost.*

12*m*"What do you think? If a man has a hundred sheep, and one of them goes astray, does he not leave the ninety-nine and go to the mountains to seek the one that is straying? 13And if he should find it, assuredly, I say to you, he rejoices more over that *sheep* than over the ninety-nine that did not go astray. 14Even so it is not the *n*will of your Father who is in heaven that one of these little ones should perish.

Dealing with a Sinning Brother

15"Moreover *o*if your brother sins against you, go and tell him his fault between you and him alone. If he hears you, *p*you have gained your brother. 16But if he will not hear, take with you one or two more, that *q*'by the mouth of two or three witnesses every word may be established.'* 17And if he refuses to hear them, tell *it* to the church. But if he refuses even to hear the church, let him be to you like a *r*heathen and a tax collector.

18"Assuredly, I say to you, *s*whatever you bind on earth will be bound in heaven, and whatever you loose on earth will be loosed in heaven.

19*t*"Again I say* to you that if two of you agree on earth concerning anything that they ask, *u*it will be done for them by My Father in heaven. 20For where two or three are gathered *v*together in My name, I am there in the midst of them."

The Parable of the Unforgiving Servant

21Then Peter came to Him and said, "Lord, how often shall my brother sin against me, and I forgive him? *w*Up to seven times?"

22Jesus said to him, "I do not say to you, *x*up to seven times, but up to seventy times seven. 23Therefore the kingdom of heaven is like a certain king who wanted to settle accounts with his servants. 24And when he had begun to settle accounts, one was brought to him who owed him ten thousand talents. 25But as he was not able to pay, his master commanded *y*that he be sold, with

* **18:11** NU-Text omits this verse. * **18:16** Deuteronomy 19:15 * **18:19** NU-Text and M-Text read *Again, assuredly, I say.*

18:3 *converted.* To be "converted" means to turn around, to take a different course (Luke 22:32).

18:10 *their angels.* This verse seems to imply that angels watch over and serve His followers on earth (Heb. 1:14).

18:16 *two or three witnesses.* The principle of witnesses is taken from Deuteronomy 19:15. Evidently, in this case they are to witness that the offended brother is acting in good faith and the right spirit in attempting to work towards reconciliation. They would also be witnesses to any agreement.

18:17 *church.* Unfortunately "discipline" has sometimes been reduced to a merely negative concept. To be sure, discipline includes the notion of punishment and correction, but church discipline in this context clearly has the restoration of the offender in view. Severe measures may sometimes need to be taken with an erring brother or sister, but restoration and reconciliation should always be the goal.

18:22 *seventy times seven.* Some translations say "seventy-seven times." Whichever number is used, the point is the same: be ready to forgive over and over again, past counting. This verse does not only apply to forgiveness for seventy times seven different sins. Sometimes, we may have to consciously decide to forgive and let go of an old hurt again and again, "seventy times seven."

18:1 *a* Luke 9:46–48; 22:24–27 **18:2** *b* Matt. 19:14 **18:3** *c* Luke 18:16 **18:4** *d* [Matt. 20:27; 23:11] **18:5** *e* [Matt. 10:42] **18:6** *f* Mark 9:42 **18:7** *g* [1 Cor. 11:19] *h* Matt. 26:24; 27:4, 5 **18:8** *i* Matt. 5:29, 30 **18:10** *j* [Heb. 1:14] *k* Luke 1:19 **18:11** *l* Luke 9:56 **18:12** *m* Luke 15:4–7 **18:14** *n* [1 Tim. 2:4] **18:15** *o* Lev. 19:17 *p* [James 5:20] **18:16** *q* Deut. 17:6; 19:15 **18:17** *r* [2 Thess. 3:6, 14] **18:18** *s* [John 20:22, 23] **18:19** *t* [1 Cor. 1:10] *u* [1 John 3:22; 5:14] **18:20** *v* Acts 20:7 **18:21** *w* Luke 17:4 **18:22** *x* Col. 3:13 **18:25** *y* 2 Kin. 4:1

his wife and children and all that he had, and that payment be made. [26]The servant therefore fell down before him, saying, 'Master, have patience with me, and I will pay you all.' [27]Then the master of that servant was moved with compassion, released him, and forgave him the debt.

[28]"But that servant went out and found one of his fellow servants who owed him a hundred denarii; and he laid hands on him and took *him* by the throat, saying, 'Pay me what you owe!' [29]So his fellow servant fell down at his feet* and begged him, saying, 'Have patience with me, and I will pay you all.'* [30]And he would not, but went and threw him into prison till he should pay the debt. [31]So when his fellow servants saw what had been done, they were very grieved, and came and told their master all that had been done. [32]Then his master, after he had called him, said to him, 'You wicked servant! I forgave you [z]all that debt because you begged me. [33]Should you not also have had compassion on your fellow servant, just as I had pity on you?' [34]And his master was angry, and delivered him to the torturers until he should pay all that was due to him.

[35]a"So My heavenly Father also will do to you if each of you, from his heart, does not forgive his brother his trespasses."*

Marriage and Divorce

19 Now it came to pass, [a]when Jesus had finished these sayings, *that* He departed from Galilee and came to the region of Judea beyond the Jordan. [2]b And great multitudes followed Him, and He healed them there.

[3]The Pharisees also came to Him, testing Him, and saying to Him, "Is it lawful for a man to divorce his wife for *just* any reason?"

[4]And He answered and said to them, "Have you not read that He who made* them at the beginning [c]'made them male and female,'* [5]and said, [d]'For this reason a man shall leave his father and mother and be joined to his wife, and [e]the two shall become one flesh'?* [6]So then, they are no longer two but one flesh. Therefore what God has joined together, let not man separate."

[7]They said to Him, [f]"Why then did Moses command to give a certificate of divorce, and to put her away?"

[8]He said to them, "Moses, because of the [g]hardness of your hearts, permitted you to divorce your [h]wives, but from the beginning it was not so. [9]i And I say to you, whoever divorces his wife, except for sexual immorality,* and marries another, commits adultery; and whoever marries her who is divorced commits adultery."

[10]His disciples said to Him, [j]"If such is the case of the man with *his* wife, it is better not to marry."

Jesus Teaches on Celibacy

[11]But He said to them, [k]"All cannot accept this saying, but only *those* to whom it has been given: [12]For there are eunuchs who were born thus from *their* mother's womb, and [l]there are eunuchs who were made eunuchs by men, and there are eunuchs who have made themselves eunuchs for the kingdom of heaven's sake. He who is able to accept *it*, let him accept *it*."

Jesus Blesses Little Children

[13]m Then little children were brought to Him that He might put *His* hands on them and pray, but the disciples rebuked them. [14]But Jesus said, "Let the little children come to Me, and do not forbid them; for [n]of such is the kingdom of heaven." [15]And He laid *His* hands on them and departed from there.

Jesus Counsels the Rich Young Ruler

[16]o Now behold, one came and said to Him, [p]"Good* Teacher, what good thing shall I do that I may have eternal life?"

[17]So He said to him, "Why do you call Me good?* No one *is* [q]good but One, *that is*, God.* But if you want to enter into life, [r]keep the commandments."

[18]He said to Him, "Which ones?"

---

* **18:29** NU-Text omits *at his feet.* • NU-Text and M-Text omit *all.* * **18:35** NU-Text omits *his trespasses.* * **19:4** NU-Text reads *created.* • Genesis 1:27; 5:2 * **19:5** Genesis 2:24 * **19:9** Or *fornication* * **19:16** NU-Text omits *Good.* * **19:17** NU-Text reads *Why do you ask Me about what is good?* • NU-Text reads *There is One who is good.*

18:35 forgive. This verse is a serious warning (1 John 4:20).

19:9 divorces his wife. When the Pharisees asked Jesus if divorce could ever be considered lawful, He did not fall into their trap. He took them back to Genesis and God's original intent in marriage, one man and one woman for life (vv. 4–5; Gen. 1:27; 2:24). In spite of the "exception clause," one thing is surely clear: God hates divorce (Mal. 2:15–16). Marriage is a divine arrangement that is intended to be permanent and inviolable. Straying from God's path always has tragic consequences.

19:12 eunuchs. The term eunuch refers to a castrated man, whether by surgery, accident, or birth.

In the ancient world, eunuchs were put in charge of harems, because they had the physical strength and endurance of a man, but would not be a sexual threat to the women of the harem.

18:32 [z] Luke 7:41–43 **18:35** [d] James 2:13 **19:1** [a] Mark 10:1–12 **19:2** [b] Matt. 12:15 **19:4** [c] Gen. 1:27; 5:2 **19:5** [d] Gen. 2:24 [e] [1 Cor. 6:16; 7:2] **19:7** [f] Deut. 24:1–4 **19:8** [g] Heb. 3:15 [h] Mal. 2:16 **19:9** [i] [Matt. 5:32] **19:10** [j] [Prov. 21:19] **19:11** [k] [1 Cor. 7:2, 7, 9, 17] **19:12** [l] [1 Cor. 7:32] **19:13** [m] Luke 18:15 **19:14** [n] Matt. 18:3, 4 **19:16** [o] Mark 10:17–30 [p] Luke 10:25 **19:17** [q] Nah. 1:7 [r] Lev. 18:5

Jesus said, s"'*You shall not murder,' 'You shall not commit adultery,' 'You shall not steal,' 'You shall not bear false witness,'* 19t'*Honor your father and your mother,'** and, u'*You shall love your neighbor as yourself.'*"*

20The young man said to Him, "All these things I have vkept from my youth.* What do I still lack?"

21Jesus said to him, "If you want to be perfect, wgo, sell what you have and give to the poor, and you will have treasure in heaven; and come, follow Me."

22But when the young man heard that saying, he went away sorrowful, for he had great possessions.

With God All Things Are Possible

23Then Jesus said to His disciples, "Assuredly, I say to you that xit is hard for a rich man to enter the kingdom of heaven. 24And again I say to you, it is easier for a camel to go through the eye of a needle than for a rich man to enter the kingdom of God."

25When His disciples heard *it*, they were greatly astonished, saying, "Who then can be saved?"

26But Jesus looked at *them* and said to them, "With men this is impossible, but ywith God all things are possible."

27Then Peter answered and said to Him, "See, zwe have left all and followed You. Therefore what shall we have?"

28So Jesus said to them, "Assuredly I say to you, that in the regeneration, when the Son of Man sits on the throne of His glory, ayou who have followed Me will also sit on twelve thrones, judging the twelve tribes of Israel. 29bAnd everyone who has left houses or brothers or sisters or father or mother or wife* or children or lands, for My name's sake, shall receive a hundredfold, and inherit eternal life. 30cBut many *who are* first will be last, and the last first.

The Parable of the Workers in the Vineyard

20 "For the kingdom of heaven is like a landowner who went out early in the morning to hire laborers for his vineyard. 2Now when he had agreed with the laborers for a denarius a day, he sent them into his vineyard. 3And he went out about the third hour and saw others standing idle in the marketplace, 4and said to them, 'You also go into the vineyard, and whatever is right I will give you.' So they went. 5Again he went out about the sixth and the ninth hour, and did likewise. 6And about the eleventh hour he went out and found others standing idle,* and said to them, 'Why have you been standing here idle all day?' 7They said to him, 'Because no one hired us.' He said to them, 'You also go into the vineyard, and whatever is right you will receive.'*

8"So when evening had come, the owner of the vineyard said to his steward, 'Call the laborers and give them *their* wages, beginning with the last to the first.' 9And when those came who *were hired* about the eleventh hour, they each received a denarius. 10But when the first came, they supposed that they would receive more; and they likewise received each a denarius. 11And when they had received *it*, they complained against the landowner, 12saying, 'These last *men* have worked *only* one hour, and you made them equal to us who have borne the burden and the heat of the day.' 13But he answered one of them and said, 'Friend, I am doing you no wrong. Did you not agree with me for a denarius? 14Take *what is* yours and go your way. I wish to give to this last man *the same* as to you. 15aIs it not lawful for me to do what I wish with my own things? Or bis your eye evil because I am good?' 16cSo the last will be first, and the first last. dFor many are called, but few chosen."*

---

* **19:19** Exodus 20:12–16; Deuteronomy 5:16–20
• Leviticus 19:18   * **19:20** NU-Text omits *from my youth.*   * **19:29** NU-Text omits *or wife.*
* **20:6** NU-Text omits *idle.*   * **20:7** NU-Text omits the last clause of this verse.   * **20:16** NU-Text omits the last sentence of this verse.

19:21 *sell what you have.* This verse does not teach salvation by works (Rom. 3:23–24; Eph. 2;8–9). Rather, Jesus was proving that the rich young man could not have truly fulfilled all of the law of Moses. If he really loved his neighbor as the law required (Lev. 19:18), he would not have had any difficulty in giving away his wealth to the poor.

19:23–24 *it is hard for a rich man to enter the kingdom.* The point of this seems to be that fear of losing one's wealth can hold a person back to the extent that they will never become saved at all. One of the things that goes with being saved is saying, "God's way, not my way."

20:3 *third hour.* This was about 9:00 A.M.

20:5 *the sixth and the ninth hour.* This was about noon and about 3:00 P.M.

20:6 *the eleventh hour.* This was about 5:00 P.M. There would be only an hour or so left in the working day.

20:16 *the last will be first.* The workers who were collected without an agreement represent the Gentiles who are made equal with the Jewish people when salvation became available to all through Jesus Christ (Rom. 11:15; Eph. 2:13–15; 3:6).

19:18 s Ex. 20:13–16   **19:19** t Ex. 20:12–16; Deut. 5:16–20   u Lev. 19:18   **19:20** v [Phil. 3:6, 7]   **19:21** w Acts 2:45; 4:34, 35   **19:23** x [1 Tim. 6:9]   **19:26** y Jer. 32:17   **19:27** z Deut. 33:9   **19:28** a Luke 22:28–30   **19:29** b Mark 10:29, 30   **19:30** c Luke 13:30   **20:15** a [Rom. 9:20, 21]   b Deut. 15:9   **20:16** c Matt. 19:30   d Matt. 22:14

Jesus a Third Time Predicts His Death and Resurrection

17eNow Jesus, going up to Jerusalem, took the twelve disciples aside on the road and said to them, 18f"Behold, we are going up to Jerusalem, and the Son of Man will be betrayed to the chief priests and to the scribes; and they will condemn Him to death, 19gand deliver Him to the Gentiles to hmock and to iscourge and to jcrucify. And the third day He will krise again."

Greatness Is Serving

20lThen the mother of mZebedee's sons came to Him with her sons, kneeling down and asking something from Him.

21And He said to her, "What do you wish?"

She said to Him, "Grant that these two sons of mine nmay sit, one on Your right hand and the other on the left, in Your kingdom."

22But Jesus answered and said, "You do not know what you ask. Are you able to drink othe cup that I am about to drink, and be baptized with pthe baptism that I am baptized with?"*

They said to Him, "We are able."

23So He said to them, q"You will indeed drink My cup, and be baptized with the baptism that I am baptized with;* but to sit on My right hand and on My left is not Mine to give, but it is for those for whom it is prepared by My Father."

24rAnd when the ten heard it, they were greatly displeased with the two brothers. 25But Jesus called them to Himself and said, "You know that the rulers of the Gentiles lord it over them, and those who are great exercise authority over them. 26Yet sit shall not be so among you; but twhoever desires to become great among you, let him be your servant. 27uAnd whoever desires to be first among you, let him be your slave— 28vjust as the wSon of Man did not come to be served, xbut to serve, and yto give His life a ransom zfor many."

Two Blind Men Receive Their Sight

29aNow as they went out of Jericho, a great multitude followed Him. 30And behold, btwo blind men sitting by the road, when they heard that Jesus was passing

by, cried out, saying, "Have mercy on us, O Lord, cSon of David!"

31Then the multitude dwarned them that they should be quiet; but they cried out all the more, saying, "Have mercy on us, O Lord, Son of David!"

32So Jesus stood still and called them, and said, "What do you want Me to do for you?"

33They said to Him, "Lord, that our eyes may be opened." 34So Jesus had ecompassion and touched their eyes. And immediately their eyes received sight, and they followed Him.

The Triumphal Entry

21 Now awhen they drew near Jerusalem, and came to Bethphage,* at bthe Mount of Olives, then Jesus sent two disciples, 2saying to them, "Go into the village opposite you, and immediately you will find a donkey tied, and a colt with her. Loose them and bring them to Me. 3And if anyone says anything to you, you shall say, 'The Lord has need of them,' and immediately he will send them."

4All* this was done that it might be fulfilled which was spoken by the prophet, saying:

5 "Tellc the daughter of Zion,
'Behold, your King is coming to you,
Lowly, and sitting on a donkey,
A colt, the foal of a donkey.'"*

6dSo the disciples went and did as Jesus commanded them. 7They brought the donkey and the colt, elaid their clothes on them, and set Him* on them. 8And a very great multitude spread their clothes on the road; fothers cut down branches from the trees and spread them on the road. 9Then the multitudes who went before and those who followed cried out, saying:

"Hosanna to the Son of David!
g'Blessed is He who comes in the name of the LORD!'*
Hosanna in the highest!"

---

* 20:22 NU-Text omits and be baptized with the baptism that I am baptized with.   * 20:23 NU-Text omits and be baptized with the baptism that I am baptized with.   * 21:1 M-Text reads Bethsphage.   * 21:4 NU-Text omits All.   * 21:5 Zechariah 9:9   * 21:7 NU-Text reads and He sat.
* 21:9 Psalm 118:26

20:26–27 whosoever desires to become great. The measure of greatness is not position, power, or prestige. It is service.

21:2 a donkey tied. This was prophesied in Zechariah 9:9.

21:9 Hosanna. Hosanna literally means "save now." The people were using it as an exclamation of joyous praise, but also they expected the Messiah to save them from the oppression of the Romans.

20:17 e Mark 10:32–34   **20:18** f Matt. 16:21; 26:47–57
20:19 g Matt. 27:2   h Matt. 26:67, 68; 27:29, 41   i Matt. 27:26
j Acts 3:13–15   k Matt. 28:5, 6   **20:20** l Mark 10:35–45
m Matt. 4:21; 10:2   n [Matt. 19:28]   **20:22** o Luke
42:42   p Luke 12:50   **20:23** q [Acts 12:2]   **20:24** r Mark
10:41   **20:26** s [1 Pet. 5:3]   t Matt. 23:11   **20:27** u [Matt.
18:4]   **20:28** v John 13:4   w [Phil. 2:6, 7]   x Luke 22:27
y [Is. 53:10, 11]   z [Rom. 5:15, 19]   **20:29** a Mark 10:46–52
20:30 b Matt. 9:27   c [Ezek. 37:21–25]   **20:31** d Matt.
19:13   **20:34** e Matt. 9:36; 14:14; 15:32; 18:27
21:1 a Luke 19:29–38   b [Zech. 14:4]   **21:5** c Zech. 9:9
21:6 d Mark 11:4   **21:7** e 2 Kin. 9:13   **21:8** f Lev. 23:40
21:9 g Ps. 118:26; Matt. 23:39

[10h]And when He had come into Jerusalem, all the city was moved, saying, "Who is this?"

[11]So the multitudes said, "This is Jesus, [i]the prophet from Nazareth of Galilee."

Jesus Cleanses the Temple

[12j]Then Jesus went into the temple of God* and drove out all those who bought and sold in the temple, and overturned the tables of the [k]money changers and the seats of those who sold doves. [13]And He said to them, "It is written, [l]'My house shall be called a house of prayer,'* but you have made it a [m]'den of thieves.'"*

[14]Then the blind and the lame came to Him in the temple, and He healed them. [15]But when the chief priests and scribes saw the wonderful things that He did, and the children crying out in the temple and saying, "Hosanna to the [n]Son of David!" they were indignant [16]and said to Him, "Do You hear what these are saying?"

And Jesus said to them, "Yes. Have you never read,

[o]'Out of the mouth of babes and nursing infants
You have perfected praise'?"*

[17]Then He left them and [p]went out of the city to Bethany, and He lodged there.

The Fig Tree Withered

[18q]Now in the morning, as He returned to the city, He was hungry. [19r]And seeing a fig tree by the road, He came to it and found nothing on it but leaves, and said to it, "Let no fruit grow on you ever again." Immediately the fig tree withered away.

The Lesson of the Withered Fig Tree

[20s]And when the disciples saw it, they marveled, saying, "How did the fig tree wither away so soon?"

[21]So Jesus answered and said to them, "Assuredly, I say to you, [t]if you have faith and [u]do not doubt, you will not only do what was done to the fig tree, [v]but also if you say to this mountain, 'Be removed and be cast into the sea,' it will be done. [22]And [w]whatever things you ask in prayer, believing, you will receive."

Jesus' Authority Questioned

[23x]Now when He came into the temple, the chief priests and the elders of the people confronted Him as He was teaching, and [y]said, "By what authority are You doing these things? And who gave You this authority?"

[24]But Jesus answered and said to them, "I also will ask you one thing, which if you tell Me, I likewise will tell you by what authority I do these things: [25]The [z]baptism of [a]John—where was it from? From heaven or from men?"

And they reasoned among themselves, saying, "If we say, 'From heaven,' He will say to us, 'Why then did you not believe him?' [26]But if we say, 'From men,' we [b]fear the multitude, [c]for all count John as a prophet." [27]So they answered Jesus and said, "We do not know."

And He said to them, "Neither will I tell you by what authority I do these things.

The Parable of the Two Sons

[28]"But what do you think? A man had two sons, and he came to the first and said, 'Son, go, work today in my [d]vineyard.' [29]He answered and said, 'I will not,' but afterward he regretted it and went. [30]Then he came to the second and said likewise. And he answered and said, 'I go, sir,' but he did not go. [31]Which of the two did the will of his father?"

They said to Him, "The first."

Jesus said to them, [e]"Assuredly, I say to you that tax collectors and harlots enter the kingdom of God before you. [32]For [f]John came to you in the way of righteousness, and you did not believe him; [g]but tax collectors and harlots believed him; and when you saw it, you did not afterward relent and believe him.

The Parable of the Wicked Vinedressers

[33]"Hear another parable: There was a certain landowner [h]who planted a vineyard and set a hedge around it, dug a winepress in it and built a tower. And he leased it to vinedressers and [i]went into

---

* **21:12** NU-Text omits of God. * **21:13** Isaiah 56:7 • Jeremiah 7:11 * **21:16** Psalm 8:2

21:19 Immediately. This does not necessarily mean instantly; it may have the idea of "very soon" as in Luke 19:11. (The account of this miracle in Mark 11:12–14,20–21 indicates some time passing.)

21:21 faith. Few if any besides our Savior will reach this kind of faith in its fullness. However, as each believer approaches such faith in prayer, his effort will be rewarded. Answers are always given, even to the feeblest prayers of faith.

21:33 planted a vineyard. The owner of the vineyard was God; the vinedressers were the people of Israel. The servants represent God's messengers, and the son is Jesus the Messiah.

21:10 [h] John 2:13, 15 **21:11** [i] John 6:14; 7:40; 9:17 **21:12** [j] Mark 11:15–18 [k] Deut. 14:25 **21:13** [l] Is. 56:7 [m] Jer. 7:11 **21:15** [n] John 7:42 **21:16** [o] Ps. 8:2 **21:17** [p] John 11:1, 18; 12:1 **21:18** [q] Mark 11:12–14, 20–24 **21:19** [r] Matt. 17:20 [u] James 1:6 [v] 1 Cor. 13:2 **21:22** [w] Matt. 7:7–11 **21:20** [s] Mark 11:20 **21:21** [t] Matt. 17:20 [u] James 1:6 [v] 1 Cor. 13:2 **21:22** [w] Matt. 7:7–11 **21:23** [x] Luke 20:1–8 [y] Ex. 2:14 **21:25** [z] [John 1:29–34] [a] John 1:15–28 **21:26** [b] Matt. 14:5; 21:46 [c] Mark 6:20 **21:28** [d] Matt. 20:1; 21:33 **21:31** [e] Luke 7:29, 37–50 **21:32** [f] Luke 3:1–12; 7:29 [g] Luke 3:12, 13 **21:33** [h] Luke 20:9–19 [i] Matt. 25:14

a far country. [34]Now when vintage-time drew near, he sent his servants to the vinedressers, that they might receive its fruit. [35]*And the vinedressers took his servants, beat one, killed one, and stoned another. [36]Again he sent other servants, more than the first, and they did likewise to them. [37]Then last of all he sent his [k]son to them, saying, 'They will respect my son.' [38]But when the vinedressers saw the son, they said among themselves, [l]"This is the heir. [m]Come, let us kill him and seize his inheritance.' [39][n]So they took him and cast him out of the vineyard and killed him.

[40]"Therefore, when the owner of the vineyard comes, what will he do to those vinedressers?"

[41][o]They said to Him, [p]"He will destroy those wicked men miserably, [q]and lease his vineyard to other vinedressers who will render to him the fruits in their seasons."

[42]Jesus said to them, "Have you never read in the Scriptures:

[r]'The stone which the builders rejected
Has become the chief cornerstone.
This was the LORD's doing,
And it is marvelous in our eyes'?*

[43]"Therefore I say to you, [s]the kingdom of God will be taken from you and given to a nation bearing the fruits of it. [44]And [t]whoever falls on this stone will be broken; but on whomever it falls, [u]it will grind him to powder."

[45]Now when the chief priests and Pharisees heard His parables, they perceived that He was speaking of them. [46]But when they sought to lay hands on Him, they [v]feared the multitudes, because [w]they took Him for a prophet.

The Parable of the Wedding Feast

22 And Jesus answered [a]and spoke to them again by parables and said: [2]"The kingdom of heaven is like a certain king who arranged a marriage for his son, [3]and sent out his servants to call those who were invited to the wedding; and they were not willing to come. [4]Again, he sent out other servants, saying, 'Tell those who are invited, "See, I have

prepared my dinner; [b]my oxen and fatted cattle are killed, and all things are ready. Come to the wedding."' [5]But they made light of it and went their ways, one to his own farm, another to his business. [6]And the rest seized his servants, treated them spitefully, and killed them. [7]But when the king heard about it, he was furious. And he sent out [c]his armies, destroyed those murderers, and burned up their city. [8]Then he said to his servants, 'The wedding is ready, but those who were invited were not [d]worthy. [9]Therefore go into the highways, and as many as you find, invite to the wedding.' [10]So those servants went out into the highways and [e]gathered together all whom they found, both bad and good. And the wedding hall was filled with guests.

[11]"But when the king came in to see the guests, he saw a man there [f]who did not have on a wedding garment. [12]So he said to him, 'Friend, how did you come in here without a wedding garment?' And he was [g]speechless. [13]Then the king said to the servants, 'Bind him hand and foot, take him away, and* cast him [h]into outer darkness; there will be weeping and gnashing of teeth.'

[14][i]"For many are called, but few are chosen."

The Pharisees: Is It Lawful to Pay Taxes to Caesar?

[15][j]Then the Pharisees went and plotted how they might entangle Him in His talk. [16]And they sent to Him their disciples with the [k]Herodians, saying, "Teacher, we know that You are true, and teach the way of God in truth; nor do You care about anyone, for You do not regard the person of men. [17]Tell us, therefore, what do You think? Is it lawful to pay taxes to Caesar, or not?"

[18]But Jesus perceived their wickedness, and said, "Why do you test Me, you hypocrites? [19]Show Me the tax money."

So they brought Him a denarius.

[20]And He said to them, "Whose image and inscription is this?"

---

* **21:42** Psalm 118:22, 23   * **22:13** NU-Text omits take him away, and.

21:42 cornerstone. The rejected stone was the Messiah, who became the head cornerstone, the one holding the whole building together (Ps. 118:22–23).
22:11 did not have on a wedding garment. Like the others, this visitor had been invited to the wedding, but he failed to prepare himself for it. In Revelation, the garment of fine linen worn by the bride of the Lamb is said to be the righteous deeds of the saints (Rev. 19:8). In this parable the garment may refer to the righteousness of Christ, graciously provided for us through His death. To refuse to put it on would mean a refusal of Christ's sacrifice.
22:14 many are called, but few are chosen. All Israel

has been invited, but only a few will accept and follow Jesus. Not all those invited will be among the chosen of God, for not all will believe.

21:35[1 Thess. 2:15]   **21:37**[k [John 3:16]
21:38[f [Heb. 1:2]   m John 11:53   **21:39**n [Acts 2:23]   **21:41**o Luke 20:16   p [Luke 21:24]   q [Acts 13:46]   **21:42**r Ps. 118:22, 23   **21:43**s [Matt. 8:12]
21:44t Is. 8:14, 15   u [Dan. 2:44]   **21:46**v Matt. 21:26
w Matt. 21:11   **22:1**a [Rev. 19:7–9]   **22:4**b Prov. 9:2
22:7c [Dan. 9:26]   **22:8**d Matt. 10:11   **22:10**e Matt. 13:38, 47, 48   **22:11**f [Col. 3:10, 12]   **22:12**g [Rom. 3:19]   **22:13**h Matt. 8:12; 25:30   **22:14**i Matt. 20:16
22:15j Mark 12:13–17   **22:16**k Mark 3:6; 8:15; 12:13

²¹They said to Him, "Caesar's."

And He said to them, ˡ"Render therefore to Caesar the things that are ᵐCaesar's, and to God the things that are ⁿGod's." ²²When they had heard *these words,* they marveled, and left Him and went their way.

The Sadducees: What About the Resurrection?

²³ᵒThe same day the Sadducees, ᵖwho say there is no resurrection, came to Him and asked Him, ²⁴saying: "Teacher, ᵩMoses said that if a man dies, having no children, his brother shall marry his wife and raise up offspring for his brother. ²⁵Now there were with us seven brothers. The first died after he had married, and having no offspring, left his wife to his brother. ²⁶Likewise the second also, and the third, even to the seventh. ²⁷Last of all the woman died also. ²⁸Therefore, in the resurrection, whose wife of the seven will she be? For they all had her."

²⁹Jesus answered and said to them, "You are mistaken, ʳnot knowing the Scriptures nor the power of God. ³⁰For in the resurrection they neither marry nor are given in marriage, but ˢare like angels of God* in heaven. ³¹But concerning the resurrection of the dead, have you not read what was spoken to you by God, saying, ³²ᵗ'I am the God of Abraham, the God of Isaac, and the God of Jacob'?* God is not the God of the dead, but of the living." ³³And when the multitudes heard *this,* ᵘthey were astonished at His teaching.

The Scribes: Which Is the First Commandment of All?

³⁴ᵛBut when the Pharisees heard that He had silenced the Sadducees, they gathered together. ³⁵Then one of them, ʷa lawyer, asked Him *a question,* testing Him, and saying, ³⁶"Teacher, which *is* the great commandment in the law?"

³⁷Jesus said to him, ˣ'"You shall love the LORD your God with all your heart, with all your soul, and with all your mind.'* ³⁸This

is *the* first and great commandment. ³⁹And *the* second is like it: ʸ'You shall love your neighbor as yourself.'* ⁴⁰ᶻOn these two commandments hang all the Law and the Prophets."

Jesus: How Can David Call His Descendant Lord?

⁴¹ᵃWhile the Pharisees were gathered together, Jesus asked them, ⁴²saying, "What do you think about the Christ? Whose Son is He?"

They said to Him, "*The* ᵇSon of David."

⁴³He said to them, "How then does David in the Spirit call Him *'Lord,'* saying:

⁴⁴ *'The*ᶜ LORD said to my Lord,
"Sit at My right hand,
Till I make Your enemies Your
    footstool" '?*

⁴⁵If David then calls Him *'Lord,'* how is He his Son?" ⁴⁶ᵈAnd no one was able to answer Him a word, ᵉnor from that day on did anyone dare question Him anymore.

Woe to the Scribes and Pharisees

23 Then Jesus spoke to the multitudes and to His disciples, ²saying: ᵃ"The scribes and the Pharisees sit in Moses' seat. ³Therefore whatever they tell you to observe,* *that* observe and do, but do not do according to their works; for ᵇthey say, and do not do. ⁴ᶜFor they bind heavy burdens, hard to bear, and lay *them* on men's shoulders; but they *themselves* will not move them with one of their fingers. ⁵But all their works they do to ᵈbe seen by men. They make their phylacteries broad and enlarge the borders of their garments. ⁶ᵉThey love the best places at feasts, the best seats in the synagogues, ⁷greetings in the marketplaces, and to be called by men, 'Rabbi, Rabbi.' ⁸ᶠBut you, do not be

* **22:30** NU-Text omits *of God.* * **22:32** Exodus 3:6, 15 * **22:37** Deuteronomy 6:5 * **22:39** Leviticus 19:18 * **22:44** Psalm 110:1 * **23:3** NU-Text omits *to observe.*

22:21 *things that are Caesar's.* When one subjects oneself to the state and accepts its protection and benefits, one is obligated to support it and obey its laws until it becomes sinful to do so (Rom. 13:1–7; 1 Pet. 2:13–17). But giving back to God what is His reaches far deeper than obedience to the state. Man has a duty to give himself to God, with all he is and all that he has.

22:42–45 *Christ . . . Whose Son is He?* The Old Testament foretold that the Messiah would come from David's royal line (2 Sam. 7:12–16; Ps. 89:3–4,34–36; Is. 9:7; 16:5; 55:3–4).

22:44 *The LORD said to my Lord.* The Hebrew text of Psalm 110:1 uses two different Hebrew words for "Lord." The first, translated "LORD," is the name Yahweh, the proper name of Israel's God. The second "Lord" means "master." David, the great king of Israel, calls one of his offspring "Lord" or "master." The implication is that Jesus, the Son of David, is divine.

23:5 *phylacteries.* Phylacteries were small boxes containing specific Scripture passages, in fulfillment of Deuteronomy 6:8 (Ex. 13:9,16; Prov. 3:3; 6:21; 7:3). They were worn on the forehead or arm. In order to be seen as especially righteous, some Pharisees wore conspicuously large phylacteries.

23:7 *Rabbi.* The title "rabbi" means "teacher."

22:21 ˡMatt. 17:25 ᵐ[Rom. 13:1–7] ⁿ[1 Cor. 3:23; 6:19, 20; 12:27] **22:23** ᵒLuke 20:27–40 ᵖActs 23:8 **22:24** ᵩDeut. 25:5 **22:29** ʳJohn 20:9 **22:30** ˢ[1 John 3:2] **22:32** ᵗEx. 3:6, 15 **22:33** ᵘMatt. 7:28 **22:34** ᵛMark 12:28–31 **22:35** ʷLuke 7:30; 10:25; 11:45, 46, 52; 14:3 **22:37** ˣDeut. 6:5; 10:12; 30:6 **22:39** ʸLev. 19:18 **22:42** ᵇMatt. 1:1; 21:9 **22:44** ᶜPs. 110:1 **22:46** ᵈLuke 14:6 ᵉMark 12:34 **23:2** ᵃNeh. 8:4, 8 **23:3** ᵇ[Rom. 2:19] **23:4** ᶜLuke 11:46 **23:5** ᵈ[Matt. 6:1–6, 16–18] **23:6** ᵉLuke 11:43; 20:46 **23:8** ᶠ[James 3:1]

called 'Rabbi'; for One is your Teacher, the Christ,* and you are all brethren. 9Do not call anyone on earth your father; *for One is your Father, He who is in heaven. 10And do not be called teachers; for One is your Teacher, the Christ. 11But *h*he who is greatest among you shall be your servant. 12*i*And whoever exalts himself will be humbled, and he who humbles himself will be exalted.

13"But *j*woe to you, scribes and Pharisees, hypocrites! For you shut up the kingdom of heaven against men; for you neither go in *yourselves*, nor do you allow those who are entering to go in. 14Woe to you, scribes and Pharisees, hypocrites! *k*For you devour widows' houses, and for a pretense make long prayers. Therefore you will receive greater condemnation.*

15"Woe to you, scribes and Pharisees, hypocrites! For you travel land and sea to win one proselyte, and when he is won, you make him twice as much a son of hell as yourselves.

16"Woe to you, *l*blind guides, who say, *m*'Whoever swears by the temple, it is nothing; but whoever swears by the gold of the temple, he is obliged *to perform it*.' 17Fools and blind! For which is greater, the gold *n*or the temple that sanctifies* the gold? 18And, 'Whoever swears by the altar, it is nothing; but whoever swears by the gift that is on it, he is obliged *to perform it*.' 19Fools and blind! For which is greater, the gift *o*or the altar that sanctifies the gift? 20Therefore he who swears by the altar, swears by it and by all things on it. 21He who swears by the temple, swears by it and by *p*Him who dwells* in it. 22And he who swears by heaven, swears by *q*the throne of God and by Him who sits on it.

23"Woe to you, scribes and Pharisees, hypocrites! *r*For you pay tithe of mint and anise and cummin, and *s*have neglected the weightier *matters* of the law: justice and mercy and faith. These you ought to have done, without leaving the others undone. 24Blind guides, who strain out a gnat and swallow a camel!

25"Woe to you, scribes and Pharisees, hypocrites! *t*For you cleanse the outside of the cup and dish, but inside they are full of extortion and self-indulgence.* 26Blind Pharisee, first cleanse the inside of the cup and dish, that the outside of them may be clean also.

27"Woe to you, scribes and Pharisees, hypocrites! *u*For you are like whitewashed tombs which indeed appear beautiful outwardly, but inside are full of dead *men's* bones and all uncleanness. 28Even so you also outwardly appear righteous to men, but inside you are full of hypocrisy and lawlessness.

29*v*"Woe to you, scribes and Pharisees, hypocrites! Because you build the tombs of the prophets and adorn the monuments of the righteous, 30and say, 'If we had lived in the days of our fathers, we would not have been partakers with them in the blood of the prophets.'

31"Therefore you are witnesses against yourselves that *w*you are sons of those who murdered the prophets. 32*x*Fill up, then, the measure of your fathers' guilt. 33Serpents, *y*brood of vipers! How can you escape the condemnation of hell? 34*z*Therefore, indeed, I send you prophets, wise men, and scribes: *a*some of them you will kill and crucify, and *b*some of them you will scourge in your synagogues and persecute from city to city, 35*c*that on you may come all the righteous blood shed on the earth, *d*from the blood of righteous Abel to *e*the blood of Zechariah, son of Berechiah, whom you murdered between the temple and the altar. 36Assuredly, I say to you, all these things will come upon this generation.

Jesus Laments over Jerusalem

37*f*"O Jerusalem, Jerusalem, the one who kills the prophets *g*and stones those who are sent to her! How often *h*I wanted to gather your children together, as a hen gathers her chicks *i*under *her* wings, but you were not willing! 38See! Your house is left to you desolate; 39for I say to you, you shall see Me no more till you say,

* **23:8** NU-Text omits *the Christ*. * **23:14** NU-Text omits this verse. * **23:17** NU-Text reads *sanctified*. * **23:21** M-Text reads *dwelt*. * **23:25** M-Text reads *unrighteousness*.

23:10 *do not be called teachers.* This verse is a warning against the human tendency to replace a personal relationship with God with following an earthly leader. No matter how dynamic or even how godly such a leader is, as soon as people start looking to that person rather than to God, they have created an idol.

23:24 *swallow a camel.* The Pharisees would literally "strain out a gnat" in order not to violate Leviticus 11:41–43, but they swallowed "a camel" by neglecting mercy, justice, and faith.

23:25–26 *but inside.* The inside of the cup represents a person's character. Sometimes those who most loudly protest the sins of others are secretly guilty of those or worse sins themselves.

23:35 *Abel . . . Zechariah.* Abel was the first person murdered in the Old Testament (Gen. 4:8); Zechariah was the last. His death is recorded in 2 Chronicles 24:20–22, the last book of the Hebrew canon.

23:9 *g* [Mal. 1:6] **23:11** *h* Matt. 10:26, 27 **23:12** *i* Luke 14:11; 18:14 **23:13** *j* Luke 11:52 **23:14** *k* Mark 12:40 **23:16** *l* Matt. 15:14; 23:24 *m* [Matt. 5:33, 34] **23:17** *n* Ex. 30:29 **23:19** *o* Ex. 29:37 **23:21** *p* 1 Kin. 8:13 **23:22** *q* Matt. 5:34 **23:23** *r* Luke 11:42; 18:12 *s* [Hos. 6:6] **23:25** *t* Luke 11:39 **23:27** *u* Acts 23:3 **23:29** *v* Luke 11:47, 48 **23:31** *w* [Acts 7:51, 52] **23:32** *x* [1 Thess. 2:16] **23:33** *y* Matt. 3:7; 12:34 **23:34** *z* Luke 11:49 *a* Acts 7:54–60; 22:19 *b* 2 Cor. 11:24, 25 **23:35** *c* Rev. 18:24 *d* Gen. 4:8 *e* 2 Chr. 24:20, 21 **23:37** *f* Luke 13:34, 35 *g* 2 Chr. 24:20, 21; 36:15, 16 *h* Deut. 32:11, 12 *i* Ps. 17:8; 91:4

i'Blessed is He who comes in the name of the LORD!' "*

Jesus Predicts the Destruction of the Temple

24 Then *a*Jesus went out and departed from the temple, and His disciples came up to show Him the buildings of the temple. **2**And Jesus said to them, "Do you not see all these things? Assuredly, I say to you, *b*not one stone shall be left here upon another, that shall not be thrown down."

The Signs of the Times and the End of the Age

3Now as He sat on the Mount of Olives, *c*the disciples came to Him privately, saying, *d*"Tell us, when will these things be? And what *will be* the sign of Your coming, and of the end of the age?"

4And Jesus answered and said to them: *e*"Take heed that no one deceives you. **5**For *f*many will come in My name, saying, 'I am the Christ,' *g*and will deceive many. **6**And you will hear of *h*wars and rumors of wars. See that you are not troubled; for all* *these things* must come to pass, but the end is not yet. **7**For *i*nation will rise against nation, and kingdom against kingdom. And there will be *j*famines, pestilences,* and earthquakes in various places. **8**All these *are* the beginning of sorrows.

9*k*"Then they will deliver you up to tribulation and kill you, and you will be hated by all nations for My name's sake. **10**And then many will be offended, will betray one another, and will hate one another. **11**Then *l*many false prophets will rise up and *m*deceive many. **12**And because lawlessness will abound, the love of many will grow *n*cold. **13***o*But he who endures to the end shall be saved. **14**And this *p*gospel of the kingdom *q*will be preached in all the world as a witness to all the nations, and then the end will come.

The Great Tribulation

15*r*"Therefore when you see the *s*'abomination of desolation,'* spoken of by Daniel the prophet, standing in the holy place" *t*(whoever reads, let him understand), **16**"then let those who are in Judea flee to the mountains. **17**Let him who is on the housetop not go down to take anything out of his house. **18**And let him who is in the field not go back to get his clothes. **19**But *u*woe to those who are pregnant and to those who are nursing babies in those days! **20**And pray that your flight may not be in winter or on the Sabbath. **21**For *v*then there will be great tribulation, such as has not been since the beginning of the world until this time, no, nor ever shall

---

* **23:39** Psalm 118:26   * **24:6** NU-Text omits *all.*
* **24:7** NU-Text omits *pestilences.*   * **24:15** Daniel 11:31; 12:11

24:1 temple. The first temple, built by Solomon, was destroyed by the Babylonians in 586 B.C. The second temple, built under the encouragement of Haggai and Zechariah, and the leadership of Zerubbabel and Joshua (Hag. 1:1), was completed after considerable delay in 516 B.C. This second temple was lavishly restored by Herod the Great, but not completed until A.D. 64. It stood completed for only six years before it was reduced to rubble by the Romans. The devastation in A.D. 70 was so complete that the precise location is still unknown today.

24:4 Take heed that no one deceives you. Jesus' warning about being deceived was especially appropriate for the disciples. The destruction of Jerusalem did not necessarily mean the nearness of the end of the age. This principle was a point of confusion for them (Luke 19:11–27; Acts 1:6–7).

24:6 must come to pass. This indicates a divine or logical necessity. Such things will happen because of the people's sin. False messiahs had existed before (Acts 5:36–38) and false preachers would come in the future (Acts 20:29; 2 Cor. 11:13–15). Verses 4–6 may describe the first part of Daniel's seventieth week (Dan. 9:25–27), but possibly they present a general picture of the present age.

24:7 famines . . . and earthquakes. These disasters are more fully described in Revelation 6:1–8; 8:5–23; 9:13–21; and 16:2–21.

24:10 Apostasy—Satan is a subtle adversary who works as an angel of light through false religious teachers (2 Cor. 11:14–15), and many will be misled. Apostasy is also the result of persecution. Jesus speaks of temporary faith, and says that a falling away often occurs when "tribulation or persecution arises because of the word" (13:21). Perseverance in faith and in the accompanying results of faith are positive evidence of a genuine Christian profession.

24:15 abomination of desolation. The abomination of desolation literally means "the abomination that makes desolate." This prophecy comes from Daniel, specifically Daniel 9:27; 11:31; 12:11. Many believe that Daniel 11:31 refers to Antiochus IV, who desecrated the temple by sacrificing a pig on its altar and setting up an idol to Zeus in it. His actions were certainly a prelude to what the ultimate "man of sin" will do. In A.D. 70, Titus destroyed Jerusalem, burned the temple, and set up an idol to mock the Jews. Significantly, Paul speaks of the Antichrist at the end times also setting himself up as a god (2 Thess. 2:3–4; Rev. 13:14–15).

24:16 flee. At the time of the war ending in the destruction of the temple in A.D. 70, many of the Christians did flee, hiding in the clefts of Petra. Some believe that the final fulfillment of this prophecy will occur in the future desecration of the temple (Dan. 9:27) and the subsequent setting up of an image of the "man of sin" in the Most Holy Place.

23:39 *i* Ps. 118:26   **24:1** *a* Mark 13:1   **24:2** *b* Luke 19:44   **24:3** *c* Mark 13:3   *d* [1 Thess. 5:1–3]   **24:4** *e* [Col. 2:8, 18]   **24:5** *f* John 5:43   *g* Matt. 24:11   **24:6** *h* [Rev. 6:2–4]   **24:7** *i* Hag. 2:22   *j* Rev. 6:5, 6   **24:9** *k* Matt. 10:17   **24:11** *l* 2 Pet. 2:1   *m* [1 Tim. 4:1]   **24:12** *n* [2 Thess. 2:3]   **24:13** *o* Matt. 10:22   **24:14** *p* Matt. 4:23   *q* Rom. 10:18   **24:15** *r* Mark 13:14   *s* Dan. 9:27; 11:31; 12:11   *t* Dan. 9:23   **24:19** *u* Luke 23:29   **24:21** *v* Dan. 9:26

be. **22**And unless those days were shortened, no flesh would be saved; wbut for the elect's sake those days will be shortened.

23x"Then if anyone says to you, 'Look, here is the Christ!' or 'There!' do not believe it. **24**For yfalse christs and false prophets will rise and show great signs and wonders to deceive, zif possible, even the elect. **25**See, I have told you beforehand.

26"Therefore if they say to you, 'Look, He is in the desert!' do not go out; or 'Look, He is in the inner rooms!' do not believe it. **27**aFor as the lightning comes from the east and flashes to the west, so also will the coming of the Son of Man be. **28**bFor wherever the carcass is, there the eagles will be gathered together.

The Coming of the Son of Man

29c"Immediately after the tribulation of those days dthe sun will be darkened, and the moon will not give its light; the stars will fall from heaven, and the powers of the heavens will be shaken. **30**eThen the sign of the Son of Man will appear in heaven, fand then all the tribes of the earth will mourn, and they will see the Son of Man coming on the clouds of heaven with power and great glory. **31**gAnd He will send His angels with a great sound of a trumpet, and they will gather together His elect from the four winds, from one end of heaven to the other.

The Parable of the Fig Tree

32"Now learn hthis parable from the fig tree: When its branch has already become tender and puts forth leaves, you know that summer is near. **33**So you also, when you see all these things, know ithat it* is near—at the doors! **34**Assuredly, I say to you, jthis generation will by no means pass away till all these things take place. **35**kHeaven and earth will pass away, but My words will by no means pass away.

No One Knows the Day or Hour

36l"But of that day and hour no one knows, not even the angels of heaven,* mbut My Father only. **37**But as the days of Noah were, so also will the coming of the Son of Man be. **38**nFor as in the days before the flood, they were eating and drinking, marrying and giving in marriage, until the day that Noah entered the ark, **39**and did not know until the flood came and took them all away, so also will the coming of the Son of Man be. **40**oThen two men will be in the field: one will be taken and the other left. **41**Two women will be grinding at the mill: one will be taken and the other left. **42**pWatch therefore, for you do not know what hour* your Lord is coming. **43**qBut know this, that if the master of the house had known what hour the thief would come, he would have watched and not allowed his house to be broken into. **44**rTherefore you also be ready, for the Son of Man is coming at an hour you do not expect.

The Faithful Servant and the Evil Servant

45s"Who then is a faithful and wise servant, whom his master made ruler over his household, to give them food in due season? **46**tBlessed is that servant whom his master, when he comes, will find so doing. **47**Assuredly, I say to you that uhe will make him ruler over all his goods. **48**But if that evil servant says in his heart, 'My master vis delaying his coming,'* **49**and begins to beat his fellow servants, and to eat and drink with the drunkards, **50**the master of that servant will come on a day when he is not looking for him and at an hour that he is wnot aware of, **51**and will cut him in two and appoint him his portion with the hypocrites. xThere shall be weeping and gnashing of teeth.

---

* **24:33** Or He * **24:36** NU-Text adds nor the Son. * **24:42** NU-Text reads day. * **24:48** NU-Text omits his coming.

24:24 signs and wonders. Miracles by themselves do not prove that something is of God (7:21–23; 2 Thess. 2:9; Rev. 13:13–15). The teaching of those who perform signs and wonders must be tested against correct doctrine (Deut. 13:1–5; 1 John 4:1–3), and by the witness of God's Spirit (John 10:3–5,27).
24:29 Immediately after. This verse moves chronologically to the close of the tribulation, a period that will be marked by monumental cosmic disturbances (Is. 13:10; 34:4; Ezek. 32:7–8; Joel 2:30–31; 3:15; Hag. 2:6; Zech. 14:6; Rev. 6:12–14).
24:34 this generation. "Generation" may mean "race," indicating that Israel as a people will not cease to exist before God fulfills His promises to them. Another possibility is that the word describes a particular era in which people will see the end times. That is, the events will occur so rapidly that all will happen within one generation. Perhaps both interpretations are true.

24:36 that day and hour no one knows. Mark 13:32 indicates that even Jesus Himself did not know the exact time of His return. When the Lord Jesus was on earth, He voluntarily limited His use of His divine attributes (John 17:4–5; Phil. 2:5–8). Therefore He became hungry, thirsty, and tired. In this instance, Jesus surrendered the use of His divine omniscience.

24:22 w Is. 65:8, 9 **24:23** x Luke 17:23
24:24 y [2 Thess. 2:9] z [2 Tim. 2:19] **24:27** a Luke 17:24
24:28 b Luke 17:37 **24:29** c [Dan. 7:11] d Ezek. 32:7
24:30 e [Dan. 7:13, 14] f Zech. 12:12 **24:31** g [1 Cor. 15:52] **24:32** h Luke 21:29 **24:33** i [James 5:9]
24:34 j [Matt. 10:23; 16:28; 23:36] **24:35** k Luke 21:33 **24:36** l Acts 1:7 m Zech. 14:7 **24:38** n [Gen. 6:3–5] **24:40** o Luke 17:34 **24:42** p Matt. 25:13
24:43 q Luke 12:39 **24:44** r [1 Thess. 5:6] **24:45** s Luke 12:42–46 **24:46** t Rev. 16:15 **24:47** u Matt. 25:21, 23 **24:48** v [2 Pet. 3:4–9] **24:50** w Mark 13:32
24:51 x Matt. 8:12; 25:30

The Parable of the Wise and Foolish Virgins

25 "Then the kingdom of heaven shall be likened to ten virgins who took their lamps and went out to meet *a*the bridegroom. 2*b*Now five of them were wise, and five *were* foolish. 3Those who *were* foolish took their lamps and took no oil with them, 4but the wise took oil in their vessels with their lamps. 5But while the bridegroom was delayed, *c*they all slumbered and slept.

6"And at midnight *d*a cry was *heard:* 'Behold, the bridegroom is coming;* go out to meet him!' 7Then all those virgins arose and *e*trimmed their lamps. 8And the foolish said to the wise, 'Give us *some* of your oil, for our lamps are going out.' 9But the wise answered, saying, 'No, lest there should not be enough for us and you; but go rather to those who sell, and buy for yourselves.' 10And while they went to buy, the bridegroom came, and those who were ready went in with him to the wedding; and *f*the door was shut.

11"Afterward the other virgins came also, saying, *g*'Lord, Lord, open to us!' 12But he answered and said, 'Assuredly, I say to you, *h*I do not know you.'

13*i*"Watch therefore, for you *j*know neither the day nor the hour* in which the Son of Man is coming.

The Parable of the Talents

14*k*"For *the kingdom of heaven is l*like a man traveling to a far country, *who* called his own servants and delivered his goods to them. 15And to one he gave five talents, to another two, and to another one, *m*to each according to his own ability; and immediately he went on a journey. 16Then he who had received the five talents went and traded with them, and made another five talents. 17And likewise he who *had received* two gained two more also. 18But he who had received one went and dug in the ground, and hid his lord's money. 19After a long time the lord of those servants came and settled accounts with them.

20"So he who had received five talents came and brought five other talents, saying, 'Lord, you delivered to me five talents; look, I have gained five more talents besides them.' 21His lord said to him, 'Well *done,* good and faithful servant; you were *n*faithful over a few things, *o*I will make you ruler over many things. Enter into *p*the joy of your lord.' 22He also who had received two talents came and said, 'Lord, you delivered to me two talents; look, I have gained two more talents besides them.' 23His lord said to him, *q*'Well *done,* good and faithful servant; you have been faithful over a few things, I will make you ruler over many things. Enter into *r*the joy of your lord.'

24"Then he who had received the one talent came and said, 'Lord, I knew you to be a hard man, reaping where you have not sown, and gathering where you have not scattered seed. 25And I was afraid, and went and hid your talent in the ground. Look, *there* you have *what is* yours.'

26"But his lord answered and said to him, 'You *s*wicked and lazy servant, you knew that I reap where I have not sown, and gather where I have not scattered seed. 27So you ought to have deposited my money with the bankers, and at my coming I would have received back my own with interest. 28So take the talent from him, and give *it* to him who has ten talents.

29*t*'For to everyone who has, more will be given, and he will have abundance; but from him who does not have, even what he has will be taken away. 30And cast the unprofitable servant *u*into the outer darkness. *v*There will be weeping and *w*gnashing of teeth.'

The Son of Man Will Judge the Nations

31*x*"When the Son of Man comes in His glory, and all the holy* angels with Him, then He will sit on the throne of His glory. 32*y*All the nations will be gathered before Him, and *z*He will separate them one from another, as a shepherd divides *his*

---

* **25:6** NU-Text omits *is coming.* * **25:13** NU-Text omits the rest of this verse. * **25:31** NU-Text omits *holy.*

25:10 *the bridegroom came.* Christ's return is often compared to a wedding (22:1–14; Rev. 19:7 8).
25:14 *delivered his goods to them.* The parable of the talents illustrates the faith required of God's servants.
25:15 *talents.* A talent was a large sum of money, about six thousand denarii.
25:23 *I will make you ruler over many things.* The first two servants received the same reward, based on their faithfulness, not on the size of their responsibilities. The smallest task in God's work may receive a great reward if we are faithful in performing it (10:42).
25:32–40 Judgment—The Final Judgment will be according to the evidence, not according to what was professed but what was practiced. It will be not according to what was said, but what was done.

These works cannot earn salvation, but they are works of love which reflect a life redeemed by the saving work of Christ through the Holy Spirit (Gal. 5:6). Love for God is demonstrated by love for man (1 John 4:20).

25:1 *a* [Eph. 5:29, 30]   **25:2** *b* Matt. 13:47; 22:10   **25:5** *c* 1 Thess. 5:6   **25:6** *d* [1 Thess. 4:16]   **25:7** *e* Luke 12:35   **25:10** *f* Luke 13:25   **25:11** *g* [Matt. 7:21–23]   **25:12** *h* [Hab. 1:13]   **25:13** *i* Mark 13:35   *j* Matt. 24:36, 42   **25:14** *k* Luke 19:12–27   *l* Matt. 21:33   **25:15** *m* [Rom. 12:6]   **25:21** *n* [1 Cor. 4:2]   *o* [Luke 12:44; 22:29, 30]   *p* [Heb. 12:2]   **25:23** *q* Matt. 24:45, 47; 25:21   *r* [Ps. 16:11]   **25:26** *s* Matt. 18:32   **25:29** *t* Matt. 13:12   **25:30** *u* Matt. 8:12; 22:13   *v* Matt. 7:23; 8:12; 24:51   *w* Ps. 112:10   **25:31** *x* [1 Thess. 4:16]   **25:32** *y* [2 Cor. 5:10]   *z* Ezek. 20:38

sheep from the goats. 33 And He will set the ᵃsheep on His right hand, but the goats on the left. 34 Then the King will say to those on His right hand, 'Come, you blessed of My Father, ᵇinherit the kingdom ᶜprepared for you from the foundation of the world: 35 ᵈfor I was hungry and you gave Me food; I was thirsty and you gave Me drink; ᵉI was a stranger and you took Me in; 36 I *was* ᶠnaked and you clothed Me; I was sick and you visited Me; ᵍI was in prison and you came to Me.'

37 "Then the righteous will answer Him, saying, 'Lord, when did we see You hungry and feed *You*, or thirsty and give *You* drink? 38 When did we see You a stranger and take *You* in, or naked and clothe *You*? 39 Or when did we see You sick, or in prison, and come to You?' 40 And the King will answer and say to them, 'Assuredly, I say to you, ʰinasmuch as you did *it* to one of the least of these My brethren, you did *it* to Me.'

41 "Then He will also say to those on the left hand, ⁱ'Depart from Me, you cursed, ʲinto the everlasting fire prepared for ᵏthe devil and his angels: 42 for I was hungry and you gave Me no food; I was thirsty and you gave Me no drink; 43 I was a stranger and you did not take Me in, naked and you did not clothe Me, sick and in prison and you did not visit Me.'

44 "Then they also will answer Him,* saying, 'Lord, when did we see You hungry or thirsty or a stranger or naked or sick or in prison, and did not minister to You?' 45 Then He will answer them, saying, 'Assuredly, I say to you, ⁱinasmuch as you did not do *it* to one of the least of these, you did not do *it* to Me.' 46 And ᵐthese will go away into everlasting punishment, but the righteous into eternal life."

The Plot to Kill Jesus

26 Now it came to pass, when Jesus had finished all these sayings, *that* He said to His disciples, 2 ᵃ"You know that after two days is the Passover, and the Son of Man will be delivered up to be crucified."

3 ᵇThen the chief priests, the scribes,* and the elders of the people assembled at the palace of the high priest, who was called Caiaphas, 4 and ᶜplotted to take Jesus by trickery and kill *Him.* 5 But they said, "Not during the feast, lest there be an uproar among the ᵈpeople."

The Anointing at Bethany

6 And when Jesus was in ᵉBethany at the house of Simon the leper, 7 ᵃa woman came to Him having an alabaster flask of very costly fragrant oil, and she poured *it* on His head as He sat *at the table.* 8 ᶠBut when His disciples saw *it,* they were indignant, saying, "Why this waste? 9 For this fragrant oil might have been sold for much and given to *the* poor."

10 But when Jesus was aware of *it,* He said to them, "Why do you trouble the woman? For she has done a good work for Me. 11 ᵍFor you have the poor with you always, but ʰMe you do not have always. 12 For in pouring this fragrant oil on My body, she did *it* for My ⁱburial. 13 Assuredly, I say to you, wherever this gospel is preached in the whole world, what this woman has done will also be told as a memorial to her."

Judas Agrees to Betray Jesus

14 ʲThen one of the twelve, called ᵏJudas Iscariot, went to the chief priests 15 and said, ˡ"What are you willing to give me if I deliver Him to you?" And they counted out to him thirty pieces of silver. 16 So from that time he sought opportunity to betray Him.

Jesus Celebrates Passover with His Disciples

17 ᵐNow on the first *day of the Feast* of the Unleavened Bread the disciples came to Jesus, saying to Him, "Where do You want us to prepare for You to eat the Passover?"

18 And He said, "Go into the city to a certain man, and say to him, 'The Teacher says, ⁿ"My time is at hand; I will keep the Passover at your house with My disciples."'"

19 So the disciples did as Jesus had directed them; and they prepared the Passover.

20 ᵒWhen evening had come, He sat down with the twelve. 21 Now as they were eating, He said, "Assuredly, I say to you, one of you will ᵖbetray Me."

22 And they were exceedingly sorrowful, and each of them began to say to Him, "Lord, is it I?"

23 He answered and said, ᵠ"He who dipped *his* hand with Me in the dish will

---

* 25:44 NU-Text and M-Text omit *Him.*
* 26:3 NU-Text omits *the scribes.*

26:14 *one of the twelve.* The enormity of Judas' sin is seen in these words: Jesus was betrayed by one of His own best friends.
26:15 *thirty pieces of silver.* Thirty pieces of silver was the price of a slave (Ex. 21:32). Zechariah prophesied this sum (Zech. 11:12–13).
26:21 *one of you will betray Me.* This statement indicates the Lord's omniscience. Repeatedly, Christ unveiled evidence of His deity to His disciples.

25:33 ᵃ [John 10:11, 27, 28] **25:34** ᵇ [Rom. 8:17] ᶜ Mark 10:40 **25:35** ᵈ Is. 58:7 ᵉ [Heb. 13:2] **25:36** ᶠ [James 2:15, 16] ᵍ 2 Tim. 1:16 **25:40** ʰ Mark 9:41 **25:41** ⁱ Matt. 7:23 ʲ Matt. 13:40, 42 ᵏ [2 Pet. 2:4] **25:45** ˡ Prov. 14:31 **25:46** ᵐ [Dan. 12:2] **26:2** ᵈ Luke 22:1, 2 **26:3** ᵇ John 11:47 **26:4** ᶜ Acts 4:25–28 **26:5** ᵈ Matt. 21:26 **26:6** ᵉ Mark 14:3–9 **26:8** ᶠ John 12:4 **26:11** ᵍ [Deut. 15:11] ʰ [John 13:33; 14:19; 16:5, 28; 17:11] **26:12** ⁱ John 19:38–42 **26:14** ʲ Mark 14:10, 11; Luke 22:3–6 ᵏ Matt. 10:4 **26:15** ˡ Zech. 11:12 **26:17** ᵐ Ex. 12:6, 18–20 **26:18** ⁿ Luke 9:51 **26:20** ᵒ Mark 14:17–21 **26:21** ᵖ John 6:70, 71; 13:21 **26:23** ᵠ Ps. 41:9

betray Me. 24The Son of Man indeed goes just ʳas it is written of Him, but ˢwoe to that man by whom the Son of Man is betrayed! ᵗIt would have been good for that man if he had not been born."

25Then Judas, who was betraying Him, answered and said, "Rabbi, is it I?"

He said to him, "You have said it."

Jesus Institutes the Lord's Supper

26ᵘAnd as they were eating, ᵛJesus took bread, blessed* and broke *it,* and gave *it* to the disciples and said, "Take, eat; ʷthis is My body."

27Then He took the cup, and gave thanks, and gave *it* to them, saying, ˣ"Drink from it, all of you. 28For ʸthis is My blood ᶻof the new* covenant, which is shed ᵃfor many for the remission of sins. 29But ᵇI say to you, I will not drink of this fruit of the vine from now on ᶜuntil that day when I drink it new with you in My Father's kingdom."

30ᵈAnd when they had sung a hymn, they went out to the Mount of Olives.

Jesus Predicts Peter's Denial

31Then Jesus said to them, ᵉ"All of you will ᶠbe made to stumble because of Me this night, for it is written:

ᵍ'I will strike the Shepherd,
And the sheep of the flock will be scattered.'*

32But after I have been raised, ʰI will go before you to Galilee."

33Peter answered and said to Him, "Even if all are made to stumble because of You, I will never be made to stumble."

34Jesus said to him, ⁱ"Assuredly, I say to you that this night, before the rooster crows, you will deny Me three times."

35Peter said to Him, "Even if I have to die with You, I will not deny You!"

And so said all the disciples.

The Prayer in the Garden

36ʲThen Jesus came with them to a place called Gethsemane, and said to the disciples, "Sit here while I go and pray over there." 37And He took with Him Peter and ᵏthe two sons of Zebedee, and He began to be sorrowful and deeply distressed. 38Then He said to them, ˡ"My soul is exceedingly sorrowful, even to death. Stay here and watch with Me."

39He went a little farther and fell on His face, and ᵐprayed, saying, ⁿ"O My Father, if it is possible, ᵒlet this cup pass from Me; nevertheless, ᵖnot as I will, but as You *will.*"

40Then He came to the disciples and found them sleeping, and said to Peter, "What! Could you not watch with Me one hour? 41ᵠWatch and pray, lest you enter into temptation. ʳThe spirit indeed *is* willing, but the flesh *is* weak."

42Again, a second time, He went away and prayed, saying, "O My Father, if this cup cannot pass away from Me unless* I drink it, Your will be done." 43And He came and found them asleep again, for their eyes were heavy.

44So He left them, went away again, and prayed the third time, saying the same words. 45Then He came to His disciples and said to them, "Are *you* still sleeping and resting? Behold, the hour is at hand, and the Son of Man is being ˢbetrayed into the hands of sinners. 46Rise, let us be going. See, My betrayer is at hand."

Betrayal and Arrest in Gethsemane

47And ᵗwhile He was still speaking, behold, Judas, one of the twelve, with a great multitude with swords and clubs, came from the chief priests and elders of the people.

48Now His betrayer had given them a sign, saying, "Whomever I kiss, He is the One; seize Him." 49Immediately he went up to Jesus and said, "Greetings, Rabbi!" ᵘand kissed Him.

50But Jesus said to him, ᵛ"Friend, why have you come?"

Then they came and laid hands on Jesus and took Him. 51And suddenly, ʷone of those *who were* with Jesus stretched out

---

* **26:26** M-Text reads *gave thanks for.*
* **26:28** NU-Text omits *new.* * **26:31** Zechariah 13:7 * **26:42** NU-Text reads *if this may not pass away unless.*

26:26–28 *My body . . . My blood.* The Lord Jesus, at this last meal with His disciples before He went to the cross, instituted this ordinance for His church throughout this age. It is called "the Lord's Supper" (1 Cor. 11:20). Using common everyday items, the bread and wine that could be found on any table, no matter how poor, He gave us a "remembrance" so that we would never forget that His broken body and shed blood bought salvation for us.

26:28 *My blood of the new covenant.* This refers to the new covenant promised in the Old Testament (Jer. 31:31–34; 32:37–44; Ezek. 34:25–31; 37:26–28).

26:36 *Gethsemane.* The name "Gethsemane" means "oil press." This garden was east of Jerusalem on the Mount of Olives. In the place where olives were crushed and ground, the Anointed One was crushed.

26:51 *one of those.* John 18:10 informs us that the impetuous swordsman was Peter. This action was performed with one of the two swords that the disciples had (Luke 22:38).

26:24 ʳ1 Cor. 15:3 ˢLuke 17:1 ᵗJohn 17:12 **26:26** ᵘMark 14:22–25 ᵛ1 Cor. 11:23–25 ʷ[1 Pet. 2:24] **26:27** ˣMark 14:23 **26:28** ʸ[Ex. 24:8] ᶻJer. 31:31 ᵃMatt. 20:28 **26:29** ᵇMark 14:25 ᶜActs 10:41 **26:30** ᵈMark 14:26–31 **26:31** ᵉJohn 16:32 ᶠ[Matt. 11:6] ᵍZech. 13:7 **26:32** ʰMatt. 28:7, 10, 16 **26:34** ⁱJohn 13:38 **26:36** ʲMark 14:32–35 **26:37** ᵏMatt. 4:21; 17:1 **26:38** ˡJohn 12:27 **26:39** ᵐ[Heb. 5:7–9] ⁿJohn 12:27 ᵒMatt. 20:22 ᵖJohn 5:30; 6:38 **26:41** ᵠLuke 22:40, 46 ʳ[Gal. 5:17] **26:45** ˢMatt. 17:22, 23; 20:18, 19 **26:47** ᵗActs 1:16 **26:49** ᵘ2 Sam. 20:9 **26:50** ᵛPs. 41:9; 55:13 **26:51** ʷJohn 18:10

his hand and drew his sword, struck the servant of the high priest, and cut off his ear.

[52]But Jesus said to him, "Put your sword in its place, [x]for all who take the sword will perish[*] by the sword. [53]Or do you think that I cannot now pray to My Father, and He will provide Me with [y]more than twelve legions of angels? [54]How then could the Scriptures be fulfilled, [z]that it must happen thus?"

[55]In that hour Jesus said to the multitudes, "Have you come out, as against a robber, with swords and clubs to take Me? I sat daily with you, teaching in the temple, and you did not seize Me. [56]But all this was done that the [a]Scriptures of the prophets might be fulfilled."

Then [b]all the disciples forsook Him and fled.

Jesus Faces the Sanhedrin

[57c]And those who had laid hold of Jesus led *Him* away to Caiaphas the high priest, where the scribes and the elders were assembled. [58]But [d]Peter followed Him at a distance to the high priest's courtyard. And he went in and sat with the servants to see the end.

[59]Now the chief priests, the elders,[*] and all the council sought [e]false testimony against Jesus to put Him to death, [60]but found none. Even though [f]many false witnesses came forward, they found none.[*] But at last [g]two false witnesses[*] came forward [61]and said, "This *fellow* said, [h]'I am able to destroy the temple of God and to build it in three days.'"

[62i]And the high priest arose and said to Him, "Do You answer nothing? What *is it* these men testify against You?" [63]But [j]Jesus kept silent. And the high priest answered and said to Him, [k]"I put You under oath by the living God: Tell us if You are the Christ, the Son of God!"

[64]Jesus said to him, "*It is as* you said. Nevertheless, I say to you, [l]hereafter you will see the Son of Man [m]sitting at the right hand of the Power, and coming on the clouds of heaven."

[65n]Then the high priest tore his clothes, saying, "He has spoken blasphemy! What further need do we have of witnesses? Look, now you have heard His [o]blasphemy! [66]What do you think?"

They answered and said, [p]"He is deserving of death."

[67q]Then they spat in His face and beat Him; and [r]others struck *Him* with the palms of their hands, [68]saying, [s]"Prophesy to us, Christ! Who is the one who struck You?"

Peter Denies Jesus, and Weeps Bitterly

[69t]Now Peter sat outside in the courtyard. And a servant girl came to him, saying, "You also were with Jesus of Galilee."

[70]But he denied it before *them* all, saying, "I do not know what you are saying."

[71]And when he had gone out to the gateway, another *girl* saw him and said to those *who were* there, "This *fellow* also was with Jesus of Nazareth."

[72]But again he denied with an oath, "I do not know the Man!"

[73]And a little later those who stood by came up and said to Peter, "Surely you also are *one* of them, for your [u]speech betrays you."

[74]Then [v]he began to curse and swear, *saying*, "I do not know the Man!"

Immediately a rooster crowed. [75]And Peter remembered the word of Jesus who had said to him, [w]"Before the rooster crows, you will deny Me three times." So he went out and wept bitterly.

---

[*] **26:52** M-Text reads *die.* [*] **26:59** NU-Text omits *the elders.* [*] **26:60** NU-Text puts a comma after *but found none,* does not capitalize *Even,* and omits *they found none.* • NU-Text omits *false witnesses.*

26:53 twelve legions of angels. A legion in the Roman army was about six thousand men. When one considers the power of one angel (Ex. 32:23; 2 Sam. 24:15–17; 2 Kin. 19:35) the power of more than 72,000 angels is beyond comprehension. Jesus had all of heaven's power at His disposal, yet He refused to use it. His Father's will was for Him to go to the cross.
26:62 Do You answer nothing? In maintaining His silence, Jesus fulfilled the prophecy of Isaiah 53:7.
26:64 Second Coming—Throughout His ministry, Jesus had applied to Himself the Old Testament prophecies that were acknowledged as messianic by the Jewish teachers. Here, Jesus answers Caiaphas the high priest by combining two well-known messianic prophecies from Psalm 110:1 and Daniel 7:13. The first describes His enthronement and the other His second coming. The final word spoken by Christ to the Jews was about the certainty of His future return. About His first coming Jesus said, "For God did not send His Son into the world to condemn the world" (John 3:17). But the time will come when all the world

will see Him enthroned at the right hand of God and given all power and majesty as the judge of the ages.
26:74 Immediately a rooster crowed. Some have detected a contradiction between this passage and the account in Mark 14:72. Others believe that seeing a contradiction is a forced reading of the text. Matthew, Luke, and John make the simple statement that a rooster would crow (Luke 22:61; John 18:27), whereas Mark, which is believed to be based on Peter's memories, would include more exact details.

26:52 [x]Rev. 13:10 **26:53** [y]Dan. 7:10 **26:54** [z]Is. 50:6; 53:2–11 **26:56** [a]Lam. 4:20 [b]John 18:15 **26:57** [c]John 18:12, 19–24 **26:58** [d]John 18:15, 16 **26:59** [e]Ps. 35:11 **26:60** [f]Mark 14:55 [g]Deut. 19:15 **26:61** [h]John 2:19 **26:62** [i]Mark 14:60 **26:63** [j]Is. 53:7 [k]Lev. 5:1 **26:64** [l]Dan. 7:13 [m]Acts 7:55] **26:65** [n]2 Kin. 18:37 [o]John 10:30–36 **26:66** [p]Lev. 24:16 **26:67** [q]Is. 50:6; 53:3 [r]Luke 22:63–65 **26:68** [s]Mark 14:65 **26:69** [t]John 18:16–18, 25–27 **26:73** [u]Luke 22:59 **26:74** [v]Mark 14:71 **26:75** [w]Matt. 26:34

Jesus Handed Over to Pontius Pilate

27 When morning came, ^aall the chief priests and elders of the people plotted against Jesus to put Him to death. ²And when they had bound Him, they led Him away and ^bdelivered Him to Pontius* Pilate the governor.

Judas Hangs Himself

^{3c}Then Judas, His betrayer, seeing that He had been condemned, was remorseful and brought back the thirty ^dpieces of silver to the chief priests and elders, ⁴saying, "I have sinned by betraying innocent blood."

And they said, "What *is that* to us? You see *to it!*"

⁵Then he threw down the pieces of silver in the temple and ^edeparted, and went and hanged himself.

⁶But the chief priests took the silver pieces and said, "It is not lawful to put them into the treasury, because they are the price of blood." ⁷And they consulted together and bought with them the potter's field, to bury strangers in. ⁸Therefore that field has been called ^fthe Field of Blood to this day.

⁹Then was fulfilled what was spoken by Jeremiah the prophet, saying, ^g"And they took the thirty pieces of silver, the value of Him who was priced, whom they of the children of Israel priced, ¹⁰and ^hgave them for the potter's field, as the LORD directed me."*

Jesus Faces Pilate

¹¹Now Jesus stood before the governor. ⁱAnd the governor asked Him, saying, "Are You the King of the Jews?"

Jesus said to him, ^j"It is as you say."

¹²And while He was being accused by the chief priests and elders, ^kHe answered nothing.

¹³Then Pilate said to Him, ^l"Do You not hear how many things they testify against You?" ¹⁴But He answered him not one word, so that the governor marveled greatly.

Taking the Place of Barabbas

^{15m}Now at the feast the governor was accustomed to releasing to the multitude one prisoner whom they wished. ¹⁶And

at that time they had a notorious prisoner called Barabbas.* ¹⁷Therefore, when they had gathered together, Pilate said to them, "Whom do you want me to release to you? Barabbas, or Jesus who is called Christ?" ¹⁸For he knew that they had handed Him over because of ⁿenvy.

¹⁹While he was sitting on the judgment seat, his wife sent to him, saying, "Have nothing to do with that just Man, for I have suffered many things today in a dream because of Him."

^{20o}But the chief priests and elders persuaded the multitudes that they should ask for Barabbas and destroy Jesus. ²¹The governor answered and said to them, "Which of the two do you want me to release to you?"

They said, ^p"Barabbas!"

²²Pilate said to them, "What then shall I do with Jesus who is called Christ?"

They all said to him, "Let Him be crucified!"

²³Then the governor said, ^q"Why, what evil has He done?"

But they cried out all the more, saying, "Let Him be crucified!"

²⁴When Pilate saw that he could not prevail at all, but rather *that* a tumult was rising, he ^rtook water and washed *his* hands before the multitude, saying, "I am innocent of the blood of this just Person.* You see *to it.*"

²⁵And all the people answered and said, ^s"His blood *be* on us and on our children."

²⁶Then he released Barabbas to them; and when ^the had scourged Jesus, he delivered *Him* to be crucified.

The Soldiers Mock Jesus

^{27u}Then the soldiers of the governor took Jesus into the Praetorium and gathered the whole garrison around Him. ²⁸And they ^vstripped Him and ^wput a scarlet robe on Him. ^{29x}When they had twisted a crown of thorns, they put *it* on His head, and a reed in His right hand. And they bowed the knee before Him and mocked Him, saying, "Hail, King of the Jews!" ^{30y}they spat on Him, and took the reed and struck Him on the head.

---

* **27:2** NU-Text omits *Pontius.* * **27:10** Jeremiah 32:6–9 * **27:16** NU-Text reads *Jesus Barabbas.* * **27:24** NU-Text omits *just.*

27:2 Pilate. Pontius Pilate was governor of Judea, Samaria, and Idumea from A.D. 26 to 36. Because the Jews did not have authority to execute Jesus, they brought Him to Pilate.

27:25 His blood be on us and on our children. The sins of the fathers are visited on their children for those who hate God. But if anyone turns to Jesus and repents, He never fails to show His lovingkindness.

27:27 the Praetorium. This was the official residence of the governor when he was in Jerusalem.

27:1 ^a John 18:28 **27:2** ^b Acts 3:13 **27:3** ^c Matt. 26:14 ^d Matt. 26:15 **27:5** ^e Acts 1:18 **27:8** ^f Acts 1:19 **27:9** ^g Zech. 11:12 **27:10** ^h Jer. 32:6–9; Zech. 11:12, 13 **27:11** ⁱ Mark 15:2–5 ^j John 18:37 **27:12** ^k John 19:9 **27:13** ^l Matt. 26:62 **27:15** ^m Luke 23:17–25 **27:18** ⁿ Matt. 21:38 **27:20** ^o Acts 3:14 **27:21** ^p Acts 3:14 **27:23** ^q Acts 3:13 **27:24** ^r Deut. 21:6–8 **27:25** ^s Josh. 2:19 **27:26** ^t [Is. 50:6; 53:5] **27:27** ^u Mark 15:16–20 **27:28** ^v John 19:2 ^w Luke 23:11 **27:29** ^x Is. 53:3 **27:30** ^y Matt. 26:67

[31]And when they had mocked Him, they took the robe off Him, put His *own* clothes on Him, [z]and led Him away to be crucified.

The King on a Cross

[32a]Now as they came out, [b]they found a man of Cyrene, Simon by name. Him they compelled to bear His cross. [33c]And when they had come to a place called Golgotha, that is to say, Place of a Skull, [34d]they gave Him sour* wine mingled with gall to drink. But when He had tasted *it*, He would not drink.

[35e]Then they crucified Him, and divided His garments, casting lots,* that it might be fulfilled which was spoken by the prophet:

> [f]"They divided My garments among them,
> And for My clothing they cast lots."*

[36g]Sitting down, they kept watch over Him there. [37]And they [h]put up over His head the accusation written against Him:

THIS IS JESUS THE KING
OF THE JEWS.

[38i]Then two robbers were crucified with Him, one on the right and another on the left.

[39]And [j]those who passed by blasphemed Him, wagging their heads [40]and saying, [k]"You who destroy the temple and build *it* in three days, save Yourself! [l]If You are the Son of God, come down from the cross."

[41]Likewise the chief priests also, mocking with the scribes and elders,* said, [42]"He [m]saved others; Himself He cannot save. If He is the King of Israel,* let Him now come down from the cross, and we will believe Him.* [43n]He trusted in God; let Him deliver Him now if He will have Him; for He said, 'I am the Son of God.'"

[44o]Even the robbers who were crucified with Him reviled Him with the same thing.

Jesus Dies on the Cross

[45p]Now from the sixth hour until the ninth hour there was darkness over all the land. [46]And about the ninth hour [q]Jesus cried out with a loud voice, saying, "Eli, Eli, lama sabachthani?" that is, [r]"My God, My God, why have You forsaken Me?"*

[47]Some of those who stood there, when they heard *that*, said, "This Man is calling for Elijah!" [48]Immediately one of them ran and took a sponge, [s]filled *it* with sour wine and put *it* on a reed, and offered it to Him to drink.

[49]The rest said, "Let Him alone; let us see if Elijah will come to save Him."

[50]And Jesus [t]cried out again with a loud voice, and [u]yielded up His spirit.

[51]Then, behold, [v]the veil of the temple was torn in two from top to bottom; and the earth quaked, and the rocks were split,

---

* **27:34** NU-Text omits *sour.*   * **27:35** NU-Text and M-Text omit the rest of this verse. • Psalm 22:18
* **27:41** M-Text reads *with the scribes, the Pharisees, and the elders.*   * **27:42** NU-Text reads *He is the King of Israel!* • NU-Text and M-Text read *we will believe in Him.*   * **27:46** Psalm 22:1

27:31 crucified. Crucifixion, a practice probably adopted from Persia, was considered by the Romans to be the cruelest form of execution. This punishment was reserved for the worst criminals. The offender usually died after two or three days of agonizing suffering, enduring not only incomprehensible pain, but also hunger, thirst, and exposure. The offender's arms were nailed to a beam that was hoisted up and fixed to a post, to which his feet were nailed.

27:32 Simon by name. Simon probably was (or later became) a follower of Christ; it is unlikely that he would be referred to by name if he were a stranger to the Christian community (Mark 15:21).

27:34 sour wine mingled with gall. It is believed that this mixture was meant to dull the victim's pain. The prophetic words of Psalm 69:21 were fulfilled here.

27:35 casting lots. The soldiers fulfilled the prophetic words of Psalm 22:18.

27:38 two robbers. This is the fulfillment of Isaiah 53:12, "He was numbered with the transgressors." Psalm 22:6 predicted the insults that would be directed at the Messiah.

27:45 the sixth hour. This would have been noon. The first hour began at sunrise (approximately 6:00 A.M.). **darkness.** The darkness could not have been due to a natural cause, such as an eclipse of the sun, since the Passover occurred during a full moon. This was a supernatural occurrence.

27:46–50 Atonement—Because God cannot tolerate sin, as Jesus took upon Himself the sin of the whole human race, God had to turn away. Jesus felt this separation, and many believe it was as much for the dread of this as for the physical pain that Jesus wept in the garden. Jesus' cry to God is a quote from Psalm 22:1, a messianic verse that the Jews should have understood.

27:50 cried out again with a loud voice. The cry referred to here by Matthew was, "It is finished" (John 19:30). This was not a cry of exhaustion, but a cry of victory. The purpose for which Jesus came into the world had been accomplished. Redemption from sin had been purchased for all mankind.

27:51 the veil of the temple was torn in two from top to bottom. The temple had two veils or curtains, one in front of the holy place and the other separating the holy place from the Most Holy Place. These curtains were heavy and very strong and thick. It was the second of these that was torn, demonstrating that through the death of Jesus, there was now open access to God. Jesus' blood covered our sins from God's sight.

27:31 [z] Is. 53:7   **27:32** [a] Heb. 13:12   [b] Mark 15:21   **27:33** [c] John 19:17   **27:34** [d] Ps. 69:21   **27:35** [e] Luke 23:34   [f] Ps. 22:18   **27:36** [g] Matt. 27:54   **27:37** [h] John 19:19   **27:38** [i] Is. 53:9, 12   **27:39** [j] Mark 15:29   **27:40** [k] John 2:19   [l] Matt. 26:63   **27:42** [m] John 3:14, 15]   **27:43** [n] Ps. 22:8   **27:44** [o] Luke 23:39–43   **27:45** [p] Mark 15:33–41   **27:46** [q] [Heb. 5:7]   [r] Ps. 22:1   **27:48** [s] Ps. 69:21   **27:50** [t] Luke 23:46   [u] [John 10:18]   **27:51** [v] Ex. 26:31

52and the graves were opened; and many bodies of the saints who had fallen asleep were raised; 53and coming out of the graves after His resurrection, they went into the holy city and appeared to many.

54wSo when the centurion and those with him, who were guarding Jesus, saw the earthquake and the things that had happened, they feared greatly, saying, x"Truly this was the Son of God!"

55And many women ywho followed Jesus from Galilee, ministering to Him, were there looking on from afar, 56zamong whom were Mary Magdalene, Mary the mother of James and Joses,* and the mother of Zebedee's sons.

Jesus Buried in Joseph's Tomb

57Now awhen evening had come, there came a rich man from Arimathea, named Joseph, who himself had also become a disciple of Jesus. 58This man went to Pilate and asked for the body of Jesus. Then Pilate commanded the body to be given to him. 59When Joseph had taken the body, he wrapped it in a clean linen cloth, 60and blaid it in his new tomb which he had hewn out of the rock; and he rolled a large stone against the door of the tomb, and departed. 61And Mary Magdalene was there, and the other Mary, sitting opposite the tomb.

Pilate Sets a Guard

62On the next day, which followed the Day of Preparation, the chief priests and Pharisees gathered together to Pilate, 63saying, "Sir, we remember, while He was still alive, how that deceiver said, c'After three days I will rise.' 64Therefore command that the tomb be made secure until the third day, lest His disciples come by night* and steal Him away, and say to the people, 'He has risen from the dead.' So the last deception will be worse than the first."

65Pilate said to them, "You have a guard; go your way, make it as secure as you know how." 66So they went and made the tomb secure, dsealing the stone and setting the guard.

He Is Risen

28 Now aafter the Sabbath, as the first day of the week began to dawn, Mary Magdalene band the other Mary came to see the tomb. 2And behold, there was a great earthquake; for can angel of the Lord descended from heaven, and came and rolled back the stone from the door,* and sat on it. 3dHis countenance was like lightning, and his clothing as white as snow. 4And the guards shook for fear of him, and became like edead men.

5But the angel answered and said to the women, "Do not be afraid, for I know that you seek Jesus who was crucified. 6He is not here; for He is risen, fas He said. Come, see the place where the Lord lay. 7And go quickly and tell His disciples that He is risen from the dead, and indeed gHe is going before you into Galilee; there you will see Him. Behold, I have told you."

8So they went out quickly from the tomb with fear and great joy, and ran to bring His disciples word.

The Women Worship the Risen Lord

9And as they went to tell His disciples,* behold, hJesus met them, saying, "Rejoice!" So they came and held Him by the feet and worshiped Him. 10Then Jesus said to them, "Do not be afraid. Go and tell iMy brethren to go to Galilee, and there they will see Me."

The Soldiers Are Bribed

11Now while they were going, behold, some of the guard came into the city and reported to the chief priests all the things that had happened. 12When they had assembled with the elders and consulted together, they gave a large sum of money to the soldiers, 13saying, "Tell them, 'His disciples came at night and stole Him away while we slept.' 14And if this comes to the governor's ears, we will appease him and make you secure." 15So they took the money and did as they were instructed; and this saying is commonly reported among the Jews until this day.

The Great Commission

16Then the eleven disciples went away into Galilee, to the mountain iwhich Jesus had appointed for them. 17When they saw Him, they worshiped Him; but some kdoubted.

---

* **27:56** NU-Text reads *Joseph.*   * **27:64** NU-Text omits *by night.*   * **28:2** NU-Text omits *from the door.*   * **28:9** NU-Text omits the first clause of this verse.

27:57 *a rich man of Arimathea.* Joseph's actions fulfilled the prophecy of Isaiah, "they made His grave with the wicked—but with the rich at His death" (Is. 53:9).

28:2 *rolled back the stone.* The tomb was not opened to allow Christ to come out; it was opened to allow others to go in and see for themselves that it was empty.

28:6 *He is risen, as He said.* Jesus predicted His resurrection to His disciples, even though they did not understand Him (12:40; 16:21; 17:9,23; 26:32).

28:7 *go quickly and tell.* This is always the divine

order: to tell others the good news that Jesus is alive (v. 19).

27:54 w Mark 15:39 x Matt. 14:33   **27:55** y Luke 8:2, 3   **27:56** z Mark 15:40, 47; 16:9   **27:57** a John 19:38–42   **27:60** b Is. 53:9   **27:63** c Mark 8:31; 10:34   **27:66** d Dan. 6:17   **28:1** a Luke 24:1–10 b Matt. 27:56, 61   **28:2** c Mark 16:5   **28:3** d Dan. 7:9; 10:6   **28:4** e Rev. 1:17   **28:6** f Matt. 12:40; 16:21; 17:23; 20:19   **28:7** g Mark 16:7   **28:9** h John 20:14   **28:10** i John 20:17   **28:16** i Matt. 26:32; 28:7, 10   **28:17** k John 20:24–29

¹⁸And Jesus came and spoke to them, saying, ˡ"All authority has been given to Me in heaven and on earth. ¹⁹ᵐGo therefore* and ⁿmake disciples of all the nations, baptizing them in the name of the Father and of the Son and of the Holy Spirit, ²⁰ₒteaching them to observe all things that I have commanded you; and lo, I am ᵖwith you always, *even* to the end of the age." Amen.*

---

* **28:19** M-Text omits *therefore*.   * **28:20** NU-Text omits *Amen.*

28:19 Why Share Our Faith—There are at least six compelling reasons for sharing our faith in Christ with those who have not experienced new life in Christ:

1. Because God has commanded us to do so (Acts 1:8).
2. Because it demonstrates our love for God. If we truly love Him we will keep His commandments (John 14:15).
3. Because all are lost without Christ (Rom. 3:10,23).
4. Because this is God's chosen method: He could use angels, but He only uses redeemed sinners to tell lost sinners about Christ (Rom. 10:14–17; 1 Tim. 1:15).
5. Because God desires to save all people (Acts 4:12; 1 Tim. 2:4; 2 Pet. 3:9).
6. Because faith grows best when each generation conscientiously strives to pass it on to the next.

28:20 *I am with you always.* Jesus is the true Immanuel, "God with us" (1:23; Heb. 13:5–6; Rev. 21:3).

28:18 ˡ [Dan. 7:13, 14] **28:19** ᵐ Mark 16:15 ⁿ Luke 24:47
28:20 ₒ [Acts 2:42] ᵖ [Acts 4:31; 18:10; 23:11]

THE GOSPEL ACCORDING TO
MARK

▶ **AUTHOR:** According to Acts 12:12, Mark's mother Mary had a large house that was used as a meeting place for believers in Jerusalem. Barnabas was Mark's cousin (Col. 4:10), but Peter may have been the person that led him to Christ (Peter called him "Mark my son" in 1 Pet. 5:13). It was this close association with Peter that lent apostolic authority to Mark's Gospel, since Peter was evidently Mark's primary source of information. It has been suggested that Mark was referring to himself in his account of a "certain young man" in Gethsemane (14:51). Since all the disciples had abandoned Jesus (14:50), this little incident may have been a firsthand account.

▶ **TIME:** C. A.D. 29–33   ▶ **KEY VERSES:** Mark 8:34–37

▶ **THEME:** Mark is the shortest and simplest of the Gospels. He doesn't seem to be telling the story in a way that appeals to a particular audience the way Matthew does. He also does not use the well-developed thematic structure that characterizes John. One of the most common terms in the book is one that is translated "immediately" or "at once." He uses this frequently as he moves from one anecdote to another. Mark's quickly paced Gospel is often confrontational, as he tells the story of the gospel as clearly as possible. He wants the reader to respond, and almost seems to be saying, "Here is the truth, believe it, and let's get on with following Jesus."

John the Baptist Prepares the Way

1 The ᵃbeginning of the gospel of Jesus Christ, ᵇthe Son of God. ²As it is written in the Prophets:*

ᶜ"*Behold, I send My messenger before Your face,*
Who will prepare Your way before You."*
3 "*Theᵈ voice of one crying in the wilderness:*
'*Prepare the way of the* LORD;
Make His paths straight.'"*

⁴ᵉJohn came baptizing in the wilderness and preaching a baptism of repentance for the remission of sins. ⁵ᶠThen all the land of Judea, and those from Jerusalem, went out to him and were all baptized by him in the Jordan River, confessing their sins.

⁶Now John was ᵍclothed with camel's hair and with a leather belt around his waist, and he ate locusts and wild honey. ⁷And he preached, saying, ʰ"There comes One after me who is mightier than I, whose sandal strap I am not worthy to stoop down and loose. ⁸I indeed baptized you with water, but He will baptize you ⁱwith the Holy Spirit."

---

* **1:2** NU-Text reads *Isaiah the prophet.* • Malachi 3:1   * **1:3** Isaiah 40:3

1:1 The beginning of the gospel of Jesus Christ. Writing three decades after the resurrection of Christ, Mark starts his narrative with a simple declaration of the good news about God's Son, the Lord Jesus Christ. The *gospel* refers to the basic story of the good news to be found in Christ's life, ministry, death, and resurrection.

1:2–3 As it is written. Other than by quoting Jesus, Mark makes only one reference to the Old Testament.

1:4 John came baptizing. The mention of John without any introduction presupposes some knowledge of the Christian faith on the part of Mark's readers. **the remission of sins.** This phrase does not mean that one is baptized in order to receive forgiveness of sins. The Greek preposition translated "of" in English probably means "with a view to," signifying that baptism looks to the forgiveness that God gives through the gift of repentance.

1:5 were all baptized by him. John's baptizing was a recurring popular event that attracted large crowds. Mark vividly portrays the continuous stream of followers who flocked to John. As each person was baptized by John, he or she would admit to his or her individual sin and need for the Messiah.

1:7 And he preached, saying. The tense of these verbs indicates continuous action in past time. John's characteristic message was to promote expectancy and acceptance of the Lord Jesus Christ.

1:8 I indeed baptized you with water. The water is a physical representation of the future life in the Spirit that people who followed the Messiah would have.

1:1 ᵃ Luke 3:22 ᵇ Matt. 14:33   **1:2** ᶜ Mal. 3:1   **1:3** ᵈ Is. 40:3   **1:4** ᵉ Matt. 3:1   **1:5** ᶠ Matt. 3:5   **1:6** ᵍ Matt. 3:4   **1:7** ʰ John 1:27   **1:8** ⁱ Acts 1:5; 11:16 ʲ Is. 44:3

John Baptizes Jesus

9k It came to pass in those days *that* Jesus came from Nazareth of Galilee, and was baptized by John in the Jordan. 10l And immediately, coming up from* the water, He saw the heavens parting and the Spirit m descending upon Him like a dove. 11 Then a voice came from heaven, n "You are My beloved Son, in whom I am well pleased."

Satan Tempts Jesus

12o Immediately the Spirit drove Him into the wilderness. 13 And He was there in the wilderness forty days, tempted by Satan, and was with the wild beasts; p and the angels ministered to Him.

Jesus Begins His Galilean Ministry

14q Now after John was put in prison, Jesus came to Galilee, r preaching the gospel of the kingdom* of God, 15 and saying, s "The time is fulfilled, and t the kingdom of God is at hand. Repent, and believe in the gospel."

Four Fishermen Called as Disciples

16u And as He walked by the Sea of Galilee, He saw Simon and Andrew his brother casting a net into the sea; for they were fishermen. 17 Then Jesus said to them, "Follow Me, and I will make you become v fishers of men." 18w They immediately left their nets and followed Him.

19 When He had gone a little farther from there, He saw James the *son* of Zebedee, and John his brother, who also *were* in the boat mending their nets. 20 And immediately He called them, and they left their father Zebedee in the boat with the hired servants, and went after Him.

Jesus Casts Out an Unclean Spirit

21x Then they went into Capernaum, and immediately on the Sabbath He entered the y synagogue and taught. 22z And they were astonished at His teaching, for He taught them as one having authority, and not as the scribes.

23 Now there was a man in their synagogue with an q unclean spirit. And he cried out, 24 saying, "Let *us* alone! b What have we to do with You, Jesus of Nazareth? Did You come to destroy us? I c know who You are— the d Holy One of God!"

25 But Jesus e rebuked him, saying, "Be quiet, and come out of him!" 26 And when the unclean spirit f had convulsed him and cried out with a loud voice, he came out of him. 27 Then they were all amazed, so that they questioned among themselves, saying, "What is this? What new doctrine *is* this? For with authority* He commands even the unclean spirits, and they obey Him." 28 And immediately His g fame spread throughout all the region around Galilee.

Peter's Mother-in-Law Healed

29h Now as soon as they had come out of the synagogue, they entered the house of Simon and Andrew, with James and John. 30 But Simon's wife's mother lay sick with a fever, and they told Him about her at once. 31 So He came and took her by the hand and lifted her up, and immediately the fever left her. And she served them.

Many Healed After Sabbath Sunset

32i At evening, when the sun had set, they brought to Him all who were sick and

* **1:10** NU-Text reads *out of.* * **1:14** NU-Text omits *of the kingdom.* * **1:27** NU-Text reads *What is this? A new doctrine with authority.*

1:9 Jesus ... was baptized by John. Because He had no sins to repent of, Jesus' baptism was unique. It showed His identity with John's work and with the sinner for whom He would die. It also foreshadowed His own death, burial, and resurrection for sinners.

1:11 a voice came from heaven. Three times during Christ's earthly ministry a voice came from heaven. Here it was the Father's testimony to Christ's unique and divine Sonship. The other two confirming incidents were at the transfiguration (9:7) and on the day of Christ's triumphal entry into Jerusalem (John 12:28).

1:13 angels ministered to Him. Mark is the only Gospel that mentions these angels.

1:15 kingdom of God. The kingdom was the subject of much Old Testament prophecy, and the theme was familiar to Jesus' listeners. **Repent, and believe.** These are both acts of faith. When a person accepts the only true and worthy object of faith, that person readily turns from inferior substitutes.

1:19 James ... John. The scenes of verses 16–20 are very colorful. Simon and Andrew are fishing when we encounter them. James and John are mending their nets. Such details indicate the testimony of an eyewitness, probably Peter.

1:21 Capernaum. This city is now in ruins, and sits beside the northern edge of the Sea of Galilee. It is mentioned 22 times in the Gospels. By contrast, only one recorded event during Christ's ministry occurred at Nazareth (Luke 4:16).

1:22 they were astonished at His teaching. Christ's teaching differed from that of scribes and Pharisees because He did not lean on the wisdom of other teachers and rabbis. His authority came from Himself.

1:28 His fame spread throughout all the region around Galilee. Mark notes the extent of recognition this great miracle brought Jesus. He also creates suspense by contrasting the people who received Christ with the Pharisees and rulers who worked to bring about His death.

1:9 k Matt. 3:13–17 **1:10** l Matt. 3:16 m Acts 10:38 **1:11** n Matt. 3:17; 12:18 **1:12** o Matt. 4:1–11 **1:13** p Matt. 4:10, 11 **1:14** q Matt. 4:12 r Matt. 4:23 **1:15** s [Gal. 4:4] t Matt. 3:2; 4:17 **1:16** u Luke 5:2–11 **1:17** v Matt. 13:47, 48 **1:18** w [Luke 14:26] **1:21** x Luke 4:31–37 y Matt. 4:23 **1:22** z Matt. 7:28, 29; 13:54 **1:23** a [Matt. 12:43] **1:24** b Matt. 8:28, 29 c James 2:19 d Ps. 16:10 **1:25** e [Luke 4:39] **1:26** f Mark 9:20 **1:28** g Matt. 4:24; 9:31 **1:29** h Luke 4:38, 39 **1:32** i Matt. 8:16, 17

those who were demon-possessed. ³³And the whole city was gathered together at the door. ³⁴Then He healed many who were sick with various diseases, and ʲcast out many demons; and He ᵏdid not allow the demons to speak, because they knew Him.

Preaching in Galilee

³⁵Now ˡin the morning, having risen a long while before daylight, He went out and departed to a solitary place; and there He ᵐprayed. ³⁶And Simon and those *who were* with Him searched for Him. ³⁷When they found Him, they said to Him, ⁿ"Everyone ᵒis looking for You."

³⁸But He said to them, ᵖ"Let us go into the next towns, that I may preach there also, because ᵠfor this purpose I have come forth."

³⁹ʳAnd He was preaching in their synagogues throughout all Galilee, and ˢcasting out demons.

Jesus Cleanses a Leper

⁴⁰ᵗNow a leper came to Him, imploring Him, kneeling down to Him and saying to Him, "If You are willing, You can make me clean."

⁴¹Then Jesus, moved with ᵘcompassion, stretched out *His* hand and touched him, and said to him, "I am willing; be cleansed." ⁴²As soon as He had spoken, ᵛimmediately the leprosy left him, and he was cleansed. ⁴³And He strictly warned him and sent him away at once, ⁴⁴and said to him, "See that you say nothing to anyone; but go your way, show yourself to the priest, and offer for your cleansing those things ʷwhich Moses commanded, as a testimony to them."

⁴⁵ˣHowever, he went out and began to proclaim *it* freely, and to spread the matter, so that Jesus could no longer openly enter the city, but was outside in deserted places; ʸand they came to Him from every direction.

Jesus Forgives and Heals a Paralytic

2 And again ᵃHe entered Capernaum after *some* days, and it was heard that He was in the house. ²Immediately* many gathered together, so that there was no longer room to receive *them,* not even near the door. And He preached the word to them. ³Then they came to Him, bringing a ᵇparalytic who was carried by four *men.* ⁴And when they could not come near Him because of the crowd, they uncovered the roof where He was. So when they had broken through, they let down the bed on which the paralytic was lying.

⁵When Jesus saw their faith, He said to the paralytic, "Son, your sins are forgiven you."

⁶And some of the scribes were sitting there and reasoning in their hearts, ⁷"Why does this *Man* speak blasphemies like this? ᶜWho can forgive sins but God alone?"

⁸But immediately, when Jesus perceived in His spirit that they reasoned thus within themselves, He said to them, "Why do you reason about these things in your hearts? ⁹ᵈWhich is easier, to say to the paralytic, 'Your sins are forgiven you,' or to say, 'Arise, take up your bed and walk'? ¹⁰But that you may know that the Son of Man has power on earth to forgive sins"—He said to the paralytic, ¹¹"I say to you, arise, take up your bed, and go to your house." ¹²Immediately he arose, took up the bed, and went out in the presence of them all, so that all were amazed and ᵉglorified God, saying, "We never saw *anything* like this!"

Matthew the Tax Collector

¹³ᶠThen He went out again by the sea; and all the multitude came to Him, and He taught them. ¹⁴ᵍAs He passed by, He saw Levi the *son* of Alphaeus sitting at the tax office. And He said to him, ʰ"Follow Me." So he arose and ⁱfollowed Him.

---

* **2:2** NU-Text omits *Immediately.*

1:35 *there He prayed.* The verb tense indicates Jesus prayed continuously. Jesus' prayer life was successful because it was planned, private, and prolonged. He got up early enough, got far enough away, and stayed at it long enough.

1:44 *say nothing to anyone.* Jesus' demand has several plausible explanations: (1) The report of Jesus' healing the man may have prejudiced the priest who needed to pronounce him clean; (2) Jesus did not want to be known primarily as a miracle worker, so He often commanded those who received His healing to remain quiet; and (3) the man's testimony would possibly have hastened the confrontation between Jesus and the religious leaders.

2:5 *saw their faith.* Not only did the four men have faith, but the paralytic himself had it too. When Jesus announced to him, "your sins are forgiven you," He was implicitly acknowledging the paralytic's trust that He was the Messiah.

2:6–7 *some of the scribes.* Mark notes the opposition

of the scribes, who under their breath accused Jesus of blasphemy. In Christ's day the scribes were commonly called lawyers.

2:11 *arise, take up your bed, and go to your house.* By healing the paralytic, Jesus made His pronouncement of forgiveness far more credible.

2:13 *He taught them.* Jesus regularly taught the multitudes in retreat settings. This is indicated by the continuous tense of the verbs used here. They kept on coming and Jesus kept on teaching.

1:34 ʲLuke 13:32 ᵏActs 16:17, 18   **1:35** ˡLuke 4:42, 43   ᵐLuke 5:16; 6:12; 9:28, 29   **1:37** ⁿJohn 3:26; 12:19   ᵒ[Heb. 11:6]   **1:38** ᵖLuke 4:43 ᵠ[Is. 61:1, 2]   **1:39** ʳMatt. 4:23; 9:35 ˢMark 5:8, 13; 7:29, 30   **1:40** ᵗLuke 5:12–14   **1:41** ᵘLuke 7:13   **1:42** ᵛMatt. 15:28   **1:44** ʷLev. 14:1–32   **1:45** ˣLuke 5:15 ʸMatt. 2:2, 13; 3:7   **2:1** ᵃMatt. 9:1   **2:3** ᵇMatt. 4:24; 8:6   **2:7** ᶜIs. 43:25   **2:9** ᵈMatt. 9:5   **2:12** ᵉ[Phil. 2:11]   **2:13** ᶠMatt. 9:9   **2:14** ᵍLuke 5:27–32   ʰJohn 1:43; 12:26; 21:22 ⁱLuke 18:28

15*j*Now it happened, as He was dining in *Levi's* house, that many tax collectors and sinners also sat together with Jesus and His disciples; for there were many, and they followed Him. 16And when the scribes and* Pharisees saw Him eating with the tax collectors and sinners, they said to His disciples, "How *is it* that He eats and drinks with tax collectors and sinners?"

17When Jesus heard *it*, He said to them, *k*"Those who are well have no need of a physician, but those who are sick. I did not come to call *the* righteous, but sinners, to repentance."*

Jesus Is Questioned About Fasting

18*l*The disciples of John and of the Pharisees were fasting. Then they came and said to Him, "Why do the disciples of John and of the Pharisees fast, but Your disciples do not fast?"

19And Jesus said to them, "Can the friends of the bridegroom fast while the bridegroom is with them? As long as they have the bridegroom with them they cannot fast. 20But the days will come when the bridegroom will be *m*taken away from them, and then they will fast in those days. 21No one sews a piece of unshrunk cloth on an old garment; or else the new piece pulls away from the old, and the tear is made worse. 22And no one puts new wine into old wineskins; or else the new wine bursts the wineskins, the wine is spilled, and the wineskins are ruined. But new wine must be put into new wineskins."

Jesus Is Lord of the Sabbath

23*n*Now it happened that He went through the grainfields on the Sabbath; and as they went His disciples began *o*to pluck the heads of grain. 24And the Pharisees said to Him, "Look, why do they do what is *p*not lawful on the Sabbath?"

25But He said to them, "Have you never read *q*what David did when he was in need and hungry, he and those with him: 26how he went into the house of God *in the days* of Abiathar the high priest, and ate the showbread, *r*which is not lawful to eat except for the priests, and also gave some to those who were with him?"

27And He said to them, "The Sabbath was made for man, and not man for the *s*Sabbath. 28Therefore *t*the Son of Man is also Lord of the Sabbath."

Healing on the Sabbath

3 And *a*He entered the synagogue again, and a man was there who had a withered hand. 2So they *b*watched Him closely, whether He would *c*heal him on the Sabbath, so that they might accuse Him. 3And He said to the man who had the withered hand, "Step forward." 4Then He said to them, "Is it lawful on the Sabbath to do good or to do evil, to save life or to kill?" But they kept silent. 5And when He had looked around at them with anger, being grieved by the *d*hardness of their hearts, He said to the man, "Stretch out your hand." And he stretched *it* out, and his hand was restored as whole as the other.* 6*e*Then the Pharisees went out and immediately plotted with *f*the Herodians against Him, how they might destroy Him.

A Great Multitude Follows Jesus

7But Jesus withdrew with His disciples to the sea. And a great multitude from Galilee followed Him, *g*and from Judea 8and Jerusalem and Idumea and beyond the Jordan; and those from Tyre and Sidon, a great multitude, when they heard how *h*many things He was doing, came to Him. 9So He told His disciples that a small boat

---

* **2:16** NU-Text reads *of the.* * **2:17** NU-Text omits *to repentance.* * **3:5** NU-Text omits *as whole as the other.*

2:18 fast. Jesus was not against fasting, if properly observed. He gave guidelines for fasting in the Sermon on the Mount (Matt. 6:16–18). Here, the Pharisees' fasting, perhaps twice each week (Luke 18:12), is contrasted with Jesus' feasting probably at Levi's house.

2:21–22 No one sews . . . no one puts. Mark records only four of Jesus' parables—two of which he includes here. The comparison implies that the newness of His message, and of the new covenant to follow, cannot fit into the old molds of Judaism. The Old Testament was preparation for the New Testament (Gal. 3:19–25).

2:24 what is not lawful on the Sabbath. The point to the Pharisees' accusation against Jesus and His disciples was that they had performed work on the Sabbath, but their charge was dubious. The act of plucking grain should not be confused with Sabbath work condemned by the law (Ex. 31:15). This incident is further proof of rising opposition to Jesus' ministry.

3:5 when He had looked around at them with

anger. It is possible, as Paul exhorts, to be angry and not sin (Eph. 4:26). Jesus demonstrated this righteous anger. He was grieved with sin but did not sin Himself by retaliating or losing control of His emotions.

3:6 Herodians. The Pharisees were religious experts who should have led the people in righteousness. Instead they plotted Jesus' death with the Herodians, their bitter enemies. They were willing to set aside differences to destroy a common foe. The Herodians were Jews who supported Rome and the Herods in particular. Herod Antipas, a son of Herod the Great, ruled Galilee during the same time that Pilate served as Roman governor over Judea and Samaria.

2:15 *j* Matt. 9:10   **2:17** *k* Matt. 9:12, 13; 18:11
2:18 *l* Luke 5:33–38   **2:20** *m* Acts 1:9; 13:2, 3; 14:23
2:23 *n* Luke 6:1–5   *o* Deut. 23:25   **2:24** *p* Ex. 20:10; 31:15
2:25 *q* 1 Sam. 21:1–6   **2:26** *r* Lev. 24:5–9   **2:27** *s* Deut. 5:14   **2:28** *t* Matt. 12:8   **3:1** *a* Luke 6:6–11   **3:2** *b* Luke 14:1; 20:20   *c* Luke 13:14   **3:5** *d* Zech. 7:12   **3:6** *e* Mark 12:13   *f* Matt. 22:16   **3:7** *g* Luke 6:17   **3:8** *h* Mark 5:19

should be kept ready for Him because of the multitude, lest they should crush Him. [10]For He healed *i*many, so that as many as had afflictions pressed about Him to *j*touch Him. [11]*k*And the unclean spirits, whenever they saw Him, fell down before Him and cried out, saying, *l*"You are the Son of God." [12]But *m*He sternly warned them that they should not make Him known.

The Twelve Apostles

[13]*n*And He went up on the mountain and called to *Him* those He Himself wanted. And they came to Him. [14]Then He appointed twelve,* that they might be with Him and that He might send them out to preach, [15]and to have power to heal sicknesses and* to cast out demons: [16]Simon,* *o*to whom He gave the name Peter; [17]James the *son* of Zebedee and John the brother of James, to whom He gave the name Boanerges, that is, "Sons of Thunder"; [18]Andrew, Philip, Bartholomew, Matthew, Thomas, James the *son* of Alphaeus, Thaddaeus, Simon the Cananite; [19]and Judas Iscariot, who also betrayed Him. And they went into a house.

A House Divided Cannot Stand

[20]Then the multitude came together again, *p*so that they could not so much as eat bread. [21]But when His *q*own people heard *about this*, they went out to lay hold of Him, *r*for they said, "He is out of His mind." [22]And the scribes who came down from Jerusalem said, *s*"He has Beelzebub," and, "By the *t*ruler of the demons He casts out demons." [23]*u*So He called them to *Himself* and said to them in parables: "How can Satan cast out Satan? [24]If a kingdom is divided against itself, that kingdom cannot stand. [25]And if a house is divided against itself, that house cannot stand. [26]And if Satan has risen up against himself, and is divided, he cannot stand, but has an end. [27]*v*No

one can enter a strong man's house and plunder his goods, unless he first binds the strong man. And then he will plunder his house.

The Unpardonable Sin

[28]*w*"Assuredly, I say to you, all sins will be forgiven the sons of men, and whatever blasphemies they may utter; [29]but he who blasphemes against the Holy Spirit never has forgiveness, but is subject to eternal condemnation"— [30]because they *x*said, "He has an unclean spirit."

Jesus' Mother and Brothers Send for Him

[31]*y*Then His brothers and His mother came, and standing outside they sent to Him, calling Him. [32]And a multitude was sitting around Him; and they said to Him, "Look, Your mother and Your brothers* are outside seeking You." [33]But He answered them, saying, "Who is My mother, or My brothers?" [34]And He looked around in a circle at those who sat about Him, and said, "Here are My mother and My brothers! [35]For whoever does the *z*will of God is My brother and My sister and mother."

The Parable of the Sower

4 And *a*again He began to teach by the sea. And a great multitude was gathered to Him, so that He got into a boat and sat *in it* on the sea; and the whole multitude was on the land facing the sea. [2]Then He taught them many things by parables, *b*and said to them in His teaching:

* 3:14 NU-Text adds *whom He also named apostles.* * 3:15 NU-Text omits *to heal sicknesses* and. * 3:16 NU-Text reads *and He appointed the twelve: Simon* .... * 3:32 NU-Text and M-Text add *and Your sisters.*

3:11–12 *He sternly warned them that they should not make Him known.* Jesus rebuked the demons who proclaimed, "You are the Son of God." This was not because the demons incorrectly identified Jesus, but because their testimony was untrustworthy.

3:16–19 *gave the name Peter.* Jesus gave Peter a new name because it was the Jewish custom to rename someone who had experienced a life-changing event. This renaming of the disciples has similarities to the renaming of Abram (Gen. 17:3–5) and of Saul (Acts 9).

3:27 *strong man.* Whoever defeats Satan must be stronger than he. Jesus implies that He Himself has come to enter the house of the strong man, Satan, to seize his goods (1 John 3:8).

3:28–30 *he who blasphemes against the Holy Spirit.* This person places himself or herself outside the redeeming grace of God. It is apparently not a single act of defiant behavior, but a continued state of opposition entered into willingly. The tense of "they said" indicates a continued action, not a one-time event. The words and works of Christ were spoken

and performed by the power of the Holy Spirit. To attribute them to Satan is to call the work of heaven a work of hell. For such perverse belief there is no remedy. How someone can commit this sin today is a difficult question to answer, but those who persist in denigrating Christ by insulting His work or by attributing it to Satan may drive themselves past a point of no return (Matt. 12:31–32).

3:31 *His brothers and His mother.* Opposition arose from Jesus' own immediate family. We are not told precisely what they wanted to say, but it likely involved a concern for Jesus' safety or reputation, since He was becoming widely known as a preaching prophet and a worker of miracles.

3:10 *i* Luke 7:21 *j* Matt. 9:21; 14:36 **3:11** *k* Luke 4:41 *l* Matt. 8:29; 14:33 **3:12** *m* Mark 1:25, 34 **3:13** *n* Luke 9:1 **3:16** *o* John 1:42 **3:20** *p* Mark 6:31 **3:21** *q* Mark 6:3 *r* John 7:5; 10:20 **3:22** *s* Matt. 9:34; 10:25 *t* [John 12:31; 14:30; 16:11] **3:23** *u* Matt. 12:25–29 **3:27** *v* [Is. 49:24, 25] **3:28** *w* Luke 12:10 **3:30** *x* Matt. 9:34 **3:31** *y* Matt. 12:46–50 **3:35** *z* Eph. 6:6 **4:1** *d* Luke 8:4–10 **4:2** *b* Mark 12:38

3"Listen! Behold, a sower went out to sow. **4**And it happened, as he sowed, *that* some *seed* fell by the wayside; and the birds of the air* came and devoured it. **5**Some fell on stony ground, where it did not have much earth; and immediately it sprang up because it had no depth of earth. **6**But when the sun was up it was scorched, and because it had no root it withered away. **7**And some *seed* fell among thorns; and the thorns grew up and choked it, and it yielded no crop. **8**But other *seed* fell on good ground and yielded a crop that sprang up, increased and produced: some thirtyfold, some sixty, and some a hundred."

9And He said to them,* "He who has ears to hear, let him hear!"

The Purpose of Parables

10c But when He was alone, those around Him with the twelve asked Him about the parable. **11**And He said to them, "To you it has been given to *d*know the mystery of the kingdom of God; but to *e*those who are outside, all things come in parables, **12**so that

f '*Seeing they may see and not perceive,*
And hearing they may hear and not
understand;
Lest they should turn,
And their sins be forgiven them.' "*

The Parable of the Sower Explained

13And He said to them, "Do you not understand this parable? How then will you understand all the parables? **14g**The sower sows the word. **15**And these are the ones by the wayside where the word is sown. When they hear, Satan comes immediately and takes away the word that was sown in their hearts. **16**These likewise are the ones sown on stony ground who, when they hear the word, immediately receive it with gladness;

17and they have no root in themselves, and so endure only for a time. Afterward, when tribulation or persecution arises for the word's sake, immediately they stumble. **18**Now these are the ones sown among thorns; *they are* the ones who hear the word, **19**and the *h*cares of this world, *i*the deceitfulness of riches, and the desires for other things entering in choke the word, and it becomes unfruitful. **20**But these are the ones sown on good ground, those who hear the word, accept *it*, and bear *j*fruit: some thirtyfold, some sixty, and some a hundred."

Light Under a Basket

21k Also He said to them, "Is a lamp brought to be put under a basket or under a bed? Is it not to be set on a lampstand? **22l**For there is nothing hidden which will not be revealed, nor has anything been kept secret but that it should come to light. **23m**If anyone has ears to hear, let him hear." **24**Then He said to them, "Take heed what you hear. *n*With the same measure you use, it will be measured to you; and to you who hear, more will be given. **25o**For whoever has, to him more will be given; but whoever does not have, even what he has will be taken away from him."

The Parable of the Growing Seed

26And He said, *p*"The kingdom of God is as if a man should scatter seed on the ground, **27**and should sleep by night and rise by day, and the seed should sprout and *q*grow, he himself does not know how. **28**For the earth *r*yields crops by itself: first the blade, then the head, after that the full grain in the head. **29**But when the grain ripens, immediately *s*he puts in the sickle, because the harvest has come."

---

* **4:4** NU-Text and M-Text omit *of the air.* * **4:9** NU-Text and M-Text omit *to them.*
* **4:12** Isaiah 6:9, 10

4:3–8 *a sower went out to sow.* The point of the parable is that the condition of the soil determines the potential for growth. The principle is true for Christians and non-Christians alike. Those who have become complacent and lackadaisical are not likely to receive the Word with benefit (James 1:2–25).

4:11 *To you it has been given to know the mystery.* In Scripture, a mystery is a truth God has revealed or will reveal at the proper time (Rom. 16:25–26). Jesus apparently used parables for several reasons. First, they are interesting and grab the listener's attention. Second, such stories are easily remembered. Third, they reveal truth to those who are ready spiritually to receive it. Fourth, they conceal truth from those who oppose Christ's message. Frequently Jesus' opponents failed to understand the lessons because of their own spiritual blindness (Matt. 21:45–46).

4:20 *hear the word, accept it, and bear fruit.* Only one soil produces fruit. Such a person recognizes God's call, determines to follow it, and experiences a profound transformation.

4:21–23 *a lamp.* These were small clay vessels that burned a wick set in olive oil. Like the lamp, Jesus' teachings reveal the motives of the human heart.

4:26–29 *The kingdom of God is as if.* Plants develop in a complex, intricate process that humans still do not fully understand even two thousand years after Jesus spoke these words. Yet plants grow and bear fruit and seeds just the same. God's kingdom likewise is growing, although we do not understand all that is happening. This parable, which appears only in Mark's Gospel, presents God's kingdom in brief, from first sowing to final reaping.

4:10 *c* Luke 8:9 **4:11** *d* [1 Cor. 2:10–16] *e* [Col. 4:5] **4:12** *f* Is. 6:9, 10; 43:8 **4:14** *g* Matt. 13:18–23 **4:19** *h* Luke 21:34 *i* 1 Tim. 6:9, 10, 17 **4:20** *j* [Rom. 7:4] **4:21** *k* Matt. 5:15 **4:22** *l* Matt. 10:26, 27 **4:23** *m* Matt. 11:15; 13:9, 43 **4:24** *n* Matt. 7:2 **4:25** *o* Luke 8:18; 19:26 **4:26** *p* [Matt. 13:24–30, 36–43] **4:27** *q* [2 Pet. 3:18] **4:28** *r* [John 12:24] **4:29** *s* Rev. 14:15

The Parable of the Mustard Seed

[30]Then He said, [t]"To what shall we liken the kingdom of God? Or with what parable shall we picture it? [31]It is like a mustard seed which, when it is sown on the ground, is smaller than all the seeds on earth; [32]but when it is sown, it grows up and becomes greater than all herbs, and shoots out large branches, so that the birds of the air may nest under its shade."

Jesus' Use of Parables

[33u]And with many such parables He spoke the word to them as they were able to hear it. [34]But without a parable He did not speak to them. And when they were alone, [v]He explained all things to His disciples.

Wind and Wave Obey Jesus

[35w]On the same day, when evening had come, He said to them, "Let us cross over to the other side." [36]Now when they had left the multitude, they took Him along in the boat as He was. And other little boats were also with Him. [37]And a great windstorm arose, and the waves beat into the boat, so that it was already filling. [38]But He was in the stern, asleep on a pillow. And they awoke Him and said to Him, [x]"Teacher, [y]do You not care that we are perishing?" [39]Then He arose and [z]rebuked the wind, and said to the sea, [a]"Peace, be still!" And the wind ceased and there was a great calm. [40]But He said to them, "Why are you so fearful? [b]How is it that you have no faith?"* [41]And they feared exceedingly, and said to one another, "Who can this be, that even the wind and the sea obey Him!"

A Demon-Possessed Man Healed

5 Then [a]they came to the other side of the sea, to the country of the Gadarenes.* [2]And when He had come out of the boat, immediately there met Him out of the tombs a man with an [b]unclean spirit, [3]who had his dwelling among the tombs; and no one could bind him,* not even with chains, [4]because he had often been bound with shackles and chains. And the chains had been pulled apart by him, and the shackles broken in pieces; neither could anyone

tame him. [5]And always, night and day, he was in the mountains and in the tombs, crying out and cutting himself with stones. [6]When he saw Jesus from afar, he ran and worshiped Him. [7]And he cried out with a loud voice and said, "What have I to do with You, Jesus, Son of the Most High God? I [c]implore You by God that You do not torment me." [8]For He said to him, [d]"Come out of the man, unclean spirit!" [9]Then He asked him, "What is your name?"

And he answered, saying, "My name is Legion; for we are many." [10]Also he begged Him earnestly that He would not send them out of the country. [11]Now a large herd of [e]swine was feeding there near the mountains. [12]So all the demons begged Him, saying, "Send us to the swine, that we may enter them." [13]And at once Jesus* gave them permission. Then the unclean spirits went out and entered the swine (there were about two thousand); and the herd ran violently down the steep place into the sea, and drowned in the sea. [14]So those who fed the swine fled, and they told it in the city and in the country. And they went out to see what it was that had happened. [15]Then they came to Jesus, and saw the one who had been [f]demon-possessed and had the legion, [g]sitting and [h]clothed and in his right mind. And they were afraid. [16]And those who saw it told them how it happened to him who had been demon-possessed, and about the swine. [17]Then [i]they began to plead with Him to depart from their region. [18]And when He got into the boat, [j]he who had been demon-possessed begged Him that he might be with Him. [19]However, Jesus did not permit him, but said to him, "Go home to your friends, and tell them what great things the Lord has done for you, and how He has had compassion on you." [20]And he departed and began to [k]proclaim in Decapolis all that Jesus had done for him; and all [l]marveled.

* 4:40 NU-Text reads Have you still no faith?
* 5:1 NU-Text reads Gerasenes. * 5:3 NU-Text adds anymore. * 5:13 NU-Text reads And He gave.

4:35 cross over to the other side. The Sea of Galilee is about eight miles wide and twelve miles long. Its unique geography produces a greatly varying climate. It is 700 feet below sea level with mountains that rise 3,000–4,000 feet around it. It is not unusual for sudden windstorms to appear during the evening hours. The warm tropical air from the lake's surface rises and meets the colder air from the nearby hills. The resulting turbulences and winds can be treacherous.

4:41 Who can this be. Mark uses the disciples' question to evoke a similar response in the minds of his readers. Mark relates the works and words of the one he calls "Jesus Christ, the Son of God" (1:1).

5:1 the country of the Gadarenes. This area is on the eastern shore of the Sea of Galilee. The form of the name varies (Matt. 8:28; Luke 8:26,37).

5:17–20 they began to plead with Him to depart from their region. Jesus was not well received in this region. His presence had cost financial loss to some, although it meant liberation to the demoniac. Jesus could have healed and saved in that region, but He was turned away by its fearful citizens. Decapolis.

4:30 [t] Matt. 13:31, 32   4:33 [u] Matt. 13:34, 35   4:34 [v] Luke 24:27, 45   4:35 [w] Luke 8:22, 25   4:38 [x] [Matt. 23:8–10] [y] Ps. 44:23   4:39 [z] Luke 4:39 [a] Ps. 65:7; 89:9; 93:4; 104:6, 7   4:40 [b] Matt. 14:31, 32   5:1 [a] Matt. 8:28–34   5:2 [b] Mark 1:23; 7:25   5:7 [c] Acts 19:13   5:8 [d] Mark 1:25; 9:25   5:11 [e] Deut. 14:8   5:15 [f] Matt. 4:24; 8:16 [g] Luke 10:39 [h] [Is. 61:10]   5:17 [i] Acts 16:39   5:18 [j] Luke 8:38, 39   5:20 [k] Ps. 66:16 [l] Matt. 9:8, 33

A Girl Restored to Life and a Woman Healed

21*m*Now when Jesus had crossed over again by boat to the other side, a great multitude gathered to Him; and He was by the sea. 22*n*And behold, one of the rulers of the synagogue came, Jairus by name. And when he saw Him, he fell at His feet 23and begged Him earnestly, saying, "My little daughter lies at the point of death. Come and *o*lay Your hands on her, that she may be healed, and she will live." 24So *Jesus* went with him, and a great multitude followed Him and thronged Him.

25Now a certain woman *p*had a flow of blood for twelve years, 26and had suffered many things from many physicians. She had spent all that she had and was no better, but rather grew worse. 27When she heard about Jesus, she came behind *Him* in the crowd and *q*touched His garment. 28For she said, "If only I may touch His clothes, I shall be made well."

29Immediately the fountain of her blood was dried up, and she felt in *her* body that she was healed of the affliction. 30And Jesus, immediately knowing in Himself that *r*power had gone out of Him, turned around in the crowd and said, "Who touched My clothes?"

31But His disciples said to Him, "You see the multitude thronging You, and You say, 'Who touched Me?' "

32And He looked around to see her who had done this thing. 33But the woman, *s*fearing and trembling, knowing what had happened to her, came and fell down before Him and told Him the whole truth. 34And He said to her, "Daughter, *t*your faith has made you well. *u*Go in peace, and be healed of your affliction."

35*v*While He was still speaking, *some* came from the ruler of the synagogue's *house* who said, "Your daughter is dead. Why trouble the Teacher any further?"

36As soon as Jesus heard the word that was spoken, He said to the ruler of the synagogue, "Do not be afraid; only *w*believe." 37And He permitted no one to follow Him except Peter, James, and John the brother of James. 38Then He came to the house of the ruler of the synagogue, and saw a tumult and those who *x*wept and wailed loudly. 39When He came in, He said to them, "Why make this commotion and weep? The child is not dead, but *y*sleeping."

40And they ridiculed Him. *z*But when He had put them all outside, He took the father and the mother of the child, and those *who were* with Him, and entered where the child was lying. 41Then He took the child by the hand, and said to her, "Talitha, cumi," which is translated, "Little girl, I say to you, arise." 42Immediately the girl arose and walked, for she was twelve years *of age*. And they were *a*overcome with great amazement. 43But *b*He commanded them strictly that no one should know it, and said that *something* should be given her to eat.

Jesus Rejected at Nazareth

6 Then *a*He went out from there and came to His own country, and His disciples followed Him. 2And when the Sabbath had come, He began to teach in the synagogue. And many hearing *Him* were *b*astonished, saying, *c*"Where *did* this Man *get* these things? And what wisdom *is* this which is given to Him, that such mighty works are performed by His hands! 3Is this not the carpenter, the Son of Mary, and *d*brother of James, Joses, Judas, and Simon? And are not His sisters here with us?" So they *e*were offended at Him.

4But Jesus said to them, *f*"A prophet is not without honor except in his own country, among his own relatives, and in his

---

This literally means "ten cities." This largely Gentile, Greek-speaking area was an important strategic link in Rome's military defense.

5:22 one of the rulers of the synagogue. Jairus was a lay leader charged with supervising services at the synagogue.

5:26 suffered many things from many physicians. Mark is not complimentary toward the physicians who had treated this woman.

5:29–30 Immediately. This word is used twice in this context. Both the woman and Jesus simultaneously knew what had happened. **Who touched My clothes?** Jesus turned when He was touched and confronted the woman before she disappeared. He wanted to correct any mistaken notion she may have had about her healing. It was not any magical quality of His clothing but His divine will that had made her well.

5:33 told Him the whole truth. Jesus' kind manner and tender words must have eased the fear this woman had of being revealed. Naturally, the time that Jesus took to care for the woman must have worried the already tense disciples.

5:34 Daughter. Jesus used this tender word to address this woman, and He noted that her faith made the difference, for it was correctly placed in Him. Faith itself does not heal—it is the proper object of that faith, Jesus, who heals.

5:43 He commanded them strictly. The command to keep the miracle a secret was a temporary measure, for certainly the girl's appearance could not be hidden very long. Such orders would, however, allow Jesus to exit quietly. Jesus did not want to be known primarily as a miracle worker, lest people seek Him for the wrong reasons.

6:4 A prophet is not without honor except in his own country. This maxim is still repeated and is still

---

5:21 *m* Luke 8:40 **5:22** *n* Matt. 9:18–26 **5:23** *o* Acts 9:17; 28:8 **5:25** *p* Lev. 15:19, 25 **5:27** *q* Matt. 14:35, 36 **5:30** *r* Luke 6:19; 8:46 **5:33** *s* [Ps. 89:7] **5:34** *t* Matt. 9:22 *u* Luke 7:50; 8:48 **5:35** *v* Luke 8:49 **5:36** *w* [John 11:40] **5:38** *x* Acts 9:39 **5:39** *y* John 11:4, 11 **5:40** *z* Acts 9:40 **5:42** *a* Mark 1:27; 7:37 **5:43** *b* [Matt. 8:4; 12:16–19; 17:9] **6:1** *a* Matt. 13:54 **6:2** *b* Matt. 7:28 *c* John 6:42 **6:3** *d* Matt. 12:46 *e* [Matt. 11:6] **6:4** *f* John 4:44

own house." 5gNow He could do no mighty work there, except that He laid His hands on a few sick people and healed *them*. 6And hHe marveled because of their unbelief. iThen He went about the villages in a circuit, teaching.

Sending Out the Twelve

7jAnd He called the twelve to *Himself*, and began to send them out ktwo *by* two, and gave them power over unclean spirits. 8He commanded them to take nothing for the journey except a staff—no bag, no bread, no copper in *their* money belts— 9but lto wear sandals, and not to put on two tunics.

10mAlso He said to them, "In whatever place you enter a house, stay there till you depart from that place. 11nAnd whoever* will not receive you nor hear you, when you depart from there, oshake off the dust under your feet as a testimony against them.* Assuredly, I say to you, it will be more tolerable for Sodom and Gomorrah in the day of judgment than for that city!"

12So they went out and preached that *people* should repent. 13And they cast out many demons, pand anointed with oil many who were sick, and healed *them*.

John the Baptist Beheaded

14qNow King Herod heard *of Him*, for His name had become well known. And he said, "John the Baptist is risen from the dead, and therefore rthese powers are at work in him."

15sOthers said, "It is Elijah."

And others said, "It is the Prophet, tor* like one of the prophets."

16uBut when Herod heard, he said, "This is John, whom I beheaded; he has been raised from the dead!" 17For Herod himself had sent and laid hold of John, and bound him in prison for the sake of Herodias, his brother Philip's wife; for he had married her. 18Because John had said to Herod, v"It is not lawful for you to have your brother's wife."

19Therefore Herodias held it against him and wanted to kill him, but she could not; 20for Herod wfeared John, knowing that he

was a just and holy man, and he protected him. And when he heard him, he did many things, and heard him gladly.

21xThen an opportune day came when Herod yon his birthday gave a feast for his nobles, the high officers, and the chief *men* of Galilee. 22And when Herodias' daughter herself came in and danced, and pleased Herod and those who sat with him, the king said to the girl, "Ask me whatever you want, and I will give it to you." 23He also swore to her, z"Whatever you ask me, I will give you, up to half my kingdom."

24So she went out and said to her mother, "What shall I ask?"

And she said, "The head of John the Baptist!"

25Immediately she came in with haste to the king and asked, saying, "I want you to give me at once the head of John the Baptist on a platter."

26aAnd the king was exceedingly sorry; *yet*, because of the oaths and because of those who sat with him, he did not want to refuse her. 27Immediately the king sent an executioner and commanded his head to be brought. And he went and beheaded him in prison, 28brought his head on a platter, and gave it to the girl; and the girl gave it to her mother. 29When his disciples heard *of it*, they came and btook away his corpse and laid it in a tomb.

Feeding the Five Thousand

30cThen the apostles gathered to Jesus and told Him all things, both what they had done and what they had taught. 31dAnd He said to them, "Come aside by yourselves to a deserted place and rest a while." For ethere were many coming and going, and they did not even have time to eat. 32fSo they departed to a deserted place in the boat by themselves.

33But the multitudes* saw them departing, and many gknew Him and ran there on foot from all the cities. They arrived before them and came together to Him.

---

* **6:11** NU-Text reads *whatever place*. • NU-Text omits the rest of this verse. * **6:15** NU-Text and M-Text omit *or*. * **6:33** NU-Text and M-Text read *they*.

---

true today. Perhaps others were jealous of Jesus' popularity and huge following. Their envy even took the form of violence against Christ (Luke 4:29).

6:14 *King Herod*. This is Herod Antipas, one of the sons of Herod the Great, the king who tried to kill the baby Jesus (Matt. 2:1–18). After Herod the Great's death in 4 B.C. his kingdom was divided between Archelaus, who received Judea and Samaria; Philip, who ruled Iturea and Trachonitis, north and east of Galilee; and Antipas, who controlled Galilee and Perea from 4 B.C. to A.D. 39. Jesus ministered largely in the territory ruled by Antipas.

6:18 *not lawful*. John's message to Herod was that his divorce was not lawful as grounds for remarriage. John's declaration could be based on Jesus' stern

words about divorce (10:11–12) or on Leviticus 20:21, which prohibits a man from taking his brother's wife.

6:23 *up to half my kingdom*. This is an expression meaning a large amount but with some limits.

6:5 g Gen. 19:22; 32:25   **6:6** h Is. 59:16   i Matt. 9:35
6:7 j Mark 3:13, 14   k [Eccl. 4:9, 10]   **6:9** l [Eph. 6:15]
6:10 m Matt. 10:11   **6:11** n Matt. 10:14   o Acts 13:51; 18:6   **6:13** p [James 5:14]   **6:14** q Luke 9:7–9   r Luke 19:37   **6:15** s Mark 8:28   t Matt. 21:11   **6:16** u Luke 3:19
6:18 v Lev. 18:16; 20:21   **6:20** w Matt. 14:5; 21:26
6:21 x Matt. 14:6   y Gen. 40:20   **6:23** z Esth. 5:3, 6, 7:2
6:26 a Matt. 14:9   **6:29** b 1 Kin. 13:29, 30   **6:30** c Luke 9:10   **6:31** d Matt. 14:13   e Mark 3:20   **6:32** f Matt. 14:13–21   **6:33** g [Col. 1:6]

³⁴ʰAnd Jesus, when He came out, saw a great multitude and was moved with compassion for them, because they were like ⁱsheep not having a shepherd. So ʲHe began to teach them many things. ³⁵ᵏWhen the day was now far spent, His disciples came to Him and said, "This is a deserted place, and already the hour *is* late. ³⁶Send them away, that they may go into the surrounding country and villages and buy themselves bread;* for they have nothing to eat."

³⁷But He answered and said to them, "You give them something to eat."

And they said to Him, ˡ"Shall we go and buy two hundred denarii worth of bread and give them *something* to eat?"

³⁸But He said to them, "How many loaves do you have? Go and see."

And when they found out they said, ᵐ"Five, and two fish."

³⁹Then He ⁿcommanded them to make them all sit down in groups on the green grass. ⁴⁰So they sat down in ranks, in hundreds and in fifties. ⁴¹And when He had taken the five loaves and the two fish, He ᵒlooked up to heaven, ᵖblessed and broke the loaves, and gave *them* to His disciples to set before them; and the two fish He divided among *them* all. ⁴²So they all ate and were filled. ⁴³And they took up twelve baskets full of fragments and of the fish. ⁴⁴Now those who had eaten the loaves were about* five thousand men.

Jesus Walks on the Sea

⁴⁵ᵠImmediately He made His disciples get into the boat and go before Him to the other side, to Bethsaida, while He sent the multitude away. ⁴⁶And when He had sent them away, He ʳdeparted to the mountain to pray. ⁴⁷Now when evening came, the boat was in the middle of the sea; and He *was* alone on the land. ⁴⁸Then He saw them straining at rowing, for the wind was against them. Now about the fourth watch of the night He came to them, walking on the sea, and ˢwould have passed them

by. ⁴⁹And when they saw Him walking on the sea, they supposed it was a ᵗghost, and cried out; ⁵⁰for they all saw Him and were troubled. But immediately He talked with them and said to them, ᵘ"Be of good cheer! It is I; do not be ᵛafraid." ⁵¹Then He went up into the boat to them, and the wind ʷceased. And they were greatly ˣamazed in themselves beyond measure, and marveled. ⁵²For ʸthey had not understood about the loaves, because their ᶻheart was hardened.

Many Touch Him and Are Made Well

⁵³ᵃWhen they had crossed over, they came to the land of Gennesaret and anchored there. ⁵⁴And when they came out of the boat, immediately the people recognized Him, ⁵⁵ran through that whole surrounding region, and began to carry about on beds those who were sick to wherever they heard He was. ⁵⁶Wherever He entered, into villages, cities, or the country, they laid the sick in the marketplaces, and begged Him that ᵇthey might just touch the ᶜhem of His garment. And as many as touched Him were made well.

Defilement Comes from Within

7 Then ᵃthe Pharisees and some of the scribes came together to Him, having come from Jerusalem. ²Now when* they saw some of His disciples eat bread with defiled, that is, with ᵇunwashed hands, they found fault. ³For the Pharisees and all the Jews do not eat unless they wash *their* hands in a special way, holding the ᶜtradition of the elders. ⁴*When they come* from the marketplace, they do not eat unless they wash. And there are many other things which they have received and hold,

---

* **6:36** NU-Text reads *something to eat* and omits the rest of this verse.   * **6:44** NU-Text and M-Text omit *about.*   * **7:2** NU-Text omits *when* and *they found fault.*

6:34 *moved with compassion.* The Gospels record several times that when Jesus saw a need He responded compassionately (1:41). That compassion led to action, despite an obvious lack of food in this instance.

6:36–37 *Send them away.* The disciples sought to avoid responsibility for the hungry multitude.

6:39–40 *in ranks, in hundreds and in fifties.* Details such as sitting on the green grass, which is possible only in late winter and early spring, and the fact that the groups were counted are indications that an eyewitness, probably Peter, recounted this story to Mark.

6:43 *twelve baskets full of fragments.* These were small baskets commonly carried by travelers. It is possible to conclude that the leftovers gave each disciple enough food for his own use.

6:51 *He went up into the boat to them.* Three miracles are contained in this brief account (vv. 47–51):

(1) In the darkness Jesus saw the disciples out in the storm miles away, (2) Jesus walked on the water, and (3) Jesus showed complete control over His creation when the wind ceased.

6:56 *Wherever He entered, into villages, cities, or the country.* Mark summarizes Jesus' healing ministry, noting how widespread it was.

7:3–4 *For the Pharisees.* These two verses explain the tradition of handwashing and various kinds of

6:34 ʰ Matt. 9:36; 14:14 ⁱ Num. 27:17 ʲ Luke 9:11
6:35 ᵏ Matt. 14:15   **6:37** ˡ 2 Kin. 4:43   **6:38** ᵐ John
6:9   **6:39** ⁿ Matt. 15:35   **6:41** ᵒ John 11:41, 42 ᵖ Matt.
15:36; 26:26   **6:45** ᵠ John 6:15–21   **6:46** ʳ Luke 5:16
6:48 ˢ Luke 24:28   **6:49** ᵗ Matt. 14:26   **6:50** ᵘ Matt. 9:2
ᵛ Is. 41:10   **6:51** ʷ Ps. 107:29 ˣ Mark 1:27; 2:12; 5:42; 7:37
6:52 ʸ Mark 8:17, 18 ᶻ Mark 3:5; 16:14   **6:53** ᵃ Matt.
14:34–36   **6:56** ᵇ Matt. 9:20 ᶜ Num. 15:38, 39
7:1 ᵃ Matt. 15:1–20   **7:2** ᵇ Matt. 15:20   **7:3** ᶜ Gal. 1:14

like the washing of cups, pitchers, copper vessels, and couches.

5dThen the Pharisees and scribes asked Him, "Why do Your disciples not walk according to the tradition of the elders, but eat bread with unwashed hands?"

6He answered and said to them, "Well did Isaiah prophesy of you ehypocrites, as it is written:

> f'This people honors Me with their lips,
> But their heart is far from Me.
> 7   And in vain they worship Me,
>   Teaching as doctrines the
>   commandments of men.'*

8For laying aside the commandment of God, you hold the tradition of men* —the washing of pitchers and cups, and many other such things you do."

9He said to them, "All too well gyou reject the commandment of God, that you may keep your tradition. 10For Moses said, h'Honor your father and your mother';* and, i'He who curses father or mother, let him be put to death.'* 11But you say, 'If a man says to his father or mother, j"Whatever profit you might have received from me is Corban"—' (that is, a gift to God), 12then you no longer let him do anything for his father or his mother, 13making the word of God of no effect through your tradition which you have handed down. And many such things you do."

14kWhen He had called all the multitude to Himself, He said to them, "Hear Me, everyone, and lunderstand: 15There is nothing that enters a man from outside which can defile him; but the things which come out of him, those are the things that mdefile a man. 16nIf anyone has ears to hear, let him hear!"*

17oWhen He had entered a house away from the crowd, His disciples asked Him concerning the parable. 18So He said to them, p"Are you thus without understanding also? Do you not perceive that whatever enters a man from outside cannot

defile him, 19because it does not enter his heart but his stomach, and is eliminated, thus purifying all foods?"* 20And He said, q"What comes out of a man, that defiles a man. 21rFor from within, out of the heart of men, sproceed evil thoughts, tadulteries, ufornications, murders, 22thefts, vcovetousness, wickedness, wdeceit, xlewdness, an evil eye, yblasphemy, zpride, foolishness. 23All these evil things come from within and defile a man."

A Gentile Shows Her Faith

24aFrom there He arose and went to the region of Tyre and Sidon.* And He entered a house and wanted no one to know it, but He could not be bhidden. 25For a woman whose young daughter had an unclean spirit heard about Him, and she came and cfell at His feet. 26The woman was a Greek, a Syro-Phoenician by birth, and she kept asking Him to cast the demon out of her daughter. 27But Jesus said to her, "Let the children be filled first, for it is not good to take the children's bread and throw it to the little dogs."

28And she answered and said to Him, "Yes, Lord, yet even the little dogs under the table eat from the children's crumbs."

29Then He said to her, "For this saying go your way; the demon has gone out of your daughter."

30And when she had come to her house, she found the demon gone out, and her daughter lying on the bed.

Jesus Heals a Deaf-Mute

31dAgain, departing from the region of Tyre and Sidon, He came through the midst of the region of Decapolis to the Sea

---

* 7:7 Isaiah 29:13   * 7:8 NU-Text omits the rest of this verse.   * 7:10 Exodus 20:12; Deuteronomy 5:16 • Exodus 21:17   * 7:16 NU-Text omits this verse.   * 7:19 NU-Text ends quotation with eliminated, setting off the final clause as Mark's comment that Jesus has declared all foods clean.   * 7:24 NU-Text omits and Sidon.

---

ceremonial uncleanness. Mark's intended readers in Rome likely needed more background on the Jewish faith to understand this controversy.

7:5 the tradition of the elders. This phrase refers to a series of rules meant to bolster the ceremonial law of the Jews. Its authority was not supported by Scripture. The question indirectly challenged Jesus, for as the disciples' teacher He was judged responsible for their actions.

7:6–7 hypocrites. The term originally referred to actors who wore masks on stage as they played different characters. Thus the Pharisees were not genuinely religious; they were merely playing a part for all to see.

7:11–13 But you say. This shows the absolute contrast between God's will and man's empty tradition. **Corban.** This was evidently a pious-sounding evasion of the requirement of honoring one's parents by supporting them financially.

7:24 the region of Tyre. This city is the farthest Jesus traveled from Israel during His public ministry.

7:27 to the little dogs. Jesus is not attempting to insult the woman by using this metaphor. In fact, He is testing her faith. Matthew records Jesus' reaction to her reply, "O woman, great is your faith" (Matt. 15:28).

7:28 And she answered. The woman understood Jesus' test and persistently replied that even during the meal the dogs consume the children's crumbs that fall from the table.

7:5 d Matt. 15:2   **7:6** e Matt. 23:13–29 f Is. 29:13   **7:9** g Prov. 1:25   **7:10** h Ex. 20:12; Deut. 5:16 i Ex. 21:17   **7:11** j Matt. 15:5; 23:18   **7:14** k Matt. 15:10 l Matt. 16:9, 11, 12   **7:15** m Is. 59:3   **7:16** n Matt. 11:15   **7:17** o Matt. 15:15   **7:18** p [Heb. 5:11–14]   **7:20** q Ps. 39:1   **7:21** r Gen. 6:5; 8:21 s [Gal. 5:19–21] t 2 Pet. 2:14 u 1 Thess. 4:3   **7:22** v Luke 12:15 w Rom. 1:28, 29 x 1 Pet. 4:3 y Rev. 2:9 z 1 John 2:16   **7:24** a Matt. 15:21 b Mark 2:1, 2   **7:25** c John 11:32   **7:31** d Matt. 15:29

of Galilee. ³²Then ᵉthey brought to Him one who was deaf and had an impediment in his speech, and they begged Him to put His hand on him. ³³And He took him aside from the multitude, and put His fingers in his ears, and ᶠHe spat and touched his tongue. ³⁴Then, ᵍlooking up to heaven, ʰHe sighed, and said to him, "Ephphatha," that is, "Be opened."

³⁵ⁱImmediately his ears were opened, and the impediment of his tongue was loosed, and he spoke plainly. ³⁶Then ʲHe commanded them that they should tell no one; but the more He commanded them, the more widely they proclaimed *it*. ³⁷And they were ᵏastonished beyond measure, saying, "He has done all things well. He ˡmakes both the deaf to hear and the mute to speak."

Feeding the Four Thousand

8 In those days, ᵃthe multitude being very great and having nothing to eat, Jesus called His disciples *to Him* and said to them, ²"I have ᵇcompassion on the multitude, because they have now continued with Me three days and have nothing to eat. ³And if I send them away hungry to their own houses, they will faint on the way; for some of them have come from afar."

⁴Then His disciples answered Him, "How can one satisfy these people with bread here in the wilderness?"

⁵ᶜHe asked them, "How many loaves do you have?"

And they said, "Seven."

⁶So He commanded the multitude to sit down on the ground. And He took the seven loaves and gave thanks, broke *them* and gave *them* to His disciples to set before *them*; and they set *them* before the multitude. ⁷They also had a few small fish; and ᵈhaving blessed them, He said to set them also before *them*. ⁸So they ate and were filled, and they took up seven large baskets of leftover fragments. ⁹Now those who had eaten were about four thousand. And He sent them away, ¹⁰ᵉimmediately got into the boat with His disciples, and came to the region of Dalmanutha.

The Pharisees Seek a Sign

¹¹ᶠThen the Pharisees came out and began to dispute with Him, seeking from Him a sign from heaven, testing Him. ¹²But He ᵍsighed deeply in His spirit, and said, "Why does this generation seek a sign? Assuredly, I say to you, ʰno sign shall be given to this generation."

Beware of the Leaven of the Pharisees and Herod

¹³And He left them, and getting into the boat again, departed to the other side. ¹⁴ⁱNow the disciples* had forgotten to take bread, and they did not have more than one loaf with them in the boat. ¹⁵ʲThen He charged them, saying, "Take heed, beware of the leaven of the Pharisees and the leaven of Herod."

¹⁶And they reasoned among themselves, saying, "*It is* because we have no bread."

¹⁷But Jesus, being aware of *it*, said to them, "Why do you reason because you have no bread? ᵏDo you not yet perceive nor understand? Is your heart still* hardened? ¹⁸Having eyes, do you not see? And having ears, do you not hear? And do you not remember? ¹⁹ˡWhen I broke the five loaves for the five thousand, how many baskets full of fragments did you take up?"

They said to Him, "Twelve."

²⁰"Also, ᵐwhen I broke the seven for the four thousand, how many large baskets full of fragments did you take up?"

And they said, "Seven."

²¹So He said to them, "How *is it* ⁿyou do not understand?"

A Blind Man Healed at Bethsaida

²²Then He came to Bethsaida; and they brought a ᵒblind man to Him, and begged Him to ᵖtouch him. ²³So He took the blind man by the hand and led him out of the town. And when ᵩHe had spit on his eyes and put His hands on him, He asked him if he saw anything.

---

* **8:14** NU-Text and M-Text read *they*.   * **8:17** NU-Text omits *still.*

7:32–35 *one who was deaf.* The healing of this deaf man (who also had a speech impediment) is one of the two miracles recorded by Mark only. (The other is the healing of the blind man in 8:22–26.)

8:8 *seven large baskets.* There was one basket for each original loaf. These baskets were much larger than the 12 small personal baskets mentioned in 6:43. It was the kind of larger basket that was used to lower Paul over the wall of Damascus (Acts 9:25).

8:10 *Dalmanutha.* This was probably on the western side of the Sea of Galilee, about three miles north of modern Tiberias and about five miles southwest of Capernaum. This is the only time it is mentioned in the New Testament.

8:11 *the Pharisees came out and began to dispute with Him.* The Pharisees' testing of Jesus was crafty and devious. Obviously these men did not heed the many signs and wonders that Jesus had already

performed. John 20:30–31 indicates that the signs were meant to produce faith. It is doubtful that the Pharisees would have changed their minds even if they had seen another miracle.

8:17–21 *How is it you do not understand?* The disciples continued to show a lack of spiritual discernment despite the miracles they had witnessed. Jesus' rebuke was intended to make them recall what God had done for them.

7:32 ᵉ Luke 11:14   **7:33** ᶠ Mark 8:23   **7:34** ᵍ Mark 6:41   ʰ John 11:33, 38   **7:35** ⁱ Is. 35:5, 6   **7:36** ʲ Mark 5:43   **7:37** ᵏ Mark 6:51; 10:26   ˡ Matt. 12:22   **8:1** ᵃ Matt. 15:32–39   **8:2** ᵇ Mark 1:41; 6:34   **8:5** ᶜ Mark 6:38   **8:7** ᵈ Matt. 14:19   **8:10** ᵉ Mark 8:13   **8:11** ᶠ Matt. 12:38; 16:1   **8:12** ᵍ Mark 7:34   ʰ Matt. 12:39   **8:14** ⁱ Matt. 16:5   **8:15** ʲ Luke 12:1   **8:17** ᵏ Mark 6:52; 16:14   **8:19** ˡ Matt. 14:20   **8:20** ᵐ Matt. 15:37   **8:21** ⁿ [Mark 6:52]   **8:22** ᵒ John 9:1 ᵖ Luke 18:15   **8:23** ᵩ Mark 7:33

²⁴And he looked up and said, "I see men like trees, walking." ²⁵Then He put *His* hands on his eyes again and made him look up. And he was restored and saw everyone clearly. ²⁶Then He sent him away to his house, saying, "Neither go into the town, ʳnor tell anyone in the town."*

Peter Confesses Jesus as the Christ

²⁷ˢNow Jesus and His disciples went out to the towns of Caesarea Philippi; and on the road He asked His disciples, saying to them, "Who do men say that I am?"

²⁸So they answered, ᵗ"John the Baptist; but some *say,* ᵘElijah; and others, one of the prophets."

²⁹He said to them, "But who do you say that I am?"

Peter answered and said to Him, ᵛ"You are the Christ."

³⁰ᵂThen He strictly warned them that they should tell no one about Him.

Jesus Predicts His Death and Resurrection

³¹And ˣHe began to teach them that the Son of Man must suffer many things, and be ʸrejected by the elders and chief priests and scribes, and be ᶻkilled, and after three days rise again. ³²He spoke this word openly. Then Peter took Him aside and began to rebuke Him. ³³But when He had turned around and looked at His disciples, He ᵃrebuked Peter, saying, "Get behind Me, Satan! For you are not mindful of the things of God, but the things of men."

Take Up the Cross and Follow Him

³⁴When He had called the people to *Himself,* with His disciples also, He said to them, ᵇ"Whoever desires to come after Me, let him deny himself, and take up his cross, and follow Me. ³⁵For ᶜwhoever desires to save his life will lose it, but whoever loses his life for My sake and the gospel's will save it. ³⁶For what will it profit a man if he gains the whole world, and loses his own soul? ³⁷Or what will a man give in exchange for his soul? ³⁸ᵈFor whoever ᵉis ashamed of Me and My words in this adulterous and sinful generation, of him the Son of Man also will be ashamed when He comes in the glory of His Father with the holy angels."

9 And He said to them, ᵃ"Assuredly, I say to you that there are some standing here who will not taste death till they see ᵇthe kingdom of God present with power."

Jesus Transfigured on the Mount

²ᶜNow after six days Jesus took Peter, James, and John, and led them up on a high mountain apart by themselves; and He was transfigured before them. ³His clothes became shining, exceedingly ᵈwhite, like snow, such as no launderer on earth can whiten them. ⁴And Elijah appeared to them with Moses, and they were talking with Jesus. ⁵Then Peter answered and said to Jesus, "Rabbi, it is good for us to be here; and let us make three tabernacles: one for You, one for Moses, and one for Elijah"— ⁶because he did not know what to say, for they were greatly afraid.

⁷And a ᵉcloud came and overshadowed them; and a voice came out of the cloud, saying, "This is ᶠMy beloved Son. ᵍHear Him!" ⁸Suddenly, when they had looked around, they saw no one anymore, but only Jesus with themselves.

⁹ʰNow as they came down from the mountain, He commanded them that they should tell no one the things they had seen,

---

* **8:26** NU-Text reads *"Do not even go into the town."*

8:27 *Caesarea Philippi.* This city is about 25 miles north of Bethsaida and the Sea of Galilee. It stands on the southern edge of Mount Hermon. One of the sources of the Jordan River springs forth from under a large rocky cliff that rises a hundred or more feet above the village. The name Philippi distinguishes this town from Caesarea on the coast.

8:29 *But who do you say that I am?* Jesus emphatically asks His disciples for their understanding. *you.* Prominent in Jesus' question is the word "you." *You are the Christ.* Peter answers for the group. Jesus wants His disciples to grasp firmly His true identity before He reveals to them the necessity of His coming death and resurrection. In Mark's Gospel, only the disciples come to understand who Jesus is.

8:30 *tell no one about Him.* Jesus' warning may seem strange. Its explanation lies in the fact that the Jews expected the Messiah to be a political liberator. Jesus' first coming was meant to accomplish another kind of liberation—release from sin. Hence Jesus was careful not to use the name Messiah publicly, for it was misunderstood by the Jewish people, their leaders, and the Roman authorities.

8:38 *when He comes in the glory.* This is the first glimpse of the fulfillment of all history (1 Cor. 15:24–28). Those who will reign with Christ invest their lives in that which will last (v. 35). Those who are willing to confess Him today will be rewarded before the Father in heaven (Matt. 5:10–12; 2 Tim. 2:11–13; Rev. 2:26–28).

9:4 *Elijah.* Elijah is mentioned in Malachi 4:5–6 in connection with the future coming of Christ. This is why people asked John the Baptist if he were Elijah (John 1:21). Moses was the lawgiver and liberator, while Elijah was the first of the great prophets. Their presence confirmed the reality that Jesus is the Messiah of Peter's confession.

8:26 ʳ Mark 5:43; 7:36 **8:27** ˢ Luke 9:18–20
8:28 ᵗ Matt. 14:2 ᵘ Luke 9:7, 8 **8:29** ᵛ John 1:41; 4:42;
6:69; 11:27 **8:30** ᵂ Matt. 8:4; 16:20 **8:31** ˣ Matt. 16:21;
20:19 ʸ Mark 10:33 ᶻ Mark 9:31; 10:34 **8:33** ᵃ [Rev. 3:19]
8:34 ᵇ Luke 14:27 **8:35** ᶜ John 12:25 **8:38** ᵈ Matt.
10:33 ᵉ 2 Tim. 1:8, 9; 2:12 **9:1** ᵃ Luke 9:27 ᵇ [Matt. 24:30]
9:2 ᶜ Matt. 17:1–8 ᵈ Dan. 7:9 **9:7** ᵉ Ex. 40:34 ᶠ Mark
1:11 ᵍ Acts 3:22 **9:9** ʰ Matt. 17:9–13

till the Son of Man had risen from the dead. [10]So they kept this word to themselves, questioning [i]what the rising from the dead meant.

[11]And they asked Him, saying, "Why do the scribes say [j]that Elijah must come first?"

[12]Then He answered and told them, "Indeed, Elijah is coming first and restores all things. And [k]how is it written concerning the Son of Man, that He must suffer many things and [l]be treated with contempt? [13]But I say to you that [m]Elijah has also come, and they did to him whatever they wished, as it is written of him."

A Boy Is Healed

[14n]And when He came to the disciples, He saw a great multitude around them, and scribes disputing with them. [15]Immediately, when they saw Him, all the people were greatly amazed, and running to *Him*, greeted Him. [16]And He asked the scribes, "What are you discussing with them?"

[17]Then [o]one of the crowd answered and said, "Teacher, I brought You my son, who has a mute spirit. [18]And wherever it seizes him, it throws him down; he foams at the mouth, gnashes his teeth, and becomes rigid. So I spoke to Your disciples, that they should cast it out, but they could not."

[19]He answered him and said, "O [p]faithless generation, how long shall I be with you? How long shall I bear with you? Bring him to Me." [20]Then they brought him to Him. And [q]when he saw Him, immediately the spirit convulsed him, and he fell on the ground and wallowed, foaming at the mouth.

[21]So He asked his father, "How long has this been happening to him?"

And he said, "From childhood. [22]And often he has thrown him both into the fire and into the water to destroy him. But if You can do anything, have compassion on us and help us."

[23]Jesus said to him, [r]"If you can believe,* all things *are* possible to him who believes."

[24]Immediately the father of the child cried out and said with tears, "Lord, I believe; [s]help my unbelief!"

[25]When Jesus saw that the people came running together, He [t]rebuked the unclean spirit, saying to it, "Deaf and dumb spirit, I command you, come out of him and enter him no more!" [26]Then *the spirit* cried out, convulsed him greatly, and came out of

him. And he became as one dead, so that many said, "He is dead." [27]But Jesus took him by the hand and lifted him up, and he arose.

[28u]And when He had come into the house, His disciples asked Him privately, "Why could we not cast it out?"

[29]So He said to them, "This kind can come out by nothing but [v]prayer and fasting."*

Jesus Again Predicts His Death and Resurrection

[30]Then they departed from there and passed through Galilee, and He did not want anyone to know *it*. [31w]For He taught His disciples and said to them, "The Son of Man is being betrayed into the hands of men, and they will [x]kill Him. And after He is killed, He will [y]rise the third day." [32z]But they did not understand this saying, and were afraid to ask Him.

Who Is the Greatest?

[33a]Then He came to Capernaum. And when He was in the house He asked them, "What was it you disputed among yourselves on the road?" [34]But they kept silent, for on the road they had [b]disputed among themselves who *would be the* [c]greatest. [35]And He sat down, called the twelve, and said to them, [d]"If anyone desires to be first, he shall be last of all and servant of all." [36]Then [e]He took a little child and set him in the midst of them. And when He had taken him in His arms, He said to them, [37]"Whoever receives one of these little children in My name receives Me; and [f]whoever receives Me, receives not Me but Him who sent Me."

Jesus Forbids Sectarianism

[38g]Now John answered Him, saying, "Teacher, we saw someone who does not follow us casting out demons in Your name, and we forbade him because he does not follow us."

[39]But Jesus said, "Do not forbid him, [h]for no one who works a miracle in My name can soon afterward speak evil of Me. [40]For [i]he who is not against us is on our* side. [41j]For whoever gives you a cup of water to

---

* 9:23 NU-Text reads "'If You can!' All things...."
* 9:29 NU-Text omits *and fasting*.   * 9:40 M-Text reads *against you is on your side.*

9:24 I believe; help my unbelief. These words express the dilemma that even those who believe can be nagged by doubt and hopelessness. This man took the correct course by appealing to Jesus for help.

9:40 For he who is not against us is on our side. Jesus is not endorsing all who claim to follow Him. Rather, this statement was meant to remind the disciples that God's work was not necessarily restricted to their small group.

9:10 [i] John 2:19–22   **9:11** [j] Mal. 4:5   **9:12** [k] Is. 53:3   [l] Phil. 2:7   **9:13** [m] Luke 1:17   **9:14** [n] Matt. 17:14–19   **9:17** [o] Luke 9:38   **9:19** [p] John 4:48   **9:20** [q] Mark 1:26   **9:23** [r] John 11:40   **9:24** [s] Luke 17:5   **9:25** [t] Mark 1:25   **9:28** [u] Matt. 17:19   **9:29** [v] [James 5:16]   **9:31** [w] Luke 9:44   [x] Matt. 16:21; 27:50   [y] 1 Cor. 15:4   **9:32** [z] Luke 2:50; 18:34   **9:33** [a] Matt. 18:1–5   **9:34** [b] [Prov. 13:10]   [c] Luke 22:24; 23:46; 24:46   **9:35** [d] Luke 22:26, 27   **9:36** [e] Mark 10:13–16   **9:37** [f] Matt. 10:40   **9:38** [g] Num. 11:27–29   **9:39** [h] 1 Cor. 12:3   **9:40** [i] [Matt. 12:30]   **9:41** [j] Matt. 10:42

drink in My name, because you belong to Christ, assuredly, I say to you, he will by no means lose his reward.

Jesus Warns of Offenses

42k"But whoever causes one of these little ones who believe in Me to stumble, it would be better for him if a millstone were hung around his neck, and he were thrown into the sea. 43lIf your hand causes you to sin, cut it off. It is better for you to enter into life maimed, rather than having two hands, to go to hell, into the fire that shall never be quenched— 44where

m'Their worm does not die
And the fire is not quenched.'*

45And if your foot causes you to sin, cut it off. It is better for you to enter life lame, rather than having two feet, to be cast into hell, into the fire that shall never be quenched— 46where

n'Their worm does not die
And the fire is not quenched.'*

47And if your eye causes you to sin, pluck it out. It is better for you to enter the kingdom of God with one eye, rather than having two eyes, to be cast into hell fire— 48where

o'Their worm does not die
And the pfire is not quenched.'*

Tasteless Salt Is Worthless

49"For everyone will be qseasoned with fire,* rand every sacrifice will be seasoned with salt. 50sSalt is good, but if the salt loses its flavor, how will you season it? tHave salt in yourselves, and uhave peace with one another."

Marriage and Divorce

10 Then aHe arose from there and came to the region of Judea by the other side of the Jordan. And multitudes gathered to Him again, and as He was accustomed, He taught them again.

2bThe Pharisees came and asked Him, "Is it lawful for a man to divorce his wife?" testing Him.

3And He answered and said to them, "What did Moses command you?"
4They said, c"Moses permitted a man to write a certificate of divorce, and to dismiss her."
5And Jesus answered and said to them, "Because of the hardness of your heart he wrote you this precept. 6But from the beginning of the creation, God d'made them male and female.'* 7e'For this reason a man shall leave his father and mother and be joined to his wife, 8and the two shall become one flesh';* so then they are no longer two, but one flesh. 9Therefore what God has joined together, let not man separate."
10In the house His disciples also asked Him again about the same matter. 11So He said to them, f"Whoever divorces his wife and marries another commits adultery against her. 12And if a woman divorces her husband and marries another, she commits adultery."

Jesus Blesses Little Children

13gThen they brought little children to Him, that He might touch them; but the disciples rebuked those who brought them. 14But when Jesus saw it, He was greatly displeased and said to them, "Let the little children come to Me, and do not forbid them; for hof such is the kingdom of God. 15Assuredly, I say to you, iwhoever does not receive the kingdom of God as a little child will jby no means enter it." 16And He took them up in His arms, laid His hands on them, and blessed them.

Jesus Counsels the Rich Young Ruler

17kNow as He was going out on the road, one came running, knelt before Him, and asked Him, "Good Teacher, what shall I ldo that I may inherit eternal life?"
18So Jesus said to him, "Why do you call Me good? No one is good but One, that is, mGod. 19You know the commandments:

* 9:44 NU-Text omits this verse.   * 9:46 NU-Text omits the last clause of verse 45 and all of verse 46.   * 9:48 Isaiah 66:24   * 9:49 NU-Text omits the rest of this verse.   * 10:6 Genesis 1:27; 5:2   * 10:8 Genesis 2:24

9:49 For everyone will be seasoned with fire. This phrase may refer to the trials and judgments that all will face—believers with trials that purify faith, unbelievers with the eternal fire of God's judgment.
10:4 a certificate of divorce. This was a document signed before witnesses. Its intent was to limit frivolous divorces. In Jesus' day, the interpretation of this custom varied widely. The disciples of Hillel allowed divorce for almost any reason, but the followers of Shammai permitted divorce only for sexual impurity.
10:11 Whosoever divorces his wife. Mark includes no exception to Christ's prohibition of divorce, nor is any exception listed in Luke 16:18, Romans 7:1–2, or 1 Corinthians 7:10–11. Compare Matthew 5:32 where the exception is made.
10:18 No one is good but One, that is, God. This

reply is a claim to deity, which Jesus asks the young ruler to recognize.
10:19 Do not. Jesus recounts the Seventh, Sixth, Eighth, Ninth, and Fifth Commandments. **Do not defraud.** Jesus inserts this phrase just before the Fifth Commandment. All of these commands concern

---

9:42 k Luke 17:1, 2   9:43 l Matt. 5:29, 30; 18:8, 9
9:44 m Is. 66:24   9:46 n Is. 66:24   9:48 o Is. 66:24
p Jer. 7:20   9:49 q [Matt. 3:11] r Lev. 2:13   9:50 s Matt. 5:13 t Col. 4:6 u Rom. 12:18; 14:19   10:1 a Matt. 19:1–9
10:2 b Matt. 19:3   10:4 c Deut. 24:1–4   10:6 d Gen. 1:27; 5:2   10:7 e Gen. 2:24   10:11 f [Matt. 5:32; 19:9]   10:13 g Luke 18:15–17   10:14 h [1 Pet. 2:2]
10:15 i Matt. 18:3, 4; 19:14 j Luke 13:28   10:17 k Matt. 19:16–30 l John 6:28   10:18 m 1 Sam. 2:2

[n]*'Do not commit adultery,' 'Do not murder,'*
'Do not steal,' 'Do not bear false witness,'
'Do not defraud,' *'Honor your father and*
*your mother.' "**
20 And he answered and said to Him,
"Teacher, all these things I have [o]kept from
my youth."
21 Then Jesus, looking at him, loved him,
and said to him, "One thing you lack: Go
your way, [p]sell whatever you have and give
to the poor, and you will have [q]treasure in
heaven; and come, [r]take up the cross, and
follow Me."
22 But he was sad at this word, and went
away sorrowful, for he had great possessions.

With God All Things Are Possible

23 [s]Then Jesus looked around and said
to His disciples, "How hard it is for those
who have riches to enter the kingdom of
God!" 24 And the disciples were astonished
at His words. But Jesus answered again
and said to them, "Children, how hard it
is for those [t]who trust in riches* to enter
the kingdom of God! 25 It is easier for a
camel to go through the eye of a needle
than for a [u]rich man to enter the kingdom
of God."
26 And they were greatly astonished, saying among themselves, "Who then can be
saved?"
27 But Jesus looked at them and said,
"With men *it is* impossible, but not [v]with
God; for with God all things are possible."
28 [w]Then Peter began to say to Him, "See,
we have left all and followed You."
29 So Jesus answered and said, "Assuredly, I say to you, there is no one who
has left house or brothers or sisters or
father or mother or wife* or children or
lands, for My sake and the gospel's, 30 [x]who
shall not receive a hundredfold now in this
time—houses and brothers and sisters
and mothers and children and lands, with
[y]persecutions—and in the age to come,
eternal life. 31 [z]But many *who are* first will
be last, and the last first."

Jesus a Third Time Predicts His Death and Resurrection

32 [a]Now they were on the road, going up
to Jerusalem, and Jesus was going before
them; and they were amazed. And as they
followed they were afraid. [b]Then He took
the twelve aside again and began to tell
them the things that would happen to Him:
33 "Behold, we are going up to Jerusalem,
and the Son of Man will be betrayed to the
chief priests and to the scribes; and they
will condemn Him to death and deliver Him
to the Gentiles; 34 and they will mock Him,
and scourge Him, and spit on Him, and kill
Him. And the third day He will rise again."

Greatness Is Serving

35 [c]Then James and John, the sons of
Zebedee, came to Him, saying, "Teacher,
we want You to do for us whatever we ask."
36 And He said to them, "What do you
want Me to do for you?"
37 They said to Him, "Grant us that we
may sit, one on Your right hand and the
other on Your left, in Your glory."
38 But Jesus said to them, "You do not
know what you ask. Are you able to drink
the [d]cup that I drink, and be baptized with
the [e]baptism that I am baptized with?"
39 They said to Him, "We are able."
So Jesus said to them, [f]"You will indeed
drink the cup that I drink, and with the
baptism I am baptized with you will be
baptized; 40 but to sit on My right hand and
on My left is not Mine to give, but *it is for*
those [g]for whom it is prepared."
41 [h]And when the ten heard *it*, they began
to be greatly displeased with James and
John. 42 But Jesus called them to *Himself*
and said to them, [i]"You know that those who
are considered rulers over the Gentiles lord
it over them, and their great ones exercise
authority over them. 43 [j]Yet it shall not be so
among you; but whoever desires to become

* **10:19** Exodus 20:12–16; Deuteronomy 5:16–20
* **10:24** NU-Text omits *for those who trust in riches.* * **10:29** NU-Text omits *or wife.*

---

the fair and ethical treatment of other people (Ex. 20:12–17).

10:25–27 ***It is easier.*** This comparison of a camel going through a needle is a literal one. In human terms, it is not just difficult, but totally impossible, for a rich man to be saved. But it is also impossible for anyone at all to be saved apart from God's grace and power. God provides the means of salvation, enlightens the sinner's understanding, and regenerates the believing soul.

10:30 ***in this time.*** This is the time between Christ's first and second comings. Mark alone mentions that persecutions will follow as well—a point his Roman readers may have already known.

10:37 ***one on Your right hand and the other on Your left.*** To be seated at a king's right hand was to take the position of the most prominence; the person seated at the left hand ranked just below that (Luke 22:24–30). Jesus had to remind the disciples again about the price of greatness in God's kingdom.

10:38 ***drink the cup that I drink . . . be baptized with the baptism.*** These phrases are references to the suffering and death that awaited Jesus (14:36). Jesus wanted His disciples to understand the mocking, scourging, beating, and torture He would have to endure.

10:19 [n] Ex. 20:12–16; Deut. 5:16–20 **10:20** [o] Phil. 3:6 **10:21** [p] [Luke 12:33; 16:9] [q] Matt. 6:19, 20; 19:21 [r] [Mark 8:34] **10:23** [s] Matt. 19:23 **10:24** [t] [1 Tim. 6:17] **10:25** [u] [Matt. 13:22; 19:24] **10:27** [v] Jer. 32:17 **10:28** [w] Luke 18:28 **10:30** [x] Luke 18:29, 30 [y] [1 Pet. 4:12, 13] **10:31** [z] Luke 13:30 **10:32** [a] Matt. 20:17–19 [b] Mark 8:31; 9:31 **10:35** [c] [James 4:3] **10:38** [d] John 18:11 [e] Luke 12:50 **10:39** [f] Acts 12:2 **10:40** [g] [Heb. 11:16] **10:41** [h] Matt. 20:24 **10:42** [i] Luke 22:25 **10:43** [j] Mark 9:35

great among you shall be your servant. ⁴⁴And whoever of you desires to be first shall be slave of all. ⁴⁵For even ^kthe Son of Man did not come to be served, but to serve, and ^lto give His life a ransom for many."

Jesus Heals Blind Bartimaeus

^{46m}Now they came to Jericho. As He went out of Jericho with His disciples and a great multitude, blind Bartimaeus, the son of Timaeus, sat by the road begging. ⁴⁷And when he heard that it was Jesus of Nazareth, he began to cry out and say, "Jesus, ⁿSon of David, ^ohave mercy on me!"

⁴⁸Then many warned him to be quiet; but he cried out all the more, "Son of David, have mercy on me!"

⁴⁹So Jesus stood still and commanded him to be called.

Then they called the blind man, saying to him, "Be of good cheer. Rise, He is calling you."

⁵⁰And throwing aside his garment, he rose and came to Jesus.

⁵¹So Jesus answered and said to him, "What do you want Me to do for you?"

The blind man said to Him, "Rabboni, that I may receive my sight."

⁵²Then Jesus said to him, "Go your way; ^pyour faith has made you well." And immediately he received his sight and followed Jesus on the road.

The Triumphal Entry

11 Now ^awhen they drew near Jerusalem, to Bethphage* and Bethany, at the Mount of Olives, He sent two of His disciples; ²and He said to them, "Go into the village opposite you; and as soon as you have entered it you will find a colt tied, on which no one has sat. Loose it and bring *it*. ³And if anyone says to you, 'Why are you doing this?' say, 'The Lord has need of it,' and immediately he will send it here."

⁴So they went their way, and found the* colt tied by the door outside on the street, and they loosed it. ⁵But some of those who stood there said to them, "What are you doing, loosing the colt?"

⁶And they spoke to them just as Jesus had commanded. So they let them go. ⁷Then they brought the colt to Jesus and threw their clothes on it, and He sat on it. ^{8b}And many spread their clothes on the road, and others cut down leafy branches from the trees and spread *them* on the road. ⁹Then those who went before and those who followed cried out, saying:

"Hosanna!
^c'Blessed *is* He who comes in the name of the LORD!'*
¹⁰ Blessed *is* the kingdom of our father David
That comes in the name of the Lord!*
^dHosanna in the highest!"

^{11e}And Jesus went into Jerusalem and into the temple. So when He had looked around at all things, as the hour was already late, He went out to Bethany with the twelve.

The Fig Tree Withered

^{12f}Now the next day, when they had come out from Bethany, He was hungry. ^{13g}And seeing from afar a fig tree having leaves, He went to see if perhaps He would find something on it. When He came to it, He found nothing but leaves, for it was not the season for figs. ¹⁴In response Jesus said to it, "Let no one eat fruit from you ever again."

And His disciples heard *it*.

* **11:1** M-Text reads *Bethsphage.* * **11:4** NU-Text and M-Text read *a.* * **11:9** Psalm 118:26 * **11:10** NU-Text omits *in the name of the Lord.*

10:45 The Ministry of Christ—
1. *He is Savior.* Sinful men to be saved (1 Tim. 1:15); Christ's qualifications to be Savior (John 10:18–38); His humiliating death (John 19:18); bodily resurrection to guarantee our salvation (1 Cor. 15:13–22); and results of salvation (John 5:24). It is no wonder that, in light of these realities, Paul speaks of Christ as "our great God and Savior" (Titus 2:13).
2. *He is High Priest.* The high priest brought the people before God on the Day of Atonement (Lev. 16:32–33). Jesus is eminently qualified to be our High Priest: appointed by God (Heb. 5:5), eternal (Heb. 7:24–25), sinless (Heb. 7:26), His offering was final (Heb. 9:28), and His mediation is effective (Rom. 8:34; Heb. 7:25; 1 John 2:1). As the only qualified High Priest for men and women, Jesus Christ thus constitutes the only way to God (1 Tim. 2:5).
3. *He is King.* King implies sovereign authority and rule over all. This right belongs only to Jesus Christ who is called "Lord of lords and King of kings" (Rev. 17:14; 19:16). He is destined to rule

as king and every knee must ultimately bow and acknowledge His authority (Phil. 2:10). Those who acknowledge Christ as King and Lord in this life will reign with Him; those who do not will be judged by Him (Rev. 20:11–15).
11:8–11 Bethany. Jesus retired there each night, perhaps staying in a friend's home. But in view of the fact that Jesus appears to have had no breakfast the next day (v. 12), He and the twelve may have camped outside this night.
11:13 it was not the season for figs. Passover always comes in March or April, and fig season is not until May or June. However, fig trees generally produce a number of buds in March, leaves in April, and ripe fruit later on. Jesus was looking for the edible buds, the lack of which indicated that the tree would be fruitless that year.

10:45 ^k [Phil. 2:7, 8] ^l [Titus 2:14] **10:46** ^m Luke 18:35–43 **10:47** ⁿ Rev. 22:16 ^o Matt. 15:22 **10:52** ^p Matt. 9:22 **11:1** ^a Zech. 9:9; Matt. 21:1–9 **11:8** ^b Matt. 21:8 **11:9** ^c Ps. 118:25, 26 **11:10** ^d Ps. 148:1 **11:11** ^e Matt. 21:12 **11:12** ^f Matt. 21:18–22 **11:13** ^g Matt. 21:19

Jesus Cleanses the Temple

15hSo they came to Jerusalem. Then Jesus went into the temple and began to drive out those who bought and sold in the temple, and overturned the tables of the money changers and the seats of those who sold idoves. 16And He would not allow anyone to carry wares through the temple. 17Then He taught, saying to them, "Is it not written, j'My house shall be called a house of prayer for all nations'?* But you have made it a k'den of thieves.'"*

18And lthe scribes and chief priests heard it and sought how they might destroy Him; for they feared Him, because mall the people were astonished at His teaching. 19When evening had come, He went out of the city.

The Lesson of the Withered Fig Tree

20nNow in the morning, as they passed by, they saw the fig tree dried up from the roots. 21And Peter, remembering, said to Him, "Rabbi, look! The fig tree which You cursed has withered away."

22So Jesus answered and said to them, "Have faith in God. 23For oassuredly, I say to you, whoever says to this mountain, 'Be removed and be cast into the sea,' and does not doubt in his heart, but believes that those things he says will be done, he will have whatever he says. 24Therefore I say to you, pwhatever things you ask when you pray, believe that you receive them, and you will have them.

Forgiveness and Prayer

25"And whenever you stand praying, qif you have anything against anyone, forgive him, that your Father in heaven may also forgive you your trespasses. 26But rif you do not forgive, neither will your Father in heaven forgive your trespasses."*

Jesus' Authority Questioned

27Then they came again to Jerusalem. sAnd as He was walking in the temple, the chief priests, the scribes, and the elders came to Him. 28And they said to Him, "By what tauthority are You doing these things? And who gave You this authority to do these things?"

29But Jesus answered and said to them, "I also will ask you one question; then answer Me, and I will tell you by what authority I do these things: 30The ubaptism of John—was it from heaven or from men? Answer Me."

31And they reasoned among themselves, saying, "If we say, 'From heaven,' He will say, 'Why then did you not believe him?' 32But if we say, 'From men'"—they feared the people, for vall counted John to have been a prophet indeed. 33So they answered and said to Jesus, "We do not know."

And Jesus answered and said to them, "Neither will I tell you by what authority I do these things."

The Parable of the Wicked Vinedressers

12 Then aHe began to speak to them in parables: "A man planted a vineyard and set a hedge around it, dug a place for the wine vat and built a tower. And he leased it to vinedressers and went into a far country. 2Now at vintage-time he sent a servant to the vinedressers, that he might receive some of the fruit of the vineyard from the vinedressers. 3And they took him and beat him and sent him away empty-handed. 4Again he sent them another servant, and at him they threw stones,* wounded him in the head, and sent him away shamefully treated. 5And again he sent another, and him they killed; and many others, bbeating some and killing some. 6Therefore still having one son, his beloved, he also sent him to them last, saying, 'They will respect my son.' 7But those vinedressers said among themselves, 'This is the heir. Come, let us kill him, and the inheritance will be ours.' 8So they took him and ckilled him and cast him out of the vineyard.

---

* **11:17** Isaiah 56:7 • Jeremiah 7:11   * **11:26** NU-Text omits this verse.   * **12:4** NU-Text omits and at him they threw stones.

11:17 den of thieves. Jesus was referring to the practice of cheating people, both Israelites and those of other nations, either through a crooked exchange of money or by selling inferior products.
11:21 The fig tree which You cursed has withered away. The passage emphasizes the power of true faith. Some have suggested that the fig tree represented Israel, which bore no fruit and would soon face the judgment of God.
11:29–30 answer Me. The intent of Jesus' question was to expose once again the insincerity of His detractors. **baptism of John.** This refers to the authority of John's baptism. **from heaven.** Was it ordained by God and worthy of obedience? **from men.** Or was it of human contrivance and void of any spiritual authority and reality?
12:1 He began to speak to them in parables.

Parables usually get across a significant truth, but the details are not meant to correspond exactly with particular spiritual realities. In this parable, the owner of the vineyard represents God, but God Himself was never so mistaken as to assume they would respect His Son. God is omniscient, whereas the vineyard owner in the parable is not. This story illustrates the immense patience God had with Israel.

11:15 h John 2:13–16 i Lev. 14:22   **11:17** j Is. 56:7 k Jer. 7:11   **11:18** l Matt. 21:45, 46 m Matt. 7:28   **11:20** n Matt. 21:19–22   **11:23** o Matt. 17:20; 21:21   **11:24** p Matt. 7:7   **11:25** q [Col. 3:13]   **11:26** r Matt. 6:15; 18:35   **11:27** s Luke 20:1–8   **11:28** t John 5:27   **11:30** u Luke 7:29, 30   **11:32** v Matt. 3:5; 14:5   **12:1** a Luke 20:9–19   **12:5** b 2 Chr. 36:16   **12:8** c [Acts 2:23]

9"Therefore what will the owner of the vineyard do? He will come and destroy the vinedressers, and give the vineyard to others. 10Have you not even read this Scripture:

d'The stone which the builders rejected
Has become the chief cornerstone.
11 This was the LORD's doing,
And it is marvelous in our eyes'?"*

12eAnd they sought to lay hands on Him, but feared the multitude, for they knew He had spoken the parable against them. So they left Him and went away.

The Pharisees: Is It Lawful to Pay Taxes to Caesar?

13fThen they sent to Him some of the Pharisees and the Herodians, to catch Him in His words. 14When they had come, they said to Him, "Teacher, we know that You are true, and care about no one; for You do not regard the person of men, but teach the gway of God in truth. Is it lawful to pay taxes to Caesar, or not? 15Shall we pay, or shall we not pay?"

But He, knowing their hhypocrisy, said to them, "Why do you test Me? Bring Me a denarius that I may see it." 16So they brought it.

And He said to them, "Whose image and inscription is this?" They said to Him, "Caesar's."

17And Jesus answered and said to them, "Render to Caesar the things that are Caesar's, and to iGod the things that are God's."

And they marveled at Him.

The Sadducees: What About the Resurrection?

18jThen some Sadducees, kwho say there is no resurrection, came to Him;

and they asked Him, saying: 19"Teacher, lMoses wrote to us that if a man's brother dies, and leaves his wife behind, and leaves no children, his brother should take his wife and raise up offspring for his brother. 20Now there were seven brothers. The first took a wife; and dying, he left no offspring. 21And the second took her, and he died; nor did he leave any offspring. And the third likewise. 22So the seven had her and left no offspring. Last of all the woman died also. 23Therefore, in the resurrection, when they rise, whose wife will she be? For all seven had her as wife."

24Jesus answered and said to them, "Are you not therefore mistaken, because you do not know the Scriptures nor the power of God? 25For when they rise from the dead, they neither marry nor are given in marriage, but mare like angels in heaven. 26But concerning the dead, that they nrise, have you not read in the book of Moses, in the burning bush passage, how God spoke to him, saying, o'I am the God of Abraham, the God of Isaac, and the God of Jacob'?* 27He is not the God of the dead, but the God of the living. You are therefore greatly mistaken."

The Scribes: Which Is the First Commandment of All?

28pThen one of the scribes came, and having heard them reasoning together, perceiving* that He had answered them well, asked Him, "Which is the first commandment of all?"

29Jesus answered him, "The first of all the commandments is: q'Hear, O Israel, the LORD our God, the LORD is one. 30And

* 12:11 Psalm 118:22, 23   * 12:26 Exodus 3:6, 15
* 12:28 NU-Text reads seeing.

12:12 they sought to lay hands on Him. Only as the final points of the parable were made did these evil men realize that Jesus was speaking of them.

12:14 You are true, and care about no one. This comment was intended as a compliment. The teachers recognized that Jesus was partial to no one. The question, however, was a lose-lose proposition: a yes answer would alienate Jews who opposed Rome, while a no answer could be taken as treason against the state.

12:18 Sadducees were an elite group of religious leaders who denied the existence of angels, the immortality of the soul, and the resurrection. They rejected the oral traditions and accepted only the validity of the Pentateuch, the first five books of the Old Testament.

12:19–22 Moses wrote to us. The custom of marrying the widow of one's brother was supported by Deuteronomy 25:5–6, but it was not absolutely binding (Deut. 25:7–10).

12:26–27 I am the God of Abraham . . . Isaac . . . Jacob. Jesus quotes from the law—the Book of Exodus—to make His point. God said I am the God of the three patriarchs mentioned, not "I was their God, but

now they are dead." He still is their God because they are still alive. Their souls not only live after death, but their bodies will be raised anew as well.

12:29 Hear, O Israel. In Judaism, these words (quoted from Deut. 6:4–5) are known as the Shema. It is described by Jews as the most important words a Jew can know. Jesus quotes these words at the beginning of answering the question, "Which is the first commandment of all?" We should be driven to the cross. There, we understand His love for us and are constantly motivated to seek to love Him better because of what He has done. We can only be thankful at the comprehensiveness of His love. Even though we sin every day of our lives, He forgives. We just need to keep coming to Him for that forgiveness.

12:10 d Ps. 118:22, 23   12:12 e John 7:25, 30, 44   12:13 f Luke 20:20–26   12:14 g Acts 18:26   12:15 h Luke 12:1   12:17 i [Eccl. 5:4, 5]   12:18 j Luke 20:27–38 k Acts 23:8   12:19 l Deut. 25:5   12:25 m [1 Cor. 15:42, 49, 52]   12:26 n [Rev. 20:12, 13] o Ex. 3:6, 15   12:28 p Matt. 22:34–40   12:29 q Deut. 6:4, 5

you shall *r*love the LORD your God with all your heart, with all your soul, with all your mind, and with all your strength.'* This *is* the first commandment.* **31**And the second, like *it, is* this: *s*'You shall love your neighbor as yourself.'* There is no other commandment greater than *t*these."

32So the scribe said to Him, "Well *said*, Teacher. You have spoken the truth, for there is one God, *u*and there is no other but He. **33**And to love Him with all the heart, with all the understanding, with all the soul,* and with all the strength, and to love one's neighbor as oneself, *v*is more than all the whole burnt offerings and sacrifices."

34Now when Jesus saw that he answered wisely, He said to him, "You are not far from the kingdom of God."

*w*But after that no one dared question Him.

Jesus: How Can David Call His Descendant Lord?

35*x*Then Jesus answered and said, while He taught in the temple, "How *is it* that the scribes say that the Christ is the Son of David? **36**For David himself said *y*by the Holy Spirit:

> *z*'The LORD said to my Lord,
> "Sit at My right hand,
> Till I make Your enemies Your
>   footstool." '*

37Therefore David himself calls Him 'Lord'; how is He *then* his *a*Son?"

And the common people heard Him gladly.

Beware of the Scribes

38Then *b*He said to them in His teaching, *c*"Beware of the scribes, who desire to go around in long robes, *d*love greetings in the marketplaces, **39**the *e*best seats in the synagogues, and the best places at feasts, **40***f*who devour widows' houses, and for a

pretense make long prayers. These will receive greater condemnation."

The Widow's Two Mites

41*g*Now Jesus sat opposite the treasury and saw how the people put money *h*into the treasury. And many *who were* rich put in much. **42**Then one poor widow came and threw in two mites,* which make a quadrans. **43**So He called His disciples to *Himself* and said to them, "Assuredly, I say to you that *i*this poor widow has put in more than all those who have given to the treasury; **44**for they all put in out of their abundance, but she out of her poverty put in all that she had, *j*her whole livelihood."

Jesus Predicts the Destruction of the Temple

13 Then *a*as He went out of the temple, one of His disciples said to Him, "Teacher, see what manner of stones and what buildings *are here!*"

2And Jesus answered and said to him, "Do you see these great buildings? *b*Not *one* stone shall be left upon another, that shall not be thrown down."

The Signs of the Times and the End of the Age

3Now as He sat on the Mount of Olives opposite the temple, *c*Peter, *d*James, *e*John, and *f*Andrew asked Him privately, **4***g*"Tell us, when will these things be? And what *will be* the sign when all these things will be fulfilled?"

5And Jesus, answering them, began to say: *h*"Take heed that no one deceives you. **6**For many will come in My name, saying, 'I am *He*,' and will deceive many. **7**But when you hear of wars and rumors of wars, do

---

* **12:30** Deuteronomy 6:4, 5 • NU-Text omits this sentence. 　 * **12:31** Leviticus 19:18 　 * **12:33** NU-Text omits *with all the soul.* 　 * **12:36** Psalm 110:1 　 * **12:42** Greek *lepta*, very small copper coins worth a fraction of a penny

---

12:35 *in the temple.* This does not refer to the sanctuary itself, where only the priests were allowed to minister. The temple environs included a number of porticos and courts. One was designated especially for women, another for men. Gentiles could view the temple from an outer area.

12:43–44 *this poor widow hath put it more than all those who have given to the treasury.* Jesus' comparison of the percentages contributed by the rich and the poor reminds us that God measures not how much we give, but how much we retain. Those with greater income have an obligation to return a larger percentage of it to God's work.

13:1–2 *what manner of stones and what buildings are here.* The disciples' excitement over the temple's tremendous construction was a natural reaction to splendid and majestic architecture; each stone weighed several tons. Josephus described its magnificence. There was nothing like it in all the world.

Begun by Herod the Great in 20 B.C., the temple was later completed by Herod's descendants some time before A.D. 66. Its beautiful white marble stones with gold ornamentation reached 100 feet high. Surrounding it were colonnaded walkways, courtyards, and stairways that filled 20 acres of the most prominent landscape in all Jerusalem.

12:30 *r* [Deut. 10:12; 30:6] 　 **12:31** *s* Lev. 19:18 　 *t* [Rom. 13:9] 　 **12:32** *u* Deut. 4:39 　 **12:33** *v* [Hos. 6:6] 　 **12:34** *w* Matt. 22:46 　 **12:35** *x* Luke 20:41–44 　 **12:36** *y* 2 Sam. 23:2 　 *z* Ps. 110:1 　 **12:37** *a* [Acts 2:29–31] 　 **12:38** *b* Mark 4:2 　 *c* Matt. 23:1–7 　 *d* Matt. 23:7 　 **12:39** *e* Luke 14:7 　 **12:40** *f* Matt. 23:14 　 **12:41** *g* Luke 21:1–4 　 *h* 2 Kin. 12:9 　 **12:43** *i* [2 Cor. 8:12] 　 **12:44** *j* Deut. 24:6 　 **13:1** *a* Luke 21:5–36 　 **13:2** *b* Luke 19:44 　 **13:3** *c* Matt. 16:18 　 *d* Mark 1:19 　 *e* Mark 1:19 　 *f* John 1:40 　 **13:4** *g* Matt. 24:3 　 **13:5** *h* Eph. 5:6

not be troubled; for *such things* must happen, but the end *is* not yet. [8]For nation will rise against nation, and [i]kingdom against kingdom. And there will be earthquakes in various places, and there will be famines and troubles.* [j]These *are* the beginnings of sorrows.

[9]"But [k]watch out for yourselves, for they will deliver you up to councils, and you will be beaten in the synagogues. You will be brought* before rulers and kings for My sake, for a testimony to them. [10]And [l]the gospel must first be preached to all the nations. [11m]But when they arrest you and deliver you up, do not worry beforehand, or premeditate* what you will speak. But whatever is given you in that hour, speak that; for it is not you who speak, [n]but the Holy Spirit. [12]Now [o]brother will betray brother to death, and a father *his* child; and children will rise up against parents and cause them to be put to death. [13p]And you will be hated by all for My name's sake. But [q]he who endures to the end shall be saved.

The Great Tribulation

[14r]"So when you see the [s]'abomination of desolation,'* spoken of by Daniel the prophet,* standing where it ought not" (let the reader understand), "then [t]let those who are in Judea flee to the mountains. [15]Let him who is on the housetop not go down into the house, nor enter to take anything out of his house. [16]And let him who is in the field not go back to get his clothes. [17u]But woe to those who are pregnant and to those who are nursing babies in those days! [18]And pray that your flight may not be in winter. [19v]For *in* those days there will be tribulation, such as has not been since the beginning of the creation which God created until this time, nor ever shall be. [20]And unless the Lord had shortened those days, no flesh would be saved; but for the

elect's sake, whom He chose, He shortened the days.

[21w]"Then if anyone says to you, 'Look, here *is* the Christ!' or, 'Look, *He is* there!' do not believe it. [22]For false christs and false prophets will rise and show signs and [x]wonders to deceive, if possible, even the elect. [23]But [y]take heed; see, I have told you all things beforehand.

The Coming of the Son of Man

[24z]"But in those days, after that tribulation, the sun will be darkened, and the moon will not give its light; [25]the stars of heaven will fall, and the powers in the heavens will be [a]shaken. [26b]Then they will see the Son of Man coming in the clouds with great power and glory. [27]And then He will send His angels, and gather together His elect from the four winds, from the farthest part of earth to the farthest part of heaven.

The Parable of the Fig Tree

[28c]"Now learn this parable from the fig tree: When its branch has already become tender, and puts forth leaves, you know that summer is near. [29]So you also, when you see these things happening, know that it* is near—at the doors! [30]Assuredly, I say to you, this generation will by no means pass away till all these things take place. [31]Heaven and earth will pass away, but [d]My words will by no means pass away.

No One Knows the Day or Hour

[32]"But of that day and hour [e]no one knows, not even the angels in heaven, nor the Son, but only the [f]Father. [33g]Take heed, watch and pray; for you do not know when

---

* **13:8** NU-Text omits *and troubles.* * **13:9** NU-Text and M-Text read *will stand.* * **13:11** NU-Text omits *or premeditate.* * **13:14** Daniel 11:31; 12:11 • NU-Text omits *spoken of by Daniel the prophet.* * **13:29** Or *He*

13:11–12 the Holy Spirit. The promise given that the Holy Spirit will guide one's speech in the hour of trial applies first to the twelve and only secondarily to others who will experience persecution. But this promise does not assure escape from persecution or even freedom from being put to death.
13:13 he who endures to the end shall be saved. This is not referring to regeneration or justification but to physical deliverance from affliction (vv. 19–20). The ones who physically endure will be delivered into Christ's messianic kingdom.
13:14 standing where it ought not. This phrase refers to the presence of an idol standing in the temple. Daniel's prediction primarily referred to placement of sacrifices to Zeus on the temple's altar by Antiochus Epiphanes. Some believe that the destruction of the Herodian temple in A.D. 70 fulfilled Jesus' prediction. Others still await its fulfillment in the blasphemous actions of the antichrist in the last days (2 Thess. 2:3–4).
13:28–29 when you see these things happening.

Jesus likened the signs of His second coming to the sprouts of growth and leaves on a fig tree. Both point to the glories to come—the full flowering of the earth and return of Christ.
13:32 But of that day and hour no one knows. As one who was fully God and at the same time fully man, Jesus possessed all the attributes of deity, including omnipotence and omniscience. He knew what was in people's hearts (2:8), and He could still the waves (4:39). When Jesus became a man, however, He voluntarily placed certain knowledge in the hands of the

13:8 [i] Hag. 2:22 [j] Matt. 24:8 **13:9** [k] Matt. 10:17, 18; 24:9 **13:10** [l] Matt. 24:14 **13:11** [m] Luke 12:11; 21:12–17 [n] Acts 2:4; 4:8, 31 **13:12** [o] Mic. 7:6 **13:13** [p] Luke 21:17 [q] Matt. 10:22; 24:13 **13:14** [r] Matt. 24:15 [s] Dan. 9:27; 11:31; 12:11 [t] Luke 21:21 **13:17** [u] Luke 21:23 **13:19** [v] Dan. 9:26; 12:1 **13:21** [w] Luke 17:23; 21:8 **13:22** [x] Rev. 13:13, 14 **13:23** [y] [2 Pet. 3:17] **13:24** [z] Zeph. 1:15 **13:25** [a] Is. 13:10; 34:4 **13:26** [b] [Dan. 7:13, 14] **13:28** [c] Luke 21:29 **13:31** [d] Is. 40:8 **13:32** [e] Matt. 25:13 [f] Acts 1:7 **13:33** [g] 1 Thess. 5:6

the time is. **34**hIt *is* like a man going to a far country, who left his house and gave iauthority to his servants, and to each his work, and commanded the doorkeeper to watch. **35**jWatch therefore, for you do not know when the master of the house is coming—in the evening, at midnight, at the crowing of the rooster, or in the morning— **36**lest, coming suddenly, he find you sleeping. **37**And what I say to you, I say to all: Watch!"

The Plot to Kill Jesus

14 After ªtwo days it was the Passover and bthe Feast of Unleavened Bread. And the chief priests and the scribes sought how they might take Him by trickery and put *Him* to death. **2**But they said, "Not during the feast, lest there be an uproar of the people."

The Anointing at Bethany

3cAnd being in Bethany at the house of Simon the leper, as He sat at the table, a woman came having an alabaster flask of very costly oil of spikenard. Then she broke the flask and poured *it* on His head. **4**But there were some who were indignant among themselves, and said, "Why was this fragrant oil wasted? **5**For it might have been sold for more than three hundred ddenarii and given to the poor." And they ecriticized her sharply.

6But Jesus said, "Let her alone. Why do you trouble her? She has done a good work for Me. **7**fFor you have the poor with you always, and whenever you wish you may do them good; gbut Me you do not have always. **8**She has done what she could. She has come beforehand to anoint My body for burial. **9**Assuredly, I say to you, wherever this gospel is hpreached in the whole world, what this woman has done will also be told as a memorial to her."

Judas Agrees to Betray Jesus

10iThen Judas Iscariot, one of the twelve, went to the chief priests to betray Him to them. **11**And when they heard *it,* they were glad, and promised to give him money. So he sought how he might conveniently betray Him.

Jesus Celebrates the Passover with His Disciples

12jNow on the first day of Unleavened Bread, when they killed the Passover *lamb,* His disciples said to Him, "Where do You want us to go and prepare, that You may eat the Passover?"

13And He sent out two of His disciples and said to them, "Go into the city, and a man will meet you carrying a pitcher of water; follow him. **14**Wherever he goes in, say to the master of the house, 'The Teacher says, "Where is the guest room in which I may eat the Passover with My disciples?"' **15**Then he will show you a large upper room, furnished *and* prepared; there make ready for us."

16So His disciples went out, and came into the city, and found it just as He had said to them; and they prepared the Passover.

17kIn the evening He came with the twelve. **18**Now as they sat and ate, Jesus said, "Assuredly, I say to you, lone of you who eats with Me will betray Me."

19And they began to be sorrowful, and to say to Him one by one, "*Is* it I?" And another *said,* "*Is* it I?"*

20He answered and said to them, "*It is* one of the twelve, who dips with Me in the dish. **21**mThe Son of Man indeed goes just as it is written of Him, but woe to that man by whom the Son of Man is betrayed! It

---

* **14:19** NU-Text omits this sentence.

Father. Of course today, glorified in heaven, Jesus now knows the day and hour of His return.

13:34–36 like a man going to a far country. Jesus' parable of the absent master of the house is unique to Mark. The point of the parable is that the master could return at any time so all servants must be vigilant and watchful (Luke 19:11–27).

14:3 alabaster. Alabaster is a translucent stone still used to make ornamented jewelry boxes and other items of value. **spikenard.** Spikenard was a precious perfume imported from India, made from plants that grow in the high elevations of the Himalayas. This perfume is mentioned in the Song of Solomon (1:12; 4:13–14).

14:7 For you have the poor with you always. Jesus' statement does not show callousness towards the poor (Deut. 15:7–11). His compassion for those overwhelmed by sickness and poverty appears frequently in the Gospels, and He encouraged others to meet their needs (10:21). But He also wanted people to give freely and of their own volition. No one can coerce a gift from another; no one should criticize another's

gift; and no one can read the heart of a giver. A giver's motive is known only to God.

14:14–15 a large upper room. There is reason to suspect that the master of the house may have been Mark's father. Mark himself may have been the young man of verses 51 and 52. Acts 12:12 indicates that this house was later used as a gathering place for many believers who prayed together. Tradition has it that this was also the "upper room" of Acts 1:13 where over 100 believers met on Pentecost.

14:19 Is it I? In Greek this is actually a negative question that implies a negative answer. The phrase means "It is not I, is it?" Matthew and John both identify the culprit as Judas, even though Mark does not (Matt. 26:25; John 13:26).

13:34 h Matt. 24:45; 25:14 i [Matt. 16:19]   **13:35** j Matt. 24:42, 44   **14:1** a Luke 22:1, 2 b Ex. 12:1–27   **14:3** c Luke 7:37   **14:5** d Matt. 18:28 e John 6:61   **14:7** f Deut. 15:11 g [John 7:33; 8:21; 14:2, 12; 16:10, 17, 28]   **14:9** h Luke 24:47   **14:10** i Matt. 10:2–4   **14:12** j Matt. 26:17–19   **14:17** k Matt. 26:20–24   **14:18** l John 6:70, 71; 13:18   **14:21** m Luke 22:22

would have been good for that man if he had never been born."

Jesus Institutes the Lord's Supper

22*n*And as they were eating, Jesus took bread, blessed and broke *it*, and gave *it* to them and said, "Take, eat;* this is My *o*body."

23Then He took the cup, and when He had given thanks He gave *it* to them, and they all drank from it. **24**And He said to them, "This is My blood of the new* covenant, which is shed for many. **25**Assuredly, I say to you, I will no longer drink of the fruit of the vine until that day when I drink it new in the kingdom of God."

26*p*And when they had sung a hymn, they went out to the Mount of Olives.

Jesus Predicts Peter's Denial

27*q*Then Jesus said to them, "All of you will be made to stumble because of Me this night,* for it is written:

r'I will strike the Shepherd,
    And the sheep will be scattered.'*

28"But *s*after I have been raised, I will go before you to Galilee."

29*t*Peter said to Him, "Even if all are made to stumble, yet I *will* not *be*."

30Jesus said to him, "Assuredly, I say to you that today, *even* this night, before the rooster crows twice, you will deny Me three times."

31But he spoke more vehemently, "If I have to die with You, I will not deny You!" And they all said likewise.

The Prayer in the Garden

32*u*Then they came to a place which was named Gethsemane; and He said to His disciples, "Sit here while I pray." **33**And He *v*took Peter, James, and John with Him, and He began to be troubled and deeply distressed. **34**Then He said to them, *w*"My soul is exceedingly sorrowful, *even* to death. Stay here and watch."

35He went a little farther, and fell on the ground, and prayed that if it were possible, the hour might pass from Him. **36**And He said, *x*"Abba, Father, *y*all things *are* possible for You. Take this cup away from Me; *z*nevertheless, not what I will, but what You *will.*

37Then He came and found them sleeping, and said to Peter, "Simon, are you sleeping? Could you not watch one hour? **38***a*Watch and pray, lest you enter into temptation. *b*The spirit indeed *is* willing, but the flesh *is* weak."

39Again He went away and prayed, and spoke the same words. **40**And when He returned, He found them asleep again, for their eyes were heavy; and they did not know what to answer Him.

41Then He came the third time and said to them, "Are you still sleeping and resting? It is enough! *c*The hour has come; behold, the Son of Man is being betrayed into the hands of sinners. **42***d*Rise, let us be going. See, My betrayer is at hand."

---

* **14:22** NU-Text omits *eat.* * **14:24** NU-Text omits *new.* * **14:27** NU-Text omits *because of Me this night.* • Zechariah 13:7

14:24 *This is My blood.* This means that the contents of this cup represented Jesus' blood that would be shed for our sins. The sprinkling of blood was required to institute the Mosaic covenant in Exodus 29:12 (Heb. 9:18–22). In the same way, Jesus' blood shed on the cross initiated the new covenant. His blood was shed for many. He died on the cross in the place of many sinners from every nation. He paid the price for all of their sins. All those who believe in Him will receive eternal life.

14:26 *And when they had sung a hymn.* What they sang was no doubt from the Psalms. Frequently Psalms 113–118 were used in connection with the Passover.

14:30 *before the rooster crows twice.* Only Mark mentions Christ's prediction of Peter's denial. The incident would have remained vivid in Peter's mind when he related the story to Mark.

14:34 *My soul is exceeding sorrowful.* The crushing realization of having to bear the sin of the world and to lose, even temporarily, the fellowship of God the Father was nearly more than Jesus' soul could bear.

14:35 *the hour might pass from Him.* This is a reference to the time Jesus would bear the punishment for the sin of the world in His own body, becoming, as it were, sin for all.

14:38 *Temptation by the Flesh—Flesh* in the Bible often means something other than the substance of the human body. It is used constantly to refer to the carnal, sinful principle within man that is opposed to

God (Rom. 8:7). The actions produced by the flesh are given in detail in Galatians 5:19–21. Among these are all types of sexual immorality, impurity, hatred, anger, envy, and drunkenness. A person whose life is characterized by these sins cannot be a true Christian and is under the wrath of God (Gal. 5:21; Eph. 2:3). Though the flesh is not eradicated for the Christian, he does have the power to deny it (Rom. 7:15–25). He possesses a new nature empowered by the Holy Spirit. The solution to the urges of the flesh lies in acknowledging that the power of sin was nullified by Jesus' death (Rom. 6:11) and in living under the control of the Spirit's power (Gal. 5:16). The latter is a moment-by-moment dependence in faith on the Spirit's power. The believer must choose by an act of his will to benefit from the Spirit's enablement.

14:39–41 *Again He went away.* The three apostles were exhorted to watch and pray several times, and no doubt truly desired to uphold their Lord in His deepest hour of need. Yet physical fatigue overcame spiritual alertness.

14:22 *n* 1 Cor. 11:23–25 *o* [1 Pet. 2:24] **14:26** *p* Matt. 26:30 **14:27** *q* Matt. 26:31–35 *r* Zech. 13:7 **14:28** *s* Mark 16:7 **14:29** *t* John 13:37, 38 **14:32** *u* Luke 22:40–46 **14:33** *v* Mark 5:37; 9:2; 13:3 **14:34** *w* John 12:27 **14:36** *x* Gal. 4:6 *y* [Heb. 5:7] *z* John 5:30; 6:38 **14:38** *a* Luke 21:36 *b* [Rom. 7:18, 21–24] **14:41** *c* John 13:1; 17:1 **14:42** *d* John 13:21; 18:1, 2

Betrayal and Arrest in Gethsemane

43ᵉAnd immediately, while He was still speaking, Judas, one of the twelve, with a great multitude with swords and clubs, came from the chief priests and the scribes and the elders. 44Now His betrayer had given them a signal, saying, "Whomever I ƒkiss, He is the One; seize Him and lead *Him* away safely."

45As soon as he had come, immediately he went up to Him and said to Him, "Rabbi, Rabbi!" and kissed Him.

46Then they laid their hands on Him and took Him. 47And one of those who stood by drew his sword and struck the servant of the high priest, and cut off his ear.

48ᵍThen Jesus answered and said to them, "Have you come out, as against a robber, with swords and clubs to take Me? 49I was daily with you in the temple ʰteaching, and you did not seize Me. But ⁱthe Scriptures must be fulfilled."

50ʲThen they all forsook Him and fled.

A Young Man Flees Naked

51Now a certain young man followed Him, having a linen cloth thrown around *his* naked *body*. And the young men laid hold of him, 52and he left the linen cloth and fled from them naked.

Jesus Faces the Sanhedrin

53ᵏAnd they led Jesus away to the high priest; and with him were ˡassembled all the ᵐchief priests, the elders, and the scribes. 54But ⁿPeter followed Him at a distance, right into the courtyard of the high priest. And he sat with the servants and warmed himself at the fire.

55ᵒNow the chief priests and all the council sought testimony against Jesus to put Him to death, but found none. 56For many bore ᵖfalse witness against Him, but their testimonies did not agree.

57Then some rose up and bore false witness against Him, saying, 58"We heard Him say, ᵠ'I will destroy this temple made with hands, and within three days I will build another made without hands.'" 59But not even then did their testimony agree.

60ʳAnd the high priest stood up in the midst and asked Jesus, saying, "Do You answer nothing? What *is it* these men testify against You?" 61But ˢHe kept silent and answered nothing.

ᵗAgain the high priest asked Him, saying to Him, "Are You the Christ, the Son of the Blessed?"

62Jesus said, "I am. ᵘAnd you will see the Son of Man sitting at the right hand of the Power, and coming with the clouds of heaven."

63Then the high priest tore his clothes and said, "What further need do we have of witnesses? 64You have heard the ᵛblasphemy! What do you think?"

And they all condemned Him to be deserving of ʷdeath.

65Then some began to ˣspit on Him, and to blindfold Him, and to beat Him, and to say to Him, "Prophesy!" And the officers struck Him with the palms of their hands.*

Peter Denies Jesus, and Weeps

66ʸNow as Peter was below in the courtyard, one of the servant girls of the high priest came. 67And when she saw Peter warming himself, she looked at him and said, "You also were with ᶻJesus of Nazareth."

68But he denied it, saying, "I neither know nor understand what you are saying." And he went out on the porch, and a rooster crowed.

69ᵃAnd the servant girl saw him again, and began to say to those who stood by, "This is *one* of them." 70But he denied it again.

ᵇAnd a little later those who stood by said to Peter again, "Surely you are *one* of them; ᶜfor you are a Galilean, and your speech shows *it*."*

71Then he began to curse and swear, "I do not know this Man of whom you speak!"

72ᵈA second time *the* rooster crowed. Then Peter called to mind the word that Jesus had said to him, "Before the rooster crows twice, you will deny Me three times." And when he thought about it, he wept.

---

* **14:65** NU-Text reads *received Him with slaps.*
* **14:70** NU-Text omits *and your speech shows it.*

14:43 with a great multitude. Judas came with a detachment of troops (John 18:3). It was one-tenth of a Roman legion or roughly 600 men.

14:50–52 young man. Only Mark tells of this incident and many believe that this young man was Mark himself. How else would he have known this story, and why else should he have included it? If it was Mark, and if the Last Supper was at his home that evening, he could easily have risen from bed, pulled on a linen sheet, and followed the disciples.

14:61 He kept silent. Jesus remained silent before Pilate and Herod Antipas. Finally they could find nothing substantial with which to charge Him. **the Christ, the Son of the Blessed.** The trial was over, and Jesus stood falsely condemned for blasphemy, which in this context means laying claim to deity. Naturally,

this is the boast of a liar or a lunatic—unless He is the Almighty God in human flesh, as Jesus was (Phil. 2:5–8; 1 John 1:1–3).

14:71–72 the rooster crowed. We are not told that Peter thought at all about Jesus' words. If he did,

14:43 ᵉLuke 22:47–53 **14:44** ƒ[Prov. 27:6]
14:48 ᵍMatt. 26:55 **14:49** ʰIs.
53:7 **14:50** ʲPs. 88:8 **14:53** ᵏMatt. 26:57–68
ˡMark 15:1 ᵐJohn 7:32; 18:3; 19:6 **14:54** ⁿJohn
18:15 **14:55** ᵒMatt. 26:59 **14:56** ᵖEx. 20:16
14:58 ᵠJohn 2:19 **14:60** ʳMatt. 26:62 **14:61** ˢIs. 53:7
ᵗLuke 22:67–71 **14:62** ᵘLuke 22:69 **14:64** ᵛJohn
10:33, 36 ʷJohn 19:7 **14:65** ˣIs. 50:6; 52:14
14:66 ʸJohn 18:16–18, 25–27 **14:67** ᶻJohn 1:45
14:69 ᵃMatt. 26:71 **14:70** ᵇLuke 22:59 ᶜActs 2:7
14:72 ᵈMatt. 26:75

Jesus Faces Pilate

15 Immediately, *a*in the morning, the chief priests held a consultation with the elders and scribes and the whole council; and they bound Jesus, led *Him* away, and *b*delivered *Him* to Pilate. 2*c*Then Pilate asked Him, "Are You the King of the Jews?"

He answered and said to him, "*It is as you say.*"

3And the chief priests accused Him of many things, but He *d*answered nothing. 4*e*Then Pilate asked Him again, saying, "Do You answer nothing? See how many things they testify against You!"* 5*f*But Jesus still answered nothing, so that Pilate marveled.

Taking the Place of Barabbas

6Now *g*at the feast he was accustomed to releasing one prisoner to them, whomever they requested. 7And there was one named Barabbas, *who was* chained with his fellow rebels; they had committed murder in the rebellion. 8Then the multitude, crying aloud,* began to ask *him to do* just as he had always done for them. 9But Pilate answered them, saying, "Do you want me to release to you the King of the Jews?" 10For he knew that the chief priests had handed Him over because of envy.

11But *h*the chief priests stirred up the crowd, so that he should rather release Barabbas to them. 12Pilate answered and said to them again, "What then do you want me to do *with Him* whom you call the *i*King of the Jews?"

13So they cried out again, "Crucify Him!"

14Then Pilate said to them, "Why, *j*what evil has He done?"

But they cried out all the more, "Crucify Him!"

15*k*So Pilate, wanting to gratify the crowd, released Barabbas to them; and he delivered Jesus, after he had scourged *Him,* to be *l*crucified.

The Soldiers Mock Jesus

16*m*Then the soldiers led Him away into the hall called Praetorium, and they called together the whole garrison. 17And they clothed Him with purple; and they twisted a crown of thorns, put it on His head, 18and began to salute Him, "Hail, King of the Jews!" 19Then they *n*struck Him on the head with a reed and spat on Him; and bowing the knee, they worshiped Him. 20And when they had *o*mocked Him, they took the purple off Him, put His own clothes on Him, and led Him out to crucify Him.

The King on a Cross

21*p*Then they compelled a certain man, Simon a Cyrenian, the father of Alexander and Rufus, as he was coming out of the country and passing by, to bear His cross. 22*q*And they brought Him to the place Golgotha, which is translated, Place of a Skull. 23*r*Then they gave Him wine mingled with myrrh to drink, but He did not take *it.* 24And when they crucified Him, *s*they divided His garments, casting lots for them *to determine* what every man should take.

25Now *t*it was the third hour, and they crucified Him. 26And *u*the inscription of His accusation was written above:

THE KING OF THE JEWS.

27*v*With Him they also crucified two robbers, one on His right and the other on His left. 28So the Scripture was fulfilled* which says, *w"And He was numbered with the transgressors."*

29And *x*those who passed by blasphemed Him, *y*wagging their heads and saying, "Aha! *z*You who destroy the temple and build *it* in three days, 30save Yourself, and come down from the cross!"

* **15:4** NU-Text reads *of which they accuse You.*
* **15:8** NU-Text reads *going up.*   * **15:28** Isaiah 53:12 ● NU-Text omits this verse.

---

maybe he tried to conceal his identity more carefully, but to no avail. Each of the other Gospel writers tells us that the cock crowed immediately upon Peter's final denial (Matt. 26:74; Luke 22:60; John 18:27). This time he thought about it, and he wept.

15:1–3 *held a consultation.* Rather than murdering Jesus privately, the Jewish politicians decided to seek Pilate's approval so they could execute the "blasphemer" legally. Their charges included many things but apparently centered on treason. Jesus claimed to be a king, thus defying Caesar (Luke 23:2). This crime was punishable in the Roman Empire by death. Pilate must have concluded that the charges against Jesus were groundless, for Mark tells us he desired to release Him.

15:15 *after he had scourged Him.* This word, used only twice in the New Testament (Matt. 27:26 and here), describes a punishment more severe than flogging or beating. The prisoner was beaten with a whip fashioned of numerous strips of leather attached to a handle. To the leather strips were tied sharp pieces of

bone and metal, which could rip and tear one's skin to shreds.

15:22 *Golgotha* is an Aramaic word. The hill may have resembled the bony features of a skull or was called this because it was a place of death. The name Calvary comes from the Latin word for skull.

15:25 *the third hour.* This was 9 A.M., using a common Jewish system of marking the day. Jesus suffered on the cross until at least 3 P.M., the ninth hour of verse 34.

15:1 *a* Ps. 2:2   *b* Acts 3:13   **15:2** *c* Matt. 27:11–14   **15:3** *d* John 19:9   **15:4** *e* Matt. 27:13   **15:5** *f* Is. 53:7   **15:6** *g* Matt. 27:15–26   **15:11** *h* Acts 3:14   **15:12** *i* Mic. 5:2   **15:14** *j* 1 Pet. 2:21–23   **15:15** *k* Matt. 27:26   *l* [Is. 53:8]   **15:16** *m* Matt. 27:27–31   **15:19** *n* [Is. 50:6; 52:14; 53:5]   **15:20** *o* Luke 22:63; 23:11   **15:21** *p* Matt. 27:32   **15:22** *q* John 19:17–24   **15:23** *r* Matt. 27:34   **15:24** *s* Ps. 22:18   **15:25** *t* John 19:14   **15:26** *u* Matt. 27:37   **15:27** *v* Luke 22:37   **15:28** *w* Is. 53:12   **15:29** *x* Ps. 22:6, 7; 69:7   *y* Ps. 109:25   *z* John 2:19–21

[31]Likewise the chief priests also, [a]mocking among themselves with the scribes, said, "He saved [b]others; Himself He cannot save. [32]Let the Christ, the King of Israel, descend now from the cross, that we may see and believe."*

Even [c]those who were crucified with Him reviled Him.

Jesus Dies on the Cross

[33]Now [d]when the sixth hour had come, there was darkness over the whole land until the ninth hour. [34]And at the ninth hour Jesus cried out with a loud voice, saying, "Eloi, Eloi, lama sabachthani?" which is translated, [e]"My God, My God, why have You forsaken Me?"*

[35]Some of those who stood by, when they heard that, said, "Look, He is calling for Elijah!" [36]Then [f]someone ran and filled a sponge full of sour wine, put it on a reed, and [g]offered it to Him to drink, saying, "Let Him alone; let us see if Elijah will come to take Him down."

[37h]And Jesus cried out with a loud voice, and breathed His last.

[38]Then [i]the veil of the temple was torn in two from top to bottom. [39]So [j]when the centurion, who stood opposite Him, saw that He cried out like this and breathed His last,* he said, "Truly this Man was the Son of God!"

[40k]There were also women looking on [l]from afar, among whom were Mary Magdalene, Mary the mother of James the Less and of Joses, and Salome, [41]who also [m]followed Him and ministered to Him when He was in Galilee, and many other women who came up with Him to Jerusalem.

Jesus Buried in Joseph's Tomb

[42n]Now when evening had come, because it was the Preparation Day, that is, the day before the Sabbath, [43]Joseph of Arimathea, a prominent council member, who [o]was himself waiting for the kingdom of God, coming and taking courage, went in to Pilate and asked for the body of Jesus. [44]Pilate marveled that He was already dead; and summoning the centurion, he asked him if He had been dead for some time. [45]So when he found out from the centurion, [p]he granted the body to Joseph. [46q]Then he bought fine linen, took Him down, and wrapped Him in the linen. And he laid Him in a tomb which had been hewn out of the rock, and rolled a stone against the door of the tomb. [47]And Mary Magdalene and Mary the mother of Joses observed where He was laid.

He Is Risen

16 Now [a]when the Sabbath was past, Mary Magdalene, Mary the mother of James, and Salome [b]bought spices, that they might come and anoint Him. [2c]Very early in the morning, on the first day of the week, they came to the tomb when the sun had risen. [3]And they said among themselves, "Who will roll away the stone from the door of the tomb for us?" [4]But when they looked up, they saw that the stone had been rolled away—for it was very large. [5d]And entering the tomb, they saw a young man clothed in a long white robe sitting on the right side; and they were alarmed.

[6e]But he said to them, "Do not be alarmed. You seek Jesus of Nazareth, who was crucified. He is risen! He is not here. See the place where they laid Him. [7]But go, tell his disciples—and Peter—that He is going before you into Galilee; there you will see Him, [f]as He said to you."

---

* **15:32** M-Text reads *believe Him.*   * **15:34** Psalm 22:1   * **15:39** NU-Text reads *that He thus breathed His last.*

15:32 *Let the Christ.* Jesus was mockingly called the Christ or Messiah by the chief priests and scribes. Their offer to believe in Christ if He would descend from the cross was not believable.

15:37 *Jesus cried out with a loud voice.* Frequently, crucifixion produced a coma or unconsciousness prior to death, but Jesus was in control of all His faculties until the moment when He voluntarily gave up His life (John 10:17–18).

15:38 *the veil of the temple.* The significance of this event is that access to God is now open to all. No longer through priests and the blood of bulls and goats do we approach God, but through the torn veil, which also symbolizes Jesus' broken and torn body (Heb. 10:20).

15:40–41 *There were also women looking on.* These women were true disciples of Christ. They had ministered to Jesus' needs and would be the first witnesses of His resurrection. Mark does not name Jesus' mother here but includes other prominent women. Three Marys were present along with many other women and Salome. She was the mother of the disciples James and John (Matt. 27:56).

15:43 *Joseph of Arimathea.* He is identified as a prominent member of the Sanhedrin. To ask Pilate for the body of Jesus was not just a gesture of kindness. It was an act of bravery, which placed Joseph in opposition to the Sanhedrin and identified him as a follower of Jesus.

16:5–6 *a young man . . . sitting on the right side.* Mark does not identify the young man with the robe as an angel, but he is there to explain the mystery

15:31 [a] Luke 18:32 [b] John 11:43, 44   **15:32** [c] Matt. 27:44   **15:33** [d] Luke 23:44–49   **15:34** [e] Ps. 22:1   **15:36** [f] John 19:29   [g] Ps. 69:21   **15:37** [h] Matt. 27:50   **15:38** [i] Ex. 26:31–33   **15:39** [j] Luke 23:47   **15:40** [k] Matt. 27:55   [l] Ps. 38:11   **15:41** [m] Luke 8:2, 3   **15:42** [n] John 19:38–42   **15:43** [o] Luke 2:25, 38; 23:51   **15:45** [p] Is. 53:9, 12   **15:46** [q] Matt. 27:59, 60   **16:1** [a] John 20:1–8   [b] Luke 23:56   **16:2** [c] Luke 24:1   **16:5** [d] John 20:11, 12   **16:6** [e] Matt. 28:6   **16:7** [f] Matt. 26:32; 28:16, 17

8So they went out quickly* and fled from the tomb, for they trembled and were amazed. gAnd they said nothing to anyone, for they were afraid.

Mary Magdalene Sees the Risen Lord

9Now when *He* rose early on the first *day* of the week, He appeared first to Mary Magdalene, hout of whom He had cast seven demons. 10iShe went and told those who had been with Him, as they mourned and wept. 11jAnd when they heard that He was alive and had been seen by her, they did not believe.

Jesus Appears to Two Disciples

12After that, He appeared in another form kto two of them as they walked and went into the country. 13And they went and told *it* to the rest, *but* they did not believe them either.

The Great Commission

14lLater He appeared to the eleven as they sat at the table; and He rebuked their unbelief and hardness of heart, because they did not believe those who had seen

Him after He had risen. 15mAnd He said to them, "Go into all the world nand preach the gospel to every creature. 16oHe who believes and is baptized will be saved; pbut he who does not believe will be condemned. 17And these qsigns will follow those who believe: rIn My name they will cast out demons; sthey will speak with new tongues; 18tthey* will take up serpents; and if they drink anything deadly, it will by no means hurt them; uthey will lay hands on the sick, and they will recover."

Christ Ascends to God's Right Hand

19So then, vafter the Lord had spoken to them, He was wreceived up into heaven, and xsat down at the right hand of God. 20And they went out and preached everywhere, the Lord working with *them* yand confirming the word through the accompanying signs. Amen.*

* **16:8** NU-Text and M-Text omit *quickly.*
* **16:18** NU-Text reads *and in their hands they will.*
* **16:20** Verses 9–20 are bracketed in NU-Text as not original. They are lacking in Codex Sinaiticus and Codex Vaticanus, although nearly all other manuscripts of Mark contain them.

---

that confronts the women. *He is risen.* In the passive voice, this indicates that an act of God accomplished the raising up of Jesus.
16:9–20 *Now when He rose.* The authenticity of these last twelve verses has been disputed. Those who doubt Mark's authorship of this passage point to two fourth-century manuscripts that omit these verses. Others believe that they should be included because even these two manuscripts leave space for all or some of these verses, indicating that their copyists knew of their existence. The difficulty is in knowing whether the space is for this longer version of Mark's ending or for one of the alternate endings found in the manuscripts. Important early church fathers endorsed this passage, and it does not seem likely that Mark would end his story on a note of fear (v. 8).

16:14 *to the eleven.* After Judas' demise (Matt. 27:3–5; Acts 1:16–18), the disciples were known for a while as the eleven. Jesus upbraided these disciples for not believing the accounts of eyewitnesses, but He pronounced a blessing on "those who have not seen and yet have believed" (John 20:29).
16:19 *He was received up into heaven.* This was the final sign that Jesus was the Son of God.

16:8 g Matt. 28:8   **16:9** h Luke 8:2   **16:10** i Luke 24:10   **16:11** j Luke 24:11, 41   **16:12** k Luke 24:13–35   **16:14** l 1 Cor. 15:5   **16:15** m Matt. 28:19   n [Col. 1:23]   **16:16** o [John 3:18, 36]   p [John 12:48]   **16:17** q Acts 5:12   r Luke 10:17   s [Acts 2:4]   **16:18** t Acts 28:3–6   u James 5:14   **16:19** v Acts 1:2, 3   w Luke 9:51; 24:51   x [Ps. 110:1]   **16:20** y [Heb. 2:4]

THE GOSPEL ACCORDING TO
LUKE

▶ **AUTHOR:** It is evident from the prologues to Luke and Acts (1:1–4; Acts 1:1–5) that both books were addressed to a man called Theophilus as a two-volume work. Acts begins with a summary of Luke and continues the story from where the Gospel of Luke concludes. Luke may have been a Hellenistic Jew, but it is more likely that he was a Gentile (this would make him the only Gentile contributor to the New Testament). It has been suggested that Luke may have been a Greek physician in a Roman family who at some point was set free and given Roman citizenship. Luke was not an eyewitness of the events in his Gospel, but he relied on the testimony of apostolic eyewitnesses and reliable written sources.

▶ **TIME:** c. 4 B.C.–A.D. 33   ▶ **KEY VERSE:** Luke 19:10

▶ **THEME:** The beginning of Luke makes reference to the fact that there was a great deal of oral tradition concerning Jesus circulating during the first century. The rapid growth of the church (over 3,000 on the Day of Pentecost alone) meant that there would have been potential for significant variety in stories about Jesus. Luke's stated agenda is reliability. Where Matthew goes to great lengths to tie Jesus' story to the history of the Jews, Luke is more interested in where the story fits in the history of the human race. Throughout the book, Christ reaches out to people from a variety of social strata, nationalities, and cultures. Luke sees Jesus as the Savior of the whole world.

Dedication to Theophilus

1 Inasmuch as many have taken in hand to set in order a narrative of those ᵃthings which have been fulfilled* among us, ²just as those who ᵇfrom the beginning were ᶜeyewitnesses and ministers of the word ᵈdelivered them to us, ³it seemed good to me also, having had perfect understanding of all things from the very first, to write to you an orderly account, ᵉmost excellent Theophilus, ⁴ᶠthat you may know the certainty of those things in which you were instructed.

John's Birth Announced to Zacharias

⁵There was ᵍin the days of Herod, the king of Judea, a certain priest named Zacharias, ʰof the division of ⁱAbijah. His ʲwife *was* of the daughters of Aaron, and her name *was* Elizabeth. ⁶And they were both righteous before God, walking in all the commandments and ordinances of the Lord blameless. ⁷But they had no child, because Elizabeth was barren, and they were both well advanced in years.

* 1:1 Or *are most surely believed*

1:1 *many have taken in hand to set in order.* Luke makes it clear that he was not the first to write a narrative of the ministry of Jesus.

1:2 *eyewitnesses.* These verses suggest that Luke was not an eyewitness to the events of Jesus' ministry, but that he had access to statements of those who were.

1:3 *orderly account.* Luke gave his narrative a basic structure. Not every part is in chronological sequence, but the broad sequence is Christ's ministry in Galilee, His travel to Jerusalem, and His struggles in Jerusalem. The order of events shows how Jesus gradually revealed Himself and how opposition to Him grew.

1:4 *the certainty.* Theophilus was likely a young Gentile believer. He not only needed to know the truth and accuracy of what the church taught, but he also

needed to be reassured. He might well have been wondering what he as a Gentile was doing in a movement which was originally Jewish.

1:5 *Herod.* He was appointed by the Roman emperor and reigned over Judea, Samaria, Galilee, Perea, and Syria from 37 to 4 B.C.

1:7 *Elizabeth was barren.* Being childless was a grave disappointment in ancient Israel (1 Sam. 1). The Scriptures record a number of times when God blessed a barren woman by giving her a son (Gen. 18:11; 21:2).

1:1 ᵃ John 20:31   1:2 ᵇ Acts 1:21, 22   ᶜ Acts 1:2   ᵈ Heb. 2:3
1:3 ᵉ Acts 1:1   1:4 ᶠ [John 20:31]   1:5 ᵍ Matt. 2:1   ʰ 1 Chr.
24:1, 10   ⁱ Neh. 12:4   ʲ Lev. 21:13, 14

8So it was, that while he was serving as priest before God in the order of his division, 9according to the custom of the priesthood, his lot fell kto burn incense when he went into the temple of the Lord. 10lAnd the whole multitude of the people was praying outside at the hour of incense. 11Then an angel of the Lord appeared to him, standing on the right side of mthe altar of incense. 12And when Zacharias saw him, nhe was troubled, and fear fell upon him. 13But the angel said to him, "Do not be afraid, Zacharias, for your prayer is heard; and your wife Elizabeth will bear you a son, and oyou shall call his name John. 14And you will have joy and gladness, and pmany will rejoice at his birth. 15For he will be qgreat in the sight of the Lord, and rshall drink neither wine nor strong drink. He will also be filled with the Holy Spirit, seven from his mother's womb. 16And he will turn many of the children of Israel to the Lord their God. 17tHe will also go before Him in the spirit and power of Elijah, 'to turn the hearts of the fathers to the children,'* and the disobedient to the wisdom of the just, to make ready a people prepared for the Lord."

18And Zacharias said to the angel, u"How shall I know this? For I am an old man, and my wife is well advanced in years."

19And the angel answered and said to him, "I am vGabriel, who stands in the presence of God, and was sent to speak to you and bring you these glad wtidings. 20But behold, xyou will be mute and not able to speak until the day these things take place, because you did not believe my words which will be fulfilled in their own time."

21And the people waited for Zacharias, and marveled that he lingered so long in the temple. 22But when he came out, he could not speak to them; and they perceived that he had seen a vision in the temple, for he beckoned to them and remained speechless.

23So it was, as soon as ythe days of his service were completed, that he departed to his own house. 24Now after those days his wife Elizabeth conceived; and she hid herself five months, saying, 25"Thus the Lord has dealt with me, in the days when He looked on me, to ztake away my reproach among people."

Christ's Birth Announced to Mary

26Now in the sixth month the angel Gabriel was sent by God to a city of Galilee named Nazareth, 27to a virgin abetrothed to a man whose name was Joseph, of the house of David. The virgin's name was Mary. 28And having come in, the angel said to her, b"Rejoice, highly favored one, cthe Lord is with you; blessed are you among women!"*

29But when she saw him,* dshe was troubled at his saying, and considered what manner of greeting this was. 30Then the angel said to her, "Do not be afraid, Mary, for you have found efavor with God. 31fAnd behold, you will conceive in your womb and bring forth a Son, and gshall call His name JESUS. 32He will be great, hand will be called the Son of the Highest; and ithe Lord God will give Him the jthrone of His kfather David. 33lAnd He will reign over the house of Jacob forever, and of His kingdom there will be no end."

34Then Mary said to the angel, "How can this be, since I do not know a man?"

---

* 1:17 Malachi 4:5, 6   * 1:28 NU-Text omits *blessed are you among women.*   * 1:29 NU-Text omits *when she saw him.*

1:8–9 the custom of the priesthood. Zacharias served for one week twice a year at the temple, one of perhaps 18,000 priests who served in a year.

1:13 Do not be afraid. Angels often calmed the fears of those to whom they appeared (v. 30; 2:10; Gen. 15:1; Dan. 10:12; Matt. 1:20; Acts 18:9; Rev. 1:17).

1:14 joy and gladness. Joy is a major theme throughout the writings of Luke (vv. 44,47,58; 2:10; 10:20; 13:17; 15:5–7; Acts 5:41).

1:15 shall drink neither wine nor strong drink. As with Samuel and Samson, a vow was imposed on the child that indicated his special consecration to the Lord. **filled with the Holy Spirit.** Being filled with the Spirit means being directed by Him and obedient to Him (Eph. 5:18).

1:17 in the spirit and power of Elijah. John was the forerunner of the Messiah. This description recalls Matthew 3:1–6. John's ministry paralleled Elijah, for both prophets called Israel to repentance (1 Kin. 17:18).

1:19 Gabriel. Two angels are named in the Bible who function as messengers. Michael is the other one (Dan. 8:16; 9:21; 10:13,21; Jude 9; Rev. 12:7).

1:25 my reproach. In ancient Israel barrenness was seen as a cause for shame. The "opening of the womb" indicated God's grace (Gen. 21:6; 30:23; 1 Sam. 1:2). In this verse, Elizabeth praises the Lord for mercifully blessing her even as He moved His plan for all of human history forward.

1:32 the Highest. This phrase is another way of referring to the majesty of God. **David.** Jesus fulfilled God's promise to David concerning an unending dynasty.

1:34 How can this be. Mary did not ask for a sign, so this remark does not reflect unbelief. She accepts her role without question in verse 38, and thus is a model of faith, even though she does not fully understand everything. The work of God in Mary introduces something unknown before or after; the birth into the human race of One who is both God and man.

1:9 k Ex. 30:7, 8   **1:10** l Lev. 16:17   **1:11** m Ex. 30:1   **1:12** n Luke 2:9   **1:13** o Luke 1:57, 60, 63   **1:14** p Luke 1:58   **1:15** q [Luke 7:24–28]   r Num. 6:3   s Jer. 1:5   **1:17** t Mal. 4:5, 6; Matt. 3:2; 11:14   **1:18** u Gen. 17:17   **1:19** v Dan. 8:16   w Luke 2:10   **1:20** x Ezek. 3:26; 24:27   **1:23** y 2 Kin. 11:5   **1:25** z Gen. 30:23   **1:27** a Matt. 1:18   **1:28** b Dan. 9:23   c Judg. 6:12   **1:29** d Luke 1:12   **1:30** e Luke 2:52   **1:31** f Is. 7:14   g Luke 2:21   **1:32** h Mark 5:7   i 2 Sam. 7:12, 13, 16   j 2 Sam. 7:14–17   k Matt. 1:1   **1:33** l [Dan. 2:44]

35And the angel answered and said to her, m"*The* Holy Spirit will come upon you, and the power of the Highest will overshadow you; therefore, also, that Holy One who is to be born will be called nthe Son of God. 36Now indeed, Elizabeth your relative has also conceived a son in her old age; and this is now the sixth month for her who was called barren. 37For owith God nothing will be impossible."

38Then Mary said, "Behold the maidservant of the Lord! Let it be to me according to your word." And the angel departed from her.

Mary Visits Elizabeth

39Now Mary arose in those days and went into the hill country with haste, pto a city of Judah, 40and entered the house of Zacharias and greeted Elizabeth. 41And it happened, when Elizabeth heard the greeting of Mary, that the babe leaped in her womb; and Elizabeth was qfilled with the Holy Spirit. 42Then she spoke out with a loud voice and said, r"Blessed *are* you among women, and blessed *is* the fruit of your womb! 43But why *is* this *granted* to me, that the mother of my Lord should come to me? 44For indeed, as soon as the voice of your greeting sounded in my ears, the babe leaped in my womb for joy. 45sBlessed *is* she who believed, for there will be a fulfillment of those things which were told her from the Lord."

The Song of Mary

46And Mary said:

t"My soul magnifies the Lord,
47   And my spirit has urejoiced in vGod my Savior.
48   For wHe has regarded the lowly state of His maidservant;
     For behold, henceforth xall generations will call me blessed.
49   For He who is mighty yhas done great things for me,
     And zholy *is* His name.
50   And aHis mercy *is* on those who fear Him
     From generation to generation.

51 bHe has shown strength with His arm;
   cHe has scattered *the* proud in the imagination of their hearts.
52 dHe has put down the mighty from *their* thrones,
   And exalted *the* lowly.
53   He has efilled *the* hungry with good things,
     And *the* rich He has sent away empty.
54   He has helped His fservant Israel,
   gIn remembrance of *His* mercy,
55 hAs He spoke to our ifathers,
   To Abraham and to his jseed forever."

56And Mary remained with her about three months, and returned to her house.

Birth of John the Baptist

57Now Elizabeth's full time came for her to be delivered, and she brought forth a son. 58When her neighbors and relatives heard how the Lord had shown great mercy to her, they krejoiced with her.

Circumcision of John the Baptist

59So it was, lon the eighth day, that they came to circumcise the child; and they would have called him by the name of his father, Zacharias. 60His mother answered and said, m"No; he shall be called John." 61But they said to her, "There is no one among your relatives who is called by this name." 62So they made signs to his father— what he would have him called. 63And he asked for a writing tablet, and wrote, saying, "His name is John." So they all marveled. 64Immediately his mouth was opened and his tongue *loosed,* and he spoke, praising God. 65Then fear came on all who dwelt around them; and all these sayings were discussed throughout all the hill country of Judea. 66And all those who heard *them* nkept *them* in their hearts, saying, "What kind of child will this be?" And othe hand of the Lord was with him.

Zacharias' Prophecy

67Now his father Zacharias pwas filled with the Holy Spirit, and prophesied, saying:

1:35 *The Holy Spirit will come upon you.* This is a direct declaration of Jesus' divine conception. The child's conception means He is uniquely set apart.
1:38 *maidservant.* This term suggests humility before the Lord and a readiness for faithful and obedient service, which should characterize every believer. Paul uses the masculine form of this word to describe himself (Rom. 1:1).
1:46 *My soul magnifies the Lord.* The following hymn gets its name, the "Magnificat," from the Latin word for *magnifies.* Mary's hymn is a recital of what God had done for her and for others in the past.
1:48 *all generations will call me blessed.* Mary went from being a poor unknown Hebrew girl to the most honored woman in the history of the world.
1:50 *mercy.* This term expresses the Old Testament concept of God's loyal, gracious, faithful love (Ps. 103).

1:51–53 *He has put down the mighty.* These verses portray a "reversal" in the end times, when those who have abused power will be judged and those who have suffered persecution will be exalted.
1:67 *Zacharias was filled with the Holy Spirit, and prophesied.* The presence of the Holy Spirit enabled

---

1:35 m Matt. 1:20   n [Heb. 1:2, 8]   **1:37** o Jer. 32:17
1:39 p Josh. 21:9   **1:41** q Acts 6:3   **1:42** r Judg. 5:24
1:45 s John 20:29   **1:46** t 1 Sam. 2:1–10   **1:47** u Hab.
3:18   v 1 Tim. 1:1; 2:3   **1:48** w Ps. 138:6   x Luke 11:27
1:49 y Ps. 71:19; 126:2, 3   z Ps. 111:9   **1:50** a Ps. 103:17
1:51 b Ps. 98:1; 118:15   c [1 Pet. 5:5]   **1:52** d 1 Sam.
2:7, 8   **1:53** e [Matt. 5:6]   **1:54** f Is. 41:8   g [Jer. 31:3]
1:55 h Gen. 17:19   i [Rom. 11:28]   j Gen. 17:7   **1:58** k [Rom.
12:15]   **1:59** l Gen. 17:12   **1:60** m Luke 1:13, 63
1:66 n Luke 2:19   o Acts 11:21   **1:67** p Joel 2:28

68 "Blessed[q] *is* the Lord God of Israel,
For [r]He has visited and redeemed His
    people,
69 [s]And has raised up a horn of salvation
    for us
In the house of His servant
    David,
70 [t]As He spoke by the mouth of His holy
    prophets,
Who *have been* [u]since the world
    began,
71 That we should be saved from our
    enemies
And from the hand of all who hate us,
72 [v]To perform the mercy *promised* to our
    fathers
And to remember His holy covenant,
73 [w]The oath which He swore to our father
    Abraham:
74 To grant us that we,
Being delivered from the hand of our
    enemies,
Might [x]serve Him without fear,
75 [y]In holiness and righteousness before
    Him all the days of our life.

76 "And you, child, will be called the
    [z]prophet of the Highest;
For [a]you will go before the face of the
    Lord to prepare His ways,
77 To give [b]knowledge of salvation to His
    people
By the remission of their sins,
78 Through the tender mercy of our God,
With which the Dayspring from on
    high has visited* us;
79 [c]To give light to those who sit in
    darkness and the shadow of
    death,
To [d]guide our feet into the way of
    peace."

80 So [e]the child grew and became strong
in spirit, and [f]was in the deserts till the day
of his manifestation to Israel.

Christ Born of Mary

2 And it came to pass in those days *that*
a decree went out from Caesar Augustus that all the world should be registered. 2[a]This census first took place while
Quirinius was governing Syria. 3So all
went to be registered, everyone to his own
city.
4Joseph also went up from Galilee,
out of the city of Nazareth, into Judea, to
[b]the city of David, which is called Bethlehem, [c]because he was of the house and
lineage of David, 5to be registered with
Mary, [d]his betrothed wife,* who was with
child. 6So it was, that while they were
there, the days were completed for her to
be delivered. 7And [e]she brought forth her
firstborn Son, and wrapped Him in swaddling cloths, and laid Him in a manger,
because there was no room for them in
the inn.

Glory in the Highest

8Now there were in the same country shepherds living out in the fields,
keeping watch over their flock by night.
9And behold,* an angel of the Lord stood
before them, and the glory of the Lord
shone around them, [f]and they were greatly afraid. 10Then the angel said to them,
[g]"Do not be afraid, for behold, I bring
you good tidings of great joy [h]which will
be to all people. 11[i]For there is born to you
this day in the city of David [j]a Savior,
[k]who is Christ the Lord. 12And this *will
be* the sign to you: You will find a Babe
wrapped in swaddling cloths, lying in a
manger."
13[l]And suddenly there was with the angel a multitude of the heavenly host praising God and saying:

---

* **1:78** NU-Text reads *shall visit.* * **2:5** NU-Text
omits *wife.* * **2:9** NU-Text omits *behold.*

Zacharias to announce God's promise. Zacharias's
hymn is called the "Benedictus" from its first word in
the Latin Vulgate translation. There are three types
of prophecy in the Bible: foretelling future events,
forth-telling the Word of God, and praising God.
Zacharias's prophecy includes all three.
1:69 horn of salvation. The horn of an ox is a symbol of power (Deut. 33:17; 1 Sam. 2:10; 2 Sam. 22:3; Ps.
75:4–5,10; 132:17; Ezek. 29:21).
1:77 knowledge of salvation. John's task was to
prepare the people by informing them of their need
to repent (3:1–14) and of the One who was coming
(3:15–18).
1:78 the Dayspring from on high has visited us. This
phrase is a reference to the coming of Messiah (Num.
24:17; Mal. 4:2).
2:1–2 Augustus. This was the Roman emperor from
31 B.C. to A.D. 14. **Quirinius.** Quirinius was the governor or administrator of a major census organized to
facilitate the collection of taxes.
2:3–4 to be registered. The registration, following
Jewish custom, took place at a person's ancestral

home (2 Sam. 24). The journey from Nazareth to Bethlehem was about 90 miles, at least a three-day trip.
2:9 glory. This word refers to evidence of God's
majestic presence, later associated with Jesus (Acts
7:55). In this scene, the glory is the appearance of light
in the midst of darkness.
2:11 Savior, who is Christ the Lord. These three titles
together summarize the saving work of Jesus and His
sovereign position. What God was called in 1:47, Jesus
is called here. The word Christ means "Anointed,"
referring to Jesus' royal, messianic position. The word
Lord was the title of a ruler.

1:68 [q] 1 Kin. 1:48 [r] Ex. 3:16 **1:69** [s] Ps. 132:17
1:70 [t] Rom. 1:2 [u] Acts 3:21 **1:72** [v] Lev. 26:42
1:73 [w] Gen. 12:3; 22:16–18 **1:74** [x] [Heb. 9:14]
1:75 [y] [Eph. 4:24] **1:76** [z] Matt. 3:3; 11:9 [a] Is. 40:3
1:77 [b] [Mark 1:4] **1:79** [c] Is. 9:2 [d] [John 10:4; 14:27;
16:33] **1:80** [e] Luke 2:40 [f] Matt. 3:1 **2:2** [a] Acts
5:37 **2:4** [b] 1 Sam. 16:1 [c] Matt. 1:16 **2:5** [d] [Matt.
1:18] **2:7** [e] Matt. 1:25 **2:9** [f] Luke 1:12 **2:10** [g] Luke
1:13, 30 [h] Gen. 12:3 **2:11** [i] Is. 9:6 [j] Matt. 1:21 [k] Acts 2:36
2:13 [l] Dan. 7:10

14 "Glory[m] to God in the highest,
   And on earth [n]peace, [o]goodwill toward
      men!"*

15So it was, when the angels had gone away from them into heaven, that the shepherds said to one another, "Let us now go to Bethlehem and see this thing that has come to pass, which the Lord has made known to us." 16And they came with haste and found Mary and Joseph, and the Babe lying in a manger. 17Now when they had seen *Him*, they made widely* known the saying which was told them concerning this Child. 18And all those who heard *it* marveled at those things which were told them by the shepherds. 19pBut Mary kept all these things and pondered *them* in her heart. 20Then the shepherds returned, glorifying and qpraising God for all the things that they had heard and seen, as it was told them.

Circumcision of Jesus

21rAnd when eight days were completed for the circumcision of the Child,* His name was called sJESUS, the name given by the angel tbefore He was conceived in the womb.

Jesus Presented in the Temple

22Now when uthe days of her purification according to the law of Moses were completed, they brought Him to Jerusalem to present *Him* to the Lord 23v(as it is written in the law of the Lord, w*"Every male who opens the womb shall be called holy to the LORD"*),* 24and to offer a sacrifice according to what is said in the law of the Lord, x*"A pair of turtledoves or two young pigeons."**

Simeon Sees God's Salvation

25And behold, there was a man in Jerusalem whose name *was* Simeon, and this man *was* just and devout, ywaiting for the Consolation of Israel, and the Holy Spirit was upon him. 26And it had been revealed to him by the Holy Spirit that he would not zsee death before he had seen the Lord's Christ. 27So he came aby the Spirit into the temple. And when the parents brought in the Child Jesus, to do for Him according to the custom of the law, 28he took Him up in his arms and blessed God and said:

29 "Lord, bnow You are letting Your
      servant depart in peace,
   According to Your word;
30 For my eyes chave seen Your salvation
31   Which You have prepared before the
      face of all peoples,
32 dA light to *bring* revelation to the
      Gentiles,
   And the glory of Your people Israel."

33And Joseph and His mother* marveled at those things which were spoken of Him. 34Then Simeon blessed them, and said to Mary His mother, "Behold, this *Child* is destined for the efall and rising of many in Israel, and for fa sign which will be spoken against 35(yes, ga sword will pierce through your own soul also), that the thoughts of many hearts may be revealed."

Anna Bears Witness to the Redeemer

36Now there was one, Anna, a prophetess, the daughter of Phanuel, of the tribe of hAsher. She was of a great age, and had lived with a husband seven years from her virginity; 37and this woman *was* a widow of about eighty-four years,* who did not depart from the temple, but served God with fastings and prayers inight and day. 38And coming in that instant she gave thanks to the Lord,* and spoke of Him to all those who jlooked for redemption in Jerusalem.

The Family Returns to Nazareth

39So when they had performed all things according to the law of the Lord, they returned to Galilee, to their *own* city,

* **2:14** NU-Text reads *toward men of goodwill.*
* **2:17** NU-Text omits *widely.* * **2:21** NU-Text reads *for His circumcision.* * **2:23** Exodus 13:2, 12, 15 * **2:24** Leviticus 12:8 * **2:33** NU-Text reads *And His father and mother.* * **2:37** NU-Text reads *a widow until she was eighty-four.* * **2:38** NU-Text reads *to God.*

2:14 *peace, goodwill toward men.* Peace is not for everyone, but for those who please God.
2:21 *when eight days.* According to the law, a Jewish boy was to be circumcised on his eighth day (Gen. 17:12; Lev. 12:3).
2:25 *Consolation of Israel.* Simeon was waiting for the comforter of Israel, a hope that parallels the hope of national deliverance expressed in the two hymns of chapter one. This deliverance would involve the work of Messiah, as verse 26 suggests.
2:32 *A light to bring revelation to the Gentiles.* This is the first explicit statement in Luke that includes both Jew and Gentile. Salvation is portrayed as light (1:79). It would be a revelation to Gentiles because they would be able to participate in God's blessing with a fullness that had not been revealed in the Old Testament (Eph. 2:11—3:7).

2:36 *there was one, Anna, a prophetess.* Anna's work as a prophetess in the temple court suggests that she addressed all who would listen to her, as did Miriam (Ex. 15:20), Deborah (Judg. 4:4), and Huldah (2 Kin. 22:14).

2:14 m Luke 19:38 n Is. 57:19 o [Eph. 2:4, 7] **2:19** p Gen. 37:11 **2:20** q Luke 19:37 **2:21** r Lev. 12:3 s [Matt. 1:21] t Luke 1:31 **2:22** u Lev. 12:2–8 **2:23** v Deut. 18:4 w Ex. 13:2, 12, 15 **2:24** x Lev. 12:2, 8 **2:25** y Mark 15:43 **2:26** z [Heb. 11:5] **2:27** a Matt. 4:1 **2:29** b Gen. 46:30 **2:30** c [Is. 52:10] **2:32** d Acts 10:45; 13:47; 28:28 **2:34** e [1 Pet. 2:7, 8] f Acts 4:2; 17:32; 28:22 **2:35** g Ps. 42:10 **2:36** h Josh. 19:24 **2:37** i 1 Tim. 5:5 **2:38** j Mark 15:43

Nazareth. [40k]And the Child grew and became strong in spirit,* filled with wisdom; and the grace of God was upon Him.

The Boy Jesus Amazes the Scholars

[41]His parents went to [l]Jerusalem [m]every year at the Feast of the Passover. [42]And when He was twelve years old, they went up to Jerusalem according to the [n]custom of the feast. [43]When they had finished the [o]days, as they returned, the Boy Jesus lingered behind in Jerusalem. And Joseph and His mother* did not know it; [44]but supposing Him to have been in the company, they went a day's journey, and sought Him among their relatives and acquaintances. [45]So when they did not find Him, they returned to Jerusalem, seeking Him. [46]Now so it was that after three days they found Him in the temple, sitting in the midst of the teachers, both listening to them and asking them questions. [47]And [p]all who heard Him were astonished at His understanding and answers. [48]So when they saw Him, they were amazed; and His mother said to Him, "Son, why have You done this to us? Look, Your father and I have sought You anxiously."

[49]And He said to them, "Why did you seek Me? Did you not know that I must be [q]about [r]My Father's business?" [50]But [s]they did not understand the statement which He spoke to them.

Jesus Advances in Wisdom and Favor

[51]Then He went down with them and came to Nazareth, and was subject to them, but His mother [t]kept all these things in her heart. [52]And Jesus [u]increased in wisdom and stature, [v]and in favor with God and men.

John the Baptist Prepares the Way

3 Now in the fifteenth year of the reign of Tiberius Caesar, [a]Pontius Pilate being governor of Judea, Herod being tetrarch of Galilee, his brother Philip tetrarch of Iturea and the region of Trachonitis, and Lysanias tetrarch of Abilene, [2]while [b]Annas and Caiaphas were high priests,* the word of God came to [c]John the son of Zacharias in the wilderness. [3d]And he went into all the region around the Jordan, preaching a baptism of repentance [e]for the remission of sins, [4]as it is written in the book of the words of Isaiah the prophet, saying:

> [f]"The voice of one crying in the wilderness:
> 'Prepare the way of the LORD;
> Make His paths straight.
> 5 Every valley shall be filled
> And every mountain and hill brought low;
> The crooked places shall be made straight
> And the rough ways smooth;
> 6 And [g]all flesh shall see the salvation of God.'"*

John Preaches to the People

[7]Then he said to the multitudes that came out to be baptized by him, [h]"Brood of vipers! Who warned you to flee from the wrath to come? [8]Therefore bear fruits [i]worthy of repentance, and do not begin to say to yourselves, 'We have Abraham as our father.' For I say to you that God is able to raise up children to Abraham from these stones. [9]And even now the ax is laid to the root of the trees. Therefore [j]every tree which does not bear good fruit is cut down and thrown into the fire."

[10]So the people asked him, saying, [k]"What shall we do then?"

[11]He answered and said to them, [l]"He who has two tunics, let him give to him who has none; and he who has food, [m]let him do likewise."

---

* **2:40** NU-Text omits in spirit. * **2:43** NU-Text reads And His parents. * **3:2** NU-Text and M-Text read in the high priesthood of Annas and Caiaphas. * **3:6** Isaiah 40:3–5

2:41 to Jerusalem every year. The annual pilgrimage to Jerusalem was customary for many who lived outside the city. The laws commanded three pilgrimages for the men each year: Passover, Pentecost, and the Feast of Tabernacles (Ex. 23:14–17; Deut. 16:16).
2:49 I must be about My Father's business. This is the first indication in Luke's Gospel that Jesus knew He had a unique mission and a unique relationship to the Father.
3:1–2 Tiberius Caesar . . . Pontius Pilate . . . Herod . . . Annas . . . Caiaphas. The various rulers that Luke lists show the complexity of the historical and political situation in Israel during Jesus' day. A first-century Israelite had to deal with the edicts of the Roman emperor, the regulations of the governor over Israel, and the judgments of the religious leaders of Israel.
3:4–6 Prepare the way of the LORD. This citation from Isaiah 40:3–5 declares the coming of God's deliverance. Luke cites the text more fully than Matthew or Mark. He carries the passage through to its mention of salvation being seen by all flesh (v. 6), thus highlighting that the gospel is for all people. The preparation for the arrival of a king typically meant that a road was prepared for his journey. This is what Isaiah compares to the arrival of God's salvation.
3:8 Therefore bear fruits. John the Baptist warned that the fruits of repentance are necessary, not the claim of an ancestral connection to Abraham. External genealogical connections would not change one's attitude to God.
3:11 two tunics. One was an undergarment, and the

2:40 [k] Luke 1:80; 2:52   **2:41** [l] John 4:20 [m] Deut. 16:1, 16   **2:42** [n] Ex. 23:14, 15   **2:43** [o] Ex. 12:15   **2:47** [p] Matt. 7:28; 13:54; 22:33   **2:49** [q] John 9:4 [r] [Luke 4:22, 32]   **2:50** [s] John 7:15, 46   **2:51** [t] Dan. 7:28   **2:52** [u] [Col. 2:2, 3] [v] 1 Sam. 2:26   **3:1** [a] Matt. 27:2   **3:2** [b] Acts 4:6 [c] Luke 1:13   **3:3** [d] Mark 1:4 [e] Luke 1:77   **3:4** [f] Is. 40:3–5   **3:6** [g] Is. 52:10   **3:7** [h] Matt. 3:7; 12:34; 23:33   **3:8** [i] [2 Cor. 7:9–11]   **3:9** [j] Matt. 7:19   **3:10** [k] [Acts 2:37, 38; 16:30, 31]   **3:11** [l] 2 Cor. 8:14 [m] Is. 58:7

[12]Then [n]tax collectors also came to be baptized, and said to him, "Teacher, what shall we do?"

[13]And he said to them, [o]"Collect no more than what is appointed for you."

[14]Likewise the soldiers asked him, saying, "And what shall we do?"

So he said to them, "Do not intimidate anyone [p]or accuse falsely, and be content with your wages."

[15]Now as the people were in expectation, and all reasoned in their hearts about John, whether he was the Christ or not, [16]John answered, saying to all, [q]"I indeed baptize you with water; but One mightier than I is coming, whose sandal strap I am not worthy to loose. He will [r]baptize you with the Holy Spirit and fire. [17]His winnowing fan is in His hand, and He will thoroughly clean out His threshing floor, and [s]gather the wheat into His barn; but the chaff He will burn with unquenchable fire."

[18]And with many other exhortations he preached to the people. [19t]But Herod the tetrarch, being rebuked by him concerning Herodias, his brother Philip's wife,* and for all the evils which Herod had done, [20]also added this, above all, that he shut John up in prison.

John Baptizes Jesus

[21]When all the people were baptized, [u]it came to pass that Jesus also was baptized; and while He prayed, the heaven was opened. [22]And the Holy Spirit descended in bodily form like a dove upon Him, and a voice came from heaven which said, "You are My beloved Son; in You I am [v]well pleased."

The Genealogy of Jesus Christ

[23]Now Jesus Himself began His ministry at [w]about thirty years of age, being (as was supposed) [x]the son of Joseph, the son of Heli, [24]the son of Matthat,* the son of

Levi, the son of Melchi, the son of Janna, the son of Joseph, [25]the son of Mattathiah, the son of Amos, the son of Nahum, the son of Esli, the son of Naggai, [26]the son of Maath, the son of Mattathiah, the son of Semei, the son of Joseph, the son of Judah, [27]the son of Joannas, the son of Rhesa, the son of [y]Zerubbabel, the son of Shealtiel, the son of Neri, [28]the son of Melchi, the son of Addi, the son of Cosam, the son of Elmodam, the son of Er, [29]the son of Jose, the son of Eliezer, the son of Jorim, the son of Matthat, the son of Levi, [30]the son of Simeon, the son of Judah, the son of Joseph, the son of Jonan, the son of Eliakim, [31]the son of Melea, the son of Menan, the son of Mattathah, the son of [z]Nathan, [a]the son of David, [32b]the son of Jesse, the son of Obed, the son of Boaz, the son of Salmon, the son of Nahshon, [33]the son of Amminadab, the son of Ram, the son of Hezron, the son of Perez, the son of Judah, [34]the son of Jacob, the son of Isaac, the son of Abraham, [c]the son of Terah, the son of Nahor, [35]the son of Serug, the son of Reu, the son of Peleg, the son of Eber, the son of Shelah, [36d]the son of Cainan, the son of [e]Arphaxad, [f]the son of Shem, the son of Noah, the son of Lamech, [37]the son of Methuselah, the son of Enoch, the son of Jared, the son of Mahalalel, the son of Cainan, [38]the son of Enosh, the son of Seth, the son of Adam, [g]the son of God.

Satan Tempts Jesus

4 Then [a]Jesus, being filled with the Holy Spirit, returned from the Jordan and [b]was led by the Spirit into* the wilderness,

---

* **3:19** NU-Text reads his brother's wife.
* **3:24** This and several other names in the genealogy are spelled somewhat differently in the NU-Text. Since the New King James Version uses the Old Testament spelling for persons mentioned in the New Testament, these variations, which come from the Greek, have not been footnoted.
* **4:1** NU-Text reads in.

---

other was an outer garment. A person did not need two when another person had none.

3:12 tax collectors. These men were Jewish agents employed by those who had purchased the right to collect taxes for the Roman state. They often added interest to cover their own expenses and to pad their income. They were disliked both for their business practices and for their support of the occupying state.

3:16–17 the Holy Spirit and fire. These two facets of Christ's work relate to His first and second comings. As a result of Christ's work at His first coming, believers are placed into one family (1 Cor. 12:13) and commended to the care of the Holy Spirit. When Christ comes a second time, He will come with the fire of judgment. **winnowing fan.** This tool was a wooden forklike shovel that lifted the grain in the air so that the wind could separate it from the chaff.

3:19–20 all the evils which Herod had done. Herod had divorced his wife to marry his own niece Herodias, who already had been the wife of his brother

Philip. Not only was the divorce a problem, so was marrying such a close relative (Lev. 18:16; 20:21).

3:22 You are My beloved Son; in You I am well pleased. This statement combines two ideas. The idea of God's Son comes from Psalm 2:7, a psalm about God's chosen King. The idea of pleasure comes from the image of the Servant in Isaiah 42:1. The fact that Jesus is both King and Servant is fundamental to Jesus' identity.

4:1–13 Temptation of Christ—Hebrews 2:18 makes the point that, because Christ was tempted, He is able to help those who are being tempted. We can see two

3:12 [n] Luke 7:29   **3:13** [o] Luke 19:8   **3:14** [p] Ex. 20:16; 23:1   **3:16** [q] Matt. 3:11, 12   [r] John 7:39; 20:22   **3:17** [s] Matt. 13:24–30   **3:19** [t] Mark 6:17   **3:21** [u] Matt. 3:13–17   **3:22** [v] 2 Pet. 1:17   **3:23** [w] [Num. 4:3, 35, 39, 43, 47]   [x] John 6:42   [y] Ezra 2:2; 3:8   **3:31** [z] Zech. 12:12   [a] 2 Sam. 5:14; 7:12   **3:32** [b] Ruth 4:18–22   **3:34** [c] Gen. 11:24, 26–30; 12:3   **3:36** [d] Gen. 11:12   [e] Gen. 10:22, 24; 11:10–13   [f] Gen. 5:6–32; 9:27; 11:10   **3:38** [g] Gen. 5:1, 2   **4:1** [a] Matt. 4:1–11   [b] Luke 2:27

2being tempted for forty days by the devil. And cin those days He ate nothing, and afterward, when they had ended, He was hungry.

3And the devil said to Him, "If You are dthe Son of God, command this stone to become bread."

4But Jesus answered him, saying,* "It is written, e'Man shall not live by bread alone, but by every word of God.' "*

5Then the devil, taking Him up on a high mountain, showed Him* all the kingdoms of the world in a moment of time. 6And the devil said to Him, "All this authority I will give You, and their glory; for fthis has been delivered to me, and I give it to whomever I wish. 7Therefore, if You will worship before me, all will be Yours."

8And Jesus answered and said to him, "Get behind Me, Satan!* For* it is written, g'You shall worship the LORD your God, and Him only you shall serve.' "*

9hThen he brought Him to Jerusalem, set Him on the pinnacle of the temple, and said to Him, "If You are the Son of God, throw Yourself down from here. 10For it is written:

> i'He shall give His angels charge over
>   you,
>   To keep you,'

11and,

> j'In their hands they shall bear you up,
>   Lest you dash your foot against a
>   stone.' "*

12And Jesus answered and said to him, "It has been said, k'You shall not tempt the LORD your God.' "*

13Now when the devil had ended every temptation, he departed from Him luntil an opportune time.

Jesus Begins His Galilean Ministry

14mThen Jesus returned nin the power of the Spirit to oGalilee, and pnews of Him went out through all the surrounding region. 15And He qtaught in their synagogues, rbeing glorified by all.

Jesus Rejected at Nazareth

16So He came to sNazareth, where He had been brought up. And as His custom was, tHe went into the synagogue on the Sabbath day, and stood up to read. 17And He was handed the book of the prophet Isaiah. And when He had opened the book, He found the place where it was written:

18 "Theu Spirit of the LORD is upon Me,
    Because He has anointed Me
    To preach the gospel to the poor;
    He has sent Me to heal the
      brokenhearted,*
    To proclaim liberty to the captives
    And recovery of sight to the blind,
    To vset at liberty those who are
      oppressed;
19 To proclaim the acceptable year of the
    LORD."*

---

* **4:4** Deuteronomy 8:3 • NU-Text omits *but by every word of God.* * **4:5** NU-Text reads *And taking Him up, he showed Him.* * **4:8** NU-Text omits *Get behind Me, Satan.* • NU-Text and NU-Text omit *For.* • Deuteronomy 6:13 * **4:11** Psalm 91:11, 12 * **4:12** Deuteronomy 6:16 * **4:18** NU-Text omits *to heal the brokenhearted.* * **4:19** Isaiah 61:1, 2

---

examples of this quite plainly. The temptations are about security and power. In becoming man, Jesus gave up both (Phil. 2:5–11). Jesus didn't cling to any of what was by nature and identity rightfully His. In doing so, He had to trust fully in the Father for His life and very being. He can truly identify with our temptations. His experience wasn't just like ours are. No one ever gave up more power. No one of greater stature has ever been in such an insecure position. He can be there for us because He has been there before us.

4:3 If You are the Son of God. This is a conditional statement. In other words, Satan was saying: "Let's assume for the sake of argument that You are the Son of God." In fact, Satan was challenging Jesus' identity and authority.

4:4 It is written. Jesus responded to Satan's temptation by quoting Deuteronomy 8:3. Jesus refused to operate independently of God. The Spirit had led Him into the wilderness to prepare Him for His ministry, so eating at Satan's instruction would have shown a lack of dependence on the Father.

4:5 all the kingdoms of the world. This temptation was an attempt to offer Jesus power by the wrong means. Satan's method involved a detour around the cross, an inducement to "take the easy way" to power.

4:10–11 He shall give His angels charge over you, to keep you. Satan cited Psalm 91:11–12, reminding Jesus of God's promise of protection. However, the

mere use of biblical words does not always reveal God's will, particularly if they are placed in the wrong context.

4:12 You shall not tempt the LORD your God. In response to Satan's third temptation, Jesus cited Deuteronomy 6:16. God is to be trusted, not tested. The Deuteronomy passage refers to Israel's attempt to test God at Meribah (Ex. 17:1–7). Jesus would not repeat the nation's error of unfaithfulness to God.

4:16–17 stood up to read. Most synagogue services had a reading from the Law and one from the Prophets, with an exposition that tied the texts together. Jesus expounded Isaiah 61.

4:18–19 He has sent Me. By citing Isaiah 61, Jesus was claiming to be a royal figure and to have a prophetic mission (v. 24). **liberty to the captives.** In the Old Testament, captivity refers to Israel's exile (1:68–74); here captivity refers to sin (1:77; 7:47; 24:47; Acts 2:38; 5:31; 10:43; 13:38; 26:18). **those who are oppressed.** This was originally the call of Israel, but

---

4:2 c Ex. 34:28 **4:3** d John 20:31 **4:4** e Deut. 8:3 **4:6** f [Rev. 13:2, 7] **4:8** g Deut. 6:13; 10:20 **4:9** h Matt. 4:5–7 **4:10** i Ps. 91:11 **4:11** j Ps. 91:12 **4:12** k Deut. 6:16 **4:13** l [Heb. 4:15] **4:14** m Matt. 4:12 n John 4:43 o Acts 10:37 p Matt. 4:24 **4:15** q Matt. 4:23 r Is. 52:13 **4:16** s Mark 6:1 t Acts 13:14–16; 17:2 **4:18** u Is. 49:8, 9; 61:1, 2 v [Dan. 9:24]

20Then He closed the book, and gave *it* back to the attendant and sat down. And the eyes of all who were in the synagogue were fixed on Him. 21And He began to say to them, "Today this Scripture is wfulfilled in your hearing." 22So all bore witness to Him, and xmarveled at the gracious words which proceeded out of His mouth. And they said, y"Is this not Joseph's son?"

23He said to them, "You will surely say this proverb to Me, 'Physician, heal yourself! Whatever we have heard done in zCapernaum,* do also here in aYour country.'" 24Then He said, "Assuredly, I say to you, no bprophet is accepted in his own country. 25But I tell you truly, cmany widows were in Israel in the days of Elijah, when the heaven was shut up three years and six months, and there was a great famine throughout all the land; 26but to none of them was Elijah sent except to Zarephath,* *in the region* of Sidon, to a woman *who was* a widow. 27dAnd many lepers were in Israel in the time of Elisha the prophet, and none of them was cleansed except Naaman the Syrian."

28So all those in the synagogue, when they heard these things, were efilled with wrath, 29fand rose up and thrust Him out of the city; and they led Him to the brow of the hill on which their city was built, that they might throw Him down over the cliff. 30Then gpassing through the midst of them, He went His way.

Jesus Casts Out an Unclean Spirit

31Then hHe went down to Capernaum, a city of Galilee, and was teaching them on the Sabbaths. 32And they were iastonished at His teaching, jfor His word was with authority. 33kNow in the synagogue there was a man who had a spirit of an unclean demon. And he cried out with a loud voice, 34saying, "Let *us* alone! What have we to do with You, Jesus of Nazareth? Did You come to destroy us? lI know who You are—mthe Holy One of God!"

35But Jesus rebuked him, saying, "Be quiet, and come out of him!" And when the demon had thrown him in *their* midst, it came out of him and did not hurt him. 36Then they were all amazed and spoke among themselves, saying, "What a word this *is!* For with authority and power He commands the unclean spirits, and they come out." 37And the report about Him went out into every place in the surrounding region.

Peter's Mother-in-Law Healed

38nNow He arose from the synagogue and entered Simon's house. But Simon's wife's mother was sick with a high fever, and they omade request of Him concerning her. 39So He stood over her and prebuked the fever, and it left her. And immediately she arose and served them.

Many Healed After Sabbath Sunset

40qWhen the sun was setting, all those who had any that were sick with various diseases brought them to Him; and He laid His hands on every one of them and healed them. 41rAnd demons also came out of many, crying out and saying, s"You are the Christ,* the Son of God!"

And He, trebuking *them*, did not allow them to speak, for they knew that He was the Christ.

Jesus Preaches in Galilee

42uNow when it was day, He departed and went into a deserted place. And the crowd sought Him and came to Him, and tried to keep Him from leaving them; 43but He said to them, "I must vpreach the kingdom of God to the other cities also, because for this purpose I have been sent." 44wAnd He was preaching in the synagogues of Galilee.*

---

* 4:23 Here and elsewhere the NU-Text spelling is *Capharnaum*. * 4:26 Greek *Sarepta* * 4:41 NU-Text omits *the Christ*. * 4:44 NU-Text reads *Judea*.

---

the nation had failed in its assignment (Is. 58:6). **the acceptable year of the Lord.** This phrase is an allusion to the year of Jubilee when every 50th year all debt was forgiven and slaves were given their freedom (Lev. 25:10).
4:20 He closed the book. Jesus closed the book in the middle of the sentence. He did not continue because the next phrase—"the day of vengeance of our God"—was not being fulfilled then.
4:34 What have we to do with You. The demon knew that Jesus possessed divine authority, and he wanted nothing to do with Him.
4:35–36 rebuked. This term in Aramaic was a technical term for calling evil into submission. Jesus' authority over evil forces is clear.
4:41 You are the Christ, the Son of God. This confession, unique to the Gospel of Luke, shows the close connection Luke makes between Jesus' sonship and messiahship.

4:43 kingdom of God. In Luke, the kingdom is referred to thirty times and six times in Acts. Jesus announced the rule of God through His person, in dealing with sin (24:47), in distributing the Spirit as He mediates blessing from God's side (24:49), and in reigning with His followers according to the Old Testament promise (Ps. 2:7–12; Acts 3:18–22).

4:21 w Acts 13:29 **4:22** x [Ps. 45:2] y John 6:42
4:23 z Matt. 4:13; 11:23 a Matt. 13:54 **4:24** b John 4:44
4:25 c 1 Kin. 17:9 **4:27** d 2 Kin. 5:1–14 **4:28** e Luke 6:11 **4:29** f John 8:37; 10:31 **4:30** g John 8:59; 10:39 **4:31** h Matt. 4:13 **4:32** i Matt. 7:28, 29 j [John 6:63; 7:46; 8:26, 28, 38, 47; 12:49, 50] **4:33** k Mark 1:23 **4:34** l Luke 4:41 m Ps. 16:10 **4:38** n Mark 1:29–31 o Mark 5:23 **4:39** p Luke 8:24 **4:40** q Matt. 8:16, 17 **4:41** r Mark 1:34; 3:11 s Mark 8:29 t Mark 1:25, 34; 3:11 **4:42** u Mark 1:35–38 **4:43** v [John 9:4] **4:44** w Matt. 4:23; 9:35

Four Fishermen Called as Disciples

5 So [a]it was, as the multitude pressed
about Him to [b]hear the word of God,
that He stood by the Lake of Gennesaret,
2and saw two boats standing by the lake;
but the fishermen had gone from them and
were washing *their* nets. 3Then He got into
one of the boats, which was Simon's, and
asked him to put out a little from the land.
And He [c]sat down and taught the multitudes from the boat.
4When He had stopped speaking, He
said to Simon, [d]"Launch out into the deep
and let down your nets for a catch."
5But Simon answered and said to Him,
"Master, we have toiled all night and
caught [e]nothing; nevertheless [f]at Your
word I will let down the net." 6And when
they had done this, they caught a great
number of fish, and their net was breaking. 7So they signaled to *their* partners
in the other boat to come and help them.
And they came and filled both the boats,
so that they began to sink. 8When Simon
Peter saw *it*, he fell down at Jesus' knees,
saying, [g]"Depart from me, for I am a sinful
man, O Lord!"
9For he and all who were with him were
[h]astonished at the catch of fish which they
had taken; 10and so also *were* James and
John, the sons of Zebedee, who were partners with Simon. And Jesus said to Simon,
"Do not be afraid. [i]From now on you will
catch men." 11So when they had brought
their boats to land, [j]they forsook all and
followed Him.

Jesus Cleanses a Leper

12[k]And it happened when He was in a
certain city, that behold, a man who was
full of [l]leprosy saw Jesus; and he fell on *his*
face and implored Him, saying, "Lord, if
You are willing, You can make me clean."
13Then He put out *His* hand and touched
him, saying, "I am willing; be cleansed."
[m]Immediately the leprosy left him. 14[n]And
He charged him to tell no one, "But go and
show yourself to the priest, and make an
offering for your cleansing, as a testimony
to them, [o]just as Moses commanded."
15However, [p]the report went around
concerning Him all the more; and [q]great
multitudes came together to hear, and to
be healed by Him of their infirmities. 16[r]So
He Himself *often* withdrew into the wilderness and [s]prayed.

Jesus Forgives and Heals a Paralytic

17Now it happened on a certain day, as
He was teaching, that there were Pharisees
and teachers of the law sitting by, who had
come out of every town of Galilee, Judea,
and Jerusalem. And the power of the Lord
was *present* to heal them.* 18[t]Then behold,
men brought on a bed a man who was paralyzed, whom they sought to bring in and
lay before Him. 19And when they could not
find how they might bring him in, because
of the crowd, they went up on the housetop
and let him down with *his* bed through the
tiling into the midst [u]before Jesus.
20When He saw their faith, He said to
him, "Man, your sins are forgiven you."
21[v]And the scribes and the Pharisees
began to reason, saying, "Who is this who
speaks blasphemies? [w]Who can forgive
sins but God alone?"
22But when Jesus [x]perceived their
thoughts, He answered and said to them,
"Why are you reasoning in your hearts?
23Which is easier, to say, 'Your sins are forgiven you,' or to say, 'Rise up and walk'?
24But that you may know that the Son of
Man has power on earth to forgive sins"—
He said to the man who was paralyzed, [y]"I
say to you, arise, take up your bed, and go
to your house."

---

* **5:17** NU-Text reads *present with Him to heal.*

5:1 *Gennesaret.* This is another name for the Sea of Galilee or the Sea of Tiberias.

5:5 *at Your word I will let down the net.* This is Peter's statement of faith. The fisherman noted that he and his companions had just failed to make a catch at the best time for fishing, the evening. The circumstances were not good for a catch at the time of Jesus' command, but Peter chose to obey His word and let down his nets anyway.

5:12 *leprosy.* This term was used broadly in the ancient world. It included psoriasis, lupus, and ringworm. Lepers were isolated from the rest of society (Lev. 13:45–46), but could be restored to the community when they recovered (Lev. 14).

5:14 *show yourself to the priest.* Jesus commanded that the regulation of Leviticus 14 be followed in silencing the healed leper. Jesus sought to avoid drawing excessive attention to His healing ministry.

5:21 *blasphemies.* The charge of the scribes and the Pharisees was that Jesus' claim dishonored God. This was a serious charge; the conviction of blasphemy would eventually lead to Jesus' death (22:70–71).

5:23 *Which is easier.* Jesus posed a riddle to His audience. From an external point of view, it would seem easier to declare sins forgiven than to actually heal a person. In reality, however, one has to possess more authority to forgive sin. Jesus linked the healing to what it represented, the forgiveness of sin. Jesus forgave the man's sins and healed him at the same time.

5:24 *Son of Man.* This is an Aramaic idiom that refers to a human being, meaning "someone" or "I." Jesus used this idiom as a title, taken from Daniel 7:13. In the Book of Daniel, the phrase "Son of Man" describes a figure who shares authority with the Ancient of Days.

5:1 [a] Mark 1:16–20 [b] Acts 13:44 **5:3** [c] John 8:2 **5:4** [d] John 21:6 **5:5** [e] John 21:3 [f] Ps. 33:9 **5:8** [g] 1 Kin. 17:18 **5:9** [h] Mark 5:42; 10:24, 26 **5:10** [i] Matt. 4:19 **5:11** [j] Matt. 4:20; 19:27 **5:12** [k] Mark 1:40–44 [l] Lev. 13:14 **5:13** [m] John 5:9 **5:14** [n] Matt. 8:4 [o] Lev. 13:1–3; 14:2–32 **5:15** [p] Mark 1:45 [q] John 6:2 **5:16** [r] Luke 9:10 [s] Matt. 14:23 **5:18** [t] Mark 2:3–12 **5:19** [u] Matt. 15:30 **5:21** [v] Mark 2:6, 7 [w] Is. 43:25 **5:22** [x] John 2:25 **5:24** [y] Luke 7:14

²⁵Immediately he rose up before them, took up what he had been lying on, and departed to his own house, ᶻglorifying God. ²⁶And they were all amazed, and they ᵃglorified God and were filled with fear, saying, "We have seen strange things today!"

Matthew the Tax Collector

²⁷ᵇAfter these things He went out and saw a tax collector named Levi, sitting at the tax office. And He said to him, ᶜ"Follow Me." ²⁸So he left all, rose up, and ᵈfollowed Him.

²⁹ᵉThen Levi gave Him a great feast in his own house. And ᶠthere were a great number of tax collectors and others who sat down with them. ³⁰And their scribes and the Pharisees* complained against His disciples, saying, ᵍ"Why do You eat and drink with tax collectors and sinners?"

³¹Jesus answered and said to them, "Those who are well have no need of a physician, but those who are sick. ³²ʰI have not come to call the righteous, but sinners, to repentance."

Jesus Is Questioned About Fasting

³³Then they said to Him, ⁱ"Why do* the disciples of John fast often and make prayers, and likewise those of the Pharisees, but Yours eat and drink?"

³⁴And He said to them, "Can you make the friends of the bridegroom fast while the ʲbridegroom is with them? ³⁵But the days will come when the bridegroom will be taken away from them; then they will fast in those days."

³⁶ᵏThen He spoke a parable to them: "No one puts a piece from a new garment on an old one;* otherwise the new makes a tear, and also the piece that was taken out of the new does not match the old. ³⁷And no one puts new wine into old wineskins; or else the new wine will burst the wineskins and be spilled, and the wineskins will be

ruined. ³⁸But new wine must be put into new wineskins, and both are preserved.* ³⁹And no one, having drunk old wine, immediately* desires new; for he says, 'The old is better.'"*

Jesus Is Lord of the Sabbath

6 Now ᵃit happened on the second Sabbath after the first* that He went through the grainfields. And His disciples plucked the heads of grain and ate them, rubbing them in their hands. ²And some of the Pharisees said to them, "Why are you doing ᵇwhat is not lawful to do on the Sabbath?"

³But Jesus answering them said, "Have you not even read this, ᶜwhat David did when he was hungry, he and those who were with him: ⁴how he went into the house of God, took and ate the showbread, and also gave some to those with him, ᵈwhich is not lawful for any but the priests to eat?" ⁵And He said to them, "The Son of Man is also Lord of the Sabbath."

Healing on the Sabbath

⁶ᵉNow it happened on another Sabbath, also, that He entered the synagogue and taught. And a man was there whose right hand was withered. ⁷So the scribes and Pharisees watched Him closely, whether He would ᶠheal on the Sabbath, that they might find an ᵍaccusation against Him. ⁸But He ʰknew their thoughts, and said to the man who had the withered hand, "Arise and stand here." And he arose and stood.

---

* **5:30** NU-Text reads *But the Pharisees and their scribes.* * **5:33** NU-Text omits *Why do*, making the verse a statement. * **5:36** NU-Text reads *No one tears a piece from a new garment and puts it on an old one.* * **5:38** NU-Text omits *and both are preserved.* * **5:39** NU-Text omits *immediately.* ● NU-Text reads *good.* * **6:1** NU-Text reads *on a Sabbath.*

5:29 with them. In ancient Israel the table was a place where spiritual points were taught and where fellowship occurred.

5:33 fast. The Pharisees fasted twice a week, on Mondays and Thursdays (18:12), as well as on the Day of Atonement (Lev. 16:29). They also fasted as an act of penitence (Is. 58:1–9) and to recall four times a year the destruction of Jerusalem (Zech. 7:3,5; 8:19). The goal of fasting was to dedicate oneself to prayer and to focus on God. John led an ascetic life, which his followers also imitated (7:24–28; Matt. 11:1–19).

5:35 the days will come. The image of the removal of the bridegroom is the first hint in Jesus' ministry of His fast-approaching death.

5:37 puts new wine into old wineskins. This would not work because as the new wine fermented, it would stretch the old skin and break it, ruining the wineskin and wasting the wine.

6:1 plucked . . . ate . . . rubbing. According to Jewish tradition, the disciples were reaping, threshing, and preparing food, and so were violating the commandment not to work on the Sabbath. It is clear that at

this point the Pharisees were watching Jesus carefully (v. 7).

6:3–4 showbread. This was bread that was taken from the twelve loaves placed on a table in the holy place and changed once a week (Ex. 25:30; 39:36; Lev. 24:5–9). Jesus pointed out that if David and his men could violate the law to satisfy their hunger, His disciples could do the same.

6:5 also Lord of the Sabbath. Regardless of the laws and customs that the Pharisees cited, Jesus has authority over the Sabbath. Jesus' claim of divine authority here is similar to His claim of authority to forgive sins in 5:21, 24.

5:25 ᶻActs 3:8 **5:26** ᵃLuke 1:65; 7:16 **5:27** ᵇMatt. 9:9–17 ᶜJohn 12:26; 21:19, 22 **5:28** ᵈMark 10:28 **5:29** ᵉMatt. 9:9, 10 ᶠLuke 15:1 **5:30** ᵍLuke 15:2 **5:32** ʰ1 Tim. 1:15 **5:33** ⁱMatt. 9:14 **5:34** ʲJohn 3:29 **5:36** ᵏMark 2:21, 22 **6:1** ᵃMatt. 12:1–8 **6:2** ᵇEx. 20:10 **6:3** ᶜ1 Sam. 21:6 **6:4** ᵈLev. 24:9 **6:6** ᵉMark 3:1–6 **6:7** ᶠLuke 13:14; 14:1–6 ᵍLuke 20:20 **6:8** ʰMatt. 9:4

⁹Then Jesus said to them, "I will ask you one thing: ʲIs it lawful on the Sabbath to do good or to do evil, to save life or to destroy?"* ¹⁰And when He had looked around at them all, He said to the man,* "Stretch out your hand." And he did so, and his hand was restored as whole as the other.* ¹¹But they were filled with rage, and discussed with one another what they might do to Jesus.

The Twelve Apostles

¹²Now it came to pass in those days that He went out to the mountain to pray, and continued all night in ʲprayer to God. ¹³And when it was day, He called His disciples to *Himself;* ᵏand from them He chose ˡtwelve whom He also named apostles: ¹⁴Simon, ᵐwhom He also named Peter, and Andrew his brother; James and John; Philip and Bartholomew; ¹⁵Matthew and Thomas; James the *son* of Alphaeus, and Simon called the Zealot; ¹⁶Judas ⁿ*the son* of James, and ᵒJudas Iscariot who also became a traitor.

Jesus Heals a Great Multitude

¹⁷And He came down with them and stood on a level place with a crowd of His disciples ᵖand a great multitude of people from all Judea and Jerusalem, and from the seacoast of Tyre and Sidon, who came to hear Him and be healed of their diseases, ¹⁸as well as those who were tormented with unclean spirits. And they were healed. ¹⁹And the whole multitude ᵠsought to ʳtouch Him, for ˢpower went out from Him and healed *them* all.

The Beatitudes

²⁰Then He lifted up His eyes toward His disciples, and said:

ᵗ"Blessed *are you* poor,
  For yours is the kingdom of God.

²¹ ᵘBlessed *are you* who hunger now,
  For you shall be ᵛfilled.
ʷBlessed *are you* who weep now,
  For you shall ˣlaugh.
²² ʸBlessed are *you* when men hate you,
  And when they ᶻexclude you,
  And revile *you,* and cast out your
    name as evil,
  For the Son of Man's sake.
²³ ᵃRejoice in that day and leap for joy!
  For indeed your reward *is* great in
    heaven,
  For ᵇin like manner their fathers did
    to the prophets.

Jesus Pronounces Woes

²⁴ "Butᶜ woe to you ᵈwho are rich,
  For ᵉyou have received your
    consolation.
²⁵ ᶠWoe to you who are full,
  For you shall hunger.
ᵍWoe to you who laugh now,
  For you shall mourn and ʰweep.
²⁶ ʲWoe to you* when all* men speak well
    of you,
  For so did their fathers to the false
    prophets.

Love Your Enemies

²⁷ʲ"But I say to you who hear: Love your enemies, do good to those who hate you, ²⁸ᵏbless those who curse you, and ˡpray for those who spitefully use you. ²⁹ᵐTo him who strikes you on the *one* cheek, offer the other also. ⁿAnd from him who takes away your cloak, do not withhold *your* tunic either. ³⁰ᵒGive to everyone who asks of you. And from him who takes away your goods do not ask *them* back. ³¹ᵖAnd just as you want men to do to you, you also do to them likewise.

---

* **6:9** M-Text reads *to kill.* * **6:10** NU-Text and M-Text read *to him.* • NU-Text omits *as whole as the other.* * **6:26** NU-Text and M-Text omit *to you.* • M-Text omits *all.*

6:11 *rage.* The term here means irrational or mindless anger. The parallels in Matthew 12:14 and Mark 3:6 make it clear that the Pharisees started to plot against Jesus in earnest after this confrontation.
6:17 *level place.* This probably refers to a plateau on a mountain. The setting and the contents of the sermon that follows suggest that Luke is providing a shorter version of the Sermon on the Mount, omitting those portions that have to do with the law.
6:20 *Blessed are you.* Blessed means "happy," referring to the special joy and favor that comes upon those who experience God's grace.
6:22 *For the Son of Man's sake.* Identification with Jesus usually leads to rejection and hardship, but the disciple who has left all to follow Jesus understands what placing Jesus first means. He or she also recognizes that God is aware of all suffering.
6:24 *woe.* A woe is a cry of pain that results from misfortune. Just as God presented blessings for obedience and curses for disobedience in Deuteronomy 28, Jesus presented blessings and woes to His disciples who were anticipating the kingdom. The same

blessings and woes apply to believers today when their works are evaluated (1 Cor. 3:12–15; 2 Cor. 5:10; 1 John 2:28; Rev. 22:12).
6:27–28 *Love your enemies.* The threat of religious persecution was very real when Jesus presented His command for extraordinary love. The reference to a cursing enemy suggests a context of religious persecution.
6:30 *do not ask them back.* The commands of verses 29 and 30 are expressed in such absolute terms that

---

6:9 ʲ John 7:23 **6:12** ʲ Mark 1:35 **6:13** ᵏ John 6:70 ˡ Matt. 10:1 **6:14** ᵐ John 1:42 **6:16** ⁿ Jude 1 ᵒ Luke 22:3–6 **6:17** ᵖ Mark 3:7, 8 **6:19** ᵠ Matt. 9:21; 14:36 ʳ Mark 5:27, 28 ˢ Luke 8:46 **6:20** ᵗ Matt. 5:3–12; [11:5] **6:21** ᵘ Is. 55:1; 65:13 ᵛ [Rev. 7:16] ˣ Ps. 126:5 **6:22** ʸ 1 Pet. 2:19; 3:14; 4:14 ᶻ [John 16:2] **6:23** ᵃ James 1:2 ᵇ Acts 7:51 **6:24** ᶜ James 5:1–6 ᵈ Luke 12:21 ᵉ Luke 16:25 **6:25** ᶠ [Is. 65:13] ᵍ [Prov. 14:13] ʰ James 4:9 **6:26** ʲ [John 15:19] **6:27** ʲ Rom. 12:20 **6:28** ᵏ Rom. 12:14 ˡ Acts 7:60 **6:29** ᵐ Matt. 5:39–42 ⁿ [1 Cor. 6:7] **6:30** ᵒ Deut. 15:7, 8 **6:31** ᵖ Matt. 7:12

32q"But if you love those who love you, what credit is that to you? For even sinners love those who love them. **33**And if you do good to those who do good to you, what credit is that to you? For even sinners do the same. **34**rAnd if you lend *to those* from whom you hope to receive back, what credit is that to you? For even sinners lend to sinners to receive as much back. **35**But slove your enemies, tdo good, and ulend, hoping for nothing in return; and your reward will be great, and vyou will be sons of the Most High. For He is kind to the unthankful and evil. **36**wTherefore be merciful, just as your Father also is merciful.

Do Not Judge

37x"Judge not, and you shall not be judged. Condemn not, and you shall not be condemned. yForgive, and you will be forgiven. **38**zGive, and it will be given to you: good measure, pressed down, shaken together, and running over will be put into your abosom. For bwith the same measure that you use, it will be measured back to you."

39And He spoke a parable to them: c"Can the blind lead the blind? Will they not both fall into the ditch? **40**dA disciple is not above his teacher, but everyone who is perfectly trained will be like his teacher. **41**eAnd why do you look at the speck in your brother's eye, but do not perceive the plank in your own eye? **42**Or how can you say to your brother, 'Brother, let me remove the speck that *is* in your eye,' when you yourself do not see the plank that *is* in your own eye? Hypocrite! First remove the plank from your own eye, and then you will see clearly to remove the speck that is in your brother's eye.

A Tree Is Known by Its Fruit

43f"For a good tree does not bear bad fruit, nor does a bad tree bear good fruit. **44**For gevery tree is known by its own fruit. For *men* do not gather figs from thorns, nor do they gather grapes from a bramble bush. **45**hA good man out of the good treasure of his heart brings forth good; and an evil man out of the evil treasure of

his heart* brings forth evil. For out iof the abundance of the heart his mouth speaks.

Build on the Rock

46j"But why do you call Me 'Lord, Lord,' and not do the things which I say? **47**kWhoever comes to Me, and hears My sayings and does them, I will show you whom he is like: **48**He is like a man building a house, who dug deep and laid the foundation on the rock. And when the flood arose, the stream beat vehemently against that house, and could not shake it, for it was founded on the rock.* **49**But he who heard and did nothing is like a man who built a house on the earth without a foundation, against which the stream beat vehemently; and immediately it fell.* And the ruin of that house was great."

Jesus Heals a Centurion's Servant

7 Now when He concluded all His sayings in the hearing of the people, He aentered Capernaum. **2**And a certain centurion's servant, who was dear to him, was sick and ready to die. **3**So when he heard about Jesus, he sent elders of the Jews to Him, pleading with Him to come and heal his servant. **4**And when they came to Jesus, they begged Him earnestly, saying that the one for whom He should do this was deserving, **5**"for he loves our nation, and has built us a synagogue."

6Then Jesus went with them. And when He was already not far from the house, the centurion sent friends to Him, saying to Him, "Lord, do not trouble Yourself, for I am not worthy that You should enter under my roof. **7**Therefore I did not even think myself worthy to come to You. But bsay the word, and my servant will be healed. **8**For I also am a man placed under cauthority, having soldiers under me. And I say to one, 'Go,' and he goes; and to another, 'Come,' and he comes; and to my servant, 'Do this,' and he does *it*."

---

* **6:45** NU-Text omits *treasure of his heart.*
* **6:48** NU-Text reads *for it was well built.*
* **6:49** NU-Text reads *collapsed.*

---

they force the listener to reflect on them by contrasting them with the normal responses people would have to such injustices.

6:35 *He is kind to the unthankful and evil.* The practice of loving one's enemies is modeled by God Himself.

6:38 *good measure.* This illustration comes from the marketplace where grain was poured out, shaken down, and then filled to overflowing so the buyer received the full amount purchased. Such is the full measure that will be returned to one who has been generous.

6:46 *Lord, Lord.* Jesus pointed out that those who called Him by this title of respect acknowledged submission to Him. However when these same people ignored His teaching, they were guilty of hypocrisy.

7:1 *Capernaum.* This city was on the northwest

shore of the Sea of Galilee. It was an important town in northern Galilee with an economy centered on fishing and agriculture. Heavily Jewish, it was the center for Jesus' Galilean ministry (4:31–44).

7:5 *built us a synagogue.* The Roman government regarded synagogues as valuable because their moral emphasis helped maintain order.

6:32 q Matt. 5:46　**6:34** r Matt. 5:42　**6:35** s [Rom. 13:10] t Heb. 13:16 u Ps. 37:26 v Matt. 5:46　**6:36** w Matt. 5:48 **6:37** x Matt. 7:1–5 y Matt. 18:21–35　**6:38** z [Prov. 19:17; 28:27] a Ps. 79:12 b James 2:13　**6:39** c Matt. 15:14; 23:16 **6:40** d [John 13:16; 15:20] e Matt. 7:3　**6:43** f Matt. 7:16–18, 20　**6:44** g Matt. 12:33　**6:45** h Matt. 12:35 i Matt. 12:34　**6:46** j Mal. 1:6　**6:47** k James 1:22–25 **7:1** a Matt. 8:5–13　**7:7** b Ps. 33:9; 107:20　**7:8** c [Mark 13:34]

[9]When Jesus heard these things, He marveled at him, and turned around and said to the crowd that followed Him, "I say to you, I have not found such great faith, not even in Israel!" [10]And those who were sent, returning to the house, found the servant well who had been sick.*

Jesus Raises the Son of the Widow of Nain

[11]Now it happened, the day after, *that* He went into a city called Nain; and many of His disciples went with Him, and a large crowd. [12]And when He came near the gate of the city, behold, a dead man was being carried out, the only son of his mother; and she was a widow. And a large crowd from the city was with her. [13]When the Lord saw her, He had [d]compassion on her and said to her, [e]"Do not weep." [14]Then He came and touched the open coffin, and those who carried *him* stood still. And He said, "Young man, I say to you, [f]arise." [15]So he who was dead [g]sat up and began to speak. And He [h]presented him to his mother.

[16][i]Then fear came upon all, and they [j]glorified God, saying, [k]"A great prophet has risen up among us"; and, [l]"God has visited His people." [17]And this report about Him went throughout all Judea and all the surrounding region.

John the Baptist Sends Messengers to Jesus

[18][m]Then the disciples of John reported to him concerning all these things. [19]And John, calling two of his disciples to *him,* sent *them* to Jesus,* saying, "Are You the Coming One, or do we look for another?"

[20]When the men had come to Him, they said, "John the Baptist has sent us to You, saying, 'Are You the Coming One, or do we look for another?'" [21]And that very hour He cured many of infirmities, afflictions, and evil spirits; and to many blind He gave sight.

[22]oJesus answered and said to them, "Go and tell John the things you have seen and heard: [p]that *the* blind [q]see, *the* lame [r]walk, *the* lepers are [s]cleansed, *the* deaf [t]hear, *the*

dead are raised, [u]*the* poor have the gospel preached to them. [23]And blessed is *he* who is not offended because of Me."

[24]vWhen the messengers of John had departed, He began to speak to the multitudes concerning John: "What did you go out into the wilderness to see? A reed shaken by the wind? [25]But what did you go out to see? A man clothed in soft garments? Indeed those who are gorgeously appareled and live in luxury are in kings' courts. [26]But what did you go out to see? A prophet? Yes, I say to you, and more than a prophet. [27]This is *he* of whom it is written:

[w]'Behold, I send My messenger before Your face,
Who will prepare Your way before You.'*

[28]For I say to you, among those born of women there is not a [x]greater prophet than John the Baptist;* but he who is least in the kingdom of God is greater than he."

[29]And when all the people heard *Him,* even the tax collectors justified God, [y]having been baptized with the baptism of John. [30]But the Pharisees and lawyers rejected [z]the will of God for themselves, not having been baptized by him.

[31]And the Lord said,* [a]"To what then shall I liken the men of this generation, and what are they like? [32]They are like children sitting in the marketplace and calling to one another, saying:

'We played the flute for you,
And you did not dance;
We mourned to you,
And you did not weep.'

[33]For [b]John the Baptist came [c]neither eating bread nor drinking wine, and you say, 'He has a demon.' [34]The Son of Man has come [d]eating and drinking, and you say, 'Look, a glutton and a winebibber, a friend of tax collectors and sinners!' [35]eBut wisdom is justified by all her children."

---

* **7:10** NU-Text omits *who had been sick.*
* **7:19** NU-Text reads *the Lord.*   * **7:27** Malachi 3:1   * **7:28** NU-Text reads *there is none greater than John.*   * **7:31** NU-Text and M-Text omit *And the Lord said.*

7:9 not even in Israel. The centurion's example of faith came from outside the nation of Israel. This is one of only two cases where Jesus "marveled" (Mark 6:6).

7:12 a dead man . . . carried out. This was a funeral procession. The cemetery was located outside the city gates. Funerals were normally held the day of death because keeping a body overnight rendered a house unclean.

7:24–26 He began to speak to the multitudes concerning John. The questions that Jesus asked were designed to emphasize that John the Baptist played a special role in God's plan. The crowds did not go out to the wilderness to see scenery or a man dressed in special clothes, but to see a prophet.

7:28 he who is least in the kingdom of God. Jesus

emphasizes the contrast between the old and new eras. John was the greatest prophet ever born. But the lowest person in the new era of God's kingdom is higher than the greatest prophet of the old era.

7:31–34 To what then shall I liken. Jesus made a comparison between children playing a game in the

7:13 [d] John 11:35   [e] Luke 8:52   **7:14** [f] Acts 9:40
7:15 [g] John 11:44   [h] 2 Kin. 4:36   **7:16** [i] Luke 1:65   [j] Luke 5:26   [k] Luke 24:19   [l] Luke 1:68   **7:18** [m] Matt. 11:2–19
7:19 [n] [Zech. 9:9]   **7:22** [o] Matt. 11:4   [p] Is. 35:5   [q] John 9:7   [r] Matt. 15:31   [s] Luke 17:12–14   [t] Mark 7:37   [u] [Is. 61:1–3]
7:24 [v] Matt. 11:7   **7:27** [w] Mal. 3:1   **7:28** [x] [Luke 1:15]
7:29 [y] Luke 3:12   **7:30** [z] Acts 20:27   **7:31** [a] Matt. 11:16   **7:33** [b] Matt. 3:1   [c] Luke 1:15   **7:34** [d] Luke 15:2
7:35 [e] Matt. 11:19

A Sinful Woman Forgiven

36ᶠThen one of the Pharisees asked Him to eat with him. And He went to the Pharisee's house, and sat down to eat. **37**And behold, a woman in the city who was a sinner, when she knew that *Jesus* sat at the table in the Pharisee's house, brought an alabaster flask of fragrant oil, **38**and stood at His feet behind *Him* weeping; and she began to wash His feet with her tears, and wiped *them* with the hair of her head; and she kissed His feet and anointed *them* with the fragrant oil. **39**Now when the Pharisee who had invited Him saw *this*, he spoke to himself, saying, ᵍ"This Man, if He were a prophet, would know who and what manner of woman *this is* who is touching Him, for she is a sinner."

40And Jesus answered and said to him, "Simon, I have something to say to you."

So he said, "Teacher, say it."

41"There was a certain creditor who had two debtors. One owed five hundred ʰdenarii, and the other fifty. **42**And when they had nothing with which to repay, he freely forgave them both. Tell Me, therefore, which of them will love him more?"

43Simon answered and said, "I suppose the *one* whom he forgave more."

And He said to him, "You have rightly judged." **44**Then He turned to the woman and said to Simon, "Do you see this woman? I entered your house; you gave Me no ⁱwater for My feet, but she has washed My feet with her tears and wiped *them* with the hair of her head. **45**You gave Me no ʲkiss, but this woman has not ceased to kiss My feet since the time I came in. **46**ᵏYou did not anoint My head with oil, but this woman has anointed My feet with fragrant oil. **47**ˡTherefore I say to you, her sins, which *are* many, are forgiven, for she loved much. But to whom little is forgiven, *the same* loves little."

48Then He said to her, ᵐ"Your sins are forgiven."

49And those who sat at the table with Him began to say to themselves, ⁿ"Who is this who even forgives sins?"

50Then He said to the woman, ᵒ"Your faith has saved you. Go in peace."

Many Women Minister to Jesus

8 Now it came to pass, afterward, that He went through every city and village, preaching and bringing the glad tidings of the kingdom of God. And the twelve *were* with Him, **2**and ᵃcertain women who had been healed of evil spirits and infirmities— Mary called Magdalene, ᵇout of whom had come seven demons, **3**and Joanna the wife of Chuza, Herod's steward, and Susanna, and many others who provided for Him* from their substance.

The Parable of the Sower

4ᶜAnd when a great multitude had gathered, and they had come to Him from every city, He spoke by a parable: **5**"A sower went out to sow his seed. And as he sowed, some fell by the wayside; and it was trampled down, and the birds of the air devoured it. **6**Some fell on rock; and as soon as it sprang up, it withered away because it lacked moisture. **7**And some fell among thorns, and the thorns sprang up with it and choked it. **8**But others fell on good ground, sprang up, and yielded a crop a hundredfold." When He had said these things He cried, ᵈ"He who has ears to hear, let him hear!"

The Purpose of Parables

9ᵉThen His disciples asked Him, saying, "What does this parable mean?"

10And He said, "To you it has been given to know the mysteries of the kingdom of God, but to the rest *it is given* in parables, that

> ᶠ'Seeing they may not see,
> And hearing they may not
> understand.'*

---

* **8:3** NU-Text and M-Text read *them*.   * **8:10** Isaiah 6:9

---

marketplace and the present generation of Israel, referring especially to the Jewish religious leaders. The leaders were like the children in that they complained no matter what tune was played. John the Baptist refused to eat bread or drink wine, and the religious leaders dismissed him as demon-possessed. In contrast, Jesus, the Son of Man was accused of living loosely and associating with sinners. No matter what the style of God's messenger was, the religious leaders complained and rejected him.

7:36 *one of the Pharisees asked Him to eat with him.* This event is not the same as the one in Matthew 26:6–13; Mark 14:3–9; and John 12:1–8. The event described in those passages occurred in the house of a leper, a place where no Pharisee would ever have gone.

7:37 *alabaster flask.* This was made of soft stone to preserve the quality of the precious and expensive perfume. There is humility and devotion in the woman's act of service, as well as a great deal of courage, as she performed the deed in front of a crowd that knew her as a sinner.

7:44–46 *Do you see this woman?* Jesus contrasted the actions of the woman with the actions of the Pharisee Simon, implying that the woman knew more about forgiveness than Simon (v. 47).

8:1–3 *Mary called Magdalene.* Because she is introduced here, it is unlikely that she was the sinful woman of 7:36–50. ***Joanna.*** This is an example of how some women of means used their wealth to benefit the work of God.

8:10 *kingdom . . . parables.* Jesus' parables both concealed and revealed truths. The disciples were

7:36 ᶠ John 11:2   **7:39** ᵍ Luke 15:2   **7:41** ʰ Matt. 18:28   **7:44** ⁱ Gen. 18:4; 19:2; 43:24   **7:45** ʲ Rom. 16:16   **7:46** ᵏ Ps. 23:5   **7:47** ˡ [1 Tim. 1:14]   **7:48** ᵐ Matt. 9:2   **7:49** ⁿ Luke 5:21   **7:50** ᵒ Matt. 9:22   **8:2** ᵃ Matt. 27:55   ᵇ Mark 16:9   **8:4** ᶜ Mark 4:1–9   **8:8** ᵈ Luke 14:35   **8:9** ᵉ Matt. 13:10–23   **8:10** ᶠ Is. 6:9

The Parable of the Sower Explained

11g"Now the parable is this: The seed is the hword of God. 12Those by the wayside are the ones who hear; then the devil comes and takes away the word out of their hearts, lest they should believe and be saved. 13But the ones on the rock are those who, when they hear, receive the word with joy; and these have no root, who believe for a while and in time of temptation fall away. 14Now the ones that fell among thorns are those who, when they have heard, go out and are choked with cares, iriches, and pleasures of life, and bring no fruit to maturity. 15But the ones that fell on the good ground are those who, having heard the word with a noble and good heart, keep it and bear fruit with jpatience.

The Parable of the Revealed Light

16k"No one, when he has lit a lamp, covers it with a vessel or puts it under a bed, but sets it on a lampstand, that those who enter may see the llight. 17mFor nothing is secret that will not be nrevealed, nor anything hidden that will not be known and come to light. 18Therefore take heed how you hear. oFor whoever has, to him more will be given; and whoever does not have, even what he seems to phave will be taken from him."

Jesus' Mother and Brothers Come to Him

19qThen His mother and brothers came to Him, and could not approach Him because of the crowd. 20And it was told Him by some, who said, "Your mother and Your brothers are standing outside, desiring to see You."

21But He answered and said to them,

"My mother and My brothers are these who hear the word of God and do it."

Wind and Wave Obey Jesus

22rNow it happened, on a certain day, that He got into a boat with His disciples. And He said to them, "Let us cross over to the other side of the lake." And they launched out. 23But as they sailed He fell asleep. And a windstorm came down on the lake, and they were filling with water, and were in jeopardy. 24And they came to Him and awoke Him, saying, "Master, Master, we are perishing!"

Then He arose and rebuked the wind and the raging of the water. And they ceased, and there was a calm. 25But He said to them, s"Where is your faith?"

And they were afraid, and marveled, saying to one another, t"Who can this be? For He commands even the winds and water, and they obey Him!"

A Demon-Possessed Man Healed

26uThen they sailed to the country of the Gadarenes,* which is opposite Galilee. 27And when He stepped out on the land, there met Him a certain man from the city who had demons for a long time. And he wore no clothes,* nor did he live in a house but in the tombs. 28When he saw Jesus, he vcried out, fell down before Him, and with a loud voice said, w"What have I to do with xYou, Jesus, Son of the Most High God? I beg You, do not torment me!" 29For He had commanded the unclean spirit to come out of the man. For it had often seized him, and he was kept under guard, bound

* 8:26 NU-Text reads Gerasenes.　* 8:27 NU-Text reads who had demons and for a long time wore no clothes.

---

privileged to learn the truths of parables. For other listeners, the parables served as judgments that concealed truth, as the reference to Isaiah 6:9 indicates. On occasion, a parable was understood by an outsider but was not accepted, thus still functioning as a message of judgment (20:9–19).

8:13 who believe for a while . . . fall away. Brief and superficial encounters with the Word of God will not stand times of testing. A person needs to meditate on the truths in Scripture and establish them as principles for living in order to withstand the trials and temptations that will inevitably come.

8:14 cares, riches, and pleasures of life. According to this parable, these three are the great obstacles to spiritual fruitfulness. The concerns of life can squelch spiritual growth. This type of "soil" is viewed as tragically unsuccessful (2 Tim. 2:4; 4:10).

8:19–20 Then his mother and brothers came to Him. Jesus' family was concerned about the direction of His ministry (Mark 3:31–35). Though some have suggested that the brothers here were sons of Joseph by a previous marriage or cousins of Jesus, most likely they were the sons of Joseph and Mary. Joseph's absence here may mean that he had died by this time.

8:23 a windstorm. The calming of the wind is the first of four miracles in verses 22–56 that demonstrate Jesus' authority over a variety of phenomena—nature, demons, disease, and death. This miracle took place on the Sea of Galilee. Cool air rushing down the ravines and hills of the area collides with warm air from the Sea of Galilee, causing sudden and strong storms.

8:25 Where is your faith? Jesus' question was a rebuke of His disciples. Because God was aware of their situation, they could trust in His protection, for He was powerful enough to control the winds and waves.

8:28 Son of the Most High God. The demon's confession recalls the angel's announcement to Mary in 1:31–32 and the demonic confessions of 4:34, 41.

8:11 g [1 Pet. 1:23]　h Luke 5:1; 11:28　8:14 i 1 Tim. 6:9, 10　8:15 j [Heb. 10:36–39]　8:16 k Luke 11:33　l Matt. 5:14　8:17 m Luke 12:2　n [2 Cor. 5:10]　8:18 o Matt. 25:29　p Matt. 13:12　8:19 q Mark 3:31–35　8:22 r Matt. 8:23–27　8:25 s Luke 9:41　t Luke 4:36; 5:26　8:26 u Mark 5:1–17　8:28 v Mark 1:26; 9:26　w Mark 1:23, 24　x Luke 4:41

with chains and shackles; and he broke the bonds and was driven by the demon into the wilderness.

30Jesus asked him, saying, "What is your name?"

And he said, "Legion," because many demons had entered him. 31And they begged Him that He would not command them to go out yinto the abyss.

32Now a herd of many zswine was feeding there on the mountain. So they begged Him that He would permit them to enter them. And He permitted them. 33Then the demons went out of the man and entered the swine, and the herd ran violently down the steep place into the lake and drowned.

34When those who fed *them* saw what had happened, they fled and told *it* in the city and in the country. 35Then they went out to see what had happened, and came to Jesus, and found the man from whom the demons had departed, asitting at the bfeet of Jesus, clothed and in his cright mind. And they were afraid. 36They also who had seen *it* told them by what means he who had been demon-possessed was healed. 37dThen the whole multitude of the surrounding region of the Gadarenes* easked Him to fdepart from them, for they were seized with great gfear. And He got into the boat and returned.

38Now hthe man from whom the demons had departed begged Him that he might be with Him. But Jesus sent him away, saying, 39"Return to your own house, and tell what great things God has done for you." And he went his way and proclaimed throughout the whole city what great things Jesus had done for him.

A Girl Restored to Life and a Woman Healed

40So it was, when Jesus returned, that the multitude welcomed Him, for they were all waiting for Him. 41iAnd behold, there came a man named Jairus, and he was a ruler of the synagogue. And he fell down at Jesus' feet and begged Him to come to his house, 42for he had an only daughter about twelve years of age, and she jwas dying.

But as He went, the multitudes thronged Him. 43kNow a woman, having a lflow of blood for twelve years, who had spent all

her livelihood on physicians and could not be healed by any, 44came from behind and mtouched the border of His garment. And immediately her flow of blood stopped.

45And Jesus said, "Who touched Me?"

When all denied it, Peter and those with him* said, "Master, the multitudes throng and press You, and You say, 'Who touched Me?'"*

46But Jesus said, "Somebody touched Me, for I perceived npower going out from Me." 47Now when the woman saw that she was not hidden, she came trembling; and falling down before Him, she declared to Him in the presence of all the people the reason she had touched Him and how she was healed immediately.

48And He said to her, "Daughter, be of good cheer;* oyour faith has made you well. pGo in peace."

49qWhile He was still speaking, someone came from the ruler of the synagogue's *house*, saying to him, "Your daughter is dead. Do not trouble the Teacher."*

50But when Jesus heard *it*, He answered him, saying, "Do not be afraid; ronly believe, and she will be made well." 51When He came into the house, He permitted no one to go in* except Peter, James, and John,* and the father and mother of the girl. 52Now all wept and mourned for her; but He said, s"Do not weep; she is not dead, tbut sleeping." 53And they ridiculed Him, knowing that she was dead.

54But He put them all outside,* took her by the hand and called, saying, "Little girl, uarise." 55Then her spirit returned, and she arose immediately. And He commanded that she be given *something* to eat. 56And her parents were astonished, but vHe charged them to tell no one what had happened.

Sending Out the Twelve

9 Then aHe called His twelve disciples together and bgave them power and authority over all demons, and to cure

---

* **8:37** NU-Text reads *Gerasenes.* * **8:45** NU-Text omits *and those with him.* • NU-Text omits *and You say, 'Who touched Me?'* * **8:48** NU-Text omits *be of good cheer.* * **8:49** NU-Text adds *anymore.* * **8:51** NU-Text adds *with Him.* • NU-Text and M-Text read *Peter, John, and James.* * **8:54** NU-Text omits *put them all outside.*

8:30 *Legion.* This name reflects the fact that the man was possessed by multiple demons. A legion was a Roman military unit of about 6,000 soldiers.

8:31 *the abyss.* This is an allusion to the underworld and the destruction of judgment (Rom. 10:7).

8:44 *her flow of blood stopped.* This condition not only would have been embarrassing, it would have made the woman unclean (Lev. 15:25–31). It took great courage for her to seek out Jesus. Note that her action was not criticized, but commended (v. 48).

8:52 *but sleeping.* Sleeping was a common

metaphor for death. Here it indicates that the girl's death was not permanent.

8:31 y [Rev. 20:1, 3]   **8:32** z Lev. 11:7   **8:35** a [Matt. 11:28]   b Luke 10:39; 17:16   c [2 Tim. 1:7]   **8:37** d Matt. 8:34   e Luke 4:34   f Acts 16:39   g Luke 5:26   **8:38** h Mark 5:18–20   **8:41** i Mark 5:22–43   **8:42** j Luke 7:2   **8:43** k Matt. 9:20   l Luke 15:19–22   **8:44** m Mark 6:56   **8:46** n Mark 5:30   **8:48** o Luke 7:50   p John 8:11   **8:49** q Mark 5:35   **8:50** r [Mark 11:22–24]   **8:52** s Luke 7:13   t [John 11:11, 13]   **8:54** u John 11:43   **8:56** v Matt. 8:4; 9:30   **9:1** a Matt. 10:1, 2   b [John 14:12]

diseases. [2c]He sent them to preach the kingdom of God and to heal the sick. [3d]And He said to them, "Take nothing for the journey, neither staffs nor bag nor bread nor money; and do not have two tunics apiece. [4e]"Whatever house you enter, stay there, and from there depart. [5f]And whoever will not receive you, when you go out of that city, [g]shake off the very dust from your feet as a testimony against them."

[6h]So they departed and went through the towns, preaching the gospel and healing everywhere.

Herod Seeks to See Jesus

[7i]Now Herod the tetrarch heard of all that was done by Him; and he was perplexed, because it was said by some that John had risen from the dead, [8]and by some that Elijah had appeared, and by others that one of the old prophets had risen again. [9]Herod said, "John I have beheaded, but who is this of whom I hear such things?" [j]So he sought to see Him.

Feeding the Five Thousand

[10k]And the apostles, when they had returned, told Him all that they had done. [l]Then He took them and went aside privately into a deserted place belonging to the city called Bethsaida. [11]But when the multitudes knew it, they followed Him; and He received them and spoke to them about the kingdom of God, and healed those who had need of healing. [12m]When the day began to wear away, the twelve came and said to Him, "Send the multitude away, that they may go into the surrounding towns and country, and lodge and get provisions; for we are in a deserted place here."

[13]But He said to them, "You give them something to eat."

And they said, "We have no more than five loaves and two fish, unless we go and buy food for all these people." [14]For there were about five thousand men.

Then He said to His disciples, "Make them sit down in groups of fifty." [15]And they did so, and made them all sit down.

[16]Then He took the five loaves and the two fish, and looking up to heaven, He [n]blessed and broke them, and gave *them* to the disciples to set before the multitude. [17]So they all ate and were filled, and twelve baskets of the leftover fragments were taken up by them.

Peter Confesses Jesus as the Christ

[18o]And it happened, as He was alone praying, *that* His disciples joined Him, and He asked them, saying, "Who do the crowds say that I am?"

[19]So they answered and said, [p]"John the Baptist, but some *say* Elijah; and others *say* that one of the old prophets has risen again."

[20]He said to them, "But who do you say that I am?"

[q]Peter answered and said, "The Christ of God."

Jesus Predicts His Death and Resurrection

[21r]And He strictly warned and commanded them to tell this to no one, [22]saying, [s]"The Son of Man must suffer many things, and be rejected by the elders and chief priests and scribes, and be killed, and be raised the third day."

Take Up the Cross and Follow Him

[23t]Then He said to *them* all, "If anyone desires to come after Me, let him deny himself, and take up his cross daily,* and follow Me. [24u]For whoever desires to save his life will lose it, but whoever loses his life

---

* **9:23** M-Text omits *daily*.

9:2 to preach...to heal the sick. The entire nation of Israel needed to see the evidence of the kingdom of God and make a decision concerning the King. Jesus commissioned His disciples to spread the word about God's kingdom through preaching and healing.

9:11 spoke...healing. Jesus had the same two-pronged ministry that the twelve disciples had: preaching and healing (v. 2). The topic of Jesus' preaching was always the kingdom of God.

9:13–17 about five thousand men. This is the only miracle of Jesus' ministry that appears in all four Gospels. The feeding of the 5,000 demonstrated Jesus' ability to provide.

9:20 The Christ of God. The emphasis here is on the messianic role of Jesus. He is the Promised One who was ushering in a new era. However, Jesus would soon reveal to the disciples that His messiahship would have elements of suffering that the disciples did not expect (vv. 22–23).

9:22 must suffer...be rejected...be killed... be raised. This is the first of several predictions in Luke of Jesus' suffering and vindication (v. 44; 12:50;

13:31–33; 17:25; 18:31–33). The disciples struggled to understand what Jesus was saying (v. 45; 18:34). They could not comprehend how Jesus' predictions fit into God's plan. Only after Jesus' resurrection and His explanation of the Scriptures to them did they begin to understand (24:25–27,44–49).

9:23 take up his cross daily. Although Jesus offered salvation as a free gift (John 1:12; 3:16–18), He also warned that following Him would entail suffering and hardship (Matt. 5:10–12; Rom. 8:17; 2 Thess. 1:5).

9:24–25 For what profit is it to a man if he gains the whole world. It makes no sense to attempt to save our lives on earth only to lose everything when

---

9:2 c Matt. 10:7, 8   **9:3** d Luke 10:4–12; 22:35
9:4 e Mark 6:10   **9:5** f Matt. 10:14   g Acts 13:51
9:6 h Mark 6:12   **9:7** i Matt. 14:1, 2   **9:9** j Luke 23:8
9:10 k Mark 6:30   l Matt. 14:13   **9:12** m John 6:1, 5
9:16 n Luke 22:19; 24:30   **9:18** o Matt. 16:13–16
9:19 p Matt. 14:2   **9:20** q John 6:68, 69   **9:21** r Matt.
8:4; 16:20   **9:22** s Matt. 16:21; 17:22   **9:23** t Matt. 10:38;
16:24   **9:24** u [John 12:25]

for My sake will save it. ²⁵vFor what profit is it to a man if he gains the whole world, and is himself destroyed or lost? ²⁶wFor whoever is ashamed of Me and My words, of him the Son of Man will be xashamed when He comes in His *own* glory, and *in His* Father's, and of the holy angels. ²⁷yBut I tell you truly, there are some standing here who shall not taste death till they see the kingdom of God."

Jesus Transfigured on the Mount

²⁸zNow it came to pass, about eight days after these sayings, that He took Peter, John, and James and went up on the mountain to pray. ²⁹As He prayed, the appearance of His face was altered, and His robe *became* white *and* glistening. ³⁰And behold, two men talked with Him, who were ªMoses and bElijah, ³¹who appeared in glory and spoke of His decease which He was about to accomplish at Jerusalem. ³²But Peter and those with him cwere heavy with sleep; and when they were fully awake, they saw His glory and the two men who stood with Him. ³³Then it happened, as they were parting from Him, *that* Peter said to Jesus, "Master, it is good for us to be here; and let us make three tabernacles: one for You, one for Moses, and one for Elijah"—not knowing what he said.

³⁴While he was saying this, a cloud came and overshadowed them; and they were fearful as they entered the dcloud. ³⁵And a voice came out of the cloud, saying, e"This is My beloved Son.* fHear Him!" ³⁶When the voice had ceased, Jesus was found alone. gBut they kept quiet, and told no one in those days any of the things they had seen.

A Boy Is Healed

³⁷hNow it happened on the next day, when they had come down from the mountain, that a great multitude met Him. ³⁸Suddenly a man from the multitude cried out, saying, "Teacher, I implore You, look on my son, for he is my only child. ³⁹And behold, a spirit seizes him, and he suddenly cries out;

it convulses him so that he foams *at the mouth*; and it departs from him with great difficulty, bruising him. ⁴⁰So I implored Your disciples to cast it out, but they could not."

⁴¹Then Jesus answered and said, "O faithless and perverse generation, how long shall I be with you and bear with you? Bring your son here." ⁴²And as he was still coming, the demon threw him down and convulsed *him*. Then Jesus rebuked the unclean spirit, healed the child, and gave him back to his father.

Jesus Again Predicts His Death

⁴³And they were all amazed at the majesty of God.

But while everyone marveled at all the things which Jesus did, He said to His disciples, ⁴⁴i"Let these words sink down into your ears, for the Son of Man is about to be betrayed into the hands of men." ⁴⁵jBut they did not understand this saying, and it was hidden from them so that they did not perceive it; and they were afraid to ask Him about this saying.

Who Is the Greatest?

⁴⁶kThen a dispute arose among them as to which of them would be greatest. ⁴⁷And Jesus, lperceiving the thought of their heart, took a mlittle child and set him by Him, ⁴⁸and said to them, n"Whoever receives this little child in My name receives Me; and owhoever receives Me preceives Him who sent Me. qFor he who is least among you all will be great."

Jesus Forbids Sectarianism

⁴⁹rNow John answered and said, "Master, we saw someone casting out demons in Your name, and we forbade him because he does not follow us."

⁵⁰But Jesus said to him, "Do not forbid *him*, for she who is not against us* is on our* side."

---

* **9:35** NU-Text reads *This is My Son, the Chosen One.* * **9:50** NU-Text reads *you.* • NU-Text reads *your.*

---

our lives quickly and inevitably pass away. The wise course is to invest our earthly resources—our time, talents, and wealth—in what is eternal.
9:31 *spoke of His decease.* This important allusion to the central Old Testament event of salvation is unique to Luke's account of the transfiguration. The comparison is made between Jesus' death and the journey to salvation that the nation of Israel experienced under Moses.
9:34 *cloud.* This is an allusion to the presence of God (Ex. 40:35).
9:41 *O faithless and perverse generation.* This rebuke suggests that the disciples lacked the faith to cast out the spirit described in verses 38–40. There is also a hint of a competitive spirit among the disciples (v. 46).
9:45 *they were afraid to ask.* The indication here is that the disciples still had much to learn. Their fear

shows that they understood something about what Jesus said, but they did not understand how and why Jesus could say such things about Himself, since He was the Messiah. The suffering of the Messiah was something the disciples did not yet understand. They would continue to be confused in their understanding of how such suffering fit into God's plan until Jesus' death and resurrection (24:25–26,43–49).

9:25 v Mark 8:36 **9:26** w [Rom. 1:16] x Matt. 10:33
9:27 y Matt. 16:28 **9:28** z Mark 9:2–8 **9:30** ª Heb.
11:23–29 b 2 Kin. 2:1–11 **9:32** c Dan. 8:18; 10:9
9:34 d Ex. 13:21 **9:35** e [Matt. 3:17; 12:18] f Acts 3:22
9:36 g Matt. 17:9 **9:37** h Mark 9:14–27 **9:44** i Matt.
17:22 **9:45** j Mark 9:32 **9:46** k Matt. 18:1–5
9:47 l Matt. 9:4 m Luke 18:17 **9:48** n Matt. 18:5 o John
12:44 p John 13:20 q Eph. 3:8 **9:49** r Mark 9:38–40
9:50 s Luke 11:23

A Samaritan Village Rejects the Savior

⁵¹Now it came to pass, when the time had come for ᵗHim to be received up, that He steadfastly set His face to go to Jerusalem, ⁵²and sent messengers before His face. And as they went, they entered a village of the Samaritans, to prepare for Him. ⁵³But ᵘthey did not receive Him, because His face was set for the journey to Jerusalem. ⁵⁴And when His disciples ᵛJames and John saw this, they said, "Lord, do You want us to command fire to come down from heaven and consume them, just as ʷElijah did?"*

⁵⁵But He turned and rebuked them,* and said, "You do not know what manner of ˣspirit you are of. ⁵⁶For ʸthe Son of Man did not come to destroy men's lives but to save them."* And they went to another village.

The Cost of Discipleship

⁵⁷ᶻNow it happened as they journeyed on the road, that someone said to Him, "Lord, I will follow You wherever You go."

⁵⁸And Jesus said to him, "Foxes have holes and birds of the air have nests, but the Son of Man ᵃhas nowhere to lay His head."

⁵⁹ᵇThen He said to another, "Follow Me." But he said, "Lord, let me first go and bury my father."

⁶⁰Jesus said to him, "Let the dead bury their own dead, but you go and preach the kingdom of God."

⁶¹And another also said, "Lord, ᶜI will follow You, but let me first go and bid them farewell who are at my house."

⁶²But Jesus said to him, "No one, having put his hand to the plow, and looking back, is ᵈfit for the kingdom of God."

The Seventy Sent Out

10 After these things the Lord appointed seventy others also,* and ᵃsent them two by two before His face into every city and place where He Himself was about to go. ²Then He said to them, ᵇ"The harvest truly is great, but the laborers are few; therefore ᶜpray the Lord of the harvest to send out laborers into His harvest. ³Go your way; ᵈbehold, I send you out as lambs among wolves. ⁴ᵉCarry neither money bag, knapsack, nor sandals; and ᶠgreet no one along the road. ⁵ᵍBut whatever house you enter, first say, 'Peace to this house.' ⁶And if a son of peace is there, your peace will rest on it; if not, it will return to you. ⁷ʰAnd remain in the same house, ⁱeating and drinking such things as they give, for ʲthe laborer is worthy of his wages. Do not go from house to house. ⁸Whatever city you enter, and they receive you, eat such things as are set before you. ⁹ᵏAnd heal the sick there, and say to them, ˡ'The kingdom of God has come near to you.' ¹⁰But whatever city you enter, and they do not receive you, go out into its streets and say, ¹¹ᵐ'The very dust of your city which clings to us* we wipe off against you. Nevertheless know this, that the kingdom of God has come near you.' ¹²But* I say to you that ⁿit will be more tolerable in that Day for Sodom than for that city.

Woe to the Impenitent Cities

¹³ᵒ"Woe to you, Chorazin! Woe to you, Bethsaida! ᵖFor if the mighty works which were done in you had been done in Tyre and Sidon, they would have repented long ago, sitting in sackcloth and ashes. ¹⁴But it will be more tolerable for Tyre and Sidon

---

* **9:54** NU-Text omits *just as Elijah did.*
* **9:55** NU-Text omits the rest of this verse.
* **9:56** NU-Text omits the first sentence of this verse. * **10:1** NU-Text reads *seventy-two others.* * **10:11** NU-Text reads *our feet.* * **10:12** NU-Text and M-Text omit *But.*

9:51 *He steadfastly set His face to go to Jerusalem.* This is the first indication that Jesus' attention was turning toward His final suffering in Jerusalem (v. 53; 13:22; 17:11; 18:31; 19:11,28,41). Luke's Gospel uniquely emphasizes this journey to Jerusalem.

9:52 *Samaritans.* These people were the descendants of Jews who had married Gentiles after the fall of the northern kingdom, Israel. The Samaritans eventually developed their own religious rites which they practiced on Mount Gerizim instead of at the temple in Jerusalem. Though there was deep hostility between Jews and Samaritans, Jesus ministered to both groups.

9:54 *command fire to come down.* James and John wanted Jesus to bring judgment upon the Samaritan villages that refused to respond to His message, just as Elijah had done in 2 Kings 1:9–16. Their demand for judgment was antithetical to Jesus' loving response (v. 56).

9:59 *let me first go and bury my father.* This aspiring disciple placed family responsibilities ahead of following Jesus. The concerns of home were this man's stumbling block.

9:62 *fit for the kingdom.* This remark of Jesus demonstrates the seriousness of commitment to Him.

10:2 *The harvest truly is great.* The picture of a great harvest suggests that a positive response awaited the laborers, even in the face of much rejection.

10:3 *lambs among wolves.* This image from Isaiah 40:11 was a popular one in Judaism.

10:13 *if the mighty works . . . had been done.* Jesus' remark was meant to wake the people up to what their rejection of Him signified.

9:51 ᵗMark 16:19 **9:53** ᵘJohn 4:4, 9 **9:54** ᵛMark 3:17 ʷ2 Kin. 1:10, 12 **9:55** ˣ[2 Tim. 1:7] **9:56** ʸJohn 3:17; 12:47 **9:57** ᶻMatt. 8:19–22 **9:58** ᵃLuke 2:7; 8:23 **9:59** ᵇMatt. 8:21, 22 **9:61** ᶜ1 Kin. 19:20 **9:62** ᵈ2 Tim. 4:10 **10:1** ᵃMark 6:7 **10:2** ᵇJohn 4:35 ᶜ2 Thess. 3:1 **10:3** ᵈMatt. 10:16 **10:4** ᵉLuke 9:3–5 ᶠ2 Kin. 4:29 **10:5** ᵍMatt. 10:12 **10:7** ʰMatt. 10:11 ⁱ1 Cor. 10:27 ʲ1 Tim. 5:18 **10:9** ᵏMark 3:15 ˡMatt. 3:2; 10:7 **10:11** ᵐActs 13:51 **10:12** ⁿMatt. 10:15; 11:24 **10:13** ᵒMatt. 11:21–23 ᵖEzek. 3:6

at the judgment than for you. 15*a*And you, Capernaum, who are *r*exalted to heaven, *s*will be brought down to Hades.* 16*t*He who hears you hears Me, *u*he who rejects you rejects Me, and *v*he who rejects Me rejects Him who sent Me."

The Seventy Return with Joy

17Then *w*the seventy* returned with joy, saying, "Lord, even the demons are subject to us in Your name."

18And He said to them, *x*"I saw Satan fall like lightning from heaven. 19Behold, *y*I give you the authority to trample on serpents and scorpions, and over all the power of the enemy, and nothing shall by any means hurt you. 20Nevertheless do not rejoice in this, that the spirits are subject to you, but rather* rejoice because *z*your names are written in heaven."

Jesus Rejoices in the Spirit

21*a*In that hour Jesus rejoiced in the Spirit and said, "I thank You, Father, Lord of heaven and earth, that You have hidden these things from *the* wise and prudent and revealed them to babes. Even so, Father, for so it seemed good in Your sight. 22*b*All* things have been delivered to Me by My Father, and *c*no one knows who the Son is except the Father, and who the Father is except the Son, and *the one* to whom the Son wills to reveal *Him*."

23Then He turned to *His* disciples and said privately, *d*"Blessed *are* the eyes which see the things you see; 24for I tell you *e*that many prophets and kings have desired to see what you see, and have not seen *it*, and to hear what you hear, and have not heard *it*."

The Parable of the Good Samaritan

25And behold, a certain lawyer stood up and tested Him, saying, *f*"Teacher, what shall I do to inherit eternal life?"

26He said to him, "What is written in the law? What is your reading *of it*?"

27So he answered and said, *g*"'You shall love the LORD your God with all your heart, with all your soul, with all your strength, and with all your mind,'* and *h*'your neighbor as yourself.'"*

28And He said to him, "You have answered rightly; do this and *i*you will live."

29But he, wanting to *j*justify himself, said to Jesus, "And who is my neighbor?"

30Then Jesus answered and said: "A certain *man* went down from Jerusalem to Jericho, and fell among thieves, who stripped him of his clothing, wounded *him*, and departed, leaving *him* half dead. 31Now by chance a certain priest came down that road. And when he saw him, *k*he passed by on the other side. 32Likewise a Levite, when he arrived at the place, came and looked, and passed by on the other side. 33But a certain *l*Samaritan, as he journeyed, came where he was. And when he saw him, he had *m*compassion. 34So he went to *him* and

* **10:15** NU-Text reads *will you be exalted to heaven? You will be thrust down to Hades!*
* **10:17** NU-Text reads *seventy-two.* * **10:20** NU-Text and M-Text omit *rather.* * **10:22** M-Text reads *And turning to the disciples He said, "All …*
* **10:27** Deuteronomy 6:5 • Leviticus 19:18

10:16 *He who hears you hears Me.* Hearing the messenger is the same as hearing the One who sent him. Authority resides not in the messenger, but in the person the messenger represents, the source of the message.

10:18 *I saw Satan.* This verse provides a commentary on what the disciples' healing ministry meant. The reversal of the effects of sin and death, which Satan introduced through his deception in Genesis 3 is portrayed graphically as Satan falling from heaven. Jesus' ministry and what grows out of it represents the defeat of Satan, sin, and death.

10:19–20 *I give you the authority.* This passage records the transmission of Jesus' power to His immediate circle of disciples. It should be noted that similar power was not given beyond that circle of disciples.

10:22 *All things have been delivered to Me.* This is Jesus' declaration of total authority as the Son of God (John 10:18; 17:2). Jesus declares His unique relationship with God the Father. The Lord reveals Himself only through Jesus. To know God, one must know His Son, Jesus.

10:25–26 *what shall I do to inherit eternal life.* The question posed by the lawyer is really a challenge, since the verse speaks of the testing of Jesus. This is a similar, though probably distinct, event from Matthew 22:34–40 and Mark 12:28–34. To inherit something is to receive it. In other words, the man was asking, "What must I do to share in the reward at the resurrection of the righteous at the end?"

10:27 *love the LORD . . . your neighbor.* The lawyer responded to Jesus' question by quoting Deuteronomy 6:5, a text that was recited twice a day by every faithful Jew. This text summarized the central ethical standard of the law.

10:28 *do this and you will live.* Jesus was not saying that righteousness is the result of works. Rather He was saying that love for and obedience to God will be a natural result of placing one's faith in the Lord.

10:29 *who is my neighbor.* This question was an attempt to limit the demands of the law by suggesting that some people are neighbors while others are not. The lawyer was looking for minimal obedience while Jesus was looking for absolute obedience.

10:30 *Jerusalem to Jericho.* This was a 17-mile journey on a road known to harbor many robbers.

10:31–33 *priest . . . Levite . . . Samaritan.* Part of the beauty of the story of the Good Samaritan is the reversal of stereotypes. The priest and Levite traditionally would have been the "good guys." The

10:15 *q* Matt. 11:23 *r* Is. 14:13–15 *s* Ezek. 26:20
10:16 *t* John 13:20 *u* 1 Thess. 4:8 *v* John 5:23
10:17 *w* Luke 10:1 **10:18** *x* John 12:31 **10:19** *y* Mark 16:18 **10:20** *z* Is. 4:3 **10:21** *a* Matt. 11:25–27
10:22 *b* John 3:35; 5:27; 17:2 *c* [John 1:18; 6:44, 46] **10:23** *d* Matt. 13:16, 17 **10:24** *e* 1 Pet. 1:10, 11
10:25 *f* Matt. 19:16–19; 22:35 **10:27** *g* Deut. 6:5 *h* Lev. 19:18 **10:28** *i* Ezek. 20:11, 13, 21 **10:29** *j* Luke 16:15
10:31 *k* Ps. 38:11 **10:33** *l* John 4:9 *m* Luke 15:20

bandaged his wounds, pouring on oil and wine; and he set him on his own animal, brought him to an inn, and took care of him. 35On the next day, when he departed,* he took out two ⁿdenarii, gave *them* to the innkeeper, and said to him, 'Take care of him; and whatever more you spend, when I come again, I will repay you.' 36So which of these three do you think was neighbor to him who fell among the thieves?"

37And he said, "He who showed mercy on him."

Then Jesus said to him, ᵒ"Go and do likewise."

Mary and Martha Worship and Serve

38Now it happened as they went that He entered a certain village; and a certain woman named ᵖMartha welcomed Him into her house. 39And she had a sister called Mary, ᑫwho also ʳsat at Jesus'* feet and heard His word. 40But Martha was distracted with much serving, and she approached Him and said, "Lord, do You not care that my sister has left me to serve alone? Therefore tell her to help me."

41And Jesus* answered and said to her, "Martha, Martha, you are worried and troubled about many things. 42But ˢone thing is needed, and Mary has chosen that good part, which will not be taken away from her."

The Model Prayer

11 Now it came to pass, as He was praying in a certain place, when He ceased, *that* one of His disciples said to Him, "Lord, teach us to pray, as John also taught his disciples."

2So He said to them, "When you pray, say:

ᵃOur Father in heaven,*
Hallowed be Your name.
Your kingdom come.*
Your will be done
On earth as *it is* in heaven.
3 Give us day by day our daily bread.

4 And ᵇforgive us our sins,
For we also forgive everyone who is indebted to us.
And do not lead us into temptation,
But deliver us from the evil one."*

A Friend Comes at Midnight

5And He said to them, "Which of you shall have a friend, and go to him at midnight and say to him, 'Friend, lend me three loaves; 6for a friend of mine has come to me on his journey, and I have nothing to set before him'; 7and he will answer from within and say, 'Do not trouble me; the door is now shut, and my children are with me in bed; I cannot rise and give to you'? 8I say to you, ᶜthough he will not rise and give to him because he is his friend, yet because of his persistence he will rise and give him as many as he needs.

Keep Asking, Seeking, Knocking

9ᵈ"So I say to you, ask, and it will be given to you; ᵉseek, and you will find; knock, and it will be opened to you. 10For everyone who asks receives, and he who seeks finds, and to him who knocks it will be opened. 11ᶠIf a son asks for bread* from any father among you, will he give him a stone? Or if *he asks* for a fish, will he give him a serpent instead of a fish? 12Or if he asks for an egg, will he offer him a scorpion? 13If you then, being evil, know how to give ᵍgood gifts to your children, how much more will *your* heavenly Father give the Holy Spirit to those who ask Him!"

A House Divided Cannot Stand

14ʰAnd He was casting out a demon, and it was mute. So it was, when the demon had

---

* **10:35** NU-Text omits *when he departed.*
* **10:39** NU-Text reads *the Lord's.* * **10:41** NU-Text reads *the Lord.* * **11:2** NU-Text omits *Our* and *in heaven.* • NU-Text omits the rest of this verse. * **11:4** NU-Text omits *But deliver us from the evil one.* * **11:11** NU-Text omits the words from *bread* through *for* in the next sentence.

Samaritan would have been a "bad guy," a person who compromised in religious matters. However, the Samaritan knew how to treat his neighbor. The neighbor here was not someone the Samaritan knew or even someone of the same race, just someone in need.

10:36 *which . . . was neighbor.* The central issue is not determining who one's neighbor is, but being a good neighbor to all.

11:1 *Lord, teach us to pray.* The Lord's Prayer illustrates the variety of requests that one can and should make to God, as well as displaying the humble attitude that should accompany prayer. The use of the plural pronoun "us" throughout the prayer shows that it is not just the prayer of one person for his or her own personal needs, but a community prayer.

11:2 *Your kingdom come.* The reference here is to God's program and promise. This is more affirmation than request, highlighting the petitioner's

submission to God's will and the desire to see God's work come to pass.

11:4 *we also forgive.* The petitioner recognizes that if mercy is to be sought from God, then mercy must be shown to others. We need to adopt the same standard that we expect others to follow. *do not lead us into temptation.* This remark is often misunderstood as suggesting that perhaps God can lead us into sin. The point is that if one is to avoid sin, one must follow where God leads. In short, the petitioner asks God for the spiritual protection necessary to avoid falling into sin.

10:35 ⁿ Matt. 20:2   **10:37** ᵒ Prov. 14:21   **10:38** ᵖ John 11:1; 12:2, 3   **10:39** ᑫ [1 Cor. 7:32–40]   ʳ Acts 22:3   **10:42** ˢ [Ps. 27:4]   **11:2** ᵈ Matt. 6:9–13   **11:4** ᵇ [Eph. 4:32]   **11:8** ᶜ [Luke 18:1–5]   **11:9** ᵈ [John 15:7]   ᵉ Is. 55:6   **11:11** ᶠ Matt. 7:9   **11:13** ᵍ James 1:17   **11:14** ʰ Matt. 9:32–34; 12:22, 24

gone out, that the mute spoke; and the multitudes marveled. [15]But some of them said, [i]"He casts out demons by Beelzebub,* the ruler of the demons."

[16]Others, testing *Him*, [j]sought from Him a sign from heaven. [17k]But [l]He, knowing their thoughts, said to them: "Every kingdom divided against itself is brought to desolation, and a house *divided* against a house falls. [18]If Satan also is divided against himself, how will his kingdom stand? Because you say I cast out demons by Beelzebub. [19]And if I cast out demons by Beelzebub, by whom do your sons cast *them* out? Therefore they will be your judges. [20]But if I cast out demons [m]with the finger of God, surely the kingdom of God has come upon you. [21n]When a strong man, fully armed, guards his own palace, his goods are in peace. [22]But [o]when a stronger than he comes upon him and overcomes him, he takes from him all his armor in which he trusted, and divides his spoils. [23p]He who is not with Me is against Me, and he who does not gather with Me scatters.

An Unclean Spirit Returns

[24q]"When an unclean spirit goes out of a man, he goes through dry places, seeking rest; and finding none, he says, 'I will return to my house from which I came.' [25]And when he comes, he finds *it* swept and put in order. [26]Then he goes and takes with *him* seven other spirits more wicked than himself, and they enter and dwell there; and [r]the last *state* of that man is worse than the first."

Keeping the Word

[27]And it happened, as He spoke these things, that a certain woman from the crowd raised her voice and said to Him, [s]"Blessed *is* the womb that bore You, and *the* breasts which nursed You!"

[28]But He said, [t]"More than that, blessed *are* those who hear the word of God and keep it!"

Seeking a Sign

[29u]And while the crowds were thickly gathered together, He began to say, "This is an evil generation. It seeks a [v]sign, and no sign will be given to it except the sign of Jonah the prophet.* [30]For as [w]Jonah became a sign to the Ninevites, so also the Son of Man will be to this generation. [31x]The queen of the South will rise up in the judgment with the men of this generation and condemn them, for she came from the ends of the earth to hear the wisdom of Solomon; and indeed a [y]greater than Solomon *is* here. [32]The men of Nineveh will rise up in the judgment with this generation and condemn it, for [z]they repented at the preaching of Jonah; and indeed a greater than Jonah *is* here.

The Lamp of the Body

[33a]"No one, when he has lit a lamp, puts *it* in a secret place or under a [b]basket, but on a lampstand, that those who come in may see the light. [34c]The lamp of the body is the eye. Therefore, when your eye is good, your whole body also is full of light. But when *your eye* is bad, your body also *is* full of darkness. [35]Therefore take heed that the light which is in you is not darkness. [36]If then your whole body *is* full of light, having no part dark, *the* whole *body* will be full of light, as when the bright shining of a lamp gives you light."

Woe to the Pharisees and Lawyers

[37]And as He spoke, a certain Pharisee asked Him to dine with him. So He went in

---

* 11:15 NU-Text and M-Text read *Beelzebul*.
* 11:29 NU-Text omits *the prophet*.

11:17–18 you say I cast out demons by Beelzebub. The attribution of Jesus' miracles to Satan was not only blasphemous, it was illogical. If Satan had cast out the demon (v. 14), he would have been destroying the result of his own work.

11:20 the finger of God. This phrase is an allusion to God's power, like that demonstrated in the Exodus (Ex. 8:19; Deut. 9:10; Ps. 8:3). **the kingdom of God has come upon you.** Jesus' miracles represented the arrival of God's power and promise—in short, His rule. That rule comes in and through Jesus. The miracles of Jesus demonstrated God's victory over the forces of evil. The kingdom program, depicted as drawing near, will be consummated at the return of Jesus when this rule is manifested over every creature.

11:22 when a stronger than he. Jesus portrays Himself as someone stronger than Satan who overruns Satan's house and gives the spoils of victory to those who are His (Eph. 4:8–9).

11:23 He who is not with Me. Jesus' ministry forces everyone to make a choice. Neutrality is not an

option. Either Jesus comes from God or He does not. Not to align with Jesus is to be against Him.

11:26 the last state. Jesus' point is that experiencing God's blessing and then ignoring it leaves one callous towards the work of God and exposed to the control of demonic forces.

11:29 the sign of Jonah. This refers to his prophetic call to repentance rather than to the resurrection foreshadowed by Jonah's return from the belly of the great fish.

11:36 your whole body is full of light. A person can become like light, a living picture of what God's Word teaches, by concentrating on the light of the truth.

11:15 [i] Matt. 9:34; 12:24   **11:16** [j] Matt. 12:38; 16:1
11:17 [k] Matt. 12:25–29 [l] John 2:25   **11:20** [m] Ex. 8:19
11:21 [n] Mark 3:27   **11:22** [o] [Is. 53:12]   **11:23** [p] Matt.
12:30   **11:24** [q] Matt. 12:43–45   **11:26** [r] [2 Pet. 2:20]
11:27 [s] Luke 1:28, 48   **11:28** [t] [Luke 8:21]   **11:29** [u] Matt.
12:38–42 [v] 1 Cor. 1:22   **11:30** [w] Jon. 1:17; 2:10; 3:3–10
11:31 [x] 1 Kin. 10:1–9 [y] [Rom. 9:5]   **11:32** [z] Jon. 3:5
11:33 [a] Mark 4:21 [b] Matt. 5:15   **11:34** [c] Matt. 6:22, 23

and sat down to eat. 38dWhen the Pharisee saw *it*, he marveled that He had not first washed before dinner.

39eThen the Lord said to him, "Now you Pharisees make the outside of the cup and dish clean, but fyour inward part is full of greed and wickedness. 40Foolish ones! Did not gHe who made the outside make the inside also? 41hBut rather give alms of such things as you have; then indeed all things are clean to you.

42i"But woe to you Pharisees! For you tithe mint and rue and all manner of herbs, and jpass by justice and the klove of God. These you ought to have done, without leaving the others undone. 43lWoe to you Pharisees! For you love the best seats in the synagogues and greetings in the marketplaces. 44mWoe to you, scribes and Pharisees, hypocrites!* nFor you are like graves which are not seen, and the men who walk over *them* are not aware of *them*."

45Then one of the lawyers answered and said to Him, "Teacher, by saying these things You reproach us also."

46And He said, "Woe to you also, lawyers! oFor you load men with burdens hard to bear, and you yourselves do not touch the burdens with one of your fingers. 47pWoe to you! For you build the tombs of the prophets, and your fathers killed them. 48In fact, you bear witness that you approve the deeds of your fathers; for they indeed killed them, and you build their tombs. 49Therefore the wisdom of God also said, q'I will send them prophets and apostles, and *some* of them they will kill and persecute,' 50that the blood of all the prophets which was shed from the foundation of the world may be required of this generation,

51rfrom the blood of Abel to sthe blood of Zechariah who perished between the altar and the temple. Yes, I say to you, it shall be required of this generation.

52t"Woe to you lawyers! For you have taken away the key of knowledge. You did not enter in yourselves, and those who were entering in you hindered."

53And as He said these things to them,* the scribes and the Pharisees began to assail *Him* vehemently, and to cross-examine Him about many things, 54lying in wait for Him, and useeking to catch Him in something He might say, that they might accuse Him.*

Beware of Hypocrisy

12 In athe meantime, when an innumerable multitude of people had gathered together, so that they trampled one another, He began to say to His disciples first of all, b"Beware of the leaven of the Pharisees, which is hypocrisy. 2cFor there is nothing covered that will not be revealed, nor hidden that will not be known. 3Therefore whatever you have spoken in the dark will be heard in the light, and what you have spoken in the ear in inner rooms will be proclaimed on the housetops.

Jesus Teaches the Fear of God

4d"And I say to you, eMy friends, do not be afraid of those who kill the body, and after that have no more that they can do. 5But I will show you whom you should fear: Fear

---

* **11:44** NU-Text omits *scribes and Pharisees, hypocrites.* * **11:53** NU-Text reads *And when He left there.* * **11:54** NU-Text omits *and seeking* and *that they might accuse Him.*

11:39 make the outside ... clean. These condemnations by Jesus are similar to those in Matthew 23. The Pharisees washed the outside of cups, making sure that the cups had not become unclean through contact with a dead insect (Lev. 11:31–38). Jesus pointed out that the Pharisees concerned themselves with outward appearances and ritual cleanness, while what was inside, what really counts, was full of selfishness and evil.

11:42 tithe mint and rue. Some Pharisees took the strictest interpretation and counted almost anything, including spices. However, they neglected two basic things that the prophets also had warned about: love and justice (Mic. 6:8; Zech. 7:8–10).

11:46 burdens. This term refers to a ship's cargo. The idea is that a heavy strain was being imposed on the people and yet, in the end, this burden did not bring them close to God. Here Jesus rebuked the tradition that had grown up around the law of Moses.

11:47–48 you build the tombs of the prophets. Jesus made a biting, ironic comparison between the current generation of Israel and the generations of the past. Jesus was saying that the current generation finished the job of slaying the prophets that the previous generation had started. The building and care of tombs was supposed to be an act of honoring the prophets, but Jesus pointed out that something else was really going on.

11:52 Woe to you lawyers. Jesus charged the lawyers with doing the opposite of what they claimed their calling to be. Rather than bringing people nearer to God, they had removed the possibility of their entering into that knowledge, and had prevented others from understanding it as well.

12:1–2 leaven. This represents the presence of corruption. Unleavened bread is what the Jews ate at Passover (Ex. 12:14–20). The corruption in view here is hypocrisy. Practicing hypocrisy is senseless because eventually all deeds—both good and evil—will be exposed.

12:4 do not be afraid of those who kill the body. This verse anticipates the presence of severe religious persecution in response to Jesus' remarks in Luke 11:39–54.

12:5 Fear Him. Even in the context of physical

11:38 d Mark 7:2, 3 **11:39** e Matt. 23:25 f Titus 1:15 **11:40** g Gen. 1:26, 27 **11:41** h [Luke 12:33; 16:9] **11:42** i Matt. 23:23 j [Mic. 6:7, 8] k John 5:42 **11:43** l Mark 12:38, 39 **11:44** m Matt. 23:27 n Ps. 5:9 **11:46** o Matt. 23:4 **11:47** p Matt. 23:29 **11:49** q Matt. 23:34 **11:51** r Gen. 4:8 s 2 Chr. 24:20, 21 **11:52** t Matt. 23:13 **11:54** u Mark 12:13 **12:1** a Mark 8:15 b Matt. 16:12 **12:2** c Matt. 10:26; [1 Cor. 4:5] **12:4** d Is. 51:7, 8, 12, 13 e [John 15:13–15]

Him who, after He has killed, has power to cast into hell; yes, I say to you, ^ffear Him!

⁶"Are not five sparrows sold for two copper coins?* And ^gnot one of them is forgotten before God. ⁷But the very hairs of your head are all numbered. Do not fear therefore; you are of more value than many sparrows.

Confess Christ Before Men

^{8h}"Also I say to you, whoever confesses Me ⁱbefore men, him the Son of Man also will confess before the angels of God. ⁹But he who ^jdenies Me before men will be denied before the angels of God.

¹⁰"And ^kanyone who speaks a word against the Son of Man, it will be forgiven him; but to him who blasphemes against the Holy Spirit, it will not be forgiven. ^{11l}"Now when they bring you to the synagogues and magistrates and authorities, do not worry about how or what you should answer, or what you should say. ¹²For the Holy Spirit will ^mteach you in that very hour what you ought to say."

The Parable of the Rich Fool

¹³Then one from the crowd said to Him, "Teacher, tell my brother to divide the inheritance with me."

¹⁴But He said to him, ⁿ"Man, who made Me a judge or an arbitrator over you?" ¹⁵And He said to them, ^o"Take heed and beware of covetousness,* for one's life does not consist in the abundance of the things he possesses."

¹⁶Then He spoke a parable to them, saying: "The ground of a certain rich man yielded plentifully. ¹⁷And he thought within himself, saying, 'What shall I do, since I have no room to store my crops?' ¹⁸So he said, 'I will do this: I will pull down my barns and build greater, and there I will store all my crops and my goods. ¹⁹And I will say to my soul, ^p"Soul, you have many goods laid up for many years; take your

ease; ^qeat, drink, *and* be merry." ' ²⁰But God said to him, 'Fool! This night ^ryour soul will be required of you; ^sthen whose will those things be which you have provided?'

²¹"So *is* he who lays up treasure for himself, ^tand is not rich toward God."

Do Not Worry

²²Then He said to His disciples, "Therefore I say to you, ^udo not worry about your life, what you will eat; nor about the body, what you will put on. ²³Life is more than food, and the body *is more* than clothing. ²⁴Consider the ravens, for they neither sow nor reap, which have neither storehouse nor barn; and ^vGod feeds them. Of how much more value are you than the birds? ²⁵And which of you by worrying can add one cubit to his stature? ²⁶If you then are not able to do *the* least, why are you anxious for the rest? ²⁷Consider the lilies, how they grow: they neither toil nor spin; and yet I say to you, even ^wSolomon in all his glory was not arrayed like one of these. ²⁸If then God so clothes the grass, which today is in the field and tomorrow is thrown into the oven, how much more *will He clothe* you, O *you* of ^xlittle faith?

²⁹"And do not seek what you should eat or what you should drink, nor have an anxious mind. ³⁰For all these things the nations of the world seek after, and your Father ^yknows that you need these things. ^{31z}But seek the kingdom of God, and all these things* shall be added to you.

³²"Do not fear, little flock, for ^ait is your Father's good pleasure to give you the kingdom. ^{33b}Sell what you have and give ^calms; ^dprovide yourselves money bags which do not grow old, a treasure in the heavens that does not fail, where no thief approaches

---

* **12:6** Greek *assarion*, a coin of very small value   * **12:15** NU-Text reads *all covetousness.*
* **12:31** NU-Text reads *His kingdom, and these things.*

---

persecution, the only One believers should fear is God, who sees how we live and judges us. Jesus was not guaranteeing physical preservation in this life, but was opening the prospect of deliverance in the next life.

12:6 two copper coins. These were the smallest coins in circulation, worth about one-sixteenth of a basic day's wages.

12:14 who made Me a judge. Jesus refuses to enter into a dispute over money, which is clearly dividing a family. Such disputes over money destroy relationships, so Jesus tells a parable that explains the danger of focusing on wealth.

12:18–19 I will do this. Including verse 17, the word "I" appears six times, showing the selfish focus this man has as a result of his fortune. His plan is to store his abundant resources for himself, as though the assets were his alone and should be hoarded. This focus on the self is what Jesus is condemning.

12:27–29 God so clothes the grass. This illustration indicates that God cares enough to provide beauty

for the parts of His creation that have a short life. Why should we worry if God takes such care of even the smallest blade of grass? The Lord knows our problems and will provide us with what we need.

12:33 Sell what you have. In contrast to the world's hoarding of possessions, the disciple must be generous with what God gives. By serving God and others, you can invest in your eternal future. You cannot take possessions with you in the next life, but you can store up an eternal treasure by giving to others (Phil. 4:17).

12:5 ^fPs. 119:120   **12:6** ^gMatt. 6:26   **12:8** ^hMatt. 10:32 ⁱPs. 119:46   **12:9** ^jMatt. 10:33   **12:10** ^k[Matt. 12:31, 32] **12:11** ^lMark 13:11   **12:12** ^m[John 14:26]   **12:14** ⁿ[John 18:36]   **12:15** ^o[1 Tim. 6:6–10]   **12:19** ^pEccl. 11:9 ^q[Eccl. 2:24; 3:13; 5:18; 8:15]   **12:20** ^rPs. 52:7 ^sPs. 39:6   **12:21** ^t[James 2:5; 5:1–5]   **12:22** ^uMatt. 6:25–33   **12:24** ^vJob 38:41   **12:27** ^w1 Kin. 10:4–7 **12:28** ^xMatt. 6:30; 8:26; 14:31; 16:8   **12:30** ^yMatt. 6:31, 32   **12:31** ^zMatt. 6:33   **12:32** ^a[Matt. 11:25, 26]   **12:33** ^bMatt. 19:21 ^cLuke 11:41 ^dMatt. 6:20

nor moth destroys. 34 For where your treasure is, there your heart will be also.

The Faithful Servant and the Evil Servant

35 [e]“Let your waist be girded and [f]*your*
lamps burning; 36 and you yourselves be
like men who wait for their master, when
he will return from the wedding, that when
he comes and knocks they may open to him
immediately. 37 [g]Blessed *are* those servants
whom the master, when he comes, will find
watching. Assuredly, I say to you that he
will gird himself and have them sit down *to*
eat, and will come and serve them. 38 And
if he should come in the second watch, or
come in the third watch, and find *them* so,
blessed are those servants. 39 [h]But know
this, that if the master of the house had
known what hour the thief would come, he
would have watched and* not allowed his
house to be broken into. 40 [i]Therefore you
also be ready, for the Son of Man is coming
at an hour you do not expect.”

41 Then Peter said to Him, “Lord, do You
speak this parable *only* to us, or to all *peo-*
ple?”

42 And the Lord said, [j]“Who then is that
faithful and wise steward, whom *his* master will make ruler over his household,
to give *them their* portion of food in due
season? 43 Blessed *is* that servant whom
his master will find so doing when he
comes. 44 [k]Truly, I say to you that he will
make him ruler over all that he has. 45 [l]But
if that servant says in his heart, ‘My master is delaying his coming,’ and begins to
beat the male and female servants, and to
eat and drink and be drunk, 46 the master
of that servant will come on a [m]day when
he is not looking for *him*, and at an hour
when he is not aware, and will cut him
in two and appoint *him* his portion with
the unbelievers. 47 And [n]that servant who
[o]knew his master’s will, and did not prepare *himself* or do according to his will,
shall be beaten with many *stripes*. 48 [p]But
he who did not know, yet committed
things deserving of stripes, shall be beat-
en with few. For everyone to whom much
is given, from him much will be required;
and to whom much has been committed,
of him they will ask the more.

Christ Brings Division

49 [q]“I came to send fire on the earth, and
how I wish it were already kindled! 50 But
[r]I have a baptism to be baptized with, and
how distressed I am till it is [s]accomplished!
51 [t]Do *you* suppose that I came to give peace
on earth? I tell you, not at all, [u]but rather
division. 52 [v]For from now on five in one
house will be divided: three against two,
and two against three. 53 [w]Father will be
divided against son and son against father, mother against daughter and daughter against mother, mother-in-law against
her daughter-in-law and daughter-in-law
against her mother-in-law.”

Discern the Time

54 Then He also said to the multitudes,
[x]“Whenever you see a cloud rising out of
the west, immediately you say, ‘A shower
is coming’; and so it is. 55 And when *you see*
the [y]south wind blow, you say, ‘There will
be hot weather’; and there is. 56 Hypocrites!
You can discern the face of the sky and of
the earth, but how *is it* you do not discern
[z]this time?

* **12:39** NU-Text reads *he would not have allowed.*

12:34 ***where your treasure is.*** What people consider valuable is where their energy will be spent. Knowing God and investing in His purposes should be the treasure we seek.

12:38 ***if he should come in the second watch, or come in the third watch.*** This verse speaks of a return at an unusually late hour. The exact time referred to depends on which system of time was used. In the Roman system the second and third watch would be 9 P.M. to 3 A.M. By the Jewish method it would be 10 P.M. to 6 A.M.

12:41 ***only to us, or to all.*** Peter asked if Jesus' teaching was for the disciples only or for all people. Jesus did not answer the question directly. Instead He described a variety of categories of servants. Servants are those who belong to the Master and have their stewardship evaluated (19:11–27). Several responses, from faithfulness to blatant disobedience, are described in verses 42–48. The issue is who lives life in a way that looks for, and takes seriously, the return of Jesus (1 John 2:28).

12:45 ***begins to beat the male and female servants.*** This servant is depicted as consciously doing the opposite of caring for others, and of treating the Master's return as irrelevant.

12:46 ***will cut him in two.*** The image of being slain indicates the severity of this judgment, especially in contrast to the whippings of verses 47 and 48.

12:49 ***I came to send fire on the earth.*** Fire is an image associated with God's judgment (Jer. 5:14; 23:29). Jesus' coming brings judgment on those who refuse to accept Him and divides the believers from the faithless.

12:54–55 ***a cloud rising out of the west.*** In Palestine, a western breeze meant moisture coming from the Mediterranean Sea. A south wind meant hot air coming from the desert.

12:56 ***Hypocrites.*** Jesus rebuked His audience for being able to discern the weather but not what God was doing through Him.

12:35 [e] [1 Pet. 1:13] [f] [Matt. 25:1–13] **12:37** [g] Matt. 24:46 **12:39** [h] Rev. 3:3; 16:15 **12:40** [i] Mark 13:33 **12:42** [j] Matt. 24:45, 46; 25:21 **12:44** [k] Matt. 24:47; 25:21 **12:45** [l] 2 Pet. 3:3, 4 **12:46** [m] 1 Thess. 5:3 **12:47** [n] Deut. 25:2 [o] [James 4:17] **12:48** [p] [Lev. 5:17] **12:49** [q] Luke 12:51 **12:50** [r] Mark 10:38 [s] John 12:27; 19:30 **12:51** [t] Matt. 10:34–36 [u] John 7:43; 9:16; 10:19 **12:52** [v] Mark 13:12 **12:53** [w] Matt. 10:21, 36 **12:54** [x] Matt. 16:2, 3 **12:55** [y] Job 37:17 **12:56** [z] Luke 19:41–44

Make Peace with Your Adversary

57"Yes, and why, even of yourselves, do you not judge what is right? **58**aWhen you go with your adversary to the magistrate, make every effort balong the way to settle with him, lest he drag you to the judge, the judge deliver you to the officer, and the officer throw you into prison. **59**I tell you, you shall not depart from there till you have paid the very last mite."

Repent or Perish

13 There were present at that season some who told Him about the Galileans whose blood Pilate had mingled with their sacrifices. **2**And Jesus answered and said to them, "Do you suppose that these Galileans were worse sinners than all *other* Galileans, because they suffered such things? **3**I tell you, no; but unless you repent you will all likewise perish. **4**Or those eighteen on whom the tower in Siloam fell and killed them, do you think that they were worse sinners than all *other* men who dwelt in Jerusalem? **5**I tell you, no; but unless you repent you will all likewise perish."

The Parable of the Barren Fig Tree

6He also spoke this parable: a"A certain *man* had a fig tree planted in his vineyard, and he came seeking fruit on it and found none. **7**Then he said to the keeper of his vineyard, 'Look, for three years I have come seeking fruit on this fig tree and find none. Cut it down; why does it use up the ground?' **8**But he answered and said to him, 'Sir, let it alone this year also, until I dig around it and fertilize *it*. **9**And if it bears fruit, *well*. But if not, after that* you can bcut it down.'"

A Spirit of Infirmity

10Now He was teaching in one of the synagogues on the Sabbath. **11**And behold, there was a woman who had a spirit of infirmity eighteen years, and was bent over and could in no way raise *herself* up. **12**But when Jesus saw her, He called *her* to *Him*

and said to her, "Woman, you are loosed from your cinfirmity." **13**dAnd He laid *His* hands on her, and immediately she was made straight, and glorified God.

14But the ruler of the synagogue answered with indignation, because Jesus had ehealed on the Sabbath; and he said to the crowd, f"There are six days on which men ought to work; therefore come and be healed on them, and gnot on the Sabbath day."

15The Lord then answered him and said, "Hypocrite!* hDoes not each one of you on the Sabbath loose his ox or donkey from the stall, and lead *it* away to water it? **16**So ought not this woman, ibeing a daughter of Abraham, whom Satan has bound—think of it—for eighteen years, be loosed from this bond on the Sabbath?" **17**And when He said these things, all His adversaries were put to shame; and all the multitude rejoiced for all the glorious things that were jdone by Him.

The Parable of the Mustard Seed

18kThen He said, "What is the kingdom of God like? And to what shall I compare it? **19**It is like a mustard seed, which a man took and put in his garden; and it grew and became a large* tree, and the birds of the air nested in its branches."

The Parable of the Leaven

20And again He said, "To what shall I liken the kingdom of God? **21**It is like leaven, which a woman took and hid in three lmeasures* of meal till it was all leavened."

The Narrow Way

22mAnd He went through the cities and villages, teaching, and journeying toward Jerusalem. **23**Then one said to Him, "Lord, are there nfew who are saved?"

* **13:9** NU-Text reads *And if it bears fruit after that, well. But if not, you can cut it down.*
* **13:15** NU-Text and M-Text read *Hypocrites.*
* **13:19** NU-Text omits *large.* * **13:21** Greek *sata,* approximately two pecks in all

---

13:1 Pilate. Pilate was known for his insensitivity to the Jewish people early in his rule. The event probably occurred during the Feast of the Passover or Tabernacles, when Galileans most likely would have been at the temple.
13:5 unless you repent. The manner in which a person dies is not a measure of righteousness; what is important is not to die outside of God's grace and care. The way to avoid such a fate is to repent, to come to God through the care of the Physician Jesus (5:32).
13:6 a fig tree. This tree often represents God's blessing, or a people who have a special relationship with God (Mic. 7:1–2). The man in this parable represents God; the fig tree represents Israel.
13:7 for three years. A fig tree was often given some time to bear good fruit since its root structure was complex and took time to develop. Three years would have been enough for the tree to yield some fruit.

13:15 Hypocrite. When the ruler of the synagogue became indignant regarding Jesus' healing on the Sabbath (vv. 10–14), Jesus pointed out that basic compassion was shown to animals on the Sabbath, so how much more compassion should be shown to a suffering woman (v. 16)?
13:18–19 mustard. A tree of the mustard family would grow to about twelve feet. The image of birds nesting in the trees is found frequently in the Old Testament (Ps. 104:12; Ezek. 17:22–24; Dan. 4:10–12).

12:58 a Prov. 25:8 b [Is. 55:6] **13:6** d Matt. 21:19 **13:9** b [John 15:2] **13:12** c Luke 7:21; 8:2 **13:13** d Acts 9:17 **13:14** e [Luke 6:6–11; 14:1–6] f Ex. 20:9; 23:12 g Mark 3:2 **13:15** h Luke 14:5 **13:16** i Luke 19:9 **13:17** j Mark 5:19, 20 **13:18** k Mark 4:30–32 **13:21** l Matt. 13:33 **13:22** m Mark 6:6 **13:23** n [Matt. 7:14; 20:16]

And He said to them, 24o"Strive to enter through the narrow gate, for Pmany, I say to you, will seek to enter and will not be able. 25qWhen once the Master of the house has risen up and rshut the door, and you begin to stand outside and knock at the door, saying, s"Lord, Lord, open for us,' and He will answer and say to you, t'I do not know you, where you are from,' 26then you will begin to say, 'We ate and drank in Your presence, and You taught in our streets.' 27uBut He will say, 'I tell you I do not know you, where you are from. vDepart from Me, all you workers of iniquity.' 28wThere will be weeping and gnashing of teeth, xwhen you see Abraham and Isaac and Jacob and all the prophets in the kingdom of God, and yourselves thrust out. 29They will come from the east and the west, from the north and the south, and sit down in the kingdom of God. 30yAnd indeed there are last who will be first, and there are first who will be last."

31On that very day* some Pharisees came, saying to Him, "Get out and depart from here, for Herod wants to kill You." 32And He said to them, "Go, tell that fox, 'Behold, I cast out demons and perform cures today and tomorrow, and the third day zI shall be perfected.' 33Nevertheless I must journey today, tomorrow, and the day following; for it cannot be that a prophet should perish outside of Jerusalem.

Jesus Laments over Jerusalem

34a"O Jerusalem, Jerusalem, the one who kills the prophets and stones those who are sent to her! How often I wanted to gather your children together, as a hen gathers her brood under her wings, but you were not willing! 35See! bYour house is left to you desolate; and assuredly,* I say to you, you shall not see Me until the time comes when you say, c'Blessed is He who comes in the name of the LORD!' "*

A Man with Dropsy Healed on the Sabbath

14 Now it happened, as He went into the house of one of the rulers of the Pharisees to eat bread on the Sabbath, that they watched Him closely. 2And behold, there was a certain man before Him who had dropsy. 3And Jesus, answering, spoke to the lawyers and Pharisees, saying, a"Is it lawful to heal on the Sabbath?"*

4But they kept silent. And He took him and healed him, and let him go. 5Then He answered them, saying, b"Which of you, having a donkey* or an ox that has fallen into a pit, will not immediately pull him out on the Sabbath day?" 6And they could not answer Him regarding these things.

Take the Lowly Place

7So He told a parable to those who were invited, when He noted how they chose the best places, saying to them: 8"When you are invited by anyone to a wedding feast, do not sit down in the best place, lest one more honorable than you be invited by him; 9and he who invited you and him come and say to you, 'Give place to this man,' and then you begin with shame to take the lowest place. 10cBut when you are invited, go and sit down in the lowest place, so that when he who invited you comes he may say to you, 'Friend, go up higher.' Then you will have glory in the presence of those who sit at the table with you. 11dFor whoever exalts himself will be humbled, and he who humbles himself will be exalted."

---

* **13:31** NU-Text reads *In that very hour.*
* **13:35** NU-Text and M-Text omit *assuredly.* •
Psalm 118:26 * **14:3** NU-Text adds *or not.*
* **14:5** NU-Text and M-Text read *son.*

13:26 We ate and drank . . . You taught. The appeal here is by people who experience Jesus' presence. The passage primarily involves those Jews who witnessed Jesus' ministry. They were trying to gain entry into God's presence based simply on the fact that they had observed Jesus. Jesus refused them, pointing out that it was not enough for them to have been close to Him. In order to have a relationship with God, one must embrace Jesus and come to know Him.

13:29 east . . . west . . . north . . . south. People would come from all corners of the earth for entrance into God's kingdom. This passage alludes to the inclusion of Gentiles.

13:30 there are last who will be first. There will be many surprises in God's kingdom. Those who are despised on earth—some Gentiles, for example—will be greatly honored in the kingdom. Conversely, those who are considered influential and powerful on earth—the Jewish religious leaders of Jesus' day, for example—will be excluded from the kingdom.

13:32 Go, tell that fox. Herod is portrayed as more curious than hostile. The reference here is to Herod's cunning. Jesus' reply seems to take the Pharisees' warning at face value.

13:34 O Jerusalem, Jerusalem. The double address indicates Jesus' deep sorrow (2 Sam. 18:33; Jer. 22:29). The city had executed many of God's messengers. Stephen makes a similar point about the nation of Israel in Acts 7:51–53.

13:35 Blessed is He. This is a citation of Psalm 118:26. The people of Israel would not see the Messiah again until they were ready to receive Him and recognize that He was sent from God. Psalm 118 reflects the greeting of a priest to a group entering the temple. Jesus used the language of this psalm to illustrate God's greeting to Him.

14:7 they chose the best places. In ancient times the best seats at a meal were those next to the host.

13:24 o [Matt. 7:13] P [John 7:34; 8:21; 13:33] **13:25** q Is. 55:6 r Matt. 25:10 s Luke 6:46 t Matt. 7:23; 25:12 **13:27** u [Matt. 7:23; 25:41] v Ps. 6:8 **13:28** w Matt. 8:12; 13:42; 24:51 x Matt. 7:23 **13:30** y [Matt. 19:30; 20:16] **13:32** z [Heb. 2:10; 5:9; 7:28] **13:34** d Matt. 23:37–39 **13:35** b Lev. 26:31, 32 c Ps. 118:26; Matt. 21:9 **14:3** d Matt. 12:10 **14:5** b [Ex. 23:5] **14:10** c Prov. 25:6, 7 **14:11** d Matt. 23:12

¹²Then He also said to him who invited Him, "When you give a dinner or a supper, do not ask your friends, your brothers, your relatives, nor rich neighbors, your, lest they also invite you back, and you be repaid. ¹³But when you give a feast, invite ᵉthe poor, *the* maimed, *the* lame, *the* blind. ¹⁴And you will be ᶠblessed, because they cannot repay you; for you shall be repaid at the resurrection of the just."

The Parable of the Great Supper

¹⁵Now when one of those who sat at the table with Him heard these things, he said to Him, ᵍ"Blessed *is* he who shall eat bread* in the kingdom of God!"

¹⁶ʰThen He said to him, "A certain man gave a great supper and invited many, ¹⁷and ⁱsent his servant at supper time to say to those who were invited, 'Come, for all things are now ready.' ¹⁸But they all with one *accord* began to make excuses. The first said to him, 'I have bought a piece of ground, and I must go and see it. I ask you to have me excused.' ¹⁹And another said, 'I have bought five yoke of oxen, and I am going to test them. I ask you to have me excused.' ²⁰Still another said, 'I have married a wife, and therefore I cannot come.' ²¹So that servant came and reported these things to his master. Then the master of the house, being angry, said to his servant, 'Go out quickly into the streets and lanes of the city, and bring in here *the* poor and *the* maimed and *the* lame and *the* blind.' ²²And the servant said, 'Master, it is done as you commanded, and still there is room.' ²³Then the master said to the servant, 'Go out into the highways and hedges, and compel *them* to come in, that my house may be filled. ²⁴For I say to you ʲthat none of those men who were invited shall taste my supper.'"

Leaving All to Follow Christ

²⁵Now great multitudes went with Him. And He turned and said to them, ²⁶ᵏ"If anyone comes to Me ˡand does not hate his father and mother, wife and children, brothers and sisters, ᵐyes, and his own life also, he cannot be My disciple. ²⁷And ⁿwhoever does not bear his cross and come after Me cannot be My disciple. ²⁸For ᵒwhich of you, intending to build a tower, does not sit down first and count the cost, whether he has *enough* to finish *it*— ²⁹lest, after he has laid the foundation, and is not able to finish, all who see *it* begin to mock him, ³⁰saying, 'This man began to build and was not able to finish'? ³¹Or what king, going to make war against another king, does not sit down first and consider whether he is able with ten thousand to meet him who comes against him with twenty thousand? ³²Or else, while the other is still a great way off, he sends a delegation and asks conditions of peace. ³³So likewise, whoever of you ᵖdoes not forsake all that he has cannot be My disciple.

Tasteless Salt Is Worthless

³⁴ᵍ"Salt *is* good; but if the salt has lost its flavor, how shall it be seasoned? ³⁵It is neither fit for the land nor for the dunghill, *but* men throw it out. He who has ears to hear, let him hear!"

The Parable of the Lost Sheep

15 Then ᵃall the tax collectors and the sinners drew near to Him to hear Him. ²And the Pharisees and scribes complained, saying, "This Man receives sinners ᵇand eats with them." ³So He spoke this parable to them, saying:

⁴ᶜ"What man of you, having a hundred

---

* 14:15 M-Text reads *dinner.*

14:17 those who were invited. In the ancient world, invitations to a feast were sent out well in advance of the meal. Then on the day of the feast, servants would announce the start of the meal. This parable is similar to the one in Matthew 22:1–4, but was probably spoken on a different occasion.

14:20 I have married a wife. While the Old Testament exempted a man from military duty because of marriage (Deut. 20:7; 24:5), marriage was not an excuse for avoiding social duties. The general point here is that the man regarded his own affairs as more important than the feast.

14:21 the poor and the maimed and the lame and the blind. This list matches that of verse 13. The maimed were excluded from full participation in Jewish worship (Lev. 21:17–23). The master's second invitation extended the scope of the offer to those who were rejected by society.

14:23 Go out into the highways. The master's second invitation extended beyond the city limits, encouraging even more people to come to the feast. This may picture the inclusion of Gentiles in God's salvation (Is. 49:6). The instruction to *compel* them

to come in does not mean to force people in, but to urge them.

14:34 Salt is good. In the ancient world, salt was often used as a catalyst for burning fuel such as cattle dung. The salt of the time was impure and could lose its strength over time, becoming useless. Jesus' point is that the same is true of a "saltless" disciple.

15:1 tax collectors . . . sinners. The three parables of chapter 15 explain why Jesus associated with despised groups while the Pharisees and scribes did not. The parables in this chapter are found only in Luke.

15:4 a hundred sheep. This was a medium-sized flock. The average herd ran from 20 to 200 head, while a flock of 300 or more was considered large.

14:13 ᵉNeh. 8:10, 12   **14:14** ᶠ[Matt. 25:34–40]
14:15 ᵍRev. 19:9   **14:16** ʰMatt. 22:1–14   **14:17** ⁱProv. 9:2, 5   **14:24** ʲ[Acts 13:46]   **14:26** ᵏDeut. 13:6; 33:9 ˡRom. 9:13 ᵐRev. 12:11   **14:27** ⁿLuke 9:23
14:28 ᵒProv. 24:27   **14:33** ᵖMatt. 19:27   **14:34** ᵍ[Mark 9:50]   **15:1** ᵃ[Matt. 9:10–13]   **15:2** ᵇGal. 2:12
15:4 ᶜMatt. 18:12–14

sheep, if he loses one of them, does not leave the ninety-nine in the wilderness, and go after the one which is lost until he finds it? ⁵And when he has found *it*, he lays *it* on his shoulders, rejoicing. ⁶And when he comes home, he calls together *his* friends and neighbors, saying to them, *d*'Rejoice with me, for I have found my sheep *e*which was lost!' ⁷I say to you that likewise there will be more joy in heaven over one sinner who repents *f*than over ninety-nine just persons who *g*need no repentance.

The Parable of the Lost Coin

⁸"Or what woman, having ten silver coins,* if she loses one coin, does not light a lamp, sweep the house, and search carefully until she finds *it*? ⁹And when she has found *it*, she calls her friends and neighbors together, saying, 'Rejoice with me, for I have found the piece which I lost!' ¹⁰Likewise, I say to you, there is joy in the presence of the angels of God over one sinner who repents."

The Parable of the Lost Son

¹¹Then He said: "A certain man had two sons. ¹²And the younger of them said to *his* father, 'Father, give me the portion of goods that falls *to me*.' So he divided to them *h*his livelihood. ¹³And not many days after, the younger son gathered all together, journeyed to a far country, and there wasted his possessions with prodigal living. ¹⁴But when he had spent all, there arose a severe famine in that land, and he began to be in want. ¹⁵Then he went and joined himself to a citizen of that country, and he sent him into his fields to feed swine. ¹⁶And he would gladly have filled his stomach with the pods that the swine ate, and no one gave him *anything*. ¹⁷"But when he came to himself, he said, 'How many of my father's hired servants have bread enough and to spare, and I perish with hunger! ¹⁸I will arise and go to my father, and will say to him, "Father, *i*I have sinned against heaven and before you, ¹⁹and I am no longer worthy to be called your son. Make me like one of your hired servants."' ²⁰"And he arose and came to his father. But *j*when he was still a great way off, his father saw him and had compassion, and ran and fell on his neck and kissed him. ²¹And the son said to him, 'Father, I have sinned against heaven *k*and in your sight, and am no longer worthy to be called your son.' ²²"But the father said to his servants, 'Bring* out the best robe and put *it* on him, and put a ring on his hand and sandals on *his* feet. ²³And bring the fatted calf here and kill *it*, and let us eat and be merry; ²⁴*l*for this my son was dead and is alive again; he was lost and is found.' And they began to be merry.

²⁵"Now his older son was in the field. And as he came and drew near to the house, he heard music and dancing. ²⁶So he called one of the servants and asked what these things meant. ²⁷And he said to him, 'Your brother has come, and because he has received him safe and sound, your father has killed the fatted calf.' ²⁸"But he was angry and would not go in. Therefore his father came out and pleaded

---

* **15:8** Greek *drachma*, a valuable coin often worn in a ten-piece garland by married women
* **15:22** NU-Text reads *Quickly bring.*

15:7 *persons who need no repentance.* This phrase is a rhetorical way of describing the scribes and Pharisees. A similar description is found in 5:31, where it is said that some do not need a physician. The scribes and Pharisees believed that they did not need to repent because they were not lost.

15:8 *ten silver coins.* A drachma was a silver coin equal to a day's wage for a basic laborer. The woman needed a lamp because she lived in a windowless house. Her broom for sweeping would have been made of palm twigs.

15:15 *to feed swine.* Feeding swine was an insulting job for a Jewish person, since pigs were unclean according to the law of Moses.

15:20 *his father saw him and had compassion.* Many scholars feel that the emphasis on the son in this parable causes people to miss the more important point, namely, the importance of the father's welcoming role. Still others think it could even be called the Parable of the Elder Brother. Interestingly, both brothers underestimate their father's love and grace. The younger brother is slow to realize the extent and permanence of his father's love. The elder brother has trouble understanding that the restored relationship with the younger son is vital to the life of the father. What makes the dramatic conversion possible is the younger son's knowledge that he will be accepted when he returns. While there are consequences to his behavior (his money is gone), he is welcomed to be a part of the family again. In many ways the welcome is even more than he could have hoped for. What is amazing about grace is that it is always more than we expect or deserve.

15:21 *no longer worthy to be called your son.* Despite his awareness of being accepted by his father, the son continued his confession of his sin. He then asked to become one of his father's servants. Similarly, a sinner realizes that he or she brings nothing to and deserves nothing from God, but must rely completely on God's mercy.

15:24 *dead . . . alive again . . . lost . . . found.* The total transformation of the prodigal son is summarized in these two contrasts. Such a transformation is a reason to celebrate. It is also the reason Jesus chose to associate with the lost.

15:28 *he was angry.* The elder brother's unhappiness over a fatted calf (v. 27) being killed to celebrate

---

15:6 *d* [Rom. 12:15] *e* [1 Pet. 2:10, 25]   **15:7** *f* [Luke 5:32] *g* [Mark 2:17]   **15:12** *h* Mark 12:44   **15:18** *i* 2 Sam. 12:13; 24:10, 17   **15:20** *j* [Eph. 2:13, 17]   **15:21** *k* Ps. 51:4   **15:24** *l* Luke 9:60; 15:32

with him. 29So he answered and said to *his* father, 'Lo, these many years I have been serving you; I never transgressed your commandment at any time; and yet you never gave me a young goat, that I might make merry with my friends. 30But as soon as this son of yours came, who has devoured your livelihood with harlots, you killed the fatted calf for him.'

31"And he said to him, 'Son, you are always with me, and all that I have is yours. 32It was right that we should make merry and be glad, *m*for your brother was dead and is alive again, and was lost and is found.'"

The Parable of the Unjust Steward

16 He also said to His disciples: "There was a certain rich man who had a steward, and an accusation was brought to him that this man was wasting his goods. 2So he called him and said to him, 'What is this I hear about you? Give an *a*account of your stewardship, for you can no longer be steward.'

3"Then the steward said within himself, 'What shall I do? For my master is taking the stewardship away from me. I cannot dig; I am ashamed to beg. 4I have resolved what to do, that when I am put out of the stewardship, they may receive me into their houses.'

5"So he called every one of his master's debtors to *him*, and said to the first, 'How much do you owe my master?' 6And he said, 'A hundred measures* of oil.' So he said to him, 'Take your bill, and sit down quickly and write fifty.' 7Then he said to another, 'And how much do you owe?' So he said, 'A hundred measures* of wheat.' And he said to him, 'Take your bill, and write eighty.' 8So the master commended the unjust steward because he had dealt shrewdly. For the sons of this world are more shrewd in their generation than *b*the sons of light.

9"And I say to you, *c*make friends for yourselves by unrighteous mammon, that when you fail,* they may receive you into

an everlasting home. 10*d*He who *is* faithful in *what is* least is faithful also in much; and he who is unjust in *what is* least is unjust also in much. 11Therefore if you have not been faithful in the unrighteous mammon, who will commit to your trust the true *riches?* 12And if you have not been faithful in what is another man's, who will give you what is your *e*own?

13*f*"No servant can serve two masters; for either he will hate the one and love the other, or else he will be loyal to the one and despise the other. You cannot serve God and mammon."

The Law, the Prophets, and the Kingdom

14Now the Pharisees, *g*who were lovers of money, also heard all these things, and they derided Him. 15And He said to them, "You are those who *h*justify yourselves *i*before men, but *j*God knows your hearts. *k*what is highly esteemed among men is an abomination in the sight of God.

16*l*"The law and the prophets *were* until John. Since that time the kingdom of God has been preached, and everyone is pressing into it. 17*m*And it is easier for heaven and earth to pass away than for one tittle of the law to fail.

18*n*"Whoever divorces his wife and marries another commits adultery; and whoever marries her who is divorced from *her* husband commits adultery.

The Rich Man and Lazarus

19"There was a certain rich man who was clothed in purple and fine linen and fared sumptuously every day. 20But there was a certain beggar named Lazarus, full of sores, who was laid at his gate, 21desiring to be fed with the crumbs which fell* from the rich man's table. Moreover the dogs came

---

* **16:6** Greek *batos*, eight or nine gallons each (Old Testament *bath*) * **16:7** Greek *koros*, ten or twelve bushels each (Old Testament *kor*) * **16:9** NU-Text reads *it fails.* * **16:21** NU-Text reads *with what fell.*

---

the return of his undisciplined brother illustrates the response of the Pharisees and scribes at the prospect of sinners becoming acceptable to God.

16:1 *a steward.* This was a servant who supervised and administered an estate. The charge brought against this steward is incompetence.

16:8 *So the master commended the unjust steward.* The master recognized the foresight in the steward's generosity. It is debatable whether the steward was dishonest and robbed the master by such reductions or was shrewd in using his authority to discount the goods (vv. 6–7). The fact that the master commended the steward may suggest that the master was not robbed and that the steward's reduction was the result of either an adherence to the law or a lowering of the steward's own commission.

16:9 *unrighteous mammon.* This is money and should be used generously to build works that last.

Money is called unrighteous because it often manifests unrighteousness and selfishness in people (1 Tim. 6:6–10,17–19; James 1:9–11; 5:1–6).

16:19 *clothed in purple.* Purple clothes were extremely expensive because they were made with a special dye extracted from a kind of snail.

16:20–21 *licked his sores.* To have his sores licked by dogs threatened Lazarus with infection as well as ritual uncleanness, since dogs fed on garbage, including dead animals.

15:32 *m* Luke 15:24   **16:2** *a* [Rom. 14:12]   **16:8** *b* [Eph. 5:8]   **16:9** *c* Dan. 4:27   **16:10** *d* Matt. 25:21   **16:12** *e* [1 Pet. 1:3, 4]   **16:13** *f* Matt. 6:24   **16:14** *g* Matt. 23:14   **16:15** *h* Luke 10:29   *i* [Matt. 6:2, 5, 16]   *j* Ps. 7:9   *k* 1 Sam. 16:7   **16:16** *l* Matt. 3:1–12; 4:17; 11:12, 13   **16:17** *m* Is. 40:8; 51:6   **16:18** *n* 1 Cor. 7:10, 11

and licked his sores. 22So it was that the beggar died, and was carried by the angels to
[o]Abraham's bosom. The rich man also died
and was buried. 23And being in torments in
Hades, he lifted up his eyes and saw Abraham afar off, and Lazarus in his bosom.
24"Then he cried and said, 'Father Abraham, have mercy on me, and send Lazarus
that he may dip the tip of his finger in water
and [p]cool my tongue; for I [q]am tormented in
this flame.' 25But Abraham said, 'Son, [r]re-
member that in your lifetime you received
your good things, and likewise Lazarus
evil things; but now he is comforted and
you are tormented. 26And besides all this,
between us and you there is a great gulf
fixed, so that those who want to pass from
here to you cannot, nor can those from
there pass to us.'
27"Then he said, 'I beg you therefore,
father, that you would send him to my father's house, 28for I have five brothers, that
he may testify to them, lest they also come
to this place of torment.' 29Abraham said to
him, [s]'They have Moses and the prophets;
let them hear them.' 30And he said, 'No, father Abraham; but if one goes to them from
the dead, they will repent.' 31But he said to
him, [t]'If they do not hear Moses and the
prophets, [u]neither will they be persuaded
though one rise from the dead.' "

Jesus Warns of Offenses

17 Then He said to the disciples, [a]"It is
impossible that no offenses should
come, but [b]woe *to him* through whom they
do come! 2It would be better for him if a
millstone were hung around his neck, and
he were thrown into the sea, than that he
should offend one of these little ones. 3Take
heed to yourselves. [c]If your brother sins
against you,* [d]rebuke him; and if he repents, forgive him. 4And if he sins against
you seven times in a day, and seven times
in a day returns to you,* saying, 'I repent,'
you shall forgive him."

Faith and Duty

5And the apostles said to the Lord, "Increase our faith."
6[e]So the Lord said, "If you have faith as
a mustard seed, you can say to this mulberry tree, 'Be pulled up by the roots and be
planted in the sea,' and it would obey you.
7And which of you, having a servant plowing or tending sheep, will say to him when
he has come in from the field, 'Come at
once and sit down to eat'? 8But will he not
rather say to him, 'Prepare something for
my supper, and gird yourself [f]and serve me
till I have eaten and drunk, and afterward
you will eat and drink'? 9Does he thank
that servant because he did the things that
were commanded him? I think not.* 10So
likewise you, when you have done all those
things which you are commanded, say, 'We
are [g]unprofitable servants. We have done
what was our duty to do.' "

Ten Lepers Cleansed

11Now it happened [h]as He went to Jerusalem that He passed through the midst of
Samaria and Galilee. 12Then as He entered
a certain village, there met Him ten men
who were lepers, [i]who stood afar off. 13And
they lifted up *their* voices and said, "Jesus,
Master, have mercy on us!"
14So when He saw *them*, He said to them,
[j]"Go, show yourselves to the priests." And
so it was that as they went, they were
cleansed.
15And one of them, when he saw that he
was healed, returned, and with a loud voice
[k]glorified God, 16and fell down on *his* face
at His feet, giving Him thanks. And he was
a [l]Samaritan.
17So Jesus answered and said, "Were
there not ten cleansed? But where *are* the
nine? 18Were there not any found who returned to give glory to God except this foreigner?" 19[m]And He said to him, "Arise, go
your way. Your faith has made you well."

The Coming of the Kingdom

20Now when He was asked by the Pharisees when the kingdom of God would

* **17:3** NU-Text omits *against you.* * **17:4** M-Text omits *to you.* * **17:9** NU-Text ends verse with *commanded;* M-Text omits *him.*

16:22 ***Abraham's bosom.*** This was the blessed place of the dead. Angelic escorts for the dead were also known in Judaism. This verse indicates that the dead know their fate immediately.
16:24 ***I am tormented in this flame.*** The rich man desired relief from his suffering. The image of thirst for the experience of judgment is common (Is. 5:13; 65:13; Hos. 2:3).
16:29 ***They have Moses and the prophets.*** Abraham made it clear that the rich man's brothers should have known what to do, since they had the message of God in the ancient writings. The point here is that generosity with money and care for the poor were taught in the Old Testament (Deut. 14:28–29; Is. 3:14–15; Mic. 6:10–11).
17:1–2 ***woe to him.*** Jesus warned that judgment awaits those who cause others to stumble. The severe form of the warning suggests that false teaching, or leading someone into apostasy, is in view here. ***a millstone.*** This was a heavy stone used in a grinding mill.
17:20 ***kingdom of God.*** In ancient Israel there was an expectation that the kingdom of God would come

16:22 [o] Matt. 8:11 **16:24** [p] Zech. 14:12 [q] [Mark 9:42–48] **16:25** [r] Luke 6:24 **16:29** [s] Acts 15:21; 17:11 **16:31** [t] [John 5:46] [u] John 12:10, 11 **17:1** [a] [1 Cor. 11:19] [b] [2 Thess. 1:6] **17:3** [c] [Matt. 18:15, 21] [d] [Prov. 17:10] **17:6** [e] [Mark 9:23; 11:23] **17:8** [f] [Luke 12:37] **17:10** [g] Rom. 3:12; 11:35 **17:11** [h] Luke 9:51, 52 **17:12** [i] Lev. 13:46 **17:14** [j] Matt. 8:4 **17:15** [k] Luke 5:25; 18:43 **17:16** [l] 2 Kin. 17:24 **17:19** [m] Matt. 9:22

come, He answered them and said, "The kingdom of God does not come with observation; [21]nnor will they say, 'See here!' or 'See there!'* For indeed, othe kingdom of God is within you."

[22]Then He said to the disciples, p"The days will come when you will desire to see one of the days of the Son of Man, and you will not see it. [23]qAnd they will say to you, 'Look here!' or 'Look there!'* Do not go after them or follow them. [24]rFor as the lightning that flashes out of one part under heaven shines to the other part under heaven, so also the Son of Man will be in His day. [25]sBut first He must suffer many things and be trejected by this generation. [26]uAnd as it vwas in the wdays of xNoah, so it will be also in the days of the Son of Man: [27]They ate, they drank, they married wives, they were given in marriage, until the yday that Noah entered the ark, and the flood came and zdestroyed them all. [28]aLikewise as it was also in the days of Lot: They ate, they drank, they bought, they sold, they planted, they built; [29]but on bthe day that Lot went out of Sodom it rained fire and brimstone from heaven and destroyed them all. [30]Even so will it be in the day when the Son of Man cis revealed.

[31]"In that day, he dwho is on the housetop, and his goods are in the house, let him not come down to take them away. And likewise the one who is in the field, let him not turn back. [32]eRemember Lot's wife. [33]Whoever seeks to save his life will lose it, and whoever loses his life will preserve it. [34]gI tell you, in that night there will be two men in one bed: the one will be taken and the other will be left. [35]hTwo women will be grinding together: the one will be taken and the other left. [36]Two men will be in the field: the one will be taken and the other left."*

[37]And they answered and said to Him, i"Where, Lord?"

So He said to them, "Wherever the body is, there the eagles will be gathered together."

The Parable of the Persistent Widow

18 Then He spoke a parable to them, that men aalways ought to pray and not lose heart, [2]saying: "There was in a certain city a judge who did not fear God nor regard man. [3]Now there was a widow in that city; and she came to him, saying, 'Get justice for me from my adversary.' [4]And he would not for a while; but afterward he said within himself, 'Though I do not fear God nor regard man, [5]byet because this widow troubles me I will avenge her, lest by her continual coming she weary me.'"

[6]Then the Lord said, "Hear what the unjust judge said. [7]And cshall God not avenge His own elect who cry out day and night to Him, though He bears long with them? [8]I tell you dthat He will avenge them speedily. Nevertheless, when the Son of Man comes, will He really find faith on the earth?"

---

* **17:21** NU-Text reverses here and there.
* **17:23** NU-Text reverses here and there.
* **17:36** NU-Text and M-Text omit verse 36.

---

with cosmic signs (Joel 2:28–32). Jesus' concept of the kingdom of God, however, was broader than the time of the final consummation.

17:21 within you. This verse indicates that there was an aspect of kingdom promise involved in Jesus' first coming. The kingdom of God is among earthly kingdoms today; but one day the kingdom of God will swallow up all rival kingdoms (Rev. 11:15). In verses 22–37, Jesus makes it clear that the kingdom has two phases—one now and one to come. In the beginning of His kingdom on earth, God first prepares a King to rule; then He gathers a people for Him to rule over; then He gives the Ruler a realm in which to reign. The kingdom of God is not the same as the church, though the church is a part of the kingdom. The kingdom now is the presence of God alongside earthly kingdoms. One day, however, Jesus will rule over all, and He will share that rule with His people (Rev. 2:26–27; 5:9–10; 20:4–6).

17:26 in the days of Noah. At that time people paid little attention to God and faced judgment as a result (Gen. 6:5–13). The same will be the case at Jesus' return.

17:32 Lot's wife. This woman represents those who are attached to earthly things, those whose hearts are still in this world. Like Lot's wife, such people will perish (Gen. 19:26).

17:34–37 one will be taken. This phrase suggests judgment such as when the soldiers took Jesus to crucify Him. Verse 37 makes it clear that those who are taken are taken to final judgment. The vultures will be gathered. When judgment comes, it will be final and terrible, with the stench of death and the presence of vultures everywhere. No one will need to look for the place of judgment; the presence of the birds will reveal where the carcasses are.

18:2 a judge. The Romans allowed the Jews to manage most of their own affairs. This judge did not fear God, and was therefore probably a secular judge, not a religious one. The dishonest judge represents corrupted power.

18:5 this widow troubles me. The persistence of the widow is the lesson of the parable. God is a counterexample to the judge. God does not begrudge answering prayer. Jesus' point is that, if an insensitive judge will respond to the continual requests of a widow, God will certainly respond to the continual prayers of believers.

17:21 n Luke 17:23 o [Rom. 14:17] **17:22** p Matt. 9:15 **17:23** q Matt. 24:23 **17:24** r Matt. 24:27 **17:25** s Mark 8:31; 9:31; 10:33 t Luke 9:22 **17:26** u Matt. 24:37–39 v [Gen. 6:5–7] w [Gen. 6:8–13] x 1 Pet. 3:20 **17:27** y Gen. 7:1–16 z Gen. 7:19–23 **17:28** a Gen. 19 **17:29** b Gen. 19:16, 24, 29 **17:30** c [2 Thess. 1:7] **17:31** d Mark 13:15 **17:32** e Gen. 19:26 **17:33** f Matt. 10:39; 16:25 **17:34** g [1 Thess.4:17] **17:35** h Matt.24:40,41 **17:37** i Matt. 24:28 **18:1** a Luke 11:5–10 **18:5** b Luke 11:8 **18:7** c Rev. 6:10 **18:8** d Heb. 10:37

The Parable of the Pharisee and the Tax Collector

9Also He spoke this parable to some ewho trusted in themselves that they were righteous, and despised others: 10"Two men went up to the temple to pray, one a Pharisee and the other a tax collector. 11The Pharisee fstood and prayed thus with himself, g"God, I thank You that I am not like other men—extortioners, unjust, adulterers, or even as this tax collector. 12I fast twice a week; I give tithes of all that I possess.' 13And the tax collector, standing afar off, would not so much as raise his eyes to heaven, but beat his breast, saying, 'God, be merciful to me a sinner!' 14I tell you, this man went down to his house justified rather than the other; hfor everyone who exalts himself will be humbled, and he who humbles himself will be exalted."

Jesus Blesses Little Children

15iThen they also brought infants to Him that He might touch them; but when the disciples saw it, they rebuked them. 16But Jesus called them to Him and said, "Let the little children come to Me, and do not forbid them; for jof such is the kingdom of God. 17kAssuredly, I say to you, whoever does not receive the kingdom of God as a little child will by no means enter it."

Jesus Counsels the Rich Young Ruler

18lNow a certain ruler asked Him, saying, "Good Teacher, what shall I do to inherit eternal life?"

19So Jesus said to him, "Why do you call Me good? No one is good but mOne, that is, God. 20You know the commandments: n'Do not commit adultery,' 'Do not murder,' 'Do not steal,' 'Do not bear false witness,' o'Honor your father and your mother.' "*

21And he said, "All pthese things I have kept from my youth."

22So when Jesus heard these things, He said to him, "You still lack one thing. qSell all that you have and distribute to the poor, and you will have treasure in heaven; and come, follow Me."

23But when he heard this, he became very sorrowful, for he was very rich.

With God All Things Are Possible

24And when Jesus saw that he became very sorrowful, He said, r"How hard it is for those who have riches to enter the kingdom of God! 25For it is easier for a camel to go through the eye of a needle than for a rich man to enter the kingdom of God."

26And those who heard it said, "Who then can be saved?"

27But He said, s"The things which are impossible with men are possible with God."

28tThen Peter said, "See, we have left all* and followed You."

29So He said to them, "Assuredly, I say to you, uthere is no one who has left house or parents or brothers or wife or children, for the sake of the kingdom of God, 30vwho shall not receive many times more in this present time, and in the age to come eternal life."

Jesus a Third Time Predicts His Death and Resurrection

31wThen He took the twelve aside and said to them, "Behold, we are going up to Jerusalem, and all things xthat are written by the prophets concerning the Son of Man will be accomplished. 32For yHe will be delivered to the Gentiles and will be mocked and insulted and spit upon. 33They will scourge Him and kill Him. And the third day He will rise again."

---

* **18:20** Exodus 20:12–16; Deuteronomy 5:16–20
* **18:28** NU-Text reads our own.

18:11–12 God, I thank You. The tone of the prayer reveals the Pharisee's problem. He uses the pronoun "I" five times in two verses. The Pharisee's attitude seems to be that God should be grateful to him for his commitment. The man obviously looked down on other people and was proud of his fasting and tithing.
18:13 God, be merciful to me a sinner. This is an example of the humble spirit of repentance that Jesus commends. The tax collector knew that he could not say or bring anything to enhance his standing with God. He knew that only God's mercy and grace, and not his own works, could deliver him.
18:16 But Jesus called them. Jesus used the thoughtlessness of his disciples to make two points: (1) all people, even little children, are important to God; and (2) the kingdom of God consists of those who respond to Him with the trust that a little child gives to a parent.
18:22 Sell all that you have and distribute to the poor. This was a radical test of the ruler's concern for others (12:33–34). Jesus was determining whether

the ruler's treasure (Matt. 6:19–21) lay with God or money (16:13). Jesus was not establishing a new requirement for being saved. He was examining the ruler's orientation to God by directly confronting him with the very thing that was hindering him—namely, his wealth.
18:24–25 For it is easier for a camel to go through the eye of a needle. Jesus used this figure of speech to emphasize the difficulty of turning from wealth to find salvation. Because many Jewish people believed that wealth was evidence of God's blessing, Jesus' statements would have been shocking to His audience.

18:9 e Luke 10:29; 16:15 **18:11** f Ps. 135:2 g Is. 1:15; 58:2 **18:14** h Luke 14:11 **18:15** i Mark 10:13–16 **18:16** j 1 Pet. 2:2 **18:17** k Mark 10:15 **18:18** l Matt. 19:16–29 **18:19** m Ps. 86:5; 119:68 **18:20** n Ex. 20:12–16; Deut. 5:16–20 o Eph. 6:2; Col. 3:20 **18:21** p Phil. 3:6 **18:22** q Matt. 6:19, 20; 19:21 **18:24** r Mark 10:23 **18:27** s Jer. 32:17 **18:28** t Matt. 19:27 **18:29** u Deut. 33:9 **18:30** v Job 42:10 **18:31** w Matt. 16:21; 17:22; 20:17 x Ps. 22 **18:32** y Acts 3:13

³⁴ᶻBut they understood none of these things; this saying was hidden from them, and they did not know the things which were spoken.

A Blind Man Receives His Sight

³⁵ᵃThen it happened, as He was coming near Jericho, that a certain blind man sat by the road begging. ³⁶And hearing a multitude passing by, he asked what it meant. ³⁷So they told him that Jesus of Nazareth was passing by. ³⁸And he cried out, saying, "Jesus, ᵇSon of David, have mercy on me!"

³⁹Then those who went before warned him that he should be quiet; but he cried out all the more, "Son of David, have mercy on me!"

⁴⁰So Jesus stood still and commanded him to be brought to Him. And when he had come near, He asked him, ⁴¹saying, "What do you want Me to do for you?"

He said, "Lord, that I may receive my sight."

⁴²Then Jesus said to him, "Receive your sight; ᶜyour faith has made you well." ⁴³And immediately he received his sight, and followed Him, ᵈglorifying God. And all the people, when they saw *it*, gave praise to God.

Jesus Comes to Zacchaeus' House

19 Then *Jesus* entered and passed through ᵃJericho. ²Now behold, *there was* a man named Zacchaeus who was a chief tax collector, and he was rich. ³And he sought to ᵇsee who Jesus was, but could not because of the crowd, for he was of short stature. ⁴So he ran ahead and climbed up into a sycamore tree to see Him, for He was going to pass that *way.* ⁵And when Jesus came to the place, He looked up and saw him,* and said to him, "Zacchaeus, make haste and come down, for today I must stay at your house." ⁶So he made haste and came down, and received

Him joyfully. ⁷But when they saw *it*, they all complained, saying, ᶜ"He has gone to be a guest with a man who is a sinner."

⁸Then Zacchaeus stood and said to the Lord, "Look, Lord, I give half of my goods to the ᵈpoor; and if I have taken anything from anyone by ᵉfalse accusation, ᶠI restore fourfold."

⁹And Jesus said to him, "Today salvation has come to this house, because ᵍhe also is ʰa son of Abraham; ¹⁰ᶦfor the Son of Man has come to seek and to save that which was lost."

The Parable of the Minas

¹¹Now as they heard these things, He spoke another parable, because He was near Jerusalem and because ʲthey thought the kingdom of God would appear immediately. ¹²ᵏTherefore He said: "A certain nobleman went into a far country to receive for himself a kingdom and to return. ¹³So he called ten of his servants, delivered to them ten minas,* and said to them, 'Do business till I come.' ¹⁴ˡBut his citizens hated him, and sent a delegation after him, saying, 'We will not have this *man* to reign over us.'

¹⁵"And so it was that when he returned, having received the kingdom, he then commanded these servants, to whom he had given the money, to be called to him, that he might know how much every man had gained by trading. ¹⁶Then came the first, saying, 'Master, your mina has earned ten minas.' ¹⁷And he said to him, ᵐ'Well *done*, good servant; because you were ⁿfaithful in a very little, have authority over ten cities.' ¹⁸And the second came, saying, 'Master, your mina has earned five minas.' ¹⁹Likewise he said to him, 'You also be over five cities.'

---

* **19:5** NU-Text omits *and saw him.*   * **19:13** The *mina* (Greek *mna*, Hebrew *minah*) was worth about three months' salary.

18:34 they understood none of these things. The disciples may have understood something of what Jesus said, but they could not understand why God's Chosen One would have to face such suffering. For those who were expecting the Promised One to be an exalted figure who would deliver God's people, it would be very difficult to reconcile such an expectation with such terrible suffering.

18:38 Son of David. Note the irony in this verse. The blind man recognized who Jesus was more clearly than many people who were blessed with physical sight. The blind man's cry for mercy demonstrated his belief that Jesus had the power to heal him.

19:2 Zacchaeus. This was the chief tax collector, which meant he most likely bid for the right to collect taxes and then hired another tax collector to actually gather the money.

19:7 they all complained. The crowd was not happy with Jesus' choice of who to honor with His fellowship. In the crowd's opinion, Zacchaeus was a sinner. Tax collectors often took for themselves a high

percentage of what they demanded. They were hated and despised in ancient Israel.

19:11 they thought. Evidently the disciples believed that Jesus' arrival in Jerusalem would signal the arrival of the kingdom of God. Jesus' parable in verses 12–27 was designed to dispel this misconception. Note that the disciples raised the same question in Acts 1:1.

19:13 ten minas. Each servant received one mina or about three months' wages for the average worker. The master, symbolizing Jesus Himself, wants to see fruit, or dividends from his investment. Did his servants put the money they received to good use?

18:34 ᶻLuke 2:50; 9:45   **18:35** ᵃMatt. 20:29–34
18:38 ᵇMatt. 9:27   **18:42** ᶜLuke 17:19   **18:43** ᵈLuke 5:26   **19:1** ᵃJosh. 6:26   **19:3** ᵇJohn 12:21   **19:7** ᶜLuke 5:30; 15:2   **19:8** ᵈ[Ps. 41:1] ᵉLuke 3:14 ᶠEx. 22:1
19:9 ᵍ[Gal. 3:7] ʰ[Luke 13:16]   **19:10** ᶦMatt. 18:11
19:11 ʲActs 1:6   **19:12** ᵏMatt. 25:14–30   **19:14** ˡ[John 1:11]   **19:17** ᵐMatt. 25:21, 23 ⁿLuke 16:10

20"Then another came, saying, 'Master, here is your mina, which I have kept put away in a handkerchief. **21**oFor I feared you, because you are an austere man. You collect what you did not deposit, and reap what you did not sow.' **22**And he said to him, p'Out of your own mouth I will judge you, you wicked servant. qYou knew that I was an austere man, collecting what I did not deposit and reaping what I did not sow. **23**Why then did you not put my money in the bank, that at my coming I might have collected it with interest?' **24**"And he said to those who stood by, 'Take the mina from him, and give it to him who has ten minas.' **25**(But they said to him, 'Master, he has ten minas.') **26**'For I say to you, rthat to everyone who has will be given; and from him who does not have, even what he has will be taken away from him. **27**But bring here those enemies of mine, who did not want me to reign over them, and slay them before me.'"

The Triumphal Entry

28When He had said this, sHe went on ahead, going up to Jerusalem. **29**tAnd it came to pass, when He drew near to Bethphage* and uBethany, at the mountain called vOlivet, that He sent two of His disciples, **30**saying, "Go into the village opposite you, where as you enter you will find a colt tied, on which no one has ever sat. Loose it and bring it here. **31**And if anyone asks you, 'Why are you loosing it?' thus you shall say to him, 'Because the Lord has need of it.'"

32So those who were sent went their way and found it just was He had said to them. **33**But as they were loosing the colt, the owners of it said to them, "Why are you loosing the colt?"

34And they said, "The Lord has need of him." **35**Then they brought him to Jesus. xAnd they threw their own clothes on the colt, and they set Jesus on him. **36**And as He went, many spread their clothes on the road. **37**Then, as He was now drawing near the descent of the Mount of Olives, the whole multitude of the disciples began to yrejoice and praise God with a loud voice for all the mighty works they had seen, **38**saying:

z"'Blessed is the King who comes in the
    name of the LORD!'*
aPeace in heaven and glory in the
    highest!"

39And some of the Pharisees called to Him from the crowd, "Teacher, rebuke Your disciples."

40But He answered and said to them, "I tell you that if these should keep silent, bthe stones would immediately cry out."

Jesus Weeps over Jerusalem

41Now as He drew near, He saw the city and cwept over it, **42**saying, "If you had known, even you, especially in this dyour day, the things that emake for your fpeace! But now they are hidden from your eyes. **43**For days will come upon you when your enemies will gbuild an embankment around you, surround you and close you in on every side, **44**hand level you, and your children within you, to the ground; and they will not leave in you one stone upon another, jbecause you did not know the time of your visitation."

Jesus Cleanses the Temple

45kThen He went into the temple and began to drive out those who bought and sold in it,* **46**saying to them, "It is written, l'My house is* a house of prayer,'* but you have made it a m'den of thieves.'"*

47And He nwas teaching daily in the temple. But othe chief priests, the scribes, and the leaders of the people sought to destroy Him, **48**and were unable to do anything; for all the people were very attentive to phear Him.

* **19:29** M-Text reads Bethsphage. * **19:38** Psalm 118:26 * **19:45** NU-Text reads those who were selling. * **19:46** NU-Text reads shall be. • Isaiah 56:7 • Jeremiah 7:11

19:20–23 I feared you. The unfaithful servant's excuse for failure reflects a negative view of the nobleman. If the servant had really feared the master, he would have done something with the money. Even putting the money in the bank would have yielded interest.
19:31–34 the Lord has need of it. Such borrowing of an animal was not as strange as it may appear. There was an ancient custom by which a political or religious leader could commandeer property for short-term use. Jesus was entering Jerusalem to celebrate the Passover and the Feast of Unleavened Bread, festivals that commemorated the great act of God's deliverance of the nation. Such feasts were often celebrated at this time with the hope that God's decisive deliverance would come.
19:41 wept over it. Jesus knew that so many of the people of Israel had rejected Him that the nation would suffer judgment, in the form of the terrible destruction that came on Jerusalem in A.D. 70.

19:43 build an embankment around you. This is a prediction of Rome's successful siege of Jerusalem under Titus. The details reflect a divine judgment for covenant unfaithfulness, similar to the Babylonian destruction of Jerusalem in 586 B.C. (Is. 29:1–4; Jer. 6:6–21, Ezek. 4.1–3).
19:45 He went into the temple. Jesus cleansed the temple in anger after seeing that the place of prayer had become an excuse for corrupt commerce.

19:21 o Matt. 25:24 **19:22** p Job 15:6 q Matt. 25:26 **19:26** r Luke 8:18 **19:28** s Mark 10:32 **19:29** t Matt. 21:1 u John 12:1 v Acts 1:12 **19:32** w Luke 22:13 **19:35** x 2 Kin. 9:13 **19:37** y Luke 13:17; 18:43 **19:38** z Ps. 118:26 a [Eph. 2:14] **19:40** b Hab. 2:11 **19:41** c John 11:35 **19:42** d Heb. 3:13 e [Acts 10:36] f [Rom. 5:1] **19:43** g Jer. 6:3, 6 **19:44** h 1 Kin. 9:7, 8 i Matt. 24:2 j [1 Pet. 2:12] **19:45** k Mark 11:11, 15–17 **19:46** l Is. 56:7 m Jer. 7:11 **19:47** n Luke 21:37; 22:53 o John 7:19; 8:37 **19:48** p Luke 21:38

Jesus' Authority Questioned

20 Now [a]it happened on one of those days, as He taught the people in the temple and preached the gospel, *that* the chief priests and the scribes, together with the elders, confronted *Him* [2]and spoke to Him, saying, "Tell us, [b]by what authority are You doing these things? Or who is he who gave You this authority?"

[3]But He answered and said to them, "I also will ask you one thing, and answer Me: [4]The [c]baptism of John—was it from heaven or from men?"

[5]And they reasoned among themselves, saying, "If we say, 'From heaven,' He will say, 'Why then* did you not believe him?' [6]But if we say, 'From men,' all the people will stone us, [d]for they are persuaded that John was a prophet." [7]So they answered that they did not know where *it was* from.

[8]And Jesus said to them, "Neither will I tell you by what authority I do these things."

The Parable of the Wicked Vinedressers

[9]Then He began to tell the people this parable: [e]"A certain man planted a vineyard, leased it to vinedressers, and went into a far country for a long time. [10]Now at vintage-time he [f]sent a servant to the vinedressers, that they might give him some of the fruit of the vineyard. But the vinedressers beat him and sent *him* away empty-handed. [11]Again he sent another servant; and they beat him also, treated *him* shamefully, and sent *him* away empty-handed. [12]And again he sent a third; and they wounded him also and cast *him* out.

[13]"Then the owner of the vineyard said, 'What shall I do? I will send my beloved son. Probably they will respect *him* when they see him.' [14]But when the vinedressers saw him, they reasoned among themselves, saying, 'This is the [g]heir. Come, [h]let us kill him, that the inheritance may be [i]ours.' [15]So they cast him out of the vineyard and [j]killed *him*. Therefore what will the owner of the vineyard do to them? [16]He will come and destroy those vinedressers and give the vineyard to [k]others."

And when they heard *it* they said, "Certainly not!"

[17]Then He looked at them and said, "What then is this that is written:

> [l]'The stone which the builders rejected
> Has become the chief cornerstone'?*

[18]Whoever falls on that stone will be [m]broken; but [n]on whomever it falls, it will grind him to powder."

[19]And the chief priests and the scribes that very hour sought to lay hands on Him, but they feared the people*—for they knew He had spoken this parable against them.

The Pharisees: Is It Lawful to Pay Taxes to Caesar?

[20][o]So they watched *Him*, and sent spies who pretended to be righteous, that they might seize on His words, in order to deliver Him to the power and the authority of the governor. [21]Then they asked Him, saying, [p]"Teacher, we know that You say and teach rightly, and You do not show personal favoritism,

---

* **20:5** NU-Text and M-Text omit *then*.
* **20:17** Psalm 118:22 * **20:19** M-Text reads *but they were afraid.*

Merchants were selling sacrificial animals in the outer court of the temple (the Court of the Gentiles) at exorbitant prices. Money changers were making an excessive profit exchanging currencies for the temple shekel. John records a temple cleansing in John 2:13–22, but it is not clear whether that event is the same as this one in Luke. Since John places the event early in Jesus' ministry, Jesus might have cleansed the temple twice.

20:4 *The baptism of John—was it from heaven or from men?* Here as throughout the Gospel of Luke, the ministries of John the Baptist and Jesus are linked. Jesus' question presented the Pharisees with a dilemma. If they recognized John's ministry as coming from heaven, they would be recognizing the same divine origin of Jesus' similar "independent" Spirit-directed ministry. But if the Pharisees denied that John was sent by God they risked angering the majority of the people, who believed that John's ministry was divinely directed (vv. 5–6).

20:9 *A certain man planted a vineyard.* The imagery of the vineyard recalls the subject of Jesus' parable in 13:6–9. This parable is also found in Matthew 21:33–44 and Mark 12:1–12, with some slight variations of detail in each account.

20:14 *This is the heir.* The vinedressers hoped that

with the son gone, the inheritance would fall to those who worked the property, a transfer that was possible in the ancient world. The details of this parable do not represent the thinking of those who crucified Jesus. The leaders of Israel thought they were stopping someone who was dangerous to Judaism, not that they were going to inherit Jesus' kingdom.

20:17 *The stone which the builders rejected.* This passage, taken from Psalm 118:22, pictures the exaltation of the Righteous One, Jesus, after His rejection. Opposition will not stop God from making the One who is rejected the center of His work of salvation.

20:18 *Whoever falls on that stone.* Jesus is the stone. Anyone who goes against the stone will be destroyed. Jesus' statement is similar to a late Jewish proverb: "If the stone falls on the pot, alas for the pot; If the pot falls on the stone, alas for the pot." The imagery for the stone is also found in 1 Peter 2:4–8.

20:1 [a] Matt. 21:23–27 **20:2** [b] Acts 4:7; 7:27
20:4 [c] John 1:26, 31 **20:6** [d] Luke 7:24–30 **20:9** [e] Mark 12:1–12 **20:10** [f] [1 Thess. 2:15] **20:14** [g] [Heb. 1:1–3] [h] Matt. 27:21–23 [i] John 11:47, 48 **20:15** [j] Luke 23:33
20:16 [k] Rom. 11:1, 11 **20:17** [l] Ps. 118:22 **20:18** [m] Is. 8:14, 15 [n] [Dan. 2:34, 35, 44, 45] **20:20** [o] Matt. 22:15
20:21 [p] Mark 12:14

but teach the way of God in truth: ²²Is it lawful for us to pay taxes to Caesar or not?"

²³But He perceived their craftiness, and said to them, "Why do you test Me?* ²⁴Show Me a denarius. Whose image and inscription does it have?"

They answered and said, "Caesar's."

²⁵And He said to them, ^q"Render therefore to Caesar the things that are Caesar's, and to God the things that are God's."

²⁶But they could not catch Him in His words in the presence of the people. And they marveled at His answer and kept silent.

The Sadducees: What About the Resurrection?

^{27r}Then some of the Sadducees, ^swho deny that there is a resurrection, came to Him and asked Him, ²⁸saying: "Teacher, Moses wrote to us *that* if a man's brother dies, having a wife, and he dies without children, his brother should take his wife and raise up offspring for his brother. ²⁹Now there were seven brothers. And the first took a wife, and died without children. ³⁰And the second* took her as wife, and he died childless. ³¹Then the third took her, and in like manner the seven also; and they left no children,* and died. ³²Last of all the woman died also. ³³Therefore, in the resurrection, whose wife does she become? For all seven had her as wife."

³⁴Jesus answered and said to them, "The sons of this age marry and are given in marriage. ³⁵But those who are ^tcounted worthy to attain that age, and the resurrection from the dead, neither marry nor are given in marriage; ³⁶nor can they die anymore, for ^uthey are equal to the angels and are sons of God, ^vbeing sons of the

resurrection. ³⁷But even Moses showed in the *burning* bush *passage* that the dead are raised, when he called the Lord ^w'*the God of Abraham, the God of Isaac, and the God of Jacob.'* ³⁸For He is not the God of the dead but of the living, for ^xall live to Him."

³⁹Then some of the scribes answered and said, "Teacher, You have spoken well." ⁴⁰But after that they dared not question Him anymore.

Jesus: How Can David Call His Descendant Lord?

⁴¹And He said to them, ^y"How can they say that the Christ is the Son of David? ⁴²Now David himself said in the Book of Psalms:

^z'The Lord said to my Lord,
"Sit at My right hand,
⁴³ Till I make Your enemies Your
  footstool." '*

⁴⁴Therefore David calls Him '*Lord*'; ^ahow is He then his Son?"

Beware of the Scribes

^{45b}Then, in the hearing of all the people, He said to His disciples, ^{46c}"Beware of the scribes, who desire to go around in long robes, ^dlove greetings in the marketplaces, the best seats in the synagogues, and the best places at feasts, ^{47e}who devour widows' houses, and for a ^fpretense make long prayers. These will receive greater condemnation."

* **20:23** NU-Text omits *Why do you test Me?*
* **20:30** NU-Text ends verse 30 here. * **20:31** NU-Text and M-Text read *the seven also left no children.* * **20:37** Exodus 3:6, 15 * **20:43** Psalm 110:1

20:22 *Is it lawful for us to pay taxes to Caesar.* This question concerned the poll tax to Rome, which was different from the taxes collected by the tax collectors. The poll tax was a citizenship tax paid directly to Rome, as an indication that Israel was subject to that Gentile nation. The Pharisees' query was a trick question. If Jesus answered yes, the people would be angry because He respected a foreign power. If He answered no, He could be charged with sedition.

20:24 *Whose image and inscription does it have?* Jesus' reply was clever. He had the Pharisees pull out a coin, indicating that they already recognized Roman sovereignty by using Roman coins themselves. A penny was a silver coin that had a picture of the emperor Tiberius on it.

20:27 *Sadducees.* The Sadducees, the Pharisees, and the Essenes were three major divisions in first-century Judaism. The Sadducees rejected the oral traditions that the Pharisees too stringently obeyed. Instead they based their teaching only on the first five books of the Old Testament. They also denied that there could be a resurrection.

20:36 *they are equal to the angels.* The everlasting life of a resurrected person makes that person something like an angel. Paul explains further that in the

resurrection we will be given resurrection bodies similar to Christ's (1 Cor. 15:25–58). This will be a new experience that will not necessarily parallel experiences on this earth, such as marriage.

20:41–42 *How can they say.* Here Jesus takes His turn at raising a theological issue. The dilemma He poses is how the Messiah could be called the Son of David, when David himself gave Him the title *Lord, my Lord*. This is a citation from Psalm 110:1. The Messiah was David's descendant and yet David gave Him the respect due to a superior, the reverse of what normally occurred in ancient times. Jesus was not denying the title *Son of David* to the Messiah, He was simply noting that the title *Lord*, meaning "Master," is more central. Even David one day will bow at the Messiah's feet and confess that He is Lord (Phil. 2:10).

20:25 ^q[1 Pet. 2:13–17] **20:27** ^rMark 12:18–27 ^sActs 23:6, 8 **20:35** ^tPhil. 3:11 **20:36** ^u[1 John 3:2] ^vRom. 8:23 **20:37** ^wEx. 3:1–6, 15 **20:38** ^x[Rom. 6:10, 11; 14:8, 9] **20:41** ^yMatt. 22:41–46 **20:42** ^zPs. 110:1 **20:44** ^aRom. 1:3; 9:4, 5 **20:45** ^bMatt. 23:1–7 **20:46** ^cMatt. 23:5 ^dLuke 11:43; 14:7 **20:47** ^eMatt. 23:14 ^f[Matt. 6:5, 6]

The Widow's Two Mites

21 And He looked up *a*and saw the rich putting their gifts into the treasury, [2]and He saw also a certain *b*poor widow putting in two *c*mites. [3]So He said, "Truly I say to you *d*that this poor widow has put in more than all; [4]for all these out of their abundance have put in offerings for God,* but she out of her poverty put in *e*all the livelihood that she had."

Jesus Predicts the Destruction of the Temple

[5]*f*Then, as some spoke of the temple, how it was adorned with beautiful stones and donations, He said, [6]"These things which you see—the days will come in which *g*not *one* stone shall be left upon another that shall not be thrown down."

The Signs of the Times and the End of the Age

[7]So they asked Him, saying, "Teacher, but when will these things be? And what sign *will there be* when these things are about to take place?"

[8]And He said: *h*"Take heed that you not be deceived. For many will come in My name, saying, 'I am *He*,' and, 'The time has drawn near.' Therefore* do not go after them. [9]But when you hear of *i*wars and commotions, do not be terrified; for these things must come to pass first, but the end *will* not *come* immediately."

[10]*j*Then He said to them, "Nation will rise against nation, and kingdom against kingdom. [11]And there will be great *k*earthquakes in various places, and famines and pestilences; and there will be fearful sights

and great signs from heaven. [12]But before all these things, they will lay their hands on you and persecute *you*, delivering *you* up to the synagogues and *m*prisons. *n*You will be brought before kings and rulers *o*for My name's sake. [13]But *p*it will turn out for you as an occasion for testimony. [14]*q*Therefore settle *it* in your hearts not to meditate beforehand on what you will answer; [15]for I will give you a mouth and wisdom *r*which all your adversaries will not be able to contradict or resist. [16]*s*You will be betrayed even by parents and brothers, relatives and friends; and they will put *t*some of you to death. [17]And *u*you will be hated by all for My name's sake. [18]*v*But not a hair of your head shall be lost. [19]By your patience possess your souls.

The Destruction of Jerusalem

[20]*w*"But when you see Jerusalem surrounded by armies, then know that its desolation is near. [21]Then let those who are in Judea flee to the mountains, let those who are in the midst of her depart, and let not those who are in the country enter her. [22]For these are the days of vengeance, that *x*all things which are written may be fulfilled. [23]*y*But woe to those who are pregnant and to those who are nursing babies in those days! For there will be great distress in the land and wrath upon this people. [24]And they will fall by the edge of the sword, and be led away captive into all nations. And Jerusalem will be trampled by Gentiles *z*until the times of the Gentiles are fulfilled.

* **21:4** NU-Text omits *for God.*   * **21:8** NU-Text omits *Therefore.*

21:2 two mites. These were the smallest currency available.

21:5 donations. These were gift offerings for the decoration of the temple and included gold and silver-plated gates, grapevine clusters, and Babylonian linen tapestries which hung from the temple veil. Even Tacitus, the Roman historian, called it an "immensely opulent temple."

21:6 not one stone shall be left upon another. Jesus noted that the beautiful place of worship was temporary and would be destroyed. He was referring to the fall of Jerusalem in A.D. 70, which itself was a picture of the destruction of the last days.

21:8 Take heed that you not be deceived. The first century and early second century were times of great messianic fervor in Judaism, as the Israelites sought freedom from Roman rule. Many people claimed to be the Messiah. Jesus warned His disciples not to be fooled by such claims.

21:12 synagogues and prisons . . . kings and rulers. These references indicate that all nations would share responsibility for the massacre of the disciples.

21:15 I will give you a mouth and wisdom. Jesus promises the disciples that the Holy Spirit will assist them in giving testimony (12:11–12). The initial fulfillment of this promise is found in Acts 4:8–14; 7:54; and 26:24–30.

21:16 You will be betrayed. The persecution of the disciples would be painful and severe. Identifying with Jesus often means risking the rejection and denunciation of family, and in some cases martyrdom.

21:20 its desolation. This passage compared the desecration of the temple to what occurred in 167 B.C., when Antiochus Epiphanes erected an altar to Zeus in the temple. A similar desecration of the temple site occurred during the destruction of Jerusalem in A.D. 70.

21:22 days of vengeance. Jerusalem had become an object of divine judgment because of its unfaithfulness. Jesus warned of this consequence throughout His ministry (13:9,34–35; 19:41–44). The premise for such judgment goes back to the curses of the Mosaic

---

21:1 *a* Mark 12:41–44   **21:2** *b* [2 Cor. 6:10]   *c* Mark 12:42   **21:3** *d* [2 Cor. 8:12]   **21:4** *e* [2 Cor. 8:12]   **21:5** *f* Mark 13:1   **21:6** *g* Luke 19:41–44   **21:8** *h* Eph. 5:6   **21:9** *i* Rev. 6:4   **21:10** *j* Matt. 24:7   **21:11** *k* Rev. 6:12   **21:12** *l* [Rev. 2:10]   *m* Acts 4:3; 5:18; 12:4; 16:24   *n* Acts 25:23   *o* 1 Pet. 2:13   **21:13** *p* [Phil. 1:12–14, 28]   **21:14** *q* Luke 12:11   **21:15** *r* Acts 6:10   **21:16** *s* Mic. 7:6   *t* Acts 7:59; 12:2   **21:17** *u* Matt. 10:22   **21:18** *v* Matt. 10:30   **21:20** *w* Mark 13:14   **21:22** *x* [Dan. 9:24–27]   **21:23** *y* Matt. 24:19   **21:24** *z* [Dan. 9:27; 12:7]

The Coming of the Son of Man

25*a*"And there will be signs in the sun, in the moon, and in the stars; and on the earth distress of nations, with perplexity, the sea and the waves roaring; 26men's hearts failing them from fear and the expectation of those things which are coming on the earth, *b*for the powers of the heavens will be shaken. 27Then they will see the Son of Man *c*coming in a cloud with power and great glory. 28Now when these things begin to happen, look up and lift up your heads, because *d*your redemption draws near."

The Parable of the Fig Tree

29*e*Then He spoke to them a parable: "Look at the fig tree, and all the trees. 30When they are already budding, you see and know for yourselves that summer is now near. 31So you also, when you see these things happening, know that the kingdom of God is near. 32Assuredly, I say to you, this generation will by no means pass away till all things take place. 33*f*Heaven and earth will pass away, but My *g*words will by no means pass away.

The Importance of Watching

34"But *h*take heed to yourselves, lest your hearts be weighed down with carousing, drunkenness, and *i*cares of this life, and that Day come on you unexpectedly. 35For *j*it will come as a snare on all those who dwell on the face of the whole earth. 36*k*Watch therefore, and *l*pray always that you may be counted *m*worthy* to escape all these things that will come to pass, and *n*to stand before the Son of Man."

37*o*And in the daytime He was teaching in the temple, but *p*at night He went out and stayed on the mountain called Olivet.

38Then early in the morning all the people came to Him in the temple to hear Him.

The Plot to Kill Jesus

22 Now *a*the Feast of Unleavened Bread drew near, which is called Passover. 2And *b*the chief priests and the scribes sought how they might kill Him, for they feared the people.

3*c*Then Satan entered Judas, surnamed Iscariot, who was numbered among the *d*twelve. 4So he went his way and conferred with the chief priests and captains, how he might betray Him to them. 5And they were glad, and *e*agreed to give him money. 6So he promised and sought opportunity to *f*betray Him to them in the absence of the multitude.

Jesus and His Disciples Prepare the Passover

7*g*Then came the Day of Unleavened Bread, when the Passover must be killed. 8And He sent Peter and John, saying, "Go and prepare the Passover for us, that we may eat."

9So they said to Him, "Where do You want us to prepare?"

10And He said to them, "Behold, when you have entered the city, a man will meet you carrying a pitcher of water; follow him into the house which he enters. 11Then you shall say to the master of the house, 'The Teacher says to you, "Where is the guest room where I may eat the Passover with My disciples?" ' 12Then he will show you a large, furnished upper room; there make ready."

13So they went and *h*found it just as He had said to them, and they prepared the Passover.

---

* 21:36 NU-Text reads *may have strength.*

---

covenant and the Old Testament prophets' warnings of coming judgment (Deut. 28:49–57; 32:35; Jer. 6:1–8; 26:1–9; Hos. 9:7).

21:27 the Son of Man coming in a cloud. The reference here is to the authoritative return of Jesus. The allusion to the cloud and the figure comes from Daniel 7:13–14, with its picture of One who receives authority from the Ancient of Days. Jesus viewed this text in terms of an apocalyptic deliverance. The image of the cloud is important, since God is identified as riding the clouds in the Old Testament (Ex. 34:5; Ps. 104:3). The Son of Man has divine authority to judge the world.

21:29–30 When they are already budding. The tender buds that appear every spring on trees show that summer is approaching; the appearance of the signs Jesus describes will warn of the coming of the end times.

21:33 will by no means pass away. The disciples had the assurance that Jesus' promises concerning the end times were more certain than creation itself. God made an unconditional and unilateral covenant, and He will keep it (Gen. 12:1–3; 15:18–21; Ps. 89).

21:34 take heed to yourselves. Though the events of the end times may not come to pass for a long time,

believers should continue to look for their arrival. The day of Jesus' return should not take us by surprise. We should live as if it is imminent.

22:1 the Feast of Unleavened Bread. This feast took place immediately following Passover (Ex. 12:1–20; Deut. 16:1–8). The two feasts were often considered as one. Passover commemorated the night of the tenth plague in Egypt. The Feast of Unleavened Bread celebrated the Exodus.

22:4 captains. These were Levites who were members of the temple guard. They were the ones who could make the arrest.

22:11–12 guest room. Such rooms were often made available to the thousands of pilgrims who came to Jerusalem for the celebration of Passover and the

21:25 *a* [2 Pet. 3:10–12] 21:26 *b* Matt. 24:29 21:27 *c* Rev. 1:7; 14:14 21:28 *d* [Rom. 8:19, 23] 21:29 *e* Mark 13:28 21:33 *f* Matt. 24:35 *g* Is. 40:8 21:34 *h* 1 Thess. 5:6 *i* Luke 8:14 21:35 *j* Rev. 3:3; 16:15 21:36 *k* Matt. 24:42; 25:13 *l* Luke 18:1 *m* Luke 20:35 *n* [Eph. 6:13] 21:37 *o* John 8:1, 2 *p* Luke 22:39 22:1 *a* Matt. 26:2–5 22:2 *b* John 11:47 22:3 *c* Mark 14:10, 11 *d* Matt. 10:2–4 22:5 *e* Zech. 11:12 22:6 *f* Ps. 41:9 22:7 *g* Matt. 26:17–19 22:13 *h* Luke 19:32

Jesus Institutes the Lord's Supper

14*i*When the hour had come, He sat down, and the twelve* apostles with Him. 15Then He said to them, "With *fervent* desire I have desired to eat this Passover with you before I suffer; 16for I say to you, I will no longer eat of it *j*until it is fulfilled in the kingdom of God."

17Then He took the cup, and gave thanks, and said, "Take this and divide *it* among yourselves; 18for *k*I say to you,* I will not drink of the fruit of the vine until the kingdom of God comes."

19*l*And He took bread, gave thanks and broke *it*, and gave *it* to them, saying, "This is My *m*body which is given for you; *n*do this in remembrance of Me."

20Likewise He also *took* the cup after supper, saying, *o*"This cup *is* the new covenant in My blood, which is shed for you. 21*p*But behold, the hand of My betrayer *is* with Me on the table. 22*q*And truly the Son of Man goes *r*as it has been determined, but woe to that man by whom He is betrayed!"

23*s*Then they began to question among themselves, which of them it was who would do this thing.

The Disciples Argue About Greatness

24*t*Now there was also a dispute among them, as to which of them should be considered the greatest. 25*u*And He said to them, "The kings of the Gentiles exercise lordship over them, and those who exercise authority over them are called 'benefactors.' 26*v*But not so *among* you; on the contrary, *w*he who is greatest among you, let him be as the younger, and he who governs as he who serves. 27*x*For who *is* greater, he who sits at the table, or he who serves? *Is* it not he who sits at the table? Yet *y*I am among you as the One who serves.

28"But you are those who have continued with Me in *z*My trials. 29And *a*I bestow upon you a kingdom, just as My Father bestowed *one* upon Me, 30that *b*you may eat and drink at My table in My kingdom, *c*and sit on thrones judging the twelve tribes of Israel."

Jesus Predicts Peter's Denial

31And the Lord said,* "Simon, Simon! Indeed, *d*Satan has asked for you, that he may *e*sift *you* as wheat. 32But *f*I have prayed for you, that your faith should not fail; and when you have returned to *Me*, *g*strengthen your brethren."

33But he said to Him, "Lord, I am ready to go with You, both to prison and to death."

34*h*Then He said, "I tell you, Peter, the rooster shall not crow this day before you will deny three times that you know Me."

Supplies for the Road

35*i*And He said to them, "When I sent you without money bag, knapsack, and sandals, did you lack anything?"

So they said, "Nothing."

36Then He said to them, "But now, he who has a money bag, let him take *it*, and likewise a knapsack; and he who has no sword, let him sell his garment and buy one. 37For I say to you that this which is written must still be accomplished in Me: *i*'And He was numbered with the transgressors.'* For the things concerning Me have an end."

38So they said, "Lord, look, here *are* two swords."

And He said to them, "It is enough."

The Prayer in the Garden

39*k*Coming out, *l*He went to the Mount of Olives, as He was accustomed, and His disciples also followed Him. 40*m*When He came to the place, He said to them, "Pray that you may not enter into temptation."

---

* **22:14** NU-Text omits *twelve*.   * **22:18** NU-Text adds *from now on.*   * **22:31** NU-Text omits *And the Lord said.*   * **22:37** Isaiah 53:12

Feast of Unleavened Bread. Such a room would contain couches for guests at the feasts to recline for the meal. Access to the room was probably gained by stairs on the outside of the home.

22:19 My body . . . do this in remembrance. Jesus instituted a new meal which is not only a memorial of His death, but also a fellowship meal of unity. It is a proclamation and a symbol of the believer's anticipation of Jesus' return, when all God's promises will be fulfilled (1 Cor. 10:16–17; 11:23–26).

22:20 This cup is the new covenant. The wine of the Lord's Supper depicts the giving of life, a sacrifice of blood, which inaugurated the new covenant for those who respond to Jesus' offer of salvation (Heb. 8:8,13; 9:11–28).

22:30 eat and drink . . . sit on thrones judging. This is a promise of future blessing and authority. The disciples were promised a seat at the banquet of victory and the right to help Jesus rule over Israel on His return (Matt. 19:28; 2 Tim. 2:12).

22:32 I have prayed for you . . . you have returned. The Greek word for *you* here is singular, referring specifically to Peter. In effect, Jesus restored Peter even before his fall (vv. 54–62), and He instructed the disciple to shepherd the saints by strengthening them.

22:37 this which is written. Jesus cited Isaiah 53:12, which describes a righteous one who suffers as a

22:14 *i* Mark 14:17   **22:16** *j* [Rev. 19:9]   **22:18** *k* Mark 14:25   **22:19** *l* Matt. 26:26   *m* [1 Pet. 2:24]   *n* 1 Cor. 11:23–26   **22:20** *o* 1 Cor. 10:16   **22:21** *p* John 13:21, 26, 27   **22:22** *q* Matt. 26:24   *r* Acts 2:23   **22:23** *s* John 13:22, 25   **22:24** *t* Mark 9:34   **22:25** *u* Mark 10:42–45   **22:26** *v* [1 Pet. 5:3]   *w* Luke 9:48   **22:27** *x* [Luke 12:37]   *y* Phil. 2:7   **22:28** *z* [Heb. 2:18; 4:15]   **22:29** *a* Matt. 24:47   **22:30** *b* [Matt. 8:11]   *c* [Rev. 3:21]   **22:31** *d* 1 Pet. 5:8   *e* Amos 9:9   **22:32** *f* [John 17:9, 11, 15]   *g* John 21:15–17   **22:34** *h* John 13:37, 38   **22:35** *i* Matt. 10:9   **22:37** *j* Is. 53:12   **22:39** *k* John 18:1   *l* Luke 21:37   **22:40** *m* Mark 14:32–42

⁴¹ⁿAnd He was withdrawn from them about a stone's throw, and He knelt down and prayed, ⁴²saying, "Father, if it is Your will, take this cup away from Me; nevertheless ᵒnot My will, but Yours, be done." ⁴³Then ᵖan angel appeared to Him from heaven, strengthening Him. ⁴⁴ᵠAnd being in agony, He prayed more earnestly. Then His sweat became like great drops of blood falling down to the ground.*

⁴⁵When He rose up from prayer, and had come to His disciples, He found them sleeping from sorrow. ⁴⁶Then He said to them, "Why ʳdo you sleep? Rise and ˢpray, lest you enter into temptation."

Betrayal and Arrest in Gethsemane

⁴⁷And while He was still speaking, ᵗbehold, a multitude; and he who was called ᵘJudas, one of the twelve, went before them and drew near to Jesus to kiss Him. ⁴⁸But Jesus said to him, "Judas, are you betraying the Son of Man with a ᵛkiss?"

⁴⁹When those around Him saw what was going to happen, they said to Him, "Lord, shall we strike with the sword?" ⁵⁰And ʷone of them struck the servant of the high priest and cut off his right ear.

⁵¹But Jesus answered and said, "Permit even this." And He touched his ear and healed him.

⁵²ˣThen Jesus said to the chief priests, captains of the temple, and the elders who had come to Him, "Have you come out, as against a ʸrobber, with swords and clubs? ⁵³When I was with you daily in the ᶻtemple, you did not try to seize Me. But this is your ᵃhour, and the power of darkness."

Peter Denies Jesus, and Weeps Bitterly

⁵⁴ᵇHaving arrested Him, they led *Him* and brought Him into the high priest's house. ᶜBut Peter followed at a distance. ⁵⁵ᵈNow when they had kindled a fire in the midst of the courtyard and sat down together, Peter sat among them. ⁵⁶And a

certain servant girl, seeing him as he sat by the fire, looked intently at him and said, "This man was also with Him."

⁵⁷But he denied Him,* saying, "Woman, I do not know Him."

⁵⁸ᵉAnd after a little while another saw him and said, "You also are of them."

But Peter said, "Man, I am not!"

⁵⁹ᶠThen after about an hour had passed, another confidently affirmed, saying, "Surely this *fellow* also was with Him, for he is a ᵍGalilean."

⁶⁰But Peter said, "Man, I do not know what you are saying!"

Immediately, while he was still speaking, the rooster* crowed. ⁶¹And the Lord turned and looked at Peter. Then ʰPeter remembered the word of the Lord, how He had said to him, ⁱ"Before the rooster crows,* you will deny Me three times." ⁶²So Peter went out and wept bitterly.

Jesus Mocked and Beaten

⁶³ʲNow the men who held Jesus mocked Him and ᵏbeat Him. ⁶⁴And having blindfolded Him, they ˡstruck Him on the face and asked Him,* saying, "Prophesy! Who is the one who struck You?" ⁶⁵And many other things they blasphemously spoke against Him.

Jesus Faces the Sanhedrin

⁶⁶ᵐAs soon as it was day, ⁿthe elders of the people, both chief priests and scribes, came together and led Him into their council, saying, ⁶⁷ᵒ"If You are the Christ, tell us."

But He said to them, "If I tell you, you will ᵖby no means believe. ⁶⁸And if I also ask *you*, you will by no means answer Me or let *Me* go.* ⁶⁹ᵠHereafter the Son of Man

* **22:44** NU-Text brackets verses 43 and 44 as not in the original text. * **22:57** NU-Text reads *denied it*. * **22:60** NU-Text and M-Text read *a rooster*. * **22:61** NU-Text adds *today*. * **22:64** NU-Text reads *And having blindfolded Him, they asked Him*. * **22:68** NU-Text omits *also* and *Me or let Me go*.

criminal. Jesus noted that His death would fulfill Isaiah's prediction.
22:42 *this cup*. This is a figure of speech for wrath (Ps. 11:6; 75:7–8; Jer. 25:15–16; Ezek. 23:31–34).
22:43 *strengthening Him*. God's answer to Jesus' prayer did not allow His Son to avoid suffering. However, God did provide angelic help for Jesus to face what was coming. Sometimes God answers prayer by eliminating trials; sometimes He answers by strengthening us in the midst of them.
22:52 *as against a robber*. The Greek term for *robber* was used of both highway bandits and revolutionaries. Jesus rebuked His captors for treating Him as though He were a dangerous lawbreaker.
22:59 *for he is a Galilean*. According to Mark 14:70, Peter's accent gave him away as being from the same region as Jesus.
22:66 *the elders of the people . . . came together*. The description here is of a major morning trial that

involved all the Jewish religious leaders, the entire council or Sanhedrin. This trial violated various Jewish legal rules given in later sources: meeting on the morning of a feast; meeting at Caiaphas's home; trying a defendant without defense; and reaching the verdict in one day instead of the two days that were required for capital cases.
22:69 *on the right hand of the power of God*. Jesus'

22:41 ⁿ Matt. 26:39 **22:42** ᵒ John 4:34; 5:30; 6:38; 8:29 **22:43** ᵖ Matt. 4:11 **22:44** ᵠ [Heb. 5:7] **22:46** ʳ Luke 9:32 ˢ Luke 22:40 **22:47** ᵗ John 18:3–11 ᵘ Acts 1:16, 17 **22:48** ᵛ [Prov. 27:6] **22:50** ʷ Matt. 26:51 **22:52** ˣ Matt. 26:55 ʸ Luke 23:32 **22:53** ᶻ Luke 19:47, 48 ᵃ [John 12:27] **22:54** ᵇ Matt. 26:57 ᶜ John 18:15 **22:55** ᵈ Mark 14:66–72 **22:58** ᵉ John 18:25 **22:59** ᶠ Mark 14:70 ᵍ Acts 1:11; 2:7 **22:61** ʰ Matt. 26:75 ⁱ John 13:38 **22:63** ʲ Ps. 69:1, 4, 7–9 ᵏ Is. 50:6 **22:64** ˡ Zech. 13:7 **22:66** ᵐ Matt. 27:1 ⁿ Acts 4:26 **22:67** ᵒ Matt. 26:63–66 ᵖ Luke 20:5–7 **22:69** ᵠ Heb. 1:3; 8:1

will sit on the right hand of the power of God."

⁷⁰Then they all said, "Are You then the Son of God?"

So He said to them, ʳ"You *rightly* say that I am."

⁷¹ˢAnd they said, "What further testimony do we need? For we have heard it ourselves from His own mouth."

Jesus Handed Over to Pontius Pilate

23 Then ᵃthe whole multitude of them arose and led Him to ᵇPilate. ²And they began to ᶜaccuse Him, saying, "We found this *fellow* ᵈperverting the* nation, and ᵉforbidding to pay taxes to Caesar, saying ᶠthat He Himself is Christ, a King."

³ᵍThen Pilate asked Him, saying, "Are You the King of the Jews?"

He answered him and said, "*It is as* you say."

⁴So Pilate said to the chief priests and the crowd, ʰ"I find no fault in this Man."

⁵But they were the more fierce, saying, "He stirs up the people, teaching throughout all Judea, beginning from ⁱGalilee to this place."

Jesus Faces Herod

⁶When Pilate heard of Galilee,* he asked if the Man were a Galilean. ⁷And as soon as he knew that He belonged to ʲHerod's jurisdiction, he sent Him to Herod, who was also in Jerusalem at that time. ⁸Now when Herod saw Jesus, ᵏhe was exceedingly glad; for he had desired for a long *time* to see Him, because ˡhe had heard many things about Him, and he hoped to see some miracle done by Him. ⁹Then he questioned Him with many words, but He answered him ᵐnothing. ¹⁰And the chief priests and scribes stood and vehemently accused Him. ¹¹ⁿThen Herod, with his men

of war, treated Him with contempt and mocked *Him*, arrayed Him in a gorgeous robe, and sent Him back to Pilate. ¹²That very day ᵒPilate and Herod became friends with each other, for previously they had been at enmity with each other.

Taking the Place of Barabbas

¹³ᵖThen Pilate, when he had called together the chief priests, the rulers, and the people, ¹⁴said to them, ᵠ"You have brought this Man to me, as one who misleads the people. And indeed, ʳhaving examined *Him* in your presence, I have found no fault in this Man concerning those things of which you accuse Him; ¹⁵no, neither did Herod, for I sent you back to him;* and indeed nothing deserving of death has been done by Him. ¹⁶ˢI will therefore chastise Him and release *Him*" ¹⁷ᵗ(for it was necessary for him to release one to them at the feast).*

¹⁸And ᵘthey all cried out at once, saying, "Away with this *Man*, and release to us Barabbas"— ¹⁹who had been thrown into prison for a certain rebellion made in the city, and for murder.

²⁰Pilate, therefore, wishing to release Jesus, again called out to them. ²¹But they shouted, saying, "Crucify *Him*, crucify Him!"

²²Then he said to them the third time, "Why, what evil has He done? I have found no reason for death in Him. I will therefore chastise Him and let *Him* go."

²³But they were insistent, demanding with loud voices that He be crucified. And the voices of these men and of the chief priests prevailed.* ²⁴So ᵛPilate gave sentence that it should be as they requested.

---

* **23:2** NU-Text reads *our.* * **23:6** NU-Text omits *of Galilee.* * **23:15** NU-Text reads *for he sent Him back to us.* * **23:17** NU-Text omits verse 17. * **23:23** NU-Text omits *and of the chief priests.*

---

reply here alludes to the regal enthronement image of Psalm 110:1. This reply is what convicted Him. Apparently what offended Jesus' audience was His claim to sit in God's presence and to exercise divine authority. In effect, His answer to their question about being the Christ was more than they expected. It was not blasphemous to claim to be Messiah. What was blasphemous was the claim to be the Judge of Jewish people, with God's authority.

23:2 began to accuse. Three charges were lodged against Jesus: (1) perverting the nation, (2) forbidding payment of taxes to Rome, and (3) claiming to be the Christ. The first charge, which was a general complaint, involved disturbing the peace. The other two charges could have been construed as challenges to Rome. The second charge was a blatant lie (20:20–26). The third charge was true, but not in the threatening sense that the prosecutors suggested. A three-part Roman procedure was followed at the trial; charges, examination, and verdict.

23:5 they were the more fierce. By mentioning the charge that Jesus stirred up the people, the leaders

suggested that Pilate risked being found derelict in his duty if he let Jesus go.

23:7 Herod's jurisdiction. Herod was responsible for Galilee, so Pilate "passed the buck" for the ruling and showed political courtesy at the same time.

23:16 chastise Him and release Him. Pilate hoped that a public whipping might satisfy the crowd and tame Jesus, avoiding the need to resort to the death penalty.

23:18–19 Away with this Man. The entire crowd is portrayed as wanting Jesus to die. Luke makes it clear that Jesus' death was not only instigated by Jewish officials but approved by the Jewish people.

22:70 ʳMatt. 26:64; 27:11   **22:71** ˢMark 14:63
23:1 ᵈJohn 18:28 ᵇLuke 3:1; 13:1   **23:2** ᶜActs 24:2
ᵈActs 17:7 ᵉMatt. 17:27 ᶠJohn 19:12   **23:3** ᵍ1 Tim. 6:13
23:4 ʰ[1 Pet. 2:22]   **23:5** ⁱJohn 7:41   **23:7** ʲLuke 3:1;
9:7; 13:31   **23:8** ᵏLuke 7:8 ˡMatt. 14:1   **23:9** ᵐJohn
19:9   **23:11** ⁿIs. 53:3   **23:12** ᵒActs 4:26, 27
23:13 ᵖMark 15:14   **23:14** ᵠLuke 23:1, 2 ʳLuke 23:4
23:16 ˢJohn 19:1   **23:17** ᵗJohn 18:39   **23:18** ᵘActs
3:13–15   **23:24** ᵛMark 15:15

25wAnd he released to them* the one they requested, who for rebellion and murder had been thrown into prison; but he delivered Jesus to their will.

The King on a Cross

26xNow as they led Him away, they laid hold of a certain man, Simon a Cyrenian, who was coming from the country, and on him they laid the cross that he might bear *it* after Jesus.

27And a great multitude of the people followed Him, and women who also mourned and lamented Him. 28But Jesus, turning to them, said, "Daughters of Jerusalem, do not weep for Me, but weep for yourselves and for your children. 29yFor indeed the days are coming in which they will say, 'Blessed *are* the barren, wombs that never bore, and breasts which never nursed!' 30Then they will begin z*to say to the mountains, "Fall on us!" and to the hills, "Cover us!"'* 31aFor if they do these things in the green wood, what will be done in the dry?"

32bThere were also two others, criminals, led with Him to be put to death. 33And cwhen they had come to the place called Calvary, there they crucified Him, and the criminals, one on the right hand and the other on the left. 34Then Jesus said, "Father, dforgive them, for ethey do not know what they do."*

And fthey divided His garments and cast lots. 35And gthe people stood looking on. But even the hrulers with them sneered, saying, "He saved others; let Him save Himself if He is the Christ, the chosen of God."

36The soldiers also mocked Him, coming and offering Him isour wine, 37and saying, "If You are the King of the Jews, save Yourself."

38jAnd an inscription also was written over Him in letters of Greek, Latin, and Hebrew:*

THIS IS THE KING OF THE JEWS.

39kThen one of the criminals who were hanged blasphemed Him, saying, "If You are the Christ,* save Yourself and us."

40But the other, answering, rebuked him, saying, "Do you not even fear God, seeing you are under the same condemnation? 41And we indeed justly, for we receive the due reward of our deeds; but this Man has done lnothing wrong." 42Then he said to Jesus, "Lord,* remember me when You come into Your kingdom."

43And Jesus said to him, "Assuredly, I say to you, today you will be with Me in mParadise."

Jesus Dies on the Cross

44nNow it was* about the sixth hour, and there was darkness over all the earth until the ninth hour. 45Then the sun was darkened,* and othe veil of the temple was torn in two. 46And when Jesus had cried out with a loud voice, He said, "Father, p*into Your hands I commit My spirit.*"* qHaving said this, He breathed His last.

47rSo when the centurion saw what had happened, he glorified God, saying, "Certainly this was a righteous Man!"

48And the whole crowd who came together to that sight, seeing what had been done, beat their breasts and returned. 49sBut all His acquaintances, and the women who followed Him from Galilee, stood at a distance, watching these things.

Jesus Buried in Joseph's Tomb

50tNow behold, *there was* a man named Joseph, a council member, a good and just man. 51He had not consented to their

* 23:25 NU-Text and M-Text omit *to them.*
* 23:30 Hosea 10:8   * 23:34 NU-Text brackets the first sentence as a later addition.   * 23:38 NU-Text omits *written* and *in letters of Greek, Latin, and Hebrew.*   * 23:39 NU-Text reads *Are You not the Christ?*   * 23:42 NU-Text reads *And he said, "Jesus, remember me.*   * 23:44 NU-Text adds *already.*   * 23:45 NU-Text reads *obscured.*
* 23:46 Psalm 31:5

23:26 Simon a Cyrenian was recruited to carry Jesus' cross. He was from a leading city of Libya.

23:28 do not weep for me. Though He was dying, Jesus pointed out that their weeping should be for Jerusalem and its inhabitants, since judgment was going to fall on the city (19:41–44). Jerusalem here represents the entire nation of Israel.

23:31 what will be done in the dry. The idea here seems to be "If this is what is done to a live tree, what will happen to the dead one?" In other words, "If Jesus, the living tree, has not been spared, how much more will dead wood not be spared." This is Jesus' final lament over the nation of Israel.

23:33 the place called Calvary. The name of the place in Aramaic is Golgotha, which means "skull." Calvary is the Latin name for Golgotha. Possibly the name referred to a geographical feature of the locale, something that resembled a skull.

23:36 sour wine. The drink referred to here was probably wine vinegar, which was inexpensive and

quenched thirst better than water. It was a drink of the poor.

23:44 sixth hour . . . ninth hour. The first hour was sunrise, so the time was 12 P.M. to 3 P.M. During these three hours, signs of creation revealed that the hour was not one of light but of darkness (22:53).

23:47 Certainly this was a righteous Man. If Jesus was righteous and innocent, then He is who He claimed to be. Thus a second figure besides the thief on the cross had insight into Jesus' death.

23:25 W Is. 53:8   23:26 X Matt. 27:32   23:29 Y Matt. 24:19   23:30 Z Hos. 10:8; Rev. 6:16, 17; 9:6   23:31 a [Jer. 25:29]   23:32 b Is. 53:9, 12   23:33 c John 19:17–24   23:34 d 1 Cor. 4:12 e Acts 3:17 f Matt. 27:35   23:35 g Ps. 22:17 h Matt. 27:39   23:36 i Ps. 69:21   23:38 j John 19:19   23:39 k Mark 15:32   23:41 l [Heb. 7:26]   23:43 m [Rev. 2:7]   23:44 n Matt. 27:45–56   23:45 o Matt. 27:51   23:46 p Ps. 31:5 q John 19:30   23:47 r Mark 15:39   23:49 s Ps. 38:11   23:50 t Matt. 27:57–61

decision and deed. *He was* from Arimathea, a city of the Jews, *u*who himself was also waiting* for the kingdom of God. 52This man went to Pilate and asked for the body of Jesus. 53*v*Then he took it down, wrapped it in linen, and laid it in a tomb *that was* hewn out of the rock, where no one had ever lain before. 54That day was *w*the Preparation, and the Sabbath drew near.

55And the women *x*who had come with Him from Galilee followed after, and *y*they observed the tomb and how His body was laid. 56Then they returned and *z*prepared spices and fragrant oils. And they rested on the Sabbath *a*according to the commandment.

He Is Risen

24 Now *a*on the first *day* of the week, very early in the morning, they, and certain *other women* with them,* came to the tomb *b*bringing the spices which they had prepared. 2*c*But they found the stone rolled away from the tomb. 3*d*Then they went in and did not find the body of the Lord Jesus. 4And it happened, as they were greatly* perplexed about this, that *e*behold, two men stood by them in shining garments. 5Then, as they were afraid and bowed *their* faces to the earth, they said to them, "Why do you seek the living among the dead? 6He is not here, but is risen! *f*Remember how He spoke to you when He was still in Galilee, 7saying, 'The Son of Man must be *g*delivered into the hands of sinful men, and be crucified, and the third day rise again.' "

8And *h*they remembered His words. 9*i*Then they returned from the tomb and told all these things to the eleven and to all the rest. 10It was Mary Magdalene, *j*Joanna, Mary *the mother* of James, and the other *women* with them, who told these things to the apostles. 11*k*And their words seemed to them like idle tales, and they did not believe them. 12*l*But Peter arose and ran to the tomb; and stooping down, he saw the linen cloths

lying* by themselves; and he departed, marveling to himself at what had happened.

The Road to Emmaus

13*m*Now behold, two of them were traveling that same day to a village called Emmaus, which was seven miles* from Jerusalem. 14And they talked together of all these things which had happened. 15So it was, while they conversed and reasoned, that *n*Jesus Himself drew near and went with them. 16But *o*their eyes were restrained, so that they did not know Him. 17And He said to them, "What kind of conversation *is* this that you have with one another as you walk and are sad?"*

18Then the one *p*whose name was Cleopas answered and said to Him, "Are You the only stranger in Jerusalem, and have You not known the things which happened there in these days?"

19And He said to them, "What things?"

So they said to Him, "The things concerning Jesus of Nazareth, *q*who was a Prophet *r*mighty in deed and word before God and all the people, 20*s*and how the chief priests and our rulers delivered Him to be condemned to death, and crucified Him. 21But we were hoping *t*that it was He who was going to redeem Israel. Indeed, besides all this, today is the third day since these things happened. 22Yes, and *u*certain women of our company, who arrived at the tomb early, astonished us. 23When they did not find His body, they came saying that they had also seen a vision of angels who said He was alive. 24And *v*certain of those who were with us went to the tomb and found *it* just as the women had said; but Him they did not see."

---

* 23:51 NU-Text reads *who was waiting.*
* 24:1 NU-Text omits *and certain other women with them.* * 24:4 NU-Text omits *greatly.*
* 24:12 NU-Text omits *lying.* * 24:13 Literally *sixty stadia* * 24:17 NU-Text reads *as you walk? And they stood still, looking sad.*

23:52 *the body of Jesus.* There is no doubt that Jesus died. Efforts to explain the resurrection as something like a return from a coma are more impossible than the idea of the resurrection itself.

23:54 *That day was the Preparation.* Jesus was buried late on Friday, on the day called Preparation when everything was made ready for the Sabbath, the day when no labor could take place.

24:2 *they found the stone rolled away.* Matthew 28:2 mentions that an earthquake moved the stone, which would have fit in a channel in front of the entrance to the tomb. Moving the stone would have been possible, though difficult, for a group of people. The earthquake settles the question of how the stone was moved.

24:11 *they did not believe them.* Skepticism reigned among the disciples. It is clear that they did not expect a resurrection. The disciples thought the women's story was nonsense.

24:12 *Peter arose and ran.* Having already experienced a fulfilled prediction of the Lord (22:54–62), Peter hurried to the tomb to check out the women's

story. It is hard to say whether Peter believed in the resurrection when he left the tomb. At that point he was probably more amazed than anything else.

24:19–21 *Jesus of Nazareth, who was a Prophet.* These disciples on the road to Emmaus regarded Jesus as the Revealer of God's way and the Doer of His work.

24:23 *He was alive.* The women reported that there was no body found in Jesus' tomb, and that angels had announced to them that Jesus lives. The fact

---

23:51 *u* Luke 2:25, 38   **23:53** *v* Mark 15:46
23:54 *w* Matt. 27:62   **23:55** *x* Luke 8:2   *y* Mark
15:47   **23:56** *z* Mark 16:1   *a* Ex. 20:10   **24:1** *a* John
20:1–8   *b* Luke 23:56   **24:2** *c* Mark 16:4   **24:3** *d* Mark
16:5   **24:4** *e* John 20:12   **24:6** *f* Luke 9:22   **24:7** *g* Luke
9:44; 11:29, 30; 18:31–33   **24:8** *h* John 2:19–22
24:9 *i* Mark 16:10   **24:10** *j* Luke 8:3   **24:11** *k* Luke
24:25   **24:12** *l* John 20:3–6   **24:13** *m* Mark
16:12   **24:15** *n* [Matt. 18:20]   **24:16** *o* John 20:14;
21:4   **24:18** *p* John 19:25   **24:19** *q* Matt. 21:11   *r* Acts
7:22   **24:20** *s* Acts 13:27, 28   **24:21** *t* Luke 1:68; 2:38
24:22 *u* Mark 16:10   **24:24** *v* Luke 24:12

25Then He said to them, "O foolish ones, and slow of heart to believe in all that the prophets have spoken! 26wOught not the Christ to have suffered these things and to enter into His xglory?" 27And beginning at yMoses and zall the Prophets, He expounded to them in all the Scriptures the things concerning Himself.

The Disciples' Eyes Opened

28Then they drew near to the village where they were going, and aHe indicated that He would have gone farther. 29But bthey constrained Him, saying, c"Abide with us, for it is toward evening, and the day is far spent." And He went in to stay with them.

30Now it came to pass, as dHe sat at the table with them, that He took bread, blessed and broke it, and gave it to them. 31Then their eyes were opened and they knew Him; and He vanished from their sight.

32And they said to one another, "Did not our heart burn within us while He talked with us on the road, and while He opened the Scriptures to us?" 33So they rose up that very hour and returned to Jerusalem, and found the eleven and those who were with them gathered together, 34saying, "The Lord is risen indeed, and ehas appeared to Simon!" 35And they told about the things that had happened on the road, and how He was known to them in the breaking of bread.

Jesus Appears to His Disciples

36fNow as they said these things, Jesus Himself stood in the midst of them, and said to them, "Peace to you." 37But they were terrified and frightened, and supposed they had seen ga spirit. 38And He said to them, "Why are you troubled? And why do doubts arise in your hearts? 39Behold My hands and My feet, that it is I Myself. hHandle Me and see, for a ispirit does not have flesh and bones as you see I have."

40When He had said this, He showed

them His hands and His feet.* 41But while they still did not believe jfor joy, and marveled, He said to them, k"Have you any food here?" 42So they gave Him a piece of a broiled fish and some honeycomb.* 43lAnd He took it and ate in their presence.

The Scriptures Opened

44Then He said to them, m"These are the words which I spoke to you while I was still with you, that all things must be fulfilled which were written in the Law of Moses and the Prophets and the Psalms concerning Me." 45And nHe opened their understanding, that they might comprehend the Scriptures.

46Then He said to them, o"Thus it is written, and thus it was necessary for the Christ to suffer and to rise* from the dead the third day, 47and that repentance and premission of sins should be preached in His name qto all nations, beginning at Jerusalem. 48And ryou are witnesses of these things. 49sBehold, I send the Promise of My Father upon you; but tarry in the city of Jerusalem* until you are endued with power from on high."

The Ascension

50And He led them out tas far as Bethany, and He lifted up His hands and blessed them. 51uNow it came to pass, while He blessed them, that He was parted from them and carried up into heaven. 52vAnd they worshiped Him, and returned to Jerusalem with great joy, 53and were continually win the temple praising and* blessing God. Amen.*

* 24:40 Some printed New Testaments omit this verse. It is found in nearly all Greek manuscripts. * 24:42 NU-Text omits and some honeycomb. * 24:46 NU-Text reads written, that the Christ should suffer and rise. * 24:49 NU-Text omits of Jerusalem. * 24:53 NU-Text omits praising and. • NU-Text omits Amen.

---

that the men were still sad indicates that they did not believe the report.

24:25 slow of heart to believe. Jesus, who at this time was still not known to the travelers, rebuked His companions and reminded them of the things that the prophets taught.

24:27 And beginning at Moses. Going from the books of Moses to the Prophets, Jesus provided an overview of God's plan in the Scriptures. This plan is present throughout the entire Old Testament (Acts 3:22–26; 10:43).

24:39 flesh and bones. Jesus pointed out that a raised body is not a disembodied spirit. The presence of His body indicates that He had been raised and that He was not a hallucination. He was raised in the same physical body in which He had been put to death. The difference was that His resurrected body is not corruptible and not subject to death.

24:46 Christ to suffer and to rise from the dead. Two parts of God's plan had been fulfilled. Jesus had been crucified and raised from the dead. Old

Testament texts that predict these events are Psalm 22 and Psalm 118:22.

24:49 the Promise of My Father. This is a reference to the baptism of the Holy Spirit at Pentecost (Acts 2:4). It was promised in Jeremiah 31:31–33, and in Joel 2:28. Peter called this coming of the Spirit "the beginning" (Acts 11:15) because the real fulfillment of God's promise of salvation would start in those people united by the Spirit to establish the church.

24:26 w Acts 17:2, 3 x [1 Pet. 1:10–12] **24:27** y [Deut. 18:15] z [Is. 7:14; 9:6] **24:28** d Mark 6:48 **24:29** b Gen. 19:2, 3 c [John 14:23] **24:30** d Matt. 14:19 **24:34** e 1 Cor. 15:5 **24:36** f Mark 16:14 **24:37** g Mark 6:49 **24:39** h John 20:20, 27 i [1 Cor. 15:50] **24:41** j Gen. 45:26 k John 21:5 **24:43** l Acts 10:39–41 **24:44** m Matt. 16:21; 17:22; 20:18 **24:45** n Acts 16:14 **24:46** o Acts 17:3 **24:47** p Acts 5:31; 10:43; 13:38; 26:18 q [Jer. 31:34] **24:48** r [Acts 1:8] **24:49** s Joel 2:28 **24:50** t Acts 1:12 **24:51** u Mark 16:19 **24:52** v Matt. 28:9 **24:53** w Acts 2:46

THE GOSPEL ACCORDING TO
JOHN

▶ **AUTHOR:** Jesus nicknamed John and his brother, James, "sons of thunder" (Mark 3:17). John was evidently among the Galileans who followed John the Baptist until they were called to follow Jesus at the outset of His public ministry. These Galileans were later called to become full-time disciples of the Lord (Luke 5:1–11), and John was among the twelve men who were selected to be apostles (Luke 6:12–16). The author of this Gospel is identified only as the disciple "whom Jesus loved" (John 13:23; 19:26; 21:7), but attention to detail concerning geography and Jewish culture in the Gospel lend credibility to the author's claim to be an eyewitness. The strong testimony of the early church relates this eyewitness to the apostle John.

▶ **TIME:** c. A.D. 29–33   ▶ **KEY VERSES:** John 20:30–31

▶ **THEME:** John is a great book for new or young Christians because it intentionally helps the reader understand the significance of Jesus. What becomes increasingly clear as you read the Gospel of John is that Jesus does not fit the image of someone who is simply a nice moral teacher. Only a lunatic would make the claims He makes for Himself unless He was who He said He was. John leaves no room for indecision. Like the many people Jesus encounters in the book, as you read, you must either reject Him or accept Him, and say in the end like Thomas: "My Lord and my God" (20:28). This Gospel is an incredibly powerful presentation of Jesus.

The Eternal Word

1 In the beginning *a*was the Word, and the *b*Word was *c*with God, and the Word was *d*God. *2eHe was in the beginning with God. *3fAll things were made through Him, and without Him nothing was made that was made. *4gIn Him was life, and *hthe life was the light of men. *5And *ithe light shines in the darkness, and the darkness did not comprehend* it.

John's Witness: The True Light

*6There was a *jman sent from God, whose name *was John. *7This man came for a *kwitness, to bear witness of the Light, that all through him might *lbelieve. *8He was not that Light, but *was sent* to bear witness of that *mLight. *9nThat was the true Light which gives light to every man coming into the world.*

* **1:5** Or *overcome*   * **1:9** Or *That was the true Light which, coming into the world, gives light to every man.*

1:1 *In the beginning.* Genesis 1:1 starts with the moment of creation and moves forward to the creation of humanity. John 1:1 starts with creation and contemplates eternity past. ***the Word was with God.*** This suggests a face-to-face relationship. In the ancient world, it was important that persons of equal station be on the same level when seated across from one another.

1:3 *All things were made through Him.* God the Father created the world (Gen. 1:1) through God the Son (Col. 1:16; Heb. 1:2). All creation was made through Him. Thus, He is the Creator God.

1:4 *light of men.* This image conveys the concept of revelation. As the light, Jesus Christ reveals both sin and God to humans (Ps. 36:9). Later in this Gospel, Christ declares Himself to be both the life (11:25) and the light (8:12). Death and darkness flee when the life and light enter.

1:5 *light shines in the darkness.* Although Satan and his forces resist the light, they cannot thwart its power. In short, Jesus is life and light; those

who accept Him are "sons of light" (12:35–36). As the creation of light was the beginning of the original creation, so, when believers receive the light, they become part of the new creation (2 Cor. 4:3–6).

1:7 *for a witness.* This phrase means "to testify" or "to declare." John uses the word translated *witness* 33 times as a verb and 14 times as a noun in his Gospel. The term is particularly important to his purpose, which is to record adequate witnesses to Jesus as the Messiah so that individuals might believe Him (20:30–31). ***believe.*** This word means "to trust." John uses this verb almost 100 times in his Gospel to express what must take place for a person to receive the gift of eternal life.

1:1 *a* 1 John 1:1 *b* Rev. 19:13 *c* [John 17:5] *d* [1 John 5:20]
1:2 *e* Gen. 1:1   **1:3** *f* [Col. 1:16, 17]   **1:4** *g* [1 John 5:11]
h John 8:12; 9:5; 12:46   **1:5** *i* [John 3:19]   **1:6** *j* Matt.
3:1–17   **1:7** *k* John 3:25–36; 5:33–35 *l* [John 3:16]
1:8 *m* Is. 9:2; 49:6   **1:9** *n* Is. 9:6

¹⁰He was in the world, and the world was made through Him, and ᵒthe world did not know Him. ¹¹ᵖHe came to His own,* and His own* did not receive Him. ¹²But ᑫas many as received Him, to them He gave the right to become children of God, to those who believe in His name: ¹³ʳwho were born, not of blood, nor of the will of the flesh, nor of the will of man, but of God.

The Word Becomes Flesh

¹⁴ˢAnd the Word ᵗbecame ᵘflesh and dwelt among us, and ᵛwe beheld His glory, the glory as of the only begotten of the Father, ʷfull of grace and truth. ¹⁵ˣJohn bore witness of Him and cried out, saying, "This was He of whom I said, ʸ'He who comes after me is preferred before me, ᶻfor He was before me.'" ¹⁶And* of His ᵃfullness we have all received, and grace for grace. ¹⁷For ᵇthe law was given through Moses, but ᶜgrace and ᵈtruth came through Jesus Christ. ¹⁸ᵉNo one has seen God at any time. ᶠThe only begotten Son,* who is in the bosom of the Father, He has declared Him.

A Voice in the Wilderness

¹⁹Now this is ᵍthe testimony of John, when the Jews sent priests and Levites from Jerusalem to ask him, "Who are you?" ²⁰ʰHe confessed, and did not deny, but confessed, "I am not the Christ."

²¹And they asked him, "What then? Are you Elijah?"
He said, "I am not."
"Are you ᶦthe Prophet?"
And he answered, "No."
²²Then they said to him, "Who are you, that we may give an answer to those who sent us? What do you say about yourself?"
²³He said: ʲ"I am

ᵏ'The voice of one crying in the wilderness:
"Make straight the way of the LORD,"'*

as the prophet Isaiah said."
²⁴Now those who were sent were from the Pharisees. ²⁵And they asked him, saying, "Why then do you baptize if you are not the Christ, nor Elijah, nor the Prophet?"
²⁶John answered them, saying, ˡ"I baptize with water, ᵐbut there stands One among you whom you do not know. ²⁷ⁿIt is He who, coming after me, is preferred before me, whose sandal strap I am not worthy to loose."
²⁸These things were done ᵒin Bethabara* beyond the Jordan, where John was baptizing.

---

* **1:11** That is, His own things or domain • That is, His own people   * **1:16** NU-Text reads *For.*   * **1:18** NU-Text reads *only begotten God.*   * **1:23** Isaiah 40:3   * **1:28** NU-Text and M-Text read *Bethany.*

1:11 receive. This means "to receive with favor" and implies "welcome." Instead of a welcome mat, Jesus had a door slammed in His face. The themes of rejection and reception (v. 12) introduced in the prologue (1:1–18) appear repeatedly throughout the Gospel of John.
1:12 He gave the right. This phrase refers to the legitimate entitlement to the position of children of God. By believing, undeserving sinners can become full members of God's family.
1:14 the Word became flesh. The Son of God who was from eternity became human, with limitations in time and space (Phil. 2:5–8). This is the doctrine of the incarnation: God became human. Nothing of the essential nature of deity was lost in this event; we might rephrase *became* as "took to Himself." John uses the word *flesh* to refer to the physical nature of humans, not to our sinful disposition. **dwelt among us.** The Greek word for *tent* or *dwelling* was also used in the Greek Old Testament for the tabernacle, where the presence of God dwelt. **only begotten.** This means unique, one of a kind.
1:16 grace for grace. The background of this doubled term, as well as the use of the term in verse 17, is found in Exodus 32–34. Moses and the people had received grace, but they were in tremendous need of more grace (Ex. 33:13).
1:18 No one has seen God. God is Spirit (4:24) and is invisible (Col. 1:15; 1 Tim. 1:17) unless God chooses to reveal Himself. Humans cannot look at God and live (Ex. 33:20). However, the Son is in intimate relationship with the Father, face-to-face with God (1:1; 6:46; 1 John 1:2). God became visible to human eyes in the man Jesus. It is through seeing the Son that we see God.

1:19–20 the Jews. This refers to the Jewish leaders or the council (the Sanhedrin), who would be responsible for examining anyone thought to be a prophet, to see if the person was true or false.
1:23 Make straight. When a king traveled, roads were built so that the royal chariot would not have to travel over rough terrain or be stuck in the mud. Isaiah was saying that before God appeared to manifest His glory, a voice would be heard, inviting Israel to make straight the way by which God Himself would come.
1:24 the Pharisees. The Pharisees were an influential sect that numbered about 6,000. As strict interpreters of the law in Israel, they were extremely zealous for ritual and tradition.
1:27 whose sandal strap I am not worthy to loose. Undoing the shoe strap was the job of a slave. The Jewish Talmud says, "Everything that a servant will do for his master, a scholar shall perform for his teacher, except the menial task of loosing his sandal thong." Thus, John was saying that "Jesus Christ is the living Lord and I am the voice, His servant and slave. Actually, I'm not even worthy to be His slave."

1:10 ᵒHeb. 1:2   **1:11** ᵖIs. 53:3; [Luke 19:14]   **1:12** ᑫGal. 3:26   **1:13** ʳ[1 Pet. 1:23]   **1:14** ˢRev. 19:13 ᵗGal. 4:4 ᵘHeb. 2:11 ᵛIs. 40:5 ʷ[John 8:32; 14:6; 18:37]   **1:15** ˣJohn 3:32 ʸ[Matt. 3:11] ᶻ[Col. 1:17]   **1:16** ᵃ[Col. 1:19; 2:9]   **1:17** ᵇ[Ex. 20:1] ᶜ[Rom. 5:21; 6:14] ᵈ[John 8:32; 14:6; 18:37]   **1:18** ᵉEx. 33:20 ᶠ1 John 4:9   **1:19** ᵍJohn 5:33   **1:20** ʰLuke 3:15   **1:21** ᶦDeut. 18:15, 18   **1:23** ʲMatt. 3:3 ᵏIs. 40:3   **1:26** ˡMatt. 3:11 ᵐMal. 3:1   **1:27** ⁿActs 19:4   **1:28** ᵒJudg. 7:24

The Lamb of God

29The next day John saw Jesus coming toward him, and said, "Behold! PThe Lamb of God qwho takes away the sin of the world! 30This is He of whom I said, 'After me comes a Man who is preferred before me, for He was before me.' 31I did not know Him; but that He should be revealed to Israel, rtherefore I came baptizing with water."

32sAnd John bore witness, saying, "I saw the Spirit descending from heaven like a dove, and He remained upon Him. 33I did not know Him, but He who sent me to baptize with water said to me, 'Upon whom you see the Spirit descending, and remaining on Him, tthis is He who baptizes with the Holy Spirit.' 34And I have seen and testified that this is the uSon of God."

The First Disciples

35Again, the next day, John stood with two of his disciples. 36And looking at Jesus as He walked, he said, v"Behold the Lamb of God!"

37The two disciples heard him speak, and they wfollowed Jesus. 38Then Jesus turned, and seeing them following, said to them, "What do you seek?"

They said to Him, "Rabbi" (which is to say, when translated, Teacher), "where are You staying?"

39He said to them, "Come and see." They came and saw where He was staying, and remained with Him that day (now it was about the tenth hour).

40One of the two who heard John *speak*, and followed Him, was xAndrew, Simon Peter's brother. 41He first found his own brother Simon, and said to him, "We have found the Messiah" (which is translated, the Christ). 42And he brought him to Jesus.

Now when Jesus looked at him, He said, "You are Simon the son of Jonah.* yYou shall be called Cephas" (which is translated, A Stone).

Philip and Nathanael

43The following day Jesus wanted to go to Galilee, and He found zPhilip and said to him, "Follow Me." 44Now aPhilip was from Bethsaida, the city of Andrew and Peter. 45Philip found bNathanael and said to him, "We have found Him of whom cMoses in the law, and also the dprophets, wrote— Jesus eof Nazareth, the fson of Joseph."

46And Nathanael said to him, g"Can anything good come out of Nazareth?"

Philip said to him, "Come and see."

47Jesus saw Nathanael coming toward Him, and said of him, "Behold, han Israelite indeed, in whom is no deceit!"

48Nathanael said to Him, "How do You know me?"

Jesus answered and said to him, "Before Philip called you, when you were under the fig tree, I saw you."

49Nathanael answered and said to Him, "Rabbi, iYou are the Son of God! You are jthe King of Israel!"

50Jesus answered and said to him, "Because I said to you, 'I saw you under the fig tree,' do you believe? You will see greater things than these." 51And He said to him, "Most assuredly, I say to you, khereafter* you shall see heaven open, and the angels of God ascending and descending upon the Son of Man."

Water Turned to Wine

2 On the third day there was a awedding in bCana of Galilee, and the cmother of Jesus was there. 2Now both Jesus and His disciples were invited to the wedding. 3And when they ran out of wine, the mother of Jesus said to Him, "They have no wine."

4Jesus said to her, d"Woman, ewhat does your concern have to do with Me? fMy hour has not yet come."

---

* 1:42 NU-Text reads *John.*   * 1:51 NU-Text omits *hereafter.*

1:29 The Lamb of God. Jesus Christ is the Lamb that God would give as a sacrifice not only for Israel, but for the whole world (Is. 52:13—53:12).

1:33 this is He who baptizes with the Holy Spirit. Seven times, the New Testament mentions this ministry of Jesus. Five are prophetic (Matt. 3:11; Mark 1:8; Luke 3:16; Acts 1:5); one is historical (Acts 11:16–18); one is doctrinal (1 Cor. 12:13).

1:42 Cephas. This is the Aramaic word for "rock" (Matt. 16:18).

1:45 Nathanael. This name is not mentioned in the Synoptic Gospels. But in every list of the apostles in Matthew, Mark, and Luke, the name Bartholomew is listed with Philip, as Nathanael is linked with Philip here. It is likely that Nathanael and Bartholomew were the same person.

1:46 Nazareth. Nathanael knew that the Old Testament prophets had predicted that the Messiah would be born in Bethlehem. Furthermore, Nazareth was an obscure village. Nathanael simply could not fathom that such a significant person as the Messiah could come from such an insignificant place as Nazareth.

1:48–49 under the fig tree. In the Old Testament, this expression often suggests being safe and at leisure (1 Kin. 4:25; Mic. 4:4; Zech. 3:10).

2:1–2 Cana. This city was about four and a half miles northwest of Nazareth. **the mother of Jesus was there. Now both Jesus and His disciples were invited.** This suggests that Jesus and His disciples were invited because of Mary. Her forwardness in asking Jesus to help when the wine ran out (v. 3) may indicate that she was in some way related to the family holding the wedding.

2:3 They have no wine. Hospitality in the East was a

1:29 P Rev. 5:6–14 q [1 Pet. 2:24]   1:31 r Matt. 3:6   1:32 s Mark 1:10   1:33 t Is. 42:1; 61:1; Matt. 3:11   1:34 u John 11:27   1:36 v John 1:29   1:37 w Matt. 4:20, 22   1:40 x Matt. 4:18   1:42 y Matt. 16:18   1:43 z John 6:5; 12:21, 22; 14:8, 9   1:44 a John 12:21   1:45 b John 21:2 c Luke 24:27 d [Zech. 6:12] e [Matt. 2:23] f Luke 3:23   1:46 g John 7:41, 42, 52   1:47 h Ps. 32:2; 73:1   1:49 i Matt. 14:33 j Matt. 21:5   1:51 k Gen. 28:12   2:1 a [Heb. 13:4] b John 4:46 c John 19:25   2:4 d John 19:26 e 2 Sam. 16:10 f John 7:6, 8, 30; 8:20

5His mother said to the servants, "Whatever He says to you, do *it*."

6Now there were set there six waterpots of stone, *g*according to the manner of purification of the Jews, containing twenty or thirty gallons apiece. 7Jesus said to them, "Fill the waterpots with water." And they filled them up to the brim. 8And He said to them, "Draw *some* out now, and take *it* to the master of the feast." And they took *it*. 9When the master of the feast had tasted *h*the water that was made wine, and did not know where it came from (but the servants who had drawn the water knew), the master of the feast called the bridegroom. 10And he said to him, "Every man at the beginning sets out the good wine, and when the *guests* have well drunk, then the inferior. You have kept the good wine until now!"

11This *i*beginning of signs Jesus did in Cana of Galilee, *j*and manifested His glory; and His disciples believed in Him.

12After this He went down to *k*Capernaum, He, His mother, *l*His brothers, and His disciples; and they did not stay there many days.

Jesus Cleanses the Temple

13*m*Now the Passover of the Jews was at hand, and Jesus went up to Jerusalem. 14*n*And He found in the temple those who sold oxen and sheep and doves, and the money changers doing business. 15When He had made a whip of cords, He drove them all out of the temple, with the sheep and the oxen, and poured out the changers' money and overturned the tables. 16And He said to those who sold doves, "Take these things away! Do not make *o*My Father's house a house of merchandise!" 17Then His disciples remembered that it was written, *p*"Zeal for Your house has eaten* Me up."*

18So the Jews answered and said to Him, *q*"What sign do You show to us, since You do these things?"

19Jesus answered and said to them, *r*"Destroy this temple, and in three days I will raise it up."

20Then the Jews said, "It has taken forty-six years to build this temple, and will You raise it up in three days?"

21But He was speaking *s*of the temple of His body. 22Therefore, when He had risen from the dead, *t*His disciples remembered that He had said this to them;* and they believed the Scripture and the word which Jesus had said.

The Discerner of Hearts

23Now when He was in Jerusalem at the Passover, during the feast, many believed in His name when they saw the *u*signs which He did. 24But Jesus did not commit Himself to them, because He *v*knew all *men*, 25and had no need that anyone should testify of man, for *w*He knew what was in man.

---

* **2:17** NU-Text and M-Text read *will eat*. • Psalm 69:9 * **2:22** NU-Text and M-Text omit *to them*.

---

sacred duty. A wedding feast often lasted for a week. To run out of wine at such an important event would have been humiliating for the bride and groom. The family of Jesus was not wealthy, and it is likely their relatives and acquaintances were not either. This may have been a "low-budget" wedding feast.

2:6 six waterpots. Each waterpot held 20–30 gallons, for a total of 120–180 gallons of the finest wine (v. 10). **manner of purification of the Jews.** Jewish tradition required several kinds of ceremonial washings. Strict Jews washed their hands before a meal, between courses, and after the meal. This "purifying" extended not only to washing hands, but also to washing cups and vessels (Mark 7:3–4).

2:11 This beginning of signs. In the Gospel of John, the miracles of Jesus are called signs, indicating that they pointed to His messiahship. This sign signified Christ's glory that is, His deity. When Jesus transformed water into wine, He demonstrated His power.

2:13 the Passover of the Jews. Every male Jew was required to go to Jerusalem three times a year—for the Feast of Passover, the Feast of Pentecost, and the Feast of Tabernacles (Ex. 23:14–19; Lev. 23). **Jerusalem.** The Synoptic Gospels concentrate on Jesus' Galilean ministry. John focuses on Jesus' ministry in Jerusalem.

2:14 And He found in the temple those who sold oxen and sheep and doves. The Synoptic Gospels place the cleansing of the temple at the conclusion of Jesus' ministry (Matt. 21:12–13), whereas John puts it at the beginning. Apparently, Jesus cleansed the temple two different times. The law of Moses required that any animal offered in sacrifice be unblemished and that every Jewish male over 19 years of age pay a temple tax (Lev. 1:3; Deut. 17:1). As a result, tax collectors and inspectors of sacrificial animals were present at the temple. However, these officials would not accept secular coins because they had an image of the Roman emperor. To put such coins into the temple treasury was thought to be an offense. Accordingly, merchants and money changers set up shop and charged high prices for changing currency and for sacrificial animals.

2:19 Destroy this temple. Jesus was not talking about the physical building; He was referring to His body, as John emphasizes in verse 21. Jesus was speaking of His death. **I will raise it up.** Note that Jesus did not say, "I will build it again." He was referring to His resurrection, three days after His death.

2:20 Forty-six years. Herod the Great began restoring the temple in 20 B.C. The work was not finished at the time of this conversation. In fact, it was not completed until around A.D. 64 under Herod Agrippa.

2:23 many believed in His name. This was saving faith. John's purpose in recording Jesus' miracles was for people to believe and have eternal life (20:30–31).

2:24 But Jesus did not commit Himself. This word

2:6 *g* [Mark 7:3] **2:9** *h* John 4:46 **2:11** *i* John 4:54 *j* [John 1:14] **2:12** *k* Matt. 4:13 *l* Matt. 12:46; 13:55 **2:13** *m* Deut. 16:1–6 **2:14** *n* Mark 11:15, 17 **2:16** *o* Luke 2:49 **2:17** *p* Ps. 69:9 **2:18** *q* Matt. 12:38 **2:19** *r* Matt. 26:61; 27:40 **2:21** *s* [1 Cor. 3:16; 6:19] **2:22** *t* Luke 24:8 **2:23** *u* [Acts 2:22] **2:24** *v* Rev. 2:23 **2:25** *w* Matt. 9:4

The New Birth

3 There was a man of the Pharisees named Nicodemus, a ruler of the Jews. [2][a]This man came to Jesus by night and said to Him, "Rabbi, we know that You are a teacher come from God; for [b]no one can do these signs that You do unless [c]God is with him."

[3]Jesus answered and said to him, "Most assuredly, I say to you, [d]unless one is born again, he cannot see the kingdom of God."

[4]Nicodemus said to Him, "How can a man be born when he is old? Can he enter a second time into his mother's womb and be born?"

[5]Jesus answered, "Most assuredly, I say to you, [e]unless one is born of water and the Spirit, he cannot enter the kingdom of God. [6]That which is born of the flesh is [f]flesh, and that which is born of the Spirit is spirit. [7]Do not marvel that I said to you, 'You must be born again.' [8][g]The wind blows where it wishes, and you hear the sound of it, but cannot tell where it comes from and where it goes. So is everyone who is born of the Spirit."

[9]Nicodemus answered and said to Him, [h]"How can these things be?"

[10]Jesus answered and said to him, "Are you the teacher of Israel, and do not know these things? [11][i]Most assuredly, I say to you, We speak what We know and testify what We have seen, and [j]you do not receive Our witness. [12]If I have told you earthly things and you do not believe, how will you believe if I tell you heavenly things? [13][k]No one has ascended to heaven but He who came down from heaven, *that is,* the Son of Man who is in heaven.* [14][l]And as Moses lifted up the serpent in the wilderness, even so [m]must the Son of Man be lifted up, [15]that whoever [n]believes in Him should not perish but* [o]have eternal life. [16][p]For God so loved the world that He gave His only begotten [q]Son, that whoever believes in Him should not perish but have everlasting life. [17][r]For God did not send His Son into the world to condemn the world, but that the world through Him might be saved.

[18][s]"He who believes in Him is not condemned; but he who does not believe is condemned already, because he has not believed in the name of the only begotten Son of God. [19]And this is the condemnation, [t]that the light has come into the world, and men loved darkness rather than light, because their deeds were evil. [20]For [u]everyone practicing evil hates the light and does not come to the light, lest his deeds should be exposed. [21]But he who does the truth comes to the light, that his deeds may be clearly seen, that they have been [v]done in God."

* **3:13** NU-Text omits *who is in heaven.*
* **3:15** NU-Text omits *not perish but.*

---

is the same Greek word translated *believe* in verse 23. There is a play on words here. These individuals trusted Jesus, but Jesus did not entrust Himself to them.

3:2 by night. The fact that Nicodemus came to Jesus at night may reveal the timidity of his faith (12:42); however, his faith was developing (7:50–51; 19:39).

3:3 unless one is born again. Jesus was explaining to Nicodemus that there is more to having a right relationship with God than being physically born a Jew. The new birth is not physical; rather, it is spiritual (v. 6). It must come by the Spirit of God if it is a spiritual birth (v. 5).

3:5 born of water and the Spirit. There are several interpretations of this phrase. (1) Jesus was referring to water baptism (Acts 10:43–47). (2) Water is to be understood as a symbol for the Holy Spirit. (3) Water is to be understood as a symbol of the Word of God. (4) Jesus used the phrase "born of water" to refer to physical birth. He then used the contrasting phrase "of the Spirit" to refer to spiritual birth. (5) Jesus used the phrase "born of water" to refer to John the Baptist's baptism. (6) Jesus used the Old Testament imagery of "water" and "wind" to refer to the work of God from above (Is. 44:3–5).

3:8 The wind. Jesus used the wind as an illustration of the work of the Holy Spirit. The Greek word translated *Spirit* also means "wind." As the wind seemingly blows where it wills, so the Holy Spirit sovereignly works. Likewise, no one knows the origin or destination of the wind, but everyone knows it is there. The same is true of the Holy Spirit.

3:12 heavenly things. This refers to events like Christ's ascension (6:61–62) and the coming of the Holy Spirit (16:7).

3:14 as Moses lifted up the serpent in the wilderness. Those who looked at it lived (Num. 21:9). So it is with the Son of Man (1:51). **lifted up.** Every time these words occur in the Gospel of John, there is a reference to Jesus' death (8:28; 12:32,34).

3:16 Belief—Belief involves understanding, knowing, living, and being committed to a relationship with God. How one does all that is so different from not doing it, it is like being born again to a new life. Nicodemus had a little knowledge. What Nicodemus failed to understand was the nature of spiritual reality. He was earthbound and didn't understand that Jesus and belief are God things. He could not get from where he was to where Jesus was on the road of his understanding. He needed to accept a new road, namely the one Jesus was walking, toward Him. Jesus draws us to that light, His light. We have to respond to it as Nicodemus did over time (7:50; 19:39). Belief involves internalizing these truths with our whole hearts and minds, being born again, letting all of ourselves be exposed to, and by, that light.

3:20 For everyone practicing evil hates the light. People offer many excuses for not accepting Christ.

3:2 [a] John 7:50; 19:39 [b] John 9:16, 33 [c] [Acts 10:38] **3:3** [d] [1 Pet. 1:23] **3:5** [e] [Acts 2:38] **3:6** [f] 1 Cor. 15:50 **3:8** [g] Eccl. 11:5 **3:9** [h] John 6:52, 60 **3:11** [i] [Matt. 11:27] [j] John 3:32; 8:14 **3:13** [k] Eph. 4:9 **3:14** [l] Num. 21:9 [m] John 8:28; 12:34; 19:18 **3:15** [n] John 6:47 [o] John 3:36 **3:16** [p] Rom. 5:8 [q] [Is. 9:6] **3:17** [r] Luke 9:56 **3:18** [s] John 5:24; 6:40, 47; 20:31 **3:19** [t] [John 1:4, 9–11] **3:20** [u] Eph. 5:11, 13 **3:21** [v] 1 Cor. 15:10

John the Baptist Exalts Christ

22After these things Jesus and His disciples came into the land of Judea, and there He remained with them wand baptized. 23Now John also was baptizing in Aenon near xSalim, because there was much water there. yAnd they came and were baptized. 24For zJohn had not yet been thrown into prison.

25Then there arose a dispute between *some* of John's disciples and the Jews about purification. 26And they came to John and said to him, "Rabbi, He who was with you beyond the Jordan, *a*to whom you have testified—behold, He is baptizing, and all *b*are coming to Him!"

27John answered and said, *c*"A man can receive nothing unless it has been given to him from heaven. 28You yourselves bear me witness, that I said, *d*'I am not the Christ,' but, *e*'I have been sent before Him.' 29*f*He who has the bride is the bridegroom; but *g*the friend of the bridegroom, who stands and hears him, rejoices greatly because of the bridegroom's voice. Therefore this joy of mine is fulfilled. 30*h*He must increase, but I *must* decrease. 31*i*He who comes from above *j*is above all; *k*he who is of the earth is earthly and speaks of the earth. *l*He who comes from heaven is above all. 32And *m*what He has seen and heard,

that He testifies; and no one receives His testimony. 33He who has received His testimony *n*has certified that God is true. 34oFor He whom God has sent speaks the words of God, for God does not give the Spirit *p*by measure. 35*q*The Father loves the Son, and has given all things into His hand. 36*r*He who believes in the Son has everlasting life; and he who does not believe the Son shall not see life, but the *s*wrath of God abides on him."

A Samaritan Woman Meets Her Messiah

4 Therefore, when the Lord knew that the Pharisees had heard that Jesus made and *a*baptized more disciples than John 2(though Jesus Himself did not baptize, but His disciples), 3He left Judea and departed again to Galilee. 4But He needed to go through Samaria.

5So He came to a city of Samaria which is called Sychar, near the plot of ground that *b*Jacob *c*gave to his son Joseph. 6Now Jacob's well was there. Jesus therefore, being wearied from *His* journey, sat thus by the well. It was about the sixth hour.

7A woman of Samaria came to draw water. Jesus said to her, "Give Me a drink." 8For His disciples had gone away into the city to buy food.

Some cite the presence of hypocrites in the church. Others claim inability to believe some of the truths about Christ or the gospel. These are merely attempts to conceal a heart in rebellion against God. The ultimate reason people do not come to Christ is that they do not want to.

3:26 they came to John. John the Baptist's disciples were loyal to him. They were deeply concerned that one of his "disciples," Jesus, was competing with and surpassing him. In their astonishment, they exaggerated the predicament, saying, "all are coming to Him." They were concerned that John was losing his audience to another preacher.

3:27 John answered. John the Baptist clarified the relationship between himself and Jesus. First, he talked about himself (vv. 27–29); then he talked about Jesus (vv. 30–36). John explained that he could not accept the position of supremacy that his disciples wanted to thrust upon him because he had not received it from heaven.

3:29 friend of the bridegroom. John compared himself to this person who was generally appointed to arrange the preliminaries of the wedding, to manage the wedding, and to preside at the wedding feast.

3:31 He who comes from above. This is a reference to Christ. **he who is of the earth.** This refers to John the Baptist. John emphasized his earthly origin and its limitations. John proclaimed divine truth on earth; Jesus, on the other hand, is from heaven and above all.

3:33 has certified. In a society where many could not read, seals were used to convey a clear message, even to the illiterate. A seal indicated ownership to all and expressed a person's personal guarantee. To receive Jesus' testimony is to certify that God is true regarding what He has sealed.

3:34 God does not give the Spirit by measure. Unlike human teachers, Jesus was not given the Spirit in a limited way (Is. 11:1–2). All three Persons of the Trinity are referred to in this verse; God the Father sent Christ the Son, and gave Him the Holy Spirit without measure.

4:1 Therefore, when. This refers the reader back to 3:22–36. Christ's success in winning disciples had created jealousy among John's followers and provoked questions among the Pharisees. Since Jesus did not want to be drawn into a controversy over baptism at this stage of His ministry, He left Judea for Galilee (v. 3).

4:4 He needed to go through Samaria. The shortest route from Judea in the south to Galilee in the north went through Samaria. The journey took three days if He wanted to travel the direct route. The Jews often avoided Samaria by going around it along the Jordan River. The hatred between the Jews and Samaritans went back to the days of the exile. Samaria was the region between Judea and Galilee. When the northern kingdom was exiled to Assyria, King Sargon repopulated the area with captives from other lands. The intermarriage of these foreigners and the Jews who had been left complicated the ancestry of the Samaritans. The Jews hated the Samaritans and considered them to be no longer "pure" Jews.

3:22 *w* John 4:1, 2   3:23 *x* 1 Sam. 9:4 *y* Matt. 3:5, 6
3:24 *z* Matt. 4:12; 14:3   3:26 *a* John 1:7, 15, 27, 34 *b* Mark
2:2; 3:10; 5:24   3:27 *c* 1 Cor. 3:5, 6; 4:7   3:28 *d* John
1:19–27 *e* Mal. 3:1   3:29 *f* [2 Cor. 11:2] *g* Song 5:1
3:30 *h* [Is. 9:7]   3:31 *i* John 3:13; 8:23 *j* Matt. 28:18
k 1 Cor. 15:47 *l* John 6:33   3:32 *m* John 3:11; 15:15
3:33 *n* 1 John 5:10   3:34 *o* Deut. 18:18; John 7:16 *p* John
1:16   3:35 *q* [Heb. 2:8]   3:36 *r* John 3:16, 17; 6:47 *s* Rom.
1:18   4:1 *a* John 3:22, 26   4:5 *b* Gen. 33:19 *c* Gen. 48:22

9 Then the woman of Samaria said to
Him, "How is it that You, being a Jew, ask a
drink from me, a Samaritan woman?" For
[d]Jews have no dealings with [e]Samaritans.
10 Jesus answered and said to her, "If you
knew the [f]gift of God, and who it is who
says to you, 'Give Me a drink,' you would
have asked Him, and He would have given
you [g]living water."
11 The woman said to Him, "Sir, You have
nothing to draw with, and the well is deep.
Where then do You get that living water?
12 Are You greater than our father Jacob,
who gave us the well, and drank from it
himself, as well as his sons and his livestock?"
13 Jesus answered and said to her, "Whoever drinks of this water will thirst again,
14 but [h]whoever drinks of the water that I
shall give him will never thirst. But the
water that I shall give him [i]will become in
him a fountain of water springing up into
everlasting life."
15 [j]The woman said to Him, "Sir, give me
this water, that I may not thirst, nor come
here to draw."
16 Jesus said to her, "Go, call your husband, and come here."
17 The woman answered and said, "I
have no husband."
Jesus said to her, "You have well said, 'I
have no husband,' 18 for you have had five
husbands, and the one whom you now have
is not your husband; in that you spoke truly."
19 The woman said to Him, "Sir, [k]I perceive that You are a prophet. 20 Our fathers
worshiped on [l]this mountain, and you *Jews*
say that in [m]Jerusalem is the place where
one ought to worship."
21 Jesus said to her, "Woman, believe Me,
the hour is coming [n]when you will neither
on this mountain, nor in Jerusalem, worship the Father. 22 You worship [o]what you
do not know; we know what we worship,
for [p]salvation is of the Jews. 23 But the hour
is coming, and now is, when the true worshipers will [q]worship the Father in [r]spirit
[s]and truth; for the Father is seeking such
to worship Him. 24 [t]God *is* Spirit, and those
who worship Him must worship in spirit
and truth."
25 The woman said to Him, "I know
that Messiah [u]is coming" (who is called
Christ). "When He comes, [v]He will tell us
all things."
26 Jesus said to her, [w]"I who speak to you
am *He*."

The Whitened Harvest

27 And at this *point* His disciples came,
and they marveled that He talked with a
woman; yet no one said, "What do You
seek?" or, "Why are You talking with her?"
28 The woman then left her waterpot,
went her way into the city, and said to the
men, 29 "Come, see a Man [x]who told me all
things that I ever did. Could this be the
Christ?" 30 Then they went out of the city
and came to Him.
31 In the meantime His disciples urged
Him, saying, "Rabbi, eat."
32 But He said to them, "I have food to eat
of which you do not know."
33 Therefore the disciples said to one another, "Has anyone brought Him *anything*
to eat?"
34 Jesus said to them, [y]"My food is to do
the will of Him who sent Me, and to [z]finish
His work. 35 Do you not say, 'There are still
four months and *then* comes [a]the harvest'?
Behold, I say to you, lift up your eyes and
look at the fields, [b]for they are already
white for harvest! 36 [c]And he who reaps receives wages, and gathers fruit for eternal
life, that [d]both he who sows and he who
reaps may rejoice together. 37 For in this
the saying is true: [e]'One sows and another
reaps.' 38 I sent you to reap that for which
you have not labored; [f]others have labored,
and you have entered into their labors."

4:14 ***a fountain of water springing up into everlasting life.*** Jesus desired a drink of water. He then directed the focus of discussion from physical water to spiritual water, pointing out the tremendous advantages of the second kind, which is obtained without cost or effort. This water satisfies completely and eternally.

4:16 ***Go, call your husband.*** Jesus mentioned the woman's husband in order to expose her sin (v. 18).

4:20 ***you Jews say that in Jerusalem.*** The Jews insisted that the exclusive place of worship was Jerusalem. But the Samaritans had set up a rival worship site on Mount Gerizim, which according to their tradition was where Abraham went to sacrifice Isaac and where later on he met Melchizedek.

4:24 ***God is Spirit . . . must worship in spirit and truth.*** God is not limited by time and space. When people are born of the Spirit, they can commune with God anywhere. *Spirit* is the opposite of what is material and earthly, for example, Mount Gerizim. Christ makes worship a matter of the heart. *Truth* is what is in harmony with the nature and will of God. The issue is not where a person worships, but how and whom.

4:29 ***all things that I ever did.*** In her excitement, the woman exaggerated. She did not report what Jesus actually told her, but what He could have told her. Note the woman's spiritual journey. She first viewed Christ as a Jew (v. 9), then as a prophet (v. 19), and finally as the Messiah.

4:36 ***receives wages.*** The reaper of a spiritual harvest receives wages—that is, fruit which brings joy. In this case, Jesus sowed by giving the message to the woman. The disciples were going to reap the harvest that He had sown.

4:9 [d] Acts 10:28 [e] 2 Kin. 17:24 **4:10** [f] [Rom. 5:15] [g] Is. 12:3; 44:3 **4:14** [h] [John 6:35, 58] [i] John 7:37, 38 **4:15** [j] John 6:34, 35; 17:2, 3 **4:19** [k] Luke 7:16, 39; 24:19 **4:20** [l] Judg. 9:7 [m] Deut. 12:5, 11 **4:21** [n] 1 Tim. 2:8 **4:22** [o] [2 Kin. 17:28–41] [p] [Rom. 3:1; 9:4, 5] **4:23** [q] [Heb. 13:10–14] [r] Phil. 3:3 [s] [John 1:17] **4:24** [t] 2 Cor. 3:17 **4:25** [u] Deut. 18:15 [v] John 4:29, 39 **4:26** [w] Matt. 26:63, 64 **4:29** [x] John 4:25 **4:34** [y] Ps. 40:7, 8 [z] [John 6:38; 17:4; 19:30] **4:35** [a] Gen. 8:22 [b] Matt. 9:37 **4:36** [c] Dan. 12:3 [d] 1 Thess. 2:19 **4:37** [e] 1 Cor. 3:5–9 **4:38** [f] [1 Pet. 1:12]

The Savior of the World

[39]And many of the Samaritans of that city believed in Him [g]because of the word of the woman who testified, "He told me all that I *ever* did." [40]So when the Samaritans had come to Him, they urged Him to stay with them; and He stayed there two days. [41]And many more believed because of His own [h]word.

[42]Then they said to the woman, "Now we believe, not because of what you said, for [i]we ourselves have heard *Him* and we know that this is indeed the Christ,* the Savior of the world."

Welcome at Galilee

[43]Now after the two days He departed from there and went to Galilee. [44]For [j]Jesus Himself testified that a prophet has no honor in his own country. [45]So when He came to Galilee, the Galileans received Him, [k]having seen all the things He did in Jerusalem at the feast; [l]for they also had gone to the feast.

A Nobleman's Son Healed

[46]So Jesus came again to Cana of Galilee [m]where He had made the water wine. And there was a certain nobleman whose son was sick at Capernaum. [47]When he heard that Jesus had come out of Judea into Galilee, he went to Him and implored Him to come down and heal his son, for he was at the point of death. [48]Then Jesus said to him, [n]"Unless you *people* see signs and wonders, you will by no means believe."

[49]The nobleman said to Him, "Sir, come down before my child dies!"

[50]Jesus said to him, "Go your way; your son lives." So the man believed the word that Jesus spoke to him, and he went his way. [51]And as he was now going down, his servants met him and told *him*, saying, "Your son lives!"

[52]Then he inquired of them the hour when he got better. And they said to him, "Yesterday at the seventh hour the fever left him." [53]So the father knew that *it was* at the same hour in which Jesus said to him, "Your son lives." And he himself believed, and his whole household.

[54]This again *is* the second sign Jesus did when He had come out of Judea into Galilee.

A Man Healed at the Pool of Bethesda

5 After [a]this there was a feast of the Jews, and Jesus [b]went up to Jerusalem. [2]Now there is in Jerusalem [c]by the Sheep *Gate* a pool, which is called in Hebrew, Bethesda,* having five porches. [3]In these lay a great multitude of sick people, blind, lame, paralyzed, waiting for the moving of the water. [4]For an angel went down at a certain time into the pool and stirred up the water; then whoever stepped in first, after the stirring of the water, was made well of whatever disease he had.* [5]Now a certain man was there who had an infirmity thirty-eight years. [6]When Jesus saw him lying there, and knew that he already had been in *that condition* a long time, He said to him, "Do you want to be made well?"

[7]The sick man answered Him, "Sir, I have no man to put me into the pool when the water is stirred up; but while I am coming, another steps down before me."

[8]Jesus said to him, [d]"Rise, take up your bed and walk." [9]And immediately the man was made well, took up his bed, and walked. And [e]that day was the Sabbath. [10]The Jews therefore said to him who was cured, "It is the Sabbath; [f]it is not lawful for you to carry your bed."

[11]He answered them, "He who made me well said to me, 'Take up your bed and walk.' "

[12]Then they asked him, "Who is the Man who said to you, 'Take up your bed and walk'?" [13]But the one who was [g]healed did not know who it was, for Jesus had withdrawn, a multitude being in *that* place. [14]Afterward Jesus found him in the temple, and said to him, "See, you have been made well. [h]Sin no more, lest a worse thing come upon you."

* 4:42 NU-Text omits *the Christ.* * 5:2 NU-Text reads *Bethzatha.* * 5:4 NU-Text omits *waiting for the moving of the water* at the end of verse 3, and all of verse 4.

4:42 *Savior of the world.* This title is used only here and in 1 John 4:14. The Jews of Jesus' day taught that to approach God, one first had to be a Jew. By including this incident in the Gospel, John demonstrates that Jesus is for all people of the world.

4:46 *a certain nobleman.* This was probably someone who was in the service of the king. Herod Antipas was technically the "tetrarch" of Galilee, but he was referred to as a king.

5:2 *the Sheep Gate.* This was a gate in the wall of Jerusalem near the temple, through which sheep were brought for sacrifice.

5:9 *took up his bed, and walked.* Carrying a bed on the Sabbath was considered a violation of the law of Moses (v. 10).

5:10 *it is not lawful.* The law of Moses taught that the Sabbath must be different from other days. On it,

neither people nor animals could work. The prophet Jeremiah had prohibited carrying burdens or working on the Sabbath (Jer. 17:21–22). Over the years, the Jewish leaders had amassed thousands of rules and regulations concerning the Sabbath. By Jesus' day, they had 39 different classifications of work. According to them, carrying furniture and even providing medical treatment on the Sabbath were forbidden. Jesus did not break the law. He violated the *traditions* of the Pharisees which had grown up around the law.

4:39 *g* John 4:29　**4:41** *h* Luke 4:32　**4:42** *i* 1 John 4:14　**4:44** *j* Matt. 13:57　**4:45** *k* John 2:13, 23; 3:2　*l* Deut. 16:16　**4:46** *m* John 2:1, 11　**4:48** *n* 1 Cor. 1:22　**5:1** *a* Deut. 16:16　*b* John 2:13　**5:2** *c* Neh. 3:1, 32; 12:39　**5:8** *d* Luke 5:24　**5:9** *e* John 9:14　**5:10** *f* Jer. 17:21, 22　**5:13** *g* Luke 13:14; 22:51　**5:14** *h* John 8:11

15The man departed and told the Jews that it was Jesus who had made him well.

Honor the Father and the Son

16For this reason the Jews *i*persecuted Jesus, and sought to kill Him,* because He had done these things on the Sabbath. 17But Jesus answered them, *j*"My Father has been working until now, and I have been working."

18Therefore the Jews *k*sought all the more to kill Him, because He not only broke the Sabbath, but also said that God was His Father, *l*making Himself equal with God. 19Then Jesus answered and said to them, "Most assuredly, I say to you, *m*the Son can do nothing of Himself, but what He sees the Father do; for whatever He does, the Son also does in like manner. 20For *n*the Father loves the Son, and *o*shows Him all things that He Himself does; and He will show Him greater works than these, that you may marvel. 21For as the Father raises the dead and gives life to *them*, *p*even so the Son gives life to whom He will. 22For the Father judges no one, but *q*has committed all judgment to the Son, 23that all should honor the Son just as they honor the Father. *r*He who does not honor the Son does not honor the Father who sent Him.

Life and Judgment Are Through the Son

24"Most assuredly, I say to you, *s*he who hears My word and believes in Him who sent Me has everlasting life, and shall not come into judgment, *t*but has passed from death into life. 25Most assuredly, I say to you, the hour is coming, and now is, when *u*the dead will hear the voice of the Son of God; and those who hear will live. 26For *v*as the Father has life in Himself, so He has granted the Son to have *w*life in Himself, 27and *x*has given Him authority to execute judgment also, *y*because He is the Son of Man. 28Do not marvel at this; for the hour is coming in which all who are in the graves will *z*hear His voice 29*a*and come forth—*b*those who have done good, to the resurrection of life, and those who have done evil, to the resurrection of condemnation. 30*c*I can of Myself do nothing. As I hear, I judge; and My judgment is righteous, because *d*I do not seek My own will but the will of the Father who sent Me.

The Fourfold Witness

31*e*"If I bear witness of Myself, My witness is not true. 32*f*There is another who bears witness of Me, and I know that the witness which He witnesses of Me is true. 33You have sent to John, *g*and he has borne witness to the truth. 34Yet I do not receive testimony from man, but I say these things that you may be saved. 35He was the burning and *h*shining lamp, and *i*you were willing for a time to rejoice in his light. 36But *j*I have a greater witness than John's; for *k*the works which the Father has given Me to finish—the very *l*works that I do—bear witness of Me, that the Father has sent

---

* **5:16** NU-Text omits *and sought to kill Him.*

5:16 the Jews persecuted Jesus. This is the first recorded declaration of open hostility toward Jesus in the Gospel of John.

5:17 My Father. Jesus is "the only begotten Son" (1:14,18; 3:16,18)—that is, the unique Son of God. Here He claims not only a unique relationship with God the Father, but also equality with God in nature. Since God continually does good works without allowing Himself to stop on the Sabbath, the Son does likewise, since He is equal with God. Certainly the Jewish leaders understood the implications of Jesus' claims (v. 18).

5:19 the Son can do nothing of Himself. Action by the Son apart from the Father is impossible because of the unity of the Father and the Son (v. 17). **whatever He does, the Son also does in like manner.** Here is a claim of deity and unity with the Father.

5:22 all judgment to the Son. The Jews recognized that God alone had the right to judge humanity. In claiming that the Father committed all judgment to Him, Jesus again claimed equality with God.

5:24 Never-Ending Life—One of the primary features of the new life that we have in Christ is that it is an eternal or everlasting life. This truth completely changes how we look at our present lives and at the future. It needs to be seen as something we possess even now (10:28). We have entered into a new, personal relationship with God that gives us a spiritual vitality and fullness of life that we lacked before (17:3). It will be completely fulfilled in the future when we are bodily redeemed (Rom. 8:23).

The greatness of this spiritual reality constitutes a wonderful incentive to vigorously proclaim the gospel to those who are still dead in trespasses and sins (Eph. 2:1).

5:26 For. This indicates that this verse explains the previous verse. Christ can give life because He Himself possesses life. He not only has a part in giving it, He is the source of it. This is another testimony to Jesus' deity because only God has life in Himself.

5:29 resurrection of life . . . resurrection of condemnation. Two separate resurrections are presented here in the fashion of the Old Testament prophets, who often grouped together events of the future without distinction of the time (Is. 61:2). Jesus was teaching the universality of resurrection, not the timing of it.

5:31–32 My witness is not true. If Christ were the only one bearing witness of what He was claiming, His witness would not be accepted. According to

5:16 *i* John 8:37; 10:39 **5:17** *j* [John 9:4; 17:4]
5:18 *k* John 7:1, 19 *l* John 10:30 **5:19** *m* John 5:30;
6:38; 8:28; 12:49; 14:10 **5:20** *n* Matt. 3:17 *o* [Matt.
11:27] **5:21** *p* [John 11:25] **5:22** *q* [Acts 17:31]
5:23 *r* 1 John 2:23 **5:24** *s* John 3:16, 18; 6:47 *t* [1 John
3:14] **5:25** *u* [Col. 2:13] **5:26** *v* Ps. 36:9 *w* 1 Cor. 15:45
5:27 *x* [Acts 10:42; 17:31] *y* Dan. 7:13 **5:28** *z* [1 Thess.
4:15–17] **5:29** *a* Is. 26:19 *b* Dan. 12:2 **5:30** *c* John 5:19
d Matt. 26:39 **5:31** *e* John 8:14 **5:32** *f* [Matt. 3:17]
5:33 *g* [John 1:15, 19, 27, 32] **5:35** *h* 2 Pet. 1:19 *i* Mark
6:20 **5:36** *j* 1 John 5:9 *k* John 3:2; 10:25; 17:4 *l* John
9:16; 10:38

Me. 37 And the Father Himself, who sent
Me, [m]has testified of Me. You have neither heard His voice at any time, [n]nor seen
His form. 38 But you do not have His word
abiding in you, because whom He sent,
Him you do not believe. 39 [o]You search the
Scriptures, for in them you think you have
eternal life; and [p]these are they which testify of Me. 40 [q]But you are not willing to come
to Me that you may have life.
41 [r]"I do not receive honor from men.
42 But I know you, that you do not have the
love of God in you. 43 I have come in My Father's name, and you do not receive Me; if
another comes in his own name, him you
will receive. 44 [s]How can you believe, who
receive honor from one another, and do not
seek [t]the honor that *comes* from the only
God? 45 Do not think that I shall accuse you
to the Father; [u]there is *one* who accuses
you—Moses, in whom you trust. 46 For if
you believed Moses, you would believe Me;
[v]for he wrote about Me. 47 But if you [w]do not
believe his writings, how will you believe
My words?"

Feeding the Five Thousand

6 After [a]these things Jesus went over the
Sea of Galilee, which is *the Sea* of [b]Ti-
berias. 2 Then a great multitude followed
Him, because they saw His signs which He
performed on those who were [c]diseased.
3 And Jesus went up on the mountain, and
there He sat with His disciples.
4 [d]Now the Passover, a feast of the Jews,
was near. 5 [e]Then Jesus lifted up *His* eyes,
and seeing a great multitude coming toward Him, He said to [f]Philip, "Where shall
we buy bread, that these may eat?" 6 But
this He said to test him, for He Himself
knew what He would do.
7 Philip answered Him, [g]"Two hundred
denarii worth of bread is not sufficient for
them, that every one of them may have a
little."
8 One of His disciples, [h]Andrew, Simon
Peter's brother, said to Him, 9 "There is a
lad here who has five barley loaves and
two small fish, [i]but what are they among
so many?"
10 Then Jesus said, "Make the people sit
down." Now there was much grass in the
place. So the men sat down, in number
about five thousand. 11 And Jesus took the
loaves, and when He had given thanks He
distributed *them* to the disciples, and the
disciples* to those sitting down; and likewise of the fish, as much as they wanted.
12 So when they were filled, He said to His
disciples, "Gather up the fragments that remain, so that nothing is lost." 13 Therefore
they gathered *them* up, and filled twelve
baskets with the fragments of the five barley loaves which were left over by those
who had eaten. 14 Then those men, when
they had seen the sign that Jesus did, said,
"This is truly [j]the Prophet who is to come
into the world."

Jesus Walks on the Sea

15 Therefore when Jesus perceived that
they were about to come and take Him
by force to make Him [k]king, He departed
again to the mountain by Himself alone.
16 [l]Now when evening came, His disciples went down to the sea, 17 got into the
boat, and went over the sea toward Capernaum. And it was already dark, and Jesus
had not come to them. 18 Then the sea arose

* **6:11** NU-Text omits *to the disciples, and the disciples.*

Jewish legal practice, a person's testimony about himself was not accepted in court. So, in this case, Jesus offered another witness—John the Baptist (v. 33).

5:42 ***the love of God.*** This love is not love from God but love for God. Love from God is evidenced in Christ (3:16; Rom. 5:8). Since God loves us, we should love Him (Deut. 6:5; 1 John 4:19).

5:45 ***you trust.*** Christ will not have to accuse the people on judgment day because the one in whom they place their trust, Moses, will. The people will be condemned by the very law they professed to keep.

5:46 ***for he wrote about Me.*** Moses wrote about Christ in the promises to the patriarchs, in the history of the deliverance from Egypt, in the symbolic institutions of the law, and in the prediction of a Prophet like himself (Luke 24:25–26). If the people had believed Moses, they would have received Jesus gladly. Over 300 Old Testament prophecies were specifically fulfilled in the first coming of Christ.

6:1 ***Sea of Galilee, which is the Sea of Tiberias.*** John's use of the name Tiberias is an indication that his Gospel was written for those outside of Palestine. The Jewish people called this body of water the Lake of Gennesaret. The Romans called it Tiberias, after the city built on its western shore by Herod Antipas and named for the Emperor Tiberius.

6:7 ***Two hundred denarii.*** One denarius was a day's wage for a laborer or field hand (Matt. 20:2). Two hundred denarii would have been almost two-thirds of a year's wages.

6:9 ***barley loaves.*** These were an inexpensive food of the common people and the poor.

6:10–11 ***in number about five thousand . . . He distributed . . . those sitting down.*** This is the only miracle of Jesus that is recounted in all four Gospels.

6:15 ***to make Him king.*** Moses had not only miraculously provided food for the Israelites, he had also led them out of bondage in Egypt. Perhaps these men felt that Jesus could lead them out of bondage to the Romans. Christ was at the zenith of His popularity, and the temptation to take the kingdom without the cross must have been great (Matt. 4:8–10).

5:37 [m] Matt. 3:17 [n] 1 John 4:12 **5:39** [o] Is. 8:20; 34:16 [p] Luke 24:27 **5:40** [q] [John 1:11; 3:19] **5:41** [r] 1 Thess. 2:6 **5:44** [s] John 12:43 [t] [Rom. 2:29] **5:45** [u] Rom. 2:12 **5:46** [v] Deut. 18:15, 18 **5:47** [w] Luke 16:29, 31 **6:1** [a] Mark 6:32 [b] John 6:23; 21:1 **6:2** [c] Matt. 4:23; 8:16; 9:35; 14:36; 15:30; 19:2 **6:4** [d] Deut. 16:1 **6:5** [e] Matt. 14:14 [f] John 1:43 **6:7** [g] Num. 11:21, 22 **6:8** [h] John 1:40 **6:9** [i] 2 Kin. 4:43 **6:14** [j] Gen. 49:10 **6:15** [k] [John 18:36] **6:16** [l] Matt. 14:23

because a great wind was blowing. [19]So when they had rowed about three or four miles,* they saw Jesus walking on the sea and drawing near the boat; and they were [m]afraid. [20]But He said to them, [n]"It is I; do not be afraid." [21]Then they willingly received Him into the boat, and immediately the boat was at the land where they were going.

The Bread from Heaven

[22]On the following day, when the people who were standing on the other side of the sea saw that there was no other boat there, except that one which His disciples had entered,* and that Jesus had not entered the boat with His disciples, but His disciples had gone away alone— [23]however, other boats came from Tiberias, near the place where they ate bread after the Lord had given thanks— [24]when the people therefore saw that Jesus was not there, nor His disciples, they also got into boats and came to Capernaum, [o]seeking Jesus. [25]And when they found Him on the other side of the sea, they said to Him, "Rabbi, when did You come here?"

[26]Jesus answered them and said, "Most assuredly, I say to you, you seek Me, not because you ate the signs, but because you ate of the loaves and were filled. [27][p]Do not labor for the food which perishes, but [q]for the food which endures to everlasting life, which the Son of Man will give you, [r]because God the Father has set His seal on Him."

[28]Then they said to Him, "What shall we do, that we may work the works of God?"

[29]Jesus answered and said to them, [s]"This is the work of God, that you believe in Him whom He sent."

[30]Therefore they said to Him, [t]"What sign will You perform then, that we may see it and believe You? What work will You do? [31][u]Our fathers ate the manna in the desert; as it is written, [v]'He gave them bread from heaven to eat.' "*

[32]Then Jesus said to them, "Most assuredly, I say to you, Moses did not give you the bread from heaven, but [w]My Father gives you the true bread from heaven. [33]For the bread of God is He who comes down from heaven and gives life to the world."

[34][x]Then they said to Him, "Lord, give us this bread always."

[35]And Jesus said to them, [y]"I am the bread of life. [z]He who comes to Me shall never hunger, and he who believes in Me shall never [a]thirst. [36][b]But I said to you that you have seen Me and yet [c]do not believe. [37][d]All that the Father gives Me will come to Me, and [e]the one who comes to Me I will by no means cast out. [38]For I have come down from heaven, [f]not to do My own will, [g]but the will of Him who sent Me. [39]This is the will of the Father who sent Me, [h]that of all He has given Me I should lose nothing, but should raise it up at the last day. [40]And this is the will of Him who sent Me, [i]that everyone who sees the Son and believes in Him may have everlasting life; and I will raise him up at the last day."

Rejected by His Own

[41]The Jews then complained about Him, because He said, "I am the bread which came down from heaven." [42]And they said, [j]"Is not this Jesus, the son of Joseph, whose father and mother we know? How is it then that He says, 'I have come down from heaven'?"

[43]Jesus therefore answered and said to them, "Do not murmur among yourselves. [44][k]No one can come to Me unless the Father who sent Me [l]draws him; and I will raise him up at the last day. [45]It is written in the prophets, [m]'And they shall all be taught by God.'* [n]Therefore everyone who has heard and learned* from the Father comes to Me.

---

* **6:19** Literally *twenty-five or thirty stadia*
* **6:22** NU-Text omits *that* and *which His disciples had entered.* * **6:31** Exodus 16:4; Nehemiah 9:15; Psalm 78:24 * **6:45** Isaiah 54:13 • M-Text reads *hears and has learned.*

6:19–21 they saw Jesus walking on the sea. This miracle, the fifth sign recorded by John, pointed to Jesus' deity. Only God could walk on water, calm the sea, and supernaturally transport the disciples to their destination.
6:27 Do not labor. The impression that one must work for eternal life is quickly corrected when Jesus adds "which the Son of Man will give you." The Son provides *life* as a gift (4:10).
6:31 He gave them bread from heaven. There was a tradition that said the Messiah would cause manna to fall from heaven as Moses did (Ex. 16:4,15). The people probably also saw this "miracle worker" as the perpetual provider of physical needs rather than spiritual ones.
6:32 My Father. The crowd misrepresented the truth, so Jesus corrected them. The manna had not come from Moses; it had been provided by God. Moreover, God still gives "true bread"—that is, eternal life (v. 33).

6:39–40 the will of the Father. This is twofold: (1) that all who come to the Son will be received and not lost; (2) that all who see and believe on the Son will have eternal life.
6:42 the son of Joseph. The religious leaders' proof that Jesus was not from heaven was that they knew His parents. To them, there was nothing supernatural about Jesus' origin.

6:19 [m] Matt. 17:6   **6:20** [n] Is. 43:1, 2   **6:24** [o] Luke 4:42   **6:27** [p] Matt. 6:19   [q] John 4:14   [r] Acts 2:22   **6:29** [s] [1 John 3:23]   **6:30** [t] Matt. 12:38; 16:1   **6:31** [u] Ex. 16:15 [v] Ex. 16:4, 15; Neh. 9:15; Ps. 78:24   **6:32** [w] John 3:13, 16   **6:34** [x] John 4:15   **6:35** [y] John 6:48, 58   [z] John 4:14; 7:37   [a] Is. 55:1, 2   **6:36** [b] John 6:26, 64; 15:24   [c] John 10:26   **6:37** [d] John 6:45   [e] 2 Tim. 2:19   **6:38** [f] Matt. 26:39   [g] John 4:34   **6:39** [h] John 10:28; 17:12; 18:9   **6:40** [i] John 3:15, 16; 4:14; 6:27, 47, 54   **6:42** [j] Matt. 13:55   **6:44** [k] Song 1:4   [l] [Phil. 1:29; 2:12, 13]   **6:45** [m] Is. 54:13   [n] John 6:37

⁴⁶ᵒNot that anyone has seen the Father, ᵖexcept He who is from God; He has seen the Father. ⁴⁷Most assuredly, I say to you, ᑫhe who believes in Me* has everlasting life. ⁴⁸ʳI am the bread of life. ⁴⁹ˢYour fathers ate the manna in the wilderness, and are dead. ⁵⁰ᵗThis is the bread which comes down from heaven, that one may eat of it and not die. ⁵¹I am the living bread ᵘwhich came down from heaven. If anyone eats of this bread, he will live forever; and ᵛthe bread that I shall give is My flesh, which I shall give for the life of the world."

⁵²The Jews therefore ʷquarreled among themselves, saying, "How can this Man give us His flesh to eat?"

⁵³Then Jesus said to them, "Most assuredly, I say to you, unless ˣyou eat the flesh of the Son of Man and drink His blood, you have no life in you. ⁵⁴ʸWhoever eats My flesh and drinks My blood has eternal life, and I will raise him up at the last day. ⁵⁵For My flesh is food indeed,* and My blood is drink indeed. ⁵⁶He who eats My flesh and drinks My blood ᶻabides in Me, and I in him. ⁵⁷As the living Father sent Me, and I live because of the Father, so he who feeds on Me will live because of Me. ⁵⁸ᵃThis is the bread which came down from heaven—not ᵇas your fathers ate the manna, and are dead. He who eats this bread will live forever."

⁵⁹These things He said in the synagogue as He taught in Capernaum.

Many Disciples Turn Away

⁶⁰ᶜTherefore many of His disciples, when they heard this, said, "This is a hard saying; who can understand it?"

⁶¹When Jesus knew in Himself that His disciples complained about this, He said to them, "Does this offend you? ⁶²ᵈWhat then if you should see the Son of Man ascend where He was before? ⁶³ᵉIt is the Spirit who gives life; the ᶠflesh profits nothing. The ᵍwords that I speak to you are spirit, and they are life. ⁶⁴But ʰthere are some of you who do not believe." For ⁱJesus knew from the beginning who they were who did not believe, and who would betray Him. ⁶⁵And He said, "Therefore ʲI have said to you that no one can come to Me unless it has been granted to him by My Father."

⁶⁶ᵏFrom that time many of His disciples went back and walked with Him no more. ⁶⁷Then Jesus said to the twelve, "Do you also want to go away?"

⁶⁸But Simon Peter answered Him, "Lord, to whom shall we go? You have ˡthe words of eternal life. ⁶⁹ᵐAlso we have come to believe and know that You are the Christ, the Son of the living God."*

⁷⁰Jesus answered them, ⁿ"Did I not choose you, the twelve, ᵒand one of you is a devil?" ⁷¹He spoke of ᵖJudas Iscariot, the son of Simon, for it was he who would ᑫbetray Him, being one of the twelve.

Jesus' Brothers Disbelieve

7 After these things Jesus walked in Galilee; for He did not want to walk in Judea, ᵃbecause the Jews* sought to kill Him. ²ᵇNow the Jews' Feast of Tabernacles was at hand. ³ᶜHis brothers therefore said to Him, "Depart from here and go into Judea, that Your disciples also may see the works that You are doing. ⁴For no one does anything in secret while he himself seeks to be known openly. If You do these things, show Yourself to the world." ⁵For ᵈeven His ᵉbrothers did not believe in Him.

⁶Then Jesus said to them, ᶠ"My time has not yet come, but your time is always ready. ⁷ᵍThe world cannot hate you, but it hates Me ʰbecause I testify of it that its

---

* **6:47** NU-Text omits in Me. * **6:55** NU-Text reads true food and true drink. * **6:69** NU-Text reads You are the Holy One of God. * **7:1** That is, the ruling authorities

---

6:47 everlasting life. The believer, possessing both peace and purpose, can rejoice even in the midst of fiery trials, knowing that God Himself will arrange the outcome for His glory and the believer's good (Rom. 8:28).

6:48–49 I am the bread of life. Those who believe in Him have life (v. 47). The manna in the wilderness did not ultimately sustain life. Those who ate it eventually died because it could not provide eternal life.

6:53–58 eats My flesh and drinks My blood. Jesus had made it abundantly clear in this context that eternal life is gained by believing (vv. 29,35,40,47). These verses teach that the benefits of Jesus' death must be appropriated, by faith, by each individual.

6:60 This is a hard saying. It was hard for the Jewish learners to accept the idea of eating flesh and drinking blood. Jews were forbidden to even taste blood.

6:63 It is the Spirit who gives life. Jesus was trying to get the religious leaders to see beyond the physical aspects of His teaching to the real issue—namely, that if they believed on Him they would have eternal life.

7:2 Feast of Tabernacles. This was one of the three great Jewish religious festivals (Passover and Pentecost were the other two). It was called the Feast of Tabernacles (Booths) because for seven days the people lived in makeshift shelters or lean-tos made of branches and leaves. The feast commemorated the days when the Israelites wandered in the wilderness and lived in tents (Lev. 23:40–43).

7:3–4 His brothers. Jesus' brothers argued, "If You

6:46 ᵒ John 1:18 ᵖ Matt. 11:27 **6:47** ᑫ [John 3:16, 18] **6:48** ʳ John 6:33, 35 **6:49** ˢ John 6:31, 58 **6:50** ᵗ John 6:51, 58 **6:51** ᵘ John 3:13 ᵛ Heb. 10:5 **6:52** ʷ John 7:43; 9:16; 10:19 **6:53** ˣ Matt. 26:26 **6:54** ʸ John 4:14; 6:27, 40 **6:56** ᶻ [1 John 3:24; 4:15, 16] **6:58** ᵃ John 6:49–51 ᵇ Ex. 16:14–35 **6:60** ᶜ John 6:66 **6:62** ᵈ Acts 1:9; 2:32, 33 **6:63** ᵉ 2 Cor. 3:6 ᶠ John 3:6 ᵍ [John 6:68; 14:24] **6:64** ʰ John 6:36 ⁱ John 2:24, 25; 13:11 **6:65** ʲ John 6:37, 44, 45 **6:66** ᵏ Luke 9:62 **6:68** ˡ Acts 5:20 **6:69** ᵐ Luke 9:20 ⁿ John 6:70 ᵒ Luke 6:13 ᵒ [John 13:27] **6:71** ᵖ John 12:4; 13:2, 26 ᑫ Matt. 26:14–16 **7:1** ᵃ John 5:18; 7:19, 25; 8:37, 40 **7:2** ᵇ Lev. 23:34 **7:3** ᶜ Matt. 12:46 **7:5** ᵈ Ps. 69:8; Mic. 7:6 ᵉ Mark 3:21 **7:6** ᶠ John 2:4; 8:20 **7:7** ᵍ [John 15:19] ʰ John 3:19

works are evil. 8You go up to this feast. I
am not yet* going up to this feast, [i]for My
time has not yet fully come." 9When He had
said these things to them, He remained in
Galilee.

The Heavenly Scholar

10But when His brothers had gone up,
then He also went up to the feast, not openly, but as it were in secret. 11Then [j]the Jews
sought Him at the feast, and said, "Where
is He?" 12And [k]there was much complaining among the people concerning Him.
[l]Some said, "He is good"; others said, "No,
on the contrary, He deceives the people."
13However, no one spoke openly of Him
[m]for fear of the Jews.
14Now about the middle of the feast
Jesus went up into the temple and [n]taught.
15[o]And the Jews marveled, saying, "How
does this Man know letters, having never
studied?"
16Jesus* answered them and said, [p]"My
doctrine is not Mine, but His who sent Me.
17[q]If anyone wills to do His will, he shall
know concerning the doctrine, whether it
is from God or *whether* I speak on My own
authority. 18[r]He who speaks from himself
seeks his own glory; but He who [s]seeks the
glory of the One who sent Him is true, and
[t]no unrighteousness is in Him. 19[u]Did not
Moses give you the law, yet none of you
keeps the law? [v]Why do you seek to kill
Me?"
20The people answered and said, [w]"You
have a demon. Who is seeking to kill You?"
21Jesus answered and said to them, "I
did one work, and you all marvel. 22[x]Moses
therefore gave you circumcision (not that it
is from Moses, [y]but from the fathers), and
you circumcise a man on the Sabbath. 23If
a man receives circumcision on the Sabbath, so that the law of Moses should not
be broken, are you angry with Me because
[z]I made a man completely well on the Sabbath? 24[a]Do not judge according to appearance, but judge with righteous judgment."

Could This Be the Christ?

25Now some of them from Jerusalem
said, "Is this not He whom they seek to
[b]kill? 26But look! He speaks boldly, and
they say nothing to Him. [c]Do the rulers
know indeed that this is truly* the Christ?
27[d]However, we know where this Man is
from; but when the Christ comes, no one
knows where He is from."
28Then Jesus cried out, as He taught in
the temple, saying, [e]"You both know Me,
and you know where I am from; and [f]I have
not come of Myself, but He who sent Me [g]is
true, [h]whom you do not know. 29But* [i]I know
Him, for I am from Him, and He sent Me."
30Therefore [j]they sought to take Him;
but [k]no one laid a hand on Him, because
His hour had not yet come. 31And [l]many
of the people believed in Him, and said,
"When the Christ comes, will He do more
signs than these which this *Man* has done?"

Jesus and the Religious Leaders

32The Pharisees heard the crowd murmuring these things concerning Him, and
the Pharisees and the chief priests sent
officers to take Him. 33Then Jesus said to
them,* [m]"I shall be with you a little while
longer, and *then* I [n]go to Him who sent Me.
34You [o]will seek Me and not find *Me,* and
where I am you [p]cannot come."
35Then the Jews said among themselves,
"Where does He intend to go that we shall
not find Him? Does He intend to go to [q]the
Dispersion among the Greeks and teach
the Greeks? 36What is this thing that He
said, 'You will seek Me and not find Me,
and where I am you cannot come'?"

The Promise of the Holy Spirit

37[r]On the last day, that great *day* of the
feast, Jesus stood and cried out, saying,
[s]"If anyone thirsts, let him come to Me and

* **7:8** NU-Text omits *yet.* * **7:16** NU-Text and M-Text read *So Jesus.* * **7:26** NU-Text omits *truly.* * **7:29** NU-Text and M-Text omit *But.* * **7:33** NU-Text and M-Text omit *to them.*

---

are really working miracles and thus claiming to be the Messiah, do not hide in obscure Galilee. If You are doing miracles at all, then do them in Jerusalem at the Feast to convince the whole nation." These words were sarcastic, as verse 5 explains.

7:14 ***the middle of the feast.*** This would have been the fourth day of the seven-day feast. During the first half of the festival, Jesus remained in seclusion (v. 10). During the second half, He began to teach publicly. This is the first mention in the Gospel of John of Jesus teaching in the temple.

7:15 ***having never studied.*** Jesus never attended a rabbinical school. Similar bewilderment was later expressed regarding Jesus' disciples (Acts 4:13).

7:28–29 ***You both know Me, and you know where I am from.*** Jesus reminded the leaders that they knew His origin. Their problem was that they did not know God, who sent Jesus. He explained to them that He knew God, was from God, and was sent by God.

7:32 ***to take Him.*** The Jewish leaders decided earlier that they wanted to kill Christ (5:16), but this is the first real attempt on His life.

7:37–39 ***that great day of the feast.*** On each day of the feast, the people came with palm branches and marched around the great altar. A priest took

7:8 [i] John 8:20 **7:11** [j] John 11:56 **7:12** [k] John 9:16; 10:19 [l] Luke 7:16 **7:13** [m] [John 9:22; 12:42; 19:38] **7:14** [n] Ps. 22:22; Mark 6:34 **7:15** [o] Matt. 13:54 **7:16** [p] John 3:11 **7:17** [q] John 3:21; 8:43 **7:18** [r] John 5:41 [s] John 8:50 [t] [2 Cor. 5:21] **7:19** [u] Deut. 33:4 [v] Matt. 12:14 **7:20** [w] John 8:48, 52 **7:22** [x] Lev. 12:3 [y] Gen. 17:9–14 **7:23** [z] John 5:8, 9, 16 **7:24** [a] Prov. 24:23 **7:25** [b] Matt. 21:38; 26:4 **7:26** [c] John 7:48 **7:27** [d] Luke 4:22 **7:28** [e] John 8:14 [f] John 5:43 [g] Rom. 3:4 [h] John 1:18; 8:55 **7:29** [i] Matt. 11:27 **7:30** [j] Mark 11:18 [k] John 7:32, 44; 8:20; 10:39 **7:31** [l] Matt. 12:23 **7:33** [m] John 13:33 [n] [1 Pet. 3:22] **7:34** [o] Hos. 5:6 [p] [Matt. 5:20] **7:35** [q] James 1:1 **7:37** [r] Lev. 23:36 [s] [Is. 55:1]

drink. **38t**He who believes in Me, as the Scripture has said, **u**out of his heart will flow rivers of living water." **39v**But this He spoke concerning the Spirit, whom those believing* in Him would receive; for the Holy* Spirit was not yet *given*, because Jesus was not yet **w**glorified.

Who Is He?

40Therefore many* from the crowd, when they heard this saying, said, "Truly this is **x**the Prophet." **41**Others said, "This is **y**the Christ."

But some said, "Will the Christ come out of Galilee? **42z**Has not the Scripture said that the Christ comes from the seed of David and from the town of Bethlehem, **a**where David was?" **43**So **b**there was a division among the people because of Him. **44**Now **c**some of them wanted to take Him, but no one laid hands on Him.

Rejected by the Authorities

45Then the officers came to the chief priests and Pharisees, who said to them, "Why have you not brought Him?"

46The officers answered, **d**"No man ever spoke like this Man!"

47Then the Pharisees answered them, "Are you also deceived? **48**Have any of the rulers or the Pharisees believed in Him? **49**But this crowd that does not know the law is accursed."

50Nicodemus **e**(he who came to Jesus by night,* being one of them) said to them, **51f**"Does our law judge a man before it hears Him and knows what he is doing?"

52They answered and said to him, "Are you also from Galilee? Search and look, for **g**no prophet has arisen* out of Galilee."

An Adulteress Faces the Light of the World

53And everyone went to his *own* house.*

8 But Jesus went to the Mount of Olives. **2**Now early* in the morning He came again into the temple, and all the people came to Him; and He sat down and **a**taught them. **3**Then the scribes and Pharisees brought to Him a woman caught in adultery. And when they had set her in the midst, **4**they said to Him, "Teacher, this woman was caught* in **b**adultery, in the very act. **5c**Now Moses, in the law, commanded* us that such should be stoned.* But what do You say?"* **6**This they said, testing Him, that they **d**might have *something* of which to accuse Him. But Jesus stooped down and wrote on the ground with *His* finger, as though He did not hear.*

7So when they continued asking Him, He raised Himself up* and said to them, **e**"He who is without sin among you, let him throw a stone at her first." **8**And again He stooped down and wrote on the ground. **9**Then those who heard *it*, **f**being convicted by *their* conscience,* went out one by one,

---

* **7:39** NU-Text reads *who believed.* • NU-Text omits *Holy.* * **7:40** NU-Text reads *some.* * **7:50** NU-Text reads *before.* * **7:52** NU-Text reads *is to rise.* * **7:53** The words *And everyone* through *sin no more* (8:11) are bracketed by NU-Text as not original. They are present in over 900 manuscripts. * **8:2** M-Text reads *very early.* * **8:4** M-Text reads *we found this woman.* * **8:5** M-Text reads *in our law Moses commanded.* • NU-Text and M-Text read *to stone such.* • M-Text adds *about her.* * **8:6** NU-Text and M-Text omit *as though He did not hear.* * **8:7** M-Text reads *He looked up.* * **8:9** NU-Text and M-Text omit *being convicted by their conscience.*

---

a golden pitcher filled with water from the pool of Siloam, carried it to the temple, and poured it on the altar as an offering to God. This dramatic ceremony was a memorial of the water that flowed from the rock when the Israelites traveled through the wilderness. On the last day of the feast, the people marched seven times around the altar in memory of the seven circuits around the walls of Jericho.

7:38 *as the Scripture has said.* The reference is not to a single passage, but to the general emphasis of such passages as Deuteronomy 18:15, Isaiah 58:11, and Zechariah 14:8. In contrast to the small amount of water poured out each day during the feast, there will be a river of water coming out of those who believe in Christ. Not only will they be satisfied themselves, but they will also become a river so that others may drink and be satisfied (v. 39).

7:40–42 *Christ comes from the seed of David.* These passages knew that the Messiah was to come from Bethlehem (Mic. 5:2). However, they did not know that Jesus had been born there. They thought He was from Galilee. They knew the Scripture, but they did not take the time to know the Messiah (5:39).

8:2 *He sat down.* Teachers in ancient Israel sat when they taught. Jesus assumed the position of an authoritative teacher.

8:3 *a woman caught in adultery.* The scribes and Pharisees were not interested in helping the woman, but in using her sinful circumstances to discredit Jesus (v. 6). His refusal to countenance the stoning of the woman does not bring Him into conflict with the law given to Moses, nor does He condone sin. The issue in the encounter was the accusers' blindness to their own sin.

8:4–5 *commanded us that such should be stoned.* Stoning was specified in certain cases of adultery (Deut. 22:23–24), though not all. (It is not clear why the authorities intended to punish the woman but not the man.) In the Greek text, the pronoun *You* is emphatic. The religious leaders were trying to trap Jesus into saying something that was contrary to the law.

8:6 *testing him.* If Jesus had said to not stone her, He would have contradicted Jewish law. If He had said to stone her, He would have run counter to Roman law, which did not permit Jews to carry out their own

---

7:38 **t** Deut. 18:15 **u** Is. 12:3; 43:20; 44:3; 55:1 **7:39** **v** Is. 44:3 **w** John 12:16; 13:31; 17:5 **7:40** **x** Deut. 18:15, 18 **7:41** **y** John 4:42; 6:69 **7:42** **z** Mic. 5:2 **a** 1 Sam. 16:1, 4 **7:43** **b** John 7:12 **7:44** **c** John 7:30 **7:46** **d** Luke 4:22 **7:50** **e** John 3:1, 2; 19:39 **7:51** **f** Deut. 1:16, 17; 19:15 **7:52** **g** [Is. 9:1, 2] **8:2** **a** John 8:20; 18:20 **8:4** **b** Ex. 20:14 **8:5** **c** Lev. 20:10 **8:6** **d** Matt. 22:15 **8:7** **e** Deut. 17:7 **8:9** **f** Rom. 2:22

beginning with the oldest *even* to the last.
And Jesus was left alone, and the woman
standing in the midst. 10 When Jesus had
raised Himself up and saw no one but the
woman, He said to her,* "Woman, where
are those accusers of yours?* Has no one
condemned you?"
11 She said, "No one, Lord."
And Jesus said to her, [g]"Neither do I condemn you; go and* [h]sin no more."
12 Then Jesus spoke to them again, saying, [i]"I am the light of the world. He who
[j]follows Me shall not walk in darkness, but
have the light of life."

Jesus Defends His Self-Witness

13 The Pharisees therefore said to Him,
[k]"You bear witness of Yourself; Your witness is not true."
14 Jesus answered and said to them,
"Even if I bear witness of Myself, My
witness is true, for I know where I came
from and where I am going; but [l]you do
not know where I come from and where
I am going. 15 [m]You judge according to
the flesh; [n]I judge no one. 16 And yet if I
do judge, My judgment is true; for [o]I am
not alone, but I *am* with the Father who
sent Me. 17 [p]It is also written in your law
that the testimony of two men is true. 18 I
am One who bears witness of Myself, and
[q]the Father who sent Me bears witness of
Me."
19 Then they said to Him, "Where is Your
Father?"
Jesus answered, [r]"You know neither Me
nor My Father. [s]If you had known Me, you
would have known My Father also."
20 These words Jesus spoke in [t]the treasury, as He taught in the temple; and [u]no
one laid hands on Him, for [v]His hour had
not yet come.

Jesus Predicts His Departure

21 Then Jesus said to them again, "I am going away, and [w]you will seek Me, and [x]will
die in your sin. Where I go you cannot come."
22 So the Jews said, "Will He kill Himself,
because He says, 'Where I go you cannot
come'?"
23 And He said to them, [y]"You are from
beneath; I am from above. [z]You are of this
world; I am not of this world. 24 [a]Therefore
I said to you that you will die in your sins;
[b]for if you do not believe that I am *He*, you
will die in your sins."
25 Then they said to Him, "Who are You?"
And Jesus said to them, "Just what I
[c]have been saying to you from the beginning. 26 I have many things to say and to
judge concerning you, but [d]He who sent
Me is true; and [e]I speak to the world those
things which I heard from Him."
27 They did not understand that He spoke
to them of the Father.
28 Then Jesus said to them, "When you
[f]lift up the Son of Man, [g]then you will know
that I am *He*, and [h]*that* I do nothing of Myself; but [i]as My Father taught Me, I speak
these things. 29 And [j]He who sent Me is with
Me. [k]The Father has not left Me alone, [l]for
I always do those things that please Him."
30 As He spoke these words, [m]many believed in Him.

The Truth Shall Make You Free

31 Then Jesus said to those Jews who believed Him, "If you [n]abide in My word, you
are My disciples indeed. 32 And you shall
know the [o]truth, and [p]the truth shall make
you free."

*8:10 NU-Text omits *and saw no one but the woman;* M-Text reads *He saw her and said.* • NU-Text and M-Text omit *of yours.* *8:11 NU-Text and M-Text add *from now on.*

---

executions (18:31). What Jesus wrote on the ground is a matter of conjecture.

8:13 *Your witness is not true.* This phrase does not mean "false"; it means "not sufficient." The Pharisees challenged Jesus on legal grounds because no man on trial in a Jewish court was allowed to testify on his own behalf. Their point was that, if Jesus were the only one testifying as to who He claimed to be, it would not be enough to prove His case.

8:14 *My witness is true.* In 5:31 Jesus argued on the basis of legality and offered other witnesses. Sometimes, however, an individual is the only one who knows the facts about himself. Thus, self-disclosure is the only way to truth (7:29; 13:3).

8:15 *according to the flesh.* This could mean either "according to appearance" or "by human standards." The religious leaders formed conclusions based on human standards and an imperfect, external, and superficial examination. Jesus did not judge according to human standards or outward appearances.

8:24 *I am He.* This was God's designation of Himself (Ex. 3:14). Jesus was claiming to be God. This assertion was not understood by the religious leaders at this time. Later, Jesus' claim to be the "I am" (v. 58) prompted the Jewish leaders to seek His life (v. 59).

8:31 God's Word Confirms—The Bible establishes the truth in our own hearts in several ways.

1. *It confirms our salvation.* In Jesus' own words in the Gospel of John: "Most assuredly, I say to you, he who hears My word and believes in Him who sent Me has everlasting life, and shall not come into judgment, but has passed from death into life" (5:24). Compare 3:16; 6:27,35,37,40; 10:27–29; Romans 8:1.
2. *It confirms the hand of God in all of life's bitter disappointments.* Romans 8:28 provides reassurance and comfort in these crucial situations:

8:11 [g] [John 3:17] [h] [John 5:14] **8:12** [i] John 1:4; 9:5; 12:35 [j] 1 Thess. 5:5 **8:13** [k] John 5:31 **8:14** [l] John 7:28; 9:29 **8:15** [m] John 7:24 [n] [John 3:17; 12:47; 18:36] **8:16** [o] John 16:32 **8:17** [p] Deut. 17:6; 19:15 **8:18** [q] John 5:37 **8:19** [r] John 16:3 [s] John 14:7 **8:20** [t] Mark 12:41, 43 [u] John 2:4; 7:30 [v] John 7:8 **8:21** [w] John 7:34; 13:33 [x] John 8:24 **8:23** [y] John 3:31 [z] 1 John 4:5 **8:24** [a] John 8:21 [b] [Mark 16:16] **8:25** [c] John 4:26 **8:26** [d] John 7:28 [e] John 3:32; 15:15 **8:28** [f] John 3:14; 12:32; 19:18 [g] [Rom. 1:4] [h] John 5:19, 30 [i] John 3:11 **8:29** [j] John 14:10 [k] John 8:16; 16:32 [l] John 4:34; 5:30; 6:38 **8:30** [m] John 7:31; 10:42; 11:45 **8:31** [n] [John 14:15, 23] **8:32** [o] [John 1:14, 17; 14:6] [p] [Rom. 6:14, 18, 22]

33They answered Him, a"We are Abraham's descendants, and have never been in bondage to anyone. How *can* You say, 'You will be made free'?"

34Jesus answered them, "Most assuredly, I say to you, rwhoever commits sin is a slave of sin. 35And sa slave does not abide in the house forever, *but* a son abides forever. 36tTherefore if the Son makes you free, you shall be free indeed.

Abraham's Seed and Satan's

37"I know that you are Abraham's descendants, but uyou seek to kill Me, because My word has no place in you. 38vI speak what I have seen with My Father, and you do what you have seen with* your father."

39They answered and said to Him, w"Abraham is our father."

Jesus said to them, x"If you were Abraham's children, you would do the works of Abraham. 40yBut now you seek to kill Me, a Man who has told you the truth zwhich I heard from God. Abraham did not do this. 41You do the deeds of your father."

Then they said to Him, "We were not born of fornication; awe have one Father—God."

42Jesus said to them, b"If God were your Father, you would love Me, for cI proceeded forth and came from God; dnor have I come of Myself, but He sent Me. 43eWhy do you not understand My speech? Because you are not able to listen to My word. 44fYou are of *your* father the devil, and the gdesires of your father you want to hdo. He was a murderer from the beginning, and idoes not stand in the truth, because there is no truth in him. When he speaks a lie, he speaks from his own *resources*, for he is a liar and the father of it. 45But because I tell the truth, you do not believe Me. 46Which of you convicts Me of sin? And if I tell the truth, why do you not believe Me? 47jHe

who is of God hears God's words; therefore you do not hear, because you are not of God."

Before Abraham Was, I AM

48Then the Jews answered and said to Him, "Do we not say rightly that You are a Samaritan and khave a demon?"

49Jesus answered, "I do not have a demon; but I honor My Father, and lyou dishonor Me. 50And mI do not seek My *own* glory; there is One who seeks and judges. 51Most assuredly, I say to you, nif anyone keeps My word he shall never see death."

52Then the Jews said to Him, "Now we know that You ohave a demon! pAbraham is dead, and the prophets; and You say, 'If anyone keeps My word he shall never taste death.' 53Are You greater than our father Abraham, who is dead? And the prophets are dead. qWho do You make Yourself out to be?"

54Jesus answered, r"If I honor Myself, My honor is nothing. sIt is My Father who honors Me, of whom you say that He is your* God. 55Yet tyou have not known Him, but I know Him. And if I say, 'I do not know Him,' I shall be a liar like you; but I do know Him and ukeep His word. 56Your father Abraham vrejoiced to see My day, wand he saw *it* and was glad."

57Then the Jews said to Him, "You are not yet fifty years old, and have You seen Abraham?"

58Jesus said to them, "Most assuredly, I say to you, xbefore Abraham was, yI AM."

59Then zthey took up stones to throw at Him; but Jesus hid Himself and went out of the temple,* agoing through the midst of them, and so passed by.

* **8:38** NU-Text reads *heard from.*   * **8:54** NU-Text and M-Text read *our.*   * **8:59** NU-Text omits the rest of this verse.

"And we know that all things work together for good to those who love God, to those who are the called according to His purpose."
3. *It confirms our forgiveness when we sin.* Repeatedly, the Bible assures us that all confessed sin is instantly and eternally forgiven (Ps. 32:5; 103:12; Is. 38:17).

8:33 have never been in bondage to anyone. The Pharisees' objection is startling. In their past, the Israelites had been in bondage to the Egyptians, the Assyrians, and the Babylonians. At the time they spoke, Israel was under the power of Rome.

8:39 Abraham is our father. The Pharisees believed that being a descendant of Abraham guaranteed them a place in heaven.

8:41 We were not born of fornication. From ancient times, this has been interpreted as a sneer, as if to say, "We are not illegitimate children, but You are." Apparently gossip followed Jesus, alleging that He had been conceived out of wedlock.

8:53 Are You greater than our father Abraham. Abraham and the prophets kept God's word and

died. Jesus was claiming not that He would prevent physical death, but that He could give eternal life. To the Jewish leaders, this was proof that Jesus was demon-possessed.

8:58–59 I AM. Jesus was not just claiming to have lived before Abraham; He was claiming eternal existence. He was claiming to be God Himself (Ex. 3:14). This time the Jewish leaders understood that Jesus

8:33 q [Matt. 3:9]   **8:34** r 2 Pet. 2:19   **8:35** s Gal. 4:30   **8:36** t Gal. 5:1   **8:37** u John 7:19   **8:38** v [John 3:32; 5:19, 30; 14:10, 24]   **8:39** w Matt. 3:9   x [Rom. 2:28]   **8:40** y John 8:37   z John 8:26   **8:41** a Is. 63:16   **8:42** b 1 John 5:1   c John 16:27; 17:8, 25   d Gal. 4:4   **8:43** e [John 7:17]   **8:44** f Matt. 13:38   g 1 John 2:16, 17   h [1 John 3:8–10, 15]   i [Jude 6]   **8:47** 1 John 4:6   **8:48** k John 7:20; 10:20   **8:49** l John 5:41   **8:50** m John 5:41; 7:18   **8:51** n John 5:24; 11:26   **8:52** o John 7:20; 10:20   p Zech. 1:5   **8:53** q John 10:33; 19:7   **8:54** r John 5:31, 32   s Acts 3:13   **8:55** t John 7:28, 29   u [John 15:10]   **8:56** v Luke 10:24   w Heb. 11:13   **8:58** x Mic. 5:2   y Rev. 1:8   **8:59** z John 10:31; 11:8   a Luke 4:30

A Man Born Blind Receives Sight

9 Now as *Jesus* passed by, He saw a man
who was blind from birth. 2 And His
disciples asked Him, saying, "Rabbi, [a]who
sinned, this man or his parents, that he was
born blind?"
3 Jesus answered, "Neither this man nor
his parents sinned, [b]but that the works of
God should be revealed in him. 4 [c]I* must
work the works of Him who sent Me while
it is [d]day; *the* night is coming when no one
can work. 5 As long as I am in the world, [e]I
am the light of the world."
6 When He had said these things, [f]He
spat on the ground and made clay with
the saliva; and He anointed the eyes of
the blind man with the clay. 7 And He said
to him, "Go, wash [g]in the pool of Siloam"
(which is translated, Sent). So [h]he went and
washed, and came back seeing.
8 Therefore the neighbors and those who
previously had seen that he was blind*
said, "Is not this he who sat and begged?"
9 Some said, "This is he." Others *said*,
"He is like him."*
He said, "I am *he*."
10 Therefore they said to him, "How were
your eyes opened?"
11 He answered and said, [i]"A Man called
Jesus made clay and anointed my eyes
and said to me, 'Go to the pool of* Siloam
and wash.' So I went and washed, and I received sight."
12 Then they said to him, "Where is He?"
He said, "I do not know."

The Pharisees Excommunicate the Healed Man

13 They brought him who formerly was
blind to the Pharisees. 14 Now it was a Sabbath when Jesus made the clay and opened
his eyes. 15 Then the Pharisees also asked
him again how he had received his sight.
He said to them, "He put clay on my eyes,
and I washed, and I see."
16 Therefore some of the Pharisees said,
"This Man is not from God, because He
does not keep the Sabbath."
Others said, [j]"How can a man who is a
sinner do such signs?" And [k]there was a
division among them.
17 They said to the blind man again,
"What do you say about Him because He
opened your eyes?"
He said, [l]"He is a prophet."
18 But the Jews did not believe concerning
him, that he had been blind and received
his sight, until they called the parents of
him who had received his sight. 19 And they
asked them, saying, "Is this your son, who
you say was born blind? How then does he
now see?"
20 His parents answered them and
said, "We know that this is our son, and
that he was born blind; 21 but by what
means he now sees we do not know, or
who opened his eyes we do not know.
He is of age; ask him. He will speak for
himself." 22 His parents said these *things*
because [m]they feared the Jews, for the
Jews had agreed already that if anyone confessed *that* He *was* Christ, he
[n]would be put out of the synagogue.
23 Therefore his parents said, "He is of age;
ask him."
24 So they again called the man who was
blind, and said to him, [o]"Give God the glory! [p]We know that this Man is a sinner."
25 He answered and said, "Whether He is
a sinner *or not* I do not know. One thing I
know: that though I was blind, now I see."
26 Then they said to him again, "What
did He do to you? How did He open your
eyes?"
27 He answered them, "I told you already,
and you did not listen. Why do you want to
hear *it* again? Do you also want to become
His disciples?"
28 Then they reviled him and said, "You
are His disciple, but we are Moses' disciples. 29 We know that God [q]spoke to [r]Mo-
ses; *as for this fellow*, [s]we do not know
where He is from."

* **9:4** NU-Text reads *We*. * **9:8** NU-Text reads *a beggar*. * **9:9** NU-Text reads *"No, but he is like him."* * **9:11** NU-Text omits *the pool of*.

---

was claiming to be God, so they took up stones to stone Him for blasphemy (Lev. 24:16).

9:1 ***a man who was blind from birth.*** Most likely he was a beggar. Beggars waited by the gates of the temple for gifts from worshipers. Therefore, it is likely that this scene took place near the temple.

9:2 ***who sinned.*** It was commonly supposed that sickness was a result of sin. It would follow that sin committed by a baby still in the womb or sin committed by parents could result in a baby being born with a disease. Jesus rejected both suggestions (v. 3).

9:7 ***pool of Siloam.*** Hezekiah had a tunnel cut through solid rock to transport water from Gihon into the city of Jerusalem, to the pool of Siloam (2 Kin. 20:20; 2 Chr. 32:30). John emphasizes that the name Siloam means "sent," because Jesus had just announced that He had been sent by God (v. 4).

9:22 ***put out of the synagogue.*** To take this action was a form of excommunication. The Jews had three types of excommunication: one lasting 30 days, during which the person could not come within six feet of anybody else; one for an indefinite time, during which the person was excluded from all fellowship and worship; and one that meant absolute expulsion forever. These judgments were very serious because no one could conduct business with a person who was excommunicated.

9:2 [a] John 9:34 **9:3** [b] John 11:4 **9:4** [c] [John 4:34; 5:19, 36; 17:4] [d] John 11:9, 10; 12:35 **9:5** [e] [John 1:5, 9; 3:19; 8:12; 12:35, 46] **9:6** [f] Mark 7:33; 8:23 **9:7** [g] Neh. 3:15 [h] 2 Kin. 5:14 **9:11** [i] John 9:6, 7 **9:16** [j] John 3:2; 9:33 [k] John 7:12, 43; 10:19 **9:17** [l] [John 4:19; 6:14] **9:22** [m] Acts 5:13 [n] John 16:2 **9:24** [o] Josh. 7:19 [p] John 9:16 **9:29** [q] Num. 12:6–8 [r] [John 5:45–47] [s] John 7:27, 28; 8:14

30The man answered and said to them, t"Why, this is a marvelous thing, that you do not know where He is from; yet He has opened my eyes! 31Now we know that uGod does not hear sinners; but if anyone is a worshiper of God and does His will, He hears him. 32Since the world began it has been unheard of that anyone opened the eyes of one who was born blind. 33vIf this Man were not from God, He could do nothing."

34They answered and said to him, w"You were completely born in sins, and are you teaching us?" And they cast him out.

True Vision and True Blindness

35Jesus heard that they had cast him out; and when He had xfound him, He said to him, "Do you ybelieve in zthe Son of God?"*

36He answered and said, "Who is He, Lord, that I may believe in Him?"

37And Jesus said to him, "You have both seen Him and ait is He who is talking with you."

38Then he said, "Lord, I believe!" And he bworshiped Him.

39And Jesus said, c"For judgment I have come into this world, dthat those who do not see may see, and that those who see may be made blind."

40Then some of the Pharisees who were with Him heard these words, eand said to Him, "Are we blind also?"

41Jesus said to them, f"If you were blind, you would have no sin; but now you say, 'We see.' Therefore your sin remains.

Jesus the True Shepherd

10 "Most assuredly, I say to you, he who does not enter the sheepfold by the door, but climbs up some other way, the same is a thief and a robber. 2But he who enters by the door is the shepherd of the sheep. 3To him the doorkeeper opens, and the sheep hear his voice; and he calls his own sheep by aname and leads them out. 4And when he brings out his own sheep, he goes before them; and the sheep follow him, for they know his voice. 5Yet they will by no means follow a bstranger, but will flee from him, for they do not know the voice of strangers." 6Jesus used this illustration, but they did not understand the things which He spoke to them.

Jesus the Good Shepherd

7Then Jesus said to them again, "Most assuredly, I say to you, I am the door of the sheep. 8All who ever came before Me* are thieves and robbers, but the sheep did not hear them. 9cI am the door. If anyone enters by Me, he will be saved, and will go in and out and find pasture. 10The thief does not come except to steal, and to kill, and to destroy. I have come that they may have life, and that they may have it more abundantly.

11d"I am the good shepherd. The good shepherd gives His life for the sheep. 12But a hireling, he who is not the shepherd, one who does not own the sheep, sees the wolf coming and eleaves the sheep and flees; and the wolf catches the sheep and scatters them. 13The hireling flees because he is a hireling and does not care about the sheep. 14I am the good shepherd; and fI know My sheep, and gam known by My own. 15hAs the Father knows Me, even so I know the Father; iand I lay down My life for the

---

*9:35 NU-Text reads Son of Man. * 10:8 M-Text omits before Me.

9:30–33 unheard of. There is no healing of a blind man recorded anywhere in the Old Testament.

9:38 Lord, I believe. Note the progression throughout this chapter of the healed man's understanding of the person of Christ. First, he called Jesus "a Man" (v. 11); then, "a prophet" (v. 17); and finally, he realized that Jesus is the Son of God (vv. 35–38).

10:1 sheepfold. A sheepfold was a walled enclosure or high fence made with stakes and having one door or gate; often the enclosure was a cave. **some other way.** The Pharisees had secured their power by illegitimate means.

10:3 the doorkeeper. The doorkeeper was the undershepherd. **calls his own sheep by name.** The naming of sheep was an ancient practice (Ps. 147:4; Is. 40:26).

10:7 I am the door. In verses 1–5, Jesus is the shepherd; here, He is the door. Some shepherds lay down across the entry of the sheepfold at night to sleep. Wild beasts would be discouraged from entering, and sheep would not exit. Thus, the shepherd was also the door.

10:10 may have it more abundantly. The thieves take life; the shepherd gives it. Abundant life includes salvation, nourishment, healing (v. 9), and much more. Life here refers to eternal life, God's life. It speaks not only of endlessness, but of quality of life. With Christ, life on earth can reach much higher quality, and then in heaven it will be complete and perfect.

10:11 The Ministry of Jesus—Jesus' most important teachings are: the kingdom of God (Matt. 5–7; 24–25); His divine authority over men (Matt. 7:28–29; Mark 2:10); His own role as God and Messiah demonstrated by miracles and signs; the significance of His death and resurrection (Matt. 16:21; Luke 24:26); the relationship which His disciples and subsequent believers are to share with Him (John 13–16); and the urgency of His commission to believers to make disciples (Matt. 28:19–20). The most significant events of His earthly life, His death and resurrection, are central to the entire Christian faith (1 Cor. 15:14).

9:30 t John 3:10   **9:31** u Zech. 7:13   **9:33** v John 3:2; 9:16   **9:34** w John 9:2   **9:35** x John 5:14 y John 1:7; 16:31   z Matt. 14:33; 16:16   **9:37** a John 4:26   **9:38** b Matt. 8:2   **9:39** c [John 3:17; 5:22, 27; 12:47]   d Matt. 13:13; 15:14   **9:40** e [Rom. 2:19]   **9:41** f John 15:22, 24   **10:3** a John 20:16   **10:5** b [2 Cor. 11:13–15]   **10:9** c [Eph. 2:18]   **10:11** d Is. 40:11   **10:12** e Zech. 11:16, 17   **10:14** f 2 Tim. 2:19   g 2 Tim. 1:12   **10:15** h Matt. 11:27   i [John 15:13; 19:30]

sheep. [16]And [j]other sheep I have which are not of this fold; them also I must bring, and they will hear My voice; [k]and there will be one flock *and* one shepherd.

[17]"Therefore My Father [l]loves Me, [m]because I lay down My life that I may take it again. [18]No one takes it from Me, but I lay it down of Myself. I [n]have power to lay it down, and I have power to take it again. [o]This command I have received from My Father."

[19]Therefore [p]there was a division again among the Jews because of these sayings. [20]And many of them said, [q]"He has a demon and is mad. Why do you listen to Him?"

[21]Others said, "These are not the words of one who has a demon. [r]Can a demon [s]open the eyes of the blind?"

The Shepherd Knows His Sheep

[22]Now it was the Feast of Dedication in Jerusalem, and it was winter. [23]And Jesus walked in the temple, [t]in Solomon's porch. [24]Then the Jews surrounded Him and said to Him, "How long do You keep us in doubt? If You are the Christ, tell us plainly."

[25]Jesus answered them, "I told you, and you do not believe. [u]The works that I do in My Father's name, they [v]bear witness of Me. [26]But [w]you do not believe, because you are not of My sheep, as I said to you.* [27][x]My sheep hear My voice, and I know them, and they follow Me. [28]And I give them eternal life, and they shall never perish; neither

shall anyone snatch them out of My hand. [29][y]My Father, [z]who has given *them* to Me, is greater than all; and no one is able to snatch *them* out of My Father's hand. [30][a]I and *My* Father are one."

Renewed Efforts to Stone Jesus

[31]Then [b]the Jews took up stones again to stone Him. [32]Jesus answered them, "Many good works I have shown you from My Father. For which of those works do you stone Me?"

[33]The Jews answered Him, saying, "For a good work we do not stone You, but for [c]blasphemy, and because You, being a Man, [d]make Yourself God."

[34]Jesus answered them, "Is it not written in your law, [e]'I said, "You are gods"'?* [35]If He called them gods, [f]to whom the word of God came (and the Scripture [g]cannot be broken), [36]do you say of Him [h]whom the Father sanctified and [i]sent into the world, 'You are blaspheming,' [j]because I said, 'I am [k]the Son of God'? [37][l]If I do not do the works of My Father, do not believe Me; [38]but if I do, though you do not believe Me, [m]believe the works, that you may know and believe* [n]that the Father *is* in Me, and I in Him." [39][o]Therefore they sought again to seize Him, but He escaped out of their hand.

---

* **10:26** NU-Text omits *as I said to you.*
* **10:34** Psalm 82:6 * **10:38** NU-Text reads *understand.*

The death of Christ was a humiliating physical death (John 19:18,33) that constituted a spiritual separation from God (Matt. 27:46). Within this moment there occurred the inexplicable mystery of the Father punishing the Son for the sins of the world (2 Cor. 5:21; 1 Pet. 3:18). The greatest crime of human history was in the plan of God (Acts 2:23) and became the basis of salvation for sinners (Is. 53:5). The resurrection of Christ demonstrated that His death, by which believing sinners are justified, was valid (1 Cor. 15:12–20). The historical evidence for the resurrection is plentiful: the many separate accounts of post-resurrection appearances, the empty tomb, and the transformed disciples. It is the power of the resurrection that empowers Christians today to live the Christian life (Eph. 1:19–20; Phil. 3:10).

10:16 *other sheep I have.* These were not Jews in heathen lands, but Gentiles. The Jewish people had asked if Jesus would go and teach the Gentiles (7:35). Jesus now declared that He had sheep among the despised heathen. ***one flock.*** This anticipates the salvation of the Gentiles and the formation of the church, in which converted Jews and Gentiles would form one spiritual body (Gal. 3:28; Eph. 2:16).

10:19–21 *many of them said . . . Others said.* After Jesus' analogy of the good shepherd, the editorial comment by John is fitting. In the analogy, Jesus was the good shepherd whose sheep hear His voice, implying that there are sheep who do not hear His voice. John's comment indicates that some believe and others do not. This is the same division that occurred in 9:16.

10:22 *the Feast of Dedication.* This festival was celebrated for eight days. In 167 B.C. Antiochus Epiphanes desecrated the temple in Jerusalem, as prophesied in Daniel 11:31. The Maccabeans restored and purified the temple. In commemoration of the restoration, the Feast of Dedication was instituted. Today it is also known as the Feast of Lights or Hanukkah.

10:27–29 *hear . . . follow.* The following of the sheep is a metaphor for faith. Other metaphors for faith in this Gospel include drinking water (4:14), eating bread (6:50–51), eating flesh, and drinking blood (6:54).

10:30 *I and My Father are one.* The Jewish opponents understood that Jesus was claiming to be God (vv. 31,33).

10:34 *You are gods.* In the Old Testament, judges were called gods. They exercised godlike judicial sovereignty. Psalm 82:6, the verse quoted here, refers to judges who violate the law. Jesus' argument was that,

---

10:16 [j] Is. 42:6; 56:8 [k] Eph. 2:13–18   **10:17** [l] John 5:20 [m] [Heb. 2:9]   **10:18** [n] [John 2:19; 5:26] [o] [John 6:38; 14:31; 17:4; Acts 2:24, 32]   **10:19** [p] John 7:43; 9:16   **10:20** [q] John 7:20   **10:21** [r] [Ex. 4:11] [s] John 9:6, 7, 32, 33   **10:23** [t] Acts 3:11; 5:12   **10:25** [u] John 5:36; 10:38 [v] Matt. 11:4   **10:26** [w] [John 8:47]   **10:27** [x] John 10:4, 14   **10:29** [y] John 14:28 [z] [John 17:2, 6, 12, 24]   **10:30** [a] John 17:11, 21–24   **10:31** [b] John 8:59   **10:33** [c] Matt. 9:3 [d] John 5:18   **10:34** [e] Ps. 82:6   **10:35** [f] Matt. 5:17, 18 [g] 1 Pet. 1:25   **10:36** [h] John 6:27 [i] John 3:17 [j] John 5:17, 18 [k] Luke 1:35   **10:37** [l] John 10:25; 15:24   **10:38** [m] John 5:36 [n] John 14:10, 11   **10:39** [o] John 7:30, 44

The Believers Beyond Jordan

⁴⁰And He went away again beyond the Jordan to the place ᵖwhere John was baptizing at first, and there He stayed. ⁴¹Then many came to Him and said, "John performed no sign, ᵠbut all the things that John spoke about this Man were true." ⁴²And many believed in Him there.

The Death of Lazarus

11 Now a certain *man* was sick, Lazarus of Bethany, the town of ᵃMary and her sister Martha. ²ᵇIt was *that* Mary who anointed the Lord with fragrant oil and wiped His feet with her hair, whose brother Lazarus was sick. ³Therefore the sisters sent to Him, saying, "Lord, behold, he whom You love is sick."

⁴When Jesus heard *that*, He said, "This sickness is not unto death, but for the glory of God, that the Son of God may be glorified through it."

⁵Now Jesus loved Martha and her sister and Lazarus. ⁶So, when He heard that he was sick, ᶜHe stayed two more days in the place where He was. ⁷Then after this He said to *the* disciples, "Let us go to Judea again."

⁸*The* disciples said to Him, "Rabbi, lately the Jews sought to ᵈstone You, and are You going there again?"

⁹Jesus answered, "Are there not twelve hours in the day? ᵉIf anyone walks in the day, he does not stumble, because he sees the ᶠlight of this world. ¹⁰But ᵍif one walks in the night, he stumbles, because the light is not in him." ¹¹These things He said, and after that He said to them, "Our friend Lazarus ʰsleeps, but I go that I may wake him up."

¹²Then His disciples said, "Lord, if he sleeps he will get well." ¹³However, Jesus spoke of his death, but they thought that He was speaking about taking rest in sleep.

¹⁴Then Jesus said to them plainly, "Lazarus is dead. ¹⁵And I am glad for your sakes that I was not there, that you may believe. Nevertheless let us go to him."

¹⁶Then ⁱThomas, who is called the Twin, said to his fellow disciples, "Let us also go, that we may die with Him."

I Am the Resurrection and the Life

¹⁷So when Jesus came, He found that he had already been in the tomb four days. ¹⁸Now Bethany was near Jerusalem, about two miles* away. ¹⁹And many of the Jews had joined the women around Martha and Mary, to comfort them concerning their brother.

²⁰Now Martha, as soon as she heard that Jesus was coming, went and met Him, but Mary was sitting in the house. ²¹Now Martha said to Jesus, "Lord, if You had been here, my brother would not have died. ²²But even now I know that ʲwhatever You ask of God, God will give You."

²³Jesus said to her, "Your brother will rise again."

²⁴Martha said to Him, ᵏ"I know that he will rise again in the resurrection at the last day."

²⁵Jesus said to her, "I am ˡthe resurrection and the life. ᵐHe who believes in Me, though he may ⁿdie, he shall live. ²⁶And whoever lives and believes in Me shall never die. Do you believe this?"

²⁷She said to Him, "Yes, Lord, ᵒI believe that You are the Christ, the Son of God, who is to come into the world."

Jesus and Death, the Last Enemy

²⁸And when she had said these things, she went her way and secretly called Mary her sister, saying, "The Teacher has come and is calling for you." ²⁹As soon as she heard *that*, she arose quickly and came to Him. ³⁰Now Jesus had not yet come into the town, but was* in the place where Martha met Him. ³¹ᵖThen the Jews who were with her in the house, and comforting her, when they saw that Mary rose up quickly and went out, followed her, saying, "She is going to the tomb to weep there."*

³²Then, when Mary came where Jesus was, and saw Him, she ᵠfell down at His feet, saying to Him, ʳ"Lord, if You had been here, my brother would not have died."

³³Therefore, when Jesus saw her weeping, and the Jews who came with her weeping,

---

* **11:18** Literally *fifteen stadia*   * **11:30** NU-Text adds *still*.   * **11:31** NU-Text reads *supposing that she was going to the tomb to weep there.*

---

if the divine name had been applied by God to mere men, there could be neither blasphemy nor folly in its application to the incarnate Son of God Himself.
11:1 *Bethany.* This was a small village on the southeast slope of the Mount of Olives. It was located about two miles from Jerusalem.
11:4 *not unto death.* This phrase means not having death as its final result.
11:6–8 *He stayed two more days.* God's purpose was to glorify His Son (v. 4) and to cause the disciples to grow (v. 15). Had Jesus immediately rushed to Lazarus' bedside and healed him, Lazarus would not have died and Jesus would not have been able to manifest His glory by raising Lazarus.

11:16 *Let us also go, that we may die with Him.* While the Lord saw their development in faith, Thomas saw their deaths. Yet, in his loyalty, he followed anyway.
11:33 *troubled.* This word means to be stirred up,

10:40 ᵖ John 1:28   **10:41** ᵠ [John 1:29, 36; 3:28–36; 5:33]
11:1 ᵃ Luke 10:38, 39   **11:2** ᵇ Matt. 26:7   **11:6** ᶜ John 10:40   **11:8** ᵈ John 8:59; 10:31   **11:9** ᵉ John 9:4; 12:35   ᶠ Is. 9:2   **11:10** ᵍ John 12:35   **11:11** ʰ Matt. 9:24   **11:16** ⁱ John 14:5; 20:26–28   **11:22** ʲ [John 9:31; 11:41]   **11:24** ᵏ [John 5:29]   **11:25** ˡ John 5:21; 6:39, 40, 44   ᵐ 1 John 5:10   ⁿ 1 Cor. 15:22   **11:27** ᵒ Matt. 16:16
11:31 ᵖ John 11:19, 33   **11:32** ᵠ Rev. 1:17   ʳ John 11:21

He groaned in the spirit and was troubled. 34And He said, "Where have you laid him?"

They said to Him, "Lord, come and see."

35sJesus wept. 36Then the Jews said, "See how He loved him!"

37And some of them said, "Could not this Man, twho opened the eyes of the blind, also have kept this man from dying?"

Lazarus Raised from the Dead

38Then Jesus, again groaning in Himself, came to the tomb. It was a cave, and a ustone lay against it. 39Jesus said, "Take away the stone."

Martha, the sister of him who was dead, said to Him, "Lord, by this time there is a stench, for he has been *dead* four days."

40Jesus said to her, "Did I not say to you that if you would believe you would vsee the glory of God?" 41Then they took away the stone *from the place* where the dead man was lying.* And Jesus lifted up *His* eyes and said, "Father, I thank You that You have heard Me. 42And I know that You always hear Me, but wbecause of the people who are standing by I said *this*, that they may believe that You sent Me." 43Now when He had said these things, He cried with a loud voice, "Lazarus, come forth!" 44And he who had died came out bound hand and foot with xgraveclothes, and yhis face was wrapped with a cloth. Jesus said to them, "Loose him, and let him go."

The Plot to Kill Jesus

45Then many of the Jews who had come to Mary, zand had seen the things Jesus did, believed in Him. 46But some of them went away to the Pharisees and atold them the things Jesus did. 47bThen the chief priests and the Pharisees gathered a council and said, c"What shall we do? For this Man works many signs. 48If we let Him alone like this, everyone will believe in Him, and the Romans will come and take away both our place and nation."

49And one of them, dCaiaphas, being high priest that year, said to them, "You know nothing at all, 50enor do you consider that it is expedient for us* that one man should die for the people, and not that the whole nation should perish." 51Now this he did not say on his own *authority*; but being high priest that year he prophesied that Jesus would die for the nation, 52and fnot for that nation only, but galso that He would gather together in one the children of God who were scattered abroad. 53Then, from that day on, they plotted to hput Him to death. 54iTherefore Jesus no longer walked openly among the Jews, but went from there into the country near the wilderness, to a city called jEphraim, and there remained with His disciples.

55kAnd the Passover of the Jews was near, and many went from the country up to Jerusalem before the Passover, to lpurify themselves. 56mThen they sought Jesus, and spoke among themselves as they stood in the temple, "What do you think—that He will not come to the feast?" 57Now both the chief priests and the Pharisees had given a command, that if anyone knew where He was, he should report it, that they might nseize Him.

The Anointing at Bethany

12 Then, six days before the Passover, Jesus came to Bethany, awhere Lazarus was who had been dead,* whom He had raised from the dead. 2bThere they made Him a supper; and Martha served, but Lazarus was one of those who sat at the table with Him. 3Then cMary took a pound of very costly oil of dspikenard, anointed the feet of Jesus, and wiped His feet with her hair. And the house was filled with the fragrance of the oil.

* **11:41** NU-Text omits *from the place where the dead man was lying.* * **11:50** NU-Text reads *you.* * **12:1** NU-Text omits *who had been dead.*

---

disturbed. Jesus was moved by the mourning of Mary and indignant at the hypocritical lamentations of His enemies.

11:37 Could not this Man. Some people misinterpreted Jesus' tears as powerlessness. They complained that He had healed others, but now was impotent.

11:43 Lazarus. Augustine once said that, if Jesus had not designated Lazarus by name, all the graves would have been emptied at His command (5:28). Raising Lazarus from the dead is the seventh sign of Jesus' messiahship, the greatest miracle of all, giving life back to the dead.

11:49–52 it is expedient. In the opinion of Caiaphas, Jesus should die rather than plunge the nation into destruction. John adds that by virtue of his office Caiaphas pronounced a message of God unconsciously. Caiaphas was a prophet in spite of himself. John also saw in Caiaphas' words a prophecy that Jesus should die not only for Israel but for the Gentiles as well.

11:53 they plotted to put Him to death. Humanly speaking, the resurrection of Lazarus was a major factor that led to the plot by the Jewish religious leaders to kill Christ. At this point the council decided informally, if not formally, to put Jesus to death. It is ironic that these men believed they could put to death permanently One who could raise the dead.

12:1 six days before the Passover. If the crucifixion took place on a Friday, this dinner occurred during the evening of the previous Saturday. Verse 12 seems to support this conclusion because the Jerusalem entry took place on Sunday.

12:3 very costly oil of spikenard. Judas Iscariot said

11:35 s Luke 19:41 **11:37** t John 9:6, 7 **11:38** u Matt. 27:60, 66 **11:40** v [John 11:4, 23] **11:42** w John 12:30; 17:21 **11:44** x John 19:40 y John 20:7 **11:45** z John 2:23; 10:42; 12:11, 18 **11:46** a John 5:15 **11:47** b Ps. 2:2 c Acts 4:16 **11:49** d Luke 3:2 **11:50** e John 18:14 **11:52** f Is. 49:6 g [Eph. 2:14–17] **11:53** h Matt. 26:4 **11:54** i John 4:1, 3; 7:1 j 2 Chr. 13:19 **11:55** k John 2:13; 5:1; 6:4 l Num. 9:10, 13; 31:19, 20 **11:56** m John 7:11 **11:57** n Matt. 26:14–16 **12:1** a John 11:1, 43 **12:2** b Mark 14:3; Luke 10:38–41 **12:3** c John 11:2 d Song 1:12

4But one of His disciples, *e*Judas Iscariot, Simon's *son*, who would betray Him, said, 5"Why was this fragrant oil not sold for three hundred denarii* and given to the poor?" 6This he said, not that he cared for the poor, but because he was a thief, and *f*had the money box; and he used to take what was put in it. 7But Jesus said, "Let her alone; she has kept* this for the day of My burial. 8For *g*the poor you have with you always, but Me you do not have always."

The Plot to Kill Lazarus

9Now a great many of the Jews knew that He was there; and they came, not for Jesus' sake only, but that they might also see Lazarus, *h*whom He had raised from the dead. 10*i*But the chief priests plotted to put Lazarus to death also, 11*j*because on account of him many of the Jews went away and believed in Jesus.

The Triumphal Entry

12*k*The next day a great multitude that had come to the feast, when they heard that Jesus was coming to Jerusalem, 13took branches of palm trees and went out to meet Him, and cried out:

"Hosanna!
l'Blessed is He who comes in the name
   of the LORD!'*
The King of Israel!"

14*m*Then Jesus, when He had found a young donkey, sat on it; as it is written:

15 *"Fear*n *not, daughter of Zion;
   Behold, your King is coming,
   Sitting on a donkey's colt."*

16*o*His disciples did not understand these things at first; *p*but when Jesus was glorified, *q*then they remembered that these things were written about Him and *that* they had done these things to Him.

17Therefore the people, who were with Him when He called Lazarus out of his tomb and raised him from the dead, bore witness. 18*r*For this reason the people also met Him, because they heard that He had done this sign. 19The Pharisees therefore said among themselves, *s*"You see that you are accomplishing nothing. Look, the world has gone after Him!"

The Fruitful Grain of Wheat

20Now there *t*were certain Greeks among those *u*who came up to worship at the feast. 21Then they came to Philip, *v*who was from Bethsaida of Galilee, and asked him, saying, "Sir, we wish to see Jesus." 22Philip came and told Andrew, and in turn Andrew and Philip told Jesus. 23But Jesus answered them, saying, *w*"The hour has come that the Son of Man should be glorified. 24Most assuredly, I say to you, *x*unless a grain of wheat falls into the ground and dies, it remains alone; but if it dies, it produces much grain. 25*y*He who loves his life will lose it, and he who hates his life in this world will keep it for eternal life. 26If anyone serves Me, let him *z*follow Me; and *a*where I am, there My servant will be also. If anyone serves Me, him *My* Father will honor.

Jesus Predicts His Death on the Cross

27*b*"Now My soul is troubled, and what shall I say? 'Father, save Me from this hour'? *c*But for this purpose I came to this hour. 28Father, glorify Your name."

---

* **12:5** About one year's wages for a worker
* **12:7** NU-Text reads *that she may keep.*
* **12:13** Psalm 118:26 * **12:15** Zechariah 9:9

---

that this perfume cost 300 denarii (v. 5). One denarius was a laborer's wage for one day. Thus, the perfume cost approximately a year's wages. *anointed the feet.* Mary also anointed Jesus' head. The custom of that time was to anoint the heads of guests. Anointing Jesus' head was an act of honor; anointing His feet was a display of devotion.
12:10–11 *the chief priests plotted to put Lazarus to death also.* The chief priests were mostly Sadducees. They had an additional reason to kill Lazarus. He was a living refutation of their doctrine that there was no resurrection (11:57; Acts 23:8). Yet this was not a meeting of the Jewish council, nor was it a formal sentence of death. The ultimate motivation for wanting to kill Lazarus was that because of him many were believing in Jesus.
12:13–15 *The King of Israel.* Until this point, Jesus had discouraged expressions of support from the people (6:15; 7:1–8). Here, He allowed public enthusiasm. He entered Jerusalem on the back of a young donkey. This act fulfilled prophecy (Zech. 9:9) and as such was a symbolic proclamation that Jesus is the Messiah.

12:20 *to worship at the feast.* This verse indicates that these Greeks were Jewish proselytes. By recording this incident, perhaps John was hinting that the salvation rejected by many of the Jews was already passing to the Gentiles.
12:24 *unless a grain of wheat . . . dies.* When a seed dies, it produces fruit. Life comes by death. This principle is not only true in nature, but it is also true spiritually. Jesus was speaking first and foremost of Himself. He is the grain of wheat. His death would produce much fruit and would result in many living for God.
12:27 *Now My soul is troubled.* Jesus' agony over His impending death was not confined to Gethsemane,

12:4 *e* John 13:26   **12:6** *f* John 13:29   **12:8** *g* Mark 14:7   **12:9** *h* John 11:43, 44   **12:10** *i* Luke 16:31   **12:11** *j* John 11:45; 12:18   **12:12** *k* Matt. 21:4–9   **12:13** *l* Ps. 118:25, 26   **12:14** *m* Matt. 21:7   **12:15** *n* Is. 40:9; Zech. 9:9   **12:16** *o* Luke 18:34   *p* John 7:39; 12:23   *q* [John 14:26]   **12:18** *r* John 12:11   **12:19** *s* John 11:47, 48   **12:20** *t* Acts 17:4   *u* 1 Kin. 8:41, 42   **12:21** *v* John 1:43, 44; 14:8–11   **12:23** *w* John 13:32   **12:24** *x* 1 Cor. 15:36   **12:25** *y* Mark 8:35   **12:26** *z* [Matt. 16:24]   *a* John 14:3; 17:24   **12:27** *b* [Matt. 26:38, 39]   *c* Luke 22:53

*d*Then a voice came from heaven, *saying,* "I have both glorified *it* and will glorify *it* again."

²⁹Therefore the people who stood by and heard *it* said that it had thundered. Others said, "An angel has spoken to Him."

³⁰Jesus answered and said, *e*"This voice did not come because of Me, but for your sake. ³¹Now is the judgment of this world; now *f*the ruler of this world will be cast out. ³²And I, *g*if I am lifted up from the earth, will draw *h*all *peoples* to Myself." ³³*i*This He said, signifying by what death He would die.

³⁴The people answered Him, *j*"We have heard from the law that the Christ remains forever; and how *can* You say, 'The Son of Man must be lifted up'? Who is this Son of Man?"

³⁵Then Jesus said to them, "A little while longer *k*the light is with you. *l*Walk while you have the light, lest darkness overtake you; *m*he who walks in darkness does not know where he is going. ³⁶While you have the light, believe in the light, that you may become *n*sons of light." These things Jesus spoke, and departed, and *o*was hidden from them.

Who Has Believed Our Report?

³⁷But although He had done so many *p*signs before them, they did not believe in Him, ³⁸that the word of Isaiah the prophet might be fulfilled, which he spoke:

q"Lord, who has believed our report?
And to whom has the arm of the LORD
been revealed?"*

³⁹Therefore they could not believe, because Isaiah said again:

⁴⁰ "He*r* has blinded their eyes and
hardened their hearts,
*s*Lest they should see with their eyes,
Lest they should understand with their
hearts and turn,
So that I should heal them."*

⁴¹*t*These things Isaiah said when* he saw His glory and spoke of Him.

Walk in the Light

⁴²Nevertheless even among the rulers many believed in Him, but *u*because of the Pharisees they did not confess *Him,* lest they should be put out of the synagogue; ⁴³*v*for they loved the praise of men more than the praise of God.

⁴⁴Then Jesus cried out and said, *w*"He who believes in Me, *x*believes not in Me *y*but in Him who sent Me. ⁴⁵And *z*he who sees Me sees Him who sent Me. ⁴⁶*a*I have come *as* a light into the world, that whoever believes in Me should not abide in darkness. ⁴⁷And if anyone hears My words and does not believe,* *b*I do not judge him; for *c*I did not come to judge the world but to save the world. ⁴⁸*d*He who rejects Me, and does not receive My words, has that which judges him—*e*the word that I have spoken will judge him in the last day. ⁴⁹For *f*I have not spoken on My own *authority;* but the Father who sent Me gave Me a command, *g*what I should say and what I should speak. ⁵⁰And I know that His command is everlasting life. Therefore, whatever I speak, just as the Father has told Me, so I *h*speak."

Jesus Washes the Disciples' Feet

13 Now *a*before the Feast of the Passover, when Jesus knew that *b*His hour had come that He should depart from this world to the Father, having loved His own who were in the world, He *c*loved them to the end.

²And supper being ended,* *d*the devil having already put it into the heart of Judas Iscariot, Simon's *son,* to betray Him, ³Jesus, knowing *e*that the Father had given all things into His hands, and that He *f*had come from God and *g*was going to God, ⁴*h*rose from supper and laid aside His garments, took a towel and girded Himself. ⁵After that, He poured water into a basin and began to wash the disciples' feet, and

---

* **12:38** Isaiah 53:1   * **12:40** Isaiah 6:10
* **12:41** NU-Text reads *because.*   * **12:47** NU-Text reads *keep them.*   * **13:2** NU-Text reads *And during supper.*

---

where He prayed for the cup to pass from Him (Matt. 26:39). He felt the agony and expressed it almost a week before Gethsemane.

12:35–36 *while you have the light.* Instead of answering the people's questions (v. 34), Jesus gave them a warning. Jesus is the light. He wanted the people to believe and abide in Him (v. 46).

12:42–43 *Nevertheless.* This word marks a stark contrast between these believers and the unbelief spoken of in verses 37–41. These men were genuine believers. Their problem was that they feared the opinions of their fellow leaders. Such believers will be ashamed at Christ's return (1 John 2:28).

12:47 *I do not judge him.* Christ will judge, but at His first coming He did not come to judge but to save (3:17).

13:1 *to the end.* This phrase means either "to the last" or "utterly and completely." What follows in verses 1–11 demonstrates Jesus' complete love. Jesus loved His disciples, even though He knew that one would betray Him, another would deny Him, and all would desert Him for a time.

12:28 *d* Matt. 3:17; 17:5   **12:30** *e* John 11:42
12:31 *f* [2 Cor. 4:4]   **12:32** *g* John 3:14; 8:28   *h* [Rom. 5:18]   **12:33** *i* John 18:32; 21:19   **12:34** *j* Mic. 4:7   **12:35** *k* [John 1:9; 7:33; 8:12]   *l* Eph. 5:8   *m* [1 John 2:9–11]   **12:36** *n* Luke 16:8   *o* John 8:59   **12:37** *p* John 11:47   **12:38** *q* Is. 53:1   **12:40** *r* Is. 6:9, 10   *s* Matt. 13:14   **12:41** *t* Is. 6:1   **12:42** *u* John 7:13; 9:22   **12:43** *v* John 5:41, 44   **12:44** *w* Mark 9:37   *x* [John 3:16, 18, 36; 11:25, 26]   *y* [John 5:24]   **12:45** *z* [John 14:9]   **12:46** *a* John 1:4, 5; 8:12; 12:35, 36   **12:47** *b* John 5:45   *c* John 3:17   **12:48** *d* [Luke 10:16]   *e* Deut. 18:18, 19   **12:49** *f* John 8:38   *g* Deut. 18:18   **12:50** *h* John 5:19; 8:28   **13:1** *a* Matt. 26:2   *b* John 12:23; 17:1   *c* John 15:9   **13:2** *d* Luke 22:3   **13:3** *e* Acts 2:36   *f* John 8:42; 16:28   *g* John 17:11; 20:17   **13:4** *h* [Luke 22:27]

to wipe *them* with the towel with which He was girded. **6**Then He came to Simon Peter. And *Peter* said to Him, *i*"Lord, are You washing my feet?"

7Jesus answered and said to him, "What I am doing you *j*do not understand now, *k*but you will know after this."

8Peter said to Him, "You shall never wash my feet!"

Jesus answered him, *l*"If I do not wash you, you have no part with Me."

9Simon Peter said to Him, "Lord, not my feet only, but also *my* hands and *my* head!"

10Jesus said to him, "He who is bathed needs only to wash *his* feet, but is completely clean; and *m*you are clean, but not all of you." **11**For *n*He knew who would betray Him; therefore He said, "You are not all clean."

12So when He had washed their feet, taken His garments, and sat down again, He said to them, "Do you know what I have done to you? **13**oYou call Me Teacher and Lord, and you say well, for *so* I am. **14**pIf I then, *your* Lord and Teacher, have washed your feet, *q*you also ought to wash one another's feet. **15**For *r*I have given you an example, that you should do as I have done to you. **16**sMost assuredly, I say to you, a servant is not greater than his master; nor is he who is sent greater than he who sent him. **17**tIf you know these things, blessed are you if you do them.

Jesus Identifies His Betrayer

18"I do not speak concerning all of you. I know whom I have chosen; but that the *u*Scripture may be fulfilled, *v*'He who eats bread with Me* has lifted up his heel against Me.'* **19**wNow I tell you before it comes, that when it does come to pass, you may believe that I am *He.* **20**xMost assuredly, I say to you, he who receives whomever I send receives Me; and he who receives Me receives Him who sent Me."

21yWhen Jesus had said these things,

*z*He was troubled in spirit, and testified and said, "Most assuredly, I say to you, *a*one of you will betray Me." **22**Then the disciples looked at one another, perplexed about whom He spoke.

23Now *b*there was leaning on Jesus' bosom one of His disciples, whom Jesus loved. **24**Simon Peter therefore motioned to him to ask who it was of whom He spoke.

25Then, leaning back* on Jesus' breast, he said to Him, "Lord, who is it?"

26Jesus answered, "It is he to whom I shall give a piece of bread when I have dipped *it.*" And having dipped the bread, He gave it to *c*Judas Iscariot, *the son* of Simon. **27**dNow after the piece of bread, Satan entered him. Then Jesus said to him, "What you do, do quickly." **28**But no one at the table knew for what reason He said this to him. **29**For some thought, because *e*Judas had the money box, that Jesus had said to him, "Buy *those things* we need for the feast," or that he should give something to the poor.

30Having received the piece of bread, he then went out immediately. And it was night.

The New Commandment

31So, when he had gone out, Jesus said, *f*"Now the Son of Man is glorified, and *g*God is glorified in Him. **32**If God is glorified in Him, God will also glorify Him in Himself, and *h*glorify Him immediately. **33**Little children, I shall be with you a *i*little while longer. You will seek Me; *j*and as I said to the Jews, 'Where I am going, you cannot come,' so now I say to you. **34**kA new commandment I give to you, that you love one another; as I have loved you, that you also love one another. **35**lBy this all will know that you are My disciples, if you have love for one another."

---

* **13:18** NU-Text reads *My bread.* • Psalm 41:9
* **13:25** NU-Text and M-Text add *thus.*

13:8 *no part with Me.* The washing was a symbol of spiritual cleansing (vv. 10–11). If Peter did not participate in the cleansing, he would not enjoy fellowship with Christ (1 John 1:9).
13:13 *Teacher and Lord.* These were the ordinary titles of respect given to a rabbi.
13:18 *has lifted up his heel.* Jesus quoted Psalm 41:9 to explain the action of Judas. Lifting up one's heel was a gesture of insult or a preparation to kick. The blow had not yet been given. This was the attitude of Judas at that moment. He was eating with the disciples, but he was ready to strike.
13:23 *leaning on Jesus' bosom.* At this time people did not generally sit at a table to eat. They reclined on the left side of a low platform, resting on the left elbow and eating with the right hand, their feet extended outward. Reclining in such a way, a man's head was near the chest of the person on his left. ***whom Jesus loved.*** The disciple is never named in Scripture, but the tradition of the early church designates him as John, the author of this Gospel.

13:33 *Little children* is an expression of tender affection used nowhere else in the Gospels. John did not forget the expression; he used it repeatedly in 1 John.
13:34 *love one another.* One of the dominant themes in the apostle John's writings is love. God loves the whole world (3:16). Jesus repeatedly demonstrates His compassion for people in general and His love for His disciples in particular (10:11; 11:3; 13:1; 15:9).
13:35 *By this.* Unbelievers recognize Jesus' disciples

13:6 *j* Matt. 3:14   **13:7** *j* John 12:16; 16:12   *k* John 13:19   **13:8** *l* [1 Cor. 6:11]   **13:10** *m* [John 15:3]   **13:11** *n* John 6:64; 18:4   **13:13** *o* Matt. 23:8, 10   **13:14** *p* Luke 22:27   *q* [Rom. 12:10]   **13:15** *r* [1 Pet. 2:21–24]   **13:16** *s* Matt. 10:24   **13:17** *t* [James 1:25]   **13:18** *u* John 15:25; 17:12   *v* Ps. 41:9   **13:19** *w* John 14:29; 16:4   **13:20** *x* Matt. 10:40   **13:21** *y* Luke 22:21   *z* John 12:27   *a* 1 John 2:19   **13:23** *b* John 19:26; 20:2; 21:7, 20   **13:26** *c* John 6:70, 71; 12:4   **13:27** *d* Luke 22:3   **13:29** *e* John 12:6   **13:31** *f* John 12:23   *g* [1 Pet. 4:11]   **13:32** *h* John 12:23   **13:33** *i* John 12:35; 14:19; 16:16–19   *j* [John 7:34; 8:21]   **13:34** *k* 1 Thess. 4:9   **13:35** *l* 1 John 2:5

Jesus Predicts Peter's Denial

³⁶Simon Peter said to Him, "Lord, where are You going?"

Jesus answered him, "Where I ᵐam going you cannot follow Me now, but ⁿyou shall follow Me afterward."

³⁷Peter said to Him, "Lord, why can I not follow You now? I will ᵒlay down my life for Your sake."

³⁸Jesus answered him, "Will you lay down your life for My sake? Most assuredly, I say to you, the rooster shall not ᵖcrow till you have denied Me three times.

The Way, the Truth, and the Life

14 "Let ᵃnot your heart be troubled; you believe in God, believe also in Me. ²In My Father's house are many mansions;* if *it were* not *so,* I would have told you. ᵇI go to prepare a place for you.* ³And if I go and prepare a place for you, ᶜI will come again and receive you to Myself; that ᵈwhere I am, *there* you may be also. ⁴And where I go you know, and the way you know."

⁵ᵉThomas said to Him, "Lord, we do not know where You are going, and how can we know the way?"

⁶Jesus said to him, "I am ᶠthe way, ᵍthe truth, and ʰthe life. ⁱNo one comes to the Father ʲexcept through Me.

The Father Revealed

⁷ᵏ"If you had known Me, you would have known My Father also; and from now on you know Him and have seen Him."

⁸Philip said to Him, "Lord, show us the Father, and it is sufficient for us."

⁹Jesus said to him, "Have I been with you so long, and yet you have not known Me, Philip? ˡHe who has seen Me has seen the Father; so how can you say, 'Show us the Father'? ¹⁰Do you not believe that ᵐI am in the Father, and the Father in Me? The words that I speak to you ⁿI do not speak on My own *authority;* but the Father who dwells in Me does the works. ¹¹Believe Me that I *am* in the Father and the Father in Me, ᵒor else believe Me for the sake of the works themselves.

The Answered Prayer

¹²ᵖ"Most assuredly, I say to you, he who believes in Me, the works that I do he will do also; and greater *works* than these he will do, because I go to My Father. ¹³ᑫAnd whatever you ask in My name, that I will do, that the Father may be ʳglorified in the Son. ¹⁴If you ask* anything in My name, I will do *it.*

Jesus Promises Another Helper

¹⁵ˢ"If you love Me, keep* My commandments. ¹⁶And I will pray the Father, and ᵗHe will give you another Helper, that He may abide with you forever— ¹⁷ᵘthe Spirit of truth, ᵛwhom the world cannot receive, because it neither sees Him nor knows Him; but you know Him, for He dwells with you ʷand will be in you. ¹⁸ˣI will not leave you orphans; ʸI will come to you.

* **14:2** Literally *dwellings* • NU-Text adds a word which would cause the text to read either *if it were not so, would I have told you that I go to prepare a place for you?* or *if it were not so I would have told you; for I go to prepare a place for you.* * **14:14** NU-Text adds *Me.* * **14:15** NU-Text reads *you will keep.*

---

not by their doctrinal distinctives, nor by dramatic miracles, nor even by their love for the lost. They recognize His disciples by their deeds of love for one another.

13:36 Lord, where are You going? This question Jesus had already addressed twice before, indicating that Peter completely missed the point of what Jesus said in verses 34 and 35.

13:37 I will lay down my life for Your sake. Peter was ready to die for Jesus. Unfortunately, he was not ready, at this point, to live for Him. Later Peter would die for Christ (21:18–19). Church tradition states that Peter was crucified upside down, at his request, for he felt himself unworthy to be crucified like his Lord.

14:3 I will come again and receive you. Peter may have failed Jesus (13:38), but Christ will not fail to return for Peter and for everyone else who has believed in Him (1 Thess. 4:16–17).

14:6 the way, the truth, and the life. Through His death and resurrection, Jesus is the way to the Father. He is also the truth and the life. As truth, He is the revelation of God. As life, He is the source of our very beings.

14:12 greater works. Jesus had accomplished the greatest works possible, including raising the dead. How could He say that believers would do greater works? The answer is seen in the extent of what the apostles did. Jesus' work on earth was confined to Palestine; the apostles would preach everywhere and see the conversion of thousands. Peter's message at Pentecost brought more followers to Jesus than did Jesus' entire earthly ministry. The disciples were able to do this work because Christ would go to the Father and send the Holy Spirit to empower them.

14:17 the Spirit of truth. This is another name for the Holy Spirit because He is truth and guides us into all truth (1 Cor. 2:13; 2 Pet. 1:21).

14:18 orphans. He would not abandon them. He would come to them. There are three suggested interpretations as to when that statement would be fulfilled: (1) after the resurrection, (2) at Pentecost, in the person of the Holy Spirit, and (3) at the second coming.

13:36 ᵐ John 13:33; 14:2; 16:5 ⁿ 2 Pet. 1:14   **13:37** ᵒ Mark 14:29–31   **13:38** ᵖ John 18:25–27   **14:1** ᵃ [John 14:27; 16:22, 24]   **14:2** ᵇ John 13:33, 36   **14:3** ᶜ [Acts 1:11] ᵈ [John 12:26]   **14:5** ᵉ Matt. 10:3   **14:6** ᶠ [Heb. 9:8; 10:19, 20] ᵍ [John 1:14, 17; 8:32; 18:37] ʰ [John 11:25] ⁱ 1 Tim. 2:5 ʲ [John 10:7–9]   **14:7** ᵏ John 8:19   **14:9** ˡ Col. 1:15   **14:10** ᵐ John 10:38; 14:11, 20 ⁿ John 5:19; 14:24   **14:11** ᵒ John 5:36; 10:38   **14:12** ᵖ Luke 10:17   **14:13** ᑫ Matt. 7:7 ʳ John 13:31   **14:15** ˢ 1 John 5:3   **14:16** ᵗ Rom. 8:15   **14:17** ᵘ [1 John 4:6; 5:7] ᵛ [1 Cor. 2:14] ʷ [1 John 2:27]   **14:18** ˣ [Matt. 28:20] ʸ [John 14:3, 28]

Indwelling of the Father and the Son

19"A little while longer and the world
will see Me no more, but [z]you will see Me.
[a]Because I live, you will live also. 20At that
day you will know that [b]I *am* in My Father,
and you in Me, and I in you. 21[c]He who has
My commandments and keeps them, it is
he who loves Me. And he who loves Me will
be loved by My Father, and I will love him
and manifest Myself to him."

22[d]Judas (not Iscariot) said to Him,
"Lord, how is it that You will manifest
Yourself to us, and not to the world?"

23Jesus answered and said to him, "If
anyone loves Me, he will keep My word;
and My Father will love him, [e]and We will
come to him and make Our home with him.
24He who does not love Me does not keep
My words; and [f]the word which you hear
is not Mine but the Father's who sent Me.

The Gift of His Peace

25"These things I have spoken to you
while being present with you. 26But [g]the
Helper, the Holy Spirit, whom the Father
will [h]send in My name, [i]He will teach you
all things, and bring to your [j]remembrance
all things that I said to you. 27[k]Peace I leave
with you, My peace I give to you; not as the
world gives do I give to you. Let not your
heart be troubled, neither let it be afraid.
28You have heard Me [l]say to you, 'I am
going away and coming *back* to you.' If
you loved Me, you would rejoice because
I said,* [m]'I am going to the Father,' for [n]My
Father is greater than I.

29"And [o]now I have told you before it
comes, that when it does come to pass, you
may believe. 30I will no longer talk much
with you, [p]for the ruler of this world is
coming, and he has [q]nothing in Me. 31But
that the world may know that I love the Father, and [r]as the Father gave Me commandment, so I do. Arise, let us go from here.

The True Vine

15 "I am the true vine, and My Father is
the vinedresser. 2[a]Every branch in Me
that does not bear fruit He takes away;* and
every *branch* that bears fruit He prunes,
that it may bear [b]more fruit. 3[c]You are already clean because of the word which I
have spoken to you. 4[d]Abide in Me, and I
in you. As the branch cannot bear fruit of
itself, unless it abides in the vine, neither
can you, unless you abide in Me.

5"I am the vine, you *are* the branches. He
who abides in Me, and I in him, bears much
[e]fruit; for without Me you can do [f]nothing.
6If anyone does not abide in Me, [g]he is cast
out as a branch and is withered; and they
gather them and throw *them* into the fire,
and they are burned. 7If you abide in Me,
and My words [h]abide in you, [i]you will* ask
what you desire, and it shall be done for
you. 8[j]By this My Father is glorified, that
you bear much fruit; [k]so you will be My
disciples.

Love and Joy Perfected

9"As the Father [l]loved Me, I also have
loved you; abide in My love. 10[m]If you keep
My commandments, you will abide in My
love, just as I have kept My Father's commandments and abide in His love.

11"These things I have spoken to you,
that My joy may remain in you, and [n]*that*
your joy may be full. 12[o]This is My [p]com-
mandment, that you love one another as I

---

* **14:28** NU-Text omits *I said.* * **15:2** Or *lifts up*
* **15:7** NU-Text omits *you will.*

14:23 ***If anyone loves Me, he will keep My word.*** In response to Judas' question (v. 22), Jesus explained that His manifestation to the disciples would be in response to their love and obedience. ***make Our home with him.*** If a believer loves and obeys the Lord, he or she will experience fellowship with God.

14:24 ***He who does not love Me.*** If a person does not love Jesus, he or she will not obey Him. Disobedience is a serious matter, for Jesus' words are the words of God.

14:30 ***has nothing in Me.*** These words indicate Jesus' sinlessness. Jesus' yielding to what was about to happen did not mean that Satan had any power over Him. Jesus would soon voluntarily yield to the death of the cross, in loving obedience to the Father (v. 31).

15:2 ***Every branch in Me.*** The emphasis of "in Me" in this passage is on deep, abiding fellowship. Jesus' purpose was to move His disciples from servants to friends (vv. 13–15). This would involve a process of discipline in regard to His commandments. ***prunes.*** This word means "cleanses." Once the fruit is on the vine, the vinedresser cleanses the fruit of bugs and diseases. The spiritual counterpart is cleansing which is done through the Word (v. 3).

15:6 ***If anyone does not abide.*** Not abiding in Christ has serious consequences: (1) the person *is cast out as a branch,* indicating the loss of fellowship; (2) the person *is withered,* indicating a loss of vitality; (3) the person is *burned,* indicating a loss of reward.

15:8 ***By this.*** Notice the striking parallel between this verse and 13:35. ***fruit.*** The love of 13:35 is pictured here. The text has come full circle in showing how strategic it is for disciples to love each other, as Christ's method of evangelizing the lost. Where there is good fruit, there are also seeds for propagation.

15:11 ***that your joy may be full.*** This phrase is an

14:19 [z] John 16:16, 22 [a] [1 Cor. 15:20] **14:20** [b] John 10:38; 14:11 **14:21** [c] 1 John 2:5 **14:22** [d] Luke 6:16 **14:23** [e] Rev. 3:20; 21:3 **14:24** [f] John 5:19 **14:26** [g] Luke 24:49 [h] John 15:26 [i] 1 Cor. 2:13 [j] John 2:22; 12:16 **14:27** [k] [Phil. 4:7] **14:28** [l] John 14:3, 18 [m] John 16:16 [n] [Phil. 2:6] **14:29** [o] John 13:19 **14:30** [p] [John 12:31] [q] [Heb. 4:15] **14:31** [r] Is. 50:5; John 10:18 **15:2** [a] Matt. 15:13 [b] [Matt. 13:12] **15:3** [c] [John 13:10; 17:17] **15:4** [d] [Col. 1:23] **15:5** [e] Hos. 14:8 [f] 2 Cor. 3:5 **15:6** [g] Matt. 3:10 **15:7** [h] 1 John 2:14 [i] John 14:13; 16:23 **15:8** [j] [Matt. 5:16] [k] John 8:31 **15:9** [l] John 5:20; 17:26 **15:10** [m] John 14:15 **15:11** [n] 1 John 1:4 **15:12** [o] 1 John 3:11 [p] Rom. 12:9

have loved you. [13]ªGreater love has no one than this, than to lay down one's life for his friends. [14]ʳYou are My friends if you do whatever I command you. [15]No longer do I call you servants, for a servant does not know what his master is doing; but I have called you friends, ˢfor all things that I heard from My Father I have made known to you. [16]ᵗYou did not choose Me, but I chose you and ᵘappointed you that you should go and bear fruit, and *that* your fruit should remain, that whatever you ask the Father ᵛin My name He may give you. [17]These things I command you, that you love one another.

The World's Hatred

[18]ʷ"If the world hates you, you know that it hated Me before *it hated* you. [19]ˣIf you were of the world, the world would love its own. Yet ʸbecause you are not of the world, but I chose you out of the world, therefore the world hates you. [20]Remember the word that I said to you, ᶻ'A servant is not greater than his master.' If they persecuted Me, they will also persecute you. ªIf they kept My word, they will keep yours also. [21]But ᵇall these things they will do to you for My name's sake, because they do not know Him who sent Me. [22]ᶜIf I had not come and spoken to them, they would have no sin, ᵈbut now they have no excuse for their sin. [23]ᵉHe who hates Me hates My Father also. [24]If I had not done among them ᶠthe works which no one else did, they would have no sin; but now they have ᵍseen and also hated both Me and My Father. [25]But *this happened* that the word might be fulfilled which is written in their law, ʰ*'They hated Me without a cause.'**

The Coming Rejection

[26]ⁱ"But when the Helper comes, whom I shall send to you from the Father, the Spirit of truth who proceeds from the Father, ʲHe will testify of Me. [27]And ᵏyou also will bear witness, because ˡyou have been with Me from the beginning.

16 "These things I have spoken to you, that you ª should not be made to stumble. [2]ᵇThey will put you out of the synagogues; yes, the time is coming ᶜthat whoever kills you will think that he offers God service. [3]And ᵈthese things they will do to you* because they have not known the Father nor Me. [4]But these things I have told you, that when the* time comes, you may remember that I told you of them.

"And these things I did not say to you at the beginning, because I was with you.

The Work of the Holy Spirit

[5]"But now I ᵉgo away to Him who sent Me, and none of you asks Me, 'Where are You going?' [6]But because I have said these things to you, ᶠsorrow has filled your heart. [7]Nevertheless I tell you the truth. It is to your advantage that I go away; for if I do not go away, the Helper will not come to you; but ᵍif I depart, I will send Him to you. [8]And when He has ʰcome, He will convict the world of sin, and of righteousness, and of judgment: [9]ⁱof sin, because they do not believe in Me; [10]ʲof righteousness, ᵏbecause I go to My Father and you see Me no more; [11]ˡof judgment, because ᵐthe ruler of this world is judged.

---

* **15:25** Psalm 69:4   * **16:3** NU-Text and M-Text omit *to you*.   * **16:4** NU-Text reads *their*.

---

expression peculiar to John (3:29; 16:24; 17:13; 1 John 1:4; 2 John 12). It describes a believer's experience of Christ's love: complete joy.
15:14 *if you do.* Jesus is our model for love (v. 13). Intimacy with Him is the motive for loving as He loves. If believers obey His command to love, they enjoy the intimacy of His friendship. Not that friendship, unlike sonship, is a once-for-all gift, but develops as the result of obeying Jesus' command to love.
15:15 *call you servants.* Until this point, Jesus had called His disciples servants (12:26; 13:13–16). A servant does what he is told and sees what his master does, but does not necessarily know the meaning or purpose of it. ***friends.*** A friend knows what is happening because friends develop deep fellowship by communicating with one another.
15:22–23 *have no sin . . . no excuse for their sin.* The world's hatred of Jesus was a sin against God, for He revealed the Father Himself to them.
15:26–27 *He will testify.* As the disciples spoke, the Holy Spirit would bring inner conviction to unbelievers concerning Christ. This in turn would make the disciples witnesses for Jesus.
16:2 *They will put you out of the synagogues.* The persecution that the disciples would face included excommunication and even execution. Excommunication had economic as well as religious implications because much of the life of an ancient Jew revolved around the synagogue.

16:7 *It is to your advantage.* The disciples must have thought, "How can it be advantageous for us to be alone? The Romans hate us because they see us as disturbers of the peace. The Jewish leaders hate us because they see us as blasphemers." Jesus explained the benefits of His departure. When Jesus left, the believers would have (1) the provision of the Holy Spirit (vv. 7–15); (2) the potential of full joy (vv. 16–24); (3) the possibility of fuller knowledge (vv. 25–28); and (4) the privilege of peace (vv. 29–33).
16:8 *convict.* The Holy Spirit would demonstrate the truth of Christ beyond the fear of contradiction. The Holy Spirit convicts unbelievers through believers who witness about Christ (15:26–27). Believers are the mouthpiece for God's voice.
16:11 *of judgment.* Satan, the ruler of the world,

15:13 ᵍ 1 John 3:16   **15:14** ʳ [Matt. 12:50; 28:20]
15:15 ˢ Gen. 18:17   **15:16** ᵗ John 6:70; 13:18; 15:19
ᵘ [Col. 1:6] ᵛ John 14:13; 16:23, 24   **15:18** ʷ 1 John 3:13
15:19 ˣ 1 John 4:5 ʸ John 17:14   **15:20** ᶻ John 13:16
ª Ezek. 3:7   **15:21** ᵇ Matt. 10:22; 24:9   **15:22** ᶜ John 9:41;
15:24 ᵈ [James 4:17]   **15:23** ᵉ 1 John 2:23   **15:24** ᶠ John
3:2 ᵍ John 14:9   **15:25** ʰ Ps. 35:19; 69:4; 109:3–5
15:26 ⁱ Luke 24:49 ʲ 1 John 5:6   **15:27** ᵏ Luke 24:48
ˡ Luke 1:2   **16:1** ª Matt. 11:6   **16:2** ᵇ John 9:22 ᶜ Acts
8:1   **16:3** ᵈ John 8:19; 15:21   **16:5** ᵉ John 7:33; 13:33;
14:28; 17:11   **16:6** ᶠ [John 16:20, 22]   **16:7** ᵍ Acts 2:33
16:8 ʰ Acts 1:8; 2:1–4, 37   **16:9** ⁱ Acts 2:22   **16:10** ʲ Acts
2:32 ᵏ John 5:32   **16:11** ˡ Acts 26:18 ᵐ [Luke 10:18]

¹²"I still have many things to say to you, ⁿbut you cannot bear *them* now. ¹³However, when He, ᵒthe Spirit of truth, has come, ᵖHe will guide you into all truth; for He will not speak on His own *authority*, but whatever He hears He will speak; and He will tell you things to come. ¹⁴ᵃHe will glorify Me, for He will take of what is Mine and declare *it* to you. ¹⁵ᵣAll things that the Father has are Mine. Therefore I said that He will take of Mine and declare *it* to you.*

Sorrow Will Turn to Joy

¹⁶"A ˢlittle while, and you will not see Me; and again a little while, and you will see Me, ᵗbecause I go to the Father."

¹⁷Then *some* of His disciples said among themselves, "What is this that He says to us, 'A little while, and you will not see Me; and again a little while, and you will see Me'; and, 'because I go to the Father'?" ¹⁸They said therefore, "What is this that He says, 'A little while'? We do not know what He is saying."

¹⁹Now Jesus knew that they desired to ask Him, and He said to them, "Are you inquiring among yourselves about what I said, 'A little while, and you will not see Me; and again a little while, and you will see Me'? ²⁰Most assuredly, I say to you that you will weep and ᵘlament, but the world will rejoice; and you will be sorrowful, but your sorrow will be turned into ᵛjoy. ²¹ʷA woman, when she is in labor, has sorrow because her hour has come; but as soon as she has given birth to the child, she no longer remembers the anguish, for joy that a human being has been born into the world. ²²Therefore you now have sorrow; but I will see you again and ˣyour heart will rejoice, and your joy no one will take from you.

²³"And in that day you will ask Me nothing. ʸMost assuredly, I say to you, whatever you ask the Father in My name He will give you. ²⁴Until now you have asked nothing in My name. Ask, and you will receive, ᶻthat your joy may be ᵃfull.

Jesus Christ Has Overcome the World

²⁵"These things I have spoken to you in figurative language; but the time is coming when I will no longer speak to you in figurative language, but I will tell you ᵇplainly about the Father. ²⁶In that day you will ask in My name, and I do not say to you that I shall pray the Father for you; ²⁷ᶜfor the Father Himself loves you, because you have loved Me, and ᵈhave believed that I came forth from God. ²⁸ᵉI came forth from the Father and have come into the world. Again, I leave the world and go to the Father."

²⁹His disciples said to Him, "See, now You are speaking plainly, and using no figure of speech! ³⁰Now we are sure that ᶠYou know all things, and have no need that anyone should question You. By this ᵍwe believe that You came forth from God."

³¹Jesus answered them, "Do you now believe? ³²ʰIndeed the hour is coming, yes, has now come, that you will be scattered, ⁱeach to his own, and will leave Me alone. And ʲyet I am not alone, because the Father

* **16:15** NU-Text and M-Text read *He takes of Mine and will declare it to you.*

---

rules in the hearts of unregenerate people and blinds their minds (1 Cor. 2:6–8). Satan was judged at the cross, and the Holy Spirit would convince people of the judgment to come. Satan has been judged, so all who side with him will be judged with them.

16:12 you. Here, this refers to the apostles. Technically, what the Lord says about the ministry of the Holy Spirit in verses 12–15 applies primarily to the apostles. That ministry was threefold: (1) He would guide them into all truth (v. 13); (2) He would tell them of the future (v. 13); and (3) He would help them glorify Christ (vv. 14–15). Jesus' words were fulfilled in the apostles' preaching and writing.

16:13 Spirit of truth. The phrase means that the Holy Spirit is the source of truth (14:17; 15:26). **guide.** The Holy Spirit would not compel or carry the disciples into truth. He would lead; their job was to follow.

16:14 glorify Me. The Holy Spirit glorifies Christ by declaring Him or making Him known. It is the work of the Holy Spirit to throw light on Jesus Christ, who is the image of the invisible God. Christ is to be on center stage; that is the desire of both the Father and the Spirit. The apostles received truth from the Holy Spirit, truth about things to come, and truth about Christ. Then, under the guidance of the Holy Spirit, they wrote those truths in documents known today as the New Testament.

16:18 A little while. The biggest question weighing on the disciples' minds was the time factor. They simply did not understand the strange intervals marked by their separation from Jesus.

16:21 A woman, when she is in labor. Jesus used the example of a pregnant woman whose sorrow is transformed into joy in the birth of a child.

16:26 I shall pray the Father for you. Because Jesus provides forgiveness of sins through His death and now intercedes for all believers at the right hand of the Father (Heb. 7:25), we have direct access to the Father. We do not need the intercession of a priest, because Jesus acts as our High Priest before God.

16:31 Do you now believe? We continue in the Christian life the same way we begin, by believing in Jesus. The more we learn of Christ, the more we have to believe. The more we place our trust in Jesus, the more we receive. The more we receive, the more we can accomplish for His glory.

16:12 ⁿ Mark 4:33   **16:13** ᵒ [John 14:17]   ᵖ John 14:26
16:14 ᵍ John 15:26   **16:15** ʳ Matt. 11:27   **16:16** ˢ John 7:33; 12:35; 13:33; 14:19; 19:40–42; 20:19   ᵗ John 13:3   **16:20** ᵘ Mark 16:10   ᵛ Luke 24:32, 41   **16:21** ʷ Is. 13:8; 26:17; 42:14   **16:22** ˣ 1 Pet. 1:8   **16:23** ʸ Matt. 7:7   **16:24** ᶻ John 17:13   ᵃ John 15:11   **16:25** ᵇ John 7:13   **16:27** ᶜ [John 14:21, 23]   ᵈ John 3:13   **16:28** ᵉ John 13:1, 3; 16:5, 10, 17   **16:30** ᶠ John 21:17   ᵍ John 17:8
16:32 ʰ Matt. 26:31, 56   ⁱ John 20:10   ʲ John 8:29

is with Me. **33**These things I have spoken to you, that *k*in Me you may have peace. *l*In the world you will* have tribulation; but be of good cheer, *m*I have overcome the world."

Jesus Prays for Himself

17 Jesus spoke these words, lifted up His eyes to heaven, and said: "Father, *a*the hour has come. Glorify Your Son, that Your Son also may glorify You, **2***b*as You have given Him authority over all flesh, that He should* give eternal life to as many *c*as You have given Him. **3**And *d*this is eternal life, that they may know You, *e*the only true God, and Jesus Christ *f*whom You have sent. **4***g*I have glorified You on the earth. *h*I have finished the work *i*which You have given Me to do. **5**And now, O Father, glorify Me together with Yourself, with the glory *j*which I had with You before the world was.

Jesus Prays for His Disciples

6*k*"I have manifested Your name to the men *l*whom You have given Me out of the world. *m*They were Yours, You gave them to Me, and they have kept Your word. **7**Now they have known that all things which You have given Me are from You. **8**For I have given to them the words *n*which You have given Me; and they have received *them*, *o*and have known surely that I came forth from You; and they have believed that *p*You sent Me.

9"I pray for them. *q*I do not pray for the world but for those whom You have given Me, for they are Yours. **10**And all Mine are Yours, and *r*Yours are Mine, and I am glorified in them. **11***s*Now I am no longer in the world, but these are in the world, and I come to You. Holy Father, *t*keep through

Your name those whom You have given Me,* that they may be one *u*as We *are*. **12**While I was with them in the world,* *v*I kept them in Your name. Those whom You gave Me I have kept;* and *w*none of them is lost *x*except the son of perdition, *y*that the Scripture might be fulfilled. **13**But now I come to You, and these things I speak in the world, that they may have My joy fulfilled in themselves. **14**I have given them Your word; *z*and the world has hated them because they are not of the world, *a*just as I am not of the world. **15**I do not pray that You should take them out of the world, but *b*that You should keep them from the evil one. **16**They are not of the world, just as I am not of the world. **17***c*Sanctify them by Your truth. *d*Your word is truth. **18***e*As You sent Me into the world, I also have sent them into the world. **19**And *f*for their sakes I sanctify Myself, that they also may be sanctified by the truth.

Jesus Prays for All Believers

20"I do not pray for these alone, but also for those who will* believe in Me through their word; **21***g*that they all may be one, as *h*You, Father, *are* in Me, and I in You; that they also may be one in Us, that the world may believe that You sent Me. **22**And the *i*glory which You gave Me I have given them, *i*that they may be one just as We are

---

* **16:33** NU-Text and M-Text omit *will*.
* **17:2** M-Text reads *shall*.   * **17:11** NU-Text and M-Text read *keep them through Your name which You have given Me*.   * **17:12** NU-Text omits *in the world*. • NU-Text reads *in Your name which You gave Me. And I guarded them;* (or *it;*).
* **17:20** NU-Text and M-Text omit *will*.

16:33 *tribulation.* This is literally "pressure" and figuratively means "affliction" or "distress."

17:1–2 *the hour has come.* Throughout the Gospel of John, Jesus referred to the cross as His "hour" (2:4; 7:30; 8:20; 12:23; 13:1). The time for Him to die had arrived. ***Glorify Your Son.*** Jesus was asking that His mission to the world would be made known through the cross. The reasons for this request are twofold: (1) that *Your Son also may glorify You.* In this request, Jesus reveals the Father to the world, that is, His love and justice, and (2) that, through Jesus' death on the cross, God would provide forgiveness of sins and *give eternal life* to all those who believe in His Son.

17:3 *that they may know You.* Eternal life consists of a growing knowledge of the only true God as opposed to false gods.

17:11 *keep through Your name.* This verse reveals Jesus' sensitivity to the plight of His disciples brought on by His departure. He was going to the Father, but they would be left behind. Jesus asked the Father to keep them true to the revelation of God that Jesus had given to them while He was with them. The disciples would have a new union with the Father and Son through the future indwelling of the Holy Spirit.

17:14–16 *of the world.* This verse has profound implications for discipleship. Our desire should not be to isolate ourselves from the world, but to use Christ's Word and the Holy Spirit's power to serve Him

while our life lasts. Yet, at the same time, we should not become like the world, succumbing to the evil influences of the world.

17:17 *Sanctify them.* This means "to set apart." There are two ways to understand this statement: (1) as separate for holiness, or (2) as set apart for service. According to the first view, Jesus was praying not only that the disciples should be kept from evil, but that they should advance in holiness.

17:21 *that they all may be one.* The present tense of the verb "to be" indicates that Jesus was praying for the unity that takes place through the sanctification of believers. This is what Jesus was commanding in 13:34–35.

17:22 *the glory.* This is the revelation of Jesus Christ

16:33 *k* [Eph. 2:14] *l* 2 Tim. 3:12 *m* Rom. 8:37   **17:1** *a* John 12:23   **17:2** *b* John 3:35 *c* John 6:37, 39; 17:6, 9, 24   **17:3** *d* Jer. 9:23, 24 *e* 1 Cor. 8:4 *f* John 3:34   **17:4** *g* John 13:31 *h* John 4:34; 19:30 *i* John 14:31   **17:5** *j* Phil. 2:6   **17:6** *k* Ps. 22:22 *l* John 6:37 *m* Ezek. 18:4   **17:8** *n* John 8:28 *o* John 8:42; 16:27, 30 *p* Deut. 18:15, 18   **17:9** *q* [1 John 5:19]   **17:10** *r* John 16:15   **17:11** *s* John 13:1 *t* [1 Pet. 1:5] *u* John 10:30   **17:12** *v* Heb. 2:13   *w* 1 John 2:19 *x* John 6:70 *y* Ps. 41:9; 109:8   **17:14** *z* John 15:19 *a* John 8:23   **17:15** *b* 1 John 5:18   **17:17** *c* [Eph. 5:26] *d* Ps. 119:9, 142, 151   **17:18** *e* John 4:38; 20:21   **17:19** *f* [Heb. 10:10]   **17:21** *g* [Gal. 3:28] *h* John 10:38; 17:11, 23   **17:22** *i* 1 John 1:3 *j* [2 Cor. 3:18]

one: 23I in them, and You in Me; kthat they may be made perfect in one, and that the world may know that You have sent Me, and have loved them as You have loved Me.

24l"Father, I desire that they also whom You gave Me may be with Me where I am, that they may behold My glory which You have given Me; mfor You loved Me before the foundation of the world. 25O righteous Father! nThe world has not known You, but oI have known You; and pthese have known that You sent Me. 26qAnd I have declared to them Your name, and will declare it, that the love rwith which You loved Me may be in them, and I in them."

Betrayal and Arrest in Gethsemane

18 When Jesus had spoken these words, aHe went out with His disciples over bthe Brook Kidron, where there was a garden, which He and His disciples entered. 2And Judas, who betrayed Him, also knew the place; cfor Jesus often met there with His disciples. 3dThen Judas, having received a detachment of troops, and officers from the chief priests and Pharisees, came there with lanterns, torches, and weapons. 4Jesus therefore, eknowing all things that would come upon Him, went forward and said to them, "Whom are you seeking?"

5They answered Him, f"Jesus of Nazareth."

Jesus said to them, "I am He." And Judas, who gbetrayed Him, also stood with them. 6Now when He said to them, "I am He," they drew back and fell to the ground.

7Then He asked them again, "Whom are you seeking?"

And they said, "Jesus of Nazareth."

8Jesus answered, "I have told you that I am He. Therefore, if you seek Me, let these go their way," 9that the saying might be fulfilled which He spoke, h"Of those whom You gave Me I have lost none."

10iThen Simon Peter, having a sword, drew it and struck the high priest's servant, and cut off his right ear. The servant's name was Malchus.

11So Jesus said to Peter, "Put your sword into the sheath. Shall I not drink jthe cup which My Father has given Me?"

Before the High Priest

12Then the detachment of troops and the captain and the officers of the Jews arrested Jesus and bound Him. 13And kthey led Him away to lAnnas first, for he was the father-in-law of mCaiaphas who was high priest that year. 14nNow it was Caiaphas who advised the Jews that it was expedient that one man should die for the people.

Peter Denies Jesus

15oAnd Simon Peter followed Jesus, and so did panother* disciple. Now that disciple was known to the high priest, and went with Jesus into the courtyard of the high priest. 16qBut Peter stood at the door outside. Then the other disciple, who was known to the high priest, went out and spoke to her who kept the door, and brought Peter in. 17Then the servant girl who kept the door said to Peter, "You are not also one of this Man's disciples, are you?"

He said, "I am rnot."

18Now the servants and officers who had made a fire of coals stood there, for it was cold, and they warmed themselves. And Peter stood with them and warmed himself.

Jesus Questioned by the High Priest

19The high priest then asked Jesus about His disciples and His doctrine. 20Jesus answered him, s"I spoke openly to the world. I always taught tin synagogues and uin the temple, where the Jews always meet,* and in secret I have said nothing. 21Why do you ask Me? Ask vthose who have heard Me what I said to them. Indeed they know what I said."

* **18:15** M-Text reads the other.   * **18:20** NU-Text reads where all the Jews meet.

through His disciples and is the means to unity. Such unity begins with belief and correct thinking about Jesus and God the Father, that is, with doctrine. But correct belief must bear fruit—a life that demonstrates God's love and produces unity between all believers.

17:23 I in them, and You in me. The mutual indwelling of the Father in the Son and the Son in the church is also the means to unity, the ultimate expression of God's love (13:35; Rom. 8:17).

18:1 Brook Kidron. A brook was located in a ravine that was between Jerusalem and the Mount of Olives.

18:3 officers. These were members of the temple police under the command of the Jewish council, the Sanhedrin.

18:13 Annas. Annas was high priest from A.D. 7 to 14. He was deposed by the Romans. Then Caiaphas, Annas' son-in-law, was appointed to the position and served from A.D. 18 to 37. However, according

to Jewish law the high priest was a lifetime position, so the Jews still considered Annas to be high priest. Therefore, they took Jesus to Annas first.

18:15 another disciple. Although this other disciple is never identified, the consensus is that he was John, the author of this Gospel.

18:21 Ask those who have heard. According to the law, the witnesses for the defense had to be called

17:23 k [Col. 3:14]   **17:24** l [1 Thess. 4:17]   m John 17:5   **17:25** n John 15:21   o John 7:29; 8:55; 10:15   p John 3:17; 17:3, 8, 18, 21, 23   **17:26** q John 17:6   r John 15:9   **18:1** a Mark 14:26, 32   b 2 Sam. 15:23   **18:2** c Luke 21:37; 22:39   **18:3** d Luke 22:47–53   **18:4** e John 6:64; 13:1, 3; 19:28   **18:5** f Matt. 21:11   g Ps. 41:9   **18:9** h [John 6:39; 17:12]   **18:10** i Matt. 26:51   **18:11** j Matt. 20:22; 26:39   **18:13** k Matt. 26:57   l Luke 3:2   m Matt. 26:3   **18:14** n John 11:50   **18:15** o Mark 14:54   p John 20:2–5   **18:16** q Matt. 26:69   **18:17** r Matt. 26:34   **18:20** s Luke 4:15   t John 6:59   u Mark 14:49   **18:21** v Mark 12:37

22And when He had said these things, one of the officers who stood by wstruck Jesus with the palm of his hand, saying, "Do You answer the high priest like that?"

23Jesus answered him, "If I have spoken evil, bear witness of the evil; but if well, why do you strike Me?"

24xThen Annas sent Him bound to yCaiaphas the high priest.

Peter Denies Twice More

25Now Simon Peter stood and warmed himself. zTherefore they said to him, "You are not also one of His disciples, are you?"

He denied it and said, "I am not!"

26One of the servants of the high priest, a relative of him whose ear Peter cut off, said, "Did I not see you in the garden with Him?"

27Peter then denied again; and aimmediately a rooster crowed.

In Pilate's Court

28bThen they led Jesus from Caiaphas to the Praetorium, and it was early morning. cBut they themselves did not go into the Praetorium, lest they should be defiled, but that they might eat the Passover. 29dPilate then went out to them and said, "What accusation do you bring against this Man?"

30They answered and said to him, "If He were not an evildoer, we would not have delivered Him up to you."

31Then Pilate said to them, "You take Him and judge Him according to your law."

Therefore the Jews said to him, "It is not lawful for us to put anyone to death," 32ethat the saying of Jesus might be fulfilled which He spoke, fsignifying by what death He would die.

33gThen Pilate entered the Praetorium again, called Jesus, and said to Him, "Are You the King of the Jews?"

34Jesus answered him, "Are you speaking for yourself about this, or did others tell you this concerning Me?"

35Pilate answered, "Am I a Jew? Your own nation and the chief priests have delivered You to me. What have You done?"

36hJesus answered, i"My kingdom is not of this world. If My kingdom were of this world, My servants would fight, so that I should not be delivered to the Jews; but now My kingdom is not from here."

37Pilate therefore said to Him, "Are You a king then?"

Jesus answered, "You say rightly that I am a king. For this cause I was born, and for this cause I have come into the world, jthat I should bear kwitness to the truth. Everyone who lis of the truth mhears My voice."

38Pilate said to Him, "What is truth?" And when he had said this, he went out again to the Jews, and said to them, n"I find no fault in Him at all.

Taking the Place of Barabbas

39o"But you have a custom that I should release someone to you at the Passover. Do you therefore want me to release to you the King of the Jews?"

40pThen they all cried again, saying, "Not this Man, but Barabbas!" qNow Barabbas was a robber.

The Soldiers Mock Jesus

19 So then aPilate took Jesus and scourged Him. 2And the soldiers

---

first. Jesus should not have been questioned until witnesses had testified.

18:27 Peter then denied again. For the third time, Peter denied the Lord, as Jesus had said he would (13:38). In the upper room, Peter had boasted that he would remain true to the Lord to the end (13:37; Matt. 26:33,35). In the garden he surrendered to the desires of his body by sleeping three times when the Lord had commanded the disciples to stay up in prayer (Mark 14:34–42). Now he submitted to the pressure of the world and denied the Lord three times.

18:28 the Praetorium. This was probably the Roman governor's official residence, the Fortress Antonia near the temple.

18:29–30 What accusation. Pilate was not ignorant of the accusation. He was merely requesting that it be formally stated.

18:31 It is not lawful for us to put anyone to death. The Romans did not allow the Jews to impose capital punishment. These Jewish leaders had no interest in a just trial; they simply wanted permission from Rome to have Jesus executed.

18:34 Are you speaking for yourself. In reply to Pilate, Jesus gave no violent protest of innocence, nor was He sullenly defiant. Jesus politely but directly asked whether Pilate was asking on his own initiative or whether the charge was secondhand. If Pilate's question originated with him, he was using king in

the Roman sense of political ruler. If not, then king was being used in the Jewish sense of the messianic king.

18:38 What is truth? This question has been interpreted as (1) a cynical denial of the possibility of knowing truth; (2) a contemptuous jest at anything so impractical as abstract truth; and (3) a desire to know what no one had been able to tell him. **no fault.** This is a legal term meaning that there were no grounds for a criminal charge.

18:39 you have a custom. It appears that some in the crowd suggested that a prisoner should be released in honor of the Passover (Mark 15:8,11). Pilate jumped at the possible compromise. By promising to release Jesus on account of the custom rather than by proclaiming Him innocent, Pilate would avoid insulting the Jewish leaders, who had already pronounced Him guilty.

18:22 w Jer. 20:2 **18:24** x Matt. 26:57 y John 11:49 **18:25** z Luke 22:58–62 **18:27** a John 13:38 **18:28** b Mark 15:1 c Acts 10:28; 11:3 **18:29** d Matt. 27:11–14 **18:32** e Matt. 20:17–19; 26:2 f John 3:14; 8:28; 12:32, 33 **18:33** g Matt. 27:11 **18:36** h 1 Tim. 6:13 i [Dan. 2:44; 7:14] **18:37** j [Matt. 5:17; 20:28] k Is. 55:4 l [John 14:6] m John 8:47; 10:27 **18:38** n John 19:4, 6 **18:39** o Luke 23:17–25 **18:40** p Acts 3:14 q Luke 23:19 **19:1** a Matt. 20:19; 27:26

twisted a crown of thorns and put *it* on His head, and they put on Him a purple robe. ³Then they said,* "Hail, King of the Jews!" And they ᵇstruck Him with their hands.

⁴Pilate then went out again, and said to them, "Behold, I am bringing Him out to you, ᶜthat you may know that I find no fault in Him."

Pilate's Decision

⁵Then Jesus came out, wearing the crown of thorns and the purple robe. And *Pilate* said to them, "Behold the Man!"

⁶ᵈTherefore, when the chief priests and officers saw Him, they cried out, saying, "Crucify *Him*, crucify *Him!*" Pilate said to them, "You take Him and crucify *Him*, for I find no fault in Him."

⁷The Jews answered him, ᵉ"We have a law, and according to our* law He ought to die, because ᶠHe made Himself the Son of God."

⁸Therefore, when Pilate heard that saying, he was the more afraid, ⁹and went again into the Praetorium, and said to Jesus, "Where are You from?" ᵍBut Jesus gave him no answer.

¹⁰Then Pilate said to Him, "Are You not speaking to me? Do You not know that I have power to crucify You, and power to release You?"

¹¹Jesus answered, ʰ"You could have no power at all against Me unless it had been given you from above. Therefore ⁱthe one who delivered Me to you has the greater sin."

¹²From then on Pilate sought to release Him, but the Jews cried out, saying, "If you let this Man go, you are not Caesar's friend. ʲWhoever makes himself a king speaks against Caesar."

¹³ᵏWhen Pilate therefore heard that saying, he brought Jesus out and sat down in the judgment seat in a place that is called *The* Pavement, but in Hebrew, Gabbatha. ¹⁴Now ˡit was the Preparation Day of the

Passover, and about the sixth hour. And he said to the Jews, "Behold your King!"

¹⁵But they cried out, "Away with *Him*, away with *Him!* Crucify Him!"

Pilate said to them, "Shall I crucify your King?"

The chief priests answered, ᵐ"We have no king but Caesar!"

¹⁶ⁿThen he delivered Him to them to be crucified. Then they took Jesus and led *Him* away.*

The King on a Cross

¹⁷ᵒAnd He, bearing His cross, ᵖwent out to a place called *the Place* of a Skull, which is called in Hebrew, Golgotha, ¹⁸where they crucified Him, and �q two others with Him, one on either side, and Jesus in the center. ¹⁹ʳNow Pilate wrote a title and put *it* on the cross. And the writing was:

JESUS OF NAZARETH, THE KING
OF THE JEWS.

²⁰Then many of the Jews read this title, for the place where Jesus was crucified was near the city; and it was written in Hebrew, Greek, *and* Latin. ²¹Therefore the chief priests of the Jews said to Pilate, "Do not write, 'The King of the Jews,' but, 'He said, "I am the King of the Jews."'"

²²Pilate answered, "What I have written, I have written."

²³ˢThen the soldiers, when they had crucified Jesus, took His garments and made four parts, to each soldier a part, and also the tunic. Now the tunic was without seam, woven from the top in one piece. ²⁴They said therefore among themselves, "Let us not tear it, but cast lots for it, whose it shall be," that the Scripture might be fulfilled which says:

---

* **19:3** NU-Text reads *And they came up to Him and said.* * **19:7** NU-Text reads *the law.*
* **19:16** NU-Text omits *and led Him away.*

19:4 I am bringing Him out to you. Perhaps Pilate was appealing to the people's compassion so that he could release Jesus.

19:7 We have a law. The Jewish leaders were telling Pilate, "If you are appealing to us, we say that, according to our law, He must die." As governor, Pilate was bound by Roman custom to respect Jewish law. **He made Himself the Son of God.** The Jewish leaders were accusing Jesus of violating the laws against blasphemy (Lev. 24:16).

19:9 Jesus gave him no answer. Three times Pilate had publicly pronounced Jesus innocent (18:38; 19:4,6).

19:12 you are not Caesar's friend. The Jews shifted their focus from the religious charge (v. 7) to the political charge (18:33), which they backed up with an appeal to Caesar's own political interest. This new plea forced Pilate to choose between yielding to an indefinite sense of right or escaping the danger of an accusation from Rome.

19:19 wrote a title. It was a Roman custom to write

the name of the condemned person and his crime on a plaque to be placed above his head at execution.

19:20 written in Hebrew, Greek, and Latin. Multilingual inscriptions were common. The title was written in the local, common, and official languages of the day. Everyone could read the message in his or her own language.

19:23 the soldiers. According to Roman law, the garments of a condemned criminal belonged to the executioners. Jesus had two items of clothing. The cloak was a large, loose garment. The tunic was a close-fitting garment that went from the neck to the knees.

19:24 cast lots. The outer garment could be

19:3 ᵇ Is. 50:6   **19:4** ᶜ John 18:33, 38   **19:6** ᵈ Acts 3:13   **19:7** ᵉ Lev. 24:16   ᶠ Matt. 26:63–66   **19:9** ᵍ Is. 53:7   **19:11** ʰ [Luke 22:53]   ⁱ Rom. 13:1   **19:12** ʲ Luke 23:2   **19:13** ᵏ 1 Sam. 15:24   **19:14** ˡ Matt. 27:62   **19:15** ᵐ [Gen. 49:10]   **19:16** ⁿ Luke 23:24   **19:17** ᵒ Mark 15:21, 22   ᵖ Num. 15:36   **19:18** q Is. 53:12   **19:19** ʳ Matt. 27:37   **19:23** ˢ Luke 23:34

t"They divided My garments among
    them,
And for My clothing they cast lots."*

Therefore the soldiers did these things.

Behold Your Mother

25uNow there stood by the cross of Jesus
His mother, and His mother's sister, Mary
the wife of vClopas, and Mary Magdalene.
26When Jesus therefore saw His mother,
and wthe disciple whom He loved standing
by, He said to His mother, x"Woman, behold
your son!" 27Then He said to the disciple,
"Behold your mother!" And from that hour
that disciple took her yto his own home.

It Is Finished

28After this, Jesus, knowing* that all
things were now accomplished, zthat the
Scripture might be fulfilled, said, "I thirst!"
29Now a vessel full of sour wine was sitting
there; and athey filled a sponge with sour
wine, put it on hyssop, and put it to His
mouth. 30So when Jesus had received the
sour wine, He said, b"It is finished!" And
bowing His head, He gave up His spirit.

Jesus' Side Is Pierced

31cTherefore, because it was the Preparation Day, dthat the bodies should not
remain on the cross on the Sabbath (for
that Sabbath was a ehigh day), the Jews
asked Pilate that their legs might be broken, and that they might be taken away.
32Then the soldiers came and broke the
legs of the first and of the other who was
crucified with Him. 33But when they came
to Jesus and saw that He was already dead,
fthey did not break His legs. 34But one of
the soldiers pierced His side with a spear,
and immediately gblood and water came
out. 35And he who has seen has testified,
and his testimony is htrue; and he knows
that he is telling the truth, so that you may

ibelieve. 36For these things were done that
the Scripture should be fulfilled, i"Not one
of His bones shall be broken."* 37And again
another Scripture says, k"They shall look
on Him whom they pierced."*

Jesus Buried in Joseph's Tomb

38lAfter this, Joseph of Arimathea, being
a disciple of Jesus, but secretly, mfor fear of
the Jews, asked Pilate that he might take
away the body of Jesus; and Pilate gave
him permission. So he came and took the
body of Jesus. 39And nNicodemus, who at
first came to Jesus by night, also came,
bringing a mixture of omyrrh and aloes,
about a hundred pounds. 40Then they took
the body of Jesus, and pbound it in strips of
linen with the spices, as the custom of the
Jews is to bury. 41Now in the place where
He was crucified there was a garden, and
in the garden a new tomb in which no one
had yet been laid. 42So qthere they laid
Jesus, rbecause of the Jews' Preparation
Day, for the tomb was nearby.

The Empty Tomb

20 Now the afirst day of the week Mary
Magdalene went to the tomb early,
while it was still dark, and saw that the
bstone had been taken away from the tomb.
2Then she ran and came to Simon Peter,
and to the cother disciple, dwhom Jesus
loved, and said to them, "They have taken
away the Lord out of the tomb, and we do
not know where they have laid Him."

3ePeter therefore went out, and the other
disciple, and were going to the tomb. 4So
they both ran together, and the other disciple outran Peter and came to the tomb
first. 5And he, stooping down and looking
in, saw fthe linen cloths lying there; yet he

* **19:24** Psalm 22:18　　* **19:28** M-Text reads seeing.
* **19:36** Exodus 12:46; Numbers 9:12; Psalm 34:20
* **19:37** Zechariah 12:10

---

conveniently divided, but the inner garment could
not. Thus, the soldiers divided the outer one and cast
lots for the inner one. Unknowingly, the soldiers fulfilled David's prophecy in Psalm 22:18.
19:30 It is finished. Having fulfilled every command of
the Father and every prophecy of Scripture, Jesus voluntarily died. This was not a cry of exhaustion, but of
completion. Jesus had done what He had agreed to do.
19:31 the Preparation Day. This day was Friday, the
day before the Sabbath. Bodies should not remain
on the cross. It is ironic that in the midst of a deliberate judicial murder the Jews were scrupulous about
keeping the ceremonial law. According to Jewish law
(Deut. 21:23), it was necessary to remove the bodies
of executed criminals before sunset. To avoid breaking the law, the Jews requested that the legs of the
condemned be broken so that the men would die
quickly and could be removed from their crosses.
With his legs broken, a victim could no longer lift his
body in order to breathe and would soon suffocate.
19:34 one of the soldiers pierced His side. After the
soldier did this, blood and water came out, indicating

that Jesus was already dead. Only blood would have
flowed from a living body.
19:35 he who has seen. John's words can be trusted
because he is giving an eyewitness account, so that
his readers will believe that Jesus is the Savior.
20:2 They have taken away the Lord. Mary Magdalene jumped to the wrong conclusion.
20:5 the linen cloths lying. No one who came to

19:24 tPs. 22:18　　**19:25** uMark 15:40 vLuke
24:18　　**19:26** wJohn 13:23; 20:2; 21:7, 20, 24 xJohn 2:4
19:27 yJohn 1:11; 16:32　　**19:28** zPs. 22:15　　**19:29** aPs.
69:21; Matt. 27:48, 50　　**19:30** bJohn 17:4　　**19:31** cMark
15:42 dDeut. 21:23 eEx. 12:16　　**19:33** f[Ex. 12:46; Num.
9:12]; Ps. 34:20　　**19:34** g[1 John 5:6, 8]　　**19:35** hJohn
21:24 i[John 20:31]　　**19:36** j[Ex. 12:46; Num.
9:12]; Ps. 34:20　　**19:37** kPs. 22:16, 17; Zech. 12:10;
13:6　　**19:38** lLuke 23:50–56 mJohn 7:13; 9:22; 12:42]
19:39 nJohn 3:1, 2; 7:50 oMatt. 2:11　　**19:40** pJohn 20:5, 7
19:42 qIs. 53:9 rJohn 19:14, 31　　**20:1** aMatt. 28:1–8
bMatt. 27:60, 66; 28:2　　**20:2** cJohn 21:23, 24 dJohn 13:23;
19:26; 21:7, 20, 24　　**20:3** eLuke 24:12　　**20:5** fJohn 19:40

did not go in. **6**Then Simon Peter came, following him, and went into the tomb; and he saw the linen cloths lying *there,* **7**and **g**the handkerchief that had been around His head, not lying with the linen cloths, but folded together in a place by itself. **8**Then the **h**other disciple, who came to the tomb first, went in also; and he saw and believed. **9**For as yet they did not know the **i**Scripture, that He must rise again from the dead. **10**Then the disciples went away again to their own homes.

Mary Magdalene Sees the Risen Lord

11j But Mary stood outside by the tomb weeping, and as she wept she stooped down *and looked* into the tomb. **12**And she saw two angels in white sitting, one at the head and the other at the feet, where the body of Jesus had lain. **13**Then they said to her, "Woman, why are you weeping?"

She said to them, "Because they have taken away my Lord, and I do not know where they have laid Him."

14k Now when she had said this, she turned around and saw Jesus standing *there,* and **l**did not know that it was Jesus. **15**Jesus said to her, "Woman, why are you weeping? Whom are you seeking?"

She, supposing Him to be the gardener, said to Him, "Sir, if You have carried Him away, tell me where You have laid Him, and I will take Him away."

16Jesus said to her, **m**"Mary!"

She turned and said to Him,* "Rabboni!" (which is to say, Teacher).

17Jesus said to her, "Do not cling to Me, for I have not yet **n**ascended to My Father; but go to **o**My brethren and say to them, **p**'I am ascending to My Father and your Father, and *to* **q**My God and your God.'"

18r Mary Magdalene came and told the disciples that she had seen the Lord,* and *that* He had spoken these things to her.

The Apostles Commissioned

19s Then, the same day at evening, being the first *day* of the week, when the doors

were shut where the disciples were assembled,* for **t**fear of the Jews, Jesus came and stood in the midst, and said to them, **u**"Peace *be* with you." **20**When He had said this, He **v**showed them *His* hands and His side. **w**Then the disciples were glad when they saw the Lord.

21So Jesus said to them again, "Peace to you! **x**As the Father has sent Me, I also send you." **22**And when He had said this, He breathed on *them,* and said to them, "Receive the Holy Spirit. **23y**If you forgive the sins of any, they are forgiven them; if you retain the *sins* of any, they are retained."

Seeing and Believing

24Now Thomas, **z**called the Twin, one of the twelve, was not with them when Jesus came. **25**The other disciples therefore said to him, "We have seen the Lord."

So he said to them, "Unless I see in His hands the print of the nails, and put my finger into the print of the nails, and put my hand into His side, I will not believe."

26And after eight days His disciples were again inside, and Thomas with them. Jesus came, the doors being shut, and stood in the midst, and said, "Peace to you!" **27**Then He said to Thomas, "Reach your finger here, and look at My hands; and **a**reach your hand *here,* and put *it* into My side. Do not be **b**unbelieving, but believing."

28And Thomas answered and said to Him, "My Lord and my God!"

29Jesus said to him, "Thomas,* because you have seen Me, you have believed. **c**Blessed *are* those who have not seen and yet have believed."

That You May Believe

30And **d**truly Jesus did many other signs in the presence of His disciples, which are

---

* **20:16** NU-Text adds *in Hebrew.*   * **20:18** NU-Text reads *disciples, "I have seen the Lord," ...*   * **20:19** NU-Text omits *assembled.*   * **20:29** NU-Text and M-Text omit *Thomas.*

---

steal the body would have taken the time to unwrap it and leave the clothes behind.
20:6 *saw the linen cloths.* The Greek term implies an intense stare, in contrast to the more casual look described in verse 5. Peter went into the tomb to get a good look. He carefully examined the place where Jesus' body had been.
20:9 *they did not know the Scripture.* The disciples believed because of what they saw in the tomb (v. 8), not because of what they knew from Old Testament passages describing the Savior's resurrection (Luke 24:25–27). Jesus had prophesied His death and resurrection in the disciples' presence, but the disciples had not understood what He was talking about.
20:17 *Do not cling to Me.* This means "to fasten oneself to" or "to hold." Mary had grabbed Christ and was holding on to Him as if she would never turn Him loose.

20:19 *Jesus came and stood in the midst.* Christ's appearance was miraculous because the doors were shut. Jesus, as God, could perform a variety of miracles without requiring a change in His humanity. Here Christ's body was a physical body, the same body in which He died and was buried. The difference is that His flesh had been changed to take on immortality and incorruptibility (1 Cor. 15:53).

20:7 *g* John 11:44   **20:8** *h* John 21:23, 24   **20:9** *i* Ps. 16:10   **20:11** *j* Mark 16:5   **20:14** *k* Matt. 28:9   *l* John 21:4   **20:16** *m* John 10:3   **20:17** *n* Heb. 4:14   *o* Heb. 2:11   *p* John 16:28; 17:11   *q* Eph. 1:17   **20:18** *r* Luke 24:10, 23   **20:19** *s* Luke 24:36   *t* John 9:22; 19:38   *u* John 14:27; 16:33   **20:20** *v* Acts 1:3   *w* John 16:20, 22   **20:21** *x* John 17:18, 19   **20:23** *y* Matt. 16:19; 18:18   **20:24** *z* John 11:16   **20:27** *a* Ps. 22:16; Zech. 12:10; 13:16; 1 John 1:1   *b* Mark 16:14   **20:29** *c* 1 Pet. 1:8   **20:30** *d* John 21:25

not written in this book; [31e]but these are written that [f]you may believe that Jesus [g]is the Christ, the Son of God, [h]and that believing you may have life in His name.

Breakfast by the Sea

21 After these things Jesus showed Himself again to the disciples at the [a]Sea of Tiberias, and in this way He showed Himself: [2]Simon Peter, [b]Thomas called the Twin, [c]Nathanael of [d]Cana in Galilee, [e]the *sons* of Zebedee, and two others of His disciples were together. [3]Simon Peter said to them, "I am going fishing."

They said to him, "We are going with you also." They went out and immediately* got into the boat, and that night they caught nothing. [4]But when the morning had now come, Jesus stood on the shore; yet the disciples [f]did not know that it was Jesus. [5]Then [g]Jesus said to them, "Children, have you any food?"

They answered Him, "No."

[6]And He said to them, [h]"Cast the net on the right side of the boat, and you will find *some.*" So they cast, and now they were not able to draw it in because of the multitude of fish.

[7]Therefore [i]that disciple whom Jesus loved said to Peter, "It is the Lord!" Now when Simon Peter heard that it was the Lord, he put on *his* outer garment (for he had removed it), and plunged into the sea. [8]But the other disciples came in the little boat (for they were not far from land, but about two hundred cubits), dragging the net with fish. [9]Then, as soon as they had come to land, they saw a fire of coals there, and fish laid on it, and bread. [10]Jesus said to them, "Bring some of the fish which you have just caught."

[11]Simon Peter went up and dragged the net to land, full of large fish, one hundred and fifty-three; and although there were so many, the net was not broken. [12]Jesus said to them, [j]"Come *and* eat breakfast." Yet none of the disciples dared ask Him, "Who are You?"—knowing that it was the Lord. [13]Jesus then came and took the bread and gave it to them, and likewise the fish.

[14]This *is* now [k]the third time Jesus showed Himself to His disciples after He was raised from the dead.

Jesus Restores Peter

[15]So when they had eaten breakfast, Jesus said to Simon Peter, "Simon, *son* of Jonah,* do you love Me more than these?"

He said to Him, "Yes, Lord; You know that I love You."

He said to him, [l]"Feed My lambs."

[16]He said to him again a second time, "Simon, *son* of Jonah,* do you love Me?"

He said to Him, "Yes, Lord; You know that I love You."

[m]He said to him, "Tend My [n]sheep."

[17]He said to him the third time, "Simon, *son* of Jonah,* do you love Me?" Peter was grieved because He said to him the third time, "Do you love Me?"

And he said to Him, "Lord, [o]You know all things; You know that I love You."

Jesus said to him, "Feed My sheep. [18p]Most assuredly, I say to you, when you were younger, you girded yourself and walked where you wished; but when you are old, you will stretch out your hands, and another will gird you and carry *you* where you do not wish." [19]This He spoke, signifying [q]by what death he would glorify God. And when He had spoken this, He said to him, [r]"Follow Me."

The Beloved Disciple and His Book

[20]Then Peter, turning around, saw the disciple [s]whom Jesus loved following, [t]who also had leaned on His breast at the supper, and said, "Lord, who is the one who betrays You?" [21]Peter, seeing him, said to Jesus, "But Lord, what *about* this man?"

[22]Jesus said to him, "If I will that he remain [u]till I come, what *is that* to you? You follow Me."

[23]Then this saying went out among the brethren that this disciple would not die. Yet Jesus did not say to him that he would not die, but, "If I will that he remain till I come, what *is that* to you?"

* **21:3** NU-Text omits *immediately.*   * **21:15** NU-Text reads *John.*   * **21:16** NU-Text reads *John.*
* **21:17** NU-Text reads *John.*

20:31 *that you may believe.* John states the purpose of his book, which was to convince his readers that Jesus is the Christ, the Messiah who fulfilled God's promises to Israel. Jesus is the Son of God, God in the flesh. By believing these things, a person obtains eternal life (1:12).

21:4 *the disciples did not know.* Perhaps the apostles did not recognize Jesus because they were preoccupied with their work, as Mary Magdalene had been with her sorrow (20:14). In addition, there was not much light at this time of day.

21:7 *Peter . . . plunged into the sea.* John was the first to recognize the Lord; Peter was the first to act.

21:17 *You know that I love You.* Peter denied the

Lord at least three times. Here, he affirmed his love for the third time.

21:20–21 *the disciple whom Jesus loved.* This is commonly considered to be John, the author of this Gospel.

20:31 [e] Luke 1:4 [f] 1 John 5:13 [g] Luke 2:11 [h] John 3:15, 16; 5:24 **21:1** [a] John 6:1 **21:2** [b] John 20:24 [c] John 1:45–51 [d] John 2:1 [e] Matt. 4:21 **21:4** [f] John 20:14 **21:5** [g] Luke 24:41 **21:6** [h] Luke 5:4, 6, 7 **21:7** [i] John 13:23; 20:2 **21:12** [j] Acts 10:41 **21:14** [k] John 20:19, 26 **21:15** [l] Acts 20:28 **21:16** [m] Heb. 13:20 [n] Ps. 79:13 **21:17** [o] John 2:24, 25; 16:30 **21:18** [p] Acts 12:3, 4 **21:19** [q] 2 Pet. 1:13, 14 [r] [Matt. 4:19; 16:24] **21:20** [s] John 13:23; 20:2 [t] John 13:25 **21:22** [u] [Rev. 2:25; 3:11; 22:7, 20]

24This is the disciple who vtestifies of these things, and wrote these things; and we know that his testimony is true.

25wAnd there are also many other things that Jesus did, which if they were written one by one, xI suppose that even the world itself could not contain the books that would be written. Amen.

21:24 *This is the disciple.* This is basically John's signature to his Gospel.

21:25 *there are also many other things that Jesus did.* The Gospel of John is truthful (v. 24), but it is not exhaustive.

21:24 v John 19:35   **21:25** w John 20:30 x Amos 7:10

THE
ACTS
OF THE APOSTLES

▶ **AUTHOR:** There are many "we" sections in Acts that imply the author was present for these events (16:10–17; 20:5—21:18; 27:1—28:16). These sections of Acts are the historical record of an eyewitness. For the remainder of this book, Luke no doubt followed the same careful investigative procedures that he used in writing his Gospel (Luke 1:1–4). As a close traveling companion of Paul, Luke had access to the principal eyewitness for chapters 13–18. It is also likely that he had opportunities to interview such key witnesses in Jerusalem as Peter and John for the information in chapters 13–28. Modern archaeological discoveries have strikingly confirmed the trustworthiness and precision of Luke as an historian.

▶ **TIME:** c. A.D. 33–62   ▶ **KEY VERSES:** Acts 2:42–47

▶ **THEME:** Acts is the record of how the events surrounding Jesus' life and death and resurrection resulted in this worldwide movement called the church. The book is certainly not a comprehensive history. Acts is more like a photo album of snapshots. It is the record of an eyewitness who wrote about what he saw and what seemed to be the critical events in the beginnings of the church and its movement out of Jerusalem to the rest of the world. One could say that the Book of Acts is an elaboration on Acts 1:8: "But you shall receive power when the Holy Spirit has come upon you; and you shall be witnesses to Me in Jerusalem, and in all Judea and Samaria, and to the end of the earth."

Prologue

1 The former account I made, O *a*Theophilus, of all that Jesus began both to do and teach, *2b*until the day in which He was taken up, after He through the Holy Spirit *c*had given commandments to the apostles whom He had chosen, *3d*to whom He also presented Himself alive after His suffering by many infallible proofs, being seen by them during forty days and speaking of the things pertaining to the kingdom of God.

The Holy Spirit Promised

*4e*And being assembled together with *them,* He commanded them not to depart from Jerusalem, but to wait for the Promise of the Father, "which," He said, "you have *f*heard from Me; *5g*for John truly baptized with water, *h*but you shall be baptized with the Holy Spirit not many days from now." *6*Therefore, when they had come together, they asked Him, saying, "Lord, will You at this time restore the kingdom to Israel?" *7*And He said to them, *i*"It is not for you to *j*know times or seasons which the Father has put in His own authority. *8k*But you shall receive power *l*when the Holy Spirit has come upon you; and *m*you shall be witnesses to Me* in Jerusalem, and in all Judea and *n*Samaria, and to the *o*end of the earth."

* **1:8** NU-Text reads *My witnesses.*

1:3 *many infallible proofs.* This is the only time the Greek word *tekmerion* occurs, emphasizing the certainty of the resurrection.
1:5 Baptism—The promised Holy Spirit (Is. 32:15; Joel 2:28–32) is a gift to believers after the glorification of Jesus (John 7:39). John baptized for forgiveness of sins, but the outpouring of the Spirit resulted from Christ's victory and exaltation to God's right hand (2:33). Believers are sealed until redemption (Eph. 1:13), made one body, and caused to drink of one Spirit (1 Cor. 12:13). The baptism of the Spirit is the immersion in the Spirit and uniting of believers into one body.
1:8 Living by Faith—God designed the Christian life to be one lived in the power of the Holy Spirit. Believers must appropriate daily, by faith, the power

of the Holy Spirit to live as Christians (Rom. 8:4–5). This means that the believer trusts the Spirit to empower him in specific instances such as resisting temptation, being faithful, and sharing one's faith. There is no secret formula that makes the Spirit's power operational in our lives. Scripture tells us that the Spirit dwells and operates in us (1 Cor. 6:9). We have to learn by experience through interaction with God to understand how that dynamic works. First the disciples received the Holy Spirit. Then He gave them

---

1:1 *a* Luke 1:3   **1:2** *b* Mark 16:19   *c* Matt. 28:19
1:3 *d* Mark 16:12, 14   **1:4** *e* Luke 24:49   *f* [John 14:16, 17, 26; 15:26]   **1:5** *g* Matt. 3:11   *h* [Joel 2:28]   **1:7** *i* 1 Thess. 5:1   *j* Matt. 24:36   **1:8** *k* [Acts 2:1, 4]   *l* Luke 24:49   *m* Luke 24:48   *n* Acts 8:1, 5, 14   *o* Col. 1:23

Jesus Ascends to Heaven

⁹ᵖNow when He had spoken these things, while they watched, ᵠHe was taken up, and a cloud received Him out of their sight. ¹⁰And while they looked steadfastly toward heaven as He went up, behold, two men stood by them ʳin white apparel, ¹¹who also said, "Men of Galilee, why do you stand gazing up into heaven? This *same* Jesus, who was taken up from you into heaven, ˢwill so come in like manner as you saw Him go into heaven."

The Upper Room Prayer Meeting

¹²ᵗThen they returned to Jerusalem from the mount called Olivet, which is near Jerusalem, a Sabbath day's journey. ¹³And when they had entered, they went up ᵘinto the upper room where they were staying: ᵛPeter, James, John, and Andrew; Philip and Thomas; Bartholomew and Matthew; James *the son* of Alphaeus and ʷSimon the Zealot; and ˣJudas *the son* of James. ¹⁴ʸThese all continued with one accord in prayer and supplication,* with ᶻthe women and Mary the mother of Jesus, and with ᵃHis brothers.

Matthias Chosen

¹⁵And in those days Peter stood up in the midst of the disciples* (altogether the number ᵇof names was about a hundred and twenty), and said, ¹⁶"Men *and* brethren, this Scripture had to be fulfilled, ᶜwhich the Holy Spirit spoke before by the mouth of David concerning Judas, ᵈwho became a guide to those who arrested Jesus; ¹⁷for ᵉhe was numbered with us and obtained a part in ᶠthis ministry."

¹⁸ᵍ(Now this man purchased a field with ʰthe wages of iniquity; and falling headlong, he burst open in the middle and all his entrails gushed out. ¹⁹And it became known to all those dwelling in Jerusalem; so that field is called in their own language, Akel Dama, that is, Field of Blood.)

²⁰"For it is written in the Book of Psalms:

ⁱ'Let his dwelling place be desolate,
And let no one live in it';*

and,

ʲ'Let* another take his office.'*

²¹"Therefore, of these men who have accompanied us all the time that the Lord

Jesus went in and out among us, ²²beginning from the baptism of John to that day when ᵏHe was taken up from us, one of these must ˡbecome a witness with us of His resurrection."

²³And they proposed two: Joseph called ᵐBarsabas, who was surnamed Justus, and Matthias. ²⁴And they prayed and said, "You, O Lord, ⁿwho know the hearts of all, show which of these two You have chosen ²⁵oto take part in this ministry and apostleship from which Judas by transgression fell, that he might go to his own place." ²⁶And they cast their lots, and the lot fell on Matthias. And he was numbered with the eleven apostles.

Coming of the Holy Spirit

2 When ᵃthe Day of Pentecost had fully come, ᵇthey were all with one accord* in one place. ²And suddenly there came a sound from heaven, as of a rushing mighty wind, and it ᶜfilled the whole house where they were sitting. ³Then there appeared to them divided tongues, as of fire, and *one* sat upon each of them. ⁴And ᵈthey were all filled with the Holy Spirit and began ᵉto speak with other tongues, as the Spirit gave them utterance.

The Crowd's Response

⁵And there were dwelling in Jerusalem Jews, ᶠdevout men, from every nation under heaven. ⁶And when this sound occurred, the ᵍmultitude came together, and were confused, because everyone heard them speak in his own language. ⁷Then they were all amazed and marveled, saying to one another, "Look, are not all these who speak ʰGalileans? ⁸And how *is it that* we hear, each in our own language in which we were born? ⁹Parthians and Medes and Elamites, those dwelling in Mesopotamia, Judea and ⁱCappadocia, Pontus and Asia, ¹⁰Phrygia and Pamphylia, Egypt and the parts of Libya adjoining Cyrene, visitors from Rome, both Jews and proselytes, ¹¹Cretans and Arabs—we hear them speaking in our own tongues the wonderful works of God." ¹²So they were all

---

* **1:14** NU-Text omits *and supplication.*
* **1:15** NU-Text reads *brethren.* * **1:20** Psalm 69:25 • Psalm 109:8 • Greek *episkopen,* position of overseer * **2:1** NU-Text reads *together.*

---

power and finally the disciples were told they would be Christ's witness to the very ends of the earth. Effective witness requires that we first learn to rely on the Spirit to help us.

1:14 *with one accord.* The disciples were like-minded; the people put aside personal positions and took on a common goal. True unity is an act of grace.

2:4 *tongues.* This means "diverse languages" and was essential to the rapid worldwide spread of the gospel. Those gathered for Pentecost came from around the known world and had various "mother tongues."

1:9 ᵖ Luke 24:50, 51 ᵠ Acts 1:2 **1:10** ʳ John 20:12 **1:11** ˢ Dan. 7:13 **1:12** ᵗ Luke 24:52 **1:13** ᵘ Acts 9:37, 39; 20:8 ᵛ Matt. 10:2–4 ʷ Luke 6:15 ˣ Jude 1 **1:14** ʸ Acts 2:1, 46 ᶻ Luke 23:49, 55 ᵃ Matt. 13:55 **1:15** ᵇ Rev. 3:4 **1:16** ᶜ Ps. 41:9 ᵈ Luke 22:47 **1:17** ᵉ Matt. 10:4 ᶠ Acts 1:25 **1:18** ᵍ Matt. 27:3–10 ʰ Mark 14:21 **1:20** ⁱ Ps. 69:25 ʲ Ps. 109:8 ᵏ Acts 1:9 ˡ Acts 1:8; 2:32 **1:23** ᵐ Acts 15:22 **1:24** ⁿ 1 Sam. 16:7 **1:25** ᵒ Acts 1:17 **2:1** ᵃ Lev. 23:15 ᵇ Acts 1:14 **2:2** ᶜ Acts 4:31 **2:4** ᵈ Acts 1:5 ᵉ Mark 16:17 **2:5** ᶠ Acts 8:2 **2:6** ᵍ Acts 4:32 **2:7** ʰ Acts 1:11 **2:9** ⁱ 1 Pet. 1:1

amazed and perplexed, saying to one another, "Whatever could this mean?"

13Others mocking said, "They are full of new wine."

Peter's Sermon

14But Peter, standing up with the eleven, raised his voice and said to them, "Men of Judea and all who dwell in Jerusalem, let this be known to you, and heed my words. 15For these are not drunk, as you suppose, *j*since it is *only* the third hour of the day. 16But this is what was spoken by the prophet Joel:

17 'And*k* it shall come to pass in the last days, says God,
  *l*That I will pour out of My Spirit on all flesh;
  Your sons and *m*your daughters shall prophesy,
  Your young men shall see visions,
  Your old men shall dream dreams.
18 And on My menservants and on My maidservants
  I will pour out My Spirit in those days;
  *n*And they shall prophesy.
19 *o*I will show wonders in heaven above
  And signs in the earth beneath:
  Blood and fire and vapor of smoke.
20 *p*The sun shall be turned into darkness,
  And the moon into blood,
  Before the coming of the great and awesome day of the LORD.
21 And it shall come to pass
  That *q*whoever calls on the name of the LORD
  Shall be saved.'*

22"Men of Israel, hear these words: Jesus of Nazareth, a Man attested by God to you *r*by miracles, wonders, and signs which God did through Him in your midst, as you yourselves also know— 23Him, *s*being delivered by the determined purpose and foreknowledge of God, *t*you have taken* by lawless hands, have crucified, and put to death; 24*u*whom God raised up, having loosed the pains of death, because it was not possible that He should be held by it. 25For David says concerning Him:

v'I foresaw the LORD always before my face,
  For He is at my right hand, that I may not be shaken.

26 Therefore my heart rejoiced, and my tongue was glad;
  Moreover my flesh also will rest in hope.
27 For You will not leave my soul in Hades,
  Nor will You allow Your Holy One to see *w*corruption.
28 You have made known to me the ways of life;
  You will make me full of joy in Your presence.'*

29"Men *and* brethren, let *me* speak freely to you *x*of the patriarch David, that he is both dead and buried, and his tomb is with us to this day. 30Therefore, being a prophet, *y*and knowing that God had sworn with an oath to him that of the fruit of his body, according to the flesh, He would raise up the Christ to sit on his throne,* 31he, foreseeing this, spoke concerning the resurrection of the Christ, *z*that His soul was not left in Hades, nor did His flesh see corruption. 32*a*This Jesus God has raised up, *b*of which we are all witnesses. 33Therefore *c*being exalted to *d*the right hand of God, and *e*having received from the Father the promise of the Holy Spirit, He *f*poured out this which you now see and hear. 34"For David did not ascend into the heavens, but he says himself:

g'The LORD said to my Lord,
  "Sit at My right hand,
35 Till I make Your enemies Your footstool."'*

36"Therefore let all the house of Israel know assuredly that God has made this Jesus, whom you crucified, both Lord and Christ."

37Now when they heard *this*, *h*they were cut to the heart, and said to Peter and the rest of the apostles, "Men *and* brethren, what shall we do?"

38Then Peter said to them, *i*"Repent, and let every one of you be baptized in the name of Jesus Christ for the remission of sins; and you shall receive the gift of the

---

* **2:21** Joel 2:28–32　* **2:23** NU-Text omits *have taken.*　* **2:28** Psalm 16:8–11　* **2:30** NU-Text omits *according to the flesh, He would raise up the Christ* and completes the verse with *He would seat one on his throne.*　* **2:35** Psalm 110:1

2:17 visions . . . dreams. The Holy Spirit was poured out on the church at the beginning of this final age of Scripture.

2:37 Conviction of the Holy Spirit—Peter's preaching was extremely effective, for it came "in power, and in the Holy Spirit and in much assurance" (1 Thess. 1:5). The result was they were "cut to the heart." Their response was, "brethren, what shall we do?" The reality was that conviction by the Holy Spirit brought about a real search for an answer. Such a consciousness of sin is an indispensable prerequisite to conversion.

2:38 Repent. Peter called the Jews to turn their backs on their former lives and change. Faith involves an action of belief by those who accept Jesus.

2:15*j* 1 Thess. 5:7　**2:17***k* Joel 2:28–32　*l* Acts 10:45　*m* Acts 21:9　**2:18***n* 1 Cor. 12:10　**2:19***o* Joel 2:30　**2:20***p* Matt. 24:29　**2:21***q* Rom. 10:13　**2:22***r* John 3:2; 5:6　**2:23***s* Luke 22:22　*t* Acts 5:30　**2:24***u* [Rom. 8:11]　**2:25***v* Ps. 16:8–11　**2:27***w* Acts 13:30–37　**2:29***x* Acts 13:36　**2:30***y* Ps. 132:11　**2:31***z* Ps. 16:10　**2:32***a* Acts 2:24　*b* Acts 1:8; 3:15　**2:33***c* [Acts 5:31]　*d* [Heb. 10:12]　*e* [John 14:26]　*f* Acts 2:1–11, 17; 10:45　**2:34***g* Ps. 68:18; 110:1　**2:37***h* Luke 3:10, 12, 14　**2:38***i* Luke 24:47

Holy Spirit. [39]For the promise is to you and [j]to your children, and [k]to all who are afar off, as many as the Lord our God will call."

A Vital Church Grows

[40]And with many other words he testified and exhorted them, saying, "Be saved from this perverse generation." [41]Then those who gladly* received his word were baptized; and that day about three thousand souls were added *to them*. [42l]And they continued steadfastly in the apostles' doctrine and fellowship, in the breaking of bread, and in prayers. [43]Then fear came upon every soul, and [m]many wonders and signs were done through the apostles. [44]Now all who believed were together, and [n]had all things in common, [45]and sold their possessions and goods, and [o]divided them among all, as anyone had need.

[46p]So continuing daily with one accord [q]in the temple, and [r]breaking bread from house to house, they ate their food with gladness and simplicity of heart, [47]praising God and having favor with all the people. And [s]the Lord added to the church* daily those who were being saved.

A Lame Man Healed

3 Now Peter and John went up together [a]to the temple at the hour of prayer, [b]the ninth *hour*. [2]And [c]a certain man lame from his mother's womb was carried, whom they laid daily at the gate of the temple which is called Beautiful, [d]to ask alms from those who entered the temple; [3]who, seeing Peter and John about to go into the temple, asked for alms. [4]And fixing his eyes on him, with John, Peter said, "Look at us." [5]So he gave them his attention, expecting to receive something from them. [6]Then Peter said, "Silver and gold I do not have, but what I do have I give you: [e]In the name of Jesus Christ of Nazareth, rise up and walk." [7]And he took him by the right hand and lifted *him* up, and immediately his feet and ankle bones received strength. [8]So he, [f]leaping up, stood and walked and entered the temple with them—walking, leaping,

and praising God. [9g]And all the people saw him walking and praising God. [10]Then they knew that it was he who [h]sat begging alms at the Beautiful Gate of the temple; and they were filled with wonder and amazement at what had happened to him.

Preaching in Solomon's Portico

[11]Now as the lame man who was healed held on to Peter and John, all the people ran together to them in the porch [i]which is called Solomon's, greatly amazed. [12]So when Peter saw *it*, he responded to the people: "Men of Israel, why do you marvel at this? Or why look so intently at us, as though by our own power or godliness we had made this man walk? [13j]The God of Abraham, Isaac, and Jacob, the God of our fathers, [k]glorified His Servant Jesus, whom you [l]delivered up and [m]denied in the presence of Pilate, when he was determined to let *Him* go. [14]But you denied [n]the Holy One [o]and the Just, and [p]asked for a murderer to be granted to you, [15]and killed the Prince of life, [q]whom God raised from the dead, [r]of which we are witnesses. [16s]And His name, through faith in His name, has made this man strong, whom you see and know. Yes, the faith which *comes* through Him has given him this perfect soundness in the presence of you all.

[17]"Yet now, brethren, I know that [t]you did *it* in ignorance, as *did* also your rulers. [18]But [u]those things which God foretold [v]by the mouth of all His prophets, that the Christ would suffer, He has thus fulfilled. [19w]Repent therefore and be converted, that your sins may be blotted out, so that times of refreshing may come from the presence of the Lord, [20]and that He may send Jesus Christ, who was preached to you before,* [21x]whom heaven must receive until the times of [y]restoration of all things, [z]which God has spoken by the mouth of all His

* **2:41** NU-Text omits *gladly.*   * **2:47** NU-Text omits *to the church.*   * **3:20** NU-Text and M-Text read *Christ Jesus, who was ordained for you before.*

2:42–47 Being in the Church—Converts were apparently immediately incorporated into the body of believers that became the church. Being involved in the Jerusalem church clearly must have changed the lives of these new believers dramatically. This was manifested in several ways: (1) they devoted themselves to new teaching; (2) they thought differently about all their possessions; (3) they became people of prayer; and (4) they ate and worshiped together with unified hearts. They weren't just saved from sin. They were saved to Christ and to this new body called the church, which of course is also His. We are called to be a part of one another's lives. We are to learn, share, pray, and worship together. As a body of believers, God expects us to have great concern for our fellow believers and to help one another mature.

3:7 strength. This account is told by a physician who describes instant healing. Before their eyes strength

is given to muscles and bones. The man's feet could instantly hold his weight.

3:19 Repent therefore and be converted. Peter challenges all to change their minds and change their courses. Not only is their sin addressed but their closed minds.

2:39 [j] Joel 2:28, 32 [k] Eph. 2:13   **2:42** [l] Acts 1:14
2:43 [m] Acts 2:22   **2:44** [n] Acts 4:32, 34, 37; 5:2   **2:45** [o] Is.
58:7   **2:46** [p] Acts 1:14 [q] Luke 24:53 [r] Acts 2:42;
20:7   **2:47** [s] Acts 5:14   **3:1** [a] Acts 2:46 [b] Ps. 55:17
3:2 [c] Acts 14:8 [d] John 9:8   **3:6** [e] Acts 4:10   **3:8** [f] Is.
35:6   **3:9** [g] Acts 4:16, 21   **3:10** [h] John 9:8   **3:11** [i] John
10:23   **3:13** [j] John 5:30 [k] John 7:39; 12:23; 13:31 [l] Matt.
27:2 [m] Matt. 27:20   **3:14** [n] Mark 1:24 [o] Acts 7:52 [p] John
18:40   **3:15** [q] Acts 2:24 [r] Acts 2:32   **3:16** [s] Matt.
9:22   **3:17** [t] Luke 23:34   **3:18** [u] Acts 26:22 [v] 1 Pet. 1:10
3:19 [w] [Acts 2:38; 26:20]   **3:21** [x] Acts 1:11 [y] Matt. 17:11
[z] Luke 1:70

holy prophets since the world began. ²²For Moses truly said to the fathers, ᵃ'The LORD your God will raise up for you a Prophet like me from your brethren. Him you shall hear in all things, whatever He says to you. ²³And it shall be that every soul who will not hear that Prophet shall be utterly destroyed from among the people.'* ²⁴Yes, and ᵇall the prophets, from Samuel and those who follow, as many as have spoken, have also foretold* these days. ²⁵ᶜYou are sons of the prophets, and of the covenant which God made with our fathers, saying to Abraham, ᵈ'And in your seed all the families of the earth shall be blessed.'* ²⁶To you ᵉfirst, God, having raised up His Servant Jesus, sent Him to bless you, ᶠin turning away every one of you from your iniquities."

Peter and John Arrested

4 Now as they spoke to the people, the priests, the captain of the temple, and the ᵃSadducees came upon them, ²being greatly disturbed that they taught the people and preached in Jesus the resurrection from the dead. ³And they laid hands on them, and put them in custody until the next day, for it was already evening. ⁴However, many of those who heard the word believed; and the number of the men came to be about five thousand.

Addressing the Sanhedrin

⁵And it came to pass, on the next day, that their rulers, elders, and scribes, ⁶as well as ᵇAnnas the high priest, Caiaphas, John, and Alexander, and as many as were of the family of the high priest, were gathered together at Jerusalem. ⁷And when they had set them in the midst, they asked, ᶜ"By what power or by what name have you done this?"

⁸ᵈThen Peter, filled with the Holy Spirit, said to them, "Rulers of the people and elders of Israel: ⁹If we this day are judged for a good deed done to a helpless man, by what means he has been made well, ¹⁰let it be known to you all, and to all the people of Israel, ᵉthat by the name of Jesus Christ of Nazareth, whom you crucified, ᶠwhom God raised from the dead, by Him this man stands here before you whole. ¹¹This is the ᵍ'stone which was rejected by you builders, which has become the chief cornerstone.'* ¹²ʰNor is there salvation in any other, for there is no other name under heaven given among men by which we must be saved."

The Name of Jesus Forbidden

¹³Now when they saw the boldness of Peter and John, ⁱand perceived that they were uneducated and untrained men, they marveled. And they realized that they had been with Jesus. ¹⁴And seeing the man who had been healed ʲstanding with them, they could say nothing against it. ¹⁵But when they had commanded them to go aside out of the council, they conferred among themselves, ¹⁶saying, ᵏ"What shall we do to these men? For, indeed, that a notable miracle has been done through them is ˡevident to all who dwell in Jerusalem, and we cannot deny it. ¹⁷But so that it spreads no further among the people, let us severely threaten them, that from now on they speak to no man in this name."

¹⁸ᵐSo they called them and commanded them not to speak at all nor teach in the name of Jesus. ¹⁹But Peter and John answered and said to them, ⁿ"Whether it

* **3:23** Deuteronomy 18:15, 18, 19   * **3:24** NU-Text and M-Text read proclaimed.   * **3:25** Genesis 22:18; 26:4; 28:14   * **4:11** Psalm 118:22

3:22 Messiah—Peter draws on the witness of the prophets who foretold the suffering of Christ. He quotes Moses, who spoke of a prophet like himself from among the Jews (Deut. 18:15–17). The crucified, risen, and ascended Jesus has fulfilled this role perfectly as God's anointed Servant sent to atone for humans. Jesus carried God's authority; the words of Jesus must be heeded since they give life to the dying sinner. A person greater than Moses has come to fulfill the prophets. Peter is proclaiming that Jesus is the deliberate fulfillment of God's promise for redemption.

4:1 Sadducees. The Sadducees were skeptics who rejected all of the Old Testament except the books of Moses, and who denied the resurrection from the dead. Peter's teaching about the resurrection challenged their beliefs and teaching.

4:5 rulers, elders, and scribes. The Sanhedrin, which consisted of 70 men plus the high priest, was the highest Jewish court. The group consisted of the wealthiest, most educated, and most powerful Jewish men in Israel.

4:8 The Filling of the Holy Spirit—This is the second description in the Book of Acts of someone being filled with the Holy Spirit (see 2:4; 4:31; 9:17; 13:9). The

initial filling accompanies the baptism in the Spirit. This filling brought boldness for God's work. Jesus had promised His disciples that they would stand before kings and rulers and that the Spirit of God within them would implant in their minds exactly what to say to these leaders (Matt. 10:16–20).

4:19 listen to you more than to God. There is no authority apart from God. When human authority rejects God's authority, it becomes twisted and loses its right to demand compliance (5:29). God's people are responsible to obey the government because it has been set in place by God, but when government directs against God's will, the Author of authority has the higher claim on our allegiance. We must resist any command that is against God's will (Ex. 1; Dan. 3; Heb. 11:23).

3:22 ᵃ Deut. 18:15, 18, 19   **3:24** ᵇ Luke 24:25
3:25 ᶜ [Rom. 9:4, 8]   ᵈ Gen. 12:3; 18:18; 22:18; 26:4; 28:14
3:26 ᵉ [Rom. 1:16; 2:9]   ᶠ Matt. 1:21   **4:1** ᵃ Matt. 22:23
4:6 ᵇ Luke 3:2   **4:7** ᶜ Matt. 21:23   **4:8** ᵈ Luke 12:11, 12
4:10 ᵉ Acts 2:22; 3:6, 16   ᶠ Acts 2:24   **4:11** ᵍ Ps. 118:22
4:12 ʰ [1 Tim. 2:5, 6]   **4:13** ⁱ [1 Cor. 1:27]   **4:14** ʲ Acts
3:11   **4:16** ᵏ John 11:47   ˡ Acts 3:7–10   **4:18** ᵐ Acts 5:28,
40   **4:19** ⁿ Acts 5:29

is right in the sight of God to listen to you more than to God, you judge. 20oFor we cannot but speak the things which pwe have seen and heard." 21So when they had further threatened them, they let them go, finding no way of punishing them, qbecause of the people, since they all rglorified God for swhat had been done. 22For the man was over forty years old on whom this miracle of healing had been performed.

Prayer for Boldness

23And being let go, tthey went to their own companions and reported all that the chief priests and elders had said to them. 24So when they heard that, they raised their voice to God with one accord and said: "Lord, uYou are God, who made heaven and earth and the sea, and all that is in them, 25who by the mouth of Your servant David* have said:

v'Why did the nations rage,
   And the people plot vain things?
26   The kings of the earth took their
      stand,
   And the rulers were gathered together
   Against the LORD and against His
      Christ.'*

27"For wtruly against xYour holy Servant Jesus, ywhom You anointed, both Herod and Pontius Pilate, with the Gentiles and the people of Israel, were gathered together 28zto do whatever Your hand and Your purpose determined before to be done. 29Now, Lord, look on their threats, and grant to Your servants athat with all boldness they may speak Your word, 30by stretching out Your hand to heal, band that signs and wonders may be done cthrough the name of dYour holy Servant Jesus." 31And when they had prayed, ethe place where they were assembled together was shaken; and they were all filled with the Holy Spirit, fand they spoke the word of God with boldness.

Sharing in All Things

32Now the multitude of those who believed gwere of one heart and one soul; hneither did anyone say that any of the things he possessed was his own, but they had all things in common. 33And with

igreat power the apostles gave jwitness to the resurrection of the Lord Jesus. And kgreat grace was upon them all. 34Nor was there anyone among them who lacked; lfor all who were possessors of lands or houses sold them, and brought the proceeds of the things that were sold, 35mand laid them at the apostles' feet; nand they distributed to each as anyone had need.

36And Joses,* who was also named Barnabas by the apostles (which is translated Son of Encouragement), a Levite of the country of Cyprus, 37ohaving land, sold it, and brought the money and laid it at the apostles' feet.

Lying to the Holy Spirit

5 But a certain man named Ananias, with Sapphira his wife, sold a possession. 2And he kept back part of the proceeds, his wife also being aware of it, and brought a certain part and laid it at the apostles' feet. 3aBut Peter said, "Ananias, why has bSatan filled your heart to lie to the Holy Spirit and keep back part of the price of the land for yourself? 4While it remained, was it not your own? And after it was sold, was it not in your own control? Why have you conceived this thing in your heart? You have not lied to men but to God."

5Then Ananias, hearing these words, cfell down and breathed his last. So great fear came upon all those who heard these things. 6And the young men arose and dwrapped him up, carried him out, and buried him.

7Now it was about three hours later when his wife came in, not knowing what had happened. 8And Peter answered her, "Tell me whether you sold the land for so much?"

She said, "Yes, for so much."

9Then Peter said to her, "How is it that you have agreed together eto test the Spirit of the Lord? Look, the feet of those who have buried your husband are at the door, and they will carry you out." 10fThen immediately she fell down at his feet and breathed her last. And the young men came in and found her dead, and carrying

---

* 4:25 NU-Text reads who through the Holy Spirit, by the mouth of our father, Your servant David.
* 4:26 Psalm 2:1, 2   * 4:36 NU-Text reads Joseph.

5:3 Filled with Satan—Satan is the father of lies (John 8:44). When Ananias and Sapphira deliberately lied, they took upon themselves the moral character of the one who is behind all lies, the devil himself. A person who is listening to Satan begins to act like Satan; his or her thoughts and actions are "filled with Satan" rather than reflecting the filling and direction of the Holy Spirit. Satan or a demon cannot possess someone who is filled with the Holy Spirit, but by listening to Satan rather than the Holy Spirit a believer can behave like one who belongs to Satan rather than one who belongs to God.

5:4 Holy Spirit—This passage confirms the deity of the Holy Spirit. The Holy Spirit is the third Person

of the triune Godhead. To lie to Him (v. 3) is to lie to God.

4:20 o Acts 1:8; 2:32   p [1 John 1:1, 3]   4:21 q Acts 5:26   r Matt. 15:31   s Acts 3:7, 8   4:23 t Acts 2:44–46; 12:12   4:24 u Ex. 20:11   4:25 v Ps. 2:1, 2   4:27 w Luke 22:2; 23:1, 8   x [Luke 1:35]   y John 10:36   4:28 z Acts 2:23; 3:18   4:29 a Acts 4:13, 31; 9:27; 13:46; 14:3; 19:8; 26:26   4:30 b Acts 2:43; 5:12   c Acts 3:6, 16   d Acts 4:27   4:31 e Acts 2:2, 4; 16:26   f Acts 4:29   4:32 g Rom. 15:5, 6   h Acts 2:44   4:33 i [Acts 1:8]   j Acts 1:22   k Rom. 6:15   4:34 l Acts 2:45   4:35 m Acts 4:37; 5:2   n Acts 2:45; 6:1   4:37 o Acts 4:34, 35; 5:1, 2   5:3 a Deut. 23:21   b Luke 22:3   5:5 c Acts 5:10, 11   5:6 d John 19:40   5:9 e Acts 5:3, 4   5:10 f Acts 5:5

her out, buried *her* by her husband. ¹¹ᵍSo great fear came upon all the church and upon all who heard these things.

Continuing Power in the Church

¹²And ʰthrough the hands of the apostles many signs and wonders were done among the people. ⁱAnd they were all with one accord in Solomon's Porch. ¹³Yet ʲnone of the rest dared join them, ᵏbut the people esteemed them highly. ¹⁴And believers were increasingly added to the Lord, multitudes of both men and women, ¹⁵so that they brought the sick out into the streets and laid *them* on beds and couches, ˡthat at least the shadow of Peter passing by might fall on some of them. ¹⁶Also a multitude gathered from the surrounding cities to Jerusalem, bringing ᵐsick people and those who were tormented by unclean spirits, and they were all healed.

Imprisoned Apostles Freed

¹⁷ⁿThen the high priest rose up, and all those who *were* with him (which is the sect of the Sadducees), and they were filled with indignation, ¹⁸ᵒand laid their hands on the apostles and put them in the common prison. ¹⁹But at night ᵖan angel of the Lord opened the prison doors and brought them out, and said, ²⁰"Go, stand in the temple and speak to the people ᑫall the words of this life."

²¹And when they heard *that*, they entered the temple early in the morning and taught. ʳBut the high priest and those with him came and called the council together, with all the elders of the children of Israel, and sent to the prison to have them brought.

Apostles on Trial Again

²²But when the officers came and did not find them in the prison, they returned and reported, ²³saying, "Indeed we found the prison shut securely, and the guards standing outside* before the doors; but when we opened them, we found no one inside!" ²⁴Now when the high priest,* ˢthe captain of the temple, and the chief priests heard these things, they wondered what the outcome would be. ²⁵So one came and

told them, saying,* "Look, the men whom you put in prison are standing in the temple and teaching the people!"

²⁶Then the captain went with the officers and brought them without violence, ᵗfor they feared the people, lest they should be stoned. ²⁷And when they had brought them, they set *them* before the council. And the high priest asked them, ²⁸saying, ᵘ"Did we not strictly command you not to teach in this name? And look, you have filled Jerusalem with your doctrine, ᵛand intend to bring this Man's ʷblood on us!"

²⁹But Peter and the *other* apostles answered and said: ˣ"We ought to obey God rather than men. ³⁰ʸThe God of our fathers raised up Jesus whom you murdered by ᶻhanging on a tree. ³¹ᵃHim God has exalted to His right hand *to be* ᵇPrince and ᶜSavior, ᵈto give repentance to Israel and forgiveness of sins. ³²And ᵉwe are His witnesses to these things, and *so* also *is* the Holy Spirit ᶠwhom God has given to those who obey Him."

Gamaliel's Advice

³³When they heard *this*, they were ᵍfurious and plotted to kill them. ³⁴Then one in the council stood up, a Pharisee named ʰGamaliel, a teacher of the law held in respect by all the people, and commanded them to put the apostles outside for a little while. ³⁵And he said to them: "Men of Israel, take heed to yourselves what you intend to do regarding these men. ³⁶For some time ago Theudas rose up, claiming to be somebody. A number of men, about four hundred, joined him. He was slain, and all who obeyed him were scattered and came to nothing. ³⁷After this man, Judas of Galilee rose up in the days of the census, and drew away many people after him. He also perished, and all who obeyed him were dispersed. ³⁸And now I say to you, keep away from these men and let them alone; for if this plan or this work is of men, it will come to nothing; ³⁹ⁱbut if it is of God, you cannot overthrow it—lest you even be found ʲto fight against God."

---

* 5:23 NU-Text and M-Text omit *outside.*
* 5:24 NU-Text omits *the high priest.* * 5:25 NU-Text and M-Text omit *saying.*

5:12 signs and wonders. These are miraculous occurrences that point to a warning, instruction, or encouragement from God. The signs and wonders which were done among the people at this time gave credibility to the apostles as messengers from God.
5:19 Angels—The word "angel" simply means "messenger." The phrase "angel of the Lord" is commonly used in the Old Testament to refer to spiritual messengers of God.
5:32 witnesses to these things. The witness of the believer is vitally related to the Holy Spirit. Jesus had said that the Holy Spirit would be a witness and that the apostles would be witnesses. The apostles were conscious that they were indwelt by the Holy Spirit of God, and that their witness depended upon this

filling. There is a tremendous lesson here for every believer. No one can be a witness for Christ and a herald of the gospel by individual initiative. Empowerment must come from the Holy Spirit.

5:11 ᵍ Acts 2:43; 5:5; 19:17 **5:12** ʰ Acts 2:43; 4:30; 6:8; 14:3; 15:12 ⁱ Acts 3:11; 4:32 **5:13** ʲ John 9:22 ᵏ Acts 2:47; 4:21 **5:15** ˡ Acts 19:12 **5:16** ᵐ Mark 16:17, 18 **5:17** ⁿ Acts 4:1, 2, 6 **5:18** ᵒ Luke 21:12 **5:19** ᵖ Acts 12:7; 16:26 **5:20** ᑫ [John 6:63, 68; 17:3] **5:21** ʳ Acts 4:5, 6 **5:24** ˢ Acts 4:1; 5:26 **5:26** ᵗ Matt. 21:26 **5:28** ᵘ Acts 4:17, 18 ᵛ Acts 2:23, 36 ʷ Matt. 23:35 **5:29** ˣ Acts 4:19 **5:30** ʸ Acts 3:13, 15 ᶻ [1 Pet. 2:24] **5:31** ᵃ [Acts 2:33, 36] ᵇ Acts 3:15 ᶜ Matt. 1:21 ᵈ Luke 24:47 **5:32** ᵉ John 15:26, 27 ᶠ Acts 2:4; 10:44 **5:33** ᵍ Acts 2:37; 7:54 **5:34** ʰ Acts 22:3 **5:39** ⁱ 1 Cor. 1:25 ʲ Acts 7:51; 9:5

40And they agreed with him, and when they had kcalled for the apostles land beaten *them*, they commanded that they should not speak in the name of Jesus, and let them go. 41So they departed from the presence of the council, mrejoicing that they were counted worthy to suffer shame for His* name. 42And daily nin the temple, and in every house, othey did not cease teaching and preaching Jesus *as* the Christ.

Seven Chosen to Serve

6 Now in those days, awhen *the number* of the disciples was multiplying, there arose a complaint against the Hebrews by the bHellenists,* because their widows were neglected cin the daily distribution. 2Then the twelve summoned the multitude of the disciples and said, d"It is not desirable that we should leave the word of God and serve tables. 3Therefore, brethren, eseek out from among you seven men of *good* reputation, full of the Holy Spirit and wisdom, whom we may appoint over this fbusiness; 4but we gwill give ourselves continually to prayer and to the ministry of the word."

5And the saying pleased the whole multitude. And they chose Stephen, ha man full of faith and the Holy Spirit, and iPhilip, Prochorus, Nicanor, Timon, Parmenas, and jNicolas, a proselyte from Antioch, 6whom they set before the apostles; and kwhen they had prayed, lthey laid hands on them.

7Then mthe word of God spread, and the number of the disciples multiplied greatly in Jerusalem, and a great many nof the priests were obedient to the faith.

Stephen Accused of Blasphemy

8And Stephen, full of faith* and power, did great owonders and signs among the people. 9Then there arose some from what is called the Synagogue of the Freedmen (Cyrenians, Alexandrians, and those from Cilicia and Asia), disputing with Stephen. 10And pthey were not able to resist the wisdom and the Spirit by which he spoke. 11aThen they secretly induced men to say, "We have heard him speak blasphemous

words against Moses and God." 12And they stirred up the people, the elders, and the scribes; and they came upon *him*, seized him, and brought *him* to the council. 13They also set up false witnesses who said, "This man does not cease to speak blasphemous* words against this holy place and the law; 14rfor we have heard him say that this Jesus of Nazareth will destroy this place and change the customs which Moses delivered to us." 15And all who sat in the council, looking steadfastly at him, saw his face as the face of an angel.

Stephen's Address: The Call of Abraham

7 Then the high priest said, "Are these things so?"

2And he said, a"Brethren and fathers, listen: The bGod of glory appeared to our father Abraham when he was in Mesopotamia, before he dwelt in cHaran, 3and said to him, d'Get out of your country and from your relatives, and come to a land that I will show you.'* 4Then ehe came out of the land of the Chaldeans and dwelt in Haran. And from there, when his father was fdead, He moved him to this land in which you now dwell. 5And *God* gave him no inheritance in it, not even *enough* to set his foot on. But even when *Abraham* had no child, gHe promised to give it to him for a possession, and to his descendants after him. 6But God spoke in this way: hthat his descendants would dwell in a foreign land, and that they would bring them into ibondage and oppress *them* four hundred years. 7i'And the nation to whom they will be in bondage I will jjudge,'* said God, l'and after that they shall come out and serve Me in this place.'* 8mThen He gave him the covenant of circumcision; nand so *Abraham* begot Isaac and circumcised him on the eighth day; oand Isaac *begot* Jacob, and pJacob *begot* the twelve patriarchs.

---

* **5:41** NU-Text reads *the name;* M-Text reads *the name of Jesus.* * **6:1** That is, Greek-speaking Jews * **6:8** NU-Text reads *grace.* * **6:13** NU-Text omits *blasphemous.* * **7:3** Genesis 12:1 * **7:7** Genesis 15:14 • Exodus 3:12

6:3 full of the Holy Spirit and wisdom. The men's lives were consistent with their confession of faith. They knew the will of God and understood how to carry it out in their lives (Eph. 5:15–18). They could be trusted with responsibility and authority.

6:6 laid hands on them. This was not done in order for the men to receive the Holy Spirit, because the seven men were already "full of the Holy Spirit" (vv. 3,5). Instead the apostles were conferring on these men the responsibility of carrying out the ministry. The laying on of hands was a meaningful tradition that dated back to the days of Moses (Num. 27:23); it identified people with the ministries to be performed.

6:8 full of faith and power. Stephen had the gifts, the boldness, and the brilliance to be a powerful witness; yet even his witness would be rejected by the

religious leaders. Hearts are opened only by God, not by our gifts, boldness, or brilliance.

7:8 circumcision. This covenant and its outward

5:40 k Acts 4:18 l Matt. 10:17 **5:41** m [1 Pet. 4:13–16] **5:42** n Acts 2:46 o Acts 4:20, 29 **6:1** a Acts 2:41; 4:4 b Acts 9:29; 11:20 c Acts 4:35; 11:29 **6:2** d Ex. 18:17 **6:3** e 1 Tim. 3:7 f 1 Tim. 3:8–13 **6:4** g Acts 2:42 **6:5** h Acts 6:3; 11:24 i Acts 8:5, 26; 21:8 j Rev. 2:6, 15 **6:6** k Acts 1:24 l [2 Tim. 1:6] **6:7** m Acts 12:24 n John 12:42 **6:8** o Acts 2:43; 5:12; 8:15; 14:3 **6:10** p Luke 21:15 **6:11** q Kin. 21:10, 13 **6:14** r Acts 10:38; 25:8 **7:2** a Acts 22:1 b Ps. 29:3 c Gen. 11:31, 32 **7:3** d Gen. 12:1 **7:4** e Gen. 11:31; 15:7 f Gen. 11:32 **7:5** g Gen. 12:7; 13:15; 15:3, 18; 17:8; 26:3 **7:6** h Gen. 15:13, 14, 16; 47:11, 12 i Ex. 1:8–14; 12:40, 41 **7:7** j Gen. 15:14 k Ex. 14:13–31 l Ex. 3:12 **7:8** m Gen. 17:9–14 n Gen. 21:1–5 o Gen. 25:21–26 p Gen. 29:31—30:24; 35:18, 22–26

The Patriarchs in Egypt

9q"And the patriarchs, becoming envious, rsold Joseph into Egypt. sBut God was with him 10and delivered him out of all his troubles, tand gave him favor and wisdom in the presence of Pharaoh, king of Egypt; and he made him governor over Egypt and all his house. 11uNow a famine and great trouble came over all the land of Egypt and Canaan, and our fathers found no sustenance. 12vBut when Jacob heard that there was grain in Egypt, he sent out our fathers first. 13And the wsecond time Joseph was made known to his brothers, and Joseph's family became known to the Pharaoh. 14xThen Joseph sent and called his father Jacob and yall his relatives to him, seventy-five* people. 15zSo Jacob went down to Egypt; aand he died, he and our fathers. 16And bthey were carried back to Shechem and laid in cthe tomb that Abraham bought for a sum of money from the sons of Hamor, the father of Shechem.

God Delivers Israel by Moses

17"But when dthe time of the promise drew near which God had sworn to Abraham, ethe people grew and multiplied in Egypt 18till another king farose who did not know Joseph. 19This man dealt treacherously with our people, and oppressed our forefathers, gmaking them expose their babies, so that they might not live. 20hAt this time Moses was born, and iwas well pleasing to God; and he was brought up in his father's house for three months. 21But jwhen he was set out, kPharaoh's daughter took him away and brought him up as her own son. 22And Moses was learned in all the wisdom of the Egyptians, and was lmighty in words and deeds.

23m"Now when he was forty years old, it came into his heart to visit his brethren, the children of Israel. 24And seeing one of them suffer wrong, he defended and

avenged him who was oppressed, and struck down the Egyptian. 25For he supposed that his brethren would have understood that God would deliver them by his hand, but they did not understand. 26And the next day he appeared to two of them as they were fighting, and tried to reconcile them, saying, 'Men, you are brethren; why do you wrong one another?' 27But he who did his neighbor wrong pushed him away, saying, n'Who made you a ruler and a judge over us? 28Do you want to kill me as you did the Egyptian yesterday?'* 29oThen, at this saying, Moses fled and became a dweller in the land of Midian, where he phad two sons.

30q"And when forty years had passed, an Angel of the Lord* appeared to him in a flame of fire in a bush, in the wilderness of Mount Sinai. 31When Moses saw it, he marveled at the sight; and as he drew near to observe, the voice of the Lord came to him, 32saying, r'I am the God of your fathers—the God of Abraham, the God of Isaac, and the God of Jacob.'* And Moses trembled and dared not look. 33s'Then the LORD said to him, "Take your sandals off your feet, for the place where you stand is holy ground. 34I have surely tseen the oppression of My people who are in Egypt; I have heard their groaning and have come down to deliver them. And now come, I will usend you to Egypt."'*

35"This Moses whom they rejected, saying, v'Who made you a ruler and a judge?'* is the one God sent to be a ruler and a deliverer wby the hand of the Angel who appeared to him in the bush. 36xHe brought them out, after he had yshown wonders and signs in the land of Egypt, zand in the Red Sea, aand in the wilderness forty years.

---

* 7:14 Or seventy (compare Exodus 1:5)
* 7:28 Exodus 2:14   * 7:30 NU-Text omits of the Lord.   * 7:32 Exodus 3:6, 15   * 7:34 Exodus 3:5, 7, 8, 10   * 7:35 Exodus 2:14

---

symbol were given to Abraham that he might never forget God's promise to bless him. Abraham was saved by faith in God (Gen. 15:6); the symbol of circumcision was an outward sign of the inward reality of his faith. God's blessing was not based on the physical fact of circumcision but on genuine faith.

7:16 Shechem. At the time of Stephen's defense, Shechem was the center of Samaritan life. Mount Gerizim, the Samaritan worship center, was located nearby. Stephen's point was not to speak against the temple in Jerusalem, but to point out that God had been speaking and moving in the lives of His people not only in Jerusalem or the temple. The most important address God made to His people was at Mount Sinai, which is nowhere near Jerusalem.

7:19 Persecution—Pharaoh enslaved and mistreated the Hebrews, and at the same time he feared their strength. It was his fear that led him to seek their destruction, persecuting them and destroying their children. It is easy to recognize the enormity and

evil of the Egyptian persecution of the Jews as a race and a nation, but the ancient Egyptians are not the only ones guilty of such sin. Some of those claiming the name of Christ in recent times have been guilty of mistreating or even enslaving those of a different ethnic background. Feelings of racial superiority have no place in the heart of a Christian.

7:9 q Gen. 37:4, 11, 28 r Gen. 37:28 s Gen. 39:2, 21, 23   **7:10** t Gen. 41:38–44   **7:11** u Gen. 41:54; 42:5   **7:12** v Gen. 42:1, 2   **7:13** w Gen. 45:4, 16   **7:14** x Gen. 45:9, 27 y Deut. 10:22   **7:15** z Gen. 46:1–7 a Gen. 49:33   **7:16** b Josh. 24:32 c Gen. 23:16   **7:17** d Gen. 15:13 e Ex. 1:7–9   **7:18** f Ex. 1:8   **7:19** g Ex. 1:22   **7:20** h Ex. 2:1, 2 i Heb. 11:23   **7:21** j Ex. 2:3, 4 k Ex. 2:5–10   **7:22** l Luke 24:19   **7:23** m Ex. 2:11, 12   **7:27** n Ex. 2:14   **7:29** o Heb. 11:27 p Ex. 2:15, 21, 22; 4:20; 18:3   **7:30** q Ex. 3:1–10   **7:32** r Ex. 3:6, 15   **7:33** s Ex. 3:5, 7, 8, 10   **7:34** t Ex. 2:24, 25 u Ps. 105:26   **7:35** v Ex. 2:14 w Ex. 14:21   **7:36** x Ex. 12:41; 33:1 y Ps. 105:27 z Ex. 14:21 a Ex. 16:1, 35

Israel Rebels Against God

37"This is that Moses who said to the children of Israel,* b'The LORD your God will raise up for you a Prophet like me from your brethren. cHim you shall hear.'*

38d"This is he who was in the congregation in the wilderness with ethe Angel who spoke to him on Mount Sinai, and with our fathers, fthe one who received the living goracles to give to us, 39whom our fathers hwould not obey, but rejected. And in their hearts they turned back to Egypt, 40isaying to Aaron, 'Make us gods to go before us; as for this Moses who brought us out of the land of Egypt, we do not know what has become of him.'* 41jAnd they made a calf in those days, offered sacrifices to the idol, and krejoiced in the works of their own hands. 42Then lGod turned and gave them up to worship mthe host of heaven, as it is written in the book of the Prophets:

n'Did you offer Me slaughtered animals
　and sacrifices during forty years
　in the wilderness,
O house of Israel?
43　You also took up the tabernacle of
　　Moloch,
　And the star of your god Remphan,
　Images which you made to worship;
　And oI will carry you away beyond
　　Babylon.'*

God's True Tabernacle

44"Our fathers had the tabernacle of witness in the wilderness, as He appointed, instructing Moses pto make it according to the pattern that he had seen, 45qwhich our fathers, having received it in turn, also brought with Joshua into the land possessed by the Gentiles, rwhom God drove out before the face of our fathers until the sdays of David, 46twho found favor before God and uasked to find a dwelling for the

God of Jacob. 47vBut Solomon built Him a house.

48"However, wthe Most High does not dwell in temples made with hands, as the prophet says:

49　'Heavenx is My throne,
　And earth is My footstool.
　What house will you build for Me?
　　says the LORD,
　Or what is the place of My rest?
50　Has My hand not ymade all these
　　things?'*

Israel Resists the Holy Spirit

51"You zstiff-necked and auncircumcised in heart and ears! You always resist the Holy Spirit; as your fathers did, so do you. 52bWhich of the prophets did your fathers not persecute? And they killed those who foretold the coming of cthe Just One, of whom you now have become the betrayers and murderers, 53dwho have received the law by the direction of angels and have not kept it."

Stephen the Martyr

54eWhen they heard these things they were cut to the heart, and they gnashed at him with their teeth. 55But he, fbeing full of the Holy Spirit, gazed into heaven and saw the gglory of God, and Jesus standing at the right hand of God, 56and said, "Look! hI see the heavens opened and the iSon of Man standing at the right hand of God!"

57Then they cried out with a loud voice, stopped their ears, and ran at him with one accord; 58and they cast him out of the city and stoned him. And jthe witnesses laid down their clothes at the feet of a young

---

* **7:37** Deuteronomy 18:15 • NU-Text and M-Text omit Him you shall hear. * **7:40** Exodus 32:1, 23 * **7:43** Amos 5:25–27 * **7:50** Isaiah 66:1, 2

7:38 The Meaning of the Church—In modern English the word church is used five ways: (1) a building designated as a place of worship; (2) all who profess faith in Christ; (3) a denomination; (4) a single organized local church; and (5) the body of Christ, that is, the universal church. While all of these may be legitimate uses for modern English, the word church is used in the New Testament in only the last two senses—a local congregation or the body of Christ, the universal church. At its root, the word church means a "called-out group." It is used for the nation of Israel (7:38), which was a group of people who were called out of the rest of the world to have a special national relationship to God. It is used for a local church (1 Thess. 1:1; Rev. 2:1) and for the universal church, the body of Christ (Col. 1:18). The universal church comprises all believers from the Day of Pentecost until God completes His plan for the world. The local church is a local, visible, temporal manifestation of the universal church.

7:44 tabernacle. The ancient tabernacle had been the focus of the Israelites' national worship. Even after the miraculous deliverance from Egypt there was a tendency among the people to forget God. The

tabernacle was a constant testimony of God's presence no matter where the people went. Paul tells us that we are the tabernacle, the temple of God (1 Cor. 3:16). We can never move beyond God's reach, for we carry His presence with us.

7:58 cast him out of the city. Because Jewish law did not allow an execution within the walls of the holy city, the religious leaders took Stephen outside the city. Jerusalem is situated in a stony area and this made Stephen's hasty (and illegal) execution easy. His executioners had plenty of rocks at hand, they only had to bend over and pick them up (see John 10:31).

7:37 b Deut. 18:15, 18, 19 c Matt. 17:5 **7:38** d Ex. 19:3 e Gal. 3:19 f Deut. 5:27 g Heb. 5:12 **7:39** h Ps. 95:8–11 **7:40** i Ex. 32:1, 23 **7:41** j Deut. 9:16 k Ex. 32:6, 18, 19 **7:42** l [2 Thess. 2:11] m 2 Kin. 21:3 n Amos 5:25–27 **7:43** o Jer. 25:9–12 **7:44** p [Heb. 8:5] **7:45** q Josh. 3:14; 18:1; 23:9 r Ps. 44:2 s 2 Sam. 6:2–15 **7:46** t 2 Sam. 7:1–13 u 1 Chr. 22:7 **7:47** v 1 Kin. 6:1–38; 8:20, 21 **7:48** w 1 Kin. 8:27 **7:49** x Is. 66:1, 2 **7:50** y Ps. 102:25 **7:51** z Ex. 32:9 a Lev. 26:41 **7:52** b 2 Chr. 36:16 c Acts 3:14; 22:14 **7:53** d Ex. 20:1 **7:54** e Acts 5:33 **7:55** f Acts 6:5 g [Ex. 24:17] **7:56** h Matt. 3:16 i Dan. 7:13 **7:58** j Acts 22:20

man named Saul. ⁵⁹And they stoned Stephen as he was calling on *God* and saying, "Lord Jesus, ᵏreceive my spirit." ⁶⁰Then he knelt down and cried out with a loud voice, ˡ"Lord, do not charge them with this sin." And when he had said this, he fell asleep.

Saul Persecutes the Church

8 Now Saul was consenting to his death. At that time a great persecution arose against the church which was at Jerusalem; and ᵃthey were all scattered throughout the regions of Judea and Samaria, except the apostles. ²And devout men carried Stephen *to his burial*, and ᵇmade great lamentation over him.

³As for Saul, ᶜhe made havoc of the church, entering every house, and dragging off men and women, committing *them* to prison.

Christ Is Preached in Samaria

⁴Therefore ᵈthose who were scattered went everywhere preaching the word. ⁵Then ᵉPhilip went down to the* city of Samaria and preached Christ to them. ⁶And the multitudes with one accord heeded the things spoken by Philip, hearing and seeing the miracles which he did. ⁷For ᶠunclean spirits, crying with a loud voice, came out of many who were possessed; and many who were paralyzed and lame were healed. ⁸And there was great joy in that city.

The Sorcerer's Profession of Faith

⁹But there was a certain man called Simon, who previously ᵍpracticed sorcery in the city and ʰastonished the people of Samaria, claiming that he was someone great, ¹⁰to whom they all gave heed, from the least to the greatest, saying, "This man is the great power of God." ¹¹And they heeded him because he had astonished

them with his sorceries for a long time. ¹²But when they believed Philip as he preached the things ⁱconcerning the kingdom of God and the name of Jesus Christ, both men and women were baptized. ¹³Then Simon himself also believed; and when he was baptized he continued with Philip, and was amazed, seeing the miracles and signs which were done.

The Sorcerer's Sin

¹⁴Now when the ʲapostles who were at Jerusalem heard that Samaria had received the word of God, they sent Peter and John to them, ¹⁵who, when they had come down, prayed for them ᵏthat they might receive the Holy Spirit. ¹⁶For ˡas yet He had fallen upon none of them. ᵐThey had only been baptized in ⁿthe name of the Lord Jesus. ¹⁷Then ᵒthey laid hands on them, and they received the Holy Spirit.

¹⁸And when Simon saw that through the laying on of the apostles' hands the Holy Spirit was given, he offered them money, ¹⁹saying, "Give me this power also, that anyone on whom I lay hands may receive the Holy Spirit."

²⁰But Peter said to him, "Your money perish with you, because ᵖyou thought that �q the gift of God could be purchased with money! ²¹You have neither part nor portion in this matter, for your ʳheart is not right in the sight of God. ²²Repent therefore of this your wickedness, and pray God ˢif perhaps the thought of your heart may be forgiven you. ²³For I see that you are ᵗpoisoned by bitterness and bound by iniquity."

²⁴Then Simon answered and said, ᵘ"Pray to the Lord for me, that none of the things which you have spoken may come upon me."

²⁵So when they had testified and

---

* 8:5 Or *a*

7:59–60 Death—Scripture affirms, and experience confirms, the universality of death. It comes to kings and commoners, saints and sinners alike. Christians die, as well as unbelievers. No one likes to think of dying violently, but Stephen's death shows that even this end can be met with courage and peace. In both life and death Stephen sought to imitate his Lord, and he departed without resentment, praying for the pardon of his foes.

8:5 *Samaria*. In the first century, the Jews and Samaritans despised one another. The Jews considered the Samaritans half-breeds and religious deviants. Following the fall of the northern kingdom of Israel in 722 B.C., Samaria had been resettled by colonists brought to the land by the Assyrians. These colonists intermarried with the remaining Jews, and the Samaritans of the New Testament era were descendants of these mixed marriages. Because of their mixed heritage and their rejection of the temple in Jerusalem and most of the Old Testament Scriptures (the Samaritans only accepted the five books of Moses), the Jews considered them to be unclean. The

amazing work of the Holy Spirit in forming one fellowship out of Jewish and Samaritan believers indicates that there is no room for racial or ethnic division in His church (Gal. 3:26–28).

8:14–15 *that they might receive the Holy Spirit.* This episode clearly showed the Samaritans that salvation did come through the Jews, and that the Scriptures they had previously rejected were actually God's message. It also showed the Jewish believers that God had accepted the Samaritan believers fully into His family. The dependence of the Samaritans upon the Jews to receive the gift of the Holy Spirit was the healing sign that the two sides were to become one.

7:59 ᵏPs. 31:5 **7:60** ˡMatt. 5:44 **8:1** ᵃActs 8:4; 11:19 **8:2** ᵇGen. 23:2 **8:3** ᶜPhil. 3:6 **8:4** ᵈMatt. 10:23 **8:5** ᵉActs 6:5; 8:26, 30 **8:7** ᶠMark 16:17 **8:9** ᵍActs 8:11; 13:6 ʰActs 5:36 **8:12** ⁱActs 1:3; 8:4 **8:14** ʲActs 5:12, 29, 40 **8:15** ᵏActs 2:38; 19:2 **8:16** ˡActs 19:2 ᵐMatt. 28:19 ⁿActs 10:48; 19:5 **8:17** ᵒActs 6:6; 19:6 **8:20** ᵖ[Matt. 10:8] q[Acts 2:38; 10:45; 11:17] **8:21** ʳJer. 17:9 **8:22** ˢ2 Tim. 2:25 **8:23** ᵗHeb. 12:15 **8:24** ᵘJames 5:16

preached the word of the Lord, they returned to Jerusalem, preaching the gospel in many villages of the Samaritans.

Christ Is Preached to an Ethiopian

26Now an angel of the Lord spoke to vPhilip, saying, "Arise and go toward the south along the road which goes down from Jerusalem to Gaza." This is desert. 27So he arose and went. And behold, wa man of Ethiopia, a eunuch of great authority under Candace the queen of the Ethiopians, who had charge of all her treasury, and xhad come to Jerusalem to worship, 28was returning. And sitting in his chariot, he was reading Isaiah the prophet. 29Then the Spirit said to Philip, "Go near and overtake this chariot."

30So Philip ran to him, and heard him reading the prophet Isaiah, and said, "Do you understand what you are reading?"

31And he said, "How can I, unless someone guides me?" And he asked Philip to come up and sit with him. 32The place in the Scripture which he read was this:

y"He was led as a sheep to the slaughter;
And as a lamb before its shearer is
   silent,
z So He opened not His mouth.
33 In His humiliation His ajustice was
   taken away,
And who will declare His
   generation?
For His life is btaken from the earth."*

34So the eunuch answered Philip and said, "I ask you, of whom does the prophet say this, of himself or of some other man?" 35Then Philip opened his mouth, cand beginning at this Scripture, preached Jesus to him. 36Now as they went down the road, they came to some water. And the eunuch said, "See, here is water. dWhat hinders me from being baptized?"

37Then Philip said, e"If you believe with all your heart, you may."

And he answered and said, f"I believe that Jesus Christ is the Son of God."*

38So he commanded the chariot to stand still. And both Philip and the eunuch went down into the water, and he baptized him. 39Now when they came up out of the water, gthe Spirit of the Lord caught Philip away, so that the eunuch saw him no more; and he went on his way rejoicing. 40But Philip was found at Azotus. And passing through, he preached in all the cities till he came to hCaesarea.

The Damascus Road: Saul Converted

9 Then aSaul, still breathing threats and murder against the disciples of the Lord, went to the high priest 2and asked bletters from him to the synagogues of Damascus, so that if he found any who were of the Way, whether men or women, he might bring them bound to Jerusalem.

3cAs he journeyed he came near Damascus, and suddenly a light shone around him from heaven. 4Then he fell to the ground, and heard a voice saying to him, "Saul, Saul, dwhy are you persecuting Me?"

5And he said, "Who are You, Lord?"

Then the Lord said, "I am Jesus, whom you are persecuting.* It is hard for you to kick against the goads."

6So he, trembling and astonished, said, "Lord, what do You want me to do?"

Then the Lord said to him, "Arise and go into the city, and you will be told what you must do."

* **8:33** Isaiah 53:7, 8   * **8:37** NU-Text and M-Text omit this verse. It is found in Western texts, including the Latin tradition. * **9:5** NU-Text and M-Text omit the last sentence of verse 5 and begin verse 6 with *But arise and go.*

8:27 *had come to Jerusalem to worship.* Many Gentiles in the first century had grown weary of the multiple gods and loose morals of their own cultures. In their search for something more, some of them came to Judaism. One who accepted Judaism, obeying all the law of Moses (including circumcision and baptism), was called a *proselyte.* Gentiles who did not become proselytes but did attend the Jewish synagogues to listen to the Scriptures were called *God-fearers.* We cannot be sure which category the Ethiopian eunuch fell into.

8:35 *preached Jesus to him.* First-century Jews did not speak much about a suffering Messiah. The Jewish people, facing the yoke of Roman rule, believed that the Messiah would come as the Lion of Judah, a delivering king, not a weak lamb. They believed and taught that the suffering One spoken of by Isaiah was the suffering nation of Israel. Philip's explanation of the passage gave a very different view, showing Jesus as the Messiah who came to suffer and die in order to redeem sinners.

9:2 *synagogues.* The early Jewish believers in Jesus were still attending the synagogues, gathering

places where Jews came together to hear the Scriptures read and expounded upon. Part of Saul's mission was apparently to let the Damascus synagogues know beyond any doubt that the followers of "the Way" did not have the approval of the Sanhedrin.

9:4–5 *Messiah*—Apparently unimpressed by the witness of the dying Stephen (7:59), Saul needed a more serious, personal jolt to awaken his spiritual awareness. The light that blinded Saul prepared him to receive the True Light that came into the world to dispel the darkness of sin. This personal encounter with the risen Christ changed Saul from a fire-breathing persecutor into a dynamic preacher who was not ashamed to publicly claim the crucified Man from Galilee as his Lord and Savior.

8:26 v Acts 6:5 **8:27** w Ps. 68:31; 87:4 x John 12:20
8:32 y Is. 53:7, 8 z John 19:9 **8:33** a Luke 23:1–25 b Luke 23:33–46 **8:35** c Luke 24:27 **8:36** d Acts 10:47; 16:33
8:37 e [Mark 16:16] f Matt. 16:16 **8:39** g Ezek. 3:12, 14 **8:40** h Acts 21:8 **9:1** a Acts 7:57; 8:1, 3; 26:10, 11
9:2 b Acts 22:5 **9:3** c 1 Cor. 15:8 **9:4** d [Matt. 25:40]

7And ethe men who journeyed with him stood speechless, hearing a voice but seeing no one. 8Then Saul arose from the ground, and when his eyes were opened he saw no one. But they led him by the hand and brought *him* into Damascus. 9And he was three days without sight, and neither ate nor drank.

Ananias Baptizes Saul

10Now there was a certain disciple at Damascus fnamed Ananias; and to him the Lord said in a vision, "Ananias."

And he said, "Here I am, Lord."

11So the Lord *said* to him, "Arise and go to the street called Straight, and inquire at the house of Judas for *one* called Saul gof Tarsus, for behold, he is praying. 12And in a vision he has seen a man named Ananias coming in and putting *his* hand on him, so that he might receive his sight."

13Then Ananias answered, "Lord, I have heard from many about this man, hhow much harm he has done to Your saints in Jerusalem. 14And here he has authority from the chief priests to bind all iwho call on Your name."

15But the Lord said to him, "Go, for jhe is a chosen vessel of Mine to bear My name before kGentiles, lkings, and the mchildren of Israel. 16For nI will show him how many things he must suffer for My oname's sake."

17pAnd Ananias went his way and entered the house; and qlaying his hands on him he said, "Brother Saul, the Lord Jesus,* who appeared to you on the road as you came, has sent me that you may receive your sight and rbe filled with the Holy Spirit." 18Immediately there fell from his eyes *something* like scales, and he received his sight at once; and he arose and was baptized.

19So when he had received food, he was strengthened. sThen Saul spent some days with the disciples at Damascus.

Saul Preaches Christ

20Immediately he preached the Christ* in the synagogues, that He is the Son of God.

21Then all who heard were amazed, and said, t"Is this not he who destroyed those who called on this name in Jerusalem, and has come here for that purpose, so that he might bring them bound to the chief priests?"

22But Saul increased all the more in strength, uand confounded the Jews who dwelt in Damascus, proving that this *Jesus* is the Christ.

Saul Escapes Death

23Now after many days were past, vthe Jews plotted to kill him. 24wBut their plot became known to Saul. And they watched the gates day and night, to kill him. 25Then the disciples took him by night and xlet *him* down through the wall in a large basket.

Saul at Jerusalem

26And ywhen Saul had come to Jerusalem, he tried to join the disciples; but they were all afraid of him, and did not believe that he was a disciple. 27zBut Barnabas took him and brought *him* to the apostles. And he declared to them how he had seen the Lord on the road, and that He had spoken to him, aand how he had preached boldly at Damascus in the name of Jesus. 28So bhe was with them at Jerusalem, coming in and going out. 29And he spoke boldly in the name of the Lord Jesus and disputed against the cHellenists, dbut they attempted to kill him. 30When the brethren found out, they brought him down to Caesarea and sent him out to Tarsus.

The Church Prospers

31eThen the churches* throughout all Judea, Galilee, and Samaria had peace and were fedified. And walking in the gfear of the Lord and in the hcomfort of the Holy Spirit, they were imultiplied.

Aeneas Healed

32Now it came to pass, as Peter went jthrough all *parts of the country*, that he also came down to the saints who dwelt in Lydda. 33There he found a certain man named Aeneas, who had been bedridden eight years and was paralyzed. 34And Peter said to him, "Aeneas, kJesus the Christ heals you. Arise and make your bed." Then he arose immediately. 35So all who dwelt at

---

* 9:17 M-Text omits *Jesus.*   * 9:20 NU-Text reads *Jesus.*   * 9:31 NU-Text reads *church ... was edified.*

9:17 Jesus, who appeared to you. Saul was not dreaming on the road to Damascus but instead had seen the resurrected Lord.

9:30 Tarsus. Saul's hometown was about three hundred miles north of Jerusalem and about ten miles inland from the Mediterranean Sea. Tarsus was a well-known university city, surpassed in educational opportunities only by Athens and Alexandria.

9:31 peace. This peace was not due solely to Saul's conversion. Tiberius, the emperor of Rome, died around this time. He was replaced by Caligula, who wanted to erect a statue of himself in the temple at Jerusalem. The attention of the Jewish religious leaders was directed towards this new threat, and

the emerging church was given a short season of respite.

9:7 e [Acts 22:9; 26:13]   **9:10** f Acts 22:12   **9:11** g Acts 21:39; 22:3   **9:13** h Acts 9:1   **9:14** i Acts 7:59; 9:2, 21   **9:15** j Eph. 3:7, 8 k Rom. 1:5; 11:13 l Acts 25:22, 23; 26:1 m Rom. 1:16; 9:1–5   **9:16** n Acts 20:23 o 2 Cor. 4:11   **9:17** p Acts 22:12, 13 q Acts 8:17 r Acts 2:4; 4:31; 8:17; 13:52   **9:19** s Acts 26:20   **9:21** t Gal. 1:13, 23   **9:22** u Acts 18:28   **9:23** v 2 Cor. 11:26   **9:24** w 2 Cor. 11:32   **9:25** x Josh. 2:15   y Acts 22:17–20; 26:20   **9:27** z Acts 4:36; 13:2   a Acts 9:20, 22   **9:28** b Gal. 1:18   **9:29** c Acts 6:1; 11:20   d 2 Cor. 11:26   **9:31** e Acts 5:11; 8:1; 16:5 f [Eph. 4:16, 29] g Ps. 34:9 h John 14:16 i Acts 16:5   **9:32** j Acts 8:14   **9:34** k [Acts 3:6, 16; 4:10]

Lydda and *l*Sharon saw him and *m*turned to the Lord.

Dorcas Restored to Life

³⁶At Joppa there was a certain disciple named Tabitha, which is translated Dorcas. This woman was full *n*of good works and charitable deeds which she did. ³⁷But it happened in those days that she became sick and died. When they had washed her, they laid *her* in *o*an upper room. ³⁸And since Lydda was near Joppa, and the disciples had heard that Peter was there, they sent two men to him, imploring *him* not to delay in coming to them. ³⁹Then Peter arose and went with them. When he had come, they brought *him* to the upper room. And all the widows stood by him weeping, showing the tunics and garments which Dorcas had made while she was with them. ⁴⁰But Peter *p*put them all out, and *q*knelt down and prayed. And turning to the body he *r*said, "Tabitha, arise." And she opened her eyes, and when she saw Peter she sat up. ⁴¹Then he gave her *his* hand and lifted her up; and when he had called the saints and widows, he presented her alive. ⁴²And it became known throughout all Joppa, *s*and many believed on the Lord. ⁴³So it was that he stayed many days in Joppa with *t*Simon, a tanner.

Cornelius Sends a Delegation

10 There was a certain man in *a*Caesarea called Cornelius, a centurion of what was called the Italian Regiment, 2*b*a devout *man* and one who *c*feared God with all his household, who gave alms generously to the people, and prayed to God always. ³About the ninth hour of the day *d*he saw clearly in a vision an angel of God coming in and saying to him, "Cornelius!"

⁴And when he observed him, he was afraid, and said, "What is it, lord?"

So he said to him, "Your prayers and your alms have come up for a memorial before God. ⁵Now *e*send men to Joppa, and send for Simon whose surname is Peter. ⁶He is lodging with *f*Simon, a tanner, whose house is by the sea.* *g*He will tell you what you must do." ⁷And when the angel who spoke to him had departed, Cornelius called two of his household servants and

a devout soldier from among those who waited on him continually. ⁸So when he had explained all *these* things to them, he sent them to Joppa.

Peter's Vision

⁹The next day, as they went on their journey and drew near the city, *h*Peter went up on the housetop to pray, about the sixth hour. ¹⁰Then he became very hungry and wanted to eat; but while they made ready, he fell into a trance ¹¹and *i*saw heaven opened and an object like a great sheet bound at the four corners, descending to him and let down to the earth. ¹²In it were all kinds of four-footed animals of the earth, wild beasts, creeping things, and birds of the air. ¹³And a voice came to him, "Rise, Peter; kill and eat."

¹⁴But Peter said, "Not so, Lord! *j*For I have never eaten anything common or unclean."

¹⁵And a voice *spoke* to him again the second time, *k*"What God has cleansed you must not call common." ¹⁶This was done three times. And the object was taken up into heaven again.

Summoned to Caesarea

¹⁷Now while Peter wondered within himself what this vision which he had seen meant, behold, the men who had been sent from Cornelius had made inquiry for Simon's house, and stood before the gate. ¹⁸And they called and asked whether Simon, whose surname was Peter, was lodging there.

¹⁹While Peter thought about the vision, *l*the Spirit said to him, "Behold, three men are seeking you. ²⁰*m*Arise therefore, go down and go with them, doubting nothing; for I have sent them."

²¹Then Peter went down to the men who had been sent to him from Cornelius,* and said, "Yes, I am he whom you seek. For what reason have you come?"

²²And they said, "Cornelius *the* centurion, a just man, one who fears God and *n*has a good reputation among all the nation of

---

* **10:6** NU-Text and M-Text omit the last sentence of this verse.   * **10:21** NU-Text and M-Text omit *who had been sent to him from Cornelius.*

10:1—11:18 The following two chapters mark an important turning point in the Book of Acts. Those who were scattered by persecution from Jerusalem had been preaching the gospel only to Jews (11:19). At this point, they began to overcome their prejudices and carry the message of Christ to the Gentiles. **10:6 *Simon, a tanner.*** God cut away Peter's prejudices by having him stay for many days with one whose trade Peter likely considered repulsive. Since a tanner (one who makes leather) is constantly working with animals dead from various causes, he would spend much of his life ceremonially "unclean." **10:15 *What God has cleansed you must not call***

common. Food may have been his first consideration, but Peter would soon understand the greater message. The vision was a sign from heaven that Jews were no longer to call Gentiles unclean.

9:35 *l* 1 Chr. 5:16; 27:29 *m* Acts 11:21; 15:19   **9:36** *n* 1 Tim. 2:10   **9:37** *o* Acts 1:13; 9:39   **9:40** *p* Matt. 9:25   *q* Acts 7:60   *r* Mark 5:41, 42   **9:42** *s* John 11:45   **9:43** *t* Acts 10:6   **10:1** *a* Acts 8:40; 23:23   **10:2** *b* Acts 8:2; 9:22; 22:12   *c* [Acts 10:22, 35; 13:16, 26]   **10:3** *d* Acts 10:30; 11:13   **10:5** *e* Acts 11:13, 14   **10:6** *f* Acts 9:43   *g* Acts 11:14   **10:9** *h* Acts 10:9–32; 11:5–14   **10:11** *i* Acts 7:56   **10:14** *j* Deut. 14:3, 7   **10:15** *k* [Rom. 14:14]   **10:19** *l* Acts 11:12   **10:20** *m* Acts 15:7–9   **10:22** *n* Acts 22:12

the Jews, was divinely instructed by a holy angel to summon you to his house, and to hear words from you." [23]Then he invited them in and lodged *them*.

On the next day Peter went away with them, [o]and some brethren from Joppa accompanied him.

Peter Meets Cornelius

[24]And the following day they entered Caesarea. Now Cornelius was waiting for them, and had called together his relatives and close friends. [25]As Peter was coming in, Cornelius met him and fell down at his feet and worshiped *him*. [26]But Peter lifted him up, saying, [p]"Stand up; I myself am also a man." [27]And as he talked with him, he went in and found many who had come together. [28]Then he said to them, "You know how [q]unlawful it is for a Jewish man to keep company with or go to one of another nation. But [r]God has shown me that I should not call any man common or unclean. [29]Therefore I came without objection as soon as I was sent for. I ask, then, for what reason have you sent for me?"

[30]So Cornelius said, "Four days ago I was fasting until this hour; and at the ninth hour* I prayed in my house, and behold, [s]a man stood before me [t]in bright clothing, [31]and said, 'Cornelius, [u]your prayer has been heard, and [v]your alms are remembered in the sight of God. [32]Send therefore to Joppa and call Simon here, whose surname is Peter. He is lodging in the house of Simon, a tanner, by the sea.* When he comes, he will speak to you.' [33]So I sent to you immediately, and you have done well to come. Now therefore, we are all present before God, to hear all the things commanded you by God."

Preaching to Cornelius' Household

[34]Then Peter opened *his* mouth and said: [w]"In truth I perceive that God shows no partiality. [35]But [x]in every nation whoever fears Him and works righteousness is [y]accepted by Him. [36]The word which *God* sent to the children of Israel, [z]preaching peace through Jesus Christ—[a]He is Lord of all— [37]that word you know, which was proclaimed throughout all Judea, and [b]began from Galilee after the baptism which John preached: [38]how [c]God anointed Jesus

of Nazareth with the Holy Spirit and with power, who [d]went about doing good and healing all who were oppressed by the devil, [e]for God was with Him. [39]And we are [f]witnesses of all things which He did both in the land of the Jews and in Jerusalem, whom they* [g]killed by hanging on a tree. [40]Him [h]God raised up on the third day, and showed Him openly, [41][i]not to all the people, but to witnesses chosen before by God, *even* to us [j]who ate and drank with Him after He arose from the dead. [42]And [k]He commanded us to preach to the people, and to testify [l]that it is He who was ordained by God *to be* Judge [m]of the living and the dead. [43][n]To Him all the prophets witness that, through His name, [o]whoever believes in Him will receive [p]remission of sins."

The Holy Spirit Falls on the Gentiles

[44]While Peter was still speaking these words, [q]the Holy Spirit fell upon all those who heard the word. [45][r]And those of the circumcision who believed were astonished, as many as came with Peter, [s]because the gift of the Holy Spirit had been poured out on the Gentiles also. [46]For they heard them speak with tongues and magnify God.

Then Peter answered, [47]"Can anyone forbid water, that these should not be baptized who have received the Holy Spirit [t]just as we *have*?" [48][u]And he commanded them to be baptized [v]in the name of the Lord. Then they asked him to stay a few days.

Peter Defends God's Grace

11 Now the apostles and brethren who were in Judea heard that the Gentiles had also received the word of God. [2]And when Peter came up to Jerusalem, [a]those of the circumcision contended with him, [3]saying, [b]"You went in to uncircumcised men [c]and ate with them!"

[4]But Peter explained *it* to them [d]in order from the beginning, saying: [5][e]"I was in the city of Joppa praying; and in a trance I saw a vision, an object descending like a great sheet, let down from heaven by

---

* **10:30** NU-Text reads *Four days ago to this hour, at the ninth hour.* * **10:32** NU-Text omits the last sentence of this verse. * **10:39** NU-Text and M-Text add *also.*

10:44 the Holy Spirit fell upon all those who heard the word. Following the plan laid out by Jesus before His ascension (1:8), the good news had reached the Jews, the Samaritans, and now the Gentiles. All were united by the same faith in the same Lord with the same gift of the Holy Spirit.

11:2 those of the circumcision. This term refers to Jewish believers in Jesus who taught that Gentiles had to become Jews (be circumcised and keep the law of Moses) in order to become Christians.

10:23 [o] Acts 10:45; 11:12 **10:26** [p] Acts 14:14, 15 **10:28** [q] John 4:9; 18:28 [r] [Acts 10:14, 35; 15:8, 9] **10:30** [s] Acts 1:10 [t] Matt. 28:3 **10:31** [u] Dan. 10:12 [v] Heb. 6:10 **10:34** [w] Deut. 10:17 **10:35** [x] [Eph. 2:13] [y] Ps. 15:1, 2 **10:36** [z] Is. 57:19 [a] Rom. 10:12 **10:37** [b] Luke 4:14 **10:38** [c] Luke 4:18 [d] Matt. 4:23 [e] John 3:2; 8:29 **10:39** [f] Acts 1:8 [g] Acts 2:23 **10:40** [h] Acts 2:24 **10:41** [i] [John 14:17, 19, 22; 15:27] [j] Luke 24:30, 41–43 **10:42** [k] Matt. 28:19 [l] John 5:22, 27 [m] 1 Pet. 4:5 [n] Zech. 13:1 [o] Gal. 3:22 [p] Acts 13:38, 39 **10:44** [q] Acts 4:31 **10:45** [r] Acts 10:23 [s] Acts 11:18 **10:47** [t] Acts 2:4; 10:44; 11:17; 15:8 **10:48** [u] 1 Cor. 1:14–17 [v] Acts 2:38; 8:16; 19:5 **11:2** [a] Acts 10:45 **11:3** [b] Acts 10:28 [c] Gal. 2:12 **11:4** [d] Luke 1:3 **11:5** [e] Acts 10:9

four corners; and it came to me. 6 When I
observed it intently and considered, I saw
four-footed animals of the earth, wild
beasts, creeping things, and birds of the
air. 7 And I heard a voice saying to me,
'Rise, Peter; kill and eat.' 8 But I said, 'Not
so, Lord! For nothing common or unclean
has at any time entered my mouth.' 9 But
the voice answered me again from heav-
en, 'What God has cleansed you must not
call common.' 10 Now this was done three
times, and all were drawn up again into
heaven. 11 At that very moment, three men
stood before the house where I was, having been sent to me from Caesarea. 12 Then
[f]the Spirit told me to go with them, doubting nothing. Moreover [g]these six brethren
accompanied me, and we entered the man's
house. 13 [h]And he told us how he had seen
an angel standing in his house, who said
to him, 'Send men to Joppa, and call for
Simon whose surname is Peter, 14 who will
tell you words by which you and all your
household will be saved.' 15 And as I began
to speak, the Holy Spirit fell upon them, [i]as
upon us at the beginning. 16 Then I remembered the word of the Lord, how He said,
[j]'John indeed baptized with water, but [k]you
shall be baptized with the Holy Spirit.' 17 [l]If
therefore God gave them the same gift as
He gave us when we believed on the Lord
Jesus Christ, [m]who was I that I could withstand God?"
18 When they heard these things they
became silent; and they glorified God, saying, [n]"Then God has also granted to the
Gentiles repentance to life."

Barnabas and Saul at Antioch

19 [o]Now those who were scattered after
the persecution that arose over Stephen
traveled as far as Phoenicia, Cyprus, and
Antioch, preaching the word to no one
but the Jews only. 20 But some of them
were men from Cyprus and Cyrene, who,
when they had come to Antioch, spoke to
[p]the Hellenists, preaching the Lord Jesus.
21 And [q]the hand of the Lord was with them,
and a great number believed and [r]turned
to the Lord.
22 Then news of these things came to the
ears of the church in Jerusalem, and they
sent out [s]Barnabas to go as far as Antioch.
23 When he came and had seen the grace of
God, he was glad, and [t]encouraged them
all that with purpose of heart they should
continue with the Lord. 24 For he was a
good man, [u]full of the Holy Spirit and of
faith. [v]And a great many people were added to the Lord.
25 Then Barnabas departed for [w]Tarsus
to seek Saul. 26 And when he had found
him, he brought him to Antioch. So it was
that for a whole year they assembled with
the church and taught a great many people.
And the disciples were first called Christians in Antioch.

Relief to Judea

27 And in these days [x]prophets came
from Jerusalem to Antioch. 28 Then one
of them, named [y]Agabus, stood up and
showed by the Spirit that there was going
to be a great famine throughout all the
world, which also happened in the days
of [z]Claudius Caesar. 29 Then the disciples,
each according to his ability, determined to
send [a]relief to the brethren dwelling in Judea. 30 [b]This they also did, and sent it to the
elders by the hands of Barnabas and Saul.

Herod's Violence to the Church

12 Now about that time Herod the king
stretched out *his* hand to harass some
from the church. 2 Then he killed James
[a]the brother of John with the sword. 3 And
because he saw that it pleased the Jews,
he proceeded further to seize Peter also.
Now it was *during* [b]the Days of Unleavened Bread. 4 So [c]when he had arrested
him, he put *him* in prison, and delivered
him to four squads of soldiers to keep him,
intending to bring him before the people
after Passover.

11:16 *baptized with the Holy Spirit.* This is found seven times in the New Testament (1:5; Matt. 3:11; Mark 1:8; Luke 3:16; John 1:33; 1 Cor. 12:13) and refers to an act by Christ for believers.

11:22–23 *Antioch.* Seleucus I founded the city of Antioch, naming it after his father. The city was cosmopolitan, attracting people of various cultures and ethnic backgrounds—including people from Persia, India, and even China. The gospel proclaimed in Antioch would have tremendous potential for reaching other areas of the world.

11:26 *called Christians.* Originally, the believers had called themselves "followers of the Way." Although the term "Christian" was apparently given to them by nonbelievers, they adopted it for themselves. Its essential meaning, "Christ-follower" is appropriate for those who have given their lives into the keeping of Jesus, the Messiah.

11:29–30 Benevolence—Christians must exercise responsibility and charity (love) towards all men, and especially to other believers (Gal. 6:10). The Christians at Antioch are an example of well implemented Christian giving. All gave in accordance with their means (2 Cor. 8:3). The gifts were placed in the charge of trustworthy Christians (2 Cor. 8:20–21), who could ensure a responsible delivery and administration of the gifts.

12:1–3 *Herod the king.* This is Herod Agrippa I, the nephew of Herod Antipas who murdered John the

11:12 [f][John 16:13] [g]Acts 10:23 **11:13** [h]Acts 10:30 **11:15** [i]Acts 2:1–4; 15:7–9 **11:16** [j]John 1:26, 33 [k]Is. 44:3 **11:17** [l][Acts 15:8, 9] [m]Acts 10:47 **11:18** [n]Rom. 10:12, 13; 15:9, 16 **11:19** [o]Acts 8:1, 4 **11:20** [p]Acts 6:1; 9:29 **11:21** [q]Luke 1:66 [r]Acts 9:35; 14:1 **11:22** [s]Acts 4:36; 9:27 **11:23** [t]Acts 13:43; 14:22 **11:24** [u]Acts 6:5 [v]Acts 5:14; 11:21 **11:25** [w]Acts 9:11, 30 **11:27** [x]1 Cor. 12:28 **11:28** [y]Acts 21:10 [z]Acts 18:2 **11:29** [a]1 Cor. 16:1 **11:30** [b]Acts 12:25 **12:2** [a]Matt. 4:21; 20:23 **12:3** [b]Ex. 12:15; 23:15 **12:4** [c]John 21:18

Peter Freed from Prison

5 Peter was therefore kept in prison, but
constant* prayer was offered to God for
him by the church. 6 And when Herod was
about to bring him out, that night Peter
was sleeping, bound with two chains between two soldiers; and the guards before
the door were keeping the prison. 7 Now
behold, [d]an angel of the Lord stood by
him, and a light shone in the prison; and
he struck Peter on the side and raised him
up, saying, "Arise quickly!" And his chains
fell off *his* hands. 8 Then the angel said to
him, "Gird yourself and tie on your sandals"; and so he did. And he said to him,
"Put on your garment and follow me." 9 So
he went out and followed him, and [e]did not
know that what was done by the angel was
real, but thought [f]he was seeing a vision.
10 When they were past the first and the
second guard posts, they came to the iron
gate that leads to the city, [g]which opened to
them of its own accord; and they went out
and went down one street, and immediately the angel departed from him.

11 And when Peter had come to himself,
he said, "Now I know for certain that [h]the
Lord has sent His angel, and [i]has delivered
me from the hand of Herod and *from* all the
expectation of the Jewish people."

12 So, when he had considered *this,* [j]he
came to the house of Mary, the mother of
[k]John whose surname was Mark, where
many were gathered together [l]praying.
13 And as Peter knocked at the door of the
gate, a girl named Rhoda came to answer.
14 When she recognized Peter's voice, because of *her* gladness she did not open the
gate, but ran in and announced that Peter
stood before the gate. 15 But they said to her,
"You are beside yourself!" Yet she kept in-
sisting that it was so. So they said, [m]"It is
his angel."

16 Now Peter continued knocking; and
when they opened *the door* and saw him,
they were astonished. 17 But [n]motioning to
them with his hand to keep silent, he declared to them how the Lord had brought
him out of the prison. And he said, "Go,
tell these things to James and to the
brethren." And he departed and went to
another place.

18 Then, as soon as it was day, there was
no small stir among the soldiers about what
had become of Peter. 19 But when Herod had
searched for him and not found him, he examined the guards and commanded that
they should be put to death.

And he went down from Judea to Caesarea, and stayed *there.*

Herod's Violent Death

20 Now Herod had been very angry with
the people of [o]Tyre and Sidon; but they
came to him with one accord, and having made Blastus the king's personal aide
their friend, they asked for peace, because
[p]their country was supplied with food by
the king's *country.*

21 So on a set day Herod, arrayed in
royal apparel, sat on his throne and gave
an oration to them. 22 And the people kept
shouting, "The voice of a god and not of a
man!" 23 Then immediately an angel of the
Lord [q]struck him, because [r]he did not give
glory to God. And he was eaten by worms
and died.

24 But [s]the word of God grew and multiplied.

Barnabas and Saul Appointed

25 And [t]Barnabas and Saul returned
from* Jerusalem when they had [u]fulfilled
their ministry, and they also [v]took with
them [w]John whose surname was Mark.

13 Now [a]in the church that was at Antioch there were certain prophets
and teachers: [b]Barnabas, Simeon who was
called Niger, [c]Lucius of Cyrene, Manaen
who had been brought up with Herod the
tetrarch, and Saul. 2 As they ministered to
the Lord and fasted, the Holy Spirit said,
[d]"Now separate to Me Barnabas and Saul
for the work [e]to which I have called them."
3 Then, [f]having fasted and prayed, and laid
hands on them, they sent *them* away.

---

* **12:5** NU-Text reads *constantly* (or *earnestly*).
* **12:25** NU-Text and M-Text read *to.*

Baptist, and the grandson of Herod the Great who had the children of Bethlehem put to death in his search for Jesus. Herod was not a Jew but an Edomite. The Jews resented the fact that a son of Edom was given the position of king of the Jews.

12:11 *delivered me from the hand of Herod.* Why was Peter's life spared while James' life was taken? The answer is the sovereign will of God. If we believe that God is good and wise, we can trust that what He allowed to happen was part of His wise plan for the good of all His people.

12:22 *The voice of a god.* The Jewish historian Josephus also provides an account of this display, informing us that in an attempted appeasement of the king the people confessed that he was "more than mortal."

13:2–4 Holy Spirit—God reveals His will to those who are sensitive to His leading. The believers in Antioch heard from the Lord as they were praying and fasting. Most often, God does not speak to us out of the blue. He speaks to us when we are listening. The Holy Spirit gave distinct direction to the listening, sensitive believers of the first century, and He leads believers in the same way today.

13:3 *laid hands on them.* The laying on of hands was

12:7 [d]Acts 5:19 **12:9** [e]Ps. 126:1 [f]Acts 10:3, 17; 11:5 **12:10** [g]Acts 5:19; 16:26 **12:11** [h][Ps. 34:7] [i]Job 5:19 **12:12** [j]Acts 4:23 [k]Acts 13:5, 13; 15:37 [l]Acts 12:5 **12:15** [m][Matt. 18:10] **12:17** [n]Acts 13:16; 19:33; 21:40 **12:20** [o]Matt. 11:21 [p]Ezek. 27:17 **12:23** [q]2 Sam. 24:16, 17 [r]Ps. 115:1 **12:24** [s]Acts 6:7; 19:20 **12:25** [t]Acts 11:30 [u]Acts 11:30 [v]Acts 13:5, 13 [w]Acts 12:12; 15:37 **13:1** [a]Acts 14:26 [b]Acts 11:22 [c]Rom. 16:21 **13:2** [d]Gal. 1:15; 2:9 [e]Heb. 5:4 **13:3** [f]Acts 6:6

Preaching in Cyprus

4So, being sent out by the Holy Spirit, they went down to Seleucia, and from there they sailed to *g*Cyprus. 5And when they arrived in Salamis, *h*they preached the word of God in the synagogues of the Jews. They also had *i*John as *their* assistant.

6Now when they had gone through the island* to Paphos, they found *j*a certain sorcerer, a false prophet, a Jew whose name *was* Bar-Jesus, 7who was with the proconsul, Sergius Paulus, an intelligent man. This man called for Barnabas and Saul and sought to hear the word of God. 8But *k*Elymas the sorcerer (for so his name is translated) withstood them, seeking to turn the proconsul away from the faith. 9Then Saul, who also *is called* Paul, *l*filled with the Holy Spirit, looked intently at him 10and said, "O full of all deceit and all fraud, *m*you son of the devil, *you* enemy of all righteousness, will you not cease perverting the straight ways of the Lord? 11And now, indeed, *n*the hand of the Lord *is* upon you, and you shall be blind, not seeing the sun for a time."

And immediately a dark mist fell on him, and he went around seeking someone to lead him by the hand. 12Then the proconsul believed, when he saw what had been done, being astonished at the teaching of the Lord.

At Antioch in Pisidia

13Now when Paul and his party set sail from Paphos, they came to Perga in Pamphylia; and *o*John, departing from them, returned to Jerusalem. 14But when they departed from Perga, they came to Antioch in Pisidia, and *p*went into the synagogue on the Sabbath day and sat down. 15And *q*after the reading of the Law and the Prophets, the rulers of the synagogue sent to them, saying, "Men *and* brethren, if you have *r*any word of exhortation for the people, say on."

16Then Paul stood up, and motioning with *his* hand said, "Men of Israel, and *s*you who fear God, listen: 17The God of this people Israel* *t*chose our fathers, and exalted the people *u*when they dwelt as strangers in the land of Egypt, and with an uplifted arm He *v*brought them out of it. 18Now *w*for a time of about forty years He put up with

their ways in the wilderness. 19And when He had destroyed *x*seven nations in the land of Canaan, *y*He distributed their land to them by allotment.

20"After that *z*He gave *them* judges for about four hundred and fifty years, *a*until Samuel the prophet. 21*b*And afterward they asked for a king; so God gave them *c*Saul the son of Kish, a man of the tribe of Benjamin, for forty years. 22And *d*when He had removed him, *e*He raised up for them David as king, to whom also He gave testimony and said, *f'I* have found David* the *son* of Jesse, *g*a man after My own heart,* who will do all My will.'* 23*h*From this man's seed, according *i*to *the* promise, God raised up for Israel *j*a Savior—Jesus—* 24*k*after John had first preached, before His coming, the baptism of repentance to all the people of Israel. 25And as John was finishing his course, he said, *l'*Who do you think I am? I am not *He.* But behold, *m*there comes One after me, the sandals of whose feet I am not worthy to loose.'

26"Men *and* brethren, sons of the family of Abraham, and *n*those among you who fear God, *o*to you the word of this salvation has been sent. 27For those who dwell in Jerusalem, and their rulers, *p*because they did not know Him, nor even the voices of the Prophets which are read every Sabbath, have fulfilled *them* in condemning *Him.* 28*a*And though they found no cause for death *in Him,* they asked Pilate that He should be put to death. 29*r*Now when they had fulfilled all that was written concerning Him, *s*they took *Him* down from the tree and laid *Him* in a tomb. 30*t*But God raised Him from the dead. 31*u*He was seen for many days by those who came up with Him from Galilee to Jerusalem, who are His witnesses to the people. 32And we declare to you glad tidings—*v*that promise which was made to the fathers. 33God has fulfilled this for us their children, in that He has raised up Jesus. As it is also written in the second Psalm:

*w'*You are My Son,
    Today I have begotten You.'*

---

* **13:6** NU-Text reads *the whole island.*
* **13:17** M-Text omits *Israel.* * **13:22** Psalm 89:20 • 1 Samuel 13:14 * **13:23** M-Text reads *for Israel salvation.* * **13:33** Psalm 2:7

---

the church's way of identifying with and affirming the mission to which God had called a particular person.
13:6–12 *Sergius Paulus.* Luke presents this man as the first Gentile ruler to believe the gospel. There is no evidence that Sergius Paulus was a God-fearer or had ever shown any interest in Judaism prior to this time. This pagan government official was amazed at the power of God and believed the truth.

13:4 *g* Acts 4:36   **13:5** *h* [Acts 13:46] *i* Acts 12:25; 15:37
13:6 *j* Acts 8:9   **13:8** *k* Ex. 7:11   **13:9** *l* Acts 2:4; 4:8

13:10 *m* Matt. 13:38   **13:11** *n* 1 Sam. 5:6   **13:13** *o* Acts 15:38   **13:14** *p* Acts 16:13   **13:15** *q* Luke 4:16 *r* Heb. 13:22   **13:16** *s* Acts 10:35   **13:17** *t* Deut. 7:6–8 *u* Acts 7:17 *v* Ex. 14:8   **13:18** *w* Num. 14:34   **13:19** *x* Deut. 7:1 *y* Josh. 14:1, 2; 19:51   **13:20** *z* Judg. 2:16 *a* 1 Sam. 3:20
13:21 *b* 1 Sam. 8:5 *c* 1 Sam. 10:20–24   **13:22** *d* 1 Sam. 15:23, 26, 28 *e* 1 Sam. 16:1, 12, 13 *f* Ps. 89:20 *g* 1 Sam. 13:14   **13:23** *h* Is. 11:1 *i* Ps. 132:11 *j* [Matt. 1:21]   **13:24** *k* [Luke 3:3]   **13:25** *l* Mark 1:7 *m* John 1:20, 27   **13:26** *n* Ps. 66:16 *o* Matt. 10:6   **13:27** *p* Luke 23:34   **13:28** *q* Matt. 27:22, 23   **13:29** *r* Luke 18:31 *s* Matt. 27:57–61   **13:30** *t* Matt. 12:39, 40; 28:6   **13:31** *u* Acts 1:3, 11   **13:32** *v* [Gen. 3:15]
13:33 *w* Ps. 2:7

34And that He raised Him from the dead, no more to return to corruption, He has spoken thus:

x'I will give you the sure mercies of
    David.'*

35Therefore He also says in another *Psalm*:

y'You will not allow Your Holy One to
    see corruption.'*

36"For David, after he had served his own generation by the will of God, zfell asleep, was buried with his fathers, and saw corruption; 37but He whom God raised up saw no corruption. 38Therefore let it be known to you, brethren, that athrough this Man is preached to you the forgiveness of sins; 39and bby Him everyone who believes is justified from all things from which you could not be justified by the law of Moses. 40Beware therefore, lest what has been spoken in the prophets come upon you:

41 'Behold,c you despisers,
    Marvel and perish!
    For I work a work in your days,
    A work which you will by no means
        believe,
    Though one were to declare it to
        you.' "*

Blessing and Conflict at Antioch

42So when the Jews went out of the synagogue,* the Gentiles begged that these words might be preached to them the next Sabbath. 43Now when the congregation had broken up, many of the Jews and devout proselytes followed Paul and Barnabas, who, speaking to them, dpersuaded them to continue in ethe grace of God.

44On the next Sabbath almost the whole city came together to hear the word of God. 45But when the Jews saw the multitudes, they were filled with envy; and contradicting and blaspheming, they fopposed the things spoken by Paul. 46Then Paul and Barnabas grew bold and said, g"It was necessary that the word of God should be spoken to you first; but hsince you reject it, and judge yourselves unworthy of everlasting life, behold, iwe turn to the Gentiles. 47For so the Lord has commanded us:

i'I have set you as a light to the Gentiles,
    That you should be for salvation to the
        ends of the earth.' "*

48Now when the Gentiles heard this, they were glad and glorified the word of the Lord. kAnd as many as had been appointed to eternal life believed. 49And the word of the Lord was being spread throughout all the region. 50But the Jews stirred up the devout and prominent women and the chief men of the city, lraised up persecution against Paul and Barnabas, and expelled them from their region. 51mBut they shook off the dust from their feet against them, and came to Iconium. 52And the disciples nwere filled with joy and owith the Holy Spirit.

At Iconium

14 Now it happened in Iconium that they went together to the synagogue of the Jews, and so spoke that a great multitude both of the Jews and of the aGreeks believed. 2But the unbelieving Jews stirred up the Gentiles and poisoned their minds against the brethren. 3Therefore they stayed there a long time, speaking boldly in the Lord, bwho was bearing witness to the word of His grace, granting signs and cwonders to be done by their hands.

4But the multitude of the city was ddivided: part sided with the Jews, and part with the eapostles. 5And when a violent attempt was made by both the Gentiles and Jews, with their rulers, fto abuse and stone them, 6they became aware of it and gfled to Lystra and Derbe, cities of Lycaonia, and to the surrounding region. 7And they were preaching the gospel there.

Idolatry at Lystra

8hAnd in Lystra a certain man without strength in his feet was sitting, a cripple from his mother's womb, who had never walked. 9This man heard Paul speaking.

* **13:34** Isaiah 55:3   * **13:35** Psalm 16:10
* **13:41** Habakkuk 1:5   * **13:42** Or *And when they went out of the synagogue of the Jews;* NU-Text reads *And when they went out, they begged.*
* **13:47** Isaiah 49:6

13:39 everyone who believes is justified from all things. "Justified" is a technical legal term declaring that a person is acquitted and absolved. Because of Jesus' death on the cross, our sin debt has been paid. Everyone who accepts this payment is justified before God, considered righteous through the blood of Christ.

13:45 the Jews. When Luke refers to "the Jews," he is not speaking of all Jewish people, but rather of the Jewish religious establishment, which opposed the gospel.

13:52 Joy—The pursuit of happiness doesn't always lead to the possession of joy. Joy does not come from circumstances but from the presence of God. It is a fruit of the Spirit, poured into a believer's life by the

grace of God. The believers in this passage were not filled with joy because their lives were comfortable, or because they were wealthy or powerful, but because they saw God working and had His Holy Spirit in their lives.

13:34 x Is. 55:3   **13:35** y Ps. 16:10   **13:36** z Acts 2:29
13:38 a Jer. 31:34   **13:39** b [Is. 53:11]   **13:41** c Hab.
1:5   **13:43** d Acts 11:23   e Titus 2:11   **13:45** f 1 Pet.
4:4   **13:46** g Rom. 1:16   h Ex. 32:10   i Acts 18:6   **13:47** i Is.
42:6; 49:6   **13:48** k [Acts 2:47]   **13:50** l 2 Tim. 3:11
13:51 m Matt. 10:14   **13:52** n John 16:22   o Acts 2:4;
4:8; 31; 13:9   **14:1** a Acts 18:4   **14:3** b Heb. 2:4   c Acts
5:12   **14:4** d Luke 12:51   e Acts 13:2, 3   **14:5** f 2 Tim. 3:11
14:6 g Matt. 10:23   **14:8** h Acts 3:2

Paul, observing him intently and seeing that he had faith to be healed, [10]said with a loud voice, [i]"Stand up straight on your feet!" And he leaped and walked. [11]Now when the people saw what Paul had done, they raised their voices, saying in the Lycaonian *language*, [j]"The gods have come down to us in the likeness of men!" [12]And Barnabas they called Zeus, and Paul, Hermes, because he was the chief speaker. [13]Then the priest of Zeus, whose temple was in front of their city, brought oxen and garlands to the gates, [k]intending to sacrifice with the multitudes.

[14]But when the apostles Barnabas and Paul heard this, [l]they tore their clothes and ran in among the multitude, crying out [15]and saying, "Men, [m]why are you doing these things? [n]We also are men with the same nature as you, and preach to you that you should turn from [o]these useless things [p]to the living God, [q]who made the heaven, the earth, the sea, and all things that are in them, [16r]who in bygone generations allowed all nations to walk in their own ways. [17s]Nevertheless He did not leave Himself without witness, in that He did good, [t]gave us rain from heaven and fruitful seasons, filling our hearts with [u]food and gladness." [18]And with these sayings they could scarcely restrain the multitudes from sacrificing to them.

Stoning, Escape to Derbe

[19v]Then Jews from Antioch and Iconium came there; and having persuaded the multitudes, [w]they stoned Paul *and* dragged *him* out of the city, supposing him to be [x]dead. [20]However, when the disciples gathered around him, he rose up and went into the city. And the next day he departed with Barnabas to Derbe.

Strengthening the Converts

[21]And when they had preached the gospel to that city [y]and made many disciples, they returned to Lystra, Iconium, and Antioch, [22]strengthening the souls of the disciples, [z]exhorting *them* to continue in the faith, and *saying*, [a]"We must through many tribulations enter the kingdom of God." [23]So when they had [b]appointed elders in every church, and prayed with fasting, they

commended them to the Lord in whom they had believed. [24]And after they had passed through Pisidia, they came to Pamphylia. [25]Now when they had preached the word in Perga, they went down to Attalia. [26]From there they sailed to Antioch, where they had been commended to the grace of God for the work which they had completed.

[27]Now when they had come and gathered the church together, [c]they reported all that God had done with them, and that He had [d]opened the door of faith to the Gentiles. [28]So they stayed there a long time with the disciples.

Conflict over Circumcision

15 And [a]certain *men* came down from Judea and taught the brethren, [b]"Unless you are circumcised according to the custom of Moses, you cannot be saved." [2]Therefore, when Paul and Barnabas had no small dissension and dispute with them, they determined that [c]Paul and Barnabas and certain others of them should go up to Jerusalem, to the apostles and elders, about this question.

[3]So, [d]being sent on their way by the church, they passed through Phoenicia and Samaria, [e]describing the conversion of the Gentiles; and they caused great joy to all the brethren. [4]And when they had come to Jerusalem, they were received by the church and the apostles and the elders; and they reported all things that God had done with them. [5]But some of the sect of the Pharisees who believed rose up, saying, "It is necessary to circumcise them, and to command *them* to keep the law of Moses."

The Jerusalem Council

[6]Now the apostles and elders came together to consider this matter. [7]And when there had been much dispute, Peter rose up *and* said to them: [f]"Men *and* brethren, you know that a good while ago God chose among us, that by my mouth the Gentiles should hear the word of the gospel and believe. [8]So God, [g]who knows the heart, acknowledged them by [h]giving them the Holy Spirit, just as *He did* to us, [9i]and made no distinction between us and them, [j]purifying their hearts by faith. [10]Now therefore,

---

14:11 *The gods have come down.* The Roman poet Ovid told of an ancient legend in which Zeus and Hermes came to the Phrygian hill country disguised as mortals seeking lodging. After being turned away from a thousand homes, they found refuge in the humble cottage of an elderly couple. In appreciation for the couple's hospitality, the gods transformed the cottage into a splendid temple and then destroyed all the houses of the inhospitable people. The people probably remembered this ancient legend, and wanted to make sure they did not make the same mistake their ancestors did.

14:23 *appointed elders.* The process outlined in 6:1–7 for selecting the seven men to serve the

Jerusalem believers may provide a clue to the process used for selecting elders here. Both the assembly and the apostles were involved in the selection process.

14:10 [i] [Is. 35:6] **14:11** [j] Acts 8:10; 28:6 **14:13** [k] Dan. 2:46 **14:14** [l] Matt. 26:65 **14:15** [m] Acts 10:26 [n] James 5:17 [o] 1 Cor. 8:4 [p] 1 Thess. 1:9 [q] Rev. 14:7 **14:16** [r] Ps. 81:12 **14:17** [s] Rom. 1:19, 20 [t] Deut. 11:14 [u] Ps. 145:16 **14:19** [v] Acts 13:45, 50; 14:2–5 [w] 2 Cor. 11:25 [x] [2 Cor. 12:1–4] **14:21** [y] Matt. 28:19 **14:22** [z] Acts 11:23 [a] [2 Tim. 2:12; 3:12] **14:23** [b] Titus 1:5 **14:27** [c] Acts 15:4, 12 [d] 2 Cor. 2:12 **15:1** [a] Gal. 2:12 [b] Phil. 3:2 **15:2** [c] Gal. 2:1 **15:3** [d] Rom. 15:24 [e] Acts 14:27; 15:4, 12 **15:7** [f] Acts 10:20 **15:8** [g] Acts 1:24 [h] Acts 2:4; 10:44, 47 **15:9** [i] Rom. 10:12 [j] Acts 10:15, 28

why do you test God ^{k}by putting a yoke on the neck of the disciples which neither our fathers nor we were able to bear? ¹¹But ^{l}we believe that through the grace of the Lord Jesus Christ* we shall be saved in the same manner as they."

¹²Then all the multitude kept silent and listened to Barnabas and Paul declaring how many miracles and wonders God had ^{m}worked through them among the Gentiles. ¹³And after they had become silent, ^{n}James answered, saying, "Men *and* brethren, listen to me: ¹⁴oSimon has declared how God at the first visited the Gentiles to take out of them a people for His name. ¹⁵And with this the words of the prophets agree, just as it is written:

¹⁶ 'After^p this I will return
    And will rebuild the tabernacle of
       David, which has fallen down;
    I will rebuild its ruins,
    And I will set it up;
¹⁷ So that the rest of mankind may seek
       the LORD,
    Even all the Gentiles who are called by
       My name,
    Says the LORD who does all these
       things.'*

¹⁸"Known to God from eternity are all His works.* ¹⁹Therefore ^{q}I judge that we should not trouble those from among the Gentiles who ^{r}are turning to God, ²⁰but that we ^{s}write to them to abstain ^{t}from things polluted by idols, ^{u}from sexual immorality,* ^{v}from things strangled, and *from* blood. ²¹For Moses has had throughout many generations those who preach him in every city, ^{w}being read in the synagogues every Sabbath."

The Jerusalem Decree

²²Then it pleased the apostles and elders, with the whole church, to send chosen men of their own company to Antioch with Paul

and Barnabas, *namely,* Judas who was also named ^{x}Barsabas,* and Silas, leading men among the brethren.

²³They wrote this *letter* by them:

The apostles, the elders, and the brethren,

To the brethren who are of the Gentiles in Antioch, Syria, and Cilicia:

Greetings.

²⁴ Since we have heard that ^{y}some who went out from us have troubled you with words, ^{z}unsettling your souls, saying, "*You must* be circumcised and keep the law"*—to whom we gave no *such* commandment— ²⁵it seemed good to us, being assembled with one accord, to send chosen men to you with our beloved Barnabas and Paul, ²⁶$a$men who have risked their lives for the name of our Lord Jesus Christ. ²⁷We have therefore sent Judas and Silas, who will also report the same things by word of mouth. ²⁸For it seemed good to the Holy Spirit, and to us, to lay upon you no greater burden than these necessary things: ²⁹$b$that you abstain from things offered to idols, ^{c}from blood, from things strangled, and from ^{d}sexual immorality.* If you keep yourselves from these, you will do well.

Farewell.

Continuing Ministry in Syria

³⁰So when they were sent off, they came to Antioch; and when they had gathered

---

* **15:11** NU-Text and M-Text omit *Christ.*
* **15:17** Amos 9:11, 12 * **15:18** NU-Text (combining with verse 17) reads *Says the Lord, who makes these things known from eternity (of old).*
* **15:20** Or *fornication* * **15:22** NU-Text and M-Text read *Barsabbas.* * **15:24** NU-Text omits *saying, "You must be circumcised and keep the law."* * **15:29** Or *fornication*

15:11 *through the grace of the Lord Jesus Christ we shall be saved.* These are the last words of Peter in the Book of Acts. He leaves us with the eternal truth that we are saved through faith by grace alone. The emphasis in the narrative now moves from Peter to Paul, and his outreach to the Gentiles.
15:13 *James.* James was the leader of the church in Jerusalem until he was stoned to death at the insistence of the high priest in A.D. 62. It is believed that this James is the Lord's brother, the son of Mary and Joseph, who did not believe until the Lord appeared to him privately after the Resurrection (1 Cor. 15:7).
15:19–20 *abstain from things polluted by idols.* The Jerusalem council understood that it was not necessary for Gentiles to keep the whole of the law in order to be believers in Jesus, but also recognized that they did not have the background of moral teaching the Jewish believers had. They needed both reassurance as to their acceptance as true Christians and teaching for a godly life. In looking at the present application of these requirements, it is important to remember that Acts is a transitional book,

documenting the beginning of the Christian movement. Sexual purity and food regulations are both addressed more thoroughly elsewhere in the New Testament (1 Cor. 6–8).
15:20 Fornication—Illicit sexual relationships were not a matter of shame or sin among the Gentiles as they were among the Jews. In fact, many pagan religious practices included prostitution and sexual orgies. This made the need for teaching on sexual purity doubly urgent for the new Gentile believers. They would be constantly presented with temptation, not only for sexual sin but for returning to their old ways of worship. They needed to hear God's strict prohibition of such behavior.

15:10 ^{k}Matt. 23:4   **15:11** ^{l}Rom. 3:4; 5:15   **15:12** ^{m}Acts 14:27; 15:3, 4   **15:13** ^{n}Acts 12:17   **15:14** ^{o}Acts 15:7   **15:16** ^{p}Amos 9:11, 12   **15:19** ^{q}Acts 15:28; 21:25 ^{r}1 Thess. 1:9   **15:20** ^{s}Acts 21:25 ^{t}[1 Cor. 8:1; 10:20, 28] ^{u}[1 Cor. 6:9] ^{v}Lev. 3:17   **15:21** ^{w}Acts 13:15, 27   **15:22** ^{x}Acts 1:23   **15:24** ^{y}Titus 1:10, 11 ^{z}Gal. 1:7; 5:10   **15:26** ^{a}Acts 13:50; 14:19   **15:29** ^{b}Acts 15:20; 21:25 ^{c}Lev. 17:14 ^{d}Col. 3:5

the multitude together, they delivered the letter. [31]When they had read it, they rejoiced over its encouragement. [32]Now Judas and Silas, themselves being [e]prophets also, [f]exhorted and strengthened the brethren with many words. [33]And after they had stayed *there* for a time, they were [g]sent back with greetings from the brethren to the apostles.*

[34]However, it seemed good to Silas to remain there.* [35][h]Paul and Barnabas also remained in Antioch, teaching and preaching the word of the Lord, with many others also.

Division over John Mark

[36]Then after some days Paul said to Barnabas, "Let us now go back and visit our brethren in every city where we have preached the word of the Lord, *and see* how they are doing." [37]Now Barnabas was determined to take with them [i]John called Mark. [38]But Paul insisted that they should not take with them [j]the one who had departed from them in Pamphylia, and had not gone with them to the work. [39]Then the contention became so sharp that they parted from one another. And so Barnabas took Mark and sailed to [k]Cyprus; [40]but Paul chose Silas and departed, [l]being commended by the brethren to the grace of God. [41]And he went through Syria and Cilicia, [m]strengthening the churches.

Timothy Joins Paul and Silas

16 Then he came to [a]Derbe and Lystra. And behold, a certain disciple was there, [b]named Timothy, [c]*the* son of a certain Jewish woman who believed, but his father *was* Greek. [2]He was well spoken of by the brethren who were at Lystra and Iconium. [3]Paul wanted to have him go on with him. And he [d]took *him* and circumcised him because of the Jews who were in that region, for they all knew that his father was Greek. [4]And as they went through the

cities, they delivered to them the [e]decrees to keep, [f]which were determined by the apostles and elders at Jerusalem. [5][g]So the churches were strengthened in the faith, and increased in number daily.

The Macedonian Call

[6]Now when they had gone through Phrygia and the region of [h]Galatia, they were forbidden by the Holy Spirit to preach the word in Asia. [7]After they had come to Mysia, they tried to go into Bithynia, but the Spirit* did not permit them. [8]So passing by Mysia, they [i]came down to Troas. [9]And a vision appeared to Paul in the night. A [j]man of Macedonia stood and pleaded with him, saying, "Come over to Macedonia and help us." [10]Now after he had seen the vision, immediately we sought to go [k]to Macedonia, concluding that the Lord had called us to preach the gospel to them.

Lydia Baptized at Philippi

[11]Therefore, sailing from Troas, we ran a straight course to Samothrace, and the next *day* came to Neapolis, [12]and from there to [l]Philippi, which is the foremost city of that part of Macedonia, a colony. And we were staying in that city for some days. [13]And on the Sabbath day we went out of the city to the riverside, where prayer was customarily made; and we sat down and spoke to the women whom we met *there*. [14]Now a certain woman named Lydia heard *us*. She was a seller of purple from the city of [m]Thyatira, who worshiped God. [n]The Lord opened her heart to heed the things spoken by Paul. [15]And when she and her household were baptized, she begged *us*, saying, "If you have judged me to be faithful to the Lord, come to my house and stay." So [o]she persuaded us.

---

* **15:33** NU-Text reads *to those who had sent them.*
* **15:34** NU-Text and M-Text omit this verse.
* **16:7** NU-Text adds *of Jesus.*

15:39 *that they parted from one another.* Even though Paul and Barnabas had a heated disagreement, it is important to note that they did not bring their disagreement into the church fellowship, forcing others to take sides and causing more dissension. Instead, they simply parted ways, each continuing to faithfully serve the Lord. Later, the disagreement was apparently resolved, for Paul wrote to Timothy when he was imprisoned, asking for Mark to be sent to him, "for he is useful to me for ministry" (2 Tim. 4:11).

16:3 *circumcised him.* According to Jewish law, Timothy should have been circumcised and raised a Jew, even with a Gentile father. For whatever reason, this had not happened, and the fact that he was an uncircumcised Jew would limit his effectiveness with Jewish Christians. The issue was not law but effectiveness.

16:12 *Philippi.* Named after the father of Alexander the Great, Philippi was a Roman colony loyal to the empire. The city itself was organized by the state of Rome and functioned as a military outpost. Because of its proximity to the sea as well as to one of the

major roads to Europe, Philippi was a commercial center in Macedonia. Its influence throughout the region made it a good place to begin preaching the gospel of Jesus Christ.

16:13 *where prayer was customarily made.* According to Jewish custom, a congregation consisted of ten households. If ten male household heads could be found in a city, a synagogue was formed. If not, a place of prayer was established. Philippi did not have a synagogue, but Paul was still able to find the God-fearers of the city.

15:32 [e] Eph. 4:11 [f] Acts 14:22; 18:23 **15:33** [g] Heb. 11:31 **15:35** [h] Acts 13:1 **15:37** [i] Acts 12:12, 25 **15:38** [j] Acts 13:13 **15:39** [k] Acts 4:36; 13:4 **15:40** [l] Acts 11:23; 14:26 **15:41** [m] Acts 16:5 **16:1** [a] Acts 14:6 [b] Rom. 16:21 [c] 2 Tim. 1:5; 3:15 **16:3** [d] [Gal. 2:3; 5:2] **16:4** [e] Acts 15:19–21 [f] Acts 15:28, 29 **16:5** [g] Acts 2:47; 5:41 **16:6** [h] Gal. 1:1, 2 **16:8** [i] 2 Cor. 2:12 **16:9** [j] Acts 10:30 **16:10** [k] 2 Cor. 2:13 **16:12** [l] Phil. 1:1 **16:14** [m] Rev. 1:11; 2:18, 24 [n] Luke 24:45 **16:15** [o] Judg. 19:21

Paul and Silas Imprisoned

16Now it happened, as we went to prayer, that a certain slave girl Ppossessed with a spirit of divination met us, who brought her masters qmuch profit by fortune-telling. 17This girl followed Paul and us, and cried out, saying, "These men are the servants of the Most High God, who proclaim to us the way of salvation." 18And this she did for many days.

But Paul, rgreatly annoyed, turned and said to the spirit, "I command you in the name of Jesus Christ to come out of her." sAnd he came out that very hour. 19But twhen her masters saw that their hope of profit was gone, they seized Paul and Silas and udragged them into the marketplace to the authorities.

20And they brought them to the magistrates, and said, "These men, being Jews, vexceedingly trouble our city; 21and they teach customs which are not lawful for us, being Romans, to receive or observe." 22Then the multitude rose up together against them; and the magistrates tore off their clothes wand commanded them to be beaten with rods. 23And when they had laid many stripes on them, they threw them into prison, commanding the jailer to keep them securely. 24Having received such a charge, he put them into the inner prison and fastened their feet in the stocks.

The Philippian Jailer Saved

25But at midnight Paul and Silas were praying and singing hymns to God, and the prisoners were listening to them. 26xSuddenly there was a great earthquake, so that the foundations of the prison were shaken; and immediately yall the doors were opened and everyone's chains were loosed. 27And the keeper of the prison, awaking from sleep and seeing the prison doors open, supposing the prisoners had fled, drew his sword and was about to kill himself. 28But Paul called with a loud voice, saying, "Do yourself no harm, for we are all here."

29Then he called for a light, ran in, and fell down trembling before Paul and Silas. 30And he brought them out and said, z"Sirs, what must I do to be saved?"

31So they said, a"Believe on the Lord Jesus Christ, and you will be saved, you and your household." 32Then they spoke the word of the Lord to him and to all who were in his house. 33And he took them the same hour of the night and washed their stripes. And immediately he and all his family were baptized. 34Now when he had brought them into his house, bhe set food before them; and he rejoiced, having believed in God with all his household.

Paul Refuses to Depart Secretly

35And when it was day, the magistrates sent the officers, saying, "Let those men go." 36So the keeper of the prison reported these words to Paul, saying, "The magistrates have sent to let you go. Now therefore depart, and go in peace." 37But Paul said to them, "They have beaten us openly, uncondemned cRomans, and have thrown us into prison. And now do they put us out secretly? No indeed! Let them come themselves and get us out." 38And the officers told these words to the magistrates, and they were afraid when they heard that they were Romans. 39Then they came and pleaded with them and brought them out, and dasked them to depart from the city. 40So they went out of the prison eand entered the house of Lydia; and when they had seen the brethren, they encouraged them and departed.

16:25 Praise—Paul and Silas were praying and singing hymns of praise to God at midnight in spite of the fact that they had been arrested, stripped naked, and beaten, confined to an inner cell and clamped into an uncomfortable position. They could praise God because their joy was not based on circumstances but on a relationship. Jesus Christ and His love and grace are the same, no matter where you are or what is happening to you.

16:31 It Begins with Faith—Paul and Silas's answer to the Philippian jailer's question is the essence of salvation: "Believe on the Lord Jesus Christ, and you will be saved." This verse raises two questions: What does it mean to believe, and what does it mean to be saved? Belief includes but is more than just an intellectual assent. Belief includes the idea of total trust, dependence, and submission of oneself to Christ as Lord (King, Master). To be saved is to be delivered. We are delivered from the very presence of sin and evil (Satan and hell) and will be delivered into the very presence of God (Christ and heaven). We receive this new life by faith—believing that we are sinful, that Jesus died for our sins, that His death was in our place, and that His payment for sin is fully acceptable in God's sight. Faith can be summarized in the acrostic:

Forsaking
All
I
Take
Him

16:33–34 Family—This man assumed spiritual leadership of his family by being the first to repent, to humble himself before God and ask for forgiveness and a change of life. By his example, the rest of his family was won. In the same way, every believing father has the responsibility to set the example of spiritual commitment, and to teach his family all he knows of following Christ.

16:37 Romans. Paul was not simply seeking self-justification, he was protecting the infant church in

16:16 P 1 Sam. 28:3, 7 q Acts 19:24 16:18 r Mark 1:25, 34 s Mark 16:17 16:19 t Acts 16:16; 19:25, 26 u Matt. 10:18 16:20 v Acts 17:8 16:22 w 1 Thess. 2:2 16:26 x Acts 4:31 y Acts 5:19; 12:7, 10 16:30 z Acts 2:37; 9:6; 22:10 16:31 a [John 3:16, 36; 6:47] 16:34 b Luke 5:29; 19:6 16:37 c Acts 22:25–29 16:39 d Matt. 8:34 16:40 e Acts 16:14

Preaching Christ at Thessalonica

17 Now when they had passed through Amphipolis and Apollonia, they came to *a*Thessalonica, where there was a synagogue of the Jews. ²Then Paul, as his custom was, *b*went in to them, and for three Sabbaths *c*reasoned with them from the Scriptures, ³explaining and demonstrating *d*that the Christ had to suffer and rise again from the dead, and *saying*, "This Jesus whom I preach to you is the Christ." ⁴*e*And some of them were persuaded; and a great multitude of the devout Greeks, and not a few of the leading women, joined Paul and *f*Silas.

Assault on Jason's House

⁵But the Jews who were not persuaded, becoming *g*envious,* took some of the evil men from the marketplace, and gathering a mob, set all the city in an uproar and attacked the house of *h*Jason, and sought to bring them out to the people. ⁶But when they did not find them, they dragged Jason and some brethren to the rulers of the city, crying out, *i*"These who have turned the world upside down have come here too. ⁷Jason has harbored them, and these are all acting contrary to the decrees of Caesar, *j*saying there is another king— Jesus." ⁸And they troubled the crowd and the rulers of the city when they heard these things. ⁹So when they had taken security from Jason and the rest, they let them go.

Ministering at Berea

¹⁰Then *k*the brethren immediately sent Paul and Silas away by night to Berea. When they arrived, they went into the synagogue of the Jews. ¹¹These were more fair-minded than those in Thessalonica, in that they received the word with all readiness, and *l*searched the Scriptures daily *to find out* whether these things were so. ¹²Therefore many of them believed, and also not a few of the Greeks, prominent women as well as men. ¹³But when the Jews from Thessalonica learned that the word of God was preached by Paul at Berea, they

came there also and stirred up the crowds. ¹⁴*m*Then immediately the brethren sent Paul away, to go to the sea; but both Silas and Timothy remained there. ¹⁵So those who conducted Paul brought him to Athens; and *n*receiving a command for Silas and Timothy to come to him with all speed, they departed.

The Philosophers at Athens

¹⁶Now while Paul waited for them at Athens, *o*his spirit was provoked within him when he saw that the city was given over to idols. ¹⁷Therefore he reasoned in the synagogue with the Jews and with the *Gentile* worshipers, and in the marketplace daily with those who happened to be there. ¹⁸Then* certain Epicurean and Stoic philosophers encountered him. And some said, "What does this babbler want to say?"

Others said, "He seems to be a proclaimer of foreign gods," because he preached to them *p*Jesus and the resurrection.

¹⁹And they took him and brought him to the Areopagus, saying, "May we know what this new doctrine *is* of which you speak? ²⁰For you are bringing some strange things to our ears. Therefore we want to know what these things mean." ²¹For all the Athenians and the foreigners who were there spent their time in nothing else but either to tell or to hear some new thing.

Addressing the Areopagus

²²Then Paul stood in the midst of the Areopagus and said, "Men of Athens, I perceive that in all things you are very religious; ²³for as I was passing through and considering the objects of your worship, I even found an altar with this inscription:

TO THE UNKNOWN GOD.

Therefore, the One whom you worship without knowing, Him I proclaim to you:

* **17:5** NU-Text omits *who were not persuaded;* M-Text omits *becoming envious.* * **17:18** NU-Text and M-Text add *also.*

Philippi. By forcing a public statement of their innocence, he minimized the possibility that the new believers would be regarded as "friends of criminals and troublemakers."

17:7 *acting contrary to the decrees of Caesar.* In A.D. 49 the Roman emperor Caligula expelled all Jews from Rome due to riots ignited by a group of zealous Jews. Paul's accusers were trying to paint him as a revolutionary who was bringing sedition to Thessalonica.

17:18 *this babbler.* This word is literally "seed picker." The philosophers were saying that Paul was like a gutter sparrow, picking up bits and scraps of knowledge without fully digesting or thinking about what he taught.

17:19 *Areopagus.* Just southwest of the Acropolis in Athens was a hill called the Hill of Ares (Mars, in Latin), the god of war. This was where court was held

concerning questions of religion and morals. In Athens, the gospel message was examined by the supposed experts of philosophy and religion.

17:23 An Unknown God—In the sixth century B.C. it was said that a poet from Crete name Epimenides turned aside a horrible plague from the people of Athens by appealing to a god of whom the people had never heard. An altar was built to honor this god, and its inscription caught Paul's attention. Knowing that the Athenians had no background in

17:1 *a* 1 Thess. 1:1 **17:2** *b* Luke 4:16 *c* 1 Thess. 2:1–16 **17:3** *d* Acts 18:5, 28 **17:4** *e* Acts 28:24 *f* Acts 15:22, 27, 32, 40 **17:5** *g* Acts 13:45 *h* Rom. 16:21 **17:6** *i* [Acts 16:20] **17:7** *j* 1 Pet. 2:13 **17:10** *k* Acts 9:25; 17:14 **17:11** *l* John 5:39 **17:14** *m* Matt. 10:23 **17:15** *n* Acts 18:5 **17:16** *o* 2 Pet. 2:8 **17:18** *p* 1 Cor. 15:12

24aGod, who made the world and everything in it, since He is rLord of heaven and earth, sdoes not dwell in temples made with hands. 25Nor is He worshiped with men's hands, as though He needed anything, since He tgives to all life, breath, and all things. 26And He has made from one blood* every nation of men to dwell on all the face of the earth, and has determined their pre-appointed times and uthe boundaries of their dwellings, 27vso that they should seek the Lord, in the hope that they might grope for Him and find Him, wthough He is not far from each one of us; 28for xin Him we live and move and have our being, yas also some of your own poets have said, 'For we are also His offspring.' 29Therefore, since we are the offspring of God, zwe ought not to think that the Divine Nature is like gold or silver or stone, something shaped by art and man's devising. 30Truly, athese times of ignorance God overlooked, but bnow commands all men everywhere to repent, 31because He has appointed a day on which cHe will judge the world in righteousness by the Man whom He has ordained. He has given assurance of this to all by draising Him from the dead."

32And when they heard of the resurrection of the dead, some mocked, while others said, "We will hear you again on this matter." 33So Paul departed from among them. 34However, some men joined him and believed, among them Dionysius the Areopagite, a woman named Damaris, and others with them.

Ministering at Corinth

18 After these things Paul departed from Athens and went to Corinth. 2And he found a certain Jew named aAquila, born in Pontus, who had recently come from Italy with his wife Priscilla (because Claudius had commanded all the Jews to depart from Rome); and he came to them. 3So, because he was of the same trade, he stayed with them band worked; for by occupation they were tentmakers. 4cAnd he reasoned in the synagogue every Sabbath, and persuaded both Jews and Greeks.

5dWhen Silas and Timothy had come from Macedonia, Paul was ecompelled by the Spirit, and testified to the Jews that Jesus is the Christ. 6But fwhen they opposed him and blasphemed, ghe shook his garments and said to them, h"Your blood be upon your own heads; iI am clean. jFrom now on I will go to the Gentiles." 7And he departed from there and entered the house of a certain man named Justus,* one who worshiped God, whose house was next door to the synagogue. 8kThen Crispus, the ruler of the synagogue, believed on the Lord with all his household. And many of the Corinthians, hearing, believed and were baptized.

9Now lthe Lord spoke to Paul in the night by a vision, "Do not be afraid, but speak, and do not keep silent; 10mfor I am with you, and no one will attack you to hurt you; for I have many people in this city." 11And he continued there a year and six months, teaching the word of God among them.

12When Gallio was proconsul of Achaia, the Jews with one accord rose up against Paul and brought him to the judgment seat, 13saying, "This fellow persuades men to worship God contrary to the law."

14And when Paul was about to open his mouth, Gallio said to the Jews, "If it were a matter of wrongdoing or wicked crimes, O Jews, there would be reason why I should

---

* **17:26** NU-Text omits *blood*.   * **18:7** NU-Text reads *Titius Justus*.

---

the Old Testament Scriptures as did the Jews in the synagogues, Paul began his discourse with what they were already familiar with: their own legends and observation.

17:31 Resurrection—Christ has been raised from the dead not only for the purpose of returning to heaven and resuming His fellowship with the Father, a fellowship interrupted only by the alienation and abandonment at the cross; He has gone from His tomb to the right hand of His Father to intercede for us. And one day the mantle of Judge will be placed on Him, and everyone will stand before Him. The world has yet to see the last of Jesus Christ.

17:32 some mocked. Though they embraced the idea of the soul living on, the Greeks were repulsed by the idea of a bodily resurrection because they considered the body to be evil. This idea, known as *dualism,* was derived from the teachings of Socrates and Plato. It held that everything physical is evil and everything spiritual is good. Therefore, they believed the body and what is done with it is not important because it will be discarded at the end of life.

18:1 Corinth. Corinth was the political capital of Achaia. It was also a center for the worship of Aphrodite, the goddess of fertility, and it housed the major temple of Apollo. Because of the sensuous nature of the religious cult of Aphrodite, Corinth had a reputation for being a city of immorality. Beginning in the fifth century B.C., the Greeks used a word meaning "to act like a Corinthian" as a symbol for sexual immorality.

18:3 tentmakers. All young rabbinical students had to learn a trade. The province of Cilicia, from which Paul came, was noted for its cloth made from goats' hair. It is likely that Paul's skill involved making such cloth.

18:7 Justus. Most Romans had three names. This man's name was Titius Justus. Based on Paul's letter to the Corinthians, it is likely that Justus was the man called Gaius mentioned in 1 Corinthians 1:14.

17:24 q Acts 14:15 r Matt. 11:25 s Acts 7:48–50
17:25 t Is. 42:5 **17:26** u Deut. 32:8 **17:27** v [Rom. 1:20] w Jer. 23:23, 24 **17:28** x [Heb. 1:3] y Titus 1:12 **17:29** z Is. 40:18, 19 **17:30** a [Rom. 3:25] b [Titus 2:11, 12] **17:31** c Acts 10:42 d Acts 2:24 **18:2** a 1 Cor. 16:19 **18:3** b Acts 20:34 **18:4** c Acts 17:2 **18:5** d Acts 17:14, 15 e Acts 18:28 **18:6** f Acts 13:45 g Neh. 5:13 h 2 Sam. 1:16 i [Ezek. 3:18, 19] j Acts 13:46–48; 28:28 **18:8** k 1 Cor. 1:14 **18:9** l Acts 23:11 **18:10** m Jer. 1:18, 19

bear with you. 15But if it is a [n]question of words and names and your own law, look *to it* yourselves; for I do not want to be a judge of such *matters*." 16And he drove them from the judgment seat. 17Then all the Greeks* took [o]Sosthenes, the ruler of the synagogue, and beat *him* before the judgment seat. But Gallio took no notice of these things.

Paul Returns to Antioch

18So Paul still remained a good while. Then he took leave of the brethren and sailed for Syria, and Priscilla and Aquila *were* with him. [p]He had *his* hair cut off at [q]Cenchrea, for he had taken a vow. 19And he came to Ephesus, and left them there; but he himself entered the synagogue and reasoned with the Jews. 20When they asked *him* to stay a longer time with them, he did not consent, 21but took leave of them, saying, [r]"I must by all means keep this coming feast in Jerusalem;* but I will return again to you, [s]God willing." And he sailed from Ephesus.

22And when he had landed at [t]Caesarea, and gone up and greeted the church, he went down to Antioch. 23After he had spent some time *there*, he departed and went over the region of [u]Galatia and Phrygia in order, [v]strengthening all the disciples.

Ministry of Apollos

24[w]Now a certain Jew named Apollos, born at Alexandria, an eloquent man *and* mighty in the Scriptures, came to Ephesus. 25This man had been instructed in the way of the Lord; and being [x]fervent in spirit, he spoke and taught accurately the things of the Lord, [y]though he knew only the baptism of John. 26So he began to speak boldly in the synagogue. When Aquila and Priscilla heard him, they took him aside and explained to him the way of God more accurately. 27And when he desired to cross to Achaia, the brethren wrote, exhorting the disciples to receive him; and when he arrived, [z]he greatly helped those who had believed through grace; 28for he vigorously refuted the Jews publicly, [a]showing from the Scriptures that Jesus is the Christ.

Paul at Ephesus

19 And it happened, while [a]Apollos was at Corinth, that Paul, having passed through [b]the upper regions, came to Ephesus. And finding some disciples 2he said to them, "Did you receive the Holy Spirit when you believed?"

So they said to him, [c]"We have not so much as heard whether there is a Holy Spirit."

3And he said to them, "Into what then were you baptized?"

So they said, [d]"Into John's baptism."

4Then Paul said, [e]"John indeed baptized with a baptism of repentance, saying to the people that they should believe on Him who would come after him, that is, on Christ Jesus."

5When they heard *this*, they were baptized [f]in the name of the Lord Jesus. 6And when Paul had [g]laid hands on them, the Holy Spirit came upon them, and [h]they spoke with tongues and prophesied. 7Now the men were about twelve in all.

8[i]And he went into the synagogue and spoke boldly for three months, reasoning and persuading [j]concerning the things of the kingdom of God. 9But [k]when some were hardened and did not believe, but spoke evil [l]of the Way before the multitude, he departed from them and withdrew the disciples, reasoning daily in the school of Tyrannus. 10And [m]this continued for two years, so that all who dwelt in Asia heard the word of the Lord Jesus, both Jews and Greeks.

---

* **18:17** NU-Text reads *they all.* * **18:21** NU-Text omits *I must* through *Jerusalem.*

18:18 ***had his hair cut off.*** Paul had his hair cut as part of a Nazirite vow he had made (see Num. 6:5). Such a vow had to be fulfilled in Jerusalem where the hair would be presented to God.

18:24 ***Apollos, born at Alexandria.*** This Jew with a Greek name was from the second largest city in the Roman Empire. Alexandria was a seaport on the northern coast of Egypt. Founded by Alexander the Great, the city was very cosmopolitan. Egyptians, Romans, and Greeks all lived there; over one quarter of the population was Jewish. The Greek translation of the Hebrew Scriptures had been produced in that city about 150 years before the birth of Jesus. The city was famous for its great library and was considered the cultural and educational center of the world.

19:3 ***John's baptism.*** Baptism was a ritual used by the Jews as a picture of cleansing and purification. Gentiles who converted to Judaism would go through the rite of purification as their first act of worship. They would dip themselves in water as a sign of being cleansed from their old way of life. Before entering into the temple to worship, Jews would dip themselves in ritual bathing pools to show their desire for purification. John's baptism was a symbol of repentance from sin and a looking ahead to the coming of the Messiah.

19:6 ***laid hands on them.*** The Holy Spirit was received without the laying on of hands in 10:44–48. By laying on his hands here, Paul was demonstrating his apostolic authority. He was also affirming the unity of the new church in Ephesus with the church in Jerusalem. Both were empowered by the Holy Spirit to speak in foreign tongues.

19:10 ***all who dwelt in Asia heard.*** From Ephesus, other churches were born in Asia Minor—in Colosse,

18:15 [n] Acts 23:29; 25:19 **18:17** [o] 1 Cor. 1:1 **18:18** [p] Acts 21:24 [q] Rom. 16:1 **18:21** [r] Acts 19:21; 20:16 [s] 1 Cor. 4:19 **18:22** [t] Acts 8:40 **18:23** [u] Gal. 1:2 [v] Acts 14:22; 15:32, 41 **18:24** [w] Titus 3:13 **18:25** [x] Rom. 12:11 [y] Acts 19:3 **18:27** [z] 1 Cor. 3:6 **18:28** [a] Acts 9:22; 17:3; 18:5 **19:1** [a] 1 Cor. 1:12; 3:5, 6 [b] Acts 18:23 **19:2** [c] 1 Sam. 3:7 **19:3** [d] Acts 18:25 **19:4** [e] Matt. 3:11 **19:5** [f] Acts 8:12, 16; 10:48 **19:6** [g] Acts 6:6; 8:17 [h] Acts 2:4; 10:46 **19:8** [i] Acts 17:2; 18:4 [j] Acts 1:3; 28:23 **19:9** [k] 2 Tim. 1:15 [l] Acts 9:2; 19:23; 22:4; 24:14 **19:10** [m] Acts 19:8; 20:31

Miracles Glorify Christ

11Now nGod worked unusual miracles by the hands of Paul, 12oso that even handkerchiefs or aprons were brought from his body to the sick, and the diseases left them and the evil spirits went out of them. 13pThen some of the itinerant Jewish exorcists qtook it upon themselves to call the name of the Lord Jesus over those who had evil spirits, saying, "We* exorcise you by the Jesus whom Paul rpreaches." 14Also there were seven sons of Sceva, a Jewish chief priest, who did so.

15And the evil spirit answered and said, "Jesus I know, and Paul I know; but who are you?"

16Then the man in whom the evil spirit was leaped on them, overpowered* them, and prevailed against them,* so that they fled out of that house naked and wounded. 17This became known both to all Jews and Greeks dwelling in Ephesus; and sfear fell on them all, and the name of the Lord Jesus was magnified. 18And many who had believed came tconfessing and telling their deeds. 19Also, many of those who had practiced magic brought their books together and burned *them* in the sight of all. And they counted up the value of them, and *it* totaled fifty thousand *pieces* of silver. 20uSo the word of the Lord grew mightily and prevailed.

The Riot at Ephesus

21vWhen these things were accomplished, Paul wpurposed in the Spirit, when he had passed through xMacedonia and Achaia, to go to Jerusalem, saying, "After I have been there, yI must also see Rome." 22So he sent into Macedonia two of those who ministered to him, zTimothy and aErastus, but he himself stayed in Asia for a time.

23And babout that time there arose a great commotion about cthe Way. 24For a certain man named Demetrius, a silversmith, who made silver shrines of Diana,* brought dno small profit to the craftsmen. 25He called them together with the workers of similar occupation, and said: "Men, you know that we have our prosperity by this trade. 26Moreover you see and hear that not only at Ephesus, but throughout almost all Asia, this Paul has persuaded and turned away many people, saying that ethey are not gods which are made with hands. 27So

not only is this trade of ours in danger of falling into disrepute, but also the temple of the great goddess Diana may be despised and her magnificence destroyed,* whom all Asia and the world worship."

28Now when they heard *this*, they were full of wrath and cried out, saying, "Great *is* Diana of the Ephesians!" 29So the whole city was filled with confusion, and rushed into the theater with one accord, having seized fGaius and gAristarchus, Macedonians, Paul's travel companions. 30And when Paul wanted to go in to the people, the disciples would not allow him. 31Then some of the officials of Asia, who were his friends, sent to him pleading that he would not venture into the theater. 32Some therefore cried one thing and some another, for the assembly was confused, and most of them did not know why they had come together. 33And they drew Alexander out of the multitude, the Jews putting him forward. And hAlexander imotioned with his hand, and wanted to make his defense to the people. 34But when they found out that he was a Jew, all with one voice cried out for about two hours, "Great *is* Diana of the Ephesians!"

35And when the city clerk had quieted the crowd, he said: "Men of Ephesus, what man is there who does not know that the city of the Ephesians is temple guardian of the great goddess Diana, and of the *image* which fell down from Zeus? 36Therefore, since these things cannot be denied, you ought to be quiet and do nothing rashly. 37For you have brought these men here who are neither robbers of temples nor blasphemers of your* goddess. 38Therefore, if Demetrius and his fellow craftsmen have a case against anyone, the courts are open and there are proconsuls. Let them bring charges against one another. 39But if you have any other inquiry to make, it shall be determined in the lawful assembly. 40For we are in danger of being called in question for today's uproar, there being no reason which we may give to account for this disorderly gathering." 41And when he had said these things, he dismissed the assembly.

* **19:13** NU-Text reads *I.* * **19:16** M-Text reads *and they overpowered.* • NU-Text reads *both of them.* * **19:24** Greek *Artemis* * **19:27** NU-Text reads *she be deposed from her magnificence.* * **19:37** NU-Text reads *our.*

Smyrna, Pergamos, Thyatira, Sardis, Philadelphia, and Laodicea. Paul and his students clearly did more than study. They must have actively evangelized as well.

19:13 *the name of the Lord Jesus.* The use of magical names in incantations was common in the ancient world. These practitioners had latched onto the name of Jesus to use as an incantation, but they discovered that it was not enough to know the name of Jesus; they needed to know Jesus personally.

19:29 *the theater.* This amphitheater seated 25,000 people.

19:40 *we are in danger.* The riot at Ephesus could

have brought the discipline of Rome down upon the city. The Pax Romana, the peace that the Roman Empire brought to the Mediterranean world, was

19:11 nMark 16:20   **19:12** oActs 5:15   **19:13** pMatt. 12:27 qMark 9:38 r1 Cor. 1:23; 2:2   **19:17** sLuke 1:65; 7:16   **19:18** tMatt. 3:6   **19:20** uActs 6:7; 12:24   **19:21** vRom. 15:25 wActs 20:22 xActs 20:1 yRom. 1:13; 15:22–29   **19:22** z1 Tim. 1:2 aRom. 16:23   **19:23** b2 Cor. 1:8 cActs 9:2   **19:24** dActs 16:16, 19   **19:26** eIs. 44:10–20   **19:29** fRom. 16:23 gCol. 4:10 **19:33** h2 Tim. 4:14 iActs 12:17

Journeys in Greece

20 After the uproar had ceased, Paul called the disciples to *himself*, embraced *them*, and ªdeparted to go to Macedonia. ²Now when he had gone over that region and encouraged them with many words, he came to ᵇGreece ³and stayed three months. And ᶜwhen the Jews plotted against him as he was about to sail to Syria, he decided to return through Macedonia. ⁴And Sopater of Berea accompanied him to Asia—also ᵈAristarchus and Secundus of the Thessalonians, and ᵉGaius of Derbe, and ᶠTimothy, and ᵍTychicus and ʰTrophimus of Asia. ⁵These men, going ahead, waited for us at ⁱTroas. ⁶But we sailed away from Philippi after ʲthe Days of Unleavened Bread, and in five days joined them ᵏat Troas, where we stayed seven days.

Ministering at Troas

⁷Now on ˡthe first *day* of the week, when the disciples came together ᵐto break bread, Paul, ready to depart the next day, spoke to them and continued his message until midnight. ⁸There were many lamps ⁿin the upper room where they* were gathered together. ⁹And in a window sat a certain young man named Eutychus, who was sinking into a deep sleep. He was overcome by sleep; and as Paul continued speaking, he fell down from the third story and was taken up dead. ¹⁰But Paul went down, ᵒfell on him, and embracing *him* said, ᵖ"Do not trouble yourselves, for his life is in him." ¹¹Now when he had come up, had broken bread and eaten, and talked a long while, even till daybreak, he departed. ¹²And they brought the young man in alive, and they were not a little comforted.

From Troas to Miletus

¹³Then we went ahead to the ship and sailed to Assos, there intending to take Paul on board; for so he had given orders,

intending himself to go on foot. ¹⁴And when he met us at Assos, we took him on board and came to Mitylene. ¹⁵We sailed from there, and the next *day* came opposite Chios. The following *day* we arrived at Samos and stayed at Trogyllium. The next *day* we came to Miletus. ¹⁶For Paul had decided to sail past Ephesus, so that he would not have to spend time in Asia; for ᑫhe was hurrying ʳto be at Jerusalem, if possible, on ˢthe Day of Pentecost.

The Ephesian Elders Exhorted

¹⁷From Miletus he sent to Ephesus and called for the elders of the church. ¹⁸And when they had come to him, he said to them: "You know, ᵗfrom the first day that I came to Asia, in what manner I always lived among you, ¹⁹serving the Lord with all humility, with many tears and trials which happened to me ᵘby the plotting of the Jews; ²⁰how ᵛI kept back nothing that was helpful, but proclaimed it to you, and taught you publicly and from house to house, ²¹ʷtestifying to Jews, and also to Greeks, ˣrepentance toward God and faith toward our Lord Jesus Christ. ²²And see, now ʸI go bound in the spirit to Jerusalem, not knowing the things that will happen to me there, ²³except that ᶻthe Holy Spirit testifies in every city, saying that chains and tribulations await me. ²⁴But ªnone of these things move me; nor do I count my life dear to myself,* ᵇso that I may finish my race with joy, ᶜand the ministry ᵈwhich I received from the Lord Jesus, to testify to the gospel of the grace of God.

²⁵"And indeed, now I know that you all, among whom I have gone preaching the kingdom of God, will see my face no more. ²⁶Therefore I testify to you this day that I *am* ᵉinnocent of the blood of all *men*. ²⁷For I have not shunned to declare to you ᶠthe

---

* **20:8** NU-Text and M-Text read *we*.   * **20:24** NU-Text reads *But I do not count my life of any value or dear to myself.*

---

very important to Rome. The Romans would not tolerate any kind of uprising or rebellion. Ephesus risked losing its freedom and being ruled directly by the Roman army.

20:2 encouraged. This word has a full range of meanings, from rebuking to comforting. It includes instruction, appeal, affirmation, exhortation, warning, and correction.

20:7 The Lord's Supper—Although the phrase "to break bread" could mean an ordinary meal, it more likely refers to the observance of the Lord's Supper in obedience to Christ's command. The "breaking of bread" appears to be the primary purpose for the gathering, with Paul's sermon rising naturally in a group of people who had gathered to remember Christ.

20:13–16 to go on foot. The distance between Troas and Assos was about thirty miles by sea, but Paul chose to go over land on foot.

20:17 elders. The words "elder" (literally, one who

is older) and "overseer" (v. 28) appear to be used in the New Testament as interchangeable terms for the leaders of a particular fellowship.

20:22 bound in the spirit. Some say that Paul was out of the will of God in going to Jerusalem after the warnings of bonds and afflictions. But there is no evidence that Paul was rebelling against God. On the contrary, Jesus Himself confirmed that the trip was part of His good and perfect will (23:11).

20:1 ª 1 Tim. 1:3   **20:2** ᵇ Acts 17:15; 18:1   **20:3** ᶜ 2 Cor. 11:26   **20:4** ᵈ Col. 4:10 ᵉ Acts 19:29 ᶠ Acts 16:1 ᵍ Eph. 6:21 ʰ 2 Tim. 4:20   **20:5** ⁱ 2 Tim. 4:13   **20:6** ʲ Ex. 12:14, 15 ᵏ 2 Tim. 4:13   **20:7** ˡ 1 Cor. 16:2 ᵐ Acts 2:42, 46; 20:11   **20:8** ⁿ Acts 1:13   **20:10** ᵒ 1 Kin. 17:21 ᵖ Matt. 9:23, 24   **20:16** ᑫ Acts 18:21; 19:21; 21:4 ʳ Acts 24:17 ˢ Acts 2:1   **20:18** ᵗ Acts 19:1, 10; 20:4, 16   **20:19** ᵘ Acts 20:3   **20:20** ᵛ Acts 20:27   **20:21** ʷ Acts 18:5; 19:10 ˣ Mark 1:15   **20:22** ʸ Acts 19:21   **20:23** ᶻ Acts 21:4, 11   **20:24** ª Acts 21:13 ᵇ 2 Tim. 4:7 ᶜ Acts 1:17 ᵈ Gal. 1:1   **20:26** ᵉ Acts 18:6   **20:27** ᶠ Luke 7:30

whole counsel of God. ²⁸ᵍTherefore take heed to yourselves and to all the flock, among which the Holy Spirit ʰhas made you overseers, to shepherd the church of God* ⁱwhich He purchased ʲwith His own blood. ²⁹For I know this, that after my departure ᵏsavage wolves will come in among you, not sparing the flock. ³⁰Also ˡfrom among yourselves men will rise up, speaking perverse things, to draw away the disciples after themselves. ³¹Therefore watch, and remember that ᵐfor three years I did not cease to warn everyone night and day with tears.

³²"So now, brethren, I commend you to God and ⁿto the word of His grace, which is able ᵒto build you up and give you ᵖan inheritance among all those who are sanctified. ³³I have coveted no one's silver or gold or apparel. ³⁴Yes,* you yourselves know ᑫthat these hands have provided for my necessities, and for those who were with me. ³⁵I have shown you in every way, ʳby laboring like this, that you must support the weak. And remember the words of the Lord Jesus, that He said, 'It is more blessed to give than to receive.' "

³⁶And when he had said these things, he knelt down and prayed with them all. ³⁷Then they all ˢwept freely, and ᵗfell on Paul's neck and kissed him, ³⁸sorrowing most of all for the words which he spoke, that they would see his face no more. And they accompanied him to the ship.

Warnings on the Journey to Jerusalem

21 Now it came to pass, that when we had departed from them and set sail, running a straight course we came to Cos, the following day to Rhodes, and from there to Patara. ²And finding a ship sailing over to Phoenicia, we went aboard and set sail. ³When we had sighted Cyprus, we passed it on the left, sailed to Syria, and landed at Tyre; for there the ship was to unload her cargo. ⁴And finding disciples,* we stayed there seven days. ᵃThey told Paul through

the Spirit not to go up to Jerusalem. ⁵When we had come to the end of those days, we departed and went on our way; and they all accompanied us, with wives and children, till we were out of the city. And ᵇwe knelt down on the shore and prayed. ⁶When we had taken our leave of one another, we boarded the ship, and they returned ᶜhome.

⁷And when we had finished our voyage from Tyre, we came to Ptolemais, greeted the brethren, and stayed with them one day. ⁸On the next day we who were Paul's companions* departed and came to ᵈCaesarea, and entered the house of Philip ᵉthe evangelist, ᶠwho was one of the seven, and stayed with him. ⁹Now this man had four virgin daughters ᵍwho prophesied. ¹⁰And as we stayed many days, a certain prophet named ʰAgabus came down from Judea. ¹¹When he had come to us, he took Paul's belt, bound his own hands and feet, and said, "Thus says the Holy Spirit, ⁱ'So shall the Jews at Jerusalem bind the man who owns this belt, and deliver him into the hands of the Gentiles.' "

¹²Now when we heard these things, both we and those from that place pleaded with him not to go up to Jerusalem. ¹³Then Paul answered, ʲ"What do you mean by weeping and breaking my heart? For I am ready not only to be bound, but also to die at Jerusalem for the name of the Lord Jesus." ¹⁴So when he would not be persuaded, we ceased, saying, ᵏ"The will of the Lord be done."

Paul Urged to Make Peace

¹⁵And after those days we packed and went up to Jerusalem. ¹⁶Also some of the disciples from Caesarea went with us, and brought with them a certain Mnason of Cyprus, an early disciple, with whom we were to lodge.

---

* **20:28** M-Text reads of the Lord and God.
* **20:34** NU-Text and M-Text omit Yes. * **21:4** NU-Text reads the disciples. * **21:8** NU-Text omits who were Paul's companions.

20:28 Church—The elders or overseers of God's flock must be men who are appointed not just by other men, but by the Holy Spirit of God. The leadership of the church is a solemn responsibility, and it should only be accepted by those who are convinced that they have been both called and equipped by the Holy Spirit to do this work. An elder has the responsibility to follow the example of our Chief Shepherd, Jesus Christ, as a servant leader.

20:35 It is more blessed to give. This saying of Jesus is not found in the Gospels, but it has been recorded here through Paul's knowledge of it.

21:2 a ship sailing over to Phoenicia. In the summer months, the wind of the Aegean Sea blows from the north, beginning very early in the morning. In the late afternoon the wind dies away. Sunset brings a dead calm, and later a gentle southerly breeze blows. If a ship was heading down the coast, it would typically anchor at evening and wait for the winds of the morning.

21:4 through the Spirit. Because of this warning,

many have thought that Paul's insistence in going to Jerusalem was disobedience to God's will. However, it is more likely that this was simply a warning to let him know what to expect in the future. Paul was obviously very sensitive to the Holy Spirit (16:6), and felt that he had received specific instructions to go to Jerusalem (20:22). Later Jesus Himself encouraged Paul concerning his decision to go (23:11).

21:10–14 bound his own hands and feet. The Holy Spirit did not forbid Paul to go to Jerusalem, but warned him of what it would cost him.

20:28 ᵍ 1 Pet. 5:2 ʰ 1 Cor. 12:28 ⁱ Eph. 1:7, 14 ʲ Heb. 9:14 **20:29** ᵏ Matt. 7:15 **20:30** ˡ 1 Tim. 1:20 **20:31** ᵐ Acts 19:8, 10; 24:17 **20:32** ⁿ Heb. 13:9 ᵒ Acts 9:31 ᵖ [Heb. 9:15] **20:34** ᑫ Acts 18:3 **20:35** ʳ Rom. 15:1 **20:37** ˢ Acts 21:13 ᵗ Gen. 45:14 **21:4** ᵃ [Acts 20:23; 21:12] **21:5** ᵇ Acts 9:40; 20:36 **21:6** ᶜ John 1:11 **21:8** ᵈ Acts 8:40; 21:16 ᵉ Eph. 4:11 ᶠ Acts 6:5 **21:9** ᵍ Joel 2:28 **21:10** ʰ Acts 11:28 **21:11** ⁱ Acts 20:23; 21:33; 22:25 **21:13** ʲ Acts 20:24, 37 **21:14** ᵏ Luke 11:2; 22:42

17l And when we had come to Jerusalem, the brethren received us gladly. 18 On the following *day* Paul went in with us to m James, and all the elders were present. 19 When he had greeted them, n he told in detail those things which God had done among the Gentiles o through his ministry. 20 And when they heard *it*, they glorified the Lord. And they said to him, "You see, brother, how many myriads of Jews there are who have believed, and they are all p zealous for the law; 21 but they have been informed about you that you teach all the Jews who are among the Gentiles to forsake Moses, saying that they ought not to circumcise *their* children nor to walk according to the customs. 22 What then? The assembly must certainly meet, for they will* hear that you have come. 23 Therefore do what we tell you: We have four men who have taken a vow. 24 Take them and be purified with them, and pay their expenses so that they may q shave *their* heads, and that all may know that those things of which they were informed concerning you are nothing, but *that* you yourself also walk orderly and keep the law. 25 But concerning the Gentiles who believe, r we have written *and* decided that they should observe no such thing, except* that they should keep themselves from *things* offered to idols, from blood, from things strangled, and from sexual immorality."

Arrested in the Temple

26 Then Paul took the men, and the next day, having been purified with them, s entered the temple t to announce the expiration of the days of purification, at which time an offering should be made for each one of them.

27 Now when the seven days were almost ended, u the Jews from Asia, seeing him in the temple, stirred up the whole crowd and v laid hands on him, 28 crying out, "Men of Israel, help! This is the man w who teaches all *men* everywhere against the people, the law, and this place; and furthermore he also brought Greeks into the temple and

has defiled this holy place." 29 (For they had previously* seen x Trophimus the Ephesian with him in the city, whom they supposed that Paul had brought into the temple.)

30 And y all the city was disturbed; and the people ran together, seized Paul, and dragged him out of the temple; and immediately the doors were shut. 31 Now as they were z seeking to kill him, news came to the commander of the garrison that all Jerusalem was in an uproar. 32 a He immediately took soldiers and centurions, and ran down to them. And when they saw the commander and the soldiers, they stopped beating Paul. 33 Then the b commander came near and took him, and c commanded *him* to be bound with two chains; and he asked who he was and what he had done. 34 And some among the multitude cried one thing and some another.

So when he could not ascertain the truth because of the tumult, he commanded him to be taken into the barracks. 35 When he reached the stairs, he had to be carried by the soldiers because of the violence of the mob. 36 For the multitude of the people followed after, crying out, d "Away with him!"

Addressing the Jerusalem Mob

37 Then as Paul was about to be led into the barracks, he said to the commander, "May I speak to you?"

He replied, "Can you speak Greek? 38 e Are you not the Egyptian who some time ago stirred up a rebellion and led the four thousand assassins out into the wilderness?"

39 But Paul said, f "I am a Jew from Tarsus, in Cilicia, a citizen of no mean city; and I implore you, permit me to speak to the people."

40 So when he had given him permission, Paul stood on the stairs and g motioned with his hand to the people. And when there was a great silence, he spoke to *them* in the h Hebrew language, saying,

---

* **21:22** NU-Text reads *What then is to be done? They will certainly.*   * **21:25** NU-Text omits *that they should observe no such thing, except.*   * **21:29** M-Text omits *previously.*

21:17 Fellowship—Fellowship means more than chatting over coffee and cookies, or sharing a potluck supper. Christian fellowship essentially means sharing one another's lives, participating in both the joy and sorrow of our brothers and sisters in Christ. Christian community extends beyond geography, class, color, and gender. As parts of one glorious whole, the body of Christ, believers rejoice in one another's joy, and reach out a helping hand for another's need.

21:25 keep themselves from. The spiritual unity of the body of believers is realized in its diversity, not in its conformity. From our diverse backgrounds and cultures we honor the same Lord.

21:28 defiled this holy place. The temple in New Testament times was surrounded by three courts. The innermost court was the Court of Israel, where Jewish men could offer sacrifices. The second court was the Court of Women where Jewish families could

gather for prayer and worship. The outer court was the Court of Gentiles, open to all who would worship God. The penalty for any Gentile who went beyond this court was death.

21:38 Are you not the Egyptian. An assassin claiming to be a prophet had come to Jerusalem in A.D. 54, and led four thousand Jews up to the Mount of

---

21:17 l Acts 15:4   **21:18** m Gal. 1:19; 2:9   **21:19** n Rom. 15:18, 19   o Acts 1:17; 20:24   **21:20** p Acts 15:1; 22:3   **21:24** q Acts 18:18   **21:25** r Acts 15:19, 20, 29   **21:26** s Acts 21:24; 24:18   t Num. 6:13   **21:27** u Acts 20:19; 24:18   v Acts 26:21   **21:28** w Acts 6:13; 24:6   **21:29** x Acts 20:4   **21:30** y Acts 16:19; 26:21   **21:31** z 2 Cor. 11:23   **21:32** a Acts 23:27; 24:7   **21:33** b Acts 24:7   c Acts 20:23; 21:11   **21:36** d John 19:15   **21:38** e Acts 5:36   **21:39** f Acts 9:11; 22:3   **21:40** g Acts 12:17   h Acts 22:2

22 "Brethren[a] and fathers, hear my defense before you now." [2]And when they heard that he spoke to them in the [b]Hebrew language, they kept all the more silent.

Then he said: [3c]"I am indeed a Jew, born in Tarsus of Cilicia, but brought up in this city [d]at the feet of [e]Gamaliel, taught [f]according to the strictness of our fathers' law, and [g]was zealous toward God [h]as you all are today. [4]I persecuted this Way to the death, binding and delivering into prisons both men and women, [5]as also the high priest bears me witness, and [i]all the council of the elders, [k]from whom I also received letters to the brethren, and went to Damascus [l]to bring in chains even those who were there to Jerusalem to be punished.

[6]"Now [m]it happened, as I journeyed and came near Damascus at about noon, suddenly a great light from heaven shone around me. [7]And I fell to the ground and heard a voice saying to me, 'Saul, Saul, why are you persecuting Me?' [8]So I answered, 'Who are You, Lord?' And He said to me, 'I am Jesus of Nazareth, whom you are persecuting.'

[9]"And [n]those who were with me indeed saw the light and were afraid,* but they did not hear the voice of Him who spoke to me. [10]So I said, 'What shall I do, Lord?' And the Lord said to me, 'Arise and go into Damascus, and there you will be told all things which are appointed for you to do.' [11]And since I could not see for the glory of that light, being led by the hand of those who were with me, I came into Damascus.

[12]"Then [o]a certain Ananias, a devout man according to the law, [p]having a good testimony with all the [q]Jews who dwelt there, [13]came to me; and he stood and said to me, 'Brother Saul, receive your sight.' And at that same hour I looked up at him. [14]Then he said, [r]'The God of our fathers [s]has chosen you that you should [t]know His will, and [u]see the Just One, [v]and hear the voice of His mouth. [15w]For you will be His witness to all men of [x]what you have seen and heard. [16]And now why are you waiting? Arise and be baptized, [y]and wash away your sins, [z]calling on the name of the Lord.'

[17]"Now [a]it happened, when I returned to Jerusalem and was praying in the temple, that I was in a trance [18]and [b]saw Him saying to me, [c]'Make haste and get out of Jerusalem quickly, for they will not receive your testimony concerning Me.' [19]So I said, 'Lord, [d]they know that in every synagogue I imprisoned and [e]beat those who believe on You. [20f]And when the blood of Your martyr Stephen was shed, I also was standing by [g]consenting to his death,* and guarding the clothes of those who were killing him.' [21]Then He said to me, 'Depart, [h]for I will send you far from here to the Gentiles.' "

Paul's Roman Citizenship

[22]And they listened to him until this word, and then they raised their voices and said, [i]"Away with such a fellow from the earth, for [j]he is not fit to live!" [23]Then, as they cried out and tore off their clothes and threw dust into the air, [24]the commander ordered him to be brought into the barracks, and said that he should be examined under scourging, so that he might know why they shouted so against him. [25]And as they bound him with thongs, Paul said to the centurion who stood by, [k]"Is it lawful for you to scourge a man who is a Roman, and uncondemned?"

[26]When the centurion heard that, he went and told the commander, saying, "Take care what you do, for this man is a Roman."

[27]Then the commander came and said to him, "Tell me, are you a Roman?"

He said, "Yes."

[28]The commander answered, "With a large sum I obtained this citizenship."

And Paul said, "But I was born a citizen."

[29]Then immediately those who were about to examine him withdrew from him; and the commander was also afraid after he found out that he was a Roman, and because he had bound him.

---

* 22:9 NU-Text omits and were afraid.
* 22:20 NU-Text omits to his death.

Olives, promising that at his word the walls of Jerusalem would fall and the Roman Empire would be destroyed. The uprising was crushed, leaving four hundred Jews dead and another two hundred as prisoners. The Egyptian escaped into the desert with some of his followers.

22:16 calling on the name of the Lord. Calling on the name of the Lord is what brings salvation, not the physical act of baptism (Rom. 10:9–13). Baptism is the public declaration of one's repentance and new life.

22:24 under scourging. The scourge was a leather whip, studded with pieces of metal or bone, fastened to a wooden handle. The victim was stretched out on the floor or bound to a pillar to be beaten. Scourging was a cruel torture, designed to maim or kill the victim.

22:28 born a citizen. Roman citizenship was

originally limited to free Romans, but later it was offered to many others in the empire, either as a reward for outstanding service, or in exchange for a high price. Because Paul's father was a Roman citizen (how he became a citizen is unknown), Paul was born

22:1 [a] Acts 7:2   **22:2** [b] Acts 21:40   **22:3** [c] 2 Cor. 11:22 [d] Deut. 33:3 [e] Acts 5:34 [f] Acts 23:6; 26:5 [g] Gal. 1:14 [h] [Rom. 10:2]   **22:4** [i] 1 Tim. 1:13   **22:5** [j] Acts 23:14; 24:1; 25:15 [k] Luke 22:66 [l] Acts 9:2   **22:6** [m] Acts 9:3; 26:12, 13   **22:9** [n] Acts 9:7   **22:12** [o] Acts 9:17 [p] Acts 10:22 [q] 1 Tim. 3:7   **22:14** [r] Acts 3:13; 5:30 [s] Acts 9:15; 26:16 [t] Acts 3:14; 7:52 [u] 1 Cor. 9:1; 15:8 [v] Gal. 1:12   **22:15** [w] Acts 23:11 [x] Acts 4:20; 26:16   **22:16** [y] Heb. 10:13 [z] Rom. 10:13 **22:17** [a] Acts 9:26; 26:20   **22:18** [b] Acts 22:14 [c] Matt. 10:14   **22:19** [d] Acts 8:3; 22:4 [e] Matt. 10:17   **22:20** [f] Acts 7:54—8:1 [g] Luke 11:48   **22:21** [h] Acts 9:15   **22:22** [i] Acts 21:36 [j] Acts 25:24   **22:25** [k] Acts 16:37

The Sanhedrin Divided

30The next day, because he wanted to know for certain why he was accused by the Jews, he released him from *his* bonds, and commanded the chief priests and all their council to appear, and brought Paul down and set him before them.

23 Then Paul, looking earnestly at the council, said, "Men *and* brethren, ªI have lived in all good conscience before God until this day." 2And the high priest Ananias commanded those who stood by him *b*to strike him on the mouth. 3Then Paul said to him, "God will strike you, *you* whitewashed wall! For you sit to judge me according to the law, and *c*do you command me to be struck contrary to the law?"

4And those who stood by said, "Do you revile God's high priest?"

5Then Paul said, *d*"I did not know, brethren, that he was the high priest; for it is written, *e*'*You shall not speak evil of a ruler of your people.'**

6But when Paul perceived that one part were Sadducees and the other Pharisees, he cried out in the council, "Men *and* brethren, *f*I am a Pharisee, the son of a Pharisee; *g*concerning the hope and resurrection of the dead I am being judged!"

7And when he had said this, a dissension arose between the Pharisees and the Sadducees; and the assembly was divided. 8*h*For Sadducees say that there is no resurrection—and no angel or spirit; but the Pharisees confess both. 9Then there arose a loud outcry. And the scribes of the Pharisees' party arose and protested, saying, *i*"We find no evil in this man; but *j*if a spirit or an angel has spoken to him, *k*let us not fight against God."*

10Now when there arose a great dissension, the commander, fearing lest Paul might be pulled to pieces by them, commanded the soldiers to go down and take him by force from among them, and bring *him* into the barracks.

The Plot Against Paul

11But *l*the following night the Lord stood by him and said, "Be of good cheer, Paul; for as you have testified for Me in *m*Jerusalem, so you must also bear witness at *n*Rome."

12And when it was day, *o*some of the Jews

banded together and bound themselves under an oath, saying that they would neither eat nor drink till they had *p*killed Paul. 13Now there were more than forty who had formed this conspiracy. 14They came to the chief priests and *q*elders, and said, "We have bound ourselves under a great oath that we will eat nothing until we have killed Paul. 15Now you, therefore, together with the council, suggest to the commander that he be brought down to you tomorrow,* as though you were going to make further inquiries concerning him; but we are ready to kill him before he comes near."

16So when Paul's sister's son heard of their ambush, he went and entered the barracks and told Paul. 17Then Paul called one of the centurions to *him* and said, "Take this young man to the commander, for he has something to tell him." 18So he took him and brought *him* to the commander and said, "Paul the prisoner called me to *him* and asked *me* to bring this young man to you. He has something to say to you."

19Then the commander took him by the hand, went aside, and asked privately, "What is it that you have to tell me?"

20And he said, *r*"The Jews have agreed to ask that you bring Paul down to the council tomorrow, as though they were going to inquire more fully about him. 21But do not yield to them, for more than forty of them lie in wait for him, men who have bound themselves by an oath that they will neither eat nor drink till they have killed him; and now they are ready, waiting for the promise from you."

22So the commander let the young man depart, and commanded *him*, "Tell no one that you have revealed these things to me."

Sent to Felix

23And he called for two centurions, saying, "Prepare two hundred soldiers, seventy horsemen, and two hundred spearmen to go to *s*Caesarea at the third hour of the night; 24and provide mounts to set Paul on, and bring *him* safely to Felix the governor." 25He wrote a letter in the following manner:

* **23:5** Exodus 22:28 * **23:9** NU-Text omits last clause and reads *what if a spirit or an angel has spoken to him?* * **23:15** NU-Text omits *tomorrow.*

a citizen. Ultimately, God used Paul's Roman citizenship to spread the gospel to Rome.

23:1 Conscience—The human conscience is given as a tool, enabling us to tell right from wrong, and to evaluate our own actions. The problem is that the conscience of fallen humans is not a reliable guide. Because humans are not "basically good," an untrained conscience will not necessarily lead toward right. The conscience must be trained by good teaching. It can be rendered useless if it is seared or defiled, it can be deadened by constantly ignoring it. In order to provide useful guidance, the conscience must be recharged by the Holy Spirit. It must be kept clear by confession of sins, and refusing to accept violations.

23:11 *witness at Rome.* Because of the earlier warnings of his friends (21:4,10–14), Paul may have begun to doubt his decision. The Lord gave Paul special encouragement at this time, that he was indeed doing just what God wanted him to do.

23:1 *a* 2 Tim. 1:3 **23:2** *b* John 18:22 **23:3** *c* Deut. 25:1, 2 **23:5** *d* Lev. 5:17, 18 *e* Ex. 22:28 **23:6** *f* Phil. 3:5 *g* Acts 24:15, 21; 26:6; 28:20 **23:8** *h* Matt. 22:23 **23:9** *i* Acts 25:25; 26:31 *j* Acts 22:6, 7, 17, 18 *k* Acts 5:39 **23:11** *l* Acts 18:9; 27:23, 24 *m* Acts 21:18, 19; 22:1–21 *n* Acts 28:16, 17, 23 **23:12** *o* Acts 23:21, 30; 25:3 *p* Acts 9:23, 24; 25:3; 26:21; 27:42 **23:14** *q* Acts 4:5, 23; 6:12; 22:5; 24:1; 25:15 **23:20** *r* Acts 23:12 **23:23** *s* Acts 8:40; 23:33

²⁶ Claudius Lysias,

To the most excellent governor Felix:

Greetings.

²⁷ ᵗThis man was seized by the Jews and was about to be killed by them. Coming with the troops I rescued him, having learned that he was a Roman. ²⁸ᵘAnd when I wanted to know the reason they accused him, I brought him before their council. ²⁹I found out that he was accused ᵛconcerning questions of their law, ʷbut had nothing charged against him deserving of death or chains. ³⁰And ˣwhen it was told me that the Jews lay in wait for the man,* I sent him immediately to you, and ʸalso commanded his accusers to state before you the charges against him.

Farewell.

³¹Then the soldiers, as they were commanded, took Paul and brought him by night to Antipatris. ³²The next day they left the horsemen to go on with him, and returned to the barracks. ³³When they came to ᶻCaesarea and had delivered the ᵃletter to the governor, they also presented Paul to him. ³⁴And when the governor had read it, he asked what province he was from. And when he understood that he was from ᵇCilicia, ³⁵he said, ᶜ"I will hear you when your accusers also have come." And he commanded him to be kept in ᵈHerod's Praetorium.

Accused of Sedition

24 Now after ᵃfive days ᵇAnanias the high priest came down with the elders and a certain orator named Tertullus. These gave evidence to the governor against Paul. ²And when he was called upon, Tertullus began his accusation, saying: "Seeing that through you we enjoy great peace, and prosperity is being brought to this nation by your foresight, ³we accept it always and in all places, most noble Felix, with all thankfulness. ⁴Nevertheless, not to be tedious to you any further, I beg you to

hear, by your courtesy, a few words from us. ⁵ᶜFor we have found this man a plague, a creator of dissension among all the Jews throughout the world, and a ringleader of the sect of the Nazarenes. ⁶ᵈHe even tried to profane the temple, and we seized him,* and wanted ᵉto judge him according to our law. ⁷ᶠBut the commander Lysias came by and with great violence took him out of our hands, ⁸ᵍcommanding his accusers to come to you. By examining him yourself you may ascertain all these things of which we accuse him." ⁹And the Jews also assented,* maintaining that these things were so.

The Defense Before Felix

¹⁰Then Paul, after the governor had nodded to him to speak, answered: "Inasmuch as I know that you have been for many years a judge of this nation, I do the more cheerfully answer for myself, ¹¹because you may ascertain that it is no more than twelve days since I went up to Jerusalem ʰto worship. ¹²ⁱAnd they neither found me in the temple disputing with anyone nor inciting the crowd, either in the synagogues or in the city. ¹³Nor can they prove the things of which they now accuse me. ¹⁴But this I confess to you, that according to ʲthe Way which they call a sect, so I worship the ᵏGod of my fathers, believing all things which are written in ˡthe Law and in the Prophets. ¹⁵ᵐI have hope in God, which they themselves also accept, ⁿthat there will be a resurrection of the dead,* both of the just and the unjust. ¹⁶ᵒThis being so, I myself always strive to have a conscience without offense toward God and men.

¹⁷"Now after many years ᵖI came to bring alms and offerings to my nation, ¹⁸ᵠin the midst of which some Jews from Asia found me ʳpurified in the temple, neither with a mob nor with tumult. ¹⁹ˢThey ought to have been here before you to

---

* **23:30** NU-Text reads *there would be a plot against the man.*   * **24:6** NU-Text ends the sentence here and omits the rest of verse 6, all of verse 7, and the first clause of verse 8.   * **24:9** NU-Text and M-Text read *joined the attack.*   * **24:15** NU-Text omits *of the dead.*

23:33 the governor. Antonius Felix governed Judea from A.D. 52 to 60. Felix had been a slave, but had gained the status of freedman under the emperor Claudius. Because Felix's brother was a friend of the emperor, Felix's political career blossomed, even though he was not popular among his peers. The writer Tacitus described him as "exercising the powers of a king with the character of a slave."
24:14 the Way. Paul openly admitted that he was a follower of "the Way" (those who followed Jesus), but he contended that he still believed the Law and the Prophets. That is, he was a follower of Judaism, a religion which enjoyed the protection of Rome.
24:16 Conscience—There is a connection between Paul's belief in future judgment and his desire to maintain a clear conscience before God and man.

The intensity of Paul's desire may be seen from the verb translated "always strive," which occurs only here in the New Testament. Paul's desire to have a

23:27 ᵗ Acts 21:30, 33; 24:7   **23:28** ᵘ Acts 22:30   **23:29** ᵛ Acts 18:15; 25:19   ʷ Acts 25:25; 26:31   **23:30** ˣ Acts 23:20   ʸ Acts 24:8; 25:6   **23:33** ᶻ Acts 8:40   ᵃ Acts 24:1; 10; 25:16   ᵈ Matt. 27:27   **24:1** ᵃ Acts 21:27   ᵇ Acts 23:2; 30, 35; 25:2   **24:5** ᶜ 1 Pet. 2:12, 15   **24:6** ᵈ Acts 21:28   ᵉ John 18:31   **24:7** ᶠ Acts 21:33; 23:10   **24:8** ᵍ Acts 23:30   **24:11** ʰ Acts 21:15, 18, 26, 27; 24:17   **24:12** ⁱ Acts 25:8; 28:17   **24:15** ᵐ Acts 23:6; 26:6, 7; 28:20   ⁿ [Dan. 12:2]   **24:16** ᵒ Acts 23:1   **24:17** ᵖ Rom. 15:25–28   **24:18** ᵠ Acts 21:27; 26:21   ʳ Acts 21:26   **24:19** ˢ [Acts 23:30; 25:16]

object if they had anything against me. [20]Or else let those who are *here* themselves say if they found any wrongdoing* in me while I stood before the council, [21]unless *it is* for this one statement which I cried out, standing among them, *t*"Concerning the resurrection of the dead I am being judged by you this day.'"

Felix Procrastinates

[22]But when Felix heard these things, having more accurate knowledge of *the* *u*Way, he adjourned the proceedings and said, "When *v*Lysias the commander comes down, I will make a decision on your case." [23]So he commanded the centurion to keep Paul and to let *him* have liberty, and *w*told him not to forbid any of his friends to provide for or visit him.

[24]And after some days, when Felix came with his wife Drusilla, who was Jewish, he sent for Paul and heard him concerning the *x*faith in Christ. [25]Now as he reasoned about righteousness, self-control, and the judgment to come, Felix was afraid and answered, "Go away for now; when I have a convenient time I will call for you." [26]Meanwhile he also hoped that *y*money would be given him by Paul, that he might release him.* Therefore he sent for him more often and conversed with him.

[27]But after two years Porcius Festus succeeded Felix; and Felix, *z*wanting to do the Jews a favor, left Paul bound.

Paul Appeals to Caesar

25 Now when Festus had come to the province, after three days he went up from *a*Caesarea to Jerusalem. [2]*b*Then the high priest* and the chief men of the Jews informed him against Paul; and they petitioned him, [3]asking a favor against him, that he would summon him to Jerusalem—*c*while *they* lay in ambush along the road to kill him. [4]But Festus answered that Paul should be kept at Caesarea, and that he himself was going *there* shortly. [5]"Therefore," he said, "let those who have authority among you go down with *me* and accuse this man, to see *d*if there is any fault in him."

[6]And when he had remained among them more than ten days, he went down to Caesarea. And the next day, sitting on the judgment seat, he commanded Paul to be brought. [7]When he had come, the Jews who had come down from Jerusalem stood about *e*and laid many serious complaints against Paul, which they could not prove, [8]while he answered for himself, *f*"Neither against the law of the Jews, nor against the temple, nor against Caesar have I offended in anything at all."

[9]But Festus, *g*wanting to do the Jews a favor, answered Paul and said, *h*"Are you willing to go up to Jerusalem and there be judged before me concerning these things?"

[10]So Paul said, "I stand at Caesar's judgment seat, where I ought to be judged. To the Jews I have done no wrong, as you very well know. [11]*i*For if I am an offender, or have committed anything deserving of death, I do not object to dying; but if there is nothing in these things of which these men accuse me, no one can deliver me to them. *j*I appeal to Caesar."

[12]Then Festus, when he had conferred with the council, answered, "You have appealed to Caesar? To Caesar you shall go!"

Paul Before Agrippa

[13]And after some days King Agrippa and Bernice came to Caesarea to greet Festus. [14]When they had been there many days, Festus laid Paul's case before the king, saying: *k*"There is a certain man left a prisoner by Felix, [15]*l*about whom the chief priests and the elders of the Jews informed me, when I was in Jerusalem, asking for a judgment against him. [16]*m*To them I answered, 'It is not the custom of the Romans to deliver any man to destruction* before the accused meets the accusers face to face, and has opportunity to answer for himself concerning the charge against

---

* **24:20** NU-Text and M-Text read *say what wrongdoing they found.*   * **24:26** NU-Text omits *that he might release him.*   * **25:2** NU-Text reads *chief priests.*   * **25:16** NU-Text omits *to destruction,* although it is implied.

---

good conscience toward God and man reflects the summary of duties of the law of love toward God and neighbor. The conscience needs to be enlightened and purified by Scripture in regard to our responsibilities toward God and man.

24:22 *having more accurate knowledge of the Way.* Felix's wife Drusilla was Jewish, and part of the Herodian family. Felix had governed Judea and Samaria for six years. He had ample opportunity to understand both Judaism and "the Way" as he must have observed the workings of the early church in Jerusalem.

24:27 *after two years.* Around A.D. 60, a riot broke out in Caesarea. Felix crushed it with such force that he was removed from office.

25:11 *appeal to Caesar.* If a Roman citizen thought

he was not getting justice in a provincial court, he could appeal to the emperor himself. If the appeal was declared valid, all other proceedings in the lower courts ceased and the prisoner was sent to Rome for the disposition of his case.

24:21 *t* [Acts 23:6; 24:15; 28:20]   **24:22** *u* Acts 9:2; 18:26; 19:9, 23; 22:4 *v* Acts 23:26; 24:7   **24:23** *w* Acts 23:16; 27:3; 28:16   **24:24** *x* [Rom. 10:9]   **24:26** *y* Ex. 23:8   **24:27** *z* Acts 12:3; 23:35; 25:9, 14   **25:1** *a* Acts 8:40; 25:4, 6, 13   **25:2** *b* Acts 24:1; 25:15   **25:3** *c* Acts 23:12, 15   **25:5** *d* Acts 18:14; 25:18   **25:7** *e* Acts 24:5, 13   **25:8** *f* Acts 6:13; 24:12; 28:17   **25:9** *g* Acts 12:2; 24:27 *h* Acts 25:20   **25:11** *i* Acts 18:14; 23:29; 25:25; 26:31 *j* Acts 26:32; 28:19   **25:14** *k* Acts 24:27   **25:15** *l* Acts 24:1; 25:2, 3   **25:16** *m* Acts 25:4, 5

him.' [17]Therefore when they had come to-gether, [n]without any delay, the next day I sat on the judgment seat and command-ed the man to be brought in. [18]When the accusers stood up, they brought no accu-sation against him of such things as I sup-posed, [19]but had some questions against him about their own religion and about a certain Jesus, who had died, whom Paul affirmed to be alive. [20]And because I was uncertain of such questions, I asked wheth-er he was willing to go to Jerusalem and there be judged concerning these matters. [21]But when Paul [p]appealed to be reserved for the decision of Augustus, I command-ed him to be kept till I could send him to Caesar."

[22]Then [q]Agrippa said to Festus, "I also would like to hear the man myself."

"Tomorrow," he said, "you shall hear him."

[23]So the next day, when Agrippa and Bernice had come with great pomp, and had entered the auditorium with the com-manders and the prominent men of the city, at Festus' command [r]Paul was brought in. [24]And Festus said: "King Agrippa and all the men who are here present with us, you see this man about whom [s]the whole assembly of the Jews petitioned me, both at Jerusalem and here, crying out that he was [t]not fit to live any longer. [25]But when I found that [u]he had committed nothing de-serving of death, [v]and that he himself had appealed to Augustus, I decided to send him. [26]I have nothing certain to write to my lord concerning him. Therefore I have brought him out before you, and especially before you, King Agrippa, so that after the examination has taken place I may have something to write. [27]For it seems to me unreasonable to send a prisoner and not to specify the charges against him."

Paul's Early Life

26 Then Agrippa said to Paul, "You are permitted to speak for yourself."

So Paul stretched out his hand and an-swered for himself: [2]"I think myself [a]hap-py, King Agrippa, because today I shall answer [b]for myself before you concerning all the things of which I am [c]accused by the Jews, [3]especially because you are expert in all customs and questions which have to do with the Jews. Therefore I beg you to hear me patiently.

[4]"My manner of life from my youth, which was spent from the beginning among my own nation at Jerusalem, all the Jews know. [5]They knew me from the first, if they were willing to testify, that according to [d]the strictest sect of our reli-gion I lived a Pharisee. [6e]And now I stand and am judged for the hope of [f]the promise made by God to our fathers. [7]To this prom-ise [g]our twelve tribes, earnestly serving God [h]night and day, [i]hope to attain. For this hope's sake, King Agrippa, I am accused by the Jews. [8]Why should it be thought in-credible by you that God raises the dead?

[9i]"Indeed, I myself thought I must do many things contrary to the name of [k]Je-sus of Nazareth. [10l]This I also did in Jeru-salem, and many of the saints I shut up in prison, having received authority [m]from the chief priests; and when they were put to death, I cast my vote against them. [11n]And I punished them often in every synagogue and compelled them to blaspheme; and being exceedingly enraged against them, I persecuted them even to foreign cities.

Paul Recounts His Conversion

[12o]"While thus occupied, as I journeyed to Damascus with authority and commis-sion from the chief priests, [13]at midday, O king, along the road I saw a light from heaven, brighter than the sun, shining around me and those who journeyed with me. [14]And when we all had fallen to the ground, I heard a voice speaking to me and saying in the Hebrew language, 'Saul, Saul, why are you persecuting Me? It is hard for you to kick against the goads.' [15]So I said, 'Who are You, Lord?' And He said, 'I am Jesus, whom you are persecut-ing. [16]But rise and stand on your feet; for I have appeared to you for this purpose, [p]to make you a minister and a witness both of the things which you have seen and of the things which I will yet reveal to you. [17]I will deliver you from the Jewish people, as well as [q]from the Gentiles, [q]to whom I now* send you, [18r]to open their eyes, in order [s]to turn them from darkness to light, and from the power of Satan to God, [t]that they may receive forgiveness of sins and [u]an inheri-tance among those who are [v]sanctified by faith in Me.'

---

* **26:17** NU-Text and M-Text omit now.

26:5 *I lived a Pharisee.* Paul was not some stranger or foreigner trying to start a new religion. He was a Jew, and a member of the religious body which took God's law most seriously.

26:6–7 Hope—Paul faced a real paradox in his trial before Agrippa. He had been a faithful Pharisee, look-ing forward to the fulfillment of their common hope, the coming of the Messiah, and eventually the resur-rection of the dead. Now that the Messiah had come, and Paul began proclaiming the truth of His atone-ment and resurrection, he was being persecuted by the very ones who had once shared his hope.

25:17 [n] Acts 25:6, 10   **25:19** [o] Acts 18:14, 15;
23:29   **25:21** [p] Acts 25:11, 12   **25:22** [q] Acts 9:15
25:23 [r] Acts 9:15   **25:24** [s] Acts 25:2, 3, 7   [t] Acts 21:36;
22:22   **25:25** [u] Acts 23:9, 29; 26:31   [v] Acts 25:11, 12
26:2 [a] [1 Pet. 3:14; 4:14]   [b] [1 Pet. 3:15, 16]   [c] Acts 21:28;
24:5, 6   **26:5** [d] Phil. 3:5   **26:6** [e] Acts 23:6   [f] Acts 13:32
26:7 [g] James 1:1   [h] 1 Thess. 3:10   [i] Phil. 3:11   **26:9** [j] 1 Tim.
1:12, 13   [k] Acts 2:22; 10:38   **26:10** [l] Acts 8:1–3; 9:13
[m] Acts 9:14   **26:11** [n] Acts 22:19   **26:12** [o] Acts 9:3–8;
22:6–11; 26:12–18   **26:16** [p] Acts 22:15   **26:17** [q] Acts
22:21   **26:18** [r] Is. 35:5; 42:7, 16   [s] 1 Pet. 2:9   [t] Luke 1:77
[u] Col. 1:12   [v] Acts 20:32

Paul's Post-Conversion Life

[19]"Therefore, King Agrippa, I was not disobedient to the heavenly vision, [20]but [w]declared first to those in Damascus and in Jerusalem, and throughout all the region of Judea, and *then* to the Gentiles, that they should repent, turn to God, and do [x]works befitting repentance. [21]For these reasons the Jews seized me in the temple and tried to kill *me*. [22]Therefore, having obtained help from God, to this day I stand, witnessing both to small and great, saying no other things than those [y]which the prophets and [z]Moses said would come— [23a]that the Christ would suffer, [b]that He would be the first to rise from the dead, and [c]would proclaim light to the *Jewish* people and to the Gentiles."

Agrippa Parries Paul's Challenge

[24]Now as he thus made his defense, Festus said with a loud voice, "Paul, [d]you are beside yourself! Much learning is driving you mad!"

[25]But he said, "I am not mad, most noble Festus, but speak the words of truth and reason. [26]For the king, before whom I also speak freely, [e]knows these things; for I am convinced that none of these things escapes his attention, since this thing was not done in a corner. [27]King Agrippa, do you believe the prophets? I know that you do believe."

[28]Then Agrippa said to Paul, "You almost persuade me to become a Christian."

[29]And Paul said, [f]"I would to God that not only you, but also all who hear me today, might become both almost and altogether such as I am, except for these chains."

[30]When he had said these things, the king stood up, as well as the governor and Bernice and those who sat with them; [31]and when they had gone aside, they talked among themselves, saying, [g]"This man is doing nothing deserving of death or chains."

[32]Then Agrippa said to Festus, "This man might have been set [h]free [i]if he had not appealed to Caesar."

The Voyage to Rome Begins

27 And when [a]it was decided that we should sail to Italy, they delivered Paul and some other prisoners to *one* named Julius, a centurion of the Augustan Regiment. [2]So, entering a ship of Adramyttium, we put to sea, meaning to sail along the coasts of Asia. [b]Aristarchus, a Macedonian of Thessalonica, was with us. [3]And the next *day* we landed at Sidon. And Julius [c]treated Paul kindly and gave *him* liberty to go to his friends and receive care. [4]When we had put to sea from there, we sailed under *the shelter of* Cyprus, because the winds were contrary. [5]And when we had sailed over the sea which is off Cilicia and Pamphylia, we came to Myra, *a city* of Lycia. [6]There the centurion found [d]an Alexandrian ship sailing to Italy, and he put us on board.

[7]When we had sailed slowly many days, and arrived with difficulty off Cnidus, the wind not permitting us to proceed, we sailed under *the shelter of* [e]Crete off Salmone. [8]Passing it with difficulty, we came to a place called Fair Havens, near the city *of* Lasea.

Paul's Warning Ignored

[9]Now when much time had been spent, and sailing was now dangerous [f]because the Fast was already over, Paul advised them, [10]saying, "Men, I perceive that this voyage will end with disaster and much loss, not only of the cargo and ship, but also our lives." [11]Nevertheless the centurion was more persuaded by the helmsman and the owner of the ship than by the things spoken by Paul. [12]And because the harbor was not suitable to winter in, the majority advised to set sail from there also, if by any means they could reach Phoenix, a harbor of Crete opening toward the southwest and northwest, *and* winter *there*.

In the Tempest

[13]When the south wind blew softly, supposing that they had obtained *their* desire, putting out to sea, they sailed close by Crete. [14]But not long after, a tempestuous

---

26:20 *that they should repent.* Repentance indicates a complete change in thinking, an "about face" of the mind and heart. Genuine repentance is evidenced by changed behavior.

26:22–23 Christ—Paul makes it clear that Jesus stood firmly in the tradition of the Hebrew Law and Prophets, and specifically identifies Him as the promised Messiah. The suffering and death of the Messiah were ordained by God and proclaimed by His prophets. The resurrection of Jesus provided evidence of the control God was exercising over the process of redemption. This triumphant event removed the purely local and national character of Christ's work, and gave His message of salvation worldwide dimensions, as had been prophesied (Is. 60:3; Mal. 1:11).

27:4 *the winds were contrary.* This happened just before the winter storms increased, and sailing became difficult. Paul was being sent to Rome by ship at the worst time of year for sailing.

26:20 [w] Acts 9:19, 20, 22; 11:26 [x] Matt. 3:8 **26:22** [y] Rom. 3:21 [z] John 5:46 **26:23** [a] Luke 24:26 [b] 1 Cor. 15:20, 23 [c] Luke 2:32 **26:24** [d] [1 Cor. 1:23; 2:13, 14; 4:10] **26:26** [e] Acts 26:3 **26:29** [f] 1 Cor. 7:7 **26:31** [g] Acts 23:9, 29; 25:25 **26:32** [h] Acts 28:18 [i] Acts 25:11 **27:1** [a] Acts 25:12, 25 **27:2** [b] Acts 19:29 **27:3** [c] Acts 24:23; 28:16 **27:6** [d] Acts 28:11 **27:7** [e] Titus 1:5, 12 **27:9** [f] Lev. 16:29–31; 23:27–29

head wind arose, called Euroclydon.* [15]So when the ship was caught, and could not head into the wind, we let *her* drive. [16]And running under *the shelter of* an island called Clauda,* we secured the skiff with difficulty. [17]When they had taken it on board, they used cables to undergird the ship; and fearing lest they should run aground on the Syrtis* *Sands,* they struck sail and so were driven. [18]And because we were exceedingly tempest-tossed, the next *day* they lightened the ship. [19]On the third *day* [g]we threw the ship's tackle overboard with our own hands. [20]Now when neither sun nor stars appeared for many days, and no small tempest beat on *us,* all hope that we would be saved was finally given up.

[21]But after long abstinence from food, then Paul stood in the midst of them and said, "Men, you should have listened to me, and not have sailed from Crete and incurred this disaster and loss. [22]And now I urge you to take heart, for there will be no loss of life among you, but only of the ship. [23][h]For there stood by me this night an angel of the God to whom I belong and [i]whom I serve, [24]saying, 'Do not be afraid, Paul; you must be brought before Caesar; and indeed God has granted you all those who sail with you.' [25]Therefore take heart, men, [j]for I believe God that it will be just as it was told me. [26]However, [k]we must run aground on a certain island."

[27]Now when the fourteenth night had come, as we were driven up and down in the Adriatic *Sea,* about midnight the sailors sensed that they were drawing near some land. [28]And they took soundings and found *it* to be twenty fathoms; and when they had gone a little farther, they took soundings again and found *it* to be fifteen fathoms. [29]Then, fearing lest we should run aground on the rocks, they dropped four anchors from the stern, and prayed for day to come. [30]And as the sailors were seeking to escape from the ship, when they had let down the skiff into the sea, under pretense of putting out anchors from the prow, [31]Paul said to the centurion and the soldiers, "Unless these men stay in the ship, you cannot be saved." [32]Then the soldiers cut away the ropes of the skiff and let it fall off.

[33]And as day was about to dawn, Paul implored *them* all to take food, saying, "Today is the fourteenth day you have waited and continued without food, and eaten nothing. [34]Therefore I urge you to take nourishment, for this is for your survival, [l]since not a hair will fall from the head of any of you." [35]And when he had said these things, he took bread and [m]gave thanks to God in the presence of them all; and when he had broken *it* he began to eat. [36]Then they were all encouraged, and also took food themselves. [37]And in all we were two hundred and seventy-six [n]persons on the ship. [38]So when they had eaten enough, they lightened the ship and threw out the wheat into the sea.

Shipwrecked on Malta

[39]When it was day, they did not recognize the land; but they observed a bay with a beach, onto which they planned to run the ship if possible. [40]And they let go the anchors and left *them* in the sea, meanwhile loosing the rudder ropes; and they hoisted the mainsail to the wind and made for shore. [41]But striking a place where two seas met, [o]they ran the ship aground; and the prow stuck fast and remained immovable, but the stern was being broken up by the violence of the waves.

[42]And the soldiers' plan was to kill the prisoners, lest any of them should swim away and escape. [43]But the centurion, wanting to save Paul, kept them from *their* purpose, and commanded that those who could swim should jump *overboard* first and get to land, [44]and the rest, some on boards and some on *parts* of the ship. And so it was [p]that they all escaped safely to land.

Paul's Ministry on Malta

28 Now when they had escaped, they then found out that [a]the island was called Malta. [2]And the [b]natives showed us unusual kindness; for they kindled a fire and made us all welcome, because of the rain that was falling and because of the cold. [3]But when Paul had gathered a bundle of sticks and laid *them* on the fire, a viper came out because of the heat, and fastened on his hand. [4]So when the natives saw the creature hanging from his hand, they said to one another, "No doubt this man is a murderer, whom, though he has escaped the sea, yet justice does not allow to live." [5]But he shook off the creature into the fire and [c]suffered no harm. [6]However, they were expecting that he would swell up or suddenly fall down dead. But after they had looked for a long time and saw no harm come to him, they changed their minds and [d]said that he was a god.

---

*27:14 NU-Text reads *Euraquilon.* * 27:16 NU-Text reads *Cauda.* * 27:17 M-Text reads *Syrtes.*

27:14 Euroclydon. This was a name given to the northeasterly storms which blow up on the Mediterranean Sea at this time of year.

27:19 [g] Jon. 1:5 **27:23** [h] Acts 18:9; 23:11 [i] Dan. 6:16 **27:25** [j] Rom. 4:20, 21 **27:26** [k] Acts 28:1 **27:34** [l] [Matt. 10:30] **27:35** [m] [1 Tim. 4:3, 4] **27:37** [n] Acts 2:41; 7:14 **27:41** [o] 2 Cor. 11:25 **27:44** [p] Acts 27:22, 31 **28:1** [a] Acts 27:26 **28:2** [b] Col. 3:11 **28:5** [c] Mark 16:18 **28:6** [d] Acts 12:22; 14:11

[7]In that region there was an estate of the leading citizen of the island, whose name was Publius, who received us and entertained us courteously for three days. [8]And it happened that the father of Publius lay sick of a fever and dysentery. Paul went in to him and [e]prayed, and [f]he laid his hands on him and healed him. [9]So when this was done, the rest of those on the island who had diseases also came and were healed. [10]They also honored us in many [g]ways; and when we departed, they provided such things as were [h]necessary.

Arrival at Rome

[11]After three months we sailed in [i]an Alexandrian ship whose figurehead was the Twin Brothers, which had wintered at the island. [12]And landing at Syracuse, we stayed three days. [13]From there we circled round and reached Rhegium. And after one day the south wind blew; and the next day we came to Puteoli, [14]where we found [j]brethren, and were invited to stay with them seven days. And so we went toward Rome. [15]And from there, when the brethren heard about us, they came to meet us as far as Appii Forum and Three Inns. When Paul saw them, he thanked God and took courage.

[16]Now when we came to Rome, the centurion delivered the prisoners to the captain of the guard; but [k]Paul was permitted to dwell by himself with the soldier who guarded him.

Paul's Ministry at Rome

[17]And it came to pass after three days that Paul called the leaders of the Jews together. So when they had come together, he said to them: "Men and brethren, [l]though I have done nothing against our people or the customs of our fathers, yet [m]I was delivered as a prisoner from Jerusalem into the hands of the Romans, [18]who, [n]when they had examined me, wanted to let me go, because there was no cause for putting me to death. [19]But when the Jews* spoke against it, [o]I was compelled to appeal to Caesar, not

that I had anything of which to accuse my nation. [20]For this reason therefore I have called for you, to see you and speak with you, because [p]for the hope of Israel I am bound with [q]this chain."

[21]Then they said to him, "We neither received letters from Judea concerning you, nor have any of the brethren who came reported or spoken any evil of you. [22]But we desire to hear from you what you think; for concerning this sect, we know that [r]it is spoken against everywhere."

[23]So when they had appointed him a day, many came to him at his lodging, [s]to whom he explained and solemnly testified of the kingdom of God, persuading them concerning Jesus [t]from both the Law of Moses and the Prophets, from morning till evening. [24]And [u]some were persuaded by the things which were spoken, and some disbelieved. [25]So when they did not agree among themselves, they departed after Paul had said one word: "The Holy Spirit spoke rightly through Isaiah the prophet to our* fathers, [26]saying,

[v]'Go to this people and say:
"Hearing you will hear, and shall not understand;
And seeing you will see, and not perceive;
[27] For the hearts of this people have grown dull.
Their ears are hard of hearing,
And their eyes they have closed,
Lest they should see with their eyes and hear with their ears,
Lest they should understand with their hearts and turn,
So that I should heal them."'*

[28]"Therefore let it be known to you that the salvation of God has been sent [w]to the Gentiles, and they will hear it!" [29]And when he had said these words, the Jews departed and had a great dispute among themselves.*

---

* **28:19** That is, the ruling authorities   * **28:25** NU-Text reads your.   * **28:27** Isaiah 6:9, 10
* **28:29** NU-Text omits this verse.

28:8 lay sick of a fever. This fever was possibly Malta fever, which was common in Malta, Gibraltar, and other Mediterranean islands. The microorganism has since been traced to the milk of the Maltese goats. The fever usually lasted four months, but sometimes could last as long as two or three years.
28:17 leaders of the Jews. By this time, the decree of the emperor Claudius (18:2) had been allowed to lapse, and Jews had returned to Rome.
28:20 Hope—The hope of Israel and the hope which Paul had found in Christ were not two different things. Wherever he went, he proclaimed Christ to the Jews as the fulfillment of their hope. That hope included not only the resurrection; it also included the Messiah and His kingdom. Paul is careful to emphasize that the hope which he now proclaims does not undermine the hope of Israel but rather

is its divine fulfillment. His devotion to the hope of the fathers was the cause that brought about his imprisonment and put him in chains. His demeanor before these Jewish leaders in Rome must have been impressive. As he stood before these men whose influence could result in life or death for him, there

28:8 [e] [James 5:14, 15]   [f] Mark 5:23; 6:5; 7:32; 16:18   **28:10** [g] Matt. 15:6   [h] [Phil. 4:19]   **28:11** [i] Acts 27:6   **28:14** [j] Rom. 1:8   **28:16** [k] Acts 23:11; 24:25; 27:3   **28:17** [l] Acts 23:29; 24:12, 13; 26:31   [m] Acts 21:33   **28:18** [n] Acts 22:24; 24:10; 25:8; 26:32   **28:19** [o] Acts 25:11, 21, 25   **28:20** [p] Acts 26:6, 7   [q] Eph. 3:1; 4:1; 6:20   **28:22** [r] [1 Pet. 2:12; 3:16; 4:14, 16]   **28:23** [s] Luke 24:27   [t] Acts 26:6, 22   **28:24** [u] Acts 14:4; 19:9   **28:26** [v] Is. 6:9, 10   **28:28** [w] Rom. 11:11

³⁰Then Paul dwelt two whole years in his own rented house, and received all who came to him, ³¹ˣpreaching the kingdom of God and teaching the things which concern the Lord Jesus Christ with all confidence, no one forbidding him.

---

was no quaking or fear. He had that hope which made him secure, whatever happened.

28:30 *two whole years.* Paul wrote four of the New Testament letters (Ephesians, Philippians, Colossians, and Philemon) during this period.

28:31 *preaching...teaching.* Apparently Paul's case had not been decided when Luke finished this book. It is thought that Paul was in fact released (there was really no case against him), and actually went to

Spain as he desired (Rom. 15:24). Titus 1:5 implies that Paul ministered on the island of Crete (something not mentioned in Acts), and many believe that Paul resumed his missionary travel for a few more years before his final arrest, condemnation, and execution, sometime around A.D. 67.

28:31 ˣ Eph. 6:19

THE EPISTLE OF PAUL THE APOSTLE TO THE
ROMANS

▶ **AUTHOR:** All critical schools agree on the Pauline authorship of this foundational book. The vocabulary, style, logic, and theological development are consistent with Paul's other epistles. He wrote Romans in A.D. 57, near the end of his third missionary journey, evidently during his three-month stay in Greece (Acts 20:3–6), more specifically, in Corinth. The church in Rome was well known (Rom. 1:8), and it had been established for several years by the time of this letter. The believers were probably numerous, and evidently they met in several places (16:1–16). The historian Tacitus even referred to the Christians who were persecuted there under Nero in A.D. 64 as an "immense multitude," as the gospel filled the gap left by the practically defunct polytheism of Roman religion.

▶ **TIME:** C. A.D. 57   ▶ **KEY VERSES:** Rom. 1:16–17

▶ **THEME:** Most scholars think that Paul probably wrote this letter from Corinth, shortly before going to Jerusalem with the relief funds for the believers there. At this point in his life and ministry, his theology has been fully developed through years of study and interaction with people as he preached the gospel. Romans systematically explains what Christ did, why He did it, and what has happened as a result. It speaks to what we are as humans and how God has interacted with us through Christ. It lays out God's plan for the world, clarifying what has happened and is still happening in biblical history. In this way, Paul forces us to deal with all the false versions of reality inspired by our fallen human nature as opposed to God's gracious, sustaining plan.

Greeting

1 Paul, a bondservant of Jesus Christ, *a*called *to be* an apostle, *b*separated to the gospel of God *2c*which He promised before *d*through His prophets in the Holy Scriptures, *3*concerning His Son Jesus Christ our Lord, who was *e*born of the seed of David according to the flesh, *4and* *f*declared *to be* the Son of God with power according *g*to the Spirit of holiness, by the resurrection from the dead. *5*Through Him *h*we have received grace and apostleship for *i*obedience to the faith among all nations *j*for His name, *6*among whom you also are the called of Jesus Christ;

*7*To all who are in Rome, beloved of God, *k*called *to be* saints:

*l*Grace to you and peace from God our Father and the Lord Jesus Christ.

Desire to Visit Rome

*8*First, *m*I thank my God through Jesus Christ for you all, that *n*your faith is spoken of throughout the whole world. *9*For *o*God is my witness, *p*whom I serve with my spirit in the gospel of His Son, that *q*without ceasing I make mention of you always in my prayers, *10*making request if, by some means, now at last I may find a way in the will of God to come to you. *11*For I long to see you, that *r*I may impart to you some spiritual gift, so that you may be established— *12*that is, that I may be encouraged together with you by *s*the mutual faith both of you and me.

*13*Now I do not want you to be unaware, brethren, that I often planned to come to you (but *t*was hindered until now), that I might have some *u*fruit among you also, just as among the other Gentiles. *14*I am a debtor both to Greeks and to barbarians,

---

1:1 bondservant. A bondservant is a slave. Paul is talking about a slavery taken voluntarily out of love (see Ex. 21:1–6), unlike the forced slavery known to so many in the Roman Empire.
1:4 declared. The word translated "declared" means "designated." Jesus did not become the Son of God by the resurrection. Instead, the resurrection proved that Jesus was the Son of God.
1:14 barbarians. Paul is referring to the non-Greek

Gentile populations, such as the northern European peoples, the Britons, the Gauls, and the Celts.

1:1 *a* 1 Tim. 1:11 *b* Acts 9:15; 13:2   **1:2** *c* Acts 26:6 *d* Gal. 3:8 **1:3** *e* Gal. 4:4   **1:4** *f* Acts 9:20; 13:33 *g* [Heb. 9:14] **1:5** *h* Eph. 3:8 *i* Acts 6:7 *j* Acts 9:15   **1:7** *k* 1 Cor. 1:2, 24 *l* 1 Cor. 1:3   **1:8** *m* 1 Cor. 1:4 *n* Rom. 16:19   **1:9** *o* Rom. 9:1 *p* Acts 27:23 *q* 1 Thess. 3:10   **1:11** *r* Rom. 15:29   **1:12** *s* Titus 1:4   **1:13** *t* [1 Thess. 2:18] *u* Phil. 4:17

both to wise and to unwise. 15So, as much as is in me, *I am* ready to preach the gospel to you who are in Rome also.

The Just Live by Faith

16For vI am not ashamed of the gospel of Christ,* for wit is the power of God to salvation for everyone who believes, xfor the Jew first and also for the Greek. 17For yin it the righteousness of God is revealed from faith to faith; as it is written, z "*The just shall live by faith.*"*

God's Wrath on Unrighteousness

18aFor the wrath of God is revealed from heaven against all ungodliness and bunrighteousness of men, who suppress the truth in unrighteousness, 19because cwhat may be known of God is manifest in them, for dGod has shown *it* to them. 20For since the creation of the world eHis invisible *attributes* are clearly seen, being understood by the things that are made, *even* His eternal power and Godhead, so that they are without excuse, 21because, although they knew God, they did not glorify *Him* as God, nor were thankful, but fbecame futile in their thoughts, and their foolish hearts were darkened. 22gProfessing to be wise, they became fools, 23and changed the glory of the hincorruptible iGod into an image made like corruptible man—and birds and four-footed animals and creeping things.

24jTherefore God also gave them up to uncleanness, in the lusts of their hearts, kto dishonor their bodies lamong themselves, 25who exchanged mthe truth of God nfor the lie, and worshiped and served the creature rather than the Creator, who is blessed forever. Amen.

26For this reason God gave them up to ovile passions. For even their women exchanged the natural use for what is against nature. 27Likewise also the men, leaving the natural use of the woman, burned in their lust for one another, men with men committing what is shameful, and receiving in themselves the penalty of their error which was due.

28And even as they did not like to retain God in *their* knowledge, God gave them over to a debased mind, to do those things pwhich are not fitting; 29being filled with all unrighteousness, sexual immorality,* wickedness, covetousness, maliciousness; full of envy, murder, strife, deceit, evil-mindedness; *they are* whisperers, 30backbiters, haters of God, violent, proud, boasters, inventors of evil things, disobedient to parents, 31undiscerning, untrustworthy, unloving, unforgiving,* unmerciful; 32who, qknowing the righteous judgment of God, that those who practice such things rare deserving of death, not only do the same but also sapprove of those who practice them.

God's Righteous Judgment

2 Therefore you are ainexcusable, O man, whoever you are who judge, bfor in whatever you judge another you condemn

---

* **1:16** NU-Text omits *of Christ.* * **1:17** Habakkuk 2:4 * **1:29** NU-Text omits *sexual immorality.* * **1:31** NU-Text omits *unforgiving.*

1:17 faith to faith. Faith is at the beginning of the salvation process, and it is the goal as well. Paul had faith that God, through the Holy Spirit, could and would build true righteousness in him. For the believer this means prayerful self-examination, prayer to do better, and careful response to those inner nudges that say, "don't say that . . . have pity . . . encourage him . . . ," etc.

1:18–19 There Are No Excuses—Someone once said there were two points they understood about God: (1) "There is a God"; and (2) "I am not Him." Theologians use the term "general revelation" to describe the concept Paul is teaching here in Romans 1. God has revealed Himself through His creation so that everyone can understand that He exists and that He has created the world and man with a purpose. God created man with an inner sense that there is something bigger out there, something that transcends mankind. That something is God and He requires recognition. The created world points us to God, but we suppress that truth, preferring to put ourselves in the place of God, in effect saying, "There is no God but me." Paul further says that, because the revelation is so clear, we have no excuse for missing it, no legitimate reason for our blindness. People who do not see it are guilty of not acknowledging the most basic reality there is.

1:25 lie. This refers to the kind of wrong thinking that led to idol worship. This "lie" refuses to honor both God's law and His authority. When people stop knowing that God created the universe, that it is His, they adopt all kinds of wrong thinking about sin, society, morality, and especially, the role of God Himself.

1:27 what is shameful. Homosexuality is sin (Lev. 18:22), and the actions that are part of this lifestyle are called "shameful" by God. In this passage Paul explains that homosexual sin is the result of men having rejected God and exchanged what is natural for the unnatural. The problems from this way of living are themselves the "penalty" for this choice.

1:29–32 being filled with all unrighteousness. These verses contain one of the most complete lists of sin in all of Scripture. This passage addresses not only the fact that God judges rightly that these sins are deserving of death, but it also addresses the idea that approving of these sins is something God judges.

2:1–4 judge. Paul points out in this passage that anyone who judges others condemns himself, for in this list of sins is something that everyone has been guilty

---

1:16 v Ps. 40:9, 10 w 1 Cor. 1:18, 24 x Acts 3:26   **1:17** y Rom. 3:21; 9:30 z Hab. 2:4   **1:18** a [Acts 17:30] b 2 Thess. 2:10   **1:19** c [Acts 14:17; 17:24] d [John 1:9]   **1:20** e Ps. 19:1–6   **1:21** f Jer. 2:5   **1:22** g Jer. 10:14   **1:23** h 1 Tim. 1:17; 6:15, 16 i Deut. 4:16–18   **1:24** j Eph. 4:18, 19 k 1 Cor. 6:18 l Lev. 18:22   **1:25** m 1 Thess. 1:9 n Is. 44:20   **1:26** o Lev. 18:22   **1:28** p Eph. 5:4   **1:32** q [Rom. 2:2] r [Rom. 6:21] s Hos. 7:3   **2:1** a [Rom. 1:20] b [Matt. 7:1–5]

yourself; for you who judge practice the same things. [2]But we know that the judgment of God is according to truth against those who practice such things. [3]And do you think this, O man, you who judge those practicing such things, and doing the same, that you will escape the judgment of God? [4]Or do you despise [c]the riches of His goodness, [d]forbearance, and [e]longsuffering, [f]not knowing that the goodness of God leads you to repentance? [5]But in accordance with your hardness and your impenitent heart [g]you are treasuring up for yourself wrath in the day of wrath and revelation of the righteous judgment of God, [6]who [h]"will render to each one according to his deeds":[*] [7]eternal life to those who by patient continuance in doing good seek for glory, honor, and immortality; [8]but to those who are self-seeking and [i]do not obey the truth, but obey unrighteousness—indignation and wrath, [9]tribulation and anguish, on every soul of man who does evil, of the Jew [j]first and also of the Greek; [10]but glory, honor, and peace to everyone who works what is good, to the Jew first and also to the Greek. [11]For [l]there is no partiality with God.

[12]For as many as have sinned without law will also perish without law, and as many as have sinned in the law will be judged by the law [13](for [m]not the hearers of the law are just in the sight of God, but the doers of the law will be justified; [14]for when Gentiles, who do not have the law, by nature do the things in the law, these, although not having the law, are a law to themselves, [15]who show the [n]work of the law written in their hearts, their [o]conscience also bearing witness, and between themselves their thoughts accusing or else excusing them) [16p]in the day when God

will judge the secrets of men [q]by Jesus Christ, [r]according to my gospel.

The Jews Guilty as the Gentiles

[17]Indeed* [s]you are called a Jew, and [t]rest on the law, [u]and make your boast in God, [18]and [v]know His will, and [w]approve the things that are excellent, being instructed out of the law, [19]and [x]are confident that you yourself are a guide to the blind, a light to those who are in darkness, [20]an instructor of the foolish, a teacher of babes, [y]having the form of knowledge and truth in the law. [21z]You, therefore, who teach another, do you not teach yourself? You who preach that a man should not steal, do you steal? [22]You who say, "Do not commit adultery," do you commit adultery? You who abhor idols, [a]do you rob temples? [23]You who [b]make your boast in the law, do you dishonor God through breaking the law? [24]For [c]"the name of God is [d]blasphemed among the Gentiles because of you,"* as it is written.

Circumcision of No Avail

[25e]For circumcision is indeed profitable if you keep the law; but if you are a breaker of the law, your circumcision has become uncircumcision. [26]Therefore, [f]if an uncircumcised man keeps the righteous requirements of the law, will not his uncircumcision be counted as circumcision? [27]And will not the physically uncircumcised, if he fulfills the law, [g]judge you who, even with your written code and circumcision, are a transgressor of the law? [28]For [h]he is not a Jew who is one outwardly,

---

* **2:6** Psalm 62:12; Proverbs 24:12   * **2:17** NU-Text reads But if.   * **2:24** Isaiah 52:5; Ezekiel 36:22

---

of in one way or another. Paul asks if the judgers realize that it is God in His goodness who leads one to repentance, and that only God can judge rightly. Only He can judge the actions of the heart and person without condemning Himself, for only He is without sin.

2:4 repentance. Literally, this means "to change one's mind." In this context it means to reject one's sinful habits and turn to God.

2:7–8 eternal life . . . doing good. According to these verses it might seem that "eternal life" can be gained by "doing good." But Romans clearly teaches justification by faith (3:22). The subject of this verse is judgment, not justification. Jesus said that "every idle word men may speak, they will give account of it in the day of judgment" (Matt. 12:36). Even Christians will see both the good and the evil that they have done. They are justified (considered righteous and therefore not punished for their sins because they have accepted Christ's death on their behalf) but they still have to see what they have done according to God's righteous judgment. Good works are a "foundation for the time to come [eternity]" (1 Tim. 6:17–19).

2:12 without law. Gentiles, who did not receive the Mosaic law, were sometimes described by this term.

2:14 by nature do the things in the law. Gentiles who still do such things as honor their parents, respond in kindness, or live honestly, show that they do have the idea of a basic moral law and the concepts of right and wrong.

2:16 secrets. According to the gospel that Paul preached, God will judge not only people's actions, but their motives, or "secrets."

2:17–25 Self-Righteousness—Paul speaks of the lamentable disparity between the truth that the Jews knew, and their practice of the truth. Boasting about having God's law, while breaking the law in their lives, brings upon them the strongest condemnation, and establishes the truth that the law can only condemn.

2:4 [c] [Eph. 1:7, 18; 2:7]   [d] [Rom. 3:25]   [e] Ex. 34:6   [f] Is. 30:18   **2:5** [g] [Deut. 32:34]   **2:6** [h] Ps. 62:12; Prov. 24:12   **2:8** [i] [2 Thess. 1:8]   **2:9** [j] 1 Pet. 4:17   **2:10** [k] [1 Pet. 1:7]   **2:11** [l] Deut. 10:17   **2:13** [m] [James 1:22, 25]   **2:15** [n] 1 Cor. 5:1   [o] Acts 24:25   **2:16** [p] [Matt. 25:31]   [q] Acts 10:42; 17:31   [r] 1 Tim. 1:11   **2:17** [s] John 8:33   [t] Mic. 3:11   [u] Is. 48:1, 2   **2:18** [v] Deut. 4:8   [w] Phil. 1:10   **2:19** [x] Matt. 15:14   **2:20** [y] [2 Tim. 3:5]   **2:21** [z] Matt. 23:3   **2:22** [a] Mal. 3:8   **2:23** [b] Rom. 2:17; 9:4   **2:24** [c] Ezek. 16:27   [d] Is. 52:5; Ezek. 36:22   **2:25** [e] [Gal. 5:3]   **2:26** [f] [Acts 10:34]   **2:27** [g] Matt. 12:41   **2:28** [h] [Gal. 6:15]

nor *is* circumcision that which *is* outward in the flesh; ²⁹but *he* is a Jew ⁱwho *is one* inwardly; and ʲcircumcision *is that* of the heart, ᵏin the Spirit, not in the letter; ˡwhose praise *is* not from men but from God.

God's Judgment Defended

3 What advantage then has the Jew, or what *is* the profit of circumcision? ²Much in every way! Chiefly because ᵃto them were committed the oracles of God. ³For what if ᵇsome did not believe? ᶜWill their unbelief make the faithfulness of God without effect? ⁴ᵈCertainly not! Indeed, let ᵉGod be true but ᶠevery man a liar. As it is written:

ᵍ"That You may be justified in Your words,
And may overcome when You are judged."*

⁵But if our unrighteousness demonstrates the righteousness of God, what shall we say? *Is* God unjust who inflicts wrath? ʰ(I speak as a man.) ⁶Certainly not! For then ⁱhow will God judge the world? ⁷For if the truth of God has increased through my lie to His glory, why am I also still judged as a sinner? ⁸And *why* not say, ʲ"Let us do evil that good may come"?—as we are slanderously reported and as some affirm that we say. Their condemnation is just.

All Have Sinned

⁹What then? Are we better *than they?* Not at all. For we have previously charged both Jews and Greeks that ᵏthey are all under sin.

¹⁰As it is written:

ˡ"There is none righteous, no, not one;
¹¹ There is none who understands;

There is none who seeks after God.
¹² They have all turned aside;
They have together become unprofitable;
There is none who does good, no, not one."*
¹³ "Theirᵐ throat is an open tomb;
With their tongues they have practiced deceit";*
ⁿ"The poison of asps is under their lips";*
¹⁴ "Whoseᵒ mouth is full of cursing and bitterness."*
¹⁵ "Theirᵖ feet are swift to shed blood;
¹⁶ Destruction and misery are in their ways;
¹⁷ And the way of peace they have not known."*
¹⁸ "Thereq is no fear of God before their eyes."*

¹⁹Now we know that whatever ʳthe law says, it says to those who are under the law, that ˢevery mouth may be stopped, and all the world may become guilty before God. ²⁰Therefore ᵗby the deeds of the law no flesh will be justified in His sight, for by the law *is* the knowledge of sin.

God's Righteousness Through Faith

²¹But now ᵘthe righteousness of God apart from the law is revealed, ᵛbeing witnessed by the Law ʷand the Prophets, ²²even the righteousness of God, through faith in Jesus Christ, to all and on all* who believe. For ˣthere is no difference; ²³for ʸall have sinned and fall short of the glory of God, ²⁴being justified freely ᶻby His grace ᵃthrough the redemption that is in

---

* **3:4** Psalm 51:4 * **3:12** Psalms 14:1–3; 53:1–3; Ecclesiastes 7:20 * **3:13** Psalm 5:9 • Psalm 140:3 * **3:14** Psalm 10:7 * **3:17** Isaiah 59:7, 8 * **3:18** Psalm 36:1 * **3:22** NU-Text omits *and on all.*

2:29 in the Spirit, not in the letter. The internal circumcision of the heart is the work of the Holy Spirit. God condemns external observance if it is not the product of a righteous heart (Is. 1:10–18).
3:2 oracles of God. The entire Old Testament, the laws and the covenants that have been given by God Himself to the nation of Israel are the "oracles," or the things that God has spoken.
3:16 Destruction and misery. In verses 10–18, Paul quotes without formal introduction a number of different verses from the Old Testament. In these passages it is shown that man not only does not seek God, but apart from Him they lack true goodness and will treat each other with violence, cursing, being quick to kill, and finding only destruction and misery.
3:18 fear of God. This is an Old Testament expression for respect and reverence for God.
3:20 justified. A legal term used of the defendant in a trial, "justified" means "declared righteous." No one will be declared righteous by doing what God requires in the law.
3:23 Universal Sin—We generally avoid the word *sin.* We want to call it something other than what it is because we don't like the implications of the word. We don't like being told we're rebels, that we're

flawed and bent in our very natures, and that there is nothing we can do about it on our own (Gen. 3:6–7). We have this innate sense that we can overcome the problem with a little more effort or maturity. Even that innate sense is an illustration of the problem. The bold hard facts always point us back to Paul's conclusions; "we're sinners," period.
3:24 redemption. Those who believe are *justified,* that is, declared righteous, freely, by God's grace or favor. Christ Jesus died to provide *redemption,* (or to "buy back," in the same way we "redeem" a promissory note). He died to pay the price required to ransom sinners. He transfers His righteousness to those who believe in Him, and on the basis of Christ's

---

2:29 ⁱ[1 Pet. 3:4] ʲPhil. 3:3 ᵏDeut. 30:6 ˡ[1 Cor. 4:5] **3:2** ᵃDeut. 4:5–8 **3:3** ᵇHeb. 4:2 [2 Tim. 2:13] **3:4** ᵈJob 40:8 ᵉ[John 3:33] ᶠPs. 62:9 ᵍPs. 51:4 **3:5** ʰGal. 3:15 **3:6** ⁱ[Gen. 18:25] **3:8** ʲRom. 5:20 **3:9** ᵏGal. 3:22 **3:10** ˡPs. 14:1–3; 53:1–3; Eccl. 7:20 **3:13** ᵐPs. 5:9 ⁿPs. 140:3 **3:14** ᵒPs. 10:7 **3:15** ᵖProv. 1:16; Is. 59:7, 8 **3:18** qPs. 36:1 **3:19** ʳJohn 10:34 ˢJob 5:16 **3:20** ᵗ[Gal. 2:16] **3:21** ᵘActs 15:11 ᵛJohn 5:46 ʷ1 Pet. 1:10 **3:22** ˣ[Col. 3:11] **3:23** ʸGal. 3:22 **3:24** ᶻ[Eph. 2:8] ᵃ[Heb. 9:12, 15]

Christ Jesus, 25whom God set forth bas a propitiation cby His blood, through faith, to demonstrate His righteousness, because in His forbearance God had passed over dthe sins that were previously committed, 26to demonstrate at the present time His righteousness, that He might be just and the justifier of the one who has faith in Jesus.

Boasting Excluded

27eWhere is boasting then? It is excluded. By what law? Of works? No, but by the law of faith. 28Therefore we conclude fthat a man is justified by faith apart from the deeds of the law. 29Or is He the God of the Jews only? Is He not also the God of the Gentiles? Yes, of the Gentiles also, 30since gthere is one God who will justify the circumcised by faith and the uncircumcised through faith. 31Do we then make void the law through faith? Certainly not! On the contrary, we establish the law.

Abraham Justified by Faith

4 What then shall we say that aAbraham our bfather has found according to the flesh?* 2For if Abraham was cjustified by works, he has something to boast about, but not before God. 3For what does the Scripture say? d"Abraham believed God, and it was accounted to him for righteousness."* 4Now eto him who works, the wages are not counted as grace but as debt.

David Celebrates the Same Truth

5But to him who fdoes not work but believes on Him who justifies gthe ungodly, his faith is accounted for righteousness, 6just as David also hdescribes the blessedness of the man to whom God imputes righteousness apart from works:

7 "Blessedi are those whose lawless deeds are forgiven,
And whose sins are covered;

8 Blessed is the man to whom the LORD shall not impute sin."*

Abraham Justified Before Circumcision

9Does this blessedness then come upon the circumcised only, or upon the uncircumcised also? For we say that faith was accounted to Abraham for righteousness. 10How then was it accounted? While he was circumcised, or uncircumcised? Not while circumcised, but while uncircumcised. 11And jhe received the sign of circumcision, a seal of the righteousness of the faith which he had while still uncircumcised, that khe might be the father of all those who believe, though they are uncircumcised, that righteousness might be imputed to them also, 12and the father of circumcision to those who not only are of the circumcision, but who also walk in the steps of the faith which our father lAbraham had while still uncircumcised.

The Promise Granted Through Faith

13For the promise that he would be the mheir of the world was not to Abraham or to his seed through the law, but through the righteousness of faith. 14For nif those who are of the law are heirs, faith is made void and the promise made of no effect, 15because othe law brings about wrath; for where there is no law there is no transgression.

16Therefore it is of faith that it might be paccording to grace, qso that the promise might be sure to all the seed, not only to those who are of the law, but also to those who are of the faith of Abraham, rwho is the father of us all 17(as it is written, s"I have made you a father of many nations"*) in

---

* **4:1** Or Abraham our (fore)father according to the flesh has found?   * **4:3** Genesis 15:6   * **4:8** Psalm 32:1, 2   * **4:17** Genesis 17:5

---

righteousness alone, believers can approach God's throne with praise.
3:25 propitiation. By His death, Christ satisfied the justice of God. The word translated "propitiation" refers to appeasement. No man can ever appease God, for His wrath over sin and His judgment of sin are totally just. But God in His mercy provided that appeasement through Jesus Christ, who died on the cross to pay for the sins of the world and to open the way for sinners to come before our Holy God.
3:27 law of faith. The "law of faith" is a kind of play on words. Paul has been talking about the fact that the law does not give people a right relationship with God. The only "law" about having this relationship is that it must be by "faith," not by deeds, whether people are Jewish or Gentile. We can never earn our salvation.
3:31 make void the law. In this passage the question of either making the law void or establishing the law means that if salvation is received by faith, it would seem like the law was of no value. But actually the

fact that Christ came, which was promised through the whole Old Testament, and that He kept the law perfectly, establishes the law as being valid. Only after salvation can people keep the law at all, as Jesus explained in Matthew 22:40, for the law is summed up in loving God and loving our neighbor.
4:1 according to the flesh. Or "by his own labor."
4:16 Abraham, who is the father of us all. God's promises to Abraham were not based on any performance or ritual, but on Abraham's belief, so Abraham is the "father" of all who believe.
4:17 gives life to the dead. The description of God

3:25 b Lev. 16:15 c Col. 1:20 d Acts 14:16; 17:30
3:27 e [1 Cor. 1:29] **3:28** f Gal. 2:16 **3:30** g [Gal. 3:8, 20] **4:1** a Is. 51:2 b James 2:21 **4:2** c Rom. 3:20, 27 **4:3** d Gen. 15:6 **4:4** e Rom. 11:6 **4:5** f [Eph. 2:8, 9] g Josh. 24:2 **4:6** h Ps. 32:1, 2 **4:7** i Ps. 32:1, 2 **4:11** j Gen. 17:10 k Luke 19:9 **4:12** l Rom. 4:18–22 **4:13** m Gen. 17:4–6; 22:17 **4:14** n Gal. 3:18 **4:15** o Rom. 3:20 **4:16** p [Rom. 3:24] q [Gal. 3:22] r Is. 51:2 **4:17** s Gen. 17:5

the presence of Him whom he believed—
God, [t]who gives life to the dead and
calls those [u]things which do not exist as
though they did; **18**who, contrary to hope,
in hope believed, so that he became the
father of many nations, according to what
was spoken, [v]"*So shall your descendants
be.*"* **19**And not being weak in faith, [w]he
did not consider his own body, already
dead (since he was about a hundred years
old), [x]and the deadness of Sarah's womb.
20He did not waver at the promise of God
through unbelief, but was strengthened
in faith, giving glory to God, **21**and being
fully convinced that what He had promised [y]He was also able to perform. **22**And
therefore [z]"*it was accounted to him for
righteousness.*"*

23Now [a]it was not written for his sake
alone that it was imputed to him, **24**but also
for us. It shall be imputed to us who believe
[b]in Him who raised up Jesus our Lord from
the dead, **25**[c]who was delivered up because
of our offenses, and [d]was raised because of
our justification.

Faith Triumphs in Trouble

5 Therefore, [a]having been justified
by faith, we have* [b]peace with God
through our Lord Jesus Christ, **2**[c]through
whom also we have access by faith into
this grace [d]in which we stand, and [e]rejoice
in hope of the glory of God. **3**And not only
that, but [f]we also glory in tribulations,
[g]knowing that tribulation produces perseverance; **4**[h]and perseverance, character;
and character, hope. **5**[i]Now hope does not
disappoint, [j]because the love of God has
been poured out in our hearts by the Holy
Spirit who was given to us.

Christ in Our Place

6For when we were still without
strength, in due time [k]Christ died for the
ungodly. **7**For scarcely for a righteous man
will one die; yet perhaps for a good man
someone would even dare to die. **8**But

[l]God demonstrates His own love toward
us, in that while we were still sinners,
Christ died for us. **9**Much more then, having now been justified [m]by His blood, we
shall be saved [n]from wrath through Him.
10For [o]if when we were enemies [p]we were
reconciled to God through the death of
His Son, much more, having been reconciled, we shall be saved [q]by His life.
11And not only *that,* but we also [r]rejoice
in God through our Lord Jesus Christ,
through whom we have now received the
reconciliation.

Death in Adam, Life in Christ

12Therefore, just as [s]through one man
sin entered the world, and [t]death through
sin, and thus death spread to all men, because all sinned— **13**(For until the law sin
was in the world, but [u]sin is not imputed
when there is no law. **14**Nevertheless death
reigned from Adam to Moses, even over
those who had not sinned according to
the likeness of the transgression of Adam,
[v]who is a type of Him who was to come.
15But the free gift *is* not like the offense.
For if by the one man's offense many died,
much more the grace of God and the gift
by the grace of the one Man, Jesus Christ,
abounded [w]to many. **16**And the gift *is* not
like *that which came* through the one who
sinned. For the judgment *which came* from
one *offense resulted* in condemnation, but
the free gift *which came* from many offenses *resulted* in justification. **17**For if by the
one man's offense death reigned through
the one, much more those who receive
abundance of grace and of the gift of righteousness will reign in life through the
One, Jesus Christ.)

18Therefore, as through one man's offense *judgment came* to all men, resulting
in condemnation, even so through [x]one
Man's righteous act *the free gift came* [y]to
all men, resulting in justification of life.

---

* **4:18** Genesis 15:5   * **4:22** Genesis 15:6
* **5:1** Another ancient reading is, *let us have peace.*

---

as one who "gives life to the dead" refers not only to
God making Abraham and Sarah's dead reproductive
systems alive, but also to the fact that God could and
did resurrect Jesus. That is the kind of God He is; belief
in the resurrection is central to Christianity, and also
to our belief in our own eternal life through Christ.
5:1 Justification—God's gracious justification of
the believer does not take place by stages or degrees.
It is an instantaneous judicial "not guilty" declaration,
based on the perfect obedience and the once-for-all
sacrifice of Christ. The believer now has peace with
God through Jesus Christ, full pardon of his sins, and
the title to eternal life. The crowning gift is an abiding
joy and peace in the Lord, which remains in spite of
outside circumstances.
5:12 one man. The "one man" is Adam.
5:13 imputed. "Imputed" means "to charge to one's
account," as by an entry made into a ledger. In other
words, sin was present in the world from Adam

to Moses, but God did not keep an account of sins
before the giving of the law because there was no
law to obey or disobey. Those after Adam and before
Moses did not sin like Adam because there were no
prohibitions similar to the law of Moses. But they did
sin, and the way we know this is that "death reigned."
They all died.

4:17 [t][Rom. 8:11]   [u]Rom. 9:26   **4:18**[v]Gen. 15:5
4:19[w]Gen. 17:17   [x]Heb. 11:11   **4:21**[y][Heb. 11:19]
4:22[z]Gen. 15:6   **4:23**[a]Rom. 15:4   **4:24**[b]Acts
2:24   **4:25**[c]Is. 53:4, 5   [d][1 Cor. 15:17]   **5:1**[a]Is. 32:17
[b][Eph. 2:14]   **5:2**[c][Eph. 2:18; 3:12]   [d]1 Cor. 15:1   [e]Heb.
3:6   **5:3**[f]Matt. 5:11, 12   [g]James 1:3   **5:4**[h][James 1:12]
5:5[i]Phil. 1:20   [j]2 Cor. 1:22   **5:6**[k][Rom. 4:25; 5:8; 8:32]
5:8[l][John 3:16; 15:13]   **5:9**[m]Eph. 2:13   [n]1 Thess. 1:10
5:10[o][Rom. 8:32]   [p]2 Cor. 5:18   [q]John 14:19   **5:11**[r][Gal.
4:9]   **5:12**[s][1 Cor. 15:21]   [t]Gen. 2:17   **5:13**[u]1 John 3:4
5:14[v][1 Cor. 15:21, 22]   **5:15**[w][Is. 53:11]   **5:18**[x][1 Cor.
15:21, 45]   [y][John 12:32]

19For as by one man's disobedience many were made sinners, so also by zone Man's obedience many will be made righteous.

20Moreover athe law entered that the offense might abound. But where sin abounded, grace babounded much more, 21so that as sin reigned in death, even so grace might reign through righteousness to eternal life through Jesus Christ our Lord.

Dead to Sin, Alive to God

6 What shall we say then? aShall we continue in sin that grace may abound? 2Certainly not! How shall we who bdied to sin live any longer in it? 3Or do you not know that cas many of us as were baptized into Christ Jesus dwere baptized into His death? 4Therefore we were eburied with Him through baptism into death, that fjust as Christ was raised from the dead by gthe glory of the Father, heven so we also should walk in newness of life.

5iFor if we have been united together in the likeness of His death, certainly we also shall be in the likeness of His resurrection, 6knowing this, that jour old man was crucified with Him, that kthe body of sin might be done away with, that we should no longer be slaves of sin. 7For lhe who has died has been freed from sin. 8Now mif we died with Christ, we believe that we shall also live with Him, 9knowing that nChrist, having been raised from the dead, dies no more. Death no longer has dominion over Him. 10For the death that He died, oHe died to sin once for all; but the life that He lives, pHe lives to God. 11Likewise you also, reckon yourselves to be qdead indeed to sin, but ralive to God in Christ Jesus our Lord.

12sTherefore do not let sin reign in your mortal body, that you should obey it in its lusts. 13And do not present your tmembers as instruments of unrighteousness to sin, but upresent yourselves to God as being alive from the dead, and your members as instruments of righteousness to God. 14For vsin shall not have dominion over you, for you are not under law but under grace.

From Slaves of Sin to Slaves of God

15What then? Shall we sin wbecause we are not under law but under grace? Certainly not! 16Do you not know that xto whom you present yourselves slaves to obey, you are that one's slaves whom you obey, whether of sin leading to death, or of obedience leading to righteousness? 17But God be thanked that though you were slaves of sin, yet you obeyed from the heart ythat form of doctrine to which you were delivered. 18And zhaving been set free from sin, you became slaves of righteousness. 19I speak in human terms because of the weakness of your flesh. For just as you presented your members as slaves of uncleanness, and of lawlessness leading to more lawlessness, so now present your members as slaves of righteousness for holiness.

20For when you were aslaves of sin, you were free in regard to righteousness. 21bWhat fruit did you have then in the things of which you are now ashamed? For cthe end of those things is death. 22But now dhaving been set free from sin, and having become slaves of God, you have your fruit to holiness, and the end, everlasting life. 23For ethe wages of sin is death, but fthe gift of God is eternal life in Christ Jesus our Lord.

Freed from the Law

7 Or do you not know, brethren (for I speak to those who know the law), that the law has dominion over a man as long as he lives? 2For athe woman who has a husband is bound by the law to her husband as long as he lives. But if the husband dies, she is released from the law of her husband. 3So then bif, while her husband lives, she marries another man, she will

---

5:19 many will be made righteous. Through the sanctifying work of the Holy Spirit, the believer who has been declared righteous by God is continually becoming more righteous in thought and action.
5:20 where sin abounded, grace abounded much more. Once the law had been revealed, the sin which was already there became much more obvious because it had been explicitly illustrated how wrong it was. But grace was even bigger than the sin. Sin can never exceed the grace provided by God, and it loses its threat when compared to the infinite grace of God.
6:6 crucified with Him. Simply put, a believer is not the same person he or she was before conversion. A believer is a new creation in Christ (2 Cor. 5:17).
6:23 New Life: A Free Gift—This passage gets at the central point of the Christian gospel. When we are separated from God, sin directs our lives and there is a wage, a consequence, for that sin: death and permanent separation from God. In stark contrast, we do not earn a wage from God. His gifts are free and abundant—the gift of eternal life. There is nothing

that one can do to earn this incredible gift. Eternal life is just that—eternal—it never ceases. All fear of death and its effects can end. Instead of being separated from God for all eternity, Christians will have union with Him. Jesus Christ accomplished all of this on the cross once and for all.
7:3 Adultery—In this passage Paul uses the marriage relationship as an illustration of the believer's relationship to the law and Christ. A wife cannot

5:19 z [Phil. 2:8]   **5:20** a John 15:22   b 1 Tim. 1:14
6:1 a Rom. 3:8; 6:15   **6:2** b [Gal. 2:19]   **6:3** c [Gal. 3:27]
d [1 Cor. 15:29]   **6:4** e Col. 2:12   f 1 Cor. 6:14   g John 2:11
h [Gal. 6:15]   **6:5** i Phil. 3:10   **6:6** j Gal. 2:20; 5:24; 6:14
k Col. 2:11   **6:7** l 1 Pet. 4:1   **6:8** m 2 Tim. 2:11   **6:9** n Rev.
1:18   **6:10** o Heb. 9:27   p Luke 20:38   **6:11** q [Rom.
6:2; 7:4, 6]   r [Gal. 2:19]   **6:12** s Ps. 19:13   **6:13** t Col.
3:5   u 1 Pet. 2:24; 4:2   **6:14** v [Gal. 5:18]   **6:15** w 1 Cor.
9:21   **6:16** x 2 Pet. 2:19   **6:17** y 2 Tim. 1:13   **6:18** z John
8:32   **6:20** o John 8:34   **6:21** b Rom. 7:5   c Rom.
1:32   **6:22** d Rom. 6:18; 8:2   **6:23** e Gen. 2:17   f 1 Pet. 1:4
7:2 a 1 Cor. 7:39   **7:3** b [Matt. 5:32]

be called an adulteress; but if her husband dies, she is free from that law, so that she is no adulteress, though she has married another man. [4]Therefore, my brethren, you also have become [c]dead to the law through the body of Christ, that you may be married to another—to Him who was raised from the dead, that we should [d]bear fruit to God. [5]For when we were in the flesh, the sinful passions which were aroused by the law [e]were at work in our members [f]to bear fruit to death. [6]But now we have been delivered from the law, having died to what we were held by, so that we should serve [g]in the newness of the Spirit and not in the oldness of the letter.

Sin's Advantage in the Law

[7]What shall we say then? Is the law sin? Certainly not! On the contrary, [h]I would not have known sin except through the law. For I would not have known covetousness unless the law had said, [i]"You shall not covet."* [8]But [i]sin, taking opportunity by the commandment, produced in me all manner of evil desire. For [k]apart from the law sin was dead. [9]I was alive once without the law, but when the commandment came, sin revived and I died. [10]And the commandment, [l]which was to bring life, I found to bring death. [11]For sin, taking occasion by the commandment, deceived me, and by it killed me. [12]Therefore [m]the law is holy, and the commandment holy and just and good.

Law Cannot Save from Sin

[13]Has then what is good become death to me? Certainly not! But sin, that it might appear sin, was producing death in me through what is good, so that sin through the commandment might become exceedingly sinful. [14]For we know that the law is spiritual, but I am carnal, [n]sold under sin.

[15]For what I am doing, I do not understand. [o]For what I will to do, that I do not practice; but what I hate, that I do. [16]If, then, I do what I will not to do, I agree with the law that it is good. [17]But now, it is no longer I who do it, but sin that dwells in me. [18]For I know that [p]in me (that is, in my flesh) nothing good dwells; for to will is present with me, but how to perform what is good I do not find. [19]For the good that I will to do, I do not do; but the evil I will not to do, that I practice. [20]Now if I do what I will not to do, it is no longer I who do it, but sin that dwells in me.

[21]I find then a law, that evil is present with me, the one who wills to do good. [22]For I [q]delight in the law of God according to [r]the inward man. [23]But [s]I see another law in [t]my members, warring against the law of my mind, and bringing me into captivity to the law of sin which is in my members. [24]O wretched man that I am! Who will deliver me [u]from this body of death? [25]v[I] thank God—through Jesus Christ our Lord! So then, with the mind I myself serve the law of God, but with the flesh the law of sin.

Free from Indwelling Sin

8 There is therefore now no condemnation to those who are in Christ Jesus,* [a]who do not walk according to the flesh, but according to the Spirit. [2]For [b]the law of [c]the Spirit of life in Christ Jesus has made me free from [d]the law of sin and death. [3]For [e]what the law could not do in that it was weak through the flesh, [f]God did by sending His own Son in the likeness of sinful flesh, on account of sin: He condemned sin in the flesh, [4]that the righteous requirement of the law might be fulfilled in us who [g]do not walk according to the flesh

* 7:7 Exodus 20:17; Deuteronomy 5:21   * 8:1 NU-Text omits the rest of this verse.

---

marry another without committing adultery, but if her husband is dead, she is free to marry another. In the same way, believers must count the law (reconciliation with God by works) dead, in order to "marry" Christ and have a new life. Believers cannot live by the law and by grace, any more than a woman can have two husbands.

7:6 newness of the Spirit . . . oldness of the letter. Believers have a new life in the Holy Spirit, not in trying to gain life by obeying ancient or old laws.

7:8 apart from the law sin was dead. Sin can exist without the law, but without a standard of right and wrong, there can be no judgment of what is sin and what is not.

7:9 when the commandment came, sin revived. Oddly enough, the very rules against certain behaviors arouse the desire to perform those evil acts.

7:13 become death to me. The problem is not the law; the problem is sin. Through the law, sin is shown for what it is, and realization that we are "dead" in sin. We cannot really "be good," even when we know what that is.

8:1 Condemnation—God's justification ("not guilty"), once pronounced, is final. Christ's death blots out the sins of His people, and when His work is applied to the believer, there is no room for condemnation, for God's justice has removed all grounds for it forever. This does not mean that the believer does not still deal with overcoming sin on a regular basis, but through the work of the Holy Spirit, he can be free from the tyranny of sin, and for the love of Christ, live in a way that pleases his Savior.

8:3 the law could not do. The law can point out sin, but it cannot do anything about sin itself.

8:4 the righteous requirement of the law might

7:4 c Gal. 2:19; 5:18 d Gal. 5:22   7:5 e Rom. 6:13 f James 1:15   7:6 g Rom. 2:29   7:7 h Rom. 3:20 i Ex. 20:17; Deut. 5:21; Acts 20:33   7:8 i Rom. 4:15 k 1 Cor. 15:56   7:10 l Lev. 18:5   7:12 m Ps. 19:8   7:14 n 2 Kin. 17:17   7:15 o [Gal. 5:17]   7:18 p [Gen. 6:5; 8:21]   7:22 q Ps. 1:2 r [2 Cor. 4:16]   7:23 s [Gal. 5:17] t Rom. 6:13, 19   7:24 u [1 Cor. 15:51, 52]   7:25 v 1 Cor. 15:57   8:1 a Gal. 5:16   8:2 b Rom. 6:18, 22 c [1 Cor. 15:45] d Rom. 7:24, 25   8:3 e Acts 13:39 f [2 Cor. 5:21]   8:4 g Gal. 5:16, 25

but according to the Spirit. [5]For [h]those who live according to the flesh set their minds on the things of the flesh, but those *who live* according to the Spirit, [i]the things of the Spirit. [6]For [j]to be carnally minded *is* death, but to be spiritually minded *is* life and peace. [7]Because [k]the carnal mind *is* enmity against God; for it is not subject to the law of God, [l]nor indeed can be. [8]So then, those who are in the flesh cannot please God.

[9]But you are not in the flesh but in the Spirit, if indeed the Spirit of God dwells in you. Now if anyone does not have the Spirit of Christ, he is not His. [10]And if Christ *is* in you, the body *is* dead because of sin, but the Spirit *is* life because of righteousness. [11]But if the Spirit of [m]Him who raised Jesus from the dead dwells in you, [n]He who raised Christ from the dead will also give life to your mortal bodies through His Spirit who dwells in you.

Sonship Through the Spirit

[12o]Therefore, brethren, we are debtors—not to the flesh, to live according to the flesh. [13]For [p]if you live according to the flesh you will die; but if by the Spirit you [q]put to death the deeds of the body, you will live. [14]For [r]as many as are led by the Spirit of God, these are sons of God. [15]For [s]you did not receive the spirit of bondage again [t]to fear, but you received the [u]Spirit of adoption by whom we cry out, [v]"Abba, Father." [16w]The Spirit Himself bears witness with our spirit that we are children of God, [17]and if children, then [x]heirs—heirs of God and joint heirs with Christ, [y]if indeed we suffer with *Him*, that we may also be glorified together.

From Suffering to Glory

[18]For I consider that [z]the sufferings of this present time are not worthy *to be compared* with the glory which shall be revealed in us. [19]For [a]the earnest expectation

of the creation eagerly waits for the revealing of the sons of God. [20]For [b]the creation was subjected to futility, not willingly, but because of Him who subjected *it* in hope; [21]because the creation itself also will be delivered from the bondage of corruption into the glorious [c]liberty of the children of God. [22]For we know that the whole creation [d]groans and labors with birth pangs together until now. [23]Not only *that*, but we also who have [e]the firstfruits of the Spirit, [f]even we ourselves groan [g]within ourselves, eagerly waiting for the adoption, the [h]redemption of our body. [24]For we were saved in this hope, but [i]hope that is seen is not hope; for why does one still hope for what he sees? [25]But if we hope for what we do not see, we eagerly wait for *it* with perseverance.

[26]Likewise the Spirit also helps in our weaknesses. For [j]we do not know what we should pray for as we ought, but [k]the Spirit Himself makes intercession for us* with groanings which cannot be uttered. [27]Now [l]He who searches the hearts knows what the mind of the Spirit *is*, because He makes intercession for the saints [m]according to *the will of* God.

[28]And we know that all things work together for good to those who love God, to those [n]who are the called according to *His* purpose. [29]For whom [o]He foreknew, [p]He also predestined [q]to be conformed to the image of His Son, [r]that He might be the firstborn among many brethren. [30]Moreover whom He predestined, these He also [s]called; whom He called, these He also [t]justified; and whom He justified, these He also [u]glorified.

God's Everlasting Love

[31]What then shall we say to these things? [v]If God *is* for us, who *can be* against us?

* 8:26 NU-Text omits *for us.*

---

be fulfilled in us. The believer gains the righteous standard of the law—love—not by means of the law, but by being in Christ and walking "according to the Spirit."

8:15 God the Father—God is the Father of all who believe in Christ in a special sense not shared by unbelievers. God is called their Father, first of all, because they have a new standing before Him. While unbelievers are the offspring of God because He created them (Acts 17:28–29), they do not have the standing of sons or daughters. Their standing is rather as condemned sinners before God the Judge (John 3:18; Rev. 20:11). When a person believes in Christ as Savior, his estate is changed from condemnation to sonship. This new standing grants to all believers the legal right and spiritual privileges of divine sonship: "heirs of God and joint heirs with Christ" (Rom. 8:17). He gives them new life (John 3:3). This relationship then is a family one involving many of the same realities that exist between an earthly father and child: birth of the child (John 3:3); partaking of the father's

nature (2 Pet. 1:4); the father's care for the child (Matt. 6:32–33; 7:9–11); and the father's discipline of the child (Heb. 12:6–8). This new Father-child relationship carries with it new brothers and sisters (Heb. 13:1). The one who believes in Christ as Savior enters into the Father-child relationship with God on the grounds of Christ's sonship (Rom. 8:17; Heb. 2:17).

8:5 [h] John 3:6 [i] [Gal. 5:22–25]   **8:6** [j] Gal. 6:8
8:7 [k] James 4:4 [l] 1 Cor. 2:14   **8:11** [m] Acts 2:24 [n] 1 Cor. 6:14   **8:12** [o] [Rom. 6:7, 14]   **8:13** [p] Gal. 6:8 [q] Eph. 4:22   **8:14** [r] [Gal. 5:18]   **8:15** [s] Heb. 2:15 [t] 2 Tim. 1:7 [u] [Is. 56:5] [v] Mark 14:36   **8:16** [w] Eph. 1:13   **8:17** [x] Acts 26:18 [y] Phil. 1:29   **8:18** [z] 2 Cor. 4:17   **8:19** [a] [2 Pet. 3:13]   **8:20** [b] Gen. 3:17–19   **8:21** [c] [2 Cor. 3:17]   **8:22** [d] Jer. 12:4, 11   **8:23** [e] 2 Cor. 5:5 [f] 2 Cor. 5:2, 4 [g] [Luke 20:36] [h] Eph. 1:14; 4:30   **8:24** [i] Heb. 11:1   **8:26** [j] Matt. 20:22 [k] Eph. 6:18   **8:27** [l] 1 Chr. 28:9 [m] 1 John 5:14   **8:28** [n] 2 Tim. 1:9   **8:29** [o] 2 Tim. 2:19 [p] Eph. 1:5, 11 [q] [2 Cor. 3:18] [r] Heb. 1:6   **8:30** [s] [1 Pet. 2:9; 3:9] [t] [Gal. 2:16] [u] John 17:22   **8:31** [v] Num. 14:9

[32]w He who did not spare His own Son, but [x]delivered Him up for us all, how shall He not with Him also freely give us all things? [33]Who shall bring a charge against God's elect? [y]It is God who justifies. [34]z Who *is* he who condemns? *It is* Christ who died, and furthermore is also risen, [a]who is even at the right hand of God, [b]who also makes intercession for us. [35]Who shall separate us from the love of Christ? *Shall* tribulation, or distress, or persecution, or famine, or nakedness, or peril, or sword? [36]As it is written:

[c]"For Your sake we are killed all day long;
We are accounted as sheep for the slaughter."*

[37]d Yet in all these things we are more than conquerors through Him who loved us. [38]For I am persuaded that neither death nor life, nor angels nor [e]principalities nor powers, nor things present nor things to come, [39]nor height nor depth, nor any other created thing, shall be able to separate us from the love of God which is in Christ Jesus our Lord.

Israel's Rejection of Christ

9 I [a]tell the truth in Christ, I am not lying, my conscience also bearing me witness in the Holy Spirit, [2]b that I have great sorrow and continual grief in my heart. [3]For [c]I could wish that I myself were accursed from Christ for my brethren, my countrymen* according to the flesh, [4]who are Israelites, [d]to whom *pertain* the adoption, [e]the glory, [f]the covenants, [g]the giving of the law, [h]the service *of God*, and [i]the promises; [5]i of whom *are* the fathers and from [k]whom, according to the flesh, Christ *came*, [l]who is over all, *the* eternally blessed God. Amen.

Israel's Rejection and God's Purpose

[6]m But it is not that the word of God has taken no effect. For [n]they *are* not all Israel who *are* of Israel, [7]o nor *are they* all children because they are the seed of Abraham; but, [p]"In Isaac your seed shall be called."* [8]That is, those who *are* the children of the flesh, these *are* not the children of God; but [q]the children of the promise are counted as the seed. [9]For this *is* the word of promise: [r]"At this time I will come and Sarah shall have a son."* [10]And not only *this*, but when [s]Rebecca also had conceived by one man, *even by* our father Isaac [11](for *the children* not yet being born, nor having done any good or evil, that the purpose of God according to election might stand, not of works but of [t]Him who calls), [12]it was said to her, [u]"The older shall serve the younger."* [13]As it is written, [v]"Jacob I have loved, but Esau I have hated."*

Israel's Rejection and God's Justice

[14]What shall we say then? [w]Is there unrighteousness with God? Certainly not! [15]For He says to Moses, [x]"I will have mercy on whomever I will have mercy, and I will have compassion on whomever I will have compassion."* [16]So then *it is* not of him who wills, nor of him who runs, but of God who shows mercy. [17]For [y]the Scripture says to the Pharaoh, [z]"For this very purpose I have raised you up, that I may show My power in you, and that My name may be

* **8:36** Psalm 44:22　* **9:3** Or *relatives*　* **9:7** Genesis 21:12　* **9:9** Genesis 18:10, 14　* **9:12** Genesis 25:23　* **9:13** Malachi 1:2, 3　* **9:15** Exodus 33:19

8:38–39 The Ultimate Security—The first chapters of Romans contain the most complete and systematic presentation of the gospel in the Scriptures. This passage is the bottom-line statement. Nothing can separate us from the love of God that is in Christ. Sadly, too often we hear those words and aren't able to apply them to how we live on a day-to-day basis. Satan is known as a deceiver. He will always try to persuade us that God's love is less than what it is. No matter what the circumstances, no matter how much we mess up, no matter how many powerful forces there are that would try to damage our relationship with Him, God will be there for us with His love.

8:39 shall be able to separate us. Christ created all things, "in heaven and . . . on earth, visible and invisible," and He was "before all things, and in Him all things consist" (Col. 1:16–17). If God, who was from the beginning, is for us, no created thing can separate us from His love. Our security in Him is absolute.

9:1 Conscience—This word is used by Paul for the witness within a person which scrutinizes, examines, and renders a verdict on behavior. Paul is saying in the passage that his conscience verifies the truthfulness of his statement that he has great grief over the Jews' rejection of the gospel. The Holy Spirit is the revealer of truth to the soul, and only as the mind and

heart are taught by Scripture and governed by the Holy Spirit is the voice of conscience a reliable guide in life.

9:6 not all Israel. What about the Jewish people? They had the law, the covenants, and the promises. God has not changed His mind about His chosen people. He always intended for them to understand His whole message, up to and including the Messiah (Christ), as Paul has just explained. But God has, throughout history, always worked with those who believed, not just according to bloodline.

9:15 I will have mercy. God does not "owe" any of us salvation. He has mercy on us in spite of the way we act, not because of the way we act.

8:32 [w] Rom. 5:6, 10　[x] [Rom. 4:25]　**8:33** [y] Is. 50:8; 9　**8:34** [z] John 3:18　[a] Mark 16:19　[b] Heb. 7:25; 9:24　**8:36** [c] Ps. 44:22　**8:37** [d] 1 Cor. 15:57　**8:38** [e] [Eph. 1:21]　**9:1** [a] 2 Cor. 1:23　**9:2** [b] Rom. 10:1　**9:3** [c] Ex. 32:32　**9:4** [d] Ex. 4:22　[e] 1 Sam. 4:21　[f] Acts 3:25　[g] Ps. 147:19　[h] Heb. 9:1, 6　[i] [Acts 2:39; 13:32]　**9:5** [j] Deut. 10:15　[k] [Luke 1:34, 35; 3:23]　[l] Jer. 23:6　**9:6** [m] Num. 23:19　[n] [Gal. 6:16]　**9:7** [o] [Gal. 4:23]　[p] Gen. 21:12　**9:8** [q] Gal. 4:28　**9:9** [r] Gen. 18:10, 14　**9:10** [s] Gen. 25:21　**9:11** [t] [Rom. 4:17; 8:28]　**9:12** [u] Gen. 25:23　**9:13** [v] Mal. 1:2, 3　**9:14** [w] Deut. 32:4　**9:15** [x] Ex. 33:19　**9:17** [y] Gal. 3:8　[z] Ex. 9:16

*declared in all the earth."** 18Therefore He
has mercy on whom He wills, and whom
He wills He [a]hardens.
19You will say to me then, "Why does He
still find fault? For [b]who has resisted His
will?" 20But indeed, O man, who are you to
reply against God? [c]Will the thing formed
say to him who formed *it*, "Why have you
made me like this?" 21Does not the [d]potter
have power over the clay, from the same
lump to make [e]one vessel for honor and
another for dishonor?
22*What* if God, wanting to show *His*
wrath and to make His power known, endured with much longsuffering [f]the vessels
of wrath [g]prepared for destruction, 23and
that He might make known [h]the riches of
His glory on the vessels of mercy, which He
had [i]prepared beforehand for glory, 24even
us whom He [j]called, [k]not of the Jews only,
but also of the Gentiles?
25As He says also in Hosea:

[l]"I will call them My people, who were
not My people,
And her beloved, who was not
*beloved."**
26 *"And[m] it shall come to pass in the place*
where it was said to them,
'You are not My people,'
There they shall be called sons of the
*living God."**

27Isaiah also cries out concerning Israel:*

[n]"Though the number of the children of
Israel be as the sand of the sea,
[o]The remnant will be saved.
28 *For He will finish the work and cut it*
short in righteousness,
[p]Because the LORD will make a short
*work upon the earth."**

29And as Isaiah said before:

[q]"Unless the LORD of Sabaoth had left*
us a seed,
[r]We would have become like Sodom,
And we would have been made like
*Gomorrah."**

Present Condition of Israel

30What shall we say then? [s]That Gentiles,
who did not pursue righteousness, have
attained to righteousness, [t]even the righteousness of faith; 31but Israel, [u]pursuing the
law of righteousness, [v]has not attained to
the law of righteousness.* 32Why? Because
they did not *seek it* by faith, but as it were,
by the works of the law.* For [w]they stumbled
at that stumbling stone. 33As it is written:

[x]"Behold, I lay in Zion a stumbling stone
and rock of offense,
And [y]whoever believes on Him will not
*be put to shame."**

Israel Needs the Gospel

10 Brethren, my heart's desire and
prayer to God for Israel* is that they
may be saved. 2For I bear them witness
[a]that they have a zeal for God, but not according to knowledge. 3For they being ignorant of [b]God's righteousness, and seeking
to establish their own [c]righteousness, have
not submitted to the righteousness of God.
4For [d]Christ *is* the end of the law for righteousness to everyone who believes.
5For Moses writes about the righteousness which is of the law, [e]*"The man who*
*does those things shall live by them."**
6But the righteousness of faith speaks in
this way, [f]*"Do not say in your heart, 'Who*
*will ascend into heaven?'"** (that is, to bring

* **9:17** Exodus 9:16 * **9:25** Hosea 2:23
* **9:26** Hosea 1:10 * **9:27** Isaiah 10:22, 23
* **9:28** NU-Text reads *For the LORD will finish the work and cut it short upon the earth.* * **9:29** Literally, in Hebrew, *Hosts* • Isaiah 1:9 * **9:31** NU-Text omits *of righteousness.* * **9:32** NU-Text reads *by works.* * **9:33** Isaiah 8:14; 28:16
* **10:1** NU-Text reads *them.* * **10:5** Leviticus 18:5
* **10:6** Deuteronomy 30:12

9:20 *reply against God.* Herein lies the divine tension. The Lord says that He does not wish for any to perish, but for all to come to repentance (2 Pet. 3:9). But He also says that no one comes to Jesus unless the Father draws him (John 6:44). He has mercy on whom He desires, and He hardens whom He desires (v. 18). Paul insists on God's right to do as He pleases. Even though God both draws and hardens, He also says that who He is and His worthiness to be worshiped are made plain in creation, so man is without excuse (Rom. 1:18–21). The question is not, "Why are some saved and some condemned?" Everyone deserves condemnation and it is only by God's grace that anyone is saved. We can be sure that whatever God does, it will be righteous, and there is a bigger picture than we can understand from our finite point of view. The only real question is, "How can I be saved?"

9:32 *stumbled.* Being committed to righteousness by works, Israel "stumbled" over the righteousness of faith offered in Christ, just as God had already seen they would and declared through the prophet Isaiah (v. 33).

10:3 Self-Righteousness—There are two things which hinder people from submitting themselves to God's plan of salvation. The first is ignorance of God's own righteous character, and the second is human pride. No one is ever a candidate for Christ's righteousness unless he sees himself as utterly devoid of all possibility of attaining it on his own merits.

10:4 *For Christ is the end of the law.* Christ fulfilled all the requirements of the law, and He is also the

9:18 [a] Ex. 4:21 **9:19** [b] 2 Chr. 20:6 **9:20** [c] Is. 29:16 **9:21** [d] Prov. 16:4 [e] 2 Tim. 2:20 **9:22** [f] [1 Thess. 5:9] [g] [1 Pet. 2:8] **9:23** [h] [Col. 1:27] [i] [Rom. 8:28–30] **9:24** [j] [Rom. 8:28] [k] Rom. 3:29 **9:25** [l] Hos. 2:23 **9:26** [m] Hos. 1:10 **9:27** [n] Is. 10:22, 23 [o] Rom. 11:5 **9:28** [p] Is. 10:23; 28:22 **9:29** [q] Is. 1:9 [r] Is. 13:19 **9:30** [s] Rom. 4:11 [t] Rom. 1:17; 3:21; 10:6 **9:31** [u] [Rom. 10:2–4] [v] [Gal. 5:4] **9:32** [w] [1 Cor. 1:23] **9:33** [x] Is. 8:14; 28:16 [y] Rom. 5:5; 10:11 **10:2** [a] Acts 21:20 **10:3** [b] [Rom. 1:17] [c] [Phil. 3:9] **10:4** [d] [Gal. 3:24; 4:5] **10:5** [e] Lev. 18:5 **10:6** [f] Deut. 30:12–14

Christ down *from above*) [7]or, [g]"*Who will descend into the abyss?*"* (that is, to bring Christ up from the dead). [8]But what does it say? [h]"*The word is near you, in your mouth and in your heart*"* (that is, the word of faith which we preach): [9]that [i]if you confess with your mouth the Lord Jesus and believe in your heart that God has raised Him from the dead, you will be saved. [10]For with the heart one believes unto righteousness, and with the mouth confession is made unto salvation. [11]For the Scripture says, [j]"*Whoever believes on Him will not be put to shame.*"* [12]For [k]there is no distinction between Jew and Greek, for [l]the same Lord over all [m]is rich to all who call upon Him. [13]For [n]"*whoever calls [o]on the name of the LORD shall be saved.*"*

Israel Rejects the Gospel

[14]How then shall they call on Him in whom they have not believed? And how shall they believe in Him of whom they have not heard? And how shall they hear [p]without a preacher? [15]And how shall they preach unless they are sent? As it is written:

[q]"*How beautiful are the feet of those
who preach the gospel of peace,*
*Who bring glad tidings of good
things!*"*

[16]But they have not all obeyed the gospel. For Isaiah says, [r]"*LORD, who has believed our report?*"* [17]So then faith *comes* by hearing, and hearing by the word of God.

[18]But I say, have they not heard? Yes indeed:

[s]"*Their sound has gone out to all the earth,
And their words to the ends of the
world.*"*

[19]But I say, did Israel not know? First Moses says:

[t]"*I will provoke you to jealousy by those
who are not a nation,
I will move you to anger by a [u]foolish
nation.*"*

[20]But Isaiah is very bold and says:

[v]"*I was found by those who did not seek
Me;
I was made manifest to those who did
not ask for Me.*"*

[21]But to Israel he says:

[w]"*All day long I have stretched out My
hands
To a disobedient and contrary people.*"*

Israel's Rejection Not Total

11 I say then, [a]has God cast away His people? [b]Certainly not! For [c]I also am an Israelite, of the seed of Abraham, *of* the tribe of Benjamin. [2]God has not cast away His people whom [d]He foreknew. Or do you not know what the Scripture says of Elijah, how he pleads with God against Israel, saying, [3e]"*LORD, they have killed Your prophets and torn down Your altars, and I alone am left, and they seek my life*"?* [4]But what does the divine response say to him? [f]"*I have reserved for Myself seven thousand men who have not bowed the knee to Baal.*"* [5g]Even so then, at this present time there is a remnant according to the election of grace. [6]And [h]if by grace, then *it is* no longer of works; otherwise grace is no longer grace.* But if *it is* of works, it is no longer grace; otherwise work is no longer work.

[7]What then? [i]Israel has not obtained what it seeks; but the elect have obtained it, and the rest were [j]blinded. [8]Just as it is written:

[k]"*God has given them a spirit of stupor,
[l]Eyes that they should not see
And ears that they should not hear,
To this very day.*"*

[9]And David says:

[m]"*Let their table become a snare and a
trap,
A stumbling block and a recompense
to them.
[10] Let their eyes be darkened, so that
they do not see,
And bow down their back always.*"*

* **10:7** Deuteronomy 30:13   * **10:8** Deuteronomy 30:14   * **10:11** Isaiah 28:16   * **10:13** Joel 2:32
* **10:15** NU-Text omits *preach the gospel of peace, Who.* • Isaiah 52:7; Nahum 1:15   * **10:16** Isaiah 53:1   * **10:18** Psalm 19:4   * **10:19** Deuteronomy 32:21   * **10:20** Isaiah 65:1   * **10:21** Isaiah 65:2   * **11:3** 1 Kings 19:10, 14   * **11:4** 1 Kings 19:18   * **11:6** NU-Text omits the rest of this verse.   * **11:8** Deuteronomy 29:4; Isaiah 29:10   * **11:10** Psalm 69:22, 23

---

opening to the only way of righteousness we can ever have.
10:8 *The word is near you.* Righteousness by faith is not far off and inaccessible, but it is as near as a person's mouth and heart.
10:11 *Whoever.* Paul emphasizes the universal offer of salvation.
11:1 *Has God cast away His people?* Paul points out that he himself is an Israelite, and was chosen by God to be a believer and an apostle. As he develops this thought, Paul reminds us that there has always been a remnant of Israelites whom God has kept true to Himself.

11:8–10 *ears that they should not hear.* Paul quotes Isaiah and David to show that Israel's spiritual indifference was a continual pattern.

10:7 [g] Deut. 30:13   **10:8** [h] Deut. 30:14   **10:9** [i] Luke 12:8   **10:11** [j] Is. 28:16   **10:12** [k] Rom. 3:22, 29   [l] Acts 10:36   [m] Eph. 1:7   **10:13** [n] Joel 2:32   [o] Acts 9:14   **10:14** [p] Titus 1:3   **10:15** [q] Is. 52:7; Nah. 1:15   **10:16** [r] Is. 53:1   **10:18** [s] Ps. 19:4   **10:19** [t] Deut. 32:21   [u] Titus 3:3   **10:20** [v] Is. 65:1   **10:21** [w] Is. 65:2   **11:1** [a] Jer. 46:28   [b] 1 Sam. 12:22   [c] 2 Cor. 11:22   **11:2** [d] [Rom. 8:29]   **11:3** [e] 1 Kin. 19:10, 14   **11:4** [f] 1 Kin. 19:18   **11:5** [g] Rom. 9:27   **11:6** [h] Rom. 4:4   **11:7** [i] Rom. 9:31   [j] 2 Cor. 3:14   **11:8** [k] Is. 29:10, 13   [l] Deut. 29:3, 4   **11:9** [m] Ps. 69:22, 23

Israel's Rejection Not Final

[11]I say then, have they stumbled that they should fall? Certainly not! But [n]through their fall, to provoke them to [o]jealousy, salvation *has come* to the Gentiles. [12]Now if their fall *is* riches for the world, and their failure riches for the Gentiles, how much more their fullness!

[13]For I speak to you Gentiles; inasmuch as [p]I am an apostle to the Gentiles, I magnify my ministry, [14]if by any means I may provoke to jealousy *those who are* my flesh and [q]save some of them. [15]For if their being cast away *is* the reconciling of the world, what *will* their acceptance *be* [r]but life from the dead?

[16]For if [s]the firstfruit *is* holy, the lump *is* also *holy;* and if the root *is* holy, so *are* the branches. [17]And if [t]some of the branches were broken off, [u]and you, being a wild olive tree, were grafted in among them, and with them became a partaker of the root and fatness of the olive tree, [18]v do not boast against the branches. But if you do boast, *remember that* you do not support the root, but the root *supports* you.

[19]You will say then, "Branches were broken off that I might be grafted in." [20]Well *said.* Because of [w]unbelief they were broken off, and you stand by faith. Do not be haughty, but fear. [21]For if God did not spare the natural branches, He may not spare you either. [22]Therefore consider the goodness and severity of God: on those who fell, severity; but toward you, goodness,* [x]if you continue in *His* goodness. Otherwise [y]you also will be cut off. [23]And they also, [z]if they do not continue in unbelief, will be grafted in, for God is able to graft them in again. [24]For if you were cut out of the olive tree which is wild by nature, and were grafted contrary to nature into a cultivated olive tree, how much more will these, who *are* natural *branches,* be grafted into their own olive tree?

[25]For I do not desire, brethren, that you should be ignorant of this mystery, lest you should be [a]wise in your own opinion, that [b]blindness in part has happened to Israel [c]until the fullness of the Gentiles has come in. [26]And so all Israel will be saved,* as it is written:

[d]"The Deliverer will come out of Zion,
    And He will turn away ungodliness
        from Jacob;
27 For [e]this is My covenant with them,
    When I take away their sins."*

[28]Concerning the gospel *they are* enemies for your sake, but concerning the election *they are* [f]beloved for the sake of the fathers. [29]For the gifts and the calling of God *are* [g]irrevocable. [30]For as you [h]were once disobedient to God, yet have now obtained mercy through their disobedience, [31]even so these also have now been disobedient, that through the mercy shown you they also may obtain mercy. [32]For God has committed them [i]all to disobedience, that He might have mercy on all.

[33]Oh, the depth of the riches both of the wisdom and knowledge of God! How unsearchable *are* His judgments and His ways past finding out!

34 "For who has known the [j]mind of the
        Lord?
    Or [k]who has become His counselor?"*
35 "Or[l] who has first given to Him
        And it shall be repaid to him?"*

[36]For [m]of Him and through Him and to Him *are* all things, [n]to whom *be* glory forever. Amen.

Living Sacrifices to God

12 I [a]beseech you therefore, brethren, by the mercies of God, that you present your bodies [b]a living sacrifice, holy, acceptable to God, *which is* your reasonable service. [2]And [c]do not be conformed to this world, but [d]be transformed by the renewing of your mind, that you may [e]prove what *is* that good and acceptable and perfect will of God.

---

* **11:22** NU-Text adds *of God.*   * **11:26** Or *delivered*
* **11:27** Isaiah 59:20, 21   * **11:34** Isaiah 40:13; Jeremiah 23:18   * **11:35** Job 41:11

11:25 *mystery.* The mystery is that Israel has been temporarily and partially hardened, but God has not rejected them.

11:26 *all Israel.* "All Israel" does not mean that every individual in the nation will turn to the Lord. It means that the nation as a whole will be saved, just as the nation as a whole (but not every individual in it) is now rejecting the Lord.

12:1 *living sacrifice.* In the Old Testament sacrificial system, the "job" of the sacrificial lamb was ended with its death. An individual or household selected an animal according to the dictated forms, and it was sacrificed to cover sins. Since Christ became the final atonement for sin, we no longer need the old system. But Paul is calling believers to consider their whole life as a sacrifice dedicated to God and His purposes, a "living" sacrifice, both holy and single-minded.

12:2 Walking in the Spirit—Confession of sin in itself is not enough to enable the believer to automatically walk in the Spirit. He or she must learn to yield their whole self to God (Rom. 6:13; James 4:7). This involves both the body (Rom. 12:1; 1 Cor. 6:20) and the mind (Rom. 12:2), since what is conceived

11:11 [n] Is. 42:6, 7   [o] Rom. 10:19   **11:13** [p] Acts 9:15; 22:21   **11:14** [q] 1 Cor. 9:22   **11:15** [r] [Is. 26:16–19]   **11:16** [s] Lev. 23:10   **11:17** [t] Jer. 11:16   [u] [Eph. 2:12]   **11:18** [v] [1 Cor. 10:12]   **11:20** [w] Heb. 3:19   **11:22** [x] 1 Cor. 15:2   [y] [John 15:2]   **11:23** [z] [2 Cor. 3:16]   **11:25** [a] Rom. 12:16   [b] 2 Cor. 3:14   [c] Luke 21:24   **11:26** [d] Is. 59:20, 21   **11:27** [e] Is. 27:9   **11:28** [f] Deut. 7:8; 10:15   **11:29** [g] Num. 23:19   **11:30** [h] [Eph. 2:2]   **11:32** [i] [Gal. 3:22]   **11:34** [j] Is. 40:13; Jer. 23:18   [k] Job 36:22   **11:35** [l] Job 41:11   **11:36** [m] Heb. 2:10   [n] Heb. 13:21   **12:1** [a] 2 Cor. 10:1–4   [b] Heb. 10:18, 20   **12:2** [c] 1 John 2:15   [d] Eph. 4:23   [e] [1 Thess. 4:3]

Serve God with Spiritual Gifts

[3]For I say, [f]through the grace given to me, to everyone who is among you, [g]not to think of himself more highly than he ought to think, but to think soberly, as God has dealt [h]to each one a measure of faith. [4]For [i]as we have many members in one body, but all the members do not have the same function, [5]so [j]we, being many, are one body in Christ, and individually members of one another. [6]Having then gifts differing according to the grace that is [k]given to us, let us use them: if prophecy, let us [l]prophesy in proportion to our faith; [7]or ministry, let us use it in our ministering; [m]he who teaches, in teaching; [8][n]he who exhorts, in exhortation; [o]he who gives, with liberality; [p]he who leads, with diligence; he who shows mercy, [q]with cheerfulness.

Behave Like a Christian

[9][r]Let love be without hypocrisy. [s]Abhor what is evil. Cling to what is good. [10][t]Be kindly affectionate to one another with brotherly love, [u]in honor giving preference to one another; [11]not lagging in diligence, fervent in spirit, serving the Lord; [12][v]rejoicing in hope, [w]patient in tribulation, [x]continuing steadfastly in prayer; [13][y]distributing to the needs of the saints, [z]given to hospitality.

[14][a]Bless those who persecute you; bless and do not curse. [15][b]Rejoice with those who rejoice, and weep with those who weep. [16][c]Be of the same mind toward one another. [d]Do not set your mind on high things, but associate with the humble. Do not be wise in your own opinion.

[17][e]Repay no one evil for evil. [f]Have regard for good things in the sight of all men. [18]If it is possible, as much as depends on you, [g]live peaceably with all men. [19]Beloved, [h]do not avenge yourselves, but

rather give place to wrath; for it is written, [i]"Vengeance is Mine, I will repay,"* says the Lord. [20]Therefore

[j]"If your enemy is hungry, feed him;
If he is thirsty, give him a drink;
For in so doing you will heap coals of
fire on his head."*

[21]Do not be overcome by evil, but [k]overcome evil with good.

Submit to Government

13 Let every soul be [a]subject to the governing authorities. For there is no authority except from God, and the authorities that exist are appointed by God. [2]Therefore whoever resists [b]the authority resists the ordinance of God, and those who resist will bring judgment on themselves. [3]For rulers are not a terror to good works, but to evil. Do you want to be unafraid of the authority? [c]Do what is good, and you will have praise from the same. [4]For he is God's minister to you for good. But if you do evil, be afraid; for he does not bear the sword in vain; for he is God's minister, an avenger to execute wrath on him who practices evil. [5]Therefore [d]you must be subject, not only because of wrath [e]but also for conscience' sake. [6]For because of this you also pay taxes, for they are God's ministers attending continually to this very thing. [7][f]Render therefore to all their due: taxes to whom taxes are due, customs to whom customs, fear to whom fear, honor to whom honor.

Love Your Neighbor

[8]Owe no one anything except to love one another, for [g]he who loves another

---

* **12:19** Deuteronomy 32:35   * **12:20** Proverbs 25:21, 22

---

in the mind is carried out by the body. One's whole being must be presented by a decisive act of the will to God for His service. Yielding leads not only to dedication but also can result in separation: "do not be conformed to this world" (Rom. 12:2). Finally, yielding includes transformation of the mind. This work is said to be accomplished through a lifetime of "renewing" the mind. Man's mind has been darkened by sin (8:7; Col. 1:21) and must be brought to the place where it thinks as God thinks (Eph. 4:23). This renewing is said to come especially through prayer in everything (Phil. 4:6–7) and through constant meditation on the Word of God (Ps. 119:1). This transformation is a lifelong process that will not be completed until we are with Christ (Phil. 1:6; 1 John 3:2).

12:4–5 Fellowship—A believer must not view himself exclusively as an individual, but must also see himself as part of the whole, as a member of "one body." Fellowship in the New Testament sense is not merely companionship, but a partnership, a responsibility to one another that is financial, practical, and spiritual.

12:6 prophecy. In its narrower sense, "prophecy" means the revealing of God's will in a particular situation (Acts 13:1–3).

12:9 love. There are three words used for love in the New Testament: "self-sacrificial love," "brotherly love," and "kindly affection," the last of which is used in this verse. The greatest proof of the truth of the gospel message and of the reality of Jesus' love is the love believers show to each other.

12:20 coals of fire. Freed from vengeance, believers can give themselves to mercy, even toward their enemies. Such unexpected acts of mercy might even bring enemies to shame and repentance.

12:3 [f]Gal. 2:9 [g]Prov. 25:27 [h][Eph. 4:7]   **12:4** [i]1 Cor. 12:12–14   **12:5** [j][1 Cor. 10:17]   **12:6** [k][John 3:27] [l]Acts 11:27   **12:7** [m]Eph. 4:11   **12:8** [n]Acts 15:32 [o][Matt. 6:1–3] [p][Acts 20:28] [q]2 Cor. 9:7   **12:9** [r]1 Tim. 1:5 [s]Ps. 34:14   **12:10** [t]Heb. 13:1 [u]Phil. 2:3   **12:12** [v]Luke 10:20 [w]Luke 21:19 [x]Luke 18:1   **12:13** [y]1 Cor. 16:1 [z]1 Tim. 3:2   **12:14** [a][Matt. 5:44]   **12:15** [b][1 Cor. 12:26]   **12:16** [c][Phil. 2:2; 4:2] [d]Jer. 45:5   **12:17** [e][Matt. 5:39] [f]2 Cor. 8:21   **12:18** [g]Heb. 12:14   **12:19** [h]Lev. 19:18 [i]Deut. 32:35   **12:20** [j]Prov. 25:21, 22   **12:21** [k][Rom. 12:1, 2]   **13:1** [a]1 Pet. 2:13   **13:2** [b][Titus 3:1]   **13:3** [c]1 Pet. 2:14   **13:5** [d]Eccl. 8:2 [e][1 Pet. 2:13, 19]   **13:7** [f]Matt. 22:21   **13:8** [g][Gal. 5:13, 14]

has fulfilled the law. 9For the commandments, h"You shall not commit adultery," "You shall not murder," "You shall not steal," "You shall not bear false witness,"* "You shall not covet,"* and if there is any other commandment, are all summed up in this saying, namely, i"You shall love your neighbor as yourself."* 10Love does no harm to a neighbor; therefore jlove is the fulfillment of the law.

Put on Christ

11And do this, knowing the time, that now it is high time kto awake out of sleep; for now our salvation is nearer than when we first believed. 12The night is far spent, the day is at hand. lTherefore let us cast off the works of darkness, and mlet us put on the armor of light. 13nLet us walk properly, as in the day, onot in revelry and drunkenness, pnot in lewdness and lust, qnot in strife and envy. 14But rput on the Lord Jesus Christ, and smake no provision for the flesh, to fulfill its lusts.

The Law of Liberty

14 Receivea one who is weak in the faith, but not to disputes over doubtful things. 2For one believes he bmay eat all things, but he who is weak eats only vegetables. 3Let not him who eats despise him who does not eat, and clet not him who does not eat judge him who eats; for God has received him. 4dWho are you to judge another's servant? To his own master he stands or falls. Indeed, he will be made to stand, for God is able to make him stand.

5eOne person esteems one day above another; another esteems every day alike. Let each be fully convinced in his own mind. 6He who fobserves the day, observes it to

the Lord;* and he who does not observe the day, to the Lord he does not observe it. He who eats, eats to the Lord, for ghe gives God thanks; and he who does not eat, to the Lord he does not eat, and gives God thanks. 7For hnone of us lives to himself, and no one dies to himself. 8For if we ilive, we live to the Lord; and if we die, we die to the Lord. Therefore, whether we live or die, we are the Lord's. 9For jto this end Christ died and rose* and lived again, that He might be kLord of both the dead and the living. 10But why do you judge your brother? Or why do you show contempt for your brother? For lwe shall all stand before the judgment seat of Christ.* 11For it is written:

m"As I live, says the LORD,
    Every knee shall bow to Me,
    And every tongue shall confess to
        God."*

12So then neach of us shall give account of himself to God. 13Therefore let us not judge one another anymore, but rather resolve this, onot to put a stumbling block or a cause to fall in our brother's way.

The Law of Love

14I know and am convinced by the Lord Jesus Pthat there is nothing unclean of itself; but to him who considers anything to be unclean, to him it is unclean. 15Yet if your brother is grieved because of your food, you are no longer walking in love. qDo not destroy with your food the one for

* **13:9** NU-Text omits "You shall not bear false witness." • Exodus 20:13–15, 17; Deuteronomy 5:17–19, 21 • Leviticus 19:18 * **14:6** NU-Text omits the rest of this sentence. * **14:9** NU-Text omits and rose. * **14:10** NU-Text reads of God. * **14:11** Isaiah 45:23

13:9 as yourself. This is not a command to love ourselves. It is a recognition that we do love ourselves, and a command to love others just as genuinely and sincerely.
13:10 Love. "Love" excludes murder, adultery, stealing, and lying. Therefore when we love, we automatically fulfill the prohibitions of the law.
14:1 weak in the faith. Those who are weak in the faith are not unbelievers, but they have not yet understood (or are not able to understand) some of the deeper thinking about the not so clearly defined situations that a Christian faces.
14:5 one day above another. This verse probably relates to the holy days of the Old Testament ceremonial law. The exhortation does not mean it is wrong to have strong convictions, but that all people must have their own convictions. Concerning "doubtful things" (v. 1), things that are not clearly defined as sin, we as Christians are supposed to think deeply about these things, and decide what we think best pleases the Lord. We are not supposed to live by default, doing what most others are doing, or being swayed by the strongest voice. We may find that we need to change our original conclusions, but we must do so thoughtfully, not impulsively. We must not condemn others who come to a different conclusion.

14:12 account of himself to God. We must give an account to God for these conclusions we have reached about how to live, and in light of that, we want to be sure that our conclusions do not cause someone else to stumble.
14:14 unclean. "Unclean" means common, and refers to the things prohibited by the Jewish ceremonial law. If anyone considers some activity to be wrong, then for him it is wrong to engage in that activity.
14:15 Selfishness—This chapter concerns weak and strong Christians and their attitudes toward each other in practical matters within the church. If a stronger brother fails to consider the scruples of the weaker brother, the stronger brother violates the

13:9 h Ex. 20:13–17; Deut. 5:17–21 i Lev. 19:18
13:10 j [Matt. 7:12; 22:39, 40] 13:11 k [1 Cor. 15:34]
13:12 l Eph. 5:11 m [Eph. 6:11, 13] 13:13 n Phil. 4:8
o Prov. 23:20 p [1 Cor. 6:9] q James 3:14 13:14 r Gal.
3:27 s [Gal. 5:16] 14:1 a [1 Cor. 8:9; 9:22]
14:2 b [Titus 1:15] 14:3 c [Col. 2:16] 14:4 d James
4:11, 12 14:5 e Gal. 4:10 14:6 f Gal. 4:10 [1 Tim. 4:3]
14:7 h [Gal. 2:20] 14:8 i 2 Cor. 5:14, 15 14:9 j 2 Cor.
5:15 k Acts 10:36 14:10 l 2 Cor. 5:10 14:11 m Is. 45:23
14:12 n 1 Pet. 4:5 14:13 o 1 Cor. 8:9 14:14 p 1 Cor.
10:25 14:15 q 1 Cor. 8:11

whom Christ died. ¹⁶ʳTherefore do not let your good be spoken of as evil; ¹⁷ˢfor the kingdom of God is not eating and drinking, but righteousness and ᵗpeace and joy in the Holy Spirit. ¹⁸For he who serves Christ in these things* ᵘis acceptable to God and approved by men.

¹⁹ᵛTherefore let us pursue the things which make for peace and the things by which ʷone may edify another. ²⁰ˣDo not destroy the work of God for the sake of food. ʸAll things indeed are pure, ᶻbut it is evil for the man who eats with offense. ²¹It is good neither to eat ᵃmeat nor drink wine nor do anything by which your brother stumbles or is offended or is made weak.* ²²Do you have faith?* Have it to yourself before God. ᵇHappy is he who does not condemn himself in what he approves. ²³But he who doubts is condemned if he eats, because he does not eat from faith; for ᶜwhatever is not from faith is sin.*

Bearing Others' Burdens

15 We ᵃthen who are strong ought to bear with the scruples of the weak, and not to please ourselves. ²ᵇLet each of us please his neighbor for his good, leading to edification. ³ᶜFor even Christ did not please Himself; but as it is written, ᵈ"The reproaches of those who reproached You fell on Me."* ⁴For ᵉwhatever things were written before were written for our learning, that we through the patience and comfort of the Scriptures might have hope. ⁵ᶠNow may the God of patience and comfort grant you to be like-minded toward one another, according to Christ Jesus, ⁶that you may ᵍwith one mind and one mouth glorify the God and Father of our Lord Jesus Christ.

Glorify God Together

⁷Therefore ʰreceive one another, just ᶦas Christ also received us,* to the glory of God. ⁸Now I say that ʲJesus Christ has become a servant to the circumcision for the truth of God, ᵏto confirm the promises made to the fathers, ⁹and ˡthat the Gentiles might glorify God for His mercy, as it is written:

> ᵐ"For this reason I will confess to You
> among the Gentiles,
> And sing to Your name."*

¹⁰And again he says:

> ⁿ"Rejoice, O Gentiles, with His people!"*

¹¹And again:

> ᵒ"Praise the LORD, all you Gentiles!
> Laud Him, all you peoples!"*

¹²And again, Isaiah says:

> ᵖ"There shall be a root of Jesse;
> And He who shall rise to reign over
> the Gentiles,
> In Him the Gentiles shall hope."*

¹³Now may the God of hope fill you with all ᑫjoy and peace in believing, that you may abound in hope by the power of the Holy Spirit.

From Jerusalem to Illyricum

¹⁴Now ʳI myself am confident concerning you, my brethren, that you also are full of goodness, ˢfilled with all knowledge, able also to admonish one another.* ¹⁵Nevertheless, brethren, I have written more boldly to you on some points, as reminding you, ᵗbecause of the grace given to me by God, ¹⁶that ᵘI might be a minister of Jesus Christ to the Gentiles, ministering the gospel of God, that the ᵛoffering of the Gentiles

---

* **14:18** NU-Text reads this. * **14:21** NU-Text omits or is offended or is made weak. * **14:22** NU-Text reads The faith which you have— have. * **14:23** M-Text puts Romans 16:25–27 here. * **15:3** Psalm 69:9 * **15:7** NU-Text and M-Text read you. * **15:9** 2 Samuel 22:50; Psalm 18:49 * **15:10** Deuteronomy 32:43 * **15:11** Psalm 117:1 * **15:12** Isaiah 11:10 * **15:14** M-Text reads others.

---

obligations of love. He is selfishly putting his own desires above the real needs of one who is weak in faith.

14:16 good be spoken of as evil. Even if you have decided that eating certain foods is in accord with your understanding of what is pleasing to God, if it causes another believer to be grieved by the choice you have made, you should be eager to change. Your freedom should not look like license or gluttony. The kingdom of God is a lot more important than the things we eat and drink.

14:21 stumbles. A believer does not have to abandon his own convictions, but love should cause him to carefully observe how what he does affects others. It is a sin (v. 23) to do something that you are really convinced is wrong, even if others think it is all right. In light of this, if a believer is influencing another to violate his conscience, even if the believer is not violating his own conscience, he has caused the other brother to "stumble," and that should not happen.

15:3 Christ. Jesus Christ is the ultimate model for the strong believer. He "did not consider it robbery to be

equal with God, but made Himself of no reputation" (Phil. 2:5–7) so that He could clearly represent God and His cause.

15:9 as it is written. Paul quotes from all three divisions of the Old Testament (the Law, the Prophets, and the Psalms) and from three great Jewish leaders (Moses, David, and Isaiah) to demonstrate that God's purpose was always to bless the Gentiles through Israel.

15:12 root of Jesse. This is a title for the Messiah (Christ). Jesse was the father of David, and the

---

14:16 ʳ [Rom. 12:17] **14:17** ˢ 1 Cor. 8:8 ᵗ [Rom. 8:6] **14:18** ᵘ 2 Cor. 8:21 **14:19** ᵛ Rom. 12:18 ʷ 1 Cor. 14:12 ˣ Rom. 14:15 ʸ Acts 10:15 ᶻ 1 Cor. 8:9–12 **14:21** ᵃ 1 Cor. 8:13 **14:22** ᵇ [1 John 3:21] **14:23** ᶜ Titus 1:15 **15:1** ᵃ [Gal. 6:1, 2] **15:2** ᵇ 1 Cor. 9:22; 10:24, 33 **15:3** ᶜ Matt. 26:39 ᵈ Ps. 69:9 **15:4** ᵉ 1 Cor. 10:11 **15:5** ᶠ 1 Cor. 1:10 **15:6** ᵍ Acts 4:24 **15:7** ʰ Rom. 14:1, 3 ᶦ Rom. 5:2 **15:8** ʲ Matt. 15:24 ᵏ 2 Cor. 1:20 **15:9** ˡ John 10:16 ᵐ 2 Sam. 22:50; Ps. 18:49 **15:10** ⁿ Deut. 32:43 **15:11** ᵒ Ps. 117:1 **15:12** ᵖ Is. 11:1, 10 **15:13** ᑫ Rom. 12:12; 14:17 **15:14** ʳ 2 Pet. 1:12 ˢ 1 Cor. 1:5; 8:1, 7, 10 **15:15** ᵗ Rom. 1:5; 12:3 **15:16** ᵘ Rom. 11:13 ᵛ [Is. 66:20]

might be acceptable, sanctified by the Holy Spirit. [17]Therefore I have reason to glory in Christ Jesus ʷin the things *which pertain* to God. [18]For I will not dare to speak of any of those things ˣwhich Christ has not accomplished through me, in word and deed, ʸto make the Gentiles obedient— [19]ᶻin mighty signs and wonders, by the power of the Spirit of God, so that from Jerusalem and round about to Illyricum I have fully preached the gospel of Christ. [20]And so I have made it my aim to preach the gospel, not where Christ was named, ᵃlest I should build on another man's foundation, [21]but as it is written:

> ᵇ*"To whom He was not announced, they shall see;*
> *And those who have not heard shall understand."** *

Plan to Visit Rome

[22]For this reason ᶜI also have been much hindered from coming to you. [23]But now no longer having a place in these parts, and ᵈhaving a great desire these many years to come to you, [24]whenever I journey to Spain, I shall come to you.* For I hope to see you on my journey, ᵉand to be helped on my way there by you, if first I may ᶠenjoy your *company* for a while. [25]But now ᵍI am going to Jerusalem to minister to the saints. [26]For ʰit pleased those from Macedonia and Achaia to make a certain contribution for the poor among the saints who are in Jerusalem. [27]It pleased them indeed, and they are their debtors. For ⁱif the Gentiles have been partakers of their spiritual things, ʲtheir duty is also to minister to them in material things. [28]Therefore, when I have performed this and have sealed to them ᵏthis fruit, I shall go by way of you to Spain. [29]ˡBut I know that when I come to you, I shall come in the fullness of the blessing of the gospel* of Christ.

[30]Now I beg you, brethren, through the Lord Jesus Christ, and ᵐthrough the love of the Spirit, ⁿthat you strive together with me

in prayers to God for me, [31]ᵒthat I may be delivered from those in Judea who do not believe, and that ᵖmy service for Jerusalem may be acceptable to the saints, [32]ᵠthat I may come to you with joy ʳby the will of God, and may ˢbe refreshed together with you. [33]Now ᵗthe God of peace *be* with you all. Amen.

Sister Phoebe Commended

16 I commend to you Phoebe our sister, who is a servant of the church in ᵃCenchrea, [2]ᵇthat you may receive her in the Lord ᶜin a manner worthy of the saints, and assist her in whatever business she has need of you; for indeed she has been a helper of many and of myself also.

Greeting Roman Saints

[3]Greet ᵈPriscilla and Aquila, my fellow workers in Christ Jesus, [4]who risked their own necks for my life, to whom not only I give thanks, but also all the churches of the Gentiles. [5]Likewise *greet* ᵉthe church that is in their house.

Greet my beloved Epaenetus, who is ᶠthe firstfruits of Achaia* to Christ. [6]Greet Mary, who labored much for us. [7]Greet Andronicus and Junia, my countrymen and my fellow prisoners, who are of note among the ᵍapostles, who also ʰwere in Christ before me.

[8]Greet Amplias, my beloved in the Lord. [9]Greet Urbanus, our fellow worker in Christ, and Stachys, my beloved. [10]Greet Apelles, approved in Christ. Greet those who are of the *household* of Aristobulus. [11]Greet Herodion, my countryman.* Greet those who are of the *household* of Narcissus who are in the Lord.

[12]Greet Tryphena and Tryphosa, who have labored in the Lord. Greet the beloved Persis, who labored much

---

* **15:21** Isaiah 52:15   * **15:24** NU-Text omits *I shall come to you* (and joins *Spain* with the next sentence).   * **15:29** NU-Text omits *of the gospel.*
* **16:5** NU-Text reads *Asia.*   * **16:11** Or *relative*

Messiah was to be the Son of David. The Messiah is both the Origin and the Offspring of David.

15:25–26 Kindness—One of the New Testament commands is that Christians display kindness toward other believers (12:10). The Macedonian believers had just gathered a love offering for the needy saints in Jerusalem. Such kindness is a response to God's wonderful kindness to us. In fact, wanting to reach out to others is an evidence of our new birth, and as we bless others in this way, we will find ourselves receiving similar blessings of kindness (Luke 6:38).

15:28 Spain. No one knows for sure if Paul ever got to Spain, but he had it on his travel itinerary.

15:29 when I come to you. Paul did get to Rome, but not in the time frame or way he had thought. God had a special plan for Paul. The Lord would give him the opportunity to testify of his faith in the emperor's court, but he would do so as a prisoner (Acts 28).

16:3–4 Priscilla and Aquila. This married couple is never mentioned separately, perhaps because they ministered so effectively together. Like Paul, they were tentmakers, and worked with him in Corinth and Ephesus (Acts 18:1–3,18,26).

16:8–10 Amplias...Urbanus...Stachys...Apelles.

15:17 ʷ Heb. 2:17; 5:1   **15:18** ˣ Acts 15:12; 21:19 ʸ Rom. 1:5   **15:19** ᶻ Acts 99:11   **15:20** ᵃ [2 Cor. 10:13, 15, 16]   **15:21** ᵇ Is. 52:15   **15:22** ᶜ Rom. 1:13   **15:23** ᵈ Acts 19:21; 23:11   **15:24** ᵉ Acts 15:3 ᶠ Rom. 1:12   **15:25** ᵍ Acts 19:21   **15:26** ʰ 1 Cor. 16:1   **15:27** ⁱ Rom. 11:17 ʲ 1 Cor. 9:11   **15:28** ᵏ Phil. 4:17   **15:29** ˡ [Rom. 1:11]   **15:30** ᵐ Phil. 2:1 ⁿ 2 Cor. 1:11   **15:31** ᵒ 2 Tim. 3:11; 4:17 ᵖ 2 Cor. 8:4   **15:32** ᵠ Rom. 1:10 ʳ Acts 18:21 ˢ 1 Cor. 16:18   **15:33** ᵗ 1 Cor. 14:33   **16:1** ᵃ Acts 18:18   **16:2** ᵇ Phil. 2:29 ᶜ Phil. 1:27   **16:3** ᵈ Acts 18:2, 18, 26   **16:5** ᵉ 1 Cor. 16:19 ᶠ 1 Cor. 16:15   **16:7** ᵍ Acts 1:13, 26 ʰ Gal. 1:22

in the Lord. [13]Greet Rufus, *i*chosen in the Lord, and his mother and mine. [14]Greet Asyncritus, Phlegon, Hermas, Patrobas, Hermes, and the brethren who are with them. [15]Greet Philologus and Julia, Nereus and his sister, and Olympas, and all the saints who are with them.

[16]*j*Greet one another with a holy kiss. The* churches of Christ greet you.

Avoid Divisive Persons

[17]Now I urge you, brethren, note those *k*who cause divisions and offenses, contrary to the doctrine which you learned, and *l*avoid them. [18]For those who are such do not serve our Lord Jesus* Christ, but *m*their own belly, and *n*by smooth words and flattering speech deceive the hearts of the simple. [19]For *o*your obedience has become known to all. Therefore I am glad on your behalf; but I want you to be *p*wise in what is good, and simple concerning evil. [20]And *q*the God of peace *r*will crush Satan under your feet shortly.

*s*The grace of our Lord Jesus Christ *be* with you. Amen.

Greetings from Paul's Friends

[21]*t*Timothy, my fellow worker, and *u*Lucius, *v*Jason, and *w*Sosipater, my countrymen, greet you.

[22]I, Tertius, who wrote *this* epistle, greet you in the Lord.

[23]*x*Gaius, my host and *the host* of the whole church, greets you. *y*Erastus, the treasurer of the city, greets you, and Quartus, a brother. [24]*z*The grace of our Lord Jesus Christ *be* with you all. Amen.*

Benediction

[25]Now *a*to Him who is able to establish you *b*according to my gospel and the preaching of Jesus Christ, *c*according to the revelation of the mystery *d*kept secret since the world began [26]but *e*now made manifest, and by the prophetic Scriptures made known to all nations, according to the commandment of the everlasting God, for *f*obedience to the faith— [27]to *g*God, alone wise, *be* glory through Jesus Christ forever. Amen.*

---

* **16:16** NU-Text reads *All the churches.*
* **16:18** NU-Text and M-Text omit *Jesus.*
* **16:24** NU-Text omits this verse.   * **16:27** M-Text puts Romans 16:25–27 after Romans 14:23.

These were common slave names. **Aristobulus.** This was a familiar Greek name, and this man may have been the owner of the previously mentioned men, if they were indeed slaves.
16:23 Gaius. "Gaius" of Corinth (1 Cor. 1:14) not only gave Paul lodging, but offered his house as a meeting place for the church.
16:25 mystery. Paul speaks of his message as a "mystery" (see 11:25) because God's complete plan of salvation was at first hidden but now was being revealed. Part of the mystery is that the church will consist of both Jews and Gentiles united in one body of Christ (Eph. 3:1–13).

16:13 *i* 2 John 1   **16:16** *j* 1 Cor. 16:20   **16:17** *k* [Acts 15:1] *l* [1 Cor. 5:9]   **16:18** *m* Phil. 3:19 *n* Col. 2:4   **16:19** *o* Rom. 1:8 *p* Matt. 10:16   **16:20** *q* Rom. 15:33 *r* Gen. 3:15 *s* 1 Cor. 16:23   **16:21** *t* Acts 16:1 *u* Acts 13:1 *v* Acts 17:5 *w* Acts 20:4   **16:23** *x* 1 Cor. 1:14 *y* Acts 19:22   **16:24** *z* 1 Thess. 5:28   **16:25** *a* [Eph. 3:20] *b* Rom. 2:16 *c* Eph. 1:9 *d* Col. 1:26; 2:2; 4:3   **16:26** *e* Eph. 1:9 *f* Rom. 1:5   **16:27** *g* Jude 25

THE FIRST EPISTLE OF PAUL THE APOSTLE TO THE
CORINTHIANS

▶ **AUTHOR:** Pauline authorship of 1 Corinthians is almost universally accepted. Instances of this widely held belief can be found as early as A.D. 95, when Clement of Rome wrote to the Corinthian church and cited this epistle in regard to the continuing problem of factions among themselves. Paul taught the word of God in Corinth for eighteen months in A.D. 51 and 52, leaving Apollos to preach and teach in his absence. When Paul was in Ephesus during his third missionary journey, he became disturbed by reports of discord in the church of Corinth. First Corinthians is a record of Paul's initial response to these problems.

▶ **TIME:** C. A.D. 56   ▶ **KEY VERSE:** 1 Cor. 1:10

▶ **THEME:** The basic theme of this epistle is the application of Christian principles to carnality in the individual as well as in the church. Paul is responding to a letter he received from the Corinthians concerning five behavioral problems that are causing dissension in one way or another: (1) divisions in the church; (2) a case of incest; (3) court cases between members; (4) the abuse of Christian "freedom"; and (5) the chaos occurring in connection with celebration of the Lord's Supper. Paul's ethical responses to the various behaviors of the Corinthian church are based on a theological understanding of what it means to be a part of the people of God in a complex multicultural, pagan environment.

Greeting

1 Paul, *a*called *to be* an apostle of Jesus Christ *b*through the will of God, and *c*Sosthenes *our* brother,

2To the church of God which is at Corinth, to those who *d*are sanctified in Christ Jesus, *e*called *to be* saints, with all who in every place call on the name of Jesus Christ *f*our Lord, *g*both theirs and ours:

3*h*Grace to you and peace from God our Father and the Lord Jesus Christ.

Spiritual Gifts at Corinth

4*i*I thank my God always concerning you for the grace of God which was given to you by Christ Jesus, 5that you were enriched in everything by Him *j*in all utterance and all knowledge, 6even as *k*the testimony of Christ was confirmed in you, 7so that you come short in no gift, eagerly *l*waiting for the revelation of our Lord Jesus Christ, 8*m*who will also confirm you to the end, *n*that you may be blameless in the day of our Lord Jesus Christ. 9*o*God *is* faithful, by whom you were called into *p*the fellowship of His Son, Jesus Christ our Lord.

Sectarianism Is Sin

10Now I plead with you, brethren, by the name of our Lord Jesus Christ, *q*that you all speak the same thing, and *that* there be no divisions among you, but *that* you be perfectly joined together in the same mind and in the same judgment. 11For it has been declared to me concerning you, my brethren, by those of Chloe's *household*, that there are contentions among you. 12Now I say this, that *r*each of you says, "I am of Paul," or "I am of *s*Apollos," or "I am of *t*Cephas,"

1:1 *through the will of God.* The Corinthian church greatly valued human wisdom. This misplaced emphasis had caused some in the church to challenge Paul's authority. They forgot that Jesus Christ Himself had called him to his ministry as an apostle of Christ.
1:2 *sanctified in Christ Jesus.* Holiness comes from our position in Christ, not from our own goodness. Jesus' death in payment for our sins makes a believer holy forever in God's eyes (Heb. 10:14). But in everyday living, sanctification involves small daily changes.
1:7 *come short in no gift.* The Corinthians were richly blessed with spiritual gifts because God was giving them everything they needed to do His will (12:14–27).
1:10 *in the same mind.* Christian unity is not uniformity of appearance, but unity of direction, and the bond of mutual love and esteem (Eph. 4:14–16).

1:1 *a* Rom. 1:1 *b* 2 Cor. 1:1 *c* Acts 18:17   **1:2** *d* [Acts 15:9] *e* Rom. 1:7 *f* [1 Cor. 8:6] *g* [Rom. 3:22]   **1:3** *h* Rom. 1:7 **1:4** *i* Rom. 1:8 **1:5** *j* [1 Cor. 12:8] **1:6** *k* 2 Tim. 1:8 **1:7** *l* Phil. 3:20 **1:8** *m* 1 Thess. 3:13; 5:23 *n* Col. 1:22; 2:7 **1:9** *o* Is. 49:7 *p* [John 15:4] **1:10** *q* 2 Cor. 13:11 **1:12** *r* 1 Cor. 3:4 *s* Acts 18:24 *t* John 1:42

or "I am of Christ." [13u]Is Christ divided? Was Paul crucified for you? Or were you baptized in the name of Paul?

[14]I thank God that I baptized [v]none of you except [w]Crispus and [x]Gaius, [15]lest anyone should say that I had baptized in my own name. [16]Yes, I also baptized the household of [y]Stephanas. Besides, I do not know whether I baptized any other. [17]For Christ did not send me to baptize, but to preach the gospel, [z]not with wisdom of words, lest the cross of Christ should be made of no effect.

Christ the Power and Wisdom of God

[18]For the message of the cross is [a]foolishness to [b]those who are perishing, but to us [c]who are being saved it is the [d]power of God. [19]For it is written:

[e]"I will destroy the wisdom of the wise,
   And bring to nothing the
      understanding of the prudent."*

[20f]Where is the wise? Where is the scribe? Where is the disputer of this age? [g]Has not God made foolish the wisdom of this world? [21]For since, in the [h]wisdom of God, the world through wisdom did not know God, it pleased God through the foolishness of the message preached to save those who believe. [22]For [i]Jews request a sign, and Greeks seek after wisdom; [23]but we preach Christ crucified, [j]to the Jews a stumbling block and to the Greeks* [k]foolishness, [24]but to those who are called, both Jews and Greeks, Christ [l]the power of God and [m]the wisdom of God. [25]Because the foolishness of God is wiser than men, and the weakness of God is stronger than men.

Glory Only in the Lord

[26]For you see your calling, brethren, [n]that not many wise according to the flesh, not many mighty, not many noble, are called. [27]But [o]God has chosen the foolish things of the world to put to shame the wise, and God has chosen the weak things of the world to put to shame the things which are mighty; [28]and the base things of the world and the things which are despised God has chosen, and the things which are not, to bring to nothing the things that are, [29]that no flesh should glory in His presence. [30]But of Him you are in Christ Jesus, who became for us wisdom from God—and [p]righteousness and sanctification and redemption—[31]that, as it is written, [q]"He who glories, let him glory in the LORD."*

Christ Crucified

2 And I, brethren, when I came to you, did not come with excellence of speech or of wisdom declaring to you the testimony* of God. [2]For I determined not to know anything among you [a]except Jesus Christ and Him crucified. [3b]I was with you [c]in weakness, in fear, and in much trembling. [4]And my speech and my preaching [d]were not with persuasive words of human* wisdom, [e]but in demonstration of the Spirit and of power, [5]that your faith should not be in the wisdom of men but in the [f]power of God.

Spiritual Wisdom

[6]However, we speak wisdom among those who are mature, yet not the wisdom of this age, nor of the rulers of this age, who are coming to nothing. [7]But we speak the wisdom of God in a mystery, the hidden wisdom which God ordained before the ages for our glory, [8]which none of the rulers of this age knew; for [g]had they known, they would not have [h]crucified the Lord of glory.

* **1:19** Isaiah 29:14   * **1:23** NU-Text reads *Gentiles.*
* **1:31** Jeremiah 9:24   * **2:1** NU-Text reads *mystery.*   * **2:4** NU-Text omits *human.*

1:14 Crispus and Gaius. Crispus was the ruler of the synagogue in Corinth when Paul began to preach there (Acts 18:8). He was instrumental in the conversion of many other Christians. Gaius may be the same person who hosted Paul and the entire church (Rom. 16:23).

1:16 Stephanas. Stephanas was one of Paul's first converts in Achaia, the region of which Corinth was the capital. Paul praised him and his household for their devotion to the ministry and for their assistance (16:15). Stephanas was one of the couriers who took correspondence to and from Corinth.

1:17 not . . . to baptize, but to preach the gospel. Paul's primary ministry was not baptism, but preaching the truth. Baptism naturally follows conversion, but is secondary in importance.

1:20 Where is the wise? All human efforts to find favor with God fall woefully short (Rom. 3:9–28). Only through faith in Christ can we be saved from our sins.

1:27 the foolish things of the world. God's plan of salvation does not conform to the world's priorities. Yet in reality, eternal salvation is more valuable than anything else.

1:28 and the base . . . are despised. Corinth had a large slave population, and many of these slaves became followers of Christ. Slaves were despised by the free-born and the well-to-do.

2:6 the rulers of this age. In some passages Paul uses the word "rulers" to refer to spiritual beings (Eph. 6:12; Col. 2:15); here it seems to be a reference to earthly rulers.

2:7 mystery. God's plan was kept hidden, known only to Him, until He chose to reveal it (Eph. 3:1–11). This is in contrast to the teachings of the Gnostics, a

1:13 [u]2 Cor. 11:4   **1:14** [v]John 4:2   [w]Acts 18:8   [x]Rom. 16:23   **1:16** [y]1 Cor. 16:15, 17   **1:17** [z][1 Cor. 2:1, 4, 13]   **1:18** [a]1 Cor. 2:14   [b]2 Cor. 2:15   [c][1 Cor. 15:2]   [d]Rom. 1:16   **1:19** [e]Is. 29:14   **1:20** [f]Is. 19:12; 33:18   [g]Job 12:17   **1:21** [h]Dan. 2:20   **1:22** [i]Matt. 12:38   **1:23** [j]Luke 2:34   [k][1 Cor. 2:14]   [l][Rom. 1:4]   [m]Col. 2:3   **1:26** [n]John 7:48   **1:27** [o]Matt. 11:25   **1:30** [p][2 Cor. 5:21]   **1:31** [q]Jer. 9:23, 24   **2:2** [a]Gal. 6:14   **2:3** [b]Acts 18:1   [c][2 Cor. 4:7]   **2:4** [d]2 Pet. 1:16   [e]Rom. 15:19   **2:5** [f]1 Thess. 1:5   **2:8** [g]Luke 23:34   [h]Matt. 27:33–50

9But as it is written:

i*"Eye has not seen, nor ear heard,*
Nor have entered into the heart of man
The things which God has prepared
*for those who love Him."**

10But jGod has revealed *them* to us through His Spirit. For the Spirit searches all things, yes, the deep things of God. 11For what man knows the things of a man except the kspirit of the man which is in him? lEven so no one knows the things of God except the Spirit of God. 12Now we have received, not the spirit of the world, but mthe Spirit who is from God, that we might know the things that have been freely given to us by God. 13These things we also speak, not in words which man's wisdom teaches but which the Holy* Spirit teaches, comparing spiritual things with spiritual. 14nBut the natural man does not receive the things of the Spirit of God, for they are foolishness to him; nor can he know *them*, because they are spiritually discerned. 15But he who is spiritual judges all things, yet he himself is *rightly* judged by no one. 16For o*"who has known the mind of the LORD that he may instruct Him?"** pBut we have the mind of Christ.

Sectarianism Is Carnal

3 And I, brethren, could not speak to you as to spiritual *people* but as to carnal, as to ababes in Christ. 2I fed you with bmilk and not with solid food; cfor until now you were not able *to receive it*, and even now you are still not able; 3for you are still carnal. For where *there are* envy, strife, and divisions among you, are you not carnal and behaving like *mere* men? 4For when one says, "I am of Paul," and another, "I *am* of Apollos," are you not carnal?

Watering, Working, Warning

5Who then is Paul, and who *is* Apollos, but dministers through whom you believed,

as the Lord gave to each one? 6eI planted, fApollos watered, gbut God gave the increase. 7So then hneither he who plants is anything, nor he who waters, but God who gives the increase. 8Now he who plants and he who waters are one, iand each one will receive his own reward according to his own labor.

9For jwe are God's fellow workers; you are God's field, *you are* kGod's building. 10lAccording to the grace of God which was given to me, as a wise master builder I have laid mthe foundation, and another builds on it. But let each one take heed how he builds on it. 11For no other foundation can anyone lay than nthat which is laid, owhich is Jesus Christ. 12Now if anyone builds on this foundation *with* gold, silver, precious stones, wood, hay, straw, 13each one's work will become clear; for the Day pwill declare it, because qit will be revealed by fire; and the fire will test each one's work, of what sort it is. 14If anyone's work which he has built on *it* endures, he will receive a reward. 15If anyone's work is burned, he will suffer loss; but he himself will be saved, yet so as through fire.

16rDo you not know that you are the temple of God and *that* the Spirit of God dwells in you? 17If anyone defiles the temple of God, God will destroy him. For the temple of God is holy, which *temple* you are.

Avoid Worldly Wisdom

18sLet no one deceive himself. If anyone among you seems to be wise in this age, let him become a fool that he may become wise. 19For the wisdom of this world is foolishness with God. For it is written, t*"He catches the wise in their own craftiness"*;* 20and again, u*"The LORD knows the thoughts of the wise, that they are futile."**

---

* **2:9** Isaiah 64:4   * **2:13** NU-Text omits *Holy.*
* **2:16** Isaiah 40:13   * **3:19** Job 5:13   * **3:20** Psalm 94:11

---

group of false religious teachers who would infiltrate the early church (1 John 2:18–27). They claimed that there existed a body of secret knowledge that was only available to those initiated into an inner circle of spiritual teachers.
2:13 *comparing spiritual things with spiritual.* These words are difficult to translate and interpret. The Greek term translated "comparing" can also mean "combining," or "interpreting." The two references to "spiritual" may mean interpreting spiritual truths to spiritual persons, or else combining spiritual truths with spiritual words (2 Tim. 3:16; 2 Pet. 1:20–21).
3:2 *I fed you with milk.* Paul did not expect the Corinthians to be mature when they first accepted Christ. Yet they should have grown in their faith—that is, become sanctified. The behavior of Christians should begin to line up with their righteous position in Christ.
3:3 *for you are still carnal.* An immature Christian naturally lacks many Christian traits, but no one

should expect this condition to last. Paul was surprised that the Corinthians had not yet grown into spiritual maturity or become able to distinguish between good and evil (Heb. 5:14).
3:13 *the Day.* This is the time when Christ will judge the merits of His servants' work (2 Cor. 5:10), not whether they receive forgiveness of sin. Likewise, the fire does not refer to the eternal fire of damnation (Rev. 20:10) but to the evaluation of believers' works (Rev. 22:12).

2:9 i [Is. 64:4; 65:17]   **2:10** j Matt. 11:25; 13:11; 16:17   **2:11** k [James 2:26]   l Rom. 11:33   **2:12** m [Rom. 8:15]   **2:14** n Matt. 16:23   **2:16** o Is. 40:13   p [John 15:15]   **3:1** a Heb. 5:13   **3:2** b 1 Pet. 2:2   c John 16:12   **3:5** d 2 Cor. 3:3, 6; 4:1; 5:18; 6:4   **3:6** e Acts 18:4   f Acts 18:24–27   g [2 Cor. 3:5]   **3:7** h [Gal. 6:3]   **3:8** i Ps. 62:12   **3:9** j 2 Cor. 6:1   k [Eph. 2:20–22]   **3:10** l Rom. 1:5   m 1 Cor. 4:15   **3:11** n Is. 28:16   o Eph. 2:20   **3:13** p 1 Pet. 1:7   q Luke 2:35   **3:16** r 2 Cor. 6:16   **3:18** s Prov. 3:7   **3:19** t Job 5:13   **3:20** u Ps. 94:11

²¹Therefore let no one boast in men. For ᵛall things are yours: ²²whether Paul or Apollos or Cephas, or the world or life or death, or things present or things to come—all are yours. ²³And ʷyou *are* Christ's, and Christ *is* God's.

Stewards of the Mysteries of God

4 Let a man so consider us, as ᵃservants of Christ ᵇand stewards of the mysteries of God. ²Moreover it is required in stewards that one be found faithful. ³But with me it is a very small thing that I should be judged by you or by a human court.* In fact, I do not even judge myself. ⁴For I know of nothing against myself, yet I am not justified by this; but He who judges me is the Lord. ⁵ᶜTherefore judge nothing before the time, until the Lord comes, who will both bring to ᵈlight the hidden things of darkness and ᵉreveal the counsels of the hearts. ᶠThen each one's praise will come from God.

Fools for Christ's Sake

⁶Now these things, brethren, I have figuratively transferred to myself and Apollos for your sakes, that you may learn in us not to think beyond what is written, that none of you may be puffed up on behalf of one against the other. ⁷For who makes you differ *from another?* And ᵍwhat do you have that you did not receive? Now if you did indeed receive *it,* why do you boast as if you had not received *it?*

⁸You are already full! ʰYou are already rich! You have reigned as kings without us—and indeed I could wish you did reign, that we also might reign with you! ⁹For I think that God has displayed us, the apostles, last, as men condemned to death; for we have been made a ⁱspectacle to the world, both to angels and to men. ¹⁰We *are* ʲfools for Christ's sake, but you *are* wise in Christ! ᵏWe *are* weak, but you *are* strong! You *are* distinguished, but we *are* dishonored! ¹¹To the present hour we both hunger and thirst, and we are poorly clothed, and beaten, and homeless. ¹²ˡAnd we labor, working with our own hands. ᵐBeing reviled, we bless; being persecuted, we endure; ¹³being defamed, we entreat. ⁿWe have been made as the filth of the world, the offscouring of all things until now.

Paul's Paternal Care

¹⁴I do not write these things to shame you, but ᵒas my beloved children I warn *you.* ¹⁵For though you might have ten thousand instructors in Christ, yet *you do* not *have* many fathers; for ᵖin Christ Jesus I have begotten you through the gospel. ¹⁶Therefore I urge you, �q imitate me. ¹⁷For this reason I have sent ʳTimothy to you, ˢwho is my beloved and faithful son in the Lord, who will ᵗremind you of my ways in Christ, as I ᵘteach everywhere ᵛin every church.

¹⁸ʷNow some are puffed up, as though I were not coming to you. ¹⁹ˣBut I will come to you shortly, ʸif the Lord wills, and I will know, not the word of those who are puffed up, but the power. ²⁰For ᶻthe kingdom of God *is* not in word but in ᵃpower. ²¹What do you want? ᵇShall I come to you with a rod, or in love and a spirit of gentleness?

Immorality Defiles the Church

5 It is actually reported *that there is* sexual immorality among you, and such sexual immorality as is not even named* among the Gentiles—that a man has his father's ᵃwife! ²ᵇAnd you are puffed up, and have not rather ᶜmourned, that he who has done this deed might be taken away from among you. ³ᵈFor I indeed, as absent in body but present in spirit, have already judged (as though I were present) him who has so done this deed. ⁴In the ᵉname of our Lord Jesus Christ, when you are gathered together, along with my spirit, ᶠwith the

---

* 4:3 Literally *day*   * 5:1 NU-Text omits *named.*

3:21 *all things are yours.* The Stoic literature of the time, which the Corinthians would have known, often spoke of the wise man as possessing everything. Everything God has done in the church, and in the entire universe, benefits all believers. There is no place for foolish boasting or competition among Christians.

4:5 *judge nothing.* While believers can benefit from the constructive evaluations of other believers, their ultimate Judge is the Lord Himself. We cannot know the whole picture, and we must be careful not to make premature evaluations of others.

4:6 *puffed up.* Greeks considered humility to be a fault, a characteristic of slaves. To the Christian, however, it exemplifies the attitude of Christ (Phil. 2:5–8).

4:10 *fools for Christ's sake.* True strength is found in understanding our weakness and Christ's sufficiency (2 Cor. 12:7–10; Phil. 4:11–13).

5:1 *sexual immorality.* The sexual immorality of incest was forbidden by Old Testament law (Lev. 18:8; Deut. 22:30) and by Roman law. The phrase "his father's wife" probably indicates that the woman was the offender's stepmother. Paul does not specify any discipline for the woman, which may indicate that she was not a believer.

5:2 *puffed up, and have not rather mourned.* The Corinthian Christians had a twisted view of grace that caused them to be proud of their tolerance of the sexual offender. They believed that, because God's grace is limitless, living in sin was no problem.

3:21 ᵛ[2 Cor. 4:5]   **3:23** ʷ2 Cor. 10:7   **4:1** ᵃCol. 1:25 ᵇTitus 1:7   **4:5** ᶜMatt. 7:1 ᵈMatt. 10:26 ᵉ1 Cor. 3:13 ᶠRom. 2:29   **4:7** ᵍJohn 3:27   **4:8** ʰRev. 3:17   **4:9** ⁱHeb. 10:33 **4:10** ʲActs 17:18; 26:24 ᵏ2 Cor. 13:9   **4:12** ˡActs 18:3; 20:34 ᵐMatt. 5:44   **4:13** ⁿLam. 3:45   **4:14** ᵒ1 Thess. 2:11   **4:15** ᵖGal. 4:19   **4:16** �q[1 Cor. 11:1]   **4:17** ʳActs 19:22 ˢ1 Tim. 1:2, 18 ᵗ1 Cor. 11:2 ᵘ1 Cor. 7:17 ᵛ1 Cor. 14:33   **4:18** ʷ1 Cor. 5:2   **4:19** ˣActs 19:21; 20:2 ʸActs 18:21   **4:20** ᶻ1 Thess. 1:5 ᵃ1 Cor. 2:4   **4:21** ᵇ2 Cor. 10:2   **5:1** ᵃLev. 18:6–8   **5:2** ᵇ1 Cor. 4:18 ᶜ2 Cor. 7:7–10 **5:3** ᵈCol. 2:5   **5:4** ᵉ[Matt. 18:20] ᶠ[John 20:23]

power of our Lord Jesus Christ, [5]^{g}deliver such a one to ^{h}Satan for the destruction of the flesh, that his spirit may be saved in the day of the Lord Jesus.*

[6]^{i}Your glorying *is* not good. Do you not know that ^{j}a little leaven leavens the whole lump? [7]Therefore purge out the old leaven, that you may be a new lump, since you truly are unleavened. For indeed ^{k}Christ, our ^{l}Passover, was sacrificed for us.* [8]Therefore ^{m}let us keep the feast, ^{n}not with old leaven, nor ^{o}with the leaven of malice and wickedness, but with the unleavened *bread* of sincerity and truth.

Immorality Must Be Judged

[9]I wrote to you in my epistle ^{p}not to keep company with sexually immoral people. [10]Yet *I* certainly *did* not *mean* with the sexually immoral people of this world, or with the covetous, or extortioners, or idolaters, since then you would need to go ^{q}out of the world. [11]But now I have written to you not to keep company ^{r}with anyone named a brother, who is sexually immoral, or covetous, or an idolater, or a reviler, or a drunkard, or an extortioner—^{s}not even to eat with such a person.

[12]For what *have* I *to do* with judging those also who are outside? Do you not judge those who are inside? [13]But those who are outside God judges. Therefore ^{t}*"put away from yourselves the evil person."**

Do Not Sue the Brethren

6 Dare any of you, having a matter against another, go to law before the unrighteous, and not before the ^{a}saints? [2]Do you not know that ^{b}the saints will judge the

world? And if the world will be judged by you, are you unworthy to judge the smallest matters? [3]Do you not know that we shall ^{c}judge angels? How much more, things that pertain to this life? [4]If then you have judgments concerning things pertaining to this life, do you appoint those who are least esteemed by the church to judge? [5]I say this to your shame. Is it so, that there is not a wise man among you, not even one, who will be able to judge between his brethren? [6]But brother goes to law against brother, and that before unbelievers!

[7]Now therefore, it is already an utter failure for you that you go to law against one another. ^{d}Why do you not rather accept wrong? Why do you not rather *let* yourselves be cheated? [8]No, you yourselves do wrong and cheat, and *you do* these things to *your* brethren! [9]Do you not know that the unrighteous will not inherit the kingdom of God? Do not be deceived. ^{e}Neither fornicators, nor idolaters, nor adulterers, nor homosexuals,* nor sodomites, [10]nor thieves, nor covetous, nor drunkards, nor revilers, nor extortioners will inherit the kingdom of God. [11]And such were ^{f}some of you. ^{g}But you were washed, but you were sanctified, but you were justified in the name of the Lord Jesus and by the Spirit of our God.

Glorify God in Body and Spirit

[12]^{h}All things are lawful for me, but all things are not helpful. All things are lawful for me, but I will not be brought under the

---

* **5:5** NU-Text omits *Jesus.* * **5:7** NU-Text omits *for us.* * **5:13** Deuteronomy 17:7; 19:19; 22:21, 24; 24:7 * **6:9** That is, catamites

---

5:6 *a little leaven.* The backdrop for this passage is the Passover (Ex. 12). In commemoration of their ancestors' hurried departure from Egypt, Jewish families would carefully remove all leaven (yeast) from their homes in preparation for the celebration of the Passover. In the New Testament, leaven is often used as a symbol of sin. Yeast spreads through a batch of dough, and unchallenged sin can soon contaminate the whole church. The sexual offender was guilty of sin, but the whole congregation was also guilty of ignoring the man's disobedience.

5:9 *my epistle.* It is believed that this refers to an earlier letter which has not been preserved.

5:10 *of this world.* Christians are called to influence the world, not to run away from it (Matt. 5:13–16). They are agents of God to carry the light of Jesus Christ into a dark world (Phil. 2:14–16; 1 Pet. 2:11–12).

6:9 *kingdom of God.* This term seems to refer to a future time when God will rule the earth in righteousness (Matt. 6:10; Luke 11:2).

6:11 *Changed Life*—The greatest proof of the new birth is a changed life. The child of God now suddenly loves the following:

1. *He loves Jesus.* Before conversion the sinner might hold Christ in high esteem, but after conversion he loves the Savior (1 John 5:1–2).

2. *He loves the Bible.* We should love God's Word as the psalmist did in Psalm 119. There he expresses his great love for God's Word 17 times.

3. *He loves other Christians.* "We know that we have passed from death to life, because we love the brethren" (1 John 3:14).

4. *He loves his enemies* (Matt. 5:43–45).

5. *He loves the souls of all people.* Like Paul, he too can cry out for the conversion of loved ones. "Brethren, my heart's desire and prayer to God for Israel is that they may be saved" (Rom. 10:1).

6. *He loves the pure life.* John says that if one loves the world, the love of the Father is not in him (1 John 2:15–17).

7. *He loves to talk to God.* "Speaking to one another in psalms and hymns and spiritual songs, singing and making melody in your heart to the Lord" (Eph. 5:19).

5:5 ^{g} 1 Tim. 1:20 ^{h} [Acts 26:18] **5:6** ^{i} 1 Cor. 3:21 ^{j} Gal. 5:9 **5:7** ^{k} Is. 53:7 ^{l} John 19:14 **5:8** ^{m} Ex. 12:15 ^{n} Deut. 16:3 ^{o} Matt. 16:6 **5:9** ^{p} 2 Cor. 6:14 **5:10** ^{q} John 17:15 **5:11** ^{r} Matt. 18:17 ^{s} Gal. 2:12 **5:13** ^{t} Deut. 17:7, 12; 19:19; 21:21; 22:21, 24; 24:7 **6:1** ^{a} Dan. 7:22 **6:2** ^{b} Ps. 49:14 **6:3** ^{c} 2 Pet. 2:4 **6:7** ^{d} [Prov. 20:22] **6:9** ^{e} Gal. 5:21 **6:11** ^{f} [1 Cor. 12:2] ^{g} Heb. 10:22 **6:12** ^{h} 1 Cor. 10:23

power of any. [13] [i]Foods for the stomach and the stomach for foods, but God will destroy both it and them. Now the body *is* not for [j]sexual immorality but [k]for the Lord, [l]and the Lord for the body. [14]And [m]God both raised up the Lord and will also raise us up [n]by His power.

[15]Do you not know that [o]your bodies are members of Christ? Shall I then take the members of Christ and make *them* members of a harlot? Certainly not! [16]Or do you not know that he who is joined to a harlot is one body *with her*? For [p]"*the two*," He says, "*shall become one flesh.*"* [17a]But he who is joined to the Lord is one spirit *with Him*.

[18]Flee sexual immorality. Every sin that a man does is outside the body, but he who commits sexual immorality sins [s]against his own body. [19]Or [t]do you not know that your body is the temple of the Holy Spirit *who is* in you, whom you have from God, [u]and you are not your own? [20]For [v]you were bought at a price; therefore glorify God in your body* and in your spirit, which are God's.

Principles of Marriage

7 Now concerning the things of which you wrote to me:

[a]*It is* good for a man not to touch a woman. [2]Nevertheless, because of sexual immorality, let each man have his own wife, and let each woman have her own husband.

[3b]Let the husband render to his wife the affection due her, and likewise also the wife to her husband. [4]The wife does not have authority over her own body, but the husband *does*. And likewise the husband does not have authority over his own body, but the wife *does*. [5c]Do not deprive one another except with consent for a time, that you may give yourselves to fasting and prayer; and come together again so that [d]Satan does not tempt you because of your lack of self-control. [6]But I say this as a concession, [e]not as a commandment. [7]For [f]I wish that all men were even as I myself. But each one has his own gift from God, one in this manner and another in that.

[8]But I say to the unmarried and to the widows: [g]It is good for them if they remain even as I am; [9]but [h]if they cannot exercise self-control, let them marry. For it is better to marry than to burn *with passion*.

Keep Your Marriage Vows

[10]Now to the married I command, *yet* not I but the [i]Lord: [j]A wife is not to depart from *her* husband. [11]But even if she does depart, let her remain unmarried or be reconciled to *her* husband. And a husband is not to divorce *his* wife.

---

* **6:16** Genesis 2:24 * **6:20** NU-Text ends the verse at *body*.

6:13 Foods for the stomach and the stomach for foods. The stomach's purpose is to digest food, but it is not the purpose of the body to commit immorality. Furthermore, by design God put restrictions on both eating and sexual activity. Eating to the point of gluttony and having sex outside of marriage both violate God's intent and are sinful.

6:15 your bodies are the members of Christ. Becoming a Christ follower is not just a "spiritual experience." Our bodies belong to Jesus as well as our souls, and nothing that we do with our bodies is apart from our relationship with Jesus Christ.

6:16 one body. God designed sex as part of the intense "one flesh" bond between husband and wife, so sex is not a one-dimensional physical act. It involves soul, spirit, and emotions as well. Broken sexual relationships tear away at a person's very being in a way that nothing else does.

6:19 The Work of the Holy Spirit—The Holy Spirit is sometimes referred to as the *Paraclete*. The first part of that word, *para*, is a preposition that means "coming alongside." As the Spirit comes alongside of us, He ministers in the following ways:

1. *The Holy Spirit indwells Christians.* The Bible teaches that believers are indwelt and are the "temple of the Holy Spirit" (1 Cor. 6:19). The purpose of this indwelling ministry is to empower the newly created nature (2 Cor. 5:17; Eph. 3:16).

2. *The Holy Spirit fills believers.* We are admonished to "be filled with the Spirit" (Eph. 5:18). We are then to be subject to the control of the Spirit in contrast to being controlled by the lures of the world.

3. *The Holy Spirit sanctifies the believer* (Rom. 15:16; 2 Thess. 2:13).

4. *The Holy Spirit produces fruit in the life of the believer.* This fruit is described by Paul: "But the fruit of the Spirit is love, joy, peace, longsuffering, kindness, goodness, faithfulness, gentleness, self-control" (Gal. 5:22–23).

5. *The Holy Spirit gives gifts to Christians* (Rom. 12:6–8; 1 Cor. 12:1–11; Eph. 4:7–12). These are abilities given to every Christian (1 Cor. 7:7; 1 Pet. 4:10). The purpose of these gifts is to glorify God (Rev. 4:11) and to edify the body of Christ (Eph. 4:12–13).

6. *The Holy Spirit teaches believers.* He will instruct us in all spiritual things as we read the Word of God (John 14:26) and abide in the Son of God (1 John 2:24–27).

6:20 bought at a price. With His death, Jesus Christ paid the cost to redeem us from our slavery to sin (Eph. 1:7; 1 Pet. 1:18–19).

7:6 concession, not as a commandment. The Corinthians seemed to be caught by two extreme false positions: the false concept that physical activity does not affect the spirit, and the opposite incorrect idea that any kind of physical relationship is evil. Sexual relationships in marriage are good and God given, yet Paul also outlines the value of celibacy.

7:11 remain unmarried. This statement is consistent with Jesus' teaching (Mark 10:9–12).

6:13 [i]Matt. 15:17 [j]Gal. 5:19 [k]1 Thess. 4:3 [l][Eph. 5:23] **6:14** [m]2 Cor. 4:14 [n]Eph. 1:19 **6:15** [o]Rom. 12:5 **6:16** [p]Gen. 2:24 **6:17** [q][John 17:21–23] **6:18** [r]Heb. 13:4 [s]Rom. 1:24 **6:19** [t]2 Cor. 6:16 [u]Rom. 14:7 **6:20** [v]2 Pet. 2:1 **7:1** [a]1 Cor. 7:8, 26 **7:3** [b]Ex. 21:10 **7:5** [c]Joel 2:16 [d]1 Thess. 3:5 **7:6** [e]2 Cor. 8:8 **7:7** [f]Acts 26:29 **7:8** [g]1 Cor. 7:1, 26 **7:9** [h]1 Tim. 5:14 **7:10** [i]Mark 10:6–10 [j][Matt. 5:32]

12But to the rest I, not the Lord, say: If
any brother has a wife who does not believe, and she is willing to live with him, let
him not divorce her. 13And a woman who
has a husband who does not believe, if he
is willing to live with her, let her not divorce him. 14For the unbelieving husband
is sanctified by the wife, and the unbelieving wife is sanctified by the husband; otherwise [k]your children would be unclean,
but now they are holy. 15But if the unbeliever departs, let him depart; a brother or
a sister is not under bondage in such *cases*. But God has called us [l]to peace. 16For
how do you know, O wife, whether you
will [m]save *your* husband? Or how do you
know, O husband, whether you will save
your wife?

Live as You Are Called

17But as God has distributed to each one,
as the Lord has called each one, so let him
walk. And [n]so I ordain in all the churches.
18Was anyone called while circumcised?
[o]Let him not become uncircumcised. Was
anyone called while uncircumcised? Let
him not be circumcised. 19[p]Circumcision
is nothing and uncircumcision is nothing,
but [q]keeping the commandments of God
is what matters. 20Let each one remain in
the same calling in which he was called.
21Were you called *while* a slave? Do not be
concerned about it; but if you can be made
free, rather use *it.* 22For he who is called
in the Lord *while* a slave is [r]the Lord's
freedman. Likewise he who is called
while free is [s]Christ's slave. 23[t]You were
bought at a price; do not become slaves
of men. 24Brethren, let each one remain
with [u]God in that *state* in which he was
called.

To the Unmarried and Widows

25Now concerning virgins: [v]I have no
commandment from the Lord; yet I give
judgment as one [w]whom the Lord in His
mercy has made [x]trustworthy. 26I suppose
therefore that this is good because of the
present distress—[y]that *it is* good for a man
to remain as he is: 27Are you bound to a
wife? Do not seek to be loosed. Are you
loosed from a wife? Do not seek a wife.
28But even if you do marry, you have not
sinned; and if a virgin marries, she has not
sinned. Nevertheless such will have trouble in the flesh, but I would spare you.

29But [z]this I say, brethren, the time *is*
short, so that from now on even those who
have wives should be as though they had
none, 30those who weep as though they did
not weep, those who rejoice as though they
did not rejoice, those who buy as though
they did not possess, 31and those who use
this world as not [a]misusing *it.* For [b]the
form of this world is passing away.

32But I want you to be without care. [c]He
who is unmarried cares for the things of
the Lord—how he may please the Lord.
33But he who is married cares about the
things of the world—how he may please
his wife. 34There is* a difference between
a wife and a virgin. The unmarried woman [d]cares about the things of the Lord, that
she may be holy both in body and in spirit. But she who is married cares about the
things of the world—how she may please
her husband. 35And this I say for your own
profit, not that I may put a leash on you, but
for what is proper, and that you may serve
the Lord without distraction.

36But if any man thinks he is behaving
improperly toward his virgin, if she is past
the flower of youth, and thus it must be, let
him do what he wishes. He does not sin; let
them marry. 37Nevertheless he who stands
steadfast in his heart, having no necessity, but has power over his own will, and
has so determined in his heart that he will
keep his virgin,* does well. 38[e]So then he
who gives *her** in marriage does well, but
he who does not give *her* in marriage does
better.

39[f]A wife is bound by law as long as her
husband lives; but if her husband dies, she
is at liberty to be married to whom she
wishes, [g]only in the Lord. 40But she is happier if she remains as she is, [h]according to
my judgment—and [i]I think I also have the
Spirit of God.

---

* **7:34** M-Text adds *also.* * **7:37** Or *virgin daughter* * **7:38** NU-Text reads *his own virgin.*

7:16 *how do you know.* First Peter 3:1–6 reminds us that consistent obedience to God can make a skeptical spouse into a believing one, but there are no guarantees.

7:17 *as the Lord has called . . . let him walk.* Social status is unimportant to God. He is interested in faithfulness.

7:27 *bound to a wife . . . loosed.* Considering the clear prohibition in verses 10–11, this verse is most likely referring to couples who are betrothed but not yet married.

7:36–38 *his virgin.* One interpretation of this verse is that this refers to a virgin daughter, although the word "daughter" is not actually in the Greek text. A second interpretation suggests that the "any man" of verse 36 refers to a fiancé who is maintaining, although with difficulty, a celibate state with a virgin he is (or has been) engaged to.

7:40 *I think I also have the Spirit of God.* The Holy Spirit enabled Paul to speak with apostolic authority and also with spiritual wisdom.

7:14 [k] Mal. 2:15 **7:15** [l] Rom. 12:18 **7:16** [m] 1 Pet. 3:1 **7:17** [n] 1 Cor. 4:17 **7:18** [o] Acts 15:1 **7:19** [p] [Gal. 3:28; 5:6; 6:15] [q] [John 15:14] **7:22** [r] [John 8:36] [s] 1 Pet. 2:16 **7:23** [t] 1 Pet. 1:18, 19 **7:24** [u] [Col. 3:22–24] **7:25** [v] 2 Cor. 8:8 [w] 1 Tim. 1:13, 16 [x] 1 Tim. 1:12 **7:26** [y] 1 Cor. 7:1, 8 **7:29** [z] 1 Pet. 4:7 **7:31** [a] 1 Cor. 9:18 [b] [1 John 2:17] **7:32** [c] 1 Tim. 5:5 **7:34** [d] Luke 10:40 **7:38** [e] Heb. 13:4 **7:39** [f] Rom. 7:2 [g] 2 Cor. 6:14 **7:40** [h] 1 Cor. 7:6, 25 [i] 1 Thess. 4:8

Be Sensitive to Conscience

8 Now ^aconcerning things offered to idols: We know that we all have ^bknowledge. ^cKnowledge puffs up, but love edifies. 2And ^dif anyone thinks that he knows anything, he knows nothing yet as he ought to know. 3But if anyone loves God, this one is known by Him.

4Therefore concerning the eating of things offered to idols, we know that ^ean idol *is* nothing in the world, ^fand that *there is* no other God but one. 5For even if there are ^gso-called gods, whether in heaven or on earth (as there are many gods and many lords), 6yet for us *there is* one God, the Father, ⁱof whom *are* all things, and we for Him; and ^jone Lord Jesus Christ, ^kthrough whom *are* all things, and ^lthrough whom we *live*.

7However, *there is* not in everyone that knowledge; for some, ^mwith consciousness of the idol, until now eat *it* as a thing offered to an idol; and their conscience, being weak, is ⁿdefiled. 8But ^ofood does not commend us to God; for neither if we eat are we the better, nor if we do not eat are we the worse.

9But ^pbeware lest somehow this liberty of yours become ^qa stumbling block to those who are weak. 10For if anyone sees you who have knowledge eating in an idol's temple, will not ^rthe conscience of him who is weak be emboldened to eat those things offered to idols? 11And ^sbecause of your knowledge shall the weak brother perish, for whom Christ died? 12But ^twhen you thus sin against the brethren, and wound their weak conscience, you sin against Christ. 13Therefore, ^uif food makes my brother stumble, I will never again eat meat, lest I make my brother stumble.

A Pattern of Self-Denial

9 Am ^aI not an apostle? Am I not free? ^bHave I not seen Jesus Christ our Lord? ^cAre you not my work in the Lord? 2If I am

not an apostle to others, yet doubtless I am to you. For you are ^dthe seal of my apostleship in the Lord.

3My defense to those who examine me is this: 4^eDo we have no right to eat and drink? 5Do we have no right to take along a believing wife, as *do* also the other apostles, ^fthe brothers of the Lord, and ^gCephas? 6Or *is it* only Barnabas and I ^hwho have no right to refrain from working? 7Who ever ⁱgoes to war at his own expense? Who ^jplants a vineyard and does not eat of its fruit? Or who ^ktends a flock and does not drink of the milk of the flock?

8Do I say these things as a *mere* man? Or does not the law say the same also? 9For it is written in the law of Moses, ^l*"You shall not muzzle an ox while it treads out the grain."** Is it oxen God is concerned about? 10Or does He say *it* altogether for our sakes? For our sakes, no doubt, *this* is written, that ^mhe who plows should plow in hope, and he who threshes in hope should be partaker of his hope. 11ⁿIf we have sown spiritual things for you, *is it* a great thing if we reap your material things? 12If others are partakers of *this* right over you, *are* we not even more?

^oNevertheless we have not used this right, but endure all things ^plest we hinder the gospel of Christ. 13^qDo you not know that those who minister the holy things eat *of the things* of the ^rtemple, and those who serve at the altar partake of *the offerings* of the altar? 14Even so ^sthe Lord has commanded ^tthat those who preach the gospel should live from the gospel.

15But ^uI have used none of these things, nor have I written these things that it should be done so to me; for ^vit *would be* better for me to die than that anyone should make my boasting void. 16For if I preach the gospel, I have nothing to boast of, for ^wnecessity is laid upon me; yes, woe is me if

---

* 9:9 Deuteronomy 25:4

8:4 there is no other God but one. The Corinthian believers who claimed to have knowledge readily admitted that an idol is nothing (Is. 37:19; Jer. 16:20; Gal. 4:8) and that there is only one God (Deut. 6:4). Therefore, since an idol is nothing, and since the whole world belongs to God, food which has been offered to idols is not contaminated (10:19,25–26).
8:7 with consciousness of the idol. Even though it is true that an idol is not a real god, a new believer leaving a life of idol worship is still accustomed to thinking of the idol as real. Because of this strong association, eating meat sacrificed to an idol might still feel like paying honor to the idol, and thus seem vile and contaminating. A person who still feels the pull of the old worship is right to flee from all remembrances of it (10:20–23).
8:12 wound their weak conscience. The believer is given responsibility for a weaker brother's conscience. It is sin to cause another to fall or to be wounded in the conscience. God is warning believers to stay away from questionable things.

9:1 an apostle. Paul could claim the title of apostle because he had seen the resurrected Lord (Acts 1:21–22), and the church in Corinth was his work in the Lord, a seal of his apostleship.
9:14 live from the gospel. God commands that ministers of the gospel be supported. Even as the priests in Israel were supported for their work, New

8:1 ^aActs 15:20 ^bRom. 14:14 ^cRom. 14:3 **8:2** ^d[1 Cor. 13:8–12] **8:4** ^eIs. 41:24 ^fDeut. 4:35, 39; 6:4 **8:5** ^g[John 10:34] **8:6** ^hMal. 2:10 ⁱActs 17:28 ^jJohn 13:13 ^kJohn 1:3 ^lRom. 5:11 **8:7** ^m[1 Cor. 10:28] ⁿRom. 14:14, 22 **8:8** ^o[Rom. 14:17] **8:9** ^pGal. 5:13 ^qRom. 14:13, 21 **8:10** ^r1 Cor. 10:28 **8:11** ^sRom. 14:15, 20 **8:12** ^tMatt. 25:40 **8:13** ^uRom. 14:21 **9:1** ^aActs 9:15 ^b1 Cor. 15:8 ^c1 Cor. 3:6; 4:15 **9:2** ^d2 Cor. 12:12 **9:4** ^e[1 Thess. 2:6, 9] **9:5** ^fMatt. 13:55 ^gMatt. 8:14 **9:6** ^hActs 4:36 **9:7** ⁱ2 Cor. 10:4 ^jDeut. 20:6 ^kJohn 21:15 **9:9** ^lDeut. 25:4 **9:10** ^m2 Tim. 2:6 **9:11** ⁿRom. 15:27 **9:12** ^o[Acts 18:3; 20:33] ^p2 Cor. 11:12 **9:13** ^qLev. 6:16, 26; 7:6, 31 ^rNum. 18:8–31 **9:14** ^sMatt. 10:10 ^tRom. 10:15 **9:15** ^uActs 18:3; 20:33 ^v2 Cor. 11:10 **9:16** ^w[Rom. 1:14]

I do not preach the gospel! [17]For if I do this willingly, [x]I have a reward; but if against my will, [y]I have been entrusted with a stewardship. [18]What is my reward then? That [z]when I preach the gospel, I may present the gospel of Christ* without charge, that I [a]may not abuse my authority in the gospel.

Serving All Men

[19]For though I am [b]free from all men, [c]I have made myself a servant to all, [d]that I might win the more; [20]and [e]to the Jews I became as a Jew, that I might win Jews; to those who are under the law, as under the law,* that I might win those who are under the law; [21]to [g]those who are without law, as without law [h](not being without law toward God,* but under law toward Christ*), that I might win those who are without law; [22]to the weak I became as* weak, that I might win the weak. [i]I have become all things to all men, [k]that I might by all means save some. [23]Now this I do for the gospel's sake, that I may be partaker of it with you.

Striving for a Crown

[24]Do you not know that those who run in a race all run, but one receives the prize? [l]Run in such a way that you may obtain it. [25]And everyone who competes for the prize is temperate in all things. Now they do it to obtain a perishable crown, but we for [m]an imperishable crown. [26]Therefore I run thus: [n]not with uncertainty. Thus I fight: not as one who beats the air. [27]But I discipline my body and [p]bring it into subjection, lest, when I have preached to others, I myself should become [q]disqualified.

Old Testament Examples

10 Moreover, brethren, I do not want you to be unaware that all our fathers were under [a]the cloud, all passed through [b]the sea, [2]all were baptized into Moses in the cloud and in the sea, [3]all ate the same [c]spiritual food, [4]and all drank the same [d]spiritual drink. For they drank of that spiritual Rock that followed them, and that Rock was Christ. [5]But with most of them God was not well pleased, for their bodies [e]were scattered in the wilderness.

[6]Now these things became our examples, to the intent that we should not lust after evil things as [f]they also lusted. [7g]And do not become idolaters as were some of them. As it is written, [h]"The people sat down to eat and drink, and rose up to play."* [8]Nor let us commit sexual immorality, as [i]some of them did, and [k]in one day twenty-three thousand fell; [9]nor let us tempt Christ, as [l]some of them also tempted, and [m]were destroyed by serpents; [10]nor complain, as [n]some of them also complained, and [o]were destroyed by [p]the destroyer. [11]Now all* these things happened to them as examples, and [q]they were written for our admonition, [r]upon whom the ends of the ages have come.

[12]Therefore [s]let him who thinks he stands take heed lest he fall. [13]No temptation has overtaken you except such as is common to man; but [t]God is faithful, [u]who will not allow you to be tempted beyond what you are able, but with the temptation will also make the way of escape, that you may be able to bear it.

Flee from Idolatry

[14]Therefore, my beloved, [v]flee from idolatry. [15]I speak as to [w]wise men; judge for

---

* **9:18** NU-Text omits of Christ.   * **9:20** NU-Text adds though not being myself under the law.   * **9:21** NU-Text reads God's law. • NU-Text reads Christ's law.   * **9:22** NU-Text omits as.   * **10:7** Exodus 32:6   * **10:11** NU-Text omits all.

Testament ministers were to be provided for as well (1 Tim. 5:17–18).

9:20 to the Jews I became as a Jew. In order to relate to the Jews in Jerusalem, Paul made a Nazirite vow in the temple (Acts 21:23–24).

9:21 under law toward Christ. Paul was not lawless; he was differentiating between the law of the old covenant and the broader law of Christ which includes great freedom and flexibility for the believer whose heart is obedient to Christ's will (11:1; Rom. 13:8; Gal. 6:2).

9:27 should become disqualified. A careful distinction should be made between the prize and the gift. The free gift of justification cannot be the result of good works (Rom. 4:1–8). The prize or crown, however, is the reward for endurance and suffering for the cause of Christ (Phil. 1:29; 2 Tim. 2:12).

10:1 under the cloud. When the ancient Israelites were wandering in the wilderness, the pillar of cloud was the visible manifestation of God's presence with them.

10:6 lust after evil things. The first failure of the Israelites was that they were not satisfied with God's provision (Num. 11:4–34). It is not that the food they craved was evil in itself, but their lack of trust in God was sin.

10:7 idolaters. The Israelites had seen God's mighty hand work on their behalf, yet they still fell into idolatry and sexual immorality. Knowledge alone does not protect against sin—obedience is a heart issue.

10:12 take heed lest he fall. The Corinthians may have had the attitude that, since they were justified by God, nothing could happen to them. The discipline of God, however, is not to be taken lightly. No one can sin without consequences (Gal. 6:7–8).

10:14 flee from idolatry. This was not a simple thing to do in ancient Greek culture, where the worship of

---

9:17 [x]1 Cor. 3:8, 14; 9:18 [y]Gal. 2:7   **9:18** [z]1 Cor. 10:33 [a]1 Cor. 7:31; 9:12   **9:19** [b]1 Cor. 9:1 [c]Gal. 5:13 [d]Matt. 18:15   **9:20** [e]Acts 16:3; 21:23–26   **9:21** [f][Gal. 2:3; 3:2] [g][Rom. 2:12, 14] [h][1 Cor. 7:22]   **9:22** [i]Rom. 14:1; 15:1 [j]1 Cor. 10:33 [k]Rom. 11:14   **9:24** [l]Gal. 2:2   **9:25** [m]James 1:12   **9:26** [n]2 Tim. 2:5   **9:27** [o][Rom. 8:13] [p][Rom. 6:18]   **9** Jer. 6:30   **10:1** [a]Ex. 13:21, 22 [b]Ex. 14:21, 22, 29   **10:3** [c]Ex. 16:4, 15, 35   **10:4** [d]Ex. 17:5–7   **10:5** [e]Num. 14:29, 37; 26:65   **10:6** [f]Num. 11:4, 34   **10:7** [g]1 Cor. 5:11; 10:14 [h]Ex. 32:6   **10:8** [i]Rev. 2:14 [j]Num. 25:1–9 [k]Ps. 106:29   **10:9** [l]Ex. 17:2, 7 [m]Num. 21:6–9   **10:10** [n]Ex. 16:2 [o]Num. 14:37 [p]Ex. 12:23   **10:11** [q]Rom. 15:4 [r]Phil. 4:5   **10:12** [s]Rom. 11:20   **10:13** [t]1 Cor. 1:9 [u]Ps. 125:3   **10:14** [v]2 Cor. 6:17   **10:15** [w]1 Cor. 8:1

yourselves what I say. [16x]The cup of blessing which we bless, is it not the communion of the blood of Christ? [y]The bread which we break, is it not the communion of the body of Christ? [17]For [z]we, *though* many, are one bread *and* one body; for we all partake of that one bread.

[18]Observe [a]Israel [b]after the flesh: [c]Are not those who eat of the sacrifices partakers of the altar? [19]What am I saying then? [d]That an idol is anything, or what is offered to idols is anything? [20]Rather, that the things which the Gentiles [e]sacrifice [f]they sacrifice to demons and not to God, and I do not want you to have fellowship with demons. [21g]You cannot drink the cup of the Lord and [h]the cup of demons; you cannot partake of the [i]Lord's table and of the table of demons. [22]Or do we [j]provoke the Lord to jealousy? [k]Are we stronger than He?

All to the Glory of God

[23]All things are lawful for me,* but not all things are [l]helpful; all things are lawful for me,* but not all things edify. [24]Let no one seek his own, but each one [m]the other's well-being.

[25n]Eat whatever is sold in the meat market, asking no questions for conscience' sake; [26]for [o]"the earth is the LORD's, and all its fullness."*

[27]If any of those who do not believe invites you *to dinner,* and you desire to go, [p]eat whatever is set before you, asking no question for conscience' sake. [28]But if anyone says to you, "This was offered to idols," do not eat it [q]for the sake of the one who told you, and for conscience' sake;* for [r]"the earth is the LORD's, and all its fullness."* [29]"Conscience," I say, not your own, but that of the other. For [s]why is my liberty judged by another *man's* conscience? [30]But if I partake with thanks, why am I evil spoken of for *the food* [t]over which I give thanks?

[31u]Therefore, whether you eat or drink, or whatever you do, do all to the glory of God. [32v]Give no offense, either to the Jews or to the Greeks or to the church of God, [33]just [w]as I also please all *men* in all *things,* not seeking my own profit, but the *profit* of many, that they may be saved.

11 Imitate[a] me, just as I also *imitate* Christ.

Head Coverings

[2]Now I praise you, brethren, that you remember me in all things and keep the traditions just as I delivered *them* to you. [3]But I want you to know that [b]the head of every man is Christ, [c]the head of woman is man, and [d]the head of Christ *is* God. [4]Every man praying or [e]prophesying, having *his* head covered, dishonors his head. [5]But every woman who prays or prophesies with *her* head uncovered dishonors her head, for that is one and the same as if her head were [f]shaved. [6]For if a woman is not covered, let

---

* **10:23** NU-Text omits *for me.* • NU-Text omits *for me.* * **10:26** Psalm 24:1 * **10:28** NU-Text omits the rest of this verse. • Psalm 24:1

---

multiple gods was deeply ingrained. There were idols on street corners and in houses. Various civic societies paid homage to their favorite gods. Cities adopted certain gods as their special protectors. The pagan temples were frequented often, especially in Corinth with its temple prostitution. Most of the food in the marketplace had been offered in worship to different gods.

10:20 sacrifice to demons. While the idols themselves are worthless, powerless, and certainly not gods, behind the statues and images is the very real evil and power of Satan and his demons. Anytime that worship is being directed at something that is not God, we can be sure that Satan is behind it.

10:22 provoke the Lord to jealousy. To participate in idolatrous activity is to deny that God is the only one worthy of worship.

10:23 All things are lawful. Though we have freedom, we also have a responsibility to help others in their Christian growth. Our first duty is to others, not to ourselves.

10:25 Eat whatever is sold. Paul himself did not ask whether meat was sacrificed in the temple, because pagan worship could not contaminate what God had made clean (Ps. 24:1; Acts 10:15).

10:28 for conscience' sake. Believers do not need to fearfully ask whether the meat they are eating has been sacrificed to idols—it doesn't make any difference to the food itself. However, a Christian may give the impression to others, by eating sacrificed food, that he himself is also still involved in idol worship.

11:3 the head. The term "head" primarily means "authority" when used in the context of human relationships, but it can also mean "source" or "origin." The relationship between men and women does not involve inferiority; in the parallel clause Christ is not inferior to God the Father. Just as Christ and God are equally divine, men and women are equal in God's image. But Jesus and God the Father have different roles in God's plan of salvation, and so also men and women are given different roles in life and in the church.

11:4 praying or prophesying. This may refer to intercessory prayer similar to that of Old Testament prophets (Gen. 20:7; 1 Sam. 12:23; Jer. 27:18) or Anna (Luke 2:36–38), or to the combination of tongues and prayer (14:13–16; Acts 2:4; 10:46). The term "prophesy" means to speak forth the words of God (14:3).

11:5 every woman who prays or prophesies. It is difficult from this passage alone to tell exactly what

---

10:16 [x]Matt. 26:26–28 [y]Acts 2:42 **10:17** [z]1 Cor. 12:12, 27 **10:18** [a]Rom. 4:12 [b]Rom. 4:1 [c]Lev. 3:3; 7:6, 14 **10:19** [d]1 Cor. 8:4 **10:20** [e]Lev. 17:7 [f]Deut. 32:17 **10:21** [g]2 Cor. 6:15, 16 [h]Deut. 32:38 [i][1 Cor. 11:23–29] **10:22** [j]Deut. 32:21 [k]Ezek. 22:14 **10:23** [l]1 Cor. 6:12 **10:24** [m]Phil. 2:4 **10:25** [n][1 Tim. 4:4] **10:26** [o]Ps. 24:1 **10:27** [p]Luke 10:7, 8 **10:28** [q]1 Cor. 8:7, 10, 12] [r]Ps. 24:1 **10:29** [s]Rom. 14:16 **10:30** [t]Rom. 14:6 **10:31** [u]Col. 3:17 **10:32** [v]Rom. 14:13 **10:33** [w]Rom. 15:2 **11:1** [a]Eph. 5:1 **11:3** [b]Eph. 1:22; 4:15; 5:23 [c]Gen. 3:16 [d]John 14:28 **11:4** [e]1 Cor. 12:10 **11:5** [f]Deut. 21:12

her also be shorn. But if it is ᵍshameful for a woman to be shorn or shaved, let her be covered. ⁷For a man indeed ought not to cover *his* head, since ʰhe is the image and glory of God; but woman is the glory of man. ⁸For man is not from woman, but woman ⁱfrom man. ⁹Nor was man created for the woman, but woman ʲfor the man. ¹⁰For this reason the woman ought to have *a symbol of* authority on *her* head, because of the angels. ¹¹Nevertheless, ᵏneither *is* man independent of woman, nor woman independent of man, in the Lord. ¹²For as woman *came* from man, even so man also *comes* through woman; but all things are from God.

¹³Judge among yourselves. Is it proper for a woman to pray to God with her head uncovered? ¹⁴Does not even nature itself teach you that if a man has long hair, it is a dishonor to him? ¹⁵But if a woman has long hair, it is a glory to her; for *her* hair is given to her* for a covering. ¹⁶But ˡif anyone seems to be contentious, we have no such custom, ᵐnor *do* the churches of God.

Conduct at the Lord's Supper

¹⁷Now in giving these instructions I do not praise *you*, since you come together not for the better but for the worse. ¹⁸For first of all, when you come together as a church, ⁿI hear that there are divisions among you, and in part I believe it. ¹⁹For ᵒthere must also be factions among you, ᵖthat those who are approved may be recognized among you. ²⁰Therefore when you come together in one place, it is not to eat the Lord's Supper. ²¹For in eating, each one takes his own supper ahead of *others*; and one is hungry and �q another is drunk. ²²What! Do you not have houses to eat and drink in? Or do you despise ʳthe church of

God and ˢshame those who have nothing? What shall I say to you? Shall I praise you in this? I do not praise *you*.

Institution of the Lord's Supper

²³For ᵗI received from the Lord that which I also delivered to you: ᵘthat the Lord Jesus on the *same* night in which He was betrayed took bread; ²⁴and when He had given thanks, He broke *it* and said, "Take, eat;* this is My body which is broken* for you; do this in remembrance of Me." ²⁵In the same manner He also *took* the cup after supper, saying, "This cup is the new covenant in My blood. This do, as often as you drink *it*, in remembrance of Me."

²⁶For as often as you eat this bread and drink this cup, you proclaim the Lord's death ᵛtill He comes.

Examine Yourself

²⁷Therefore whoever eats ʷthis bread or drinks *this* cup of the Lord in an unworthy manner will be guilty of the body and blood* of the Lord. ²⁸But ˣlet a man examine himself, and so let him eat of the bread and drink of the cup. ²⁹For he who eats and drinks in an unworthy manner* eats and drinks judgment to himself, not discerning the Lord's* body. ³⁰For this reason many *are* weak and sick among you, and many sleep. ³¹For ʸif we would judge ourselves, we would not be judged. ³²But when we are judged, ᶻwe are chastened by the Lord, that we may not be condemned with the world.

---

* **11:15** M-Text omits *to her.*   * **11:24** NU-Text omits *Take, eat.* • NU-Text omits *broken.*
* **11:27** NU-Text and M-Text read *the blood.*
* **11:29** NU-Text omits *in an unworthy manner.* • NU-Text omits *Lord's.*

---

a woman's role is to be in the Christian assembly, but it appears that women did minister to other believers through prayer and prophecy (see also 1 Tim. 2:11–14). **shaved.** For a woman to have her head shaved was a sign of public disgrace.
11:9 woman for the man. This does not mean that women are inferior to men; it refers only to the purposes of God for men and women in the creative order, and the woman's God-given role of helper (Gen. 2:20).
11:10 authority. Some think that this might be a symbol of the woman's authority to prophesy in the new church age; others believe that it might refer to a symbol of the man's authority over the woman and her willingness to submit to God's order. **because of the angels.** Evidently God's angels are present at the meetings of the church and actually learn of God's work of grace through the lives and worship of God's people (Eph. 3:10).
11:11 neither . . . independent. Men and women need each other, and as creatures of God, both depend on Him. Neither man nor woman can have any claim to special status other than what God has purposed for them as their Creator.
11:19 those who are approved. Paul is here being sarcastic, suggesting that some individuals within

the church felt that they alone were truly approved of by the Lord, and trying to separate themselves from other believers whom they felt to be unapproved or less approved by God than themselves. He condemns this attitude in these verses.
11:20 the Lord's Supper. The Lord's Supper was the centerpiece of early Christian worship. Gathered around one table, fellow believers met with the Lord and with each other in unity. Christ had expressed this type of humility and unity when He instituted the Supper (Matt. 26:26–30; Mark 14:22–26; Luke 22:14–23).
11:26 you proclaim the Lord's death till He comes. The Lord's Supper looks back to Christ's death and forward to His second coming (Matt. 26:29; Mark 14:25; Luke 22:18).
11:30 sleep. The death of Christians is often referred

11:6 ᵍ Num. 5:18   **11:7** ʰ Gen. 1:26, 27; 5:1; 9:6
11:8 ⁱ Gen. 2:21–23   **11:9** ʲ Gen. 2:18   **11:11** ᵏ [Gal. 3:28]
11:16 ˡ 1 Tim. 6:4   ᵐ 1 Cor. 7:17   **11:18** ⁿ 1 Cor. 1:10–12;
3:3   **11:19** ᵒ 1 Tim. 4:1   ᵖ [Deut. 13:3]   **11:21** q Jude
12   **11:22** ʳ 1 Cor. 10:32   ˢ James 2:6   **11:23** ᵗ 1 Cor. 15:3
ᵘ Matt. 26:26–28   **11:26** ᵛ John 14:3   **11:27** ʷ [John
6:51]   **11:28** ˣ 2 Cor. 13:5   **11:31** ʸ [1 John 1:9]
11:32 ᶻ Ps. 94:12

33 Therefore, my brethren, when you ^acome together to eat, wait for one another. 34 But if anyone is hungry, let him eat at home, lest you come together for judgment. And the rest I will set in order when I come.

Spiritual Gifts: Unity in Diversity

12 Now ^aconcerning spiritual *gifts*, brethren, I do not want you to be ignorant: 2 You know ^bthat* you were Gentiles, carried away to these ^cdumb idols, however you were led. 3 Therefore I make known to you that no one speaking by the Spirit of God calls Jesus accursed, and ^dno one can say that Jesus is Lord except by the Holy Spirit.

4 ^eThere are diversities of gifts, but ^fthe same Spirit. 5 ^gThere are differences of ministries, but the same Lord. 6 And there are diversities of activities, but it is the same God ^hwho works all in all. 7 But the manifestation of the Spirit is given to each one for the profit *of all:* 8 for to one is given ⁱthe word of wisdom through the Spirit, to another ^jthe word of knowledge through the same Spirit, 9 ^kto another faith by the same Spirit, to another ^lgifts of healings by the same* Spirit, 10 ^mto another the working of miracles, to another ⁿprophecy, to another ^odiscerning of spirits, to another ^pdifferent kinds of tongues, to another the interpretation of tongues. 11 But one and the same Spirit works all these things, ^qdistributing to each one individually ^ras He wills.

Unity and Diversity in One Body

12 For ^sas the body is one and has many members, but all the members of that one body, being many, are one body, ^tso also is Christ. 13 For ^uby one Spirit we were all baptized into one body—^vwhether Jews or Greeks, whether slaves or free—and ^whave

all been made to drink into* one Spirit. 14 For in fact the body is not one member but many.

15 If the foot should say, "Because I am not a hand, I am not of the body," is it therefore not of the body? 16 And if the ear should say, "Because I am not an eye, I am not of the body," is it therefore not of the body? 17 If the whole body *were* an eye, where *would be* the hearing? If the whole *were* hearing, where *would be* the smelling? 18 But now ^xGod has set the members, each one of them, in the body ^yjust as He pleased. 19 And if they were all one member, where *would* the body *be?*

20 But now indeed *there are* many members, yet one body. 21 And the eye cannot say to the hand, "I have no need of you"; nor again the head to the feet, "I have no need of you." 22 No, much rather, those members of the body which seem to be weaker are necessary. 23 And those *members* of the body which we think to be less honorable, on these we bestow greater honor; and our unpresentable *parts* have greater modesty, 24 but our presentable *parts* have no need. But God composed the body, having given greater honor to that *part* which lacks it, 25 that there should be no schism in the body, but *that* the members should have the same care for one another. 26 And if one member suffers, all the members suffer with *it;* or if one member is honored, all the members rejoice with *it.*

27 Now ^zyou are the body of Christ, and ^amembers individually. 28 And ^bGod has appointed these in the church: first ^capostles, second ^dprophets, third teachers, after that ^emiracles, then ^fgifts of healings, ^ghelps, ^hadministrations, varieties of tongues. 29 *Are* all apostles? *Are* all prophets? *Are*

* **12:2** NU-Text and M-Text add *when.* * **12:9** NU-Text reads *one.* * **12:13** NU-Text omits *into.*

---

to as "sleep" (15:18; 1 Thess. 4:15–16). In this passage, it refers to untimely death, a punishment suffered by some Christians who failed to examine themselves at the Lord's Supper (v. 28).
12:1–10 Using Spiritual Gifts—Spiritual gifts are discussed in detail in four passages of the New Testament: Romans 12:3–8; 1 Corinthians 12:1–10; Ephesians 4:11–12; and 1 Peter 4:10–11. These lists are not exhaustive but are to be regarded as representative of spiritual gifts. They are given by the Spirit of God to accomplish God's purpose in the world and for the edification of the church, the body of Christ. Every believer has been given spiritual gifts (Rom. 12:5–6; 1 Cor. 12:7; 1 Pet. 4:10). The gifts belong to God and are given for the believer to use for the glory of God (1 Pet. 4:11).
12:3 accursed . . . Lord. A person speaking by the Holy Spirit will never curse Jesus; by the same token, no one can genuinely proclaim the lordship of Jesus without the enabling of the Spirit.
12:4 gifts. These gifts are spiritual capacities that God gives to individual Christians, through which He may strengthen His people.

12:13 by one Spirit. "By" here may also be translated "in," speaking of location. Christ places each new member of the body in the Holy Spirit for His care and safekeeping (2 Cor. 1:22).
12:18 God has set the members. We should neither boast in what we do nor think too little of ourselves. Each one of us is important to God and has a mission to accomplish here on earth.
12:28 apostles. The term "apostle" or "sent one" refers generally to missionaries (15:7; Rom. 16:7; 2 Cor. 11:5; 12:11; Gal. 1:17–19). Other times the term is limited to the small group who witnessed the

11:33 ^a 1 Cor. 14:26   **12:1** ^a 1 Cor. 12:4; 14:1, 37
12:2 ^b Eph. 2:11   ^c Ps. 115:5   **12:3** ^d Matt. 16:17
12:4 ^e Rom. 12:3–8   ^f Eph. 4:4   **12:5** ^g Rom. 12:6
12:6 ^h 1 Cor. 15:28   **12:8** ⁱ 1 Cor. 2:6, 7   ^j Rom. 15:14
12:9 ^k 2 Cor. 4:13   ^l Mark 3:15; 16:18   **12:10** ^m Mark 16:17   ⁿ Rom. 12:6   ^o 1 John 4:1   ^p Acts 2:4–11   **12:11** ^q Rom. 12:6   ^r John 3:8]   **12:12** ^s Rom. 12:4, 5   ^t [Gal. 3:16]
12:13 ^u [Rom. 6:5]   ^v Col. 3:11   ^w [John 7:37–39]
12:18 ^x 1 Cor. 12:28   ^y Rom. 12:3   **12:27** ^z Rom. 12:5   ^a Eph. 5:30   **12:28** ^b Eph. 4:11   ^c [Eph. 2:20; 3:5]   ^d Acts 13:1   ^e 1 Cor. 12:10, 29   ^f 1 Cor. 12:9, 30   ^g Num. 11:17   ^h Rom. 12:8

all teachers? *Are* all workers of miracles? ³⁰Do all have gifts of healings? Do all speak with tongues? Do all interpret? ³¹But ⁱearnestly desire the best* gifts. And yet I show you a more excellent way.

The Greatest Gift

13 Though I speak with the tongues of men and of angels, but have not love, I have become sounding brass or a clanging cymbal. ²And though I have *the gift of* ᵃprophecy, and understand all mysteries and all knowledge, and though I have all faith, ᵇso that I could remove mountains, but have not love, I am nothing. ³And ᶜthough I bestow all my goods to feed *the poor,* and though I give my body to be burned,* but have not love, it profits me nothing.

⁴ᵈLove suffers long *and* is ᵉkind; ᶠlove does not envy; love does not parade itself, is not puffed up; ⁵does not behave rudely, ᵍdoes not seek its own, is not provoked, thinks no evil; ⁶ʰdoes not rejoice in iniquity, but ⁱrejoices in the truth; ⁷ʲbears all things, believes all things, hopes all things, endures all things.

⁸Love never fails. But whether *there are* prophecies, they will fail; whether *there are* tongues, they will cease; whether *there is* knowledge, it will vanish away. ⁹ᵏFor we know in part and we prophesy in part. ¹⁰But when that which is perfect has come, then that which is in part will be done away.

¹¹When I was a child, I spoke as a child, I understood as a child, I thought as a child; but when I became a man, I put away childish things. ¹²For ˡnow we see in a mirror, dimly, but then ᵐface to face. Now I know in part, but then I shall know just as I also am known.

¹³And now abide faith, hope, love, these three; but the greatest of these *is* love.

Prophecy and Tongues

14 Pursue love, and ᵃdesire spiritual *gifts,* ᵇbut especially that you may prophesy. ²For he who ᶜspeaks in a tongue does not speak to men but to God, for no one understands *him;* however, in the spirit he speaks mysteries. ³But he who prophesies speaks ᵈedification and ᵉexhortation and comfort to men. ⁴He who speaks in a tongue edifies himself, but he who prophesies edifies the church. ⁵I wish you all spoke with tongues, but even more that you prophesied; for* he who prophesies *is* greater than he who speaks with tongues, unless indeed he interprets, that the church may receive edification.

Tongues Must Be Interpreted

⁶But now, brethren, if I come to you speaking with tongues, what shall I profit you unless I speak to you either by ᶠrevelation, by knowledge, by prophesying, or by teaching? ⁷Even things without life, whether flute or harp, when they make a sound, unless they make a distinction in the sounds, how will it be known what is piped or played? ⁸For if the trumpet makes an uncertain sound, who will prepare for battle? ⁹So likewise you, unless you utter by the tongue words easy to understand, how will it be known what is spoken? For you will be speaking into the air. ¹⁰There are, it may be, so many kinds of languages in the world, and none of them *is* without significance. ¹¹Therefore, if I do not know the meaning of the language, I shall be a foreigner to him who speaks, and he who speaks *will be* a foreigner to me. ¹²Even so you, since you are zealous for spiritual *gifts, let it be* for the edification of the church *that* you seek to excel.

* **12:31** NU-Text reads *greater.*   * **13:3** NU-Text reads *so I may boast.*   * **14:5** NU-Text reads *and.*

---

resurrected Christ and were given a special mission by Him as His representatives (9:1; 15:5,8).

12:31 *earnestly desire the best gifts.* This phrase has generally been interpreted as Paul's exhortation to the Corinthians to seek after the more spiritually profitable gifts, yet it is possible that Paul is stating that the Corinthians were improperly desiring the gifts that would bring attention to themselves. In other words, he would be telling them that, although they desire this sort of gift, he wants to show them a more excellent way.

13:1–13 *Love*—The more one reads 1 Corinthians 13, the more one has to face the fact that we don't naturally have that kind of love in us. The only way to get it is to get it from God. Love comes from God (1 John 4:7). We're not very good at this kind of loving, and the only way we can be is through the empowering work of the Holy Spirit. It is tough because it means dependency on God for that which we cannot do by ourselves. It is tough because the objects of our love often act in unlovable ways or they reject our love when we give it. It is tough because we have to keep coming back with more love, even when it is rejected.

13:8 *Love never fails.* This uncompromising and bold affirmation introduces the contrast with the spiritual gifts which will not last. Paul wants the Corinthians to know that the gifts would one day no longer be needed, but love.

13:10 *when that which is perfect has come.* The Greek word for "perfect" means "end" or "completion." Most likely, this is a reference to the second coming of Christ and the completion of all things, but some have interpreted this as referring to the completion of the New Testament canon.

14:3 *prophesies.* In this sense, prophecy incorporates all speaking gifts that edify the church (Rom. 12:6; 1 Pet. 4:11).

14:11 *I do not know the meaning.* Paul underlines the original purpose of all spiritual gifts: they must

12:31 ⁱ 1 Cor. 14:1, 39   **13:2** ᵃ 1 Cor. 12:8–10, 28; 14:1   ᵇ Matt. 17:20; 21:21   **13:3** ᶜ Matt. 6:1, 2   **13:4** ᵈ Prov. 10:12; 17:9   ᵉ Eph. 4:32   ᶠ Gal. 5:26   **13:5** ᵍ 1 Cor. 10:24   **13:6** ʰ Rom. 1:32   ⁱ 2 John 4   **13:7** ʲ Gal. 6:2   **13:9** ᵏ 1 Cor. 8:2; 13:12   **13:12** ˡ Phil. 3:12   ᵐ [1 John 3:2]   **14:1** ᵃ 1 Cor. 12:31; 14:39   ᵇ Num. 11:25, 29   **14:2** ᶜ Acts 2:4; 10:46   **14:3** ᵈ Rom. 14:19; 15:2   ᵉ 1 Tim. 4:13   **14:6** ᶠ 1 Cor. 14:26

13Therefore let him who speaks in a tongue pray that he may ginterpret. 14For if I pray in a tongue, my spirit prays, but my understanding is unfruitful. 15What is *the conclusion* then? I will pray with the spirit, and I will also pray with the understanding. hI will sing with the spirit, and I will also sing iwith the understanding. 16Otherwise, if you bless with the spirit, how will he who occupies the place of the uninformed say "Amen" jat your giving of thanks, since he does not understand what you say? 17For you indeed give thanks well, but the other is not edified.

18I thank my God I speak with tongues more than you all; 19yet in the church I would rather speak five words with my understanding, that I may teach others also, than ten thousand words in a tongue.

Tongues a Sign to Unbelievers

20Brethren, kdo not be children in understanding; however, in malice lbe babes, but in understanding be mature. 21mIn the law it is written:

n"With men of other tongues and other
    lips
 I will speak to this people;
 And yet, for all that, they will not hear
    Me,"*

says the Lord.

22Therefore tongues are for a osign, not to those who believe but to unbelievers; but prophesying is not for unbelievers but for those who believe. 23Therefore if the whole church comes together in one place, and all speak with tongues, and there come in *those who are* uninformed or unbelievers, pwill they not say that you are out of your mind? 24But if all prophesy, and an unbeliever or an uninformed person comes in, he is convinced by all, he is convicted by all. 25And thus* the secrets of his heart are revealed; and so, falling down on *his* face,

he will worship God and report qthat God is truly among you.

Order in Church Meetings

26How is it then, brethren? Whenever you come together, each of you has a psalm, rhas a teaching, has a tongue, has a revelation, has an interpretation. sLet all things be done for edification. 27If anyone speaks in a tongue, *let there be* two or at the most three, *each* in turn, and let one interpret. 28But if there is no interpreter, let him keep silent in church, and let him speak to himself and to God. 29Let two or three prophets speak, and tlet the others judge. 30But if *anything* is revealed to another who sits by, ulet the first keep silent. 31For you can all prophesy one by one, that all may learn and all may be encouraged. 32And vthe spirits of the prophets are subject to the prophets. 33For God is not *the author* of confusion but of peace, was in all the churches of the saints.

34xLet your* women keep silent in the churches, for they are not permitted to speak; but *they are* to be submissive, as the ylaw also says. 35And if they want to learn something, let them ask their own husbands at home; for it is shameful for women to speak in church.

36Or did the word of God come *originally* from you? Or *was it* you only that it reached? 37zIf anyone thinks himself to be a prophet or spiritual, let him acknowledge that the things which I write to you are the commandments of the Lord. 38But if anyone is ignorant, let him be ignorant.*

39Therefore, brethren, adesire earnestly to prophesy, and do not forbid to speak with tongues. 40bLet all things be done decently and in order.

---

* **14:21** Isaiah 28:11, 12   * **14:25** NU-Text omits *And thus.*   * **14:34** NU-Text omits *your.*
* **14:38** NU-Text reads *if anyone does not recognize this, he is not recognized.*

---

serve the church (vv. 13–14; 12:7). Tongues must convey meaning or else they fail to help those who listen.
14:16 Amen. The word "amen" means "truly" or "so be it" (John 3:5). Saying "amen" indicated agreement with what was being said (Deut. 27:14–26; Rev. 5:14).
14:29 two or three. The meetings of the church should be characterized by orderliness and moderation. *judge.* No one, not even a person exercising a spiritual gift, is exempt from accountability to the church (6:5; 11:29–31).
14:32 subject to the prophets. Paul anticipated that some might excuse disorder by claiming that they could not prevent themselves from prophesying when God brought a revelation to them. He explained that the Holy Spirit does not overpower the person through whom He speaks.
14:34 women keep silent. This command is the subject of much debate, for it seems to contradict the fact that Paul spoke of women prophesying in 1 Corinthians 11:5. It has been suggested that Paul was addressing a particular problem in the Corinthian church, a group of women who were disruptive,

but the prohibition is repeated at a different time to a different group of people (1 Tim. 2:11–12). This verse has also been interpreted as a prohibition on women interpreting prophecy, judging the prophets, or speaking in tongues. Others believe that women do prophesy and minister, but only to other women, or in a setting other than public church meetings, such as Priscilla and Aquila instructing Apollos (Acts 18:24–28).
14:40 decently and in order. This verse is the key to all church practice. In worship and teaching, as in all of life, believers should demonstrate self-control and consideration.

14:13 g 1 Cor. 12:10   **14:15** h Col. 3:16 i Ps. 47:7
14:16 j 1 Cor. 11:24   **14:20** k Ps. 131:2 l [1 Pet. 2:2]
14:21 m John 10:34 n Is. 28:11, 12   **14:22** o Mark 16:17
14:23 p Acts 2:13   **14:26** r 1 Cor. 12:8–10;
14:6 s [2 Cor. 12:19]   **14:29** t 1 Cor. 12:10   **14:30** u [1 Thess.
5:19, 20]   **14:32** v 1 John 4:1   **14:33** w 1 Cor. 11:16
14:34 x 1 Tim. 2:11 y Gen. 3:16   **14:37** z 2 Cor. 10:7
14:39 a 1 Cor. 12:31   **14:40** b 1 Cor. 14:33

The Risen Christ, Faith's Reality

15 Moreover, brethren, I declare to you the gospel *a*which I preached to you, which also you received and *b*in which you stand, ²*c*by which also you are saved, if you hold fast that word which I preached to you—unless *d*you believed in vain.

³For *e*I delivered to you first of all that *f*which I also received: that Christ died for our sins *g*according to the Scriptures, ⁴and that He was buried, and that He rose again the third day *h*according to the Scriptures, ⁵*i*and that He was seen by Cephas, then *j*by the twelve. ⁶After that He was seen by over five hundred brethren at once, of whom the greater part remain to the present, but some have fallen asleep. ⁷After that He was seen by James, then *k*by all the apostles. ⁸*l*Then last of all He was seen by me also, as by one born out of due time.

⁹For I am *m*the least of the apostles, who am not worthy to be called an apostle, because *n*I persecuted the church of God. ¹⁰But *o*by the grace of God I am what I am, and His grace toward me was not in vain; but I labored more abundantly than they all, *p*yet not I, but the grace of God *which was* with me. ¹¹Therefore, whether *it was* I or they, so we preach and so you believed.

The Risen Christ, Our Hope

¹²Now if Christ is preached that He has been raised from the dead, how do some among you say that there is no resurrection of the dead? ¹³But if there is no resurrection of the dead, *q*then Christ is not risen. ¹⁴And if Christ is not risen, then our preaching *is* empty and your faith *is* also empty. ¹⁵Yes, and we are found false witnesses of God, because *r*we have testified of God that He raised up Christ, whom He did not raise up—if in fact the dead do not rise. ¹⁶For if *the* dead do not rise, then Christ is not risen. ¹⁷And if Christ is not risen, your faith *is* futile; *s*you are still in your sins! ¹⁸Then also those who have fallen *t*asleep in Christ have perished. ¹⁹*u*If in this life only we have hope in Christ, we are of all men the most pitiable.

The Last Enemy Destroyed

²⁰But now *v*Christ is risen from the dead, *and* has become *w*the firstfruits of those who have fallen asleep. ²¹For *x*since by man *came* death, *y*by Man also *came* the resurrection of the dead. ²²For as in Adam all die, even so in Christ all shall *z*be made alive. ²³But *a*each one in his own order:

15:3–4 Gospel Message—Paul makes it clear here that evangelism should be centered on the gospel of Christ. The central point of the good news is Christ's death and resurrection. The four key points about that gospel are:

1. God's Word says all are sinners, condemned to hell (Is. 53:6; Rom. 3:10–11,23; 5:8,12; Rev. 20:15).
2. There is nothing a sinner can do on his own to save himself (Is. 64:6; Eph. 2:9).
3. Christ was born, crucified, and resurrected to save lost people from their sin (John 3:16; 1 Tim. 1:15).
4. To be saved, a sinner must believe God's Word and invite Christ into his or her heart by faith (John 5:24; Acts 16:31).

15:3 *according to the Scriptures.* Christ lived and died in accordance with the prophecies about Him in the Old Testament (Ps. 16:10; Is. 53:8–10).

15:8 *born out of due time.* This is probably Paul's comment on the unique way that he became an apostle. Unlike the other apostles, who had the benefit of an initial training period with Christ, Paul became an apostle abruptly, with no opportunity for earthly contact with Christ or His teaching.

15:9 *persecuted the church.* The story of Paul's persecuting and conversion is told in Acts 9; 22; Ephesians 3:8; 1 Timothy 1:15–16.

15:12 *no resurrection.* These opponents of Paul may have been denying the reality of Christ's resurrection. They may also have been teaching that resurrection is only spiritual and not physical; or they may have been teaching that the resurrection had already happened (2 Tim. 2:18). Whatever the case, they contradicted the essential teaching that Christ had been physically raised from the dead and that all believers in Him will someday also be resurrected.

15:15 *false witnesses.* In verses 5–8 Paul listed several people, including himself, who had witnessed the resurrected Christ. To deny the resurrection was to call these people liars.

15:17 Resurrection—There are many biblical scholars these days who say that the resurrection was an invented story out of some kind of "faith" process. They relegate the critical event that defines Christianity to the imaginations of some well-meaning but deluded Palestinian peasants. Paul goes to great pains to put the resurrection in the realm of fact, not opinion or imagination. He talks about the eyewitness testimony of hundreds (v. 6). He references his own story of personal confrontation with Christ (v. 8). In the end he says that if the resurrection isn't a fact, then he is absolutely lost (v. 19). This sounds like a man who staked his entire life on an indisputable fact.

15:19 *pitiable.* If Christ did not rise, then He is just another dead prophet with no power over sin or death, and the Christian's hope of eternal life is a lie.

15:20 *firstfruits.* The "firstfruits" is the first installment of a crop, which anticipates and guarantees the ultimate offering of the whole crop (16:15; Rom. 8:23). Because Christ rose from the dead, those who are asleep in Christ (1 Thess. 4:15–16) have a guarantee of their own resurrection.

15:21 *by man came death.* The first man, Adam, transgressed God's law and brought sin and death into the world (Gen. 2:17; 3:19; Rom. 5:12–21); the second man, Jesus Christ, was the perfect sacrifice to take away sin and to bring life and resurrection to those who believe in Him (Rom. 5:15–21).

15:23 *each one in his own order.* The believers who

15:1 *a* [Gal. 1:11] *b* [Rom. 5:2; 11:20] **15:2** *c* Rom. 1:16 *d* Gal. 3:4 **15:3** *e* 1 Cor. 11:2, 23 *f* [Gal. 1:12] *g* Ps. 22:15 **15:4** *h* Ps. 16:9–11; 68:18; 110:1 **15:5** *i* Luke 24:34 *j* Matt. 28:17 **15:7** *k* Acts 1:3, 4 **15:8** *l* [Acts 9:3–8; 22:6–11; 26:12–18] **15:9** *m* Eph. 3:8 *n* Acts 8:3 **15:10** *o* Eph. 3:7, 8 *p* Phil. 2:13 **15:13** *q* [1 Thess. 4:14] **15:15** *r* Acts 2:24 **15:17** *s* [Rom. 4:25] **15:18** *t* Job 14:12 **15:19** *u* 2 Tim. 3:12 **15:20** *v* 1 Pet. 1:3 *w* Acts 26:23 **15:21** *x* Rom. 5:12; 6:23 *y* John 11:25 **15:22** *z* [John 5:28, 29] **15:23** *a* [1 Thess. 4:15–17]

Christ the firstfruits, afterward those *who are* Christ's at His coming. 24Then *comes* the end, when He delivers *b*the kingdom to God the Father, when He puts an end to all rule and all authority and power. 25For He must reign *c*till He has put all enemies under His feet. 26*d*The last enemy *that* will be destroyed *is* death. 27For *e*"He has put *all things under His feet."** But when He says "all things are put under *Him*," *it is* evident that He who put all things under Him is excepted. 28*f*Now when all things are made subject to Him, then *g*the Son Himself will also be subject to Him who put all things under Him, that God may be all in all.

Effects of Denying the Resurrection

29Otherwise, what will they do who are baptized for the dead, if the dead do not rise at all? Why then are they baptized for the dead? 30And *h*why do we stand in jeopardy every hour? 31I affirm, by *i*the boasting in you which I have in Christ Jesus our Lord, *j*I die daily. 32If, in the manner of men, *k*I have fought with beasts at Ephesus, what advantage *is it* to me? If *the* dead do not rise, *l*"Let us eat and drink, for tomorrow we die!"*

33Do not be deceived: *m*"Evil company corrupts good habits." 34*n*Awake to righteousness, and do not sin; *o*for some do not have the knowledge of God. *p*I speak *this* to your shame.

A Glorious Body

35But someone will say, *q*"How are the dead raised up? And with what body do they come?" 36Foolish one, *r*what you sow is not made alive unless it dies. 37And what you sow, you do not sow that body that shall be, but mere grain—perhaps wheat or some other *grain.* 38But God gives it a body as He pleases, and to each seed its own body.

39All flesh *is* not the same flesh, but there is one *kind of* flesh* of men, another

flesh of animals, another of fish, *and* another of birds.

40*There are* also celestial bodies and terrestrial bodies; but the glory of the celestial *is* one, and the *glory* of the terrestrial *is* another. 41*There is* one glory of the sun, another glory of the moon, and another glory of the stars; for *one* star differs from *another* star in glory.

42*s*So also *is* the resurrection of the dead. *The body* is sown in corruption, it is raised in incorruption. 43*t*It is sown in dishonor, it is raised in glory. It is sown in weakness, it is raised in power. 44It is sown a natural body, it is raised a spiritual body. There is a natural body, and there is a spiritual body. 45And so it is written, *u*"The first man *Adam became a living being."** *v*The last Adam *became wa life-giving spirit.

46However, the spiritual is not first, but the natural, and afterward the spiritual. 47*x*The first man *was* of the earth, *y*made of dust; the second Man *is* the Lord* *z*from heaven. 48As was the *man* of dust, so also *are* those *who are made* of dust; *a*and as *is* the heavenly *Man,* so also *are* those *who* are heavenly. 49And *b*as we have borne the image of the *man* of dust, *c*we shall also bear* the image of the heavenly *Man.*

Our Final Victory

50Now this I say, brethren, that *d*flesh and blood cannot inherit the kingdom of God; nor does corruption inherit incorruption. 51Behold, I tell you a mystery: *e*We shall not all sleep, *f*but we shall all be changed— 52in a moment, in the twinkling of an eye, at the last trumpet. *g*For the trumpet will sound, and the dead will be raised incorruptible, and we shall be changed. 53For this corruptible must put on incorruption, and *h*this mortal *must* put on immortality.

---

* **15:27** Psalm 8:6   * **15:32** Isaiah 22:13
* **15:39** NU-Text and M-Text omit *of flesh.*
* **15:45** Genesis 2:7   * **15:47** NU-Text omits *the Lord.*   * **15:49** M-Text reads *let us also bear.*

---

have died will be the first to rise at Christ's coming and be reunited with their physical bodies. Following this is the removal of all living Christians from the earth (1 Thess. 4:13–18).

15:29 baptized for the dead. It may be that some of the Corinthians had for some reason been baptized on behalf of others who had died without baptism. Paul does not address whether this practice was right or wrong (although his use of "they" rather than "we" indicates that he did not participate), but makes the point that their own actions are inconsistent with their beliefs. There would be no point in doing anything for the dead if there is no resurrection.

15:30 in jeopardy. If this life is all there is, it would make more sense to take the position of the Epicureans, seeking pleasure and avoiding pain.

15:32 beasts at Ephesus. This may be a figurative reference to Paul's enemies at Ephesus (Acts 19).

15:36 unless it dies. Difficulty understanding the nature of the resurrection should not cause a person

to doubt its reality any more than not understanding how a seed becomes a plant should cause disbelief in the coming harvest.

15:44 natural body . . . spiritual body. The contrast is not between a material body and an immaterial body, but between a body subject to death and a body that is immortal.

15:24 *b* [Dan. 2:44; 7:14, 27]   **15:25** *c* Ps. 110:1
15:26 *d* [2 Tim. 1:10]   **15:27** *e* Ps. 8:6   **15:28** *f* [Phil. 3:21]   *g* 1 Cor. 3:23; 11:3; 12:6   **15:30** *h* 2 Cor. 11:26
15:31 *i* 1 Thess. 2:19   *j* Rom. 8:36   **15:32** *k* 2 Cor. 1:8
l Is. 22:13; 56:12   **15:33** *m* [1 Cor. 5:6]   **15:34** *n* Rom. 13:11   *o* [1 Thess. 4:5]   *p* I Cor. 6:5   **15:35** *q* Ezek. 37:3
15:36 *r* John 12:24   **15:42** *s* [Dan. 12:3]   **15:43** *t* [Phil. 3:21]   **15:45** *u* Gen. 2:7   *v* John 5:21;
6:57   **15:47** *x* John 3:31   *y* Gen. 2:7; 3:19   *z* John 3:13   **15:48** *a* Phil. 3:20   **15:49** *b* Gen. 5:3   *c* Rom. 8:29
15:50 *d* [John 3:3, 5]   **15:51** *e* [1 Thess. 4:15]   *f* [Phil. 3:21]
15:52 *g* Matt. 24:31   **15:53** *h* 2 Cor. 5:4

[54]So when this corruptible has put on incorruption, and this mortal has put on immortality, then shall be brought to pass the saying that is written: [i]*"Death is swallowed up in victory."**

[55] *"O[j] Death, where is your sting?** O Hades, where is your victory?"**

[56]The sting of death *is* sin, and [k]the strength of sin *is* the law. [57]But thanks *be* to God, who gives us [m]the victory through our Lord Jesus Christ.

[58n]Therefore, my beloved brethren, be steadfast, immovable, always abounding in the work of the Lord, knowing [o]that your labor is not in vain in the Lord.

Collection for the Saints

16 Now concerning [a]the collection for the saints, as I have given orders to the churches of Galatia, so you must do also: [2b]On the first *day* of the week let each one of you lay something aside, storing up as he may prosper, that there be no collections when I come. [3]And when I come, [c]whomever you approve by *your* letters I will send to bear your gift to Jerusalem. [4d]But if it is fitting that I go also, they will go with me.

Personal Plans

[5]Now I will come to you [e]when I pass through Macedonia (for I am passing through Macedonia). [6]And it may be that I will remain, or even spend the winter with you, that you may [f]send me on my journey, wherever I go. [7]For I do not wish to see you now on the way; but I hope to stay a while with you, [g]if the Lord permits.

[8]But I will tarry in Ephesus until [h]Pentecost. [9]For [i]a great and effective door has opened to me, and [j]there are many adversaries.

[10]And [k]if Timothy comes, see that he may be with you without fear; for [l]he does the work of the Lord, as I also *do.* [11m]Therefore let no one despise him. But send him on his journey [n]in peace, that he may come to me; for I am waiting for him with the brethren.

[12]Now concerning *our* brother [o]Apollos, I strongly urged him to come to you with the brethren, but he was quite unwilling to come at this time; however, he will come when he has a convenient time.

Final Exhortations

[13p]Watch, [q]stand fast in the faith, be brave, [r]be strong. [14s]Let all *that* you *do* be done with love.

[15]I urge you, brethren—you know [t]the household of Stephanas, that it is [u]the firstfruits of Achaia, and *that* they have devoted themselves to [v]the ministry of the saints— [16w]that you also submit to such, and to everyone who works and [x]labors with *us.*

[17]I am glad about the coming of Stephanas, Fortunatus, and Achaicus, [y]for what was lacking on your part they supplied. [18z]For they refreshed my spirit and yours. Therefore [a]acknowledge such men.

Greetings and a Solemn Farewell

[19]The churches of Asia greet you. Aquila and Priscilla greet you heartily in the Lord, [b]with the church that is in their house. [20]All the brethren greet you.

[c]Greet one another with a holy kiss.

[21d]The salutation with my own hand—Paul's.

---

* **15:54** Isaiah 25:8 * **15:55** Hosea 13:14 • NU-Text reads *O Death, where is your victory? O Death, where is your sting?*

15:54 *Death is swallowed up in victory.* Satan's apparent victories in the garden of Eden (Gen. 3:13) and at the cross (Mark 15:22–24) were reversed by Jesus' death and resurrection (Col. 2:13–15).

15:58 *your labor is not in vain.* We are looking forward to eternal life because of the hope of the resurrection; everything we do on this earth matters for eternity.

16:2 *the first day of the week.* It appears that the custom of believers meeting on the first day of the week began early in Christian history. *lay something aside.* The Old Testament tithe was not adopted by the New Testament church, though certainly Christ practiced it. New Testament believers were encouraged to give liberally, but never a specified amount or percentage (Rom. 12:8). Considering the New Testament teachings on generosity and self-sacrifice, believers should probably expect to give much more than ten percent.

16:13 *be brave.* This emphasizes courage as well as maturity. Paul's command to do everything with love serves as a balance to these strong exhortations.

16:17 *Stephanas, Fortunatus, and Achaicus.* These were probably the ones who confirmed the bad report brought by Chloe's household in 1 Corinthians 1:11.

16:19 *Aquila and Priscilla.* Aquila and Priscilla were tentmakers who had met Paul in Corinth. They followed him to Ephesus and made their house available for the meetings of the church (Rom. 16:3–5). They would have been known to many in the Corinthian church.

16:20 *holy kiss.* In the ancient world (as in many

15:54 [i] Is. 25:8 **15:55** [j] Hos. 13:14 **15:56** [k] [Rom. 3:20; 4:15; 7:8] **15:57** [l] [Rom. 7:25] [m] [1 John 5:4] **15:58** [n] 2 Pet. 3:14 [o] [1 Cor. 3:8] **16:1** [a] Gal. 2:10 **16:2** [b] Acts 20:7 **16:3** [c] 2 Cor. 3:1; 8:18 **16:4** [d] 2 Cor. 8:4, 19 **16:5** [e] 2 Cor. 1:15, 16 **16:6** [f] Acts 15:3 **16:7** [g] James 4:15 **16:8** [h] Lev. 23:15–22 **16:9** [i] Acts 14:27 [j] Acts 19:9 **16:10** [k] Acts 19:22 [l] Phil. 2:20 **16:11** [m] 1 Tim. 4:12 [n] Acts 15:33 **16:12** [o] 1 Cor. 1:12; 3:5 **16:13** [p] Matt. 24:42 [q] Phil. 1:27; 4:1 [r] [Eph. 3:16; 6:10] **16:14** [s] [1 Pet. 4:8] **16:15** [t] 1 Cor. 1:16 [u] Rom. 16:5 [v] 2 Cor. 8:4 **16:16** [w] Heb. 13:17 [x] [Heb. 6:10] **16:17** [y] 2 Cor. 11:9 **16:18** [z] Col. 4:8 [a] Phil. 2:29 **16:19** [b] Rom. 16:5 **16:20** [c] Rom. 16:16 **16:21** [d] Col. 4:18

²²If anyone ᵉdoes not love the Lord Jesus Christ, ᶠlet him be accursed.* ᵍO Lord, come!*

²³ʰThe grace of our Lord Jesus Christ *be* with you. ²⁴My love *be* with you all in Christ Jesus. Amen.

* **16:22** Greek *anathema* • Aramaic *Maranatha*

---

cultures still today), a kiss was a common form of friendly or affectionate greeting.
16:22 *accursed.* Paul does not condemn unbelievers, but rather unbelievers condemn themselves by ignoring the claims of the Creator on their lives.

16:22 ᵉEph. 6:24 ᶠGal. 1:8, 9 ᵍJude 14, 15 **16:23** ʰRom. 16:20

THE SECOND EPISTLE OF PAUL THE APOSTLE TO THE
CORINTHIANS

▶ **AUTHOR:** External and internal evidence amply support the Pauline authorship of this letter. There is an interval of about a year between these two letters to the Corinthians. Since Paul's first letter, the Corinthian church had been swayed by false teachers who stirred the people against Paul. They claimed he was fickle, arrogant, unimpressive in appearance and speech, and unqualified to be an apostle of Jesus Christ. During this time Paul has paid them what must have been an unpleasant visit and then wrote them another letter, which we do not have (2:1–4). Paul wrote 2 Corinthians in A.D. 56 in Macedonia and sent the letter to the church with Titus and another brother (8:16).

▶ **TIME:** C. A.D. 56   ▶ **KEY VERSES:** 2 Cor. 4:5–6

▶ **THEME:** As Paul writes this letter, he is looking forward to yet another visit, and it appears that the Corinthians have listened to him and things are getting on the right track. But there are still some problems. The key issue seems to be Paul's leadership. He spends a good deal of the letter establishing his authority and the need to exercise it, which makes the letter intensely personal. In it we can see the depth of his relationship with the Corinthians, and we get an understanding of the hardships Paul went through for these people on his missionary journeys. Most importantly we see a faith that is so focused that Paul is ready to endure anything to see it spread.

Greeting

1 Paul, *a*an apostle of Jesus Christ by the will of God, and *b*Timothy *our* brother,

To the church of God which is at Corinth, *c*with all the saints who are in all Achaia:

2*d*Grace to you and peace from God our Father and the Lord Jesus Christ.

Comfort in Suffering

3*e*Blessed *be* the God and Father of our Lord Jesus Christ, the Father of mercies and God of all comfort, 4who *f*comforts us in all our tribulation, that we may be able to comfort those who are in any trouble, with the comfort with which we ourselves are comforted by God. 5For as *g*the sufferings of Christ abound in us, so our consolation also abounds through Christ. 6Now if we are afflicted, *h*it *is* for your consolation and salvation, which is effective for enduring the same sufferings which we also suffer.

Or if we are comforted, *it is* for your consolation and salvation. 7And our hope for you *is* steadfast, because we know that *i*as you are partakers of the sufferings, so also *you will partake* of the consolation.

Delivered from Suffering

8For we do not want you to be ignorant, brethren, of *j*our trouble which came to us in Asia: that we were burdened beyond measure, above strength, so that we despaired even of life. 9Yes, we had the sentence of death in ourselves, that we should *k*not trust in ourselves but in God who raises the dead, 10*l*who delivered us from so great a death, and does* deliver us; in whom we trust that He will still deliver *us,* 11you also *m*helping together in prayer for us, that thanks may be given by many persons on our* behalf *n*for the gift *granted* to us through many.

* **1:10** NU-Text reads *shall.*   * **1:11** M-Text reads *your behalf.*

1:4 *comforts us in all our tribulation.* God comforts us for our own encouragement and also to make us comforters of others. The comfort that God gives to us becomes a gift that we can give to others (7:6; Acts 9:10–19).
1:5 *the sufferings of Christ.* Jesus warned His disciples that they would experience the same kind of suffering that He did for the sake of the gospel (John 15:20).

1:8 *Asia.* This is the Roman province in western Asia Minor, present day Turkey. The trouble that Paul speaks of is likely the riots in Ephesus (Acts 19:23–41).

1:1 *a* 2 Tim. 1:1 *b* 1 Cor. 16:10 *c* Col. 1:2 **1:2** *d* Rom. 1:7	
1:3 *e* 1 Pet. 1:3 **1:4** *f* Is. 51:12; 66:13 **1:5** *g* 2 Cor. 4:10	
1:6 *h* 2 Cor. 4:15; 12:15 **1:7** *i* [Rom. 8:17] **1:8** *j* Acts 19:23 **1:9** *k* Jer. 17:5, 7 **1:10** *l* [2 Pet. 2:9] **1:11** *m* Rom. 15:30 *n* 2 Cor. 4:15; 9:11	

Paul's Sincerity

12For our boasting is this: the testimony of our conscience that we conducted ourselves in the world in simplicity and °godly sincerity, ᵖnot with fleshly wisdom but by the grace of God, and more abundantly toward you. 13For we are not writing any other things to you than what you read or understand. Now I trust you will understand, even to the end 14(as also you have understood us in part), ᵠthat we are your boast as ʳyou also *are* ours, in the day of the Lord Jesus.

Sparing the Church

15And in this confidence ˢI intended to come to you before, that you might have ᵗa second benefit— 16to pass by way of you to Macedonia, ᵘto come again from Macedonia to you, and be helped by you on my way to Judea. 17Therefore, when I was planning this, did I do it lightly? Or the things I plan, do I plan ᵛaccording to the flesh, that with me there should be Yes, Yes, and No, No? 18But *as* God *is* ʷfaithful, our word to you was not Yes and No. 19For ˣthe Son of God, Jesus Christ, who was preached among you by us—by me, ʸSilvanus, and ᶻTimothy—was not Yes and No, ᵃbut in Him was Yes. 20ᵇFor all the promises of God in Him *are* Yes, and in Him Amen, to the glory of God through us. 21Now He who establishes us with you in Christ, and ᶜhas anointed us *is* God, 22who ᵈalso has sealed us and ᵉgiven us the Spirit in our hearts as a guarantee.

23Moreover ᶠI call God as witness against my soul, ᵍthat to spare you I came no more to Corinth. 24Not ʰthat we have dominion over your faith, but are fellow workers for your joy; for ⁱby faith you stand.

2 But I determined this within myself, ᵃthat I would not come again to you in sorrow. 2For if I make you ᵇsorrowful, then who is he who makes me glad but the one who is made sorrowful by me?

Forgive the Offender

3And I wrote this very thing to you, lest, when I came, ᶜI should have sorrow over those from whom I ought to have joy, ᵈhaving confidence in you all that my joy is *the joy* of you all. 4For out of much affliction and anguish of heart I wrote to you, with many tears, ᵉnot that you should be grieved, but that you might know the love which I have so abundantly for you.

5But ᶠif anyone has caused grief, he has not ᵍgrieved me, but all of you to some extent—not to be too severe. 6This punishment which *was inflicted* ʰby the majority *is* sufficient for such a man, 7ⁱso that, on the contrary, you *ought* rather to forgive and comfort *him*, lest perhaps such a one be swallowed up with too much sorrow. 8Therefore I urge you to reaffirm *your* love to him. 9For to this end I also wrote, that I might put you to the test, whether you are ʲobedient in all things. 10Now whom you forgive anything, I also *forgive*. For if indeed I have forgiven anything, I have forgiven that one* for your sakes in the presence of Christ, 11lest Satan should take advantage of us; for we are not ignorant of his devices.

Triumph in Christ

12Furthermore, ᵏwhen I came to Troas to *preach* Christ's gospel, and ˡa door was opened to me by the Lord, 13ᵐI had no rest in my spirit, because I did not find Titus my brother; but taking my leave of them, I departed for Macedonia.

14Now thanks *be* to God who always leads us in triumph in Christ, and through us diffuses the fragrance of His knowledge in every place. 15For we are to God the fragrance of Christ ⁿamong those who are being saved and ᵒamong those who are perishing. 16ᵖTo the one *we are* the aroma

* **2:10** NU-Text reads *For indeed, what I have forgiven, if I have forgiven anything, I did it.*

1:12 *godly sincerity.* The Corinthians certainly were well acquainted with Paul's character, since he had spent 18 months with them (Acts 18:11).

1:19 *not Yes and No.* Paul's preaching was not inconsistent or contradictory. Instead, his preaching reflected the truthfulness and faithfulness of God, because his teaching was based on the Scriptures and the teachings of Christ.

1:21 *anointed us.* God confirmed Paul and his fellow workers by anointing them, the special mark of service to God which was given to kings and priests in the Old Testament. This anointing probably refers to special empowerment by the Holy Spirit, similar to the anointing that John described in 1 John 2:20, 27.

1:22 *sealed us.* Sealing indicates ownership and security. The *sealing* and the *giving* of the Holy Spirit are also linked. The Holy Spirit is a guarantee, the down payment that there is more spiritual blessing to come and that the believer will receive eternal life.

2:5 *caused grief.* This is probably a reference to the incestuous man of 1 Corinthians 5.

2:7 *forgive and comfort him.* The purpose of church

discipline is repentance and restoration. Forgiveness should always follow the correction, just as Christ instructed (Matt. 18:15–35).

2:12 *Troas.* Troas was a city on the Aegean coast, where Paul had received his call to preach the gospel in Macedonia (Acts 16:8).

2:16 *death leading to death.* The gospel message gives life to those who choose to accept it, but it represents death and judgment to those who reject it.

1:12 º 2 Cor. 2:17 ᵖ [1 Cor. 2:4]   **1:14** ᵠ 2 Cor. 5:12 ʳ Phil. 2:16 **1:15** ˢ 1 Cor. 4:19 ᵗ Rom. 1:11; 15:29   **1:16** ᵘ 1 Cor. 16:3–6   **1:17** ᵛ 2 Cor. 10:2; 11:18   **1:18** ʷ 1 John 5:20   **1:19** ˣ Mark 1:1 ʸ 1 Pet. 5:12 ᶻ 2 Cor. 1:1 ᵃ [Heb. 13:8]   **1:20** ᵇ [Rom. 15:8, 9]   **1:21** ᶜ [1 John 2:20, 27]   **1:22** ᵈ [Eph. 4:30] ᵉ [Eph. 1:14]   **1:23** ᶠ Gal. 1:20 ᵍ 1 Cor. 4:21   **1:24** ʰ [1 Pet. 5:3] ⁱ Rom. 11:20   **2:1** ᵃ 2 Cor. 1:23   **2:2** ᵇ 2 Cor. 7:8   **2:3** ᶜ 2 Cor. 12:21 ᵈ Gal. 5:10   **2:4** ᵉ [2 Cor. 2:9; 7:8, 12]   **2:5** ᶠ [1 Cor. 5:1] ᵍ Gal. 4:12   **2:6** ʰ 1 Cor. 5:4, 5   **2:7** ⁱ Gal. 6:1   **2:9** ʲ 2 Cor. 7:15; 10:6   **2:12** ᵏ Acts 16:8 ˡ 1 Cor. 16:9   **2:13** ᵐ 2 Cor. 7:6, 13; 8:6   **2:15** ⁿ [1 Cor. 1:18] ᵒ [2 Cor. 4:3]   **2:16** ᵖ Luke 2:34

of death *leading* to death, and to the other the aroma of life *leading* to life. And ^qwho *is* sufficient for these things? ¹⁷For we are not, as so many,* ^rpeddling the word of God; but as ^sof sincerity, but as from God, we speak in the sight of God in Christ.

Christ's Epistle

3 Do ^awe begin again to commend ourselves? Or do we need, as some *others*, ^bepistles of commendation to you or *letters* of commendation from you? ^{2c}You are our epistle written in our hearts, known and read by all men; ³clearly you are an epistle of Christ, ^dministered by us, written not with ink but by the Spirit of the living God, not ^eon tablets of stone but ^fon tablets of flesh, *that is*, of the heart.

The Spirit, Not the Letter

⁴And we have such trust through Christ toward God. ^{5g}Not that we are sufficient of ourselves to think of anything as *being* from ourselves, but ^hour sufficiency *is* from God, ⁶who also made us sufficient as ⁱministers of ^jthe new covenant, not ^kof the letter but of the Spirit;* for ^lthe letter kills, ^mbut the Spirit gives life.

Glory of the New Covenant

⁷But if ⁿthe ministry of death, ^owritten *and* engraved on stones, was glorious, ^pso that the children of Israel could not look steadily at the face of Moses because of the glory of his countenance, which *glory* was passing away, ⁸how will ^qthe ministry of the Spirit not be more glorious? ⁹For if the ministry of condemnation *had* glory, the ministry ^rof righteousness exceeds

much more in glory. ¹⁰For even what was made glorious had no glory in this respect, because of the glory that excels. ¹¹For if what is passing away *was* glorious, what remains *is* much more glorious.

¹²Therefore, since we have such hope, ^swe use great boldness of speech— ¹³unlike Moses, ^twho put a veil over his face so that the children of Israel could not look steadily at the end of what was passing away. ¹⁴But ^vtheir minds were blinded. For until this day the same veil remains unlifted in the reading of the Old Testament, because the *veil* is taken away in Christ. ¹⁵But even to this day, when Moses is read, a veil lies on their heart. ¹⁶Nevertheless ^wwhen one turns to the Lord, ^xthe veil is taken away. ¹⁷Now ^ythe Lord is the Spirit; and where the Spirit of the Lord is, there is ^zliberty. ¹⁸But we all, with unveiled face, beholding ^aas in a mirror ^bthe glory of the Lord, ^care being transformed into the same image from glory to glory, just as by the Spirit of the Lord.

The Light of Christ's Gospel

4 Therefore, since we have this ministry, ^aas we have received mercy, we ^bdo not lose heart. ²But we have renounced the hidden things of shame, not walking in craftiness nor handling the word of God deceitfully, but by manifestation of the truth ^ccommending ourselves to every man's conscience in the sight of God. ³But even if our gospel is veiled, ^dit is veiled to those who are perishing, ⁴whose minds ^ethe god of this age ^fhas blinded, who do not believe, lest ^gthe light of the gospel of the glory of Christ, ^hwho is the image of

---

* 2:17 M-Text reads *the rest*.   * 3:6 Or *spirit*

3:2 You are our epistle. Paul sometimes did use letters of recommendation (8:22; Rom. 16:1; 1 Cor. 16:10; Col. 4:10), but he did not need one for the Corinthians. They already knew him personally and had personally benefited from his ministry. Paul's love for the Corinthians was known to all who were acquainted with him. One of the qualifications for ministry is love for people, both God's people and the lost.

3:6 not of the letter. The "letter" is the old covenant of law. The "letter" kills because no one can be perfect enough to keep the whole law all the time, and the penalty for breaking it is death.

3:7 ministry of death. Though the law itself is holy (Rom. 7:12), the ministry of the law is the ministry of death because the law defines and convicts of sin but offers no salvation.

3:9 ministry of righteousness. God declares righteous those who believe in His Son, and then the Holy Spirit empowers the believer to live righteously. This first work of God is called justification, and the second is called sanctification.

3:11 what remains. The new covenant supersedes the old covenant established at Mount Sinai between God and the nation of Israel.

3:18 from glory to glory. As believers behold the glory of God in the Word of God, the Spirit of God changes their hearts and actions to make them more and more like Jesus Christ.

4:2 handling the word of God deceitfully. Apparently Paul had been accused of being crafty (12:16) and of being deceitful in the way that he preached. In fact, his ministry was based on the truthfulness of the word of God.

4:4 the god of this age has blinded. Because of Satan's deception, sometimes what the world thinks is obviously true is painfully wrong (Prov. 14:12). *image of God.* Jesus Christ is God's Son, and He perfectly reveals God the Father to us. Human beings have been created in the image of God, but through sin they have fallen from a perfect relationship with God. Jesus Christ is restoring believers to what they were originally created to be (3:18; Gen. 1:26).

2:16 ^q[1 Cor. 15:10]   **2:17** ^r2 Pet. 2:3 ^s2 Cor. 1:12
3:1 ^a2 Cor. 5:12; 10:12, 18; 12:11 ^bActs 18:27   **3:2** ^c1 Cor. 9:2   **3:3** ^d1 Cor. 3:5 ^eEx. 24:12; 31:18; 32:15 ^fPs. 40:8
3:5 ^g[John 15:5] ^h1 Cor. 15:10   **3:6** ⁱ1 Cor. 3:5 ^jJer. 31:31 ^kRom. 2:27 ^lGal. 3:10 ^mJohn 6:63   **3:7** ⁿRom. 7:10 ^oEx. 34:1 ^pEx. 34:29   **3:8** ^q[Gal. 3:5]   **3:9** ^r[Rom. 1:17; 3:21]   **3:12** ^sEph. 6:19   **3:13** ^tEx. 34:33–35 ^u[Gal. 3:23]   **3:14** ^vActs 28:26   **3:16** ^wRom. 11:23 ^xIs. 25:7
3:17 ^y[1 Cor. 15:45] ^zGal. 5:1, 13   **3:18** ^a1 Cor. 13:12 ^b[2 Cor. 4:4, 6] ^c[Rom. 8:29, 30]   **4:1** ^a1 Cor. 7:25 ^b2 Cor. 4:16   **4:2** ^c2 Cor. 5:11   **4:3** ^d[1 Cor. 1:18]   **4:4** ^eJohn 12:31 ^fJohn 12:40 ^g[2 Cor. 3:8, 9] ^h[John 1:18]

God, should shine on them. [5i]For we do not preach ourselves, but Christ Jesus the Lord, and [j]ourselves your bondservants for Jesus' sake. [6]For it is the God [k]who commanded light to shine out of darkness, who has [l]shone in our hearts to give the light of the knowledge of the glory of God in the face of Jesus Christ.

Cast Down but Unconquered

[7]But we have this treasure in earthen vessels, [m]that the excellence of the power may be of God and not of us. [8]We are [n]hardpressed on every side, yet not crushed; we are perplexed, but not in despair; [9]persecuted, but not [o]forsaken; [p]struck down, but not destroyed— [10q]always carrying about in the body the dying of the Lord Jesus, [r]that the life of Jesus also may be manifested in our body. [11]For we who live [s]are always delivered to death for Jesus' sake, that the life of Jesus also may be manifested in our mortal flesh. [12]So then death is working in us, but life in you.

[13]And since we have [t]the same spirit of faith, according to what is written, [u]"I believed and therefore I spoke,"[*] we also believe and therefore speak, [14]knowing that [v]He who raised up the Lord Jesus will also raise us up with Jesus, and will present us with you. [15]For [w]all things are for your sakes, that [x]grace, having spread through the many, may cause thanksgiving to abound to the glory of God.

Seeing the Invisible

[16]Therefore we [y]do not lose heart. Even though our outward man is perishing, yet the inward man is [z]being renewed day by day. [17]For [a]our light affliction, which is but for a moment, is working for us a far more exceeding and eternal weight of glory,

[18b]while we do not look at the things which are seen, but at the things which are not seen. For the things which are seen are temporary, but the things which are not seen are eternal.

Assurance of the Resurrection

5 For we know that if [a]our earthly house, this tent, is destroyed, we have a building from God, a house [b]not made with hands, eternal in the heavens. [2]For in this [c]we groan, earnestly desiring to be clothed with our habitation which is from heaven, [3]if indeed, [d]having been clothed, we shall not be found naked. [4]For we who are in this tent groan, being burdened, not because we want to be unclothed, [e]but further clothed, that mortality may be swallowed up by life. [5]Now He who has prepared us for this very thing is God, who also [f]has given us the Spirit as a guarantee.

[6]So we are always confident, knowing that while we are at home in the body we are absent from the Lord. [7]For [g]we walk by faith, not by sight. [8]We are confident, yes, [h]well pleased rather to be absent from the body and to be present with the Lord.

The Judgment Seat of Christ

[9]Therefore we make it our aim, whether present or absent, to be well pleasing to Him. [10i]For we must all appear before the judgment seat of Christ, [j]that each one may receive the things done in the body, according to what he has done, whether good or bad. [11]Knowing, therefore, [k]the terror of the Lord, we persuade men; but we are well known to God, and I also trust are well known in your consciences.

---

[*] 4:13 Psalm 116:10

4:8 yet not crushed. As believers we will face trials, but we must remember that God controls trials and uses them to strengthen His people. God's glory is manifested through broken vessels, through people who endure troubles by relying on His power.

4:9 struck down. This literally happened (Acts 14:19). In Lystra a crowd stoned Paul, leaving him for dead. But the Lord spared his life so that he could continue to preach the gospel and testify to God's deliverance.

4:12 life in you. Had Paul not been willing to risk death to bring the gospel to Corinth, the Corinthians would not have received eternal life.

4:17 working for us. Afflictions produce glory, but the glory is far greater than the affliction (Mark 10:30).

5:2 we groan. Along with the rest of creation, our spirits cry out for what we were meant to be (Rom. 8:22–23).

5:5 a guarantee. The Holy Spirit's work in believers' lives can be compared to a down payment, or earnest money (1:22). The presence of the Holy Spirit assures believers that God has purchased them. They are no longer slaves to sin, but are now His children.

5:8 be present with the Lord. This is one of the passages indicating where believers will go after death; they will be with Jesus in heaven (Luke 23:43; Phil. 1:23).

5:9 we make it our aim. Pleasing the Lord should always be our first concern in this life, since it is the only thing which will carry over into the next life.

5:10 according to what he has done. The believer will either be approved or ashamed (5:3; Luke 19:11–26; 1 Cor. 3:14–15; 9:27; 1 John 2:28; 2 John 7–8).

5:11 terror of the Lord. This is the fear of standing before the Lord and having one's life exposed and evaluated. The reality of giving an account to the Lord motivated Paul to persuade people, in this context meaning to convince the Corinthians of his sincerity and integrity.

4:5 [i] 1 Cor. 1:13 [j] 1 Cor. 9:19 **4:6** [k] Gen. 1:3 [l] 2 Pet. 1:19 **4:7** [m] 1 Cor. 2:5 **4:8** [n] 2 Cor. 1:8; 7:5 **4:9** [o] [Heb. 13:5] [p] Ps. 37:24 **4:10** [q] Phil. 3:10 [r] Rom. 8:17 **4:11** [s] Rom. 8:36 **4:13** [t] 2 Pet. 1:1 [u] Ps. 116:10 **4:14** [v] [Rom. 8:11] **4:15** [w] Col. 1:24 [x] 2 Cor. 1:11 **4:16** [y] 2 Cor. 4:1 [z] [Is. 40:29, 31] **4:17** [a] Rom. 8:18 **4:18** [b] [Heb. 11:1, 3] **5:1** [a] Job 4:19 [b] Mark 14:58 **5:2** [c] Rom. 8:23 **5:3** [d] Rev. 3:18 **5:4** [e] 1 Cor. 15:53 **5:5** [f] Rom. 8:23 **5:7** [g] Heb. 11:1 **5:8** [h] Phil. 1:23 **5:10** [i] Rom. 2:16; 14:10, 12 [j] Eph. 6:8 **5:11** [k] [Heb. 10:31; 12:29]

Be Reconciled to God

12 For [l]we do not commend ourselves
again to you, but give you opportunity [m]to
boast on our behalf, that you may have *an
answer* for those who boast in appearance
and not in heart. 13 For [n]if we are beside
ourselves, *it is* for God; or if we are of
sound mind, *it is* for you. 14 For the love
of Christ compels us, because we judge
thus: that [o]if One died for all, then all
died; 15 and He died for all, [p]that those who
live should live no longer for themselves,
but for Him who died for them and rose
again.

16 [q]Therefore, from now on, we regard no one according to the flesh. Even
though we have known Christ according
to the flesh, [r]yet now we know *Him thus*
no longer. 17 Therefore, if anyone [s]*is* in
Christ, *he is* [t]a new creation; [u]old things
have passed away; behold, all things have
become [v]new. 18 Now all things *are* of
God, [w]who has reconciled us to Himself
through Jesus Christ, and has given us the
ministry of reconciliation, 19 that is, that
[x]God was in Christ reconciling the world
to Himself, not imputing their trespasses
to them, and has committed to us the word
of reconciliation.

20 Now then, we are [y]ambassadors for
Christ, as though God were pleading
through us: we implore *you* on Christ's behalf, be reconciled to God. 21 For [z]He made
Him who knew no sin *to be* sin for us, that
we might become [a]the righteousness of
God in Him.

Marks of the Ministry

6 We then, *as* [a]workers together *with Him*
also [b]plead with *you* not to receive the
grace of God in vain. 2 For He says:

> [c]*"In an acceptable time I have heard you,*
> *And in the day of salvation I have*
> *helped you."**

Behold, now *is* the accepted time; behold,
now *is* the day of salvation.

3 [d]We give no offense in anything, that
our ministry may not be blamed. 4 But in
all *things* we commend ourselves [e]as ministers of God: in much patience, in tribulations, in needs, in distresses, 5 [f]in stripes,
in imprisonments, in tumults, in labors, in
sleeplessness, in fastings; 6 by purity, by
knowledge, by longsuffering, by kindness,
by the Holy Spirit, by sincere love, 7 [g]by the
word of truth, by [h]the power of God, by [i]the
armor of righteousness on the right hand
and on the left, 8 by honor and dishonor, by
evil report and good report; as deceivers,
and *yet* true; 9 as unknown, and [j]*yet* well
known; [k]as dying, and behold we live; [l]as
chastened, and *yet* not killed; 10 as sorrowful, yet always rejoicing; as poor, yet making many [m]rich; as having nothing, and *yet*
possessing all things.

Be Holy

11 O Corinthians! We have spoken openly
to you, [n]our heart is wide open. 12 You are

* **6:2** Isaiah 49:8

5:14 ***love of Christ.*** This phrase can mean either Christ's love for us or our love for Christ.
5:15 ***for Him.*** Believers are united with Jesus both in His death and in His resurrection, and therefore they participate in the new creation. That is, they receive the benefits of being restored by Christ to what God had originally created them to be (Gen. 1:26; 1 Cor. 15:45–49).
5:17 Our New Nature—The term "new nature" refers to the spiritual transformation that occurs within people when they believe in Christ as Savior. New does not mean renewed, renovated, reformed, or rehabilitated. It means completely and distinctly new, with a new family, a new set of values, new motivations, and a whole new life. The old man is still present in the new life and expresses himself in sinful deeds such as lying (Eph. 4:22; Col. 3:9). The new man, to be visible, must be *put on,* as one would put on a new suit of clothes (Col. 3:10). In other words, the new nature must be cultivated or nurtured by spiritual decisiveness to grow in Christ. We must not revert to putting on the old suit of the former life; rather, we must continue to grow in this new life (Eph. 5:8).
5:18 ***ministry of reconciliation.*** Reconciliation is the change of relation from enmity to peace. We who have been reconciled to God through Christ have the privilege of telling others that they can be reconciled to Him as well.
5:19 ***reconciling the world to Himself.*** God could change His relationship toward us because our sins have been imputed (charged) to Christ instead of to us. If we believe in Jesus, God counts Jesus' righteousness as our righteousness (v. 21).
5:20 ***ambassadors.*** Ambassadors are representatives of the sovereign who sends them, the "stand in" for their own ruler in a foreign country. Christians have been called by their King to serve as ambassadors in a world that is in rebellion against Him, with the responsibility to bring a message of peace and of reconciliation.
6:1 ***in vain.*** Believers who live for themselves may have received the grace of God, but they will miss out on a heavenly reward for their service to Him. Paul encourages those who have been saved to work out or develop their salvation (Phil. 2:12). The Corinthians were failing at this very point. They were saved and stuck, so to speak.
6:4 ***in much patience.*** Believers must not expect that it will be easy or comfortable to be a disciple, but it will be more deeply fulfilling than anything else could be.

5:12 [l] 2 Cor. 3:1 [m] 2 Cor. 1:14 **5:13** [n] 2 Cor. 11:1, 16; 12:11 **5:14** [o] [Rom. 5:15; 6:6] **5:15** [p] [Rom. 6:11] **5:16** [q] 2 Cor. 10:3 [r] [Matt. 12:50] **5:17** [s] [John 6:63] [t] [Rom. 8:9] [u] Is. 43:18; 65:17 [v] [Rom. 6:3–10] **5:18** [w] Rom. 5:10 **5:19** [x] [Rom. 3:24] **5:20** [y] Eph. 6:20 **5:21** [z] Is. 53:6, 9 [a] [Rom. 1:17; 3:21] **6:1** [a] 1 Cor. 3:9 [b] 2 Cor. 5:20 **6:2** [c] Is. 49:8 **6:3** [d] Rom. 14:13 **6:4** [e] 1 Cor. 4:1 **6:5** [f] 2 Cor. 11:23 **6:7** [g] 2 Cor. 7:14 [h] 1 Cor. 2:4 [i] 2 Cor. 10:4 **6:9** [j] 2 Cor. 4:2; 5:11 [k] 1 Cor. 4:9, 11 [l] Ps. 118:18 **6:10** [m] [2 Cor. 8:9] **6:11** [n] 2 Cor. 7:3

not restricted by us, but °you are restricted by your *own* affections. ¹³Now in return for the same ᵖ(I speak as to children), you also be open.

¹⁴ᵃDo not be unequally yoked together with unbelievers. For ʳwhat fellowship has righteousness with lawlessness? And what communion has light with darkness? ¹⁵And what accord has Christ with Belial? Or what part has a believer with an unbeliever? ¹⁶And what agreement has the temple of God with idols? For ˢyou* are the temple of the living God. As God has said:

> ᵗ*"I will dwell in them*
> *And walk among them.*
> *I will be their God,*
> *And they shall be My people."**

¹⁷Therefore

> ᵘ*"Come out from among them*
> *And be separate, says the Lord.*
> *Do not touch what is unclean,*
> *And I will receive you."**
> ¹⁸ *"I* ᵛ*will be a Father to you,*
> *And you shall be My* ʷ*sons and daughters,*
> *Says the* LORD *Almighty."**

7 Therefore,ᵃ having these promises, beloved, let us cleanse ourselves from all filthiness of the flesh and spirit, perfecting holiness in the fear of God.

The Corinthians' Repentance

²Open *your hearts* to us. We have wronged no one, we have corrupted no one, ᵇwe have cheated no one. ³I do not say *this* to condemn; for ᶜI have said before that you are in our hearts, to die together and to live together. ⁴ᵈGreat *is* my boldness of speech toward you, ᵉgreat *is* my boasting on your behalf. ᶠI am filled with comfort. I am exceedingly joyful in all our tribulation.

⁵For indeed, ᵍwhen we came to Macedonia, our bodies had no rest, but ʰwe were troubled on every side. ⁱOutside *were* conflicts, inside *were* fears. ⁶Nevertheless ʲGod, who comforts the downcast, comforted us by ᵏthe coming of Titus, ⁷and not only by his coming, but also by the consolation with which he was comforted in you, when he told me of your earnest desire, your mourning, your zeal for me, so that I rejoiced even more.

⁸For even if I made you ˡsorry with my letter, I do not regret it; ᵐthough I did regret it. For I perceive that the same epistle made you sorry, though only for a while. ⁹Now I rejoice, not that you were made sorry, but that your sorrow led to repentance. For you were made sorry in a godly manner, that you might suffer loss from us in nothing. ¹⁰For ⁿgodly sorrow produces repentance *leading* to salvation, not to be regretted; °but the sorrow of the world produces death. ¹¹For observe this very thing, that you sorrowed in a godly manner: What diligence it produced in you, *what* ᵖclearing of *yourselves, what* indignation, *what* fear, *what* vehement desire, *what* zeal, *what* vindication! In all *things* you proved yourselves to be ᵠclear in this matter. ¹²Therefore, although I wrote to you, *I did* not *do it* for the sake of him who had done the wrong, nor for the sake of him who suffered wrong, ʳbut that our care for you in the sight of God might appear to you.

The Joy of Titus

¹³Therefore we have been comforted in your comfort. And we rejoiced exceedingly more for the joy of Titus, because his spirit ˢhas been refreshed by you all. ¹⁴For if in anything I have boasted to him about you, I am not ashamed. But as we spoke all things to you in truth, even so our boasting to Titus was found true. ¹⁵And his affections are greater for you as he remembers ᵗthe obedience of you all, how with fear and trembling you received him. ¹⁶Therefore I rejoice that ᵘI have confidence in you in everything.

---

* **6:16** NU-Text reads *we.* • Leviticus 26:12; Jeremiah 32:38; Ezekiel 37:27 * **6:17** Isaiah 52:11; Ezekiel 20:34, 41 * **6:18** 2 Samuel 7:14

6:14 unequally yoked together with unbelievers. This verse has most often been applied to the subject of marriage, warning believers not to bind themselves for life to one who does not love the Lord.

6:15 Belial. This term for Satan occurs only here in the New Testament. It refers to one who is vile and wicked and who causes destruction.

6:16 you are the temple. This reference to Leviticus 26:11–12 and Ezekiel 37:27 reminds believers of their relationship with God. Since the Holy Spirit is living in them, they are God's new dwelling place (1 Cor. 6:19).

6:17 be separate. Paul was not encouraging isolation from unbelievers (1 Cor. 9:5–13) but discouraging compromise with their sinful values and practices. He was urging them (and us) to maintain integrity in the world just as Christ did (John 15:14–16; Phil. 2:14–16).

7:1 perfecting holiness. This means dedicating ourselves to Christ and living righteously (Heb. 6:1).

7:3 you are in our hearts. Paul was not throwing his weight around or trying to be controlling. He loved the Corinthians and wanted the very best for them.

7:10 produces repentance. A person can be sorry that he or she was caught in sin, or sorry to have to bear the consequences, without repenting of sin. True sorrow leads to a change of heart and a turning to God. Repentance means changing direction, and results in spiritual deliverance.

6:12 °2 Cor. 12:15 **6:13** ᵖ1 Cor. 4:14 **6:14** ᵠ1 Cor. 5:9 ʳEph. 5:6, 7, 11 **6:16** ˢ[1 Cor. 3:16, 17; 6:19] ᵗEzek. 37:26, 27 **6:17** ᵘIs. 52:11 **6:18** ᵛ2 Sam. 7:14 ʷ[Rom. 8:14] **7:1** ᵃ[1 John 3:3] **7:2** ᵇActs 20:33 **7:3** ᶜ2 Cor. 6:11, 12 **7:4** ᵈ2 Cor. 3:12 ᵉ1 Cor. 1:4 ᶠPhil. 2:17 **7:5** ᵍ2 Cor. 2:13 ʰ2 Cor. 4:8 ⁱDeut. 32:25 **7:6** ʲ2 Cor. 1:3, 4 ᵏ2 Cor. 2:13; 7:13 **7:8** ˡ2 Cor. 2:2 ᵐ2 Cor. 2:4 **7:10** ⁿMatt. 26:75 °Prov. 17:22 **7:11** ᵖEph. 5:11 ᵠ2 Cor. 2:5–11 **7:12** ʳ2 Cor. 2:4 **7:13** ˢRom. 15:32 **7:15** ᵗ2 Cor. 2:9 **7:16** ᵘ2 Thess. 3:4

Excel in Giving

8 Moreover, brethren, we make known to you the grace of God bestowed on the churches of Macedonia: ²that in a great trial of affliction the abundance of their joy and ᵃtheir deep poverty abounded in the riches of their liberality. ³For I bear witness that according to *their* ability, yes, and beyond *their* ability, *they were* freely willing, ⁴imploring us with much urgency that we would receive* the gift and ᵇthe fellowship of the ministering to the saints. ⁵And not *only* as we had hoped, but they first ᶜgave themselves to the Lord, and *then* to us by the ᵈwill of God. ⁶So ᵉwe urged Titus, that as he had begun, so he would also complete this grace in you as well. ⁷But as ᶠyou abound in everything—in faith, in speech, in knowledge, in all diligence, and in your love for us—*see* ᵍthat you abound in this grace also.

Christ Our Pattern

⁸ʰI speak not by commandment, but I am testing the sincerity of your love by the diligence of others. ⁹For you know the grace of our Lord Jesus Christ, ⁱthat though He was rich, yet for your sakes He became poor, that you through His poverty might become ʲrich.

¹⁰And in this ᵏI give advice: ˡIt is to your advantage not only to be doing what you began and ᵐwere desiring to do a year ago; ¹¹but now you also must complete the doing of it; that as *there was* a readiness to desire *it*, so *there* also *may be* a completion out of what *you* have. ¹²For ⁿif there is first a willing mind, *it is* accepted according to what one has, *and* not according to what he does not have.

¹³For I do not *mean* that others should be eased and you burdened; ¹⁴but by an equality, *that* now at this time your abundance *may supply* their lack, that their abundance also may *supply* your lack— that there may be equality. ¹⁵As it is written, ᵒ"He who gathered much had nothing left over, and he who gathered little had no lack."*

Collection for the Judean Saints

¹⁶But thanks *be* to God who puts* the same earnest care for you into the heart of Titus. ¹⁷For he not only accepted the exhortation, but being more diligent, he went to you of his own accord. ¹⁸And we have sent with him ᵖthe brother whose praise *is* in the gospel throughout all the churches, ¹⁹and not only *that*, but who was also ᵠchosen by the churches to travel with us with this gift, which is administered by us ʳto the glory of the Lord Himself and *to show* your ready mind, ²⁰avoiding this: that anyone should blame us in this lavish gift which is administered by us— ²¹ˢproviding honorable things, not only in the sight of the Lord, but also in the sight of men.

²²And we have sent with them our brother whom we have often proved diligent in many things, but now much more diligent, because of the great confidence which *we have* in you. ²³If *anyone* inquires about ᵗTitus, *he is* my partner and fellow worker concerning you. Or if our brethren *are inquired about, they are* ᵘmessengers of the churches, the glory of Christ. ²⁴Therefore show to them, and* before the churches, the proof of your love and of our ᵛboasting on your behalf.

Administering the Gift

9 Now concerning ᵃthe ministering to the saints, it is superfluous for me to write to you; ²for I know your willingness, about which I boast of you to the Macedonians, that Achaia was ready a ᵇyear ago; and your zeal has stirred up the majority. ³ᶜYet I have sent the brethren, lest our boasting of you should be in vain in this respect, that, as I said, you may be ready; ⁴lest if *some* Macedonians come with me and find you unprepared, we (not to mention you!) should be ashamed of this confident boasting.* ⁵Therefore I thought it necessary to exhort the brethren to go to you ahead of time, and prepare your generous gift beforehand, which *you had* previously promised, that it may be ready as *a matter of* generosity and not as a grudging obligation.

---

*8:4 NU-Text and M-Text omit *that we would receive*, thus changing text to *urgency for the favor and fellowship ....* *8:15 Exodus 16:18 *8:16 NU-Text reads *has put.* *8:24 NU-Text and M-Text omit *and.* *9:4 NU-Text reads *this confidence.*

8:1 *Macedonia.* Macedonia corresponds to the northern part of present day Greece. Paul had established churches in the Macedonian cities of Philippi, Thessalonica, and Berea.

8:8 *testing the sincerity of your love.* Generosity is the natural result of sincere love.

8:9 *you ... might become rich.* Jesus offers forgiveness, justification, regeneration, eternal life, and glorification. He purchased us from slavery to sin, giving us the position of children of God with free access to His presence.

8:10 *advantage.* Giving in this life is an investment for eternity (Matt. 6:19–21).

9:4 *Macedonians.* Paul was in Macedonia when he wrote this letter (2:13; 7:5). When he made his visit to Corinth he would no doubt bring traveling companions from Macedonia.

8:2 ᵈ Mark 12:44 **8:4** ᵇ Rom. 15:25, 26 **8:5** ᶜ [Rom. 12:1, 2] ᵈ [Eph. 6:6] **8:6** ᵉ 2 Cor. 8:17; 12:18 **8:7** ᶠ [1 Cor. 1:5; 12:13] ᵍ 2 Cor. 9:8 **8:8** ʰ 1 Cor. 7:6 **8:9** ⁱ Phil. 2:6, 7 ʲ Rom. 9:23 **8:10** ᵏ 1 Cor. 7:25, 40 ˡ [Heb. 13:16] ᵐ 2 Cor. 9:2 **8:12** ⁿ Mark 12:43, 44 **8:15** ᵒ Ex. 16:18 **8:18** ᵖ 2 Cor. 12:18 **8:19** ᵠ 1 Cor. 16:3, 4 ʳ 2 Cor. 4:15 **8:21** ˢ Rom. 12:17 **8:23** ᵗ 2 Cor. 7:13, 14 ᵘ Phil. 2:25 **8:24** ᵛ 2 Cor. 7:4, 14; 9:2 **9:1** ᵃ Gal. 2:10 **9:2** ᵇ 2 Cor. 8:10 **9:3** ᶜ 2 Cor. 8:6, 17

The Cheerful Giver

⁶ᵈBut this *I say:* He who sows sparingly will also reap sparingly, and he who sows bountifully will also reap bountifully. ⁷*So let* each one *give* as he purposes in his heart, ᵉnot grudgingly or of necessity; for ᶠGod loves a cheerful giver. ⁸ᵍAnd God *is* able to make all grace abound toward you, that you, always having all sufficiency in all *things,* may have an abundance for every good work. ⁹As it is written:

> ʰ "He has dispersed abroad,
> He has given to the poor;
> His righteousness endures forever."*

¹⁰Now may* He who ⁱsupplies seed to the sower, and bread for food, supply and multiply the seed you have *sown* and increase the fruits of your ʲrighteousness, ¹¹while *you are* enriched in everything for all liberality, ᵏwhich causes thanksgiving through us to God. ¹²For the administration of this service not only ˡsupplies the needs of the saints, but also is abounding through many thanksgivings to God, ¹³through the proof of this ministry, they ᵐglorify God for the obedience of your confession to the gospel of Christ, and for *your* liberal ⁿsharing with them and all *men,* ¹⁴and by their prayer for you, who long for you because of the exceeding ᵒgrace of God in you. ¹⁵Thanks *be* to God ᵖfor His indescribable gift!

The Spiritual War

10 Now ᵃI, Paul, myself am pleading with you by the meekness and gentleness of Christ—ᵇwho in presence *am* lowly among you, but being absent am bold toward you. ²But I beg *you* ᶜthat when I am present I may not be bold with that confidence by which I intend to be bold against some, who think of us as if we

walked according to the flesh. ³For though we walk in the flesh, we do not war according to the flesh. ⁴ᵈFor the weapons ᵉof our warfare *are* not carnal but ᶠmighty in God ᵍfor pulling down strongholds, ⁵ʰcasting down arguments and every high thing that exalts itself against the knowledge of God, bringing every thought into captivity to the obedience of Christ, ⁶ⁱand being ready to punish all disobedience when ʲyour obedience is fulfilled.

Reality of Paul's Authority

⁷ᵏDo you look at things according to the outward appearance? ˡIf anyone is convinced in himself that he is Christ's, let him again consider this in himself, that just as he *is* Christ's, even so ᵐwe *are* Christ's.* ⁸For even if I should boast somewhat more ⁿabout our authority, which the Lord gave us* for edification and not for your destruction, ᵒI shall not be ashamed— ⁹lest I seem to terrify you by letters. ¹⁰"For *his* letters," they say, "*are* weighty and powerful, but ᵖhis bodily presence *is* weak, and *his* ᵠspeech contemptible." ¹¹Let such a person consider this, that what we are in word by letters when we are absent, such *we will* also *be* in deed when we are present.

Limits of Paul's Authority

¹²ʳFor we dare not class ourselves or compare ourselves with those who commend themselves. But they, measuring themselves by themselves, and comparing themselves among themselves, are not wise. ¹³ˢWe, however, will not boast beyond measure, but within the limits of the sphere which God appointed us—a sphere

* **9:9** Psalm 112:9   * **9:10** NU-Text reads *Now He who supplies … will supply….*   * **10:7** NU-Text reads *even as we are.*   * **10:8** NU-Text omits *us.*

9:6–8 Giving—There is no better indicator of growth in the new life than in the area of giving. This passage and others deal with several aspects of giving:

1. Giving should be done generously, even extravagantly (2 Cor. 9:6).
2. Giving should be done cheerfully (2 Cor. 9:7).
3. Giving should be regular (1 Cor. 16:2).
4. Giving should be systematic (1 Cor. 16:2).
5. Giving should be proportionate (2 Cor. 8:3).

God is not primarily concerned about the amount of the gift, but with the motive that lies behind it. The person who fails to honor God with his money actually robs God (Mal. 3:8), not because it impoverishes God but because it denies the God-ordained means for the support of His work and His ministers. For the child of God who honors God with his money, God promises abundant blessing (Mal. 3:10; Luke 6:38) and the provision of his every need (Phil. 4:19).

9:6 reap sparingly. The law of the harvest is referred to repeatedly in Scripture (Prov. 11:24–25; 19:17; Luke 6:38; Gal. 6:7). If you do not plant, you will have no harvest.

9:8 God is able. God sees to it that the generous giver will not suffer want. Instead, God generously provides for those who give so that they can continue to do so.

9:15 indescribable gift. Our gifts can never compare with God's sacrifice for us.

10:4 our warfare. The world is hostile to Christ and His followers because the world is following Satan. The life of a believer is not one of ease but a constant spiritual battle.

10:8 edification. Paul's exhortation was aimed at correcting abuses, not the tearing down of the church.

9:6 ᵈ Prov. 11:24; 22:9   **9:7** ᵉ Deut. 15:7   ᶠ Rom. 12:8   **9:8** ᵍ [Prov. 11:24]   **9:9** ʰ Ps. 112:9   **9:10** ⁱ Is. 55:10   ʲ Hos. 10:12   **9:11** ᵏ 2 Cor. 1:11   **9:12** ˡ 2 Cor. 8:14   **9:13** ᵐ [Matt. 5:16]   ⁿ [Heb. 13:16]   **9:14** ᵒ 2 Cor. 8:1   **9:15** ᵖ [James 1:17]   **10:1** ᵃ Rom. 12:1   ᵇ 1 Thess. 2:7   **10:2** ᶜ 1 Cor. 4:21   **10:4** ᵈ Eph. 6:13   ᵉ 1 Tim. 1:18   ᶠ Acts 7:22   ᵍ Jer. 1:10   **10:5** ʰ 1 Cor. 1:19   **10:6** ⁱ 2 Cor. 13:2, 10   ʲ 2 Cor. 7:15   **10:7** ᵏ [John 7:24]   ˡ 1 Cor. 1:12; 14:37   ᵐ 1 Cor. 3:23   **10:8** ⁿ 2 Cor. 13:10   ᵒ 2 Cor. 7:14   **10:10** ᵖ Gal. 4:13   ᵠ 2 Cor. 11:6   **10:12** ʳ 2 Cor. 5:12   **10:13** ˢ 2 Cor. 10:15

which especially includes you. [14]For we are not overextending ourselves (as though *our authority* did not extend to you), [f]for it was to you that we came with the gospel of Christ; [15]not boasting of things beyond measure, *that is,* [u]in other men's labors, but having hope, *that* as your faith is increased, we shall be greatly enlarged by you in our sphere, [16]to preach the gospel in the *regions* beyond you, *and* not to boast in another man's sphere of accomplishment.

[17]But [v]"he who glories, let him glory in the LORD."* [18]For [w]not he who commends himself is approved, but [x]whom the Lord commends.

Concern for Their Faithfulness

11 Oh, that you would bear with me in a little [a]folly—and indeed you do bear with me. [2]For I am [b]jealous for you with godly jealousy. For [c]I have betrothed you to one husband, [d]that I may present *you* [e]*as* a chaste virgin to Christ. [3]But I fear, lest somehow, as [f]the serpent deceived Eve by his craftiness, so your minds [g]may be corrupted from the simplicity* that is in Christ. [4]For if he who comes preaches another Jesus whom we have not preached, or *if* you receive a different spirit which you have not received, or a [h]different gospel which you have not accepted—you may well put up with it!

Paul and False Apostles

[5]For I consider that [i]I am not at all inferior to the most eminent apostles. [6]Even though [j]I *am* untrained in speech, yet *I am* not [k]in knowledge. But [l]we have been thoroughly manifested* among you in all things.

[7]Did I commit sin in humbling myself that you might be exalted, because I preached the gospel of God to you [m]free of charge? [8]I robbed other churches, taking wages *from them* to minister to you. [9]And when I was present with you, and in need,

[n]I was a burden to no one, for what I lacked [o]the brethren who came from Macedonia supplied. And in everything I kept myself from being burdensome to you, and so I will keep *myself.* [10][p]As the truth of Christ is in me, [q]no one shall stop me from this boasting in the regions of Achaia. [11]Why? [r]Because I do not love you? God knows!

[12]But what I do, I will also continue to do, [s]that I may cut off the opportunity from those who desire an opportunity to be regarded just as we are in the things of which they boast. [13]For such [t]are false apostles, [u]deceitful workers, transforming themselves into apostles of Christ. [14]And no wonder! For Satan himself transforms himself into [v]an angel of light. [15]Therefore *it is* no great thing if his ministers also transform themselves into ministers of righteousness, [w]whose end will be according to their works.

Reluctant Boasting

[16]I say again, let no one think me a fool. If otherwise, at least receive me as a fool, that I also may boast a little. [17]What I speak, [x]I speak not according to the Lord, but as it were, foolishly, in this confidence of boasting. [18]Seeing that many boast according to the flesh, I also will boast. [19]For you put up with fools gladly, [y]since you *yourselves* are wise! [20]For you put up with it [z]if one brings you into bondage, if one devours *you,* if one takes *from you,* if one exalts himself, if one strikes you on the face. [21]To *our* shame [a]I say that we were too weak for that! But [b]in whatever anyone is bold—I speak foolishly—I am bold also.

Suffering for Christ

[22]Are they [c]Hebrews? So *am* I. Are they Israelites? So *am* I. Are they the seed of

---

* **10:17** Jeremiah 9:24   * **11:3** NU-Text adds *and purity.*   * **11:6** NU-Text omits *been.*

10:16 *regions beyond you.* Paul states in Romans that his ambition was to preach the gospel in Spain (Rom. 15:24).

11:2 *jealous.* Usually jealousy has a negative connotation to us—we confuse jealousy with envy or spite. The word has the same root as "zealous," and it can mean a sincere and energetic protection of the rights or purity of a person or place.

11:3 *simplicity.* In this sense, simplicity indicates sincerity or lack of double motives or cunning.

11:6 *untrained in speech.* Paul may have lacked gifts as a professional speaker, but he did not lack knowledge since he had received direct revelation from the Lord (Gal. 1:11–12).

11:7 *free of charge.* Professional philosophers and teachers in Greek society charged for teaching.

11:14 *transforms himself into an angel of light.* Don't make the mistake of believing that evil always appears grotesque, ugly, or repulsive. Satan's main tool is deception and he is quite capable of making evil appear beautiful.

11:17 *I speak not according to the Lord.* This kind of boasting was not characteristic of the Lord. Jesus Christ was an example of humility (Phil. 2:5–11).

11:18 *according to the flesh.* The false apostles measured themselves by their own standards rather than by God's.

11:21 *too weak.* Paul's critics had accused him of being weak (10:10). He sarcastically said that he was too weak to rule the Corinthians harshly as the false apostles had done.

10:14 [r] 1 Cor. 3:5, 6   **10:15** [u] Rom. 15:20   **10:17** [v] Jer. 9:24   **10:18** [w] Prov. 27:2   [x] Rom. 2:29   **11:1** [a] 2 Cor. 11:4, 16, 19   **11:2** [b] Gal. 4:17   [c] Hos. 2:19   [d] Col. 1:28   [e] Lev. 21:13   **11:3** [f] Gen. 3:4, 13   [g] Eph. 6:24   **11:4** [h] Gal. 1:6–8   **11:5** [i] 2 Cor. 12:11   **11:6** [j] [1 Cor. 1:17]   [k] [Eph. 3:4]   [l] [2 Cor. 12:12]   **11:7** [m] 1 Cor. 9:18   **11:9** [n] Acts 20:33   [o] Phil. 4:10   **11:10** [p] Rom. 1:9; 9:1   [q] 1 Cor. 9:15   **11:11** [r] 2 Cor. 6:11; 12:15   **11:12** [s] 1 Cor. 9:12   **11:13** [t] Phil. 1:15   [u] Phil. 3:2   **11:14** [v] Gal. 1:8   **11:15** [w] [Phil. 3:19]   **11:17** [x] 1 Cor. 7:6   **11:19** [y] 1 Cor. 4:10   **11:20** [z] [Gal. 2:4; 4:3, 9; 5:1]   **11:21** [a] 2 Cor. 10:10   [b] Phil. 3:4   **11:22** [c] Phil. 3:4–6

Abraham? So *am* I. ²³Are they ministers of Christ?—I speak as a fool—I *am* more: ᵈin labors more abundant, ᵉin stripes above measure, in prisons more frequently, ᶠin deaths often. ²⁴From the Jews five times I received ᵍforty ʰ*stripes* minus one. ²⁵Three times I was ᶦbeaten with rods; ʲonce I was stoned; three times I ᵏwas shipwrecked; a night and a day I have been in the deep; ²⁶*in* journeys often, *in* perils of waters, *in* perils of robbers, ˡ*in* perils of *my own* country-men, ᵐ*in* perils of the Gentiles, *in* perils in the city, *in* perils in the wilderness, *in* perils in the sea, *in* perils among false brethren; ²⁷in weariness and toil, ⁿin sleeplessness often, ᵒin hunger and thirst, in ᵖfastings often, in cold and nakedness— ²⁸besides the other things, what comes upon me dai-ly: ۹my deep concern for all the churches. ²⁹ʳWho is weak, and I am not weak? Who is made to stumble, and I do not burn *with indignation?*

³⁰If I must boast, ˢI will boast in the things which concern my infirmity. ³¹ˡᵗThe God and Father of our Lord Jesus Christ, ᵘwho is blessed forever, knows that I am not lying. ³²ᵛIn Damascus the governor, under Aretas the king, was guarding the city of the Damascenes with a garrison, desiring to arrest me; ³³but I was let down in a basket through a window in the wall, and escaped from his hands.

The Vision of Paradise

12 It is doubtless* not profitable for me to boast. I will come to ᵃvisions and ᵇrevelations of the Lord: ²I know a man ᶜin Christ who fourteen years ago—whether in the body I do not know, or whether out of the body I do not know, God knows—such a one ᵈwas caught up to the third heaven. ³And I know such a man—whether in the body or out of the body I do not know, God knows— ⁴how he was caught up into

ᵉParadise and heard inexpressible words, which it is not lawful for a man to utter. ⁵Of such a one I will boast; yet of myself I will not ᶠboast, except in my infirmities. ⁶For though I might desire to boast, I will not be a fool; for I will speak the truth. But I refrain, lest anyone should think of me above what he sees in me *to be* or hears from me.

The Thorn in the Flesh

⁷And lest I should be exalted above mea-sure by the abundance of the revelations, a ᵍthorn in the flesh was given to me, ʰa messenger of Satan to buffet me, lest I be exalted above measure. ⁸ᶦConcerning this thing I pleaded with the Lord three times that it might depart from me. ⁹And He said to me, "My grace is sufficient for you, for My strength is made perfect in weakness." Therefore most gladly ʲI will rather boast in my infirmities, ᵏthat the power of Christ may rest upon me. ¹⁰Therefore ˡI take plea-sure in infirmities, in reproaches, in needs, in persecutions, in distresses, for Christ's sake. ᵐFor when I am weak, then I am strong.

Signs of an Apostle

¹¹I have become ⁿa fool in boasting;* you have compelled me. For I ought to have been commended by you; for ᵒin nothing was I behind the most eminent apostles, though ᵖI am nothing. ¹²۹Truly the signs of an apostle were accomplished among you with all perseverance, in signs and ʳwon-ders and mighty ˢdeeds. ¹³For what is it in which you were inferior to other churches, except that I myself was not burdensome to you? Forgive me this wrong!

* **12:1** NU-Text reads *necessary, though not profitable, to boast.*   * **12:11** NU-Text omits *in boasting.*

11:23 *as a fool.* Paul acknowledged the silliness of such bragging. He knew that only God had made his preaching and service effective. Paul's credentials were superior to those of the false teachers, but even so his ministry had authority only because he received it from God.

12:1 *visions and revelations.* This boasting may have been to counter similar claims by the false teachers.

12:2 *fourteen years.* Paul wrote 2 Corinthians in A.D. 56; 14 years earlier would have been A.D. 42, probably when he was in Antioch (Acts 11:26). ***third heaven.*** It was common to speak of three "heavens": The first is the atmosphere where the birds fly; the second is the place of the sun, moon, and stars; the third is where God dwells.

12:7 *thorn in the flesh.* Most commentators inter-pret Paul's thorn as a physical ailment, and many suggest that it was eye trouble on the basis of Gala-tians 4:15. It is also possible that "flesh" is a reference to the fallen human nature, in which case the thorn could be a temptation, or it could refer to persecution

or opposition. ***messenger of Satan.*** God permitted Satan to afflict Paul as he did Job (Job 1–2).

12:11 *compelled me.* Only the fact that the Corin-thians had listened to the silly slander against Paul had made him waste time on boasting.

12:12 *signs of an apostle.* God has often used mir-acles as supernatural evidences of His authority in a new work (Acts 14:3).

11:23 ᵈ 1 Cor. 15:10 ᵉ Acts 9:16 ᶠ 1 Cor. 15:30 **11:24** ᵍ Deut. 25:3 ʰ 2 Cor. 6:5 **11:25** ᶦ Acts 16:22, 23; 21:32 ʲ Acts 14:5, 19 ᵏ Acts 27:1–44 **11:26** ˡ Acts 9:23, 24; 13:45, 50; 17:5, 13 ᵐ Acts 14:5, 19; 19:23; 27:42 **11:27** ⁿ Acts 20:31 ᵒ 1 Cor. 4:11 ᵖ Acts 9:9; 13:2, 3; 14:23 **11:28** ۹ Acts 20:18 **11:29** ʳ [1 Cor. 8:9, 13; 9:22] **11:30** ˢ [2 Cor. 12:5, 9, 10] **11:31** ˡ 1 Thess. 2:5 ᵘ Rom. 9:5 **11:32** ᵛ Acts 9:19–25 **12:1** ᵃ Acts 16:9; 18:9; 22:17, 18; 23:11; 26:13–15; 27:23 ᵇ [Gal. 1:12; 2:2] **12:2** ᶜ Rom. 16:7 ᵈ Acts 22:17 **12:4** ᵉ Luke 23:43 **12:5** ᶠ 2 Cor. 11:30 **12:7** ᵍ Ezek. 28:24 ʰ Job 2:7 **12:8** ᶦ Matt. 26:44 **12:9** ʲ 2 Cor. 11:30 ᵏ [1 Pet. 4:14] **12:10** ˡ [Rom. 5:3; 8:35] ᵐ 2 Cor. 13:4 **12:11** ⁿ 2 Cor. 5:13; 11:1, 16; 12:6 ᵒ 2 Cor. 11:5 ᵖ 1 Cor. 3:7; 13:2; 15:9 **12:12** ۹ Rom. 15:18 ʳ Acts 15:12 ˢ Acts 14:8–10; 16:16–18; 19:11, 12; 20:6–12; 28:1–10

Love for the Church

14tNow *for* the third time I am ready to come to you. And I will not be burdensome to you; for uI do not seek yours, but you. vFor the children ought not to lay up for the parents, but the parents for the children. 15And I will very gladly spend and be spent wfor your souls; though xthe more abundantly I love you, the less I am loved.

16But be that *as it may,* yI did not burden you. Nevertheless, being crafty, I caught you by cunning! 17Did I take advantage of you by any of those whom I sent to you? 18I urged Titus, and sent our zbrother with *him.* Did Titus take advantage of you? Did we not walk in the same spirit? Did *we* not *walk* in the same steps?

19aAgain, do you think* that we excuse ourselves to you? bWe speak before God in Christ. cBut *we do* all things, beloved, for your edification. 20For I fear lest, when I come, I shall not find you such as I wish, and *that* dI shall be found by you such as you do not wish; lest *there be* contentions, jealousies, outbursts of wrath, selfish ambitions, backbitings, whisperings, conceits, tumults; 21lest, when I come again, my God ewill humble me among you, and I shall mourn for many fwho have sinned before and have not repented of the uncleanness, gfornication, and lewdness which they have practiced.

Coming with Authority

13 This *will be* athe third *time* I am coming to you. b"By the mouth of two or three witnesses every word shall be established."* 2cI have told you before, and foretell as if I were present the second time, and now being absent I write* to those dwho have sinned before, and to all the rest, that if I come again eI will not spare— 3since you seek a proof of Christ fspeaking in me,

who is not weak toward you, but mighty gin you. 4hFor though He was crucified in weakness, yet iHe lives by the power of God. For jwe also are weak in Him, but we shall live with Him by the power of God toward you.

5Examine yourselves *as to* whether you are in the faith. Test yourselves. Do you not know yourselves, kthat Jesus Christ is in you?—unless indeed you are ldisqualified. 6But I trust that you will know that we are not disqualified.

Paul Prefers Gentleness

7Now I* pray to God that you do no evil, not that we should appear approved, but that you should do what is honorable, though mwe may seem disqualified. 8For we can do nothing against the truth, but for the truth. 9For we are glad nwhen we are weak and you are strong. And this also we pray, othat you may be made complete. 10pTherefore I write these things being absent, lest being present I should use sharpness, according to the qauthority which the Lord has given me for edification and not for destruction.

Greetings and Benediction

11Finally, brethren, farewell. Become complete. rBe of good comfort, be of one mind, live in peace; and the God of love sand peace will be with you.

12tGreet one another with a holy kiss. 13All the saints greet you.

14uThe grace of the Lord Jesus Christ, and the love of God, and vthe communion of the Holy Spirit *be* with you all. Amen.

---

* **12:19** NU-Text reads *You have been thinking for a long time....* * **13:1** Deuteronomy 19:15 * **13:2** NU-Text omits *I write.* * **13:7** NU-Text reads *we.*

12:14 the third time. It is not clear whether Paul had already made two previous visits to Corinth, or whether this refers to the third attempt to visit. We know that he had tried to come and had been prevented at least once (1:15–16,23; 2:1–4).
13:4 in weakness. Christ appeared to be weak when He was crucified, but He was raised by the power of God; similarly, Paul was weak, but by the power of God he would live with Christ in strength toward them.
13:5 Examine yourselves. Paul did not doubt that they were true believers (1:1,24; 7:1; 8:1; 12:14). He wanted them to ask themselves whether they were walking according to the gospel that they professed. He wanted them to apply the same standard to themselves that they were applying to him.
13:9 complete. The Greek word for "complete" was used to describe the setting of bones and the reconciliation of alienated friends.
13:14 the communion of the Holy Spirit. At the end

of his letter, Paul identifies the solution to many of the Corinthians' problems. The Holy Spirit, who dwelled in each of them, could empower them to live righteously. Furthermore, the Spirit could reconcile them to each other. They could love and encourage each other instead of fighting each other (12:20). They needed God's grace, not selfishness; God's love, not anger; and communion, not conflict.

12:14 t 2 Cor. 1:15; 13:1, 2 u [1 Cor. 10:24–33] v 1 Cor. 4:14 **12:15** w [2 Tim. 2:10] x 2 Cor. 6:12, 13 **12:16** y 2 Cor. 11:9 **12:18** z 2 Cor. 8:18 **12:19** a 2 Cor. 5:12 b [Rom. 9:1, 2] c 1 Cor. 10:33 **12:20** d 1 Cor. 4:21 **12:21** e 2 Cor. 2:1, 4 f 2 Cor. 13:2 g 1 Cor. 5:1 **13:1** a 2 Cor. 12:14 b Deut. 17:6; 19:15 **13:2** c 2 Cor. 10:2 d 2 Cor. 12:21 e 2 Cor. 1:23; 10:11 **13:3** f Matt. 10:20 g [1 Cor. 9:2] **13:4** h [1 Pet. 3:18] i [Rom. 1:4; 6:4] j [2 Cor. 10:3, 4] **13:5** k [Gal. 4:19] l 1 Cor. 9:27 **13:7** m 2 Cor. 6:9 **13:9** n 1 Cor. 4:10 o [1 Thess. 3:10] **13:10** p 1 Cor. 4:21 q 2 Cor. 10:8 **13:11** r Rom. 12:16, 18 s Rom. 15:33 **13:12** t Rom. 16:16 **13:14** u Rom. 16:24 v Phil. 2:1

THE EPISTLE OF PAUL THE APOSTLE TO THE

GALATIANS

▶ **AUTHOR:** The Pauline authorship and the unity of this epistle are virtually unchallenged. The first verse clearly identifies the author as, "Paul, an apostle" as does 5:2, "I, Paul, say to you." In fact, Paul actually wrote, or at least finished, Galatians by his own hand (6:11) instead of dictating it to a secretary, as was his usual practice. There is some controversy as to whether Paul was writing to the northern Galatians or the southern Galatians. If the former theory is correct, this epistle was written sometime during Paul's third missionary journey in A.D. 53–56. If the latter theory is correct, this epistle was written before the Jerusalem council (Acts 15) in A.D. 49, right after the first missionary journey. Regardless of the timing of its writing, Galatians affords us a clear glimpse into the ministry and theology of Paul as a Jewish Christian.

▶ **TIME:** C. A.D. 49–53   ▶ **KEY VERSES:** Gal. 2:20–21

▶ **THEME:** The big question for the church in its first generation was, "Did a person have to become a Jew before they could be a Christian?" There were many Jews who thought this was the case. Three things happened to move the church away from this perspective: Peter's vision as recorded in Acts 10; the decision of the Jerusalem council in Acts 15 that Gentiles didn't need to adopt all the Jewish customs; and Paul's received revelation that he was to deliver to the Gentiles. Even with all this evidence, there were still some Jews who followed Paul around and attempted to teach Jewish regulations to his newly planted churches. Paul was furious at these events and used this letter to set the record straight. Christ brought freedom and died for people of all cultures, an idea that was a new paradigm for many of the Jews who were stuck in a "God loves us most" mode. Paul goes to great lengths to review with the Galatians what he had taught them and where this teaching had come from.

Greeting

1 Paul, an apostle (not from men nor through man, but *a*through Jesus Christ and God the Father *b*who raised Him from the dead), ²and all the brethren who are with me,

To the churches of Galatia:

³Grace to you and peace from God the Father and our Lord Jesus Christ, ⁴*c*who gave Himself for our sins, that He might deliver us *d*from this present evil age, according to the will of our God and Father, ⁵to whom *be* glory forever and ever. Amen.

Only One Gospel

⁶I marvel that you are turning away so soon *e*from Him who called you in the grace of Christ, to a different gospel, ⁷*f*which is not another; but there are some *g*who trouble you and want to *h*pervert the gospel of Christ. ⁸But even if *i*we, or an angel from

1:1 *an apostle.* Paul calls himself this title to assert his divinely given authority to speak to the problem confronting the Galatian churches. *through Jesus Christ and God the Father.* Paul makes reference to his unique call to be an apostle (vv. 15–16) which came to him at the same time as his salvation on the road to Damascus (Acts 26:12–18).
1:2 *To the churches of Galatia.* Galatians is a circular letter, intended for several churches.
1:3 *Grace to you and peace.* These words are a variation from the standard greeting of ancient letters in Paul's time. Paul adds the Greek word for the traditional Hebrew greeting, "peace."
1:4 *deliver us from this present evil age.* This passage is similar to Colossians 1:13, which states, "He has delivered us from the power of darkness and

conveyed us into the kingdom of the Son of His love." Both passages develop this truth based on Christ's redemptive work (Col. 1:14), implying that the word "deliver" refers to sanctification in the face of temptations of this present age.
1:6–7 *marvel.* Use of this word reveals Paul's ongoing shock at the Galatians' defection from the gospel of God's undeserved grace. The Galatians had unwittingly fallen for a different message.
1:8–9 *If anyone.* Paul's concern for the purity of the gospel message is revealed by his assertion that he

1:1 *a* Acts 9:6 *b* Acts 2:24   **1:4** *c* [Matt. 20:28] *d* Heb. 2:5   **1:6** *e* Gal. 1:15; 5:8   **1:7** *f* 2 Cor. 11:4 *g* Gal. 5:10, 12 *h* 2 Cor. 2:17   **1:8** *i* 1 Cor. 16:22

heaven, preach any other gospel to you than what we have preached to you, let him be accursed. 9As we have said before, so now I say again, if anyone preaches any other gospel to you *i*than what you have received, let him be accursed.

10For *k*do I now *l*persuade men, or God? Or *m*do I seek to please men? For if I still pleased men, I would not be a bondservant of Christ.

Call to Apostleship

11*n*But I make known to you, brethren, that the gospel which was preached by me is not according to man. 12For *o*I neither received it from man, nor was I taught *it*, but *it came* *p*through the revelation of Jesus Christ.

13For you have heard of my former conduct in Judaism, how *q*I persecuted the church of God beyond measure and *r*tried to destroy it. 14And I advanced in Judaism beyond many of my contemporaries in my own nation, *s*being more exceedingly zealous *t*for the traditions of my fathers.

15But when it pleased God, *u*who separated me from my mother's womb and called *me* through His grace, 16*v*to reveal His Son in me, that *w*I might preach Him among the Gentiles, I did not immediately confer with *x*flesh and blood, 17nor did I go up to Jerusalem to those *who were* apostles before me; but I went to Arabia, and returned again to Damascus.

Contacts at Jerusalem

18Then after three years *y*I went up to Jerusalem to see Peter,* and remained with

him fifteen days. 19But *z*I saw none of the other apostles except *a*James, the Lord's brother. 20(Now *concerning* the things which I write to you, indeed, before God, I do not lie.)

21*b*Afterward I went into the regions of Syria and Cilicia. 22And I was unknown by face to the churches of Judea which *c*were in Christ. 23But they were *d*hearing only, "He who formerly *e*persecuted us now preaches the faith which he once *tried to* destroy." 24And they *f*glorified God in me.

Defending the Gospel

2 Then after fourteen years *a*I went up again to Jerusalem with Barnabas, and also took Titus with *me*. 2And I went up by revelation, and communicated to them that gospel which I preach among the Gentiles, but *b*privately to those who were of reputation, lest by any means *c*I might run, or had run, in vain. 3Yet not even Titus who *was* with me, being a Greek, was compelled to be circumcised. 4And *this occurred* because of *d*false brethren secretly brought in (who came in by stealth to spy out our *e*liberty which we have in Christ Jesus, *f*that they might bring us into bondage), 5to whom we did not yield submission even for an hour, that *g*the truth of the gospel might continue with you.

6But from those *h*who seemed to be something—whatever they were, it makes no difference to me; *i*God shows personal favoritism to no man—for those who

* 1:18 NU-Text reads *Cephas*.

---

would condemn to destruction anyone who taught a false gospel.
1:10 *seek to please men.* This was neither Paul's motivation nor the source of his authority (v. 1). Paul continually sought the approval of God. He did not base his decisions on the opinions of other people. Instead he single-mindedly aimed at pleasing God (Phil. 3:14).
1:13–14 *Judaism.* This refers to the Jewish way of life, which was based partly on the Old Testament and partly on additional traditions (Matt. 15:2).
1:15–17 *separated me . . . called me through His grace.* Paul related that God had chosen him to be an apostle (v. 1) before his birth, not unlike Jeremiah's call to be a prophet (Jer. 1:5). Paul, like the Judaizers in Galatia, had previously tried to earn his salvation by works (v. 14). He needed no human validation because of the way he had received his message.
1:19 *James, the Lord's brother.* This reference indicates that the "apostles" were not always restricted to the Twelve.
2:1 *fourteen years.* This timeframe may refer to twelve full years plus fractions of the first and last years (1:18). The span could date from Paul's previous visit to Jerusalem, but more likely from his conversion.
2:3 *Titus.* One of Paul's companions was a kind of "test-case" Gentile. ***circumcised.*** This term introduces a central topic of the Jewish false teachers, one which Paul addresses repeatedly in Galatians

(5:2–3,6). Unlike Timothy, whom Paul had circumcised because Timothy's mother was Jewish, Titus was not circumcised. Circumcising him would have been a sign to all other Gentiles that following Jewish law was required for a person to become a Christian. As Paul explains in this letter, circumcising Titus would be a rejection of the good news that salvation is God's gift to those who believe in His Son.
2:4 *false brethren.* This phrase apparently indicates that, although these people passed themselves off convincingly as Christians, there was reason to view their profession as a sham. These pseudo-Christians did not announce their purpose, which was to curtail Christian liberty (5:1,13).
2:6 *those who seemed to be something.* While Paul recognized the leadership roles of James, Peter, and John, he pointed out that they were in no way superior to him in their understanding of the gospel.

1:9 *i* Deut. 4:2   **1:10** *k* 1 Thess. 2:4   *l* 1 Sam. 24:7   *m* 1 Thess. 2:4   **1:11** *n* 1 Cor. 15:1   **1:12** *o* 1 Cor. 15:1   *p* [Eph. 3:3–5]   **1:13** *q* Acts 9:1   *r* Acts 8:3; 22:4, 5   **1:14** *s* Acts 26:9   *t* Jer. 9:14   **1:15** *u* Is. 49:1, 5   **1:16** *v* [2 Cor. 4:5–7]   *w* Acts 9:15   *x* Matt. 16:17   **1:18** *y* Acts 9:26   **1:19** *z* 1 Cor. 9:5   *a* Matt. 13:55   **1:21** *b* Acts 9:30   **1:22** *c* Rom. 16:7   **1:23** *d* Acts 9:20, 21   *e* Acts 8:3   **1:24** *f* Acts 11:18   **2:1** *a* Acts 15:2   **2:2** *b* Acts 15:1–4   *c* Phil. 2:16   **2:4** *d* Acts 15:1, 24   *e* Gal. 3:25; 5:1, 13   *f* Gal. 4:3, 9   **2:5** *g* [Gal. 1:6; 2:14; 3:1]   **2:6** *h* Gal. 2:9; 6:3   *i* Acts 10:34

seemed *to be something* iadded nothing to me. 7But on the contrary, kwhen they saw that the gospel for the uncircumcised lhad been committed to me, as *the gospel* for the circumcised *was* to Peter 8(for He who worked effectively in Peter for the apostleship to the mcircumcised nalso oworked effectively in me toward the Gentiles), 9and when James, Cephas, and John, who seemed to be ppillars, perceived qthe grace that had been given to me, they gave me and Barnabas the right hand of fellowship, rthat we *should go* to the Gentiles and they to the circumcised. 10*They desired* only that we should remember the poor, sthe very thing which I also was eager to do.

No Return to the Law

11tNow when Peter* had come to Antioch, I withstood him to his face, because he was to be blamed; 12for before certain men came from James, uhe would eat with the Gentiles; but when they came, he withdrew and separated himself, fearing those who were of the circumcision. 13And the rest of the Jews also played the hypocrite with him, so that even Barnabas was carried away with their hypocrisy.

14But when I saw that they were not straightforward about vthe truth of the gospel, I said to Peter wbefore *them* all, x"If you, being a Jew, live in the manner of Gentiles and not as the Jews, why do you* compel Gentiles to live as Jews?* 15yWe *who are* Jews by nature, and not zsinners of the Gentiles, 16aknowing that a man is not justified by the works of the law but bby faith in Jesus Christ, even we have believed in Christ Jesus, that we might be justified

by faith in Christ and not cby the works of the law; for by the works of the law no flesh shall be justified.

17"But if, while we seek to be justified by Christ, we ourselves also are found dsinners, *is* Christ therefore a minister of sin? Certainly not! 18For if I build again those things which I destroyed, I make myself a transgressor. 19For I ethrough the law fdied to the law that I might glive to God. 20I have been hcrucified with Christ; it is no longer I who live, but Christ lives in me; and the *life* which I now live in the flesh iI live by faith in the Son of God, jwho loved me and gave Himself for me. 21I do not set aside the grace of God; for kif righteousness *comes* through the law, then Christ died in vain."

Justification by Faith

3 O foolish Galatians! Who has bewitched you that you should not obey the truth,* before whose eyes Jesus Christ was clearly portrayed among you* as crucified? 2This only I want to learn from you: Did you receive the Spirit by the works of the law, aor by the hearing of faith? 3Are you so foolish? bHaving begun in the Spirit, are you now being made perfect by cthe flesh? 4dHave you suffered so many things in vain—if indeed *it was* in vain? 5Therefore He who supplies the Spirit to you and works miracles among you, *does He do it* by the works of the law, or by the

* 2:11 NU-Text reads *Cephas.* * 2:14 NU-Text reads *how can you.* • Some interpreters stop the quotation here. * 3:1 NU-Text omits *that you should not obey the truth.* • NU-Text omits *among you.*

2:7–10 uncircumcised . . . circumcised. There were not two different gospels. Rather, the primary scope of Paul's apostolic ministry was to the Gentiles (Rom. 11:13), while Peter's apostleship was, first and foremost, targeted toward the Jews. **remember the poor.** Almost certainly, this is a reference to the poor among the church in Judea (Acts 11:29–30).

2:11–12 Antioch. This city was the largest of the Roman province of Syria. It became a center for missionary outreach to other Gentile cities in Asia Minor and Macedonia (Acts 13:1–3).

2:14 they were not straightforward about the truth. Peter's hypocritical example implied that Gentiles had to behave like Jews in order to receive God's grace. It had already been decided (vv. 1–5) that it was not proper to compel Gentiles to live as Jews, because salvation was through faith alone.

2:15–17 We who are Jews by nature. Paul is not denying that those who are Jews by birth are sinners, as are all Gentiles (Rom. 3:23). Rather he is implying that Jews enjoy spiritual privileges (Rom. 9:4–5) that should make them more knowledgeable about how to be justified before God (3:6; Gen. 15:6). The Jews should have been aware that no person can be declared righteous or justified by obedience to the law of Moses (3:10–21).

2:17–19 is Christ therefore a minister of sin. Paul strongly rejects the erroneous conclusion that being

justified by faith in Christ actually made Jews sinners. Those who attempt to be justified through "the works of the law" are "cursed" (3:10). If anyone attempts to reassert the "works of the law" as having any part in the justification before God, the law itself convicts that person. The law itself is not sinful; its purpose is to convince individuals of their personal, spiritual deadness in sin outside of faith in Christ (Rom. 7:7–13).

3:1 O foolish Galatians. This phrase does not indicate lack of intelligence, but lack of wisdom. Paul wonders whether something like an evil spell had prevented the Galatians from recalling the gospel of the crucified Christ.

3:3 Having begun in the Spirit . . . made perfect by the flesh. The Galatians were mistakenly trying to achieve perfection through their own efforts, especially through circumcision.

2:6j 2 Cor. 11:5; 12:11 **2:7**k Acts 9:15; 13:46; 22:21 l 1 Thess. 2:4 **2:8**m 1 Pet. 1:1 n Acts 9:15 o [Gal. 3:5] **2:9**p Matt. 16:18 q Rom. 1:5 r Acts 13:3 **2:10**s Acts 11:30 **2:11**t Acts 15:35 **2:12**u [Acts 10:28; 11:2, 3] **2:14**v Gal. 1:6; 2:5 w 1 Tim. 5:20 x [Acts 10:28] **2:15**y [Acts 15:10] z Matt. 9:11 **2:16**a Acts 13:38, 39 b Rom. 1:17 c Ps. 143:2 **2:17**d [1 John 3:8] **2:19**e Rom. 8:2 f [Rom. 6:2, 14; 7:4] g [Rom. 6:11] **2:20**h [Rom. 6:6] i 2 Cor. 5:15 j Eph. 5:2 **2:21**k Heb. 7:11 **3:2**d Rom. 10:16, 17 **3:3**b [Gal. 4:9] c Heb. 7:16 **3:4**d Heb. 10:35

hearing of faith?— 6just as Abraham [e]*"believed God, and it was accounted to him
for righteousness."** 7Therefore know that
only [f]those who are of faith are sons of
Abraham. 8And [g]the Scripture, foreseeing that God would justify the Gentiles by
faith, preached the gospel to Abraham beforehand, *saying,* [h]*"In you all the nations
shall be blessed."** 9So then those who *are*
of faith are blessed with believing Abraham.

The Law Brings a Curse

10For as many as are of the works of the
law are under the curse; for it is written,
[i]*"Cursed is everyone who does not continue
in all things which are written in the book
of the law, to do them."** 11But that no one
is justified by the law in the sight of God *is*
evident, for [j]*"the just shall live by faith."**
12Yet [k]the law is not of faith, but [l]*"the man
who does them shall live by them."**
13[m]Christ has redeemed us from the
curse of the law, having become a curse for
us (for it is written, [n]*"Cursed is everyone
who hangs on a tree"**), 14[o]that the blessing
of Abraham might come upon the [p]Gen-
tiles in Christ Jesus, that we might receive
[q]the promise of the Spirit through faith.

The Changeless Promise

15Brethren, I speak in the manner of
men: [r]Though *it is* only a man's covenant,
yet *if it is* confirmed, no one annuls or adds
to it. 16Now to Abraham and his Seed were
the promises made. He does not say, "And
to seeds," as of many, but as of [s]one, [t]*"And
to your Seed,"** who is [u]Christ. 17And this
I say, *that* the law, [v]which was four hundred and thirty years later, cannot annul
the covenant that was confirmed before
by God in Christ,* [w]that it should make
the promise of no effect. 18For if [x]the inheritance *is* of the law, [y]*it is* no longer of
promise; but God gave *it* to Abraham by
promise.

Purpose of the Law

19What purpose then *does* the law *serve?*
[z]It was added because of transgressions,
till the [a]Seed should come to whom the
promise was made; *and it was* [b]appointed
through angels by the hand [c]of a mediator.
20Now a mediator does not *mediate* for one
only, [d]but God is one.
21Is the law then against the promises of
God? Certainly not! For if there had been
a law given which could have given life,
truly righteousness would have been by
the law. 22But the Scripture has confined
[e]all under sin, [f]that the promise by faith in
Jesus Christ might be given to those who
believe. 23But before faith came, we were
kept under guard by the law, kept for the
faith which would afterward be revealed.
24Therefore [g]the law was our tutor *to bring
us* to Christ, [h]that we might be justified by

---

*3:6 Genesis 15:6 *3:8 Genesis 12:3; 18:18; 22:18; 26:4; 28:14 *3:10 Deuteronomy 27:26 *3:11 Habakkuk 2:4 *3:12 Leviticus 18:5 *3:13 Deuteronomy 21:23 *3:16 Genesis 12:7; 13:15; 24:7 *3:17 NU-Text omits *in Christ.*

3:6 *believed God.* There are several reasons for Paul's reference to Abraham's faith as an example: (1) Abraham was the father of the Jewish nation (Gen. 12:1–3); (2) Abraham is the clearest example of justification in the Old Testament; and (3) the Judaizers almost certainly were pointing back to Abraham, probably in connection with circumcision (2:3; 5:2–3). The example of Abraham's faith is also developed in Romans 4 and Hebrews 11.

3:7 *who are of faith.* These are the spiritual sons of Abraham, even if they are not Jews. They are part of God's people.

3:8–9 *Scripture.* Here, Scripture is personified as a preacher who foretells that Abraham and his example of faith (Gen. 15:6) would become a life-changing blessing to all nations (Gen. 12:3; Matt. 28:19) as the gospel spread. All who have faith, as Abraham did, join in his "blessed" status.

3:10 *Cursed is everyone.* The quotation from Deuteronomy 27:26 says that those who do not keep the whole law are cursed, proving that all are cursed who follow the law, because all fall short of the law's standards (Rom. 1:17; 3:10,18,23).

3:13 *the curse of the law.* Paul knew that many of his readers would perceive that they were actually under the curse of the law. For them, as for us, it is incredibly comforting to know that Christ became that curse for us on the cross (Deut. 21:23).

3:16 *to Abraham and his Seed.* Jesus Christ is the fulfillment of the covenant (v. 15) God made with Abraham. Although in one sense all Jews are the physical seed of Abraham, Christ is the final focus of God's promises, the ultimate Seed.

3:19–20 *What purpose then does the law serve?* The purpose of the law of Moses was not to justify man in God's eyes (2:16). Rather, the law was added after God's promise to Abraham to clarify the issue of sin until Christ, the Seed, came.

3:21–22 *Is the law then against the promises of God?* The relationship of the law and the promises is one of need and fulfillment. The law was not designed by God to give eternal life and righteousness. Rather, the law showed humanity's need for the promise of life through faith in Jesus Christ (v. 9; 2:16).

3:23–25 *kept under guard . . . tutor.* Paul gives two different illustrations concerning the function of the law until Christ came (4:4–5). The law acted as a jailor to hold humankind in custody until faith in Christ was revealed. But the law also served as a tutor. A tutor in ancient Greek culture would accompany the children

3:6 [e] Gen. 15:6 **3:7** [f] John 8:39 **3:8** [g] Rom. 9:17 [h] Gen. 12:3; 18:18; 22:18; 26:4; 28:14 **3:10** [i] Deut. 27:26 **3:11** [j] Hab. 2:4 **3:12** [k] Rom. 4:4, 5 [l] Lev. 18:5 **3:13** [m] [Rom. 8:3] [n] Deut. 21:23 **3:14** [o] Gen. 12:3; 22:18; [Rom. 4:1–5, 9, 16] [p] Is. 49:6; Rom. 3:29, 30 [q] Is. 32:15 **3:15** [r] Heb. 9:17 **3:16** [s] Gen. 22:18 [t] Gen. 12:3, 7; 13:15; 24:7 [u] [1 Cor. 12:12] **3:17** [v] Ex. 12:40 [w] [Rom. 4:13] **3:18** [x] [Rom. 8:17] [y] Rom. 4:14 **3:19** [z] John 15:22 [a] Gal. 4:4 [b] Acts 7:53 [c] Ex. 20:19 **3:20** [d] [Rom. 3:29] **3:22** [e] Rom. 11:32 [f] Rom. 4:11 **3:24** [g] Rom. 10:4 [h] Acts 13:39

faith. 25 But after faith has come, we are no longer under a tutor.

Sons and Heirs

26 For you [i]are all sons of God through faith in Christ Jesus. 27 For [j]as many of you as were baptized into Christ [k]have put on Christ. 28 [l]There is neither Jew nor Greek, [m]there is neither slave nor free, there is neither male nor female; for you are all [n]one in Christ Jesus. 29 And [o]if you *are* Christ's, then you are Abraham's [p]seed, and [q]heirs according to the promise.

4 Now I say *that* the heir, as long as he is a child, does not differ at all from a slave, though he is master of all, 2 but is under guardians and stewards until the time appointed by the father. 3 Even so we, when we were children, [a]were in bondage under the elements of the world. 4 But [b]when the fullness of the time had come, God sent forth His Son, [c]born* [d]of a woman, [e]born under the law, 5 [f]to redeem those who were under the law, [g]that we might receive the adoption as sons.

6 And because you are sons, God has sent forth [h]the Spirit of His Son into your hearts, crying out, "Abba, Father!" 7 Therefore you are no longer a slave but a son, [i]and if a son, then an heir of* God through Christ.

Fears for the Church

8 But then, indeed, [j]when you did not know God, [k]you served those which by nature are not gods. 9 But now [l]after you have known God, or rather are known by God, [m]how *is it that* you turn again to [n]the weak and beggarly elements, to which you desire again to be in bondage? 10 [o]You observe days and months and seasons and years. 11 I am afraid for you, [p]lest I have labored for you in vain.

12 Brethren, I urge you to become like me, for I *became* like you. [q]You have not injured me at all. 13 You know that [r]because of physical infirmity I preached the gospel to you at the first. 14 And my trial which was in my flesh you did not despise or reject, but you received me [s]as an angel of God, [t]*even* as Christ Jesus. 15 What* then was the blessing you *enjoyed?* For I bear you witness that, if possible, you would have plucked out your own eyes and given them to me. 16 Have I therefore become your enemy because I tell you the truth?

17 They [u]zealously court you, *but* for no good; yes, they want to exclude you, that you may be zealous for them. 18 But it is good to be zealous in a good thing always, and not only when I am present with you. 19 [v]My little children, for whom I labor in birth again until Christ is formed in you, 20 I would like to be present with you now and to change my tone; for I have doubts about you.

* **4:4** Or *made* * **4:7** NU-Text reads *through God* and omits *through Christ.* * **4:15** NU-Text reads *Where.*

---

in his care, instructing and disciplining them when necessary. The law was like a tutor because it both corrected and instructed the Israelites in God's ways until Christ was revealed and such a schoolmaster was no longer needed (4:1–2).

3:28 *There is neither Jew nor Greek.* The context of this verse is justification by faith in Christ Jesus. Racial, social, and gender distinctions that so easily divide in no way hinder a person from coming to Christ in order to receive His mercy. All people equally can become God's heirs and recipients of His eternal promises (4:5–7).

4:1–2 *until the time appointed by the father.* In ancient society a child had to wait until the proper time before he could inherit what was his. Paul uses this idea to explain why God delayed Jesus Christ's coming, leaving people with His law as a guide (3:23–25).

4:4–5 *born under the law.* This means Christ was subject to the Jewish law (Matt. 5:17–19), further establishing His identification with all people who are subject to the law. ***redeem.*** This verb was used in the context of buying from a slave market. It describes Christ's supreme and final payment for the sins of humanity. His death on the cross frees those who believe in Him from the curse of the law and slavery to sin. This decisive payment and resulting freedom clear the way for Christians to become God's sons.

4:6 *God has sent forth the Spirit.* Just as "God sent forth His Son" in "fullness of the time" in world history (v. 4), so God has also sent the Spirit at just the right time for every person who believes in Christ.

4:9 *how is it that you turn again.* The Galatians had come to know God through faith in Jesus Christ (John 17:2–3). He had adopted them as His own sons, but they were turning back to the law that had once enslaved them.

4:12 *I urge you.* To get beyond the present dilemma, Paul appeals to the Galatians to follow his example (1 Cor. 11:1). He had abandoned the ceremonial rules and regulations connected with Judaism so that he could freely preach the gospel of Christ to Jew and Gentile alike in the cities of Galatia. They too should not hinder the gospel of Christ with laws and regulations.

4:17–18 *they want to exclude you.* Paul was strongly implying that the false teachers in Galatia were making the same mistake he had made prior to his conversion. Their zeal for the law was blinding them to the freedom and truth to be found in Jesus Christ.

4:19 *My little children.* Paul calls the Galatians children because of their lack of spiritual growth and depth. The apostle also portrays himself as the Galatians' "spiritual mother." He was feeling the labor

3:26 [i]John 1:12 **3:27** [j][Rom. 6:3] [k]Rom. 10:12; 13:14 **3:28** [l]Col. 3:11 [m][1 Cor. 12:13] [n][Eph. 2:15, 16] **3:29** [o]Gen. 21:10 [p]Rom. 4:11; Gal. 3:7 [q]Gen. 12:3; 18:18; Rom. 8:17 **4:3** [a]Col. 2:8, 20 **4:4** [b][Gen. 49:10] [c][John 1:14] [d]Gen. 3:15; [Is. 7:14; Matt. 1:25] [e][Matt. 5:17]; Luke 2:21, 27 **4:5** [f][Matt. 20:28] [g][John 1:12] **4:6** [h][Rom. 5:5; 8:9, 15, 16] **4:7** [i][Rom. 8:16, 17] **4:8** [j]Eph. 2:12 [k]Rom. 1:25 **4:9** [l][1 Cor. 8:3] [m]Col. 2:20 [n]Heb. 7:18 **4:10** [o]Rom. 14:5 **4:11** [p]1 Thess. 3:5 **4:12** [q]2 Cor. 2:5 **4:13** [r]1 Cor. 2:3 **4:14** [s]Mal. 2:7 [t][Luke 10:16] **4:17** [u]Rom. 10:2 **4:19** [v]1 Cor. 4:15

Two Covenants

21Tell me, you who desire to be under the law, do you not hear the law? 22For it is written that Abraham had two sons: wthe one by a bondwoman, xthe other by a freewoman. 23But he *who was* of the bondwoman ywas born according to the flesh, zand he of the freewoman through promise, 24which things are symbolic. For these are the* two covenants: the one from Mount aSinai which gives birth to bondage, which is Hagar—25for this Hagar is Mount Sinai in Arabia, and corresponds to Jerusalem which now is, and is in bondage with her children—26but the bJerusalem above is free, which is the mother of us all. 27For it is written:

c"Rejoice, O barren,
You who do not bear!
Break forth and shout,
You who are not in labor!
For the desolate has many more children
Than she who has a husband."*

28Now dwe, brethren, as Isaac *was*, are echildren of promise. 29But, as fhe who was born according to the flesh then persecuted him *who was born* according to the Spirit, geven so *it is* now. 30Nevertheless what does hthe Scripture say? i"Cast out the bondwoman and her son, forjthe son of the bondwoman shall not be heir with the son of the freewoman."* 31So then, brethren, we are not children of the bondwoman but of the free.

Christian Liberty

5 aStand fast therefore in the liberty by which Christ has made us free,* and do not be entangled again with a byoke of bondage. 2Indeed I, Paul, say to you that cif you become circumcised, Christ will profit you nothing. 3And I testify again to every man who becomes circumcised dthat he is a debtor to keep the whole law. 4eYou have become estranged from Christ, you who *attempt to* be justified by law; fyou have fallen from grace. 5For we through the Spirit eagerly gwait for the hope of righteousness by faith. 6For hin Christ Jesus neither circumcision nor uncircumcision avails anything, but ifaith working through love.

Love Fulfills the Law

7You jran well. Who hindered you from obeying the truth? 8This persuasion does not *come* from Him who calls you. 9kA little leaven leavens the whole lump. 10I have confidence in you, in the Lord, that you will have no other mind; but he who troubles you shall bear his judgment, whoever he is.

---

* 4:24 NU-Text and M-Text omit *the.* * 4:27 Isaiah 54:1 * 4:30 Genesis 21:10 * 5:1 NU-Text reads *For freedom Christ has made us free; stand fast therefore.*

---

pains of their birth all over again because they had fallen into serious error.

4:21–22 bondwoman . . . freewoman. To clinch his argument about the bondage of the law and freedom found in Christ, Paul uses as examples the two sons of Abraham, Ishmael and Isaac. Ishmael was born of a bondwoman, Hagar, and Isaac was born of Sarah, a freewoman (Gen. 16:15; 21:2). Paul counters the Jewish false teachers' zeal for the law with an argument based on the Law, the Pentateuch. He uses allegory to prove his point because it was a rhetorical technique the false teachers used. In other words, Paul was demonstrating that he could argue from the law just as well as they could, but to prove that the law of Moses pointed to the Messiah, Jesus Christ.

4:26 Jerusalem above. This phrase represents the Jewish hope of heaven finally coming to earth (Rev. 21–22). Paul was strongly implying that the question at hand was not allegiance to Jerusalem, but allegiance to which Jerusalem—the new or the old? Would the Galatians follow the shortsighted present Jerusalem and its legalism or the liberty of the heavenly Jerusalem?

4:28–30 Now we, brethren, as Isaac was, are children of promise. This portion of Paul's allegory is based on Genesis 21:9–10. Isaac was continually persecuted by his older half brother Ishmael. Eventually, Ishmael and his mother Hagar were expelled because Ishmael had no standing in God's eyes as an heir of Abraham. In creating a parallel between the story from Genesis and the Galatians' situation, Paul points out that (1) the persecution by the Jewish legalists of his day was not unexpected, and (2) it would not go

on indefinitely because the legalists would soon be cast out.

4:31—5:1 So then. This phrase represents the conclusion of the previous section, while "therefore" signals that Paul is going to apply this spiritual truth to the lives of the Galatian believers.

5:2–3 if you become circumcised. The legalistic Jewish teachers in Galatia were urging believers to be circumcised (6:12–13). Paul points out that circumcision would change the entire orientation of salvation away from God's grace to one's own actions. One who is circumcised in an attempt to gain God's acceptance is obligated to keep the whole law, which history has abundantly demonstrated no one can do (Rom. 3:10–18).

5:5 hope of righteousness. We can be assured that we will be declared righteous before the Lord on that last day because we have a foretaste of that righteousness from the Spirit who lives within us (2 Cor. 5:5).

5:9–10 leaven. This symbolizes the intruders, with their false doctrine and its sinister influence. They were taking the gospel of free forgiveness away from the Galatians. The one who causes such harm will experience God's judgment (2 Cor. 5:10).

4:22 w Gen. 16:15 x Gen. 21:2 **4:23** y Rom. 9:7, 8 z Heb. 11:11 **4:24** a Deut. 33:2 **4:26** b [Is. 2:2] **4:27** c Is. 54:1 **4:28** d Gal. 3:29 e Acts 3:25 **4:29** f Gen. 21:9 g Gal. 5:11 **4:30** h [Gal. 3:8, 22] i Gen. 21:10, 12 j [John 8:35] **5:1** a Phil. 4:1 b Acts 15:10 **5:2** c Acts 15:1 **5:3** d [Rom. 2:25] **5:4** e [Rom. 9:31] f Heb. 12:15 **5:5** g Rom. 8:24 **5:6** h [Gal. 6:15] i 1 Thess. 1:3 **5:7** j 1 Cor. 9:24 **5:9** k 1 Cor. 5:6

¹¹And I, brethren, if I still preach circumcision, ˡwhy do I still suffer persecution? Then ᵐthe offense of the cross has ceased. ¹²ⁿI could wish that those ᵒwho trouble you would even cut themselves off! ¹³For you, brethren, have been called to liberty; only ᵖdo not *use* liberty as an ᑫopportunity for the flesh, but ʳthrough love serve one another. ¹⁴For ˢall the law is fulfilled in one word, *even* in this: ᵗ*"You shall love your neighbor as yourself."* ¹⁵But if you bite and devour one another, beware lest you be consumed by one another!

Walking in the Spirit

¹⁶I say then: ᵘWalk in the Spirit, and you shall not fulfill the lust of the flesh. ¹⁷For ᵛthe flesh lusts against the Spirit, and the Spirit against the flesh; and these are contrary to one another, ʷso that you do not do the things that you wish. ¹⁸But ˣif you are led by the Spirit, you are not under the law. ¹⁹Now ʸthe works of the flesh are evident, which are: adultery,* fornication, uncleanness, lewdness, ²⁰idolatry, sorcery, hatred, contentions, jealousies, outbursts

of wrath, selfish ambitions, dissensions, heresies, ²¹envy, murders,* drunkenness, revelries, and the like; of which I tell you beforehand, just as I also told *you* in time past, that ᶻthose who practice such things will not inherit the kingdom of God. ²²But ᵃthe fruit of the Spirit is ᵇlove, joy, peace, longsuffering, kindness, ᶜgoodness, ᵈfaithfulness, ²³gentleness, self-control. ᵉAgainst such there is no law. ²⁴And those *who are* Christ's ᶠhave crucified the flesh with its passions and desires. ²⁵ᵍIf we live in the Spirit, let us also walk in the Spirit. ²⁶ʰLet us not become conceited, provoking one another, envying one another.

Bear and Share Burdens

6 Brethren, if a man is overtaken in any trespass, you who *are* spiritual restore such a one in a spirit of ᵃgentleness, considering yourself lest you also be tempted. ²ᵇBear one another's burdens, and so fulfill ᶜthe law of Christ. ³For ᵈif anyone thinks himself to be something, when ᵉhe

* **5:14** Leviticus 19:18   * **5:19** NU-Text omits *adultery.*   * **5:21** NU-Text omits *murders.*

5:11 *the offense of the cross.* The cross is offensive to people because it proclaims God's unmerited grace and leaves no place for people's good works.

5:13 *liberty.* Christian liberty is the freedom to serve one another in love (vv. 5–6). As we grow in our knowledge of the Word of God, understand and apply its meaning, we should increasingly be involved in serving God and our fellow believers. The Spirit of God has given us spiritual gifts, but those gifts are worthless unless they are used in the service of God and His church. Paul often uses the figure of the human body to show the importance of each part serving the others (Rom. 12:4–5; 1 Cor. 12:12–31). While some parts of the body have more prominent places of service than others, all are equally important. To maintain strength, health, and vitality, every part of the body must function and serve all the other parts of the body. This is also true of the spiritual or new life. We will grow in the new life, become strong, and maintain good spiritual health as we use the talents and abilities that God has given us to meet the needs of the other parts of the body.

5:14 *all the law.* The Christian does not live under the law of Moses, but instead under "the law of Christ" (6:2). Living in Christ empowers us to love others, which is the fulfillment of the law (Matt. 22:36–40).

5:16 *Walk in the Spirit.* The only consistent way to overcome the sinful desires of our human nature (the flesh) is to live step-by-step in the power of the Holy Spirit as He works through our spirit.

5:17 *the flesh lusts against the Spirit.* The potential of the flesh energized by Satan in the life of the Christian should not be underestimated. Given free rein, the flesh will direct our choices, making us do what we know we should not do. This inner conflict between the flesh and the Spirit is very real. Although the precise meaning of "flesh" is unclear, Paul's intent is plain. The desires of our flesh are at odds with what the Holy Spirit desires for us: to be free from sin.

5:19–21 The Human Condition—The last part of Galatians 5 contrasts *works of the flesh* with *fruit of the*

Spirit. The works of the flesh here are represented by those kinds of activities that are characteristic of our old natures. Without God, our lives are dominated by these more obvious sins and less obvious sinful attitudes. It is our sinful nature to be this way. Those who operate with these sins as a regular part of their lives, with no sense of guilt, demonstrate their need for salvation. It is the role of the Spirit to change these sinful behaviors. Paul points out that, if changes are not occurring, then there is a need for the Spirit that comes with the gift of salvation.

5:22–24 The New Nature—While the deeds of the flesh portray a disintegrating life, the fruit of the Spirit describes a life where things are working harmoniously. It points to qualities of personality and to behaviors that make us function as better people. It points to what God wants to see in us and should see in us as we mature in the faith.

5:22 *fruit of the Spirit.* This analogy is reminiscent of Jesus' teaching on the vine, branches, and fruitful harvest.

5:24 *have crucified the flesh.* Those who have mastered these sinful desires are those who have kept their focus on God (Jer. 9:23–24; Dan. 11:32; John 17:3; Heb. 12:1–3).

6:1 *restore such a one in a spirit of gentleness.* A believer devastated by sin needs to be approached gently by fellow believers.

6:2 *the law of Christ.* This phrase is probably referring to the summation of the law: "Love your neighbor" (5:14; Matt. 22:39; John 13:34–35). Bearing the

---

5:11 ˡ 1 Cor. 15:30   ᵐ [1 Cor. 1:23]   **5:12** ⁿ Josh. 7:25   ᵒ Acts 15:1, 2   **5:13** ᵖ 1 Cor. 8:9   ᑫ 1 Pet. 2:16   ʳ 1 Cor. 9:19   **5:14** ˢ Matt. 7:12; 22:40   ᵗ Lev. 19:18   **5:16** ᵘ Rom. 6:12   **5:17** ᵛ Rom. 7:18, 22, 23; 8:5   ʷ Rom. 7:15   **5:18** ˣ [Rom. 6:14; 7:4; 8:14]   **5:19** ʸ Eph. 5:3, 11   **5:21** ᶻ 1 Cor. 6:9, 10   **5:22** ᵃ [John 15:2]   ᵇ [Col. 3:12–15]   ᶜ Rom. 15:14   ᵈ 1 Cor. 13:7   **5:23** ᵉ 1 Tim. 1:9   **5:24** ᶠ Rom. 6:6   **5:25** ᵍ [Rom. 8:4, 5]   **5:26** ʰ Phil. 2:3   **6:1** ᵃ Eph. 4:2   **6:2** ᵇ Rom. 15:1   ᶜ [James 2:8]   **6:3** ᵈ Rom. 12:3   ᵉ [2 Cor. 3:5]

is nothing, he deceives himself. 4But ^f let each one examine his own work, and then he will have rejoicing in himself alone, and ^g not in another. 5For ^h each one shall bear his own load.

Be Generous and Do Good

6^i Let him who is taught the word share in all good things with him who teaches.

7Do not be deceived, God is not mocked; for ^j whatever a man sows, that he will also reap. 8For he who sows to his flesh will of the flesh reap corruption, but he who sows to the Spirit will of the Spirit reap ^k everlasting life. 9And ^l let us not grow weary while doing good, for in due season we shall reap ^m if we do not lose heart. 10^n Therefore, as we have opportunity, ^o let us do good to all, ^p especially to those who are of the household of faith.

Glory Only in the Cross

11See with what large letters I have written to you with my own hand! 12As many as desire to make a good showing in the flesh, these *would* compel you to be circumcised, ^q only that they may not suffer persecution for the cross of Christ. 13For not even those who are circumcised keep the law, but they desire to have you circumcised that they may boast in your flesh. 14But God forbid that I should boast except in the ^r cross of our Lord Jesus Christ, by whom* the world has been crucified to me, and ^s I to the world. 15For ^t in Christ Jesus neither circumcision nor uncircumcision avails anything, but a new creation.

Blessing and a Plea

16And as many as walk according to this rule, peace and mercy *be* upon them, and upon the Israel of God.

17From now on let no one trouble me, for I bear in my body the marks of the Lord Jesus.

18Brethren, the grace of our Lord Jesus Christ *be* with your spirit. Amen.

* **6:14** Or *by which* (the cross)

---

burdens of one another is precisely what Christ expects of all believers. The Greek word for *burdens* refers to something beyond the normal capacity to carry, as opposed to a "load" (v. 5), which is what a person could be expected to carry.

6:7–8 he who sows to his flesh. The principle of sowing and reaping was known to everyone in a largely agricultural society. It would be foolish for Christians to think that they could escape the harvest of destruction and judgment if they persist in sin. *corruption.* This is a term used for a field in which the produce is too rotten to harvest (Heb. 6:8). *he who sows to the Spirit will of the Spirit reap everlasting life.* This does not mean that everlasting life is earned by works. Rather, Paul is saying that everlasting life is the glorious end of those who follow the guidance of the Spirit (Rom. 6:22). Jesus said that He came so that we might have life and have it more abundantly (John 10:10). In this life, through the indwelling of the Spirit, Christians are developing a capacity to experience Christ to the fullest in the life to come.

6:9 doing good. The apostle has argued at length that such works cannot justify (2:16) or sanctify (3:3) anyone. However, good works are, in fact, an important fruit of the life of faith (5:5) that God has planned for each believer (Eph. 2:8–10).

6:12 make a good showing. The Judaizers were trying to appear spiritual by becoming circumcised and demanding that others become circumcised (5:2–12). By teaching that all Christians should become circumcised, the Judaizers were trying to make Christianity into a sect of Judaism. This would have two advantages. First, they could counter the persecution that they suffered from the zealous Jews. Second, they could include themselves with an officially sanctioned religion of the Roman Empire, Judaism.

6:13 not even those . . . keep the law. The Judaizers knew that they were unable to keep the entire law even though they were required to do so. They still attempted to persuade the Galatians to be circumcised so that they could boast about having them as their followers.

6:16 the Israel of God. This probably refers to the remnant of believing Jews (Rom. 11:1–2,7). They are Abraham's spiritual descendants (3:6–9) because they believe in God and rely on His grace.

6:17 I bear in my body. Paul's scars branded him as a slave for Christ (Rom. 1:1). Such marks far outweighed the "mark" of circumcision so valued by the false teachers in Galatia (vv. 12–15).

6:4 ^f 1 Cor. 11:28 ^g Luke 18:11 **6:5** ^h [Rom. 2:6]
6:6 ^i 1 Cor. 9:11, 14 **6:7** ^j [Rom. 2:6] **6:8** ^k [Rom. 6:8]
6:9 ^l 1 Cor. 15:58 ^m [James 5:7, 8] **6:10** ^n Prov. 3:27
^o Titus 3:8 ^p Rom. 12:13 **6:12** ^q Gal. 5:11 **6:14** ^r [1 Cor. 1:18] ^s Col. 2:20 **6:15** ^t 1 Cor. 7:19

THE EPISTLE OF PAUL THE APOSTLE TO THE
EPHESIANS

▶ **AUTHOR:** All internal and external evidence strongly supports the Pauline authorship of Ephesians. In recent years, however, critics have turned to internal grounds to challenge this unanimous ancient tradition. It has been argued that the vocabulary and style are different from other Pauline epistles, but this overlooks Paul's flexibility under different circumstances (as in Romans and 2 Corinthians). The theology of Ephesians in some ways reflects a later development, but this must be attributed to Paul's own growth and meditation on the church as the body of Christ. Ephesians was written during his first Roman imprisonment in A.D. 60–62, perhaps around the same time as Philippians, Colossians, and Philemon.

▶ **TIME:** C. A.D. 60–61   ▶ **KEY VERSES:** Eph. 4:1–3

▶ **THEME:** Ephesians is like a grand landscape whose subject is the whole world. Paul paints a richly textured picture of God's plan to bless the world through Christ. God is bringing light to darkness, healing to brokenness and reconciliation to the separated. Central to this teaching is the role of the church in the world and the gifts God has given it. God will bring about these things through the church. Once we understand and believe all that God has done and is doing, it is our responsibility to obey and live in light of His actions. Paul gives us much more than the theory in Ephesians. He makes critical connections between big-picture theology and the practical implications for living the day-to-day Christian life.

Greeting

1 Paul, an apostle of Jesus Christ by the will of God,

To the saints who are in Ephesus, and faithful in Christ Jesus:

2Grace to you and peace from God our Father and the Lord Jesus Christ.

Redemption in Christ

3aBlessed *be* the God and Father of our Lord Jesus Christ, who has blessed us with every spiritual blessing in the heavenly *places* in Christ, 4just as bHe chose us in Him cbefore the foundation of the world, that we should dbe holy and without blame before Him in love, 5ehaving predestined us to fadoption as sons by Jesus Christ to Himself, gaccording to the good pleasure of His will, 6to the praise of the glory of His grace, hby which He made us accepted in ithe Beloved.

7In Him we have redemption through His blood, the forgiveness of sins, according to kthe riches of His grace 8which He made to abound toward us in all wisdom and prudence, 9lhaving made known to us the mystery of His will, according to His

---

1:1–2 saints. In the New Testament all believers are set apart by God in Christ. *Grace to you and peace.* The salutations in the New Testament epistles follow the form of the typical first-century letter. The writer is mentioned first and the recipient next, followed by a blessing or best wishes for good health. The difference here lies in the content of the blessing: pagan letters mentioned nonexistent gods and goddesses such as Diana or Apollo; the apostles call upon the one true God and His Son Jesus Christ to bless their readers.
1:3 every spiritual blessing. God does not guarantee health, wealth, and prosperity to the New Testament believer. The blessings of Christianity are largely spiritual.
1:4–5 love. In this instance the Greek *agape* is used. That love is a love that is by choice or one's will, not just a sentimental feeling. *having predestined us.* Predestination is not a cold-hearted determinism or set fate, but rather a loving choice on God's part.

1:6 the Beloved. This title is messianic, referring to God's Son, Jesus.
1:7 redemption. The word means "buy back" or "ransom." In ancient times, one could buy back a person who was sold into slavery. In the same way, Christ through His death bought us from our slavery to sin. *His blood.* The blood of Christ is the means by which our redemption comes. The Old Testament and the New both clearly teach that there is no forgiveness without the shedding of blood.
1:9 the mystery. This is not a puzzle to solve, or knowledge only for the few and the initiated, as in the mystery religions of Paul's day. In Paul's use, the

1:3 a 2 Cor. 1:3   **1:4** b Rom. 8:28 c 1 Pet. 1:2 d Luke 1:75
1:5 e [Rom. 8:29] f John 1:12 g [1 Cor. 1:21]   **1:6** h [Rom. 3:24] i Matt. 3:17   **1:7** j [Heb. 9:12] k [Rom. 3:24, 25]
1:9 l [Rom. 16:25]

good pleasure [m]which He purposed in
Himself, 10 that in the dispensation of [n]the
fullness of the times [o]He might gather together in one [p]all things in Christ, both*
which are in heaven and which are on
earth—in Him. 11 [q]In Him also we have obtained an inheritance, being predestined
according to [r]the purpose of Him who
works all things according to the counsel
of His will, 12 [s]that we [t]who first trusted
in Christ should be to the praise of His
glory.
13 In Him you also *trusted*, after you
heard [u]the word of truth, the gospel of your
salvation; in whom also, having believed,
[v]you were sealed with the Holy Spirit of
promise, 14 [w]who* is the guarantee of our
inheritance [x]until the redemption of [y]the
purchased possession, [z]to the praise of His
glory.

Prayer for Spiritual Wisdom

15 Therefore I also, [a]after I heard of your
faith in the Lord Jesus and your love for all
the saints, 16 [b]do not cease to give thanks
for you, making mention of you in my
prayers: 17 that [c]the God of our Lord Jesus
Christ, the Father of glory, [d]may give to
you the spirit of wisdom and revelation in
the knowledge of Him, 18 [e]the eyes of your
understanding* being enlightened; that
you may know what is [f]the hope of His
calling, what are the riches of the glory of
His inheritance in the saints, 19 and what
is the exceeding greatness of His power
toward us who believe, [g]according to the
working of His mighty power 20 which He
worked in Christ when [h]He raised Him
from the dead and [i]seated *Him* at His right
hand in the heavenly *places*, 21 [j]far above
all [k]principality and power and might and
dominion, and every name that is named,
not only in this age but also in that which
is to come.
22 And [l]He put all *things* under His feet,
and gave Him [m]*to be* head over all *things* to
the church, 23 [n]which is His body, [o]the fullness of Him [p]who fills all in all.

By Grace Through Faith

2 And [a]you *He made alive,* [b]who were
dead in trespasses and sins, 2 [c]in which
you once walked according to the course of
this world, according to [d]the prince of the
power of the air, the spirit who now works
in [e]the sons of disobedience, 3 [f]among
whom also we all once conducted ourselves in [g]the lusts of our flesh, fulfilling
the desires of the flesh and of the mind, and
[h]were by nature children of wrath, just as
the others.
4 But God, [i]who is rich in mercy, because
of His [j]great love with which He loved us,
5 [k]even when we were dead in trespasses,
[l]made us alive together with Christ (by
grace you have been saved), 6 and raised *us*
up together, and made *us* sit together [m]in
the heavenly *places* in Christ Jesus, 7 that
in the ages to come He might show the exceeding riches of His grace in [n]*His* kindness
toward us in Christ Jesus. 8 [o]For by grace
you have been saved [p]through faith, and
that not of yourselves; [q]*it is* the gift of God,
9 not of [r]works, lest anyone should [s]boast.

* **1:10** NU-Text and M-Text omit *both.* * **1:14** NU-Text reads *which.* * **1:18** NU-Text and M-Text read *hearts.*

word *mystery* refers to an aspect of God's will that was once hidden or obscure, but now was being revealed by God (Rom. 11:25).

1:14 *the guarantee of our inheritance.* The Greek word for *guarantee* can also be used to indicate an engagement ring. As Christ is the bridegroom and the church is the bride, so the Holy Spirit is the down payment, the earnest money in the long-awaited marriage of the two (Rev. 19:7). ***purchased possession.*** The Old Testament described the nation of Israel as God's special treasure, one He had purchased by His mighty acts of deliverance during the Exodus (Ex. 19:5). Here Paul describes Christians as a purchased possession, bought with the blood of Christ.

1:18–19 *the eyes of your understanding.* This phrase refers to spiritual understanding. To describe this, Paul uses words that picture eyes that have been brightened with divine illumination.

1:21 *not only in this age but also in that which is to come.* The Jews of Christ's time understood the end times to be divided into two time periods, the age in which they were living and the coming age. The Messiah, called "the Coming One," would rule in the age which is to come.

2:2 *you once walked.* Walking is a biblical expression that pictures a believer's steady normal progress with God (Ps. 1:1). Believers are saved so that they can have a lifestyle characterized by good works (v. 10). ***prince of the power of the air.*** This is a reference to Satan.

2:4–7 *we were dead in trespasses.* Because of Adam's sin, the entire human race is spiritually dead. Only God can grant new life and save us from this predicament. Out of His mercy, God gave His Son for us while we were yet His enemies. He loved us long before we loved Him (1 John 4:9–10).

2:8–10 *you have been saved through faith.* The grace of God is the source of salvation; faith is the channel, not the cause. God alone saves. Salvation never originates in the efforts of people; it always arises out of the lovingkindness of God. ***the gift of God.*** We cannot do anything to earn our salvation.

1:9 [m] [2 Tim. 1:9] **1:10** [n] Gal. 4:4 [o] 1 Cor. 3:22 [p] [Col. 1:16, 20] **1:11** [q] Rom. 8:17 [r] Is. 46:10 **1:12** [s] 2 Thess. 2:13 [t] James 1:18 **1:13** [u] John 1:17 [v] [2 Cor. 1:22] **1:14** [w] 2 Cor. 5:5 [x] Rom. 8:23 [y] [Acts 20:28] [z] 1 Pet. 2:9 **1:15** [a] Col. 1:4 **1:16** [b] Rom. 1:9 **1:17** [c] John 20:17 [d] Col. 1:9 **1:18** [e] Acts 26:18 [f] Eph. 2:12 **1:19** [g] Col. 2:12 **1:20** [h] Acts 2:24 [i] Ps. 110:1 **1:21** [j] Phil. 2:9, 10 [k] [Rom. 8:38, 39] **1:22** [l] Ps. 8:6; 110:1; Matt. 28:18; 1 Cor. 15:27 [m] Heb. 2:7, 8 **1:23** [n] Rom. 12:5 [o] Col. 2:9 [p] [1 Cor. 12:6] **2:1** [a] Col. 2:13 [b] Eph. 4:18 **2:2** [c] Col. 1:21 [d] Eph. 6:12 [e] Col. 3:6 **2:3** [f] 1 Pet. 4:3 [g] Gal. 5:16 [h] [Ps. 51:5] **2:4** [i] Rom. 10:12 [j] John 3:16 **2:5** [k] Rom. 5:6, 8 [l] [Rom. 6:4, 5] **2:6** [m] Eph. 1:20 **2:7** [n] Titus 3:4 **2:8** [o] [2 Tim. 1:9] [p] Rom. 4:16 [q] [John 1:12, 13] **2:9** [r] Rom. 4:4, 5; 11:6 [s] Rom. 3:27

[10]For we are [t]His workmanship, created in Christ Jesus for good works, which God prepared beforehand that we should walk in them.

Brought Near by His Blood

[11]Therefore remember that you, once Gentiles in the flesh—who are called Uncircumcision by what is called [u]the Circumcision made in the flesh by hands— [12]that at that time you were without Christ, being aliens from the commonwealth of Israel and strangers from the covenants of promise, having no hope and without God in the world. [13]But now in Christ Jesus you who once were far off have been brought near by the blood of Christ.

Christ Our Peace

[14]For He Himself is our peace, who has made both one, and has broken down the middle wall of separation, [15]having abolished in His flesh the enmity, *that is,* the law of commandments *contained* in ordinances, so as to create in Himself one [v]new man *from* the two, *thus* making peace, [16]and that He might [w]reconcile them both to God in one body through the cross, thereby [x]putting to death the enmity. [17]And He came and preached peace to you who were afar off and to those who were near. [18]For [y]through Him we both have access [z]by one Spirit to the Father.

Christ Our Cornerstone

[19]Now, therefore, you are no longer strangers and foreigners, but fellow citizens with the saints and members of the household of God, [20]having been [a]built [b]on the foundation of the [c]apostles and prophets, Jesus Christ Himself being [d]the chief corner*stone,* [21]in whom the whole building, being fitted together, grows into [e]a holy temple in the Lord, [22][f]in whom you also are being built together for a [g]dwelling place of God in the Spirit.

The Mystery Revealed

3 For this reason I, Paul, the prisoner of Christ Jesus for you Gentiles— [2]if indeed you have heard of the dispensation of the grace of God [a]which was given to me for you, [3][b]how that by revelation [c]He made known to me the mystery (as I have briefly written already, [4]by which, when you read, you may understand my knowledge in the mystery of Christ), [5]which in other ages was not made known to the sons of men, as it has now been revealed by the Spirit to His holy apostles and prophets: [6]that the Gentiles [d]should be fellow heirs, of the same body, and partakers of His promise in Christ through the gospel, [7][e]of which I became a minister [f]according to the gift of the grace of God given to me by [g]the effective working of His power.

Purpose of the Mystery

[8]To me, [h]who am less than the least of all the saints, this grace was given, that I should preach among the Gentiles [i]the unsearchable riches of Christ, [9]and to make all see what is the fellowship* of the mystery, which from the beginning of the ages has been hidden in God who [j]created all things through Jesus Christ;* [10][k]to the intent that now [l]the manifold wisdom of God might be made known by the church [m]to the principalities and powers in the heavenly *places,* [11][n]according to the eternal purpose which He accomplished in Christ Jesus our Lord, [12]in whom we have boldness and access [o]with confidence through faith in Him. [13][p]Therefore I ask that you do not lose heart at my tribulations for you, [q]which is your glory.

Appreciation of the Mystery

[14]For this reason I bow my knees to the [r]Father of our Lord Jesus Christ,* [15]from whom the whole family in heaven and

---

* **3:9** NU-Text and M-Text read *stewardship* (dispensation). • NU-Text omits *through Jesus Christ.*
* **3:14** NU-Text omits *of our Lord Jesus Christ.*

2:14 *the middle wall of separation.* This was vividly portrayed by an actual partition in the temple area, with a sign warning that any Gentile going beyond the Court of the Gentiles would receive swift and sudden death.
2:15 *one new man.* In the early days of Christianity, the church was largely made up of Jews. But, under the direction of God's Spirit, the believers witnessed to Gentiles (Acts 10), who then soon outnumbered the Jewish members. As the two groups learned to work together, they became something completely new.
2:20 *the apostles and prophets.* The early church was established on the teaching and preaching of the apostles. They were the foundation of the church.
2:21 *fitted together.* This idea pictures the process in Roman construction whereby laborers would turn huge rocks around until they fit each other perfectly.
3:5–6 *the Gentiles should be fellow heirs.* In Old Testament times people had only partial knowledge of God and His works. While Genesis pointed to the

fact that God's grace would come to the Gentiles (Gen. 12:3), no one understood that they would also be fully equal with the Jews.
3:10 *manifold wisdom.* God's ways are not only "mysterious," but also varied. Angels are also learning about God's wisdom as they watch His grace working in us (1 Cor. 11:10).

2:10 [r] Is. 19:25   **2:11** [u] [Col. 2:11]   **2:15** [v] Gal. 6:15
2:16 [w] [Col. 1:20–22]   [x] [Rom. 6:6]   **2:18** [y] John 10:9
[z] 1 Cor. 12:13   **2:20** [a] 1 Pet. 2:4   [b] Matt. 16:18; 1 Cor. 3:10,
11   [c] 1 Cor. 12:28   [d] Ps. 118:22; Luke 20:17   **2:21** [e] 1 Cor.
3:16, 17   **2:22** [f] 1 Pet. 2:5   [g] John 17:23   **3:2** [a] Acts
9:15   **3:3** [b] Acts 22:17, 21; 26:16   [c] [Rom. 11:25; 16:25]
3:6 [d] Gal. 3:28, 29   **3:7** [e] Rom. 15:16   [f] Rom. 1:5   [g] Rom.
15:18   **3:8** [h] [1 Cor. 15:9]   [i] [Col. 1:27; 2:2, 3]   **3:9** [j] Heb.
1:2   **3:10** [k] 1 Pet. 1:12   [l] [1 Tim. 3:16]   [m] Col. 1:16; 2:10,
15   **3:11** [n] [Eph. 1:4, 11]   **3:12** [o] Heb. 4:16; 10:19, 35
3:13 [p] Phil. 1:14   [q] 2 Cor. 1:6   **3:14** [r] Eph. 1:3

earth is named, [16]that He would grant you, [s]according to the riches of His glory, [t]to be strengthened with might through His Spirit in [u]the inner man, [17v]that Christ may dwell in your hearts through faith; that you, [w]being rooted and grounded in love, [18x]may be able to comprehend with all the saints [y]what is the width and length and depth and height— [19]to know the love of Christ which passes knowledge; that you may be filled [z]with all the fullness of God.

[20]Now [a]to Him who is able to do exceedingly abundantly [b]above all that we ask or think, [c]according to the power that works in us, [21d]to Him be glory in the church by Christ Jesus to all generations, forever and ever. Amen.

Walk in Unity

4 I, therefore, the prisoner of the Lord, beseech you to [a]walk worthy of the calling with which you were called, [2]with all lowliness and gentleness, with longsuffering, bearing with one another in love, [3]endeavoring to keep the unity of the Spirit [b]in the bond of peace. [4c]There is one body and one Spirit, just as you were called in one hope of your calling; [5d]one Lord, [e]one faith, [f]one baptism; [6g]one God and Father of all, who is above all, and [h]through all, and in you* all.

Spiritual Gifts

[7]But [i]to each one of us grace was given according to the measure of Christ's gift. [8]Therefore He says:

[j]"When He ascended on high,
He led captivity captive,
And gave gifts to men."*

* **4:6** NU-Text omits you; M-Text reads us.
* **4:8** Psalm 68:18

3:17 Christ may dwell in your hearts. Christ actually resides or makes His home in the believer's heart.

3:21 The Purpose of the Church—The ultimate purpose of the church is to bring honor and glory to Jesus Christ. It does this as it fulfills its three purposes related to God's plan for the world.

Worship—As the church worships, it continually declares to believers and the world God's view of reality. God is the world's Creator and Sustainer. Through Jesus Christ, God has redeemed the world and provided a way of salvation for people who rebel against Him.

Evangelism—The Great Commission in Matthew 28 clearly points to evangelism as a primary purpose for the church. "Teaching" implies that there is more to evangelism than simply declaring the good news. Evangelism should lead to discipleship, which involves the work of helping the new believer reach full maturity in Christ. This happens much as a parent raises children, nurturing them in every way possible so that they can grow. Christ makes baptism an important element in this process. In baptism, one indicates that he has been identified with Christ in His death, burial, and resurrection and that he wishes to be identified with the church.

Edification—Ephesians 4:12 points to the fact that the saints need to be built up (that is equipped) to fully do the work of the church, namely the ministry of Christ to the world. This involves making believers aware of everything they have in Christ and how the Spirit's gifts enable them to serve the body of Christ effectively.

4:1 therefore . . . walk worthy of the calling with which you were called. The second half of Ephesians, like that of a number of Paul's epistles, emphasizes the behavior that should result from the doctrines or beliefs taught in the first half.

4:2 lowliness and gentleness, with longsuffering. These are the attitudes that Jesus demonstrated when He was on earth (Phil. 2:5–8). These attitudes do not come naturally, but must be cultivated by the determination to place others above ourselves. Only the Spirit can empower us to treat people this way consistently.

4:3 The Person of the Holy Spirit—Many people make the serious error of thinking of the Holy Spirit as only some kind of vague principle or influence. On the contrary, the Holy Spirit is as much a person

(individual existence of a conscious being) as the Father and the Son.

1. *The personality of the Holy Spirit.* The Bible speaks of the mind (Rom. 8:27) and will (1 Cor. 2:11) of the Spirit. He is often described as speaking directly to men in the Book of Acts. During Paul's second missionary journey, the apostle was forbidden by the Spirit to visit a certain mission field (Acts 16:6–7) and then was instructed to proceed toward another field of service (Acts 16:10). It was God's Spirit who spoke directly to Christian leaders in the Antioch church, commanding them to send Paul and Barnabas on their first missionary journey (Acts 13:2).

2. *The deity of the Holy Spirit.* He is not only a distinct being, but He is also God. As is God the Father, He too is everywhere at once (Ps. 139:7). As the Son is eternal, the Holy Spirit has also existed forever (Heb. 9:14). He is often referred to as God in the Bible (Acts 5:3–4). Finally, the Holy Spirit is equal with the Father and Son. This is seen during the baptism of Christ (Matt. 3:16–17) and is mentioned by Jesus Himself just prior to His ascension from the Mount of Olives (Matt. 28:19–20).

4:7 grace was given according to the measure of Christ's gift. Like Peter (1 Pet. 4:10), Paul taught that all Christians have a spiritual gift or gifts. The gifts are given sovereignly by the ascended Christ in order to build up the church (1 Cor. 12:11). Thus the body of Christ is to function like a machine in which every part is essential for getting a job done. But, unlike a machine, the body of Christ should maintain itself and build every one of its members up so that they can do good works (1 Cor. 12:7).

4:8 When He ascended on high. Paul quotes Psalm 68:18 to picture the ascended Messiah triumphant over Satan and his hosts, distributing spiritual gifts to His people.

3:16 [s][Phil. 4:19] [t]Col. 1:11 [u]Rom. 7:22 **3:17** [v]John 14:23 [w]Col. 1:23 **3:18** [x]Eph. 1:18 [y]Rom. 8:39 **3:19** [z]Eph. 1:23 **3:20** [a]Rom. 16:25 [b]1 Cor. 2:9 [c]Col. 1:29 **3:21** [d]Rom. 11:36 **4:1** [a]1 Thess. 2:12 **4:3** [b]Col. 3:14 **4:4** [c]Rom. 12:5 **4:5** [d]1 Cor. 1:13 [e]Jude 3 [f][Heb. 6:6] **4:6** [g]Mal. 2:10 [h]Rom. 11:36 **4:7** [i][1 Cor. 12:7, 11] **4:8** [j]Ps. 68:18; Mark 16:19; Acts 1:9; [1 Cor. 12:4–11]

[9]k(Now this, *"He ascended"*—what does it mean but that He also first* descended into the lower parts of the earth? [10]He who descended is also the One lwho ascended far above all the heavens, mthat He might fill all things.)

[11]And He Himself gave some *to be* apostles, some prophets, some evangelists, and some pastors and teachers, [12]for the equipping of the saints for the work of ministry, nfor the edifying of othe body of Christ, [13]till we all come to the unity of the faith pand of the knowledge of the Son of God, to qa perfect man, to the measure of the stature of the fullness of Christ; [14]that we should no longer be rchildren, tossed to and fro and carried about with every wind of doctrine, by the trickery of men, in the cunning craftiness of sdeceitful plotting, [15]but, speaking the truth in love, may grow up in all things into Him who is the thead—Christ— [16]ufrom whom the whole body, joined and knit together by what every joint supplies, according to the effective working by which every part does its share, causes growth of the body for the edifying of itself in love.

The New Man

[17]This I say, therefore, and testify in the Lord, that you should vno longer walk as the rest of* the Gentiles walk, in the futility of their mind, [18]having their understanding darkened, being alienated from the life of God, because of the ignorance that is in them, because of the wblindness of their heart; [19]xwho, being past feeling, yhave given themselves over to lewdness, to work all uncleanness with greediness.

[20]But you have not so learned Christ, [21]if indeed you have heard Him and have been taught by Him, as the truth is in Jesus: [22]that you zput off, concerning your former

conduct, the old man which grows corrupt according to the deceitful lusts, [23]and abe renewed in the spirit of your mind, [24]and that you bput on the new man which was created according to God, in true righteousness and holiness.

Do Not Grieve the Spirit

[25]Therefore, putting away lying, c"Let each one of you speak truth with his neighbor,"* for dwe are members of one another. [26]e"Be angry, and do not sin".* do not let the sun go down on your wrath, [27]fnor give place to the devil. [28]Let him who stole steal no longer, but rather glet him labor, working with *his* hands what is good, that he may have something hto give him who has need. [29]iLet no corrupt word proceed out of your mouth, but jwhat is good for necessary edification, kthat it may impart grace to the hearers. [30]And ldo not grieve the Holy Spirit of God, by whom you were sealed for the day of redemption. [31]mLet all bitterness, wrath, anger, clamor, and nevil speaking be put away from you, owith all malice. [32]And pbe kind to one another, tenderhearted, qforgiving one another, even as God in Christ forgave you.

Walk in Love

5 Thereforea be imitators of God as dear bchildren. [2]And cwalk in love, das Christ also has loved us and given Himself for us, an offering and a sacrifice to God efor a sweet-smelling aroma.

[3]But fornication and all funcleanness or gcovetousness, let it not even be named among you, as is fitting for saints; [4]hneither

---

* **4:9** NU-Text omits *first*.   * **4:17** NU-Text omits *the rest of*.   * **4:25** Zechariah 8:16
* **4:26** Psalm 4:4

4:11 apostles . . . prophets . . . evangelists . . . pastors and teachers. Apostles, meaning "envoys" or "ambassadors," in its strict sense refers to those who saw Christ in resurrected form and were specially chosen by Christ to tell others about Him from their eyewitness accounts. Prophets delivered direct revelations from God. They foretold God's actions in the future and they proclaimed what God had already said in the Scriptures. Evangelists play a major role in bringing people into the body of Christ. Pastors function as shepherds. They feed, nurture, care for, and protect the members of the body. The Greek ties in teacher with pastor.

4:12–13 equipping of the saints for the work of ministry, for the edifying of the body of Christ. Three stages of growth are presented here. Leaders are responsible to equip. The well-equipped saints do the work of the ministry, and the result is that the body is built up. The final goal is maturity, truth, and love.

4:16 every joint . . . every part. There are no insignificant parts in the body (1 Cor. 12:14–27). Anything that builds up believers and the church can be said to be edifying.

4:22–24 you put off . . . the old man. Paul compares

the Christian life to stripping off the dirty clothes of a sinful past and putting on the snowy white robes of Christ's righteousness.

4:30 the Holy Spirit of God. We should never push away, ignore, or reject the Holy Spirit. If we would remember that the One who lives in us is God's own Spirit, we would be much more selective about what we think, read, watch, say, and do.

5:1 imitators of God. Believers are to follow the example of God's actions. He loved us when we were still His enemies.

4:9 k John 3:13; 20:17   **4:10** l Ps. 68:18; Acts 1:9
m [Acts 2:33; Eph. 1:23]   **4:12** n 1 Cor. 14:26   o Col. 1:24
4:13 p Col. 2:2   q 1 Cor. 14:20   **4:14** r 1 Cor. 14:20   s Rom.
16:18   **4:15** t Eph. 1:22   u Col. 2:19   **4:17** v Eph.
2:2; 4:22   **4:18** w Rom. 1:21   **4:19** x 1 Tim. 4:2   y 1 Pet. 4:3
4:22 z Col. 3:8   **4:23** a [Rom. 12:2]   **4:24** b [Rom. 6:4;
7:6; 12:2]   **4:25** c Zech. 8:16   d Rom. 12:5   **4:26** e Ps. 4:4;
37:8   **4:27** f [Rom. 12:19]   **4:28** g Acts 20:35   h Luke 3:11
4:29 i Col. 3:8   j 1 Thess. 5:11   k Col. 3:16   **4:30** l Is. 7:13
4:31 m Col. 3:8, 19   n James 4:11   o Titus 3:3   **4:32** p 2 Cor.
6:10   q [Mark 11:25]   **5:1** a Luke 6:36   b 1 Pet. 1:14–16
5:2 c 1 Thess. 4:9   d Gal. 1:4   e 2 Cor. 2:14, 15   **5:3** f Col.
3:5–7   g [Luke 12:15]   **5:4** h Matt. 12:34, 35

filthiness, nor *i*foolish talking, nor coarse jesting, *j*which are not fitting, but rather *k*giving of thanks. **5**For this you know,* that no fornicator, unclean person, nor covetous man, who is an idolater, has any *l*inheritance in the kingdom of Christ and God. **6**Let no one deceive you with empty words, for because of these things the wrath of God comes upon the sons of disobedience. **7**Therefore do not be *m*partakers with them.

Walk in Light

8For you were once darkness, but now *you are* *n*light in the Lord. Walk as children of light **9**(for *o*the fruit of the Spirit* *is* in all goodness, righteousness, and truth), **10**pfinding out what is acceptable to the Lord. **11**And have *q*no fellowship with the unfruitful works of darkness, but rather expose *them.* **12**rFor it is shameful even to speak of those things which are done by them in secret. **13**But *s*all things that are exposed are made manifest by the light, for whatever makes manifest is light. **14**Therefore He says:

t"Awake, you who sleep,
  Arise from the dead,
And Christ will give you light."

Walk in Wisdom

15uSee then that you walk circumspectly, not as fools but as wise, **16**vredeeming the time, *w*because the days are evil.

17xTherefore do not be unwise, but *y*understand *z*what the will of the Lord *is.* **18**And *a*do not be drunk with wine, in which is dissipation; but be filled with the Spirit, **19**speaking to one another *b*in psalms and hymns and spiritual songs, singing and making *c*melody in your heart to the Lord, **20**dgiving thanks always for all things to God the Father *e*in the name of our Lord Jesus Christ, **21**fsubmitting to one another in the fear of God.*

Marriage—Christ and the Church

22Wives, *g*submit to your own husbands, as to the Lord. **23**For *h*the husband is head of the wife, as also *i*Christ is head of the church; and He is the Savior of the body. **24**Therefore, just as the church is subject to Christ, so *let* the wives *be* to their own husbands *j*in everything.

25kHusbands, love your wives, just as Christ also loved the church and *l*gave

* **5:5** NU-Text reads *For know this.* * **5:9** NU-Text reads *light.* * **5:21** NU-Text reads *Christ.*

5:12 *in secret.* This verse effectively bans Christians from indulging in the modern preoccupation with examining the lurid details of evils such as the occult and other perverted practices.
5:16 *redeeming the time.* This means taking advantage of opportunities for service. Paul exhorts us to use as much time as is possible for advancing Christ's purposes in this world.
5:18 *drunk with wine.* Just as a person who is drunk is under the control of alcohol, so a Spirit-filled believer is controlled by the Spirit. *filled.* Filling is a step beyond the sealing of the Holy Spirit (1:13). Sealing is an action God took at the point of our new birth. The tense of the Greek word translated *filled* indicates that filling is a moment-by-moment repeatable action. To be filled with the Spirit is to be controlled by the Spirit and is therefore crucial to successfully living the Christian life. The imperative says that the believer is to be filled with the presence of the Spirit so that he comes to know God in all His fullness, living in relationship with Him. Out of this relationship, the believer is able to manifest Christlike character. The certainty of being filled with the Spirit may be confirmed by the believer's faith and life. The believer must, of course, believe God's Word that meeting the conditions will result in the filling. The Spirit-filled person will exhibit the Christlike character described in Galatians 5:22–23 as the fruit of the Spirit. Included in that list are all the vibrant, attractive qualities desired by all Christians. Any Christian may be transformed by the filling of the Spirit and possess these qualities.
5:19 *singing and making melody.* Most believe that these words refer to three larger categories: (1) the 150 psalms in the Psalter, (2) hymns or compositions addressed directly to God, and (3) spiritual songs, hymns about the Christian experience.
5:21–22 *submitting.* Verse 21 completes the thought of the previous verses (vv. 18–20), which

address how being filled with the Spirit manifests itself in the believer's life. It also introduces the next section (5:22—6:4), about how members of a Christian family should relate to each other. The Greek word for *submit* does not refer to being under the absolute control of another but to voluntarily placing oneself under the authority of another.
5:22–24 *Wives, submit.* Just as Christ is not inferior to the Father, but is the second Person in the Trinity, so wives are equal to their own husbands. Yet, in a marriage relationship, a husband and wife have different roles. A wife's voluntary submission arises out of her own submission to Christ.
5:25 *Husbands, love.* Paul does not emphasize the husband's authority; instead, he calls on husbands to love self-sacrificially. Husbands are to emulate Christ's love, the kind of love that is willing to lay down one's life for another. *Christ also loved the church.* The relationship between Christ and the church was initiated by Christ, who loved the church and gave Himself for it. The details of that relationship are described with seven images:
  1. *The Shepherd and the sheep* emphasizes both the warm leadership and protection of Christ and the helplessness and dependency of believers (John 10:1–18).
  2. *The vine and the branches* points out the necessity for Christians to depend on Christ's sustaining strength for growth (John 15:1–8).

5:4 *i* Titus 3:9 *j* Rom. 1:28 *k* Phil. 4:6 **5:5** *l* 1 Cor. 6:9, 10 **5:7** *m* 1 Tim. 5:22 **5:8** *n* 1 Thess. 5:5 **5:9** *o* Gal. 5:22 **5:10** *p* [Rom. 12:1, 2] **5:11** *q* 2 Cor. 6:14 **5:12** *r* Rom. 1:24 **5:13** *s* [John 3:20, 21] **5:14** *t* [Is. 26:19; 60:1] **5:15** *u* Col. 4:5 **5:16** *v* Col. 4:5 *w* Eccl. 11:2 **5:17** *x* Col. 4:5 *y* [Rom. 12:2] *z* 1 Thess. 4:3 **5:18** *a* Prov. 20:1; 23:31 **5:19** *b* Acts 16:25 *c* James 5:13 **5:20** *d* Ps. 34:1 *e* [1 Pet. 2:5] **5:21** *f* [Phil. 2:3] **5:22** *g* Col. 3:18—4:1 **5:23** *h* [1 Cor. 11:3] *i* Col. 1:18 **5:24** *j* Titus 2:4, 5 **5:25** *k* Col. 3:19 *l* Acts 20:28

Himself for her, [26]that He might sanctify and cleanse her [m]with the washing of water [n]by the word, [27o]that He might present her to Himself a glorious church, [p]not having spot or wrinkle or any such thing, but that she should be holy and without blemish. [28]So husbands ought to love their own wives as their own bodies; he who loves his wife loves himself. [29]For no one ever hated his own flesh, but nourishes and cherishes it, just as the Lord *does* the church. [30]For [q]we are members of His body,* of His flesh and of His bones. [31r]*"For this reason a man shall leave his father and mother and be joined to his wife, and the [s]two shall become one flesh."** [32]This is a great mystery, but I speak concerning Christ and the church. [33]Nevertheless [t]let each one of you in particular so love his own wife as himself, and let the wife *see* that she [u]respects *her* husband.

Children and Parents

6 Children, [a]obey your parents in the Lord, for this is right. [2b]*"Honor your father and mother,"* which is the first commandment with promise: [3]*"that it may be well with you and you may live long on the earth."** [4]And [c]you, fathers, do not provoke your children to wrath, but [d]bring them up in the training and admonition of the Lord.

Bondservants and Masters

[5e]Bondservants, be obedient to those who are your masters according to the flesh, [f]with fear and trembling, [g]in sincerity of heart, as to Christ; [6h]not with eyeservice, as men-pleasers, but as bondservants of Christ, doing the will of God from the heart, [7]with goodwill doing service, as to the Lord, and not to men, [8i]knowing that whatever good anyone does, he will receive the same from the Lord, whether *he is a* slave or free.

[9]And you, masters, do the same things to them, giving up threatening, knowing that your own [j]Master also* is in heaven, and [k]there is no partiality with Him.

---

* **5:30** NU-Text omits the rest of this verse.
* **5:31** Genesis 2:24   * **6:3** Deuteronomy 5:16
* **6:9** NU-Text reads *He who is both their Master and yours.*

---

3. *Christ as high priest* and *the church as a kingdom of priests* stress the joyful worship, fellowship, and service which the church can render to God through Christ (Heb. 5:1–10; 7:1; 8:6; 1 Pet. 2:5–9).

4. *The cornerstone and building stones* (Matt. 21:42) accents the foundational value of Christ to everything the church is and does, as well as Christ's value to the unity of believers. Love is to be the mortar which solidly holds the living stones together (1 Cor. 3:9; 13:1–13; Eph. 2:19–22; 1 Pet. 2:5).

5. *The head and many-membered body,* the church is a vibrant organism, not merely an organization; it draws its vitality and direction from Christ, the Head, and each believer has a unique and necessary place in its growth (1 Cor. 12:12–13,27; Eph. 4:4).

6. *The last Adam and new creation* presents Christ as the initiator of a new creation of believers as Adam was of the old creation (1 Cor. 15:22,45; 2 Cor. 5:17).

7. *The bridegroom and bride* beautifully emphasizes the intimate fellowship and co-ownership existing between Christ and the church (Eph. 5:25–33; Rev. 19:7–8; 21:9).

5:31 the two shall become one flesh. Paul quotes Genesis 2:24, which teaches that the special union between husband and wife supersedes the original family ties.

5:32 This is a great mystery. A sacred secret revealed here is that Christian marriage parallels the union that exists spiritually between Christ and His bride, the church.

6:1–4 Children, obey . . . fathers, do not provoke. This paragraph has the beautiful balance we expect to find in God's Word: children are to obey their parents, and parents are to treat their children in such a way that the children will want to obey.

6:4 Parenting—The father is the parent responsible for setting the pattern for the child's obedience in the family. The father's responsibility is set forth in two ways: First, what the father is *not to do*—"do not provoke your children to wrath." He is not to over-discipline them or rule the household in such a way that the child can only react in a rage. Second, what the father *is to do*—"but bring them up in the training and admonition of the Lord." "Bring them up" involves three ideas:

a. It is a continuous job. As long as the child is a dependent, the father is to be responsible for providing for the child so that he becomes what God wants him to be.

b. It is a loving job. To "bring up" means literally to nourish tenderly; children should be objects of tender, loving care.

c. It is a job that involves nurture and admonition. The child needs to be nurtured physically and spiritually. He also needs corrective discipline that will be effective in bringing about obedience to the Word of God (Prov. 13:24; 19:18; 29:15–17).

6:5 Bondservants, be obedient. Bondservants made up a large percentage of the population of the Roman Empire. These people were considered mere property and could be abused and even killed by their masters with no resulting investigation by the state. In the church, wealthy slave owners and their slaves broke bread together at the Lord's Table as equals.

6:6 not with eyeservice. Servants and employees should serve faithfully even when no one is looking. After all, God sees all that we do.

5:26 [m] John 3:5 [n] [John 15:3; 17:17] **5:27** [o] Col. 1:22 [p] Song 4:7 **5:30** [q] Gen. 2:23 **5:31** [r] Gen. 2:24 [s] [1 Cor. 6:16] **5:33** [t] Col. 3:19 [u] 1 Pet. 3:1, 6 **6:1** [a] Col. 3:20 **6:2** [b] Deut. 5:16 **6:4** [c] Col. 3:21 [d] Gen. 18:19 **6:5** [e] [1 Tim. 6:1] [f] 2 Cor. 7:15 [g] 1 Chr. 29:17 **6:6** [h] Col. 3:22 **6:8** [i] Rom. 2:6 **6:9** [j] Col. 4:1 [k] Rom. 2:11

The Whole Armor of God

[10]Finally, my brethren, be strong in the Lord and in the power of His might. [11]lPut on the whole armor of God, that you may be able to stand against the wiles of the devil. [12]For we do not wrestle against flesh and blood, but against [m]principalities, against powers, against [n]the rulers of the darkness of this age,* against spiritual *hosts* of wickedness in the heavenly *places*. [13]oTherefore take up the whole armor of God, that you may be able to withstand [p]in the evil day, and having done all, to stand.

[14]Stand therefore, [q]having girded your waist with truth, [r]having put on the breastplate of righteousness, [15]sand having shod your feet with the preparation of the gospel of peace; [16]above all, taking [t]the shield of faith with which you will be able to quench all the fiery darts of the wicked one. [17]And [u]take the helmet of salvation, and [v]the sword of the Spirit, which is the word of God; [18]wpraying always with all prayer and supplication in the Spirit, [x]being watchful to this end with all perseverance and [y]supplication for all the saints— [19]and for me, that utterance may be given to me, [z]that I may open my mouth boldly to make known the mystery of the gospel, [20]for which [a]I am an ambassador in chains; that in it I may speak boldly, as I ought to speak.

A Gracious Greeting

[21]But that you also may know my affairs *and* how I am doing, [b]Tychicus, a beloved brother and [c]faithful minister in the Lord, will make all things known to you; [22]dwhom I have sent to you for this very purpose, that you may know our affairs, and *that* he may [e]comfort your hearts.

[23]Peace to the brethren, and love with faith, from God the Father and the Lord Jesus Christ. [24]Grace *be* with all those who love our Lord Jesus Christ in sincerity. Amen.

---

* **6:12** NU-Text reads *rulers of this darkness.*

6:11 *the whole armor of God.* This equipment is the believer's protection against evil and the devil. Paul presented the extended metaphor of the battle dress roughly according to the order in which the various pieces were put on.

6:12 *For we do not wrestle.* The real battle is not with human cultists, false religionists, atheists, agnostics, and pseudo-Christians, but with the demonic beings working through them.

6:14 *truth.* This is a reference to integrity, a life of practical truthfulness and honesty. ***breastplate.*** In Roman times this went completely around the body and was made of hard leather or metal. ***righteousness.*** This is not the righteousness of Christ, which all believers possess, but the practical, righteous character and deeds of the believer.

6:15 *the preparation of the gospel of peace.* This may mean either that the gospel is the firm foundation on which Christians are to stand or that the Christian soldier should be ready to go out to defend and spread the gospel.

6:16 *shield of faith.* The Christian's shield offers protection against all forms of evil. Flaming arrows could not penetrate the fireproof shield of the ancient Roman soldier, nor can the assaults of Satan penetrate to the believer who places his or her faith in God.

6:17 *the sword of the Spirit.* This is the only offensive weapon in the believer's armor. This weapon is not necessarily the Bible as a whole, but the specific word that needs to be spoken in a specific situation.

6:21–24 *that you also may know my affairs.* The last verses of Ephesians reveal Paul's appreciation of the ministry of others, especially the ministry of Tychicus (Col. 4:7). The fact that this letter does not conclude with personal greetings, as Paul's other letters do, may indicate that this was a circular letter, one intended for a number of churches around Ephesus.

6:11 *l* [2 Cor. 6:7]   **6:12** *m* Rom. 8:38   *n* Luke 22:53
6:13 *o* [2 Cor. 10:4]   *p* Eph. 5:16   **6:14** *q* Is. 11:5   *r* Is. 59:17
6:15 *s* Is. 52:7   **6:16** *t* 1 John 5:4   **6:17** *u* 1 Thess. 5:8
v [Heb. 4:12]   **6:18** *w* Luke 18:1   *x* [Matt. 26:41]   *y* Phil. 1:4
6:19 *z* Col. 4:3   **6:20** *a* 2 Cor. 5:20   **6:21** *b* Acts 20:4
c 1 Cor. 4:1, 2   **6:22** *d* Col. 4:8   *e* 2 Cor. 1:6

THE EPISTLE OF PAUL THE APOSTLE TO THE
PHILIPPIANS

▶ **AUTHOR:** The external and internal evidence for the Pauline authorship of Philippians is very strong, and there is scarcely any doubt that anyone but Paul wrote it. Paul's "Macedonian call" in Troas during his second missionary journey led to his ministry in Philippi with the conversion of Lydia and others. Internal evidence suggests that the epistle was written from Rome (1:3; 4:22), although some commentators argue for Caesarea or Ephesus. It seems that during the writing of this letter Paul's life was at stake, and he was evidently awaiting the verdict of the imperial court (2:20–26).

▶ **TIME:** c. A.D. 62   ▶ **KEY VERSES:** Phil. 4:4–7

▶ **THEME:** Even though Paul probably wrote this letter while imprisoned in Rome, the letter is often called the Epistle of Joy. It gives us valuable insight into key areas of the Christian life by helping understand how we should identify with Christ in a variety of circumstances. We gain some insight into what Christian relationships should look like and what the content of our prayers for each other should be. Philippians also provides great insight in setting spiritual direction and determining practical priorities. Christians desiring to mature in the Lord will return to study it often.

Greeting

1 Paul and Timothy, bondservants of Jesus Christ,

To all the saints in Christ Jesus who are in Philippi, with the bishops* and ᵃdeacons:

²Grace to you and peace from God our Father and the Lord Jesus Christ.

Thankfulness and Prayer

³ᵇI thank my God upon every remembrance of you, ⁴always in ᶜevery prayer of mine making request for you all with joy, ⁵ᵈfor your fellowship in the gospel from the first day until now, ⁶being confident of this very thing, that He who has begun ᵉa good work in you will complete it until the day of Jesus Christ; ⁷just as it is right for me to think this of you all, because I have you in my heart, inasmuch as both in my chains and in the defense and confirmation of the gospel, you all are partakers with me of grace. ⁸For God is my witness, how greatly I long for you all with the affection of Jesus Christ.

---

* 1:1 Literally *overseers*

1:1–11 To all the saints. This term means "holy ones" (those who are separated to God) and refers to all the believers in Philippi. **bishops.** This refers to those who watch over the spiritual welfare of the local church. **deacons.** This is a reference to those who serve the congregation in special service capacities. They were charged with handling the physical and material concerns of the church (Acts 6:1–7). In the first few verses, Paul reveals his great love for the Philippians. He thinks of them often (vv. 3–6), he is concerned about them (vv. 7–8), and he regularly prays for them (vv. 9–11).
1:3 I thank. The tense of the Greek verb indicates that Paul was continually thankful to God for the Philippian Christians. **upon every remembrance of you.** Every time God brought them to his mind, Paul gave thanks.
1:4 joy. This is the first of five uses of the Greek word for *joy* in the letter (v. 25; 2:2,29; 4:1). Paul also uses the Greek word for *rejoice* eight times in this letter (v. 18; 2:17–18,28; 3:1; 4:4).
1:5 fellowship. This term is a commercial term for a joint-partnership in a business venture in which all parties actively participate to ensure the success of the business. In the Christian community, the word expresses intimacy with Christ (1 Cor. 1:9).
1:6 until. This word can also be translated "as far as." It expresses progress toward a goal and indicates that a time is coming when God will completely finish His work among the Philippian Christians.
1:7 right. This word conveys a sense of moral uprightness and is often translated throughout the New Testament as "righteous." In this context, the word indicates that Paul's thoughts regarding the Philippians were in perfect accord with God's will. **confirmation.** Used only here and in Hebrews 6:16 in the New Testament, this word is a legal and commercial term meaning "a validating guarantee."
1:8 the affection of Jesus Christ. The word translated "affection" literally means the internal organs, regarded by the first century reader as the center of

---

1:1 *ᵃ* [1 Tim. 3:8–13]   **1:3** *ᵇ* 1 Cor. 1:4   **1:4** *ᶜ* Eph. 1:16
1:5 *ᵈ* [Rom. 12:13]   **1:6** *ᵉ* [John 6:29]

⁹And this I pray, that your love may abound still more and more in knowledge and all discernment, ¹⁰that you may approve the things that are excellent, that you may be sincere and without offense till the day of Christ, ¹¹being filled with the fruits of righteousness ᶠwhich *are* by Jesus Christ, ᵍto the glory and praise of God.

Christ Is Preached

¹²But I want you to know, brethren, that the things *which happened* to me have actually turned out for the furtherance of the gospel, ¹³so that it has become evident ʰto the whole palace guard, and to all the rest, that my chains are in Christ; ¹⁴and most of the brethren in the Lord, having become confident by my chains, are much more bold to speak the word without fear.

¹⁵Some indeed preach Christ even from envy and strife, and some also from goodwill: ¹⁶The former* preach Christ from selfish ambition, not sincerely, supposing to add affliction to my chains; ¹⁷but the latter out of love, knowing that I am appointed for the defense of the gospel. ¹⁸What then? Only *that* in every way, whether in pretense or in truth, Christ is preached; and in this I rejoice, yes, and will rejoice.

To Live Is Christ

¹⁹For I know that ⁱthis will turn out for my deliverance through your prayer and the supply of the Spirit of Jesus Christ, ²⁰according to my earnest expectation and hope that in nothing I shall be ashamed, but ʲwith all boldness, as always, so now also Christ will be magnified in my body, whether by life ᵏor by death. ²¹For to me, to live *is* Christ, and to die *is* gain. ²²But if *I* live on in the flesh, this *will mean* fruit from *my* labor; yet what I shall choose I cannot tell. ²³For* I am hard-pressed between the two, having a ˡdesire to depart and be with Christ, *which is* ᵐfar better. ²⁴Nevertheless to remain in the flesh *is* more needful for you. ²⁵And being confident of this, I know that I shall remain and continue with you all for your progress and joy of faith, ²⁶that ⁿyour rejoicing for me may be more abundant in Jesus Christ by my coming to you again.

Striving and Suffering for Christ

²⁷Only ᵒlet your conduct be worthy of the gospel of Christ, so that whether I come and see you or am absent, I may hear of your

---

* **1:16** NU-Text reverses the contents of verses 16 and 17.   * **1:23** NU-Text and M-Text read *But.*

---

the deepest feelings. Whereas the heart is the seat of reflection, Paul now speaks of his deep feelings for the believers. His feelings for the Philippians were like those of Jesus Christ, who loved them and died for them.

1:9 love. The kind of love that Paul sought for the believers is the highest form of Christian love, based on a lasting, unconditional commitment, not on an unstable emotion. *knowledge.* The first of two terms on which a directed love is built, knowledge suggests an intimate understanding based on a relationship with a person. Here the focus of this knowledge is God. *discernment.* Found only here in the New Testament, the Greek word means moral or ethical understanding based on both the intellect and the senses.

1:10 that you may approve. This verb is used in ancient literature for the testing of gold to determine its purity and for trying oxen to assess their usefulness for the task at hand.

1:12 furtherance. This phrase could suggest a pioneer beating or cutting a path through a densely forested area. Paul's imprisonment was a strategic advance in the kingdom of God because it was clearing the way for the gospel to penetrate the ranks of the Roman military.

1:13 palace guard. This is a reference to the praetorian guard, a force consisting of several thousand highly trained, elite soldiers of the Roman Empire who were headquartered at Rome. For the one to two years that Paul had been under house arrest in Rome, different soldiers had taken turns guarding him. Although Paul could not go to the world to preach, in this way God brought the world to Paul. In an ironic twist, they were the captives and Paul was free to preach.

1:18 in pretense or in truth. Whether the preaching was done for false motives or pure, whether for

appearance's sake or for the sake of what was right, Paul was pleased that the gospel was being spread.

1:19 deliverance. In the New Testament this word is used for physical healing, rescue from danger or death, justification, sanctification, and glorification.

1:20 be magnified. Paul was committed to ensuring that Christ would be made even more conspicuous in his own life than ever. He was not relying on himself to magnify Christ but looked to the Holy Spirit (v. 19) to magnify Christ in him (John 16:14).

1:21 Christ . . . gain. Paul would experience gain in his own death because he would be with Christ (v. 23). In fact, Paul may have been expressing his confidence that his imprisonment had furthered the gospel; God would also use his death to further His kingdom.

1:22 what I shall choose I cannot tell. Paul was in a dilemma because he clearly saw the advantages of both life and death, for the Christian life meant an opportunity to minister to people like the Philippians (v. 24), while death meant being with Christ his Savior.

1:25 your progress. Paul was not satisfied that the Philippian Christians should simply be saved, but that they should advance to maturity in Christ.

1:27 let your conduct. The word used could refer to discharging the obligations of a citizen. Because Philippi held the privileged status of a Roman colony, its citizens understood the responsibilities associated with citizenship. Paul here commanded them to shift their perspective from the earthly realm to the heavenly one. They should live in this world as citizens of another world, the heavenly kingdom. Their conduct should reveal their heavenly citizenship.

1:11 ᶠCol. 1:6 ᵍJohn 15:8   **1:13** ʰPhil. 4:22   **1:19** ⁱJob 13:16, LXX   **1:20** ʲEph. 6:19, 20 ᵏ[Rom. 14:8]   **1:23** ˡ[2 Cor. 5:2, 8] ᵐ[Ps. 16:11]   **1:26** ⁿ2 Cor. 1:14   **1:27** ᵒEph. 4:1

affairs, that you stand fast in one spirit, ᵖwith one mind �q̱striving together for the faith of the gospel, ²⁸and not in any way terrified by your adversaries, which is to them a proof of perdition, but to you of salvation,* and that from God. ²⁹For to you ʳit has been granted on behalf of Christ, ˢnot only to believe in Him, but also to ᵗsuffer for His sake, ³⁰ᵘhaving the same conflict ᵛwhich you saw in me and now hear *is* in me.

Unity Through Humility

2 Therefore if *there is* any consolation in Christ, if any comfort of love, if any fellowship of the Spirit, if any ᵃaffection and mercy, ²ᵇfulfill my joy ᶜby being likeminded, having the same love, *being* of ᵈone accord, of one mind. ³ᵉ*Let* nothing *be done* through selfish ambition or conceit, but ᶠin lowliness of mind let each esteem others better than himself. ⁴g̱Let each of you look out not only for his own interests, but also for the interests of ʰothers.

The Humbled and Exalted Christ

⁵ⁱLet this mind be in you which was also in Christ Jesus, ⁶who, ʲbeing in the form of God, did not consider it robbery to be equal with God, ⁷ᵏbut made Himself of no reputation, taking the form ˡof a bondservant, *and* ᵐcoming in the likeness of men. ⁸And being found in appearance as a man, He humbled Himself and ⁿbecame ᵒobedient to *the point of* death, even the death of the cross. ⁹ᵖTherefore God also q̱has highly exalted Him and ʳgiven Him the name which is above every name, ¹⁰ˢthat at the name of Jesus every knee should bow, of those in heaven, and of those on earth, and of those under the earth, ¹¹and ᵗ*that* every tongue should confess that Jesus Christ *is* Lord, to the glory of God the Father.

Light Bearers

¹²Therefore, my beloved, ᵘas you have always obeyed, not as in my presence only, but now much more in my absence, ᵛwork out your own salvation with ʷfear and trembling; ¹³for ˣit is God who works in you both to will and to do ʸfor *His* good pleasure.

¹⁴Do all things ᶻwithout complaining

---

* **1:28** NU-Text reads *of your salvation.*

1:28 terrified. This word is a strong term that is used for the terror of a panicked horse. The Philippians are not to be terror-stricken in the face of their enemies.
1:29 to suffer for His sake. Suffering matures us as Christians in the present (James 1:2–4) and enables us to be glorified with Christ in the future (Rom. 8:17).
2:1 if . . . if . . . if. The conditional clauses in this verse indicate certainties, not "maybes." Each *if* here expresses the idea of "since," and each following clause may be considered to be true.
2:2 being like-minded. In this verse the apostle sets forth a fourfold appeal that expresses one major idea—namely, the unity of the church. Paul is strongly emphasizing the unity that should exist between believers and how they must single-mindedly strive together to advance the gospel of Jesus Christ.
2:3 esteem others better than himself. This verb indicates a thorough analysis of the facts in order to reach a correct conclusion about the matter. In other words, each Philippian Christian was to properly assess himself or herself. Such an assessment would lead to valuing others.
2:5 Let this mind. All godly action begins with the renewing of our minds. Right thinking produces right actions. Our actions are the fruit of our deepest thoughts. *in you.* Thinking and being like Christ are requirements not only for an individual but also for the corporate body of believers. Together, we need to think and act like one being, like the Person of Jesus Christ.
2:6 did not consider it robbery. Because Christ was God, He did not look on sharing God's nature as "robbery," as though He did not already possess it, or as "a thing to be retained," as though He might lose it.
2:7 made Himself of no reputation. Christ did this by taking on the form of a servant. In doing this, He did not empty Himself of any part of His essence as God. Instead, He gave up His privileges as God and took upon Himself existence as a man. While remaining completely God, He became completely human.

form. Jesus added to His divine essence (v. 6) a servant's essence, that is, the essential characteristics of a human being seeking to fulfill the will of another. Paul does not say that Christ exchanged the form of God for the form of a servant, involving a loss of deity or the attributes of deity. Rather, in the incarnation, Christ continued in the very nature of God but added to Himself the nature of a servant.
2:8 He humbled Himself. Jesus willingly took the role of a servant; no one forced Him to do it. **obedient.** Although He never sinned and did not deserve to die, He chose to die so that the sins of the world could be charged to His account. Subsequently, He could credit His righteousness to the account of all who believe in Him (2 Cor. 5:21; Gal. 1:4). **even the death of the cross.** Paul describes the depths of Christ's humiliation by reminding his readers that Christ died by the cruelest form of capital punishment, crucifixion. The Jews viewed death on a cross as a curse from God (Deut. 21:23; Gal. 3:13).
2:11 confess. The term Paul uses is a strong, intensive verb, which means "agree with" or "say the same thing." Essentially Paul is saying that everyone will unanimously affirm what God the Father has already stated (Is. 45:23): that Jesus Christ is Lord.
2:12 work out. The Greek term speaks of the present deliverance of the Philippians. The word translated *work out* is used by a first century author to speak of digging silver out of silver mines. Thus, salvation

---

1:27 ᵖEph. 4:3 q̱Jude 3 **1:29** ʳ[Matt. 5:11, 12] ˢEph. 2:8 ᵗ[2 Tim. 3:12] **1:30** ᵘCol. 1:29; 2:1 ᵛActs 16:19–40 **2:1** ᵃCol. 3:12 **2:2** ᵇJohn 3:29 ᶜRom. 12:16 ᵈPhil. 4:2 **2:3** ᵉGal. 5:26 ᶠRom. 12:10 **2:4** g̱1 Cor. 13:5 ʰRom. 15:1, 2 **2:5** ⁱ[Matt. 11:29] **2:6** ʲ2 Cor. 4:4 **2:7** ᵏPs. 22:6 ˡIs. 42:1 ᵐ[John 1:14] **2:8** ⁿMatt. 26:39 ᵒHeb. 5:8 **2:9** ᵖHeb. 2:9 q̱Ps. 68:18; 110:1; Is. 52:13; Acts 2:33 ʳEph. 1:21 **2:10** ˢIs. 45:23 **2:11** ᵗJohn 13:13; [Rom. 10:9; 14:9] **2:12** ᵘPhil. 1:5, 6; 4:15 ᵛJohn 6:27, 29 ʷEph. 6:5 **2:13** ˣHeb. 13:20, 21 ʸEph. 1:5 **2:14** ᶻ1 Pet. 4:9

and ᵃdisputing, ¹⁵that you may become blameless and harmless, children of God without fault in the midst of a crooked and perverse generation, among whom you shine as ᵇlights in the world, ¹⁶holding fast the word of life, so that ᶜI may rejoice in the day of Christ that ᵈI have not run in vain or labored in ᵉvain.

¹⁷Yes, and if ᶠI am being poured out *as a drink offering* on the sacrifice ᵍand service of your faith, ʰI am glad and rejoice with you all. ¹⁸For the same reason you also be glad and rejoice with me.

Timothy Commended

¹⁹But I trust in the Lord Jesus to send ᶦTimothy to you shortly, that I also may be encouraged when I know your state. ²⁰For I have no one ʲlike-minded, who will sincerely care for your state. ²¹For all seek their own, not the things which are of Christ Jesus. ²²But you know his proven character, ᵏthat as a son with *his* father he served with me in the gospel. ²³Therefore I hope to send him at once, as soon as I see how it goes with me. ²⁴But I trust in the Lord that I myself shall also come shortly.

Epaphroditus Praised

²⁵Yet I considered it necessary to send to you ˡEpaphroditus, my brother, fellow worker, and ᵐfellow soldier, ⁿbut your messenger and ᵒthe one who ministered to my need; ²⁶ᵖsince he was longing for you all, and was distressed because you had heard that he was sick. ²⁷For indeed he was sick almost unto death; but God had mercy on him, and not only on him but on me also, lest I should have sorrow upon sorrow. ²⁸Therefore I sent him the more eagerly, that when you see him again you may rejoice, and I may be less sorrowful. ²⁹Receive him therefore in the Lord with all gladness, and hold such men in esteem; ³⁰because for the work of Christ he came close to death, not regarding his life, �q to supply what was lacking in your service toward me.

All for Christ

3 Finally, my brethren, ᵃrejoice in the Lord. For me to write the same things to you *is* not tedious, but for you *it is* safe.

²ᵇBeware of dogs, beware of ᶜevil workers, ᵈbeware of the mutilation! ³For we are ᵉthe circumcision, ᶠwho worship God in the Spirit,* rejoice in Christ Jesus, and have no confidence in the flesh, ⁴though ᵍI also might have confidence in the flesh. If anyone else thinks he may have confidence in the flesh, I ʰmore so: ⁵circumcised the eighth day, of the stock of Israel, ᶦof the tribe of Benjamin, ʲa Hebrew of the Hebrews; concerning the law, ᵏa Pharisee;

---

* **3:3** NU-Text and M-Text read *who worship in the Spirit of God.*

---

can be compared to a huge gift that needs to be unwrapped for one's thorough enjoyment. Note that Paul is encouraging the Philippians to develop and *work out* their salvation, but not to work *for* their salvation.

2:15 crooked and perverse generation. Paul describes the world as being the opposite of Christian. On the one hand, the world is turned away from the truth, while on the other hand, it exerts a corrupting influence that is opposed to the truth.

2:17 poured out. Paul was probably saying that he was presently being offered as a living sacrifice on behalf of the faith of the Philippians. *sacrifice.* This means primarily the act of offering something to God.

2:19 Timothy. He had accompanied Paul on his second missionary journey, during which time they had established the church at Philippi. Timothy was apparently well loved by the Philippians, and he in turn exhibited a great concern for them.

2:22 as a son with his father. In New Testament times a son who served his father did so to learn the family trade. Serving in this way meant learning all about the business and being willing to obey the teacher in order to become as skillful as possible in the work.

2:25 Epaphroditus. He was a Philippian Christian sent by the church in Philippi to take a gift to Paul and to assist Paul in his ministry.

2:27 sick almost unto death. Paul was making certain that the Philippians understood the effort that Epaphroditus had made for the cause of Christ. His condition had been far worse than perhaps they had imagined. Paul viewed Epaphroditus's healing as God's direct intervention.

3:2 Beware of dogs. In New Testament times, dogs were hated scavengers. The term came to be used for all who had morally impure minds. **the mutilation.** Paul here points sarcastically and specifically to those who desire to reinstate Jewish religious practices as necessary for salvation. He chooses a term that literally means "to cut." By doing so, he suggests that these people do not even understand the truth about the Old Testament practice of circumcision.

3:3 the circumcision. Paul defines this as a matter of the heart and not of the flesh. He reveals three aspects: (1) worshiping God in the Spirit; (2) rejoicing in Christ; and (3) placing no confidence in any human honor or accomplishment as a means to reach God.

3:5 eighth day. Paul's parents obeyed God's law and had Paul circumcised on the appropriate day after his birth (Lev. 12:2–3). **tribe of Benjamin.** This tribe was highly regarded because it had produced the first king of Israel and had remained loyal to David. **Hebrew of the Hebrews.** This description of Paul may indicate that (1) both his parents were Jews, (2) he was a model Jew, or (3) he was educated completely as a Jew. **Pharisee.** They rigorously followed and defended the letter of the Jewish law.

2:14 ᵃRom. 14:1 **2:15** ᵇMatt. 5:15, 16 **2:16** ᶜ2 Cor. 1:14 ᵈGal. 2:2 ᵉ1 Thess. 3:5 **2:17** ᶠ2 Tim. 4:6 ᵍRom. 15:16 ʰ2 Cor. 7:4 **2:19** ᶦRom. 16:21 **2:20** ʲ2 Tim. 3:10 **2:22** ᵏ1 Cor. 4:17 **2:25** ˡPhil. 4:18 ᵐPhilem. 2 ⁿ2 Cor. 8:23 ᵒ2 Cor. 11:9 **2:26** ᵖPhil. 1:8 **2:30** q 1 Cor. 16:17 **3:1** ᵃ1 Thess. 5:16 **3:2** ᵇGal. 5:15 ᶜPs. 119:115 ᵈRom. 2:28 **3:3** ᵉDeut. 30:6 ᶠRom. 7:6 **3:4** ᵍ2 Cor. 5:16; 11:18 ʰ2 Cor. 11:22, 23 **3:5** ᶦRom. 11:1 ʲ2 Cor. 11:22 ᵏActs 23:6

⁶concerning zeal, *l*persecuting the church; concerning the righteousness which is in the law, blameless.

⁷But *m*what things were gain to me, these I have counted loss for Christ. ⁸Yet indeed I also count all things loss *n*for the excellence of the knowledge of Christ Jesus my Lord, for whom I have suffered the loss of all things, and count them as rubbish, that I may gain Christ ⁹and be found in Him, not having *o*my own righteousness, which *is* from the law, but *p*that which *is* through faith in Christ, the righteousness which is from God by faith; ¹⁰that I may know Him and the *q*power of His resurrection, and *r*the fellowship of His sufferings, being conformed to His death, ¹¹if, by any means, I may *s*attain to the resurrection from the dead.

Pressing Toward the Goal

¹²Not that I have already *t*attained, or am already *u*perfected; but I press on, that I may lay hold of that for which Christ Jesus has also laid hold of me. ¹³Brethren, I do not count myself to have apprehended; but one thing *I do*, *v*forgetting those things which are behind and *w*reaching forward to those things which are ahead, ¹⁴*x*I press toward the goal for the prize of *y*the upward call of God in Christ Jesus.

¹⁵Therefore let us, as many as are *z*mature, *a*have this mind; and if in anything you

think otherwise, *b*God will reveal even this to you. ¹⁶Nevertheless, to *the degree* that we have already attained, *c*let us walk *d*by the same rule,* let us be of the same mind.

Our Citizenship in Heaven

¹⁷Brethren, *e*join in following my example, and note those who so walk, as *f*you have us for a pattern. ¹⁸For many walk, of whom I have told you often, and now tell you even weeping, *that they are* *g*the enemies of the cross of Christ: ¹⁹*h*whose end *is* destruction, *i*whose god *is their* belly, and *j*whose* glory *is* in their shame—*k*who set their mind on earthly things. ²⁰For *l*our citizenship is in heaven, *m*from which we also *n*eagerly wait for the Savior, the Lord Jesus Christ, ²¹*o*who will transform our lowly body that it may be *p*conformed to His glorious body, *q*according to the working by which He is able even to *r*subdue all things to Himself.

4 Therefore, my beloved and *a*longed-for brethren, *b*my joy and crown, so *c*stand fast in the Lord, beloved.

Be United, Joyful, and in Prayer

²I implore Euodia and I implore Syntyche *d*to be of the same mind in the Lord. ³And* I urge you also, true companion,

---

* **3:16** NU-Text omits *rule* and the rest of the verse.
* **4:3** NU-Text and M-Text read *Yes*.

3:7 *loss.* This word indicates that which is damaged or of no further use (v. 8). Those things that Paul thought to be important became unimportant after confronting the resurrected Messiah.

3:8 *rubbish.* This word means anything that is detestable or worthless. All things of this world are dung compared to Christ. Even our righteousness is like filthy rags (Is. 64:6).

3:10 *power of His resurrection.* Paul does not say the power "in" His resurrection, which would specify the power of the one-time event of His resurrection. Rather, Paul seeks the ongoing power that is the day-to-day experience of being in Christ. *fellowship of His sufferings.* Paul sees the value of participating in the persecutions or struggles that naturally accompany one who is in partnership with Christ and His sufferings. *being conformed to His death.* Paul desires to imitate Christ—even in His death. In other words, Paul wants to be completely obedient to God the Father, just as Jesus was obedient to His Father's will (Luke 22:42).

3:12 *perfected.* The Greek term means mature or complete, finished. It does not specifically mean a moral or sinless perfection. Paul is not speaking of moral perfection or righteousness but of reaching the state of completion as a Christian. *lay hold.* This phrase adds the idea of overtaking by surprise to the sense of seizing some object. Paul urgently wants to "grab hold of" God as God had laid hold of him.

3:13 *forgetting.* Paul was indicating that it is an ongoing process. He might even be implying that he wanted to forget everything so that he would not rest on his past successes in Christ, but continue to labor for the Lord.

3:16 *let us walk.* Paul commands the Philippians to conduct themselves as soldiers who "march in line" together, organized each in his proper position.

3:17 *example.* The word indicates an exact representation of the original. The example of Paul's life is so evident that one can readily see it and use it as a pattern for living.

3:19 *glory is in their shame.* The things in which they take pride actually are the things that will bring disgrace or humiliation to them, things of which they should have been ashamed.

3:20 *citizenship is in heaven.* Here Paul presents a direct contrast to the earthly focus of enemies of the cross in verse 19. The eager desire of Christians is not earthly things, but a heavenly Person, the Savior.

3:21 *conformed to His glorious body.* Our bodies now are weak and susceptible to sin, disease, and death. But God will change our bodies to resemble Christ's glorious resurrection body.

4:2 *Euodia . . . Syntyche.* What is written here is all that is known about the two women and their dispute. Paul does not take sides in the argument, but instead encourages them to be reconciled.

3:6 *i* Acts 8:3; 22:4, 5; 26:9–11 **3:7** *m* Matt. 13:44 **3:8** *n* Jer. 9:23 **3:9** *o* Rom. 10:3 *p* Rom. 1:17 **3:10** *q* Eph. 1:19, 20 *r* [Rom. 6:3–5] **3:11** *s* Acts 26:6–8 **3:12** *t* [1 Tim. 6:12, 19] *u* Heb. 12:23 **3:13** *v* Luke 9:62 *w* Heb. 6:1 **3:14** *x* 2 Tim. 4:7 *y* Heb. 3:1 **3:15** *z* 1 Cor. 2:6 *a* Gal. 5:10 *b* Hos. 6:3 **3:16** *c* Gal. 6:16 *d* Rom. 12:16; 15:5 **3:17** *e* [1 Cor. 4:16; 11:1] *f* Titus 2:7 **3:18** *g* Gal. 1:7 **3:19** *h* 2 Cor. 11:15 *i* 1 Tim. 6:5 *j* Hos. 4:7 *k* Rom. 8:5 **3:20** *l* Eph. 2:6, 19 *m* Acts 1:11 *n* 1 Cor. 1:7 **3:21** *o* [1 Cor. 15:43–53] *p* 1 John 3:2 *q* Eph. 1:19 *r* [1 Cor. 15:28] **4:1** *a* Phil. 1:8 *b* 2 Cor. 1:14 *c* Phil. 1:27 **4:2** *d* Phil. 2:2; 3:16

help these women who ᵉlabored with me in the gospel, with Clement also, and the rest of my fellow workers, whose names *are* in ᶠthe Book of Life.

⁴ᵍRejoice in the Lord always. Again I will say, rejoice!

⁵Let your gentleness be known to all men. ʰThe Lord *is* at hand.

⁶ⁱBe anxious for nothing, but in everything by prayer and supplication, with ʲthanksgiving, let your requests be made known to God; ⁷and ᵏthe peace of God, which surpasses all understanding, will guard your hearts and minds through Christ Jesus.

Meditate on These Things

⁸Finally, brethren, whatever things are ˡtrue, whatever things *are* ᵐnoble, whatever things *are* ⁿjust, ᵒwhatever things *are* pure, whatever things *are* ᵖlovely, whatever things *are* of good report, if *there* is any virtue and if *there* is anything praiseworthy—meditate on these things. ⁹The things which you learned and received and heard and saw in me, these do, and ᑫthe God of peace will be with you.

Philippian Generosity

¹⁰But I rejoiced in the Lord greatly that now at last ʳyour care for me has flourished again; though you surely did care, but you lacked opportunity. ¹¹Not that I speak in regard to need, for I have learned in whatever state I am, ˢto be content: ¹²ᵗI know how to be abased, and I know how to abound. Everywhere and in all things I have learned both to be full and to be hungry, both to abound and to suffer need. ¹³I can do all things ᵘthrough Christ* who strengthens me.

¹⁴Nevertheless you have done well that ᵛyou shared in my distress. ¹⁵Now you Philippians know also that in the beginning of the gospel, when I departed from Macedonia, ʷno church shared with me concerning giving and receiving but you only. ¹⁶For even in Thessalonica you sent *aid* once and again for my necessities. ¹⁷Not that I seek the gift, but I seek ˣthe fruit that abounds to your account. ¹⁸Indeed I have all and abound. I am full, having received from ʸEpaphroditus the things *sent* from you, ᶻa sweet-smelling aroma, ᵃan acceptable sacrifice, well pleasing to God. ¹⁹And my God ᵇshall supply all your need according to His riches in glory by Christ Jesus. ²⁰ᶜNow to our God and Father *be* glory forever and ever. Amen.

Greeting and Blessing

²¹Greet every saint in Christ Jesus. The brethren ᵈwho are with me greet you. ²²All the saints greet you, but especially those who are of Caesar's household.

²³The grace of our Lord Jesus Christ be with you all.* Amen.

* 4:13 NU-Text reads *Him who.*   * 4:23 NU-Text reads *your spirit.*

4:4 Rejoice in the Lord. The joy of Christians is not based on agreeable circumstances; instead, it is based on their relationship to God. Christians will face trouble in this world, but they should rejoice in the trials they face because they know God is using those situations to improve their character.
4:6 Be anxious for nothing. Paul prohibits the Philippians from worrying about their own problems. Instead, they are to commit their problems to God in prayer, trusting that He will provide deliverance.
4:7 will guard. Paul's choice of a military term "guard" implies that the mind is in a battle zone and needs to be protected by a "military guard" since the purpose of such a guard in a wartime situation is either to prevent a hostile invasion or to keep the inhabitants of a besieged city from escaping.
4:9 learned. This verb conveys not only the concept of "increasing in intellectual knowledge," but also the idea of "learning by habitual practice." In some areas of their Christian development, the Philippians had been excellent disciples of Paul, practicing what he had taught.
4:11 content. The word literally means "self-sufficient." In Stoic philosophy this Greek word described a person who dispassionately accepted whatever

circumstances brought. For the Greeks, this contentment came from personal sufficiency. But for Paul, true sufficiency is found in the strength of Christ.
4:17 account. Paul uses business terminology. The Philippians' gift was producing spiritual profit, just as money deposited in a bank account accrues interest. But Paul was not as concerned with their gift as with the development in the Philippians of the spiritual ability to give.
4:20 Amen. The Jewish practice of closing prayers with the word *amen* carried over to the Christian church as well. When found at the end of a sentence, as it is here, the word can be translated "so be it" or "may it be fulfilled." At the beginning of a sentence, it means "surely," "truly," or "most assuredly."

4:3 ᵉRom. 16:3 ᶠLuke 10:20   **4:4** ᵍRom. 12:12
4:5 ʰ[James 5:7–9]   **4:6** ⁱMatt. 6:25 ʲ[1 Thess. 5:17, 18]
4:7 ᵏ[John 14:27]   **4:8** ˡEph. 4:25 ᵐ2 Cor. 8:21 ⁿDeut.
16:20 ᵒ1 Thess. 5:22 ᵖ1 Cor. 13:4–7   **4:9** ᑫRom. 15:33
4:10 ʳ2 Cor. 11:9   **4:11** ˢ1 Tim. 6:6, 8   **4:12** ᵗ1 Cor. 4:11
4:13 ᵘJohn 15:5   **4:14** ᵛPhil. 1:7   **4:15** ʷ2 Cor. 11:8, 9
4:17 ˣTitus 3:14   **4:18** ʸPhil. 2:25 ᶻHeb. 13:16 ᵃ2 Cor.
9:12   **4:19** ᵇPs. 23:1   **4:20** ᶜRom. 16:27   **4:21** ᵈGal. 1:2

THE EPISTLE OF PAUL THE APOSTLE TO THE
COLOSSIANS

▶ **AUTHOR:** The external testimony to the Pauline authorship of Colossians is ancient and consistent, and the internal evidence is also very good. It not only claims to be written by Paul (1:1,23; 4:18), but the personal details and close parallels with Ephesians and Philemon make the case even stronger. It is evident from 1:4–8 and 2:1 that Paul had never visited the church at Colosse, which was founded by Epaphras. On his third missionary journey, Paul devoted almost three years to an Asian ministry centered in Ephesus (Acts 19:10; 20:31), and Epaphras probably came to Christ during this time. He then carried the gospel to cities like Colosse in the Lycus Valley. Epaphras visited Paul in prison (4:12) and his report concerning the church in Colosse prompted this epistle.

▶ **TIME:** C. A.D. 60–61   ▶ **KEY VERSES:** Col. 2:9–10

▶ **THEME:** The problem of the Colossian church was similar to what we experience in many churches today. This is often called syncretism, the tendency to regard other philosophies and religions as equally valid as Christianity. The people in Colosse wanted to believe Christian truth, but they also wanted to hang on to their old beliefs by blending them with the gospel. Paul's purpose in this letter is to settle once and for all the issue of Christ's centrality and supremacy. He writes to restore Jesus, the Messiah, to the center of these believers' lives. Here we can see Paul's unwavering confidence in the incomparability of Christ, as it has completely shaped his views on all of life. He writes to introduce the Colossians to this same vision.

Greeting

1 Paul, [a]an apostle of Jesus Christ by the will of God, and Timothy our brother,

[2]To the saints [b]and faithful brethren in Christ who are in Colosse:

[c]Grace to you and peace from God our Father and the Lord Jesus Christ.*

Their Faith in Christ

[3d]We give thanks to the God and Father of our Lord Jesus Christ, praying always for you, [4e]since we heard of your faith in Christ Jesus and of [f]your love for all the saints; [5]because of the hope [g]which is laid up for you in heaven, of which you heard before in the word of the truth of the gospel, [6]which has come to you, [h]as it has also in all the world, and [i]is bringing forth fruit,* as it is also among you since the day you heard and knew [j]the grace of God in truth; [7]as you also learned from [k]Epaphras, our dear fellow servant, who is [l]a faithful minister of Christ on your behalf, [8]who also declared to us your [m]love in the Spirit.

Preeminence of Christ

[9n]For this reason we also, since the day we heard it, do not cease to pray for you,

---

* **1:2** NU-Text omits *and the Lord Jesus Christ.*
* **1:6** NU-Text and M-Text add *and growing.*

1:1 *an apostle.* Paul calls himself an apostle, a word whose root means "to send." The Greek word was first used for a cargo ship or fleet, but later denoted a commander of a fleet. The New Testament employs the word to signify an approved spokesman sent as a personal representative.
1:2 *saints.* The Greek term means "holy people." The essence of "holiness" is being set apart to God. All believers are saints, not because they are perfect, but because they belong to God. *in Christ.* This is a favorite expression of the apostle Paul, used some 80 times in his letters.
1:4–8 *faith . . . love . . . hope.* Paul often uses these three terms together (Rom. 5:2–5; 1 Cor. 13:13;

1 Thess. 1:3; 5:8). Faith is in Christ. Love flows from faith and proves the genuineness of one's faith (James 2:14–26). Hope refers to the result of faith, the treasure laid up in heaven.
1:9 *all wisdom and spiritual understanding. Wisdom* is the practical outworking of knowledge (James 3:17), and that knowledge cannot be separated from the *spiritual understanding* that comes through the discernment given by the Holy Spirit.

1:1 [a] Eph. 1:1 **1:2** [b] 1 Cor. 4:17 [c] Gal. 1:3 **1:3** [d] Phil. 1:3 **1:4** [e] Eph. 1:15 [f] [Heb. 6:10] **1:5** [g] [1 Pet. 1:4] **1:6** [h] Matt. 24:14 [i] John 15:16 [j] Eph. 3:2 **1:7** [k] Philem. 23 [l] 2 Cor. 11:23 **1:8** [m] Rom. 15:30 **1:9** [n] Eph. 1:15–17	

and to ask [o]that you may be filled with [p]the
knowledge of His will [q]in all wisdom and
spiritual understanding; 10[r]that you may
walk worthy of the Lord, [s]fully pleasing
Him, [t]being fruitful in every good work
and increasing in the [u]knowledge of God;
11[v]strengthened with all might, according
to His glorious power, [w]for all patience and
longsuffering [x]with joy; 12[y]giving thanks to
the Father who has qualified us to be partakers of [z]the inheritance of the saints in
the light. 13He has delivered us from [a]the
power of darkness [b]and conveyed *us* into
the kingdom of the Son of His love, 14[c]in
whom we have redemption through His
blood,* the forgiveness of sins.
15He is [d]the image of the invisible God,
[e]the firstborn over all creation. 16For [f]by
Him all things were created that are in
heaven and that are on earth, visible and
invisible, whether thrones or [g]dominions
or principalities or powers. All things
were created [h]through Him and for Him.
17[i]And He is before all things, and in Him
[j]all things consist. 18And [k]He is the head
of the body, the church, who is the beginning, [l]the firstborn from the dead, that in
all things He may have the preeminence.

Reconciled in Christ

19For it pleased *the Father that* [m]in Him
all the fullness should dwell, 20and [n]by Him
to reconcile [o]all things to Himself, by Him,
whether things on earth or things in heav-
en, [p]having made peace through the blood
of His cross.
21And you, [q]who once were alienated and
enemies in your mind [r]by wicked works,
yet now He has [s]reconciled 22[t]in the body
of His flesh through death, [u]to present you
holy, and blameless, and above reproach in
His sight— 23if indeed you continue [v]in the
faith, grounded and steadfast, and are [w]not

* **1:14** NU-Text and M-Text omit *through His blood.*

1:10 ***walk worthy of the Lord.*** Paul wanted the Colossians to live in a manner that adequately reflected what God had done for them and was doing in them. Being "worthy of God" is a phrase that occurs in ancient pagan inscriptions throughout Asia. It pictures someone's life being weighed on scales to determine its worth.

1:12 ***qualified us.*** This means to be able or qualified for a task. Believers can never be qualified on their own; instead, God must make them sufficient through Jesus Christ. The tense of the verb points to "qualifying" as an act in the past rather than a process.

1:13 ***delivered . . . conveyed.*** God has liberated believers from the dominion of darkness. The apostle uses the common symbolism of light and darkness for good and evil, for God's kingdom and Satan's kingdom, that is found throughout the New Testament. The kingdom from which believers have been rescued is the kingdom of darkness.

1:14 ***redemption.*** The Greek word points naturally to the payment of a price or ransom for the release of a slave. They are freed from bondage to sin by forgiveness through the blood of Jesus (Eph. 1:7).

1:15 ***firstborn over all creation.*** Verses 15–20 are thought to be an early Christian hymn celebrating the supremacy of Christ. *Firstborn* could denote a priority in time or in rank. The word does not describe Christ as the first being created in time because the hymn proclaims that all things were "created by Him" and that "He is before all things." Being firstborn referred more to rank and privilege than to order of birth.

1:16 ***All things were created through Him and for Him.*** Not only did Jesus create all things, everything was created for His purposes (Heb. 1:2, where Christ is said to be the "heir of all things").

1:18 ***head of the body.*** No one should underestimate the significance of the church, for it is in fact Christ's body. The sovereign Creator of the universe, as Head of the church, provides leadership and oversight over it.

1:19 ***fullness.*** The opponents of Paul, and later the Greek Gnostics, seem to have used this word as a technical term for the sphere between heaven and earth where a hierarchy of angels lived. The Gnostics viewed Christ as one of many spirits existing in this hierarchy between God and all people. However, Paul used the term *fullness* to refer to the complete embodiment of God.

1:20–22 Jesus Pays the Price—Salvation is a free gift, but it is not a cheap one. It costs us nothing, but it cost God dearly—it cost Jesus His life. In physically dying on the cross, Jesus sacrificed Himself and satisfied the debt that we had incurred through sin, so that it is possible for God and man to be reconciled. As Jesus hung on the cross, He cried, "My God, My God, why have You forsaken Me?" (Matt. 27:46). Jesus was separated from God the Father so that we do not have to be. This is the heart of the atonement (becoming *at one* with God). The marvel of it all is that He did this while we were His enemies: "But God demonstrates His own love toward us, in that while we were still sinners, Christ died for us" (Rom. 5:8).

1:20–21 ***reconcile all things.*** This phrase shows the significance of Christ's work on the cross. It does not mean that all people will be saved, since many passages clearly say that unbelievers will suffer eternal separation from God (Matt. 25:46).

1:22 ***holy, and blameless, and above reproach.*** We who were once enemies of God and alienated by our own wicked works will one day be presented as above reproach on account of Christ's death for us.

1:23 ***if indeed you continue in the faith.*** The perseverance of the Colossians was proof of the reconciling work of Christ on their behalf. ***every creature under heaven.*** Paul uses this exaggeration to illustrate the rapid spread of the gospel. Compare Acts 17:6 where the apostles are said to have turned the world upside down, even though their ministry, up to that point,

1:9 [o] 1 Cor. 1:5 [p] [Rom. 12:2] [q] Eph. 1:8 **1:10** [r] Eph. 4:1 [s] 1 Thess. 4:1 [t] Heb. 13:21 [u] 2 Pet. 3:18 **1:11** [v] [Eph. 3:16; 6:10] [w] Eph. 4:2 [x] [Acts 5:41] **1:12** [y] [Eph. 5:20] [z] Eph. 1:11 **1:13** [a] Eph. 6:12 [b] 2 Pet. 1:11 **1:14** [c] Eph. 1:7 **1:15** [d] 2 Cor. 4:4 [e] Rev. 3:14 **1:16** [f] Heb. 1:2, 3 [g] [Eph. 1:20, 21] [h] Heb. 2:10 **1:17** [i] [John 17:5] [j] Heb. 1:3 **1:18** [k] Eph. 1:22 [l] Rev. 1:5 **1:19** [m] John 1:16 **1:20** [n] Eph. 2:14 [o] 2 Cor. 5:18 [p] Eph. 1:10 **1:21** [q] [Eph. 2:1] [r] Titus 1:15 [s] 2 Cor. 5:18, 19 **1:22** [t] 2 Cor. 5:18 [u] [Eph. 5:27] **1:23** [v] Eph. 3:17 [w] [John 15:6]

moved away from the hope of the gospel
which you heard, [x]which was preached to
every creature under heaven, [y]of which I,
Paul, became a minister.

Sacrificial Service for Christ

24[z]I now rejoice in my sufferings [a]for
you, and fill up in my flesh [b]what is lacking in the afflictions of Christ, for [c]the
sake of His body, which is the church,
25of which I became a minister according
to [d]the stewardship from God which was
given to me for you, to fulfill the word of
God, 26[e]the mystery which has been hidden
from ages and from generations, [f]but now
has been revealed to His saints. 27[g]To them
God willed to make known what are [h]the
riches of the glory of this mystery among
the Gentiles: which* is [i]Christ in you, [j]the
hope of glory. 28Him we preach, [k]warning
every man and teaching every man in all
wisdom, [l]that we may present every man
perfect in Christ Jesus. 29To this *end* I also
labor, striving according to His working
which works in me [m]mightily.

Not Philosophy but Christ

2 For I want you to know what a great
[a]conflict I have for you and those in Laodicea, and *for* as many as have not seen
my face in the flesh, 2that their hearts may
be encouraged, being knit together in love,
and *attaining* to all riches of the full assurance of understanding, to the knowledge
of the mystery of God, both of the Father
and* of Christ, 3[b]in whom are hidden all the
treasures of wisdom and knowledge.
4Now this I say [c]lest anyone should
deceive you with persuasive words. 5For
[d]though I am absent in the flesh, yet I am
with you in spirit, rejoicing to see [e]your
good order and the [f]steadfastness of your
faith in Christ.
6[g]As you therefore have received Christ
Jesus the Lord, so walk in Him, 7[h]rooted
and built up in Him and established in the
faith, as you have been taught, abounding
in it* with thanksgiving.
8Beware lest anyone cheat you through
philosophy and empty deceit, according
to [i]the tradition of men, according to the
[j]basic principles of the world, and not according to Christ. 9For [k]in Him dwells all
the fullness of the Godhead bodily; 10and
you are complete in Him, who is the [l]head
of all principality and power.

Not Legalism but Christ

11In Him you were also [m]circumcised
with the circumcision made without hands,
by [n]putting off the body of the sins* of the
flesh, by the circumcision of Christ, 12[o]bur-
ied with Him in baptism, in which you also
were raised with *Him* through [p]faith in the
working of God, [q]who raised Him from
the dead. 13And you, being dead in your
trespasses and the uncircumcision of your
flesh, He has made alive together with
Him, having forgiven you all trespasses,
14[r]having wiped out the handwriting of
requirements that was against us, which
was contrary to us. And He has taken

* **1:27** M-Text reads *who*. * **2:2** NU-Text omits *both of the Father and*. * **2:7** NU-Text omits *in it*. * **2:11** NU-Text omits *of the sins*.

---

had been limited to a small portion of the eastern Mediterranean region.

1:24 *my sufferings for you.* Paul is making the point that a Christian will endure the sufferings that Christ would be enduring if He were still in the world (2 Cor. 1:5; 4:11).

1:26–27 *mystery.* In Greek pagan religions, a mystery was a secret teaching reserved for a few spiritual teachers who had been initiated into an inner circle. Paul uses the word to refer to knowledge that had been "hidden from ages and from generations" but was now being revealed by God. The mystery is that Christ now lives within Gentile believers.

2:1 *Laodicea.* It was a sister city of Colosse about 11 miles away. The two churches were to share their letters from Paul.

2:2–3 *the knowledge of the mystery of God.* Paul reminds the Colossians that true knowledge will be acknowledged by bringing people together in Christian love in the church. The Gnostics thought only certain "knowledgeable" people could join their elite group; Paul teaches that every believer has access to complete wisdom found in Christ.

2:8 *philosophy.* This verse has been used at times to teach that Christians should not study or read philosophy. This is not Paul's meaning. Paul himself was adept at philosophy, evidenced by his interaction with the Stoic and Epicurean philosophers in Athens (Acts 17:1–34). Paul was warning the believers not to be taken in by any philosophy that does not conform to a proper knowledge of Christ. The false teachers at Colosse had combined worldly philosophies with the gospel.

2:9 *dwells all the fullness of the Godhead bodily.* In this verse Paul clearly proclaims the incarnation, the fact that God became a man bodily. This contradicts the Gnostic idea of the inherent evil of physical bodies and the claim that Jesus is merely a spirit.

2:10 *you are complete.* Paul emphasizes the sufficiency of Christ in order to refute the Gnostics and the Judaizers who respectively believed that special knowledge or works were necessary to make a Christian complete.

2:12–13 *buried with Him in baptism.* Baptism is the symbol of the believer's association with Christ's death on the cross. Water baptism itself does not bring forgiveness of sins, but Paul uses the rite to help explain the work of the Spirit. The early church would never have understood the idea of an unbaptized Christian.

1:23 [x]Col. 1:6 [y]Col. 1:25 **1:24** [z]2 Cor. 7:4 [a]Eph. 3:1, 13 [b][2 Cor. 1:5; 12:15] [c]Eph. 1:23 **1:25** [d]Gal. 2:7 **1:26** [e][1 Cor. 2:7] [f][2 Tim. 1:10] **1:27** [g]2 Cor. 2:14 [h]Rom. 9:23 [i][Rom. 8:10, 11] [j]1 Tim. 1:1 **1:28** [k]Acts 20:20 [l]Eph. 5:27 **1:29** [m]Eph. 3:7 **2:1** [a]Phil. 1:30 **2:3** [b]1 Cor. 1:24, 30 **2:4** [c]Rom. 16:18 **2:5** [d]1 Thess. 2:17 [e]1 Cor. 14:40 [f]1 Pet. 5:9 **2:6** [g]1 Thess. 4:1 **2:7** [h]Eph. 2:21 **2:8** [i]Gal. 1:14 [j]Gal. 4:3, 9, 10 **2:9** [k][John 1:14] **2:10** [l][Eph. 1:20, 21] **2:11** [m]Deut. 10:16 [n]Rom. 6:6; 7:24 **2:12** [o]Rom. 6:4 [p]Eph. 1:19, 20 [q]Acts 2:24 **2:14** [r][Eph. 2:15, 16]

it out of the way, having nailed it to the cross. [15s]Having disarmed [t]principalities and powers, He made a public spectacle of them, triumphing over them in it.

[16]So let no one [u]judge you in food or in drink, or regarding a festival or a new moon or sabbaths, [17v]which are a shadow of things to come, but the substance is of Christ. [18]Let no one cheat you of your reward, taking delight in *false* humility and worship of angels, intruding into those things which he has not* seen, vainly puffed up by his fleshly mind, [19]and not holding fast to [w]the Head, from whom all the body, nourished and knit together by joints and ligaments, [x]grows with the increase *that is* from God.

[20]Therefore,* if you [y]died with Christ from the basic principles of the world, [z]why, as *though* living in the world, do you subject yourselves to regulations— [21a]"Do not touch, do not taste, do not handle," [22]which all concern things which perish with the using—[b]according to the commandments and doctrines of men? [23c]These things indeed have an appearance of wisdom in self-imposed religion, *false* humility, and neglect of the body, *but are* of no value against the indulgence of the flesh.

Not Carnality but Christ

3 If then you were [a]raised with Christ, seek those things which are above, [b]where Christ is, sitting at the right hand of God. [2]Set your mind on things above, not on things on the [c]earth. [3d]For you died, [e]and your life is hidden with Christ in God. [4f]When Christ *who is* [g]our life appears, then you also will appear with Him in [h]glory.

[5i]Therefore put to death [j]your members which are on the earth: [k]fornication,

uncleanness, passion, evil desire, and covetousness, [l]which is idolatry. [6m]Because of these things the wrath of God is coming upon [n]the sons of disobedience, [7o]in which you yourselves once walked when you lived in them.

[8p]But now you yourselves are to put off all these: anger, wrath, malice, blasphemy, filthy language out of your mouth. [9]Do not lie to one another, since you have put off the old man with his deeds, [10]and have put on the new *man* who [q]is renewed in knowledge [r]according to the image of Him who [s]created him, [11]where there is neither [t]Greek nor Jew, circumcised nor uncircumcised, barbarian, Scythian, slave *nor* free, [u]but Christ *is* all and in all.

Character of the New Man

[12]Therefore, [v]as *the* elect of God, holy and beloved, [w]put on tender mercies, kindness, humility, meekness, longsuffering; [13x]bearing with one another, and forgiving one another, if anyone has a complaint against another; even as Christ forgave you, so you also *must do.* [14y]But above all these things [z]put on love, which is the [a]bond of perfection. [15]And let [b]the peace of God rule in your hearts, [c]to which also you were called [d]in one body; and [e]be thankful. [16]Let the word of Christ dwell in you richly in all wisdom, teaching and admonishing one another [f]in psalms and hymns and spiritual songs, singing with grace in your hearts to the Lord. [17]And [g]whatever you do in word or deed, *do* all in the name of the Lord Jesus, giving thanks to God the Father through Him.

* **2:18** NU-Text omits *not.*   * **2:20** NU-Text and M-Text omit *Therefore.*

2:15 *principalities and powers.* These words allude to Satan and the fallen angels. Paul is describing Christ's victory on the cross over the powers that opposed Him and that were against God's faithful people. To describe this victory, Paul uses the spectacle of the military triumph, when prisoners of war were stripped and paraded before the populace behind the conquering general.

2:16–19 *false humility.* People who do not champion salvation in Christ alone often appear to be humble. But their search for a new spiritual experience or advocacy of some work as necessary for salvation is actually human pride. They do not want to submit to God's plan of salvation.

2:20–23 *subject yourselves to regulations.* Since believers have been released from ritualistic observances, why should they let others bind them down again (Rom. 6:3–14)? No human work can be added to the merit of Christ's death. His work on the cross is the only acceptable work in God's eyes.

3:1–4 *Set your mind on things above.* The false teachers were instructing the Colossians to concentrate on temporal observances; in contrast, Paul instructs them to concentrate on the eternal realities of heaven. The Greek verb for *set* emphasizes an ongoing decision. Christians must continually discipline themselves to focus on

eternal realities instead of the temporal realities of this earth.

3:9–10 *old man . . . new man.* These two terms do not refer to the Christian's fleshly and spiritual natures. Instead, Paul describes our former unredeemed life as the old man and our life as God's child as the new man. The new man has the image of the new creation in Christ, just as the old man bears the image of our fallen nature. The old man is under an old master, Satan, while the new man has a new master, the Spirit of God living within.

3:11 *barbarian.* In the Roman Empire a person who did not speak Greek was despised. *Scythian.* An

2:15 [s] [Is. 53:12] [t] Eph. 6:12 **2:16** [u] Rom. 14:3
2:17 [v] Heb. 8:5; 10:1 **2:19** [w] Eph. 4:15 [x] Eph. 1:23;
4:16 **2:20** [y] Rom. 6:2–5 [z] Gal. 4:3, 9 **2:21** [a] 1 Tim.
4:3 **2:22** [b] Titus 1:14 **2:23** [c] 1 Tim. 4:8 **3:1** [d] Col.
2:12 [b] Ps. 68:18; 110:1; Eph. 1:20 **3:2** [c] [Matt. 6:19–21]
3:3 [d] [Rom. 6:2] [e] [2 Cor. 5:7] **3:4** [f] [1 John 3:2] [g] John
14:6 [h] 1 Cor. 15:43 **3:5** [i] [Rom. 8:13] [j] [Rom. 6:13]
[k] Eph. 5:3 [l] Eph. 4:19; 5:3, 5 **3:6** [m] Rom. 1:18 [n] [Eph.
2:2] **3:7** [o] 1 Cor. 6:11 **3:8** [p] Eph. 4:22 **3:10** [q] Rom.
12:2 [r] [Rom. 8:29] **3:11** [s] [Eph. 2:10] [t] Gal. 3:27, 28 [u] Eph.
1:23 **3:12** [v] [1 Pet. 1:2] [w] 1 John 3:17 **3:13** [x] [Mark
11:25] **3:14** [y] 1 Pet. 4:8 [z] [1 Cor. 13] [a] Eph. 4:3
3:15 [b] [John 14:27] [c] 1 Cor. 7:15 [d] Eph. 4:4 [e] [1 Thess. 5:18]
3:16 [f] Eph. 5:19 **3:17** [g] 1 Cor. 10:31

The Christian Home

18hWives, submit to your own husbands, ias is fitting in the Lord.

19jHusbands, love your wives and do not be kbitter toward them.

20lChildren, obey your parents min all things, for this is well pleasing to the Lord.

21nFathers, do not provoke your children, lest they become discouraged.

22oBondservants, obey in all things your masters according to the flesh, not with eyeservice, as men-pleasers, but in sincerity of heart, fearing God. 23pAnd whatever you do, do it heartily, as to the Lord and not to men, 24qknowing that from the Lord you will receive the reward of the inheritance; rfor* you serve the Lord Christ. 25But he who does wrong will be repaid for what he has done, and sthere is no partiality.

4 Masters,a give your bondservants what is just and fair, knowing that you also have a Master in heaven.

Christian Graces

2bContinue earnestly in prayer, being vigilant in it cwith thanksgiving; 3dmeanwhile praying also for us, that God would eopen to us a door for the word, to speak fthe mystery of Christ, gfor which I am also in chains, 4that I may make it manifest, as I ought to speak.

5hWalk in iwisdom toward those who are outside, jredeeming the time. 6Let your speech always be kwith grace, lseasoned with salt, mthat you may know how you ought to answer each one.

Final Greetings

7nTychicus, a beloved brother, faithful minister, and fellow servant in the Lord, will tell you all the news about me. 8oI am sending him to you for this very purpose,

that he* may know your circumstances and comfort your hearts, 9with pOnesimus, a faithful and beloved brother, who is one of you. They will make known to you all things which are happening here.

10qAristarchus my fellow prisoner greets you, with rMark the cousin of Barnabas (about whom you received instructions: if he comes to you, welcome him), 11and Jesus who is called Justus. These are my only fellow workers for the kingdom of God who are of the circumcision; they have proved to be a comfort to me.

12sEpaphras, who is one of you, a bondservant of Christ, greets you, always tlaboring fervently for you in prayers, that you may stand uperfect and complete* in all the will of God. 13For I bear him witness that he has a great zeal* for you, and those who are in Laodicea, and those in Hierapolis. 14vLuke the beloved physician and wDemas greet you. 15Greet the brethren who are in Laodicea, and Nymphas and xthe church that is in his* house.

Closing Exhortations and Blessing

16Now when ythis epistle is read among you, see that it is read also in the church of the Laodiceans, and that you likewise read the epistle from Laodicea. 17And say to zArchippus, "Take heed to athe ministry which you have received in the Lord, that you may fulfill it."

18bThis salutation by my own hand— Paul. cRemember my chains. Grace be with you. Amen.

---

* 3:24 NU-Text omits for.　* 4:8 NU-Text reads you may know our circumstances and he may.　* 4:12 NU-Text reads fully assured.　* 4:13 NU-Text reads concern.　* 4:15 NU-Text reads Nympha … her house.

---

uncultured person who came from the area around the Black Sea.

3:18–23 submit. See notes at Ephesians 5:19–31.

3:22–25 the reward of the inheritance. The strong motivation to serve someone well is found in the future reward that Christ gives to those who are faithful in this service. We normally think we receive eternal rewards for spiritual practices like reading the Bible, prayer, or evangelism. Here, Paul asserts that all work done to the honor of Christ will bring an eternal reward (1:22–23; 2:18).

4:5 Walk in wisdom toward those who are outside. Early Christians were often viewed with suspicion, distrust, and disdain. They were considered atheists because they would not worship the gods of Rome and Greece. Many labeled them as unpatriotic because they would not burn incense before the image of the emperor. Some even accused the early Christians of participating in orgies because of their talk of "love feasts" (Jude 12). Others harbored suspicions that Christians were really cannibals who ate and drank the blood and body of the Lord. With such misrepresentations of Christian belief and practice running rampant, it was very important for misunderstandings to be dispelled by the virtuous and impeccable lives of Christian believers.

4:9 Onesimus. This slave of Philemon probably accompanied Tychicus to Colosse. Paul's letter to Philemon would have been carried along with the letter to the Colossians. It dealt with a personal situation between Onesimus and his master.

4:10–15 Mark. This is the author of the Gospel of Mark.

4:18 This salutation by my own hand. The apostle dictated his letters to a secretary, but it was his custom to give a greeting in his own handwriting at the end (2 Thess. 2:1; 3:17). This served to personalize and authenticate the letter.

3:18h 1 Pet. 3:1　i[Eph. 5:22—6:9]　**3:19**j[Eph. 5:25] kEph. 4:31　**3:20**lEph. 6:1　mEph. 5:24　**3:21**nEph. 6:4　**3:22**oEph. 6:5　**3:23**p[Eccl. 9:10]　**3:24**qEph. 6:8　r1 Cor. 7:22　**3:25**sRom. 2:11　**4:1**aEph. 6:9 **4:2**bLuke 18:1　cCol. 2:7　**4:3**dEph. 6:19　e1 Cor. 16:9 fEph. 3:3, 4; 6:19　gEph. 6:20　**4:5**hEph. 5:15　i[Matt. 10:16]　jEph. 5:16　**4:6**kEccl. 10:12　lMark 9:50　m1 Pet. 3:15　**4:7**n2 Tim. 4:12　**4:8**oEph. 6:22　**4:9**pPhilem. 10　**4:10**qActs 19:29; 20:4; 27:2　r2 Tim. 4:11 **4:12**sPhilem. 23　tRom. 15:30　uMatt. 5:48　**4:14**v2 Tim. 4:11　w2 Tim. 4:10　**4:15**xRom. 16:5　**4:16**y1 Thess. 5:27　**4:17**zPhilem. 2　a2 Tim. 4:5　**4:18**b1 Cor. 16:21 cHeb. 13:3

THE FIRST EPISTLE OF PAUL THE APOSTLE TO THE
THESSALONIANS

▶ **AUTHOR:** First Thessalonians went unchallenged as a Pauline epistle until the nineteenth century, when radical critics claimed that its lack of doctrinal content made its authenticity suspect. But this is a weak objection on two counts: (1) the proportion of doctrinal teaching in Paul's epistles varies widely, and (2) 4:13—5:11 is a foundational passage for New Testament eschatology (future events). Paul had quickly grounded the Thessalonians in Christian doctrine, and the only problematic issue when this epistle was written concerned the matter of Christ's return. Paul planted the Thessalonian church on his second missionary journey, and wrote this epistle as a response to a good report regarding the church from Timothy in A.D. 51.

▶ **TIME:** c. A.D. 51   ▶ **KEY VERSES:** 1 Thess. 3:12–13

▶ **THEME:** Since Paul's time in Thessalonica was cut short, Paul used these letters to clarify some of his teaching. After a review of the basics, the primary issues covered in 1 Thessalonians are what happens when people die and the timing of the second coming of Christ. In that there were so many people around at that time that had seen Jesus, the promise of His return was met with anxious expectation. We tend to be blasé about it because we have watched so many predictions concerning the end times come and go, but this book will help us to sharpen and renew our expectations.

Greeting

1 Paul, ᵃSilvanus, and Timothy,

To the church of the ᵇThessalonians in God the Father and the Lord Jesus Christ:

Grace to you and peace from God our Father and the Lord Jesus Christ.*

Their Good Example

2 ᶜWe give thanks to God always for you all, making mention of you in our prayers,

3 remembering without ceasing ᵈyour work of faith, ᵉlabor of love, and patience of hope in our Lord Jesus Christ in the sight of our God and Father, 4 knowing, beloved brethren, ᶠyour election by God. 5 For ᵍour gospel did not come to you in word only, but also in power, ʰand in the Holy Spirit ⁱand in much assurance, as you know what kind of men we were among you for your sake.

* **1:1** NU-Text omits *from God our Father and the Lord Jesus Christ.*

1:1 Silvanus. Silvanus is the Roman form of the name Silas. After Paul had separated from Barnabas (Acts 15:36–40), Silas became Paul's traveling companion on the second missionary journey, and he may have served as Paul's secretary. He was a leader of the Jerusalem church (Acts 15:22–23), and he accompanied Paul and Barnabas to Antioch to deliver the decree of the Jerusalem council (Acts 15:22–23). He and Paul suffered a beating at Philippi (Acts 16:22–24), and he had helped found the church at Thessalonica (Acts 17:1–4). **Timothy.** Timothy was also with Paul on the second missionary journey. Paul considered him like a son and loved him dearly (Acts 16:3; 1 Tim. 1:2). This letter is a response to Timothy's report from the church in Thessalonica. **To the church.** The Greek word *ekklēsia* was a familiar term meaning any gathering or assembly. In its New Testament usage this word calls to mind the relationship of believers in Thessalonica as a body.
1:3 patience of hope. The believers at Thessalonica fixed their hope solidly on the return of Jesus Christ

(v. 10). Notice that each of the virtues has Christ as its object. Jesus is constantly the focus. This is a good standard for evaluating any Christian service.
1:5 our gospel. Paul had preached the gospel to them clearly when he was with them. For three weeks he had "reasoned with them from the Scriptures, explaining and demonstrating that the Christ had to suffer and rise again from the dead" (Acts 17:2–3). This message was far different from the messianic expectations that Paul knew from his own training as a Pharisee. The Jews of that day were not looking for a suffering savior but a conquering champion.
1:5 Sharing Our Faith—In order to share our faith successfully, we must keep the following rules in mind:

1:1 ᵃ 1 Pet. 5:12 ᵇ Acts 17:1–9   **1:2** ᶜ Rom. 1:8
1:3 ᵈ John 6:29 ᵉ Rom. 16:6   **1:4** ᶠ Col. 3:12   **1:5** ᵍ Mark 16:20 ʰ 2 Cor. 6:6 ⁱ Heb. 2:3

6And [j]you became followers of us and
of the Lord, having received the word in
much affliction, [k]with joy of the Holy Spirit, 7so that you became examples to all in
Macedonia and Achaia who believe. 8For
from you the word of the Lord [l]has sounded
forth, not only in Macedonia and Achaia,
but also [m]in every place. Your faith toward
God has gone out, so that we do not need to
say anything. 9For they themselves declare
concerning us [n]what manner of entry we
had to you, [o]and how you turned to God
from idols to serve the living and true God,
10and [p]to wait for His Son from heaven,
whom He raised from the dead, *even* Jesus
who delivers us [q]from the wrath to come.

Paul's Conduct

2 For you yourselves know, brethren, that
our coming to you was not in vain. 2But
even* after we had suffered before and
were spitefully treated at [a]Philippi, as you
know, we were [b]bold in our God to speak
to you the gospel of God in much conflict.
3[c]For our exhortation *did* not *come* from
error or uncleanness, nor *was it* in deceit.

4But as [d]we have been approved by God
[e]to be entrusted with the gospel, even so we
speak, [f]not as pleasing men, but God [g]who
tests our hearts. 5For [h]neither at any time
did we use flattering words, as you know,
nor a cloak for covetousness—[i]God *is* witness. 6[j]Nor did we seek glory from men,
either from you or from others, when [k]we
might have [l]made demands [m]as apostles of
Christ. 7But [n]we were gentle among you,
just as a nursing *mother* cherishes her own
children. 8So, affectionately longing for
you, we were well pleased [o]to impart to you
not only the gospel of God, but also [p]our
own lives, because you had become dear to
us. 9For you remember, brethren, our [q]labor
and toil; for laboring night and day, [r]that
we might not be a burden to any of you, we
preached to you the gospel of God.

10[s]You *are* witnesses, and God *also*, [t]how
devoutly and justly and blamelessly we behaved ourselves among you who believe;
11as you know how we exhorted, and comforted, and charged* every one of you, as
a father *does* his own children, 12[u]that you
would walk worthy of God [v]who calls you
into His own kingdom and glory.

Their Conversion

13For this reason we also thank God
[w]without ceasing, because when you [x]re-
ceived the word of God which you heard
from us, you welcomed *it* [y]not *as* the word
of men, but as it is in truth, the word of
God, which also effectively [z]works in you
who believe. 14For you, brethren, became
imitators [a]of the churches of God which
are in Judea in Christ Jesus. For [b]you also
suffered the same things from your own
countrymen, just as they *did* from the Judeans, 15[c]who killed both the Lord Jesus
and [d]their own prophets, and have persecuted us; and they do not please God [e]and

---

* **2:2** NU-Text and M-Text omit *even*. * **2:11** NU-Text and M-Text read *implored*.

First, we must be clean vessels. God reminds Isaiah the prophet of this: "Be clean, you who bear the vessels of the LORD" (Is. 52:11). David prays for forgiveness and cleansing, and a willing spirit. He states, "Then I will teach transgressors Your ways, and sinners shall be converted to You (Ps. 51:13).

We must be able to clearly give out the simple facts of the gospel without getting bogged down with profound theological concepts. Philip the evangelist demonstrated how to do this when he dealt with the Ethiopian eunuch in the desert. "Then Philip opened his mouth, and beginning at this Scripture, preached Jesus to him" (Acts 8:35).

We must avoid arguments and stick to the basic issues of man's sin and Christ's sacrifice.

We must use the Word of God. Paul's tremendous success as an evangelist can be linked directly to his constant use of God's Word (Acts 17:2; 18:28; 2 Tim. 2:15; 3:14–17).

We must depend upon the Spirit of God (John 3:15; Acts 6:10; 1 Cor. 2:4).

1:6 ***followers of us.*** As we focus on Jesus we will reflect His image to others (2 Cor. 3:18).

1:8 ***sounded forth.*** Since Thessalonica was a port city on the much-traveled Egnatian Way, those who saw the virtuous life and persistent faith of the Thessalonian Christians would spread the word throughout the entire region.

1:10 ***delivers us from the wrath to come.*** Because Christ endured God's wrath at Calvary, all who are in Christ will escape that wrath. They have nothing to fear.

2:2 ***at Philippi.*** Paul and Silas were beaten and put in the stocks in Philippi (Acts 16:22–24).

2:5 ***flattering words.*** Far from flattering, Paul preached boldly that everyone was a sinner who needed to be saved by the grace of God.

2:9 ***labor.*** This word indicates strenuous work that produces weariness. Paul made tents to provide for his financial needs (Acts 18:3), showing that his ministry was motivated by an unselfish desire to promote the well-being of others rather than to advance his own needs.

2:13 ***effectively works.*** Gentile Christians in Thessalonica could contrast the pure Word of God, with its transforming effect, with the immoral pagan religions, which only perverted people even more. Likewise, Jewish believers could contrast the love and grace of God in the gospel to the legalism and pride often produced by the Jewish religion.

1:6 [j] 1 Cor. 4:16; 11:1 [k] Acts 5:41; 13:52 **1:8** [l] Rom. 10:18 [m] Rom. 1:8; 16:19 **1:9** [n] 1 Thess. 2:1 [o] 1 Cor. 12:2 **1:10** [p] [Rom. 2:7] [q] Rom. 5:9 **2:2** [a] Acts 14:5; 16:19–24 [b] Acts 17:1–9 **2:3** [c] 2 Cor. 7:2 **2:4** [d] 1 Cor. 7:25 [e] Titus 1:3 [f] Gal. 1:10 [g] Prov. 17:3 **2:5** [h] 2 Cor. 2:17 [i] Rom. 1:9 **2:6** [j] 1 Tim. 5:17 [k] 1 Cor. 9:4 [l] 2 Cor. 11:9 [m] 1 Cor. 9:1 **2:7** [n] 1 Cor. 2:3 **2:8** [o] Rom. 1:11 [p] 2 Cor. 12:15 **2:9** [q] Acts 18:3; 20:34, 35 [r] 2 Cor. 12:13 **2:10** [s] 1 Thess. 1:5 [t] 2 Cor. 7:2 **2:12** [u] Eph. 4:1 [v] 1 Cor. 1:9 **2:13** [w] 1 Thess. 1:2, 3 [x] Mark 4:20 [y] [Gal. 4:14] [z] [1 Pet. 1:23] **2:14** [a] Gal. 1:22 [b] Acts 17:5 **2:15** [c] Acts 2:23 [d] Matt. 5:12; 23:34, 35 [e] Esth. 3:8

are contrary to all men, [16f]forbidding us to speak to the Gentiles that they may be saved, so as always [g]to fill up *the measure* of their sins; [h]but wrath has come upon them to the uttermost.

Longing to See Them

[17]But we, brethren, having been taken away from you for a short time [i]in presence, not in heart, endeavored more eagerly to see your face with great desire. [18]Therefore we wanted to come to you—even I, Paul, time and again—but [j]Satan hindered us. [19]For [k]what *is* our hope, or joy, or [l]crown of rejoicing? *Is it* not even you in the [m]presence of our Lord Jesus Christ [n]at His coming? [20]For you are our glory and joy.

Concern for Their Faith

3 Therefore, when we could no longer endure it, we thought it good to be left in Athens alone, [2]and sent [a]Timothy, our brother and minister of God, and our fellow laborer in the gospel of Christ, to establish you and encourage you concerning your faith, [3b]that no one should be shaken by these afflictions; for you yourselves know that [c]we are appointed to this. [4d]For, in fact, we told you before when we were with you that we would suffer tribulation, just as it happened, and you know. [5]For this reason, when I could no longer endure it, I sent to know your faith, [e]lest by some means the tempter had tempted you, and [f]our labor might be in vain.

Encouraged by Timothy

[6g]But now that Timothy has come to us from you, and brought us good news of your faith and love, and that you always have good remembrance of us, greatly desiring to see us, [h]as we also *to see* you— [7]therefore, brethren, in all our affliction and distress [i]we were comforted concerning you by your faith. [8]For now we live, if you [j]stand fast in the Lord.

[9]For what thanks can we render to God for you, for all the joy with which we rejoice for your sake before our God, [10]night and day praying exceedingly that we may see your face [k]and perfect what is lacking in your faith?

Prayer for the Church

[11]Now may our God and Father Himself, and our Lord Jesus Christ, [l]direct our way to you. [12]And may the Lord make you increase and [m]abound in love to one another and to all, just as we *do* to you, [13]so that He may establish [n]your hearts blameless in holiness before our God and Father at the coming of our Lord Jesus Christ with all His saints.

Plea for Purity

4 Finally then, brethren, we urge and exhort in the Lord Jesus [a]that you should abound more and more, [b]just as you received from us how you ought to walk and to please God; [2]for you know what commandments we gave you through the Lord Jesus.

[3]For this is [c]the will of God, [d]your sanctification: [e]that you should abstain from sexual immorality; [4f]that each of you should know how to possess his own vessel in sanctification and honor, [5g]not in passion of lust, [h]like the Gentiles [i]who do not know

---

2:16 *always to fill up the measure of their sins.* The implication is that God will allow a nation, group, or individual to go only so far in sin before He brings judgment upon them (Gen. 15:16).

2:18 *Satan hindered us.* Satan has a vested interest in hindering the spread of the gospel, and we may be sure that when we are engaged in the Lord's work, we will experience spiritual attacks and opposition of various kinds.

3:1 *Athens.* When forced to leave Thessalonica, Paul and Silas went to Berea, the next city west of Thessalonica. The Thessalonian Jews who had opposed Paul learned that he was at Berea, and went there also to stir up opposition. Paul's friends then escorted him south to Athens (Acts 17:13–15).

3:3 *shaken by these afflictions.* The Bible teaches that those who live godly lives should expect persecution (2 Tim. 3:12). In fact, Christ warned His disciples that they would experience the same type of rejection He had experienced (John 15:18–21). But such suffering should not make us depressed. Instead we should rejoice that we are allied with His name (Matt. 5:10–12).

3:12 *increase and abound in love to one another.* Christ had told His disciples that His followers would be identified by their love for one another (John 13:35).

3:13 *all His saints.* The word saints means "holy ones" or "those set apart." It can be used to apply to

believers, or to holy angels. Angels will participate in the second coming (4:16; Jude 14; Rev. 19:14).

4:1 *how you ought to walk.* The Christian life not only begins with faith, but it continues as a daily walk of faith. Christians are not to live like unsaved Gentiles (Eph. 4:17); instead they are to walk worthy of their calling from God (Eph. 4:1). John exhorts Christians to walk in the light, that is, in the revealed will of God (1 John 1:7).

4:3 *abstain from sexual immorality.* A major problem for the early church was maintaining sexual purity (1 Cor. 5:1,9–11). Pagan religions often included sexual orgies as part of their rites of worship, and temple prostitutes were dedicated to various gods. In contrast, Christianity taught that the body is God's temple (1 Cor. 6:18–20). The body should be honored as created by God and should be sanctified in keeping with its holy purpose.

2:16 [f]Luke 11:52 [g]Gen. 15:16 [h]Matt. 24:6 **2:17** [i]1 Cor. 5:3 **2:18** [j]Rom. 1:13; 15:22 **2:19** [k]2 Cor. 1:14 [l]Prov. 16:31 [m]Jude 24 [n]1 Cor. 15:23 **3:2** [a]Rom. 16:21 **3:3** [b]Eph. 3:13 [c]Acts 9:16; 14:22 **3:4** [d]Acts 20:24 **3:5** [e]1 Cor. 7:5 [f]Gal. 2:2 **3:6** [g]Acts 18:5 [h]Phil. 1:8 **3:7** [i]2 Cor. 1:4 **3:8** [j]Phil. 4:1 **3:10** [k]2 Cor. 13:9 **3:11** [l]Mark 1:3 **3:12** [m]Phil. 1:9 **3:13** [n]2 Thess. 2:17 **4:1** [a]1 Cor. 15:58 [b]Phil. 1:27 **4:3** [c][Rom. 12:2] [d]Eph. 5:27 [e][1 Cor. 6:15–20] **4:4** [f]Rom. 6:19 **4:5** [g]Col. 3:5 [h]Eph. 4:17, 18 [i]1 Cor. 15:34

God; 6that no one should take advantage of
and defraud his brother in this matter, because the Lord [j]*is* the avenger of all such, as
we also forewarned you and testified. 7For
God did not call us to uncleanness, [k]but in
holiness. 8[l]Therefore he who rejects *this*
does not reject man, but God, [m]who has
also given* us His Holy Spirit.

A Brotherly and Orderly Life

9But concerning brotherly love you have
no need that I should write to you, for [n]you
yourselves are taught by God [o]to love one
another; 10and indeed you do so toward all
the brethren who are in all Macedonia. But
we urge you, brethren, [p]that you increase
more and more; 11that you also aspire to
lead a quiet life, [q]to mind your own business, and [r]to work with your own hands, as
we commanded you, 12[s]that you may walk
properly toward those who are outside, and
that you may lack nothing.

The Comfort of Christ's Coming

13But I do not want you to be ignorant,
brethren, concerning those who have fall-
en asleep, lest you sorrow [t]as others [u]who
have no hope. 14For [v]if we believe that Jesus
died and rose again, even so God will bring
with Him [w]those who sleep in Jesus.*

15For this we say to you [x]by the word of
the Lord, that [y]we who are alive *and* remain until the coming of the Lord will by
no means precede those who are asleep.
16For [z]the Lord Himself will descend from
heaven with a shout, with the voice of an
archangel, and with [a]the trumpet of God.
[b]And the dead in Christ will rise first.
17[c]Then we who are alive *and* remain shall
be caught up together with them [d]in the
clouds to meet the Lord in the air. And
thus [e]we shall always be with the Lord.
18[f]Therefore comfort one another with
these words.

The Day of the Lord

5 But concerning [a]the times and the seasons, brethren, you have no need that
I should write to you. 2For you yourselves
know perfectly that [b]the day of the Lord
so comes as a thief in the night. 3For when
they say, "Peace and safety!" then [c]sudden
destruction comes upon them, [d]as labor
pains upon a pregnant woman. And they
shall not escape. 4[e]But you, brethren, are
not in darkness, so that this Day should
overtake you as a thief. 5You are all [f]sons
of light and sons of the day. We are not of
the night nor of darkness. 6[g]Therefore let
us not sleep, as others *do*, but [h]let us watch
and be sober. 7For [i]those who sleep, sleep
at night, and those who get drunk [j]are
drunk at night. 8But let us who are of the
day be sober, [k]putting on the breastplate
of faith and love, and *as* a helmet the hope

* **4:8** NU-Text reads *who also gives.* * **4:14** Or *those who through Jesus sleep*

4:10 ***increase more and more.*** These believers already had a good record of loving one another, but Paul desired that love to increase. This was the commandment of Jesus (John 13:34–35; 15:12,17) and is an important basis of evangelism. In a world that is filled with self-serving individuals, the genuine love of Christians should attract others to the faith.

4:11 ***aspire to lead a quiet life.*** This does not refer to a lack of activity but rather to an inner quietness and peace befitting the Christian faith (2 Thess. 3:12; 1 Tim. 2:11). ***work with your own hands.*** Usually people who are busy running other people's affairs do not run their own affairs well. A Christian's house should be in order as a testimony to others.

4:14 ***those who sleep in Jesus.*** Some believe this phrase indicates that departed Christians are unconscious until the second coming. But the Bible indicates that to be absent from our present body is to be present with the Lord Jesus (5:10; 2 Cor. 5:8; Phil. 1:23).

4:16 ***descend from heaven with a shout.*** Accompanying the descent of Christ from heaven will be the voice of an archangel, perhaps Michael, who is portrayed as the leader of the army of God (Dan. 10:13,21; Jude 9; Rev. 12:7–9). The only other angel named in Scripture is Gabriel, who is given a prominent role as a messenger of God (Dan. 8:16; 9:21; Luke 1:19,26). ***the dead in Christ will rise.*** Clearly this will be a physical resurrection in which bodily existence will be restored, as confirmed in 1 Corinthians 15:51–53. The resurrected bodies of Christians will be like the body of Christ (1 John 3:2), incorruptible and immortal, and yet they will be bodies of flesh and bone (Luke 24:39–40; John 20:20,25,27).

4:17 ***caught up.*** The English word *rapture* comes from the Latin for "caught up."

5:2 ***the day of the Lord.*** This expression was familiar to those who knew the Hebrew Scriptures. The day of the Lord in the Old Testament was characterized by two phases: God's judgment against sinful people and God's eternal reign over His people. God's judgment will be a time of darkness and an expression of His wrath (Joel 2:1–2; Amos 5:18–20; Zeph. 1:14–15). His reign will also be a time of blessing (Is. 2:1–3; 11:1–9; 30:23–26; Zech. 14:1,7–11,20–21; Matt. 19:28; Acts 3:19–21).

5:4 ***not in darkness.*** Though the day of the Lord will overtake the unsaved world unexpectedly, it will not overtake Christians, because they will be looking forward to and expecting it. The fact that Christ could come at any moment should motivate unbelievers to accept His forgiveness, and believers to live daily for Him.

5:8 ***sober.*** A sober life is not only free from drunkenness, but awake to spiritual realities.

4:6 [j] 2 Thess. 1:8 **4:7** [k] Lev. 11:44 **4:8** [l] Luke 10:16 [m] 1 Cor. 2:10 **4:9** [n] [Jer. 31:33, 34] [o] Matt. 22:39 **4:10** [p] 1 Thess. 3:12 **4:11** [q] 2 Thess. 3:11 [r] Acts 20:35 **4:12** [s] Rom. 13:13 **4:13** [t] Lev. 19:28 [u] [Eph. 2:12] **4:14** [v] 1 Cor. 15:13 [w] 1 Cor. 15:20, 23 **4:15** [x] 1 Kin. 13:17; 20:35 [y] 1 Cor. 15:51, 52 **4:16** [z] [Matt. 24:30, 31] [a] [1 Cor. 15:52] [b] [1 Cor. 15:23] **4:17** [c] [1 Cor. 15:51–53] [d] Acts 1:9 [e] John 14:3; 17:24 **4:18** [f] 1 Thess. 5:11 **5:1** [a] Matt. 24:3 **5:2** [b] [2 Pet. 3:10] **5:3** [c] Is. 13:6–9 [d] Hos. 13:13 **5:4** [e] 1 John 2:8 **5:5** [f] Eph. 5:8 **5:6** [g] Matt. 25:5 [h] [1 Pet. 5:8] **5:7** [i] [Luke 21:34] [j] Acts 2:15 **5:8** [k] Eph. 6:14

of salvation. [9]For [l]God did not appoint us to wrath, [m]but to obtain salvation through our Lord Jesus Christ, [10][n]who died for us, that whether we wake or sleep, we should live together with Him.

[11]Therefore comfort each other and edify one another, just as you also are doing.

Various Exhortations

[12]And we urge you, brethren, [o]to recognize those who labor among you, and are over you in the Lord and admonish you, [13]and to esteem them very highly in love for their work's sake. [p]Be at peace among yourselves.

[14]Now we exhort you, brethren, [q]warn those who are unruly, [r]comfort the fainthearted, [s]uphold the weak, [t]be patient with all. [15][u]See that no one renders evil for evil to anyone, but always [v]pursue what is good both for yourselves and for all.

[16][w]Rejoice always, [17][x]pray without ceasing, [18]in everything give thanks; for this is the will of God in Christ Jesus for you.

[19][y]Do not quench the Spirit. [20][z]Do not despise prophecies. [21][a]Test all things; [b]hold fast what is good. [22]Abstain from every form of evil.

Blessing and Admonition

[23]Now may [c]the God of peace Himself [d]sanctify you completely; and may your whole spirit, soul, and body [e]be preserved blameless at the coming of our Lord Jesus Christ. [24]He who calls you is [f]faithful, who also will [g]do it.

[25]Brethren, pray for us.

[26]Greet all the brethren with a holy kiss.

[27]I charge you by the Lord that this epistle be read to all the holy* brethren.

[28]The grace of our Lord Jesus Christ be with you. Amen.

* **5:27** NU-Text omits *holy.*

5:9 did not appoint us to wrath. There will be wrath at the day of the Lord, but it will be God's wrath on the unbelieving world that has spurned and mocked Christ (Rev. 6:12–17).

5:12 And we urge you. Significantly, Paul combines prophecy with practical teachings for the Christian life. God never intended prophecy to just be a field for academic debate, but to be a truth that would provide believers hope and direction in their lives.

5:16 Rejoice always. Regardless of difficult circumstances, a Christian always has grounds for rejoicing. The Lord is a sovereign Ruler and will accomplish His purpose. Christian joy is not based on circumstances, but on a growing awareness of God and the certain future of eternal life with Christ (Rev. 21:1–7).

5:17 pray without ceasing. To pray without ceasing seems impossible, but a person can develop an attitude and habit of constant prayer. No matter what else is going on, we should be aware of God's presence with us, and turn to Him with every thought and action.

5:23 spirit, soul, and body. Every part of the Christian life should bear evidence that we are set apart as holy to God.

5:26 a holy kiss. A kiss was a customary greeting among friends (as it still is in some cultures), something like our modern handshake.

5:9 [l] Rom. 9:22 [m] [2 Thess. 2:13] **5:10** [n] 2 Cor. 5:15 **5:12** [o] 1 Cor. 16:18 **5:13** [p] Mark 9:50 **5:14** [q] 2 Thess. 3:6, 7, 11 [r] Heb. 12:12 [s] Rom. 14:1; 15:1 [t] Gal. 5:22 **5:15** [u] Lev. 19:18 [v] Gal. 6:10 **5:16** [w] [2 Cor. 6:10] **5:17** [x] Eph. 6:18 **5:19** [y] Eph. 4:30 **5:20** [z] 1 Cor. 14:1, 31 **5:21** [a] 1 John 4:1 [b] Phil. 4:8 **5:23** [c] Phil. 4:9 [d] 1 Thess. 3:13 [e] 1 Cor. 1:8, 9 **5:24** [f] [1 Cor. 10:13] [g] Phil. 1:6

THE SECOND EPISTLE OF PAUL THE APOSTLE TO THE
THESSALONIANS

▶ **AUTHOR:** The external attestation to the authenticity of 2 Thessalonians as a Pauline epistle is even stronger than that for 1 Thessalonians. Internally the vocabulary, style, and doctrinal content support the claims in 1:1 and 3:17 that it was written by Paul. This letter was probably written a few months after 1 Thessalonians, while Paul was still in Corinth with Silas and Timothy (1:1; Acts 18:5).

▶ **TIME:** c. A.D. 51   ▶ **KEY VERSES:** 2 Thess. 2:2–3

▶ **THEME:** This letter to the Thessalonians appears to have been written fairly soon after the first one. He provides some further clarification on some of the same issues he addressed in the first letter. There appears to still be some confusion about the events of the end times, which he clarifies. He also wisely encourages the believers in the basics he has taught them in his role as a caring pastor.

Greeting

1 Paul, Silvanus, and Timothy,

To the church of the Thessalonians in God our Father and the Lord Jesus Christ:

2ᵃGrace to you and peace from God our Father and the Lord Jesus Christ.

God's Final Judgment and Glory

3We are bound to thank God always for you, brethren, as it is fitting, because your faith grows exceedingly, and the love of every one of you all abounds toward each other, 4so that bwe ourselves boast of you among the churches of God cfor your patience and faith din all your persecutions and tribulations that you endure, 5which is emanifest evidence of the righteous judgment of God, that you may be counted worthy of the kingdom of God, ffor which you also suffer; 6gsince it is a righteous thing with God to repay with tribulation those who trouble you, 7and to give you who are troubled hrest with us when ithe Lord Jesus is revealed from heaven with His mighty angels, 8in flaming fire taking vengeance on those who do not know God, and on those who do not obey the gospel of our Lord Jesus Christ. 9iThese shall be punished with everlasting destruction from the presence of the Lord and kfrom the glory of His power, 10when He comes, in that Day, lto be mglorified in His saints and to be admired among all those who believe,* because our testimony among you was believed. 11Therefore we also pray always for you that our God would ncount you worthy of this calling, and fulfill all the good pleasure of His goodness and othe work of faith with power, 12pthat the name of our Lord Jesus Christ may be glorified in you, and you in Him, according to the grace of our God and the Lord Jesus Christ.

* 1:10 NU-Text and M-Text read *have believed.*

1:1 *Silvanus, and Timothy.* Silvanus (Latin for Silas) had been Paul's traveling companion ever since the start of the second missionary journey. He had participated in the founding of the church at Thessalonica (Acts 17:1–4). Timothy also accompanied Paul on his second missionary journey. His report from the Thessalonian church had been the occasion for writing 1 Thessalonians (1 Thess. 3:6–8). ***To the church.*** The Greek word *ekklēsia* means "gathering" or "assembly." **1:5 *counted worthy of the kingdom of God.*** If believers handle their persecutions properly, they will be counted worthy of great reward in the coming kingdom of God (Matt. 5:12; 1 Pet. 2:19–20). Christians are called to endure suffering in this world, for they will receive a far greater reward in the next (2 Tim. 2:12). **1:7–8 *when the Lord Jesus is revealed.*** Presently the Lord Jesus is enthroned in glory at the right hand of the Father (John 17:5). Stephen saw this glory before he was martyred (Acts 7:55–56), but one day, and it may be soon, "every eye will see Him" (Rev. 1:7). ***in flaming fire.*** Some believe that this is the fulfillment of John the Baptist's prophecy of the One who would "baptize with fire" (Matt. 3:11–12; Luke 3:16–17). **1:8 *do not know . . . do not obey.*** Those who do not know are the unbelieving Gentiles, those who do not obey are the unbelieving Jews who knew about God and rejected His Son (Rom. 10:1,16). **1:12 *glorified in you.*** Christ will be glorified not only among, but also in the saints, for believers reflect His glory.

1:2ᵃ 1 Cor. 1:3   **1:4**ᵇ 2 Cor. 7:4 ᶜ 1 Thess. 1:3 ᵈ 1 Thess. 2:14   **1:5**ᵉ Phil. 1:28 ᶠ 1 Thess. 2:14   **1:6**ᵍ Rev. 6:10   **1:7**ʰ Rev. 14:13 ⁱ Jude 14   **1:9**ʲ Phil. 3:19 ᵏ Deut. 33:2   **1:10**ˡ Matt. 25:31 ᵐ John 17:10   **1:11**ⁿ Col. 1:12 ᵒ 1 Thess. 1:3   **1:12**ᵖ [Col. 3:17]

The Great Apostasy

2 Now, brethren, ªconcerning the coming of our Lord Jesus Christ ᵇand our gathering together to Him, we ask you, 2ᶜnot to be soon shaken in mind or troubled, either by spirit or by word or by letter, as if from us, as though the day of Christ* had come. ³Let no one deceive you by any means; for *that Day will not come* ᵈunless the falling away comes first, and ᵉthe man of sin* is revealed, ᶠthe son of perdition, 4who opposes and ᵍexalts himself ʰabove all that is called God or that is worshiped, so that he sits as God* in the temple of God, showing himself that he is God.

⁵Do you not remember that when I was still with you I told you these things? ⁶And now you know what is restraining, that he may be revealed in his own time. ⁷For ⁱthe mystery of lawlessness is already at work; only He* who now restrains *will do so* until He* is taken out of the way. ⁸And then the lawless one will be revealed, ʲwhom the Lord will consume ᵏwith the breath of His mouth and destroy ˡwith the brightness of His coming. ⁹The coming of the *lawless one* is ᵐaccording to the working of Satan, with all power, ⁿsigns, and lying wonders, ¹⁰and with all unrighteous deception among ᵒthose who perish, because they did not receive ᵖthe love of the truth, that they

might be saved. ¹¹And ᑫfor this reason God will send them strong delusion, ʳthat they should believe the lie, ¹²that they all may be condemned who did not believe the truth but ˢhad pleasure in unrighteousness.

Stand Fast

¹³But we are bound to give thanks to God always for you, brethren beloved by the Lord, because God ᵗfrom the beginning ᵘchose you for salvation ᵛthrough sanctification by the Spirit and belief in the truth, ¹⁴to which He called you by our gospel, for ʷthe obtaining of the glory of our Lord Jesus Christ. ¹⁵Therefore, brethren, ˣstand fast and hold ʸthe traditions which you were taught, whether by word or our epistle.

¹⁶Now may our Lord Jesus Christ Himself, and our God and Father, ᶻwho has loved us and given *us* everlasting consolation and ᵃgood hope by grace, ¹⁷comfort your hearts ᵇand establish you in every good word and work.

Pray for Us

3 Finally, brethren, ªpray for us, that the word of the Lord may run *swiftly* and be

* **2:2** NU-Text reads *the Lord.* * **2:3** NU-Text reads *lawlessness.* * **2:4** NU-Text omits *as God.* * **2:7** Or *he* • Or *he*

2:1 *concerning the coming.* After writing 1 Thessalonians, Paul had received word that the believers in Thessalonica were being misled by false teachers who were confusing the believers with erroneous ideas about the second coming. ***gathering together to Him.*** This will be the first time that the whole church, including every believer, will be gathered before the Lord to worship Him. The phrase seems to refer to the event described in 1 Thessalonians 4:17, where Paul speaks of meeting the Lord in the air.
2:2 *the day of Christ had come.* The false teaching was that the day of the Lord (1 Thess. 5:2–4) had already come, bringing with it the tribulations they were experiencing. Thus, some Thessalonian believers thought that they had missed the second coming.
2:3 *the falling away.* The Greek word translated "falling away" is the word commonly used to describe a military rebellion. In the Scriptures, the word is used of rebellion against God. Some have therefore interpreted this verse to refer to a general defection from the truth, perhaps even by those professing to be the church. This rebellious apostasy would prepare the way for the antichrist. ***the man of sin.*** Paul does not use the title "antichrist" for this man, but his description parallels John's description of the antichrist (1 John 2:18; Rev. 13). The man of sin will lead the world into rebellion against God (v. 10), perform wonders through Satan's power (v. 9), and finally will present himself as a god to be worshiped (v. 4).
2:4 *he sits as God in the temple.* This is the ultimate fulfillment of the "abomination of desolation" spoken of by Daniel (Dan. 7:23; 9:26; 11:31,36–37; 12:11) and Jesus (Matt. 24:15; Mark 13:14).
2:7 *is already at work.* The evil and deception that the man of sin embodies already exist in this world

(1 John 2:18). Anyone who opposes Christ and His church and seeks to deceive others into worshiping false gods is against Christ (antichrist). ***taken out of the way.*** Many believe that this verse refers to the rapture of the church (1 Thess. 4:16–17), and the cessation of the Holy Spirit working through believers to restrain the power of sin in this world. There are a variety of other interpretations for the identity of the restrainer, including the Roman state, or the principle of law and government embodied in the state.
2:8 *whom the Lord will consume . . . and destroy.* Although the man of lawlessness will be revealed as extremely powerful (Rev. 13:7), he will be destroyed by Christ and cast into the lake of fire when the Lord comes (Rev. 19:19–20).
2:14 *obtaining of the glory.* The Thessalonians have already been saved (v. 13), and called, but they must respond to God's work in them. Through the power of the Holy Spirit (v. 13), believers on this earth prepare for a future with Christ by living in a holy manner (1:10; 1 Thess. 4:1–2).
2:17 *comfort your hearts and establish.* It is interesting to note that Paul uses the singular form of these verbs, with the plural subject of "Jesus Christ and God our Father," supporting the trinity and equality of God (1 Thess. 3:11).

2:1 ª [1 Thess. 4:15–17] ᵇ Matt. 24:31 **2:2** ᶜ Matt. 24:4 **2:3** ᵈ 1 Tim. 4:1 ᵉ Dan. 7:25; 8:25; 11:36 ᶠ John 17:12 **2:4** ᵍ Is. 14:13, 14 ʰ 1 Cor. 8:5 **2:7** ⁱ 1 John 2:18 **2:8** ʲ Dan. 7:10 ᵏ Is. 11:4 ˡ Heb. 10:27 **2:9** ᵐ John 8:41 ⁿ Deut. 13:1 **2:10** ᵒ 2 Cor. 2:15 ᵖ 1 Cor. 16:22 **2:11** ᑫ Rom. 1:28 ʳ 1 Tim. 4:1 **2:12** ˢ Rom. 1:32 **2:13** ᵗ Eph. 1:4 ᵘ 1 Thess. 1:4 ᵛ [1 Pet. 1:2] **2:14** ʷ 1 Pet. 5:10 **2:15** ˣ 1 Cor. 16:13 ʸ 1 Cor. 11:2 **2:16** ᶻ [Rev. 1:5] ª 1 Pet. 1:3 **2:17** ᵇ 1 Cor. 1:8 **3:1** ª Eph. 6:19

glorified, just as *it is* with you, ²and ᵇthat we may be delivered from unreasonable and wicked men; ᶜfor not all have faith.

³But ᵈthe Lord is faithful, who will establish you and ᵉguard *you* from the evil one. ⁴And ᶠwe have confidence in the Lord concerning you, both that you do and will do the things we command you.

⁵Now may ᵍthe Lord direct your hearts into the love of God and into the patience of Christ.

Warning Against Idleness

⁶But we command you, brethren, in the name of our Lord Jesus Christ, ʰthat you withdraw ⁱfrom every brother who walks ʲdisorderly and not according to the tradition which he* received from us. ⁷For you yourselves know how you ought to follow us, for we were not disorderly among you; ⁸nor did we eat anyone's bread free of charge, but worked with ᵏlabor and toil night and day, that we might not be a burden to any of you, ⁹not because we do not have ˡauthority, but to make ourselves an example of how you should follow us. ¹⁰For even when we were with you, we commanded you this: If anyone will not work, neither shall he eat. ¹¹For we hear that there are some who walk among you in a disorderly manner, not working at all, but are ᵐbusybodies. ¹²Now those who are such we command and exhort through our Lord Jesus Christ ⁿthat they work in quietness and eat their own bread.

¹³But *as for* you, brethren, ᵒdo not grow weary *in* doing good. ¹⁴And if anyone does not obey our word in this epistle, note that person and ᵖdo not keep company with him, that he may be ashamed. ¹⁵�q Yet do not count *him* as an enemy, ʳbut admonish *him* as a brother.

Benediction

¹⁶Now may ˢthe Lord of peace Himself give you peace always in every way. The Lord *be* with you all.

¹⁷ᵗThe salutation of Paul with my own hand, which is a sign in every epistle; so I write.

¹⁸ᵘThe grace of our Lord Jesus Christ *be* with you all. Amen.

---

* **3:6** NU-Text and M-Text read *they.*

3:2 *unreasonable and wicked men.* These may have been the unbelieving Jews in Corinth who were persecuting Paul at the time he wrote this letter (Acts 18:12–13). Justice in this world may never come for Christians, but they can certainly pray for deliverance from the wicked.

3:5 *direct your hearts.* The heart, the seat of a person's will and emotions, is the place where spiritual renewal begins. There God plants love and patience, traits that will produce a harvest of good works.

3:6 *command.* This is not just a friendly suggestion, but a binding order with the authority of Jesus Christ. ***withdraw.*** Among other things, this would include not allowing the person to participate in love feasts and the Lord's Supper (Matt. 18:15–17; 1 Cor. 5:9–12).

3:9 *not because we do not have authority.* It is right for the church to financially support those who do the Lord's work (Luke 10:7; 1 Cor. 9:6–14; Gal. 6:6; 1 Tim. 5:17–18).

3:11 *not working at all.* Some Thessalonians, apparently using the impending return of the Lord as an excuse, had refused to work and were expecting others in the church to feed them. In his previous letter,

Paul had already exhorted them to work (1 Thess. 4:11–12). Since they had not heeded, the time had come to take further steps. While believers must always act with gentleness and love toward one another, it is wrong to enable another person to continue in sin.

3:12 *they work in quietness.* The cure for gossips and busybodies is hard work. There is much truth in the saying "Satan finds work for idle hands."

3:15 *as a brother.* The disobedient one is not an enemy, but one who needs compassionate correction.

3:18 *our Lord Jesus Christ.* Not only is Jesus our ultimate hope, it is He who lovingly strengthens us to endure trials.

3:2 ᵇ Rom. 15:31 ᶜ Acts 28:24   **3:3** ᵈ 1 Cor. 1:9 ᵉ John 17:15   **3:4** ᶠ 2 Cor. 7:16   **3:5** ᵍ 1 Chr. 29:18   **3:6** ʰ Rom. 16:17 ⁱ 1 Cor. 5:1 ʲ 1 Thess. 4:11   **3:8** ᵏ 1 Thess. 2:9   **3:9** ˡ 1 Cor. 9:4, 6–14   **3:11** ᵐ 1 Pet. 4:15   **3:12** ⁿ Eph. 4:28   **3:13** ᵒ Gal. 6:9   **3:14** ᵖ Matt. 18:17   **3:15** �q Lev. 19:17 ʳ Titus 3:10   **3:16** ˢ Rom. 15:33   **3:17** ᵗ 1 Cor. 16:21   **3:18** ᵘ Rom. 16:20, 24

THE FIRST EPISTLE OF PAUL THE APOSTLE TO
TIMOTHY

▶ **AUTHOR:** The external evidence solidly supports the position that Paul wrote the letters to Timothy and Titus. Only Romans and 1 Corinthians have better attestation among the Pauline Epistles. Pauline authorship of the Pastoral Epistles requires Paul's release from his Roman imprisonment (Acts 28), the continuation of his missionary endeavors, and his imprisonment for a second time in Rome. Unfortunately, the order of events can only be reconstructed from hints, because there is no concurrent history paralleling Acts to chronicle the last years of the apostle. It is most probable that Paul wrote 1 Timothy from Macedonia in A.D. 62 or 63 while Timothy was serving as his representative in Ephesus.

▶ **TIME:** C. A.D. 62–63   ▶ **KEY VERSES:** 1 Tim. 3:15–16

▶ **THEME:** The letters to Timothy and Titus are generally called "the Pastoral Epistles." They are pastoral in tone and in the subject matter they address. While covering much of the apostolic instruction on the life and doctrine of the church, they also provide some guidelines on how Christians in the church should relate to society. One of the overriding concerns of the books is that truth be valued and guarded. Too often today, truth is subjective and culturally conditioned to the point where people don't even have problems believing mutually contradictory ideas. Paul speaks of the value of truth in his own apostolic role, and he stands against false teachers who would distort the truth for their own ends.

Greeting

1 Paul, an apostle of Jesus Christ, by the commandment of God our Savior and the Lord Jesus Christ, our hope,

2 To Timothy, a *a*true son in the faith:

*b*Grace, mercy, *and* peace from God our Father and Jesus Christ our Lord.

No Other Doctrine

3 As I urged you *c*when I went into Macedonia—remain in Ephesus that you may charge some *d*that they teach no other doctrine, 4*e*nor give heed to fables and endless genealogies, which cause disputes rather than godly edification which is in faith. 5Now *f*the purpose of the commandment is love *g*from a pure heart, *from* a good conscience, and *from* sincere faith, 6from which some, having strayed, have turned aside to *h*idle talk, 7desiring to be teachers of the law, understanding neither what they say nor the things which they affirm.

8But we know that the law *is* *i*good if one uses it lawfully, 9knowing this: that the law is not made for a righteous person, but for *the* lawless and insubordinate, for *the* ungodly and for sinners, for *the* unholy and profane, for murderers of fathers and murderers of mothers, for manslayers, 10for fornicators, for sodomites, for kidnappers, for liars, for perjurers, and if there is any other thing that is contrary to sound doctrine, 11according to the glorious gospel of the *j*blessed God which was *k*committed to my trust.

1:1 apostle of Jesus Christ. The Greek word for "apostle" means "sent one." Paul was an ambassador sent by Christ (Acts 9).

1:2 Timothy. Timothy was a young believer from Lystra who traveled with Paul during his second and third missionary journeys.

1:3 that you may charge. Paul's request that Timothy stay in Ephesus to minister to the believers there demonstrates Paul's confidence in the young man.

1:4 fables and endless genealogies. The errors that Paul left Timothy to correct in Ephesus appear to have been primarily Jewish in nature. The Jews tended to place a lot of importance on the genealogies and also on allegorical interpretations of the law.

1:6 idle talk. Gossip, speculation, and criticism should not come from the lips of believers.

1:8 law. The proper function of the law is to make sinners aware of their sinfulness (Rom. 3:20).

1:10 perjurers. The term "perjure" is more significant than simply "lie," as it deals with false promises. To swear an oath and then not carry through is a serious thing indeed.

1:2 *a* Titus 1:4   *b* Gal. 1:3   **1:3** *c* Acts 20:1, 3   *d* Gal. 1:6, 7   **1:4** *e* Titus 1:14   **1:5** *f* Rom. 13:8–10   *g* Eph. 6:24   **1:6** *h* 1 Tim. 6:4, 20   **1:8** *i* Rom. 7:12, 16   **1:11** *j* 1 Tim. 6:15   *k* 1 Cor. 9:17

Glory to God for His Grace

[12]And I thank Christ Jesus our Lord who has [l]enabled me, [m]because He counted me faithful, [n]putting me into the ministry, [13]although [o]I was formerly a blasphemer, a persecutor, and an insolent man; but I obtained mercy because [p]I did it ignorantly in unbelief. [14q]And the grace of our Lord was exceedingly abundant, [r]with faith and love which are in Christ Jesus. [15s]This is a faithful saying and worthy of all acceptance, that [t]Christ Jesus came into the world to save sinners, of whom I am chief. [16]However, for this reason I obtained mercy, that in me first Jesus Christ might show all longsuffering, as a pattern to those who are going to believe on Him for everlasting life. [17]Now to [u]the King eternal, [v]immortal, [w]invisible, to God [x]who alone is wise,* [y]be honor and glory forever and ever. Amen.

Fight the Good Fight

[18]This charge I commit to you, son Timothy, according to the prophecies previously made concerning you, that by them you may wage the good warfare, [19]having faith and a good conscience, which some having rejected, concerning the faith have suffered shipwreck, [20]of whom are [z]Hymenaeus and [a]Alexander, whom I delivered to Satan that they may learn not to [b]blaspheme.

Pray for All Men

2 Therefore I exhort first of all that supplications, prayers, intercessions, and giving of thanks be made for all men, [2a]for kings and [b]all who are in authority, that we may lead a quiet and peaceable life in all godliness and reverence. [3]For this is [c]good and acceptable in the sight [d]of God our Savior, [4e]who desires all men to be saved [f]and to come to the knowledge of the truth. [5g]For there is one God and [h]one Mediator between God and men, the Man Christ Jesus, [6i]who gave Himself a ransom for all, to be testified in due time, [7i]for which I was appointed a preacher and an apostle—I am speaking the truth in Christ* and not lying—[k]a teacher of the Gentiles in faith and truth.

---

* **1:17** NU-Text reads to the only God.   * **2:7** NU-Text omits in Christ.

1:13 but I obtained mercy. Paul found mercy and forgiveness even after his intense persecution of the church. God surely offers salvation to all people (2:4).
1:14 grace. Grace is God's undeserved, unearned, freely given favor.
1:15–16 Believing Jesus—Jesus came to earth to save sinners. Paul knew this firsthand. When he became a Christian, Paul realized the extent of his sin in terms of both his past sins and his current tendencies. But he also knew exactly where he stood in Christ as a believer. The mercy of God can only be acquired through belief. Paul reminds Timothy here of God's perfect patience and mercy and urges others to come to faith and receive the benefit of new and everlasting life, as he has. Eternal life can only begin with belief. It is an active choice of the individual. We must believe that Jesus is the saving Christ or reject Him. Paul says, "I obtained mercy, that in me first Jesus Christ might show all longsuffering, as a pattern to those who are going to believe on Him for everlasting life." If you have never believed in Jesus, take this opportunity to tell God how you feel. Believe in Jesus as Savior and begin on the path of a new life.
1:16 believe on Him. As stated over 185 times in the New Testament, the sole condition for salvation is belief, having faith or trust in Jesus Christ. The gospel (or "good news") is that Jesus Christ, God's Son, gave up His heavenly kingdom for a time to become a human. As a man, He died for our sins, was buried, and rose on the third day. All who place their trust in Jesus will be saved from the coming judgment and from the present power of sin. To add any other condition to faith for salvation is to make it dependent on our own works (Rom. 11:6; Gal. 2:16).
1:20 delivered to Satan. Paul did not have some sort of authority over these men to have them "delivered" in the sense that they would now belong to Satan. Rather, Paul had stopped trying to exhort them, or show them the way they should go. They would not listen, so Paul had to say, "So be it, go your own way."

2:4 desires all men to be saved. God desires that all men would be saved, although this does not mean that He will force this to happen. Only those who believe in Christ will receive salvation (Rom. 1:16–17; 3:21–26; 5:17). Christ died for the sins of the entire world, but only those who believe will receive the benefits of His sacrifice. **to come to the knowledge of the truth.** God not only wants our salvation (justification), He also wants us to grow in truth (sanctification) so that we will not be led astray by false teachers.
2:5 one God. This is the central truth of the Hebrew Scriptures. The only living God desires that all should be saved. He is the only one to whom our prayers should be addressed. **Mediator.** This is a concept that came from the ceremonial worship in the Old Testament. In the tabernacle and later in the temple, the priests mediated between God and Israel by offering sacrifices to atone for the sins of the people. In their position of mediator, the priests were the only ones eligible to enter into the holy place, the place where God had made His presence known. When Jesus came, He came as the Mediator between man and God. Through Him we can be eligible to enter into God's holy presence.
2:6 ransom. The Greek word translated "ransom" is found only here in the New Testament. It specifically refers to a ransom paid for a slave.
2:7 in faith and truth. Paul was called not only to preach the gospel to the Gentiles, but also to guide their growth in truth.

1:12 [l] 1 Cor. 15:10 [m] 1 Cor. 7:25 [n] Col. 1:25   **1:13** [o] Acts 8:3 [p] John 4:21   **1:14** [q] Rom. 5:20 [r] 2 Tim. 1:13; 2:22   **1:15** [s] 2 Tim. 2:11 [t] Matt. 1:21; 9:13   **1:17** [u] Ps. 10:16 [v] Rom. 1:23 [w] Heb. 11:27 [x] Rom. 16:27 [y] 1 Chr. 29:11   **1:20** [z] 2 Tim. 2:17, 18 [a] 2 Tim. 4:14 [b] Acts 13:45   **2:2** [a] Ezra 6:10 [b] [Rom. 13:1]   **2:3** [c] Rom. 12:2 [d] 2 Tim. 1:9   **2:4** [e] Ezek. 18:23, 32 [f] [John 17:3]   **2:5** [g] Gal. 3:20 [h] [Heb. 9:15]   **2:6** [i] Mark 10:45   **2:7** [i] Eph. 3:7, 8 [k] [Gal. 1:15, 16]

Men and Women in the Church

8I desire therefore that the men pray *l*everywhere, *m*lifting up holy hands, without wrath and doubting; 9in like manner also, that the *n*women adorn themselves in modest apparel, with propriety and moderation, not with braided hair or gold or pearls or costly clothing, 10*o*but, which is proper for women professing godliness, with good works. 11Let a woman learn in silence with all submission. 12And *p*I do not permit a woman to teach or to have authority over a man, but to be in silence. 13For Adam was formed first, then Eve. 14And Adam was not deceived, but the woman being deceived, fell into transgression. 15Nevertheless she will be saved in childbearing if they continue in faith, love, and holiness, with self-control.

Qualifications of Overseers

3 This *is* a faithful saying: If a man desires the position of a bishop,* he desires a good work. 2A bishop then must be blameless, the husband of one wife, temperate, sober-minded, of good behavior, hospitable, able to teach; 3not given to wine, not violent, not greedy for money,* but gentle, not quarrelsome, not covetous; 4one who rules his own house well, having *his* children in submission with all reverence 5(for if a man does not know how to rule his own house, how will he take care of the church of God?); 6not a novice, lest being puffed up with pride he fall into the *same* condemnation as the devil. 7Moreover he must have a good testimony among

* **3:1** Literally *overseer*   * **3:3** NU-Text omits *not greedy for money.*

2:8 men. The Greek word translated "men" in this verse refers specifically to males as distinguished from females. Some believe that this verse means specifically public worship, while others believe it refers to life in general. **lifting up holy hands.** This is a Hebrew way of praying (1 Kin. 8:22; Ps. 141:2). "Holy" means morally and spiritually clean.

2:9 in modest apparel. Modesty means more than just covering up enough. It means not flaunting one's wealth, and one's jewels, or one's name brands, as well as not flaunting one's body. **propriety.** This word means reverence and respect, shrinking away from what is inappropriate.

2:10 good works. A Christian woman's beauty should be found in her godly character and her love for the Lord as demonstrated in all types of good works.

2:11 in silence with all submission. These verses are not easy to understand, and there are many differences of opinion as to their meaning. The Scripture here does actually say just what it looks like: that women must be silent and submissive. It is universally accepted that this is referring to times of public worship, although the Bible makes it clear that a woman must submit to her husband (Eph. 5:22; Col. 3:18), but the concept of submission also applies to all believers. Philippians 4:5 says, "Let your gentleness be known to all men. The Lord is at hand." Being submissive means not being unruly or argumentative. There are times when it is proper for a woman to teach, pray, or prophesy (1 Cor. 11), but apparently this is not supposed to happen in public worship.

2:12 to teach or to have authority. It seems best to understand this passage as saying that women may exercise their spiritual gifts in a variety of ministries in the local assembly, as long as those gifts are exercised under the appropriate leadership of men. We have problems understanding the roles of men and women in the church. Often we want to ignore the subject altogether and say that men and women are entirely equal, the alternative being that men become despotic and tyrannical, while women become spiritually weak with no teaching and no opportunity to use their God-given gifts. Men and women are equal in God's eyes in terms of their value as people and eligibility for spiritual growth and relationship with God, but He created this difference in roles. Many tend to feel that this role difference is because of the fall, but God did create men and women to be different. The mess and confusion we have with our God-given positions is the result of the fall.

2:14 Adam was not deceived. This seems to point to the fact that Adam sinned with his eyes open; he knew what he was doing. Eve sinned because she was deceived. Paul's arguments from creation and the fall seem to indicate that the prohibitions in verses 9–12 are permanent, not cultural.

2:15 will be saved in childbearing. This is a very difficult verse to understand and no one agrees about what it means. We know that it does not mean "saved" in terms of receiving eternal life, because the Bible elsewhere makes it very clear we are saved by faith alone (John 3:15–18; Rom. 1:16–17; 3:23–26). Some think that it has to do with daily sanctification and the woman's special task of bearing children. Others say it is referring to being delivered from the desire to dominate by recognizing one's appropriate place in God's creation order. Still others believe that it refers specifically to the birth of Jesus Christ, the seed born of woman prophesied in Genesis 3:15.

3:1 bishop. This means a person who oversees a congregation. The words "bishop" and "elder" are used interchangeably for the same office (Titus 1:5–7).

3:2 blameless. The idea is not that an overseer is sinless, but that he displays mature consistent Christian conduct that gives no reason for anyone to accuse him of anything. **husband of one wife.** This phrase is also subject to much disagreement. Many feel that it means "a one-woman kind of man," indicating a lifestyle of fidelity. Others feel that it is more specific, and prohibits a divorced and remarried man from the elder position. Certainly it is an exclusion of anyone who is sexually immoral or a polygamist.

3:3 violent. An overseer is not to be a quarrelsome man.

3:7 good testimony. An overseer must have a good reputation in the community. A non-Christian should not be able to reproach or insult an elder because of his behavior. The elder's good testimony avoids the traps of Satan.

2:8 *l* Luke 23:34   *m* Ps. 134:2   **2:9** *n* 1 Pet. 3:3
2:10 *o* 1 Pet. 3:4   **2:12** *p* 1 Cor. 14:34

those who are outside, lest he fall into reproach and the ᵃsnare of the devil.

Qualifications of Deacons

⁸Likewise deacons *must be* reverent, not double-tongued, ᵇnot given to much wine, not greedy for money, ⁹holding the mystery of the faith with a pure conscience. ¹⁰But let these also first be tested; then let them serve as deacons, being *found* blameless. ¹¹Likewise, *their* wives *must be* reverent, not slanderers, temperate, faithful in all things. ¹²Let deacons be the husbands of one wife, ruling *their* children and their own houses well. ¹³For those who have served well as deacons ᶜobtain for themselves a good standing and great boldness in the faith which is in Christ Jesus.

The Great Mystery

¹⁴These things I write to you, though I hope to come to you shortly; ¹⁵but if I am delayed, *I write* so that you may know how you ought to conduct yourself in the house of God, which is the church of the living God, the pillar and ground of the truth. ¹⁶And without controversy great is the mystery of godliness:

ᵈGod* was manifested in the flesh,
ᵉJustified in the Spirit,
ᶠSeen by angels,
ᵍPreached among the Gentiles,
ʰBelieved on in the world,
ⁱReceived up in glory.

The Great Apostasy

4 Now the Spirit expressly says that in latter times some will depart from the faith, giving heed ᵃto deceiving spirits and doctrines of demons, ²ᵇspeaking lies in hypocrisy, having their own conscience ᶜseared with a hot iron, ³forbidding to marry, *and commanding* to abstain from foods which God created to be received with thanksgiving by those who believe and know the truth. ⁴For every creature of God *is* good, and nothing is to be refused if it is received with thanksgiving; ⁵for it is sanctified by the word of God and prayer.

A Good Servant of Jesus Christ

⁶If you instruct the brethren in these things, you will be a good minister of Jesus Christ, ᵈnourished in the words of faith and of the good doctrine which you have carefully followed. ⁷But ᵉreject profane and old wives' fables, and ᶠexercise yourself toward godliness. ⁸For ᵍbodily exercise profits a little, but godliness is profitable for all things, ʰhaving promise of the life that now is and of that which is to come. ⁹This *is* a faithful saying and worthy of all acceptance. ¹⁰For to this *end* we both labor and suffer reproach,* because we trust in the living God, ⁱwho is *the* Savior of all men, especially of those who believe. ¹¹These things command and teach.

---

* **3:16** NU-Text reads *Who.* * **4:10** NU-Text reads *we labor and strive.*

3:8 deacons. Deacons fill a second leadership position in the local assembly. The Greek word for deacon means "servant." **not double-tongued.** This speaks specifically of the dangers of gossip, especially changing sides or changing a story to fit the audience.

3:9 mystery of the faith. The mystery of the faith is the coming of God in the flesh (v. 16). The Son of God becoming a human in order to serve humanity (Mark 10:43–45) is the embodiment of service.

3:11 their wives. Some believe here that Paul is speaking of another office in the local body, that of "deaconess," godly women who serve under the leadership of the elders. Others, however, believe that this verse refers to the wives of the deacons, and not to an office. It could be assumed that both are true, and that the deacon and his wife are supposed to work together as a team, serving the church. The original language leaves the verse open to interpretation, since the Greek uses one word to mean both woman and wife.

3:15 pillar and ground of the truth. Misconduct and disorder in the local church weaken the support of God's truth in the world. We as believers have a tremendous responsibility to keep the name of our Lord without spot or criticism from the nonbelieving world.

3:16 manifested in the flesh. This refers to Christ's incarnation, the fact that Jesus became man (John 1:14). **Justified in the Spirit.** This is the work of the Holy Spirit in Jesus' ministry and resurrection (Matt. 3:15–17; John 16:7–10; Rom. 1:4). **Seen by angels.** This refers to the angelic witness of Christ's ministry and resurrection. **Preached among the Gentiles.**

This refers to the preaching of Christ to the Gentiles (Col. 1:23). **Believed on in the world.** This is the response of individuals to God's plan of salvation (Col. 1:18–25). **Received up in glory.** Christ ascended to heaven and is seated at God's right hand there (Acts 1:9; Heb. 1:3–4).

4:1 the Spirit expressly says. When Paul speaks of the Holy Spirit's words here, he may be referring to various prophecies inspired by the Holy Spirit concerning defection from God's truth (Dan. 7:25; 8:23; Matt. 24:4–12), or also he may have been referring to a revelation the Spirit had given him.

4:5 sanctified. Sanctified means "set apart," or "made holy." Paul is saying that God has sanctified all the good things He created, from marriage to the food we eat. Nothing is less in accord with God than to begin forbidding the good things He made for us.

4:7 old wives' fables. This is not to say that such fables are appropriate for old women either. Paul is merely using the term "old wives' fables" to describe the superstitions and thoughtless beliefs that were prevalent.

4:8 profits a little. This contrasts the short-term value of physical exercise with the long-term benefits of godliness for all things.

4:10 Savior of all men. This describes God as the One who gives life, breath, and existence to all.

3:7 ᵃ 2 Tim. 2:26 **3:8** ᵇ Ezek. 44:21 **3:13** ᶜ Matt. 25:21 **3:16** ᵈ John 1:14] ᵉ [Matt. 3:16] ᶠ Matt. 28:2 ᵍ Rom. 10:18 ʰ Col. 1:6, 23 ⁱ Luke 24:51 **4:1** ᵃ Rev. 16:14 **4:2** ᵇ Matt. 7:15 ᶜ Eph. 4:19 **4:6** ᵈ 2 Tim. 3:14 **4:7** ᵉ 2 Tim. 2:16 ᶠ Heb. 5:14 **4:8** ᵍ 1 Cor. 8:8 ʰ Ps. 37:9 **4:10** ⁱ Ps. 36:6

Take Heed to Your Ministry

¹²Let no one despise your youth, but be an ʲexample to the believers in word, in conduct, in love, in spirit,* in faith, in purity. ¹³Till I come, give attention to reading, to exhortation, to doctrine. ¹⁴ᵏDo not neglect the gift that is in you, which was given to you by prophecy ˡwith the laying on of the hands of the eldership. ¹⁵Meditate on these things; give yourself entirely to them, that your progress may be evident to all. ¹⁶Take heed to yourself and to the doctrine. Continue in them, for in doing this you will save both yourself and those who hear you.

Treatment of Church Members

5 Do not rebuke an older man, but exhort him as a father, younger men as brothers, ²older women as mothers, younger women as sisters, with all purity.

Honor True Widows

³Honor widows who are really widows. ⁴But if any widow has children or grandchildren, let them first learn to show piety at home and ᵃto repay their parents; for this is good and* acceptable before God. ⁵Now she who is really a widow, and left alone, trusts in God and continues in supplications and prayers ᵇnight and day. ⁶But she who lives in pleasure is dead while she lives. ⁷And these things command, that they may be blameless. ⁸But if anyone does not provide for his own, ᶜand especially for those of his household, ᵈhe has denied the faith ᵉand is worse than an unbeliever.

⁹Do not let a widow under sixty years old be taken into the number, *and not unless*

she has been the wife of one man, ¹⁰well reported for good works: if she has brought up children, if she has lodged strangers, if she has washed the saints' feet, if she has relieved the afflicted, if she has diligently followed every good work.

¹¹But refuse *the* younger widows; for when they have begun to grow wanton against Christ, they desire to marry, ¹²having condemnation because they have cast off their first faith. ¹³And besides they learn *to be* idle, wandering about from house to house, and not only idle but also gossips and busybodies, saying things which they ought not. ¹⁴Therefore I desire that *the* younger *widows* marry, bear children, manage the house, give no opportunity to the adversary to speak reproachfully. ¹⁵For some have already turned aside after Satan. ¹⁶If any believing man or* woman has widows, let them relieve them, and do not let the church be burdened, that it may relieve those who are really widows.

Honor the Elders

¹⁷Let the elders who rule well be counted worthy of double honor, especially those who labor in the word and doctrine. ¹⁸For the Scripture says, ᶠ*"You shall not muzzle an ox while it treads out the grain,"* and, ᵍ*"The laborer is worthy of his wages."** ¹⁹Do not receive an accusation against an elder except ʰfrom two or three witnesses. ²⁰Those who are sinning rebuke in the presence of all, that the rest also may fear.

---

* **4:12** NU-Text omits *in spirit.*   * **5:4** NU-Text and M-Text omit *good and.*   * **5:16** NU-Text omits *man or.*   * **5:18** Deuteronomy 25:4 • Luke 10:7

4:12 be an example. Timothy, in spite of youth, was to set an example in five areas: "in word," meaning his speech; "in conduct," or behavior; "in love, in spirit" which is the love of God; "in faith," meaning trust in God; "in purity," both in thought and action. These are qualities every believer should strive after, practice, and desire.

4:16 save both yourself. This is not a reference to justification by works, but to sanctification, which is the Christian's daily walk of faith (Mark 8:34–38; John 12:25–26). Timothy's example and hard work in teaching would serve to help others with their walk also.

5:2 all purity. Believing men must respect the purity of a young woman as the purity of a sister.

5:3 really widows. This refers to a woman who when widowed is left with no family at all, as opposed to those widows who still have living children or other relations.

5:4 show piety at home. Piety is respect, reverence, or obligation. Honoring our parents includes caring for them physically and financially as they grow older.

5:8 does not provide for his own. A believer is to provide for his family and this seems to include any of his relatives that need help. Failure to do this denies the faith he has said to believe in and smirches the name of Christianity.

5:9 taken into the number. Many believe the list

referred to here was a list of widows whom the church was to assist. Some have maintained that this was an official order of widows. These women were to pray for the church and practice works of charity (vv. 5,10).

5:13–14 idle...gossips and busybodies. An old saying tells us, "Idle hands are the devil's workshop." Do not allow yourself to become so idle that you begin to gossip. As odd as it may sound, it will happen. Employ yourself with the tasks God has set before you. Look around. There are lots of things we as believers should be doing.

5:18 Scripture says. Paul quotes two passages: Deuteronomy 25:4 and Luke 10:7. The quotation from Luke is especially interesting as it shows that Paul considered the Gospels to be Scripture as well as the Old Testament.

5:19 an accusation against an elder. Charges against elders are to be factual, not based on a single opinion or rumor.

5:20 Those who are sinning. This seems to refer to elders who fail in their leadership, whether in the church, in their social relationships, or in their home life. Public rebuke is to serve as a warning to other

4:12 ʲ 1 Pet. 5:3   **4:14** ᵏ 2 Tim. 1:6   ˡ Acts 6:6   **5:4** ᵃ Gen. 45:10   **5:5** ᵇ Acts 26:7   **5:8** ᶜ Is. 58:7   ᵈ 2 Tim. 3:5   ᵉ Matt. 18:17   **5:18** ᶠ Deut. 25:4   ᵍ Luke 10:7   **5:19** ʰ Deut. 17:6; 19:15

²¹I charge you before God and the Lord Jesus Christ and the elect angels that you observe these things without ⁱprejudice, doing nothing with partiality. ²²Do not lay hands on anyone hastily, nor ʲshare in other people's sins; keep yourself pure.

²³No longer drink only water, but use a little wine for your stomach's sake and your frequent infirmities.

²⁴Some men's sins are ᵏclearly evident, preceding them to judgment, but those of some men follow later. ²⁵Likewise, the good works of some are clearly evident, and those that are otherwise cannot be hidden.

Honor Masters

6 Let as many ᵃbondservants as are under the yoke count their own masters worthy of all honor, so that the name of God and His doctrine may not be blasphemed. ²And those who have believing masters, let them not despise them because they are brethren, but rather serve them because those who are benefited are believers and beloved. Teach and exhort these things.

Error and Greed

³If anyone teaches otherwise and does not consent to ᵇwholesome words, even the words of our Lord Jesus Christ, ᶜand to the doctrine which accords with godliness, ⁴he is proud, knowing nothing, but is obsessed with disputes and arguments over words, from which come envy, strife, reviling, evil suspicions, ⁵useless wranglings* of men of corrupt minds and destitute of the truth, who suppose that godliness is a means of gain. From ᵈsuch withdraw yourself.*

⁶Now godliness with ᵉcontentment is great gain. ⁷For we brought nothing into this world, and it is ᶠcertain* we can carry nothing out. ⁸And having food and clothing, with these we shall be ᵍcontent. ⁹But those who desire to be rich fall into temptation and a snare, and into many foolish and harmful lusts which drown men in destruction and perdition. ¹⁰For the love of money is a root of all kinds of evil, for which some have strayed from the faith in their greediness, and pierced themselves through with many sorrows.

The Good Confession

¹¹But you, O man of God, flee these things and pursue righteousness, godliness, faith, love, patience, gentleness. ¹²Fight the good fight of faith, lay hold on eternal life, to which you were also called and have confessed the good confession in the presence of many witnesses. ¹³I urge you in the sight of God who gives life to all things, and before Christ Jesus ʰwho witnessed the good confession before Pontius Pilate, ¹⁴that you keep this commandment without spot, blameless until our Lord Jesus Christ's appearing, ¹⁵which He will manifest in His own time, He who is the blessed and only Potentate, the King of kings and Lord of lords, ¹⁶who alone has immortality, dwelling in ⁱunapproachable light, ʲwhom no man has seen or can see,

---

* 6:5 NU-Text and M-Text read *constant friction.* • NU-Text omits this sentence.   * 6:7 NU-Text omits *and it is certain.*

---

believers. Sin is a serious matter, especially for those who are in leadership, setting an example for others (1 Pet. 4:14).

5:22 hastily. This verse is believed to be warning against too quickly restoring a leader who has fallen. Correction in love and restoration to fellowship should occur as soon as possible, but restoration to leadership should not be made without time and biblical evaluation. Not only does this apply to former leaders, it is a caution not to share responsibility for someone else's sin by restoring or appointing someone who is not qualified.

5:25 evident . . . cannot be hidden. Unnoticed good works always come to light, if not in this life, at the judgment seat, but even sins hidden from men cannot be concealed from God.

6:1 bondservants. This serves as an example of how believers should act in the workplace. We are Christians, who are to represent our faith, and Christ Himself. If we do this badly, we minimize not only our faith, but the power and testimony of Christ.

6:2 these things. "These things" probably are best understood as the contents of the entire letter to Timothy.

6:9 those who desire to be rich. Inside of every man there is a "God-shaped void." Many unbelievers try to

fill this inner longing with wealth and possessions. Greed drives people to temptation and foolish and harmful desires. This is not an ailment of unbelievers only. Many believers also try to gain material things rather than the imperishable things of righteousness, godliness, faith, love, perseverance, and gentleness (v. 11). These are the things we should pursue with all of our being.

6:10 love of money. Money in and of itself is not a problem, but the love of money is. Christians can be so blinded by greed that they no longer see the need for holy living. A life focused on material things brings only pain.

6:12 lay hold on eternal life. Use the hope of everlasting life with the Savior as your lifeline, your comfort, and your guide.

6:14 our Lord Jesus Christ's appearing. The imminent return of Christ should be a motive for godly living (1 John 2:28).

6:16 immortality. This may also be translated "without death." The glorified Christ can never die.

5:21 ⁱDeut. 1:17   **5:22** ʲEph. 5:6, 7   **5:24** ᵏGal. 5:19–21   **6:1** ᵃEph. 6:5   **6:3** ᵇ2 Tim. 1:13   ᶜTitus 1:1   **6:5** ᵈ2 Tim. 3:5   **6:6** ᵉHeb. 13:5   **6:7** ᶠJob 1:21   **6:8** ᵍProv. 30:8, 9   **6:13** ʰJohn 18:36, 37   **6:16** ⁱDan. 2:22   ʲJohn 4:46

to whom *be* honor and everlasting power. Amen.

Instructions to the Rich

[17]Command those who are rich in this present age not to be haughty, nor to trust in uncertain [k]riches but in the living God, who gives us richly all things [l]to enjoy. [18]*Let them* do good, that they be rich in good works, ready to give, willing to share, [19][m]storing up for themselves a good foundation for the time to come, that they may lay hold on eternal life.

Guard the Faith

[20]O Timothy! [n]Guard what was committed to your trust, [o]avoiding the profane *and* idle babblings and contradictions of what is falsely called knowledge— [21]by professing it some have strayed concerning the faith.

Grace *be* with you. Amen.

6:20 *falsely called knowledge.* Gnosticism (from the Greek word for knowledge) is a heresy that teaches that salvation comes through secret knowledge of spiritual mysteries.
6:21 *Grace be with you.* The Greek word for "you" here is plural, including the whole church. God's grace to us as sinners is indeed amazing.

6:17 [k] Jer. 9:23; 48:7 [l] Eccl. 5:18, 19 **6:19** [m] [Matt. 6:20, 21; 19:21] **6:20** [n] [2 Tim. 1:12, 14] [o] Titus 1:14

THE SECOND EPISTLE OF PAUL THE APOSTLE TO
TIMOTHY

▶ **AUTHOR:** Fearing for their own lives, the Asian believers failed to support Paul after this second Roman imprisonment and his first defense before the imperial court (1:15; 4:16). Now he was in a cold Roman cell (4:13) without hope of acquittal in spite of the success of his initial defense. Under these conditions, Paul wrote this epistle in the fall of A.D. 67, hoping that Timothy would be able to visit him before the approaching winter (4:21).

▶ **TIME:** c. A.D. 66–67   ▶ **KEY VERSES:** 2 Tim. 3:14–17

▶ **THEME:** This is likely the last of Paul's writings that we have. He writes this letter from a prison cell where he is being kept like a common criminal. He knows that his work on earth is nearing its conclusion, and these are then his last words of counsel to his trusted companion in ministry. One can sense his weariness, but also his strongly held conviction about what is necessary for the continued growth of the church. One can also clearly see the hope that sustains him as he looks forward to going home to Christ.

Greeting

1 Paul, an apostle of Jesus Christ* by the will of God, according to the *a*promise of life which is in Christ Jesus,

2 To Timothy, a *b*beloved son:

Grace, mercy, *and* peace from God the Father and Christ Jesus our Lord.

Timothy's Faith and Heritage

3 I thank God, whom I serve with a pure conscience, as *my* *c*forefathers *did*, as without ceasing I remember you in my prayers night and day, 4greatly desiring to see you, being mindful of your tears, that I may be filled with joy, 5when I call to remembrance *d*the genuine faith that is in you, which dwelt first in your grandmother Lois and *e*your mother Eunice, and I am persuaded is in you also. 6Therefore I remind you *f*to stir up the gift of God which is in you

through the laying on of my hands. 7For *g*God has not given us a spirit of fear, *h*but of power and of love and of a sound mind.

Not Ashamed of the Gospel

8*i*Therefore do not be ashamed of *j*the testimony of our Lord, nor of me *k*His prisoner, but share with me in the sufferings for the gospel according to the power of God, 9who has saved us and called *us* with a holy calling, *l*not according to our works, but *m*according to His own purpose and grace which was given to us in Christ Jesus *n*before time began, 10but *o*has now been revealed by the appearing of our Savior Jesus Christ, *who* has abolished death and brought life and immortality to light through the gospel, 11*p*to which I was appointed a preacher, an apostle, and a

---

* **1:1** NU-Text and M-Text read *Christ Jesus.*

1:1 the promise of life. This message of life stands in ironic contrast to the fact that Paul was writing from a Roman prison, facing his execution.
1:3 my forefathers. Paul's forefathers were the patriarchs of the faith: Abraham, Isaac, and Jacob. Paul had great love for Israel (Rom. 9:1–5). The reason that he connects himself to Israel's forefathers may be to demonstrate that he is not advocating a new religion but one of which the godly of the past are also a part.
1:5 Lois … Eunice. The prayers, witness, and faith of his godly mother and grandmother were central factors in the spiritual development of Timothy (1 Tim. 2:15).
1:8 do not be ashamed of the testimony. Testimony is the witness of the Lord; the Greek term is the source of the English word *martyr*. Church tradition says that most of the apostles died as martyrs.

1:9 not according to our works. It is impossible for people to earn their way into heaven. Salvation is by grace, the unearned and undeserved favor of God.
1:10 abolished death. Knowing that leaving our earthly bodies simply means that we will live forever with the Lord effectively robs death of its dread. The same gospel that offers us the forgiveness of sins and draws us to holy living also announces life and immortality. Believing the gospel, we begin to live in the power of an endless life (1 John 5:11–13,20).

1:1 *a* Titus 1:2 **1:2** *b* 1 Tim. 1:2 **1:3** *c* Acts 24:14	
1:5 *d* 1 Tim. 1:5; 4:6 *e* Acts 16:1 **1:6** *f* 1 Tim. 4:14	
1:7 *g* Rom. 8:15 *h* [Acts 1:8] **1:8** *i* [Rom. 1:16] *j* 1 Tim. 2:6	
k Eph. 3:1 **1:9** *l* [Rom. 3:20] *m* Rom. 8:28 *n* Rom. 16:25	
1:10 *o* Eph. 1:9 **1:11** *p* Acts 9:15	

teacher of the Gentiles.* ¹²For this reason I also suffer these things; nevertheless I am not ashamed, ᵍfor I know whom I have believed and am persuaded that He is able to keep what I have committed to Him until that Day.

Be Loyal to the Faith

¹³ʳHold fast ˢthe pattern of ᵗsound words which you have heard from me, in faith and love which are in Christ Jesus. ¹⁴That good thing which was committed to you, keep by the Holy Spirit who dwells in us.

¹⁵This you know, that all those in Asia have turned away from me, among whom are Phygellus and Hermogenes. ¹⁶The Lord grant mercy to the ᵘhousehold of Onesiphorus, for he often refreshed me, and was not ashamed of my chain; ¹⁷but when he arrived in Rome, he sought me out very zealously and found *me*. ¹⁸The Lord ᵛgrant to him that he may find mercy from the Lord ʷin that Day—and you know very well how many ways he ˣministered to *me** at Ephesus.

Be Strong in Grace

2 You therefore, ᵃmy son, ᵇbe strong in the grace that is in Christ Jesus. ²And the things that you have heard from me among many witnesses, commit these to faithful men who will be able to teach others also. ³You therefore must ᶜendure* hardship ᵈas a good soldier of Jesus Christ. ⁴ᵉNo one engaged in warfare entangles himself with the affairs of *this* life, that he may please him who enlisted him as a soldier. ⁵And also ᶠif anyone competes in athletics, he is not crowned unless he competes according to the rules. ⁶The hardworking farmer must be first to partake of the crops. ⁷Consider what I say, and may* the Lord ᵍgive you understanding in all things.

⁸Remember that Jesus Christ, ʰof the seed of David, ⁱwas raised from the dead ʲaccording to my gospel, ⁹ᵏfor which I suffer trouble as an evildoer, ˡ*even* to the point of chains; ᵐbut the word of God is not chained. ¹⁰Therefore ⁿI endure all things for the sake of the elect, ᵒthat they also may obtain the salvation which is in Christ Jesus with eternal glory.

¹¹ *This is* a faithful saying:

For ᵖif we died with *Him*,
We shall also live with *Him*.
¹² ᵍIf we endure,
We shall also reign with *Him*.
ʳIf we deny *Him*,
He also will deny us.
¹³ If we are faithless,
He remains faithful;
He ˢcannot deny Himself.

Approved and Disapproved Workers

¹⁴Remind *them* of these things, ᵗcharging *them* before the Lord not to strive about words to no profit, to the ruin of the hearers. ¹⁵ᵘBe diligent to present yourself approved to God, a worker who does not need to be ashamed, rightly dividing the word of truth. ¹⁶But shun profane *and* idle babblings, for they will increase to more ungodliness. ¹⁷And their message will spread like cancer. ᵛHymenaeus and Philetus are of this sort, ¹⁸who have strayed concerning the truth, ʷsaying that the resurrection is already past; and they overthrow the faith of some. ¹⁹Nevertheless ˣthe solid foundation of God stands, having this seal: "The Lord ʸknows those

---

* **1:11** NU-Text omits *of the Gentiles.* * **1:18** *To me* is from the Vulgate and a few Greek manuscripts. * **2:3** NU-Text reads *You must share.* * **2:7** NU-Text reads *the Lord will give you.*

1:12 *what I have committed.* It is certain that God will keep our "deposit" safe. Paul was preparing for imminent death, but in spite of this he was hopeful. He had spent his time, resources, and even his life proclaiming the gospel, and this investment in Christ's kingdom would bring him an abundant reward in eternity (Luke 19:15; 1 Cor. 3:10–15; Rev. 11:15,18).
1:14 *That good thing.* This is the truth of the kingdom of God (Matt. 13:44–45; 1 Tim. 6:20).
2:1 *strong in the grace that is in Christ Jesus.* The emphasis is on the strength of Christ, not on Timothy's own power. If we trust in ourselves, we are doomed to fail.
2:2 *commit these to faithful men.* Since the time of Christ, there has been an endless chain of Christian discipleship (Matt. 28:18–20).
2:8 *seed of David.* Jesus is the fulfillment of all the promises that God gave to David (2 Sam. 7:11–16).
2:11 *if we died . . . shall also live.* Believers are united with Christ in His death and resurrection (Rom. 6:3–11).
2:12 *If we endure.* Persevering in our faith, even in the face of hardship or persecution, will result in a reward when Christ returns (Luke 19:11–27; Rom. 8:17; Rev. 3:21).

2:13 *faithless.* This word describes an immature believer who lives for self and not for the Savior (1 Cor. 3:1–3,15). *He remains faithful.* For Christ to abandon us would be contrary to His faithful nature (John 10:27–30; Heb. 10:23; 13:5).
2:15 *Be diligent.* The position of teaching God's word is a position of great responsibility, not to be taken lightly (James 3:1).
2:18 *already past.* This was probably an early form of Gnosticism, a body of teaching which emphasized the "spiritual," and considered the physical world and the human body unreal and unimportant.

1:12 ᵍ 1 Pet. 4:19 **1:13** ʳ Titus 1:9 ˢ Rom. 2:20; 6:17 ᵗ 1 Tim. 6:3 **1:16** ᵘ 2 Tim. 4:19 **1:18** ᵛ Mark 9:41 ʷ 2 Thess. 1:10 ˣ Heb. 6:10 **2:1** ᵃ 1 Tim. 1:2 ᵇ Eph. 6:10 **2:3** ᶜ 2 Tim. 4:5 ᵈ 1 Tim. 1:18 **2:4** ᵉ [2 Pet. 2:20] **2:5** ᶠ [1 Cor. 9:25] **2:7** ᵍ Prov. 2:6 **2:8** ʰ Rom. 1:3, 4 ⁱ 1 Cor. 15:4 ʲ Rom. 2:16 **2:9** ᵏ Acts 9:16 ˡ Eph. 3:1 ᵐ Acts 28:31 **2:10** ⁿ Eph. 3:13 ᵒ 2 Cor. 1:6 **2:11** ᵖ Rom. 6:5, 8 **2:12** ᵍ [Rom. 5:17; 8:17] ʳ Matt. 10:33 **2:13** ˢ Num. 23:19 **2:14** ᵗ Titus 3:9 **2:15** ᵘ 2 Pet. 1:10 **2:17** ᵛ 1 Tim. 1:20 **2:18** ʷ 1 Cor. 15:12 **2:19** ˣ [1 Cor. 3:11] ʸ [Nah. 1:7]

who are His," and, "Let everyone who names the name of Christ* depart from iniquity."

20But in a great house there are not only ᶻvessels of gold and silver, but also of wood and clay, some for honor and some for dishonor. **21**Therefore if anyone cleanses himself from the latter, he will be a vessel for honor, sanctified and useful for the Master, ᵃprepared for every good work. **22**ᵇFlee also youthful lusts; but pursue righteousness, faith, love, peace with those who call on the Lord out of a pure heart. **23**But avoid foolish and ignorant disputes, knowing that they generate strife. **24**And ᶜa servant of the Lord must not quarrel but be gentle to all, ᵈable to teach, ᵉpatient, **25**ᶠin humility correcting those who are in opposition, ᵍif God perhaps will grant them repentance, ʰso that they may know the truth, **26**and *that* they may come to their senses *and* ⁱescape the snare of the devil, having been taken captive by him to *do* his will.

Perilous Times and Perilous Men

3 But know this, that ᵃin the last days perilous times will come: **2**For men will be lovers of themselves, lovers of money, boasters, proud, blasphemers, disobedient to parents, unthankful, unholy, **3**unloving, unforgiving, slanderers, without self-control, brutal, despisers of good, **4**ᵇtraitors, headstrong, haughty, lovers of pleasure rather than lovers of God, **5**ᶜhaving a form of godliness but ᵈdenying its power. And ᵉfrom such people turn away! **6**For ᶠof this sort are those who creep into households and make

captives of gullible women loaded down with sins, led away by various lusts, **7**always learning and never able ᵍto come to the knowledge of the truth. **8**ʰNow as Jannes and Jambres resisted Moses, so do these also resist the truth: ⁱmen of corrupt minds, ʲdisapproved concerning the faith; **9**but they will progress no further, for their folly will be manifest to all, ᵏas theirs also was.

The Man of God and the Word of God

10ˡBut you have carefully followed my doctrine, manner of life, purpose, faith, longsuffering, love, perseverance, **11**persecutions, afflictions, which happened to me ᵐat Antioch, ⁿat Iconium, ᵒat Lystra—what persecutions I endured. And ᵖout of *them* all the Lord delivered me. **12**Yes, and ᑫall who desire to live godly in Christ Jesus will suffer persecution. **13**ʳBut evil men and impostors will grow worse and worse, deceiving and being deceived. **14**But you must ˢcontinue in the things which you have learned and been assured of, knowing from whom you have learned *them*, **15**and that from childhood you have known ᵗthe Holy Scriptures, which are able to make you wise for salvation through faith which is in Christ Jesus.

16ᵘAll Scripture *is* given by inspiration of God, ᵛand *is* profitable for doctrine, for reproof, for correction, for instruction in righteousness, **17**ʷthat the man of God may be complete, ˣthoroughly equipped for every good work.

---

* 2:19 NU-Text and M-Text read *the Lord.*

2:21 Master. This is a strong term for God's authority over the lives of believers, regardless of their level of spiritual maturity.

2:22 Flee... pursue. When we run toward righteousness, we are running away from sin. The two are completely opposite, and a person cannot follow both at once.

2:25 in humility correcting. The aim of instruction is repentance or a change of thinking, not self-justification or the pleasure of argument.

2:26 come to their senses. False teaching has an intoxicating effect that dulls the mind to God's truth.

3:5 a form of godliness. This is an outward appearance of reverence for God. Denying its power describes religious activity that is not connected to a living relationship with Jesus Christ. This kind of religion provokes God's anger (Is. 1:10–18; Matt. 23:25–28).

3:8 Jannes and Jambres. They are not named in the Old Testament, but according to Jewish tradition, Jannes and Jambres were two of the Egyptian magicians who opposed Moses (Ex. 7:11).

3:12 will suffer persecution. God does not promise deliverance *from* persecution, but deliverance *through* it. Persecution is one of the means that God uses to bring about our growth and sanctification (2:12; Matt. 5:10–12; Rev. 2:10).

3:16 inspiration of God. This is literally "God-breathed." Scripture was freely produced by human writers, but the original Author is God Himself. God "breathed out" the Scriptures so that they are not only human words, but simultaneously and ultimately the very utterances of God. Thus, Scripture is true in all it affirms and is completely authoritative (1 Pet. 1:20–21). The Bible not only "contains God's words," it *is* God's Word. Therefore the Scriptures are fully consistent and inerrant, authoritative and trustworthy.

3:17 every good work. Paul emphasizes the essential link between knowing God's Word and applying it to one's daily life. Right doctrine should produce right practice.

2:20 ᶻ Rom. 9:21 **2:21** ᵃ 2 Tim. 3:17 **2:22** ᵇ 1 Tim. 6:11
2:24 ᶜ Titus 3:2 ᵈ Titus 1:9 ᵉ 1 Tim. 3:3 **2:25** ᶠ Gal. 6:1
ᵍ Acts 8:22 ʰ 1 Tim. 2:4 **2:26** ⁱ 1 Tim. 3:7 **3:1** ᵃ 1 Tim.
4:1 **3:4** ᵇ 2 Pet. 2:10 **3:5** ᶜ Titus 1:16 ᵈ 1 Tim.
5:8 ᵉ 2 Thess. 3:6 **3:6** ᶠ Matt. 23:14 **3:7** ᵍ 1 Tim.
2:4 **3:8** ʰ Ex. 7:11, 12, 22; 8:7; 9:11 ⁱ 1 Tim. 6:5 ʲ Rom.
1:28 **3:9** ᵏ Ex. 7:11, 12; 8:18; 9:11 **3:10** ˡ 1 Tim. 4:6
3:11 ᵐ Acts 13:44–52 ⁿ Acts 14:1–6, 19 ᵒ Acts 14:8–20
ᵖ Ps. 34:19 **3:12** ᑫ [Ps. 34:19] **3:13** ʳ 2 Thess. 2:11
3:14 ˢ 2 Tim. 1:13 **3:15** ᵗ John 5:39 **3:16** ᵘ [2 Pet. 1:20]
ᵛ Rom. 4:23; 15:4 **3:17** ʷ 1 Tim. 6:11 ˣ 2 Tim. 2:21

Preach the Word

4 I [a]charge *you* therefore before God and the Lord Jesus Christ, [b]who will judge the living and the dead at* His appearing and His kingdom: [2]Preach the word! Be ready in season *and* out of season. [c]Convince, [d]rebuke, [e]exhort, with all longsuffering and teaching. [3][f]For the time will come when they will not endure [g]sound doctrine, [h]but according to their own desires, *because* they have itching ears, they will heap up for themselves teachers; [4]and they will turn *their* ears away from the truth, and [i]be turned aside to fables. [5]But you be watchful in all things, [j]endure afflictions, do the work of [k]an evangelist, fulfill your ministry.

Paul's Valedictory

[6]For [l]I am already being poured out as a drink offering, and the time of [m]my departure is at hand. [7][n]I have fought the good fight, I have finished the race, I have kept the faith. [8]Finally, there is laid up for me [o]the crown of righteousness, which the Lord, the righteous [p]Judge, will give to me [q]on that Day, and not to me only but also to all who have loved His appearing.

The Abandoned Apostle

[9]Be diligent to come to me quickly; [10]for [r]Demas has forsaken me, [s]having loved this present world, and has departed for Thessalonica—Crescens for Galatia, Titus for Dalmatia. [11]Only Luke is with me. Get [t]Mark and bring him with you, for he is useful to me for ministry. [12]And [u]Tychicus I have sent to Ephesus. [13]Bring the cloak that I left with Carpus at Troas when you come—and the books, especially the parchments.

[14][v]Alexander the coppersmith did me much harm. May the Lord repay him according to his works. [15]You also must beware of him, for he has greatly resisted our words.

[16]At my first defense no one stood with me, but all forsook me. [w]May it not be charged against them.

The Lord Is Faithful

[17][x]But the Lord stood with me and strengthened me, [y]so that the message might be preached fully through me, and *that* all the Gentiles might hear. Also I was delivered [z]out of the mouth of the lion. [18][a]And the Lord will deliver me from every evil work and preserve *me* for His heavenly kingdom. [b]To Him *be* glory forever and ever. Amen!

Come Before Winter

[19]Greet [c]Prisca and Aquila, and the household of [d]Onesiphorus. [20][e]Erastus stayed in Corinth, but [f]Trophimus I have left in Miletus sick.

[21]Do your utmost to come before winter. Eubulus greets you, as well as Pudens, Linus, Claudia, and all the brethren.

Farewell

[22]The Lord Jesus Christ* be with your spirit. Grace be with you. Amen.

---

* 4:1 NU-Text omits *therefore* and reads *and by* for at. * 4:22 NU-Text omits *Jesus Christ*.

4:2 longsuffering. Longsuffering and doctrine are two necessary components of an effective ministry. True spiritual growth occurs over a period of time, through consistent teaching and application of God's Word.

4:6 drink offering. An offering performed by pouring wine out on the ground or altar (Num. 28:11–31). Paul's life was already being poured out in service to Christ.

4:7 fought the good fight. Paul did not make these comments until the end of his race, when he was about to die. He did not presume or rely on his past service. Instead, he persevered, struggled, and served God until the end (1 Cor. 9:24–27).

4:8 loved His appearing. These are the believers who have lived faithfully in the hope of His return (Titus 2:11–15; 1 John 2:28).

4:11 Mark. Mark's desertion of Paul in Pamphylia on his first missionary journey had led to the separation of Paul and Barnabas at the beginning of Paul's second missionary journey (Acts 15:36–40). Later Paul and Mark were reconciled, and Mark served Paul in the ministry (Col. 4:10). It is believed that Mark later wrote the Gospel of Mark.

4:12 Tychicus. Tychicus was Paul's faithful co-worker (Acts 20:4; Eph. 6:21; Col. 4:7).

4:14 Alexander. This may be the person named in 1 Timothy 1:20 or Acts 19:33, who caused harm to Paul's ministry in Ephesus.

4:19 Prisca and Aquila. Prisca is a form of the name Priscilla. Paul had met Priscilla and Aquila in Corinth on his second missionary journey (Acts 18:1–3), and they had assisted in God's work in Ephesus (Acts 18:18–19).

4:20 Trophimus. Trophimus, a member of the church of Ephesus (Acts 21:29), had traveled with Paul to Jerusalem (Acts 20:4).

4:1 [a] 1 Tim. 5:21 [b] Acts 10:42 **4:2** [c] Titus 2:15 [d] 1 Tim. 5:20 [e] 1 Tim. 4:13 **4:3** [f] 2 Tim. 3:1 [g] 1 Tim. 1:10 [h] 2 Tim. 3:6 **4:4** [i] 1 Tim. 1:4 **4:5** [j] 2 Tim. 1:8 [k] Acts 21:8 **4:6** [l] Phil. 2:17 [m] [Phil. 1:23] **4:7** [n] 1 Cor. 9:24–27 **4:8** [o] James 1:12 [p] John 5:22 [q] 2 Tim. 1:12 **4:10** [r] Col. 4:14 [s] 1 John 2:15 **4:11** [t] Acts 12:12, 25; 15:37–39 **4:12** [u] Acts 20:4 **4:14** [v] 1 Tim. 1:20 **4:16** [w] Acts 7:60 **4:17** [x] Acts 23:11 [y] Acts 9:15 [z] 1 Sam. 17:37 **4:18** [a] Ps. 121:7 [b] Rom. 11:36 **4:19** [c] Acts 18:2 [d] 2 Tim. 1:16 **4:20** [e] Rom. 16:23 [f] Acts 20:4; 21:29

THE EPISTLE OF PAUL THE APOSTLE TO
TITUS

▶ **AUTHOR:** Titus was one of Paul's Gentile converts. He probably worked with Paul during his time at Ephesus on his third missionary journey. Later he also worked in Corinth and this letter indicates that Paul is commissioning him to work on the island of Crete. Paul wrote this letter about A.D. 63, perhaps from Corinth, taking advantage of the journey of Zenas and Apollos (3:13), whose destination would take them by way of Crete.

▶ **TIME:** c. A.D. 63   ▶ **KEY VERSE:** Titus 3:8

▶ **THEME:** Paul's instructions to Titus are similar to those he gives to Timothy. He gives him instructions about the leadership and organization of the church and guidance in dealing with the opposition of those who would contradict his teaching. His tone is that of a seasoned leader passing on the essential instructions to a valued disciple.

Greeting

1 Paul, a bondservant of God and an apostle of Jesus Christ, according to the faith of God's elect and *a*the acknowledgment of the truth *b*which accords with godliness, ²in hope of eternal life which God, who *c*cannot lie, promised before time began, ³but has in due time manifested His word through preaching, which was committed to me according to the commandment of God our Savior;

⁴To *d*Titus, a true son in *our* common faith:

Grace, mercy, *and* peace from God the Father and the Lord Jesus Christ* our Savior.

Qualified Elders

⁵For this reason I left you in Crete, that you should *e*set in order the things that are lacking, and appoint elders in every city as I commanded you— ⁶if a man is blameless, the husband of one wife, *f*having faithful children not accused of dissipation or insubordination. ⁷For a bishop* must be blameless, as a steward of God, not self-willed, not quick-tempered, *g*not given to wine, not violent, not greedy for money, ⁸but hospitable, a lover of what is good, sober-minded, just, holy, self-controlled,

* **1:4** NU-Text reads *and Christ Jesus.*   * **1:7** Literally *overseer*

1:2 We Can Trust God—Often Christians will doubt our position with God simply because we do not *feel* saved. We don't understand that the basis for our standing is the promise of God and not emotional feelings. One helpful way to see these promises is in relation to the Trinity:

1. *The promise and work of the Father.* He has promised to graciously accept in Christ all repenting sinners (Eph. 1:6 and Col. 3:3). This means a Christian has the right to be in heaven someday, for he is in Christ. God guarantees us that He will work out all things for our ultimate good (Rom. 8:28).

2. *The promise and work of the Son.* He has promised us eternal life (John 5:24) and abundant life (John 10:10). This promise covers not only our final destiny in heaven, but also our present Christian service here on earth. He is, in fact, right now praying for us and ministering to us at His Father's right hand (Heb. 8:1; 9:24).

3. *The promise and work of the Holy Spirit.* The Holy Spirit is said to indwell the believer (John 14:16). In addition, He places all believing sinners into the body of Christ, thus assuring us of union with God's family (1 Cor. 12:13).

1:3 preaching. Paul places the emphasis on the message, not on the messenger. Christ is the center of our faith, not any one preacher (1 Cor. 9:16; 2 Cor. 4:5).

1:5 appoint elders. The Greek words for "elder" and "bishop" (literally, overseer) seem to have been used interchangeably by Paul (v. 7). "Elder" perhaps speaks more of the office and its authority, while "bishop" may speak more of the person's function and the ministry of oversight (Acts 20:17).

1:6 husband of one wife. The exact application of this phrase is debated; some believe that it merely forbids polygamy, while others believe that it also prohibits a man who is divorced and remarried. It is clearly emphasizing the importance of marital faithfulness (Matt. 19:5). *faithful children.* The man must have a good relationship with his wife, and he should also have children who demonstrate faithfulness to God. If a man has children who reject the ways of God, or who are out of control, this reflects on the father's ability to lead others outside his home.

1:1 *d* 2 Tim. 2:25 *b* [1 Tim. 3:16]   **1:2** *c* Num. 23:19   **1:4** *d* 2 Cor. 2:13; 8:23   **1:5** *e* 1 Cor. 11:34   **1:6** *f* 1 Tim. 3:2–4   **1:7** *g* Lev. 10:9

9holding fast the faithful word as he has been taught, that he may be able, by sound doctrine, both to exhort and convict those who contradict.

The Elders' Task

10For there are many insubordinate, both idle htalkers and deceivers, especially those of the circumcision, 11whose mouths must be stopped, who subvert whole households, teaching things which they ought not, ifor the sake of dishonest gain. 12jOne of them, a prophet of their own, said, "Cretans are always liars, evil beasts, lazy gluttons." 13This testimony is true. kTherefore rebuke them sharply, that they may be sound in the faith, 14not giving heed to Jewish fables and lcommandments of men who turn from the truth. 15mTo the pure all things are pure, but to those who are defiled and unbelieving nothing is pure; but even their mind and conscience are defiled. 16They profess to nknow God, but oin works they deny Him, being abominable, disobedient, pand disqualified for every good work.

Qualities of a Sound Church

2 But as for you, speak the things which are proper for sound doctrine: 2that the older men be sober, reverent, temperate, sound in faith, in love, in patience; 3the older women likewise, that they be reverent in behavior, not slanderers, not given to much wine, teachers of good things— 4that they admonish the young women to love their husbands, to love their children, 5to be discreet, chaste, ahomemakers, good, bobedient to their own husbands, cthat the word of God may not be blasphemed.

6Likewise, exhort the young men to be sober-minded, 7in all things showing yourself to be da pattern of good works; in doctrine showing integrity, reverence, eincorruptibility,* 8sound speech that cannot be condemned, that one who is an opponent may be ashamed, having nothing evil to say of you.*

9Exhort fbondservants to be obedient to their own masters, to be well pleasing in all things, not answering back, 10not pilfering, but showing all good fidelity, that they may adorn the doctrine of God our Savior in all things.

Trained by Saving Grace

11For gthe grace of God that brings salvation has appeared to all men, 12teaching us that, denying ungodliness and worldly lusts, we should live soberly, righteously, and godly in the present age, 13hlooking for the blessed ihope and glorious appearing of our great God and Savior Jesus Christ,

---

* **2:7** NU-Text omits incorruptibility.   * **2:8** NU-Text and M-Text read us.

1:9 convict. The word convict here means to rebuke in such a way as to produce repentance and confession of sin (John 16:8). A rebuke can have the positive results of producing change in a person's life.
1:10 those of the circumcision. Apparently there were Jewish Christians in the churches of Crete who were limiting the Christian freedom of Gentile Christians by requiring an adherence to Jewish laws (Gal. 3).
1:12 Cretans are always liars. Paul is quoting the Cretan poet Epimenides, who wrote these words around 600 B.C. The Cretans were so much regarded as liars in the Mediterranean world that the expression "to Cretanize" meant "to lie."
1:14 Jewish fables. These were probably legends about Old Testament figures, like some that survive to this day in non-biblical writings.
1:15 To the pure . . . to those who are defiled. Paul highlights the mistaken asceticism of the Cretan false teachers. They had identified certain foods and practices as defiled when in reality it was their minds that were defiled and unbelieving. On the other hand, to the pure, all things are pure. The Cretan believers had placed their trust in Christ, focusing their minds on Him, and therefore they would be empowered by God's Spirit to lead pure lives. Jesus taught the same principle in Matthew 15:11. Physical objects or external practices do not defile a person, but a mind focused on evil thoroughly corrupts.
2:1 sound doctrine. "Sound" means "healthy." Right thinking is the raw material for right actions (Ps. 119:11; Prov. 23:7; Rom. 12:2; James 1:13–15). Our actions will naturally reveal the direction of our thoughts.
2:2 older men. Maturity is not determined simply by age or even by how much a person knows; it is

determined by how skilled a person is in applying the truth to life and in distinguishing good from evil (Heb. 5:13–14).
2:4 love their husbands . . . their children. This is not just romantic or emotional love, but the commitment of a woman to the welfare of her husband and children.
2:5 obedient to their own husbands. Women are not under the authority of men in general, but rather the authority of their own husbands (Eph. 5:21). **not be blasphemed.** The older women are to teach the younger women so that their actions will glorify God, build His kingdom, and strengthen the family. Failure to follow Paul's instructions will result in the word of God being maligned in the pagan community.
2:6 young men. Young men are to pursue the character qualities that older men should possess already.
2:7 pattern of good works. More people will learn from our daily actions than from what we say.
2:11 appeared. Christ came the first time in grace to save men from their sins; the second time He will come in glory to reign (v. 13).
2:13 looking for the blessed hope. Paul reminded Timothy that there is a special crown awaiting all who "have loved His appearing" (2 Tim. 4:8). **great God and Savior Jesus Christ.** This is one of the strongest statements of the deity of Christ in the New Testament.

1:10 h James 1:26   **1:11** i 1 Tim. 6:5   **1:12** j Acts 17:28
1:13 k 2 Cor. 13:10   **1:14** l Is. 29:13   **1:15** m 1 Cor. 6:12
1:16 n Matt. 7:20–23; 25:12   o [2 Tim. 3:5, 7]   p Rom. 1:28
2:5 a 1 Tim. 5:14   b 1 Cor. 14:34   c Rom. 2:24   **2:7** d 1 Tim.
4:12   e Eph. 6:24   **2:9** f 1 Tim. 6:1   **2:11** g [Rom. 5:15]
2:13 h 1 Cor. 1:7   i [Col. 3:4]

14iwho gave Himself for us, that He might redeem us from every lawless deed kand purify for Himself lHis own special people, zealous for good works.

15Speak these things, mexhort, and rebuke with all authority. Let no one despise you.

Graces of the Heirs of Grace

3 Remind them ato be subject to rulers and authorities, to obey, bto be ready for every good work, 2to speak evil of no one, to be peaceable, gentle, showing all humility to all men. 3For cwe ourselves were also once foolish, disobedient, deceived, serving various lusts and pleasures, living in malice and envy, hateful and hating one another. 4But when dthe kindness and the love of eGod our Savior toward man appeared, 5fnot by works of righteousness which we have done, but according to His mercy He saved us, through gthe washing of regeneration and renewing of the Holy Spirit, 6hwhom He poured out on us abundantly through Jesus Christ our Savior, 7that having been justified by His grace iwe should become heirs according to the hope of eternal life.

8iThis is a faithful saying, and these things I want you to affirm constantly, that those who have believed in God should be careful to maintain good works. These things are good and profitable to men.

Avoid Dissension

9But kavoid foolish disputes, genealogies, contentions, and strivings about the law; for they are unprofitable and useless. 10lReject a divisive man after the first and second admonition, 11knowing that such a person is warped and sinning, being self-condemned.

Final Messages

12When I send Artemas to you, or mTychicus, be diligent to come to me at Nicopolis, for I have decided to spend the winter there. 13Send Zenas the lawyer and nApollos on their journey with haste, that they may lack nothing. 14And let our people also learn to maintain good works, to meet urgent needs, that they may not be unfruitful.

Farewell

15All who are with me greet you. Greet those who love us in the faith.

Grace be with you all. Amen.

2:14 redeem. "Redeem" means "to purchase." With His death on the cross, Christ paid the price to release us from the bondage of sin (Rom. 6:6–7,17,20; Eph. 1:7). God's purpose in redeeming us is not only to save us from hell; He also wants to free us from sin so that we can produce good works that glorify Him (Eph. 2:8–10).

3:1 Remind them. The Cretans notoriously lacked the virtue of good citizenship (1:12). Disobedience permeated the Cretan's lifestyle, both in the church (v. 10) and in government. Believers who got along with civil authorities and who lived peacefully with their neighbors would reflect positively on their faith and would glorify God.

3:5 not by works of righteousness. Paul has been exhorting Titus to emphasize good works in his ministry with the Cretans, and he wants to make it clear that such good works have no value in saving a person. It is solely on the basis of God's mercy that we are delivered from the penalty of our sin. **washing of regeneration.** This phrase refers to the work of the Holy Spirit, in whom we are "born again" (John 3:3,6), given a new nature and cleansed from old sin. **renewing of the Holy Spirit.** There are three works performed by the Holy Spirit in preparing nonbelievers to become Christians. (1) The Holy Spirit restrains. Satan would enjoy nothing more than to destroy people before they make their decision to accept Christ as Savior. But the Holy Spirit prevents this from occurring (Is. 59:19). (2) The Holy Spirit convicts. Mankind's sin and righteousness are exposed by the Holy Spirit (John 16:8). Two examples of such conviction

are Felix, a Roman governor who "trembled" under conviction (Acts 24:25), and King Agrippa, who was almost persuaded in Acts 26:28. (3) The Holy Spirit regenerates. When a repenting sinner accepts Christ as Savior, he is given a new nature by the Holy Spirit (2 Cor. 5:17). Jesus carefully explained this ministry of the Holy Spirit to Nicodemus (John 3:3–7).

3:7 we should become heirs. God justifies believers so that they might become co-heirs with Jesus Christ in His coming reign (Rom. 8:17; 2 Tim. 2:12).

3:10 Reject a divisive man. A sinner must always be given ample opportunity to repent, but if he insists on continuing in sin, the church is required to let him go (Matt. 18:15–17; 2 Thess. 3:14–15).

3:12 Tychicus. Tychicus, one of Paul's assistants, is also mentioned in Acts 20:4; Ephesians 6:21; Colossians 4:7; 2 Timothy 4:12.

3:13 Apollos. Apollos was a fellow worker of Paul's (1 Cor. 16:12), an Alexandrian who had been taught by Priscilla and Aquila and who had eloquently preached the gospel at Ephesus and Corinth (Acts 18:24—19:1).

3:14 not be unfruitful. Justification is a free gift from God, but we will be rewarded according to what we do on this earth (Rev. 22:12). It would be tragedy to stand ashamed at Christ's return (1 John 2:28).

2:14 i Gal. 1:4 k [Heb. 1:3; 9:14] l Ex. 15:16 **2:15** m 2 Tim. 4:2 **3:1** a 1 Pet. 2:13 b Col. 1:10 **3:3** c 1 Cor. 6:11 **3:4** d Titus 2:11 e 1 Tim. 2:3 **3:5** f [Rom. 3:20] g John 3:3 **3:6** h Ezek. 36:26 **3:7** i [Rom. 8:17, 23, 24] **3:8** j 1 Tim. 1:15 **3:9** k 2 Tim. 2:23 **3:10** l Matt. 18:17 **3:12** m Acts 20:4 **3:13** n Acts 18:24

THE EPISTLE OF PAUL THE APOSTLE TO
PHILEMON

▶ **AUTHOR:** Though some critics deny its authenticity, the general consensus of scholarship recognizes Philemon as Paul's work. There could have been no doctrinal motive for its forgery, and it is supported externally by consistent tradition and internally by no less than three references to Paul (Philem. 1,9,19).

▶ **TIME:** c. A.D. 60–61   ▶ **KEY VERSES:** Philem. 16–17

▶ **THEME:** Paul wrote this letter to a slave owner in the church at Colosse. Apparently, Onesimus, the slave of Philemon had stolen from him and had run away, an act punishable by death under Roman law. Onesimus had since met Paul and become a Christian. Paul's letter is a personal appeal in an effort to help them reconcile and renew their relationship.

Greeting

Paul, a ᵃprisoner of Christ Jesus, and Timothy *our* brother,

To Philemon our beloved *friend* and fellow laborer, ²to the beloved* Apphia, ᵇArchippus our fellow soldier, and to the church in your house:

³Grace to you and peace from God our Father and the Lord Jesus Christ.

Philemon's Love and Faith

⁴ᶜI thank my God, making mention of you always in my prayers, ⁵ᵈhearing of your love and faith which you have toward the Lord Jesus and toward all the saints, ⁶that the sharing of your faith may become effective ᵉby the acknowledgment of ᶠevery good thing which is in you* in Christ Jesus. ⁷For we have* great joy* and consolation in your love, because the hearts of the saints have been refreshed by you, brother.

The Plea for Onesimus

⁸Therefore, though I might be very bold in Christ to command you what is fitting,

⁹yet for love's sake I rather appeal *to you*—being such a one as Paul, the aged, and now also a prisoner of Jesus Christ— ¹⁰I appeal to you for my son ᵍOnesimus, whom I have begotten *while* in my chains, ¹¹who once was unprofitable to you, but now is profitable to you and to me.

¹²I am sending him back.* You therefore receive him, that is, my own heart, ¹³whom I wished to keep with me, that on your behalf he might minister to me in my chains for the gospel. ¹⁴But without your consent I wanted to do nothing, ʰthat your good deed might not be by compulsion, as it were, but voluntary.

¹⁵For perhaps he departed for a while for this *purpose*, that you might receive him forever, ¹⁶no longer as a slave but more than a slave—a beloved brother, especially to me but how much more to you, both in the ⁱflesh and in the Lord.

---

*2 NU-Text reads *to our sister Apphia.*   *6 NU-Text and M-Text read *us.*   *7 NU-Text reads *had.* • M-Text reads *thanksgiving.*   *12 NU-Text reads *back to you in person, that is, my own heart.*

1–2 To Philemon . . . and to the church. Paul addresses the letter to Philemon and the Colossian church, but this intensely personal epistle uses the singular "I" and "you," demonstrating that the letter is Paul's personal plea to Philemon. It was written at the same time as the letter to the Colossians, and doubtless carried by the same messenger.

2 Apphia . . . Archippus. Apphia may have been the wife of Philemon; Archippus may have been Philemon's son, or perhaps an elder in the Colossian church (Col. 4:17).

6 faith may become effective. Working faith is a sharing faith; it is the acknowledgment of what Christ has done in the believer's life (Eph. 3:17–19).

9 Paul, the aged. The apostle is either speaking of his old age, or of the office of an elder.

11 unprofitable . . . profitable. Paul uses an interesting play on words here. Having mentioned Onesimus, whose name means "useful," the apostle describes him as someone who was formerly useless, but who has become useful through the work of Christ in his life.

14 not . . . by compulsion. Service for Christ is never forced. Paul has given Philemon several good reasons to forgive Onesimus, but here he returns to the foundation of his argument: Philemon's actions must proceed from his own love (v. 9).

---

1 ᵃEph. 3:1   **2** ᵇCol. 4:17   **4** ᶜ2 Thess. 1:3   **5** ᵈCol. 1:4   **6** ᵉPhil. 1:9   ᶠ[1 Thess. 5:18]   **10** ᵍCol. 4:9   **14** ʰ2 Cor. 9:7   **16** ⁱCol. 3:22

Philemon's Obedience Encouraged

17If then you count me as a partner, receive him as *you would* me. **18**But if he has wronged you or owes anything, put that on my account. **19**I, Paul, am writing with my own *j*hand. I will repay—not to mention to you that you owe me even your own self besides. **20**Yes, brother, let me have joy from you in the Lord; refresh my heart in the Lord.

21*k*Having confidence in your obedience, I write to you, knowing that you will do even more than I say. **22**But, meanwhile, also prepare a guest room for me, for *l*I trust that *m*through your prayers I shall be granted to you.

Farewell

23*n*Epaphras, my fellow prisoner in Christ Jesus, greets you, **24***as do* *o*Mark, *p*Aristarchus, *q*Demas, *r*Luke, my fellow laborers.

25*s*The grace of our Lord Jesus Christ *be* with your spirit. Amen.

---

18 wronged you. Onesimus had probably stolen something from Philemon when he left. **put that on my account.** This accounting imagery reminds us of the theological truth that our sins were charged over to Christ even though He had not earned them. Forgiveness is costly (Is. 53:6).
19 my own hand. Paul wrote this personal letter himself, and therefore it could be considered a legal document obligating him to pay the damages that Onesimus had caused.
22 prepare a guest room. It is believed that Paul wrote this letter during his imprisonment in Rome (Acts 28), and that he was released shortly afterwards. He was probably not at liberty for very long, but it is possible that he was able to visit Colosse before his second imprisonment and execution.
23–24 Epaphras . . . Mark, Aristarchus, Demas, Luke. These five co-workers are also mentioned in Colossians 4:10–14.

---

19 *j* 1 Cor. 16:21   **21** *k* 2 Cor. 7:16   **22** *l* Phil. 1:25; 2:24   *m* 2 Cor. 1:11   **23** *n* Col. 1:7; 4:12   **24** *o* Acts 12:12, 25; 15:37–39   *p* Acts 19:29; 27:2   *q* Col. 4:14   *r* 2 Tim. 4:11   **25** *s* 2 Tim. 4:22

THE EPISTLE TO THE
HEBREWS

▶ **AUTHOR:** The origin of Hebrews is unknown. Uncertainty plagues not only its authorship, but also its date and its readership. Hebrews 13:18–24 tells us that this book was not anonymous to the original readers; they evidently knew the author. For some reason however, early church tradition is divided over the identity of the author. Part of the church attributed it to Paul, others preferred Barnabas, Luke, or Clement, and some chose anonymity. Some aspects of the language style and theology of Hebrews are very similar to Paul's epistles. However, significant stylistic differences have led the majority of biblical scholars to reject Pauline authorship of this book.

▶ **TIME:** c. A.D. 64–68   ▶ **KEY VERSES:** Heb. 4:14–16

▶ **THEME:** Hebrews was written for a group of Jewish Christians who were thinking about returning to their original faith. The author goes to great lengths to convince them to stay with their new faith. Point by point he goes through a whole series of arguments showing how Judaism was a foreshadowing of Christ. Everything promising about Old Testament Judaism is fulfilled in Christ. The new way is the superior way, as Christ and the faith that He established supersedes what has gone before. Understanding Jewish faith and practice, and the role of Moses and Aaron in biblical history is a prerequisite to understanding Hebrews.

God's Supreme Revelation

1 God, who at various times and ᵃin various ways spoke in time past to the fathers by the prophets, ²has in these last days spoken to us by *His* Son, whom He has appointed heir of all things, through whom also He made the worlds; ³ᵇwho being the brightness of *His* glory and the express ᶜimage of His person, and ᵈupholding all things by the word of His power, ᵉwhen He had by Himself* purged our* sins, ᶠsat down at the right hand of the Majesty on high, ⁴having become so much better than the angels, as ᵍHe has by inheritance obtained a more excellent name than they.

The Son Exalted Above Angels

⁵For to which of the angels did He ever say:

ʰ "You are My Son,
   Today I have begotten You"?*

And again:

ⁱ "I will be to Him a Father,
   And He shall be to Me a Son"?*

⁶But when He again brings ʲthe firstborn into the world, He says:

---

* **1:3** NU-Text omits *by Himself.* • NU-Text omits *our.*   * **1:5** Psalm 2:7 • 2 Samuel 7:14

1:2 by His Son. This could be rephrased as "in such a person as a Son." The emphasis rests on the character of the revelation. It is a revelation of the Son, a revelation not so much in what He has said as in who He is and what He has done.
1:3 brightness of His glory. The author of Hebrews is emphasizing that this is not a reflected brightness like the light of the moon. Instead, this is an inherent brightness like a ray from the sun. Jesus' glorious brightness comes from being essentially divine. ***express image.*** In Greek literature the word was used for stamping a coin from the die. **upholding.** This means to "bear" or "carry," referring to movement and progress toward a final end. The Son not only created the universe by His powerful word, but also maintains and directs its course. He is the Governor of the universe. **sat down.** This suggests the formal act of assuming the office of High Priest and implies a contrast to the Levitical priest, who never finished his work and sat down (10:11–13).
1:5 Today I have begotten You. This probably refers to the day Christ sat down at the Father's right hand after He accomplished His work as the Messiah.
1:6 when He again brings the firstborn. This is a reference to the second coming. "Firstborn" refers to rank, meaning one who ranks above all others (Ps. 89:27).

1:1 ᵃ Num. 12:6, 8   **1:3** ᵇ John 1:14 ᶜ 2 Cor. 4:4 ᵈ Col. 1:17 ᵉ [Heb. 7:27] ᶠ Ps. 110:1   **1:4** ᵍ [Phil. 2:9, 10]   **1:5** ʰ Ps. 2:7 ⁱ 2 Sam. 7:14   **1:6** ʲ [Rom. 8:29]

k "Let all the angels of God worship Him."*

⁷And of the angels He says:

l "Who makes His angels spirits
And His ministers a flame of fire."*

⁸But to the Son He says:

m "Your throne, O God, is forever and ever;
A scepter of righteousness is the scepter of Your kingdom.

9   You have loved righteousness and hated lawlessness;
Therefore God, Your God, *n*has anointed You
With the oil of gladness more than Your companions."*

¹⁰And:

o "You, Lord, in the beginning laid the foundation of the earth,
And the heavens are the work of Your hands.

11 *p*They will perish, but You remain;
And *q*they will all grow old like a garment;

12 Like a cloak You will fold them up,
And they will be changed.
But You are the *r*same,
And Your years will not fail."*

¹³But to which of the angels has He ever said:

s "Sit at My right hand,
Till I make Your enemies Your footstool"?*

¹⁴*t*Are they not all ministering spirits sent forth to minister for those who will *u*inherit salvation?

Do Not Neglect Salvation

2 Therefore we must give the more earnest heed to the things we have heard, lest we drift away. ²For if the word *a*spoken through angels proved steadfast, and *b*every transgression and disobedience received a just reward, ³*c*how shall we escape if we neglect so great a salvation, *d*which at the first began to be spoken by the Lord, and was *e*confirmed to us by those who heard Him, ⁴*f*God also bearing witness *g*both with signs and wonders, with various miracles, and *h*gifts of the Holy Spirit, *i*according to His own will?

The Son Made Lower than Angels

⁵For He has not put *j*the world to come, of which we speak, in subjection to angels. ⁶But one testified in a certain place, saying:

k "What is man that You are mindful of him,
Or the son of man that You take care of him?

7   You have made him a little lower than the angels;
You have crowned him with glory and honor,*
And set him over the works of Your hands.

8   *l*You have put all things in subjection under his feet."*

For in that He put all in subjection under him, He left nothing that is not put under him. But now *m*we do not yet see all things

---

* **1:6** Deuteronomy 32:43 (Septuagint, Dead Sea Scrolls); Psalm 97:7   * **1:7** Psalm 104:4
* **1:9** Psalm 45:6, 7   * **1:12** Psalm 102:25–27
* **1:13** Psalm 110:1   * **2:7** NU-Text and M-Text omit the rest of verse 7.   * **2:8** Psalm 8:4–6

1:7 ministers. The Son is superior to angels because He is the Sovereign who is worshiped, while the angels are *ministers,* that is, servants of God. The author of Hebrews quotes Psalm 104 because that psalm places angels in a long list of created objects which God sovereignly controls.
1:9 companions. This term comes from a word that means "close associates" or "partners." The concept of believers being partners with Christ is key in Hebrews (3:1,14; 6:4; 12:8). The term refers to those who will be participants with Christ in His reign.
1:10–12 You, Lord. The context of Psalm 102 here indicates that the Lord is the One who would appear in the future to Israel and the nations (Ps. 102:12–16).
1:14 those who will inherit salvation. Salvation here is not justification because it is in the future, not in the past. The reference is to believers who inherit the kingdom or rule in God's kingdom as a reward for their service to the Son (9:28; Col. 3:24).
2:1 drift away. The author's audience was marked by immaturity and spiritual sluggishness (5:11–12). The author warned them not to be carried away by the popular opinions that surrounded them. Instead, they were to hold fast to Christ's words because they were the words of God.

2:3 how shall we escape. If the people who heard the message delivered through angels were justly punished when they disobeyed the law, how can believers expect to escape punishment when they neglect the even greater message delivered through the greater Messenger, the Son?
2:4 signs and wonders. This phrase refers to the miracles performed by the Holy Spirit through the Lord and His apostles in fulfillment of the ancient promises regarding the coming of the Messiah (Acts 2:22,43; 4:30; 5:12; 6:8; 14:3; 15:12; 1 Cor. 12:12).
2:6–8 set him over the works of Your hands. Since the Son's humanity might appear to be an obstacle to the claim of His superiority, the author of Hebrews cites Psalm 8, a lyrical reflection on Genesis 1, to prove that God has placed humanity over all created things, which includes the angelic world.

1:6 *k* Deut. 32:43, LXX, DSS; Ps. 97:7   **1:7** *l* Ps. 104:4   **1:8** *m* Ps. 45:6, 7   **1:9** *n* Is. 61:1, 3   **1:10** *o* Ps. 102:25–27   **1:11** *p* [Is. 34:4]   *q* Is. 50:9; 51:6   **1:12** *r* Heb. 13:8   **1:13** *s* Ps. 110:1   **1:14** *t* Ps. 103:20   *u* Rom. 8:17   **2:2** *a* Acts 7:53   *b* Num. 15:30   **2:3** *c* Heb. 10:28   *d* Matt. 4:17   *e* Luke 1:2   **2:4** *f* Mark 16:20   *g* Acts 2:22, 43   *h* 1 Cor. 12:4, 7, 11   *i* Eph. 1:5, 9   **2:5** *j* [2 Pet. 3:13]   **2:6** *k* Ps. 8:4–6   **2:8** *l* Matt. 28:18   *m* 1 Cor. 15:25, 27

put under him. 9 But we see Jesus, [n]who was
made a little lower than the angels, for the
suffering of death [o]crowned with glory and
honor, that He, by the grace of God, might
taste death [p]for everyone.

Bringing Many Sons to Glory

10 For it was fitting for Him, [q]for whom
are all things and by whom *are* all things,
in bringing many sons to glory, to make the
captain of their salvation [r]perfect through
sufferings. 11 For [s]both He who sanctifies
and those who are being sanctified [t]*are*
all of one, for which reason [u]He is not
ashamed to call them brethren, 12 saying:

[v]*"I will declare Your name to My*
brethren;
In the midst of the assembly I will sing
*praise to You."**

13 And again:

[w]*"I will put My trust in Him."**

And again:

[x]*"Here am I and the children whom God*
*has given Me."**

14 Inasmuch then as the children have
partaken of flesh and blood, He [y]Himself
likewise shared in the same, [z]that through
death He might destroy him who had the
power of [a]death, that is, the devil, 15 and
release those who [b]through fear of death
were all their lifetime subject to bondage.
16 For indeed He does not give aid to angels,
but He does give aid to the seed of Abraham. 17 Therefore, in all things He had [c]to
be made like *His* brethren, that He might
be [d]a merciful and faithful High Priest in
things *pertaining* to God, to make propitiation for the sins of the people. 18 [e]For
in that He Himself has suffered, being
tempted, He is able to aid those who are
tempted.

The Son Was Faithful

3 Therefore, holy brethren, partakers
of the heavenly calling, consider the
Apostle and High Priest of our confession,
Christ Jesus, 2 who was faithful to Him who
appointed Him, as [a]Moses also *was faith-*
ful in all His house. 3 For this One has been
counted worthy of more glory than Moses,
inasmuch as [b]He who built the house has
more honor than the house. 4 For every
house is built by someone, but [c]He who
built all things *is* God. 5 [d]And Moses indeed
was faithful in all His house as [e]a servant,
[f]for a testimony of those things which
would be spoken *afterward*, 6 but Christ as
[g]a Son over His own house, [h]whose house

*__2:12__ Psalm 22:22 *__2:13__ 2 Samuel 22:3; Isaiah 8:17 • Isaiah 8:18

2:10 ***captain of their salvation.*** The Greek word here means "leader" or "originator." The word describes a pioneer or pathfinder. Jesus' endurance of sufferings on this earth makes Him our leader. He not only endured them but also triumphed over sin, death, and Satan through them.

2:12 ***to My brethren.*** Psalm 22 is quoted here. In it, the Messiah refers to "My brethren," identifying Himself with all those who place their faith in God.

2:14–16 ***He might destroy . . . release.*** Having established the unity between the Son and believer, the author concludes that there are two purposes of this close identification. The Son became human so that He could destroy the devil and release those who were in bondage to sin.

2:16 ***seed of Abraham.*** The author may have used the expression because the recipients of this letter were primarily Jewish believers. The author is pointing out that Christ came to the aid of Abraham's sons, not the angelic hosts.

2:17 ***in things pertaining to God.*** Jesus participated in our nature and in our sufferings on earth so that He could be a sympathetic Mediator between God and humanity. He understands our weaknesses and intercedes for us in the presence of God the Father. ***make propitiation.*** This term refers to the satisfaction of the claims of a holy and righteous God against sinners who have broken His law. Christ appeased God's righteous wrath by dying on the cross in our place (Rom. 3:21–26). Although completely sinless, Christ voluntarily submitted to the penalty of sin, His agonizing death on the cross. This voluntary sacrifice of Himself for our welfare satisfied the justice and holiness of God. The benefits of His sacrifice are applied to all who place their faith in Him.

2:18 ***He Himself has suffered, being tempted.*** Christ's suffering included temptation. He experienced the lure of sin, but He never surrendered Himself to it. He knows what it is like to be tempted, so He knows how to assist those who are being tempted.

3:2 ***in all His house.*** This phrase is taken from Numbers 12:7. "House" refers to the tabernacle, the center of Israelite worship. Moses had faithfully obeyed God's instructions concerning the tabernacle. In the same way, Jesus had been obedient to the mission the Father had given Him. Through obedience, God established a new house of God, the church.

3:3–4 ***worthy of more glory than Moses.*** The implication is that the covenant established through Jesus' death is more glorious than the covenant established at Mount Sinai.

3:5 ***as a servant.*** The author of Hebrews continues the comparison between Moses and Jesus. While Moses was faithful as a servant, Christ's faithfulness was greater because it was performed by a Son. ***things which would be spoken afterward.*** Moses' work pointed forward to Christ (9:10; 10:3). The regulations of the law of Moses pointed out both the sin of humanity and the need for a perfect sacrifice to reconcile people to their holy Creator.

2:9 [n]Phil. 2:7–9 [o]Acts 2:33; 3:13 [p][John 3:16] **2:10** [q]Col. 1:16 [r]Heb. 5:8, 9; 7:28 **2:11** [s]Heb. 10:10 [t]Acts 17:26 [u]Matt. 28:10 **2:12** [v]Ps. 22:22 **2:13** [w]2 Sam. 22:3; Is. 8:17 [x]Is. 8:18 **2:14** [y]John 1:14 [z]Col. 2:15 [a]2 Tim. 1:10 **2:15** [b][Luke 1:74] **2:17** [c]Phil. 2:7 [d][Heb. 4:15; 5:1–10] **2:18** [e][Heb. 4:15, 16] **3:2** [a]Num. 12:7 **3:3** [b]Zech. 6:12, 13 **3:4** [c][Eph. 2:10] **3:5** [d]Heb. 3:2 [e]Ex. 14:31 [f]Deut. 18:15, 18, 19 **3:6** [g]Heb. 1:2 [h][1 Cor. 3:16]

we are [i]if we hold fast the confidence and the rejoicing of the hope firm to the end.*

Be Faithful

[7]Therefore, as [j]the Holy Spirit says:

[k]"Today, if you will hear His voice,
[8] Do not harden your hearts as in the
      rebellion,
      In the day of trial in the wilderness,
[9] Where your fathers tested Me, tried
      Me,
      And saw My works forty years.
[10] Therefore I was angry with that
      generation,
      And said, 'They always go astray in
      their heart,
      And they have not known My ways.'
[11] So I swore in My wrath,
      'They shall not enter My rest.'"*

[12]Beware, brethren, lest there be in any of you an evil heart of unbelief in departing from the living God; [13]but exhort one another daily, while it is called "Today," lest any of you be hardened through the deceitfulness of sin. [14]For we have become partakers of Christ if we hold the beginning of our confidence steadfast to the end, [15]while it is said:

[l]"Today, if you will hear His voice,
      Do not harden your hearts as in the
      rebellion."*

Failure of the Wilderness Wanderers

[16m]For who, having heard, rebelled? Indeed, was it not all who came out of Egypt, led by Moses? [17]Now with whom was He angry forty years? Was it not with those who sinned, [n]whose corpses fell in the wilderness? [18]And [o]to whom did He swear that they would not enter His rest, but to those

who did not obey? [19]So we see that they could not enter in because of [p]unbelief.

The Promise of Rest

4 Therefore, since a promise remains of entering His rest, [a]let us fear lest any of you seem to have come short of it. [2]For indeed the gospel was preached to us as well as to them; but the word which they heard did not profit them,* not being mixed with faith in those who heard it. [3]For we who have believed do enter that rest, as He has said:

[b]"So I swore in My wrath,
      'They shall not enter My rest,'"*

although the works were finished from the foundation of the world. [4]For He has spoken in a certain place of the seventh day in this way: [c]"And God rested on the seventh day from all His works";* [5]and again in this place: [d]"They shall not enter My rest."*

[6]Since therefore it remains that some must enter it, and those to whom it was first preached did not enter because of disobedience, [7]again He designates a certain day, saying in David, "Today," after such a long time, as it has been said:

[e]"Today, if you will hear His voice,
      Do not harden your hearts."*

[8]For if Joshua had [f]given them rest, then He would not afterward have spoken of another day. [9]There remains therefore a rest for the people of God. [10]For he who has entered His rest has himself also ceased from his works as God did from His.

---

* **3:6** NU-Text omits *firm to the end.*   * **3:11** Psalm 95:7–11   * **3:15** Psalm 95:7, 8   * **4:2** NU-Text and M-Text read *profit them, since they were not united by faith with those who heeded it.*   * **4:3** Psalm 95:11   * **4:4** Genesis 2:2   * **4:5** Psalm 95:11   * **4:7** Psalm 95:7, 8

3:7–11 *Do not harden your hearts.* The author of Hebrews quotes Psalm 95:7–11 to warn the Jewish Christians about hardening their hearts to God and the salvation He offers. Moses' generation had refused to trust in God to provide for their needs in the wilderness (Ex. 17:1–7), and the readers of this letter were also in danger. *My rest.* This is a key concept in Hebrews. In the Old Testament, the conquest of the Promised Land and the cessation of fighting in the land was viewed as a form of rest (Deut. 3:20; 12:9; 25:19; Josh. 11:23; 21:44; 22:4). In the New Testament, "rest" speaks of the believer's eternal home and the joy that he or she will experience in Jesus' presence (4:1).

3:12–13 *heart of unbelief.* In essence, unbelief is a stubborn refusal to trust in the truthfulness of His word. It is a grave sin because it leads us away from God.

3:14 *partakers of Christ.* This is the same word translated *companions* in 1:9. Believers will be partners with Christ in His future kingdom (Rev. 2:26–27).

3:15–19 *with whom was He angry.* The Jewish Christians to whom this letter was addressed were in danger of following in their ancestors' footsteps.

They were tempted to doubt the words of Jesus. With the rhetorical questions in these verses, the author of Hebrews was encouraging them to place their faith firmly in Christ.

4:2 *the gospel was preached.* This is the translation of a single Greek word meaning "the good news was announced."

4:4 *God rested.* The theme of rest has its beginning in God's own rest after creation. The fact that Genesis makes no mention of the evening of the seventh day of creation provides a basis for some Jewish commentators to conclude that the rest of God lasts throughout all history.

4:9 *rest.* The word used here is different from the word used in verses 1, 3, 5, 10–11; 3:11, 18. Jews commonly taught that the Sabbath foreshadowed the world to come, and they spoke of "a day which shall be all Sabbath."

3:6 [i][Matt. 10:22]   **3:7** [j]Acts 1:16   [k]Ps. 95:7–11   **3:15** [l]Ps. 95:7, 8   **3:16** [m]Num. 14:2, 11, 30   **3:17** [n]Num. 14:22, 23   **3:18** [o]Num. 14:30   **3:19** [p]1 Cor. 10:11, 12   **4:1** [a]Heb. 12:15   **4:3** [b]Ps. 95:11   **4:4** [c]Gen. 2:2   **4:5** [d]Ps. 95:11   **4:7** [e]Ps. 95:7, 8   **4:8** [f]Josh. 22:4

The Word Discovers Our Condition

11gLet us therefore be diligent to enter that rest, lest anyone fall according to the same example of disobedience. 12For the word of God is hliving and powerful, and isharper than any jtwo-edged sword, piercing even to the division of soul and spirit, and of joints and marrow, and is ka discerner of the thoughts and intents of the heart. 13lAnd there is no creature hidden from His sight, but all things are mnaked and open to the eyes of Him to whom we must give account.

Our Compassionate High Priest

14Seeing then that we have a great nHigh Priest who has passed through the heavens, Jesus the Son of God, olet us hold fast our confession. 15For pwe do not have a High Priest who cannot sympathize with our weaknesses, but qwas in all points tempted as we are, ryet without sin. 16sLet us therefore come boldly to the throne of grace, that we may obtain mercy and find grace to help in time of need.

Qualifications for High Priesthood

5 For every high priest taken from among men ais appointed for men in things pertaining to God, that he may offer both gifts and sacrifices for sins. 2He can have compassion on those who are ignorant and going astray, since he himself is also subject to bweakness. 3Because of this he is required as for the people, so also for chimself, to offer sacrifices for sins. 4And no man takes this honor to himself, but he who is called by God, just as dAaron was.

A Priest Forever

5eSo also Christ did not glorify Himself to become High Priest, but it was He who said to Him:

f"You are My Son,
   Today I have begotten You."*

6As He also says in another place:

g"You are a priest forever
   According to the order of
      Melchizedek";*

7who, in the days of His flesh, when He had hoffered up prayers and supplications, iwith vehement cries and tears to Him jwho was able to save Him from death, and was heard kbecause of His godly fear, 8though He was a Son, yet He learned lobedience by the things which He suffered. 9And mhaving been perfected, He became the author of eternal salvation to all who obey Him, 10called by God as High Priest n"according to the order of Melchizedek," 11of whom owe have much to say, and hard to explain, since you have become pdull of hearing.

Spiritual Immaturity

12For though by this time you ought to be teachers, you need someone to teach you again the first principles of the oracles of God; and you have come to need qmilk and not solid food. 13For everyone who partakes only of milk is unskilled in the word of righteousness, for he is ra babe. 14But solid food belongs to those who are of full age, that is, those who by reason of use have their senses exercised sto discern both good and evil.

* **5:5** Psalm 2:7   * **5:6** Psalm 110:4

4:11 be diligent to enter that rest. The rest is not automatic. Determined diligence is required. The danger is that believers today, like the Israelites of the past, will not stand, but will fall in disobedience.
4:13 naked and open. This phrase suggests complete exposure and defenselessness before God.
4:15 sympathize. This word means "to suffer with" and expresses the feeling of one who has entered into suffering.
4:16 come. This command strongly contrasts with God's command at Mount Sinai: "Do not go up to the mountain or touch its base" (Ex. 19:12). Because of Christ's priestly work, believers can approach God's presence. **boldly.** This word carries with it the idea of "fearlessness" or "courageousness." Believers should boldly approach God in prayer because His Son is our gracious High Priest who sits at God's right hand interceding for us.
5:1–4 high priest. He represents the people and thus must identify with their human nature. But he also represents God to the people and thus must be called by God to his office.
5:2 ignorant, and going astray. This phrase describes those who unintentionally sin (Num. 15:30–36).
5:8 He learned obedience. Jesus experienced all of what a person goes through on this earth. He knows

how difficult it is to obey God completely, just as He understands the attraction of temptation (2:18).
5:9 having been perfected. This phrase does not suggest that Jesus had not been perfect before. It means that He successfully carried out God's plan for Him. He endured suffering and temptation so that He could truly function as our High Priest, understanding our weaknesses and interceding before God for us.
5:12 first principles. The phrase refers to the letters of the alphabet in writing or to addition and subtraction tables in arithmetic. They are principles out of which everything else develops.
5:13 unskilled in the word of righteousness. The readers of this letter did not necessarily lack information concerning righteousness; they lacked experience in practicing the information they had.

4:11 g 2 Pet. 1:10   **4:12** h Ps. 147:15 i Is. 49:2 j Eph. 6:17 k 1 Cor. 14:24, 25   **4:13** l Ps. 33:13–15; 90:8 m Job 26:6   **4:14** n Heb. 2:17; 7:26 o Heb. 10:23   **4:15** p Is. 53:3–5 q Luke 22:28 r 2 Cor. 5:21   **4:16** s [Eph. 2:18] **5:1** a Heb. 2:17; 8:3   **5:2** b Heb. 7:28   **5:3** c Lev. 9:7; 16:6 **5:4** d Ex. 28:1   **5:5** e John 8:54 f Ps. 2:7   **5:6** g Ps. 110:4 **5:7** h Matt. 26:39, 42, 44 i Ps. 22:1 j Matt. 26:53 k Matt. 26:39   **5:8** l Phil. 2:8   **5:9** m Heb. 2:10   **5:10** n Ps. 110:4 **5:11** o [John 16:12] p [Matt. 13:15]   **5:12** q 1 Cor. 3:1–3 **5:13** r Eph. 4:14   **5:14** s Is. 7:15

The Peril of Not Progressing

6 Therefore, *a*leaving the discussion of the elementary *principles* of Christ, let us go on to perfection, not laying again the foundation of repentance from *b*dead works and of faith toward God, 2*c*of the doctrine of baptisms, *d*of laying on of hands, *e*of resurrection of the dead, *f*and of eternal judgment. 3And this we will* do if God permits.

4For *it is* impossible for those who were once enlightened, and have tasted *g*the heavenly gift, and *h*have become partakers of the Holy Spirit, 5and have tasted the good word of God and the powers of the age to come, 6if they fall away,* to renew them again to repentance, *i*since they crucify again for themselves the Son of God, and put *Him* to an open shame.

7For the earth which drinks in the rain that often comes upon it, and bears herbs useful for those by whom it is cultivated, *j*receives blessing from God; 8*k*but if it bears thorns and briers, *it is* rejected and near to being cursed, whose end *is* to be burned.

A Better Estimate

9But, beloved, we are confident of better things concerning you, yes, things that accompany salvation, though we speak in this manner. 10For *l*God *is* not unjust to forget *m*your work and labor of* love which you have shown toward His name, *in that* you have *n*ministered to the saints, and do

minister. 11And we desire that each one of you show the same diligence *o*to the full assurance of hope until the end, 12that you do not become sluggish, but imitate those who through faith and patience *p*inherit the promises.

God's Infallible Purpose in Christ

13For when God made a promise to Abraham, because He could swear by no one greater, *q*He swore by Himself, 14saying, *r*"Surely blessing I will bless you, and multiplying I will multiply you."* 15And so, after he had patiently endured, he obtained the *s*promise. 16For men indeed swear by the greater, and *t*an oath for confirmation *is* for them an end of all dispute. 17Thus God, determining to show more abundantly to *u*the heirs of promise *v*the immutability of His counsel, confirmed *it* by an oath, 18that by two immutable things, in which it *is* impossible for God to *w*lie, we might* have strong consolation, who have fled for refuge to lay hold of the hope *x*set before *us*. 19This *hope* we have as an anchor of the soul, both sure and steadfast, *y*and which enters the *Presence* behind the veil, 20*z*where the forerunner has entered for us, *even* Jesus, *a*having become High Priest forever according to the order of Melchizedek.

* **6:3** M-Text reads *let us do.*   * **6:6** Or *and have fallen away*   * **6:10** NU-Text omits *labor of.*   * **6:14** Genesis 22:17   * **6:18** M-Text omits *might.*

6:1 *repentance from dead works.* This phrase refers to a change of mind about the demands of the law of Moses (9:14). Even though the law was good (1 Tim. 1:8), it was weak because of the weakness of our sinful nature (Rom. 8:3). What is needed for salvation is not lifeless works that cannot save, but faith directed toward God.

6:2 *laying on of hands.* This action was used to impart the Holy Spirit (Acts 8:17–18; 19:6). It was also used for ordination of the ministry (Acts 6:6; 13:3). This practice is also found in the Old Testament in commissioning someone to a public office (Num. 27:18,23; Deut. 34:9) or in the context of presenting a sacrificial offering to the Lord (Lev. 1:4; 3:2; 4:4; 8:14; 16:21). *eternal judgment.* This refers to the belief that everyone will be judged by the great Judge.

6:4–6 *if they fall away.* This difficult passage has been interpreted in various ways. Some insist that the author is speaking of nominal Christians who heard the truth and appeared to believe in Christ but were not sincere in their faith. Others view these verses as a hypothetical argument. In other words, the author is using this hypothetical case to warn the spiritually immature. These two positions are supported by passages that speak of God's consistency in His work, that nothing can separate us from His love (John 6:39–40; 10:27–29; Rom. 8:28–30). But another group of commentators insists that the author is speaking of genuine Christians who renounce Christ. They point out that those who "tasted the heavenly gift" fall away. Passages such as 2 Corinthians 11:1–4; 2 Timothy 2:17–18; 1 John 2:21–25 are in support of this position. Whatever way

one interprets this passage, it is clear that the author of Hebrews has given us a clear warning not to renounce Christ or spurn His offer of salvation.

6:6 *renew.* This word means "restore." In other words, it is impossible for continuous effort on the part of anyone in the Christian community to restore an apostate back to fellowship with God. Continuing Christian immaturity is dangerous.

6:13–15 *Abraham.* Here is an example of faith and patience in God's promise (v. 12). He waited 25 years from the time the promise was first made until Isaac, the promised son, was born (Gen. 12:3–4; 15:4; 18:10; 21:5).

6:18 *two immutable things.* These things are God's Word and God's oath. Since God does not lie and since He is all-powerful, He will fulfill all His promises.

6:20 *forerunner.* This word was used in the second century A.D. for the smaller boats sent into the harbor by larger ships unable to enter due to the buffeting of the weather. These smaller boats carried the anchor through the breakers inside the harbor and dropped it there, securing the larger ship. *Forerunner* also

6:1 *a* Heb. 5:12 *b* [Heb. 9:14]   **6:2** *c* Acts 19:3–5 *d* [Acts 8:17] *e* Acts 24:25   **6:4** *g* [John 4:10] *h* [Gal. 3:2, 5]   **6:6** *i* Heb. 10:29   **6:7** *j* Ps. 65:10   **6:8** *k* Is. 5:6   **6:10** *l* Rom. 3:4 *m* 1 Thess. 1:3 *n* Rom. 15:25   **6:11** *o* Col. 2:2   **6:12** *p* Heb. 10:36   **6:13** *q* Gen. 22:16, 17   **6:14** *r* Gen. 22:16, 17   **6:15** *s* Gen. 12:4; 21:5   **6:16** *t* Ex. 22:11   **6:17** *u* Acts 24:25 *v* Rom. 11:29   **6:18** *w* Num. 23:19 *x* [Col. 1:5]   **6:19** *y* Lev. 16:2, 15   **6:20** *z* [Heb. 4:14] *a* Heb. 3:1; 5:10, 11

The King of Righteousness

7 For this ^aMelchizedek, king of Salem, priest of the Most High God, who met Abraham returning from the slaughter of the kings and blessed him, ²to whom also Abraham gave a tenth part of all, first being translated "king of righteousness," and then also king of Salem, meaning "king of peace," ³without father, without mother, without genealogy, having neither beginning of days nor end of life, but made like the Son of God, remains a priest continually.

⁴Now consider how great this man *was,* to whom even the patriarch Abraham gave a tenth of the spoils. ⁵And indeed ^bthose who are of the sons of Levi, who receive the priesthood, have a commandment to receive tithes from the people according to the law, that is, from their brethren, though they have come from the loins of Abraham; ⁶but he whose genealogy is not derived from them received tithes from Abraham ^cand blessed ^dhim who had the promises. ⁷Now beyond all contradiction the lesser is blessed by the better. ⁸Here mortal men receive tithes, but there he *receives them,* ^eof whom it is witnessed that he lives. ⁹Even Levi, who receives tithes, paid tithes through Abraham, so to speak, ¹⁰for he was still in the loins of his father when Melchizedek met him.

Need for a New Priesthood

¹¹*f*Therefore, if perfection were through the Levitical priesthood (for under it the people received the law), what further need *was there* that another priest should rise according to the order of Melchizedek, and not be called according to the order of Aaron? ¹²For the priesthood being changed, of necessity there is also a change of the law. ¹³For He of whom these things are spoken belongs to another tribe, from which no man has officiated at the altar.

¹⁴For *it is* evident that ^gour Lord arose from ^hJudah, of which tribe Moses spoke nothing concerning priesthood.* ¹⁵And it is yet far more evident if, in the likeness of Melchizedek, there arises another priest ¹⁶who has come, not according to the law of a fleshly commandment, but according to the power of an endless life. ¹⁷For He testifies:*

> ⁱ"You are a priest forever
> According to the order of
> Melchizedek."*

¹⁸For on the one hand there is an annulling of the former commandment because of ^jits weakness and unprofitableness, ¹⁹for ^kthe law made nothing perfect; on the other hand, *there is the* bringing in of ^la better hope, through which ^mwe draw near to God.

Greatness of the New Priest

²⁰And inasmuch as *He was* not *made* priest without an oath ²¹(for they have become priests without an oath, but He with an oath by Him who said to Him:

> ⁿ"The LORD has sworn
> And will not relent,
> 'You are a priest forever*
> According to the order of
> Melchizedek'"),*

²²by so much more Jesus has become a surety of a ^obetter covenant.

²³Also there were many priests, because they were prevented by death from continuing. ²⁴But He, because He continues forever, has an unchangeable priesthood.

---

* **7:14** NU-Text reads *priests.*   * **7:17** NU-Text reads *it is testified.* • Psalm 110:4   * **7:21** NU-Text ends the quotation here. • Psalm 110:4

---

presupposes that others will follow. Thus, Jesus is like a runner boat that has taken our anchor into port and secured it there.

7:1 *Melchizedek.* The name means "king of righteousness." *Salem* means "peace." The ideal king rules in righteousness, which assures peace (Is. 32:17).

7:3 *without father, without mother, without genealogy.* Genesis, a book with many genealogies, has none for Melchizedek. The author is not saying that Melchizedek was born without a father and mother, only that there is no record of his birth in the genealogies of Genesis. This description of Melchizedek prefigures the eternal priesthood of Jesus. Like Melchizedek, Jesus is both a Priest and a King belonging to a righteous priesthood that is independent of Aaron's.

7:4 *patriarch.* In the Greek text this word is emphatic. The greatness of Abraham, the one who possessed the promises of God (v. 6), underscores the even greater rank of Melchizedek, the priest of righteousness.

7:8–10 *mortal men receive tithes.* Melchizedek was not only superior to Abraham, but he was also superior to the Levitical priesthood in two ways: first, the Levitical priests were mortal. In contrast, Melchizedek seems to be immortal. At least, the Old Testament does not record his death. Second, in a sense, Levi paid tithes to Melchizedek through Abraham's gift. Because he was descended from Abraham, he is counted as having paid tithes to Melchizedek.

7:12 *changed.* This word means removal (12:27). If the Melchizedek priesthood removed the Levitical priesthood, then the Mosaic law is also removed. In short, the believer is not under the law but instead relies on the righteousness of Christ (Rom. 6:14; Gal. 3:24–25).

7:15–18 *according to the power of an endless life.* This point is proved by Psalm 110:4, quoted in verse 17. Jesus is a different kind of priest, another indication that the law has been changed. There has been an *annulling,* a putting away, of the law.

7:1 ^aGen. 14:18–20   **7:5** ^bNum. 18:21–26   **7:6** ^cGen. 14:19, 20 ^d[Rom. 4:13]   **7:8** ^eHeb. 5:6; 6:20   **7:11** ^fHeb. 7:18; 8:7   **7:14** ^gIs. 1:1 ^hMatt. 1:2   **7:17** ⁱPs. 110:4   **7:18** ^j[Rom. 8:3]   **7:19** ^k[Acts 13:39] ^lHeb. 6:18, 19 ^mRom. 5:2   **7:21** ⁿPs. 110:4   **7:22** ^oHeb. 8:6

25Therefore He is also *p*able to save to the uttermost those who come to God through Him, since He always lives *q*to make intercession for them.

26For such a High Priest was fitting for us, *r*who is holy, harmless, undefiled, separate from sinners, *s*and has become higher than the heavens; 27who does not need daily, as those high priests, to offer up sacrifices, first for His *t*own sins and then for the people's, for this He did once for all when He offered up Himself. 28For the law appoints as high priests men who have weakness, but the word of the oath, which came after the law, *appoints* the Son who has been perfected forever.

The New Priestly Service

8 Now *this is* the main point of the things we are saying: We have such a High Priest, *a*who is seated at the right hand of the throne of the Majesty in the heavens, 2a Minister of *b*the sanctuary and of *c*the true tabernacle which the Lord erected, and not man.

3For *d*every high priest is appointed to offer both gifts and sacrifices. Therefore *e*it is necessary that this One also have something to offer. 4For if He were on earth, He would not be a priest, since there are priests who offer the gifts according to the law; 5who serve *f*the copy and *g*shadow of the heavenly things, as Moses was divinely instructed when he was about to make the tabernacle. For He said, *h*"See that you make all things according to the pattern shown you on the mountain."* 6But now

*i*He has obtained a more excellent ministry, inasmuch as He is also Mediator of a *j*better covenant, which was established on better promises.

A New Covenant

7For if that *k*first *covenant* had been faultless, then no place would have been sought for a second. 8Because finding fault with them, He says: *l*"Behold, the days are coming, says the LORD, when I will make a new covenant with the house of Israel and with the house of Judah—9not according to the covenant that I made with their fathers in the day when I took them by the hand to lead them out of the land of Egypt; because they did not continue in My covenant, and I disregarded them, says the LORD. 10For this is the covenant that I will make with the house of Israel after those days, says the *m*LORD: I will put My laws in their mind and write them on their hearts; and *n*I will be their God, and they shall be My people. 11oNone of them shall teach his neighbor, and none his brother, saying, 'Know the *p*LORD,' for all shall know Me, from the least of them to the greatest of them. 12For I will be merciful to their unrighteousness, *q*and their sins and their lawless deeds* I will remember no more."*

13rIn that He says, "A new covenant," He has made the first obsolete. Now what is becoming obsolete and growing old is ready to vanish away.

---

* **8:5** Exodus 25:40   * **8:12** NU-Text omits *and their lawless deeds.* • Jeremiah 31:31–34

7:25 He is also able to save. Christ is able to save because He is fully God and fully human (2:18; 4:15). Since this verse speaks to Jesus' present intercession for us, the word *save* in this verse speaks of our sanctification, the continuing process by which we are freed from the power of sin. This continuing process of salvation will eventually be completed in our glorification, when we are saved from the presence of sin.

7:26–28 daily, as those high priests. The high priest offered an annual sacrifice on the Day of Atonement for the atonement of the people's sins (9:7; 10:1), but the priests also offered sacrifices every day before the Lord (Ex. 29:36). In contrast, Jesus offered Himself once, a perfect, sinless sacrifice for the sins of all. Since Jesus is perfect, He did not have to offer sacrifices for His own sins.

8:2 sanctuary. This word refers to the heavenly reality represented by the Most Holy Place (9:2,8,24; 10:19; 13:11). The reality is the presence of God. Our High Priest serves there and desires to bring us there (10:19).

8:8 a new covenant. This covenant is the "better covenant" of verse 6. This covenant was made with Israel and Judah, yet the church enjoys the spiritual blessings of this covenant now. The Abrahamic covenant was made with Abraham and his physical descendants (Gen. 17:7). Yet the Abrahamic covenant also contained a spiritual promise (Gen. 12:3) in which the church participates (Rom. 11:11–27;

Gal. 3:13–14). The new covenant in fact is a fulfillment of the spiritual redemption promise in the Abrahamic and Davidic covenants (Matt. 26:26–29; Luke 22:20).

8:10–12 after those days, says the LORD. There are four provisions of the new covenant: (1) God's law will be written on believers' minds and hearts. (2) Believers will have a relationship with God fulfilling the promise of Leviticus 26:12 (2 Cor. 6:16). (3) All will know God. No longer will Pharisees and scribes have to teach the intricacies of the law to the people. (4) God will forgive the sins of believers and remember them no more. The continual sacrifice of animals for the atonement of sin will cease.

8:13 obsolete and growing old. At the time the author of Hebrews wrote these words, the ceremonies of the Mosaic covenant were still being conducted in the temple in Jerusalem. In A.D. 70 the Roman general Titus destroyed the temple, fulfilling these words.

7:25 *p* Jude 24 *q* Rom. 8:34   **7:26** *r* Heb. 4:15 *s* Eph. 1:20   **7:27** *t* Lev. 9:7; 16:6   **8:1** *a* Col. 3:1   **8:2** *b* Heb. 9:8, 12 *c* Heb. 9:11, 24   **8:3** *d* Heb. 5:1; 8:4 *e* [Eph. 5:2]   **8:5** *f* Heb. 9:23, 24 *g* Col. 2:17 *h* Ex. 25:40   **8:6** *i* [2 Cor. 3:6–8] *j* Heb. 7:22   **8:7** *k* Ex. 3:8; 19:5   **8:8** *l* Jer. 31:31–34   **8:10** *m* Jer. 31:33 *n* Zech. 8:8   **8:11** *o* Is. 54:13 *p* Jer. 31:34   **8:12** *q* Rom. 11:27   **8:13** *r* [2 Cor. 5:17]

The Earthly Sanctuary

9 Then indeed, even the first *covenant* had ordinances of divine service and *a*the earthly sanctuary. [2]For a tabernacle was prepared: the first *part*, in which *was* the lampstand, the table, and the showbread, which is called the sanctuary; [3b]and behind the second veil, the part of the tabernacle which is called the Holiest of All, [4]which had the *c*golden censer and *d*the ark of the covenant overlaid on all sides with gold, in which *were* *e*the golden pot that had the manna, *f*Aaron's rod that budded, and *g*the tablets of the covenant; [5]and *h*above it were the cherubim of glory overshadowing the mercy seat. Of these things we cannot now speak in detail.

Limitations of the Earthly Service

[6]Now when these things had been thus prepared, *i*the priests always went into the first part of the tabernacle, performing the services. [7]But into the second part the high priest *went* alone *j*once a year, not without blood, which he offered for *k*himself and *for* the people's sins *committed* in ignorance; [8]the Holy Spirit indicating this, that *l*the way into the Holiest of All was not yet made manifest while the first tabernacle was still standing. [9]It *was* symbolic for the present time in which both gifts and sacrifices are offered *m*which cannot make him who performed the service perfect in regard to the conscience— [10]*concerned* only with *n*foods and drinks, *o*various washings, *p*and fleshly ordinances imposed until the time of reformation.

The Heavenly Sanctuary

[11]But Christ came *as* High Priest of *q*the good things to come,* with the greater and more perfect tabernacle not made with hands, that is, not of this creation. [12]Not *r*with the blood of goats and calves, but *s*with His own blood He entered the Most Holy Place *t*once for all, *u*having obtained eternal redemption. [13]For if *v*the blood of bulls and goats and *w*the ashes of a heifer, sprinkling the unclean, sanctifies for the purifying of the flesh, [14]how much more shall the blood of Christ, who through the eternal Spirit offered Himself without spot to God, *x*cleanse your conscience from *y*dead works *z*to serve the living God? [15]And for this reason *a*He is the Mediator of the new covenant, by means of death, for the redemption of the transgressions under the first covenant, that *b*those who are called may receive the promise of the eternal inheritance.

The Mediator's Death Necessary

[16]For where there *is* a testament, there must also of necessity be the death of the testator. [17]For *c*a testament *is* in force after men are dead, since it has no power at all while the testator lives. [18d]Therefore not even the first *covenant* was dedicated without blood. [19]For when Moses had spoken every precept to all the people according to the law, *e*he took the blood of calves and goats, *f*with water, scarlet wool, and hyssop, and sprinkled both the book itself and all the people, [20]saying, *g*"This is the *h*blood of the covenant which God has commanded you."* [21]Then likewise *i*he sprinkled with blood both the tabernacle and all the vessels of the ministry. [22]And according to the law almost all things are purified with blood, and *j*without shedding of blood there is no remission.

---

* **9:11** NU-Text reads *that have come.*　　* **9:20** Exodus 24:8

9:2–5 *a tabernacle was prepared.* These verses simply describe the furniture of the tabernacle. The tabernacle courtyard contained an altar for animal sacrifice and a laver for ceremonial washings. The tabernacle was divided into two rooms by a veil. The first part was the sanctuary or holy place, housing the lampstand, the table for the showbread, and the altar of incense. The second room was the Most Holy Place, containing the ark of the covenant, in which were stored the symbols of the Mosaic covenant.

9:7–8 *once a year.* In the provisions of the Mosaic covenant, access to God was limited. The fact that the high priest had such little access himself indicates the striking failure of the Mosaic covenant to bring believers into the presence of God.

9:9 *cannot make him who performed the service perfect.* The Mosaic covenant covered sins of ignorance (v. 7), but not premeditated sins or the sinful nature of all people (Ps. 51). In other words, the old system was lacking. It did not completely reconcile the people to God.

9:12 *with His own blood.* Christ obtained eternal redemption. His sacrifice never has to be repeated because it is perfect.

9:13 *ashes of a heifer.* These were mixed with water and were used to cleanse a person who had become ceremonially defiled by touching a corpse (Num. 19:11–13). The author of Hebrews points out that these ceremonies could purify only a person's exterior, not a person's heart.

9:14 *the eternal Spirit.* All three persons of the Trinity are involved in cleansing. The defilement is internal, not external (v. 13). Christ's death has the power to purify a person's mind and soul.

9:15 *redemption.* Christ paid the price to free us from our own sin. His death substitutes for our death, the penalty of our sins. Like the Israelites, believers receive an inheritance, but our inheritance is eternal (v. 14).

9:1 *a* Ex. 25:8　**9:3** *b* Ex. 26:31–35; 40:3　**9:4** *c* Lev. 16:12 *d* Ex. 25:10 *e* Ex. 16:33 *f* Num. 17:1–10 *g* Ex. 25:16; 34:29 **9:5** *h* Lev. 16:2　**9:6** *i* Num. 18:2–6; 28:3　**9:7** *j* Ex. 30:10 *k* Heb. 5:3　**9:8** *l* [John 14:6]　**9:9** *m* Heb. 7:19 **9:10** *n* Col. 2:16 *o* Num. 19:7 *p* Eph. 2:15　**9:11** *q* Heb. 10:1　**9:12** *r* Heb. 10:4 *s* Eph. 1:7 *t* Zech. 3:9 *u* [Dan. 9:24]　**9:13** *v* Lev. 16:14, 15 *w* Num. 19:2　**9:14** *x* 1 John 1:7 *y* Heb. 6:1 *z* Luke 1:74　**9:15** *a* Rom. 3:25 *b* Heb. 3:1 **9:17** *c* Gal. 3:15　**9:18** *d* Ex. 24:6　**9:19** *e* Ex. 24:5, 6 *f* Lev. 14:4, 7　**9:20** *g* [Matt. 26:28] *h* Ex. 24:3–8　**9:21** *i* Ex. 29:12, 36　**9:22** *j* Lev. 17:11

Greatness of Christ's Sacrifice

23Therefore *it was* necessary that *k*the copies of the things in the heavens should be purified with these, but the heavenly things themselves with better sacrifices than these. 24For *l*Christ has not entered the holy places made with hands, *which are* copies of *m*the true, but into heaven itself, now *n*to appear in the presence of God for us; 25not that He should offer Himself often, as *o*the high priest enters the Most Holy Place every year with blood of another— 26He then would have had to suffer often since the foundation of the world; but now, once at the end of the ages, He has appeared to put away sin by the sacrifice of Himself. 27*p*And as it is appointed for men to die once, *q*but after this the judgment, 28*r*Christ was *s*offered once to bear the sins *t*of many. To those who *u*eagerly wait for Him He will appear a second time, apart from sin, for salvation.

Animal Sacrifices Insufficient

10 For the law, having a *a*shadow of the good things to come, *and* not the very image of the things, *b*can never with these same sacrifices, which they offer continually year by year, make those who approach perfect. 2For then would they not have ceased to be offered? For the worshipers, once purified, would have had no more consciousness of sins. 3But in those *sacrifices there is* a reminder of sins every year. 4For *c*it is not possible that the blood of bulls and goats could take away sins.

Christ's Death Fulfills God's Will

5Therefore, when He came into the world, He said:

d"Sacrifice and offering You did not desire,
But a body You have prepared for Me.

6 In burnt offerings and sacrifices for sin
You had no pleasure.
7 Then I said, 'Behold, I have come—
In the volume of the book it is written of Me—
To do Your will, O God.'"*

8Previously saying, "Sacrifice and offering, burnt offerings, and offerings for sin You did not desire, nor had pleasure in them" (which are offered according to the law), 9then He said, "Behold, I have come to do Your will, O God."* He takes away the first that He may establish the second. 10*e*By that will we have been sanctified *f*through the offering of the body of Jesus Christ once *for all.*

Christ's Death Perfects the Sanctified

11And every priest stands *g*ministering daily and offering repeatedly the same sacrifices, which can never take away sins. 12*h*But this Man, after He had offered one sacrifice for sins forever, sat down *i*at the right hand of God, 13from that time waiting *j*till His enemies are made His footstool. 14For by one offering He has perfected forever those who are being sanctified.

15But the Holy Spirit also witnesses to us; for after He had said before, 16*k*"This is the covenant that I will make with them after those days, says the LORD: I will put My laws into their hearts, and in their minds I will write them,"* 17then He adds, *l*"Their sins and their lawless deeds I will remember no more."* 18Now where there is remission of these, *there is* no longer an offering for sin.

* **10:7** Psalm 40:6–8   * **10:9** NU-Text and M-Text omit *O God.*   * **10:16** Jeremiah 31:33
* **10:17** Jeremiah 31:34

9:24 Christ has not entered the holy places made with hands. Christ's sacrifice was better than sacrifices made under the Mosaic covenant because Christ did not enter a man-made sanctuary, which was a copy; instead, He entered the true sanctuary, which is in heaven, the very presence of God.
9:26 but now, once. Christ's sacrifice was better than the sacrifices made under the Mosaic covenant because He did not offer an annual sacrifice of animals but offered Himself once for all time.
10:1–4 not the very image of the things. The sacrifices of the Mosaic covenant prefigured Christ's ultimate sacrifice of Himself. Therefore, these imperfect sacrifices of mere animals could not completely purify the person who offered them. If they had been able to, these sacrifices would have ceased. Instead of thoroughly atoning for the sins of the people, the annual sacrifice on the Day of Atonement was a visible reminder of the people's sins.
10:5–7 To do Your will. The Old Testament prophets had warned the Israelites that sacrifices alone would not please God. He desired obedience as well (Ps. 51:16–17; Is. 1:13–17; Mark 12:33). This messianic

psalm indicates that Jesus' obedience to God the Father was one of the reasons His sacrifice was better than the Old Testament sacrifices.
10:8–9 He takes away the first that He may establish the second. The author is explaining Psalm 40. The verb translated "takes away" means "abolishes." The imperfect sacrifices were abolished so that the perfect Sacrifice could impart true life.
10:11–12 sat down. Sitting indicates that His work of atonement is finished. His final words on the cross, "It is finished," declare this spiritual reality (John 19:30).
10:16–18 I will remember no more. This phrase does not mean to forget, but not to hold sin against us any longer.

9:23 *k* Heb. 8:5   **9:24** *l* Heb. 6:20   *m* Heb. 8:2   *n* Rom. 8:34   **9:25** *o* Heb. 9:7   **9:27** *p* Gen. 3:19   *q* [2 Cor. 5:10]   **9:28** *r* Rom. 6:10   *s* 1 Pet. 2:24   *t* Matt. 26:28   *u* Titus 2:13   **10:1** *a* Heb. 8:5   *b* Heb. 7:19; 9:9   *c* Mic. 6:6, 7   **10:5** *d* Ps. 40:6–8   **10:10** *e* John 17:19   *f* [Heb. 9:12]   **10:11** *g* Num. 28:3   **10:12** *h* Col. 3:1   *i* Ps. 110:1   **10:13** *j* Ps. 110:1   **10:16** *k* Jer. 31:33, 34   **10:17** *l* Jer. 31:34

Hold Fast Your Confession

19Therefore, brethren, having mboldness to enter nthe Holiest by the blood of Jesus, 20by a new and oliving way which He consecrated for us, through the veil, that is, His flesh, 21and *having* a High Priest over the house of God, 22let us pdraw near with a true heart qin full assurance of faith, having our hearts sprinkled from an evil conscience and our bodies washed with pure water. 23Let us hold fast the confession of *our* hope without wavering, for rHe who promised *is* faithful. 24And let us consider one another in order to stir up love and good works, 25snot forsaking the assembling of ourselves together, as *is* the manner of some, but exhorting *one another,* and tso much the more as you see uthe Day approaching.

The Just Live by Faith

26For vif we sin willfully wafter we have received the knowledge of the truth, there xno longer remains a sacrifice for sins, 27but a certain fearful expectation of judgment, and yfiery indignation which will devour the adversaries. 28Anyone who has rejected Moses' law dies without mercy on the *testimony of* two or three zwitnesses. 29aOf how much worse punishment, do you suppose, will he be thought worthy who has trampled the Son of God underfoot, bcounted the blood of the covenant by which he was sanctified a common thing, cand insulted the Spirit of grace? 30For we know Him who said, d*"Vengeance is Mine, I will repay,"** says the Lord.* And again, e*"The LORD will judge His people."** 31fIt is a fearful thing to fall into the hands of the living God.

32But grecall the former days in which, after you were illuminated, you endured a great struggle with sufferings: 33partly while you were made ha spectacle both by reproaches and tribulations, and partly while iyou became companions of those who were so treated; 34for you had compassion on me* jin my chains, and kjoyfully accepted the plundering of your goods, knowing that lyou have a better and an enduring possession for yourselves in heaven.* 35Therefore do not cast away your confidence, mwhich has great reward. 36nFor you have need of endurance, so that after you have done the will of God, oyou may receive the promise:

37 *"For* pyet a little while,
    And qHe* who is coming will come
         and will not tarry.
38 Now rthe* just shall live by faith;
    But if anyone draws back,
    My soul has no pleasure in him."**

39But we are not of those swho draw back to perdition, but of those who tbelieve to the saving of the soul.

By Faith We Understand

11 Now faith is the substance of things hoped for, the evidence aof things not seen. 2For by it the elders obtained a *good* testimony.

---

* **10:30** Deuteronomy 32:35 • NU-Text omits *says the Lord.* • Deuteronomy 32:36 * **10:34** NU-Text reads *the prisoners* instead of *me in my chains.* • NU-Text omits *in heaven.* * **10:37** Or *that which* * **10:38** NU-Text reads *My just one.* • Habakkuk 2:3, 4

10:19 Therefore. The author has spent five chapters explaining the superiority of Christ's priesthood to the Levitical priesthood and the superiority of the new covenant to the Mosaic covenant. Unlike the Israelites, who approached God at Mount Sinai with fear and trembling (Ex. 20:18–21), believers can approach God with boldness (3:6; 4:16; 10:35) because we possess Christ's righteousness and not our own.
10:20 His flesh. The Old Testament high priest passed through a veil to get to the Most Holy Place. Now, believers enter God's presence through Christ's flesh, meaning His sacrificial death.
10:22 our hearts sprinkled . . . our bodies washed. Our consciences can be cleansed through the blood of Christ (9:14). Just as the high priest washed before entering the Most Holy Place (Lev. 16:3–4), so believers are cleansed before they come before the Holy One.
10:24–25 stir up love and good works. The Greek word translated "stir up" means "convulse." In this context the word speaks forcefully of the tremendous impact believers can have on each other. That is why the author exhorts the Hebrews to gather together. Evidently, some believers had stopped attending the worship services of the church, perhaps because they feared persecution.
10:26 sin willfully. The reference here is not to an occasional act of sin (which can be confessed and forgiven) but to a conscious rejection of God. The Old Testament speaks in Numbers 15:30–31 of committing

willful sin. A person who sinned presumptuously was to be cut off from the people. To sin deliberately after receiving the knowledge of the truth is apostasy. If a Christian rejects God's provision for his or her salvation, there is no other remedy for sins, since forgiveness for sins can only be found in Christ's perfect sacrifice.
10:29 Spirit of grace. This is a reference to the Holy Spirit, the agent of God's gracious gift of salvation. A believer who commits these offenses will be judged with a punishment worse than physical death.
10:35 do not cast away your confidence. For the recipients of Hebrews to return to the safety of Judaism would mean a loss of eternal reward at the judgment seat of Christ.
11:1 Now faith is. This verse is not a definition of faith, but a description of what faith does. **substance.** This means "essence" or "reality." Faith treats things hoped

---

10:19 m [Eph. 2:18] n Heb. 9:8, 12 **10:20** o John 14:6 **10:22** p Heb. 7:19; 10:1 q Eph. 3:12 **10:23** r 1 Cor. 1:9; 10:13 **10:25** s Acts 2:42 t Rom. 13:11 u Phil. 4:5 **10:26** v Num. 15:30 w 2 Pet. 2:20 x Heb. 6:6 **10:27** y Zeph. 1:18 **10:28** z Deut. 17:2–6; 19:15 **10:29** a [Heb. 2:3] b 1 Cor. 11:29 c [Matt. 12:31] **10:30** d Deut. 32:35 e Deut. 32:36 **10:31** f [Luke 12:5] **10:32** g Gal. 3:4 **10:33** h 1 Cor. 4:9 i Phil. 1:7 **10:34** j 2 Tim. 1:16 k Matt. 5:12 l Matt. 6:20 **10:35** m Matt. 5:12 **10:36** n Luke 21:19 o [Col. 3:24] **10:37** p Luke 18:8 q Hab. 2:3, 4 **10:38** r Rom. 1:17 **10:39** s 2 Pet. 2:20 t Acts 16:31 **11:1** a Rom. 8:24

3By faith we understand that [b]the worlds were framed by the word of God, so that the things which are seen were not made of things which are visible.

Faith at the Dawn of History

4By faith [c]Abel offered to God a more excellent sacrifice than Cain, through which he obtained witness that he was righteous, God testifying of his gifts; and through it he being dead still [d]speaks.

5By faith Enoch was taken away so that he did not see death, [e]*"and was not found, because God had taken him"*;* for before he was taken he had this testimony, that he pleased God. 6But without faith *it is* impossible to please *Him*, for he who comes to God must believe that He is, and *that* He is a rewarder of those who diligently seek Him.

7By faith [f]Noah, being divinely warned of things not yet seen, moved with godly fear, [g]prepared an ark for the saving of his household, by which he condemned the world and became heir of [h]the righteousness which is according to faith.

Faithful Abraham

8By faith [i]Abraham obeyed when he was called to go out to the place which he would receive as an inheritance. And he went out, not knowing where he was going. 9By faith he dwelt in the land of promise as *in* a foreign country, [j]dwelling in tents with Isaac and Jacob, [k]the heirs with him of the same promise; 10for he waited for [l]the city which has foundations, [m]whose builder and maker *is* God.

11By faith [n]Sarah herself also received strength to conceive seed, and [o]she bore a child* when she was past the age, because she judged Him [p]faithful who had promised. 12Therefore from one man, and him as good as [q]dead, were born *as many* as the [r]stars of the sky in multitude—innumerable as the sand which is by the seashore.

The Heavenly Hope

13These all died in faith, [s]not having received the [t]promises, but [u]having seen them afar off were assured of them,* embraced *them* and [v]confessed that they were strangers and pilgrims on the earth. 14For those who say such things [w]declare plainly that they seek a homeland. 15And truly if they had called to mind [x]that *country* from which they had come out, they would have had opportunity to return. 16But now they desire a better, that is, a heavenly *country*. Therefore God is not ashamed [y]to be called their God, for He has [z]prepared a city for them.

The Faith of the Patriarchs

17By faith Abraham, [a]when he was tested, offered up Isaac, and he who had received the promises offered up his only begotten *son*, 18of whom it was said, [b]*"In Isaac your seed shall be called,"** 19concluding that God [c]*was* able to raise *him* up, even from the dead, from which he also received him in a figurative sense.

20By faith [d]Isaac blessed Jacob and Esau concerning things to come.

21By faith Jacob, when he was dying, [e]blessed each of the sons of Joseph, and worshiped, *leaning* on the top of his staff.

22By faith [f]Joseph, when he was dying, made mention of the departure of the children of Israel, and gave instructions concerning his bones.

The Faith of Moses

23By faith [g]Moses, when he was born, was hidden three months by his parents, because they saw *he was* a beautiful child; and they were not afraid of the king's [h]command.

* **11:5** Genesis 5:24 * **11:11** NU-Text omits *she bore a child.* * **11:13** NU-Text and M-Text omit *were assured of them.* * **11:18** Genesis 21:12

---

for as reality. ***evidence.*** This means "proof." Faith itself proves that what is unseen is real, such as the believer's rewards at the return of Christ (2 Cor. 4:18).

11:4 *a more excellent sacrifice than Cain.* Evidently, Cain offered his sacrifice without faith (Gen. 4). ***still speaks.*** Abel still speaks to us because his righteous deeds have been recorded in Scripture.

11:6 *comes.* This word is used repeatedly in Hebrews to refer to the privilege of drawing near to God (4:16; 7:25; 10:1,22). Here, the author of Hebrews explains that faith is mandatory for those who approach Him. ***rewarder.*** God rewards not only those who seek Him, but also those who do good works in the Holy Spirit's power (Rev. 22:12).

11:8 *not knowing where he was going.* Abraham placed his trust in God. Faith means obediently stepping into the unknown (v. 1). Abraham did this, and God considered him righteous because of it (Gen. 15:6; Rom. 4:1–12).

11:15 *opportunity to return.* The patriarchs and Sarah did not return to Ur, even though they could have if they had wanted to. The recipients of Hebrews were to follow the patriarchs' example and refuse to return to the religion of their ancestors, a religious system that no longer provided atonement for sin (8:7–13).

11:17–19 *Abraham . . . tested.* Abraham believed that God could raise Isaac from the dead (Gen. 22:5), if necessary. The incident is figurative of what God has done for us. Isaac was as good as dead, but God provided a ram to sacrifice in his place (Gen. 22:9–14).

11:3 [b] Ps. 33:6 **11:4** [c] Gen. 4:3–5 [d] Heb. 12:24 **11:5** [e] Gen. 5:21–24 **11:7** [f] Gen. 6:13–22 [g] 1 Pet. 3:20 [h] Rom. 3:22 **11:8** [i] Gen. 12:1–4 **11:9** [j] Gen. 12:8; 13:3, 18; 18:1, 9 [k] Heb. 6:17 **11:10** [l] [Heb. 12:22; 13:14] [m] [Rev. 21:10] **11:11** [n] Gen. 17:19; 18:11–14; 21:1, 2 [o] Luke 1:36 [p] Heb. 10:23 **11:12** [q] Rom. 4:19 [r] Gen. 15:5; 22:17; 32:12 **11:13** [s] Heb. 11:39 [t] Gen. 12:7 [u] John 8:56 [v] Ps. 39:12 **11:14** [w] Heb. 13:14 **11:15** [x] Gen. 11:31 **11:16** [y] Ex. 3:6, 15; 4:5 [z] [Rev. 21:2] **11:17** [a] James 2:21 **11:18** [b] Gen. 21:12 **11:19** [c] Rom. 4:17 **11:20** [d] Gen. 27:26–40 **11:21** [e] Gen. 48:1, 5, 16, 20 **11:22** [f] Gen. 50:24, 25 **11:23** [g] Ex. 2:1–3 [h] Ex. 1:16, 22

²⁴By faith ⁱMoses, when he became of age, refused to be called the son of Pharaoh's daughter, ²⁵choosing rather to suffer affliction with the people of God than to enjoy the passing pleasures of sin, ²⁶esteeming ʲthe reproach of Christ greater riches than the treasures in* Egypt; for he looked to the ᵏreward.

²⁷By faith ˡhe forsook Egypt, not fearing the wrath of the king; for he endured as seeing Him who is invisible. ²⁸By faith ᵐhe kept the Passover and the sprinkling of blood, lest he who destroyed the firstborn should touch them.

²⁹By faith ⁿthey passed through the Red Sea as by dry *land, whereas* the Egyptians, attempting to do so, were drowned.

By Faith They Overcame

³⁰By faith ᵒthe walls of Jericho fell down after they were encircled for seven days. ³¹By faith ᵖthe harlot Rahab did not perish with those who did not believe, when �qshe had received the spies with peace.

³²And what more shall I say? For the time would fail me to tell of ʳGideon and ˢBarak and ᵗSamson and ᵘJephthah, also of ᵛDavid and ʷSamuel and the prophets: ³³who through faith subdued kingdoms, worked righteousness, obtained promises, ˣstopped the mouths of lions, ³⁴ʸquenched the violence of fire, escaped the edge of the sword, out of weakness were made strong, became valiant in battle, turned to flight the armies of the aliens. ³⁵ᶻWomen received their dead raised to life again.

Others were ᵃtortured, not accepting deliverance, that they might obtain a better resurrection. ³⁶Still others had trial of mockings and scourgings, yes, and ᵇof chains and imprisonment. ³⁷ᶜThey were stoned, they were sawn in two, were tempted,* were slain with the sword.

ᵈThey wandered about ᵉin sheepskins and goatskins, being destitute, afflicted, tormented— ³⁸of whom the world was not worthy. They wandered in deserts and mountains, ᶠin dens and caves of the earth.

³⁹And all these, ᵍhaving obtained a good testimony through faith, did not receive the promise, ⁴⁰God having provided something better for us, that they should not be ʰmade perfect apart from us.

The Race of Faith

12 Therefore we also, since we are surrounded by so great a cloud of witnesses, ᵃlet us lay aside every weight, and the sin which so easily ensnares *us,* and ᵇlet us run ᶜwith endurance the race that is set before us, ²looking unto Jesus, the author and finisher of *our* faith, ᵈwho for the joy that was set before Him ᵉendured the cross, despising the shame, and ᶠhas sat down at the right hand of the throne of God.

The Discipline of God

³ᵍFor consider Him who endured such hostility from sinners against Himself, ʰlest you become weary and discouraged in your souls. ⁴ⁱYou have not yet resisted to bloodshed, striving against sin. ⁵And you have forgotten the exhortation which speaks to you as to sons:

ʲ"My son, do not despise the chastening of the LORD,
    Nor be discouraged when you are rebuked by Him;
6   For ᵏwhom the LORD loves He chastens,
    And scourges every son whom He receives."*

---

* **11:26** NU-Text and M-Text read *of.*   * **11:37** NU-Text omits *were tempted.*   * **12:6** Proverbs 3:11, 12

11:26 the reproach of Christ. This phrase refers to the earthly disgrace Christ received. Like Christ, Moses chose to suffer the indignities associated with God's people, instead of embracing the worldly pleasures of Pharaoh's court.

11:28 sprinkling of blood. God told Moses to sprinkle blood on the doorposts. Moses believed God's word and heeded His warning, and, as a result, the firstborn of every Israelite family was saved (Ex. 12:1–13).

11:35 Women received their dead. This is probably a reference to the raising of the son of the widow of Zarephath (1 Kin. 17:17–24) and of the Shunammite woman (2 Kin. 4:32–37). But the author of Hebrews also points out that not all who had faith won victories, at least not in the same hour. **tortured.** This is usually understood to be an allusion to the heroic martyrs of Maccabean times, who were well known.

11:40 made perfect. This phrase means "made complete." This completion, the realization of all of God's promises in Christ's coming kingdom, awaits all believers.

12:1 cloud of witnesses. This refers to the people of faith mentioned in chapter 11. They are not actually spectators watching us; they are witnesses testifying to the truth of the faith (11:2,4–6).

12:2 finisher. Christ has done everything necessary for us to endure in our faith. He is our example and model. **the joy that was set before Him.** His attention was not on the agonies of the cross, but on the crown, not on the suffering, but on the reward.

12:3 consider. This thought involves the idea of comparison, as an accountant would compare the various columns of a balance sheet. Believers should compare their sufferings to the torture Christ endured on their behalf (v. 4).

11:24 ⁱEx. 2:11–15   **11:26** ʲHeb. 13:13 ᵏRom. 8:18
11:27 ˡEx. 10:28   **11:28** ᵐEx. 12:21   **11:29** ⁿEx. 14:22–29   **11:30** ᵒJosh. 6:20   **11:31** ᵖJosh. 2:9; 6:23
�q Josh. 2:1   **11:32** ʳJudg. 6:11; 7:1–25 ˢJudg. 4:6–24
ᵗ Judg. 13:24—16:31 ᵘJudg. 11:1–29; 12:1–7 ᵛ 1 Sam. 16; 17
ʷ 1 Sam. 7:9–14   **11:33** ˣDan. 6:22   **11:34** ʸDan. 3:23–28
11:35 ᶻ 1 Kin. 17:22 ᵃActs 22:25   **11:36** ᵇGen. 39:20
11:37 ᶜ 1 Kin. 21:13 ᵈ2 Kin. 1:8 ᵉZech. 13:4   **11:38** ᶠ 1 Kin. 18:4, 13; 19:9   **11:39** ᵍHeb. 11:2, 13   **11:40** ʰHeb. 5:9
12:1 ᵃCol. 3:8 ᵇ1 Cor. 9:24 ᶜRom. 12:12   **12:2** ᵈLuke 24:26 ᵉPhil. 2:8 ᶠPs. 110:1   **12:3** ᵍMatt. 10:24 ʰGal. 6:9
12:4 ⁱ[1 Cor. 10:13]   **12:5** ʲProv. 3:11, 12   **12:6** ᵏRev. 3:19

7[If* you endure chastening, God deals with you as with sons; for what ^mson is there whom a father does not chasten? 8But if you are without chastening, ⁿof which all have become partakers, then you are illegitimate and not sons. 9Furthermore, we have had human fathers who corrected *us*, and we paid *them* respect. Shall we not much more readily be in subjection to ^othe Father of spirits and live? 10For they indeed for a few days chastened *us* as seemed *best* to them, but He for *our* profit, ^pthat *we* may be partakers of His holiness. 11Now no chastening seems to be joyful for the present, but painful; nevertheless, afterward it yields ^qthe peaceable fruit of righteousness to those who have been trained by it.

Renew Your Spiritual Vitality

12Therefore ^rstrengthen the hands which hang down, and the feeble knees, 13and make straight paths for your feet, so that what is lame may not be dislocated, but rather be healed.

14sPursue peace with all *people*, and holiness, ^twithout which no one will see the Lord: 15looking carefully lest anyone ^ufall short of the grace of God; lest any ^vroot of bitterness springing up cause trouble, and by this many become defiled; 16lest there *be* any ^wfornicator or profane person like Esau, ^xwho for one morsel of food sold his birthright. 17For you know that afterward, when he wanted to inherit the blessing, he was ^yrejected, for he found no place for repentance, though he sought it diligently with tears.

The Glorious Company

18For you have not come to ^zthe mountain that* may be touched and that burned with fire, and to blackness and darkness* and tempest, 19and the sound of a trumpet and the voice of words, so that those who

heard *it* ^abegged that the word should not be spoken to them anymore. 20(For they could not endure what was commanded: ^b*"And if so much as a beast touches the mountain, it shall be stoned* or shot with an arrow."* 21And so terrifying was the sight *that* Moses said, ^c*"I am exceedingly afraid and trembling."*)

22But you have come to Mount Zion and to the city of the living God, the heavenly Jerusalem, to an innumerable company of angels, 23to the general assembly and church of ^dthe firstborn ^ewho are registered in heaven, to God ^fthe Judge of all, to the spirits of just men ^gmade perfect, 24to Jesus ^hthe Mediator of the new covenant, and to ⁱthe blood of sprinkling that speaks better things ^jthan *that of* Abel.

Hear the Heavenly Voice

25See that you do not refuse Him who speaks. For ^kif they did not escape who refused Him who spoke on earth, much more *shall we not escape* if we turn away from Him who *speaks* from heaven, 26whose voice then shook the earth; but now He has promised, saying, ^l*"Yet once more I shake* not only the earth, but also heaven."* 27Now this, *"Yet once more,"* indicates the ^mremoval of those things that are being shaken, as of things that are made, that the things which cannot be shaken may remain.

28Therefore, since we are receiving a kingdom which cannot be shaken, let us have grace, by which we may* ⁿserve God acceptably with reverence and godly fear. 29For ^oour God *is* a consuming fire.

---

* **12:7** NU-Text and M-Text read *It is for discipline that you endure; God … .* • **12:18** NU-Text reads *to that which.* • NU-Text reads *gloom.* * **12:20** NU-Text and M-Text omit the rest of this verse. • Exodus 19:12, 13 * **12:21** Deuteronomy 9:19 * **12:26** NU-Text reads *will shake.* • Haggai 2:6 * **12:28** M-Text omits *may.*

12:8 *then you are illegitimate and not sons.* In Roman society an illegitimate son was one who had no inheritance rights.

12:11 *the peaceable fruit of righteousness.* This phrase suggests that the result of God's discipline is peace and righteousness.

12:18–24 *For you have not come to the mountain.* In these verses, the author of Hebrews contrasts the Mosaic covenant with the new covenant by contrasting two mountains: Mount Sinai and Mount Zion. At Mount Sinai, the Israelites received the law from God with fear and trembling, for God displayed at that time His awesome power (Ex. 19:10—20:26). In contrast, Christian believers have come to a heavenly Jerusalem on Mount Zion through Jesus' blood. This mountain is a celebration of the Holy One, attended by angels, believers, and righteous people. The author makes the contrast between the two covenants vivid and then once again exhorts his readers not to reject Christ's offer of salvation (vv. 25–29).

12:23 *just men made perfect.* This phrase refers to all believers who have died. They are just because

they have been justified or made righteous and perfect because they are now "complete" in heaven.

12:25 *Him who speaks from heaven.* This is a reference to Christ, who spoke on earth and is now in heaven.

12:29 *our God is a consuming fire.* The author concludes his lengthy warning to those who are tempted to abandon the faith (2:1—12:29) with a vivid description of God's judgment (Deut. 4:24). The Lord will judge His people (10:27,30).

12:7 *l* Deut. 8:5 *m* Prov. 13:24; 19:18; 23:13 **12:8** *n* 1 Pet. 5:9 **12:9** *o* [Job 12:10] **12:10** *p* Lev. 11:44 **12:11** *q* James 3:17, 18 **12:12** *r* Is. 35:3 **12:14** *s* Ps. 34:14 *t* Matt. 5:8 **12:15** *u* Heb. 4:1 *v* Deut. 29:18 **12:16** *w* [1 Cor. 6:13–18] *x* Gen. 25:33 **12:17** *y* Gen. 27:30–40 **12:18** *z* Deut. 4:11; 5:22 **12:19** *a* Ex. 20:18–26 **12:20** *b* Ex. 19:12, 13 **12:21** *c* Deut. 9:19 **12:23** *d* [James 1:18] *e* Luke 10:20 *f* Ps. 50:6; 94:2 *g* [Phil. 3:12] **12:24** *h* Heb. 8:6; 9:15 *i* Ex. 24:8 *j* Gen. 4:10 **12:25** *k* Heb. 2:2, 3 **12:26** *l* Hag. 2:6 **12:27** *m* [Is. 34:4; 54:10; 65:17] **12:28** *n* Heb. 13:15, 21 **12:29** *o* Ex. 24:17

Concluding Moral Directions

13 Let [a]brotherly love continue. **2**[b]Do not forget to entertain strangers, for by so *doing* [c]some have unwittingly entertained angels. **3**[d]Remember the prisoners as if chained with them—those who are mistreated—since you yourselves are in the body also.

4[e]Marriage *is* honorable among all, and the bed undefiled; [f]but fornicators and adulterers God will judge.

5*Let your* conduct *be* without covetousness; *be* content with such things as you have. For He Himself has said, [g]*"I will never leave you nor forsake you."** **6**So we may boldly say:

> [h]*"The LORD is my helper;*
> *I will not fear.*
> *What can man do to me?"**

Concluding Religious Directions

7Remember those who rule over you, who have spoken the word of God to you, whose faith follow, considering the outcome of *their* conduct. **8**Jesus Christ is [i]the same yesterday, today, and forever. **9**Do not be carried about* with various and strange doctrines. For *it is* good that the heart be established by grace, not with foods which have not profited those who have been occupied with them.

10We have an altar from which those who serve the tabernacle have no right to eat. **11**For the bodies of those animals, whose blood is brought into the sanctuary by the high priest for sin, are burned outside the camp. **12**Therefore Jesus also, that He might sanctify the people with His own blood, suffered outside the gate. **13**Therefore let us go forth to Him, outside the camp, bearing [j]His reproach. **14**For here we have no continuing city, but we seek the one to come. **15**[k]Therefore by Him let us continually offer [l]the sacrifice of praise to God, that is, [m]the fruit of *our* lips, giving thanks to His name. **16**[n]But do not forget to do good and to share, for [o]with such sacrifices God is well pleased.

17[p]Obey those who rule over you, and be submissive, for [q]they watch out for your souls, as those who must give account. Let them do so with joy and not with grief, for that would be unprofitable for you.

Prayer Requested

18[r]Pray for us; for we are confident that we have [s]a good conscience, in all things desiring to live honorably. **19**But I especially urge *you* to do this, that I may be restored to you the sooner.

---

* **13:5** Deuteronomy 31:6, 8; Joshua 1:5
* **13:6** Psalm 118:6   * **13:9** NU-Text and M-Text read *away*.

13:2 *entertained angels.* This is a reference to men in the Old Testament who encounter heavenly beings. These men included Abraham (Gen. 18), Lot (Gen. 19), and Gideon (Judg. 6). The idea is that, when you practice hospitality, you may be helping a messenger of God without realizing it.

13:5 *I will never leave you nor forsake you.* This quotation is one of the emphatic statements in the New Testament. In Greek it contains two double negatives, similar to saying in English, "I will never, ever, ever forsake you." Jesus uses the same technique to express the certainty of eternal life for believers (John 10:28).

13:9 *strange doctrines.* This implies ideas foreign to the gospel message. Many of the ideas which the author was confronting were Jewish in origin—pertaining to ritual observances, sacrificial feasts, and various laws identifying what was clean and unclean.

13:11 *burned outside the camp.* The believer has a sacrifice, Jesus Christ. He atoned for the sins of humanity with His death on the cross. But, unlike the high priests from the Old Testament, believers receive their sustenance from Christ in a symbolic way, by believing in Him (John 6:41–58).

13:15–16 *sacrifice of praise.* Although the Old Testament sacrifices are now obsolete (8:13), believers are to offer spiritual sacrifices which include their praise, their possessions, and even their lives (Rom. 12:1–2).

13:15 Worship—Since worship encompasses thought, feeling, and deed, there are many expressions of it. Worship especially includes praise and thanksgiving which may be expressed privately or publicly, whether by grateful declarations (Heb. 13:15) or by joyful singing (Ps. 100:2; Eph. 5:19; Col. 3:16). Portions of early Christian hymns of worship have been preserved in the New Testament (Phil. 2:5–11; 1 Tim. 3:16; 2 Tim. 2:11–13). One very important expression of worship for the church is remembering the death of Christ through the Lord's Supper (1 Cor. 11:26). The Lord's Supper was instituted by Christ Himself (Matt. 26:26–28) and judged by Paul to be taken very seriously (1 Cor. 11:28–32). Since worship means giving something to God, the cheerful giving of money to God's work is certainly an act of worship (2 Cor. 9:7). The exercise of one of the spiritual gifts in ministry to the body of Christ constitutes worship as service (1 Cor. 12) as does faithfully occupying a church office (Eph. 4:11; 1 Tim. 3:1–13; Titus 1:5–9). In fact, presenting ourselves (mind and body) to God to serve in any context is described as an act of worship in Romans 12:1. In this manner our whole lives become acts of worship.

13:1 [a] Rom. 12:10   **13:2** [b] Matt. 25:35   [c] Gen. 18:1–22; 19:1   **13:3** [d] Matt. 25:36   **13:4** [e] Prov. 5:18, 19   [f] 1 Cor. 6:9   **13:5** [g] Deut. 31:6; Josh. 1:5   **13:6** [h] Ps. 27:1; 118:6   **13:8** [i] Heb. 1:12   **13:13** [j] 1 Pet. 4:14   **13:15** [k] Eph. 5:20   [l] Lev. 7:12   [m] Hos. 14:2   **13:16** [n] Rom. 12:13   [o] Phil. 4:18   **13:17** [p] Phil. 2:29   [q] Ezek. 3:17   **13:18** [r] Eph. 6:19   [s] Acts 23:1

Benediction, Final Exhortation, Farewell

20Now may tthe God of peace uwho brought up our Lord Jesus from the dead, vthat great Shepherd of the sheep, wthrough the blood of the everlasting covenant, 21make you complete in every good work to do His will, xworking in you* what is well pleasing in His sight, through Jesus Christ, to whom be glory forever and ever. Amen.

22And I appeal to you, brethren, bear with the word of exhortation, for I have written to you in few words. 23Know that our brother Timothy has been set free, with whom I shall see you if he comes shortly.

24Greet all those who rule over you, and all the saints. Those from Italy greet you.

25Grace be with you all. Amen.

---

* 13:21 NU-Text and M-Text read us.

13:20 great Shepherd of the sheep. Having laid down His life for them (John 10:15) and now continuing to make intercession for them (7:25), this is another description of Jesus' ministry.

13:22 word of exhortation. This phrase refers to the whole epistle to the Hebrews. It is an exhortation not to depart from the living God (3:12), but to go on to maturity (6:1) and endure in the faith to the end (3:6,14).

13:24 Those from Italy. This phrase may refer to people living in Italy, or else to people from there who were now living elsewhere. Because of its ambiguity, this phrase does not reveal the location of the author or of the recipients.

13:20 t Rom. 5:1, 2, 10; 15:33 u Rom. 4:24 v 1 Pet. 2:25; 5:4 w Zech. 9:11 **13:21** x Phil. 2:13

THE EPISTLE OF
JAMES

▶ **AUTHOR:** Four men are named James in the New Testament, one of which is the Lord's brother (Matt. 13:55; Mark 6:3; Gal. 1:19). Tradition points to this prominent figure as the author of the epistle, and this best fits the evidence of Scripture. The brevity and limited doctrinal emphasis of James kept it from wide circulation, and by the time it became known in the church as a whole, there was uncertainty about the identity of the James in 1:1. Growing recognition that it was written by the Lord's brother led to its acceptance as a canonical book.

▶ **TIME:** c. A.D. 46–49   ▶ **KEY VERSES:** James 1:19–22

▶ **THEME:** James is for the practical person. While most of Paul's epistles have a theological and practical section, there isn't much theoretical or systematic theology in this book. The subject matters covered in James are the issues we face daily if not hourly. How do we respond to trials and temptation? What are we doing with our money? Do we keep our tongues under control? Are we acting on our faith? What are we doing with our prayer lives? The main point of all these questions James raises is that saving faith needs to result in changed behavior.

Greeting to the Twelve Tribes

1 James, *a* a bondservant of God and of the Lord Jesus Christ,

To the twelve tribes which are scattered abroad:

Greetings.

Profiting from Trials

2My brethren, *b* count it all joy *c* when you fall into various trials, 3*d* knowing that the testing of your faith produces patience. 4But let patience have *its* perfect work, that you may be perfect and complete, lacking nothing. 5*e* If any of you lacks wisdom, *f* let him ask of God, who gives to all liberally and without reproach, and *g* it will be given to him. 6*h* But let him ask in faith, with no doubting, for he who doubts is like a wave of the sea driven and tossed by the wind. 7For let not that man suppose that he will receive anything from the Lord; 8*he is* *i* a double-minded man, unstable in all his ways.

The Perspective of Rich and Poor

9Let the lowly brother glory in his exaltation, 10but the rich in his humiliation, because *j* as a flower of the field he will pass away. 11For no sooner has the sun risen with a burning heat than it withers the grass; its flower falls, and its beautiful appearance perishes. So the rich man also will fade away in his pursuits.

Loving God Under Trials

12*k* Blessed *is* the man who endures temptation; for when he has been approved, he will receive *l* the crown of life *m* which the

1:1 *To the twelve tribes.* This salutation probably means the letter is for Jewish Christians living outside of Palestine. The letter was not intended for one specific church but was to be passed around among various local assemblies.
1:2 *trials.* These are outward circumstances—conflicts, sufferings, and troubles—encountered by all believers. Trials are not pleasant and may be extremely grievous, but believers are to consider them as opportunities for rejoicing. Troubles and difficulties are a tool which refines and purifies our faith, producing patience and endurance.
1:3 *testing of your faith.* The word that is translated into this phrase occurs only here and in 1 Peter 1:7. The term was used for coins that were genuine and not debased. The aim of testing is not to destroy or afflict, but to purge and refine. "Patience" here transcends the idea of bearing affliction; it includes the

idea of standing fast under pressure, with a staying power that turns adversities into opportunities.
1:5 *wisdom.* The starting point for wisdom is a genuine reverence for the Almighty (Ps. 111:10; Prov. 9.10) and a steadfast confidence that God controls all circumstances, guiding them to His good purposes (Rom. 8:28).
1:8 *double-minded.* This person is literally one with "two souls." If one part of a person is set on God and the other is set on this world (Matt. 6:24), there will be constant conflict within.
1:12 *will receive the crown of life.* The Bible describes the believer's reward (2 Cor. 5:10; Rev. 22:12)

1:1 *a* Acts 12:17   **1:2** *b* Acts 5:41   *c* 1 Pet. 1:6   **1:3** *d* Rom. 5:3–5   **1:5** *e* 1 Kin. 3:9   *f* Matt. 7:7   *g* Jer. 29:12
1:6 *h* [Mark 11:23, 24]   **1:8** *i* James 4:8   **1:10** *j* Job 14:2
1:12 *k* James 5:11   *l* [1 Cor. 9:25]   *m* Matt. 10:22

Lord has promised to those who love Him. [13]Let no one say when he is tempted, "I am tempted by God"; for God cannot be tempted by evil, nor does He Himself tempt anyone. [14]But each one is tempted when he is drawn away by his own desires and enticed. [15]Then, [n]when desire has conceived, it gives birth to sin; and sin, when it is full-grown, [o]brings forth death.

[16]Do not be deceived, my beloved brethren. [17p]Every good gift and every perfect gift is from above, and comes down from the Father of lights, [q]with whom there is no variation or shadow of turning. [18r]Of His own will He brought us forth by the [s]word of truth, [t]that we might be a kind of first-fruits of His creatures.

Qualities Needed in Trials

[19]So then,* my beloved brethren, let every man be swift to hear, [u]slow to speak, [v]slow to wrath; [20]for the wrath of man does not produce the righteousness of God.

Doers—Not Hearers Only

[21]Therefore [w]lay aside all filthiness and overflow of wickedness, and receive with meekness the implanted word, [x]which is able to save your souls.

[22]But [y]be doers of the word, and not hearers only, deceiving yourselves. [23]For [z]if anyone is a hearer of the word and not a doer, he is like a man observing his natural face in a mirror; [24]for he observes himself, goes away, and immediately forgets what kind of man he was. [25]But [a]he who looks into the perfect law of liberty and continues in it, and is not a forgetful hearer but a doer of the work, [b]this one will be blessed in what he does.

[26]If anyone among you* thinks he is religious, and [c]does not bridle his tongue but deceives his own heart, this one's religion is useless. [27d]Pure and undefiled religion before God and the Father is this: [e]to visit orphans and widows in their trouble, [f]and to keep oneself unspotted from the world.

Beware of Personal Favoritism

2 My brethren, do not hold the faith of our Lord Jesus Christ, [a]the Lord of glory, with [b]partiality. [2]For if there should come into your assembly a man with gold rings, in fine apparel, and there should also come in a poor man in filthy clothes, [3]and you pay attention to the one wearing the fine clothes and say to him, "You sit here in a good place," and say to the poor man, "You stand there," or, "Sit here at my footstool," [4]have you not shown partiality among yourselves, and become judges with evil thoughts?

[5]Listen, my beloved brethren: [c]Has God not chosen the poor of this world to be [d]rich in faith and heirs of the kingdom [e]which He promised to those who love Him? [6]But [f]you have dishonored the poor man. Do not the rich oppress you [g]and drag you into the courts? [7]Do they not blaspheme that noble name by which you are [h]called?

[8]If you really fulfill the royal law according to the Scripture, [i]"You shall love your neighbor as yourself,"* you do well; [9]but if you show partiality, you commit sin, and are convicted by the law as [j]transgressors. [10]For whoever shall keep the whole law, and yet [k]stumble in one point, [l]he is guilty

* 1:19 NU-Text reads Know this or This you know.
* 1:26 NU-Text omits among you.   * 2:8 Leviticus 19:18

---

under various vivid images, such as precious metals (1 Cor. 3:8–14), garments (Rev. 3:5,18; 19:7–8), and crowns (1 Cor. 9:25; Rev. 2:10; 3:11).

1:13 nor does He Himself tempt anyone. Enticement to sin does not come from God. God will never deliberately lead a person to commit sin because that would not only go against His nature, but it would also be opposed to His purpose of molding His creation into His holy image. Yet, God does sometimes place His people in adverse circumstances for the purpose of building godly character (Gen. 22:1,12).

1:19 swift to hear, slow to speak, slow to wrath. These three exhortations reveal the outline of this letter (1:21—2:26 for "swift to hear"; 3:1–18 for "slow to speak"; 4:1—5:18 for "slow to wrath").

1:21 receive with meekness the implanted word. The believer should have a teachable spirit—without resisting, disputing, or questioning. Receiving God's Word this way will save the believer's soul.

1:22 be doers of the word, and not hearers only. Believers who hear the Word of God (v. 19) must receive it with a teachable spirit (v. 21), applying it to their daily lives. To hear and not obey is to be deceived.

1:25 the perfect law of liberty. Loving God and loving one's neighbor sum up the law (Rom. 13:8–10).

But it is Christ's love (Eph. 3:17–19) which frees us from our sins to truly love others (John 8:36–38; Gal. 5:13).

1:27 orphans and widows. These people were among the most unprotected and needy classes in ancient societies (Ezek. 22:7). Pure religion does not merely give material goods for the relief of the distressed; it also oversees their care (Acts 6:1–7).

2:5 heirs of the kingdom. This inheritance means more than entering the kingdom; it also involves ruling with Christ (1 Cor. 6:9; Gal. 5:21; 2 Tim. 2:12).

2:9 if you show partiality, you commit sin. James alludes to Leviticus 19:15, which prohibits favoritism to either the poor or the rich.

2:10 he is guilty of all. God does not allow selective

1:15 [n] Job 15:35   [o] [Rom. 5:12; 6:23]   1:17 [p] John 3:27   [q] Num. 23:19   1:18 [r] John 1:13   [s] [1 Pet. 1:3, 23]   [t] [Eph. 1:12, 13]   1:19 [u] Prov. 10:19; 17:27   [v] Prov. 14:17; 16:32   1:21 [w] Col. 3:8   [x] Acts 13:26   1:22 [y] Matt. 7:21–28   1:23 [z] Luke 6:47   1:25 [a] James 2:12   [b] John 13:17   1:26 [c] Ps. 34:13   1:27 [d] Matt. 25:34–36   [e] Is. 1:17   [f] [Rom. 12:2]   2:1 [a] 1 Cor. 2:8   [b] Lev. 19:15   2:5 [c] 1 Cor. 1:27   [d] Luke 12:21   [e] Ex. 20:6   2:6 [f] 1 Cor. 11:22   [g] Acts 13:50   2:7 [h] 1 Pet. 4:16   2:8 [i] Lev. 19:18   2:9 [j] Deut. 1:17   2:10 [k] Gal. 3:10   [l] Deut. 27:26

of all. 11For He who said, m"Do not commit adultery,"* also said, n"Do not murder."* Now if you do not commit adultery, but you do murder, you have become a transgressor of the law. 12So speak and so do as those who will be judged by othe law of liberty. 13For pjudgment is without mercy to the one who has shown qno rmercy. sMercy triumphs over judgment.

Faith Without Works Is Dead

14tWhat does it profit, my brethren, if someone says he has faith but does not have works? Can faith save him? 15uIf a brother or sister is naked and destitute of daily food, 16and vone of you says to them, "Depart in peace, be warmed and filled," but you do not give them the things which are needed for the body, what does it profit? 17Thus also faith by itself, if it does not have works, is dead.

18But someone will say, "You have faith, and I have works." wShow me your faith without your* works, xand I will show you my faith by my* works. 19You believe that there is one God. You do well. Even the demons believe—and tremble! 20But do you want to know, O foolish man, that faith without works is dead?* 21Was not Abraham our father justified by works ywhen he offered Isaac his son on the altar? 22Do you see zthat faith was working together with his works, and by aworks faith was made perfect? 23And the Scripture was fulfilled which says, b"Abraham believed God, and it was accounted to him for righteousness."* And he was called cthe friend of God. 24You see then that a man is justified by works, and not by faith only.

25Likewise, dwas not Rahab the harlot also justified by works when she received the messengers and sent them out another way?

26For as the body without the spirit is dead, so faith without works is dead also.

The Untamable Tongue

3 My brethren, alet not many of you become teachers, bknowing that we shall receive a stricter judgment. 2For cwe all stumble in many things. dIf anyone does not stumble in word, ehe is a perfect man, able also to bridle the whole body. 3Indeed,* fwe put bits in horses' mouths that they may obey us, and we turn their whole body. 4Look also at ships: although they are so large and are driven by fierce winds, they are turned by a very small rudder wherever the pilot desires. 5Even so gthe tongue is a little member and hboasts great things.

See how great a forest a little fire kindles! 6And ithe tongue is a fire, a world of iniquity. The tongue is so set among our members that it jdefiles the whole body, and sets on fire the course of nature; and it is set on fire by hell. 7For every kind of beast and bird, of reptile and creature of the sea, is tamed and has been tamed by mankind. 8But no man can tame the tongue. It is an unruly evil, kfull of deadly poison. 9With it we bless our God and Father, and with it we curse men, who have been made lin the similitude of God. 10Out of the same mouth proceed blessing and cursing. My brethren, these things ought not to be so.

---

* 2:11 Exodus 20:14; Deuteronomy 5:18 • Exodus 20:13; Deuteronomy 5:17   * 2:18 NU-Text omits your. • NU-Text omits my.   * 2:20 NU-Text reads useless.   * 2:23 Genesis 15:6   * 3:3 NU-Text reads Now if.

---

obedience. We cannot choose to obey the parts of the law that are to our own liking and disregard the rest. Some of the Pharisees were guilty of this. They carefully observed some of the requirements of the law, such as keeping the Sabbath, and ignored others, such as honoring their parents (Matt. 15:1–7). Sin is a violation of the perfect righteousness of God, who is the Lawgiver. James is saying that the whole divine law has to be accepted as an expression of God's will for His people. The violation of even one commandment separates an individual from God and His purposes.

2:14 What does it profit. James is implying in this verse that faith in Christ will demonstrate itself in love for others (John 13:34–35).

2:19 Even the demons believe—and tremble. While they believe, the demons do not love Him (Matt. 8:29). Their kind of belief does not lead to love, submission, and obedience; instead, it leads to hatred, rebellion, and disobedience.

2:21 justified. James is using the word justified to mean "proved." We prove to others our genuine faith in Christ through our works. But the justification that comes through faith is before God, and we do not "prove" ourselves to Him; instead, God declares us righteous through our association with Christ, the One who died for our sins (Rom. 3:28).

2:22 faith . . . works. These two should be together; there is a close relationship between the two. Faith produces faith; and works make faith perfect, meaning "mature" or "complete."

3:1 we shall receive a stricter judgment. James does not give the warning of condemnation to others without applying it to himself.

3:7–8 no man can tame the tongue. The instincts of animals can be subdued through conditioning and punishment, but the sinful nature that inspires evil words is beyond our control. Only the work of the Holy Spirit within us can bring this destructive force under control.

3:9 we bless our God and Father. James is pointing out the inconsistency of blessing God while cursing people who are created in His image.

2:11 m Ex. 20:14; Deut. 5:18 n Ex. 20:13; Deut. 5:17
2:12 o James 1:25   2:13 p Job 22:6 q Prov. 21:13 r Mic.
7:18 s Rom. 12:8   2:14 t Matt. 7:21–23, 26; 21:28–32
2:15 u Luke 3:11   2:16 v [1 John 3:17, 18]   2:18 w Heb.
6:10 x James 3:13   2:21 y Gen. 22:9, 10, 12, 16–18
2:22 z Heb. 11:17 a John 8:39   2:23 b Gen. 15:6 c 2 Chr.
20:7   2:25 d Heb. 11:31   3:1 a [Matt. 23:8] b Luke
6:37   3:2 c 1 Kin. 8:46 d Ps. 34:13 e [Matt. 12:34–37]
3:3 f Ps. 32:9   3:5 g Prov. 12:18; 15:2 h Ps. 12:3; 73:8
3:6 i Prov. 16:27 j [Matt. 12:36; 15:11, 18]   3:8 k Ps. 140:3
3:9 l Gen. 1:26; 5:1; 9:6

11Does a spring send forth fresh *water* and
bitter from the same opening? 12Can a [m]fig
tree, my brethren, bear olives, or a grapevine bear figs? Thus no spring yields both
salt water and fresh.*

Heavenly Versus Demonic Wisdom

13[n]Who *is* wise and understanding
among you? Let him show by good conduct *that* his works *are done* in the meekness of wisdom. 14But if you have [o]bitter
envy and self-seeking in your hearts, [p]do
not boast and lie against the truth. 15[q]This
wisdom does not descend from above, but
is earthly, sensual, demonic. 16For [r]where
envy and self-seeking *exist,* confusion and
every evil thing *are* there. 17But [s]the wisdom that is from above is first pure, then
peaceable, gentle, willing to yield, full of
mercy and good fruits, [t]without partiality
[u]and without hypocrisy. 18[v]Now the fruit
of righteousness is sown in peace by those
who make peace.

Pride Promotes Strife

4 Where do wars and fights *come* from
among you? Do *they* not *come* from
your *desires for* pleasure [a]that war in your
members? 2You lust and do not have. You
murder and covet and cannot obtain. You
fight and war. Yet* you do not have because you do not ask. 3[b]You ask and do not
receive, [c]because you ask amiss, that you
may spend *it* on your pleasures. 4Adulter-
ers and* adulteresses! Do you not know
that [d]friendship with the world is enmity
with God? [e]Whoever therefore wants to
be a friend of the world makes himself an
enemy of God. 5Or do you think that the
Scripture says in vain, [f]"The Spirit who
dwells in us yearns jealously"?
6But He gives more grace. Therefore He
says:

[g]*"God resists the proud,*
*But gives grace to the humble."**

Humility Cures Worldliness

7Therefore submit to God. [h]Resist the
devil and he will flee from you. 8[i]Draw
near to God and He will draw near to you.
[j]Cleanse *your* hands, *you* sinners; and
[k]purify *your* hearts, *you* double-minded.
9[l]Lament and mourn and weep! Let your
laughter be turned to mourning and *your*
joy to gloom. 10[m]Humble yourselves in the
sight of the Lord, and He will lift you up.

Do Not Judge a Brother

11[n]Do not speak evil of one another,
brethren. He who speaks evil of a brother
[o]and judges his brother, speaks evil of the
law and judges the law. But if you judge
the law, you are not a doer of the law but
a judge. 12There is one Lawgiver,* [p]who is
able to save and to destroy. [q]Who* are you
to judge another?*

Do Not Boast About Tomorrow

13Come now, you who say, "Today or tomorrow we will* go to such and such a city,

* **3:12** NU-Text reads *Neither can a salty spring produce fresh water.* * **4:2** NU-Text and M-Text omit *Yet.* * **4:4** NU-Text omits *Adulterers and.* * **4:6** Proverbs 3:34 * **4:12** NU-Text adds *and Judge.* • NU-Text and M-Text read *But who.* • NU-Text reads *a neighbor.* * **4:13** M-Text reads *let us.*

3:16 *confusion.* On the other hand, God brings harmony and wisdom (1 Cor. 14:33). Anyone who is involved in envy and strife is confused. This confusion corrupts human relationships. It is likely that the Jewish Christians to whom James was writing were going through turmoil because of sinful acts like the ones mentioned here. James wanted his readers to set aside their petty attitudes and seek reconciliation.

4:1 *wars and fights.* The source of problems is the conflict between desires for pleasure and the desire for God's will, an attitude that the Holy Spirit has placed within us.

4:3 *you ask amiss.* Some might have protested James's admonition (vv. 1–2) by claiming that they had not received an answer to their prayers (Matt. 7:7). James responds by suggesting that they were praying for the wrong things. Instead of praying for their sinful desires, they should have been praying for God's good will for them.

4:4 *Whoever therefore wants.* This verse does not speak of God's attitude toward the believer, but of the believer's attitude toward God. The difference between the world and God is so vast that, as we move toward the world, we alienate ourselves from God. In the world, sin is considered acceptable and pleasurable. Ultimately the world has lost its awareness of sin, and thus sin has become habitual.

4:6 *God resists the proud.* James quotes from Proverbs 3:34 to prove his point. Those who submit to divine wisdom will receive the necessary grace from God to put into practice the kind of life James describes (3:13–18). On the other hand, those who elevate themselves will face a formidable foe (v. 4). God Himself will fight against their plans, because they are not on His side.

4:9 *Lament and mourn and weep.* When a believer who has fallen into sin responds to God's call for repentance, he or she should place laughter and joy aside to reflect on the sin with genuine sorrow (2 Cor. 7:9–10). In this verse, laughter seems to refer to the loud revelry of pleasure-loving people. They immerse themselves in a celebration of their sins in an effort to forget God's judgment. A Christian should never laugh at sin. However, Christian sorrow leads to repentance; repentance leads to forgiveness; and forgiveness leads to true joy over one's reconciliation with God (Ps. 32:1; 126:2; Prov. 15:13).

4:13 *we will go . . . and make a profit.* The problem here is not the plan or the concept of planning; it is leaving God out of the plan (v. 15).

3:12 [m] Matt. 7:16–20 **3:13** [n] Gal. 6:4 **3:14** [o] Rom. 13:13 [p] Rom. 2:17 **3:15** [q] Phil. 3:19 **3:16** [r] 1 Cor. 3:3 **3:17** [s] 1 Cor. 2:6, 7 [t] James 2:1 [u] Rom. 12:9 **3:18** [v] Prov. 11:18 **4:1** [a] Rom. 7:23 **4:3** [b] Job 27:8, 9 [c] [Ps. 66:18] **4:4** [d] 1 John 2:15 [e] Gal. 1:4 **4:5** [f] Gen. 6:5 **4:6** [g] Prov. 3:34 **4:7** [h] [Eph. 4:27; 6:11] **4:8** [i] 2 Chr. 15:2 [j] Is. 1:16 [k] 1 Pet. 1:22 **4:9** [l] Matt. 5:4 **4:10** [m] Job 22:29 **4:11** [n] 1 Pet. 2:1–3 [o] [Matt. 7:1–5] **4:12** [p] [Matt. 10:28] [q] Rom. 14:4

spend a year there, buy and sell, and make a profit"; [14]whereas you do not know what *will happen* tomorrow. For what *is* your life? [r]It is even a vapor that appears for a little time and then vanishes away. [15]Instead you *ought* to say, [s]"If the Lord wills, we shall live and do this or that." [16]But now you boast in your arrogance. [t]All such boasting is evil.

[17]Therefore, [u]to him who knows to do good and does not do *it*, to him it is sin.

Rich Oppressors Will Be Judged

5 Come now, *you* [a]rich, weep and howl for your miseries that are coming upon *you!* [2]Your [b]riches are corrupted, and [c]your garments are moth-eaten. [3]Your gold and silver are corroded, and their corrosion will be a witness against you and will eat your flesh like fire. [d]You have heaped up treasure in the last days. [4]Indeed [e]the wages of the laborers who mowed your fields, which you kept back by fraud, cry out; and [f]the cries of the reapers have reached the ears of the Lord of Sabaoth.* [5]You have lived on the earth in pleasure and luxury; you have fattened your hearts as* in a day of slaughter. [6]You have condemned, you have murdered the just; he does not resist you.

Be Patient and Persevering

[7]Therefore be patient, brethren, until the coming of the Lord. See *how* the farmer waits for the precious fruit of the earth, waiting patiently for it until it receives the early and latter rain. [8]You also be patient. Establish your hearts, for the coming of the Lord is at hand.

[9]Do not grumble against one another, brethren, lest you be condemned.* Behold, the Judge is standing at the door! [10]g My brethren, take the prophets, who spoke in the name of the Lord, as an example of suffering and [h]patience. [11]Indeed [i]we count them blessed who [j]endure. You have heard of [k]the perseverance of Job and seen [l]the end *intended by* the Lord—that [m]the Lord is very compassionate and merciful.

[12]But above all, my brethren, [n]do not swear, either by heaven or by earth or with any other oath. But let your "Yes" be "Yes," and *your* "No," "No," lest you fall into judgment.*

Meeting Specific Needs

[13]Is anyone among you suffering? Let him [o]pray. Is anyone cheerful? [p]Let him sing psalms. [14]Is anyone among you sick? Let him call for the elders of the church, and let them pray over him, [q]anointing him with oil in the name of the Lord. [15]And the prayer of faith will save the sick, and the Lord will raise him up. [r]And if he has committed sins, he will be forgiven. [16]Confess *your* trespasses* to one another, and pray for one another, that you may be healed. [s]The effective, fervent prayer of a righteous man avails much. [17]Elijah was a man [t]with a nature like ours, and [u]he prayed earnestly that it would not rain; and it did not rain on the land for three years and six months. [18]And he prayed [v]again, and the heaven gave rain, and the earth produced its fruit.

Bring Back the Erring One

[19]Brethren, if anyone among you wanders from the truth, and someone [w]turns him back, [20]let him know that he who turns a sinner from the error of his way [x]will save a soul* from death and [y]cover a multitude of sins.

---

* **5:4** Literally, in Hebrew, *Hosts*   * **5:5** NU-Text omits *as.*   * **5:9** NU-Text and M-Text read *judged.*   * **5:12** M-Text reads *hypocrisy.*   * **5:16** NU-Text reads *Therefore confess your sins.*   * **5:20** NU-Text reads *his soul.*

5:2–3 *your garments.* In the ancient world, food, costly clothing, and precious metals were conspicuous signs of wealth. James pronounces judgment and destruction on all three.
5:12–13 *do not swear.* James is not forbidding a believer from taking an oath in court or invoking God as witness to some significant statement (1 Thess. 2:5). Instead, he is prohibiting the ancient practice of appealing to a variety of different objects to confirm the veracity of one's statement. This practice was extremely close to idolatry, for it implied that such objects contained spirits. The warning in these verses can serve as a reminder to us to watch what we say. We should not use God's name in a reckless manner, and we should be careful to speak the truth.
5:14 *anointing him with oil.* This may refer to medicinal treatment (Luke 10:34). Yet, in this passage, it most likely refers to the healing power of the Holy Spirit, for verse 15 speaks of prayer saving the person.

In either case, there is no indication that calling the elders excludes the use of a physician or medicine.
5:15 *the prayer of faith.* Whether a believer is healed through medicine or through miraculous means, all healing is ultimately from the Lord. That is why prayers should be consistently offered for the sick.
5:16 *The effective, fervent prayer.* This can mean that (1) prayer is effective when it is used, or (2) fervent prayer accomplishes great results.

4:14 [r] Job 7:7   4:15 [s] Acts 18:21   4:16 [t] 1 Cor. 5:6   4:17 [u] [Luke 12:47]   5:1 [a] [Luke 6:24]   5:2 [b] Matt. 6:19   [c] Job 13:28   5:3 [d] Rom. 2:5   5:4 [e] Lev. 19:13   [f] Deut. 24:15   5:10 [g] Matt. 5:12   [h] Heb. 10:36   5:11 [i] [Ps. 94:12]   [j] [James 1:12]   [k] Job 1:21, 22; 2:10   [l] Job 42:10   [m] Num. 14:18   5:12 [n] Matt. 5:34–37   5:13 [o] Ps. 50:14, 15   [p] Eph. 5:19   5:14 [q] Mark 6:13; 16:18   5:15 [r] Is. 33:24   5:16 [s] Num. 11:2   5:17 [t] Acts 14:15   [u] 1 Kin. 17:1; 18:1   5:18 [v] 1 Kin. 18:1, 42   5:19 [w] Gal. 6:1   5:20 [x] Rom. 11:14   [y] [1 Pet. 4:8]

THE FIRST EPISTLE OF
PETER

▶ **AUTHOR:** The early church universally acknowledged the authenticity and authority of 1 Peter. It is likely that Peter used Silvanus as his scribe (5:12). This epistle was addressed to Christians throughout Asia Minor, indicating the spread of the gospel in regions not evangelized when Acts was written. It was written from Babylon (5:13), but scholars are divided as to whether this refers literally to Babylon in Mesopotamia or symbolically to Rome. It is probably the latter as tradition consistently indicates that Peter spent the last few years of his life in Rome.

▶ **TIME:** c. A.D. 63–64   ▶ **KEY VERSES:** 1 Pet. 4:12–13

▶ **THEME:** First Peter was probably written to the Roman provinces of Turkey at the beginning of Nero's persecutions of Christians. Its primary message is one of comfort, hope, and encouragement. He asks the readers to hold fast to the faith in the midst of the coming persecution. In these letters we get a picture of a mature Peter who has incorporated Christ's crucifixion and death and resurrection into his thinking about suffering. He fully understands, and even looks forward to, the glory that is to come after the sufferings of this life.

Greeting to the Elect Pilgrims

1 Peter, an apostle of Jesus Christ,

To the pilgrims ªof the Dispersion in Pontus, Galatia, Cappadocia, Asia, and Bithynia, 2belect ccording to the foreknowledge of God the Father, din sanctification of the Spirit, for eobedience and fsprinkling of the blood of Jesus Christ:

gGrace to you and peace be multiplied.

A Heavenly Inheritance

3hBlessed be the God and Father of our Lord Jesus Christ, who iaccording to His abundant mercy jhas begotten us again to a living hope kthrough the resurrection of Jesus Christ from the dead, 4to an inheritance incorruptible and undefiled and that does not fade away, lreserved in heaven for you, 5mwho are kept by the power of God through faith for salvation ready to be revealed in the last time.

6nIn this you greatly rejoice, though now ofor a little while, if need be, pyou have been grieved by various trials, 7that qthe genuineness of your faith, being much more precious than gold that perishes, though rit is tested by fire, smay be found to praise, honor, and glory at the revelation of Jesus Christ, 8twhom having not seen* you love. uThough now you do not see Him, yet

* 1:8 M-Text reads known.

1:1 *pilgrims.* This term conveys the idea of being dispersed, much like the Jewish exiles of the Old Testament who were not living in their homeland but in Babylon.

1:2 *sanctification of the Spirit.* Sanctification is the ongoing process whereby the Holy Spirit works in believers, making their lives holy, separated from their old ways and to God in order to be more like Him. *sprinkling of the blood.* This concept, the second reason why God chooses us, draws our attention to three situations in the Old Testament when the Israelites were sprinkled with the blood of animals: (1) Moses' sprinkling of blood on the Israelites at Mount Sinai to symbolize their initiation into the covenant (Ex. 24:5–8); (2) the sprinkling of Aaron and his sons to be the priests of Israel (Ex. 29:19–21); and (3) the sprinkling of the blood performed by priests over healed lepers to symbolize their cleansing (Lev. 14:1–9). Any of these three cases could be the one that Peter has in mind here.

1:3 *according to His abundant mercy.* Our salvation is grounded in God's mercy, His act of compassion toward us despite our condition of sinfulness. *has begotten us again.* God has given believers a new, spiritual life that enables us to live in an entirely different dimension than the one our physical birth allowed.
1:4 *inheritance.* The Greek word here suggests both a present and a future reality. God has already determined what we will one day experience in its totality. *reserved.* God has set aside in heaven a wonderful inheritance that is waiting for us even now.
1:7 *that the genuineness of your faith.* As the purity of gold is brought forth by intense heat, so the reality

1:1 ª James 1:1   **1:2** b Eph. 1:4   c [Rom. 8:29]   d 2 Thess. 2:13   e Rom. 1:5   f Heb. 10:22; 12:24   g Rom. 1:7   **1:3** h Eph. 1:3   i Gal. 6:16   j [John 3:3, 5]   k 1 Cor. 15:20   **1:4** l Col. 1:5   **1:5** m John 10:28   **1:6** n Matt. 5:12   o 2 Cor. 4:17   p James 1:2   **1:7** q James 1:3   r Job 23:10   s [Rom. 2:7]   **1:8** t 1 John 4:20   u John 20:29

believing, you rejoice with joy inexpressible and full of glory, **9**receiving the end of your faith—the salvation of *your* souls.

10Of this salvation the prophets have inquired and searched carefully, who prophesied of the grace *that would come* to you, **11**searching what, or what manner of time, ʋthe Spirit of Christ who was in them was indicating when He testified beforehand the sufferings of Christ and the glories that would follow. **12**To them it was revealed that, not to themselves, but to us* they were ministering the things which now have been reported to you through those who have preached the gospel to you by the Holy Spirit sent from heaven—things which ʷangels desire to look into.

Living Before God Our Father

13Therefore gird up the loins of your mind, be sober, and rest *your* hope fully upon the grace that is to be brought to you at the revelation of Jesus Christ; **14**as obedient children, not ˣconforming yourselves to the former lusts, *as* in your ignorance; **15**ʸbut as He who called you *is* holy, you also be holy in all *your* conduct, **16**because it is written, ᶻ*"Be holy, for I am holy."**

17And if you call on the Father, who ªwithout partiality judges according to each one's work, conduct yourselves throughout the time of your stay *here* in fear; **18**knowing that you were not redeemed with corruptible things, *like* silver or gold, from your aimless conduct *received* by tradition from your fathers, **19**but ᵇwith the precious blood of Christ, ᶜas of a lamb without blemish and without spot.

20ᵈHe indeed was foreordained before the foundation of the world, but was manifest ᵉin these last times for you **21**who through Him believe in God, ᶠwho raised Him from the dead and ᵍgave Him glory, so that your faith and hope are in God.

The Enduring Word

22Since you ʰhave purified your souls in obeying the truth through the Spirit* in sincere ⁱlove of the brethren, love one another fervently with a pure heart, **23**ʲhaving been born again, not of corruptible seed but incorruptible, ᵏthrough the word of God which lives and abides forever,* **24**because

ˡ"All flesh is as grass,
  And all the glory of man* as the flower
    of the grass.
  The grass withers,
    And its flower falls away,
25 ᵐBut the word of the LORD endures
    forever."*

ⁿNow this is the word which by the gospel was preached to you.

2 Therefore, ªlaying aside all malice, all deceit, hypocrisy, envy, and all evil speaking, **2**ᵇas newborn babes, desire the pure ᶜmilk of the word, that you may grow thereby,* **3**if indeed you have ᵈtasted that the Lord is gracious.

---

* **1:12** NU-Text and M-Text read *you*. * **1:16** Leviticus 11:44, 45; 19:2; 20:7 * **1:22** NU-Text omits *through the Spirit.* * **1:23** NU-Text omits *forever.* * **1:24** NU-Text reads *all its glory.* * **1:25** Isaiah 40:6–8 * **2:2** NU-Text adds *up to salvation.*

---

and purity of our faith are revealed as a result of the fiery trials we face. Ultimately the testing of our faith not only demonstrates our final salvation but also develops our capacity to bring glory to the Lord Jesus Christ when He comes into His kingdom and we reign with Him (Rom. 8:17; 2 Tim. 2:12; Rev. 5:9–12).

1:10 the prophets. Peter indicates that the Old Testament prophets knew of the gracious salvation we would one day receive and, as a result, studied it carefully and intensively.

1:12 by the Holy Spirit. Although humans may preach God's message of salvation, ultimately the Holy Spirit is the One who proclaims these great truths. Even the angels are amazed at what a wonderful salvation God has enacted on our behalf (Eph. 3:10).

1:13 gird up the loins of your mind. Just as people in biblical times would gather up their long robes and tie them around their waists so that they could move quickly and freely, we need to do whatever it takes to focus our thoughts on those things that allow us to serve God successfully, all the while eliminating any thoughts that would trip us up (Heb. 12:1). **be sober.** Peter's concern here is primarily using mentally or spiritually sound judgment. **hope fully.** We need to exhibit confidence that God will accomplish all that He promised He would do (v. 3; Rom. 8:24–25).

1:17 in fear. For Christians, this phrase should be understood as something between terror and reverential awe. We need to remember that God is both

our merciful Savior (vv. 3,18–21) and our holy Judge (vv. 15–17).

1:19 a lamb. Peter describes Christ as the ultimate sacrificial Lamb, who is offered in our place to pay the price for our sins. The analogy here may be a reference either to the Passover lamb (Ex. 12:3–6) or to the many lambs without blemish that were offered as part of the Old Testament sacrificial system (Lev. 23:12; Num. 6:14; 28:3).

1:20 foreordained. God has known (v. 2) the One who would bring salvation, even as He has known those to whom that salvation is offered and secured (Rom. 11:2). **but was manifest.** This phrase contrasts with the first half of the verse. What was known only to God before the creation of the world is now made known to us.

1:22 purified your souls. We accomplish the purification of our souls by obedience to God's truth.

2:2 that you may grow thereby. The purpose of studying God's truth is not only to learn more, but to become mature in the faith.

1:11 ʋ 2 Pet. 1:21 **1:12** ʷ Eph. 3:10 **1:14** ˣ [Rom. 12:2] **1:15** ʸ [2 Cor. 7:1] **1:16** ᶻ Lev. 11:44, 45; 19:2; 20:7 **1:17** ª Acts 10:34 **1:19** ᵇ Acts 20:28 ᶜ Ex. 12:5 **1:20** ᵈ Rom. 3:25 ᵉ Gal. 4:4 **1:21** ᶠ Acts 2:24 ᵍ Acts 2:33 **1:22** ʰ Acts 15:9 ⁱ Heb. 13:1 **1:23** ʲ John 1:13 ᵏ James 1:18 **1:24** ˡ Is. 40:6–8 **1:25** ᵐ Is. 40:8 ⁿ [John 1:1] **2:1** ª Heb. 12:1 **2:2** ᵇ [Matt. 18:3; 19:14] ᶜ 1 Cor. 3:2 **2:3** ᵈ Heb. 6:5

The Chosen Stone and His Chosen People

4Coming to Him *as to* a living stone, *e*rejected indeed by men, but chosen by God *and* precious, 5you also, as living stones, are being built up a spiritual house, a holy priesthood, to offer up spiritual sacrifices acceptable to God through Jesus Christ. 6Therefore it is also contained in the Scripture,

f "Behold, I lay in Zion
A chief cornerstone, elect, precious,
And he who believes on Him will by
no means be put to shame."*

7Therefore, to you who believe, *He is* precious; but to those who are disobedient,*

g "The stone which the builders rejected
Has become the chief cornerstone,"*

8and

h "A stone of stumbling
And a rock of offense."*

*i*They stumble, being disobedient to the word, *j*to which they also were appointed.
9But you *are* a chosen generation, a royal priesthood, a holy nation, His own special people, that you may proclaim the praises of Him who called you out of *k*darkness into His marvelous light; 10*l*who once *were* not a people but *are* now the people of God,

who had not obtained mercy but now have obtained mercy.

Living Before the World

11Beloved, I beg *you* as sojourners and pilgrims, *m*abstain from fleshly lusts *m*which war against the soul, 12*n*having your conduct honorable among the Gentiles, that when they speak against you as evildoers, *o*they may, by *your* good works which they observe, glorify God in the day of visitation.

Submission to Government

13*p*Therefore submit yourselves to every ordinance of man for the Lord's sake, whether to the king as supreme, 14or to governors, as to those who are sent by him for the punishment of evildoers and *for the praise* of those who do good. 15For this is the will of God, that by doing good you may put to silence the ignorance of foolish men— 16*q*as free, yet not *r*using liberty as a cloak for vice, but as bondservants of God. 17Honor all *people.* Love the brotherhood. Fear *s*God. Honor the king.

Submission to Masters

18*t*Servants, *be* submissive to *your* masters with all fear, not only to the good and

---

* **2:6** Isaiah 28:16   * **2:7** NU-Text reads *to those who disbelieve.* • Psalm 118:22   * **2:8** Isaiah 8:14

2:4 living stone. This phrase anticipates the Old Testament quotations in verses 6–8. Jesus, as a living stone, is superior to the Old Testament temple.
2:5 stones. Christians are part of God's great spiritual building project. Referenced here are stones that are shaped and ready for use in construction, as opposed to natural rock. **a holy priesthood.** Unlike the Old Testament priesthood, in which only those who were born into a certain tribe could be priests, all who are reborn into God's family, that is, all believers, are priests who have the privilege and responsibility of offering spiritual sacrifices to God (Rom. 12:1–2; Heb. 13:15–16).
2:6 A chief cornerstone . . . precious. Jesus is the foundation stone from which the placement of all other living stones in the spiritual house (v. 5) is determined (Is. 28:16). In ancient buildings, the cornerstone was first situated on the foundation and then all of the other stones were aligned to it. Thus as part of the house of God, we need to keep our focus on our Cornerstone (Heb. 12:2).
2:9 a chosen generation. God has not left to chance who will be part of a unique body of people, a group who will serve Him. **a royal priesthood.** Believers are transformed not only internally (v. 5), which describes us as being made into a "holy priesthood" but also externally. We are a priesthood that functions in a ruling capacity, as kings. **a holy nation.** Believers are a unified group of people who are set apart for God's use. **special people.** God protects those whom He has adopted into His family.
2:11 sojourners and pilgrims. With these words, Peter reminds believers (1:1) that this earth is not our home. We are foreigners here, traveling to our eternal home, heaven.

2:12 day of visitation. This term probably refers to the final day of judgment when all people, believers and unbelievers alike, will fall on their knees and acknowledge who Jesus Christ is and what He has done through His people.
2:13 every ordinance of man. This phrase suggests that the submission of Christians is not to be exercised solely in relation to civil authorities (v. 14), but to all kinds of rules that Christians encounter (2:18; 3:1).
2:13 Our Responsibility to Human Government—As children of God, our responsibility to human government is threefold:

1. We are to recognize and accept that the powers that be are ordained by God (Rom. 13:1). This truth even applies to governments that are anti-Christian. If a given law is clearly anti-scriptural, the believer is required to obey God rather than man (Dan. 3; 6; Acts 4:18–20).
2. We are to pay our taxes to human governments (Matt. 17:24; 22:21; Rom. 13:7).
3. We are to pray for the leaders in human government (1 Tim. 2:1–3).

2:16 as a cloak for vice. This may be understood either as an excuse made up before the fact, or after the fact.
2:18 be submissive . . . with all fear. Workers are to take their responsibilities seriously, even when serving the worst of bosses.

2:4 *e* Ps. 118:22   **2:6** *f* Is. 28:16   **2:7** *g* Ps. 118:22
2:8 *h* Is. 8:14   *i* 1 Cor. 1:23   *j* Rom. 9:22   **2:9** *k* [Acts 26:18]
2:10 *l* Hos. 1:9, 10; 2:23   **2:11** *m* James 4:1   **2:12** *n* Phil.
2:15   *o* Matt. 5:16; 9:8   **2:13** *p* Matt. 22:21   **2:16** *q* Rom.
6:14, 20, 22   *r* Gal. 5:13   **2:17** *s* Prov. 24:21   **2:18** *t* Eph.
6:5–8